f
Z
00
74
ndex
v. 37-46

Bookman's Price Index

CUMULATIVE INDEX TO VOLUMES 37-46

ISSN 0068-0141

Bookman's Price Index
CUMULATIVE INDEX TO VOLUMES 37-46

A Consolidated Index to More Than
200,000 Citations Describing
Antiquarian Books Offered For
Sale by Leading Dealers

Edited by
Anne F. McGrath

 **Gale Research Inc.** • *DETROIT* • *WASHINGTON, D.C.* • *LONDON*

Anne F. McGrath, *Editor*

Linda Bell, Richard Grazide, Kathy Hinkle, and Tony Mobley, *Contributing Editors*

Gale Research Inc. Staff

Donna Wood, *Coordinating Editor*
Erin E. Holmberg, Jacqueline L. Longe, Matt Merta, Gerda-Ann Raffaelle,
and Bradford J. Wood, *Contributors*

Benita L. Spight, *Data Entry Supervisor*
Gwendolyn S. Tucker, *Data Entry Group Leader*
Kenneth D. Benson Jr., Merrie Ann Carpenter, Edgar C. Jackson, Beverly Jendrowski,
Nancy K. Sheridan, Fredrick L. Penn Jr., *Data Entry Associates*

Mary Beth Trimper, *Production Director*
Shanna Heilveil, *Production Assistant*

Cynthia D. Baldwin, *Art Director*
Nicholas Jakubiak, *Graphic Designer*

Theresa Rocklin, *Supervisor of Systems and Programming*
Joe Krutulis, *Programmer*

∞™ The paper used in this publication meets the minimum requirements
of American National Standard for Information Sciences-Permanence Paper for
Printed Library Materials, ANSI Z39.48-1984.

♻ This book is printed on recycled paper that meets Environmental
Protection Agency Standards.

Copyright © 1994
Gale Research Inc.
835 Penobscot Bldg.
Detroit, MI 48226-4094

ISBN 0-8103-9554

Printed in the United States of America

Published simultaneously in the United Kingdom
by Gale Research International Limited
(An affiliated company of Gale Research Inc.)

The trademark **ITP** is used under license.

Contents

This work provides speedy access to the 250,000 book titles contained in Volumes 37-46 of the *Bookman's Price Index*. Additional information is available about these titles in the individual volumes.

Introduction

The *Bookman's Price Index (BPI)*, published since 1964, indicates the availability and price of antiquarian books in the United States, Canada, and the British Isles. Since the *BPI* now numbers 47 volumes, searching for specific titles has become a time consuming task for the user.

This volume is a "cumulative index to the index." It references the entries in the last ten issues, Volumes 37 through 46. Since each *BPI* volume includes over 25,000 entries, this work provides access to about 250,000 entries from the rare book dealer catalogs published over the past five years.

What is Included?

Since the primary purpose of this volume is speedy access to 250,000 book titles, the complete entry in the original *BPI* volume is not repeated here. Such a repetition would necessarily negate the ability to include all this information in one volume, thus defeating its purpose of quick and easy access.

Sufficient information is included here for rapid identification of a specific title including the author with birth and death dates, if available; date of publication; and place of publication, followed by a list of all the *BPI* volumes in which that book is included.

BPI's regular volumes provide extensive information so that the user can identify a rare book and get some indication of how the particular dealer arrived at its price. This information, taken from rare book dealer catalogs, includes not only the author, title, date and place of publication, publisher, edition and price, but a thorough description of the book and notes on its condition. The description and condition information includes physical size, illustrations, binding, authors' signatures, general physical condition, specific flaws, and relative scarcity whenever this information has been given by the dealer listing the book.

Arrangement

Entries appear in a single alphabetic sequence, based on the name of the author: in cases of personal authorship, the author's last name; in cases of books produced by corporate bodies such as governments of countries or states, the name of that entity; in cases of anonymous books, the title; and in cases of anonymous classics such as *Arabian Nights*, the customary or well-known title.

Extensive efforts were made to standardize the names of authors so that all titles belonging to the same author appeared together. However, in combining ten volumes of the *BPI*, some inconsistencies appeared in the way the authors' names were presented. The editors have brought as much consistency as possible to this index, but in certain cases, changing an author's name for the sake of consistency might have made it impossible for the user to find the entry in the original *BPI* volume. Therefore, some latitude is necessary when searching for a specific author.

Under the author's name, individual works are arranged in alphabetical sequence according to the first word of the title, excluding initial articles. In addition, a method was developed by the editors so that references to the same title, regardless of the variations used to represent that title, are grouped together, even if users may not, at first, think of these various titles as the same. This same method of arranging entries was also employed for the collected works of an author. Therefore, it may appear, at times, that entries are not logically arranged. Different editions of a single work are arranged according to the date of publication, with the earliest dates first. If the date of publication is the same but the place of publication is different, these entries are then organized alphabetically by the place of publication. Bearing all of this in mind, it would be advisable for users to scan the entire list of an author's works so as not to miss locating information on a specific title.

User's Guide

The following sample illustrates the components of a typical entry:

(2)

(1) **DE QUINCY, THOMAS** 1785-1859   (4)   (5)
(3) *Confessions of an English Opium Eater.* Oxford: 1930.
V. 38; 39; 40; 43; 45 (6)

(1) Author's name
(2) Life dates of the author
(3) Title
(4) Place of publication
(5) Date of publication
(6) Volumes of the *BPI* in which the complete descriptive entry for copies of this edition can be found

Acknowledgments

My thanks to Donna Wood, coordinating editor at Gale Research Inc., for her guiding hand throughout this project, to Richard Grazide for his assistance in research and editing, and to Kathy Hinkle, Linda Bell, and Tony Mobley for their many hours of reviewing and correcting some 250,000 entries in order to bring consistency to this index.

Suggestions

Suggestions are always welcome. This index volume is, in part, a result of the suggestions of *BPI* users. The editor invites all comments, especially those that might improve the usefulness of the *Bookman's Price Index.*

Anne F. McGrath
Editor

Bookman's Price Index

CUMULATIVE INDEX TO VOLUMES 37-46

A

THE A, B, C, with the Church of England Catechism.. Philadelphia: 1785. V. 38; 39

A., D.

The Whole Art of Converse . . . London: 1683. V. 44; 46

A., T.

A Rich Storehouse or Treasure for the Diseased Wherein are Many Approved Medicines. London: 1630. V. 44

AALBORG, NIELS MIKKELSEN

Medicin Eller Laege-Boog, Deelt udi Fem smaa Boger . . . Copenhagen. V. 44

AARANDA, ANTONIO DE

Verdadera Inofrmacion de la Tierra Sancta. Alcala: 1584. V. 37

ABAD Y ARAMBURU, J.

Oracion Funebre, que en el Sufragio Solemme que Ofrecieron por el Alma de el Senor Don Josef Escandon . . . Mexico: 1812. V. 39

ABADIE, HILARIAN

A French Grammar, or Theoretical and Practical Lessons in the French Langauge. Philadelphia: 1823. V. 41

ABAILARD, PIERRE 1079-1142

The Letters of Abelard and Heloise. London: 1925. V. 42

ABARBANEL, DON YITZHAK

Merkevet H'Mishne (commentary on Deuteronomy). Sabbioneta: 1551. V. 37

ABATI, BALDUS ANGELUS

De Admirabili Viperae Natura, et de Mirificis Eiusdem Facultatibus Liber. Urbini: 1589. V. 41; 43

ABBADIE, JACQUES

The History of the Late Conspiracy Against the King and the Nation, with a Particular Account of the Lancashire Plot . . . London: 1696. V. 46

A Panegyric On Our Late Sovereign Lady Mary Queen of England, Scotland, France and Ireland . . . London: 1695. V. 42

ABBAT, RICHARD

A Treatise on the Calculus of Variations. London: 1841. V. 40

ABBATT, RICHARD

A Treatise on the Calculus of Variations. London: 1836. V. 45

ABBE, DOROTHY

The Dwiggins Marionettes . . . New York: 1970. V. 44; 45; 46

The Dwiggins Marionettes. New York: 1969. V. 37

Stencilled Ornament and Illustration. Hingham: 1979. V. 39

ABBE, ELFRIEDE

Plants of Virgil's Georgics. Part I, Trees and Shrubs. Part II, Herbs & Other Small Plants. Ithaca: 1962. V. 37

The Plants of Virgil's Georgics. New York: 1962, 1965. V. 42

THE ABBEY of Weyhill, a Romance; Interspersed with Poetry. N.P.: 1832. V. 40

ABBEY, EDWARD

Appalachian Wilderness. New York: 1970. V. 43; 46

Beyond the Wall. New York: 1984. V. 44; 46

Black Sun. New York: 1971. V. 44

Cactus Country. New York: 1973. V. 44

Desert Images. New York: 1979. V. 46

Desert Solitaire. New York: 1968. V. 43; 44; 45; 46

Down the River. New York: 1982. V. 46

Fire on the Mountain. New York: 1962. V. 45; 46

Fool's Progress. New York: 1988. V. 44; 45; 46

Good News. New York: 1980. V. 44

In Praise of Mountain Lions. Albuquerque: 1984. V. 44

Jonathan Troy. New York: 1954. V. 38; 42; 44; 46

The Journey Home. New York: 1977. V. 44; 45; 46

The Monkey Wrench Gang. Philadelphia: 1975. V. 38; 39; 42; 44; 46

The Monkey Wrench Gang. Edinburgh: 1978. V. 43

The Monkey Wrench Gang. Salt Lake City: 1985. V. 44; 46

One Life at a Time, Please. New York: 1988. V. 44; 45

Slickrock. San Francisco/New York: 1971. V. 43; 44

Slumgullion Stew. New York: 1984. V. 44; 45

Vox Clamantis in Deserto. Santa Fe: 1989. V. 42; 43; 44; 45

ABBEY, EDWIN AUSTIN

Old Songs. New York: 1889, 1888. V. 41

ABBEY, HENRY

The Poems of . . . Kingston: 1886. V. 40

ABBEY, JOHN ROLAND

Catalogue of Valuable Printed Books and Fine Bindings from the Celebrated Collection of . . . London: 1965. V. 37; 39; 40; 41; 42; 44

Catalogue of Highly Important Modern French Illustrated Books and Bindings. London: 1970. V. 41

English Bindings 1490-1940 in the Library of J. R. Abbey. London: 1940. V. 39; 42; 45

Life in England in Aquatint and Lithography 1770-1860. London: 1953. V. 37; 42; 45

Life in England in Aquatint and Lithography 1770-1860. Scenery of Great Britain and Ireland in Aquatint and Lithography 1770-1860. Travel in Aquatint and Lithography 1770-1860. San Francisco: 1991. V. 46

Scenery of Great Britain and Ireland in Aquatint and Lithography 1770-1860. (with) Life in England in Aquatint . . . London: 1952/53. V. 42

Scenery of Great Britain and Ireland in Aquatint and Lithography, 1770-1860. With Life In England. With Travel. London: 1952/53/56/57. V. 39

Scenery of Great Britian, and Ireland in Aquatint and Lithography, 1770-1860. (with) Life in England in Aquatint and Lithography. (with) Travel in Aquatint and Lithography. London: 1952/53/57. V. 41

Scenery of Great Britian and Ireland in Aquatint and Lithography, 1770-1860 From (His) Library. London: 1972. V. 40; 41; 42; 44

Travel in Aquatint and Lithography 1770-1860 from the Library of J. R. Abbey. London: 1956-57. V. 43

Travel in Aquatint and Lithography, 1770-1860, from (His) Library. London: 1972. V. 40; 41; 42

ABBOT, ABIEL

Letters Written in the Interior of Cuba, Between the Mountains of Arcana to the East and of Cusco to the West . . . in 1828. Boston: 1829. V. 38; 40; 42; 43

ABBOT, CHARLES CONRAD

Ten Years' Diggings in Lenape Land, 1901-1911. Trenton: 1912. V. 44

ABBOT, GEORGE

A Brief Description of the Whole World. London: 1620. V. 41

Sketches About Kurrah, Mannickpore. London: 1831. V. 41; 44

ABBOT, GORHAM D.

Mexico, and the United States: Their Mutual Relations and Common Interests. New York: 1869. V. 44

ABBOT, HENRY L.

Professional Papers Corps of Engineers No. 14 Siege Artillery in the Campaigns Against Richmond with Notes on the 15 Inch Gun. Washington: 1867. V. 44

Report Upon Experiments and Investigations to Develop a System of Submarine Mines for Defending the Harbors of the United States. Washington: 1881. V. 42

ABBOT, J. WILLIS

Panama and the Canal, in Picture and Prose. London & New York: 1913. V. 39

ABBOT, JACOB

China and English. London: 1836. V. 46

The Harper Establishment; or, How the Story Books are Made. New York: 1855. V. 40

The Teacher: or Moral Influences Employed in the Instruction and Government of the Young . . . Boston: 1833. V. 39

ABBOT, JOHN

The Natural History of the Rarer Lepidopterous Insects of Georgia, Including Their Systematic Characters, the Particulars of Their Systematic Characters, the Particulars of Their Several Metamorphoses and the Plants on Which they Feed. London: 1797. V. 37

ABBOT, JOHN S. C.

The Mother at Home; or, the Principles of Material Duty. London: 1835. V. 45

ABBOT, ROBERT

The True Ancient Roman Catholike. London: 1611. V. 44

ABBOT, W. J.

The Panama Canal. London: New York: 1914. V. 46

ABBOT, WILLIS J.

The Naval History of the United States . . . New York: 1896. V. 42

ABBOTSFORD CLUB

Compota Domestica Familiarum de Buckingham et d'Angouleme . . . Edinburgh: 1836. V. 38

ABBOTT, BERENICE

Greenwich Village: Today and Yesterday. V. 42

A Guide to Better Photography. New York: 1941. V. 41; 46

The World of Atget. New York: 1964. V. 37; 39; 40

ABBOTT, CARLISLE S.

Recollections of a California Pioneer. New York: 1917. V. 46

ABBOTT, CHARLES

Recollections of a California Pioneer. New York: 1917. V. 39

ABBOTT, CHARLES C.

Primitive Industry . . . Salem: 1881. V. 46

ABBOTT, CHARLES CONRAD

Ten Years' Digging in Lenape Land 1901-1911. Trenton: 1912. V. 42

ABBOTT, CHARLES D.

Howard Pyle. A Chronicle. New York: 1925. V. 37; 39; 41; 42; 44; 46

ABBOTT, CLAUDE COLLEER

The Life and Letters of George Darley - a Poet and Critic. London: 1928. V. 41

ABBOTT, E. C.

We Pointed Them North. New York: 1939. V. 39; 42; 43

ABBOTT, EDWIN ABBOTT 1838-1926

Flatland: a Romance of Many Dimensions. London: 1884. V. 42

Flatland. A Romance of Many Dimensions. By A Square. Boston: 1885. V. 37; 46

ABBOTT, F. H.

The Adminstration of Indian Affairs in Canada. Washington: 1915. V. 37

ABBOTT, FREDERIC V.

History of the Class of 'Seventy-Nine at the U.S. Military Academy of West Point. New York: 1884. V. 37; 46

ABBOTT, GEORGE

Broadway. Los Angeles: 1929. V. 45

ABBOTT, JACOB

McDonner; or Truth through Fiction. Boston: 1839. V. 38

ABBOTT, JAMES

Narrative of a Journey from Heraut to Khiva, Moscow, and St. Petersburgh, During the Late Russian Invasion of Khiva . . . London: 1843. V. 40

ABBOTT, JOHN

Exposition of the Principles of Abbott's Hydraulic Engine, with Tables & Engravings . . . Boston: 1835. V. 39

ABBOTT, LAWRENCE F.

Impressions of Theodore Roosevelt. Garden City: 1919. V. 37

ABBOTT, LYMAN

The House and Home. A Practical Book. By Dr. Lyman Abbott . . . *H.C. Candee* . . . *Constance Cary Harrison* . . . *Kate Douglas Wiggin.* New York: (1894-1896). V. 37

ABBOTT, MAUDE

Appreciations and Reminiscences of Sir William Osler. Montreal: 1926. V. 42; 45

Atlas of Congenital Cardiac Disease. New York: 1936. V. 42

Atlas of Congenital Cardiac Disease. New York: 1954. V. 42; 46

Classified and Annotated Bibliography of Sir William Osler's Publications. Montreal: 1939. V. 45

ABBOTT, T. K.

Catalogue of Fifteenth Century Books in the Library of Trinity College, Dublin and in Marsh's Library, Dublin, etc. Dublin: 1905. V. 43

Celtic Ornaments from the Book of Kells. Dublin: 1895. V. 37; 38

ABBOTT, THOMAS KINGSMILL 1829-1913

Celtic Ornaments from the Book of Kells. Dublin: 1892-95. V. 41; 42

ABBREGE de l'Histoire Francoise, avec Les Effigies des Roys, Depuis Pharamond Iusques au Roy Henry III, Tirees des Plus Rares & Excellentz Cabinetz de la France. Paris: 1595. V. 40

ABD AL-WAHHAB IBN IBRAHIM

Liber Tasriphi Compositio et Senis Alemani. Rome: 1610. V. 44

ABD AR-RAZZAK, IBN NEDSCHEI KULI

History of the Khadjar Dynasty. Tabriz: 1825. V. 43

ABDIAS

De Historia Certaminis Apostolici, Libri Decem, Ivlio Africano Interprete. B. Mathiae Apostoli Vita, ex Hebraica Lingua Incerto Interprete Versa. Beatorvm, Marci, Clementis, Cypriani & Apollinaris Historiae, ex Scriniis & Archiuis Primitiuae . . . Paris: 1560. V. 39

ABDULKURREEM, KHOJEH

The Memoirs of Khojeh Abdulkurreem, a Cashmerian of Distinction. Calcutta: 1788. V. 43

ABDY, EDWARD S.

Journal of a Residence and Tour in the United States of North American from April 1833 to October 1834. London: 1835. V. 41; 42; 43

ABDY, ROWENA MEEKS

Old California. Being Ten Reproductions of Original Watercolors, Painted by Rowena Meeks Abdy. San Francisco: 1924. V. 38

A'BECKETT, GILBERT ABBOTT 1811-1856

The Comic Blackstone. London: 1887. V. 38

The Comic History of England. London: 1886. V. 39

The Comic History of England. The Comic History of Rome. London: 1848. V. 43

The Comic History of England. (with) The Comic History of Rome. London: 1847/48. V. 37; 38; 40; 41; 45; 46

The Comic History of England. (with) the Comic History of Rome. London: 1847-51. V. 42

The Comic History of Rome. London: 1851. V. 37; 38; 39; 40; 41; 46

The Comic History of Rome. (with) The Comic History of England. London: 1852. V. 42

Table Book. London: 1845. V. 37; 40

ABEEL, DAVID

Journal of a Residence in China and the Neighboring Countries, from 1829 to 1833. New York: 1834. V. 42; 43

Journal of a Residence in China, and the Neighbouring Countries . . . New York: 1836. V. 37; 39; 42; 45; 46

ABEEL, JOHN N.

A Discourse . . . *In the Middle Dutch Church Before the New York Missionary Society.* New York: 1801. V. 42

ABEL, ANNIE HELOISE

The American Indian as Slaveholder and Secessionist an Omitted Chapter in the Diplomatic History of the Confederacy. Cleveland: 1915. V. 42

Chardon's Journal at Fort Clark 1834-1839. Pierre: 1932. V. 44

ABEL, CLARKE

Narrative of a Journey in the Interior of China, and of a Voyage to and from that Country, in the Years 1816 and 1817 . . . London: 1818. V. 38; 41

Narrative of a Journey in the Interior of China, and of a Voyage to and From That Country, in the Years 1816 and 1817 . . . London: 1819. V. 45

ABEL, MARTIN

Harry Kurnitz 1909-1968. (New York: 1968). V. 37

ABEL, THOMAS

Subtensial Plain Trigonometry, Wrought with a Sliding-Rule, with Gunter's Lines . . . Philadelphia: 1761. V. 40; 41

ABELING, JAMES

The History of Roche Abbey Yorkshire From Its Foundation to Its Dissolution. London: 1870. V. 40

ABELL, L. G., MRS.

Skillful Housewife's Book . . . New York: 1852. V. 45

ABELL, WILLIAM

Copie. The Copie of a Letter (in Verse) Sent from the Roaring Boyes in Elizium; to the Two Arrant Knights of the Grape, in Limbo, Alderman Abell and M. Kilvert, the Two Great Projectors for Wine . . . London: 1641. V. 45

A Dialogue or Accidental Discourse Betwixt Mr. Alderman Abell, and Richard Kilvert, the Two Main Projectors for Wine . . . London: 1641. V. 45

The Last Discourse Betwixt Master Abel and Master Richard Kilvert, Interrupted at the First by an Ancient and Angry Gentlewoman . . . London: 1641. V. 45

ABERCONWAY, CHRISTABEL

The Story of Mr. Korah. London: 1954. V. 44

ABERCROMBIE, JOHN 1726-1806

The Garden Mushroom: its Nature and Civilisation. London: 1780.
V. 41; 42; 46

The Garden Mushroom, Its Most Effectual General Culture Thoroughly Displayed . . . London: 1802. V. 45

A General System of Trees and Shrubs For All Useful and Ornamental Plantations . . . London. V. 45; 46

The Hot-House Gardener on the General Culture of the Pine-Apple. London: 1789. V. 37; 45

Inquiries Concerning the Intellectual Powers, and the Investigation of Truth. New York: 1825. V. 39

Inquiries Concerning the Intellectual Powers and the Investigation of Truth. London: 1830. V. 42; 43; 45

Inquiries Concerning the Intellectual Powers and the Investigation of Truth. Edinburgh: 1830. V. 37; 42; 43

Inquiries concerning the Intellectual Powers and the Investigation of Truth. Edinburgh: 1832. V. 37; 38

Pathological and Practical Researches on Diseases of the Brain and Spinal Cord. Philadelphia: 1831. V. 42

Pathological and Practical Researches On Diseases of the Brain and Spinal Cord. Philadelphia: 1843. V. 42

The Philosophy of the Moral Feelings. London: 1833. V. 39; 40; 42; 43; 45

ABERCROMBIE, LASCELLES

An Essay Towards a Theory of Art. London: 1922. V. 43

Interludes and Poems. London: 1908. V. 46

Lyrics and Unfinished Poems. London: 1940. V. 40

Lyrics and Unfinished Poems. Newtown: 1940. V. 41; 42; 43; 46

The Sale of Saint Thomas. London: 1930. V. 40

ABERCROMBIE, P.

Cumbrian Regional Planning Scheme, Prepared for the Cumbrian Regional Joint Advisory Scheme. Liverpool: 1932. V. 45

ABERCROMBIE, PATRICK

A Civic Survey and Plan for the City & Royal Burgh of Edinburgh. Edinburgh: 1949. V. 45

ABERCROMBIE, W. R.

Alaska 1899. Copper River Exploring Expedition. Washington: 1900. V. 40

Copper River Exploring Expedition. Washington: 1900. V. 37; 39

ABERCROMBY, DAVID

A Moral Discourse of the Power of Interest. London: 1690. V. 40

ABERCROMBY, PATRICK

The Advantages of the Act of Security, Compar'd with These of the Intended Union . . . N.P.: Edinburgh?: 1706. V. 41; 42

The Martial Achievments of the Scots Nation. Edinburgh: 1711-15. V. 42; 44

ABERDEEN, GEORGE, EARL OF

An Enquiry into the Principles of Beauty in Architecture. London: 1822. V. 37

ABERDEEN, LADY

The Canadian Journal of Lady Aberdeen, 1893-1898. Toronto: 1960. V. 37

ABERG, NILS

The Anglo Saxons in England During the Early Centuries Under the Invasion . . . Uppsala: 1926. V. 45

ABERIGH-MACKAY, GEORGE ROBERT

A Manual of Indian Sport. Bombay: 1876. V. 40

ABERNATHY, JOHN R.

In Camp with Theodore Roosevelt, or the Life of John R. (Jack) Abernathy. Oklahoma City: 1933. V. 45

ABERNETHY, JOHN 1764-1831

Introductory Lectures, Exhibiting Some of Mr. Hunter's Opinions Respecting Life and Diseases . . . London: 1823. V. 42; 43

Surgical Observations on the Constitutional Origin and Treatment of Local Diseases; and on Aneurysms. London: 1809. V. 42; 43

Surgical Observations on the Constitutional Origin and Treatment of Local Diseases; and On Aneurisms, on Diseases Resembling Syphilis; and on Diseases of the Urethra. Philadelphia: 1811. V. 42

The Surgical and Physiological Works of . . . London: 1830. V. 46

Surgical Observations on Diseases Resembling Syphilis; and on Diseases of the Urethra. London: 1810. V. 43; 44

Surgical Observations on Injuries to the Head; and on Miscellaneous Subjects. London: 1810. V. 43

Surgical Observations on Tumours and on Lumbar Abscesses. London: 1811. V. 43; 44

ABERT, JAMES WILLIAM

Message . . . Communicating a Report of an Expedition Led by Lieut. Abert, on the Upper Arkansas and through the Country of the Camanche Indians, in the Fall of the Year 1845. Washington: 1846. V. 37; 38; 39; 40; 41; 43; 45

. . . A Report and Examination of New Mexico, Made by Lieut. J. W. Abert, Of the Topographical Corps. 1848. V. 41

A Report and Map of the Examination of New Mexico. Washington: 1848. V. 38; 39; 42; 46

A Report and Map of the Examination of New Mexico, Made by Lieutenant J. W. Abert, of the Topographic Corps, Feb. 20, 1848. Washington: 1848. V. 43

Report of the Secretary of War Communicating . . . a Report and Map of the Examination of New Mexico. Washington: 1848. V. 37; 38; 42; 43; 45

Through the Country of the Comanche Indians in the Fall of the Year 1845, the Journal of a U.S. Army Expedition Led by Lieut. James W. Abert of the Topographical Engineers. San Francisco: 1970. V. 37; 38; 39; 40; 41; 42; 43

Western America in 1846-1847. San Francisco: 1966. V. 39; 43; 44; 46

ABERT, JOHN JAMES 1788-1863

Report of the Chief Topographical Engineer for the Year 1858 (and) Report of the Chief Topographical Engineer (for the Year 1859). Washington: 1858-59. V. 41; 42

ABERTI, LEONE BATTISTA

L'Architettura . . . Venice: 1565. V. 37

ABINGDON, ALEXANDER

More Boners. Compiled from Classrooms and Examination Papers by Alexander Abingdon, Illustrated by Dr. Seuss. New York: 1931. V. 37; 39; 45

ABINGDON, WILLOUGHBY BERTIE, EARL OF

Thoughts on the Letter of Edmund Burke, Esq. to the Sheriffs of Bristol, on the Affairs of America. Oxford: 1777. V. 45

ABISH, WALTER

Duel Site. New York: 1970. V. 44

ABNEY, WILLIAM DE WIVELESLIE 1843-1920

Colour Vision. Being the Tyndall Lectures Delivered in 1894 at the Royal Instutition. London: 1895. V. 42; 45

Instruction in Photography. London: 1892. V. 39

Thebes and Its Five Greater Temples. London: 1876. V. 44

THE ABORIGINAL Portfolio. Philadelphia: 1835-36. V. 44

ABOTT, ABOTT A.

The Assassination and Death of Abraham Lincoln, President of the United States of America at Washington, on the 14th of April, 1865. New York: 1865. V. 40; 44

ABRAHALL, H. A. HOSKYNS, MRS.

English Minstrelsy. London: 1860. V. 38

ABRAHALL, JOHN HOSKYNS

Western Woods and Waters: Poems and Illustrative Notes. London: 1864. V. 37

ABRAHAM A SANTA CLARA

Neu-Eroeffnete Welt Galleria. Nurenberg: 1703. V. 39; 41

ABRAHAM, ASHLEY P.

Rock-Climbing in Sky. London: 1908. V. 43

ABRAHAM, GEORGE

Rock-Climbing in North Wales. Keswick: 1906. V. 37; 43

ABRAHAM, HAROLD

Extinct Medical Schools of 19th Century Philadelphia. Philadelphia: 1966. V. 45

ABRAHAM, JAMES JOHNSTON

Lettsom. His Life, times, Friends and Descendants. London: 1933. V. 38; 39; 45

ABRAHAM, R. D.

Notes on Chinese Painting, with Reproductions from My Collection. Shanghai: 1932? V. 42

ABRAHAM, RICHARD

A Catalogue of Italian, Flemish, Spanish, Dutch, French and English Pictures; Which Have Been Collected in Euorpe and Brought to this Country by Mr. Richard Abraham, of New Bond Street, London. New York: 1830. V. 39

ABRAHAM Trueman's Letter to James the Scribe. Dublin: 1760. V. 41

ABRAHAMS, PETER

Tell Freedom: Memories of Africa. New York: 1954. V. 42

ABRAMS, ALEXANDER ST. CLAIR

The Trials of the Soldier's Wife. Atlanta: 1864. V. 44

ABRAMS, HERBERT L.

Angiography. Boston: 1961. V. 43

ABRANTES, MIGUEL CALMON DU PIN E ALMEIDA, MARQUES DE 1794-1865

Americus. Cartas Politicas Extrahidas do Padre Amaro. London: 1825-26. V. 39

ABRAVANEL, JUDAH c. 1465-1535

Dailoghi di Amore, Composti per Leone Medico Hebreo. Venice: 1549. V. 45

ABREU DE GALINDA, JUAN DE

The History of the Discovery, and Conquest of the Canary Islands. London: 1764. V. 39

ABREU DE GALINDO, JUAN DE

The History of the Discovery and Conquest of the Canary Islands . . . London: 1767. V. 45

ABREU, SEBASTIAO D'

Vida, e Virtudes do Admiravel Padre Joam Cardim da Companhia de Jesu . . . Evora: 1659. V. 38

AN ABRIDGEMENT of the Secret History of Crete. London: 1711. V. 37

AN ABRIDGMENT of the Regulations for the Formation and Movements of the Cavalry . . . London: 1833. V. 41

AN ABSTRACT of All the Claims on the New Forest, in the County of Southampton. Salisbury: 1776. V. 41

ABSTRACT of the Corn Acts: With Extracts from the Report of the Select Committee Appointed to Take into Consideration an Act made in the Twenty-First Year of the Reign of His Present Majesty . . . London: 1785. V. 41

AN ABSTRACT of the Evidence Delivered Before a Select Committee of the House of Commons in the Years 1790 and 1791 . . . Abolition of the Slave Trade. London: 1791. V. 38; 40

ABSTRACT of the Goods, Wares and Merchandise Exported from the Several States from the 1st of October 1791 to 30th September 1792. Also an Abstract of Duties . . . New York: 1793. V. 41

AN ABSTRACT of the Most Curious and Excellent Thoughts in Seigneur de Montaigne's Essays . . . London: 1701. V. 45

ABSTRACT of the Plans and Arrangements, Adopted and Acted Upon, by His Majesty's Government, for Insuring a Regular Supply of Bread to His Majesty's Forces in Case of Invasion . . . N.P.: 1797-8. V. 43

ABSTRACTS of Wills on File in the Surrogate's Office. City of New York 1665-1801. New York: 1892-1908. V. 40

ABU BAKR IBN AL-TUFAIL

The Improvement of Human Reason Exhibited in the Life of Hai Ebn Yokdhan . . . London: 1708. V. 43

The Life and Surprizing Adventures of Don Antonio de Trezzanio, Who was Self-Educated and Lived Forty Five Years in an Uninhabited Island in the East-Indies. London: 1761. V. 43

ABU MA'SHAR 805 or 806-886

De Magnis Coniunctionibus. Augsburg: 1489. V. 43

ABU OBEYD

The Celebrated Romance of the Stealing of the Mare. Newtown: 1930. V. 43

ABULCACIM Tarif Abentarique, La Verdadera Historia del Rey Don Rodrigo . . . Valencia: 1606. V. 45

ABULFEDA 1273-1331

Ismael Abu'l Feda, de Vita et Rebus Gestis Mohammedis, Moslemicae re Religionis Auctoris, et Imperii Saracenici Fundatoris. Oxford: 1723. V. 39

THE ABUSED Prisoner. London: 1831. V. 38

ABU TALEB, MIRZA

The Travels of Mirza Abu Taleb Khan, in Asia, Africa and Europe, During the Years 1799, 1800, 1801, 1802 and 1803. London: 1810. V. 37

ABU TALIB IBN MUHAMMAD, ISFAHANI 1752-1806?

The Travels of Mirza Abu Taleb Khan, in Asia, Africa, and Europe, During the Years 1799, 1800, 1801, 1802 and 1803. London: 1810. V. 39

ACADEMIE DES BEAUX-ARTS, PARIS.

Memoires de l'Institut National des Science et Arts . . . Literature et Beaux-Arts. Paris: 1798-1804. V. 44

ACADEMIE DES SCIENCES, PARIS.

The Philosophical History and Memoirs of the Royal Academy of Sciences at Paris. London: 1742. V. 40

ACADEMIE ROYALE DES SCIENCES

Divers Ouvrages de Mathematique et de Physique . . . Paris: 1693. V. 46

Memoires de Mathematique et de Physique . . . Paris: 1750/76/80-86. V. 41

ACADEMY OF PACIFIC COAST HISTORY

Publications. Berkeley: 1910-11. V. 41

Publications. Berkeley: 1910-19. V. 44

THE ACADEMY of Pleasure. London: 1656. V. 42

THE ACADIAN Code of Signals . . . Calculated for the Various Numerical and Alphabetical Symbols Used at Sea and by Land. London: 1817. V. 40

A CAMPBELL, ARCHIBALD b. 1787

A Voyage Around the World, From 1806 to 1812. New York: 1817. V. 40

ACARETE DU BISCAY

A Relation of Mr. R. M.'s Voyage to Buenos-Ayres: and From Thence by Land to Potosi. London: 1716. V. 40

ACCADEMIA Degli Intronati. Il Sacrificio Comedia . . . Celebrato ne i Giovochi di uno Carnevale in Siena. Venice: 1585. V. 37

ACCADEMIA DEL CIMENTO

Essays of Natural Experiments Made in the Academie del Cimento, Under the Protection of the Most Serene Prince Leopold of Tuscany. London: 1684. V. 38

ACCARIAS DE SERIONNE, JACQUES

Les Interets des Nations de l'Europe . . . Leiden: 1766. V. 38

La Richesse de la Hollande, Ouvrage dans Lequel on Expose, l'Origine du Commerce et de la Puissance des Hollandois . . . Londres: 1778. V. 46

ACCOLTI, PIETRO

Lo Inganno Degli'occhi, Prospetiva Pratica . . . Florence: 1625. V. 40

ACCOUNT of a Shooting Excursion (of Negroes) on the Mountains Near Dromilly Estate, in the Parish of Trelawny, and Island of Jamaica, in the Month of October, 1824!!! London: 1825. V. 38

AN ACCOUNT Of a Strange and Prodigious Storm of Thunder, Lightening and Hail, Which Happened in and About London, on Tuesday, the Eighteenth of This Instant May; Wherein There Fell some Hail-stones as Big as a Pullets Egg and Others Five & Seven Inches . . . London: 1680. V. 45; 46

AN ACCOUNT of a Voyage to India, China &c. in His Majesty's Ship Caroline, Performed in the Years 1803-4-5 . . . By an Officer of the Caroline. London: 1806. V. 40

AN ACCOUNT of Louisiana, Being an Abstract of Documents, in the Office of the Departments of State, and of the Treasury. Philadelphia: 1803. V. 37; 44

AN ACCOUNT of Mr. Francis Charlton's Surrendering Himself to the Bishop of Oxford, As Also a Copy of the Letter Sent by the Bishop to Madam Charlton, Touching the Same . . . London: 1683. V. 42

AN ACCOUNT of Monsieur De Quesne's Late Expedition at Chio; Together with the Negotiation of Monsieur Guilleragues the French Ambassador at the Port. In a Letter Written by an Officer of the Grand Vizir's to a Pacha. London: 1683. V. 37

AN ACCOUNT of Portugal, As It Appeared in 1776 to Dumouriez . . . London: 1797. V. 43

AN ACCOUNT of Some of the Bloody Deeds of General Jackson. N.P.: 1828. V. 40

AN ACCOUNT of Some Remarkable Passages in the Life of a Private Gentleman . . . London: 1711. V. 46

AN ACCOUNT of the Antiquities, Modern Buildings and Natural Curiosities in the Province of Moray, Worthy of the Attention of the Tourist. Edinburgh: 1813. V. 37; 40

AN ACCOUNT of the Arraignments and Tryals of Col. Richard Kirkby, Capt. John Constable . . . for Cowardice, Neglect of Duty, Breach of Orders, and Other Crimes, Committed by Them in a Fight at Sea, Commence the 19th of August, 1702, Off of St. Martha . . . London: 1703. V. 37; 40

AN ACCOUNT of the Arrangements and Procedure in Westminster Hall Friday 7 May 1937, on the Occasion of the Luncheon of the Empire Parliamentary Association at Which H. M. King George VI Welcomed the Prime Ministers & Other Delegates to the Imperial Confer.. Cambridge: 1937. V. 41

AN ACCOUNT of the Convincement, Exercises, Services and Travel of that Ancient Servant of the Lord, Richard Davies. Newtown: 1928. V. 45; 46

AN ACCOUNT of the Convincement Exercises, Services and Travels of that Ancient Servant of the Lord, Richard Davies. 1928. V. 38

AN ACCOUNT of the Dedication of the West Window of St. John's Church, Beverly Farms, Whitsunday, Mar thirty-first MDCCCCXXV. V. 39

AN ACCOUNT of the Dedication of the West Window of St. John's Church, Beverly Farms Whitsunday, May Thirty First MCCCCXXV. Boston: 1925. V. 41

AN ACCOUNT of the Designs of the Associates of Dr. Bray, With an Abstract of Their Proceedings. London: 1763. V. 42

AN ACCOUNT of the Expedition to Carthagena, with Explanatory Notes and Observations. London: 1743. V. 41

ACCOUNT of the Experiments Tried by the Board of Agriculture in the Composition of Various Sorts of Bread anno 1795. London: 1795. V. 42; 43

AN ACCOUNT of the Extraordinary Abstinence of Ann Moor, of Tutbury, Staffordshire, Who Has, for More Than Two Years . . . Philadelphia: 1810. V. 44

AN ACCOUNT of the Gifts and Legacies that Have Been Given and Bequeathed to Charitable Uses, in the Town of Ipswich. Ipswich: 1819. V. 38

AN ACCOUNT of the Grand Fancy Dress Ball, at Stockport, for the Benefit of the Stockport Dispensary and House of Recovery . . . Stockport: 1828. V. 40

ACCOUNT of the Late Aeronautical Expedition from London to Weilburg, Accomplished by Robert Hollond, Esq., Monck Mason, Esq., and Charles Green, Aeronaut. New York: 1837. V. 37; 40; 43
ACCOUNT Of the Late Aeronautical Expedition from London to Weilburg, Accomplished by Robert Hollond, Esq., Monck Mason, Esq., and Charles Green, Aeronaut. New York: 1837. V. 37

AN ACCOUNT of the Late Proceedings in the Council of the Royal Society, in Order to Remove from Gresham-College into Crane-Court, in Fleet-Street. London: 1710. V. 41

AN ACCOUNT of the Late Terrible Earthquake in Sicily. London: 1793. V. 40

AN ACCOUNT of the Life of that Ancient Servant of Christ, John Richardson, etc. London: 1774. V. 42

AN ACCOUNT of the Loss of His Majesty's Ship Deal Castle. London: 1787. V. 46

AN ACCOUNT of the Manner in Which the Persons Confined in the Prisons of Paris Were Tried and Put to Death, on the 2d and 3d of September Last. London: 1793. V. 42

AN ACCOUNT of the Martyrs at Smyrna and Lyons, in the Second Century. Edinburgh: 1776. V. 40

ACCOUNT of the Most Dangerous Voyage . . . by . . . Capt. John Monck in the Years 1619 and 1620 by the Special Command of Christian IV, King of Denmark, Norway, etc., to Hudson's Straits in Order to Discover a Passage . . . to the West Indies. London: 1704. V. 46

AN ACCOUNT of the Mutinous Seizure of the Bounty. Guilford: 1987. V. 41; 43

AN ACCOUNT of the Operations of the 18th (Indian) Division in Mesopotamia. December 1917 to December 1918. With the Names of all the Units Which Served with the Division and a Nominal Roll of All the Officers and an Introductory Note . . . . 1919. V. 45

AN ACCOUNT of the Origin, Proceedings, and Intentions of the Society for the Promotion of Industry, in the Southern District of the parts of Lindsey, in the County of Lincoln . . . the third edition . . . To this edition is also added . . . Louth: (1790). V. 37

AN ACCOUNT of the Origin, Symptoms, and Cure of the Influenza or Epidemic Catarrh. Philadelphia: 1832. V. 37

AN ACCOUNT Of the Petititioners for the Rev. Mr. Hetherington's Charity. N.P.: 1775. V. 46

AN ACCOUNT of the Proceedings of the Dinner by Mr. George Peabody to the Americans Connected with the Great Exhibition at the London Coffee House Ludgate Hill on the 27th October 1851. London: 1851. V. 41

AN ACCOUNT of the Proceedings on the Trial of Susan B. Anthony, on the Charge of Illegal Voting, at the Presidential Election in Nov., 1872 and on the Trial of Beverly W. Jones, Edwin T. Marsh and William B. Hall, the Inspectors of Election . . . Rochester: 1874. V. 45

AN ACCOUNT of the Progress of an Epidemical Madness. In a Letter to the President and Fellows of the College of Physicians. London: 1735. V. 42

AN ACCOUNT of the Reasons of the Nobility and Gentry's Invitation of His Highness the Prince of Orange Into England. London: 1688. V. 42

AN ACCOUNT of the Rise and Present Establishment of the Lunatick Hospital, in Manchester. Manchester: 1771. V. 42

AN ACCOUNT of the Rise, Progress and Present State of the Society for the Discharge and Relief of Persons Imprisoned for Small Debts Throughout England. London: 1799. V. 40

ACCOUNT of the Siamese Twin Brothers, From Actual Observations. London: 1830. V. 40

AN ACCOUNT of the Spanish Settlements in America in Four Parts. Edinburgh: 1762. V. 40

AN ACCOUNT of the Strata of Northumberland and Durham as Proved by Borings and Sinkings. Newcastle-upon-Tyne: 1878-97. V. 38

ACCOUNT OF THE Terrific and Fatal Riot at the New York Astor Place Opera House, on the Night of May 10, 1849 . . . New York: 1849. V. 41

ACCOUNT Of the Terrific and Fatal Riot at the New York Astor Place Opera House, On the Night of May 10th . . . New York: 1849. V. 43

AN ACCOUNT of the Visit of His Royal Highness The Prince Regent and Their Imperial . . . Majesties The Emperor of Russia and the King of Prussia to the University of Oxford In June MDCCCXIV. Oxford: 1815. V. 37

AN ACCOUNT of the Visit of His Royal Higness, the Prince Regent, with Their Imperial and Royal Majesties the Emperor of all the Russias and the King of Prussia . . . London: 1815. V. 46

ACCOUNTS and Extracts of the Manuscripts in the Library of the King of France. London: 1789. V. 46

ACCUM, FRIEDRICH CHRISTIAN 1769-1838

Chemical Amusement, Comprising a Series of Curious and Instructive Experiments in Chemistry . . . London: 1817. V. 40

Culinary Chemistry, Exhibiting the Scientific Principles of Cookery . . . London: 1821. V. 40

Description of the Process of Manufacturing Coal Gas, for the Lighting of Streets, and Public Buildings, with Elevations . . . London: 1820. V. 42

Description of the Process of Manufacturing Coal Gas for the Lighting of Streets and Public Buildings. London: 1820. V. 38; 40

Elements of Crytallography, After the Method of Hauy. London: 1813. V. 38

A Practical Treatise on Gas-Light . . . London: 1815. V. 44; 45; 46

A Practical Treatise on Gas-Light. London: 1816. V. 37; 38

A Practical Treatise on Gas-Light, Exhibiting a Summary Description of the Apparatus and Machinery Best Calculated for Illuminating Streets, Houses, and Manufactories, with Carburetted Hydrogen or Coal Gas . . . London: 1818. V. 45

A Practical Treatise on the Use and Application of Chemical Tests . . . London: 1818. V. 40; 46

A System of Theoretical and Practical Chemistry. London: 1803. V. 40

A Treatise on Adulterations of Food, and Culinary Poisons, Exhibiting the Fradulent Sophistications of Bread, Beer, Wine, Spirituous Liquors . . . London: 1820. V. 37; 38; 39; 40; 42; 43

A Treatise on the Art of Brewing. London: 1821. V. 38; 39

A Treatise on the Art of Making Wine from Native Fruits . . . London: 1820. V. 43

AN ACCURATE and Impartial Narrative of the War, by an Officer of the Guards . . . London: 1796. V. 40

ACERBI, JOSEPH

Travels through Sweden, Findland and Lapland to the North Cape. London: 1802. V. 37; 38; 40; 41; 42; 43; 44; 45; 46

ACHEBE, CHINUA

No Longer at Ease. New York: 1960. V. 44

Things Fall Apart. New York: 1959. V. 42

ACHESON, JAMES

Chinese Imperial Maritime Customs. Hong Kong: 1884. V. 40

ACHILLES TATIUS

De Clitophontis et Leucippes Amoribus Libri VIII. Heidelberg: 1606. V. 45

De Clitophontis. Leyden: 1606. V. 46

The Loves of Clithophon and Leucippe. Oxford: 1923. V. 39; 46

ACKER, J. M.

Catalogue of a Cabinet of Minerals, Presented for Exhibition at the Industrial Fair of the American Institute by Capt. J. M. Acker of Coulterville, Mariposa Col. Ca. San Francisco: 1865. V. 43

ACKER, KATHY

I Dreamt I Became a Nymphomaniac!: Imagining. San Francisco: 1974. V. 45

ACKERLEY, CHARLES HENRY

A Plan for the Better Security of Vessels Navigating the River Thames. A La Haye: 1834. V. 38

ACKERLEY, J. R.

E. M. Forster a Portrait . . . London: 1970. V. 39

Hindoo Holiday. London: 1932. V. 40; 41; 45

My Dog Tulip. London: 1956. V. 46

Poems by Four Authors. Cambridge: 1923. V. 37

The Prisoners of War - a Play in Three Acts. London: 1925. V. 37; 40; 42; 46

We Think the World of You. London: 1960. V. 46

ACKERMAN, JAMES S.

The Architecture of Michelangelo. London: 1961. V. 44

The Architecture of Michelangelo. New York: London: 1961/64. V. 44

ACKERMANN, RUDOLPH 1764-1834

Ackermann's Repository. London: 1809-28. V. 41

Book of Landscapes and Ruins. London: 1800. V. 42

The History of the Abbey Chura of St. Peter's Westminster, Its Antiquities and Monuments. London: 1812. V. 37; 39; 41; 42; 43; 45; 46

A History of Cambridge, Its Colleges, Halls, Public Buildings. London: 1814-15. V. 46

The History of the College of Winchester. London: 1816. V. 38

The History of the Colleges of Winchester, Eton and Westminster; with the Charter-House, The Schools of St. Paul's Merchant Taylors, Harrow, and Rugby and the Free-School of Christ's Hospital. London: 1816. V. 40

History of Eton College. London: 1816. V. 41

A History of the University of Oxford, Its Colleges, Halls and Public Buildings. London: 1814. V. 42

A History of the University of Oxford, Its Colleges, Halls and Public Buildings. London: 1814. V. 37; 40; 41; 44; 45

A History of the University of Oxford, Its Colleges, Halls and Public Buildings. London: 1814. V. 43

A History of the University of Oxford, Its Colleges, Halls and Public Buildings. (with) A History of the University of Cambridge, Its Colleges, Halls and Public Buildings. (with) the History of the Colleges of Winchester, Eton and Westminster . . . London: 1814-16. V. 45

A History of the University of Cambridge, Its Colleges, Halls and Public Buildings. London: 1815. V. 38; 39; 40; 41; 42

Loyal Volunteers of London and Environs. Infantry and Cavalry in their Respective Uniforms. Introduction by John King. Facsimile of original 1798 Edition. London: 1972. V. 37

The Microcosm of London. London: 1808-10. V. 37; 40; 46

The Microcosm of London. London: 1810. V. 45; 46

Microcosm of London. London: 1904. V. 38; 40

Observations on Ackermann's Patent Moveable Axles for Four Wheeled Carriages. London: 1819. V. 45

Poetical Magazine: Dedicated to the Lovers of the Muse, by the Agent of the Goddess. London: 1809-11. V. 39; 41

Public Schools for Charterhouses, Eton Harrow, Rugby, Winchester. Guildford: 1958. V. 41

The Repository of Arts, Literature, Commerce, Manufactures, Fashions and Politics. London: 1809-15. V. 41

Theatre of Anatomy. London: 1815. V. 37

The Writing School, Christ Hospital. V. 44

ACKLAND, VALENTINE

Later Poems. N.P.: 1970. V. 40

ACKLEY, MARY E.

Crossing the Plains and Early Days in California. San Francisco: 1928. V. 40; 43; 45

ACKROYD, PETER

Country Life. London: 1978. V. 44; 45

Dickens. London: 1990. V. 43

London Lickpenny. London: 1973. V. 42

ACLAND, HENRY

The Oxford Museum. London: 1859. V. 45

ACLAND-TROYTE, C. E.

From the Pyrenees to the Channel in a Dogcart. London: 1887. V. 46

ACOSTA, JOSE DE 1539-1600

Concilium Limense. Celebratum Anno 1583 Sub Gregorio XIII . . . Madrid: 1591. V. 38; 40

Histoire Naturelle et Morale des Indes, tant Orientales qu-Occidentales. Paris: 1600. V. 43

Histoire Naturelle et Morale des Indes, Tant Orientales qu' Occidentales. Paris: 1616. V. 39

Historia Natural y Moral de las Indias, en Que se Tratan las Cosas Notables del Cielo, y Elementos, Metales, Plantas, y Animales Dellas . . . Seville: 1590. V. 45

Historia Naturale, e Morale delle Indie . . . Venice: 1596. V. 40

De Natura de Novi Orbis. Cologne: 1596. V. 38; 39

The Naturall and Morall Historie of the East and West Indies . . . London: 1604. V. 38; 40; 41; 45

The Natural and Moral History of the Indies . . . London: 1880. V. 43

ACOSTA, MANUEL

Rerum a Societate Jesu in Oriente Gestarum . . . De Japonicis Rebus Libri IV. Dilingen: 1571. V. 38

ACRELIUS, ISRAEL

Beskrifning Om de Swenska Forsamlingarnas Forna Och Narwarande Tilstand, Uti Det Sa Kallade Nya Swerige, Sedan Nya Nederland, Men Nu for Tiden Pensylvanien . . . Stockholm: 1759. V. 39; 40; 41; 42; 43; 44; 45

AN ACT, for Securing Certain Estates and Property, for the Support and Uses of the Ministers of the Roman Catholic Religion. Baltimore: 1793? V. 41

THE ACT of Tonnage and Poundage, and rates of Merchandize . . . Digested into an Easie Method, Whereby in one View may be found the several Duties upon each particular Commodity . . . etc. London: 1726. V. 37

AN ACT Relative to Bonds, Due Bills and Other Instruments of Writing and Making them Assignable. Approved, April 20, 1850. (San Jose): (1850). V. 37

ACTA Canonizationis Sanctorum Pii V., Pont, Max., Andreae Avellini, Felicis a Catolicio & Catharinae de Bononia. Rome: 1720. V. 38

ACTIUS, THOMAS

De Ludo Sacchorum in Legali Methodo Tractatus. Pesauro: 1583. V. 40

ACTIVE Anthology. London: 1933. V. 46

ACTON, ELIZA

Modern Cookery, In all Its Branches. London: 1848. V. 41

Modern Cookery in All Its Branches . . . London: 1853. V. 39

Modern Cookery. London: 1858. V. 42

Modern Cookery In All Its Branches. Philadelphia: 1880. V. 39

Modern Cookery in all Its Branches . . . London: 1847. V. 37

ACTON, HAROLD 1904-

Cornelian. London: 1928. V. 37; 39; 41

Five Saints and an Appendix. London: 1927. V. 44

Glue and Lacquer. London: 1941. V. 41

Humdrum. 1928. V. 40

The Last of the Medici. Florence: 1930. V. 42; 46

The Last Medici. London: 1932. V. 41; 43; 46

The Last Bourbons of Naples. London: 1961. V. 38

Memoirs of an Aesthete. London: 1948. V. 38

Old Lamps for New. London: 1965. V. 38; 44

ACTON, JOHN

An Essay on Shooting. London: 1789. V. 43; 45

An Essay on Shooting. London: 1791. V. 39; 42; 45

ACTON, ROGER

The Abyssinian Expedition and the Life and Reign of King Theodore. London: 1868. V. 42

ACTON, WILLIAM

The Functions and Disorders of the Reproductive Organs in Childhood, Youth, Adult Age, and Advanced Life, Considered in Their Physiological, Social and Moral Relations. Philadelphia: 1865. V. 40

THE ACTOR; or, a Peep Behind the Curtain. New York: 1846. V. 40

THE ACTOR; or, Guide to the Stage, Exemplifying the Whole Art of Acting . . . London: 1821. V. 46

THE ACTS and Deeds of the Most Famous and Valiant Champion Sir William Wallace, Knight of Ellerslie. Edinburgh: 1758. V. 45

ACUNA, CHRISTOVAL D'

Voyages and Discoveries in South America. The First Up the River Amazons to Quito in Peru, and Back Again to Brazil, Performed at the Command of the King of Spain . . . London: 1698. V. 38; 40

ADAIR-FITZGERALD, S. J.

The Zankiwank and the Blethwitch. London: 1896. V. 40

ADAIR, JAMES

Adair's History of the American Indians. Johnson City: 1930. V. 38

The History of the American Indians. London: 1775. V. 38; 39; 40; 41; 42; 43; 44; 45

ADAIR, JOHN

Discussions of the Law of Libels as at Present Received, in Which Its Authenticity is Examined . . . London: 1785. V. 42

ADAMS, ELEANOR B.

Missions of New Mexico, 1776. 1956. V. 45

The Missions of New Mexico, 1776. Albuquerque: 1956. V. 38; 42

Missions of New Mexico, 1776. Albqerque: 1975. V. 45

The Missions of New Mexico, 1776: A Description by Fray Francisco Atanasio Dominguez. Albuquerque: 1956, 1975. V. 37

ADAMS, EMMA H.

To and Fro, Up and Dwon in Southern California, with Sketches in Arizona, New Mexico. Cincinnati: 1887. V. 39

To and Fro, Up and Down in Southern California, Oregon, and Washington Territory, with Sketches in Arizona, New Mexico, and British Columbia. Cincinnati: 1888. V. 38; 43; 44

ADAMS, EPHRIAM D.

British Diplomatic Correspondence Concerning the Republic of Texas, 1838-1846. Austin: 1917. V. 42

ADAMS, ERIC

Francis Danby Varities of Poetic Landscape. New Haven: 1973. V. 46

ADAMS, FRANCES COLBURN

Manuel Pereira; or, the Sovereign Rule of South Carolina. Washington: 1853. V. 39; 44

ADAMS, FRANCIS

A Child of the Age. London: 1894. V. 37

ADAMS, FRANCIS COLBURN

The Von Toodelburgs; or, the History of a Very Distinguished Family. Philadelphia: 1868. V. 42

ADAMS, FRANCIS OTTWELL

The History of Japan from the Earliest Period to the Present Time. London: 1874-75. V. 40

ADAMS, FRANK

Old Time Rhymes. London: 1915. V. 42; 45

ADAMS, FRANK DAVID

Ancestors and Descendants of Elias Adams: the Pioneer. Kayesville: 1929. V. 42

ADAMS, FREDERICK B.

Homage to the Book. N.P.: 1968. V. 41

Radical Literature in America: an Address . . . to Which is Appended a Catalogue of an Exhibition Held at the Grolier Club in New York City . . . Stamford: 1939. V. 42

To Russia with Frost. Boston: 1963. V. 37; 40; 41; 42; 45

ADAMS, G. MERCER

Toronto, Old and New: a Memorial Volume. Toronto: 1891. V. 43

ADAMS, GEORGE 1750-1795

Astronomical and Geographical Essays. London: 1789. V. 43

Astronomical and Geographical Essays. London: 1790. V. 40; 42

Astronomical and Geographical Essays . . . London: 1812. V. 40

An Essay on Electricity. London: 1784. V. 38

An Essay on Electricity, Explaining the Theory and Practice of that Useful Science, and the Mode of Applying it to Medical Purposes. London: 1787. V. 39

An Essay on Vision, Briefly Explaining the Fabric of the Eye, and the Nature of Visions . . . London: 1792. V. 39

Essays on the Microscope. London: 1787. V. 40; 44; 45

Essays on the Microscope. London: 1798. V. 38

Geometrical and Graphical Essays. London: 1797. V. 45

Lectures on Natural and Experimental Philosophy . . . London: 1794. V. 40

Lectures On Natural and Experimental Philosophy, Considered In Its Present State of Improvement . . . London: 1799. V. 40; 46

Micrographia Illustrata, or, the Knowledge of the Microscope Explain'd. London. V. 38

Plates for the Essays on the Microscope. London: 1787. V. 45

A Treatise Describing and Explaining the Construction and Use of New Celestial and Terrestrial Globes. London: 1766. V. 45; 46

A Treatise Describing the Construction and Explaining the Use of New Celestial and Terrestial Globes; . . . By George Adams. London: 1810. V. 37

ADAMS, H.

The General of Recent mollusca. London: 1853-1858. V. 37

ADAMS, H. C.

Who Was Philip? London: 1886. V. 39; 46

ADAMS, H. G. 1811-1891

Humming Birds Described and Illustrated. London. V. 42

Humming Birds Described and Illustrated. London. V. 45

Humming Birds Described and Illustrated. London. V. 43

Humming Birds, Described and Illustrated. London: 1856. V. 39

Humming Birds. London: n.d. V. 37

Humming Birds. Described and illustrated with eight hand coloured plates. London: (n.d.). V. 37

The Smaller British Birds. London: 1874. V. 37

ADAMS, H. ISABEL

Wild Flowers of the British Isles. London: 1910. V. 46

ADAMS, H. M.

Catalogue of Books Printed on the Continent of Europe, 1501-1600 in Cambridge Libraries. Volume II N-Z. Cambridge: 1967. V. 39

ADAMS, HANNAH 1755-1831

An Abridgement of the History of New England, for the Use of Young Persons. Boston: 1807. V. 40

A Memoir of Miss Hannah Adams, Written by Herself. Boston: 1832. V. 44; 45; 46

A Summary History of New England, From the First Settlement at Plymouth, to the Acceptance of the Federal Constitution. Dedham: 1799. V. 39; 42; 43

The Truth and Excellence of the Christian Religion Exhibited. Boston: 1804. V. 40; 44; 45

A View of Religions, In Two Parts. Boston: 1791. V. 44; 45

A View of Religions. Boston: 1801. V. 45

A View of Religions, in Two Parts. Boston: 1801. V. 37; 42; 43; 44

ADAMS, HELEN

Selected Poems and Ballads. New York: 1975. V. 39

ADAMS, HENRY 1838-1918

Democracy, an American Novel. New York: 1880. V. 39; 40; 41; 43

Democracy, an American Novel . . . London: 1882. V. 40; 43

Documents Relating to New England Federalism, 1800-1815. Boston: 1877. V. 39; 42

The Education of Henry Adams. Washington: 1907. V. 44

The Education of Henry Adams: an Autobiography. Boston: 1944. V. 46

Historical Essays. New York: 1891. V. 39; 42; 43

History of the United States of America, 1801-1813. New York: 1889-90. V. 39

History of the United States . . . During the Administration of Thomas Jefferson (1801-1817). New York: 1921. V. 46

Kansas Territory. Woodson Town Association . . . Greenwood: 1856. V. 42

A Letter to American Teachers of History. Washington: 1910. V. 38

Letters to a Niece and Prayer to the Virgin of Chartres. Boston & New York: 1920. V. 40

The Life of Albert Gallatin. Philadelphia: 1879. V. 41; 42

The Life of George Cabot Lodge. Boston: 1911. V. 38; 40

Memoirs of Arii Taimai E Marama of Eimeo, Teriirere of Tooarai. Paris: 1901. V. 39; 40; 44

Mont Saint Michel and Chartres. Washington: 1912. V. 39

Mont-Saint Michel and Chartes. New York: 1957. V. 46

Mont-Saint-Michel and Chartres. Boston;: 1919. V. 37

The Tendency of History. Washington: 1896. V. 41

ADAMS, HERBERT M.

Catalogue of the Books printed on the Continent of Europe 1501-1600 in Cambridge Libraries. Cambridge: 1967. V. 46

ADAMS, J. G.

Our Day. Boston: 1848. V. 43

ADAMS, JAMES A.

Pioneering in Cuba. Concord: 1901. V. 42

ADAMS, JAMES H.

Reports of the Committee to Whom Was Referred the Message of Governor James H. Adams, Relating to Slavery and the Slave Trade. Columbia: 1857. V. 45

ADAMS, JAMES TRUSLOW 1879-1949

Album of American History. New York: 1944-48. V. 46

Atlas of American History. New York: 1943. V. 38

Dicationary of American History. New York: 1940. V. 46

History of the United States. New York: 1933. V. 42; 44; 46

Memorials of Old Bridgehampton. Bridgehampton: 1916. V. 46

ADAMS, JEREMY DUQUESNAY

A Leaf from the Letters of St. Jerome: First Printed by Sixtus Reissinger, Rome, c. 1466-1467. Los Angeles: 1981. V. 37

ADAMS, JOHN

V. 46

ADAMS, JOHN continued

An Address of the Convention, for Framing a New Constitution of Government, for the State of Massachusetts Bay, to Their Constituents. Boston: 1780. V. 37; 39; 41; 44

Analysis of Horsemanship: Teaching the Whole Art of Riding in the Manege, Military, Hunting, Racing, or Travelling System. London: 1799. V. 45

Authentic Copies of the Correspondence of Charles Cotesworth Pinckney, John Marshall and Ellbridge Gerry, Esqrs . . . London: 1798. V. 46

The Constitution or Frame of Government for the Commonwealth of Massachusetts. Boston: 1781. V. 37

Correspondence Between the Hon. John Adams . . . and the Late Wm. Cunningham. Boston: 1823. V. 39; 42

A Defence of the Constitutions of Government of the United States of America. London: 1787. V. 37; 39

A Defence of the Constitutions of Governemnt of the United States of America. London: 1787-88. V. 39

A Defence of the Constitutions of Government of the United States of America. Philadelphia: 1788. V. 41

A Defence of the Constitutions of Government of the United States of America, Against the Attack of M. Turgot in His Letters to Dr. Price . . . London: 1794. V. 43

A Defence of the Constitutions of Government of the United States of America, Against the Attack of M. Turgot in His Letter to Dr. Price, dated the Twenty-Second Day of March, 1778. Philadelphia: 1797. V. 37; 38

Diary and Autobiography of John Adams. Cambridge: 1962. V. 44

The Flowers of Ancient History . . . Dublin: 1789. V. 46

The Flowers of Ancient History . . . London: 1790. V. 41

The Flowers of Modern Travels; Being, Elegant, Entertaining and Instructive Extracts Selected from the Works of the Most Celebrated Travellers . . . Boston: 1797. V. 44; 45

Index Villaris; or, an Alphabetical Table of all the Cities, Market-Towns, Parishes, Vilages and Private Seats in England and Wales. London: 1680. V. 38; 41

Novanglus & Massuchesettensis, or Political Essays Published in the Years 1774 and 1775. Boston: 1819. V. 39

Poems on Several Occasions, Original and Translated. Boston: 1745. V. 37

Sketches of the History, Genius, Disposition, Accomplishments, Employments, Customs, Virtues and Vices of the Fair Sex . . . Philadelphia: 1797. V. 45

Sketches of the History, Genius, Disposition, Accomplishments, Employments, Customs, Virtues and Vices of the Fair Sex. Boston: 1807. V. 44

Twenty Six Letters, Upon Interesting Subjects Respecting the Revolution in America. London: 1786. V. 42

Woman: Sketches of the History, Genius, Disposition, Accomplishments, Employments, Customs and Importance of the Fair Sex, In All Parts of the World. London: 1790. V. 45

The Works of John Adams, Second President of the U.S . . . Boston: 1856. V. 46

ADAMS, JOHN COLEMAN

Nature Studies in Berkshire, by John Coleman Adams. New York: 1899. V. 37; 42

ADAMS, JOHN QUINCY 1767-1848

Argument . . . Before the Supreme Court of the United States, in the Case of the United States . . . vs. Cinque . . . Captured in the Schooner Amistad. New York: 1841. V. 46

Boundary on the Pacific Ocean: Correspondence with the British Government. Washington: 1826. V. 37

A Catalogue of the Books of John Quincy Adams in the Boston Athenaeum with Notes on Books, Adams Seals and Bookplates. Boston: 1938. V. 41

Commissioners Under the Treaty of Ghent: Proceedings of the Joint Commission of Indemnities. Washington: 1826. V. 37

Dermot Mac Morrogh, or the Conquest of Ireland. Columbus: 1834. V. 40

The Duplicate Letters, The Fisheries and the Mississippi. Washington: 1822. V. 37; 43

The Duplicate Letters, the Fisheries and the Mississippi. Louisville: 1823. V. 42

An Inaugural Oration, Delivered at the Author's Installation, as Boylston Professor of Rhetorick and Oratory at Harvard Unviersity. Boston: 1806. V. 41

Lectures on Rhetoric and Oratory, Delivered to the Classes of Senior and Junior Sophisters in Harvard University. Cambridge: 1810. V. 37

Memoirs of . . . Philadelphia: 1874. V. 46

Observations on Paine's Rights of Man, in a Series of Letters, by Publicola. Edinburgh: 1792. V. 41

Oration on the Life and Character of Gilbert Motier de Lafayette. Delivered at the Request of Both Houses of Congress of the United States, Before Them, in the House of Representatives at Washington, on 31st of Dec. 1834. Washington: 1835. V. 39; 41

An Oration Delivered Before the Inhabitants of the Town of Newburyport . . . on the Sixty-First Anniversary of the Declaration of Independence July 4, 1837. Newburyport: 1837. V. 42

Poems of Religion and Society. Auburn: 1850. V. 41

Speech (Suppressed by the Previous Question) of . . . of Massachusetts, on the Removal of the Public Deposites, and Its Reasons. Washington: 1834. V. 41; 44

Speech . . . Relating to the Annexation of Texas. Washington: 1838. V. 37

Texas. Washington: 1842. V. 38; 39

Writings, 1779-1823. New York: 1913-17. V. 39; 40; 46

ADAMS, JOSEPH

Memoirs of the Life and Doctrines of the Late John Hunter, Esq. Founder of the Hunterian Museum . . . London: 1817. V. 38; 39; 40

Memoirs of the Life and Doctrines of the Late John Hunter, Esq. Founder of the Hunterian Museum at the Royal College of Surgeons in London. London: 1818. V. 41; 42

Observations on Morbid Poisons, Chronic and Acute. London: 1807. V. 42

Observations on Morbi Poisons, Phagedaena, and Cancer. London: 1795. V. 37

ADAMS, LEONIE

Those Not Elect. New York: 1925. V. 39; 41; 42

ADAMS, MARY M.

The Choir Visible. Chicago: 1897. V. 38

ADAMS, MARYLINE POOLE

Mistletoe: Legends, Myths and Folk Lore. Berkeley: 1984. V. 39

ADAMS, MAURICE S. R.

Modern Decorative Art. London: 1930. V. 44

ADAMS, MICHAEL

Province of New Brunswick. Fredericton: 1879. V. 46

ADAMS, N.

A Voyage Around the World. Boston: 1871. V. 41

ADAMS, NATHANIEL

Annals of Portsmouth. Comprising a Period of Two Hundred Years from the First Settlement of the Town. Portsmouth: 1825. V. 42; 43

ADAMS, OSCAR FAY

The Story of Jane Austen's Life. Boston: 1897. V. 41; 43; 45

ADAMS, RAMON F.

The Adams One Fifty: a Checklist of the 150 Most Important Books on Western Outlaws and Lawmen. (with) Six Score: the 120 Best Books on the Range Cattle Industry. Austin: 1976. V. 44; 45; 46

A Bibliography of Books and Pamphlets on Western Outlaws and Gunmen. Six Guns and Saddle Leather. Norman: 1969. V. 40

Burrs Under the Saddle. Norman: 1964. V. 42; 43; 44

Burrs Under the Saddle. Norman: 1966. V. 43

Charles M. Russell. The Cowboy Artist. A Biography. Pasadena: 1948. V. 45; 46

The Old-Time Cowhand. New York: 1961. V. 42

Rampaging Herd, a Bibliography of Books & Pamphlets on Men and Events in the Catle Industry. Norman: 1959. V. 37; 39; 40; 42; 44; 46

Six Guns & Saddle Leather. Norman: 1954. V. 39; 42; 43; 44; 46

Six-Guns and Saddle Leather. Norman: 1969. V. 37; 38; 42

ADAMS, RANDOLPH G.

The Headquarters Papers of the British Army in North America During the War of the American Revolution. Ann Arbor: 1926. V. 40; 44

ADAMS, RICHARD

The Girl in a Swing. London: 1980. V. 37; 40; 46

The Ledgend of Te Tuna. Los Angeles: 1982. V. 38

Watership Down. New York. V. 41

Watership Down. London: 1972. V. 37; 39; 40; 42; 43; 45; 46

Watership Down. New York: 1972. V. 41; 43; 45

Watership Down. Sydney: 1972. V. 44; 45

Watership Down. New York: 1974. V. 37; 40; 43

Watership Down. London: 1976. V. 41

Watership Down. Middlesex: 1976. V. 39

Watership Down. New York: 1974, c. 1972. V. 37

Watership Down. By Richard Adams. Illustrated by John Lawrence. 1976. V. 37

Watership Down. With many illustrations throughout, a number full page, both in black and white and full colour from the Originals by John Lawrence. Paradine: 1976. V. 37

ADAMS, RICHARD C.

A Delaware Indian Legend and the Story of Their Troubles. Washington: 1899. V. 38; 39

ADAMS, ROBERT

The Narrative of, Who Was Wrecked in the Year 1810 on the Western Coast of Africa, was Detained Three Years in Slavery by the Arabs and Resided Several Months in the City of Tombuctoo. London: 1816. V. 39

ADAMS, SAMUEL

An Appeal to the World or a Vindication of the Town of Boston, from Many false and Malicious Asperions Contained in Certain Letters and Memorials . . . London: 1770. V. 45; 46

An Oration Delivered at the State-House in Philadelphia, to a Very Numerous Audience; on . . . the 1st of August, 1776; By Samuel Adams . . . Philadelphia: 1776. V. 41

The Writings of . . . . (1764-1802). New York: 1904-08. V. 46

The Writings of . . . 1764-1802. New York: 1904. V. 37

ADAMS, SAMUEL H.

Average Jones. 1911. V. 39

ADAMS, SEBASTIAN C.

illustrated Panorama of History. V. 44

ADAMS, THOMAS

The Humble Petititon of the Worshipful Thomas Adams, John Langham and James Bunce, Aldermen of London, Presented to the Lords . . . April 25, 1648. London: 1648. V. 43

ADAMS, THOMAS F.

Typographia: a Brief Sketch of the Origin, Rise and progress of the Typographic Art: with Practical Directions for Conducting Every Department in an Office. Philaelphia: 1837. V. 39

Typographia: or the Printer's Instructor; a Brief Sketch of the Origin, Rise and Progress of the Typographic Art. Philadelphia: 1844. V. 39

Typographia. Philadelphia: 1853. V. 39

Typographia . . . New York: 1856. V. 44

ADAMS, THOMAS R.

The American Controversy, A Bibliographical Study of the British Pamphlets About the American Disputes 1764-1783. Providence: 1980. V. 43

ADAMS, W. H. DAVENPORT

Windsor Castle and the Water-Way Thither. London: 1880. V. 44

ADAMS, W. L.

Centennial Address Delivered by Dr. W.L. Adams, of Portland, Oregon at the Oregon State Fair October 13th, 1876. Portland: 1876. V. 37

ADAMS, WILLIAM

Lectures on the Pathology and Treatment of Lateral and Other Forms of Curvature of the Spine. London: 1865. V. 42

Sacred Allegories. London: 1859. V. 42; 44

ADAMS, WILLIAM BRIDGES 1797-1872

English Pleasure Carriages. London: 1837. V. 38; 39; 45; 46

The Producing Man's Companion . . . London: 1833. V. 41

ADAMS, WILLIAM TAYLOR 1822-1897

Across India or Live Boys in the Far East. Boston. V. 41

Hatchie, the Guardian Slave; or, The Heiress of Bellevue. Boston: 1853. V. 43

ADAMSON, C. E.

Haltwhistle. A History of the Manor and the Church of Haltwhistle. South Shields. V. 45

ADAMSON, JAMES

Sketches of Our Information as to Rail-Roads. Also, an Account of the Stockton and Darlington Rail-Way, with Observations on Rail-Ways. Newcastle: 1826. V. 46

ADAMSON, JOHN 1787-1855

Bibliotheca Lusitana . . . Forming a Part of the Library of . . . Newcastle on Tyne: 1836. V. 37; 42

Lusitania Illustrada: Notices on the History, Antiquities, Literature &c. of Portugal. Newcastle-upon-Tyne: 1842-46. V. 45

Memoirs of the Life and Writings of Luis de Camoens. London: 1820. V. 45

ADAMSON, THOMAS

Englands Defence. A Treatise Concerning Invasion: or, a Brief Discourse of What Orders Were Best for Repulsing of Foreign Forces. (with) An Account of Such Stores of War, and other Materials as are Requisite for the Defence of a Fort . . . London: 1680. V. 38

ADAMUS, MELCHIOR

The Life and Death of Dr. Martin Luther. London: 1641. V. 40

ADANSON, MICHEL

Histoire Naturelle du Senegal Coquillages . . . Paris: 1757. V. 38; 40

A Voyage to Senegal, in the Isle of Goree, and the River Gambia. London: 1759. V. 43

ADCOCK, A. ST. JOHN

The Glory that Was Grub Street. London: 1920's. V. 41

Gods of Modern Grub Street. Impressions of Contemporary Authors. London. V. 43

ADCOCK, FLEUR

The Eye of the Hurricane. Wellington: 1964. V. 43

ADCOCK, HENRY

Adcock's Syllabus of a Course of Eight Lectures in Mechanical Philosophy, Including Numerous Rules, Tables and Data with Illustrative Remarks for Practical Application. Leeds: 1832. V. 45

ADDA, GIOACHIMO D'

La Metropolitana di Milano e Dettagli Rimarcabili di Questo Edificio . . . Milan: 1824. V. 38

ADDAMS, CHARLES

Creature Comforts. New York: 1981. V. 45; 46

ADDAMS, JANE

Hull House Maps and Papers, a Presentation of Nationalities and Wages in a Congested District of Chicago, Together With Comments and Essays on problems Growing Out of the Social Conditions. New York & Boston: 1895. V. 40

The Second Twenty Years at Hull-House, September 1909 to September 1929; With a Record of a Growing World Consciousness. New York: 1930. V. 42; 44

Twenty Years at Hull-House. New York: 1910. V. 40; 42; 43; 44

ADDERLEY, H. A.

History of the Warwickshire Yeomnry Cavalry. Warwick,: 1896. V. 38

ADDINGTON, A. C.

The Royal House of Stuart: The Descendants of King James VI of Scotland (James I of England). London: 1971. V. 46

The Royal House of Stuart: The Descendants of King James VI of Scotland (James I of England). London: (1971). V. 37

ADDINGTON, WILLIAM

An Abridgement of Penal Statutes, Which Exhibits at One View. London: 1786. V. 37; 44

An Abridgment of the Penal Statues, Which Exhibit at One View the Offences, and the Punishments or Penalties in Consequence of Those Offences . . . London: 1812. V. 39; 42; 43; 46

An Abridgment of the Penal Statutes, Which Exhibit at One View the Offences and the Punishments or Penalties in Consequence to Those Offences . . . London: 1812. V. 46

ADDISON, ALEXANDER

Analysis of the Report of the Committee of the Virginia Assembly. Philadelphia: 1800. V. 41

ADDISON, CHARLES G.

Damascus and Palmyra, a Journey to the East. London: 1838. V. 37; 39; 40; 44; 45

The History of the Knights Templars, the Temple Church and the Temple. London: 1842. V. 38; 39

ADDISON, FRANK

The Wellcome Excavations in the Sudan. London: 1949-51. V. 40; 44

ADDISON, HENRY ROBERT

Paris Social. A Sketch of Every-Day Life in the French Metropolis. London: 1866. V. 38

ADDISON, JOSEPH 1672-1719

The Campaign, a Poem to His Grace the Duke of Marlborough. Edinburgh: 1705. V. 41; 45

The Campaign, a Poem, to His Grace the Duke of Marlborough. London: 1705. V. 37

Cato, a Tragedy. In Firenze. V. 42

Cato. London: 1713. V. 37; 38; 45

Cato. A Tragedy. Florence: 1725. V. 38

The Drummer; or, the Haunted House. London: 1716. V. 38

The Free Holder. London: 1716. V. 41

The Free-Holder, or Political Essays. London: 1716. V. 38

The Free-Holder, or Political Essays. London: 1716. V. 45; 46

The Free-Holder; or, Political Essays. London: 1758. V. 38; 39; 41

Interesting Anecdotes, Memoirs, Allegories, Essays and Poetical Fragments. London: 1796. V. 40

Le Mentor Moderne, ou Discours sur les Moeurs du Siecle. Amsterdam: 1727. V. 39

Miscellaneous Works in Verse and Prose. London: 1726. V. 43

Miscellaneous Works . . . (with) Remarks on Several Parts of Italy &c. in the Years 1701, 1702, 1703. London: 1736/33. V. 43

The Miscellaneous Works. London: 1765. V. 37; 38; 40; 43; 46

The Miscellaneous Works, in Verse and Prose. Dublin: 1773. V. 41; 43

The Miscellaneous Works in Verse and Prose of . . . London: 1777. V. 38; 43

Miscellanies in Prose and Verse, in Three Volumes. Glasgow: 1754. V. 46

The Papers of Joseph Addison, Esq. in the Tatler, Spectator, Guardian and Freeholder . . . Edinburgh: 1790. V. 45

ADDISON, JOSEPH 1672-1719 continued

Poems on Several Occasions. With a Dissertation Upon the Roman Poets. London: 1719. V. 38; 43; 45

Poems on Several Occasions. London: 1719/1718. V. 41; 43

Remarks On Several Parts of Italy, Etc. in the years 1701, 1702, 1703. V. 38

Remarks on Several Parts of Italy. London: 1705. V. 37; 40; 41; 42; 44

Remarks on Several Parts of Italy in the Years 1701, 1702, 1703. London: 1745. V. 46

Rosamond. London: 1707. V. 45

The Sir Roger de Coverly Papers, from the Spectator, 1711-1712. New York: 1945. V. 43

The Works of the Right and Honourable Joseph Addison, Esq. London: 1721. V. 37; 38; 39; 45; 46

The Works. Dublin: 1722-23. V. 43

Works. Birmingham: 1761. V. 38; 39; 40; 42; 45; 46

The Works of the Right Honourable . . . London: 1804. V. 40

The Works. London: 1811. V. 38; 40

The Works . . . New York: 1860. V. 40

The Works. London: 1887. V. 42; 46

The Works . . . London: 1730. V. 37

ADDISON, LANCELOT

West Barbary, or A Short Narrative of the Revolution of the Kingdoms of Fez and Morocco. Oxford: 1671. V. 41

West Barbary, or a Short Narrative of the Revolutions of the Kingdoms of Fez and Morocco. Oxford: 1671. V. 38; 41; 43; 45

ADDISON, THOMAS

A Collection of the Published Writings. London: 1868. V. 37; 38; 40; 41; 42; 43

On The Constitutional and Local Effects of Disease of the Supra-Renal Capsules. London: 1968. V. 38

On the Constitutional and Local Effects of Disease of the Supra-Renal Capsules. London: 1968. V. 43

On the Constitutional and Local Effects of Disease of the Supra-renal Capsules. London: 1855. V. 37

ADDISON, WILLIAM 1802-1881

On Healthy and Diseased Structure and the True Principles of Treatment for the Cure of Disease . . . London: 1849. V. 39

ADDITIONAL Papers Relative to the Arctic Expedition Under the Orders of Captain Austin and Mr. William Penny. London: 1851. V. 45

ADDRESS and Regulations of the Astronomical Society of London: Established February 8, 1820. London: 1821. V. 39

AN ADDRESS Before the 'Mystic Fraternity' at Thetford, Vt. On the Death of Brother Levi Root, Who Departed This Life, Sept. 4, 1826. Haverhill: 1826. V. 44

ADDRESS from the Carrier of the Herald, to His Friends and Patrons, Wishing Them a Happy New Year. Newburyport: 1825. V. 39

AN ADDRESS from the Independent Freeholders of the P---v---ce of M--ns---r, to Sir R----- C------ Baronet. London: 1754. V. 45

AN ADDRESS Of Great Importance (at least in the Opinion of the Writer), to the Natives of England, the Emigrants from France, and the Rulers of Both Countries. London: 1798. V. 39

AN ADDRESS of Thanks to the Broad Bottoms, for the Good Things They Have Done, and the Evil Things They Have Not Done, Since Their Elevation. London: 1745. V. 40; 41; 42; 43; 45

ADDRESS of the Atlanta Register to the People of the Confederate States. Atlanta: 1864. V. 44

ADDRESS of the Carrier of the Newburyport Herald at the Commencement of the New Year. To His Friends and patrons, with the Compliments of the Season. Newburyport: 1826. V. 39

ADDRESS of the Carriers of Poulson's American Daily Advertiser, To Its Patrons, ont he Commencment of the Year 1808. Philadelphia: 1807. V. 40

AN ADDRESS of the Convention for Framing a New Constitution of Government, for the State of Massachusetts Bay, to Their Constituents. Boston: 1780. V. 37; 44

ADDRESS of the Friends of the Domestic Industry, Assembled in Convention, at New York, October 26, 1831, to the People of the United States. Baltimore: 1831. V. 42

ADDRESS of the Louisiana Native American Association, to the Citizens of Louisiana and the Inhabitants of the United States. New Orleans,: 1839. V. 37

THE ADDRESS of the Minority in the Virginia Legislature to the People of that State . . . Richmond: 1799. V. 37; 41

AN ADDRESS to a Young Lady on Her Entrance into the World. London: 1796. V. 38

AN ADDRESS to Britons. London: 174-. V. 41

AN ADDRESS to Such of the Electors of Great Britain, as ARe Not Makers of Cyder and Perry. London: 1763. V. 38; 39; 40

AN ADDRESS to the Associated Friends of the People. Edinburgh: 1792. V. 40

AN ADDRESS To the Citizens of the United States, on the Subject of Slavery. N.P.: 1838. V. 42

AN ADDRESS to the Committee of the Merchant's Society. Dublin: 1761. V. 40

AN ADDRESS to the Jurymen of London. London: 1752. V. 41

AN ADDRESS to the Labourers on the Subject of Destroying Machinery. London: 1830. V. 42

AN ADDRESS to the People of Maine, on the Question of Separation, by the Convention of Delegates, Assembled at Brunswick, August 1, 1816. Brunswick: 1816. V. 42

ADDRESS to the People of New Jersey, Relative to a Bridge Over the Delaware River at Trenton and a Rail-Road from Trenton to New Brunswick. N.P.: 1834. V. 46

AN ADDRESS to the People of the United States, on the Policy of Maintaining a Permanent Navy. Philadelphia: 1802. V. 45

AN ADDRESS to the Proprietors of India Stock, Shewing from the Political State of Indostan, the Necessity of Sending Commissioners to Regulate and Direct Their Affairs Abroad . . . London: 1769. V. 41

AN ADDRESS to the Proprietors of the South-Sea Capital. London: 1732. V. 37; 39; 41

AN ADDRESS to the Public, from the Society for the Improvement of Naval Architecture. London: 1791. V. 41

AN ADDRESS to the Quarterly, Monthly and Preparative Meetings and the members Thereof, Composing the Yearly Meeting of Friends, Held in Philadelphia . . . Philadelphia: 1839. V. 45

AN ADDRESS to the Worshipful Company of Barbers in Oxford . . . Oxford: 1749. V. 42

ADDRESSES and Recommendations to the States by the United States in Congress Assembled. Philadelphia: 1783. V. 44

ADDRESSES, Remonstrances and Petitions; Commencing the 24th of June, 1769, Presented to the King and Parliament, from the Court of Common Council, and Livery in Common Hall Assembled with His Majesty's Answers . . . London: 1778. V. 39

ADE, GEORGE

Circus Day. New York: & Chicago: 1896. V. 42

Fables in Slang. Chicago & New York: 1900. V. 43; 46

Forty Modern Fables. New York: 1901. V. 39

One Afternoon with Mark Twain. Chicago: 1939. V. 43

People You Know. Illustrated by John T. McCutcheon and Others. New York: 1903. V. 37

The Strenuous Lad's Library Number 2. Clarence Allen The Hypnotic Boy Journalist or the Mysterious Disappearance of the United States Government Bonds. Phoenix: 1903. V. 40

Thirty Fables in Slang. New York: 1933. V. 39

True Bills. New York: 1904. V. 39

ADELMAN, SEYMOUR

The Adelman Collection. Bryn Mawr: 1976. V. 46

ADELMANN, HOWARD

Marcello Malpighi and the Evolution of Embryology. Ithaca: 1966. V. 37; 38; 41; 42; 45; 46

ADELMANN, HOWARD B.

The Correspondence of Marcello Malpighi, edited by Howard B. Adelmann. Ithaca: 1975. V. 37

Marcello Malpighi and the Evolution of Embryology. New York: 1966. V. 45

ADELUNG, JOHANN CHRISTOPH 1732-1806

Geschichte der Philosophie fur Liebhaber. Leipzig: 1786-87. V. 40

Leipziger Wochenblatt fur Kinder. Leipzig: 1773-4. V. 40

Mithradetes Oder Allgemeine Sprach Enkunde Mit dem Vater Unser Als Sprachprobe in Beynahe Funfhundert Sprachen und Mundarten . . . Berlin: 1806-17. V. 40

Three Philological Essays. London: 1798. V. 37

Versuch Eines Vollstandigen Grammatisch-Kritischen Worterbuches Der Hochdeutschen Mundart mit Bestandiger Vergleichung der Ubrigen Mundarten . . . Leipzig: 1774-80. V. 39

ADELUNG, JOHANN CHRISTOPH 1732-1806 continued

Versuch Eines Vollstandigen Grammatisch-Kritischen Worterbuches der Hochdeutschen Mundart mit Bestandiger Vergleichung der Ubrigen Mundarten, Besonders aber der Oberdeutschen. Leizpig: 1774-86. V. 40; 41; 43

ADEMOLA, FRANCES

Reflections. Lagos: 1962. V. 42

ADES, DAWN

Dada and Surrealism Reviewed. London: 1978. V. 39; 42; 46

ADHEMAR, J.

Toulouse-Lautrec, His Complete Lithographs and Drypoints. New York: 1965. V. 46

ADHEMAR, JEAN

Degas: the Complete Etchings, Lithographs and Monotypes. New York: 1975. V. 37; 40

Edgar Degas: Gravures et Monotypes. Paris: 1973. V. 43

Toulouse-Lautrec: His Complete Lithographs and Drypoints. New York. V. 37; 40; 44

ADIMARI, ALESSANDRO 1579-1649

La Calliope Overo XXXXX Sonetti Morali . . . Florence: 1641. V. 43

ADLAM, GLADYS M.

Forty Years of Bull Terriers. London: 1952. V. 40

ADLARD, JOHN

Owen Seaman: His Life and Work. London: 1977. V. 41

ADLER, BRUNO

Utopia. Dokumente der Wirklichkeit. Weimar: 1921. V. 40

ADLER, ELMER

Catalogue of an Exhibition of Portraitures by James McNeill Whistler. The Memorial Art Gallery, Rochester. Rochester: 1915. V. 44

Quarto Club Papers 1928, 1929. New York: 1930. V. 39

ADLER, MICHAEL

British Jewry Book of Honour. London: 1922. V. 46

ADLER, STAN

Sagebush Strokes. Yarns of the Southwestern Range. Bisbee: 1938. V. 39

ADLRICH, THOMAS BAILEY 1836-1907

The Story of a Bad Boy. Boston: 1870. V. 37

ADLUM, JOHN

A Memoir on the Cultivation of the Vine in America, and the Best Mode of Making Wine. Washington: 1828. V. 38; 39

ADMINISTRATION Dissected. In Which the Grand National Culprits, Are Laid Open for the Public Inspection. London: 1779. V. 37

ADMIRAL Mathew's Charge Against Vice-Admiral Lestock Dissected and Confuted, by a King's Letterman. London: 1745. V. 40; 41

ADOLPHUS, J. H.

A Correct, Full and Impartial Report, of the Trial of Her Majesty, Caroline, Queen Consort of Great Britain, Before the House of Peers . . . London: 1820. V. 46

ADOLPHUS, JOHN

Memoirs of John Bannister, Comedian. London: 1839. V. 43

ADOMEIT, RUTH E.

The Miniature Book Collector. Woodstock: 1960-63. V. 41

An Original Leaf from the Newberry Bible, 1780. Los Angeles: 1980. V. 41

ADONIA, a Desultory Story. London: 1801. V. 38; 41

ADORNO, THEODOR W.

The Authoritarian Personality. New York: 1950. V. 44

ADRIAN, E. D.

The Basis of Sensation, The Action of the Sense Organs. London: 1928. V. 37

ADRIANO, D. C.

Trace Elements in the Terrestrial Environment. Berlin: 1986. V. 37

ADRIANUS CARTHUSIENSIS

De Remediis Utriusque Fortunae. Cologne: 1470. V. 42

ADSHEAD, JOSEPH

On Juvenile Criminals, Reformatories, and the Means of Rendering the Perishing and Dangerous Classes Serviceable to the State. Manchester: 1856. V. 42

Our Present Gaol System Deeply Depraving to the Prisoner and a Positive Evil to the Community. N.P.: 1847. V. 42

Prisons and Prisoners. London: 1845. V. 41; 42

ADSONVILLE: Marrying Out. Albany: 1824. V. 45

ADVANCES in Insect Physiology. 1963-1978. V. 38

THE ADVANTAGES of Deliberation; or, the Folly of Indiscretion. London: 1772. V. 42

THE ADVANTAGES of the Difinitive (sic) Treaty, to the People of Great Britain, Demonstrated. London: 1749. V. 46

THE ADVANTAGES of the Hanover Succession, and English Ingratitude Freely and Impartially Considered and Examined. London: 1744. V. 41

ADVANTAGES of the Revolution Illustrated by a View of the Present State of Great Britain, in a Letter to a member of Parliament. London: 1753. V. 44

THE ADVENTURER. London: 1752-54. V. 44
THE ADVENTURER. London: 1753-54. V. 40; 45
THE ADVENTURER. London: 1754. V. 39
THE ADVENTURER. London: 1777. V. 44
THE ADVENTURER. London: 1778. V. 41; 46
THE ADVENTURER. Dublin: 1788. V. 41
THE ADVENTURER. London: 1794. V. 38; 46
THE ADVENTURER. London: 1797. V. 43

ADVENTURES In Americana, 1492-1897 . . . Being a Selection of Books from the Library of Herschel V. Jones . . . New York: 1928. V. 37

ADVENTURES of a Gold Finder. London: 1850. V. 42; 43

ADVENTURES of an Austalian Traveler in Search of the Marvelous. New York: 1867. V. 38

THE ADVENTURES of Congo in Search of His Master: an American Tale. London: 1823. V. 46

THE ADVENTURES of Doctor Comicus, or the Frolicks of Fortune. London: 1815. V. 44

ADVENTURES of Hunters and Travellers, and Narratives of Border Warfare. Philadelhpia: 1852. V. 38; 44

ADVENTURES of Jackey Jingle and Sukey Single. London: 1830. V. 39

ADVENTURES of Little Julia. London: 1841. V. 39

THE ADVENTURES of My Obadiah Oldbuck. New York: 1852. V. 39

THE ADVENTURES of Old Dame Trot and Her Comical Cat. London: 1830. V. 39

THE ADVENTURES of Paul Jones, English Pirate. London: 1790. V. 42

ADVENTURES of (Vasily) Michailow, a Russian Captive; Among the Kalmucs, Kirghiz, and Kiwenses. London: 1822. V. 37

ADVICE from a Lady of Quality to Her Children; in the Last State of a Lingering Illness. London: 1779. V. 43; 46

THE ADVICE of a father or, Counsel to a Child. London: 1688. V. 38

THE ADVICE of a Friend, to the Army and People of Scotland. N.P.,: 1744. V. 38

ADVICE on the Study of the Law, With Directions for the Choice of Books, and Additional Notes for the American Student. Baltimore: 1811. V. 40

ADVICE to a Minister, on the Present Posture of Affairs. London: 1748. V. 41

ADVICE to a Painter. N.P.: 1679? V. 40

ADVICE to Proprietors, on the Care of Valuable Pictures Painted in Oil, with Instructions for Preserving, Cleaning and Restoring Them, When Damaged or Decayed. London: 1835. V. 38; 44

ADVICE to the Officers of the British Navy. London: 1785. V. 39

ADVICE to the Unwary; or, an Abstract of Certain Penal Laws Now in Force Against Smuggling in General, and the Adulteration of Tea, with Some Remarks . . . London: 1780. V. 41; 42

ADVICE to Unmarried Women. London: 1791. V. 39

ADYE, JOHN

Sitana: A Mountain Campaign on the Borders of Afghanistan in 1863. London: 1867. V. 37

ADYE, RALPH WILLETT

The Bombardier, and Pocket Gunner. Boston & Charlestown: 1804. V. 41

AEAU, BARTHELEMY

Picta Poesis. Ut Pictura Poesis Erit. Lyon: 1556. V. 42

AEGIDIUS, PETRUS CORBOLENSIS

Carmina de Urinarum Judiciis . . . cum Expositione et Commento Magistri Gentilis de Fulgineo . . . 1515. V. 45

Carmina de Urinarum Judiciis . . . Lugd.: 1515. V. 44

Carmina de Urinarum Judiciis . . . cum Expositione et Commento Magistri Gentilis de Fulgineo . . . Lugd. per Jacobum Myt.: 1515. V. 46

AELFRIC

The Homilies of the Anglo-Saxon Church. London: 1844-46. V. 44

AELFRIC, GRAMMATICUS, ABBOT OF EYNSHAM

An English-Saxon Homily on the Birthday of St. Gregory . . . London: 1709. V. 43

AELIAN

Aeliani Variae Historiae Libri XIII . . . Romae: 1545. V. 44

The Tacktics of Aelian Or Art of Embattailing an Army After ye Grecian Manner . . . London: 1616. V. 38; 44

AELIANUS

A Registre of Hystories . . . Written in Greeke by Aelianus a Romaine . . . London: 1576. V. 37; 39

AELIANUS, CLAUDIUS

Ex Aeliani Historia per Petrum Gyllium Latini Facti, Itemque ex Porphyrio, Heliodoro, Oppiano, Eiusdem Gylii Liber Unus. Lyon: 1535. V. 40

Opera, quae Extant Omnia. Zurich: 1556. V. 44

Variae Historiae Libri XIII. Lyon: 1587. V. 44

AEMILIUS, PAULUS

De Rebus Gestis Francorum. Paris: 1520. V. 37

AEMYLIUS, PAULUS

Historiae . . . de Rebus Gestis Francorum, a Pharamundo Primo Rege Usque ad Carolum Octavum, Libri X. Basle: 1569. V. 45

AENEAS, and His Two Sons. London: 1746. V. 41; 45

AERO CLUB OF AMERICA

Navigating the Air. A Scientific Statement of the Progress of Aeronautical Science up to the Present Time. London: 1907. V. 37

AESCHINES

Graeciae Excellentium Oratorum Aeschinis & Demosthenis. Col: Haganoae,: 1522. V. 38

AESCHUYLUS

(Six Lines in Greek). Aeschyli Tragoediae VII. Geneva: 1557. V. 37

AESCHYLUS

The Agamemnon of Aeschylus. London: 1831. V. 42

Agamemnon. N.P.: 1869. V. 39

Agamemnon, Choephoroi, Eumenides. Greenbrae: 1982 & 1983. V. 37; 39

The House of Atreus: Being the Agamemnon . . . of Aeschylus. London: 1901. V. 37

Opera. Paris: 1552. V. 41

Oresteia. London: 1904. V. 41

The Oresteia. New York: 1978. V. 46

The Oresteia of Aeschylus. New York: 1978. V. 38

The Oresteian Trilogy: Agamemnon, Volume I; Choephoroi, the Libation Bearers and Eumenides, the Furies. Volume II. 1982-83. V. 41

The Oresteian Trilogy. Greenbrae: 1982/83. V. 45

The Oresteian Trilogy. Greenbrae: 1982/83. V. 46

The Oresteian Trilogy. Greenbrae: 1983. V. 44

The Oresterian Trilogy. Greenbrae: 1982, 1983. V. 40

Prometheus Bound. Translated from the Greek of Aeschylus. And Miscellaneous Poems, by the Translator. London: 1833. V. 39

Tentmen de Metris ab Aeschylo in Choricis Cantibus Adhibitis, in Latin and Greekn. Cambridge: 1809. V. 44

Tragedie di Eschilo, Tradotti da Felice Bellotti. Milano: 1821. V. 45

Tragedies. Glasgow: 1746. V. 39; 40

The Tragedies. Norwich: 1777. V. 39

Tragedies (Greek title). Glasgow: 1795. V. 46

Aeschyli Tragoediae Sex. Colophon: Venetiis: 1518. V. 38

Tragoediae. Venice: 1518. V. 43; 46

Tragoediae Quae Supersunt. Cambridge: 1809. V. 41

Tragoediae. Berlin: 1925. V. 43

AESCULAPIUS

The Umbrella of Aesculapius. Highlands: 1975. V. 44

AESOPUS

Aesop's Fables Versified and Arranged for the Piano Forte. London. V. 45

The Eagle and the Robin. London: 1709. V. 42

The Fables. London. V. 39

Esopi Appologi Sive Mythologi cum Quibusdam Carminum et Fabularum Additionibus Sebastiani Brant. Basle: 1501. V. 38

Fabularum Quae Hoc Libro Continentur Interpretes, Atque Authores Sunt Hii. Vienna: 1520. V. 40

Fables (Fabellae Graece & Latine, Cum Aliis Opusculis, Quorium Index Proxima Refertur Pagella). Basileae: 1530. V. 38

Aesopi Phrygis Fabulae Graece et Latine. Basileae: 1541. V. 41; 42

Aesopi Phrygis Vita & Fabulae, Plures & Emendatiores, ex Vetustissimo Codice Bibliothecae Regiae. Lutetiae: 1546. V. 38

Fabulae Graece et Latine, cum aliis Quibusdam Opusculis. Antwerp: 1567. V. 37

Fabulae Variorum Auctorum, Nempe Aesopi Fabulae Graeco-Latinae CCXCVII. Frankfurt: 1660. V. 38

Fabulae. Edinburgh: 1676. V. 38

Fables of Aesop and Other Eiminent Mythologists. London: 1694. V. 37; 38; 39; 42; 43

Fabularum Aescopicarum Delectus. Oxoniae: 1698. V. 40

Fables and Storyes Moralised. London: 1699. V. 38

Aesop's Fables, in English and Latin. London: 1703. V. 38

Aesop's Fables in English and Latin. London: 1723. V. 46

Aesop's Fables, with Instructive Morals and Reflections, Abstracted from All Party Considerations . . . London: 1749. V. 44

Fables of Aesop and Others. London: 1754. V. 45

Aesop's Fables. London: 1760. V. 46

Select Fables of (A)esop and Other Fabulists. Birmingham: 1761. V. 37; 39; 43

Fables of Aesop and Others . . . London: 1775. V. 37

Fables Choisies d'Esope, Mises en Chansons. A Samos: 1782. V. 38

Select Fables, in Three Parts. Newcastle: 1784. V. 40

Fabulae Aesopi Selectae, or Select Fables of Aesop. Boston: 1787. V. 42

Aesop's Fables. York: 1790. V. 42

The Fables of Aesop, with a Life of the Author. London: 1793. V. 37; 39; 43

Aesop's Fables: With His Life, Morals, and Remarks. Glasgow: 1794. V. 42

Aesop's Fables: With His Life, Morals and Remarks. Glasgow: 1794. V. 42; 44

Aesopus Fables. London: 1798. V. 41

Fables of Aesop and Others. London: 1805. V. 37; 40

The Fables of Aesop and Others. Newcastle: 1818. V. 37; 40; 43; 45; 46

The Fables of Aesop, and Others, with Designs on wood by Thomas Bewick. Newcastle-upon-Tyne: 1818. V. 44

Select Fables. Together with a memoir; and a descriptive Catalogue of the works of Messrs. Bewick. Newcastle: 1820. V. 37

Select Fables; with cuts, designed and engraved by Thomas and John Bewick, And Others, previous to the year 1784: together with a Memoir; and a Descriptive Catalogue of the Works of Messrs. Bewick. Newcastle/London: 1820. V. 37

The Fables of Aesop and Others. London: 1823. V. 42

The Fables of Aesop. Newcastle: 1823. V. 42; 43; 46

The Fables of Aesop and Others. Newcastle-upon-Tyne: 1823. V. 40; 44

Esop's Fables Written in Chinese by the Learned Mun Mooy Seen-Shang, and Compiled in Their Present Form (with a Free and Literal Translation) by His Pupil, Sloth, pseud. Canton: 1840. V. 41

Fables. London: 1848. V. 39

Aesops Fables: a New Version, Chiefly from Original Sources. London: 1848. V. 37; 40

Fables of Aesop and other Eminent Mythologists, with Morals and Reflections by Sir Roger L'Estrange, Kt. London: 1869? V. 39

Select Fables of Aesop and Others in Three Parts. London: 1878. V. 37

Some of Aesop's Fables with Modern Instances . . . From New Translations by Alfred Caldecott . . . London;: 1883. V. 37

The Fables of Aesop. London: 1887. V. 46

The Fables. London: 1909. V. 38

The Fables of Aesop. London: 1909. V. 43; 46

The Fables of Aesop. New York: 1909. V. 45

Fables. London: 1912. V. 37

Aesop's Fables. London: 1912. V. 37; 38; 39; 40; 41; 44

Aesop's Fables. London: & New York: 1912. V. 46

Aesop's Fables. New York: 1912. V. 44

The Fables of Esope. Newtown: 1921. V. 44

The Fables of Aesop. 1926. V. 37

The Fables of Aesop. N.P.: Waltham St. Lawrence: 1926. V. 45

The Begynning of the Book of the Subtyl Historyes and Fables of Esope Which Were Translated Out of Frensshe into Englysshe by William Caxton in the Year MCCCLXXXIII. San Francisco: 1929. V. 38

Fables of Aesop. New York: 1931. V. 38; 42; 45

The Fables of Esope. Newtown: 1931. V. 43

Fables of Aesop According to Sir Roger L'Estrange. Paris: 1931. V. 44

Aesop's Fables. London: 1933. V. 38; 41

Aesop's Fables. New York: 1933. V. 44

Aesop's Fables. New York: 1933. V. 38; 41; 44; 45

AESOPUS continued

Fables. Oxford: 1933. V. 45

Aesop's Fables. London: 1936. V. 37; 40; 42; 44

Fables, Translated by Sir Roger L'Estrange. London: 1936. V. 40

Fables. London: 1936. V. 37; 43; 45; 46

Aesop's Fables. Ithaca: 1950. V. 44

Twelve Fables of Aesop. New York: 1954. V. 37; 38; 40

Twelve Fables of Aesop. Narrated by Glenway Wescott. New York: (1954). V. 37

Aesop's Fables. London: 1963. V. 44

Aesop's Fables. London: 1967. V. 41

The Fables of Aesop. Verona: 1973. V. 37; 40; 41; 42

A Selection of Aesop's Fables. Portland: 1984. V. 41

Fabulae Elegantissimis Eiconibus Veras Animalium Species ad Viuum Adumbrantes. Leiden: 1582. V. 41

Fabulae Variorum Auctorum Nempe Aesopi Fabulae Graeco-Latine CCXCVII . . . Frankfurt: 1660. V. 45

Fabulae Aesopi Selectae, or Select Fables of Aesop. Boston: 1787. V. 42

Mythologia Aesopica: In Qua Aesopi Fabulae Graece-Latine CCXCVII. London: 1682. V. 45

Phaedri. Aug. Liberti Fabularum Aesopiarum Libri V. Notis Illustravit in Usum Serenissimi Principis . . . Amsterdamp: 1701. V. 43

Select Fables of Aesop and Other Fabulists. London: 1764. V. 45

Select Fables of Esop and Other Fabulists. Philadelphia: 1798. V. 40

Select Fables of Aesop and Others. London: 1871. V. 43

A Selection of Fables. 1984. V. 38

A Selection of Aesop's Fables. Portland: 1984. V. 44

The Subtyl Historyes and Fables of Esope. San Francisco: 1930. V. 45

Tales of Aesop and Others. Derby: 1772. V. 43

AETIUS OF AMIDA 502-575

Contractae ex Veteribus Medicinae Tetrabiblios. Basel: 1542. V. 44; 46

AFBEELDING der marmor Sorten . . . Amsterdam: 1776. V. 45; 46

AFFAIRS of the Mexican Kickapoo Indians. Hearings Before the Subcommittee of the . . . In Three Volumes. Washington: 1908. V. 37

THE AFFECTING Case of the Queen of Hungary; in Relation Both to Friends and Foes; Being a Fair Specimen of Modern History. London: 1742. V. 41

AN AFFECTING History of the Captivity and Sufferings of Mrs. Mary Gerard. Boston: 1810. V. 43

AN AFFECTING History of the Captivity and Sufferings of Mrs. Mary Velnet, an Italian Lady, Who Was Seven Years a Slave in Tripoli. Boston: 1804? V. 43

AN AFFECTIONATE Address to the Inhabitants of the British Colonies in America.. Philadelphia: 1766. V. 37; 46

THE AFFIANCED One. London: 1832. V. 45

AFLALO, A. G.

The Sportsman's Book of India. London: 1904. V. 45

AFLALO, F. G.

The Sportsman's Book for India. 1904. V. 42

AFLALO, FREDERICK GEORGE

The Encyclopaedia of Sport. London: 1897. V. 46

AFRICA, J. SIMPSON

History of Huntington and Blair Counties, Pennsylvania. Philadelphia: 1883. V. 41

AN AFRICAN Folktale. Guildford, Surrey: 1979. V. 44

AFRICAN Lessons. London: 1823. V. 43

THE AFRICAN Repository and Colonial Journal. Washington: 1825-26. V. 40

AGAR, HERBERT

Who Owns America? Boston: 1936. V. 44

AGASSIZ, ALEXANDER

A Contribution to American Thalassography. Three Cruises of the United States Coast and Geodetic Survey Steamer 'Blake' in the Gulf of Mexico, in the Caribbean Sea, and Along the Atlantic Coast of the United States, from 1877 to 1889. Boston/New York: 1888. V. 37

Coral Reefs of Fiji, Cruise of the Screw Steamer Yaralla for the Zoological Study of the Islands in the South Pacific Feejee Archipelago, Based on Wilkes 1855 Charats and Admiralty Surveys. Cambridge: 1899. V. 38

General Report of the Expedition from the Memoirs of the Museum of Comparative Zoology at Harvard College. Cambride. V. 40

Hawaiian and Other Pacific Echini. Cambridge: 1907-17. V. 37

The Panamic Deep Sea Echini. Cambridge: 1904. V. 37

Three Cruises of the United States Coast and Geodetic Survey Steamer 'Blake' in the Gulf of Mexico in the Caribbean Sea, and Along the Atlantic Coast of the United States from 1877 to 1880. London: 1888. V. 39; 46

AGASSIZ, ELIZABETH C.

Seaside Studies in Natural History. Boston: 1865. V. 38

AGASSIZ, LOUIS 1807-1873

Bibliographia Zoologiae et Geologies; a General Catalogue of all Books, Tracts, and Memoirs on Zoology and Geology. London: 1848-54. V. 38

Contributions to the Natural History of the United States of America. Boston: 1857-62. V. 38

Etudes sur Les Glaciers. Neuchatel: 1840. V. 38; 43

Histoire Naturelle des Poissons d'eau douce de l'Europe Centrale. Neuchatel: 1839-42. V. 42

A Journey in Brazil. Boston: 1868. V. 40; 45; 46

Lake Superior; Its Physical Character, Vegetation and Animals, Compared with Those of Other and Similar Regions. Boston: 1850. V. 39; 42; 43

Nomenclator Zoologicus, Continens Nomina Systematica Generum Animalium. Soleure: 1842-46. V. 38

Notice of a Collection of Fishes from the Southern Bend of the Tennessee River, Alabama. New Haven: 1854. V. 44

Outlines of Comparative Physiology, Touching the Structure and Development of the Races of Animals, Living and Extinct. London: 1851. V. 38; 40; 45

AGATE, JAMES

Kingdoms for Horses. London: 1936. V. 39

Responsibility. London: 1919. V. 38

Their Hour Upon the Stage. Cambridge: 1930. V. 38

AGATE, JMAES

L. of C. (Lines of Communication). Being the Letters of a Temporary Officer in the Army Service Corps. Toronto. V. 39

AGATE, W.

The Diary of a Tour in South Africa. Paisley: 1912. V. 37

AGATHA, SISTER

Texas Prose Writing. Dallas: 1936. V. 38

Texas Prose Writing. Dallas: 1936. V. 38

THE AGE of Intellect: or Clerical Showfolk, and Wonderful Layfolk. London: 1819. V. 39

THE AGE of Johnson. Essays Presented to C. B. Tinker on His Retirement from Teaching. New Haven: 1949. V. 39; 40; 46

AGEE, JAMES 1909-1955

Agee on Film. New York: 1958. V. 39

Agee on Film. New York: 1960. V. 37; 42

A Death in the Family. New York: 1957. V. 37; 39; 40; 42; 45

A Death in the Family. London: 1958. V. 45

Four Early Stories. Iowa City: 1963. V. 39

Four Early Stories. West Branch: 1964. V. 40; 42

Let Us Now Praise Famous Men. Boston: 1941. V. 38; 39; 40; 42; 45; 46

Let Us Now Praise Famous Men. Boston: 1960. V. 39

The Morning Watch. Boston: 1951. V. 39; 41

Permit Me Voyage. New Haven: 1934. V. 38; 40; 42; 46

A Way of Seeing. New York: 1965. V. 44

AGEND Buchlein Fur Die Pfar-Herren auff Dem Land. Nuremberg: 1543. V. 38

THE AGENT, and His Natural Son: a New and True Story. London: 1808. V. 43

AGG, JOHN

The General Post Bag; or, News. London: 1814. V. 42

Lord Byron's Farewell to England; with Three Other Poems. London: 1816. V. 39

A Month in Town. London: 1815. V. 37; 41; 43

AGGADA

The Haggadah. London: 1939. V. 44

AGLIONBY, WILLIAM

Painting Illustrated in Three Diallogues, Containing Some Choice Observations Upon the Art. London: 1685. V. 38; 42; 44; 45

AGNER, DWIGHT

The Books of WAD. A Bibliography of the Books Designed by W. A. Dwiggins. Baton Rouge: 1974. V. 37; 41; 43

AGNES Arlington: Life, Times, Troubles, Tribulations and Sad End of Agnes Arlington, the Cotton Planter's Daughter . . . Baltimore: Philadelphia: 1854. V. 43

AIKEN, CONRAD continued

Turns and Movies and Other Tales in Verse. Boston: 1916. V. 37

Ushant; an Essay. New York: 1971. V. 38

AIKEN, JOAN

The Cuckoo Tree. London: 1971. V. 45

A Goose on Your Grave. London: 1987. V. 45

The Ribs of Death. London: 1967. V. 45

The Shadow Guests. London: 1980. V. 45

The Stolen Lake. London: 1981. V. 45

A Touch of Chill - Stories of Horror, Suspense and Fantasy. London: 1979. V. 45

Trouble with Product X. London: 1966. V. 45

Voices in an Empty Room. London: 1975. V. 45

A Whisper in the Night - Stories of Horror, Suspense and Fantasy. London: 1982. V. 45

The Whispering Mountain. London: 1968. V. 45

The Windscreen Wipers and Other Tales of Horror, Suspense and Fantasy. London: 1969. V. 45

AIKEN, JOHN

England Delineated; or, a Geographical Description of Every County in England and Wales... London: 1788. V. 42

Essays on Song Writing. London: 1772. V. 41

A View of Character and Public Services of the Late John Howard, Esq. London: 1792. V. 43; 46

A View of the Life, Travels and Philanthropic Labors of the Late John Howard. Philadelphia: 1794. V. 43

The Wolves of Willoughby Chase. London: 1962. V. 42

AIKEN, PETER FREELAND

A Comparative View of the Constitutions of Great Britain and the United States of America, in Six Lectures. London: 1842. V. 39; 40; 41

AIKEN, South Carolina: a Description of the Climate, Soils and the Nature of the Products in the Vicinity of Aiken, S.C.... New York: and Aiken: 1870. V. 38; 44

AIKIN, A.

A Dictionary of Chemistry and Mineralogy... (with) An Account of the Most Important Recent Discoveries and Improvements in Chemistry and Mineralogy... London: 1807-14. V. 42

AIKIN, ARTHUR

Journal of a Tour through North Wales and Part of Shropshire. London: 1797. V. 38

AIKIN, EDMUND

An Essay on the Doric Order of Architecture, containing a Historical View of Its Rise and Progress Among the Ancients. London: 1810. V. 38

AIKIN, J.

A Description of the Country from Thirty to Forty Miles Round Manchester; Containing Its Geography, Natural and Civil... London: 1795. V. 41

Miscellaneous Pieces in Prose. London: 1773. V. 37

AIKIN, JAMES

The Journal of... Norman: 1919. V. 39

AIKIN, JOHN 1747-1822

A Description of the Country from Thirty to Forty Miles Round Manchester. London: 1795. V. 39; 42

An Essay on the Application of natural History to Poetry. Warrington: 1777. V. 38

Essays on Song Writing... London: 1772. V. 39; 42; 45; 46

Essays on Song-Writing... London: 1772? V. 42; 45

Essays on Song-Writing with a Collection of English Songs as Are Most Eminent for Poetical Merit. London: 1774. V. 42

Essays on Song Writing. Warrington: 1774. V. 40; 42; 44; 45; 46

Evenings at Home. Philadelphia: 1802. V. 45

Letters from A Father to a Son on Various Topics. London: 1794/1800. V. 44

Letters from a Father to His Son, on Various Topics. London: 1796-1800. V. 39; 40; 42; 45

Letters to a Young Lady on a Course of English Poetry. London: 1807. V. 42

Letters to a Young Lady on a Course of English Poetry. London: 1807. V. 38; 46

Observations on the External Use of Preparations of Lead, with some General Remarks on Topical Medicines. London: 1771. V. 38

A View of the Life, Travels and Philanthropic Labours of the Late John Howard. New York: 1814. V. 45

The Woodland Companion. London: 1802. V. 45

The Woodland Companion, or a Brief Description of British Trees. London: 1820. V. 40; 46

AIKIN, LUCY

Juvenile Correspondence, or Letters Designed as Examples of the Epistolary Style, for Children o Both Sexes. London: 1811. V. 38

Memoir of John Aikin. London: 1823. V. 39

Memoirs of the Court of King James the First. London: 1822. V. 38; 43; 46

Memoirs of the Court of Queen Elizabeth. London: 1879. V. 42; 46

Poems. London: 1773. V. 37; 39

AIKMAN, JAMES

Disappointment; and Other Poems. Edinburgh: 1826. V. 40

Poems, Chiefly Lyrical, Partly in the Scottish Dialect. Edinburgh: 1816. V. 42

AIKMAN, LOUISA SUSANNAH WELLS

The Journal of a Voyage from Charlestown, S.C. to London Undertaken During the American Revolution.... in the Year 1778. New York: 1906. V. 41; 42

AIMARD, GUSTAV

V. 45

AIMARD, GUSTAVE 1818-1883

The Border Rifles. Philadelphia. V. 45

The Freebooters. London. V. 45

The Pirates of the Prairies. Adventures in the American Desert. London: 1861. V. 41

AIMO, BAPTISTA

De Alluvionibus... In quo Incremento et Decremento Fluminum, ad Fundorum Vicinorum Commoda et Incommoda, Cum Naturali Acquistione et Amissione Dominiorum et Possessionum... Venetiis: 1599. V. 38

AIN Schoner Dialogus von Zwayen Gutten Gesellen... Sagendt vom Antechrist und Seynen Jungern. Augsburg: 1523. V. 43

AINGER, ARTHUR CAMPBELL

Eton Songs. London: 1891-92. V. 40

AINSLIE, ANN MARIA

Letters from the Dead to the Living; and Moral Letters. Edinburgh: 1812. V. 46

AINSLIE, DOUGLAS

Chosen Poems. London: 1926. V. 38

AINSLIE, JOHN

A Comprehensive Treatise on Land Surveying... Edinburgh: 1842. V. 38

The Gentleman and Farmer's Pocket Companion and Assistant... Edinburgh: 1802. V. 37

AINSLIE, KATHELEEN

Catharine Susan and Me Goes Abroad. London: 1905. V. 41

AINSLIE, KATHLEEN

Lady Tabitha and Us. London: 1905. V. 43

AINSLIE, ROBERT

Views in Egypt... with Historical Observations, and Incidental Illustrations of the Manners and Customs of the Natives of that Country. London: 1801. V. 39

AINSLIE, WHITELAW

Materia Indica. London: 1826. V. 40; 42; 43; 45

Medical, Geographical, and Agricultural Report... Into the Causes of the Epidemic Fever Which Prevailed in the Provinces of Coimbatore, Madura, Dindigul &... London: 1816. V. 43

Observations on the Cholera Morbus of India. London: 1825. V. 43

AINSWORTH, DANFORTH H.

Recollections of a Civil Engineer. Newton: 1899. V. 38

AINSWORTH, E.

Golden Checkerboard. Palm Desert: 1965. V. 45

Golden Checkerboard. Palm Desert: 1965. V. 38; 41; 43; 45; 46

AINSWORTH, EDWARD

Golden Checkerboard. Palm Desert: (1965). V. 37

AINSWORTH, HARRISON

Works. London: 1885. V. 37

AINSWORTH, ROBERT

An Abridgement of Ainsworth's Dictionary of the latin Tongue (from the Folio Edition)., by Mr. N. Thomas. London: 1758. V. 37

AINSWORTH, WILLIAM

Triplex Memoriale; or, the Substance of Three Commemoration Sermons... London: 1650. V. 45

AINSWORTH, WILLIAM FRANCIS 1807-1896

A Personal Narrative of the Euphrates Expedition. London: 1888. V. 39

Researches in Assyria, Babylonia and Chaldaea . . . London: 1838. V. 37; 45

Travels and Researches in Asia Minor, Mesopotamia, Chaldea, and Armenia. London: 1842. V. 40

AINSWORTH, WILLIAM HARRISON 1805-1882

Ainsworth's Magazine: a Miscellany of Romance, General Literature and Art. London: 1842-52. V. 42

Auriol. London: 1850. V. 38

Ballads: Romantic, Fantastical and Humorous. London: 1855. V. 41

Beatrice Tyldesley. London: 1878. V. 40

Boscobel; or, the Royal Oak. London: 1872. V. 41; 46

Cardinal Pole. London: 1863. V. 41; 42; 43

Catalogue of the Library of the Late Celebrated Novelist William Harrison Ainsworth, Esq . . . . Which Will be Sold by Auction, by Messrs. Sotheby, Wilkinson and Hodge. London: 1882. V. 40

Chetwynd Calverley. London: 1876. V. 40; 42

The Collected Novels. London: 1900. V. 42

The Constable de Bourbon. London: 1866. V. 40; 41

Crichton. London: 1837. V. 38; 45

December Tales. London: 1823. V. 41

The Fall of Somerset. London: 1877. V. 40

The Goldsmith's Wife. London: 1875. V. 39; 40

The Good Old Times: The Story of the Manchester Rebels of '45. London: 1873. V. 38

Hilary St. Ives. London: 1870. V. 40

Historical Romances. Philadelphia: 1900. V. 38; 40

Historical Romances. Philadelphia: 1920. V. 42; 44

Jack Sheppard. London: 1839. V. 38; 40; 43; 44; 46

Jack Sheppard. London: 1854. V. 41; 44

The Lancashire Witches. London: 1849. V. 42

The Leaguer of Lathom. London: 1876. V. 40

Life of Jack Sheppard the Housebreaker. (with) Turpin's Ride to York. London: 1840/1839. V. 42

The Lord Major of London: or, City Life in the Last Century. London: 1862. V. 39; 43; 46

The Maid's Revenge; and, a Summer Evening's Tale . . . London: 1823. V. 44

Merry England; or, Nobels and Serfs. London: 1874. V. 40; 43

Mervyn Clitheroe. London: 1858. V. 46

Novels. New York: 1903. V. 42

Old Saint Paul's: a Tale of the Plague and the Fire. London: 1841. V. 38; 45; 46

Old Saint Paul's; a Tale of the Plague and the Fire. London: 1847. V. 42; 46

Old Court. London: 1867. V. 37; 40

Old Saiant Paul's: A Tale of the Plague and the Fire. London: 1847. V. 37

Ovingdean Grange. London: 1860. V. 40; 43; 46

Pictorial Life and Adventures of Jack Sheppard . . . Philadelphia: 185-. V. 45

Preston Fight, or, the Insurrection of 1715. London: 1875. V. 40

Rockwood, a Romance. London: 1834. V. 39

Rockwood, a Romance. London: 1836. V. 37; 45

Rookwood: a Romance. London: 1873. V. 46

Saint James's: Or, The Court of Queen Anne. London: 1844. V. 43

St. James's; or the Court of Queen Anne. London: 1844. V. 41

Sir John Chiverton. London: 1826. V. 40; 44

The Spendthrift. London: 1857. V. 38

Stanley Brereton. London: 1839. V. 43

Stanley Brereton. London: 1881. V. 37; 40

The Star-Chamber; an Historical Romance. London: 1854. V. 46

The Tower of London. London: 1840. V. 37; 38; 39; 40; 41; 43; 44; 46

Windsor Castle. London: 1843. V. 41

Windsor Castle. London: 1844. V. 41

Windsor Castle. London: 1862. V. 39

Works. London: n.d. V. 37

The Works. London: 1875. V. 37

The Works of . . . London: 1901. V. 44

The Works of . . . Author's Copyright Edition. London: (c. 1901). V. 37

AINSWORTH'S Magazine. London: 1842-1850. V. 37

AIRCRAFT of the Fighting Powers. Volumes I-VII (all published, the complete set). Compiled by H.J. Cooper, O.G. Thetford, C.B. Maycock, and E.J. Riding. Edited by D.A. Russell. Leicester: 1941-46. V. 37

AIRES DO CASAL, MANUEL

Corografia Brazilica . . . Rio de Janeiro: 1817. V. 39

AIRY, OSMUND

Charles II. London: 1901. V. 46

AISLABIE, JOHN

Mr. Aislabie's Two Speeches Considered: with His Tryal at Large in Both Houses of Parliament, Wherein the Learned Speeches for and Against Him, in the Several Debates . . . London: 1721. V. 41

AISNWORTH, C. W.

Excursion of South Dakota Editiors and Their Families to Chicago, Indianapolis . . . Chattanooga, Atlanta, Savannah . . . Ocala, Inverness, Lakeland, Port Tampa . . . Orlando, Sanford . . . St. Augustine, Jacksonville . . . Plankinton, S.C.: (1892). V. 37

AITCHISON, G. U.

A Collection of Treaties, Engagements and Sanads Relating to India and Neighbouring Countries. Volume XI. Delhi: 1933. V. 40

AITKEN, JAMES

From the Clyde to California with Jottings by the Wary. (with the supplement) A Run through the States: Supplemntary to from the Clyde to California. Greenock: 1882, 1894. V. 41

From the Clyde to California with Jottings by the Way. Greenock: 1882/1894. V. 45

From the Clyde to California with Jottings by the Way. Greenock: 1882 & 1894. V. 38

A Genuine Account of the Life, Transactions, Confession and Execution, of James Aitken, Alias John Hill, Commonly Called John the Painter, Who Was Tried at the Castle of Winchester, on Thursday the 7th of March 1777, and Convicted . . . London: 1777. V. 42

The Trial (at Large) of James Hill; Otherwise, James Hind; Otherwise James Actzen; for . . . Setting Fire to the Rope-House, In His Majesty's Dock-Yard at Portsmouth . . . London: 1777. V. 37; 40

AITKEN, R. B.

Gret Game Animals of the World. London: 1969. V. 38

AITKEN, WILLIAM

Echoes from the Iron Road and Other Poems. Glasgow: 1893. V. 46

AITON, WILLIAM

A Treatise on the Origin, Qualities and Cultivation of Moss-Earth . . . 1811. V. 42

A Treatise on the Origin, Qualities and Cultivation of Moss-Earth, with Directions for Converting It Into Manure . . . Air: 1811. V. 43

A Treatise on the Origin, Qualitites and Cultivation of Moss-Earth, with Directions for Converting It into Manure. London: 1811. V. 38

AITZEMA, LION

Notable Revolutions . . . London: 1653. V. 44

AKEN, DAVID

Pioneers of the Black Hills; or, Gordon's Stockade Party of 1874. Milwaukee: 1920. V. 40; 43; 44

AKENSIDE, MARK 1721-1770

An Epistle to Cruio. London: 1744. V. 38; 42

An Ode to the Right Honorable the Earl of Huntingdon. London: 1748. V. 39

Odes on Several Subjects. London: 1745. V. 42

The Pleasures of Imagination. London: 1744. V. 37; 38; 39; 40; 41; 43; 45; 46

The Pleasures of Imagination. London: 1769. V. 40; 41

The Pleasures of Imagination, and Other Poems. London: 1788. V. 42

The Pleasures of Imagination. Glasgow: 1825. V. 42

Poems. London: 1772. V. 37; 38; 39; 41; 45

The Poetical Works. London: 1825. V. 46

AKERLY, J.

Voltaire and Rousseau Against the Atheists; or Essays and Detached Passages from Those Writers, in Relation to the Being . . . of God. New York: 1845. V. 40

AKERMAN, JOHN YONGE

A Glossary of Provincial Words and Phrase in Use in Wiltshire. London: 1842. V. 41

Remains of Pagan Saxondom. London: 1855. V. 39; 41

Spring Tides, or, the Angler and His friends. London: 1805. V. 46

Spring-Tide; or, the Angler and His Friends. London: 1852. V. 42

Tales of Other Days. London: 1830. V. 40; 41

AKERMAN, LUCY EVELINA

Nothing by Leaves, a Poem. Philadelphia: 1868. V. 42

AKHMATOVA, ANNA

Forty Seven Love Poems. London: 1927. V. 41; 42

AKIN, JAMES

Journal of James Akin, Jr. Norman: 1919. V. 42; 43

AKINS, THOMAS B.

Selections from the Public Documents of the Province of Nova Scotia . . . Halifax: 1869. V. 42

AKIYAMA, TERUKAZU

Arts of China: Volume I - Neolithic Cultures to the T'ang Dynasty, Recent Discovers. Volume II - Budhist Cave Temples, New Researches, Volume III - Paintings in Chinese Museums, New Collections. Tokyo: 1968-70. V. 39

AKKADIAN

A Babylonian Anthology. North Hill: 1966. V. 41

AKURGAL, EKREM

The Art of the Hittites. New York. V. 41

The Art of the Hittites. New York. V. 38

The Art of the Hittites. New York: 1962. V. 40; 41; 42; 44; 46

The Art of the Hittites. Photographs by Max Hirmer. New York: (1962). V. 37

Etting-Hausen. Treasures of Turkey. N.P.: 1966. V. 45

AKVAREZ DE PAZ, DIEGO

De Vita Spirtuali . . . Mainz: 1614-19. V. 37

AL IDRISI

Geographia Nubiensis Idest Accuratissima Totius Obis in Septem Climata Divisi Descripto Continens Praesertium Exactam Universae Asiae & Africae . . . Paris: 1619. V. 45

AL-MAQRIZI, AHMD IBN ALI

Historia Monete rabicae e Codice Escorialensi, cum Vriis Duorum Codd. Leidensium Lectionibus et Exceprtis Anecdotis. Rostochii: 1797. V. 38

AL-MUBASHSHIR IBN FATIK, ABU AL-WAFA

The Dictes and Sayings of the Philosophers. London: 1877. V. 44

Dictes and Sayings of the Philosophers. Detroit: 1901. V. 46

AL-RAZI, ABU BAKR MUHAMMAD IBN ZAKARIYA 865?-925?

A Treatise on the Small-Pox and Measles . . . London: 1848. V. 43

ALABAMA. CONSTITUTION - 1819

Constitution of the State of Alabama. Washington: 1819. V. 38

ALABAMA. CONSTITUTIONAL CONVENTION - 1901

Official Proceedings of the Constitutional Convention of the State of Alabama, May 21st, 1901 to September 3rd, 1901. Wetumpka: 1940. V. 42

ALAGONA, PETRUS

Compendium Manualis Navarri. Lyon: 1593. V. 37

ALAMANNI, LUIGI

La Coltivatione. Florence: 1546. V. 40

La Coltivatione di Luigi Alamanni al Christianissimo Re Francesco Primo. Parigi: 1546. V. 37; 39

La Coltivazione del Sig. Lvigi Alamanni & Le Api Del S. Giovanni Rvcellai . . . Fiorenza: 1590. V. 39

Gyrone il Cortese. Paris: 1548. V. 37

ALARCON, PEDRO ANTONIO DE 1833-1891

The Three Cornered Hat. New York: 1944. V. 40

THE ALARM. London: 1719. V. 46

ALARM to the Patriots. London: 1749. V. 41; 46

THE ALARM. To Which is Subjoined Great News from Abroad. N.P.: 1745? V. 39

ALASKA COMMERCIAL CO.

Hon. Phineas W. Hitchcock, Chairman Committee on Territories, United States Senate: Sir: The Alaska Commercial Company of San Francisco, California, Respectfully Protests Against the Passage of Senate Bill no. 67. N.P.: 1874? V. 46

ALASKA Tours to the National Wonderland. Chicago: 1898. V. 45

ALASKAN BOUNDARY TRIBUNAL

Atlas of Award: Twenty-Five Sectional Maps and Index Map Showing the Line Fixed by the Tribunal. Washington: 1904. V. 39

Proceedings of the . . . Convened at London, Under the Treaty Between the U.S.A. nd Great Britain, Concluded at Washington, January 24, 1903, for the Settlement of Questions Between the Two Countries . . . Washington: 1904. V. 38

United States Atlas. Maps and Charts Accompanying the Case and Counter Case of the United States. Washington: 1904. V. 39

ALASTAIR

Fifty Drawings by Alastair. New York: 1925. V. 37; 44

ALBANI, ANGELO fl. 1615-1630

Innamoramento di Due Fedeli Amanti Paris et Vienna . . . Viterbo: 1670. V. 46

ALBANI, FRANCESCO

Pitture . . . Rome: 1704. V. 45

ALBANIS BEAUMONT, JEAN FRANCOIS

Select Views of the Antiquities and Harbours in the South of France . . . London: 1794. V. 40; 43; 45

Travels through the Rhaetian Alps in the Year 1786. From Italy to Germany through Tyrol. London: 1792. V. 46

ALBEE, EDWARD 1928-

A Delicate Balance. New York: 1966. V. 38

Seascape. New York: 1975. V. 43

Tiny Alice. New York: 1965. V. 43

Who's Afraid of Virginia Woolf? 1962. V. 42

Who's Afraid of Virginia Woolf? New York: 1962. V. 42

Who's Afraid of Virginia Woolf. London: 1964. V. 38

The Zoo Story et al. New York: 1960. V. 37; 39; 42; 43; 44; 45

The Zoo Story and Other Plays. London: 1962. V. 45; 46

ALBEE, FRED HOUDLETT

Bone-Graft Surgery. Philadelphia: 1915. V. 41; 42; 43

Injuries and Diseases of the Hip. New York: 1937. V. 40

Orthopedic and Reconstructive Surgery. Philadelphia: 1919. V. 41; 42; 43

ALBEE, LOUISE RANKIN

The Bartlett Collection: A List of Books on Angling, Fishes and Fish Culture in Harvard College Library. Cambridge: 1896. V. 37

ALBEMARLE, GEORGE MONCK, DUKE OF

The Lord General Monck His Speech Delivered by Him in the Parliament on Munday, Feb. 6, 1659. London: 1660. V. 46

Observations Upon Military and Political Affairs. London: 1796. V. 46

The Speech and Declaration of His Excellency the Lord Generall Monck Delivered at White-hall Upon Tuesday the 21 of February 1699 to the Members of Parliament at Their Meeting There, Before the Re-admission of the Formerly Secluded Members . . . London: 1659. V. 46

ALBEMARLE, GEORGE THOMAS KEPPEL, 6TH EARL OF 1799-1891

Personal Narrative of a Journey from India to England, by Bussorah, Bagdad, the Ruins of Babylon, Curdistan, the Court of Persia . . . London: 1827. V. 43

ALBERICI, JACOB

Historiarum Sanctissimae, et Gloriosiss (sic), Virginis Deiparae de Populo Almae Urbis Compendium. Rome: 1599. V. 38

ALBERS, ANNIE

On Weaving. Middletown: 1965. V. 43

ALBERS, JOSEF

Despite Straight Lines: an Analysis of His Graphic Constructions by F. Bucher. New Haven: 1961. V. 46

Her Royal Highness and His Majesty Cupid. New Haven: 1958. V. 39

Poems and Drawings. New Haven: 1958. V. 41

ALBERT, ALLEN DIEHL

History of the Forty-Fifth Regiment Pennsylvania Veteran Volunteer Infantry 1861-1865. Williamsport: 1912. V. 42

ALBERT Camus and the Men of the Stone. San Francisco: 1971. V. 40

ALBERT, GEORGE D.

History of the County of Westmoreland, Pennsylvania, with Biographical Sketches of Many of Its Prominent Men. Philadelphia: 1882. V. 41

ALBERT, HEINRICH

Arien Theils Geist-Licher, Theils Weltlicher . . . Lieder, Zum Singen & Spelen Gesetzt. Koenigsberg: 1650-54. V. 41

ALBERT, HONORE THEODORIC

Metaponte. Paris: 1833. V. 38

ALBERT, JAMES

A Narrative of the Most Remarkable Particulars in the Life of James Albert, Akawsaw, Granwasa; as Dictated to Himself. Catskill: 1810. V. 41

ALBERT, JOHN

The Fatal Book Opened! Otley: 1830. V. 46

THE ALBERT Memorial. London: 1870. V. 37

ALBERT, VICTOR

Prince of Wales: The Cruise of her Majesty's SHip 'Bacchante', 1879-1882, compiled from the Private Journals, Letters, Note-Books of . . . 1886. V. 37

ALBERTA. DEPARTMENT OF AGRICULTURE - 1925

Alberta Horse and Cattle Brands, Being Brands Allotted for First Time and Old Brands Renewed, Changed or Reissued During the Years 1921-1922-1923 and 1924. Edmonton: 1925. V. 38

ALBERTANUS CAUSIDICUS BRIXIENSIS

Tractatus de Doctrina Dicendi et Tacendi. Strassburg: 1476. V. 40

Tractatus de Arte Loquendi et Tacendi. Leipzig: 1491. V. 37

ALBERTANUS DE BRIXIA

Dis ist der Brunndes Rates, aus Welchem ein ekummerter Ocder Betrupter Mensch Trost, Radt und Weissheit Empfahet, das Manchem Dick Radt not ist, was Redt Sey, Warumb et rat Heiss, von Wem Rat Zu Fordern Sey. Strassburg: 1508. V. 37

ALBERTI, LEANDRO 1479-1552

Descrittione di Tutta Italia. Bologna: 1550. V. 39; 42

Descrittione di Tutta Italia, Nella, Quale si Contiene il lito (sic) di Essa, l'Origine, & le Signorie Delle Citta, & de' Castelli co' Nomi Antichi, & Moderni . . . Vinegia: 1588. V. 39

Vita della Beata Colomba da Rieto. (Bologna: 1521). V. 37

ALBERTI, LEON BATTISTA 1404-1472

L'Architettura. Venice: 1565. V. 40

Della Architectura Della Pittura e Della Statua . . . Bologna: 1782. V. 37

I Dieci Libri della Architettura. Rome: 1784. V. 40

I Dieci Libri de l'Architecttura. Venice: 1546. V. 37; 40; 44

Opera Nonnulla. Florence: 1499. V. 40

ALBERTI, LEON BATTTISTA 1404-1472

De Re Aedificatoria Libri Decem. Strasbourg: 1541. V. 37

ALBERTI, RAFAEL

A Spectre is Haunting Europe: Poems of Revolutionary Spain. New York: 1936. V. 46

ALBERTI, SALOMON

Historia Plerarunque Partium Humani Corporis . . . Wittenberg: 1585. V. 45

ALBERTINI, FRANCESCO DEGLI

Opusculu (M) D (E) Mirabilibus Nove & Veteris Urbis Rome. V. 45

Opusculum de Mirabilibus Novae et Veteris Urbis Romae. Rome: 1510. V. 37

ALBERTINUS, FRANC.

Septem Mirabilia Orbis et Urbis Romae et Florentinae Civitatis. Romae: 1510. V. 38

ALBERTS, SIDNEY S.

A Bibliography of the Works of Robinson Jeffers. New York: 1933. V. 46

ALBERTUS, FRA

So This Then is the Appreciation of Ali Baba of East Aurora. 1899. V. 40

ALBERTUS MAGNUS 1193?-1280

Alberti Magni Physica Sive De Physico Auditu Libri Octo. Venetiis: 1494. V. 40

De Animalibus. Rome: 1478. V. 39

De Animalibus Libri Vigintisex. Venice: 1495. V. 37; 38; 40

Compendium Theologice Veritatis. Venice: 1510. V. 46

Enchiridion Verae Perfectaeque Virtutis cum Eiusdem Inductiuis Signis ac Argumentis Paradisus Animae Merito Nuncupatum. Coimbra: 1553. V. 41

Liber de Laudibus Gloriosissime Dei Genetricis Mariae Semper Virginis. Basle: 1474. V. 37; 38; 40; 41

Opera Spiritvale di Alberto Magno Intitolata Paradiso dell'Anima. Fiorenza: 1556. V. 39

Sermones de Tempore et de Sanctis. Ulm: 1478-80. V. 40

ALBIN, E.

A Natural History of Spiders, and Other Curious Insects. London: 1736. V. 43

A Natural History of English Song-Birds. London: 1741. V. 37

ALBIN, ELEAZAR

Aranel, or a Natural History of Spiders . . . London: 1793. V. 40

A Natural History of English Insects. London: 1720. V. 44

ALBINUS, BERNARD S.

Tables of the Skeleton and Muscles of the Human Body. London: 1749. V. 40

THE ALBION Hotel Traveller's Guide for River St. Lawrence and the Cities of montreal, Quebec & Ottawa. 1869. V. 38

ALBON, CLAUDE CAMILLE FRANCOIS, COMTE D'

Discours Politiques, Historiques et Critiques sur Quelques Gouverremens de l'Europe. Neuchatel: 1779. V. 38

ALBORGHETTI, GUISEPPE

Poesie. Rome: 1802. V. 40

ALBRIGHT, WILLIAM FOXWELL

Eretz-Israel: Archaeological Historical and Geographical Studies. Jerusalem: 1969. V. 40

The Excavation of Tell Beit Mirsim in Palestine. New Haven: 1932. V. 40; 42; 44

The Excavation of Tell Beit Mirsim. New Haven: 1932-43. V. 42

ALBRIZZI, GIOVANNI BATTISTA

Forastiero Illuminato Intorno Le Cose Piu Rare e Curiose Antiche e Moderne Della Citta di Venezia e Dell'Isole Circonvicine . . . Venezia: 1796. V. 46

ALBRIZZI, ISABELLA

The Work of Antonio Canova in Sculpture and Modelling . . . Boston: 1876. V. 45

ALBUCASIS

De Chirurgia. Arabice et Latine . . . Cura Johannis Channing . . . Oxonii: 1778. V. 37

On Surgery and Instruments. 1973. V. 41

On Surgery and Instruments, a Definitive Edition of the Arabic Text with English Translation and Commentary . . . London: 1973. V. 45

THE ALBUM. London: 1822-25. V. 46
THE ALBUM. New York: 1824. V. 43; 44

ALBUM de la Decoration. Paris. V. 45

ALBUM de Poemes Tires du Livre de Jade. London: 1911. V. 44

ALBUM Mexicano, Colleccion de Paisajes, Monumentos, Costumbres y Ciudades Principales . . . Mexico: 1885. V. 38

AN ALBUM of Mayan Architecture. Washington. V. 45

ALBUM of the Finest Birds of All Countries. Philadelphia: 1850's. V. 42

ALBUM Typographique de l'Imprimerie Royale. Paris: 1830. V. 41

THE ALBUM Wreath and Bijou Litteraire . . . London: 1834. V. 44

ALBUMASAR

Flores Astrologiae. Augsburg: 1495. V. 38

De Magnis Coniunctionibus. Augsburg: 1489. V. 41; 42

ALBUQUERQUE, ALFONSO D'

Commentarios do Grande . . . Alfonso Dalboquerque, Capitam Geral que foy das Indias Orientaes, Em Tempo do Muito Poderoso Rey dom Manuel, o Primeiro deste nome. Lison: 1576. V. 38

ALBUQUERQUE DE OLIVEIRA, PEDRO ERNESTO

Pathogenesia Homoeopathica Brasileira . . . Rio de Janeiro: 1856. V. 39

ALCALA, PEDRO DE

Arte Para Ligeramente Saber la Lengua Araviga . . . (with): Vocabulista Aravigo en Letra Castellana. Granada: 1505. V. 39

ALCARAZ, RAMON

The Other Side: Notes for the History of the War Between Mexico and the United States. New York: 1850. V. 40

ALCEDO Y HERRERA, DIONISIO

Compendio Historico de la Provincia, Partidos, Ciudades, Astilleros, Rios, y Puerto de Guayaquil en las Costas de la Mar del Sur . . . Madrid: 1741. V. 38

ALCHABITIUS

Libellus Isagogicus Seu Introductorium. Venice: 1485. V. 40

ALCHIMIA Opuscula Complura Veterum Philosophorum . . . (Part II: Rosarium Philosophorum Secunda Pars Alchimiae de Lapido Philosophico Vero Modo Preparando . . .) Frankfurt: 1550. V. 46

ALCIATI, ANDREA

Diverse Imprese . . . Nella Lingua Italiana Non Piu Tradotte.. Lyon: 1551. V. 39

Duello de lo Eccellentissimo . . . Andrea Alciato Fatto di Latino in Italiano . . . Tre Consigli Appresso della Materia Medesima, uno de' Detto Alciato gl'altri de Mariano Socino . . . Venezia: 1545. V. 38

Dvello . . . Fatto di Latino Italiano a Commune Vtilita. Venetia: 1544. V. 42

Emblemata. Lyons: 1551. V. 37; 43

Emblemata. Frankfurt: 1567. V. 40

Emblemata. Lyon: 1614. V. 38; 40

Emblemata cum Commentariis Claudii Minois I. C. Francisci Sanctii Broncensis, & notis Laurentii Pignorii Patavini. Padua: 1621. V. 45

Emblemata Cvm Commentariis Clavdii Minois I.C., Francisci Sanctii Brocensis, & Notis Lavrentii Pignorii Patavini. Patauij: 1621. V. 39

Emblemata Cum Commentarius . . . Padua: 1661. V. 39

Emblematum Libri Duo. Lyon: 1554. V. 45

ALCIATI, ANDREA continued

Emblemes en Latin et Francois, Vers pour Vers. Paris: 1561. V. 38

Francisci Sanctii Brocensis in Inclyta Salmaticensi Academia Rhetoricae . . . Lyon: 1573. V. 40

Omnia Andreae Alciati V. C. Emblemata. Frankfurt: 1602. V. 39

Omnia Andreae Alciati V.C. Emblemata. Paris: 1602. V. 40; 45

De Verborvm Significatione Libri Qvatvor. Eiusdem, in Tractatum Eius Argumenti Ueterum Iureconsultor, Commentaria. Lyon: 1530. V. 40

ALCIATI, ANDREAS

Emblemata. Lyons: 1551. V. 37

ALCIBIADES

The Dream of Alcibiades. London: 1749. V. 44

ALCOCK, ALFRED WILLIAM

A Naturalist in Indian Seas or, Four Years with the Royal Indian Marine Survey Ship 'Investigator'. London: 1902. V. 45

ALCOCK, G. W.

Fifty Years of Railway Trade Unionism. London: 1922. V. 41

ALCOCK, JOHN

Harmonia Festi, or a Collection of Canons; Cheerful and Serious Glees and Catches; For Four and Five Voices in Score, Never Before Publish'd. Lichfield: 1791. V. 46

ALCOCK, R. C.

The Postmarks of Great Britain and Ireland . . . from 1660 to 1940. Cheltenham. V. 43

ALCOCK, RUTHERFORD

The Capital of the Tycoon: a Narrative of a Three Years' Residence in Japan. London: 1863. V. 45; 46

ALCOCK, THOMAS

Lectures on Practical and Medical Surgery, Comprising Observations and Reflections on Surgical Education . . . London: 1830. V. 42

Observations on the Defects of the Poor Laws, and the Causes and Consequences of the Great Increase and Burden of the Poor. London: 1752. V. 40

Travels in Russia, Persia, Turkey and Greece, in 1828-1829 . . . London: 1831. V. 39

ALCORTA, L. J.

Reglamento del Estado Mayor del Ejercito que debe Operar Sobre Tejas . . . Mexico: 1844. V. 42

ALCOTT, AMOS BRONSON 1799-1888

A. Bronson Alcott His Life and Philosophy. Boston: 1893. V. 37

Concord Days. Boston: 1872. V. 37

Concord Lectures on Philosophy. Cambridge: 1883. V. 40

Emerson. Cambridge: 1865. V. 40

New Connecticut. Boston: 1881. V. 40

Observations on the Principles and Methods of Infant Instruction. Boston: 1830. V. 39; 44

Table Talk. Boston: 1877. V. 41

Tablets. Boston: 1868. V. 41; 44

ALCOTT, LOUISA MAY 1832-1888

Aunt Jo's Scrap-Bag. Shawl-Straps. Boston: 1872. V. 42; 43

Comic Tragedies. Boston: 1893. V. 42; 44

Eight Cousins; or the Aunt Hill . . . Boston: 1875. V. 39

The Frost King. Boston: 1887. V. 40

Hospital Sketches. Boston: 1863. V. 38; 45

Hospital Sketches and Camp and Fireside Stories. Boston: 1869. V. 42; 43; 44

Kitty's Class Day. Boston: 1868. V. 43

Life, Letters and Journals. Boston: 1889. V. 45

Little Women. Boston: 1868. V. 38

Little Women, or Meg, Jo, Beth and Amy. (and) Little Women Part the Second. Boston: 1868, 1869. V. 40

Little Women. Boston: 1871. V. 42

Little Women. London: 1922. V. 46

Little Women. Boston: 1869. V. 37; 42; 45

Little Women. Boston: 1915. V. 37

Little Women. Racine: 1934. V. 45

Little Women Series. Boston: 1892-93. V. 41

A Modern Mephistopheles. Boston: 1877. V. 41; 44

Moods. Boston: 1865. V. 43

An Old Fashioned Girl. London: 1870. V. 40; 45

An Old Fashioned Girl. Boston: 1907. V. 46

An Old Fashioned Girl. Boston: 1916. V. 43

The Rose Family. Boston: 1864. V. 43

Rose in Bloom. Boston: 1876. V. 44

Silver Pitchers and Independence. A Centennial Love Story. Boston: 1876. V. 39; 42; 44

Spinning-Wheel Stories. Boston: 1884. V. 42; 44

ALCOTT, WILLIAM ANDRUS

The Young Mother, or Management of Children in Regard to Health. Boston: 1836. V. 41

ALCYONIUS, PETRUS 1487-1527

Medices Legatus De Exilio. Venice: 1522. V. 37; 45

ALDAM, W. H.

A Quaint Treatise on 'Felles and the Art a' Artyfichall Flee Making.' London: 1876. V. 39; 40

ALDEN, JOHN

European Americana: a Chronological Guide to Works Printed in Europe Relating to the Americas 1493-1776. New York: 1980. V. 45

European Americana. New York: 1980/82. V. 42; 44

ALDEN, TIMOTHY

An Account of Sundry Missions Performed Among the Senecas and Munsees: in a Series of Letters. New York: 1827. V. 45

A Collection of American Epitaphs and Inscriptions with Occasional Notes. New York: 1814. V. 38; 40; 41

The Glory of America. Portsmouth: 1801. V. 45

ALDEN, WILLIAM C.

The Quaternary Geology of Southeastern Wisconsin with a Chapter on the Older Rock Formations. Washington: 1918. V. 45

ALDEN'S Home Atlas of the World. New York: 1888. V. 45

ALDER, J.

A Monograph of the British Nudibranchiate Mollusca. London: 1844-45. V. 37

THE ALDERMAN'S Feast. A New Alphabet. London: 1845. V. 44

ALDERSON, A. H.

With the Mounted Infantry and the Mashonaland Field Force - 1896. London: 1898. V. 40; 42

ALDERSON, JOHN

An Essay on Apparitions, In Which Their Appearance is Accounted for by Causes Wholly Independent of Preternatural Agency. London: 1823. V. 38; 41

ALDERSON, RALPH

A Chemical Analysis and Medical Treatise on the Sharp Saw, in Westmoreland . . . Kendal: 1828. V. 38

A Chemical Analysis and Medical Treatise on the Shap Spaw in Westmoreland with Some Remarks on a Peculiar Affection of the Heart, The Consequence of Dyspepsia . . . London: 1828. V. 40

ALDIN, CECIL

Aldin's Merry Party . . . New York: 1913. V. 42

An Artist's Models. London: 1930. V. 46

An Artist's Models. London: (n.d.). V. 37

Berkshire Vale: Poems by Wilfrid Howe-Nurse. Illustrated by . . . Oxford: 1927. V. 37

Cecil Aldin's Happy Family, Being the Adventures of Hugry Peter; The Pig Rufus; The Cat; Humpty & Dumpty; the Rabbits; Rags, the Dog; Master Quack, the Dockling; and Forager, the Puppy. New York: 1912. V. 42

Dogs of Character. London: 1927. V. 41; 45

Dogs of Every Day. London: 1933. V. 41

Dogs of Character. London: 1937. V. 41

Just Among Friends. London: 1934. V. 41

Old Manor Houses. London: 1923. V. 44

Puppy-Day Frolics. London. V. 42

The Puppy Book. London: 1905. V. 41

Ratcatcher to Scarlet. London: 1932. V. 41

The Romance of the Road. London: 1928. V. 41; 44

The Romance of the Road. London: 1933. V. 39

Rough and Tumble. London. V. 38

Scarlet to M. F. H. New York: 1933. V. 46

Sleeping Partners, a Series of Episodes. London: 1929. V. 44

'Spot'. An Autobiography. London: 1894. V. 45

Time I Was Dead. London: 1934. V. 41

The White Puppy Book. London: 1909. V. 46

Who's Who in the Zoo. Boston: 1933. V. 42

THE ALDINE Edition of British Poetry. London: 1830-45. V. 37

ALDINE Poets. The Aldine Edition of the British Poets. London: 1866. V. 37

THE ALDINE Press, a Typographic Journal. New York: 1871. V. 38

ALDINGTON, JOHN HENRY

The Cyclopaedia of Law; or, the Correct British Lawyer . . . London: 1820. V. 45

ALDINGTON, RICHARD

All Men Are Enemies. London: 1933. V. 37; 38; 39; 40; 41

Balls. Westport: 1932. V. 44

The Colonel's Daughter. London: 1931. V. 40

Death of a Hero. London: 1929. V. 41; 42

Death of a Hero. London: 1930. V. 44

Death of a Hero. Paris: 1930. V. 37; 43

The Eaten Heart. 1929. V. 43; 45

The Eaten Heart. Chapelle-Reanville: 1929. V. 42; 45

Euripides. Alcestis. 1930. V. 37

Exile and Other Poems. London: 1923. V. 40

Images (1910-1915). London: 1915. V. 40

Images Old and New. Boston: 1916. V. 43

Images. London: (1919). V. 37

Images of Desire. London: 1919. V. 40

Last Straws. Paris: 1930. V. 39; 41; 45

Love and the Luxembourg. New York: 1930. V. 43

Movietones Invented and Set Down by Richard Aldington 1928 - 1929. (N.P.): (ca. 1932). V. 37

Roads to Glory. London: 1930. V. 43; 44; 46

Soft Answers. London: 1932. V. 41; 42; 43

Stepping Heavenward. Florence: 1931. V. 37; 39; 43; 46

Two Stories. N.P.: 1930. V. 43

A Wreath for San Gemignano. (Hove): 1980. V. 37

ALDINI, GIOVANNI 1762-1834

Essai Theorique et Experimental sur Le Galvanisme, avec une Serie d'Experiences Faites en Presence des Commisaires de L'Institut National France . . . Paris: 1804. V. 37; 39; 42; 46

ALDIS, CHARLES 1775?-1863

On the Nature and Cure of Glandular Diseases, Especially Those Denominated Cancer, with the Mode of Treatment; and On the Too Frequent Use of Mercury . . . London: 1832. V. 44; 46

ALDISS, BRIAN

Hothouse. London: 1962. V. 38

ALDISS, BRIAN W.

The Brightfount Diaries. London: 1955. V. 45

ALDRICH, HENRY

The Elements of Civil Architecture, According to Virtruvius and Other Ancients, and the Most Approved Practice of Modern Authors. Oxford: 1824. V. 41

ALDRICH, LORENZO D.

A Journal of the Overland Route to California & the Gold Mines. Los Angeles: 1950. V. 40

ALDRICH, THOMAS BAILEY 1836-1907

The Ballad of Babie Bell and Other Poems. New York: 1859. V. 45

The Bells, a Collection of Chimes. New York: 1855. V. 42; 46

Friar Jerome's Beautiful Book. Boston: 1881. V. 41; 43

Friar Jerome's Beautiful Book. Boston: 1896. V. 41; 42; 44

Friar Jerome's Beautiful Book. Bronxville: 1952. V. 42; 46

Friar Jerome's Beautiful Book. Boston: (1896). V. 37

The Little Violinist. Massachusetts: 1880. V. 43

The Little Violinist. 1880. V. 37

Marjorie Daw. Boston and New York: 1908. V. 46

Prudence Palfrey. Boston: 1874. V. 37; 45

A Sea Turn and Other Matters. Boston and New York: 1902. V. 46

The Stillwater Tragedy. Boston: 1880. V. 46

The Story of a Bad Boy. Boston: 1870. V. 38; 43; 44

Works. Cambridge: 1897. V. 42

The Works of Thomas Bailey Aldrich. Boston: 1897-1907. V. 44; 46

The Writings. Boston & New York: 1907. V. 46

ALDRIDGE, REGINALD

Life on a Ranch, Ranch Notes in Kansas, Colorado, the Indian Territory, and Northern Texas. New York: 1884. V. 37; 39

Ranch Notes in Kansas, Colorado, the Indian Territory and Northern Texas. London: 1884. V. 37; 45

ALDRIDGE, T. J.

The Sherebo and Its Hinterland. London: 1901. V. 43; 44; 45

ALDROVANDI, ULISSE 1522-1605

Dendrologiae Naturalis Scilicet Arborum Historiae Libri Duo. Bolonga: 1668. V. 46

Monstrorum Historia. Cum Paralipomenis Historiae Omnium Animalium Bartholomaeus Ambrosinus. Bologna: 1642. V. 37

Musaeum Metallicum in Libros IIII Distribution. colophon: Bologna: 1648. V. 46

Ornithologiae, Hoc Est de Avibus Historiae Libri XII. Bologna: 1599. V. 43

Ornithologiae Hoc Est de Avibus Historiae Libri XII . . . Bononiae: 1599-1603. V. 42

De Quadrupedibus Solidipedibus Volumen Integrum Ioannes Cornelius Uterverius In Gymnasic Bononiensi Simplicium Medicamento . . . Bononiae: 1616. V. 42

De Quadrupedibus Solidipedibus Volumen Integrum. Bologna: 1616. V. 39; 46

De Quadrupedibus Solidipedibus. Frankfurt: 1623. V. 41

De Quadrupedibus Solidipedibus. Volumen Integrum. Bologna: 1639. V. 45

De Religuis Animalibus Exanguibus Libri Quator, Post Mortem Eius Editi . . . Bononiae: 1606. V. 44

ALECHINKSY, PIERRE

Pierre Alechinsky. New York: 1977. V. 39; 46

ALEIXANDRE, VICENTE

World Alone. 1982. V. 41

ALEMAN, MATEO 1547-1610

The Rogue: or the Life of Guzman de Alfarache. London: 1622. V. 42

The Rogue; or, The Life of Guzman de Alfarache. London: 1634. V. 41; 45

The Rogue; or the Life of Guzman de Alfarache. London: 1924. V. 41; 46

The Rogue: or the Life of Guzman de Alfarache. London: 1623. V. 37

The Rogve; or, The Life of Gvzman de Alfarache. Oxford: 1630. V. 40

Vida y Hechos del Picaro Guzman de Alfarache. Atalaya de la Vida Humana. Antwerp: 1681. V. 37

Vita del Picaro Gusmano d'Alfarace, Osservatore della Vita Humana. Venice: 1615. V. 37

Vita del Picaro Gusmano d'Alfarace, Osservatore della Vita Humana . . . Milan: 1621. V. 37

ALEMANNI, NICCOLO

De Lateranensibus Parietinis . . . . Dissertatio Historica. Rome: 1625. V. 38

ALEMBERT, JEAN LE ROND D' 1717-1783

An Account of the Destruction of the Jesuits in France. London: 1766. V. 41; 43

Essai d'une Nouvelle Theorie de la Resistance des Fluides. Paris: 1752. V. 38

Oeuvres. Paris: 1821-22. V. 40; 43

Select Eulogies of Members of the French Academy. London: 1799. V. 42

Traite de Dynamique, Dans Lequel Les Loix de l'Equilibre & du Mouvement des Corps sont Reduites au Plus Petit Nombre Possible . . . Paris: 1758. V. 38

ALEMBIC PRESS

Payhembury Marbled Papers Sampler. Winchester: 1987. V. 42; 45

Plant Papers' Paper Plants. Oxford: 1989. V. 41

ALEN, LUKE

A Plan for the Better Organization of West India Troops Suggested by Major Luke Alen . . . for the Consideration of the Commander in Chief in the Windward and Leeward Islands. Antigua: 1806. V. 40

ALENCAR, J. DE

Iracema. The Honey-Lips. London: 1886. V. 45

ALENCAR, JOSE MARTINIANO DE

As Minas de Prata. Romance. Rio de Janeiro: 1865-66. V. 45

ALENCE, JOACHIM D' d. 1707?

Traitez des Barometres, Thermometres et Notiometres ou Hygrometres. Amsterdam: 1688. V. 42

ALER, F. VERNON

Aler's History of Martinsburg & Berkeley County, West Virginia. Hagerstown: 1888. V. 38

ALES, PIERRE

De Recta Vivendi Ratione . . . (with) De Utroque Jesu Christ Adventu . . . Paris: 1547/52. V. 46

ALESSIO ROBLES, VITO

Nicolas de Lafora: Relacion del Viaje Que Hizo a Los Presidios Internos Situados en la Frontera de la America Septentrional. Mexico: 1939. V. 38

ALEXANDER AB, ALEXANDRO d. 1503

Dies Geniales. Romae: 1522. V. 40

ALEXANDER, ALEXANDER

The Life, Written by Himself. Edinburgh: 1830. V. 38

ALEXANDER, ARCHIBALD

A Discourse Occasioned by the Burning of the Theatre in . . . Richmond, Virginia . . . by Which Awful Calamity a Large Number of Valuable Lives Were Lost . . . Philadelphia: 1812. V. 45

ALEXANDER, BOYD

From the Niger to the Nile. V. 39

From the Niger to the Nile. London: 1907. V. 37; 41; 44; 45; 46

ALEXANDER, C. G.

Francesca Alexander. A 'Hidden Servant'. Memories. Cambridge: 1927. V. 39

ALEXANDER, CALEB

A Grammatical Institute of the Latin Language. Worcester: 1794. V. 39

A Grammatical System of the Grecian Language. Worcester: 1796. V. 45

ALEXANDER, CHARLES BEATTY

Major William Ferguson, Member of the American Philosophical Society, Officer in the Army of the Revolution and In the Army of the United States. New York: 1908. V. 44

ALEXANDER, CHARLES W.

The Soldier's Casket. Philadelphia: 1865. V. 45

ALEXANDER, CONSTANCE M.

Baghdad in Bygone Days from the Journals and Correspondence of Claudius Rich, Traveller, Artist, Linguist, Antiquary and British Resident at Baghdad, 1808-1821. London: 1928. V. 45

ALEXANDER, DISNEY

An Answer to the Enquiry If It Is to Be the Duty of Every Person to Study the Preservation of His Health. Manchester: 1804. V. 39; 42

ALEXANDER, DOROTHY

The German Single-Leaf Woodcut, 1600-1700. New York: 1977. V. 41

ALEXANDER, E. P.

Military Memoirs of a Confederate. New York: 1907. V. 37

ALEXANDER, ESTHER FRANCES

The Story of Ida. New York: 1883. V. 44

ALEXANDER, EVELINE MARTIN

Among the Pimas. Albany: 1893. V. 39; 41; 45

ALEXANDER, GABRIEL

Robert Bruce, the Hero-King of Scotland. London: 1852. V. 43

alexander, gross

Steve P. Holcombe, the Converted Gambler; His Life and Work. Louisville: 1888. V. 46

ALEXANDER, HARTLEY BURR

Bertram Grosvenor Goodhue - Architect and Master of Many Arts. New York: 1925. V. 44

Sioux Indian Painting . . . Nice: 1938. V. 39; 43

Sioux Indian painting: Part I Paintings of the Sioux and Other Tribes of the Great Plains. Nice: 1938. V. 38; 41

ALEXANDER, J. A.

The Life of George Chaffey: a Story of Irrigation Beginnings in California and Australia. Melbourne: 1928. V. 43

ALEXANDER, J. E.

Salmon-Fishing in Canada, by a Resident. London: 1860. V. 39

ALEXANDER, J. H.

Report on the Manufacture of Iron; Addressed to the Governor of Maryland. Annapolis: 1840. V. 44

ALEXANDER, JAMES E.

L'Acadie; or, Seven Years' Explorations in British America. London: 1849. V. 44

Bush Fighting. London: 1873. V. 42

Incidents of the Maori War. New Zealand in 1860-61. London: 1863. V. 42

ALEXANDER, JAMES EDWARD

Narrative of a Voyage of Observation Among the Colonies of Western Africa, in the Flag-Ship Thalia; and a Campaign in Kaffir-Land . . . London: 1837. V. 46

Passages in the Life of a Soldier, or, Military Service in the East and West. London: 1857. V. 43; 46

Sketches in Portugal During the Civil War of 1834. London: 1835. V. 41

Transatlantic Sketches, Comprising Visits to the Most Interesting Scenes in North and South America, and the West Indies . . . London: 1833. V. 37; 38; 41

Transatlantic Sketches, a 16,000 Mile Survey of the 'New World', a One-Year Narrative of Voyages and Travels from Guiana to the West Indies, up the Mississippi and Ohio Rivers from New Orleans, through Canada, through Philadelphia . . . Philadelphia: 1833. V. 38; 43

Travels From India to England. London: 1827. V. 41; 45

ALEXANDER, JAMES MC KINNEY

Mission Life in Hawaii. Oakland: 1888. V. 46

ALEXANDER, JOHN

Boys Scouts. Orange: 1911. V. 37

ALEXANDER, JOHN A.

Mosby's Men. New York: 1907. V. 44

ALEXANDER, JOHN H.

Mosby's Men. New York/Washington: 1908. V. 37

ALEXANDER, JONATHAN JAMES GRAHAM

The Italian Manuscripts in the Library of Major J. R. Abbey. London: 1969. V. 39; 40

ALEXANDER, L.

The Book of Three. London: 1966. V. 39

ALEXANDER, LLOYD

Border Hawk; August Bondi. New York: 1958. V. 46

ALEXANDER MAGNUS, KING OF MACEDON

Alexandri Magni Historia pa Swenska Rijm aff Latinen . . . Tryckt pa Wilisingzborg: 1672. V. 38

ALEXANDER, MARY CHARLOTTE

William Patterson Alexnder. In Kentucky, the Marquesas, Hawaii. Honolulu: 1934. V. 38

ALEXANDER OF APHRODISIAS

(Greek) In Topica Aristotelis Commentarii. Venice: 1513. V. 37

ALEXANDER, PATRICK PROCTOR

Mill and Carlyle. An Examination of Mr. John Stuart Mill's Doctrine of Causation in Relation to Moral Freedom. Edinburgh: 1866. V. 39; 40; 42

ALEXANDER, RUSSELL GEORGE

The Engraved Work of F. L. Griggs. Stratford-upon-Avon: 1928. V. 37; 39; 40; 43; 46

ALEXANDER, SAMUEL

Space, Time and Deity. London: 1920. V. 46

ALEXANDER TRALLIANUS

De ARte Medica. Libri Duodecim, Graeci et Latini. Basel: 1556. V. 37; 42; 44

Libri Duodecim. Razae de Pestilentia Liberllus . . . Argentorati: 1549. V. 38; 39

ALEXANDER, WILLIAM

The Costume of the Russian Empire. London: 1803. V. 38

An Experimental Enquiry Concerning the Causes Which Have Generally Been Said to Produce Putrid Diseases. London: 1771. V. 44

The History of Women, from the Earliest Antiquity to the Present Time . . . London: 1779. V. 38; 44; 45; 46

Histoire des Femmes Depuis la Plus Haute Antiquite Jusqu'a Nos Jours. Paris: 1794. V. 43

The History of Women, from the earliest Antiquity, to the present time, giving some account of almost every interesting particular concerning that sex, among all Nations, ancient and modern. 1779. V. 37

A Journey to Beresford Hall, the Seat of Charles Cotton Esq. London: 1841. V. 39; 44

Picturesque Representations of the Dress and Manners of the English. London: 1814. V. 39; 41

Picturesque Representations of the Dress and Manners of the Russians. London: 1814. V. 39; 41; 44

Picturesque Representations of the Dress and Manners of the Austrians. London: 1814. V. 44

Picturesque Representations of the Dress and Manners of the Austrians, with Descriptions. London: 1814. V. 39

Picturesque Representations of the Dress and Manners of the Russians. London: 1815. V. 39

Picturesque Representations of the Dress and Manners of the Turks . . . London: 1814. V. 44

The Poetical Works of . . . Glasgow: 1870-72. V. 40; 46

ALEXANDER, WILLIAM D.

A Brief History of the Hawaiian People. New York: 1891. V. 38; 40

He Olelo No Ko Ke Akua Ano A Me Na Mea Ana I Kauoha Mai Ai I Kanaka . . . Honolulu: 1861. V. 39; 43

ALEXANDER, WILLIAM D. continued

History of Later Years of the Hawaiian Monarchy and the Revolution of 1893. Hawaii: 1896. V. 40; 43

History of Later Years of the Hawaiian Monarchy . . . Honolulu: 1896. V. 38; 39

History of Later years of the Hawaiian Monarchy . . . and the Revolution of 1893. (Honolulu): 1896. V. 37

ALEXANDERSON, GUNNAR

World Shipping, an Economic Geography of Ports and Seaborne Trade by 465 Internationally Quoted Authors, a Voluminous Work on Ports and Places Around the World. Stockholm: 1963. V. 38

ALEXANDRE, ARSENE 1859-1937

L'Art Decoratif de Leon Bakst. Paris: 1913. V. 39; 45

The Decorative Art of Leon Bakst. London: 1913. V. 38

Frank Boggs. Paris: 1929. V. 39

The Modern Poster. New York: 1895. V. 40; 42; 43; 44; 46

ALEXANDRE DE VILLEDIEU

The 'Costerian' Doctrinale. London: 1938. V. 38

ALEXANDRE, PHILIP

Alexandre's . . . Compendium. Facts About Oklahoma City in Detail, Oklahoma Territory in General, Kiowa & Comanche Country in Particular. Oklahoma City: 1901. V. 42; 44

ALEXIS; or, the Young Adventurer. London: 1746. V. 39; 41

ALEYN, CHARLES

The Battailes of Crescey and Poictiers, Under the Fortunes and Valour of King Edward the Third of that Name, and His Sonne Edward Price of Wales, Named the Black. London: 1633. V. 37; 46

The Battailes of Crescey and Poictiers, Under the Fortunes and Valour of King Edward the Third of that Name . . . London: 1733. V. 43

ALFIERI, VITTORIO

Memoirs of the Life and Writings of Victor Alfieri. London: 1810. V. 44

ALFONSO X, KING OF CASTILE AND LEON

Tabulae et L. Gaurici . . . Theoremata . . . In Calce Huius Libri Seorsum Annexe Sunt Tabulae Elisabeth Reginae Nuper Castigae and in Ordinem Recatae per L. Gauricum cum Additionibus & Novis Problematibus Eiusdem Gaurici. colophon: Venice: 1524. V. 43

ALFORD, HENRY 1810-1871

The Riviera: Pen and Pencil Sketches from Cannes to Genoa. By the Dean of Canterbury. London: 1870. V. 39

ALFORD, MARIAN M.

Needlework As Art. London: 1886. V. 44

ALFRED, H. J.

A Complete Guide to Spinning and Trolling Shewing How and Where to Take Pike and Jack with Instructions in the Art of Sprinning for Trout and Perch. London: 1860. V. 43

ALFRED, Lord Tennyson and His Friends. London: 1893. V. 44

ALGAROTTI, FRANCESCO, COUNT

An Essay on Painting. London: 1763. V. 42; 44

An Essay on Painting Written in Italain. London: 1764. V. 38; 40

An Essay on Opera. London: 1767. V. 45

Letters . . . to Lord Hervey and the Marquis Scipio Maffei, Containing the State of the Trade, Revenues and Forces of the Russian Empire . . . London: 1769. V. 38

ALGER, HORATIO

Ben, the Luggage Boy; or, Among the Wharves. Boston: 1870. V. 43

Fame and Fortune; or, the Progress of Richard Hunter. Boston: 1868. V. 43

Mark, the Match Boy; or, Richard Hunger's Ward. Boston: 1870. V. 39

Mark Mason's Victory. The Trials and Triumphs of a Telegraph Boy. New York: 1899. V. 41; 43

Ragged Dick; or Street Life in New York with the Boot Blacks. Boston: 1868. V. 39

Under Fire, or Fred Worthington's Campaign. New York: 1890. V. 37; 38

The Young Miner or, Thom Nelson in California. San Francisco: 1965. V. 42; 46

The Young Miner; or, Tom Nelson in California. San Francisco: Adrian Wilson: 1965. V. 37

ALGER, R. A.

Preliminary Examination of Reservoir Sites in Wyoming and Colorado. Letter From . . . Transmitting a Letter from the Chief Engineers Together with a Report from Captain Chittenden of a Preliminary Examination Made by Him . . . Washington: 1897. V. 37; 39

ALGER, WILLIAM REUNSEVILLE

A Critical History of the Doctrine of a Future Life. Philadelphia: 1864. V. 40

ALGREN, NELSON

Chicago: City on the Make. Garden City: 1951. V. 40; 46

Chicago: City on the Make. New York: 1951. V. 46

The Man With the Golden Arm. Garden City: 1949. V. 37; 39; 43; 45

Der Mann Mit Dem Goldenen Arm. Hamburg: 1952. V. 43

The Neon Wilderness. Garden City: 1947. V. 39; 43

The Neon Wilderness. New York: 1960. V. 46

Never Come Morning. New York: 1942. V. 46

Somebody in Boots. New York: 1935. V. 42; 46

A Walk on the Wild Side. New York: 1956. V. 40; 42; 45; 46

Who Lost an American? New York: 1963. V. 39; 43

ALGUE, P. JOSE

Atlas de Filipinas. Washington: 1900. V. 43

ALI IBN ISA

Memorandum Book of a Tenth Century Oculist for the Use of Modern Ophthalmologists. Chicago: 1936. V. 41

ALI, S.

Handbook of the Birds of India and Pakistan. Delhi: 1978-87. V. 38

ALI, SALIM

Handbook of the Birds of India and Pakistan; Together with Those of Bangladesh, Nepal, Bhutan and Sri Lanka. London: 1969-80. V. 40

Handbook of the Birds of India and Pakistan. London: 1968-74. V. 37

ALI, SHAHAMAT

The Skin and Afghans, In Connexion with India and Persia, Immediately Before and After the Death of Ranjeet Singh; from the Journal of an Expedition to Kabul, through the Panjab and the Khaibar Pass. London: 1847. V. 40

ALICE Neel. Atlanta: 1975. V. 46

ALIMARI, DOROTHEO

Longitudinis aut Terra Aut Mari Investigandae Methodus. London: 1715. V. 38

ALINGTON, HENRY, LORD

Catalogue of the Library of Crichel House, Dorset and Alington House, London . . . Southampton & Winchester: 1900. V. 45

ALISON, ARCHIBALD

England in 1815 and 1845; and the Monetary Famine of 1847; or, a Sufficient and a Contracted Currency. Edinburgh etc.: 1847. V. 41

England in 1815 and 1845: or, a Sufficient and a COntracted Currency. 1846. V. 37

Essays on the Nature and Principles of Taste. Boston: 1812. V. 41; 43

Essays on the Nature and Principles of Taste. Edinburgh: 1812. V. 44; 45

Essays on the Nature and Principles of Taste. Edinburgh: 1817. V. 42; 45

Essays on the Nature and Principles of Taste. New York: 1844. V. 40

History of Europe from the Commencement of the French Revolution in 1789 to the Restoration of the Bourbons in 1815. Edinburgh: 1839-42. V. 42

History of Europe from the Commencement of the French Revolution to the Restoration of the Bourbons, 1815. Edinburgh & London: 1849. V. 39

History of Europe from the Commencement of the French Revolution (to the Accession of Louis Napoleon in 1852). London: 1849-59. V. 42

Lives of Lord Castlereagh and Sir Charles Stewart the Second and Third Marquesses of Londonderry. London: 1861. V. 39

Remarks on the Administration of Criminal Justice in Scotland, and the Changes Proposed to be Introduced into It. Edinburgh: 1825. V. 37

Travels in France, During the Years 1814-15. Edinburgh: 1815. V. 42

ALKEN, HENRY 1751-1831

The Art and Practice of Etching. London: 1849. V. 41; 43; 45

The Beauties and Defects in the Figure of the Horse Comparatively Delineated in a Series of Engravings. Boston: 1830. V. 40; 41

The Beauties and Defects in the Figure of the Horse Comparatively Delineated. London: 1881, 1866. V. 39

Doing the Thing, and the Thing Done by Ben Tally Ho! London: 1818. V. 41

Illustrations for Landscape Scenery. London: 1821. V. 39; 40; 44

Illustrations to Popular Songs. London: 1825. V. 42

The Knights of the Tournament. London: 1831. V. 46

The National Sports of Great Britain. London: 1820. V. 39

The National Sports of Great Britain. London: 1821. V. 39; 40; 45; 46

The National Sports of Great Britain. London: 1825. V. 37; 38

The Progress of Human Life, Exibiting the Manner, Costume, Amusement & Field Sports of the English People. London: 1930. V. 39

Qualified Horses and Unqualified Riders, or the Reverse of Sporting Phrases Taken from the Work. London: 1815/21. V. 44

Real Life in London(. . .) London: 1821(-22). V. 37

Scraps from the Sketch-Book of . . . London: 1825. V. 40

ALKEN, HENRY 1751-1831 continued

Specimens of Riding Near London, Drawn from Life. London: 1821. V. 37; 42

Sporting Anecdotes. London: 1833-37. V. 46

The Sporting Repository . . . London: 1904. V. 42

The Sporting Repository. Containing Horse Racing, Hunting, Coursing, Shooting, Archery, Trotting, and Tandem Matches, Cooking, Pedestrianism, Pugilism; Anecdotes on Sporting Subjects interspersed with Essays, Tales and a great Variety of . . . London: 1822. V. 37

A Touch at the Fine Arts. London: 1824. V. 37; 38; 39; 41; 42; 44

Tutor's Assistant. London: 1823. V. 44

ALKEN, SAMUEL FL. 1780-1796

Sixteen Views of the Lakes from Drawings by J. Smith and J. Emes. London: 1795. V. 40

Sixteen views of the lakes in Cumberland and Westermorland; engraved by S. Alken, from drawings by J. Smith and J. Emes. London: c. 1800. V. 37

ALL About Alaska. San Francisco: 1888. V. 37

ALL About Northfield, Minn., Directory of Names and Business Firms, Information in Regard to the City, Advantages Shown Up. Northfield: 1889. V. 45

ALL About the Telephone and Phonograph. London: 1878. V. 44

THE ALL-ROUND Route Guide. The Hudson River; Trenton Falls; Niagara; Toronto; the Thousand Islands and the River St. Lawrence . . . Second Edition. Montreal: 1869. V. 37; 38; 40

ALLACCI, LEONE

Hellas, In Natales Delphini Gallici. (bound with) (Greek) Ourbanou tou Trismegistou Akrou Archiereos Andrias. Rome: 1642, 1640. V. 37

ALLAN, GEORGE

Life of Sir Walter Scott, Baronet . . . Edinburgh: 1834. V. 46

ALLAN, J. T.

Central and Western Nebraska and the Experiences of Its Stock Growers. Omaha: 1883. V. 38; 42

Nebraska and Its Settlers. Omaha: 1882. V. 38

ALLAN, JOHN HAY

The Bridal of Caolchairn and Other Poems. London: 1822. V. 43

ALLAN-OLNEY, M.

The Private Life of Galileo. London: 1870. V. 40

ALLAN, ROBERT

The Sportsman in IReland. London: 1840. V. 40

ALLAN, THOMAS

Mineralogical Nomenclature Alphabetically Arranged . . Edinburgh: 1814. V. 38

ALLAN, WILLIAM

The Army of Northern Virginia in 1862. Boston: 1892. V. 39

ALLARD, WILLIAM ALBERT

Vanishing Breed. Photographs of the Cowboy and the West. Photographs by William Albert Allard. Foreword by Thomas McGuane. Boston: (1982). V. 37

ALLARDICE, ROBERT BARCLAY 1779-1854

Agricultural Tour in the United States and Upper Canada. Edinburgh: 1842. V. 44; 45

Agricultural Tour in the United States and Upper Canada, with Miscellaneous Notices. Edinburgh & London: 1842. V. 40; 42

Agricultural Tour in the United States and Upper Canada, with Miscellaneous Notices. London: 1842. V. 42

ALLARDYCE, ALEXANDER

Balmoral. Edinburgh: 1893. V. 38; 43; 46

Balmoral; a Romance of the Queen's Country. Edinburgh & London: 1893. V. 42

ALLBUTT, CLIFFORD 1836-1925

On the Use of the Ophthalmoscope in Diseases of the Nervous System and the Kidneys; and in Certain Other General Disorders. London: 1871. V. 40

ALLBUTT, T. CLIFFORD 1836-1925

The Historical Relations of medicine and Surgery to the End of the 16th Century. London: 1905. V. 41

ALLBUTT, THOMAS CLIFFORD 1836-1925

Greek Medicine in Rome. The Fitzpatrick Lecture on the History of Medicine Delivered at the Royal College of Physicians of London in 1909-1910. With Other Historical Essays. London: 1921. V. 45

ALLDAY, JOSEPH

'Truth is Stranger than Fiction.' Birmingham: 1853. V. 46

ALLDRIDGE, T. J.

The Sherbro and Its Hinterland. London: 1901. V. 41

ALLEMAGNE, HENRY RENE D'

La Toile Imprimee et les Indiennes de Traite. Paris: 1942. V. 41

ALLEMAGNE, HENRY RENE DE

Recreations et Passe-Temps. Paris: 1906. V. 41

ALLEN, A. J.

Ten Years in Oregon. Ithaca: 1848. V. 38; 42

ALLEN, A. S.

The City of Seattle, 1900. Seattle: 1900. V. 45

ALLEN, ALBERT ARTHUR

Alo Studies. Oakland: 1919-23. V. 37

ALLEN, ALEXANDER V. G.

Life and Letters of Phillips Brooks. New York: 1901. V. 37

ALLEN, ANDREW H.

Report Upon the Official Relations of the United States with the Hawaiian Islands, from the First Appointment of a Counsular Officer. Washington: 1895. V. 37

ALLEN, ANDREW J.

The American Pioneer; with a New and Useful Plan to Establish Free Labor, in the United States. Boston: 1855. V. 42; 43

ALLEN, ANN H.

The Housekeeper's Assistant . . . Boston: 1845. V. 37

ALLEN, B. SPRAGUE

Tides in English Taste (1619-1800). New York: 1969. V. 41

ALLEN, BRASSEYA JOHNSON

Pastorals, Elegies, Odes, Epistles, and Other Poems. Abingdon: 1806. V. 45; 46

ALLEN, CHARLES

A New and Improved History of England, from the invasion of Julius Caesar to the end of the thirty-seventh year of the Reign of King George the Third. The Second Edition. London: 1798. V. 37

The Operator for the Teeth, Shewing How to Preserve the Teeth and Gums from all the Accidents They are Subject To. London: 1969. V. 44

ALLEN Crane, the Gold Seeker. Troy: 1850's. V. 39; 45

ALLEN, DOUGLAS

The Collected Paintings, Illustrations and Murals of N. C. Wyeth. New York: 1972. V. 39

ALLEN, EDWARD B.

Early American Wall Paintings. New Haven: 1926. V. 46

ALLEN, ETHAN

Historical Notices of St. Ann's Parish in Ann Arundel County, Maryland . . . 1649-1857. Baltimore: 1857. V. 46

ALLEN, FIFIELD

An Account of the Behaviour of Mr. James Maclaine, from the Time of His Condemnation to the Day of His Execution, October 3, 1750. London: 1750. V. 46

ALLEN, FRANCIS

A Complete English Dictionary. London: 1765. V. 41

ALLEN, FRANCIS H.

A Bibliography of Henry David Thoreau. Boston and New York: 1908. V. 42

ALLEN, FRED H.

The Great Cathedrals of the World. Boston: 1886. V. 38

ALLEN, GARDNER WELD

Massachusetts Privateers of the Revolution. Boston: 1927. V. 41

ALLEN, GEORGE

An Appeal to the People of Massachusetts, on the Texas Question. Boston: 1844. V. 37; 41

The Complaint of Texas and Conspiracy Against Liberty. Boston: 1843. V. 45

ALLEN, GLOVER M.

The Whalebone Whales of New England. Boston: 1916. V. 41; 42

ALLEN, GRACIE

How to Become President. New York: 1940. V. 41; 46

ALLEN, GRANT

An African Millionaire. London: 1897. V. 42

The British Barbarians. London: 1895. V. 38; 41

The Evolutionist at Large. London: 1881. V. 43

Falling in Love. With Other Essays or More Exact Branches of Science. London: 1889. V. 43

In All Shades. London: 1886. V. 43

The White Man's Foot. London: 1888. V. 41; 43

ALLEN, HARRISON

A System of Human Anatomy. Philadelphia: 1882. V. 40

A System of Human Anatomy. Including its Medical and Surgical Relations. Philadelphia: 1882-83. V. 37

ALLEN, HENRY T.

Report of an Expedition to the Copper, Tanana, and Koyukuk Rivers, in the Territory of Alaska, a Voyage and Travel, Reconnaissance by Coastal Mail Steamer Idaho to Sitka, and Portage Overland by Canoe . . . Washington: 1887. V. 38

ALLEN, HENRY W.

Address to the Citizens of New Orleans. Shreveport: 1864. V. 40

ALLEN, HENRY WATKINS

Official Report Relative to the Conduct of Federal Troops in Western Louisiana During the Invasions of 1863 and 1864. Shreveport: 1865. V. 40

Official Report Relative to the Conduct of Federal Troops in Western Louisian, During the Invasions of 1863 and 1864. New Orleans: 1939. V. 45

ALLEN, HERVEY

Anthony Adverse. New York: 1933. V. 39

Anthony Adverse. New York: 1934. V. 40; 41

Anthony Adverse. New York: 1937. V. 43

Israfel, the Life and Times of Edgar Allan Poe. New York: 1926. V. 43; 45

New Legends. New York: 1929. V. 46

Sarah Simon. Character Atlantean. Garden City: 1929. V. 39

Wampum and Old Gold. New Haven: 1921. V. 39; 46

ALLEN, IRA

A Concise Summary of the Second Volume of the Olive Branch . . . Philadelphia: 1806. V. 45

A Concise Summary of the Second Volume of the Olive Branch . . . Philadelphia: 1807. V. 45

A Narrative of the Transactions Relative to the Capture of the American Ship Olive Branch. Philadelphia?: 1804. V. 45

The Natural and Political History of the State of Vermont . . . to Which is Added, An Appendix Containing Answers to Sundry Queries Addressed to the Author. London: 1798. V. 39; 45

The State of Vermont, in Account-Current with the Hon. Samuel Mattocks, Esq. as Treasurer . . . the State of Vermont in Account with Ira Allen, Esq. as Treasurer of Said State . . . ?Rutland: 1795. V. 45

ALLEN, J. A.

American Bisons, Living and Extinct. 1876. V. 39

Ontogenetic and Other Variations in Muskoxen. 1913. V. 46

ALLEN, J. T.

Nebraska and its Settlers. What they have done and how they do it. Its crops and people. Omaha, Neb.: 1882. V. 37

ALLEN, JACOB D.

The Musings of Uncle Jake. London: 1866. V. 42

ALLEN, JAMES

At a Meeting of the West Indian Planters and Merchants Resolved, that the Following Considerations on the Present State of the Intercourse Between His Majesty's Sguar Colonies and the Dominions of the United States of America, . . . London: 1784. V. 46

Considerations on the Present State of the Intercourse Between His Majesty's Sugar Colonies and the Dominions of the United States of America. London: 1784. V. 41

Expedition to the Northwest Indians . . . 1832. Washington: 1834. V. 42

Schoolcraft and Allen - Expedition to Northwest Indians. Washington: 1834. V. 40; 41; 42; 45

ALLEN, JAMES LANE

Flute and Violin and Other Kentucky Tales and Romances. New York: 1891. V. 43

A Kentucky Cardinal and Aftermath. New York: 1900. V. 40; 43

A Kentucky Cardinal. A Story. New York: 1895. V. 37

ALLEN, JEREMIAH C.

Subject Index of the General Orders of the War Department from January 1 1809 to December 31, 1860. Washington: 1886. V. 41

ALLEN, JOEL A.

American Bisons, Living & Extinct. Cambridge: 1876. V. 38; 41

American Bisons, Living & Extinct. Cambridge, MA: 1876. V. 37

Notes on the Natural History of Portions of Montana and Dakota . . . Boston: 1874. V. 42

ALLEN, JOHN 1771-1839

Modern Judaism. London: 1816. V. 40; 41; 43

Modern Judaism; or, a Brief Account of the Opinions, Traditions, Rites and Ceremonies. London: 1830. V. 42

Principles of Modern Riding, for Gentlemen. London: 1825. V. 37

Synopsis Medicine: or, a Summary View of the Whole Practice of Physick. London: 1749. V. 40

ALLEN, JOSEPH

Battles of the British Navy. London: 1852. V. 38

Topographical and Historical Sketches of the Town of Northborough . . . Worcester: 1826. V. 46

ALLEN, L. L.

A Thrilling Sketch of the Life of the Distinguished Chief Okah Tubbee Alias, Wm. Chubbee, Son of the Head Chief, Mosholeh Tubbee, Of the Choctaw Nation of Indians. New York: 1848. V. 37; 39; 45

ALLEN, LEWIS

The Allen Press Bibliography. Facsimile with Original Leaves and Additions to Date Including a Checklist of Ephemera. Greenbrae: 1981. V. 44

The Allen Press Bibliography, a Facsimile with Original Leaves and Additions to Date Including a Checklist of Ephemera. San Francisco: 1985. V. 37; 39

Printing with the Handpress. Kentfield: 1969. V. 37; 38; 40; 41; 42; 45

ALLEN, MARY ADELE

Around a Village Green Sketches of Life in Amherst. Northampton: 1939. V. 45

ALLEN, MRS.

Pastorals, Elegies, Odes, Epistles and Other Poems. Abingdon: 1806. V. 37

ALLEN, N. I.

Diary of a March through Sinde and Afghanistan, with the Troops Under the Command of General William Nott, and Sermons Delivered on Various Occasions During the Campaign of 1842. London: 1843. V. 38

ALLEN, NATHAN

The Opium Trade; Including a Sketch of Its History, Extent, Effects, etc. Lowell: 1853. V. 43

ALLEN, PAUL

A History of the American Revolution . . . Baltimore: 1819. V. 42; 43

A History of the American Revolution. Baltimore: 1822. V. 42

History of the Expedition Under the Command of Captains Lewis and Clarke . . . New York: 1843. V. 45

Original Poems, Serious and Entertaining. Salem: 1801. V. 43

ALLEN, PHOEBE

Glimory: a Novel. London: 1876. V. 42

ALLEN PRESS

The Allen Press Bibliography. Greenbrae: 1981. V. 41

The Allen Press Bibliography. San Francisco: 1985. V. 38; 39; 40; 41

The Brothers. By Terence. 27 Drawings by Albrecht Durer. Kentfield, Calif.: 1968. V. 37

THE ALLEN Press Bibliography. Greenbrae: 1981. V. 43; 46
THE ALLEN Press Bibliography. San Francisco: 1985. V. 45; 46

ALLEN, R. R.

Tennessee Imprints 1791-1875. Knoxville: 1987. V. 39

ALLEN, RICHARD

A Souvenir of Newstead Abbey, Formerly the Home of Lord Byron. Nottingham: 1874. V. 43

ALLEN, SARAH

A Narrative of the Shipwreck and Unparalleled Sufferings of Mrs. Sarah Allen on Her Passage in May Last from New York to New Orleans . . . Boston: 1816. V. 41

ALLEN, T.

Hell Upon Earth; or, Devils Let Loose . . . London: 1822. V. 42

ALLEN, THOMAS

The Commerce and Navigation of the Valley of the Mississippi . . . St. Louis: 1847. V. 45

The History and Antiquities of London, Westminster, Southwark and Parts Adjacent. London: 1827-28. V. 39; 45

A New and Complete History of the County of York. London: 1828. V. 41

A New and Complete History of the County of York. London: 1828-31. V. 38; 43

ALLEN, THOMAS continued

Pacific Railroad Commenced. Address of Thomas Allen, Esq., of St. Louis to the Board of Directors of the Pacific Railroad Company . . . St. Louis: 1850. V. 39; 42; 45

ALLEN, THOMAS GEORGE

Egyptian Stelae in Field Museum of Natural History. Chicago: 1936. V. 40

ALLEN, VALENTINE COLLINS

Rhea and Meigs Counties (Tennessee) in the Confederate War. N.P.: 1908. V. 46

ALLEN, W.

Don't Drink the Water. 1967. V. 43

Getting Even. 1971. V. 45

ALLEN, W. E. D.

Caucasian Battlefields. A History of the Wars on the Turco-Caucasian Border 1828-1921. 1953. V. 37

David Allens. The History of a Family Firm, 1857-1957. London: 1957. V. 43

ALLEN, W. W.

California Gold Book. San Francisco: 183. V. 40

California Gold Book. San Francisco: 1893. V. 39; 43

California Gold Book. San Francisco & Chicago: 1893. V. 39; 40; 42

ALLEN, WALTER

Roaring Queen. London: 1973. V. 41; 42

ALLEN, WILKES

The History of Chelmsford . . . Memoir of the Pawtuckett Tribe of Indians. Haverhill: 1820. V. 37

ALLEN, WILLIAM

Five Years in the West . . . By Texas Preacher. Nashville: 1884. V. 37; 38

Five Years in the West . . . With Reminiscences and Sketches of Real Life, by a Texas Preacher. Nashville: 1884. V. 38

A Narrative of the Expedition Sent by Her Majesty's Government to the River Niger in 1841, under the Command of Capt. H.D. Trotter. London: 1848. V. 43

ALLEN, WILLIAM A.

Adventures with Indians and Game or Twenty Years in the Rocky Mountains. Chicago: 1903. V. 37; 40; 43; 45

The Sheep Eaters. New York: 1913. V. 37

ALLEN, WILLIAM HERVEY 1889-1949

Ballads of the Border. The Weakling and Other Pictures of Mobilization. El Paso: 1916. V. 37; 42

Israfel. The Life and Times of Edgar Allan Poe. New York: 1926. V. 37

Wampum and Old Gold. New Haven: 1921. V. 37

ALLEN, WOODY

Don't Drink the Water. New York: 1967. V. 43

Without Feathers. New York: 1975. V. 39

ALLEN, ZACHARIAH

The Practical Tourist, or Sketches of the State of the Useful Arts and of Society, Scenery, &c, &c. in Great Britain, France and Holland . . . Boston: 1832. V. 40

ALLENBY, E. H. H.

Brief Record of the Advance of the egyptian Expeditionary Force, July 1917 to October 1918. Cairo: 1919. V. 40

ALLENBY, EDMUND

A Brief Record of the Advance of the Egyptian Expeditionary Force July 1917 to October 1918 . . . Cairo: 1919. V. 46

ALLENDE, ISABEL

The House of Spirits. New York: 1985. V. 46

ALLERTON, R. G.

Brook Trout Fishing. An Account of a Trip of the Oquossoc Angling Association. New York: 1869. V. 44

ALLESTREE, RICHARD 1619-1681

The Art of Contentment. Oxford: 1675. V. 43; 45

The Causes of the Decay of Christian Piety. London: 1668. V. 40

The Gentleman's Calling. London: 1660. V. 41

The Gentleman's Calling. London: 1668. V. 40

The Gentleman's Calling. London: 1677. V. 38; 39

The Gentleman's Calling. London: 1696. V. 39; 41

The Ladies Calling. Oxford: 1673. V. 38; 41; 43; 45; 46

The Ladies Calling in Two Parts. Oxford: 1677. V. 44

The Lively Oracles Given to Us. Oxford: 1678. V. 45

The New Whole Duty of Man. London: 1813. V. 38; 39

The Whole Duty of man. Necessary for Families. London: 1673. V. 41

The Whole Duty of Man. London: 1675. V. 43

The Whole Duty of Man. Necessary for Families. 1673. V. 37

The Works of the Learned and Pious Author of the Whole Duty of Man. 1687. V. 42; 45

ALLETZ, PONS AUGUSTIN

Les Ornemens de la Memoire. Detroit: 1811. V. 42; 43; 46

ALLEY, GEORGE

Observations on the Hydrargyria; of That Vescular Disease Arising from the Exhibition of Mercury. London: 1810. V. 39

ALLEY, JEROME

The Judge; an Estimate of the Importance of the Judicial Character, Occasioned by the Death of the Late Lord Clare, Lord Chancellor of Ireland. London: 1803. V. 43

ALLEY, PETER

Public-Spirit, a Lyric Poem. London: 1793. V. 40

ALLEYN, CHARLES

The Historie of that Wise and Fortunate Prince, Henrie of that Name the Seventh, King of England . . . London: 1638. V. 40

ALLEYNE, JAMES

A New English Dispensatory, in Four Parts. London: 1733. V. 38; 39

ALLHANDS, JAMES LLEWELLYN

Boll Weevil - Recollections of the Trinity and Brazos Valley Railway. Houston: 1946. V. 42

Gringo Builders. 1931. V. 42; 44

Gringo Builders. Iowa City: 1931. V. 46

ALLIACO, PETRUS

Meditationes in Septem, Psalmos Poenitentiales. Paris: 1548. V. 37

ALLIACO, PETRUS DE

Tractatus et Sermones. Strassburg: 1490. V. 37; 40

ALLIBONE, SAMUEL AUSTIN

A Critical Dictionary of English Literature and British and American Authors Living and Deceased . . . Philadelphia: 1870-71. V. 43

A Critical Dictionary of English Literature and British and American Authors . . . Philadelphia: 1877. V. 42

A Critical Dictionary of English Literature and British and American Authors . . . Philadelphia & London: 1877. V. 39

A Critical Dictionary of English Literature and British and American Authors Living and Deceased, from the Earliest Accounts to the Latter Half of the Nineteenth Century. Detroit: 1965. V. 40

Dictionary of British and American Authors. London: 1859-1896. V. 37

ALLIENE, JOSEPH

An Alarm to Unconverted Sinners. Boston: 1764. V. 45; 46

THE ALLIES' Fairy Book. London & Philadelphia: 1916. V. 37; 38

ALLIN, E. S.

Rules for the Management and Cleaning of the Rifle Musket. Philadelphia: 1858. V. 41

ALLING, KENNETH SLADE

Core of Fire. New York: 1939. V. 38; 41

ALLINGHAM, E. G.

A Romance of the Rostrum. London: 1924. V. 38; 40

ALLINGHAM, H.

Letters to William Allingham. London: 1911. V. 39

ALLINGHAM, HELEN

Happy England. As painted by Helen Allingham, R.W.S. with Memoir and Descriptions by Marcus B. Huish. London: 1903. V. 37

ALLINGHAM, WILLIAM 1824-1889

The Ballad Books, A Selection of the Choicest British Ballads. London: 1864. V. 37

Day and Night Songs; and the Music Master. London: 1860. V. 38; 42

Day and Night Songs. London: 1884. V. 43

Evil May-Day etc. London: 1882. V. 43

Fairyland. Pictures From the Elf World. With a Poem by William Allingham. London: 1870. V. 37; 41

Flower Pieces and Other Poems. London: 1888. V. 37

Irish Songs and Poems. London: 1901. V. 43

Irish Songs and Poems. Ballyshannon: 1910. V. 38; 43

Laurence Bloomfield in Ireland. London: 1864. V. 43

ALLINGHAM, WILLIAM 1824-1889 continued

The Music Master, a Love Story. London: 1855. V. 39; 43; 45

Nightingale Valley. A Collection, including a great number of the choicest lyrics and short poems in the Enlgish Language. Edited by Giraldus. London: (1860). V. 37

Rhymes for the Young Folks. London: 1887. V. 43

Sixteen Poems by . . . Dundrum: 1905. V. 38

Sixteen Poems by William Allingham. Dundrum : 1905. V. 39

Ye Dirty Old Man (Dirty Dick). A Legend of Bishopsgate, from Household Words, Conducted by Charles Dickens. London: 1859. V. 37

ALLIS, OSCAR

An Inquiry into the Difficulties Encountered in the Reduction of Dislocations of the Hip. Philadelphia: 1896. V. 40; 42

Scoliosis: a New Study of an Old Problem. Philadelphia: 1938. V. 42

ALLIS, OSCAR H.

An Inquiry into the Difficulties Encountered in the Reduction of Dislocations of the Hip . . . Philadelphia: 1896. V. 41

ALLISON, DRUMMON

The Yellow Night. London: 1944. V. 37; 40

ALLISON, WILLIAM

The British Thoroughbred Horse. London: 1907. V. 42

The British Thoroughbred Horse. London: 1901. V. 37

ALLIX, SUSAN

The Beach, a Short Story. London: 1989. V. 41

Poems of Wyatt and Petrarch. Sonnets and Lyric Poems in English and Italian. London: 1989. V. 44

A South Italian Journey. London: 1985. V. 40

ALLMAN, GEORGE JAMES

A Monograph of the Fresh-Water Polyzoa . . . London: 1856. V. 43

A Monograph of the Gymnoblastic or Tubularian Hydroids. London: 1871. V. 42; 43

ALLNUTT, HENRY

The Auctioneer's Manual of the Manual of the Method of Keeping Accounts at Sales by Auction of Furniture, Cattle, etc. London: 1873. V. 37

ALLOM, T.

Forty-Six Views of Tyrolese Scenery, Beautifull Engraved on Steel from the Original Drawings. London: 1830. V. 44

Lake and Mountain Scenery. London. V. 41

ALLOM, THOMAS 1804-1872

China, in a Series of Views, Displaying the Scenery, Architecture and Social Habits of that Ancient Empire, with Historical and Descriptive Notices by the Rev. G. N. Wright. 1843. V. 44

Constantinople and the Scenery of the Seven Churches of Asia Minor Illustrated. London. V. 43

Picturesque Rambles in Westmorland, Cumberland, Durham and Northumberland. London: 1847. V. 39

Views in the Tyrol. London: 1836. V. 46

Westmorland, Cumberland, Durham and Northumberland Illustrated. London. V. 46

Westmorland, Cumberland, Durham and Northumberland Illustrated. London. V. 38; 40; 42

Westmorland, Cumberland, Durham and Northumberland Illustrated. London: 1832. V. 39

Westmorland, Cumberland, Durham and Northumberland Illustrated. London: 1840. V. 44

ALLOT, ROBERT

Wits Theater of the Little World. London: 1599. V. 37

ALLOT, WILLIAM

Thesaurus Bibliorum . . . Antwerp: 1581. V. 43

ALLOWAY, L.

Roy Lichtenstein. 1983. V. 46

ALLOWAY, LAWRENCE

Christo. New York: 1969. V. 43

ALLPORT, ELLEN

The Desire of the Moth. London: 1895. V. 43

ALLRIDGE, W. J.

The Universal Merchant, In Theory and Practice: Improved and Enlarged. Philadelphia: 1797. V. 39

ALLSOP, ROBERT OWEN

The Turkish Bath: Its Design and Construction . . . London: 1890. V. 38

ALLSOP, THOMAS

Letters, Conversations and Recollections of S. T. Coleridge. London: 1836. V. 42

ALLSOPP, FRED W.

Folklore of Romantic Arkansas. New York: 1931. V. 37; 38; 39; 40

ALLSTON, JOSEPH BLYTHE

Sumter. Columbia?: 1874. V. 39

ALLSTON, WASHINGTON

Monaldi: a Tale. Boston: 1841. V. 43

Outlines and Sketches. Boston: 1850. V. 39; 46

The Sylphs of the Seasons, with Other Poems. Boston: 1813. V. 45

ALLWOERDEN, HENRICUS

Historia Michaelis Serveti. Helmstadt: 1728. V. 37

ALLYN, AVERY

A Ritual, and Illustrations of Free-Masonry, and the Orange and Odd-Fellow's Societies . . . Devon: 1835. V. 38

ALLYN, GURDON L.

The Old Sailor's Story, or a Short Account of the Life, Adventures and Voyages of Captain Gurdon L. Allyn. Norwich: 1879. V. 38; 41; 42

ALLYN, JOSEPH PRATT

By Horse, Stage and Packet. San Francisco: 1988. V. 39; 40

ALMA-TADEMA, LAURENCE

Songs of Womanhood. London: 1903. V. 44

ALMACK, EDWARD

The Cavalier Soldier's Vade-Mecum. London: 1900. V. 40

Fine Old Bidnings with Other Interesting Miscellanea in Edward Almack's Library. London: 1913. V. 40; 41

The History of the Second Dragoons 'Royal Scots Greys'. London: 1908. V. 37

The Stuart Series. London: 1902-04. V. 41

ALMANACH der Wiener Werkstatte. Vienna & Leipzig: 1911. V. 43
ALMANACH der Wiener Werkstatte. Wien & Leipzig: 1911. V. 41

ALMANACH des Spectacles par K.Y.Z. Paris: 1818-25. V. 39

ALMANACH du Marriage pour l'Annee 1734 . . . Paris: 1734. V. 39

ALMANACH fur Das Jahr 1887. Vienna: 1886. V. 38

ALMANACH Pour l'Annee Bissextile 1820. Liege: 1820. V. 39

ALMANACH Royal. Paris: 1762. V. 40
ALMANACH Royal. Paris: 1782. V. 40
ALMANACH Royal. Paris: 1784. V. 40

ALMANACK. 1841. London: 1841. V. 46

ALMANACK 1929. London: 1929. V. 38

ALMANACK for 1793. London. V. 44

AN ALMANACK for the Year of Our Lord God MDCCXXXIV. London: 1734. V. 46

ALMANAK Statistico da Provincia d'Angola e Suas Dependencias Para o Anno de 1852. 1a publicacao. Loanda: 1851. V. 41

ALMAR, GEORGE

Oliver Twist. A Serio-Comic Burletta, in Three Acts. London: 1838? V. 40

ALMELOVEEN, THEODOR JANSSON VON

Inventa Nov-Antiqua. Id est Brevis Enarratio Ortus & Progressus Artis Medicae . . . Amsterdam: 1684. V. 42

ALMELOVEEN, THEODORE JANSSON VAN

De Vitis Stephanorum Celebrium Typographorum Dissertatio . . . Amsterdam: 1683. V. 38; 40; 41

ALMON, JOHN

Anecdotes of the Life of the Right Hon. William Pitt, Earl of Chatham and of the Principal Events of His Time, with His Speeches in Parliament . . . London: 1792. V. 43

An Asylum for Fugitive Pieces in Prose and Verse . . . London: 1785. V. 39

Biographical, Literary and Political Anecdotes of Several of the Most Eminent Persons of the Present Age. London: 1797. V. 40; 44; 46

A Collection of Interesting, Authentic Papers relative to the Dispute between Great Britain and America, shewing the causes and progress of that Misunderstanding from 1764 to 1775. 1777. V. 39

The Correspondence of the Late John Wilkes, with His Friends, Printed from the Original Manuscripts, in which are introduced Memoirs of His Life, by John Almon. London: 1805. V. 37

The History of the Late Minority. London: 1766. V. 38; 39; 41

ALMON, JOHN continued

A Letter Concerning Libels, Warrants, and the Seizure of Papers. London: 1764. V. 40

A Letter to the Right Honourable George Grenville, Occasioned by His Publication of the Speech He made in the House of Commons on the Motion for Expelling Mr. Wilkes . . . London: 1769. V. 38

Prior Documents. London: 1777. V. 38

The Remembrancer; or, Impartial Repository of Public Events. London: 1775-84. V. 46

A Review of Lord Bute's Administration. London: 1763. V. 46

ALMON, ROBERT

Distinguished Air (Grim Fairy Tales). Paris: 1925. V. 37

ALMONTE, JUAN N.

Noticia Estadistica Sobre Tejas. Mexico: 1835. V. 38

ALMORAN and Hamet: An Oriental Tale. London: 1761. V. 37

ALONSO Y DE LOS RUYZES DE FONTECHA, JUAN

Diez Privilegios Para Mugeres Prenadas . . . Alcala de Henaraes: 1606. V. 38

ALOPHE, MENUT

Les Danseuses de L'Oper. Costumes des Principaux Ballets. Paris: 1860. V. 38

Les Danseuses de L'Opera. Costumes des Principaux Ballets. Paris: (1860). V. 37

ALPAGO-NOVELLO, A.

Art and Architecture in medievel Georgia. 1980. V. 37

ALPATOV, M. W.

Art Treasures of Russia. New York. V. 38; 42

THE ALPHABET of Flowers. London: 1848. V. 46

AN ALPHABET; Being a Book of Designs & Rhymes by Students of the Applied Art School, Working Men's College, Melbourne. Melbourne: 1932. V. 41

THE ALPHABET of Creation. An Ancient Legend from the Zohar with Drawings by Ben Shahn. New York: (1954). V. 37

THE ALPHABET of Francesco Torniello Da Novara (1517) Followed by a Comparison with the Alphabet of Fra Luca Pacioli. Verona: 1971. V. 43

AN ALPHABETICAL Abridgment of the Laws for the Prevention of Smuggling. 1816. London: 1816. V. 38; 40

AN ALPHABETICAL List 'of the Names, Descriptions and Places of Abode of all Persons Subscribing to the Amount of 2,000 and Upwards to Any Railway Subscription Contract Deposited in the Private Bill Office During the Present Session of Parliament . . . London: 1846. V. 46

ALPHABETS Plain, Ornamented and Illuminated, a Selection from the Best Ancient and Modern Styles . . . Boston: 1880. V. 46

ALPHABETUM Graecum. Paris: 1560. V. 37

ALPHAND, A.

Les Promenades de Paris. Histoire - Descrip/tion des Embellissements - Depenses de Creation et d'Entretien des Bois de Boulogne et de Vincennes (etc.). Paris: 1867-73. V. 38

ALPHERAKY, SERGIUS

The Geese of Europe and Asia. London: 1905. V. 45; 46

ALPHONSO di Borgo; or, a Sentimental Correspondence of the Sixteenth Century. London: 1800. V. 40; 41

ALPHONSO; or, the Hermit. Cambridge: 1773. V. 40

ALPHONSUS DE SPINA

Fortalitium Fidei. Nuremberg: 1485. V. 38; 42; 44

ALPINI, PROSPER 1553-1617

De Plantis Aegypti Liber . . . Venice: 1592. V. 38

De Praesagienda Vita, et Morte Aegrotantium. Frankfurt: 1601. V. 38

De Praesagienda Vita et Morte Aegrotantium. Libri Septem. Francofurti & Lipsiae: 1754. V. 38

De Preaesagienda vita, et moret aegrotantiu,. Frankfurt: 1601. V. 37

Historiae Aegypti Naturalis, pars prima qua Continetur, Rerum Aegyptarum Libri Quatuor. Opus Postumum - Pars Secunda sive de Plantis Aegypti . . . Leyden: 1735. V. 38

Historiae Aegypti Naturalis: Part 1: Rerum Aegyptiarum. Part II: De Plantis Aegypti. Leyden: 1735. V. 37

De Medicina Aegyptiorum. Paris: 1645. V. 40

De Plantis Aegypti Liber . . . Venetiis: 1592. V. 45

De Plantis Aegypti Liber . . . Venice: 1592. V. 40

De Plantis Aegypti Liber . . . Venice: 1952. V. 43

De Praesagienda Vita et Morte Aegrotantium Libri Septem . . . Venetiis: 1751. V. 39

ALPOIM, JOSE FERNANDES PINTO DE

Exame de Artilheiros que Comprehende Arithmetica, Geometria, e Artilharia, com Quatro Appendices . . . Lisbon: 1744. V. 41

ALQUIE, FRANCOIS SAVINIEN D' fl. 1669-1681

La Science et L'Ecole des Amans . . . Amsterdam: 1677. V. 46

ALSEXANDRE, ARSENE

The Modern Poster. New York: 1895. V. 44

ALSION, ARCHIBALD

Essays on the Nature and Principles of Taste. Edinburgh: 1812. V. 42

ALSON, ARCHIBALD

History of Europe from the Commencement of the French Revolution (to the Accession of Louis Napoleon 1852). London: 1849-59. V. 39

ALSOP, ANTHONY

Odarum Libri Duo. 1752. V. 38

ALSOP, GEORGE

A Character of the Province of Maryland. Cleveland: 1902. V. 45

ALSOP, RICHARD

The Echo. New York: 1807. V. 37; 40; 45

A Narrative of the Adventures and Sufferings of John R. Jewitt: only Survivor of . . . the Ship Boston, During a Captivity of Nearly Three Years . . . Middletown: 1815. V. 40

The Political Greenhouse, for the Year 1798. Hartford;: 1799. V. 44

ALSTON, A. H.

Seamanship, and Its Associated Duties in the Royal Navy . . . Together with a Treatise on Nautical Surveying . . . London: 1860. V. 41

ALSTON, CHARLES

A Third Disseration on Quick-Lime and Lime Water. Edinburgh: 1757. V. 45; 46

ALSTON, J. W.

Hints to Young Practioners, in the Study of Landscape Painting. London: 1804. V. 38; 42

Hints to Young Practioners, in the Study of Landscape Painting. London: 1804. V. 42

Hints to Young Practitioners in the Study of Landscape Painting. London: 1805. V. 43

Hints to Young Practitioners in the Study of Landscape Painting . . . London: 1820. V. 44

ALT, CHARLES

Specimen of Wood Engravings, Presented by Charles Alt, Engraver on Wood, 318, Broadway, New York. New York: 1886. V. 43

ALTAMIRANO, PEDRO I.

Informe Historico, Canonico, Y Real, Por las Missiones de la Compania de Jesus de la Nueva Espana . . . Madrid?: 1751-57. V. 40

ALTER, J. CECIL

James Bridger, Trapper, Frontiersman, Scout and Guide. Salt Lake City: 1925. V. 39; 40; 42; 45

James Bridger: Trapper, Frontiersman, Scout and Guide. Columbus: 1951. V. 40

James Bridger: Trapper, Frontiersman, Scout and Guide. Salt Lake City: (1925). V. 37

ALTHAMER, ANDREAS 1498-1540

Diallage, Hoc Est, Concillatio Locorum Scripturae. Nuremberg: 1528. V. 40; 42; 44

ALTIERI, FERDINANDO

Dizionario Italiano ed Ingelese. A Dictionary of Italian and English . . . London: 1749. V. 42

A New Grammar, Italian-English and English-Italian Which Contains a True and Easy Method for Acquiring These Two Languages. London: 1728. V. 42; 46

ALTOUNYAN, E. H. R.

Ornament of Honour. Cambridge: 1937. V. 41

ALUFSEN, O.

Through the Unknown Pamirs. The Second Danish Pamir Expedition. London: 1904. V. 40

ALUNNO, FRANCESCO

Della Fabrica Del Mondo. Venice: 1568. V. 44

Della Fabrica del Mondo, Libri Dieci . . . con un Nuovo Vocabulario in Fine . . . Venice: 1588. V. 45

ALVARADO Y VELAUSTEGUI, FELIX ROMAN DE

Senores, Vale mas Perdonaar a Mil Culpados que Condenar a un Inocente. Madrid: 1824. V. 38

ALVARES, FRANCISCO

Historia de las Cosas de Etiopia, en la Qual se Cuenta Muy Copiosamente, el Estado y Potencia del Emperador Della . . . Antwerp: 1557. V. 41

ALVAREZ DE ABREU, JOSEPH

Extracto Historial del Expediente que Pende en el Consejo Real y Supremo de las Indias, a Instancia de la Ciudad de Manila, y Demas de las Islas Philipinas . . . Madrid: 1736. V. 40

ALVAREZ, WALTER C.

The Mechanics of the Digestive Tract. New York: 1928. V. 44

ALVENSLEBEN, MAX, BARON VON

With Maximilian in Mexico, from the Note-Book of a Mexican Officer. London: 1867. V. 42

ALVES, ROBERT

Odes. Edinburgh: 1778. V. 40

Poems. Edinburgh: 1782. V. 40; 42

Time, an Elegy. Aberdeen: 1766. V. 41

ALVORD, CLARENCE W.

The First Explorations of the Trans-Allegheny Region by the Virginians 1650-1674. Cleveland: 1912. V. 38; 45

The Mississippi Valley in British Politics. Cleveland: 1917. V. 37; 38; 42; 43; 46

ALY, MOHAMED, PRINCE

Breeding of Pure Bred Arab Horses. Cairo: 1935. V. 43

AMADEO OF SAVOY, LUIGI

On the 'Polar Star' in the Arctic Sea. London: 1903. V. 44

AMADIO, NADINE

Orpheus: The Song of Forever. New South Wales: 1983. V. 39

AMADO, JORGE

Gabriela, Clove and Cinnamon. New York: 1962. V. 44

Vida De Luiz Carlos Prestes. Buenos Aires: 1942. V. 45

AMALTEO, GIAMBATTISTA 1525-1573

Canzone..Sopra la Vittoria Seguita l'Armata Turchesca. Venice: 1572. V. 45

AMANO, YOSHITARO

Textiles of the Andes: Catalog of Amano Collection. San Francisco: 1979. V. 40

AMARAL, MELCHIOR ESTACIO DO

Tratado das Batalhas e Sucessos do Galeam Santiago com Os Olandezes na Ilha de Santa Elena. Lisbon: 1736. V. 40; 43

AMARALL, ANTHONY

Mustang, Life and Legends of Nevada's Wild Horse. Reno: 1977. V. 46

AMARI, MICHELE

History of the War of the Sicilian Vespers. London: 1850. V. 37; 39; 42

AMAT, CARLOS OQUENDO DE

Five Meters of Poems. Isla Vista: 1986. V. 38

AMATEUR Gems. By amateur Authors. Winchendon: 1878. V. 41

AMATEUR, PSEUD.

Real Life in London; or, the Rambles and Adventures of Bob Tallyho, Esa. and His Cousin the Hon. Tom Dashall Through the Metropolis . . . London: 1821-23. V. 41

AMAZON

Exploration of the Valley of the Amazon. Washington: 1854. V. 37

amberg, george

Art in Modern Ballet. New York: 1946. V. 45

THE AMBIGU of Prose and Poetry, Original and Select. London: 1825. V. 44

THE AMBITIOUS Practices of France: or, A Relation of the Ways and Methods Used by Them to Attain to the Supream Grandeur. London: 1689. V. 39

AMBLER, CHARLES

Reports of Cases Argued and Determined in the Hight Court of Chancery, with some Few In Other Courts . . . London: 1790. V. 38; 45

AMBLER, CHARLES HENRY

History of Transporation in the Ohio Valley . . . Glendale: 1932. V. 37; 40; 41; 42; 44

AMBLER, ERIC

The Ability to Kill. London: 1962. V. 37; 40; 46

The Ability to Kill. London: 1963. V. 45

Background to Danger. 1937. V. 37; 39

Background to Danger. New York: 1937. V. 37; 43

The Care of Time. New York: 1981. V. 42; 44; 45

Cause for Alarm. 1939. V. 39

A Coffin for Dimitrios. New York: 1939. V. 39

Epitaph for a Spy. London: 1938. V. 40

The Intercom Conspiracy. London: 1969. V. 40

The Jealous God. London: 1964. V. 46

Journey into Fear. 1940. V. 39

Passage of Arms. New York: 1950. V. 41

Passage of Arms. London: 1959. V. 45

Passage of Arms. New York: 1960. V. 42; 43; 45

The Schirmer Inheritance. New York: 1953. V. 45

AMBLER, LOUIS

The Old Halls and Manor Houses of Yorkshire. London: 1913. V. 46

AMBROSE, ISAAC

Prima, Edia & Ultima: The First, Middle and Last Things, in Three Treatises . . . London: 1654. V. 44; 45

AMBROSE, SAINT, ABP. OF MILAN

Christian Offices Crystall Glasse. London: 1637. V. 45

Omnia Opera Accuratissime Revisa; Atque in tres Partes Nitidissime Excusa. Basle: 1516. V. 40

AMBROSIUS, SAINT, ABP. OF MILAN

Epistolae. Milan: 1491. V. 38; 45

Expositio in Corpus Lucae Evangelistae. Augsburg: 1476. V. 41; 43

AMBROSIUS, SAINT, BP. OF MILAN

De Officiis (with other tracts). Milan: 1474. V. 41

AMEDEO, LUIGI, OF SAVOY, DUKE OF THE ABRUZZI

On the 'Polar Star' in the Arctic Sea. London: 1903. V. 44; 46

AMELIA, or the Distress'd Wife; A History Founded on Real Circumstances. London: 1751. V. 41

AMELIA; or, The Faithless Briton. Boston: 1798. V. 39

AMELOT DE LA HOUSSAYE, ABRAHAM NICOLAS

The History of the Government of Venice. London: 1677. V. 42

AMELUNG, PETER

. . . Johann Zainer the Elder and Younger. Los Angeles: 1985. V. 37; 38; 42; 46

AMERICA, An Ode. To the People of England. London: 1776. V. 37; 38; 43

AMERICA Esoterica. New York: 1927. V. 39

AMERICAN ACADEMY OF ARTS AND SCIENCES

Memoirs of the American Academy of Arts and Sciences (Old Series, Volumes One through Four). Boston & Cambridge: 1785-93-1809-18. V. 37

Memoirs. To The End of the Year 1783. Boston: 1785. V. 37

AMERICAN ACADEMY OF FINE ARTS

A Catalogue of Italian, Flemish, Spanish, Dutch, French and English Pictures. New York: 1830. V. 40

AMERICAN Anecdotes, Characters and Incidents; Revolutionary and Miscellaneous. Original and Selected. Philadelphia: 1823. V. 37

AMERICAN ANTIQUARIAN SOCIETY

Archaeologia Americana. Transactions and Collections of the American Antiquarian Society. Volume Two. Cambridge: 1836. V. 37

AMERICAN ART ASSOCIATION, NEW YORK.

Illustrated Catalogue of a Grand Collection of Beautiful Old Chinese Rugs and Carpets (Collection of) the Tiffany Studios. 1916. V. 45

AMERICAN ARTISTS' CONGRESS

America Today: a Book of 100 Prints. New York: 1936. V. 41

First Annual Membership Exhibition. Mezzanine Galleries, International Building, 630 Fifth Ave. Rockefeller Center, New York, April 16th to April 29th 1937. New York: 1937. V. 42

Third Annual Membership Exhibition. Art in a Skyscraper, 6th Floor, 444 Madison Ave., New York: Feb. 5-26, 1939. New York: 1939. V. 42

THE AMERICAN Bee . . . Leominster: 1797. V. 44

THE AMERICAN Bee: A Collection of Entertaining Histories. Leonminster: 1797. V. 43

THE AMERICAN Book Collector. Metuchen: 1932-35. V. 46

AMERICAN Book Prices Current . . . 1984. New York: 1984. V. 40

AMERICAN Book Prices Current . . . 1985. New York: 1986. V. 40

AMERICAN Book Prices Current . . . 1986. New York: 1986. V. 40

AMERICAN Book Prices Current . . . 1987. New York: 1987. V. 40

AMERICAN Book-Prices Current. Index 1955-1960. New York: 1961. V. 40; 41

AMERICAN Book Prices Current . . . Index 1960-1965. New York: 1968. V. 40; 41

AMERICAN Book Prices Current . . . Index 1965-1970. New York: 1974. V. 40
AMERICAN Book Prices Current. Index 1965-1970. New York: 1974. V. 43

AMERICAN Book Prices Current . . . Index . . . 1970-1975. New York: 1976. V. 40

AMERICAN Book Prices Current . . . Index . . . 1975-1979. New York: 1980. V. 40

AMERICAN Book Prices Current . . . Index . . . 1979-1983. New York: 1984. V. 40

THE AMERICAN BOY'S Book of Sports and Games. New York: 1864. V. 40

AMERICAN BRIDGE CO.

Standards for Structural Details. Pittsburgh: 1901. V. 44

AMERICAN Caravan IV. New York: 1931. V. 41

AMERICAN COLONIZATION SOCIETY

Information About Going to Liberia: With Things Which Every Emigrant Ought to Know. Washington: 1852. V. 39

THE AMERICAN Comic Almanack for 1831. Boston: 1830. V. 40

THE AMERICAN Cyclopedia. New York: 1881. V. 40

AMERICAN Decade. Cummington: 1943. V. 37

AMERICAN Dictionary of Printing and Bookmaking. New York: 1894. V. 39
AMERICAN Dictionary of Printing and Bookmaking. New York: 1894. V. 41; 42

THE AMERICAN Dream Book, or the Origin, Interpretation and History of Dreams. Philadelphia: 1850? V. 45

AMERICAN ELECTRO-THERAPEUTIC ASSOCIATION

Transactions of the American Electro-Therapeutic Association, 4th Annual Meeting. New York: 1894. V. 42

AMERICAN ETHNOLOGICAL SOCIETY

Transactions of the . . . New York: 1845, 1848. V. 38

Transactions of the American Ethnological Society, Volume I. New York: 1845. V. 37

THE AMERICAN Fowl-Breeder. Boston: 1850. V. 40

THE AMERICAN Guide: Comprising the Declaration of Independence; the Articles of Confederation; the Constitution of the United States; and the Constitutions of the Several States Composing the Union. Philadelphia: 1828. V. 44

AMERICAN HISTORICAL ASSOCIATION

Annual Report of the . . . Washington: 1908. V. 46

Annual Report of the American Historical Association for the Year 1893. Washington: 1894. V. 37

AMERICAN Imprints Inventory. A Check List of Wisconsin Imprints, 1833-1863. Madison: 1942. V. 42

AMERICAN INSTITUTE OF ELECTRICAL ENGINEERS

Catalogue of the Wheeler Gift of Books, Pamphlets and Periodicals in the Library of . . . . New York: 1909. V. 43

Transactions of the American Institute of Electrical Engineers, Volume XXXV. New York: 1916. V. 37

THE AMERICAN Jest Book, Being a Chaste Collection of Anecdotes, Bon Mots and Epigrams, Original and Selected, for the Amusement of the Young and Old of Both Sexes. Philadelphia: 1833. V. 40

AMERICAN Jest Book: Containing a Choice Selection of Jests, Anecdotes, Bon Mots, Stories, &c. Harrisburgh: 1796. V. 43

AMERICAN JEWISH PUBLICATION SOCIETY

Constitution and By-Laws of the American Jewish Publication Society . . . Adopted at Philadelphia on Sunday, Nov. 30, 1845. Philadelphia: (1845). V. 38

Constitution and By-Laws of the American Jewish Publication Society. Philadelphia: (i.e.1845). V. 37

Constitution and By-Laws of the American Jewish Publication Society . . . Adopted at Philadelphia . . . November 30, 1845. Philadelphia: 1845. V. 37

THE AMERICAN Journal of Syphilography and Dermatology. Volumes 1 through 4. New York: 1870-1873. V. 37

AMERICAN Journal of the Medical Sciences, Volume 1. Philadelphia: 1827. V. 40; 43

THE AMERICAN Laborer. New York: 1842-1843. V. 38; 40

AMERICAN LITERATURE

Eccentricities of Literature & life, or the Recreative Magazine. Boston: 1822. V. 37

AMERICAN Lumbermen. The Personal History and Public and Business Achievements of One Hundred Eminent Lumbermen of the United States. Chicago: 1905. V. 46
AMERICAN Lumbermen. The Personal History and Public and Business Achievements of One Hundred Eminent Lumbermen of the United States. Chicago: 1906. V. 46

THE AMERICAN Magazine of Wit; a Collection of Anecdotes, Stories and Narratives . . . New York: 1808. V. 44

AN AMERICAN Medical Lexicon, on the Plan of Quincy's Lexicon Physico Medicum, with Many Retrenchments . . . New York: 1811. V. 40

THE AMERICAN Medical Recorder. Philadelphia: 1823. V. 40; 42

AN AMERICAN Memorial to Keats. London: 1894. V. 42

THE AMERICAN Mercury. New York: 1924. V. 43

THE AMERICAN Military Pocket Atlas. London: 1776. V. 38; 39
THE AMERICAN Military Pocket Atlas. London: 1776. V. 38

AMERICAN MISSIONARY ASSOCIATION

History of the American Missionary Association: Its Churches and Educational Institutions Among the Freedman, Indians and Chinese. New York: 1874. V. 38

THE AMERICAN Museum: or, Repository of Ancient and Modern Fugitive Pieces. Philadelphia: 1789. V. 39

THE AMERICAN Musical Miscellany. Northampton: 1798. V. 39

AMERICAN Newspaper Directory 1776. New York: 1876. V. 45

AMERICAN PHARMACEUTICAL ASSOCIATION

The National Formulary of Unofficial Preparations. N.P.: 1888. V. 40

AMERICAN PHILOSOPHICAL SOCIETY

Conditions of the Magellanic Premium. Philadelphia: 1806. V. 45

Transactions of the American Philosophical Society, Held at Philadelphia, for Promoting Useful Knowledge. Philadelphia: 1786. V. 38; 40

Transactions of the American Philosophical Society, Held at Philadelphia, for Promoting Useful Knowledge. Philadelphia: 1793. V. 38; 40

AMERICAN PHYTOPATHOLOGICAL SOCIETY

Phytopathological Classics. Nos. 1-5. Lancaster, Pa.: 1926-1934. V. 37

AMERICAN Poems, Selected and Original. Litchfield: 1793. V. 38; 41; 44

AMERICAN Poetry - a Miscellany. New York: 1922. V. 38; 39; 41

AMERICAN Poets: an Anthology of Seven Young Contemporary Poets. Prairie City: 1941. V. 39

AMERICAN PRINTING HISTORY ASSOCIATION

The Journal of the American Printing History Association. New York: 1979-86. V. 40

AMERICAN Race Horses: a Review of the Breeding and Performance of the Outstanding Thoroughbreds of the year Engaged in Racing, Steeplechasing and Hunt Races. New York: 1936-56. V. 46

AMERICAN Railway Guide, and Pocket Companion, for the United States . . . New York: 1851. V. 45

THE AMERICAN Register; or Summary Review of History, Politics and Literature. Philadelphia: 1817. V. 39

AMERICAN Resistance Indefensible. A Sermon, Preached on Friday, December 13, 1776, Being a Day Appointed for a General Fast. London: 1776. V. 37

THE AMERICAN Review of History and Politics. Philadelphia. V. 38

AMERICAN School of Classical Studies at Athens. Gennadius Library Catalogue of the Gennadius Library. Boston: 1968-1981. V. 40

AMERICAN School of Classical Studies at Athens. Gennadius Library Catalogue of the Library. (with) First Supplement . . . Boston: 1968-73. V. 39

AMERICAN SCHOOL OF ORIENTAL RESEARCH IN JERUSALEM

The Annual of the . . . New Haven: 1920. V. 44

THE AMERICAN Ship-Master's Daily Assistant, or, Compendium of Marine Law and Mercantile Regulations and Customs. Portland: 1807. V. 42

AMERICAN SHIPMASTERS' ASSOCIATION

Rules for Building and Classing Vessels, 1888. N.P.: 1888. V. 41

THE AMERICAN Shooter's Manual, Comprising, Such Plain and Simple Rules, as Are Necessary to Introduce the Inexperienced Into a Full Knowledge of all that Relates to the Dog, and the Correct Use of the Gun. Philadelphia: 1827. V. 39; 46

THE AMERICAN Shooter's Manual: Comprising Such Plain and Simple Rules as are Necessary to Introduce the Inexperienced Into a Full Knowledge of All That Relates to the Dog, and the Correct Use of the Gun; also a Description of the Game of This Country. New York: 1928. V. 44

AMERICAN SOCIETY FOR THE PROMOTION OF TEMPERANCE

First Annual report of the Executive Committee of the American Society for the Promotion of Temperance for the Year Ending November, 1827. Andover: 1828. V. 39

AMERICAN SOCIETY OF CHURCH HISTORY

Paapers of the . . . Second Series Volumes 1-9. New York: 1913-14. V. 37

AMERICAN SOCIETY OF LANDSCAPE ARCHITECTS

Illustrations of Work of Members. New York: 1934. V. 45

THE AMERICAN Stage of To-day Biographies and Photographs of One Hundred Leading Actos and Actresses. New York: 1910. V. 37; 45

AMERICAN Stuff: An Anthology of Prose and Verse by Members of the Federal Writers' Project. New York: 1937. V. 44

AMERICAN Taxation, &c. or Verses Composed on the Causes, Progress, Glorious Termination, and Happy Consequences of Our Revolutionary War, in 1776-1782. N.P.: 1782 or 1783? V. 41

THE AMERICAN Timber Supply. Statement of the Property in Timber Lands Belonging to the New Hampshire Land Company . . . Boston: 1880. V. 42

THE AMERICAN Tour of Messrs Brown, Jones and Robinson. Being the History of what they saw & did in the United States, Canada and Cuba. By Toby. New York: 1872. V. 37

AMERICAN TRACT SOCIETY

Proceedings of the First Ten Years of the American Tract Society, Instituted at Boston, 1814. N.P.: 1824. V. 40

AMERICAN Turf Register and Sporting Magazine. Baltimore & New York: 1829-44. V. 43
AMERICAN Turf Register and Sporting Magazine. New York: 1829-44. V. 43

AMERICAN TYPE FOUNDERS

American Specimen Book of Type Styles. New Jersey: 1912. V. 46

American Specimen Book of Type Styles. N.P.: 1912. V. 42

American Line Type Book, Borders, Ornaments, Price List Printing Material and Machienry. Jersey City: 1906. V. 38

American Specimen Book of Type Styles, Complete Catalogue of Printing Machinery and Printing Supplies. New York: 1912. V. 38

Desk Book of Printing Types. Boston: 1898. V. 42

Desk Book of Type Specimens, Borders, Ornaments, Brass Rules and Cuts. N.P.: 1900. V. 42

Desk Book of of Printing Types to Which is Appended a Condensed Catalogue and Price List of Printing Machinery and Materials. Boston: 1898. V. 38

Initials, Headpieces and Tailpieces, Embellishments and Ornamentations for the Printer and Publisher. N.P.: 1900. V. 42

Pacific Coast Blue Book: Containing Specimens of Type, Printing Machinery, Printing Material. San Francisco & Portland: 1896. V. 42

Specimen Book and Catalogue. N.P.: 1923. V. 42

AMERICAN TYPE FOUNDERS CO.

American Line Type Book, Borders, Ornaments, Price List Printing Material and Machinery, 1906. Jersey City: 1906. V. 40; 44

Specimen Book and Catalogue. Jersey City: 1923. V. 39

AMERICAN TYPE FOUNDERS COMPANY

Catalogue of Body Type Faces Both Modern Roman and Oldstyle, Together with a Showing of body Type Sundries, List of Accents, Miscellaneous Signs, Etc. N.P.: 1913. V. 44

Wood Type. N.P.: 1896. V. 44

THE AMERICAN'S Guide Comprising the Declaration of Independence; the Articles of Confederation; the Constitution of the United States and the Constitutions of the Several States Composing the Union. Philadelphia: 1843. V. 39

L'AMERIQUIADE. Poeme, pur la Benefice de l'Auteur. Philadelphia: 1780. V. 46

L'AMERIQUIADE. Poeme, Pour le Benefice de l'Auteur. Philadelphie: 1780. V. 40; 46

AMERY, L. S.

The Times History of the War in South Africa. London: 1900-09. V. 39; 40; 41; 44; 45

AMES, AZEL

The May-Flower and Her Log, July 15, 1620-May 6, 1621. Boston: 1901. V. 41; 46

AMES, DANIEL T.

Ames Book of Flourishes. New York: 1890. V. 40

Compendium of Practical and Ornamental Penmanship. New York: 1883. V. 40

AMES, FISHER

An Oration on the Sublime Virtues of General George Washington Pronounced at the Old South Meeting-House in Boston, Before His Honor the Lieutenant-Governor, the Council and the Two Branches of the Legislature . . . 1800. Boston: 1800. V. 46

The Speech of Mr. Ames in the House of Representatives of the United States . . . Thursday April 28, 1796, In Support of the Following Motion: Resolved, That It Is Expedient to Pass the Laws Necessary to Carry Into Effect the Treaty Lately Concluded . . . Philadelphia: 1796. V. 44

AMES, HERBERT BROWN

Thee City Below the Hill. A Sociological Study of a portion of the City of Montreal, Canada. Montreal: 1897. V. 37

AMES, JAMES BARR

Lectures on Legal History and Miscellaneous Legal essays. Cambridge: 1913. V. 40; 44

Lectures on Legal History and Miscellaneous Legal Essays. 1925. V. 40

AMES, JOSEPH

A Catalogue of English Heads; or, an Account of About Two Thousand Prints. London: 1748. V. 38; 46

A List of Various Editions of the Bible, and Parts Thereof, in English from the Year 1526 to 1766. London: 1788. V. 40

Typographical Antiquities: or an Historical Account of the Origin and Progress of Printing in Great Britain and Ireland . . . London: 1785. V. 44

Typographical Antiquities: or an Historical Account of the Origin and Progress of Printing in Great Britain and Ireland. London: 1785-90. V. 40

Typographical Antiquities: or, the History of Printing in England, Scotland and IReland . . . London: 1810-19. V. 46

Typographical Antiquities . . . (with) An Index to Dibdin's Edition of the Typographical Antiquities. London: 1810-19/99. V. 42

Typographical Antiquities or the History of Printing in England, Scotland and Ireland. London: 1969. V. 39

AMES, LILIAN

Lilian Ames Fables. Fleetwood: 1935. V. 46

AMES, NATHANIEL 1708-1764

An Astronomical Diary; or, Almanack for the Year of Our Lord Christ, 1763 . . . Boston: 1762. V. 42

An Astronomical Diary; or, Almanack for the Year of Our Lord Christ, 1764. Boston: 1764. V. 38

An Astronomical Diary . . . for . . . 1756 . . . 1767 . . . 1770 . . . 1771 . . . 1772. Boston: 1755-71. V. 37

An Astronomical Diary, or an Almanack, or the Year of Our Lord Christ, 1760. Boston: 1759. V. 38

AMESBURY, JOSEPH 1795-1864

Practical Remarks on the Nature and Treatment of Fractures of the Trunk and Extremities . . . London: 1831. V. 45

AMEY, FRANCIS

Catalogue of the Major and Minor Libraries of Christ Church, Belfast, Established 1836. Belfast: 1837. V. 43

AMHERST, ALICIA

A History of Gardening in England. London: 1896. V. 37

AMHERST Express. Extra. Williams and Amherst Base Ball and Chess! Muscle and Mind!! July 1st and 2nd, 1859. N.P.: Amherst: 1859. V. 39

AMHURST, NICHOLAS

The British General. London: 1722. V. 39; 40; 42; 45

The British General. London: 1722. V. 42

AMHURST, NICHOLAS continued

Oculus Britanniae; an Heroi-Panegyrical Poem on the University of Oxford. London: 1724. V. 37; 42

Strephon's Revenge: a Satire on the Oxford Toasts. London: 1720. V. 41

Terrae-Filius; or, The Secret History of the University of Oxford, in Several Essays. London: 1726. V. 37; 39; 42; 43; 46

AMI, BEN

Jingle Book for Jewish Children. 1947. V. 41

AMICIS, EDMONDO DE 1846-1908

Holland and Its People. New York: 1885. V. 39; 40

Holland. Philadelphia: 1894. V. 42

L'AMICO de' Poveri Che Insegna il Vero Modo di Fare il Pane Venale Col Quale Possono Arricchire i Fornaj Onesti, Intelligenti, e Practici delle Regole del Loro Mestiere . . . Firenze: 1773. V. 39

AMICO, BERNARDINO

Trattato Delle Piante & Immagini de Sacri Edifizi di Terra Santa Disegnate in Jerusalemme . . . Firenza: 1620. V. 44

AMIENT, PIERRE

Art of the Ancient Near East. New York: 1980. V. 37; 38; 40; 41; 44

AMIOT, JOSEPH MARIE

Memoires Concernant l'Histoire, les Sciences, les Artes, les Moeurs, les Usages, &c. des Chinois . . . Paris: 1776-91/1814. V. 45

AMIRAN, RUTH

Ancient Pottery of the Holy Land from Its Beginnings in the Neolithic Period to the End of the Iron Age. Jersualem: 1969. V. 44

Ancient Pottery of the Holy Land from Its Beginnings in the Neolithic Period to the End of the Iron Age. N.P.: 1970. V. 41

Early Arad: the Chalcolithic Settlement and Early Bronze City. Jerusalem: 1978. V. 37; 40; 42

AMIS ET AMILES

The Friendship of Amis and Amile. 1894. V. 45

The Story of Amis and Amile. Portland: 1899. V. 44

AMIS, KINGSLEY 1922-

The Alteration. London: 1976. V. 38

Bright November. London: 1947. V. 38; 44

Bright November. London: 1947. V. 38

Bright November. London: 1947. V. 44

A Case of Samples - Poems 1946-1956. London: 1956. V. 43

The Darkwater Hall Mystery. Edinburgh: 1978. V. 42; 45; 46

The Egyptologists. London: 1965. V. 38; 46

A Frame of Mind. 1953. V. 38

A Frame of Mind. Eighteen Poems. Reading: 1953. V. 37

Girl 20. London: 1971. V. 40

I Like It Here. London: 1958. V. 38

Lucky Jim. London: 1953. V. 44; 46

Lucky Jim. Garden City: 1954. V. 41; 45

Lucky Jim. London: 1954. V. 44

Lucky Jim. New York: 1954. V. 37; 38; 40; 42; 43; 45

New Maps of Hell - a Survey of Science Fiction. New York: 1960. V. 38

The Old Devil. London: 1986. V. 38; 40; 41; 43; 46

The Riverside Villas Murder. London: 1973. V. 44

That Uncertain Feeling. London: 1955. V. 43

AMIS, MARTIN

Dead Babies. London: 1975. V. 40; 41; 44; 46

Einstein's Monsters. London: 1987. V. 46

Invasion of the Space Invaders. London: 1982. V. 38; 45

London Fields. London: 1989. V. 42; 45

Money. London: 1984. V. 40

The Moronic Inferno and Other Visits to America. London: 1986. V. 38

Other People: a Mystery Story. London: 1981. V. 45; 46

The Rachel Papers. London: 1973. V. 37; 40; 42; 46

The Rachel Papers. New York: 1974. V. 44

The Rachel Papers. New York: 1984. V. 43

Success. London: 1978. V. 43; 45

Time's Arrow. London: 1991. V. 46

AMMAN, JOST

Stand und Orden der Heil. Romischen Catholischen Kirchen Darinn Aller Geistlichen Personen, H. Rittern, und Dero Verwandten Herkommen, Constitution Regeln, Habit und Kleidung Beneben Schomen . . . Frankfurt: 1585. V. 38; 39; 40; 41

AMMANN, O. H.

First (and second) Progress Report on Kill Van Kull Bridge Between Bayonne, N.J. and Port Richmond, Staten Island, N.Y. New York: 1931. V. 43

AMMEN, DANIEL

The Old Navy and the New. Philadelphia: 1891-98. V. 39

AMMIANI, MARCELLINUS 325-391

Rerum Gestarum Qui de XXXI supersunt, Libri XVIII. Lugd. Bat.: 1693. V. 37

AMMIANUS MARCELLINUS 325-391

Delle Gverre de Romani. Venice: 1550. V. 45

Rerum Gestarum. Leiden: 1693. V. 38; 40

Rerum Gestarum qui de XXXI supersunt Libri XVIII. Ope Mss. Codicum Emendati ab Frederico Lindenbrogio & Henrico Hadrianque Valesis . . . Leyden: 1693. V. 41

The Roman Historie . . . London: 1609. V. 45; 46

AMMIRATO, SCIPIONE

Discorsi Del Signor Scipione Ammirato Sopra Cornelio Tacito. Florence: 1598. V. 39

AMMON, WOLFGANG

Neuw Gesangbuch Teutsch und Lateinisch/Darinn die Fuernembste Psalmen und Gesaenge der Kirchen Augsp. Confession . . . Frankfurt: 1581. V. 38

AMMONIUS

In Quinque Voces Porphyrii per Pomponium Gauricum Neapolitanum. Venice: 1504. V. 39; 40

AMMONS, ARCHIE RANDOLPH

Pecker's Peak; or Piker's Pique. V. 42

Shit List. V. 42

AMONG the Mountains: A Guide Book to Colorado Springs and the Scenery in the Neighborhood, including Soda Springs at Manitou, Canan and Falls of the Fountain, the Ute Pass . . . Colorado Springs, Co.: 1873. V. 37; 39

AMONTONS, GUILLAUME

Remarques et Experiences Physiques sur la Construction d'une Nouvelle Clepsidre sur les Barometres, Termonetres & Higrometres. Paris: 1695. V. 45

THE AMOROUS Jester, or, the Wit's Companion; Being a Banquet of Fun, Mirth, Glee and Gallantry; to Which is Added, Witty Stories, Songs, Poems, Epigrams, Riddles, Toasts, Sentiments, &c. London: 1785. V. 46

AMORY, CLEVELAND

Vanity Fair Selections . . . 1920's and 1930's. New York: 1960. V. 45

AMORY, ESMERIE

The Epistolary Flirt, in Four Expousures. Chicago: 1896. V. 46

AMORY, HUGH

The Descendants, of, by Gertrude Euphemia Meredith. London: 1901. V. 37

AMORY, KATHERINE GREENE

The Journal of . . . 1775-1777 With Letters from Her Father Rufus Greene 1759-1777. Boston: 1923. V. 39

AMORY, ROBERT

A Treatise on Electrolysis and Its Applications to Therapeutical and Surgical Treatise in Disease. New York: 1886. V. 44

AMORY, THOMAS

The Life of John Buncle Esq. London: 1756. V. 38

The Life of John Buncle, Esq. London: 1756/66. V. 40; 43

The Life of John Buncle, Esq. London: 1766. V. 39; 40; 42; 44

The Life of John Buncle, Esq. London: 1825. V. 43; 44

The Life of John Buncle Esq.; Containing Various Observations & Reflections Made In Several Parts of the World . . . LondonL: 1766. V. 37

AMOS, SHELDON

A Comparative Survey of the Laws in Force for the Prohibition, Regulation and Licensing of Vice in England and Other Countries. London: 1877. V. 42

AMOS, WILLIAM

Minutes in Agriculture and Planting . . . Boston: 1804. V. 40

LES AMOURS de Mirtil. Constantinople: 1761. V. 39

THE AMOURS of Lais: or, the Misfortunes of Love. London: 1766. V. 37; 38

AMPEL en Breed Verhaal Van de Jongst-Gewesene Aardbevinge tot Port-Royal in Jamaica, Op den 7 17 Juny 1692. Rotterdam: 1692. V. 39

AMPHIAREO, VESPASIANO

Opera di Frate Vespasiano, Amphiareo da Ferrara Dell'Ordine Minore Conventvale Nella Quale si Insegna a Scrivere Varie Sorti di Lettere et Massime Vna Lettera Bastarda da LVI Novamente con Sva Indvstria Ritrovata . . . Venetia: 1580. V. 40

Opera . . . Nella Quale si Insegna a Scrivere Varie Sorti di Lettere, et Massime Una Lettera Bastarda . . . Venice: 1596. V. 38; 40

AN AMPLE Disquisition into the Nature of Regalities and Heretable Jurisdiction. London: 1747. V. 41; 45

AMPUDIA, PEDRO DE

El Ciudadano General Pedro de Ampudia Ante el Tribunal Respetable de la Opinion Publica, Por Los Primeros Sucesos Ocurridos en la Guerra a Que Nos Provoca Decreta, Y Sostiene el Gobierno de los Estados-Unidos de America. San Luis Potosi: 1846. V. 39

AMSBARY, WALLACE BRUCE

The Ballads of Bourbonnais. Indianapolis: 1904. V. 44

AMSDEN, CHARLES AVERY

Navaho Weaving. Santa Ana: 1934. V. 38; 39; 44

AMSDORFF, NICOLAUS

Von Auff Die Kuenstliche Spoettische und Bitterhoenische Oration so D. Ziegler Zu Leipzig Am Oster Montag Widder Die Bestendigen Lutherischen Recitirt Hat. Magdeburgk: 1549. V. 41; 44

AMSDORFF, NICOLAUS VON

Deren Zu Magdeburgk so Widder Die Adiaphora Geschrieben Haben . . . N.P.: 1551. V. 41

AMUCHASTEGUI, A.

Some Birds and Mammals of North America. London: 1971. V. 37; 40; 42

Some Birds and Mammals of Africa. London: 1979. V. 38

Some Birds and Mammals of South America. London: 1966. V. 37

Studies of Animals and Birds of South America. London: 1967. V. 37

AMUCHASTEGUI, AXEL

Some Birds and Mammals of North America. London: 1971. V. 38; 39; 45

Some Birds and Mammals of Africa. London: 1979. V. 43; 44

Some Birds and Mammals of Africa. London: 1979. V. 45

Some Birds and Mammals of South America. London: 1966. V. 45

AMUCHASTGEGUI, AXEL

Some Birds and Mammals of South Africa. London: 1966. V. 37; 45

THE AMULET: a Tale of Spanish California. London: 1865. V. 39; 45

AMUNDSEN, ROALD

The Northwest Passage . . . New York: 1908. V. 42

The Northwest Passage, Being the Record of a Voyage of Exploration of the Ship 'Gjoa' 1903-1907. New York & London: 1908. V. 38

Our Polar Flight: the Amundsen-Ellsworth Polar Flight. New York: 1925. V. 45

The South Pole. London: 1912. V. 40; 41; 43

The South Pole. New York: 1913. V. 38; 42

AMUSING History of Little Jack Horner. London: 1830. V. 39

THE AMUSING Instructer (sic). London: 1727. V. 37; 41; 45

THE AMUSING Story of the Unselfish Children. London: 1850. V. 39

AMYRAUT, MOSES 1596-1664

A Treatise Concerning Religions, in Refutation of the Opinion Which Accounts all Indifferent. London: 1660. V. 39

AMYX, D. A.

Corinthian Vase-Painting of the Archaic Period. Berkeley: 1989. V. 42; 44

ANACONDA COPPER MINING CO.

Report of the . . . for the Year Ended December 31st, . . . 1920-3/27-9-31. V. 39

ANACREON

Anacreon Done into English Out of the Original Greek. Oxford: 1683. V. 40

Anacreon Teius . . . (Poems). Cambridge: 1721. V. 40

Anacreon. London: 1906. V. 46

Anacreon, Done Into English Out of the Original Greek. London: 1923. V. 44

Anacreon done Into English Out of the Original Greek by Abraham Cowley and S.B., 1683. London: 1923. V. 37; 40; 44; 46

Anacreon; Done Into English Out of the Original Greek by Abraham Cowley. Soho: 1923. V. 38; 41; 44; 46

Anacreontis Teij Odae. Paris: 1554. V. 38; 44

Anacreontis Teii Odaria Praefixo Commentario Quo Poetae Genus Traditur et Bibliotheca Anacreonteia . . . Parma: 1785. V. 41

Five Odes of Anacreon. 1985. V. 40; 45

Five Odes of Anacreon. Shropshire: 1985. V. 37; 39

(Odae). Praefixon Commentario Quo Poetae Genus Traditur et Bibliothecae Anacreonteia Adumbratur. Parma: 1791. V. 40; 45

Odaria. London: 1802. V. 41

Odae in Easdem Henr. Stephani Observationes (2nd part: Odae, ab Heilia Andrea Latinae Factae). Paris: 1556. V. 40

Odaria. Bodoni: 1784-85. V. 45

Odes, Inscriptions, Epitaphes, Epitaphalames et Fragments . . . Paris: 1794. V. 40

Odes of Anacreon. London: 1800. V. 37; 40

The Odes of Anacreon. V. 43

Odes. Paris: 1810. V. 45

Odes of Anacreon. London: 1806. V. 37

Opera Graece, cum Versione Latina, Notis et Indice. London: 1725. V. 45

The Works of Anacreon, Sappho, Bion, Moschus and Musaeus. London: 1760. V. 38

The Works of Anacreon and Sappho, with Pieces from Ancient Authors; and Occasional Essays . . . London: 1768. V. 41

ANAGNOS, JULIA R.

Stray Chords. Boston: 1883. V. 40; 41

ANAHEIM

Ordinances of the Town of Anaheim, County of Los Angeles, State of California. Anaheim: 1877. V. 40

AN ANALYSIS of C. W. Raines' Bibliography of Texas. Waco: 1961. V. 46

AN ANALYSIS of C. W. Raines' Bibliography of Texas. Waco: 1962. V. 40

AN ANALYTICAL Digest of the Cases Published in the Law Journal, and in All the Reports of Decisions in the Courts of Common Law and Equity, in the Ecclesiastical and Admiralty Courts, by the Twelve Judges . . . London: 1831/1835. V. 40

ANATOMY of Murder - Famous crimes Critically Considered by Members of the Detection Club. London: 1936. V. 46

ANAVIAN, RAHIM

Royal Persian and Kashmir Brocades. Kyoto: 1975. V. 39

ANAWALT, PATRICIA RIEFF

Indian Clothing Before Cortes. Norman: 1981. V. 45

ANBUREY, THOMAS

Journal d'un Voyage fait dans l'Interieur de l'Amerique Septentrionale. Paris: 1793. V. 39

Travels through the Interior Parts of America. London: 1789. V. 37; 38; 39; 41; 42; 43; 44; 45; 46

Travels Through the Interior Parts of America. London: 1791. V. 38

Travels Though the Interior Parts of America. Boston: 1923. V. 42

ANCARANO, PIETRO GIOVANNI D'

Familiarium Iuris Quaestionum Libri Tres. Venetiis: 1580. V. 37; 38; 40

ANCELL, SAMUEL

A Journal of the Blockade and Siege of Gibraltar . . . Cork: 1793. V. 42

THE ANCESTOR. London: 1902-05. V. 41

THE ANCIENT British Drama. (with) The Modern British Drama. London: 1810-11. V. 38

THE ANCIENT Code of Military Laws, for the Government of the English Army, Under King Henry the Fifth, Enacted at Manuce. With Some Additional Ordinances, Made by the Earl of Salisbury. London: 1784. V. 37

ANCIENT English Metrical Romances. London: 1802. V. 41

ANCIENT Harmony Revived. Symphonia Grandaeva Rediviva. Boston: 1850. V. 40

ANCIENT Irish Histories. The Works of Spencer, Campion, Hammer and Marleburrough. Dublin: 1809. V. 46

ANCIENT Scottish Ballads. New Castle: 1810. V. 38

ANCILLON, CHARLES

Eunuchism Display'd. London: 1718. V. 45

ANCKARSWARD, M. G.

Sweriges Markwardigaste Ruiner . . . Stockholm: 1828. V. 45

ANCOURT, D' ABBE

The lady's Preceptor. London: 1743. V. 39; 40; 43

ANCOURT, D' ABBE continued

The Lady's Preceptor. London: 1752. V. 37

ANCOURT, D'ABBE

The Lady's Preceptor. London: 1745. V. 43

ANDALUSIAN Annual, for MDCCCXXXVII. London: 1836. V. 41

ANDERDON, J. L.

The River Dove, with some Quiet Thoughts on the Happy Practice of Angling. London: 1847. V. 37

ANDERS, ALEXANDER D.

The Silver Country; or, The Great Southwest: A Review of the mineral and Other Wealth, the Attractions and material Development . . . The Mexican Cessions to the United States in 1848 and 1853. New York: 1877. V. 37

ANDERS, FRANK L.

Custer Trail, a Narrative of the Line of March of Troops Serving in the Department of Dakota in the Campaign Against Hostile Sioux 1876, Fort Abraham Lincoln to the Montana Line. Glendale: 1983. V. 38

ANDERSEN, HANS CHRISTIAN 1805-1875

Andersen's Fairy Tales. New York: (1942). V. 37

A Christmas Greeting to My English Friends. London: 1847. V. 42

The Compleat Andersen: All of the 168 Stories. New York: 1949. V. 37; 38; 40; 41; 44

Danish Fairy Legends and Tales. London: 1846. V. 39; 43

Danish Fairy Legends and Tales . . . London: 1853. V. 39

Eventyr Og Historier. Copenhagen: 1862-3. V. 41

Fairy Tales. London. V. 40; 43

Fairy Tales by Hans Andersen. London. V. 37; 40; 41; 45

The Fairy Tale of My Life. New York. V. 41

Fairy Tales. London: 1872. V. 41; 43

Fairy Tales. Chicago: 1883. V. 43

The Fairy Tales. London: 1899. V. 41

Fairy Tales. London: 1900. V. 43

Fairy Tales from Hans Christian Andersen. London: 1901. V. 42

Faery Tales. London: 1910. V. 43; 45

Hans Andersen's Fairy Tales. London: 1911. V. 46

Fairy Tales. London: 1913. V. 41; 42

Fairy Tales. New York: 1914. V. 43

Fairy Tales. London: 1916. V. 41; 46

Fairy Stories. London: 1917. V. 46

Fairy Tales. London: 1922. V. 46

Fairy Tales. London: 1924. V. 38; 39; 40; 41; 43; 44; 45; 46

Fairy Tales. New York: 1924. V. 37; 45; 46

Fairy Tales. London: 1925. V. 40; 46

Fairy Tales. London: 1930. V. 43

Fairy Tales. London: 1931. V. 44

Fairy Tales. London: 1932. V. 37; 39; 40; 41; 44; 45; 46

Fairy Tales. Philadelphia: 1932. V. 45

Fairy Tales and Legends. London: 1935. V. 38; 40; 41; 42; 44; 45

Fairy Tales. New York: 1942. V. 45

Four Tales by Hans Andersen . . . Cambridge: 1935. V. 44

Gedichte. Vienna & Leipzig: 1917. V. 41

Gessamelte marchen (Fairy Tales). Leipzig: 1849. V. 37

The Improvisatore. London. V. 40

The Improvisaiore; or Life in Italy. London: 1845. V. 40; 42; 44

Little Thumb, a Fairy Story. London: 1880. V. 39

The Maker of Fairy Tales. New York: 1942. V. 38

A New Translation by Mrs. H.B. Paull, Editor of 'Grimm's Fairy Tales'. London/New York: (c.1880). V. 37

The Nightingale. Berlin: 1947. V. 37

Only a Fiddler; and O.T. or, Life in Denmark. London: 1847. V. 43

A Picture Book Without Pictures . . . From the German translation of De La Motte Fouqué by Meta Taylor. London: 1847. V. 39; 42

A Poet's Bazaar. London: 1846. V. 43

A Poet's Day Dreams. London: 1853. V. 39

Rambles in the Romantic Regions of the Hartz Mountains . . . London: 1848. V. 46

The Red Shoes. Bristol: 1928. V. 37; 38; 39

The Sand-Hills of Jutland. Boston: 1860. V. 42

The Shadow and Other Tales. London: (n.d.). V. 37

66 Stories from Hans Andersen. London: 1920's. V. 42

The Snow Queen and Other Stories. New York: & London: 1910. V. 46

Stories from . . . . London. V. 39; 41

Stories and Tales. London: 1871. V. 45

Stories and Fairy Tales. London: 1893. V. 41; 44; 46

Stories. London: 1911. V. 41; 43; 44; 46

Stories. New York: & London: 1911. V. 45

Stories from Hans Andersen. London: 1920. V. 42

Tales from Hans Andersen. London: 1929. V. 42

To Be Or Not to Be. London: 1857. V. 45

The True Story of My Life. Translated to English by Mary Howitt. London: 1847. V. 37

The Ugly Duckling. London: 1894. V. 42

Wonderful Tales from Denmark. New York: 1850. V. 44

Wonderful Tales from Denmark. 1864. V. 44

ANDERSEN, HENDRIK CHRISTIAN

Creation of a World Centre of Communication. Paris: 1913. V. 45

Creation of a World Centre of Communication. Paris: 1918. V. 38

ANDERSON, ABRAHAM C.

The Pioneer Life of George W. Goodhart. Caldwell: 1940. V. 39

Trails Of Early Idaho, The Pioneer Life of George W. Goodhart. Caldwell: 1940. V. 43

Trails of Early Idaho-The Pioneer Life of George W. Goodhart. Caxton: 1940. V. 39

ANDERSON, ADAM 1692?-1765

An Historical and Chronological Deduction of the Origin of Commerce. London: 1764. V. 39; 45

Historical and Chronological Deduction of the Origin of Commerce, from the Earliest Accounts. London: 1787. V. 39; 42

An Historical and Chronological Deduction of the Origin of Commerce, from the Earliest Accounts. London: 1787-89. V. 38; 45

Historical and Chronological Deduction of the Origin of Commerce, From the Earliest Accounts. Dublin: 1790. V. 42

An Historical and Chronological Deduction of the Origin of Commerce. London: 1801. V. 43

ANDERSON, AENEAS

A Narrative of the British Embassy to China, in the Years 1792, 1793 and 1794. London: 1795. V. 46

ANDERSON, ALAN

The Tragara Press - a Bibliography 1954-1979. Edinburgh: 1979. V. 42

ANDERSON, ALEXANDER

Exercitationum Mathematicarum Decas Prima. Paris: 1619. V. 44

Joseph the Book-Man, a Heroi-Comical Poem in Five Cantos . . . Edinburgh: 1821. V. 38

The Lumiere. Containing A Variety of Topographical Views in Europe and America. New York: 1831. V. 37

ANDERSON, ALEXANDER CAULFIELD

The Dominion at the West. Victoria: 1872. V. 41; 43

ANDERSON, ALEXANDER D.

The Silver Country or the Great Southwest. New York: 1877. V. 39; 41; 42; 44

The Tehuantepec Inter-Ocean Railroad . . . New York: 1881. V. 43

ANDERSON, ANNE

The Betty Book. London: 1910. V. 46

The Betty Book. London: 1917. V. 46

The Betty Book. Nelson: (ca. 1912). V. 37

My Favourite Fairy Tales. London: 1920. V. 38

My Own Box of Books. 1934. V. 43

The Patsy Book. London: 1919. V. 46

ANDERSON, C. L. G.

Old Panama and Castilla Del Oro with Maps and Illustrations. Washington: 1911. V. 45

ANDERSON, CHARLES C.

Fighting by Southen Federals. New York: 1912. V. 39; 42

ANDERSON, CHRISTOPHER

The Annals of the English Bible. London: 1845. V. 39; 45

Historical Sketches of the Ancient Irish and Their Descendents . . . Edinburgh: 1828. V. 46

ANDERSON, DAVID

Charge Delivered to the Clergy of the Diocese of Rupert's Land, at His Primary Visitation. London: 1851. V. 46

Notes on the Flood at the Red River, by the Bishop of Rupert's Land. London: 1852. V. 38

ANDERSON, EDMUND 1530-1605

Les Reports des Mults Principals Cases ARgues & Adjuges en le Temps del Jadid Roign Elizabeth Cibien en le Common-Bank . . . London: 1664-1665. V. 40

ANDERSON, ELBERT

The Skylight and the Dark-Room: a Complete Textbook on Portrait Photography. Philadelphia: 1872. V. 37

ANDERSON, ERICA

The World of Albert Schweitzer: a Book of Photographs. New York: 1955. V. 44

ANDERSON, FLORENCE MARY

The Rainbow Twins. London: 1919. V. 40

The Rainbow Twins. London: 1919. V. 40; 45

ANDERSON, FREDERICK IRVING

Adventures of the Infallible Godhal. New York: 1914. V. 42

ANDERSON, FULTON

Addresses Delivered Before the Virginia State Convention By . . . February 1861. Richmond: 1861. V. 37; 39; 42

ANDERSON, GEORGE WILLIAM

A Collection of Voyages Round the World . . . London: 1790. V. 45

A New, Authentic and Complete Collection of Voyages Around the World . . . The Complete History of Captain Cook's First, Second, Third and last Voyages . . . To which will be added, genuine narratives of other voyages of discovery around the . . . London: (1784-86). V. 37

A New, Authentic and Complete Collection of Voyages Round the World, containing a Complete Historical Account of Captain Cook's First, Second, Third and last Voyages . . . to which are added Narratives of Lord Bryron, Capt. Wallis, . . . London: 1784. V. 37

ANDERSON, GREGG

Recollections of the Grabhorn Press. Los Angeles: 1935. V. 37

ANDERSON, HENRY

An Enquiry Into the Natural Right of Mankind to Debate Freely Concerning Religion. London: 1737. V. 45

ANDERSON, J. CORBET

Monuments and Antiquities of the Old Parish Church of St. John the Baptist at Croydon. and The Parish Church . . . As It Was Rebuilt . . . London: 1871. V. 40; 44

The Parish Church of St. John the Baptist at Croydon, Surrey, as It Was Rebuilt During the Years MDCCCLXVII-IX after the Designs of G. Gilbert Scott, R.A. London: 1871. V. 38

ANDERSON, J. L.

The Life of Thomas Ken, Bishop of Bath and Wells. London: 1851. V. 42

ANDERSON, J. MARTIN

Cartoons, Social and Political. London: 1893. V. 39

Cartoons Social and Political. London: 1893. V. 37

Symbols and Metaphors. London: 1892. V. 37; 39

ANDERSON, JAMES

Ancient Scottish Weapons. Edinburgh & London: 1881. V. 40; 44

Constitutions of the Antient Fraternity of Free and Accepted Masons. London: 1784. V. 38

Essays Relating to Agriculture and Rural Affairs . . . Edinburgh: 1775. V. 41

Essays relating to Agriculture and Rural Affairs. The Third Edition. Edinburgh/London: 1784. V. 37

A Genealogical History of the House of Yvery. London: 1742. V. 38; 40

The New Book of Constitutions of the Antient and Honourable Fraternity of Free and Accepted Masons. London: 1738. V. 38; 41; 43; 46

The New Practical Gardener and Modern Horticulturist. London: 1880. V. 39

The New Practical Gardener and Modern Horticulturist. London: c. 1870. V. 37

Recreations in Agriculture, Natural-History, Arts and Miscellaneous Literature. London: 1799-1802. V. 39

Royal Genealogies: or, the Genealogical Tables of Emperors, Kings and Princes, from Adam to These Times. London: 1732. V. 39

Royal Genealogies: or the Genealogical Tables of Emperors, Kings and Princes fro Adam to these Times . . . 1732. V. 37

Selectus Diplomatum et Numismatum Scotiae Thesaurus. Edinburgh: 1739. V. 41; 44; 46

ANDERSON, JAMES H.

Life and Letters of Judge Thomas J. Anderson and Wife, Mostly Written During the Civil War. Columbus: 1904. V. 41; 42

ANDERSON, JOHAN

Nachrichten Von Island, Gronland Und der Strasse Davis. Hamburg: 1746. V. 38; 40

ANDERSON, JOHN

A Defence of the Church-Government Faith, Worship & Spirit of the Presbyterians in Answer to a Late Book Intituled An Apology for Mr. Thomas Rhind. Glasgow: 1714. V. 38

Dura Den. A Monograph of the Yellow Sandstone and Its Remarkable Fossil Remains. Edinburgh: 1859. V. 37

Mandalay to Momien: A Narrative of the Two Expeditions to Western China of 1868 and 1875 Under Colonel Edward B. Sladen and Colonel Horace Browne. London: 1876. V. 39; 45

Prize Essay on the State of Society and Knowledge in the Highlands of Scotland, Particulary in the Northern Counties, at the Period of the Rebellion in 1745 . . . Edinburgh: 1827. V. 42; 45

Sketch of the Comparative Anatomy of the Nervous System . . . London: 1838. V. 42

The Unknown Turner. New York: 1926. V. 39; 40; 44

Wanderings in the Land of Israel and Through the Wilderness of Sinai, in 1850 and 1851. London: 1851. V. 45

ANDERSON, JOHN CORBETT

Monuments and Antiquities of Croydon Church in the County of Surrey, Comprising Its History, also Exterior and Interior Views of the Structure . . . Croydon: 1855. V. 38

ANDERSON, JOHN L.

Night of the Silent Drums. plus The Glossary of Native. New York: 1975. V. 38

The River Dore, With Some Quiet Thoughts on the Happy Practice of Angling. London: 1847. V. 39; 40

ANDERSON, MABEL WASHBOURNE

Life of General Stand Waite. 1915. V. 44

The Life of General Stand Waite . . . Pryor: 1915. V. 42

The Life of General Stand Waite; the Only Indian Brigadier General of the Confederate Army and the Last General to Surrender. Pryor: 1931. V. 44

ANDERSON, MARIAN

My Lord What a Morning: an Autobiography. New York: 1956. V. 42

ANDERSON, MAXWELL

Valley Forge. Washington: 1934. V. 43

Winterset. Culver City: 1935. V. 39

ANDERSON, MELVILLE BEST

The Florence of Dante Alighieri. San Francisco: 1929. V. 43

ANDERSON, P.

The High Crusade. New York: 1960. V. 43

Murder Bound. 1962. V. 39

Star Wars. 1957. V. 43

Three Hearts and Three Lions. 1961. V. 39

ANDERSON, PATRICK

A Tent for April. Montreal: 1945. V. 43; 44

ANDERSON, POUL

Agent of the Terran Empire. Philadelphia & New York: 1965. V. 44

Brain Wave. London: 1955. V. 44

Tau Zero. New York: 1970. V. 44

Twilight World. New York: 1961. V. 40; 42

ANDERSON, R. B.

The Flatey Book and Recently Discovered Vatican Manuscripts Concerning America as Early as the Tenth Century. London, Stockholm, etc.: 1908. V. 41

ANDERSON, R. C. B.

History of the Argyll and Sutherland Highlanders. First Battalion, 1909-1939-1954. London: 1954-1956. V. 37

ANDERSON, ROBERT

An Artillery Officer in the Mexican War 1846-7. New York: 1911. V. 42

By Direction of the Secretary of War, Instruction for Field Artillery, Horse and Foot. Philadelphia: 1839. V. 43

A Catalogue of Foreign and Native Forest Trees, Evergreens and Flowering Shrubs; Also Fruit Trees of All Kinds, Hot-House and Green-House Plants, Flower Roots &c . . . Edinburgh: 1780. V. 38; 40

The Life of Samuel Johnson, LL.D. London: 1795. V. 38; 43

The Life of Rev. Robert Anderson . . . The Young Men's Guide, or the Brother in White. Macon: 1892. V. 44

The Poetical Works . . . Carlisle: 1820. V. 42

A Practical Exposition of St. Paul's Epistle to the Romans. London: 1833. V. 43

Tea and Sympathy. New York: 1953. V. 45

ANDERSON, ROBERT A.

Fighting the Mill Creeks. Chico: 1909. V. 37; 41

ANDERSON, RUFUS

The Hawaiian Islands: Their Progress and Condition Under Missionary Labors. Boston: 1864. V. 38; 40; 41

History of the Sandwich Islands Mission. Boston: 1870. V. 38; 41

History of the Sandwich Islands Mission (and) History of the Missions of the Hawaiian Islands. Boston: 1870-1875. V. 37

ANDERSON, RUFUS continued

Kapiolani, the Heroine of Hawaii. New York: 1866. V. 40

A Memoir of Catherine Brown, a Christian Indian of the Cherokee Nation. Boston: 1825. V. 37

ANDERSON, SHERWOOD 1876-1941

Alice and the Lost Novel. London: 1929. V. 37; 39; 43; 46

Dark Laughter. New York: 1925. V. 38; 39; 40; 41; 42; 45

Hello Towns. New York: 1929. V. 41; 42; 43; 44

Home Town. New York: 1940. V. 40

Horses and Men. New York: 1923. V. 41; 42; 43

Kit Brandon: a Portrait. New York: 1936. V. 40

Many Marriages. New York: 1923. V. 42; 43

Marching Men. New York: 1917. V. 38; 43

Mid-American Chants. New York: 1918. V. 43; 44; 45

The Modern Writer. San Francisco: 1925. V. 37; 39; 46

Nearer the Grass Roots. San Francisco: 1929. V. 37; 38; 40

A New Testament. New York: 1927. V. 39

No Swank. Philadelphia: 1934. V. 41; 43

Notebook. New York: 1926. V. 39; 45

Poor White. New York: 1920. V. 43

Puzzled America. New York: 1935. V. 38; 41; 42; 43; 44

Puzzled America. New York: 1935. V. 44

Sherwood Anderson's Notebook. New York: 1926. V. 43; 46

6 Mid-American Chants. Highlands: 1964. V. 44

A Story Teller's Story. New York: 1924. V. 39; 40; 42; 43

Tar. New York: 1926. V. 39; 40; 41; 42

Tar. New York: 1926. V. 43

The Triumph of the Egg. New York: 1921. V. 39; 41; 42; 46

Windy McPherson's Son. London: 1916. V. 43

Windy McPherson's Sons. New York: 1916. V. 46

Windy McPherson's Sons. New York & London: 1916. V. 38; 39

Winesburg, Ohio. New York: 1919. V. 39; 42

Winesburg, Ohio. New York: 1978. V. 37; 46

ANDERSON, T. C.

Ubique: War Services of all the Officers of H.M.'s Bengal Army, Exhibiting the Rank and Various Services of Every Officer in the Army . . . Calcutta: 1863. V. 41

ANDERSON, T. SCOTT

Holloas from the Hills. Jedburgh: 1899. V. 43

ANDERSON, W. J.

C. E. Holiwell's New Tourist Guide to the City and Environs of Quebec for the Year 1872. Quebec: 1872. V. 41

ANDERSON, WILLIAM

Japanese and Chinese Paintings in the British Museum. London: 1886. V. 43; 46

Japanese Wood Engravings: Their History, Technique and Characteristics. London: 1905. V. 38

Sketch of the Mode of Manufacturing Gunpowder at the Ishapore Mills in Bengal. London: 1862. V. 40

The Speeches and Judgement of the Right Honourable the Lords of Council and Session in Scotland, Upon the Important Cause. Edinburgh: 1768. V. 42

System of Surgical Anatomy. New York: 1822. V. 44; 45

ANDERSON, WILLIAM C.

The Gooney Bird. New York: 1968. V. 44

ANDERSON, WILLIAM J.

Architectural Studies in Italy. Glasgow: 1889. V. 40; 44

Architectural Studies in Italy. Glasgow: 1890. V. 39

ANDERSON, WILLIAM JAMES

The Life of F.M., H.R.H. Edward, Duke of Kent, Illustrated by His Correspondence With the De Salaberry Family, Never Before Published . . . Ottawa and Toronto: 1870. V. 37

ANDERSON, WILLIAM JOHN

The Causes, Symptoms and Treatment of Eccentric Nervous Affections. London: 1850. V. 40

The Causes, Symptoms and Treatment of Hysterical, Hypochondriacal, Epileptic and Other Nervous Affections. London: 1850. V. 40

ANDERSON, WILLIAM M.

Adventures in the Rocky Mountains in 1834. New York: 1951. V. 40

ANDERSON, WILLIAM WEMYSS

Jamaica and the Americans. New York: 1851. V. 45

ANDERSSON, C. J.

The Lion and the Elephant. London: 1873. V. 37

ANDERSSON, CHARLES J.

Explorations and Discoveries During Four Years' Wanderings in the Wilds of South Western Africa . . . Philadelphia: 1859. V. 43

ANDERSSON, CHARLES JOHN

Lake Ngami; or, Explorations and Discoveries, During Four Years' Wanderings in the Wilds of South Western Africa. London: 1856. V. 38

The Okavango River. London: 1861. V. 38

ANDERSSON, J. G.

Researches into the Prehistory of the Chinese. Stockholm: 1943. V. 42

ANDERSSON, KARL JOHAN

Lake Ngami; or, Explorations and Discoveries, During Four Years' Wanderings in the Wild of South Western Africa. London: 1856. V. 41; 42; 46

Lake Ngami; or, Explorations and Discoveries During Four Years' Wanderings in the Wilds of Southwestern Africa. New York: 1857. V. 42; 45

Notes of Travel in South-Western Africa. New York: 1875. V. 40

Notes of Travel in South Western Africa. New York: 1882. V. 42

The Okavango River. New York: 1861. V. 45

ANDERTON, BASIL

Catalogue of the Bewick Collection (Pease Bequest). Newcastle-upon-Tyne: 1904. V. 44

ANDRADA, JACINTO FREIRE DE

The Life of Dom John De Castro, the Fourth Vice-Roy of India. London: 1693. V. 45

ANDRADA LEITAO, FRANCISCO DE

Discurso Politico Sobre o se Aver de Largar a Coroa de Portugal Angola, S. Thome & Maranhao, Exclamado aos Altos & Poderosos Estados de Olanda. Lisbon: 1642. V. 41

ANDRADE, ANTONIO DE

Lettere Annue del Tiber del MCXCCVI. E Della Cina del MDCXXIV. Scritte al M.R.P. Mutio Vitelleschi Generale della Compagnia di Giesu. Roma: 1628. V. 45

ANDRADE DE FIGUEIREDO, MANUEL DE

Nova Escola Para Aprender, a ler Escrever, e Contar . . . Primeira Parte (all published). Lisboa Occidental: 1722. V. 41

Nova Escola Para Aprender a ler, Escreber, e Contar . . . Lisbon: 1722. V. 39; 40; 41; 42

Novo Escola Para Aprender . . . Lisboa: 1772. V. 38

ANDRADE, MANOEL CARLOS DE

Luz da Liberal, e Nobre Arte da Cavallaria, Offerecida ao Senhor D. Joao Principe do Brazil. Lisbon: 1790. V. 45

ANDRAE, WALTER

Coloured Ceramics from Ashur and Earlier Ancient Assyrian Wall-Paintings. London: 1925. V. 37; 38; 46

ANDRAL, G.

Medical Clinic: Diseases of the Encephalon, with Extracts from Ollivier's Work on Diseases of the Spinal Cord and Its Membranes. Philadelphia: 1843. V. 42; 45; 46

Medical Clinic: Diseases of the Chest. Philadelphia: 1843. V. 40

ANDRAL, GABRIEL

A Treatise on Pathological Anatomy. Dublin: 1829. V. 43; 46

A Treatise on Pathological Anatomy . . . New York: 1832. V. 44

ANDRASY, EMANUEL, COUNT

Reise in Ostindien. Pest: 1859. V. 46

ANDRASY, MANO

Hazai Vadaszatok es Sport Magyarorszagon. Budapest: 1857. V. 44

ANDRE, EDOUARD

L'Art des Jardins. Paris: 1879. V. 38

ANDRE, GEORGE G.

A Practical Treatise on Coal Mining. London: 1875. V. 37

ANDRE, JOHN

Andre's Journal. Boston: 1903. V. 37; 38; 39; 41; 42; 43; 44; 45

The Cow Chase. London: 1781. V. 42

The Cow Chace: a Poem in Three Cantos. Albany: 1866. V. 38

Proceedings of a Board of General Officers, Held by Order of His Excellency Gen. Washington . . . Respecting Major John Andre, Adjutant General of the British Army . . . Philadelphia: 1780. V. 41

ANDREA, ALESSANDRO

De la Guerra de Campana de Rome, y del Reyno de Napoles, en el Pontificado de Paulo IIII, Ano de MDLVI y LVII Tres Libros. Madrid: 1589. V. 45

ANDREADES, A.

A History of the Bank of England. London: 1909. V. 41

ANDREAE, BERNARD

The Art of Rome. Translated form the German by Robert Erich Wolf. New York: (1977). V. 37

ANDREAE, JOHANN LUDWIG

Mathematische und Historische Beschreibung des Welt-Gebaudes. Nurnberg: 1718. V. 45

ANDREAE, JOHANNES

Super Arboribus Consanguinitatis et Affinitatis. 1474. V. 42

Super Arboribus Consanguinitatis et Affinitatis. Nuremberg: 1476. V. 42; 45

Super Arboribus Consanguinitatis, Affinitatis et Cognationis Spiritualis et Legalis. Leipzig: 1498. V. 38; 40; 42; 44

ANDREAS, A. T.

History of the State of Kansas. Chicago: 1883. V. 46

History of Chicago. From the Earliest Period to the Present Time. Chicago: 1884-5-6. V. 39; 42

History of Chicago from the Earliest Period to the Present Time. Chicago: 1884. V. 37; 39

ANDREAS, ALFRED THEODORE

Atlas Map of Vigo County, Indiana. Chicago: 1874. V. 44

History of Cook County, Illinois. Chicago: 1884. V. 45

History of Chicago. Chicago: 1884-86. V. 42

Illustrated Historical Atlas of the State of Iowa. Chicago: 1875. V. 45

ANDREAS DE NOVO CASTRO

Primum Scriptum Sententiarum. Paris: 1514. V. 40

ANDREAS, VALERIUS

Bibliotheca Belgica. Louvain: 1623. V. 41; 46

ANDREE, JOHN

An Account of the Tilbury Water. London: 1740. V. 42

ANDREE, R. JOHN

Vocabulary in Six Languages (English, Latin, Italian, French, Spanish and Portugese) arranged after a New Method to Show the Dependance (sic) of the Four Last Upon Latin and Their Mutual Analogy to Each Other . . . London: 1725. V. 40

ANDREE, S. A.

The Andree Diaries. London: 1931. V. 44

Andree's Story, with Complete Record of His Polar Flight, 1897. New York: 1930. V. 46

ANDRELINUS, PUBLIUS FAUSTUS

Buccolica Fausti. colophon: 1501. V. 43

Liuia. Paris: 1498. V. 40

Livia Fausti sine Commento. Paris: 1493. V. 46

ANDREOLI, PASQUALE

Descrizione Dell 'Aerostato 'La Speranza', Costruito a Forli Nell 'Anno 1809. Forli: 1808. V. 37

ANDREONI, JOAO ANTONIO 1650-1716

Cultura e Opulencia do Brazil, por Suas Drogas e Minas . . . Rio de Janeiro: 1837. V. 41

ANDREOSSY, F.

Histoire du Canal du Midi, ou Canal de Languedoc, Consideres Sous Les Rapports d'Invention, d'Art, d'Administration, d'Irrigation, et dans ses Relations avec les Etangs de l'Interieur des Terres qui l'Avoisinent. Paris: 1804. V. 39

ANDREW, CHRISTOPHER

Secret Service. The Making of the British Intelligence Community. London: 1985. V. 40

ANDREW, HENRY C.

Coloured Engravings on Heths. London: 1802-30. V. 42

ANDREW, JAMES O.

Miscellanies: Comprising Letters, Essays and Addresses . . . Nashville: 1855. V. 41

ANDREW, OF WYNTOUN 1350?-1420?

De Orygynale Cronykil of Scotland. London: 1795. V. 39; 44

ANDREW, THOMAS

A Cyclopedia of Domestic Medicine and Surgery . . . Glasgow: 1845. V. 44

ANDREW, WILLIAM

A Comprehensive Synopsis of the Elements of Persian Grammar; with Some Remarks on the Arabic. London: 1803. V. 44

Constitution of Nature. Milwaukee: 1863. V. 43

Euphrates Valley Route in India, in Connection with the Central Asian and Egyptian Questions. Lecture Delivered at the National Club on the 16th June, 1882. London: 1882. V. 37

ANDREWES, LANCELOT

The Adoration of the Magi: an Excerpt from a Sermon Preached by Lancelot Andrewes, Lord Bishop of Winchester on Christmas Day MDCXXII, Before King James the First at Whitehall. Philadelphia: 1960. V. 41

A Manual of Private Devotions and Meditations. London: 1692. V. 44

XCVI Sermons. London: 1641. V. 38

XCVI Sermons . . . London: 1661. V. 46

The Pattern of Catechistical Doctrine at Large . . . London: 1650. V. 44; 46

A Patterne of Catechisticall Doctrine, Wherein Many Profitable Questions Touching Christian Religion are Handled. London: 1630. V. 41

ANDREWS & CO.

Strangers Guide in the City of Philadelphia 1851. Philadelphia: 1851. V. 42

ANDREWS, BYRON

The Facts About the Candidate. Chicago: 1904. V. 39

ANDREWS, C. C.

History of the Campaign of Mobile. New York: 1867. V. 42

ANDREWS, C. L.

The Story of Sitka - The Historic Outpost of the Northwest Coast. Seattle: 1922. V. 39; 40

ANDREWS, CAROL A. R.

Catalogue of Eygptian Antiquities in the British Museum VI. London: 1981. V. 44

ANDREWS, CHARLES

A Full and Authentick Narrative of the Intended Horrid Conspiracy and Invasion. London: 1715. V. 39; 46

The Prisoners' Memoirs, or Dartmoor Prison . . . New York: 1852. V. 42

ANDREWS, CHARLES M.

The Colonial Period of American History. New Haven: 1935. V. 44

The Colonial period in American History. New Haven: 1939-43. V. 46

The Colonial Period of American History. New Haven: 1947-49. V. 41

ANDREWS, CHARLES W.

A Monograph of Christmas Island (Indian Ocean); Physical Features and Geology . . . London: 1900. V. 43

ANDREWS, CHRISTOPHER COLUMBUS

History of the Campaign of Mobile. New York: 1867. V. 37

ANDREWS, EDWARD D.

Shaker Furniture: The Craftsmanship of an American Communal Sect. New Haven: 1937. V. 44

ANDREWS, EMERSON

Living Life; or, Autobiography of Rev. Emerson Andrews . . . Boston: 1872. V. 43

ANDREWS, ETHAN ALLEN

Slavery and the Domestic Slave-Trade in the United States in a Series of Letters Addressed to the Executive Committee of the American Union for the Relief and Improvement of the Colored Race. Boston: 1836. V. 39

ANDREWS, EVANGELINE WALKER

Journal of a Lady of Quality; Being a Narrative of a Journey from Scotland to the West Indies, North Carolina and Portugal in the Years 1774 to 1776. New Haven: 1923. V. 42

ANDREWS, G. H.

Modern Husbandry. London: 1853. V. 39; 42

ANDREWS, H. FRANKLIN

The Hamlin Family: a Genealogy of Capt. Giles Hamlin of Middletown, Connecticut, 1654-1900. Exira: 1900. V. 46

ANDREWS, HENRY C.

Colored Engravings of heaths. London: 1802-30. V. 39

Coloured Engravings of Heaths. London: 1802-09. V. 40

Coloured Engravings of Heaths, with Drawings Taken from Living Plants Only. London: 1802-09 (1828?) V. 42

The Heathery. London: 1804-06. V. 39

ANDREWS, HENRY C. continued

The Heathery; or a Monograph of the Genus Erica; Containing Colour Engravings with Latin and English Dissections, Etc. of All Known Species of that Extensive and Distinguished Trible of Plants. London: 1804-c.1830. V. 39; 40; 42; 43; 45; 46

The heathery; or a Monograph of the Genus Erica . . . London: 1845. V. 37

ANDREWS, ISRAEL D.

Communication from the Secretary of the Treasury (Hon. Thoms Corwin) Transmitting, in Compliance with a Resolution of the Senate of March 8, 1851, the Report of Israel D. Andrews (Consul of the United States for Canada & New Brunswick) . . . Washington: 1853. V. 38

Communication from the Secretary of the Treasury, Transmitting in Compliance with a Resolution of the Senate of March 8, 1851, the Report of Israel D. Andrews, Consul of the United States for Canada and New Brunswick, On the Trade and Commerce of . . . Washington: 1854. V. 44

North American Colonies and Trade of the Great Lakes and Rivers . . . Washington: 1853. V. 41

ANDREWS, JAMES PETTIT

Anecdotes &c. Antient and Modern. London: 1789. V. 45

Anecdotes, &c. Antient and Modern With Observations. London: 1790. V. 39; 43

The History of Great Britain, Connected with the Chronology of Europe . . . London: 1794-95. V. 39

History of Great Britain from the Death of Henry VIII to the Accession of James VI of Scotland to the Crown of England. London: 1796. V. 41

The History of Great Britain, Connected with the Chronology of Europe: with Notes, Containing Anecdotes of the Times, Lives of the Learned, and Specimens of their Works. By James Pettit Andrews. London: 1794. V. 37; 39

ANDREWS, JANE

Ten Boys Who Lived on the Road from Long Ago to Now. Boston: 1886. V. 46

ANDREWS, JOHN

An Account of the Character and Manners of the French; with Occasional Observations on the English. London: 1770. V. 40

A Comparative View of the French and English Nations in their Manners, Politics and Literature. London: 1785. V. 42; 46

History of the War with America, France, Spain and Holland. London: 1785-86. V. 39; 41; 42; 43; 45

History of the War with America, France, Spain and Holland: Commencing in 1775 and Ending in 1783. London: 1785-89. V. 44

Letters of a Young Gentleman, On His Setting Out for France. London: 1784. V. 41; 42; 45

Remarks on the French and English Ladies in a Series of Letters . . . Dublin: 1783. V. 40; 42; 45; 46

Remarks on the French and English Ladies, in a Series of Letters . . . London: 1783. V. 37; 38; 40; 42; 45; 46

A Review of the Characters of the Principal Nations in Europe. London: 1770. V. 42; 46

ANDREWS, JOHN PETIT

Anecdotes, Etc. Antient and Modern. Dublin: 1789. V. 46

ANDREWS, KENNETH R.

English Privateering Voyages to the West Indies, 1588-1595. Cambridge: 1959. V. 45

ANDREWS, L. F.

Pioneers of Polk County, Iow & Reminiscences of Early Days. Des Moines: 1908. V. 38; 46

ANDREWS, LANCELOT

A Manuel of the Private Devotions and Meditations of . . . Lancelot Andrews . . . London: 1682. V. 39

ANDREWS, LORRIN

A Dictionary of the hawaiian Language, to Which is Appended an English-Hawaiian Vocabulary and a Chronological Table of Remarkable Events. Honolulu, H.I.: 1865. V. 37

Grammar of the Hawaiian Language. Honolulu: 1854. V. 38; 44

A Vocabulary of Words in the Hawaiian Language. Lahainaluna: 1836. V. 38; 40; 41; 43

ANDREWS, MATTHEW PAGE

The Generall Historie of Virginia. Glasgow: 1907. V. 46

History of Maryland: Province and State. New York: 1929. V. 37

Virginia, the Old Dominion. New York: 1937. V. 39

ANDREWS, MICHAEL

Machu Picchu. Hermosa Beach: 1978. V. 38; 44; 46

River Run. Hermosa Beach: 1977. V. 38; 44; 46

ANDREWS, R. C.

Whale Hunting with Gun and Camera. New York: 1916. V. 45

ANDREWS, ROBERT H.

If I Had a Million; Movie Title of 'Windfall'. New York: 1931. V. 39

ANDREWS, ROY C.

Ends of the Earth. London: 1929. V. 38

ANDREWS, ROY CHAPMAN

The New Conquest of Central Asia, a Narrative of the Explorations of the Central Asiatic Expeditions in Mongolia and China, 1921-1930. V. 41

The New Conquest of Central Asia a Narrative of the Explorations of the Central Asiatic Expeditions in Mongolia and China 1921-1930. New York: 1932. V. 43

ANDREWS, STEPHEN PEARL

Discoveries in Chinese or Symbolism of the Primitive Chracters of the Chinese System of Writing as a Contribution to Philology and Ethnology and a Practical Aid in the Acquisition of the Chinse Langauge. New York: 1854. V. 40

Love, Marriage and Divorce, and the Sovereignty of the Individual. Boston: 1889. V. 43; 46

The Phonographic Reader; a Complete Course of Inductive Reading Lessons in Phonography. Boston: 1845. V. 42

The Science of Society. - No. 1. The Constitution of Government in the Sovereignty of the Individual, as the Final Development of Protestantism, Democracy and Socialism. New York: 1851. V. 45

ANDREWS, W. S.

Andrews' Illustrations of the West Indies. London: 1850. V. 37

ANDREWS, WILLIAM

Bygone Punishments. London: 1899. V. 40

The Doctor in History, Literature, Folk-Lore, etc. London: 1896. V. 41

ANDREWS, WILLIAM A.

Columbus Outdone, Narrative of the Voyage of the Yankee Skipper Capt. William A. Andrews in the Boat 'Sapolio' . . . . New York: 1893. V. 42

A Daring Voyage Across the Atlantic Ocean from Boston to LeHavre in a 19 foot Gloucester dory 'Nautilus', a 48 Day Voyage in 1878 of the Two Brothers Andrews. New York: 1879. V. 38

ANDREWS, WILLIAM LORING

Among My Books. New York: 1894. V. 38; 40; 42; 43; 45

The Bradford Map. New York: 1893. V. 39; 42; 43

A Choice Collection of Books from the Aldine Presses in the Possession of . . . New York: 1885. V. 40

Continental Insurance Company of New York, 1853-1905. New York: 1906. V. 43

An English XIX Century Sportsman, Bibliopole and Binder of Angling Books. New York: 1906. V. 39

An English XIX Century Sportsman. V. 44

An English XIX Century Sportsman Bibliopole and Binder of Angling Books. London: 1906. V. 41

An Essay on the Portraiture of the American Revolutionary War. New York: 1896. V. 42

Fragments of American History, Illustrated Soley by the Works of Those of Our Own Engravers Who Flourished in the XVIIIth Century. New York: 1898. V. 43

Gossip About Book Collecting. New York: 1900. V. 37; 40; 42

The Heavenly Jerusalem. New York: 1908. V. 40; 43

The Iconography of the Battery and Castle Garden. New York: 1901. V. 42; 43

Jacob Steendam noch Vaster. A Memoir of the First Poet in New Netherland with Translations of His Poems Descriptive of the Colony. New York: 1908. V. 37; 39; 40; 42; 43

James Lyne's Survey or, As It Is More Commonly Known the Bradford Map a Plan of the City of New York at the Time of the Granting of the Montgomery Charter in 131. New York: 1900. V. 37; 39; 40; 42; 43

Jean Grolier, De Servier Viscount d'Aguisy, Some Account of His Life and of His Famous Library. New York: 1892. V. 41

New Amsterdam, New Orange, New York, A Chronologically Arranged Account of Engraved Views of the City From the First Picture Published in MDCLI Until the Year MDCCC. New York: 1897. V. 40

New York as Washington Knew It After the Revolution. New York: 1905. V. 37; 39; 40; 42; 43; 46

The Old Booksellers of New York and Other Papers. New York: 1895. V. 37; 39; 40

A Prospect of the Colleges in Cambridge in New England. New York: 1897. V. 46

Roger Payne and His Art. New York: 1892. V. 40

Sextodecimos et Infra. New York: 1899. V. 41

A Trio of Eighteenth Century French Engravers of Portraits in Miniature. New York: 1898. V. 39; 44

A Trio of Eighteenth Century French Engravers of Portraits in Miniature. New York: 1899. V. 43; 46

ANDREY, NICHOLAS

Account of the Breeding of Worms in Human Bodies . . . London: 1701. V. 43

ANDREYEV, LEONID

Abyss. 1929. V. 38; 40; 43

Abyss. Berkshire: 1929. V. 46

Abyss . . . London: 1929. V. 40

Aybss. Waltham St. Lawrence: 1929. V. 45

ANDRONICOS, MANOLIS

Thessalonike Museum, a New Guide to the Archaeological Treasures. Athens: 1987. V. 45

ANDROS, EDMUND

The Andros Tracts. Boston: 1868. V. 45

The Andros Tracts. Boston: 1868/69. V. 44

ANDROS, R. S. S.

Chocorua, and Other Sketches. Fall River: 1838. V. 44

ANDROS, THOMAS

The Old Jersey Captive: or a Narrative of the Captivity of Thomas Andros . . . On Board the Old Jersey Prison Ship at New York, 1781. Boston: 1833. V. 41

ANDROS Tracts: Being a Collection of Pamphlets and Official Papers Issued During the Period Between the Overthrow of the Andros Government and the Establishment of the Second Charter of Massachusetts. Boston: 1868-74. V. 38

ANDROUET DU CERCEAU, JACQUES

Iacobus Androvetius Du Cerceau. Lectoribus. S. Veteri Convetvdine Institutoque Nostro . . . Aureliae: 1551. V. 38

Lecons de Perspective Positive. Paris: 1576. V. 41; 42

Livre d'Architecture . . . Auquel Sont Contenues Diverses Ordonnances de Plants 7 Elevations de Bastiments Pour Seigneurs, Gentilshommes & Autres Qui Voudront Bastir Aux Champs. Paris: 1648. V. 38

ANDRY, NICHOLAS

An Account of the Breeding of Worms in Human Bodies. London: 1701. V. 37; 46

ANDRY, NICOLAS

Orthopaedia. Philadelphia: 1961. V. 41; 42

AN ANECDOTE Concerning a Cherry-Tree and George Washington. Stanford University: 1932. V. 46

ANECDOTES of a Convent. London: 1771. V. 39

ANECDOTES of Eminent Persons, Comprising Also Many Interesting Literary Fragments, Biographical Sketches, Dialogues, Letters, Characters, etc. in Prose and Verse. London: 1804. V. 38

ANECDOTES of the House of Bedford from the Norman Conquest to the Present Period. London: 1796? V. 39

ANECDOTES on the Origin and Antiquity of Horse-Racing from the Earliest Times. London: 1825. V. 42; 43

ANELAY, HENRY

The Mother's Picture Alphabet. London: 1830. V. 39

ANGAS, GEORGE FRENCH 1822-1886

The Kafirs Illustrated. London: 1849. V. 38

The Kafirs Illustrated. Cape Town: 1974. V. 45

The New Zealanders. London: 1842. V. 44

The New Zealanders. London: 1846-47. V. 43

The New Zealanders Illustrated. London: 1847. V. 41; 45

Polynesia; a Popular Description of the Physical Features, Inhabitants, Natural History and Productions of the Islands of the Pacific. London: 1866. V. 37; 41

Savage Life and Scenes in Australia and New Zealand . . . London: 1847. V. 46

ANGEL, MYRON

History of Nevada with Illustrations and Biographical Sketches of Its Prominent Men and Pioneers. Oakland: 1881. V. 42

Reproduction of Thompson & West's History of Nevada, 1881. Berkeley: 1958. V. 38

ANGELETTUS, ANDREAS

Vita ac Miracula S. Canuti Mart(iri) Regis Daniae Vel Danemarciae. Rome: 1667. V. 37; 40

ANGELI, PIETRO 1517-1596.

Poemata Omnia. Florence: 1568. V. 37

ANGELIC PRESS

Wood Types of the Angelica Press. Brooklyn: 1975. V. 45

ANGELICA PRESS

Wood Type of the Angelica Press. New York: 1976. V. 40; 42

Wood Type of the Angelica Press. N.P.: 1976. V. 44

ANGELICA'S Ladies Library; or, Parents and Guardians Present. London: (1794). V. 37

ANGELIS, FRANCESCO-MARIA

Collis Paradisi Amoenitas, Seu Sacri Conventus Assisiensis Historiae. Montefalisco: 1704. V. 38; 40; 44

ANGELL, JOSEPH K.

An Index to All the English Reports, Now in General Use Which Contain Cases Adjudged by the Courts of King's Bench, Common Pleas, Nisi Prius, Chancery, etc. and Which are Chronologically Arranged from 1280 to 1820 Inclusvie. (with) A Correspondent . . . Providence: 1823. V. 38

ANGELL, ROGER

The Summer Game. New York: 1972. V. 42

ANGELL, SAMUEL

Sculptured Metopes Discovered Amongst the Ruins of the Temples of the Ancient City of Selinus in Sicily by William Harris & Samuel Angell. London: 1826. V. 38; 40

ANGELL, T.

Birds of Prey. Seattle: 1972. V. 39

Marine Birds and Mammals of Puget Sound. 1984. V. 39

Owl. Seattle: 1974. V. 39

ANGELO, DOMENICO 1717-1804

The School of Fencing . . . London: 1765. V. 45

The School of fencing, with a General Explanation of the Principal Attitudes and Postitions Peculiar to the Art. London: 1787. V. 39

ANGELO, E. A.

A Letter to the Hon. H. G. Bennett, M.P. Upon His Presenting a Petition to Parliament Complaining of the Administration of Government in the Ionian Island While Under the Command of Lieut. General Campbell. London: 1818. V. 45

ANGELO, HENRY

Angelo's Pic-Nic; or Table Talk. London: 1905. V. 40

Bayonet Exercise. London: 1853. V. 42

Reminiscences . . . With Memoirs of His Late Father and Friends . . . London: 1828-30. V. 42

Reminiscences of Henry Angelo . . . London: 1830. V. 46

The Reminiscences of . . . London: 1904. V. 46

ANGELO, R. R. F. F. MICHAEL

A Curious and Exact Account of a Voyage to Congo in the Years 1666 and 1667. London: 1704. V. 46

ANGELO, VALENTI

Albert Camus, September 15th, 1937. Bronxville: 1963. V. 37

Author-Illustrator-Printer. A Checklist of His Work from 1926 to 1970. Bronxville: 1970. V. 44

A Battle in Washington Square. New York: 1942. V. 44; 46

The Bells of Bleecker Street. New York: 1949. V. 44

The Canticle of the Sun. New York: (1951). V. 37

Golden Gate. New York: 1939. V. 44

Hill of Little Miracles. New York: 1942. V. 44

Nino. New York: 1938. V. 38; 40; 43; 44

Of the Most Holy Miracle of Saint Francis in Taming the Fierce Wolf of Gubbio. New York: 1949. V. 38

Original Book Marks Designed and Printed by Valenti Angelo. New York: 1951. V. 41

Paradise Valley. New York: 1940. V. 44

The Sermon on the Mount . . . of the Gospel According to St. Matthew. Bronxville. V. 37

True Charity. An Example of San Bernardino of Siena. (Bronxville): 1979. V. 37

Valenti Angelo, Author, Illustrator, Printer. San Francisco: 1976. V. 37; 38; 40

Valenti Angelo: Author, Illustrator, Printer. A Checklist of his Work from 1926 to 1970. Bronxville: 1970. V. 37

ANGELOMUS, O. S. B.

Ennarationes in Quatuor Libros Regum. Cologne: 1530. V. 46

ANGELOU, MAYA

I Know Why the Caged Bird Sings. New York: 1969. V. 46

Oh Pray My Wings are Gonna Fit Me Well. New York: 1975. V. 45

ANGELSEA FISHING CLUB OF NEW JERSEY

Constitution, By-Laws and Rules of the . . . Philadelphia: 1883. V. 38

ANGELUS DE CLAVASIO

Summa Angelica de Casibus Conscientiae. Nuremberg: 1492. V. 40

ANGELUS DE CLAVASIO continued

Summa Angelica de Casibus Conscientie Correcta fm Primum Exemplar.. Colophon: 1512. V. 38

ANGERIANO, GIROLAMO

Epotoiiaetnion. Paris: 1526? V. 45

Erotopaegnion. Paris: 1526. V. 40

ANGERSTEIN, JOHN JULIUS

Catalogue of the Celebrated Collection of Pictures of the Late John Julius Angerstein, Esq. London: 1823. V. 41; 44; 45

Catalogue of the Celebrated Collection of Pictures of the Late John Julius Angerstein, Esq. London: 1823. V. 44

ANGHIERA, PIETRO MARTIRE D' 1455-1526

De Rebus Oceanicis et Novo Orbe . . . et Item de Rebus Aethiopicis, Indicis, Lusitanicis & Hispanici . . . Cologne: 1574. V. 40

ANGHIERA, PIETRO MATIRE 1455-1526

De Rebus Oceanicis & Orbe Novo decades Tres . . . Basel: 1533. V. 38

ANGHIERA, PIETRO MATIRE D' 1455-1526

The Common Places of the Most Famous and Renowned Diuine Doctor Peter Martyr, Diuided into Foure Principall Parts . . . London: 1583. V. 41

ANGIOLIERI, CECCO

Sonette. 1944. V. 40; 45

Sonette. Verona: 1944. V. 44

THE ANGLER; a Poem in Ten Cantos. London: 1820. V. 38

THE ANGLER'S Pocket-Book; or Compleat English Angler. London: 1805. V. 39; 40

ANGLESEY, ARTHUR ANNESLEY, 1ST EARL OF 1614-1686

The Privileges of the House of Lords and Commons Argued and Stated in Two Conferences Between Both Houses April 19, and 22, 167. (with) A Discourse . . . Wherein the Rights of the House of Lords are Truly Asserted with Learned Remarks on . . . L: 1702. V. 40

ANGLESY, BARON

The Military Mentor. Being a Series of Letters Recently Written by a General Officer to His Son, On His Entering the Army . . . Salem: 1808. V. 40

THE ANGLICAN Friar, and the Fish Which He Took by Hook and by Crook. London: 1851. V. 39

ANGLIOLIERI, CECCO

Sonette. Verona: 1944. V. 46

ANGLO American First Editions 1826-1900 . . . London: 1935. V. 40; 42

THE ANGLO-BOER War, 1899-1900. Cape Town: 1901. V. 42

ANGOLA

Regulations for the Port of Loanda. Loanda: 1849. V. 41

ANGRESTEEN, J.

A Circumstantial Account of all the Barbarities Practised by the Monsters! London: 1790. V. 42

ANGSTROM, ANDERS JONAS

Recherches sur le Spectre Solaire . . . Spectre Normal du Soleil . . . Atlas. Upsala: 1868. V. 41

ANGUILBERT, THEOBALD

Mensa Philosophica. Cologne: 1485. V. 38

ANGUILLARA, GIO. ANDREA

Edippo Tragedia. Padua: 1565. V. 41

ANGUS, W.

The Seats of the Nobility and Gentry, in Great Britain and Wales in a Collection of Select Views, Engraved by W Angus. London: 1787-1815. V. 38

The Seats of the Nobility and Gentry in Great Britain and Wales in a Collection of Select Views. London: 1815. V. 37

ANGUS, W. CRAIBE

The Printed Works of Robert Burns. Glasgwo: 1899. V. 39

ANGUS, WILLIAM

The Seats of the Nobility and Gentry in Great Britain and Wales. London: 1787. V. 39

ANIMADVERSIONS Upon the Present Laws of England; or, An Essay to Render Them More Useful and Less Expensive . . . London: 1750. V. 41

ANIMADVERSIONS Upon Those Notes Which the Late Observator Hath Published Upon the Seven Doctrines and Positions, Which the King by Way of Recapitulation (hee saith) Lays Open so Offensive. London: 1642. V. 43

THE ANIMAL Model Book. London: 1910. V. 45

ANIMAL Nursery Rhymes. London: 1910. V. 46

ANIMAL Stories for Little People. Philadelphia: 1902. V. 38

ANIMATED Nursery Tales. New York: 1943. V. 46

ANJOU, GUSTAVE

Ulster County, New York Probate Records in the Office of the Surrogate, and in the County Clerk's Office at Kingston, New York. New York: 1906. V. 44

ANKENBRAND, FRANK

Fireflies: a Collection of Haiku. Evanston: 1965. V. 41

The House of Vanity. Philadelphia: 1928. V. 38

ANKER, J.

Bird Books and Bird Art, an Outline of the Literary History and Iconography of Descriptive Orinthology, Based Principally on the Collection in the University Library at Copenhagen. Copenhagen: 1938. V. 37

ANKER, JEAN

Bird Books and Bird Art. The Hague: 1973. V. 45

Bird Books and Bird Art. Amsterdam: 1979. V. 41

ANKER, MOSES

A Hurray-Graph of Colorado and Its Silver Mines. Baltimore: 1870. V. 44

ANLEY, CHARLOTTE

Influence: a Moral Tale for Young People. London: 1822. V. 38

Miriam: or, The Power of Truth. London: 1826. V. 45

Miriam; or, The Power of Truth. London: 1826. V. 43; 45

ANLEY, MARY DE LA RIVIERE

Secret Memoirs and Manners of Several Persons of Both Sexes. London: 1720. V. 37

ANNABEL, RUSSELL

Tales of a Big Game Guide. New York: 1938. V. 44

Tales of A Big Game Guide. By Russell Anabel. New York: (1938). V. 37

ANNALES de Pomologie Belge et Etrangere; Publiees par la Commission Royale de Pomologie. Brussels: 1853-60. V. 42

THE ANNALS and Magazine of Natural History. London: 1844-45. V. 38

ANNALS of Applied Biology. London: 1937-75. V. 37

ANNALS of Archaeology and Anthropology. Liverpool: 1932-1933. V. 40

ANNALS of Botany. London: 1906-70. V. 38

ANNALS of Ireland. Three Fragments, Copied from Ancient Sources by Dubhaltach Mac Firbisigh. Dublin: 1860. V. 43; 44

ANNALS of Medical History. New York: 1917-42. V. 42

A Complete run of this journal extending from 1917 to 1942. V. 37

ANNALS of Phrenology; to Consist Articles from the Edinburgh, Paris and London Phrenological Journals, and of Such Original Papers as May be Selected and Apparovaed by the 'Boston Phrenological Society.' Boston: 1833-35. V. 37

ANNALS Of Pioneer Settlers On the Whitewater and Its Tributaries, in the Vicinity of Richmond, Indiana from 1804 to 1830. Richmond: 1875. V. 42

THE ANNALS of Sporting and Fancy Gazette . . . London: 1822-28. V. 39; 42; 43; 46

ANNALS OF THE FOUR MASTERS

The Annls of Ireland. Dublin: 1846. V. 38

Annals of the Kingdom of Ireland by the Four Masters . . . Dublin: 1856. V. 43

ANNALS of the Troubles in the Netherlands from the Accession of Charles V, Emperor of Germany . . . A Proper and Seasonable Mirror for the Present Americans. Hartford: 1778. V. 38

ANNAN, THOMAS

The Old Country Houses of the Old Glasgow Gentry. Glasgow: 1878. V. 39

Photographic Views of Loch Katrine and of Some of the Principal Works Constructed for Introducing the Waters of Loch Katrine into the City of Glasgow. Glasgow: 1877. V. 40

ANNAND, DOUGLAS

Drawings and Paintings in Australia. Sydney: 1944. V. 41

ANNANDALE, THOMAS

The Malformations, Diseases and Injuries of the Fingers and Toes and Their Surgical Treatment. Edinburgh: 1865. V. 42

Observations and Cases in Surgery. Edinburgh: 1865. V. 42

ANNENBERG, MAURICE

Type Foundries of America and Their Catalogs. Baltimore: 1975. V. 37; 39; 41

Type Foundries of America and Their Catalogs. Baltimore & Washington: 1975. V. 42

ANNESLEY, ALEXANDER

A Compendium of the Law of Marine Insurances, Bottomry, Insurance on Lives, and of Insurance Against Fire. London: 1808. V. 38

ANNESLEY, EARL OF

Beautiful and Rare Trees and Plants. London: 1903. V. 38

ANNESLEY, JAMES

Memoirs of an Unfortunate Young Nobleman, Return'd from a Thirteen Years Slavery in America Where He Had Been Sent by the Wicked Contrivances of His Cruel Uncle. London: 1743. V. 37; 39; 41

The Trial in Ejectment . . . . Between Campbell Craig, Lessee of James Annesley, Esq . . . and the Right Honourable Richard Earl of Anglesey. London: 1744. V. 38; 39; 40

ANNESLEY, SAMUEL

The Morning-Exercise at Cripplegate . . . London: 1664. V. 42

ANNESLEY, WILLIAM

A Description of William Annesley's New System of Naval Architecture, as Secured to Him . . . London: 1818. V. 38; 45

ANNEXATION of Texas: Opinions of Messrs. Clay, Polk, Benton & Van Buren on the Immediate Annexation of Texas. N.P.: 1844. V. 39

ANNIGONI, PIETRO

Spanish Sketchbook. London: 1957. V. 38

ANNIUS, JOHANNES

Auctores Vetustissimi Nuper in Lucem Editi. Venice: 1498. V. 43

ANNIVERSARY Lectures. Washington: 1949. V. 44

PENNSYLVANIA Society for the Promotion of Internal Improvements in the Commonwealth The First Annual Report of the Acting Committe of the Society for the Promotion of Internal Improvement in the Commonwealth of Pennsylvania. Philadelphia: 1826. V. 39

AN ANNUAL Abstract of the Sinking Fund, for Michaelmas 1718, Whien It Was First Stated to Parliament, to the 10th of October, 1763. London: 1764. V. 38; 46

THE ANNUAL Anthology. Bristol: 1799-1800. V. 38

THE ANNUAL Miscellany: for . . . 1694. Being the Foruth Part of Miscellany Poems. Containg Great Variety of New Translations and Original Copies by . . . Eminent Hands. London: 1708. V. 37

AN ANNUAL of New Poetry 1917. London: 1917. V. 37

THE ANNUAL Register; or A View of the History, Politicks, and Literature of the Year. 1758-1851. London: 1762-1852. V. 39

THE ANNUAL Register; or a View of the History, Politicks, and Literature of the Year. 1780 to 1797. and 1801. London: 1784-1802. V. 39

THE ANNUAL Register, or a View of the History, Politics and Literature for the Year 1758-92. London: 1777-92. V. 45

THE ANNUAL Register, or a View of the History, Politics and Literature, for the Year 1758 (to the Year 1782). London: 1777-83, 1784. V. 39

THE ANNUAL Register, or a View of the History, Politics and Literature for the Year 1776. London: 1777. V. 44
THE ANNUAL Register, or, A View of the History, Politics and Literature, for the Year 1776. London: 1777. V. 37; 41

THE ANNUAL Register, or, a View of the History, Politics, and Literature for the Year(s) 1758-(1888). London: 1771-89. V. 41

ANNUAL Reunion of Pegram Battalion Association . . . Mary 21st, 1886, When the Battle-Flag of the Battalion was Presented by Capt. W. Gordon McCabe, Adjutant. Richmond: 1886. V. 37

ANNUAL Review. History of the City of St. Louis, Commercial Statistics, Improvements of the Year and Account of Leading Manufactories, &c. From the Missouri Republican, January 10, 1854. St. Louis: 1854. V. 40

ANNUAL Review of the Commerce, Manufactures, Public and Private Improvement of Chicago, for the Year 1854, with a Notice of Her System of Railroads. Chicago: 1855. V. 45

ANONYMOUS Fairy Tales. London: 1851. V. 45

ANOTHER Common Place Book. San Francisco: 1956. V. 41; 45; 46

ANQUETIL, LOUIS PIERRE

A Summary of Universal History . . . Exhibiting the Rise, Decline, and Revolutions of the Different Nations of the World. London: 1800. V. 45

ANSEL Adams: Images 1923-1974. Boston: 1974. V. 46

ANSELL, CHARLES 1794-1881

A Treatise on Friendly Societies, in Which the Doctrine of Interest of Money, and the Doctrine of Probability, are Practically Applied to the Affairs of Such Societies. London: 1835. V. 37; 38

ANSELM, SAINT, BP. OF CANTERBURY 1033-1109

Opuscula. Basel: 1497. V. 39; 45

ANSHELM, VALERIUS

Catalogus Annorum et Principium Geminus, ab Homine Condito Usque ad Presentem a Nato Christo 1540 annum. Berne: 1540. V. 38; 40

ANSON, GEORGE

A voyage Round the World, in the Years MDCCXL, I, II, III, IV. London: 1748. V. 38

A Voyage Round the World, in the Years MDCCXL, I, II, III, IV . . . London: 1748. V. 37; 38

A Voyage Round the World, in the Years MDCCXL, I, II, III, IV. London: 1756. V. 38

A Voyage Round the World, in the Years MDCCXL, I, II, III, IV. London: 1776. V. 38

ANSORGE, W. J.

Under the African Sun. London: 1899. V. 39; 40

ANSTAD, DAVID THOMAS

The Ionian Islands in the Year 1863. London: 1863. V. 37; 39; 40; 45

ANSTED, DAVID THOMAS

Geology, Introductory, Descriptive and Practical. London: 1844. V. 40
The Gold Seekers Manual. London: 1849. V. 42; 45
Scenery, Science and Art. London: 1854. V. 40; 46
Water and Water Supply, Chiefly in Reference to the British Islands - Surface Waters. London: 1878. V. 45

ANSTELL, T.

Hand-Book of the Useful Arts. New York: 1852. V. 40

ANSTER, JOHN MARTIN

Xenolia. Poems . . . Dublin: 1837. V. 41

ANSTEY, CHRISTOPHER 1724-1805

An Election Ball. Bath: 1776. V. 42

An Election Ball In Poetical Letters in the Zomerzetshire Dialect from Mr. Inkle Freeman of Bath to his Wife at Gloucester with a Poetical Address to John Miller, Esq., at Bath-Easton Villa. Dublin: 1776. V. 37

The New Bath Guide; or Memoirs of the B-R-D Family. London: 1766. V. 41

The New Bath Guide. London: 1784. V. 43

The New Bath Guide: or Memoirs of the B.N.R.D. Family: in a Series of Political Epistles. Bath: 1807. V. 39

The New Bath Guide; or Memoirs of the B-N-R-D Family . . . London: 1830. V. 38

The New Bath Guide; or Memoirs of the B-n-r-d Family, in a Series of Poetical Epistles . . . London: 1832. V. 38

The Patriot, a Pindaric Address to Lord Buckhorse. Cambridge: 1767. V. 38

Poetical Amusements at a Villa Near Bath. Bath and London: 1775-81. V. 39

The Poetical Works. London: 1808. V. 37; 39; 42; 46

The Priest Dissected; a Poem, Addressed to the Rev. Mr. ---, Author of Regulus, Toby, Caesar and Other Satirical Pieces in the Public Papers. Bath: 1774. V. 41; 44; 46

ANSTEY, F.

Vice Versa; or, a Lesson to Fathers. London: 1882. V. 39; 40

ANSTEY, JOHN d. 1819

The Pleader's Guide, a Didactic Poem, in Two Books. London: 1796. V. 40
The Pleader's Guide. Philadelphia: 1803. V. 39; 40; 43
The Pleader's Guide, a Didactic Poem, in two Parts. London: 1808. V. 38

ANSTEY, T. CHISHOLM

Crime and Government at Hong Kong. London: 1859. V. 45

ANSTIE, F. E.

The Uses of Wines in Health and Disease. New York: 1870. V. 40

ANSTRUTHER, G. ELLIOT

The Bindings of Tomorrow. London: 1902. V. 41; 43; 44; 45

AN ANSWER Addressed to Those Who Have Read Sir John Dalrymple's Pamphlet, in Support of a Tax and Permission to Export Raw Wool, by A Plain Matter of Fact Man. London: 1782. V. 40

AN ANSWER (in verse) of Coleman's Ghost, to H(enry) N(evill)'s Poetick Offering. N.P.: 1679. V. 42

THE ANSWER of the Sutro Tunnell Company to the Complaint of Divers Companies Working Mines on the Comstock Lode. Washington: 1876. V. 37

AN ANSWER to a Letter Address'd to the Archbishop of York, Containing a Vindication of His Grace's Speech at the York Association, the Causes to Which the Faults Complained of in the Present Administration May be Most Properly Imputed . . . Edinburgh: 1745. V. 39

AN ANSWER to a Pamphlet Entitled. Observations on the Mutiny Bill. Dublin: 1781. V. 45

AN ANSWER to a Pamphlet entitled Taxation no Tyranny. London: 1775. V. 42

AN ANSWER to a Pamphlet Entitled Taxation no Tyranny. Addressed to the Author and to Persons in Power. London: 1773. V. 41

AN ANSWER to a Paper, Entituled, the Grievances of His Majesty's Subjects Residing with the Principality of Wales, in Respect of the Court of the Council in the Marches of Wales. London: 1689. V. 40

AN ANSWER to Dr. Baker's Essay Concerning the Cause of the Endemial Colic of Devonshire, Wherein the Cyder of that County is Exculpated from the Accusations Brought Against it by that Gentelman. Exeter: 1767. V. 38

AN ANSWER to Mr. Eton's Charges Against the Turkey Company. London: 1799. V. 46

AN ANSWER to Mr. Pitt's Attack Upon Earl St. Vincent, and the Admiralty, on His Motion for an Enquiry into the State of the naval Defence of the Country, on the 15th March, 1804. London: 1804. V. 42

AN ANSWER to the Declaration of the King of England, Respecting His Motives for Carrying on the Present War . . . Paris: 1791. V. 44

AN ANSWER to the Declaration of the King of England, Respecting His Motives for Carrying on the Present War; and His Conduct Towards France. Paris: 1793. V. 39; 43

AN ANSWER to the Right Hon. Edmund Burke's Reflections on the Revolution in France, with Some Remarks on the Present State of the Irish Constitution. By an Irishman. Dublin: 1791. V. 38

AN ANSWER to the Second Part of Rights of Man. London: 1792. V. 39; 42

ANSWERS to Questions Concerning the Mammoth . . . Admittance One Shilling. London: 1802. V. 46

ANTAR

Antar, a Bedoueen Romance. London: 1820. V. 39; 45

ANTHEIL, GEORGE

Bad Boy of Music. Garden City: 1945. V. 44

ANTHEMS to be Sung at the Coronation of Their Majesties King George III and Queen Charlotte, in the Abbey Church of St. Peter, Westmisnter, on Tuesday the 22nd of September 1761. London: 1761. V. 41

ANTHING, FREDERICK

History of the Campaigns of Count Alexander Suworow Rymnikski . . . London: 1799. V. 43

ANTHING, JOHANN FRIEDRICH

Collection de Cent Silhouettes des Personnes Illustres et Celebres. Gotha: 1791. V. 42

Collection de Cent Silhouettes des Personnes Illustres et Celebres Dessinees d'Apres les Originaux. Gotha: 1793. V. 38; 40

ANTHOENSEN, FRED

Types and Bookmaking. Portland: 1943. V. 44

ANTHOLOGIA Graeca. Florence: 1494. V. 39

ANTHOLOGIA Graeca Florilegium Diversorum Epigrammatum in Septem Libros. Venice: 1503. V. 43

ANTHOLOGIAS Diaphoron Epigrammaton. Raccolta di Varii Epigrammi in Sette Libri. Napoli: 1788-96. V. 38

ANTHOLOGIE Dada No. 4-5. Zurich: 1915. V. 39

AN ANTHOLOGY Of Magazine Verse for 1923-1927. Boston: 1923-27. V. 40

ANTHOLOGY of Verse. Columbus: 1926. V. 43

AN ANTHOLOGY of Younger Poets. Philadelphia: 1922. V. 45
AN ANTHOLOGY of Younger Poets. Philadelphia: 1932. V. 40; 45; 46

ANTHON, JOHN

The Law of Nisi Prius, Being Cases Determined at Nisi Prius in The Sutpreme Court of New York, with Notes and Commentaries on Each Case. New York: 1820. V. 37

ANTHONY, GEORGE

The Scholar Dance. Boston: 1951. V. 42; 44

ANTHONY, GORDON

Alicia Markova: a Photographic Survey of the Great Ballerina. London: 1951. V. 39

Ballet: Camera Studies. London: 1937. V. 43

Sleeping Princess: Camera Sutdies. London: (1940). V. 37

ANTHONY, SUSAN B. 1820-1906

History of Woman Suffrage. Volume II 1861-876. Rochester: 1881. V. 45

History of Woman Suffrage. Volume III. 1861-1876. Rochester: 1886. V. 45

The History of Woman Suffrage. Volume IV. 1883-1900. Rochester: 1902. V. 45

THE ANTI-GALLICAN; or, Standard of British Loyalty, Religion and Liberty. London: 1804. V. 42

THE ANTI-JACOBIN; or Weekly Examiner. London: 1797-98. V. 40

THE ANTI-SLAVERY Alphabet. Philadelphia: 1847. V. 37

THE ANTI-WEESILS. A Poem Giving an Account of Some Historical and Argumental Passages Happening in the Lyon's Court. London: 1691. V. 40

THE ANTICHRIST of Nietzsche. A New Version in English by P.R. Stephenson. London: (1928). V. 37

ANTIDOTARII Romani Sev De Modo Componendi Medicamenta Quae Sunt in Vsu, Opus Pharmacopolis, Medicisque Non Minus Vtile q Necessarium. Rome: 1853. V. 43

THE ANTIDOTE for the Poison: Abstract of Speeches and Documents Against the Parsons Bulkhead Bill. San Francisco: 1860. V. 37; 39

AN ANTIDOTE to Expel the Poison Contained in an Anonymous Pamphlet, Lately Published, Entitled, A Detection of the Proceedings and Practices of the Directors of the Royal African Company of England. London: 1749. V. 41

THE ANTIENT and Present State of Military Law in Great Britain Consider'd: With a Review of the Debates of the Army and Navy Bills. London: 1749. V. 41

THE ANTIGALLICAN; or, Strictures on the Present Form of Government Established in France. London: 1793. V. 38

ANTIGALLICUS, TITUS, PSEUD.

An Ode for the Thanksgiving. N.P.,: 1749. V. 40

THE ANTIQUARIAN and Topographical Cabinet. London: 18179-19. V. 40

ANTIQUARIAN Lust. Angelopolis: 1973. V. 39

THE ANTIQUITIES of St. Peter's, or, the Abbey-Church of Westminster . . . London: 1741. V. 43

ANTOINE, JEAN

Traite d'Architecture, ou Proportions des Trois Ordres Grecs sur un Module de Douze Parties. Treves: 1768. V. 38

ANTOMMARCHI, F.

The Last Days of the Emperor Napoleon. London: 1825. V. 45

ANTON, FERDINAND

Art of Maya. New York: 1970. V. 45

The Art of Ancient Peru. New York: 1972. V. 40

Primitive Art. New York: 1979. V. 42

Primitive Art. Pre Columbian, North American Indian, African, Oceanic. New York: (1979). V. 37

ANTONIN Raymond, Architectural Details. New York: 1947. V. 46

ANTONINI, CARLO

Manuale di Vari Ornamenti Tratti Dalle Fabbriche, e Frammenti Antichi Per Uso, e Commodo de Pittori, Scultori, Architetti, Scaarpellini, Stuccatori, Intalgiatori de Pietre, e Legni (etc.). Rome: 1781. V. 37

ANTONINTUS, BROTHER 1912-

The Blowing Seed. New Haven: 1966. V. 45

ANTONINUNS, BROTHER

Who is She that Looketh forth as the Morning. By Brother Antoninus. Santa Barbara: 1972. V. 37

ANTONINUS, AUGUSTUS

Iter Britanniarum Commentariis Illustratum Thomae Gale . . . London: 1719. V. 40

ANTONINUS, BROTHER 1912-

Birth of a Poet. Santa Barbara: 1982. V. 39; 43

Black Hills. 1973. V. 45

Black Hills. N.P.: 1973. V. 44

Black Hills. San Francisco: 1973. V. 42

Blackbird Sundown. Northridge: 1978. V. 45

Blame It on the Jet Stream! Ode: The First Commencement, June 17, 1973 Kresge College, The University of California Santa Cruz. Santa Cruz: 1978. V. 37; 42

The Blowing of the Seed. New Haven: 1966. V. 39; 41; 42; 46

A Canticle to the Waterbirds. Berkeley: 1968. V. 39; 40; 41; 42; 44; 46

Eastward the Armies. Torrance: 1980. V. 37; 39

The High Embrace. Los Angeles: 1986. V. 42; 46

In the Fictive Wish. Oyez: 1967. V. 39

In Medioas Res. Canto One of an Autobiographical Epic: Dust Shall Be the Serpent's Food. San Francisco: 1984. V. 41; 43; 44; 45; 46

The Last Crusade. Berkeley: 1969. V. 42

The Last Crusade. Oakland: 1969. V. 39

The Last Crusade. Oyez: 1969. V. 39

A Man Who Prints. V. 44

A Man Who Prints. Los Angeles: 1980. V. 39; 45

The Masks of Drought. Santa Barbara: 1980. V. 44; 46

The Mate-Flight of Eagles. Blue Oak: 1977. V. 39

The Mate-Flight of Eagles: Two Poems on the Love-Death of the Cross. Newcastle: 1977. V. 40; 44

Novum Psalterium Pii XII. Los Angeles: 1955. V. 45

Poems: MCMXIII. Waldport: 1944-45. V. 45

Poems: MCMXLII. Waldport: 1945. V. 39

The Poet is Dead. San Francisco: 1964. V. 42; 44

The Poet Is Dead. A Memorial for Robinson Jeffers. Santa Cruz: 1987. V. 42

A Privacy of Speech. Berkeley: 1949. V. 46

Rattlesnake August: a Poem. Northridge: 1978. V. 37

Renegade Christmas. Northridge: 1984. V. 42

The Residual Years. New York: 1948. V. 42

River Root. Berkeley: 1976. V. 39; 40; 42; 44

San Joaquin. Los Angeles: 1939. V. 43; 44

San Joaquin. Los Angeles: 1939. V. 44

Single Source. Berkeley: 1966. V. 39; 41

The Springing of the Blade. Reno: 1968. V. 39

The Springing of the Blade. 1968. V. 39

Ten War Elegies. Waldport: 1943. V. 45

Tendril in the Mesh. Aptos: 1973. V. 42

Tendril in the Mesh. San Francisco: 1973. V. 39; 46

There Will Be Harvest. N.P.: 1960. V. 42

Triptych for the Living. Oakland: 1951. V. 42; 44; 46

Triptych for the Living. Oakland: 1955. V. 42

The Veritable Years 1949-1966. 1978. V. 39

The Veritable Years, 1949-1966. Santa Barbara: 1978. V. 40

Waldport Poems. Waldport: 1944. V. 37; 40; 45

War Elegies. Waldport: 1944. V. 45

Who Is She That Looketh Forth as the Morning. 1972. V. 39

Who Is She that Looketh Forth as the Morning. Santa Barbara: 1972. V. 37; 39; 40; 42; 43; 44; 46

Who Is She That Looketh Forth as the Morning. Santa Barbara: 1972. V. 46

The Year's Declension. Berkeley: 1961. V. 39

ANTONINUS FLORENTINUS

Confessionale. Strassbourg: 1490. V. 40

Summa Theologia. Venice: 1480. V. 42

ANTONINUS, FLORENTINUS, SAINT

De Censuris. De Sponsalibus et Matrimonio. Venice: 1474. V. 40

ANTONINUS FLORENTIUS

Summae Secunda Pars. Venice: 1477. V. 41

ANTONINUS, SAINT, ABP. OF FLORENCE

Suma de Confession llamada Defecerunt. Toledo: 1511. V. 37

Summa de Confession llamada Defecerunt. Seville: 1537. V. 38

ANTONIO DA SYLVA, P.

Sol do Orient S. Francisco Xavier da Companhia de Jesu. Lisbon: 1665. V. 45

ANTONIO DE VIGA, DIEGO

Por la Jurisdicion, Patronato y Regalia de su Magestad, el Licenciado Don Diego Antonio de Viga . . . Manila: 1678. V. 43

ANTONIUS DE BALOCCO DE VERCELLIS

Sermones Quadragesimales de XII Mirabilibus Christianae Fidei Excellentiis. Venice: 1492/93. V. 37; 44

ANTONIUS DE VERCELLIS

Sermones Quadragesimales de xii Mirabilibus Christianae Fidei Excellentiis. Venice: 1492-93. V. 38

ANTRAM, C. B.

Butterflies of India. Calcutta & Simia: 1924. V. 38

ANTRIM, BENAJAH J.

Pantography, or Universal Drawings. Philadelphia: 1843. V. 37; 40; 41; 43

ANTRIM, JOSHUA

History of Champaign & Logan Counties, From Their First Settlement. Bellefontaine, Ohio: 1872. V. 37

ANTROBUS, CLARA LOUISA

Wildersmoor: a Novel. London: 1895. V. 44

ANVILLE, JEAN BAPTISTE BOURGUIGNON D' 1697-1782

A Complete Body of Ancient Geography . . . London: 1818. V. 40

APEL, JOHANN AUGUST

Der Freischutz Travestie. London: 1824. V. 41

APES, WILLIAM

Indian Nullification of the Unconstitutional Laws of Massachsetts, Relative to the Marshpee Tribe; or, The Pretended Riot Explained. Boston: 1835. V. 39; 41

A Son of the Forest. New York: 1829. V. 39; 40; 42; 45

APGAR, JOHN F.

Frank E. Schoonover, Painter-Illustrator, a Bibliography. N.P.: 1969. V. 43

APHORISMS for Youth, with Observations and Reflections, Religious, Moral, Cirtical and Characteristic . . . London: 1801. V. 46

APHORISMS on Education; Selected from the Works of the Most Celebrated English, French and Latin Writers . . . Intended as A Vade-Mecum for Parents . . . London: 1800. V. 41

APHRODITE a Mythical Journey in Eight Episodes. London: 1970. V. 43

APHTHONIUS OF ANTIOCH

(Greek title) Aphthonivs, Hermogens & Dionysivs Longinvs, Praestantissimi Artis Rheotrices Magistri, Francisci Porti Cretensis Opera Industriaque Illustrati Atque Exploiti. Geneva: 1570-1569. V. 39

APIANUS, PETER

Astronomicum Caesareum. New York: 1969. V. 42

APIANUS, PETRUS

Cosmographia . . . Antwerp: 1564. V. 41

Cosmographia Petri Apiani. Paris: 1551. V. 37

Cosmographie, ou Description des Quatre Parties du Monde . . . Antwerp: 1581. V. 37

Inscriptiones Sacrosanctae Vetustatis non Illae Quidem Romanae, sed Totius Fere Orbis . . . Ingolstadt: 1534. V. 37; 38

APICIUS

Cookery and Dining in Imperial Rome. Chicago: 1936. V. 44

In Hoc Opere Contenta. Apicii Caelii de Opsoniis et Condimentis, Sive Arte Coquinaria, Libri X. Zurich: 1542. V. 41

APICIUS COELIUS

Caelii Apitii . . . de re Culinaria Libri Decem B. Platinae Cremonensis de Tuenda Valetudine . . . Libri X. Pauli Aeginetae de Facultatibus Alimentorum Tractatus, Albano Torino Interprete. Lyons: 1541. V. 42

In Hoc Opere C(ontenta) Apicii Caelii de Opsoniis et Condimentis, sive Arte Coqvina. Ria, Libri X . . . Zurich: 1542. V. 42

APOLLINAIRE, GUILLAUME 1880-1918

The Cubist Painters. New York: 1949. V. 39

Le Flaneur des Deux Rives. Paris: 1918. V. 46

L'Oeuvre du Marquis de Sade - Pages Choisis. Paris: 1909. V. 37

Les Mamelles de Tiresias. Paris: 1918. V. 40

Oeuvres Completes de Guillaume Apollinaire. Paris: 1965-66. V. 42

Les Peintres Cubistes. Paris: 1913. V. 44

The Poet Assassinated. New York: 1923. V. 39

Sept Calligrammes. Paris: 1967. V. 41

Zone. Dublin & London: 1972. V. 41

Zone. London: 1972. V. 39; 43

APOLLINARIS, BP. OF LAODICAEA

(Greek title: then) Apolinari (sic) Interpretatio Psalmonum, Versibus Heroicis. Ex Bibliotheca REgia. Paris: 1552. V. 43

APOLLINARIS SIDONIUS, CAIUS SOLLIUS

Opera. Parisiis: 1598. V. 42; 46

Opera . . . Io. Savaro . . . Multo Quam Antea Castigatius, Recognovit & Librum Commentarium Adiecit. Paris: 1599. V. 40

APOLLINARIUS

Apolinarij Interpretatio Psalmorum. Londini: 1590. V. 37

APOLLONIUS

Historia Appllonii Regis Tyri. Translated from the Latin by Paul Turner. London: 1956. V. 37

APOLLONIUS OF PERGA

Locorum Planorum Libri II. Glasgow: 1749. V. 40

APOLLONIUS OF RHODES

(Greek title then) Agronauticon, Libri IIII. Paris: 1574. V. 38

Argonautica. New York: 1957. V. 44; 46

APOLLONIUS OF TYRE

Apollonius of Tyre. Waltham St. Lawrence: 1956. V. 40

Historia Apollonii Regis Tyri. London: 1956. V. 41; 42

Historia Apolloni Regis Tyri. Waltham St. Lawrence: 1956. V. 44

The Patterne of Painefull Adventures . . . New York: 1903. V. 43

APOLLONIUS RHODIUS

Argonautica. Venice: 1521. V. 37

Argonauticon. Geneva: 1574. V. 40

The Argonautics of . . . Dublin: 1803. V. 41

Medea and Jason. A Poem, in three books translated from the Greek of Apollonius Rhodius's Argonautics. London: 1772. V. 41

AN APOLOGY for the Conduct of a Late Celebrated Second-Rate Minister, from the Year 1729, at Which Time he Commenc'd Courtier, Till Within a Few Weeks of His Death, in 1746. London: 1757. V. 46

APOLOGY for the Conduct of a Late Second-Rate Minister, from the Year 1729, at which time he commenc'd Courtier, till within a few Weeks of His Death in 1746. London: 1747. V. 41; 42; 46

AN APOLOGY for the Conduct of the Present Administration, As to Foreign Affairs Generally, and Particularly With Regard to France . . . In a Letter to a Noble Lord in the Opposition. London: 1744. V. 41

AN APOLOGY for the Failures Charg'd on the Rev. Mr. George Walker's Printed Account of the Siege of Derry, in a Letter to the Undertaker of a More Accurate Narrative of that Siege. London. V. 38; 43

AN APOLOGY of the Protestants of Ireland. London: 1689. V. 38

APONIUS

Commentariorvm In Cantica Canticorvm Solomonis Libri Sex: Quo Hucusqz . . . Erasmi Roterodami Testimonio, Unaqua Scripsit in Eadem Cantica: Opus iam Primum et Situ ac Squalore Erutum, & in Lcem Aeditum . . . Freiburg im Breisagu: 1538. V. 39

AN APPEAL from the New to the Old Whigs, in Consequence of Some Late Discussions in Parliament, Relative to the Reflections on the French Revolution. Dublin: 1791. V. 38

APPEAL of the Day Labourers, to the Landowners of England. London: 1832. V. 43

APPEAL to the California Delegation in Congress Upon the Goat Island Grant to the Central Pacific R.R. Co. San Francisco: 1872. V. 40

AN APPEAL to the Candour and Justice of the People of England, in Behalf of the West India Merchants . . . London: 1792. V. 46

AN APPEAL to the Consciences of Christians on the Subject of Dress. Darlington: 1816. V. 43

AN APPEAL to the Impartial Public by the Society of Christian Independents, Congregating in Gloucester. Boston: 1785. V. 44

AN APPEAL to the Imperial Public by the Society of Christian Independents, Congregating in Gloucester. Boston: 1785. V. 40

APPEAL to the Moral and Religious of all Denominations; or, an Exposition of Some of the Indiscretions of General Andrew Jackson, as Copied from the Records, and Certified by the Clerk of Mercer County, Kentucky. New York: 1828. V. 46

AN APPEAL to the Public; in Relation to the Tobacco ***; and a Revival of the Old Project, to Establish a General Excise. London: 1751. V. 41
AN APPEAL To the Public: in Relation to the Tobacco ***: and a Revival of the Old Project, to Establish a General Excise. London: 1751. V. 45

AN APPEAL to the Public, or Strictures on Certain Characters Concerned in the Recent Proceedings of the Whitby Union Mill Society. Whitby: 1815. V. 40

APPEL, KAREL

Works on Paper. New York: 1980. V. 41

AN APPENDIX or, Further Reasons in Support of the Plan or Proposals for the Easy and Effectual Amendment of the Roads. London: 1753. V. 43

AN APPENDIX to the Rowfant Library. London: 1900. V. 45

APPERLEY, CHARLES JAMES 1777-1843

The Chace, The Turf, and the Road. London: 1837. V. 37; 38; 39; 40; 41; 42

The Chace, the Turf, and the Road. London: 1853. V. 39; 43

The Condition of Hunters. London: 1908. V. 40

The Horse and the Hound Their Various Uses and Treatment . . . Edinburgh: 1842. V. 43

The Life of John Mytton Esq. London. V. 38; 40

The Life of John Mytton. London: 1870. V. 44

The Life of John Mytton Esq. London: 1877. V. 38

The Life of a Sportsman. London: 1905. V. 39

The Life of a Sportsman. London: 1842. V. 37

The Life of a Sportsman. Downey: 1901. V. 37

The Life of a Sportsman. London: 1914. V. 37

The Life of a Sportsman, by Nimrod. London: 1901. V. 37; 40

The Life of John Mytton, Esa. of Halston, Shropshire. London: 1869. V. 37

The Life of John Mytton, Esq., of Halston, Shropshire. London: 1870. V. 37

Memoirs of the Life of the Late John Mytton, Esq . . . London: 1835. V. 37; 40; 45

Memoirs of the Life of the Late John Mytton, Esq. London: 1837. V. 37; 39; 40; 42; 44

Memoirs of the Life of the Late John Mytton, Esq. of Halston, Shropshire, Formerly M.P. for Shrewsbury . . . London: 1837. V. 43

Memoirs of the Late John Mytton. London: 1851. V. 37; 38; 39; 40

Memoirs of the Life of the Late John Mytton, Esq. Downey: 1899. V. 37

Nimrod's Hunting Tours. London: 1903. V. 46

Nimrod's Hunting Tours, Interspersed with Characteristic Anecdotes, Sayings, and Doings of Sporting Men, Including Notices of the principal crack riders of England . . . To which are added Nimrod's Letters on riding th Hounds. London: 1835. V. 37

Remarks on the Condition of Hunters, the Choice of Horses and Their management. London: 1837. V. 39; 40; 44

Sporting. London: 1838. V. 37

APPERT, NICHOLAS

The Art of Preserving All Kinds of Animal and Vegetable Substances for Several Years. London: 1811. V. 45

APPERT, NICOLAS

The Art of Perserving All Kinds of Animal and Vegetable Substances for Several Years . . . London: 1812. V. 40

Book For All Households, or The Art of Preserving Animal and Vegetable Substances for Many Years. Chicago: 1920. V. 39

APPIAN

Romanorum Historiarum - ex Bibliotheca Regia. Paris: 1551. V. 44

APPIANUS, OF ALEXANDRIA

Appiani Alexandrini Romanarum Historiarum. Lutetiae: 1551. V. 38; 40

An Avncient Historie and Exquisite Chronicle of the Romanes Warres, Both Ciuile and Foren . . . London: 178. V. 46

De Bellis Civilibus Romanis etc. Venice: 1472. V. 40

De Ciuilibus Romanorum Bellis Historiarum Libri Quinque Eiusdem Libri Sex . . . Lvgdvni: 1560. V. 44

De Civilibus Romanorum Bellis Historiarum . . . Paris: 1538. V. 46

Delle Gverre Civili et Esterne de Romani. In Vinegia: 1551. V. 44

(Historia Romana), Cum: De Bellis Civilibus. Venice: 1500. V. 46

Illyrica. Augsburg: 1599. V. 40

Romanarum Historiarum. Paris: 1551. V. 37

(Greek title: then) Romanorum Historiam Celtica . . . ex Bibliotheca Regia. Paris: 1551. V. 43

Romanorum Historiarum. Amstelodami: 1670. V. 46

APPIER, JEAN (CALLED HANZELET)

Recveil de Plusieurs Machines Militaires, et Feux Artificiels Pour la Guerre, & Recreation. Pont a Mousson: 1620. V. 37

APPLEBY, BROTHERS

Appleby's Illustrated Hand-Book of Machinery and Iron Work, with the cost, the Working expenses, and Results obtained, in the use of Steam and Hand Cranes, pumps, Fixed and portable steam Engines, and Various other . . . London: 1869. V. 37

ARABIAN NIGHTS continued

Sinbad the Sailor and Other Stories from the Arabian Nights. V. 40

The Book of the Thousand Nights and a Night. V. 40

Dalziel's Illustrated Arabian Nights' Entertainments. London. V. 44

Arabian Nights. London. V. 43

The Book of the Thousand Nights and a Night, a Plain and Literal Translation. London. V. 40

Sinbad the Sailor and Other Stories from the Arabian Nights. London. V. 39; 40

Arabian Nights Entertainments. London. V. 39

The Arabian Nights. New York. V. 44

Le Livre des Mille Nuits et Une Nuit. Paris. V. 41

Thousand and One Days: Persian Tales. London: 1738. V. 41

Tales, Anecdotes and Letters. Translated from the Arabic and Persian By Jonathan Scott. Shrewsbury: 1800. V. 38

The Arabian Nights, in Five Volumes. London: 1802. V. 40

The Arabian Nights. London: 1802. V. 46

The Arabian Nights Entertainment. London: 1811. V. 40; 44; 46

The Arabian Nights Entertainments. Philadelphia: 1826. V. 46

Arabian Nights Entertainments. Glasgow: 1828. V. 42

The Thousand and One Nights, Commonly Called in England, the Arabian Nights Entertainments. London: 1839/40/41. V. 44

The Thousand and One Nights, Commonly Called, in England, the Arabian Nights' Entertainments. London: 1839-41. V. 41

The Arabian Nights' Entertainments. London: 1839/41. V. 43

The Arabian Night's Entertainments. London: 1841. V. 39

Arabian Night's Entertainments. London: 1865. V. 43

Alaadin; or, the Wonderful Lamp. London: 1880. V. 39

The Arabian Nights Entertainments. London: 1883. V. 46

The Book of the Thousand Nights and a Night. London: 1885. V. 40

A Plain and Literal Translation of the Arabian Nights' Entertainments, Entitled the Book of the Thousand Nights and a Night. Benares: 1885-1888. V. 40

Aladdin and the Wonderful Lamp. London: 1890. V. 39

Arabian Nights: The Thousand and One Nights or Arabian Nights Entertainments. London: 1896. V. 41

The Arabian Nights . . . Kamashastra Version. London: 1897. V. 41

The Book of the Thousand Nights and a Night. London: 1897. V. 41

The Arabian Nights. London: 1899. V. 46

The Child's Arabian Nights. London: 1903. V. 40

A Plain and Literal Translation of the Arabian Nights' Entertainment, Now Entitled the Book of a Thousand and One Nights. London: 1903-04. V. 42

Stories from the Arabian Nights. London: 1907. V. 40

The Arabian Nights: Their Best Known Tales. New York: 1909. V. 40; 45

The Book of the Thousand Nights and a Night. N.P.: 1910. V. 39

Stories from the Arabian Nights. London: 1911. V. 40

The Arabian Nights. London: 1913. V. 41; 42

The Arabian Nights Entertainments. 1914. V. 46

Sinbad the Sailor and Other Stories from the Arabian Nights. London: 1914. V. 41

Des Contes des Mille Nuits et Une Nuit. Histoire d'Aladdin et de la Lampe Magique. Paris: 1914. V. 42

Ali Baba & Aladdin. London: 1918. V. 40

The Arabian Nights. London: 1924. V. 44; 46

Arabian Nights. Philadelphia: 1928. V. 43; 45

The Book of the Thousand Nights and One Night. London: 1929. V. 39

The Seven Voyages of Sinbad the Sailor, from the Arabian Nights Entertainment. Park Ridge: 1939. V. 41

The Arabian Nights Entertainments . . . Ipswich: 1954. V. 41; 46

The Book of a Thousand Nights and One Night. London: 1958. V. 39

Ali Baba and the Forty Thieves. Chicago and Skokie: 1962. V. 41

The Book of the Thousand Nights and One Night. London: 1973. V. 39

Arabian Nights. London: 1988. V. 39

The Book of the Thousand Nights and a Night. (with) Supplemental Nights, to the Book of the Thousand Nights and a Nigth. Benares. V. 37

Sinbad the Sailor and Other Stories from the Arabian Nights. London. V. 37

The Books of the Thousand Nights and One Night. London. V. 38

The Book of a Thousand Nights and a Night. London. V. 38

Arabian Tales: or, a Continuation of the Arabian Nights Entertainments. Edinburgh: 1792. V. 38

New Arabian Nights' Entertainments, Selected from the Original Oriental MS. London: 1826. V. 38

The Thousand and One Nights, Commonly called in England, The Arabian Nights' Entertainment. London: 1839-41. V. 37

The Thousand and One Nights. London: 1841. V. 38

The Thousand and One Nights, the Arabian Nights Entertainments. London: 1883. V. 37

The Book of the Thousand Nights and a Night. (with) Supplemental Nights. Benares: 1885-86. V. 37

The Thousand and One Nights; or Arabian Night's Entertainment, translated by Edward William Lane. London: 1896. V. 38

The Book of the Thousand Nights and a Night. London: 1899. V. 38

Stories from the Arabian Nights. Retold by Laurence Housman. London: 1907. V. 37

The Book of the Thousand Nights and One Night. London: 1923. V. 37

The Book of the Thousand Nights and One Night. London: 1929. V. 38

The Book of the Thousand Nights and a Night. New York: 1934. V. 38

The Book of the Thousand Nights and a Night. London. V. 42; 44; 46

The Book of the Thousand Nights and A Night. n.d. V. 42

The Book of the Thousand Nights and a Night. (with Supplemental Nights, with Notes. Denver: 1889-1901. V. 46

The Book of the Thousand Nights and a Night. Benares (London): 1897. V. 43

The Book of the Thousand Nights and a Night. London: 1897. V. 44

The Book of a Thousand Nights and a Night. 1900. V. 46

The Book of the Thousand Nights and One Night. New York: 1923. V. 41; 42

The Book of the Thousand Nights and a Night. N.P.: 1925. V. 46

The Book of the Thousand Nights and One Night. London: 1929. V. 46

The Book of the Thousand Nights and One Night. New York: 1930. V. 46

The Book of the Thousand Nights and a Night. New York: 1934. V. 42; 43; 45

The Book of the Thousand Nights and One Night. London: 1958. V. 42

The Thousand and One Nights, commonly called, in England, the Arabian Nights' Entertainments. A new translation from the Arabic, with copious notes, by Edward William Lane. Illustrated by many hundred engravings on wood, from original designs by William.. London: 1839-41. V. 37

The Book of the Thousand Nights and a night. A Plain and literal translation of the Arabian Nights Entertainments . . . with Introduction explanatory notes . . . and a terminal essay upon the history of The Nights . . . London: 1885. V. 37

The Book of the Thousand and One Nights. Version of Dr. J.C. Mardrus collated with other sources by E. Powys Mathers. London: ca. 1930. V. 37

The Book of the Thousand Nights and a Night. Translated from the Arabic by R.F. Burton . . . Reprinted from the Original Edition and Edited by Leonard C. Smithers. Illustrated . . . by Albert Letchford. London: 1897. V. 37

Fairy Tales from the Arabian Nights. London: 1893. V. 43; 46

The Magic Horse - from the Arabian Nights. 1930. V. 38

Persian Stories from the Arabian Nights. Greenbrae: 1980. V. 41

A Plain and Literal Translation of the Arabian Nights' Entertainments, Now Entituled The Book of the Thousand Nights and a Night . . . Benares: 1885-88. V. 46

A Plain and Literal Translation of the Arabian Nights. 1910. V. 45

The Sailor and Other Stories from the Arabian Nights. London: 1914. V. 46

The Seven Voyages of Sinbad the Sailor. New York: 1949. V. 43

Sinbad the Sailor and Other Stories from the Arabian Nights. London. V. 45

Sinbad the Sailor and Other Stories from the Arabian Nights. London: 1914. V. 42

Stories from the Arabian Nights Retold by Laurence Housman. London. V. 46

Stories from the Arabian Nights by Laurence Housman. London: 1907. V. 44

Stories from the Arabian Nights Retold by Laurence Housman. London: 1908. V. 42

Tales, Anecdotes and Letters. Shrewsbury: 1800. V. 46

The Thousand and One Days; Persian Tales. London: 1722. V. 43

The Thousand and One Nights, Commonly Called, . . . The Arabian Nights' Entertainments. London: 1839-41. V. 46

3 Persian Stories. 1980. V. 44

Two Tales from the Arabian Nights. Princeton: 1983. V. 42

THE ARABIAN Stud Book. Voluem XIII. Chicago: 1963. V. 38

ARAGAON, LOUIS

Henri Matisse. New York: 1972. V. 46

ARAGO, D. FRANCOIS J.

Popular Astronomy. London: 1855-58. V. 42

ARAGO, DOMENIQUE FRANCOIS JEAN

Atlas. V. 45

ARAGO, DOMINIQUE FRANCOIS JEAN

Eloge Historique de James Watt. Paris: 1839. V. 43

Historical Eloge of James Watt. London: 1839. V. 43

Oeuvres . . . Paris: 1854-57. V. 44

Popular Astronomy. London: 1855-58. V. 43

ARAGO, FRANCOIS 1786-1853

Popular Astronomy . . . London: 1855. V. 40

ARAGO, JACQUES ETIENNE VICTOR

Narrative of a Voyae Round the World, in the Uranie and Physicienne Corvettes, Commanded by Captain Freycinet, During the Yearas 1817, 1818, 1819 and 1820 . . . London: 1823. V. 38; 40

ARAGON

Henri Matisse. London: 1971. V. 44

ARAGON, LOUIS

The Blue Dream, a Poem Written for Man Ray. Nancy: 1981. V. 39

Feu de Joie. 1920. V. 44

Le Grande Gaite. 1929. V. 44

Henri Matisse. Paris. V. 46

Henri Matisse: a Novel. New York: 1972. V. 39

Le Mouvement Perpetuel. 1926. V. 44

The Red Front. Chapel Hill: 1933. V. 37; 39

ARAN, F. A.

Practical Manual of the Diseases of the Heart and Great Vessels. Philadelphia: 1843. V. 44

ARANDA, EMANUEL D'

The History of Algiers and Its Slavery. London: 1666. V. 41

ARAPAHOE CATTLE AND LAND COMPANY

The Arapahoe Cattle and Land Company . . . Incorporated Under the L. V. 39

ARATOS OF SOLI

Phaenomena et Prognostica. Cologne: 1569. V. 40

ARATUS

Hug. Grotii Batavi Syntagma Arateorum: Opus Antiquitatis et Astronomiae Studiois Utilisimum . . . Leyden: 1600. V. 43

Phenomena. N.P.: 1975. V. 46

ARATUS OF SOLI

Phaenomena et Prognostica . . . C. Iulii Hygini Astronomicon . . . Cologne: 1569. V. 38

ARAUJO CARNEIRO, HELIODOR JACINTO DE

Cartas, e Factos, Para Servirem de Introducam ao Conhecimento do Egoismo, Inconsideracaeo, e Despotismo em Londres. London: 1811. V. 39

ARBEAU, THOINOT

Orchesography, a Treatise in the Form of a Dialogue . . . London: 1925. V. 37

ARBER, A.

Herbals, Their Origin and Exolution, a Chatper in the History of Botany 1470-1670. Cambridge: 1938. V. 37

ARBER, AGNES

Herbals; Their Origin and Evolution. Cambridge: 1938. V. 39; 40; 41; 42; 45

ARBER, E.

The Term Catalogues 1668-1709. New York: 1965. V. 44

ARBER, EDWARD

English Reprints. London. V. 39

An English Garner in Gatherings from Our History and Literature. London: 1897. V. 46

A List, Based on the Registers of Stationer's Company of 837 London Publishers . . . Between 1553- and 1640 . . . Birmingham: 1890. V. 38; 40

The Term Catalogues, 1668-1709 A.D. . . . . London: 1903-05-06. V. 43

The Term Catalogues, 1668-1709. London: 1903-06. V. 38; 40; 43

The Term Catalogues, 1668-1709 A. D. with a Number for Easter Term 1711 A.D. . . . . New York: 1965. V. 43

A Transcript of the Registers of the Company of Stationers of London: 1554-1640. (and) The Registers . . . from 1640-1708. Gloucester: 1967. V. 42

A Transcript of the Rgisters of the Company of Stationers of London: 1554-1640 A.D. (with) . . . 1640-1708. Gloucester: 1967, 1950. V. 39

ARBERRY, A. J.

Catalogue of the Library of the India Office. Volume II - Part VI. London: 1937. V. 44

ARBERT, EDWARD

The First Three English Books on America. Birmingham: 1885. V. 39

ARBLAY, FRANCES BURNEY D'

V. 46

Brief Reflections Relative to the Emigrant French Clergy . . . London: 1793. V. 41

Camilla. London: 1796. V. 38; 39; 40; 41; 42; 43; 44; 45; 46

Camilla. London: 1796. V. 40

Camilla; or, a Picture of Youth. London: 1796. V. 45

Camilla; or, a Picture of Youth. London: 1802. V. 40

Cecilia. London: 1773. V. 40

Cecilia, or Memoirs of an Heiress. London: 1782. V. 43

Cecila. London: 1782. V. 38; 40; 43; 44

Cecilia, or Memoirs of an Heiress. London: 1786. V. 41; 42

Cecilia, or Memoirs of an Heiress. London: 1791. V. 40; 42

Cecilia. London: 1810. V. 43

Cecilia, or Memoirs of an Heiress. London: 1825. V. 40

Diary and Letters of Madame d'Arblay . . . London: 1842. V. 43

Diary and Letters. London: 1842-46. V. 38; 39; 40; 41; 42; 43; 45; 46

Diary and Letters of Madame D'Arblay. London: 1843-46. V. 38; 41

Diary and Letters of Madamde D'Arblay. London: 1854. V. 38; 40; 42; 44; 46

Diary and Letters of Madame D'Arblay. London: 1891. V. 40

Diary and Letters of Madame D'Arblay. London: 1892. V. 45; 46

Diary and Letters of (1778-1840). London: 1904. V. 45

The Early Diary of Frances Burney 1768-1778 with a Selection from Her Correspondence and from the Journals of Her Sisters, Susan and Charlotte Burney. London: 1889. V. 39

Evelina. V. 43

Evelina, or a Young Lady's Entrance Into the World. London: 1778. V. 45

Evelina, or a Young Lady's Entrace Into the World. London: 1779. V. 44

Evelina. London: 1779-83. V. 38

Evelina. London: 1784. V. 38; 41

Evelina; or the History of a Young Lady's Entrance Into the World. London: 1794. V. 42; 46

Evelina, eller et Ungt Freuntimmers Indtraelse i Verden. Copenhagen: 1812. V. 45; 46

Evelina; or the History of a Young Lady's Introduction to the World. London: 1821. V. 45

Evelina. London: 1825? V. 40

Evelina . . . London: 1826. V. 43

Memoirs of Dr. Burney. London: 1832. V. 45; 46

The Wanderer. London: 1814. V. 38; 39; 44; 46

ARBOUSSET, T.

Narrative of an Exploratory Tour to the North-East of the Colony of the Cape of Good Hope. Cape Town: 1846. V. 41

ARBUCKLE'S Illustrated Atlas of the United States of America. New York: 1889. V. 45

ARBUTHNOT, JAMES

A True Method of Treating Light Hazely Ground. Edinburgh: 1811. V. 39

ARBUTHNOT, JOHN 1667-1735

Annus Mirabilis; or the Wonderful Effects of the Approaching Conjunction of the Planets Jupiter, Mars and Saturn. London: 1722. V. 45

An Appendix to John Bull Still in His Senses . . . London: 1712. V. 45

The Congress of Bees; or, Political Remarks on the Bees Swarming at St. James's . . . London: 1728. V. 42

An Essay on the Usefulness of Mathemtical Learning, In a Letter from a Gentlemn in the City to His Friend in Oxford. Oxford: 1701. V. 38

An Essay Concerning the Nature of Aliments and the Choice of Them According to the Different Constitutions of Human Bodies. London: 1731. V. 39; 40

An Essay Concerning the Nature of Aliments, and the Choice of Them, According to the Different Constitutions of Human Bodies . . . London: 1756. V. 37

John Bull in His Senses; Being the Second Part of Law Is a Bottomless Pit. London: 1712. V. 45

John Bull Still In His Senses; Being the Third Part of Law is a Bottomless Pit. London: 1712. V. 45

Law is a Bottomless Pit. London: 1712. V. 45

Lewis Baboon Turned Honest and John Bull Politician. London: 1712. V. 45

The Miscellaneous Works. Glasgow: 1751. V. 42

Miscellaneous Works . . . with an Account of the Author's Life. London: 1770. V. 38; 41

Of the Laws of Chance, or, a Method of Calculation of the Hazards of Game, Plainly Demonstrated, and Applied to Games at Present Most in Use . . . London: 1738. V. 41

Tables of the Grecian, Roman and Jewish Measures, Weights and Coins . . . London: 1705? V. 38; 41

Tables of Ancient Coins, Weights and Measures. London: 1727. V. 37; 40; 41; 44; 46

Tables of Antient Coins, Weights and Measures, Explained and Exemplified in Several Dissertations . . . London: 1754. V. 38

Tables of the Grecian, Roman and Jewish Measures. London: ?1705. V. 37

Tables of the Grecian, Roman and Jewish Measures, Weights and Coins . . . London: 1705? V. 41

ARBUTHNOTT, BARBARA E. F. BLAIR

The Henwife, Her Own Experience in Her Own Poultry-Yard. Edinburgh: 1861. V. 43; 44

ARCADY: A National Playground. New York: 1929. V. 40

ARCAMBEAU, EDME

The Book of Bridges. Glasgow: 1911. V. 39

The Book of Bridges. London: 1911. V. 44

ARCANDAM, PSEUD.

The Most Excellent, Profitable & Pleasant Book of the Famous Doctor, and Expert Astrologian, Arcandam or Alcandrin . . . London: 1670. V. 44

ARCANGELI, FRANCESCO

Graham Sutherland. New York: 1975. V. 39; 43; 46

ARCE, HECTOR

Groucho. New York: 1979. V. 45

ARCHAEOLOGIA. Or, Miscellaneous Tracts Relating to Antiquity. Volume XXIV. London: 1832. V. 39

ARCHAEOLOGICAL INSTITUTE OF GREAT BRITIAN AND IRELAND

Memoirs Illustrative of the History and Antiquities of Wiltshire and the City of Salisbury. London: 1851. V. 41

ARCHBOLD, JOHN FREDERICK 1785-1870

Peel's Acts, Lord Lansdowne's Act, and the Recent Acts relating to Poaching, Smuggling, Personating, etc. London: 1830. V. 40

ARCHDALE, HENRY BLACKWOOD

Memoirs of Archdales, with the Descents of Some Allied Families. Enniskillen: 1925. V. 37; 43

ARCHDALE, JOHN

A New Description of that Fertile and Pleasant Province of Carolina: with a brief account of its discovery and settling . . . Charleston, S.C.: 1822. V. 37

ARCHDALL, MERVYN

Monasticen Hibernicum or a History of the Abbey, Priories and Other Religious Houses in Ireland. Dublin: 1873. V. 46

Monasticon Hibernicum, or a History of the Abbies, Priories and Other Religious Houses in Ireland. Dublin: 1786. V. 38

Proposals for Printing by Subscription, Monasticon Hibernicum; or, an History of the Abbies, Priories, and Other Religious Houses in Ireland . . . Dublin: 1785. V. 41

ARCHDALL, N.

An Alarum to the People of Great Britain and Ireland: In Answer to a Late Proposal for Uniting These Kingdoms. Dublin: 1751. V. 42

ARCHER, GEOFFREY

The Birds of British Somaliland and the Gulf of Aden, Their Life Histories, Breeding Habits and Eggs. London: 1937-61. V. 37; 39; 40; 42; 46

The Birds of Somaliland and the Gulf of Aden. Edinburgh & London: 1961. V. 39

The Birds of British Somaliland and the Gulf of Aden. London: 1961. V. 37

ARCHER, M.

British Drawings in the India Office Library. London: 1969. V. 39

William Hedley, The Invention of Locomotion on the Present Principle. Newcastle-upon-Tyne: 1882. V. 39; 46

ARCHER, THOMAS

Charles Dickens: a Gossip About His Life, Works and Characters . . . London: 1874? V. 43

Charles Dickens: A Gossip About His Life, Works and Characters . . . London: 1884. V. 40

Charles Dickens: a Gossip About His Life, Works and Characters with Eighteen Full Page Character Sketches . . . by Frederick Barnard . . . . London: 1894? V. 40; 41

The Frog's Parish and Clerk; and His Adventures in Strange Lands. London: 1866. V. 44

Pictures and Royal Portraits Illustrative of English and Scottish History. London: 1878. V. 42

The War in Egypt and the Soudan, an Episode in the History of the British Empire . . . London: 1887. V. 40; 41

ARCHER, W. G.

Indian Miniatures. London: 1960. V. 39

Indian Miniatures. Greenwich: 1966. V. 38; 41

ARCHER, WILLIAM

The Divine Adventure - Iona: by Sundown Shores - Studies in Spiritual History. London: 1900. V. 44

Masks on Faces: a Study in the Psychology of Acting. London: 1888. V. 45

THE ARCHER'S Guide: Containing Full Instruction for the Use of That Ancient and Noble Instrument the Bow . . . London: 1833. V. 41; 42

THE ARCHER'S Manual; or the Art of Shotting with the Long Bow, as Practised by the United Bowmen of Philadelphia. Philadelphia: 1830. V. 45

ARCHIBALD, A. G.

Letter from A. G. Archibald, Esq., M.P.P. 85 Oxford Terrace, London, 24th Nov. 1866 to the People of Nova Scotia. V. 46

ARCHIBOLD, ANN

A Book for the Married and Single. East Plainfield: 1850. V. 42

ARCHIBOLD, JOHN FREDERICK

The Justice of the Peace, and Paris Officer . . . London: 1840. V. 38

ARCHILOCHUS

Carmina Archilochi. Berkeley: 1964. V. 39

ARCHIMEDES

Archimedes Quae Supersunt Omnia cum Eutocii Ascalonitae Commentariis . . . Oxford: 1792. V. 41; 45

Archimedis Syracusani Arenarius, et Dimensio Circuli. Oxford: 1676. V. 41

Oeuvres . . . Paris: 1807. V. 40

Opera . . . . colophon: 1543. V. 43

Opera non Nulla a Federico Commandino Urbinate Nuper in Latinum Conversa, et Commentariis Illustrata . . . Venice: 1558. V. 38

Quae Supersunt Omnia cum Eutocii Ascalonitae Commentariis, ex Recensione Josephi Torelli, Veronensis . . . Oxford: 1792. V. 38

ARCHIPENKO, ALEXANDER

Archipenko: Fifty Creative Years 1908-1958. New York: 1960. V. 46

ARCHIPENKO, ALEXANDRE

Son Oeuvre. Berlin: 1923. V. 44

ARCHITECTURAL Ornaments, or a Collection of Capitals, Friezes, Roses, Entablatures, Mouldings &c., Drawn on Stone from the Antique. London: 1820-21. V. 37; 39

ARCHITECTURAL PUBLICATION SOCIETY

The Dictionary of Architecture. London: 1853-92. V. 39; 45

THE ARCHITECTURAL Review. London: 1896-97. V. 41; 44

THE ARCHITECTURE of Paul Rudolph. New York: 1970. V. 46

ARCHIV fur den Thierischen Magnetismus. Altenburg und Leipzig: 1817-24. V. 46

ARCHIVES of Maryland. Baltimore and Annapolis: 1883-1972. V. 40

ARCHIVES of Science. Burlington: 1870-1874. V. 40

ARCLAIS DE MONTAMY, DIDIER D'

Traite des Couleurs pour La Peinture en Email et sur La Porcelaine . . . Paris: 1765. V. 42

ARCTIC Rewards and Their Claimants. London: 1856. V. 41

THE ARCTIC World: Its Plants, Animals, and Natural Phenomena. London: 1876. V. 40

ARCTIC CLUB

The Arctic Club Manual. Published for the Members. New York: 1906. V. 38

ARCTIC INSTITUTE OF NORTH AMERICA

Arctic Bibliography, Prepared for . . . The Department of Defense. Washington: 1953. V. 42

Arctic Bibliographhy. Washington: 1953-. V. 39

Arctic Bibliography. Washington: 1953-. V. 39; 40

ARCULARIUS, DANIEL

Commentarius in Acta Apostolaroum Reverendi et Clarissimi Viri, daniel Arcularii . . . Francofurti: 1607. V. 44

ARDEBEILI, ACHMED

A Series of Poems, Containing the Plaints, Consolations and Delights of Achmed Ardebeili, a Persian Exile. Bristol: 1797. V. 46

A Series of Poems, Containing the Plaints, Consolations and Delights of Achmed Ardebeili, a Persian Exile. London: 1797. V. 41; 46

ARDEN the Unfortunate Stranger, who was Tried for the Murder of Miss Harriet Finch; but was Acquitted through the Interposition of a Young Lady whom he Afterwards Married. New York: 1822. V. 37

ARDITTI, J.

Orchid Biology, Review and Perspectives. New York: 1977-84. V. 37; 38

ARDIZZONE, EDWARD

Little Tim and the Grave Sea Captain. New York: 1936. V. 46

ARDIZZONE, EDWARD continued

Some Words and Drawings from Edward Ardizzone's Indian Diary, 1952-53. London: 1983. V. 46

The Tale of an Old Tweed Jacket. London. V. 41

Tim to the Rescue. 1949. V. 46

Visiting Dieppe. London: 1981. V. 42

ARDLICKA, ALES

Anthropological Survey in Alaska. Washington: 1930. V. 39

ARENBERG, CHARLES D' 1593-1669

Flores Seraphici . . . Sive Icones Vitae Et Gesta Virorum Illustrium . . . Coloniae Agrippiane,: 1640/42. V. 43

ARENTS, GEORGE

The Arents Catalogue. Tobacco, Its History Illustrated by the Books, Manuscripts and Engravings in the Library of George Arents, Jr. New York: 1937/1958-69. V. 40

The Arents Catalogue. Tobacco, Its History Illustrated by the Books, Manuscripts and Engravings in the Library of George Arents, Jr. New York: 1937-52/58-69. V. 39

Tobacco Its History Illustrated by Books, Manuscripts and Engravings in the Library of George Arents, Jr . . . New York: 1937. V. 42

Tobacco. Its History Illustrated by the Books, Manuscripts and Engravings in the Library of George Arents, Jr. New York: 1937-52/58-58, V. 46

Tobacco: Its History Illustrated by Books, Manuscripts and Engravings in the Library of George Arents, Jr. New York: 1937-69. V. 42

Tobacco, its History. Illustrated Jerome E. Banks, from the books, manuscripts and engravings in the Library of New York, 1958-1962, with Supplementary Catalog Part I-VIII. New York: 1962. V. 37

ARESKINE, CHARLES

Information for the East India Company of Holland, of the Chamber of Zeland. N.P.: 1729. V. 42

ARETAEUS

Aretaei Capadocis Medici Lib. VIII. Ruffi Ephesii de Hominis Partib. Li. III. Parisiis: 1554. V. 46

ARETINO, PIETRO 1492-1557

Aretino Pentito, si o e Parafrasi Sovra i Sette Salmi della Penitenza di Davide. Lyon: 1648. V. 37

Del Primo (-Sesto) Libro de le Lettere di M. Pietro Areatino. Parigi: 1609. V. 37

Pornodidascalus, seu Colloquium Muliebre . . . Demonstrataoris. Frankfurt am Main: 1623. V. 37

Quattro Comedie Cioe Il Marescalco. London: 1588. V. 42

The Ragionamenti or Dialogues. Paris: 1889. V. 38; 46

Vita di Maria Vergine Descritta en tre Libri da Partenio Etiro. Venice: 1642. V. 37

ARFWEDSON, C. D.

The United States and Canada in 1832, 1833 and 1934. London: 1834. V. 46

ARGAN, GIULIO CARLO

Henry Moore. New York: 1971. V. 39

ARGELANDER, FRIEDRICH WILHELM AUGUST

DLX Stellarum Fixarum Positiones Mediae Ineunte Anno 1830 . . . Helsinki: 1835. V. 44

Uranometria Nova. Berlin: 1843. V. 45

ARGELATUS, PHILPPUS

Scriptorum Mediolanensium seu Acta, et Elogia Virorum Omnigena Eruditione Illustrium, qui in Metropoli Insubriae, Oppidisque Circumjacentibus Orti Sunt. Mediolani: 1745. V. 37

ARGELLATA, PIETRO D'

Cirurgia. Venice: 1497. V. 42

ARGENS, JEAN BAPTISTE DE BOYER, MARQUIS D' 1704-1771

The Jewish Spy. London: 1739-40. V. 40

The Jewish Spy. London: 1766-5. V. 38

New Memoirs Establishing a True Knowledge of Mankind, by Discovering the Affections of the Heart, and the Operations of the Understanding, in the Various Scenes of Life. London: 1747. V. 39; 40; 45

ARGENSOLA, BARTOLOME LEONARDO DE

Conquista de Las Islas Malucas. Madrid: 1609. V. 40

ARGENSOLA, BARTOLOMME LEONARDO DE

Rimas. Saragossa: 1634. V. 45

ARGENTERIO, GIOVANNI 1513-1572

De Consultationibus Medicis sive (ut Vulgus Vocat) de Collegian di Ratione Liber. Florence: 1551. V. 41; 45

De Somno et Vigilia Libri Duo . . . Florentiae: 1556. V. 40; 43; 46

ARGENTERIUS, JOANNES

Opera Omnia. Venice: 1607-06. V. 38

Varia Opera de la Medica . . . Florentiae: 1550. V. 38

ARGENTI, PHILIP

Chius Vincta or the Occupation of the Chios by the Turks (1566) & Their Administration of the Island (1566-1912). Cambridge: 1941. V. 37

ARGENTI, PHILIP P.

Chius Liberata, or the Occupation of Chios by the Greeks in 1912 . . . London: 1933. V. 45

The Expedition of Colonel Fabvier to Chios, Described in Contemporary Diplomatic Reports. London: 1933. V. 45

The Expedition of the Florentines to Chios (1599). London: 1934. V. 45

The Religious Minorities of Chios, Jews and Roman Catholics. Cambridge: 1970. V. 45

ARGENTINA Past and Present. London: 1914. V. 46

ARGENTINE. An Auto-biography. London: 1839. V. 39

ARGOLI, ANDREA

De Diebus Criticis et de Aegrorum Decubitu. Patavii: 1639. V. 37

Tabulae Primi Mobilis . . . Quibus Veterum Reiectis Prolixitatibus Directiones Facillime Componuntur . . . Rome: 1610. V. 45

ARGOLI, ANDREAS

De Diebus Criticis et Aegrorum Decubitu Libri Duo . . . Padua: 1639. V. 37

THE ARGOSY, a Magazine of Tales, Travels, Essays and Poems. London: 1866. V. 38

AN ARGUMENT in Defence of the Exclusive Right Claimed by the Colonies to Tax Themselves, with a Review of the Laws of England . . . London: 1774. V. 37

ARGUMENTS and Materials for a Register of Estates. London: 1698. V. 39

THE ARGUMENTS Of Sir Richard Hutton . . . and Sir George Croke . . . in the Cases Made Touching Ship-Money. London: 1641. V. 37

ARGUMENTUM Anti-Normannicum; Or an Argument Proving from Ancient Histories and Records, that William, Duke of Normandy, Made No Absolute Conquest of England by the Sword; in the Sense of Our Modern Writers. London: 1682. V. 40

ARGYLE, ANNIE

Cupid's Album. New York: 1866. V. 37

ARGYLE, ARCHIBALD CAMBPELL

Instructions to a Son. 1661. V. 38

ARGYLE, ARCHIE

Cupid's Album. New York: 1866. V. 43

ARGYLL, ARCHIBALD CAMPBELL, MARQUIS OF d. 1661

Instructions to a Son, Containing the Rules of Conduct in Publick and Private Life. Glasgow: 1743. V. 39

ARGYLL, JOHN DOUGLAS SUTHERLAND, DUKE OF

V.R.I.: Her Life and Empire. London: 1901. V. 38

ARGYLL, JOHN GEORGE EDWARD HENRY DOUGLAS SUTHERLAND 1845-1914

Canadian Pictures, Drawn with Pen and Pencil. London: 1885. V. 42

ARIAS MONTANO, BENITO

Humanae Salutis Monumenta. Antwerp: 1571. V. 45

ARIAS, P. E.

A History of 1000 Years of Greek Vase Painting. London: 1961. V. 44

History of 1000 Years of Greek Vase Painting. New York: 1961. V. 39

A History of 1000 Years of Greek Vase Painting. New York: 1962. V. 40

THE ARIEL. Philadelphia: 1829. V. 40

ARIEL Poems. London: 1928/1929. V. 37

ARIES, ROBERT S.

Mane-Katz 1894-1962. The Complete Works. 1970. V. 42

ARIETI, SILVANO

American Handbook of Psychiatry. New York: 1974-86. V. 43

ARIOSTO, LODOVICO 1474-1533

L'Arioste Francoes de Jean de Boessiers de montferrand en Auvernie. Lyon: 1580. V. 37

Orlando Furioso. Venice: 1554. V. 40

Orlando Furioso . . . In Venetia: 1556. V. 38

ARIOSTO, LODOVICO 1474-1533 continued

Orlando Furioso. Venice: 1562. V. 40

Orlando Furioso . . . Venice: 1565. V. 40

Orlando Furioso di M. Lodovico Ariosto. Venetia: 1584. V. 46

Orlando Furioso in English Heroical Verse. London: 1634. V. 43

Orlando Furioso. London: 1634. V. 39; 43; 46

Orlando Furioso. Venice: 1730-31. V. 39

Orlando Furioso. Parigi: 1795. V. 44

The Orlando Furioso. London: 1823-31. V. 39

Orlando Furioso. Venice: 1772-73. V. 37

Orlando Furioso, Dirigido al Principe Don Philipe Nuestro Senor, Traduzido en Romance Castellano por don Jeronymo de Urrea. Lyon: 1550. V. 37

Orlando Furioso, Tutto Ricorretto, et di Nuove Figure Adornatao . . . di Nuovo Aggiuntovi. Venice: 1572. V. 37

Le Satire . . . Milan: 1558. V. 45

ARIOSTO, LUDOVICO

Delle Satire e Rime di M. Ludovico Ariosto Libri Due. Londra: 1716. V. 38

Orlando Furioso. Venice: 1556. V. 46

Orlando Furioso. Birmingham: 1773. V. 41; 42

Orlando Furioso Di Lodovico Ariosto. Birmingham: 1773. V. 46

Orlando Furioso. London: 1783. V. 40; 46

Orlando Furioso. London: 1785. V. 41

The Orlando . . . Reduced to XXIV Books . . . London: 1791. V. 41

Orlando Furioso. London: 1799. V. 40; 41; 44

The Orlando Furioso. London: 1823. V. 42

The Orlando Furioso, Translated into English Verse from the Italian of Ludovico Ariosto. With Notes by William Stewart Rose. London: 1823-31. V. 37

The Satires of Ludovico Ariosto. London: 1759. V. 41

ARISPHANES

Comoediae Novem Cum Commentariis Antiquis Admodum Utilibus, Duaeq, Sine Commentariis . . . Basileae: 1547. V. 45

ARISTA, MARIANO

El Ciudadano Mariano Arista General en Gefe de la Division . . . a Los Habitantes de Los Departameentos de Tamaulipas, Coahuila Y Nuevo Leon. Saltillo,: 1839. V. 40

ARISTAENETOS

(Greek title then): Epistolae Ertikai. Antwerp: 1566. V. 43

ARISTAENETUS

The Love Epistles of Aristaenetus. London: 1771. V. 39; 41; 44; 46

ARISTEAS

Aristeas' Epistle. Aristea de Settanta due Interpreti. Florence: 1550. V. 37

The Auncient History of the Septuagint. London: 1633. V. 40

The History of the Seventy Two Interpreters . . . Their Version of the Septuagint. London: 1715. V. 41; 42

ARISTIDES

Orationes. Florence: 1517. V. 40; 45

ARISTIDES, AELIUS

Orationes. Florence: 1517. V. 37

Orationum Tomi Tres . . . Huc Accessit Orationum Tomus Quartus. Basel: 1566. V. 37

ARISTOMENES: A Grecian Tale. London: 1838. V. 43

ARISTOPHANES

Aristophanis facetissimi comoediae undecim. Basel: 1532. V. 37

Facetissimi Comoediae Undecim. Basle: 1532. V. 40

Aristophanes, Veteris Comoediae Princeps: Poeta Longe Facetissimus & Eloquentissimus; Repurgatus a Mendis & Imitatione Plauti & Terentii Interpretatus . . . Frankfurt: 1586. V. 38

Comoediae Undecim, Graece & Latine. Lvdvni Batavorvm: 1624. V. 38

Comoedia Plutus. Harlingae: 1744. V. 40

The Comedies. London: 1820-22. V. 40; 41

The Eleven Comedies, Literally and Completely Translated. New York: 1926. V. 38

The Eleven Comedies Literally and Completely Translated . . . New York: 1928. V. 39; 40; 41; 43; 44; 46

(Greek title: then) Comoediae Novem cum Commentariis Antiquis Admodum Utilibus, Duaeque sine Commentariis . . . Basle: 1547. V. 43

Comoediae. Lipsiae: 1860. V. 44

Facetissimi Comoediae Undecim. Basle: 1532. V. 45

The Frogs. Oxford: 1780. V. 42

The Frogs, a Comedy. Oxford: 1785. V. 37; 40

The Lysistrata. London: 1896. V. 37; 43

The Lysistrata. London: 1896. V. 37

Lysistrata. London: 1926. V. 38; 40; 41; 44; 45; 46

The Lysistrata. Paris: 1931. V. 46

Lysistrata. New York: 1934. V. 42; 44

A Metrical Version of the Acharnians The Knights and the Birds in the Last of Which a Vein of Peculiar Humour and Character is for the First Time Detected and Developed. London: 1840. V. 37; 38; 41

The Plutus of Aristohanes. London: 1847. V. 37

(Greek title) Plvtvs. Nurnberg: J. Petri (after 20 July), 1531. Nurnberg: 1531. V. 40

Women in Parliament. London: 1919. V. 41

Women in Parliament. London: 1929. V. 38; 39; 41; 44; 46

ARISTOPHANES, Being a Classic Collection of True Attic Wit, Containing the Jests, Gibes, Bon-Mots, Witticisms, and Most Extraordinary Anecdotes of Samuel Foote, Esq., the Lords Chesterfield, Tyrwaley, Messrs. Churchill, Thornton . . . London: 1778. V. 37

ARISTOTELES 384-322 BC

De Anima Historium Libri X. Frankfurt: 1587. V. 38; 39

L'Anima. La Cognition Della Qvale e Necessaria Molto all'Intelligenza del l'Ethica per Esser Materia Conguinta, & Breuemente Raccolta. Venice: 1551. V. 38

De Animalbius. (De Natura Animalium. Departibus Animalium. De Genertione Animalium). Venice: 1498. V. 37; 38; 40

Aristotelis Stagyrite Dialectica. Augsburg: 1516-May 1517. V. 44

Aristotelis Stagiritae Politica, ab Iacobo Lodoico Strebaeo a Graeco Conversa. Paris: 1549. V. 41

Aristotelis et Theophrasti Historiae, cum de Natura Animalium, tum de Plantis & Earum Causis . . . Lugduni: 1552. V. 42

Aristotelis Politicorum Libri Octo ex Dion. Basileae: 1582. V. 37

Commentarii Collegii Conimbricensis Societatis Jesu. Lyon: 1594. V. 42

Aristotle's Compleat Masterpiece. London: 1768. V. 43

Ethics (In Greek, then) Aristotelis de Moribus, ad Nicomachium Libri Decem. Heidelbergae: 1560. V. 38; 40

Aristotle's Ethics and Politics, Comprising His Practical Philosophy. London: 1797. V. 41; 42; 44; 45

Insigne Artificium Aristotelis . . . London: 1702. V. 41

Introductio Physica. (with) Primus Physicorum. (with) Libri Quatuor de Coelo. (with) De Anima Libri Tres. (with) De Sensu & Sensili, de Memoria & Reminiscentia, de Somno & Vigilia, de Insomniis, de Divinatione in Somno. Paris: 1535-36. V. 37

Libri Politicorum cum Commento Multum Utili et Comprendioso Magistri Johannis Versoris. Cologne: 1497. V. 38

Logica. Lugduni: 1584. V. 38; 40

The Metaphysics. London: 1801. V. 37; 38

Aristotle's Metaphysics. Oxford: 1966. V. 44

The Nicomachean ethics of Aristotle. Oxford: 1836. V. 40; 41

Aristotelis Opera Omnia Quae Extant, Graece & Latine. Paris: 1629. V. 42; 43; 45

Opera. Berlin: 1831-70. V. 40

Organum: Hoc est Libri Omnes ad Logicam Pertinentes Graece & Latine. Frankfurt: 1592. V. 40

Parva Naturalia. Venetus: 1512. V. 37; 42

De Physica Auscultatione, Lib. 8. Frankfurt: 1577. V. 38; 41

Physices Akroaseos Biblia Octo. Naturalis Auscultationis Libri Octo, Nova Recognitione Emendati. Venice: 1546. V. 38

De Poetica Liber. Londini: 1621. V. 42; 44; 46

Aristotelis de Poetica. Glasgow: 1745. V. 39

(Greek Title) De Poetica. Oxford: 1794. V. 42

Politicorum et Oeconomicorum Libri Qui Extant. Frankfurt: 1587. V. 43

Politics and Poetics. 1964. V. 40; 45

Politics and Poetics. Lunenburg: 1964. V. 46

Politics and Poetics. New York: 1964. V. 43; 46

Posteriorum Resolutioriorum, Libri Duo, cum Averrois Commentariis, Triplici Interpretatione Distinctis. Venetiis: 1562. V. 41

The Problems of Artistotle; with Other Philosohers and Physicians. London: 1704. V. 38; 40

Questiones Magistri Johannis Versoris Super Libros Ethicorum Aristotelis et Textus Eiusdem cum Singulari Diligentia Correcte. Cologne: 1494. V. 38

(Greek Title) De Rehtorica. London: 1619. V. 42

Rettorica, et Poetica d'Aristotile. Firenze: 1549. V. 41

Rettorica et Poetica d'Aristotle Tradotte di Greco in Lingua Vulgare Fiorentina da Bernardo Segni. Venice: 1551. V. 43

Rettorica, D'Aristotile. Fatta in Lingua Toscana dal Commendatore Annibal Caro. Venice: 1570. V. 38

Aristoteles Rhetoric; or the True Grounds and Principles of Oratory . . . London: 1686. V. 46

Aristotele's Rhetoric; or the True Grounds and Principles of Oratory . . . London: 1693. V. 46

De Rhetorica. London: 1619. V. 38

Aristotelis De Rhetorica Seu Arte Dicendi Libri Tres, Graecolat, Contextu Graeco . . . London: 1696. V. 43

Rhetoricorum ad Theodecten Libri Tres. Lyon: 1541. V. 42

ARISTOTELES 384-322 BC continued

Sententiae Omnes Undiquaque Selectissimae. Lugduni: 1570. V. 38; 40; 42; 44

Sententiae Omnes Undiquaque Selectissimae. Lugduni: 1570. V. 40

Aristotelis Stagiritae Politica, ab Iacobo Lodoico Strebaeo a Graeco Conversa. Paris: 1549. V. 45

Aristotelis Stagyritae Acroases Physicae Libri VIII. Augsburg: 1518-20. V. 45

Trattato Dei Governi di Aristotile. Venice: 1551. V. 46

A Treatise on Government. London: 1778. V. 39

ARISTOTLE, PSEUD.

Aristotle's Master-Piece, or the Secrets of nature Displayed in the Generation of Man . . . Worcester: 1801. V. 41

The Complete Master-Piece of Aristotle, the Famous Philosopher . . . Philadelphia: 1798. V. 37; 41

Theologia, Sive Mistica Phylosophia Secundum Aegyptios Noviter Reperta & in Latinum Redacta. Rome: 1519. V. 38

The Works of Aristotle. London: 1798. V. 42

The Works of Aristotle, the Famous Philosopher in Four Parts. New England: 1813. V. 37

ARISTOTLE'S Last Legacy, Unfolding the Mysteries of Nature in the Generation of Man. London: 1749. V. 38

De Anima Historium Libri X. Frankfurt: 1587. V. 37

The Metaphysics fo Aristotle, translated from the Greek: with Copious Notes, in which the Pythagoric an platonic Dogmas respecting numbers and ideas are unfolded from antient sources. To which is added a dissertation on Nullitites and . . . London: 1801. V. 37

The Complete Works of Aristotle. London: 1984. V. 37

ARIZE, I. DE

Senores. Encargado Por Una Ley de Estado de Dar Cumplimiento . . . Mexico: 1827. V. 39

ARIZONA AL, PSEUD.

If You Wanta Ride Herd on the Arizona Market, You'll Haf'ta Lissen to Arizona Al. Phoenix: 1934. V. 38

ARIZONA. CONSTITUTION - 1910

The Proposed Constitution for the State of Arizona, Adopted by the Constitutional Convention Held at Phoenix. Phoenix: 1910. V. 39

ARIZONA. CONSTITUTION - 1912

The Proposed Constitution for the State of Arizona . . . N.P.: 1912. V. 39

ARIZONA HISTORICAL SOCIETY

Charter, Constitution and By-Laws of the Arizona Historical Society, Incorporated and Organized, November, 1864. Prescott: 1864. V. 37

ARIZONA Illustrated. History-Mining-Railroads-Lands. Facts for Tourists. Chicago: 1880. V. 38; 39

ARIZONA. LIVE STOCK SANITARY BOARD.

Brand Book of the State of Arizona. Ordered, Compiled and Printed by the Arizona Live Stock Sanitary Board at the Meeting Held at Phoenix, May 8th 1920. Phoenix: 1920. V. 39

Brands and Marks of Cattle, Horses, Sheep, Goats and Hogs as They Appear of Recorod in the Offie of the Live Stock Sanitary Board of Arizona at Phoenix, Arizona. Phoenix: 1908. V. 39

ARIZONA. (TERRITORY). CONSTITUTIONAL CONVENTION - 1910

Minutes of the Constutional Convention of the Territory of Arizona, 1910. Phoenix: 1910. V. 39

ARIZONA. (TERRITORY). CONSTITUTIONAL CONVENTION - 1941

Minutes of the Constitutional Convention of the Territory of Arizona Session Began on the Tenth Day of October, A.D. 1910. Phoenix: 1911? V. 42

ARIZONA. (TERRITORY). LAWS, STATUTES, ETC. - 1866

Acts, Resolutions and Memorials, Adopted by the Second Legislative Assembly of the Territory of Arizona. Prescott: 1866. V. 38; 40; 43

ARIZONA. (TERRITORY). TERRITORIAL PRISON COMMISSIONERS

Biennial Report of the Territorial Prison to the Governor of Arizona 1897-1898. Phoenix: 1899. V. 38

ARJUNBA, SAKHARAM

Principles and Practice of Medicine Designed for the Students of the Vernacular Class, Grant Medical College. Bombay: 1869. V. 40; 41; 44; 45

ARKANSAS: an Accurate and Reliable Description of the State of Arkansas for the Information of the Farmer, the Home Seeker and the Investor. St. Louis: 1891. V. 43

ARKANSAS. CONSTITUTION

Constitution of Arkansas, and Memorial of the Convention, Praying for the Admission of Arkansas into the Union as a State. Washington: 1836. V. 39

ARKANSAS. GEOLOGICAL SURVEY, 1857-1858.

First Report of a Geological Reconnoissance of the Northern Counties of Arkansas, Made During the Years 1857 and 1858. Little Rock: 1858. V. 39

ARKANSAS. LAWS, STATUTES, ETC.

Acts, Resolutions, Memorials of the General Assembly of the State of Arkansas, Jan. 13, 1879-March 13, 1879. Little Rock: 1879. V. 37

ARKANSAS: Statistics and Information Showing the Agricultural and Mineral Resources. N.P.: 1888. V. 42

THE ARKANSAW Grant. A Brief History from the Time the Grant Was Made by the Mexican Government in 1832 . . . Washington: 1901. V. 41

ARKELL, A. J.

Early Khartoum: an Account of the Excavation of an Early Occupation Site Carried Out by the Sudan Government Antiquities Service in 1944-5. London: 1949. V. 42; 44

Shaheinab: an Account of the Excavation of a Neolithic Occupation Site Carried Out for the Sudan Antiquities Service in 1949-50. London: 1953. V. 42; 44

Wanyanga and an Archaeological Reconnaissance of the South-West Libyan Desert. London: 1964. V. 44

ARKELL, W. J.

A Monograph of British Corallian Lamellibranchia. London: 1927-37. V. 38

ARKHAM HOUSE

100 Books by August Derleth. With a Foreword by Donald Wandrei. Sauk City: 1962. V. 37

ARKIN, DAVID

Architektura Sovremennogo Zapada. The Architecture of the Contemporary West. Moscow: 1932. V. 38

ARKWRIGHT, RICHARD

The Trial of a Cause . . . to Repeal a Patent, Granted on the Sixteenth Day of December 1775, to Mr. Richard Arkwright, for an Invention of Certain Instruments and Machines for Preparing Silk, Cotton, Flax and Wool for Spinning . . . London: 1785. V. 40

ARKWRIGHT, WILLIAM

The Pointer and His Predecessors. London: 1902. V. 38; 42; 44

The Pointer and His Predecessors. London: 1906. V. 40

ARLAND, MARCEL

Maternite. Paris: 1926. V. 41

ARLEGUI, JOSE

Chronica De La Provincia de N. S. P. S. Francisco De Zacatecas . . . Mexico: 1737. V. 41

ARLEN, MICAHEL

The Crooked Coronet: and Other Misrepresentations of the Real Facts of Life. London: 1937. V. 39

ARLEN, MICHAEL

The Crooked Coronet and other Misrepresentations of the Real Facts of Life. London: (1937). V. 37

The Green Hat. London: 1924. V. 40; 42; 45

Hell! Said the Duchess - a Bed Time Story. London: 1934. V. 41

May Fair. London: 1925. V. 38

ARLINGTON, HENRY BENNET, 1ST EARL OF

The Right Honourable the Earl of Arlington's Letters to Sir W. Temple, Bar, From Jul6 1665. London: 1701. V. 45

ARLINGTON, L. C.

The Chinese Drama, From the Earliest Times Until Today . . . Shanghai: 1930. V. 45; 46

Through the Dragon's Eyes, Fifty Years' Experience of a Foreigner in the Chinese Government Service. London: 1931. V. 46

ARLOT, M.

A Complete Guide for Coach Painters Translated from the French . . . Philadelphia: 1888. V. 41

ARLOTT, JOHN

Clausentum. London: 1946. V. 41

L'ARMEE Francaise. Paris: 1885-89. V. 46

ARMENGAUD, JACQUES EUGENE

The Practical Draughsman's Book of Industrial Design. London: 1853. V. 39

ARMENINI, GIOVANNI BATTISTA

De' Veri Precetti Della Pittura Libri tre. Ravenna: 1587. V. 37; 40

ARMES, ETHEL

Story of Coal and Iron in Alabama. Birmingham: 1910. V. 37; 38

Stratford Hall: The Great House of the Lees. Richmond: 1936. V. 46

ARMES, GEORGE

Ups and Downs of an Army Officer. Washington: 1900. V. 38; 39; 40; 42; 45

ARMFIELD, MAXWELL

The Hanging Garden and Other Verse. London: 1914. V. 43

THE ARMIES of Europe Illustrated. London: 1890. V. 41

ARMIGER, CHARLES

The Sportsman's Vocal Cabinet. London: 1831. V. 39

ARMISTEAD, WILSON

A Tribute for the Negro . . . Manchester: 1848. V. 45

ARMITAGE, GILBERT

Banned in England. An examination of the Law Relating to Obscene Publications. London: 1932. V. 40

ARMITAGE, JOHN

The History of Brazil, from the Period of the Arrival of the Braganza Family in 1808, to the Abdication of Don Pedro the First in 1831. London: 1836. V. 41; 45

ARMITAGE, MERLE

The Art of Edward Weston. New York: 1932. V. 41

Designed Books, Books and Typography Designed by Merle Armitage . . . New York: 1938. V. 38

George Gershwin. New York: 1938. V. 46

The Lithographs of Richard Day. New York: 1932. V. 44; 46

Rockwell Kent. New York: 1932. V. 38; 39; 42

Warren Newcombe. New York: 1932. V. 37

The Work of Maier-Krieg. New York: 1932. V. 44

ARMITT, M. L.

Rydal. Kendal: 1916. V. 41

ARMOUR, ALEXANDER WILLIAM

Notables and Autographs. New York: 1939. V. 41

ARMOUR and Ramsay's Canadian School Atlas . . . Montreal: 1840. V. 37

ARMOUR, G. D.

Humour in the Hunting Field as Seen by G. D. Armour. London: 1928. V. 37; 43

A Huntin Alphabet. London: 1929. V. 37

Sport 'And There's the Humour Of It'. V. 42

ARMOUR, J. OGDEN

The Packers, The Private Car Lines, and the People. Philadelphia: 1906. V. 37; 42; 44

ARMOUR, MARGARET

The Eerie Book. London: 1898. V. 44

ARMS and Armour at Sandringham. The Indian Collection Presented by the Princes, Chiefs and Nobles of India to His Majesty King Edward VII, When Prince of Wales, on the Occasion of His Visit to India in 1875-1876. London: 1910. V. 41

ARMS and the Man, I Sing. N.P.: 1746. V. 39

ARMS and the Man, I Sing. A Ballad. N.P., n.d.: 1746? V. 40

ARMS and the Man, I Sing. A Ballad. (Part Two). N.P.: 1746? V. 40

ARMS, DOROTHY NOYES

Churches of France. New York: 1929. V. 40; 42

Hill Towns and Cities of Northern Italy. New York: 1932. V. 46

ARMS, JOHN TAYLOR

Modern American Etchers: Arthur William Heintzelman. New York: 1927. V. 41; 42

THE ARMS of the Colleges and Halls of the Univesity of Oxford, Emblazoned. Oxford: 1869. V. 42

ARMSTEAD, HUGH W.

The Artistic Anatomy of the Horse. London: 1900. V. 39

ARMSTRONG, A. N.

Oregon: Comprising a Brief History and Full Description of the Territories of Oregon and Washignton. Chicago: 1857. V. 37; 38; 39; 40; 42; 44; 45; 46

ARMSTRONG, ALEXANDER

A Personal Narrative of the Discovery of the North-West Passage . . . During Nearly Five Years' Continous Service in the Arctic Regions While in Search of the Expedition Under Sir John Franklin . . . London: 1857. V. 45

ARMSTRONG, AMBROSE N.

Oregon: Comprising a Brief History and Full Description of the Territories of Oregon and Washington. Chicago: 1857. V. 41

ARMSTRONG, ANTHONY

The Story of Cocktails. London: 1932. V. 43

ARMSTRONG, BENJAMIN C.

Early Life of Among the Indians. Ashland: 1892. V. 39; 42; 45

ARMSTRONG, E. A.

Axel Herman Haig and His Work, Illustrated from His Etchings, Pencil-Drawings and Water-Colours, with a Biography and Descriptive Catalogue of His Etched Works. London: 1905. V. 39; 41

The Wren. London: 1955. V. 37

ARMSTRONG, ELIZABETH

Robert Estienne, Royal Printer. Cambridge: 1954. V. 39; 40; 42; 44

ARMSTRONG, GEORGE D.

Introductory Lecture to a Course of Chemistry, Delivered in Washington College, Lexington, Va. Richmond: 1838. V. 41

ARMSTRONG, GEORGE DODD

The Good Hand Of Our God Upon Us. A Thanksgiving Sermon, Preached On Occasion of the Victory of Manassas, July 21st, 1861, in the Presbyterian Church, Norfolk, Va. Norfolk: 1861. V. 44

ARMSTRONG, HARRY

Aero-Space Medicine. Baltimore: 1961. V. 42

ARMSTRONG, HENRY JAMES GOLDSMITH

Euancondit. London: 1895. V. 39

ARMSTRONG, JAMES L.

Reminiscences; or an Extract from the Catalogue of General Jackson's Juvenile Indiscretions, Between the Ages of 23 and 60. N.P.: 1828? V. 44

ARMSTRONG, JAMES LESLIE

Scenes in Craven: in a Series of Letters . . . York: 1835. V. 45

ARMSTRONG, JOHN 1709-1779

The Art of Preserving Health. London: 1744. V. 37; 38; 39; 40; 41

The Art of Preserving Health: a Poem. London: 1748. V. 42; 45

The Art of Preserving Health: a Poem. London: printed.: 1757. V. 37

A Day: an Epistle to John Wilkes, of Aylesbury, Esq. London: 1761. V. 39

Facts and Observations, and Practical Illustrations Relative to the Puerperal Fever, Scarlet Fever, Pulmonary Consumption and Measles. Hartford: 1823. V. 37; 40; 43

Facts, Observations and Practical Illustrations, Relative to Puerperal Fever, Scarlet Fever, Pulmonary Consumption and Measles . . . Philadelphia: 1826. V. 42

Hints to Young Generals. Kingston: 1812. V. 37

The History of the Island of Minorca. London: 1752. V. 38; 43

The History of the Island of Minorca. London: 1756. V. 40; 41

Miscellanies. London: 1770. V. 38; 39; 40; 42; 45

Notices of the War of 1812. New York: 1840. V. 38

The Oeconomy of Love. London: 1739. V. 40

Of Benevolence: an Epistle to Eumenes. London: 1751. V. 40; 42

Practical Illustrations of Typhus Fever of the Common Continued Fever and of Inflammatory Diseases, &c, &c. From the Last London Edition. With Notes by an American Physician. New York: 1824. V. 37

Taste: an Epistle to a Young Critic. London: 1753. V. 38

ARMSTRONG, JOHN M. C. 1784-1829

Practical Illustrations of Typhus Fever . . . Philadelphia: 1822. V. 37

ARMSTRONG, KOSCIUSZKO

Examination of Thomas L. McKenney's Reply to the Review of His Narrative. New York: 1847. V. 41; 45

Review of T. L. McKenney's Narrative of the Causes Which, in 1814, Led to General Armstrong's Resignation of the War Office. (with) Examination of Thomas L. McKenney's Reply to the Review of His Narrative, etc. New York: 1846, 1847. V. 39

ARMSTRONG, LOUIS

Swing That Music. London: 1936. V. 41; 45

ARMSTRONG, M. J.

An Actual Survey of the Great Post Roads Between London and Edinburgh . . . London: 1783. V. 42

ARMSTRONG, MARGARET

Murder in Stained Glass. New York: 1939. V. 45

ARMSTRONG, MARTIN

Desert - a Legend. London: 1926. V. 43; 44

54 Conceits - a Collection of Epigrams and Epitaphs Serious and Comic. London: 1933. V. 38

Saint Hercules and other Stories. London: 1927. V. 41; 42; 46

ARMSTRONG, MOSTYN JOHN

An Actual Survey of the Great Post Roads. London: 1777. V. 45

ARMSTRONG, N. A. D.

After Big Game in the Upper Yukon. London: 1937. V. 38; 39

After on Sporting Big Game in the Upper Yukon. London: 1937. V. 37

ARMSTRONG, NEIL

First On the Moon. 1970. V. 44

ARMSTRONG, P. A.

The Piasa, or, the Devil Among the Indians. Morris: 1887. V. 40

ARMSTRONG, PERRY A.

The Sauks and the Black Hawk War. Springfield: 1887. V. 42

ARMSTRONG, RICHARD

No Cause to Mourn for the Pious Dead, a Sermon Preached at the Funeral of Angeline L., Wife of S. N. Castle, an Assistant Missionary. Honolulu: 1841. V. 40

ARMSTRONG, ROBERT

Through the Ages to Netwonabbey. Belfast. V. 43

ARMSTRONG, T. B.

Journal of Travels in the Seat of War, During the Last Two Campaigns of Russia and Turkey. London: 1831. V. 46

ARMSTRONG, T. L.

The City of London and County of Middlesex Directory for 1871-72 . . . Strathroy: 1871. V. 44

ARMSTRONG, W.

Turner. London: 1902. V. 39

ARMSTRONG, W. G.

A Record of the Opera in Philadelphia. Philadelphia: 1884. V. 37; 40

ARMSTRONG, WALTER

Sir Joshua Reynolds, First President of the Royal Academy. London: 1900. V. 40; 44

Turner. London: 1902. V. 38; 41

ARMSTRONG, WILLIAM

Practical Observations on the Errors Committed by Generals and Field Officers Commanding Armies and Detachments . . . from the Year 1743 to the Present Time. London: 1808. V. 38

ARMSTRONG, WILLIAM GEORGE

Electric Movement in Air and Water With Theoretical Inferences. London: 1897. V. 45

ARMSTRONG, WILLIAM H., & CO.

Catalogue of Surgical Instruments, Deformity Apparatus, Aseptic Furniture and Hospital Supplies. Indianapolis: 1901. V. 42

ARMSTRONG, WILLIAM LORD

Three Reports on the Use of the Steam Coals of the 'Hartley District' of Northumberland in Marine Boilers. London & Newcastle: 1858. V. 40

THE ARMY and Navy Prayer Book. Richmond: 1864. V. 44

THE ARMY Register of the United States . . . Corrected Up to the 1st Day of June, 1814. Boston: 1814. V. 45

THE ARMY'S Plea for Their Present Practice: Tendered to the Consideration of All Ingenuous and Impartial Men. London: 1659. V. 43

ARNAL, JUAN PEDRO

Descubrimiento de los Pavimentos de Rielves. Madrid: 1787-88. V. 40

ARNALDI, CONTE ENEA 1716-1794

Idea Di Un Teatro Nelle Principali Sue Parti Simile a'Teatri Antichi. Venice: 1762. V. 37; 42; 44; 45

Idea di un Teatro, Nelle Principali sue Parti Simile a Teatri Antichi, all'uso Moderno Accomodato . . . Vicenza: 1762. V. 40

Idea di Un Teatro Nelle Principali sue Parti Simile a'Teatri Antichi all'Uso Moderno Accomodato. Vicenza: 1762. V. 42

ARNALDO OF VILLANOVA

Regimen Sanitatis Cum Expositione Magistri Arnaldi de Villa Nova Cathellano Noviter Impressus. Venetiis: 1500? V. 43

ARNALL, WILLIAM 1699 or 1700-1736

The Complaint of the Children of Israel, Representing Their Grievances Under the Penal Laws . . . London: 1736. V. 43

Opposition no Proof of Patriotism; With Some Observations and Advice Concerning Party-Writings. London: 1735. V. 39

ARNASON, H. H.

The Sculptures of Houdon. London: 1975. V. 43

ARNASON, JON

Icelandic Legends. London: 1864. V. 44

ARNAUD, E. R.

Introduction a la Chymie, ou a la Vraye Physique. Lyon: 1655. V. 38

ARNAULD, ANTOINE

The Art of Speaking . . . London: 1676. V. 46

The Art of Speaking. London: 1708. V. 43; 45

A General and Rational Grammar, Containing the Fundamental Principles of the Art of Speaking . . . London: 1753. V. 41

Logic, or the Art of Thinking. London. V. 46

Logic; or, the Art of Thinking; Containing (Besides the Common Rules) Many New Observations, That Are of Great Use in Forming an Exactness of Judgment. London: 1717. V. 42; 43; 46

La Logique ou lArt de Penser: Contenant, Outre les Regles communes, Plusieurs Observations Nouvelles Propres a Former le Jugement. Paris: 1650. V. 37

ARNAULT, ANTOINE VINCENT

Memoirs of the Public and Private Life of Napoleon Buonaparte . . . London: 1826. V. 42

ARND, JOHANN

Des Gottseligen und Hocherleuchten Lehrers Hrn Johann Arnds Weiland General-Superintendentens des Furstenhums Luneburg . . . Germantown: 1765. V. 40

ARNDT, H. R.

A System of Medicine Based Upon the Law of Homoeopathy. Philadelphia: 1885-86. V. 41

ARNE, T. J.

Excavations at Shah Tepe, Iran. Stockholm: 1945. V. 37

ARNE, THOMAS AUGUSTINE

The Words of the Favourite Catches and Glees, Which Will be Performed at the Theatre-Royal in the Hay-Market. London?: 1772. V. 37

ARNELL, J. C.

Atlantic Mails: a History of the Mail Service Between Great Britain and Canada to 1889. Ottawa: 1980. V. 45

ARNETT, JOHN ANDREWS

Bibliopegia; or the Art of Bookbinding. London: 1835. V. 39; 41

An Inquiry into the Nature and Form of the Books of the Ancients. London: 1837. V. 37; 40

ARNETT, ROSS H.

American Insects: a Handbook of the Insects of America North of mexico. 1985. V. 39

ARNO, PETER

Whoops Dearie. New York: 1927. V. 38

ARNO Werner. One Man's Work. Easthampton: 1982. V. 39; 44

ARNOBIUS

Afer, Arnobii Disputationum Adversus Gentes Libri Octo. Romae: 1542. V. 40

ARNOBIUS, AFER

Arnobii Disputationum Adversus Gentes Libri Octo. Romae: 1542. V. 38

ARNOBIUS OF AFER fl. 284-305

Disputationum Adversus Gentes. Rome: 1542. V. 43

ARNOLD, A. S.

Broughton, a Novel. London: 1890. V. 43

ARNOLD, C. D.

Official Views of the World's Colombian Exposition. Chicago: 1893. V. 40

ARNOLD, CARL

The Kansas Inferno: a Study of the Criminal Problem by a Life Prisoner. Wichita: 1906. V. 40

ARNOLD, CARL continued

The Kansas Inferno A Study of the Criminal Problem by a Life Prisoner. Witchita: 1906. V. 45

ARNOLD, CHANNING

The American Egypt. New York: 1909. V. 44

ARNOLD, E. C.

British Waders. Cambridge: 1924. V. 40

ARNOLD, EDWIN 1832-1904

Japonica. New York: 1891. V. 38; 44

The Light of Asia, or the Great Renunciation. London: 1889. V. 43

The Light of the World, or The Great Consummation. London: 1893. V. 37; 38

The Light of Asia Being the Life and Teaching of Gautama, Prince of India . . . Connecticut: 1976. V. 41; 44

The Light of Asia. London: 1890. V. 37

Poems, Narrative and Lyrical. Oxford: 1853. V. 40

The Song Celestial or Bhagavad-Gita. Philadelphia: 1934. V. 37

The Voyage of Ithobal. London: 1901. V. 42

ARNOLD, EDWIN LESTER

The Wonderful Adventures of Phra the Phoenician. London: 1891. V. 41

ARNOLD-FORSTER, FRANCES

Studies in Church Dedications or England's Patron Saints. London: 1899. V. 44

ARNOLD, GOTTFRIED

A Bibliographical Sketch of the Life of Talerus, a Popular Preacher of the Fourteenth Century. Richmond: 1836. V. 40

ARNOLD, ISAAC N.

The Life of Benedict Arnold: His Patriotism and His Treason. Chicago: 1880. V. 39

ARNOLD, JOHN P.

Origin and History of Beer and Brewing, from Prehistoric Times to the Beginning of Brewing Science and Technology, a Critical Essay. Chicago;: 1911. V. 37

ARNOLD, JOSIAS

Poems. Providence: 1797. V. 40; 42; 43

ARNOLD, MATHEW 1822-1888

Works of . . . London: 1861-95. V. 46

ARNOLD, MATTHEW 1822-1888

Cromwell: a Prize Poem. V. 41

Cromwell: a Prize Poem, Recited in the Theatre, Oxford; June 28, 1843. Oxford: 1843. V. 38

Culture and Anarchy. London: 1894. V. 43

Culture and Anarchy; an Essay in Political and Social Criticism. London: 1869. V. 45

Discourses in America. London: 1896. V. 37

Empedocles on Etna and Other Poems. London: 1852. V. 38

Empedocles on Etna: a Dramatic Poem. 1896. V. 40

Empedocles on Etna. London: 1896. V. 37; 38; 41; 43; 44; 46

Empedocles on Etna. Portland: 1900. V. 39

Essays in Criticism. London: 1865. V. 40; 41

Essays in Criticism. London and Cambridge: 1865. V. 39

Essays In Criticism. (with) Essays in Criticism. Second Series. London: 1888. V. 43

Essays in Cirticism. (with) Essays in Criticism. Second Series. London & Cambridge: 1865, 1888. V. 37; 38

The Forsaken Merman. London: 1900. V. 37

A French Eton; or, Middle Class Education and the State. London: 1864. V. 45

A French Eton; or, Middle Class Education and the State. London and Cambridge: 1864. V. 42

Laudes Creaturarum. Hammersmith: 1910. V. 42

The Letters of Matthew Arnold, 1848-1888. London: 1895. V. 39

Literature and Dogma. London: 1873. V. 42

Merope. London: 1858. V. 37; 39

New Poems. London: 1867. V. 40

On Translating Homer. London: 1862. V. 40

On Translating Homer: Three Lectures Given at Oxford. (and) On Translating Homer: Last Words. London: 1861, 1862. V. 37

The Oxford Poems. Oxford: 1890. V. 40

Poems, Second Series. London: 1855. V. 40; 42; 44

Poems. London: 1857. V. 37

Poems. London: 1881. V. 37

Poems. New York: 1883. V. 44

Poems. London: 1885. V. 38

Poems. London: 1895. V. 37

Poems of Matthew Arnold. London: 1900. V. 42

Poems. A New Edition. London: 1853. V. 37

Poetical Works. London: 1893. V. 46

The Scholar Gipsy & Thyrsis. London: 1910. V. 40

Selected Poems of . . . London: 1880. V. 37

The Strayed Reveller and Other Poems. London: 1849. V. 40

Works of . . . London: 1861-1895. V. 40

The Works. London: 1903. V. 42; 44

Works. London: 1903-04. V. 37; 41; 42; 44; 46

Works. London: 1903-04. V. 42

ARNOLD, OREN

Hot Irons Heraldry of the Range. New York: 1940. V. 38; 39; 40; 45

ARNOLD, R. LLOYD

High on the Wild with Hemingway. Caldwell: 1968. V. 46

ARNOLD, R. ROSS

Indian Wars of Idaho. Caldwell: 1932. V. 44

ARNOLD, RICHARD

The Customs of London, Otherwise Called Arnold's Chronicle. London: 1811. V. 41

ARNOLD, SAMUEL 1740-1802

Inkle and Yarico: an Opera in Three Acts. London: 1787. V. 40

ARNOLD, T. W.

The Islamic Book. Paris: 1929. V. 44

ARNOLD, THOMAS

History of Rome. London: 1840. V. 38

History of Rome. London: 1857. V. 43; 46

History of Roman. (with) History of the Later Roman Commonwealth, from the Second Punic War to the Death of Julius Caesar, and of the Reign of Augustus: with a Life of Trajan. London: 1844-45. V. 37

An Inaugural Lecture on the Study of Modern History. Oxford: 1841. V. 39

Introductory Lectures on Modern History. London: 1862. V. 39

A Manual of English Literature, Historical and Critical. London: 1888. V. 41

Observations on the Nature, Kinds, Causes and Prevention of Insanity, Lunacy, or Madness. Leicester: 1782. V. 45

Oneirokriton Biblia Pente-De Somniorum Interpretatione Libre Quinque. Venetiis: 1518. V. 45

The Scouring of the White Horse. Cambridge: 1859. V. 39

ARNOLD, THOMAS W.

Bihzad and His Paintings in the Zafar-Namah MS. London: 1930. V. 38; 42; 43; 46

Painting in Islam. A Study of the Place of Pictorial Art in Muslim Culture. 1928. V. 46

Painting in Islam. Oxford: 1928. V. 46

ARNOLD, THOMAS WALKER

The Islamic Book. London: 1929. V. 43

The Islamic Book. A Contribution to Its Art and History from the VII-XVIII Century. (London): 1929. V. 37

Painting in Islam. A Study of the Place of Pictorial Art in Muslim Culture. Oxford: 1928. V. 43

ARNOLD, WILLIAM HARRIS

A Record of First Editions Collected by . . . New York: 1901. V. 38; 42; 44

ARNOLDI, E., COUNT

Descrizione Delle Architetture. Vicenza: 1779. V. 46

ARNOLDUS DE VILLA NOVA

Opera Ultissima di Conservare la Sanita pur Hora Tradotto di Latino in Buono Lingua Italiana. Venice: 1549. V. 38

ARNOT, F. S.

Bihe and Garenganze; or, Four Years' Further Work and Travel in Central Africa. London: 1893. V. 42

ARNOT, HUGO

A Collection and Abridgement of Celebrated Criminal Trials in Scotland from A.D. 1536 to 1784. Edinburgh: 1784. V. 40

A Collection and Abridgement of Celebrated Criminal Trials in Scotland from A.D. 1536-1784. Edinburgh: 1785. V. 37; 38; 41; 42

An Essay on Nothing. London and Edinburgh: 1776. V. 38

An Essay on Nothing. A Discourse Delivered in A Society. London: 1776. V. 37

ARNOTT, HENRY

Cancer: Its Varieties, Their Histology and Diagnosis. Philadelphia: 1872. V. 40

ARNOTT, JAMES A.

The Petit Trianon Versailles. London: 1908. V. 39

ARNOTT, NEIL

Elements of Physics, or Natural Philosophy, General and Medical, Explained Independently of Technical Mathematics. London: 1827-29. V. 38

On Warming and Ventilating; with Directions for Making and Using the Thermometer-Stove, or Self-Regulating Fire. London: 1838. V. 39

On the Smokeless Fire-Place, Chimney-Valves, and Other Means, Old and New of Obtaining Healthful Warmth and Ventilation. London: 1855. V. 37

ARNOUX, CHARLES A D'BERTALL

The Communists of Paris: 1871. London: 1873. V. 46

ARNOW, HARRIETTE

The Dollmaker. New York: 1954. V. 39; 42; 43

The Kentucky Trace. New York: 1974. V. 42

ARNOW, HARRIETTE SIMPSON

Seedtime on the Cumberland. New York: 1960. V. 44; 46

ARNSTEIN, FLORA

A Legacy of Hours. San Francisco: 1927. V. 37; 42

ARNWAY, JOHN

The Tablet or Moderation of Charles the First Martyr. London: 1661. V. 39; 43

ARNY, W. F. M.

Centennial Celebration, 'Santa Fe New Mexico - The Oldest City in North America . . . . Santa Fe: 1876. V. 40

Interesting Items Regarding New Mexico: Its Agricultural Pastoral and Mineral Resources. Santa Fe: 1873. V. 40

AROMATARI, GIUSEPPE

Dialoghi Di Falcidio Melampodio in Risposta a gli Auuertimenti Dati Sotto Nome di Crescentio Pepe . . . Intorno alle Risposte fatte da lui Alle Considerationi del Sig. Alessandro Tassoni Sopra le Rime del Petrarco. Venice: 1613. V. 39

ARONS, REBECCA

'There Are Monsters In My Hair.' Pelham: 1989. V. 42

ARONSON, BORIS

Sovremennaya Evreiskaya Graphika. (Contemporary Jewish Graphics). Berlin: 1924. V. 41

AROUND Pike's Peak. Colorado Springs: 1895. V. 42

ARP, HANS

7 Arpaden von Hans Arp. Zweite Mappe des Merzverlages. Hannover: 1923. V. 42

ARP, HANS JEAN

Onze Peintres vus par Arp: Taeuber, Kandinsky, Leuppi, Vordemberge, Arp, Delaunay, Schwitters, Kiesler, Morris, Magnelli, ERnst. Zurich: 1949. V. 41

ARP, JEAN

On My Way. Poetry & Essays 1912-1947. New York: 1948. V. 39; 41; 43

Soleil Recercle. Paris: 1966. V. 39

ARPASIA; or, The Wanderer. London: 1786. V. 43

ARQUERIUS, JEAN

Dictionarivm Theologicum . . . in quo Omnia Fere Nomina Virorum, Mulierum, Populorum, Vrbium, Montium, Fluuiorum & Eiusmodo Locorum . . . Basle: 1567. V. 40

THE ARRAIGNMENT and Examination of Mary Moders, Otherwise Stedman, Now Carleton (Stiled the German Princess) at the Sessions-House in the Old-Bayly, Being Brought Prisoner from the Gate-House Westmisnter, for Having Two Husbands. London: 1663. V. 46

ARREST Du Conseil D'Estat Portant que le Livre Intitule: Ludovici Montaltii Litterae Provinciales &c, Sera Lacere & Brusle par les Mains de l'Executeur de la Haute Justice. Paris: 1660. V. 37

ARREST James N. Taggart, Embezzler . . . Philadelphia: 1887. V. 39

THE ARREST, Trial and Release of Daniel Webster, a Fugitive Slave. Philadelphia: 1859. V. 45

ARRIANN Historici et Philosophi . . . Lugduni apud Bartholomaeum: 1577. V. 45

ARRIANUS

De Rebus gestis Alexandri Regis. Pesaro: 1508. V. 38

ARRIANUS, FLAVIUS

Arriani & Hannonis Periplus . . . Basel: 1533. V. 41; 42; 43

Ars Tactica . . . Liber de Venatione, Epicteti Enchiridion . . . Amsterdam: 1683. V. 39

Les Faicts & Conquestes d'Alexandre le Grand, Roy des Macedoniens. Paris: 1581. V. 37

ARRICIVITA, J. D.

Cronica Serafica . . . Mexico: 1792. V. 38

ARRILLAGA, BASILIO DE

Recopilacion de Leyes, Decretos, Bandos, Reglamentos, Circulares y Providencias de Los Supremos Poderes y Otras Autoridades de la Republica Mexicana. Mexico: 1829-39. V. 37; 40; 42

ARRINGTON, A. H.

To the Voters of the 5th Congressional District of North Carolina, Composed of the Counties of Orange, Granville, Wake, Franklin, Warren and Nash. Hilliardston: 1863. V. 39; 40

To the Voters of the 5th Congressional District of North Carolina. N.P.: 1863. V. 42

ARRINGTON, A. W.

The Rangers and Regulations of Tanaha; or, Life Among the Lawless: a Tale of the Republic of Texas. New York: 1856. V. 39

ARROW, SIMON

County Fanny's Nuptials: Being the Story of a Courtship. London: 1907. V. 44

ARROWSMITH, A.

A Comparative Atlas of Ancient and Modern Geography. London: 1828. V. 40; 46

ARROWSMITH, H. W.

The House Decorator and Painter's Guide. London: 1840. V. 37; 38; 40

ARROWSMITH, JOHN

The Crimea Chiefly from Surveys Made by ORder of the Russian Government (with) Southern Portion of the Crimea. London: 1854. V. 46

ARROWSMITH, JOSEPH

The Reformation: a Comedy. London: 1672. V. 42

The Reformation. London: 1673. V. 37; 38; 40; 41; 44; 46

ARROYO DE LA CUESTA, FELIPE

Grammar of the Mutsun Language, Spoken at the Mission of San Juan Bautista, Alta California. New York: 1861. V. 37; 38; 39

A Vocabulary or Phrase Book of the Mustun Language of Alta California. New York: 1862. V. 39; 42

ARS Moriendi. Augsburg: 1473. V. 37; 38

Speculu Artis Bene Moriendi . . . Cologne: 1495. V. 37

ARS Orientalis: the Arts of Islam and the East. Volume 2. Washington: 1957. V. 38; 41

ARS Orientalis: The Arts of Islam and the East. Volume 3. Washington: 1959. V. 38; 41

ARS Orientalis: The Arts of Islam and the East. Volume 5. Washington: 1964. V. 38; 41

ARS Orientalis: The Arts of Islam and the East. Volume I. Washington: 1954. V. 38; 41

ARS Typographica. New York: 1925-26. V. 41

ARSEMIOS OF MONEMVASIA

Scholia in Septem Euripidis Tragoedias ex Antiquis Exemplaribus . . . Venice: 1534. V. 46

ARSENIEV, V. K.

Dersu the Trapper. New York: 1941. V. 45

ARSENIOS, ABP. OF MONEMBASIA

Scholia ton Panu Dokimon eis hepta Tragoidias tou Euripidou. Scholia in Septem Euripidis Tragoedias ex Antiquis Exemplaribus. Venice: 1534. V. 37

ARSLAN, EDOARDO

Gothic Architecture in Venice. London: 1971. V. 38; 44

THE ART of Painting in Oil, Rendered Familiar to Every Capacity. London: 1801. V. 44

THE ART OF Confectionery. Boston: 1866. V. 38

THE ART Album. London: 1861. V. 44

ART and Architecture Thesaurus. 1990. V. 44

ART and Letters. An Illustrated Review, September 1889. London: 1889. V. 46

ART DIRECTORS CLUBS OF MONTREAL AND TORONTO

The Howard Smith Portfolio of Letterheads. N.P.. V. 45

ART et Decoration Revue Mensuelle d'art Moderne Publie sous la Direction de MM. Puvis de Chavannes, Vaudremer, Grasset, Jean Paul Laurens, Cazin, L-O Merson, Fermiet, Roty, Lucien Magne. Paris: 1910. V. 38

ART for All - London Transport Posters 1908-1949. London: 1949. V. 41

ART in Australia. Sydney: 1916-21. V. 41
ART in Australia. Sydney: 1916-42. V. 41

ART in California. San Francisco: 1916. V. 38; 46
ART in California. Irvine: 1988. V. 40; 44; 45

ART in California, a Survey of American Art with Special Reference to Californian Painting, Sculpture and Architecture . . . San Francisco: 1916. V. 37; 41; 43

ART in Photography. London: Paris: New York: 1905. V. 45

THE ART Journal Illustrated Catalogue: The Industry of all Nations, 1851. London: (1851). V. 37

THE ART of Anastatic Printing. London. V. 37
THE ART of Anastatic Printing. 1986. V. 40; 45
THE ART of Anastatic Printing. Kidlington: 1986. V. 42; 44

ART of Drawing and Painting in Water-Colours. London: 1763. V. 41
THE ART of Drawing and Painting in Water-Colours. Dublin: 1778. V. 43

ART of Drawing and Painting in Water-Colours. Wherein the Principles of Drawing are Laid Down, After a Natural and Easy Manner . . . London: 1779. V. 46

ART of Flower Painting: A Series of Progressive Lessons, Intended to Elucidate the Art of Flower Painting in Watercolours. London: 1815. V. 42

THE ART of Hunting, Trapping and Fishing. New York: 1874. V. 39

THE ART of Improving the Voice and Ear . . . London: 1825. V. 46

THE ART of Joking; or, an Essay on Witticism; in the Manner of Mr. Pope's Essay on Criticism . . . London: 1774? V. 42

THE ART of Making Fireworks, Improved to the Modern Practice . . . Derby: 1820? V. 46

THE ART Of Manual Defence; or, System of Boxing . . . London: 1799. V. 37; 43

THE ART of Manual Defence; or, System of Boxing: Perspictuously Explained in a Series of Lessons . . . London: 1789. V. 46

THE ART of marbling. North Hills: 1980. V. 40

THE ART of Painting in Miniature . . . London: 1752. V. 41; 45; 46

THE ART of Papermaking: a Guide to the Theory and Practice of the Manufacture of Paper. London: 1876. V. 40

THE ART of Preserving the Feet; or Practical Instructions for the Prevention and Cure of Corns, Bunions, Callosites, Chilblains, etc., with Observations on the Dangers Arising from Improper Treatment, Advice to Pedestirans . . . London: 1818. V. 45

THE ART of Singing; or, a Short and Easy Method, for Obtaining a Perfect Knowledge of the Gregorian Note. London: 1748. V. 45

THE ART of Swimming; containing Instructions . . . London: 1819? V. 38

THE ART of the Book. A Review of Some Recent European and American Work in Typography, Page Decoration and Binding. London: 1914. V. 39

THE ART of the Bookbinder and Gilder. Translated into English by Richard Atkinson. Leeds: 1977. V. 37

THE ART of the French Book from Early Manuscripts to the Present. London: 1947. V. 39

THE ART of the World Illustrated in the Paintings, Statuary and Architecture of World's Colombian Exposition. New York: 1894-95. V. 37

ART Present. Paris: 1947. V. 46

ART Studies from Nature, As Applied to Design: for the Use of Architects, Designers and Manufacturers. London: 1872. V. 39

ART UNION OF LONDON

Thirty Illustrations of Childe Harold. London: 1855. V. 39

ART Work of McKeesport, Braddock and Homestead. Chicago: 1894. V. 45

ART Work of Middlesex County, New Jersey. Chicago: 1896. V. 46

ART Work of Newark Illustrated. Chicago: 1892. V. 44

ART Work of Tacoma and Vicinity. Racine: 1907. V. 46

ART Work of Terre Haute, Indiana Published in Nine Parts. Chicago: 1907. V. 46

ART Work of Washtenaw County. Chicago: 1893. V. 40

ART Work on British Columbia. N.P.: 1900. V. 44

ARTAMONOV, M. I.

Treasures from Scythian Tombs in the Hermitage Museum, Leningrad. London: 1969. V. 40

ARTAUD, ANTONIN

Artaud Le Momo. Paris: 1947. V. 46

ARTAUD DE MONTOR, ALEXIS F.

The Lives and Times of the Popes . . . New York: 1911. V. 39

ARTE de Escribir, por Reglas y sin Muetras. Madrid: 1781. V. 40

DE ARTE Gymnastica Libri Sex. 1601. V. 42

ARTE Nova, e Curiosa Para Conserveiros, Confeiteiros, e Copeiros, e Mais Pessoas Que se Occupao em Fazer Doces . . . Lisbon: 1788. V. 45

ARTEMIDORUS

De Sominorum Interpretatione, Libri Quinge, a Iano Cornario . . . Latina Lingua Conscripti. Bail: 1544. V. 37

ARTEMY, ARARATSKY

Memoirs of the Life of Artemi, of Wagarschapat, Near Mount Ararat. London: 1822. V. 39

ARTHUR, ARCHIBALD

Discourses on Theological & Literary Subjects . . . with an account of some particulars of his life and character, by William Richardson, M.A. Professor of Humanity in the University of Glasgow. Glasgow/Edinburgh: 1803. V. 37

ARTHUR, CHESTER A.

Message From . . . Relative to Certain Lands in the Indian Territory Acquired by Treaty from the Creek and Seminole Indians. Washington: 1885. V. 37

Papers Relating to the War in South America, and Attempts to Bring About Peace. Washington: 1882. V. 42

ARTHUR, ERIC

Moose Factory, 1673-1947. Toronto: 1947. V. 42

ARTHUR, ERIC R.

Small Houses of the Late 18th and Early 19th Centuries in Ontario. Toronto: 1927. V. 44

ARTHUR, GEORGE C.

Bushwacker, A Story of Missouri's Most Famous Desperadoe. Rolla: 1938. V. 46

ARTHUR, GLEN DORA FOWLER 1858-

Annals of the Fowler Family . . . in Virginia, Carolina, Tennessee, Kentucky, Alabama, Mississippi, California and Texas. Austin: 1901. V. 37; 39; 42

ARTHUR, JAMES J., MRS.

Annals of the Fowler Family . . . in Virginia, Carolina, Tennessee, Kentucky, Alabama, Mississippi, Calfiornia and Texas. Austin: 1901. V. 38

ARTHUR, JOHN

Dark Metropolis. Boston: 1926. V. 42

ARTHUR, JOHN P.

Western North Carolina: a History (From 1730 5o 1913). Raleigh: 1914. V. 37; 39; 42

ARTHUR, KING, (Romances, etc.)

The Legend of King Arthur. New York: 1917. V. 42

The Most Ancient and Famous History of the Renowed Prince Arthur King of Britaine . . . London: 1634. V. 45

The Romance of King Arthur and His Knights of the Round Table. New York: 1917. V. 38; 41

The Story of the Grail and the Passing of Arthur. New York: 1910. V. 41

ARTHUR, LADY

The Dream of Little Hazy Cream and Other Rhymes. London: 1900. V. 40

ARTHUR, MRS. JAMES J.

Annals of the Fowler Family . . . In Virginia, Carolina, Tennessee, Kentucky, Alabama, Mississippi, California and Texas. Austin: 1901. V. 37

ARTHUR, ROBERT

A Treatise on the Use of Adhesive Gold Foil. Philadelphia: 1857. V. 41; 45

Treatment and Prevention of Decay of the Teeth. Philadelphia: 1871. V. 39

ARTHUR, STANLEY

The Story of the West Florida Rebellion. St. Francisville: 1935. V. 46

ARTHUR, STANLEY C.

Audubon an Intimate Life of the American Woodsman. New Orleans: 1937. V. 39

Jean Laffite, Gentleman Rover. New Orleans: 1952. V. 39

ARTHUR, T. S.

Stories for Good Boys. New York: 1850. V. 39

ARTHUR, TIMOTHY SHAY

The Bar-Rooms at Brantley; or, the Great Hotel Speculation. Philadelphia: 1877. V. 45

A Book About Boys. London: 185-? V. 45

The Mother. Philadelphia: 1846. V. 43

Temperance Tales. Philadelphia: 1844. V. 44

Ten Nights in a Bar Room and What I Saw There. Philadelphia: 1854. V. 43; 44

The Young Wife's Book . . . Philadelphia: 1836. V. 46

ARTHUR, WILLIAM

italy in Transition: Public Scenes and Private Opinions in the Spring of 1860 . . . London: 1860. V. 46

ARTHURS, STANLEY

The American Historical Scene, As Depicted by Stanley Arthurs and Ineterpreted by Fifty Authors. Philadelphia: 1935. V. 39

ARTHY, ELLIOT

The Seaman's Medical Advocate; or, An Attempt to Shew that Five Thousand Seamen Are, Annually, During War, Lost to the British Nation . . . Through Yellow Fever . . . London: 1798. V. 42

ARTIC Miscellanies. A Souvenir of the late Polar Search. London: 1852. V. 37

ARTICLES Exhibited Against Lord Archibald Hamilton, Late Governour of Jamaica. London: 1717. V. 40

ARTIS, EDMUND TYRELL

Antediluvian Phytology. London: 1838. V. 38; 42

ARTISAN Expedition to the World's Fair, Chicago, Organized by the Dundee Courier and the Dundee Weekly News. Dundee: 1893. V. 37; 38; 42

THE ARTIST and the Book: 1860-1960. Boston: 1961. V. 39
THE ARTIST and the Book, 1860-1960. Boston: 1962. V. 40

LES ARTISTES du Livre. Paris: 1928-33. V. 38; 40

ARTISTIC Japan: Illustrations and Essays. London: 1889. V. 37

ARTISTOELES

Parva Naturalia. Venetus: 1512. V. 44

ARTISTOTELES

Politics and Poetics. New York: 1964. V. 44

ARTMAN, WILLIAM

Beauties and Achievements of the Blind. Rochester: 1879. V. 46

ARUNDEL MARBLES

Marmora Arundelliana: sive Saxa Graece Incisa ex Venerandis Priscae Orientis Gloriae Ruderibus . . . Londini: 1629. V. 41

ARUNDELL, F. V. J.

Discoveries in Asia Minor . . . London: 1834. V. 42

ARUNDELL, FRANCIS VYVIAN JAGO 1780-1846

Discoveries in Asia Minor: Including a Description of the Ruins of Several Ancient Cities . . . London: 1834. V. 38; 40; 43

ARUNDELL, THOMAS

Historical Reminiscences of the City of London and Its Livery Companies. London: 1869. V. 44

ARUNDELL, V. J.

A Visit to the Seven Chruches of Asia. London: 1828. V. 38; 41

ARVIEUX, LAURENT D'

Voyage dans la Palestine, Vers le Grand Emir, Chef des Princes Arabes du Desert, Connus Sous le Nom de Bedouins . . . Avec la Description Generale de l'Arabie . . . Amsterdam: 1718. V. 39; 45

ARWAKER, EDMUND

Truth in Fiction: or, Morality in Masquerade. London: 1708. V. 45

The Vision: a Pindarick Ode . . . (with) The Second Part of the Vision. London: 1685. V. 41; 45

ARWAS, VICTOR

Art Deco. New York: 1980. V. 44; 45

AS No Other Dare Fail. For Samuel Beckett on His 80th Birthday By His Friends and Admirers. London: 1986. V. 40; 42

ASBJORNSEN, PETER CHRISTEN

East of the Sun and West of the Moon . . . London. V. 42

East of the Sun and West of the Moon. Old Tales from the North. London: 1914. V. 41; 42; 46

East of the Sun and West of the Moon. London: 1912. V. 40

ASBJORNSEN, PETER CHRISTIAN 1812-1885

East of the Sun and West of the Moon. New York: 1913-14. V. 42; 46

ASBOTH, J. DE

An Offical Tour through Bosnia and Herzegovnia with an Account of the History, Antiquities, Agrarian Conditions, Religions, Ethnology, Folklore, and Social Life of the People. London: 1890. V. 41

ASBURY, FRANCIS

An Extract from the Journal of Francis Asbury, Bishop of the Methodist-Episcopal Church in America, from August 7, 1771 to December 29, 1778. Philadelphia: 1792. V. 39

The Journal of . . . , Bishop of the Methodist Episcopal Church, from Aug. 7, 1771 to December 7, 1815. New York: 1821. V. 42

Journal. New York: 1900. V. 42

The Journal and Letters of . . . London: & Nashville: 1958. V. 46

ASBURY, H.

Sucker's Progress. An Informal History of Gambling in America From the Colonies to Canfield. New York: 1938. V. 41

ASBURY, HENRY

Reminiscences of Quincy, Illinois, Containing Historical Events . . . Quincy: 1882. V. 45

ASBURY, HERBERT

Carry Nation. New York: 1929. V. 39

Up from Methodism. New York: 1926. V. 42; 44

ASCANIUS or the Young Adventurer. London: 1746. V. 38

ASCH, NATHAN

Love in Chartres. London: 1927. V. 46

ASCH, SHOLEM

The Nazarene. New York: 1939. V. 41

ASCHAM, ANTHONY

Of the Confusions and Revolutions of Governments . . . London: 1649. V. 38

ASCHAM, ROGER

Apologia Pro Caena Dominica. London: 1577. V. 41

Disertissimi Viri Rogeri Aschami Angli, Regiae Olim Maiestate A Latinis Epistolis, Familiarum Epistolarum Libri Tres, Magna Orationis Elegantia Conscripti. Londini: 1590. V. 45

Dissertissimi Viri Rogeri Aschami Angli . . . . Londini: 1578. V. 40

The English Works of Roger Ascham. London: 1767. V. 38; 39

English Works: Toxophilus, Report of the Affaires and State of Germany, the Scholemaster. Cambridge: 1904. V. 41

The English Works of Roger Ascham. London: 1761. V. 37; 38

The English Works of Roger Ascham . . . With Notes and Observations and the Author's Life by James Bennet. London: (1767). V. 37

Epistolarum Libri Quatuor. Oxford: 1703. V. 39

An Report and Discourse Written by Roger Ascham, of the Affaires and State of Germany and the Emperour Charles His Court, Durying Certaine Yeares While the Sayd Roger Was There. London: 1570? V. 41

A Report and Discourse Written by Roger Ascham, of the Affaires and State of Germany and the Emperour Charles His Court, Duryng Certaine Yeares While the Sayd Roger Was There. London: 1571. V. 41

The Scholemaster, or Plaine and Perfite Way of Teaching Children . . . London: 1573. V. 42; 43

The Scholemaster, or Plain and Perfite Way of Treating Children to Understand, Write and Speak the Latin Tong. London: 1579. V. 42

The Scholemaster. London: 1743. V. 39; 42; 46

The Schole Master. London: 1570. V. 40

The Schoolemaster. London: 1589. V. 39

The Schoolmaster; or, a Plain and Perfect Way of Teaching Children to Understand, Write and Speak the Latin Tongue . . . London: 1711. V. 41

Toxophilus: The Schole of Shootinge. London: 1545. V. 42; 43

Toxophilus. London: 1571. V. 43

Toxophilus, the Schole, or Parititons, of Shooting. Wrexham: 1788. V. 37; 38; 41; 44; 45; 46

The English Works. London: 1767. V. 40

ASCONIUS PAEDIANUS, QUINTUS

Expositio in Ill. Orationes M. Tvllii Cic. Contra C. Verrem &c. Venice: 1522. V. 37

ASEEV, NIKOLAI

Zor. Moscow: 1914. V. 42; 45

ASGILL, JOHN

An Argument, Proving That According to the Covenant of Eternal Life Revealed in the Scriptures, Many May be Translated from Hence into that Eternal Life, Without Passing through Death, Altho the Humane Nature of Christ Himself Could Not Be Thus . . . London: 1700. V. 40; 42; 43; 45

A Collection of Tracts. London: 1715. V. 38

An Essay on a Registry for Title of Lands. London: 1698. V. 38; 43; 46

The Pretender's Declaration English'd. London: 1715. V. 41

Remarks on the Proceedings of the Commissioners for Putting in Execution the Act Passed Last Sessions, for Establishing a Land Bank. London: 1696. V. 41

ASH, CHARLES BOWKER

The Poetical Works. London: 1831. V. 45

ASH, EDMUND C.

Dogs: Their History and Devlopment. London: 1927. V. 39; 41

ASH, EDWARD C.

Dogs: Their History and Development. Boston: 1927. V. 38; 43

The Practical Dog Book. New York: 1931. V. 43

ASH, JOHN

The Easiest Introduction to Dr. Lowth's English Grammar, Designed for the Use of Children Under Ten Years of Age . . . London: 1768. V. 41; 43

Grammatical Institutes: or, an Easy Introduction to Dr. Lowth's English Grammar . . . London: 1786. V. 41; 43

Grammatical Institutes; or, an Easy Introduction to Dr. Lowth's Grammar . . . London: 1796. V. 46

The New and Complete Dictionary of the English Language. London: 1775. V. 37; 39; 41; 42; 43

ASHBEE, C. R.

The Private Press: A Study in Idealism. To Which is added, a Bibliography of the Essex House Press. London: 1909. V. 37

The Trinity Hospital in Mile End: An Object Lesson in Natural History. London: 1896. V. 37

ASHBEE, CHARLES ROBERT

American Sheaves and English Seed Corn: Being a Series of Addresses Mainly Delivered in the United States, 1900-1901. V. 43

American Sheaves and English Seed Corn. London: 1901. V. 37; 38; 42; 46

American Sheaves & English Seed Corn: Being a Series of Addresses Delivered in the United States 1900-1901. (London): 1901. V. 37

American Sheaves and English Seed Corn: Being a Series of Addresses mainly Delivered in the United States, 1900-1901, by C. R. Ashbee. (London: 1901). V. 37

Conradin: a Philosophical Ballad. Gloucestershire: 1908. V. 38; 41; 43; 46

Conradin: a Philsophical Ballad. London: 1908. V. 41

Craftsmanship in Competitive Industry. London. V. 40

A Dialogue in an English Garden. London: 1934. V. 38

Echoes from the City of the Sun. London: 1905. V. 38; 44; 46

An Endeavour Towards the Teaching of John Ruskin and William Morris. London: 1901. V. 38; 39; 40; 42; 43; 44; 46

The Essex House Song Book. London: 1904. V. 45

Frank Lloyd Wright: The Early Work. New York: 1968. V. 41

From Whitechapel to Camelot. London: 1892. V. 40; 41

Grannie. A Victorian Cameo. Oxford: 1939. V. 41; 46

Jerusalem, 1920-1922. London: 1924. V. 45

The Kings of Min Zaman. London: 1938. V. 41

The Last Records of a Cotswold Community . . . 1904. V. 45

Last Records of a Cotswold Community. London: 1904. V. 46

Lyrics of the Nile. London: 1938. V. 40; 41

The Manual of the Guild and School of Handicraft . . . London: 1892. V. 43

The Masque of the Edwards of England; Being a Coronation Pageant to Celebrate the Crowning of the King. 1902. V. 39; 43

The Masque of the Edwards of England. London: 1902. V. 37; 41; 43; 44; 46

Modern English Silverwork: An Essay by C.R. Ashbee, Together with a Series of Designs by the Author Drawn Upon a Hundred Separate Lithograph Plates and Coloured By Hand, with a Descriptive Index. A New Edition with introductory essays by . . . London: 1974. V. 37; 43

A Report by C. R. Ashbee to the Council of the National Trust for Places of Historic Interest and Natural Beauty. London: 1901. V. 46

Socialism and Politics: a Study in the Readjustment of the Values of Life. Campden, Gloucestershire: 1906. V. 39

Socialism and Politics. London: 1906. V. 38; 42

Transactions of the Guild and School of Handicraft. Essex House, Mile End. E: 1890. V. 42

The Trinity Hospital in Mile End. London: 1896. V. 40; 43

Where the Great City Stands. London: 1917. V. 38; 42; 43

ASHBEE, H. S.

A Bibliography of Tunisia from the Earliest Times to the End of 1888. London: 1889. V. 39

My Secret Life. New York: 1966. V. 45

ASHBEE, HENRY SPENCER

A Sunday in Coney Island. London: 1882. V. 40

ASHBERRY, JOHN

Apparitions. Northridge: 1981. V. 45

The Deadlier Sex. New York: 1961. V. 45

Murder in Montmartre. New York: 1960. V. 45

ASHBERY, JOHN

The Double Dream of Spring. New York: 1970. V. 39; 45

Fragment. 1969. V. 37; 38

Fragment. Los Angeles: 1969. V. 37

A Nest of Ninnies. New York: 1969. V. 45; 46

Rivers and Mountains. New York: 1966. V. 39; 45; 46

Selected Poems. London: 1967. V. 38

Self-Portrait in a Convex Mirror. Poems. New York: 1975. V. 46

Self-Portrait in a Convex Mirror. San Francisco: 1984. V. 40

Some Trees. New Haven: 1956. V. 37; 39; 41; 42; 44; 45; 46

Sunrise in Suburbia. New York: 1968. V. 39

The Tennis Court Oath. Middletown: 1962. V. 39; 44; 45

Three Madrigals. New York: 1968. V. 39

A Vermont Notebook. Los Angeles: 1975. V. 37; 39

ASHBURNER, JOHN 1793-1878

Notes and Studies in the Philosophy of Animal Magnetism, With Observations Upon Catarrh, Bronchitis, Rheumatism, Gout, Scrofula . . . and Spiritualism. London: 1867. V. 39; 46

ASHBURNHAM, JOHN

A Narrative by John Ashburnham of His Attendance on King Charles the First. London: 1830. V. 38

ASHBURTON, ALEXANDER BARING, 1ST BARON 1774-1848

An Inquiry into the Causes and Consequences of the Orders in Council and an Examination of the Conduct of Great Britain Towards the Neutral Commerce of America. London: 1808. V. 41

ASHBURTON, RICHARD BARR, LORD

Genealogical Memoirs of the Royal House of France . . . London: 1825. V. 38

ASHBY, JOHN

The Account Given by Sir John Asby Vice-Admiral and Reere Admiral Rooke to the Lords Commissioners of the Engagement at Sea Between the English, Dutch and French Fleets June the 30th, 1690 . . . London: 1691. V. 42

ASHBY, PROFESSOR

Helen Howard, or the Bankrupt and Broker. Boston: 1845. V. 45

Viola: the Redeemed. Boston: 1845. V. 43

ASHBY, THOMAS

The Aqueducts of Ancient Rome. Oxford: 1935. V. 37

ASHBY, THOMAS ALMOND

Life of Turner Ashby. New York: 1914. V. 38

ASHBY, W. ROSS

Design for a Brain. London: 1952. V. 42

Design for a Brain. London: 1960. V. 45

ASHBY, WILLIAM

New Zealand the Land of Health, Wealth and Prosperity. Its Present Position and Future Prospects. London: 1889. V. 38

ASHCAM, ANTHONY

A Discourse: Wherein is Examined What is Particularly Lawfull During the Confusions and Revolutions of Government. London: 1648. V. 39

ASHE, JOHN

A Perfect Relation of all the Passages and Proceedings of the Marquesse Hartford, the Lord Paulet, and the Rest of the Cavelleers, that Were With them in Wels. London: 1642. V. 43

A Second Letter Sent . . . to the Honourable William Lenthall . . . concerning Divers Messages and Passages Between the Marquesse Hartford, Lord Pawlet, Lord Seymour, Lord Coventry and Other His Majesties Commissioners . . . London: 1642. V. 45

ASHE, MAJOR

The Story of the Zulu Campaign. London: 1880. V. 41

ASHE, R. P.

Chronicles of Uganda. London: 1894. V. 42

ASHE, SIMEON

Living Loves Betwixt Christ and Dying Christians. London: 1654. V. 45

ASHE, THOMAS

History of the Azores of Western Islands. 1813. V. 41

History of the Azores, or Western Islands . . . Sherwood: 1813. V. 44

History of the Azores, or Western Islands . . . etc. (By Capt. Thos. Ashe). London: 1813. V. 37

Memoirs and Confessions of Captain Ashe. London: 1815. V. 39; 40; 42; 43

Le Primier (and Second) Volume del Promptuarie, ou Repertory Generall de les Annales et Plusors Auters Livres del Common Ley d'Engleterre. London: 1614. V. 46

The Spirit of 'The Book'; or, Memoirs of Caroline, Princess of Hasburgh, a Political and Amatory Romance. London: 1811. V. 38; 42; 46

Travels in America, Performed in 1806, for the Purpose of Exploring the Rivers Alleghany, Monogahela, Ohio and Mississippi. London: 1808. V. 37; 38; 39; 45

Travels in America, Performed in 1806, for the Purpose of Exploring the Rivers Alleghny, Monongahela, Ohio, and Mississippi, and Ascertaining the Produce and Condition of Their Banks and Vicinity. Newburyport: 1808. V. 37; 38

Travels in America, 1806, for the Purpose of Exploring the Rivers Alleghany, Monongahela, Ohio and Mississippi . . . London: 1809. V. 39; 44; 46

ASHENDEN, THOMAS

The Presbyterian Pater Noster, Creed and Commandments. London: 1681. V. 42

ASHENDENE PRESS

The Ashendene Press, Announcement of the Last Books to Be Issued from the Press. Shelley House, Chelsea: 1933. V. 39

A Chronological List, with Prices of he Forty Books Printed at the Ashendene Press, MDCCCXCV-MCMXXXV. 1935. V. 42; 45

A Chronological List, with Prices of the Forty Books Printed at the Ashendene Press, 1905-1935. Chelsea: 1935. V. 37; 39; 41

A Chronological List, with Prices of the Forty Books Printed at the Ashendene Press: MDCCCXCV-MCMXXXV. London: 1935. V. 43

A Chronological List, with Prices, of the Forty Books. London. V. 37

A Descriptive Bibliography of the Books Printed at the Ashendene Press, 1895-1935. Chelsea: 1935. V. 37; 41; 44

A Descriptive Bibliography of the Books Printed at the Ashendene Press, 1895-1935. London: 1935. V. 39; 45

A Descriptive Bibliography of the Books Printed at the Ashendene Press MDCCCXCV-MCMXXXV. London: 1976. V. 39

A Hand-List. Chelsea: 1925. V. 41; 43; 45; 46

A Hand-List of the Books Printed at the Ashendene Press MDCCCXCV-MCMXXV. Shelley House, Chelsea: 1925. V. 43

A Hand-List of the Books Printed at the Ashendene Press MDCCCXCV-MCMXXV. London: 1925. V. 40

Specimens of Types Used at the Ashendene Press. Chelsea: 1925. V. 37

ASHENHURST, THOMAS R.

Design in Textile Fabrics. London: 1885. V. 40

ASHER, ADOLF

A Bibliographical Essay on the Scriptores Rerum Germanicarum. London: 1843. V. 44

ASHER & ADAMS

Asher & Adams' New Topographical Atlas and Gazetteer of New York . . . New York: 1870. V. 39

ASHER & Adams' New Commercial and Statistical Atlas and Gazetteer of the United States . . . New York: 1872. V. 45

ASHER, G. M.

A Bibliographical and Historical Essay on the Dutch Books and Pamphlets Relating to New NEtherland, and to the Dutch West-India Company and to Its Possessions in Brazil, Angola, &c . . . Amsterdam: 1854-67. V. 37

ASHFIELD, C. R.

The Protestant Cause, and Other Poems. Aylesbury: 1829. V. 39

ASHFORD, DAISY

The Young Visiters. London: 1919. V. 42

ASHFORD, FAITH

Poor Man's Pence. A Book of Verses. Ditchling, Sussex: 1917. V. 46

Poor Man's Pence. Ditchling: 1917. V. 37

A Soul Cake. Ditchling, Sussex: 1919. V. 46

Things Unseen. Ditchling, Sussex: 1924. V. 46

ASHHURST, JOHN

Injuries of the Spine, with an Analysis of nearly Four Hundred Cases. Philadelphia: 1867. V. 42

Transactions of the International Medical Congress of Philadelphia 1876. Philadelphia: 1877. V. 40

ASHLEIGH, CHARLES

Rambling Kid. London: 1930. V. 42

ASHLEY, CLIFFORD W.

Whaleships of New Bedford. Boston & New York: 1929. V. 42

The Yankee Whaler. Boston & New York: 1926. V. 38; 41; 42

The Yankee Whaler. Boston: 1938. V. 41

ASHLEY, DORIS

Children's Stories from French Fairy Tales. Philadelphia. V. 45

ASHLEY, JOHN

The Present State of the British and French Trade to Africa and America Consider'd and Compar'd: . . . . London: 1745. V. 41; 45

A Supplement to the Second Part of the Memoirs . . . London: 1744. V. 45

ASHLEY, JONATHAN

The Great Duty of Charity, Considered and Applied in a Sermon, Preached at the Church in Brattle Street, Boston, on the Lord's Day, November 28, 1742. Boston: 1742. V. 43; 44

ASHLEY, WILLIAM H.

(To Thomas Hart Benton) In Senate of the United States, January 9, 1828. Washington: 1828. V. 40

The West of William H. Ashley. Denver: 1963. V. 38; 41

The West of William H. Ashley. Denver: 1964. V. 38; 42; 44

The West of William H. Ashley. Denver: 1964. V. 42

The West of William H. Ashley; the International Struggle for the Fur Trade of the Missouri, the Rocky Mountains, & The Columbia, with Explorations Beyond the Continental Divide, Recorded in the Diaries & Letters of William H. Ashley & His . . . Denver: 1964. V. 37

ASHMEAD, HENRY G.

Historical Sketch of Chester, Pennsylvania, on Delaware. Chester: 1883. V. 42

History of Delaware County, Pennsylvania. Philadelphia: 1884. V. 41

ASHMOLE, BERNARD

Olympia: the Sculptures of the Temple of Zeus. London: 1967. V. 44

ASHMOLE, ELIAS

The Antiquities of Berkshire. London: 1719. V. 39

Autobiographical and Historical Notes, Correspondence and other Contemporary Sources relating to his Life and Work. Edited and biographical introduciton by C.H. Josten. London: 1966. V. 37

The Institution, Laws & Ceremonies of the Most Noble Order of the Garter. London: 1672. V. 38; 39; 41; 45

The Institution, Laws and Ceremonies of the Most Noble Order of the Garter. London: 1693. V. 38

ASHMOLEAN MUSEUM

Catalogue of the Collection of Drawings. 1938/56/80/82; V. 46

ASHMORE, HARRIETTE

Narrative of a Three Month's March i India; and a Residence in the Dooab. London: 1841. V. 46

ASHPITEL, ARTHUR

Treatise on Architecture Including the Arts of Construction, Building, Stone-Masonry, Arch, Carpentry, Roof Joinery and Strength of Materials. Edinburgh: 1867. V. 43

ASHTON, DORE

Richard Lindner. New York: 1969. V. 43; 46

ASHTON, JOHN

A Century of Ballads. London: 1887. V. 38

Chap-Books of the Eighteenth Century. London: 1882. V. 41; 46

Curious Creatures in Zoology. London: 1890. V. 43

English Caricature and Satire on Napoleon I. New York: 1884. V. 41

The Fleet: Its River, Prison and Marriages. London: 1888. V. 38

A History of English Lotteries. London: 1893. V. 38; 39; 40; 41; 42

A History of English Lotteries now for the First Time Written. 1893. V. 37

Humour, Wit and Saitre of the Seventeenth Century. London: 1883. V. 38

Old Times, a Picture of Social Life at the End of the Eighteenth Century. New York: 1885. V. 46

Real Sailor-Songs. London: 1891. V. 37; 42; 46

Real Sailor Songs Collected and Edited by . . . London & New York: 1891. V. 38

A Right Merrie Christmasse! London: 1890. V. 41; 43

ASHTON, LEIGH

The Art of India and Pakistan: A Commemorative Catalogue of the Exhibition Held at the Royal Academy of Arts, London, 1947-48. New York. V. 38

The Art of India and Pakistan: a Commemorative Catalogue of the Exhitition Held at the Royal Academy of Arts. London: 1950. V. 41; 43

The Art of India and Pakistan. London: (1950). V. 37

An Introduction to the Study of Chinese Sculpture. London: 1924. V. 38; 41; 42

ASHTON, T. J.

On the Diseases, Injuries and Malformations of the Rectum and Anus, with Remarks on Habitual Constipation. Philadelphia: 1860. V. 42

ASHTON, THOMAS

Sermons on Several Occasions. London: 1770. V. 38

ASHURST, JOHN

The Principles and Practice of Surgery. Philadelphia: 1871. V. 42

ASHURST, W. H.

Facts and Reasons in Support of Mr. Rowland Hill's Plan for a Universal Penny Postage. London: 1838. V. 45

ASHWAL, STEPHEN

The Founders of Child Neurology. San Francisco: 1990. V. 45

ASHWIN, E. ALLEN

The Letters of a Portuguese Nun. 1929. V. 39

ASHWORTH, CALEB

Reflections on the Fall of a Great Man. A Sermon Preached to a Congregation of Protestant Dissenters at Daventry in Northamptonshire, on Occasion of the Death of the Late Reverend Isaac Watts, D.D. London: 1749. V. 40; 41

ASHWORTH, HENRY

A Tour in the United States, Cuba and Canada. London & Manchester,: 1861. V. 38

ASHWORTH, JOHN HENRY

Rathlynn, (a novel). London: 1864. V. 37; 43

The Saxon in Ireland; or the Rambles of an Englishman in Search of a Settlement in the West of IReland. London: 1851. V. 44

ASHWORTH, THOMAS

The Salmon Fisheries of England, 1868. London: 1868. V. 39; 44

ASIATIC INSURANCE CO.

Articles of Agreement of the Asiatic Insurance Co. Calcutta: 1812. V. 40

ASIATIC SOCIETY OF JAPAN

Transactions of the Asiatic Society of Japan from 30th October, 1872 (-22nd June 1878). Yokohama: 1874-78. V. 40

ASIMOV, ISAAC 1920-1992

The Currents of Space. New York: 1952. V. 39

Triangle. Collecting the Currents of Space, Pebble in the Sky & the Stars Like Dust. New York: 1961. V. 44

The Currents of Space. 1952. V. 37

Fantastic Voyage. Boston: 1966. V. 39; 40; 41

Fantastic Voyage II. New York: 1987. V. 37; 39; 41; 43; 44; 45; 46

Fantastic Voyage II. 1987. V. 37; 39

Foundation. New York: 1951. V. 37; 39; 40; 41; 45

Foundation. New York: (1951). V. 37

Foundation. Foundation and Empire. & Second Foundation. 1951-53. V. 45

Foundation and Empire. New York: 1952. V. 45

Foundation. 1953. V. 39

Foundation. Foundation and Empire and Second Foundation. 1962. V. 39

Foundation and Earth. 1986. V. 39

Foundation and Earth. 1986. V. 37; 43

Foundation and Empire. 1952. V. 43

Foundation. Foundation & Empire. Second Foundation. New York: 1962. V. 37; 43

Foundations Edge. 1982. V. 39

Foundations Edge. New York: 1982. V. 43; 45

I, Robot. London: 1952. V. 44

The Martian Way. New York: 1955. V. 39

The Naked Sun. London: 1958. V. 44

Nemesis. New York: 1989. V. 44

Nightfall and Other Stories. Garden City: 1969. V. 39

Pebble in the Sky. New York: 1950. V. 45

Pebble in the Sky. Garden City: 1950. V. 37

Prelude to Foundation. New York: 1988. V. 43

Robot Dreams. Berkeley: 1986. V. 45

The Robots of Dawn. Huntington Woods: 1983. V. 46

Robots and Empire. 1985. V. 39; 45

The Robots of Dawn. 1983. V. 39

The Stars Like Dust. 1951. V. 37; 39

3 by Asimov: Three Science Fiction Tales. 1981. V. 43

3 by Asmiov. New York: 1981. V. 43

Toward the Foundation. (Part 1). 1984. V. 37; 39

Triangle. Garden City: 1961. V. 39

Triangle. New York: (1961). V. 37

A Whiff of Death. New York: 1968. V. 39

ASIMOV, ISACC 1920-1992

Second Foundation. New York: 1953. V. 45; 46

ASIMOV, ISSAC 1920-1992

Robot Dreams. 1986. V. 37

ASKEW, ANTHONY

Bibliotheca Askeviana. London: 1774. V. 37

Bibliotheca Askeviana Manuscripta. London: 1785. V. 37

ASKIN, JOHN

John Askin Papers. 1747-1820. Detroit: 1928-31. V. 38; 44

ASLANAPA, O

Turkish Art and Architecture . . . London: 1971. V. 44

THE ASMAT: The Michael C. Rockefeller Expeditions. New York: (1967). V. 37

ASPIN, JEHOSAPHAT

Cosmorama: The Manners, Customs, and Costumes, of all Nations of the World, Described. London: 1834. V. 37

ASPINALL, A.

The Later Correspondence of George III. Cambridge: 1966-70. V. 46

ASPINALL-OGLANDER, C. F.

Gallipoli. London: 1929-32. V. 46

ASPLUND, JOHN

The Annual Register of the Baptist Denomination in North America, Containing an Account of the Churches and Their Constitutions. Norfolk: 1791. V. 39

The Annual Register of the Baptist Denomination, in North America; to the First of November 1790. Southampton County: 1791. V. 40

The Annual Register of the Baptist Denomination, in North America, to the First of November, 1790. Richmond: 1791? V. 44; 45

The Annual Register of the Baptist Denomination, In North America, to the Past of November 1790. Ricmond: 1792? V. 41

ASPLUND, KARL

Anders Zorn: His Life and Work. London: 1921. V. 40; 44

ASQUITH, MARGOT

The Autobiography of Margot Asquith. London: 1920. V. 46

ASSALINI, PAOLO

Observations on the Disease Called the Plague, on the Dysentery; The Opthalmy of Egypt, and on the Means of Prevention. New York: 1806. V. 41

ASSASSINATION of Abraham Lincoln & the Attempted Assassination of William H. Seward & Frederick W. Seward: Expressions of Condolence & Sympathy Inspired by These Events. Washington: 1867. V. 37; 44

ASSHETON, WILLIAM

The Cry of Royal Innocent Blood, Heard and Answered: Being a True and Impartial Account of God's Extra-Ordinary and Signal Judgments Upon Regicides. London: 1683. V. 41

THE ASSIENTO; or Contract for Allowing to the Subjects of Great Britain and the Liberty of Importing Negroes into the Spanish America . . . London: 1713. V. 41

ASSOCIATE-REFORMED CHURCH IN NORTH AMERICA

The Constitution and Standards of the Associate-Reformed Church in North America. New York: 1799. V. 39

ASSOCIATE-REFORMED SYNOD

The Constitution of the Associate-Reformed Synod . . . Philadelphia: 1783. V. 44

ASSOCIATED FABRICS CORP., NEW YORK.

Associated Fabrics: Costume Material Guide. 1937. V. 43

ASSOCIATION for Promoting the Discovery of the Interior Parts of Africa. London. Proceedings of the Association for Promoting the Discovery of the Interior Parts of Africa. London: 1790. V. 38; 40

ASSOCIATION FOR THE BENEFIT OF COLORED ORPHANS
Fifth Annual Report. New York: 1841. V. 43

ASSOCIATION OF AMERICAN LAW SCHOOLS
Selected Essays on Constitutional Law. Chicago: 1938. V. 43

ASTBURY, ANTHONY
My W. S. Graham Wall. Warwick: 1989. V. 40; 41

ASTBURY, WILLIAM THOMAS
Fundamentals of Fibre Structure. Oxford: 1933. V. 42

ASTELL, MARY
The Christian Religion, as Profess'd by a Daughter of the Church of England. London: 1705. V. 41
An Essay in Defence of the Female Sex. London: 1696. V. 39; 40; 41; 43; 44; 45; 46
An Essay in Defence of the Female Sex. London: 1697. V. 37; 39; 42; 44
A Serious Proposal to the Ladies, for the Advancement of Their True and Greatest Interest. London: 1695. V. 39; 41; 43; 45
A Serious Proposal to the Ladies for the Advancement of Their True and Greatest Interest. (with) A Serious Proposal to the Ladies, Part II. London: 1696/97. V. 44
A Serious Proposal to the Ladies, for the Advancement of Their True and Greatest Interest. London: 1697/1701/1697. V. 38
Some Reflections Upon Marriage, Occasion'd by the Duke and Dutchess of Mazarine's Case. London: 1700. V. 39

ASTESANUS DE AST. d. 1330
Summa de Casibus Conscientiae. Nuremberg: 1482. V. 42

ASTESANUS De Ast. Summa de Casibus Conscientiae. Nuremberg: 1482. V. 41

ASTESANUS DE AST
Summa De Casibus Conscientiae. Venice: 1478. V. 37

ASTESANUS DE ASTI
Summa de Casibus Conscientiae. Strasburg: 1480. V. 39

ASTLE, THOMAS
Calendarium Totulorum Patentium in Turri Londinensi. London: 1802. V. 41
The Origin and Progress of Writing. London: 1784. V. 37; 38; 39; 40; 42; 43; 44
The Origin and Progress of Writing, as well Hieroglyphic and Elementary Illustrated by Engravings Taken from Marbles, Manuscripts and Charters, Ancient and Modern. London: 1784. V. 38
The Origin and Progress of Writing, as Well Hieroglyphic as Elementary . . . London: 1876. V. 39; 46
The Origin and Progress of Writing, as well Hieroglyphic as Elementary, Illustrated by Engravings taken from Marbles, manuscripts and Charters, Ancient and Modern: also some account of the Origin and Progress of Printing. Second Edition . . . London: 1803. V. 37

ASTLEY, FRANCIS DUKINFIELD
Hints to Planters, Collected from Various Authors of Esteemed Authority, and from Actual Observation. Manchester: 1807. V. 38

ASTLEY, JOHN
The Art of Riding, Set Foorth in a Breefe Treatise. London: 1584. V. 37; 44; 45

ASTLEY, PHILIP
Astley's System of Equestrian Education. London: 1801. V. 39
Astley's System of Equestrian Education. Dublin: 1802. V. 39; 40; 43

ASTLEY, THOMAS
A New General Collection of Voyages and Travels . . . London: 1745-47. V. 42; 46

ASTOCRACY Versus Popular Government. N.P.: 1860? V. 42

ASTON, FRANCIS W.
Isotopes. London: 1922. V. 38; 42; 45; 46

ASTON, FRANCIS WILLIAM
Isotopes. New York: 1923. V. 38

ASTON, J. J.
The Law of Pauper Lunacy and Pauper Lunatic Asylums. London: 1849. V. 37

ASTON, ROBERT
Placita Latine Rediviva: A Book of Entries. London: 1673. V. 40

ASTON, W. G.
A Grammar of the Japanese Written Language. London: 1872. V. 38

ASTOR, WILLIAM WALDORF
Valentino. New York: 1885. V. 44

THE ASTROLOGER of the Nineteenth Century. London: 1825. V. 40

ASTROM, PAUL
The Late Cypriote Bronze Age; Other Arts and Crafts. Lund: 1972. V. 40
The Middle Cypriote Bronze Age. Lund: 1972. V. 40

ASTRONOMICAL Diary: or an Almanack for the Year of Our Lord Christ, 1755. Boston: 1754. V. 45

ASTRONOMICAL Observations Made . . . at the National Observatory, Washington. Washington: 1846-51-3-7-9. V. 41

ASTRUC, JEAN
A General and Compleat Treatise on all Diseases Incident to Children from Their Birth to the Age of Fifteen. London: 1746. V. 37
Tractatus Therapeuticus et Pathologicus. Venice: 1748. V. 42
A Treatise on the Diseases of Women . . . London: 1762. V. 38

ASTRUC, JOHANNES 1685-1766
De Morbis Venereis Libri Novem. Paris: 1740. V. 46

ASTRUC, JOHN 1685-1766
A General and Compleat Treatise on All the Diseases Incident to Children. London: 1746. V. 40; 46
A Treatise on the Venereal Disease . . . London: 1737. V. 43

ASTRUC, JON
A Treatise of Venereal Diseases in Nine Books . . . London: 1754. V. 44

ASTRUP, E.
With Peary Near the Pole. London: 1898. V. 46

ATALANTA'S Garland. Edinburgh: 1926. V. 45

ATCHELEY, SHIRLEY CLIFFORD
Wild Flowers of Africa. Oxford: 1939. V. 41

ATCHERLEY, R. J.
A Trip to Boerland; or, a Year's Travel, Sport and Gold Digging in the Transvaal and Colony of Natal. London: 1879. V. 39; 40

ATCHESON, NATHANIEL
A Compressed View of the Points to Be Discussed in Treating with the United States of America; A.D. 1814. London: 1814. V. 37

ATCHISON, J.
The Zoology of the Afghan Delimitation Commission. London: 1889. V. 43

ATCHISON, TOPEKA & SANTA FE RAILWAY
Oklahoma: Cherokee Strip Country, Kiowa and Commanche, Wichita, Otoe and Ponca Reservations. Chicago. V. 46

ATCHISON, TOPEKA, SANTA FE RAILROAD
The Atchison, Topeka, and Santa Fe Railroad . . . to the Rocky Mountains! . . . The Land Hunters, Gold-Hunters and Buffalo Hunters Road. The Only direct route to the San Juan Mines. (St Louis: 1876). V. 37

ATCHLEY, DANA
ABC Design. New York: 1965. V. 46

ATCHLEY, S. C.
Wild Flowers of Attica. London: 1938. V. 37; 43; 44

ATEN, IRA
Six and One-Half years in the Ranger Service: the Memoirs of Ira Aten, Sergeant Company D, Texas Rangers. Bandera: 1945. V. 46

ATGET
Visions of Paris. New York: 1963. V. 38; 39; 41

ATGET, EUGENE
A Vision of Paris: The Photographs of Eugene Atget. New York: 1963. V. 37; 42; 44

ATHANASIUS, SAINT, BP. OF ALEXANDERIA c. 296-373
Opera Quae Reperiuntur Omnia. Heidelberg: 1601, 1600. V. 39

ATHENAEUM CLUB, LONDON. LIBRARY
A Catalogue of the Library of the Athenanaeaum. London: 1845. V. 45
A Catalogue of the Library of the Athenaeum. With a Supplement to the Catalogue . . . With a Classified Index of Subjects. London: 1845-51. V. 39

ATHENAEUS
Deipnosophiston Biblia Pentekaideka. Deipnosophistarum . . . Liv. XV. Basel: 1535. V. 37; 39; 44
Dipnosophistarum sive Coenae Libri XV. Venice: 1556. V. 41
Dipnosophistarum Sive Coenae Sapientium Libri XV. Lyon: 1556. V. 41

ATHENAGORAS

Opera. Oxonii: 1682. V. 44

ATHENIAN Letters. Dublin: 1792. V. 45

ATHENIAN Letters; or, the Epistolary Correspondence of an Agent of the King of Persia. London: 1810. V. 38; 40; 43

ATHERLEY, EDMOND GIBSON

A Practical Treatise of the Law of Marriage and Other Family Settlements. London: 1813. V. 38

ATHERTON, CHARLES

The Capability of Steam Ships, Based on the Mutual Relations of Displacement, Power and Speed . . . Woolwich: 1853. V. 42

ATHERTON, FAXON DEAN

The California Diary of Faxon Dean Atherton, 1836-1839. San Francisco: 1964. V. 43; 44; 46

ATHERTON, GERTRUDE

Ancestors. New York: 1907. V. 46

The Conqueror: Being the True and Romantic Story of Alexander Hamilton. New York: 1902. V. 42

The Splendid Idle Forties. New York: 1902. V. 43; 44

The Splendid Idle Forties. Kentfield: 1960. V. 37; 38

ATHERTON, J. G.

The Tomato Crop. London: 1986. V. 37

ATHERTON, JOHN

The Fly and the Fish. New York: 1951. V. 39

ATHERTON, WILLIAM

Narrative of the Suffering & Defeat of the North-Western Army, Under General Winchester. Frankfort: 1842. V. 37; 39; 42; 43; 45

Narrative of the Suffering & Defeat of the North-Western Army, Under General Winchester . . . Frankfort, Ky.: 1842. V. 37

ATKIN, G. DUCKWORTH

House Scraps. London: 1887. V. 38; 44

ATKINS, EDWIN F.

Sixty Years in Cuba. Cambridge: 1926. V. 44

ATKINS, HENRY MARTIN

Ascent to the Summit of Mont Blanc, on the 22nd and 23rd of August, 1837. London: 1838. V. 43

ATKINS, JOHN

The Navy Surgeon; or Practical System of Surgery. London: 1742. V. 43

A Voyage to Guinea, Brasil, and the West-Indies; In His Majesty's Ships, the Swallow and Weymouth. London: 1735. V. 41

ATKINS, ROBERT

Parliamentary and Political Tracts. London: 1741. V. 39; 42

ATKINS, SAMUEL ELLIOTT

Some Account of the Company of Clockmakers. London: 1881. V. 42; 44; 45

ATKINS, WILLIAM

The Art and Practice of Printing. London: 1920s. V. 38; 43; 44

The Art and Practice of Printing . . . London: 1931. V. 45

The Art and Practice of Printing. London: 1932. V. 46

The Art and Practice of Printing. London: 1932-33. V. 37; 39; 41

ATKINSON, A.

Ireland Exhibited to England, in a Political and Moral Survey of Her Population and in a Statistical and Scenographic Tour of Certain Districts . . . London: 1823. V. 40; 43

The Irish Tourist . . . Dublin: 1815. V. 38

ATKINSON, BLANCHE

The Real Princess. London: 1894. V. 45

ATKINSON, C. T.

The Queen's Own Royal West Kent Regiment. 1914-1919. London: 1914. V. 45

The South Wales Borderers, 24th Foot 1689-1937. Cambridge: 1937. V. 40

ATKINSON, CHRISTOPHER

The Trial of Christopher Atkinson, Esq. Member of Parliament for Heydon in Yorkshire, the Late Cornfactor of His Majesty's Victualling-Board for Perjury . . . London: 1783. V. 46

ATKINSON, CHRISTOPHER WILLIAM

A Guide to New Brunswick, British Nroth America &c. Edinburgh: 1843. V. 43

A Historical and Statistical Account of New Brunswick, B.N.A. with Advice to Emigrants. Edinburgh: 1844. V. 41; 42; 45

ATKINSON, E. MILES

Abscess of the Brain: Its Pathology, Diagnosis and Treatment. London: 1934. V. 42

ATKINSON, FRANK H.

Sign Painting Up to Now. Chicago: 1909. V. 40

ATKINSON, FREDERICK

The Banquet of Thalia, or the Fashionable Songsters Pocket Memorial . . . York? London?. V. 42

The Banquet of Thalia, or the Fashionable Songsters Pocket Memorial . . . York: 1790. V. 45

ATKINSON, G. C.

Journal of an Expedition to the Feroe and Westman Islands and Iceland, 1833. Newcastle-upon-Tyne. V. 42

ATKINSON, G. F.

Curry and Rice. London: 1911. V. 40

ATKINSON, G. H.

The Northwest Coast, Including Oregon, Washington and Idaho . . . Portland: 1878. V. 45

ATKINSON, GEORGE FRANCKLIN

The Campaign in India, 1857-58. London: 1859. V. 39; 45

'Curry and Rice'. London: 1859. V. 46

ATKINSON, GEORGE H.

Address Delivered . . . Before the Chamber of Commerce of the State of New York, Upon the Possession, Settlement, Climate and Resources of Oregon and the Northwest Coast, Including Some Remarks Upon Alaska. New York: 1868. V. 41; 44

Address . . . Upon the Possession, Settlement, Climate and Resources of Oregon and the North-West Coast Including Some Remarks Upon Alaska. New York: 1868. V. 39; 42

The Northwest Coast, Including Oregon, Washington and Idaho. Portland: 1878. V. 41

ATKINSON, HENRY

Expedition Up the Missouri. Washington: 1826. V. 37; 40; 42

ATKINSON, HENRY GEORGE

Letters on the Laws of Man's Nature and Development. London: 1851. V. 39; 42

ATKINSON, HERBERT

Cock Fighting and Game Fowl. Bath: 1938. V. 40

ATKINSON, J. A.

Sixteen Scenes Taken from the Miseries of Human Life. London: 1807. V. 43

ATKINSON, J. C.

Forty Years in a Moorland Parish. London: 1891. V. 38; 41

Glossary of the Cleveland Dialect. London: 1866. V. 40

A Glossary of the Cleveland Dialect . . . London: 1868. V. 45

ATKINSON, JAMES

A Compleat System of Navigation. Dublin: 1767. V. 38; 40

A Compleat System of Navigation: In Two Parts. I: Atkinson's Epitome. II: Navigation New-Modell'd; Or, the whole Art performed, without Tables or Instruments, by a New Method, never yet published . . . etc. London: 1767. V. 37

Epitome of the Art of Navigation; or, a Short, Easy and Methodical Way to Become a Compleat Navigator . . . London: 1765. V. 45

The Expedition into Affghanistan: Notes and Sketches Descriptive of the Country. London: 1842. V. 41

Medical Bibliography. London: 1834. V. 42

Sketches in Afghaunistan. London: 1842. V. 39

ATKINSON, JOHN

Epitome of the Whole Art of Navigation: or, A Short, Easy, and Methodical Way to Become An Astronomer and A Complete Navigator . . . use of Mercator's Chart, Hadley's Octant and Sextant . . . Revised by John Adams. London;: 1782. V. 37

ATKINSON, JOHN AUGUSTUS

The Cutter, in Five Lectures upon the Art and Practice of Cutting Friends, Acquaintances, and Relations. London: 1808. V. 37

A Pictuesque Representation of the Manners, Customs and Amusements of the Russians . . . London: 1812. V. 37; 38

ATKINSON, MINNE

Hinckley Township or Grand Lake Plantation. Newburyport: 1920. V. 39

ATKINSON, NANCY BATES

Biography of Rev. G. H. Atkinson, D.D . . . . Portland: 1893. V. 43

ATKINSON, S.

The Effects of the New System of Free Trade Upon Our Shipping, Colonies and Commerce, Exposed in a Letter to the Right Hon. W. Huskisson. London: 1827. V. 38; 45

ATKINSON, STEPHEN

The Discoverie and Historie of the Gold Mynes in Scotland by Stephen Atkinson. Edinburgh: 1825. V. 37

ATKINSON, T. D.

Excavations at Phylakopi in Melos Conducted by the British School at Athens. London: 1904. V. 40; 44

ATKINSON, THOMAS

On the Causes of our National Troubles: A Sermon. Wilmington, NC: 1861. V. 37

ATKINSON, THOMAS WITLAM 1799-1861

Oriental and Western Siberia. London: 1858. V. 39; 40; 41; 42; 43; 46

Oriental and Western Siberia . . . New York: 1858. V. 42

Travels in the Regions of the Upper and Lower Amoor and the Russian Acquisitions on the Confines of India and China . . . London: 1860. V. 37; 39; 40; 45

Travels in the Regions of the Upper and Lower Amoor and the Russian Acquistions on the Confines of India and China. New York: 1860. V. 44; 46

Travels in the Regions of the Upper and Lower Amoor and the Russian Acquisitions on the Confines of India and China. London: 1861. V. 40; 42

ATKINSON, W. CHRISTOPHER

A Historical and Statistical Account of new Brunswick, B. N. A. With Advice to Emigrants. Edinburgh: 1844. V. 37; 38

ATKINSON, WILLIAM

Views of Picturesque Cottages with Plans, Selected from a Collection of Drawings Taken in Different Parts of England, and Intended as Hints for the Improvement of Village Scenery. London: 1805. V. 41

ATKINSON, WILLIAM B.

The Physicians and Surgeons of the United States. Philadelphia: 1878. V. 41; 42

ATKYNS, JOHN TRACY

Reports of Cases Argued and Determined in the Hight Court of Chancery in the Time of Lord Chancellor Hardwicke. London: 1794. V. 38; 39

ATKYNS, RICHARD 1615-1677

The Kings Grant of Privilege for Sole Printing Common-Law-Books, Defended; and the Legality Thereof Asserted. London: 1669. V. 39

ATKYNS, ROBERT

The Ancient and Present State of Gloucestershire. London: 1768. V. 40
The Ancient and Present State of Gloucestershire. London: 1974. V. 42

ATLANTIC AND PACIFIC RAILROAD CO.

Annual Report Atlantic and Pacific Railroad Co. to the Stockholders. New York: 1875. V. 37

The Atlantic & Pacific Railroad Co.: The Route and Its Advantages . . . Boston: 1870. V. 37

THE ATLANTIC and South Atlantic, Telegraphs. London: 1859. V. 45

THE ATLANTIC Club-Book: Being Sketches in Prose and Verse, by Various Authors. New York: 1834. V. 37

ATLANTIC MINING CO.

Report of the . . . for 1882-(1897). New York: 1883-98. V. 39

THE ATLANTIC Souvenir. New York: 1859. V. 43; 46

THE ATLANTIC Souvenir: A Christmas and New Year's Offering, 1828. Philadelphia: 1827. V. 43

THE ATLANTIC Souvenir for MDCCCXXX. Philadelphia: 1830. V. 38

ATLANTIC Tales, a Collection of Stories from the Atlantic Monthly. Boston: 1866. V. 46

ATLAS of Blair and Huntingdon Counties, Pennsylvania, From Actual Surveys by and Under the Direction of Beach Nichols. Philadelphia: 1873. V. 41

AN ATLAS of Boone, Kenton and Campbell Counties Kentucky. Philadelphia: 1883. V. 45

ATLAS of Cumberland County, Pennsylvania. New York: 1872. V. 41

ATLAS of Early American History. The Revolutionary Era. Chicago: 1976. V. 39

ATLAS of Edible Fishes. Tokyo?: 1883. V. 39

ATLAS of Hunterdon County, New Jersey . . . Flemington: 1977. V. 41

ATLAS of Hunterdon County, New Jersey. From Recent and Actual Surveys and Records Under the Superintendence of F. W. Beers. New York: 1873. V. 46

ATLAS Of Ionia Co. Michigan from Recent and Actual Surveys and Records Under the Superintendence of F. W. Beers. New York: 1875. V. 39

ATLAS Of Israel: Cartography, Physical Geography, Human and Economic Geography, History. Jerusalem & Amsterdam: 1970. V. 43

ATLAS OF Kalamazoo Co. Michigan From Recent and Actual Surveys and Records Under the Superintendence of F. W. Beers. New York: 1873. V. 39

ATLAS of Lenawee County, Michigan. 1893. V. 39

ATLAS Of Logan County, Ohio. Philadelphia: 1890. V. 39

ATLAS of Monmouth Co., New Jersey. From Recent and Actual Surveys and Records Under the Superintendence of F. W. Beers. New York: 1873. V. 46

ATLAS of Ports, Cities and Localities of the Island of Cuba. Washington: 1898. V. 39

ATLAS Of Russia Made Up of Nineteen Special Maps Respresenting the Russian Empire with Its Frontier Countries Composed According to the Geographic Rules and New Observations with the Addition of a General Map of the Great Empire. St. Petersburg: 1745. V. 45

ATLAS of Susquehanna County, Pennsylvania. New York: 1872. V. 41

ATLAS of the City of Worcester, Massachusetts. Springfield: 1896. V. 45

ATLAS of the City of Worcester, Worcester County, Massachusetts from Actual Surveys by and Under the Direction of F. W. Beers . . . New York: 1870. V. 45

ATLAS of the International Boundary Between the United States and Canada Arctic Ocean to Mount St. Elias. Washington: 1918. V. 40

ATLAS of the International Boundary Between the United States and Canada Arctic Ocean to Mount St. Elias . . . Washington: 1918. V. 42

AN ATLAS of the United States of North America. London: 1832. V. 46
AN ATLAS of the United States of North America. Philadelphia: 1832. V. 45

ATLAS PORTLAND CEMENT CO.

Reinforced Concrete in Factory Construction. New York: 1907. V. 44

ATLAS PORTLAND CEMENT COMPANY

Concrete Country Residences. New York: 1905. V. 42

ATLAS to Accompany A Monograph on the Geology and Mining Industry of Leadville, Colorado. Washington: 1883. V. 37

ATLAS to Accompany the Official Records of the Union and Confederate Armies . . . Washington: 1891-1895. V. 39

ATLEE, PHILIP

The Inheritors. New York: 1940. V. 37; 38; 39; 40

ATLEE, WASHINGTON

General and Differential Diagnosis of Ovarian Tumor, With Special Reference tot he Operation of Ovariotomy and Occasional Pathological and Therapeutical Considerations. Philadelphia: 1873. V. 42

ATSON, WILLIAM

Heart Whispers; or, A Peep Behind the Family Curtain, Interspersed with Sketches of a Tour Through Nine Southern States . . . Philadelphia: 1859. V. 41; 45

ATTAWAY, WILLIAM

Blood on the Forge. Garden City: 1941. V. 45; 46

Calypso Song Book. New York: 1957. V. 46

Let Me Breathe Thunder. Garden City: 1939. V. 43

AN ATTEMPT . . . Third edition, with very considerable additions. London: (1825). V. 37

ATTEMPTS for the Instruction and Conversion of the Jews Seriously Recommended to the Attention of All Christians. London: 1817. V. 42

ATTENDOLI, DARIO

Il Dvello. Venetia: 1564-66. V. 42

ATTERBURY, FRANCIS 1663-1732

The Epistolary Correspondence, Visitation Charges, Speeches and Miscellanies. London: 1783-87. V. 42

Some Proceedings in the Convocation, A.D., 1705. London: 1708. V. 39

ATTERIDGE, A. HILLIARD

Towards Khartoum. The Story of the Soudan War of 1896. London: 1897. V. 41

THE ATTORNEY and Solicitor's Companion; or, Compleat Affidavit-Man. London: 1725. V. 38; 40

THE ATTORNEY'S Compleat Pocket-Book. Dublin: 1791. V. 37

THE ATTORNEY'S Compleat Pocket-Book: Containing Near 350 of Such Choice and Approved Precedents in Law, Equity and Conveyancing, as an Attorney May Have Occasion for, When Absent from His Office . . . London: 1741. V. 40

AN ATTORNEY'S Practice Epitomized; or the Method, Times and Expences of Proceeding in the Courts of King's Bench and Common Pleas (etc.). London: 1759. V. 45

THE ATTRACTIVE Picture Book. London: 1867. V. 42

ATTWELL, MABEL LUCIE

Lucie Attwell's Fairy Book. London: 1932. V. 45

ATTWOOD, THOMAS 1783-1856

Observations on Currency, Population and Pauperism, in Two Letters to Arthur Young, Esq. Birmingham: 1818. V. 37

ATWATER, CALEB

Description of the Antiquities Discovered in the State of Ohio and Other Western States Communicated to the President of the American Antiquarin Society. V. 46

An Essay on Education. Cincinnati: 1841. V. 45

Remarks Made on a Tour to Prairie du Chien; Thence to Washington City in 1829. Columbus: 1831. V. 37; 38; 39; 41; 44; 45

The Writings of Caleb Atwater. Columbus: 1833. V. 37

ATWATER, H. COWLES

Incidents of a Southern Tour; or, the South, as Seen with Northern Eyes. Boston: 1857. V. 39; 41; 42; 43

ATWOOD, DANIEL T.

Atwood's Country and Suburban Houses. New York: 1871. V. 42

ATWOOD, DANIEL TOPPING

Atwood's Modern American Homesteads. New York: 1876. V. 41; 44

ATWOOD, F. T.

An Account of the Endowed Charities and Benefactions of the Parish of Hammersmith, Showing Their Origin, Progress, Present Amount of Funds and Mode of Distribution. Hammersmith: 1856. V. 39

ATWOOD, MARGARET

The Animals in that Country. Boston: 1968. V. 42

The Animals in that Country. Toronto: 1968. V. 45

Bluebeard's Egg. London: 1987. V. 45

Bodily Harm. Toronto: 1981. V. 45

Bodily Harm. New York: 1982. V. 42; 45

Double Peresphone. Toronto: 1961. V. 44

The Edible Woman. Boston: 1969. V. 41; 44

The Edible Woman. Toronto: 1969. V. 37; 39

Encounters with the Element Man. Concord: 1982. V. 39; 45

Hurrican Hazel and Other Stories. Helsiniki: 1987. V. 45

The Journals of Susanna Moodie. Toronto: 1970. V. 43

Lady Oracle. Toronto: 1976. V. 45

Life Before Man. Toronto: 1979. V. 45

Notes Toward a Poem that Can Never Be Written. 1981. V. 42

Notes Towards a Poem that Can Never Be Written. Toronto: 1981. V. 45

Power Politics: Poems. Toronto: 1971. V. 45

Procedures for Underground. Toronto: 1970. V. 45

Snake Poems. Toronto: 1983. V. 45

Surfacing. Toronto: 1972. V. 43; 45

Unearthing Suite. Toronto: 1983. V. 45

ATWOOD, THOMAS 1783-1856

A Letter to . . . on the Creation of Money and On Its Action Upon National Prosperity. Birmingham: 1817. V. 41

ATWOOD, WILLIAM d. 1705

Jus Anglorum ab Antiquo; or, Confutation of an Impotent Libel Against the Government by Kings, Lords and Commons, Under Pretence of Answering Mr. Petyt and the author of Jani Anglorum . . . London: 1681. V. 40

AUBANEL, ANTOINE

Catalogue Des Livres, de Hazard Qui se Trouvent chez Antoine Aubanel & Neveu, Libraires rue des Orfevres a Avignon, Avec le Juste Prix. 1775. Avignon: 1775. V. 40

AUBER, PETER

An Analysis of the Constitution of the East-India Company, and of the Laws passed by Parliament for the Government of their Affairs at home and abroad. (with) A Brief History of the Company and of the rise and progress of the . . . Kingsbury: 1826. V. 37

AUBERT DE VERTOT D'AUBEUF, RENE

The History of the Revolutions in Sweden and Portugal. Dublin: 1727. V. 38

AUBERTIN, J. J.

A Fight with Distances the States the Hawaiian Islands, Canda, British Columbia, Cuba the Bahamas. London: 1888. V. 37; 38

AUBERY DU MAURIER, LOUIS

The Lives of all the Princes of Orange, from William the Great . . . London: 1693. V. 39; 42

AUBERY, JAMES

36th Wisconsin Volunteer Infantry. N.P.: 1900. V. 39

AUBIGNAC, FRANCOIS HEDELIN, ABBE D'

The Whole Art of the Stage. London: 1684. V. 43; 46

AUBIGNE, THEODORE AGRIPPA D'

L'Histoire Universelle . . . Maille: 1616-18. V. 40

AUBIN, NICHOLAS

The Cheats and Illusions of Romish Priests and Exorcists. London: 1703. V. 37; 46

AUBIN, NICOLAS

Cruels Effets de la Vengeance du Cardinal de Richelieu, ou Histoire es Diables de Loudun. Amsterdam: 1716. V. 42

AUBORN, A. D'

The French Convert: Being a True Relation of the Happy Conversion of a Noble French Lady, from the Errors and Superstitions of Popery, to the Reformed Religion . . . London: 1745? V. 42

The French Convert: Being a True Relation of the Happy Conversion of a Noble Lady, from the Errors and Superstitions of Popery . . . Also Her Wonderful Deliverance, From Two Assassins, Hired by a Popish Priest to Murder Her . . . Hartford: 1798. V. 41; 45

AUBREY, F.

King of the Dead. 1903. V. 44

AUBREY, JOHN

Gulnitzl a Dantisc Ulysses. 1631. V. 45

Letters Written by Eminent Persons in the Seventeenth and Eighteenth Centuries; to which are added, Hearne's Journeys to Reading, and to Whaddon Hall, the Seat of Brown Willis and Lives of Eminent Men by John Aubrey. London: 1813. V. 37

Miscellanies. London: 1696. V. 42

Miscellanies, Upon the Follow Subjects. Day Fatality. II. Local Fatality. III. Ostenta. IV. Omens. V. Dreams. VI. Apparitions . . . London: 1721. V. 37; 42; 45

Monumenta Britannica. Boston: 1980. V. 41; 43; 46

The Natural History of Wiltshire. London: 1847. V. 37

Wiltshire; The Topographical Collections of John Aubrey, F.R.S., A.D. 1659-70, with illustrations. Corrected and Enlarged by John Edward Jackson. London: 1862. V. 37

AUBURN COPYING CO.

Catalogue and Price List of the Auburn Copying Co.'s Celebrated Berlin Photographs, India Ink, Water Colored and Oil Portraits and Photograph Frames, for Agents. Aubrun: 1877. V. 46

AUCASSIN AND NICOLETTE

Aucassin et Nicolete. 1903. V. 37

The Song-Story of Aucassin & Nicolette. (Lexington: 1957. V. 37

AUCASSIN E NICOLETE

C'Est d'Aucassin et de Nicolete. London: 1903. V. 42

AUCASSIN ET NICOLETE

C'est D'Aucassin et de Nicolete. Hammersmith: 1903. V. 41; 43

AUCASSIN ET NICOLETTE

Aucassin and Nicolete. London. V. 40

Aucassin and Nicolette Done from the Old French by Michael West . . . New York. V. 42

Aucassin and Nicolete. London: 1887. V. 41

Aucassin and Nicolete. Chicago: 1896. V. 38

The Song-Story of Aucassin and Nicolette. 1900. V. 41

Of Aucassin and Nicolette and Amabel and Amoris. London: 1902. V. 41

C'Est D'Aucassin et de Nicolete. Hammersmith: 1903. V. 38; 41; 43

C'est d'Aucassin et de Nicolete. London: 1903. V. 39; 40; 44; 46

Aucassin and Nicolette. London: 1914. V. 40; 46

AUCASSIN ET NICOLETTE continued

Aucassin and Nicolette. New York: 1931. V. 41

Aucassin and Nicolete. Praha: 1931. V. 43

Of Aucassin and Nicolette and Amabel and Amoris. London: 1902. V. 38; 43

Of Aucassion and Nicolette. London: 1925. V. 45; 46

The Song-Story of Aucassin and Nicolete. Chelsea: 1900. V. 46

AUCHAMPAUGH, PHILIP GERALD

James Buchanan and His Cabinet on the Eve of Secession. Duluth: 1926. V. 45

AUCHER, F. PASCHAL

A Grammar Armenian and English. Venice: 1819. V. 38; 40

AUCHER, PASCHAL

Grammar, English and Armenian. Venice: 1817. V. 39

A Grammar Armeian and English. Venice: 1832. V. 39

AUCHINCLOSS, LOUIS

The Indifferent Children. New York: 1947. V. 39; 46

The Injustice Collectors. Boston: 1950. V. 46

Life, Law and Letters. Boston: 1979. V. 39

AUCHINCLOSS, WILLIAM S.

Ninety Days in the Tropics, or Letters from Brazil. Wilmington: 1874. V. 39

AUCKLAND, WILLIAM EDEN, 1ST BARON

Four Letters to the Earl of Carlisle. On Certain Perversions of Political Reasoning . . . London. V. 38

Four Letters to the Earl of Carlisle. Edinburgh: 1779. V. 41

Principles of Penal Law. London: 1771. V. 38; 40

The Substance of a Speech, Made in the House of Peers on Tuesday, 8th Jan. 1799, on the Third Reading of the 'Bill for Granting Certain Duties Upon Income.' London: 1799. V. 42; 46

THE AUCTION: a Poem. London: 1770. V. 38

AUCTION Sale of the Milton Abbey Estate. Blandford: 1932. V. 40

AUDA, DOMENICO

Breve Compendio di Maaraviglioso Secreti. Venetia & Bassano: 1690. V. 38

AUDEBERT, J. B.

Histoire Naturelle des Singes et des Makis. Paris: 1800. V. 41

Oisseaux Dores ou a Reflets Metalliques. Paris: 1800?-02. V. 41

AUDEN, J. E.

A Short History of the Albrighton Hunt. London: 1905. V. 42

AUDEN, WYSTAN HUGH 1907-1973

The Age of Anxiety. New York: 1947. V. 38

Another Time. London: 1940. V. 45

The Ascent of F6 - a Tragedy in Two Acts. London: 1936. V. 40; 41

The Ascent of F6. New York: 1937. V. 39; 44; 45; 46

Auden: Five Poems. Cedar Falls: 1984. V. 40

A Certain World: A Commonplace Book. New York: 1970. V. 37

A Choice of Dryden's Verse. London: 1973. V. 37

City Without Walls and Other Poems. London: 1969. V. 46

City Without Walls. New York: 1969. V. 39

The Collected Poetry of W. H. Auden. New York: 1945. V. 39

Collected Shorter Poems 1930-1944. London: 1950. V. 44

Collected Shorter Poems 1927-1957. London: 1956. V. 45

Collected Shorter Poems 1927-1957. New York: 1967. V. 46

Collected Longer Poems. London: 1968. V. 46

Collected Longer Poems. New York: 1969. V. 45

The Dance of Death. London: 1933. V. 37; 40; 44; 45

The Dog Beneath the Skin or Where is Francis? London: 1935. V. 41; 45; 46

The Double Man. New York: 1941. V. 43

The Dyer's Hand, and Other Essays. London: 1963. V. 38

Education Today and Tomorrow. London: 1939. V. 38

The Enchafed Flood. New York: 1950. V. 39

Eyes Look Into the Well. Let the Florid Music. That Night When Joy. To You Simply. What's in Your Mind. Grasse: 1982. V. 38

Five Poems. Cedar Falls: 1983. V. 46

Five Poems. 1984. V. 40

Five Poems. Cedar Falls: 1984. V. 37; 38; 39; 42

Five Poems. (Cedar Falls): 1983. V. 37

Good-Bye to the Mezzogiorno. Milan: 1958. V. 38

Homage to Clio. London: 1960. V. 44

Journey to War. London: 1939. V. 43

Letters from Iceland. London: 1937. V. 38; 41; 43; 45

Litany and Anthem for S. Matthew's Day. Northampton: 1946. V. 40

Litany and Anthem for S. Matthew's Day, 1946. Written for the Church of: 1946. V. 38

Look Stranger! London: 1936. V. 40; 45

Look, Stranger! London: (1936). V. 37

Louis Macneice: a Memorial Address, Delivered at All Souls, Langham Place on 17 October, 1963. V. 39

Louis MacNeice - a Memorial Address. London: 1963. V. 38; 40; 41; 42; 45; 46

Louis Macneice: a Memorial Address, Delivered at All Souls, Langham Place on 17 October, 1963. V. 42

A Mosaic for Marianne Moore. V. 45

New Year Letter. London: 1941. V. 45

Nones. New York: 1950. V. 37

Nones. New York: 1951. V. 46

the Old Man's Road. New York: 1956. V. 37; 43; 45

On This Island. New York: 1937. V. 41; 44

On the Frontier. London: 1938. V. 37; 39; 42; 45

The Orators - an English Study. London: 1932. V. 38; 39; 42; 45; 46

The Orators - an English Study. London: 1932. V. 42

The Orators. New York: 1967. V. 45

Our Hunting Fathers. Cambridge: 1935. V. 44

The Platonic Blow: a Poem. 1965. V. 43

Platonic Blow. New York: 1965. V. 40; 43; 45

Poems. London: 1930. V. 38; 39; 40; 42; 43; 45

Poems. London: 1930. V. 37

Poems. London: 1933. V. 39; 42

Poems. London: (1933). V. 37

Poems. New York: 1934. V. 45

Poems. New York: 1974. V. 40; 45

The Poets Tongue. London: 1935. V. 45

Selected Poems. London: 1938. V. 42

Selections from Poems by Auden. London: 1974. V. 37; 40; 43; 45

The Shield of Achilles. New York: 1955. V. 39

Slick But Not Streamlined - Poems and Short Pieces. New York: 1947. V. 45

Some Poems. London: 1940. V. 39; 45

Spain. London: 1937. V. 40; 41; 42; 43; 45; 46

Thank You, Fog: Last Poems. London: 1974. V. 40

Three Songs for St. Cecilia's Day. New York. V. 39

Three Unpublished Poems. New York: 1986. V. 37; 40; 43

Two Songs. New York: 1968. V. 45

AUDIGUIER, VITAL D'

Histoire des Amours de Lysandre et de Caliste. Amsterdam: 1679. V. 37

AUDSLEY, G. A.

Keramic Art of Japan. Liverpool: 1875. V. 45

AUDSLEY, GEORGE A.

Keramic Art of Japan. London: 1881. V. 37; 41; 44

AUDSLEY, GEORGE ASHDOWN

The Art of Chromolithography. New York: 1883. V. 38; 43

Gems of Japanese Art and Handicraft. London: 1913. V. 44

Keramic Art of Japan. Liverpool: 1875. V. 39

The Organ of the Twentieth Century. New York: 1919. V. 46

The Ornamental Arts of Japan. New York: 1883-1884. V. 39

AUDSLEY, W.

Cottage, Lodge and Villa Architecture. London: 1860. V. 43

Cottage, Lodge and Villa Architecture. London & Glasgow: 1868. V. 39

Guide to the Art of Illuminating and Missal Painting. London: (c. 1870). V. 37

AUDSLEY, WILLIAM JAMES

Cottage, Lodge and Villa Architecture. London: 1870. V. 38; 39; 44

Cottage, Lodge and Villa Architecture. London: 1868. V. 37; 39; 40; 44

Cottage, Lodge and Villa Architecture. London: 1872. V. 38

Handbook of Christian Symbolism . . . London: 1865. V. 44

Outlines of Ornament in the Leading Styles. London: 1881. V. 38

Polychromatic Decoration As Applied to Buildings in the Mediaeval Styles. London: 1882. V. 38; 39; 44

AUDUBON, JOHN JAMES 1785-1851

Audubon and His Journals. New York: 1897. V. 39; 43; 44

The Birds of America. New York: 1840-44. V. 44; 45; 46

The Birds of America. New York & Philadelphia: 1840-44. V. 38; 39; 41; 42; 43

AUDUBON, JOHN JAMES 1785-1851 continued

the Birds of America. New York: 1856. V. 44

The Birds of America . . . New York: 1856. V. 45

The Birds of America, From Drawings Made in the United States and Their Territories. New York: 1871. V. 39

The Birds of America. London: 1973. V. 40

The Birds of America. London & Leipzig: 1972. V. 37

Delineations of American Scenery and Character. New York: 1926. V. 39; 44

Journal of John James Audubon Made During His Trip to New Orleans in 1820-1821. (with) *Journal of John James Audubon . . . 1840-1843.* Boston: 1929. V. 38; 39; 42; 43; 45

Journal of John James Audubon Made During His Trip to New Orleans in 1820-1821. (with) *Journal of John James Audubon Made While Obtaining Subscriptions to His Birds of America 1840-1843.* Cambridge: 1929. V. 44

Letters 1826-1840. Boston: 1930. V. 37; 39; 41; 42; 43

The Original Bird Paintings of John James Audubon. London: 1966. V. 37; 38; 44; 45

Original Water Color Paintings by J. J. Audubon for the Birds of America. New York: 1966. V. 37; 39; 40; 42; 43; 46

Ornithological Biography. Edinburgh: 1831-39. V. 38

The Quadrupeds of North America. London: 1849-51-54. V. 42; 43

The Quadrupeds of North America. New York: 1849-54. V. 39

The Quadrupeds of North America. New York: 1851-51-54. V. 38; 39; 41; 42

The Quadrupeds of North America. New York: 1851-54. V. 39; 46

The Quadrupeds of North America. New York: 1851/54/n.d. V. 43

The Quadrupeds of North America. New York: 1854. V. 39

The Quadrupeds of North America. New York: 1849. V. 37

The Quadrupeds of North America. New York: 1854, 1854. V. 38

The Quadrupeds of North America. New York: 1870. V. 37

Six Plates from Birds of America. London: 1985-87. V. 37

A Synopsis of the Birds of North America. Edinburgh: 1839. V. 43; 45

The Vivaporous Quadrupeds of North America. New York: J. J. Audubon,: 1851-53. V. 37

Audubon's Western Journal: 1849-1850. Cleveland: 1906. V. 38

Works. Kent: 1977-80. V. 41; 43

The Complete Works of Audubon. Kent: 1978-80. V. 40

AUDUBON, JOHN WOODHOUSE

Audubon's Western Journal: 1849-1850. Cleveland: 1906. V. 38; 40; 41; 44; 45

The Drawings Audubon Illustrating His Adventures through Mexico and California 1849-1850. San Francisco: 1957. V. 38; 39; 40; 41; 42; 43

Illustrated Notes of an Expedition through Mexico and California. New York: 1852. V. 41

AUDUBON, MARIA R.

Audubon and His Journals. New York: 1897. V. 37; 38; 39; 42

Audubon and His Journals . . . New York: 1900. V. 45

AUDUBON, MARIE R.

Audubon and His Journals. New York: 1896. V. 38

AUEL, JEAN M.

The Clan of the Cave Bear. New York: 1980. V. 37; 40; 42

The Clan of the Cave Bear. The Valley of Horses. The Mammoth Hunters. New York: 1980/82/85. V. 41

AUENBRUGGER, L.

Manuel des Pulmoniques, ou Traite Complet des Maladies de la Poitrine. Paris: 1770. V. 44

Nouvelle Methode Pour Reconnaitre les Maladies Internes de la Poitrine par la Percussion de Cete Cavite. Paris: 1808. V. 41; 42

AUENBRUGGER, LEOPOLD

Inventum Novum ex Percussione Thoracis Humani ut Signo Abstursos Interni Pectoris Morbos Detegendi. Vienna: 1761. V. 42

Nouvelle Methode Pour Reconnaitre Les Maladies Internes de la Portrine Par La Percussion de Cette Cavite . . . Paris: 1808. V. 42

AUER, ALOIS

Der Polygraphische Apparat Oder die Verschiedenen Kunstfacher der k k Hof- und Staatsdruckerei zu Wien. Vienna: 1853. V. 41; 45

Die Entdeckung des Naturselbstdruckes Oder die Erfindung . . . wien: 1853. V. 39

The Discovery of the Natural Printing Process. Wien: 1854. V. 37

AUER, ALOIS VON WELSBACH

Die Entdeckung des Naturselbstdruckes . . . Vienna: 1854. V. 42

AUERBACH-LEVY, WILLIAM

Is That Me? A Book About Caricatures. New York: 1947. V. 38

AUFFGEBOT und Warnungsschrifft, so Die Chur, und Fursten zu Sachssen etc. an alle irer Gnaden . . . N.P.: 1541. V. 37

AUGE, DANIEL D'

Deux Dialogues de l'Invention Poetique, de la Vraye Congnoissance de l'Histoire, de l'Art Oratoire, et de la Fiction de la Fable. Paris: 1560. V. 37

AUGEREAN, YAROUTHIUN

Grammr English and Armenian. Venice: 1817. V. 46

AUGSBURG. CATHOLISCHE GYMNASIUM SANTA ANNA

Instrvction, und Ordnung/Fur die Herrn Rectorem, und Praeceptores dess Evangelischen Gymnasij bey S. Anna. Augsburg: 1634. V. 42

AUGSBURG, DIOCESE OF

Statuta Diocesana Reuerendissimi in Chr(ist)o Patris et D(omi)ni Henrich Ep. Augusten(sis). Augsburg: 1506. V. 44

AUGSBURG. GYMNASIUM SOCIETATIS JESU

Ritterlicher Kampff/In Welchem der Heylige Wencesslaus/Hertzog inn Boehem/Wider den Tyrannen Radisslaum/von den Englen beschutzt Und Verfochten Worden. Augsburg: 1636. V. 42

AUGUSTIN, ANTOINE

De Emmendatione Gratiani, Dialogorum Libri Duo . . . ad Haec Andreae Schotti Oratio in Funere. Paris: 1607. V. 45

AUGUSTIN, JAMES M.

In Memory of the Late Joseph Numa Augustin, Jr., Lieutenant of the 274th U.S. Infantry Regiment, Who Fell At . . . San Juan Hill . . . New Orleans: 1898. V. 46

AUGUSTIN, JOHN ALCEE

War Flowers, Reminiscences of Four Years' Campaigning. Respectfully Dedicated to the Ladies of New Orleans. New Orleans: 1865. V. 37; 38; 39

AUGUSTINE, AURELIUS

Incomentiano li Solliloquij . . . in Uolgare. Milan: 1480. V. 37

AUGUSTINE, AURELIUS, SAINT, BP. OF HIPPO

S. Aurelli Augustini di Civitate del Libri XXII. N.P.: 1930. V. 45

AUGUSTINIAN d. 1639

Les Oeuvres Spirituelles. Tournay: 1665. V. 39

AUGUSTINIUS, AURELIUS, SAINT, BP. OF HIPPO

Confessionum. Coloniae Agrippinae: 1629. V. 39

Epistole Pulcherrime. Venice: 1490. V. 39

Opusculum Multarum Bonarum . . . Venice: 1516. V. 45

Pious Breathings. Being the Meditations of St. Augustine, His Treatise of the Love of God, Soliloquies and Manual. London: 1708. V. 39

AUGUSTINUS, AURELIUS

Les Confessions. Paris: 1656. V. 38

De Agone Christiano. De Sermone Domini in Monte. Cologne: 1470. V. 37

De Civitate Dei. Libri xxii . . . (cum) Commentariis per Joan. Lodovicum Vivem. Paris: 1544. V. 37

AUGUSTINUS, AURELIUS, SAINT, BP. OF HIPPO

Confessioni di Sant'Aurelio Agostino, Vescova d'Ippona . . . Venezia: 1775. V. 44

The Confessions of St. Augustine. London: 1900. V. 41; 44

De Civitate Dei. Naples: 1477. V. 45

Epistole Pulcherrime. Venice: 1490. V. 44

Explanatione Libri Psalmorum. Basle: 1489. V. 40

Manuell; or, Little Book of the Contemplation of Christ, or of Gods Worde . . . London: 1575. V. 43

Meditationes, Soliloquia & Manuale. Cologne: 1584. V. 40

Of the Citie of God; with the Learned Comments of Io. Lod. Vives. London: 1610. V. 42

Opuscula . . . cum Duplici Indicio. Paris: 1513. V. 40

A Pretious Booke of Heavenlie Meditations. London: 1612. V. 44

Sermones de Tempore. (with) *Sermones de Sactis and; Opus Quinquaginta Homiliarum.* Basel: 1494-5. V. 41

Sermones de Tempore. (with) *Sermones de Sanctis and: Opus Quinquaginta Homiliarum.* Basel: 1494-95. V. 42

AUGUSTINUS TRIUMPHUS DE ANCONA

Summa de Potestate Ecclesiastica. Augsburg: 1743. V. 46

AUGUSTUS, JOHN

Fifty-Two Drawings. With an Introduction by Lord David Cecil. 1957. V. 37

AULDJO, JOHN

Journal of a Visit to Constantinople, and Some of the Greek Islands in the Spring and Summer of 1833. London: 1835. V. 38; 39; 44; 45; 46

AULDJO, JOHN continued

Narrative of an Ascent to the Summit of Mont Blanc, on the 8th and 9th August 1827. London: 1827. V. 41

Sketches of Vesuvius, with Short Accounts of Its Principle Eruptions, From the Commencement of the Christian Era to the Present Time. Naples: 1832. V. 45

AULISIO, DOMENICO 1639-1717

Opuscula de Gymnasii Constructione, Mausolei Architectura, Harmonia Timaica & Numeris Medicis. Naples: 1694. V. 40

AULNOY, MARIE CATHERINE JUMELLE DE BERNEVILLE, COMTESSE D' 1650-1705

The History of Several of the Spanish Nobility Now Living . . . London: 1704. V. 39

The Lady's Travels into Spain; or a Genuine Relation of the Religion, Laws, Commerce, Customs and Manners of that Country. London: 1774. V. 46

Memoirs of the Present State of the Court and Councils of Spain . . . London: 1701. V. 43

Memoirs of the Court of France, and the City of Paris . . . London: 1702. V. 42; 45

Memoirs of the Court of England. London: 1707. V. 37; 40

The Prince of Carency. London: 1719. V. 38; 40; 41; 45; 46

AULNOY, MARIE CATHERINE JUMELLE DE BERNEVILLE, COMTESSE DE d. 1705

The Lady's Travels into Spain; or, a Genuine Relation of the Religion, Laws, Commerce, Customs and Manners of that Country . . . London: 1774. V. 45

AULNOY, MARIE CATHERINE JUMELLE DE BERNVILLE, COMTESSE D' 1650-1705

L'Oranger et l'Abeille, Conte; Suivi de Florine, Reine de l'Isle des Fleurs, Conte. Caen: 1798. V. 39

AULNOY'S Fairy Tales. Philadelphia: 1923. V. 45

AULOY, MARIE CAHTERINE JUMELLE DE BERNEVILLE, COMTESSE D' 1650-1705

The History of the Earl of Warwick, Surnamed the Kingmaker; Containing his Amours, and other Memorable Transactions . . . To which is added, the Remaining Part of the unknown Lady's Pacquet of Letters, Taken from her by a French Privateer . . . London: 1708. V. 37

AULT & WIEBORG CO.

Efficient Inks: The Ault & Wieborg Co. New York: 1930's. V. 39

AULT, NORMAN

The Podgy Book of Tales. London: 1907. V. 45; 46

AUNGERVILLE, RICHARD 1281-1345

The Liber Epistolaris of Richard de Bury. Oxford: 1950. V. 40

Philobiblion. New York. V. 40

Philobiblion. New York: 1889. V. 37; 39; 41

Philobiblon, a Treatise on the Love of Books. Albany: 1861. V. 41

The Philobiblon of Richard De Bury, Bishop of Durham, Treasurer and Chancellor of Edward III. London: 1888. V. 41

The Philobiblon of Richard de Bury. New Rochelle: 1901. V. 40; 41; 44; 46

Philobiblon. San Francisco: 1925. V. 42; 46

Philobiblon of Richard De Bury, Bishop of Durham. San Francisco: 1925. V. 41

The Philobiblon of Richard De Bury. New York: 1945. V. 41

AUNT Babette's Cook Book, Foreign and Domestic Receipts for the Household. Cincinnati: 1893. V. 45

AUNT FANNY

Fanny's Birth-Day. Buffalo: 1866. V. 41

AUNT LAURA

The Bunch of Grapes. Buffalo: 1863. V. 38

Little Katy and Her Mother. Buffalo: 1863. V. 41

A Talk with the Little Folks. Buffalo: 1863. V. 41

AUNT Louisa's Gift Book: The Zoological Gardens. New York: 1882. V. 45

AUNT Louisa's Nursery Favourite. London: 1870. V. 46

AURA Lea, or the Maid with Golden Hair. Richmond: 1864. V. 39; 41

AUREA Biblia. Ulm: 1475. V. 40

AURELIANUS, CAELIUS

Caelii Aureliani Siccensis Tardarum Passionum Libri V.D. Basileae: 1529. V. 44; 45

On Acute Diseases and On Chronic Diseases. Chicago: 1950. V. 45

Tardarum Passionum Libri V. D. Oribasii Sardi Iuliani Caesaris Archiatri Euporiston . . . Basel: 1529. V. 45

AURELIUS ANTONINUS, EMPEROR OF ROME 121-180

The Golden Boke (Book). London: 1553. V. 46

AURELIUS ANTONINUS, MARCUS, EMPEROR OF ROME 121-180

The Commentaries of the Emperor Marcus Antoninus. London: 1747. V. 43

The Emperor Marcus Antoninus His Conversation with Himself . . . London: 1701. V. 41; 43; 46

The Emperor Marcus Antoninus: His Conversation with Himself. London: 1701. V. 38

Marcus Aurelius Antoninus the Roman Emperor, His Meditations Concerning Himself . . . London: 1673. V. 43

Marcus Aurelius Antoninus the Roman Emperour, His Meditations Concerning Himselfe. London: 1635. V. 38

Meditations concerning Himself: Treating of a Naturall Mans Happinesse . . . London: 1635. V. 46

The Meditations of Emperor Marcus Aurelius Antoninus. Glasgow: 1742. V. 42; 45

The Meditations of the Emperor Marcus Aurelius Antoninus. Glasgow: 1752. V. 42; 45

Reflexions Morales. Amsterdam: 1691. V. 43

The Roman Emperor, His Meditations, Concerning Himself. London: 1673. V. 40

The Thoughts of the Emperor Marcus Aurelius. London: 1897. V. 43

The Thoughts of the Emperor Marcus Aurelius Antoninus. London: 1902. V. 42; 44

The Thoughts of the Emperor Marcus Aurelius Antoninus. London: 1909. V. 38; 39

The Thoughts of the Emperor Marcus Aurelius Antoninus. 1909. V. 40; 42; 45

Thoughts. London: 1909. V. 39

The Thoughts of the Emperor Marcus Aurelius Antoninus. London: 1909. V. 46

The Thoughts of the Emperor Marcus Antoninus. London: 1912. V. 37

The Thoughts of the Emperor Marcus Aurelius Antonius. Translated by George Long. London: 1909. V. 37

AURELIUS VICTOR

Historiae Romanae Breviarium. Ex Bibliotheca Andreae Schotti: Cuiuseriam Notae Adiectae sunt. (bound with) DE Vita et Moribus Imperatorum Romanorum. Antwerp: 1579. V. 37

AURORA Australis. Auckland: 1988. V. 40; 45

AUSCHER, E. S.

A History and Description of French Porcelain. London: 1905. V. 37; 41; 44

AUSLANDER, JOSEPH

Five American Immortals. Worcester: 1940. V. 38

Letters to Women. New York: 1929. V. 42; 43

AUSMO, NICOLAUS DE d. 1454

Supplementum Pisanellae et Canones Poenitentiales Fratris Astensis. Liber qui Dicitur Supplementum. Venice: 1473. V. 43

AUSONIUS, DECIMUS MAGNUS

Opera in Meliorem Ordinem Digesta. Lyon: 1575, 1574. V. 38

Patchwork Quilt. Poems. London. V. 43

Patchwork Quilt - Poems. London: 1930. V. 38

AUSONIUS, DECIUS MAGNUS

Omnia Opera Nuper Maxima Diligentia Recognita Atque Excusa. Florentiae: 1517. V. 39

Opera, Tertiae Fere Partis Complemento Auctiora, et Diligentiore Quam Hactenus, Censura Recognita . . . Lugduni: 1558. V. 39

AUST, FELIX

Cash as Cash Can. Jagstfeld: 1990. V. 45

AUST, SRAH MAESE MURRAY 1744-1811

A Companion and Useful Guide to the Beauties of Scotland, to the Lakes of Westmorland, Cumberland and Lancashire and to the Curiosities of Cravern in the West Riding of Yorkshire . . . London: 1799. V. 42

AUSTEN, J.

Three Evening Prayers. 1940. V. 43

AUSTEN, JAMES

The Loiterer. Oxford: 1789-90. V. 43

The Loiterer . . . Dublin: 1792. V. 42

AUSTEN, JANE 1775-1817

Charades. London: 1895. V. 46

Collected Novels. London: 1988. V. 46

The Complete Novels. London;: (1928). V. 37

Emma. London: 1816. V. 37; 38; 39; 40; 42; 43; 44; 45; 46

Emma: a Novel. Philadelphia: 1833. V. 39

Emma. New York: 1906. V. 40

AUSTEN, JANE 1775-1817 continued

Emma. London: 1954/1948. V. 42; 44

Emma. New York: 1964. V. 46

Five Letters from Jane Austen to Her Niece Fanny Knight Printed in Facsimile. Oxford: 1924. V. 41; 43; 44

The Horrid Novels. The Northanger Set of Jane Austen's Horrid Novels. London: 1968. V. 45

Jane Austen's Letters to Her Sister Cassandra and Others. Oxford: 1932. V. 40

Jane Austen's Letters to Her Sister Cassandra. Oxford: 1964. V. 41; 42

Lady Susan. Oxford: 1925. V. 41; 43

Love and Friendship and Other Early Works. New York: 1922. V. 41; 43

Mansfield Park. London: 1814. V. 38; 42; 45; 46

Mansfield Park; a Novel. Philadelphia: 1832. V. 44

Mansfield Park. London: 1833. V. 38; 40; 46

Mansfield Park. London: 1851. V. 44

Mansfield Park. London: 1856. V. 40; 42

Mansfield Park. New York: 1906. V. 40

Northanger Abbey; and Persuasion. London: 1818. V. 37; 38; 39; 40; 45

Northanger Abbey; and Persuasion. London: 1818. V. 40

Northanger Abbey. London: 1833. V. 40

Northanger Abbey, and Persuasion. London: 1850. V. 44

Northanger Abbey. New York: 1906. V. 40

The Northanger Set of Jane Austen Horrid Novels. London: 1968. V. 42

Northanger Abbey. New York: 1971. V. 45

Novels of . . . London. V. 38

The Novels. London: 1833-36. V. 37; 39

The Novels of . . . Philadelphia: 1838. V. 45

Novels. London: 1875. V. 41

Novels. London: 1879-83. V. 44

The Novels. London: 1895-96. V. 43

The Novels. London: 1895-97. V. 42

The Novels in Ten Volumes. London: 1896-97. V. 39

The Novels. London: and New York: 1897-98. V. 45

The Novels. Edinburgh: 1898. V. 45

The Novels of . . . London: 1898. V. 46

The Novels. London: & New York: 1898-1901. V. 45

The Novels. London: 1902-04. V. 39

The Novels. London: 1903-07. V. 39; 41

The Novels. Boston: 1905. V. 42

The Novels . . . Edinburgh: 1905. V. 46

Novels and Letters. New York: 1906. V. 39; 40; 45

The Novels. London: 1906/07/29. V. 39; 41

The Novels. Edinburgh: 1911. V. 42

The Novels. Edinburgh: 1911-12. V. 37; 42

The Novels of Jane Austen. Edinburgh: 1911-12. V. 37; 44

The Novels. Illustrated with Charming Color Plates by Charles E. Brock. London: 1922. V. 37

Novels. Oxford: 1923. V. 37; 39; 40; 41; 42; 44

Novels. Letters. Oxford: 1923-32. V. 42

The Novels. Oxford: 1926. V. 39

The Complete Novels of . . . London: 1928. V. 46

Novels. Oxford: 1932. V. 40

The Novels. Oxford: 1943. V. 42

The Novels. Oxford: 1948-49. V. 44

The Novels of . . . London: 1974. V. 43

The Novels of Jane Austen. London: 1978. V. 46

The Novels, and Shorter Works. London: 1984. V. 38

Persuasion. New York: 1906. V. 40

Plan of a Novel, According to Hints from Various Quarters . . . Oxford: 1926. V. 44

Pride and Prejudice. London: 1813. V. 44; 45; 46

Pride and Prejudice. London: 1817. V. 37; 38; 42; 44; 45

Pride and Prejudice. London: 1833. V. 38

Pride and Prejudice. London: 1853. V. 40; 42

Pride and Prejudice, a Novel. London: 1870. V. 43

Pride and Prejudice. London: 1894. V. 38

Pride and Prejudice. New York: 1894. V. 41

Pride and Prejudice. London: 1897. V. 39

Pride and Prejudice. Boston: 1940. V. 41; 45

Pride and Prejudice. New York: 1940. V. 43

Pride and Prejudice. London: 1957. V. 40

(Sandition) Fragment of a Novel . . . Now First Printed from the Manuscript. Oxford: 1925. V. 37; 39; 41; 43

Sense and Sensibility. London: 1811. V. 43; 45; 46

Sense and Sensibility. London: 1813. V. 38; 42; 44

Sense and Sensibility. London: 1833. V. 37; 43

Sense and Sensibility. Philadelphia: 1833. V. 38; 40

Sense and Sensibility. London: 1850. V. 39; 41

Sense and Sensibility. London: 1856. V. 40; 42

Sense and Sensibility. London: 1870. V. 38; 43

Sense and Sensibility. London: 1886. V. 45

Sense and Sensibility. London: 1947. V. 46

Sense and Sensibility. New York: 1957. V. 38

The Series of English Idylls. London: 1908-09. V. 41

Two Chapters of 'Persuasion' Printed From Jane Austen's Autograph. Oxford: 1926. V. 45

Volume the First. 'Now First Printed from the Manuscript In the Bodleian Library.' Oxford: 1933. V. 37

The Watsons. Oxford: 1927. V. 37; 39; 41; 42; 43

The Works. London. V. 38; 45

Works. New York: 1859. V. 39

Works. New Edition. London: 1866-71. V. 37

Works. London: 1907-09. V. 37

The Works . . . London: 1907-1909. V. 37

Works. London: 1910. V. 42

Works. London: (1923). V. 37

The Works. Boston: 1930. V. 43

Works. London: 1930-31. V. 39; 42

Works. London: (1930-31). V. 37

The Works. London: 1933-34. V. 37

Works. London: 1957-62. V. 41

Works. London: 1975. V. 42

Works. London: (ca. 1910). V. 37

AUSTEN, JOHN

Daphnis & Chloe. Translated out of the Greek of Longus by George Thornley in 1657. London: 1925. V. 37

The Novels of . . . Edinburgh: 1906. V. 46

The Novels. London: 1922. V. 38

The Works. Boston: 1930. V. 44

AUSTEN-LEIGH, J. E.

A Memoir. London: 1870. V. 37; 39; 41; 43; 45; 46

AUSTEN-LEIGH, JAMES EDWARD

Memoir of Jane Austen . . . Oxford: 1926. V. 37

AUSTEN, RALPH

A Treatise of Fruit-Trees. (with) The Spirituall Use of an Orchard, or Garden of Fruit-Trees. (with) Observations Upon Some of Sir Francis Bacon's Naturall History as it Concernes, Fruit-Trees, Fruits and Flowers. Oxford: 1657. V. 38

A Treatise of Fruit Trees, Shewing the Manner of Grafting, Planting, Pruning and Ordering of Them in all Respects. (with) The Spirituall Use of an Orcharad, or Garden of Fruit Trees. (with) Observations Upon Some Part of Sir Francis Bacon's . . . Oxford: 1657-58. V. 38; 41

AUSTEN, SARAH

The Story Without an End. London: 1912. V. 43

AUSTER, PAUL

Disappearances. Woodstock: 1988. V. 44

A Little Anthology of Surrealist Poems. New York: 1972. V. 46

Unearth. 1974; V. 43

Unearth. Weston: 1974. V. 46

Wall Writing. Berkeley: 1976. V. 46

AUSTIN, ALFRED

Lamia's Winter Quarters. London: 1907. V. 44

AUSTIN, BENJAMIN

Constitutional Republicanism in Opposition to Fallacious Federalism, as Published Occasionally in the Independent Chronicle, under the signature of Old-South. To which is added, a Prefatory Address to the Citizens of the U.S . . . . Boston: 1803. V. 37; 38; 43

AUSTIN, DAVID

The Millennium; or, The Thousand Years of Prosperity, Promised to the Church of God . . . Shortly to Commence . . . Elizabeth Town: 1794. V. 42

AUSTIN, EMILY M.

Mormonism: or, Life Among the Mormons. Madison,: 1882. V. 39

AUSTIN, GABRIEL

Four Oaks Farm Together With Four Oaks Library. Somerville: 1967. V. 42

Four Oaks Farm and Four Oaks Farm Library. Somerville, NJ: 1967. V. 37

The Library of Jean Grolier. New York: 1971. V. 46

AUTHENTIC Memoirs, Memorandums and Confessions. London: 1800? V. 41

AUTHENTIC Narrative of the Loss of His Majesty's Frigate Apollo. London: 1804. V. 46

AUTHENTIC Papers from America: Submitted to the Dispassioante Consideration of the Public. London: 1775. V. 45

AUTHENTIC Papers Relataive to the Expedition Against the Charibbs, and the Sale of Lands in the Island of St. Vincent. London: 1773. V. 37; 46

AUTHENTIC Papers Relating to the Expedition Against Carthagena . . . London: 1744. V. 45

AN AUTHENTICK Account of the Conduct of the Young Chevalier, from His First Arrival in Paris, After His Defeat at Cullodden, to the Conclusion of the Peace at Aix-La-Chapelle . . . London: 1749. V. 41

AN AUTHENTICK Copy of the Acts of the Processe Against the English at Amboyna. London: 1632. V. 39

AUTHORS CLUB, NEW YORK.

Liber Scriptorium. New York: 1893. V. 39; 40; 41

The Second Book of the Author's Club: Liber Scriptorum. New York: 1921. V. 40; 41

THE AUTHOR'S Printing and Publishing Assistant. London: 1842. V. 38

AUTHORS Take Sides on Vietnam. New York: 1967. V. 44

AUTOBIOGRAPHY of Barnum or the Opening of the Oyster. Danbury: 1889. V. 38

THE AUTOBITURARY of a West Pointer. New York: 1882. V. 40

AUTOGRAPH Leaves of Our Country's Authors. Baltimore: 1864. V. 45

AUTOGRAPHS for Freedom. Auburn & Rochester: 1854. V. 43

AUTOMOBILE CLUB OF GREAT BRITAIN & IRELAND

Official Programme of the 1,000 Mile Motor Vehicle Trial, Starting from London on Monday April 23rd, 1900 . . . 1900. V. 40

AUTOMOBILE CLUB OF SOUTHERN CALIFORNIA

A Pictorial Story of Transportation in the Southwest. (with) A Descriptive Leaflet by John S. Gorby. Los Angeles: 1930. V. 41

THE AUTOMOBILE Handbook and Guide, an Illustrated Treatise on Petrol, Steam and Electric Cars for all Puroses. London: 1900. V. 44

AUTOMOBILE MANUFACTURING CO.

The Automobile Handbook and Guide. London: 1900. V. 46

AUTON, RICHARD

Essays and Sketches of Character by the late Richard yton, Esq. With a Memoir of his Life. London: 1825. V. 37

AUVIGNY, J. DU CASTRE D'

Memoirs of Madame de Barneveldt. London: 1796. V. 46

AVANCINUS, NICHOLAS 1612-1685

Imperium Romanao-Germanicum sive Quinquaginta Imperatorum ac Germaniae Regum Elogia . . . Vienna: 1663. V. 43

AVE Vale Robinson Jeffers . . . This Little Volume Pays Homage to a Man Who Has Left Us a Legacy That Will Be Recorded in the Annals of Literature As One of the Greatest . . . San Francisco: 1962. V. 43

AVEBURY, JOHN LUBBOCK

The Origin of Civilisation and the Primitive Condition of Man. New York: 1870. V. 39

AVEBURY, JOHN LUBBOCK, BARON 1834-1913

The Scenery of England and the Causes to Which It Is Due. London: 1902. V. 43

AVEDON, RICHARD

In the American West. New York: 1985. V. 45; 46
Nothing Personal. New York: 1964. V. 37; 38
Observations. Photographs. New York: 1959. V. 37
Photographies 1947-77. Paris: 1977. V. 41
Portraits. New York: 1976. V. 44; 45; 46
Portraits. New York: 1977. V. 38

AVEIRO, PANTALIAO DE

Itinerario de Terra Sancta, e Todas Suas Particularidades . . . Lisbon: 1596. V. 45

AVELING, E. M.

Shelley's Socialism. London: 1888. V. 42

AVELLA, GIOVANNI D' fl. 1657

Regole di Musica . . . Rome: 1657. V. 46

AVENARIUS, JOHANN

(Hebrew) Hoc est Liber Radicum seu Lexicon Ebraicum, in Quo Omnium Vocabulorum Bibliocorum . . . Wittenberg: 1588. V. 45; 46

AVENARIUS, JOHANNES 1477-1534

Liber Radicum seu Lexicon Ebraicum . . . Wittenberg: 1568. V. 37; 38
Liber Radicum Seu Lexicon Ebraicum. Wittenberg: 1589. V. 40

AVENTINUS, JOANNES 1477-1534

Annalium Boiorum Libri VII. Basle: 1580. V. 38; 41

AVENTURES et Espiegleries de Lazarille de Tormes, Ecrites par lui-me. Paris: 1801. V. 45

AVERILL, ESTHER

Daniel Boone. Paris: 1931. V. 46

AVERMAETE, ROGER

Frans Masereel. London: 1977. V. 45; 46

AVERY, C. LOUISE

American Silver of the XVII & XVIII Centuries. New York: 1920. V. 38

AVERY, DAVID

Two Sermons on the Nature and Evil of Professors of Religion Not Bridling the Tongue. Boston: 1791. V. 43

AVERY, GILES B.

A Juvenile Guide, or Manual of Good Manners. Canterbury: 1844. V. 40

AVERY, OSWALD

Studies on the Chemical nature of the Substance Including Transformation of Pneumococcal Types . . . V. 40

AVERY, P. O.

History of 4th Illinois Cavlary Regt. Humboldt: 1903. V. 39

AVERY, RUFUS

Narrative of Jonathan Rathbun, with Accurate Accounts of the Capture of Groton Fort, the Massacre that Followed and the Sacking and Burning of New London, September 6, 1781. New London?: 1840. V. 42; 45

AVERY, S. W.

The Dyspeptic's Monitor, or, The Nature, Causes and Cure of . . . Dyspepsia, Indigestion, Liver Complaint, Hypochondriasis, Melancholy &c. New York: 1830. V. 40

AVERY, SAMUEL PUTNAM

Catalogue Raisonnee. Works on Bookbinding Practical and Historical. New York: 1903. V. 46

THE AVIARY; or, Magazine of British Melody. London: 1744. V. 43

AVICENNA

Canon of Medicine. Rome: 1593. V. 38

AVICENNA, IBN SINA

Canon Medicinae . . . Rome: 1593. V. 42

AVICULTURE, a Treatise on the Manaagement of Foreign and British Birds in Captivity. Hertford: 1936, 1931. V. 37

AVICULTURE, A Treatise on the Management of Foreign and British Birds in Captivity. Hertford: 1925-31. V. 37; 38

AVILA, FRANCISCO DE

Conciones in Sacrum Quadragesimae Tempus & in Dies Dicatos Sanctis illo Tempore Occurrentes. Alcala: 1589. V. 37

AVILA, JUAN DE, SAINT 1500-1569

The Audi Filia, or a Rich Cabinet Full of Spirituall Jewells . . . N.P.: 1620. V. 45
The Audi Filia, or a Rich Cabinet Full of Spiritual Jewels. St. Omer: 1620. V. 37; 40; 45
Triumph Uber die Welt, das Fleisch und den Teufel. Munich: 1601. V. 46

AVILA Y ZUNIGA, LUIS DE

Brieve Commentario . . . Nella Guerra Della Germania Fatta dal Felicissimo & Maximo Imperadore Carlo. 1548. V. 42

AVILER, AUGUSTIN CHARLES D'

Cours d'Architecture . . . Paris: 1691. V. 42

AVILLEZ JUSARTE DE SOUSA TAVARES, JORGE D'

Manifesto aos Cidadaos do Rio de Janeiro. Rio de Janeiro: 1822. V. 39

AVINOFF, ANDREY

Nationality Rooms of the University of Pittsburgh. Pittsburgh: 1947. V. 46

AVIRETT, JAMES B.

The Memoirs of General Turn Asby and His Compeers. Baltimore: 1867. V. 37

AVISON, CHARLES

An Essay on Musical Expression. London: 1752. V. 39

An Essay on Musical Expression with Alterations and Large Additions to Which is Added a Letter to the Author Concerning the Music of the Ancients . . . London: 1775. V. 38; 40

AVOGADRO DI QUAREGNA E DI CERRETO, LORENZO ROMANO AMEDEO

Traite Elementaire de Physique. V. 46

AVVISI Del Giapone De Gli Anni MDLXXXII, LXXXIII, et LXXXIV. Con Alcuni Altri Della Cina dell' LXXXIII. et LXXXIV . . . Roma. V. 43

aWASSON, R. GORDON

Soma; Divine Mushroom of Immortality. New York: (1968). V. 37

AWDLAWY, JOHN

Alia Cantalena de Sancta Maria. Long Crendon: 1926. V. 44; 46

AWDLAY, JOHN

Alia Cantalena de Sancta Maria. Lon Crendon, Bucks: 1926. V. 42

Alia Cantalena de Sancta Maria. Long Crendon, Bucks: 1926. V. 39

AWFUL Calamities; or, the Shipwrecks of December 1839, Being a Full Account of the Dreadful Hurricane of Dec. 15, 21 & 27 on the Coast of Massachusetts . . . Boston: 1840. V. 43

AWSITER, JOHN

An Essay on the Effects of Poium Considered as a Poison. London: 1763. V. 37

AXE, J. WORTLEY

The Horse. Its Treatment in Health and Disease. London: 1905-08. V. 39; 44

The Horse: Its Treatment in Health and Disease. London: 1906. V. 37; 40

AXELROD, GEORGE

The Seven Year Itch. New York: 1953. V. 39; 45

AXENFELD

The Bacteriology of the Eye . . . London: 1908. V. 44

AXFORD, LAVONNE BRADY

English Language Cookbooks, 1600-1973. Detroit: (1976). V. 39

English Language Cookbooks, 1600-1973. Detroit: 1976. V. 37

AXON, ERNEST

Bygone Lancashire. London: 1892. V. 39

AXON, WILLIAM

The Suspected Spy; or, the Mysterious Stranger. Chester: 1844. V. 45

AYER, A. J.

More of My Life. London: 1984. V. 40

AYER, I. WINSLOW

Life in the Wilds of America, and Wonders of the West in and Beyond the Bounds of Civilization. Grand Rapids, Mich.: 1880. V. 37

AYERS, JOHN

The Bauer Collection, Geneva: Japanese Ceramics. Geneve: 1982. V. 42

AYLIFFE, JOHN

The Ancient and Present State of the University of Oxford. London: 1723. V. 39

The Case of Dr. Ayliffe, at Oxford. London: 1716. V. 38

AYLING, AUGUSTUS

Revised Register of the Soldiers and Sailors of New Hampshire in the War of the Rebellion 1861-1866. Concord: 1895. V. 42

AYLING, STEPHEN

Photographs from Sketches by Augustus Welby N. Pugin. London: 1865. V. 38; 39; 42

AYLMER, EDWARD

Memoirs of George Edwards, Alias Wards, the Acknowledged Spy, and Principal Instigator in the Cato-Street Plot . . . London: 1820. V. 38

AYLMER, F. J.

The Aylmers of Ireland. London: 1931. V. 38

AYLMER, FENTON

A Cruise in the Pacific. London: 1860. V. 38

AYLOFFE, JOSEPH

Calendars of the Ancient Charters, and of the Welch and Scottish Rolls, Now Remaining in the Tower of London. London: 1774. V. 40

An Historical Description of an Ancient Picture in Windsor Castle, Representing the Interview Between King Henry VIII and the French King Francis I Between Guines and Ardres in the Year 1520. London: 1773. V. 38; 42; 46

AYLWARD, ALFRED

The Transavaal of To-Day: War, Witchcraft, Sport and Spoils in South Africa. London: 1878. V. 42; 43; 44; 45

AYMONIN, GERARD G.

The Besler Florilegium, Plants of the Four Seasons. New York: 1989. V. 45

AY MORNAY, DE SEIGNEUR DU PLESSIS-MARLY, CALLED DU PLESSIS-MORN 1549-1623

Memoires. Amsterdam: 1652-1651. V. 37

A Work Concerning the Trunesse of Christian Religion, Written in French. London: 1604. V. 37

AYRAULT, PIERRE

Rerum ab Omni Antiquitate Judicatarum Pandectae, Recognitae a Philippo Andrea Oldenburgeror. Genevae: 1677. V. 38

AYRE, JOSEPH

Pathalogical Researches into the Nature and Treatment of Dropsy of the Brain, Chest, Abdomen, Ovarium and Skin . . . London: 1829. V. 40; 41; 44; 45

AYRE, WILLIAM

The Life of Alexnder Pope, Esq. London: 1754. V. 38

Memoirs of the Life and Writings of Alexander Pope. London: 1745. V. 38

AYRES, ATLEE B.

Mexican Architecture. New York: 1926. V. 40; 41; 42; 46

AYRES, DANIEL

Contributions to Practical Surgery. New York: 1857. V. 44

AYRES, GEORGE B.

How to Paint Photographs in Water Colors, and In Oil . . . New York: 1878. V. 42

AYRES, PHILIP

Emblems of Love, in Four Dialogues. London: 1687. V. 42; 44

Emblems of Love in Four Languages. London: 1690. V. 38; 39

Lyric Poems, Made in Imitation of the Italians. Of which, many are Translations from Other Languages. London: 1687. V. 37

AYRES, PHILLIP

Emblems of Love, in Four Languages. London: 1683. V. 42; 46

AYRES, WILLIAM P.

The Garden Companion and Florists' Guide. January to October, 1852. London: 1852. V. 46

AYRTON, EDWARD

Pre-Dynastic Cemetery at El Mahasna. London: 1911. V. 37; 40

AYRTON, ELIZABETH

Royal Favourites - Recipes from Palace Kitchens. London: 1971. V. 40

AYRTON, JOHN

Philosophy in Sport Made Science in Earnest . . . (By John Ayrton. Paris). London: 1827. V. 37

AYRTON, M. C.

Child-Life in Japan, and Japanese Child-Stories. London. V. 38

AYRTON, MAXWELL

Wrought Iron and Its Decorative Use. London: 1929. V. 38

AYRTON, MICHAEL

Fabrications. London. V. 41

Fabrications. London: 1972. V. 44

Giovanni Pisano, Sculptor. London: 1969. V. 42; 44

Summer's Last Will and Testament. London: 1946. V. 37

AYRTON, WILLIAM

The Adventure of a Salmon in the River Dee. London: 1853. V. 43

Mr. Barnacle and His Boat. N.P.: 1855. V. 39; 44

AYSCOUGH, GEORGE EDWARD

Letters from an Officer in the Guards to His Friend in England. London: 1778. V. 45

AYSCOUGH, JAMES

Optician: a Short Account of the Nature and Use of Spectacles. London: 1750. V. 39

A Short Account of the Eye and Nature of Vision. London: 1752. V. 39; 42

A Short account of the nature and use of spectacles. In which is recommended, a kind of glass for spectacles, preferable to any hiterto made use of for that purpose. 1750. V. 37

AYSCOUGH, SAMUEL

An Index to the Remarkable Passages and Words Made Use of by Shakespeare. London: 1790. V. 38; 40

AYTON, RICHARD

A Voyage Round Great Britain Undertaken . . . 1813 and 1823, With a Series of Views Illustrative of the Character and Prominent Features of the Coast . . . London: 1978. V. 39

AYTOUN, WILLIAM E.

Lays of the Scottish Cavaliers and Other Poems. Edinburgh: 1881. V. 39

AYTOUN, WILLIAM EDMONDSTOUNE

Lays of the Scottish Cavaliers and Other Poems. Edinburgh: 1865. V. 41

AYTOUN, WILLIAM EDMONSTOUNE

The Book of Ballads. London: 1849. V. 38

Firmilian; or the Student of Badajoz. London: 1854. V. 45

Lays of the Scottish Cavaliers, and Other Poems. Edinburgh: 1870. V. 38

AZARA, FELIX DE

Descripcion e Historia del Paraguay y del Rio de la Plata. Madrid: 1847. V. 38

Viaggi nell' America Meridionale . . . Milan: 1817. V. 38

AZEGLIO, MASSIMO D'

The Challenge of Barletta. London: 1880. V. 44

AZEREDO COUTINHO, JOSE JOAQUIM DA CUNHA DE

Allegacao Juridica, Na Qual se Mostra, que Sao do Padroado da Coroa, e Nao da Ordem Militar de Cristo, as Igrejas, Dignidades, e Beneficios dos Bispados do Cabo de Bojador Para o Sul, em Que se Compreendem os Bispados de Cabo Verde . . . Lisbon: 1804. V. 39

Copia da Carta que a Sua Magestade o Senhor Rey D. Joao Vi . . . London: 1817. V. 38

Discurso Sobre o Estado Actual das minas do Brazil . . . Lisbon: 1804. V. 38

AZERO, RAYMUNDO

Premios de la Obedienciaa Castigos de la Inobediencia . . . Santa Fe de Bogota: 1782. V. 38

AZMI, IFTIKHAR

The Garden of the Night. 1979. V. 40

AZNAR DE POLANCO, JUAN CLAUDIO

Arte Nuevo de Escribir Por Preceptos Gometircos y Reglas Mathematicas . . . Mardid: 1719. V. 46

AZUELA, MARIANO

The Underdog. New York: 1929. V. 42

AZUNI, DOMENICO ALBERTO 1740-1827

The Maritime Law of Europe. New York: 1806. V. 38; 40; 45

B

B., A.

Copy of a Letter from Paris, December 20, 1748. N.P.: 1748. V. 43

A Letter from a Friend in Abingdon, to a Gentleman in London, Concerning the Election of Burgesses for the Ensuing Parliament. 1679. V. 44; 45

The Life or the Ecclesiastical Historie of S. Thomas, Archbhishop of Canterby. Colloniae: 1639. V. 46

The Treaty of Seville and the Measures That Have Been Taken for the Four Last Years, Impartially Considered. In a Letter to a Friend. London: 1730. V. 41

B., G.

The Advantages of the Revolution Illustrated, by a View of the Present State of Great Britain. London: 1753. V. 42

B., H.

Political Sketches &c. London: 1829-51. V. 46

B., H. M.

Mad Minstrel; or, the Irish Exile; and Other Poems. London: 1812. V. 41; 42

B., J.

The Pet Lamb in Rhyme, and the Ladder of Learning. London: 1829. V. 39

B., T.

The Loyalty of the Last Long Parliament. London: 1681. V. 39

BAAS, JOHANNES HERMANN

Outlines of the History of Medicine and the Medical Profession. New York: 1889. V. 45

BAAZ, JAN

Inventarium Ecclesiae Sveo-Gothorum Continens Integram Historiam Eccles. Svec. Libris VIII Descriptam . . . ad Praesentem Annum Christi MDC.XLII. Lyncoping: 1642. V. 39

BABB, T. A.

In the Bosom of the Comanches . . . Savage Indian Life, Massacre and Captivity, Truthfully Told by a Surviving Capative. Amarillo: 1923. V. 46

In the Bosom of the Comanches, a Thrilling Tale of Savage Indian Life, Massacre and Captivity Truthfull Told by a Surviving Captive. Amarillo: 1912. V. 37

BABBAGE, CHARLES 1792-1871

The Ninth Bridgewater Treatise. London: 1837. V. 41

The Ninth Bridgewater Treatise. London: 1838. V. 38

On the Economy of Machinery and Manufactures. London: 1832. V. 37; 38; 39; 41; 42; 44

On the Economy of Machinery and Manufactures. London: 1832, 1833. V. 39

On the Economy of Machinery and Manufactures. London: 1833. V. 37; 38; 40; 42; 43; 45

On the Economy of Machinery and Manufactures. London: 1835. V. 37; 38; 41

On the Economy of Machinery and Manufactures. London: 1832 (1833). V. 37

Passages from the Life of a Philosopher. London: 1864. V. 42

Passages from the Life of a Philosopher. London: 1864. V. 41

Passages from the Life of a Philosopher. London: 1864. V. 37; 38; 41; 42; 43

Passages from the Life of a Philosopher. London: 1854. V. 37

Reflections on the decline of Science in England and On Some of Its Causes. London: 1830. V. 41

Tables of the Logarithms of the Natural Numbers from 1 to 1080000. London: 1844. V. 38

BABBITT, CHARLES H.

Early Days at Council Bluffs. Washington: 1916. V. 42; 45

BABBITT, E. L.

The Allegheny Pilot . . . Freeport: 1855. V. 44

BABBITT, EDWIN D.

The Principles of Light and Color. New York: 1878. V. 38

BABBITT, IRVING

On Being Creative. And Other Essays. London: 1932. V. 37

BABCOCK, A. E.

Military Posts . . . a Report of Inspection of Military Posts. Washington: 1867. V. 39

BABCOCK, CHARLES A.

Venango County Pennsylvania; Her Pioneers and People Embracing a General History of the County. Chicago: 1919. V. 41; 42

BABCOCK, HAVILAH

The Education of Pretty Boy. N: 1960. V. 37; 44; 46

I Don't Want to Shoot an Elephant. New York: 1958. V. 39

My Health is Better in November. Columbia: 1947. V. 43

My Heath is Better in November: Thirty-Five Stories of Hunting and Fishing in the South. New York: 1952. V. 37

Tales of Quails 'n Such. New York: 1951. V. 43

BABCOCK, LOUIS M.

The Denver Annual. Denver: 1890. V. 39; 43

Our American Resorts. Washington: 1883. V. 45

BABCOCK, PHILIP H.

Falling Leaves. New York: 1937. V. 39

BABCOCK, RUFUS

Forty Years of Pioneer Life. Philadelphia: 1864. V. 41; 43

BABCOCK, WILLOUGHBY M.

Selections from the Letters and Diaries of Brevet Brigadie General Willoughby Babcock of the Seventy Fifth New York Volunteers. Albany: 1922. V. 42

BABER, JOHN

To the King, Upon the Queens Being Deliver'd of a Son, June the 10th, MDCLXXXVIII. London: 1688. V. 43

BABER, ZEHIR-ED-DIN MUHAMMED, EMPEROR OF HINDUSTAN

Memoirs . . . Written by Himself . . . London: 1826. V. 39

THE BABES in the Wood. London: 1849. V. 44
THE BABES in the Wood. London: 1854. V. 45
THE BABES in the Wood. London: 1861. V. 43

BABEUF, FRANCOIS NOEL

The Defense of Gracchus Babeuf Before the High Court of Vendome. Northampton: 1964. V. 37

BABEUF, GRACCHUS

The Defense of Gracchus Babeuf Before the High Court of Vendome. Northampton: 1964. V. 37

BABINGTON, C. C.

Flora Bathoniensis . . . Plants Indigenous to the Vicinity of Bath. Bath & Bristol: 1834. V. 43

BABINGTON, CHURCHILL 1821-1889

The Influence of Christianity in Promoting the Abolition of Slavery in Europe. Cambridge: 1846. V. 42; 45

BABINGTON, GERVASE

The Works. London: 1637. V. 45

BABINGTON, THOMAS

Practical View of Christian Education In Its Early Stages. London: 1814. V. 41; 45

BABINGTON, WILLIAM

Outlines of a Course of Lectures on the practice of Medicine, as delivered in the Medical School of Guy's Hospital by William Babington, MD, FRS, and James Curry, MD, FAS . . . London: 1802-06. V. 37

A Syllabus of a Course of Chemical Lectures Read at Guy's Hospital. London: 1802. V. 43

BABINGTON, ZACHARY

Advice to Grand Jurors in Cases of Blood. London: 1677. V. 46

BABLET, DENIS

The Revolution of Stage Design in the 20th Century. Paris/New York: (1977). V. 37

BABSON, GRACE K.

A Descriptive Catalogue of the Grace K. Babson Collection of the Works of Sir Isaac Newton and the Material Relating to Him in the Babson Inst. Library. New York: 1950. V. 37; 39

A Descriptive Catalogue . . . (with) A Supplement to the Catalogue . . . New York and Babson Park,: 1950-55. V. 37

DES BABSTS und Kayserlicher Wayestat Bundinuss, auss dem Latein, ins Teutstch Transferiert. N.P.: 1546. V. 44

BABY, WILLIAM LEWIS

Souvenirs of the Past, with illustrations. An instructive and amusing work, giving a correct account of the customs and habits of the pioneers of Canada . . . Windsor, Ontario: 1896. V. 37

BABYLONIAN Anthology. North Hills: 1966. V. 37; 38; 44; 45

BACA, MANUEL CABEZA DE

Vicente Silva and His 40 Bandits. Washington: 1947. V. 45; 46

BACALL, LAUREN

By Myself. New York: 1979. V. 45

BACCANELLI, GIOVANNI BATTISTA

De Consensu Medicorum . . . Ejusdem de Consensu Medicorum in Cognoscendis Simplicibus Liber. Venice: 1556. V. 38

BACCHETONI, HIERONYMUS LEOPOLD

Anatomia Medicinae Theoreticae et Practicae Ministra, Cautelisque in Praxi Observandis Illustrata. Oeniponti (Innsbruck): 1740. V. 46

BACCI, ANDREA

Del Tevere Libri Tre. Ne' Quale si Tratta della Natura, & Bonta dell'acque & Specialmente del Tevere & dell'acque Antiche de Roma . . . Venice: 1576. V. 41

De Naturali Vinorum Historia de Vinis Italiae de Convivijs Antiquorum Libri Septem Andreae Baccii Elpidiani Medici atq . . . Romae: 1596. V. 39

De Thermis. Venice: 1571. V. 39; 42; 43; 45

De Thermis. Venice: 1571. V. 43

BACH, JOHANN CHRISTIAN

A Third Collection of Favorite Songs. London: 1771. V. 40

BACH, JOHANN SEBASTIAN

Motetten in Partitur. Leipzig: 1803. V. 40

BACHAUS, THEODORE

Private Presses of San Serriffe. 1980. V. 43

BACHE, A. D.

Observations at the Magnetic and Meteorological Observatory, at the Girgard College, Pennsylvania. Washington: 1845. V. 42; 44

BACHE, FRANKLIN

The Pharmacopoeia of the United States of America. 4th Decennial Revision. Philadelphia: 1863. V. 40

BACHE, JULES S.

A Catalogue of Paintings in the Collection of Jules S. Bache. New York: 1929. V. 44; 45

BACHE, RICHARD

Notes on Colombia, Taken in the Years 1822-3. Philadelphia: 1827. V. 41

BACHELLER, IRVING

Eben Holden. Boston: 1900. V. 43

The Story of Passion. East Aurora: 1901. V. 44

THE BACHELOR'S Own Book, Being the Progress of Mr. Lambkin, (gent.) in the Persuit (sic) of Pleasure and Amusement (sic), nd also in Serch of Health and Happiness. London: 1844. V. 38

BACHER, ROBERT FOX

Atomic Engery States, as Derived from the Analyses of Optical Spectra. New York & London: 1932. V. 42

BACHHOFER, LUDWIG

Early Indian Sculpture. Calcutta: (1929). V. 37

BACHMAIR, JOHN JAMES

A Complete German Grammar. London: 1771, V. 44; 46

A German Grammar, Containing the Theory of the Language through all the parts of Speech . . . Philadelphia: 1788. V. 37

BACHMAN, C. L.

John Bachman. Charleston: 1888. V. 37

BACHMAN, JOHN

Doctrine of the Unity of the Human Race Examined on the Principles of Science. Charleston: 1850. V. 38; 45

Vindication of Rev. Dr John Bachman, of Charleston, S.C. N.P.: 1868. V. 39

BACHMAN, WALTER

Continental Confectionery. London: 1955. V. 39

BACHMANN, C. G.

Ansichten Geschmackvoller Stadt und Landhauser zur Auswahl fur Baulustige und Baugewerken: Vues de Maisons de Ville ou de Campagne . . . Leipzig: 1820. V. 38; 40; 44

BACHOFEN, J. J.

Res Sancta/Res Sacrae. Lexington: 1961. V. 44

BACK, GEORGE 1796-1878

Narrative of the Arctic Land Expedition to the Mouth of the Great Fish River, and Along the Shores of the Arctic Ocean, in the Years 1833, 1834 and 1835. London: 1836. V. 37; 38; 40; 42; 43; 44; 45; 46

Narrative of the Arctic Land Expedition to the Mouth of the Great Fish River, and Along the Shores of the Arctic Ocean, 1833-35. Paris: 1836. V. 42

Narrative of the Arctic Land Expedition to the Mouth of the Great Fish River and Along the Shores of the Arctic Ocean, in the Years 1833, 1834 and 1835. Paris: 1836. V. 37; 42

Narrative of the Arctic Land Expedition to the Mouth of the Great Fish River, and Along the Shores of the Arctic Ocean, in . . . 1833, 1834 and 1835. Philadelphia: 1836. V. 37; 39; 40; 41; 42; 44

Narrative of the Arctic Land Expedition to the Mouth of the Great River, and Along the Shores of the Arctic Ocean in the Years 1833, 34 and 35. Philadelphia: 1836. V. 41; 42

Narrative of an Expedition in H.M.S. Terror, Undertaken With a View to Geographical Discovery on the Arctic Shores, in the Years 1836-7. London: 1838. V. 37; 40; 45

BACKHOUSE, JAMES 1794-1869

Extracts from the Letters of James Backhouse, Now Engaged in a Religious Visit to Van Dieman's Land and New South Wales. London: 1838-41. V. 41

A Narrative of a Visit to the Australian Colonies. London: 1843. V. 46

A Narrative of a Visit to Mauritius and South Africa. 1844. V. 43

A Narrative of a Visit to Mauritius and South Africa. Hamilton,: 1844. V. 44

A Narrative of a Visit to Mauritius and South Africa. London: 1844. V. 39; 40; 42; 45

BACKHOUSE, JANET

John Scottowe's Alphabet Books. London: 1974. V. 39

The Madresfield Hours, a Fourteenth century Manuscript. London: 1975. V. 39

The Madresfield Hours, a 14th century Manuscript in the Library of Earl Beauchamp. Oxford: 1975. V. 37; 38

BACKUS, ISAAC 1724-1806

The Diary of Isaac Backus. Providence: 1979. V. 42

BACON, ANTHONY

A Short Address to the Government, the Merchants, Manufacturers, and the Colonists in America, and the Sugar Islands, On the Present State of Affairs. London: 1775. V. 41; 42

BACON, DELIA SALTER

The Birds of Fort Edward, Founded on an Incident of the Revolution. New York: 1839. V. 43; 44

The Philosophy of The Plays of Shakespere Unfolded. Boston: 1857. V. 43; 44

Tales of the Puritans. New Haven: 1831. V. 45; 46

BACON, E. M.

Narragansett Bay, Historic Associations and Picturesque Setting, the Men and Their Ships from the Earliest Colonial Times to the Present Era of Yachting. New York: 1904. V. 41

BACON, EDGAR MAYHEW

The Hudson River, from Ocean to Source. New York: 1902. V. 38

BACON, EDWARD R.

Catalogue of Chinese Art Objects, Including Porcelains, Potteries, Jades, Bronzes, and Cloisonne Enamels Collected by Edward R. Bacon. New York: 1919. V. 38

BACON, EPHRAIM

Abstract of a Jounral Kept by . . . Assistant Agent of the United States to Africa . . . Philadelphia: 1824. V. 41

Abstract of a Journal Kept by E. Bacon, United States Assistant Agent for the Reception of Recaptured Negroes on the Coast of Africa . . . Philadelphia: 1834. V. 42

BACON, FRANCIS, VISCOUNT ST. ALBANS 1561-1626

Apophthegmes New and Old. London: 1626. V. 38; 41

Baconiana. London: 1679. V. 37; 38; 40; 41; 42; 45

Baconis de Verulam Angliae Cancellarii De Augmentis Scientiarum Lib IX. Leyden: 1562. V. 45

A Brief Discourse of the Happy Union of the Kingdoms of England and Scotland, with Certain Articles Concerning the Same. London: 1700. V. 43

A Brief Discourse of the Happy Union of the Kingdoms of Scotland and England, with Certain Articles Concerning the Same. London: 1702. V. 38

Certaine Considerations Touching the Better Pacification and Edification of the Church of England. London: 1640. V. 40; 44

The Charge of Sr. Francis Bacon, Kt. His Majesties Attourney General, Touching Duells. London: 1670. V. 40

De Dignitate et Augmentis Scientiarum Libri IX. Parisiis: 1624. V. 38

BACON, FRANCIS, VISCOUNT ST. ALBANS 1561-1626 continued

De Dignitate & Augmentis Scientiarum, Libri IX. (with) Novum Organum Scientiarum. Leiden: 1645. V. 43

De Avgmentis Scientiarvm Lib. IX. Argentorati: 1654. V. 45

The Element sof the Common Lavves of England, Branched into a Double Tract . . . The Other The Vse of the Law Provided for Prefervation of Our Persons, Goods and Good Names . . . London: 1636 & 1635. V. 44

The Elements of the Common Lawes of England . . . London: 1639. V. 37; 38; 40; 45

The Essayes, or Covnsels, Civill and Morall. London: 1629. V. 45

The Essayes or Counsels, Civill and Morall . . . London: 1632. V. 37; 38; 39; 41; 42; 45

The Essayes or, Counsels Civill and Morall: of Francis Lo. Verulam, Viscount St. Alban. With a table of the Colours, or Apparances of Good and Evill, and their degrees, as places of Persuasion, and DIssuation, and their severall . . . 1639. V. 37

The Essayes or, Covnsels, Civill and Morall . . . London: 1639. V. 40; 45; 46

The Essayes, or Covnsels, Civill and Morall. London: 1664. V. 45

The Essayes, or Covnsels, Civill and Morall. London: 1673. V. 45

The Essays or Counsels, Civil and Moral . . . London: 1680. V. 42

The Essays or Councils, Civil and Moral. To this edition is added the Character of Queen Elizabeth; Never Before Printed in English. London: 1696. V. 37; 38; 41; 43

The Essays, or Councils, Cicil and Moral of . . . London: 1701. V. 42; 43

The Essays, or Councils, Civil and Moral . . . London: 1718. V. 40; 43

The Essays on Civil, Moral, Literary and Political Subjects Together with the Life of that Celebrated Writer. London: 1787. V. 38; 39

The Essays, or Counsels Civil and Moral, and Wisdom of the Ancients. London: 1852. V. 45

Essays with Annotations by Richard Whately. London: 1886. V. 41

Essays and Apothegms. London: 1894. V. 40

The Essays of Francis Bacon, from the First edition, 1625. Munich: 1920. V. 40

The Essays. Tolz: 1920. V. 38; 44; 45

The Essayes or Counsels, Civill and Morall. London: 1927. V. 41; 42; 46

Essayes or Counsels Civill and Morall of Francis Lord Verulam, Viscount St. Alban. London: 1928. V. 39; 40; 45

The Essayes or Counsels, Civill & Morall. New York: 1944. V. 37; 38; 44; 45

Historia Naturalis et Experimentalis de Ventis etc. Leiden: 1638. V. 39

History Natural and Experimental of Life and Death. London: 1638. V. 40; 44; 45

Historia Naturalis & Experimentalis De Ventis Uc. Leyden: 1648. V. 42; 43; 45

The Historie of the Raigne of King Henry the Seventh. London: 1622. V. 44

Historie Dv Regne De Henry VII, Roy D'Angleterre. Paris: 1627. V. 38; 44

The Historie of the Reigne of King Henry the Seventh. London: 1629. V. 40; 45

The History of the Reigns of Henry the Seventh, Henry the Eighth, Edward the Sixth, and Queen Mary. London: 1676. V. 44; 45

Historia Vitae et Mortis. Lugduni Batavorum (Leiden): 1636. V. 46

Instauratio Magna (Novum Organum). London: 1620. V. 43

Law Tracts . . . London: 1741. V. 39

Letters. London: 1702. V. 38; 41; 43

Letters. London: 1702. V. 41; 44

Letters, Memoirs, Parliamentary Affairs, State Papers & with Some Curious Pieces in Law and Philosophy . . . London: 1736. V. 41

Letters, Speeches, Charges, Advices &c. of Francis Bacon . . . Now First Published by Thomas Birch, D.D . . . . London: 1763. V. 37

The Naturall and Experimentall History of Winds, &c. London: 1653. V. 39; 40; 41; 46

Novum Organum. London: 1850. V. 45

Novum Organum Instauratio Magna. London: 1620. V. 44

Novum Organum Scientiarum. Leyden: 1650. V. 42

Novum Organum Scientiarum. Amstelaedami: 1660. V. 42

Novum Organum Scientiarum. Amsterdam: 1660. V. 43

Of Gardens, an Essay. 1902. V. 40; 45

Of Gardens. Bronxville: 1959. V. 43; 44; 45

Of Gardens. Northampton: 1959. V. 37

Of the Advancement and Proficience of Learning. Oxford: 1640. V. 37; 41; 45

Of the Advancement and Proficience of Learning. London: 1674. V. 38; 43; 45

Of the Advancement of Proficiency of Learning . . . London: 1974. V. 41

Of the Proficience and Advancement of Learning. London: 1851. V. 45

Of Truth, Beautye and Goodness. Chelsea: 1926. V. 45

The Reading Upon the Statute of Uses. London: 1804. V. 40

Resuscitatio or, Bringing into Publick Light Several Pieces of the Works Civil, Historical, Philsophical and Theological, Hitherto Sleeping . . . London: 1671, 1670. V. 38; 40

Resuscitatio, or, Bringing into Publick Light Severall Pieces of the Works, Civil, Historical, Philosophical and Theological . . . London: 1657. V. 46

Resucitatio, o, Bringing into PUblic Light Severall Pieces of the Works . . . London: 1671. V. 45

Scripta in Naturali et Vniversali Philosophia. Amsterodami: 1653. V. 37

Sermones Fideles, Ethici, Politici, Oeconomici. 1644. V. 45

Sir Francis Bacon His Apologie, In Certaine Imputations Concerning the Late Earle of Essex. London: 1642. V. 44

Sylva Sylvarum; or, a Naturall Historie. London: 1635. V. 39; 46

Sylva Sylvarum. (with) New Atlantis, a work unfinished; London: 1635. V. 39

Sylva Sylvarum. (with) New Atlantis, an Unfinished Work. London: 1635 & n.d. V. 41

Sylva Sylvarum; or, a Naturall Historie. London: 1639. V. 37; 42

Sylva Sylvarum, Sive Historia Naturalis . . . Lvg. Batavor. (Leyden): 1648. V. 37

Sylva Sylvarum; or, a Naturall History. London: 1651. V. 45

Sylva Sylvarum . . . London: 1658. V. 46

Sylva Sylvarum; or, a Natural History . . . London: 1664. V. 43

Sylva Sylvarum, Or a Natural History, in Ten Centuries. London: 1670. V. 46

Three Speeches of. London: 1641. V. 44

The Two Bookes of Sr Francis Bacon, of the Proficience and Advancement of Learning, Divine and Humane. (with) The Essayes or Counsels, Civill and Morall . . . Oxford. V. 45

The Tvvoo Bookes of Francis Bacon. Of the Proficience and Aduancement of Learning, Divine and Humane. Tot he King. London: 1605. V. 37; 42; 43; 44; 46

The Two Bookes of Sr. Francis Bacon. Of the Proficience and Advancement of Learning, Divine and Humane. London: 1629. V. 42

The Two Bookes of Sr. Francis Bacon, of the Proficience and Advancement of Learning, Divine and Humane. Oxford: 1633. V. 38; 39; 40; 43; 44; 45; 46

The Two Books of Francis Bacon. Of the Proficience and Advnacement. London: 1747. V. 43

Opera Omnia. London: 1730. V. 41; 46

Certain Miscellany Works. London: 1629. V. 45

Opervm Moralivm et Civilivm. Londini: 1638. V. 45; 46

Opuscula Varia Posthuma, Philosophica, Civila, et Theologica . . . Amstelodami: 1663. V. 45

Opera Omnia Quae Extant: Philosophica, Moralia, Politica, Historica. Francofurt ad Moenum: 1665. V. 44

Francisci Baconi . . . Opera Omnia . . . Frankfurt: 1665. V. 41

Opera Omnia. Frankfurt: 1665. V. 45

Opera Omnia. Londini: 1730. V. 39; 42; 43; 44; 45

Opera Omnia. Londini: 1730. V. 46

The Works of the Lord Bacon. London: 1730. V. 37; 43

The Philosophical Works . . . London: 1733. V. 37; 38

The Works of Francis Bacon, Baron of Verulam . . . London: 1740. V. 37; 38; 39; 44

The Works. London: 1765. V. 40; 42

The Works of Francis Bacon, Baron of Verulam, Viscount St. Alban and Lord High Chancellor of England. London: 1803. V. 45

The Works of . . . London: 1807. V. 44; 46

The Works. London: 1807. V. 46

The Works of Francis Bacon . . . London: 1817. V. 37; 42

The Works of . . . Baron of Verulam . . . London: 1819. V. 37; 38; 39; 40

The Works of Francis Bacon, Baron of Verulam, Viscount of St. Albans and Lord High Chancellor of England. London: 1824. V. 39

The Works. London: 1825-34. V. 37; 39; 42

The Works. London: 1826. V. 38

The Works. London: 1858-62. V. 42

The Works of . . . Boston: 1861-74. V. 40

The Works. London: 1868-1901. V. 39

The Works. London: 1879. V. 38

BACON, G. W.

Bacon's Guide to America for the Capitalist, Tourist, or Emigrant. London: 1871. V. 38

BACON, GENERAL

The British Cavalry at Balaklava. London: 1855. V. 41

BACON, GEORGE W.

New Large Scale Atlas of the British Isles. London: 1883. V. 46

BACON, HENRY M.

New Light in Old Paths. Chicago: 1860. V. 43

BACON, JOHN

Liber Regis vel Thesaurus Rerum Ecclesiasticarum . . . London: 1786. V. 41

Memoirs of John Bacon, R.A. London: 1801. V. 46

BACON, LEONARD

Review of Pamphlets on Slavery and Colonization. New Haven: 1833. V. 42

BACON, M. A.

Flowers and Kindred Thoughts. London: 1848. V. 38; 42; 44

Fruits from the Garden and Field. London: 1850. V. 43; 44

Winged Thoughts. London: 1851. V. 37; 39; 44

BACON, MATTHEW

The Compleat Arbitrator; or the Law of Awards. London: 1770. V. 39

A New Abridgement of the Law. London: 1759/62/66. V. 38

A New Abridgment of the Law. London: 1762/59/66. V. 40

A New Abridgment of the Law. Dublin: 1786. V. 39

A New Abridgment of the Law. London: 1807. V. 40

BACON, NATHANIEL 1593-1660

An Historical Discourse of the Uniformity of the Government of England. London: 1647, 1651. V. 39

An Historical Discourse of the Government of England. (with) The Continuation of an Historical Discourse . . . Until the end of the Reign of Queen Elizabeth. London: ptd. for Matthew: 1672. V. 43

An Historical and Political Discourse of the Laws of Government of England . . . London: 1739. V. 38; 39

An Historical and Political Discourse of the Laws and Government of England, from the First Times to the End of the Reign of Queen Elizabeth. With a Vindication of the Antient Way of Parliaments in England. London: 1760. V. 41

An Historical Discourse of the Uniformity of the Government of England. The First Part. From the first Times till the Reign of Edward the Third. London: 1651. V. 37

A Journal of Meditations For Every Day in the Year. St. Omer: 1674. V. 37

BACON, PEGGY

Cat Calls. New York: 1935. V. 39

Funerealities. New York. V. 44

Funerealities. New York: 1925. V. 41

Off With Their Heads. New York: 1934. V. 44

BACON, R. H.

Benin, the City of Blood. London: 1897. V. 42

The Dover Patrol, 1915-1917, a study of naval actions, strategy and tactics in WW I in the Dover Straits. 45 miles of moor-nets, waters continually swept by mine trawlers. New York/London: (ca. 1920). V. 37

BACON, R. N.

A Report of the Transactions of the Holkham Sheep-Shearing, on Monday, Tuesday, Wednesday and Thursday, July 2, 3, 4 and 5 , being the Forty-Third Anniversary of that Meeting. Norwich: 1821. V. 46

BACON, ROGER

The Mirror of Alchemy. Los Angeles: 1975. V. 42

Opus Majus. London: 1738. V. 43

The Opus Majus. Oxford: 1897. V. 40

The Opus Majus. Philadelphia: 1928. V. 41; 42; 46

BACON, THOMAS

First Impressions and Studies from Nature in Hindostan . . . London: 1837. V. 41; 44

Laws of Maryland at Large, with Proper Indexes, Now First Collected into One Compleat Body, and Published from the Original Acts and Records . . . Annapolis: 1765. V. 39

BACONTHORPE, JOHN

Quodlibeta Joannis Bachonisanglici Carmelite Theologi Profundissimi . . . Venice: 1527. V. 41

BACOU, ROSELINE

Bresdin to Redon: Six Letters, 1870 to 1881. London: 1969. V. 41

BACQUEVILLE DE LA POTHERIE, C. C. LEROY

Histoire de l'Amerique Septentrional . . . Paris: 1722. V. 44

BACQUIER, J.

Le Style Empire Mobilier, Bronzes, Decorations, Exterieures et Interieures. Paris: 1924-34. V. 45

BAD HEART BULL, AMOS

Pictographic History of the Ogala Sioux. Lincoln: 1967. V. 38

A Pictographic History of the Oglala Sioux. Lincoln: 1968. V. 43

Sioux Indian Painting. Paris: 1938. V. 39

BADAWY, ALEXANDER

Ancient Egyptian Architectural Design . . . Berkeley & Los Angeles: 1965. V. 44

A History of Egyptian Architecture: From the Earliest Times to the End of the Old Kingdom. Giza: 1954. V. 42

A History of Egyptian Architecture: the Empire (the New Kingdom) from the Eighteenth Dynasty to the End of the Twentieth Dynasty 1580-1085 BC. Berkeley & Los Angeles: 1968. V. 40; 42; 44

A History of Egyptian Architecture: The First Intermediate Period, the Middle Kingdom, and the Second Intermediate Period. Berkeley & Los Angeles: 1966. V. 40; 42; 44

BADCOCK, JOHN

Conversations on Conditioning. London: 1829. V. 39; 43

A Living Picture of London for 1828, and Stranger's Guide Through the Streets of the Metropolis. London: 1828. V. 40

BADCOCK, LOVELL

Rough Leaves from a Journal Kept in Spain and Portugal, During the Years 1832, 1833 and 1834. London: 1835. V. 38

BADCOCK, WILLIAM

A Touch-Stone for Gold and Silver Wares; or, a Manual for Goldsmiths, and all other Persons. London: 1677. V. 37

BADDELEY, JOHN

The London Angler's Book, or Waltonian Chronicle . . . London: 1834. V. 42

BADDELEY, JOHN F.

The Rugged Flanks of Caucasus. London: 1940. V. 40

The Rugged Flanks of the Caucasus. Oxford: 1940. V. 42

Russia, Mongolia, China: Being Some Record of the Relations Between Them. New York. V. 43

Russia, Mongolia, China, Being Some Record of the Relations Between Them from the Beginning of the XVIIth Century to the Death of the Tsar Alexei Mikhailovich A.D. 1602-1676. London: 1919. V. 46

Russia in the 'Eighties' Sport and Politics. London: 1921. V. 43

BADDELEY, RICHARD

The Life of Dr. Thomas Morton, Late Bishop of Duresme. York: 1669. V. 42

BADE, WILLIAM FREDERIC

The Life and Letters of John Muir. Boston & New York: 1924. V. 45

The Life and Letters of John Muir. Boston: 1934. V. 44

BADEAU, ADAM

Military History of Ulysses S. Grant, from April 1861 to April 1865. New York. V. 42

Military History of Ulysses S. Grant from April 1861 to April 1865. New York: 1881. V. 37; 43

BADEN-POWELL, AGNES

How Girls Can Help Their Country. New York: 1917. V. 46

BADEN-POWELL, BADEN HENRY

The Indian Village Community Examined with Reference to the Physical, Ethnographic and Historical Conditions of the Provicnes . . . London: 1896. V. 38

BADEN-POWELL, GEORGE

New Homes for the Old Country. London: 1872. V. 39; 45

BADEN-POWELL, R. S. S.

The Matabele Campaign 1896. London: 1897. V. 40

Pigsticking or Hoghunting. London: 1889. V. 43

Sketches in Making and East Africa. London: 1907. V. 37

BADEN-POWELL, ROBERT

The Downfall of Prempeh, A Diary of Life with the Native Levy in Ashanti 1895-96 . . . London: 1898. V. 43; 44; 45

Indian Memories - Recollections of Soldiering, Sport, Etc. London: 1915. V. 45

Quick Training for War - a Few Practical Suggestions Illustrated by Diagrams. London: 1914. V. 45

Rovering to Success. London: 1922. V. 42

Sketches in Mafeking and East Africa. London: 1907. V. 42; 43; 44; 45

BADEN, WOLDEMAR

Switzerland Its Mountains and Valleys with 418 illustrations by Bauenfeind. Braith. &c. London: 1878. V. 45

BADESLADE, THOMAS

Chorographia Britanniae. London: 1742. V. 39

BADGER, B.

The Naval Temple. Boston: 1816. V. 40

BADGER, C. M., MRS.

Floral Belles From the Green-House and Garden, Painted From Nature. New York: 1867. V. 38; 39; 40; 42; 43

Wild Flowers Drawn and Colored from Nature. New York: 1859. V. 45

Wild Flowers Drawn and Colored from Nautre. New York: 1860. V. 37; 38

Wild Flowers Drawn and Colored from Nature. New York: 1860. V. 37

BADGER, JOHN

A Collection of Remarkable Cures of the King's Evil. London: 1748. V. 37; 38; 39; 40; 41; 45

BADGER, JOSEPH

A Memoir of Rev. Joseph Badger: Containing an Augobiography and Selections from His Private Journal and Correspondence. Hudson: 1851. V. 46

BADHAM, CHARLES DAVID 1806-1857

Prose Haleutics of Ancient and Modern Fish Tatlle. London: 1854. V. 43

A Treatise on the Esculent Funguses of England. London: 1847. V. 37; 41; 42; 43; 44; 45

A Treatise on the Esculent Funguses of England. London: 1863. V. 38; 39

BADHAM, HERBERT

A Gallery of Australian Art. Sydney: 1954. V. 37; 38

A Study of Australian Art. Sydney: 1949. V. 41

THE BADIANUS Manuscript. Baltimore: 1940. V. 40

BADIN, STEPHEN THEODORE

Origine et Progres de la Mission du Kentucky. Paris: 1821. V. 39; 45

BAEDEKER

Greece. Panorama of Athens. Leipsic: 1889. V. 37

BAEDEKER, FRANZ

Egypt. Part Second: Upper Egypt, with Nubia as Far as the Second Cataract and the Western Oases. Leipsic & London: 1892. V. 39

Egypt and the Sudan. Leipzig: 1929. V. 39

A Handbook for Travelers on the Rhine, from Switzerland to Holland . . . London & Coblenz: 1864. V. 39

Russia. Leipzig: 1914. V. 39

BAEDEKER, KARL

The Dominion of Canada with New-foundland and an Excursion to Alaska. Leipsic: 1894. V. 44

The Dominion of Canada With New-foundland and an Excursion to Alaska. Leipsic: 1900. V. 44

The Dominion of Canada with New-foundland and an Excursion to Alaska. Leipzig: 1907. V. 44

Egypt: Handbook for Travellers. Leipsic: 1892-95. V. 46

Egypt. Handbook for Travellers. Leipsic: 1902. V. 44; 46

Egypt and the Sudan. Leipzig: & London: 1914. V. 44

Egypt and the Sudan. Leipzig: 1929. V. 45

Grece Panorama of Athens. Leipzig: 1910. V. 45

Greece. Handbook for Travellers. Leipsic: 1894. V. 45

Palestine and Syria, with the Chief Routes through Mesopotamia and Babylonia. Leipzig: 1906. V. 45

Palestine and Syria, with Routes through Mesopotamia and Babylonia and the Island of Cyprus. Leipzig: 1912. V. 45

The Rhine from Rotterdam to Constance. Coblenz & Leipsic: 1873. V. 46

Russia, with Teheran, Port Arthur and Peking. Leipzig: 1914. V. 41

The United States with an Excursion Into Mexico. Leipsic: 1893. V. 38; 42

The United States, with Excursions to Mexico, Cuba, Porto Rico and Alaska. Leipzig: 1909. V. 42

BAENA, JOHAN ALFON DE

Cancionero de Baena. New York: 1926. V. 46

BAER, ELIZABETH

Seventeenth Century Maryland. Baltimore: 1949. V. 42; 43; 44; 46

BAER, WARREN

The Duke of Sacramento: a Comedy in Four Acts . . . San Francisco: 1934. V. 43

BAERENTZEN, E. M.

Denmark. Copenhagen: 1856. V. 38

BAERLANDUS, ADRIAAN VAN

Dialogi Omnes Sane Quam Elegantes ac Lepidi, Admodum Pueris Utiles Futuri. Paris: 1535. V. 42

BAERLE, KASPER VAN

Blyde Inkonst der Allerdoorluchighste Koninginne Maria de Medicis t'Amsterdam, Vertaelt uit het Latijn . . . Amsterdam: 1639. V. 46

BAERNREITHER, J. M.

English Associations of Working Men. London: 1889. V. 46

BAGBY, GEORGE WILLIAM 1828-1883

For Virginians Only. What I Did with My Fifty Millions. Philadelphia: 1874. V. 37

Hepsidam. Richmond: 1879. V. 41

A Week in Hepsidam. Richmond: 1879. V. 37

BAGE, ROBERT

Hermsprong; or, Man as He Is Not. London: 1796. V. 39; 43

Man as He Is. London: 1792. V. 41

Man as he is. A Novel in Four VOlumes. London: 1796. V. 37

BAGEHOT, WALTER 1826-1877

The Collected Works. London: 1986. V. 41

Economic Studies. London: 1880. V. 40; 43

The English Constitution. London: 1872. V. 45

Essays on Parliamentary Reform. London: 1883. V. 40; 43

Estimates of Some Englishmen and Scotchmen . . . London: 1858. V. 37; 45

The History of the Unreformed Parliament, and Its Lessons. London: 1860. V. 37

Literary Studies . . . London: 1879. V. 45

Lombard Street: a Description of the Money Market . . . London: 1873. V. 46

Lombard Street. London: 1892. V. 43

Physics and Politics, or Thoughts on the Application of the Principles of 'Natural Selection' and 'Inheritance' to Political Society. London: 1872. V. 41

The Postulates of English Political Economy. New York: 1885. V. 39; 41

The Works. Hartford: 1891. V. 45

The Works and Life. London: 1915. V. 38; 41; 46

BAGENAL, PHILIP H.

Vicissitudes of an Anglo Irish Family. 1530-1800. London: 1925. V. 38

BAGES, JOSE RAMON

Tratado Practico de Astronomia Nautica Y Pilotage . . . Habana: 1842. V. 43

BAGG, A. C.

Birds of the Connecticut Valley in Massachusetts. Northampton: 1937. V. 39

BAGLEY, CLARENCE B.

The Acquisition and Pioneering of Old Oregon. Seattle: 1924. V. 38; 39; 42; 45

History of Seattle from the Earliest Settlement to the Present Time; Chicago: 1916. V. 45

History of King County, Washington. Chicago: 1929. V. 45

BAGLEY, GEORGE

A Guide to the Tongues, Antient and Modern . . . Shrewsbury: 1804. V. 41

BAGLIVI, GIORGO 1668-1707

Opera Omnia Medico-Practica et Anatomica. Venice: 1754. V. 37

The Practice of Physick, Reduc'd to the Ancient Way of Observations Containing a Just Parallel Between the Wisdom and Experience of the Ancients, and the Hypothesis's of Modern Physicians. London: 1704. V. 39

The Practice of Physick. London: 1723. V. 40; 45

De Praxi Medica Ad Priscam Observandi Rationem Revocanda, Libri Duo. Lyons: 1699. V. 44

BAGNOLD, ENID

Early Poems. Gloucestershire: 1987. V. 37; 41

Enid Bagnold Letters to Frank Harris & Other Friends. London: 1980. V. 43; 46

Letters to Frank Harris and Other Friends. Andoversford/London: 1980. V. 37; 39

BAGOT, DANIEL

A Full Report of a Meeting Held in Newry, on Monday, the 24th, January, 1848 to Celebrate the Laying the First Stone of the First District National Model School in that Town. Dublin: 1848. V. 45

BAGROW, LEO

History of Cartography. Cambridge: 1964. V. 38; 40; 42

History of Cartography. Harvard: 1964. V. 46

History of Cartography. Cambridge: 1966. V. 38

Imago Mundi . . . Yearbook of Old Cartography. Amsterdam: 1974-87. V. 40

BAGSHAW, EDWARD

The Rights of the Crown of England As It Is Established by Law. London: 1660. V. 42

BAGSHAW, WILLIAM

On Man: His Motives, Their Rise, Operations, Opposition and Results. London: 1833. V. 42

BAGSTER, SAMUEL

The Management of Bees. London: 1834. V. 38; 42

BAGWELL, RICHARD

Ireland under the Tudors, with a succinct account of the Earlier History. London: 1885. V. 37

BAHR, A. W.

Early Chinese Paintings from the A. W. Bahr Collection. London: 1938. V. 39; 42

Old Chinese Porcelain and Works of Art in China. London: 1911. V. 39; 42; 46

BAHR, HERMANN

Expressionism. London: 1925. V. 38

BAHR, JEROME

All Good American. New York: 1937. V. 37; 40

BAHRDT, KARL FRIEDRICH

Handbuch der Moral fur den Burgerstand. Halle: 1789. V. 39

BAIF, LAZARE DE d. 1546

De re Vestiaria Libellus . . . In Adolescentulorum Gratiam Atque Utilitatem. Paris: 1541. V. 41

Lazari Bayfii Annotationes inL. II de Captivis, et Postlimino Reversis. Paris: 1536. V. 40; 44; 45

Opus de re Vestimentaria ab Authore Ipso Diligenter Recognitum. Venice: 1535. V. 45

BAIGELL, MATTHEW

Charles Burchfield. New York: 1976. V. 44; 45; 46

BAIKIE, JAMES

Great Ones of Ancient Egypt. London: 1929. V. 42
Great Ones of Ancient Egypt. London: (1929). V. 37

BAIKIE, WILLIAM BALFOUR

Narrative of an Exploring Voyage Up the Rivers Kwo'ra and Bi'nue. London: 1856. V. 39; 45

BAIKOV, N.

Big Game Hunting in Manchuria. London: 1936. V. 43

BAILEY, A.

Milwaukee City Directory of 1862. Milwaukee: 1862. V. 46

BAILEY, A. M.

Birds of Colorado. Denver: 1965. V. 39

BAILEY, ALICE COOPER

Katrina and Jan. New York: 1923. V. 45

BAILEY, ALICE WARD

Flower Fancies. Boston: 1889. V. 38

BAILEY, ARTHUR

Songs of Saguenay and Other Poems. Quebec: 1927. V. 43

BAILEY, C. T. P.

Knives and Forks. London and Boston: 1927. V. 39

BAILEY, CAROLYN SHERWIN

Finnegan II. His Nine Lives. New York: 1953. V. 39

BAILEY, D. M.

A Catalogue of the Lamps in the British Museum. London: 1975-1980. V. 42

BAILEY, DANIEL

The Essex Harmony Containing a New and Concise Introduction to Musick. Newbury Port: 1770. V. 44

BAILEY, E. B.

Tertiary and Post-Tertiary Geology of Mull, Loch Aline, Oban. London: 1924. V. 46

BAILEY, F. M.

Comprehensive Catalogue of Queensland Plants, Both Indigenous and Naturalised . . . Brisbane: 1909-13. V. 38

BAILEY, FLORENCE

Birds of New Mexico. Socorro: 1928. V. 45

BAILEY, FLORENCE MERRIAM

Birds of New Mexico. New Mexico: 1928. V. 39
Birds of New Mexico. Santa Fe: 1928. V. 39

BAILEY, GEORGE W.

A Private Chapter of the War, 1861-65. St. Louis: 1880. V. 46

BAILEY, H. C.

The Red Castle Mystery. Garden City: 192. V. 46

BAILEY, H. H.

The Birds of Florida. Baltimore: 1925. V. 39; 46

BAILEY, HAROLD H.

The Birds of Florida. 1925. V. 46
The Birds of Florida. Maryland: 1925. V. 45

BAILEY, ISAAC

American Naval Biography . . . Providence: 1815. V. 37
A Poem. Delivered Before the Philermenian Society of Brown University . . . Providence: 1812. V. 43

BAILEY, J.

A General View of the Agriculture of the County of Northumberland. Newcastle: 1800. V. 39

A General View of the Agriculture on the County of Northumberland with Observations on the means of Its Improvement. Newcastle: 1800. V. 37; 39; 44

BAILEY, J. A.

Biology and Moleculara Biology of Plant Pathogen Interactions. Berlin: 1986. V. 37

BAILEY, J. W., & SONS

Catalogue for Carpenters and Builders. Boston: 1886. V. 42

BAILEY, JAMES DAVIS

Commanders at Kings Mountain. Gaffnev: 1926. V. 42; 46
Some Heroes of the American Revolution. Spartanburg: 1924. V. 46

BAILEY, JOHN

A Folio of a Shakespeare Engravings Taken from the Drawings by Henry William Bunbury and Presented to H.R.H. the Duchess of York. London: 1978. V. 43

General View of the Agriculture of the County of Cumberland . . . London: 1794. V. 40

BAILEY, JOHN C.

Waldimara. New York: 1834. V. 37

BAILEY, JOSEPH W.

Proceedings and Reports of the Bailey Investigation Committee. Austin: 1907. V. 37

BAILEY, KENNETH P.

The Ohio Company of Virginia and the Westward Movement 1748-1792 . . . Glendale: 1939. V. 38; 45

BAILEY, LIBERTY HYDE

Cyclopedia of American Horticulture. New York: 1906. V. 46
Cyclopedia of American Agriculture, a Popular Survey of Agricultural Conditions, Practices and Ideals in the Unites States and Canada. London: 1909. V. 46
Cyclopedia of American Agriculture. New York: 1909-10. V. 42
Cyclopedia of American Horticulture. London: 1900. V. 37
Hortus Third, a Concise Dictionary of Gardening, General Horticulture and Cultivated Plants in North America. New York: 1976. V. 45
The Standard Cyclopedia of Horticulture . . . New York: 1922. V. 45
The Standard Cyclopedia of Horticulture. New York: 1925. V. 40
The Standard Cyclopedia of Horticulture, a Discussion for the Amateur and the Professional and Commercial Grower. New York: 1928. V. 45
The Standard Cyclopedia of Horticulture. London: 1933. V. 38
The Standard Cyclopedia of Horticulture. New York & London: 1925. V. 37

BAILEY, MATTHEW

The Morbid anatomy of Some of the Most Important Parts of the Human Body. Albany: 1795. V. 39

BAILEY, NATHANIEL

Dictionarium Britannicum; or a More Compleat Universal Etymological Dictionary Than Any Extant . . . London: 1730. V. 41
Dictionarium Britannicum . . . London: 1736. V. 38; 41
English and Latin Exercises for School Boys, Comprising All the Rules of Syntax. Leeds: 1800. V. 39
An Universal Etymological English Dictionary. London. V. 38
An Universal Etymological English Dictionary. London: 1721. V. 39
An Universal Etymological English Dictionary . . . London: 1731. V. 41; 43
An Universal Etymological Dictionary . . . London: 1733. V. 42
The Universal Etymological English Dictionary. London: 1737. V. 40
An Universal Etymological English Dictionary . . . London: 1745. V. 41
An Universal Etymological English Dictionary. London: 1749. V. 41
An Universal Etymological English Dictionary . . . London: 1753. V. 41
An Universal Etymological English Dictionary . . . London: 1759. V. 45
An Universal Etymological English Dictionary. London: 1759. V. 39; 40
An Universal Etymological Dictionary . . . London: 1763. V. 42

BAILEY, NATHANIEL continued

An Universal Etymological English Dictionary . . . London: 1782. V. 41; 42; 43

An Universal Etymological English Dictionary . . . London: 1789. V. 41

BAILEY, O. F.

The Kensingtons' 13th London Regiment. 1935. V. 43; 46

BAILEY, PEARCE

Accident and Injury, Their Relations to the Diseases of the Nervous System. New York: 1899. V. 42

BAILEY, PERCIVAL 1892-1973

A Classification of the Tumors of the Glioma Group on a Histo-Genetic Basis with a Correlated Study of Prognosis. Philadelphia: 1926. V. 42; 44

Studies in Acromegaly: VII. The Microscopical Structure of the Adenomas in Aromegalic Dyspituitarism. Boston: 1928. V. 44

BAILEY, ROBERT G.

Hell's Canyon. Lewiston: 1943. V. 38; 44

River of No Return. Lewiston: 1935. V. 41

River of No Return, Historical Stories of Idaho. Lewiston: 1947. V. 44

BAILEY, ROSALIE FELLOWS

Pre-Revolutionary Dutch Houses and Families in Northern New Jersey and Southern New York. New York: 1936. V. 46

BAILEY, SAMUEL

Discourses on Various Subjects; Read Before Literary and Philosophical Societies. London: 1852. V. 38; 39; 40

Essays on the Formation and Publication of Opinions, and On Other Subjects. London: 1821. V. 40

Essays on the Formation and Publication of Opinions, and Other Subjects. London: 1826. V. 38

Essays on the Pursuit of Truth, on the Progress of Knowledge, and on the Fundamental Principle of All Evidence and Expectation. London: 1829. V. 40; 42

Essays on the Formation and Publication of Opinions . . . London: 1837. V. 40

Letters on the Philosophy of the Human Mind . . . *First Series (Second Series, Third Series).* London: 1855/58/63. V. 38

The Rationale of Political Representation. London: 1835. V. 46

BAILEY, THOMAS

Annals of Nottinghamshire: History of the County of Nottingham Including the Borough. London: 1852-1855. V. 39; 40

BAILEY, VERNON

North American Fauna No. 25; Biological Survey of Texas. Washington: 1905. V. 44

BAILEY, WILLIAM

The Advancement of Arts, Manufactures and Commerce. Munich: 1773. V. 40

The Advancement of Arts, Manufactures, and Commerce . . . London: 1776. V. 43

Records of Patriotism and Love of Country. Washington, DC: 1826. V. 37

BAILIE, H. W.

Report on the Health of the County Borough of Belfast for 1906. Belfast: 1907. V. 43

BAILLAIRGE, CHARLES

Key to Baillairge's Stereometrical Tableau. Quebec: 1876. V. 44

BAILLET, ADRIEN

Auteurs Desguisez, Sous Des Noms Etrangers; Empruntez, Supposez, Feints a Plaisir, Chiffrez, Renversez, Retournez, ou Changez d'une Langue en une Autre. Paris: 1690. V. 39

BAILLIE, ALEXANDER F.

The Oriental Club and Hanover Square. London: 1901. V. 42

BAILLIE, G. H.

Watches, Their History, Decoration and Mechanism. London: 1929. V. 42; 45

BAILLIE-GROHMAN, W. A.

Camps in the Rockies. Being a Narrative of Life on the Frontier, and Sport in the Rocky Mountains, with an Account of the Cattle Ranches of the West. London: 1882. V. 38; 41

Fifteen Years' Sport and Life in the Hunting Grounds of Western America and British Columbia. London: 1900. V. 43; 45

Sport in the Alps in the Past and Present. London: 1896. V. 41

BAILLIE-GROHMAN, WILLIAM

A Sport in Art an Iconography of Sport Illustrating the Field Sports of Europe . . . London: 1919. V. 37; 40; 44

BAILLIE-GROHMAN, WILLIAM A.

Sport in Art. London. V. 42

BAILLIE, J.

Advice to Mothers, on the best means of promoting the health, strength, beauty and intellectual improvement of their offspring; with instructions respecting their own health and happiness . . . Newcastly-upon-Tyne: 1812. V. 37

BAILLIE, J. W.

Home Letters from the Crimea. London: 1900. V. 41

BAILLIE, JOANNA 1762-1851

A Collection of Poems, Chiefly Manuscript, and from Living Authors. London: 1823. V. 38; 41; 46

Dramas. London. V. 37

Dramas. London: 1836. V. 42

Epilogue, to the Theatrical Representation at Strawberry Hill. N.P.. V. 42

Epilogue to the Theatrical Representation at Strawberry Hill. N.P.: 1800. V. 42

Epilogue to the Theatrical Representation at Strawberry Hill. N.P.: 1804? V. 44

Metrical Legends of Exalted Characters. London: 1821. V. 46

Miscellaneous Plays. London: 1804. V. 39; 46

A Series of Plays: In Which It Is Attempted to Delineate the Stronger Passions of the Mind . . . London: 1799. V. 42

A Series of Plays; In Which It Is Attempted to Delineate the Stronger Passions of the Mind. London: 1800-2-12. V. 40

A Series of Plays . . . London: 1802. V. 43; 46

BAILLIE, JOHN

A Letter to Dr. ----- in Answer to a Tract in the Bibliotheque Ancienne & Moderne, Relating to Some Passages in Dr. Freind's History of Physick . . . London: 1728. V. 44; 45

BAILLIE, MARIANNE 1795?-1830

First Impressions on a Tour Upon the Continent in the Summer of 1818 . . . London: 1819. V. 37; 38; 42; 46

First Impressions on a Tour Upon the Continent in the Summer of 1818, through Parts of France, Italy, Switzerland, the Borders of Germany, and a Part of French Flanders. London: 1819. V. 38

Guy of Warwick. Kingsbury: 1818. V. 39

Lisbon in the Years 1821, 1822 and 1823. London: 184. V. 43

BAILLIE, MATTHEW 1761-1823

An Account of a Particular Change of Structure in the Human Ovarium. Extracted from the Philosophical Transations. (London): 1789. V. 37

The Morbid Anatomy of Some of the Most Important Parts of Human Body. (with) A Series of Engravings, Accompanied with Explanations . . . London: 1797/1812. V. 43

The Morbid Anatomy of Some of the Most Important Parts of the Human Body. (with) A Series of Engravings, Accompanied with Explanations; Which are Intended to Illustrate the Morbid Anatomy . . . . London: 1812. V. 45

The Morbid Anatomy of Some of the Most Important Parts of the Human Body. London: 1797. V. 37

The Works . . . to Which is Prefixed, and Account of His Life, Collected from Authentic Sources, by James Wardrop . . . London: 1825. V. 41

BAILLIE SCOTT, M. H.

Furniture Made at the Pyghtle Works Bedford by John P. White Designed by M. H. Baillie Scott. Derby: 1901. V. 42

BAILLIE, THOMAS

A Solemn Appeal to the Public . . . London: 1779. V. 37

BAILLOU, GUILLAUME DE 1538-1616

Consiliorum Medicinalium Libri II . . . Paris: 1635-36. V. 46

De Convulsionibus, Libellus . . . Paris: 1640. V. 42

BAILLY, JEAN SYLVAIN

The Ancient History of Asia, and Remarks on the Atlantis of Plato. London: 1814. V. 38

Essai sur la Theorie des Satellites de Jupiter, Suivi des Tables de Leurs Mouvemens Deduits du Principe de la Gravitation Universelle . . . Paris: 1766. V. 42; 44

Histoire de l'Astronomie Ancienne, Deupis Son Origine Jusqu'a l'Establissement de l'Ecole d'Alexandrie . . . (with) *Histoire de l'Astronomie Moderne Depuis la Fondation de l'Ecole d'Alexandrie* . . . (with) *Traite de l'Astronomie Indienne et Orientale Ouvrage* . . . Paris: 1781/85/87. V. 38

BAILY, FRANCIS

The Catalogue of the Stars of the British Association for the Advancement of Science. London: 1845. V. 40

The Doctrine of Life-Annuities and Assurances Analytically Investigated and Practically Explained . . . Liverpool: 1864. V. 40

BAILY, JOHN

Central America; Describing Each of the States of Guatemala, Honduras, Salvador, Nicaragua and Costa Rica. London: 1850. V. 39

BAILY, LAURENCE R.

General Average, and the Losses and Expenses Resulting from General Average Acts . . . (with) General Average . . . London: 1851/56. V. 46

BAILY, WILLIAM HELLIER

Figures of Charactersitic British Fossils . . . Volume I - Palaezoic. London: 1875. V. 41

BAIN, ALEXANDER

The Emotions and the Will. London: 1859. V. 39

The Emotions and the Will. London: 1865. V. 44

The Emotions and the Will. London: 1875. V. 39

John Stuart Mill. A Criticism, with Personal Recollections. London: 1882. V. 39; 41; 42; 43; 45

Mental and Moral Science; a Compendium of Psychology and Ethics. London: 1868. V. 40

The Senses and the Intellect. London: 1855. V. 37

BAIN, FRANCIS WILLIAM 1863-1940

Body and Soul, or the Method of Economy. London: 1894. V. 39

The Digit of the Moon Series. London: 1899-09/1911-19. V. 42

The Digit of the Moon Series. London: 1899-1909. V. 37

The Indian Stories. London: 1913. V. 37; 42; 44

On the Principle of Wealth Creation . . . London: 1892. V. 41

BAIN, IAIN

The Watercolors and Drawings of Thomas Bewick and His Workshop Apprentices. Cambridge: 1981. V. 39; 43

The Watercolour Drawings of Thomas Bewick and His Workshop Apprentices. London: 1981. V. 42

The Watercolours and Drawings of Thomas Bewick. 1981. V. 46

BAIN, R. NISBET

Wierd Tales from Northern Seas - from the Danish of Jonas Lie. 1893. V. 37

BAIN, WILLIAM T.

Letters and Meditations on Religious and Other Subjects. Raleigh: 1839. V. 39

BAINBRIDGE, BERYL

Another Part of the World. London: 1968. V. 39

A Weekend with Claud. London: 1967. V. 41; 42; 43; 44; 46

BAINBRIDGE, GEORGE COLE

The Fly Fisher's Guide, . . . Liverpool: 1816. V. 39; 44; 45

The Fly Fisher's Guide. London: 1840. V. 45

BAINBRIDGE, H. C.

Twice Seven. London: 1933. V. 40

BAINBRIDGE, HENRY CHARLES

Peter Carl Faberge. London: 1949. V. 39; 40; 46

Peter Charles Fabrege Goldsmith and Jeweller to the Russian Imperial Court and the Principal Crowned Heads of Europe . . . New York: 1949. V. 41

BAINE, ALBERT BIGELOW

Mark Twain. A Biography. New York: 1912. V. 40

BAINE, JAMES

The Theatre Licentious and Perverted. Edinburgh: 1770. V. 46

BAINES, EDWARD

A Companion to the Lakes of Cumberland, Westmoreland, and Lancashire. London: 1830. V. 39; 42

A Companion to the Lakes of Cumberland, Westmoreland and Lancashire . . . London: 1834. V. 45

History, Directory and Gazetter of the County of York . . . Leeds: 1822. V. 45

History, Directory and Gazetteer of the County of York . . . Volume I: West Riding. London: 1822. V. 41

History, Directory and Gazeteer of the County Palatine of Lancaster, with a VAriety of Commercial and Statistical Information. Liverpool: 1825. V. 41

History of the Cotton manufacture in Great Britain: with a notice of its early history in the East, and in all the quarters of the globe; a description of the great mechanical inventions . . . and a view of the present state of manufacture. (1835). V. 37

History of the Cotton Manufacture in Great Britain . . . London: 1835. V. 39

The History of the County Palatine and Duchy of Lancaster. London: 1868. V. 39

History of the Wars of the French Revolution 1792-1815 . . . Leeds: 1817. V. 39

History of the Wars of the French Revolution. London: 1817. V. 40

Letters to the Right Hon. Lord John Russell, First Lord of the Treasury, on Education . . . London: 1847. V. 43; 46

BAINES, FREDERIC EBENEZER

Forty Years at the Post Office. London: 1895. V. 42

BAINES, THOMAS 1806-1881

Explorations in South-West Africa. London: 1864. V. 38; 41

The Gold Regions of South Eastern Africa. London: 1877. V. 40

The Gold Regions of South Eastern Africa. London: 1877. V. 39; 40; 46

History of the Commerce and Town of Liverpool . . . London: 1852. V. 38; 40

Lancashire and Cheshire Past and Present. London. V. 38

Lancashire and Cheshire, Past and Present. London: 1867. V. 39

Lancashire and Cheshire Past and Present. London: 1868-69. V. 38; 40; 41; 42; 46

Nature and Art. London: 1866-67. V. 45

The Northern Goldfields Diaries of . . . First (&) Second Journeys 1869-1872. London: 1946. V. 37; 39

Observations on the Present State of the Affairs of the River Plate. Liverpool: 1845. V. 38

Shifts and Expedients of Camp Life, Travel and Exploration. London: 1876. V. 44

The Victoria Falls, Zambesi River . . . London: 1865. V. 45

Yorkshire Past and Present. London. V. 38; 45

Yorkshire. Past and Present: a History and Description . . . London: 1871-77. V. 42

BAINTON, GEORGE

The Art of Authorship. London: 1890. V. 39

BAIRD, HENRY CAREY 1825-1912

General Washington and General Jackson on Negro Soldiers. Philadelphia: 1863. V. 46

The Painter, Gilder and Varnisher's Companion . . . Philadelphia: 1858. V. 44

BAIRD, JOSEPH

California's Pictorial Letter Sheets 1849-1869. 1967. V. 44

BAIRD, JOSEPH ARMSTRONG

California's Pictorial Letter Sheets, 1849-1869. San Francisco: 1967. V. 37; 39; 42; 43; 45; 46

Time's Wondrous Changes. San Francisco Architecture 1776-1915. San Francisco: 1962. V. 44

BAIRD, NEWTON D.

An Annotated Bibliography of California Fiction, 1664-1970. Georgetown: 1971. V. 38; 40

BAIRD, ROBERT

Impressions and Experiences of the West Indies and North America in 1819. Philadelphia: 1850. V. 39

Religion in the United States of America, or An Account of the Origin, Progress, Relations to the State . . . Glasgow & Edinburgh: 1844. V. 39; 42; 43

View of the Valley of the Mississippi . . . Philadelphia: 1832. V. 42

View of the Valley of the Mississippi or the Emigrant's and Traveller's Guide to the West . . . Philadelphia: 1834. V. 41

BAIRD, SPENCER FULLERTON 1823-1887

The Birds of North America. New York: 1860. V. 42

The Birds of North America. Philadelphia: 1860. V. 41; 42; 45

The Birds of North American. Salem: 1870. V. 40; 41

The Birds (of North America). Washington: 1858. V. 37

A History of North American Birds. Boston: 1805. V. 45

A History of North American Birds. Boston: 1874. V. 40

A History of North American Birds: Land Birds. Boston: 1875. V. 37

BAIRD, W.

John Thomson of Duddingston. Pastor Painter. Edinburgh: 1895. V. 39

BAIRNSFATHER, BRUCE

Bullets and Billets. London: 1917. V. 37

BAIRNSFATHER, P. R.

Sport and Nature in the Himalayas. London: 1914. V. 40

BAIRO, PIETRO 1468-1558

Secreti Medicinali. In Venetia: 1562. V. 38

BAISHER, JAMES CAMILLE

Travels in the Air. London: 1871. V. 44

BAITSELL, GEORGE A.

Science in Progress. New Haven: 1939-47. V. 46

BAJA California Travel Series. Los Angeles: 1965-84. V. 39; 46

BAK, BRONISLAW M.

Homo Sum. Chicago: 1967. V. 38

BAKAER, WILLIAM M.

The Life and Labours of the Rev. Daniel Baker . . . Philadelphia: 1589. V. 37

A BAKE-PAN for the Dough-Faces. Burlington: 1854. V. 46

BAKELAND, GEORGE

Journal of Fishing and Shooting. N.P.: 1945-53. V. 39

BAKER, A. I.

Ruins of Kenilworth Castle. London: 1822. V. 38; 45

BAKER, ALF

Applied Arts in Iberia 1880-1920. Canterbury: 1988. V. 40; 45

BAKER, ANN ELIZABETH

Glossary of Northamptonshire Words and Phrases. London: 1854. V. 41

BAKER, C. ALICE

True Stories of new England Captives Carried to Canada During the Old French and Indian Wars. Cambridge: 1897. V. 39; 42; 43; 45

True Stories of New England Captives Carried to Canada During the Old French and Indian Wars. Cambridge: 1897. V. 43

BAKER, CHARLES

Charles Baker's Treatise for Preventing of the Smut in Wheat. Bristol: 1797. V. 41; 42

Contributions to Publications of the Society for the Diffusion of Useful Knowledge and the Central Society of Education. Doncaster: 1842. V. 42

BAKER, CHARLES H.

The Gentleman's Companion. New York: 1939. V. 39; 41; 43

BAKER, CHARLES HENRY COLLINS 1880-

Catalogue of the Petworth Collection of Pictures. London: 1920. V. 38; 40

Crome. London: 1921. V. 39; 42; 44

English Painting of the Sixteenth and Seventeenth Centuries. Paris: 1930. V. 44

BAKER, DAVID ERSKINE 1730-1767

Biographia Dramatica, or, A Companion to the Playhouse. Dublin: 1782. V. 41; 42

Biographia Dramatica, or, A Companion to the Playhouse Containing Historical and Critical Memoirs . . . London: 1782. V. 40; 42; 43

Biographia Dramatica . . . London: 1812. V. 38; 43

Biographica Dramatica, or, a Companion to the Playhouse . . . London: 1782. V. 43

The Companion to the Play-House. London: 1764. V. 38; 40

BAKER, EDWARD CHARLES STUART

The Fauna of British India. Birds. London: 1922-30. V. 37; 38; 39; 43; 44; 46

The Game Birds of India, Burma, and Ceylon. Volume 2: Snipe, Bustards and Sand-Grouse. London: 1921. V. 37; 38

The Game Birds of India, Burma and Crylon. London: 1921-30. V. 37; 38; 40; 43

The Game Birds of India, Burma and Ceylon. London: 1929 & 1930. V. 40

The Identification of Birds of the Indian Empire. London: 1932-35. V. 43

The Indian Ducks and Their Allies. 1908. V. 44; 46

Indian Ducks and Their Allies. Bombay: 1898-1900. V. 43

The Indian Ducks and Their Allies. London: 1908. V. 39; 42; 43

Indian Pigeons and Doves. London: 1913. V. 37; 39; 43

BAKER, ERNEST A.

The History of the English Novel. New York: 1967-79. V. 37; 42

The Netherworld of Mendip, Explorations in the great caverns of Somerset, Yorkshire, Derbyshire and elsewhere. London: 1907. V. 37

BAKER, ESEKIEL

Remarks on Rifle Guns . . . London: 1829. V. 46

BAKER, GEORGE

De Affectibus Animi et Morbis inde Oriundis Dissertatio . . . Cambridge: 1755. V. 41

Britannica Curiosa: or a Description of the Most Remarkable Curiosities, Natural and Artificial of the Island of Great Britain . . . London: 1777. V. 44

A Catalogue of the . . . Collection of Prints and Drawings . . . the Works of Hogarth (and) Woollett, Drawings by Reynolds, Gainsborough, Hearne, Gilpin and Books of Prints . . . London: 1825. V. 45

The History and Antiquities of the County of Northampton. London: 1822-41. V. 39; 44

The New Sad Sack. New York: 1946. V. 38

Opuscula Medica, Iterrum Edita. London: 1771. V. 45

BAKER, H. BARTON

Strafford, a Romance. London: 1878. V. 46

BAKER, H. R.

The Birds of Southern India. Madras: 1930. V. 42; 43

BAKER, HARRIET

The Organ Grinder; or, Struggles After Holiness. Boston: 1862. V. 44

BAKER, HENRY

An Attempt Towards a Natural History of the Polype . . . London: 1743. V. 46

Employment for the Microscope. London: 1753. V. 42

Employment for the Microscope. London: 1764. V. 38; 39

Medulla Poetarum Romanorum; or the Most Beautiful and Instructive Passages of the Roman Poets . . . London: 1737. V. 42; 43

The Microscope Made Easy. London: 1754. V. 38

The Microscope Made Easy; or, the Nature, Uses and Magnifying Powers of the best kinds of Microscopes Described, Calculated and Explained: for the Instruction of such, particularly, as desire to search in the Wonders of th Minute Creation . . . London: 1769. V. 37

Of Miscroscopes, and the Discoveries Made Thereby. London: 1785. V. 38

The Universe; a Philosophical Poem . . . Taunton: 1808. V. 38

BAKER, HENRY BARTON

Our Old Actors. London: 1878. V. 43

BAKER, HENRY H.

A Reminiscent Story of the Great Civil War. Second Paper. New Orleans: 1911. V. 38; 39

BAKER, HOLLIS S.

Furniture in the Ancient World. London: 1966. V. 46

Furniture of the Ancient World. New York: 1966. V. 42

BAKER, HUMFREY

The Well Spring of Sciences. London: 1602. V. 46

The Well-Spring of Sciences . . . London: 1617. V. 41; 42

The Well-Spring of Sciences. London: 1631. V. 40

BAKER, INEZ

Yesterday in Hall County, Texas. Memphis: 1940. V. 42

BAKER, J.

A Brief Narrative of the French Invasion, Near Fishguard Bay. Worcester: 1797. V. 41

Multum in Parvo. London: 1802. V. 45

BAKER, JAMES

The Imperial Guide, with picturesque plans of the great post roads, containing miniature likenesses . . . London: 1802. V. 37

Turkey in Europe. London: 1877. V. 46

BAKER, JAMES H.

The Relative Position of the South, 1860-1930. San Marcos,: 1940. V. 39

BAKER, JANE

Love Intrigues; or, the History of the Amours of Bosvil and Galesia. London: 1713. V. 39

BAKER, JOHN GILBERT

North Yorkshire: Studies of Its Botany, Geology, Climate and Physical Geography. London: 1863. V. 46

BAKER, JOHN REMIGIUS

The Valuable and Extraordinary Collection of Books from the Library of Genl. Geo. Washington . . . Collected by John R. Baker, Sr., of Philadelphia. Philadelphia: 1891. V. 39; 42

BAKER, JOHN WYNN

A New Plan for more effectually Propagating the Knowledge of Husbandry in the Kingdom Ireland, reducing it to a Rational and Intelligible System. Dublin: 1764. V. 39

To His Excellency Rt. Hon. Lord, Visc. Townsend, Ltd. Gen. and General Governor of Ireland. Dublin: 1769. V. 43

BAKER, JOSEPH BROGDEN

The History of Scarborough, from the Earliest Date. London: 1882. V. 45

BAKER, JOSEPHINE

Memoiren. Munchen: 1928. V. 44

BAKER Lake, N.W.T., 1870-1970. N.P.: 1971. V. 42

BAKER, LEWIS

The Percys of Mississippi. Baton Rouge: 1983. V. 44

BAKER, MRS.

Nursery Rhymes and Pretty Little Stories. London: 1830. V. 45; 46

BAKER, NICOLAS

Aldus Manutius and the Development of Greek Script and Type in the Fifteenth Century. Sandy Hook: 1985. V. 37

BAKER, OLIVER

Black Jacks and Leather Bottells, Being Some Account of Leather Drinking Vessel in England . . . London: 1921. V. 42

Black jacks and Leather Botells . . . Stratford-on-Avon: 1921. V. 42

BAKER, P. W.

Catalogue of . . . Furniture, Pictures and Prints, the Cellar of Choice Wines and Other Effects. London. V. 40

Catalogue of . . . Furniture, Pictures and Prints, the Cellar of Choice Wines and Other Effects . . . London: 1817. V. 44

BAKER, PETER C.

European Recollections. New York: 1861. V. 42; 44; 45

BAKER, R. T.

Building and Ornamental Stones of Australia. Sydney: 1915. V. 43

A Research on the Pines of Australia. Sydney: 1910. V. 38

BAKER, RICHARD

The Australian Flora in Applied Art. Part I. The Waratah. Sydney: 1915. V. 38

A Chronicle of the Kings of England from the Time of the Romans Government Unto the Reign of King Charles . . . London: 1653. V. 44

A Chronicle of the Kings of England. London: 1684. V. 38; 44; 46

A Chronicle of the Kings of England from the Time of the Romans Government to the Death of King James the First. London: 1733. V. 44

BAKER, RICHARD CHAFFEY

A Manual of Reference to Authorities for the Use of the Members of the National Australasian Convention Which Will Assemble at Sydney on March 2, 1891, for the Purpose of Drafting a Constitution for the Dominion of Australia. Adelaide: 1891. V. 45

BAKER, S. JOSEPHINE

The Division of Child Hygiene of the Department of Health of the City of New York. New York: 1912. V. 45

BAKER, S. S. T.

Aunt Friendly's Picture Book. London. V. 46

BAKER, SAMUEL

Cast Up by the Sea - Cornwall Village . . . New York: 1869. V. 39

BAKER, SAMUEL W.

A Narrative of the Expedition to Central Africa for the Suppression of the Slave Trade. London: 1874. V. 42

BAKER, SAMUEL WHITE

The Albert N'Yanza Great Basin of the Nile . . . London: 1866. V. 38; 41; 42; 43; 44; 45; 46

The Albert N'Yanza, Great Basin of the Nile, and Explorations of the Nile Sources. London: 1867. V. 45

Cyprus as I Saw It in 1879. London: 1879. V. 45

Eight Years' Wanderings in Ceylon. London: 1855. V. 39; 46

Exploration of the Nile Tributaries of Abyssinia. Hartford: 1868. V. 43

Ismailia: a Narrative of the Expedition to Central Africa for the Suppression of the Slave Trade. London: 1874. V. 38; 41; 43; 44; 46

Ismailia: a Narrative of the Expedition to Central Africa for the Suppression of the Slave Trade. New York: 1875. V. 42; 43

The Nile Tributaries of Abyssinia, and the Sword Hutners of the Hamran Arabs. London: 1867. V. 38; 39; 40; 43; 45; 46

The Nile Tributaries of Abyssinia, and the Sword Hunters of the Hamran Arabs. London: 1868. V. 45; 46

The Nile Tributaries of Abyssinia, and the Sword Hunters of the Hamran Arabs. Philadelphia: 1868. V. 38

Reminiscences of Europe, Asia, Africa and America. London: 1874. V. 43

The Tributaries of Abyssinia, and the Sword Hunters of the Hamran Arabs. London: 1867. V. 37

Wild Beasts and Their Ways - Reminiscences of Europe, Asia, Africa and America. London: 1890. V. 43

Wild Beasts and Their Ways. London: 1891. V. 40

Wild Beasts and Their Ways. London: 1898. V. 39

BAKER, SARAH S. TUTHILL

The Children on the Plains. London: 1873. V. 37

The Children on the Plains. A Story of Travel and Adventure from the Missouri to the Rocky Mountains. London: 1865. V. 37

BAKER SILVER MINING CO.

Annual Report of the Baker Silver Mining Co. of Colorado. Philadelphia: 1869. V. 41

The Baker Silver Mining Co. of Colorado . . . Philadelphia: 1867. V. 41

BAKER SILVER MINING COMPANY

Annual Report of the Baker Silber Mining Co. of Colorado. Philadelphia: 1869. V. 37

BAKER, THOMAS

An Act at Oxford. A Comedy. London: 1704. V. 38

An Act at Oxford. A Comedy. London: 1794. V. 41

The Geometrical Key. London: 1684. V. 41

Reflections Upon Learning; Wherein is Shewn the Insufficiency Thereof, In Its Several Particulars . . . London: 1576. V. 38

Reflections Upon Learning, Wherein is Shewn the Insufficiency Thereof, In Its Several Particulars. London: 1700. V. 40

Reflections Upon Learning, Wherein is Shewn the Insufficiency thereof, in Its Several Particulars. London: 1708. V. 41; 44

Reflections Upon Learning. London: 1738. V. 38

Tunbridge-Walks; or, the Yeoman of Kent. London: 1703. V. 38; 43

BAKER, W. S.

Bibliotheca Washingtonia: A Descriptive List of the Biographies and Biographical Sketches of George Washington. Philadelphia: 1889. V. 39

The Engraved Portraits of Washington, with Notices of the Originals and Brief Biographical Sketches of the Painters. Philadelphia: 1880. V. 41

Medallic Portraits of Washington with Historical and Critical Notes and a Descriptive Catalogue of the Coins, Medals, Tokens and Cards. Philadelphia: 1885. V. 40; 46

BAKER, WILLIAM SPOHN 1824-1897

Early Sketches of George Washington. Philadelphia: 1894. V. 38

The Origin and Antiquity of Engraving. Philadelphia: 1872. V. 38

BAKER, WILLIAM WASHINGTON

Memoirs of Service with John Yates Beall. Richmond: 1910. V. 44

BAKEWELL, ROBERT 1768-1843

An Introduction to Geology, Illustrative of the General Structures of the Earth. London: 1815. V. 39; 44; 46

Observations on the Influence of Soile and Climate upon Wook; from which is deduced a certain and easy method of improving the quality of English Clothing wools and preserving the Health of Sheep; with hints for . . . 1808. V. 37

Travels, Comprising Observations Made During a Residence in the Tarentaise and Various Parts of the Grecian and Pennine Alps, and in Switzerland and Auvergne . . . London: 1823. V. 40; 41; 42; 44

BAKOUNINE, MICHAEL

God and the State. Boston: 1890. V. 40

BAKST, LEON

Bakst, The Story of the Artist's Life. London: (1923). V. 37

The Decorative Art. London: 1913. V. 44

The Designs of Leon Bakst for the Sleeping Princess. Preface by Andre Levinson. With a portrit of Leon Bakst by Picasso. London: 1923. V. 37; 42; 46

BAKUNIN, MICHAEL

God and State. Boston: 1983. V. 42

BALASHEV, P. I.

Collection of Views of the Locality of Valaamo Island Drawn from Nautre. St. Petersburg: 1863. V. 46

BALBI, GASPARO

Viaggio dell'Indie Orientali. Venice: 1590. V. 40

BALBIN, BOHUSLAV 1621-1688

Vita S. Joannis Nepomuceni . . . Augsburg: 1730. V. 46

BALBIRNIE, WILLIAM

An Account, Historical and Genealogical from Earliest Days Till the Present Time, of the Family of Vance in Ireland etc.. 1908. V. 43

BALBO, CESARE

The Life and Times of Dante Alighieri. London: 1852. V. 39

BALCARRES, COLIN LINDSAY, 3RD EARL OF 1654-1722

An Account of the Affairs of Scotland Relating to the Revolution of 1688 . . . London: 1714. V. 38; 39; 41; 45; 46

Memoirs Touching the Revolution in Scotland. Edinburgh: 1841. V. 46

BALCH, D. S.

Lexington. St. Anthony: 1857. V. 45

BALCH, H. E.

Wookey Hole, Its Caves and Cave Dwellers. 1914. V. 38; 46

Wookey Hole, Its Caves and Cave Dwellers . . . London: 1914. V. 42

Wookey Hole, Its Caves and Cave Dwellers. Oxford: 1914. V. 40

BALCH, THOMAS

The French in Ameica During the War of Independence of the United States 1777-1783. Philadelphia: 1891. V. 45

Letters and Papers Relating Chiefly to the Provincial History of Pennsylvania . . . Philadelphia: 1855. V. 37; 41; 42

BALD Eagle Club of Amateur Fishermen. Yonkers: 1865. V. 39

BALDASS, LUDWIG

Giorgione. New York: 1965. V. 44

Jan Van Eyck. London: 1952. V. 42; 44

BALDASS, LUDWIG VON

Hieronymus Bosch. Muchen: 1959. V. 46

BALDELLI, G. B.

Il Milione de Marco Polo, Testo di Lengua de Secolo Decimoterzo. Firenze: 1827. V. 39

BALDERSTON, JOHN

Berkeley Square: a Play in Three Acts. New York: 1929. V. 41

BALDERSTON, KATHARINE C.

A Census of the Manuscripts of Oliver Goldsmith. New York: 1926. V. 39

BALDI, BALDO

Disquisitio Iatro-Physica ad Textum. Rome: 1637. V. 38

BALDI, BERNARDINO 1553-1617

Versi E Prose. Venice: 1590. V. 38; 39; 45

BALDINUCCI, FILIPPO

Cominciamento, e Progresso dell' Arte Dell' Intagliare in Rame, Colle Vite di Molti d' Piu Eccellenti Maestri Della Stessa Professione . . . Firenze: 1686. V. 41

Vita Del Cavaliere Gio. Lorenzo Bernino, Scultore, Architetto, et Pittore . . . Florence: 1682. V. 44

BALDIT, MICHEL fl. 1651-1666

Speculum Sacro-Medicum Octagonum . . . Lyon: 1666. V. 40

BALDRY, A.

Modern Mural Decoration. London: 1902. V. 38

BALDRY, A. L.

Hubert von Herkomer, R.A. A Study and a Biography. London: 1901. V. 46

BALDRY, ALFRED LYS

Albert Moore. His Life and Works. London: 1894. V. 39

BALDUIN, CHRISTIAN ADOLPH

Aurum Superius & Inferius Aurae Superioris & Inferioris Hermeticum. (with) Phosphorus Hermeticus, sive Magnes Luminaris. Frankfurt & Leipzig: 1675. V. 38

BALDUINUS, FRANCOIS 1520-1573.

De institutione hisoriae universae. Paris: 1561. V. 37

BALDUNG, HIERONYMUS

Aphorismi Compunctionis Theologicales. Strassburg: 1497. V. 42; 45

BALDWIN, ALICE B.

Memoirs of Major General Frank D. Baldwin. Los Angeles: 1929. V. 45

BALDWIN, CALEB C.

A Manual of the Foochow Dialect . . . Foochow: 1871. V. 41; 42; 43; 44

BALDWIN, CHARLES N.

A Universal Biographical Dictionary, Containing the Lives of the Most Celebrated Characters of Every Age and Nation . . . Richmond: 1826. V. 42

BALDWIN, EBENEEZER

Annals of Yale College in New Haven, Connecticut from Its Foundation to the Year 1831. New Haven: 1831. V. 38

BALDWIN, F. G. C.

The History of the Telephone in the United Kingdom. London: 1938. V. 42

The History of the Telephone in the United Kingdom. With a Foreword by Frank Gill, O. B. E., M. Inst. C.E., M.I.E.E., Engineer-in-Chief, 1902-1913, the National Telephone Co., Ltd., Past President of the Institution of . . . London: 1925. V. 37

BALDWIN, GEORGE P.

The Black Hills Illustrated. Philadelphia: 1904. V. 42

BALDWIN, HENRY

A General View of the Origin and Nature of the Constitution and Government of the United States . . . from 1744 Until 1788. Philadelphia: 1837. V. 38

BALDWIN, JAMES 1924-

Another Country. New York: 1962. V. 46

Blues for Mister Charlie. New York: 1964. V. 46

The Devil Finds Work. New York: 1976. V. 46

A Dialogue. Philadelphia: 1973. V. 46

Evensong and a Celebration Honoring James Baldwin. 1974. V. 46

The Fire Next Time. New York: 1963. V. 46

Giovanni's Room. New York: 1956. V. 40; 42; 45; 46

Giovanni's Room. London: 1957. V. 41; 46

Go Tell It On the Mountain. New York: 1953. V. 37; 39; 41; 43; 44

Go Tell It On the Mountain. London: 1954. V. 45

Go Tell It On the Mountain. New York: 1963. V. 46

Go Tell It On the Mountain. Franklin Center: 1979. V. 44

Gypsy and Other Poems. Leeds: 1989. V. 45; 46

Gypsy and Other Poems. N.P.: 1989. V. 42

If Beale Street Could Talk. New York: 1974. V. 39; 45; 46

In Black, White and Gray. New York: 1964. V. 46

Le Jour ou J'Etais Perdu. Paris: 1973. V. 46

Just Above My Head. New York: 1978. V. 41

Just Above My Head. New York: 1979. V. 38; 39; 40; 41; 43; 44; 45; 46

The Negro Protest. Boston: 1963. V. 46

No Name in the Street. New York: 1972. V. 42

Nobody Knows My Name. New York: 1961. V. 43; 45; 46

Notes of a Native Son. Boston: 1955. V. 41; 45

Nothing Personal. New York: 1964. V. 37; 39; 40; 45

Nothing Personal. New York: 1965. V. 46

The Price of the Ticket. New York: 1985. V. 43

A Rap on Race. Philadelphia: 1971. V. 46

The Story of Siegfried. New York: 1882. V. 40

Tell Me How Long the Train's Been Gone. New York: 1968. V. 42; 46

BALDWIN, JAMES MARK 1861-1934

Dictionary of Philosophy and Psychology: Including Many fo the Principal Conceptions of Ethics, Logic, Aesthetics, Philosophy of Religion, Mental Pathaology, Antropolgy, Biology, Neurology Physiology . . . Gloucester, Mass: 1960. V. 37

BALDWIN, JOSEPH G.

The Flush Times of Alabama and Mississippi. New York: 1853. V. 45

The Flush Times of Alabama and Mississippi. A Series of Sketches. New York: 1853. V. 37

BALDWIN, LOAMMI 1780-1830

Thoughts on the study of Political Economy, as connected with the Population, Industry and Paper currency of the United States. Cambridge: 1809. V. 37

BALDWIN LOCMOTIVE WORKS

History of the Baldwin Locmotive Works 1831-1923. Philadelphia: 1924. V. 46

BALDWIN LOCOMOTIVE WORKS

Baldwin Locomotive Works: Illustrated Catalogue of Locomotives. Philadelphia: 1881. V. 38

Illustrated Catalogue of Locomotives. Philadelphia: 1871. V. 41

BALDWIN LOCOMOTIVES

Dimensions, Weights and Tractive Power of Narrow-Gauge Locomotives, Manufactures by the Baldwin Locomotive Works. Burnham, Parry, Williams & Company. (Philadelphia): 1877. V. 37

BALDWIN, OLIVER P.

Eulogy, Upon the Life and Character of General Zachary Taylor, Delivered at the African Church, on the 10th of August, 1850. Richmond: 1850. V. 41; 45

BALDWIN, THOMAS

Narrative of the Massacre, by the Savages, of the Wife and Children of Thomas Baldwin, Who, Since the Melancholy Period of the Destruction of His Unfortunate Family . . . New York: 1835. V. 37; 39; 45

A New and Complete Gazeteer of the United States. Philadelphia: 1854. V. 38; 42; 44

A Universal Pronouncing Gazeteer . . . Philadelphia: 1845. V. 45

BALDWIN, WILLIAM CHARLES

African Hunting and Adventure from Natal to the Zambesi Including Lake Ngami, the Kalahari Desert, &c. from 1852 to 1860. London: 1863. V. 41; 44; 45; 46

African Hunting and Adventure from Natal to the Zambesi . . . London: 1894. V. 39; 41; 43; 44; 45

BALDWYN, GEORGE AUGUSTUS

A New, Royal, Authentic, Complete and Universal System of Geography. London: 1794. V. 39

BALE, EDWARD E.

Wagon Road from Fort Defiance to the Colorado River. Washington: 1858. V. 37

BALE, EDWARD F.

Wagon Road, Fort Smith to Colorado River. Washington: 1860. V. 44

BALE, JOHN

A Brefe Chronycle Concernynge the Examincayon and Death of the Blessed Martyr of Christ syr Johan Öldecastell the Lorde Cobham. N.P.: 1544. V. 43

A Brefe Chronycle Concernynge the Examinacyon and Death of the Blessed Martyr of Christ syr Johan Öldecastell the lorde Cobham. N.P.: 1544. V. 45

A Brefe Chronycle Concernynge the Examynacyon and Death of the Blessed Martyr of Christ Syr Johan Oldecastell the Lorde Cobham. London: 1729. V. 43

The First Two Partes of the Actes or Unchast Examples of the Englysh Votaryes, Gathered Out of Their Owne Legendes . . . London: 1551. V. 43

The First Two Partes of the Actes or Vnchaste Examples of the Englyshe Votaryes. Colophon: 1560. V. 45

Illustrium Maioris Britanniae Scriptorum . . . Ipswich: 1548. V. 38

The Image of Both Churches. London: 1570. V. 44

Scriptorum Illustriu(m) Maioris Brytannie . . . Catalogus. Basle: 1557-59. V. 38; 41; 46

BALFOUR, ALEXANDER

Characters Omitted in Crabbe's Parish Register. Edinburgh: 1825. V. 38; 41; 44

Contemplation, with Other Poems. Edinburgh: 1820. V. 42

BALFOUR, ALICE BLANCHE

Twelve Hundred Miles in a Waggon. London: 1895. V. 45

BALFOUR, C. L.

Moral Heroism. London: 1848. V. 46

BALFOUR, CLARA LUCAS

A Mother's Lessons on the Lord's Prayer. London: 1860. V. 38; 39

BALFOUR, E.

Cyclopaedia of India. Dehra Dun: 1985. V. 38

BALFOUR, FRANCIS

A Collection of Treatises on the Effects of Sol-Lunar Influence on Fevers . . . 1815. V. 44

A Collection of Treatises on the Effects of Sol-Lunar Influence on Fevers; with an Improved Method of Curing Them. Cupar: 1815. V. 37

BALFOUR, JAMES

A Delineation of the Nature and Obligation of Morality. Edinburgh: 1753. V. 42; 43; 45

BALFOUR, MARY

Hope, a Poetical Essay; With Various Other Poems. Belfast: 1810. V. 37

BALGARNIE, R.

Sir Titus Salt, His Life and Its Lessons. London: 1877. V. 37

BALGUY, THOMAS

Divine Benevolence Asserted, and Vindicated from the Objections of Ancient and Modern Sceptics. London: 1781. V. 37

BALKWILL, F. H.

Mechanical Dentistry in Gold and Vulcanite. London: 1880. V. 40

BALKWILL, HELEN

On Dress, Viewed in Connection with the Society of Friends. Philadelphia: 1873. V. 45

BALL, A. W.

The Journal of the Ethnological Society of London. London: 1869. V. 37

BALL, B. L.

Rambles in Eastern Asia. Boston: 1855. V. 43

Three Days on the White Mountains. Boston: 1877. V. 39

BALL, CHARLES

The History of the Indian Mutiny . . . London: 1858, 1859. V. 39

The History of the Indian Mutiny: Giving a Detailed Account of the Sepoy Insurrection in India. London: 1858-59. V. 37; 42; 44

The History of the Indian Mutiny. London: 1859. V. 42

Slavery in the United States: a Narrative of the Life and Adventures of Charles Ball, a Black Man. Lewistown: 1836. V. 45

BALL, EDWARD I.

Duties Payable on Goods, Wares and Merchandize, Imported Into the United States of America, from and After the 30th June, 1800. The Duties of Tonnage, Rates of Fees, Drawbacks, etc. New York: 1803. V. 41

BALL, EDWARDS

Hounds will meet. London: 1931. V. 37

BALL, ELIZA CRAUFURD

The Christian Armour. New York: 1866. V. 37; 38; 44

BALL, HENRY WILLIAM

The Social History and Antiquities of Barton-Upon-Humber. Barton-on-Humber: 1856. V. 41

BALL, ISAAC

An Analytical View of the Animal Economy, Calculated for the Students of Medicine, As Well as Private Gentlemen . . . New York: 1808. V. 38; 42

BALL, J.

Peaks, Passes and Glaciers. A Series of Excursions by Members of the Alpine Club. First & Second Series. London: 1859, 1862. V. 37

BALL, JAMES MOORE

Andreas Vesalius. The Reformer of Anatomy. St. Louis: 1910. V. 38; 39; 40; 41

BALL, JOHN

A Friendly Triall of the Grounds Tending to Separation; In a Plain and Modest Dispute Touching the Lawfulness of a Stinted Liturgie and Set Form of Prayer . . . Cambridge: 1640. V. 46

John Ball: Member of the Wyeth Expedition to the Pacific Northwest, 1832 . . . Glendale: 1925. V. 40

A New Compendious Dispensatory. London: 1769. V. 41

BALL, JOHN T.

Historical Review of the Legislative Systems Operative in Ireland, From the Invasion of Henry the Second to the Union (1172-1800). London: 1889. V. 41

BALL, JOHNSON

Paul and Thomas Sandby Royal Academicians. Bath: 1985. V. 42; 44

Paul and Thomas Sandby, Royal Academicians. Cheddar: 1985. V. 39

BALL, KATHERINE M.

Bamboo: Its Cult and Culture, Paintings by Wang Tseng-Tsu, Imperial Prince Painter. Berkeley: 1945. V. 41; 46

Decorative Motives of Oriental Art. London: 1927. V. 39; 42; 44; 45; 46

BALL, NICHOLAS

The Pioneers of '49. A History of the Excurison of the Society of California Pioneers of New England From Boston tot he Leading Cities of the Golden State, April 10-May 17, 1890. Boston: 1891. V. 37; 42; 43

Voyages of Nicholas Ball, from 1838 to 1853 . . . Boston: 1895. V. 46

BALL, RICHARD

Astrology Improv'd; or, a Compendium of the Whole Art of the Most Noble Science. London: 1723. V. 39

BALL, ROBERT STAWELL

A Popular Guide to the Heavens. London: 1925. V. 40

BALL, THOMAS

Two Books of Elegies. London: 1697. V. 40

BALL, W. W. ROUSE

An Essay on Newton's 'Principia'. London: 1893. V. 45

BALL, WILLIAM

The Transcript; also, The Memorial and Other Poems. N.P.: London: 1853. V. 43

THE BALLAD Book, a Selection of the Choicest British Ballads. Editor William Allingham. London: 1864. V. 37; 40

THE BALLAD of a Little Musgrove and Lady Barnet: a Poem. 1986. V. 40; 45

BALLADS Weird and Wonderful. London: 1912. V. 46

BALLANCE, CHARLES ALFRED 1856-1936

Essays on the Surgery of the Temporal Bone. London: 1919. V. 42

Some Points in the Surgery of the Brain and Its membranes. London: 1907. V. 39; 42

Some Points in the Surgery of the Brain and Its Membranes. London: 1908. V. 45

A Treatise on the Ligation of the Great Arteries in Continuity. London: and New York: 1891. V. 40; 45

BALLANO, ANTONIO

Diccionario de Medicina y Cirugia o Biblioteca Manual Medico Quirurgica. Madrid: 1805-7. V. 37; 39; 41

BALLANTINE, JAMES

The Life of David Roberts, R.A. Edinburgh: 1866. V. 39

BALLANTINE, JAMES continued

One Hundred Songs. Glasgow: 1866. V. 41

A Treatise on Painted Glass, Shewing Its Applicability to Every Style of Architecture. London: 1845. V. 40

BALLANTYNE, A. RANDAL

Robert Hancock and His Works. London: 1885. V. 39

BALLANTYNE, J.

Refutation of the Mistatements and Calumnies Contained in Mr. Lockhart's Life of Sir Walter Scott, Bart, Respecting the Messrs. Ballantyne. London: 1838-39. V. 44

BALLANTYNE, JAMES ROBERT

A Grammar of the Hindustani Language; Followed by a Series of Grammatical Exercises for the Use of the Scottish Naval and Military Academy. London: 1838. V. 44

Principles of Persian Calligraphy. London: 1844. V. 40

BALLANTYNE, JANE B.

Aseop's Fables in Verse. Edinburgh: 1877. V. 37

BALLANTYNE, JOHN

An Examination of the Human Mind. Edinburgh: 1828. V. 45

BALLANTYNE, JOHN A.

Refutation of the Mistatements and Calumnies Contained in Mr. Lockhart's Life of Sir Walter Scott, Bart . . . Edinburgh: 1838. V. 44

BALLANTYNE, R. M.

The Dog Crusoe and His Master. London: 1914. V. 41

BALLANTYNE, ROBERT MICHAEL

The Butterfly's Ball and the Grasshopper's Feast. London: 1857. V. 46

The Coral Island; a Tale of the Pacific Ocean. London: 1858. V. 37; 39

Hudson's Bay. Edinburgh: 1848. V. 40

Hudson's Bay: or Every-Day Life in the Wilds of North America, During Six Years' Residence in the Territories of the Hon. Hudson's Bay Co. Boston: 1859. V. 40; 44; 46

Hudson's Bay: or Everyday Life in the Wilds of North America. Boston: 1859. V. 44

Snowflakes and Sunbeams; or, the Young Fur Traders. London: 1856. V. 38; 46

The Three Little Kittens. Edinburgh & New York: 1857. V. 39

BALLANTYNE, ROBERT MONTGOMERY

Hudson's Bay; or Every-Day Life in the Wilds of Old North America. Edinburgh & London: 1848. V. 37

BALLARD, ELLIS AMES

Catalogue Intimate and Descriptive of My Kipling Collection. Philadelphia: 1935. V. 44

BALLARD, GEORGE

Memoirs of Several Ladies of Great Britain, Who Have Been Celebrated for Their Writings or Skill in the Learned Languages Arts and Sciences. Oxford: 1752. V. 44; 45

Memoirs of British Ladies Who Have Been Celebrated for Their Writing or Skill in the Learned Languages, Arts and Sciences. London: 1775. V. 37; 41; 46

BALLARD, H. C.

Poems. Chicago: 1870. V. 46

BALLARD, J.

The Empire of the Sun. 1984. V. 37

BALLARD, J. G.

The Atrocity Exhibition. London: 1970. V. 45

The Atrocity Exhibition. London: 1970. V. 41; 43; 45; 46

Chronopolis and Other Stories. New York: 1971. V. 41; 42; 46

Concrete Island. London: 1974. V. 41; 46

Crash. London: 1973. V. 41; 45

The Crystal World. London: 1966. V. 40; 41; 46

Crystal World. London: 1966. V. 46

The Day of Creation. London: 1987. V. 38; 40; 41; 42; 43; 44

The Day of Forever: Stories. London: 1967. V. 41

The Disaster Area: Stories. London: 1967. V. 39; 41; 45

The Drought. London: 1965. V. 40; 41; 46

The Drowned World. London: 1962. V. 41; 44

The Drowned World and the Wind from Nowhere. 1965. V. 43

The Empire of the Sun. 1984. V. 39

The Empire of the Sun. London: 1984. V. 40; 41; 42; 43; 45

Empire of the Sun. New York: 1984. V. 38; 39; 40; 42; 43

The Four-Dimensional Nightmare. London: 1963. V. 40

Hello America. London: 1981. V. 41

High Rise. London: 1975. V. 41; 43; 45

Love and Napalm: Export U.S.A. New York: 1972. V. 41

Low-Flying Aircraft and Other Stories. London: 1976. V. 41

Myths of the Near Future: Stories. London: 1982. V. 41

News from the Sun. London: 1982. V. 41

The Terminal Beach: Stories. London: 1964. V. 41

The Unlimited Dream Company. London: 1979. V. 40

Vermilion Sands: Stories. London: 1973. V. 41

Why I Want to Fuck Ronald Reagan. Bright: 1968. V. 41

BALLAU, MATURIN M.

History of Cuba. New York: 1854. V. 40

BALLENGER, EDGAR

History of Urology. Baltimore: 1933. V. 41; 42; 45

BALLENTINE, GEORGE

Autobiography of an English Soldier in the United States Army. London: 1853. V. 37; 38; 40; 42; 44; 45

Autobiography of an English Solider in the United States Army. London: 1853. V. 37

The Mexican War, by an English Solider. New York. V. 41

BALLEYDIER, AUGUSTIN

Album Jacquard, Flore des Dessinateurs. Paris: 1856. V. 39

BALLIN, ADA S.

The Science of Dress in Theory and Practice. London: 1885. V. 45

BALLINGER, JOHN

Catalogue of Printed Literature in the Welsh Department. Cardiff: 1898. V. 44

BALLIVET, SUZANNE

Restif de la Bretone. Monsieur Nicolas: ou le Coeur Humain Devoile. Avec es ligthographies originales de Suzanne Ballivet. (Paris): 1956. V. 37

BALLOU, ADIN

A Concise Exposition of the Hopedale Community. N.P.: 1853. V. 37

An Elaborate History and Genealogy of the Ballous in America . . . Providence: 1888. V. 46

An Exposition of Views Respecting the Principal Facts, Causes and Peculiarities Involved in Spirit Manifestations . . . London: 1852. V. 41

History of Hopedale Community, From Its Inception to Its Virtual Submergence in the Hopedale Parish. Lowell: 1897. V. 46

History of the Town of Milford, Worcester County, Massachusetts, from Its Earliest Settlement to 1881. Boston: 1882. V. 37; 46

An Oration, Delivered July 4, 1827. Boston: 1827. V. 40

Practical Christian Socialism . . . Fundamental Principles, Constitutional Polity, Superiority to Other Systems. Hoedale: 1854. V. 37; 41

The True Scriptual Doctrine of the Second Advent; an Effectual Antidote to Millerism, and all Other Kindred Errors. Hopedale: 1843. V. 38; 39

Violations of the Federal Constitution, in the 'Irrepressible Conflict' Between the Pro-Slavery and Anti-Slavery Sentiments of the American People. Hopedale: 1861. V. 42

BALLOU, MATURIN

Biography of Rev. Hosea Ballou. Boston: 1852. V. 45

BALLOU, MATURIN MURRAY

Due South, or Cuba Past and Present. Boston & New York: 1885. V. 38; 41; 44

Fanny Campbell, The Female Pirate Captain. Boston: 1845. V. 37

History of Cuba, or, Notes of a Traveller in the Tropics. Boston: 1854. V. 40

The Spanish Musketeer. Boston: 1852. V. 44

Under the Southern Cross; or Travels in Australia, Tasmania, new Zealand, Samoa and Other Pacific Islands. Boston: 1888. V. 41

BALLOU, ROBERT

Early Klickitat Valley Days. Goldendale: 1938. V. 39; 42

BALMANNO, MRS.

Pen and Pencil. New York: 1858. V. 39

BALME, J. R.

American States, Churches and Slavery. London: 1863. V. 39

BALMIS, FRANCISCO JAVIER

Demostracion de la Efficaces Virtudes Nuevamente Descubiertas en Las Raices de Los Plantas de Nueva-Espana Especies de Agave Y De Begonia, Para La Curacion Del Vicio Venero Y Escrofuloso, Y de Otras Graves Enfer-Medades . . . Madrid: 1794. V. 40

BALSTON, T.

The Cambridge University Press Collection of Private Press Types, Kelmscott, Ashendene, Eragny, Cranach. Cambridge: 1951. V. 40; 41; 45; 46

BALSTON, THOMAS

The Cambridge University Press Collection of Private Press Types, Kelmscott, Ashendene, Eragny, Cranch. London: 1951. V. 38; 46

English Wood engraving, 1900-1950. London: 1951. V. 42

Sitwelliana 1915-1927. London: 1928. V. 40

William Balston: Paper Maker, 1759-1849. L: 1954. V. 40

William Balston, Paper Maker 1759-1849. London: 1954. V. 44

BALTARD, V.

Monographie des Halles Centrales de Paris Construites sous le Regne de Napoleon III et Sous l'Administration de M. le Baron Haussmann. Paris: 1873. V. 38

BALTES, F. W.

The Cost of Printing, A System in Practical Operation, with Forms and Books Especially Adapted to Large and Small Printing Concerns. Portland: 1894. V. 43

BALTHASAR, J. A.

Carta . . . en que da Noticia de la Exemplar Vida, Religiosas Virtudes, y Apostolicos Trabajos del Fervoroso Missionero el Venerable P. Francisco Mario Picolo. Mexico: 1752. V. 38; 40

Catalogus Peronarum & Domiciliorum . . . Mexico: 1751. V. 38; 40; 42

BALTHASAR, JUAN ANTONIO

Carta Del P. Provincial Juan Antonio Balthassar, en Que da Noticia de la Exemplar Vida, Religiosas Virtudes, y Apostolicos Trabajos del Seroroso . . . Mexico: 1752. V. 45

THE BALTIMORE Book, a Christmas and New Year's Present. Baltimore: 1838. V. 39

BALTIMORE CATECHISM

Catechism of Christian Doctrine Prepared and Enjoined by Order of the Third Plenary Council of Baltimore. Translated into Flat-Head. Woodstock College: 1891. V. 38; 39; 43

BALTIMORE, FREDERICK CALVERT, 6TH BARON

A Tour to the East, In the Years 1763 and 1764. London: 1767. V. 38; 40

BALTIMORE Furniture. The Work of Baltimore and Annapolis Cabinetmakers from 1760 to 1810. Baltimore: 1947. V. 39

BALTIMORE. MUSEUM OF ART

The History of Bookbinding. 525-1950 A.D. An Exhibition Held at the Baltimore Museum of Art, November 12, 1957 to January 12, 1958. Baltimore: 1957. V. 40; 41; 42; 43; 45

BALTZ, LEWIS

The New Industrial Parks Near Irvine, California. New York: 1974. V. 45

BALZAC, HONORE

La Comedie Humaine. Boston: 1896. V. 42

La Comedie Humaine. Boston: 1898-99. V. 42

La Comedie Humaine. Boston: 1901. V. 38

Droll Stories. New York: 1928. V. 37; 42

Droll Stories Collected from the Abbeys of Touraine. London: (1874). V. 37

La Fille Aux Yeaux d'Or. (The Girl with Golden Eyes). London: 1896. V. 38

The Girl with the Golden Eyes. London. V. 40

The Hidden Treasures; or, The Adventures of Maitre Cornelius. Kentfield: 1953. V. 43

The Human Comedy. Philadelphia: 1895. V. 46

The Novels. Philadelphia: 1899. V. 38

Old Goriot. New York: 1948. V. 39; 45

The Physiology of Marriage . . . London: 1925. V. 44

Ten Droll Tales. London: 1926. V. 41

Une Passion dans le Desert. Paris: 1949. V. 38; 41

The Works. Philadelphia: 1901. V. 39; 40

The Works of . . . New York: 1915. V. 37; 39

BALZAC, JEAN LOUIS GUEZ, SIEUR DE 1594-1654

Aristippus, or Monsr. de Balsac's Masterpiece. Being a Discourse concerning the Court. With an exact Table of the Principall Matter, Englished by R. W. London: 1659. V. 37; 44

The Letters of Monsieur de Balzac. London: 1634. V. 42

The Letters of Movnsievr de Balzac. London: 1638. V. 38; 43

Lettres Choises. Amsterdam: 1656. V. 37

Le Prince. Paris: 1631. V. 45

BAMFIELD, ROBERT WILLIAM

A Practical Treatise on Tropical Dysentery, More Particularly as It Occurs in the East Indies . . . London: 1819. V. 42

BAMFORD, FRANCIS

Dear Miss Heber - an Eighteenth Century Correspondence. London: 1936. V. 46

BAMFORD, SAMUEL 1788-1872

The Dialect of South Lancashire. London: 1854. V. 38; 40

Early Days. London: 1849. V. 38; 41

Hours in the Bowers. Manchester: 1834. V. 38

Passages in the Life of a Radical. London: 1840-44. V. 39

Passages in the Life of a Radical. London: 1844. V. 38

BANBURY Chap Books and Nursery Tory Book Literature of the 18th and early 19th Centuries . . . London: 1890. V. 42

BANCKS, JOHN

The Weavers Miscellany; or, Poems on Several Subjects. London: 1730. V. 38; 41

BANCROFT, A. L.

Bancroft's Tourist Guide to the Geysers. San Francisco: 1871. V. 42

BANCROFT, AARON

The Life of George Washington. Boston: 1826. V. 40; 44

BANCROFT, ANNE

The Memorable Lives of Bummer & Lazarus: Citizens of San Francisco 185?-1865. Los Angeles: 1939. V. 39

BANCROFT, EDWARD

An Essay on the Natural History of Guiana, in South America. London: 1769. V. 39; 40; 41

Experimental Researches Concerning the Philosophy of Permanent Colours. London: 1794. V. 38

Experimental Researches Concerning the Philosophy of Permanent Colours. London: 1813. V. 38; 40

Experimental Researches Concerning the Philosophy of Permananet Colours, and the Best Means of Producing Them, by Dyeing, Calico Printing, &c. Philadelphia: 1814. V. 38; 40; 41; 42; 45; 46

BANCROFT, GEORGE

History of the American Revolution. London: 1852. V. 40; 42

History of the Colonization of the United States . . . Boston: 1854. V. 42

History of the United States of America: From the Discovery of the Continent. New York: 1891. V. 42

History of the Colonization of the United States. Boston: 1838-40. V. 40

Memorial Address on the Life and Character of Abraham Lincoln . . . 1866. San Francisco: 1929. V. 45

Poems. Cambridge: 1823. V. 43; 46

BANCROFT, GEORGE WOOD

Gold: Its Sources, and Methods of Obtaining It. Durban: 1868. V. 40

BANCROFT, HUBERT HOWE 1832-1918

Achievements of Civilization. The Book of Wealth. New York: 1896-1900. V. 46

Achievements of Civilization. New York: 1896-1904. V. 40

Alaska 1730-1885. San Francisco: 1866. V. 44

The Book of the Fair, an Historical and Descriptive Presentation of the World's Science, Art and Industry as Viewed through the Columbian Exposition at Chicago in 1893. Chicago & San Francisco: 1893. V. 37

The Book of the Fair: An Historical and Descriptive Presentation of the World's Science, Art and Industry, as Viewed through the Columbian Exposition at Chicago in 1893. Chicago: 1895. V. 40

Chronicles of the Builders of the Commonwealth: Historical Character Study. San Francisco: 1891. V. 40

Hand-Book Almanac for the Pacific States: an Offical Register and Year-Book of Facts, for the Years 1862. San Francisco: 1862. V. 40

The Historical Works of Hubert Howe Bancroft In Their Relation tot he Progress and Destiny of the Pacific States. San Francisco: 1885. V. 41

History of Alaska 1730-1885. San Francisco: 1886. V. 42

History of California. Santa Barbara: 1963-1970. V. 40

History of California. Santa Barbara: 1964-70. V. 38

History of California. 1969. V. 42

History of Central America. San Francisco: 1883-87. V. 37

History of Mexico - 1516-1887. San Francisco: 1883-88. V. 38; 42

History of the Northwest Coast, 1543-1846. San Francisco: 1884. V. 39; 44

History of the Northwest Coast. San Francisco: 1886. V. 37

History of Oregon. San Francisco: 1886/88. V. 44

History of Oregon, 1834-1888. San Francisco: 1886. V. 37; 43

History of the Pacific States of North America: Volume XXVII, British Columbia 1792-1887. San Francisco: 1887. V. 37

History of Texas and North Mexican States. San Francisco: 1890. V. 38; 40

History of the Life of Lroenzo Sawyer: A Character Study. San Francisco: 1891. V. 37

BANCROFT, HUBERT HOWE 1832-1918 continued

History of the North Mexican States and Texas, 1521-1889. San Francisco: 1883-1889. V. 42; 44; 45

History of Utah, 1540-1886. San Francisco: 1889. V. 38

History of Utah 1540-1887. San Francisco: 1890. V. 42; 45

Index to the Chronicles of the Builders of the Commonwealth. San Francisco: 1892. V. 43

Index to Bancroft's History of California. Glendale: 1985. V. 46

The Native Races of the Pacific States of North America. New York: 1875. V. 40

Native Races of the Pacific States. New York: 1875-76. V. 45

The Native Races. San Francisco: 1882-86. V. 39; 44

The Native Races. San Francisco: 1883. V. 43

The Northwest Coast. San Francisco: 1884. V. 44

The Works of . . . San Francisco: 1882-90. V. 44

Bancroft's Works. San Francisco: 1882-91. V. 45

Works. San Francisco: 1882-91. V. 42; 45

Works. San Francisco: 1883-1890. V. 38

The Works of Hubert Howe Bancroft. San Francisco: 1883-1890. V. 39; 42

The Works of . . . San Francisco: 1883-90. V. 39

The Works. San Francisco: 1886-90. V. 41; 42

The Works of Hubert Howe Bancroft. San Francisco: 1886-90. V. 45

The Works . . . . New York: 1967. V. 40

BANCROFT, JOHN

Henry the Second, King of England, with the Death of Rosamond. London: 1693. V. 39

King Edward the Third, With the Fall of Mortimer Earl of March. London: 1691. V. 38; 41

The Tragedy of Sertorius. London: 1679. V. 39; 44; 46

BANCROFT, JOSEPH

Census of the City of Savannah, Together with Statistics, Relating to the Trade, Commerce, Mechanical Arts and Health of the Same . . . Savannah: 1848. V. 40

BANCROFT, SIDNEY C.

Report of Some of the Proceedings in the Case of Oliver Earle and Others, in Equity, Against William Wood and Others; in the Supreme Judicial Court of the Commonwealth of Massachusetts. Boston: 1855. V. 38

BANCROFT, THOMAS

The Poetical Correspondent; or Sketches of Manchester in Verse . . . Manchester: 1777. V. 40

Two Bookes of Epigrammes and Epitaphs. London: 1639. V. 43

BANCROFT'S Tourist Gide. The Geysers. San Francisco and ARound the Bay. (North). San Francisco: 1871. V. 39; 45

BANDALIER, ADOLPH F.

Historical Introduction to Studies Among the Sedentary Indians of New Mexico. Boston: 1881. V. 42

BANDEL, EUGENE

Frontier Life in the Army, 1854-1861. Glendale: 1932. V. 41; 44

BANDELIER, ADOLF FRANCIS ALPHONSE 1840-1914

Contributions to the History of the Southwestern Portion of the United States. Cambridge: 1890. V. 37; 39; 40; 42; 43

The Southwestern Journals of . . . 1966/70/75/84. V. 43

BANDELIER, ADOLPH FRANCIS ALPHONSE 1840-1914

The Delight Makers. New York: 1890. V. 37; 38; 40; 45

Final Report of Investigations Among the Indians of the Southwestern United States. Cambridge: 1890. V. 38; 39; 42

Historical Introduction to Studies Among the Sedentary Indians of New Mexico. Boston: 1881. V. 43

A History of the Southwest. 1969. V. 38

Indians of the Rio Grande Valley. Albuquerque: 1937. V. 44

The Islands of TIticaca and Koati. (Bolivia), New York: 1910. V. 37

The Islands of Titicaca and Koati. New York: 1910. V. 42

Report of an Archaeological Tour in Mexico in 1881. V. 42

Report of an Arachaeological Tour in Mexico in 1881. Boston: 1884. V. 45

BANDELLO, MATTEO

Certain Tragical Discourses. London: 1898. V. 46

Histoires Tragiques. Lyon & Paris. V. 44

The Novels. London: 1890. V. 40

BANDINEL, JAMES

The Star of Lovell; a Tale of the Poor Clery. London: 1862. V. 40

BANDINELLI, R. B.

Hellenistic-Byzantine Miniatures of the Iliad. Olten: 1955. V. 39

BANDINELLI, RANUCCIO BIANCHI

Rome: the Late Empire. Roman Art A.D. 200-400. London: 1971. V. 40; 42; 44

Rome: the Centre of Power. London: 1970. V. 40

Rome: the Late Empire. Roman Art A.D. 200-400. New York: (1971). V. 37

BANDINI, ANGELO MARIA

Collectio Veterum Aliquot Monumentorum . . . Arezzo: 1752. V. 38

BANDINI, RALPH

Veiled Horizons. Stories of Big Game Fish of the Sea. New York: 1939. V. 39; 43; 46

BANERJI, M. L.

The Orchids of Nepal Himalaya. London: 1984. V. 46

The Orchids of Nepal Himalaya. Vaduz: 1984. V. 37; 38

BANFIELD, RAFAELIO DE

Lord Byron's Love Letter. New York: 1955. V. 39

BANFIELD, T. C.

The Organization of Industry, Explained in a Course of Lectures Delivered in the University of Cambridge in Easter Term 1844. London: 1848. V. 42; 46

BANGS, J. K.

The General Idiot. New York: 1908. V. 45

The Genial Idiot. New York: 1908. V. 44

BANGS, JOHN KENDRICK

Alice in Blunderland. New York: 1907. V. 43

Echoes of Cheer. Boston: 1912. V. 42

The Idiot. New York: 1895. V. 38; 46

The Mantel-Piece Minstrels, and Other Stories. New York: 1896. V. 43

R. Holmes & Co. New York: 1906. V. 46

R. Holmes & Co. New York/London: 1906. V. 41

BANIER, ANTOINE, ABBE

The Mythology and Fables of the Ancients, Explain'd from History. London: 1739-40. V. 46

BANIM, JOHN

The Anglo-Irish of the Nineteenth Century. London: 1828. V. 46

The Boyne Water, a Tale, by the O'Hara Family. London: 1826. V. 43

Father Connell, by the O'Hara Family. London: 1842. V. 43

The Smuggler; a Tale. London: 1831. V. 43

Tales, by the O'Hara Family: Containing Crohoore of the Bill-Hook, The Fetches and John Doe. London: 1825. V. 37; 43; 45; 46

BANK OF ENGLAND

An Historical Catalogue of Engravings and Paintings in the Bank of England. London: 1928. V. 38; 40; 44

BANK OF IRELAND

A Copy of the Charter of the Corporation of the Governor and Company of the Bank of Ireland. Dublin: 1798. V. 42

BANKART, GEORGE P.

The Art of the Plasterer. London: 1908. V. 44

BANKES, THOMAS

Royal System of Universal Geography - Antient and Modern - history of all countries and voyages and travels. London: 1787. V. 37

BANKOFF, GEORGE

The Story of Plastic Surgery. London: 1952. V. 41; 45

BANKS, CHARLES EUGENE

The Artistic Guide to Chicago and the World's Columbian Exposition. N.P.: 1893. V. 46

BANKS, EDGAR JAMES

Bismya or the Lost City of Adab. New York: 1912. V. 40

BANKS, HENRY

The Vindication of John Banks, of Virginia, Against Foul Calumnies Published by Judge Johnson of Charleston, South Carolina . . . Frankfort: 1826. V. 44

BANKS, IAIN

The Player of Games. London: 1988. V. 45

The Wasp Factory. London: 1984. V. 41; 45; 46

The Wasp Factory. 1984. V. 37

BANKS, ISABELLA VARLEY 1821-1897

The Manchester Man. London: 1876. V. 43

The Slowly Grinding Mills. London: 1893. V. 40

BANKS, JOHN

The Albion Queens; or the Death of Mary Queen of Scotland. London: 1704. V. 40

Cyrus the Great; or, the Tragedy of Love. London: 1696. V. 38; 41

An Epitome of a Course of Lectures on Natural and Experimental Philosophy. Kendal: 1775. V. 38

The History of the Life and Reign of the Czar Peter the Great, Emperor of All Russia. London: 1740. V. 41; 42

The Innocent Usurper; or, the Death of Lady Jane Grey. London: 1694. V. 38

On the Power of Machines, etc., Including Doctor Barker's Mill . . . Kendal: 1803. V. 44; 46

A Short Critical Review of the Political Life of Oliver Cromwell, Lord-Protector of the Commonwealth of England, Scotland and Ireland. London: 1739. V. 39

A Short Critical Review of the Political Life of Oliver Cromwell, Lord Protector of the Commonwealth of England, Scotland and Ireland . . . London: 1747. V. 46

A Treatise on Mills in Four Parts. London: 1795. V. 38; 40; 45; 46

The Unhappy Favourite. London: 1682. V. 38; 41

Vertue Betray'd: or, Anna Bullen. London: 1682. V. 37; 45

BANKS, JOSEH

A Short Account of the Cause of the Disease in Corn, Called by Farmers the Blight, the Mildew and the Rust. London: 1805. V. 43

BANKS, JOSEPH

Illustrations of the Botany of Captain Cook's Voyage Round the World in H.M.S. Endeavour in 1768-71. (Volume 3 titled 'Illustrations of Australian Plants Collected in 1770 During Captain Cook's Voyage Round the World in H.M.S. Endeavour). London: 1900-05. V. 42

Illustrations of Australian Plants Collected in 1770 During Captain Cook's Voyage Round the World in H.M.S. Endeavour. London: 1905. V. 42

Joseph Banks in Newfoundland and Labrador, 1766. Berkeley and Los Angeles: 1971. V. 46

Journal of the Right Hon. Sir Joseph Banks During Captain Cook's First Voyge in H.M.S. Endeavour in 1768-71 . . . London: 1896. V. 37; 38

The Journal of Joseph Banks in the Endeavour, 1768-1771. Guildford: 1980. V. 41; 43; 46

Letters on Iceland . . . Dublin: 1780. V. 42

The Propriety of Allowing a Qualified Exportation of Wool Discussed Historically. London: 1782. V. 40; 43

A Short Account of the Cause of the Disease in Corn, called by farmers the Blight, the Mildew, and the Rust. London: 1805. V. 39; 40

BANKS, LANGLEY

The Joiner's Compaion to a New System of Handrailing, Namely the Square Cut. Manchester: 1853. V. 40

BANKS, LOUIS A.

Censor Echoes; or, Words That Burned, and Speeches of Some of the Prominent Temperance Workers of Oregon and Washington. Portland: 1882. V. 42

BANKS, LYNNE REID

The L-Shaped Room. London: 1960. V. 38

BANKS, ROBERT WEBB

The Battle of Franklin, November 30, 1864, the Bloodiest Engagement of the War Between the States. New York: 1908. V. 44

BANKS, RUSSELL

Waiting to Freeze. Northwood Narrows: 1969. V. 45

BANKS, THOMAS C.

History of the Ancient Noble Family of Marmyun, their singular office of King's Champion . . . also other dignitorial tenures, and the services of London, Oxford, &c., on the Coronation-Day. London: 1817. V. 37

BANKS, THOMS CHRISTOPHER 1765-1854

The Dormant and Extinct Baronage of England . . . from the Norman Conquest to the Year 1809. London: 1807-1809. V. 38

BANKS, W. L.

Flora Exotica; or, Companion to the Green-House. London: 1893. V. 43

BANKS, WILLIAM

The English Master; or Student's Guide to Reasoning and Composition . . . London: 1829. V. 42

BANKS, WILLIAM MITCHEL

A Narrative of the Voyage of the Argonauts in 1880. N.P.: Edinburgh: 1881. V. 42

BANNAN, T.

Pioneer Irish of Onondaga, c. 1776-1847. New York: 1911. V. 37; 43

BANNARD, JOHN

A Defence of Several Proposals for Raising of Three Millions for the Service of the Government for the Year 1746. London: 1746. V. 41

BANNATYNE CLUB

Notices Relative to the Bannatyne Club . . . February 1823, Including Critiques on Some Of Its Publications. Edinburgh: 1836. V. 39

BANNATYNE, GEORGE

Ancient Scottish Poems. Edinburgh: 1770. V. 43; 46

The Bannatyne Manuscript: 1568. N.P.: 1896. V. 40

THE BANNER of Truth. Hackensack: 1866-78. V. 38

BANNERMAN, ANNE

Tales of Superstition and Chivalry. London: 1802. V. 39

BANNERMAN, DAVID ARMITAGE

The Birds of Tropical West Africa . . . London: 1930-51. V. 43

Birds of the Atlantic Islands. London: 1963-68. V. 37; 38; 39

Birds of the Atlantic Islands. London: 1963-68. V. 38

The Birds of the British Isles. Edinburgh: 1953. V. 38; 42

The Birds of the British Isles. London: 1953-1963. V. 37; 39; 44

Birds of the British Isles. Edinburgh: 1953-62. V. 39

The Birds of the British Isles. Edinburgh: 1953-63. V. 45

The Birds of the British Isles. Edinburgh: 1953-63. V. 46

The Birds of the British Islands. London: 1953-63. V. 42; 45

The Birds of the British Isles. London: 1956. V. 38

The Birds of the British Isles. Volume 5 - Birds of Prey. London: 1956. V. 45

Birds of Cyprus. Edinburgh: 1958. V. 44

Birds of Cyprus. Edinburgh: 1958. V. 38; 41

Birds of Cyprus. Edinburgh: 1958. V. 39

Birds of Cyprus. London: 1958. V. 37; 38; 40; 46

The Birds of Tropical West Africa with Special Reference to those of Gambia, Sierra Leone, the Gold Coast and Nigeria. London: 1930. V. 41

The Birds of Tropical West Africa with Special Reference to Those of Gambia, Sierra Leone, the Gold Coast and Nigeria. London: 1930-51. V. 37; 38; 39; 40; 43; 46

The Birds of Tropical West Africa. Volume 7: Weaver Birds. London: 1949. V. 37; 38

The Birds of West and Equatorial Africa. London: 1952. V. 39; 40

The Birds of West and Equatorial Africa. Edinburgh: (1953). V. 37

The Birds of West Equatorial Africa. Edinburgh & London: 1953. V. 39

Birds of West & Equatorial Africa. London: 1953. V. 39

The Birds of West and Equatorial Africa. London: 1953. V. 43; 44

The Canary Islands, Their History, Natural History and Scenery. London: 1922. V. 38; 46

History of the Birds of the Azores. London: 1966. V. 37

History of the Birds of the Cape Verde Islands. London: 1968. V. 37

BANNERMAN, HELEN

Little Degchie-head An Awful Warning to Bad Babas. London: 1903. V. 41; 46

Little Degchie-Head. London: 1903. V. 41

Little Black Mingo. London: 1901. V. 45; 46

The Story of Little Black Mingo. 1902. V. 46

Little Black Quibba. London: 1902. V. 45

Little Black Sambo. N.P.. V. 46

The Story of Little Black Sambo. London: 1899. V. 42; 44; 46

The Story of Little Black Sambo. London: 1901. V. 46

The Story of Little Black Sambo. London: 1902 (1899). V. 46

The Story of Little Black Sambo. London: 1903. V. 45

Little Black Sambo. Chicago: 1905. V. 43

Little Black Sambo. 1919. V. 46

Little Black Sambo. 1927. V. 46

The Story of Little Black Sambo. 1931. V. 46

The Story of Little Black Sambo. London: 1932. V. 45

The Story of Sambo and the Twins. London: 1937. V. 46

Little Black Sambo. 1940. V. 46

Little Black Sambo. Arkansas: 1940. V. 38

The Story of Little Black Sambo. London: 1941. V. 46

Little Black Sambo. New York: 1943. V. 46

The Story of Little Black Sambo. Berkeley: 1983. V. 38

BANNET, IVOR

The Amazons. 1948. V. 44

The Amazons. 1948. V. 40

The Amazons. 1948. V. 38

The Amazons. London: 1948. V. 37; 39; 40; 46

The Amazons. Waltham St. Lawrence: 1948. V. 41; 45

BANNING, KENDALL

Bypaths in Arcady: a Book of Love Songs. Chicago: 1915. V. 37; 45

BANNING, KENDALL continued

Songs of the Love Uneding Sonnet Sequence. Chicago: 1912. V. 41

BANNING, WILLIAM

Six Horses. New York: 1930. V. 43; 45

BANTA, RICHARD ELWELL 1904-

Indiana Books and Their Authors, 1816-1980. Crawfordsvile: 1949-1980. V. 38; 40

BANTOCK, MILES

On Many Greens. New York: 1901. V. 46

BANVARD, JOHN

Description of Banvard's Panorama of the Mississippi River, Painted on Three Miles of Canvas, Exhibiting a View of Country 1200 Miles in Length, Extending from the Mouth of the Missouri River to the City of New Orleans . . . Boston: 1847. V. 37; 38; 39; 44; 45

Description of Banvard's Panorama of the Mississippi River, Painted on Three Miles of Canvas . . . Boston: 1847. V. 38

Description of Banvard's Panroama of the Mississippi and Missouri Rivers . . . London: 1848. V. 39

BANVARD, JOSEPH

Tragic Scenes in the History of Maryland and the Old French War. Boston: 1856. V. 46

BANVILLE, JOHN

Long Lankin. London: 1970. V. 42

BANYER, HENRY

Pharmacopoeia Pauperum; or, The Hosptial Dispensatory. London: 1718. V. 41

BAPTIST CHURCH. GEORGIA. LOWER CANOOCHEE ASSOCIATION

Minutes of the Lower Canoochee Association in Session with the Church at Upper Black Creek, Bulloch County Georgia . . . N.P.: 1862? V. 45

BAPTIST MISSIONARY AND EDUCATION CONVENTION

Minutes of the Eighth Annual Meeting of the Baptist Missionary & Education Convention of Indian Territory. Atoka: 1890. V. 38

BAPTIST MISSIONARY AND EDUCATIONAL COVNENTION

Minutes of the Tenth Annual Meeting of the Baptist Missionary and Education Covnention . . . Oklahoma City: 1892. V. 38

BAPTISTA, JUAN

Sermonario en Lengua Mexicana . . . Primera Parate. Mexico: 1606. V. 37

BAPTISTA MANTUANUS 1448-1516

F. Baptiste Mantuani Carmelite Theologi; Aureum Contra Impudice Scribentes Opusculum . . . Paris: 1510. V. 43

Opera. Paris: 1513. V. 39

Opera Omnia. Antwerp: 1576. V. 42

De Patientia. Basel: 1499. V. 45

BAQUET, CAMILLE

History of the First Brigade, New Jersey Volunteers, from 1861 to 1865. Trenton: 1910. V. 42

BAR-ADON, PESSAH

The Cave of the Treasure. The Finds from the Caves in Nahal Mishmar. Jerusalem: 1980. V. 37

THE BAR, With Sketches of Eminent Judges, Barristers &c. London: 1825. V. 45

BARABINO, CARLO

Piante e Prospetti del Teatro Carlo Felice di Genova . . . Genova: 1827. V. 37

BARAG, D.

Catalogue of Western Asiatic Glass in the British Museum. London: 1985. V. 42

BARAGA, F.

A Dictionary of the Otchipwe Language, Explained in English. Montreal: 1881. V. 42

BARAGA, R. R. BISHOP

A Dictionary of the Otchipwe Language, Explained in English. Montreal: 1878-80. V. 37

A Theoretical and Practical Grammar of the Otchipwe Language for the Use of Missionaries and Other Persons Living Among the Indians . . . (with) A Dictionary of the Otchipwe Language Explained in English . . . Montreal: 1878. V. 41

BARAKA, AMIRI

Confirmation: an Anthology of African American Women. New York: 1983. V. 46

BARAKAT GALLERY

The Barakat Gallery: a Catalogue of the Collection. Beverly Hills: 1985. V. 40; 44

BARAMKI, D. C.

The Coin Collection of the American University of Beirut Museum. Beirut: 1974. V. 37

BARATARIANA. A Select Collection of Fugitive Politcal Pieces, Published During the Administration of Lord Townshend in Ireland. Dublin: 1777. V. 37; 39

BARATTIERI, G. B.

Architettura d'Acque. Piacenzo: 1699. V. 37

BARBA, ALVARO ALONSO

Arte de los Metales . . . Reimpreso por el Real Tribunal de Mineria de Esta Capital de Orden del Excmo. Sr. Virey. Lima: 1817. V. 41

BARBA, POMPEO DE LA d. 1582.

I discorsi filosofici . . . Venice: 1553. V. 37

Spositione d'un Sonetto Plantonico, Fatto Sopra il Primo Effecto d'Amore . . . Florence: 1554. V. 38; 39; 40

BARBARIAN PRESS

Sorts & Founts. A Showing of Typefaces Held at Barbarian Press. Columbia: 1983. V. 39

Sorts and Founts: A Showing of Typefaces Held at Barbarian Press, Set & Printed by Hand at the Press in Steelhead B.C. June MCMXXCIII. Mission: 1983. V. 41

BARBARITIES of the Enemy Exposed in a Report and the Documents Accompanying Said Report. Troy: 1813. V. 41
BARBARITIES of the Enemy Exposed in a Report . . . and the Documents Accompanying Said Report. Troy: 1813. V. 37; 42; 45

BARBARITIES of the Enemy, Exposed in a Report of the Committee of the House of Representatives of the United States, Appointed to Enquire Into the Spirit and Manner in Which the War Has Been Waged by the Enemy, and the Documents Accompanying Said . . . Worcester: 1814. V. 37; 39; 42; 46

BARBARO, DANIEL

La Pratica Della Perspettiva. Venetia: 1569 (1568). V. 37

BARBARO, DANIELE

La Practica Della Perspettiva . . . Opera Molto Utile a Pittori, a Scultori & Ad Architetti. 1568. V. 42

La Practica della Perspettiva . . . Opera Molto Utile a Pittori, a Scultori & ad Architettti. Venice: 1569. V. 40; 44; 45

La Pratica della Perspettiva . . . Opera Molto Utile a Pittori, a Scultori & ad Architetti. Venetia: 1568. V. 41

BARBARO, IOSAPHAT

Viaggi Fatti Da Venetia, Alla Tana, in Persia, in India et in Constantinopoli. Venice: 1543. V. 40

BARBARUS, APULEIUS

The Herbal of . . . 1925. V. 44

THE BARBARY Voyage of 1638. Philadelphia: 1929. V. 46

BARBAULD, ANNA LAETITIA AIKIN 1743-1825

Epistle to William Wilberforce, Esq. On the rejection of the Bill for Abolishing the Slave Trade . . . The Second Edition. London: 1791. V. 37

A Legacy for Young Ladies, Consisting of Miscellaneous Pieces, in Prose and Verse. New York: 1826. V. 37

Pastoral Lessons, and Parental Conversations. London: 1803. V. 39

Poems. London: 1773. V. 37; 38; 40; 42; 44; 45

Poems. Warrington: 1773. V. 46

Remarks on Mr. Giblert Wakefield's Enquiry into the Expediency and Propriety of Public or Social Worship. London: 1792. V. 39

Selections from the Spectator, Tatler, Guardian and Freeholder . . . London: 1804. V. 46

The Works with a Memoir by Lucy Aikin. London: 1825. V. 41; 42; 43; 46

BARBAULD, ANNA LETITIA AIKIN 1743-1825

Poems. London: 1777. V. 41

The Works, with a Memoir by Lucy Aikin. London: 1825. V. 42

The Works . . . Boston: 1826. V. 42

BARBAULT, JEAN

Les Plus Beaux Monuments de Rome Ancienne, Ou Recueil des Plus Beaux Morceau de l'Antiquite Romaine Qui Existent Encore . . . Rome: 1761. V. 37; 46

BARBE DE MARBOIS, FRANCOIS, MARQUIS DE

The History of Louisiana, Particularly of the Cession of that Colony to the United States of America. Philadelphia: 1830. V. 37; 38; 39; 40; 42

BARBEAU, MARIUS

Cornelius Krieghoff, Pioneer Painter of North America. Toronto: 1934.
V. 37; 41

Haida Myths Illustrated in Argillite Carvings. 1953. V. 43

Haida Myths: Illustrated with Argillite Carvings. Ottawa: 1953. V. 39

Haida Carvers in Argillite. Ottawa: 1957. V. 37

Indian Days in the Canadian Rockies. Toronto: 1923. V. 40; 45

Mountain Cloud. Caldwell: and Toronto: 1944. V. 45

Totem Poles. Ottawa. V. 38

Totem Poles. Ottawa: 1950. V. 39

Totem Poles. Ottawa: 1964. V. 43

BARBER, EDWARD C.

The Crack Shot; or, Young Rifleman's Complete Guide . . . New York:
1868. V. 42

BARBER, EDWIN A.

The Maiolica of Mexico. Philadelphia: 1908. V. 46

Tulip Ware of the Pennsylvania German Potters. Philadelphia: 1903.
V. 39; 46

BARBER, EDWIN ATLEE

The Pottery and Porcelain of the United States. New York: 1901. V. 41

BARBER, EDWIN ATLEY

The Pottery and Porcelain of the United States. New York and London:
1901. V. 40

BARBER, GEORGE, & CO.

Wire Works, Chester Street. Birmingham: 1875. V. 37

BARBER, J. T.

A Journey throughout South Wales and Monmouthsire. London: 1803. V. 39

A Tour throughout South Wales and Monmouthshire, Comprehending a
General Survey of the Piecturesque Scenery, Remains of Antiquity,
Historical Events, Peculiar Manners and Commercial Situations, of that
Interesting Portion of the British Empire. London: 1803. V. 41

BARBER, JOHN WARNER 1798-1885

Historical Collections of the State of New Jersey . . . Newark: 1855. V. 42

Historical Collections of New Jersey: Past and Present . . . New Haven:
1868. V. 46

Historical Collections of the State of New Jersey. New York: 1844. V. 37

History and Antiquites of New Haven . . . From Its Earliest Settlement to the
Present Time. New Haven: 1831. V. 37; 38; 39; 43

History and Antiquities of New Haven, Conn. New Haven: 1856. V. 40

The History and Antiquities of New England, New York, New Jersey and
Pennsylvania. Hartford: 1844. V. 37

Interesting Events in the History of the United States. New Haven: 1828.
V. 39

Views in New-Haven and Its Vicinity; with a Particular Description to Each
View. New Haven: 1825. V. 41

BARBER, MARJORIE

A Short History of Holy Trinity Church, Sloane St., Chelsea, P.P.
Letchworth: 1958? V. 44

BARBER, MARY

Poems on Several Occasions. London: 1734. V. 38; 40; 41; 42; 45

Some Drawings of Ancient Embroidery. London: 1880. V. 37; 44

The True Narrative of the Five Years' Suffering & Perilous Adventures by
Miss Barber . . . Philadelphia: 1872. V. 37; 45

The True Narrative of the Five Years' Suffering and Perilous Adventures, by
Miss Barber, Wife of 'Squatting Bear', a Celebrated Sioux Chief.
Philadelphia: 1873. V. 41

The True Narrative of the Five Years' Suffering and Perilous Adventures
By . . . Philadelphia: 1880. V. 45

BARBER, THOMAS

Barber's Picturesque Illustrations, of the Isle of Wight . . . London: 1835.
V. 41; 44

Barber's Picturesque Illustrations of the Isle of Wight Comprising Views of
Every Object of Interest on the Island . . . London: 1834. V. 37; 41

Picturesque Illustrations of the Isle of Wight. London. V. 42

Picturesque Illustrations of the Isle of Wight. London: 1830. V. 45

BARBER, WILLIAM HENRY

The Case of Mr. W. H. Barber . . . London: 1849. V. 42

BARBERINI, FRANCESCUS

Maphaei S.R.E. Card Barberini nunc Urbani PP VIII Poemata. Rome: 1631.
V. 39

BARBEY D'AUREVILLY, JULES AMEDEE

What Never Dies. Paris: 1902. V. 42

BARBIER, ANTOINE 1765-1825

Catalogue des Livres de la Bibliotheque du Conseil d'Etat. Paris: 1802.
V. 40

BARBIER, GEORGE

Album Dedie a Tamara Karsavina. Pris: 1914. V. 38

Designs on the Dances of Vaslav Nijinsky. London: 1913. V. 39

Falbalas & Fanfreluches. Paris: 1921-25. V. 43

The Romance of Perfume. New York: 1928. V. 37

BARBIER, MARCEL N.

Mining and Arts. Paris: 1956. V. 42

BARBOSA RODRIGUES, J.

Genera et Species Orchideaarum Novarum. Rio de Janeiro: 1877-81-82.
V. 38

BARBOSA, VINCENTE

Compendia da Relacam, que Veyo da India o Anno de 1691 . . . Lisbon:
1692. V. 41

BARBOUR, JOHN

The Bruce, or the History of Robert I, King of Scotland. London: 1790.
V. 40

The Buik of Alexander or the Buik of the Most Noble and Valiant
Conqueror Alexander the Grit. Edinburgh: 1921-29. V. 43

BARBOUR, PHILIP L.

The Jamestown Voyages Under the First Charter 1606-1609. Cambridge:
1969. V. 45

BARBOUR, PHILIP NORBOURNE

Journals of the Late Brevet Major Philip Norbourne Barbour, Captain in the
Third Regiment. New York: & London: 1936. V. 46

BARBOUR, T.

The Herpetology of Cuba. Cambridge: 1919. V. 37

BARBUT, J.

The Genera Insectorum of Linnaeus Exemplified. London: 1781. V. 38; 43

BARCENA, MANUEL

Manifesto Al Mundo. La Justicia Y La Necesidad de la Indepedencia de la
Nueva Espana. Puebla: 1821. V. 39

BARCIA, ANDRES GONZALES DE

Ensayo Cronologico, Para la Historia General de la Florida, Contienne los
Descubrimientos, y Principales Sucesos . . . Madrid: 1723. V. 39; 45

BARCLAY, ALEXANDER 1475-1552

The Shepheards Kalender . . . London: 1656. V. 43

BARCLAY, ANDREW

Life of Captain Andrew Barclay of Cambock, Near Launceston, Van
Diemen's Land. Edinburgh: 1854. V. 43

BARCLAY, ANTHONY

Wilde's Summer Rose; or the Lament of the Captive. Savannah: 1871.
V. 41

BARCLAY, C. N.

The History of the Cameronians (Scottish Rifles). Volume III (1933-1946).
1947. V. 40

The Regimental History of the 3rd Queen Alexandra's Own Gurkha Rifles.
Volume II 1927 to 1947. London: 1953. V. 41

BARCLAY, D.

A Book of South African Flowers - a Second Book of South African
Flowers. Cape Town: 1925-36. V. 37

BARCLAY, E. N.

Big Game Shooting Records. Together with Biographical Notes and
Anecdotes on the Most Prominent Big Game Hunters of Ancient and
Modern Times. London: 1932. V. 39

BARCLAY, EDGAR

Stonehenge and Its Earth-Works. London: 1895. V. 37; 42

BARCLAY, JAMES

A Complete and Universal English Dictionary. London: 1792. V. 39

A Complete and Universal Dictionary of the English Language . . . London:
1848. V. 45

The Greek Rudiments; in Which all the Grammatical Difficulties of That
Language, Are Adapted to the Capacities of Children . . . Edinburgh: 1754.
V. 42

A Treatise on Education: or, an Easy Method of Acquiring Lanuage, and
Introducing Children to the Knowledge of History, Geography, Mythology,
Antiquities, etc. Edinburgh: 1743. V. 37

Barclay's Complete and Universal English Dictionary. Liverpool: 1810. V. 40

The Universal English Dictionary. London: 1845. V. 40

BARCLAY, JAMES continued

Barclay's Universal English Dictionary. London: 1850. V. 39

BARCLAY, JAMES T.

The City of the Great King. Philadelphia: 1857. V. 38

BARCLAY, JAMES W.

Mormonism Exposed (Unveiled). The Other Side. Salt Lake City?: 1884-85. V. 42

BARCLAY, JOHN 1582-1621

His Argenis. London: 1625. V. 42; 44

John Barclay His Argenis. London: 1628. V. 46

Jo. Barclaii Argenis. Leiden: 1630. V. 42; 44

Barclay, His Argenis . . . London: 1636. V. 42; 43

Argenis, Figuris Aeneis Adillustrata, Suffixo Clave, Hoc Est, Nominum Propriorum Explicatione . . . Noribergae: 1673. V. 39; 41; 46

Arenis. Stockholm: 1740. V. 40

Argenis, pa Swenskio ofwersatt . . . Stockholm: 1740. V. 43

Argensis. Paris: 1621. V. 44

John Barclay, His Argensis. London: 1629. V. 44

Barclay His Argenis. London: 1636. V. 46

Euphormionis Lusinini, Sive . . . Satyricon, nunc Primum in Sex Paartes Dispertitum, & Notis Illustratum, cum Clavi. Leyden: 1674. V. 38

Euphormionis Luisinini, Sive Jo. Barclaii, Satyricon . . . Lugd. Batavorum: 1674. V. 39

Euphormio's Satyricon. London: 1954. V. 46

The Mirror of Minds or Barclay's Icon Animorum. London: 1633. V. 41

A New Anatomical Nomenclature, Relating to the Germs Which are Expressive of Position and Aspect in the Animal System. Edinburgh: 1803. V. 44

A Series of Engravings, Representing the Bones of the Human Skelton . . . Edinburgh: 1820. V. 41

BARCLAY, RACHEL

Select Pieces of Poetry, Intended to Promote Piety and Virtue in the Minds of Young People. London: 1795. V. 41; 42

BARCLAY, ROBERT

Agricultural Tour in the United States and Upper Canada, with Miscellaenous Notices. London: 1842. V. 39

The Anarchy of the Ranters, and Other Libertines . . . Philadelphia: 1757. V. 42

An Aplogy for the True Christian Divinity, being an explanation and vindication of the principals and doctrines of the people called Quakers. Birmingham: 1765. V. 37; 44

Apologie Oder Vertheidigungs-Schrift der Wahren Christlichen Gottesglahreit . . . Germantown: 1776. V. 43

An Apology for the True Christian Divinity, as the Same is Held Forth, and Preached by the People Called, in Scorn, Quakers. London: 1678. V. 38; 42

Robert Barclay's Apology for the True Christian Divinity Vindicated from John Brown's Examination and Pretended Confutation Thereof in the Book Called Quakerism in the Path-Way to Paganisme. London: 1679. V. 41

An Apology for the True Christian Divinity, As the Same is Held Forth and Preached by the People Called in Scorn, Quakers . . . Newport: 1729. V. 41

An Apology for the Christian Divinity as the Same Is Held Forth and Preached, by the People Called in Scorn, Quakers. London: 1736. V. 45

An Apology for The True Christian Divinity, Being an Explanation and Vindication of the Principles an Doctrines of the People Called Quakers . . . Birmingham: 1765. V. 38; 43; 45; 46

An Apology for the True Christian Divinity, Being an Explanation and Vindication . . . of the People Called Quakers . . . Birmingham: 1765. V. 45

An Apology for the True Christian Divinity. New York: 1832. V. 44

An Apology for the True Christian Divinity, as the Same is Held Forth, and Preached by the People, called, in Scorn, Quakers . . . Aberdeen: 1678. V. 37

A Catechism and Confession of Faith, Approved of, and Agreed Unto, by the General Assembly of the Patriarchs, Prophets and Apostles . . . Newport: 1752. V. 41; 44

Complete Narrative of all the Surprising Performances of Captain Barclay. London. V. 38

Theologiae Vere Christianae Apologia. 1676. V. 41

Theologiae vere Christianae Apologia. Amstelodami: 1676. V. 39

BARCLAY'S Universal Dictionary. London: 1850. V. 38

BARCROFT, JOSEPH 1872-1947

The Respiratory Function of the Blood. Cambridge: 1914. V. 45

BARD, PHILIP

Diencephalic Control of the Sympathetic Nervous System. Boston: 1927. V. 42

BARD, SAMUEL

A Guide for Young Shepards of Facts and Observations on the Character and Value of Merino Sheep. New York: 1811. V. 41

A Guide for Young Shepherds; or, Facts and Observations on the Character and Value of Merino Sheep. V. 37

Tentamen Medicum Inaugurale, de Viribus Opii. Edinburgh: 1765. V. 37

BARD, WAYNE

Sam Bass. Boston: 1936. V. 37

BARDAISAN

The Hymn of Bardaisan Rendered into English by F. Crawford Burkitt. London: 1899. V. 37

BARDAISAN. The Hymn, Rendered Into English by F. Crawford Burkitt. Colophon: 1899. V. 44

BARDE, FREDERICK S.

Life of 'Billy' Dixon Plainsman, Scout and Pioneer . . . Dallas: 1927. V. 39

Life and Adventures of 'Billy' Dixon of Adobe Walls, Texas Panhandle . . . A Narrative in which is Described Many Things Relating to the Early Southwest . . . Guthrie: (1914). V. 37; 38; 42; 44; 46

BARDEEN, CHARLES

Anatomy in America. Madison: 1905. V. 41

BARDI, GIROLAMO

Dichiaratione di Tutte le Istorie che si Contengono Nei Quadri Posti Novamente Nelle Sale Dello Scrutino & del Gran Consiglio del Palagio Ducale Nella Serenissima Republica di Vinegia. Venice: 1587. V. 40

Dichiaratione di Tutte le Istorie, che Si Contengono ne i Quadri Posti Nuovamente nelle Sale dell Scrutinio & del Gran Consiglio del Palagio Ducale della Serenissima Republica di Vinegia . . . Venice: 1601? V. 38; 39

Vittoria Navale Ottenvta Dalla Repvblica Venetiana Contra Othone Figlivolo Di Federigo. Venice: 1584. V. 37

BARDI, P. M.

Marino Mrini: Graphic Work and Painting. New York: 1960. V. 39

BARDSLEY, JAMES LOMAX 1801-1876

Dissertatio Medica Inauguralis, de Rabie Canina. Edinburgi: 1823. V. 39

Hospital Facts and Observations, Illustrative of the Efficacy of the new Remedies, Strychnia, Brucia,Acetate of Morphia, Veratria, Iodine, &c. London: 1830. V. 38

BARDSLEY, SAMUEL A.

Medical Reports of Cases and Experiments, with Observations, chiefly Derived from Hospital Practice. London: 1807. V. 41

BARDUZZI, BERNARDINO

A Letter in Praise of Verona (1489) in the Origin Latin Text, with an English translation by Betty Radice. Verona: 1974. V. 38; 40; 41; 42; 44; 45; 46

BARDWELL, THOMAS

Practical Treatise on Painting in Oil-Colours. London: 1795. V. 46

BARENTZEN, E. M.

Denmark. Copenhagen: 1856. V. 42

BARERE DE VIEUZAC, BERTRAND

Memoirs . . . London: 1896. V. 46

BARETTI, GIUSEPPE MARCO ANTONIO 1719-1789

An Account of the Manners and Customs of Italy with Observations on the Mistakes of Some Travellers with Regard to that Country. London: 1768. V. 41; 46

An Account of the Manners and Customs of Italy; with Observations on the Mistakes of Some Travellers . . . London: 1769. V. 42; 43

The Carmen Seculare of Horace. N.P.: London: 1779. V. 39

A Dictionary, Spanish and English and English and Spanish. London: 1778. V. 45

Easy Phraseology, for the Use of Young Ladies, Who Intend to Learn the Colloquial Part of the Italian Language. London: 1775. V. 39

A Grammar of the Italian Language. London: 1762. V. 41; 42; 45

An Introduction to the Most Useful European Languages, Consisting of Select Passages, from the Most Celebrated English, French, Italian and Spanish Authors. London: 1772. V. 40; 43

The Italian Library. London: 1757. V. 39; 42; 43; 45

A Journey from London to Genoa, through England, Portugal, Spain and France. London: 1770. V. 40; 41; 44; 45; 46

Opere Di Giuseppe Baretti. Milano: 1838-39. V. 39; 40; 41

Tolondron. London: 1786. V. 42

The Works, with a Memoir by Lucy Aikin. London: 1770. V. 43

BARETTI, JOSEPH

A Dictionary of the English and Italian Languages . . . To Which is Prefixed, an Italian and English Grammar. London: 1790. V. 38

Dictionary of the English and Italian Languages . . . London: 1824. V. 39

A Journey from London to Genoa, through England, Portugal, Spain and France. Dublin: 1770. V. 37

BARFIELD, OWEN

Danger, Ugliness and Waste. London: 1922-24. V. 43

The Silver Trumpet. London: 1925. V. 41; 46

BARFORD, RICHARD

The Assembly: an Heroi-comical Poem in Five Cantos. London: 1726. V. 38; 40; 42

The Virgin Queen. Dublin: 1728. V. 39

The Virgin Queen. London: 1729. V. 39; 41

BARGAGLI, GIROLAMO

Dialogo De'Givocchi Che nelle Vegghie Sanesi di Fare, Del Materiale Intronato. Siena: 1572. V. 38

Dialogo de' Givochi che Nelle Veghie Sanesi si Usano di Fare. Venice: 1574. V. 38

BARGIOCCHI, GIOVANNI BAPTISTA

Epigrammata Sacra, Moralia & Demonstrativa. Rome: 1624. V. 45

BARHAM, HENRY

An Essay Upon the Silk-Worm. London: 1719. V. 38

BARHAM, RICHARD HARRIS 1788-1845

The Ingoldsby Legends. London: 1840-42-47. V. 38; 46

The Ingoldsby Legends or Mirth and Marvels by Thomas Ingoldsby, Esquire. London: 1840. V. 43

The Ingoldsby Legends; or, Mirth and Marvels. London: 1840-2-7. V. 43

The Ingoldsby Legends or Mirth and Marvels. First, Second and Third Series. London: 1840-42-47. V. 38

The Ingoldsby Legends of Myrth and Marvels. London: 1840/42/47. V. 42

The Ingoldsby Legends. London: 1843-47. V. 38

The Ingoldsby Legends or Mirth and Marvels . . . London: 1852. V. 41

The Ingoldsby Legends. London: 1855. V. 38; 40; 41

The Ingoldsby Legends or Mirth and Marvels. London: 1855. V. 41

The Ingoldsby Legends. London: 1865. V. 38

The Ingoldsby Legends . . . London: 1867. V. 39

The Ingoldsby Legends or Mirth and Marvels. London: 1869. V. 46

The Ingoldsby Legends of Mirth and Marvel. London: 1878. V. 46

The Ingoldsby Legends, or Mirth and Marvels. London: 1882. V. 42

The Ingoldsby Legends. London: 1894. V. 38

The Ingoldsby Legends or Mirth and Marvels . . . London: 1894. V. 38

The Ingoldsby Legends or Mirths and Marvels. London: 1898. V. 40

The Ingoldsby Legends. London: 1907. V. 38

The Ingdoldsby Legends. London: 1907. V. 38; 39; 40; 41; 42; 43; 45

The Ingoldsby Legends or Mirth & Marvels by Thomas Ingoldsby. London: 1907. V. 37; 38; 40; 42; 43; 44; 45; 46

The Ingoldsby Legends Mirth and Marvels by Thomas Ingoldsby, Esqre. London: 1907. V. 39; 40; 41; 46

The Ingdoldsby Legends. London: 1909. V. 41

The Ingoldsby Legends of Mirth and Marvels. New York: 1911. V. 39

The Ingoldsby Legends. London: 1913. V. 41

The Ingoldsby Legends. London: 1920. V. 46

The Ingoldsby Legends. London: 1920. V. 39

The Ingoldsby Legends or Myth and Marvels. London: 1922. V. 40

The Ingoldsby Legends. London: 1929. V. 43

Ingoldsby Legends or Mirth & Marvels. London: 1930. V. 40

The Ingoldsby Legends. London: 1930. V. 40

The Ingoldsby Legends. London: 1870. V. 37

The Ingoldsby Legends. London: 1876. V. 37

The Ingoldsby Legends. London: 1898. V. 37

Ingoldsby Legends, or Mirth & Marvels, by Thomas Ingoldsbly. Illustrated by Arthur Rackham. London: 1930. V. 37

The Jackdaw of Rheims. London: 1913. V. 38; 39; 44; 45; 46

The Life and Remains of Theodore Edward Hook. London: 1849. V. 38

BARHAM, WILLIAM

Descriptions of Niagara; Selected from Various Travellers . . . Gravesend: 1847. V. 42; 43

BARILLI, GUISEPPE

Miranda! London: 1858-60. V. 43; 44

BARING, ALEXANDER

An Inquiry Into the Causes and Consequences of the Orders in Council; and of an Examination of the Conduct of Great Britain Towards the Neutral Commerce of America. London: 1808. V. 42; 45

BARING, DANIEL EBERHARD

Clavis Diplomaticus . . . Hanover: 1754. V. 40

BARING, EVELYN

Modern Egypt. New York: 1909. V. 38

BARING, FRANCIS 1740-1810

Brief Observations on a Late Letter Addressed to the Rt. Hon. W. Pitt by W. Boyd, Esq., etc. on the Stoppage of Issues in Specie by the Bank of England. London: 1801. V. 38; 41

Observations on the Establishment of the Bank of England, and on the Paper Circulation of the Country. London: 1797. V. 39

BARING-GOULD, SABINE 1834-1924

A Book of Fairy Tales. London: 1894. V. 41

A Book of Nursery Songs and Rhymes. London: 1895. V. 41

The Chorister, a Tale of King's College Chapel in the Civil Wars. Cambridge: 1855? V. 45

The Deserts of Southern France. An Introduction to the Limestone and Chalk Plateaux of Ancient Aquitaine. London: 1894. V. 37

Guavas the Tinner. London: 1897. V. 44

Iceland: Its Scenes and Sagas. London: 1863. V. 42; 43

In Exitu Israel. London: 1870. V. 38; 42; 43

In the Roar of the Sea. London: 1892. V. 38

Legends of Old Testament Characters, From the Talmud and Other Sources. London: 1871. V. 43

The Lives of the Saints. London: 1872-7. V. 46

The Lives of the Saints. London: 1897. V. 42

The Lives of the Saints. Edinburgh: 1914. V. 38

The Lives of the Saints. London: 1897-98. V. 37

Old English Fairy Tales. London: 1896. V. 41

Richard Cable. The Lightshipman. London: 1888. V. 43

Siegfried. London: 1904. V. 40; 43

The Silver Store. London: 1868. V. 43

BARING, MAURICE

Algae: an Anthology of Phrases. (with) Algae . . . Second Series. London: 1928/29. V. 37; 43

Poems: 1914-1919. London: 1920. V. 43

Sarah Bernhardt. New York & London: 1934. V. 41

Sonnets and Short Poems. Oxford and London: 1906. V. 37

The Story of Forget-Me-Not and Lily of the Valley. London: 1910. V. 40

Translations Ancient and Modern. V. 37

BARINSFATHER, BRUCE

The Bystander's Fragments from France. London: 1915-17. V. 43

Fragments from France. New York & London: 1917. V. 43

BARJAUD, J. B.

Description de Londres et de ses Edifices. Paris, London: 1810. V. 40

BARKER, A. S.

Deep Sea Sounding - A Brief Account of the Work Done by the U.S.S. Enterprise on a Round the World Curise During 1883-86 . . . New York: 1892. V. 39

BARKER, B. FORDYCE

The Puerperal Diseases. New York: 1874. V. 44

BARKER, BENJAMIN

Emily Elwood, or the Hermit of the Crags. Boston: 1845. V. 43

The Fine Arts. Forty-Eight Aquatint Colored Engravings by Theodore Fielding, from a Work Containing Forty-Eight Subjects of Landscape Scenery, Principally Views in and Near Bath, Painted in Oil, by Benjamin Barker. 1824. V. 38

Francisco, or, the Pirate of the Pacific. Boston: 1845. V. 44

Mornilva; or, the Outlaw of the Forest. Boston: 1846. V. 45

BARKER, C.

Books of Blood. 1984. V. 45

The Damnation Game. 1985. V. 37

BARKER, CECILY M.

Autumns Songs with Music From Flower Fairies of the Autumn. London: and Glasgow: 1910. V. 45

Summer Songs with Music. London: and Glasgow: 1910. V. 45

BARKER, CICLEY M.

The Book of the Flower Fairies. London. V. 46

A Flower Fairy Alphabet. London. V. 46

BARKER, CLIVE

Books of Blood. 1984. V. 42; 43

Books of Blood. Santa Cruz: 1985. V. 40

Books of Blood IV. Los Angeles: 1987. V. 44; 46

Cabal. New York: 1985. V. 43

Cabal. New York: 1988. V. 41; 42; 43

BARKER, CLIVE continued

The Damnation Game. New York: 1985. V. 39; 43

The Damnation Game. New York: 1987. V. 38; 43

In the Flesh. New York: 1985. V. 43

The Inhuman Condition. New York: 1986. V. 41; 43

Weaveworld. London: 1987. V. 38; 41; 42; 45

BARKER, ELLIOTT

A Fine Madness. New York: 1964. V. 42

BARKER, EUGENE

Mexico and Texas 1821-1835 . . . . Causes of the Texas Revoltuion. Dallas: 1928. V. 40

BARKER, EUGENE C.

Life of Stephen F. Austin. Nashville: 1925. V. 45

The Life of Stephen F Austin, Founder of Texas. Nashville & Dallas: 1925. V. 37; 38; 39; 40; 42; 44

Mexico and Texas, 1821-1835 . . . the Causes of the Texas Revolution. Dallas: 1928. V. 38; 42

BARKER, F. D.

The Angler's Paradise, Recollections of Twenty Years with Rod and Line In Ireland. London: 1929. V. 40

BARKER, GEORGE

Elegy on Spain. Manchester: 1939. V. 40

His Manuscript Diary for 1968. V. 46

Janus. London: 1935. V. 40

Poems. London: 1935. V. 43; 46

Roentgen Rays, Memoirs by Roentgen, Stokes and J. J. Thomson. New York: 1899. V. 41

Selected Poems. New York: 1941. V. 41

Thirty Preliminary Poems. London: 1930. V. 41; 43

Thrilling Adventures of the Whaler Alcyone - Killing Man-Eating Sharks in the Indian Ocean, Hunting Kangaroos in Australia. Peabody: 1916. V. 39

The True Confession of George Barker. London: 1950. V. 44

BARKER, H. M.

Tough Yarns: a Series of Naval Tales to Please All Hands . . . London: 1835. V. 44

BARKER, HENRY

The Polite Gentleman; or, Reflections Upon the Several Kings of Wit . . . London: 1700. V. 42

BARKER, HENRY ASTON

Description of the View of Athens and Surroudning Country . . . N.P.: n.d.: 1818. V. 43

BARKER, J. N.

Marmion; or, The Battle of Flodden Field. New York: 1816. V. 39

BARKER, JACOB

Jacob Barker's Letters, Developing the Conspiracy Formed in 1826 for His Ruin. New York: 1827. V. 37; 42

The Rebellion: Its Consequences, and the Congressional Committee, Denominated the Reconstruction Committee, with Their Action. New Orleans: 1866. V. 37; 42

BARKER, JAMES N.

Sketches of the Primitive Settlements on the River Delaware. Philadelphia: 1827. V. 45

BARKER, JAMES P.

The Log of a Limejuicer, experiences sailing square riggers around Cape Horn forty-one times in thirty-one times in thirty years. New York: 1933. V. 37

BARKER, JANE

Poetical Recreations. London: 1688. V. 39; 42; 44; 46

BARKER, JOHN

An Inquiry into the Nature, Cause and Cure of the Present Epidemic Fever. London: 1742. V. 43

An Inquiry into the Nature, Cause and cure of the Present Epidemic Fever. Together with Some General Observations Concerning the Difference Betwixt Nervous and Inflammatory Fevers . . . London: 1742. V. 41; 43

BARKER, LEWELLYS

Endocrinology and Metabolism Presented in Their Scientific and Practical Clincial Aspects by Ninety-Eight Contributors. New York: 1922-24. V. 40

The Nervous System and Its Constituent Neurons. New York: 1899. V. 45

The Nervous System and Its Constituent Neurones. New York: 1899. V. 42; 46

The Nervous System and Its Constituent Neurons . . . New York: 1901. V. 40; 41

BARKER, MATTHEW 1619-1698

Flores Intellectaules; or (8 Centuries of) Select Notions, Sentences and Observations . . . London: 1691. V. 46

BARKER, MATTHEW HENRY 1788-1839

Evenings at Sea. London: 1853. V. 37

Greenwich Hospital. A Series of Naval Sketches. London: 1826. V. 37; 38; 39; 41; 44

Jem Bunt, By an Old Sailor. London: 1841. V. 38

Jem Bunt: a Tale of the Land and the Ocean. London: 1846. V. 46

Land and Sea Tales. London: 1836. V. 41

The Old Sailor's Jolly Boat, Lade with Tales and Yarns, To Please All Hands. London: 1850. V. 42

Tough Yarns: a Series of Naval Tales and Sketches to Please all Hands . . . London: 1835. V. 38

BARKER, N.

An Account of his work by J. Dreyfus. 1966. V. 37

BARKER, NICHOLAS

The Printer and the poet. An account of the printing of 'The Tapestry' based upon correspondence between Stanley Morison and Robert Bridges. Cambridge: 1970. V. 37

BARKER, NICOLAS

Aldus Manutius and the Development of Greek Script and Type in the 15th Century. 1985. V. 45

Aldus Manutius and the Development of Greek script and Type. Connecticut: 1985. V. 39

Aldus Manutius and the Development of Greek Script and Type in the Fifteenth Century with Original Leaves from the First Aldine Editions of Aristotle, 1497; Cratonus' Dictionarium Graecum 1497; Euripides 1503; and the Septuagint, 1518. Sandy Hook: 1985. V. 37; 39; 41; 43; 44

Bibliotheca Lindesiana. 1978. V. 42; 44

The Printer and the Poet. Cambridge: 1970. V. 41

The Printer and the Poet, and Account of the Printing of 'The Tapestry' based Upon Correspondence Between Stanley Morison and Robert Bridges. Cambridge: 1970. V. 39; 40; 41; 45

The Publications of the Roxburghe Club. Cambridge: 1964. V. 38; 40

BARKER, RAYMOND H.

From Lake Erie to the Golden Gate. Brooklyn Village: 1888. V. 43

BARKER, T. W.

Handbook to the Natural History of Carmarthenshire. Carmarthen: 1905. V. 43

BARKER, THOMAS

Barker's Delight; or, the Art of Angling. London: 1820. V. 39; 40; 43

Forty Lithographic Impressions from Drawings by Thomas Barker Selected from His Studies of Rustic Figures After Nature. Bath: 1813. V. 39; 41; 43; 45

A Poem, Dedicated to the Memory of Dr. Joseph Beaumont. Cambridge: 1700. V. 38

Reflections Upon Learning, Wherein is Shewn the Insufficiency Thereof, in Its Several Particulars . . . London: 1714. V. 42

BARKER, W. B.

Lares and Penates; or Cilicia and Its Governors: Being a Short Historical Account of that Province from the Earliest Times to the Present Day. London: 1853. V. 39

BARKER, W. G. M. JONES

The Three Days of Wensleydale. London: 1854. V. 40; 42

BARKLEY, ARCHIBALD HENRY

Kentucky's Pioneer Lithotomists. Cincinnati: 1913. V. 42

BARKLEY, FANNY A.

Among the Boers and Basutos. 1893. V. 43

Among the Boers and Basutos. London: 1893. V. 44

Among Boers and Basutos and with Barkly's Horse, the Story of Our Life on the Frontier . . . Westminster: 1896. V. 42; 45

BARKLEY, HENRY C.

Between the Danube and the Black Sea, or Five Years in Bulgaria. London: 1876. V. 45

BARKSDALE, CLEMENT

A Remembrancer of Excellent Men. I. Dr. John Reynolds. II. Mr. Richard Hooker. III. Dr. William Whitaker. IV. Dr. Andrew Willet. V. Dr. Daniel Featley. VI. Walter Norban, Esq. VII. Mr. John Gregory. VIII. Bishop Duppa. IX. Archbishop Bramhall . . . . London: 1670. V. 41

BARLA, J. B.

Flore Illustree de Nice et des Alpes-Maritimes, Iconographie des Orchidees. Nice: 1868. V. 39

BARLAAM AND JOASAPH

Barlaam and Josaphat. 1986. V. 44

BARLAAM & JOSAPHAT

Barlaam & Josaphat: a Christian Legend of the Buddha. 1986. V. 45

Vita di San Giosafat Convertito da Barlaam Nuouamento Corretto, Tistampato, e Di Belle Figure Adornato. Padua: 1700. V. 44

BARLAAM and Josaphat: a Christian Legend of the Buddha. Greenbrae: 1986. V. 40; 42; 46

BARLACE, JAMES GEORGE

An Historical Sketch of the Progress of Knowledge in England, from the Conversion of the Anglo-Saxons, to the End of the Reign of Queen Elizabeth. London: 1819. V. 38

BARLAEUS, CASPAR

Rerum per Octennium in Brasilia et Alibi Gestarum.. Cleves: 1660. V. 37; 39; 45

BARLANDUS, HADRIAN

Ducum Brabantiae Chronica . . . Antwerp: 1600. V. 41

BARLAS, JOHN EVELYN

Bird Notes. Chelmsford: 1887. V. 45

Holy of Holies - Confessions of an Anarchist. Chelmsford: 1887. V. 45

Love Sonnets. Chelmsford: 1889. V. 45

Phantasmagoria - 'Dream-Fugues'. Chelmsford: 1887. V. 45

Songs of a Bayadere and Songs of a Troubadour. Dundee: 1893. V. 45

BARLER, MILES

Early Days in Llano. Llano: 1905. V. 37; 45

BARLEZIO, MARINO

Des Aller Steyttbartsen und Theursten . . . Georgen Castioten, Genannt Scanderbeg, Herzog zu Epyro . . . Ritterl. Tathen. Frankfurt: 1561. V. 45

BARLOW, ALFRED

The History and Principles of Weaving by Hand and Power. London: 1878. V. 45

BARLOW, EDWARD

Barlow's Journal of His Life at Sea in King's Ships. London: 1934. V. 38; 44; 45; 46

Meteorologial Essays, Concerning the Origin of Springs, Generation of Rain, and Production of Wind . . . London: 1715. V. 40

BARLOW, FRANCIS

Aesop's Life. London: 1687. V. 46

BARLOW, JANE

The Battle of the Frogs and Mice. London: 1894. V. 43

BARLOW, JOEL

Advice to the Priviledged Orders in the Several States of Europe, Resulting from the Necessity and Propriety of a General revolution in the Principles of Government. London: 1792. V. 39

The Columbiad, a Poem. Philadelphia: 1807. V. 39; 45; 46

A Letter to the National Convention of France, on the Defects in the Constitution of 1791 . . . London: 1792. V. 42

The Vision of Columbus: A Poem in Nine Books. Hartford: 1787. V. 38; 39; 40; 43

The Vision of Columbus: a Poem, in Nine Books. London: 1787. V. 41; 43

The Vision of Columbus. Paris: 1793. V. 37; 39

BARLOW, JOHN W.

Letter from the Secretary of War, Accompanying an Engineer Report of a Reconnaissance of the Yellowstone River in 1871. Washington: 1872. V. 42

Letter from . . . Accompanying an Engineer Report of a Reconnaissance of the Yellowstone River in 1871. Washington: 1872. V. 40; 43

BARLOW, P. W.

Kaipara or Experiences of a Settler in North New Zealand. London: 1888. V. 38

BARLOW, PETER

The Encyclopaedia of Arts, Manufactures and Machinery . . . London: 1848. V. 42

Experiments on the Transverse Strength and Other Properties of Malleable Iron, with Reference to Its Uses for Railway Bars . . . London: 1835. V. 44; 46

Second Report Addressed to the Directors and Proprietors of the London and Birmingham Railway Company, Founded on an Inspection of, and Experiments Made on the Liverpool and Manchester Railway. London: 1835. V. 44

A Treatise on the Strength of Timber, Cast Iron, Malleable Iron and Other Materials . . . London: 1837. V. 44

A Treatise on the Strength of Timber, Cast and Malleable Iron, and Other Materials . . . London: 1851. V. 44

A Treatise on the Strength of Materials . . . London: 1867. V. 44

BARLOW, SAMUEL LATHAM MITCHILL

Catalogue of the American Library . . . New York: 1889. V. 45

BARLOW, T. D.

The Medieval World Picture and Albert Durer's Melancholia. Cambridge: 1950. V. 44

BARLOW, THOMAS

Brutum Fulmen: or, the Bull of Pope Pius V, Concerning the Damnation, Excommunication and Deposition of Q. Elizabeth, as also the Absolution of Her Subjects of Their Oath of Allegiance. London: 1681. V. 38

The Genuine Remains of that Learned Prelate . . . Late Lord Bishop of Lincoln. London: 1693. V. 43

Popery; or, the Principles and Positions Approved by the Church of Rome . . . In the Savoy: 1679. V. 46

BARLOW, WILLIAM

Advice to the Would-Be Private Pressman. Piedmont: 1962. V. 41

A Brand, Titio Erepta. On the fifth day of November last, before the Honouralbe Lordes of his Maiesties Privie Concell, and the grave Judges of the Law, &c. this sermon preached By the Reverend Father in Christ, William, Lord Bishoppe of Rochester. London: 1607. V. 37

Magneticall Advertisements: or Divers Pertinent Observations, and Approved Experiments Concerning the Nature and Properties of the Load-Stone. London: 1616. V. 38

The Sermon Preached at Paules Crosse, the Tenth Day of November, Being the Next Sunday after the Discoveries of this Late Horrible Treason. London: 1606-05. V. 46

The Summe and Substance of the Conference . . . at Hampton Court, January 14, 1603. London: 1604. V. 39

The Summe and Substance of the Conference Which, It Pleased His Excellent Maiestie to Have with the Lords Bishops, and Other of His Cleargie . . . at Hampton-Court January 14, 1603. London: 1605. V. 38; 39; 42

The Summe and Substance of the Conference Which, It Pleased His Excellent Maiestie to Have with the Lords Bishops, and Other of His Clergie . . . at Hampton-Court January 14, 1603. London: 1605. V. 38

The Summe and Substance of the Conference. London: 1638. V. 40

The Svmme and Svbstance of the Conference Which Is Pleased His Excellent Majestie to Have with the Lords Bishops and Others of His Clergie . . . London: 1638. V. 46

A Treatise on Fornication: Shewing What the Sin Is. London: 1690. V. 43

BARLOW, WILLIAM P.

The Allen Press Bibliography. San Francisco: 1985. V. 37

The Felicities of Book Collecting. Piedmont: 1958. V. 38

BARMAN, CHRISTIAN

The Bridge, a Chapter in the History of Building. London: 1926. V. 39; 40

BARMBY, JOHN GOODWYN

A Prospectus for the Establishment of a Concordium; or an Industry Harmony College. London: 1841. V. 39

BARNACLES from Many Bottoms. Scaped and Gathered for BR by the Typophiles. New York: 1935. V. 37

BARNARD, E.

Virtue the Source of Pleasure. London: 1757. V. 43

Virtue the Source of Pleasure. London: 1757. V. 39; 42; 46

BARNARD, FREDERICK

A Series of Character Sketches from William Makepeace Thackeray. Philadelphia: 1888. V. 38

A Series of Sketches from Dickens. New York: 1900. V. 40

BARNARD, GEORGE

Drawing from Nature: a Series of Progressive Instructions in Sketching, to Which are Appended Lectures on Art Delivered at Rugby School. London: 1877. V. 39; 44

Drawing from Nature: A Series of Progressive Instructions in Sketching . . . with Examples from Switzerland and the Pyrenees, to which are Appended Lectures on Art Delivered at Rugby School. London: 1865. V. 38; 40; 41

Handbook of Foliage and Foreground Drawing. London: 1853. V. 39

Handbook of Foliage and Foreground Drawing. London: 1876. V. 39; 44

The Theory and Practice of Landscape Painting in Water Colours. London: 1855. V. 46

The Theory and Practice of Landscape Painting in Water Colors. London: 1858. V. 42

The Theory and Practice of Landscape Painting in Water-Colours. London: 1871. V. 39

The Theory and Practice of Landscape Painting in Water Colours. London: 1885. V. 44

BARNARD, HENRY

School Architecture; or Contributions to the Improvement of School Houses in the United States. New York: 1849. V. 46

School Architecture; or Contributions to the Improvement of School-Houses in the United States . . . New York: 1849. V. 45

School Architecture; or, Contributions to the Improvement of School-Houses in the United States. New York: 1854. V. 38; 39; 40; 41

BARNARD, J. G.

The Phenomena of the Gyroscope, Analytically Examined. New York: 1858. V. 37; 44

A Report on the General Defenses of Washington, to the Chief of Engineers, U.S. Army. Washington: 1871. V. 45

BARNARD, J. H.

Dr. J.H. Barnard's Journal, a Composite of Known Versions of One of the Surgeons of Fannin's Regiment, December 1835, to June 5, 1836. Goliad: 1836. V. 37

BARNARD, JOHN 1685-1764

Considerations on the Proposal for Reducing the Interest on the National Debt. London: 1750. V. 39

A Defence of Several Proposals for Raising of Three Millions for the Service of the Government, for the Year 1746. London: 1746. V. 39; 41; 42; 45

A Present for an Apprentice. Philadelphia: 1774. V. 40

Sin Testify'd Against by Heaven and Earth. A Sermon Preached on the Friday After the Great and Terrible Earthquake, Which Occur'd on the Lord's-Day-Evening, Between the 29th and 30th of October, 1727. Boston: 1727, 1728. V. 39

BARNARD, JOHN GROSS

Professional Papers of the Corps of Engineers U.S. Army. No. 20. A Report on the Defenses of Washington, to the Chief of Engineers U.S. Army. Washington: 1871. V. 37; 39

Report on the Fabrication of Iron for Defensive Purposes and Its Uses in Modern Fortification. Washington: 1871. V. 42

BARNARD, K. H.

South Africa in Print. Catalogue of an Exhibition of Books, Atlases and Maps Held in the South African Library. Cape Town: 1952. V. 40

BARNARD, NOEL

Early Chinese Art and Its Possible Influence in the Pacific Basin. New York: 1972. V. 39

BARNARD, R. N.

A Three Years' Cruise in the Mozambique Channel, for the Suppression of the Slave Trade. London: 1848. V. 38

BARNARD, THOMAS

An Historical Character Relating to the Holy & Exemplary Life of . . . Elisabeth Hastings; to which are added . . . one of the codicils of her last will, setting forth her devise of lands to the Provost & Scholars of Queen's College in Oxford . . . Leeds: 1742. V. 37; 42; 45; 46

A Letter to . . . Lord Bishop of Durham . . . on the Principle and Detail of the Measures Under the Consideration of Parliament, for Promoting and Encouraging Industry, and for the Relief and Regulation of the Poor. London: 1807. V. 42

BARNAUD, NICHOLAS d. 1605

Le Cabinet du Roy de France . . . Paris: 1581. V. 40; 46

Le Reveille-Matin des Francois et de Leurs Voisins. Edinburgh: 1574. V. 44

BARNEBY, W. HENRY

The New Far West and the Old Far East . . . London: 1889. V. 43

BARNEBY, WILLIAM HENRY

Life and Labour in the Far, Far West: Being Notes of a Tour in the Western States, British Columbia, Manitoba, and the North-West Territory. London: 1884. V. 38

BARNES, A. A. S.

On Active Service with the Chinese Regiment. London: 1902. V. 41

BARNES, A. C.

Mechanical Processes for the Extraction of Palm Oil. 195. V. 46

BARNES, C. H.

History of the 142nd Infantry of the 36th Division, 1917-1919, Including a Sketch of the 1st Oklahoma Infantry and 7th Texas Infantry. N.P.: 1922. V. 38

BARNES, CARL LEWIS

The Art and Science of Embalming, Descriptive and Operative. N.P.: 1905. V. 41; 46

BARNES, DEMAS

From the Atlantic to the Pacific, Overland. A Series of Letters . . . Describing a Trip from New York, Via Chicago, Atchison, the Great Plains, Denver, The Rocky Mountains, Central City, Colorado, Dakota, Pike's Peak, Laramie Park, Bridger's Pass . . . New York: 1866. V. 37; 38; 42; 45; 46

BARNES, DJUNA 1892-

The Book of Repulsive Women: 8 Rhythms and 5 Drawings. New York: 1915. V. 41; 43; 44

Nightwood. London: 1936. V. 38; 43

Nightwood. New York: 1937. V. 43

Nightwood. New York: 1961. V. 42

Ryder. 1928. V. 45

Ryder. New York: 1928. V. 39

BARNES, GEORGE

A Statistical Account of Ireland, Founded on Historical Fact. Dublin: 1811. V. 42

BARNES, GILBERT H.

Letters of Theodore Dwight Weld, Angelina Grimke Weld and Sarah Grimke, 1822-1844. New York: 1934. V. 46

BARNES, HENRY

The Guerilla-Bride: a Poem. Bellefontaine: 1858. V. 42

BARNES, JOHN

A Tour through the Whole of France; or, New Topographical and Historical Sketch of All Its Most Important Cities, Towns, (etc) . . . London: 1815. V. 37

BARNES, JOHN S.

The Logs of the Serapis -- Alliance -- Ariel Under the Command of John Paul Jones 1779-1780. New York: 1911. V. 42

BARNES, JOSEPH K.

The Medical And Surgical History of the War and the Rebellion (1861-65). Washington: 1875. V. 41; 43

A Medical and Surgical History of the War of the Rebellion. Volume I, Part I. Washington: 1883. V. 37; 41; 42

BARNES, JOSHUA

The History of that Most Victorious Monarch Edward IIId, King of England and France, and Lord of Ireland. Cambridge. V. 43

The History of that Most Victorious Monarch Edward IIId. Cambridge: 1688. V. 37

The History of that Most Victorious Monarch Edward IIId . . . together with that of His Most Renowed Son Edward, Prince of Wales and of Aquitain, Sirnamed the Black Prince. Cambridge: 1688. V. 37; 38; 45; 46

A New Discovery of a Little Sort of People, Anciently Discoursed of, Called Pygmies . . . London: 1750. V. 40; 43; 46

BARNES, JULIAN

Before She Met Me. London: 1982. V. 45

Duffy. London: 1980. V. 45; 46

Duffy. London: 1980. V. 46

Fiddle City. London: 1981. V. 45

Flaubert's Parrot. London: 1984. V. 38; 40; 45

A History of the World in 10 1/2 Chapters. London: 1989. V. 45

Metroland. London: 1980. V. 45

Putting the Boot In. London: 1985. V. 45

Staring at the Sun. London: 1986. V. 38; 45

Talking It Over. New York: 1991. V. 46

BARNES, ROBERT

The Supplication of Doctour BArnes Unto the Most Gracyous Kynge Henrye the Eyght . . . London: 1550? V. 44

Vitae Romanorum Pontificum . . . Basle: 1535? V. 40

BARNES, THOMAS

A New Method of Propagating Fruit Trees, and Flowering Shrubs . . . London: 1759. V. 41

BARNES, WARNER

A Bibliography of Elizabeth Barret Browning. 1967. V. 42

BARNES, WILL C.

Tales from the X-Bar Horse Camp. Chicago: 1920. V. 37; 42; 43

Western Grazing Grounds and Forest Ranges, Breeders Gazette. Chicago: 1913. V. 37; 46

BARNES, WILLIAM

A Grammar and Glossary of the Dorset Dialect, with the History, Outspreadings and Bearings of south Western English. Berlin: 1863. V. 41; 42; 46

Homely Rhymes. London: 1859. V. 45

Poems, Partly of Rural Life. Dorchester printed: 1846. V. 46

Poems of Rural Life, in the Dorset Dialect. London: 1848. V. 42

Poems in the Dorset Dialect. London: 1862. V. 44

Poems of Rural Life in the Dorset Dialect. London: 1862-63. V. 38

Poems, Partly in Rural Life (Written in National English). London: 1864. V. 40

BARNES, WILLIAM continued

Poems of Rural Life in the Dorset Dialect. London: 1879. V. 43; 44

Poems of Rural Life, in the Dorset Dialect. London: 1887. V. 46

Poems Partly of Rural Life. London: 1846. V. 38

BARNES, WILLIAM C.

A Collation of Facts Relative to Fast Typesetting Together With Portraits and Biographies of the More Famous Swift Compositors . . . New York: 1887. V. 41

BARNETT, CHARLES ZACHARY

A Christmas Carol. London: 1872? V. 40

BARNETT, JOEL

A Long Trip in a Prairie Schooner. Whittier: 1928. V. 39; 40; 42; 43; 46

BARNETT, JOHN

Systems and Singing Masters . . . London: 1842. V. 45

BARNETT, P. NEVILLE

Pictorial Book-Plates: Their Origin and Use in Australia. Sydney: 1931. V. 41

Souvenir of Japanese Colour-Prints. Sydney: 1936. V. 37; 40; 41

BARNETT, RICHARD D.

Assyrian Sculpture in the British Museum. Toronto: 1975. V. 40; 42

A Catalogue of the Nimrud Ivories with other examples of Ancient Near Eastern Ivories in the British Museum. London: 1957. V. 37

The Sculptures of Assur-Nasir-Apli II (883-859) B.C. London: 1962. V. 40; 42

Sculptures from the North Palace of Ashurbanipal at Nineveh (668-627 B.C.). London: (1976). V. 37

BARNEY, JOSHUA

Letter from the Secretary of War . . . A Report of the Survey . . . of a Route from St. Louis to the Big Bend of the Red River. Washington: 1852. V. 37; 45

. . . Report of the Survey . . . of a Route from St. Louis to the Big Bend of the Red River. Washington: 1852. V. 38; 39; 41

BARNEY, LIBEUS

Letters of the Pike's Peak Gold Rush . . . San Jose: 1959. V. 40

BARNEY, MARY

A Biographical Memoir of the Late Commodore Joshua Barney from Autobiographical Notes and Journals in Possession of His Family and Other Authentic Sources . . . Boston: 1832. V. 37; 38; 40; 42; 45

BARNEY, MARY CHASE

Mrs. Barney's Letter to President Jackson, Baltimore, June 13th, 1829. N.P.: 1829. V. 44

BARNEY, NATALIE CLIFFORD

The One Who is Legion. London: 1930. V. 42; 43

Poems & Poemes. New York: 1920. V. 46

Poems and Poemes. Paris: 1920. V. 41

Poems and Poemes. Paris & New York: 1920. V. 39

BARNEY, WILLIAM B.

William B. Barney to His Fellow Citizens. Baltimore: 1830. V. 43

BARNHART BROS. & SPINDLER

Great Western Type Foundry, Pony Spcimen Book and Price List from Barnhardt Bros. & Spindler . . . Chicago: 1893-1899. V. 38

Great Western Type Foundry, Pony Specimen Book and Price List from Barnhart Bros. & Spindler. Chicago: 1898. V. 38

Specimen Book of Type. Chicago: 1900. V. 38

Superior Copper-Mixed Type. Barnharts Big Blue Book. Chicago: 1896. V. 38

BARNHART BROTHERS

Catalog 25-A Type Faces Border Designs, Typecast Ornaments, Brass Rule. Chicago: 1925. V. 40

BARNHART BROTHERS & SPINDLER

Book of Type Specimens. Chicago: 1907. V. 42

Catalog 25: Type Faces, Border Designs, Typecast Ornaments, Brass Rules. Chicago: 1925. V. 42

Pony Specimen Book. Chicago: 1893-99. V. 42

Specimen Book of Type. Chicago: 1900. V. 42

BARNHART, JOHN D.

Indiana, from Frontier to Industrial Commonwealth. New York: 1954. V. 39

BARNHART, NANCY

The Wind in the Willows. By Kenneth Grahame. New York: 1933. V. 37

BARNHILL, JOHN

Surgical Anatomy of the Nead and Neck. Baltimore: 1937. V. 42

BARNIM, ADALBERT VON

Des Freiherrn Adalbert Von Barnim Durch Nord-Ost Afrika in den Jahren 1859 und 1860 Beschrieben von Seinem Begleiter . . . Berlin: 1863. V. 45

BARNS, C. R.

Switzler's Illustrated History of Missouri, from 1541 to 1877. Saint Louis: 1879. V. 44

BARNS, FLORENCE E.

A Texas Calendar. Dallas: 1935. V. 37

BARNS, T. ALEXANDER

The Wonderland of the Eastern Congo. London: 1922. V. 42; 43; 44

The Wonderland of the Eastern congo. London: & New York: 1922. V. 45

BARNUM, FRANCIS

Grammatical Fundamentals of the Innuit Language as Spoken by the Eskimo of the Western Coast of Alaska. Boston: 1901. V. 39; 44

BARNUM, PHINEAS TAYLOR 1810-1891

Autobiography of Barnum or the Opening of the Oyster. Danbury: 1889. V. 41

Dollars and Sense or How to Get On. Chicago: 1890. V. 44

The Humbugs of the World. New York: 1866. V. 40

Life of P. T. Barnum. Buffalo: 1888. V. 43

The Life of P. T. Barnum. New York: 1855. V. 37

Struggles and Triumphs. Hartford: 1869. V. 38

Struggles and Triumphs; or, Forty Years' Recollections of P.T. Barnum. London: 1870. V. 41; 46

The Struggles and Triumphs; or Forty Years' Recollections. Buffalo: 1879. V. 38; 39

Struggles and Triumphs; or, Forty Years' Recollections of P. T. Barnum. Buffalo: 1882. V. 41

BAROLI, COSIMO

Del Modo di Misurare le Distantie, le Superficie, I Corpi, le Piante, Le Prouincie, le Prospettiue & Tutte le Altre Cose Terrene, Che Possono Occorrere a Gli Huomini. Venetia: 1589. V. 41

BAROLUS A SAXOFERRATO

In Secundam Digesti Veteris Partem Comentaria (etc.). Lugduni: 1544. V. 43

BARON And Feme. A Treatise of Law and Equity, Concerning Husbands and Wives. Savoy: 1738. V. 39

BARON, JOHN

The Life of Edward Jenner, M.D. London: 1827. V. 37; 43

The Life of Edward Jenner, M.D. London: 1838. V. 37; 39; 43

Scudamore Organs, or Practical Hints Respecting Organs for Village Churches and Small Chancels, on Improved Principles. London: 1862. V. 38

BARON, ROBERT

Mirza. London: 1655. V. 40

BARON, RON

Mystery of Love and other Optical Illusions. (Los Angeles: 1974). V. 37

Mystery of Love and Other Optical Illusions. (Los Angeles: 1974). V. 37

BARON, S.

A Description of the Kingdom of Tonqueen. London: 1734. V. 45

BARON, WENDY

The Camden Town Group. London: 1979. V. 44

Sickert. London: 1973. V. 39; 46

BARONIO, GIUSEPPE

Degli Innesti Animali. Milan: 1804. V. 42

On Grafting in Animals. Boston: 1985. V. 38; 42

BAROZZI, FRANCESCO

Cosmographia in Quatros Libros Distributa Symmo Ordine, Miraq, Facilitatem ac Brevitate ad maagnam Ptolemaei Mathematicam Constructionem . . . Venetiis: 1598. V. 45

BARR, ALFRED H.

Fantastic Art, Dada, Surrealism. New York: 1936. V. 39

Fantastic Art, Dada, Surrealism. New York: 1946. V. 39

Matisse: His Art and His Public. New York: 1951. V. 44

BARR, AMELIA

All the Days of My Life. New York & London: 1913. V. 41

A Knight of the Nets. New York: 1896. V. 41; 43

BARR, JOHN

Natural Wonders. Easthampton: 1991. V. 44

BARR, LOUISE FARROW

Presses of Northern California and Their Books 1900-1933. Berkeley: 1934. V. 44

Presses of Northern California and Their Books, 1900-1933. Berkeley: 1934. V. 43

BARR, MARY MARGARET H.

A Bibliography of Writings on Voltaire, 1825-1925. New York & London: 1925. V. 38

A Bibliography of Writings on Voltaire, 1825-1925. New York: 1929. V. 41

BARRA, E. I.

A Tale of Two Oceans; a New Story by an Old Californian. San Francisco: 1893. V. 44; 46

BARRABUS, HERMOLUS 1454-1493

In C. Plinii Naturalis Historiae Libros Castigationes. Basileae: 1534. V. 38

BARRANTES, VICENTE

Guerras Piraticas de Filipinas Contra Mindanaos Y Joloanos . . . Madrid: 1878. V. 40

BARRAS, PAUL, COMTE DE

Memoirs of Barras, Member of the Directorate. London: 1895. V. 37

BARRAT, JOSEPH

The Indian of New-England, and the North-Eastern Provinces. Middleton;: 1851. V. 37; 38; 40

BARRATT, ALFRED

Physical Ethics of the Science of Action. London: 1869. V. 38

BARRATT, N. S.

Freemasonry in Pennsylvania, 1727-1907. Philadelphia: 1908-19. V. 41; 42

BARRATT, THOMAS J.

The Annals of Hampstead. London: 1912. V. 37; 38; 40; 42

BARRAUD, PHILIP

A New Book of Single Cyphers, Comprising Six Hundred Invented and Engraved. London: 1805. V. 42

BARRAUD, WILLIAM

Men and Women of the Day. A Picture Gallery of Contemporary Portraiture. London: 1888-94. V. 44; 45

BARRAULT & BRIDEL

Le Palais de l'Industrie et ses Annexes. Paris: 1857. V. 43

BARRE, UTTERE

Avon of Avondale. London: 1877. V. 40

BARRELL, GEORGE

Notes of Voyages and Incidents Connected Therewith in a Career of Thirty Years at Sea, with Other Miscellaneous Matter. Springfield: 1890. V. 42

BARREME, FRANCOIS BERTRAND

La Livre Necessaire a Toute Sorte de Conditions . . . Paris: 1671. V. 41

BARRERE, ALBERT

Argot and Slang: a New French and English Dictionary of the Cant Words, Quaint Expressions, Slang Terms and Flash Phrases Used in the High and Low Life of Old and New Paris. London: 1887. V. 41

A Dictionary of Slang, Jargon, Cant Embracing English, American and Anglo-Indian Slang, Pidgin English, Tinkers' Jargon and Other Irregular Phraseology. London: 1889-90. V. 41

A Dictionary of Slang, Jargon & Cant . . . London: 1897. V. 41

BARRERE, PIERRE

Nouvelle Relation de la France Equinoxiale . . . Paris: 1743. V. 39

BARRES, FERANUD

Les Transformateurs d'Energie, Generateurs, Accumulateurs, Moteurs . . . Paris: 1910. V. 44

BARRETT, ALFRED

The Life of the Rev. John Hewgill Bumby. Who Was Drowned in the River Thames, New Zealand, June 26th 1840. London: 1852. V. 41; 43

BARRETT, C. G.

The Lepidoptera of the British Islands. London: 1892-1907. V. 37

BARRETT, C. R. B.

The 85th King's Light Infantry. London: 1913. V. 37; 42

The 7th (Queen's Own) Hussars. London: 1914. V. 41

BARRETT, CHARLES

Art of the Australian Aboriginal. Melbourne: 1943. V. 41

The Lepidoptera of the British Islands. London: 1893-1902. V. 43

BARRETT, CHARLES G.

The Leipdoptera of the British Islands. London: 1893-1907. V. 42; 45; 46

BARRETT, CHARLES RAYMOND BOOTH

Essex: Highways, Byways and Waterways. London: 1892-93. V. 39

BARRETT, CHARLES SIMON

The Mission, History and Times of the Farmer's Union: a Narrative of the Greatest Industrial, Agricultural Organization . . . and Its Makers. Nashville: 1909. V. 45

BARRETT, DAVID B.

World Christian Encyclopedia: a Comparative Study of Churches and Religions in the Modern World AD 1900-2000. 1982. V. 39

BARRETT, DOUGLAS

Early Cola Bronzes. Bombay: 1965. V. 41

BARRETT, EATON STANNARD

All the Talents; A Satirical Peom in three dialogues. By Polypus (and) All the Talents . . . Dialogue the Fourth. Embellished with a frontispiece. London: 1807. V. 37; 39

The Heroine, or Adventures of a Fair Romance Reader. London: 1813. V. 41

The Heroine, or Adventures of Cherubina. London: 1814. V. 38; 42

The Heroine, or Adventures of Cherubine. London: 1815. V. 39

Six Weeks at Long's. London: 1817. V. 41

BARRETT, ELLEN C.

Baja California, 1535-1956. Los Angeles: 1957. V. 46

Baja California, 1535-1956: A Bibliography of Historical, Geographical and Scientific Literature Relating to the Peninsula of Baja California and to the Adjacent Islands . . . (with) Baja California II, 1535- 1964 . . . Los Angeles: 1957, 1967. V. 38; 40; 41

Baja California 1535-1968. Los Angeles: 1957-68. V. 40

Baja California 1535-1956. Los Angeles: 1957-68. V. 39

Baja California 1535-1956 (and), 1535-1964: a Bibliography of Historical, Geographical and Scientific Literature . . . Los Angeles: 1967. V. 40

BARRETT, FRANCIS

The Magus, or Celestial Intelligencer, Being a Complete System of Occult Philosophy. London: 1801. V. 42; 46

BARRETT, FRANK

The Admirable Lady Biddy Fane: Her Surprising Curious Adventures . . . London: 1888. V. 40

Fettered for Life. London: 1889. V. 43

BARRETT, FRANKLIN A.

Caughley and Coalport Porcelain. Leigh-on-Sea: 1951. V. 42; 44

Caughley and Coalport Porcelain. London: 1951. V. 42

BARRETT-HAMILTON, G. E. H.

A History of British Mammals. Continued by M. A. C. Hinton. London: 1910-21. V. 37; 38

BARRETT, JOHN

An Essay on the Earlier Part of the Life of Swift . . . London: 1808. V. 37; 45

BARRETT, JOSEPH O.

History of 'Old Abe' the Live War Eagle of the Eighth Regiment Wisconsin Volunteers. Chicago: 1865. V. 37; 39; 42; 43; 44; 45

BARRETT-LENNARD, C.

Travels in British Columbia, with the Narrative of a Yacht Voyage Round Vancouver's Island. London: 1862. V. 44

BARRETT, S. A.

Material Aspects of Pomo Culture. V. 39

Pomo Myths. 1933. V. 39

BARRETT, SOLOMON

The Principles of Grammar: Being a Compendious Treatise on the Languages, English, Latin, Greek, German, Spanish and French. Boston: 1866. V. 37

BARRETT, TIMOTHY

Early vs. Modern Handmade Papers. 1990. V. 43

Nagashizuki, the Japanese Craft of Hand Papermaking. North Hills: 1979. V. 39; 40; 41; 42; 46

BARRETT, W. A.

Flowers and Festivals, or Directions for the Floral Decoration of Churches. London: 1868. V. 38; 40

BARRETT, WALTER

The Old Merchants of New York City. New York: 1870. V. 39

BARRI, GIACOMO

The Painters Voyage of Italy. London: 1679. V. 38

BARRI, GIRALDUS DE

Itinerarium Cambriae Seu Laboriosae Baldvini Cantuariensis Archiepiscopi per Walliam Legationis Auccurata... Londini: 1804. V. 45

The Itinery of Archbishop Baldwin through Wales.... London: 1806. V. 45

BARRIE, JAMES MATTHEW 1860-1937

The Admirable Crichton. London: 1910. V. 41

The Admirable Crichton. London: 1914. V. 45; 46

Auld Licht Idylls. London: 1888. V. 38

Auld Licht Idylls. London: 1895. V. 39; 42

Better Dead. London: 1888. V. 38

Better Dead. London: 1891. V. 43

Better Dead. London: 1887. V. 37

Biography of Rev. Hosea Ballou. Boston: 1852. V. 45

Courage; an Address. London: 1922. V. 40

Don't Count On It: a Note on the Number of the 1001 Nights. Northridge: 1984. V. 43

An Edinburgh Eleven - Pencil Portraits From Colonial Life. London: 1889. V. 37; 39; 40; 42

The Greenwood Hat, being a Memoir of James Anon 1885-1887. London: 1930. V. 37

Half Hours. London: 1916. V. 45

Jane Annie; or, the Good Conduct Prize. London: 1893. V. 39; 41; 43

The Little Minister. London: 1891. V. 37; 38; 39; 42; 43; 44; 45; 46

The Little Minister... London: Paris & Melbourne: 1891. V. 43

The Little Minister. New York: 1898. V. 38

The Little White Bird or Adventures in Kensington Gardens. New York: 1902. V. 42

The Little White Bird. By J.M. Barrie. London: 1902. V. 37

My Lady Nicotine. London: 1890. V. 39; 43

The Novels, Tales and Sketches of J. M. Barrie. New York: 1896-1911. V. 46

The Novels, Tales and Sketches. New York: 1912. V. 42

Novels, Tales and Sketches. New York: 1913. V. 38

Novels, Tales and Sketches. New York: 1927. V. 45

The Novels, Tales & Sketches. New York: 1896. V. 37

The Novels, Tales and Sketches. London: 1896-1902. V. 37

Peter Pan in Kensington Gardens. London. V. 44

Peter Pan in Kensington Gardens. London: 1906. V. 37; 38; 40; 41; 44; 45; 46

Peter Pan in Kensington Gardens. New York: 1906. V. 43; 44

Peter Pan in Kensington Gardens. New York: 1907. V. 39; 40

Piter Pan dans les Jardins de Kensington. Paris: 1907. V. 37; 43

Peter Pan and Wendy. London: 1908. V. 40

Peter Pan in Kensington Gardens. London: 1910. V. 39; 45

Peter and Wendy. London: 1911. V. 45

Peter Pan and Wendy. New York: 1911. V. 44

Peter Pan in Kensington Gardens. London: 1912. V. 37; 39; 40; 41; 46

Peter Pan In Kensington Gardens. New York: 1925. V. 40

Peter Pan: or the Boy Who Would Not Grow Up. New York: 1928. V. 38; 46

Peter Pan and Wendy. London: 1929. V. 46

Peter and Wendy. London: 1939. V. 46

Peter Pan and Wendy. New York: 1940. V. 45

Peter Pan dans les Jardins de Kensington. Paris: 1907. V. 37

The Plays of J. M. Barrie. London: 1928. V. 39; 45

Quality Street. V. 40

Quality Street. London. V. 40

Quality Street. London. V. 41

Quality Street. London. V. 42

Quality Street. London. V. 45

Quality Street. London. V. 38

Quality Street. N.P.. V. 39

Quality Street. London: 1901. V. 37; 45

Quality Streeter. N.P.: 1901. V. 46

Quality Street. London: 1910. V. 43

Quality Street. London: 1912. V. 40; 46

Quality Street. Boston: 1913. V. 44

Quality Street. London: 1913. V. 41

Quality Street. London: (c. 1913). V. 37

Scotland's Lament: Robert Louis Stevenson. London: 1918. V. 44

Sentimental Tommy. New York: 1896. V. 43

Sentimental Tommy. London, Paris & Melbourne: 1896. V. 37

Tommy and Grizel. London: 1900. V. 45

Two of Them. New York: 1893. V. 37

Walker London. London: 1907. V. 43

The Plays of J. M. Barrie: What Every Woman Knows. London, New York & Toronto: 1918. V. 38

When a Man's Single. London: 1888. V. 38; 40; 43; 45

A Window in Thurms. London: 1889. V. 40

A Window in Thrums. London: 1892. V. 37

The Kirriemuir Edition of the Works of... London: 1913. V. 38

Works. London: 1913. V. 42; 46

Works. New York: 1929. V. 42

The Works. New York: 1929-31. V. 41; 43

The Works. London: 1930. V. 38; 42

BARRIENTOS, BARTOLOME

Pedro Menendez de Aviles: Founder of Florida. Gainesville: 1965. V. 38

BARRIERE, DOMINICUS

Villa Aldobrandina Tusculana Sive Varii Illius Hortorum et Fontium Prospectus. Rome: 1647. V. 37

BARRIFFE, WILLIAM

Military Discipline or the Young Artillery-Man. London: 1643. V. 45

BARRINGTON, DAINES 1727-1800

Additional Instances of Navigators Who Have Reached High Northern Latitudes... London: 1775. V. 40; 42

Additional Instances of Navigators, Who have Reached High Northern Latitudes... London: 1775. V. 37

Miscellaneies. London: 1781. V. 39; 40; 41; 45; 46

Miscellanies. London: 1781. V. 37; 41; 46

The Naturalist's Journal. London: 1766-67. V. 41

The Naturalist's Journal. London: 1775. V. 43

Observations on the Statutes, Chiefly the More Ancient from Magna Charta to the Twenty-First of James the First. London: 1766. V. 39

Observations Upon the Statutes, Chiefly the More Ancient from Magna Charta to the 21st of James I. Dublin: 1767. V. 38; 40

Observations Upon the Statutes, Chiefly the More Ancient from Magna Charta to the 21st of James I. London: 1769. V. 38

The Possibility of Approaching the North Pole Asserted. London: 1818. V. 38; 40; 42; 43; 44; 46

The Possibility of Approaching the North Pole Asserted... New York: 1818. V. 46

The Possibility of Approaching the North Pole Asserted, a new edition, with an appendix containing papers on the same subject and on the Northwest Passage by Col. Beaufoy. London/New York: 1818. V. 37

BARRINGTON, EMILIE ISABEL d. 1933

The Life, Letters and Work of Frederic Leighton. London: 1906. V. 41; 42; 43

BARRINGTON, GEORGE

The Genuine Life and Trial of George Barrington, from His Birth... to the Time of His Conviction. London: 1791. V. 40

A Voyage to Botany Bay, with a Description of the Country Manners, Customs, Religion &c. of the Natives... (with) A Sequel to Barrington's Voyage to New South Wales... London: 1795/1801. V. 40

A Voyage to New South Wales; With a Description of the Country. Philadelphia: 1796. V. 40; 45

Voyage a Botany Bay. Paris: 1798. V. 40; 43; 46

BARRINGTON, GEORGE, PSEUD.

Barrington's New London Spy... London: 1810. V. 43

BARRINGTON, JOHN SHUTE 1678-1734

The Revolution and Anti-Revolution Principles Stated and Compar'd, the Constitution Explain'd and Vindicated, and the Justice and Necessity of Excluding the Pretender... London: 1714. V. 39

BARRINGTON, JONAH

Historic Memoirs of Ireland, Comprising Secret Records of the National Convention, The Rebellion and the Union... London: 1833. V. 43

Personal Sketches of His Own Times. London: 1827. V. 41

Personal Sketches of His Own Times. London: 1830. V. 38

Rise and Fall of the Irish Nation. Paris: 1835. V. 46

BARRINGTON, RICHARD

The Migration of Birds as Observed at Irish Lighthouses and Lightships, Including the Original Reports from 1888-97. London & Edinburgh: 1900. V. 39

BARRON, ARCHIBALD F.

Vines and Vine Culture. et. London: 1900. V. 46

BARRON, SAMUEL BENTON

The Lone Star Defenders. New York & Washington: 1908. V. 39; 46

The Lone Star Defenders. Waco: 1964. V. 46

BARRON, WILLIAM

History of the Colonization of the Free States of Antiquity Applied to the Present Contest Between Great Britain and Her American Colonies. London: 1777. V. 37; 39; 42; 43

History of the Colonization of the Free States of Antiquity, Applied to the Present Contest Between Great Britain and Her American Colonies. London: 1777/80. V. 41; 43

BARROUGH, PHILIP

The Method of Physick . . . London: 1617. V. 42

BARROW, ALBERT STEWART

More Shires & Provinces. London: 1928. V. 39; 46

BARROW, ISAAC

Euclide's Elements; the Whole Fifteen Books, Compendiously Investigated; with Archimedes's Theorems of the Sphere and Cylinder, Investigated by the Method of Indivisibles . . . London: 1751. V. 42

The Mathematical Works of Isaac Barrow, D.D. Cambridge: 1860. V. 45

The Theological Works. Oxford: 1818. V. 40

The Theological Works of . . . Oxford: 1830. V. 46

A Treatise of the Pope's Supremacy. To Which is Added a Discourse Concerning the Unity of the Church. London: 1680. V. 41

The Works of Dr. Isaac Barrow . . . London: 1830. V. 39

The Works, with a Life of the Author of James Hamilton. Edinburgh: 1841-42. V. 39

BARROW, JOHN 1764-1848

An Account of Travels into Southern Africa in the years 1797 and 1798. London: 1801-04. V. 38; 41

A Chronological History of the Voyages into the Arctic Regions . . . London: 1815. V. 42

A Chronological History of Voyages into the Arctic Regions. London: 1818. V. 37; 38; 41; 43; 46

A Chronological History of Voyages into the Arctic Regions . . . London: 1819. V. 46

Dictionarium Polygraphicum; or, the Whole Body of the Arts. London: 1735. V. 41; 46

The Eventful History of the Mutiny and Piratical Seizure of H. M. S. Bounty: Its Cause and Consequences. London: 1831. V. 41

Excursions in the North of Europe, Through Parts of Russia, Finland, Sweden, Denmark and Norway. London: 1835. V. 43

Expeditions on the Glaciers: Including an Asent of Mont Blanc, Monte Rusa, Col du Geant, and Mont Buet. London: 1864. V. 38

The Life of Richard Earl Howe, Admiral of the Fleet and General of Marines. London: 1838. V. 38

The Life and Correspondence of Admiral Sir Sidney Smith. London: 1848. V. 46

Mountain Ascents in Westmoreland and Cumberland. London: 1886. V. 38

Navigatio Britannica; or a Complete System of Navigation . . . London: 1750. V. 41

A New and Universal Dictionary of Arts and Sciences . . . wtih a Supplement. London: 1751-54. V. 40

Some Account of the Public Life, and a Selection from the Unpublished writings of the Earl of Macartney. London: 1807. V. 38; 41; 45

A Tour Round Ireland, through the Sea Coast Counties in the Autumn of 1835. London: 1836. V. 43

Travels in China. London: 1806. V. 43; 45; 46

Travels into the Interior of Southern Africa, 1797-1798. London: 1801. V. 42; 43; 44

Travels in China. London: 1804. V. 41

Travels in China, Containing Descriptions, Observations and Comparisons, Made and Collected in the Course of a Short Residence at the Imperial Palace of Yuen-Min-Yuen, and on a Subsequent Journey through the Country from Pekin to Canton . . . London: 1804. V. 40; 41

Travels in China, Containing Descriptions, Observations and Comparisons, Made and Collected in the Course of a Short Residence at the Imperial Palace of Yuen-Min-Yuen, and a Subsequent Journey through the Country from Pekin to Canton. London: 1806. V. 38; 41; 45

Travels into the Interior of Southern Africa. London: 1806. V. 43

Travels in China . . . London: 1806. V. 37

A Visit to Iceland, by Way of Tronyem, in the 'Flower of Yarrow' Yacht in the Summer of 1834. London: 1835. V. 39; 43

A Voyage to Cochin China in the Years 1792 and 1793 . . . London: 1806. V. 38; 41; 43; 45; 46

Voyages of Discovery and Research Within the Arctic Regions, from the Year 1818 to the Present Time. London: 1846. V. 37; 39; 41; 42; 45; 46

Voyages of Discovery and Research within the Arctic Regions, from the Year 1818 to the Present Time, Under the Command of the Several Naval Officers Employed by Sea and Land in Search of a Northwest Passage from the Atlantic to the Pacific . . . New York: 1846. V. 38

BARROW, PHILIP

The Methode of Physicke. London: 1583. V. 37

BARROW, W. J.

Manuscripts and Documents. Their Deterioration and Restoration. Charlottesville: 1955. V. 42

Manuscripts and Documents. Their Deterioration and Restoration. Charlottesville: 1955. V. 39; 40

BARROW, WILLIAM

An Essay on Education; in which are particularly considered the Merits and the Defects of the Discipline and Instruction in our Academies. London: 1802. V. 37

BARROWS, JOHN R.

Ubet. Caldwell: 1934. V. 43

BARROWS, R. M.

The Kit Book for Soldiers, Sailors and Marines: Favorite Stories . . . Chicago: 1943. V. 44

BARROWS, WILLIAM

The General; or, Twelve Nights in the Hunters' Camp. Boston: 1869. V. 40; 45

The General; or, Twelve Nights in the Hunters' Camp. Boston;: 1869. V. 37; 40

BARRUEL, AUGUSTIN

Memoirs Illustrating the History of Jacobinism Written in French . . . London: 1798. V. 39; 41; 43

BARRUEL, AUGUSTIN DE

The History of the Clergy during the French Revolution; in Three Parts . . . Third Edition-Frst American. Burlington: 1794. V. 37

Memoirs Illustrating the History of Jacobinism. A Translated from the French. Hartford, New York: 1799. V. 37

BARRUS, CLARA

Our Friend John Burroughs. Boston & New York: 1914. V. 45

BARRY, ALFRED

The Life and Works of Sir Charles Barry, R. A., F.R.S. London: 1867. V. 39; 45; 46

Memoir of the Life and Works of the Late Sir Charles Barry. London: 1870. V. 43; 46

BARRY, EDWARD

Observations Historical, Critical, and Medical, on the Wines of the Ancients, and the Analogy between them and Modern Wines. . . . . and in particular those of Bath. London: 1775. V. 39; 42

Observations Historical, Critical and medical on the Wines of the Ancients and the Analogy Between Them and Modern Wines, with General Observations on the Principles and Qualities of Water and in Particular Those of Bath. London: 1775. V. 37

The Present Practice of a Justice of the Peace; and a Complete Library of Parish Law. London: 1790. V. 40

A Treatise on the Three Different Digestions and Discharges of the Human Body. London: 1759. V. 37; 38; 44

BARRY, GEORGE

The History of the Orkney Islands . . . Edinburgh: 1805. V. 46

The History of the Orkney Islands . . . With Their Agriculture, Manufactures, Fisheries, Etc. London: 1808. V. 38; 39; 40; 44; 46

BARRY, JAMES

A Description of the Series of Pictures Painted by James Barry and Preserved in the Great Room of the Society . . . fro the Encouragement of Art, Manufactures and Commerce. London: 1808. V. 44

A Letter to the Right Honourable the President, Vice-Presidents, and the Rest of the Nobleman and Gentlemen of the Society for the Encouragement of the Arts, Manufactures and Commerce . . . London: 1793. V. 40

A Letter to the Dilettanti Society Respecting the Obtention of Certain Matters Essentially Necessary for the Improvement of Public Taste, and for Accomplishing the Original Views of the Royal Academy of Great Britain. London: 1799. V. 41

BARRY, JOHN

A Tribute to Albert M. Bender. San Francisco: 1938. V. 37; 40

BARRY, JOHN WOLFE

The Tower-Bridge. A Lecture. London: 1894. V. 43

BARRY, MARTIN

Ascent to the Summit of Mont Blanc, 16th-18th of 9th Month (Septr.) 1834. 1835. V. 43

Ascent to the Summit of Mont Blanc in 1834. Edinburgh: 1836. V. 40; 43

BARRY, PATRICK

The Theory and Practice of the International Trade of the United States and England and of the Trade of the United States and Canada . . . Chicago: 1858. V. 45

BARRY, T. A.

Men and Memories of San Francisco, in the 'Spring of '50'. San Francisco: 1873. V 37; 40; 44; 45

BARRY, WILLIAM E.

Chronicles of Kennebunk. Being Scenes and Episodes in an Old Maine Village and Vicinity. N. P.: 1923. V. 37

BARRYMORE, LIONEL

Mr. Cantonwine: a Moral Tale. Boston: 1953. V. 45

BARSCHAMP, IVO

Sterbekunst: Disputatio und Gesprech Zwischen Einem Krancken Menschen und dem Versucher. Erfurt: 1561. V. 37

BARSKY, ARTHUR

Plastic Surgery. Philadelphia: 1938. V. 42

BARSTOW, WILLIAM A.

Annual Message of William A. Barstow, Governor of the State of Wisconsin . . . January 11, 1856. Madison: 1845. V. 37

BARTELL, EDMUND

Cromer, Considered as a Watering Place; with Observations on the Picturesque Scenery in the Neighbourhood. London: 1806. V. 45

Hints for Picturesque Improvements in Ornamented Cottages. London: 1804. V. 38; 44

BARTER, CHARLOTTE

Alone Among the Zulus, by a Plain Woman. London: 1866. V. 45

BARTER, S.

Manual Instruction. Woodwork (The English Sloyd). London: 1892. V. 38

BARTER, WILLIAM GEORGE THOMAS

Poems Original and Translated. London: 1850. V. 38

BARTH, F. G.

Neurobiology of Arachnids. Berlin: 1985. V. 37

BARTH, HENRY

Travels and Discoveries in North and Central Africa. New York: 1857. V. 41

Travels and Discoveries in North and Central Africa. Being a Journal of an Expedition Undertaken Under the Auspices of H.B.M.'s Government in the Years 1849-1855. New York: 1857. V. 39; 45

Travels and Discoveries in North and Central Africa: Being a Journal of an Expedition . . . in the Years 1849-1855. London: 1857-58. V. 42; 43; 45

Travels and Discoveries in North and Central Africa. New York: 1857-59. V. 38; 41; 44

BARTH, JOHN 1930-

Chimera. New York: 1972. V. 37; 39; 40; 41; 42; 43; 44

Don't Count On It: a Note on the Number of the 1001 Nights. Northridge: 1984. V. 43

The End of the Road. Garden City: 1958. V. 39; 42; 44; 45; 46

The End of the Road. Garden City: 1958. V. 42

The End of the Road. London: 1962. V. 38; 40; 42; 45

The Floating Opera. New York: 1956. V. 37; 38; 39; 40; 41; 42; 44; 45; 46

Floating Opera. London: 1962. V. 44; 45

The Floating Opera. London: 1968. V. 37; 42

The Floating Opera. New York: 1956. V. 37

Giles Goat Boy. Garden City: 1966. V. 37; 40; 41; 42; 44; 45

Giles Goat Boy. New York: 1966. V. 37; 41; 45

Letters. New York: 1979. V. 39; 41; 42; 43

Lost in the Funhouse. Garden City: 1968. V. 37; 42; 44; 45; 46

The Sot Weed Factor. Garden City: 1960. V. 42; 44

The Sot-Weed Factor. London: 1961. V. 37; 40; 44; 45; 46

Todd Andrews to the Author. Northridge: 1979. V. 37; 40; 42; 43

BARTH, JOSEPH

Anfangsgrunde der Muskellehre. Wien: 1786. V. 40

Muskellehre . . . Vienna: 1819. V. 41

BARTH, M.

A Practical Treatise on Auscultation. Edinburgh: 1842. V. 40

A Practical Treatise on Ausculation. Philadelphia: 1845. V. 42

BARTHELEMY, ABBE

Travels in Italy . . . in a Series of Letters Written to County Caylus. London: 1802. V. 37

Travels of Anacharsis the Younger in Greece, During the Middle of the Fourth Century before the Christian Aera. Boudn with Maps, Plans, Vues & Coins Illustrative of the Travels . . . London: 1796. V. 37

BARTHELEMY, JEAN JACQUES

Carite and Polydorus. London: 1799. V. 44

Maps, Plans, Views and Coins, Illustrative of the Travels of Anacharsis the Younger in Greece . . . London: 1791. V. 43

Travels in Italy . . . London: 1802. V. 42; 45

Voyage du Jeune Anacharis en Grece. Paris: 1817. V. 38; 44

Voyage de Jeune Anacharsis en Grece . . . Paris: 1822. V. 40

BARTHELME, DOANLD

Sixty Stories. New York: 1981. V. 45

BARTHELME, DONALD

City Life. New York: 1970. V. 45

Come Back Dr. Caligari. Boston: 1964. V. 37; 44; 45; 46

Come Back Dr. Caligari. London: 1966. V. 37; 45

The Dead Father. New York: 1975. V. 45

Here in the Village. Northridge: 1978. V. 37; 43

Sadness. New York: 1972. V. 45

Sixty Stories. New York: 1981. V. 43

Unspeakable Practices, Unnatural Acts. New York: 1968. V. 45

BARTHES, ROLAND

Critical Essays. Evanston: 1972. V. 46

Image/Music/Text. New York: 1977. V. 46

Mythologies. New York: 1972. V. 46

The Pleasure of the Text. New York: 1975. V. 46

S/Z. New York: 1974. V. 46

Sade/Fourier/Loyola. New York: 1976. V. 46

BARTHEZ, PAUL JOSEPH

Nouvelle Mechanique Mouvements de l'Homme et des Animaux. Carcassonne: 1798. V. 38

Oratio Academica de Principio Vitali Hominis. (with) Nova Doctrina de Functionibus Naturae Humanae. Montpellier: 1773 & 1774. V. 41

BARTHOLEMEW, ALFRED

Specifications for Practical Architecture, Preceded by an Essay on the Decline of Excellence in the Structure and in the Science of Modern English Buildings. London: 1840. V. 38

BARTHOLIN, CASPAR

De Tibiis Veterum & Earum Antiquo Usu. Rome: 1677. V. 46

BARTHOLIN, THOMAS 1616-1680

. . . Anatome ex Omnium Veterum Recentinorumque Observationibus . . . as Circulationem . . . Lugduni Batavorum: 1673-74. V. 43

Antiquitatum Danicarum de Causis Contemptae a Danis adhuc Gentilibus Mortis Libri Tres. Hafniae: 1689. V. 44

De Medicina Danorum Domestica Dissertationes X. Copenhagen: 1666. V. 41; 45

BARTHOLINUS, CASPAR

Casp. Bartholini . . . Institutiones Anatomicae, Novis Recentiorum Opinionibus . . . 1645. V. 42

De Tibiis Veterum, et Earum Antiquo Usu Libri Tres. Amsterdam: 1679. V. 40

BARTHOLINUS, PETRUS

Apologia Pro Observationibus, et Hypothesibus Astronomicis Nobilissimi Viri Dn. Tychonis Brahe Dani . . . Hafniae: 1632. V. 40

BARTHOLINUS, THOMAS

De Peregrinatione Medica ad Cl. V. Oligerum Jacobaeum Nepotem Suum et Filios Casparum Bartholinum, Christoph. Bartholinum. Hafniae: 1674. V. 37

Defensio Vasorum Lacteorum et Lymphaticum Adversus Joannem Riolanum Celeberrimum Lutetiae Anatomicum. Hafniae: 1655. V. 40

Dissertatio Prima de Theriaca in Officina Christophori Heerford Sen. Pharmacop . . . Dissertatio Secunda . . . Hafniae: 1671. V. 40

De Unicornu Obervationes Novae. Amstelaedami: 1678. V. 38; 40; 44; 46

BARTHOLOMAEUS ANGLICUS

Le Grand Proprietaire de Toutes Choses, Contenant Plusieurs Maladies et Dont ils Procedent & Aussi les Remedes. Paris: 1556. V. 40

BARTHOLOMEW, A. T.

Richard Bentley, D. D. A Bibliography of His Works and of all the Literature Called forth y His Acts or His Writings. Cambridge: 1908. V. 37

BARTHOLOMEW, E.

Biographical Album of Western Gunfighters Containing More than 1,000 Biographical Entries, With Over 600 Rare Photographs of the Most Famous Sheriffs, Outlaws, Marshalls and Celebrated Personalities in the History of the Western Frontier. Houston: 1958. V. 37; 42

Wyatt Earp, the Untold Story and the Man and the Myth. Toyahville: 1963 & 1964. V. 43

BARTHOLOMEW, GEORGE W.

Record of the Bartholomew Family (In America), historicla, genealogical and biographical. London: 1885. V. 37

BARTHOLOMEW, HENRY SAGER KNAPP

Pioneer History of Elkhart County, Indiana, with Sketches and Stories. Goshen: 1930. V. 42

BARTHOLOMEW, JOHN

Oxford Advanced Atlas. London: 1924. V. 46

BARTHOLOMEW, JOHN G.

The XXth Century Citizen's Atlas of the World . . . London: 1902. V. 45

Zell's Descriptive Hand Atlas of the World. Philadelphia/New York: 1871. V. 45

BARTHOLOMEW, W. N.

Bartholomew's Sketches from Nature. Boston: 1860-63. V. 37

BARTHOLOW, ROBERTS 1831-1904

The Treatment of Diseases by the Hypodermic Method . . . Philadelphia: 1879. V. 44

BARTISCH, GEORG

Ophthalmo-Douleia, das Ist Augendienst . . . Dresden: 1583. V. 41; 43

BARTLET, JOHN

The Gentleman's Farriery. London: 1753. V. 38; 40

BARTLET, WILLIAM S.

The Frontier Missionary: a Memoir of the Life of the Rev. Jacob Bailey, A. M., Missionary at Pownalborough, Maine; Cornwallis and Annapolis, N.S. Boston: 1853. V. 42

BARTLETT, DAVID VANDEWATER GOLDEN 1828-1912

The Life and Public Services of Hon. Abraham Lincoln . . . and Hon. Hannibal Hamlin . . . Boston: 1860. V. 40

The Life and Public Services of Hon. Abraham Lincoln. Indianapolis: 1860. V. 39

BARTLETT, E.

A Monograph of the Weaver-Birds, Ploceidae and Arboreal and Terrestrial Finches, Fringillidae. Maidstone: 1888-89. V. 43

BARTLETT, EDWARD EVERETT

The Typographic Treasures in Europe and a Study of Contemporaneous Book Production in Great Britain, France, Italy, Germany, Holland and Belgium. New York: 1925. V. 41; 44

BARTLETT, ELISHA

The History, Diagnosis and Treatment of Typhoid and Typhus Fever. Philadelphia: 1842. V. 38; 42

Simple Settings in Verse . . . from Mr. Dickens Gallery. Boston: 1855. V. 45; 46

BARTLETT, GEORGE HARTNELL

Pen and Ink Drawing. Cambridge: 1903. V. 44

BARTLETT, HENRIETTA C.

A Census of Shakespeare's Plays in Quarto, 1594-1709. New Haven: 1916. V. 38; 40; 41; 42

A Census of Shakespeare's Plays in Quarto, 1594-1709. New Haven: 1916. V. 41

A Census of Shakespeare's Plays in Quarto 1594-1709. London: 1916. V. 39

BARTLETT, JAMES H.

The Manufacture, Consumption and Production of Iron, Steel and Coal, in the Dominion of Canada. Montreal: 1885. V. 39

BARTLETT, JOHN

Catalogue of Books on Angling Including Ichthyology, Pisciculture, Fisheries and Fishing Laws. Cambridge: 1882. V. 42

A Collection of Familiar Quotations, with Complete Indices of Authors and Subjects. Cambridge: 1855. V. 43; 44

BARTLETT, JOHN R.

Official Despatches . . . Connected with the Commission to . . . Mark the Boundary Between the United States and Mexico. Washington: 1852. V. 40

BARTLETT, JOHN RUSSELL 1805-1886

Dictionary of Americanisms. Boston: 1859. V. 40

Genealogy of that Branch of the Russell Family Which Comprises the Descendants of John Russell, of Woburn, Massachusetts. 1640-1878. Providence: 1879. V. 46

The Literature of the Rebellion. Boston: 1866. V. 43; 44

Personal Narrative of Explorations and Incidents in Texas, New Mexico, California, Sonora and Chinuaha with the U.S. Boundary Commission. New York & London: 1856. V. 38

Personal Narrative of Explorations and Incidents in Texas, New Mexico, California, Sonora and Chihuha, Connected with the United States and Mexican Boundary Commission, During the Years 1850, 51, 52, and 53. New York: 1854. V. 37; 38; 39; 41; 42; 43; 45

Personal Narrative of Explorations and Incidents in Texas, New Mexico, California, Sonora and Chihuahua, Connected with the United States and Mexican Boundary Commission . . . London: 1854. V. 39

Personal Narrative of Explorations and Incidents in Texas, New Mexico, California, Sonora and Chihuahua, Connected with the United States . . . New York: 1854. V. 45

Personal Narrative of Explorations and Incidents in Texas, New Mexico, California, Sonora and Chihuahua . . . New York: 1856. V. 45

Personal Narrative of Explorations and Incidents in Texas, New Mexico, California, Sonora, and Chihuahua, Connected with the United States and Mexican Boundary commission. London: 1854. V. 37

Personal Narrative of Explorations and Incidents in Texas, New Mexico, California, SOnora, and Chihuahua with the U.S. Boundary Commission. New York/London: 1856. V. 37; 39

Report of the Secretary of the Interior . . . A Report from Mr. Bartlett on the Subject of the Boundary Line Between the United States and Mexico. Washington: 1853. V. 43

BARTLETT, JOHN S. 1790-1863

Maize or Indian Corn, Its Advantages as a Cheap and Nutritious Article of Food, with Directions For Its Use. London: 1846. V. 45

BARTLETT, JOSEPH

Aphorisms on Man, Manners, Principles & Things. Portsmouth: 1810. V. 37

BARTLETT, JOSIAH

Speech of . . . at a Meeting of Citizens Opposed to the Re-election of Andrew Jackson, Holden at Portsmouth, N.H. Oct., 15, 1832. Portsmouth: 1832. V. 42

BARTLETT, ROBERT A.

The Last Voyage of the Karluk, Flagship of Vilhajalmar Stefansson's Canadian Arctic Expedition of 1913-16. Boston: 1916. V. 45

The Log of Bob Bartlett. New York: & London: 1928. V. 43

BARTLETT, THOMAS

A Treatise on British Mining. London: 1850. V. 39

BARTLETT, W. H.

Canadian Scenery Illustrated. London: 1842. V. 44

BARTLETT, WASHINGTON A.

A Reply of Washington A. Bartlett to the Testimony Taken Before the Naval Committee. Washington: 1856. V. 39; 40; 42

BARTLETT, WILLIAM

The Beauties of the Bosphorus. London. V. 46

Syria, the Holy Land, Asia Minor &c. London: 1836. V. 40

BARTLETT, WILLIAM HENRY 1809-1854

American Scenery; or Land, Lake and River. London: 1852. V. 45

Canadian Scenery Illustrated. London: 1842. V. 45

The Danube; Its History, Scenery and Topography. London: 1844. V. 42

Footsteps of Our Lord and His Apostles, in Syria, Greece, and Italy, a Succession of Visits to the Scenes of New Testament Narrative. London: 1852. V. 44

Forty Days in the Desert, on the Tracks of the Israelites. London: 1845. V. 39

Forty Days in the Desert, On the Track of the Israelites. London: 1850. V. 38; 39; 42

Forty Days in the Desert, on the Track of the Israelites, or, a Journey from Cairo, by Wady Feiran, to Mount Sinai and Petra. London: 1862. V. 44

The Nile Boat. London: 1849. V. 38; 42

The Nile Boat; or, Glimpses of the Land of Egypt. London: 1850. V. 39; 43

The Nile Boat: or, Glimpses of the Land of Egypt. New York: 1851. V. 37; 38

Pictures from Sicily. London: 1853. V. 39

The Pilgrim Fathers. London: 1853. V. 38; 40

The Pilgrim Fathers; or, the Founders of New England in the Reign of James the First. London: 1853. V. 39; 45; 46

The Scenery and Antiquities of Ireland. London: 1850. V. 43

The Scenery and Antiquities of Ireland. London: 1855. V. 37; 38; 41; 44

Walks About the City and Environs of Jerusalem. London: 1844. V. 39; 44

Walks about the City and Environs of Jerusalem. London: (ca. 1850). V. 37; 39

BARTLETT, WILLIAM S.

The Frontier Missionary: a Memoir of the Life of the Rev. Jacob Bailey, A.M., Missionary at Pownalborough, Maine: Cornwallis and Annapolis, N.S. Boston: 1853. V. 39

BARTOL, B. H.

A Treatise on the Marine Boilers of the United States. Philadelphia: 1851. V. 45

BARTOLETTI, FABRIZIO

Encyclopaedia Hermetico-Dogmatica; sive, Orbis Doctinarum Medicarum Physiologiae, Hygiinae Pathologiae . . . Bologna: 1619. V. 40; 43

BARTOLI, COSIMO 1503-1572

Del Modo di Misvrare le Distantie, le Superficie, i Corpi, le Plante, le Prouincie, le Prospettiue & Tutte le Altre Cose Terrene, che Possono Occorrere a Gli Huomini, Secondo le Vere Regole d'Euclide . . . Francesco: 1589. V. 42

Del Modo di Misurare . . . 1614. V. 42

Discorsi Historici Universali. Venice: 1569. V. 39

BARTOLI, DANIELLO

Del Suono de' Tremori Armonici e delludiot. Rome: 1679. V. 37

La Tensione, e la Pressione Disputanti . . . Venice: 1678. V. 42

BARTOLI, PIETRO SANTI 1635-1700

Parerga Atque Ornamenta, ex Raphaelis Sanctii Prototypis, a Ioanne Nannio Utienensi, in Vaticani Palatii Xystis . . . Rome: 1690. V. 40

Picturae Antiquae Cryptarum Romanarum et Sepulcri Nasonum . . . Rome: 1750. V. 38

Le Pitture Antiche del Sepolcro de Nasoni . . . Rome: 1680. V. 40

BARTOLOZZI, FRANCESCO

Prints Engraved by F. Bartolozzi and From the Original Drawings of Guercino in the Collection of His Majesty. London: 1800. V. 40

BARTOLUS, DE SAXOFERRATO 1314-1357

Commentaria Omnium Legum. Venice: 1520. V. 45

In Primam Digesti, Novi Partem Praelectiones. Lyons: 1546. V. 38; 40

La Tiberiade . . . del Modo di Dividere l'Alluvioni, l'Isole, & gli'Aluei, Con l'Annotationi, et Espositioni di Claudio Tobaldutii da Montalboddo. Rome: 1587. V. 38; 40

BARTON, B. H.

The British Flora Medica. London: 1877. V. 37

BARTON, B. S.

Elements of Botany. Philadelphia: 1827. V. 38

BARTON, BENAJMIN SMITH

Elements of Botany: or Outlines of the Natural History of Vegetables. Philadelphia: 1803. V. 40

BARTON, BENJAMIN SMITH

Fragments of the Natural History of Pennsylvania. Philadelphia: 1799. V. 42; 43; 45

A Memoir Concerning the Fascinating Faculty Which Has Been Ascribed to the Rattle Snake, and Other American Serpents. Philadelphia: 1796. V. 43

BARTON, BERNARD

Devotional Verses; Founded On and Illustrative of Select Texts of Scripture. London: 1826. V. 40

Memoir, Letters and Poems. Philadelphia: 1850. V. 44

Poems . . . London: 1820. V. 42

Poetic Vigils . . . London: 1824. V. 42

Selections from the Poems and Letters of Bernard Barton. London: 1849. V. 37; 38

A Suffolk Yeoman's Memorial. Ipswich or Woodbridge?: 1847. V. 40

BARTON, BERTRAM FRANCIS

Some Account of the Family of Burton, Drawn from Manuscripts and Records . . . Dublin: 1902. V. 38

BARTON, BRUCE

Unkown. 1931. V. 38

BARTON, CAROL JUNE

Everyday Road Signs. 1988. V. 45

BARTON, CHARLES 1768-1843

An Historical Treatise of a Suit in Equity. London: 1796. V. 37; 40

BARTON, CLARA 1821-1912

The Red Cross of the Geneva Convention: What It Is . . . Dansville: 1881. V. 38

The Red Cross in Peace and War. Washington: 1899. V. 41; 42; 45

Report of Red Cross Relief Galveston Texas. Meriden: 1901. V. 41

BARTON, CUTTS

Modern Characters from Shakespear, Alphabetically Arranged. London: 1778. V. 41

BARTON, E.

Miscellaneous Traacts. Volume I. Containing Recent Scenes; Miracles, a Rhapsody . . . Dublin: 1824. V. 38

BARTON, G. B.

Literature in New South Wales. Sydney: 1866. V. 45

BARTON, GEORGE AARON

Haverford Library Collection of Cuneiform Tablets. Philadelphia: 1907. V. 40

BARTON, JAMES L.

Address on the Early Reminiscences of Western New York and the Lake Region of Country. Buffalo: 1848. V. 45

BARTON, LUCAS

Bernard Barton and His Friends.. London: 1893. V. 45

BARTON, RICK

Musical Instruments. San Francisco: 1958. V. 45

Sausalito Boat Harbor. San Francisco: 1959. V. 45

BARTON, ROSE

Familiar London. London: 1904. V. 40

BARTON, WILLIAM

A Dissertation on the Freedom of Navigation and Maritime Commerce . . . the Law of Nations. Philadelphia: 1802. V. 37

Memoirs of the Life of David Rittenhouse, LLD. F.R.S., Late President of the AMerican Philosophical Society . . . Philadelphia: 1813. V. 39; 42; 43

BARTON, WILLIAM PAUL CRILLON

Compendium Florae Philadelphicae . . . Philadelphia: 1918. V. 41

Compendium Florae Phildelphicae: Containing a Description of the Plants Found Within a Circuit of Ten Miles Around Philadelphia. Philadelphia: 1818. V. 37; 41; 42; 44

A Flora of North America. Philadelphia: 1821-22-23. V. 38; 40

Vegetable Materia Medica of the United States, of Medical Botany. Philadelphia: 1818, 1825. V. 38; 45; 46

BARTRAM, JOHN

An Account of East-Florida, with a Journal, Kept by John Bartram of Philadelphia . . . London: 1766. V. 43

Observations on the Inhabitants, Climate Soil, Rivers, Productions, Animals and Other Matters Worthy of Notice. London: 1751. V. 37; 39; 40; 41; 44

BARTRAM, WILLIAM

Botanical and Zoological Drawings 1756-1788. Philadelphia: 1968. V. 40

Observations on the Creek and Cherokee Indians.. New York: 1909. V. 42

Travels through North and South Carolina, Georgia, East and West Florida, the Cherokee Country, the Extensive Territories of the Muscogulges, or Creek Confederacy, and the Country of the Chactaws. Philadelphia: 1791. V. 37; 38; 39; 42; 44; 45

Travels Through North and South Carolina, Georgia, East and West Florida, The Cherokee Country, the Extensive Territories of the Muscogulges of Creek Confederacy, and the Country of the Choctaws. London: 1792. V. 37; 39; 41; 42; 43; 45

Travels Through North and South Carolina, Georgia, East and West Florida, the Cherokee Country, the Extensive Territories of the Muscogulges or Creek Confederacy, and the Country of the Chactaws. Dublin: 1793. V. 39

Travels through North and South Carolina, Georgia, East and West Florida, the Cherokee Country, the Extensive Territories of the Muscogulges or Creek Confederacy, and the Country of the Chactaws (sic) . . . London: 1794. V. 38

Voyage dans les Parties Sud de l'Amerique Septentrionale; Savior; Les Carolines Septentrinale et Meridionale, la Georgie, les Florides Orientale et Occidentale, le Pays des Chactaws . . . Paris: 1801. V. 39; 42

Voyage dans les Parties Sud de l'Amerique Septentrionale . . . Paris: 1801. V. 42

BARTRUM, MRS.

A Widow's Reminiscences of the Siege of Lucknow. London: 1858. V. 38

BARTRUM, PETER C.

Welsh Genealogies A.D. 300-1400. 1974, 1980. V. 38

BARTTELOT, W. G.

The Life of Edmund Musgrave Barttelot. London: 1890. V. 41

BARWELL, RICHARD

A Treatise on Diseases of the Joints. 1861. V. 42

BARWICK, GEORGE F.

A Book Bound for Mary Queen of Scots: Being a Description of the Binding of a Copy of the Geographia of Ptolemy Printed at Rome, 1490, With Notes on Other Books Bearing Queen Mary's Insignia. 1901. V. 39

BARWICK, JOHN

Querela Cantabrigiensis; or, a Remonstrance by Way of Apologie, for the Banished Members of the Late Flourishing University of Cambridge. 1647. V. 45

Querela Cantabrigiensis: London: 1647. V. 45

BARWICK, PETER

The Life of Dr. John Barwick, Dean of Durham and St. Paul's. London: 1724. V. 39

Vita Johannis Barwick, S.T.P. London: 1721. V. 44; 46

BARZINI, LUIGI

Pekin to Paris. An Account of Prince Borghese's Journey across Two Continents in a Motor-Car. Translated by L.P. de Castelvecchio. With an Introduction by Prince Borghese. London: 1907. V. 37

BARZIZIUS, GASPARINI

Epistole. Paris: 1499. V. 40

BARZUN, JACQUES

A Book of Prefaces to Fifty Classics of Crime Fiction 1900-1950. New York: 1976. V. 38

BASAN, F.

Cabinet Poullain ou Collection de Cent-vingt Estampes . . . Paris: 1781. V. 44

BASBEE, C.

Six Views of Windsor Castle. Windsor: 1831. V. 41
Six Views of Windsor Castle. Windsor: 1835. V. 41

BASCOM, LEE

A God of Gotham. New York: 1891. V. 43

BASEDOW, HERBERT

Journal of the Government North-West Expedition. London: 1914. V. 41

BASEILHAC, JEAN

Nouvelle Methode d'Extraire la Pierre de la Vessie Urinaire par-Dessus le Pubis. Brussels: 1779. V. 38

BASHKIRTSEFF, MARIE 1860-1884

The Journal of Marie Bashkirtseff. London: Paris & Melbourne: 1890. V. 43
The Journal of Marie Bashkirtseff. Melbourne: 1890. V. 45

BASHO, MATSURA

The Records of a Weather-Exposed Skeleton. London: 1969. V. 46
Traveler, My Name: Haiku. 1984. V. 40

BASILE, GIAMBATTISTA

Stories from the Pentamerone. V. 39

BASILE, GIOVANNI BATTISTA 1575 ca. - 1632

Il Pentamerone. London: 1893. V. 38
Stories from the Pentamerone. London: 1911. V. 37; 38; 40; 41
Stories from the Pentamerone. London: 1991. V. 44

BASILEON. Cambridge: 1900-1909. V. 41

BASILIUS, SAINT, THE GREAT, ABP. OF CAESAREA 330ca. - 379

Opera Graeca Quae ad Nos Extant Omnia. Basle: 1551. V. 40
Opera Quaedam . . . Tractatus Ethicorum Regula . . . De Virginitate, Contra Eunomium, Item Sermones & Epistolae . . . Venice: 1535. V. 37
Orationes de Moribus XXIII. Simone Magistro Auctore. (with) Conciones de Vita et Moribus. Latinae Factae Simone a Maille. Paris: 1556/58. V. 41

BASILIUS VALENTINUS

Of Natural and Supernatural Things. 1671. V. 46

BASKERVILLE, CHARLES

Radium and Radio-Active Substances. Philadelphia: 1905. V. 38

THE BASKERVILLE Club: No. 1. Handlist. Cambridge: 1904. V. 45

BASKET, JAMES

History of the Island of St. Domingo, from Its First Discovery by Columbus to the Present Period. London: 1818. V. 37; 39; 42
History of the Island of St. Domingo, From Its First Discovery by Columbus to the Present Period. New York: 1824. V. 41
History of the Island of St. Domingo, from its First Discovery by Columbus to the Present Period. London: 1818. V. 37

BASKETT, JOHN

English Drawings and Water Colours 1550-1850. New York: 1972. V. 42

BASKIN, LEONARD

An ABC with Best Wishes from Esther and Leonard Baskin. Northampton: 1958. V. 37
Ars Anatomica. New York. V. 39
Ars Anatomica. New York: 1972. V. 37; 38; 40; 41; 42; 45; 46
Blake and the Youthful Ancients. Northampton: 1956. V. 40
Caprices and Grotesques. Northampton: 1965. V. 37; 45
Demons, Imps & Fiends. Northampton: 1976. V. 38; 39; 40; 41; 42; 44; 46
An Exhibition of the Wood Cuts and Wood Engravings of Leonard Baskin. London: 1962. V. 40
Fancies Bizarreries & Ornamented Grotesques. Leeds: 1989. V. 45
Fifteen Woodcuts. Boston: 1962. V. 46
Figures of Dead men. 1968. V. 41

Icones Librorum Artifices. Northampton: 1988. V. 43; 44; 45; 46
Iconologia. New York: 1988. V. 42
Irises. A Book of Etchings. Leeds: 1988. V. 45; 46
Leonard Baskin - Woodcuts and Wood Engravings. London: 1962. V. 45
Mokomaki: Thirteen Etchings of Shunken and Tatooed Maoriheads. Leeds: 1985. V. 38; 44; 46
Mokomaki. Leeds: 1985. V. 38
To Colour Thought. 1967. V. 44
To Colour Thought. New Haven: 1967. V. 40; 41; 42; 45; 46
To Colour Thought. The Graphic Arts in Yale University Library. Verona: 1967. V. 39; 41
Twelve Sculptors. Leeds: 1988. V. 43; 44; 45
Unknown Dutch Artists. N.P: 1983. V. 38
Unknown Dutch Artists. N.P.: 1983. V. 44

BASKIN, O. L.

History of the City of Denver, Arapahoe County and Colorado. Chicago: 1880. V. 37

BASNAGE, JACQUES

Histoir et du Vieux et du Nouveau Testament. Amsterdam: 1705. V. 42
The History of the Jews. London: 1708. V. 44

BASOLI, ANTONIO

Raccolta di Prospettive Serie, Rustiche, e di Paesaggio. Bologna: 1810. V. 37

BASON, FREDERICK T.

A Bibliography of the Writings of William Somerset Maugham. London: 1931. V. 40

BASS, HERMANN

Outlines of the History of Medicine and the Medical Profession. New York: 1889. V. 39

BASS, MICHAEL T.

Street Music in the Metropolis. London: 1864. V. 43

BASS, WILLIAM WALLACE

Adventures in the Canyons of the Colorado by Two of Its Earliest Explorers, James White and W. W. Hawkins . . . Grand Canyon: 1920. V. 37; 39; 40

BASSANI, ANTONIO

Viaggio a Roma Della S.R.M. di Maria Casimira Regina di Polonia . . . Rome: 1700. V. 46

BASSETT, JOHN

The Medical Reports of John Y. Bassett, M.D.: The Alabama Student. Springfield: 1941. V. 37; 38; 41; 42; 45

BASSETT, THOMAS

A Catalogue of the Common and Statute Law-Books of this Realm. London: 1671. V. 40

BASSHAW, EDWARD

A True and Perfect Narrative of the Differences Between Mr. Busby and Mr. Bagshawe . . . London: 1659. V. 42

BASSHE, EMJO

Earth. New York: 1927. V. 46

BASSI, GIULIO

Arimmetica, e Geometria Pratica . . . Libri Otto . . . Piacenza: 1666. V. 45

BASSING, EILLEN

Home Before Dark. New York: (1957). V. 37

BASSO, HAMILTON

Relics and Angels. New York: 1929. V. 37

THE BASTARD; or, The History of Mr. Greville. London: 1784. V. 39

BASTIAN, H. CHARLTON

The Modes of Origin of Lowest Organisms: including a Discussion of the Experiments of M. Pasteur, and a Reply to Some Statements by Professors Huxley and Tyndall. London: 1871. V. 37

BASTIAT, FREDERIC

Economic Sophisms. Edinburgh: 1873. V. 39; 41
Essays on Political Economy. Part 1. Capital and Interest. II. That Which is Seen, and That Which is Not Seen. Part III. Government. What is Money? Part IV. The Law. London: 1853. V. 39
Harmonies of Political Economy. London: 1860. V. 38; 41; 42
Harmonies of Political Economy. with Part II . . . London: 1860, 1870. V. 39
Harmonies of Political Economy. Edinburgh: 1880's. V. 41
Oeuvres Completes. Paris: 1855-1860. V. 38

BASTON, THOMAS

The Cambridge Unviersity Press Collection of Private Press Types . . . Cambridge: 1951. V. 39

BASTWICK, JOHN

Flagellum Pontificis & Episcoporum Latialium: Sive Tractatus, De Jurisdictione Episcopali . . . Holland: 1635. V. 45

BASWELL, RICHARD

Ireland Under the Tudors, with a Succinct Account of the Earlier History. London: 1885. V. 43

BATAES, J. H.

Notes of a Tour in Mexico and California. New York: 1897. V. 38

BATCHELDER, GEORGE

A Sketch of the History and Resources of Dakota Territory. Yankton: 1870. V. 37; 38; 39; 42; 45

BATCHELDER, GEORGE A.

A Sketch of the History and Resources of Dakota Territory. Yankton: 1876. V. 39; 43

BATCHELDER, J. P.

Thoughts on the Connection of Life, Mind and Matter, in Respect to Education. Utica: 1845. V. 41

BATCHELDER, JAMES b. 1828

Multim in Parvo. London: 1802. V. 39

Multum in Parvo: Notes from the Life and Travels of a Retired Locomotive Engineer. San Francisco: 1892. V. 37; 39

BATCHELDER, ROGER

Watching and Waiting on the Border. Boston: 1917. V. 43

BATCHELOR, JOHN

Sea-Girt Yezo. Glimpses at Missionary Work in North Japan. London: 1902. V. 38

BATCHELOR, JOHN CALVIN

The Further Adventures of Halley's Comet. N.P.: 1980. V. 42

BATCHELOR, S.

The Cabinet of Gems, or Vocabulary of Precious Stones, Arranged According to Their Comparative Value . . . N.P.: 1846. V. 41

THE BATCHELOR'S DIRECTORY... London: 1694. V. 43

BATE, C. SPENCE

A History of British Sessile-Eyed Crustacea. London: 1863-68. V. 37; 43

BATE, GEORGE

Elenchi Motuum Nuperorum in Anglia. London: 1661-63. V. 45

Elenchi Motum Nuperorum in Anglia Pars Prima (and) Pars Secunda . . . Londini: 1663. V. 46

Elenchus Mortuum Nuperorum in Aanglia, Simul ac Juris Regii et Parliamentarii . . . A.2455. Paris: 1658. V. 38

Pharmacopoeia Bateana. In Qua, Octingenta Circiter Pharmaca . . . Londini: 1688. V. 38

BATE, JOHN

Mysteries of Nature and Art . . . London: 1635. V. 43

BATE, PERCY

The English Pre-Raphaelite Painters. London: 1899. V. 42

Modern Scottish Portrait Painters. Edinburgh: 1910. V. 43; 46

BATEMAN, CHARLES SOMERVILLE LATROBE

First Ascent of the Kasai . . . London: 1889. V. 42; 43

BATEMAN, FREDERIC

Darwinism Tested by Language . . . London: 1877. V. 43

BATEMAN, GERALD COOPER

A Countryman's Calendar. Ditchling, Sussex: 1928. V. 37; 46

A Countryman's Calendar. Sayings for the Months compiled by Gerald Bateman. Ditchling: 1927. V. 37; 39

BATEMAN, J.

A Monograph of Odontoglossum. London: 1864-74. V. 40; 41

BATEMAN, J. F. LA TROBE

History and Description of the Manchester Waterworks. Manchester: 1884. V. 37; 42

BATEMAN, JAMES

A Second Century of Orchidaceous Plants. London: 1867. V. 44; 45

BATEMAN, JOHN FREDERIC

On the Supply of Water to London from the Sources of the River Severn. London: 1865. V. 37; 40

BATEMAN, THOMAS

A Practical Synopsis of Cutaneous Diseases, According to the Arrangements of Dr. Willan, Exhibiting a Concise View, etc. Philadelphia;: 1818. V. 37; 38; 42

Reports on the Diseases of London, and the State of the Weather, from 1804-1816 . . . London: 1819. V. 38

A Succinct Account of the Contagious Fever of this Country, Exemplified in the Epidemic Now Prevailing in London. London: 1818. V. 39

BATENHAM, GEORGE

Etchings of Churches, Gates &c. in Chester. London: 1880. V. 41

BATES, A. C.

An Early Connecticut Engraver and His Work. Hartford: 1906. V. 39

BATES, ALFRED

The Drama: Its History, Literature and Influence on Civlization. London: 1903. V. 42

BATES, BARNABAS

Peculiarities of the Shakers . . . New York: 1832. V. 39

BATES, CADWALLADER JOHN

The Border Holds of Northumberland. Newcastle: 1891. V. 38; 40; 44

BATES, D. B., MRS.

Incidents on Land and Water, or Four Years on the Pacific Coasat. Boston: 1857. V. 38; 45

BATES, F. A.

Graves: Memoirs of the Civil War Compiled from 17th Century Records. London: 1927. V. 38

BATES, F. A. GRAVES

Memoirs of the Civil War . . . London: 1927. V. 41

BATES, GEORGE WASHINGTON

Sandwich Island Notes. New York: 1854. V. 38; 42; 44; 46

BATES, HENRY WALTER 1825-1892

Illustrated Travels: a Record of Discovery, Geography and Adventure. London: 1880. V. 41; 46

The Naturalist on the River Amazons, a Record of Adventures, Habits of Animals, Sketches of Brazilian and Indian Life and Aspects of Nature Under the Equator. London: 1863. V. 40; 42; 46

The Naturalist on the River Amazon. London: 1892. V. 40

The Naturalist on the River Amazons . . . London: 1910. V. 41

The Naturalist on the River Amazons. London: 1863. V. 42

The Naturalist on the River Amazons. New York: 1892. V. 41

BATES, HERBERT ERNEST 1905-1974

Achilles the Donkey. London: 1962. V. 42

Achilles and the Twins. London: 1964. V. 38

An Aspidistra in Babylon. London: 1960. V. 43

The Beauty of the Dead and Other Stories. London: 1940. V. 38

The Black Boxer - Tales. London: 1932. V. 37; 38; 40; 44; 46

A Breath of French Air. London: 1959. V. 41; 43

Catherine Foster. London: 1929. V. 37; 38; 40; 46

Charlotte's Row. London: 1931. V. 37; 38; 42; 43; 44; 46

Charlotte's Row. London: 1931. V. 46

Colonel Julian and Other Stories. London: 1951. V. 43

Country Tales - Collected Short Stories. London: 1940. V. 40

The Country Heart. London: 1949. V. 38

The Cruise of the Breadwinner. 1946. V. 37

Cut and Come Again - Fourteen Stories. London: 1935. V. 38; 43

The Darling Buds of May. London: 1958. V. 43

Day of the Tortoise. London: 1961. V. 43

Day's End and Other Stories. London: 1928. V. 37; 38; 39; 44; 46

Death of a Huntsman. Four Short Novels. London: 1957. V. 41; 43

Down the River. London: 1937. V. 42; 43; 44

Down the River. New York: 1937. V. 45

The Duet. London: 1935. V. 39

The Fabulous Mrs. V. London: 1964. V. 37; 43

The Face of England. London: 1952. V. 40

Fair Stood the Wind for France. London: 1944. V. 37; 44

The Fallow Land. London: 1932. V. 38; 40; 43; 44; 46

Flowers and Faces. 1935. V. 40

Flowers and Faces. 1935. V. 45

Flowers and Faces. London: 1935. V. 37; 41

BATES, HERBERT ERNEST 1905-1974 continued

Flowers and Faces. Waltham St. Lawrence: 1935. V. 44; 45

The Flying Goat. London: 1939. V. 40

A German Idyll. 1932. V. 42

A German Idyll. Waltham St. Lawrence: 1932. V. 44; 46

The Golden Oriole. London: 1962. V. 43

The Hessian Prisoner. London: 1930. V. 38; 41; 42; 46

Holly and Sallow. 1931. V. 46

The House with the Apricot and Two Other Tales. London: 1933. V. 38; 46

A House of Women. London: 1936. V. 38

The Last Bread. A Play in One Act. London: 1926. V. 37; 40; 43; 45

The Last Bread: a Play. London: 1926. V. 40

The Last Bread: a Play. London: 1926. V. 37

Love for Lydia. London: 1952. V. 41

Mrs. Esmond's Life. London: 1931. V. 37; 38; 40; 41; 46

The Modern Short Story - a Critical Survey. London: 1941. V. 45

A Moment in Time. London: 1964. V. 43

My Uncle Silas. London: 1939. V. 38; 43

My Uncle Silas. 1939. V. 37

Pastoral on Paper. Maidstone. V. 43

The Poacher. London: 1935. V. 38; 40; 43; 46

Sally Go Round the Moon. London: 1932. V. 43

Sea Days, Sea Flowers; from 'O More than Happy Countryman.' 1984. V. 45

Sea Days, Sea Flowers: from 'O More than Happy Countryman.' 1984. V. 40

The Seekers. London: 1926. V. 37; 38; 43; 44

Seven Tales and Alexander. London: 1929. V. 37; 38; 43; 44; 45

Seven Tales and Alexander. London: 1929. V. 38

Seven by Five. London: 1963. V. 43

Songs of Exile. Boston: 1896. V. 40; 41

The Story Without an End and the Country Doctor. London: 1932. V. 37; 38; 44; 46

Thirty Tales. London: 1934. V. 46

A Threshing Day. London: 1931. V. 37; 41; 44

Through the Woods: The English Woodland - April to April. London: 1936. V. 41

The Tinkers of Elstow - The Story of the Royal Ordnance Factory Managed by J. Lyons and Co. Limited for the Ministry of Supply During the World War of 1939-1945. London: 1946. V. 40

The Tinkers of Elstow - the Story of the Royal Ordance Factory managed by J. Lyons and Company Limited for the Ministry of Supply During the World War of 1939-1945. (1946). V. 37

The Triple Echo. London: 1970. V. 43

The Two Seekers. London: 1926. V. 43

The Two Sisters. London: 1926. V. 37; 38; 44; 45; 46

The Two Sisters. London: 1926. V. 38

The Vanished World. London: 1969. V. 43

The Wedding Party. London: 1965. V. 43

The Wild Cherry Tree. London: 1968. V. 43

The Woman Who Had Imagination - Fourteen Stories. London: 1934. V. 38; 40; 42; 46

BATES, J. H.

Notes of a Tour in Mexico and California. New York: 1887. V. 37; 42

BATES, JOSEPH

Autobiography of Elder Joseph Bates: Embracing a Long Life on Shipboard, with Sketches of Voyages on the Atlantic and Pacific Oceans, the Baltic and Mediterranean Seas . . . Battle Creek: 1868. V. 38; 42

Life of Joseph Bates: An Autobiography. Takoma Park: 1927. V. 44

BATES, JOSEPH CLEMENT

History of the Bench and Bar of California. San Francisco: 1912. V. 38

BATES, KATHERINE LEE

America the Beautiful and Other Poems. New York: 1911. V. 43; 46

BATES, LOIS

Kindergarten Guide. London: 1897. V. 38

BATES, ORIC

The Eastern Libyans: an Essay. London: 1914. V. 37; 40; 42

BATES, RALPH

Rainbow Fish - Four Short Novels. London: 1937. V. 38

BATES, RALPH D.

Billy and Dick from Andersonville Prison to the White House. Santa Cruz: 1910. V. 42

BATES, SAMUEL P.

History of the Pennsylvania Volunteers, 1861-65. Harrisburg: 1869. V. 42

BATES, W.

The Airs, Overture &c in the Prelude Called the Theatrical Candidates As Now Performing with Universal Applause at the Theatre Royal, Drury Lane. London: 1775. V. 42; 46

BATES, WALTER

The Mysterious Stranger, or the Adventures of Henry More Smith, Containing a Descriptive Account of His Life and Adventures from the Time of His Appearance in Windsor, N.S. in 1812, Until His Confinement in Toronto, Upper Canada. Charlottetown: 1855. V. 39; 40

BATES, WILLIAM

A Funeral-Sermon for the Reverend, Holy and Excellent Divine, Mr. Richard Baxter, Who Deceased Decemb. 8, 1691. London: 1692. V. 42

The Harmony of the Divine Attributes in the Contrivance and Accomplishment of Man's Redemption by the Lord Jesus Christ. London: 1771. V. 44

BATESON, FREDERICK WILSE 1901-

The Cambridge Bibliography of English Literature. Cambridge: 1940. V. 39; 43

The Cambridge Bibliography of English Literature. (with) Supplement. Cambridge: 1940-66/1975. V. 41

The Cambridge Bibliography of English Literature. New York & Cambridge: 1941. V. 38; 41

Cambridge Bibliography of English Literture. Cambridge: 1966. V. 39

Cambridge Bibliography of English Literature. London: 1940. V. 37

BATESON, GREGORY

Balinese Character: A Photographic Analysis. By Gregory Bateson and Margaret Mead. New York: 1942. V. 37

BATESON, MARGARET

Professional Women Upon Their Professions. London: 1895. V. 46

BATESON, W.

Materials for the Study of Variation. London: 1894. V. 38

BATESON, WILLIAM

Mendel's Principles of Heredity. Cambridge: 1909. V. 37; 40

Mendel's Principles of Heredity. A Defence. Cambridge: 1902. V. 37; 40

Problems of Genetics. New Haven: 1913. V. 40

Reports to the Evolution Committe of the Royal Society. London: 1902-10. V. 39

BATH AGRICULTURAL SOCIETY

Letters and Papers on Agriculture, Planting &c. Selected from the Correspondence of the Bath and West of England Society, for the Encouragement of Agriculture, Arts, Manufactures and Commerce. Bath: 1802. V. 45

BATH Anecdotes and Characters: by the Genus Loci. London: 1782. V. 38; 43

BATH, WILLIAM PULTENEY, EARL OF 1684-1764

The Case of the Revival of the Salt Duty, Fully Started and Considered, with Some Remarks on the Present State of Affairs. London: 1732. V. 42

The Conduct of the Late and Present M-----ry Compared. With an Impartial Review of Public Transaction Since the Resignation of . . . the Earl of Orford . . . In a Letter to a Friend. London: 1742. V. 41

An Enquiry Into the Conduct of Our Domestick Affairs, From the Year 1721 to the Present Time. London: 1734. V. 42; 46

The Politicks on Both Sides, With Regard to Foreign Affairs . . . With Some Observations on the Present State of Affairs in Great Britain. London: 1734. V. 41; 45

A Proper Answer to the By-Stander. Wherein Is Shewn I, That There is No Necessity For, but Infallible Ruin in the Maintenance of a Large Regular (or Mercenary) Land Force in this Island. II That by Keeping a Standing Army for Preventing an Invasion . . . London: 1742. V. 41; 45

A Review of All That Hath Pass'd Between the Courts of Great Britain and Spain, Relating to Our Trade and Navigation from the Year 1721 to the Present Convention; with Some Particular Observations Upon It. London: 1739. V. 41; 42; 45

A Short View of the State of Affairs, with Relation to Great Britain, for Four Years Past; with Some Remarks on the Treaty Lately Published and a Pamphlet Intituled 'Observations' Upon It. London: 1730. V. 37; 39

Some Considerations on the National Debts, the Sinking Fund, and the State of Publick Credit: in a Letter to a Friend in the Country. London: 1729. V. 39; 45

BATHE, GREVILLE

Oliver Evans. A Chronicle of Early American Engineering. Philadelphia: 1935. V. 39; 42; 43; 46

Oliver Evans. A Chronicle of Early American Engineering. Philadelphia: 1935. V. 39

THE BATHROOM: a New Interior. Pittsburgh: 1931. V. 43; 45

BATHURST, CHARLES

Notes on Nets. Cirencester: 1837. V. 38

Notes on Nets; or, The Quincunx Practically Considered. London: 184-. V. 39

BATHURST, EARL

Catalogue of the Bathurst Collection of Pictures. London: 1908. V. 40

Supplement to the Foxhound Kennel Stud Book. London: 1928. V. 43

BATHURST, HENRY BATHURST, 2ND EARL OF 1714-1794

An Introduction to the Law Relative to Trials at Nisi Prius. Dublin: 1768. V. 38; 40

BATHURST, HENRY, EARL OF

The Genuine Speech of the Hon. Mr. ----- at the Late Trial of Miss Blandy, Which Contains a Summary of all the Proofs Against Her . . . London: 1752. V. 45

BATONI, POMPEO

A Complete Catalogue of His Works. London: 1985. V. 40

BATRAWI, AHMED M. EL

Report on the Human Remains. Cairo: 1935. V. 37

BATTAGLINI, MARCO

Istoria Vniversale di Tvtti i Concili Generali, e Particolari Celebrati nella Chiesa. Venezia: 1689. V. 37

BATTELL, JOSEPH

The Morgan Horse and Register. 1894-1939. V. 39

BATTELY, JOHN

Opera Posthuma viz; Antiquitates Rutupinae et Antiquitates S. Edmundi Nurgi ad annum 1272 Perductae. Oxoniae: 1745. V. 40

BATTEN, A.

Flowers of Southern Africa. Sandton: 1986. V. 37; 38; 42

BATTERSBY, D.

Battersby's Dominion Pocket Railway and Travellers Guide. Montreal: 1855. V. 45

BATTERSHALL, FLETCHER

Bookbinding for Bibliophiles, Being Notes on Some Technical Features of the Well Bound Book for the Aid of Connoisseurs, Together with A Sketch of Gold Tooling, Ancient and Modern. Greenwich: 1905. V. 37

BATTEY, THOMAS C.

The Life and Adventures of a Quaker Among the Indians. Boston: 1875. V. 46

The Life and Adventures of a Quaker Among the Indians. New York: 1876. V. 38; 40; 45

BATTINE, CECIL

The Crisis of the Confederacy: a History of Gettysburg and the Wilderness. London: 1905. V. 42

BATTISCOMBE, C. F.

The Relics of Saint Cuthbert. Oxford: 1956. V. 40; 42; 45

THE BATTLE of the Frogs and Mice. 1988. V. 40

BATTLE, J. H.

History of Columbia and Montour Counties, Pennsylvania. Chicago: 1887. V. 41; 42

BATTLE, KEMP P.

The Early History of Raleigh. Raleigh: 1893. V. 37

BATTLE of Nashville. December 15-16, 1864. Nashville: 1864. V. 40

THE BATTLE of the Frogs and Mice. 1988. V. 45

THE BATTLE of the Two Philosophies. London: 1866. V. 41; 45

BATTLES and Leaders of the Civil War. New York: 1884-87. V. 37; 42

BATTLES and Leaders of the Civil War - By Union and Confederate Officers. New York: 1887. V. 37

THE BATTLES of America by Sea and Land. With biographical sketches of great Naval and Military Commanders. New York: (1875). V. 37

BATTLES of the Civil War 1861-1865. The Complete Kurz and Allison. Birmingham: 1976. V. 39

BATTLES of the Civil War, A Pictorial Presentation. London: 1960. V. 46

BATTS, JOHN HERRIDGE

Dr. Barnardo: The Foster-Father of 'Nobody's Children' . . . London: 1904. V. 45

BATTUTA, IBN

The Travels of Ibn Battuta, A.D. 1325-1354. London: 1958/62/71. V. 39

BATTY, BEATRICE

Forty-Two Years Amongst the Indians and Eskimor Pictures from the Life of the Right Reverend John Horden First Bishop of Moosonee. London: 1895. V. 37; 42; 44; 46

BATTY, ELIZABETH FRANCES

Italian Scenery From Drawings Made in 1817. London: 1820. V. 37; 38; 39; 40

BATTY, ROBERT d. 1848

Campaign of the Left Wing of the Allied Army, in the Western Pyranees and South of France, in the Years 1813-1814, Under Field Marshal the Marquess of Wellington. London: 1823. V. 39

European Scenery . . . London: 1820-23. V. 42

European Scenery. London: 1820-29. V. 41; 44

French Scenery from Drawings Made in 1819 by Captain Batty of the Grenadier Guards. London: 1822. V. 40; 41; 43; 44; 46

Scenery of the Rhine, Belgium and Holland from Drawings Made by Captn. Batty of the Grenadier Guards, F.R.S. London: 1826. V. 45

Welsh Scenery. London: 1825. V. 41; 44

BATTYE, CHRISTINE

The Brewhouse Private Press, 1963-1983. Wymondham: 1984. V. 37; 39; 41

BATTYE, J. S.

Western Australia. Oxford: 1924. V. 37; 41

BAUD-BOVY, DANIEL

In Greece. Journeys by Mountain and Valley. Geneva: 1920. V. 45

BAUDELAIRE, CHARLES

Les Fleurs du Mal. Paris: 1858. V. 39

Les Fleurs du Maul. Paris: 1910. V. 44

Les Fleurs du Mal. Paris: 1928. V. 41

Fleurs du Mal. London: 1929. V. 44

Les Fleurs du Mal. Paris: 1930. V. 41

Flowers of Evil. New York: 1971. V. 38

Intimate Journals. London: 1930. V. 40; 42

Little Poems in Prose. Paris: 1928. V. 40

The Voyage and Other Versions of Poems by Baudelaire. London: 1968. V. 41; 46

BAUDIER, MICHAEL

The History of the Administration of Cardinal Ximenes, Great Minister of State in Spain. London: 1671. V. 42

BAUDIER, MICHEL

Histoire de l'Administration du Cardinal d'Ambroise . . . Paris: 1634. V. 41

BAUDIN, NICOLAS

Baudin in Australian Waters. Oxford: 1988. V. 40

BAUDOUIN, ALEXANDRE

The Man of the World's Dictionary. London: 1822. V. 41

BAUDOUIN, FRANCOIS

Ad Edicta Veterum Principum Rom. de Christianis. (with) Ad Leges de Iuri Civili, Voconiam, Falcidiam, Iuliam Papiam Poppaeam . . . Basle: 1557/59. V. 45

BAUDRY DES LOZIERES, LOUIS NARCISSE

Voyage a la Louisiane, et sur le Continent d l'Amerique Septentrionale, Fait Dans les Annees 1794-1798 . . . Paris: 1802. V. 37; 38; 39

BAUER, K. H.

Surgery: General and Special Fiat Review of German Science 1939-1946. Wiesbaden: 1948. V. 41

BAUER, LOUIS

Outlines of the Principles and Practice Adopted in the Orthopaedic Institution of Brooklyn. New York: 1854. V. 42

BAUER, MAX

Precious Stones, Popular Account of Their Characters, Occurrence and Applications with an Introduction to Their Determintions.. London: 1904. V. 38

BAUER, WOLFGANG

Romeo and Julia. Drama in 5 Bildern, by Wolfgang Bauer. (Munich/Berlin: 1969). V. 37

BAUGHMANN, ROBERT W.

Kansas in Maps. Topeka: 1981. V. 37

BAUHIN, CASPAR

Theatri Botanici sive Index in theophrasti Dioscoridis Plinii et Botanicorum qui a Seculo Scripserunt Opera... Basel: 1623. V. 46

BAUHIN, JEAN

De Plantis a Divis Sanctis've Nomen Habentibus... Basle: 1591. V. 37

Historia Plantarum Universalis, Nova et Absolutissima, cum Consensu et Dissensu Circa Eas... Yverdon: 1650-51. V. 43

Historiae Plantarum Generalis Novae et Absolutiss. Quinquaginta Annis Elaboratae iam Prelo Commissae... Yverdon: 1619. V. 42; 45; 46

BAUHIN, JOHANN

Historia Novi et Admirabilis Fontis Balneique Bolensis in Ducatu Wirtembergico ad Acidulas Gooepingenses... Montbeliard: 1598. V. 38

BAUHIN, KASPAR

Theatrum Anatomicum. Frankfurt am Main: 1605. V. 42

BAUHINUS, CASPAR

Pinax Theatri Botanici sive Index in Theophrasti, Dioscorides, Plinii et Botanicorum qui a Seculo Scripserunt Opera. Basileae: 1623. V. 37

BAUM, JULIUS

Romanesque Architecture in France. London: 1928. V. 44

BAUM, LYMAN FRANK

American Fairy Tales. Chicago: 1901. V. 46

The Army Alphabet. Chicago: 1900. V. 45

Aunt Jane's Nieces at Milville. 1908. V. 37; 39

Babes in Birdland. Chicago: 1911. V. 46

Baum's American Fairy Tales. Indianapolis: 1908. V. 40; 41; 46

The Daring Twins: A Study for Young Folk. Chicago: (1911). V. 37; 41; 46

Dorothy and the Wizard in Oz. Chicago: 1908. V. 37; 38; 39; 41; 46

Dorothy and the Wizard in Oz. Chicago: 1916. V. 43

Dorothy and the Wizard of Oz. 1925. V. 46

Dot and Tot of merryland. Chicago: 1901. V. 45

Dot and Tot of Merryland. Indianapolis: 1903. V. 41; 46

The Emerald City of Oz. Chicago: 1910. V. 41; 44; 45; 46

The Enchanted Island of Yew. Indianapolis: 1903. V. 37; 41; 43; 46

The Enchanted Island of Yew. Indianpolis: 1920. V. 46

Father Goose: His Book. Chicago: 1899. V. 45

Father Goose's Year Book. Chicago: 1907. V. 44

Glinda of Oz. Chicago: 1920. V. 38; 41; 46

John Dough and the Cherub. Chicago: 1906. V. 40; 41; 45; 46

L. Frank Baum's Juvenile Speaker. Readings and Recitations in Prose and Verse, Humorous and Otherwise. Chicago: 1910. V. 46

The Land of Oz. Chicago: 1919. V. 42

The Land of Oz. Chicago: 1939. V. 39

The Last Egyptian - a Romance of the Nile. 1907. V. 44

The Last Egyptian - a Romance of the Nile. 1908. V. 43

The Life and Adventures of Santa Claus. Indianapolis: 1902. V. 37; 45

Little Wizard Stories of Oz. 1914. V. 43

The Lost Princess of Oz. Chicago: 1917. V. 38; 46

The Magic of Oz. Chicago: 1919. V. 42

The Magic of Oz. 1925. V. 38; 46

The Magical Monarch of Mo. V. 40

The Wonderful Wizard of Oz. V. 45

The Marvelous Land of Oz Being an Account of the Further Adventures of the Scarecrow and Tin Woodman. Chicago: 1904. V. 37; 43; 45

The Master-Key: an Electrical Fairy Tale. Indianapolis: 1901. V. 37; 41; 44; 46

Mother Goose in Prose. Chicago: 1897. V. 45

The Navy Alphabet. Chicago: 1900. V. 45

A New Wonderland, Being the First Account Ever Printed of the Beautiful Valley and the Wonderful Adventures of Its Inhabitants. New York: 1900. V. 42

The New Wizard of Oz. Indianapolis: 1903. V. 39; 41; 42; 46

The New Wizard of Oz. Indianapolis: 1904. V. 42

The New Wizard of Oz. Indianapolis: 1920. V. 43

The New Wizard of Oz. Indianapolis: 1930. V. 41

Ozma and the Little Wizard. Chicago: 1932. V. 44

The Patchwork Girl of Oz. Chicago: 1913. V. 38; 41; 43

Policeman Bluejay. 1907. V. 45

Queen Zixi of Ix, or the Story of the Magic Cloak. New York: 1905. V. 41

The Road to Oz. Chicago: 1909. V. 46

Rinkitink in Oz. Chicago: 1916. V. 38; 45

The Road to Oz. Chicago: 1909. V. 41; 44; 46

The Royal Book of Oz. Chicago: 1921. V. 38; 45

The Scarecrow of Oz. Chicago: 1919. V. 45

The Scarecrow of Oz. Chicago: 1915. V. 38

The Sea Fairies. Chicago: 1911. V. 40; 43

Sky Island. Chicago: 1912. V. 41; 44; 45

The Songs of Father Goose. 1900. V. 46

The Songs of Father Goose. Indianpolis: 1909. V. 45

Sugar Loaf Mountain. Chicago: 1906. V. 42; 46

The Surprising Adventures Magical Monarch of Mo. Indianapolis: 1920. V. 46

Tik-Tok of Oz. Chicago: 1914. V. 41

The Tin Woodman of Oz. Chicago: 1918. V. 38; 46

The Twinkle Tales. Chicago: 1915. V. 45

The Wonderful Wizard of Oz. Chicago: 1900. V. 38; 42; 43

The Wonderful Wizard of Oz. Chicago & New York: 1900. V. 38; 40; 41; 45

The Wonderful Wizard of Oz. Illustrated by Barry Mosher, with an Appreciation by Justin G. Schiller. West Hatfield, MA.: 1985. V. 37; 38; 44; 45; 46

BAUM, R. K.

Antique Maps of Leicestershire. Loughborough: 1972. V. 44

BAUMANN, GUSTAVE

Frijoles Canyon Pictographs. Santa Fe: 1939. V. 38

Pirates! or, The Cruise of the Black Revenge. Chicago: 1916. V. 41

BAUMER, LEWIS

Did You Ever? London: 1903. V. 46

BAUMGARTEL, ELISE J.

The Cultures of Prehistoric Egypt. Oxford: 1947-60. V. 37; 40

The Cultures of Prehistoric Egypt. Oxford: 1960. V. 40; 42; 44

BAUMGARTNER, LEONA

A Bibliography of the Poem 'Syphilis sive marbus gallicus' by Girolamo Fracastoro of Verona. New Haven: 1935. V. 39; 40

BAUNGARTNER, K. H.

Kranken-Physiognomik. Stuttgart: 1842. V. 42

BAUR, J. I. H.

New Art in America. Greenwich: 1957. V. 46

BAUR, P. V. C.

The Lamps. New Haven: 1947. V. 40

BAURENFEIND, MICHAELE 1680-1753

Vollkomene Wieder-Herstellung... in ... Schreib-Kunst. Nuremberg: 1716. V. 43

BAUSMAN, JOSEPH H.

History of Beaver County, Pennsylvania. New York: 1904. V. 41; 42

BAUSMAN, LETTIE M.

A Bibliography of Lancaster County, Pennsylvania, 1745-1912. Philadelphia: n.d.: 1916. V. 42

BAUTHMEL, RICHARD

The Roman Antiquities of Overborough. London: 1746. V. 46

The Roman Antiquities of Overborough. 1824. V. 41

BAVALLIUS, CARL

Nicaraguan Antiquities. Stockholm: 1886. V. 39

THE BAWD: a Poem. London: 1781? V. 37; 38; 42; 43

BAWDEN, EDWARD

English as She is Spoke. 1960. V. 42

Take the Broom. London: 1944. V. 45

BAWDEN, WILLIAM

Dom. Boc. A Translation of the Record Called Domesday, So Far as Relates to the County of York. Doncaster: 1809. V. 39; 44

BAX, CLIFFORD

Florence Farr, Bernard Shaw and W. B. Yeats. Dublin: 1941. V. 39; 46

The Golden Hind. London: 1922-July 1923. V. 46

BAX, E. BELFORT

A Short Account of the Commune of Paris. London: 1886. V. 46

BAXANDALL, D.

Catalogue of the Collections in the Science Museum South Kensington. London: 1926. V. 37

BAXLEY, H. W.

What I Saw on the West Coast of South and North America, and the Hawaiian Islands. New York: 1865. V. 38; 39; 42; 43; 46

BAXLEY, H. WILLIS

Spain: Art-Remains and Art Realities, Painters, Priests and Princes. London: 1875. V. 41

BAXTER, ALBERT

History of the City of Grand Rapids, Michigan. (with an Appendix - History of Lowell, Michigan). New York: & Grand Rapids: 1891. V. 46

BAXTER, ANDREW

An Inquiry into the Nature of the Human Soul. London: 1737. V. 37; 38; 45

Matho; or the Cosmotheoria Puerilis a Dialogue. London: 1740. V. 40

Matho; or, the Cosmotheoria Puerilis, a Dialogue in Which the First Principles of Philosophy and Astronomy are Accomodated to the Capacity of Young Persons . . . London: 1740. V. 37; 39; 40

BAXTER, D. W. C.

The Volunteer's Manual: Containing Full Instructions for the Recruit . . . Philadelphia: 1861. V. 46

BAXTER, DOREEN

Fairyland Frolics. London: 1950. V. 40

BAXTER, E. V.

The Birds of Scotland, Their History, Distribution and Migration. London: 1953. V. 38

BAXTER, EVELYN V.

The Birds of Scotland. Their History, Distribution and Migration. Edinburgh: 1953. V. 37; 38; 43; 45

BAXTER, FRANCIS WILLOUGHBY

Percy Lockhart; or, the Hidden Will. London: 1872. V. 45; 46

BAXTER, G. R. WYTHEN

The Book of the Bastiles; or, the History of the Working of the New Poor Law. London: 1841. V. 43

BAXTER, GEORGE

The Centary Baxter Book . . . Together with a Catalogue Resume of His Works. Royal Leamington Spa: 1936. V. 44

The Flower Garden, With Selected Lists of Annual, Biennial and Perennial Flowering Plants. London: 1838. V. 39

The Pictorial Album; or, Cabinet of Paintings Containing Eleven Designs, Executed in Oil Colours by . . . London: 1836. V. 39

The Pictorial Album, or Cabinet of Paintings for the Year 1837. London: 1837. V. 40; 42

The Pictorial Album or Cabinet of Paintings for the Year 1837. London: 1837/36. V. 42

The Pictorial Album; or, Cabinet of Paintings. London: 1838. V. 38

BAXTER, GLEN

Glen Baxter: His Life. London: 1983. V. 46

BAXTER, J.

The Sister Arts, or a Concise and Interesting View of the Nature and History of Paper-Making, Printing and Bookbinding. Lewes: 1809. V. 41

BAXTER, J. H.

Statistics, Medical and Anthropological, of the Provost-Marshall-General's Bureau, Derived From the Records of the Examination for Military Service in the Armies of the United States During the Late War of the Rebellion, of Over a Million Recruits . . . Washington: 1875. V. 41

BAXTER, JAMES K.

The Fallen House - Poems. Chirstchurch: 1953. V. 40

BAXTER, JAMES PHINNEY 1831-1921

Christopher Levett of York the Pioneer Colonist in Casco Bay. Portland: 1893. V. 37; 42; 43

A Memoir of Jacques Cartier Sieur de Limooilou His Voyages to the Saint Lawrence a Bibliography and a facsimile of the Manuscript of 1534 with Annotations. New York: 1906. V. 39; 42; 43

Sir Ferdinando Georges and His Province of Maine. Boston: 1890. V. 38; 39; 45

The Trelawny Papers. Portland: 1884. V. 43

BAXTER, JOHN M.

Life of John M. Baxter Being a Brief Account of His Experiences as a Pioneer, Missionary, Bishop and Stake President . . . Salt Lake City: 1932. V. 42

BAXTER, RICHARD

A Breviate of the Life of Margaret, the Daughter of Francis Charlton of Apply in Shropshire, Esq; and Wife of Richard Baxter. London: 1681. V. 42

The Catechizing of Families. London: 1683. V. 39; 43

The Crucifying of the World. London: 1658. V. 37

Gilda Salvianus: the Reformed Pastor. London: 1657. V. 40; 42

A Key for Catholicks, to Open the Jugling of the Jesuits, and Satisfie all That are but Truly Willing to Understand Whether the Cause of the Roman or Reformed Churches Be of God. London: 1659. V. 39; 45

The Life of Faith. London: 1670. V. 40

A Petition for Peace; with the Reformation of the Liturgy . . . London: 1661. V. 45

The Poetical Fragments of Richard Baxter. London: 1821. V. 41

The Quakers Catechism, or, the Quakers Questioned, Their Questions Answered, and Both. London: 1655. V. 42

The Reasons of the Christian Religion. London: 1667. V. 42

Reliquiae Baxterianae; or, a Narrative of the Most Memorable Passges of His Life and Times. London: 1696. V. 40; 41; 45

The Saints Everlasting Rest. London: 1653. V. 40

The Saints Everlasting Rest; or, a Treatise of the Blessed State of the Saints in Their Enjoyment of God in Glory . . . London: 1659. V. 44

A Treatise of Self Denyall . . . London: 1660. V. 44

BAXTER, VIDA S.

H. M. Vandeveer & Company One Hundred and Fifty Years of the Vandeveer Family. Taylorville: 1979. V. 40

BAXTER, W.

British Phaenogamous Botany; or Figures and Descriptions . . . Oxford: 1834-43. V. 38; 39; 44; 45; 46

BAXTER, WILLIAM

Glossarium Antiquitatum Britannicarum sive Syllabus Etymologicus Antiquitatum Veteris Britanniae Atque Iberniae Temporibus Romanorum. London: 1719. V. 42; 46

Glossarium Antiquitatum Britannicarum, Sive Syllabus Eymologicus Antiquitatum Veteris Britanniae Atque Iberniae, Temporibus Romanorum. London: 1733. V. 39

Impressions of Central and Southern Europe . . . London: 1950. V. 45

BAXTER, WILLIAM EDWARD

Impressions of Central and Southern Europe. London: 1850. V. 37; 39

BAY, JENS CHRISTIAN

Handful of Western Books. A Second Handful . . . A Third Handful . . . Cedar Rapids: 1935/36/36. V. 38

Three Handfuls of Western Books. Cedar Rapids: 1941. V. 46

BAYARD, HIPPOLYTE

Bayard. Paris: 1943. V. 41

BAYARD, JAMES ASHETON

Speech of the Honorable . . . of Delaware, on the Bill Received from the Senate, Entitled 'An Act to Repeal Certain Acts Respecting the Organization of the Court of the United States.' Hartford: 1802. V. 40

BAYARD, SAMUEL JOHN

A Sketch of the Life of Com. Robert F. Stockton; with His Correspondence with the Navy Department respecting His Conquest of California, etc. and His Speeches in the Senate of the U.S. New York: 1856. V. 37; 38; 39; 40; 41; 42; 45; 46

BAYARD, THOMAS F.

Cattle and Dairy Farming. Letter from . . . Transmitting . . . Reports from the Consuls of the United States on Cattle and Dairy Farming and the Markets for Cattle, Beef and Dairy Products in Their Several Districts. Washington: 1887. V. 39; 44

BAYARDI, OTTAVIO ANTONIO

The Antiquities of Herculaneum. London: 1773. V. 45

BAYE, J. DE

The Industrial Arts of the Anglo-Saxons. New York: 1893. V. 38

BAYER, HERBERT

Bauhaus 1919-1928. New York: 1938. V. 39; 41; 46

Visual Communication, Architecture, Painting. New York: 1967. V. 46

BAYFIELD, HENRY WOLSEY

The St. Lawrence Survey Journals of Captain Henry Wolsey Bayfield 1829-1853. Toronto: 1984-86. V. 37; 42

BAYFIUS, LAZARUS

V. 39

Opus de re Vestimentaria ab Autore Ipso . . . Recognitum. Basileae: 1531. V. 38

BAYLDON, J. S.

Bayldon's Art of Valuing Rents nd Tillages, and the Tenant's Right on Entering and Quitting Farms, Explained by Several Specimens of Valuations, and Remarks on Cultivations Pursued on Soils in Different Situations. London: 1844. V. 38

BAYLDON, OLIVER

The Paper Makers Craft. Leicester: 1965. V. 37; 38; 39; 40; 41; 42; 43; 44; 46

BAYLDON, OLIVER continued

The Paper Makers Craft. Cambridge: 1965. V. 37

BAYLE, ALJ

A Manual of General Anatomy, containing a concise description of the elemenatary tissues of the human body. From the French of . . . by S.D. Gorss, MD. Philadelphia: 1828. V. 37

BAYLE, FRANCISCI

Tractatus de Apoplexia. (with) Dissertationes Physicae in quibus Principia Proprietatum in Mistis, Oeconomia Corporum in Plantis & Animalius . . . Hagae-Comitis: 1678. V. 38

BAYLE, GASPARD LAURENT

Recherches sur la Phthisie Pulmonaire. Paris: 1810. V. 38

BAYLE, PIERRE 1647-1706

An Historical and Critical Dictionary . . . London: 1710. V. 39

Dictionnaire Historique et Critique. Rotterdam: 1720. V. 38; 39; 40; 41; 42

A General Dictionary, Historical and Critical. London: 1734/41. V. 39

Dictionnaire Historique et Critique. Paris: 1820. V. 40

The Dictionary Historical and Critical of Mr. Peter Bayle . . . to which is prefixed, the Life of the Author. London: 1734-38. V. 37

Dictionnaire Historique et Critique. Amsterdam: 1730. V. 38; 45

The Dictionary Historical and Critical. London: 1734-38. V. 38; 39; 40; 41; 42

Dictionnaire Historique et Critique. Paris: 1820. V. 41

Dictionnaire Historique et Critique. Rotterdam: 1697. V. 37

An Historical and Critical Dictionary, Selected and Abridged from the Great Work of Peter Bayle. London: 1826. V. 43

Lettre a M. L. A. D. C. Docteur de Sorbonne. Cologne: 1682. V. 44

Oeuvres Diverses de Mr. Pierre Bayle, Professeur en Philosophie, et en Histoire, a Rotterdam: Contenant Tout ce Que cet Auteur a Publie sur des Matieres de Theologie, de Philosophie, de Critque, d'Histoire & de Litterature . . . La Haye: 1727-31. V. 41; 43; 45

A Philosophical Commentary on These Words of the Gospel, Luke XIV. 23. Compel Them to Come in, That My House May be Full. London: 1708. V. 40

BAYLES, F. H.

The Race Courses of Great Britain and Ireland. London: 1908. V. 37

The Racehorse Atlas of Great Britain and Ireland. London: 1903. V. 37

BAYLES, GEORGE JAMES

Women and the Law. New York: 1901. V. 44

BAYLES, RICHARD M.

History of Newport County, Rhode Island. From the Year 1638 to the Year 1887. New York: 1888. V. 46

History of Providence County, Rhode Island. New York: 1891. V. 46

BAYLEY, ANSELM 1719-1794

The Sacred Singer. London: 1771. V. 40

BAYLEY, F. W. M.

Four Years' Residence in the West Indies, During the Years 1826, 7, 8 and 9. London: 1833. V. 38; 40; 42

BAYLEY, FRANK W.

Five Colonial Artists of New England. Joseph Badger, Joseph Blackburn, John Singleton Copley, Robert Feke, John Smibert. Boston: 1929. V. 37; 38; 41

The Life and Works of John Singleton Copley. Boston: 1915. V. 46

A Sketch of the Life and a List of Some of the Works of John Singleton Copley. Boston: 1910. V. 46

BAYLEY, FREDERICK W. N.

Four Years Residence in the West Indies, During the Years 1826, 7, 8, and 9. London: 1833. V. 39

The New Tale of a Tub: an Adventure in Verse. London: 1841. V. 39

BAYLEY, HAROLD

A New Light on the Renaissance, Displayed in Contemporary Emblems. London. V. 38; 44

A New Light on the Renaissance. London: 1909. V. 42

BAYLEY, JOHN

The History and Antiquities of the Tower of London. London: 1825. V. 45

A Short Treatise on the Law of the Bills of Exchange, Cash Bill, and Promissory Notes. Dublin: 1789. V. 37

BAYLEY, JOSEPH

An Inaugural Dissertation on the Origin and Propagation of the Yellow Fever. New York: 1802. V. 42

BAYLEY, NATHAN

English and Latine Exercises for School-Boys, Comprising All the Rules of Syntasxis . . . Boston: 1720. V. 41

BAYLEY, PETER

Idwal; a Poem. London: 1824. V. 43

BAYLEY, RICHARD

Letters from the Health-Office, Submitted to the Common Council, of the City of New York. New York: 1799. V. 45

BAYLEY, THOMAS

The Royal Charter Granted unto Kings, by God Himself; and Collected Out of His Holy Word, in Both Testaments . . . 1649. London: 1649. V. 39; 44

BAYLIE, THOMAS

Certamen Religiosum; or, a Conference Between His Late Majestie Charles King of England and Henry Late Marquess and Earl of Worcester, Concerning His Religion. London: 1649. V. 39

BAYLIES, FRANCIS

Exploration of the Northwest Coast: Report . . . Washington: 1826. V. 39; 41; 42

Narrative of Major General Wool's Campaign in Mexico, in the Years 1846, 1847 & 1848. Albany: 1851. V. 37; 38; 39; 40; 42; 45

Northwest Coast of America . . . As Respects the Establishment of a Military Post at the Mouth of the Columbia River . . . Washington: 1826. V. 39; 40

BAYLIES, WILLIAM

Practical Reflections on the Uses and Abuses of Bath Waters Made from Actual Experiments and Observations. London: 1757. V. 40

BAYLISS, GARLAND E.

Public Affairs in Arkansas, 1874-1896. Austin. V. 39; 42

BAYLISS, M. F.

The Matriarchy of the American Turf, 1875-1930. London: 1931. V. 42

BAYLISS, MARGUERITE F.

Bolinvar. New York: 1937. V. 42

BAYLISS, WILLIAM

Intravenous Injection in Wound Shock. London: 1918. V. 40

Principles of General Physiology. London: 1915. V. 42

The Vaso-Motor System. London: 1923. V. 42

BAYLISS, WYKE

Five Great Painters of the Victorian Era: Leighton, Millais, Burne-Jones, Watts, Holman Hunt. New York: 1902. V. 38; 40

BAYLOR, ARMISTEAD KEITH

Abdul, an Allegory. New York: 1930. V. 39; 43

BAYLOR, GEORGE

Bull Run to Bull Run; or, Four Years in the Army of Northern Virginia. Richmond. V. 42

BAYLY, ANSELM

An Introduction to Languages, Literary and Philosophical. London: 1758. V. 41

A Practical Treatise on Singing and Playing with Just Expression and Real Elegance. London: 1771. V. 41; 42; 46

BAYLY, THOMAS HAYNES

Songs, Ballads and Other Poems. London: 1844. V. 42

BAYMA, JOSEPH

The Elements of Molecular Mechanics. London: 1866. V. 42; 43

BAYNARD, EDWARD

Health: a Poem. London: 1716. V. 46

BAYNE, A. D.

Royal Illustrated History of Eastern England . . . Yarmouth: 1872. V. 40

BAYNE, MARIE

Toy Soldiers. London: 1915. V. 45

BAYNE, PETER

The Life and Letters of Hugh miller. London: 1871. V. 37

Two Great Englishwomen Mrs. Browning and Charlotte Bronte; With an Essay on Poetry, Illustrated from Wordworth, Burns and Byron. London: 1881. V. 41; 43; 45

BAYNE, R.

Historical Sketch of Rickmansworth and the Surrounding Parishes. London: & Aylesbury,: 1870. V. 44

BAYNES, JOHN

An Archaeological Epistle to the Reverend and Worshipful Jeremiah Milles, D.D., Dean of Exeter, President of the Society of Antiquaries . . . London: 1782. V. 40

BAYS, PETER

A General History of Negro Slavery, Collected from the Most Respectable Evidence and Unquestionable Authorities by a Late President in the West Indies . . . Cambridge: 1826. V. 41

BAZ, GUSTAVO

History of the Mexican Railway. Mexico: 1876. V. 39; 41

BAZIN, G. A.

The Natural History of Bees. London: 1744. V. 38; 42; 43

BAZIN, GERMAIN

The History of World Sculpture. Greenwich: 1968. V. 41

BAZIRE, EDMOND

Manet. Paris: 1884. V. 38

BE Thou My Vision. Dublin: 1941. V. 43

BEACH, CHARLES

Lost Lenore; or, the Adventures of a Rolling Stone. London: 1864. V. 44; 46

BEACH, JOSEPH PERKINS

The Log of Apollo: Joseph Perkins Beach's Journal of the Voyage of the Ship Apollo from New York to San Francisco 1849. San Francisco: 1986. V. 37; 40; 43

BEACH, MOSES S.

The Ely Ancestry: Lineage of Richard Ely of Plymouth, England Who Came to Boston, Mass., About 1655 . . . New York: 1902. V. 46

BEACH, REX

The Looting of Alaska. The True Story of a Robbery by Law. New York: 1906. V. 46

The Spoilers. New York: 1906. V. 38; 44; 45

BEACH, S. A.

The Apples of New York. Albany: 1905. V. 44; 45

BEACH, SYLVIA

Ulysses in Paris. New York: 1956. V. 41

BEACH, THOMAS

Eugenio: or Virtuous and Happy Life. London: 1737. V. 42

BEACH, W.

The American Practice Condensed, or the Family Physician . . . New York: 1848. V. 42

The British and American Reformed Practice of Medicine, Embracing a Treatise of the Causes, Symptoms and Treatment of Diseases Generally on Eclectic Principles. Birmingham: 1859. V. 40

BEACH, W. W.

The Indian Miscellany. Albany: 1877. V. 39; 44

BEACH, WILLIAM

Visit of His Royal Highness the Duke of Edinburgh . . . to Hong Kong in 1869. Hong Kong: 1869. V. 41

BEACH, WILLIAM WITHER

Abradates and Panthea: a Tale Extracted from Xenophon. Salisbury: 1765. V. 37

BEACH, WOOSTER

An Improved System of Midwifery, Adapted to the Reformed Practice of Medicine. New York: 1848. V. 42; 44

A Treatise on Anatomy, Physiology and Health, Designed for Students, Schools and Popular Use. New York: 1847. V. 40

BEACHARD, JOHN

Some Opinions of Mr. Hobbs Considered in a Second Dialogue Between Philautus and Timothy. London: 1673. V. 42

BEACON Priory; or, Memoirs of the Rockalba Family. Including the Melancholy Deaths of the Earl of Rusport, and Sophia, Countess of Rockabala. London: 1810. V. 44

BEADLE, CLAYTON

Chapters on Papermaking. London: 1908-9-7-7-8. V. 38; 46

BEADLE, D. W.

Canadian Fruit, Flower, and Kitchen Gardener. Toronto: 1872. V. 37

BEADLE, DELOS W.

The American Lawyer and Business-Man's Form-Book; Containing Forms and Instructors . . . New York: 1851. V. 39; 42; 43

BEADLE, J. H.

Western Wilds and the Men Who Redeem Them. Cincinnati: 1878. V. 37

BEADLE, JOHN HANSON 1840-1897

Life in Utah; or, The Mysteries and Crimes of Mormonism. Being an Expose of the Secret Rites and Ceremonies of the Latter-Day Saints. Philadelphia: 1870. V. 37; 39; 40; 41; 42; 44; 45

Western Wilds, and the Men Who Redeem Them. Detroit: 1877. V. 42

Western Wilds and the Men Who Redeem Them. Cincinnati: 1878. V. 39; 41

Western Wilds, and the Men Who Redeem Them. Cincinnati: 1879. V. 42

BEAGLE, PETER

The Fantasy Worlds of Peter Beagle. New York: 1978. V. 43

The Last Unicorn. New York: 1968. V. 39; 42; 43

BEAGLE, PETER S.

A Fine & Private Place. New York: 1960. V. 37

BEAL, M. D.

A History of Southeastern Idaho . . . Caldwell: 1942. V. 42

BEALE, ANNE

Gladys, the Reaper. London: 1860. V. 44

Nothing Venture, Nothing Have. London: 1864. V. 44

BEALE, BARTHOLOMEW

An Essay Attempting a More Certain and Satisfactory Discovery Both of the True Causes of all Diseases, Proceeding from Vicious Bloods, and the Genuine Operations of all Remedies Used Interanlly in Their Cures. London: 1706. V. 37

BEALE, CLARE HUTTON

Memorials of the Old Meeting House and Burial Grounds, Birmingham. Birmingham: 1882. V. 38

BEALE, EDWARD F.

Wagon Road - Fort Smith to Colorado River. Washington: 1860. V. 38; 40; 41; 43; 45

Wagon Road From Fort Defiance to the Colorado River. Letter from the Secretary of War . . . Washington: 1858. V. 37; 39; 40; 41; 45

BEALE, G. W.

A Lieutenant of Cavalry in Lee's Army. Boston: 1918. V. 38

BEALE, JAMES

The Battle Flags of the Army of the Potomac At Gettysburg, July 1, 2, 3, 1863. Philadelphia: 1887. V. 46

BEALE, JOSEPH HENRY

A Bibliography of Early English Law Books. Cambridge: 1926. V. 37; 46

A Selection of Cases and Other Authorities Upon Ciminal Law. Cambridge: 1915. V. 38; 40

BEALE, LIONEL J.

A Treatise on Deformities Exhibiting a Concise View of the Nature and Treatment of the Principal Distortions and Contractions of the Limbs, Joints and Spine. London: 1830. V. 42

BEALE, LIONEL S.

The Microscope In Its Application to Practical Medicine. Philadelphia: 1866. V. 40; 42; 45

The Physiological Anatomy and Physiology of Man. London: 1866-71. V. 38; 40

BEALE, R. L. T.

History of the Ninth Virginia Cavalry in the War Between the States. Richmond: 1899. V. 38

BEALE, ROBERT

A Report on the Trial of Commodore David Porter, Before a General Court-Martial, July, 1825 . . . Washington: 1825. V. 38

BEALE, THOMAS

The Natural History of the Sperm Whale . . . To Which is Added, A Sketch of a South-Sea Whaling Voyage . . . London: 1839. V. 40

BEALL, JOHN Y.

Trial of John Y. Beall, As a Spy and Guerrillero. By a Military Commission. New York: 1865. V. 37; 39; 42; 44

BEALS, C. S.

Science, History and Hudson Bay. Ottawa: 1968. V. 45

BEALS, CARLETON

The Crime of Cuba. Philadelphia: 1933. V. 37

BEAMAN, CHARLES C.

The National and Private 'Alabama Claims' and Their 'Final and Amicable Settlement'. Washington City: 1871. V. 46

BEAMISH, NORTH L.

The Discovery of America by the Northmen. London: 1841. V. 42

BEAMISH, RICHARD

Memoir of the Life of Sir Marc Isamabard Brunel. London: 1862. V. 39; 40; 41; 42; 43

The Psychonomy of the Hand; or, The Hand an Index of Mental Development According to MM. d'Arpentigny and Desbarolles . . . London: 1865. V. 38

BEAMISH, T. M.

Beamish. A Genealogical Study of a Family in County Cork and Elsewhere. London: 1950. V. 38

BEAN, C. E. W.

The Official History of Australia in the War 1914-1918. Volume IV: The Australian Imperial Force in France. 1917. 1933. V. 44; 45

The Official History of Australia in the War 1914-1918. Volume VI. The Australian Imperial Force in France During the Spring Offensive, 1918. 1942. V. 45

BEAN, ELLIS P.

Memoir of Col. Ellis P. Bean Written by Himself. Dallas: 1930. V. 37; 38; 42; 44

BEAN, LOWELL JOHN

Diaries and Accounts of the Romero Expeditions in Arizona and California, 1823-1826. Los Angeles: 1962. V. 39; 40; 44

BEAN, ORESTES U.

Corianton, an Aztec Romance. N.P.: 1902? V. 41

BEAN, PERCY

The Chemistry and Practice of Finishing. Manchester: 1926. V. 38; 40; 46

BEAN, THEODORE W.

History of Montgomery County, Pennsylvania. Philadelphia: 1884. V. 41; 42

BEAN, W. J.

Trees and Shrubs Hardy in the British Isles. London: 1976. V. 38

Trees and Shrubs Hardy in the British Isles. London: 1970-80. V. 37

BEAR, D.

Russell Cowles. Los Angeles: 1946. V. 46

BEAR, JOHN W.

The Life and Travels of . . . 'The Buckeye Blacksmith.' Written by Himself. Baltimore: 1873. V. 37

BEARCROFT, PHILIP

An Historical Account of Thomas Sutton Esq., and His Foundation in Charter House. London: 1737. V. 37; 38; 39; 40; 41; 45

BEARD, C. R.

A Catalogue of the Collection of Martinware Formed by Mr. Frederick John Nettlefold . . . London: 1936. V. 37

BEARD, CHARLES H.

Ophthalmic Surgery. A Treatise on Surgical Operations Pertaining to the Eye and Its Appendages . . . Philadelphia: 1910. V. 44

BEARD, DAN

Imaginotions. Truthless Tales. By Tudor Jenks. New York: 1894. V. 37

Moonblight and Six Feet of Romance. New York: 1892. V. 46

BEARD, G.

Dictionary of English Furniture Makers 1660-1840. London: 1986. V. 37

BEARD, GEORGE

Hay-Fever; or, Summer Catarrh: Its Nature and Treatment. New York: 1876. V. 40

Stimulants and Narcotics; Medically, Philosophically and Morally Considered. New York: 1871. V. 40; 42

BEARD, GEORGE M. 1839-1883

American Nervousness Its Causes and Consequences: a Supplement to Nervous Exhaustion . . . New York: 1881. V. 43; 46

A Practical Treatise on Nervous Exhaustion (Neurasthenia). New York: 1880. V. 38

BEARD, JAMES

K.K.K. Sketches, Humorous and Didactic, Treating the More Important Events of the Ku-Klux-Klan Movement in the South . . . Philadelphia: 1877. V. 37; 39

BEARD, JOHN

A Diary of Fifteen Years' Hunting, viz from 1796 to 1811 . . . Bath: 1813. V. 43

BEARD, JOHN R.

The Life of Toussaint L'Ouverture, The Negro Patriot of Hayti. London: 1853. V. 39

BEARD, JOHN RELLY 1800-1876

Toussaint L'Ouverture: a Biography and Autobiography. Boston: 1863. V. 40; 44

BEARD, MARK

Manhattan Third Year Reader. New York: 1984. V. 44; 45

Utah Reader. New York: 1986. V. 44; 45

BEARD, PETER

The End of the Game. London: 1965. V. 38; 44

Eyelids of Morning. The Mingled Destinies of Crocodiles and Man. Greenwich: 1973. V. 37

BEARD, WILLIAM HOLBROOK

On the Prairie. New York: 1869. V. 39

BEARDSELL, HELENA

Pillow Fancies in Silver Grey. N.P.: 1901. V. 37

BEARDSLEY, AUBREY VINCENT 1872-1898

Aubrey Beardsley's Drawings. A Catalogue and List of Criticisms by A. E. Gallatin. New York: 1903. V. 37

Beardsley Prints Etc. London: 1898. V. 43

a Book of Fifty Drawings. London: 1897. V. 37; 46

The Early Work. The Later Work. The Uncollected Work. London: 1899/1901/1925. V. 40

The Early Work of Aubrey Beardsley . . . (with) the Uncollected Work . . . London: 1899/1901/25. V. 39

The Early Work of Aubrey Beardsley. London: 1912. V. 39

The Early Work of . . . (with) The Work. London: 1920. V. 46

Early Work; Later Work. London: 1920. V. 39

Fifty Drawings . . . Selected from the Collection Owned by Mr. H. S. Nichols. New York: 1920. V. 41; 42; 43

Keynotes Series of Novels and Short Stories. London: 1896. V. 41; 43

Last Letters of Aubrey Beardsley. London: 1904. V. 38

The Later Work of Aubrey Beardsley. London: 1912. V. 39; 43

The Later Works. London: 1920. V. 37; 40; 46

Letters from Aubrey Beardsley to Leonard Smithers. London: 1937. V. 37; 41; 45

The Morte d'Arthur Portfolio Being Eleven Designs Omitted From the First Edition of Le Morte D'Arthur Illustrated by Aubrey Beardsley and published in MDCCCXCIII (1893). London: 1927. V. 40; 41

A Portfolio of Aubrey Beardsley's Drawings Illustrating 'Salome' by Oscar Wilde. London: 1907. V. 37; 39; 40; 43; 44

A Portfolio of . . . Drawings Illustrating 'Salome' by Oscar Wilde. London: 1912. V. 44

Reproductions of Eleven Designs Omitted from the First Editions of Le Morte D'Arthur . . . also those Made for the Covers of the Issue in Parts and a Facsimile Print of the Merlin Drawing. London: 1927. V. 39; 44; 45

Salome. A Portfolio of Aubrey Beardsley's Illustrating Salome by Oscar Wilde. London: 1907. V. 41

A Second Book of Fifty Drawings. London: 1899. V. 37; 38; 40; 41; 44

Some Unknown Drawings of Aubrey Beardsley, Collected and Annotated. London: 1923. V. 37; 39

The Story of Venus and Tannhauser. London: 1907. V. 37; 40; 41; 42; 43; 46

The Story of Venus and Tannhauser. New York: 1927. V. 41

The Uncollected Work. London: 1925. V. 37; 39; 41; 42; 43; 44; 45; 46

Under the Hill and Other Essays. London: 1904. V. 37; 40; 41; 43

Under the Hill and Other Essays in Prose and Verse with Illustrations. London & New York: 1904. V. 37; 41

Under the Hill and Other Essays in Prose and Verse. London: 1934. V. 39

BEARDSLEY, CHARLES E.

The Victims of Tyranny, a Tale. Buffalo: 1847-47. V. 37

BEARDSLEY, D. B.

History of Hancock County, From Its Earliest Settlement to the Present Time. Together with Reminiscences of Pioneer Life, Incidents, Statistical Tables and Biographical Sketches. Springfield: 1881. V. 46

BEARDSLEY, LEVI

Reminiscences Personal and Other Incidents . . . New York: 1852. V. 40

BEARON, HENRY BRADSHAW

Sketches of America. London: 1818. V. 39

BEASLAI, PIARAS

Michael Collins and the Making of a New Ireland. Dublin: 1926. V. 38; 43

BEASLEY, DELILAH L.

The Negro Trail Blazers of California. Los Angeles: 1919. V. 37; 38

BEASLEY, GERTRUDE

My First Thirty Years. Paris: 1925. V. 38; 42

My First Thirty Years. Austin: 1989. V. 43; 46

BEASLEY, HENRY

The Druggist's General Receipt Book. London: 1854. V. 40

BEASLEY, ROBERT E.

A Plan to Stop the Present and Prevent Future Wars. Rio Vista: 1864. V. 46

BEASTS and Men, Folk Tales Collected in Flanders. London: 1918. V. 46

BEATON, ALEXANDER

A New System of Cultivation, Without Lime, or Dung, or Summer Fallows as Practised at Knowle-Farm, in the County of Sussex. London: 1820. V. 39

BEATON, CECIL

Ashcombe - The Story of a Fifteen Year Lease. London: 1949. V. 38

Ballet. London. V. 45

Ballet. London: 1951. V. 41; 46

The Book of Beauty. London: 1930. V. 38

Cecil Beaton's Scrapbook. London: 1937. V. 39

Cecil Beaton's New York. London: 1938. V. 44

Cecil Beaton's My Fair Lady. New York: (1964). V. 37

The Face of the World: an International Scrapbook of People and Places. New York: 1957. V. 40; 42

History Under Fire - 52 Photographs of Air Raid Damage to London Buildings, 1940-1941. London: 1941. V. 38

India. Bombay: 1945. V. 40; 41

The Restless Years: Diaries 1955-63. London: 1976. V. 40

Scrapbook. London: 1937. V. 41

Winged Squadrons. London. V. 45

BEATRICE, PRINCESS

A Birthday Book. Designed by Her Royal Highness the Princess Beatrice. London: 1881. V. 37; 41; 42

BEATSON, ALEXANDER

Tracts Relative to the Island of St. Helena. London: 1816. V. 41

A View of the Origin and Conduct of the War with Tippoo Sultaun. London: 1800. V. 40; 42; 43

BEATSON, ROBERT

A Chronological Register of Both Houses of the British Parliament, from the Union in 1708, to the Third Parliament of the United Kingdom of Great Britain and Ireland in 1807. London: 1807. V. 42

A Political Index to the Histories of Great Britain and Ireland. London: 1788. V. 38

A Political Index to the Histories of Great Britain and Ireland. London: 1806. V. 39

BEATTIE, ALEXANDER

Poems: Containing the History of the Patriarch Joseph . . . Edinburgh: 1832. V. 44

BEATTIE, ANN

Chilly Scenes of Winter. New York: 1976. V. 45; 46

Distortions. Garden City: 1976. V. 45; 46

Jacklighting. 1981. V. 39

BEATTIE, GEORGE

Heritage of the Valley. Pasadena: 1939. V. 46

BEATTIE, JAMES 1735-1803

Dissertations Moral and Critical. On Memory and Imagination. On Dreaming. The Theory of Language. On Fable and Romance. On the Attachments of Kindred Illustrations on Sublimity. London: 1783. V. 40; 42; 43; 45

Elements of Moral Science . . . to Which is Now Added, a Complete Index. Edinburgh: 1817. V. 43

An Essay on the Nature and Immutability of Truth in Opposition to Sophistry and Scepticism. London: 1772. V. 38

An Essay on the Nature and Immutability of Truth, In Opposition to Sophistry and Scepticism. Edinburgh: 1773. V. 42

An Essay on the Nature of Truth in Opposition to Sophistry and Scepticism. Edinburgh: 1774. V. 38

An Essay on the Nature and Immutability of Truth, in Opposition to Sophistry and Scepticism. London: 1774. V. 44

An Essay on the Nature and Immutability of Truth. London: 1778. V. 42; 45

An Essay on the Nature and Immutability of Truth, in Opposition to Sophistry and Scepticism. Philadelphia: 1809. V. 41

An Essay on the Nature and Immutability of Truth, in Opposition to Sophsitry and Scepticism. London: 1823. V. 46

An Essay on the Nature and Immutability of Truth in Opposition to Sophistry and Scepticism. London: 1774. V. 37

Essays. On the Nature and Immutability of Truth, in Opposition to Sophistry and Scepticism. Edinburgh: 1776. V. 42

Essays on the Nature and Immutability of Truth, in Opposition to Sophistry and Scepticism . . . Dublin: 1778. V. 37; 42; 43; 45

Essays: on Poetry and Music, as They Affect the Mind; on Laughter, and Ludicrous Composition; on the Utility of Classical Learning. Edinburgh: 1778. V. 38; 42; 46

Essays on Poetry and Music, As They Affect the Mind. London: 1779. V. 43

The Judgment of Paris. London: 1765. V. 38

The Minstrel; or, the Progress of Genius. London: 1771-74. V. 43

The Minstrel; or, the Progress of Genius. A Poem. London: 1771/74. V. 37; 38; 41

The Minstrel or the Progress of Genius. London: 1806. V. 41

The Minstrel. London: 1816. V. 45

The Minstrel, or the Progress of Genius. With some other Poems. Edinburgh: 1807. V. 37

Original Poems and Translations. London: 1760. V. 45

The Philosophical and critical Works. London: 1974-75. V. 39

Poems on several occasions. Edinburgh: 1796. V. 37

Scoticisms, Arranged in Alphabetical Order, Designed to Correct Improprieties of Speech and Writing. Edinburgh: 1787. V. 38

Verses Occasioned by the Death of the Revd. Mr. Charles Churchill. London: 1765. V. 41

BEATTIE, WILLIAM

Caledonia illustrated in a series of views . . . by W.H. Bartlett, T. Allom and Others (In Two Volumes). London: (c. 1840). V. 37

The Castles and Abbeys of England. London: 1842. V. 46

The Castles and Abbeys of England . . . London: 1845. V. 37; 40

The Castles and Abbeys of England, from the National Records, Early Chronicles and Other Standard Authors. London: 1870. V. 44

The Danube, its History, Scenery, and Topography . . . London: 1840. V. 41

The Danube. London: 1844. V. 37; 38; 39; 40

The Danube: Its History, Scenery and Topography. London: 1850. V. 37

Journal of a Residence in Germany. London: 1831. V. 37

Lay of the Graduate. Edinburgh: 1819. V. 39

Life and Letters of Thomas Campbell. London: 1849. V. 38

Life and Letters of Thomas Campbell. London: 1850. V. 39; 42

The Ports, Harbours, Watering Places and Coast Scenery of Great Britain. London: 1842. V. 39

Scotland, Illustrated in a Series of Views Taken Expressly for this Work by Messrs. T. Allom, W. Bartlett and H. M'Culloch. London: 1838. V. 38; 39; 41; 44; 45; 46

Scotland Illustrated, in a Series of Views Taken Expressly for This Work by Messrs. Allom, Bartlett &c. London: 1842. V. 44

Scotland Illustrated in a Series of Views Taken Expressly for This Work by Messrs. T. Allom, W. H. Bartlett and H. M'Culloch. London: 1847. V. 45

Scotland, Illustrated in a Series of Views Taken Expressly for this Work by Thomas Allom. London. V. 37

Switzerland, Illustrated in a Series of Views Taken Expressly for This Work. London: 1836. V. 37; 38; 39; 40; 42; 43; 44; 45; 46

The Waldenes, or Protestant Valleys of Piedmont and Dauphiny and Ban De La Roche . . . London: 1838. V. 39; 40; 41; 42; 43

BEATTY, A. CHESTER

Catalogue of the Renowned Collection of Western (Medieval) Manuscripts. The Property of . . . London: 1932-33. V. 38

BEATTY, ADAM

Essays on Practical Agriculture, Including His Prize Essays, Carefully Revised. Maysville: 1844. V. 42

BEATTY, ALFRED CHESTER 1875-

Catalogue of the Renowned Collection of Western Manuscripts, the Property of A. Chester Beatty. London: 1932-33. V. 43

A Catalogue of the Armenian Manuscripts. Dublin: 1958. V. 39

The Chester Beatty Library. A Handlist of the Arabic Manuscripts. Dublin: 1955-66. V. 39

The Chester Beatty Library, a Catalogue of the Armenian Manuscripts. Dublin: 1958. V. 39

The Library of A. Chester Beatty. Description of a Hieratic Papyrus with a Mythological Story, Love-Songs and Other Miscellaneous Texts. London: 1931. V. 40; 42

BEATTY, CHARLES

The Journal of a Two Months Tour: With a View of Promotin Religion Among the Frontier Inhabitants of Pennsylvania, and of Introducing Christianity Among the Indians to the Westward of the Alegh-geny Mountains. London: 1768. V. 37; 38; 39; 40; 42

The Journal of a Two Months Tour. Edinburgh: 1798. V. 41

The Journal of a Two-Months Tour. Edinburgh: 1798. V. 37; 38; 41; 42; 43; 45

The Journal of a Two-Months Tour . . . Edinburgh: 1798. V. 43

BEATUS RHENANUS

Rerum Germanicarum Libri Tres . . . Quibus Praemissa est Vita Beati Rhenani . . . Basle: 1551. V. 38

THE BEAU BOOK. New York: 1926-27. V. 46

BEAUCHAMP, WILLIAM M.

History of the New York Iroquois Now Commonly Called the Six Nations. Albany: 1905; V. 39

BEAUCLERK, CHARLES

Lithographic Views of Military Operations in Canada Under His Excellency Sir John Colborne, G. C. B. London: 1840. V. 45

Military Operations in Canada, 1837-8-9. Belleville: 1980. V. 42

BEAUCLERK, G.

A Journey to Morocco in 1826. London: 1828. V. 40

BEAUCLERK, HELEN

The Love of the Foolish Angel. London: 1929. V. 38; 41

BEAUCLERK, TOPHAM

Bibliotheca Beauclerkiana. A Catalogue of the Large and Valuable Library of the Late Honourable Topham Beauclerk, F.R.S. Which will be Sold by Auction . . . by Mr. Paterson, On Mday April 9 1781, and Forty-Nine following Days . . . London: 1781. V. 39

BEAUCOUR, FERNAND

The Discovery of Egypt. Paris: 1990. V. 44

BEAUFORT, DANIEL A.

Memoir of a Map of Ireland . . . account of its present State. Dublin: 1792. V. 37

BEAUFORT, DUKE OF

Yachting. London: 1894. V. 39

BEAUFORT, FRANCIS

Karamania, or a Brief Description of the South Coast of Asia Minor and of the Remains of Antiquity. London: 1818. V. 39; 41; 46

BEAUFORT, HENRIETTA

The Heiress in Her Minority; or, the Progress of Character. London: 1850. V. 41

BEAUFORT, JAMES

Hoyle's Games Improved . . . 1788. V. 44

BEAUFOY, HENRY

Scloppetaria; or Considerations on the Nature and Use of Rifled Barrel Guns . . . London: 1808. V. 42

BEAUFOY, MARK

Nautical and Hydraulic Experiments, with Numerous Scientific Miscellanies. London: 1834. V. 38; 39; 40; 43; 46

BEAUGRAND, NICOLAS

Le Mareschal Expert Taictant du Naturel des Chevaux, des Marques de Leur Bonte & Remedes a Toutes Leurs Maladies. Paris: 1639. V. 41

BEAUGUE, JEAN DE

L'Histoire de la Guerre d'Escosse, Traitant Comme le Royaume fut Assailly & en Grande Partie Occupe par les Anglois & Depuis Rendu Paisible a sa Reyne & reduit en son Ancien Estat & Dignite . . . Paris: 1556. V. 41; 42

BEAUJOUR, FELIX DE

Sketch of the United States of North America . . . From 1800 to 1810. London: 1814. V. 39; 42; 43

BEAUMARCHAIS, ARNOULD

Le Genese du Barbier de Seville. Dublin: 1965. V. 42

BEAUMARCHAIS, PIERRE AUGUSTIN CARON DE

Le Barbier de Seville. Neuchatel: 1775. V. 37

La Folle Journee, ou le Mariage de Figaro. Paris: 1785. V. 40

The Follies of a Day; or, the Marriage of Figaro. London: 1785. V. 38

BEAUMONT

The Works. The Text Formed from a New Collection of the Early Editions. With Notes and a Biographical Memoir by the Rev. Alexander Dyce. London: 1843. V. 37

BEAUMONT, C. W.

New Papers 1917-1918. London: 1918. V. 37

L'Oiseau de Feu - Impressions of the Russian Ballet. London: 1919. V. 38

BEAUMONT, CHARLES

Charles Beaumont: Selected Stories. 1988. V. 43

The Hunger and Other Stories. London: 1957. V. 43

BEAUMONT, CYRIL

The First Score an Account of the Foundation and Dvelopment of the Beaumont Press and Its First Twenty Publications. London: 1927. V. 44

The Romantic Ballet in Lithographs of the Time. London: 1938. V. 42

BEAUMONT, CYRIL W.

Carnaval. London: 1918. V. 40

The First Score: an Account of the Foundation and Development of the Beaumont Press and Its First Twenty Publications. London: 1927. V. 44

The History of Harlequin. London: 1926. V. 45

Impressions of the Russian Ballet. London: 1918-1921. V. 37

Toys. Rhymes by . . . London: 1930. V. 37

BEAUMONT, FRANCIS 1584-1616

V. 45

Comedies and Tragedies. London: 1647. V. 38; 40; 42; 43; 44; 46

Comedies and Tragedies . . . London: Printed by J.: 1679. V. 37

Cvpids Revenge. London: 1630. V. 37

The Dramatic Works of Beaumont and Fletcher. London: 1778. V. 45

The Dramatick Works Collataed with all the Former Editions, and Corrected. London: 1778. V. 38

The Dramatic Works of Beaumont and Fletcher. London: 1811. V. 37

Fifty Comedies and Tragedies. London: 1679. V. 37; 38; 41; 44

A King and No King. London: 1661. V. 45

A King and No King. London: 1639. V. 37

The Knight of the Burning Pestle. London. V. 45

The Maides Tragedy. New York: 1932. V. 39

Philaster, or Love Lies a Bleeding. London: 1687. V. 39; 44; 46

Philaster Or Love Lies a Bleeding. London: 1639. V. 37

Philaster; or, love lies bleeding; The Fifth Impression. London: 1652. V. 37

Salmacis and Hermaphorditus. London: 1951. V. 41; 42; 46

The Scornfull Lady. London: 1639. V. 37; 40

Songs and Lyrics from the Plays of Beaumont and Fletcher. London: 1928. V. 37

Wit Without Money. London: 1639. V. 42

The Works of Mr. Francis Beaumont and Mr. John Fletcher. London: 1711. V. 42; 43; 45

The Works. Edinburgh: 1812. V. 37; 38; 39; 40; 41; 42; 43; 44; 46

The Works. Edinburgh: 1812. V. 39

The Works of Beaumont and Fletcher. London: 1843. V. 41; 45

The Works of Beaumont and Fletcher. London: 1843-46. V. 39; 41; 46

The Works of Beaumont and Fletcher. London: 1875. V. 44

The Works. 1905-12. V. 46

BEAUMONT, FRANICS 1584-1616

Songs and Lyrics from the Plays of Beaumont and Fletcher. London: 1928. V. 39

BEAUMONT, JOHN

Bosworth Field. London: 1629. V. 44

An Historical, Physiological and Theological Treatise of Spirits, Apparitions, Witchcrafts and other Magical Practices. London: 1705. V. 40

BEAUMONT, JOSEPH

The Complete Poems of Dr. Joseph Beaumont. London: 1880. V. 41

Original Poems in English and Latin . . . to which is prefixed an Account of His Life and Writings. Cambridge: 1749. V. 38

Psyche; or Loves Mysteri in XX Canto's. London: 1648. V. 43

Psyche, or Love's Mystery, in XXIV Cantos. Cambridge: 1702. V. 40; 42; 44; 45

Psyche: or Loves Mysterie in XX Cantos. London: 1648. V. 38

The Works. Edinburgh: 1812. V. 42

The Works of Beaumont and Fletcher. London: 1843-46. V. 44

BEAUMONT, ROBERTS

Colour in Woven Design. London: 1890. V. 38

Colour in Woven Design. London: 1890. V. 44

BEAUMONT, W. WORBY

Motor Vehicles and Motors. London: 1902. V. 41

BEAUMONT, WILLIAM

A Diary of a Journey from Warrington to the East in the Autumn of 1854. Warrington: 1855. V. 45

Experiments and Observations on the Gastric Juice, and the Physiology of Digestion. Plattsburgh: 1833. V. 37; 38; 39; 40; 41; 42; 45

Experiments and Observations on the Gastric Juice, and the Physiology of Digestion. Boston: 1834. V. 37; 40; 45

Experiments and Observations On the Gastric Juice and the Physiology of Digestion. Edinburgh: 1838. V. 41; 43; 44; 45; 46

Experiments and Observations on the Gastric Juice and the Physiology of Digestion. Boston: 1929. V. 41

Experiments and Observations on the Gastric Juice, and the physiology of Digestion, Reprinted from the Plattsburgh Edition, with notes by Andrew Combe. Edinburgh: 1839. V. 37

The Physiology of Digestion, with Experiments on the Gastric Juice. Burlington: 1847. V. 37; 38; 40; 41; 42

BEAUPRE, MORICHEAU

A Treatise on the Effects and Properties of Gold, with a Sketch, Historical and Medical, of the Russian Campaign. Edinburgh: 1826. V. 45

BEAURAIN, JEAN LE CHEVALIER DE

Histoire Militaire de Flandre Depuis L'Annee 1690, Jusqu'en 1694 . . . Paris: 1755. V. 43

BEAURDELEY, MICHEL

Porcelain of the East India Companies. London: 1962. V. 42

BEAUREGARD, NETTIE H.

Illustrations of Colonel Lindbergh's Decorations and Some of His Trophies Received Following His Transatlantic Flight of May 20-21, 1927. St. Louis: 1933. V. 40

BEAUREGARD, P. G. T.

General Orders. No. 61. Head Quarters, 1st Corps, Army of the Potomac. Fairfax: 1861. V. 41

THE BEAUTIES of Ancient Poetry. London: 1794. V. 38

THE BEAUTIES of Biography; Containing the Lives of the Most Illustrious Persons Who Have Flourished in Great Britain, France, Italy and Other Parts of Europe. London: 1777. V. 41; 46

BEAUTIES of English Poets. Venice: 1852. V. 45

THE BEAUTIES of Poetry Display'd. Dublin: 1757. V. 42

THE BEAUTIES of the English Stage: Consisting of the Most Affecting and Sentimental Passages, Soliloquies, Similes, Descriptions, etc. in the English Plays, Ancient and Modern . . . London: 1756. V. 41

THE BEAUTIES of the Rambler, Adventurer, Connoisseur, World and Idler. London: 1787. V. 37

BEAUTIES of Windsor. London: 1840. V. 45
BEAUTIES of Windsor. Windsor: 1840. V. 41

BEAUTY and the Beast. London: 1875. V. 44

BEAUTY'S Awakening, a Masque of Winter and of Spring. London: 1899. V. 37; 41

BEAUTY'S Awakening: a Masque of Winter and Spring. N.P.: 1899. V. 46

BEAUTY'S Triumph: or, the Superiority of the Fair Sex Invincibly Proved. London: 1751. V. 46

BEAUVALLET, P. N.

Fragmens d'Arichtecture, Sculpture et Peinture, dans le Style Antique. Paris: 1804. V. 40

BEAUVILLIERS, ANTOINE

L'Art du Cuisinier. Paris: 1814. V. 40

BEAUVOIR, SIMONE DE

Le Deuxieme Sexe. Paris: 1649. V. 45
Le Deuxieme Sexe. Paris: 1949. V. 40; 41
The Mandarins. Cleveland: 1956. V. 44
The Second Sex. New York: 1953. V. 42; 46

BEAUX and Belles of England. London. V. 38

BEAUX, CECILIA

Background with Figures. Boston and New York: 1930. V. 37; 44

BEAVER, JOHN

Letter to the Lords Commissioners for Trade and Plantations Concerning the Advantage of Gibraltar to the Trade of Great Britain. London: 1720. V. 38; 40; 43

BEAVER, PHILIP

African Memoranda: Relative to an Attempt to Establish a British Settlement on the Island of Bulama, on the Western Coast of Africa, in the Year 1792. London: 1805. V. 39

BEAWES, WYNDHAM

Lex Mercatoria Rediviva. Dublin: 1773. V. 38
Lex Mercatoria Rediviva. London: 1813. V. 38
Lex Mercatoria Rediviva; or, The Merchant's Directory. London: 1970. V. 38

BEAZLEY, J. D.

Attic Red-figured Vases in American Museums. Cambridge: 1918. V. 44
Attic Red-Figure Vase Painters. Oxford: 1963. V. 37; 40; 42
Attic Red-Figured Vases in American Museums. Cambridge: 1918. V. 40
Etruscan Vase-Painting. Oxford: 1947. V. 46
Greek Vases in Poland. Oxford: 1928. V. 40
Paralipomena: Additions to Attic Black-figure Vase Painters and to Attic Red-figure Painters. Oxford: 1971. V. 44

BEAZLEY, JOHN DAVIDSON

Etruscan Vase-Painting. Oxford: 1947. V. 42
Herodotus at the Zoo. Oxford: 1911. V. 42

BEBEL, AUGUST 1840-1913

Woman in the Past, Present and Future. London: 1885. V. 43; 45

BEBEL, HEINRICH 1472-1518

Opera. (with) Opuscula Nova. Pforzheim: 1509. V. 39

BECATI, GIOVANNI

The Art of Ancient Greece and Rome from the Rise of Greece to the Fall of Rome. New York: 1967. V. 41

BECCADELLI, LODOVICO

Vita Reginaldi Poli, Britanni S.R.E. Cardinalis, et Cantuariensis Archiepiscopi. Venice: 1563. V. 38

Vita Reginaldi Poli, Cardinalis et Cantuarensis Archiepiscopi; et Acta Disceptationis Inter Legatos Angliae & Galliae in Concilio Constatiensi. Londini: 1690. V. 40; 44; 46

BECCARI, O.

Asiatic Palms: Lepidocaryae. Corypheae. Calcutta: 1908-33. V. 39

BECCARI, ODOARDO

Wanderings in the Great Forests of Borneo. London: 1904. V. 42

BECCARIA, CESARE BONESANA, MARCHESE DI 1738-1794

An Essay on Crimes and Punishments . . . London: 1767. V. 39
An Essay on Crimes and Punishments. Glasgow: 1770. V. 37; 41
An Essay on Crimes and Punishments . . . London: 1770. V. 38; 42; 45
An Essay on Crimes and Punishments With A Commentary attributed to Mons. de Voltaire. Philadelphia: 1778. V. 41
An Essay on Crimes and Punishments. London: 1785. V. 38
An Essay on Crimes and Punishments. Edinburgh: 1788. V. 40
An Essay on Crimes and Punishments . . . Philadelphia: 1793. V. 39; 45
An Essay on Crimes and Punishments. London: 1804. V. 40
An Essay on Crimes and Punishments . . . Edinburgh: 1807. V. 39
An Essay on Crimes and Punishments . . . To Which is Added a Commentary . . . Philadelphia: 1819. V. 40
An Essay on Crimes and Punishments. London: 1767. V. 37; 38; 39; 41

BECCATELLI, LODOVICO

The Life of Cardinal Pole. London: 1766. V. 42; 44

BECCEGA, TOMASO CARLO

Sull'Architettura Greco-Romana Applicata Alla Construzione del Teatro Moderno Italiano e Sulle Macchine Teatrali. Venice: 1817. V. 45

BECCUTI, FRANCESCO

Cicalamenti Del Grappa Intorno Al Sonetto 'Poi che Mia Speme e Lunga a Venir Troppe'. Dove si'Ciarlia Allvngo Delle Lodi Delle Donne et Del Mal Francioso. Mantua: 1545. V. 38

BECH, BIRGER

Five Years in a Sailor's Life. Toronto: 1886. V. 38

BECHER, H. C. R.

A Trip to Mexico, Being Notes of a Journey from Lake Erie to Lake Tezcuco and Bakc, with an Appendix. Toronto: 1880. V. 38; 42; 44
A Trip to Mexico, Being Notes of a Journey from Lake Erie to Lake Tezcuco and Back . . . Toronto: 1880. V. 46

BECK, CARL

The Crippled Hand and Arm. Philadelphia: 1925. V. 42

BECK, I. LOWTHIAN

The Iron Trade of the United Kingdom Compared with that of the Other Chief Iron Making Nations. London: 1866. V. 44

BECK, JOHANN JODOCUS

Tractatus de Juribus Judaeorum, von Recht der Juden. Nuremberg: 1731. V. 42

BECK, LEWIS C.

A Gazetteer of the States of Illinois and Missouri. Albany: 1823. V. 37; 39

BECK, LEWIS CALEB

Adulterations of Various Substances Used in Medicine and the Arts, with the Means of Detecting Them. New York: 1846. V. 42

BECK, MAURICE

The Modern Motor Car. London: 1937. V. 42

BECK, RICHARD

A Treatise on the Construction, Proper Use, and Capabilities of Smith, Beck and Beck's Achromatic Microscopes. London: 1865. V. 38

BECK, S. WILLIAM

Gloves, Their Annals and Associations: a Chapter of Trade and Social History. London: 1883. V. 40; 46

BECK, THEODRIC ROMEYN 1791-1855

An Inaugural Dissertation on Insanity . . . New York: 1811. V. 43

BECKER, BERNARD H.

Disturbed Ireland: Being the Letters Written During the Winter of 1880-81 by . . . London: 1881. V. 39

BECKER, DANIEL

Historische Bescreibund Preussichen Messerschluckers. Konigsberg: 1643. V. 37

BECKER, ETHEL ANDERSON

Klondike '98. Portland: 1949. V. 45

BECKER, FRIEDRICH

The Successful Female Lines in the Breeding of the Thoroughbred Horse. Hamburg: 1922-27. V. 42

BECKER, G. C.

Fishes of Wisconsin. Madison: 1983. V. 37; 38

BECKER, GEORGE F.

Geology of the Comstock Lode and the Washoe District. Washington: 1882. V. 46

BECKER, GEORGE J.

Becker's Ornamental Penmanship. Philadelphia: 1854. V. 41

BECKER, GEORGE M.

Atlas to Accomapany the Geology of the Comstock Lode and the Washoe District. Washington: 1882. V. 41

BECKER, JOHN P.

The Sexagenary, or Reminiscences of the American Revolution. Albany: 1833. V. 41

BECKER, JOSEPH ERNEST DE

The Nightless City or The 'History of the Yoshiwara Yukwaku.' Yokohama: 1899. V. 38

BECKER, LYDIA E.

Autobiography. London: 1873. V. 45

Liberty, Equality, Fraternity. Manchester: 1874. V. 45

BECKER, R. Z.

Bildnisse der Urheber and Beforderer, auch Einiger Gegner der Relitions-und Kirchenverbesserung in 16. Gotha: 1817. V. 45

BECKER, ROBERT H.

Designs on the Land, Disenos of California Ranchos and Their Makers. San Francisco: 1969. V. 39; 40; 41; 43; 44; 45

Designs on the Land; Disenos of California Ranchos and Their Makers. San Francisco: 1969. V. 38; 40; 43

Disenos of California Ranchos. San Francisco: 1965. V. 38

Disenos of California Ranchos - Maps of Thirty-Seven Land Granats, 1822-1846, from the Records of the U.S. District Court, San Francisco. San Francisco: 1964. V. 37; 39; 45; 46

The Plains and the Rockies . . . San Francisco: 1982. V. 37

BECKER, SMITH & PAGE, INC., PHILADELPHIA.

Trade Catalogue of Wallpaper for 1912. V. 43

BECKER, STEPHEN

Comic Art in America. New York: 1959. V. 38

BECKER, WILHELM GOTTLIEB

Der Plauische Grund bei Dresden, mit Hinsicht auf Naturgeschichte und Schone Gartenkunst. Nurnberg: 1799. V. 46

BECKET, ANDREW

Shakespeare's Himself Again; or the Language of the Poet Asserted. London: 1815. V. 41

BECKET, THOMAS

Materials for the History of Thomas Becket, Archbishop of Canterbury . . . London: 1875-85. V. 44

BECKETT, JOSEPH

Elements and Practice of Mensuration and Land Surveying, Adapted Both to Public and Private Instruction. London: 1804. V. 43; 46

BECKETT, R. B.

Hogarth. London: 1949. V. 37; 39; 44

Lely. London. 1951. V. 39

BECKETT, S. B.

Guide Book of the Atlantic and St. Lawrence, and St. Lawrence and Atlantic Rail Roads, Including a Full Description of all the Interesting Features of the White Mountains. Sanborn: 1853. V. 42

BECKETT, SAMUEL 1906-1989

All That Fall. London: 1957. V. 46

All That Fall. New York: 1957. V. 37; 44

All That Fall. London: 1959. V. 46

All Strange Away. New York: 1976. V. 37; 39; 45; 46

Assez. Paris: 1966. V. 41

Beginning to End. New York: 1987. V. 38

Beginning to End: A Selection from the Works of Samuel Beckett. New York: 1988. V. 40; 41; 42; 43; 45; 46

Berceuse Suivi de Impromptu d'Ohio. Paris: 1982. V. 41

Bing. Paris: 1966. V. 43

Breath and Other Shorts. London: 1971. V. 39; 45

Catastrophe et autres Dramaticules. Paris: 1982. V. 41

Catastrophe. N.P.: 1983. V. 46

The Collected Works: Waiting for Godot. New York: 1970. V. 45

Come and Go - Dramaticule. London: 1967. V. 37; 39

Come and Go. London: 1967. V. 40; 43

Comedie et Actes Divers. Paris: 1966. V. 41

Comment C'Est. Paris: 1961. V. 41; 42

Compagnie. Paris: 1980. V. 41

Company. London: 1980. V. 45

Company. Iowa City: 1985. V. 39; 42; 44

Company. Iowa City: 1985. V. 40

Le Depeupleur. Paris: 1970. V. 39; 41

Drunken Boat. Reading: 1976. V. 42

Echo's Bones and Other Precipitates. Paris: 1935. V. 44; 46

Echo's Bones and Other Precipitates. Paris: 1935. V. 37; 38

Endgame - a Play . . . London: 1958. V. 42

Film. Paris: 1972. V. 42

Fin de Partie. 1957. V. 43; 44

First Love. London: 1973. V. 37; 44

Foirade, Foirades II and III, Foirades Iv & V in Minuit Nos. 1, 2 and 4. Paris: 1972-73. V. 46

Footfalls. 1976. V. 41

Happy Days - a Play in Two Acts. London: 1962. V. 44

How It Is. London: 1964. V. 37; 39; 40; 43; 45

How It Is. London: 1964. V. 45

How It Is . . . New York: 1964. V. 41

Il Seen, Il Said. Northridge: 1982. V. 43

Ill seen, Ill Said. 1982. V. 43; 46

Ill Seen Ill Said. 1982. V. 43

Ill Seen Ill Said. 1982. V. 42

Ill Seen Ill Said. 1982. V. 39

Ill Seen Ill Said. 1982. V. 46

Ill Seen, Ill Said. 1982. V. 46

Ill Seen, Ill Said. 1982. V. 46

Ill Seen Ill Said. 1982. V. 45

Ill Seen, Ill Said. California: 1982. V. 43

Imagination Dead Imagine. London: 1965. V. 39

Imagination Dead Imagine. London: 1965. V. 37; 43; 45

Imagination Morte Imaginez. Paris: 1965. V. 41; 43

Krapp's Last Tape and Embers. London: 1959. V. 45

Lessness. London: 1970. V. 37; 39

L'Issue. Paris: (1968). V. 37

The Lost Ones. London: 1972. V. 39; 42; 43; 46

The Lost Ones. Stamford: 1984. V. 37

Malone Dies. New York: 1956. V. 37; 45

Malone Dies. New York: 1956. V. 44

Mercier et Camier. Paris: 1970. V. 41

Molloy. Paris: V. 45

Molloy. 1951. V. 37

Molloy. Paris: 1951. V. 37; 40; 41; 42; 43; 44

Molloy. New York: 1955. V. 37; 39

Molloy. Paris: 1955. V. 40; 41; 42; 43; 45

Molloy/ Malone Dies/ The Unnamable. New York: 1955-58. V. 43

Molloy, Malone Meurt, l'Innommable. Paris: 1951/1951/1953. V. 37

Molloy, Malone Dies, the Unnamable. New York: 1959. V. 45

Molly. Malone Dies. The Unnamable. Paris: 1959. V. 45

Le Monde et la Pantalon. Paris: 1989. V. 46

More Pricks than Kicks. London: 1970. V. 42; 43

Murphy. London: 1938. V. 39; 41; 42

BECKETT, SAMUEL 1906-1989 continued

Murphy. New York: 1957. V. 37; 41

The Negress in the Brothel. London: 1989. V. 42

Nohow On. 1989. V. 42

The North. London: 1972. V. 37; 42; 45

No's Knife: Collected Shorter Prose, 1945-1966. London: 1967. V. 37; 39; 40; 42; 43

Not I. London: 1973. V. 43; 45

Nouvelles et Textes Pour Rien. Paris: 1958. V. 41; 44

Our Exagmination Round His Factification for Incamination of Work of Progress. (1936). V. 37

Pas Moi. Paris: 1975. V. 41

Poemes. Paris: 1968. V. 41

Poems in English. London: 1961. V. 39; 45

Premier Amour. Paris: 1970. V. 41

Proust. London: 1931. V. 37; 40; 42; 43; 44; 46

Proust. New York: 1931. V. 40

Proust. New York: 1957. V. 44

Proust & Three Dialogues. London: 1965. V. 39

Quatre Poemes :Four Songs. Poestenkill: 1986. V. 38

Samuel Becktt Exhibition Catalogue. London: 1971. V. 39

Sans. Paris: 1972. V. 42

Sejour. Paris: 1970. V. 41

Stirrings Still. New York/London: 1989. V. 42

Tetes-Mortes. Paris: 1967. V. 41

Tous Ceux qui Tombent. Paris: 1957. V. 41; 46

Waiting for Godot. New York: 1954. V. 39

Waiting for Godot. London: 1956. V. 40; 42; 43

Watt. London: 1953. V. 40

Watt. Olympia: 1953. V. 46

Watt. New York: 1959. V. 43

Whoroscope. Paris: 1930. V. 37; 38; 41

Zone. London: 1972. V. 39; 46

BECKETT, SYLVESTER BREAKMORE

Guide Book of the Atlantic and St. Lawrence and St. Lawrence and Atlantic Rail Roads, Including a Full Description of all the Interesting Features of the White Mountains. Portland: 1853. V. 46

BECKFORD, PETER

Familiar Letters from Italy, to a Friend in England. Salisbury: 1805. V. 37; 40

Thoughts on Hunting. London. V. 43

Thoughts on Hunting. Salisbury: 1781. V. 42; 44

Thoughts in Hunting in a Series of Familiar Letters to a Friend. Sarum: 1781. V. 39

Thoughts Upon Hunting. Sarum (Salisbury): 1782. V. 37; 39; 44

Thoughts on Hunting. London: 1784. V. 39

Thoughts Upon Hare and Fox Hunting . . . Also an Account of the Most Celebrated Dog Kennels in the Kingdom. London: 1796. V. 37; 38; 39; 44

Thoughts on Hunting, in a Series of Familiar Letters to a Friend . . . London: 1798. V. 43; 44

Thoughts on Hunting in a Series of familiar Letters to a Friend. London: 1810. V. 40

Thoughts on Hunting in a Series of Familiar Letters to a Friend. London: 1820. V. 39

Thoughts on Hunting, in a Series of Familiar Letters to a Friend. Sarum: 1781. V. 37

Thoughts upon Hunting . . . London: 1810. V. 37

BECKFORD, WILLIAM 1759-1844

An Arabian Tale. London: 1786. V. 37; 38; 40; 41; 42; 44; 45

Biographical Memoirs of Extraordinary Painters. London: 1780. V. 37; 38; 41; 43; 44

Biographical Memoirs of Extraordinary Painters. London: 1834. V. 43; 45; 46

Catalogue of a Portion of the Library . . . London: 1817. V. 45

Catalogue of the Magnificent, Rare, and Valuable Library of Books in Fonthill Abbey. 1823. V. 39

Catalogue of the First (to Fourth) Portion of the Beckford Library, Removed From Hamilton Palace. With Catalogue of the Hamilton Library. London: 1882/3/3/4/4. V. 39

A Descriptive Account of the Island of Jamaica. London: 1790. V. 37; 41

The Hamilton Palace Libraries. Catalogue of the First (to Fourth) Portion of the Beckford Library, removed from Hamilton Palace. Which Will be Sold by Auction by Messrs. Sotheby, Wilkinson & Hodge. 1882-83. V. 39; 42; 45; 46

Italy. London: 1834. V. 39; 40

Italy; with Sketches of Spain and Portugal. London: 1834. V. 37; 38; 40; 42

Memoirs of Extraordinary Painters. London: 1780. V. 40

Recollections of an Excursion to the Monasteries of Alcobaca and Batalha. London: 1835. V. 38; 39; 40; 41; 43; 45; 46

The Story of Al Raoui, a Tale from the Arabic. London: 1799. V. 37

Thoughts on Hunting in a Series of Familiar Letters to a Friend. Poultry, England: 1810. V. 38

Travel Diaries. London: 1928. V. 39

An Arabian Tale . . . (The History of the Caliph Vathek. V. 39

Vathek; an Arabian Tale. London: 1786. V. 41

Vathek. Paris: 1787. V. 44

Vathek. Lausanne: 1787/86. V. 46

Vathek. Lausanne: 1797-86. V. 43

Vathek. Londres: 1815. V. 41; 45

Vathek. London: 1823. V. 43

Vathek. London: 1893. V. 40

Vathek. New York: 1928. V. 39

Vathek. Bloomsbury: 1929. V. 37

Vathek, with The Episodes of Vathek. London: 1929. V. 39

Vathek. London: 1929. V. 44

Vathek. New York: 1945. V. 45

Vathek: an Arabian Tale. N.P.: 1945. V. 43

The Vision. Liber Veritatis. London: 1930. V. 39

BECKHART, BENJMAIN H.

The New York Money Market. New York: 1979. V. 40

BECKHER, DANIEL

Historische Bescreibund Preussischen Messerschluckers. Konigsberg: 1643. V. 38

BECKINGHAM, C. F.

The Preseter John of the Indies. Cambridge: 1961. V. 45

BECKINGHAM, CHARLES

The Life of Mr. Richard Savage. London: 1727. V. 43; 46

Scipio Africanus: a Tragedy. London: 1718. V. 38

The Tragedy of Henry IV of France: As It is Acted by His Majesty's Servants. London: 1720. V. 45

BECKINGTON, THOMAS

A Journal by One of the Suite of Thomas Beckington . . . During an Embassy to Negociate a Marriage Between Henry VI and a Daughter of the Count of Armagnac. London: 1828. V. 40

BECKIUS, MATTHIA FRIDERICO

Ephemerides Persarum per Totum Annum, Juxta Epochas Celebriores Orientis, Alexandream, Christi, Diocletiani, Hegirae, Jesdegirdicam et Gelalaeam . . . Augsburg: 1695-96. V. 37

BECKMAN, ERNST

Fran Nya Verlden Reseskildringar Fran Amerikas Forenta Stater. Stockholm: 1877. V. 46

BECKMANN, JOHANN

A Concise History of Ancient Institutions, Inventions and Discoveries in Science and Mechanic Art. London: 1823. V. 38; 42; 43

A History of Inventions and Discoveries. London: 1814. V. 42; 43

A History of Inventions and Discoveries. London: 1817. V. 42; 44

History of Inventions, Discoveries and Origins. London: 1846. V. 40; 44

BECKSON, KARL

Henry Harland. His Life and Work. London: 1978. V. 41

BECKWITH, EDWIN G.

Report of Exploration of a Route for the Pacific Railroad . . . From the mouth of the Kansas to Sevier River, in the Great Basin. (Washington: 1855). V. 37

Report of Explorations for the Pacific Railroad, On the Life of the Forty-First Parallel of North Latitude. (Washington: 1854). V. 37

BECKWITH, GEORGE CONE 1800-1870

The peace Manual: or, War and its Remedies. Boston: 1847. V. 37

BECKWITH, H. W.

History of Fountain County. Chicago: 1881. V. 44

BECKWITH, LEONARD F.

Report on Beton-Coignet, Its Fabrication and Uses . . . Washington: 1868. V. 44

BECKWITH, PAUL

Creoles of St. Louis. St. Louis: 1893. V. 37; 38

BECKWITH, WILLIAM

Letter to Sir Samuel Romilly, on the Necessity of an Immediate Enquiry into the Causes of Delay in Chancery Proceedings and of Arrears of Appeals in the House of Lords. London: 1810. V. 42; 45

BECKWOURTH, JAMES PIERSON 1798-ca. 1867.

The Life and Adventures of James P. Beckwourth, Mountaineer, Scout and Pioneer, and Chief of the Crow Nation of Indians. With Illustrations. Written from his own Dictation, by T.D. Bonner. New York: 1856. V. 37

BECLARD, P. A.

Additions to the General Anatomy of Xavier Bichat. Boston: 1823. V. 42

Elements of General Anatomy. Edinburgh: 1830. V. 37; 38; 39; 40; 41; 44; 45; 46

BECLARD, PIERRE AUGSTINE

Additions to the General Anatomy of Xavier Bichat ... Boston: 1823. V. 43; 44

BECLARD, PIERRE AUGUSTIN 1785-1825

Pathological Anatomy. The Last Course of Xavier Bichat from an Autograph Manuscript of P. A. Beclard ... Philadelphia: 1827. V. 44

BECQUEREL, ALEXANDRE EDMOND

La Lumiere ses Causes et ses Effets ... Paris: 1867-68. V. 41; 45

La Lumiere ses Causes et ses Effets. Paris: 1867-8. V. 38; 45

BECQUEREL, ANTOINE CESAR

Traite Experimental de l'Electricite et du Magnetisme, et de Leurs Rapports avec les Phenomenes Naturels. Paris: 1834-40. V. 40

BEDDARD, FRANK E.

A Book of Whales. London & New York: 1900. V. 38; 41

BEDDIE, M. K.

Bibliography of Captain James Cook. 1970. V. 45

BEDDOES, THOMAS

Alexander's Expedition Down the Hydaspes and the Indus to the Indian Ocean. London: 1792. V. 42

Essay on the Causes, Early Signs, and Prevention of Pulmonary Consumption for the Use of Parents and Preceptors. Bristol: 1799. V. 38

Hygeia; or Essays Moral and Medical on the causes Affecting the Personal State of Our Middling and Affluent Classes. Bristol: 1802-03. V. 45

A Lecture Introductory to a Course of Popular Instruction on the Constitution and Management of the Human Body. Bristol: 1797. V. 38

A Lecture Introductory to a Course of Popular Instruction on the Constitution and Management of the Human Body. Bristol: 1798. V. 40

A Letter to Erasmus Darwin, M.D. on a New Method of Treating Pulmonary Consumption, and Some Other Diseases Hitherto Found Incurable. Bristol: 1793. V. 40

Observations on the Medical and Domestic Management of the Consumptive, on the Powers of Digitalis Purpurea ... Troy: 1801. V. 40

Observations on the Medical and Domestic Management of the Consumptive. New York: 1803. V. 38

Observations on the Medical and Domestic Management of the Consumptive, on the Powers of Digitalis Purpurea and on the Cure of Schrophula. Troy: 1803. V. 37; 38; 39

Observations of the Medical and Domestic Management of the Consumptive; on the Powers of Digitalis Purpurea and on the Cure of Scrofula. London: 1801. V. 37; 38; 40

Observations on the Nature and Cure of Calculus, Sea Scurvy, Consumption, Catarrh and Fever. London: 1793. V. 38

Observations on the Nature and Cure of Calculus, Sea Scurvy, Consumption, Catarrh and Fever: Together with Conjectures Upon Several Other Subjects of Physiology and Pathology. London: 1793. V. 37

Observations on the Nature and Cure of Calculus, Sea Scurvy, Consumption, Catarrh and Fever Together with Conjectures Upon Several Other Subjects of Physiology and Pathology. Philadelphia: 1797. V. 37; 38

Researches Anatomical and Practical Concerning Fever, as Connected with Inflammation. London: 1807. V. 38

BEDDOES, THOMAS LOVELL 1803-1849

The Brides' Tragedy. London: 1822. V. 38; 42

The Complete Works. 1928. V. 39; 40; 43; 44

Death's Jest Book or the Fool's Strategy. London: 1850. V. 44

Dream Pediary. Edinburgh: 1968. V. 43

The Letters of Thomas Lovell Beddoes. London: 1894. V. 41

The Poetical Works of Thomas Lovell Beddoes. London: 1890. V. 40; 44

The Works of Beddoes. 1935. V. 37

BEDDOME, R. H.

The Ferns of British India. Madras: 1865-70. V. 43

The Ferns of Southern India. Madras: 1873. V. 37; 38

The Ferns of Southern India, Being Descriptions and Plates of the Ferns of the Madras Presidency. Madras: 1863. V. 37; 38

The Flora Sylvatica for Southern India. Madras: 1869-73. V. 43

Supplement to the Ferns of Southern India. Madras: 1876. V. 37

BEDE, VENERABLE 673-735

Ecclesiasticae Historiae Gentis Anglorum. Cologne: 1601. V. 44

Historia Ecclesiastica Gentis Anglorum. Strassburg: 1473-75. V. 44

The Historie of the Church of England. London: 1622. V. 43

The History of the Church of Englande. Antwerp: 1565. V. 43

The History of the Church of Englande. 1930. V. 40

the History of the Church of Englande. London: 1930. V. 45

The History of the Church of Englande. Oxford: 1930. V. 37; 39; 41; 45; 46

The History of the Church of Englande Compiled by Venerable Bede Englishman. Stratford-upon-Avon: 1930. V. 41

Homiliae in D. Paul Epistolas ... Cologne: 1535. V. 40

Homiliae Hyemales & Aestivales de Tempore & De Sanctis. Cologne: 1541. V. 37

De Natura Rerum Libri Duo. Basle: 1529. V. 45

Opera Historica. Londini: 1841. V. 45

BEDE, WILLIAM LEMAN

The Royal Rake, and Adventures of Alfred Chesterton. London: 1842. V. 38

BEDELET, LEONIE C.

Le Monde en Estampes Types et Costumes des Principaux Peuples de L'Univers ... Paris: 1858? V. 41; 43

BEDELL, ARTHUR J.

Photographs of the Fundus Oculi. Philadelphia: 1929. V. 39

BEDFORD, ADELINE MARIE SOMERS-COCKS RUSSELL, DUCHES OF 1852-1920

Biographical Catalogue of the Pictures at Woburn Abbey. London: 1890/92. V. 44

BEDFORD, ARTHUR

The Evil and Danger of Stage-Plays ... London: 1706. V. 42; 46

The Scripture Chronology Demonstrated by Astronomical Calculations and also by the Year of Jubilee, and the Sabbatical Year Among the Jews; or an Account of Time from the Creation of the World ... London: 1730. V. 46

Serious Reflections on the Scandalous Abuse and Effects of the Stage ... Bristol: 1705. V. 42

BEDFORD, EVAN

The Evan Bedford Library of Cardiology. Catalogue of Books, Pamphlets and Journals. London: 1977. V. 44; 45; 46

BEDFORD, F.

A Chart of Anglican Churdh Architecture arranged chronologically. York: 1844. V. 37

Sketches in York. York: 1841. V. 41

BEDFORD, FRANCIS

Catalogue of the Choice Library of the Late Eminent Bookbinder Mr. Francis Bedford. London: 1884. V. 41

Outline Engravings and Descriptions of the Woburn Abbey Marbles. London: 1822. V. 38; 40

Photographic Views of North Wales. Chester: 1865? V. 38

The Treasury of Ornamental Art. London: 1856. V. 38

The Treasury of Ornamental Art. London: 1859. V. 44

BEDFORD, H. G.

Texas Indian Troubles. Dallas: 1905. V. 42

BEDFORD, HILIAH

The Hereditary Right of the Crown of England Asserted; the History of the Succession Since the Conquest ... London: 1713. V. 38; 40

BEDFORD, JESSE

Cornish Diamonds. London: 1895. V. 42

BEDFORD, JOHN RUSSELL, 6TH DUKE OF 1766-1839

A Catalogue of Miniature Portraits in Enamel by Henry Bone Esq. R.A. in the Collection of the Duke of Beford at Woburn Abbey. London: 1825. V. 39

A Descriptive Catalogue of the Portraits in the Collection of John, Duke of Bedford ... London: 1834. V. 38

Hortus Ericaeus Woburnensis; or, a Catalogue of Heaths, in the Collection of the Duke of Bedford, at Woburn Abbey ... London: 1825. V. 39

Outline Engravings and Descriptions of the Woburn Abbey Marbles. London: 1822. V. 40

BEDFORD, JOHN RUSSELL, DUKE OF 1766-1839

Pinetum Woburnense: or, a Catalogue of Coniferous Plants in the Collection of the Duke of Bedford, at Woburn Abbey. London: 1839. V. 37

BEDFORD, PAUL

Recollections and Wanderings of Paul Bedford. London: 1864. V. 43

BEDFORD, SYBILLE

Aldous Huxley: a Biography. London: 1973. V. 40

BEDFORD, W. K. RILAND

The Blazon of Episcopacy. The arms borne by the Archibishops and Bishops of England and Wales; with an ordinary of the coats. London: 1897. V. 37; 39

BEDICHEK, ROY

Adventures with a Texas Naturalist. Garden City: 1947. V. 37; 40

BEDINGFIELD, THOMAS

Poetry, Fugitive and Original. Newcastle: 1815. V. 40

BEDLINGTON, JOHN

An Address to the Proprietors of Collieries on the Rivers Tyne and Wear, on the Subject of Ventilation. Newcastle: 1814. V. 40

BEDOLLIERRE, EMILE DE LA

Les Industriels. Paris: 1842. V. 38

BEDORTHA, N.

Practical Medication, or the Invalid's Guide; with Directions for the Treatment of Disease. Albany: 1860. V. 42

THE BEE, a Selection of Poetry from the Best Authors. Dublin: 1796. V. 41; 42

THE BEE, Fire-Side Companion and Evening Tales. Liverpool: 1820. V. 43

BEEBE, CHARLES WILLIAM 1877-1962

The Arcturus Adventures. London: 1926. V. 40
The Arcturus Adventure. New York: 1926. V. 40; 43; 46
Galapagos: World's End. New York: 1924. V. 42; 46
Galapagos World's End. New York: & London: 1924. V. 45
Monograph of Pheasants. London: 1918-22. V. 39; 42; 44; 45; 46
Pheasants. Their Lives and Homes. New York: 1926. V. 41
Pheasants: Their Lives and Homes. Garden City: 1931. V. 40
Pheasants: Their Lives & Homes. Garden City: 1931. V. 39
Pheasants: Their Lives and Homes. New York: 1931. V. 45
Pheasants, Their Lives and Homes. 1936. V. 46
Pheasants, Their Lives and Homes. USA: 1936. V. 45; 46
Pheasants: Thier Lives & Homes. Garden City: 1926. V. 37
Pheasants. V. 45
Two Bird-Lovers in Mexico. Boston/New York: 1905. V. 37; 38; 40

BEEBE, LUCIUS

Virginia & Truckee, a Story of Virginia City and Comstock Times. Oakland: 1949. V. 46

BEEBE, LUCIUS M.

Fallen Stars. Boston: 1921. V. 37; 38
Mr. Pullman's Elegant Palace Car. New York: 1961. V. 38

BEEBE, RUSSELL

Memorial to the Legislature. (Little Rock): 1852. V. 37

BEECH, M. W. H.

The Suk: Their Language and Folklore . . . Oxford: 1911. V. 38

BEECHER, CATHARINE E.

The American Woman's Home: or, Principles of Domestic Science; Being a Guide to the Formation and Maintenance of Economical, Healthful, Beautiful and Christian Homes. New York: 1869. V. 37; 39
Domestic Receipt Book. New York: 1869. V. 40
Letters on the Difficulties of Religion. Hartford: 1836. V. 44
Letters to the People on Health and Happiness. New York: 1855. V. 42
Miss Beecher's Domestic Receipt Book. New York: 1846. V. 41
A Treatise on Domestic Economy, for the Use of Young Ladies at Home and at School. Boston: 1841. V. 45

BEECHER, CATHERINE E.

The American Woman's Home. New York: 1870. V. 38

BEECHER, EDWARD

Narrative of Riots at Alton. Alton: 1838. V. 42
Narrative of Riots at Alton; In Connection with the Death of Rev. Elijah P. Lovejoy. Alton: 1838. V. 37; 40; 41; 42; 44; 45

BEECHER, EUNICE WHITE

Letters from Florida. New York: 1879. V. 41

BEECHER, HARRIS H.

Record of the 114th Regiment N.Y.S.V. Where It Went, What It Saw and What It Did. Norwich: 1866. V. 42; 43

BEECHER, HENRY WARD

Eyes and Ears. Boston: 1862. V. 44

Norwood; or, Village Life in New England. London: 1867. V. 43
Notes from Plymouth Pulpit. New York: 1858. V. 43
Seven Lectures to Young Men on Various Important Subjects . . . Indianapolis: 1844. V. 44
Star Papers: Or, Experience of Art and Nature. New York: 1855. V. 43; 45

BEECHER, JOHN

Here I Stand. New York: 1941. V. 41; 42

BEECHEY, FREDERICK WILLIAM 1796-1856

Narrative of a Voyage to the Pacific and Beering's Strait, to Co-operate with the Polar Expeditions . . . London: 1831. V. 37; 42

BEECHEY, FREDERICK WILLIAM 1796-1856

An Account of a Visit to California 1826-'27 Reprinted from a Narrative of a Voyage to the Pacific and Beering's Strait Performed in His Majesty's Ship Blossom Under the Command of Capt. F. W. Beechey in 1825, '26, '27, '28. San Francisco: 1941. V. 41; 42; 43
Narrative of a Voyage to Pacific and Beering's Strait, to Co-Operate with the Polar Expeditions . . . in the Years 1825, 26, 27, 28. London: 1831. V. 37; 38; 39; 40; 41; 42; 43; 44; 45; 46
Narrative of a Voyage to the Pacific and Beering's Strait, to Co-Operate with the Polar Expeditions: Performed in His Majesty's Ship Blossom . . . Philadelphia: 1832. V. 37; 38
Proceedings of the Expedition to Explore the Northern Coast of Africa, from Tripoly Eastward, in MDCCCXXI and MDCCCXXII. London: 1828. V. 37; 46
A Voyage of Discovery Towards the North Pole, Performed in His Majesty's Ships Dorothea and Trent, Under the Command of Captain David Buchan, R. N.; 1818 . . . London: 1843. V. 41; 45

BEECHING, H. C.

A Book of Christmas Verse. London: 1895. V. 37; 41; 43; 44

BEECROFT, GEORGE

Companion to the Iron Trade, Etc., Being a General Assistant to the Iron Master and Merchant . . . London: 1851. V. 42; 43

BEEDHAM, R. JOHN

Wood Engraving. Ditchling, Sussex: 1920. V. 38; 40; 46
Wood Engraving. Ditchling: 1925. V. 39; 41; 42
Wood Engraving. Ditchling, Sussex: 1925. V. 37; 43; 46

BEEDOME, THOMAS

Select Poems, Divine and Humane. Bloomsbury: 1928. V. 41; 46
Select Poems Divine and Humane. London: 1928. V. 44

BEEF and Butt Beer, Against Mum and Pumpernickle. London: 1743. V. 38; 45

BEEHLER, WILLIAM HENRY

The Cruise of the 'Brooklyn' a Journal of the Principal Events of a Three Years' Cruise . . . Philadelphia: 1885. V. 46

BEEKMAN, E. M.

Carnal Lent. Easthampton: 1975. V. 38
A Narcissus. A Poem. Easthampton: 1974. V. 38
Narcissus. Northampton: 1974. V. 42
Totem. N.P.: 1973. V. 38

BEEKMAN, GEORGE C.

Early Dutch Settlers on Monmouth County, New Jersey. Freehold: 1915. V. 39

BEELER, JOE

Cowboys and Indians. V. 39
Joe Beeler Portfolio. Flagstaff: 1978. V. 38; 40; 45; 46

BEER, EDWIN

Collected Papers, 1904-1929. New York: 1931. V. 42

BEER, GEORG JOSEPH

The Art of Preserving the Sight Unimpaired to an Extreme Old AGe . . . London: 1816. V. 41; 43
Art of Preserving the Sight Unimpaired to an Extreme Old Age . . . London: 1822. V. 45
Lehre von den Augenkrankheiten als Leitfaden zu Seinen Oeffentlichen. Viena: 1813/17. V. 42

BEER, GEORGE JOSEPH

The Art of Preserving the Sight Unimpaired to an Extreme Old Age and of Re-Establishing and Strengthening It When It Becomes Weak . . . London: 1815. V. 37; 44
Art of Preserving the Sight Unimpaired to An Extreme Old Age . . . London: 1824. V. 41

BEER, THOMAS

Hanna. New York: 1929. V. 42
Stephen Crane, a Study in American Letters. New York: 1923. V. 43

BEERBOHM, MAX 1872-1956

And Even Know. London: 1920. V. 37; 39; 41; 43; 44

Caricatures of Twenty-Five Gentlemen. London: 1896. V. 37; 39; 46

Caricatures of Twenty-Five Gentlemen. London & New York: 1897. V. 37

Cartoons: 'The Second Childhood of John Bull.' London: 1901. V. 38

Cartoons: 'The Second Childhood of John Bull.' London: 1911. V. 45

Catalogue of an Exhibition of Caricatures by 'Quiz'. London: 1923. V. 46

A Christmas Garland. London: 1912. V. 39; 40; 42; 46

The Dreadful Dragon of Hay Hill. London: 1928. V. 39

The Fetish of Speed. London: 1936. V. 46

Fifty Caricatures. London: 1913. V. 37; 39; 40; 41; 43; 46

The Happy Hypocrite. New York: 1897. V. 40; 43

Happy Hypocrite. New York: & London: 1897. V. 43

The Happy Hypocrite. London: 1914. V. 40

The Happy Hypocrite. London: 1915. V. 40

The Happy Hypocrite. London: 1915. V. 41; 42; 46

The Happy Hypocrite. London: 1918. V. 41

Heroes and Heroines of Bitter Sweet. London: 1931. V. 40

Leaves from the Garland. New York: 1926. V. 38; 40

Catalogue: The Library and Literary Mss. of the Late Sir Max Beerbohm, Removed from Rapallo. London. V. 41

A Luncheon. V. 37

More. London: 1899. V. 41

More. London: 1899. V. 41; 43; 46

More. New York: 1922. V. 41

Observations. London: 1925. V. 38; 41; 45

Observations. London: 1926. V. 39; 41

A Peep Into the Past. London: 1923. V. 40; 43; 44

The Poet's Corner. London: 1904. V. 37; 39; 40; 41; 43; 44; 46

The Poet's Corner. New York: 1904. V. 46

Rossetti and His Circle. London: 1922. V. 39; 41; 42

The Second Childhood of John Bull. London: 1901. V. 38

Seven Men. London: 1919. V. 40; 41; 43; 45; 46

Seven Men. New York: 1920. V. 43

Sherlockiana. Tempe: 1948. V. 46

A Survey. London: 1921. V. 37; 38; 39; 40; 41; 43; 45; 46

A Survey. New York: 1921, 1922. V. 41

Things New and Old: Caricatures. London: 1923. V. 38; 39; 40; 41; 43; 44; 46

The Works. With a Bibliography by John Lane. London: 1896. V. 37; 41

The Works. London: 1896. V. 42; 43; 46

Works of . . . London: & New York: 1896. V. 43

The Works of Max Beerbohm. New York: 1896. V. 39; 41; 43; 44; 45

The Works of . . . London: 1922. V. 46

The Works. London: 1922. V. 44

The Works. London: 1922-28. V. 37

The Works. London: 1922-28. V. 41

Yet Again. London: 1909. V. 39

Zuleika Dobson. London: 1911. V. 42

Zuleika Dobson. London: 1911. V. 43

Zuleika Dobson or an Oxford Love Story. London: 1911. V. 37; 38; 40; 41; 42; 43; 45; 46

Zuleika Dobson. Oxford: 1975. V. 43; 44

The Illustrated Zuleika Dobson. London: 1985. V. 39

Zuleika Dobson or an Oxford Love Story. By Max Beerbohm. With a foreword and illustrations by Osbert Lancaster. Oxford: 1975. V. 37; 41; 46

BEERBOHM TREE, HERBERT

Thoughts After Thoughts. London: 1913. V. 41

BEERS, ANDREW

Beer's Almanac and Ephemeris . . . for the Year 1793 . . . Hartford: 1792. V. 44; 45

BEERS, ETHEL LYNN 1827-1879

All Quiet Along the Potomac and Other Poems. Philadelphia: 1879. V. 41; 43

BEERS, F. W.

Atlas of Chemung Co. New York. New York: 1869. V. 46

Atlas of Calhoun Co., Michigan from Recent and Actual Surveys and Records. New York: 1873. V. 38

Atlas of Kalamzoo County, Michigan. New York: 1873. V. 38

BEERS, HENRY P.

The Western Military Frontier, 1815-1846. Philadelphia: 1935. V. 42

BEERS, T.

George Bellows. His Lithographs. New York: 1928. V. 39

BEESLEY, EDWARD SPENCER

The Postitivist Review. London: 1893-1920. V. 37

BEESON, JOHN

A Plea for the Indians, with Facts and Features of the Late War in Oregon. New York: 1857. V. 37; 38; 39

A Plea for the Indians; with Facts and Features of the Late War in Oregon. New York: 1858. V. 39; 42; 43

BEETHOVEN, LUDWIG VON

Messa a Quattro Voci Cool'Accompgnamento del'Orchestra. Leipzig: 1812. V. 38

BEETON, ISABELLA

Beeton's Housewife's Treasury of Domestic Information. London: 1890. V. 38

The Book of Household Management; Comprising Information for the Mistress, Housekeeper, Cook, etc. London: 1861. V. 42; 46

The Book of Household Management. London: 1864. V. 38; 40

The Book of Household Management . . . London: 1868. V. 40; 43

The Book of Household Management. London: 1869. V. 38

The English Woman's Cookery Book. London: 1863. V. 37

BEETON, ISABELLA MARY

Beeton's Every-Day Cookery and Housekeeping Book. London: 1891. V. 42

The Book of Household Management . . . London. V. 42

BEETON'S Book of Needlework. London: 1870. V. 41

BEEVOOR, CHARLES E.

The Croonian Lectures on Muscular Movements and Their Representation in the Central Nervous System. London: 1904. V. 39

BEGBIE, HAROLD

The Struwwelpeter Alphabet. London: 1900. V. 46

BEGER, LORENZ

Spicilegium Antiquitatis, Sive Variarum Ex Antiquitate Elegantiarum . . . Berlin: 1692. V. 40

Thesaurus Brandenburgicus Selectus, sive Gemmarum et Numismatum Graecorum . . . Colonia: 1696-1701. V. 40

BEGG, ALEXANDER

Alexander Begg's Red River Journal and Other Papers Relative to the Red River Resistance 1869-70. Toronto: 1956. V. 39

The Creation of Manitoba; or, a History of the Red River Troubles. Toronto: 1871. V. 38; 41; 43; 44

'Dot It Down'. A Story of Life in the North-West. Toronto: 1871. V. 44

History of British Columbia. Toronto: 1894. V. 40; 42; 44

History of British Columbia from Its Earliest Discovery to the Present Time. Toronto: 1894. V. 37; 42

History of the North-West. Toronto: 1894-95. V. 38

Ten Years in Winnipeg. Manitoba: 1879. V. 44

Ten Years in Winnipeg. Winnipeg: 1879. V. 39

BEGG, RICHARD

History of the North-West. Toronto: 1894. V. 37

BEGGS, THOMAS

An Inquiry into the Extent and Causes of Juvenile Depravity. 1849. V. 40

BEGIN, EMILE

Voyage Pittoresque en Suisse en Savoie et sur les Alpes. Paris: 1855. V. 38; 45

BEGLEY, JOHN

The Diocese of Limerick from 1691 to the Present Time. Dublin: 1938. V. 38

The Diocese of Limerick, Ancient and Medieval. Dublins: 1906. V. 37; 46

BEGUIN, JEAN

Tyrocinium Chymicum Johannis Beguini, Regis Galliae Eleemonsynarii, Antehac a Viris Clariss . . . Wittenburg: 1640. V. 45

Tyrocinium Chymicum . . . Geneva: 1659. V. 46

Tyrocinium Chymicum, Commentario Illustratum a Gerardo Blasio . . . Amsterdam: 1669. V. 46

BEHAM, HANS SEBALD 1500-1550

Biblisch Historien, Figurlich Furgebildet, Durch den Wolberuemten Sebald Behem von Nueremberg, 1533. V. 40

BEHAN, BRENDAN 1923-1964

Brendan Behan's Island. New York: 1962. V. 39

The Hostage. London: 1958. V. 39

BEHAN, BRENDAN 1923-1964 continued

The Quare Fellow. New York: 1956. V. 40

The Quare fellow. New York: 1956. V. 37; 38; 40; 42; 44

The Quare Fellow. New York: 1957. V. 43

BEHN, APHRA 1640-1689

Abdelazer; or, The Moor's Revenge. London: 1693. V. 43

All the Histories and Novels . . . Entire in One Volume . . . London: 1705. V. 42; 43

All the Histories and Novels Written by . . . London: 1751. V. 44

The Debauchee: or, The Credulous Cuckhold, a Comedy. London: 1677. V. 37

The Emperor of the Moon: a Farce. London: 1687. V. 39; 41; 42

The Histories and Novels of the Late Ingenious Mrs. Behn. (with) Histories, Novels and Translations Written by the Most Ingenious Mrs. Behn; The Second Volume. London: 1718. V. 38

Love Letters Between a Nobleman (Forde Lord Grey of Werk) and His Sister (Lady Henrietta Berkeley). London: 1708. V. 39; 42

The Plays, Histories and Novels of the Ingenious Mrs. Aphra Behn With Life and Memoirs. London: 1871. V. 46

Plays Written by the Late Ingenious Mrs. Behn . . . London: 1724. V. 37; 42

A Poem Humbly dedicated to the Great Patern of Piety and Virtue, Catherine Queen Dowager, on the Death of Her Dear Lord and Husband King Charles II. London: 1685. V. 38

Poems Upon Several Occasions; with a Voyage to the Island of Love. London: 1684. V. 37; 38; 39; 41; 42; 44; 46

The Rover; or, the Banish't Cavaliers. (with) The Second Part of the Rover. London: 1681. V. 39

The Royal Slave and Other Novels. London: 1905. V. 42

The Works of . . . London: 1871. V. 40

The Works of Mrs. Aphra Behn. London: 1915. V. 37; 38; 40; 41

The Young King; or, the Mistake. London: 1683. V. 39

The Younger Brother; or, the Amorous Jilt. London: 1696. V. 40

BEHRENS, CHARLES

Atomic Medicine. New York: 1949. V. 42; 45

BEHRENS, GEORG HENNING

The Natural History of Hartz-Forest . . . London: 1730. V. 42; 43

BEHRMAN, SAMUEL NATHANIEL 1893-1943

Three Plays: Serena Blandish; Meteor; The Second Man. New York: 1934. V. 37; 39; 45

The Worcester Account. New York: 1954. V. 37; 39

BEIER, ADRIAN

De Varii Generis Instrumentis . . . Jena: 1691. V. 37

BEIER, AGNES

Court Theatres of Drottningholm and Gripsholm. 1972. V. 37

BEIGELMAN, M. N.

400 Books from a Private Library. Los Angeles: 1967. V. 41

BEIJER, AGNE

Court Theatres of Drottningholm and Gripsholm. Malmo: 1933. V. 40; 44

BEIKE, CHARLES TILSTONE

The Sources of the Nile . . . London: 1860. V. 46

BEISSEL, JOHANN CONRAD

Paradisisches Wunder-Spiel, Welches sich in Diesen Letzten Zeiten und Tagen in Denen Abendlandischen Welt-Theilen . . . Ephrata: 1766. V. 40

BEKAERT, P. J.

A Treatise on the Pronunciation of the French Language; with an Appendix of the Genders of Nouns. London: 1820. V. 43; 46

BEKE, CHARLES

Discoveries in Sinai in Arabia and of Midian. London: 1878. V. 37

BEKE, CHARLES T.

The Sources of the Nile: Being a General Survey of the Basin of the River, and of Its Head-Streams; with This History of Nilotic Discovery. London: 1860. V. 39

BEKKER, BALTHASAR 1634-1698

De Betoverde Weereld, Zynde een Grondig Ondersoek van't Gemeen Gevoelen Aangaande de Geesten . . . Amsterdam: 1715. V. 46

Die Bezauberte Welt: Older eine Grundliche Untersuchung des Allgemeinen Aberglaubens, Betreffen die Arth und das Vermogen, Gewalt und Wirkung des Satans und der Bosen Geister uber den Menschen. Amsterdam: 1693. V. 37

Le Monde Enchantee ou Examen des Communs Sentimens Touchant les Esprits, Leur Nature Leur Pouvoir, Leur Administration & Leurs Operations . . . Amsterdam: 1694. V. 40

BEKKER, BALTHAZAR

The World Bewitch'd. London: 1695. V. 40; 42

BELASCO, DAVID

Six Plays. Boston: 1928. V. 37

BELCHER, C. R.

A Trip to Mexico, Being Notes of a Journey from Lake Erie to Lake Tezuco and Back . . . Toronto: 1880. V. 45

BELCHER, DIANA

The Mutineers of the Bounty and Their Descendants in Pitcairn and Norfolk Island. London: 1870. V. 38

The Mutineers of the Bounty and Their Descendants in Pitcairn and Norfolk Islands. New York: 1871. V. 41

BELCHER, EDWARD

The Last of the Arctic Voyages; Being a Narrative of the Expedition in H.M.S. Assistance . . . in Search of Sir John Franklin During the Years 1852-53-54. London: 1855. V. 39; 40; 41; 42; 43; 45; 46

Narrative of a Voyage Round the World, Performed in Her Majesty's Ship Sulphur, During the Years 1836-1842. London: 1843. V. 37; 38; 40; 42; 43; 45; 46

Narrative of the Voyage of H.M.S. Samarang, During 1843-46, Employed Surveying the Islands of the Eastern Archipelago . . . London: 1848. V. 38; 40

BELCHER, HENRY

Illustrations of the Scenery on the Line of the Whitby and Pickering Railway, in the North Eastern Part of Yorkshire. London: 1836. V. 41; 44

BELCHER, JOHN

The Institute of Chartered Accountants in England and Wales. Moorgate Place, E C. John Belcher, architect. London: 1893. V. 38

Later Renaisance Architecture in England. London: 1901. V. 38; 41; 45

BELCHER, LADY

The Mutineers of the Bounty and Their Descendants in Pitcairn and Norfolk Islands. London: 1870. V. 45

BELCHER, T. W.

Memoir of Sir Patrick Dun (Knt) M.D.: M.P.; Physician-General to the Army . . . Dubin: 1866. V. 42; 43

BELCOURT, G. A.

Department of Hudson Bay: Addressed to His Excellency, Alex. Ramsey President of the Minnesota Historical Society. St. Paul: 1853. V. 46

BELDEN, ALBERT LORD

The Fur Trade of America and Some of the Men Who Made and Maintain It. New York: 1917. V. 42; 43

BELDEN & CO.

Illustrated Atlas of the Dominion of Canada . . . Toronto: 1880. V. 42

Illustrated Atlas of the Dominion of Canada. Toronto: 1881. V. 42

BELDEN, BAUMAN L.

Indian Peace Medals Issued in the United States. New York: 1927. V. 37; 39

BELDEN, DAVID

Life of David Belden. New York: 1891. V. 46

BELDEN, E. PORTER

New York: Past, Present and Future; Comprising a History of the City of New York, a Description of Its Present Condition, and an Estimate of its Future Increase. (with) New York As It Is . . . (with) The American Advertiser . . . New York: 1851. V. 41

BELDEN, H.

Illustrated Atlas of the Dominion of Canada, Containing Authentic and Complete Maps of all the Provinces, The North-West Territories and the Island of Newfoundland . . . Toronto: 1881. V. 37

BELDEN, H. M.

Ballads and Songs Collected by the Missouri Folk-Lore Society. Columbia: 1940. V. 43

BELDEN, JESSIE PERRY VAN ZILE

Concerning Some of the Ancestors and Descendants of Royal Denison Belden and Olive Cadwell Belden. Philadelphia: 1898. V. 40; 46

BELDEN, LEMUEL W. 1801-1839

An Account of Jane C. Rider, The Springfield Somnambulist: the Substance of Whcih was Delivered as a Lecture Before the Springfield Lyceum, Jan. 22, 1834. Springfield: 1834. V. 39

BELDHAM, GEORGE W.

Great Golfers, Their Methods at a Glance . . . London: 1904. V. 45

BELFAST MEDICAL LIBRARY

Catalogue of the Belfast Medical Library. Belfast: 1829. V. 45

BELFOUR, JOHN

Fables on Subjects Connected with Literature. London: 1804. V. 43

Spanish Heroism; or, the Battle of Roncesvalles. London: 1809. V. 45

BELG, IGNACE J.

Hittite Hieroglyphs I-III. Chicago: 1931-42. V. 44

BEL GEDDES, NORMAN

Horizons. Boston: 1932. V. 44; 46

Magic Motorways. New York: 1940. V. 44

Magic Motorways. (New York): (1940). V. 37

BELGIUM and Nassau, or the Continental Tourist. L: 1835. V. 41
BELGIUM and Nassau; or the Continental Tourist. London: 1835. V. 44

BELGRAVE, C. DALRYMPLE

Siwa - the Oasis of Jupteter Ammon. London: 1923. V. 45

BELIDOR, BERNARD FOREST DE

Architecture Hydraulique. Paris: 1737-39/50-53. V. 38; 42

La Science des Ingenieurs dans la Conduite des Travaux de Fortification et d'Archtiecture Civile. Paris: 1729. V. 38; 40; 41; 42

La Science des Ingenieurs dans la Conduite des Travaux de Fortification . . . Paris: 1729. V. 41

THE BELIEVER'S Daily Treasure; or, Texts of the Scripture, Arranged for Every Day of the Year. London: 1841. V. 45

BELISARIO, A. M.

A Report of the Trial of Arthur Hodge, Esq. at the Island of Tortola, on the 25th April, 1811. Middletown: 1812. V. 42

BELISLE, DAVID A.

The American Family Robinson; or, The Great Adventures of a Family Lost in the Great Desert of the West. Philadelphia: 1854. V. 37

BELITT, BEN

Graffiti. V. 44

BELITZ, GEORGE FREDERICK

A Memorials of the Order of the Garter From Its Foundation to the Present Time with Biographical Notices of the Knights in the Reigns of Edward III and Richard II. London: 1841. V. 41

BELKNAP, JEREMY

A Discourse Intended to Commemorate the Discovery of America by Christopher Columbus; Delivered at the Request of the History Society in Massachusetts, on the 23rd day of October, 1792 . . . Boston: 1792. V. 38; 40

A Plain and Earnest Address from a Minster to a Parishioner, on the Neglect of the Public Worship . . . Salem: 1771. V. 44

The Foresters, an American Tale. Boston: 1792. V. 39; 42; 43; 44

The Foresters, an American Tale. Boston: 1792. V. 39

The Foresters, an American Tale: Being a Sequel to the History of John Bull the Clothier. Boston: 1792. V. 37; 38; 41

The Foresters, an American Tale. Boston: 1796. V. 39

The History of New Hampshire. Philadelphia; Boston;: 1784/91/92. V. 39

The History of New Hampshire. Philadelphia: 1784 & 1791/92. V. 39; 42; 45

The History of New Hampshire . . . from the Discovery of the River Pascataqua . . . to 1790 . . . etc. Boston: 1813. V. 42

BELKNAP, WILLIAM W.

Congressional Record; Containing the Proceedings of the Senate Sitting for the Trail of William W. Belknap, Late Secretary of War, on the Articles of Impeachment Exhibited by the House of Represenatives. Wasington: 1876. V. 40

Proceeding of the Senate Sitting for the Trial of William W. Belknap, Late Secretary of War, on the Articles of Impeachment Exhibited by the House of Representatives. Washington: 1876. V. 42

THE BELL. Dublin: 1940-54. V. 38

BELL, A.

Letter from . . . Transmitting . . . Certain Papers Relating to the Private Land Claim in the Territory of Arizona Known as El Sopori. Washington: 1884. V. 38; 39

BELL, A. C.

A History of the Blockade of Germany and Of Countries Associated with Her in the Great War: Austria-Hungary, Bulgaria, and Turkey 1914-1918. London: 1937. V. 40

BELL, A. MORTON

Locomotives. Their Construction, Maintenance and Operation, with Notes on Electric and Internal Combustion Locomotives. London: 1946. V. 37; 43; 45

BELL, A. N.

Climatology and Mineral Waters of the United States. New York: 1885. V. 40; 41; 42; 45; 46

BELL, ADRIAN

Men and the Fields. London: 1939. V. 38; 41; 42

Poems. London: 1935. V. 41

BELL, ALEXANDER

A Daughter of Maryland Was the Mother of Texas. Mrs. Jane Herbert (Wilkinson) Long. Washington: 1920. V. 44

BELL, ALEXANDER GRAHAM

Address Upon the Condition of Articulation Teaching in American Schools for the Deaf. Boston: 1893. V. 45

The Mechanism of Speech. Lectures Delivered Before the American Association to Promote the Teaching of Speech to the Deaf, to Which is Appended a paper (on) Vowel Theories Read Before the National Academy of Arts and Sciences. New York: 1907. V. 40

Memoir Upon the Formation of a Deaf Variety of the Human Race. 1883. V. 39

Memoir Upon the Formation of a Deaf Variety of the Human Race. Washington: 1884. V. 38; 43

The Mystic Oral School. Washington: 1897. V. 45

The Telephone. A Lecture Entitled Researches in Electric Telephony. London & New York: 1878. V. 42

BELL, ANDREW

Extract of a Sermon on the eduction of the Poor, Under an Appropriate System; Preached at St. Mary's, Lambeth, 28 June 1807 . . . London: 1807. V. 43; 45

History of Canada, from the Time of Its Discovery till the Union Year 1840-41. Montreal: 1865. V. 38

The Madras School, or Elements of Tuition . . . London: 1808. V. 43

Men and Things in America; Being the Experience of a Year's Residence in the United States, in a Series of Letters to a Friend. London: 1838. V. 38

Mutual Tuition and Moral Discipline . . . London: 1823. V. 44

BELL, ANNE

A Most Circumstantial Account of that Unfortunate Lady Miss Bell, Otherwise Sharpe, who Died at Marylebone on Sat. Oct. 4 . . . London: 1760. V. 41

BELL, BENJAMIN

A System of Surgery. Edinburgh: 1787-88. V. 43

A System of Surgery. Philadelphia: 1791. V. 42

A Treatise on the Theory and Management of Ulcers. Edinburgh: 1791. V. 38

A Treatise on Gonorrhoea Virulenta and Lues Venera. Philadelphia: 1795. V. 37; 39

A Treatise on the Theory and Management of Ulcers; With a Dissertation on White Swellings of the Joints. Boston: 1797. V. 42

A Treatise on the Theory and Management of Ulcers . . . . Boston: 1979. V. 40

A Treatise on the Theory and Management of Ulcers. With a Dissertation on White Swellings of the Joints. To which is Prefixed, an Essay on the Chirurgical Treatment of Inflammation and its Consequences. Edinburgh: 1778. V. 37; 42

BELL, C. N.

Our Northern Waters; a Report presented to the Winnipeg Board of Trade Regardign the Hudson's Bay and Strait. Winnipeg: 1884. V. 37; 43; 46

BELL, CATHERINE D.

The Children's Mirror. London: 1859. V. 40; 45

BELL, CHARLES 1774-1842

The Anatomy of the Brain, Explained in a Series of Engravings. London: 1802. V. 37; 38; 42

The Anatomy of the Brain, Explained in a Series of Engravings. (with) A Series of Engravings, Explaining the Course of Nerves. London: 1802/1803. V. 43; 46

The Anatomy and Philosophy of Expression as Connected with the Fine Arts. London: 1844. V. 38

The Anatomy and Philosophy of Expression as Connected with the Fine Arts. London: 1847. V. 38; 39; 42

The Anatomy and Philosophy of Expression as Connected with the Fine Arts. London: 1865. V. 41; 43

The Anatomy and Philosophy of Expression as Connected With The Fine Artists Sixth Edition. London: 1872. V. 41

Animal Mechanics. Cambridge: 1902. V. 38

Charles Bell par le Pr. Viggo Christian . . . Paris: 1922. V. 41

Engravings of the Arteries . . . London: 1801. V. 42

Engravings of the Arteries . . . . Philadelphia: 1812. V. 41

Essays on the Anatomy and Philosophy of Expression. London: 1824. V. 38; 41; 45

The Hand - Its Mechanism and Vital Endowments as Evincing Design. London: 1833. V. 42

BELL, CHARLES 1774-1842 continued

The Hand, Its Mechanism and Vital Endowments, as Evincing Design. Philadelphia: 1833. V. 43

The Hand Its Mechanism and Vital Endowments as Evincing Design. London: 1834. V. 41; 44; 45

The Hand, Its Mechanism and Vital Endowments as Evincing Design. London: 1837. V. 40; 43; 44

The History of the Indian Mutiny. London: 1880. V. 37

The History of the Indian Mutiny: A Detailed account of the Sepoy Insurrection in India; and a concise history of the great Military Events . . . 1870. V. 37

Illustrations of the Great Operations of Surgery. London: 1821. V. 37

Letters Concerning the Diseases of the Urethra. Boston: 1811. V. 46

Letters of Sir Charles Bell . . . London: 1870. V. 41

The Nervous System of the Human Body. Washington: 1833. V. 40; 41

The Nervous System of the Human Body. Edinburgh: 1836. V. 43

The Nervous System of the Human Body . . . London: 1844. V. 42

Practical Essays . . . 1. On the Powers of Life to Sustain Surgical Operations . . . II. On the Questionable Practice of Bleeding in all Apoplectic Affections . . . III. On Squinting - Its Causes . . . IV. On the Action of Purgatives . . . Edinburgh: 1841. V. 38

A Series of Engravings, Explaining the Course of the Nerves. With an Address to Young Physicians on the Study of the Nerves. Philadelphia: 1818. V. 37; 38; 41; 42

A System of Operative Surgery, Founded on the Basis of Anatomy. Hartford: 1812. V. 42

Tibet Past and Present. Oxford: 1924. V. 44

BELL, CHARLES DENT

The Four Seasons at the Lakes. London: 1870. V. 39; 44

The Four Seasons on the Lakes. London: 1878. V. 38

The Four Seasons at the Lakes. London: 1885. V. 41

BELL, CHARLES H.

John Wheelwright: His Writings, Including His Fast-Day Sermon 1637; and His Mercurius Americanus, 1645; with a Paper Upon the Genuineness of the Indian Deed of 1629, and a Memoir. Boston: 1876. V. 46

BELL, CLIVE

An Account of French Painting. London: 1931. V. 44

The Legend of Monte della Sibilla, or, Le Paradis de la Rine Sibille; a poem. Richmond: 1923. V. 37; 39; 40; 45

Poems. Richmond: 1921. V. 37; 38; 45

Proust. London: 1928. V. 46

BELL, DEWITT

Ravenwood and Other Poems. Hanover: 1963. V. 42; 43; 44

BELL, EDWARD

George Bell, Publisher. London: 1924. V. 41

BELL, EDWARD ALLEN

A History of Giggleswick School, from Its Foundation 1499 to 1912. Leeds: 1912. V. 44

BELL, ERNEST A.

Fighting the Traffic In Young Girls, or War on the White Slave Trade. N.P.: 1911. V. 42

BELL, EVANS

Retrospects and Prospects of Indian Policy. London: 1868. V. 39

BELL, FLORENCE HOPE

Savoury Dishes. Dumfires, J. Anderson &: 1899. V. 44

BELL, FRED A.

Hand-Book of Practical Directions for Sugar Cane Planting, Sugar Making and the Distillation of Rum . . . Sydney: 1866. V. 40

BELL, G. J.

A Practical Treatise on Segmental and Elliptical Oblique or Skew Arches Setting Forth the Principles and Details of Construction . . . Carlisle: 1906. V. 40

BELL, G. M.

The Philosophy of Joint-Stock Banking. London: 1855. V. 39

BELL, GEORGE

Descriptive and Other Miscellaneous Pieces in Verse. Penrith: 1835. V. 46

A Sermon Preach'd at the Cathedral Church of St. Peter in York, Before the Honourable Baron Page at the Assizes. London: 1722. V. 45

BELL, GERTRUDE

The Arab War - Confidential Information for General Headquarters from Gertrude Bell. London: 1940. V. 41; 44

Persian Pictures. London: 1928. V. 46

BELL, GERTRUDE LOWTHIAN

Amurath to Amurath. London: 1911. V. 46

BELL, H. W.

Baker Street Studies. London: 1934. V. 38; 43

Sherlock Holmes and Dr. Watson. The Chronology of Their Adventures. London: 1932. V. 42; 43

Sherlock Holmes and Dr. Watson. New York: 1953. V. 44

BELL, HENRY

An Historical Essay on the Original of Painting. London: 1728. V. 38

The Perfect Painter; or, a Compleat History of the Original, Progress and Improvement of Painting. London: 1730. V. 38; 40; 44

BELL, HENRY G.

An Account of the Burman Empire. Calcutta: 1852. V. 40

BELL, HENRY GLASSFORD

Summer and Winter Hours. London: 1831. V. 41; 42

BELL, HENRY NUGENT

The Huntingdon Peerage . . . London: 1821. V. 46

BELL, HERBERT C.

History of Northumberland County, Pennsylvania. Chicago: 1891. V. 41; 42

BELL, HORACE

Reminiscences of a Ranger; or, Early Times in Southern California. Los Angeles: 1881. V. 38

BELL, I. LOWTHIAN

Principles of the Manufacture of Iron and Steel, with Some Notes on the Economic Conditions of their Production. London: 1884. V. 44

BELL, J. J.

Jack of All Trades. London: 1900. V. 44

BELL, J. JONES

The Red River Expedition, by J. Jones Bell, an Officer in Lord Wolseley's Expedition. Toronto. V. 45

BELL, J. MUNRO

The Castles of the Lothians. Edinburgh: 1893. V. 41

BELL, JACOB

Historical Sketch of the Progress of Pharmacy in Great Britain. London: 1880. V. 39; 44

BELL, JAMES

Influence of Physical Research on Mental Philosophy. Edinburgh: 1839. V. 40

BELL, JAMES MUNRO

Furniture Designs of Chippendale, Hepplewhite and Sehraton. London: 1910. V. 39

BELL, JAMES STANISLAUS

Journal of a Residence in Circassia. London: 1840. V. 40

Journal of a Residence in Circassia During the Years 1837, 1838 and 1839. London: 1840. V. 39; 40; 42

BELL, JOHN

An Address Delivered at Nasville, T., October 5th, 1830, Being the First Anniversary of the Alumni Society of the University of Nashville. Nashville: 1830. V. 44

All the Material Facts in the History of Epidemic Cholera . . . Philadelphia: 1832. V. 42

The Anatomy and Physiology of the Human Body. New York: 1817. V. 41

The Anatomy and Physiology of the Human Body. New York: 1822. V. 42

The Anatomy and Physiology of the Human Body. London: 1823. V. 42

The Anatomy of the Human Body. London: 1811. V. 37

Bell's Edition, the Poets of Great Britain. London: 1807. V. 39

Bell's British Theatre . . . (with) Supplement to Bell's British Theatre. London: 1776-81/84. V. 44

Bell's British Theatre. London: 1791-92. V. 39; 42

Discourses on the Nature and Cure of Wounds. Edinburgh: 1795. V. 45; 46

Discourses on the Nature and Cure of Wounds. Edinburgh: 1800. V. 41

Discourses on the Nature and Cure of Wounds. Walpole: 1807. V. 41; 42

Engravings Explaining the Anatomy of the Bones, Muscles and Joints. Edinburgh: 1794. V. 40

Engravings of the Bones, Muscles and Joints . . . Part First . . . Philadelphia: 1816. V. 43

The Engravings of Bones, Muscles and Joints. Philadelphia: 1817. V. 45

Engravings of the Bones, Muscles and Joints. Part First. (and) Part Second. Philadelphia: 1816, 1815. V. 37

BELL, JOHN continued

Engravings of the Bones, Muscles and Joints. Part Second containing Engravings of the Muscles and the Joints. The First American Edition from the Second London Edition. Philadelphia: 1816. V. 37; 38; 43; 45

Observations on Italy. Edinburgh: 1825. V. 44

Observations on Italy . . . Naples: 1834. V. 45

Observations on Italy. London: 1825. V. 37

Principles of Surgery. New York: 1810. V. 42

The Principles of Surgery, as They Relate to Wounds, Ulcers, Fistulae, Aneurisms, Wounded Arteries, Fractures of the Limbs, Tumors, the Operations of Trepan and Lithotomy. London: 1826. V. 40

Rhymes of Northern Bards . . . Newcastle-upon-Tyne: 1812. V. 42

Travels from St. Petersburg in Russia, to Diverse Parts of Asia. Glagow: 1763. V. 42; 43; 45

BELL, JULIAN

We Did Not Fight - 1914-1918 Experiences of War Resisters. London: 1935. V. 41

Winter Movement and Other Poems. London: 1930. V. 44

Work for the Winter - More or Less for Christmas. London: 1935. V. 42

BELL, LANDON C.

Cumberland Parish Lunenburg County, Virginia, 1746-1816: Vestry Book, 1746-1816. Richmond: 1930. V. 42

The Old Free State: a Contribution to the History of Lunnenburg County and Southside Virginia. Richmond: 1927. V. 42

BELL, LILIAN

About Miss Mattie Morning-Glory. Chicago: 1916. V. 39

BELL, LILLIAN

The Runaway Equator. New York: 1911. V. 37

BELL, MAC KENZIE

Christina Rossetti - a Biographical and Critical Study. London: 1898. V. 43

BELL, MADISON SMARTT

The Washington Square Ensemble. New York: 1983. V. 42; 44; 46

BELL, MALCOLM

Edward Burne-Jones. A Record and Review. London: 1892. V. 42; 44

Edward Burne-Jones. A Record and Review. London: 1893. V. 38

Sir Edward Burne Jones. London. V. 44

BELL, MARCUS

Message of Love. Atlanta: 1860. V. 42

BELL, MARVIN

Things We Dreamt We Died For. Iowa City: 1966. V. 46

BELL, NANCY

The Saints in Christian Art. London: 1901-04. V. 39

BELL, NANCY R. E. MEUGENS d. 1933

Representative Painters of the XIXth Century. London: 1899. V. 38; 41

BELL, QUENTIN

Those Impossible English. London: 1952. V. 38; 39; 40; 42

BELL, ROBERT

Golden Leaves from the Works of the Poets and Painters. London: 1863. V. 38; 40

The Ladder of Gold, an English Story. London: 1850. V. 37; 39; 40; 41; 44

The Life of the Rt. Hon. George Canning. London: 1846. V. 45

A Treatise on the Election Laws, As They Relate to the Representation of Scotland, in the Parliament of the United Kingdom of Great Britain and Ireland. Edinburgh: 1812. V. 43

BELL, SOLOMON

Tales of Travels West of the Mississippi. Boston: 1830. V. 46

BELL, T.

A History of the British Stalk-Eyed Crustacea. London: 1853. V. 37

BELL, T. J.

Into Action with the 12th Field. N.P.. V. 40

Into Action with the 12th Field 1940-1945. Utrecht: 1945. V. 41

BELL, THOMAS

The Anatomy, Physiology and Diseases of the Teeth. London: 1829. V. 37; 45

The Anatomy, Physiology and Diseases of the Teeth. Philadlephia: 1830. V. 43

The Anatomy, Physiology and Diseases of the Teeth. London: 1835. V. 38; 41

The Anatomy, Physiology and Diseases of the Teeth. London: 1855. V. 43

The Anatomy, Physiology and Diseases of the Teeth. Philadelphia: 1831. V. 37

A History of British Quadrupeds. London: 1837. V. 43; 44; 45

A History of British Reptiles. London: 1839. V. 38

A History of the British Stalk-Eyed Crustacea. London: 1853. V. 43

The Ruins of Liveden. London: 1847. V. 39

BELL, THOMAS J.

into Action with the 12th Field . . . Utrecht: 1945. V. 45

BELL, VANESSA

Notes on Virginia's Childhood - a Memoir. New York: 1974. V. 45

BELL, W.

A New Compendious Grammar of the Greek Tongue. London: 1775. V. 41

BELL, WALTER DALRYMPLE MAITLAND 1800-1851

Bell of Africa. London: 1960. V. 38

Karamojo Safari. New York: 1949. V. 39; 40; 44; 45

The Wanderings of an Elephant Hunter. London: 1923. V. 39; 40; 43; 44; 45

BELL, WALTER G.

The Thames from Chelsea to the Nore . . . London: 1907. V. 44

BELL, WHITFIELD J.

Early American Science Needs and Opportunities for Study. Williamsburg: 1955. V. 42

BELL, WILLIAM 1780-1844

Papers Relative to the Regalia of Scotland. Edinburgh: 1829. V. 42; 45

Papers Relative to the Regalia of Scotland. Edinburgh: 1829. V. 45

Poetry from Oxford in Wartime. London: 1945. V. 39

BELL, WILLIAM A.

New Tracks in North America: a Journal of Travel and Adventure Whilst Engaged in the Survey for a Southern Railroad to the Pacific Ocean During 1857-8. London: 1869. V. 37; 38; 39; 43; 44; 45

New Tracks in North America. A Journal of Travel and Adventure Whilst Engaged in the Survey for a Southern Railroad to the Pacific Ocean during 1867-8. London/New York: 1870. V. 37; 38

BELL, WILLIAM E.

Carpentry Made Easy; or, the Science and Art of Framing, on a New and Improved System. Philadelphia: 1868. V. 41

Carpentry Made Easy; or, the Science and Art of Framing, on a New and Improved System. Philadelphia: 1883. V. 38; 40; 42; 45

Carpentry Made Easy or Science and Art of Framing, On a New and Improved System. Philadelphia: 1885. V. 42

BELL, WILLIAM H.

The Quiddities of an Alaskan Trip. Portland, C.A.: 1873. V. 37; 39

BELLA, STEAFANO DELLA

Orazione Recitata da Lui Pubbli . . . Nell'Esequie Celebrate Alla Impre. Ferdinando II . . . Florence: 1637. V. 38; 39

BELLA, STEFANO DELLA

Views of the Gardens of the Villa Pratolino. Florence. V. 44

BELLAIRS, BLANCHE ST. JOHN, LADY

The Transvaal War 1880-81. London: 1887. V. 41

BELLAIRS, GEORGE

Death in Desolation. London: 1967. V. 44

Fatal Alibi. London: 1968. V. 44

Intruder in the Dark. London: 1966. V. 44

Single Ticket to Death. London: 1967. V. 44

BELLAMNY, DANIEL

Miscellànies in Prose and Verse . . . London: 1741-1740. V. 45

BELLAMY, DANIEL

Ethic Amsuements . . . London: 1768. V. 38; 40; 43

Ethic Amusements. London: 1768, 1770. V. 38; 42

BELLAMY, EDWARD 1850-1898

Equality. New York: 1897. V. 37

Looking Backward, 2000-1887. Boston: 1888. V. 37; 39; 41; 42

Looking Backward 2000-1887. London: 1890. V. 42

BELLAMY, GEORGE ANNE

Memoirs of George Anne Bellamy, including all her Intrigues; with geniune anecdotes of all her public and private connections. By a Gentleman of Covent-Garden Theatre. London: 1785. V. 37; 42

BELLAMY, J. C.

The Natural History of South Devon. Plymouth: 1839. V. 37; 38; 43

BELLAMY, JOHN

The Opinion; or the Theology of the Serpent, and the Unity of God. London: 1811. V. 46

BELLAMY, JOSEPH 1719-1790

An Essay on the Nature and Glory of the Gospel of Jesus Christ . . . Boston: 1762. V. 44

True Religion Delineated; or, Experimental Religion, As Distinguished from Formality on the One Hand, and Enthusiasm on the Other . . . Boston: 1750. V. 44

BELLARMIN, ROBERT

De Officio Principis Christiani. Rome: 1619. V. 37; 40

De Scriptoribus Ecclesiasticis . . . Rome: 1613. V. 38

BELLARMINE, ROBERT

Arrest de la Cour de Parlement de Paris, Contre le Livre du Cardinal Bellarmin . . . Paaris: 1611. V. 38

Institutiones Linguae Hebraicae. Antwerp: 1616. V. 44

BELLARMINO, ROBERTO

De Officio Principis Christiani Libri Tres . . . Roma: 1619. V. 37

BELLASIS, EDWARD

Westmorland Church Notes. Kendal: 1888-89. V. 41

BELLASIS, GEORGE HUTCHINS

Views of Saint Helena. London: 1815. V. 40

THE BELLE Epoque of French Jewellery 1850-1910: Jewellery Making in Paris 1850-1910. London: 1911. V. 46

BELLECOUR, ABBE

The Academy of Play. London: 1769? V. 38

BELLEMARE, LUIS DE

The Wood Rangers. London: 1860. V. 46

BELLENDEN, WILLIAM

De Statu Libri Tres. N.P.: 1787. V. 44

BELLERBY, FRANCES

Selected Poems. London: 1970. V. 41

BELLERS, E. V. R.

The History of the 1st King George V's Own Gurkha Rifles (The Malaun Regiment). Volume II: 1920-1947. Aldershot: 1956. V. 41

BELLERS, FETTIPLACE

A Delineation of Universal Law. London: 1754. V. 37

BELLERS, JOHN 1654-1725

An Essay Towards the Improvement of Physick. London: 1714. V. 38

BELLESHEIM, A.

History of the Catholic Church in Scotland. Edinburgh: 1887. V. 38; 39

BELLEVIEW Marion County Florida. Lynn: 1885. V. 45

BELLEW, CHRISTOPHER D.

A Catalogue of the Mount Bellew Library. Dublin: 1814. V. 39

BELLEW, FRANK

The Art of Amusing. New York: 1866. V. 38

BELLEW, H. W.

Journal of a Political Mission to Afghanistan, in 1857, Under Major (now Colonel) Lumsden; with an Account of the Country and People. London: 1862. V. 41; 45

BELLEW, HENRY WALTER

The Races of Afghanistan, Being a Brief Account of the Principal Natiaons Inhabiting the Country. Calcutta: 1880. V. 37

BELLI, MELVIN M.

The Law Revolt, a Summary of Trends in Modern Criminal and Civil Law. Bellville: 1968. V. 44

BELLI, SILVIO

Libro del Misurar con la Vista. Domenico de' Nicolini,: 1565. V. 42

Quattro Libri Geometrici . . . del Misurare con la Vista . . . della Proportione e Proportionalita Communi Passioni del Quanto. Venice: 1595. V. 37; 39

BELLIER DE LA CHAVIGNERIE

V. 46

BELLIN, J. N.

Description Geographic des Isles Antilles Possedees par les Anglois. Paris: 1758. V. 38; 39; 42

BELLINGER, LUCIUS

Stray Leaves From the Port-Folio of a Methodist Local Preacher. Macon: 1870. V. 45

BELLINGHAM, WILLIAM

The Diary of a Working Man . . . in Central Africa December 1884 to October 1887. London: 1888. V. 39

BELLINGSHAUSEN, THADDEUS

The Voyage of Captain Bellingshausen to the Antarctic Seas 1819-21. London: 1945. V. 40; 46

BELLINI, LORENZO

Opuscula Aliquot ad Archibaldum Pitcarnium Professorem Lugduno-Batavm. Pistoia: 1695. V. 37; 45

BELLOC, HILAIRE 1870-1953

Advice to the Rich. London: 1925. V. 39; 40

The Aftermath; or, Gleanings from a Busy Life . . . London: 1920. V. 45

The Bad Child's Book of Beasts. London: 1896. V. 40; 44; 46

Belinda - a Tale of Affection in Youth and Age. London: 1928. V. 38; 44

But Soft - We Are Observed! London: 1928. V. 37

Cautionary Tales for Children - Designed for the Admonition of Children Between the Ages of Eight and Fourteen Years. London: 1908. V. 41

The Chanty of the Nona. London: 1928. V. 40

Characters of the Reformation. New York: 1936. V. 45

Charles the First - King of England. London: 1933. V. 38

Counsels for 1927. London: 1927. V. 39

The Cruise of the 'Nona'. London: 1925. V. 43

The Emerald. 1926. V. 37

The Emerald of Katherine the Great. New York: 1926. V. 45

Four Cautionary Tales and a Moral. London: 1909. V. 46

A General Sketch of the European War . . . The First Phase . . . The Second Phase. London: 1915-16. V. 44

The Great Inquiry. London: 1903. V. 40

The Haunted House. 1927. V. 37

An Herioc Poem in Praise of Wine. London: 1932. V. 37; 43

The Highway and Its Vehicles. London: 1926. V. 39; 40; 41; 43

Ladies and Gentlemen: for Adults Only, and Mature at That. London: 1932. V. 44

Lambkin's Remains. Oxford: 1900. V. 44; 45

The Man Who Made Gold. London: 1930. V. 44

The Missing Masterpiece. London: (1929). V. 37; 41

Mr. Clutterbuck's Election. London: 1908. V. 37

The Modern Traveller. London: 1898. V. 37; 40; 42; 44

A Moral Alphabet. London: 1899. V. 37; 44

More Beasts. London: 1897. V. 44

New Cautionary Tales. London: 1930. V. 38; 39; 44; 45

New Cautionary Tales. London: 1930. V. 38

The Party System. London: 1911. V. 43

Pongo and the Bull. London: 1910. V. 38; 40; 41; 42

The Post-Master General. London: 1932. V. 37

The Priase of Wine, an Heroic Poems. London: 1931. V. 39; 40

Return to the Baltic. London: 1938. V. 41

Robespierre. A Study. New York. V. 41

Shadowed! New York: 1929. V. 37

Short Talks with the Dead and Others. London: 1926. V. 40

The Stane Street: a Monograph. London: 1913. V. 46

Sussex. London: 1913. V. 40

Why Eat? N.P.. V. 40

Wolsey. London: 1930. V. 40

BELLORI, GIOVANNI PIETRO

Le Antiche Lucerne Sepolcrali Figurate Raccolte Dalle Caue Sotterranee, e Grotte di Roma . . . Roma: 1691. V. 44

Fragmenta Vestigii Veteris Romae ex Lapidibus Farnesianis. Rome: 1673. V. 40

Veteres Arcus Augustorum Triumphis Insignes Ex Reliquiis Que Romae Adhuc Supersunt cum Imaginibus Triumphalibus Restituti Antiquis Nummis Notisque. Rome: 1690. V. 44

BELLOSTE, AUGUSTIN

Le Chirurgien d'Hopital . . . Paris: 1696. V. 37

BELLOW, SAUL 1915-

The Adventures of Augie March. New York: 1953. V. 37; 38; 39; 43; 45

Dangling man. London: 1946. V. 37; 40; 41; 42; 45

Dangling Man. New York: 1944. V. 42; 43; 45

BELLOW, SAUL 1915- continued

The Dean's December. New York: 1982. V. 39; 43; 45; 46

Henderson, the Rain King. London: 1959. V. 45

Henderson the Rain King. New York: 1959. V. 38; 40; 43; 45

Herzog. New York: 1964. V. 45; 46

Him With His Foot In His Mouth and Other Stories. New York: 1984. V. 45

humboldt's Gift. New York: 1975. V. 45

The Last Analysis. New York: 1965. V. 39

Mr. Sammler's Planet. New York: 1970. V. 45

More Die of Heartbreak. New York: 1987. V. 42

Nobel Lecture. New York: 1979. V. 43; 46

Seize the Day. New York: 1956. V. 38; 39

Seize the Day. London: 1957. V. 45

A Silver Dish. New York: 1979. V. 41; 42; 45; 46

The Victim. London: 1948. V. 37; 38; 40; 45

BELLOWS, EMMA S.

George Bellows: His Lithographs. New York: 1928. V. 39; 42; 43; 45; 46

BELLOWS, GEORGE

George W. Bellows, His Lithographs. Preface by Thomas Beers. New York: 1927. V. 37

His Lithographs. New York: 1928. V. 41

BELL'S British Theatre. London: 1791. V. 38

BELL'S British Theatre. Printed Under Direction of John Bell, for the Proprietors. London: 1791-1797. V. 44

BELL'S New Pantheon; or Historical Dictionary of the Gods, Demi-Gods, Heroes, and Fabulous Persoanges of Antiquity . . . London: 1790. V. 39; 41

BELL'S New Pantheon; or Historical Dictionary of the Gods, Demi-Gods, Heroes and Fabulous Personages of Antiquity . . . . London: 1790. V. 41

BELMONT, AUGUST

A Few Letters and Speeches of the Late Civil War. New York: 1870. V. 37; 38; 42; 44

Letters and Address of . . . from the Hauge, on the Causes and Conduct of the Civil War, on the Financial Policy of the United States, on the Principles and Policy of the Democratic Party . . . New York: 1890. V. 46

BELMORE, EARL OF

The History of the Two Ulster Manors of Finagh, Co. Tyrone and Coole, Manor Atkinson, Co. Fermanagh and of their Owners. London: 1881. V. 43

Parliamentary Memoirs of Fermanagh County and Borough, from 1613 to 1885. Dublin: 1885. V. 43

BELOE, W.

Anecdotes of literature and scarce books. 1808-12. V. 37

BELOE, WILLIAM

Anecdotes of Literature and Scarce Books. London: 1807. V. 44

Anecdotes of Literature and Scarce Books. London: 1807-12. V. 37; 38; 41; 44; 46

Anecdotes of Literature and Scarce Books. London: 1814/8/10/11/12. V. 46

Poems and Translations. London: 1788. V. 44

The Sexagenarian; or, Recollections of a Literary Life. London: 1817. V. 37; 38; 39; 41; 42; 43; 46

BELON DU MANS, PIERRE

La Nature & Diversite des Poissons . . . 1555. V. 46

Les Observations de Plusieurs Singularitez & Choses Memorables . . . Paris: 1555. V. 46

BELON, P.

L'Histoire de la Nature des Oyseaux, Avec Leurs Descriptions, et Naifs Portraicts. Paris: 1555. V. 41

BELON, PIERRE

De Aquatilibus. Libri Duo . . . Paris: 1553. V. 40

BELOT, JEAN

L'Oeuvre des Oeuvres, ou le Plus Parfaict des Sciences Steganographiques Paulines, Armadelles & Lullistes, par Lesquelles Facilement se Comprend, s'apprend, & l'on Cognoist son Genie, & par Iceluy la Perfection de Toutes les Sciences . . . Paris: 1622. V. 38

BELSHAM, THOMAS 1750-1829

Elements of the Philosophy of the Mind and of Moral Philosophy, To Which is Prefixed a Compendium of Logic. London: 1801. V. 37; 40; 41; 43; 45

BELSHAM, W.

Essays Philosophical and Moral, Historical and Literary. London: 1799. V. 38

BELSHAM, WILLIAM

Essays, Philosophical, Historical and Literary. London: 1789/91. V. 41; 42; 45

Essays, Philosophical, Historical and Literary. Dublin: 1790/91. V. 42

Memoirs of the Reign of George III to the Session of Parliament Ending A.D. 1793. London: 1795. V. 45

BELT, T.

The Naturalist in Nicaragua. London: 1874. V. 38

The Naturalist in Nicaragua. London: 1888. V. 37; 43

BELTRAMI, GIACOMO C.

A Pilgrimage in Europe and America, Leading to the Discovery of the Sources of the Mississippi and Bloody River; with a Description of the Whole Course of the Former, and of the Ohio. London: 1828. V. 37; 38; 39; 40; 41; 43; 45

BELZONI, G.

Narrative of the Operations and Recent Discoveries . . . in Egypt and Nubia; and of a Journey to the Coast of the Red Sea, In Search of the Ancient Berenice. London: 1821. V. 40

Narrative of the Operations and Recent Discoveries Within the Pyramids, Temples, Tombs and Excavations, in Egypt and Nubia; and of a Journey to the Coast of the Red Sea, In Search of Ancient Berenice. London: 1822. V. 38; 40

BELZONI, GIOVANNI BATTISTA

Narrative of the Operations and Recent Discoveries within the Pyramids, Temples, Tombs and Excavations, in Egypt and Nubia . . . (with) Plates Illustrative of the Researches and Operations of G. Belzoni in Egypt and Nubia. London: 1820. V. 42

Narrative of the Operations and Recent Discoveries Within the Pyramids, Temples, Tombs and Excavations, in Egypt and Nubia . . . Brussels: 1835. V. 40; 42

BEMAN, DAVID

The Mysteries of Trade, or the Great Sources of Wealth. Boston: 1825. V. 43

BEMBO, PIETRO

Rerum Venetarum Historiae Libri XII. Paris: 1551. V. 38; 39; 40

Rerum Venetarum Historiae Libri XII. Paris: 1551. V. 40

BEMBO, PIETRO, CARDINAL 1470-1547

De Aetna Liber, On Etna. Verona: 1969. V. 42

De Aetna Liber, On Etna. Verona: 1969. V. 43

De Gliasolani. Venice: 1530. V. 37

Della Istoria Viniziana . . . Vinegia: 1790. V. 46

Epistolae, Omnes Quotquot Extant, Latinae Puritatis Studiosis ad Imitandum Utilissimae . . . Padua: 1535. V. 46

Bembi Epistolarum Leonis Decimi Pont. Max. Nomine Scriptarum Libri XVI. Lugduni: 1540. V. 40

Epistolarum Leonis X Nomine Scriptarum Libri XV. Lyon: 1540. V. 38; 39

Epistolarum Leonis Decimi Pontificis Max. Nomine Scriptarum, Libri XVI. Basle: 1547. V. 45

Epistolarum Familiarum Libri VI. Venice: 1552. V. 40

Gli Asolani. Venice: 1505. V. 43

Gli Asolani. In Vinegia: 1553. V. 44

De Gliasolani di M. Pietro Bembo Nqvali si Ragiona d'Amore. Colophon: 1530. V. 42

Historiae Venetae Libri XII. Venice: 1551. V. 37; 42

Letters Between Lucrezia Borgia and Pietro Bembo. London: 1985. V. 46

Messer Pietro Mio: The Letters Between Lucrezia Borgia and Pietro Bembo, 1503-1515. 1985. V. 40

Petri Bembi De Aetna Liber & Pietro Bembo on Etna. Verona: 1969. V. 40

Prose Nelle Quali Si Ragiona Sulla Volgar Lingua Scritte al Cardinale Da Medici. Venice: 1525. V. 37; 38; 40; 41

Prose . . . Nell Equali si Ragiona Della Volgar Lingua Scritte al Cardinale de Medici . . . Divise in tre Libri. Florence: 1549. V. 45

Rime. Colophon: 1540. V. 40

BEMELMANS, LUDWIG

The Donkey Inside. New York: 1941. V. 40; 43

Father, Dear Father. New York: 1953. V. 38; 39; 40; 42; 43

Hotel Splendide. New York: 1941. V. 40; 42; 44

Madeline. New York: 1939. V. 40; 45

Madeline and the Bad Hat. New York: 1956. V. 46

My War with the United States. New York: 1937. V. 39

Now I Lay Down to Sleep. New York: 1943. V. 37; 39; 42; 44; 45

Small Beer. New York: 1939. V. 37; 40

Sunshine: a Story About the City of New York. New York: 1950. V. 42

BEMENT, C. N.

The American Poulterer's Companion. New York: 1856. V. 41

BEMIS, A. F.

The Evolving House. 1933/34/36. V. 46

BEMISS, ELIJAH

The Dyer's Companion. London: 1805. V. 37; 39; 42

The Dyer's Companion. New York: 1815. V. 39; 42; 43

BEMROSE, WILLIAM

The Life and Works of Joseph Wright, A.R.A., Commonly Called 'Wright of Derby.' London: 1885. V. 39

Longton Hall Porcelain. London & Derby: 1906. V. 41

Manual of Buhl-Work and Marquetry. London: 1860. V. 40; 41; 44

Manual of Buhl-Work and Marquetry with Practical Instructions for Learners and Ninety Coloured Designs. London: 1880. V. 44

Manual of Buhl-Work and Marquetry . . . London: 1887. V. 42

Manual of Wood Carving. London: 1862. V. 37

Mosaicon; or, Paper Mosaic. London: 1870. V. 39; 41; 44

Mosaicon: or Paper Mosaic, and How to Make It . . . London: 1876. V. 38

BENAVEN, JEAN MICHAEL

Le Caissier Italien, ou l'Art de Connoitre Toutes les Monnoies Actuelles d'Italie . . . Lyon: 1787. V. 38

BENAVIDES, ALONSO DE

The Memorial of Fray Alonso de Benaavides, 1630. Chicago: 1916. V. 38; 39; 44

The Memorial of Fray Alonso de Benavides, 1630. Chicago: 1926. V. 43

BENAVIDES, ALONZO FRAY

The Memorial of . . . Chicago: 1916. V. 37

BENAVIDES, FRAY ALONSO DE

Benavides's Revised memorial of 1634. Albuquerque: 1945. V. 45

BENCHELY, ROBERT

Of All Things. New York: 1921. V. 42

BENCHLEY, ROBERT

No Poems. New York: 1932. V. 43

BENDA, JULIEN

The Great Betrayal. London: 1928. V. 41

BENDER, ALBERT M.

George Sterling, the Man: A Tribute. 1929. V. 38

BENDINELLI, SCIPIO

Pro Universalib. Carmelitarum Congregationis Mantuanae Comitiis Oratio . . . Lucca: 1598. V. 45; 46

BENDIRE, CHARLES

Life Histories of No. American Birds with Special Reference to Their Breeding Habits and Eggs. Washington: 1892-95. V. 37; 38; 39; 45

BENEATH White Tents. Buffalo: 1894. V. 37

BENECKE, LOUIS

Some Light Upon a Chariton County Episode of '64. N.P.: 1895. V. 38

BENEDETTA, MARY

The Street Markets of London. London: 1936. V. 44

BENEDETTI, GIOVANNI BATTISTA 1530-1590

De Gnomonum Umbrarumque Solarium Usu Liber . . . Turin: 1574. V. 38; 42

BENEDETTI, L'ABBATE ELPIDIO

Pompa Funebre nell' Esequie Celebrate in Roma al CArdinal Mazarini. Rome: 1661. V. 46

BENEDETTO, SANTISSIMO

Il Padre San Benedetto con l'Espositione d'il R. Padre Frate Rogiero di Barletta, Monacho Celestino. Bologna: 1539. V. 39

Regola del Padre Santissimo Benedetto, Dall'idioma Latino Tradotta in Toscano & Commentata dal Reueren . . . Fiorenza: 1574. V. 39

BENEDICT, CARL PETERS

A Tenderfoot Kid on Gyp Water. Austin: 1943. V. 43

A Tenderfoot Kid on Gyp Water. Austin and Dallas: 1943. V. 39

BENEDICT, DAVID A.

General History of the Baptist Denomination in American and other Parts of the World. Boston: 1813. V. 37; 38

BENEDICT, ERASTUS C.

A Run through Europe. New York: 1860. V. 44

BENEDICT, FRANCIS

Metabolism in Diabetes Mellitus. Washington: 1910. V. 40

Muscular Work. Washington: 1913. V. 40

BENEDICT, PIERCE E. 1844-1912

History of Beverly Hills. Beverly Hills: 1934. V. 42

BENEDICT, WILLIAM H.

New Brunswick in History. New Brunswick: 1925. V. 44

BENEDICT XII, POPE d. 1342

Lettres Communes. Paris: 1903-11. V. 39

BENEDICTUS, JOHANNES

Pindari Olympia, Pythia, Nemea Isthmia ad Metri Rationem, Variorum Exempliarum Fidem . . . Salmurii (Samaur, France): 1620. V. 46

BENESCH, OTTO

The Drawings of Rembrandt. London: 1954. V. 46

Drawings of Rembrandt. London: 1973. V. 46

BENESE, RICHARD

The Boke of Measurying of Lande, Newly Invented and Compyled. London: 1563. V. 40

BENESKI, CHARLES DE

A Narrative of the Last Moments of the Life of Don Augustine de Iturbide. New York: 1825. V. 42

BENET, LAURA

Enchanting Jenny Lind. New York: 1939. V. 41; 42; 43; 44

BENET, S. V. 1827-1895

A Treatise on Military Law and Practice of Courts-Martial. New York: 1862. V. 38; 40

BENET, STEPHEN VINCENT 1898-1943

The Ballad of the Duke's Mercy. New York: 1939. V. 38; 41

Ballads and Poems, 1915-1930. Garden City: 1931. V. 39; 43

The Barefoot Saint. New York: 1929. V. 41

The Beginning of Wisdom. New York: 1921. V. 37; 43

The Bishop's Beggar, by Stephen Vincent Benet. (Flemington, NJ: 1968). V. 37

A Book of Americans. New York: 1933. V. 43

Burning City. New York: 1936. V. 37; 38; 43

The Devil and Daniel Webster. New York: 1937. V. 39

The Devil and Daniel Webster. Kingsport: 1945. V. 45

Five Men and Pompey. Boston: 1915. V. 37; 38; 42; 43; 44; 46

James Shore's Daughter. Garden City: 1934. V. 38; 39; 43

Jean Huguenot. New York: 1923. V. 38

John Brown's Body. New York: 1928. V. 37; 38; 39; 43

John Brown's Body. New York: 1980. V. 42

John Brown's Body, a Poem. New York: 1948. V. 37; 40

Johnny Pye and the Fool-Killer. Weston: 1938. V. 43

King David. 1923. V. 43

Spanish Bayonet. New York: 1926. V. 38

Tales Before Midnight. New York: 1939. V. 38; 41

Tiger Joy. New York: 1925. V. 41; 44

BENET, WILLIAM ROSE

The Dust Which is God. New York: 1941. V. 43

The Flying King of Kurio: a Story for Children. New York: 1926. V. 41; 43; 44

Merchants from Cathay. New York: 1913. V. 43

The Oxford Anthology of American Literature. New York: 1938. V. 43

BENEZET, ANTHONY 1713-1784

The Case of Our Fellow-Creatures, the Oppressed Africans, Respectfully Recommended to the Serious Consideration of the Legislature of Great Britain, By the People called Quakers. London: printed Philadelphia: 1784. V. 37; 41; 42

A Caution to Great Britain and Her Colonies, in a Short Representation of the Calamitous State of the Enslaved Negroes in the British Dominions. London: 1767. V. 40; 42

A Caution to Great Britain and Her Colonies, in a Short Representation of the Calamitous State of the Enslaved Negroes in the British Dominions. London: 1785. V. 40

A Caution to Great Britain and Her Colonies, in a Short Representation of the Calamitous State of the Enslaved Negroes in the British Dominions. Philadelphia Printed: 1785. V. 37; 43

A Caution to Great Britain and Her Colonies, in a Short Representation of the Calamitous State of the Enslaved Negroes in the British Dominions. Philadelphia & London: 1785. V. 37

The Mighty Destroyer Displayed, in Some Account of the Dreadful Havock Made by the Mistaken Use as Well as Abuse of Distilled Spirituous Liquors. Philadelphia: 1774. V. 40

BENNET, JOHN

Pomes on Several Occasions. London: 1774. V. 37; 40

BENNET, R. H. A.

Catalogue of the Duplicates of the Two Libraries . . . London: 180. V. 45

BENNET, ROBERT

King Charle's (sic) Trial Iustified; or, Eight Objections Against the Same Fully Answered and Cleared, by Scripture, Law, History and Reason. London: 1649. V. 40

BENNET, THOMAS 1673-1728

A Paraphrase with Annotations Upon the Book of Common Prayer. London: 1708. V. 39

A Short Account of Dr. Bentley's Humanity and Justice. London: 1699. V. 38

BENNET, WHITMAN

A Practical Guide to American Nineteenth Century Color Plate Books. New York: 1949. V. 39

BENNET, WILLIAM

Owain Goch: a Tale of the Revolution. London: 1827. V. 43

BENNETT, A. W.

The Flora of the Alps. London: 1896. V. 37; 38

The Flora of the Alps. London: 1897. V. 38; 40; 42

The Flora of the Alps. London: 1898. V. 38

BENNETT, AGNES MARIA

Anna; or Memoirs of a Welch Heiress. Dublin: 1786. V. 43

The Beggar Girl and Her Benefactors. London: 1797. V. 40

Les Imprudences de la Jeunese. A Londres: 1788. V. 41

BENNETT, ARNOLD 1867-1931

Anna of the Five Towns. London: 1902. V. 40

The Author's Craft. London: 1914. V. 42

The Bright Island. London: 1924. V. 37; 38; 39; 40; 42; 43; 44; 46

Buried Alive. By Arnold Bennet. Introduction by John Wain. Illustrated with pen drawings by Moira Stephenson. Oxford: 1987. V. 37; 42; 45

The Clayhanger Family. London: 1925. V. 43; 44

The Clayhanger Family. London: 1935. V. 44

Don Juan Marana: a Play in Four Acts. London: 1923. V. 40; 41; 44; 46

Elsie and the Child. London: 1929. V. 45

Elsie and the Child. London: 1929. V. 37; 40; 43; 44; 45

Elsie and the Child. London: 1920. V. 37

The Glimpse: An Adventure of the Soul. London: 1912. V. 43; 44

The Grand Babylon Hotel: a Fantasia on Modern Themes. London: 1902. V. 46

The Grim Smile of the Five Towns. London: 1907. V. 45

Hilda Lessways. London: 1911. V. 40

Imperial Palace. London: 1930. V. 43

Journalism for Women. A Practical Guide. London and New York: 1898. V. 39

The Journals of Arnold Bennett 1896-1928. London: 1933. V. 44

Literary Taste . . . New York: 1910. V. 42

Lord Raingo. London: 1926. V. 43

The Man from the North. London: 1898. V. 38; 39; 43

A Man from the North. London: & New York: 1898. V. 46

The Old Wive's Tale. London: 1908. V. 39; 40; 41; 46

The Old Wives' Tale. London: 1927. V. 37; 39; 42; 44; 46

The Old Wives' Tale. New York: 1941. V. 43

The Old Wives' Tale. Oxford: 1941. V. 39; 40; 41

The Old Wives' Tale. New York: 1909. V. 37

The Old Wives' Tales. London: 1908. V. 37

Our Women: Chapters on the Sex-Discord. London: 1920. V. 42

Riceyman Steps. London: 1923. V. 43

These Twain. London: 1916. V. 40

Venus Rising from the Sea. London: 1931. V. 37; 40; 42; 46

BENNETT, C H.

Shadow & Substance. London: 1860. V. 38

BENNETT, CHARLES

Quarles Emblems. London: 1861. V. 44

Shadows. Second Series. (ca. 1860). V. 37

BENNETT, CHARLES H.

The Book of Blockheads. London: 1863. V. 46

Lightsome and the Little Golden Lady. London: 1867. V. 46

Shadow and Substance. London: 1859. V. 45

Shadow and Substance. London: 1860. V. 41; 45; 46

BENNETT, CHRISTOPHER

Tabidorum Theatrum: Sive, Pthisios, Atrophiae & Hecticae Xenodochium. London: 1656. V. 44

BENNETT, D. M.

Trial of D. M. Bennett, in the United States Circuit Court. New York: 1879. V. 41

BENNETT, DOUGLAS

Irish Georgian Silver. London: 1972. V. 43

BENNETT, EDWARD TURNER 1797-1836

The Gardens and Menagerie of the Zoological Society Delineated. London: 1830-31. V. 38

The Gardens and Menagerie of the Zoological Society Delineated. Chiswick: 1831. V. 37; 39; 45

BENNETT, EMERSON

The Bandits of the Osage. Cincinnati: 1847. V. 45

The Border Lily. N.P.: 1873? V. 41

The Border Robert. Philadelphia: 1857. V. 41

The Border Rover. Philadelphia: 1857. V. 41

The Fair Rebel; A Tale of Colonial Times. Cincinnati: 1853. V. 40

The Heiress of Bellefont. Philadelphia: 1855. V. 40

The Outlaw's Daughter. Philadelphia: 1871. V. 44

BENNETT, FRANK M.

The Steam Navy of the United States, The History of the Growth of the Steam Vessel of War from Fulton's 'Demologus' 1815 to the Steel Torpedo Boats, 1896. Pittsburgh: 1896. V. 38; 44

BENNETT, FREDERICK DEBELL

Narrative of a Whaling Voyage Round the Globe, from the year 1833 to 1836. London: 1840. V. 38; 39

BENNETT, GEORGE

Gatherings of a Naturalist in Australasia: Being Obervations Principally on the Animal and Vegetable Productions of New South Wales, New Zealand, and some of the Austral Islands. London: 1860. V. 39; 41; 43; 44

The History of Bandon and the Principal Towns in the West Riding of Cork. Cork: 1869. V. 37; 42; 43

Wanderings in New South Wales, Batavia, Pedir Coast, Singapore and China: Being the Journal of a Naturalist in Those Countries During 1832, 1833 and 1834. London: 1834. V. 38; 45

BENNETT, GEORGE F.

Early Architecture of Delaware. Wilmington: 1932. V. 46

BENNETT, GEORGIANA

Woman and Her Duties. London: 1860. V. 45

BENNETT, H.

The Chemical Formulary, a Condensed Collection of Valuable, Timely, Practical Formulae for Making Thousands of Products in all Fields of Industry. Brooklyn & London: 1933-41. V. 37

BENNETT, H. S.

English Books and Readers. Cambridge: 1952/65/70. V. 42

Quia Amore Langueo. 1927. V. 37

BENNETT, J. E.

The Law of Titles to Indian Lands. Oklahoma City: 1917. V. 38

BENNETT, J. W.

The Coco-Nut Tree, Its Uses and Cultivation . . . with a View to the Encouragement of a More Extensive Cultivation of this Invaluable Palm in the British and West African Colonies. London: 1830. V. 39

Gene Manipulation in Fungi. London: 1985. V. 37

A Selection of Rare and Curious Fishes Found Upon the Coast of Ceylon. London: 1851. V. 42

BENNETT, JAMES

The History of Tewksbury. Tewksbury: 1830. V. 41

Overland Journey to California. Journal of James Bennett Whose Party Left New Harmony in 1850 and Crossed the Plains and Mountains Until the Golden West Was Reached. New York: 1932. V. 42; 43

BENNETT, JOHN

Letters to a Young Lady, On a Variety of Useful and Interesting Subjects . . . Hartford: 1792. V. 44

Letters to a Young Lady, on a Variety of Useful and Interesting Subjects, Calculated to Improve the Heart, to Form the Manners, and Enlighten the Understanding. London: 1795. V. 42; 43; 46

Letters to a Young Lady, on a Variety of Useful and Interesting Subjects . . . Hartford: 1798. V. 45

Letters to a Young Lady, on a Variety of Useful and Interesting Subjects. New York: 1816. V. 44

Letters to a Young Lady, On a Variety of Useful and Interesting Subjects . . . New York: 1816. V. 45

BENNETT, JOHN continued

Strictures on Fremale Education; Chiefly As It Relates to the Culture of the Heart. Dublin: 1798. V. 41

BENNETT, JOHN C.

Poultry Book: a Treatise on Breeding & General Management of Domestic Fowls; with Numerous Original Descriptions and Portraits from Life. Boston: 1850. V. 39

BENNETT, JOHN MIZRA

Letters from England. El Paso: 1946. V. 46

BENNETT, MARY

The Cottage Girl; or, The Marriage Day. N.P.: 1867. V. 44

BENNETT, MELBA BERRY

Robinson Jeffers and the Sea. San Francisco: 1936. V. 38; 46

BENNETT, PAUL A.

Postscripts on Dwiggins. New York: 1960. V. 38

BENNETT, RICHARD

Catalogue of the Collection of Old Chinese Porcelain Formed by Richard Bennett Esq. of Thornby Hall, Northampton Purchased and Exhibited by Gorer. Gorer. V. 40; 46

Catalogue of the Collection of Old Chinese Porcelain Formed by Richard Bennett Esq., Thornby Hall, Northampton. Purchased and Exhibited by Gorer, New Bond St. London. V. 38

A Catalogue of the Early Printed Books and Illuminated Manuscripts Collected by Richard Bennett. Guildford: 1900. V. 39

Catalogue of the Collection of Old Chine Porcelains Formed by Richard Bennett, Esq., Thornby Hall, Northampton. London: 1920. V. 42

History of Corn Milling. London: 1898-1904. V. 39

The Story of Bovil. London: 1953. V. 40

BENNETT, ROBERT

The Wrath of John Steinbeck. Los Angeles: 1939. V. 39; 41; 44

BENNETT, SAMUEL

A New Explanation of the Ebbing and Flowing of the Sea, Upon the Principles of Gravitation. New York: 1816. V. 42

BENNETT, THOMAS

A Short Introduction of Grammar. London: 1707. V. 45

BENNETT, W. A.

A Practical Guide to American Book Collecting (1663-1940). New York: 1941. V. 41

BENNETT, WENDELL

The Tarahumara, an Indian Tribe of Northern Mexico. Chicago: 1935. V. 44; 45

BENNETT, WHITMAN

A Practical Guide to American Book Collecting (1663-1940). New York: 1941. V. 38

Practical Guide to American Nineteenth Century Color Plate Books. New York: 1949. V. 42

BENNETT, WILLIAM

Builders of British Columbia. Vancouver: 1937. V. 39

BENNETT, WILLIAM C.

The Worn Wedding Ring. London: 1861. V. 44; 45; 46

BENNETT, WILLIAM P.

The Sky-Sifter The Great Chieftainess and 'Medicine Woman' of the Mohawks. N.P.: 1892. V. 39; 40

BENNI, CYRIL BENHAM

The Tradition of the Syriac Church in Antioch. London: 1871. V. 37

BENNISON, W.

The Cause of the Money Crisis Explained in Answer to the Pamphlet of Mr J. Horsley Palmer; and Remedy Pointed Out. London: 1837. V. 38; 41

BENOIS, ALEXANDRE

The Russian School of Painting. New York: 1916. V. 41; 42

BENOIST, ELIE

The History of the Famous Edict of Nantes . . . London: 1694. V. 44

BENOIT, P. J.

Voyage a Surinam. Description Des Possessions Neerlandaises Dans La Guyane. Bruxelles: 1839. V. 40

BENROSE, C.

Life Histories of North American Birds with Special Reference to Their Breeding habits and Eggs. Washington: 1892-95. V. 39

BENSCHOTER, GEORGE E.

Book of Facts Concerning the Early Settlement of Sherman County, Descriptive of Its Present Business and Agricultural Developments and Natural Advantages. Loup City: 1897. V. 39

BENSON, ARTHUR CHRISTOPHER 1862-1925

The Book of the Queen's Dolls' House (and) The Book of the Queen's Dolls' House Library. London: 1924. V. 38; 40; 45

Le Cahier Jaune Poems. Eton: 1892. V. 43

Lord Vyet and Other Poems. London: 1897. V. 40

BENSON, D. R.

Irene, Good-Night. New York: 1982. V. 46

BENSON, EGBERT

Memoir, Read Before the Historical Society of the State of New York, 31st December, 1816. New York: 1817. V. 46

Vindication of the Captors of Major Andre. New York: 1865. V. 39; 42

Vindication of the Captors of Major Andre. New York: 1817. V. 37

BENSON, FRANK W.

American Etchers. Volume XII: Frank W. Benson. New York: 1931. V. 40; 45

BENSON, HENRY C.

Life Among the Choctaw Indians, and Sketches of the South West. Cincinnati: 1860. V. 37; 39; 42; 43; 45

BENSON, JAMES W.

Time and Time-Tellers. London: 1875. V. 39

BENSON, JOSEPH

The Battle of Flodden-Field . . . London: 1774. V. 41; 42

The Battle of Flodden-Field: which was fought between the English under the Earl of Surrey, (in the Absence of King Henry VIII) and the Scots under their valiant King James IV who was Slain on the Field of Battle in the . . . Lacaster: 1805. V. 37

The Life of Rev. John W. de la Flechere . . . London: 1805. V. 45

BENSON, L.

The Cacti of the United States and Canada. Stanford: 1982. V. 37; 38; 39

BENSON, MARGARET

The Temple of Mut in Asher. London: 1899. V. 44

BENSON, NATHANIEL A.

Modern Canadian Poetry. Ottawa: 1930. V. 37

Poems. Toronto: 1927. V. 37

BENSON, RICHARD

Morni; and Irish Bardic Story, in Three Cantos: and The Pilgrim of Carmel; an Eastern Tale, in One Canto. Dublin: 1815. V. 37; 41

BENSON, ROBERT

The Holford Collection Dorchester House. With 200 illustrations from the twelfth to the end of the nineteenth century. In Two Volumes. London: 1927. V. 37

Sketches of Corsica; or, a Journal Written During a Visit to that Island, in 1823. London: 1825. V. 37

BENSON, THOMAS

Vocabularium Anglo-Saxonicum, Lexico Gul. Somneri Magna Parte Auctius. Oxoniae: 1701. V. 43; 46

BENSON, WILLIAM

Principles of the Science of Colour Concisely Stated to Aid and Promote Their Useful Application in the Decorative Arts. London: 1876. V. 45

Virgil's Husbandry, Or an Essay on the Georgics: Being the First Book. Translated into English Verse. To which are added the latin Text and Mr. Dryden's Version. With Notes critical & Rustick. London: 1725. V. 37

Virgil's Husbandry, or an essay on the Georgics: being the second book translated into English verse. To which are added the Latin Text, and Mr. Dryden's version. With notes . . . London: 1724. V. 37

BENSUSAN, A. D.

Silver Images. Cape Town: 1966. V. 44

BENSUSAN, S. L.

Morocco. London: 1904. V. 38; 44

BENT, A. C.

Life Histories of North American Birds. Washington: 1971. V. 39

BENT, CHARLES

History of Whiteside County, Illinois, from Its First Settlement to the Present Time. Morrison: 1877. V. 38; 42

BENT, NEWELL

American Polo. New York: 1929. V. 43

BENT, W.

A General Catalogue of Books in all Languages, Arts and Sciences, Printed in Great Britain and Published in London, from the Year MDCC to MDCCLXXXVI... London: 1786. V. 41

BENTALOU, PAUL

Pulaski Vindicated From an Unsupported Charge Inconsiderately or Malignantly Introduced in Judge Johnson's Sketches of the Life and Correspondence of Major Gen. Nathaniel Green. Baltimore: 1824. V. 42

Reply to Judge Johnson's Remarks on an Article in the North American Review, Relating to Count Pulaski. Baltimore: 1826. V. 45

BENTHAM, EDWARD

De Tumultibus Americanis Deque Eorum Concitatoribus Meditatio Senilis. Oxford: 1776. V. 45

BENTHAM, G.

Flora Australiensis; a Description of the Plants of the Australian Territory. Amsterdam: 1966. V. 37; 39

BENTHAM, GEORGE

Outline of a New System of Logic, with Critical Examination of Dr. Whately's Elements of Logic. London: 1827. V. 41

BENTHAM, JAMES

The History and Antiquities of the Coventual and Cathedral Church of Ely; from the Foundation of the Monastery, A.D. 673, to the Year 1771. Norwich: 1812. V. 44

BENTHAM, JEREMY 1748-1832

Benthamiana; or, Select Extracts from the Works of ... Edinburgh: 1843. V. 45

The Book of Fallacies: from Unfinished Papers of Jeremy Bentham. London: 1824. V. 37; 38; 39; 41; 42; 43; 45

Church-of-Englandism and Its Catechism Examined: Preceded by Strictures on the Exclusionary System, as Pursued in the National Society's Schools: Interspersed with Parallel Views of the English and Scottish Established and Non Established Churches... London: 1818. V. 37; 38; 39; 42

The Correspondence of Jeremy Bentham: Volume 9: January 1817 to June 1820. Oxford: 1990. V. 44

Defence of Usury; Shewing the Impolicy of the Present Legal Restraints on the Terms of Pecuniary Bargains. Dublin: 1788. V. 41; 43; 44; 45

Defence of Usury ... London: 1790. V. 45

Defence of Usury. London: 1790. V. 41

Defense of Usury: Shewing the Impolicy of the Present Legal Restraints on the Terms of Pecuniary Bargains. To Which is Added, a Letter to Adam Smith, Esq. LL.D... Philadelphia: 1796. V. 39

Defence of Usury; Shewing the Impolicy of the Present Legal Restraints on the Terms of Pecuniary Bargains ... London: 1816. V. 39

Defence of Usury; Shewin the Impolicy of the Present Leal Restraints on the Terms of Pecuniary Bargains. London: 1818. V. 38; 39

Defense de l'Usure, ou Lettres sur les Inconvenients des Lois, qui Fixent le Taux de l'Interet de l'Argent ... Paris: 1828. V. 41

Deontology; or, the Science of Morality ... London: 1834. V. 39

Draught of a New Plan for the Organisation of the Judicial Establishment in France: Proposed as a Succedaneum to the Draught Presented, for the Same Purpose, by the Committee of Constitution, to the National Assembly, Dec. 21st. 1789 ... 1790. V. 37

Jeremy Bentham's Economic Writings. London: 1952-54. V. 39

Emancipate Your Colonies! London: 1830/1793. V. 42

Emancipate Your Colonies Addressed to the National Convention of France ... London: 1830. V. 37

A Fragment on Government; Being an Examination of What is Delivered, On the Subject of Government in General, in the Introduction to Sir William Blackstone's Commentaries ... Dublin: 1776. V. 45

A Fragment of Government. London: 1776. V. 37; 40; 41; 42; 45

A Fragment on Government. London: 1823. V. 39

A Fragment on Government. Oxford: 1891. V. 38; 39

An Introduction to the Principles of Morals and Legislation. London: 1823. V. 37; 38; 45

Jeremy Bentham on His Fellow Citizens of France on Death Punishment. London: 1834. V. 42

Jeremy Bentham's Economic Writing. London: 1952-54. V. 38; 41

Justice and Codification Petitions ... London: 1829. V. 43

Observations on the Restrictive and Prohibitory Commercial System ... London: 1821. V. 37; 38; 43

Observations on Mr. Secretary Peel's House of Commons Speech, 21st March 1825, introducing his Police Magistrates' Salary Raising Bill. Date of Order for Printing, 24the March 1825. Also on the announced Judges' Salary Raising Bill ... 1825. V. 37

Official Aptitude Maximized. London: 1830. V. 39

De l'Organisation Judiciare, et de la Codification, Extraits de Divers Ouvrages. Paris: 1828. V. 41

Panopticon: or the Inspection-House. Dublin: 1791. V. 37

Papers Relative to Codification and Public Instruction. (with) Supplement to Papers ... London: 1817. V. 37

Plan of Paliamentary Reform in the Form of a Catechism, with Reasons of Each Article, with an Introduction, Shewing the Necessity of Radical and the Inadequacy of Moderate Reform. London: 1817. V. 37; 38; 39; 41

Plan of Parliamentary Reform, in the Form of a Catechishm, With Reasons for Each Article. London: 1818. V. 39; 41; 42; 43; 46

The Rationale of Reward. London: 1825. V. 38; 39

Rationale of Judicial Evidence, Specially Applied to English Practice ... London: 1827. V. 42

Rhyme and Reason; or, a Fresh Stating of the Arguments Against an Opening through the Wall of Queen's Square, Westminster. London: 1780. V. 42

Scotch Reform; Considered, with Reference to the Plan, Proposed in the Late Parliament, for the Regulation of the Courts, and the Administration of Justice, in Scotland ... London: 1811. V. 45

'Swear Not at All;' Containing an Exposue of the Needlessness and Mischievousness, as Well as Antichristianity, of the Ceremony of an Oath. London: 1817. V. 37; 45

Tactique des Assemblees Legisltives, Suivie d'un des Sophismes Politiques. Geneva: 1816. V. 38

Theorie des Peines et des Recompenses. Paris: 1818. V. 43

Theorie des Peines et des Recompenses, Ouvrage Extrait des Manuscrits ... Paris: 1825. V. 42

Theory of Legislation. London: 1864. V. 43

Traite des Preuves Judiciaires, Ouvrage Extrait des Manuscrits ... Paris: 1830. V. 42

Traites de Legislation Civile et Penale. Paris: 1820. V. 38

Truth Versus Ashhurst; or Law As It Is, Contrasted with What It Is Said to Be. London: 1823. V. 39; 45

The Works of Jeremy Bentham. Edinburgh & London: 1838-43. V. 38

Works: Published Under the Superintendance of His Executor John Bowring. Edinburgh: 1843. V. 40

BENTHAM, MARY MATILDA 1776-1852

A Biographical Dictionary of the Celebrated Women of Every Age and Country. London: 1804. V. 42

BENTHAM, T.

An Illustrated Catalogue of the Asiatic Horns and Antlers in the Collection of the Indian Museum. Calcutta: 1908. V. 45

BENTINE, MICHAEL

The Long Banana Skin. London: 1975. V. 44; 45

BENTIVOGLIO, GUIDO

The History of the Warrs of Flanders. London: 1678. V. 37; 43

BENTLEY, E. C.

Baseless Biography. London: 1939. V. 37

More Biography. London: (1929). V. 37

Trent Intervenes. London: 1938. V. 40

Trent's Last Case. London: 1913. V. 37; 43; 44; 46

Trent's Own Case. London: 1936. V. 37; 40; 44

BENTLEY, G. E.

Blake Books Annotated. Catalogues of William Blake's Writings in Illuminated Printing in Conventional Typography and in Manuscript. Oxford: 1977. V. 41; 42; 46

BENTLEY, GEORGE

Mr. Dickens and Mr. Bentley. London: 1871. V. 38; 43; 45

BENTLEY, H. C.

The Legend of the Black Loch. Fores: 1890's. V. 39; 40

Songs and Verses. London: 1892. V. 39

BENTLEY, HARRY C.

Bibliography of Works on Accounting by American Authors. Boston: 1934, 1935. V. 39; 41; 42

Leonard Bibliography of Works on Accounting by American Authors. Boston: 1934. V. 41

BENTLEY, JOHN

Halifax and Its Gibbet-Law Placed in a True Light. Halifax: 1761. V. 42

BENTLEY, JOSEPH

Education; As It Is, Ought to Be, and Might Be ... London: 1862. V. 42

BENTLEY, RICHARD 1662-1742

Callimachi Hymni, Epigrammata, et Fragmenta ex Recensione Theordoi J.G.F. Graevii ... Commentarius et Annotationes Ezechielis Spanhemii. Utrecht: 1697. V. 37

Collected Works. London: 1836-38. V. 37

Designs for Six Poems by Mr. T. Gray. London: 1753. V. 39

A Dissertation Upon the Epistles of Phalaris, Themistocles, Socrates, Euripides and Others. London: 1697. V. 38; 41

A Dissertation Upon Epistles of Phalaris. London: 1699. V. 37; 40; 45

The Folly and Unreasonableness of Atheism (and Eight Other Sermons). London: 1693. V. 38

A List of the Principal Publications Issued from New Burlington St. During the Last Three Months of the Year 1829 (-During Part of the Year 1898). London: 1893-1920. V. 41; 45

BENTLEY, RICHARD 1662-1742 continued

Old 'Miscellany' Days. London: 1885. V. 38

Patriotism, a Mock Heroic. London: 1763. V. 38

Reflections Upon Ancient and Modern Learning. London: 1697. V. 40

Remarks Upon a Late Discourse of Free-Thinking. London: 1716. V. 38; 39; 41

Remarks Upon a Late Discourse of Free-Thinking . . . London: 1716-7. V. 44

Remarks Upon a Late Discourse of Free-Thinking in a Letter to N. N. by Phileleutherus Lipsiensis . . . Cambridge: 1725. V. 41

Remarks Upon a Late Discourse of Free-Thinking; in a Letter to N. N. by Phileleutherus Lipsiensis. London: 1727. V. 42

Richard Bentley & Son. London: 1886. V. 42; 43

BENTLEY, RICHARD, & SON

A List of the Principal Publications Issued from New Burlington St. During the Three Months of the Year 1829 (-during part of the year 1898) . . . London: 1893-1920. V. 38

BENTLEY, ROBERT

Medicinal Plants. London: 1880. V. 38

Medicinal Plants, Being Descriptions with Original Figures of the Principal Plants Employed in Medicine and an Account of the Characters, Properties and Uses of Their Parts and Products of medicinal Value. London: 1875-80. V. 37

BENTLEY, W. A.

Snow Crystals. New York: 1931. V. 41

Snow Crystals. New York: & London: 1931. V. 37; 40; 44

BENTLEY, W. HOLMAN

Pioneering on the Congo. London: 1900. V. 37

BENTLEY, WILLIAM

Diary of . . . , Pastor of the East Church Salem, Massachusetts, April 1784-December 1819. Salem: 1905-14. V. 46

BENTLEY'S Ballads. London: 1858. V. 37

BENTLEY'S History, Guide and Directory of the Borough of Worcester. Birmingham: 1840. V. 37

BENTLEY'S Miscellany. London: 1837-39. V. 40

BENTON, FRANK

Cowboy Life on the Sidetrack . . . Denver: 1903. V. 44

BENTON, JOEL

In the Circle with Some Account of the Poe-Chivers Controversy. New York: 1899. V. 40

BENTON, JOSEPH AUGUSTINE

The California Pilgrim: a Series of Lectures. Sacramento: 1853. V. 38; 39; 45

BENTON, JOSIAH HENRY

John Baskerville: Type-Founder and Printer 1706-1775. Boston: 1914. V. 37; 43

Warning Out in New England, 1656-1817. Boston: 1911. V. 44

BENTON, L.

A Check List of the Publications of Thomas Bird Mosher. Amherst: 1966. V. 44

BENTON, NATHANIEL S.

History of Herkimer County, Including the Upper Mohawk Valley from the Earliest Period to the Present Time . . . Albany: 1856. V. 38; 40

BENTON, THOMAS

From the Committe on Indian Affairs, Reported a Bill 'For the Better Regulation of the Fur Trade'. Washington: 1826. V. 43

BENTON, THOMAS HART 1889-

Abridgement of the Debates of Congress, from 1789-1856. New York: 1857-1861. V. 42; 44

An Artist in America. New York: 1937. V. 38; 45

Highway from the Mississippi to Pacific Ocean. Speech . . . in the Senate of the U.S. February 7, 1849. Washington: 1849. V. 37

In Senate of the United States . . . Mr. Benton, from the Committee on Indian Affairs, Communicating the Following Documents. Washington: 1824. V. 37; 40; 41; 43

In Senate of the United States . . . Resolved, That the Committee on Indian Affairs be Instructed to Inquire Into the Present State of the Fur Trade . . . Mr. Benton Made the Following Report . . . Washington: 1829. V. 37; 40; 41; 43

Letter from Col. Benton to the People of the Missouri. Central National Highway from the Mississippi River to the Pacific. N.P.: 1850. V. 37; 41

Mr. Benton's Letter to Maj. Gen. Davis, of the State of Mississippi, Declining the Nomination of the Convention of That State . . . Washington: 1835. V. 41

The Oregon Trail. Garden City: 1945. V. 45

Speech Delivered at Fayette, Howard County, Missouri, on Saturday the First of September, 1849. Jefferson City: 1849. V. 39

Thirty Years' View; or, a History of the Working of the American Government for Thirty Years, from 1820 to 1850. New York: 1854. V. 37; 39; 44; 45

Thirty Year's View; or, a History of the Working of the American Government for Thirty Years, from 1820 to 1850 . . . New York: 1854-56. V. 39

Thirty Years' View; or, A History of the Working of the American Government for Thirty Years from 1820 to 1850. New York & London: 1856. V. 40

BENVENUTO

Il Passagiore. The Passenger. London: 1612. V. 44

BENY, ROLOFF

Persia: Bridge of Turquoise. Boston: 1975. V. 45

The Thrones of Earth and Heaven. New York: 1959. V. 37

BENYOWSKY, MAURITIUS AUGUSTUS, COUNT

Memoirs and Travels of Mauritius Augustus, Count de Benyowsky . . . London: 1790. V. 41

BENZ, ADOLPH CHRISTOPH

Theasaurus Processuum Chimicorum. Nurnberg: 1715. V. 42; 44

BENZ, CARL FRIEDRICH

Particulars of the Management and Working of Benz's Carriage. London: 1901. V. 43

BENZONE, HIERONYMO

Historia Indiae Occidentalis. Geneva: 1586. V. 39; 45

BENZONI, GIROLAMO

Novae Novi Orgis Historiae, id est, Rerum ab Hispanis in India Occidentali Hactenus Gestanum, & Acerbo Illorum in Eas Gentes Dominatu . . . Geneva: 1578. V. 38; 40; 41

BEOWULF

The Tale of Beowulf: Done Out of the Old English Tongue by William Morris and A. J. Wyatt. Hammersmith: 1895. V. 38

Beowulf. New York: 1932. V. 38; 45

The Tale of Beowulf. London: 1895. V. 41

BEOWULF. Translated by John Porter. Shropshire: 1984. V. 37; 44

BEQUAERT, J.

A Revision of the Vespidae of the Belgian Congo based on the collection of the American Museum Congo Expedition, with a list of Ethiopian Diploterous Wasps. Bulletin of the American Museum of Natural History, Volume,. XXXIX, Art, I, pp. 1-384. New York: 1918. V. 37; 43

BERAIN, JEAN

Ornemens de Peinture et de Sculpture, qui Sont dans la Galerie d'Apollon au Chaateau du Louvre et dans le Grand Appartment du Roy, au Palais des Tuileries. Paris: 1719. V. 38

BERALDI, HENRI

Les Graveurs Du XIXe Siecle. Paris: 1885-92. V. 40

BERDMORE, THOMAS

A Treatise on the Disorders and Deformities of the Teeth and Gums. London: 1768. V. 46

BERDOE, MARMADUKE

An Inquiry into the Influence of the Electric-Fluid, in the Structure and Formation of Animated Beings. Bath: 1771. V. 39

BEREA, DIMITRI

Dimitri Berea at De Young Memorial Musuem. Lausanne: 1965. V. 41

BERENDSEN, ANNE

Tiles, a General History. New York: 1967. V. 44

BERENDSOHN, WALTER A.

Selma Lagerlof, Her Life and Work. London: 1931. V. 39; 41

BERENGARIO DA CARPI, GIACOMO

De Frctura Cranii Liber Aureus. Leiden: 1629. V. 38; 39

BERENGARIO, GIACOMO

. . . or, a Description of the Body of Man: Being a Practical Anatomy Shewing the Manner of Anatomiing From Part to Part . . . London: 1664. V. 41

BERENGER, RICHARD

The History and Art of Horsemanship. London: 1771. V. 37; 38; 41

BERENGER, T.

Collections de Tous Les Voyages Fait Autour du Monde. Lausanne: 1788-89. V. 44

BERENS, EDWARD

Christmas Stories. Oxford: 1823. V. 40

BERENS, S. L.

Nansen in the Frozen World. Philadelphia: 1897. V. 44

BERENSON, BERNARD

The Drawings of the Florentine Painters, Classified, Criticised and Studied as Documents in the History and Appreciation of Tuscan Art. New York: 1913. V. 39; 41

The Drawings of the Florentine Painters. Chicago: 1938. V. 38

Homeless Paintings of the Renaissance. Bloomington: 1970. V. 44

The Italian Painters of the Renaissance. Garden City: 1953. V. 44

Italian Pictures of the Renaissance, a List of the Principal Artists and Their Works . . . London: 1957. V. 38; 39

The Italian Painters of the Renaissance. London: 1959. V. 39

Studies in Medieval Painting. New Haven: 1930. V. '7

Three Essays in Method. Oxford: 1927. V. 44

BERESFORD, CHARLES

Nelson and His Times . . . London: 1906. V. 42

BERESFORD, JAMES 1764-1840

Bibliosophia: of Book-Wisdom. (with) A Course of Reading. London: 1810. V. 41; 46

The Miseries of Human Life. London: 1806. V. 41

The Miseries of Human Life; or the Groans of Samuel Sensitive, and Timothy Testy . . . (with) The Last Groans . . . In Nine Additional Dialogues . . . London: 1806/7. V. 37; 40; 42

The Miseries of Human Life; Or the Groans of Samuel Sensitive . . . (with) Miseries of Human Life; or, the Last Groans . . . London: 1807. V. 38; 42

The Miseries of Human Life. London: 1810. V. 46

The Pleasures of Human Life. London: 1807. V. 39

Sixteen Scenes Taken from the Miseries of Human Life. London: 1807. V. 45

BERESFORD, MAX

Belhaven. London: 1892. V. 37

BERESFORD, WILLIAM C.

El Comandante Britanico, con el Fin de Que el Comercio de Esta Plaza Pueda omar Toda in Actividad de Que Son Subceptibles las Presentes Circunstancias del Pais . . . Buenos Aires: 1806. V. 40; 46

BERG, ADAM

New Muntz Buech Darinnen Allerley Gross unnd Kleine, Silberne und Guldene Sorten . . . Munich: 1597-96-96. V. 42

New Muntz Buech Darinnen Allerley Gross unnd Kleine, Silberne und Guldene Sorten . . . Munich: 1604. V. 38

BERG, WALTER G.

Berg's Complete Timber Test Record. London: 1895. V. 44

BERGEN, TEUNIS G.

Register . . . of the Early Settlers of Kings County, Long Island, New York . . . New York: 1881. V. 44

BERGER, ABBE

Encyclopedie Methodique. Paris: 1730. V. 37

BERGER, H.

Mele Hawaii. Honolulu: 1893. V. 46

BERGER, LORENZ

Theasaurus Bradenburgicus Selectus, Sive Gemmarum, et Numismatum Graecorum . . . Colonia Marchia,: 1696-1701. V. 44

BERGER, THOMAS

Crazy in Berlin. New York: 1958. V. 39; 42; 43; 45

Killing Time. New York: 1967. V. 45

Little Big Man. New York: 1964. V. 37; 39; 43; 44; 45

Reinhart in Love. New York: 1962. V. 39; 42; 46

Siamese Twins. New York. V. 45

BERGERON, PIERRE

Voyages Fait Principalement En Asie Dans Les XII, XIII, XIV, et XV Siecles. The Hague: 1735. V. 41

BERGEY, DAVID HENDRICKS

Genealogy of the Bergey Family . . . New York: 1925. V. 46

BERGH, PETER

The Art of Ogden M. Pleissner. Boston: 1984. V. 39; 43

BERGHAUS, JOHANN ISAAK

Geschichte der Schiffahrtskunde bey den Vornehmsten Volkern des Alterthums . . . Leipzig: 1792. V. 43

BERGHOLD, ALEXANDER

The Indian Revenge: or Days of Horror Some Appalling Events in the History of the Sioux. San Francisco: 1891. V. 37; 40; 42; 45

BERGIER, NICOLAS

Histoire des Grands Chemins de l'Empire Romain. Brussels: 1728. V. 37

BERGILIUS, POLYDORUS

De Inventoribus Rerum libri tres. M. Antonii Sabellici de Artium Inventoribus, ad Baffum carmen elegantissimus. N.P.: n.d. V. 37

BERGMAN, RAY

Fresh Water Bass. New York: 1942. V. 39; 43; 44

BERGMAN, TORBERN OLOF 1735-1784

A Dissertation on Elective Attractions . . . London: 1785. V. 40; 42

Physical and Chemical Essays. London & Edinburugh;: 1788-1791. V. 38

BERGMANN, E. VON

A System of Practical Surgery. New York: 1904. V. 42

BERGSON, HENRI LOUIS 1859-1941

Creative Evolution. London: 1911. V. 45

An Introduction to Metaphysics. New York: 1912. V. 42

BERGSTROM, INGVAR

Dutch Still-Life Painting in the Seventeenth Century. London: 1956. V. 37; 38; 43

BERING SEA TRIBUNAL

Proceedings of the Tribunal of Arbitration, Convened at Paris Under the Treaty Between the United States of America and Great Britain Concluded at Washington Feb. 29, 1892 for the Determination of Questions Between the Two Governments . . . Washington: 1895. V. 40; 42; 45

BERINGTON, JOSEPH 1746-1827

The History of the Lives of Abeillard & Heloisa . . . with Their Geuine Letters from the Collection of Amboise. Birmingham: 1787. V. 40; 41; 42; 45

The History of the Lives of Abeillard and Heloisa. Birmingham: 1788. V. 38; 40

The History of the Reign of Henry II and of Richard and John, His Sons . . . Birmingham: 1790. V. 41

A Literary History of the Middle Ages. London: 1814. V. 40

The Memoirs of Gregorio Panzani . . . Birmginham: 1793. V. 44

BERINGTON, SIMON

The Adventures of Sigr. Gaudentio di Lucca. London: 1748. V. 42

The Adventures of Sigr. Gaudentio di Lucca. London: 1748. V. 42; 44; 45

The Adventures of Sig. Gaudentio Di Lucca . . . London: 1776. V. 44

The Memoirs of Sigr. Gaudentio di Lucca. London: 1748. V. 42

A Modest Enquiry How Far Catholicks Are Guilty of the Horrid Tenets Laid to Their Charge. London: 1749. V. 42

A Popish Pagan the Fiction of a Protestant Heathen (Conyers Middleton). London: 1743. V. 41

BERJEAU, J. P.

Early Dutch, German and English Printers' Marks. London: 1866. V. 40; 45

BERJEAU, JEAN PHILIBERT

The Bookworm. London: 1866-70. V. 39

BERKELEY, CHARLES GRANTLEY FITZHARDINGE 1800-1881

My Life and Recollections. London: 1865. V. 46

BERKELEY, G. H. F.

The Irish Batallion in the Papal Army of 1860. Dublin: 1929. V. 38

BERKELEY, GEORGE BERKELEY, 1ST EARL OF 1628-1698

Historical Applications and Occasional Meditations Upon Several Subjects. London: 1670. V. 38; 41; 42; 44; 45

BERKELEY, GEORGE, BP. OF CLOYNE 1685-1753.

Alchiphron, or the Minute Philosopher: In Seven Dialogues. New Haven, Conn: 1803. V. 37

Alchiphron, or the Minute Philosopher, in Seven Dialogues. Dublin: 1732. V. 43

Alciphron: or, the Minute Philosopher. London: 1732. V. 43

Alciphron: or, the Minute Philosopher. London: 1732. V. 38; 39; 40; 41; 42; 43; 44; 45; 46

Alciphron. London: 1752. V. 42

Alciphron; or, The Minute Philosopher in Seven Dialogues . . . Dublin: 1755. V. 40

Alciphron, or the Minute Philosopher, in Seven Dialogues. New Haven: 1803. V. 41; 42; 45; 46

BERKELEY, GEORGE, BP. OF CLOYNE 1685-1753. continued

The Analyst; or, a Discourse Addressed to an Infidel Mathematician. London: 1734. V. 41; 43; 45

A Discourse Addressed to Magistrates and Men in Authority. Dublin: 1738. V. 45

An Essay Towards a New Theory of Vision. Dublin: 1709. V. 38

The Medicinal Virtues of Tar Water Fully Explained. London: 1744. V. 41

The Medicinal Virtues of Tar Water Explained . . . together with a plain explanation of the Bishop's Physical Terms. Dublin printed: 1744. V. 37

A Miscellany, Containing Several Tracts on Various Subjects. London: 1752. V. 41

A Miscellany, Containing Several Tracts on Various Subjects. London: 1752. V. 41

A Miscellany, Containing Tracts on Various Subjects. London: 1752. V. 39

Philosophical Commentaries, Generally Called the Commonplace Book. London: 1944. V. 40; 41; 42; 43; 45

Philosophical Commentaries . . . London & elsewhere: 1944. V. 42; 45

Philosophical Reflexions and Inquiries Concerning the Virtues of Tar War, and Divers Other Subjects Connected Together and Arising One from Another. London: 1744. V. 43; 45

A Proposal for the Better Supplying of Churches in Our Foreign Plantations, and for Converting the Savage Americans to Christianity, by a College to be Erected in the Summer Islands . . . London: 1725. V. 40

The Querist, Containing Several Queries, Proposed to the Consideration of the Public. London: 1750. V. 41; 42; 43; 45

Recherches sur les Vertus de l'Eau de Goudron, Ou l'on a Joint des Reflexions Philosophiques fur Divers Uatres Sujets Importans . . . Amsterdam: 1745. V. 41

Samlung der Vornehmsten Schriftseller die die Wurklichkeit Ihres Eignen Korpers und der Ganzen Korperwelt Laugnen. Rostock: 1756. V. 41; 45

Siris. Dublin: 1744. V. 41; 44

Siris: a Shain of Philosophical Reflexions and Inquiries Concerning the Virtues of Tar Water and Divers Other Subjects . . . Dublin: 1744. V. 42; 44

Siris: A Chain of Philosophical Reflexions and Inquiries Concerning the Virtues of Tar Water, and Divers Other Subjects Connected Together and Arising One From Another. London: 1744. V. 37; 38; 39

(Siris). Recherches sur les Vertus de l'Eau de Goudron, Ou l'on a Joint des Reflexions Philosophiques fur Divers Autres Sujets Importans . . . Amsterdam: 1745. V. 40

The Theory of Vision, or Visual Language, Shewing the Immediate Presence and Providence of a Deity, Vindicted and Explained. London: 1733. V. 41

Three Dialogues Between Hylas and Philonous. London: 1725. V. 41; 45; 46

A Treatise Concerning the Principles of Human Knowledge. Dublin: 1710. V. 41

A Treatise Concerning the Principles of Human Knowledge. London: 1734. V. 41; 45

The Works of George Berkeley. To Which is Added, an Account of His Life and Several of His Letters to Thomas Prior. London: 1820. V. 38; 39

The Works of George Berkeley, to Which is Added, An Account of His Life and Several of His Letters to Thomas Prior. London: 1820. V. 40; 42

The Works of Bp. George Berkeley, D.D., Bishop of Cloyne . . . Oxford: 1871. V. 38

The Works. Oxford: 1871. V. 37

The Works of . . . Oxford at the: 1871. V. 46

The Works . . . Oxford: 1901. V. 42

BERKELEY, GEORGE, BP. PF CLOYNE 1685-1753

Alciphron; or, the Minute Philosopher. London: 1752. V. 39

BERKELEY, GEORGE CHARLES GRANTLEY FITZHARDINGE 1800-1881

The English Sportsman in the Western Prairies. London: 1861. V. 37; 38; 39; 41

My Life and Recollections. London: 1865-66. V. 39; 46

Sandron hall, or the Days of Queen Anne. London: 1840. V. 45; 46

BERKELEY, GEORGE MONCK 1763-1793

Literary Relics . . . London: 1789. V. 40; 42

BERKELEY, M. J.

The Fungi. London: 1836. V. 38

Handbook of British Mosses. London: 1863. V. 45

Outlines of British Fungology . . . London: 1860. V. 40; 46

BERKELEY, ROBERT

The Judges Resolution on the Bench in Westminster Hall, the 20. of Octob. 1642. London: 1642. V. 40

BERKENHOUT, JOHN

Synopsis of the Natural History of Great-Britain and Ireland. London: 1780. V. 42

Three Original Poems; Being the Posthumous Works of Pendavid Bitterzwigg, Esq. To Which is added, the Very Remarkable Last Will and Testament of that Well-Known Author. Oxford: 1751. V. 38

A Volume of Letters from Dr. Berkenhout to His Son at the University. Cambridge: 1790. V. 37; 38; 39; 44

BERKMAN, ALEXANDER

Prison Memoirs of an Anarchist. New York: 1920. V. 37

BERKOWITZ, DAVID S.

In Remembrance of Creation: Evolution of Art and Scholarship in the Medieval and Renaissance Bible. Waltham: 1968. V. 46

THE BERKSHIRE Tragedy or the Lover's Farewell to the World. N.P.. V. 42

BERLAND, MICHEL

Sommaire des Loix Statuts et Ordonnances Royaulx . . . Paris: 1548. V. 44

BERLANDIER, J. L.

Diario de Viage de la Comision de Limites que Puso el Gobierno de la Republica, Baja la Direccion del Exmo. Sr. D. Manuel de Mier y Teran. Mexico: 1850. V. 38; 39; 41

Journey to Mexico, 1826-1834. Austin: 1980. V. 38; 39; 42; 46

BERLE, KASPAR VAN

Poematum Editio Nova. Leyden: 1631. V. 38

BERLIC-MAZURANIC, I.

Croatian Tales of Long Ago. London: 1924. V. 42; 45

BERLIN, IRVING

Songs From 'Follow the Fleet.' New York: 1936. V. 45

Songs from Irving Berlin's 'Alexander's Ragtime Band'. New York: 1938. V. 45

Songs from 'On the Avenue.' New York: 1937. V. 45

Songs from 'Top Hat.' New York: 1935. V. 45

BERLIN, SVEN

Alfred Wallis Primitive. London: 1949. V. 43; 44

BERLINER Astronomisches Jahrbuch fur 1830-1900, Mit Genchmhaltung der Koniglicher Akademie der Wissenschaften. Berlin: 1828-1898. V. 45

BERLINER, M. L.

Biomicroscopy of the Eye. New York: 1943-49. V. 39

Biomicroscopy of the Eye, Slit Lamp Microscopy of the Living Eye. New York: 1949. V. 42; 43

BERLINGH, AMBROSIUS

Schat Kamer van Vorscheyde Geschriften . . . Amsterdam: 1682. V. 40

BERLIOZ, HECTOR

Autobiography of Hector Berlioz, Member of the Institute of France, from 1803 to 1865. London: 1884. V. 41

BERLU, J. J.

The Treasury of Drugs Unlock'd. London: 1724. V. 44

BERLYN, ALFRED MRS.

Sunrise-Land. Rambles in Eastern England. London: 1894. V. 37; 42

BERLYN, ANNIE

Sunrise Land. London: 1895, 1898. V. 40

BERMAN, EUGENE

Imaginary Promenades in Italy. New York: 1956. V. 38; 42; 44

BERMAR, A. L.

The Thalamus and Basal Telencephalon of the Cat. Madison: 1981. V. 37

BERNACCHI, LOUIS

To the South Polar Regions Expedition of 1898-1900. London: 1901. V. 39; 41

BERNAL, IGNACIO

Ancient Mexico in Colour. New York: 1968. V. 39

BERNAL, RALPH

Catalogue of the Celebrated Collection of Works of Art, from the Byzantine Period to that of Louis Seize, of the Distinguished Collector Ralph Bernal . . . also, of the Beautiful Decorative Furniture and Service of Plate . . . London: 1855. V. 41

BERNANOS, GEORGES

The Diary of a Country Priest. New York: 1986. V. 38; 39

BERNANTZ, JOHANN MARTIN

Bilder Aus Athiopen . . . Hamburg: 1854. V. 45

BERNARD, AUGUSTE

Geoffroy Tory, Painter and Engraver: First Royal Printer . . . Boston: 1909. V. 38

Geoffroy Tory, Painter and Engraver: First Royal Printer: Reformer of Orthography and Typography Under Francois I, An Account of His Life and Works. Cambridge: 1909. V. 37; 39; 40; 41; 44; 45

BERNARD, AUGUSTE continued

Geoffroy Tory, Painter and Engraver: First Royal Printer, Reformer of Orthography and Typography Under Francois I. An Account of His Life and Works . . . Translated by George B. Ives. Boston: 1901. V. 37

Geofroy Tory, Painter and Engraver . . . V. 45

BERNARD, CLAUDE

Illustrated Manual of Operative Surgery and Surgical Anatomy. New York: 1855. V. 41

Introduction a l'Etude de la Medecine Experimentale. Paris: 1865. V. 40; 42

An Introduction to the Study of Experimental Medicine. New York: 1927. V. 42

Lecons Sur la Physiologie et la Pathologie du Systeme Nerveux. Paris: 1858. V. 38

Lecons sur les Proprietes des Tissus Vivants. Paris: 1866. V. 40

Lecons sur les Anesthesiques et sur l'Asphyxie. Paris: 1875. V. 38; 45

Lecons sur la Diabete et la Glycogenese Animale. Paris: 1877. V. 38

Lecons sur la Physiologie et la Pathologie du Systeme Nerveux. Paris: 1858. V. 37

BERNARD, DAVID

Light on Masonry . . . Utica: 1829. V. 42

BERNARD DE CLAIRVAUX, SAINT 1091?-1153

Ad Sororem: Modus Bene Vivendi. Venice: 1492. V. 40

Divi Bernardi Abbatis Ad Sororem Modus Bene Viuendi in Christiana Religionem. Impr. Venetijs: 1502. V. 39

Flores Operum D. Bernardi Abbatis Clarevallensis. Lyons: 1570. V. 40

Liber Meditationu. Paris: 1493. V. 39

Liber Meditationu.. Paris: 1943. V. 44

Melliflui Devotique Doctoris Sancti Bernardi Abbatis Clarevallen . . . Paris: 1513. V. 46

Modus Bene Vivendi in Christianum Religionem. Venice: 1492. V. 45

Opus Super Cantica Canticoru Salomonis . . . Multa Diligentia Castigatum ac Emendatum per Magistru Johannem Rouauld. Paris: 1494. V. 40

Opuscula ('Flores Sancti Bernardi'). Venetiis: 1503. V. 38; 40

Sancti Bernardi Abbatis Primi Clarae-Vallensis Opera . . . Venice: 1781. V. 39

Les Sermons sur les Principales Festes & Solennitez de Toute l'Annee. Louvain: 1577, 1576. V. 38

BERNARD DU HAUTCILLY, AUGUSTE

Viaggio Intorno al Blogo Principalmente alla California ed Alle Isole Sandwich Negli Anni 1826 . . . Torino: 1841. V. 45

BERNARD, EDWARD

De Mensuris et Ponderibus Antiquis Libri Tres. Oxoniae: 1688. V. 39; 44

BERNARD, FRANCIS 1712-1779

Letters to the Rt. Hon. the Earl of Hillsborough, from Governor Bernard, General Gage and the Hon. His Majesty's. Boston: 1769. V. 39; 41

Letters to . . . the Earl of Hillsborough. Boston: (c. 1769). V. 37

Select Letters on the Trade and Government of America; and the Principles of Law and Policy Applied to the American Colonies. London: 1774. V. 43; 46

BERNARD, GEORGE S.

War Talks of Confederate Veterans. Petersburg: 1892. V. 43; 44; 46

BERNARD, J. F.

Recueil de Voiages au Nord, Contenant Divers Memoires Tres Utiles au Commerce et a La Navigation. Amsterdam: 1715-27. V. 40; 42; 43

BERNARD, J. H.

O Livro de Oracao Commum . . . na Egreja Lusitana . . . 1884. V. 43

BERNARD, JEAN FREDERIC

The Praise of Hell. London: 1760. V. 40

BERNARD, JOHN

The Anatomie of the Common-Prayer Book, Wherein is Remonstrated the Unlawfulness of It. London: 1661. V. 42

Considerations Upon a Proposal for Lowering the Interest of all the Redeemable national Debts to Three Per Cent per Annum. London: 1737. V. 45

Retrospection of the Stage. London: 1830. V. 39; 40; 46

Retrospections of the Stage. Boston: 1832. V. 42

BERNARD, JULES

Natural History. Cambridge: 1960. V. 44

BERNARD KARL, DUKE OF SAXE-WEIMAR EISENACH 1792-1862

Travels Through North America, During the Years 1825 and 1826. Philadelphia: 1828. V. 37

BERNARD, M.

The Praise of Hell-or a Discovery of the Infernal World Describing the Advantages of that Place . . . London: 1765. V. 44

BERNARD, NICHOLAS

The Life and Death of the most Reverend and learned father of our Church Dr. James Usher, late Arch-Bishop of Armagh, and Primate of all Ireland. London: 1656. V. 37; 43

The Whole Proceedings of the Siege of Drogheda, to Which is Added a True Account of the Siege of Londonderry. Dublin: 1726. V. 43

The Whole Proceedings of the Siege of Drogheda, to Which is Added a True Account of the Siege of Londonderry. Dublin: 1736. V. 43

BERNARD, P.

Le Jardin des Plantes Description Complete, Historique et Pittoresque du Museum d'Histoire Naturelle, de la Menagerie, des Serres des Galeries de Mineralogie et d'Anatomie, et de la Vallee Suisse. Paris: 1842-43. V. 46

BERNARD, PIERRE JOSEPH

L'Art D'Aimer. Parma: 1798. V. 41

BERNARD, RICHARD

The Isle of Man. London: 1648. V. 45

Thesaurus Biblicus Seu Promptuarium Sacrum. London: 1644. V. 44; 45

Thesaurus Biblicus . . . (with) The Bibles Abstract and Epitomie, the Capitall Heads, Examples, Setnences and Precepts . . . London: 1644/42. V. 44

BERNARD, THOMAS

Spurinna or the Comforts of Old Age. London: 1816. V. 42

BERNARDES, DIOGO

Varias Rimas ao bom Iesus, e a Virgem Gloriosa Sua May & a Sanctos Particulares. Lisbon: 1622. V. 41

BERNARDIN DE SAINT-PIERRE, JACQUES HENRI

Studies of Nature. London: 1796. V. 44

BERNARDISTON, SAM

Tryal and Conviction of Sir Sam. Bernardiston, Bart. for High Misdemeanor . . . Before the Rt. Hon. Sir George Jeffreys, Lord Chief Justice of England, Feb. 14, 1683. London: 1684. V. 38; 44

BERNARDUS, JOHANNES

Vocabulista Ecclesiastico Latino & Volgare. Milan: 1480. V. 37

BERNDT, RONALD M.

Australian Aboriginal Art. Sydney: 1964. V. 41

BERNERS, JULIANA, DAME b. 1388?

The Boke of Saint Alabans . . . London: 1881. V. 37; 39; 42; 43; 45; 46

An Older Form of the Treatyse of Fysshynge wyth an Angle. London: 1883. V. 43

A Treataise of Fysshyng Wyth an Angle. Chelsea: 1903. V. 37; 38; 40; 42; 43; 44; 46

A Treatise of Fysshynge with an Angle . . . being a facsimile reproduction of the first book on the subject of fishing printed in England by Wynkyn de Worde at Westminster in 1496. With a Introduction by Rev. M.G. Watkins. Stock: 1880. V. 37

A Treatyse of Fysshynge wyth an Angle. Edinburgh: 1885. V. 38; 39

The Book Containing the Treatises of Hawking; Hunting; Coat-Armour; Fishing and Blasing of Arms. As printed at Westminster by Wynkyn de Worde. London: 1810. V. 37

The Threatyse of Fysshynge wyth an Angle. London: 1827. V. 46

Treatyse of Fysshynge wyth an Angle. 1875. V. 43

A Treatyse of Fysshynge with an Angle. New York: 1875. V. 40; 42

A Treatyse of Fysshynge wyth an Angle. London: 1880. V. 38; 39

A Treatyse of Fysshynge wyth an Angle. London: 1883. V. 37; 45

A Treatyse of Fysshynge with an Angle. London: 1903. V. 39; 40; 41

The Treatyse of Fysshynge Wyth an Angel From the Book of St. Albans . . . New York: 1903. V. 41

BERNERS, LORD

Percy Wallingford and Mr. Pidger. Oxford: 1941. V. 39

BERNHARD KARL, DUKE OF SAXE-WEIMAR EISENBACH 1792-1862

Reise Sr. Hoheit des Herzogs Bernhard . . . durch Nord-Amerika in den Jahren 1825 und 1826. Weimar: 1828. V. 39; 43

Travels Through North America During the Years 1825 and 1826. Philadelphia: 1828. V. 38; 42; 45

BERNHARD, WILLIAM JOHN

The Jewel Merchants in Lino-Cuts. N.P.: 1928. V. 37; 39

Jurgen in Lino Cuts. N.P.: 1926. V. 37; 39

BERNHARDT, C.

Indian Raids in Lincoln County, Kansas 1864 and 1869. Lincoln: 1910. V. 42

BERNHARDT, F. A.

Questions Relating to Fires in General, the Draught of Smoke, and the Saving of Fueld. London: 1835. V. 39

BERNHARDT, SARAH

Dans Les Nuages. Paris: 1878. V. 46

The Idol of Paris. New York: 1922. V. 42

Ma Double Vie. Memoires de Sarah Bernhardt. Paris: 1907. V. 40

BERNHEIM, BERTRAM

Blood Transfusion Hemorrhage and the Anaemias. Philadelphia: 1917. V. 40

BERNHEIM, G. D.

History of the German Settlements and of the Lutheran Church in North and South Carolina from the Earliest Period of the Colonization of the Dutch, German and Swiss Settlers to the Close of the First Half of the Present Century. Philadelphia: 1872. V. 39; 40; 42

BERNHEIM, H. M.

Suggestive Therapeutics; a Treatise on the Nature and Uses of Hypnotism . . . translations from the Second and Revised French edition by Christian A. Herter, M.D. New York: (1889). V. 37; 42; 46

BERNHEIM, HIPPOLYTE 1840-1919

Die Suggestion und Ihre Heilwirkung. Leipzig und Wien: 1888/89. V. 46

BERNIER, F.

The History of the Late Revolution of the Empire of the Great Mogol . . . London: 1676. V. 46

BERNIER, FRANCIS

Travels in the Mogul Empire. London: 1826. V. 40

BERNIER, FRANCOIS

The History of the Late Revolution of the Empire of the Great Mogol; Together with the Most Considerable Passages, for 5 Years Following in that Empire . . . London: 1671. V. 39

BERNIER, J. E.

Master Mariner and ARctic Explorer. A Narrative of Sixty Years at Sea from the Logs and Yarns of Captain J. E. BErnier. Ottawa: 1939. V. 37; 42; 44

Report of the Dominion Government Expedition to the Nothern Waters and Arctic Archipelago of the D.G.S. 'Arctic' in 1910. Ottawa: 1910. V. 37; 42; 44

BERNIER, R. L.

Art in California: a Survey of American Art with Special Reference to California Painting, Sculpture and Architecture Past and Present . . . San Franscisco: 1916. V. 46

BERNOUILLI, JACQUES I.

Dissertatio de Gavitate Aetheris. Amstelaedami: 1683. V. 40

BERNOULLI, DANIEL 1700-1782

Hydrodynamica, Sive de Viribus et Motibus Fluidorum Commentarii. Strasbourg: 1738. V. 42

BERNOULLI, JACOB

Ars Conjectandi, Opus Posthumun. Accedit Tractatus de Seriebus Infinitis ex Epistola Gallice scripta de Ludo Pilae Reticularis. Basle: 1713. V. 37; 39; 42

BERNOULLI, JAKOB

L'Art de Conjecturer. Caen: 1801. V. 38

BERNOULLI, JOHANN 1667-1748

Opera Omnia. Lausanne & Geneva: 1742. V. 46

A Sexcentenary Table; Exhibiting, at Sight the Result of Any Proportion . . . Published by Order of the Dommissioners of Longitude. London: 1779. V. 43

BERNSTEIN, ALINE

An Actor's Daughter. New York: 1941. V. 45

The Blue Suits. New York: 1933. V. 37; 45

The Journey Down. New York & London: 1938. V. 39

Three Blue Suits. New York: 1933. V. 37; 42; 43; 45

BERNSTEIN, LEONARD 1918-

Candide, a Comic Operatta Based on Voltaire. New York: 1957. V. 39

BERNT, WALTHER

The Netherlandish Painters of the Seventeenth Century. London: 1970. V. 43

BEROALDO, PHILIPPUS

Carmen Philippi Beroaldo de Die Dominice Passionis Eiusdem que Peanes Sive Canticum Beate Virginis. Paris: 1500. V. 43

Declamatio Lepidissima Ebriosi, Scoratoris, et Aleatoris de Vitiositate Disceptantium. Bologna: 1499. V. 38; 44

Libellus de Optimo Satu. Paris: 1500. V. 41

BEROALDUS, PHILIPPUS

Declamatio Philosophi Medici Oratoris de Excellentia, De Optimo Statu et Principe. Colophon: Bologna: 1497. V. 39; 40

De Felicitate. Bologna: 1495. V. 42

De Felicitate Opusculum. Bononiae: 1495. V. 39

Opusculum Eruitum Quo Continentur Declamatio Philosophi Medici Oratoris de Excellentia Disceptantium. Bologna: 1497. V. 38

Varia Opuscula. (with) Orataiones Prelectiones. Paris: 1508. V. 37

BEROALDUS, PHILLIPUS

Enarrationes Vocum Priscarum in Libris De Re Rustica per Goergium Alexandrinum. Lyon: 1541. V. 45

BEROSSUS

I Cinque Libri dele Antichita. Venetia: 1550. V. 41

BERQUIN, ARNAUD

The Bird's Egg, an Instructive Story. Windsor: 1810. V. 40

The Children's Friend. London: 1787. V. 37

The Children's Friend. Volume I-All Published. Middletown: 1801. V. 37; 42

The Family Book, or Children's Journal. Detroit: 1812. V. 43

Le Livre de Famille ou Journal des Enfans . . . The Family Book, or Children's Journal . . . I Partie . . . Nouvelle edition (with) II. Partie . . . Detroit: 1812. V. 39; 40; 41

The Looking Glass for the Mind . . . London: 1787. V. 38

The Looking-Glass for the Mind; or Intellectual Mirror. Dublin: 1788. V. 46

The Looking-Glass for the Mind; or, Intellectual Mirror . . . London: 1792. V. 45

The Looking-Glass for the Mind; or, Intellectural Mirror. London: 1798. V. 46

The Looking-Glass for the Mind. London: 1809. V. 38

The Looking Glass for the Mind, or the Juvenile Friend. Philadelphia: 1819. V. 37; 40

BERQUIN-DUVALLON

Travels in Louisiana and the Floridas, in the Year 1802 . . . New York: 1806. V. 45

Vue de la Colonie Espagnole du Mississipi, ou des Provinces de Louisiane et Floride Occidentale en l'annee 1802. Paris: 1803. V. 39; 40; 45

BERRIDGE, E. W.

Complete Repertory of the Homoeopathic Materia Medica. London. V. 40

BERRIGAN, DANIEL

Lost and Found. 1989. V. 43

Lost and Found. Montclair: 1989. V. 45; 46

BERRIGAN, TED

Train Ride. New York: 1971. V. 43

BERRINGTON, JOSEPH

The Rights of Disseneters from the Established Church, In Relation, Principally, to English Catholics. Birmingham: 1789. V. 39

BERROW, CAPEL

A Pre-Existent Lapse of Human Souls. London: 1762. V. 42

BERRY, CHESTER D.

Loss of the Sultana and Reminiscences of Survivors. History of a Diaster where over one thousand five hundred Human Beings were lost, most of them being exchanged Prisoners of war on their way home after Privation and Suffering . . . Lansing, MI: 1892. V. 37

BERRY, DON

A Majority of Scoundrels: an Informal History of the Rocky Mountain Fur Company. New York: 1961. V. 41

A Majority of Scoundrels: An Informal History of the Rocky Mountain Fur Company. New York: (1961). V. 37

BERRY, EDWARD

Authentic Narrative of the Proceedings of His Majesty's Squadron, Under the Command of Rear Admiral Sir Horatio Nelson, from Its Sailing to Gilbraltar, to the Conclusion of the Glorious Battle of the Nile . . . Edinburgh: 1798. V. 39

An Authentic Narrative of the Proceedings of His Majesty's Squadron, Under the Command of Rear Admiral Sir Horatio Nelson, From Its Sailing from Gibraltar to the Conclusion of the Glorious Battle of the Nile . . . London: 1798. V. 40

BERRY, FRANK B.

Thoracic Surgery. Washington: 1963. V. 42

BERRY-HILL, HENRY

Chinnery and China Coast Paintings. Leigh-on-Sea: 1970. V. 39

BERRY, MARY

The Berry Papers, Being the Correspondence Hitherto Unpublished of Mary and Agnes Berry. London: 1914. V. 40

BESANT, ANNIE

In the High Court of Justice. Queen's Bench Division. June 18th 1877. The Queen v. Charles Bradlaugh and Annie Besant . . . London: 1883. V. 44

Marriage; as It Was, as It Is and As It Should Be. New York: 1879. V. 44; 45

Occult Chemistry. Madras: 1908. V. 39

BESANT, WALTER

All in a Garden Fair. The Simple Story of Three Boys and a Girl. London: 1883. V. 37

The Chaplain of the Fleet. London: 1881. V. 38

Dorothy Forster. London: 1884. V. 41

For Faith and Freedom. London: 1889. V. 41

Herr Paulus. His Rise, His Greatness and His Fall. London: 1888. V. 41; 43

The Master Craftsman. London: 1896. V. 43

The Survey of London. London: 1903-25. V. 45

The World Went Very Well Then. London: 1887. V. 43

BESBECQ, ALGIER GHISLAIN DE

Travels Into Turkey . . . London: 1744. V. 46

BESCHE, LUCIEN

A Girl's Anticipiation and Realization of Marriage. London: 1889. V. 45

BESCHKE, WILLIAM

The Dreadful Sufferings and Thrilling Adventures of an Overland Party of Emigrants to California . . . St. Louis: 1850. V. 44

To All American Patriots. Washington: 1858. V. 44

BESCHREIBUNG der Feierlichkeiten . . . er Kaiser Alexander und Napoleon und Mehrerer Gekronten Haupter in Weimar und Jena . . . Weimar: 1809. V. 46

BESCHRYVINGE Van de Ry-Bende Ofte Cavalcade . . . Brussels: 1770. V. 38

BESCIANI, MARIN

Li Trastulli Guerrieri . . . Besica: 1668. V. 45

BESHOAR, MICHAEL

All About Trinidad and Las Animas County Colorado. Denver: 1882. V. 37

BESLER, B.

The Besler Florilegium, Plants of the Four Seasons. New York: 1989. V. 46

BESOLD, CHRISTOPH

Recapitulatio Monetalium Quaestionum. Ferduckt zu Franckfurt: 1624. V. 37

BESPALOFF, RACHEL

On the Iliad. 1947. V. 44

BESS o' Bedlam's Love to Her Brother Tom: With a Word in Behalf of Poor Brother Ben Hoadly. London: 1709. V. 45

BESSARABOFF, NICHOLAS

Ancient European Musical Instruments. Cambridge: 1941. V. 38

BESSE, JOSEPH

A Brief Account of Many of the Prosectuions of the People Call'd Quakers in the Exchequer, Ecclesiastical and Other Courts, for Demands Recoverable by the Acts Made in the 7th and 8th Years of the Reign of King William the Third . . . London: 1736. V. 38; 43

A Collection of the Sufferings of the People Called Quakers . . . . London: 1752. V. 41

A Collection of the Suffferings of the People Called Quakers, for the Testimony of a Good Conscience . . . London: 1753. V. 42; 46

Life and Posthumous Work of Joseph Claridge . . . London: 1726. V. 38; 40

BESSEL, FRIEDRICH WILHELM

Untersuchungen Uber Die Scheinbare und Wahre Bahn des im Jahre 1807 Erschienenen Grossen Kometen. Konigsberg: 1810. V. 45

BESSEMER, ALFRED GEORGE

On the Dangers and Difficulties Inseparable from the Methods at Present Employed in Rescuing Persons from Dwelling Houses When on Fire . . . N.P.: 1895. V. 38

BESSEMER, HENRY

Sir Henry Bessemer, F.R.S. An Autobiography. London: 1905. V. 39; 44

BESSEUS, PETRUS 1567-1639

Conciones Sive Conceptus Theologici. Cologne: 1614. V. 38

BESSIE, ALVAH C.

Dwell in the Wilderness. New York: 1935. V. 43

Dwell in the Wilderness. London: 1936. V. 41

BESSON, JACQUES

Teatro de los Instrumentos y Figuras Matematicas y Mecanicas. Lyon: 1602. V. 40

Theatre des Instrumens Mathematiques and Mechaniques de Laques Besson Dauphinois, Docte Mathematicien. Lyons: 1579. V. 46

Theatrum Instrumentorum et Machinarum. Lugduni: 1578. V. 42; 44

BESSON, MAURICE

The Scourge of the Indies Buccaneers, Corsairs and Filibusters. London: 1929. V. 42; 45

BEST American Short Stories 1981. Boston: 1981. V. 45

THE BEST American Short Stories 1982. Boston: 1982. V. 42

THE BEST American Short Stories, 1984. Boston: 1984. V. 46

THE BEST and Easiest Method of Preserving Uninterrupted Health to Extreme Old Age: Established Upon the Justest Laws of Animal Oeconomy . . . London: 1748. V. 38

THE BEST and Most Approved Method of Curing White-Herrings and All Kinds of White-fish. London: 1750. V. 40; 41; 45

BEST, CHARLES

Selected Papers of Charles H. Best. Toronto: 1963. V. 41; 42; 45

THE BEST of the Pips: A Collection of the Writings About the Writings by the Members of the Five Orange Pips Scion Society of the Baker Street Irregulars. New York: 1955. V. 39; 44

BEST, R. I.

The Commentary on the Psalms, with Glosses in Old-Irish Preserved in the Ambrosian Library. Dublin: 1936. V. 43

THE BEST Short Stories of 1923. Boston: 1923. V. 43
THE BEST Short Stories of 1923. Boston: 1924. V. 43

BEST, THOMAS

The Art of Angling, Confirmed by Actual Experience with Several Recent Discoveries . . . London: 1822. V. 41

A Concise Treatise on the Art of Angling. London: 1787. V. 39; 43; 45

A Concise Treatise on the Art of Angling. London: 1794. V. 39; 40

A Concise Treatise on the Art of Angling. London: 1798. V. 39; 40

A Concise Treatise on the Art of Angling. London: 1802. V. 39; 40

BESTE, JOHN RICHARD

The Wabash; or, Adventures of an English Gentleman's Family in the Interior of America. London: 1855. V. 37; 42

BESTE, RICHARD

Alcazar; or, the Dark Ages. London: 1857. V. 43

BESTER, A.

The Demolished Man. 1953. V. 43; 44; 45

Tiger! Tiger! 1956. V. 43

BESTERMAN, THEODORE

Old Art Books, Collected and Catalogued By . . . London: 1975. V. 39

The Pilgrim Fathers. Waltham St. Lawrence: 1939. V. 43

The Pilgrim Fathers, a Journal of Their Coming in the Mayflower to New England . . . London: 1939. V. 37; 44; 45; 46

The Publishing Firm of Cadell & Davies: Select Correspondence and Accounts 1793-1836. London: 1938. V. 40

A World Bibliography of Bibliographies and of Bibliographical Catalogues, Calendars, Abstracts, Digest, Indexes and the Like. Geneve: 1955. V. 39

A World Bibliography of Bibliographies and of Bibliographical Catalogues, Calendars, Abstracts, Digests, Indexes and the Like. New York: 1955. V. 39; 44

World Bibliography of Bibliographies and of Bibliographical Catalogues, Calendars, Abstracts, Digests, Indexes and the Like. Totowa: 1971. V. 42

A World Bibliography of Bibliographies and of Bibliographical Catalogues, Calendars, Abstracts, Digest, Indexes, and the Like. Totowa: 1980. V. 41

BESTON, HENRY

Five Bears and Miranda. New York: 1939. V. 41; 42; 43; 44

The Outermost House: a Year in the Life on the Great Beach of Cape Cod. Garden City: 1929. V. 44; 45

BETAGH, WILLIAM

A Voyage Round the World Being an Account of a Remarkable Enterprise Begun in the Year 1719, Chiefly to Cruise on the Spaniards in Great South Ocean Relating the True Historical Facts of the Whole Affair. London: 1728. V. 40; 41

BETHAM, MARY MATILDA 1776-1852

A Biographical Dictionary of the Celebrated Women of Every Age and Country. London: 1804. V. 37; 38; 39; 41; 43

The Lay of Marie: a Poem. London: 1816. V. 43

BETHAM, WILLIAM

The Baronetage of England, or the History of the English Baronets and Such Baronets of Scotland, as are of English Faamilies. Ipswich: 1801-05. V. 38

Irish Antiquarian Researches. Dublin: 1826-27. V. 43; 44

BETHEL, BREVET

Modern Guns and Gunnery, 1910. A Practical Manual for Officers of the Horse, Field and Mountain-Artillery. Entirely Re-Written, with Numerous Additional Plates and Illustrations. Woolwich: 1910. V. 37

BETHEL, SLINGSBY 1617-1697

The Interest of Princes and States. London: 1680. V. 37; 39; 40; 41; 42; 43

The World's Mistake in Oliver Cromwell; or a Short Political Discourse, Shewing that Cromwell's Mal-adminstration . . . London: 1668. V. 39; 42; 44; 45

BETHUNE, GEORGE W.

British Female Poets with Biographical and Critical Notices. Philadlephia: 1849. V. 37; 44; 45

BETHUNE, JOHN DRINKWATER 1762-1844

A History of the Late Siege of Gibraltar. Dublin: 1793. V. 40

BETHUNE, JOHN ELLIOT DRINKWATER

Specimens of Swedish and German Poetry. London: 1848. V. 38; 43

BETJEMAN, JOHN 1906-1984

Architecture. London: 1950. V. 45

Buckinghamshire Guide. London: 1948. V. 46

A Catalogue of Works by Sir John Betjeman from the Collection of Ray Carter with an Unpublished Poem. London: 1983. V. 45

Church Poems. London: 1981. V. 37; 38; 40; 41; 43; 45

John Betjeman's Collected Poems. London: 1958. V. 37; 38; 40; 41; 43; 46

Continual Dew - A Little Book of Bourgeois Verse. London: 1937. V. 39; 40; 41; 45

Cornwall Illustrated. London: 1934. V. 42

Cornwall. London: 1964. V. 44

English Cities and Small Towns. London: 1943. V. 40

English, Scottish and Welsh Landscape 1700-c.1860. London: 1944. V. 41

An Exhibition of Works by Sir John Betjeman from the Collection of Ray Carter. London: 1983. V. 37

A Few Late Chrysanthemums. London: 1954. V. 41; 43; 44

A Few Late Chrysnthemums. London: 1955. V. 38

First and Last Loves. London: 1952. V. 41; 45; 46

Gastly Good Taste or, a depressing story of the rise and fall of English Architecture. London: 1933. V. 37; 41; 42; 43

Ghastly Good Taste . . . London: 1938. V. 42

Ghastly Good Taste or, a Depressing Story of Rise and Fall of English Architecture. London: 1913. V. 38

Ghastly Good Taste. London: 1970. V. 43; 45

Ghastly Good Taste. London: 1933. V. 37

Ground Plan to Skyline. London: 1960. V. 37

High and Low. London: 1966. V. 38

John Betjeman's Collected Poems. London: 1958. V. 45

Lord Mount Prospect. Edinburgh: 1981. V. 41; 43

Metro Land. London: 1977. V. 39; 40; 43; 46

Mount Zion or In Touch with the Infinite (Verse). London: 1931. V. 37; 38; 43

New Bats in Old Belfries. London: 1945. V. 37; 40

A Nip in the Air. London: 1974. V. 37; 39; 40; 41; 44; 45

Old Lights for New Chancels. London: 1940. V. 38

An Oxford University Chest. London: 1938. V. 38; 40

A Pictorial History of English Architecture. London: 1972. V. 38

Ode on the Marriage of H.R.H. Prince Charles to the Lady Diana Spencer in St. Paul's Cathedral on 29 July 1981. London: 1981. V. 45

Selected Poems. London: 1948. V. 40

Shropshire - a Small Guide. London: 1951. V. 41

Summoned by Bells. London: 1960. V. 37; 40; 41; 45

Temples of Power. Burford: 1979. V. 37; 42

Uncollected Poems. London: 1982. V. 37; 38; 40; 45; 46

A Wembley Lad and the Crem. London: 1971. V. 45

BETON, SAMUEL ORCHART

Beeton's Housewife's Treasury of Domestic Information. Comprising complete and practical instructions on the House and its Furniture . . . Economy . . . Children - Etiquett - Domestic and Fancy . . . London: (c. 1890?). V. 37

BETRAND, JEAN

Essays on the Spirit of Legislation in . . . Ppulation, Manufactures and Commerce. Newark: 1800. V. 38

BETT, W. R.

Tribute to Walter de la Mare on His 75th Birthday. London: 1948. V. 43

BETTANY, G. T.

Eminent Doctors: Their Lives and Their Work. London: 1885. V. 41; 42

BETTAUER, H.

The City Without Jews. 1926. V. 43; 44

BETTELHEIM, BRUNO

The Children of the Dream. New York: 1969. V. 45

BETTEN, H. L.

Upland Game Shooting. V. 44

BETTERTON, THOMAS

The History of the English Stage, from the Restauration to the Present Time. London: 1741. V. 38

BETTISON, S.

The History of Cheltenham and Visitor's Guide . . . Cheltenham: 1830. V. 41

BETTONI, EUGENIO

Storia Naturale Degli Uccelli che Nidificano in Lombardia ad Illustrazione della Raccolta Ornithologica dei Fratelli Ercole et Ernesto Turati . . . Milan: 1865-68. V. 39

BETTRIDGE, WILLIAM

A Brief History of the Church in Upper Canada. London: 1838. V. 40

BETTS, DORIS

The Gentle Insurection. New York: 1954. V. 38; 40; 44; 45; 46

Heading West. New York: 1981. V. 41

BETUSSI, GIUSEPPE

Descrizione del Cataio Luogo del Marchese Pio Enea Degli Obizi . . . Fatta . . . l'Anno MDLXXII. Ferrara: 1669. V. 37

BETZKY

Les Plans et les Statuts des Differents Etablissements Ordonnes par sa Majeste Imperiale, Catherine II, pour l'Education de la Jeunesse . . . Amsterdam: 1775. V. 44

BETZKY, IVAN

Systeme Complet d'Education Publique, Physique et Morale, pour l'un et l'autre Sexe. Neuchatel: 1777. V. 38

BEUDANT, F. S.

Voyage Mineralogique et Geologique en Hongrie. Paris: 1822. V. 40

BEUDERLEY, MICHEL

Porcelain of the East India Companies. London: 1962. V. 46

BEUGHEM, CORNELIUS VAN

Apparatus and Historiam Literariam, Qui est Bibliographia ERuditorum. Amsterdam: 1689. V. 45

BEURDELEY, CECILE

A Connoisseur's Guide to Chinese Ceramics. New York: (1974). V. 37

BEURDELEY, MICHEL

Chinese Trade Porcelain. Rutland: 1963. V. 41

BEURHUSIUS, FRIEDRICH 1536-1609

De R. Rami Dialecticae Praecipuis Capitibus Disputationes Scholasticae. Dortmund: 1581. V. 40

BEUST, JOACHIM VON

Christiados Libellus. Wittenberg: 1572. V. 38

BEUTEL, TOBIAS

Electorale Saxonicum Perpetuo Viridans Densissimum & Celsissimum Cedretum . . . Dresden: 1683. V. 37

Mathematische Schoonheiten und Auffgestechte Coronides . . . Leipzig: 1666. V. 46

BEUTTNER, JOHANN CARL

Narrative of Johann Carl Buettner in the American Revolution. New York: 1912. V. 42

BEUVES DE HANSTONE

Sir Beves of Hamptoun: a Metrical Romance. Edinburgh: 1838. V. 39

BEVAN, EDWARD

The Honey-Bee; Its Natural History, Physiology and Management. London: 1827. V. 42; 46

BEWICK, THOMAS 1753-1828 continued

21 Engravings. St. Charles: 1951. V. 42

Vignettes from Birds, Quadrapeds and Fables. Chicago: 1971. V. 46

The Watercolours and Drawings of Thomas Bewick and His Workshop Apprentices. 1981. V. 39

The Watercolours and Drawings of Thomas Bewick and his Workshop Appprentices. Itnroduced and with Editorial Notes by Iain Bain. Cambridge, Mass.: 1981. V. 37; 38; 39; 41

The Watercolours and Drawings of Thomas Bewick and His Workshop Apprentices. London: 1981. V. 37; 39; 40; 41

The Watercolours and Drawings of Thomas Bewick. USA: 1981. V. 45

Wood Engravings of Thomas Bewick. L: 1953. V. 41; 42

The Works of Thomas Bewick. Newcastle: 1822. V. 45

The Works. London: 1885-87. V. 44

Works. Newcastle-upon-Tyne: 1885-87. V. 37; 41

BEWICK, WILLIAM

Life and Letters of William Bewick. London: 1871. V. 37; 45

THE BEWILDERING Thread. Wallingford: 1986. V. 39; 41; 42

THE BEWITCHED Princess. London: 1881. V. 39

BEXLEY, NICHOLAS VANSITTART, 1ST BARON 1766-1851

Substance of Two Speeches . . . in the Committee of the House of Commons, to which the Report of the Bullion Committee was Referred. London: 1811. V. 38

BEYARD, NICHOLAS

Journal of the Late Actions of the French at Canada . . . New York: 1868. V. 37

BEYER, ADOLPH

Otia Metallica oder Bergmannische Neben-Stunden Darinnen Verschiedene Abhandlungen von Berg-Sachen aus denen Geschichten, Berg-Rechten, Natur-Lehre auch Anderen Wissenschafften. Schneeberg: 1748-51-58. V. 43

BEYER, HARTMANN

Quaestiones Novae in Libellum de Sphaera. Parisiis: 1551. V. 46

BEYLE, MARIE HENRI 1783-1842

L'Amour. Paris: 1853. V. 46

Five Short Novels. New York: 1958. V. 40

The Life of Haydn, in a Series of Letters Written at Vienna. London: 1817. V. 42; 43

Oeuvres Completes de Stendhal. Paris: 1913-40. V. 46

The Private Journals of Stendahl, 1811-1817. Kentfield: 1954. V. 37; 38; 41; 42; 46

Red and Black. New York: 1947. V. 45

Rome, Naples and Florence in 1817. London: 1818. V. 45

BEZA, THEODORE 1519-1605

Confessio Christianae Fidei, et Ejusdem Collatio cum Ppisticis Haeresibus . . . Genevae: 1570. V. 38

L' Histoire Ecclesiastiqve des Eglises Reformees Av Royavme de France. Antwerp: 1580. V. 37

Icones, id est Verae Imagines Virorum Doctrina Simul et Pietate Illustrium . . . Geneva: 1580. V. 43; 45

BEZOLD, WILHELM VON

The Theory of Color In Its Relation to Art and Art Industry. Boston: 1876. V. 40

BEZOUT, ETIENNE

Theorie Generale des Equations Algebriques. Paris: 1779. V. 38

BEZZI, GUILIANO

Il Fuoco trionfante. Forli: 1637. V. 37

BHAAGAVAD Gita, The Song Celestial. Bombay: 1964. V. 37

BHAGAVAD-GITA

The Song of God Bhagavad-Gita. Hollywood: 1951. V. 38

BHAVNANI, ENAKSHI

The Dance in India . . . Bombay: 1965. V. 45

BHITTKOWER, RUDLOF

Gian Lorenzo Berini, the Sculptor of the Roman Baraque. London: 1955. V. 44

BHUSHAN, JAMILA

Indian Jewellery, Ornaments and Decorative Designs. Bombay: 1955. V. 46

BIANCANI, GUISEPPE

Sphaera Mundi, seu Cosmographia, Demonstrativa, ac Facili Methodo Tradita . . . Modena: 1653-54. V. 38

BIANCARDI, THEODORO JOSE

Cartas Americans. Lisboa: 1820. V. 46

BIANCHI BANDINELLI, RANUCCIO

Rome: the Late Empire. Roman ARt A.D. 200-400. New York: 1971. V. 46

BIANCHI, GIOVANNI BAPTISTAE

De Naturali in Humano Corpore, Vitiosa Morabasaque Generatione Historia. Turin: 1741. V. 37

BIANCO, MARGERY WILLIAMS

Poor Cecco. The Wonderful Story of Wonderful Wooden Dog Who Was the Jolliest Toy in the House Until He Went Out to Explore the World. London: 1925. V. 38

Poor Cecco. New York: 1925. V. 39; 41; 42; 45; 46

Poor Cecco. New York: (1925). V. 37

BIANCO, PAMELA

Flora, A Book of Drawings by . . . London: 1919. V. 38

BIANCONI, GIOVANNI LODOVICO

Descrizione dei Circhi Particolarmente di Quello di Caracalla . . . Roma: 1789. V. 40; 45

BIANCUZZI, BENEDETTO

Institutiones Lingvam Sanctam Hebraicam. Romae: 1608. V. 37

BIBB, GEORGE M.

An Exposition of the Meaning of the Clause in the Constitution of the United States That 'No State Shall Pass Any Ex Post Facto Law, or Law Impairing the Obligation of Contracts' . . . Frankfort: 1824. V. 44

BIBB, HENRY

Narrative of the Life and Adventures of Henry Bibb, an American Slave . . . New York: 1849. V. 42

THE BIBELOT. New York. V. 41
THE BIBELOT. Portland: 1890-1903. V. 39
THE BIBELOT. Portland: 1895-1914. V. 37; 44

BIBER, EDWARD

Life and Trials of Henry Pestalozzi. Philadelphia: 1833. V. 39

BIBESCO, MARTHE

Churchill ou le Coruage. Paris: 1965. V. 42

BIBIENA, FERDINANDO GALLI

Architetture, e Prospettive. Vienna: 1740. V. 37

Direzioni a'Giovani Studenti nel Disegno dell'Architettura Civile, nell'Accademia Clementina dell'Instituto delle Scienze. Bologna: 1764, 1753. V. 37

THE BIBLE in Miniature. London: 1780. V. 38

BIBLE. AMHARIC - 1870

Novum Testamentum . . . In Linguam Amharicam Vertit Abu Ruhh Habessinus. 1870. V. 46

BIBLE. ARABIC - 1590

(Title in Arabic). Evangelium Sanctum Domini Nostri Iesu Christi . . . Rome: 1591. V. 45

BIBLE. ARABIC - 1591

(Title in Arabic) Evangelium Sanctum Domini Nostri Iesu Christi . . . Rome: 1591. V. 38; 44

BIBLE. ARABIC - 1614

Liber Psalmorvm Davidis Regis Et Prophetae Ex Arabico Idiomate in Latinum Translatus.. Rome: 1614. V. 39

BIBLE. ARABIC - 1725

Psalter (Arabic). London: 1725. V. 37

BIBLE. ARABIC - 1727

Bible in Arabic--New Testament. London: 1727. V. 41

BIBLE. ARABIC - 1811

Old and New Testaments, Arabic. Newcastle-Upon-Tyne: 1811. V. 37; 46

BIBLE Atlas and Gazetteer. New York: 1862. V. 45

BIBLE Beasts and Birds. London: 1886. V. 38

BIBLE. BENGALI - 1838

Gospel of Matthew, in Bengali. N.P.: 1838? V. 40

BIBLE. CARELIAN - 1820

New Testament, St. Matthew's Gospel, Carelian. St. Petersburg: 1820. V. 37

BIBLE. CHEROKEE - 1825

The Lord's Prayer in Cherokee. Boston?: 1825? V. 39

BIBLE. CHEROKEE - 1844

(New Testament in Cherokee). Park Hill: 1844-60. V. 42

BIBLE. CHEROKEE - 1849

The Epistles of Paul to Timothy. Park Hill: 1849. V. 41

BIBLE. CHEROKEE - 1853

Exodus: or, The Second Book of Moses. Park Hill: 1853. V. 37

BIBLE. CHEROKEE - 1856

Genesis, or the First Book of Moses. Translated into the Cherokee Language. Park Hill: 1856. V. 41

BIBLE. CHEROKEE - 1860

Cherokee Testament (title in Cherokee). New York: 1860. V. 37

BIBLE. CHIPPEWA - 1833

Kekitchemanitomehahn Gehbemahjeinmunk Jesus Christ . . . Albany: 1833. V. 37; 46

BIBLE. CHIPPEWA - 1878

The Gospels of the Four Evangelists, St. Matthew, St. Mark, St. Luke and St. John translated into the Language of the Chipewyan Indians of North-West America. London: 1878. V. 39

BIBLE. CHOCTAW - 1886

The Book of Psalms, Translated Into the Choctaw Language. New York: 1886. V. 45

BIBLE. CREE - 1876.

Nikumoowe Mussinahikun. The Book of Pslams Translated Into the Language of the Cree Indians of North-West America. London: 1876. V. 46

BIBLE. CREE - 1877

Oo Meyo Achimoowin St. Mathew. The Gospel According to St. Matthew, translated into the Language of the Cree Indians, of the Diocese of Rupert's Land . . . London: 1877. V. 41; 44; 46

BIBLE. CREOLE DUTCH - 1818

Die Nywe Testament von ons Heer Jesus Christus ka set over in Die Creols Tael en ka Giev na Die Ligt Tot Dienst vna Die Mission in America. Copenhagen: 1818. V. 38; 45

BIBLE. DAKOTA - 1887

The Holy Bible in the Language of the Dakotas. New York: 1887. V. 44; 45

BIBLE. DANISH - 1524

Thette Ere Thet Nove Testamenth Paa Dansk ret Effter Latinen Vdsatthe. Wittenberg: 1524. V. 38

BIBLE. DANISH - 1632

Biblia det er den Gannste Hellige Scrifft paa Danske Igien Offuerseet oc Prentet Effter vor Allernaadigste Herris oc Kongis K. Christian IV. Copenhagen: 1632-33. V. 45

BIBLE. DUTCH - 1599

Biblia Sacra Dat is de Geheele Heylighe Schrifture bedeylt int Oudt Ende Nieu Testament. Antwerp: 1599. V. 42

BIBLE. DUTCH - 1663

Biblia, dat is de Gantsche Heylige Schrifture . . . Leiden: 1663. V. 38

BIBLE. DUTCH - 1780

Bible. Haarlem: 1780. V. 43

BIBLE. DUTCH - 1793

De Kleine Print-Bybel. Amsterdam: 1793. V. 41; 42

BIBLE. ENGLISH

Apocrypha. N.P.: n.d. V. 37
The Holy bible Containing the Old and New Testaments. Oxford. V. 37

BIBLE. ENGLISH -

The Holy Bible Containing the Old and New Testaments and the Apocrypha. Boston. V. 43
The Holy Bible . . . London. V. 42
The Holy Bible, Containing the Old and New Testaments . . . London. V. 41
The Holy Bible. London: & New York. V. 44
Ecclesiastes, or the Preacher and the Songs of Solomon. V. 41; 45
The Four Gospels of Matthew, Mark, Luke and John. Mt. Vernon. V. 46
Psalm XXIII - 'the Lord is My Shepherd, I Shall Not Want.' New York. V. 44
Sermon on the Mount. Bronxville. V. 45
The Song of Songs Which is Solomons. N.P.. V. 38; 40

The Ten Commandments. Japan. V. 45

BIBLE. ENGLISH - 1380

The Gospel According to Saint Mark, As Translated into English in 1380 by John Purvey. SHropshire: 1981. V. 37

BIBLE. ENGLISH - 1510

The Ten Commandments. Jhesus. The Floure of the Commandments of God. London: 1510. V. 39

BIBLE. ENGLISH - 1541

Psalms of David. Parisiis: 1541. V. 46

BIBLE. ENGLISH - 1582

New Testament . . . Translated Faithfully into English . . . 1582. V. 39
The New Testament of Iesus Christ. Rhemes: 1582. V. 38; 40; 41

BIBLE. ENGLISH - 1594

The Whole Booke of Psalmes. Collected into English meetre by Thomas Sternhold, John Hopkins and others. London: 1594. V. 37

BIBLE. ENGLISH - 1603

The Bible. London: 1603. V. 40

BIBLE. ENGLISH - 1606

Bible; That is, The Holy Scriptures Conteined in the Old and New Testament. London: 1605. V. 41

BIBLE. ENGLISH - 1607

The Whole Book of Psalmes. London: 1607. V. 38

BIBLE. ENGLISH - 1609

The Holie Bible . . . faithfully translated . . . by the English College of Doway. Douai: 1609-10. V. 38

BIBLE. ENGLISH - 1611

The Holy Bible, Conteyning the Old Testament and the New . . . 1611. V. 39
The Bible. London: 1611. V. 46
The Book of Ezra and Nehemiah. V. 44
The Holy Bible and the pocrypha Reprinted According to the Authorised Version 1611. With copper plate engragins by Stephen Gooden. London: 1924-1927. V. 37
Book of Ruth, King James Bible. London. V. 45

BIBLE. ENGLISH - 1612

The Whole Booke of Davids Psalmes, Both in Prose and Meetre. London: 1612. V. 42

BIBLE. ENGLISH - 1616

The Holy Bible, Containing the Old Testament and the New. London: 1616. V. 37

BIBLE. ENGLISH - 1619

The New Testament. (with) The Whole Booke of Psalmes. London: 1619-20. V. 37; 39; 45
The New Testament of Our Lord and Saviour Jesus Christ. (with) The Whole Booke of Psalms. London: Imprinted by Bonham: 1620. V. 39

BIBLE. ENGLISH - 1620

The Holy Bible Containing the Old Testament and the New . . . London: 1620. V. 41

BIBLE. ENGLISH - 1628

The Holy Bible, Containing the Old Testament and the New. London: 1628. V. 43

BIBLE. ENGLISH - 1630

The Whole Book of Psalmes. London: 1630. V. 38

BIBLE. ENGLISH - 1631

Containing the Old Testament and the Nevv: Nevvly tranflated out of the Original Tongues . . . London. V. 45

BIBLE. ENGLISH - 1632

The Holy Bible, Containing the Old Testament and the Nevv . . . London: 1632. V. 46

BIBLE. ENGLISH - 1633

The New Testament of Jesus Christ. Rouen: 1633. V. 39; 40; 41

BIBLE. ENGLISH - 1634

The Holy Bible Containing the Old Testament and New. London: 1634. V. 41; 46

BIBLE. ENGLISH - 1637

The Whole Book of Psalmes: Collected into English Meter by Tho. Sternhold, Jo Hopkins, W. Whittingham and others . . . London: 1637. V. 37; 43

BIBLE. ENGLISH - 1638

The Holy Bible. 1638. V. 40

BIBLE. ENGLISH - 1639

The Holy Bible: Containing the Old Testament and New . . . . London: 1639. V. 46

BIBLE. ENGLISH - 1641

The Whole Book of Psalms. London: 1641. V. 39

BIBLE. ENGLISH - 1643

The Whole Book of Davids Pslames. London: 1643. V. 42

BIBLE. ENGLISH - 1644

The Whole Booke of Psalmes. Edinburgh: 1644. V. 41

BIBLE. ENGLISH - 1648

Containing the Old Testament and the New Newly Translated Out of the Original Tongues . . . London: 1648. V. 46

BIBLE. ENGLISH - 1651

The Psalms of David. London: 1651. V. 41

BIBLE. ENGLISH - 1652

The Holy Bible. (with) The Whole Book of Psalms. London: 1652-53/54. V. 40

BIBLE. ENGLISH - 1653

The Holy Bible . . . Newly Translated . . . and with the Former Translations . . . Compared and Revised. London: 1653. V. 43

BIBLE. ENGLISH - 1658

The Holy Bible. London: 1658. V. 40

BIBLE. ENGLISH - 1660

The Holy bible . . . London: 1660. V. 42; 43; 44

The Whole Book of Psalms in Meter, According to the Art of Short Writing Written by Jeremiah Rich . . . London: 1660. V. 42

BIBLE. ENGLISH - 1667

The New Testament of Our Lord and Saviour Jesus Christ, Newly Translated Out of the Original Greek . . . Savoy: 1667. V. 42

BIBLE. ENGLISH - 1670

The Holy Bible Containing the Old Testament and the New Newly Translated . . . . Cambridge: 1670. V. 46

BIBLE. ENGLISH - 1674

The Holy Bible Containing the Books of the Old & New Testament. Cambridge: 1674. V. 37; 39

BIBLE. ENGLISH - 1675

The Holy Bible. Cambridge: 1675. V. 38

BIBLE. ENGLISH - 1677

The Testament of the Twelve Patriarchs, the Sons of Jacob. London: 1677. V. 44

BIBLE. ENGLISH - 1678

The Holy Bible Containing the Old Testament and the New . . . London: 1685. V. 46

BIBLE. ENGLISH - 1679

The Holy Bible. London: 1679. V. 46

BIBLE. ENGLISH - 1683

The Holy Bible.. Amsterdam?: 1683. V. 37

The Holy Bible Containing the Old Testament and the New Newly Translated . . . Cambridge: 1683. V. 46

BIBLE. ENGLISH - 1687

The Holy Bible in Shorthand. Colophon: 1687. V. 44

BIBLE. ENGLISH - 1690

The Holy Bible Containing the Old Testament and the New. London: 1690. V. 38

BIBLE. ENGLISH - 1694

The Holy Bible, Containing the Old and New Testaments . . . (with) The Psalms of David in Meeter . . . Edinburgh: printed by the: 1694, 1693. V. 41

BIBLE. ENGLISH - 1695

The Holy Bible, Containing the Old and New Testaments. Oxford: 1695. V. 42

BIBLE. ENGLISH - 1696

The New Testament of Our Lord and Saviour Jesus Christ. Oxford: 1696. V. 43

A New Version of the Psalms of David. London: 1696. V. 38

BIBLE. ENGLISH - 1698

The Holy Bible, Containing the Old and New Testaments . . . London: 1698. V. 46

Heptateuchus. Oxford: 1698. V. 38

BIBLE. ENGLISH - 1704

The Holy Bible Containing the Old and New Testaments. London: 1704. V. 42

BIBLE. ENGLISH - 1728

The Whole Book of Psalm-Tunes in Four Parts. London: 1728. V. 40

BIBLE. ENGLISH - 1730

The CXIXth Psalm Paraphras'd in English Verse. London: 1730. V. 40

The Holy Bible, Containing the Old and New Testaments . . . Oxford: 1730. V. 41

BIBLE. ENGLISH - 1733

The Whole Book of Psalms. London: 1733. V. 39

BIBLE. ENGLISH - 1743

The Holy Bible. Edinburgh: 1743. V. 39; 41

BIBLE. ENGLISH - 1744

The Holy Bible, Containing the Old and New Testaments . . . Edinburgh: 1744/46. V. 46

BIBLE. ENGLISH - 1750

The Holy Bible Translated from the Latin Vulgat . . . Dublin?: 1750. V. 38

BIBLE. ENGLISH - 1751

The Holy Bible, Containing the Old and New Testaments. London: 1751. V. 39

BIBLE. ENGLISH - 1758

The Holy Bible. Dublin: 1758. V. 39; 40

The Holy Bible, Containing the Old and New Testaments. Edinburgh: 1758. V. 38

The Universal Bible. London: 1758. V. 38

BIBLE. ENGLISH - 1763

The Holy Bible Containing the Old Testament and the New . . . Cambridge: 1763. V. 37; 41; 43; 44

BIBLE. ENGLISH - 1764

Holy Bible. Edinburgh: 1764. V. 38

The Song of Solomon. London: 1764. V. 39; 41

BIBLE. ENGLISH - 1765

The Psalms, Translated or Paraphrased in English Verse. Reading: 1765. V. 38

BIBLE. ENGLISH - 1767

The Holy Bible, Containing the Old and New Testaments. London: 1767. V. 40

The Holy Bible. and Psalms (untitled). Cambridge: 1767. V. 45

BIBLE. ENGLISH - 1768

The Holy Bible, Containing the Old and New Testament . . . Cambridge: 1768. V. 44

BIBLE. ENGLISH - 1769

The Holy Bible. Birmingham: 1769. V. 39

The Holy Bible. Birmingham: 1769-72. V. 38

An Illustration of the Holy Bible, Containing the Sacred Texts of The Old Testament and the New; together with the Apocrypha. Birmingham: Boden & Adams,: 1770. V. 44

BIBLE. ENGLISH - 1772

The Holy Bible Containing the Old and New Testaments. London: 1772. V. 46

BIBLE. ENGLISH - 1774

The New Testament of Our Lord and Saviour Jesus Christ. Oxford: 1774. V. 43; 45

The New Testament of Our Lord and Saviour Jesus Christ. Oxford: 1774. V. 43

BIBLE. ENGLISH - 1775

Holy Bible, Containing the Old Testament and the New, Translated Out of the Original Tongues and with the Former Translations Diligently Compared and Revised. Cambridge: 1775. V. 44

BIBLE. ENGLISH - 1776

Holy Bible. London: 1776. V. 45

The Psalms of David, Imitated in the Language of the New Testament. (with) Hymns and Spiritual Songs in Three Books. London: 1776. V. 42

BIBLE. ENGLISH - 1780

The Bible in Miniature . . . London: 1780. V. 40; 42; 43; 44

An Original Leaf from the Newbery Bible 1780, with an essay by Ruth E. Adomeit. Los Angeles: 1980. V. 37

The Psalms of David, fitted to the Tunes used in Churches by N. Brady and N. Tate. London: 1780. V. 37

BIBLE. ENGLISH - 1781

A Poetical Translation of the Song of Solomon, from the Original Hebrew, with a Preliminary Discourse and Notes, Historical, Critical and Explanatory. London: 1781. V. 39

BIBLE. ENGLISH - 1786

The Holy Bible, Containing the Old and New Testaments. Philadelphia: 1786. V. 39

The Psalms of David, Imitated in the Language of the New Testament . . . Worcester: 1786. V. 42

BIBLE. ENGLISH - 1787

The Holy Bible . . . With Practical Observations on Each Chapter by Mr. Ostervald. Newcastle-upon-Tyne: 1787-86. V. 39

BIBLE. ENGLISH - 1791

The Holy Bible, Containing the Old and New Testaments. Trenton: 1791. V. 37; 40; 43; 45

BIBLE. ENGLISH - 1792

The Self Interpreting Bible: Containing the Sacred Text of the Old and New Testaments . . . by the Late Reverend John Brown . . . New York: 1792. V. 41

BIBLE. ENGLISH - 1793

The Holy Bible, Containing the Olde and New Testaments: Translated out of the Original Tongues: and with the Former Translations Diligently Compared and Revised. Trenton: 1793/94. V. 37

BIBLE. ENGLISH - 1794

The Holy Bible, Containing the Old Testament and the New, Translated Out of the Original Tongues, and With the Former Translations Diligently Compared and Revised. Oxford: 1794. V. 44

BIBLE. ENGLISH - 1795

The Holy Bible. Ornamented with Engravings by James Fittler From Celebrated Pictures by Old Masters. London: 1795. V. 40

The Holy Bible. London: 1795. V. 41; 44

BIBLE. ENGLISH - 1797

The Holy Bible Abridged; or, The History of the Old and New Testament. Wilmington: 1797. V. 38

BIBLE. ENGLISH - 1798

A Translation of the New Testament from the Original Greek Humbly Attempted by Nathaniel Scarlett Assisted by Men of Piety and Literature. London: 1798. V. 41

BIBLE. ENGLISH - 1800

The Old (& New) Testament, Embellished with Engravings from Pictures and Designs by the Most Eminent English Artists. London: 1800. V. 39; 46

The Old Testament and the New Testament. London: 1800. V. 38; 39

The Holy Bible. Oxford: 1800. V. 40

BIBLE. ENGLISH - 1802

Bible in Miniature. London: 1802-07. V. 38

BIBLE. ENGLISH - 1805

The Holy Bible Containing the Old and New Testaments . . . Heptinstall,. V. 37

The Holy Bible, Containing the Old and New Testaments. Boston: 1805. V. 40; 41

The Psalms of David. London: 1805. V. 43

BIBLE. ENGLISH - 1806

The Holy Bible, Containing the Old and New Testaments Translated Out of the Original Tongues. London: 1806. V. 39

BIBLE. ENGLISH - 1807

Old and New Testaments . . . Observations by the Pious and Reverend Mr. Ostervald . . . Carmarthen: 1807. V. 38

BIBLE. ENGLISH - 1808

The Old Covenant Commonly Called the Old Testament: translated from the Septuagint. Philadelphia: 1808. V. 39

BIBLE. ENGLISH - 1809

The Holy Bible for the Use of Families. London: 1809. V. 37

New Testament. London: 1809. V. 37; 39; 40

BIBLE. ENGLISH - 1810

The Holy Bible, Containing the Old and New Testaments. Edinburgh: 1810. V. 39

The Psalms of David, Imitated in the Language of the New Testament and Applied to the Christian State and Worship. London: 1810. V. 45

BIBLE. ENGLISH - 1811

The Holy Bible Abridged. Boston: 1811. V. 40; 44

BIBLE. ENGLISH - 1812

Epistles and Gospels for All Sundays and Holidays throughout the Year. Detroit: 1812. V. 40; 42

BIBLE. ENGLISH - 1815

The Holy Bible, Containing the Old and New Testaments and the Apocrypha. London: 1815. V. 43; 45

The Holy Bible, Containing the Old and New Testaments. Oxford: 1815. V. 37; 44

BIBLE. ENGLISH - 1816

Miniature Bible. Brattleborough: 1816. V. 38

Containing the Old Testament and the New. London: 1816. V. 37; 46

BIBLE. ENGLISH - 1817

The Holy Bible. Oxford: 1817. V. 46

Vetus Testamentum ex Versione Septuaginta Interpretum Secundum Exemplar, Vaticarnum Romae Editum . . . Oxford: 1817. V. 39

The Holy Bible, according to the authorzied Version. Oxford: 1834. V. 37

BIBLE. ENGLISH - 1820

The Psalms of David, Imitated in the Language of the New Testament . . . Chiswick: 1820. V. 45

BIBLE. ENGLISH - 1823

The Holy Bible, Containing the Old and New Testaments; Together with the Apocrypha . . . New York: 1823. V. 44

The Psalmes of David. 1823. V. 44

BIBLE. ENGLISH - 1824

The Holy Bible, Containing the Old and New Testament . . . Oxford: 1824. V. 46

BIBLE. ENGLISH - 1825

The Holy Bible. Cambridge: 1825. V. 42

History of the Bible. Lansingburgh: 1825. V. 37

BIBLE. ENGLISH - 1826

The New Testament, with Explanatory Notes. London: 1826. V. 42

The Self Interpreting Bible, with an Evangelical Commentary by the Late Rev. John Brown . . . New York: 1826. V. 44

BIBLE. ENGLISH - 1828

The Holy Bible, Containing the Old and New Testaments. Oxford: 1828. V. 37

The Sacred Writings of the Apostles and Evangelists of Jesus Christ, Commonly Styled the New Testament. Bethany: 1828. V. 40

BIBLE. ENGLISH - 1830

The Holy Bible According to the Authorized Version. Cambridge: 1830. V. 40

The Holy Bible. London: 1830. V. 43

BIBLE. ENGLISH - 1832

The First Epistle of Paul The Apostle to Timothy. London: 1832. V. 37

The Sacred Writings of the Apostles and Evangelists of Jesus Christ, Commonly Styled the New Testament. Bethany: 1832. V. 38

BIBLE. ENGLISH - 1833

Book of the Prophet Isaiah. London: 1833. V. 46

BIBLE. ENGLISH - 1834

The Holy Bible: Containing the Old and New Testaments. London: 1834. V. 37

BIBLE. ENGLISH - 1835

A Miniature of the Holy Bible. Sandbornton: 1835. V. 40; 41

The Bible in Miniature for Children. Worcester: 1835. V. 38; 41

Illustrations of the Bible (with) The New Testament by Westall and Martin. London: 1835/36. V. 46

BIBLE. ENGLISH - 1841

The English Hexapla. Exhibiting the Six Important English Translations of the New Testament Scriptures . . . London: 1840. V. 38

BIBLE. ENGLISH - 1844

The Sermon on the Mount. London: 1844. V. 40; 44

BIBLE. ENGLISH - 1845

The Epistles of Paul to the Galatians, Ephesians, Philippians, Colossians, Thessalonians; and to Timothy, Titus & Philemon. London: 1845. V. 37

The Sermon on the Mount. London: 1845. V. 38; 46

BIBLE. ENGLISH - 1846

The Holy Bible, Containing the Old and New Testaments and the Apocrypha, King James Version. 1846. V. 37

BIBLE. ENGLISH - 1847

The Good Shunammite. ii. Kings, chap. iv v viii. London: 1847. V. 45

The Parables of Our Lord. London: 1847. V. 38; 41; 43; 45

BIBLE. ENGLISH - 1848

The Holy Bible - Old and New Testaments, together with the Apocrypha: King James Version. 1848. V. 37

The New Testament . . . Translated by John Wycliffe . . . London: 1848. V. 45

The Miracles of Our Lord. London: 1848. V. 43

Parables of Our Lord. New York: 1848. V. 41

BIBLE. ENGLISH - 1849

The Preacher. London: 1849. V. 38; 43

The Song of Songs. London: 1849. V. 38; 41; 42; 43; 44

The Song of Songs. N.P.: 1861. V. 43

BIBLE. ENGLISH - 1850

The Book of Ruth, from Holy Scriptures. London: 1850. V. 38; 42; 44

BIBLE. ENGLISH - 1851

The Life of Christ as Told in Selections from the New Testament. New York: 1951. V. 43

BIBLE. ENGLISH - 1852

The Holy Bible (King James). Oxford: 1852. V. 41

BIBLE. ENGLISH - 1853

The Holy Bible. Philadelphia: 1853. V. 37

BIBLE. ENGLISH - 1854

The New Testament. New York: 1854. V. 37

BIBLE. ENGLISH - 1855

Psalms 1-149. London: 1855. V. 46

BIBLE. ENGLISH - 1857

The Holy Bible, Containing the Old and New Testaments . . . London: 1857. V. 46

Our Saviour's Sermon on the Mount. New Bedford: 1857. V. 39

BIBLE. ENGLISH - 1858

The National Comprehensive Family Bible . . . London: 1858. V. 45

BIBLE. ENGLISH - 1860

Cassel's Family Bible - Old and New Testaments. London: 1860/61. V. 39

The 104th Psalm. London: 1860's. V. 44

BIBLE. ENGLISH - 1861

The New Testament of Our Lord and Saviour Jesus Christ . . . Nashville: 1861. V. 39; 44

The Penitential Psalms. London: 1861. V. 40; 41; 45

The Psalms of David Illuminated. London: 1861. V. 43

Old Testament: Psalms. London: 1861. V. 37

The Sermon on the Mount. 1861. V. 44

The Sermon on the Mount. London: 1861. V. 37; 41; 45; 46

Victoria Psalter. (Psalms of David). London: 1861-62. V. 41; 43

The Wisdom of Solomon. London: 1861. V. 38

BIBLE. ENGLISH - 1862

The Holy Bible, Containing the Old and New Testaments. London: 1862. V. 40

The First New Testament printed in the English Language (1525 or 1526). Translated from the Greek by Willim Tyndale reproduced in facsimile. Bristol: 1862. V. 38

The New Testament and Psalms. Augusta: 1862. V. 43

The New Testament of Our Lord and Saviour Jesus Christ. Augusta: Confederate States: 1862. V. 37; 38

The Psalms of David. London: 1862. V. 37; 40; 42; 43; 44; 46

BIBLE. ENGLISH - 1863

The Psalms of David. London: 1863. V. 38

BIBLE. ENGLISH - 1865

The New Testament of Our Lord and Saviour Jesus Christ. London: 1865. V. 46

The Penitential Psalms. London: 1865. V. 44

BIBLE. ENGLISH - 1866

Nehemiah, in Embossed Type for the Blind. London: 1866. V. 45; 46

The Twenty-Third Psalm. New York: 1866. V. 43; 45

BIBLE. ENGLISH - 1869

The Holy Bible . . . Published with the Approbation of the Right Rev. Dr. Denvir. With: The New Testament. London: 1869. V. 42

BIBLE. ENGLISH - 1870

The Bible in Miniature for Children. Boston: 1870. V. 41

The Holy Bible. London: 1870's. V. 44

Parables of Our Lord. London: 1870. V. 40

The Self-Interpreting Bible, Containing the Old and New Testaments. London: 1870. V. 45

Twelve Parables of Our Lord Illustrated and Illuminated. London: 1870. V. 38; 40; 41; 42; 44

BIBLE. ENGLISH - 1874

The Gospel According to Saint Matthew. The Gospel According to Saint Mark. The Gospel According to Saint Luke. The Gospel According to Saint John. London: 1874/75/77/78. V. 39

The Gospel According to Mark. (Halifax, Nova Scotia: 1874). V. 37

BIBLE. ENGLISH - 1875

Isaiah XL-LXVI, with the Shorter Prophecies Allied to It. London: 1875. V. 38; 40

BIBLE. ENGLISH - 1876

The Holy Bible. Hartford: 1876. V. 38; 45; 46

BIBLE. ENGLISH - 1877

The Holy Bible: Containing the Old and New Testaments, King James Version, 1877. Includes Cruden's Complete Concordance, a comprehensive Bible dictionary, the Apocrypha an Psalms, and a history of all religious denominations. 1877. V. 37

BIBLE. ENGLISH - 1880

The Holy Bible, containing the Old and New Testaments. London: 1880. V. 37

BIBLE. ENGLISH - 1883

The Holy Bible containing the Old and new Testaments, according to the Authorised Version. With illustrations by Gustave Dore. London: (c. 1883). V. 37

BIBLE. ENGLISH - 1885

The Holy Bible, Containing the Old and New Testaments. Oxford: 1881. V. 39

BIBLE. ENGLISH - 1889

The Holy Bible . . . London: 1889-92. V. 43

BIBLE. ENGLISH - 1894

Psalmi Penitentiales. 1894. V. 39

Psalmi Penitentiales. Hammersmith: 1894. V. 45; 46

PSALMI Penitentiales. London: 1894. V. 38

BIBLE. ENGLISH - 1895

New Testament. Glasgow: 1895. V. 41

The New Testament of the Lord and Savior Jesus Christ. Glasgow: 1895. V. 38

BIBLE. ENGLISH - 1896

Ecclesiastes. The Journal of Koheleth . . . East Aurora: 1896. V. 42

The Book of Job. London: 1896. V. 37; 46

The Book of Job. With designs by Herbert Granville Fell and an introduction by Joseph Jacobs. London/New York: 1896. V. 37

The Journal of Koheleth, Being a Reprint of the Ecclesiastes. East Aurora: 1896. V. 40; 45

Book of Ruth and the Book of Esther. London: 1896. V. 46

BIBLE. ENGLISH - 1897

The Book of Ruth and the Book of Esther. New York: 1897. V. 45; 46

The Song of Solomon. With twelve full-page plates and various decorations by H. Granville Fell. London: 1897. V. 37

BIBLE. ENGLISH - 1898

The New Testament. Edinburgh: 1898. V. 42

BIBLE. ENGLISH - 1900

The Holy Bible Containing the Old and New Testaments and the Apocrypha. London: 1900. V. 44

The Psalms of David. Chicago: 1900. V. 38

BIBLE. ENGLISH - 1901

The Holy Bible, Containing the Old and New Testaments: . . . Appointed to be Read in Churches. Glasgow: (1901). V. 37

The Revelation of Saint John the Divine. Detroit: 1901. V. 45

BIBLE. ENGLISH - 1902

Ecclesiastes; or, the Preacher and The Song of Solomon. 1902. V. 43

BIBLE. ENGLISH - 1902 continued

Ecclesiastes; or the Preacher, and the Song of Solomon. London: 1902. V. 38; 41; 42; 44; 46

The Book of Job. Edinburgh: 1902. V. 40

The Book of Job. London: 1902. V. 43; 46

The Psalter or Psalms of David from the Bible of Archbishop Cranmer. London: 1902. V. 40; 41; 43; 44; 46

The Song of Songs Which is Solomon's. Chelsea: 1902. V. 40

Song of Songs. New York: 1902. V. 43

BIBLE. ENGLISH - 1903

The English Bible. Hammersmith: 1903-05. V. 37; 39; 40; 41; 42; 43; 44; 45; 46

The English Bible. London: 1903-05. V. 40; 42

The Parables from the Gospels. London: 1903. V. 38; 39; 40; 41; 44

BIBLE. ENGLISH - 1904

The Holy Bible Containing the Old and New Testaments and the Apocrypha. Boston: 1904. V. 46

The Old Testament. Paris: 1904. V. 44

A Book of Songs and Poems from the Old Testament and the Apocrypha. Chelsea: 1904. V. 40

A Book of Songs and Poems from the Old Testament and the Apocrypha. London: 1904. V. 45

The Ninety-First Psalm. Hingham: 1904. V. 41

The Book of Ruth. Indianapolis: (1904). V. 37; 40

BIBLE. ENGLISH - 1905

The English Bible. 1905. V. 42

BIBLE. ENGLISH - 1907

The Book of Ruth and the Book of Esther. New York: 1907. V. 42

BIBLE. ENGLISH - 1909

The Song of Songs which is Solomon's. London: 1909. V. 37; 44

The Song of Solomon's. Now printed in the Authorised Version. London: 1909. V. 37

BIBLE. ENGLISH - 1911

Ecclesiastes or the Pracher. Boston: 1911. V. 39

Ecclesiastes. Boston & New York: 1911. V. 45

In Principio. (The First Chapter of Genesis). Hammersmith: 1911. V. 44; 46

The Sermon on the Mount. London: 1911. V. 42; 45

BIBLE. ENGLISH - 1912

The Old and New Testament. London: 1912. V. 40

The Book of Psalms. London: 1912. V. 46

BIBLE. ENGLISH - 1913

The Apocrypha and Pseudepigrapha of the Old Testament in English. Oxford: 1913. V. 41

BIBLE. ENGLISH - 1914

The Book of Genesis. London: 1914. V. 37; 40; 43; 46

The Lamentations of Jeremiah. Newtown: 1914. V. 40

BIBLE. ENGLISH - 1915

The Book of Ruth. San Francisco: 1915. V. 44

BIBLE. ENGLISH - 1916

The Book of Job. London: 1916. V. 37

BIBLE. ENGLISH - 1918

Woes. Being Extracts from the New Testament of Our Lord and Saviour Jesus Christ as Translated from the Latin Vulgate by the English College at Rheims, 1582. Ditchling: 1918. V. 40; 42

BIBLE. ENGLISH - 1919

The Holy Bible. Edinburgh: 1919. V. 46

The Holy Bible Containing the Old and New Testaments. Glasgow: 1919. V. 41

The Holy Bible, Containing the Old and New Testaments . . . Appointed to be Read in Churches. New York: (1919). V. 37

BIBLE. ENGLISH - 1922

The Song of Songs. San Francisco;: 1922. V. 40; 44; 45

BIBLE. ENGLISH - 1923

The Book of Ruth. London: 1923. V. 38; 44; 45; 46

BIBLE. ENGLISH - 1924

The Apocrypha. London: 1924. V. 37; 45

The Holy Bible, Reprinted According to the Authorized Version 1611, together with The Apocrypha. London: 1924-1927. V. 37

The Holy Bible, Reprinted According to the Authorised Version . . . London: 1924-25. V. 44; 45

The Holy Bible and Apocrypha. London: 1924-27. V. 37; 38; 39; 41; 42; 43; 44; 45

Genesis. London: 1924. V. 37

Genesis. Soho: 1924. V. 45

Sermon on the Mount. San Francisco: 1924. V. 45

The Sermon on the Mount. San Francisco: 1924. V. 43

BIBLE. ENGLISH - 1925

The Birth of Christ from the Gospel According to Saint Luke. 1925. V. 44

The Birth of Christ from the Gospel According to Saint Luke. Berkshire: 1925. V. 46

The First Christmas as Recorded in the Second Chapter of the Gospel According to St. Matthew. New York: 1925. V. 44

Samson and Delilah, from the Book of Judges. 1925. V. 37; 38

Samson and Delilah. Berkshire: 1925. V. 46

Samson and Delilah, from the Book of Judges . . . Waltham St. Lawrence: 1925. V. 37; 39; 40; 42; 45

The Song of Songs: Called by Many the Canticle of Canticles. 1925. V. 37

The Song of Songs. Berkshire: 1925. V. 46

The Song of Songs. Waltham St. Lawrence: 1925. V. 37; 41; 42; 43; 45

BIBLE. ENGLISH - 1926

The Book of Job. According to the Authorized Version of 1611. San Francisco: 1926. V. 45

The Book of Jonah Taken from the Authorized Version of King James I. 1926. V. 38

The Book of Jonah, Taken from the Authorised Version of King James I. Waltham Saint Lawrence: 1926. V. 37; 39; 45

The Passion of the Lord Jesus Christ: Being Chapters XXVI and XXVII of Saint Matthew's Gospel Printed from the Latin Vulgate. Waltham St. Lawrence: 1926. V. 45

The Book of Ruth. 1926. V. 42

The Book of Ruth. (San Francisco: 1926). V. 37; 38; 46

BIBLE. ENGLISH - 1927

The Gentle Cynic: Being a Translation of the Book of Koheleth Known as Ecclesiastes. San Francisco: 1927. V. 39; 45

The Psalter or Psalms of David. Waltham St. Lawrence: 1927. V. 46

The Book of Ruth. San Francisco: 1927. V. 37; 38; 45; 46

BIBLE. ENGLISH - 1928

Judith. Reprinted from the Revised Version of the Apocrypha . . . London: 1928. V. 38; 39; 46

The Pslams of David. Cambridge: 1928. V. 40; 45

BIBLE. ENGLISH - 1929

Apocrypha ccording to the Authorized Version. London: 1929. V. 37; 38; 40; 41; 43; 44

The Psalms of the Singer David. San Francisco: 1929. V. 38; 41; 43; 44; 46

The Story of the Birth of Jesus Christ According to the Gospels of Saint Matthew and Saint Luke. N.P.: 1929. V. 44

Book of Tobit and the History of Susanna. London: 1929. V. 39; 40; 46

BIBLE. ENGLISH - 1930

The Holy Bible Containing the Old and New Testaments. Oxford: 1930. V. 43

The Book of Psalms from the Version of the Miles Coverdale as Published in the 'Great Bible' of 1539. Westminster: 1930. V. 45

The Story of How Amnon Ravished His Sister Thamar for Which Absalom Killed Him as it Is Written in the Second Book of Kings. 1930. V. 40

BIBLE. ENGLISH - 1931

The Four Gospels. 1931. V. 38

The Four Gospels of the Lord Jesus Christ According to the Authorized Version of King James I. Berkshire: 1931. V. 38; 43; 46

The Four Gospels of the Lord Jesus Christ According to the Authorized Version of King James I. London: 1931. V. 40

The Four Gospels of the Lord Jesus Christ . . . Waltham St. Lawrence: 1931. V. 37; 39; 43; 44; 46

The Book of Ruth. San Francisco: 1931. V. 45

The Song of Songs. New York: 1931. V. 39; 40; 41

The Book of Tobit from the Apocrypha According to the Authorised Version. With wood engravings by Horace Walter Bray. Middlesex: 1931. V. 37; 42

BIBLE. ENGLISH - 1932

Ecclesiasticus. London: 1932. V. 42

The Four Gospels. Leipzig: 1932. V. 40; 43

The People's New Testament. Monrovia: 1932. V. 38

The Revelation of Saint John the Divine. Newtown: 1932. V. 43

The Wisdom of Jesus the Son of Sirach Commonly Called Ecclesiasticus. 1932. V. 37; 45

The Wisdom of Jesus the Son of Sirach, Commonly Called Ecclesiasticus. Chelsea: 1932. V. 37; 38; 44; 45; 46

BIBLE. ENGLISH - 1932 continued

The Wisdom of Jesus the Son of Sirach Commonly Called Ecclesiasticus. London: 1932. V. 39; 42; 43; 44; 45

BIBLE. ENGLISH - 1933

The Lamentations of Jeremiah. Newtown: 1933. V. 44

BIBLE. ENGLISH - 1934

The Aldine Bible. The New Testament. London: 1934. V. 40

New Testament. London: 1934-36. V. 46

Ecclesiastes, or, The Preacher. London: 1934. V. 38

Ecclesiastes or the Preacher. Waltham St. Lawrence: 1934. V. 41; 42; 45

The Book of Ruth. London: 1934. V. 44

BIBLE. ENGLISH - 1935

The King James Version of the Holy Bible, Containing the Old and New Testament Together with the Apocrypha. New York: 1935. V. 38; 43

The Holy Bible. Containing the Old and New Testaments. Oxford: 1935. V. 41; 43

Ecclesiastes or the Preacher. Eugene: 1935. V. 39

The Book of Esther. New York: 1935. V. 45; 46

BIBLE. ENGLISH - 1936

The Second Chapter from the Gospel According to Saint Matthew. Mount Vernon: 1936. V. 46

The Song of Songs. The Authorised Version Together with a New Translation, an Introduction and Notes by W.O.E. Oesterley, Prof. of Hebrew and Old Testament Exegesis, King's College, Univ. of London. (London): 1936. V. 37

The Song of Songs: The Authorized Version. Together with a new translation and introduction and notes by W.O.E. Oesterley, Prebendary of St. Pauls, with engravings on copper by Lettice Sandford. Waltham Saint Lawrence: 1936. V. 37

BIBLE. ENGLISH - 1937

The Psalms of David. New York: 1937. V. 44; 46

The Song of Songs. London: 1937. V. 44

The Song of Songs. N.P.: 1937. V. 37; 44; 46

The Song of Solomon; According to the Authorised Version. London: 1937. V. 45

BIBLE. ENGLISH - 1940

The Book of Psalms. Jerusalem: 1940's. V. 46

BIBLE. ENGLISH - 1941

New Testament, Translated from the Latin Vulgate, a Revision of the Challoner-Rheims Version. Patterson: 1941. V. 40

Ecclesiastes, reprinted from the Authorised Version. 1941. V. 40

BIBLE. ENGLISH - 1944

The Book of Job from the King James Bible. Cummington: 1944. V. 37; 43

The Ninety First Psalm. London: 1944. V. 37

BIBLE. ENGLISH - 1946

The Book of Job. 1946. V. 37; 40; 41

The Book of Job. New York: 1946. V. 40; 41; 43; 44; 45; 46

BIBLE. ENGLISH - 1947

The Book of Job. From the Translation Prepared at Cambridge, 1611, for King James I. New York: 1947. V. 46

The Book of Psalms. Utrecht: 1947. V. 45

The Book of Ruth. 1947. V. 37; 39; 40; 46

The Book of Ruth. New York: 1947. V. 43; 44; 46

The Ten Commandments. Philadelphia: 1947. V. 38

BIBLE. ENGLISH - 1948

The Book of Job. Leigh-on-Sea: 1948. V. 37; 40

BIBLE. ENGLISH - 1949

The Holy Bible. Cleveland: 1949. V. 38

The World Bible. Cleveland & New York: 1949. V. 40; 45

The Book of Ruth and Boaz According to the King James Version of the Holy Bible. Bronxville: 1949. V. 38; 46

The Book of Ruth and Boaz According to the King James Version of the Holy Bible. New York: 1949. V. 39

BIBLE. ENGLISH - 1950

The Song of Songs. London: 1950. V. 39

BIBLE. ENGLISH - 1951

St. Mark's Gospel. London: 1951. V. 44; 45

BIBLE. ENGLISH - 1954

The Four Gospels from William Tyndale's Translation of the New Testament, 1526. Lexington;: 1954-55. V. 38

The Holkham Bible Picture Book. London: 1954. V. 38; 39

BIBLE. ENGLISH - 1955

The New Testament. M.D.XXVI. The Gospel of S. Luke. Lexington: 1955. V. 40; 42; 45

The Four Gospels. Lexington: 1955. V. 46

BIBLE. ENGLISH - 1961

The New English Bible, New Testament. 1961. V. 37

The New English Bible. New Testament. Oxford: 1961. V. 40

The New English Bible, New Testament. Oxford and Cambridge: 1961. V. 39; 43

The Song of Songs. Chicago and Skokie: 1961. V. 41

BIBLE. ENGLISH - 1962

The Holy Gospel According to Matthew, Mark, Luke and John. 1962. V. 45

The Holy Gospel According to Matthew, Mark, Luke and John. Verona: 1962. V. 37; 40; 42; 43; 44; 46

BIBLE. ENGLISH - 1963

The Holy Bible (King James Version) in Facsimile. Cleveland: 1963. V. 41

The Holy Bible. The Old Testament. London: 1963. V. 46

The Holy Bible. London: 1963. V. 37; 40; 42; 44; 45

The Holy Bible. London and New York: 1963. V. 42

Book of Proverbs. New York: 1963. V. 45

BIBLE. ENGLISH - 1965

Ecclesiastes; or, the Preacher. 1965. V. 38; 45

Genesis. Boston: 1965-66. V. 38

BIBLE. ENGLISH - 1967

Ecclesiastes. or the Preacher . . . Paris: 1967. V. 40; 41; 44

BIBLE. ENGLISH - 1968

The Book of Ecclesiastes. New York: 1968. V. 46

The Song of Solomon: from the Old Testament. Guildford: 1968. V. 37; 41

The Song of Solomon, from the Old Testament. With original screen images designed and printed by Ronald King. Surrey: 1968. V. 37; 39

BIBLE. ENGLISH - 1969

The Book of Jonah from the Authorized King James Version of the Holy Bible. Bronxville: 1969. V. 38

The Stonyhurst Gospel of Saint John. London: 1969. V. 38

BIBLE. ENGLISH - 1970

The Book of Genesis . . . Kentfield: 1970. V. 39; 44; 46

The Jerusalem Bible. Garden City: 1970. V. 43; 46

BIBLE. ENGLISH - 1972

The Book of the Prophet Ezekiel. Los Angeles: 1972. V. 46

BIBLE. ENGLISH - 1974

The Book of Kells: Reproductions from the Manuscript in Trinity College Dublin. New York: 1974. V. 46

The Twenty-Third Psalm, a Psalm of David. Esher: 1974. V. 44

BIBLE. ENGLISH - 1975

Acts of Samson. Lexington: 1975/76. V. 45

The Byble . . . Faythfull Translated into Englyshe. London: 1975. V. 37; 38; 40

BIBLE. ENGLISH - 1977

The Psalms of David. 1977. V. 38

The Psalms of David. Cambridge: 1977. V. 46

The Psalms of Daivd. London: 1977. V. 40; 45

The First Separate Edition of the Psalms of David and Others. San Francisco: 1977. V. 38; 39

The Psalms of David and Others. San Francisco: 1977. V. 46

The Sermon on the Mount. Oxford: 1977. V. 43

The Song and Story of the Three Holy Children: Shadrach Meshach & Abel nego. Lexington: 1977/78. V. 45

The Song of Solomon. London: 1977. V. 40

BIBLE. ENGLISH - 1978

The Psalm Book. Pownal: 1978. V. 38; 40

BIBLE. ENGLISH - 1979

The Book of the Prophet Isaiah. 1979. V. 38; 39

The Book of the Prophet Isaiah, in the King James Version. New York: 1979. V. 38; 41; 43; 45; 46

The Book of Jonah, Taken from the Authorised Version of King James I. 1979. V. 37; 42

The Book of Jonah. Cambridge: 1979. V. 46

The Book of Jonah; Taken from the Authorised Version of King James I. London: 1979. V. 40; 44

BIBLE. ENGLISH - 1980

Holy Bible. New York: 1980. V. 40

Jonah, Judith, Ruth. 1980. V. 44

Gospel According to Saint Mark. 1980. V. 38

BIBLE. ENGLISH - 1981

The Gospel According to Saint Mark, as Translated into English in 1830 by John Purvey. Shropshire: 1981. V. 39

BIBLE. ENGLISH - 1984

Jonah, Judith, Ruth. Greenbrae: 1984. V. 37; 38; 40; 44; 46

BIBLE. ENGLISH - 1985

The Holy Bible. 1985. V. 39

The Holy Bible. An Exact Reprint in Rome Type, Page for Page of the Authorized Version Published in the Year 1611. Oxford: 1985. V. 39

BIBLE. ENGLISH - 1987.

The Four Gospels of the Lord Jesus Christ According to the Authorized Version of King James I. Wellingborough: 1987. V. 42

BIBLE. ENGLISH - 1990

The Song of Songs. Covelo: 1990. V. 45

BIBLE. ESKIMO - 1813

The Gospels According to St. Matthew, St. Mark, St. Luke, and St. John Translated into the Language of the Esquimaux Indians, on the Coast of Labrador. London: 1813. V. 38

BIBLE. ESKIMO - 1840

Testamentetak Tamedsa: Nalegapta Piulijipta Jesusib Kristusib Apostelingitalo Pinniarningit Okausingillo. London: 1840. V. 37

BIBLE. ESKIMO - 1876

Testamentitak Tamaedsa Nalegapta Piulijipta Jesusib Kristusib Apostelinitalo Piniarningit Ajokertusingillo. Stolpen: 1876. V. 39

Testamentitak Tamaedsa Nalegapta Piulijipta Jesusib Kristusib Apostelingitalo Piniarningit Ajokertusingillo. Stolpen: 1876-78. V. 39

BIBLE. ESKIMO - 1915

The Gospel According to Mark in the Eskimo Language of the Kuskokwim District, Alaska. Herrnhut: 1915. V. 39

BIBLE. ETHIOPIC - 1826

Novum Testamentum . . . Aethiopice. London: 1826. V. 46

BIBLE. FRENCH - 1535

La Bible qui est Toute la Saincte Escripture. Neuchatel: 1535. V. 38

BIBLE. FRENCH - 1553

Quadrins Historiques d'Exode (and other books). Lyon: 1553. V. 39

BIBLE. FRENCH - 1560

La Sainte Bible. Geneva: 1560. V. 44

BIBLE. FRENCH - 1574

Evangiles et Epistres Comme on a de Costume de Tenir par Tout en Leglise Chrestienne Toutes les Festes et Dimenche. Antwerp: 1574. V. 38

BIBLE. FRENCH - 1605

La Bible, Qui est Tonte La Saincte. Geneve: 1605. V. 45

BIBLE. FRENCH - 1635

La Bible, qui est toute la Saincte Escriture. Amsterdam: 1635. V. 37

BIBLE. FRENCH - 1654

Le Nouveau Testament. (with) Les Pseaumes de David. La Haye: 1654, 1664. V. 39

BIBLE. FRENCH - 1667

Les Pseaumes de David, Mise en Rime Francoise Par Clement Marot et Theodore e Beze. Charenton: 1667. V. 40

Le Nouveau Testament de Nostre Seigneur Jesus Christ, Traduit et Francais selon l'edition Vulgate . . . Mons: 1667. V. 39

BIBLE. FRENCH - 1669

La Sainte Bible. Amsterdam: 1669. V. 40; 46

Le Nouveau Testament . . . (with) Les Pseaumes de David. (with) La Forma Des Prieres Ecclesiastiques. Leyden: 1669. V. 40

BIBLE. FRENCH - 1677

Le Nouveau Testament de Nostre Seigneur Jesus Christ. Mons: 1677. V. 40

BIBLE. FRENCH - 1694

Le Nouveau Testament . . . de la Traduction des Docteurs de Louvain. Paris: 1694. V. 39

BIBLE. FRENCH - 1743

La Sainte Bible, ou le Vieux et le Nouveau Testament; avec un Commentaire Litteral Compose de Notes Choisies & Tirees . . . La Haye-Utrecht: 1743-90. V. 39

BIBLE. FRENCH - 1810

Le Nouveau Testament de Notre Seigneur Jesus Christ, en Francaois, sur la Vulgate. Boston: 1810. V. 41

BIBLE. FRENCH - 1811

Le Nouveau Testament de Notre Seigneur Jesus Christ . . . Boston: 1811. V. 41

BIBLE. FRENCH - 1837

Les Evangiles, Traduction de la Maistre de Sacy. Paris: 1837. V. 39

BIBLE. FRENCH - 1866

La Sainte Bible. Tours: 1866. V. 39

BIBLE. FRENCH - 1873

Les Saints Evangiles. Translated into French by Bossuet. Paris: 1873. V. 37

BIBLE. GAELIC - 1685

Leabhuir na Seintiomna . . . the Books of the Old Testament. London: 1685. V. 41

BIBLE. GERMAN - 1516

Teutsch Ervangeli (sic) und Epistel. (Arranged liturgically). Hagenau: 1516? V. 37

BIBLE. GERMAN - 1522

Die Zwo Episteln Sant Peters. Augsburg: 1522. V. 41

BIBLE. GERMAN - 1530

Das Newe Testament Mar. Luthers. Wittenberg: 1530. V. 40

BIBLE. GERMAN - 1548

Dat Nye Testament Jhesu Christi/Dorch D. Mar. Luth. Na dem Grekeschen Recht Gruntlick Vordudescht/Und vpt nve vth der Bybelen Mith Flyte Thorgerichter. Rostock: 1548. V. 43

BIBLE. GERMAN - 1650

Biblia Mit der Ausslegung. Luneburg: 1650. V. 44

BIBLE. GERMAN - 1683

Biblia, Das ist; Die Gantze Heilige Schrifft . . . Luneburg: 1683. V. 41

BIBLE. GERMAN - 1739

Der Heiligen Schrifft Siebender Theil, (. . . Achter Theil). Berlenburg: 1739/42. V. 44

Der Heiligen Schrifft Siebender Theil, (. . . Achter Theil). Berlenburg: 1742. V. 44

BIBLE. GERMAN - 1743

Biblia das Ist; Die Heilige Schrift Altes und Neues Testaments, nach der Deutschen Uebersetzung D. martin Luthers mit Jedes Capitels Kurtzen Summarien . . . Germantown: 1743. V. 38; 40

BIBLE. GERMAN - 1763

Biblia, Das Ist; Die Heilige Schrift Alles und Neues Testaments, Nach der Teutschen . . . Germantown: 1763. V. 40; 41; 42; 43

BIBLE. GERMAN - 1775

Das Neue Testament Unsers Herrn und Heylandes Jesu Christi . . . Germantown: 1775. V. 43

BIBLE. GERMAN - 1776

Biblia; Das ist; Die Ganze Gottliche Heillge Schrift Alten und Neuen Testamentis . . . Germantown: 1776. V. 39; 41

BIBLE. GERMAN - 1787

Das Neue Testament . . . Germantown: 1797. V. 44

BIBLE. GERMAN - 1805

Biblia, Das ist: Die Ganze Gottliche Heilige Schrift Alten und Neuen Testaments . . . Reading: 1805. V. 44

BIBLE. GERMAN - 1813

Biblia, Das Ist: Die Ganze Gottliche Heilige Schrifft . . . Somerset: 1813. V. 44

BIBLE. GERMAN - 1814

Das Neue Testament unser Herr und Heilandes Jesu Christi. Somerset: 1814. V. 44

BIBLE. GERMAN - 1819

Biblia Das Ist Die Ganze Heilige Schrift Alten und Neuen Testaments. Lancaster: 1819. V. 44

BIBLE. GERMAN - 1840

Das Neue Testament. Stuttgart: G. Liesching,: 1840. V. 43

BIBLE. GERMAN - 1908

Die Bergpredigt Jesu Christi. Leipzig: 1908. V. 38

BIBLE. GERMAN - 1910

Das Buch Judith. Berlin: 1910. V. 41; 46

BIBLE. GERMAN - 1917

Das Buch Hiob, mit Original-Lithographien von Willi Jaeckel. Berlin: 1917. V. 41

BIBLE. GERMAN - 1926

Biblia: Das ist: Die Gantze Heilige Schrifft-Deudsch, D. Martin Luther. N.P.: 1926. V. 45

Biblia. Das ist: Die Gantze Heilige Schrift-Deutsch. D. Martin Luther. 1926-28. V. 45

Biblia. Das Ist: Die Gantze Helige Schrifft. Munich: 1926-8. V. 38; 46

BIBLE. GERMAN - 1927

Die Bibel Oder die Gange Heilige Schrift Deutsch von Doctor Martin Luther. Berlin: 1927. V. 38

BIBLE. GOTHIC - 1665

Quatuor D.N. Jesu Christi Evangeliorum Versiones Perantiquae Duae, Gothica scil. et Anglo-Saxonica: Quarum Illam ex Celeberrimo Codice Argenteo nunc Primum Depromsit Franciscus Junius . . . Dordrecht: 1665. V. 38

BIBLE. GREBO - 1852

The Gospel According to St. John. New York: 1852. V. 43

BIBLE. GREEK -

Novum Testamentum ad Exemplar Millianum . . . London. V. 42

BIBLE. GREEK - 1524

(Greek title, then): Noui Testamenti Omnia. Basle: 1524. V. 45

Novvm Testamentvm Graece. Strassburg: 1524. V. 38

BIBLE. GREEK - 1526

Tes Theias Grapahes Palaias Delade Kai Neaus Hapanta. Divinae Scripturae, Veteris Noveaque Omnia. Strassburg: 1526. V. 38

BIBLE. GREEK - 1534

New Testament, Greek. Paris: 1534. V. 40; 45

BIBLE. GREEK - 1543

(Greek) Psalterion Prophetou Kai Basileos tou David. Paris: 1543. V. 43

BIBLE. GREEK - 1548

Novvm Testmentvm Cvm Indice. Venetiis: 1548. V. 44

BIBLE. GREEK - 1550

Novum Iesu Christi D. N. Testamentum. Ex Bibliotheca Regia. Paris: 1550. V. 38; 42

BIBLE. GREEK - 1553

(Greek title, then): Novum Iesu Christi Domini Nostri Testamentum. Geneva: 1553. V. 40; 45

BIBLE. GREEK - 1559

Novum Jesu Christi Domini Nostri Testamentum. Zurich: 1559. V. 41

BIBLE. GREEK - 1570

Novum Testmentum Iesu Christi Filii Dei, ex Versione Erasmi . . . Basilea: 1570. V. 44

BIBLE. GREEK - 1601

Novum Iesu Christi dn. Nostri Testamentum. Frankfurt: 1601. V. 40

BIBLE. GREEK - 1628

Novum Iesu Christi Domini Nostri Testamentum, ex Regiis Aliisque Optimis Editionibus Cum Cura Expressum. Sedan: 1628. V. 40; 41

Novum Testamentum (in Greek). Sedan: 1628-29. V. 38; 40

BIBLE. GREEK - 1632

(Greek Title, then:) Novum Testamentum. Cambirdge: 1632. V. 38

BIBLE. GREEK - 1633

New Testament in Greek. Amsterdam: 1633. V. 38; 40

BIBLE. GREEK - 1641

He Kaine Diatheke. Novum Testamentum. Leyden: 1641. V. 38

BIBLE. GREEK - 1642

Novum Testamentum, Sive Novum Foedus, Cujus Graeco Contextui Respondent Interpretationes Duae . . . Cambridge: 1642. V. 39

BIBLE. GREEK - 1649

Novum Jesu Christi Testamentum. Paris: 1649. V. 44

BIBLE. GREEK - 1653

Vetus Testamentum Graecum Ex Versione Septuginta Interpretum, Justa Exemplar Vaticanum Romae Editum . . . Londini: 1653. V. 39; 42

Novi Testamenti Libri Omnes . . . Londini: 1653. V. 46

BIBLE. GREEK - 1664

Biblos Tes Demosias Eyches Kai Teleseos Mysterion (Printed entirely in Greek). Psalterion Tou David. Cambridge: 1665, 1664. V. 38

BIBLE. GREEK - 1675

Novi Testamenti Libri Omnes. Oxford: 1675. V. 41; 44

BIBLE. GREEK. - 1678

Psalterion (Greek letters). Oxoniae: 1678. V. 44

BIBLE. GREEK - 1697

Vetus Testamentum Graecum. (with) Novi Testamenti Libri Omnes. Lipsiae: 1697, 1697. V. 39

BIBLE. GREEK - 1707

Novum Testamentum. Oxford: 1707. V. 39

BIBLE. GREEK - 1723

Novum Testamentum Graecum. Leipzig: 1723. V. 45

BIBLE. GREEK - 1759

Novum Testamentum. Glasguae: 1759. V. 41; 45

BIBLE. GREEK - 1763

New Testament (in Greek). Oxford: 1763. V. 37; 38; 39; 41; 44; 45

BIBLE. GREEK - 1785.

Novum Jesu-Christi Testamentum. Paris: 1785. V. 44; 46

BIBLE. GREEK - 1800

Kaine Diatheke: Novum Teatamentum, Juxta Exemplar Joannis Milii Aceuratissime Impressum. Wigorniae (Worcester): 1800. V. 37; 40; 46

BIBLE. GREEK - 1813

Novum Textamentum . . . London: 1813. V. 41

BIBLE. GREEK - 1814

Novuum Testamentum. Boston: 1814. V. 40

BIBLE. GREEK - 1821

Bible. Greek. Moscow: 1821. V. 37

BIBLE. GREEK - 1932

The Four Gospels in the Original Greek. Oxford: 1932. V. 37; 41; 46

BIBLE. HAIDA - 1893

Old Testament Stories in the Haida Language. London: 1893. V. 39

BIBLE. HAWAIIAN - 1828

Ka Euanelio a Mataio: oia Ka Moo Olelo Hemolele no ko Kakou Haku e Ola'i no Iesu Kristo i Laweia i Olelo Hawaii. New York: 1828. V. 38

BIBLE. HAWAIIAN - 1837

Ke Kauoha Hou a Ko Kakou Haku e Olai (Bible: the New Testatment). Honolulu: 1837. V. 38

BIBLE. HAWAIIAN - 1843

Ka Palapala Hemolele e Iehova Ko Kaku Akua o Ke Kauoha Kahiko a Me Ke Kauoha Hou I Unuhia Mailoko Mai o Na Olelo Kahiko . . . Oahu & Honolulu: 1843. V. 40; 43

BIBLE. HAWAIIAN - 1847

Ke Kauoha Hou a Ko Kakou Haku E Olai (Bible: The New Testament). Honolulu: 1837. V. 40

BIBLE. HAWAIIAN - 1860

Ke Kauoha Hou . . . The New Testament. New York: 1860. V. 37

BIBLE. HEBREW - 1557

Torat ha-Mashi'ah. Evangelium Secundum Matthaeum in Lingua Hebraica cum Versione Latina, atque Annotationibus Seb. Munsteri. Una cum Epistola D. Pauli and Hebraeos, Hebraice & Latine. Basel: 1557. V. 37

BIBLE. HEBREW - 1580

Bible, Hewbrew. Antwerp: 1580-82. V. 38

BIBLE. HEBREW - 1608

Psalmi Davidis Hebraici, cum Interlineari Versione Xantis Pagnini, Ben . . . (with) Proverbia Salomonis . . . Leyden: 1608-15. 1608. V. 44

BIBLE. HEBREW - 1630

(Title in Hebrew). Amsterdam: 1630-31. V. 40

BIBLE. HEBREW - 1649

Liber Psalmorum Hebraice Cum Versione Latina Santis Pagnini. Basil: 1649. V. 44

BIBLE. HEBREW - 1699

Biblica Hebraica. Berlin: 1699. V. 38

BIBLE. HEBREW - 1701

Biblia Hebraica. Amstelaedami: Gerardus: 1701. V. 37

BIBLE. HEBREW - 1705

Biblia Hebraica. Utrecht: 1705. V. 38

BIBLE. HEBREW - 1709

Bibla Hebraica cum Optimis Impressis & Manuscriptis Codicibus in Extra Germaniam . . . Kiel: 1709. V. 44

BIBLE. HEBREW - 1720

Biblia Hebraica . . . Halae Magdeburgicae: 1720. V. 46

BIBLE. HEBREW - 1739

Biblia Hebraica, ad optimos Qusque Editiones Expressa cum Notis Masorethicis et Numeris Distinctionum . . . Leipzig: 1739. V. 38

BIBLE. HEBREW - 1802

The Psalms in the Sacred Language. Gothenburgh: 1802. V. 42

BIBLE. HEBREW - 1815

The Hebrew Bible; from the Edition of Everardo van der Hooght. Nos. 1 and 2. New York: 1815. V. 39

BIBLE. HIEROGLYPHIC - 1788

A Curious Hieroglyphick Bible. London: 1788. V. 39

A Curious Hieroglyphick Bible; or, Select Passages in the Old and New Testaments. Worcester: 1788. V. 44

BIBLE. HIEROGLYPHIC - 1789

A Curious Hieroglyphick Bible . . . Dublin: 1789. V. 42

A Curious Hieroglyphick Bible. London: 1789. V. 41

BIBLE. HIEROGLYPHIC - 1796

A Curious Hieroglyphick Bible . . . London: 1796. V. 42

BIBLE. HIEROGLYPHIC - 1814

The Hieroglyhick Bible; or Selected Passages in the Old and New Testaments . . . Boston: 1814. V. 45

BIBLE. HIEROGLYPHIC - 1888

Hieroglyphic Bible. London & New York: 1888. V. 40

BIBLE History. Boston: 1814. V. 38

BIBLE. IRISH - 1685

Old Testament. Translated into Irish by the Care and Diligence of Dr. William Bedel . . . London: 1685. V. 38

BIBLE. IRISH. 1740

The Pslams of David in Metre . . . Dublin: 1740. V. 43

BIBLE. IRISH - 1852

The Holy Bible, Translated from the Latin Vulgate. Belfast: 1852. V. 43

BIBLE. ITALIAN - 1541

Il Nuovo Testamento di Christo Giesu Signore Salvatore Nostro. London: 1541. V. 40

BIBLE. ITALIAN - 1554

Figure del Vecchio Testamento, con Versi Toscani per Damian Maraffi . . . Lyon: 1554. V. 38; 39

BIBLE. ITALIAN - 1559

Figure del Nuovo Testamento, Illustrate da Versi Vulgari Italiani. Lyon: 1559. V. 45

BIBLE. ITALIAN - 1588

I Salmi di David. Tradotti dalla Lingua hebrea Nella Italiana. Divisi in Cinque Parti. Di Novo Ricorretti & Emendati. Paris: 1588. V. 38

BIBLE. KANARESE - 1820

The Gospel of St. Luke. No titlepage or colophon;. V. 40

BIBLE. KHASI - 1856

The Four Gospels with the Acts of the Apostles. Translated into Khasi from the Original Greek. Calcutta: 1856. V. 42

BIBLE. LATIN - 1476

Epla bti Hieronymi psbyteri ad Damasu Papam in Quatuor Euagelistas. Paris: 176/7. V. 40

BIBLE. LATIN - 1478

Biblia Latina. Venice: 1478. V. 45; 46

BIBLE. LATIN - 1480

Biblia Latina. Ulm: 1480. V. 42; 43

Bible in Latin. Venice: 1480. V. 42

BIBLE. LATIN - 1485

The New Testament with Commentary by Nicholas de Lyra. Nurnberg: 1485. V. 39

BIBLE. LATIN - 1487

Biblia Ltaina cum Postillis Nicolai de Lyra . . . in Omnes Prologos S. Hieronymi et Editionibus Pauli Burgensis Replicisque Matthiae Doering. Nuremberg: 1487. V. 46

BIBLE. LATIN - 1495

Biblia Integra . . . Utriusque Testamenti Concordantiis Illustrata. Basle: 1495. V. 38

BIBLE. LATIN - 1498

Biblia Cum Tabula Nuper Impressa et Cum Summariis Noviter Editis. Venice: 1498. V. 45

BIBLE. LATIN - 1514

Biblia cum Summarioru(m) Apparato Pleno Quadruplicique Repetorio Insignita. Lugduni: 1514. V. 39

BIBLE. LATIN - 1519

Liturgical Epistles and Gospels. Basel: 1519. V. 38

BIBLE. LATIN - 1520

Biblia cum Concordantiis Veteris et Noui Testamenti et Sacrorum Canorum.. Lyons: 1520. V. 38

BIBLE. LATIN - 1521

Biblia cum Concordantiis Veteris & Novi Testamenti et Sacrorum Canonum. Lyon: 1521. V. 38

BIBLE. LATIN - 1526

Sacra Biblia ad LXX, Interpretum Fideum Diligentissime Tralata. Basel: 1526. V. 43

Textus Bibliae. MDXXVI. Biblia cum Concordantiis veteris et Novi Testamenti et Sacrorum Canonum. Lyon: 1526. V. 38

BIBLE. LATIN - 1527

Bibla. Habes in hoc Libro Prudens Lector Utriusque Instrumenti Novam Translatione Aeditam a Sancte Pagnino . . . Colophon: Lyon: 1528. V. 39

BIBLE. LATIN - 1528

Liber Psalmorum. Paris: 1528. V. 38

BIBLE. LATIN - 1538

Biblia Utriusque Testamenti Iuxta Vulgatam Translationem . . . Lyon: 1538. V. 38

BIBLE. LATIN - 1541

Novi Testamenti Vulgata Quidem Aeditio. Venice: 1541. V. 37

Sanctum Iesv Christi Evangelivm . . . Acta Apostolorvm (with) Pavli Apostoli Epistolae . . . Epistolae Catholicae . . . Apocalypsis Beati Ioannis Apostoli. Paris: 1540. V. 38; 40

BIBLE. LATIN - 1542

Psalterium Paraphrasibus Illustratum. (Paraphrases by Reinier Snoy). Lyon: 1542. V. 37

Biblia Sacra ex Santis Pagnini Tralatione, sed ad Hebraicae Linguae Amussim Nouissime ita Recognita & Scholiis Illustrata, ut Plane Noua Editio Uideri Possit . . . Lyons: 1542. V. 39

BIBLE. LATIN - 1543

Novum Testamentum. Paris: 1543. V. 37

Evangelium. Paris: 1543. V. 38

BIBLE. LATIN - 1545

Biblia Quid in Hac Editione Praestitutim sit, Vide in Ea Qum Operi Praeposuimus, ad Lectorem Epistola. Paris: 1545. V. 39; 40

BIBLE. LATIN - 1546

Liber Psalmorum Davidis. Annotationes in eosdem ex Hebraeorum Commentariis. Paris: 1546. V. 37

BIBLE. LATIN - 1550

Psalterium Davidis Carmine Redditum. Salomonis Ecclesiastes, Annotationibus Viti Theodori. Paris: 1550. V. 38

BIBLE. LATIN - 1551

Biblia Sacrosancta Veteris & Novi Testamenti . . . Lyons: 1551. V. 45

BIBLE. LATIN - 1552

Biblia Sacra Iuxta Vulgatam Quam Dicunt Editionem a mendis Quibus Innumeris . . . Paris: 1552. V. 38

BIBLE. LATIN - 1554

Psalterium, Reliqva qve Sacrarum Literarum Carmina & Precationes . . .
Basel: 1554. V. 45

Bibla Sacra. Lyon: 1554. V. 45

BIBLE. LATIN - 1556

Biblia Sacra and Optima Quaeque Veteris . . . Lyon: 1556. V. 43

BIBLE. LATIN - 1557

Nouum D. N. Iesu Chrsti Testamentum. Latine iam Olim a Veteri Interprete, nunc denuo a Theodoro Beza. Geneva: 1557. V. 37

BIBLE. LATIN - 1558

Psalmista Secundrum Conseuetudinem Sanctae Romanae Ecclesiae, cum Hymnis. Venice: 1558. V. 37

BIBLE. LATIN - 1573

Biblia, Sacra Veteris et Novi Testamenti Juxta Vulgatam Editionem: Ab Aliquot Theologis Parisiensibus Accurate Recognita & Emendata . . . Paris: 1573. V. 41

BIBLE. LATIN - 1576

Biblia ad Vetustissima Exemplaria Nunc Recens Castigata . . . Venice: 1576. V. 40; 46

BIBLE. LATIN - 1581

Testamenti Veteris Biblia Sacra . . . Accesserunt Libri qui Vulgo Dicuntur Apocryphi . . . London: 1581. V. 45

BIBLE. LATIN - 1582

Iesv Christi D. N. Nouum te Teftamentum, Fiue Nouum Foedus. Geneve: 1582. V. 45

BIBLE. LATIN - 1586

Le Pseavltier de David, Contenant cent Cinquante Pseaumes. Paris: 1586. V. 40

BIBLE. LATIN - 1587

Biblia, ad Vetustissima Exemplaria Nunc Recens Castigata . . . Venetiis: 1587. V. 39

BIBLE. LATIN - 1599

Biblia Sacra Vulgatae Editionis Sixti Quinti Pont. Antwerpiae: 1599. V. 42

BIBLE. LATIN - 1605

Biblia Sacra. 1605. V. 45

Biblia Sacra Vulgatae Editionis. Antverpiae: 1605. V. 42

BIBLE. LATIN - 1608

Biblia Sacra, Vulgatae Editionis. Antwerp: 1608. V. 38

BIBLE. LATIN - 1618

Biblia Sacra Vulgatae. Rome: 1618. V. 44

BIBLE. LATIN - 1651

Biblia Sacra. Sive Testamentum Vetus Ab Im. Tremellio et Iunio ex Hebraeo . . . Amsterdam: 1651. V. 45

BIBLE. LATIN - 1659

Biblia Sacra Vulgatae Editionis Sixti V. Pont. Max. Iussu Recognita, et Clementis VIII Auctoritate Edita. Coloniae Agrippinae: 1659. V. 37; 38; 42

Biblia Sacra Vulgatae Editionis Sixti V. Pont. Max. Iussu Recognita, et Clementis VIII uctoritate Edita. Coloniae: 1659. V. 38

BIBLE. LATIN - 1678

Biblia Sacra Vulgate. Cologne: 1678-9. V. 45

BIBLE. LATIN - 1690

Bibla Sacra Vulgatae Editionis Sixti V. Venice: 1690. V. 45

BIBLE. LATIN - 1691

Biblia Sacra Vulgatae Editionis. Paris: 1691. V. 39

BIBLE. LATIN - 1693

Decapla in Psalmos, Sive Commentarius ex Decem Linguis. London: 1693. V: 38

BIBLE. LATIN - 1697

Biblia Sacra sive Testamentum Vetus et Novum ex Linguis Originalibus in Linguam Latinam Translatum. Strassburg: 1697. V. 44

BIBLE. LATIN - 1706

Biblia Sacra Vulgatae Editionis. Venice: 1706. V. 39

BIBLE. LATIN - 1731

Biblia Sacra Vulate Editionis Sixti V. & Cleme. VIII Pont. Max. Auctoritate Recognita. Venice: 1731. V. 38

BIBLE. LATIN - 1778

Biblia Sacra. Vulgatae Editionis, Sixti V. & Clementis VIII. Pont. Max Auctoritate Recognita, Cum Annotationibus I. B. Du-Hamel . . . Madrid: 1778. V. 41; 42

BIBLE. LATIN - 1788

Biblia Cum Summariorum Apparatu. Lyons: 1512. V. 39

BIBLE. LATIN - 1794

Biblia Sacra. Vulgatae Editionis . . . Bassani & Venice: 1794. V. 39

BIBLE. LATIN - 1894

Biblia Pauperum. London: 1894. V. 46

BIBLE. LATIN - 1913

Bible in Latin. Leipzig: 1913-14. V. 38

BIBLE. LATIN - 1921

A Noble Fragment, Being a Leaf of the Gutenberg Bible, with a Bibliographical Essay by A. Edward Newton. New York: 1921. V. 40

BIBLE. LATIN - 1926

Passio Domini Nostri Jesu Christi: Being Chapters XXVI and XXVII of Saint Matthew's Gospel Printed from the Latin Vulgate. London: 1926. V. 39

BIBLE. LATIN - 1968

A Facsimile of the Gutenberg Bibe. New York: 1968. V. 37

BIBLE. LATIN - 1985

Facsimile of the Gutenberg Bible. Paris: 1985. V. 46

BIBLE. MANUSCRIPTS

The Book of Kells. London & New York: 1952. V. 40

BIBLE. MANUSCRIPTS - 1923

The Lindisfarne Gospels. London: 1923. V. 39

BIBLE. MANUSCRIPTS - 1960

Book of Durrow. Codex Durmachensis. Olten: 1960. V. 39

Evangeliorum Quattuor Codex Durmachensis (The Book of Durrow). Olten: 1960. V. 39

BIBLE. MANUSCRIPTS - 1967

The Lorsch Gospels. New York: 1967. V. 41

BIBLE. MANUSCRIPTS - 1974

The Book of Kells. New York: 1974. V. 43

BIBLE. MAORI - 1838

Book of Job (Ko Te Pikapuka O Hopa). Hoklanga: 1838. V. 41

BIBLE. MICMAC - 1863

Tan Teladakadidjik Apostalewidjik. Bath: 1863. V. 38

BIBLE. MICMAC - 1871

Pela Kesagunoodumumkawa Tan Tula Uksakumamenoo Westowoolkw Sasoogoole Clistawit Ootenink Megumoweesimk. Halifax: 1871. V. 42

BIBLE. MICMAC - 1874

The Gospel According to Mark. Halifax: 1874. V. 37; 42

BIBLE. MOHAWK - 1831

Ne Raorihwadogenhti ne Shongwayaner Yesus Keristus, Jinihorihoten ne Royatadogenhti Matthew. New York: 1831. V. 40

BIBLE. MOHAWK - 1836

The Epistle of Paul the Apostle to the Hebrews. Translated into the Mohawk Language. New York: 1836. V. 38; 41

The Gospel of Our Lord and Saviour Jesus Christ According to Saint Matthew, Translated into the Mohawk Language. New York: 1836. V. 38; 39; 41

BIBLE. MPONGWE - 1850

The Gospel of Matthew; in the Mpongwe Language. Gaboon: 1850. V. 40; 43

The Gospel of St. Matthew in the Mpongwe Language. Gaboon: 1850. V. 43

BIBLE. MPONGWE - 1852

The Gospel According to St. John. New York: 1852. V. 43

BIBLE. NAVAHO - 1917

God Bizad. New York: 1917. V. 38; 44

BIBLE. OJIBWA - 1844

The New Testament of Our Lord and Saviour Jesus Christ. New York: 1844. V. 37

BIBLE. OJIBWA - 1866

Iu Otoshki-Kikinoiuin Au Tebeniminung Gaie Bemajiinung Jesus Christ . . . The New Testament of Our Lord and Saviour Jesus Christ, translated into the language of the Ojibwa Indians. New York: 1856. V. 46

BIBLE. POLYGLOT - 1516

Psalterium Hebreum, Grecum, Arabicum & Chaldeum, cum Tribus Latinis Interpretationibus & Glossis. Genoa: 1516. V. 38; 42

BIBLE. POLYGLOT - 1519

Scroscancta Quator Iesu Christi D. N. Evangelia Arabice Scripta . . . Rome: 1619. V. 38

BIBLE. POLYGLOT - 1528

Precationes Aliquot Celebriores, e Sacris Bibliis Desumptae. Lyons: 1528. V. 41

BIBLE. POLYGLOT - 1545

Psalterium Davidicum Graecolatinum . . . Paris: 1545. V. 38; 43

BIBLE. POLYGLOT - 1549

Evangelia et Epistolae Graece et Latine . . . Basle: 1549. V. 43

BIBLE. POLYGLOT - 1558

Il Testamento . . . Latino & Volgare . . . Gradotto dal Testo Greco. Lyon: 1558. V. 40

BIBLE. POLYGLOT - 1562

Les Espistres Sainct Paul. Les Epistres Catholiques de Sainct Jacques, Sainct Pierre & S. Jean. L'Apocalypse ou Revelation de Sainct Jean. Lyon: 1562. V. 37

BIBLE. POLYGLOT - 1569-1571

Biblia Sacra Hebraice, Chaldaice, Graece & Latine. Antwerp: 1569 -71. V. 45

BIBLE. POLYGLOT - 1570

Novum Testamentum Iesu Christi Filii Dei, ex Versione Erasami. Basel: 1570. V. 37

BIBLE. POLYGLOT - 1571

Novvm Testamentvm Iesv Christi, Graece et Latine, Primo Quidem Studio & Industris Des Erasmi Roter . . . Basil: 1571. V. 46

BIBLE. POLYGLOT - 1583

Nouum Iesu Christi D. N. Testamentum. Paris: 1583. V. 40

BIBLE. POLYGLOT - 1584

Biblia Hebraica. Eorundem Latina Interpretatio Xantis Pagnini Lucensis, Recenter Benedicti Ariae Montani . . . Novum Testamentum Graecum, cum Vulgata Interpretatione . . . Apocryphi . . . Antwerp: 1584. V. 39; 40

Bible in the Original Tongues. Antwerp: 1854. V. 40

BIBLE. POLYGLOT - 1588

Jesu Christi Domini Nostri Novum Testamentum . . . Th. Bezae Annotationes. Geneva: 1588. V. 41

BIBLE. POLYGLOT - 1591

Evangelia Arabice, cum Interpretatione Latina Antonii Sionitae. Colophon: 1591. V. 40

BIBLE. POLYGLOT - 1609

Novum Testamentum Gracecum, cum Vulgata Interpretatione Latina Graeci Contextus Lineas Inserta . . . Biblia Hebraica, Eorundem Latina Interpretatio Xantis Pagnini Lucensis . . . Geneva: 1609. V. 39

BIBLE. POLYGLOT - 1612

*Bibliorum Pars Graeca Quae Hebraice non Inventur: cum Interlineari Interpretatione Latina, ex Biblis Complutensibus Depromta. *Novum Testamentum Graece, cum Vulgate Interpretatione Latina, Graeci Contextus Lineis Inserta.* Antwerp: 1612-13. V. 38

BIBLE. POLYGLOT - 1629

Biblia. 1. Hebraica. 2. Samaritana. 3. Chaldaica. 4. Graeca. 5. Syriaca. 6. Latina. 7. Arabica. Paris: 1629-45. V. 40

BIBLE. POLYGLOT - 1635

Novum Testamentum. Wittemberg: 1635, 1636. V. 40

BIBLE. POLYGLOT - 1744

Bible (Psalms, Coptic and Arabic). Rome: 1744. V. 37

BIBLE. POLYGLOT - 1772

Daniel Secundum Septuaginta ex Tetraplis Origenis. Nunc Primum Editus e Singulari Chisiano Codice. Rome: 1772. V. 39

BIBLE. POLYGLOT - 1788

Daniel Secundum Editionem LXX Interpretum. Milan: 1788. V. 38

BIBLE. POLYGLOT - 1818

The Three Epistles of the Apostle John. Translated into Delaware Indian by C. F. Dencke. New York: 1818. V. 41; 42

BIBLE. POLYGLOT - 1822

The Fifth Book of Moses, Called Deuteronomy. London: 1822. V. 40

BIBLE. POLYGLOT - 1845

Polyglot Bible. Hartford;: 1845. V. 37

The Law of God. Philadelphia: 1845. V. 46

BIBLE. POLYGLOT - 1860

The New Testament of Our Lord and Savior Jesus Christ, Translated Out of the Original Greek and with the Fromer Translations Diligently Compared and Revised. New York: 1860. V. 39

BIBLE. POLYGLOT - 1864

Ke Kauoha Hou . . . the New Testament. New York: 1860. V. 38

BIBLE. POLYGLOT - 1922

The Apocalypse in Latin and French. Oxford: 1922. V. 40

BIBLE. POLYGLOT - 1923

The Song of Songs. Berlin: 1923. V. 44

BIBLE. POLYGLOT - 1925

Le Livre D'Esther. Paris: 1925. V. 45

BIBLE. POLYGLOT - 1940

Hebrew Bible with English Translation. Jerusalem. V. 45

BIBLE. PORTUGUESE - 1839

O Novo Testamento de Nosso Senhor Jesu Christo . . . New York: 1839. V. 41

BIBLE Promises for Every Day. Specially issued for the Sunday Companion. Glasgow: 1890. V. 37

BIBLE. ROMANSCH - 1733

Pslams da David. Strada: 1733. V. 37

BIBLE. SCOTTISH GAELIC - 1767

Tiomnadh Nuadh . . . . Dun Eudain: 1767. V. 45

BIBLE. SHORTHAND - 1687

The Holy Bible in Shorthand. Colophon: 1687. V. 40

BIBLE. SINHALESE - 1776

De Algemeene Sendbrieven der Heiligen Apostelen. Colombo: 1776. V. 44

BIBLE. SPANISH - 1556

El Testamento Nuevo. Geneva: 1556. V. 46

BIBLE. SPANISH - 1569

La Biblia que es los Sacros Libros del Vieio y Nuevo Testament. Basel: 1569. V. 40; 41

BIBLE. SPANISH - 1824

La Biblia Sagrada, a Saber . . . Neuva York: 1824. V. 41

BIBLE. SYRIAC - 1625

Psalmi Davidis Regis & Prophetae Lingua Syriaca. Leyden: 1625. V. 43

BIBLE. TAMIL - 1852

Bible. New Testament. Madras: 1852. V. 43; 44

BIBLE. TONGAN - 1852

Koe Tohi Oe Fuakava Foou. London: 1852. V. 46

BIBLE. TUKUDH - 1874

Nuwheh Kukwadhud Jesus Christ Vih Kwunduk Nirzi Matthew, Mark, Luke, John. London: 1874. V. 44

BIBLE. TURKISH - 1819

New Testament in Turkish. St. Petersburg: 1819. V. 37

BIBLE. WELSH - 1620

Y Bibl Cyssegr-Lan, sef yr Hen Testament a'r Newydd. Printedig yn Llundain gan: 1620. V. 37

BIBLE. WELSH - 1927

Llyfr y Pregeth-wr (The Book of Ecclesiastes). London: 1927. V. 40

Llyfr y Pregeth-wr (The Book of Ecclesiastes). Newtown: 1927. V. 42

BIBLE. WELSH - 1929

Psalmau Dafydd. Newtown: 1929. V. 37; 45

BIBLIANDER, THEODORUS

Dee Ratione Communi Linguarum & Literaru Commentarius Theodori Bibliandri. Zurich: 1548. V. 37

THE BIBLICAL Keepsake: or Landscape Illustrations of the Most Remkarable Places Mentioned in the Holy Scriptures . . . London: 1835. V. 37

THE BIBLIOGRAPHER. London: 1881-81. V. 46
THE BIBLIOGRAPHER. London: 1882-84. V. 38; 39

THE BIBLIOGRAPHER. A Journal of Book-Lore. London: 1881-83. V. 39

BIBLIOGRAPHIANA, by a Society of Gentlemen . . . Manchester: 1817. V. 45

BIBLIOGRAPHICA: Papers on Books, Their History and Art. London: 1895-97. V. 38; 39; 40; 41; 45; 46
BIBLIOGRAPHICA: Papers on Books, Their History and Art. Westport: 1970. V. 46

THE BIBLIOGRAPHICAL and Retrospective Miscellany. London: 1830. V. 38; 42

BIBLIOGRAPHICAL Catalog of First Editions, Proof Copies and Manuscripts of Books by Lord Byron. 1925. V. 38; 40

BIBLIOGRAPHICAL SOCIETY, LONDON.
Hand-Lists of Books Printed by London Printers, 1501-1556. London: 1913. V. 39

BIBLIOGRAPHICAL SOCIETY OF THE UNIVERSITY OF VIRGINIA
Studies in Bibliography: Papers . . . Charlottesville: 1948-70. V. 42

BIBLIOGRAPHY of American Literature. Volume 8: Charles Warren Stoddard to Susan B. Warner. London: 1990. V. 46

A BIBLIOGRAPHY of the Books Issued by Hacon & Ricketts. London: 1904. V. 41; 42

BIBLIOGRAPHY of the British History: The Eighteenth Century, 1714-1789. Oxford: 1951. V. 41

BIBLIOGRAPHY of the Hawaiian Islands. New York: 1962. V. 45

A BIBLIOGRAPHY of the Writings of Harvey Cushing. Springfield: 1939. V. 45
A BIBLIOGRAPHY of the Writings of Harvey Cushing. Springfield: 1939. V. 42; 45

A BIBLIOGRAPHY of the Writings of Harvey Cushing Prepared on the Occasion of His Seventieth Brithday April 8, 1939. Springfield: 1940. V. 39; 40

THE BIBLIOPHILE. London: 1908-09. V. 39

BIBLIOPHILE'S Delight. A Book About Books. V. 44

BIBLIOTHECA Americana. London: 1789. V. 39; 42

BIBLIOTHECA Anatomica, Medica, Chirurgica &c. London: 1711. V. 41; 43

BIBLIOTHECA Diatomologica. Braunschweig: 1983-87. V. 38

BIBLIOTHECA Topographia Britannica. 1780-90. V. 39

BIBLIOTHEQUE DU CHATEAU DE MOUCHY
Catalogue de la Bibliotheque du Chateau de Mouchy. Paris: 1872. V. 38

BIBLIOTHEQUE du Magnetisme Animal. Paris: Vol. I Imprimerie de: 1817-19. V. 40

BIBLIOTHEQUE Portative Du Voyager. Paris: 1802-12. V. 41

BICHAT, MARAIE FRANCOIS XAVIER 1771-1802
Anatomie Generale, Appliquee a la Medecine. (Additions a l'Anatomie Generale . . . Par P. A. Beclard). Paris: 1801, 1821. V. 37

BICHAT, MARIE FRANCOIS XAVIER
General Anatomy, Applied to Physiology and Medicine. Boston: 1822. V. 40
General Anatomy, Applied to Physiology and the Practice of Medicine. London: 1824. V. 42
Physiological Researches on Life and Death . . . Boston: 1827. V. 42; 44
Physiological Researches on Life and Death. Boston: 1827. V. 39
Traite d'Anatomie Descriptive. Paris: 1801-03. V. 38
A Treatise on the Membranes in General, and on Different Membranes in Particular . . . Paris: 1802. V. 44
A Treatise on the Membranes in General and on Different Membranes in Particular. Boston: 1813. V. 39; 40; 42

BICK, EDGAR
Source Book of Orthopaedics. Baltimore: 1937. V. 42

BICK, MALCOLM W.
Poems. Northampton: 1965. V. 45

BICKELL, L.
Bookbinding from the Hessian Historical Exhibition Illustrating the Art of Bookbinding from the XVth to the XVIIIth Centuries. Leipzig: 1893. V. 37; 46

BICKELL, R.
The West Indies as They Are. London: 1825. V. 40

BICKERDYKE, JOHN
Curiosities of Ale and Beer. London: 1890. V. 46

BICKERSTAFF, ISAAC d. 1812
Love in a Village. London: 1765. V. 38
Predictions for the Year 1708. London: 1708. V. 41
Songs Introduc'd in the New Dramatic Entertainment Called the Sultan; or, a Peep into Seraglio. N.P.: London: 1775? V. 45

BICKERSTAFF, LAURA
Pioneer Artists of Taos. Denver: 1955. V. 43

BICKERSTETH, EDWARD
A Treatise on Prayer. London: 1819. V. 37

BICKERSTETH, J. B.
History of the 6th Cavalry Brigade, 1914-1991. London. V. 46

BICKERTON, THOMAS H.
A Medical History of Liverpool from the Earliest Days to the Year 1920 From the Data Collected by the Late Thomas H. Bickerton. London: 1936. V. 40

BICKFORD, JAMES
The Authentic Life of Mrs. Mary Ann Bickford, Who Was Murdered in the City of Boston on the 27th of October, 1845. Boston: 1846. V. 45

BICKHAM, GEORGE
ABC; or Alphabets, In All the Usual Hands Now Practis'd. &c. London: 1743. V. 40
The British Monarchy. London: 1743, 1748. V. 39
Delicaiae Britannicae; or, the Curiosities of Kensington, Hampton Court and Windsor Castle . . . London: 1755? V. 43
Deliciae Britannice; or, the Curiosities of Kensington, Hampton Court and Windsor Castle, Delineated; with Occasional Reflections. London. V. 38
A Description of All the Cities and Borough Towns, in England and Wales. London: 1740? V. 46
A Description of the Gardens and Buildings at Kew . . . (and) A Short Account of the Principal Seats and Gardens in and About Richmond and Kew. Brentford: 1770. V. 37
Penmanship In Its Utmost Beauty and Extent, a New Copy-Book. London: 1731. V. 45
The Universal Penman. London: 1741. V. 40; 46
The Universal Penman. London: 1743. V. 37; 43; 44
The Universal Penman. New York: 1941. V. 43

BICKHAM, JOHN
Fables and Other Short Poems Collected from the Most Celebrated English Authors the Whole Curiously Engrav'd for the Practice and Amusement of Young Gentlemen and Ladies in the Art of Writing. London: 1731. V. 37; 38; 40

BICKHAM, WILLIAM D.
From Ohio to the Rocky Mountains. Editorial Correspondence of the Dayton (Ohio) Journal. Dayton: 1879. V. 37; 38; 42
Rosecran's Campaign with the 14th Army. Cincinnati: 1863. V. 45

BICKLEY, A. C.
Midst Surrey Hills. London: 1890. V. 42

BICKLEY, F.
The Adventures of Harlequin. London: 1923. V. 38

BICKMORE, ALBERT S.
Travels in the East Indian Archipelago. London: 1868. V. 45
Travels in the East Indian Archipelago. New York: 1869. V. 37; 40

BICKNELL, A. C.
Travel and Adventure in Northern Queensland. London: 1895. V. 38

BICKNELL, AMOS JACKSON
Bicknell's Village Builder. (with) Supplement. Troy & Springfield: 1871. V. 43
Bicknell's Village Builder. (with) Supplement to Bicknell's Village Builder. New York: 1872/71. V. 44
Bicknell's Street, Store & Bank Fronts. New York: 1878. V. 39

BICKNELL, ARTHUR C.
Travel and Adventure in Northern Queensland. London: 1895. V. 39; 41; 45

BICKNELL, C.

Flowering Plants and Ferns of the Riviera and Neighbouring Mountains. London: 1885. V. 38; 39

BICKNELL, EDMUND

Ralph's Scrap Book. Lawrence: 1905. V. 38

BICKNELL, JOHN L.

Musical Travels through England. London: 1775. V. 42

BICKNELL, LES

13 Potential Poems: the Incomplete Works. London: 1986. V. 46

BICKNELL, THOMAS W.

Circular: New England Colony Association for Dakota. Boston: 1887. V. 39

BICKNELL, W. I.

The Natural History of the Sacred Scriptures and a Guide to General Zoology. London: 1850-51? V. 37; 38

BICKSHAM, W. D.

From Ohio to the Rocky Mountains. Dayton: 1879. V. 45

BIDDELL, HERMAN

The Suffolk Stud-Book: a History and Register of the County Breed of Cart Horses . . . London: 1880. V. 39

BIDDLE, A. J. DREXEL

The Land of the Wine Being an Account of the Madeira Islands at the beginning of the Twentieth Century and from a New Point of View. Philadelphia: 1901. V. 40

BIDDLE, CLEMENT

The Philadelphia Directory. Philadelphia: 1791. V. 41; 42; 43

BIDDLE, EDWARD

The Life and Works of Thomas Sully (1783-1872). Philadelphia: 1921. V. 46

BIDDLE, ELLEN MC GOWAN

Reminiscences of a Soldier's Wife. Philadelphia: 1907. V. 39; 42; 45

BIDDLE, LOUIS

A Memorial Containing Travels through Life or Sundry Incidents in the Life of Dr. Benjamin Rush . . . Philadelphia: 1905. V. 46

BIDDLE, MONCURE & CO.

A Christmas Letter. Philadelphia: 1940-45. V. 39

BIDDLE, NICHOLAS

An Ode to Bogle, July 16, 1829. Philadelphia: 1865. V. 37; 42

BIDDLE, RICHARD

Captain Hall in America. Philadelphia: 1830. V. 38
A Memoir of Sebastian Cabot . . . London: 1831. V. 46

BIDDULPH, E.

Some Account of the Case Between Elizabeth Cannning, and Mary Squires . . . London: 1754. V. 46

BIDDULPH, JOHN

The Pirates of Malabar and an English-Woman in India Two Hundred Years Ago. London: 1907. V. 41

BIDEN, W. D.

The History and Antiquities of the Ancient and Royal Town of Kingston-upon-Thames. Kingston: 1852. V. 41

BIDIE, GEORGE

Report on Neilgherry Loranthaceous Parasitical Plants Destructive to Exotic Forest and Fruit Trees. Madras: 1874. V. 43

BIDLAKE, JOHN

The Country Parson, a Poem. London: 1797. V. 41
The Sea: a Poem. In Two Books. London: 1796. V. 41
The Summer's Eve; a Poem. London: 1800. V. 41
The Year, a Poem. London: 1813. V. 42

BIDLOO, G.

Anatomia Humani Corporis, Centum et Quinque Tabulis Per Artificiosiss. Amsterdam: 1685. V. 41; 42; 45
Komste van Zyne majesteit Willem III Koning van Groot Britanje, enz. in Holland. 'sGravenhaage: 1691. V. 37
Relation du Voyage de sa Majeste Britannique en Hollande et de la Reception qui Luy e Ete fait. La Haye: 1692. V. 42; 46
Relation du Voyage de Sa Majeste Britannique en Hollande, et de la Reception qui luy a ete Faite. La Haye: 1672. V. 37

BIDPAI

The Fables of Pilay. London: 1818. V. 43

The Fables of Pilay. London: 1818. V. 46
Kalila and Dima, or the Fables of Bidpai. Oxford: 1819. V. 37

BIDWELL, ANNE KENNEDY

An Example of Indian Civilization. N.P.: 1891. V. 45

BIDWELL, BARNABUS

The Susquehannah Title Stated and Examined in a Series of Numbers. Catskill: 1796. V. 45

BIDWELL, CHARLES TOLL

The Isthumus of Panama. London: 1865. V. 39

BIDWELL, GEORGE H.

Treatise on the Imposition of Forms. New York: 1865. V. 37

BIDWELL, JOHN

A Bibliophile's Los Angeles: Essays for the International Association of Bibliophiles on the Occasion of Its XIVth Congress. Los Angeles: 1985. V. 37
Echoes of the Past. Chicago: 1914. V. 37; 42
Gen. Bidwell's Letter of Acceptance. N.P.: 1892. V. 37; 41
Journey to California with Observations About the Country . . . . San Francisco: 1937. V. 38; 41; 42; 45

BIEBER, MARGARETE

Ancient Copies: Contributions to the History of Greek and Roman Art. New York: 1977. V. 37; 40
The History of the Greek and Roman Theater. Princeton: 1961. V. 37; 42; 44
The Sculpture of the Hellenistic Age. New York: 1967. V. 44

BIEBER, RALPH P.

Exploring Southwestern Trails 1846-54. Glendale: 1938. V. 41; 44
Marching With the Army of the West, 1846-1848. Glendale: 1936. V. 40; 41; 44; 45
Southern Trails to California in 1849. Glendale: 1937. V. 45
The Southwest Historical Series. Glendale: 1931-43. V. 40
The Southwest Historical Series. Glendale: 1943. V. 46

BIEDERMAN, CHARLES

Art as the evolution of Visual Knowledge. Red Wing: 1948. V. 37; 40; 41; 42; 44

BIEGEL, PETER

Peter Biegels racing Pictures. London: 1983. V. 39

BIEHL, EDITH

Bookbinding, Its Background and Technique. New York: 1946. V. 46

BIEL, GABRIEL

Sacri Canonis Misse tam Mystica Quam Litteralis Expositio (with the text); Basel: 1510. V. 37
Treatise on the Power and Utility of Moneys . . . Lately Done into English by Robert Belle Burke for Josiah Harmar Penniman . . . Phildelphia: 1930. V. 38

BIELEFELD, CHARLES FREDERICK

On the Use of the Improved Papier-Mache in Furniture, in the Interior Decoration of Buildings . . . London: 1843. V. 38; 40; 44

BIEN, HERMAN M.

Oriental Legends and Other Poems. New York: 1883. V. 44

BIENATUS, AURELIUS

Oratio in Funere Laurentii Medice Neapoli Habita. Milan: 1492. V. 41

BIENSAN, R. DE

Conduct of a Contact Squadron. London & Aldershot: 1883. V. 41

BIER, JOHANN JACOB

Oryktographia (in Greek) Norica, sive Rerum Fossilium et ad Minerale Regnum Pertinentium, in Territorio Norimbergensi Eiusque Vicinia Observatarum Succincta Descrptio. Nuremberg: 1798. V. 38

BIERCE, AMBROSE 1842-1914

Battle Sketches. London: 1930. V. 38; 42; 46
Battle Sketches. Oxford: 1930. V. 37
Black Beetles in Amber. San Francisco: 1892. V. 43; 46
Black Beetles in Amber. San Francisco & New York: 1892. V. 37; 39; 43; 44; 45; 46
Cobwebs from an Empty Skull. London & New York: 1874. V. 38; 40; 41; 43
Cobwebs from an Empty Scull. New York: 1874. V. 41
The Collected Works. New York: & Washington: 1908-12. V. 46
The Collected Works. New York & Washington: 1909-12. V. 39
The Cynic's Word Book. New York: 1906. V. 38; 43

BIERCE, AMBROSE 1842-1914 continued

The Dance of Death. San Francisco: 1877. V. 43; 46

The Dance of Life. San Francisco: 1877. V. 43

Fantastic Fables. New York: 1899. V. 40; 42; 43; 45

Fantastic Fables. New York & London: 1899. V. 43

The Fiend's Delight. London: 1872. V. 40

The Fiend's Delight. London: 1873. V. 37; 42

The Fiend's Delight. New York: 1873. V. 43; 44; 45

In the Midst of Life. London: 1892. V. 38

In the Midst of Life. New York: 1898. V. 39; 43

In the Midst of Life. New York: & London: 1901. V. 43

An Invocation. San Francisco: 1928. V. 37

The Letters of Ambrose Bierce. San Francisco: 1922. V. 37; 45

The Monk and the Hangman's Daughter. Chicago: 1892. V. 37; 42; 43

The Monk and the Hangman's Daughter. New York & Washington: 1907. V. 43

My Favorite Murder. New York: 1916. V. 39; 43

Nuggets and Dust Panned Out in California by Dod Grile. London: 1873. V. 37; 38; 43; 46

The Shadow of the Dial and Other Essays. San Francisco: 1909. V. 38; 39; 43; 44; 45; 46

Shapes of Clay. San Francisco: 1903. V. 38; 43

A Son of the Gods & a Horseman in the Sky. 1907. V. 39

A Son of the Gods and a Horseman in the Sky. San Francisco: 1907. V. 43; 46

Tales of Soldiers and Civilians. 1891. V. 43

Tales of Soldiers and Civilians. San Francisco: 1891. V. 37; 39; 40; 41; 43; 44; 45; 46

Ten Tales. London: 1925. V. 39

Twenty-One Letters of Ambrose Bierce. Cleveland: 1922. V. 38; 43

The Collected Works. New York: 1909. V. 40; 42

Write It Right. New York: 1909. V. 39; 43; 44

BIERCE, LUCIUS V.

Historical Reminiscences of Summit County. Akron;: 1854. V. 37; 45

BIERSTADT, CHARLES

Gems of American Scenery Consisting of Stereoscopic Views Among the White Mountains. Niagara Falls: 1875. V. 39

BIERSTADT, EDWARD

Picturesque St. Augustine: Views in the Old City Printed in Permanent inks. New York: 1891. V. 42

BIERSTADT, O. A.

The Library of Robert Hoe. A Contribution to the History of Bibliophilism in America. New York: 1895. V. 43

BIERUT, BOLESLAW

The Six Year Plan for the Reconstruction of Warsaw. Warsaw: 1951. V. 39

BIESE, NICOLAS

De Methodo Medicine Liber Unus. Antwerp: 1564. V. 46

BIESELE, R. L.

The History of the German Settlements in Texas. Austin: 1930. V. 41; 42

BIESELE, RUDOLPH

The History of the German Settlements in Texas, 1831-1861. Austin: 1930. V. 37; 38; 43

THE BIG Book of Fables. London: 1912. V. 43

BIGALAND, JOHN

A Natural History of Animals (. . . Birds, Fishes, Reptiles and Insects). Philadelphia: 1828. V. 43

BIGELOW, ABIJAH 1775-1860

Essays on Various Subjects: to Which is Added, a Short Treatise on the Art of Praising One's Self; and Several Poetical Fragments. Leonminster: 1801. V. 39

BIGELOW, ANDREW

Leaves from a Journal; Sketches of Rambles in North Britain and Ireland. Edinburgh: 1824. V. 37

BIGELOW, H. E.

North American Species of Clitocybe. London: 1982-85. V. 37

BIGELOW, HENRY J.

Ether and Chloroform. Boston: 1848. V. 37; 38; 41; 42; 45

Litholapaxy or Rapid Lithotrity with Evacuation. Boston: 1878. V. 44

BIGELOW, HORATIO

Gunnerman. New York: 1939. V. 39; 44

An International System of Electro-Therapeutics. Philadelphia: 1895. V. 38; 41; 42; 45

BIGELOW, JACOB 1787-1879

American Medical Botany. Boston: 1817-20. V. 38; 40

American Medical Botany 1817-1821. Boston: 1979. V. 39

A Collection of Plants of Boston . . . Boston: 1824. V. 40

A Discourse on Self-Limited Diseases. Delivered Before the Massachusetts Medical Society at Their Annual Meeting, May 27, 1835. Boston: 1835. V. 44

Elements of Technology. Boston: 1829. V. 38; 44

Elements of Technology . . . Boston: 1831. V. 40

Eolopoesis. New York: 1855. V. 43

Florula Bostoniensis. Boston: 1824. V. 45

Modern Inquiries: Classical, Professional and Miscellaneous. Boston: 1867. V. 40; 44; 45

Nature in Disease. Boston: 1854. V. 38; 45

A Treatise on the Materia Medica, Intended as a Sequel to the Pharmacopoeia of the United States. Boston: 1822. V. 37

BIGELOW, JOHN

American Men of Letters: William Cullen Bryant. Boston & New York: 1890. V. 46

The Farewell Banquet to Mr. John Bigelow, Envoy Extraordinary and Minister Plenipotentiary of the United States to France. Paris: 1867. V. 40

Memoir of the Life and Public Services of John Charles Fremont. New York: 1856. V. 40; 41; 44; 46

Retrospections of an Active Life, 1817-1879. New York: 1909-13. V. 38; 39; 42

BIGELOW, JOSEPH

Elements of Technology Taken Chiefly from a Course of Lectures Delivered at Cambridge, on the Application of the Sciences to the Useful Arts Now Published . . . Boston: 1829. V. 38

BIGELOW, TIMOTHY

Journal of a Tour to Niagara Falls in the Year 1805. With an Introduction by a Grandson. Boston: 1876. V. 37

An Oration Pronounced at Cambridge, Before the (Greek letters) Phi Beta Kappa at their Annual Meeting on Thursday, July 21, 1796. Boston: 1797. V. 43; 46

BIGG, JOHN STANYAN

The Sea-King. London: 1848. V. 37

BIGG, R. HEATHER

The Amputations Which Afford the Most Appropriate Stumps in Civil and Military Surgery. London: 1869. V. 40

BIGGAR, H. P.

The Early Trading Companies of New France. Toronto: 1901. V. 44

The Percursors of Jacques Cartier 1497-1534. Ottawa: 1911. V. 44

Voyages of Jacques Cartier. Ottawa: 1924. V. 38

BIGGE, THOMAS

Considerations on the State of Parties, and the Means of Effecting a Reconciliation Between Them. London: 1793. V. 41

BIGGERS, DON H.

German Pioneers in Texas. Fredericksburg: 1925. V. 37; 42; 44

BIGGERS, DON HAMPTON

A Biggers Chronicle. Lubbock: 1961. V. 40; 45

BIGGERS, EARL DERR

Behind that Curtain. 1928. V. 39

Charlie Chan Carries On. Indianapolis: 1903. V. 39

Charlie Chan Carries On. Indianapolis: 1926. V. 44

Charlie Chan Carries On. 1930. V. 39

Charlie Chann Carries On. Indianpolis: 1930. V. 45

Charlie Chan Carries on. New York: 1931. V. 37; 39; 45

Keeper of the Keys. 1932. V. 39

Keeper of the Keys. Indianapolis: 1932. V. 39

Seven Keys to Baldplate. 1913. V. 39

BIGGS, JAMES

The History of Don Francisco de Miranda's Attempt to Effect a Revolution in South America, in a Series of Letters. Boston: 1811. V. 45

BIGGS, JOSEPH

A Concise History of the Kehukee Baptist Association from Its Original Rise to the Present Time. Tarboro: 1834. V. 45

BIGGS, WILLIAM

Narrative of the Captivity of William Biggs Among the Kickapoo Indians in Illinois in 1788. New York: 1922. V. 37

BIGHAM, CLIVE

The Roxburgh Club. Its History and Its Members, 1812-1927. Oxford: 1928. V. 44; 46

BIGHAM, ROBERT W.

California, Gold Field Scences: Selections from Quien Sabe's Gold field Manuscripts. Nashville: 1886. V. 37; 42

BIGLAND, JOHN

Letters on the Modern History and Political Aspect of Europe . . . London: 1806. V. 46

A Natural History of Animals. Philadelphia: 1834. V. 37

A Topographical and Historical Description of the County of York . . . London: 1819. V. 41

BIGLAND, RALPH

Observations on Marriages, Baptisms and Burials, as Preserved in Parochial Registers . . . London: 1764. V. 40; 43

BIGLER, JOHN

Governor's Annual Message to the Legislature of the State of California, Assembled at Scaramento Jan. 1, 1855. Sacramento: 1855. V. 40

Second Inaugural Address of His Excellency . . . Governor of the State of California. Benicia: 1854. V. 42

BIGLY, CANTELL A.

Aurifodina: or, Adventures in the Gold Region. New York: 1849. V. 37

BIGMORE, E. C.

A Bibliography of Printing. London: 1880-4-6. V. 38

A Bibliography of Printing. New York: 1945. V. 37; 41; 42; 44; 45

A Bibliography of Printing. New York: 1945. V. 37

BIGNEY, T. O.

A Month With the Muses. Pueblo: 1875. V. 37; 38; 39; 40; 41

BIGNON, JEAN PAUL

The Adventures of Abdalla, Son of Hanif, Sent by the Sultan of the Indies, to Make a Discovery of the Island of Borico. London: 1729. V. 41

The Adventures of Abdalla, son of Hanif; sent by the Sultan of the Indies, to make a discovery of the Island of Borico. By Mr. DeSandisson done into English by William Hatchett. The Second Edition. London: 1730. V. 37

BIGSBY, JOHN JEREMIAH 1792-1881

The Shoe and Canoe; or, Pictures of Travel in the Canadas, Illustrative of their Scenery and of Colonial Life: With facts and Opinions on Emigration, State Policy, and other Points of Public Interest . . . London: 1850. V. 37; 38

BIGSBY, ROBERT

Historical and Topographical Description of Repton, in the County of Derby. London: 1854. V. 38

Old Places Revisited; or, the Antiquarian Enthusiast. London: 1851. V. 44

BIGUS, RICHARD

The Mystique of Vellum. Boston: 1984. V. 38; 39; 42; 44

BIHALJI-MERIN, OTO

Adventure of Modern Art. New York: 1966. V. 44

Adventures of Modern Art: Similarities and Differences in Art Images, Primitive, Ancient and Modern. New York. V. 39

Art Treasures of Yugoslavia. New York. V. 38; 42

BIJOU Illustrations of Christ's Life. London;: 1850. V. 46

BIJOU Illustrations of the Holy Land. Philadelphia: 1850. V. 39; 44

BIJOU Illustrations of the United States. London: (1845). V. 37

BIKER, JULIO FIRMINO JUDICE

Colleccao de Tratados e Concertos de Pazes que a Estado da India Portugueza fez com os Reis e Senhores com quem teve Relacoes nas Partes da Asia e Africa Oriental Desde o Principio da Conquista ate ao Firm do Seculo XVIII. Lisbon: 1881-87. V. 46

BIKLAKE, F. T.

Cycling. London: 1896. V. 37

BILGUER, JOHANN ULRICH VON

A Dissertation of the inutility of the amputation of the limbs. Written in latin . . . Augmented with the notes of Mr. Tissot, physician at Lausanne. Now first translated into English, by a surgeon. London: 1764. V. 37

BILIBIN, IVAN YAKOLOVICH

Little Ivanushka and His Sister Alyonushka. St. Petersburg: 1903. V. 45

BILL, HENRY

A Chart of National Flags. V. 46

BILL, LEDYARD

Minnesota: Its Character and Climate. New York: 1871. V. 43

THE BILL of Indictment Exhibited Against John Giles, . . . for His Barbarous Attempt Upon the Body of Justice Arnold; for Which He Was Then Tryed, and Found Guilty. N.P.: 1680. V. 41

A BILL to Authorise the Election of Sheriffs in the Indiana Territory. Washington: 1811. V. 37

BILLCLIFFE, ROGER

Charles Rennie Mackintosh. The Complete Furniture, Furniture Drawings and Interior Designs. London: 1986. V. 39

BILLET, ANNE LOUISE FRANCOISE

Historical Memoirs of Stepahnie Louise de Bourbon Conti. Newbern: 1801. V. 37; 45

BILLETS in the Low Countries, 1814 to 1817. London: 1818. V. 46

BILLIARDS Simplified . . . London: 1890. V. 39

BILLIG, KURT

Pre-stressed Reinforced Concrete. London: 1944. V. 44

BILLING, ARCHIBALD

The Science of Gems, Jewels, Coins and Medals, Ancient and Modern. London: 1867. V. 44

The Science of Gems, Jewels, Coins and Medals, Ancient and Modern. London: 1875. V. 41

BILLINGHURST, GEORGE

Arcana Clericalia, or the Mysteries of Clerkship as to the Sure Settlements of Estates by Deeds, Fines, Recoveries, etc. London: 1674. V. 40

BILLINGS, C. K. G.

Fort Tryon Hall, a Descriptive and Illustrated Catalogue. Washington Heights: 1910. V. 44

BILLINGS, E. R.

Tobacco: Its History, Varieties, Culture, Manufacture and Commerce. Hartford: 1875. V. 37; 38; 39

BILLINGS, JOHN D.

Hardtack and Coffee, or the Unwritten Story of Army Life. Boston: 1888. V. 42; 46

BILLINGS, JOHN S. 1838-1913

Circular No. 4 . . . A Report on Barracks and Hospitals, with Descriptions of Military Posts. Washington: 1870. V. 45

The Composition of Expired Air and Its Effects Upon Animal Life. Washington: 1895. V. 38

Description of the Johns Hopkins Hospital. Baltimore: 1890. V. 38

Physiological Aspects of the Liquor Problem. Boston: 1903. V. 42

A Report on the Hygiene of the United States Army, With Descriptions of Military Posts. Washington: 1875. V. 41; 44; 45

A Report on the Hygiene of the United States Army with Descriptions of Military Posts. New York: 1974. V. 45

BILLINGS, JOSH

Old Probability, Perhaps Rain, Perhaps Not. New York: 1879. V. 43; 44

BILLINGS, ROBERT WILLIAM

The Baronial and Ecclesiastical Antiquities of Scotland. London: 1848. V. 39; 45

The Baronial and Ecclesiastical Antiquities of Scotland. London: 1848. V. 39

Illustrations of Geometric Tracery, from the paneling Belonging to Carlisle Cathedral. (and) The Geometric Tracery of Branceperth Church. London: 1842, 1845. V. 37; 40; 44

Illustrations of Architectural Antiquities of the County of Durham . . . Durham: 1846. V. 45

The Power of Form Applied to Geometric Tracery. One hundred designs and their foundations resulting from one diagram. Edinburgh: 1851. V. 37

BILLINGS, WILLIAM

Music in Miniature. Boston: 1779. V. 40

BILLINGSLEY, JOHN

General View of the Agriculture of the County of Somerset. London: 1794. V. 41

General View of the Agriculture of the County of Somerset, with Observations on the Means of Its Improvement. Bath: 1797. V. 42; 44

BILLINGTON, JOHN

The Architectural Director and Glossary of Architecture. London: 1834. V. 38

BILLIS, R. V.

Pastoral Pioneers of Port Phillip. Melbourne: 1932. V. 41

BILLMEIR, J. A.

A Catalogue of Scientific Instruments from the 13th to the 19th Centuries. Oxford: 1955. V. 42

BILLON, FREDERIC L.

Annal of St. Louis in Its Early Days. St. Louis: 1886-1888. V. 41; 45

Annals of St. Louis In Its Territorial Days from 1804 to 1821 . . . St. Louis: 1888. V. 40; 45

BILLOT, C. P.

Melbourne: an Annotated Bibliography to 1850. Greelong: 1970. V. 41

BILLROTH, THEODOR

Clinical Surgery. Extracts from the Reports of Surgical Practice Between the Years 1860-1876. London: 1881. V. 42

General Surgical Pathology and Therapeutics. New York: 1874. V. 42

Lectures on Surgical Pathology and Therapeutics. London: 1877-78. V. 42

BILLY, JACQUES DE

Locvtionvm raecarvm In Commvnes Locos Per Alphabeti Ordinem Digestarum Volumen. Paris: 1578. V. 38; 44

BILLYNG, WILLIAM

The Five Wounds of Christ. Manchester: 1814. V. 45

BILSON, BENJAMIN

The Hunters of Kentucky; or the Trials and Toils of Trappers and Traders. New York: 1847. V. 40; 41; 43

BILSON, THOMAS

The Effect of Certaine Sermons Touching the Full Redemption of Mankind by the Death and Bloud of Christ Jesus . . . London: 1599. V. 37; 40; 43; 45

The Perpetual Government of Christes Church. London: 1593. V. 40

The True Difference Between Christian Subjection and Unchristian Rebellion . . . Oxford: 1585. V. 46

The True Difference Betweene Christian Subjection and Unchristian Rebellion. London: 1586. V. 42; 44

BILSTONE, JOHN

Preparing for the Press, from an Ancient MS De Fucorum Ordinibus Continued by a Modern Hand: a Complete History of the Mallardians From Their Rise to the Present Time. London: 1752. V. 41

BILTON, WILLIAM

The Angler in Ireland, or an Englishman's Rambles through Connaught and Munster . . . 1833. London: 1834. V. 38

BINDER, JOSEPH

Colour in Advertising. London: 1934. V. 45

Colour in Advertising. London & New York: 1934. V. 43

THE BINDINGS of Tomorrow A Record of the Work of the Guild of Women-Binders and of the Hampstead Bindery. London: 1902. V. 44

BINDLEY, CHARLES

Stable Talk and Table Talk. London: 1845, 1846. V. 39; 42

BINDLEY, JAMES

The Bindley Granger. London: 1819. V. 45

BINDON, DAVID

A Letter from a Merchant Who Has Left Off Trade to a Member of Parliament. London: 1738. V. 43

A Letter from a Merchant Who Has Left Off Trade, to a member of Parliament. London: 1753. V. 43; 46

BING, S.

Artistic Japan. London: 1888. V. 44

Artistic Japan. London: 1888-91. V. 42

BINGFIELD, WILLIAM

The Travels and Adventures of William Bingfield, Esq. London: 1853. V. 45

BINGHAM BROTHERS CO.

Everything for the Printer. New York: 1902. V. 41; 44

BINGHAM, C. T.

The Fauna of British India Including Ceylon and Burma: Hymenoptera. London: 1897-1913. V. 38

BINGHAM, CAPTAIN

The Bastille. New York: 1901. V. 41

BINGHAM, CLIFTON

The Animals' Rebellion. London: 1900. V. 45; 46

Funny Doings in Animal Land. London: 1854 (sic). V. 38

The Puzzle Picture Book. V. 40

The Puzzle Picture Book. London: 1890. V. 45

Something New for Little Folk. London: 1900. V. 46

BINGHAM, D.

The Bastille. New York: 1901. V. 37; 38

BINGHAM, HIRAM

Lost City of the Incas. New York: 1948. V. 38; 45

Machu Picchu. A Citadel of the Incas. New Haven: 1930. V. 40

A Residence of Twenty-One Years in the Sandwich Islands . . . History . . . Civilization Among the Hawaiian People . . . Hartford: 1849. V. 38

A Residence of 21 Years in the Sandwich Islands; . . . Civil, Religious and Political History. Hartford: 1847. V. 37; 38; 42

A Residence of Twenty-One Years in the Sandwich Islands; or the Civil, Religious and Political History of Those Islands. Hartford: 1848. V. 38; 39; 42; 43

Te Boki N Anene Ao Aiabai Kiritaian, Ni Karaoiroa to Atua. Colophon: 1863. V. 40

BINGHAM, JOHN

Argument of . . . Special Judge Advocate in Reply to the Arguments of the Several Counsel for Mary E. Surratt, David E. Herold, Lewis Payne, George A. Atzerodt . . . Washington: 1865. V. 43

BINGHAM, JOHN A.

Trial of the Conspirators for the Assassination of President Lincoln, &c. Washington: 1865. V. 40

BINGHAM, JOSEPH

A New Practical digest of the Law of Evidence. London: 1797. V. 40

Origines Ecclesiasticae; or, the Antiquities of the Christian Church. London: 1710-22. V. 46

Origines Ecclesiasticae. London: 1829. V. 39

BINGHAM, PEREGRINE

The Pains of Memory, a Poem. London: 1811. V. 39

The Pains of Memory. London: 1812. V. 43

BINGHAM, RICHARD

The Whole of the Trial of the Hon. Richard Bingham, for Adultery with Lady Elizabeth Howard, Wife of B. E. Howard, Esq. Presumptive Heir to the Duke of Norfolk, and Daughter to the Earl of Fauconberg. London: 1794. V. 37

BINGHAM, ROBERT J.

Photogenic Manipulation. London: 1847, 1848. V. 40

BINGLEY, BARBARA

The Painted Cup. London: 1935. V. 41; 42

BINGLEY, J.

Select Vocalist Containing Songs, Glees, Duets &c. by Eminent Composers. London: 1840. V. 41

BINGLEY, JAMES

Bingley's Select Vocalist Containing Songs, Glees, Duets &c. London: 1830? V. 44

BINGLEY, W.

Memoirs of British Quadrupeds . . . (with) A Synopsis of British Quadrupeds. London: 1809, & n.d. V. 39

North Wales: Including Its Scenery, Antiquities, Customs and Some Sketches of the Natural History . . . London: 1804. V. 45

BINGLEY, WILLIAM

Correspondence Between Frances, Countess of Hartford (afterwards Duchess of Somerset) and Henrietta Louisa, Countess of Pomfret, Between the Years 1738 and 1741. London: 1805. V. 43; 46

A Tour Round North Wales, Performed During the Summer of 1798. London: 1800. V. 41

A Tour Round North Wales Performed During the Summer of 1798. Cambridge: 1800. V. 37; 40

Useful Knowledge. Philadelphia: 1818. V. 39

BINION, SAMUEL AUGUSTUS

Ancient Egypt or Mizraim. New York: 1887. V. 38

BINKERD, A. C.

The Mammoth Cave and Its Denizens: A Complete Descriptive Guide. Cincinnati: 1869. V. 38; 45

The Mammoth Cave and its Denizens: A Complete Descriptive Guide. Cincinnati: 1896. V. 37

BINKLEY, WILLIAM CAMPBELL

The Expansionist Movement in Texas, 1836-1950. Berkeley: 1925. V. 37; 38; 39; 42

BINKOWSKI, F. P.

North American Sturgeons: Biology and Aquaculture Potential. Milwaukee: 1985. V. 37

BINNEY, AMOS

The Terrestrial Air-Breathing Mollusks of the United States and the Adjacent Territories of North America. Boston: 1859. V. 46

BINNEY, EARLE

Now is Time. Toronto: 1945. V. 42

BINNEY, HORACE

The Opinion of Mess. Binney and Chauncey, on the Acts of the Legislature of New Jersey, Respecting the Delaware and Raritan Canal, and Camden and Amboy Rail Road Companies. Trenton: 1834. V. 41; 44

BINNEY, THOMAS 1798-1874

Lights and Shadows of Church Life in Australia . . . London: 1860. V. 42

BINNS, JOHN

Monumental Inscriptions (Sacred to the Memory of John Harris . . . David Hunt . . . Edward Lind (et al). N.P.: 1828. V. 44

BINYON, LAURENCE 1869-1943

Asiatic Art in the British Museum (Sculpture and Painting). Paris: 1925. V. 38; 41

Ayuli - a Play in Three Acts and an Epilogue. Oxford: 1923. V. 43

Brief Candles. London: 1938. V. 37; 38

Brief Candles. Waltham St. Lawrence: 1938. V. 43; 45

Catalogue of Drawings by British Artists and Artists of Foreign Origin Working in Great Britain . . . London: 1898/1900/02/07. V. 42

Catalogue of the Loan Collection of English Water-Colour Drawings Held at the Institute of Art Research, Ueno, Tokyo, 1929. Tokyo: 1929. V. 43

A Catalogue of Japanese and Chinese Woodcuts . . . London: 1916. V. 44

The Court Painters of the Grand Moguls. London: 1921. V. 44

The Court Painters of the Grand Moguls. Oxford: 1921. V. 38; 40; 42

The Drawings and Engravings of William Blake. London: 1922. V. 37; 46

Dream-Came True. Hammersmith: 1905. V. 39; 43

Dream Come True. London: 1905. V. 43; 44; 46

The Engraved Designs of William Blake. London: 1926. V. 39; 41; 44; 46

The Followers of William Blake. London: 1925. V. 39; 42

The Followers of William Blake. Edward Calvert, Samuel Palmer, George Richmond and Their Circle. London & New York: 1925. V. 39

Japanese Colour Prints. London: 1923. V. 42

Japanese Colour Prints. Boston: 1960. V. 38; 41

John Crome & John Sell Cotman. London: 1897. V. 37; 38; 40

Painting in the Far East. London: 1913. V. 38

Painting in the Far East. London: 1923. V. 44

Persian Miniature Painting, Including a Critical and Descriptive Catalogue of the Miniatures Exhibited at Burlington House, Jan.-March, 1931. London: 1933. V. 45

Poems. Oxford: 1895. V. 42

The Sirens. Chelsfield: 1924. V. 41

Three Poems. Derby: 1934. V. 41; 46

The Wonder Night. New York: 1927. V. 43; 44

BINZ, C.

Lectures on Pharmacology. London: 1895-97. V. 44

BIOGRAPHIA Britannica. London: 1973. V. 39
BIOGRAPHIA Britannica. London: 1974. V. 39

BIOGRAPHIA Britannica; or the Lives of the Most Eminent Persons Who Have Flourished in Great Britain and Ireland, from the Earliest Ages, Down to the Present Times. London: 1747-66. V. 37; 38; 39; 42; 46

BIOGRAPHIA Britannica: or, The Lives of the Most Eminent Persons Who Have Flourished in Great Britain and Ireland, from the Earliest Ages, to the Present Times. London: 1747-66. V. 37

BIOGRAPHIA Britannica; or, The Lives of the Most Eminent Persons Who Have Flourished in Great Britain and Ireland, from the Earliest Ages, to the Present Times . . . London: 1778-93. V. 39

BIOGRAPHIA Classica. London: 1750. V. 42

BIOGRAPHIA Gallica: or, the Lives of the Most Eminent French Writers of Both Sexes, in Divinity, Philosophy, Mathematics, History, Poetry, etc. London: 1752. V. 37

BIOGRAPHICAL and Genalogical History of the City of Newark, Essex Co., New Jersey. New York: 1898. V. 46

BIOGRAPHICAL and Genalogical History of Morris County, New Jersey. New York: 1899. V. 46

BIOGRAPHICAL and Historical Memoirs of Northwest Louisiana Comprising a Large Fund of biography of Actual Residents and an Interesting Historical Sketch of Thirteen Counties. Nashville: 1890. V. 41

BIOGRAPHICAL Anecdotes of the Founders of the French Republic . . . London: 1797-98. V. 38

BIOGRAPHICAL Annals of Franklin County, Pennsylvania, Containing Genealogical Records . . . Chicago: 1905. V. 42

BIOGRAPHICAL Annals of Franklin County, Pennsylvania Containing Genealogical Records . . . Early Settlers, etc . . . Chicago: 1905. V. 41

THE BIOGRAPHICAL Encyclopedia of New Jersey in the Nineteenth Century. Philadelphia: 1877. V. 42; 46

BIOGRAPHICAL Encyclopedia of Texas. New York: 1880. V. 38

BIOGRAPHICAL, Genealogical and Descriptive History of the First Congressional District of New Jersey. V. 39

A BIOGRAPHICAL History with Portraits of Prominent Men of the Great West. Chicago: 1894. V. 37

THE BIOGRAPHICAL Magazine, Containing Portraits and Characters of Eminent and Ingenious Persons of Every Age and Nation. London: 1794. V. 41

BIOGRAPHICAL Review . . . Containing Life Sketches of Leading Citizens of Burlington and Camden Counties, New Jersey. Boston: 1897. V. 42

BIOGRAPHICAL Review of the Leading Citizens of Cumberland County, N.J. Boston: 1896. V. 39; 41

A BIOGRAPHICAL Sketch of the Celebrated Salem Murderer, Who fro Ten Years Has Been the Terror of Essex County, Mass. Boston: 1830. V. 42

BIOGRAPHICAL Souvenir of the Counties of Buffalo, Kearney, Phelps, Harlan, and Franklin, Nebraska. Containing Portraits and Biographies of all the President of the U.S., and the Governors of that State . . . Chicago: 1890. V. 37

BIOGRAPHICAL Souvenir of the State of Texas, Containing Biographical Sketches of the Representative Public, and Many Early Settled Families. Chicago: 1889. V. 37; 38; 42; 44; 45; 46

BIOGRAPHIE Moderne. Lives of Remarkable Characters, Who Have Distinguished Themselves from the Commencement of the French Revolution to the Present Time. London: 1811. V. 46

BIOGRAPHIE Universelle, Ancienne et Moderne. Paris: 1862. V. 46

BIOGRAPHY of Joseph Lane . . . Washington: 1852. V. 40; 43

BION, NICOLAS 1652-1733

The Construction and Principal Uses of Mathematical Instruments. London: 1723. V. 40; 42

The Construction and Principal Uses of Mathematical Instruments. London: 1758. V. 45

L'Usage des Globes Celestes et Terestres, et des Spheres Suivant les Differens Systemes du Monde, Precede d'un Traite de Cosmographie. Paris: 1699. V. 40

L'Usage des Globes. Paris: 1751. V. 42

BION, OF SMYRNA

Idylles . . . Paris: 1794/95. V. 40

Idyllia. Londini: 1795. V. 38

Illustrabat et Emendabat Gilbertus Wakefield. London: 1795. V. 40

BIONDI, GIOVANNI FRANCESCO

Eromena, or, Love and Revenge. London: 1632. V. 39

BIONDO da Forli Roma Trionfante . . . Venice: 1549. V. 40

BIONDO, FLAVIO

Le Historie de la Declinatione de l'Imperio di Roma . . . Venice: 1547. V. 45

BIRCH, GEORGE H.

London Churches of the XVIIth and XVIIIth Centuries. London: 1896. V. 38

BIRCH, JOHN

An Essay on Medical Application of Electricity. London: 1803. V. 37; 40

Examples of Labourers' Cottage, with Plans for Improving the Dwellings of the Poor in Large Towns. London: 1871. V. 38

Examples of Labourers' Cottages etc., with Plans for Improving the Dwellings of the Poor in Large Towns. Edinburgh and London: 1892. V. 38

Examples of Stables, Hunting-Boxes, Kennels, Racing Establishments &c. Edinburgh & London: 1892. V. 39; 42

Examples of Labourers' Cottages, &c. London: 1892. V. 39; 41

BIRCH, JONATHAN

Fifty-One Original Fables. London: 1833. V. 41; 43

BIRCH, S.

Fac-similes of the Egyptian Relics, Discovered at Thebes, in the Tomb of Queen Aah-Hotep (circa B.C. 1800). London: 1863. V. 44

BIRCH, SAMUEL

Catalogue of the Collection of Egyptian Antiquities at Alnwick Castle. London: 1880. V. 40; 42

History of Ancient Pottery. London: 1858. V. 38; 41

Records of the Past: Being English Translations of the Assyrian and Egyptian Monuments. London: 1873-81. V. 38

BIRCH, THOMAS 1705-1766

An Historical View of the Negotiations. London: 1749. V. 42

The History of the Royal Society of London for Improving of Natural Knowledge from Its First Rise . . . London: 1756-57. V. 42

An Inquiry into the Share King Charles I had in the Transactios of the Earl of Glamorgan . . . for bringing over a body of Irish Rebels in the years of 1645 and 1646, in which Mr. Carte's imperfect account and use of . . . London: 1756. V. 37

An Inquiry into the Share which King Charles I had in the Transactions of the Earl of Glamor-Glamorgan . . . bringing over a body of Irish Rebels, 1645-6. London: 1747. V. 37

The Life of the Honourable Robert Boyle. London: 1744. V. 37; 38; 39; 40; 41; 46

The Life of Henry Prince of Wales, Eldest Son of King James I. London: 1760. V. 45

Memoirs of the Reign of Queen Elizabeth, from the Year 1581 till Her Death. London: 1754. V. 37; 38

BIRCH, W.

A Journal of a Voyage Up the Mediterranean. London: 1818. V. 40

BIRCH, WALTER DE GRAY

History of Scottish Seals from the Eleventh to the Seventeenth Century. London: 1905-07. V. 44

BIRCH, WILLIAM

Delices de la Grande Bretagne. London: 1791. V. 41

BIRCH, WILLIAM Y.

A New and Practical Work. A Proposal . . . for Publishing in Volumes, by Subscription . . . The Domestic Encyclopedia . . . Philadelphia: 1802. V. 37

BIRCKBEK, SIMON

The Protestants Evidence. London: 1635. V. 37

BIRD & BULL PRESS

A Babylonian Anthology . . . North Hills, Pa.: 1966. V. 37

Bird & Bull Number 13. North Hills: 1972. V. 37; 39; 40; 41

Bird and Bull Pepperpot. North Hills: 1979. V. 39

The Bird & Bull Commonplace Book. North Hills: 1971. V. 37; 38; 40; 44

Chinese Decorated Papers. Newtown: 1987. V. 44

A Collection of Receipts in Cookery, Physick and Surgery . . . By Several Hands..as Published by mary Kettibly in London, 1724. Philadelphia: 1958. V. 37

The Fortas Catalogue; A Facsimile, With an Introduction by Lessing J. Rosenwald. North Hills: 1970. V. 37

A Pair on Printing. Atkyn's The Original and Growth of Printing, and William Caslon and the First English type specimen book. Reproduced in facsimile, with introductions by Cary S. Bliss. North Hills: 1982. V. 37

Thirty Years of Bird & Bull. A Bibliography, 1958-1988. Newtown: 1988. V. 40

BIRD, ANNIE

Boise - The Peace Valley. Caldwell: 1934. V. 37

BIRD, D. T.

Catalogue of Sixteenth Century Medical Books in the Edinburgh Libraries. Edinburgh: 1982. V. 39; 44; 46

BIRD, F. J.

The American Practical Dyer's Companion. Philadelphia: 1882. V. 37; 40; 45

BIRD, H. E.

Chess Masterpieces . . . London: 1875. V. 45

BIRD, JAMES

Dunwich. A Tale of the Splendid City. London: 1828. V. 41; 42

The Emigrant's Tale. London: 1832. V. 41

Machin; or, the Discovery of Madeira. London: 1821. V. 46

Poetical Memoirs. The Exile, a Tale. London: 1823. V. 39; 46

BIRD, JAMES B.

The Laws Respecting Landlords, Tenants and Lodgers, Laid Down in a Plain, Easy and Familiar Manner . . . London: 1808. V. 40; 43

BIRD, JOSEPH

Gleanings from the History of Music, from the Earliest Ages to the Commencement of the Eighteenth Century. Boston: 1850. V. 39

BIRD, ROBERT MONGOMERY 1806-1854

Peter Pilgrim: or, a Rambler's Recollections. London: 1839. V. 44

BIRD, ROBERT MONTGOMERY 1806-1854

The Adventures of Robin Day. Philadelphia: 1839. V. 43

Calavar; or, the Knight of the Conquest. Philadelphia: 1834. V. 43

The Hawks of Hawk-Hollow. Philadelphia: 1835. V. 43

The Hawks of Hawk-Hollow: a Tradition of Pennsylvania. London: 1839. V. 44

The Infidel; or the Fall of Mexico. Philadelphia: 1835. V. 38; 40; 43; 44

Nick of the Woods; or, the Jibbenainosay. Philadelphia: 1837. V. 43

Nick of the Woods: a Story of Kentucky. London: 1837. V. 37

Peter Pilgrim; or a Rambler's Recollections. Philadelphia: 1838. V. 43

Sheppard Lee. New York: 1836. V. 43; 44

BIRD, S. DOUGAN

On Australasian Climates and Their Influence in the Prevention and Arrest of PUlmonary Consumption. London: 1863. V. 40

BIRD Study. London: 1954-86. V. 37; 38

BIRD, WILL R.

A Century at Chignecto: the Key to Old Acadia. Toronto: 1928. V. 42

Maid of the Marshes. Amherst: 1935. V. 43

BIRD, WILLIAM

The Magazine of Honour . . . London: 1642. V. 38; 39; 40; 45

BIRDS of the Kruger and Other National Parks. Volume I. Cape Town: 1959. V. 40

BIRDS of the World. London: 1969-71. V. 37

BIRDSEYE, SIDNEY H.

Informe Detallodo de la Comision Tecnica de Demaracion de la Frontera entre Guatemala y Honduras . . . Washington: 1937. V. 40

BIRDSONG, JAMES C.

Brief Sketches of the North Carolina State Troops in the War Between the States. Raleigh, NC: 1894. V. 37

BIRDWOOD, GEORGE

The Register of Letters etc. of the Governour and Company of Merchants of London trading into the East Indies 1600-1619. London: 1893. V. 37

BIRELLI, GIAMBATISTA

Opere, Tomo Primo, Nel Qual si Tratta dell' Alchimia, Suoi Membri, Utili, Curiosi & Dilletevoli, con la Vita d'Hermete . . . Florence: 1601. V. 46

BIRELLI, GIAMBATISTSA

Alchiminia Nova, das Ist, Die Guldene Kunst Selbst, Oder Aller Kunsten Gutter . . . Frankfurt: 1603. V. 46

BIRGE, JULIUS C.

The Awakening of the Desert. Boston: 1912. V. 42

BIRGITT, SAINT

Von den Syben Sondern Frewden Marie die Sie Hie in Zeyt Gehabt, Und von Syben Sondern Frewden die Sie Yetz zu Himmel Hat. N.P.: 1510-20. V. 38

BIRGITTA, SAINT

Revelationes, Niederdeutsch. Lubeck: 1478. V. 40

Revelationes. Romae: MDLVII. V. 44

BIRINGUCCIO, VANNOCCIO

La Pyrotechnie, ou Art de Feu, contneant dix livres, ausqeuls est amplement traicte de toutes sortes et diversite de minieres, fusions et separations des metaux . . . traduite d'Italien en Francois par feu maistre Jaques Vincent. Paris: 1572. V. 37; 39; 41

The Pirotechnia. 1942. V. 37

The Pirotechnia . . . New York: 1942. V. 42; 45

BIRINGUCCIO, VANNUCCIO

De la Pirotechnia. Libri X . . . Venetia: 1540. V. 38

Pirotechnia. Vinegia: 1558 (1559). V. 37

Pirotechnia. 1559. V. 42

BIRKBECK, MORRIS

Letters from Illinois. Dublin: 1818. V. 37; 42

Letters from Illinois. London: 1818. V. 39; 42; 46

Letters from Illinois . . . Illustrated by a Map of the United States . . . Philadelphia: 1818. V. 39; 42; 43; 45

Notes on a Journey through France. London: 1815. V. 37; 38; 39

Notes on a Journey in America from the Coast of Virginia to the Territory of Illinois, with Proposals for a Colony. Philadelphia: 1817. V. 39; 42

Notes on a Journey in America, from the Coast of Virginia to the Territory of Illinois. London: 1818. V. 37; 41; 42; 45

BIRKBECK, ROBERT

The Birkbecks of Westmorland and Their Descendants. London: 1900. V. 44

BIRKELAND, KNUT B.

The Whalers of Akutan. New Haven: 1926. V. 40; 41; 44; 45

BIRKETT, JOHN

The Diseases of the Breast, and Their Treatment. London: 1850. V. 42; 43

BIRKHIMER, W. E.

Letter from the Secretary of War Transmitting . . . Report of . . . Washington: 1889. V. 42

BIRKHIMER, WILLIAM EDWARD

Historical Sketch of the Organization, Administration, Material and Tactics of the Artillery, United States Army. Washington: 1884. V. 37; 46

BIRKMIRE, WILLIAM H.

The Planning and Construction of American Theatres. New York: 1901. V. 37

BIRMINGHAM, ENGLAND. ASSAY OFFICE. LIBRARY

Catalogue of the Books in the Library at the Assay Office. Birmingham: 1914. V. 39

Catalogue of the Books in the Library at the Assay Office, Birmingham. London: 1914. V. 44

BIRMINGHAM, G. A.

Irishmen All. London & Edinburgh: 1913. V. 41

BIRMINGHAM LIBRARY

Catalogue of Books Belonging to the Birmingham Library. Birmingham: 1849. V. 38

BIRNBAUM, MARTIN

Aubrey Vincent Beardsley. New York: 1911. V. 40

BIRNEY, CATHERINE

Sarah and Angelina Grimke. Boston: 1885. V. 43

BIRNEY, EARLE

Down the Long Table. Toronto: 1955. V. 45

Now Is Time. Toronto: 1945. V. 41; 43; 44

BIRNEY, JAMES G.

Correspondence Between Hon. F. H. Elmore, One of the South Carolina Delegation in Congress, and James G. Birney, One of the Secretaries of the American Anti-Slavery Society. New York: 1838. V. 42

Narrative of the Late Rioutous Proceedings Against the Liberty of the Press, in Cincinnati. Cincinnati: 1836. V. 37; 40

BIRNEY, JAMES GILLESPIE

Letters . . . 1831-1857. New York: 1938. V. 46

BIRRELL & GARNETT

Catalogue of Typefounders' Specimens, Books Printed in Founts of Historic Importance, Works on Typefounding, Printing and Bibliography. London: 1928. V. 38

BIRRELL, AUGUSTINE

Frederick Locker-Lampson. A Character Sketch. London: 1920. V. 45

BIRREN, FABER

Monument to Color. New York: 1938. V. 44

BIRT, SAMUEL

A Catalogue of Books Printed for and sold by Samuel Birt, bookseller at the Bible and Ball in Ave-mary-lane. London: 1736. V. 41

BIRTH, J. C.

Our Kin Across the Sea. London: 1888. V. 41

THE BIRTH-PLACE, or Thoughts on a Visit Made To It. London: 1775. V. 42

BIRTHS, Marriages and Deaths. London: 1954. V. 37

BIRTWHISTLE, JOHN

Vision of Wat Tyler: a Long Poem. 1972. V. 40; 45

BISACCIONI, MAJOLINO

Guerras Civiles de Inglaterra, Tragica Muerte de su Rey Carlos. Madrid: 1659. V. 38

BISANI, ALESSANDRO

A Picturesque Tour through Part of Europe, Asia and Africa . . . London: 1793. V. 39; 41; 45

BISBEE, WILLIAM H.

Through Four American Wars. Boston: 1931. V. 45

BISCHOFF, HERMANN

Deadwood to the Big Horns 1877. Bismarck, North Dakota,: 1931. V. 37; 40

BISCHOFF, JAMES

Sketch of the History of Van Dieman's Land . . . and an Account of the Van Diemen's Land Company. London: 1832. V. 39

BISHOP, A.

Na Huaolelo a Me Na Olelo Kikeke Ma Ka Olelo Beritania, A Me Ka Olelo Hawaii (English and Hawaiaan Phrase Book). Honolulu: 1871. V. 39

BISHOP, A. W.

Loyalty on the Frontier. St. Louis: 1863. V. 37; 38; 39; 42; 44

BISHOP, ABRAHAM

An Oration on the Extent and Power of Political Delusion. Delivered in New Haven . . . September 1800. Newark: 1800. V. 37; 45

Oration, in Honor of the Election of President Jefferson, and the Peaceable Acquisition of Louisiana, Delivered at the National Festival, in Hartford, on the 11th of May, 1804. Hartford: 1804. V. 44

Oration in Honor of the Election of President Jefferson, and the Peaceable Acquisition of Louisiana . . . New Haven: 1804. V. 41; 45

BISHOP, ALBERT W.

Loyalty on the Frontier, or Sketches of Uion Men of the South West . . . St. Louis: 1863. V. 45

BISHOP, CORTLANDT F.

The Cortlandt F. Bishop Library. New York: 1938/38/38/39. V. 39

The Library. American Art Association, Anderson Galleries and part 5 Kende Galleries. New York: 1938-48. V. 39

BISHOP, ELIZABETH 1911-

The Ballad of the Burglar of Babylon. New York: 1908. V. 39

The Complete Poems. New York: 1969. V. 39; 40; 42

North and South. Boston: 1946. V. 39; 42; 45

North Haven in Memoriam: Robert Lowell. 1979. V. 46

Poem. New York: 1973. V. 39; 40

Poems - North and South - a Cold Spring. Boston: 1955. V. 37; 44; 45

Poems. London: 1956. V. 38; 41; 44

BISHOP, GEORGE

New England Judged, by the Spirit of the Lord . . . London: 1703-02. V. 37; 38; 40; 45

New England Judged, Not by Man's, but the Spirit of the Lord . . . London: 1661. V. 39

Observations, Remarks and Means to Prevent Smuggling, Humbly Submitted to the Consideration of the Rt. Honourable the House of Peers, and the Honourable House of Commons . . . Maidstone: 1782. V. 42

BISHOP, H. G.

Bishop's Specimens of Job Work for Printers, Being Suggestions for Setting Up . . . business Cards, Letter Heads . . . Bill Heads . . . Oneonta: 1890. V. 41

BISHOP, HARRIET E.

Floral Home; or, First Years of Minnesota. New York: 1857. V. 37; 39; 42

Minnesota: Then and Now. St. Paul: 1869. V. 37

BISHOP, HENRY R.

Narcisse et Les Graces. The Last Grand Anacreontic Ballet . . . London: 1806. V. 40

Tamerlane et Bajazet. A New Grand Heroic Ballet as Performed at the King's Theatre Haymarket . . . London: 1806. V. 40

BISHOP, ISABELLA LUCY BIRD 1831-1904

The Englishwoman in America. London: 1856. V. 44

The Golden Cheronese and the Way Thither. London: 1883. V. 40; 41; 44

The Hawaiian Archipelago. London: 1880. V. 40

The Hawaiian Archipelago: Six Months Among the Palm Groves, Coral Reefs, and Volcanoes of the Sandwich Islands, from First Impressions to Its History. London: 1882. V. 39

Journeys in Persia and Kurdistan . . . New York: 1891. V. 42

Six Months Among the Palm Groves, Coral Reefs and Volcanoes of the Sandwich Islands. London: 1882. V. 40

Six Months Among the Palm Groves, Coral Reefs and Volcanoes of the Sandwich Islands. New York: 1903. V. 38

Unbeaten Tracks in Japan. London: 1880. V. 41; 44

Unbeaten Tracks in Japan. New York: 1880? V. 40; 46

Unbeaten Tracks in Japan. New York: 1881. V. 39; 43; 45

Unbeaten Tracks in Japan. London: 1900. V. 39; 44; 45

The Yangtze Valley & Beyond. An Account of Journeys in China, Chiefly in the Province of Sze Chuan & Among the Man-Tze of the Somo Territory. New York: 1900. V. 46

BISHOP, J. G.

A Peep into the Past. Brighton: 1880. V. 38

BISHOP, J. LEANDER

A History of American Manufactures from 1608 to 1860. Philadelphia: 1864. V. 37; 39

A History of American Manufactures from 1608 to 1860: Exhibiting the Origin and Growth of the Principal Mechanic Arts and Manufactures, from the Earliest Colonial Period to the Adoption of the Constitution; and Comprising Annals of the . . . London/Philadelphia: 1868. V. 37

BISHOP, JAMES

The Painted Picture Play-Book. London: 1830. V. 46

BISHOP, JOHN GEORGE

The Brighton Chain Pier: I Memoriam, Its History from 1823 to 1896. Brighton: 1897. V. 37; 42

BISHOP, JOHN PEALE

Act of Darkness. New York: 1935. V. 42; 46

Minute Particulars. New York: 1935. V. 37; 39; 40; 41; 42; 44

Selected Poems. New York: 1941. V. 41

BISHOP, JOHN S.

A Concise History of the War. Indianapolis: 1864. V. 42

BISHOP, MORRIS

The Odyssey of Cabeza de Vaca. New York: 1933. V. 42

BISHOP, NATHANIEL H.

Four Months in a Sneak Box, a Boat Voyage 2600 Miles Down the Ohio and Mississippi Rivers. Boston: 1879. V. 38; 39; 45

Voyage of the Paper Canoe. Boston: 1878. V. 39; 43

Voyage of the Paper Canoe. Boston: 1889. V. 43

Voyage of the Paper Canoe: a Geographical Journey of 2500 Miles from Quebec to the Gulf of Mexico, During the Years 1874-5. Boston: 1978. V. 40

BISHOP, RICHARD E.

Bishop's Wildfowl. Minneapolis: 1948. V. 44

Bishop's Wildfowl. St. Paul: 1948. V. 39; 40

Bishop's Wildfowl. USA: 1948. V. 45

BISHOP, RICHARD EVETT

Bishop's Birds. London: 1936. V. 39

Bishop's Birds. Philadelphia: 1936. V. 39

Bishop's Wildfowl. 1948. V. 46

BISHOP, SAMUEL

Feriae Poetica: Sive Carmina Anglicana Elegiaci Plerumque Arumenti Latine Reddita . . . Londini: 1766. V. 39; 40; 45

Poems on Various Subjects. London: 1802. V. 41; 42

BISHOP, STERENO EDWARDS

Why Are the Hawaiians Dying Out? Or Elements of Disability for Survival Among the Hawaiian People. Honolulu: 1888. V. 41

BISHOP, WILLIAM HENRY

Old Mexico and Her Lost Provinces. London: 1883. V. 43

Old Mexico and Her Lost Provinces . . . New York: 1883. V. 42

BISHOP, ZEALIA

The Curse of Yig. Sauk City: 1953. V. 42; 43; 45

THE BISHOP'S Fund and Phoenix Bonus. New Haven: 1816. V. 40

BISIKER, WILLIAM

Across Iceland. London: 1902. V. 40

BISLAND, ELIZABETH

The Life and Letters of Lafcadio Hearn. Boston: 1906. V. 40

BISSANI, ALESSANDRO

A Picturesque Tour through Part of Europe, Asia, and Africa. London: 1793. V. 38

BISSEL, JOHANN

Icaria. Ingolstadt: 1637. V. 45

BISSEL, JOHANNES

Argonauticon Americanorum, sive, Historiae Periculorum Petri de Victoria ac Sociorum Eius Libri Vi. Munich: 1647. V. 40

BISSELL, RICHARD

7 1/2 Cents. Boston: 1953. V. 37; 45

BISSET, JAMES

A Poetic Survey Round Birmingham . . . Birmingham: 1800. V. 42

BISSET, JOHN

Sport and War; or, Recollections of Fighting and Hunting in South Africa from the Years 1834 to 1867 . . . London: 1875. V. 45

BISSET, ROBERT 1759-1805

A Biographical Sketch of the Authors of the Spectator; Comprehending Addison Steele, Parnell, Hughes, Eusdon, Budgell, Tickell, Pope. With Critical Remarks. London: 1793. V. 37

Douglas; or, the Highlander. London: 1800. V. 40

The History of the Reign of George III to the Termination of the Late War, to Which is Prefixed, a View of the Progressive Improvement of England. London: 1803. V. 39

The History . . . with a View of the Progressive Improvement of England, In Prosperity and Strength, to the Accession of His Majesty. London: 1820. V. 41

The History of the Reign of George III. Philadelphia: 1822. V. 39

The Life of Edmund Burke. London: 1800. V. 42

A Sketch of Democracy. London: 1796. V. 38

Sketch of Democracy. Dublin: 1798. V. 43

BISSETT, CLARK PRESCOTT

Abraham Lincoln, a Universal Man. San Francisco: 1923. V. 38

BITTER ROOT VALLEY IRRIGATION COMPANY

The Bitter Root Valley Montana. Hamilton: 1900's. V. 46

BITTER to Sweet End. London: 1877. V. 43

BITTING, KATHERINE GOLDEN

Gastronomic Bibliography. San Francisco: 1939. V. 37; 38; 39

Gastronomic Bibliography. San Francisco: 1939. V. 37

BIVINS, VIOLA COBB

Memoirs. Longview?: 1942. V. 42

BIXBY, L.

A Statistical and Chronological View of the United States and Territories, and Traveler's Guide through the United States. Utica: 1842. V. 42

BIXBY, W. K.

Unpublished Letters of John Paul Jones in W. K. Bixby Collection, with . . . Remarks by Gen. Horace Porter and Franklin B. Sandborn. Boston: 1905. V. 42

BIZARI, PIETRO

Historia di Pietro Bizari Della Guerra Fatta in Ungheria dall'inuittissimo Imperatore de Christiani, contra Quello de Turchi. Lyon: 1568. V. 37

BIZOZERI, SIMPLICIANO

Ungria Restaurada. Compendiosa Noticia, de dos Tiempos . . . Barcelona: 1688. V. 38

BJERREGAARD, C. H. A.

Sufi Interpretations of the Quatrains of Omar Khayyam and Fitzgerald. New York: 1902. V. 45

BJORNSON, BJORNSTJERNE

Arne. London: and New York: 1866. V. 45

BJORNSTROM, FREDRIK

Hypnotism: Its History and Present Development . . . New York: 1887. V. 42

BLACHFORD, ROBERT

The New West-India Pilot. London: 1818. V. 37; 40

BLACHMAN, N. M.

A Survey of Automatic Digital Computers. 1953. Washington: 1953. V. 37

BLACK, A.

Black's Picturesque Tourist and Road-Book of England and Wales. Edinburgh: 1847. V. 45

BLACK, ADAM

Black's General Atlas of the World. Edinburgh: 1867. V. 45

Report of the Proceedings at the Entertainment Given to Adam Black, Esq. in the Waterloo Rooms, Edinburgh on 25th November 1840 in Connexion with the Cause of Civil and Religious Liberty. Edinburgh: 1840. V. 43

THE BLACK Art. London: 1962-64. V. 41

THE BLACK Book of Conscience; or, God's Hight-Court of Justice in the Soul of Man. Preston: 1790. V. 41

BLACK Canyon Not I and Other Stevensoniana. New York: 1899. V. 44

BLACK CAT PRESS

Bibliography of the Miniature Books and Ephemera Issued by the Black Cat Press. Chicago and Skokie: 1977. V. 41

BLACK, CHAUNCEY F.

Some Account of the Work of Stephen J. Field as a Legislator, state Judge, and Justice of the Supreme Court of the United States, with an Introductory Sketch by J. Norton Pomeroy. 1881. and an Appendix . . . by Hon. George C. Gorham. (New York?): 1895. V. 37

BLACK, DAVID D.

The History of Brechin to 1864. Edinburgh and Brechin: 1867. V. 40

BLACK, DAVIDSON

Fossil Man in China: The Choukoutien Cave Deposits with a Synopsis of Our Present Knowledge of the Late Cenozoic in China. Peiping: 1933. V. 42

BLACK, DOROTHY

Merry Times with Louis Wian. London. V. 45

BLACK, FRANCIS

A Treatise on the Principles and Practice of Homeopathy. London: 1842. V. 38

BLACK, GEORGE F.

A Gypsy Bibliography. London: 1914. V. 42; 46

BLACK, GLENN A.

Angel Site: an Archaeological, Historical and Ethnological Study. Indianapolis: 1967. V. 42; 43; 44

BLACK HAWK

Life of Ma-ka-Tai-Me-She-Kia-Kiak or Black Hawk. Cincinnati: 1833. V. 45

Life of Ma-ka-Tai-Me-She-Kia-Kiak or Black Hawk . . . with an Account of the Cause and Gen'l. History of the Late War, His Surrender and Confinement at Jefferson Barracks . . . Dictated by Himself. Boston: 1834. V. 42

THE BLACK Hills as Sung by Dick Brown. San Francisco: 187-. V. 39

THE BLACK Hills: Their Wonderful Mineral Wealth and Products . . . Chicago: 1883. V. 41; 43; 45

BLACK, JOHN

An Authentic Narrative of the Mutiny on Board the Lady Shore; with particulars of a Journey through Part of Brazil. Ipswich: 1798. V. 41

Life of Torquato Tasso; with an Historical and Critical Account of His Writings. Edinburgh: 1810. V. 39

A Sermon on National Righteousness and Sin, Delivered in . . . Pittsburgh, April 3, 1827, Before a Large Assembly, Convened for the Purpose of Adopting Resolutions Against Duelling. Pittsburgh: 1827. V. 40

BLACK, JOSEPH 1728-1799

Lectures on the Elements of Chemistry Delivered in the University of Edinburgh Now Published from His Manuscripts by John Robinson. Edinburgh: 1803. V. 38; 46

Lectures on the Elements of Chemistry, Delivered in the University of Edinburgh. Philadelphia: 1807. V. 40

BLACK, NORMAN FERGUS

History of Saskatchewan and the Old North West. Reigna: 1913. V. 42; 44

BLACK, ROBERT

A Memoir of Abraham Lincoln, President Elect of the United States . . . London: 1861. V. 37

BLACK, SAMUEL

A Journal of a Voyage from Rocky Mountains Portage in Peace River to the Sources of Finlay's Branch and North West Ward in Summer 1824. London: 1955. V. 43; 44; 46

BLACK SUN PRESS

Books of the Black Sun Press. New York: & Paris: 1930. V. 46

BLACK, W. H.

Bibliothecae Colfanae Catalogus, Catalogue of the Library in the Free Grammar-School at Lewisham . . . London: 1831. V. 38; 40

BLACK, WILLIAM

The Beautiful Wretch. The Four Macnicols. The Pupil of Aurelius. Three Stories. London: 1881. V. 38; 41; 43

The Beautiful Wretch. London: 1981. V. 45

Green Pastures and Piccadilly. London: 1877. V. 43

Judith Shakespeare. London: 1884. V. 43

The Privileges of the Royal Burrows as Contained in Their Particular Rights. Edinburgh: 1707. V. 39

Reflections on the Relicks of Ancient Grandeur and the Pleasing Retirements of South Wales. London: 1823. V. 46

Sabina Zembra. London: 1887. V. 38; 43

Shandon Bells. London: 1883. V. 38; 39; 43

A Short View of Our Present Trade and Taxes, Compared with These Taxes May Amount to After the Union, Even Tho Our Trade Should not Augment One Sixpence. Edinburgh: 1706. V. 41

The Strange Adventure of a Phaeton. London: 1872. V. 43

The Strange Adventures of a Phaeton. London: 1874. V. 39

Sunrise: a Story of These Times. London: 1881. V. 43

White Wings. London: 1880. V. 41; 43

White Heather. London: 1885. V. 43

Yolande. The Story of a Daughter. London: 1883. V. 43

BLACK, WILLIAM HENRY

The Worshipful Company of Leathersellers of the City of London - The History & Antiquities of . . . London: 1871. V. 43

BLACK WONDER GOLD AND SILVER MINING COMPANY

Prospectus of the Black Wonder Gold and Silver Mining Co. of Hinsdale County, Col. Boston: 1892. V. 39

BLACKALL, JOHN

Observations on the Nature and Cure of Dropsies, and Particularly on the Presence of the Coagulable Part of the Blood in Dropsical Urine. London: 1818. V. 42

Observations on the Nature and Cure of Dropsies, and Particularly on the Presence of the Coagulable Part of the Blood in Dropsical Urine; To Which is Added, an Appendix . . . Philadelphia: 1825. V. 42

BLACKALL, OFFSPRING, BP. OF EXETER 1654-1716

The Works . . . London: 1723. V. 38

BLACKBEARD. a Page from the Colonial History of Philadelphia. New York: 1835. V. 41

BLACKBIRD, A. J.

History of the Ottawa and Chippewa Indians of Michigan. Ypsilanti: 1887. V. 39

BLACKBURN, D.

The Detection of Forgery. London: 1909. V. 40

BLACKBURN, H.

Academy Notes. 1880-1889. London: 1880-89. V. 39

BLACKBURN, HENRY

Breton Folk: an Artistic Tour in Britanny. London: 1880, 1879. V. 41

The Harz Mountains: a Tour in the Toy Country. London: 1873. V. 45

The Pyrenees: a Description of Summer Life at French Watering Places. London: 1867. V. 41

Randolph Caldecott. London: 1886. V. 41; 43

BLACKBURN, HUGH, MRS.

Birds from Moidart and Elsewhere, Drawn from Nature. Edinburgh: 1895. V. 38

BLACKBURN, ISAAC W.

Illustrations of the Gross Morbid Anatomy of the Brain in the Insane. Washington: 1908. V. 38; 42; 44; 45; 46

BLACKBURN, JAMES KNOX POLK

Reminiscences of the Terry Rangers. Austin: 1919. V. 44

BLACKBURN, JANE

Birds Drawn from Nature. Edinburgh: 1862. V. 46

BLACKBURN, JANE J. B.

The Crows of Shakespeare. Edinburgh: 1899. V. 42

BLACKBURN, PAUL

The Dissolving Fabric. Mallorca: 1955. V. 37; 46

Early Selected Y Mas. Los Angeles: 1972. V. 46

Gin: Four Journal Pieces. Mt. Horeb. V. 46

Guillem de Poitou, His Eleven Extant Poems. Mt. Horeb: 1976. V. 44; 45

The Journals: Blue Mounds Entries. Mt. Horeb: 1971. V. 46

The Nets. New York: 1961. V. 46

The Omitted Journals. 1983. V. 40; 45

The Omitted Journals. Mt. Horeb: 1983. V. 38; 46

Proensa. Palma de Mallorca: 1953. V. 37; 43

The Selection of Heaven. Mt. Horeb: 1980. V. 39

Sing - Song. New York: 1966. V. 46

BLACKBURN, WILLIAM

One and Twenty: Duke Narrative and Verse. Durham: 1945. V. 39

BLACKBURNE, EDWARD L.

Sketches Graphic and Descriptive for a History of the Decorative Painting Applied to English Architecture During the Middle Ages. London: 1845. V. 38

BLACKBURNE, EDWARD LUSHINGTON

Sketches Graphic and descriptive Uc. for a History of the Decorative Painting Applied to English Architecture During the Middle Ages. London: 1847. V. 40; 42

BLACKBURNE, FRANCIS

Considerations on the Present State of the Controversy Between the Protestants and Papists of Great Britain and Ireland . . . London: 1768. V. 43

A Critical Commentary on Archbishop Secker's Letter to the Right Honourable Walpole, Concerning Bishops in America. London: 1770 (1769). V. 37

Remarks on Johnson's Life of Milton. London: 1780. V. 41; 42; 45

BLACKBURNE, G. L.

Decorative Painting. London: 1847. V. 42

BLACKER, J. F.

Nineteenth Century Ceramic Art. London. V. 41

BLACKER, W.

Art of Angling and Complete System of Fly Making. London: 1842. V. 40

BLACKER, WILLIAM

The Claims of the Landed Interests to Legislative Protection Considered; with Reference to the Manner in Which the Manufacturing, Commercial and Agricultural Classes Contribute . . . London: 1836. V. 43

Prize Essay on the Management of Landed Property in Ireland. Dublin: 1834. V. 40

BLACKERBY, SAMUEL

The Justice of the Peace His Companion, or A Summary of All the Acts of Parliament, Whereby One, Two, or More Justices of the Peace, are Authorised to Act . . . London: 1723. V. 44

The Second Part of the Justice of Peace His Companion. V. 40

BLACKETT, T. OSWALD

An Essay on the Use of the Spirit Level, as Applied to Engineering and Other Purposes. Newcastle-upon-Tyne: 1838. V. 43

BLACKFOOT Catechism and Prayers. Calgary: 1920. V. 39

BLACKFOOT Hymns. N.P.: 1921. V. 39

BLACKFORD, CHARLES M.

Annals of the Lynchburg Home Guard. Lynchburg: 1891. V. 37; 45

Campaign and Battle of Lynchburg, Va. Lynchburg: 1901. V. 42

BLACKIE, JOHN STUART

On Beauty: Three Discourses Delivered in the University of Edinburgh. Edinburgh: 1858. V. 37; 44

BLACKIE, W. G.

The Comprehensive ATlas and Geography of the World . . . London: 1882. V. 44

BLACKINGTON, R. & CO.

Silversmiths. Factory: North Attleborough, Mass. New York: 1900. V. 37

BLACKLEY, W.

The Diplomatic Respondence of the Right Hon. Richard Hill. London: 1845. V. 39

BLACKLOCK, THOMAS 1721-1791

A Collection of Original Poems. By the Rev. Mr. Blacklock, and other Scotch Gentlemen. Edinburgh: 1760. V. 37

Poems on Several Occasions. Edinburgh: 1754. V. 40; 41; 42

Praclesis; or, Consoloations Deduced from Natural and Revealed Religion. Edinburgh: 1767. V. 38

BLACKMAN, ALYWARD M.

The Temple of Derr. Le Caire: 1930. V. 37

BLACKMAN, AYLWARD M.

The Rock Tombs of Meir I-III. London: 1914-15. V. 40

The Rock Tombs of Meir Parts 1-6. London: 1914-1953. V. 37; 40; 42; 44

The Temple of Dendur. Le Caire: 1911. V. 37; 40; 42

The Temple of Derr. Le Caire: 1913. V. 37

BLACKMAR, FRANK W.

Kansas: A Cyclopedia of State History, Embracing Events, Institutions, Industries, Counties, Cities, Towns, Prominent Persons. Chicago: 1912. V. 39

Spanish Institutions of the Southwest. Baltimore: 1891. V. 37; 42; 43; 45

BLACKMER, HENRY MYRON

Greece and the Levant: The Catalogue of the Henry Myron Blackmer Collection of Books and Manuscripts. London: 1989. V. 43

BLACKMORE, EDWIN GORDON

The Story of the South Australian Bushmen's Corps. Adelaide: 1900. V. 41

BLACKMORE, JOHN

Views on the Newcastle and CArlisle Railway, from Original Drawings by J. W. Carmichael . . . Newcastle: 1836-8. V. 46

BLACKMORE, RICHARD 1650-1729

Alfred, An Epick Poem. London: 1723. V. 42

A Collection of Poems on Various Subjects. London: 1718. V. 43

A Discourse on the Plague. London: 1722. V. 42

Eliza an Epick Poem. London: 1705. V. 38

Essays Upon Several Subjects. London: 1716-17. V. 42; 43

Essays Upon Several Subjects. London: 1717. V. 38; 41; 46

King ARthur. London: 1697. V. 41; 45

Prince Arthur. London: 1695. V. 37; 38; 41

Prince Arthur. London: 1696. V. 45; 46

A Short History of the Last Parliament. London: 1699. V. 37; 38

A Treatise of Consumptions and Other Distempers Beloning to the Breast and Lungs. London: 1724. V. 37; 43; 45

A Treatise of Consumptions and Other Distempers Belonging to the Breast and Lungs. London: 1725. V. 43

BLACKMORE, RICHARD DODDRIDGE 1825-1900

Christowell. London: 1882. V. 43

Christowell. London: 1893. V. 39

Clara Vaughan. London: 1864. V. 46

Clara Vaughan. London: 1893. V. 39

Cradock Nowell. London: 1873. V. 38

Dariel. Edinburgh: 1897. V. 46

Erema, or My Father's Sin. London: 1877. V. 42

Fringilla. Cleveland: 1895. V. 37; 39; 40; 42; 43; 44; 45

Fringilla, Some Tales in Verse. London: 1895. V. 37; 45

Lorna Doone. London: 1869. V. 42; 44; 45; 46

Lorna Doone . . . London: 1870. V. 42

Lorna Doone. Philadelphia: 1882. V. 41

Lorna Doone. London: 1893. V. 39

The Picture Story of Lorna Doone. London: 1933. V. 42; 44

The Maid of Sker. Edinburgh: 1872. V. 41; 43

Perlycross: a Tale of the Western Hills. London: 1894. V. 45

Slain by the Doones and Other Stories. New York: 1895. V. 44; 46

Springhaven. London: 1887. V. 43

Tales from the Telling-House. I. Slain by the Doones. 2. Frida: or the Lover's Leap. e. George Bowring. 4. Crocker's Hole. London: 1896. V. 38

BLACKMORE, S.

Pollen and Spores: Form and Function. London: 1986. V. 37; 46

BLACKMORE, WILLIAM

Colorado: Its Resources, Parks and Prospects as a New Field for Emigration. London: 1869. V. 37; 39; 42; 43; 45

BLACKMUR, FRANK W.

Spanish Institutions of the Southwest. Baltimore: 1891. V. 38

BLACKMUR, R. P.

The Double Agent. New York: 1935. V. 39; 40

The Expense of Greatness. New York: 1940. V. 46

From Jordan's Delight. New York: 197. V. 46

The Good European. 1947. V. 39

The Good European. Cummington: 1947. V. 46

The Second World. 1942. V. 39

The Second World. Cummington: 1942. V. 43

BLACK'S General Atlas comprehending sixty-one maps . . . engraved on steel . . . by Sidney Hall, William Hughes &c. New Edition . . . Edinburgh: 1852. V. 37

BLACKSTOCK, CHARITY

Dewey Death. 1956. V. 39

BLACKSTON, W. A.

The Illustrated Book of Canaries and Cage-Birds; British and Foreign. London: (c. 1880). V. 37

BLACKSTONE, HARRY

Blackstone's Modern Card Tricks. New York: 1932. V. 43

BLACKSTONE, WILLIAM 1723-1780

An Analysis of the Laws of England. Oxford: 1757. V. 40

An Analysis of the Laws of England. Oxford: 1771. V. 38

Blackstone Economized: Being a Compendium of the Laws of England to the Present Time. London: 1873. V. 40

The Case for the Late Election for the County of Middlesex, Considered on the Principles of the Constitution, and the Authorities of Law. London: 1769. V. 37; 38; 41; 42

Commentaries on the Laws of England. Oxford: 1765/66/68/69. V. 44

Commentaries on the Laws of England. Oxford: 1765-69. V. 38; 46

Commentaries on the Laws of England. Oxford: 1766-69. V. 40; 41; 43; 45

BLAGDON, FRANCIS WILLIAM continued

The French Interpreter; Consisting of Copious and Familiar Conversations on Every Topic Which Can be Useful . . . London: 1819. V. 41

BLAGRAVE, JOHN

The Epitomie fo the Art of Husbandry. London: 1685. V. 46

BLAGRAVE, JOSEPH 1610-1682

Blagrave's Astrological Practice of Physick. London: 1689. V. 43; 46

The Epitome of the Art of Husbandry. London: 1669. V. 42

Introduction to Astrology. London: 1682. V. 40; 42; 44

BLAIKIE, FRANCIS

On the Conversion of Arable Land into Pasture, and on Other Rural Subjects. Burnham: 1817. V. 42

A Treatise on Mildew, and the Cultivation of Wheat Including Hints on the Application of Lime, Chalk, Marl, Clay, Gypsum &c. London: 1820. V. 42

A Treatise on Smut in Wheat, with Means of Prevention . . . Norfolk: 1821. V. 42

A Treatise on the Management of Hedges, and Hedge-Row Timber. London: 1820. V. 42

BLAINE, DELABERE P.

Canine Pathology or a Full Description of the Diseases of Dogs, With Their Causes, Symptoms and Mode of Cure . . . London: 1817. V. 42

Canine Pathology; or, a Description of the Diseases of Dogs, . . . London: 1841. V. 40; 46

An Encyclopaedia of Rural Sports. London: 1840. V. 40; 41

An Encyclopaedia of Rural Sports. London: 1858. V. 45

An Encyclopaedia of Rural Sports or Complete Account (Historical, Practical and Descriptive) of Hunting, Shooting, Fishing, Racing &c . . . London: 1870. V. 39

BLAINVILLE, H. M. D. DE

Manual de Malacologie et de Conchyliologie. Paris: 1825. V. 38

BLAIR, CHARLES

Indian Famines. Their Historical, Financial and Other Aspects. Edinburgh & London: 1874. V. 40

BLAIR, CLAUDE

Arms, Armour and Base-Metalwork. The James A. Rothschild Collection at Waddesdon Manor. London: 1974. V. 41

BLAIR, DAVID

The History of Australasia. Glasgow, Melbourne, Dunedin: 1879. V. 39

BLAIR, EMMA H.

The Indian Tribes of the Upper Mississippi Valley and Region of the Great Lakes . . . Cleveland: 1911-12. V. 39; 42

BLAIR, EMMA HELEN

The Indian Tribes of the Upper Mississippi Valley and Region of the Great Lakes. Cleveland: 1911. V. 38; 44

BLAIR, GEORGES

Lectures on Rhetoric and Belles Lettres. Philadelphia: 1784. V. 39; 40

BLAIR, HUGH

An Abridgement of Lectures on Rhetoric. Cambridge: 1802. V. 43; 45

A Critical Dissertation on the Poems of Ossian, the Son of Fingal. London: 1763. V. 37

Lectures on Rhetoric and Belle Lettres. Dublin: 1783. V. 39

Lectures on Rehtoric and Belles Lettres. London: 1783. V. 40; 45

Lectures on Rhetoric and Belles Lettres. London: 1793. V. 43

Lectures on Rhetoric and Belles Lettres. London: 1796. V. 46

Lectures on Rhetoric and Belles Lettres. Edinburgh: 1813. V. 40

Lectures on Rhetoric and Belles Lettres. London: 1817. V. 42; 43; 45

Lectures on Historic and Belles Lettres. Philadelphia: 1784. V. 38

Sermons with the Life and Character of the Author by James Finlayson. London: 1837. V. 38

BLAIR, JOHN I.

Statement of the Affairs of the Cedar Rapids and Missouri River Railroad Company to December 25th 1865. Blairstown: 1865. V. 41

BLAIR, LEWIS H.

The Propserity of the South Dependent Upon the Elevation of the Negro. Richmond: 1889. V. 44

BLAIR, M.

The Paisley Shawl and the Men Who Produced It. Paisley: 1904. V. 37

BLAIR, ROBERT 1699-1746

The Grave, a Poem. New York. V. 41

The Grave. London: 1743. V. 41

The Grave. Edinburgh: 1747. V. 43

The Grave. Perth: 1799. V. 42

The Grave, a Poem. London: 1808. V. 37; 39; 40; 41; 42

The Grave. London: 1813. V. 40

The Grave, a Poem. New York: 1847. V. 39

The Grave. Edinburgh: 1858. V. 40

A Poem Dedicated to the Memory of the Late Learned and Eminent Mr. William Law, Professor of Philosophy in the University of Edinburgh. N.P.: 1728. V. 37; 40

Scientific Aphorisms, Being the Outline of an Attempt to Establish Fixed Principles of Science . . . Edinburgh: 1827. V. 40; 45; 46

BLAIR, V. P.

Surgery and Diseases of the Mouth and Jaws. St. Louis: 1914. V. 42

BLAIR, W. L.

Pasadena Community Book. Pasadena: 1947. V. 39

BLAIR, WALTER A.

A Raft Pilot's Log: a History of the Great Rafting Industy on the Upper Mississippi, 1840-1915. Cleveland: 1930. V. 42; 44; 46

BLAIR, WILLIAM

An Opium-Eater in America and the Fratricide's Death. With an introduction by R.C. Aurora. New York: (1941). V. 37

BLAIZOT, C.

Pierre-Lucien Martin. Brussels: 1987. V. 41

BLAKE, E. R.

Manual of Neotropical Birds. Chicago: 1977. V. 39

BLAKE, E. VALE

Arctic Experiences: Containing Capt. George E. Tyson's wonderful drift on the Ice-Floe . . . New York: 1874. V. 43; 44; 46

BLAKE, EMMET R.

Manual of Neotropical Birds. Volume 1: Spheniscidae (Penguins) to Laridae (Gulls and Allies). Chicago: 1977. V. 40

BLAKE, EUPHEMIA YALE

Arctic Experiences . . . New York: 1874. V. 42

BLAKE, J. A.

Colorado Business Directory and Annual Register for 1876. Denver: 1876. V. 37; 40

Hand-Book of Colorado with Maps and Illustrations. Denver: 1872. V. 42; 45

Hand Book of Colorado, with Maps and Illustrations. Denver: 1874. V. 37; 38; 39

Handbood of Colorado for Citizen and Traveler. Denver: 1873. V. 37; 40

Handbook of Colorado, with Maps and Illustrations. Denver: 1874. V. 38

BLAKE, JOHN L.

A Geographical, Chronological and Historical Atlas . . . New York: 1826. V. 41

BLAKE, JOHN W.

Northern Ireland in the Second World War. Belfast: 1956. V. 37; 43

BLAKE, LILLIE DEVEREUX

Fettered for Life; or, Lord and Master. New York: 1874. V. 46

BLAKE, MARION ELIZABETH

Ancient Roman Construction in Italy from the Prehistoric Period to Augustus. Washington: 1947. V. 40

Roman Construction in Italy from Tiberius through the Flavians. Washington: 1959. V. 40

BLAKE, NELSON MOREHOUSE

William Mahone of Virginia, Soldier and Political Insurgent. Richmond: 1935. V. 38

BLAKE, NICHOLAS

A Question of Proof. 1935. V. 39

BLAKE, ROBERT

Blake's Remarks on Com. Johnstone's Account of His Engagement with a French Squadron, Under the Command of Mons. de Suffrein, on April 16, 1781, in Port Praya Road in the Island of St. Jago. London: 1782. V. 43

An Essay on the Structure and Formation of the Teeth in Man and Various Animals. Dublin: 1801. V. 37

A True Relation of the Late Great Seafight As It Was Sent in a Letter to . . . the Lord General Cromwell . . . London: 1653. V. 43

BLAKE, W. H.

Brown Waters and Other Sketches. Toronto: 1915. V. 44

Brown Waters. Toronto: 1940. V. 45

BLAKE, WILLIAM 1757-1827 continued

Songs of Innocence. London: 1927. V. 37; 40

Songs of Innocence. London: 1954. V. 37; 38; 39; 40; 43; 44; 46

Songs of Innocence and Experience . . . London: 1839. V. 42; 46

Songs of Innocence and Experience With Other Poems. London: 1866. V. 38; 41

Songs of Innocence and of Experience. London: 1868. V. 38; 39; 44

Songs of Innocence and of Experience. Edmonton: 1885. V. 39

Songs of Innocence and Experience. London: 1955. V. 41; 43

Songs of Innocence and of Experience. London: 1955. V. 40

Songs of Innocence and of Experience. New York: 1967. V. 42

There is No Natural Religion. London: 1971. V. 37; 40

There is No Natural Religion. Paris: 1971. V. 38

Tyger! Tyger! 1974. V. 45

Visions of the Daughters of Albion. 1959. V. 40

Visions of the Daughters of Albion. London: 1959. V. 37; 40; 42

The Works of William Blake, Poetic, Symbolic and Critical. London: 1893. V. 42; 46

The Works . . . Edited . . . by Edwin John Ellis and William Butler Yeats. London: 1893. V. 37

Writings. London: 1925. V. 37; 38; 40; 41; 42; 44

The Writings. Edited in Three Volumes by Geoffrey Keynes. (and) The Life of Blake by Mona Wilson. London: 1925-27. V. 37; 45

William Blake's Writings. Oxford: 1978. V. 39

Writings. Oxford: 1978. V. 39; 40

BLAKE, WILLIAM J.

The History of Putnam County, New York. New York: 1849. V. 40; 45

BLAKE, WILLIAM P.

Geographical Notes Upon Russian America and the Stickeen River, Being a Report Addressed to Secretary of State Seward. Washington: 1868. V. 41; 45

Report Upon the Gold Placers of a Part of Lumpkin County, Georgia, and the Practicability of Working Them by the Hydraulic Method. New York: 1858. V. 44; 45

BLAKENEY, EDWARD HENRY

The Angel of the Hours and Other Poems. London: 1907. V. 42

BLAKENEY, ROBERT

A Boy in the Peninsular War. London: 1899. V. 42

BLAKENEY, WILLIAM

The New Manual Exercise, by General Blakeney. To which is added, The Evolutions of the Foot, by General Blank. There is also added, The Act of Assembly to Regulate the Militia of the Colony of New York. New York: 1754. V. 37

On the Coasts of Cathay and Cipango Forty Years Ago. London: 1902. V. 40

BLAKESTON, OSWELL

Death While Swimming. London: 1932. V. 39

BLAKEWAY, J. BRICKDALE

The Sheriffs of Shropshire, With their Armorial Bearings and Notices Genealogical and Biographical, of their Families. Shrewsbury: 1831. V. 39

BLAKEY, DOROTHY

The Minerva Press, 1790-1820. London: 1939. V. 40; 43; 44

The Minerva Press, 1790-1820. Oxford: 1939. V. 45

BLAKEY, ROBERT

The Angler's Song Book. London: 1855. V. 40

Hints on Angling, With Suggestions for Angling Excursions in France and Belgium . . . by Palmer Hackle. London: 1846. V. 40;`41

Historical Sketch of Logic, from the Earliest Times to the Present Day. London: 1851. V. 43

Historical Sketch of the Angling Literature of all Nations to Which is Added a Bibliography. London: 1856. V. 39; 40; 46

The History of Political Literature from the Earliest Times. London: 1855. V. 39

Shooting: a Manual of Practical Information on This Branch of British Fields Sports. London: 1854. V. 39

BLAKISTON, ELEANOR FRANCIS

Do Well and Doubt Not. London: 1867. V. 38

BLAKISTON, JOHN

Twelve Years' Military Adventures in Three Quarters of the Globe, or, Memoirs of an Officer Who Served in the Armies of His Majesty and of the East India Company, Between the Years 1802 and 1814 . . . London: 1829. V. 38

Twelve Years' Military Adventure in Three Quarters of the Globe. London: 1840. V. 42

BLAKISTON, PEYTON

Practical Observations on Certain Diseases of the Chest and on the Principles of Auscultation. Philadelphia: 1848. V. 45

BLAKSTON, W. A.

Illustrated Book of Canaries and Cage Birds, British and Foreign. London: 1870. V. 38

Illustrated Book of Canaries and Cage-Birds, British and Foreign. London: 1877-80. V. 39

The Illustrated Book and Canaries and Cage-Birds, British and Foreign. London: 1880. V. 45

BLAMEY, PETER

Flowers of the Countryside. London: 1980. V. 43

BLANC, CHARLES

The Grammar of Painting and Engraving. New York: 1874. V. 38; 40; 44

BLANC, LOUIS

1848. Historical Revelations: Inscribed to Lord Normanby. London: 1858. V. 42

BLANCARD, STEPHEN

The Physical Dictionary. London: 1702. V. 44

BLANCH, LESLEY

The Nine-Tiger Man. New York: 1965. V. 45

BLANCHARD, CHARLES

Counties of Morgan, Monroe and Brown, Indiana. Chicago: 1884. V. 46

BLANCHARD, EDWARD LEMAN

Bradshaw's Guide through London and Its Environs. London: 1857. V. 40

BLANCHARD, J.

A Debate on Slavery Held on the First, Second, Third and Sixth Days of october, 1845, in the City of Cincinnati Between . . . Cincinnati: 1846. V. 39; 42

BLANCHARD, JEAN PIERRE

Journal and Certificates of the Fourth Voyage of Mr. Blanchard, who ascended from the Royal Military Academy, at Chelsea the 16th of october 1784 . . . London: 1784. V. 37

BLANCHARD, P.

San Juan de Ulua ou Relation de l'Expedition Francaise au Mexique, Sous les Ordres de M. Le Contre-Amiral Baudin . . . Paris: 1839. V. 37; 38; 39; 45

BLANCHARD, R. H.

Handbook of Egyptian Gods and Mummy Amulets. Cairo: 1909. V. 44

BLANCHARD, RUFUS

Citizen's Guide for the City of Chicago. 1869. V. 38

The Discovery and Conquest of the Northwest: Including the Early History of Chicago, Detroit, Vincennes, St. Louis, Ft. Wayne, Praitie du Chien, Marietta, Cincinnati, Cleveland. Chicago: 1880. V. 42

BLANCHARD, STEPHEN

A Letter Addressed to Ethan Smith, the Congregational Minister in Hopkinton, N.H. Concord: 1817. V. 45

The Physical Dictionary. London: 1702. V. 40

The Physical Dictionary Wherein the Terms of Anatomy, the Names and Causes of Diseases, Chirurgical Instruments and Their Use . . . London: 1726. V. 45; 46

BLANCHARD, SYDNEY

Mr. Punch: His Origin and Career. London: 1870. V. 38; 46

BLANCHARD, WILLIAM ISAAC

The Complete Instructor of short Hand. London: 1786? V. 37

BLANCHEMAIS, PROSPER 1816-1879

Les Fanfreluches Contes & Gauloiseries. Bruxelles: 1879. V. 38

BLANCHET, F. H.

Hisorical Sketches of the Catholic Church in Oregon and the Northwest. Ferndale, Wa.: 1910. V. 37

BLANCK, JACOB

Bibliography of American Literature. New Haven. V. 40; 43

Merle Johnson's American First Editions. New York: 1936. V. 45

BLANCKLEY, THOMAS RILEY

A Naval Expositor, Shewing and Explaining the Words and Terms of Art Belonging to he Parts, Qualities and Proportion of Building, Rigging, Furnishing & Fitting a Ship for Sea. London: 1750. V. 41

BLANCO, AMANDA

The Many Faces of Jake Zeitlin. Northridge: 1978. V. 37; 40

BLANCO, AMANDA continued

Type Faces: a Photographic Study of Ward Ritchie. Northridge: 1988. V. 39; 41

BLANCO WHITE, JOSEPH

Letters from Spain. London: 1822. V. 38

BLAND, ALEXANDER

The Royal Ballet: the First 50 Years. London: 1981. V. 45

BLAND, DAVID

A History of Book Illustration; the Illuminated Manuscript and the Printed Book. Berkeley. V. 40

A History of Book Illustration: The Illuminated Manuscript and the Printed Book. Cleveland: 1958. V. 43

A History of Book Illustration. 1969. V. 46

A History of Book Illustration. Berkeley & Los Angeles: 1969. V. 40

A History of Book Illustration. London: 1969. V. 42; 45

A History of Book Illustration; The Illuminated Manuscript and the Printed Book. Berkeley. V. 37

A History of Book Illustration, the Illuminated Manuscript and the Printed Book. London: 1959. V. 37

BLAND, E.

Annals of Southport and District: A Chronological History of North Meols. Southport: 1903. V. 39

BLAND, HUMPHREY

An Abstract of Military Discipline; More Particularly with Regard to the Manual Exercise, Evolutions and Firings of the Foot. Boston: 1747. V. 37; 39

An Abstract of Military Discipline; More Particularly with Regard to the manual Exercise, Evolutions and Firings of the Foot. Boston: 1755. V. 37

A Treatise of a Military Discipline. London: 1734. V. 41

A Treatise of a Military Discipline. London: 1762. V. 41

BLAND, JANE COOPER

Currier & Ives. A Manual for Collectors. Garden City: 1931. V. 43; 46

BLAND, JOHN SALKELD

The Vale of Lyvennet. Kendal: 1910. V. 41

BLAND-SUTTON, JOHN

Tumours Innocent and Malignant: Their Clinical Features and Appropriate Treatment. Philadelphia: 1893. V. 42

BLAND, T. A.

Life of Albert B. Meacham. Washington: 1883. V. 46

BLAND, W.

Hints on the Principles Which Should Regulate the Form of Ships and Boats; Derived from Original Experiments. London: 1863. V. 41

BLAND, WILLIAM

Experimental Essays on the Principles of Construction in Arches, Piers, Buttresses &c. London: 1839. V. 43

BLANDEN, CHARLES G.

The Unremembered God and Other Poems. Chicago: 1903. V. 40; 41

BLANDFORD, GEORGE FIELDING 1829-1911

Insanity and Its Treatment: Lectures on the Treatment, Medical and Legal, of Insane Patients. Edinburgh: 1871. V. 43

Insanity and Its Treatment: Lectures on the Treatment, Medical and Legal, of Insane Patients. Philadelphia: 1871. V. 42; 45

BLANDIN, PHILIPPE FREDERIC

De L'Autoplatie. These Presentee et Soutenue le 19 Fevrier 1836, au Concours Pour une Chaire de Clinique Chirurgicale Vacante a la Vaculte de Medecine de Paris. Paris: 1836. V. 40

Traite d'Anatomie Topographique ou Anatomie des Regions du Corps Humain. Paris: 1826. V. 37; 38; 39; 40; 41

BLANDING, STEPHEN F.

Recollections of a Sailor Boy, or, The Cruise of the Gunboat Louisiana. Providence: 1886. V. 37; 42

BLANDY, MARY

A Candid Appeal to the Publick Concerning the Case of Miss Mary Blandy, Wherein All the Ridiculous and False Assertions Contained in a Pamphlet. London: 1752. V. 43

The Genuine Tryal at Large of Mary Blandy, Spinster, for Poisoning Her Late Father Francis Blandy, gent. London: 1752. V. 43

Miss Mary Blandy's Own Account of the Affair Between Her and Mr. Cranstoun. London: 1752. V. 38; 45

BLANE, GILBERT

Elements of Medical Logick. London: 1819. V. 38

BLANE, WILLIAM

Cynegetica; or, Essays on Sporting; Consisting of Observations on Hare Hunting . . . London: 1788. V. 43

Essays on Hunting. Southampton: 1781. V. 37; 46

Essays on Hunting. Southampton: 1782. V. 39

BLANEY, HENRY R.

Photogravure. New York: 1895. V. 38

BLANFORD, WILLIAM THOMAS

Observations on the Geology and Zoology of Abyssinia, Made During the Progress of the British Expedition to that Country in 1867-68. London: 1870. V. 37; 40; 46

BLANKAART, NIKOLAUS

Panegyricvs Pro Ivbileo Sev Festo Secvlari, Ivssv Procervm, In Templo Academico. Franeker: 1685. V. 40

BLANKAART, STEVEN

Collectanea Medico-Physica, Oft Hollands Jaar-Register der Genees-en Natuur-kundige Aanmer-kingen van Gantisch Europa &c. Amsterdam: 1680-88. V. 45

The Physical Dictionary. London: 1708. V. 41; 42

BLANKENBERG-VAN DELDEN, C.

The Large Commemorative Scarabs of Amenhotep III. Leiden: 1969. V. 44

BLANKENSHIP, GEORGE E., MRS.

Early History of Thurston County, Washington. Together with Biographies and Reminiscences of Those Identified with Pioneer Days. Olympia: 1914. V. 42

BLANQUI, JEROME ADOLPHE

Voyage a Madrid. Paris: 1826. V. 43

BLANTON, LINDSAY HUGHES

Well Done Thou God and Faithful Servant. Funeral Sermon on the Death of Rev. John W. Griffin, Chaplain of the 19th Va. Regt. August 1st, 1864. Lynchburg: 1865. V. 44

BLANTON, THOMAS LINDSAY

Pictorial Supplement to Interwoven. Albany: 1953. V. 39; 42

BLANTON, WYNDHAM

Medicine in Virginia in the Seventeenth Century. Richmond: 1930. V. 41

Medicine in Virginia in the Eighteenth Century. Richmond: 1931. V. 42

Medicine in Virginia in the Eighteenth Century. Richmond: 1931. V. 40; 45; 46

Medicine in Virginia in the Nineteenth Century. Richmond: 1933. V. 40; 41; 42; 45

BLAQUIERE, EDWARD

Narrative of a Second Visit to Greece Including Facts Connected with the Last Days of Lord Byron . . . London: 1825. V. 42

BLASCHE, BERNHARD

The Art of Working in Pasteboard Upon Scientific Principles; to Which is added, an appendix, Containing Directions for Constructing Architectural Models . . . London: 1827. V. 42; 44

Papyro-Plastics, or the Art of Modelling Paper. London: 1825. V. 40

BLASCO IBANEZ, VICENTE

Mare Nostrum (Our Sea). New York: 1919/1918. V. 45

BLASE, ARCHILLE DE

The Development of Successful Thoroughbred Sire Lines in England and France. Milan: 1961. V. 37

BLASER, W.

Drawings in Collection of Moma. New York: 1969. V. 46

BLASERNA, PIETRO

The Theory of Sound In Its Relation to Music. London: 1876. V. 41

BLASHFIELD, EDWIN HOWLAND

Italian Citites. New York: 1902. V. 44

BLASHILL, THOMAS

Sutton-in-Holderness, the Manor and the Berewic and the Village Community. Hull and London: 1896. V. 44

BLASINGAME, IKE

Dakota Cowboy. My Life in the Old Days. New York: 1958. V. 42

BLASIUS, GERARD

Miscellanea Anatomica Hominis . . . Amsterdam: 1673. V. 41; 45

BLASQUEZ DE VALVERDE, JUAN

Alegacion en Derecho, en Defensa de la Iurisdiccion Ecclesiastica. Lima: 1647. V. 45

BLAST I, II & III. Santa Barbara: 1981, 1984. V. 37; 40

BLATCHFORD, ROBERT
Merrie England: a Series of Letters on the Labour Problem. London: 1893.
V. 42

BLATCHLY, CORNELIUS
An Essay on Common Wealths. New York: 1822. V. 40

THE BLATHWAYT Atlas . . . Providence: 1970. V. 40; 45

BLATTER, E.
Beautiful Flowers of Kashmir. London: 1928-29. V. 38; 45

BLATTY, WILLIAM PETER
The Exorcist. New York: 1971. V. 45; 46

BLAUVELT, LOUIS L.
The Blauvelt Family Genealogy. N.P.: 1957. V. 37

BLAYLOCK, J.
Paper Dragons. 1986. V. 44

BLAYNEY, ANDREW THOMAS
Narrative of a Forced Journey through Spain and France, as a Prisoner of
War, in the Years 1810 to 1814. London: 1814. V. 39; 40

BLEASCO, DAVID
The Merchant of Venice. New York: 1922. V. 45

BLEDSOE, ALBERT T.
Three Lectures on Rational Mechanics; or, the Theory of Motion.
Philadelphia: 1854. V. 37

BLEECKER, ANN ELIZA
The History of Maria Kittle In a Letter to Miss Ten Eyck. Hartford: 1802.
V. 42

BLEECKER, ANN ELIZA SCHUYLER
The Posthumous Works of . . . New York: 1793. V. 43

BLEEKER, LEONARD
The Order Book of Capt. Leonard Bleeker, Major of Brigade in the Early
Part of the Expedition Under Gen. James Clinton, Against the Indian
Settlements of Western New York, in the Campaign of 1779. New York:
1865. V. 45

BLEEKER, P.
Atlas Ichthyologique des Indes Orientales Neerlandaises. Washington: 1983.
V. 37

BLEGEN, CARL W.
Korakou: a Prehistoric Settlement Near Corinth. Boston and New York:
1921. V. 37; 42; 44
The Palace of Nestor at Pylos in Western Messenia. Princeton: 1966. V. 44
The Palace of Nestor at Pylos in Western Messenia. Princeton: 1966-73.
V. 40
Prosymna: the Helladic Settlement Preceding the Argive Heraeum.
Cambridge: 1937. V. 37; 40; 44
Troy. Princeton: 1950-1963. V. 37
Troy. Princeton: 1951. V. 42
Troy. Princeton: 1953. V. 42
Troy I-(IV). 1950-63. V. 37
Zygouries: a Prehistoric Settlement in the Valley of Cleonae. Cambridge:
1928. V. 37

BLEGNY, ETIENNE DE
Les Elemens ou Premieres Instructions de la Jeunesse . . . Paris: 1712.
V. 38; 40

BLEI, E.
In Memoriam Oscar Wilde. Leipzig: 1904. V. 38

BLENKARN, JOHN
Practical Specifications of Works Executed in Architecture. London: 1865.
V. 37; 40; 44

BLENKINSOP, ADAM
Paddiana; or, Scraps and Sketches of Irish Life, Present and Past. London:
1848. V. 39

BLENKOW, JOHN
Michaels Combat with the Divel; or, Moses His Funerall. London: 1640.
V. 41

BLENNERHASSETT, LADY
Madame de Stael. Her Friends and Her Influence In Politics and Literature.
London: 1889. V. 42

BLES, JOSEPH
Rate English Drinking Glasses of the XVII & XVIII Centuries. 1925. V. 37

BLESH, RUDI
Shining Trumpets: a History of Jazz. New York: 1946. V. 45

BLESSINGTON, J. J.
The Campaigns of Walker's Texas Division, by a Private Soldier. New York:
1875. V. 37; 38; 39; 40; 42; 43; 46

**BLESSINGTON, MARGUERITE POWER FARMER GARDINER,
COUNTESS OF** 1789-1849
The Belle of a Season. London: 1840. V. 38; 42
The Book of Beauty, or Gegal Gallery for 1849. London: 1849. V. 42
Catalogue of the Costly and Elegant Effects . . . London: 1849. V. 38; 40
The Confessions of an Elderly Gentleman. London: 1836. V. 43
The Confessions of an Elderly Lady. London: 1838. V. 44
Conversations of Lord Byron with the Countess of Blessington. London:
1850. V. 39
Gore House, Upper Kensington. A Catalogue of the Costly and Elegant
Effects, Comprising all the Magnificent Furniture, Rare Porcelain, Sculpture
in Marble, Broznes and an Assemblage of Objects of Art and
Decoration . . . London: 1849. V. 41; 44
The Idler in Italy. Paris: 1839. V. 42; 44
The Magic Lantern; or sketches of scenes in the Metropolis. London: 1822.
V. 37
Memoirs of a Femme de Chambre. London: 1846. V.`38

**BLESSINGTON, MARGUERITE POWER FRAMER GARDINER,
COUNTESS OF** 1789-1849
The Lottery of Life. London: 1844. V. 37

**BLESSINGTON, MARGUERTIE POWER FARMER GARDINER,
COUNTESS OF** 1789-1849
Rambles in Waltham Forest. London: 1827. V. 40

BLEULER, PAUL EUGEN 1857-1939
Dementia Praecox Oder Gruppen der Schizophrenien. Leipzig und Wien:
1911. V. 45
The Theory of Schizophrenic Negativism. New York: 1912. V. 45

BLEW, WILLIAM C. A.
Brighton and Its Coaches, a History of the London and Bright Road . . .
London: 1894. V. 39; 42; 45
A History of Steeple Chasing. London: 1901. V. 42
The Quorn Hunt and Its Masters. London: 1899. V. 39; 42
Racing. London: 1900. V. 44

BLEWETT, DUNCAN B.
Handbook for the Therapeutic Use of Lysergic Acid Diethylamide-25 . . .
Regina: 1958? V. 43

BLEWITT, GEORGE
An Enquiry Whether a General Practice of Virtue Tends to the Wealth or
Poverty, Benefit or Disadvantage of a People? London: 1725.
V. 38; 42; 43

BLEWITT, M.
Surveys of the Seas. Great Britain: 1957. V. 40

BLEWITT, MARY
Surveys of the Seas. A Brief History of British Hydrography. Great Britain:
1956. V. 39
Surveys of the Seas: a Brief History of British Hydrography. London: 1957.
V. 42

BLEWITT, REGINALD JAMES
The Court of Chancery; a Satirical Poem. London: 1827. V. 42

BLIGH, ERIC W.
Sir Kenelm Digby and His Venetia. London: 1932. V. 44

BLIGH, JOHN
Hints and Examples Illustrative of the Theory and Practice of Analytic
Teaching . . . London: 1835. V. 45

BLIGH, WILLIAM 1754-1817
The Bligh Notebook. Canberra: 1986. V. 40; 45
Bligh's Voyage in the Resource from Coupang to Batavia, Together with
the Log of His Subsequent Pssage to England in the Dutch Packet Vlydt
and His Remarks on Morrison's Journal. 1937. V. 38
Bligh's Voyage in the Resource, from Coupang to Batavia, Together with
the Log of His Subsequent Passage to England . . . Waltham St.
Lawrence: 1937. V. 46
Bligh's Voyage in the Resource. London: 1937. V. 37
The Log of the Bounty . . . London: 1927. V. 44
The Log of the H.M.S. Providence 1791-1793. Guildford: 1976. V. 41; 43

IGH, WILLIAM 1754-1817 continued

Lieutenant W. Bligh, log of the Proceedings of His Majesty's Armed Vessel Bounty in a Voyage to the South Seas to take the Breadfruit from the Society Islands to the West Indies. Guilford: 1975/1976. V. 37

The Log of the 'Bounty', being Lt. Bligh's Log of the Proceedings of H.M. Armed Vessel 'Bounty' in a voyage to the South Seas, to take the Bread Fruit from the Society Islands to the West Indies. Now published for the time from . . . London: 1937. V. 37

Narrative of the Mutiny on the Bounty . . . N.P.,. V. 39

A Narrative of the Mutiny, On Board His Majesty's Ship Bounty. London: 1790. V. 37; 39; 41; 45; 46

A Voyage to the South Sea, Undertaken by Command of His Majesty, for the Purpose of Conveying the Bread-Fruit Tree to the West Indies, in His Majesty's Ship the Bounty . . . London: 1792. V. 37; 41; 45; 46

A Voyage to the South Sea . . . for the Purpose of Conveying the Bread-Fruit Tree to the West Indies . . . London: 1792. V. 45

The Voyage of the Bounty's Launch as Related in William Bligh's Despatch to the Admiralty and the Journal of John Fryer with an Introduction by Owen Rutter . . . London: 1934. V. 41

A Voyage to the South Seas. Adelaide: 1975. V. 44

A Voyage to the South Seas . . . in His Majesty's Ship Bounty . . . New York: 1975. V. 38

BLIGHTED Life. London: 1880. V. 40

LINN, CAROL J.

Arno Werner: One Man's Work. Easthampton: 1982. V. 43

The Fabric. Easthampton: 1989. V. 44

A Fowl Letter Book. Easthampton: 1989. V. 41; 42; 43; 44; 46

From Stripper to Publisher, or, How Printing Changed My Life . . . 1986. V. 45

From Stripper to Publisher; or, How Printing Changed My Life. Northampton: 1986. V. 38; 44

From Stripper to Publisher or, How Printing Changed My Life. Two Lectures by Carol J. Blinn. (Easthampton: 1986). V. 37

On Becoming Three and Thirty. Easthampton: 1976. V. 39

A Poultry Piece. Easthampton: 1978. V. 44

LINN, HENRY C.

The Life and Gospel Experience of Mother Ann Lee. East Canterbury: 1901. V. 40

LISH, HELEN H.

Pictographic History of the Oglala Sioux. Lincoln: 1967. V. 40; 42; 44

LISH, J.

A Case of Conscience. London: 1959. V. 44

A Case of Conscience. 1969. V. 39

The Frozen Year. 1957. V. 43

Jack of Eagles. New York: 1952. V. 44

LISS, C. N.

Investigation of Affairs at the Kiowa, Comanche, and Apache Indian Reservation. Washington: 1897. V. 46

Proposed Removal of the Northern Cheyenne Indians. Washington: 1899. V. 38

LISS, C. V. FORSTER

The Clerical Guide and Churchman's Directory. An Annual Register for the Clergy and Laity of the Anglican Church in British North America. 1877. Ottawa: 1877. V. 38

BLISS, CAREY S.

Bibliography of Cheney Miniatures. Los Angeles: 1975. V. 41

Julius Firmicus Maternus and the Aldine Edition of the Scriptores Astonomici Veteres. Los Angeles: 1981. V. 38; 40; 41; 42; 46

A Leaf from the 1583 Rembert Dodoens Herbal Printed by Christian Plantin. San Francisco: 1977. V. 37; 39; 40; 41; 42; 44; 46

the Willow Dale Press, 1879. Los Angeles: 1975. V. 41; 44

BLISS, D. E.

The Biology of the Crustacea. London: 1982-86. V. 37; 38

BLISS, DOUGLAS PERCY

The Devil in Scotland: Being Four Great Scottish Stories of Diablerie . . . London: 1934. V. 37

Edward Bawden. London: 1979. V. 43

Edward Bawden. Surrey: 1979. V. 37; 40; 42

A History of Wood Engraving. London: 1928. V. 39; 40; 41; 43; 45

BLISS, FRANK B.

A Catalogue of the Etchings, Drypoints and Lithographs by Professor Alphonse Legros . . . in the Collection of Frank B. Bliss. London: 1923. V. 37; 38

BLISS, FRANK C.

St. Paul: Its Past and Present . . . St. Paul: 1888. V. 39; 44

BLISS, FRANK E.

The Life of the Hon. William F. Cody Known as Buffalo Bill. Hartford: 1879. V. 37; 45

BLISS, FREDERICK JONES

Excavations at Jerusalem 1894-1897. London: 1898. V. 39; 40

Excavations in Palestine During the Years 1898-1900. London: 1902. V. 40

BLISS, GEORGE

An Address to Members of the Bar of the Counties of Hampshire, Franklin and Hampden, at their Annual Meeting at Northampton, September 1826. Springfield: 1827. V. 38; 40

BLISS, MRS.

Practical Cook Book . . . Philadelphia: 1851. V. 45

BLISS, ROBERT WOODS

Robert Woods Bliss Collection Pre-Columbian Art. New York: 1957. V. 44

BLISS, WILLIAM D.

The Encyclopedia of Social Reform. New York: & London: 1897. V. 40

BLISS, WILLIAM R.

Paradise in the Pacific . . . New York: 1873. V. 42; 43; 46

BLITH, WALTER

The English Improver Improved or the Survey of Husbandry Surveyed . . . London: 1652. V. 42

BLIXEN-FINECKE, BROR VON FRIHERRE 1886-

African Hunter. London: 1937. V. 39

African Hunter. New York: 1938. V. 42

BLIXEN, KAREN

Out of Africa. London: 1937. V. 44

BLOCH, E. MARUICE

George Caleb Bingham: the Evolution of an Artist . . . Berkeley: 1967. V. 45

BLOCH, E. MAURICE

George Caleb Bingham, River Portratist. Berkeley: 1967. V. 44

BLOCH, R.

A Portfolio of Some Rare and Exquisite Poetry by the Bard of Bards. 1937 or 1938. V. 44

BLOCH, ROBERT

Blood Runs Cold. New York: 1961. V. 45

The Eighth Stage of Fandom. 1962. V. 43

The Opener of the Way. Sauk City: 1945. V. 37; 39; 42; 43; 45

Pleasant Dreams. Sauk City: 1960. V. 39

Psycho. New York: 1959. V. 39; 42

The Scarf. New York: 1947. V. 43; 45

The Trunk Murders. 1974. V. 42; 43

BLODGET, LORIN

Climatology of the United States. Philadelphia: 1857. V. 40; 42; 43; 44; 46

BLODGET, W. P.

Rocky Mountain song Book, Published for the Use of the Fremont Flying Artillery of Providence. Providence: 1856. V. 40

BLODGET, WILLIAM

Facts and Arguments Respecting the Great Utility of an Extensive Plan of Inland Navigation in America. Philadelphia: 1805. V. 38

BLOEDE, VICTOR G.

The Reducer's manual, and Gold and Silver Worker's Guide . . . New York: 1867. V. 45

BLOEMART, ABRAHAM

Fondamenten der Teeken-Kunst. V. 45

BLOGG, MINNIE WRIGHT

Bibliography of the Writings of Sir William Osler . . . Baltimore: 1921. V. 45

BLOIS, JOHN T.

Gazetteer of the State of Michigan . . . Detroit: 1838. V. 37; 39; 45

Gazetteer of the State of Michigan. Detroit & New York: 1838. V. 38; 42; 45

BLOIS, LOUIS DE

Psychagogia, hoc Est Animae Recreatio Quatuor Libris Distincta. Rome: 1585. V. 37

BLOK, ALEXANDER 1880-1921

The Twelve. London: 1920. V. 42

BLOK, ALEXANDER 1880-1921 continued

The Twelve. New York: 1920. V. 46

The Twelve. New York: 1931. V. 41; 42; 43; 44; 45

BLOM, FRANS

Tribes and Temples. A Record of the Expedition to Middle America Conducted by the Tualne University of Louisiana in 1925. New Orleans: 1926. V. 41

Tribes and Temples . . . New Orleans: 1926-27. V. 44

Tribes and Temples: a Record of the Expedition to Middle America Conducted by the Tulane University of Louisianna in 1925. Tulane: 1926-27. V. 42

BLOMBERG, CARL JOHANN

An Account of Livonia. London: 1701. V. 38

BLOME, RICHARD d. 1705

L'Amerique Angloise, ou Description des Isles et Terres du Roi d'Angleterre, dans l'Amerique. Amsterdam: 1688. V. 37; 38; 40; 43; 45

Britannia; or, a Geographical Description of the Kingdoms of England, Scotland, and Ireland. London: 1673. V. 39

A Description of the Island of Jamaica; with the Other Isles and Territories in America, To Which the English are Related . . . London: 1678. V. 41

Hawking or Faulconry. London: 1929. V. 39; 43

The Present State of His Majesties Isles and Territories in America . . . London: 1687. V. 43; 44; 45

Questions Propounded to George Whitehad and George Fox, Who Disputed by Turns Against one University-Man in Cambr. Aug. 29, 1659. N.P.: 1659. V. 39; 45

BLOMEFIELD, FRANCIS 1705-1752

Collectanea Cantabrigiensia, or Collections Relating to Cambridge, University, Town, and County. Norwich: 1750. V. 45

An Essay Towards a Topographical History of the County of Norfolk . . . London: 1805-10. V. 42; 45

BLOMFIELD, EZEKIEL

Lectures on the Philosophy of History, Accompanied With Notes and Illustrative Engravings. London: 1819. V. 42

BLOMFIELD, JAMES

Rod, Gun and Palette in the High Rockies. Chicago: 1914. V. 43

BLOMFIELD, REGINALD

Architectural Drawing and Draughtsmen. London: 1912. V. 37

The Formal Garden in England. London: 1892. V. 45

A History of Renaissance Architecture in England, 1500-1800. London: 1897. V. 39; 42

A History of French Architecture from the Reign of Charles VIII till the Death of Mazarin. London: 1911. V. 38

A History of French Architecture 1494-1774. London: 1911-21. V. 46

A History of French Architecture, from the Death of Mazarin Till the Death of Louis XV, 1661-1774. London: 1921. V. 42; 46

BLONDEL, DAVID

A Treatise of the Sibyls, So Highly Celebrated, As Well by the Antient Heathens, as the Holy Fathers of the Church. London: 1661. V. 42

BLONDEL, JACQUES FRANCOIS

Cours d'Architecture, ou Traite de la Decoration, Distribution and Construction des Batiments . . . Paris: 1771-1777. V. 41; 45

BLONDUS, FLAVIUS

Roma Ristavrata, et Italia Illustrata . . . Vinegia: 1558. V. 37

BLONDUS, MICHAELUS ANGELUS 1497-1565

Dialogus De Invidia. Rome: 1539. V. 38

BLONG, R. J.

Volcanic Hazards, a Source-Book on the Effects of Eruptions. London: 1984. V. 37

BLOODGOOD, SIMEON DEWITT

The Sexagenary, or Reminiscences of the American Revolution. Albany: 1833. V. 37; 38

BLOODSTOCK RESEARCH & STATISTICAL BUREAU

American Produce Records 1930-1971. Lexington: 1972. V. 39

THE BLOODY Massacre Perpetrated in King-Street, Boston, on March 5th 1770 by a Party of the 29th Regiment. Together with a Print of the Event Taken from the Plate Engraved by Paul Revere . . . Barre: 1970. V. 39

BLOOM, VERA

Empress Eugenia 1920. New York: 1923. V. 42

BLOOMFIELD, ARTHUR L.

A Bibliography of Internal Medicine. Chicago: 1958. V. 38; 42

BLOOMFIELD, LIN

Vincent Brown: Life and Work. North Sydney: 1980. V. 41

BLOOMFIELD, MAX

Bloomfield's Illustrated Historical Guide, Embracing an Account of the Antiquities of St. Augustine Florida . . . St. Augustine: 1884. V. 41

BLOOMFIELD, NATHANIEL

An Essay on War, in the Blank Verse; Honington Green, a Ballad; The Culprit, an Elegy; and Other Poems on Various Subjects. Bury. V. 45

BLOOMFIELD, ROBERT

The Banks of Wye. London: 1811. V. 39; 40; 46

The Farmer's Boy. London: 1800. V. 39; 40

The Farmer's Boy. (with) Rural Tales. London: 1800-02. V. 38

Good Tidings; or News from the Farm. London: 1804. V. 41; 42; 45

May Day with the Muses. London: 1822. V. 40

Rural Tales, Ballads and Songs. London: 1802. V. 40; 43; 44; 46

Wild Flowers; or Pastoral and Local Poetry. London: 1806. V. 37; 39; 40

BLOOMFIELD, WILLIAM

The Servant's Companion; or, Practical Housemaid's and Footman's Guide. Devonport: 1830. V. 42; 46

BLOOMSBURY, S. B.

Butleriana. London: 1932. V. 44

BLORE, EDWARD

The Monumental Remains of Noble and Eminent Persons, Comprising the Sepulchral Antiquities of Great Britain. London: 1824-26. V. 38; 45

The Monumental Remains of Noble and Eminent Persons, Comprising the Sepulchral Antiquities of Great Britain. London: 1826. V. 38

BLORE, THOMAS

A Guide to Burghley House, Northamptonshire, the Seat of the Marquis of Exeter; Containing a Catalogue of All the Paintings, Antiquities &c. Stamford: 1815. V. 37; 41

BLOUNDELLE-BURTON, J.

His Own Enemy: The Story of a Man of the World. London: 1887. V. 42; 43

BLOUNT, CHARLES 1654-1693

Anima Mundi; or, an Historical Narration of the Opinions of the Ancients Concerning Man's Soul After This Life. London: 1679. V. 43

King William and Queen Mary Conquerors; or, a Discourse Endeavouring to Prove Their Side, Against the Late King, the Principle Reasons That Make Conquest a Good Title. London: 1693. V. 37; 41

The Miscellaneous Works. London: 1695. V. 38; 40; 41; 43; 45

Religio Laici. London: 1683. V. 38

BLOUNT, GODFREY

The Story of the Sower. London: 1900. V. 44

The Story of the Sower. London: 1910. V. 42

BLOUNT, HENRY

A Voyage to the Levant. London: 1636. V. 39

A Voyage into the Levant. London: 1638. V. 37

BLOUNT, JOHN GRAY

Papers. (1764-1833). Raleigh: 1952-82. V. 37

BLOUNT, THOMAS

The Academie of Eloquence. London: 1654. V. 41

Boscobel; or the History of His Sacred Majesties Most Miraculous Prservation after the Battle of Worcester, 3 Sept. 1651. London: 1660. V. 46

Fragmenta Antiquitatis; or, Ancient Tenures of Land and Jocular Customs of Some Manors. York: 1784. V. 37; 40; 42; 43

Glossographia. In the Savoy: 1674. V. 41

Glossographia; or, a Dictionary, Interpreting the Hard Words of Whatsoever Language, Now Used In Our Refined English Tongue . . . London: 1674. V. 43

BLOUNT, THOMAS POPE 1649-1697

Censura Celebriorum Authorum: sive Tractatus in Quo Varia Virorum Doctorum de Clarissimis Cujusque Seculi Scriptoribus Judicia Traduntur. Londini: 1690. V. 41

De Re Poetica: or, Remarks Upon Poetry. London: 1694. V. 37; 38; 43

Essays on Several Subjects. London: 1692. V. 37; 45

Essays on Several Subjects. London: 1697. V. 40; 43

Essays on Several Subjects. London: 1691. V. 37

A Natural History Containing Many Not Common Observations, Extracted Out of the Best Modern Writers. London: 1693. V. 38; 39; 40; 42; 43

BLUNT, ANTHONY

Neapolitan Baroque and Rococo Architecture. 1975. V. 39; 43

Nicolas Poussin. New York: 1967. V. 37; 38; 40; 44

The Paintings of Nicholas Poussin, Together with Nicholas Poussin; The A. W. Mellon Lecutres in fine Arts. London: & New York: 1958/66/67. V. 46

The Paintings of Nicolas Poussin: A Critical Catalogue. London: 1966. V. 37; 40; 44

BLUNT, D. E.

Elephant. London: 1933. V. 39

BLUNT, EDMUND M.

The American Coast Pilot. New York: 1817. V. 42; 43

The American Coast Pilot . . . New York: 1850. V. 42

The American Coast Pilot . . . New York: 1864. V. 42

Blunt's Stranger's Guide to the City of New York . . . New York: 1871. V. 45

The Merchant and Seaman's Expeditious Measurer . . . New York: 1825. V. 42

BLUNT, HENRY

A Voyage into the Levant. London: 1664. V. 39

BLUNT, JOHN ELIJAH

A History of the Establishment and Residence of the Jews in England; with An Enquiry into their Civil Disabilities. London: 1830. V. 40

BLUNT, JOHN JAMES

Vestiges of Ancient Manners and Customs, Discoverable in Modern Italy and Sicily. London: 1823. V. 41; 43; 44

BLUNT, JOSEPH

A Historical Sketch of the Fomration of the Confederacy, . . . New York: 1825. V. 39; 42; 45

The Merchant's and Shipmaster's Assistant . . . New York: 1822. V. 44

BLUNT, REGINALD

Mrs. Montagu, Queen of the Blues. Boston: 1923. V. 44

BLUNT, ROSAMOND

Aunt Chloe, a Faithful Virginia Slave. Richmond: 1890. V. 42

BLUNT, SAMUEL, PSEUD.

A Voyage to Cackogallinia . . . London: 1727. V. 42

BLUNT, WILFRED SCAWEN 1840-1922

Esther; a Young Man's Tragedy Together with the Love Sonnets of Proteus. Boston: 1895. V. 39; 41

My Diaries Being a Personal Narrative of Events 1888-1914. London: 1919 & 1920. V. 42

BLUNT, WILFRID 1901-

The Art of Botanical Illustration. London: 1950. V. 39; 45

The Art of Botanical Illustrations. London: 1951. V. 37; 45; 46

Tulips and Tulipomania. London: 1977. V. 37

BLUNT, WILFRID SCAWEN 1840-1922

The Celebrated Romance of the Stealing of the Mare. Newtown: 1930. V. 45

In Vinculis: Poems. London: 1889. V. 43

The Land War in Ireland, Being a Personal Narrative of Events. London: 1912. V. 38

The Love Sonnets of Proteus. London: 1881. V. 39

The Love-Lyrics & Songs of Proteus. Hammersmith: 1892. V. 45

The Love-Lyrics & Songs of Proteus . . . with the Love-Sonnets of Proteus . . . London: 1892. V. 37; 38; 41; 46

My Diaries, Being a Personal Narrative of Events, 1888-1914. London: 1919. V. 38; 39

A New Pilgrimage and Other Poems. London: 1889. V. 43

Proteus and Amadeus, a Correspondence. London;: 1878. V. 39

Secret History of the English Occupation of Egypt . . . London: 1907. V. 42

The Seven Golden odes of Pagan Arabia, Known Also as the Moallakat. London: 1903. V. 39

Sonnets and Songs. By Proteus. London: 1875. V. 37; 40

The Wind and The Whirlwind. London: 1883. V. 39

BLUNTSCHLI, J. K.

The Theory of the State. Oxford: 1885. V. 43

BLY, ROBERT

Mirabai. New York: 1980. V. 42; 44

Visiting Emily Dickinson's Grave and Other Poems. Madison: 1979. V. 42; 44

BLYDEN, EDWARD W.

Liberia; Past, Presen and Future. An Address Delivered July 26, 1866, on Mount Lebanon, Syria . . . Washington City: 1869. V. 42

BLYGENBURGIUS, DAMASUS

Veneres Blyenburgicae, Sive Amorum Hortus. Dordraci: 1600. V. 40

BLYTH & TYNE RAILWAY. NEWBIGGIN BRANCH.

Form of Tender and Schedule of Quantities. Newcastle: 1871. V. 46

BLYTH, E.

The Natural History of the Cranes. London: 1881. V. 37; 45

B'NAI B'RITH

Constitution of the Independent Order B'nai B'rith. Adopted in the General Convention of the Order, Held in the City of New York July 19-27, 1868. New York: 1868. V. 43

BNKS, IAIN M.

Consider Phelbas. London: 1987. V. 38

BO', THEODORE SAINT

Wilfred and Mary; or, Father and Daughter. Edinburgh: 1861. V. 39

BOADBY, ROBERT

An Apology for the Life of Mr. Bampfylde-Moore Carew, Commonly Call'd the King of the Beggars . . . London: 1750? V. 46

BOADEN, JAMES

An Inquiry Into the Authenticity of Various Pictures and Prints . . . London: 1824. V. 37; 43

The Life of Mrs. Jordan. London: 1831. V. 37; 38; 39; 41; 42

The Maid of Bristol. New York: 1803. V. 44

Memoirs of the Life of John Philip Kemble, Esq . . . London: 1825. V. 38; 45

BOAISTUAU, PIERRE

Histoires Prodigievses, Extraictes de Plvsievrs Famevx Avthevrs, Grecs & Lains . . . Paris: 1564. V. 44

Histoires Prodigieuses. Paris: 1566. V. 38; 39

BOAK, ARTHUR E. R.

Karanis: Topographical and Architectural Report of Excavations During the Seasons of 1924-28. Ann Arbor: 1931. V. 42

BOAKE, BARCROFT

Where the Dead Men Lie and Other Poems. Sydney: 1897. V. 42

BOAM, H. J.

British Columbia: Its History, People, Commerce, Industries and Resources. London: 1912. V. 43

THE BOARDING School Romps. London: 1771. V. 42; 43

BOARDMAN, JOHN

Art and Architecture. New York: 1967. V. 41

Catalogue of the Engraved Gems and Finger Rings: I. Greek and Etruscan. Oxford: 1978. V. 40; 42; 44

The Cretan Collection in Oxford. The Dictaean Cave and Iron Age Crete. London: 1961. V. 43

The Cretan Collection in Oxford. Oxford: 1961. V. 40; 42; 44

Excavations at Torca 1963-1965.. London: 1966-73. V. 37; 40

Greek Gems and Finger Rings: Early Bronze Age to Late Classical. New York. V. 38; 42

Greek Art and Architecture. New York: 1967. V. 40; 42

Greek Gems and Finger Rings. Early Bronze Age to Late Classical. London: 1970. V. 40; 42; 44

Greek Gems and Finger Rings: early Bronze Age to Late Classical. New York: 1970? V. 46

BOARDMAN, MABEL THORP

Under the Red Cross Flag at Home and Abroad. Philadelphia & London: 1915. V. 45

BOARDMAN, W. A.

Boardman's Discourses on the Principles and Philosophy of the Universe. Chicago: 1862. V. 42

BOAS, FRANZ

Ethnology of the Kwakiutl. Washington: 1921. V. 37

Handbook of American Indian Languages. Washington: 1922. V. 38

Handbook of American Indian Languaages. Washington: 1911. V. 38

Handbook of the American Indian Languages. Washington: 1911-1922. V. 37

Kwakiutl Texts. New York: 1902. V. 38

The Religion of the Kwakiutl Indians. New York: 1930. V. 41; 44

Tsimshian Texts. Washington: 1902. V. 43

BOATE, GERARD

A Natural History of Ireland. Dublin: 1726. V. 45; 46

BOAZ, HERMAN

The Angler's Progress: a Poem. London: 1820. V. 39; 43; 45

BOB-LYNN Against Franck-Lynn: or, A Full History of the Controversies and Dissentions in the Family of the Lynn's. London: 1732. V. 39

BOBBIN, TIMOTHY

Human Passions Delineated in above 120 Figures, Droll, Satyrical and Humourous . . . London: 1809. V. 37

BOBBIO

Statuta Communis Bobij Impensa Dicti Communis Impressa ac Instantia Domini rancisco Coleri Sindici et Procuratoris Predicte Civitatis de Mandato Donnorum de Consilio et Presidentium Negotiis Publicis Dicte Civitatiis Bobij . . . Placentiae (Piacenza): 1527. V. 38

BOBRINKSY, A. A., COUNT

Russian Peasant Art. New York: 1922. V. 41

BOBYNET, PIERRE

L'Horographie Curieuse. 1643. V. 44

BOCAGE, MADAME DU

Letters Concerning England, Holland and Italy . . . London: 1770. V. 45

BOCANEGRA, J. M.

Memoria Del Secretario de Estado y Del Despachio de Relaciones Exteriores Y Gobernacion de la Republica Mexicana. Mexico: 1844. V. 45

BOCCACCIO, GIOVANNI 1313-1375

Ameto Over Comedia Delle Nimphe Fiorentine. Venice: 1524. V. 40; 43

Ameto. Florence: 1529. V. 37

Ameto. Venice: 1558. V. 40

Amorosa Visione, Nuovamente Ritrovata . . . *Apologia di H. Claricio.* Milan: 1521. V. 37

Amorous Flammetta. London: 1929. V. 37; 38; 39; 45; 46

Comedie del Excelentissimo Poeta Miser Johanni Boccatio da Certaldo. Venice: 1503. V. 37

Contes et Nouvelles. Cologne: 1702. V. 42

Il Corbaccio. Paris: 1569. V. 37

Il Corbaccio . . . Novellamente Stampato e con Riscontri di Testi. Firenze: 1594. V. 37; 40

The Decameron. Philadelphia. V. 41; 43; 44

Il Decamerone Di M. Giovanni Boccaccio. Florence: 1527. V. 45

Il Decameron . . . Firenze: 1582. V. 41; 43

Il Decameron . . . Florence: 1587. V. 40; 45

Il Decamerone di Messer Giovanni Boccaccio . . . Venice: 1588. V. 45

The Decameron. London: 1620. V. 37; 43; 44

Il Decameron . . . Amsterdam: 1665. V. 37

Il Decameron. London: 1725. V. 39

Il Decamerone Di M. Giovanni Boccaccio . . . Firenze: per li heredi di: 1729. V. 45

Il Decamerone. Venice: 1729. V. 37; 38; 40; 42

Il Decamerone. Londra: i.e. Paris,: 1757. V. 37

Le Decameron de Jean Boccace. Londres: 1757-61. V. 42

Decamerone Di Giovanni Boccaccio Cognominate Principe Galeotto . . . da Vincenzio Martinelli. Londra: 1762. V. 40

Il Decameron. Firenze: 1820. V. 38

Il Decameron. Florence: 1820. V. 45

Il Decameron. Firenze: 1822. V. 40

Decameron. London: 1825. V. 37

The Decameron . . . London: 1886. V. 43

Decameron. London: (1893). V. 37; 45

Il Decameron. 1902. V. 40

Il Decameron. Chelsea: 1920. V. 40; 46

The Decameron. London: 1920. V. 42; 45; 46

The Decameron. New York: 1925. V. 45

The Decameron. Philadelphia: 1928. V. 43

The Decameron. New York: 1930. V. 38; 39; 41; 42; 43; 44

The Decameron. London: 1932. V. 46

The Decameron. Oxford: 1934. V. 37; 39; 41; 42; 45; 46

Boccaccio's Decameron. Oxford: 1934-35. V. 41

The Decameron. New York: 1940. V. 46

The Decameron. Garden City: 1949. V. 38; 39; 42; 46

Philippi Beroaldi Carmen de Duobus Amantibus (-Fabula Tancredi ex Boccatio in Latinum Versa). Leipzig: ?1510. V. 38

Della Geneologia de Gli Dei . . . Venice: 1627. V. 40; 45

La Genealogia de Gli Dei Gentili . . . Venice: 1574. V. 40

Genealogiae Deoru Gentilium Libri XV. Venice: 1472. V. 42

Genealogie Deorum. Venetiis: 1495. V. 38; 40

Life of Dante. 1904. V. 45

Life of Dante. Boston: 1904. V. 39; 46

Life of Dante. San Francisco: 1922. V. 43

The Novels and Tales of the Renowned John Boccaccio . . . London: 1684. V. 43; 46

The Nymphs of Fiesole. Verona: 1952. V. 37; 39; 40; 41; 42; 43; 44

Boccaccio's Olympia. London: 1913. V. 40

Il Philocholo. Venetia: 1514. V. 37; 38

Philocholo. Colophon: 1520. V. 39

Le Plaisant Liure Auquel il Traicte des Faictz & Gestes des Illustres & Cleres Dames . . . Paris: 1538. V. 43

The Story of Griselda. London: 1909. V. 38; 46

Thirteene Most Pleasaunt and Delectable Questions. London: 1927. V. 45

The Three Admirable Accidents of Andrea de Piero: From the First Englyshed Edition of the Decameron. Lexington: 1954. V. 46

The Tragedies . . . of All Such Princes As Fell from Theyr Estates. London: 1554? V. 45; 46

The Tragedies, Gathered by Jhon (sic) Bochas . . . London: 1555? V. 44

A Treatise Excellent and Compe(n)dious, Shewing and Declaring, in Maner of Tragedye, the Falles of Sondry Most Notable Princes and Princesses with Other Nobles . . . 1554. V. 39

A Treatise Excellent and Compendious, Shewing and Declaring, in Maner of Tragedye the Salies of Sondry Most Notable Princes and Princesses with Other Nobles . . . London: 1554. V. 40; 45

BOCCALINI, TRAJANO

I Ragguagli di Parnasso; or Advertisements from Parnassus . . . London: 1657. V. 43

BOCCHI, ACHILLE

Symbolicarum Quaestionum . . . Libri Quinque. Bologna: 1574. V. 38; 39; 41

BOCCHI, FRANCESCO

Le Bellezze Della Citta Di Firenze . . . Firenze: 1677. V. 46

BOCCHI, OTTAVIO

Osservazioni Sopra un Antico Teatro Scoperto in Adria . . . Venice: 1739. V. 38

BOCCIUS, GOTTLIEB

Fish in Rivers and Streams: a Treatise on the Production and Management of Fish in Freshwaters, by Artificial Spawning, Breeding and Rearing. London: 1848. V. 39; 41

A Treatise on the Management of Fresh-Water Fish, with a View to Making Them a Source of Profit to Landed Proprietors. London: 1841. V. 37

BOCCONE, PAOLO

Icones et Descriptiones Rariorum Plantarum Siciliae, Melitae, Galliae, & Italiae. Oxford: 1674. V. 37

BOCHART, SAMUEL 1599-1667

Opera Omnia. Leiden and Utrecht: 1692. V. 40

BOCK, MICHAEL

Apothecary. Innen Beschreibene und Durch Unzahliche Proben Probat Befundene Medicamenta . . . s.l., s.n.: 1750. V. 39

BOCKETT, ELIAS

Geneva: a Poem. London: 1729. V. 43

BOCKLER, GEORG ANDREAS

Architectura Curiosa Nova . . . Explicata & Vernaculo Idiomate Descripta . . . Nuremberg: 1664. V. 39

BOCKSTOCE, JOHN R.

American Whalers in the Western Arctic . . . Fairhaven: 1982. V. 41; 44

BODDAM-WHETHAM, J. W.

Western Wanderings. A Record of Travel in the Evening Land. London: 1874. V. 38; 39; 41; 42

BODDIE, JOHN B.

Seventeenth Century Isle of Wight County Virginia. Chicago: 1938. V. 46

BODDIE, JOHN BENNETT

Historical Southern Families. Redwood City: 1957. V. 44

BODDIE, WILLIAM W.

History of Williamsburg (SC). Columbia: 1923. V. 40

BODDINGTON, J. W.

Catalogue of Works of Art, Curiosities and Antiquities, Chinese Works of Art and . . . Drawings . . . London: 1838. V. 44

BODE, CLEMENT AUGUSTUS DE

Travels in Luristan and Arabistan. London: 1845. V. 42; 45

BODE, JOHANN ELERT

Anleitung zur Allgemeinen Kenntniss der Erdkugel . . . Berlin: 1803. V. 44

BODE, W.

The Complete Work of Rembrandt. History, Description and Heliographic Reproduction of all the Master's Pictures With a Study of His Life and His Art . . . Paris: 1897-1906. V. 39

BODE, WINSTON

A Portrait of Pancho. Austin: 1965. V. 37; 38; 42

BODEFROID DE BUILLON 1058?-1100

The History of Godefrey of Boloyne. Hammersmith: 1893. V. 46

BODELSEN, MERETE

Gauguin's Ceramics: a Study in the Development of His Art. London: 1964. V. 37; 40

BODENHAMER, WILLIAM

A Practical Treatise on the Aetiology, Pathology and Treatment of the Congenital Malformations of the Rectum and Anus. New York: 1860. V. 41

Practical Observations on the Aetiology, Pathology, Diagnosis and Treatment of Anal Fissure. New York: 1868. V. 42

BODENHEIM, MAXWELL

Minna and Myself. New York: 1918. V. 38

BODENHEIMER, F. S.

Animal and Man in Bible Lands. Leiden: 1960. V. 44

BODENS, CHARLES

The Modish People. London: 1732. V. 46

BODENSTEIN, ANDREAS VON KARLSTADT

Missius von der Aller Hochsten Tugent Gelassenhait. Augsburg: 1519. V. 37

BODFISH, HARTSON H.

Chasing the Bowhead . . . . Recorded for Him by Joseph Chase Allen. Cambridge: 1936. V. 39; 41; 43; 44

BODGE, GEORGE M.

Soldiers in King Philip's War Containing Lists of the Soldiers of Massachusetts Colony Who Served in the Indian War of 1675-1677. Boston: 1891. V. 42

BODIAM Castle, a Poem, in Six Cantos. London: 1818. V. 42

BODIN, JEAN 1530-1596

De la Demonomanie des Sorciers. Antwerp: 1593. V. 38

Demonomanie des Sorciers . . . Paris: 1598. V. 46

Les six livres de la republique . . . Paris: 1577. V. 37

De Magorum Daemonomania. Strassburg: 1586. V. 38

De Magorum Daemonomania . . . Francofurti: 1590. V. 46

De Republica Libri Sex. Frankfurt: 1591. V. 38

BODINGTON, GEORGE

An Essay On the Treatment and Cure of Pulmonary Consumption. Lichfield: 1906. V. 37; 38

BODIO, STEPHEN

Atlantic Salmon. Easthampton: 1988. V. 40

BODKIN, THOMAS

Hugh Lane and His Pictures. 1932. V. 40; 45

BODLEY, JOHN BEALE

Gleanings from the Most Celebrated Books on Husbandry, Gardening and Rural Affairs, from the London edition of 1803 . . . Philadelphia: 1803. V. 37

BODLEY, JOHN EDWARD

The Coronation of Edward the Seventh - a Chapter of European and Imperial History. London: 1903. V. 46

BODLEY, TEMPLE A.

Richard A. Robinson: a Memoir. Louisville: 1903. V. 43

BODLEY, THOMAS

The Life of Sir Thomas Bodley, Written By Himself. London: 1894. V. 39

BODMER, JOHANN JACOB

Noah. London: 1770. V. 38

BODONI, GIOVANNI BATTISTA 1740-1813

Del Solenne Battesimo di S.A.R. Ludovico Principe Primogenito di Parma Inscrizioni Esotiche e Caratteri Novellamente Incisi e Fusi. Parma: 1774. V. 45

Epithalamia Exoticis Linguis Reddita. Parma: 1775. V. 39; 45

G. B. Bodoni's Preface to the Manuale Tipografico of 1818 . . . London: 1925. V. 37; 44

Manuale Tipografico del Cavaliere . . . London: 1960. V. 45

Manuale Tipografico, 1788. Verona: 1968. V. 40; 44; 45

Oratio Dominica in CLV Linguas Versa et Exoticis Characteribus Plenumque Expressa. Parmae: 1806. V. 39; 40; 41

Pel Solenne Battesimo di S.A.R. Ludovico Principe Primogenite di Parma . . . Parma: 1774. V. 39; 40; 41

Prose, E Versi per Onorare le Memoria di Livia Doria Caraffa, Principessa del S.R. Imp. e della Rocella . . . Parma: 1784. V. 45

THE BODY, Mind and Spirit; or, the Life of Nature, of Reason and of Heaven, Separately Traced in Man. London: 1853. V. 41

BOECE, HECTOR 1465?-1536

Scotorum Historiae a Prima Gentis Origine . . . Libri XIX . . . Paris: 1574. V. 41

BOECK, WILHELM

Picasso. New York. V. 46

Picasso. New York: 1955. V. 37; 41

Picasso. New York and Amsterdam: 1955. V. 41

Picasso Linoleum Cuts: Bacchanals, Women, Bulls and Bullfighters. New York: 1962. V. 41

BOECKLER, GEORG ANDREAS

Theatrum Machinarum Novum. Nurenberg: 1661. V. 40; 44

Theatrum Machinarum Novum. Coloniae Agrippinae: 1662. V. 40

BOEHME, JACOB 1575-1624

Morgenroete im Aufgang. Amsterdam: 1682. V. 38

Mysterium Magnum. London: 1654. V. 46

The Second Booke. Concerning the Three Principles of the Divine Essence of the Eternall, Dark, Light and Temporary World . . . London: 1648. V. 42; 44

The Third Booke of the Author Being the High and Deep Searching Out of the Threefold Life of Man. London: 1650. V. 45

BOEHN, MAX VON

Dolls and Puppets. London: 1932. V. 41

BOELTER, HOMER H.

Portfolio of Hopi Kachinas. Hollywood: 1969. V. 38; 39; 45

BOEMUS, JOHANNES

The Manners, Lawes and Customs of all Nations. London: 1611. V. 38; 40; 43; 44

Mores, Leges et Ritus Omnium Gentium, per Ioannem Boemum Aubanum. Lugduni (Lyon): 1556. V. 45

Mores, Leges, et Ritus Omnium Gentium. Lyon: 1582. V. 37; 43

THE BOER War, 1899-1900. From the Ultimatum to the Occupation of Bloemfontein. London: 1900. V. 45

BOERHAAVE, HERMAN 1668-1738

Aphorismi de Cognoscendis et Curandies Morbis. Edinburgh: 1744. V. 42

Aphorisms; Concerning the Knowledge and Cure of Diseases. London: 1724. V. 43

Aphorisms: Concerning the Knowledge and Cure of Diseases. London: 1742. V. 42

Aphorisms: Concerning Knowledge and Cure of Diseases. London: 1755. V. 37

Aphorisms: Concerning the Knowledge and Cure of Diseases. London: 1735. V. 37

De Cognoscendis et Curandis Morbis Aphorismi. Leipzig & Frankfurt: 1758. V. 42

The Commentaries upon the Aphrisms of Dr. Herman Boerhaave . . . concerning the knowledge and cure of the several diseases incident to the human body. By Gerard Van Swieten, MD. London: 1759-54-65. V. 37

Elementa Chemiae Quae Anniversario Labore Docuit . . . London: 1732. V. 45; 46

Elements of Chemistry. London: 1735. V. 40; 45

Institutiones Medicae, in Usus Annuae Exercitationis Domesticos Digestae. Lugduni Batavorum: 1708. V. 40

Libellus de Materie Medica et Remediorum Formulis . . . (with) Aphorismi de Cognoscendis et Curandis Morbis in Usum Doctrinae Domesticae Digesti. Nuremberg:r: 1747/48. V. 46

Methodus Discendi Artem Medicam. London: 1734. V. 45

A New Method of Chemistry. London: 1741. V. 40

Opuscula Omnia. The Hage: 1738. V. 44

Praelectiones Publicae de Morbis Oculorum ex Codice M.S. Venice: 1748. V. 41; 45

BOERICKE, WILLIAM

A Compend of the Principles of Homoeopathy as Taught by Hahnemann, and Verified by a Century of Clinical Application. San Francisco: 1896. V. 45

BOESCH, GOTTFRIED

The Glory of the Rose. London: 1965. V. 41

BOESEN, GUDMUND

Old Danish Silver. Copenhagen: 1949. V. 41

BOETCHER, J. G.

A Geographical, Historical and Political Description of the Empire of Germany, Holland, the Netherlands, Switzerland, Prussia, Italy, Sicily, Corsica and Sardinia. London: 1800. V. 40

BOETERO, GIOVANNI

Della Ragion di Stato, Libri Dieci. Ferrara: 1590. V. 45

BOETHEL, PAUL C.

A History of Lavaca County. Austin: 1979. V. 42

BOETHIUS d. 524

The Consolation of Philosophy, in Five Books. London: 1730. V. 40; 45

De Consolatione Philosophiae Liber cum Optimo Commento Beati Thome. Deventer: 1497. V. 38

Boetii Viri Celeberrimi de Consolatione Philosophiae. Cologne: 1500. V. 38

Consolatione Philosophiae. Oxford: 1663. V. 39

De Consolatione Philosophiae. Venice: 1694. V. 39

Consolationis Philosophiae Libri V. Anglo Saxonice Redditi ab alfredo, Inclyto Anglo Saxonum Rege. Oxoniae: 1698. V. 46

Consolationis Philosophiae. Glasguae: 1751. V. 41

In Topica Ciceronis Anitii Manlii Severini Boetii Commentarius. col. V. 43

De Philosophico Consolatu Sive de Consolatione Philosophiae. Strassburg: 1501. V. 46

De Consolatione Philosophiae, cum Commento. Colonia: 1482. V. 37

De Philosophiae Consolatione Eivsdem Scholastaica Disciplina, qui Alii Qvoqve Avtori a Nonnvllis Adscribitvr. Venetiis: 1516. V. 37

The Five Books on the Consolation of Philosophy. Edinburgh: 1789. V. 37

BOETHIUS, ANICIUS MANLIUS SEVERINUS

Arithmetica, Geometria, et Musica. Venice: 1492. V. 42

BOETHIUS, AXEL 1889-

Etruscan and Roman Architecture. Harmondsworth: (1970). V. 37; 40; 42

Etruscan Culture, Land and People. New York: 1962. V. 40; 42; 44

BOETHIUS, HECTOR

The History and Chronicles of Scotland. Edinburgh: 1822. V. 41

BOGAN, LOUISE

Body of this Death. New York: 1923. V. 37; 39; 42; 45

Collected Poems: 1923-53. New York: 1954. V. 39

Collected Poems 1923-1953. London: 1956. V. 41

Dark Summer. Poems. New York: 1929. V. 38; 42; 44

The Sleeping Fury. Poems. New York: 1937. V. 37

BOGARDUS, A. H.

Field, Cover and Trap Shooting. New York: 1894. V. 37

BOGATZKY, C. H. V.

A Golden Treasury for the Children of God, Whose Treasure Is in Heaven . . . London. V. 44

BOGDANOVICH, PETER

Fritz Lang in America. London: 1967. V. 45

BOGENG, G. A. E.

Geschichte der Buchdruckerkunst. Hellerau: 1930-35, 1941. V. 40

BOGERT, C. M.

Gila Monster and Its Allies. New York: 1956. V. 39

BOGG, A. CLARKE

Insulin in General Practice. London: 1924. V. 40

BOGG, EDMUND

From Eden Vale to the Plains of York. Leeds & York: 1894. V. 40

Nidderdale; and the Vale of the Nidd from Num Monkton to Great Whernside . . . Leeds. V. 41

Richmondshire and the Vale of Mowbray. Leeds: 1906-08. V. 37

Two Thousand Miles Wandering in the Border County, Lakeland and Ribblesdale. Leeds and York: 1898. V. 39

Two Thousand Miles of Wandering in the Border Country, Lakeland and Ribblesdale. Leeds: 1898. V. 37

BOGGS, JEAN SUTHERLAND

The National Gallery of Canada. Toronto: 1971. V. 43

Portraits by Degas. Berkeley: 1962. V. 40; 43

BOGGS, MAE HELEN BACON

My Playhouse Was a Concord Coach. Oakland: 1942. V. 37; 38; 39; 40; 42; 43; 44; 45; 46

My Playhouse Was a Concord Coach. San Francisco: 1942. V. 38

BOGGS, MARION ALEXANDER

The Alexander Letters 1787-1900. Savannah: 1910. V. 44

BOGUE, DAVID

History of Dissenters, from the Revolution in 1688 to the year 1808. London: 1808-9-10-12. V. 39

BOGUET, HENRY

Examen of Witches Drawn from Various Trials of Many of This Sect in the District of Saint Oyan de Joux Commonly Known as Saint Claude in the County of Burgundy . . . London: 1929. V. 46

BOGUS, RICHARD

Fine Printing, Publishing and Bookselling in the U.S.A. 1980. Port Clarendon: 1980. V. 42

BOGY, JOSEPH

Petition of Joseph Bogy, Praying Compensation for Spoilations On His Property by the Choctaw Indians . . . Washington: 1835. V. 45

BOHAIRE

Catalogue Des Livres & Pieces De Theatre A Vendre a Un Prix Modere, ou a Lire par Abonnement, Chez Bohaire, Libraire, rue PuitsGalliot No. 26. Paris: 180?. V. 39

BOHLER, LORENZ

The Treatment of Fractures. Vienna: 1919. V. 39

BOHM-BAWERK, EUGEN VON

Capital and Interest a Critical History of Economical Theory . . . (with) The Positive Theory of Capital . . . London & New York: 1890 & 1891. V. 38

The Positive Theory of Capital. London: 1891. V. 39

BOHN, H. G.

Catalogue of the Pictures, Miniatures and Art Books Collected During the Last Fifty Years . . . London: 1884. V. 45

The Standard Library Atlas of Classical Geography . . . London: 1861. V. 45

BOHN, HENRY

Polyglot of Foreign Proverbs. London: 1857. V. 46

BOHN, HENRY G.

The Biography and Bibliography of Shakespeare. London: 1863. V. 43; 45

A Catalogue of Books. London: 1841. V. 39; 42; 46

The Paper Duty Considered in Reference to Its Action on the Literture and Trade of Great Britain; Showing the Abolition on the Terms Now Proposed in Parliament would be Prejudicial to Both. London: 1861. V. 37

BOHN, JOHN

A Catalogue of an Extensive and Valuable Collection of Books. London: 1818. V. 39

BOHNE, PALL W.

Highlights in the History of American Whaling. Rosemead: 1968. V. 41

BOHNY, NICHOLAS

The New Picture Book. Edinburgh: 1858. V. 46

The New Picture Book. Edinburgh: 1860. V. 43

BOHR, HARALD

Collected Mathematical Works. Copenhagen: 1952. V. 45

BOHR, NIELS

On the Quantum Theory of Line-spectra. Copenhagen: 1928. V. 45

BOHROD, AARON

A Decade of Still Life. Madison: 1966. V. 41

BOHTLINGK, OTTO VON

Sanskrit-Worterbuch . . . St. Petersburg. V. 43; 46

BOHUN, EDMUND

An Address to the Freemen and Freeholders of the Nation. London: 1683/2. V. 39

A Geographical Dictionary . . . London: 1695. V. 42

A Geograpical Dictionary. London: 1691. V. 37

The History of the Desertion, or An Account of All the Publick Affairs in England, From the Beginning of September 1688 to the Twelfth of February Following. London: 1689. V. 38

BOHUN, RALPH

A Discourse Concerning the Origine and Properties of Wind . . . Oxford: 1671. V. 40

BOHUN, WILLIAM

A Collection of Debates, Reports, Orders, and Resolutions of the House of Commons, Touching the Right of Electing Members to Serve in Parliament, for the Several Counties, Cities and Boroughs and Towns Corporate, in England and Wales . . . London: 1700. V. 38

Privilegia Londini. London: 1723. V. 38; 40; 41

BOIARDO, MATTEO MARIA

The Expedition of Gradasso; a Metrical Romance. Dublin: 1812. V. 37; 44

Orlando Inamorato . . . Rifatto Tutto di Nuovo da M. Francesco Berni . . . Aggiunte in Questa Seconda Editione Molte Stanze del Autore che nel Altra Mancavano. Venice: 1545. V. 40

Orlando Innamorato. Dublin: 1784. V. 38

BOID, EDWARD

A Concise History and Analysis of all the Principal Styles of Architecture . . . to which is added . . . Architecture of England Down to the Present Time. London: 1828. V. 38; 40

A Concise History and Analysis of All The Principal Styles of Architecture . . . London: 1829. V. 44

BOILEAU, D.

The Art of Working in Pasteboard. London: 1827. V. 45

BOILEAU, DANIEL

An Introduction to the Study of Political Economy . . . London: 1811. V. 38; 42

BOILEAU-DESPREAUX, NICOLAS

Boileau's Lutrin: a Mock-Heroic Poem. London: 1708. V. 38; 40; 42; 43; 44; 46

Medailles sur les Principaux Evenements du Regne Entier de Louis Le Grand, avec des Explications Historiques. Paris: 1723. V. 40

Les Oeuvres . . . Paris: 1740. V. 41

Oevvres. Glasgow: 1759. V. 45

BOILEAU, G.

Papyro-Plastics, or the Art of Modelling in Paper . . . London: 1830. V. 43

BOILEAU, JACQUES 1635-1716

Histoire des Flagellans ou l'on Fair Voir le Bon et le Mauvais Usage des Flagellations Parmi les Chretiens. V. 40

The History of the Flagellants: Otherwise of Religious Flagellations Among Different Nations and Especially Among Christians . . . London: 1783. V. 46

A Just and Seasonable Reprehension of Naked Breasts & Shoulders. London: 1678. V. 38; 46

BOIS-REYMOND, EMIL

Untersuchungen Uber Thierische Elektricitat. Berlin: 1848/49/84. V. 37

BOISGELIN DE KERDU, PIERRE MARIE LOUIS DE

Travels through Denmark and Sweden. London: 1810. V. 38; 40; 43

BOISGUILBERT, PIERRE LE PESANT DE 1646-1714

Le Detail de la France, Sous le Regne de Louix XIV. N.P.: 1697. V. 38

BOISSARD, J. J.

Wahre Abbildungen der Turkischen Kayser und Persischen Fursten. Frankfurt: 1648. V. 46

BOISSARD, JEAN JACQUES 1528-1602

Bibliotheca Chalcographica Illustrium Virtute Atque Eruditione in Tota Europa Clarissimorum Virorum . . . Frankfurt: 1669. V. 40

De Divinatione & Magicis Praestigiis, Quarum Veritas ac Vanitas Solide Exponitur per Descriptionem Deorum Fatidicorum Qui Olim Responsa Dederunt . . . Oppenheim: 1615. V. 45

Emblematum Liber . . . Frankfurt a.M.: 1593. V. 38; 39

Traite des Monoyes, de Leurs Circonstances et Depdances. Paris: 1692. V. 39

BOISSEAU, JEAN

Genealogie . . . De La Royalle Tres Ancienne et Avgvste Famille De France Auec vn Abrege Chronologique des faits Memorables et Heroiques des Descendans d'Icelles . . . Paris: 1641. V. 40

BOISSELIER, JEAN

The Heritage of Thai Sculpture. New York: 1975. V. 41

Thai Painting. Tokyo: 1976. V. 38; 41

BOISSIERE, J.

Propos d'un Intoxique. V. 38

BOITARD, P.

Les Pigeons de Voliere et de Colombier, ou Histoire Naturelle et Monographie des Pigeons Domestiques, Renfermant la Nomenclature et la Description de Toutes les Races et Varietes . . . Paris: 1824. V. 42

BOIVIN, MARIE ANNE VICTOIRE 1773-1841

Traite Pratique des Maladies de l'Uterus et de ses Annexes, Fonde sur un Grand Nombre d'Observations Cliniques. Paris: 1833. V. 42

BOIZARD, JEAN

Traite des Monoyes, de Leurs Circonstances & Dependances. Paris: 1692. V. 42

BOK, CURTIS

Commonwealth V. Gordon, Et Al.: The Opinion of Judge Bok, March Eighteenth 1949. (San Francisco: 1949). V. 37

BOK, EDWARD W.

Beecher Memorial: Contemporaneous Tributes to the Memory of Henry Ward Beecher. Edited by Edward W. Bok. Brooklyn, N.Y.: 1887. V. 37

The Young Man in Business. Philadelphia: 1894. V. 42

BOK, H.

Why Artists Go But Grey. V. 44

THE BOKE of Noblesse: Addressed to King Edward the Fourth on His Invasion of France in 1475. London: 1860. V. 40

BOKER, GEORGE H. 1823-1890

The Book of the Dead. Philadelphia: 1882. V. 41; 43; 44

Konigsmark the Legend of the Hounds and Other Poems. Philadelphia: 1869. V. 44

The Legend of the Hounds. New York: 1929. V. 40

The Podesta's Daughter and Other Miscellaneous Poems. Philadelphia: 1852. V. 44

BOLAINE, BETTY

History of Betty Bolaine the Canterbury Miser, Containing an Account of Her Avarice, Whimsical Amours, and Wonderful Escapes from Matrimony. Rochester: 1825. V. 40; 42

BOLAN, WILLIAM

Coloniae Anglicanae Illustrate; or, the Acquest of Dominion, and the Planatation of Colonies, Made by the English in America . . . London: 1762. V. 38

BOLAND, EVAN

New Territory. Dublin: 1967. V. 43

23 Poems. Dublin: 1962. V. 40

BOLD, MICHAEL

Paradisus Amissa. Poema, Anglice Scriptum Johanne Milton. London: 1702. V. 42

BOLDGETTER, GEORGE B.

Early Settlers of Rowley, Massachusetts: a Genealogical Record of the Families Who Settled in Rowley Before 1700 with Several Generations of Their Descendants. Rowley: 1933. V. 46

BOLDUC, JEAN BAPTISTE ZACHARIE

Mission de la Colombie. Lettre et Journal De Mr. J.-B. Z. Bolduc, Missionnaire de la Colombie. Quebec: 1843. V. 45

BOLIN, JOHANN

Beskrifning Ofwer Nord-Amerika Forenta Stater . . . Wexjo, Sweden: 1853. V. 38

BOLINGBROKE, HENRY 1785-1855

Voyage to Demerary, Containing a Statistical Account of the Settlements There, and Of Those on the Essequebo, the Berbice and Other Contiguous River of Guyana. London: 1807. V. 43

A Voyage to the Demerary, Containing a Statistical Account of the Settlements There and of Those on the Essequebo, The Berbice, and Other Contiguous Rivers of Guyana. London: 1809. V. 39

BOLINGBROKE, HENRY ST. JOHN, 1ST VISCOUNT 1678-1751

A Collection of Political Tracts. London: 1748. V. 42

A Collection of Political Tracts. London: 1769. V. 42

The Craftsman Extraordinary. London: 1729. V. 38; 41; 43; 44; 45

A Dissertation upon (Political) Parties; in Several Letters to Caleb D'Anvers. Dedicated to the Rt. Hon. Sir Robert Walpole. London: 1754. V. 37

The Freeholder's Political Catechism. London: 1733. V. 45

French Counsels Destructive to Great-Britain; or Seaonsable Advice to Sir R--- W---- in the Present Conjecture in Seven Letters. London: 1739. V. 41

L--d B-------ke's Speech Upon the Convention. To the Tune of a Cober There Was. London: 1739. V. 42

The Last Will and Testament of . . . To Which is Added, a Copy of an Original Letter from His Lordship to a Noble Peer, Giving His Reasons for Leaving the Kingdom in March 1715. London: 1752. V. 41

BOLINGBROKE, HENRY ST. JOHN, 1ST VISCOUNT 1678-1751 continued

A Letter to Sir William Windham. II. Some Reflections on the Present State of the Nation (with regard to Taxes and Debts). III. A Letter to Mr. Pope. London: 1753. V. 39; 41; 42

Letters on the Spirit of Patriotism . . . London: 1749. V. 37; 38; 42; 43; 44; 46

Letters on the Spirit of Patriotism. London: 1750. V. 40

Letters on the Study and the Use of History. London: 1752. V. 38; 39; 40; 42; 44

Letters and Correspondence, Public and Private of . . . During the Time He Was Secretary of State to Queen Anne. London: 1798. V. 38; 46

Briefe von dem Geist des Patriotismus, dem Bilde Eines Patriotischen Konis und dem Zustande der Paratheyen . . . Jena: 1765. V. 38; 41

Memoires secrets . . . sur les Affaires d'Angleterre Depuis 1710 Jusqu'en 1716. Londres: 1754. V. 41

The Misscellaneous (sic) Works. Edinburgh: 1768. V. 39

The Philosophical Works of the Late Right Honourable Henry St. John Lord Viscount Bolingbroke. London: 1754. V. 39; 42

Remarks on the History of England. From the Minutes of Humphrey Oldcastle, Esq. London: 1743. V. 37

Some Farther Remarks on a Late Pamphlet, Intitled, Observations on the Conduct of Great Britain . . . London: 1729. V. 41; 45; 46

Works: A Letter to Sir William Windham; Reflections on the Present State of the Nation; A Letter to Mr. Pope. London: 1753. V. 43

Works: A Letter to Sir William Windham; Reflections on the Present State of the Nation; A Letter to Mr. Pope. London: 1753. V. 46

The Works of Henry St. John, Lord Viscount Bolingbroke. London: 1754. V. 37; 38; 39; 41; 42; 43; 44; 46

Works. London: 1754-88. V. 37

Works. (with) Letters, Correspondence, Public and Private . . . London: 1754-98. V. 40; 43

The Works . . . Dublin: 1793. V. 45

The Works . . . London: 1809. V. 42

The Works. London: 1968. V. 39

The Works . . . With the Life of Lord Bolingbroke by Dr. Goldsmith. London: 1809. V. 37

BOLIO, ANTONIO MEDIZ

The Land of the Pheasant and the Deer. Mexico: 1935. V. 37

BOLITHO, HECTOR

A Batsford Century: The Record of a Hundred Years of Publishing and Bookselling. London: 1943. V. 44

A Biographer's Notebook. London: (1950). V. 37

BOLL, HEINRICH

Adam, Where Art Thou? London: 1955. V. 44

Billiards at Half Past Nine. London: 1961. V. 40

BOLLAERT, WILLIAM

Antiquarian, Ethnological and Other Researches in New Granada, Ecuador, Peru and Chile, with Observations on the Pre-Incarial, Incarial and Other Monuments of Peruvian Nations. London: 1860. V. 41

BOLLAM, WILLIAM

The Importance and Advantage of Cape Breton, Truly Stated, and Impartially Considered. London: 1746. V. 43

BOLLAN, WILLIAM

Coloniae AnglicanaeIllustratae. London: 1762. V. 40

The Importance and Advantage of Cape Breton, Truly Stated, and Impartially Considered. London: 1746. V. 41

BOLLAND, WILLIAM

Cricket Notes. London: 1851. V. 44

Saint Paul at Athens. Cambridge: 1800. V. 39; 42

BOLLER, HENRY A.

Among the Indians. Eight Years in the Far West: 1858-1866. Embracing Sketches of Montana and Salt Lake. Philadelphia: 1868. V. 37; 39; 40; 42; 43; 45

BOLLER, WILLY

Masterpiece of the Japanese Color Woodcut. Boston: 1957. V. 42; 44

Masterpieces of the Japanese Color Woodcut. Boston: V. 38; 41

Masterpieces of the Japanese Color Woodcut. London: 1957. V. 41

BOLLI, H. M.

Plankton Stratigraphy. Cambridge: 1985. V. 37

BOLSEC, JEROME HERMES

De Ioannis Calvini . . . Vita, Moribus, Rebus Gestis, Studiis, ac Denique Morte Historia. (with) Historia de Vita, Moribus, Doctrina et Rebus Gestis Theodori Bezae. Cologne: L. Alectorius &: 1584. V. 37

BOLT, ROBERT

A Man For All Seasons . . . London: 1961. V. 43

BOLTON, A. C.

Game Shooting in Africa. London: 1919. V. 40

BOLTON, ARTHUR T.

The Architecture of Robert and James Adam, 1758-1794. London. V. 38

The Architecture of Robert & James Adam (1758-1794). London: 1922. V. 37; 38; 39; 40; 42; 44; 45

The Architecture of Robert and James Adam (1758-1794). 1984. V. 42

The Gardens of Italy, with Historical and Descriptive Notes by E. March Phillips. London: 1919. V. 39

The Portrait of Sir John Soane, R.A. (1753-1837). London: 1927. V. 44

BOLTON, CHARLES K.

The Founders. Boston: 1919-26. V. 46

BOLTON, CHARLES KNOWLES

On the Wooing of Martha Pitkin. Boston: 1894. V. 37; 41; 43

BOLTON, CLAIRE

DeLittle: The First Years in a Century of Wood Letter Manufacture. London: 1988. V. 40; 41; 42

BOLTON, EDMUND

The Elements of Armories. London: 1610. V. 44

BOLTON, ETHEL STANWOOD

American Samplers. 1921. V. 37; 46

BOLTON, H. C.

A Catalogue of Scientific and Technical Periodicals 1665-1895 Together with Chronological Tables. Washington: 1897. V. 37

A Select Bibliography of Chemistry 1492-1892. With the Two supplements to 1902 and Section VIII Academic Dissertations. Washington: 1893-1904. V. 37; 46

BOLTON, HENRY CARRINGTON

The Counting-Out Rhymes of Children. London: 1888. V. 44

BOLTON, HERBERT EUGENE 1870-1953

Anza's California Expedition. Berkeley: 1930. V. 38; 39; 43; 44

Anza's California Expeditions . . . New York: 1966. V. 37

Athanase De Mazieres and the Louisiana-Texas Frontier 1768-1780. Cleveland: 1914. V. 39; 44

Coronado on the Turquoise Trail: Knight of Pueblos and Plains. Albuquerque: 1949. V. 39; 42; 46

Drake's Plate of Brass; Evidence of His Visit to California in 1579. San Francisco: 1937. V. 38

Font's Complete Diary. Berkeley: 1931. V. 38; 45

Font's Complete Diary. Berkeley: 1933. V. 43; 45

Fray Juan Crespi, Missionary Explorer on the Pacific Coast, 1769-1774. Berkeley: 1927. V. 39; 43; 44; 45; 46

Guide to Materials for the History of the United States in the Principal Archives of Mexico. Washington: 1913. V. 43

Kino's Historical Memoir of Pimeria Alta. Berkeley: 1948. V. 45

New Spain and the Anglo-American West. Lancaster: 1932. V. 46

New Spain and the Anglo-American West. Los Angeles: 1932. V. 44

On the Turquoise Trail. Knight of Pueblos and Plains. Albuquerque: 1949. V. 38

Outpost of Empire. New York: 1931. V. 44

Rim of Christendom. New York: 1936. V. 37; 39; 40; 44; 45

Spanish Exploration in the Southwest, 1542-1706. New York: 1916. V. 37

Texas in the Middle Eighteenth Century. Berkeley: 1915. V. 37; 41; 43; 44

BOLTON, J.

Filices Britannicae; an History of the British Proper Ferns. Leeds: 1785. V. 41; 42

An History of Fungusses Growing About Halifax. Halifax and Huddersfield,: 1788. V. 43

BOLTON, JAMES

Harmonia Ruralis; or, an Essay Towards a Natural History of British Birds. 1794. V. 46

Harmonia Ruralis; or, an Essay Towards a Natural History of British Song Birds. Halifax: 1794-96. V. 39; 44

Harmonia Ruralis; or an Essay Towards a Natural History of British Song Birds. London: 1794-96. V. 39

Harmonia Ruralis; or, an Essay Towards a Natural History of British Song Birds. London: 1845. V. 42

Harmonia Ruralis; or, an Essay Towards a Natural History of British Song Birds. London: 1824. V. 37

BOLTON, JOHN

Geological Fragments Collected Principally From Rambles Among the Rocks of Furness and Cartmel. Ulverston: 1869. V. 40; 41; 46

Geological Fragments Collected Principally from Rambles Along the Rocks of Furness and Cartmel. 1978. V. 37; 40

BOLTON, M. P. W.

Examination of the Principles of the Scoto-Oxonian Philosophy. London: 1861. V. 43

Examination of the Principles of the Scoto-Oxonian Philosophy (with) Reply to a Critique in the Saturday Review . . . (&) Remarks on Certain Replies attempted by Dr. Mansel. London: 1861-62-69. V. 38

Inquisitio Philosohica. London: 1866. V. 38; 45

BOLTON, R. P.

Indian Life of Long Ago in the City of New York. New York: 1934. V. 38

BOLTON, REGINALD

Indian Paths in the Great Metropolis. Indian Notes and Monographs. New York: 1922. V. 37

BOLTON, RICHARD

A Justice of Peace for Ireland. Dublin: 1750. V. 38

BOLTON, ROBERT 1697-1762

An Answer to the Question, Where Are Your Arguments Against What You Call, Lewdness, If You Make No Use of the Bible? London: 1755. V. 41; 42

The Ghost of Ernest, Great Grandfather of . . . the Princess Dowager of Wales. London: 1757. V. 39

History of the Several towns, Manors & Patents of the County of Westchester, From Its First Settlement to the Present Time. New York: 1848. V. 38

The History of the Several Towns, Manors and Patents of the County of Westchester. New York: 1881. V. 44

History of the Several Towns, Manors & Patents of the County of Westchester, from Its First Settlement. New York: 1905. V. 38

Letters and Tracts on the Choice of Company and Other Subjects. London: 1761. V. 42; 44

Letters and Tracts on the Choice of Company and Other Subjects. London: 1762. V. 42; 46

A Short and Private Discourse Betweene Mr. Bolton and One M.S. Concerning Usury. London: 1637. V. 39

BOLTON, SOLOMON

The Extinct Peerage of England. London: 1769. V. 39

BOLTON, WILLIAM

A Narrative of the Last Cruise of the U.S. Steam Frigate Missouri, from the Day She Left Norfolk, Until the Arrival of Her Crew in Boston. New York: 1844. V. 44

BOLUS, HARRY

Icones Orchidearum Austro-Africanarum Extra-Tropicarum; or, Figures, with Descriptions of Extra Tropical South African Orchids. London: 1893-1913. V. 37

BOLZANIO, URBANO

Institutionum in Linguam Graecam Grammaticarum, Libri Duo. Basle: 1535. V. 40; 45

Institutionum in Linguam Graecam Grammaticarum Libri Duo. Paris: 1543. V. 46

Institutionum in Linguam Graecam Grammaticarum, Libri Duo. Basel: 1536. V. 37

BOLZANO, BERNARD

Lehrbuch der Religionswissenschaft, ein Abdruck der Vorlesungshefte Eines Ehemaligen Religionslehrers an Einer Katholischen Universitat . . . Sulzbach: 1834. V. 40; 41

Paradoxien des Unendlichen, Herausgeben aus dem Schriftlichen Nachlasse des Verfassers von Dr. Fr. Prihonsky. Leipzig: 1851. V. 39

BOMBELLI, RAFAEL 1526-1572

L'Algebra Opera. Bologna: 1579. V. 42

BOMBERG, DAVID

Russian Ballet. London: 1919. V. 38

BOMBET, L. A. C.

The Life of Haydn, in a Series of Letters Written at Vienna. London: 1817. V. 41

BOMTEMPO, JOAO DOMINGOS

Elementos de Musica e Methodo de Tocar Picano Forte . . . Obra 19. London: 1815-16? V. 38

BONA, GIOVANNI

A Guide to Heaven Containing the Marrow of the Holy Fathers and Ancient Philosophers. London: 1672. V. 42

BONACINA, MARTIN d. 1631

Opera Omnia. Antwerp: 1635. V. 39

Opera Omnia: Sive Tractatio Absolutissima Omnium Conscientiae Casuum & Multorum ad Forum Externum Attinentium . . . Paris: 1645. V. 46

BONACOSSA, HIPPOLITO

De Servis, vel Famulis Tractatus. Venetiis (Venice): 1575. V. 38

BONAL, STEPHEN

Edward Fitzgerald Beale A Pioneer in the Path of Empire. New York: 1912. V. 42

BONANNI, FILIPPO

Gabinetto Armonico Pieno d'Istromenti Sonori Indicati . . . Offerto al Santore Daivd. Roma: 1722. V. 41

BONAPARTE, CARLO LUCIANO, PRINCE

Iconografia della Fauna Italica per le Quattro Classi Degli Animali Vertebrati. Rome: 1832-41. V. 41

BONAPARTE, CHARLES LUCIEN

Monographie des Loxiens. Leiden & Dusseldorf: 1850. V. 39; 42

BONAPARTE, CHARLES LUCIEN JULES LAURENT

Iconographie des Pigeons Non Figures par Mme. Knip . . . Dans les Deux Volumes de MM. Temminck et Florent Prevost. Paris: 1857-58. V. 42; 43; 45

BONAR, ANDREW A.

Narrative of a Mission of Inquiry to the Jews from the Church of Scotland in 1839. Edinburgh: 1848. V. 37

BONAR, ANDREW ALEXANDER

Narrative of a Mission of Inquiry to the Jews from the Church of Scotland in 1839. Philadelphia: 1843. V. 41

BONAR, HORATIUS

The Land of Promise . . . London: 1858. V. 42

BONAR, JAMES 1852-1941

Thomas Robert Malthus and His Work. London: 1885. V. 39

BONARDO, GIOVANNI MARIA

La Grandezza, Larghezza, e Distanza di Tutte le Sfere, Ridotte a Nostre Miglia . . . Venice: 1589. V. 42

La Grandezza, Larghezza, e Distanze di Tutte le Sfere, Ridotte a Nostre Miglia. Venice: 1859. V. 40

BONARELLI, GUIDUBALDO

Filli di Sciro, Favola Pastorale. Ferrara: 1607. V. 37

BONATI, WALTER

On the Heights. London: 1964. V. 44

BONAVENTURA, PSEUDO

Diaeta Salutis. Paris: 1500. V. 45

BONAVENTURA, SAINT, CARDINAL 1221-1274

Breuiloqui Theologie; Quo Omnis Laus. Paris: 1500. V. 44

Breviloquium. Augsburg: 1476. V. 42; 45

Centiloquium . . . Noviter Impressum. Paris: 1503. V. 37

Legenda de Sancto Francesco . . . Reducta in Vulgare. Venice: 1522. V. 45

The Life of Saint Francis of Assisi. San Francisco: 1924. V. 38

The Life of Francis of Assisi. San Francisco: 1931. V. 46

Meditationi Deuotissime Sopra la Passione Del Nostro Signore Jesu Christa. Venice: 1537. V. 38

Opuscula. Strassburg: 1495. V. 42

Quaestiones Super IV Libros Sententiarum Petri Lombardi. Nuremberg: 1491. V. 40; 43

Soliloquium de Quattuor Exercitis. Paris: 1520. V. 45

Stimulus Duini Amoris. Paris: 1498-1500. V. 44

Tractatus de Profectu Religiosorum. Paris: 1516. V. 45

Vita Christi . . . Barcelona: 1522. V. 40

BONAVERI, DOMENICO MARIA

Freggi Dell Architetura Dedicati . . . N.P.. V. 44

BOND, A. L.

Three Gems in One Setting. London: 1860. V. 38

BOND, ALVAN

Memoir fo the Rev. Pliny Fisk, A. M., Late Missionary to Palestine. Boston: 1828. V. 45

BOND, E.

Leaves from a Christmas Bough. London: 1867. V. 39; 44

BONNER, T. D.

The Life and Adventures of James P. Beckwourth, Mountaineer, Scout and Pioneer. New York: 1856. V. 37; 38; 39; 40; 41; 42; 43; 45

BONNET, CHARLES 1720-1793

Essai Analytique sur les Facultes de l'Ame. Copenhagen: 1760. V. 40

BONNET, JACQUES 1638-1708

Histoire Generale de la Danse. Paris: 1724. V. 40

BONNET, M. E.

Tableau des Etats-Unis de l'Amerique, Au Commencement Dux XIX Siecle. Paris: 1816. V. 43

BONNEVAL, CLAUDIUS ALEXANDER DE

Memoirs of the Bashaw Count Bonneval, from His Birth to His Death . . . London: 1750. V. 39; 44; 46

BONNEY, EDWARD

The Banditti of the Prairies, or the Murder's Doom! Chicago: 1853. V. 42
The Banditti of the Prairies. Chicago: 1856. V. 42; 45

BONNEY, H. K.

Historic Notices in Reference to Fotheringay. Oundle: 1821. V. 40

BONNEY, THERESE

Europe's Children: 1939-1943. New York: 1943. V. 44

BONNEY, THOMAS GEORGE

The Alpine Regions of Switzerland and the Neighbouring Countries . . . Cambridge: 1868. V. 43
Cathedrals, Abbeys and Churches of England and Wales. London. V. 46
Cathedrals, Abbeys and Churches of England and Wales. London: 1885. V. 38
Flowers from the Upper Alps, with Glimpses of Their Homes. London: 1869. V. 43
Lake and Mountain Scenery from the Swiss Alps. London: 1874. V. 41; 46
Outline Sketches in the High Alps of Dauphine. London: 1865. V. 46

BONNEY, W. P.

History of Pierce County, Washington. Chicago: 1927. V. 45

BONNYCASTLE, JOHN

An Introduction to Astronomy. London: 1796. V. 44
An Introduction to Astronomy. London: 1803. V. 45
An Introduction to Astronomy, in a Series of Letters, from the Preceptor to His Pupil . . . London: 1822. V. 38

BONNYCASTLE, RICHARD HENRY

Canada, As It Was, Is and May Be. London: 1842. V. 45
The Canadas in 1841. London: 1841. V. 43
The Canadas in 1841. London: 1842. V. 42
Spanish America; or a Descriptive, Historical and Geographical Account of the Dominions of Spain in the Western Hemisphere . . . London: 1818. V. 45

BONOLA, ROBERTO

Non-Euclidean Geometry. Chicago: 1912. V. 38

BONOMI, JOSEPH

Egypt, Nubia and Ethiopia. London: 1862. V. 39
Nineveh and Its Palaces. London: 1852. V. 40; 42; 44
Nineveh and Its Palaces. London: 1853. V. 37; 39
The Porportions of the Human Figure . . . London: 1857. V. 38; 44
The Proportions of the Human Figure. London: 1880. V. 38

BONOMO, GIOVANNI COSIMO

Osservazioni Intorno a Pellicelli del Corpo Umano con Altre Osservazioni Scritte in Una Lettera all'Illustriss. Firenze: 1687. V. 37; 40

BONONCINI, GIOVANNI 1672-1750

The Anthem Which Was Performed in King Henry the Seventh's Chapel, at the Funeral of the Most Noble and Victorious Prince, John, Duke of Marlborough. London: 1737. V. 40

BONSAL, STEPHEN

Edward Fitzgerald Beale: a Pioneer in the Path of Empire, 1822-1903. New York: 1912. V. 37; 45

BONSER, WILFRID

An Anglo-Saxon and Celtic Bibliography (450-1087). Berkeley: 1957. V. 39

BONTEMPS, ARNA

We Have Tomorrow. Boston: 1945. V. 42; 45

BONTOUS, J. J.

L'Auguste Piete de la Royale Maison de Bourbon . . . Avignon: 1750. V. 46

BONVALOT, GABRIEL

Across Thibet. New York: 1892. V. 41; 46
Through the Heart of Asia. London: 1889. V. 43; 46

BONWICK, JAMES

Discovery and Settlement of Port Phillip. Melbourne: 1856. V. 41; 43
First Twenty Years of Australia. London: 1882. V. 40
Irish Druids and Old Irish Religions. London: 1894. V. 37
John Batman the Founder of Victoria. Melbourne: 1868. V. 41
The Last of the Tasmanians; or, The Black War of Can Diemen's Land. London: 1870. V. 38; 45
Port Phillip Settlement. London: 1883. V. 41
The Wild White Man and The Blacks of Victoria. Melbourne: 1863. V. 41; 46

BONYNGE, RICHARD

Joan Sutherland: Designs for a prima Donna. New South Wales: 1985. V. 39

BONYTHON, KIM

Modern Australian Painting and Sculpture, a Survey of Australian Art from 1950 to 1960. Adelaide: 1960. V. 41

BOO-BOO the Barrage Balloon. London: 1940. V. 44

BOOK ARTS PRESS

Specimens of Wood Type. New York: 1980. V. 38; 41; 42; 44

BOOK-AUCTION Records. London: 1924-72. V. 41

BOOK-AUCTION Records, A Priced and Annotated Quarterly Record of London, Edinburgh, Glasgow and Dublin Book-Auctions. London: 1944-78. V. 43

BOOK CLUB OF CALIFORNIA

Book Club of California Keepsakes for the Years 1954, 56, 57, 58, 59, 60, 61, 62, 63, 64, 65, 66, 67, 69, 70, 71 and 72. V. 39

BOOK Collecting World. Chicago: 1961-65. V. 43

THE BOOK-COLLECTOR. London: 1952-88. V. 41

THE BOOK-COLLECTOR'S Hand Book. A Modern Library Companion. London: 1845. V. 38

BOOK Collector's Quarterly. London: 1930-Oct. 1932. V. 40

BOOK, F. H.

M. C. Escher. His Life and Complete Graphic Work. New York: 1982. V. 46

BOOK for Sensei. Pacifica: 1990. V. 45

BOOK-LORE, a Magazine Devoted to Old Time Literature. London: 1885-87. V. 39

BOOK-LOVER'S Almanac for the year 1893 (through 1897 inclusive, all published). New York: 1893-97. V. 38

THE BOOK Of Ballads. Edinburgh & London: 1859. V. 39

THE BOOK of Beasts. London: 1954. V. 38

BOOK of Biographies . . . Biographical Sketches of leading Citizens of Bucks County, Pennsylvania. Buffalo: 1899. V. 41

THE BOOK of Book-Plates. Edinburgh: 1900/01. V. 41

THE BOOK of Bubbles, a Contribution to the New York Fair in Aid of the Sanitary Commission. New York: 1864. V. 37

THE BOOK of Christmas. London: 1836. V. 44

A BOOK of Christmas Verse. London: 1895. V. 40; 43

THE BOOK of Conversation and Behaviour. London: 1754. V. 45

A BOOK of Drawing, Limning, Washing or Colouring of Maps and Prints: and the Art of Painting, with the Names and Mixtures of Colours Used by the Picture-Drawers, or the Young-mans Time Well Spent. London: 1652. V. 38

THE BOOK of Fate. Boston: 1835. V. 45

BOOK of Favourite Modern Ballads. London: 1860. V. 39
BOOK of Favourite Modern Ballads. London: 1867. V. 39

BOOK OF FENAGH

The Book of Fenagh in Irish and English Originally Compiled by St. Caillin, Archbishop, Abbot and Founder of Fenagh. Dublin: 1875. V. 39

THE BOOK of Games; or, a History on Juvenile Sports Practiced at the Kingston Academy . . . New York: 1822. V. 40

THE BOOK of Gems. London: 1866. V. 38

THE BOOK of Gems from the Poets and Artists of the Great Britain. London: 1873. V. 44

THE BOOK of Gems. The Poets and Artists of Great Britain. London & Paris: 1844. V. 40

THE BOOK of Glasgow Cathedral, a History and Description. Glasgow: 1898. V. 45

BOOK of Goblins. A Collection of Fairy Tales. London: 1934. V. 41

BOOK OF HY MANY

The Book of Ui Maine, Otherwise Called 'The Book of the O'Kelly's'. Dublin: 1942. 39; 43

THE BOOK of Knowledge. Hartford: 1855. V. 38

THE BOOK of Martyrs, or, Christian Martyrology: . . . Persecutions Against the Church of Christ, From the Death of Abel to the Beginning of the Nineteenth Century . . . Liverpool: 1807. V. 37

BOOK OF MORMON

The Book of Mormon. New York: 1830. V. 39

The Book of Mormon. Palmyra: 1830. V. 39; 40; 43; 44; 45

The Book of Mormon. Nauvoo: 1840. V. 40

The Book of Mormon. Nauvoo: 1842. V. 45

Il Libro di Mormon: Ragguagilo Scritto per Mano di Mormon. London: 1852. V. 40

The Book of Mormon. Liverpool: 1854. V. 45

The Book of Mormon. New York: 1859-61? V. 42

The Book of Mormon, Upon Plates Taken from the Plates of Nephi. New York: 1869. V. 37; 40

The Book of Mormon. Salt Lake City: 1871. V. 42

The Book of Mormon . . . Salt Lake City: 1888. V. 42

The Book of Mormon. Salt Lake City: 1891. V. 42

Ko Te Pukapuka a Mormona . . . Akarana: Henare Perete,: 1889. V. 43

BOOK OF MORMON - 1904

Te Buka a Moromona: Te Parau I Papaihia e Te Rima O Moromona, I Nia I Te Mau Api I Irithia No Nia Mai I Te Mau Api a Nephi. Salt Lake City: 1904. V. 37

BOOK OF MORMON - 1905

Ka Buke a Moramona He Moolelo I Kakauia Ma Ka Lima O Moramona Maluna Iho O Na Papa I Laweia Mailoko Mai o Na Papa o Nepai. Salt Lake City;: 1905. V. 37

THE BOOK of Oddities; or, Agreeable Variety for Town and Country. Dublin: 1790. V. 41

A BOOK of Old Ballads. London: 1934. V. 42; 46

THE BOOK of Ornamental, Architectural, and Monumental Designs, Rare Alphaabets, etc. N.P.: 1853. V. 38

THE BOOK of Parlour Games.. Philadelphia: 1853. V. 39

BOOK of Picture Alphabets. London: 1880. V. 39

BOOK of Prayers. Latin and French. Paris: 1500-10. V. 41

A BOOK of Remembrance: Being a Short Summary of the Srevice and Sacrifice Rendered to the Empire During the Great War by One of the Many Patriotic Families of Wessex: The Popes of Wracleford Co. Dorset. London: 1919. V. 46

A BOOK of Romantic Ballads. London: 1901. V. 42

A BOOK of Simple Toys: a Facsimile. Bryn Mawr: 1982. V. 46

A BOOK of Songs and Poems form the Old Testament and the Apocrypha. 1904. V. 41

A BOOK of Special Pleadings: Containing Precedents . . . also the Forms of Entries in Writs of Error, Utlaries, General Issues and Judgments . . . Together with a Table. London: 1674. V. 40

THE BOOK of Sports British and Foreign. London: 1843. V. 46

A BOOK of Sundry Draughts, Principally Serving for Glasiers. London: 1898. V. 40

BOOK of the Alamo: The Only Official Railway and Hotel Guide Published in Texas. San Antonio: 1908. V. 37; 38

THE BOOK of the Bench. London: 1909. V. 38; 40

THE BOOK of the Dead. London: 1898. V. 40; 42; 44

Book of the Dead. London: 1894. V. 39

The Egyptian Book of the Dead: The Most Ancient and the Most Important of the Extant Religious Texts of Ancient Egypt. New York & London: 1894. V. 40; 41

The Book of the Dead. New York: 1972. V. 40; 42

BOOK of the First City Troop, Philadelphia City Cavalry, 1774-1914. Philadelphia: 1915. V. 41

THE BOOK of the Household; or, Family Dictionary of Everything Connected with Housekeeping and Domestic Medicine . . . London: 1857. V. 42

THE BOOK of the Household or Family Dictionary of Everything Connected with Housekeeping and Domestic Medicine . . . London: 1858. V. 42

THE BOOK Of the Martyrs of Tolpuddle 1834-1934. London: 1934. V. 38; 39

THE BOOK of the Orphic Hymns . . . London: 1827. V. 40

THE BOOK of the Poet's Club. London: 1915. V. 44

THE BOOK of the Rhymers Club. London: 1892. V. 37

THE BOOK of Trades: or, Circle of the Useful Arts. Glasgow: 1835. V. 42

THE BOOK of Trades or Library of the Useful Arts. London: 1805, 1806. V. 41

THE BOOK of Trades, or Library of the Useful Arts. London: 1806. V. 42

THE BOOK of Trinity College Dublin, 1591-1891. Belfast: 1892. V. 42; 43

A BOOK of Verses. Oakland: 1910. V. 41

BOOK of Wedding Days. London: 1889. V. 43; 46

THE BOOKBINDER. London: 1889. V. 40

BOOKBINDERS & MACHINE RULERS CONSOLIDATED UNION

The Bookbinding Trades Journal. London: 1904-14. V. 41

The Bookbinding Trades Journal. London: 1904, 1913. V. 41

BOOKBINDER'S GUILD OF CALIFORNIA

First Annual Exhibition of the Bookbinder's Guild of California. San Francisco: 1902. V. 44

THE BOOKBINDERS Pricie-Book, Calculated for the Different Modes of Bindin g, as Agreed Upon at a General Meeting of the Trade, in December 1812 . . . to Commence January 1st, 1813. London: 1813. V. 37

THE BOOKCOLLECTOR'S Handbook. A Modern Library Companion. London: 1845. V. 40

BOOKE of Armorie Otherwise Called the Barrons Booke Appertayneth to the Right Worshipfull Sir William Stone Knight of the Cittie of London, 1603. London: 1603. V. 42

A BOOKE of Christmas Carols. London: 1845. V. 39

A BOOKE of Presidents. London: 1607. V. 40

A BOOKE of Proclamations, Published Since the Beginning of His Ma(je)sties Most Happy Reigne Over England, etc. Untill This Present Moneth of Febr. 3. Anno Dom . . . to 5th Feb. 1612. London: 1613. V. 40

BOOKER, LUKE

Malvern, a Descriptive and Historical Poem. Dudley: 1798. V. 43

BOOKMAKING on the Distaff Side. N.P.: 1937. V. 45

BOOKMAKING on the Distaff Side. V.P.: 1937. V. 39

BOOKS Which Have Influenced Me. London: 1897. V. 40

BOOLE, GEORGE 1815-1864

An Investigation of the Laws of Thought, on Which are Founded the Mathematical Theories of Logic and Probabilities. London: 1854. V. 42; 43; 45

A Treatise on Differential Equations. Cambridge: 1859. V. 42; 43; 45

A Treatise on the Calculus of Finite Differences. Cambridge: 1860. V. 37

BOON, EDWARD P.

Catalogue of Books and Pamphlets Principally Relating to America. New York: 1870. V. 40; 46

BOON, K. G.

Rembrandt, the Complete Etchings. New York: 1963. V. 46

BOONE AND CROCKET CLUB

Records of North American Big Game. New York: 1964. V. 37

BOONE AND CROCKETT CLUB

Hunting Trails on Three Continents. New York: 1933. V. 39

BOONE, ANNA B.

The Increase of Crime, and Its Cause. Boston: 1871. V. 37; 44; 45

BOONE, DANIEL

Adventures of Col. Daniel Boon (sic). Hartford: 1794. V. 44

BOORDE, ANDREW 1490?-1549

The Vreviarie of Health . . . London: 1598. V. 43

The Forst Boke of the Introduction of Knowledge Made by Andrew Borde . . . London: 1870. V. 40

BOORN, AMOS

An Account of a Late Conversation with the Dead and How the Following Strange Event Came into Writing in Order to be Printed. Boston: 1812. V. 40

BOOSEY, THOMAS

Piscatorial Reminiscences and Gleanings by an Old Angler and Bibliopolist. London: 1835. V. 42

BOOT, W. H. J.

Trees, and How to Paint Them in Watercolours. London: 1883. V. 39

BOOTH, A.

Examen Legum Angliae; or, the Law of England Examined. London: 1656. V. 45

BOOTH, B. F.

Dark Days of the Rebellion, or . . . Life in Southern Military Prisons . . . Indianola, Iowa: 1897. V. 37

BOOTH, CHARLES

Life and Labour of the People in London. London: 1902-03. V. 44

BOOTH, DAVID

The Art of Brewing, on Scientific Principles. London: 1826. V. 38

The Art of Wine-Making, in All Its Branches. London: 1834. V. 39; 45

The Art of Brewing on Scientific Principles Adapted to the Use of Brewers and Private Families . . . London: 1852. V. 46

A Letter to the Rev. T. R. Malthus, M.A., F.R.S. Being an Answer to the Criticism on Mr. Godwin's Work on Population, Which was Inserted in the LXXth Number of the Edinburgh Review . . . London: 1823. V. 45

BOOTH, EDWARD THOMAS

Rough Notes on the Birds Observed During Twenty Five Year's Shooting and Collected in the British Islands. London: 1881-87. V. 37; 42

BOOTH, EDWIN

In War Time. Philadelphia: 1885. V. 42

BOOTH, EDWIN CARTON

Australia Illustrated with Drawings by S. Prout, N. Chevalier, J. C. Armytage, O. W. Brierly, T. Baines, J. Carr. London: 1873-76. V. 46

BOOTH, G. R.

A Popular Treatise on the Strength and Application of Materials Used in Buildings in General Shewing the Advantages to be Derived from the Principles of the Patent of Messrs. R. Witty & Co . . . London: 1836. V. 44

BOOTH, GENERAL

In Darkest England. London: 1890. V. 44

BOOTH, GEORGE

Cranbrook Papers . . . Detroit: 1901. V. 38

BOOTH, GEORGE G.

The Cranbrook Press. Detroit: 1902. V. 42

BOOTH, GEORGE WILSON

Personal Reminiscences of a Maryland Soldier in the War Between the States, 1861-1865. Baltimore: 1898. V. 43

BOOTH, HENRY

An Account of the Liverpool and Manchester Railway, Comprising a History of the Parliamentary Proceedings, Prepatory to Passing of the Act, a Description of the Railway, in an Excursion from Liverpool to Manchester . . . Liverpool: 1831. V. 39

BOOTH, J. P.

Ship Ventilation or, Sea-Sickness Mitigated, by Supplying Pure Air in Ships, Patented by J. P. Booth. Cork: 1859. V. 39

BOOTH, JOHN

The Battle of Waterloos, with Circumstantial Details, Previous and After the Battle. London: 1815/16. V. 41

A Near Observer. The Battle of Waterloo, Containing the Series of Accounts Published by Authority . . . London: 1815. V. 46

BOOTH, JUNIUS BRUTUS

Memoirs of the Life of Mr. Booth, Containing a True Statement of All the Circumstances Attending His Engagement at the Rival Theatres . . . London: 1817. V. 42

BOOTH, STEPHEN

The Book Called Holinshed's Chronicles. San Francisco: 1968. V. 38; 39; 40; 46

BOOTH, WILLIAM

In Darkest England and the Way Out. London: 1890. V. 37; 38; 40; 41; 42; 43

BOOTHBY, BROOKE

A Letter to the Right Honourable Edmund Burke. London: 1791. V. 39

Observations on the Appeal from the New to the Old Whigs, and on Mr. Paine's Rights of Man. London: 1792. V. 39

Sorrows: Sacred to the Memory of Penelope. London: 1796. V. 40

BOOTHBY, GUY NEWELL 1867-1905

Doctor Nikola. London: 1896. V. 42

Farewell Nikola. London: 1901. V. 42

The Lust of Hate. London: 1898. V. 42

BOOTHROYD, BENJAMIN

The History of the Ancient Borough of Pontefract, Containing an Interesting Account of Its Castle, and the Three Different Sieges It Sustained, During the Civil War, with Notes and Pedigrees, of Some of the Most Distinguished Royalists & Parliamentarians . . . Pontefract: 1807. V. 41

BOOTHROYD, NORMAN

Apes and Peacocks. London. V. 38; 40

BOOTS, JOHN MERCER

Powder River Invasion War on the Rustlers in 1892. N.P.: 1923. V. 46

BOOTT, F.

Illustrations fo the Genus Carex. London: 1968. V. 38; 46

BOPP, FRANZ 1791-1867

A Comparative Grammar. London: 1856. V. 38

BOPPE, AUGUSTE

Les Vignettes Emblematiques Sous la Revolution. Paris and Nancy: 1911. V. 45

BORADBENT, WILLIAM

Selections from the Writings Medical and Neurological of Sir William Broadbent. London: 1908. V. 40

BORAH, W. E.

Haywood Trial. Closing Argument of William E. Borah. Boise: 1906. V. 39

BORASTON, J. H.

Sir Douglas Haig's Despatches. (December 1915-April 1919). London: 1920. V. 43; 44; 46

BORBA DE MORAES, RUBENS

Bibliographia Brasiliana. Amsterdam & Rio de Janeiro: 1958. V. 38

Bibliographia Brasiliana. Los Angeles: 1983. V. 37

BORCH, OLE

Hermetis, Aegyptiorum, et Chemicorum Sapientia, ab Hermanni Conringii Animadversionibus Vindicata per Olaum Borrichium. Hafniae: 1674. V. 40; 44

BORCHARDT, LUDWIG

Works of Art from the Egyptian Museum at Cairo. Cairo: 1908. V. 37; 40; 42; 44

BORCHGREVINK, CARSTENS E.

First on the Antarctic Continent Being an Account of the British Antarctic Expedition 1898-1900. London: 1901. V. 42; 43; 45

BORCKE, HEROS VON

Zwei Jahre Im Sattel und am Feinde . . . Berlin: 1886. V. 44

BORDALO, FRANCISCO MARIA

Trinta Annos de Perigrinacao (1821-1851). Manuscrito Achado na Gruta de Camoes. Macaeo: 1852. V. 41

BORDE, ANDREW

The Breviarie of Health . . . London: 1598. V. 45

The Pleasant Tales of the Wise Men of Gotham. Newcastle. V. 45

BORDEAUX, WILLIAM J.

Custer's Conqueror. Sketch of Crazy Horse. 1952. V. 45

BORDELON, LAURENT

The Management of the Tongue Under the Following Very Important and Useful Heads . . . Boston: 1814. V. 38

BORDELON, LOUIS

The Management of the Tongue. London: 1706. V. 42

BORDEN, JOHN

Log of the Auxiliary Schooner Yacht Northern Light . . . Chicago: 1929. V. 37; 45

BORDEN, JOHN W.

Thomas Bewick and the Fables of Aesop. San Francisco: 1983. V. 37; 46

BORDEN, W. W.

Borden's Leadville. New Albany: 1879. V. 37; 39; 40; 42; 45

BORDEN, WILLIAM C.

The Use of Rontgen Ray by the Medical Department of the United States Army in the War with Spain (1898). Washington: 1900. V. 38; 39; 40; 41; 42; 44; 45; 46

BORDER Ballads. London: 1895. V. 41

BORDEUX, WILLIAM J.

Conquering the Mighty Sioux. Sioux Falls: 1929. V. 45

BORDLEY, JOHN BEALE

A Summary View of the Courses of Crops, in the Husbandry of England and Maryland. Philadelphia: 1784. V. 37; 38

BORDONA, J. D.

Spanish Illumination. Florence: 1930. V. 39

BORDONE, BENEDETTO

Isolario di . . . Nel Qual si Ragiona di Tutte le Isole Del Mondo, Con I Lor Nomi Antichi & Moderni, Historie, Fauole . . . Venice: 1565. V. 40

Libro di Benedetto Bordone nel Qual si Ragiona de Tutte l'Isole del Mondo con li lor Nomi Antichi & Moderni, Historie, Favole, Modi del Loro Vivere, & in Qual Parte del Mare Stanno, & in Qual Parallelo & Clima Giacciono. Venice: : 1528. V. 45

BOREAU DELANDES, ANDRE FRANCOIS

An Essay On Maritime Power and Commerce; Particularly Those of France. London: 1743. V. 41

BOREDEU, THEOPHILE DE

Recherches sur les Maladies Chroniques, Leurs Rapports Avec les Maladies Aigues . . . Paris: 1775. V. 45

BOREIN, EDWARD

Ed Borein's West. Santa Barbara: 1952. V. 37; 39; 46

Ed Borein's West: Leaves from the Sketchbook of the Last Artist of the Longhorn Era. Santa Barbara: 1952. V. 38; 41

Edward Borein Drawing and Paintings of the Old West. Volume I: The Indians. Flagstaff: 1968. V. 37; 39; 46

Etchings of the West. Santa Barbara: 1950. V. 46

BOREL, PETRI 1620-1689

Historiarum & Observationum Medicophysicarum, Centurie IV . . . Frankfurt: 1670. V. 42

BORELLI, GIOVANNI ALFONSO

De Vi Percussionis Liber. Bologna: 1667. V. 39; 41; 43

De Vi Percussionis, et Motionibus Naturalibus a Gravitate Pendentibus . . . Leiden: 1686. V. 38

Historia et Meteorologia Incendi Aetnaei Anni 1669. Regio Iulio: 1670. V. 40; 41

BORELLI, GIOVANNI ALPHONSO 1608-1679

De Motu Animalium. Rome: 1680-81. V. 37; 42

De Motu Animalium. Leiden: 1685. V. 37

BOREMAN, THOMAS

A Compendious Account of the Whole Art of Breeding, Nursing and Right Ordering of the Silkworm. London: 1733. V. 38; 39

A Description of Three Hundred Animals . . . London: 1774. V. 46

A Description of Above Three Hundred Animals, viz. Beasts, Birds, Fishes, Serpents and Insects, with Particular Account of the Manner of Catching Whales in Greenland, Extracted from the Best Authors. Edinburgh: 1797. V. 37

BORENIUS, T.

English Medieval Painting. Florence: 1921. V. 39

BORENIUS, TANCRED

Catalogue of the Pictures and Drawings at Harwood House and Elsewhere in the Collection of the Earl of Harewood. Oxford: 1936. V. 40

Drawings by Old Masters. London: 1930. V. 46

Florentine Frescoes. Edinburgh. V. 46

Forty London Statues and Public Monuments. London: 1926. V. 38; 41

The Picture Gallery of Andrea Vendramin. London: 1923. V. 46

BORG, CARL OSCAR

The Great Southwest: Etchings. N.P.: 1936. V. 40

BORG, JOHN

Descriptive Flora of the Maltese Islands, Including the Ferns and Flowering Plants. London: 1927. V. 39

Descriptive Flora of the Maltese Islands . . . Malta: 1927. V. 40

BORGES, JORGE LUIS

Borges on Writing. New York: 1973. V. 46

Chronicles of Buster Domecq. New York: 1976. V. 40; 42; 44; 46

The Congress of the World. Milan: 1981. V. 38

Deathwatch on the Southside. New York: 1968. V. 43

Deathwatch on the Southside. Cambridge: 1969. V. 43

Doctor Brodie's Report. New York: 1972. V. 44

Dreamtigers. Austin: 1964. V. 45

Extraordinary Tales. New York: 1971. V. 46

Ficciones. Buenos Aires: 1944. V. 45

Ficciones. New York: 1984. V. 38; 39; 40; 43; 44; 45

Ficciones. N.P.: 1984. V. 44

Ficciones. New York: 1985. V. 39

Homage to Walt Whitman. University: 1969. V. 45

In Praise of Darkness. London: 1975. V. 44; 46

Inquisiciones. Buenos Aires: 1925. V. 44

Irish Strategies. N.P.. V. 43

Irish Strategies. Dublin: 1975. V. 42

Labyrinths. Selected Stories and Other Writings. 1962. V. 39

Labyrinths. New York: 1962. V. 45

Labyrinths. Norfolk: 1962. V. 42

Obras Completas. Buenos Aires: 1974. V. 43

Other Inquisitions. Austin: 1964. V. 44; 46

A Personal Anthology. New York: 1967. V. 44; 46

Poems. Dublin: 1969. V. 45

Six Problems for Don Isidro Parodi. New York: 1981. V. 40

El Tamano de Mi Esperanza. Buenos Aires: 1926. V. 41

Texas. Austin: 1975. V. 42

BORGESEN, F.

The Marine Algae of the Danish West Indies. Copenhagen: 1913-20. V. 37

BORGHI, PIETRO d. 1491

Libro de Abacho. Venice: 1534. V. 42

BORGHINI, RAFFAELLO

Il Riposo . . . in Cui Della Pittura e Della Scultura si Favella, de'piu Illustri Pittori, e Scultori, e delle Piu Famose Opere Loro si fa Mentione . . . Florence: 1584. V. 40; 44

BORGIA, STEFANO, CARDINAL

Letters from the Cardinal Borgia and the Duke of York. London: 1799-1800. V. 46

BORGLUM, SOLON HANNIBAL

Sound Construction a Comparative: Analysis of Natural Forms and Their Relation to the Human Figure . . . New York: 1923. V. 44

BORINGDON, HENRY V. PARKER, VISCOUNT

Some Account of Lord Boringdon's Accident, on 21st July, 1817 and Its Consequences. London: 1818. V. 42

BORIS Grigoriev, Faces of Russia. London: 1924. V. 46

BORLAND, FRANCIS

Memoirs of Darien, Giving a Short Description of that Country, with an Account of the Attempt of the Company of Scotland to Settle a Colonie in that Place. Glasgow: 1715. V. 39

BORLASE, EDMOND d. 1682

The History of the Excrable Irish Rebellion . . . to Grand Eruption, 23 Oct. 1641 and Thence Pursued to the Act of Settlement, 1662. London: 1680. V. 43

BORLASE, EDMUND d. 1682

The Reduction of Ireland to the Crown of England. London: 1675. V. 38; 42

BORLASE, EDWARD

The History of the Irish Rebellion traced to 1641, an thence pursuant to the Act of Settlement, 1662, etc. etc. Dublin: 1743. V. 37

BORLASE, WILLIAM 1695-1772

Antiquities, Historical and Monumental, of the County of Cornwall. London: 1769. V. 41

The Natural History of Cornwall. London: 1758. V. 46

The Natural History of Cornwall. Oxford: 1758. V. 37; 39; 41

Observations on the Antiquities Historical and Monumental of the County of Cornwall . . . . Oxford: 1754. V. 41

BORLASE, WILLIAM 1695-1772 continued

Observations on the Ancient and Present State of the Islands of Scilly, and Their Importance to the Trade of Great Britain. Oxford: 1756. V. 41; 43

BORLASE, WILLIAM COPELAND

The Dolmens of Ireland, Their Distribution, Structural Characteristics and Affinities in Other Countries; Together with the Folk-Lore Attaching to Them; Supplemented by Considerations on the Anthropology, Ethnology and Traditions of the Irish People. London: 1897. V. 37

Naenia Cornubiac, a Descriptive Essay. London: & Truro: 1872. V. 40; 43

BORN, IGNAZ VON

New Process of Amalgamation of Gold and Silver Ores, and Other Metallic Mixtures . . . London: 1791. V. 42

BORN, INIGO, BARON

Travels through the Bannat of Temeswar, Transylvania and Hungary, in the Year 1770. London: 1777. V. 46

BORNEMAN, HENRY S.

Pennsylvania German Illuminated Manuscripts. Norristown: 1937. V. 39; 41; 44

Pennsylvania German Bookplates. Philadelphia: 1953. V. 38; 41; 42

BORRA, GIAMBATISTA

Trattato Della Cognizione Pratica delle Resistenze, Geometricamente Dimostrato dall'Architetto Giambatista Borra ad Uso d'Orgni Sorta d'Edifizi, Coll'Aggiunta di Varie Maniere di Coperti, Volte, ed altre Cose di tal Genere. Turin: 1748. V. 39

BORRA, GIOVANNI BATTISTA

Trattao della Cognizione Pratica Delle Resistenze Geometricamente Dimostrato . . . Turin: 1748. V. 40

BORRER, WILLIAM

The Birds of Sussex. London: 1891. V. 43; 46

BORRICHIUS, OLAUS

Hermetis, Aegyptiorum, et Chemicorum Sapientia ab Hermanni Conringii Animadversionibus Vindicata. Copenhagen: 1674. V. 46

Hermetis, Aegyptiorum, et Chemicorum Sapientia ab Hermanni Conringii Animadversionibus Vindicata . . . Hafniae: 1674. V. 42; 43; 45; 46

BORROMINI, FRANCESCO

Opera del Caval . . . (with) Opus Architectonicum Equitis Francisci Boromini ex Ejusdem Exemplaribus Petitum . . . Rome: 1720/25. V. 37; 41

Opera del Caval. (with) Opus Architectonicum Equitis Francisci Boromini ex ejusdem Exemplaribus Petitum . . . Rome: 1720, 1725. V. 37

BORROW, GEORGE HENRY 1803-1881

The Bible in Spain. London: 1843. V. 40; 42; 46

The Bible in Spain . . . London: 1849. V. 42

The Bible in Spain; Lavengro; Romano Lavolil; The Romany Rye; Wild Wales and the Zincali. London: 1907-14. V. 44

Celebrated Trials and Remarkable Cases of Criminal Jurisprudence from the Earliest Records to the Year 1825. New York: 1928. V. 41

Celebrated Trials, and Remarkable Cases of Criminal Jurisprudence from the Earliest Records to the Year 1825. London: 1825. V. 38

Collection of works by . . . comprising: Lavengro: The Romany Rye: Romano Lavo-LiL . . . : Wild Wales: The Bible of Spain. London: 1907. V. 37

The Death of Balder. London: 1889. V. 39

Lavengro. London: 1851. V. 37; 38; 39; 40; 42; 43; 44; 46

Lavengro. New York: 1936. V. 41; 45

Romano Lavo-Lil. London: 1874. V. 37; 39; 40; 41; 42; 43

Romantic Ballads. London: 1826. V. 38; 39; 40

Romantic Ballads. Norwich: 1826. V. 41; 42

The Romany Rye. London: 1857. V. 43

The Romany Rye. London: 1858. V. 40

The Sleeping Bard. London: 1860. V. 40

Tales of the Wild and the Wonderful. London: 1825. V. 46

Targrum, or Metrical Translations from Thirty Languages and Dialects. St. Petersburg: 1835. V. 43

Targrum; or, Metrical Translations from Thirty Languages and Dialects. London: 1892. V. 38; 39; 43

Wild Wales. London: 1862. V. 39; 40; 42; 43

Works (The Zincali; The Bible in Spain; Lavengro; The Romany Rye; Wild Wales; Romano Lavo-Lil). London: 1901-06. V. 39

The Works. London: 1907. V. 43

The Works. London: 1923. V. 38; 42

Works. New York: 1923. V. 38

Works. London: 1923-24. V. 37; 38; 42; 44; 46

Collected Works. London: & New York: 1923-24. V. 46

Works. London: 1923-31. V. 41; 44

The Zincali. London: 1841. V. 39; 40

The Zincali; or, an Account of the Gypsies of Spain. London: 1841. V. 43

The Zincali or an Account of the Gypsies of Spain . . . London: 1843. V. 38; 42

BORROWINGS. San Francisco: 1889. V. 41

BORSCH-SUPAN, HELMUT

Caspar David Friedrich. London: 1973. V. 44

Caspar David Friedrich. New York: 1974. V. 40

BORSOOK, EVE

The Mural Painters of Tuscany, from Cimabue to Andrea Del Sarto. London: 1960. V. 44

BORTHWICK, GEORGE

A Treatise Upon the Extraction of the Crystalline Lens. Edinburgh: 1775. V. 42

BORTHWICK, J. D.

Cyclopaedia of History and Geography. Montreal: 1859. V. 38; 40

Three Years in California. Edinburgh: 1857. V. 42

Three Years in California. Edinburgh & London: 1857. V. 37; 38; 39; 42; 45

BORUWLASKI, JOSEPH

Memoirs of the Celebrated Dwarf . . . a Polish Gentleman . . . London: 1788. V. 44

BORY DE ST. VINCENT, J. B. G. M.

Voyage dans les Quatre Principales Iles des Mers d'Afrique, Fait Par Ordre du Gouvernement . . . Paris: 1804. V. 40

BORY DE ST.VINCENT, J. B. G. M.

Voyage To and Travels Through the Four Principal Islands of the African Seas, Performed by Order of the French Government During the Years 1801 and 1802, With a Narrative of the Passage of Captain Baudin to Port Louis in the Mauritius. London: 1805. V. 40

BOSANQUET, BERNARD 1848-1923

A History of Aesthetic. London: 1934. V. 39

Logic or the Morphology of Knowledge. Oxford: 1888. V. 39; 40; 41; 43

Logic, or the Morphology of Knowledge. Oxford: 1911. V. 38

BOSANQUET, CHARLES B. P.

London: Some Account of Its Growth, Charitable Agencies, and Wants. London: 1868. V. 40

BOSANQUET, HELEN

The Strength of the People. London: 1903. V. 43

BOSANQUET, JOHN BERNARD

Reports of Cases Argued and Determined in the Courts of Common Pleas, and Exchequer Chamber and in the House of Lords from 1796-1804. London: 1800-04. V. 38; 40

BOSANQUET, S. R.

A New System of Logic and Development of the Principles of Truth and Reasoning. London: 1839. V. 43; 45

BOSANQUET, THEODORE

Henry James at Work. London: 1924. V. 38

BOSC, CLAUDE DU

The Military History of the Late Prince Eugene of Savoy, and of the Late John Duke of Marlborough . . . London: 1736-37. V. 42

BOSCAN, JUAN

Las Obras. Alcala: 1575. V. 37

BOSCANA, GERONIMO

Chinigchinich (Chi-nich-nich). Santa Ana: 1933. V. 37; 40; 41

BOSCHINI, MARCO

L'Arcipelago Con Tutte Le Isole . . . Venice: 1658. V. 40

La Carta del Navegar Pitoresco Dialogo . . . Comparti in Otto Venti . . . Con i Argumentidi del Volonteroso Academico Delfico. Venice: 1660. V. 45

Il Regno Tutto di Candia Delineato a Parte, a Parte, et Intagliato da . . . Venice: 1651. V. 37; 46

Le Ricche Minere Della Pittura Veneziana. Venice: 1664. V. 40

BOSCHIUS, JACOBUS

Symbolographia, sive De Arte Symbolica . . . Quibus Accessit Sylloge Celebriorum Symbolorum in Quatuor Divisa Classes. Augsburg/Dillingen: 1701. V. 40

BOSCHLOO, A. W. A.

Annibale Carracci in Bologna: Visible Reality in Art after the Council of Trent. The Hague: 1974. V. 37

BOSCOVIC, RUDJER JOSIP 1711-1787

A Theory of Natural Philosophy. Chicago: 1922. V. 42

BOSE, SHIB CHUNDER

The Hindoos as They Are. Calcutta: 1881. V. 39

BOSKOVIC, RUDJER JOSIP 1711-1787

De Continuitatis Lege et Ejus Consectariis Pertinentibus ad Prima Materiae Elementa Eorumque Vires Dissertatio Habita a Patribus Societatis Jesu in Collegio Romano die 7 Augusti anno 1754. Rome: 1754. V. 38; 41; 45

Dissertationes Quinque ad Dioptricam Pertinentes . . . Vienna: 1767. V. 38; 41

Observationibus Astronomicis, et Quo Pertingat Earundem Certitudo Dissertatio Habita in Seminario Romano Societatis Jesu . . . Rome: 1742. V. 38; 41

BOSMAN, WILLIAM

A New and Accurate Description of the Coast of Guinea, Divided into the Gold, the Slave and the Ivory Coasts. London: 1705. V. 41

A New and Accurate Description of the Coast of Guinea. London: 1721. V. 38; 42; 45; 46

BOSQUET, ALAIN

Jafar Islah. Works from 1967 to 1983. Kuwait: 1984. V. 42

BOSQUI, EDWARD

Memoirs of Edward Bosqui. Oakland: 1952. V. 38; 43

BOSS, HENRY R.

Sketches of the History of Ogle County, Ill., and the Early Settlement of the Northwest. Polo: 1859. V. 37

BOSS, MAE H. B.

My Playhouse Was a Concord Coach. Oakland: 1942. V. 43

BOSS, MEDARD

Meaning and Content of Sexual Perversions: . . . New York: 1949. V. 43

BOSS, W.

The Stormont, Dundas and Glengarry Highlanders 1783-1951. Ottawa: 1952. V. 42

BOSSAN, PIERRE

L'Oeuvre . . . Contenant 450 motifs d'Architecture Reproduit en Heliogravure. Paris & Montbrison: 1891. V. 38

BOSSCHERE, JEAN DE 1878-1953

Beasts and Men. London: 1918. V. 43

Christmas Tales of Flanders. London: 1917. V. 43; 44; 45

The City Curious. New York: 1920. V. 42

The City Curious. London: 1920. V. 41; 43

The Fairies Up to Date. London. V. 41

Folk Tales of Flanders. New York: 1918. V. 46

The Golden Asse of Lucius Apuleius. London: 1923. V. 37

Marthe and the Madman. New York: 1928. V. 42; 43

12 Occupations. London: 1916. V. 40

Weird Islands. London: 1921. V. 46

BOSSE, ABRAHAM

Maniere Universelle de Mr. Desargues Pour Pratiquer la Perspective par Petit-Pied . . . Ensemble les Places et Proportions des Fortes et Foibles Touches, Teintes ou Couleurs. Paris: 1648. V. 40

Sentimens sur la Distinction des Diverses Manieres de Peinture, Dessin et Gravure. Paris: 1649. V. 39

Traite des Manieres de Dessiner les Ordres de l'Architecture. (with) Representations Geometrales de Plusieurs Parties de Bastiments. Paris: 1688. V. 38

BOSSERT, HELMUTH THEODOR

An Encyclopaedia of Colour Decoration. Berlin: 1928. V. 41; 46

Ornament in Applied Art. New York: 1924. V. 42

Ornament in Applied Art . . . New York: 1924. V. 42

Peasant Art in Europe. London: 1927. V. 39; 41

Peasant Art in Europe. New York: 1927. V. 42

Volkskunst in Europa. New York: 1927. V. 46

Volkskunst in Europa. Berlin: 1938. V. 41

BOSSEWELL, JOHN

Works of Armorie, Deuyded into three Bookes, Entiutled, the Concordes of Armorie, the Armorie of Honour, and of Coates and Crestes. London: 1572. V. 37

BOSSHUT, CHARLES 1730-1814

A General History of Mathematics from the Earliest Times, to the Middle of the Eighteenth Century. London: 1803. V. 46

BOSSIL, C.

Laura et Lenza. A Grand Ballet, as Performed at the King's Theatre. London: 1805/6? V. 40

BOSSOM, ALFRED

Building to the Skies. London: 1934. V. 38

BOSSOM, ALFRED C.

The Architectural Pilgrimage in Old Mexico. New York: 1924. V. 39; 42

BOSSU, JEAN BERNARD

Nouveaux Voyages aux Indes Occidentales . . . Paris: 1768. V. 38; 39; 45

Travels through Part of North America Formerly Called Louisiana . . . London: 1771. V. 37; 38; 39; 40; 42; 43; 44; 45

BOSSUET, J. B.

An Exposition of the Doctrine of the Catholic Church in Matters of Controversie. London: 1686. V. 38

BOSSUET, JACQUES 1627-1704

De Nova Quaestione Tractatus Tres. Paris: 1698. V. 43

BOSSUET, JACQUES BENIGNE

A Treatise of Communion Under Both Species. Paris: 1685. V. 40

BOSSUS, MATTHAEUS

Epistolae Familiares et Secundae. Mantua: 1498. V. 37

BOSSUT, CHARLES

A General History of Mathematics from the Earliest Times to the Middle of the Eighteenth Century. London: 1803. V. 45

Traite Elementaire d'Hydrodynamique. Paris: 1751. V. 38

Traite Elementaire de Mechanique et de Dinamique . . . Charleville: 1763. V. 45

Traite Elementaire d'Hydrodynamique . . . Paris: 1771. V. 41; 45

BOSTOCK, JOHN

An Elementary System of Physiology. Boston: 1825-1828. V. 38

BOSTON & MONTANA CONSOLIDATED COPPER & SILVER MINING CO.

Report of the . . . for the Year Ending June 30 . . . . 1890/1893-1900. V. 39

BOSTON ARTISTS' ASSOCIATION

The Constitution of the Boston Artists' Association with a Catalogue of the First Public Exhibition . . . Boston: 1842. V. 43

THE BOSTON Book, Being Specimens of Metropolitan Literature. Boston: 1850. V. 45

BOSTON, CHARLES K.

The Silver Jackass by Charles K. Boston. New York: (1941). V. 37

BOSTON. COMMITTEE OF CORRESPONDENCE

The Votes and Proceedings of the Freeholders and Other Inhabitants of the Town of Boston, in Town Meeting Assembled, According to Law . . . to which is Prefixed, as Introductory, an Attested Copy of a Vote of the Town at a Preceding Meeting. Boston: 1772. V. 41

THE BOSTON Directory, Embracing the City Record, a General Directory of the Citizens and Business Directory. Boston: 1874. V. 46

THE BOSTON Directory; (for 1826) . . . Boston: 1826. V. 39; 43

BOSTON FEMALE ANTI-SLAVERY SOCIETY

Annual Report . . . Being a Concise History of the Cases of the Slave Child Med, and of the Women Demanded as Slaves . . . Boston: 1836. V. 42

BOSTON FIRE DEPARTMENT

Rules and Regulations for the Engine, Hose, Hook and Ladder and Other Companies, Attached to the Boston Fire Department, Established by the Board of Alderman, Oct. 23, 1837. Boston: 1837. V. 40

BOSTON. MARINE INSURANCE CO. CHARTERS

An Act to Incorporate the Boston Marine Insurance Co. Boston: 1799. V. 44

BOSTON MARINE INSURANCE COMPANY

An Act to Incorporate . . . Boston: 1799. V. 41

BOSTON Medical and Surgical Journal 1880-1890. 1800-1890. V. 42

BOSTON. MUSEUM OF FINE ARTS.

Illustrated Catalogue of a Special Loan Exhibition of Art Treasures from Japan, Held in Conjunction with the Tercentenary Celebrations of Harvard University. September - October, 1936. Boston: 1936. V. 38; 44

THE BOSTON Musical Miscellany. Boston: 1811. V. 37

BOSTON Prize Poems and Other Specimens of Dramatic Poetry. Boston: 1824. V. 37

BOSTON, THOMAS

Human Nature in Its Fourfold State of Primitive Integrity, Entire Depravation, Begun Recovery and Consummate Happiness or Misery . . . Edinburgh: 1756. V. 40

BOSWELL Again by 'Philalethes.' London: 1878. V. 40

BOSWELL, ALEXANDER

Edinburgh, or, The Ancient Royalty; a Sketch of Former Manners. Edinburgh: 1810. V. 40

Ane Oratioune Set Furth be Master Quintine Kennedy, Commendatour of Corsraguell ye Zeir of Gode 1561. Edinburgh: 1812. V. 40; 45

Clan-Alpin's Vow: a Fragment. Edinburgh: 1811. V. 42

The Poetical Works Now First Collected and Edited . . . Glasgow: 1871. V. 37; 39; 40; 42; 45; 46

BOSWELL, EDWARD

The Civil Division of the County of Dorset . . . Dorchester: 1833. V. 42

BOSWELL, JAMES 1740-1795

An Account of Corscia, the Journal of a Tour to that Island, and Memoirs of Pascal Paoli. Dublin: 1768. V. 39; 41; 43; 44

An Account of Corsica, the Journal of a Tour to That Island. Glasgow: 1768. V. 37; 38; 40; 41; 43; 45

An Account of Corsica. London: 1768. V. 37; 38; 40; 41; 43; 44; 45; 46

An Account of Corsica, the Journal of a Tour to that Island and Memoirs of Pascal Paoli. Dublin: 1769. V. 38; 40

An Account of Corsica, The Journal of a Tour to That Island . . . Glasgow: 1786. V. 45

Boswell in Holland 1763-1764 Including His Correspondence with Belle de Zuylen (Zelide). London: 1952. V. 41

Boswell in Holland 1763-1764. New York: 1952. V. 41

Boswell on the Grand Tour: Germany and Switzerland 1764. London: 1953. V. 41; 42

Boswell on the Grand Tour: Italy, Corsica and France, 1765-1766. London: 1955. V. 42; 43

Boswell in Search of a Wife. London: 1957. V. 42

Boswell for the Defence. London: 1960. V. 42

Boswell Papers: Boswell's Journal of a Tour to the Hebrides with Samuel Johnson, LL.dust jacket. 1962. V. 40

Boswell Papers: Boswell the Ominous Years 1774-76. London: 1963. V. 40; 45

Boswelliana. The Commonplace Book of James Boswell with a Memoir and Annotations by the Rev. Charles Rogers . . . London: 1876. V. 37

Boswelliana. The Commonplace Book of James Bowell. With a Memoir & nnotations by the Rev. Charles Rogers, LL.D. And Introductory Remarks by the Right Hon. Lord Houghton. London: 1874. V. 37

Boswell's London Journal 1762-1763 Together with Journal of My Jaunt Havest 1762. London: 1951. V. 41

Boswell's London Journal 1762-1763. New York: (1950). V. 37; 42

Boswell's London Journal 1762-1763 . . . London: (1950). V. 37

Boswell's Note Book, 1776-1777 . . . London: 1925. V. 42

British Essays in Favour of the Brave Corsicans . . . London: 1769. V. 43; 46

The Correspondence of James Boswell with David Garrick, Edmund Burke and Edmund Malone. London: 1986. V. 40

Dr. Johnson's Table-Talk: Containing Aphorisms on Literature, Life, and Manners; with Anecdotes of Distinguished Persons: Selected and Arranged from Mr. Boswell's Life of Johnson. London: 1798. V. 37

The Essence of the Douglas Cause. London: 1767. V. 43

The Hypochondriack, Being the Seventy Essays by the Celebrated, Biographer, James Boswell, Appearing in the London Magazine, from November 1777 to August, 1783, and here First Reprinted. 1928. V. 39

The Hypochondriack: Being the Seventy Essays by . . . Stanford: 1928. V. 42

The Journal of a Tour to the Hebrides with Samuel Johnson, LL.D. The Second Edition revised and corrected. 1785. V. 37

The Journal of a Tour to the Hebrides with Samuel Johnson, Containing Some Poetical Pieces by Dr. Johnson Relative to the Tour and Never Before Published. Dublin: 1785. V. 37; 38; 39; 40; 41; 43; 44

The Journal of a Tour to the Hebrides, with Samuel Johnson, LL.D. London: 1785. V. 37; 38; 39; 40; 41; 42; 43; 44; 45; 46

The Journal of a Tour to the Hebrides with Samuel Johnson. London: 1786. V. 37; 38; 40; 45; 46

The Journal of a Tour to the Hebrides with Samuel Johnson. London: 1807. V. 39; 40; 41; 45

The Journal of a Tour to the Hebrides with Samuel Johnson. London: 1810. V. 46

The Journal of a Tour to the Hebrides with Samuel Johnson. New York: 1810. V. 40; 45

The Journal of a Tour to the Hebrides with Samuel Johnson, LL.D. New York & Boston: 1810. V. 38

The Journal of a Tour to the Hebrides . . . London: 1813. V. 39

The Journal of a Tour to the Hebrides with Samuel Johnson. London: 1936. V. 40

The Journal of a Tour to the Herbrides with Samuel Johnson, LL.D. New York: 1959. V. 41

The Journal of a Tour to the Hebrides . . . 1962. V. 39

The Journal of a Tour to the Hebrides with Samuel Johnson. 1964. V. 38; 39; 43; 44

The Journal of A Tour to the Hebrides with Samuel Johnson, LL.D. London: 1964. V. 37

The Journal of a Tour to the Hebrides with Samuel Johnson, LL.D. 1974. V. 42

The Journal of a Tour to the Hebrides with Samuel Johnson. Avon: 1974. V. 46

The Journal of a Tour to the Hebrides with Samuel Johnson . . . Bloomfield: 1974. V. 39; 40

A Letter to Robert MacQueen, Lord Braxfield, on His Promotion to be one of the Judges of the High Court of Justiciary. London: 1784. V. 39

A Letter to Robert MacQueen, Lord Braxifield, on his Promotion to be one of the Judges of the High Court of Justiciary. Edinburgh: 1789. V. 37

A Letter to the People of Scotland, on the Present State of the Nation. Edinburgh: 1784. V. 37

Letters Between the Honourable Andrew Erskine and James Boswell. London: 1763. V. 39

Letters of James Boswell Addressed to the Rev. W. J. Temple. London: 1857. V. 41; 46

Letters . . . Addressed to the Rev. W. J. Temple. London: 1857, 1856. V. 40

Letters Between the Honourable Andrew Erskine and James Boswell. (with) His Journal of a Tour to Corsica. London: 1879. V. 39

Letters of James Boswell to the Rev. W. J. Temple. London: 1908. V. 39

Letters of James Boswell. Oxford: 1924. V. 38; 41; 42; 46

Letters between the Honourable Andrew Erskine and James Bowell. London: 1763. V. 37

Letters, Edited by Chauncey Brewster Tinker. Oxford: 1924. V. 37

The Life of Samuel Johnson, LL.D. London: 1783. V. 45

The Life of Samuel Johnson. London: 1791. V. 37; 38; 39; 40; 41; 43; 44; 45; 46

The Life of Samuel Johnson, LL.D. London: 1791. V. 45

The Life of Samuel Johnson, LL.D. Dublin: 1792. V. 38; 41; 42; 43; 46

The Life of Samuel Johnson, LL.D. Dublin: 1793. V. 41

The Life of Samuel Johnson, LL.D. London: 1793. V. 37; 38; 39; 40; 44; 46

The Life of Samuel Johnson, LL.D. London: 1799. V. 42; 43

Life of Samuel Johnson. London: 1804. V. 40; 42; 46

The Life of Samuel Johnson. Boston: 1807. V. 37; 38; 40; 42; 43; 44; 46

The Life of Samuel Johnson. London: 1807. V. 42; 43

The Life of Samuel Johnson. London: 1811. V. 40; 41; 45; 46

The Life of Samuel Johnson, LL.D. London: 1819. V. 43

The Life of Samuel Johnson, LL.D. London: 1822. V. 39; 40; 46

The Life of Samuel Johnson. London: 1823. V. 37; 42

The Life of Samuel Johnson. London: 1824. V. 41; 42; 45; 46

The Life of Samuel Johnson, LL.D. London: 1825. V. 38; 42

The Life of Samuel Johnson, LL.D. London: 1826. V. 39; 40; 41; 42

The Life of Samuel Johnson. Oxford: 1826. V. 38; 39; 40; 42; 43

The Life of Samuel Johnson. Oxford & London: 1826. V. 38; 39; 41

The Life of Samuel Johnson, LL.D. Oxford: 1827. V. 42

The Life of Samuel Johnson, LL.D. London: 1831. V. 37; 39; 40; 46

The Life of Samuel Johnson, LL.D., Including a Journal of a Tour to the Hebrides. London: 1831-36. V. 37

Life of Johnson. London: 1835. V. 40; 41; 43; 46

The Life of Samuel Johnson, LL.D. London: 1835-1844. V. 46

Boswell's Life of Samuel Johnson. London: 1844. V. 41; 46

The Life of Johnson. London: 1851. V. 39; 40; 43

The Life of Samuel Johnson, LL.D together with the Journal of a Tour to the Hbrides. New Editions with Notes and Appendices by Alexander Napier. London: 1884. V. 37

The Life of Samuel Johnson. London: 1885. V. 39

The Life of Samuel Johnson. New York: 1887. V. 43

Boswell's Life of Johnson Including Boswell's Journal of a Tour to the Hebridges and John's' Diary of a Journey into North Wales. Oxford: 1887. V. 38; 39; 40; 41; 42; 45; 46

The Life of Samuel Johnson, LL.D. London: 1888. V. 37; 39; 44

The Life of Samuel Johnson, LL.D. London: 1890. V. 39

The Life of Samuel Johnson, LL.D. New York: 1891. V. 40; 45; 46

Life of Johnson. Westminster: 1896. V. 37

The Life of Samuel Johnson. London: 1897. V. 43

The Life of Samuel Johnson. London: 1901. V. 39; 42; 45

The Life of Samuel Johnson. London/New York: 1901. V. 43

The Life of Samuel Johnson. London: 1907. V. 37; 38; 39; 40; 42; 45; 46

The Life of Samuel Johnson. New York: 1909. V. 37; 38; 40; 41; 43; 46

The Life of Dr. Johnson. New York: 1922. V. 38; 39; 41; 42; 43; 45; 46

The Life of Samuel Johnson. London: 1924. V. 39; 43

The Life of Samuel Johnson. Bath: 1925. V. 38; 46

The Life of Samuel Johnson. Boston: 1925. V. 39; 40; 41; 42; 45

The Life of Samuel Johnson. London: 1925. V. 39; 43; 45

The Life of Samuel Johnson, LL.D. Oxford and London: 1926. V. 44

The Life of Samuel Johnson, LL.D. (with) Tour to the Hebrides. London: 1930. V. 39

BOSWELL, JAMES 1740-1795 continued

The Life of Samuel Johnson, LL.D. Oxford: 1934-1950. V. 39; 40; 42; 45; 46

The Life of Samuel Johnson. 1938. V. 43

The Life of Samuel Johnson. London: 1938. V. 38

The Life of Johnson. London: 1953. V. 37; 44

The Life of Samuel Johnson. New York: 1963. V. 39; 40; 43; 45; 46

The Life of Samuel Johnson, LL.D. 1968. V. 39

The Life of Samuel Johnson, LL.D. London: 1971. V. 38

The Life of Samuel Johnson, LL.D. Oxford: 1971-75. V. 45

The Life of Samuel Johnson, LL.D. Oxford: 1979. V. 40

The Life of Samuel Johnson, LL.D. London: 1816. V. 38

The Life of Samuel Johnson, LL.D. 1818. V. 46

On the Profession of a Player, Three Essays.. London: 1929. V. 39

On the Grand Tour: Germany and Switzerland, 1764. London: 1953. V. 43

The Principal Corrections and Additions to the First Edition of Mr. Boswell's Life of Johnson. London: 1793. V. 45

Privte Papers of James Boswell from Malahide Castle. London & New York: 1928-37. V. 40

Private Papers of James Boswell: Number One- London: 1951. V. 40; 46

The Private Papers of James Boswell. London: 1951-60. V. 40; 43

The Yale Edition of the Private Papers of James Boswell. Volume Three: Boswell on the Grand Tour, Germany and Switzerland, 1764. London: 1953. V. 45; 46

The Yale Edition of the Private Papers of James Boswell: Boswell in Search of a Wife. 1766-1769. London: 1957. V. 46

Reproduction of some of the Original Proof Sheets of Boswell's Life of Johnson. Buffalo: 1923. V. 41

The Works of the Honourable Robert Boyle. London: 1772. V. 41

BOSWELL, JOHN

The Case of the Royal Martyr Considered with Candour . . . London: 1758. V. 45

BOSWELL, SAMUEL

Letters of Samuel Boswell. Oxford: 1924. V. 39

BOSWELL, WINTHROP PALMER

Hisperica Famina: The Garden of God. The 'Prologue' and a part of the 'Book of Days,: translated by Winthrop Palmer Boswell. San Francisco: 1974. V. 37

BOSWORTH, CLARENCE E.

Breeding Your Own: How to Raise and Train Colts for Pleasure and Profit. New York: 1939. V. 41

BOSWORTH, J.

A Compendious Anglo-Saxon and English Dictionary. London: 1860. V. 38

A Dictionary of the Anglo-Saxon Language . . . London: 1838. V. 43

BOSWORTH, JOSEPH

A Compendious Grammar of the Primitive English or Anglo-Saxon Language, a Knowledge of Which is Essential to Every Modern English Grammarian . . . London: 1826. V. 41

BOSWORTH, N.

A Treatise on the Rifle, Musket, Pistol and Fowling Piece. New York: 1846. V. 38

BOSWORTH, NEWTON

The Accidents of Human Life. London: 1813. V. 40; 42; 44

The Accidents of Human Life; with Hints for Their Preservation, and the Removal of Their Consequences. New York: 1814. V. 37

The Accidents of Human Life; with Hints for Their Prevention, or the Removal of Their Consequences. London: 1834. V. 39

Hochelaga Depicta: The Early History and Present State of the City and Island of Montreal. Montreal: 1839. V. 37; 44

BOTANICAL Specimens Copied from Nature and Designed as Simple Illustrations of the Twenty-Four Classes into Which, According to the Linnaean System of Arrangement, all Plans are Divided. Liverpool: 1828. V. 37

THE BOTANIST'S Calendar; and Pocket Flora; Arranged According to the Linnaean System. London: 1797. V. 41; 42

BOTCHKAREVA, MARIA

Yashka, My Life as a Peasant Exile and Soldier as Set Down by Isaac Don Levine. London: 1919. V. 44; 45

BOTELLO DE MORAES Y VASCONCELOS, FRANCISCO

El Alphonso . . . Paris: 1712. V. 38

BOTERO, GIOVANNI

Aggiunta Alla Quarta Parte Dell' Indie . . . Venice: 1618. V. 45

Della Ragione di Stato, Libri Dieci . . . (with) Aggiunte . . . alla Sua Ragion di Stato . . . Venice: 1598. V. 41

Della Ragion di Stato Libri Dieci, Con Tre Libri delle Cause della Grandezza, e Magnificenza delle Citta . . . In Venetia: 1589. V. 37

Delle Relatione Universali. Ferrara: 1592. V. 40; 45

Relations of the Most Famous Kingdoms and Common-Weales Thorovgh the World . . . London: 1689. V. 40; 43

BOTFIELD, BERIAH

Journal of a Tour through the Highlands of Scotland During the Summer of MDCCCXXIX. London: 1830. V. 40

Stemmata Botevilliana. London: 1858. V. 37; 39; 42

BOTHMER, MARY VON, COUNTESS

Aut Caesar Aut Nihil. London: 1883. V. 43; 44

BOTOSANEANU, L.

Stygofauna Mundi, A Faunistic, Distributional and Ecological Synthesis of the World Fauna Inhabiting Subterranean Waters. Leiden: 1986. V. 37

BOTSCHANTZEVA, Z. P.

Tulips, Morphology, Cytology, Phytogeography and Physiology. Rotterdam: 1982. V. 37

BOTT, EDMUND

Decisions of the Court of King's Bench, Upon the Laws Relating to the Poor. London: 1793. V. 40

The Statutes at Large Concerning the Provision for the Poor, Being a Collection of all the Acts of Parliament Relating There Now In Force. (with) A Table for All the Said Acts, Digested into Alphabetical Order. London: 1752. V. 40

BOTTA, CHARLES

History of the War of Independence of the United States of America. Philadelphia: 1820. V. 39; 42

BOTTA, PAUL EMILE

Illustrations of Discoveries at Nineveh. London: 1850. V. 40; 42

BOTTARELLI, FERDINANDO

Exercises Upon the Different Parts of Italian Speech; With Reference to Veneroni's Grammar. London: 1778. V. 41

The New Italian, English and French Pocket-Dictionary . . . London: 1777. V. 45

BOTTAZZO, GIOVANNI JACOPO d. c. 1575

Dialogi Martimi. Mantua: 1547. V. 40; 45

BOTTICELLI, SANDRO

Drawings by . . . for Dante's Divina Commedia. Reduced Facsimiles after the originals in the Royal Museum Berlin and in the Vatican Library . . . London: 1896. V. 37

BOTTOMLEY, EDWIN

An English Settler in Pioneer Wisconsin; The Letters of Edwin Bottomley, 1842-1850. Madison: 1918. V. 42

BOTTOMLEY, GEORGE

Lyric Plays. London: 1932. V. 43

BOTTOMLEY, GORDON

Chambers of Imagery. First and Second Series. London: 1907-1912. V. 40

The Gate of Smaragdus. London: 1904. V. 42; 43

Gruach and Britain's Daughter. London: 1921. V. 40; 41

King Lear's Wife and Other Plays. London: 1920. V. 45

Midsummer Eve. Harting: 1905. V. 38; 40

Poems of Thirty Years. London: 1925. V. 44

The Riding to Lithend. Flansham: 1909. V. 43

Scenes and Plays. London: 1929. V. 40; 43

A Stage for Poetry: My Purpose with My Plays. Kendal: 1948. V. 44

A Vision of Giorgione Three Variations on a Theme. London: 1922. V. 37

BOTTOMLEY, SAMUEL

Greenfield, a Poem. Saddleworth,: 1820. V. 40

Greenfield, a Poem. Manchester: 1822? V. 45

BOTTSCHILD, SAMUEL

Alphabet. Germany: 1690? V. 38

BOTURINI BENADUCI, LORENZO

Idea de Una Nueva Historia General de la America Septentrional. Madrid: 1746. V. 43

BOUCARD, A.

Catalogus Avium. London: 1876. V. 43

Travels of a Naturalist. London: 1894. V. 38; 40

BOUCAUT, JAMES PENN

The Arab and the Horse of the Future. London. V. 43

The Arab, the Horse of the Future. London: 1905. V. 39

BOUCHER, ANTHONY

The Case of the Baker Street Irregulars. New York: 1940. V. 40

BOUCHER, FRANCOIS

A History of Costume in the West. London: 1967. V. 44

20,000 Years of Fashion. The History of Costume and personal Adornment. New York: (1967). V. 37

BOUCHER, JOHN

The Volunteer Rifleman and the Rifle. London: 1859. V. 46

BOUCHER, JONATHAN

View of the Causes and Consequences of the American Revolution. London: 1797. V. 37; 44; 45

BOUCHER, PIERRE

Canada in the Seventeenth Century, from the French of . . . Montreal: 1883. V. 44

BOUCHEREAU, A.

Statement of the Sugar Crop Made in louisiana, 1894-95, With an Appendix (1894-95; 1895-96; 1897-98; 1900-01; 1904-05). New Orleans: 1895-1905. V. 37

BOUCHET, GUILLAUME 1526-1606

Les Serees de Guillaume Bouchet Sieur de Broncourt. Lyon: 1614. V. 39

BOUCHET, JEAN

Les Annales d'Aquitaine. Poitiers: 1557. V. 41

Les Triumphes de la Noble et Amovrevse Dame, et l'Art de Honnestement Aymer, Compose par le Trauerseur des Voyes . . . Paris: 1545. V. 45

BOUCHETTE, JOSEPH

The British Dominions in North America. London: 1832. V. 37; 38; 39; 42; 45

Tables, Showing the Difference of Longitude in Time, at the Most Important Places Between the Atlantic and Pacific Oceans, in the British North American Dominions, and the Northern Section of the United States. Toronto: 1857. V. 38

A Topographical Description of the Province of Lower Canada. London: 1815. V. 38; 39; 42; 43; 44

A Topographical Dictionary of the Province of Lower Canada. London: 1832. V. 37; 38; 42; 43; 45

BOUCHOR, J. F.

To Our Heroic Allies. Lyons: 1917. V. 43; 44

BOUCHOT, HENRI

Catherine de Medicis. Paris: 1899. V. 38

The Printed Book. Its History, Illustration, and Adornment. New York: 1887. V. 39

BOUCICAULT, DION

The Octroon; or, Life in Louisiana. N.P.: 1861? V. 37

BOUDIER DE VILLEMERT, PIERRE JOSEPH

The Friend of Women. Philadelphia: 1803. V. 37

The Ladies Friend: Being a Treatise on the Virtues and Qualifications Which are the Brightest Ornaments of the Fair Sex, and Render them Most Agreeable to the Sensible Part of Mankind. New Haven: 1784. V. 40

The Ladies Friend; Being a Treatise on the Virtues and Qualifications Which are the Brightest Ornaments of the Fair Sex, and Render Them Most agreeable to the Sensible Part of Mankind. New Haven: 1789. V. 40

BOUDIER, E.

Icones Mycologicae ou Iconographie des Champignons de France Principalement Discomycetes. Lausanne: 1905-11. V. 40

Icones Mycologicae ou Iconographie des Champignons de France. Paris: 1905-11. V. 39; 41

BOUDINOT, ELIAS 1740-1821

Address of the New-Jersey Bible Society to the Public with an Appendix. New Brunswick: 1810. V. 43

Documents in Relation to the Validity of the Cherokee Treaty of 1835. Washington: 1838. V. 46

Journal, or, Historical Recollections of American Events During the Revolutionary War. Philadelphia: 1894. V. 42; 44

The Life, Public Services, Addresses and Letters of Elias Boudinot, LL.D. President of the Continental Congress. Boston: 1896. V. 39

Memoirs of the Life of the Rev. William Tennent . . . Wilmington: 1819. V. 43

The Second Advent, or Coming of the Messiah in Glory, Shown to be a Scripture Doctrine, and Taught by Divine Revlation from the Beginning of the World. Trenton: 1815. V. 37; 39; 43

A Star in the West; or, a Humble Attempt to Discover the Long Lost Ten Tribes of Israel . . . Trenton: 1816. V. 37; 40; 41; 42; 43; 45

BOUGAINVILLE, LOUIS ANTOINE DE

Voyage Autour du Monde, par la Fregate du Roi la Boudeuse, et la Flute l'Etoile, en 1766, 1767, 1768 & 1769. Paris: 1771. V. 37; 45

A Voyage Round the World. London: 1772. V. 40; 41; 42; 43

Voyage Autour du Monde, par la Fregate du Roi, la Boudeuse et la Flute l'Etoile, En 1766, 1767, 1768 and 1769. Paris: 1772. V. 38; 40; 41; 42

BOUGHTON, ALICE

Photographing the Famous. New York: 1920. V. 37

BOUGHTON, J. S.

The Kansas Hand Book with Map. Lawrence: 1878. V. 38; 39

The Lawrence Massacre by a Band of Missouri Ruffians, August 21, 1863. Lawrence: 1884. V. 42

BOUGUER, PIERRE

De La Mature des Vaisseaux Medit. Super Problemate Nautico. De La Mature des Vasseaux. Paris: 1727-28-28. V. 39

Traite du Navire, de sa Construction, et de ses Mouvemens. Paris: 1746. V. 40; 44; 45

Traite d'Optique sur la Gradation de la Lumiere. Paris: 1760. V. 38; 41

BOUHOURS, DOMINICK

The Life of St. Ignatius, Founder of the Society of jesus. London: 1686. V. 38; 43

BOUHOURS, DOMINIQUE

The Arts of Logick and Rhetorick, Illustrated by Examples Taken Out of the Best Authors, Antient and Modern, In all the Polite Languages. London: 1728. V. 42

Histoire de Pierre d'Aubusson, Grand-Maistre de Rhodes. Paris: 1676. V. 37

BOUHOURS, PERE DOMINIQUE

La Vie de S. Francois Xavier. Paris & Liege: 1788. V. 40

BOUILHET, LOUIS

Melaenis. Evreux: 1900. V. 40

BOUILLAUD, JEAN BAPTISTE

Nouvelle Recherches sur le Rhumatisme . . . Paris: 1836. V. 38

BOUILLE DU CHARIOL, FRANCOIS CLAUDE AMOUR DE, MARQUIS

Memoirs Relating to the French Revolution. London: 1797. V. 42

BOUILLON, HENRI DE LA TOUR D'AUVERGNE, VICTOMTE DE TURENNE, DUC DE 1555-1623 Military Memoirs and Maxims of Marshall Turenne Interspersed with Others, Taken from the Best Authors and Observation with Remarks. London: 1740. V. 40

BOUILLON-LAGRANGE, EDME JEAN BAPTISTE

A Manual of a Course of Chemistry. London: 1800. V. 40; 41

BOUILLY, JEAN NICHOLAS

Deaf and Dumb. London: 1801. V. 40

BOUILLY, JEAN NICOLAS

Explication des Douze Ecussons quie Representent les Emblemes et les Symboles des Douze Grades Philosophiques du Rite Ecossais dit Ancient et Accepte. Paris: 1835. V. 37

BOULAINVILLIERS, HENRI, COMTE DE

Etat de I France, Dans Lequel on Voit Tout ce qui Regarde le Gouvernement Ecclesiastique, le Militire, la Justice, les Finances, le Commerce, les Manufactures, le Nombre des Habitans, & en General tout ce qui peut faire connoitre a fond cette Monarchie.. Londres. V. 38

An Historical Account of the Ancient Parliaments of France, or States General of the Kingdom. London: 1739. V. 38; 40

La Vie De Mahomed. Londres: 1730. V. 43

BOULDEN, JAMES E. P.

Medicine: or, The Legitimists and the Illegitimists. Baltimore: 1870. V. 37

BOULDER and Surroundings. Boulder: 1887. V. 41

BOULENGER, G. A.

Catalogue of the Lizards in the British Museum. London: 1885-87. V. 38

Catalogue of the Fresh-Water Fishes of Africa. London: 1909-16. V. 43

Catalogue of the Lizards in the British Museum. London: 1885-87, 1965. V. 37

The Fishes of the Nile. Volume 2: Zoology of Egypt. London: 1965. V. 38

BOULENGER, JACQUES

Miroir a Deux Faces. Paris: 1933. V. 43

BOULET, JACQUES

Nouvelles Remarques sur les Germanismes. Halle: 1773. V. 39

BOULGER, DEMETRIUS C.

The Battle of the Boyne, Together with an Account Based on French and Other Unpublished Records of the War in Ireland, 1688-91. London: 1911. V. 38; 39

History of China. London: 1881-84. V. 39

BOULGER, DEMETRIUS C. continued

The History of China. London: 1898. V. 42; 44; 45

BOULGER, G. S.

British Flowering Plants. London: 1914. V. 39; 43

BOULGER, JOHN

The Master Key to Public Offices and Candidate's Complete Instructor. London: 1860. V. 40; 43

BOULT, SWINTON

Trade and Partnership; the Relative Duties and Proper Liabilities of the Merchant and the State. London: 1855. V. 46

BOULTER, HUGH

Letters Written by His Excellency Hugh Boulter, D.D. Lord Primate of Ireland etc. To Several Ministers of State in England and Some Others Containing an Account of the Most Interesting Transactions Which Passed in Ireland from 1724-1728. Dublin: 1770. V. 39; 42; 46

BOULTON, M. P. W.

Examination of the Principles of the Scoto-oxonian Philosophy. London: 1861. V. 40

Remarks on Some Evidence Recently Communicated to the Photographic Society. London. V. 40

Remarks on Some Evidence Recently Communicated to the Photographic Society. (with) Remarks Concerning Certain Photographs Supposed to be of Early Date. London: 1863-64. V. 42

Remarks Concerning Certain Pictures Supposed to be Photographs of Early Date. London: 1865. V. 43

BOULTON, MATTHEW PIERS WATT

On Aerial Locomotion. London: 1864. V. 38

BOULTON, REG

The Sculptures of Kilpeck. Hereford: 1987. V. 45

BOULTON, RICHARD

Physico-Chyrurgical Treatises of the Gout, the King's Evil and the Lues Venera . . . London: 1714. V. 39

BOULTON, WILLIAM B.

The Amusements of Old London. London: 1891. V. 39

The Amusements of Old London. Boston: 1901. V. 43

BOUNDINOT, E. C.

Colonel Boudinot's Letter, Showing the Status of the United States Lands in Indian Territory. Baltimore: 1879. V. 40

BOUQUET, HENRY

Orderly Book of Colonel Henry Bouquet's Expedition Against the Ohio Indians, 1764. Pittsburgh: 1960. V. 46

BOURCHIER, THOMAS

Historia Ecclesiastica de Martyrio Fratrum Ordinis Divi Francisci. Paris: 1586. V. 44

BOURCHIER, WILLIAM

Narrative of a Passage from Bombay to England, Describing the Author's Shipwreck in the 'Nautilus', the Red Sea . . . London: 1834. V. 38; 41

BOURDALOUE, LOUIS

Sermons. N.P.: 1675. V. 40

BOURDE DE VILLEHUET, JACQUES

The Manoeuverer, or Skilful Seaman. London: 1788. V. 38

BOURDET, BERNARD

Soins Faciles Pour la Proprete de la Bouche, et Pour la Conservation des Dents. Paris: 1759. V. 41

BOURDILLON, F. W.

Ailes d'Alouette. Oxford: 1902. V. 41

Through the Gateway. London: 1900. V. 38

Young Maids and Old China. London: 1880's. V. 42

Young Maids and Old China. London: 1888. V. 38

BOURDOIN, W. G.

James McNeill Whistler, the Man and His Work. New York & London: 1901. V. 39

BOURDON, DAVID

Christo: Running Fence, Sonoma and Marin Counties, California 1972-1976. New York: 1978. V. 39; 42; 43

BOUREAU DELANDES, A. F.

An Essay on Maritime Power and Commerce . . . London: 1743. V. 45

BOUREAU DESLANDES, A. F.

The Art of Being Easy at All Times, and In all Places. London: 1724. V. 44

BOURGADE LA DARDY, E. DE

Paraguay; the Land and the Poeple, Natural Wealth and Commercial Capabilities. London: 1892. V. 44

BOURGELAT, CLAUDE

A New System of Horsemanship. London: 1754. V. 37

BOURGEOIS, C.

Views in Switzerland Drawn from Nature by C. Bourgeois, and on Stone by A. Aglio. London: 1822. V. 40; 43

BOURGEOIS, LOUISE 1563-1636

Observations Diverses sur la Sterilite Perte de Fruict Fecondite Accouchements et Maladies des Femmes et Enfants Nouveaux Naiz . . . Paris: 1609. V. 43

Observations Diverses sur la Sterilite Perte de Fruict Foecondite Accouchements et Maladies des Femmes et Enfants Nouveau Naiz . . . (issued with) Recueil des Secrets . . . Auquel sont Contenues ses Plus Rares Experiences Pours Diverses Maladies . . . Paris: 1642-44/35. V. 46

BOURGEOIS, NICOLAS

Voyages Interessans Dans Colonies Francaises Espagnoles, Anglaises, Uc. Contenant des Observations Importantes. Londres: 1788. V. 39

BOURGET, PAUL

Cruelle Enigme. Paris: 1893. V. 46

A Saint and Others. London: 1892. V. 43

BOURGOGNE, ANTOINE DE

Lingvae Vitia & Remedia Emblematice Expressa per Illustrem ac Reuer. Antverpiae. V. 38

Mundi Lapis Lydius sive Vanitas per Veritate Falso Accusata & Convicta. Antwerp: 1639. V. 41; 42

BOURGOIN, JULES

Les Arts, Arabes. Architecture, Menuiserie, Bronzes, Plafonds, Revetements, Marbres, Pavements, Vitraux etc . . . Paris: 1873. V. 41

BOURGOING, J. DE

English Miniature. London: 1928. V. 39

BOURGOING, JEAN FRANCOIS DE

Travels in Spain: Containing a New, Accurate, and Comprehensive View of that Country. London: 1789. V. 37

BOURGUET, PIERRE DU

Early Christian Art. New York: 1971. V. 38

BOURIGNON, ANTONIA

An Abridgement of the Light of the World. London: 1786. V. 44

BOURINOT, JOHN GEORGE

Builders of Nova Scotia. Toronto: 1900. V. 44

Canadian Studies in Comparative Politics. Montreal: 1890. V. 41

Parliamentary Procedure and Practice With an Introductory Account of the Origin and Growth of Parliamentary Insitutions in the Dominion of Canada. Montreal: 1884. V. 41

BOURJAILEY, VANCE

The End of My Life. New York: 1947. V. 43

BOURKE, ALGERNON

Catalogue of Prints after Morland in the Possession of the Hon. Algernon Bourke. London: 1894. V. 46

BOURKE, HANNAH MARIA

O'Donoghue, Prince of Killarney: a Poem. Dublin: 1830. V. 37; 42

BOURKE, JOHN G.

Apache Campaign. New York: 1886. V. 42; 43; 45; 46

Notes and News. N.P.: 1895. V. 41

On the Border with Crook. New York: 1891. V. 37; 38; 39; 41; 42; 43; 44; 45; 46

On the Border with Crook. London: 1892. V. 41

On the Border with Crook. New York: 1892. V. 39; 41

Scatalogic Rites of All Nations. Washington: 1891. V. 39; 42; 44

The Snake-Dance of the Moquis of Arizona. London: 1884. V. 38; 39

The Snake Dance of the Moquis of Arizona. New York: 1884. V. 37; 43

The Urine Dance of the Zuni Indians of New Mexico. Ann Arbor: 1855. V. 38

The Urine Dance of the Zuni Indians of New Mexico. Ann Arbor: 1885. V. 37; 38; 39; 41; 42

BOURKE, JOHN GREGORY

On the Border with Crook. New York: 1891. V. 37

BOURKE, RICHARD S.

St. Petersburg and Moscow; a Visit to the Court of the Czar. London: 1846. V. 46

BOURKE, THOMAS

A Concise History of the Moors in Spain; from Their Invasion of that Kingdom to Their Final Expulsion from It. London: 1811. V. 43

BOURKE, ULICK J.

The College Irish Grammar. Dublin: 1865. V. 39

BOURKE-WHITE, MARGARET

Dear Featherland, Rest Quietly. New York: 1946. V. 37

Eyes on Russia. New York: 1931. V. 45

Shooting the Russian War. New York: 1942. V. 37

BOURN, BENJAMIN

A Sure Guide to Hell. London: 1750. V. 46

BOURN, DANIEL

Some Brief Remarks Upon Mr. Jacob's Treatise on Wheel Carriages. London: 1773. V. 38

A Treatise Upon Wheel-Carriages. London: 1763. V. 38

BOURNE, BENJAMIN FRANKLIN

The Captive in Patagonia; or, Life Among the Giants. Boston: 1853. V. 37; 40; 45

BOURNE, C. E.

The Heroes of African Discovery and Adventure Since the Death of Livingstone. London: 1900. V. 40

BOURNE, CHARLES

The Trial of Lieutenant Charles Bourne, Upon the Prosecution of Sir James Wallace, Knt. for an Assault . . . London: 1793. V. 42

BOURNE, EULALIA

Blue Colt. Flagstaff: 1979. V. 39

BOURNE, GEORGE

Change in the Village. London: 1912. V. 40

A Condensed Anti-Slavery Bible Argument by a Citizen of Virginia. New York: 1845. V. 42

The Picture of Quebec. Quebec: 1829. V. 38

BOURNE, HENRY

The History of Newcastle upon Tyne. Newcastle upon Tyne: 1736. V. 45

BOURNE, JOHN C.

Bourne's London & Birmingham Railway. London: 1970. V. 40

A Catechism of the Steam Engine . . . London: 1868. V. 41

Drawings of the London and Birmingham Railway . . . London: 1839. V. 37; 39; 41; 46

The History and Description of the Great Western Railway. London: 1843. V. 38

A Treatise on the Steam Engine In Its Application to Mines, Mills, Steam Navigation, and Railways. London: 1846. V. 40; 45

A Treatise on the Screw Propeller, with Various Suggestions of Improvement. London: 1852. V. 40

A Treatise on the Steam Engine and Its Application to . . . Steam Navigation . . . London: 1866. V. 39

BOURNE, RANDOLPH

History of a Literary Radical and Other Essays. New York: 1920. V. 38

BOURNE, VINCENT

Miscellaneous Poems . . . London: 1772. V. 42; 43; 45

Poematia, Latine Partim Scripta. London: 1764. V. 38

BOURQUIE, M.

Refutation d'une Lettre Anonime qui a Pour Titre Response a la Lettre au Sujet des Accouchemens des Femmes fits par les Hommes. Brussels: 1755. V. 38

BOURRIENNE, LOUIS ANTOINE FAUVELET DE

Memoirs of Napoleon Bonaparte. Edinburgh: 1830. V. 38; 39

Memoirs of Napoleon Bonaparte. London: 1836. V. 41; 46

Memoirs of Napoleon Bonaparte. Glasgow: 184-? V. 42

Memoirs of Napoleon Bonaparte. London: 1885. V. 38

BOURRIT, MARC THEODORE

A Relation of a Journey to the Glaciers in the Dutchy of Savoy . . . Norwich: 1775. V. 43

A Relation of a Journey to the Glaciers in the Dutchy of Savoy. Norwich: 1776. V. 43

BOUTCHER HALLORAN, L.

Rescued Fragments of Cabin Memorandums. Plymouth: 1826. V. 40

BOUTCHER, WILLIAM

A Treatise on Forest Trees. Edinburgh: 1775. V. 38; 39; 40; 46

A Treatise on Fruit-Trees . . . Dublin: 1776. V. 43

A Treatise on Forest Trees . . . Dublin: 1784. V. 37; 44

BOUTELL, CHARLES

Monumental Brasses and Slabs. London: 1847. V. 39; 41

The Monumental Brasses of England. London: 1849. V. 41; 42; 43

BOUTELL'S Heraldry. London: and New York: 1958. V. 46

BOUTERWEK, FRIEDRICH

Immanuel Kant. Hamburg: 1805. V. 40; 41; 45

BOUTET, CLAUDE

The Art of Painting in Miniature . . . London: 1752. V. 45

BOUTET DE MONVEL, MAURICE 1851-1926

Jeanne d'Arc. Paris: 1896. V. 45

BOUTHILLIER, DENIS

Responce des Vrays Catholiqves Francois, a l'Avertissement des Catholiques Anglois, pour l'Exclusion du Roy de Nauarre de la Couronne de France. Paris?: 1588. V. 44

BOUTIER, PIERRE DE

Traicte de la Navigation et des Voyages de Descouverte & Conqueste Modernes & Principalement des Francois. V. 45

BOUTLER, HUGH

Letters Written by His Excellency, Hugh Boulter, D.D., Lord Primate of All Ireland, to Several an Account of the Most Interesting Transactions Which Passed in Ireland . . . Oxford: 1769/70. V. 43

Letters . . . to Several Ministers of State in England, and Some Others. Dublin: 1770. V. 43

BOUTLON, M. P. W.

Remarks Concerning Certain Pictures Supposed to be Photographs of Early Date. London: 1865. V. 38

BOUTON, NATHANIEL

Provincial and State Papers of New Hampshire . . . 1867-1943. V. 42

BOUTRAYS, RAOUL 1552-1630

Lvtetia . . . Adiuncta est Descriptio Lutetiae Parisiorum, Authore Eustathio a Knobelsdorf Pruteno. Paris: 1611. V. 37; 39

BOUVERIE, BARTHOLEMEW

The Eton Miscellany . . . Eton: 1827. V. 40

bouvet, f.

bONNARD: THE cOMPLETE gRAPHIC wORK. London. V. 46

Bonnard: the Complete Graphic Work. London: 1981. V. 46

BOVA, B.

The Star Conquerors. 1959. V. 44

BOVELL, J. R.

Report of the Results Obtained on the Experimental Fields, at Dodds Reformatory, 1895. Barbados: 1896. V. 39

BOVILL, E. W.

Missions to the Niger. 1964-66. V. 43; 46

BOVILLE, E. W.

Missions to the Niger. London: 1964, 1966. V. 39

BOVINI, GIUSEPPE

Ravena Mosaics. 1956. V. 42

BOVSHOVER, JOSEPH 1873-1915

To the Toilers and Other Verses. Berkeley Heights: 1929. V. 41

THE BOW in the Cloud; or, the Negro's Memorial. London: 1834. V. 37

BOWDEN, AMBROSE

A Treatise on Dry Rot, In Which are Described, The Nature and Causes of that Disease in Ships, Houses, Mills, &c . . . London: 1815. V. 39; 46

BOWDEN, J.

Observations by a Protestant on a Profession of Catholic Faith by a Clergyman from Baltimore, and with the Authority of the Right Rev. Bishop Carroll. New York: 1816. V. 43

BOWDEN, JAMES

The History of the Society of Friends in America. London: 1850. V. 40

BOWDEN, JOHN

A Letter, from John Bowden . . . to the Reverend Ezra Stiles, D.D., LL.D., President, Yale College. Occasioned by Some Passages Concerning Church Government, in an Ordination Sermon, Preached at New-London . . . (with) A Second Letter from John Bowden . . . New Haven: 1788, 1789. V. 38

BOWDEN, W.

Peculiar Mode of Treatment of the Cucumber During the Winter Season. Wallingford. V. 39

BOWDICH, T. E.

An Introduction to the Ornithology of Cuvier for the Use of Students and Travellers. Paris: 1821. V. 43

BOWDICH, THOMAS EDWARD 1791-1824

An Essay on the Superstitions, Customs and Arts, Common to the Ancient Abyssinians, and Ashanties. Paris: 1821. V. 41; 44

Excursions in Madeira and Porto Santo, During the Autumn of 1823, While on His Third Voyage to Africa . . . London: 1824. V. 38; 41

Excursions in Madeira and Porto Santo, During the Autumn of 1823, While on His Third Voyage to Africa. London: 1825. V. 38; 45

Mission from Cape Coast Castle to Ashantee. London: 1819. V. 46

Mission from Cape Coast Castle to Ashantee . . . London: 1819. V. 45

Taxidermy . . . for the Use of Museums and Travellers. London: 1820. V. 38

BOWDITCH, CHARLES

The Numeration, Calendar Systems and AStronomical Knowledge of the Maya. Cambridge: 1910. V. 37; 39

BOWDITCH, HENRY I.

Consumption in New England and Elsewhere or Soil-Moisture One of Its Chief Causes. Boston: 1868. V. 44

BOWDITCH, HENRY INGERSOLL 1808-1892

Memoir of Nathaniel Bowditch by His Son. Boston: 1839. V. 38

Memoir of Nathaniel Bowditch by His Son. Boston: 1840. V. 38

BOWDITCH, HENRY J.

Memoir of Nathaniel Bowditch - Prepared for the Young . . . Boston: 1841. V. 42

BOWDITCH, NATHANIAL

The Ether Controversy. Vindication of the Hospital Report of 1848. Boston: 1848. V. 46

BOWDITCH, NATHANIEL 1773-1838

Bowditch's Useful Tables. New York: 1844. V. 43

Methods of Computing the Orbit of a Comet or Planet. Boston: 1834. V. 37; 44

The New American Practical Navigator. Newburyport: 1802. V. 38; 39; 45

The New American Practical Navigator. Newburyport: 1807. V. 40

The New American Practical Navigator. New York: 1817. V. 41

The New American Practical Navigator . . . New York: 1821. V. 42

The New American Practical Navigator . . . New York: 1848. V. 46

The New American Practical Navigator . . . New York: 1863. V. 41; 42

BOWDITCH, NATHANIEL I.

Memoir of Nathaniel Bowditch. By His Son. Boston: 1840. V. 37; 42; 45

Memoir of Nathaniel Bowditch. By His Son. Cambridge: 1884. V. 37

BOWDITCH, NATHANIEL INGERSOLL

A History of the Massachusetts General Hospital. With a Continuation to 1872. Boston: 1872. V. 45

BOWDITCH, THOMAS EDWARD

Excursions in Madeira and Porto Santo, During the Autumn of 1823, While on His Third Voyage to Africa. London: 1825. V. 42

BOWDLER, JANE

Poems and Essays. Dublin: 1787. V. 40

Poems and Essays . . . Bath: 1798. V. 42

Poems and Essays, by the Late Miss Bowdler. Bath: 1807. V. 42

BOWDLER, JOHN

Select Pieces in Verse and Prose. London: 1816. V. 39; 42

Select Pieces in Verse and Prose. London: 1817. V. 37; 40

BOWDLER, THOMAS

Anecdotes of the Late Lieut. Genl. Villettes Commander of the Forces and Lieutenant Governor of the Island of Jamaica. Jamaica?: 1808? V. 40

Letters Written in Holland, in the Months of September and October, 1787. London: 1788. V. 43

A Short View of the Life and Character of Lieutenant General Villettes, Late Lieutenant-Governor and Commander of the Forces in Jamaica. Bath: 1815. V. 38; 42

BOWDOIN COLLEGE. ATHENAEAN SOCIETY. LIBRARY.

Catalogue of the Library of the Athenaean Society of Bowdoin College. August, 1830. Brunswick: 1830. V. 39

BOWDOIN, JAMES

A Philosophical Discourse, Addressed to the American Academy of Arts and Sciences . . . Boston: 1780. V. 39; 40

BOWDOIN, W. G.

The Rise of the Bookplate, Being an Exemplification of the Art, Signified by Various Bookplates from Its Earliest to Most Recent Practice. New York: 1910. V. 41

BOWE, NICOLA GORDON

Hary Clark: His Graphic Art. Mountrath: 1983. V. 37; 39

BOWEN, A. W.

A Portrait and Biographical Record of Allen and van Wert Counties, Ohio. Chicago: 1896. V. 37

BOWEN, ABEL

Naval Monument . . . Boston: 1816. V. 42

BOWEN, C. E.

Pussy's London Life. London. V. 42

BOWEN, CATHERINE DRINKER

John Adams and the American Revolution. Boston: 1950. V. 39

BOWEN, CLARENCE W.

The History of Woodstock, Connecticut. Norwood: 1926. V. 46

BOWEN, CLARENCE WINTHROP

The Boundary Disputes of Connecticut. Boston: 1882. V. 44

The History of the Centennial Celebration of the Inauguration of George Washington. New York: 1892. V. 38

BOWEN, DANIEL

History of Philadelphia. Philadelphia: 1839. V. 41; 42; 43

BOWEN, ELE

The Coal Regions of Pennsylvania. Pottsville: 1848. V. 42

BOWEN, ELIZABETH

Ann Lee's and Other Stories. London: 1926. V. 38

Collected Impressions. New York: 1950. V. 46

The Death of the Heart. London: 1938. V. 37

Encounters: Stories. London: 1923. V. 38; 45

The Faber Book of Modern Stories. London: 1937. V. 41

The Hotel. London: 1927. V. 40

The Hotel. New York: MCMXXVIII. V. 37

The House in Paris. London: 1935. V. 40

Joining Charles and Other Stories. London: 1929. V. 40; 43; 45

The Last September. London: 1929. V. 45

Seven Winters. Dublin: 1942. V. 39

BOWEN, EMANUEL

Britannia Depicta. London: 1730. V. 40

BOWEN, FRANCIS 1811-1890

The Principles of Political Economy applied to the Condition, the Resources and the Institutions of the American People. Boston: 1859. V. 37

BOWEN, FRANK C.

America Sails to the Seas. New York: 1938. V. 42

The Golden Age of Sail. London: 1925. V. 39; 41

Mail and Passenger Steamships of the 19th Century . . . London: 1928. V. 41

The Sea. Its History and Romance. London. V. 45

The Sea: Its History and Romance. London: 1924-26. V. 41

The Sea, Its History and Romance. New York: 1927. V. 37

BOWEN, H.

The Life and Times of 'Ali Ibn 'Isa. 'The Good Vizier'. Cambridge: 1928. V. 39

BOWEN, JAMES LORENZO

History of the Thirty-Seventh Regiment, Mass., Volunteers in the Civil War . . . Holyoke: 1884. V. 42

BOWEN, MELESINA

Ystradffin, a descriptive poem, with an appendix, containing historical and explanatory notes. London: 1839. V. 37

BOWEN, NATHANIEL

A Pastoral Letter, on the Religious Instruction of the Slaves of Members of the Protestant Episcopal Church in the State of South Carolina. Charleston: 1835. V. 43

BOWEN, THOMAS

An Historical account of the Origin, Progress and Present State of Bethelm Hospital . . . London: 1783. V. 39; 44

An Historical Statement of Treatment for Insanity as It was Carried Out in the Late 18th Century. London: 1783. V. 38

An Historical Account of the Origin, Progress and Present State of Bethlem Hospital . . . N.P.: 1783. V. 41

BOWER, ALEXANDER

An Account of the Life of James Beattie, LL.D. Professor of Moral Philosophy and Logic, Aberdeen. In which are occasionally given characters of the principal literary men, and a sketch of the state of literature in Scotland during . . . London: 1804. V. 37

BOWER, ARCHIBALD 1686-1766

The History of the Popes, from the Foundation of the See of Rome, to the Present Time. London: 1749-66. V. 44

BOWERBANK, J. S.

A Monograph of the British Spongiadae. London: 1882. V. 38

A Monograph of the British Spongiadae. London: 1864-82. V. 37; 38; 43

BOWERS, C. G.

Rhododendrons and Azaleas, Their Origins, Cultivation and Development. New York: 1936. V. 46

BOWERS, EDGAR

The Form of Loss. Denver: 1956. V. 38

BOWERS, FREDSON

Principles of Bibliographical Description. Princeton;: 1949. V. 41

BOWERS, GEORGE M.

Bulletin of the United States Fish Commission. Volume XXIII for 1903. Washington: 1905. V. 46

BOWERS, PAUL C.

Richard Henry Lee and the Continental Congress 1774-1779. Durham. V. 43

BOWERS, RONALD

The Selznick Players. New York: 1976. V. 45

BOWES, JAMES L.

Japanese Marks and Seals. London: 1882. V. 38

Japanese Pottery with Notes Describing the Thoughts and Subjects Employed in Its Decoration and Illustrations from Examples in the Bowes Collection. Liverpool: 1890. V. 42; 45

A Vindication of the Decorated Pottery of Japan. 1891. V. 44

BOWIE, THEODORE

The Carrey Drawings of the Parthenon Sculptures. Bloomington: 1971. V. 40; 42; 44

BOWIE, WILLIAM

The Black Book of Taymouth with Other Papers from the Breadalabane Charter Room. Edinburgh: 1855. V. 41

BOWLE, JOHN

Miscellaneous Pieces of Antient English Poesie. London: 1764. V. 37

BOWLER, GEORGE

Chapel and Church Architecture, with Designs for Parsonages. Boston: 1856. V. 41

BOWLER, THOMAS WILLIAM

The Kafir Wars and the British Settlers in South Africa. London: 1865. V. 39

BOWLES & CARVER

Bowles Universal Display of the Naval Flags of All Nations in the World. London: 1790. V. 41

BOWLES, CARINGTON

The Art of Drawing Without a Master, from the French of the Sieur P.B. London: 1770-75. V. 37

BOWLES, CARRINGTON

Bowles's New Preceptor in Drawing . . . London: 1764. V. 45

Bowles's Compleat Drawing Book. London: 1773. V. 46

The Whole Art of Painting in Water-Colours . . . London: 1773. V. 41

BOWLES, E. A.

My Garden Spring. (with) My Garden in Summer. (with) My Garden in Autumn and Winter. London: 1914-15. V. 46

My Garden in Spring; My Garden in Summer; My Garden in Autumn and Winter. 1914-15. V. 37

BOWLES, EDWARD

Plaine English; or, a Discourse Concerning the Accomodation. London: 1643. V. 42

BOWLES, JANE

In the Summer House. New York: 1954. V. 42

Plain Pleasures. London: 1966. V. 37; 45

BOWLES, JOHN

A Protest Against T. Paine's 'Rights of Man' Addressed to Members of a Book Society, in Consequence of the Vote of Their Committee . . . London: 1792. V. 37; 39

Remarks on Modern Female Manners, as Distinguished by Indifference to Character, and Indecency of Dress. London: 1802. V. 42

A Short Answer to the Declaration of the Persons Calling Themselves the friends of the Liberty of the Press. London: 1793. V. 41

A Third Letter to a British Merchant . . . London: 1797. V. 39

Two Letters Addressed to a British Merchant, a Short Time Before the Meeting of the New Parliament in 1796. London: 1796. V. 39

BOWLES, PAUL

Collected Stories 1939-1976. Santa Barbara: 1979. V. 39; 45; 46

The Delicate Prey: and Other Stories. New York: 1950. V. 39; 46

The Hours After Noon. London: 1959. V. 43

Let It Come Down. New York: 1952. V. 42; 44; 45

A Little Stone. London: 1950. V. 41; 43; 44; 45

Midnight Mass. Santa Barbara: 1981. V. 43; 46

Next to Nothing: Collected Poems 1926-77. Santa Barbara: 1981. V. 43; 46

Scenes. Los Angeles: 1968. V. 45

The Sheltering Sky. 1949. V. 45

The Sheltering Sky. London: 1949. V. 37; 38; 42

The Sheltering Sky. New York: 1949. V. 41; 43; 44; 45

The Sheltering Sky. Norfolk: 1949. V. 37; 39

The Spider's House. New York: 1955. V. 39; 44; 45

The Spider's House. Santa Barbara: 1982. V. 42; 43; 44

The Thicket of Spring. Los Angeles: 1972. V. 45

Things Gone and Things Still Here. Santa Barbara: 1977. V. 43

Two Poems. New York: 1933. V. 44

Two Years Beside the Strait - Tangier Journal 1987-1989. London: 1990. V. 44

Yallah. New York: 1957. V. 37; 43; 45; 46

BOWLES, SAMUEL

Across the Continent . . . New York: 1865. V. 42

Across the the Continent: A Summer's Journey to the Rocky Mountains, the Mormons, and the Pacific States. Springfield: 1865. V. 40; 41; 42; 45

Across the Continent: A Summers Journey to the Rocky Mountains. Springfield/New York: 1865. V. 38; 39

Our New West. Hartford: 1869. V. 39

A Summer Vacation in the Parks and Mountains of Colorado. Springfield: 1869. V. 45

BOWLES, WILLIAM LISLE

Days Departed; or, Banwell Hill; a Lay of the Severn Sea. London: 1828. V. 40; 44

Elegy Written at the Hot-Well, Bristol. Bath: 1791. V. 39; 41; 42; 45

A Final Appeal to the Literary Public, Relative to Pope, in Reply to Certain Observations of Mr. Roscoe, in His edition of that Poet's Works. London: 1825. V. 37

The Grave of Howard. Salisbury: 1790. V. 39; 41; 42; 45

Lessons in Criticism to William Roscoe, Esq . . . . London: 1826. V. 42; 43

Letters to Lord Byron on a Question of Poetical Criticism. London: 1822. V. 42

Monody, Written at Matlock, October 1791. Salisbury: 1791. V. 39; 42

The Parochial History of Bremhill, in the County of Wilts . . . London: 1828. V. 43

The Picture Verses Written in London, May 28, 1803, Suggested by a Magnificent Landscape of Rubens, in Possession of Sir George Beaumont. London: 1803. V. 37

The Plain Bible, and the Protestant Church of England. Bath: 1818. V. 42

A Poetical Address to the Right Honourable Edmund Burke. London: 1791. V. 39

St. Michaels Mount. Salisbury: 1798. V. 38

St. John in Patmos; a Poem. London: 1832. V. 42

Sonnets (Third Edition), with Other Poems. Bath: 1794. V. 38

Sonnets, and Other Poems. Bath: 1796. V. 40

Sonnets Written Chiefly on Picturesque Spots During a Tour . . . Bath: 1789. V. 37; 38; 39; 41; 42

Two Letters to the Right Hourable Lord Byron, in Answer to His Lordship's Letter . . . . . London: 1821. V. 41

BOWLES, WILLIAM LISLE continued

Verses to John Howard, F.R.S. on His State of Prisons and Lazarettos. Bath: 1789. V. 39; 42

Verses on the Venevolent Institution of the Philanthropic Society, for Protecting and Educating the Children of Vagrants and Criminals. Bath: 1790. V. 39; 42

A Vindication of the Late Editor of Pope's Works, From Some Charges Brought Against Him . . . London: 1821. V. 42

A Voice from St. Peter's and St. Paul's; Being a Few Plain Words Addressed to . . . London: 1823. V. 42

A Word on Cathedral-Oratorios, and Clergy-Magistrates, Addressed to Lord Mountcashel. London: 1830. V. 42

BOWLKER, CHARLES d. 1779

The Art of Angling, and Compleat Fly-Fishing. Birmingham: 1774. V. 42; 43

The Art of Angling, and Compleat Fly-Fishing . . . Birmingham: 1774. V. 39; 43

The Art of Angling; or Compleat Fly-Fisher . . . Birmingham: 1792. V. 43; 46

Bowlker's Art of Angling, Greatly Enlarged and Improved. Ludlow: 1826. V. 39

The Art of Angling. London: 1833. V. 40

The Art of Angling. Ludlow: 1833. V. 39; 42; 45

The Art of Angling. London: 1854. V. 39; 43

The Art of Angling, Rock and Sea-Fishing . . . London: 1740. V. 42

Bowlker's Art of Angling. Ludlow: 1854. V. 43

Bowlker's Art of Angling. Ludlow: 1854. V. 40

BOWMAN, A. S.

The New Skating Rink Journal. Philadelphia: 1884. V. 43

BOWMAN, AMOS

Maps of the Principal Auriferous Creeks in the Cariboo Mining District, British Columbia. Ottawa: 1895. V. 43

BOWMAN, ANNE

Adventures, Wanderings and Sufferings of the Merton Family; or, Life Scenes among the South American Indians. Philadelphia: 1860. V. 37

BOWMAN, F. H.

The Structure of the Wool Fibre in Its Relation to the Use of Wood for Technical Purposes. Manchester: 1885. V. 44

BOWMAN, HENRY

The Churches of the Middle Ages, Being Select Specimens of Early and Middle Pointed Structures With a Few of the Purest Late Pointed Examples. London: 1845-53. V. 39

BOWMAN, HILDEBRAND

The Travels of Hildebrand Bowman, Esquire, into Carnovirria, Taupiniera, Olfactaria, and Auditante, in New Zealand. London: 1778. V. 41

BOWMAN, ROBERT I.

The Galapagos. Berkeley & Los Angeles: 1966. V. 45

BOWMAN, S. M.

Sherman and His Compaigns: a Military Biography. New York: 1865. V. 45

BOWMAN, WILLIAM

Lectures on the Parts Concerned in the Operations on the Eye, and on the Structure of the Retina, Delivered at the Royal Opthalmic Hospital, Moorfields, June, 1847. London: 1849. V. 43

Muscle and Muscular Motion . . . London: 1842. V. 43

Muscle and Muscular Motion. London: 1942. V. 41

BOWNAS, SAMUEL 1676-1753

An Account of the Life, Travels and Christian Experiences in the Ministry of Samuel Bownas. London: 1756. V. 37; 38; 40; 41; 42; 43; 44; 45

An Account of the Life, Travels and Christian Experiences in the Work of the Ministry of . . . Philadelphia: 1759. V. 42

An Account of the Life, Travels and Christian Experiences in the Work of the Ministry of . . . Stanford: 1805. V. 37; 39; 42; 45

An Account of the Captivity of Elizabeth Hanson, Late of Kachecky in New-England: Who, With Four of Her Children, and Servant Maid, was Taken Captive by the Indians, and Carried into Canada. London: 1787. V. 37

BOWNESS, A.

The Complete Sculpture of Barbara Hepworth 1960-69. London: 1971. V. 39; 43; 46

BOWNESS, W.

Rustic Studies, in the Westmorland Dialect . . . London: 1868. V. 45

BOWNMAN, HEATH

Hoosier. Illustrated from Photographs by the Author. Indianapolis/New York: (1941). V. 37

BOWNOCKER, JOHN ADAMS

The Occurrence and Exploitation of Petroleum and Natural Gas in Ohio. Columbus: 1903. V. 44

BOWRING, JOHN

The Decimal System in Numbers, Coins and Accounts: Especially with Reference to the Decimalisation of the Currency and Accountancy of the United Kingdom. London: 1854. V. 41

The Kingdom and People of Siam; with a Narrative of the Mission to that Country in 1855. London: 1857. V. 38; 41; 42; 43; 45

Matins and Vespers; with Hymns and Occasional Devotional Pieces. London: 1823. V. 42

Matins and Vespers: With Hymns and Occasional Devotional Pieces. London: 1828. V. 37

Minor Morals for Young People. London: 1834-35-39. V. 43

Minor Morals for Young People. London: & Edinburgh: 1834/35/39. V. 46

Mirror Morals for Young People. London & Edinburgh: 1834-39. V. 38

Poetry of the Magyars, Preceded by a Sketch of the Language and Literature of Hungary and Transylvania. London: 1830. V. 45; 46

Servian Popular Poetry. London: 1827. V. 37

Specimens of the Russian Poets: With Preliminary Remarks and Biographical Notices. London: 1821. V. 41

Specimens of the Russian Poets, with Preliminary Remarks and Biographical Notices. Boston: 1822. V. 41

Specimens of Russian Poets. London: 1821/1823. V. 37

Specimens of the Polish Poets; With Notes . . . On the Literature of Poland. London: 1827. V. 37

A Visit to the Philippine Islands by the Late Governor of Hong Kong, H.B.M.'s Plenipotentiary in China . . . London: 1859. V. 38; 40

BOWYER, ROBERT

An Illustrated Record of Important Events in the Annals of Europe During the Years 1812-15. London: 1815-16. V. 45

An Impartial Historical, Narrative of Those Momentous Events Which Have Taken Place in this Country During the Period from the Year 1816 to 1823. London: 1823. V. 38; 40

BOX, CHARLES

The Theory and Practice of Cricket, from Its Origin to the Present Time; with Critical and Explanatory Notes Upon the Laws of the Game. London: 1868. V. 38

BOX, EDGAR

Death Before Bedtime. New York: 1953. V. 43

BOX, JAMES

Adventures and Explorations in New and Old Mexico. New York: 1869. V. 39

BOX, MICHAEL JAMES

Capt. James Box's Adventures and Explorations in New and Old Mexico. New York: 1869. V. 37; 38; 40; 43; 45

BOXER, C. R.

The Dutch Seaborne Empire 1600-1800. London: 1965. .V. 43

Fidalgos in the Far East 1550-1770. The Hague: 1948. V. 41

The Great Ship from Amacon: Annals of Macao and the Old Japan Trade, 1555-1640. Lisbon: 1959. V. 37; 42

Jan Compagnie in Japan 1600-1850. An Essay on the Cultural, Artistic and Scientific Influence Exercised by the Hollanders in Japan from the Seventeenth to the Nineteenth Centuries. The Hague: 1950. V. 41

BOXER, CHARLES R.

The Tragic History of the Sea, 1589-1622. (with) Further Selections from the Tragic History of the Sea, 1559-1565. Cambridge: 1959/68. V. 46

BOXER, F. N.

Hunter's Hand Book of the Victoria Bridge, Illustrated with Wood-Cuts. Montreal: 1860. V. 43

BOXHORN, MARCUS ZUERIUS

Arcana Imperii Detecta . . . London: 1701. V. 42

BOXWOOD & GRAVER

A Miscellany of Blocks. London: 1958. V. 46

A Miscellany of Blocks. Westerham: 1958. V. 41

BOYAJIAN, ZABELLE C.

Gilgamesh. A Dream of the Eternal Quest. London: 1924. V. 45

BOYCE, A. P.

Boyce's Modern Ornaments and Interior Decorator. Boston: 1874. V. 37

BOYCE, J.

A Vindication of the Rev. Mr. Alexander Osborn in Reference to the Affairs of the North of Ireland in Which Some Mistakes Concerning Him . . . London: 1690. V. 43

BOYCEAU, JACQUES

Traite du Jardinage Selon les Raisons de la Nature et de l'Art. Paris: 1638. V. 38

BOYD, AGNES

The Belfast Boy, by J.A.P. London: 1912. V. 37

BOYD, BELLE

Belle Boyd in Camp and Prison. London: 1865. V. 37
Belle Boyd in Camp and Prison. New York: 1865. V. 37

BOYD, CHARLES

The Turkish Interpreter or a New Grammar of the Turkish Language Respectfully Inscribed to the Right Honorable the Earl of Aberdeen K.T. Secretary of State for Foreign Affairs. Paris & London: 1842. V. 38; 43

BOYD, DAVID

A History: Greeley and the Union Colony of Colorado. Greeley: 1890. V. 40

BOYD, E.

Saints and Saint Makers of New Mexico. Santa Fe: 1946. V. 37; 42; 43

BOYD, E. R.

A Yarn of War. Palestine and France 1917-1918. Glasgow: 1919. V. 45

BOYD HARTE, GLYNN

Les Sardines a l'Huile de Glynn Boyd Harte. 1985. V. 40
Temples of Power: The Architecture of Electricity in London. 1979. V. 40; 45

BOYD, HENRY

Poems, Chiefly Dramatic and Lyric, by . . . Dublin & London: 1793-1805. V. 38

BOYD, HUGH

The Indian Observer. Calcutta: 1795. V. 40; 41
The Indian Observer . . . London: 1798. V. 40

BOYD, JAMES

Drums. New York: 1928. V. 37; 41; 42; 43; 44; 46
The Free Company Presents: a Collection of Plays About the Meaning of America. New York: 1941. V. 39
Long Hunt. New York: 1930. V. 39

BOYD, JAMES D.

The Drawings of Sir Frank Brangwyn, R.A. 1867-1956. Leigh-on-Sea, England: 1967. V. 44

BOYD, JAMES P.

Recent Indian Wars, Under the Lead of Sitting Bull and Other Chiefs . . . N.P.: 1891. V. 40

BOYD, JOHN G.

Faraday Induction Electric Light: a Simple Story of Incandescent Electric Lighting. St. Louis: 1904. V. 38

BOYD, JOHN P.

Documents and Facts, Relative to Military Events During the Late War. Boston?: 1816? V. 41

BOYD, JULIAN P.

Indian Treaties Printed by Benjamin Franklin 1736-1762. Philadelphia: 1938. V. 37

BOYD, LOUISE A.

The Coast of Northeast Greenland. New York: 1948. V. 43

BOYD, MARK

Reminiscences of Fifty Years. London: 1871. V. 43

BOYD, NANCY

Distressing Dialogues. New York: 1924. V. 46

BOYD, PETER

History of Northern West Virginia Panhandle Embracing Ohio, Marshall, Brooke and Hancock Counties. Indianpolis: 1927. V. 46

BOYD, ROBERT

Grace and Truth; or, Appeals to the Heart. Chicago: 1870. V. 43
The Office, Powers and Jurisdiction of His Majesty's Justices of the Peace, and Commissioners of Supply. Edinburgh: 1787. V. 38

BOYD SMITH, E.

So Long Ago. Boston: 1944. V. 41

BOYD, WILLIAM

Brazzaville Beach. London: 1990. V. 43; 45
A Good Man in Africa. London: 1981. V. 38; 46

A Good man in Africa. New York: 1982. V. 42; 44
An Ice Cream War. London: 1982. V. 45; 46
An Ice Cream War. New York: 1983. V. 44
The New Confessions. New York: 1988. V. 41; 46
On the Yankee Station and Other Stories. London: 1981. V. 38
On the Yankee Station. New York: 1984. V. 41
School Ties: a Play. London: 1985. V. 41
Stars and Bars. London: 1984. V. 46

BOYD, WILLIAM H.

Boyd's Co-Partnership and Residence Business Directory of Philadelphia City..1895. Philadelphia: 1895. V. 41

BOYDELL, J.

Mr. Boydell's Exhibition of Drawings from Many of the Most Capital Pictures in England . . . London: 1780. V. 40

BOYDELL, JOHN

A Catalogue of that Magnificent and Truly Valuable Collection of Pictures (with the Prices they sold for, and name of the purchasers) Being the Productions of the Greatest Artists of the British School . . . London: 1805. V. 38; 41
A Collection of Prints from the Pictures Painted for the Purpose of Illustrating the Dramatic Works of Shakespeare by the Artists of Great Britain. London: 1803. V. 41
An History of the River Thames. London: 1794. V. 45
A History of the River Thames. London: 1794-96. V. 42; 45

BOYDEN, CHARLES M.

The Cruise of the Snapshot, Chicago to Memphis 1897. Chicago?: 1898. V. 44

BOYER, A.

The Royal Dictionary/ Le Dictionnaire Royal, French and English, English and French. London: 1796. V. 46

BOYER, ABEL

Characters of the Virtues and Vices of the Age. London: 1695. V. 40
The Compleat French Master, for Ladies and Gentlemen. London: 1699. V. 46
The Complete French Master for Ladies and Gentlemen. London: 1756. V. 38
The Complete French Master for Ladies and Gentlemen. London: 1764. V. 41
Dictionnaire Royal, Francois et Anglois. La Haye: 1702. V. 39
The English Theoprastus: of the Manners of the Age, being the Modern Chracters of the Court, the Town, and the City. London: 1706. V. 37
Memoirs of the Life and Negociations of Sir W. Temple, Bar. London: 1714. V. 40; 42; 43
The Royal Dictionary Abridged. London: 1751. V. 41
The Wise and Ingenious Companion, French and English. London: 1707. V. 45

BOYER, ALEXIS

The Lectures of Boyer Upon Diseases of the Bones, Arranged into a Systematic Treatise by A. Richerand . . . Philadelphia: 1805. V. 41
A Treatise on Surgical Diseases, and the Operations Suited to Them. New York: 1815-16. V. 44; 45; 46

BOYER, C. S.

The Diatomaceae of Philadelphia Vicinity. Philadelphia: 1916. V. 38

BOYER, JEAN BAPTISTE DE

The Jewish Spy. London: 1739. V. 38

BOYER, JOHN

A Journal of Wayne's Campaign. Cincinnati: 1866. V. 45

BOYER, LANSON

From the Orient to the Occident; or L. Boyer's Trip Across the Rocky Mountains in April 1877. New York: 1878. V. 43

BOYER, MARY G.

Arizona in Literature. Glendale: 1934. V. 38

BOYKIN, EDWARD M.

The Boys and Girls Stories of the War. Richmond: 1863? V. 39; 43
The Falling Flag. Evacuation of Richmond, Retreat and Surrender at Appomattox. New York: 1874. V. 37

BOYLE, ANDREW

The Climate of Treason. London: 1979. V. 40

BOYLE, CHARLES

Dr. Bentley's Dissertation on the Epistles of Phalaris, and the Fables of Aesop, Examin'd. London: 1698. V. 40; 45

BOYLE, E. M.

Records of the Town of Limavady, 1609-1808. Londonderry: 1912. V. 37

BOYLE, E. V.

Days and Hours in a Garden . . . London: 1896. V. 41

BOYLE, ELEANOR VERE

Beauty and the Beast. London: 1875. V. 42

Child's Play. London: 1852. V. 45

Child's Play. London: 1864. V. 42

A Dream Book. London: 1870. V. 37; 45

BOYLE, FREDERICK

Camp Notes. Stories of Sport and Adventure in Asia, Africa and America. London: 1874. V. 46

Ride Across a Continent: a Personal Narrative of Wanderings through Nicaragua and Costa Rica. London: 1868. V. 38; 46

Through Fanteeland to Coomassie. London: 1874. V. 39

BOYLE, J. R.

The Early History of the Town and Port of Hedon in the East Riding of the County of York. Hull and York: 1895. V. 45

The Lost Towns of the Humber. Hull: 1889. V. 41; 44

BOYLE, JACK

Boston Blackie. 1919. V. 39

BOYLE, KAY 1903-

The Crazy Hunter. New York: 1940. V. 41; 42; 46

Death of a Man. London: 1936. V. 38

Fifty Stories. New York: 1980. V. 41; 42

The First Lover and Other Stories. New York: 1933. V. 41

A Glad Day. Norfolk: 1938. V. 37

Monday Night. New York: (19138). V. 37

Plagued by the Nightingale. New York: 1931. V. 39; 41; 42

A Statement (for El Greco and William Carlos Williams). 1932. V. 39

The Underground Woman. Garden City: 1975. V. 41; 42

Wedding Day and Other Stories. New York: 1930. V. 38; 42

The White Horses of Vienna and Other Stories. New York: 1936. V. 46

Year Before Last. New York: 1932. V. 41; 42

BOYLE, MARY

Aesop Redivivus. London: 1890. V. 41; 43

BOYLE, MARY LOUISA

The State Prisoner. London: 1837. V. 45; 46

BOYLE, P.

Museum Britannicum; or, A Display in Thirty-Two Plates, in Antiquities and Natural Curiosities. London: 1791. V. 38

BOYLE, PETER

Boyle's Court and Country Guide, and Town Visiting Directory, Corrected Up to January 16, 1804. (with) Boyle's City & Commercial Companion to the Court Guide . . . London: 1804. V. 40

The Publican's Daily Companion; or, Plain and Interesting Advice tot he Keepers of Public Houses on Subjects of the Greatest Improtance to Their Own Welfare and to the Health . . . London: 1795. V. 46

BOYLE, ROBERT 1627-1691

The Aerial Noctiluca; or Some New Phoenomena . . . (with) New Experiments, and Observations, Made Upon the Icy Noctiluca. London: 1680/81-82. V. 45

The Aerial Noctiluca . . . (with) New Experiments and Observations, Made Upon the Icy Noctiluca. London: 1681-82. V. 41

Certain Physiological Essays and Other Tracts. London: 1669. V. 38

Continuation of New Experiments Physico-Mechanical, Touching the Spring and Weight of the Air, and Their Effects. Oxford: 1669. V. 44

A Defence of Natural and Revealed Religion . . . London: 1737. V. 41; 43; 45

A Disquisition About the Final Causes of Natural Things Wherein It Is Inquir'd Whether, and (If At All) With What Cautions, a Naturalist Should Admit Them? London: 1688. V. 40; 41; 42

Essays of the Strange Subtilty Determinate Nature Great Efficacy of Effluviums. London: 1673. V. 39; 46

Experiments and Considerations Touching Colours . . . London: 1664. V. 42

Experiments and Considerations Touching Colours . . . London: 1670. V. 42

Experiments, Notes &c. About the Mechanical Origine or Production of Divers Particular Duties. London: 1676. V. 37; 39

Experiments and Considerations About the Porosity of Bodies, in Two Essays. London: 1684. V. 41; 45

General Heads for the Natural History of a Country, Great or Small . . . London: 1692. V. 42

The General History of the Air, Designed and Begun. London: 1692. V. 39

The Hon. Robert Boyle's 'Occasionall Reflections.' London: 1808. V. 40

Hydrosatical Paradoxes. Oxford: 1666. V. 39; 40

Introductio ad Historiam Qualitatum Particularium. Geneva: 1680. V. 40; 43

The Martyrdom of Theodora, and of Didymus. London: 1687. V. 43

Medicina Hydrostatica; or, Hydrostaticks Applyed to the Materia Medica. London: 1690. V. 38; 45

Medicinal Experiments . . . London: 1712. V. 37

The Method of Learning to Draw in Perspective Made Easy and Fully Explained. London: 1735. V. 45

New Experiments, and Observations, Made Upon the Icy Noctiluca. London: 1682. V. 38

New Experiments Physico-Mechanical Touching the Air. London: 1682. V. 37; 40

New Experiments and Observations Touching Cold, or, An Experimental History of Cold, Begun. London: 1683. V. 40; 43

Occasional Reflections Upon Several Subjects. London: 1665. V. 39; 40; 42; 43; 44; 45; 46

Of the Reconcileableness of Specific Medicines to the Corpuscular Philosophy. London: 1685. V. 40; 41; 45

Of the High Veneration Man's Intelelct Owes to God; Peculiarly fro His Wisedom and Power. London: 1685. V. 37

The Origine of Formes and Qualities. Oxford: 1666. V. 42

Paradoxa Hydrostatica Novis Experimentis (Maximam Partem Physicis ac Facilibus Evicta . . . Nuper ex Anglico Sermone in Latinum Versa. Oxonii: 1669. V. 38

The Philosophical Works of . . . London: 1725. V. 44

The Philosophical Works . . . abridged, methodized and disposed under the general heads of physics, statics, pneumatics, natural history, chymistry, and medicine. The whole illustrated with notes, containing the improvements made in the several parts . . . London: 1738. V. 37

Salt Water Sweetened. London: 1683. V. 38

The Sceptical Chymist . . . Oxford: 1680. V. 41

The Sceptical Chymist; or, Chymico-Physical Doubts and Paradoxes. London: 1965. V. 40

Short Memoirs for the Natural Experimental History of Mineral Waters. London: 1684-5. V. 43

Some Motives and Incentives to the Love of God. London: 1659. V. 38

Some Considerations Touching the Usefulnesse of Experimental Naturall Philosophy . . . Oxford: 1662/63. V. 42

Some Motives and Incentives to the Love of God, Pathetically Discours'd of in a Letter to a Friend. London: 1663. V. 43

Some Considerations Touching the Usefulnesse of Experimental Natruall Philosophy . . . Oxford: 1663. V. 37; 41; 45

Some Motives and Incentives to the Love of God, Pathetically Discours'd of in a Letter to a Friend. (with) Som Considerations Touching the Style of the H. Scriptures. London: 1663-61. V. 38

Some Considerations Touching the Usefulnesse of Experimental Natural Philosophy. Oxford: 1664. V. 42

Some Considerations Touching the Usefulness of Experimental Philosophy (with) . . . the Second Tome. Oxford: 1664, 1671. V. 38; 42; 46

Some Considerations Touching the Usefulnesse of Experimental Natural Philosophy Propos'd in a Familiar Discourse to a Friend by Way of Invitation to the Study of It . . . Oxford: 1664-1671. V. 37; 41

Some Considerations About the Reconcileableness of Reason and Religion. London: 1675. V. 41; 42

Some Motives and Incentives to the Love of God, Pathetically Discours'd of in a Letter to a Friend. London: 1678. V. 39

Some Considerations Touching the Style of the H. Scriptures. London: 1661. V. 37

Tentamina Quaedam Physiologica Diversis Temporibus & Occasionibus Conscripta, Cum Historia Fluiditatis et Firmitatis. Genevae: 1680. V. 40

The Theological Works . . . London: 1715. V. 43

Tracts . . . About Cosmicall Qualities of Things; Cosmicall Suspicions; The Temperature of the Subetrraneall Regions; The Temperature of the Submarine Regions; The Bottom of the Sea . . . Oxford: 1671. V. 39

Tracts . . . Containing New Experiments, Touching the Relation Betwixt Flame and Air. 1672. V. 38; 45

Tracts . . . Containing New Experiments, Touching the Relation Betwixt Flame and Air. London: 1672. V. 37; 40; 41; 42; 45

Tracts . . . Containing New Experiments, Touching the Relations Between Flame and Air, . . . London: 1672. V. 38

Tracts: Containing I. Suspicions About Some Hidden Qualities of the Air; with an Appendix Touching Celestial magnets and Some Other Particulars. II. Animadversions Upon Mr. Hobbe's Problemata de Vacuo. III. A Discourse of the Cause of Attraction by . . . London: 1674. V. 46

Tracts Consisting of Observations About the Saltiness of the Sea. London: 1674. V. 38; 40; 41; 42; 43; 45

The Works. London: 1744. V. 37; 38; 41

The Works. London: 1772. V. 42; 45; 46

The Works. London: 1965-66. V. 39

BOYLE, ROBERT & SON

The 'Boyle' System of Ventilation. London: 1899. V. 42

BOYLE, ROGER

Poems on most of the Festivals of the Church. (Lodnon): 1681. V. 37

BOYLE, T. CORAGHESSAN

Descent of Man. 1979. V. 43

Descent of Man. Boston: 1979. V. 42; 45; 46

Water Music. Boston: 1981. V. 42; 44

Water Music. London: 1981. V. 45

World's End. New York: 1987. V. 43

BOYLE, VIRGINIA FRAZER

Robert Edward Lee, the South's Gift to Fame: a Poem. Memphis: 1910. V. 39

BOYNE, WILLIAM

Trade Tokens Issued in the Seventeenth Century in England, Wales and Ireland . . . London: 1889-91. V. 40; 41; 43; 44

Trade Tokens Issued in the Seventeenth Century in England, Wales, and Ireland, By Corporations, Merchants, Tradesmen, Etc. London: 1889-99. V. 41

BOYNTON, CHARLES B.

The History of the Navy During the Rebellion. New York: 1867. V. 39; 42

The History of the Navy During the Rebellion. New York: 1867-78. V. 42

History of the Navy During the Rebellion - the Action of the Union Forces with an Overall Naval Account of the Civil War 1861-5. New York: 1870-69. V. 42

A Journey through Kansas, With Sketches of Nebraska. Cincinnati: 1855. V. 37; 39; 40; 41; 42; 43; 45

BOYNTON, H. V.

Sherman's Historical Raid. The Memoirs in the Light of the Record. Cincinnati: 1875. V. 41

BOYNTON, HENRY VAN NESS

Was General Thomas Slow at Nashville? New York: 1896. V. 42

BOYNTON, JOHN PRIESTLEY

Delight. N.P.: 1978. V. 37

BOYNTON, S. R.

The Painter Lady: Grace Carpenter Hudson. Eureka: 1978. V. 46

THE BOY'S Book of Trades and the Tools Used in them; Comprising; Brickmaker . . . Manufacture of Gas . . . Blacksmith, Brass-founder . . . tinman . . . hotpress . . . Baker . . . Gun-maker . . . etc . . . London: (c. 1880). V. 37

BOYS, EDWARD

Narrative of a Captivity and Adventures in France and Flanders Between the Years 1803 and 1809. London: 1827. V. 43

Narrative of a Captivity and Adventures in France and Flanders: Between the Years 1803 and 1809. London: 1831. V. 37

BOYS, JOHN

General View of the Agriculture of the County of Kent . . . London: 1805. V. 45

BOYS, THOMAS S.

Original Views of London As It Is. Guildford: 1594. V. 44

Original Views of London As It is . . . London: 1842. V. 39

Original Views of London as It Is. Guildford: 1954. V. 46

Original Views of London As It Is. 1972. V. 41; 44

BOYS, WILLIAM

Testacea Minuta Rariora. Nuperrime Detecta in Arena Littori Sandvicensis. (English title:) A Collection of the Minute and Rare Shells, Lately Discovered in the Sand of the Sea Shore near Sandwich . . . London: 1784. V. 37

BOYSE, SAMUEL

Deity: a Poem. London: 1749. V. 45

An Impartial History of the Late Rebellion in 1745. Dublin: 1748. V. 38

The New Pantheon: or, Fabulous History of the Heathen Gods, Godesses, Heroes, etc. Salisbury: 1760. V. 38; 39

The New Pantheon; or Fabulous History of the Heathen Gods, Goddesses, Heroes, etc. Dublin: 1769. V. 41

Ode Inscribed to the Royal Company of Archers, on Their March, July 8, 1734. Edinburgh: 1734. V. 46

BOYSS, MATTHAEUS

Tractatus Varii Atque Utiles de Monetis . . . 1574. V. 45

BOZIO, TOMMASO

De Antiqvo e Novo Italiae Statv Libri Qvatvor. Romae: 1594. V. 37

BOZMAN, JOHN LEEDS

The History of Maryland, From Its First Settlement in 1633 to the Restoration in 1660. Baltimore: 1837. V. 37; 45

A Sketch of the History of Maryland, During the Three First Years After Its Settlement. Baltimore: 1811. V. 43; 45

BRAASCH, WILLIAM

Pyelography (Pyelo-Ureterography). A Study of the Normal and Pathologic Anatomy of the Renal Pelvis and Ureter. Philadelphia: 1915. V. 42

BRABANT, A. J.

Vancouver Island and Its Missions 1874-1900. New York: 1900. V. 39

BRABAZON, WALLOP

The Deep Sea and Coast Fisheries of Ireland, with Suggestions for Working of a Fishing Company. Dublin: 1848. V. 38; 39; 40; 43

BRABOURNE, WYNDHAM WENTWORTH KNATCHBULL HUGESSON, BARON

The Birds of South America. London: 1912-17. V. 37; 38; 39

The Birds of South America. London: 1917. V. 37; 42

BRABY, FREDERICK, & CO. LTD.

London, Liverpool and Glasgow: Zinc, Galvanzied Iron and Felt Manufacturers, Metal Perforators, Engineers and Contractors for Zinc Roofing . . . London: 1879. V. 37

BRACE, CHARLES L.

The New West; or, California in 1867-1868. New York: 1869. V. 39; 40; 44; 46

BRACE, CHARLES LORING

The Dangerous Classes of New York, and Twenty Years Work Among Them. New York: 1872. V. 42

BRACHET, J.

The Cell: Biochemistry, Physiology, Morphology. London: 1959-64. V. 37

BRACHT, V. F.

Texas in Jahre 1848. Elberfeld & Iserlohn: 1849. V. 40

BRACHT, VIKTOR

Texas in 1848. San Antonio: 1931. V. 37; 38

BRACKEN, HENRY 1697-1764

Every Man His Own Farrier. Philadelphia: 1843. V. 45

Farriery Improved; or, A Compleat Treatise Upon the Art of Farriery. London: 1737. V. 43

Farriery Improv'd; or, a Compleat Treatise Upon the Art of Farriery. London: 1738. V. 38; 41

Farriery Improv'd. London: 1739. V. 38

Farriery Improv'd . . . London: 1742. V. 43

Farriery Improv'd; or, A Compleat Tratise Upon the Art of Farriery. London: 1742/40. V. 46

Farriery Improv'd; or, a Compleat Treatise Upon the Art of Farriery. London: 1745. V. 39

Ten Minutes Advice to Every Gentleman Going to Purchase a Horse Out of a Dealer, Jockey, or Groom's Tables. Philadelphia: 1775. V. 45

BRACKENBURY, GEORGE

The Campaign in the Crimea. London: 1855-56. V. 40

BRACKENBURY, HENRY

The Ashanti War. Edinburgh: 1874. V. 38; 41

The Nearest Guard. A History of Her Majesty's Body Guard of the Honourable Corps of Gentlemen-At-Arms, from their Institution in 1509 to the year 1892. London: 1892. V. 37

BRACKENRIDGE, HENRY

Views of Louisiana, Together with a Journal of a Voyage Up the Missouri in 1811. Pittsburgh: 1814. V. 37; 44

BRACKENRIDGE, HENRY MARIE 1786-1871

History of the Late War, Between the United States and Great Britain . . . Baltimore: 1817. V. 45

History of the Western Insurrection in Western Pennsylvania. Pittsburgh: 1859. V. 42; 43; 45

Istoria della Guerra Fra Gli Stati Uniti d'America e l'Inghilterra. Milan: 1821. V. 40

Journal of a Voyage up the River Missouri; Performed in Eighteen Hundred and Eleven. Baltimore: 1816. V. 37; 41

Recollections of Persons and Palces in the West. Philadlephia: 1834. V. 39; 40; 43; 45

South America. A Letter on the Present State of that Country, Addressed to James Monroe, President of the United States. London: 1818. V. 43

Speeches on the Jew Bill, in the House of Delegates of Maryland . . . Philadelphia: 1829. V. 45

Views of Louisiana; Together with a Journal of a Voyage Up the Missouri River in 1811. Pittsburgh: 1811. V. 40

Views of Louisiana: Together with a Journal of a Voyage Up the Mississippi River in 1811. Pittsburgh: 1814. V. 42

Views of Louisiana. Pittsburgh: 1814. V. 37

Views of Louisiana, Together with a Journal of a Voyage Up the Missouri in 1811. Pittsburgh: 1814. V. 38; 39; 40; 41; 42; 43; 45

BRACKENRIDGE, HENRY MARIE 1786-1871 continued

Views of Louisiana; Containing Geographical, Statistical and Historical Notices of that Vast and Important Portion of America. Baltimore: 1817. V. 37; 38

Voyage to South America, Peformed by Order of the American Government, in the Years 1817 and 1818, in the Frigate Congress. Baltimore: 1819. V. 38; 40; 41

Voyage to South America, Peformed by Order of the Government in the Years 1817 and 1818 in the Frigate Congress. London: 1820. V. 42; 43

Voyage to South America . . . 1817-1818, in the Frigate Congress. Baltimore: 1819. V. 37

BRACKENRIDGE, HUGH HENRY

The Death of General Montgomery at the Siege of Quebec. Philadelphia: 1777. V. 37

Incidents of the Insurrection in the Western Parts of Pennsylvania in the year 1794. Philadelphia: 1795. V. 44

Modern Chivalry . . . Phila: John M'Culloch, 1792,: 1792. V. 42

Modern Chivalry . . . Philadelphia: 1804-07. V. 44

Modern Chivalry . . . Pittsburgh: 1819. V. 38; 46

BRACKETT, ALBERT G.

History of the United States Cavalry, from the Formation of the Federal Government to the 1st of June, 1863. New York: 1865. V. 41; 45

BRACKETT, CHARLES

Entirely Surrounded. New York: 1934. V. 37; 41; 42; 43; 44

BRACKETT, GEORGE A.

A Winter Evening's Tale. New York: 1880. V. 44; 45

BRACKETT, J. WARREN

The Ghost of Law, or Anarchy and Despotism. Hanover: 1803. V. 41

BRACKETT, L.

The Long Tomorrow. 1955. V. 39

BRACKETT, OLIVER

Thomas Chippendale. London. V. 38

Thomas Chippendale. London: 1924. V. 46

Thomas Chippendale, a Study of His Life, Work and Influence. London: 1930. V. 39; 42

BRACTON, HENRI DE d. 1268

De Legibus et Consuetudinibus Angliae, Libri Quinq. London: 1569. V. 40; 45

De Legibus et Consuetudinibus Angliae. London: 1878-83. V. 43

BRACTON, HENRY DE C. 1268

De Legibus et Consuetudinibus Angliae Libri Quinq. London: 1640. V. 38; 40

BRADBOURNE, LORD

The Birds of South America. London: 1912. V. 45

BRADBURY, CHARLES

A Cabinet of Jewels Opened to the Curious. Berwick: 1785. V. 39

History of Kennebunk Port, From Its First Discovery by Bartholomew Gosnold, May 14, 1602, to . . . 1837. Kennebunk: 1837. V. 46

BRADBURY, FREDERICK

History of Old Sheffield Plate. London: 1912. V. 37; 40; 42

History of Old Sheffield Plate. Sheffield: 1968. V. 42

BRADBURY, HENRY

Printing: Its Dawn, Day and Destiny. London: 1858. V. 39; 42

BRADBURY, JOHN

Travels in the Interior of America, in the Years 1809, 1810 and 1811. Liverpool: 1817. V. 37; 38; 39; 40; 41; 42; 43; 45

Travels in the Interior of America, in the Years 1809, 1810, and 1811. London: 1817. V. 42

BRADBURY, MALCOLM

Eating People is Wrong. London: 1959. V. 38; 46

Stepping Westward. London: 1965. V. 38

What is a Novel? London: 1969. V. 37

BRADBURY, OLIVER G.

Ten Good Poems. 1972. V. 38

BRADBURY, OSGOOD

Mettallak; the Lone Indian of the Magalloway. Boston: 1844. V. 40

BRADBURY, RAY

About Norman Corwin. Northridge: 1979. V. 37

The Anthem Sprinters. New York: 1963. V. 44; 45

The Aqueduct. 1979. V. 45

Dandelion Wine. Garden City: 1957. V. 39; 44; 45

Dark Carnival. Sauk City: 1947. V. 43; 44; 45; 46

Dark Carnival. 1948. V. 37; 39

Dark Carnival. London: 1948. V. 38; 39; 40; 41; 42

The Day It Rained Forever. 1959. V. 43; 45

The Day It Rained Forever. London: 1959. V. 41; 42; 43; 45

Death is a Lonely Business. New York: 1985. V. 40; 43; 44; 45

Death is a Lonely Business. 1985. V. 37

The Dragon. 1988. V. 45

Fahrenheit 451. New York: 1953. V. 37; 43; 45

Fahrenheit 451. London: 1954. V. 39; 44; 46

Fahrenheit 451. New York: 1967. V. 44

Fahrenheit 451. 1982. V. 38

Fahrenheit 451. New York: 1982. V. 39; 40; 42; 43; 45

Fahrenheit 451. San Francisco: 1982. V. 38; 40

The Golden Apples of the Sun. Garden City: 1953. V. 37; 40; 43

The Golden Apples of the Sun. London: 1953. V. 41

The Golden Apples of the Sun. New York: 1953. V. 43

The Halloween Tree. New York: 1972. V. 43

Hollerbochen Comes Back or the Voyage of the Neuralgia. 1938. V. 43

Hollerbochen Comes Back or the Voyage of the Neuralgia. Los Angeles: 1938. V. 45

I Sing the Body Electric. New York: 1969. V. 46

The Illustrated Man. Garden City: 1951. V. 37; 45; 46

The Illustrated Man. New York: 1951. V. 43

The Illustrated Man. London: 1952. V. 45

The Last Circus & The Electrocution. Northridge, CA: 1980. V. 37

The Last Good Kiss. Northridge: 1984. V. 37; 40; 42; 43; 46

Long After Midnight. New York: 1976. V. 43; 45

The Machineries of Joy: Short Stories. V. 43

The Machineries of Joy. New York: 1964. V. 42; 43; 44; 45

Man Dead? Then God is Slain! Northridge: 1977. V. 40; 41

Martian Chronicles. Garden City: 1950. V. 43

The Martian Chronicles. New York: 1950. V. 44; 45

The Martian Chronicles. Garden City: 1958. V. 38

The Martian Chronicles. 1974. V. 38; 44; 45

The Martian Chronicles. Avon: 1974. V. 38; 46

The Martian Chronicles. New York: 1974. V. 39

A Medicine for Melancholy. Garden City: 1959. V. 37; 39

The October Country. 1955. V. 43; 44

The October Country. London: 1956. V. 39

The Pedestrian. Glendale: 1964. V. 40

The Pedestrian. N.P.: 1964. V. 38

R is for Rocket. Garden City: (1962). V. 37

Ray Bradbury Review. 1988. V. 43

S is For Space. Garden City: 1966. V. 37; 43

The Silver Locusts. 1951. V. 45

The Silver Locusts. London: 1951. V. 42

Something Wicked this Way Comes. 1962. V. 43

Something Wicked This Way Comes. New York: 1962. V. 42; 46

Something Wicked This Way Comes. London: 1963. V. 45

The Son of Richard III. A Birth Announcement. N.P.: 1974. V. 38

The Stories of Ray Bradbury. London: 1980. V. 43

Switch on the Night. 1955. V. 39

Switch on the Night. New York: 1955. V. 45

This Attic Where the Meadow Greens. Northridge: 1979. V. 37; 39

The Toynbee Convector. 1988. V. 45

The Toynbee Convector. New York: 1988. V. 39

Twice 22. Garden City: 1966. V. 37

Twin Hieroglyphs that Swin the River Dust. Northridge: 1978. V. 37

BRADBY, JAMES

A Treatise on the Law of Distresses. London: 1808. V. 40

BRADCOCK, JOHN

The Groom's Oracle and Pocket Stable Directory . . . Philadelphia: 1831. V. 45

BRADDON, ELIZABETH MADDOX

Eleanor's Victory. London: 1863. V. 38

BRADDON, LAWRENCE

Essex's Innocency and Honour Vindicated. London: 1690. V. 37; 41; 43

BRADDON, MARGARET ELIZABETH

Lady Audley's Secret. London: 1862. V. 37

BRADDY, HALDEEN

Hamlet's Wounded Name; a Unique Item of Shakespearana. El Paso. V. 40

Hamlet's Wounded Name . . . El Paso: 1964. V. 43

BRADE, DANIEL

Picturesque Sketches of Italy. London: 1886. V. 45

BRADELEY, JOHN F.

The Rugged Flanks of the Caucasus. Oxford: 1940. V. 45

BRADFIELD, WESLEY

Cameron Creek Village: a Site in the Mimbres Area in Grant County New Mexico. Santa Fe: 1931. V. 43

BRADFORD, A. W.

American Antiquities and Researches into the Origin and History of the Red Race. New York: 1841. V. 38

BRADFORD, ALDEN

History of Massachusetts from 1764 (..to 1820). Boston: 1822-25-29. V. 44

History of Massachusetts, for Two Hundred Years from the Year 1620 to 1820. Boston: 1835. V. 44

Memoir of the Life and Writings of Rev. Jonathan Mayhew, D.D. Boston: 1838. V. 37; 44

BRADFORD, ALEXANDER

American Antiquities and Researches in to the Origin and History of the Red Race. New York: 1843. V. 45

BRADFORD, CLARA

Ethel's Adventures in the Doll Country. London: 1890. V. 45

BRADFORD, EDWARD

Orthopedic Surgery. New York: 1911. V. 42

A Treatise on Orthopedic Surgery. New York: 1890. V. 42

BRADFORD, JOHN

John Bradford's Historical Etc. Notes on Kentucky from the Western Miscellany. San Francisco: 1932. V. 37; 38; 46

Tales of the Moor. London: 1841. V. 40

BRADFORD, ROARK

Let the Bank Play Dixie and Other Stories. New York: 1934. V. 39; 41

Ol'Man Adam an' His Chillun. New York: & London: 1928. V. 46

Ol'King David an the Philistine Boys. New York: 1930. V. 41

This Side of Jordan. New York: 1929. V. 39; 41

The Three-Headed Angel. New York: 1937. V. 41

BRADFORD, ROBERT H.

Expostion of the Nullity of Mrs. Myra Clark Gaines' Pretensions to the City of New Orelans . . . New Orleans: 1870. V. 37

BRADFORD, SAMUEL

The Credibility of the Christian Revelation, from its Intrinsick Evidence. London: 1700. V. 37

BRADFORD, T. G.

A Comprehensive Atlas Geogrphical, Historical and Commercial. Boston: 1835. V. 42

A Comprehensive Atlas Geographical, Historical and Commercial. Boston, New York: 1835. V. 37

BRADFORD, THOMAS LINDSLEY

The Bibliographer's Manual of American History. Philadelphia: 1907-10. V. 41; 43

BRADFORD, WARD

Biographical Sketches of the Life of Major Ward Bradford, (Old Pioneer) as Related by the Author. Fresno: 1892? V. 45

BRADFORD, WILLIAM

History of Plymouth Plantation. 1620-1647. 1912. V. 46

Sketches of the Country, Character and Costume in Portugal and Spain, Made During the Campaign and on the Route of the British Army in 1808 and 1809. London: 1809. V. 39

Sketches of the Country, Character and Costume in Portugal and Spain, Made During the Campaign and on the Route of the British Army in 1808 and 1809, 1812. (with) Chronological and Historical Retrospect of the Events of the War in the Peninsula 1813. London: 1813. V. 42

Sketches of the Country, Character, and Costume in Portugal and Spain . . . London: 1824. V. 42

BRADFORD, WILLIAM J. A.

Notes on the Northwest, or Valley of the Upper Mississipi (sic) . . . New York: 1846. V. 37; 40; 42; 45

BRADLAW, PAUL

Observations on the Development of the Alphabet and Printing. Norwich: 1940. V. 45

BRADLEE, FRANCIS B.

Blockade Running During the Civil War and the Effect of Land and Water Transportation on the Confederacy. Salem: 1925. V. 38; 39

BRADLEY, CUTHBERT

The Foxhound of the Twentieth Century. London: 1914. V. 41

BRADLEY, CUTHERT

The Reminiscences of Frank Gillard with Bilvior Hounds. London: 1898. V. 37

BRADLEY, DAVID

The Chaneysville Incident. New York: 1981. V. 40; 42

South Street. 1975. V. 42; 43

South Street. New York: 1975. V. 41; 42; 43; 44

BRADLEY, E. R., MRS.

Elementary Tables and Lessons in the Siamese Language. Bangkok: 1860. V. 38

BRADLEY, EDWARD 1827-1889

The Adventures of Mr. Verdant Green. London. V. 44

The Adventures of Mr. Verdant Green. (with) An Little Mr. Bouncer and His Friend Verdant Green. Boston: 1893. V. 38

The Adventures Of Mr. Verdant Green. London: 1853. V. 37

The Adventures of Mr. Verdant Green. The Further Adventures of Mr. Verdant Green. Mr. Verdant Green Married and Done for. Tales of. V. 43

Glencraggan: or, a Highland Home in Cantire. London: 1861. V. 39; 42; 43; 46

Photographic Pleasures. London: 1855. V. 43; 46

Photographic Pleasures Popularly Portrayed with Pen and Pencil. London: 1863. V. 40

BRADLEY, FRANCIS HERBERT 1846-1924

Appearance and Reality. A Metaphysical Essay. London: 1893. V. 37; 39

Collected Essays. Oxford: 1935. V. 40

Collected Essays. Oxford: 1935. V. 41

Essays on Truth and Reality. Oxford: 1914. V. 39; 40

Ethical Studies. London: 1876. V. 37; 39; 43; 45

The Principles of Logic. London: 1883. V. 38; 45

BRADLEY, GEORGE GRANVILLE

Lectures on Ecclesiastes Delivered in Westminster Abbey. Oxford: 1885. V. 37; 38

BRADLEY, GERTRUDE M.

The Run-a-way Puff-Puff, About a Baby Puffy-Train. London: 1905. V. 45

BRADLEY, JOHN

A Narrative of Travel and Sport in Burmah, Siam and the Malay Peninsula. London: 1876. V. 45

BRADLEY, JOSHUA

Accounts of Religious Revivals in Many Parts of the United States, from 1815 to 1818. Albany: 1819. V. 43

BRADLEY, R. T.

The Outlaws of the Border or the Lives of Frank and Jesse James. St. Louis. V. 43

BRADLEY, RICHARD d. 1732

A Course of Lectures, Upon the Materia Medica, Antient and Modern. London: 1730. V. 38

The Gentleman and Farmer's Guide Abridg'd. London: and Dublin: 1729. V. 43

The Great Improvement of Commons That are Enclosed, for the Advantage of the Lords of Manors, the Poor, and the Publick. London: 1732. V. 41

Improvements of Planting and Gardening, Both Philosphical and Practical. London: 1724. V. 37; 38; 40; 41; 43; 46

New Improvements of Planting and Gardening, Both Philosophical and Practical . . . London: 1726. V. 41

New Improvements of Planting and Gardening, Both Philosophical and Practical. London: 1731. V. 42

New Improvements of Planting and Gardening, both Philosophical and Practical. London: 1739. V. 37; 38; 43; 46

A Philosophical Account of the Works of Nature. London: 1721. V. 37; 41; 42

The Plague at Marseilles Consider'd; With Remarks Upon the Plague in General, Shewing Its Cause and Nature of Infection. London: 1721. V. 39; 41; 42

The Science of Good Husbandry . . . London: 1727. V. 43

Ten Practical Discourses Concerning Earth and Water, Fire and Air . . . Westminster: 1727. V. 37; 39

BRADLEY, THOMAS

Report . . . Examiner of State Claims, on the Claims of States Against the United States . . . Washington: 1880. V. 42; 44

BRADLEY, THOMAS H.

O'Toole's Mallet; or the Resurrection of the Second National City of the United States of America. Seattle: 1894. V. 42

BRADLEY, WILL

The American Chap-Book. Jersey City: 1904-05. V. 39; 42

Bradley, His Book. Springfield: 1896. V. 37; 38; 41

Bradley His Book. Springfield: 1896-97. V. 41

Bradley, His Book. Volume 1. N.P.: 1896. V. 39

Bradley, His Book. Volume II, 3. N.P.: 1897. V. 39

The Delectable Art of Printing. Everywhere: 1904. V. 45

Memories: 1875-1895. Happenings Here and There Along the Trail, or 'The World Went Very Well Then.' Pasadena: 1949. V. 37; 45

Peter Poodle. New York: 1906. V. 46

The Printer Man's Joy, Being the Book of Chap-Book Cuts & Borders, with Sundry Goodly Types. (Cover title). 1905. V. 37

Strathmore Expressive Printing Papers are Part of the Picture. (Cover title). (Sprinfield): 1954). V. 37

Will Bradley His Work and Exhibition. San Marino: 1951. V. 41

The Wonderbox Stories. New York: 1906. V. 38

The Wonderbox Stories. New York: 1916. V. 37

BRADLEY'S Atlas of the World for Commercial and Library Reference. Philadelphia: 1886. V. 45

BRADLOW, EDNA

Thomas Bowler of the Cape of Good Hope, His Life and Works, with a Catalogue of Extant Paintings . . . Cape Town/Amsterdam: 1955. V. 42; 44

BRADO, E.

Cattle Kingdom. Early Ranching in Alberta. Vancouver: 1984. V. 43

BRADSBY, HENRY C.

History of Bureau County, Illinois. Chicago: 1885. V. 42

History of Bradford County, Pennsylvania. Chicago: 1891. V. 41; 42

History of Luzerne County, Pennsylvania. Chicago: 1893. V. 41; 42

BRADSHAW, AUGUSTUS CAVENDISH

The Trial at Large of an Action for Damages, Brought in His Majesty's Court of Exchequer, Before the Right Hon. Lord Chief Baron Yelverton and a Jury of Citizens on Saturday the 20th of Feb. 1796. by the Right Hon. George Fred. Earl of Westmeath, Against . . . Dublin;: 1796. V. 46

BRADSHAW, GEORGE

Bradshaw's Railway Companion . . . Manchester: 1841. V. 46

Bradshaw's Railway Time Tables and Assistant to Railway Travelling with Illustrative Maps and Plans. London: 1839. V. 46

Bradshaw's Railway Time Tables and Assistant to Railway Travelling with Illustrative Maps and Plans. London: 1901. V. 46

BRADSHAW, H.

A Catalogue of the Bradshaw Collection of Irish Books in the University Library, Cambridge. Cambridge: 1916. V. 39

BRADSHAW, HENRY

Collected Papers. 1889. V. 38

Collected Papers. Cambridge: 1889. V. 40

BRADSHAW, JOHN

Martin Ffrench. London: 1886. V. 41; 43

New Zealand As It Is. London: 1883. V. 43

BRADSHAW, PERCY V.

The Art of the Illustrator. V. 46

Art in Advertising. London. V. 40

The Art of the Illustrator. London: 1920's. V. 38; 41; 44

Art in Advertising: a Study of British and American Pictorial Publicity. London: 1925. V. 46

BRADSHAW, THOMAS

Belfast General and Commercial Directory for 1819 . . . Belfast: 1819. V. 43

BRADSHAW'S Railway Companion. London: 1840. V. 38
BRADSHAW'S Railway Companion. Manchester: 1841. V. 38

BRADSHAW'S Railway Manual . . . for 1867. Volume XIX. London: 1867. V. 42

BRADSHAW'S Railway Manual . . . for 1868. Volume XX. London: 1868. V. 42

BRADSHAW'S Railway Manual . . . for 1870. Volume XXII. London: 1870. V. 42

BRADSHAW'S Railway Manual . . . for 1871. Volume XXIII. London: 1871. V. 42

BRADSHAW'S Railway Manual . . . for 1872. Volume XXIV. London: 1872. V. 42

BRADSHAW'S Railway Manual . . . for 1873. Volume XXV. London: 1873. V. 42

BRADSHAW'S Railway Manual . . . for 1874. Volume XXVI. London: 1874. V. 42

BRADSHAW'S Railway Manual . . . for 1879. Volume XXXI. London: 1879. V. 42

BRADSHAW'S Railway Manual . . . for 1880. Volume XXXII. London: 1880. V. 42

BRADSHAW'S Railway Manual . . . for 1881. Volume XXXIII. London: 1881. V. 42

BRADSHAW'S Railway Manual, Shareholder's Guide and Official Directory for 1866 . . . London: 1866. V. 42

BRADSHAW'S Railway Manual, Shareholder's Guide and Official Directory for 1872. Manchester: 1872. V. 38

BRADSTREET, ANNE

Alas All's Vanity, or a Leaf from the First American edition of Several Poems by Anne Bradstreet, printed at Boston, anno 1678. New York: 1942. V. 40; 43

The Tenth Muse Lately Sprung Up in America, or Severall Poems. London: 1650. V. 42

Works in Prose and Verse. Charlestown: 1867. V. 37; 41; 42; 43; 45

BRADSTREET'S Pocket Atlas of the United States. New York: 1879. V. 45
BRADSTREET'S Pocket Atlas of the United States. New York: 1880. V. 45

BRADSTREET'S Pocket Atlas of the United States . . . New York: 1882. V. 38; 41; 43

BRADWARDINE, THOMAS

Geometria Speculativa . . . Paris: 1495. V. 40

Geometria Speculativa. Paris: 1511. V. 38

BRADY, BUCKSIN

Stories and Sermons. Toronto: 1905. V. 40

BRADY, EDWIN J.

Australia Unlimited. Melbourne: 1918. V. 46

BRADY, G. STEWARDSON

A Monograph of the Free and Semi-Parasitic Copepoda of the British Islands. London: 1878-80. V. 43

BRADY, JOHN

Clavis Calendaria; or a Compendious Analysis of the Calendar. London: 1812. V. 39

Clavis Calendaria; or a Compendious Analysis of the Calendar. London: 1814. V. 41

BRADY, NICHOLAS

A New Version of the Psalms of David Fitted to the Tunes Used in Churches. London: 1749. V. 41

A New Version of the Psalms of David, Fitted to the Tunes Used in Churches. London: 1815. V. 42

New Version of the Psalms of David: Fitted to the Tunes Used in Churches. By N. Brady and N. Tate. London: 1824. V. 37

Select Sermons on Practical Subjects, Preach'd Before the Queen and On Other Occasions. London: 1713. V. 41

BRADY, ROBERT

A Complete History of England, from the First Entrance of the Romans . . . (with) A Continuation of the Complete History of England . . . (with) An Introduction to the Old English History . . . In the Savoy. V. 43

A Complete History of England, from the First Entrance of the Romans Under the Conduct of Julius Caesar, Unto the End of the Reign of Henry III . . . all Delivered in Plain Matter of Fact, Without any Reflections or Remarques. London: 1685. V. 42

An Introduction to the Old English History. London: 1684. V. 37; 41; 42

BRADY, W. MAZIERE

The Irish Reformation, or, the Alleged Conversion of the Irish Bishops at the Accession of Queen Elizabeth. London: 1867. V. 39

State Papers Concerning the Irish Church in the Time of Queen Elizabeth. London: 1868. V. 39

BRADY, WILLIAM

Glimpses of Texas: Its Divisions, Resources, Development and Prospects. Houston: 1871. V. 42

The Kedge-Anchor; or, Young Sailor's Assistant . . . Second Edition . . . New York: 1847. V. 37

BRADY, WILLIAM A.

The Fighting Man. Indianpolis: 1916. V. 43

BRADY, WILLIAM MAZIERE

Clerical and Parochial Records of Cork, Cloyne and Ross, Taken from Diocesan and Parish Registers, . . . Dublin: 1863. V. 43

Clerical and Parochial Records of Cork, Cloyne and Ross . . . Dublin: 1863-63-64. V. 37; 43

BRAGA

Constituicoes do Arcebispado de Braga. Lisbon: 1538. V. 45

BRAGANZA, RONALD LOUIS SILVEIRA DE

The Hill Collection of Pacific Voyages. San Diego: 1974. V. 37

BRAGDON, OREN D.

Facts and Figures: or, Useful and Important Information for the People of Louisiana. New Orleans: 1872. V. 43; 45

BRAGG, BENJAMIN, PSEUD.

Voyage to the North Pole, Accompanied by His Friend, Captain Slapperwhack . . . London: 1817. V. 44; 45

BRAGG, BRAXTON

Headquarters Department No. 2, General Orders No. 124. Chattanooga: 1862. V. 39

BRAGG, G. F.

Progressive Sketches for the Lead Pencil. London: 1835. V. 45

BRAGG, GEORGE F.

Afro-American Church Work and Workers. Baltimore: 1904. V. 44

BRAGG, JEFFERSON DAVIS

Louisiana in the Confederacy. Baton Rouge: 1941. V. 37

BRAGG, ROBERT

The Journey of Dr. Robert Bongout and His Lady to Bath Performed in the Year 177-. London: 1778. V. 40

BRAGG, WILLIAM HENRY

An Introduction to Crystal Analysis. New York: 1929. V. 40

X-Rays and Crystal Structure. London: 1915. V. 40

BRAGGE, FRANCIS b. 1690

A Full and Impartial Account of the Discover of Sorcery and Witchcraft, Practis'd by Jane Wenham of Walkerne in Hertfordshire, Upon the Bodies of Anne Thorn, Anne Street, &c. London: 1712. V. 46

A Practical Treatise of the Regulation of the Passions. London: 1708. V. 37; 41

BRAGGE, W.

List of Ornamented Book-Covers Belonging to W. Bragge . . . Lent to the Warrington Art Gallery. Birmingham: 1877. V. 41

BRAHAM, ALLAN

The Drawings at Windsor Castle. London: 1977. V. 44

BRAHE, TYCHO 1546-1601

Astronomiae Instauratae Mechanica. Nuremberg: 1602. V. 45

Epistolarum Astronomicarum Libri. Uraniborg: 1610. V. 44

Historia Coelestis. Colophon: Augsburg: 1666. V. 44

Learned Ticho Brahae His Astronomicall Coniectur of the New and Much Admired (Star) Which Appeared in the Year 1572 . . . London: 1632. V. 38

Opera Omnia. Hanau: 1913-29. V. 40

BRAID, JAMES 1795-1860

Braid on Hypnotism: Neurypnology, or the Rationale of Nervous Sleep Considered in Relation to Animal Magnetism or Mesmerism . . . London: 1899. V. 46

Neurypnology; or, the Rationale of Nervous Sleep, Considered in Relation with Animal Magnetism. London: 1843. V. 37; 41; 42; 43; 46

The Physiology of Fascination and the Critics Criticised. Manchester: 1855. V. 45

BRAIKENRIDGE, GEORGE WEARE

Catalogue of the Library at Claremont, Clevedon and 16 Royal Crescent, Bath, Collected by . . . London: 1894. V. 45

BRAIKENRIDGE, GULIELMO

Exercitatio Geometrica de Descriptione Linearum Curvarum. London: 1733. V. 39

BRAINARD, JOHN G. C.

The Poems . . . Hartford: 1842. V. 40; 44

BRAINE, JOHN

Room at the Top. London: 1957. V. 37; 40

BRAINE, S.

Moving Animals. London. V. 46

BRAINE, SHEILA E.

In Nurseryland. London. V. 45

Pleasant Surprises a Novel Picture Book. London: 1890. V. 45

BRAINERD, DAVID

An Abridgment of Mr. David Brainerd's Journal Among the Indians. London: 1748. V. 41

Memoirs of the Rev. David Brainerd, Missionary to the Indians on the Boders of New York, New Jersey and Pennsylvania . . . New Haven: 1822. V. 39

Mirabilia Dei Inter Indicos, or the Rise and Progress of a Remarkable Work of Grace Among a Number of the Indians, in the Provinces of New Jersey and Pennsylvania . . . Worcester: 1793. V. 45

BRAINERD, GEORGE W.

The Archaeological Ceramics of Yucatan. Berkeley: 1958. V. 42; 44

BRAINERD, THOMAS

The Life of John Brainerd, The Brother of David Brainerd, and His Successor as Missionary to the Indians of New Jersey. Philadelphia: 1865. V. 37

BRAISTED, WILLIAM

Report of the Japanese Naval Medical and Sanitary Features of the Russo Japanese War to the Surgeon-General, U.S. Navy. Washington: 1906. V. 41; 42; 44

BRAITHWAITE, R.

The British Moss Flora. London: 1887-1905. V. 37

BRAITHWAITE, ROBERT 1824-1917

The Sphagnaceae or Peat-Mosses of Europe and North America. London: 1880. V. 43

BRAITHWAITE, WILLIAM STANLEY 1878-1962

Our Lady's Choir. A Contemporary Anthology of Verse by Catholic Sisters. Foreword by The Rev. Hugh Francis Blunt. Introduction by Ralph Adams Cram. Boston: 1931. V. 37

BRAIVE, MICHEL F.

The Photograph: a Social History. New York: 1966. V. 44

BRAKE, HEZEKIAH

On Two Continents. A Long Life's Experience. Topeka: 1896. V. 45; 46

BRAKHAGE, JANE

From the Book of Legends. 1989. V. 45

BRAMAH, ERNEST SMITH

Kai Lung Beneath the Mulberry Tree. 1940. V. 43

BRAMAN, D. E. E.

Braman's Information About Texas. Philadelphia: 1857. V. 41; 42

Braman's Information About Texas. Philadelphia: 1858. V. 37; 38; 43; 46

BRAMBLE, CHARLES A.

The ABC of Mining: A Handbook for Prospectors . . . Chicago/New York: (1898). V. 37

BRAME, HERBERT

Pony Express Courier. Placerville: 1934-38. V. 44

BRAMHALL, JOHN

A Just Vindication of the Church of England, from the Unjust Aspersion of Criminal Schisme . . . London: 1654. V. 40

BRAMLEY, HENRY RAMSDEN

Christmas Carols New and Old. London: 1880. V. 38; 40

BRAMMER, WILLIAM

The Gay Place. V. 42

The Gay Place. 1961. V. 45

The Gay Place. Boston: 1961. V. 37; 42; 45

BRAMSEN, JOHN

Travels in Egypt, Syria, Cyprus, The Morea, Greece, Italy, &c . . . (with) Remarks on the North of Spain. London: 1820-23. V. 37

BRAMSTON, JAMES d. 1744

The Art of Politicks, in Imitation of Horace's Art of Poetry. London: 1729. V. 38; 40; 41; 42; 43; 44; 45

The Man of Taste. London: 1733. V. 38; 40; 41; 42; 43; 44; 45

BRAMWELL, BYROM

Atlas of Clinical Medicine. Edinburgh: 1892-6. V. 38; 45

The Diseases of the Spinal Cord. Edinburgh: 1882. V. 44; 45

BRANAGAN, THOMAS

Avenia, or a Tragical Poem, on the Oppression of the Human Species ... Philadelphia: 1810. V. 42

The Excellency of the Female Character Vindicated ... Harrisburgh: 1828. V. 44; 45

BRANCA, G.

Manuale d'architettura. Roma: 1773. V. 37

BRANCA, GIOVANNI

Le Machine ... Rome: 1629. V. 37

BRANCACCIO, LELIO

I Carichi Militari. Venetia: 1620. V. 42

BRANCATIO, GIULIO C.

Della Nvova Disciplina & Vera Arte Militare Libri VIII. - Secondo I Precetti di Cesare ... Venetia: 1585. V. 42

BRANCH, DOUGLAS

The Cowboy and His Interpreters. London: 1926. V. 46
The Cowboy and His Interpreters. New York: 1926. V. 44

BRANCH, THOMAS fl. 1750

Thoughts on Dreaming. London: 1738. V. 42; 43

BRANCH, WILLIAM

Life, a Poem in Three Books ... Richmond: 1819. V. 44

BRANCHARDIERE, RIEGO DE LA

The Crochet Book. London: 1849-53. V. 39

BRAND, CHARLES

Journal of a Voyage to Peru: A Passage Across the Cordillera of the Andes in the Winter of 1827 ... London: 1828. V. 42

BRAND, CHRISTIANNA

London Particular. London: 1952. V. 43

BRAND, DONALD D.

So Live the Works of men: Seventieth Anniversary Volume Honoring Edgar Lee Hewett. Albuquerque: 1939. V. 39

BRAND, FITZJOHN

A Defence of the Pamphlet Ascribed to John Reeves, Esq. and Entitled 'Thoughts on the English Government', Addressed to Members of the Loyal Associations Atainst Republicans and Levellers. London: 1796. V. 39

BRAND, J.

A Determination of the Average Depression of the Price of Wheat in War ... London: 1808. V. 45

BRAND, JOHN

Bibliotheca Brandiana. A Catalogue of Unique, Scarce, Rare, Curious and Numerous Collections of Works on the Antiquity, Topography, and Decayed Intelligence of Great Britain and Ireland ... London: 1807. V. 40

A Brief Description of Orkney, Zetland, Pightland-Firth & Caithness, wherein, After a short Journal of the Author's Voyage thither, These Northern Places are first more Generally Described; then a Particular View is given of the several Isles ... Edinburgh: 1701. V. 37

A Catlaogue of the Unique, Scarce, Rare, Curious and Numerous Collection of Works ... of the Late Rev. John Brand. London: 1807. V. 44

Observations on Popular Antiquities. London: 1810. V. 38; 39; 42; 43; 44

Observations on Popular Antiquities. London: 1813. V. 39; 43; 44; 46

On Illicit Love. Newcastle-upon-Tyne: 1775. V. 37; 39; 40; 45

BRAND, M.

The Happy Valley. 1931. V. 45

BRAND, MAX

The Streak. New York: 1937. V. 46

The Ten-Foot Chain or Can Love Survive the Shackless? New York: 1920. V. 37

Twenty Notches. New York: 1932. V. 46

BRANDARD, ROBERT

Scraps of Nature. London: 1864. V. 39; 43

BRANDAU, R. S.

History of Homes and Gardens of Tennessee. Nashville: 1936. V. 42; 45
History of Homes and Gardens of Tennessee. New York:.P.: 1936. V. 46
History of Homes and Gardens of Tennessee. Nashville: 1964. V. 45

BRANDE, WILLIAM THOMAS

A Manual of Chemistry. London: 1819. V. 40
Manual of Chemistry ... New York: 1821. V. 45
Outlines of Geology; Being the Substance of a Course of Lectures Delivered in ... the Royal Institution ... London: 1817. V. 46

BRANDEIS, LOUIS D.

Fatigue and Efficiency. New York: 1912. V. 43

BRANDES, GEORG

Main Currents in 19th Century Literature. New York: 1901-05. V. 42

BRANDOLINUS, AURELIO

De Hvmanae Vitae Conditione, Et Toleranda Corporis Aegritudine, Avreolvs Libellus. Paris: 1562. V. 43

BRANDON, ISAAC

Fragments: In the Manner of Sterne. London: 1797. V. 45

BRANDON, J. A.

The Open Timber Roofs of the Middle Ages. London: 1849. V. 38

BRANDON, JOHN

Fifty Queries, Seriously Propounded to Those that Question, or Deny Infants Right to Baptism. London: 1675. V. 42; 43

BRANDON, RAPHAEL

An Analysis of Gothic Architecture. London: 1847. V. 40; 42

An Analysis of Gothick Architecture. London: 1860. V. 39

An Analysis of Gothic Architecture. Illustrated by a series of upwards of seven hundred examples ... (in two volumes). Edinburgh: 1903. V. 37

The Open Timber Roofs of the Middle Ages. London: 1849. V. 38; 42

The Open Timber Roofs of the Middle Ages. London: 1850. V. 38

The Open Timber Roofs of the Middle Ages. London: 1860. V. 44

Parish Churches; Being Perspective Views of English Ecclesiastical Structures ... London: 1848. V. 44

Parish Churches, Being Perspective Views Accompanied by Plans Drawn to a Uniform Scale, and Letter-Press Descriptions. London: 1858. V. 37; 38; 40; 43; 44

BRANDT, BILL

The English at Home. London: 1936. V. 46

Perspective of Nudes. London: 1961. V. 40; 45

Perspective of Nudes. New York: 1961. V. 41

BRANDT, FRANCIS FREDERICK

'Habet!' A Short Treatise on the Law of the Land as It Affects Pugilism. London: 1857. V. 38; 39; 43; 45

BRANDT, GERARD

Het Leven en Bedryf van den Heere Michiel du Ruiter, Hertog, Ritter &c .... Amsterdam: 1701. V. 41

History of the Reformation and Other Ecclesiastical Transactions In and About the Low Countries, from the Beginning of the 8th Century to the Synod of Dort. London: 1720-23. V. 37; 39; 46

BRANDT, HERBERT

Alaska Bird Trails. Cleveland: 1943. V. 38; 39

Arizona and Its Bird Life. Cleveland: 1951. V. 39

Texas Bird Adventures in the Chisos Mountains and on the Northern Plains. Cleveland: 1940. V. 41; 42

BRANDT, SEBASTIAN

The Shyp of Fooles. Seal Harbor. V. 44

The Shyp of Fooles. Seal Harbor: 1982. V. 45

BRANGWYN, FRANK

A Book of Bridges. V. 37

Bookplates. London: 1920. V. 42; 45

The British Empire Panels Designed for the House of Lords. London: 1933. V. 38; 39

Catalogue of the Etched Work of Frank Brangwyn. London: 1912. V. 41

The Decorative Art of Frank Brangwyn. London: 1924. V. 40; 44

The Etchings of Frank Brangwyn, R.A. London: 1926. V. 41

The Pageant of Venice. London: 1922. V. 40

Ten Woodcuts Cut and Printed in Colour by Yoshijiro Urushibara after Designs by Brangwyn. London: 1924. V. 40

The Way of the Cross. London: 1935. V. 39

BRANIGAN, KEITH

Aegean Metalwork of the Early and Middle Bronze Age. Oxford: 1974. V. 40; 42; 44

BRANKSTON, A. D.

Early Ming Wares of Chingechen. Peking: 1938. V. 41

BRANN, W. C.

The Complete Works of Brann the Iconoclast. New York: 1919. V. 38; 40; 41

BRANNAGAN, THOMAS

The Excellency of the Female Character Vindicated. Harrisburg: 1828. V. 37

BRANNAN, JOHN

Official Letters of the Military and Naval Officers of the United States, During the War with Great Britain in the Years 1812, 13, 14, & 15. Washington: 1823. V. 44

BRANNAN, NOAH

Festive Wine. Ancient Japanese Poems from the Kinkafu. New York: & Tokyo: 1969. V. 43

Festive Wine: Ancietn Japanese Poems from the kinkafu. Woodblock prints by Haku Maki. New York: (1969). V. 37

BRANNER, R.

Manuscript painting in Paris during the region of Saint Louis. A Study of Styles. Berkeley: (1977). V. 37

BRANNON, G.

Vectis Scenery . . . 1830. V. 42

Vectis Scenery, Being a Series of Original and Select Views . . . London: 1830. V. 45

BRANNON, GEORGE

Vectis Scenery. Isle of Wight: 1829. V. 39; 40

Vectis Scenery. London: 1829. V. 38

Vectis Scenery. Newport: 1868. V. 44

BRANNT, WILLIAM T.

Petroleum: Its History, Origin, Occurrence, Production, Physical and Chemical Technology . . . Philadelphia: 1895. V. 42

BRANSBY, B.

Surgical Essays: The Result of Clinical Observations Made Guy's Hospital. London: 1843. V. 40

BRANSBY, J.

The Ipswich Magazine. Ipswich: 1799. V. 37

BRANT, JOSEPH

Memoir of the Distinguished Mohawk Chief, Sachem & Warrior, Capt. Joseph Brant. Brantford: 1872. V. 38; 41; 45

BRANT, SEBASTIAN 1458-1528

The Ship of Fools. Edinburgh: 1874. V. 40; 44

Stultifera Navis. Basle: 1497. V. 40

Stultifera Navis. In laudatissima Germani urbe: 1497. V. 40

Stultifera Navis. Lyon: 1498. V. 38

Stultifera Navis . . . The Ship of Fooles, Wherein is Shewed the Folloy of all States, with Divers Other Workes Adjoyned. London: 1570. V. 38; 45

BRANTEGHEM, WILLEM VAN

Pomarium Mysticu(m) Tu(m) Nouorum Tu(m) Veteru(m) Fructuu(m) Animae Christianae Imagu(n)culis Aliquot Nascentis Mundi Exordia, Necq(ue) non Totius Pene Vit(a)e Christi Decursum Referentibus . . . Antwerp: 1535. V. 38

BRANTFORD ENGINE WORKS

Illustrated Catalogue of Steam Engines, Saw and Grist Mill Machinery, Waterous' Improved System of Fire Protection and Water Supply, Saws and Saw Mill Furnishings. Toronto: 1873. V. 42

BRANTNER, C. F.

351st Infantry. First Call 1917. St. Paul: 1919. V. 41

BRANTOME, PIERRE DE BOURDEILLE, SEIGNEUR DE

Spanish Rhodomontades. London: 1741. V. 41

BRANWELL, BYROM

Diseases of the Spinal Cord. New York: 1882. V. 42

Diseases of the Spinal Cord. Edinburgh: 1884. V. 42

BRAQUE, GEORGES

Aout. Suite d'Estampes Originales. Paris: 1958. V. 42

Cahier de Georges Braque, 1917-1949 (-1955). Paris: 1947/56. V. 42

Cahier de Georges Braque, 1917-1947. New York: 1948. V. 46

The Intimate Sketchbooks of G. Braque. New York: 1955. V. 38; 45

BRASH, RICHARD R.

The Ogam Inscribed Monuments of the Gaedhill.. London: 1879. V. 37; 38; 43; 44

BRASHER, REX

Birds and Trees of North America Done in Chickadee Valley Near Kent. Connecticut: 1929-32. V. 41

Birds and Trees of North America. New York: 1961-62. V. 43; 44; 45

Birds & Trees of North America. New York: 1961. V. 37

BRASHLER, WILLIAM

The Bingo Long Traveling All-Stars and Motor Kings. New York: 1973. V. 46

BRASS, BARTH

Type Specimen. Breslau: 1760. V. 46

BRASSBRIDGE, JOSEPH

Fruits of Experience; or, Memoir . . . London: 1824. V. 46

BRASSEY, ANNIE ALLNUTT, BARONESS

In the Trades, the Tropics & the Roaring Forties. London: 1885. V. 38

The Last Voyage. London: 1887. V. 38; 45

The Last Voyage. London: 1889. V. 39; 41; 45

Sunshine and the Storm in the East, or Cruises to Cyprus and Constantinople. London: 1880. V. 45

Tahiti. London: 1882. V. 45

Voyage in the 'Sunbean'. London: 1878. V. 43

A Voyage in the 'Sunbeam' Our Home on the Ocean for Eleven Months. London: 1880. V. 38

BRASSEY, THOMAS

Foreign Work and English Wages Considered with Reference to the Depression of Trade. London: 1879. V. 38

Voyages and Travels . . . from 1862 to 1894. London: 1895. V. 40

Work and Wages Practically Illustrated. London: 1871. V. 46

Work and Wages Practically Illustrated. London: 1872. V. 37; 38

BRASSINGTON, W. SALT

Historic Bindings in the Bodleian Library, Oxford. London: 1891. V. 40

A History of the Art of Bookbinding. London: 1894. V. 40; 41; 42; 43; 45; 46

BRATHWAITE, RICHARD 1588?-1673

The Arcadian Princesse. London: 1635. V. 39

Barnabae Itinerarium or Barnabee's Journal. London: 1818. V. 40

Baranabae Itinearium, or Barnabee's JOurnal . . . London: 1820. V. 39; 40; 42; 45; 46

A Comment Upon the Two Tales of . . . Sr. Jeffray Chaucer . . . London: 1665. V. 39; 42

Drunken Barnaby's Four Journeys to the North of England. London: 1716. V. 40; 45; 46

Drunken Barnaby's Four Journeys to the North of England. London: 1723. V. 38; 41; 46

Drunken Barnaby's Four Journeys to the North of England. Dublin: 1762. V. 46

Drunken Barnaby's Four Journeys. London: 1805. V. 38

Drunken Barnaby's Four Journeys to the North of England. London: 1822. V. 46

The English Gentleman. London: 1633. V. 37; 38; 39

The English Gentleman. London: 1630. V. 37

The English Gentlewoman. London: 1631. V. 37

A Survey of History; or, A Nursery for Gentry. 1638. V. 44

A Survey of History. London: 1638. V. 39; 40; 42; 46

BRATT, JOHN

Trails of Yesterday. Lincoln: 1921. V. 37; 45

BRATTLE, WILLIAM

Sundry Rules and Directions for Drawing Up a Regimen, Posting the Officers, &c. Taken from the Best and Latest Authority; for the Use and Benefit of the First Regiment of Militia in the County of Middlesex. Boston: 1733. V. 37

BRAUN, G.

Civitates Orbis Terrarum. Cleveland & New York: 1966. V. 40

BRAUN, IOHANNES 1628-1709

Selecta Sacra. Amsterdam: 1700. V. 46

BRAUN, J.

Circular-Schreiben an die Deutschen Einwohner von Rockingham und August, und den Benachbarten Caunties. Harrisonburg: 1818. V. 40

Vorweisung Verschiedener Deutsch-u Franzosischer Schriften. Mulhausen: 1774. V. 40

BRAUN-RONSDORF, MARGARETE

Mirror of Fashion. New York: 1964. V. 44

BRAUN, THOMAS 1876-

L'An, Poemes, par Thomas Braun. Brussels: 1897. V. 39

Le Livre des Benedictions. Brussels: & Paris: 1900. V. 46

BRAUN, U.

A Monograph of the Erysiphles (Powdery Mildews). 1987. V. 38

BRAUND, J.

Illustrations of Furniture, Candelabra, Musical Instruments from the Great Exhibitions of London and Paris. London: 1858. V. 45

BRAUNE, WILHELM

An Atlas of Topographical Anatomy After Plane Sections of Frozen Bodies. Philadelphia: 1877. V. 42

BRAUNS, REINHARD

The Mineral Kingdom. Esslingen: 1912. V. 42

BRAUTIGAN, RICHARD

A Confederate General from Big Sur. 1964. V. 42

A Confederate General from Big Sur. New York: 1964. V. 46

Dreaming of Babylon: a Private Eye Novel 1942. N.P.: 1977. V. 46

Karma Repair Kit: Items 1-4. San Francisco: 1967. V. 43

Knock on Wood (Part Two). Lexington: 1979. V. 45

The Pill Versus the Springhill Mine Disaster. London: 1970. V. 46

Please Plant this Book. San Francisco: 1968. V. 42; 44

The San Francisco Weather Report. N.P.: 1968. V. 43

The San Francisco Weather Report. San Francisco: 1968. V. 44

So the Wind Won't Blow It All Away. New York: 1982. V. 46

The Tokoyo-Montana Express. 1979. V. 43

The Tokyo-Montana Express. New York: 1979. V. 43; 44; 45; 46

The Tokyo-Montana Express. New York: 1980. V. 45

Trout Fishing in America. London: 1970. V. 46

BRAVO, FRANCISCO

The Opera Medicinalia. Folkestone & London: 1970. V. 39

BRAVONIUS, FLORENTIUS

Chronicon ex Chronicis, ab Initio Mundi Vsque ad Annum 1118, Deductum, Auctore Florentio Wigorniensi Monacho. Londini: 1592. V. 45

BRAY, ANN ELIZA

Henry de Pomeroy; or, the Eve of St. John. A Legend of Cornwall and Devon. London: 1844. V. 38

BRAY, ANNA ELIZA

De Foix, or Sketches of the Manners and Customs of the Fourteenth Century. London: 1826. V. 40

Life of Thomas Stothard, RA. London: 1851. V. 39; 40; 43; 45

Traditions, Legends, Superstitions, and Sketches of Devonshire on the Borders of the Tamar and the Tavy . . . London: 1838. V. 39; 42

Works. London: 1833. V. 37

BRAY, ARTHUR

The Clue of the Postage Stamp. London: and Dublin: 1913. V. 45

BRAY, CHARLES

The Philosophy of Necessity . . . London: 1863. V. 45

BRAY, MARY M.

A Sea Trip in Clipper Ship Days. Boston: 1920. V. 44

BRAY, N. N. E.

Shifting Sands. The True Story of the Arab Revolt. London: 1934. V. 38

BRAY, THOMAS 1656-1730

Bibliotheca Parochialis. London: 1697. V. 38

Papal Usurpation and Persecution, As It Has Been Exercis'd in Ancient and Modern Times. London: 1712-11. V. 39

A Sermon Preached Before the Honourable House of Commons at St. Margaret's Westminster on Monday, January 31, 1763. London: 1763. V. 39

BRAY, WILLIAM

Sketch of a Tour into Derbyshire and Yorkshire. London: 1783. V. 37; 40

BRAYBROOKE, RICHARD

The History of Audley End. London: 1836. V. 37; 39; 41

BRAYER, HERBERT

William Blackmore. Denver: 1949. V. 45

BRAYLEY, E. W.

A Concise Account, Historical and Descriptive of Lambeth Palace. London: 1806. V. 45

BRAYLEY, EDWARD WEDLAKE 1773-1854

Illustrations of Her Majesty's Palace at Brighton; Formerly the Pavilion . . . London: 1838. V. 39

Londiniana; or, Reminiscences of the British Metropolis . . . . London: 1829. V. 44

A Topographical History of Surrey. Dorking: 1841-48. V. 40

A Topographical History of Surrey. London: 1850. V. 37; 41; 44; 46

A Topographical History of Surrey. London: 1860. V. 44

A Topographical History of Surrey. London. V. 38

The Utility of the Knowledge of Nature Considered. London: 1831. V. 38

BRAYNARD, FRANK O.

The Leviathan: The World's Greatest Ship. New York: (1972-78). V. 37

BRAYSHAW, THOMAS

A History of the Ancient Parish of Giggleswick . . . London: 1932. V. 45

BRAYTON, MATTHEW

The Indian Captive. Cleveland: 1860. V. 44; 45

The Indian Captive. Fotoria: 1896. V. 37

BRAYTON, PATIENCE

A Short Account of the Life and Religious Labours of Patience Brayton, Late of Swansey in the State of Massachusetts. New Bedford: 1801. V. 40

BRAZER, ESTHER STEVENS

Early American Decoration. Springfield: 1947. V. 41; 42

BRAZIL

Regimento da Iunta do Comercio Geral do Estado do Brasil. Lisbon: 1673. V. 45

BREADALBANE, MARCHIONESS

The High Tops of Black Mount. V. 38

BREAKENRIDGE, WILLIAM M.

Helldorado. Boston: 1928. V. 45

Helldorado. Bringing the Law to the Mesquite. Boston and New York: 1928. V. 37; 45

BREAKFAST in Perigord. London: 1968. V. 46

BREASTED, JAMES HENRY

Ancient Records of Egypt. Chicago: 1906-20. V. 41

Ancient Records of Egypt. Chicago: 1927. V. 44

Ancient Records of Egypt: Chicago: 1906-07. V. 37; 42

The Edwin Smith Surgical Papyrus. Chicago: 1930. V. 39; 40; 42; 44

Egypt through the Stereoscope: a Journey through the Land of the Pharaohs. New York: 1905. V. 40

Egyptian Servant Statues. Washington: 1948. V. 40; 44

A History of Egypt from the Earliest Times to the persian Conquest. London: (1956). V. 37

Kings and Queens of Ancient Egypt. London: 1925. V. 42

Oriental Forerunners of Byzantine Painting: First-Century Wall Paintings from the Fortress of Dura on the Middle Euphrates. Chicago: 1924. V. 38

BREAZEALE, J. W. M.

Life as It Is; or Matters and Things in General . . . Knoxville: 1842. V. 37; 38; 39

BREBEUF, JEAN DE

Travels and Sufferings Among the Hurons of Canada, as Described by Himself. 1938. V. 38

The Travels and Sufferings of Father Jean de Brebeuf Among the Hurons of Canada. London: 1938. V. 37; 46

The Travels and Sufferings of Father Jean De Brebeuf Among the Hurons of Canada as Described by Himself. Waltham St. Lawrence: 1938. V. 40

The Travels and Sufferings of . . . Among the Hurons of Canada. Waltham St. Lawrence: 1938. V. 41

The Travels and Sufferings of Father Jean de Brebeuf Among the Hurons of Canada as Described by Himself. London: 1955. V. 41

BRECHT, BERTOLT

A Penny for the Poor. New York: 1938. V. 44

The Threepenny Opera. 1982. V. 38

The Threepenny Opera. New York: 1982. V. 41; 43; 44; 45; 46

BRECHT, SAMUEL K.

The Genealogical Record of the Schwenkfelder Families. Pennsburg: 1923. V. 46

BRECK, CHARLES

The Fox Chase. New York: 1808. V. 40

The Trust. New York: 1808. V. 37

BRECK, SAMUEL 1771-1862

Historical Sketch of Continental Paper Money. Philadelphia: 1843. V. 37

Sketch of the Internal Improvements Already Made by Pennsylvania . . . Philadelphia: 1818. V. 43; 45

BRECKINRIDGE, ROBERT J.

Memoranda of Foreign Travel. Philadelphia: 1839. V. 40

BRECKNOCK, TIMOTHY

Poems and Odes, After the Manner of Anacreon. London: 1746. V. 45

BRECKWITH, WILLIAM

Letter to Sir Samuel Romilly, on the Necessity of an Immediate Enquiry into the Causes of Delay in Chancery Proceedings. London: 1810. V. 39

BREDENBURG, JOHANNES

Enervatio Tractatus Theologico-Plitici: Una Cum Demonstratione, Geometrico Ordine Diposita, Naturam non esse Deum . . . Rotterdam: 1675. V. 41; 45

BREDON, JULIET

Peking a Historical and Intimate Description of Its Chief Places of Interest . . . Shanghai: 1922. V. 45

BREE, CHARLES ROBERT

A History of the Birds of Europe, Not Observed in the British Isles. London: 1859-63. V. 37; 38; 40; 41; 43

A History of the Birds of Europe, Not Observed in the British Isles. London: 1863. V. 39; 41

History of the Birds of Europe Not Observed in the British Isles. London: 1875-76. V. 39; 42

A History of the Birds of Europe. London: 1863-60-62-63. V. 37

BREE, JOHN

Saint Herbert's Isle: a Legendary Poem in Five Cantos. London: 1832. V. 45

BREE, JOSEPH

The Cursory Sketch of the State of the Naval, Military and Civil Establishment, Legislative, Judicial and Domestic Economy of this Kingdom, During the 14th Century with a Particular Account of the Campain of King Edward the Third In Normandy & France . . . London: 1791. V. 39

BREED, W. P.

The Theatre. Philadelphia: 1868. V. 46

BREEN, HENRY H.

St. Lucia: Historical, Statistical and Descriptive. London: 1844. V. 42; 45

BREEN, PATRICK

The Diary of Patrick Breen. San Francisco: 1946. V. 37; 40; 41; 42; 43

BREENWOOD, JAMES

The Hatchet Throwers. London: 1866. V. 39

BREES, S. C.

Appendix to Railway Practice . . . London: 1839. V. 46

First (-fourth) Series of Railway Practice: a Collection of Working Plans and Practical Details of Construction in the Public Works of the Most Celebrated Engineers (etc.). London: 1847. V. 46

Railway Practice. London: 1837. V. 46

Second Series of Railway Practice: a Collection of Working Plans and Practical Details of Construction in the Public Works . . . . London: 1840. V. 46

BREESE, LOUIS V.

Some Unwritten Laws of Organized Foxhunting and Comments on the Usage of the Sport of Riding to Hounds in America. N.P.: 1900. V. 43

Some Unwritten Laws of Organized Foxhunting and Comments on the Usage of the Sport of Riding to Hounds in America. N.P.: 1909. V. 39

BREESE, SIDNEY

Reports of Cases at Common Law in the Chancery, Argued an Determined in the Supreme Court of the State of Illinois, from its First Organization in 1819 to the end of December Term 1830. Kaskaskia: 1831. V. 37

BREESKIN, ADELYN DOHME 1896-

The Graphic Work of Mary Cassatt: a Catalogue Raisonne. New York: 1948. V. 42; 45; 46

Mary Cassatt. A Catalogue Raisonne of the Graphic Work. Washington: 1979. V. 39

BREEZE, THOMAS HAMILTON

Round Table Sonnets. San Francisco: 1934. V. 43

BREGER, DAVE

Private Breger in Britain. London: 1944. V. 45

BREHM, ALFRED EDMUND

Bird Life, Being a History of the Bird, Its structure and habits. London: 1874. V. 37

Cassell's Book of Birds. London: 1869-73. V. 46

From North Pole to Equator: Studies of Wild Life and Scenes in Many Lands. London. V. 40

From the North Pole to Equator: Studies of Wild Life and Scenes in Many Lands - in Lapland, Siberia and Africa. London: 1890. V. 39

From the North Pole to the Equator: Studies of Wild Life and Scenes in Many Lands. London: 1895. V. 43

From North Pole to Equator. London: 1896. V. 41

Ornithology; or, the Science of Birds. Columbus: 1878. V. 37; 43

BREHMER, JOHANNA

The Year in Flowers with Poetical Mottoes. Wandsbeck: 1874. V. 39

BREINTNAL, JOSEPH

The Death of King George Lamented in Pennsylvania; Being Part of a Letter to the Author's Country Friend. Philadelphia: 1727. V. 41

BREIT, MARQUITA

Thomas Merton: a Comprehensive Bibliography. New York: 1986. V. 41

BREITENBACH, J.

Fungi of Switzerland. Luzern: 1981-85. V. 37

BRELSFORD, C. E. H.

It's All in the Draw. N.P.: 1895. V. 42

BRELSFORD, W. V.

The Story of the Northern Rhodesia Regiment. Lusaka: 1954. V. 42

BREMER, FREDERIKA

The Homes of the New World: Impressions of America . . . London: 1853. V. 37; 42; 46

The Homes of the New World: Impressions of America. New York: 1854. V. 40; 46

The President's Daughters . . . London: 1843. V. 43

BREMER, FREDRIKA

Greece and the Greeks. The Narrative of a winter residence and summer travel in Greece and its inlands. London: 1863. V. 37

Works. London: 1848-92. V. 39

BREMMER, ROBERT

Excursions in the Interior of Russia; Including Sketches of the Character and Policy of the Emperor Nicholas, Scenes in St. Petersburg. London: 1839. V. 42

BREMNER, DAVID

The Industries of Scotland, Their Rise, Progress and Present Condition. Edinburgh: 1869. V. 39; 41

BREMNER, ROBERT

Excursions in Denmark, Norway and Sweden, Including Notices of the State of Public Opinion in Those Countries, and Anecdotes of Their Courts. London: 1840. V. 39

The Rudiments of Music . . . to which is added, a Collection of the Best Church-Tunes. Edinburgh: 1756. V. 38

BREMOND, GABRIEL DE

L'Heureux Esclve, Nouvelle, 'Cologne, Chez Pierre Marteau, 1677' and (Second Partie) . . . (Troisieme et Derniere Partie). Paris: 1677. V. 38

BRENAN, GERALD

Dr. Partridge's Almanack for 1935. London: 1934. V. 41; 42

The Face of Spain. London: 1950. V. 38

Jack Robinson: a Picturesque Novel. New York: 1934. V. 40

The Lighthouse Always Says Yes. London: 1966. V. 38

Spanish Scene. London: 1946. V. 38

BRENAN, MARTIN

Schools of Kildare and Leighlin, 1775-1835. Dublin: 1935. V. 37; 41; 43; 44

BRENCHLEY, JULIUS L.

Jottings During the Crusie H.M.S. Curacoa Among the South Sea Islands in 1865. London: 1873. V. 41

BRENCKMAN, FRED

History of Carbon County, Pennsylvania. Harrisburg: 1913. V. 41

BREND, GAVIN

My Dear Holmes. A Study in Sherlock. London: 1951. V. 44

BRENNAN, CHRIS

Twenty Three Poems. 1938. V. 42

BRENNAN, J. P.

Scream at Midnight. 1963. V. 44

BRENNAN, JOSEPH PAYNE

The Borders Just Beyond. 1986. V. 46

Nine Horrors and a Dream. Sauk City: 1958. V. 42; 43; 45

BRENNAN, M. J.

An Ecclesiastical History of Ireland from the Introduction of Christianity into that Country to the Year 1829. Dublin: 1864. V. 39

BRENNER, ANITA

The Wind that Swept Mexico: the History of the Mexican Revolution 1910-1942. New York & London: 1943. V. 40

BRENNER, ANITA continued

The Wind that Swept Mexico. History of the Mexican Revolution, 1910-1942. New York: 1943. V. 37

BRENS, S. L.

The 'Fram' Expedition. Nansen in the Frozen World . . . and His Journey Across Northern Greenland with Lieut. R. E. Peary, U.S.N. Philadelphia: 1897. V. 46

BRENT, CHARLES

The Compendious Astronomer . . . London: 1741. V. 43

BRENT, J. THEODORE

How the Republic Rose and Fell. London: 1881. V. 45

BRENTEL, GEORG

Quadrantis Astronomici et Geometrici Utilitates. Lauingen: 1611. V. 38

BRENTON, EDWARD PELHAM

The Naval History of Great Britain, from the Year MDCCLXXXIII to MDCCCXXXVI. London: 1837. V. 42

BRENZ, JOHANN 1499-1570

Ein Evangelion, quod Inscribitur, Secudeum Lucam, Duodecim Priora Capita, Homiliae Centum & Decem, Autore Ionne Brentio. Eisudem Homilie Octoginta in Dudecim Posteriora Capita . . . Francoforti: 1556. V. 38

Ein Evangelion, Quod Inscribitur, Secundum Lucam, Duodecim Priora Capita, Homiliae Centum & Decem, Autore Ioanne Brentio. Francofurti: 1557/56. V. 44

BRERA, VALERIAN LEWIS

A Treatise on Verminous Diseases, Preceded by the Natural History of Intestinal Worms, and their Origin in the Human Body. Boston: 1817. V. 37; 38; 39; 40; 41

BRERETON, F. S.

With Shield and Assegai. A Tale of the Zulu War. London: 1900. V. 39

BRERETON, FREDERICK

An Anthology of War Poems. London: 1930. V. 41

BRERETON, THOMAS

Charnock's Remains; or, S--------l His Coronation. London: 1713. V. 41

BREREWOOD, EDWARD

Enquiries Touching the Diversity of Languages, and Religions through the Cheife Parts of the World. London: 1614. V. 40

Enquiries Touching the Diveristy of Languages and Religions through the Chief Parts of the World. London: 1674. V. 37; 38; 43

Tractatus Quidam Logici de Praedicabilibus, et Praedicamentis . . . Oxford: 1659. V. 41

BRESADOLA, G.

Iconographia Mycologica. London: 1981-82. V. 38

BRESADOLA, GIACOMO

Iconographia Mycologia. Milan: 1927-41. V. 39

BRESLAUER, B. H.

Count Heinrich IV Zu Castel. Austin: 1987. V. 38; 39; 40; 41; 42

BRESLAY, PIERRE

L'Anthologie Ov Recveil de Plvsievrs Discovrs Notables, Tirez de Diuers Bons Autheurs Grecs & Latins. Paris: 1574. V. 39

BRESSANI, FRANCESCO

Breve Relatione d'Alcune Missioni de' PP. Dellas Compagania di Giesu Nella Nuova Francia. Macerata: 1653. V. 37; 38; 39; 40; 42; 44

Breve Relatione d'Alcune Missioni de' PP. Dellas Compagania di Giesu Nella Nuova Francia. Macerata: 1653. V. 44

BRESTED, JAMES HENRY

Oriental Forerunners of Byzantine Painting: First-Century Wall Paintings from the Fortress of Dura on the Middle Euphrates. Chicago: 1924. V. 41

BRETEZ, LOUIS

La Perspective Pratique de l'Architecture . . . Paris: 1706. V. 40; 44; 45

BRETON, ANDRE 1896-1966

Entretiens, 1913-1952. Paris. V. 46

Les Manifestes du Surrealisme. Paris: 1955. V. 38

Manifesto du Surrealisme. 1924. V. 42

Ode A Charles Fourier. Paris: 1961. V. 38

Le Revolver A Cheveux Blancs. Paris: 1932. V. 38

Manifeste du Surrealisme/Poisson Soluble. Paris: 1924. V. 41

Le Surrelaisme et la Peinture. New York: 1945. V. 38

What is Surrealism? London: 1936. V. 37

Young Cherry Trees Secured AGainst Hares. New York: 1946. V. 46

Yves Tanguy. New York: 1946. V. 39

BRETON DE LA MARTINIERE, JEAN BAPTISTE JOSEPH

China: Its Costume, Arts, Manufactures, Etc. London: 1812. V. 41

BRETON, NICHOLAS 1545-1626

Breton's Longing of a Blessed Heart . . . Kent: 1814. V. 43

Englands Selected Characters, Describing the Good and Bad Worthies of This Age. London: 1643. V. 43

A Mad World My Masters and Other Prose Works . . . London: 1929. V. 43

Melancholike Humours. Kent: 1815. V. 41

Phillida and Coridon and Other Pastorals. New York: 1927. V. 45

The Twelve Moenths. London: 1927. V. 46

The Twelve Moenths . . . Waltham St. Lawrence: 1927. V. 38; 44

The Twelve Moneths and Christmas Day from Fantastickes'. New York: 1951. V. 37; 40; 41; 45

The Works in Verse and Prose . . . London: 1879. V. 41

BRETON, RAYMOND

Petit Catechisme ou Sommaire des Trois Premieres Parties de la Doctrine Chrestienne. Auxerre: 1664. V. 45

BRETON, WILLIAM HENRY

Scandinavian Sketches. London: 1835. V. 38

BRETON'S Longing of a Blessed Heart. 1814. V. 38
BRETON'S Longing of a Blessed Heart. Lee Priory: 1814. V. 40

BRETSCHNEIDER, E.

History of European Botanical Discoveries in China. Leipzig: 1981. V. 37; 38

BRETT, EDWIN J.

A Pictorial and Descriptive Record of the Origin and Development of Arms and Armour. London: 1894. V. 37; 46

BRETT, GERARD

The Great Palace of the Byzantine Emperors. 1947-58. V. 43

The Great Palace of the Byzantine Emperors. Oxford: 1947-58. V. 42

BRETT, JOHN

The Judgement of Truth; or Common Sense and Good Nature, on Behalf of Irish Roman Catholics, Occasioned by an Apology Printed for Them in London and an Answer Entitled Considerations etc. by Rev. Mr. Blackburne, Arch Deacon of Cleaveland. Dublin: 1770. V. 46

BRETT, JOHN WATKINS

The Illustrated Sale Catalogue of the Valuable Collection of Pictures and Other Works of Art of the Egyptian, Greek, Roman and Mediaeval Periods . . . of that Eminent Connoisseur John Watkins Brett . . . London: 1864. V. 44

BRETT, THOMAS

An Account of Church Government and Governors. London: 1701. V. 38; 44; 45

Some Considerations on the Times Wherein Marriage is Said to Be Prohibited . . . London: 1709. V. 42

BRETT, W. H.

The Indian Tribes of Guiana; Their Condition and Habits . . . London: 1868. V. 40; 43; 45

BRETTIELL, RICHARD

Catalogue of Drawings by Camille Pissarro in the Ashmolean Museum, Oxford. Oxford: 1980. V. 46

BRETTON, JAMES J.

Voices from the Press; A Collection of Sketches, Essays, and Poems by Practical Printers. New York: 1850. V. 37; 44

BRETZ, J. HARLAN

The Grand Coulee. New York: 1932. V. 45

BREUE Chronicon Rervm Memorablilivm, In Saxonicae Lingvae Gentibus & Vicinis Actuarum, Anno MDLXXX MDLXXXI et Sequentibus Usq(ue) ad Praesentem annum 1586. Upper Germany: 1586. V. 38

BREUER, JOSEF

Studies in Hysteria. New York: 1936. V. 42

BREUIL, ABBE HENRI

Rock Paintings of Southern Andalusia. London: 1929. V. 44

BREUIL, H.

Four Hundred Centuries of Cave Art. Montignac: 1952. V. 46

BREUIL, HENRI

Rock Paintings of Southern Andalusia. Oxford: 1929. V. 42

BREVAL, JOHN DURANT

The Art of Dress. London: 1717. V. 37; 41; 43; 45

Mac-Dermot; or, the Irish Fortune Hunter. London: 1717. V. 46

Mac-Dermont: or, the Irish Fortune-Hunter. London: 1719. V. 45

The Strolers. London. V. 42

The Strolers. London: 1727. V. 42

BREVIER, ABRAHAM G.

The Indians: or, Narratives of Massacres and Depredations on the Frontier, in Wawasink and Its Vicinity, During the American Revolution . . . Rondout: 1846. V. 37

BREVOORT, ELIAS

New Mexico. Her Natural Resources (sic) and Attractions, being a Collection of Facts, Mainly Concerning Her Geography, Climate, Population, Schools, Mines and Minerals, Agricultural and Pastoral Capacities, Prospective Railroads, Public . . . Santa Fe: 1874. V. 37; 38; 39; 40; 42; 43; 45

BREVOORT, HENRY

The Letters of Henry Brevoort to Washington Irving. New York: 1916. V. 39; 40; 41

BREWER, A. T.

History 61st Regiment, Pennsylvania Volunteers, 1861-65. Pittsburgh: 1911. V. 42

BREWER, D. S.

The Thornton Manuscript. 1978. V. 37

BREWER, E. COBHAM

Dictionary of Phrase and Fable. London: 1900. V. 46

BREWER, FRANCES J.

The Fables of Jean De La Fontaine. Los Angeles: 1964. V. 37; 38; 42; 44; 46

BREWER, GEORGE

The Juvenile Lavater or . . . The Passions of Le Brun . . . London: 1813. V. 44

The Juvenile Lavater, or a Familiar Explanation of the Passions of Le Brun. London: 1810. V. 38

The Juvenile Lavater; or, a familiar explanation of the passions of Le Brun . . . London: (1812?). V. 37

The Life of Rolla: a Peruvian Tale. London: 1800. V. 45

BREWER, J. NORRIS

The Beauties of England and Wales; or Delineations Topographical, Historical and Descriptive. London: 1801-18. V. 41

BREWER, JAMES NORRIS fl. 1799-1829

The Beauties of Ireland, Being Original Delineations, Topographical, Historical and Biographical of Each County. London: 1825. V. 37; 40; 43

A Descriptive and Historical Account of Various Palaces, and Public Buildings, English and Foreign. London: 1810. V. 38; 43

A Descriptive and Historical Account of Various Palaces. London: 1821. V. 37; 38; 40; 44; 45

Histrionic Topography; or, the Birthplaces, Residences, and Funeral Monuments of the Most Distinguished Actors. London: 1818. V. 42; 44

The Picture of England; or Historical and Descriptive Delineations of the Most Curious Works of nature and Art in Each County . . . London: 1820. V. 42; 44

BREWER, JOSIAH

Patmos, and the Seven Churches of Asia, Together with Places in the Vicinity, from the Earliest Records to the Year 1850. Bridgeport: 1851. V. 39

A Residence at Constantinople, in the Year 1827. New Haven: 1830. V. 37; 39; 40; 45

A Residence at Constantinople, in the Year 1827. New York: 1830. V. 38

BREWER, LUTHER

My Leigh Hunt Library. The First Edtiions. Collected and Described by Luther A. Brewer. With 100 Illustrations. Cedar Rapids, Iowa: 1932. V. 37

BREWER, LUTHER A.

My Leigh Hunt Library. Cedar Rapids: 1932. V. 45

BREWER, NICHOLAS R.

Trails of a Paintbrush. Boston: 1938. V. 41

BREWER, THOMAS M.

North American Oology, Being an Account of the Habits and Geographical Distribution of the Birds of North America During Their Breeding Season. Washington City: 1857. V. 39

BREWER, WILLIAM HENRY 1838-1910

Such a Landscape! N.P.: 1987. V. 45

Such a Landscape! A Narrative of the 1864 California Geological Survey Exploration of Yosemite, Sequoia and Kings Canyon . . . Yosemite: 1987. V. 38; 39; 41; 44

Up and Down California in 1860-1864. New Haven: 1930. V. 37; 38; 39; 40; 41; 44; 45

BREWERTON, G. DOUGLAS

The War In Kansas: a Rough Trip to the Border Among the New Homes and a Strange People. New York: 1856. V. 46

BREWINGTON, M. V.

The Marine Paintings and Drawings in the Peabody Museum. Salem: 1968. V. 39

Marine Paintings and Drawings in the Peabody Museum. Salem: 1981. V. 45

BREWINGTON, MARION VERNON

Kendall Whaling Museum Paintings. & Kendall Whaling Museum Prints. Sharon: 1965/69. V. 42

BREWSTER, ABEL

Free Man's Companion. Hartford: 1827. V. 37

BREWSTER, CHARLES W.

Rambles About Portsmouth. First Series. Portsmouth: 1873. V. 39

BREWSTER, DAVID

The Kaleidoscope: Its History, Theory and Construction, with Its Application to the Fine and Useful Arts. London: 1858. V. 38

Letters on Natural Magic. New York: 1832. V. 42; 46

Letters on Natural Magic, Addressed to Sir Walter Scott, Bart. London: 1834. V. 42

Letters on Natural Magic. London: 1834, 1837? V. 39

The Life of Sir Isaac Newton. London: 1831. V. 38; 40; 41; 42; 43; 44; 45; 46

Memoirs of Life, Writings and Discoveries of Sir Isaac Newton. Edinburgh: 1855. V. 38; 39; 40; 41; 42; 43; 45; 46

Memoirs of the Life, Writings and Discoveries of Sir Isaac Newton. Edinburgh: 1860. V. 40; 41; 44

The Stereoscope: Its History, Theory and Construction. London: 1856. V. 38; 41

A Treatise on New Philosophical Instruments, for Various Purposes in the Arts and Sciences, with Experiments on Light and Colours. Edinburgh: 1813. V. 38; 43

A Treatise on the Kaleidoscope. Edinburgh: 1819. V. 43

Treatise on Optics Drawn Up for the Edinburgh Encyclopaedia. Edinburgh: 1821. V. 44

A Treatise on Optics. London: 1831. V. 46

A Treatise on Magnetism . . . Edinburgh: 1838. V. 45

Treatise on the Kaleidoscope. Edinburgh & London: 1813. V. 37

BREWSTER, GEORGE

Lectures on Education. Columbus: 1833. V. 39

BREWSTER, JOHN

The Parochial History and Antiquities of Stockton upon Trees . . . Stockton: 1796. V. 37; 41

A Secular Essay: Containing a Retrospective View of Events, Connected With the Ecclesiastical History of England . . . London: 1802. V. 42

BREWSTER, MARGARET MARIA

Letters from Cannes and Nice. Edinburgh: 1857. V. 43

BREWSTER, SAMUEL

A Brief Method of the Law. London: 1680. V. 38; 40

BREWSTER, WILLIAM H.

Official Proceedings of the Second Session of the Columbia Waterway Convention Held at Vancouver, W.T., October 14th, 1886. Vancouver: 1886. V. 43

BREYER, SAMUEL

The Cadet. A Military Treatise. London: 1762. V. 37

BREYNE, JACOB

Exoticarum Aliarumque Minus Cognitarum Plantarum Centuria Prima, cum Figuris Aeneis Summo Studio Elaboratis. Danzig: 1674-1678. V. 37; 42

Exoticarum Aliarumque Minus Cognitarum Plantarum Centuria Prima . . . Danzig (Gdansk): 1678. V. 45

BRIALMONT, ALEXIS H.

Combat Tactics of Cavalry by . . . Being the Second Part of His Work Entitled Combat Tactics of the Three Arms . . . Fort Leavenworth: 1893. V. 40

BRIALMONT, M.

The History and Life of Arthur Duke of Wellington. London: 1858. V. 41

BRIANCOURT, MATHIEU

Organization of Labor and Association. New York: 1847. V. 42

BRIANT, C. C.

History of the Sixth Regiment, Indiana Volunteer Infantry. Indianapolis: 1891. V. 39

BRIANTE, JOHN GOODALE

The Old Root and Herb Doctor, Or The Indian Method of Healing. Claremont, N.H.: 1870. V. 37

BRICCIO, GIOVANNI

Breve Narratione de Martirio di Cinque Persiani . . . Rome: 1623. V. 45

BRICE, JAMES F.

Castle Crosier, (Revised) a Romance . . . Annapolis: 1839. V. 44

BRICKDALE, ELEANOR FORTESCUE

Golden Book of Famous Women. London: 1919. V. 44

BRICKELL, JOHN

The Natural History of North Carolina. Dublin: 1737. V. 39; 40; 43; 45

BRICUSSE, LESLIE

Christmas 1993 or Santa's Last Ride. London: 1987. V. 46

A BRIDAL Gift. Liverpool: 1848. V. 38

THE BRIDAL Souvenir. London: 1857. V. 38; 39; 45

BRIDE, THOMAS FRANCIS

Letters from Victorian Pioneers. Melbourne: 1898. V. 41

BRIDGE, B.

A Treatise on Mechanics . . . London: 1814. V. 45

BRIDGE, FREDERICK

The Form and Order of the Service That is to Be Performed and of the Ceremonies Thate are to Observed in the Corontation of Their Majesties King George V and Queen Mary, in the Abbey Church of S. Peter, Westminster. London: 1911. V. 45

BRIDGE, GEORGE

A Treatise on the Nature and Cultivation of Mangel Wurzel; with Practical Observations on the Method and Utility of Steaming Food for Cattle. Birmingham: 1828. V. 42

BRIDGE, HORATIO

Journal of an African Cruiser. New York: 1845. V. 43; 44

Journal of an African Cruiser: Comprising Sketches of the Canaries, the Cape De Verds, Liberia, Madeira, Sierra Leone, and other Places of Interest on the West Coast of Africa. By an Officer of the U.S. Navy . . . London: 1845. V. 37

BRIDGEMAN, CHARLES

General Plan of the Woods, Park and Gardens of STowe the Seat of the Right Honourable the Lord Viscount Cobham with Several Perspective Views in the Garden. London: 1739. V. 44

BRIDGEMAN, GEORGE

A Description of Bridgeman's Rotary Railway. New York: 1829. V. 42

BRIDGEMAN, T.

The Kitchen Gardener's Instructor . . . New York: 1840. V. 37; 39; 44; 45

The Young Gardener's Assistant . . . New York: 1837. V. 45

BRIDGENS, R.

Furniture with Candelabra and Interior Decoration, Designed by . . . London: 1838. V. 44

BRIDGENS, RICHARD H.

Sefton Church with Part of the Interior Decorations. London: 1822. V. 38

Sefton Church with Part of the Interior Decorations. London: 1835. V. 37

BRIDGER, C. M.

Floral Belles from the Green-House and Garden, Painted from Nature. New York: 1867. V. 37

BRIDGER, CHARLES

An Index to Printed Pedigrees, Contained in County and Local Histories, the Heralds' Visitations, and in the More Important Genealogical Collections. London: 1867. V. 40

BRIDGES, E. LUCAS

Uttermost Part of the Earth. London: 1948. V. 43

BRIDGES, E. S.

Round the World in Six Months. London: 1879. V. 45

BRIDGES, GEORGE WILSON

Alpine Sketches, Comprising a Short Tour through Parts of Holland, Flanders, France, Savoy, Switzerland, and Germany, During the Summer of 1814. London: 1814. V. 43

The Annals of Jamaica. London: 1827 & 1828. V. 40

BRIDGES, HORATIO 1806-1893

Journal of an African Cruiser; Comprising Sketches of the Canaries The Cape De Verds, Liberia, Madeira, Sierra Leone, and Other Places of Interest on the West Coast of Africa. By an Officer of the U.S. Navy. Edited by Nathaniel Hawthorne. New York/London: 1845. V. 37

BRIDGES, JOHN HENRY

The Unity of Comte's Life and Doctrine. London: 1866. V. 45

BRIDGES, ROBERT 1844-1930

Eros and Psyche: a Poem in XII Measures. 1935. V. 42

A Tract on the Present State of English Pronunciation. 1913. V. 46

BRIDGES, ROBERT SEYMOUR 1844-1930

Collected Essays, Papers & Etc. of . . . London: 1927. V. 39

Collected Essays, Papers, Etc. London: 1928. V. 43

Eight Plays. London: 1885-94. V. 39

Eros and Psyche; a Poem in XII Measures. London: 1935. V. 40

Eros and Psyche. Newtown: 1935. V. 37; 38; 40; 41; 43; 45

Eros and Psyche, by Robert Bridges. (Newton, Mont. Wales): 1935. V. 37

The Feast of Bacchus. Oxford. V. 41

The Feast of Bacchus: a Play. Oxford: 1889. V. 37; 40

Hymns. 1899. V. 45

Hymns. Oxford: 1899. V. 37; 41; 42; 44; 46

The Message of One of England's Greatest Poets to a Printer . . . (London: 1931). V. 37

Milton's Prosody. Oxford: 1893. V. 44

New Verse Written in 1921 . . . . Oxford: 1925. V. 42; 43; 45

Now in Wintery Delights. Oxford: 1903. V. 46

October and Other Poems, With Occasional Verses on the War. London: 1920. V. 39

Peace Ode Written On the Conclusion of the Three Years' War. London: 1903. V. 44

Poems. London: 1873. V. 43; 46

Poems. London: 1879. V. 38; 39; 42; 43

Poems. Oxford: 1884. V. 42

Poetical Works. London: 1898-1905. V. 38

The Poetical Works. London: 1912. V. 46

Prometheus the Firegiver. London: 1884. V. 42; 45

Purcell Ode and Other Poems. Chicago: 1896. V. 38; 40; 41

Shorter Poems of Robert Bridges. Oxford: 1893-94. V. 39

The Small Hymn-Book. The Word-Book of the Yattendon Hymnal. Oxford: 1899. V. 38

S(ociety for) P(ure) E(nglish) Tract No. 1: Preliminary A. V. 45

The Testament of Beauty: a Poem in Four Books. New York: 1929. V. 43; 46

The Testament of Beauty. Oxford: 1929. V. 40; 45

BRIDGES, ROY

From Silver to Steel. The Romance of the Broken Hill Proprietary. Melbourne: 1920. V. 37

BRIDGES, THOMAS

A Burlesque Translation of Homer. London: 1774. V. 41

Yamana-English: a Dictionary of the Speech of Tierra del Fuego. 1933. V. 46

BRIDGET, SAINT

Revelationes Stae. Brigittae. Rome: 1628. V. 41; 46

BRIDGEWATER, FRANCIS HENRY EGERTON, 8TH DUKE OF

The First Part (and Second) Part of a Letter to the Parisians, and, The French Nation, Upon Inland Navigation, Containing a Defence of the Public Character of Francis Egerton, Late Duke of Bridgewater . . . N.P.: 1819-20. V. 40

The First Part [and Second] Part of a Letter to the Parisians, and, The French Nation, upon Inland Navigation, containing a Defence of the Public Character of Francis Egerton, late Duke of Bridgewater, &c. &c. Paris: 1819-20. V. 39

BRIDGEWATER, JOHN 1532?-1596?

Concertatio Ecclesiae Catholicae in Anglia Adversus Calvinopapistas et Puritanos sub Elizabetha Regina . . . . Trier: 1594. V. 43

BRIDGLAND, A. S.

The Modern Tailor, Outfitter and Clothier. London: 1920's. V. 39

The Modern Tailor, Outfitter and Clothier. London: (1920). V. 37

BRIDGMAN & Fanning's Illustrated Gazetteer of the United States . . . New York: 1855. V. 45

BRIDGMAN, ELIJAH COLEMAN

Description of the City of Canton. Canton: 1839. V. 40

BRIDGMAN, FREDERICK ARTHUR

Winters in Algeria. New York: 1890. V. 38

BRIDGMAN, JOHN

An Historical and Topographical Sketch of Knole, in Kent, with a Brief Genealogy of the Sackville Family. London: 1817. V. 41

BRIDGMAN, ORLANDO

Conveyances; Being Select Precedents of Deeds and Instruments Concerning the most Considerable Estates in England. London: 1689. V. 38

BRIDGMAN, PERCY

Collected Experimental Papers. Cambridge: 1964. V. 38; 41

BRIDGMAN, RAYMOND L.

Concord Lectures on Philosophy Comprising Outlines of All the Lectures at the Concord Summer School of Philosophy in 1882 with an Historical Sketch . . . Cambridge: 1883. V. 44

BRIDGMAN, RICHARD WHALLEY

A Short View of Legal Bibliography Containing Some Critical Observations on the Authority of the Reporters and Other Law Writers . . . London: 1807. V. 46

BRIDLE, WILLIAM

A Narrative of the Rise and Progress of the Improvements Effected in His Majesty's Gaol at Ilchester, in the County of Somerset, Between July 1808 and November 1821 . . . Bath: 1822. V. 45

A BRIEF Account of the Life and Family of Miss Jenny Cameron, the Reputed Mistress of the Pretendr's Eldest Son. London: 1746. V. 44

A BRIEF Account of the Chronometer, With Remarks on Those Furnished by Parkinson, and Frodsham to the Expeditions of Captain Ross, Parry, Sabine, King, Lyon, Foster and Other Distinguished Navigators with the Rate of Others Tried . . . London: 1832. V. 43

A BRIEF Account of the Execution of the Six Militia Men. N.P.: 1828. V. 45

A BRIEF Account of the Life and Family of Miss Jenny Cameron, The Reputed Mistress of the Pretender's Eldest Son. London: 1746. V. 38

A BRIEF Account of the Proceedings of the Committee, Appointed by the Yearly Meeting of Friends, Held in Baltimore, for Promoting the Improvement and Civilization of the Indian Natives. London: 1806. V. 44

A BRIEF and True Representation of the Posture of Our Affairs . . . London: 1745. V. 45

A BRIEF and True Representation of the Posture of Our Affairs: Containing a Particular Account of the Dangers to Be Apprehended From the Present Invasion . . . London: 1745. V. 41

A BRIEF Description and a Few Testimonials Concerning the Corn Belt of South Dakota . . . Yankton: 1893. V. 44

A BRIEF Description of the Province of Carolina on the Coasts of Florida, and More Particularly of a New-Plantation Begun by the English at Cape-Feare. London: 1666. V. 38

BRIEF Description of the Works Executed in the Drainage and Sanitation of the City of Mexico for the American Society of Civil Engineers in Its XXXIX Annual Convention. Mexico: 1907. V. 38

A BRIEF Discourse on Wine; Embracing an Historical and Descriptive Account of the Vine, Its Culture and Produce in All Countries, Ancient and Modern. London: 1861. V. 40

A BRIEF Historical Account of the Romance of British Columbia. 1934. V. 38

A BRIEF Memoir Concerning Abel Thomas, a Minister of the Gospel of Christ in the Society of Friends. Philaelphia: 1824. V. 46

A BRIEF Memoir of Bernard Bolingbroke Woodward, Librarian in the Ordinary to the Queen and Keeper of the Prints and Drawings at Windsor Castle. London: 1873. V. 42

A BRIEF Record of the Advance of the Egyptian Expeditionary Force . . . Cairo: 1919. V. 37; 42

A BRIEF Record of the Advance of the Egyptian Expeditionary Force Under the Command of Sir H. H. Allenby . . . London: 1919. V. 42

BRIEF Recueil de Tovtes Les Sortes de Ievx, Qu' Avoient les Anciens Graecz & Romains, et Comment Ilz Vsoient d'Iceulx. Paris: 1542. V. 44

BRIEF Remarks on the Slave Registry Bill: and Upon a Special Report of the African Institution Recommending the Measure. London: 1816. V. 37

A BRIEF Reply to Mr. Gill's Doctrine of the Trinity; Being a Defence of a Small Piece, Intitled, the Great Concern of Jew and Gentile. London: 1743. V. 41

A BRIEF Sketch of the Morris Movement and of the Firm Founded by William Morris to Carry Out His Designs and the Industries Revived or Started by Him. London: 1911. V. 38

BRIEGER, PETER

illuminated Manuscripts of the Divine Comedy. Princeton: 1969. V. 46

BRIEGER, PETER H.

The Trinity College Apocalypse, An Introduction and Description. London: 1967. V. 40

BRIELLAT, THOMAS

Trial of Thomas Briellat, for Seditious Words, Before Mr. Mainwaring, at the Sessions-House, Clerkenwell-Green, December 6, 1793. London: 1794. V. 45

BRIER CREEK ASSOCIATION

Minutes of the Forty-Third Annual Session of the Brier Creek Association, Convened at Grassy Knob Meeting House, Iredell County, N.C . . . in Sept. 1864. N.P.: 1864. V. 44

BRIERLEY, BEN

'Ab-o'th-Yate' Sketches and Other Short Stories. Oldham: 1896. V. 41

BRIERLEY, BENJAMIN

'Ab-o'th'-Yate' Sketches and Other Short Stories. Oldham: 1896. V. 41; 42; 43

Irkdale; or, the Odd House in the Hollow. London: 1865. V. 37

BRIERLY, BEN

Ab-O-th-Yate. Sketches and Other Short Stories. Oldham: 1896. V. 43

BRIERRE DE BOISMONT, ALEXANDRE J. F. 1798-1881

Hallucinations; or, the Rational History of Apparitions, Dreams, Ecstasy, Magnetism and Somnambulism. Philadelphia: 1853. V. 43; 45; 46

BRIFFAULT, ROBERT

The Mothers: a Study of the Origins of Sentiments and Institutions. New York: 1927. V. 41; 44; 45

THE BRIGAND, or, A Tale of the West Done into Rhyme. Georgetown: 1845. V. 37; 40

BRIGANTI, GIULIANO

The View Painters Europe. London: 1970. V. 43; 46

THE BRIGANTINE; or, Admiral Lowe. New York: 1839. V. 43; 45

BRIGDEN, F. H.

Canadian Landscape. Toronto: 1944. V. 39

BRIGGS, ARTHUR

Catalogue of the Library . . . Being a Collection of . . . Books, Mostly Preserved in Splendid Bindings by Bedford, Zaehnsdorf, Riviere, Mackenzie, Kalthoeber, etc. Bradford: 1893. V. 38

Catalogue of the Library . . . Being a Collection of . . . Books, Mostly Preserved in Splendid Bindings by Bedford, Zaehnsdorf, Riviere, Mackenzie, Kalthoebe, etc . . . London: 1893. V. 40

BRIGGS, CHARLES

The Reign of Terror in Kansas. Boston: 1856. V. 37; 38; 39

BRIGGS, E. C.

Address to the Saints in Utah and California. Plano: 1869. V. 42

BRIGGS, EMILY EDSON

Ellen Parry; or, Trials of the Heart. New York: 1850. V. 43

BRIGGS, HENRY

Mathematical Tables, Contrived after a Comprehensive Method . . . London: 1726. V. 40

BRIGGS, HORACE

Letters from Alaska and the Pacific Coast. Buffalo: 1889. V. 39

BRIGGS, J.

The Lonsdale Magazine, or, Provincial Repository . . . Kendall: 1820-22. V. 41

BRIGGS, L. CABOT

Bullterriers, the Biography of a Breed. New York: 1940. V. 39; 43

BRIGGS, LLOYD VERNON

Arizona and New Mexico 1882, California 1886, Mexico 1891. Boston: 1932. V. 38; 39; 41; 42; 43; 44; 45; 46

Around Cape Horn to Honolulu on the Bark 'Amy Turner' 1880. Boston: 1926. V. 37; 38; 39; 44

California and the West, 1881 and Later. Boston: 1931. V. 37; 38; 41; 46

Experiences of a Medical Student in Honolulu and on the Island of Oahu, 1881. Boston: 1926. V. 44

BRIGGS, LLOYD VERNON continued

History of Shipbuilding on North River, Plymouth County, Massachusetts. Boston: 1889. V. 45

The Manner of Man That Kills. Boston: 1921. V. 43; 45

BRIGGS, MARTIN SHAW

Muhammadan Architecture in Egypt and Palestine. Oxford: 1924. V. 44

BRIGGS, RAYMOND

Father Christmas. London: 1973. V. 41

Fungus the Bogeyman. London: 1977. V. 41

Gentleman Jim. London: 1980. V. 41

The Snowman. London: 1978. V. 41

BRIGGS, RICHARD

The New Art of Cookery, According to the Present Practice. Philadelphia: 1792. V. 39

BRIGGS, SOPHIA

The Gitana. London: 1845. V. 40

BRIGHAM, AMARIAH 1798-1849

A Letter from Doctor Brigham to David M. Reese, M.D. N.P.: 1836? V. 45; 46

Observations on the Influence of Religion Upon the Health and Physical Welfare of Mankind. Boston: 1835. V. 39

Remarks on the Influence of Mental Cultivation and Mental Excitment Upon Health. Philadelphia: 1845. V. 43

BRIGHAM, CHARLES B.

Surgical Cases. Cambridge: 1876. V. 39

BRIGHAM, CLARENCE S.

History and Bibliography of American Newspapers, 1690-1820. Worcester: 1947. V. 38; 39; 40; 42

Paul Revere's Engraving. Worcester: 1954. V. 41; 42; 43; 44; 46

BRIGHAM, JOHNSON

Iowa, Its History and Its Foremost Citizens. Chicago: 1915. V. 38

BRIGHAM, LALA MALOY

The Story of Council Grove on the Santa Fe Trail. N.P.: 1921. V. 46

BRIGHAM, WILLIAM T.

Guatemala the Land of the Quetzal. New York: 1887. V. 40

A Handbook for Visitors to the Bernice Pauahi Bishop Museum. Honolulu: 1903. V. 37

Mat and Basket Weaving of the Ancient Hawaiians Described and Compared with the Basketry of the Other Pacific Islanders. Honolulu: 1906. V. 38

The Volcanoes of Kilauea and Mauna Loa on the Island of Hawaii. Their Variously Recorded History to the Present Time. Honolulu: 1909. V. 37

BRIGHOUSE, J. H.

Old Klimber Hal. London: 1884. V. 41

BRIGHT, C. D.

Discords. London: 1894. V. 43

BRIGHT, CHARLES

Submarine Telegraphs, Their History, Construction and Working. London: 1898. V. 40

BRIGHT, P. M.

A Monograph of the British Aberrations of the Chalkhill Blue Butterfly Lysander Coridon. Bournemouth: 1938. V. 39

A Monograph of the British Aberrations of the Chalk-hill Blue Butterfly Lysandra Cordion. Bournemouth: 1938-41. V. 38

BRIGHT, RICHARD 1789-1858

Clinical Memoirs on Abdominal Tumors and Intumescence by the Late Dr. Bright. London: 1860. V. 42; 45

Reports of Medical Cases . . . London: 1827. V. 40; 43

Travels from Vienna Through Lower Hungary; with Some Remarks on the State of Vienna During the Congress, in the Year 1814. Edinburgh: 1818. V. 37; 41; 42; 45

BRIGHTWELL, CECILIA LUCY

Heroes of the Laboratory and the Workshop, by Cecilia Lucy Brightwell. London: 1860. V. 37

Memorials of the Life of Amelia Opie. Norwich: 1854. V. 42; 44; 45

BRIGITTA, SAINT

Revelationes. Nuremberg: 1500. V. 37

BRILL, CHARLES J.

Conquest of the Southern Plains. Oklahoma City: 1938. V. 37; 46

BRILLAT-SAVARIN, JEAN ANTHELME 1755-1826

Aphorismes, Menus et Varietes. 1961. V. 44

The Handbook of Dining. New York: 18675. V. 40

Physiologie du Gout ou Meditations de Gastronomie Transcendante; Ouvrage Theorique, Historique et a l'Ordre du Jour, Dedie Aux Gastronomes Parisiens, par un Professeur . . . Paris: 1826. V. 45

The Physiology of Taste. Philadelphia: 1854. V. 39; 40; 43

The Physiology of Taste. London: 1925. V. 37; 42

Physiology of Taste, or Meditations on Transcendental Gastronomy. Garden City: 1926. V. 39

The Physiology of Taste. New York: 1949. V. 40; 41; 44; 46

BRILLIANT, RICHARD

Pompeii A.D. 79: The Treasure of Rediscovery. Kent: 1979. V. 43

BRILL'S First Encyclopedia of Islam, 1913-1936. 1987. V. 37

BRIM, CHARLES

Medicine in the Bible, the Pentateuch, Torah. New York: 1936. V. 38; 41

BRIMFIELD, Mass. Gospel Congregational Church & Society. Ecclesiastical Council, 1801. Authentic Copy of the Result of the Ecclesiastical Council, Convened in Brimfield, March 12, 1801. Worcester: 1801. V. 43

BRIMMER, MARTIN

Egypt: Three Essays on the History, Religion and Art of Ancient Egypt. Cambridge: 1892. V. 40; 42; 44

BRIN, D.

Startide Rising. 1985. V. 39

The Uplift War. 1987. V. 43; 44

BRINCKERHOFF, SIDNEY B.

Lancers for the King: a Study of the Frontier Military System of Northern New Spain. Phoenix: 1965. V. 41

BRINCKLE, WILLIAM D.

Hoffy's North American Pomologist, Containing Numerous Finely Colored Drawings. Philadelphia: 1860. V. 39; 44

BRINCKMANN, A. E.

Barock-Bozzetti: Italian Sculptors. Frankfurt: 1923. V. 42

BRINDLEY, GEORGE

Catalogue of the American Library of the Late Mr. George Brindley. Hartford: 1878-93. V. 40

BRINDLEY, JAMES

The History of Inland Navigations. London. V. 39

The History of Inland Navigations. London: 1766. V. 42

The History of Inland Navigations. London: 1769. V. 42

Reports Relative to a Navigable Communication Betwist the Firths of Forth and Clyde. Edinburgh: 1768. V. 39

BRINDLEY, JOSEPH

The New System of Naval Archiecture, to Present Ships Foundering at Sea. London: 1824. V. 41

BRINDLEY, WILLIAM

Ancient Sepulchral Monuments. London: 1887. V. 39; 42

BRINE, LINDESAY

Travels Amongst American Indians, Their Ancient Earthworks and Temples, Including a Journey in Guatemala, Mexico and Yucatan, and a Visit to the Ruins of Patinamit, Utatlan, Palenque and Uxmal. V. 39

Travels Amongst American Indians, Their Ancient Earthworks and Temples, including a Journey in Guatemala, Mexico, and Yucatan, and a Visit to the Ruins of Patinamit, Utatlan, Palenque and Uxmal. London: 1894. V. 37

BRINE, MARY DOW

Somebody's Mother. Baltimore: 1967? V. 41

BRINGAS DE MANZANEDA Y ENCINAS, DIEGO MIGUEL

Sermon que en las Solemnes Honras Celebradas en Obsequio de los vv. pp. Predicadores Apostolicos fr. Francisco Tomas Hermenegildo Garces . . . Misioneros . . . Madrid: 1819. V. 39; 40; 45

Sermon Que en las Solemnes Honras Celebradasen Obsquio de los VV.PP. Predicadores Apostolicos Fr. Francisco Tomas Hermenegildo Garces. Madrid: 1890. V. 43

BRINGHAM, WILLIAM T.

Ka Hana Kapa. The Making of Bark Cloth in Hawaii. Honolulu: 1911. V. 43

BRININSTOOL, E. A.

Crazy Horse - Greatest Fighting Chief of the Ogalalla Sioux - His Tragic End. Los Angeles: 1949. V. 37

Dull Knife. Hollywood: 1935. V. 45

BRININSTOOL, E. A. continued

A Trooper with Custer, and Other Historic Incidents of the Battle of the Little Big Horn. Columbus: 1925. V. 46

BRINISTOOL, E. A.

The Custer Fight. Capt. Benteen's Story of the Little Big Horn June 25-26, 1876. Hollywood: 1933. V. 45

BRINK, L. P.

A Vocabulary of the Navaho Language. St. Michaels: 1912. V. 40; 42; 44

BRINKERHOFF, SIDNEY B.

Lancers for the King. Phoenix: 1965. V. 39; 40

BRINKEY, FRANK

Japan. Boston: 1897. V. 43

BRINKLEY, FRANK

A History of the Japanese People from the Earliest Times to the End of the Meiji Era. New York & London: 1914. V. 39

Japan Described and Illustrated by the Japanese. Boston: 1897-98. V. 40

Japan: Its History Arts and Literature. Boston: 1901-02. V. 46

Japan: Its History, Arts and Literature. Boston & Tokyo: 1901-02. V. 39

Japan and China. Their History Arts and Literature. London: 1903-04. V. 46

Oriental Series: Japan and China. Boston & Tokyo: 1901. V. 40

Oriental Series: Japan and China. Boston & Tokyo: 1901-02. V. 40

Oriental Series: Japan and China. Boston & Tokyo: 1901-03. V. 46

BRINKLEY, JOHN

Oriental Series: Japan and China. Tokyo. V. 46

BRINLEY, GEORGE

Catalogue of the American Library of the Late Mr. George Brinley. New York: 1879-93. V. 43

BRINNIN, JOHN MALCOLM

Dylan Thomas in America. London: 1956. V. 41; 42

BRINSMADE, PETER ALLEN

Report of the Case of Peter Allen Brinsmade, of the Firm of Ladd & Co. Versus James Jackson Jarves, Editor of the Polynesian, for Alledged (sic) Libelous Publications . . . Honolulu;: 1846. V. 40

BRINSTOOL, E. A.

Major Reno Vindicated. Hollywood: 1935. V. 45

BRINTON, ANNA COX

A Pre-Raphaelite Aeneid of Virgil in the Collection of Mrs. Edward Laurence Doheny of Los Angeles. Being an Essay in Honor of the William Morris Centenary by . . . Los Angeles: 1934. V. 38

BRINTON, DANIEL G.

American Hero-Myths. Philadelphia: 1882. V. 42

The Annals of the Cakchiquels, the Original Text, with a Translation, Notes and Introduction. Philadelphia: 1885. V. 39

A Guide Book of Florida and the South. Philadelphia: 1869. V. 41

The Lenape and Their Legends: With the Complete Text and Symbols of the Walum Olum, a New Translation . . . Philadelphia: 1885. V. 43

A Lenape-English Dictionary from an Anonymous Ms. in the Archives of the Moravian Church at Bethlehem, Pa. Philadelphia: 1888. V. 43

The Maya Chronicles. Philadelphia: 1882. V. 39

Notes on the Floridan Peinsula, Its Literary History, Indian Tribes and Antiquities. Philadelphia: 1859. V. 37; 39; 40; 41; 45

Rig Veda Americanus - Sacred Songs of the Ancient Mexicans, with a Gloss in Nahuatl. Philadelphia: 1890. V. 39

BRINTON'S LIMITED

Seamless Carpets. Catalogues 1938-41. London: 1938-41. V. 37

BRION DE LA TOUR, LOUIS

Atlas General Civil et Ecclesiastique. Paris: 1767. V. 38; 41

THE BRIQUET Album, a Miscellany on Watermarks, Supplementing Dr. Briquet's Les Filigranes, by Various Paper Scholars. Hilversum: 1952. V. 41

BRIQUET, C. M.

Briquet's Opuscula, the Complete Works of Dr. C. M. Briquet Without Les Filigranes. Hilversum: 1955. V. 41

Les Filigranes, Dictionnaire Historique des Marques du Papier. Hildesheim: 1984. V. 38

BRISBANE, ALBERT

A Concise Exposition of the Doctrine of Association, or Plan for Re-Organization of Society . . . New York: 1843. V. 37

Social Destiny of Man. Philadelphia: 1840. V. 38; 39; 43; 45

BRISBANE, CHARLES

A Communication from . . . Governor of Saint Vincent, to the House of Assembly of that Colony, Enclosing Lord Bathurst's Dispatch of the 9th of July, with the Joint reply of the Council and Assembly: and a Letter Depicting the . . . (London): 1823. V. 37

BRISBANE, JOHN

The Anatomy of Painting; or a short and Easy Introduction to Anatomy . . . London: 1769. V. 44

BRISBANE, THOMAS MAKDOUGALL

Reminiscences. Edinburgh: 1860. V. 38; 40

BRISBIN, JAMES S.

The Beef Bonanza or How to Get Rich on the Plains. Philadelphia: 1881. V. 37; 38; 45

BRISCOE, JOHN

A Discourse of Money. London: 1696. V. 37; 38

BRISDON, G. D. R.

Natural History Manuscript Resources in the British isles. London: 1980. V. 37

BRISEUX, CHARLES ETIENNE 1660-1754

Traite du Beau Essentiel Dans les Arts Applique Particulierement a l'Architecture. Paris: 1752. V. 38; 45

BRISOL, ELIZABETH HERVEY, COUNTESS OF

An Authentic Detail of Particulars Relative to the Late Duchess of Kingston, During Her Connection with the Duke . . . London: 1790. V. 45

BRISSAUD, EDOUARD

Anatomie du Cerveau de l'Homme Morphologie des Hemispheres Cerebraux ou Cerveau Propremeni Du Texte et Figures. Atlas. Paris: 1893. V. 44

BRISSON, BARNABE

De Regio Persarum Principatu Libri Tres. Heidelberg: 1595. V. 41

BRISSON, MATHURIN-JACQUES

The Physical Principles of Chemistry. To which is added, a Short Appendix by the Translator. Translated from the French. London: 1801. V. 37

BRISSON, PIERRE RAYMOND DE

An Account of the Shipwreck and Captivity of M. de Brisson; Containing a Description of the Deserts of Africa, from Senegal to Morocco. London: 1789. V. 45

An Historical Narrative of the Shipwreck and Captivity of Mr. de Brisson, an Officer Belonging to the Administration of the French Colonies. Perth: by R. Morison, Jr.,: 1789. V. 37

BRISSOT DE WARVILLE, JACQUES PIERRE 1754-1793

The Commerce of America with Europe. New York: 1795. V. 39; 42; 43; 45

Examen Critique des Voyages dans l'Amerique Septentrionale, de M. le Marquis de Chatellux (sic); ou Lettre a M. le Marquis de Chatellux, Dans Laquelle on Refute Principalement ses Opinions sur les Quakers, sur les Negres . . . Londres: i.e. Paris: 1786. V. 39

New Travels in the United States of America. Peformed in 1788. Dublin: 1792. V. 45

New Travels in the United States of America. Performed in 1788. London: 1792. V. 39

New Travels in the United States of America Performed in 1788. New York: 1792. V. 39; 42

New Travels in the United States of America. London: 1794. V. 37; 39; 42

New Travels in the United States, Performed in 1788. Boston: 1797. V. 46

Nouveau Voyage dans les Etats-Unis. Paris: 1791. V. 37; 42; 44

To His Constituents, on the Situation of the National Convention; On the Influence of the Anarchists. London: 1794. V. 37; 39

BRISTED, CHARLES ASTON

The Upper Ten Thousand: Sketches of American Society. London: 1852. V. 37

BRISTED, JOHN

America and Her Resources. London: 1818. V. 39; 42

Anthroplanomenos; or a Pedestrian Tour through Part of the Highlands of Scotland in 1801. London: 1803. V. 44

Les Etats-Unis d'Amerique; ou, Tableau de l'Agriculture, du Commerce, des Manufactures, des Finances, de la Politique. Paris: 1826. V. 38

Hints on the National Bankruptcy of Britain, and On Her Resources to Maintain the Present Contest with France. New York: 1809. V. 41

An Oration on the Utility of Literary Establishments. New York: 1814. V. 45

The Resources of the United States of America. New York: 1818. V. 37; 40; 46

BRISTOL, J.

Fancyclopedia. (with) Fancyclopedia #2. 1944. V. 39

BRISTOW, AMELIA

The Orphans of Lissau, and Other Interesting Narratives, Immediately Connected with Jewish Customs, Domestic and Religious, with Explanatory Notes. London: 1830. V. 45

BRISTOW, BENJAMIN HELM

Memorial of Benjamin Helm Bristow. Cambridge: 1897. V. 44

BRISTOW, GWEN

Deep Summer. New York: 1937. V. 42; 45

Deep Summer. New York: (1937). V. 37

BRISTOW, H. W.

The Geology of the Isle of Wight. London: 1889. V. 46

BRISTOW, JAMES

A Narrative of the Sufferings of James Bristow, Belonging to the Bengal Artillery (sic) During Ten Years Captivity with Hyder Ally and Tippoo Saheb. Calcutta Printed: 1794. V. 45

A Narrative of the Sufferings of James Bristow, Belonging to the Bengal Artillery, During Ten Years Captivity with Hyder Ally and Tippoo Saheb. London: 1794. V. 43

BRISTOWE, JOHN S.

The Physiological and Pathological Relations of the Voice and Speech. London: 1880. V. 37; 38; 39

BRITAINE, WILLIAM DE

The Dutch Usurpation. London: 1672. V. 37

The Interest of England in the Present War with Holland. London: 1672. V. 37

BRITAIN'S Mistakes (with) A Supplement to Britain's Mistakes in the Commencement and Conduct of the Present War. London: 1740. V. 41; 45

BRITANNIA Illustrata or Views of Several of the Queens Palaces As Also of the Principal Seats of the Nobility and Gentry of Great Britain Curiously Engraven on 80 Copper Plates. London: 1709. V. 42

BRITANNIA in Mourning; or, a Review of the Politicks and Conduct of the Court of Great Britain with Regard to France, the Ballance of Power, and the True Interest of These Nations . . . London: 1742. V. 41; 45

BRITANNIA TRIUMPHANT. Or An Account of the Seafights and Victories of the English Nation. London: 1777. V. 41

BRITANNIAE Speculum, or, a Short View of the Ancient and Modern State of Great Britian. London: 1683. V. 41

BRITANNICA Curiosa; or, a Description of the Most Remarkable Curiosities, Natural and Artifical of the Island of Great Britain, in the Several Counties, Cities, Towns, Villages, etc. London: 1777. V. 39

BRITANNICUS, MENTOR

An Heroic Epistle (in verse) Addressed to G.L. Wardle, Esq. M.P. on the Charges Preferred by Him Against His Royal Highness the Duke of York and Foundation of Those Charles, by Mentor Britannicus. London: 1809. V. 39

BRITIAN'S Industrial Future. London: 1928. V. 38

THE BRITISH Album. Containing the Poems of Della Crusca, Anna Matilda, Arley, Benedict, the Bard &c. London: 1792. V. 37

THE BRITISH American Guide-Book . . . New York: 1859. V. 42

BRITISH AND FOREIGN SCHOOL SOCIETY

Education in Greece: An Appeal to the Public from the British and Foreign School Society, On the Subject of Education in Greece. London. V. 43

THE BRITISH Apollo, or, Curious Amusements for the Ingenious. To Which are Added the Most Material Occurrences Foreign and Domestick. London: 1708-09. V. 39

BRITISH Artisan Expedition to the World's Fair, Chicago, organised by the DUndee Courrier and the Dundee Weekly News. Dundee: 1893. V. 37

BRITISH Artists at the Front. Paul Nash. London: 1918. V. 46

BRITISH Castles; or, a Compendious History of the Ancient Military Structures of Great Britain. London: 1825. V. 45

BRITISH Classics. London. V. 46

BRITISH COLUMBIA

Coiled Basketry in British Columbia . . . by Haberlin, Roberts and Teit. Washington: 1928. V. 37

BRITISH Columbia, Canada's Most Westerly Province: Its Position, Advantages, Resources, and Climate. N.P.: 1899. V. 42

BRITISH COLUMBIA. DEPARTMENT OF LANDS

British Columbia. 1912. Victoria: 1912. V. 44

BRITISH COLUMBIA. HOUSE OF ASSEMBLY

Report of the Committee on Crown Lands of Vancouver Island. Victoria: 1864. V. 46

BRITISH COLUMBIA. LANDS & WORKS DEPT.

British Columbia. Columbia River Expedition 1866. Reports and Journals Relating to the Government Exploration of the Country Lying Between the Shuswap and Okanagan Lakes and the Rocky Mountains. Victoria: 1869. V. 40

BRITISH COLUMBIA. LAWS, STATUTES, ETC. - 1858

Proclamation by His Excellency James Douglas, (issuing) An Act to Provide for the Government of British Columbia, (2d August, 1858). Fort Langly: 1858. V. 40

BRITISH Columbia Pictorial and Biographical. Winnipeg: 1914. V. 45

THE BRITISH Critic, A New Review, for May (1793 to December 1796). London: 1793-96. V. 40

BRITISH Curiosities in Nature and Art . . . London: 1713. V. 42; 46

THE BRITISH Drama; A Collection of the Most Esteemed Tragedies, Comedies, Operas and Farces, in the English Language. London: 1824-26. V. 39; 42

THE BRITISH Encyclopaedia . . . Manchester: 1806. V. 39

BRITISH ENTOMOLOGICAL AND NATURAL HISTORY SOCIETY

Proceedings and Transactions. London: 1968-1984. V. 38

THE BRITISH Flag Triumphant! or The Wooden Walls of Old England. London: 1806. V. 42

BRITISH Flowering Plants. London: 1914. V. 41

BRITISH GUIANA. LAWS STATUTES, ETC.

An Act for More Fully Ascertaining the Slave Population of the United Colony of Demerary and Essequebo; and for Other Purposes. Georgetown: 1817. V. 40

BRITISH Hunts and Huntsmen. Compiled in conjunction with Sporting Life. London: 1898-1911. V. 37

BRITISH Hunts and Huntsmen . . . Containing a Short History of Each Fox and Stag Hunt in the British Isles . . . London: 1908-11. V. 39

BRITISH INSTITUTION FOR PROMOTING THE FINE ARTS

An Historical Catalogue of Portraits, Representing Distinguished Persons in the History and Literature of the United Kingdom. London: 1820. V. 40

THE BRITISH Lithographer. A Journal for Lithographers, Artists, Draughtsmen, Phototypers, Wood, Steel and Copperplate Engravers, &c. London: 1891-95. V. 41

THE BRITISH Magazine or Monthly Repository for Gentlemen and Ladies. London: Vol.: 1760-66. V. 38

THE BRITISH Military Library. London: 1804. V. 39

BRITISH MUSEUM.

The American Drawings of John White 1577-1590 with Drawing sof European and Oriental Subjects by Paul Hulton and David Beers Quinn. 1964. V. 46

The Buildings of the British Museum. London: 1914. V. 37

Catalogue of Printed Maps, Charts and Plans, Photographic Edition Complete to 1964 . . . (with) . . . Ten Year Supplement 1965-1974. London: 1967 & 1978. V. 40

Carchemish. Report on the Excavations at Djerabis on Behalf of the British Museum. London: 1914. V. 41

Catalogue of Printed Maps, Plans and Charts in the British Museum. London: 1885. V. 45

A Catalogue of Japanese and Chinese Woodcuts. London: 1916. V. 44

Catalogue of Western Manuscripts in the Old Royal and King's Collections by Sir George F. Warner, D. Litt., F.B.A. and Julius P. Gilson, M.A. London: 1921. V. 45

A Catalogue of the Works of Linnaeus (and Publications More Immediately Relating Thereto) Preserved in the Libraries of the British Museum. London: 1933. V. 41

Catalogue of Books Printed in the XVth Century Now in the British Museum. London: 1963-71. V. 45

Catalogue of Egyptian Antiquities in the British Museum. II. Wooden Model Boats. London: 1972. V. 41

A Catalogue of the Lamps in the British Museum. London: 1975-1980. V. 40

Catalogue of Birds. London: 1875-98. V. 37

Catalogue of Birds. Volume 9, Cinnyrimorphae; Nectariniidae and Meliphagidaae. London: 1884. V. 37

Catalogue of Birds. Volume 11, Fringilliformes, part 2: Coerebidae, Tanagridae and Icteridae. London: 1886. V. 37

BRITISH MUSEUM. continued

Catalogue of Birds. Volume 12. Fringilliformes, part 3; Fringillidae. London: 1888. V. 37

Catalogue of Birds, Volume 15, Tracheophonae; Dendrocolaptidae, Formicariidae, Conopophagidae and Pteroptochidae. London: 1890. V. 37

Catalogue of Birds, Volume 18, Scansores; Picidae. London: 1890. V. 37

Catalogue of Books Printed in the XVth Century Now in the British Museum. London: 1963-71. V. 46

Catalogue of Books Printed in the XVth Century now in the British Museum. Part 1 (to VIII); London: 1963. V. 44

A Catalogue of Early German and Flemish Woodcuts Preserved in the Department of Prints in the British Museum. London: 1903/11. V. 44

Catalogue of Egyptian Antiquities in the British Museum IV: Glass. London: 1976. V. 44

Catalogue of English Porcelain Earthenware Enamels and Glass Collected by Charles Schreiber and the Lady Charlotte Elizabeth Schreiber and Presented to the Museum in 1884. London: 1924-30. V. 46

Catalogue of Engraved British Portraits Preserved in the Department of Prints and Drawings in the British Museum. London: 1908-25. V. 44

Catalogue of the Books, Manuscripts, Maps and Drawings in the British Museum (Natural History). London: 1903-15. V. 46

Catalogue of the Books, Manuscripts, Maps and Drawings in the British Museum (Natural History). London: 1992. V. 46

Catalogue of the Fifty Manuscripts & Printed Books Bequeathed to the British Museum by Alfred H. Huth. London: 1912. V. 46

A Catalogue of the Works of Linnaeus (and Publications More Immediately Relating Thereto) Preserved in the Libraries of the British Museum . . . London: 1933. V. 46

A Description of the Collection of Ancient Terracotta in the British Museum. London: 1810. V. 41; 44

A Description of the Collection of Ancient Marbles in the British Museum. London: 1818-61. V. 46

A Guide to the Beauties of the British Museum, Being a Critical and Descriptive Account of the Principal Works of Art . . . London: 1826. V. 40; 44

Guide to the Principal Coins of the Greeks from Circ. 700 B.C. to A.D. 270, Based on the Work of Barclay V. Head. London: 1959. V. 45

Hieroglyphic Texts from Egyptian Stelae, etc. Part 1. London: 1961. V. 41

Inscriptions in the Hieratic and Demotic Character, from the Collections of the British Museum. London: 1868. V. 44

The Lumley Library; the Catalogue of 1609. London: 1956. V. 46

Prints in the Dotted Manner and Other Metal Cuts of the XV Century in the Department of Prints and Drawings. London: 1937. V. 41

BRITISH MUSEUM. DEPARTMENT OF MANUSCRIPTS

British Museum. Catalogue of Western Manuscripts in the Old Royal and King's Collections. London: 1921. V. 39

A Catalogue of the Harleian Manuscripts in the British Museum. London: 1801-1812. V. 39

A Catalogue of the Harlean Manuscripts in the British Museum. London: 1808-12. V. 38

Catalogue of the Harleian Manuscripts in the British Museum, with Indexes of Persons, Places and Matters. London: 1973. V. 39

Reproductions from Illuminated Manuscripts. London: 1907-65. V. 39

BRITISH MUSEUM. DEPARTMENT OF PRINTED BOOKS

Catalogue of the Manuscripts in the Cottonian Library. London: 1802. V. 38; 46

A Catalogue of the Lansdowne MSS. London: 1812-19. V. 38

Catalogue of Books in the Library of the British Museum Printed in England, Scotland and Ireland, and of Books in English Printed Abroad, to the Year 1640. London: 1884. V. 38

General Catalogue of Printed Books. Bible. London: 1936. V. 39

General Catalogue of Printed Books to 1955. (with) Supplement 1956-65. (with) Supplement 1966-70. (with) Supplement 1971-75. New York: 1955-80. V. 39

Librorum Impressorum qui in Museo Britannico Adservantur Catalogus. Londini: 1813-19. V. 38

A Short Title Catalogue of French Books 1601-1700 in the Library of the British Museum, by V.F. Goldsmith. 173. V. 39

BRITISH MUSEUM. DEPARTMENT OF PRINTS AND DRAWINGS

Italian Drawings in the Department of Prints and Drawings in the British Museum, 14th & 15h Centuries. London: 1950. V. 39

Prints in the Dotted Manner and Other Metal-Cuts of the XV Century in . . . the British Museum. London: 1937. V. 39; 43

BRITISH MUSEUM. DEPARTMENT OF ZOOLOGY

British Museum Catalogue of Birds. London: 1875-98. V. 38

Catalogue of the Collection of Birds' Eggs. London: 1901-12. V. 38

BRITISH MUSEUM. DEPT. OF BRITISH & MEDIAEVAL ANTIQUITIES

Catalogue of Early Christian Antiquities and Objects from the Christian East in the Department of British and Mediaeval Antiquities and Ethnography of the British Museum. London: 1901. V. 43

BRITISH MUSEUM. DEPT. OF EGYPTIAN & ASSYRIAN ANTIQUITIES

Assyrian Sculptures in the British Museum. Reign of Arthur-Nashir-Pal. B.C. 885-860 B.C. London: 1914. V. 40; 43

Catalogue of Egyptian Scarabs, etc. in the British Museum. London: 1913. V. 40

Catalogue of Demotic Papyri in the British Musuem. Volume I: A Theban Archive of the Reign of Ptolemy I, Soter. London: 1939. V. 40

Catalogue of Egyptian Antiquities in the British Museum IV: Glass. London: 1976. V. 40

Catalogue of Egyptian Antiquities in the British Museum, VI: Jewellery I, From the Earliest Times to the Seventeenth Dynasty. London: 1981. V. 40

Coptic and Greek Texts of the Christian Period from Ostraka, Stelae, etc. in the British Museum. London: 1905. V. 40

Egyptian Texts of the Earliest Period from the Coffin of Amamu in the British Museum. London: 1886. V. 40

Egyptian Sculptures in the British Museum. London: 1914. V. 42

Egyptian Texts of the Earliest Period From the Coffin of Amamu in the British Museum. London: 1886. V. 42

Hieroglyphic Texts from Egyptian Stelae, &c. in the British Museum. London: 1911-1987. V. 40

Hieroglyphic Texts from Egyptian Stelae, &c. in the British Museum. London: 1939. V. 40

Inscriptions in the Hieratic and Demotic Character, From the Collections of the British Museum. London: 1868. V. 42

Inscriptions in the Phoenician Character, Now Deposited in the British Museum, Discovered in the Site of Carthage, During Researches Made by Nathan Davis, Esq. at the Expense of Her Majesty's Government, in the Years 1856, 1857 & 1858. London: 1863. V. 40

BRITISH MUSEUM. DEPT. OF GREEK & ROMAN ANTIQUITIES

Catalogue of the Greek and Etruscan Vases in the British Museum. London: 1893-25. V. 37; 42; 44

Catalogue of the Greek, Etruscan and Roman Paintings and Mosaics in the British Museum. 1933. V. 40

Catalogue of the Terracottas in the Department of Greek and Roman Antiquities, British Museum: Greek, 730-330 B.C. London: 1969-70. V. 40; 42

A Catalogue of Sculpture in the Department of Greek and Roman Antiquities, British Museum. London: 1892-1904. V. 40

A Description of the Collection of Ancient Marbles in the British Museum. London: 1812-61. V. 40

BRITISH MUSEUM. DEPT. OF MANUSCRIPTS

Catalogue of the Manuscripts in the Cottonian Library . . . London: 1802. V. 40

Facsimile of the Rhind Mathematical Papyrus. London: 1898. V. 40

BRITISH MUSEUM. DEPT. OF PRINTED BOOKS

A Catalogue of the Works of Linnaeus . . . London: 1933. V. 40

A Catalogue of the Works of Linnaeus preseved in the Libraries of the British Museum (Nat. History). (with) An Index to the Authors (other than Linnaeus) Mentioned in the Catalogue. London: 1933-36. V. 40

General Catalogue of Printed Books to 1955. Compact Edition . . . (with) Ten Year Supplement 1956-65 (and) . . . Five Year Supplement 1966-1970. New York: 1967. V. 40

A List of the Books of Reference in the Reading Room of the British Museum. London: 1871. V. 40

List of Catalogues of English Book Sales 1676-1900 Now in the British Museum. London: 1915. V. 42

A Short Title Catalogue of French Books 1601-1700 in the Library of the British Museum. London: 1969-73. V. 42

Three Hundred Notable Books Added to the Library of the British Museum Under the Keepership of Richard Garnett, 1890-1899. London: 1899. V. 42

BRITISH MUSEUM. DEPT. OF PRINTS AND DRAWINGS

Catalogue of Drawings by Dutch and Flemish Artists Preserved in the Department of Prints and Drawings in the British Museum. London: 1915-32. V. 43

A Catalogue of Japanese & Chinese Woodcuts. London: 1916. V. 42

Catalogue of Drawings by Dutch and Flemish Artists Preserved in the Department of Prints and Drawings in the British Museums. London: 1923-1931. V. 43

BRITISH MUSEUM. DEPT. OF WESTERN ASIATIC ANTIQUITIES

Catalogue of the Western Asiatic Seals in the British Museum. London: 1974. V. 40

Catalogue of Western Asiatic Glass in the British Museum. London: 1985. V. 40

BRITISH MUSEUM. (NAT. HISTORY). DEPT. OF GEOLOGY

Descriptive and Illustrated Catalogue of the Fossil Reptilia of South Africa in the Collection of the British Museum. London: 1876. V. 40

BRITISH MUSEUM. (NAT. HISTORY). DEPT. OF ZOOLOGY

A Catalogue of the British Non-Parasitical Worms in the Collection of the British Museum. London: 1865. V. 40

Catalogue of the British Bees in the Collection of the British Museum. London: 1876. V. 40

BRITISH MUSEUM. (NAT. HISTORY). DEPT. OF ZOOLOGY continued

Catalogue of the Heads and Horns of Indian Big Game Bequeathed by A. O. Hume, C. B., to the British Museum (Natural History). London: 1913. V. 40

Catalogue of the Ungulate Mammals in the British Museum (Natural History). London: 1913-16. V. 40

BRITISH MUSEUM. NATURAL HISTORY

History of the Collections. London: 1904-12. V. 38

BRITISH MUSEUM. (NATURAL HISTORY). DEPARTMENT OF GEOLOGY

Descriptive and Illustrated Catalogue of the Fossil Reptilia of South Africa in the Collection of the British Museum. London: 1876. V. 39

BRITISH MUSEUM. (NATURAL HISTORY). DEPARTMENT OF ZOOLOGY

Catalogue of Shield Reptiles in the Collection of the British Museum. Pt. 1- Testudinata (Tortoises) with suppt. London: 1855-72. V. 39

Catalogue of the Fishes of the British Museum. New Delhi: 1981. V. 39

Gigantic Land-Tortoises (Living and Extinct) in the Collection of the British Museum. London: 1877. V. 39

BRITISH MUSEUM. (NATURAL HISTORY). DEPTARTMENT OF ZOOLOGY

Catalogue of the Lizards in the British Museum. London: 1885-87. V. 39

THE BRITISH Novelists. London: 1810-16. V. 38

BRITISH ORNITHOLOGIST UNION

Ibis, Journal of the British Ornithologist's Union. London: 1861-1986. V. 38

Ibis, Journal of the British Ornithologists' Union. London: 1896-1918. V. 38

Ibis, Journal of the British Ornithologists' Union. London: 1933-78. V. 38

THE BRITISH Orpheus. Stourport: 1810. V. 40

THE BRITISH Poets. London. V. 44
BRITISH Poets. London: 1807/1811. V. 37
THE BRITISH Poets. Boston: 1865-1866. V. 40
THE BRITISH Poets. London: 1866. V. 42

BRITISH REINFORCED CONCRETE ENGINEERING CO.

Applications of the B.R.C. System of Reinforced Concrete Construction. London: 1917. V. 44

B.R.C. Structures. A Photographic Record of the Use of the Reinforced Concrete in Modern Building Construction. London: 1923. V. 44

THE BRITISH Roll of Honour. The Roll of Honour of the Empire's Heroes. London. V. 41

THE BRITISH Satirist, Comprising the Best Satires of the Most Celebrated Poets, from Pope to Byron. Glasgow: 1826. V. 42

BRITISH SOCIETY FOR PROMOTING THE REFORMATION OF FEMALE PRISONERS

Sketch of the Origin and Results of Ladies' Prison Associations, with Hints for the Formation of Local Associations, with Hints for the Formation of Local Associations. London: 1827. V. 43

BRITISH Sports and Sportsmen: The Story of Shipping. London: 1921. V. 41

THE BRITISH Union Catalogue of Early Music Printed Before the Year 1801. London: 1957. V. 42

BRITISH Wines. Approved Receipts and Directions for Making Wines, Shrubs &c., from English Fruits, Flowers &c. Lancaster: 1816. V. 37

BRITNELL COMPANY

V. 45

BRITO, BERNARDO DO

Primeyra Parte (all published) da Chronica de Cister, onde se Contam as Cousas Principais Desta Religiam com Muytas Antiguidades, Assi de Reyno de Portugal como de Outros Muytos da Christandale. Lisbon: 1602. V. 38

BRITTAIN, HARRY

Canada There and Back. London: 1908. V. 46

BRITTAIN, VERA

Testament of Youth. London: 1933. V. 43

Verses of a V.A.D. London: 1918. V. 42

BRITTAINE, GEORGE

The Election. Dublin: 1840. V. 39; 42; 43

BRITTEN, BENJAMIN

Children's Crusade. Kinderkreuzzug, Op. 82. London: 1973. V. 38

BRITTEN, EMMA HARDINGE

Modern American Spiritualism. New York: 1870. V. 45

BRITTEN, F. J.

Old Clocks and Watches and Their Makers. London: 1911. V. 40

Old Clocks and Watches and Their Makers, a Historical and Descriptive Account of the Different Styles of Clocks and Watches of the Past in England and Abroad Containing a List of Nearly Fourteen Thousand Makers. London: 1956. V. 39

BRITTON, H.

Fiji in 1870; Being the Letters of 'The Argus' Special Correspondent. Melbourne: 1870. V. 41

BRITTON, J.

Cambridge, Cheshire and Cornwall. London: 1801. V. 40

Durham, Essex and Gloucestershire. London: 1803. V. 40

Illustrations of the Public Buildings of London. London: 1825. V. 39

Kent. London: 1808. V. 40

Monmouth, Norfolk and Northamptonshire. London: 1810. V. 40

BRITTON, JOHN 1771-1857

The Architectural Antiquities of Great Britain Represented and Illustrated in a Series of Views, Elevations, Plans, Sections and Details, of Various Ancient English Edifices . . . London: 1807. V. 46

The Architectural Antiquities of Great Britain Represented and Illustrated in a Series of Views. London: 1807-09-12. V. 46

The Architectural Antiquites of Great Britain. London: 1835. V. 42; 46

The Authorship of the Letters of Junius. London: 1848. V. 37

The Autobiography of John Britton. Together with A Descriptive Account of the Literary Works of John Britton. London: 1846-50. V. 38; 39; 40

The Beauties of England and Wales. London: 1801-15. V. 46

The Beauties of England and Wales, or Delineations, Topographical Historical and Descriptive of Each County. London: 1801-18. V. 40; 43; 46

The Beauties of England and Wales; or Delineations, Topographical, Historical and Descrptive of Each County. Volume 3: Cumberland, Isle of Man and Derbyshire. London: 1802. V. 45

The Beauties of England and Wales. London: 1803. V. 42

The Beauties of England and Wales: Volume IV, Devonshire and Dorset. London: 1803. V. 39

The Beauties of England and Wales . . . London: 1808. V. 46

The Beauties of England and Wales. London: 1810-16. V. 44; 46

Beauties of England and Wales. Volume 2: Cambridgeshire, Cheshire and Cornwall. London: 1801. V. 38

Beauties of England and Wales. Volume 1: Bedfordshire, Berkshire and Buckingham. London: 1801. V. 38

Beauties of England and Wales. Volume 3: A Topographical and Historical Description of the County of Cumberland. London: 1813. V. 38

The Beauties of Wiltshire, Displayed in Statistical, Historical and Descriptive Sketches. London: 1801. V. 38

The Beauties of Wiltshire, Displayed in Statistical, Historical and Descriptive Sketches, Illustrated by Views of the Principal Seats &c. London: 1801-25. V. 46

Britton. London: 1640. V. 37; 45

Britton (On the Laws of England). London: 1640. V. 40

Catalogue of Books, Prints, Maps, Acts of Parliament, &c . . . London: 1851. V. 45

Cathedral Antiquities. London: 1836. V. 38; 41

Chronological History and Graphic Illustrations of Christian Architecture in England. London: 1826. V. 38

Descrptive Sketches of Tunbridge Wells and the Calverley Estate. London: 1832. V. 37; 40

Devonshire and Cornwall Illustrated. London: 1832. V. 44

English Cathedrals. (with) An Historical and Architectural Essay Relating to Redcliffe Church. (with) History and Antiquities of Bath Abbey Church. London: 1813-35. V. 39

The Fine Arts of the English School. London: 1812. V. 41; 46

Graphic Illustrations, with Historical and Descriptive Accounts, of Toddington, Gloucestershire, the Seat of Lord Sudeley. London: 1840. V. 38

Graphical and Literary Illustrations of Fonthill Abbey, Wilshire; with Heraldical and Genealogical Notices of the Beckford Family. London: 1823. V. 37; 38; 40

An Historical Account of Corsham House, in Wiltshire; the Seat of Paul Cobb Methuen . . . London: 1806. V. 38; 40; 41

An Historical and Architectural Essay Relating to Redcliffe Church, Bristol. London: 1813. V. 37; 38; 40; 46

Historical Notices of Fonthill Abbey. London: 1836. V. 41

The History and Antiquities of the Metropolitical Church of York.. London: 1819. V. 46

The History and Antiquities of the Cathedral Church of Canterbury . . . . London: 1824. V. 46

The History and Antiquities of Bath Abbey Church, Including Biographical Anecdotes . . . London: 1825. V. 38; 42

The History and Antiquities of the Abbey, and Cathedral Chruch of Bristol. London: 1830. V. 44

The History and Antiquities of the Cathedral Church in Worcester. London: 1835. V. 40

The History and Description with Graphic Illustrations of Cassiobury Park, Hertfordshire, the Seat of the Earl of Essex. London: 1837. V. 37; 39; 44

BRITTON, JOHN 1771-1857 continued

The History and Antiquites of the Cathedral Churh of Wells. London: 1824. V. 38; 44

The History and Antiquties of Bath Abbey Church . . . Continued to the Present Time . . . Bath: 1887. V. 38

Illustrations of the Public Buildings of London: With Historical and Descriptive Accounts of Each Edifice. London: 1825. V. 37; 39

Illustrations of the Public Buildings of London. With historical and descriptive accounts of each edifice. London: 1825-1828. V. 37; 38; 40

Memoirs of the Tower of London. London: 1830. V. 37

Picturesque Antiquities of the English Cities. London: 1830. V. 41

Picturesque Antiquities of the English Cities. London: 1836. V. 39

The Pleasures of Human Life: Investigate cheerfully, elucidated satirically, promulgated explicitly, and discussed philosophically . . . by Hilaris Benevolus, & Co. London: 1807. V. 37

The Union of Architecture, Sculpture and Painting, Exemplified by a Series of Illustrations . . . London: 1827. V. 42

The Union of Architecture, Sculpture and Painting . . . London: 1827. V. 41

The Union of Architecture, Sculpture and Painting . . . with Descriptive Accounts of the House and Galleries of John Soane. London: 1827. V. 37

BRITTON, NATHANIEL LORD

The Cactaceae, Desciptions and Illustrations of Plants of the Cactus Family. Los Angeles: 1931-35-37-37. V. 46

The Cactaceae. Descriptions and Illustrations of Plants of the Cactus Family. Washington: 1919-23. V. 37; 43

An Illustrated Flora of the Northern United States, Canada, and the British Possessions. New York: 1896-98. V. 40

North American Trees, Being Descriptions and Illustrations of the Trees Growing Independently of Cultivation in North America, North of Mexico and the West Indies. New York: 1908. V. 46

BRITTON, WILEY

Memoirs of the Rebellion on the Border, 1863. Chicago: 1882. V. 41

The Union Brigade in the Civil War. Kansas City: 1922. V. 42

The Union Indian Brigade in the Civil War. Kansas City: 1922. V. 39; 42; 46

BRITWELL COURT (CHRISTIE-MILLER) LIBRARY

The Britwell Hand-List or Short Title Catalogue of the Principal Volumes from the Time of Caxton to the Year 1800 Formerly in the Library of Britwell Court, Buckinghamshire. London: 1933. V. 46

BRIX, MAURICE

List of Philadelphia Silversmiths and Allied Artificers from 1682 to 1850. Philadelphia: 1920. V. 46

BRIXIANI, LAVRENTII GAMBARAE

De Navigatione Christophori Columbi Libri Qvatvor. Rome: 1535. V. 46

BROAD, AMOS

The Trial of Amos Broad and His Wife, on the Several Indictments for Assaulting and Beating Betty, a Slave, and Her Little Female Child Sarah, Aged Three Years . . . New York: 1809. V. 45

BROAD, C. D.

Examiantion of McTaggart's Philosophy. Cambridge: 1933. V. 45

Examination of McTaggart's Philosophy. Cambridge: 1933/38. V. 41; 42; 43

BROADBENT, JOHN

The Australian Botanic Guide. Melbourne: 1889. V. 41

BROADBENT, WILLIAM

Heart Disease: With Special Reference to Prognosis and Treatment. New York: 1898. V. 42

Selections from the Writings Medical and Neurological of Sir William Broadbent. London: 1908. V. 38; 41; 42; 45

BROADFOOT, ALEXANDER

The Case of the King Against Alexander Broadfoot (Indicted for the Murder of Cornelius Calahan a Sailor Belonging to His Majesty's Ship the Mortar Sloop), at the Sessions of Oyer and Terminer and Goal Delivery Held for the City of Bristol and County of the.. Oxford: 1758. V. 42

BROADFOOT, W.

The Career of Major George Broadfoot, C.B. in Afghanistan and the Punjab . . . London: 1888. V. 38

BROADLEY, A. M.

Napoleon in Caricature 1795-1821. London: 1911. V. 45

BROADLEY, ALEXANDER M.

How We Defended Arabi and His Friends. London: 1884. V. 43

A BROADSIDE. Dundrum: 1908-May 1913. V. 41

BROADSIDE Ballads of the Restoration Period from the Jersey Collection Known as the Osterley Park Ballads. London: 1930. V. 44; 46

THE BROADWAY. A Miscellany of Original Literature. London: & New York: 1868. V. 46

BROADWOOD, LUCY E.

Songs from Alice in Wonderland and Through the Looking Glass. London: 1921. V. 42

BROCA, PAUL

Du Siege de la Faculte du Langage Articule dans l'Hemisphere Gauche du Cerveau . . . 1865. V. 46

Memoires d'Anthropologie. Paris: 1871-77. V. 44

Remarques sur le Siege, le Diagnostic et la Nature De L'Aphemie. 1863. V. 46

BROCAS, BERNARD

Military Antiquities etc. etc. A Catalogue of the Most Extensive and Instructive Collection of Ancient Arms and Armour . . . the Property of Bernard Brocas Esq . . . the Whole to be sold by Auction by Mr. George Robins at the Queen's Bazaar, Oxford St . . . London. V. 37

BROCH, HERMANN

The Death of Virgil. London: 1946. V. 41

The Sleepwalkers - a Trilogy. London: 1932. V. 41

The Sleepwalkers. 1947. V. 44

BROCK & COMPANY

Standard Atlas of Stutsman County North Dakota. Chicago: 1930. V. 45

BROCK, C. E.

The Series of English Idylls. London and New YorK;: 1904-06. V. 39

BROCK, H. M.

The Book of Fairy Tales. Puss in Boots, Jack & the Beanstalk, Hop O'My Thumb, Beauty & Beast. London: (1914). V. 37

A Book of Old Ballads. Selected and with an introduction by Beverly Nichols and illustrated by H.M. Brock. London: 1934. V. 37

BROCK, J. K.

Fortetsa: Early Greek Tombs Near Knossos. Cambridge: 1957. V. 40; 42; 44

BROCK, R. A.

The History of the Virginia Federal Convention of 1788, with Some Account of . . . Members of the Body . . . Richmond: 1890. V. 42; 44; 45

BROCKBANK, EDWARD

Sketches of the Lives and Work of the Honorary Medical Staff of the Manchester Infirmary. Manchester: 1904. V. 41; 42; 45

BROCKEDON, WILLIAM 1787-1854

Egypt and Nubia, 1846. Holland. V. 43

Finden's Illustrations of the Life and Works of Lord Byron. London: 1833. V. 40; 42

Finden's Illustrations of the Life and Works of Lord Byron, with Original and Selected Information on the Subjects of the Engravings by W. Brockedon. London: 1833-34. V. 39; 44

Illustrations of the Passes of the Alps, by Which Italy Communicates with France, Switzerland, and Germany . . . London: 1828. V. 40; 43

Illustrations of the Passes of the Alps. London: 1828, 1829. V. 39

Illustrations of the Passes of the Alps, By Which Italy Communicates with France, Switzerland and Germany. London: 1877. V. 43

Journals of Excursions in the Alps; The Pennine, Graian, Cottian, Rhetian, Leopontian, and Berense. London: 1833. V. 37

Road Book from London to Naples. London: 1835. V. 44; 46

BROCKETT, JOHN TROTTER

A Catalogue of the Very Valuable and Extensive Collection of Ancient Coins and Medals Collected by, and the Property of . . . Which Will be sold by Auction by Mr. Sotheby at his House, Wellington Street . . . On Wednesday, June 4th, 1823 & Nine Following Days. London: 1823. V. 45

Selecta Numismata Aurea Imperatorum Romanorum . . . Newcastle: 1822. V. 44

BROCKETT, L. P.

Battle-Field and Hospital; or, Lights and Shadows of the Great Rebellion. Philadelphia: 1888. V. 45

The Commercial Traveller's Guide Book . . . New York: 1871. V. 42

Epidemic and Contagious Diseases . . . New York: 1873. V. 45

Our Western Empire; or, the New West Beyond the Mississippi. Philadelphia: 1881. V. 43; 44

Woman: Her Rights, Wrongs, Privileges and Responsibilities. Hartford: 1869. V. 44

Woman's Work in the Civil War: a Record of Heroism, Patriotism and Patience. Philadelphia: 1867. V. 42

BROCKETT, PAUL

Bibliography of Aeronautics, 1909-1916. Washington: 1921. V. 41

BROCKLEHURST, THOMAS U.

Mexico To-Day: A Country with a Great Future, and a Glance at the Prehistoric Remains and Antiquaties of the Montezumas. New York: 1883. V. 39

BROCKLEHUSRT, H. C.

Game Animals of the Sudan, their Habits and distribution. London: 1931. V. 37; 40; 43; 44; 45

BROCKWAY, WALLACE

The Albert D. Lasker Collection: Renoir to Matisse. New York: 1957. V. 41

BROCKWELL, MAURICE W.

A Catalogue of Some of the Paintings of the British School in the Collection of Henry Edwards Huntington at San Marino, California. New York: 1925. V. 40

BROCQUIERE, BERTRANDON DE LA

The Travels of . . . to Palestine and His Return from Jerusalem Overland to France, During the Years 1432 & 1433. 1807. V. 39

BRODE, CATHERINE BIGHAM

Ludlow - Ross Genealogy; the Ancestors of Lydia Ludow and Ogden Ross and Their Descendants With Allied Families. Walla Walla: 1932. V. 42

BRODER, PATRICIA JANIS

The American West. The Modern Vision. New York: 1984. V. 38

Bronzes of the American West. New York: 1973. V. 39; 44

Bronzes of the American West. New York: 1974. V. 41; 44

BRODERICK, GWENDOLYN

Au Front (At the Front). London: 1920. V. 46

BRODERIP, FRANCES FREELING HOOD 1830-1878

Tiny Tadpoles and other Tales. London: 1862. V. 40

BRODHEAD, EDWARD H.

Report of the Engineer Upon the Preliminary Surveys for the Ousatonic Railroad. New Haven: 1836. V. 37

BRODIE, BENJAMIN COLLINS 1783-1862

Lectures on Diseases of the Urinary Organs. London: 1832. V. 39; 42; 43; 46

Lectures on Diseases of the Urinary Organs. Philadelphia: 1843. V. 40

Pathological and Surgical Observations on Diseases of the Joints. Philadelphia: 1821. V. 42

Pathological and Surgical Observations on the Diseases of the Joints. London: 1836. V. 39; 42

Psychological Inquires: in A Series of Essays . . . London: 1854. V. 43; 45

BRODIE, FAWN M.

No Man Knows My History. New York: 1945. V. 45

BRODIE, GEORGE

History of the British Empire, from the Accession of Charles I. to the Restoration . . . Edinburgh: 1822. V. 39

BRODIE, P. B.

A History of the Fossil Insects in the Secondary Rocks of England . . . London: 1845. V. 40

BRODIE, WALTER

Pitcairn's Island, and the Islanders in 1850 . . . London: 1851. V. 42

BRODIE, WILLIAM

An Account of the Trial of William Brodie and George Smith . . . August 1788 . . . Edinburgh: 1788. V. 43

BRODKEY, HAROLD

First Love and Other Sorrows. New York: 1957. V. 39; 42; 44; 45; 46

BRODMAN, ESTELLE

The Development of Medical Bibliography. Baltimore: 1954. V. 38; 41

BRODNAX, JOHN H.

Memorial of the Creek Nation of Indians. Washington: 1832. V. 39

BRODRICK, ST. JOHN

Some Remarks Upon the Late Act of Resumption of the Irish Forfeitures and Upon the Manner of Putting that Act in Execution. London: 1701. V. 46

BRODRICK, THOMAS

a Compleat History of the Late War. In the Netherlands. Together with an Abstract of the Treaty at Utrecht. London: 1713. V. 40; 41; 44; 45

BRODSKY, DANIEL

Faulkner: A Comprehensive Guide to the Brodsky Collection. Jackson: 1982-85. V. 37

BRODSKY, JOSEPH

1972. Purchase: 1989. V. 46

Selected Poems. New York: 1973. V. 43

To Urania. New York: 1988. V. 46

BRODTMAN, CARL JOSEPH

Naturhistorische Bilder-Gallerie aus dem Thierreiche. Zurich: 1810. V. 42

BRODZKY, HORACE

Henri Gaudier-Brzeska - 1891-1915. London: 1933. V. 40

BROGGER, A. W.

The Viking Ships, Their Ancestry and Evolution. Oslo: 1951. V. 44

BROGGER, W. C.

Fridtiof Nansen 1861-1893. London: 1896. V. 40

BROINOWSKI, GRACIUS JOSEPH

The Birds of Australia. Melbourne: 1887-91. V. 37; 46

The Cockatoos and Nestors of Australia and New Zealand. Melbourne: 1981. V. 38

The Cockatoos and Nestors of Australia and New Zealand. Melbourne: 1888, 1981. V. 37

BROKE, ARTHUR DE CAPELL BART 1791-1858

Sketches in Spain and Morocco. London: 1831. V. 43

Travels through Sweden, Norway, and Finmark, to the North Cape, in the Summer of 1820. London: 1823. V. 38; 39; 41

Winter Sketches in Lapland . . . London: 1826. V. 38

A Winter in Lapland and Sweden, with Various Observations Relating to Finmarak and its Inhabitants . . . London: 1827. V. 38

BROKEN Mirrors. Minneapolis: 1928. V. 37

BROMBERG, RUTH

Canaletto's Etchings: A Catalogue and Study Illustrating and Describing the Known States, Including Those Hitherto Unrecorded. London: 1974. V. 37; 45

BROME, ALEXANDER

a Congratulatory Poem on the Miraculous and Glorious Return of the Unparallel'd King Charls (sic) The II May 29, 1660. London: 1660. V. 43

Rump; or an Exact Collection of the Choycest Poems and Songs Relating to the Late Times. London: 1662. V. 38; 40; 45

Songs and Other Poems. London: 1661. V. 44

Songs and Other Poems. London: 1664. V. 46

Songs and Other Poems. London: 1668. V. 46

BROME, JAMES

An Historical Account of Mr. Brome's Three Years Travels Over England, Scotland and Wales. London: 1700. V. 43

BROME, RALPH

The Letters of Simpkin the Second, Poetic Recorder, of All the Proceedings, Upon the Trial of Warren Hastings, Esq. in Westmisnter Hall. London: 1789. V. 39; 42

BROME, RICHARD

The Antipodes. London: 1640. V. 37

The City Wit, or, The VVoman Wears the Breeches. London: 1653. V. 46

The Dramatic Works . . . London: 1873. V. 39

Five New Playes. viz. The Madd Couple Well Matcht. The Novella. The Court Beggar. The City Witt. The Damoiselle. London: 1653. V. 42

Five New Plays, viz. The English Moor, or The Mock Marriage. The Love-Sick Court, or The Ambitous Politique. Covent Garden Weeded. The New Academy, or the New Exchange. The Queen and Concubine. London: 1659. V. 40

The Northern Lasse, a Comoedie. London: 1632. V. 37

BROMFIELD, M.

A Brief Account of the Most Reigning Disease the Scurvy, with Infallible Directions for Its Cure. London: 1680. V. 40; 41

BROMLEY-DAVENPORT, W.

Sport: Fox-Hunting: Salmon-Fishing: Covert-Shooting: Deer-Stalking. London: 1885. V. 45

BROMLEY, EDWARD A.

Minneapolis Album. Minneapolis: 1890. V. 39

BROMLEY, GEORGE TISDALE

The Long Ago and The Later On or Recollections of Eighty Years. San Francisco: 1904. V. 40; 45

BROMLEY, GEORGE W.

Atlas of the City of Philadelphia 23rd and 35th Wards, from Actual Surveys and Official Plans by . . . Philadelphia: 1894. V. 42

BROMLEY, HENRY

A Catalogue of Engraved British Portraits from Egbert the Great to the Present Time. London: 1793. V. 38

BROMLEY, THOMAS 1629-1691

The Way to the Sabbath of Rest. Germantown: 1759. V. 44

The Way to the Sabbath of Rest. London: 1759. V. 39

The Way to the Sabbath of Rest, etc. London: 1761. V. 39

BROMLEY, WILLIAM

Remarks Made in Travels through France and Italy, with many Public Inscriptions, Lately Taken by a person of Quality. London: 1693. V. 46

Several Years Travels through Portugal, Spain, Italy, Germany, Prussia, Sweden, Denmark and the United Provinces. London: 1702. V. 42; 43; 44; 45; 46

BROMLEY'S Sabbath of Rest, or the Soul's Progress in the Work of the New Birth. London: 1761. V. 40

BROMLEY'S Sabbath of Rest, or the Soul's Progress in the Work of the New Birth, etc. London: 1762. V. 41

BROMME, TRAUGOTT

Die Berfaffungen der Vereinigien Staaten, Der Freistaaten Pennsylvania und Texas. Stuttgart: 1848. V. 39

Rathgeber fur Auswanderungslustige. Wie und Wohin Sollen Wir Auswandern; nach den Vereinigten Staaten oder Britisch Nord-Amerika . . . Stuttgart: 1846. V. 38; 40

Die Verfassungen der Vereinigten Staaten von Nord-Amerika der Freistaaten Pennsylvania und Texas, der Koenigreiche Belgien und Norwegen.. Stuttgart: 1848. V. 38

BROMMER, FRANK

The Sculptures of the Parthenon: Metopes, Frieze, Pediments, Cult-Statue. London: 1979. V. 44

BRONEER, OSCAR

Corinth. Volume IV, Part II: Terracotta Lamps. Cambridge: 1930. V. 40

Corinth. Volume X, the Odeum. Cambridge: 1932. V. 40

BRONK, WILLIAM

Careless Love and Its Atmospheres. New York: 1985. V. 44

Careless Love and Its Apostrophes. New York: 1985. V. 42

The Force of Desire. Verona: 1979. V. 41; 43; 46

Light in a Dark Sky. Concord: 1982. V. 41; 42; 43; 44

BRONOWSKI, JACOB

The Face of Violence. London: 1954. V. 45

The Face of Violence. New York: 1955. V. 45

BRONSON, EDGAR BEECHER

In Closed Territory. Chicago: 1910. V. 43

Reminiscences of a Ranchman. New York: 1908. V. 43

BRONSON, GEORGE WHITFIELD

The Ann Maria . . . Fall River: 1869. V. 41

Glimpses of the Whaleman's 'Cabin.' Boston: 1855. V. 42

BRONSON, J.

The Domestic Manufacturer's Assistant and Family Directory, in the Arts of Weaving and Dyeing. Utica: 1817. V. 38; 39; 40

BRONSON, M.

A Spelling Book and Vocabulary, in English, Asamese, Singpho and Naga. Jaipur: 1839. V. 39

BRONSTED, J.

Early English Ornament. Copenhagen/London: 1924. V. 42

BRONSTED, PETER OLUF

Reisen und Untersuchungen in Griechenland, Nebst Darstellung und Erklarung Vieler Neuentdeckten Denkmaler Griechischen Style. Paris: 1826-30. V. 39

Voyages et Recherches dans la Grece . . . Paris: 1826-30. V. 44

BRONTE, ANNE 1820-1849

The Tenant of Wildfell Hall. London: 1854. V. 41; 43

BRONTE, CHARLOTTE 1816-1855

Jane Eyre. London: 1847. V. 45

Jane Eyre. London: 1848. V. 38; 46

Jane Eyre: a Autobiography. London: 1848. V. 44

Jane Eyre. New York: 1848. V. 41; 43; 44; 45; 46

Jane Eyre. Leipzig: 1850, 1857. V. 38

Jane Eyre. London: 1857. V. 44

Jane Eyre. London: 1857. V. 40

Jane Eyre. New York: 1857. V. 44

Jane Eyre. London: 1858. V. 38

Jane Eyre, ou Les Memoires d'une Institutrice . . . Paris: 1858. V. 43

Jane Eyre ou Les Memoires d'une Institutrice. Paris: 1860. V. 41

Jane Eyre. Paris: 1923. V. 43

Jane Eyre. New York: 1943. V. 42

Legends of Angria. New Haven: 1933. V. 40; 43

Miscellaneous and Unpublished Writings. London: 1936. V. 41; 43

The Novels. London: 1922. V. 40

The Complete Poems. New York: 1923. V. 41

The Professor. London: 1857. V. 37; 39; 40; 42; 43; 44; 45; 46

The Professor. A Tale. By Currer Bell. London: 1857. V. 37; 41; 44; 45; 46

The Professor. New York: 1857. V. 40; 43; 45

The Professor, a Tale. London: 1857/59. V. 44

The Professor. London: 1860. V. 42

The Professor. New York: 1957. V. 43

Shirley, a Tale. Leipzig: 1849. V. 45

Shirley, a Tale. London: 1849. V. 37; 38; 39; 41; 43; 45; 46

Shirley. New York: 1850. V. 43

Shirley. London: 1860. V. 45

Shirley. London: 1894. V. 45

A Tale. By Currer Bell. London: 1849. V. 37

Thackeray and Charlotte Bronte. Being Some Hitherto Unpublished Letters to Her Publisher by Charlotte Bronte. London: 1919. V. 41

The Twelve Adventures and Other Stories. London: 1925. V. 46

Two Tales 'The Secret Hart' and 'Lily Hart'. 1978. V. 41

Vilette. New York: 1853. V. 39; 41; 43; 44; 45

Villette. London: 1853. V. 37; 38; 40; 41; 42; 43; 44; 45

Villette. New York: 1857. V. 44

BRONTE, EMILY 1818-1848

The Complete Poems of . . . London: 1923. V. 41

The Complete Poems of . . . New York: 1923. V. 41

The Professor by Currer Bell. London: 1857. V. 37

Two Poems. Austin: 1934. V. 43; 44

Wuthering Heights. London: 1931. V. 41; 42

Wuthering Heights. New York. V. 38

Wuthering Heights. New York: 1848. V. 42

Wuthering Heights by Ellis Bell; and Agnes Grey, by Acton Bell. London: 1858. V. 38

Wuthering Heights. London: 1924. V. 37; 42

Les hauts de Hurle-Vent. Paris: 1925. V. 43; 45

Wuthering Heights. New York: 1931. V. 37; 39; 42

Wuthering Heights. London: 1947. V. 37

BRONTE, PATRICK 1777-1861

Bronteana: His Collected Works and Life . . . London: 1898. V. 41

Cottage Poems. Halifax. V. 43

Cottage Poems. Halifax: 1811. V. 42; 44; 46

The Cottage in the Wood; or the Art of Becoming Rich and Happy. Bradford: 1818. V. 46

Two Sermons Preached in the Church of Haworth. Haworth: 1885. V. 43

Two Sermons Preached in the Church at Haworth . . . . (also, A Phenomenon, or, an Account in Verse of the Extraordinary Disruption of a Bog . . . London: 1885. V. 41

BRONTE, SISTERS

Poems by Currier, Ellis and Acton Bell. London: 1846. V. 41

BRONTE Sisters: The Brontes, Their Lives, Friendships and Correspondence. London: 1932. V. 40

BRONTE, THE SISTERS

A Bronte Bibliography. London: 1978. V. 37

The Complete Novels, with Mrs. Gaskell's Life of Charlotte Bronte. Edinburgh: 1911. V. 37; 39; 42

The Life and Works of the Sisters Bronte. New York. V. 42

Life and Works of Charlotte Bronte and Her Sisters. London: 1876-79. V. 42

Life and Works of Charlotte Bronte and Her Sisters. London: 1882-85. V. 46

The Life and Works of Charlotte Bronte and Her Sisters. London: 1884-85. V. 42

Life and Works. London: 1889-91. V. 40

Life and Works of the Sisters Bronte. New York: 1899. V. 42

Life and Works of Charlotte Bronte and Her Sisters. London: 1899-1900. V. 42; 46

Life and Works. London: 1899-1900. V. 46

Life and Works of the Sisters Bronte. New York: 1900. V. 40; 46

The Life and Works of Charlotte Bronte and Her Sisters. London: 1906-20. V. 46

BRONTE, THE SISTERS continued

The Life and Works. London: 1910. V. 45

Life and Works of Charlotte Bronte and her Sisters. London: 1876-79. V. 37

Novels of the Sisters Bronte. London: 1898. V. 38

Novels of the Sisters Bronte (with the final volume containing Gaskell's Life of Charlotte Bronte). London: 1898-1901. V. 45

The Novels of . . . Including Mrs. Gaskell's Life of Charlotte Bronte . . . New York: 1899. V. 41

The Novels of . . . Including Mrs. Gaskell's Life of Charlotte Bronte . . . London: 1899/1910. V. 41

The Novels of . . . Together with Mrs. Gaskell's Life of Charlotte Bronte. London: 1900. V. 43

The Novels of . . . New York: 1900 1902. V. 41; 43

The Complete Novels with Mrs. Gaskell's Life of Charlotte Bronte. Edinburgh: 1905. V. 39

Novels. Edinburgh: 1905. V. 38; 40; 45; 46

The Novels of Charlotte, Emily and Anne Bronte. London, New York: 1905. V. 42

The Novels of the Sisters Bronte in Ten Volumes. New York: 1905. V. 43

The Novels of the Sisters Bronte. London: 1905-11. V. 41

The Novels of . . . With Mrs. Gaskell's Life of Charlotte Bronte. Edinburgh: 1907. V. 43

Novels of the Sisters Bronte. Edinburgh: 1907. V. 41; 42

Novels. Edinburgh: 1911. V. 40; 42; 43

The Novels of . . . London: 1920/1922. V. 41

The Novels of . . . London: 1922. V. 38; 44

The Novels. London: 1922. V. 44

The Novels of . . . New York: 1922. V. 41; 43

The Complete Novels, with Mrs. Gaskell's Life of Charlotte Bronte. Edinburgh: 1924. V. 39; 46

The Novels. Edinburgh: 1924. V. 38; 39; 42; 43; 44; 46

The Novels. Oxford: 1931. V. 42; 44; 46

Novels. London: 1966-70. V. 37

The Novels. Edited by Temple Scott. Edinburgh: 1911. V. 37

Poems. London: 1846. V. 38

Poems by Currer, Ellis and Action Bell. London: 1846. V. 37; 38; 39; 40; 42; 43; 44; 45; 46

Poems. London: 1846, 1848. V. 41

Poems. Philadelphia: 1848. V. 40; 46

The Shakespeare Head Bronte. Oxford: 1931. V. 41; 42

The Shakespeare Head Bronte. Oxford: 1931-36. V. 46

Works . . . (with) Life of Charlotte Bronte . . . London: 1889. V. 44

Works. London: 1893. V. 38

The Works of Charlotte, Emily and Anne Bronte. London: 1893-96. V. 41; 43; 44; 45

The Works of . . . London: 1900. V. 43

The Works of . . . Edinburgh: 1905. V. 46

Works of the Bronte Sisters. New York: 1926. V. 42

The Shakespeare Head Bronte. Boston & New York: 1931. V. 38

The Works. Their Lives. Friendships, Correspondence. Miscellaneous and Unpublished Writings. Poems. Oxford: 1931-18. V. 42

The Complete Works. 1931/33. V. 41

The Complete Works. London: 1931/33. V. 43

The Works. Oxford: 1931-38. V. 44

Works of . . . London: 1933. V. 44

Works. London: 1949. V. 37; 42; 44; 45

BRONTES, THE SISTERS

Life and Works of Charlotte Bronte and Her Sisters. London: 1872-78. V. 45

The Novels. London: 1905-13. V. 45

THE BRONTES - *Their Lives, Friendships and Correspondence.* London: 1932. V. 41

BROOK, G.

Catalogue of the Madreporarian Corals in the British Museum. London: 1893-1928. V. 37; 38

BROOK, RICHARD

Cyclopaedia of Botany. London. V. 40; 42

New Cyclopaedia of Botany and Complete Book of Herbs. Huddersfield: 1853. V. 40; 46

New Cyclopedia of Botany and Complete Book of Herbs: Forming a History and Description of All Plants British or Foreign. London: 1865. V. 45

BROOK, STEPHEN

A Bibliography of the Gehenna Press 1942-1975. 1975. V. 39

A Bibliography of the Gehenna Press, 1942-1975. Northampton: 1976. V. 42

BROOKE, CHARLOTTE

Reliques of Irish Poetry, Consisting of Heroic Poems, Odes, Elegies and Songs . . . Dublin: 1789. V. 43

BROOKE, EMILY FRANCES

The Heir Without a Heritage: a Novel. London: 1887. V. 41; 43

BROOKE, FRANCES MOORE

The History of Emily Montague. London: 1769. V. 42

The History of Lady Julia Mandeville. London: 1773. V. 42; 43

The History of Charles Mandeville. Dublin: 1790. V. 38

Louisa et Maria, ou les Illusions de la Jeunesse. Paris: 1819. V. 43

BROOKE, FULKE GREVILLE, 1ST BARON 1554-1628

Caelica. London: 1936. V. 40

Caelica. Newtown: 1936. V. 37; 40; 45

Caelica. Newtown: 1936. V. 37. V. 39

Certaine Learned and Elegant Workes of the Right Honorable Fulke Lord Brooke, Written In His Youth, and Familiar Exercise with Sir Philip Sidney. London: 1633. V. 37; 38; 39; 40; 42; 43; 44; 46

Maxims, Characters, and Reflections, Critical, Satyrical and Moral. London: 1756. V. 39; 40

The Remains of Sir Fulk Greville Lord Brooke: Being Poems of Monarchy and Religion. London: 1670. V. 40; 42; 44; 46

BROOKE, GEOFFREY

The Way of a Man with a Horse. London: 1929. V. 37; 39

BROOKE, HENRY 1703-1783

The Fool of Quality: or the History of Henry Earl of Moreland. London. V. 43

The Fool of Quality: or the History of Henry Earl of Moreland. London. V. 41

The Fool of Quality: or the History of Henry Earl of Moreland. London. V. 40

The Fool of Quality; or, the History of Henry Earl of Moreland. London. V. 41

The Fool of Quality, or the History of Henry Earl of Moreland. London. V. 44

The Fool of Quality, or the History of Henry Earl of Moreland . . . London: 1767-69. V. 38

The Fool of Quality; or, the History of Henry, Earl of Moreland. London: 1767-70. V. 37; 39; 42; 45

The Fool of Quality, or the History of Henry Earl of Moreland. Dublin: 1770. V. 39; 40

The Fool of Quality; or, The History of Henry Earl of Moreland. London: 1777. V. 38

The Fool of Qaulity; or the History of Henry Earl of Moreland. London: 1782. V. 39

The Fool of Quality; or the History of Henry Earl of Morleand. London: 1792. V. 40

Gustavus Vasa the Deliverer of his Country, a Tragedy as it was to have been acted at the Theatre Royal in Drury Lane. London: 1739. V. 37; 38; 39; 40

Juliet Grenville: or, the History of the Human Heart. London: 1774. V. 39; 40; 42; 45

Liberty and Common-Sense to the People of Ireland, Greeting. Dublin: 1760. V. 41

The Poetical Works. Dublin: 1792. V. 38

The Tryal of the Cause of the Roman Catholics; On a Special Commission Directed to Lord Chief Justice Reason, Lord Chief Baron Interest, and Mr. Justice Clemency, Wednesday, August 5th, 1761 . . . Dublin: 1761. V. 43

BROOKE, JAMES 1803-1868

Narrative of Events in Borneo and Celebes down to the Occupataion of Labuan. London: 1848. V. 38

BROOKE, JAMES, RAJAH OF SARAWAK 1803-1868

The Private Letters of Sir James Brooke, K.C.B., Rajah of Sarawak, Narrating the Events of His Life from 1838 to the Present Time. London: 1853. V. 40; 45

BROOKE, JAMES WILLIAMSON

The Democrats of Marylebone. London: 1839. V. 40

BROOKE, JOCELYN

The Birth of a Legend - a Reminiscence of Arthur Machen and John Ireland. London: 1964. V. 41; 44

The Crisis in Bulgaria or Ibsen to the Rescue. London: 1956. V. 38

The Elements of Death and Other Poems. Aldington: 1952. V. 44

A Mine of Serpents. London: 1949. V. 38; 42

The Wild Orchids of Britain. London: 1950. V. 37; 38; 40; 42; 45

BROOKE, JOHN R.

Civil Report of Major General John R. Brooke U.S. Army Military Governor Island of Cuba. Havanna: 1899. V. 46

BROOKS, ELISHA

A Pioneer Mother of California. San Francisco: 1922. V. 37; 40

BROOKS, ELIZABETH

Prominent Women of Texas. Akron: 1896. V. 37; 39

BROOKS, GEORGE

Industry and Property. Suffolk: 1892? 1894? V. 38

BROOKS, GEORGE G.

The China Collector's Assistant. London: 1860. V. 46

BROOKS, GEORGE R.

The Southwest Expedition of Jedediah S. Smith. His Personal Account of the Journey to California, 1826-1827. Edited and with an Introduction by . . . Glendale: 1977. V. 37

BROOKS, GEWNDOLYN

Report from Part One. Detroit: 1972. V. 42

BROOKS, GWENDOLYN

Annie Allen. New York: 1949. V. 43; 44; 45
Bronzeville Boys and Girls. New York: 1956. V. 38; 40; 42; 43; 45; 46
Maud Martha. New York: 1953. V. 38
Selected Poems. New York: 1963. V. 46
A Street in Bronzeville. New York: 1945. V. 39; 46

BROOKS, HENRY

A History and Description of the Colony, Including Its Natural Features, Productions, Industrial Condition and Prospects. London: 1876. V. 42
Natal. A History and Description of the Colony. London: 1876. V. 41

BROOKS, J. TYRWHITT, PSEUD.

Four Months Among the Gold-Finders in Alta California; Being the Diary of an Expedition from San Francisco to the Gold Districts. London: 1849. V. 37; 46

BROOKS, JOHN

The Life and Times . . . In Which are Contained a History of the Great Revival in Tennessee . . . Nashville: 1848. V. 41

BROOKS, JUANITA

John Doyle Lee Zealot-Pioneer Builder-Scapegoat. Glendale: 1961. V. 40
The Moutain Meadows Massacre. Stanford: 1950. V. 46

BROOKS, NOAH

The Fairport Nine. New York: 1880. V. 39
Our Base Ball Club and How It Won the Championship. New York: 1884. V. 37; 39
The Transition: a Poem Recited at the Sixth Annual Fair of the Northern District Agricultural Society. Marysville Sept. 6, 1866. San Francisco: 1866. V. 37; 39; 43; 46

BROOKS, S. A.

Claims of the South for Settlement. West Point?: 187-. V. 40

BROOKS, SAMUEL H.

Designs for Cottage and Villa Architecture . . . London: 1839. V. 39; 42
Select Designs for Public Buildings: Plans, Elevations, Perspective Views, Sections and Details, of Churches, Chapels, Schools, Alms-Houses, Gas-Works, Markets and other Buildings. London: 1842. V. 38; 39

BROOKS, SARAH W.

Alamo Ranch-A Story of New Mexico. Cambridge: 1903. V. 39

BROOKS, SHIRELY

Gordian Knot: a Story of Good and of Evil. London: 1860. V. 38

BROOKS, SHIRLEY

Sooner or Later. London: 1868. V. 38

BROOKS, ULYSSES ROBERT

Butler and His Cavalry in the War of Secession 1861-1865. Columbia: 1909. V. 40; 42

BROOKS, VAN WYCK

The Flowering of New England. Boston: 1941. V. 39
From a Writer's Notebook. Worcester: 1955. V. 45
New England: Indian Summer 1865-1915. New York: 1940. V. 42

BROOKS, W. A.

Practical and Ornamental Delineations of Select Specimens of the Castellated, Monastic and Domestic Architecture of Great Britain . . . Nos. 1 and 2, Containing Raglan Castle and Tynterne Abbey, Monmouthshire. London: 1826. V. 37

BROOKSHAW, GEORGE

Groups of Flowers, Drawn and Accurately Coloured After Nature, with full Directions for the Young Artist . . . London: 1817. V. 45
The Horticultural Repository . . . London: 1823. V. 39
A New Treatise on Flower Painting, Or Every Lady Her Own Drawing Master . . . London: 1816. V. 38; 41; 46
Pomona Britannica. London: 1817. V. 38
Pomona Britannica. Leipzig: 1975. V. 39; 42

BROOM Volume 1, Number 4. Rome: 1922. V. 37

BROOME, A.

A History of the Rise and Progress of the Bengal Army. Calcutta: 1850. V. 38

BROOME, RALPH

The Letters of Simpkin the Second, Poetic Recorder, of all the Proceedings. London: 1789. V. 38
Simkin Redivivus to Simon: a Satirical and Poetical Epistle, Describing Edmund Burke's Letter to a Noble Lord in Defence of His Pension. London: 1796. V. 40; 42; 45

BROOME, WILLIAM

The Oak and the Dunghill. London: 1728. V. 40
Poems on Several Occasions. London: 1727. V. 40; 45
Poems on Several Occasions. London: 1750. V. 40; 43; 45

BROPHY, JOHN

Fanfare and Other Poems. London: 1930. V. 41

BROPHY, TRUMAN

Cleft Lip and Palate. Philadelphia: 1923. V. 42
Oral Surgery: a Treatise on the Diseases, Injuries and Malformations of the Mouth and Associated Parts. Philadelphia: 1915. V. 42

BROSSARD, CHANDLER

Who Walk in Darkness. London: 1952. V. 38

BROSSES, CHARLES DE

Histoire des Navigations aux Terres Australes Contenant ce que l'on Scait des Meours & des Productions des Contrees . . . Paris: 1756. V. 41; 45; 46

THE BROTHER to the Moon's Visit to the Court of Queen Vic. London: 1843. V. 37

BROTHERHEAD, WILLIAM

Forty Years Among the Old Booksellers of Philadelphia, with Bibliographical Remarks. Philadelphia: 1891. V. 39
General Fremont, and the Injustice Done Him. Philadelphia: 1862. V. 40

BROTHERS, A.

Photography: Its History, Processes, Apparatus and Materials, Comprising Working Details of all the More Important Methods. London: 1892. V. 38

THE BROTHERS Dalziel. A Record of Fifty Years' Work in Conjunction with Many of the Most Distinguished Artists of the Period, 1840-1890. London: 1901. V. 38; 39

BROTHERS, MARY HUDSON

A Pecos Pioneer. Albuquerque: 1943. V. 40; 43

BROTHERS, RICHARD

A Revealed Knowledge of the Prophecies and Times, Particularly of the Present Time, the Present War, and the Prophecy Now Fulfilling . . . Philadelphia: 1795. V. 40; 44

BROTHWELL, DON

Diseases in Antiquity. A Survey of the Diseases, Injuries and Surgery of Early Populations. Springfield: 1967. V. 39

BROUGH, ROBERT

The Vacant Frame. Oxfordshire: 1983. V. 41

BROUGH, ROBERT B.

The Life of Sir John Falstaff. London: 1858. V. 38; 39; 40; 41; 43; 44

BROUGH SMYTH, R.

The Aborigines of Victoria: with Notes Relating to the Habits of the Natives of Other Parts of Australia and Tasmania. Melbourne: 1878. V. 40

BROUGHAM AND VAUX, HENRY PETER BROUGAM, 1ST BARON 1778-1868

Lives of Men of Letters and Science, Who Flourished in the Time of George III. London: 1845. V. 38

BROUGHAM AND VAUX, HENRY PETER BROUGHAM, 1ST BARON 1778-1868

Albert Lunel, or the Chateau of Languedoc. London: 1844. V. 38
Analytical View of Sir Isaac Newton's Principia. London: 1855. V. 38; 44

BROUGHAM AND VAUX, HENRY PETER BROUGHAM, 1ST BARON
1778-1868 continued

Contributions to the Edinburgh Review. London: 1856. V. 43

General Theorems, Chiefly Porisms, in the Higher Geometry. London: 1798. V. 38

Historical Sketches of Statesmen Who Flourished in the Time of George III. London: 1839-43. V. 40; 41

Historical Sketches of Statesmen Who Flourished in the Time of George III. London: 1840/1839. V. 39; 41

The Life and Times, Written by Himself. London: 1871. V. 39

Lives of Men of Letters and Science Who Flourished in the Time of George III. London: 1845. V. 39; 41

Lives of Men of Letters and Science, Who Flourished in the Time of George III. London: 1845-46. V. 39; 43

Opinions of . . . on Negro Slavery. London: 1830. V. 42

Practical Observations Upon the Education of the People, Addressed to the Working Classes and Their Employers. Manchester: 1825. V. 45

Present State of Law. The Speech in the House of Commons, on February 7, 1828. London: 1828. V. 38; 40; 45

Speech Delivered on the Trial of the Cause: the King Versus J. A. Williams, for a Libel on the Clergy, at the Durham Summer Assizes, August 6th, 1822. Durham. V. 39

Speech . . . . on the Second Reading of the Reform Bill, Delivered in the House of Lords on the Memorable Night of Friday, the 7th Oct. 1831. London: 1831. V. 43

Tracts, Mathematical and Physical. London & Glasgow: 1860. V. 40

BROUGHAM, HENRY

An Inquiry into the Colonial Policy of the European Powers. Edinburgh: 1803. V. 37

BROUGHAM, HENRY PETER 1778-1868

Historical Sketches of Statesmen who flourished in the Time of George III; to which is added, remarks on Party and an Appendix. London: 1840-1839. V. 37

BROUGHAM, JOHN

David Copperfield: a Drama in Two Acts. New York: 1880? V. 43

Dombey and Son. Dramatized from Dickens' Novel. New York: 1875. V. 40; 43

BROUGHAN, HENRY

Lives of Men of Letters & Science, Who Flourished in the Time of George III. With Portraits engraved on steel. London: 1845. V. 37

BROUGHTON, ARTHUR

Dissertatio Medica Inauguralis, de Vermibus Intestinorum. Edinburgh: 1779. V. 41

BROUGHTON, BRIAN

Six Picturesque Views in North Wales, Engraved in Aquatints by Alden, from Drawings Made on the Spot . . . London: 1801. V. 41

BROUGHTON, HENRY

Historical Sketches of Statesmen Who Flourished in the Times of George III to Which are Added Remarks on the French Revolution. Third Series. London: 1843. V. 37

BROUGHTON, JAMES

A Long Undressing. Collected Poems 1949-1969. New York: 1971. V. 37; 40; 42; 44

BROUGHTON, JOHN

A Letter to a Member of the Present Honourable House of Commons, Relating to the Credit of Our Government and of the Nation in General. London: 1705. V. 41

A Letter to a Member of the Present Honourable House of Commons, Relating to the Credit of Our Government and of the Nation in General. London: 1795. V. 45

Poems: Moral, Sentimental and Satirical. Skipton: 1828. V. 45

BROUGHTON, JOHN CAM HOBHOUSE 1786-1869

Contemporary Account of the Separation of Lord and Lady Byron. Also of the Destruction of Lord Byron's Memoirs. London: 1870. V. 38

BROUGHTON, JOHN CARR HOBSON, IST BARON 1786-1869.

A Journey Through Albania, and Other Provinces of Turkey in Europe and Asia, During the Years 1809 and 1810. Philadelphia: 1817. V. 37

BROUGHTON-MAINWARING, ROWLAND

Historical Record of the Royal Welch Fusiliers Late the Twenty-Third Regiment, or, Royal Welsh Fusiliers . . . Piccadilly: 1889. V. 40

BROUGHTON, RHODA 1840-1920

Alas! A Novel. London: 1890. V. 41; 43

Belinda. London: 1883. V. 37; 39; 41; 43; 45

Cometh Up As a Flower. London: 1878. V. 45

Dear Faustina. London: 1897. V. 43

The Game and the Candle. London: 1899. V. 43

Mrs. Bligh, a Novel. London: 1892. V. 42; 43

BROUGHTON, THOMAS

Broughton's Patent Appliances for Erecting All Classes of Concrete Buildings, Walling &c . . . London: 1875. V. 44

An Historical Dictionary of all Religions from the Creation of the World to the Present Time. London: 1745. V. 39

BROUGHTON, THOMAS DUER

The Costume, Character, Manners, Domestic Habits and Religious Ceremonies of the Mahrattas. London: 1813. V. 40; 44

BROUGHTON, U. H. R.

The Dress of the First Regiment of Life Guards in Three Centuries. London: 1925. V. 38

BROUGHTON, WILLIAM ROBERT

The Voyage of Discovery to the North Pacific Ocean . . . London: 1804. V. 40; 45

BROUILETT, J. B. A.

Authentic Account of the Murder of Dr. Whitman and Other Missionaries, by the Cayuse Indians of Oregon in 1847 and the Causes Which Led to that Horrible Catastrophe. Portland: 1869. V. 41; 43

BROUMAS, OLGA

Beginning with O. New Haven: 1977. V. 37

BROUN, ANDREW

A Vindicatory Schedule, Concerning the New Cure of Fevers. Edinburgh: 1691. V. 39

BROUNER, WALTER BROOKS

Chinese Made Easy. With an Introduction by Herbert A. Giles. New York: 1904. V. 37

BROUSSAIS, F. J. V.

History of Chronic Phlegmasiae, or Inflamations, Founded on Clinical Experience and Pathological Anatomy. Philadelphia: 1831. V. 40; 42

BROUSSAIS, FRANCOIS JOSEPH VICTOR 1772-1838

On Irritation and Insanity. Columbia: 1828. V. 45

BROUSSON, H. F.

Practical Help to Amateurs and Artists for Painting and Decorating all Latest Productions in Pottery . . . London: 1886. V. 38

BROUSSONET, P. M. A.

Ichthyologia Sistens Piscium Descriptiones et Icones. London: 1782. V. 39

BROUZET, PIERRE 1713-1772

An Essay on the Medicinal Education of Children; and the Treatment of Their Diseases. London: 1755. V. 42

BROWELL & Co.'s Discovery for Preventing Mildew in Sail Cloth, Awnings, Tents and Canvas of Every Description, for Sails and Stores, 23, Aldermanbury, London. London: 1822. V. 43

BROWER, CHRISTOPHER

Fuldensium Antiquitatum Libri III. Antwerp: 1612. V. 38; 40; 44

BROWER, DAVID

The Place No One Knew: Glen Canyon on the Colorado. San Francisco: 1963. V. 41

BROWER, J. V.

Minnesota: Discovery of its Area, 1540-1665. St. Paul: 1903. V. 44

The Mississippi River and Its Source. Minneapolis: 1893. V. 44

BROWER, KENNETH

Galapagos: The Flow of Wilderness: Discovery, Prospect. San Francisco: 1968. V. 41

BROWINOWSKI, GRACIUS J.

The Birds of Australaia; Melbourne: 1890. V. 42

BROWN, A.

The Brook. Newcastle-upon-Tyne: 1880. V. 42

BROWN, A. J.

History of Newton County Mississippi, from 1834 to 1894. Jackson: 1894. V. 45

BROWN, AARON V.

Message of Governor . . . to the Tennessee Legislature, At Its October Session, 1847. Nashville: 1847. V. 42

Texas and Oregon. Letter and Speeches, in Reply to J. Q. Adams on the Annexation of Texas, and on the Bill for the Organization of a Territorial Government Over Orgeon. Washington: 1845. V. 45

BROWN, ABBIE FARWELL

The Lonesomest Doll. Boston and New York: 1928. V. 42

BROWN, ALEXANDER

The Genesis of the United States. Boston: 1890. V. 39

The Genesis of the United States . . . London: 1890. V. 42

The Genesis of the United States. Boston: 1892. V. 39

BROWN, ALFRED

Old Masterpieces in Surgery. Omaha: 1926. V. 41

Old Masterpieces in Surgery Being a Collection of Thoughts and Observations Engendered by A Perusal of Some of the Works of Our Forbears in Surgery. Omaha: 1928. V. 37; 38; 39; 41; 45

BROWN, ALICE

Fools of Nature. Boston: 1887. V. 41; 43; 44

The Road to Castalay. Boston: 1896. V. 43

The Road to Castalay. New York: 1917. V. 41; 43; 44

BROWN, ANDREW

History of Glasgow; and of Paisley, Greenock and Port Glasgow. Glasgow: 1795-97. V. 39

History of Glasgow: and of Paisley, Greenock, and Port-Glasgow. Glasgow: 1795. V. 37

BROWN, ARTHUR

Tennyson's Brook Illustrated by Arthur Brown, with Photographic Views Taken at Saltburn-by-the-Sea, Yorkshire. Newcastle-upon-Tyne: 1879. V. 39; 45

BROWN, BARRON

Comanche. The Sole Survivor of all the Forces in Custer's Last Stand. The Battle of the Little Big Horn. Kansas City: 1935. V. 45

BROWN, BASIL

Astronomical Atlases, Maps, and Charts, an Historical and General Guide. London: 1932. V. 37; 42; 43

Astronomical-Atlases, Maps and Charts. London: 1932. V. 43

Astronomical Atlases, Maps and Charts, an Historical and General Guide. London: 1932. V. 37

BROWN, BENJAMIN

Testimonies for the Truth; a Record of Manifestations of the Power of God, Miraculous and Providential, Witnessed in the Travels and Experience of . . . High Priest in the Church of Jesus Christ of Latter Day Saints. Liverpool: 1853. V. 41; 42; 43; 45

BROWN, BETSEY

Foaks an' Peeople; or, Three Years in Millbrook. Chicago: 1888. V. 45

BROWN, BOB

Demonics. Cagnes-Sur-Mer: 1931. V. 37; 38

Gems a Censored Anthology. Cagnes-sur-Mer: 1931. V. 37

Homemade Hilarity. Weston: 1938. V. 37; 40

Let There Be Beer. New York: 1932. V. 38; 40; 42

Tahiti. 10 Rhythms. New York: 1915. V. 37

You Gotta Live. London: 1932. V. 41; 42; 46

BROWN, C. BARRINGTON

Fifteen Thousand Miles on the Amazon and Its Tributaries. London: 1878. V. 40

BROWN, C. F.

The Turf Expositor . . . London: 1829. V. 46

BROWN, C. H.

The Optician's Manual. Philadelphia: 1908. V. 40

BROWN, CARLETON

A Register of Middle English Religious and Didactic Verse. Part I: List of Manuscripts. Part II: Index of First Lines and Index of Subjects and Titles. Oxford: 1916 & 1920. V. 37; 42; 46

BROWN, CHARLES

Narrative of the Expedition to South America, Which Sailed from England at the Close of 1817, for the Service of the Spanish Patriots. London: 1819. V. 39

BROWN, CHARLES BARRINGTON

Fifteen Thousand Miles on the Amazon and Its Tributaries. London: 1878. V. 39; 42

BROWN, CHARLES BROCKDEN 1771-1810

An Address to the Government of the United States, on the Cession of Louisiana to the French; and on the Late Breach of Treaty by the Spaniards, including a Translation of a Memorial, on the War of St. Domingo, and Cession of the Mississippi to . . . Philadelphia: 1803. V. 37; 44; 45

Alcuin: a Dialogue. Northampton: 1970. V. 44

Arthur Mervyn; or Memoirs of the Year 1793. Philadelphia: 1799. V. 43

Arthur Mervyn; or Memoirs of the Year 1793. (and) Arthur Mervyn, or, Memoirs of the Year 1793, Second Part. Philadelphia &: 1799/1800. V. 43

The British Treaty. Philadelphia: 1807. V. 45

Jane Talbot. Philadelphia: 1801. V. 43

Charles Brockden Brown's Novels. Philadelphia: 1887. V. 41; 43

The Novels of Charles Brockden Brown . . . with a Memoir of the Author. Boston: 1827. V. 38

Ormond; or, the Secret Witness. London: 1822. V. 40; 41; 43

Wieland; or the Transformation. New York: 1798. V. 37; 41; 42; 43; 45

BROWN, CHARLES CARROLL

Directory of American Cement Industries and Hand-Book for Cement Uses. Indianapolis: 1902. V. 44

BROWN, CORNELIUS

The Annals of Newark Upon Trent Comprising the History, Curiosities and Antiquities of the Borough. London: 1879. V. 41

The Annals of Newark-upon-Trent Comprising the History, Curiosities and Antiquities of the Borough. Newark: 1879. V. 42

BROWN, D. C., MRS.

Memoir of the Late Rev. Lemuel Covell, Missionary to the Tuscarora Indians and the Province of Upper Canada . . . Brandon: 1839. V. 42; 43; 44; 45

BROWN, DANIEL J.

The Sylva Americana . . . Boston: 1832. V. 41

BROWN, DAVID BLAYNEY

Ashmolean Museum Oxford. Catalogue of the Collection of Drawings. Volume IV. The Earlier British Drawings. Oxford: 1982. V. 39

BROWN, DAVID PAUL

The Forum; or, Forty Years Practice at the Philadelphia Bar. Philadelphia: 1856. V. 41

BROWN, DEE

Trail Driving Days. New York: 1952. V. 37

BROWN, EDWARD M.

An Ocean Voyage. N.P.: 1900. V. 41; 42

BROWN, ERASTUS

Hymns and Spiritual Songs . . . Calculated for the Entertainment of Youth and Other Serious Persons. Stockbridge: 1823. V. 45

BROWN, FRANCIS F.

Volunteer Grain. Chicago: 1895. V. 41; 44; 46

BROWN, FRED R.

History of the Ninth U. S. Infantry 1799-1909. Chicago: 1909. V. 39; 42; 45

BROWN, FREDERIC

And the Gods Laughed. 1987. V. 43

Angels and Spaceships. New York: 1954. V. 44

The Bloody Moonlight. New York: 1949. V. 46

Death Has Many Doors. New York: 1951. V. 45

The Deep End. New York: 1952. V. 44

The Deep End. New York: 1952. V. 43

The Fabulous Clipjoint. 1947. V. 43; 46

Here Comes a Candle. New York: 1950. V. 43; 44

His Name Was Death. 1954. V. 39

The Lights in the Sky are Stars. New York: 1953. V. 44

Martians, Go Home. New York: 1955. V. 37

The Office. 1958. V. 39

The Office. New York: 1961. V. 44

Space on My Hands. 1951. V. 43

Space on My Hands. Chicago: 1951. V. 46

Space on My Hands. Shasta: 1951. V. 45

Space on My Hands. 1951. V. 37

We All Killed Grandma. 1932. V. 39

What Mad Universe. New York: 1949. V. 41; 42; 44

BROWN, GEORGE

Arithmetica infinita, or the Accurate Accomptant's Best Companion. N.P.: 1718. V. 37

Australian Merino Studs. Melbourne: 1904. V. 46

The New English Letter-Writer; or, Whole Art of General Correspondence. London: 1780? V. 38

The Surgery of Oral Diseases and Malformations. Philadelphia: 1912. V. 42

BROWN, GEORGE D.

From Coast to Coast: Narrative of the Only Man to Drive a Single Horse Across the Continent. Simsbury: 1923. V. 40

BROWN, GEORGE LEE

Brown's Industrial Gazetteer and Hand-Book of the Atchison Topeka & Santa Fe R. R. Hamilton: 1881. V. 40

BROWN, GEORGE MACKAY

Stone: Poems. 1987. V. 40

Stone. Verona: 1987. V. 45

BROWN, GEORGE W.

Old Times in Oildom . . . Being a Series of Chapters in Which are Related the Writer's Many Personal Experiences, During Fifty Years of Life in the Oil Regions. Oil City: 1911. V. 44

BROWN, GLENN

History of the United States Capitol. Washington: 1900. V. 38

BROWN, H. C.

The Lordly Hudson. New York: 1937. V. 38

BROWN, HENRY

The History of Illinois, From Its First Discovery and Settlement, to the Present . . . . New York: 1844. V. 43

BROWN, HENRY A.

Narrative of the Anti-Masonick Excitment, in the Western Part of the State of New York During the Years 1826, '7, '8, and Part of 1829. Batavia: 1829. V. 42; 45

BROWN, HENRY COLLINS

The Lordly Hudson. New York: 1937. V. 39; 41; 43

BROWN, HORATIO

Studies in the History of Venice. New York: 1907. V. 41

BROWN, HORATIO F.

The Venetian Printing Press, an Historical Study based Upon Documents for the Most Part Hitherto Unpublished. London: 1891. V. 38; 39; 40; 42

The Venetian Printing Press, an Historical Study Based Upon Documents for the Most Part Hitherto Unpublished. New York: 1891. V. 44

BROWN, HUGH

The Covenanters: and Other Poems. Glasgow: 1838. V. 37

BROWN, ISAAC BAKER

On Some Diseases of Women admitting of Surgical Treatment. Philadelphia: 1856. V. 37

On the Curability of Certain Forms of Insanity, Epilepsy, Catalepsy and Hysteria in Females. London: 1866. V. 37

BROWN, ISAAC V.

Memoirs of the Rev. Robert Finely, D.D. Late Pastor of the Prebystrian Congregation at Basking Ridge New Jersey, and President of Franklin College, Located at Athens . . . Georgia. With Brief Sketches of some . . . New Brunswick: 1819. V. 37

BROWN, J. H.

Spectropia. London: 1864. V. 40; 46

Spectropia; or, Surprising Spectral Illusions. New York: 1864. V. 43

Spectropia; or, Surprising Spectral Illusions Showing Ghosts Everywhere, and of Any Colour. London: 1865. V. 39

BROWN, J. MORAY

In the Days When We Went Hog-Hunting. London: 1891. V. 39; 40; 46

Stray Sport. Edinburgh: 1893. V. 40

BROWN, JAMES

The Forester: a practical treatise on the planting, rearing, and general management of forest trees with an improved process for transplantation of trees of large size. Edinburgh: 1851. V. 37; 39; 45

BROWN, JAMES B.

Views of Canada and the Colonists. Edinburgh: 1851. V. 41

BROWN, JAMES BALDWIN

An Historical Account of the Laws Enacted Against the Catholics Both in England and Ireland of the Ameborations Which They Have Undergone During the Present Reign and of Their Existent State. London: 1813. V. 46

Memoirs of the Public and Private Life of John Howard, the Philanthropist . . . London: 1818. V. 41; 42

Memoirs of the Public and Private Life of John Howard, the Philanthropist. London: 1823. V. 39

BROWN, JAMES CABELL

Calabazas; or, Amusing Recollections of an Arizona City. San Francisco: 1892. V. 37; 38; 45

BROWN, JAMES S.

Life of a Pioneer Being the Autobiography of . . . Salt Lake City: 1900. V. 44

BROWN, JANE

Fulbrook: the Sketchbook, Letters, Specifications of Works and Accounts for a House by Edward Lutyens 1896-1899. 1989. V. 44

BROWN, JESSE

The Black Hills Trails A History of the Struggles of the Pioneers in the Winning of the Black Hills. Rapid City: 1924. V. 37; 39; 43; 45

BROWN, JOHN

Anecdotes and Characters of the House of Brunswick, Illustrative of the Courts of Hanover and London. London: 1821. V. 37

Arthur H. Hallam. Edinburgh: 1862. V. 46

The Cure of Saul. London: 1763. V. 46

Divine Help Implored Under the Loss of Godly and Faithful Men. Boston: 1726. V. 40

The Elements of Medicine; or, a Translation of the Elementa Medicinae Brunonis. Philadelphia. 1791. V. 42

The Elements of Medicine. Philadelphia: 1795. V. 38

The Elements of Medicine. Portsmouth: 1803. V. 37

An Essay on Satire: Occasion'd by the Death of Mr. Pope. London: 1745. V. 45

Essays on the Characteristics. London: 1751. V. 38; 41; 42; 43; 45

Essays on the Characteristics (of the Earl of Shaftesbury). Dublin: 1752. V. 38

An Estimate of Manners and Principles of the Times. London: 1757. V. 37; 39; 41; 42

An Estimate of the Manners and Principles of the Times. London: 1758. V. 46

An Explanatory Defence of the Estimate of Manners and Principles of the Times. London: 1758. V. 37; 42

The History of the Rise and Progress of Poetry Through It's Several Species. Newcastle: 1764. V. 46

Honour. London: 1743. V. 45

Horae Subsecivae. Edinburgh: 1858-1861-82. V. 40; 46

Horae Subsecivae. Edinburgh: 1861. V. 40

Horae Subsecivae. First, Second and Third Series. London: 1897. V. 41; 42; 44; 45

Letters Upon Poetry and Music of the Italian Opera. Edinburgh: 1789. V. 38; 40

The Life, Trial and Execution of Captain John Brown . . . New York: 1859. V. 42

The Life and Trial of Capt. John Brown. Boston: 1859. V. 37

The North-West Passage, and the Plans for the Search for Sir John Franklin. London: 1858. V. 46

Notes on an Excursion into the Highlands of Scotland, in Autumn 1818. Edinburgh: 1819. V. 37

Rab and His Friends. V. 45

Testimonies of Capt. John Brown, at Harper's Ferry, with His Address to the Court. New York: 1860. V. 42

Thoughts on Civil Liberty, on Licentiousness and Faction. Newcastle-upon-Tyne: 1765. V. 39

Thoughts on Civil Liberty, on Licentiousness, and Faction. By the Author of Essays on the Characteristics, &c. The Second Edition. London: 1765. V. 37

Twenty-Five Years a Parson in the Wild West Being the Experience of Parson Ralph Riley. Fall River, Mass.: 1896. V. 37; 41; 42; 45

BROWN, JOHN CARTER 1797-1874

Biblioteca Americana. Catalogue of the John Carter Brown Library. Providence & Milwood: 1963-75. V. 40

Bibliotheca Americana Catalogue of the John Carter Brown Library. Providence: 1921-22-23. V. 39

Bibliotheca Americana. Catalogue of the John Carter Brown Library in Brown University, Providence, R.I. New York: 1975. V. 40

BROWN, JOHN E.

Memoirs of an American Gold Seeker. V. 45

Memoirs of a Forty-Niner. New Haven: 1907. V. 37; 40; 43

Memoirs of an American Gold Seeker. Experiences of a 'Forty Niner' During his Journey across the Continent on Horseback . . . (N.P.): 1908. V. 37

BROWN, JOHN H.

Indian Wars and Pioneers of Texas. Austin: 1988. V. 41

Reminiscences and Incidents of 'The Early Days' of San Francisco. San Francisco: 1886. V. 43

BROWN, JOHN HENRY

The Encyclopedia of the New West . . . . Texas, Arkansas, Colorado, New Mexico and Indian Territory. Marshall: 1881. V. 39; 41; 42; 45

History of Texas from 1685 to 1892. St. Louis: 1892. V. 37; 44; 46

Indian Wars and Pioneers of Texas. 1896. V. 42

Indian Wars and Pioneers. Austin: 1896. V. 37; 38; 39; 42; 46

Life and Times of Henry Smith, the First American Governor of Texas. Dallas: 1887. V. 37; 44; 45

Reminiscences and Incidents of Early Days of San Francisco (1845-50). San Francisco: 1933. V. 42; 45

BROWN, JOHN MASON

The Political Beginnings of Kentucky . . . Up to the Time of Its Admission into the American Union. Louisville: 1889. V. 38; 39; 42

BROWN, JOHN, philomath

The Practical Gauger, Arithmetical and Instrumental. London: 1678. V. 43

BROWN, JONATHAN

The History and Present Condition of St. Domingo. Philadelphia: 1837/1839. V. 42

The History and Present Condition of St. Domingo. Boston: 1839. V. 42

BROWN, JOSEPH E.

Senator Brown's Argument Before the Governor in Defense of Dade Coal Company on the Convict Question. N.P.: 1887. V. 45

BROWN, JOSEPH N.

The Battle of the Bloody Angle (Spotsylvania Court House, Virginia). Anderson: 1910. V. 44

BROWN, JOSEPHINE

Biography of an American Bondman, by His Daughter. Boston: 1856. V. 42

BROWN, KEITH MACARTHUR

Medical Practice in Old Parramatta. Sydney: 1937. V. 40

BROWN, L.

Eagles, Hawks and Falcons of the World. London: 1968. V. 37

BROWN, L. H.

The Birds of Africa. Volume 2: Galliformes, Gruiformes, Charadriiformes and Columbiformes. London: 1986. V. 37; 38

BROWN, LAWRENCE L.

The Episcopal Church in Texas, 1838-1874: From Its Foundation to the Division of the Diocese. Austin: 1963. V. 39

BROWN, LEE

Trail Driving Days. New York: 1952. V. 46

BROWN, LLOYD A.

The Story of Maps. Boston: 1949. V. 40

BROWN, LOUISE NORTON

Block Printing and Book Illustration in Japan. London: 1924. V. 43; 44

BROWN, M.

Address to the Graduates in Jefferson College, Delivered on the Day of Commencement, Sept. 27, 1838. Washington, Mississippi: 1839. V. 40

BROWN, MAGGIE

The Book of Betty Barber. Boston: 1910. V. 42

BROWN, MARIAN

Bath Night and the Chained Tree. Oxford: 1983. V. 41

BROWN, MARION

San Francisco, Old and New. San Francisco: 1939. V. 41

BROWN, MISS

The Foreign Tour of the Misses Brown, Jones and Robinson. London: 1878. V. 39

BROWN, MOSES

The Compleat Angler. London: 1759. V. 41

Piscatory Eclogues. London: 1729. V. 40

BROWN, N. E.

The Book of Nacogdoches County. Nacogdoches: 1927. V. 42

BROWN, NORMAN O.

Life Against Death. 1947. V. 44

Love's Body. New York: 1966. V. 41

BROWN, O. PHELPS

The Complete Herbalist; or, the People Their Own Physicians by the Use of Nature's Remedies . . . Jersey City: 1867. V. 42

BROWN, OLIVER MADOX

The Dwale Bluth, Hebditch's Legacy and Other Literary Remains. London: 1876. V. 43; 45

BROWN, P.

Indian Paintings Under the Mughals, A. D. 1550 to A.D. 1750. Oxford: 1924. V. 37

BROWN, P. L.

The Narrative of George Russel of Golf Hill, with Russellania and Selected Papers. London: 1935. V. 41

BROWN, PAUL

Aintre, Grand Nationals - Past and Present. New York: 1930. V. 39; 42; 43

Good Luck and Bad. New York: 1940. V. 43

Spills and Thrills. New York: 1933. V. 39; 42

Ups and Downs. New York: 1936. V. 42; 43

BROWN, PERCY

American Martyrs to Science through the Roentgen Rays. Springfield: 1936. V. 45

BROWN, PETER

New Illustrations of Zoology. London: 1776. V. 39

BROWN, R.

Miscellaneous Botanical Works. London: 1866-68. V. 38

A Naturalist at the Poles, the Life Work and Voyages of Dr. W. S. Bruce. London: 1923. V. 43

On the Organs and Mode of Fecundation in Orchideae and Asclepiadae. London: 1833. V. 42; 43

Prodromus Florae Novae Hollandiae et Insulae Van Diemen. London: 1810. V. 43

BROWN, R. C. LUNDIN

British Columbia. New Westminster: 1863. V. 39

BROWN, R. N.

The Voyage of the 'Scotia' Being the Records of a Voyage of Exploration in Atarctic Seas. London: 1906. V. 43

BROWN, R. N. RUDMOSE

The Voyage of the Scotia Being the Record of a Voyage of Exploration in Antarctic Seas. Edinburgh: 1906. V. 37

BROWN, RICHARD

Domestic Architecture: Containing a History of the Science, and the Principles of Designing Public Edifices, Private Dwelling Houses, Country Mansions and Suburban Villas. London: 1842. V. 38; 40; 44; 45

The London Bookshop. Pinner: 1971-77. V. 40

Memorabilia Curliana Mabensia. Dumfries: 1830. V. 37

The Principles of Practical Perspective, or Scenographic Projection . . . to Which are Added Rules for Shadowing and the Elements of painting . . . London: 1815. V. 44

Sacred Architecture, Its Rise, Progress and Present State. London: 1845. V. 38

BROWN, RICHARD BLAKE

The Blank Cheque. London: 1934. V. 40

BROWN, RICHARD C. A.

History of Accounting and Accountants. Edinburgh: 1905. V. 42

BROWN, RITA MAE

Rubyfruit Jungle. Planfield: 1973. V. 44

BROWN, ROBERT

The Book of the Landed Estate Containing Directions for the Management and Development of the Resources of Landed Property. 1869. V. 38

The Book of the Landed Estate containing directions for the Managment and Development of the Resources of Landed Property. London: 1869. V. 37

The Countries of the World . . . London: 1885-90. V. 42

General View of the Agriculture of the West Riding of Yorkshire, Surveyed by Messrs. Rennie, Brown & Shirreff, 1793. Edinburgh: 1790. V. 39

General View of the Agriculture of the West Riding of Yorkshire . . . London: 1793. V. 45

General View of the Agriculture of the West Riding of Yorkshire. London: 1799. V. 37

The Miscellaneous Botanical Works of Robert Brown. London: 1866-68. V. 37; 43

On the Geographical Distribution and Physical Characteristics of the Coal-Fields of the North Pacific Coast. Edinburgh: 1869. V. 45

On the Nature of the Discoloration of the Artic Seas. Edinburgh: 1868. V. 37

Poems; Principally on Sacred Subjects. London: 1826. V. 41; 42

Science for All. London: 1880. V. 40

Vancouver Island. Exploration. Victoria: 1865. V. 43

BROWN, ROBERT CARLTON 1886-1959

The Remarkable Adventures of Christopher Poe. Chicago: 1913. V. 43; 44; 46

BROWN, ROBERT E.

The Book of the Landed Estate, Containing Directions for the Management and Development of the Resources of Landed Property. Edinburgh: 1869. V. 42

The Book of the Landed Estate Containing Directions for the Management and Development of the Resources of Landed Property. London: 1869. V. 40; 44

BROWN, ROBERT E. continued

The Book of the Landed Estate, Containing Directions for the Management and Development of the Resources of Landed Property. Edinburgh & London: 1869. V. 37; 40

BROWN, ROBERT NEAL RUDMOSE 1879-

A Naturalist at the Poles the Life and Work and Voyages of Dr. W. S. Bruce the Polar Explorer. London: 1923. V. 41

The Voyage of the 'Scotia' Being the Record of a Voyage of Exploration in Antarctic Seas by Three of the Staff. Edinburgh: 1906. V. 45

BROWN, S.

Alpine Flora of the Canadian Rocky Mountains. New York: and London: 1907. V. 45

BROWN, S. S.

Catalogue of Short-Horn Cattle the Property of S.S. Brown, Hazelwood Farm, Galena, Jo Daviess Co. Illinois. Galena: 1876. V. 45

BROWN, SAMUEL

Lectures on the Atomic Theory and Essays Scientific and Literary. Edinburgh: 1858. V. 40

BROWN, SAMUEL R.

Views of the Campaigns of the North-Western Army, &c . . . Troy: 1814. V. 45

Views of the Campaigns of the North-western Army &c . . . Philadelphia: 1815. V. 45

The Western Gazeteer; or Emigrant's Directory, Containing a Geographical Description of the Western States and Territories, Viz. The States of Kentucky, Indiana, Louisiana, Ohio, Tennessee and Mississippi: and the Territories of Illinois, Missouri . . . Auburn, N.Y.: 1817. V. 37; 38; 42; 43; 45

BROWN, SOLYMAN

The Birth of Washington, a Poem. New York: 1822. V. 40

BROWN, T.

Miscellaneous Botanical Works. London: 1866-68. V. 37

BROWN, T. BURTON

Excavations in Azarbaijan, 1948. London: 1951. V. 40

BROWN, T. JULIAN

The Stonyhurst Gospel of St. John. Oxford: 1969. V. 41

BROWN, TARLETON

Memoirs of Tarleton Brown, a Captain in the Revolutionary Army. New York: 1862. V. 45

BROWN, THEODORE M.

The Work of G. Rietveld, Architect. Utrecht: 1958. V. 37

BROWN, THOMAS b. 1766

An Account of the People Called Shakers . . . New York: 1812. V. 42

An Account of the People Called Shakers: Their Faith, Doctrines and Practice, Exemplified in the Life, Convesations and Experience of the author During the Time He Belonged to the Society. Troy: 1812. V. 46

An Atlas of the Fossil Conchology of Great Britain and Ireland With Descriptions of all the Species. London: 1889. V. 38; 42

The Book of Butterflies, Sphinxes and Moths. London & Edinburgh: 1832-34. V. 38

The Book of Butterflies, Sphinges and Moths. London & Edinburgh: 1832. V. 37

The Elements of Conchology . . . London: 1816. V. 43

Illustrations of the Land and Fresh Water Conchology of Great Britain and Ireland. London: 1845. V. 38

An Inquiry Into the Relation of Cause and Effect. Edinburgh: 1818. V. 40

Lectures on the Philosophy of the Human Mind. Edinburgh: 1820. V. 42; 45

Lectures on the Philosophy of the Human Mind. Edinburgh: 1824. V. 42; 43

Lectures on the Philosophy of the Human Mind. Philadelphia: 1824. V. 44

Lectures on the Philosophy of the Human Mind. Edinburgh: 1830. V. 42

Lectures on Ethics. Edinburgh: 1846. V. 43

Lectures on the Philosophy of the Human Mind: with a Memoir of the Author, by David Welsh. London: 1858. V. 43; 45

Lectures on Philosophy of the Human Mind. Boston,: 1826. V. 38

Legacy for the Ladies. London: 1705. V. 45; 46

Letters from the Dead to the Living by Mr. Tho. Brown, Capt. Ayloff, Mr. Hen. Barker &c. London: 1702. V. 37; 38; 40; 46

Letters from the Dead to the Living. London: 1707. V. 39; 40

Miscellanea Aulica; or, a Collection of State-Treatises, Never Before Publish'd . . . London: 1702. V. 42

Nature's Cabinet Unlock'd. London: 1657. V. 44

Novus Reformator Vapulans; or, the Welch Levite Tossed in a Blanket. London: 1691. V. 42

Observations on the Zoonomia of Erasmus Darwin, M.D. Edinburgh: 1798. V. 38; 40; 41; 42; 43; 45

On Dreams. London. V. 45

The Paradise of Coquettes, a Poem. London: 1814. V. 40; 42

The Reasons of Mr. Bays Changing His Religion. London: 1688. V. 41; 44; 45

The Reminiscences of an Old Traveller throughout Different Parts of Europe. London: 1835. V. 41

Treatise on the Philosophy of the Human Mind. Cambridge: 1827. V. 41

The Weesils, a Satyrical Tale, Giving an Account of Some Argumental Passages Happening in the Lion's Court About Wessilon's Taking the Oaths. London: 1691. V. 38; 40; 46

The Works . . . Serious and Comical, in Prose and Verse. London: 1721. V. 42

The Works of Mr. Thomas Brown, Serious and Comical, in Prose and Verse: With His Remains. London: 1760. V. 41; 43; 44

BROWN, THOMAS HENDERSON

The Romance of Everyday Life. Mitchell: 1923. V. 40

BROWN UNIVERSITY

Catalogue of Books in the Library. Providence: 1826. V. 38

The Laws of Rhode-Island College. Enacted by the Fellows and Trustees. (with) Supplement to the Laws of Rhode-Island College. Providence: 1803. V. 39

BROWN UNIVERSITY. JOHN CARTER BROWN LIBRARY

Bibliotheca Americana. Millwood: & Providence: 1975/1973. V. 42

Bibliotheca Americana. Catalogue of the John Carter Brown Library . . . Milwood: 1973. V. 37

BROWN, VARINA D.

A Colonel at Gettysburg and Spotslyvania. Columbia: 1931. V. 39; 42

BROWN, VINCENT

My Brother. London: 1896. V. 41

BROWN, W. HENRY

Co-Operation in a University Town. London: 1939. V. 43

BROWN, W. LLEWELLYN

The Etruscan Lion. London: 1960. V. 40

BROWN, W. M.

A Tale of the Early Days of Bruce County. London: 1932. V. 44

BROWN, W. WELLS

A Fugitive Slave . . . London: 1852. V. 42

BROWN, WALTER

Fables by Walter Brown. London: 1884. V. 38; 40

BROWN, WILLIAM

The Carpenter's Assistant . . . Worcester: 1852. V. 42

A Compendious and Accurate Treatise of Fines Upon Writs of Covenant; and Recoveries Upon Writs of Entry in the Post. London: 1693. V. 38; 40

The National History of the Salmon. Glasgow: 1862. V. 39; 40; 41; 45

BROWN, WILLIAM F.

Retriever Gun Dogs. West Hartford: 1945. V. 43

BROWN, WILLIAM GEORGE

Six Month's Residence and Travels in Mexico. London: 1824. V. 39

BROWN, WILLIAM H.

An Historical Sketch of the Early Movement in Illinois for the Legalization of Slavery. Chicago: 1856. V. 37

Portrait Gallery of Distinguished American Citizens, with Biographical Sketches and Facsimiles of Original Letters. New York: 1931. V. 38; 39; 44

BROWN, WILLIAM HARVEY

On the South African Frontier. New York: 1899. V. 39

BROWN, WILLIAM HENRY 1808-1883

The History of the First Locomotives in America: from Original Documents and the Testimony of Living Witnesses. New York: 1871. V. 37; 39; 46

BROWN, WILLIAM HILL

The Power of Sympathy; or, the Triumph of Nature. Boston: 1789. V. 43

BROWN, WILLIAM LAWRENCE

An Essay on the Natural Equality of Men . . . Philadelphia: 1793. V. 37

BROWN, WILLIAM ROBINSON

The Horse of the Desert. New York: 1929. V. 37; 39

Horse of the Desert. N.P.: 1936. V. 38

BROWN, WILLIAM WELLS

The American Fugitive in Europe, Sketches of Places and People Abroad. Boston: 1855. V. 40; 42

BROWN, WILLIAM WELLS continued

The Black Man, His Antecedents, His Genius and His Achievements. New York: 1863. V. 39; 42

Narrative of William W. Brown, a Fugitive Slave. Boston: 1847. V. 39

The Rising Son; or, the Antecedents and Advancement of the Colored RAce. Boston: 1874. V. 42

Sketches of Places and People Abroad. Boston: 1855. V. 42

BROWNBILL, JOHN

West Kirby and Hilbre. Liverpool: 1928. V. 44

BROWNE, A. K.

The Story of the Kearsage and Alabama. San Francisco: 1868. V. 46

BROWNE, ABBIE FARWELL

The Lonesomest Doll. Boston & New York: 1928. V. 40

BROWNE, C. M.

Bombay Ducks. Bombay: 1876. V. 42

BROWNE, CHARLES FARRAR 1834-1867

Artemus Ward in London and Other Papers. Montreal: 1868. V. 45

BROWNE, CHARLES FRANCIS

Artemus Ward's Lecture. (As Delivered at the Egyptian Hall, London.) London & New York: 1869. V. 37

BROWNE, D. J.

The American Bird Fancier. New York: 1860. V. 38

Sylva Americana; or, a Description of the Forest Trees Indigenous to the United States. Boston: 1832. V. 42

BROWNE, E. G.

A Year Amongst the Persians. London: 1893. V. 44

BROWNE, EDGAR

Phiz and Dickens as they Appeared to Edgar Browne. London: 1913. V. 37; 40

BROWNE, EDWARD 1644-1708

An Account of Several Travels through a Great Part of Germany. London: 1677. V. 41; 45

Arabian Medicine. Cambridge: 1921. V. 45

A Brief Account of Some Travels in Hugaria, Servia, Bulgaria, Macedonia, Thessaly, Austria, Styria, Carinthia, Carniola & Friuli. London: 1673. V. 38

A Brief Account of Some Travels in Hugaria, Servia, Bulgaria, Macedonia, Thessaly, Austria, Styria, Carinthia, Carniola and Fruili. (with) An Account of Several Travels through a Great Part of Germany ... London: 1673/77. V. 41; 46

A Brief Account of Some Travels in Divers Parts of Europe. London: 1685. V. 37; 39; 45

BROWNE, EDWARD G.

A Literary History of Persia. London: 1929-51. V. 39

A Literary History of Persia. Cambridge: 1951. V. 39

The Persian Revolution of 1905-1909. Cambridge: 1910. V. 39

The Press and Poetry of Modern Persia. Cambridge: 1914. V. 39

A Year Amongst the Persians: Impressions as to the Life, Character and Thought of the People of Persia, Received During Twelve Months' Residence in that Couuntry in the Years 1887-8. London: 1893. V. 38; 41

BROWNE, F. F.

Volunteer Grain. 1895. V. 45

BROWNE, FRANCIS F.

Volunteer Grain. Chicago: 1895. V. 38

BROWNE, FREDERICK W.

My Service in the U.S. Colored Cavalry. Cincinnati: 1908. V. 43

BROWNE, G. ST. J. ORDRE

The Vanishing Tribes of Kenya. Philadelphia: 1925. V. 39

BROWNE, G. WALDO

A Daughter of Maryland. New York: 1895. V. 44

Japan. The Place and the People. Boston: 1904. V. 39

The Paradise of the Pacific ... Boston: 1900. V. 44

BROWNE, G. WASHINGTON

Pugin Studentship Drawings. Edinburgh: 1837. V. 44

Pugin Studentship Drawings Being a Selection from Sketches, Measured Drawings, and Details of Domestic and Ecclesiastical Buildings in England and Scotland. Edinburgh: 1887. V. 38; 46

BROWNE, GEORGE Y.

Browne's Arithmetical Tables, Combined with easy lessons in mental arithmetic, for beginners. Atlanta: 1865. V. 37; 39

BROWNE, HABLOT KNIGHT

The Chronicles of Crimes; or The New Newgate Calendar. A Series of memoirs and Anecdotes of Notorious Characters Who Have Outraged the Laws of Great Britain from the Earliest Periods to 1841. London: 1886. V. 37

Four Plates Engraved Under the Superintendence to Hablot K. Browne and Robert Young, to Illustrate the Cheap Edition of the Old Curiosity Shop. London: 1848. V. 40

Four Plates Engraved Under the Superintendence of Hablot K. Browne and Robert Young to Illustrate the Cheap Edition of Barnaby Rudge. London: 1849. V. 40

Home Pictures, Sixteen Domestic Scenes of Childhood Drawn and Etched. London: 1851. V. 39; 44

BROWNE, IRVING

Ballads of A Book-Worm. 1899. V. 39

BROWNE, ISAAC HAWKINGS

De Anima Immortalitate. Poemata. London: 1754. V. 38; 40

BROWNE, ISAAC HAWKINS

Poems Upon Various Subjects, Latin and English ... London: 1768. V. 38; 39; 40; 42; 43; 46

BROWNE, J.

The Circus: or, British Olympicks. A Satyr on the Ring in Hyde-Park. London: 1709. V. 39

BROWNE, JAMES

A History of the Highlands and Highland Clans. Glasgow: 1837-38. V. 37; 41; 45

A History of the Highlands and of the Highland Clans. Glasgow: etc.,: 1838. V. 42

History of Scotland, Its Highlands, Regiments and Clans. Edinburgh: 1909. V. 44

A History of the Higlands and of the Highland Clans. Glasgow: 1839. V. 37

Picturesque Views of Edinburgh. Edinburgh: 1825. V. 40

BROWNE, JOHN

A Collection of Tracts, Concerning the Present State of Ireland, with Respect to Its Riches, Revenues, Trade and Manufacture. London: 1729. V. 45

A Compleat Treatise of the Muscles, As They Appear in the Humane Body, and Arise in Dissection; London: 1681. V. 40

The History of the Edifice of the Metropolitan Church of St. Peter, York ... London: 1847. V. 37

Myographia Nova or Graphical Description of all the Muscles in the Human Body. V. 38

Myographia Nova or Graphical Description of All the Muscles in the Human Body. V. 41

Myographia Nova: or, a Graphical Description of all the Muscles in the Humane Body, As They Arise in Dissection ... New York. V. 41

Myographia Nova Sive Musculorum Omnium ... London: 1684. V. 46

Myographia Nova Sive Musculorum Omnium. Leyden: 1687. V. 37; 38

Myographia Nova. 1970. V. 38

A Treatise on the Steam Engine in its Application to Mines, Steam Navigation, and Railways. London: 1846. V. 37

BROWNE, JOHN ROSS 1821-1875

Adventures in the Apache Country; a Tour Through Arizona and Sonora. New York: 1868. V. 37; 40

Adventures in Apache Country: a Tour through Arizona and Sonora. New York: 1869. V. 38; 39; 41; 42; 43; 45; 46

Adventures in the Apache Country: a Tour through Arizona and Sonora with Notes on the Silver Regions of Nevada. New York: 1878. V. 44

Crusoe's Island: a Ramble in the Footsteps of Alexander Selkirk. New York: 1864. V. 38; 46

Crusoe's Island a Ramble in the Footsteps of Alexander Selkirk. New York: 1864. V. 38

Crusoe's Island; A Ramble in the Footsteps of Alexander Selkirk. New York: 1867. V. 41

Etchings of a Whaling Cruise, With Notes of a Sojourn on the Island of Zanzibar; and a Brief History of the Whale Fishery, In Its Past and Present Condition. London: 1846. V. 39; 40

Etchings of a Whaling Cruise ... New York: 1850. V. 46

Etchings of A Whaling Cruise, with Notes of a Sojourn on the Island of Zanzibar. To which is Appended a Brief History of the Whale Fishery, its Past and Present Condition. New York: 1846. V. 37; 40; 41; 46

Letter from the Secretary of the Treasury, Transmitting Report upon the Mineral Resources of the States of Territories West of the Rocky Mountains. Washington: 1867. V. 37

The Mariposa Estate Its Past, Present and Future. New York: 1868. V. 43

Report of the Debates in the Convention of California, on the Formation of the State Constitution, in September & October, 1849. Washington: 1850. V. 37; 38; 39; 42; 43; 46

Report of J. Ross Browne on the Mineral Resources of the States and Territories West of the Rocky Mountains. San Francisco: 1868. V. 46

Report on the Mineral Resources of the States and Territories West of the Rocky Mountains. Washington: 1868. V. 40

BROWNE, JOHN ROSS 1821-1875 continued

Reports on the Mineral Resources of the United States. Washington: 1867. V. 40

Reports of the Mineral Resources of the United States. Washington: 1868. V. 46

A Sketch of the Settlement and Exploration of Lower California. San Francisco: 1869. V. 45

Yusef; or the Journey of the Frangi. New York: 1865. V. 43

Usef; or the Journey of the Frangi. New York: 1867. V. 44

BROWNE, JOSEPH

St. James's Park. London: 1709. V. 40; 45

BROWNE, MAGGIE

The Book of Betty Barber. London: (1910). V. 37

The Surprising Adventures of Tuppy and Tue. London: 1904. V. 43

Two Old Laides, Two Foolish Fairies and a Tom Cat. London: 1897. V. 37; 46

BROWNE, MARY ANN

Repentance; and Other Poems. London: 1829. V. 42

BROWNE, MOSES

Angling Sports: in Nine Piscatory Eclogues . . . London: 1773. V. 39; 40; 42; 46

BROWNE, P. W.

Where the Fishers Go. New York: 1909. V. 44

BROWNE, PATRICK

The Civil and Natural History of Jamaica . . . London: 1789. V. 38; 39; 40; 43

BROWNE, PETER d. 1735

The Procedure, Extent and Limits of Human Understanding. London: 1729. V. 40; 45

The Procedure, Extent, and Limits of Human Understanding. London: 1737. V. 37

Things Divine and Supernatural Conceived by Analogy with Things Natural and Human. London: 1733. V. 37; 40; 41

BROWNE, PETER A.

A Lectures on the Oregon Territory. Philadelphia: 1843. V. 37

Trichologia Mammalium; or, a Treatise on the Organization, Properties and Uses of Hair and Wool; Together with an Essay Upon the Raising and Breeding of Sheep. Philadelphia: 1853. V. 40; 42; 43; 45; 46

BROWNE, T. A.

Rolf Boldrewood, ps. Robbery Under Arms. London: 1888. V. 44

BROWNE, T. H.

History of the English Turf 1904-1930. New York: 1931. V. 43

BROWNE, THOMAS 1605-1682

Certain Miscellany Tracts. London: 1684. V. 37; 38; 39; 40; 42; 43; 44; 45

Christian Morals . . . With a Life of the Author by Samuel Johnson . . . London: 1756. V. 37; 38; 42; 46

Christian Morals. With a Life of the Author by Samuel Johnson. London: 1765. V. 41

Pseudoxia Epidemica. London: 1650. V. 37

Pseudoxia Epidemica. 1984. V. 37

Hydriotaphia, Urne-Buriall . . . With the Garden of Cyrus. London: 1568. V. 37

Hydriotaphia. Urne-Buriall, or, a Discourse of the Sepulchrall Urnes Lately Found in Norfolk. Together with the Garden of Cyrus, or the Quincunciall Lozenge, or Net-work Plantations of the Ancients, Artificially, Naturally, Mystically Considered . . . London: 1658. V. 37; 38; 40; 42; 43; 46

Hydriotaphia Urn Burial . . . London: 1893. V. 45

Hydriotaphia or Urne-Buriall. Boston: 1907. V. 38; 40; 46

Hydriotaphia: Urne Buriall, or, a Discourse of the Sepulchrall Urnes . . . Cambridge: 1907. V. 39

A Letter to a Friend Upon Occasion of the Death of His Intimate Friend. London: 1690. V. 38

A Letter to a Friend Upon the Occasion of the Death of His Intimate Friend. Boston: 1971. V. 46

Of Garlands and Coronary or Garland Plants . . . to John Evelyn. Northampton: 1962. V. 39

Of Unicornes Hornes. Williamsburg: 1984. V. 40

On Dreams . . . London: 1915. V. 46

The Parson's Handbook. Dublin: 1831. V. 46

The Parson's Horn Book. Dublin: 1831. V. 38; 40

Poems on Several Occasions. Manchester: 1800. V. 40

Posthumous Works. London: 1712. V. 40; 45

Pseudodexia Epidemica . . . Whereunto are new added two Discourses The one of Urne Burial . . . The other of the Garden of Cyrus. London: 1658. V. 38; 39; 40; 41

Pseudodoxia Epidemica. London: 1646. V. 38; 39; 42; 45; 46

Pseudodoxia Epidemica; or, Enquiries into Very Many Received Tenents, and Commonly Presumed Truths. London: 1646. V. 41; 44; 46

Pseudodoxia Epidemica. London: 1650. V. 40; 41; 43; 44; 46

Pseudodoxia Epidemica; or, Enquiries into Very Many Received Tenets, and Commonly Presumed Truths. London: 1650. V. 45

Pseudodoxia Epidemica; or, Enquiries into Very Many Received Tenents . . . London: 1659. V. 45

Pseudodoxia Epidemica. London: 1669. V. 38

Pseudodoxia Epidemica. London: 1672. V. 38

Pseudodoxia Epidemica. 1981. V. 44

Pseudodoxia Epidemica. Oxford: 1981. V. 39

Pseudodoxia Epidemica. 1984. V. 40

Pseudodoxia Epidemica. 1984. V. 40

Pseudodoxia Epidemica. 1984. V. 38

Pseudodoxia Epidemica. 1984. V. 39

Pseudodoxia Epidemica; of Unicornes Hornes. Easthampton: 1984. V. 42; 46

Pseudodoxia Epidemica; or Unicornes Hornes. Easthampton: 1984. V. 41; 43

Pseudodoxia Epidemica: Of Unicornes Hornes. Illustrated with sixteen wood engravings by Alan James Robinson. (Williamsburg, MA.): 1984. V. 37

Pseudodoxia; Epidemica: or, Enquiries into Very many Received Tenents and commonly Presumed Truths. The Second Edition, Corrected and much Enlarged by the Author. Together with some Marginall Observations, and a . . . London: 1650. V. 37

Religio Medici. London: 1642. V. 39

A True and Full Copy of that Which Was Most Imperfectly and Surreptitiously Printed Before Under the Name of Religio Medici. London: 1643. V. 39

Religio Medici. 1644. V. 46

Religio Medici. Leyden: 1644. V. 41

Religio Medici. London: 1645. V. 40

Religio Medici. London: 1656. V. 40

Religio Medici. London: 1659. V. 37; 40; 41

Religio Medici cum Annotationibus. London: 1665. V. 39

Religio Medici . . . With Annotations Never Before Published Upon all the Obscure Passages Therein. London: 1678. V. 38; 42

Religio Medici . . . London: 1678. V. 40

Religio Medici. London: 1678. V. 46

Religio Medici. London: 1682. V. 41; 45

Religio Medici. London: 1736. V. 38; 39; 44

Religio Medici, a Letter to a Friend, Christian Morals, Urn Burial and Other Papers. Boston: 1862. V. 37; 38; 41; 42; 46

Religio Medici and Urn Burial. London: 1897. V. 45

Religio Medici. London: 1898. V. 43; 45

Sir Thomas Browne's Religio Medici. Letter to a Friend and Christian Morals. London: 1898. V. 44

Religio Medici, Urn Burial, Christian Morals and Other Essays. 1902. V. 39

Religio Medici and Other Essays. London: 1902. V. 41

Religio Medici, Urn Burial, Christian Morals and Other Essays. London: 1902. V. 37; 39; 43; 44

Religio Medici and Digby's Observations. Oxford: 1909. V. 41; 42; 44

Religio Medici and Other Essays. London: 1911. V. 44

Religio Medici. Letter to a Friend and Christian Morals. London: 1923. V. 41; 44

Religio Medici. The Sixth Edition, Corrected and Amended. With Annotations Never before published, upon all the obscure passages therein. Also Observations by Sir Kenelm Digby, now newly added. London: 1669. V. 37

Religio Medici. A New Edition. Corrected and Amended. With Notes and Annotations Never before published, upon all the obscure Passages therein to which is added the life fo the author. London: 1736. V. 37

The Story of the Ordination of Our First Bishops in Queen Elizabeth's Reign of the Nag's Head Tavern in Cheapside, Thoroughly Examined . . . London: 1731. V. 41

The Union Dictionary, Containing all That is Truly Useful in the Dictionaries of Johnson, Sheridan and Walker, the Orthography and Explanatory Matter Selected from Dr. Johnson . . . London: 1800. V. 38

The Union Dictionary. London: 1810. V. 41

The Last Chapter of Urne Burial. Cambridge: 1946. V. 40

Urne Buriall and The Garden of Cyrus. Edited with an Introduction by John Carter. Illustrated with 30 Hand-Coloured Drawings by Paul Nash. London: 1932. V. 37; 39; 40; 41; 45

The Works. London: 1686. V. 38; 42; 43; 46

The Works. Containing I. Enquiries into Vulgar & Common Errors. II. Religio Medici: With Annotations & Observations upon it. III. Hydrotaphia, or, Urn-Burial: Together with The Garden of Cyrus. IV. Certain Miscellany Tracts. London: 1686. V. 37

The Works of the Learned Sir. Thomas Brown . . . Containing I. Enquiries into Vulgar and Common Errors. II. Religio Medici . . . III. Hydrotaphia; or, Urn-Burial: . . . London : 1686. V. 37; 38; 39; 40; 41; 44

Alle De Werken Van Thomas Brown . . . Amsterdam: 1688. V. 46

Posthumous Works. London: 1712. V. 37

BROWNE, THOMAS 1605-1682 continued

The Works of Sir Thomas Browne edited by Geoffrey Keynes. London: 1828-31. V. 37

Works. London: 1836. V. 38; 39; 40; 41; 42; 45; 46

Works, edited by Simon Wilkins. London: 1836. V. 37

Works, Including His Life and Correspondence. London: 1836-35. V. 40; 45

Works. London: 1836-5. V. 38

The Works of . . . London: 1852. V. 39

The Works of . . . London: 1904-07. V. 39

The Works. Edinburgh: 1927. V. 46

The Works of Sir Thomas Browne, Edited by Charles Sayle. Edinburgh: 1927. V. 37

Works. London: 1928. V. 42

The Works. London: 1928-31. V. 46

The Works of Sir Thomas Browned, Edited in Six Volumes by Geoffrey Keynes. London: 1928-31. V. 37; 38; 41; 43

The Works. London: 1964. V. 38

The Works of Sir Thomas Browne. London: 1964. V. 39; 40; 41

Works. Including his Life and Correspondence. Edited by Simon Wilkin, F.L.S. London: 1836-5. V. 37

BROWNE, THOMAS ALEXANDER

A Modern Buccaneer. London: 1894. V. 38; 46

Old Melbourne Memories. Melbourne: 1884. V. 40

Robbery Under Arms. London: 1888. V. 40

BROWNE, W. A. F.

Sisterhoods in Asylums. London: 1866. V. 40

BROWNE, WILLIAM

Britannia's Pastorals. London: 1616? V. 40; 42; 44

Britannia's Pastorals. London: 1625. V. 40; 42

Circe and Ulysses. Waltham St. Lawrence. V. 44

Circe and Ulysses. The Inner Temple Masque Presented by the Gentlemen There January 13, 1614. London: 1954. V. 42

The Works . . . containing Britannia's Pastorals: With Notes . . . by W. Thompson . . . The Shepherd's Pipe . . . The Inner Temple Masque, never published before; and other poems. With the Life of the Author. London: 1772. V. 37; 38; 43

BROWNE, WILLIAM ALEXANDER FRANCIS

What Asylums were, are, and ought to be: being the substance of Five Lectures delivered before the Managers of the Montrose Royal Lunatic Asylum. Edinburgh: 1837. V. 37

BROWNE, WILLIAM B.

The Babbitt Family History, 1643-1900. Taunton: 1912. V. 46

BROWNELL CAR COMPANY

How A Good Car Differs from a Poor One and How to Get It. St. Louis: 1895. V. 39; 41

BROWNELL, CHARLES DE WOLF

The Indian Races of America . . . Boston: 1855. V. 41

The Indian Races of North and South America. Hartford: 1860. V. 38

The Indian Races of North and South America. Hartford: 1865. V. 39

BROWNELL, F. C.

The Teacher's Guide to Illustration: a Manual to Accompany Holbrook's School Apparatus. Chicago: 1867. V. 38

BROWNING, COLIN ARROTT

An Address to the Women, Who Debarked at Sydney, New South Wales, from the Transport Ship 'Margaret', on the 26th August 1840. Sydney: 1841. V. 46

The Convict Ship, and England's Exiles. London: 1849. V. 42

BROWNING, ELIZABETH BARRETT 1806-1861

Aurora Leigh. London: 1857. V. 37; 38; 40; 41; 44; 46

Aurora Leigh. New York: 1857. V. 40; 44; 45; 46

Casa Guidi Windows: a Poem. London: 1851. V. 40; 42; 45; 46

A Drama of Exile: and Other Poems. New York: 1845. V. 41; 43; 44; 46

The Earlier Poems . . . 1826-1833. London: 1878. V. 40

Elizabeth Barrett Browning: Hitherto Unpublished Poems and Stories with an Inedited (sic) Autobiography. Boston: 1914. V. 37; 40

An Essay on Mind, with Other Poems. London: 1826. V. 40; 45

An Essay on Mind with Other Poems; Miscellaneous POems. London: 1880. V. 46

The Greek Christian Poets and the English Poets. London: 1863. V. 43; 44; 46

Last Poems. London: 1862. V. 39; 43; 45; 46

Last Poems. New York: 1862. V. 46

Last Poems. London: 1962. V. 46

Love Sonnets. London: 1913. V. 37

A Musical Instrument. New Preston: 1924. V. 44

Napoleon III in Italy and Other Poems. New York: 1860. V. 46

Only a Curl. Baltimore: 1861. V. 41

Poems. London: 1844. V. 37; 38; 39; 40; 41; 43; 44; 46

Poems. London: 1845. V. 43

Poems. London: 1850. V. 37; 38; 40

Poems. London: 1853. V. 40

Poems Before Congress. London: 1860. V. 37; 39; 40; 41; 42; 43; 46

Poems. New York: 1865. V. 42

The Poetical Works of . . . New York. V. 46

The Poetical Works. London: 1889-1894. V. 43

Poetical Works. New York: 1896. V. 40

The Poetical Works. London: 1897. V. 37

Prometheus Bound. London: 1833. V. 42

Prometheus Bound and Other Poems. New York: 1854. V. 46

Promethus Bound, and Other Poems . . . New York: 1851. V. 42

The Religious Opinions of Elizabeth Barrett Browning, As Expressed in Three Letters to Wm. Merry, Esq. London: 1896. V. 39

The Runaway Slave at Pilgrim's Point. London: 1894. V. 38

The Seraphim and Other Poems. London: 1838. V. 37; 40; 41; 42; 43; 45; 46

Sonnets from the Portuguese. Boston: 1896. V. 43; 46

Sonnets from the Portugese. New Rochelle: 1900. V. 41; 42

Sonnets from the Portuguese. New York: 1902. V. 38

Sonnets from the Portuguese. Montagnola: 1925. V. 40; 42; 45; 46

Sonnets from the Portuguese. San Francisco: 1925. V. 37; 38; 40; 41; 42; 43

Sonnets from the Portugese . . . San Francisco: 1927. V. 38; 42

Sonnets from the Portuguese. New York: & London: 1932. V. 41; 43

Sonnets from the Portuguese. Cambridge: 1939. V. 41; 44

Sonnets from the Portuguese. Oxford: 1945. V. 37

Sonnets from the Portuguese, by Elizabeth Barrett Browning. Portland: 1899. V. 37

Two Poems. London: 1854. V. 37; 40; 42; 46

BROWNING, FRED G.

Fighting and Farming in South Africa. London: 1880. V. 41

BROWNING, GEORGE

The Domestic and Financial Condition of Great Britain . . . London: 1834. V. 42

BROWNING, ROBERT 1812-1889

Asolando: Fancies and Facts. London: 1890. V. 41; 46

Bishop Blougram's Apology. London: 1931. V. 38; 43

Christmas Eve and Easter Day. London: 1850. V. 37; 38; 41; 43; 46

Dramatic Idylls with Dramatic Idylls Second Series. London: 1879, 1880. V. 38; 41; 43; 45

Dramatic Idyls (First and Second Series): Jocoseria. London: 1889. V. 45

Dramatic Romances and Lyrics. 1899. V. 38; 40; 41; 43; 44; 46

Dramatis Personae. London: 1864. V. 38; 41; 43; 46

Dramatis Personae; & Dramatic Romances & Lyrics. London: 1909. V. 41

Dramatis Personae. Hammersmith: 1910. V. 39; 42; 43; 44; 46

Dramatis Personae. London: 1910. V. 37; 38; 40; 43

Ferishtah's Fancies. London: 1884. V. 44; 45

Fifine at the Fair. London: 1872. V. 41; 43; 46

The Flight of the Duchess. 1905. V. 39

The Flight of the Duchess. 1905. V. 40

The Flight of the Duchess. 1905. V. 38

Flight of the Duchess. London: 1905. V. 43; 45

The Flight of the Duchess. 1905. V. 37

Fra Lippo Lippi. New York: 1949. V. 46

Gold Hair: a Legend of Pornic. N.P.: 1864. V. 41

In a Balcony. Chicago: 1902. V. 40

The Inn Album. London: 1875. V. 43

Jocoseria. London: 1883. V. 40; 46

The Last Ride Together. New York: 1906. V. 38; 40; 43

The Last Ride, by Robert Browning. East Aurora: 1900. V. 37

Letters of . . . to Miss Isa Blagden. Waco: 1923. V. 46

Men and Women. London: 1855. V. 37; 38

Men and Women. Boston: 1856. V. 44; 45

Men and Women. Hammersmith: 1908. V. 38; 39; 40; 42; 44; 45; 46

Men and Women. London: 1908. V. 39; 44

Men and Women. 1908. V. 37

New Poems by Robert Browning and Elizabeth Barrett Browning. London: 1914. V. 46

Pacchiarotto and How He Worked in Distemper, with Other Poems. London: 1876. V. 45

BROWNING, ROBERT 1812-1889 continued

Paracelsus. London: 1835. V. 37; 38; 39; 40; 41; 43; 45; 46

Paracelsus. London: 1904. V. 44

Parleyings with Certain People of Importance in Their Day. London: 1887. V. 43; 44

Pauline: a Fragment of a Confession. London: 1886. V. 41; 43; 45

Pictor Ignotus, Fra Lippo Lippi, Andrea del Sarto. Berkshire: 1925. V. 46

Pictor Ignotus Fra Lippo Lippi. Waltham St. Lawrence: 1925. V. 43; 44; 46

Pictor Ignotus, Frag Lippo Lippi, Andrea Del Sarto. London: 1925. V. 37

The Pied Piper of Hamelin. London: & New York. V. 44

The Pied Piper of Hamelin. London: 1888. V. 44; 45

The Pied Piper of Hamelin. London: 1889. V. 39

The Pied Piper of Hamelin. London: 1898. V. 38; 40; 43; 45

The Pied Piper of Hamelin. London: 1900. V. 42

The Pied Piper of Hamelin. Chicago & New York: 1910. V. 42

The Pied Piper of Hamelin. London: 1934. V. 37; 38; 39; 40; 41

The Pied Piper of Hamlin. 1980. V. 41

The Pied Piper of Hamlin. Portland: 1980. V. 44

The Pied Piper of Hamelin. London. V. 37

The Pied Piper of Hamelin by Robert Browning. Illustrated by Kate Greenaway. New York/London: n.d. V. 37

Pippa Passes. London: 1898. V. 43

Pippa Passes. New York: 1901. V. 43

Pippa Passes and Men and Women. London: 1908. V. 40

Poems. Boston: 1850. V. 44; 45

Poems. London: 1930. V. 43

The Poems of Robert Browning. Cambridge: 1969. V. 44; 46

The Poems. New York: 1969. V. 38

Poems . . . 1833-1865. London: 1907. V. 37

The Poetical Works of Robert Browning. London: 1868. V. 37; 46

Poetical Works. London: 1888-94. V. 37; 38; 39; 40; 46

Poetical Works. London: 1889. V. 46

The Poetical Works. London: 1897. V. 37; 38

The Poetical Works. London: 1905. V. 37

The Poetical Works. Oxford: 1983-84. V. 37

Prince Hohenstiel-Schwangau, Saviour of Society. London: 1871. V. 37; 41; 45

Rabbi Ben Ezra. Concord. V. 41; 43

Rabbi Ben Ezra. Concord: 1904. V. 37; 40; 41; 44

The Ring and the Book. London: 1868. V. 38; 40; 41; 42; 43; 46

The Ring and the Book. London: 1868-69. V. 37; 41; 45; 46

The Ring and the Book. 1869. V. 43

The Ring and the Book. London: 1869-69. V. 43

The Ring and the Book. 1949. V. 40

The Ring and the Book. Los Angeles: 1949. V. 41

The Ring and the Book. New York: 1949. V. 38; 44; 46

La Saizaiz; the Two Poets of Corsica. London: 1878. V. 43; 44; 45

Saul. Boston: 1890. V. 46

Selections from the Poetry. New York: 1883. V. 41; 43

Selections from the Poetical Works of Robert Browning. New York/Boston: 1886. V. 37

So This Then is Christmas Eve. East Aurora: 1899. V. 44

So Here Then is the Last Ride, by Robert Browning. East Aurora, New York: 1900. V. 37; 43

Some Poems. 1904. V. 41

Some Poems by . . . Hammersmith: 1904. V. 39; 40; 43; 45

Some Poems. 1904. V. 37

Sordello. London: 1840. V. 38; 39; 42; 43; 45; 46

Stafford: an Historical Tragedy. London: 1837. V. 38; 39; 45; 46

Strafford. London: 1837. V. 45

Summum Bonum. New York: 1923. V. 40; 46

Complete Works. New York: 1910. V. 42; 46

The Works. London: 1912. V. 41; 42

The Works. London: 1965. V. 46

BROWNLOW, JOHN

The History and Objects of the Foundling Hospital. London: 1805. V. 40

BROWNLOW, WILLIAM GANNAWAY

Americanism Contrasted with Foreignism, Romanism and Bogus Democracy, in the Light of Reason, History and Scripture . . . Nashville: 1856. V. 42; 45

The Helps to the Study of Presbyterianism . . . to which is Added a Brief Account of the Life and Travels of the Author. Knoxville: 1834. V. 37; 38; 39; 40; 42; 46

Helps to the Study of Presbyterianism to Which is Added A Brief Account of the Life and Travels of the Author. Knoxville: 1834. V. 40

Message and Inaugural Address of Gov. Wm. G. Brownlow, to the Senate and House of Representatives of Tennessee. Session 1865. Nashville: 1865. V. 44

A Political Register Setting Forth the Principles of the Whig and Locofoco Parties in the United States, with the Life and Public Services of Henry Clay. Jonesborough: 1844. V. 38

BROWNLOW, WWILLIAM GANNAWAY 1805-1877

Sketches of the Rise, Progress and Decline of Seccesion; with a Narrative of Personal Adventures Among the Rebels. Philadelphia: 1862. V. 40

BROWNRIGG, WILLIAM

The Art of Making Common Salt, as Now Practised in Most Parts of the World . . . London: 1748. V. 42; 43

BROWNSMITH, JOHN

The Dangers of a Lee Shore. N.P.: 1759. V. 40

The Dramatic Time-Piece. London: 1767. V. 38

BROWNSON, JOHN W.

The Vermont Disciplinarian: Containing a System of Instructions in the Rudiments of Military Science . . . Bennington: 1805. V. 43

BROWNSON, ORESTES

New Views of Christianity, Society and the Church. Boston: 1836. V. 44

BROWNSON, ORESTES A.

The Works . . . Detroit: 1882-87. V. 40

BROWSE, LILLIAN

Degas Dancers. London: 1949. V. 37; 46

Degas Dancers. Boston: 1949? V. 41

BRROKSHAW, GEORGE

Pomona Britannica. London: 1817. V. 37

BRTIISH COLUMBIA. LANDS & WORKS DEPARTMENT

British Columbia. Columbia River Expedition, 1866. Reports and Journals Relating to the Government Exploration of the Country Lying Between the Shuswap and Okanagan Lakes and the Rocky Mountains. Victoria: 1869. V. 39

BRUCCOLI, MATTHEW J.

Ernest Hemingway, Club Reporter: Kansas City Star Stories. Pittsburgh: 1970. V. 46

First Printings of American Authors: Contributions Toward Descriptive Checklists. Detroit: 1977-79. V. 46

Hemingway at Auction 1930-1973. Detroit: 1973. V. 45

The Romantic Egoists. New York: 1974. V. 43

BRUCE, CHARLES GRANVILLE

The Assault on Mount Everest 1922 by . . . and Other Members of the Expedition. London: 1923. V. 41; 44

The Assault on Mount Everest, 1922. New York: 1923. V. 44; 46

Catalogue of the Books . . . in His Library at Totenham in the County of Wiltes. Oxford: 1733. V. 38

Stirring Adventures in Afrian Travel. London: 1892. V. 40

Twenty Years in the Himalaya. London: 1910. V. 42

BRUCE, F. COLLINGWOOD

A Hand-Book to Newcastle-on-Tyne. London: 1863. V. 39

BRUCE, GEORGE

Poems, Ballads and Songs, on Various Occasions. Edinburgh: 1813. V. 39; 42

BRUCE, GEORGE A.

The Twentieth Regiment of Massachusetts Volunteer Infantry 1861-1865. Boston: 1906. V. 46

BRUCE, H. A.

Life of General Sir William Napier, K.C.B. London: 1864. V. 39; 46

BRUCE, J.

Travels of the Birds of New Zeland. London: 1872-73. V. 41

Travels to Discover the Source of the Nile, in the Years 1768-73. London: 1790. V. 42

BRUCE, JAMES 1730-1794

Interesting Narrative of Travels of James Bruce, Esq., into Abyssinia, to Discover the Source of the Nile. Boston: 1798. V. 40

An Interesting Narrative of the Travels of . . . Esq. into Abyssinia, to Discover the Source of the Nile. London: 1800. V. 40

Travels to Discover the Source of the Nile, In the Years 1768, 1769, 1770, 1771, 1772 and 1773. Edinburgh: 1790. V. 37; 38; 41; 43; 44

Travels to Discover the Source of the Nile, in the Years 1768, 1769, 1770, 1771, 1772 and 1773. Dublin: 1790-91. V. 43; 45

Travels to Discover the Source of the Nile in the Years 1768, 1769, 1770, 1771, 1772 & 1773. Edinburgh: 1804. V. 39

BRUCE, JAMES 1730-1794 continued

Travels Between the Years 1768 and 1773, through Part of Africa, Syria, Egypt and Arabia into Abyssinia . . . Glasgow: 1818. V. 44; 45

Travels to Discover the Source of the Nile, in 6 Volumes. Dublin: 1790. V. 37

BRUCE, JOHN

Annals of the Honorable East-India Company, from Their Establishment by the Charter of Queen Elizabeth, 1600, to the Union of the London and English East-India Companies 1707-8. London: 1810. V. 44

Historical View of Plans, for the Government of British India, and Regulation of Trde to the East Indies. London. V. 38

The History of Brighton, with the Latest Improvements to 1835. Brighton: 1835. V. 37; 40

Report on the Events and Circumstances Which Produced the Union of the Kingdoms of England and Scotland . . . London: 1799. V. 46

Report on the Negociation, Between the Honourable East-India Company and the Public, Respecting the Renewal of the Company's Exclusive Privileges of Trade for Twenty Years from March, 1794 . . . London: 1811. V. 38

Review of the Events and Treaties Which Established the Balance of Power in Europe, and the Balance of Trade in Favor of Great Britain. N.P.: 1796. V. 43

BRUCE, LEWIS

The Happiness of Man the Glory of God. A Sermon Preached Before the Honourable Trustees for Establishing the Colony of Georgia in America, and the Associates of the Late Rev. Dr. Bray . . . London: 1744. V. 45

BRUCE LOCKHART, ROBERT

My Rod, My Comfort. London: 1949. V. 38; 40

BRUCE, M. E. CUMMING

Family Records of the Bruces and the Cumyns, with an Historical Introduction and Appendix . . . Edinburgh: 1870. V. 39; 42; 44

BRUCE, MICHAEL

Poems on Several Occasions. Edinburgh: 1782. V. 39

Poems on Several Occasions. A New Edition. Edinburgh: 1796. V. 37

BRUCE, MINER W.

Alaska: Its History and Resources, Goldfields, Routes and Scenery. Seattle: 1895. V. 37; 38; 39; 42; 43; 45

BRUCE, PETER HENRY

Memoirs of Peter Henry Bruce, Esq . . . London: 1782. V. 42

BRUCE, THOMAS

Southwest Virginia and Shenandoah Valley, an Inquiry Into the Causes of the Rapid Growth and Wonderful Development . . . and Sketches of the Principal Cities and Towns. Richmond: 1891. V. 42

BRUCE'S NEW TYPE FOUNDRY

Specimens of Printing Types . . . Established in 1813. V. 45

BRUCH, R. M.

Colour Printing and Colour Printers . . . New York: 1911. V. 39

BRUCHNER, C.

Een Klein Woordenboek de Hollandische, Engelsche en Javaansche Talen. A Vocabulary of the Dutch, English and Javanese Languages. Batavia: 1842. V. 43

BRUCKNER, JOHN

A Philosophical Survey of the Animal Creation, an Essay. Wherein the general Devastation and Carnage that reign among the different Classes of Animals are considered from a new Point of View; and the vast Increase of Life . . . London: 1768. V. 37

BRUEHL, ANTON

Photographs of Mexico. New York: 1933. V. 39; 41

BRUEL, WALTER

Praxis Medicinae, or, the Physicians Practice. London: 1632. V. 44; 45

BRUFF, J. GOLDSBOROUGH

Gold Rush. The Journals, Drawings and Other Papers of J. Goldsborough Bruff . . . New York: 1949. V. 44; 46

The Journals, Drawings, and Other Papers of J. Goldsborough Bruff, Captain, Washington City and California Mining Association April 2, 1849 - July 20, 1851. Edited by Georgia Willis Read and Ruth Gaines. With a Foreword by F.W. Hodge. New York: 1944. V. 37; 41

BRUFF, PETER

A Treatise on Engineering Field-Work. London: 1838. V. 37

BRUFFEY, GEORGE A.

Eighty-One Years in the West. Butte: 1925. V. 37; 38; 42; 43; 45

BRUGHIERE, FRANCIS

The Evanescent City. San Francisco: 1916. V. 37

BRUGHLEY, WILLIAM CECIL, BARON

The Execution of Iustice in England for Maintenaunce of Publique and Christian Peace, Against Certeine Stirrers of Sedition and Adherents to the Traytors and Enemies of the Realme . . . London: 1583. V. 46

BRUGMANS, ANTON

Philosophische Versuche Uber die Magnetische Materie, und Deren Wirkung in Eisen und Magnet. Leipzig: 1784. V. 40

BRUGUIERE, ANTOINE ANDRE, BARON DE SORSUM 1773-1823

The Voyager. N.P.: 1828. V. 43

BRUGUIERE, FRANCIS

San Francisco. San Francisco: 1918. V. 37; 44; 45

BRUHN, ADA

Oltos and Early Red-Figure Vase Painting. Copenhagen: 1943. V. 40

BRULEFER, ETIENNE 1460-1500.

In quattour sancti Bonaventurae . . . sententiarum libros . . . (Basel: 1501). V. 37

BRUMBACH, MARTIN G.

The Life and Works of Christopher Dock . . . Philadelphia: 1908. V. 42

BRUMBAUGH, GAIUS MARCUS

Revolutionary War Records: Volume I, Virginia. Washington: 1936. V. 42; 46

BRUMMELL, GEORGE BRYAN

Male and Female Costume. Garden City: 1932. V. 38

BRUMOY, PIERRE

The Greek Theatre of Father Brumoy. London: 1759, 1760. V. 40

BRUNE, JOHAN DE

Emblemata of Zinnewerck . . . Amsterdam: 1624. V. 41

Emblemata of Zinne-Werke. Den Tweeden Druck Met Nieuwe Plaeten Vermeerdert. Amsterdam: 1661. V. 41

BRUNET, ALEXANDER

The Regal Armorie of Great Britain, from the Time of the Ancient Britons to the Reign of . . . Queen Victoria. London: 1839. V. 46

BRUNET, DAVID G.

To Messrs. Anthony dey, Wm. H. Sumner and George Curtis, Esquires. In Compliance with Your Request to Furnish a Brief Account of Texas, and More Particularly of the Colonies of Messrs. Zavala, Vehlein and Burnet . . . New York: 1830? V. 37

BRUNET, GILBERT

History of His Own Time. London: 1725-34. V. 37

BRUNET, JACOB

Notes on the Early Settlement of the North-Western Territory. Cincinatti: 1847. V. 46

BRUNET, JACQUES CHARLES

Manuel du Libraire et de l'Amateur. Paris: 1860-80. V. 46

BRUNET, JOHN 1784-1868

An Essay on the Education of the Eye with Reference to Painting. London: 1837. V. 44

Notions Pratiques sur l'Art de la Peinture, Enrichies d'Exemples d'Apres les Grands Maitres des Ecoles Italienne, Flamande et Hollndaise. Paris: 1833. V. 41

Practical Hints on Colour in Painting, Illustrated by Examples from the Works of the Venetian, Flemish and Dutch Schools. London: 1827. V. 45

BRUNET, THOMAS

Homerides; or, a Letter to Mr. Pope, Occasion'd by His Intended Translation of Homer. London: 1715. V. 38

BRUNETTI, GAETANO

Sixty Different Sorts of Ornaments, Invented by . . . London: 1736-37. V. 45

BRUNFELS, OTTO

Contrafayt Kreuterbuch nach Rechter Vollkommener Art und Beschreibungen der Alten Besstberumpten Artzt, Vormals in Teutscher Sprach, Der Masszen Nye Geshen, Noch im Truck Auszgangen . . . Strasbourg: 1532. V. 39

BRUNHOF, JEAN DE

Babar the King. London: 1936. V. 42; 46

Babar and Father Christmas. New York: 1940. V. 46

BRUNHOFF, JEAN DE

Babar's Friend Zephir. London: 1937. V. 42

BRUNI, LEONARDO ARETINO 1369-1444

De Bello Punico Libro Duo, Quorum Prior Bellum Inter Romanos et Carthaginenses Primum Continent . . . London: 1537. V. 40

Libro della Guerra de Ghotti . . . Fatto Vulgare da Lodovico Petroni Cavaliere Senese Nuovamente Stampato. Florence: 1526. V. 40

Libro della Prima Guerra Delli Carthaginesi con li Romani. Florence: 1526. V. 45; 46

BRUNI, TEOFILO 1569-1638

Frutti Singolari della Geometria. Vicenza: 1623. V. 43

BRUNKER, H. M. E.

Story of the Campaign in Eastern Virginia, Including Stonewall Jackson's 'Operations in the Valley, April 1861 to May 1863'. London: 1904. V. 38

BRUNNER, A. W.

Cottages, or Hints on Economical Building . . . to which is added a Chapter on the Water Supply, Drainage, Sewerage, Heating and Ventilation, and other Sanitary Questions Relating to Country Houses by Wm. Paul Gerhard. New York: 1884. V. 38; 46

BRUNNER, DAVID B.

The Indians of Berks County, Pennsylvania, Being a Summary of All the Tangible Records of the Aborigines of Berks County . . . Reading: 1881. V. 42

The Indians of Berks County, Pennsylvania. Reading: 1897. V. 41; 42; 45

BRUNNER, JOHANN CONRAD

Experimenta Nova Circa Pancreas. Amstelaedami: 1683. V. 38

BRUNNER, JOHN

The Brink. London: 1959. V. 45

Stand on Zanzibar. Garden City NY: 1968. V. 37; 45

While There's Hope. Richmond: 1982. V. 38

BRUNNICH, M. T.

Ornithologia Borealis. Copenhagen: 1764. V. 43

BRUNO, GIORDANO

De Triplici Minimo et Mensura ad Trium Speculativarum Scientiarum & Multarum Activarum Artium Principia, Libri V . . . Frankfurt: 1591. V. 38

BRUNO, GUIDO

Adventures in American Bookshops, Antique Stores and Auction Rooms. Detroit: 1922. V. 38

BRUNO, SAINT

Brunonis Carthusianorum . . . Opera & Vita Post Indicem Serie Literaria Indicanda. 1524. V. 40

BRUNO SPINELLI, G. B.

Economia Nelle Fabriche, e Regola di Tutti li Materiali per Costruire Ogni Fabrica . . . Bologna: 1708. V. 38

BRUNS, HENRY P.

Angling Books of the Americas . . . Atlanta: 1975. V. 43

BRUNSCHWIG, HIERONYMUS

New Vollkommen Distillerbuch. Franckfurt am Mayn: 1597. V. 44

BRUNSON, JOSEPH W.

Historical Sketch of the Pee Dee Light Artillery, Army Northern Virginia, by Orderly Sergeant J. W. Brunson, Together with a Roll of McIntosh's Battery Artillery. Winston Salem: 1927. V. 44

BRUNSON, R. J.

Historical Pulaski: Birthplace of the Ku Klux Klan: Scene of Execution of Sam Davis. N.P.: 1913. V. 39

BRUNTON, GUY

The Badarian Civilization and predynastic remains near Badari. London: 1928. V. 37

Gurob. London: 1927. V. 44

Lahun I: The Treasure. London: 1920. V. 44

Matmar. British Museum Expedition to Middle Egypt 1929-1931. London: 1948. V. 42

Mostagedda and the Tasian Culture. London: 1937. V. 44

Qua and Badri I (only). London: 1927. V. 44

Qua and Badari I-II. London: 1927-29. V. 44

BRUNTON, MARY J.

Discipline. Edinburgh: 1815. V. 41

Discipline, a Novel. Edinburgh: 1814. V. 37; 42

Emmeline. Edinburgh: 1819. V. 43; 45; 46

Self-Control. Edinburgh: 1811. V. 37; 41; 42; 45

BRUNTON, T. LAUDER

Collected Papers on Circulation and Respiration. London: 1906. V. 45

Collected Papers on Circulation and Respiration. First Series. London: 1907. V. 41

Lectures on the Actions of Medicines. New York: 1897. V. 42

Pharmacology and Therapeutics; or, Medicine Past and Present. London: 1880. V. 42; 45

BRUNTON, W.

Description of a Practical and Economical Method of Excavating Ground and Forming Embankments for Railways, &c . . . London: 1836. V. 43

BRUNUS, FRANCISCUS 1447-1508

De Indiciis et Tortura. Tractatus de Inciis Tortura. Venice: 1502. V. 38; 40

BRUSCHELLI, DOMENICO

Asisi Citta Serafica, e Santuarii che la Decorano ad Istruzione e Guida de Forestieri . . . Orvieto: 1824. V. 38

BRUSH, JOHN C.

A Small Tract Entitled A Candid and Impartial Exposition of the Various Opinions on the Subject of Wheat and Flour in the Northern and Southern Sections of the United States, with a View to Develop the True Sense of the Difference. Washington City: 1820. V. 46

BRUSHFIELD, T. N.

A Bibliography of Sir Walter Raliegh Knt. Exeter: 1908. V. 41

BRUSONI, LUCIO fl. 1518

Facetiarum Exemplorumque Libri VII. Rome: 1518. V. 44

BRUSONIUS, LUCIUS DOMITIUS

Facetiarum Exemplorumque Libri VII. Lyon: 1562. V. 45

BRUSSEL, I. R.

Anglo-American First Editions 1826-1900 East to West Describing First Editions of English Authors Whose Books were Published in America Before their Publication in England. London: 1935. V. 38

Anglo-American First Editions, Part Two West to East 1786-1930. London: 1936. V. 42; 43

Anglo-American First Editions. New York: 1981. V. 40

Anglo-American First Editions 1826-1900, East to West. (with) Anglo-American First Editions, West to East. New York: 1981. V. 39; 40; 42; 43; 44

A Bibliography of the Writings of James Branch Cabel.. Philadelphia: 1932. V. 46

BRUSSEL-SMITH, BERNARD

Bernard Brussel-Smith, an Exhibition of Wood Engravings. Madison: 1983. V. 43

BRUSSEY, I. R.

Anglo-American First Editions 1826-1900 East to West Describing First Editions of English uthors Whose Books Were Published in America Before Their Publication in England. London: 1935-36. V. 38

BRUTCHER, CHARLES

Joshua: a Man of the Finger Lakes Region. N.P.: 1927. V. 39

BRUTON, H. W.

Catalogue of a Collection of the Works of George Cruikshank . . . The Property of H. W. Bruton, Esq. 1897. V. 37

BRUWER, ANDRE

Classic Descriptions in Diagnostic Roentgenology. Springfield: 1964. V. 41

Classic Descriptions in Diagnostic Roentgenology. Springfield: 1964. V. 41; 42; 45

BRUYERE, L.

Etudes Relatives a l'Art des Constructions. Paris: 1823-28. V. 38

BRUYERINUS CAMPEGIUS, JOHANNES

De Re Cibaria Libri XXII. Omnium Ciborum Genera, Omnium Gentium Moribus & Usu Probata Complectentes. Lyon: 1560. V. 38

BRUYN, CORNELIS DE 1652-1726 or 7

Expressions of the Passions of the Soul. London: 1750. V. 45

Travels into Muscovy, Persia, and Part of the East Indies. London: 1737. V. 40; 45

BRUYN, NICHOLAS DE

Animalium Quadrupedum and Volatilium Varii Generis Effigies. Antwerp: 1594. V. 46

BRY, DORIS

Alfred Stieglitz: Photographer. Boston: 1965. V. 41

BRY, JOHANN THEODOR DE 1528-1598

Admiranda Narratio Fida Tamen de Commodis et Incoloarum Ritibus Virginae. Frankfurt: 1590. V. 43

Brevis Narratio Eorum Quae in Florida Americae Provicia Gallis Acciderunt. Frankfurt: 1591. V. 40

BRY, JOHANN THEODOR DE 1528-1598 continued

Florilegium Novum, hoc Est: Variorum Maximeque Rariorum Florum ac Plantarum Singularium una Cum Suis Radicibus & Cepis . . . Oppenheim: 1611. V. 40; 42

Funffter Theil der Orientalischen Indien. Frankfurt: 1601. V. 40; 43

Indiae Orientalis Parts I to XI. Frankfurt: 1598-1613. V. 39

Indiae Orientalis Pars X. Qua Continetur, Historica Relatio Sive Descriptio Novi Aquilonem Transitus, Supra Terras Americanas Nem Chinam atq . . . Frankfurt: 1613. V. 40

Olandus Caravellam, & Casas Aedificare Curat. XIX. (Frankfort: 1594). V. 37

Petit Voyages - Part VI. Frankfurt: 1603. V. 40

Sechster Theil der Orientalischen Indien. Frankfurt: 1603. V. 40; 43

BRYAN, C. D. B.

Friendly Fire. New York: 1976. V. 45

BRYAN, DANIEL

The Mountain Muse: Comprising the Adventures of Daniel Boone, and the Power of Virtuous Refined Beauty. Harrisonburgh;: 1813. V. 37; 38; 43; 45

BRYAN, FRANCIS T.

Report Concerning the Operations of a Party Assigned to Explore the Route from Fort Riley to Bridger Pass. Washington: 1857. V. 44

Report Concerning the Operations of a Party Assigned to Explore the Route from Fort Riley to Bridger's Pass. Washington: 1858. V. 43

BRYAN, GUY M.

Speech . . . for the Relief of the Infant Daughter of Susannah and Almiron Dickinson. Austin?: 1849. V. 39

BRYAN, J. E.

Bulbs. Portland: 1989. V. 45

BRYAN, JOHN A.

Missouri's Contribution to American Architecture. N.P.: 1928. V. 46

BRYAN, JOHN STEWART

Joseph Bryan: His Times, His Family, His Friends. Richmond: 1935. V. 40; 41; 44

BRYAN, L. C.

The World Has But One Florida, and Florida But one Indian River! Savannah: 1886. V. 41

BRYAN, MARGARET

A Compendious System of Astronomy. London: 1797. V. 41; 43; 45

Lectures on Natural Philosophy . . . London: 1806. V. 42

BRYAN, MICHAEL

A Biographical and Critical Dictionary of Painters and Engravers, from the Revival of the Art Under Cimabue, and the Alleged Discovery of Engraving by Finiguerra, to the Present Time. London: 1816. V. 41; 42

Dictionary of Painters and Engravers. London: 1903-05. V. 39; 46

Dictionary of Painters and Engravers. London: 1905-19. V. 39

Bryan's Dictionary of Painters and Engravers. New York: 1964. V. 39

A Catalogue of the Whole Valuable Contents of Mr. Bryan's Celebrated Gallery of Original Pictures . . . London: 1804. V. 38; 40

BRYAN, WILLIAM ALANSON

Natural History of Hawaii. Being an Account of the Hawaiian People, the Geology and Geography of the Islands. And the native and itnroduced plants and Animals of the Group . . . Honolulu: 1915. V. 37

BRYAN, WILLIAM JENNINGS

A Tale of Two Conventions, Being an Account of the Republican and Democratic national Conventions and the Progressive Convention. New York: 1912. V. 38

BRYAN, WILLIAM S.

A History of the Pioneer Families of Missouri. St. Louis: 1876. V. 42; 43

Our Islands and Their People As Seen with Camera and Pencil. St. Louis: 1899. V. 42; 46

BRYAN'S Dictionary of Painters and Engravers. London: 1913-19. V. 42

BRYAN'S Dictionary Paintes and Engravers. London: 1913-15. V. 46

BRYANT, CHARLES

Flora Diaetetica; or, History of Esculent Plants, Both Domestic and Foreign. London: 1783. V. 43; 45

BRYANT, CHARLES S.

A History of the Great Massacre by the Sioux Indians, in Minnesota, Including Narratives of Many Who Escaped. Cincinnati: 1868. V. 41

A History of the Great massacre by the Sioux Indians in minnesota, Including the Personal Narratives of Many who Escaped. Cincinnati: 1864. V. 37; 42; 44; 45

BRYANT, EDWIN

What I Saw in California: Being the Journal of a Tour, by the Emigrant Route and South Pass of the Rocky Mountains . . . in the Years 1846, 1847. New York: 1848. V. 38; 39

What I Saw in California: Its Soil, Climate, Productions and Gold Mines. London: 1849. V. 45

What I Saw in California, Being the Journal of a Tour. New York: 1849. V. 46

What I Saw in California, Being the Journal of a Tour by the Emigrant Route and South Pass of the Rocky Mountains, Across the Continent of North America, the Great Basin and Through California, in the Years 1846, 1847. Santa Ana: 1936. V. 38

BRYANT, G. E.

The Chelsea Porcelain Toys, Scentbottles, Bonbonnieres, Etuis, Seals and Statuettes, Made at the Chelsea Factory 1745-1769 and Derby, Chelsea, 1770-1784. London & Boston: 1975. V. 42

The Chelsea Porcelain Toys. London and Boston: 1925. V. 37

The Chelsea Porcelain Toys: Scent-Bottles, Bonbonnieres, Etuis, Seals and Statuettes, Made at the Chelsea Factory, 1745-1769, & Derby Chelsea, 1770-1784. London: 1925. V. 37; 38; 39

BRYANT, JACOB

A Dissertation Concerning the War of Troy and the Expedition of the Grecians . . . London: 1796. V. 46

A New System, or n Analysis of Ancient Mythology. London: 1775-76. V. 38

A New System, or an Analysis of Ancient Mythology. London: 1807. V. 40; 41; 43; 44

A New System, or, an Analysis of Ancient Mythology. London: 1774-7. V. 37

A New System, or, an Analysis of Ancient Mythology. London: 1775-77. V. 37

Observations and Inquiries Relating to Various Parts of Ancient History . . . Cambridge: 1767. V. 42; 44; 46

Observations Upon the Poems of Thomas Rowley, In Which the Authenticity of Those Poems is Ascertained. London: 1781. V. 37; 42; 44

BRYANT, JOSEPH

Manual of Operative Surgery. New York: 1884. V. 42

BRYANT, JOSEPH D.

American Practice of Surgery. New York: 1906-11. V. 38

BRYANT, JOSHUA

Account of an Insurrection of the Negro Slaves in the Colony of Demerara, Which Broke Out on the 18th of August 1823. Demerara: 1824. V. 40

Progressive Lessons in Landscape. London: 1807. V. 38

BRYANT, S.

Liberty, Order and Law Under the Native Irish Rule. London: 1923. V. 43

BRYANT, W. N.

Bryant's Railroad Guide! Austin: 1875. V. 45

BRYANT, WILLIAM CULLEN 1794-1878

The Embargo; or, Sketches of the Times. Boston: 1809. V. 37; 40

The Fountain and Other Poems. New York: & London: 1842. V. 40; 46

Hymns. New York: 1864. V. 41; 43

Picturesque Americana. New York. V. 38

Picturesque America. New York: 1872. V. 37; 39; 41; 46

Picturesque America. New York: 1872-74. V. 37; 39; 42

Picturesque America . . . London: 1894-5-6-7. V. 44; 46

Picturesque America. New York: 1872-74. V. 37

Poems. Cambridge: 1821. V. 37; 40; 41; 42; 43

Poems. London: 1832. V. 46

Poems. New York: 1832. V. 40; 43

Poems. London: 1874. V. 37

Poems . . . New York: 1875. V. 43

A Popular History of the United States. New York: 1876. V. 38

The Story of the Fountain. New York: 1872. V. 38; 44

Tales of Glauber-Spa by Several American Authors. New York: 1832. V. 43

Thanatopsis: a Poem . . . . San Francisco: 1927. V. 41

Thirty Poems. New York: 1864. V. 41; 42; 43; 46

Thirty Poems. New York: 1864. V. 46

The White Footed Deer and Other Poems. New York: 1844. V. 37; 42; 44

BRYCE, DAVID

The Smallest English Dictionary in the World. Glasgow: 1900. V. 41

The Smallest French and English Dictionary in the World. Glasgow: 1900. V. 41

Witty, Humorous and Merry Thoughts. New York: 1900. V. 45

BRYCE, GEORGE

A History of Manitoba. Toronto & Montreal: 1906. V. 40

BRYCE, GEORGE continued

Manitoba: Its Infancy, Growth and Present Condition. London: 1882. V. 44

The Siege and Conquest of the North Pole - Fourteen Attempts and Voyages of Discovery to the North West, from Parry's Expedition of 1827 to Peary, 1909. London: 1910. V. 39; 42; 44

BRYCE, JAMES

An Account of the Yellow Fever, with a Successful Method of Cure . . . Edinburgh: 1796. V. 37

The American Commonwealth. London: 1888. V. 37; 39; 41; 42; 43; 44

Practical Observations on the Inoculation of Cowpox . . . Edinburgh: 1809. V. 38; 43; 46

BRYCE, VISCOUNT

The Treatment of Armeians in the Ottoman Empire 1915-1916. London: 1916. V. 45

BRYCE, WILLIAM MOIR

The Scottish Grey Friars. London: 1909. V. 39

BRYCE'S Thumb English Dictionary. Glasgow: 1890. V. 44

BRYDALL, JOHN

Camera Regis: or, The Present State of the City of London viewed. Containing the Antiquity, Fame, Walls, Bridge, River, Gates, Tower, Cathedral, Officers, Courts, Customs, Franchises, &c. of that City. London: 1678. V. 37

Jus Sigilli; or, the Law of England. London: 1673. V. 44

Jus Imaginis Apud Anglos; or the Law of England Relating to the Nobility & Gentry. London: 1675. V. 46

BRYDEN, HENRY ANDERSON 1854-

Great and Small Game of Africa. London: 1899. V. 39; 40; 42; 44; 46

Gun and Camera in Southern Africa a Year of Wanderings in Bechuanaland, the Kalahari Desert, and the Lake River Country, Ngamiland, with Notes on Colonisation, Natives, Natural History and Sport. London: 1893. V. 39; 40; 41; 44; 45

Kloof & Karoo In Cape Colony, Sport, Legend, Natural History. London: 1889. V. 37; 38; 45

BRYDEN, R.

Some Woodcuts of Men of Letters of the 19th Century. London: 1899. V. 38

BRYDEN, ROBERT

Ayrshire Monuments. London: 1915. V. 38

BRYDGES, CHARLES

The Letters of Charles John Brydges: 1889-1882, Hudson's Bay Company Land Commissioner. Winnipeg. V. 45

BRYDGES, EGERTON

The Ruminator containing a Series of Moral, Critical and Sentimental Essays. London: 1813. V. 37

BRYDGES, HARFORD JONES

The Dynasty of the Kajars. London: 1833. V. 43

BRYDGES, SAMUEL EGERTON, BART 1762-1837

Archaica. London: 1815. V. 44

The Autobiography, Times, Opinions and Contemporaries of Sir Egerton Brydges. London: 1834. V. 41; 42; 44; 45

The British Bibliographer. London: 1810-14. V. 39; 40; 41; 42

Censura Literaria. London: 1815. V. 39; 45

Imaginative Biography. London: 1834. V. 38

Letters from the Continent. Kent: 1821. V. 46

Letters on the Character and Poetical genius of Lord Byron. London: 1824. V. 44

Occasional Poems, Written in the year MDCCCXI. Kent: 1814. V. 43

Occasional Poems, Written in the Year MDCCCLI. Kent: 1814. V. 44

Polyanthea Librorum Vetustiorum: Italicorum, Gallicorum, Hispanicorum, Anglicanorum, et Latinorum. Geneva;: 1822. V. 39

Recollections of Foreign Travel, on Life, Literature and Self-Knowledge. London: 1825. V. 38

Restituta; or, Titles, Extracts and Characters of Old Books in English Literature. London: 1814. V. 38; 41; 45

Restituta; or Titles, Extracts and Characters of Old Books in English Literature Revived. London: 1814. V. 41

Restituta; or, Titles, Extracts and Chracters of Old books in English Literature, Revived. London: 1814-16. V. 40

Restituta; or, Titles, Extracts and Characters of Old Books in English Literature Revived. London: 1814/16. V. 44

The Ruminator Containing a Series of Moral, Critical and Sentimental Essays. London: 1813. V. 39; 40; 45

Select Poems. Ickham: 1814. V. 44

Select Poems, with a Preface. London: 1814. V. 39; 44; 46

Sonnets and Other Poems. London: 1785. V. 38; 41; 45

Topographical Miscellanies . . . London: 1792. V. 38

What is Luxury? London: 1829. V. 45

BRYDGES, THOMAS

A Burlesque Translation of Homer. London: 1797. V. 38

BRYDONE, PATRICK 1736-1818

A Tour Through Sicily and Malta in a Series of Letters to William Beckford, Esq. London: 1773. V. 37; 38; 41; 42

A Tour through Sicily and Malta in a Series of Letters to William Beckford of Somerly in Suffolk. Dublin: 1774. V. 39

A Tour through Sicily and Malta in a Series of Letters to William Beckford of Somerly in Suffolk. London: 1774. V. 37; 39; 43

A Tour through Sicily and Malta. London: 1776. V. 44

A Tour through Sicily and Malta in a Series of Letters to William Beckford of Somerly in Suffolk. London: 1790. V. 39

A Tour Through Sicily and Malta in a Series of Letters to William Beckford . . . London: 1806. V. 43

BRYDSON, A. P.

Some Records of Two Lakeland Townships. London. V. 41

BRYHER, WINIFRED 1894-

Arrow Music. N.P.: 1922. V. 46

Civilians. Territet: 1927. V. 40; 41

Development. London: 1920. V. 39; 42

Development a Novel. New York: 1920. V. 38

Film Problems of Soviet Russia. Territet: 1929. V. 39; 42

The Fourteenth of October. London: 1954. V. 41

The Player's Boy. New York: 1953. V. 41

Visa for Avalon. New York: 1965. V. 39

West. London: 1925. V. 39; 44

BRYK, FELIX

Circumcision in Man and Woman, Its History, Psychology and Ethnology. New York: 1934. V. 41

BRYMER, JOHN

Gammon and Spinach. London: 1915. V. 40

BRYON, GEORGE GORDON NOEL 1788-1824

The Corsair; A Tale. London: 1814. V. 37

The Works of Lord Byron. A New, Revised and enlarged edition. With Illustrations. London: 1902. V. 37

BUBIER, E. T.

How to Build Automobiles. Lynn: 1904. V. 46

BUBSY, THOMAS

A General History of Music, from the earliest times to the present; comprising the lives of eminent composers and musical writers. The whole acompanied with notes and observations, critical and illustrative. London: 1819. V. 37

BUC-HOZ, PIERRE JOSEPH

The Toilet of Flora; or A Collection of the Most Simple and Approved Methods of Preparing Baths . . . London: 1772. V. 44

BUCH, LEOPOLD VON

Travels through Norway and Lapland, During the Years 1806, 1807 and 1808; London: 1813. V. 37; 38; 40; 43; 46

DAS BUCH vom Kaiser. Budapest, Vienna, Leipzig: 1909. V. 40

BUCHAN, A. P.

Practical Observations on Sea Bathing. To Which are Added Remarks on the Use of the Warm Bath. London: 1804. V. 38

BUCHAN, ALEXANDER PETER

Bionomia. Opinions Concerning Life and Health, Introductory to a Course of Lectures on the Physiology of Sentient Beings. London: 1811. V. 45

BUCHAN, JOHN 1875-1940

The African Colony. Edinburgh: 1903. V. 43

The African Colony. Studies in the Reconstruction. London: 1903. V. 41; 43

The Blanket of the Dark. London: 1931. V. 43

Castle Gay. London: 1930. V. 40; 44; 46

Castle Gay. London: 1930. V. 40

Courts of the Morning. London: 1929. V. 40

The Dancing Floor. London: 1925. V. 44

The Dancing Floor. 1926. V. 43

Francis and Riversdale Grenfell: A Memoir. London: 1920. V. 37; 43; 46

the Free Fishers. London: 1934. V. 38; 46

The Gap in the Curtain. London: 1932. V. 40

Gordon at Khartoum. N.P.: 1934. V. 44

Greenmantle. London: 1916. V. 40; 41; 43; 44

Grey Weather. London: 1899. V. 42

BUCHAN, JOHN 1875-1940 continued

A History of the Great War. London: 1921. V. 42

A History of the Great War. Boston: 1922. V. 45; 46

A History of the Great War. Boston and New York: 1922. V. 46

Homilies and Recreations. London: 1916. V. 41

Homilies and Recreations. London: 1926. V. 46

The Island of Sheep. 1936. V. 43; 46

The King's Grace: 1910-1935. London: 1935. V. 37; 38; 41

A Lost Lady of Old Years. London: 1899. V. 40; 44

The Magic Walking Stick. London: 1932. V. 44

The Man from the Norlands. Boston: 1936. V. 46

The Massacre of Glencoe. London: 1933. V. 40

The Massacre of Glencoe. N.P.: 1933. V. 44

Musa Piscatrix. London: 1896. V. 42

Oliver Cromwell. London: 1934. V. 41

The Path of the King. London: 1925. V. 38

Prester John. London: 1910. V. 45

A Prince of the Captivity. London: 1933. V. 41; 46

The Runagates Club. 1928. V. 37

Scholar Gipsies. London: 1896. V. 38

Sir Quixote of the Moors - Being Some Account of an Episode in the Life of the Sieur de Rohaine. London: 1895. V. 38; 44

The Thirty-Nine Steps. Edinburgh & London: 1915. V. 44

The Thirty-Nine Steps. London: 1915. V. 43

The Thirty-Nine Steps. 1915. V. 37

The Three Hostages. 1924. V. 45

Witch Wood. London: 1927. V. 40; 44

Some Eighteenth Century Essays. Edinburgh & London: 1908. V. 43

BUCHAN, PETER 1790-1854

An Historical and Authentic Account of the Ancient and Noble Family of Keith . . . all the Scottish Noblemen who Lost Their Titles and Estates in 1715 and 1745. Peterhead: 1820. V. 38

Scriptural and Philosophical Arguments; or, Cogent Proofs from Reason and Revelation that Brutes Have Souls . . . Peterhead: 1824. V. 46

BUCHAN, SUSAN

Funeral March of a Marionette - Charlotte of Albany. London: 1935. V. 38; 44

BUCHAN, WILLIAM 1729-1805

Advice to Mothers, on the Subject of Their Own Health; and on the Means for Promoting the Health, Strength and Beauty of Their Offspring. London: 1802. V. 45; 46

Advice to Mothers, on the Subject of Their Own Health . . . London: 1803. V. 43

Advice to Mothers, On the Subject of Their Own Health; and on the Means for Promoting the Health, Strength and Beauty of Their Offspring. Philadelphia: 1804. V. 45; 46

Domestic Medicine. Edinburgh: 1769. V. 39

Domestic Medicine; or, the Family Physician. Edinburgh: 1769. V. 37; 38; 39; 46

Domestic Medicine. London: 1772. V. 39; 40; 41; 44

Domestic Medine. Philadelphia: 1784. V. 45

Domestic Medicine; or, a Treatise on the Prevention and Cure of Diseases by Regimen and Simple Medicines. Hartford: 1789. V. 42

Domestic Medicine. London: 1792. V. 38; 39; 40

Domestic Medicinae; or, a Treatise on the Prevention and Cure of Diseases by Regimen and Simple Medicines. London: 1797. V. 44; 45

Domestic Medicine. Philadelphia: 1797. V. 38

Domestic Medicine. Waterford: 1797. V. 39; 42

Domestic Medicine. Fairhaven: 1798. V. 45

Domestic Medicine . . . Philadelphia: 1805. V. 45

Domestic Medicine. London: 1825. V. 38

Domestic medicine, or A Treatise . . . with observations concerning sea-bathing and the use of mineral waters . . . London: 1807. V. 37

The New Domestic Medicine . . . to which is added, Memoirs of the Life of Dr. Buchan.. London: 1836. V. 37

BUCHANAN, BRIGGS

Catalogue of Ancient Near Eastern Seals in the Ashmolean Museum. Oxford: 1966-84. V. 42

BUCHANAN, CLAUDIUS

Christian Rsearches in Asia with Notices of the Translation of the Scriptures into the Oriental Languages . . . London: 1812. V. 44

Christian Researches in Asia; with Notices on the Translation of the Scriptures Into the Oriental Languages. Lexington: 1813. V. 44

Christian Researches in Asia . . . Philadelphia: 1813. V. 44

Colonial Ecclesiastical Establishment: beign a brief view of the state of the colonies of Great Britain, and of her Asiati empire, in respect to religious instruction: prefaced by some considerations on the . . . London: 1813. V. 37

Two Discourses Preached Before the University of Cambridge, on Commencement Sunday July 1, 1810, and a Sermon Preached Before the Society for Missions to Africa and the East . . . Boston: 1811. V. 39; 41

Two Discourses Preached Before the University of Cambridge . . . To Which are added: Christian Researches in Asia. Boston: 1811. V. 45

BUCHANAN, DONALD W.

The Growth of Canadian Painting. London & Toronto: 1950. V. 41

James Wilson Morrice. A Biography. Toronto: 1936. V. 43; 44

BUCHANAN, GEORGE 1506-1582

Ane Detectiovn of the Duinges of Marie Quene of Scottes, Touchand the Murder of Hir Husband and Her Conspiracie, Adulterie, and Pretensed Mariage with the Erle Bothwell. London: 1571. V. 38

The History of Scotland. London: 1690. V. 38

The History of Scotland . . . to Which is Annexed a Genealogy of all the Kings from Fergus I to James VI. Aberdeen: 1799. V. 40

The History of Scotland. Glasgow: 1827. V. 37; 41; 46

Jephtha. Paisley: 1903. V. 37

De Jure Regni apud Scotos, Dialogus. N.P., n.p.,: 1579. V. 40

De Maria Scotorum Regina . . . plena et Tragica Plane Historia. N.P.,: 1571. V. 44

Opera Omnia, ad Optimorum Codicum Fidem Summo Studio Recognita & Castigata . . . Edinburgi: 1715. V. 45

Poemata Quae Extant. Amsterdam: 1687. V. 39

Rerum Scoticarum Historia. Edinburgh: 1582. V. 38

Rerum Scoticarum Historia. Frankfurt: 1584. V. 39

Rerum Scoticarum Historia. Ultrajecti: 1668. V. 40

Rerum Scoticarum Historia. Cui Accessit Eusdem Authoris Dialogus, De Jure Regni. Edinburgh: 1700. V. 38; 39

Rervm Scoticarvm Historia. Edinbvrgi, but London?: 1583. V. 44

Tyrannical-Government Anatomized: or, a Discourse Concerning Evil Councellors. London: 1642. V. 37

The Very Learned Scotsman, Mr. George Buchanan's Fratres Fraterrimi, Three Books of Epigrams, and Book of Miscellanies, in English Verse. Edinburgh: 1708. V. 41; 42

BUCHANAN, ISAAC

The Relations of the Industry of Canada, with the Mother Country and the United States. Montreal: 1864. V. 43; 44

BUCHANAN, JAMES

The British Grammar; or, an Essay, in Fourt Parts. London: 1762. V. 41

Difficulties on Southwestern Frontier. Washington: 1860. V. 42

Execution of Colonel Crabb and Associates. Washington: 1858. V. 42

The First Six Books of Milton's Paradise Lost, Rendered Into Grammatical Construction. Edinburgh: 1783. V. 41

Last Letter of Mr. Buchanan to Mr. Parkeham, on the American Title to Oregon. Baltimore: 1845. V. 43; 45

Linguae Britannicae Vera Pronunciatio; or, A New English Dictionary . . . London: 1757. V. 41

Message of . . . Communicating . . . Information in Relation to the Massacre at Mountain Meadows, and Other Massacres in Utah Territory. Washington: 1860. V. 43

A Regular Syntax. London: 1767. V. 38

Sketches of the History, Manners, and Customs of the North American Indians. London: 1824. V. 39; 42

Sketches of the History, Manners and Customs, of the North American Indian, with a plan for Their Melioration. New York: 1824. V. 37; 45

Utah Territory. Washington: 1860. V. 43

BUCHANAN-JARDINE, JOHN

Hounds of the World. London: 1937. V. 37

BUCHANAN, JOHN LANE

Travels in the Western Hebrides: from 1782 to 1790. London: 1793. V. 39; 42; 45

BUCHANAN, ROBERT

Ballad Stories of the Affections. London: 1866. V. 42

The City of Dreams; an Epic Poem. London: 1888. V. 40

A Comprehensive Atals of Modern Geography. Edinburgh: 1829. V. 45

The Fleshly School of Poetry and Other Phenomena of the Day. London: 1872. V. 37; 39; 42; 43; 44

The Heir of Linne. London: 1888. V. 38

The Land of Lorne, Including the Cruise of the 'Tern' to the Outer Hebrides. London: 1871. V. 39; 44

North Coast and Other Poems. London: 1868. V. 38; 39; 42; 43; 45

The Piper of Hamelin: A Fantastic Opera. London: 1893. V. 37; 45

Poems on Several Occasions. Edinburgh: 1797. V. 43

The Poetical Works. London: 1874. V. 43; 45

BUCHANAN, ROBERT WILLIAMS

The Moment After; a Tale of the Unseen. London: 1890. V. 46

Undertones. London: 1863. V. 46

BUCHANAN, T. R.

Bookbinding in the Library of All Souls College. Oxford: 1880. V. 41

BUCHANN, ROBERTSON

An Essay on the Warming of Mills and Other Buildings by Steam. Glasgow: 1807. V. 38

BUCHERL, W.

Venomous Animals and their Venoms. London: 1968-71. V. 37; 38

BUCHHEIM, LOTHER-GUNTHER

The Graphic Art of German Expressionism. New York: 1960. V. 46

BUCHIUS, PAULUS

The Divine Being and Its Attributes Philosophically Demonstrated from the Holy Scriptures and Original Nature of Things According to the Principles of F. N. B. of Helmont. London: 1693. V. 40

BUCHNER, D.

Defenders and Offenders. New York: 1888. V. 38

BUCHNER, GEORG

Woyzeck. Leipzig: 1920. V. 41

BUCHNER, JOHANN SIEGMUND

Theoria et Praxis Artilleriae. Oder: Deutliche Beschreibung der Bey Itziger Zeit Brauchlichen Artillerie.. Nurnberg: 1682-83. V. 39

Theoria et Praxis Artilleriae. Oder, Beschreibung der Bey Itziger Zeitbrauch-Lichen Artillerie. Nurnberg: 1685-90. V. 39

BUCHNER, LUDWIG

Kraft und Stoff. Empirisch-naturphilosophische Studien. Frankfurt: 1855. V. 41

BUCHON, J. A.

Atlas Geographique, Statistique, Historique et Chronologique des Deux Ameriques et des Isles Adjacentes . . . Paris: 1825. V. 45

BUCHOZ, M.

The Toilet of Flora. London: 1772. V. 38

BUCHOZ, PIERRE JOSEPH

Premiere (et Seconde) Centurie de Planches Enluminees et non Enluminees Representant au Naturel ce Qui se Trouve de Plus Interessant et de Plus Curieux Parmi les Animaux . . . Paris: 1775-81. V. 42

The Toilet of Flora: or, a collection of the most simple and approved methods of preparing baths, essences, pomatums, powders, perfumes, and sweet scented waters, with receipts for cosmetics of every kind . . . for the use of the ladies. A new . . . London: 1779. V. 37

BUCK, ALBERT

A Reference Handbook of the Medical Sciences being a Complete and convenient work of Reference for Information upon topics belonging to the Entire range of Scientific and Practical Medicine . . . New York: 1885. V. 37

A Treatise on Hygiene and Public Health. New York: 1879. V. 38; 41; 45

BUCK, DANIEL

Indian Outbreaks. Mankato: 1904. V. 39; 41; 42; 43; 45

BUCK, GEORGE

The History of the Life and Reigne of Richarad the Third. London: 1647. V. 37

BUCK, GEORGE W.

A Practical and Theoretical Essay on Oblique Bridges. London: 1839. V. 37; 39; 42

A Practical and Theoretical Essay on Oblique Bridges. London: 1857. V. 43

BUCK, PEARL SYDENSTRICKER 1892-1973

All Men are Brothers. New York: 1948. V. 45

The Good Earth. New York: 1931. V. 38; 42

The Good Earth. Culver City: 1936. V. 45

The Good Earth. London: 1931. V. 37

Pavilion of Women. New York: (1946). V. 37

Sons. New York: 1932. V. 45

BUCK, S.

The Castles, Abbeys and Priories of Cumberland . . . Carlisle: 1837. V. 38; 40

BUCK, SAMUEL

Buck's Famous Views of the Old Castles in the County of Durham . . . N.P.: 1840. V. 45

BUCK, W. C.

New Indian Territory in Oregon. Memorial of the Board of Managers of the American Indian Mission Association. Washington: 1846. V. 45

BUCK, WILLIAM J.

History of Bucks County . . . Doylestown: 1855. V. 42

History of Montgomery County Within the Shuylkill Valley. Norristown: 1859. V. 42

History of the Indian Walk Performed for the Proprietaries of Pennsylvania in 1737. Philadelphia: 1886. V. 41; 42

Local Sketches and Legends Pertaining to Bucks and Montgomery Counties, Pennsylvania. N.P.: 1887. V. 42

Local Sketches and Legends Pertaining to Bucks and Montgomery Counties, Pennsylvania. N.P.: 1887. V. 41

Local Sketches and Legends Pertaining to Bucks and Montgomery Counties, Pennsylvania. N.P.: 1887. V. 37

BUCKBEE, EDNA BRYAN

The Sage of Old Tuolumne. New York: 1935. V. 44; 46

BUCKE, C.

On the Beauties, Harmonies and Sublimities of Nature; with Notes, Commentaries nd Illustrations . . . London: 1837. V. 38

BUCKE, CHARLES

On the Beauties, Harmonies, and Sublimities of Nature. London: 1821. V. 38; 39; 40

The Philosophy of Nature, or the Influence of Scenery on the Mind and Heart. London: 1813. V. 45

BUCKE, RICHARD MAURICE

Cosmic Consciousness . . . Philadelphia: 1901. V. 44

BUCKELL, JOHN

Avon. Birmingham: 1758. V. 40

BUCKELMUELLER, H. HOMER

Litho Media, A Demonstration of the Selling Power of Lithography. New York: 1939. V. 45

BUCKHAM, E. W.

Personal Narrative of Adventures in the Peinsula During the War in 1812-13. London: 1827. V. 42

BUCKINGHAM & CHANDOS, RICHARD PLANTAGENET, 2ND DUKE OF 1797-1861

Memoirs of the Court of England During the Regency. London: 1856. V. 39

BUCKINGHAM, CLARENCE

Japanese: The Clarence Buckingham Collection of Japanese Prints. Volume 2. Harunobu, Koryusai, Shigemasa, Their Followers and Contemporaries. Chicago: 1905. V. 42

Japanese Prints: The Clarence Buckingham Collection, Harunobu, Koryusai, Shigemasa, Their Followers and Contemporaries. Volume II. Chicago: 1965. V. 41

BUCKINGHAM, GEORGE VILLERS, DUKE OF

The Rehearsal. London: 1692. V. 45

BUCKINGHAM, GEORGE VILLIERS, 1ST DUKE OF 1592-1628

The Chances, a Comedy: As It Was Acted at the Theatre Royal. London: 1682. V. 40

BUCKINGHAM, GEORGE VILLIERS, 2ND DUKE OF 1628-1687

The Rehearsal. London: 1675. V. 41

The Genuine Works . . . With Memoirs of His Life and Writings. Edinburgh: 1754. V. 41

BUCKINGHAM, J. T.

Golden Sentiments: Being an Address to the Native Americans of New York. Boston: 1844. V. 45

BUCKINGHAM, JAMES SILK

America, Historical, Statistic and Descriptive. London: 1841. V. 37; 38; 39; 41; 42

Autobiography of . . . London: 1855. V. 37

Canada, Nova Scotia, New Brunswick, and Other British Provinces in North America . . . London & Paris: 1843. V. 42

National Evils and Practical Remedies, with the Plan of a Model Town. London: 1850. V. 37

The Slave States of America. London: 1842. V. 38; 42

Travels Among the Arab Tribes Inhabiting the Countries East of Syria and Palestine, Including a Journey from Nazareth to the Mountains Beyond the Dead Sea, and from Thence through the Plains of the Hauran . . . London: 1825. V. 37

Travels in Assyria, Media and Persia, Including a Journey from Bagdad by Mount Zagros, to Hamadan, the Ancient Ecbatana, Researches in Ispahan and the Ruins of Persepolis, and from Thence by Shiraz and Shapoor to the Sea Shore . . . London: 1830. V. 37; 39; 45

Travels in Mesopotamia. London: 1827. V. 37; 39; 45

Travels in Palestine, through the Countries of Bashan and Gilead, East of the River Jordan. London: 1821. V. 37; 39; 45

BUCKINGHAM, JOHN SHEFFIELD, 1ST DUKE OF 1648-1721

Poems on Several Occasions. Glasgow: 1752. V. 42

The Temple of Death, a Poem, by the Right Honourable the Marquess of Normanby . . . London: 1709. V. 39

The Works of John Sheffield, Earl of Mulgrave, Marquis of Normanby and Duke of Buckingham. London: 1723. V. 39; 40; 41

The Works of . . . London: 1726. V. 39

BUCKINGHAM, JOHN SHEFFIELD, THIRD DUKE OF

The Works of John Sheffield, Earl of Mulgrave, Marquis of Normanby, and Duke of Buckingham. London: 1729. V. 37; 42

BUCKINGHAM, NASH

Blood Lines, Tales of Shooting and Fishing. New York: 1938. V. 43; 44; 46

De Shootinest Gent'man and Other Tales . . . New York: 1934. V. 43

Game bag; Tales of Shooting and Fishing. Illustrations by H.P.A.M. Hoecker. New York: (1945). V. 37; 39; 41; 42; 43; 44; 46

Hallowed Years. Harrisburg: 1955. V. 39

Mark Right! Tales of Shooting and Fishing. New York: 1936. V. 41; 43; 44; 45

Ole Miss' . . . New York. V. 43

Ole-Miss.' New York: 1937. V. 39; 44; 45

Tattered Coat. New York: 1944. V. 39; 45

BUCKLAND, FRANCIS

Curiosities of Natural History. London: 1900. V. 39

BUCKLAND, W.

Geology and Mineralogy Considered with Reference to Natural Theology. London: 1837. V. 37; 42; 43; 44; 46

BUCKLAND, WILLIAM 1784-1856

Geology and Mineralogy Considered with Reference to Natural Theology. London: 1836. V. 46

Geology and Mineralogy Considered with Reference to Natural Theology. Philadelphia: 1837. V. 42

Geology and Mineralogy Considered with Reference to Natural Theology. London: 1858. V. 43; 45

Reliquae Diluvianae; or Observations on the Organic Remains Contained in Caves, Fissures, Diluvial Gravel and on Other Geological Phenomena . . . London: 1824. V. 42; 43; 45

Reliquiae Diluvianae; or, Observations on the Organic Remains Contained in Caves, Fissures and Diluvial Gravel, and On Other Geological Phenomena, Attesting the Action an Universal Deluge. London: 1823. V. 37; 38; 42; 43

BUCKLAND WRIGHT, JOHN

Seven Book-Cover Designs. Haarlem: 1977. V. 38

BUCKLE, A.

Yorkshire Etchings with Sonnets and Descriptions. Leeds: 1885. V. 40

BUCKLE, RICHARD

Jacob Epstein, Sculptor. London: 1963. V. 43

BUCKLER, BENJAMIN 1718-1780

A Philosophical Dialogue Concerning Decency. Oxford: 1751. V. 45; 46

Stemmata Chicheleana; or a Genealogical account of Some of the Familes derived From Thomas Chichele, of Higham Ferrers in the County of Northampton. Oxford: 1765. V. 44

Stemmata Chicheleana; or, a Genealogical Account of Some of the Families Derived from Thomas Chichele, in the County of Northampton. (with) a Supplement to the Stemmata Chicheleana . . . Oxford: 1765-75. V. 37; 39

Stemmata Chicheleana: or, A Genealogical Account of some of the Families Derived from Thomas Chichele, of Higham-Ferrers in the County of Northampton. Oxford: 1765-75. V. 37

BUCKLER, ERNEST

The Cruelest Month. Toronto: 1963. V. 43

The Mountain and the Valley. New York: 1952. V. 43

Ox Bells and Fireflies. Toronto: 1968. V. 43

BUCKLER, J.

Views of Eaaton Hall in Cheshire. London: 1826. V. 38; 42

BUCKLER, W. H.

Anatolian Studies Presented to Sir William Mitchell Ramsay. Manchester: 1923. V. 44

BUCKLER, WILLIAM

The Larvae of the British Butterflies and Moths. London: 1886-1901. V. 37; 38; 39

The Larvae of British Butterflies and Moths. London: 1887-89. V. 42

The Larvae of the British Butterflies and Moths. Volume 1: The Butterflies. London: 1886. V. 37; 38

BUCKLEY, ARABELLA B.

Life and Her Children. New York: 1881. V. 46

BUCKLEY, CHARLES BURTON

An Anecdotal History of Old Times in Singapore . . . From the Foundation of the Settlement Under the Honourable the East Indian Company, on February 6th, 1819 to the Transfer to the Colonial Office as Part of the Colonial Possessions of the Crown . . . Singapore: 1902. V. 39

A Digest of Scripture, Consisting of Extracts from the Old and New Testaments: on the Plan of Brown's 'Selection of Scripture Passages.' Maulmain: 1840. V. 39

BUCKLEY, FRANCIS

A History of Old English Glass. London: 1925. V. 44; 46

BUCKLEY, HAROLD

Squadron 95. Paris: 1933. V. 43

BUCKLEY, SAMUEL

A Letter to Dr. Mead, concerning a New Edition of Thuanus's History. London: 1728/1729. V. 45

BUCKLEY, W.

Aert Sohouman and the Glasses that He Engraved. London: 1931. V. 37

Big Game Hunting in Central Africa. London: 1930. V. 40

European Glass. London: 1926. V. 37

BUCKLEY, WILFRED

The Art of Glass, Illustrated from the . . . Collection in the Victoria and Albert Museum. London: 1939. V. 39; 45

BUCKLEY, WILLIAM EDWARD

Catalogue of the Valuable and Extensive Library of the Late Rev. William Edward Buckley. London: 1893. V. 39

BUCKLIN, SOPHRONIA

In Hospital and Camp: a Woman's Record of Thrilling Incidents Among the Wounded in the Late War. Philadelphia: 1869. V. 41

BUCKMAN, GEORGE REX

Colorado Springs, Colroado and Its Famous Scenic Environs. Colorado Springs: 1893. V. 42

BUCKMAN, JAMES 1816-1884

Illustration of the Remains of Roman Art, in Cirencester, the Site of Antient Corinium. London: 1850. V. 38

BUCKMAN, S. S.

Type Ammonites. London: 1972-76. V. 37; 38

BUCKMINSTER, JOSEPH

A Discourse, Occasioned by the Late Desolating Fire. Portsmouth: 1803. V. 45

BUCKNALL, JOHN

Calendarium Pastoris; or, The Shepherd's Almanack. London: 1677. V. 43

BUCKNALL, THOMAS SKIP DYOT

The Orchardist: or, A System of Close Pruning and Medication, for Establishing the Science of Orcharding . . . London: 1805. V. 45

BUCKNER, H. F.

A Grammar of the Maskoke, or Creek Language. Marion: 1860. V. 38

BUCKNILL, JOHN

The Psychology of Shakespeare. London: 1859. V. 42; 45

BUCKNILL, JOHN CHARLES 1817-1897

The Care of the Insane and Their Legal Control. London: 1880. V. 45

A Manual of Psychological Medicine. London: 1858. V. 38

A Manual of Psychological Medicine . . . Philadelphia: 1858. V. 40; 43

The Medical Knowledge of Shakespeare. London: 1860. V. 43

Notes on Asylums for the Insane in America. London: 1876. V. 45

The Psychology of Shakespeare. London: 1859. V. 39; 43

BUCKTON, A. M.

Eager Heart. A Christmas Merry Play. London: 1931. V. 46

BUCKTON, ALICE MARY

Through Human Eyes. Oxford: 1901. V. 38; 42

BUCKTON, GEORGE BOWDLER

Monograph of the British Cicadae or Tettigidae. London: 1890. V. 43

Monograph of the British Cicadae or Tettigae. London: 1890-91. V. 37; 41; 43; 45

BUCQUET, JEAN BAPTISTE MICHEL 1746-1780

Introduction a l'Etude des Corps Naturels, Tires du Regne Mineral. Paris: 1771. V. 43

BUCY, PAUL C.

The Precentral Motor Cortex. Urbana: 1949. V. 42

BUDAEUS, GUILELMUS

Libri V De Asse et Partibus Eius . . . Venetiis: 1522. V. 38

BUDAPEST. SZEPMUVESZETI MUSEUM

Master Drawings from the Collection of the Budapest Museum of Fine Arts: 14th-18th Centuries; 19th and 20th Centuries. New York: 1957, 1958. V. 39

BUDD, GEORGE

On the Organic Diseases and Functional Disorders of the Stomach. New York: 1856. V. 42

On Diseases of the Liver. Philadelphia: 1857. V. 42

BUDD, THOMAS

Good Order Established in Pennsylvania and New Jersey in America . . . New York: 1865. V. 45

Good Order Established in Pennsylvania and New Jersey . . . Cleveland: 1902. V. 45

BUDD, WILLIAM

Typhoid Fever: Its Nature, Mode of Spreading and Prevention. London: 1873. V. 42

Typhoid Fever: Its Nature, Mode of Spreading and Prevention. New York: 1931. V. 41; 45

BUDDEN, CHARLES W.

An Introduction to the Ancient Churches of the Liverpool Diocese. Liverpool: 1929. V. 39

BUDDEN, LIONEL B.

The Book of the Liverpool School of Architecture. Liverpool: 1932. V. 37; 38

BUDDEN, MARIA 1780?-1832

Hofer the Tyrolese. London: 1824. V. 44

BUDDEN, MARIA E.

Thoughts on Domestic Education, the Result of Experience. London: 1826. V. 46

BUDDEN, MRS.

Key to Knowledge or Things in Common Use Simply and Shortly Explained by a Mother. London: 1820. V. 45

BUDE, GUILLAMUME 1468-1540

Commentarii Lingua Graecae, Guilelmo Budaeo, Consiliario Regio, Supplicum Que Libelloru in Regia Magistro, Auctore. Paris: 1548. V. 41; 46

BUDE, GUILLAUME 1468-1540

Commentarii Linguae Graecae. Paris: 1529. V. 43

Commentarii Linguae Graecae. Ab Eodem Accurate Recognita, Atque Amplius Tertia Parte Aucti. Paris: 1548. V. 39; 44

De Transitu Hellenismi ad Christianismum, Libri Tres. Paris: 1535. V. 37; 40

G. Budaei Consiliarii Regii, Supplicumque Libellorum in Regia Magistri Epostolarum Latinarum. Paris: 1531. V. 45

Libri V. de Asse et Partibus Eius . . . ab Eodem Ipson Budaeo Castigati. Venice: 1522. V. 39; 43

BUDGE, ERNEST ALFRED WALLIS 1857-1934

Amulets and Superstitions. London: 1930. V. 37; 40

The Babylonian Story of the Deluge and the Epic of Gilgamesh . . . London: 1920. V. 40

Coptic Apocrypha in the Dialect of Upper Egypt. London: 1913. V. 40

The Divine Origins of the Craft of the Herbalist. London: 1928. V. 40

The Gods of the Egyptians. London: and Chicago: 1904. V. 40

Osiris and the Egyptian Resurrection. London: 1911. V. 38

BUDGE, ERNEST ALFRED WALLIS THOMPSON 1857-1934

Assyrian Sculptures in the British Msueum. Reign of Ashur-Nasir-Pal 885-860 BC. London: 1914. V. 42; 44; 46

The Book of Paradise, Being the Histories and Sayings of the Monks and Ascetics of the Egyptian Desert by Palladius . . . London: 1904. V. 42

The Book of the Cave of Treasures. London: 1927. V. 42

By Nile and Tigris: A Narrative of Journeys in Egypt and Mesopotamia on Behalf of the British Museum Between the Years 1886 and 1913. London: 1920. V. 40; 42; 43

Cook's Handbook for Egypt and the Egyptian Sudan. London: 1921. V. 41

The Decrees of Memphis and Canopus in Three Volumes (complete). London: 1904. V. 38; 44

The Dwellers on the Nile. London: 1926. V. 45

Egypt in the Neolithic and Archaic Periods. London: 1902. V. 42

An Egyptian Reading Book for Beginners. London: 1896. V. 46

The Egyptian Sudan. Philadelphia: 1907. V. 43; 44

Egyptian Sculptures in the British Museum. London: 1914. V. 40; 44

Facsimiles of Egyptian Hieratic Papyri in the British Museum with Descriptions, Summaries of Contents, etc. London: 1923. V. 44

First Steps in Egyptian: a Book for Beginners. London: 1895. V. 44

From Fetish to God in Ancient Egypt. 1934. V. 45

From Fetish to God in Ancient Egyt. London: 1934. V. 37; 40; 42; 45

From Fetish to God in Ancient Egypt. Oxford: 1934. V. 46

A History of Ethiopia, Nubia & Abyssinia (According to the Hieroglyphic Inscriptions of Egypt and Nubia, and the Ethopian Chronicles). London: 1928. V. 37

The Life and Exploits of Alexander the Great . . . London: 1896. V. 45

The Life of Takla Haymanot in the Version of Dabra Libanos, and The Miracles of Takia Haymanot, in the Version of Dabra Libanos, and the Book of the Riches of Kings. London: 1906. V. 37; 38; 40; 44

The Liturgy of Funerary Offerings. London: 1909. V. 42

The Monks of Kublai Khan Empeor of China. London: 1928. V. 42

The Mummy: Chapters on Egyptian Funereal Archaeology. Cambridge: 1894. V. 42

The Mummy. A Handbook of Egyptian Funerary Archaeology. 1925. V. 38

The Mummy: a Handbook of Egyptian Funerary Archaeology. Cambridge: 1925. V. 40; 42

The Mummy: Chapters on Egyptian Funeral Archaeology. Cambridge: 1893. V. 37; 40

The Mummy: Chapters on Egyptian Funeral Archaeology. 1894. V. 40

On the Hieratic Papyrus of Nesl-Amsu, a Scribe in the Temple of Amen-Ra at Thebes. Westminster: 1891. V. 40

Osiris and the Egyptian Resurrection. 1911. V. 40

Osiris and the Egyptian Resurrection. London: 1911. V. 37; 38; 42

The Papyrus of Ani . . . London: 1913. V. 44

The Papyrus of Ani . . . New York: 1913. V. 44

The Paradise or Gardens of the Holy Fathers . . . New York: 1909. V. 43

The Rise and Progress of Assyriology. London: 1925. V. 44

The Rosetta Stone in the British Museum. London: 1929. V. 42

The Rosetta Stone in the British Museum: the Greek, Demotic and Hieroglyphic Texts of the Decree Described on the Rosetta Stone . . . London: 1929. V. 40; 42

The Sarcophagus of Anchnesraneferab, Queen of Ahmes II, King of Egypt. London: 1885. V. 44

Some Account of the Collection of Egyptian Antiquities in the Possession of Lady Meux, of Theobald's Park, Waltham Cross. London: 1896. V. 40; 42; 44

Some Account of the Collection of Egyptian Antiquities in the possession of Lady Meux, of Theobald's Park, Waltham Cross. London: 1893. V. 37

Tutankhamen: Amenism, Atenism and Egyptian Monotheism . . . New York: 1923. V. 38

BUDGE, J.

The Practical Miner's Guide; Comprising a Set of Trigonomical Tables Adapted to all the Purposes of Oblique or Diagonal, Vertical, Horizontal and Traverse Dialling . . . Devonport: 1825. V. 44

The Practical Miner's Guide . . . London: 1825. V. 42

BUDGE, JESSE R. S.

The Life of William Budge By His Son. Salt Lake City: 1915. V. 42; 43

BUDGELL, EUSTACE

A Letter to Cleomenes King of Sparta. London: 1731. V. 38; 44

Memoirs of the Life and Character of the Late Earl of Orrery and the Family of Boyles. London: 1732. V. 38; 39; 41

A Short History of Prime Ministers in Great Britain. London: 1733. V. 41; 42

Verses and His Scribblers; a Satire in Three Cantos. London: 1732. V. 40; 42

BUDGEN, L. M.

Episodes of Insect Life. London: 1849-51. V. 37; 38; 45

Episodes of Insect Life. First, Second and Third Series. London: 1849/51/51. V. 45

Episodes of Insect Life. By 'Acheta Domestica'. First---Second---Third Series. London: 1849. V. 37

Live Coals; or, Faces from the Fire. London: 1867. V. 43

THE BUDGET; or Humble Attempts at Immortality. Hallowell: 1830. V. 44

BUDGETT, H. M.

Hunting by Scent. London: 1933. V. 37

BUDS and Flowers of Childish Life. London: 1870. V. 45

BUECHNER, FREDERICK

Bred in the Bone: An Anthology. Edited by Henry Fischer and Bruce Berlind. Poems by Berlind, Buechner, Fischer, and others. Princeton: 1945. V. 37; 42

A Long Day's Dying. New York: 1950. V. 44

BUECHNER, THOMAS S.

Norman Rockwell, Artist and Illustrator. New York: 1970. V. 41

Norman Rockwell: Artist and Illustrator. New York: 1970. V. 41; 46

BUEL, J. W.

The Border Outlaws. St. Louis: 1881. V. 38

BUEL, JAMES W.

Heroes of the Plains or Lives and Wonderful Adventures of Wild Bill, Buffalo Bill, Kit Carson, Capt. Payne, Capt. Jack, Texas Jack, California Joe . . . St. Louis: 1882. V. 39; 44

Heroes of the Plains or Lives and Wonderful Adventures of Wild Bill, Buffalo Bill, Kit Carson, Capt. Payne, Capt. Jack, Texas Jack, California Joe, and Other Celebrated Indian Fighters . . . St. Louis: 1881. V. 37; 39

Life and Marvelous Adventures of Wild Bill, the Scout, Being a True and Exact History of all the Sanguinary Combats and Hair-Breadth Escapes of the Most Famous Scout and Spy America Ever Produced. Chicago: 1880. V. 39; 46

BUELL, AUGUST C.

Paul Jones Founder of the American Navy, A History and Biography . . . New York: 1900. V. 42

BUELL, AUGUSTUS

The Cannoneer, Recollections of Service in the Army of the Potomac. Washington: 1890. V. 46

BUELL, P. L.

A Guide to Phrenology, Designed to Illustrate the Science of the Human Mind as Manifested through the Brain, Embracing the Fundamental Principles of Phrenology . . . Woodstock: 1842. V. 44

BUELL, SAMUEL

A Faithful Narrative of the Remarkable Revival of Religion in the Congregation of Easthampton, on Long Island, in the Year of Our Lord 1764; with some Reflections . . . and also an Account of the Revival of Religion in Bridgehampton and Easthampton . . . Sag Harbor: 1808. V. 41

BUENTING, HEINRICH

Itinerarium Totius Sacrae Scripturae. London: 1619. V. 38

BUERGER, LEO

The Circulatory Distrubances of the Extremities, Including Gangrene, Vasomot and Trophic Disorders. Philadelphia, London: 1924. V. 45

BUETTNER, DAVID S. 1660-1719

Rudera Diluvii Testes. Leipzig: 1710. V. 43

BUETTNER, JOHANN CARL

Narrative of Johann Carl Buettner in the American Revolution. New York: 1912. V. 38; 39

BUFANO, BENIAMINO

Bufano: Sculpture, Mosaics, Drawings. Introduction by Henry Miller. Tokyo: n.d. V. 37

BUFFA, JOHN

Travels through the Empire of Morocco. London: 1810. V. 38

BUFFALO

Charter of the City of Buffalo, with the Several Amendments to Which are Added the Laws and Ordinances of the City of Buffalo. Buffalo: 1839. V. 42

THE BUFFALO Business Directory, with Alphabetical and Classified Index. Buffalo: 1855. V. 39; 43

BUFFALO City Directory for 1840. Buffalo: 1840. V. 39

BUFFALO, NEW YORK

Buffalo. Charter of the City of Buffalo, with the Several Amendments: to which are adeed the Laws of Ordinances of the City of Buffalo, Revised Jan. 1839. Buffalo: 1839. V. 37

BUFFET, BERNARD

Pages Choisies des Voyages Fantastiques de Cyrano de Bergerac. Bourg Le Reine: 1958. V. 41

BUFFIER, CLAUDE 1661-1737

First Truths, and the Origin of Our Opinions Explained . . . London: 1780. V. 43; 45

BUFFON, GEORGE LOUIS MARIE LE CLERC, COMTE DE

Buffon's Natural History. London: 1797. V. 41; 43; 46

The Natural History of Quadrupeds . . . Edinburgh: 1830. V. 44

BUFFON, GEORGE LOUIS MARIE LECLERC, COMPTE DE 1707-1788

Buffon's Natural History Abridged. London: 1792. V. 38; 39; 45

Natural History of Birds, Fish, Insects and Reptiles. London: 1793. V. 39; 42

BUFFON, GEORGE LOUIS MARIE LECLERC, COMTE DE

Histoires Naturelles. Textes Choisis. Lausanne: 1954. V. 41

Natural History, General and Particular. London: 1791-93. V. 42; 45

The Natural History of Insects . . . Perth: 1792. V. 42

BUFFON, GEORGES LOUIS MARIE LECLERC, COMPTE DE 1707-1788

Natural History, General and Particular. London: 1791. V. 39

BUFFON, GEORGES LOUIS MARIE LECLERC, COMTE DE

Histoire Naturelle, Generale et Particuliere avec la Description du Cabinet du Roi. Paris: 1749-67. V. 40; 43

Histoire Naturelle des Oiseaux. Paris: 1770-83. V. 38

The History of Singing Birds. Edinburgh: 1791. V. 37

Natural History, General and Particular. London: 1812. V. 37; 41; 42; 46

Oeuvres Completes de Buffon. Paris: 1855-57. V. 38

BUFFUM, E. GOULD

Six Months in the Gold Mines; from a Journal of Three Years' Residence in Upper and Lower California. Philadelphia: 1850. V. 38; 39; 42; 43; 45

BUFFUM, GEORGE T.

On Two Frontiers. Boston: 1918. V. 41

BUFFUM, W. A.

The Tears of the Heliades or Amber as a Gem. London: 1898. V. 44

BUGBEE, LESTER G.

Slavery in Early Texas. Boston: 1898. V. 37

BUGENHAGEN, JOHANNES 1485-1558

Unnderricht Deren so In Kranckhheiten und Todts Noeten Ligen, von dem Hailigen Sacrament des Leybs und Bluts Christi . . . Augsburg: 1527. V. 38

BUGLER, ARTHUR

H.M.S. Victory - Building, Restoration and Repair, and Extensive Reconstruction Since 1945. London: 1966. V. 42

BUGNEY, T. O.

A Month with the Muses, Colorado Tales and Legends of the Earlier Days. Pueblo: 1875. V. 44

BUHADOOR, NUWAB MOOST-UJAB KHAN

The Life of Hafiz-Moolk, Hafiz Rehmut Khan . . . London: 1831. V. 44

BUHL, MARIE-LOUISE

The late Egyptian Anthropoid Stone Sarcophagi. Kobenhavn: 1959. V. 37; 40

BUHLER, KATHRYN C.

American Silver 1655-1825 in the Museum of Fine Arts. Boston: 1972. V. 37

American Silver. Garvan and Other Collections in the Yale University Art Gallery. 1970. V. 37

American Silver: Garvan and other Collections in the Yale University Art Gallery. New Haven/London: 1970. V. 37

THE BUILDER'S Dictionary; or, Gentleman and Architect's Companion. London: 1734. V. 39

THE BUILDER'S Magazine. London: 1774-1786. V. 38

THE BUILDER'S Magazine: or Monthly Companion for Architects, Carpentes, Masons, Bricklayers, etc. London: 1776. V. 38

THE BUILDER'S Practical Director. Leipzig & Dresden: 1850. V. 38

THE BUILDER'S Practical Director or Buildings for All Classes . . . (plus) Supplementary Series. Leipzig and London: 1858-58. V. 37

THE BUILDER'S Practical Directory. Or, Building for all Classes, bound with the Supplemental Series. Two Volumes in One. Leipzig/Dresden: (1855-1858). V. 37; 39; 41

THE BUILDER'S Price-Book. London: 1794. V. 40

BUIST, ROBERT

The Rose Manual: Containing Accurate Descriptions of All the Finest Varities of Roses. Philadelphia: 1847. V. 41

BUKDAHL, JORGEN

Scadinavia, past and present. 1959. V. 37

BUKE, BASIL WILSON

Morgan's Cavalry. New York: and Washington: 1906. V. 44

BUKOWSKI, CHARLES

An V. 46

All the Assholes in the World and Mine. Bensenville: 1966. V. 39

At Terror Street and Agony Way. Los Angeles: 1968. V. 43; 46

Confessions of a Man Insane Enough to Live with Beasts. Bensenville: 1965. V. 46

Crucifix in a Deathhand. New Orleans: 1965. V. 39

Crucifix in a Deathhand. New Poems 1963-1965. New York: 1965. V. 37; 39; 46

BUKOWSKI, CHARLES continued

The Curtains are Waving and People Walk Through the Afternoon Here and in Berlin and in New York City and in Mexico. 1967. V. 42

Dangling in Tournefortia. Santa Barbara: 1981. V. 37; 38; 39

The Days Run Away Like Wild Horses Over the Hills. Los Angeles: 1969. V. 38; 42

Ham on Rye. Santa Barbara: 1982. V. 37; 38; 41; 42; 44

Horsemeat. Santa Barbara: 1982. V. 39

Hot Water Music. Toronto & Santa Barbara: 1983. V. 42; 43

Hot Water Music. Santa Barbara: 1983. V. 38; 42

It Catches My Heart in Its Hands. New and Selected Poems 1955-1963. New Orleans: 1963. V. 39; 41

On Going Out to Get the Mail. 1966. V. 42

Play the Piano Drunk Lie a Percussion Instrument Until the Fingers . . . Santa Barbara: 1979. V. 40

Poems Written Before Jumping Out of an 8 Story Window. Glendale. V. 46

The Rooming-House Madrigals: Early Selected Poems 1946-1966. Santa Rosa: 1988. V. 39; 41

Sparks. Santa Barbara: 1983. V. 37

A Visitor Complains of My Disenfranchise. Los Angeles: 1987. V. 45

War All the Time: Poems 1981-1984. 1984. V. 42

BULA, N'ZAU

Travel and Adventures in the Congo Free State and it's Game Shooting. London: 1894. V. 37

BULAU, ALWIN E.

Footprints of Assurance. New York: 1953. V. 37; 38

BULFINCH, S. G.

Poems. Charleston: 1834. V. 41; 45

BULFINCH, THOMAS

The Age of Fable. Boston: 1855. V. 39; 41

BULGARIN, THADDEUS

Ivan Vejeeghen; or, Life in Russia . . . Philadelphia: 1832. V. 42

BULGER, GEORGE E.

Leaves from the Records of St. Hubert's Club; or, Reminiscences of Sporting Expeditions in Many Lands. London: 1864. V. 43; 45

BULKELEY, J.

The Last Day. A Poem, in XII Books. London: 1720. V. 38

BULKELEY, JOHN

A Voyage to the South Seas, in the Years 1704-01. London: 1743. V. 39; 40; 42

A Voyage to the South Seas in the Years 1740-1. London: 1757. V. 43

A Voyage to the South Seas, in the Years 1740-1. Philadelphia: 1757. V. 41; 42; 45

BULKLEY, ABBY ISABEL BROWN

The Chad Browne Memorial Consisting of Genealogical Memoirs of a Portion of the Descendants of Chad and Elizabeth Browne. Brooklyn: 1888. V. 41

BULKLEY, CHARLES

A Vindication of My Lord Shfaftesbury, on the Subject of Ridicule. London: 1751. V. 38

A Vindication of My Lord Shaftesbury, on the Subject of Morality and Religion. London: 1752. V. 38

BULKLEY, DUNCAN

Eczema and Its Management. New York: 1882. V. 42

BULL, FREDERICK W.

A Sketch of the History of the Town of Kettering Together with Some Account of Its Worthies . . . Kettering: 1891-1908. V. 42

BULL, GEORGE

Defensio Fidei Nicaenae. Oxonii: 1685. V. 42

The Works. (with) *The Life of Bishop Bull by Robert Nelson.* Oxford: 1827. V. 39

The Works of . . . Late Bishop of St. David's . . . Concerning the Holy Trinity . . . Translated into English: with the Notes of Dr. Grabe. And some Reflections upon the late Controvertists . . . By Fr. Holland . . . Chaplain to . . . Viscount Weymouth. London: 1725. V. 37

BULL, H. J.

The Cruise of the 'Antarctic' to the South Polar Regions. London: 1896. V. 40

BULL, HENDRIK J.

The Cruise of the 'Antarctic' to the South Polar Regions. London: 1898. V. 42

BULL, HENRIK J.

the Cruise of the 'Antarctic' to the South Polar Regions. London/New York: 1896. V. 38; 39

BULL, HENRY GRAVES

The Heredordshire Pomona . . . Hereford: 1876-85. V. 46

BULL, JOHN

Poems and Translations. London: 1814. V. 42

Report of the Interesting Trial and Aquittal of . . . John Bull..for Attacking, Forcibly Entering Copenhagen, and Seizing Various Ships, naval Stores, &c. &c . . . London: 1807. V. 45

BULL, ROGER

Grobianus; or, the Compleat Booby. London: 1739. V. 40; 42; 43

BULL, WILLIAM PERKINS

From Rattlesnake Hunt to Hockey: the History of Sports in Canada and of the Sportsmen of Peel 1798 to 1834. Toronto: 1934. V. 44

From Brock to Currie. The Military Development and Exploits of Canadians in General and of the Men in Particular, 1791 to 1930. Toronto: 1935. V. 37; 40; 42

From Humming Bird to Eagle. Toronto: 1936. V. 43

From Oxford to Ontario. A History of the Downsview Community. Toronto: 1941. V. 37

Spadunk or from Paganism to Davenport United. Toronto: 1935. V. 44

BULLANT, JEAN

Reigle Generalle d'Architecture de cinq Manieres de Colonnes . . . Paris: 1568. V. 37

BULLAR, JOHN

Historaical Particulars Relating to Southampton. Southampton: 1820. V. 39

BULLAR, JOSEPH

A Winter in the Azores; and a Summer at the Baths of Furnas. London: 1841. V. 42; 43; 45

BULLARD, ARTEMAS

A Sermon, Preached in the First Presbyterian Church of Saint Louis, Missouri, on the Death of William Henry Harrison . . . Saint Louis: 1841. V. 45

BULLART, ISAAC

Academie des Sciences et des Arts, Contenant les Vies et les Eloges Historiques des Hommes Illustres . . . Brussels: 1682. V. 42

BULLEID, ARTHUR

The Glastonbury Lake Village. 1911. V. 42

The Glastonbury Lake Village. Glastonbury: 1911. V. 46

The Meare Lake Village. Taunton: 1948-53. V. 42; 46

BULLEIN, WILLIAM

Bulwark of Defence Against all Sicknesse, Soarnesse and Woundes. London: 1579. V. 44

BULLEN, A. H.

A Christmas Garland; Carols and Poems from the Fifteenth Century to the Present Time. London: 1885. V. 38

Davison's Poetical Rhapsody. London: 1890-91. V. 37

England's Helicon. A Collection of Lyrical and Pastoral Poems: Published in 1600. London: 1887. V. 44

England's Helicon. Lyrics from the Song Books of the Elizabethan Age. More Lyrics . . . Lyrics from the Dramatists of the Elizabethan Age. Poems, Chiefly Lyrical, from Romances and Prose Tracts of the Elizabethan Age. Davison's Poetical Rhapsody. London: 1887-90. V. 37; 38

More Lyrics from the Song Books of the Elizabethan Age. Edited by A.H.Bullen. London: 1888. V. 37

BULLEN, FRANK T.

The Cruise of the 'Cachalot' Round the World After Sperm Whales. London: 1898. V. 37; 40; 41; 42; 43

The Cruise of the Chachalot Round the World After Sperm Whales. New York: 1899. V. 41

The Log of a Sea-Waif, Being the First Four Years of My Sea Life. London: 1899. V. 41; 43

The Log of a Sea-Waif Being Recollections of the First Four Years of My Sea Life. New York: 1899. V. 46

BULLEN, GEORGE

Caxton Celebration, 1877. Catalogue of the Loan Collection of Antiquities, Curiosities and Appliances, Connected with the Art of Printing South Kensington. London: 1877. V. 44; 46

BULLEN, HENRY LEWIS

The Nurenberg Chronicle Or, The Book of Chronicles from the Beginning of the World . . . 1930. V. 38

BULLEN, HENRY LOUIS

Nicolaus Jensen, Printer of Venice. San Francisco: 1926. V. 38

BULLER, A. H. R.

Researches on Fungi. London: 1909-50. V. 38

BULLER, FRANCIS

The Charge of Sir Francis Buller, Bart. Dublin: 1798. V. 42

An Introduction to the Law Relative to Trials at Nisi Prius. London: 1775. V. 40

An Introduction to the Law Relative to Trials at Nisi Prius . . . London: 1781. V. 45

BULLER, W. L.

A History of the Birds of New Zealand. London: 1873-73. V. 42

A History of the Birds of New Zealand. London: 1888. V. 40

Manual of the Birds of New Zealand. Wellington: 1882. V. 38

BULLER, WALTER L.

A History of the Birds of New Zealand. 1967. V. 46

A History of the Birds of New Zealand. 1967. V. 46

A History of the Birds of New Zealand. New Zealand: 1967. V. 45

BULLER, WALTER LAWRY

A History of the Birds of New Zealand. London: 1888-1905. V. 37; 41

Manual of the Birds of New Zealand. New Zealand: 1882. V. 41

Manual of the Birds of New Zealand. Wellington: 1882. V. 37

BULLETS & Billets. London: 1916. V. 46

BULLFINCH, T.

Legends of Charlemagne. 1924. V. 43

BULLFINCH, THOMAS

Legends of Charlemagne. New York: 1924. V. 45

Works. Boston: 1863. V. 40; 46

BULLINGBROOKE, EDWARD

An Abridgement of the Public Statutes of IReland, Now in Force and of General Use . . . (with) An Appendix to the Abridgement of the Statutes of Ireland . . . Dublin: 1768. V. 46

An Abridgment of the Statautes of Ireland from the First Session of Parliament in (1310) to (1752) and of all the English and British Statutes which extend to and bind Ireland, etc. Dublin: 1754. V. 38

The Duty and Authority of Justices of the Peace and Parish-Officers for Ireland. Dublin: 1766. V. 44; 45

BULLOCH, J. M.

The House of Gordon. Aberdeen: 1903/1907. V. 38

BULLOCH, JAMES D.

The Secret Service of the Confederate States, a voluminous work written by the naval representative of the Confederate States in Europe during the Civil War, the building and equipment of the ships, with errata slip. London;: 1883. V. 37

BULLOCH, JOHN

George Jamesone, the Scottish Vandyck. Edinburgh: 1885. V. 40

BULLOCH, JOHN MALCOLM

Territorial Soldiering in the North-East of Scotland During 1759-1814. Aberdeen: 1914. V. 41

BULLOCH, JOSEPH GASTON BAILLIE

A History and Genealogy of the Habersham Family. Columbia: 1901. V. 40

BULLOCH, WILLIAM

Treasury of Human Inheritance. Parts V and VI. Section SIVa Haemophilia. London: 1911. V. 45; 46

BULLOCK, A. E.

Grinling Gibbons and His Compeers Illustrated by Sixty Phototypes of the Principal Carvings in the Churches of Saint James's Piccadilly and Saint Paul's Cathedral. London: 1914. V. 37; 44

BULLOCK, BARBARA

Wynn Bullock. San Francisco: 1971. V. 46

BULLOCK, CHRISTOPHER

The Per-Juror. London: 1717. V. 40

BULLOCK, HANNAH ANN

History of the Isle of man. London: 1816. V. 40

BULLOCK, JOHN

The American Cottage Builder . . . Philadelphia: 1868. V. 42

The Rudiments of Architecture and Building, for the Use of Architects, Builders. New York: 1855. V. 42

BULLOCK, RUFUS B.

Address of Rufus B. Bullock to the People of Georgia. N.P.: 1872. V. 41

Letter from His Excellency Governor Bullock of Georgia, in Reply to the Honorable John Scott, U. S. Senator, Chairman of Joint Select Committee into the Condition of the Late Insurrectionary States. Atlanta: 1871. V. 38; 42

BULLOCK, SHAN F.

Dan the Dollar. Dublin: 1905. V. 43

BULLOCK, W. H.

Across Mexico in 1865 . . . London: & Cambridge: 1866. V. 44

BULLOCK, WILLIAM

A Companion to the London Museum and Pantherion . . . London: 1813. V. 43

A Companion to the London Museum and Pantherion Containing a Brief Description of Upwards of 15,000 Natural and Foreign Curiosities . . . London: 1816. V. 44

A Description of the Unique Exhibition, Called Ancient Mexico . . . London: 1823. V. 39

Six Months' Residence and Travels in Mexico; Containing Remarks on the Present State of New Spain. London: 1824. V. 37; 38; 39; 42; 43

Six Months Residence and Travels in Mexico . . . London: 1825. V. 45

Six Months' Residence and Travels in Mexico. London: 1925. V. 42

Sketch of a Journey through the Western States of North America, from New Orleans, by the Mississippi, Ohio, City of Cincinnati and Falls of Niagara, to New York, in 1827. London: 1827. V. 37; 38; 39; 40; 42

BULLOCK, WYNN

The Widening Stream. Poems by Richard Mack. (San Francisco): 1965. V. 37; 44

Wynn Bullock. San Francisco: 1971. V. 41

BULLSTICKER, IMOGEN

A Study of Dionsaurs in the Comparative Method, for Students, Amateurs, Fanciers and Breeders. Andoversford: 1988. V. 42; 45

BULMER, T.

History, Topography and Directory of North Yorkshire . . . Preston: 1890. V. 46

BULOW, ERNIE

Words, Weather and Wolfmen: Conversations with Tony Hillerman. Gallup. V. 45

Words, Weather and Wolfmen: Conversations with Tony Hillerman. Gallup. V. 45

BULSTRODE, RICHARD

Memoirs and Reflections Upon the Reign and Government of King Charles the 1st and King Charles the IId . . . London: 1721. V. 39; 42

BULSTRODE, WHITELOCKE 1650-1724

An Essay of Transmigration, In Defence of Pythagoras; or a DIscourse of Natural Philosophy. London: 1692. V. 42

BULWER, EDWARD LORD LYTTON

The Coming Race. Edinburgh/London: 1871. V. 37

BULWER, ELIZABETH BARBARA

The Abbey De La Trappe. London: 1826. V. 42

BULWER, HENRY LYTTON

France, Social, Literary, Political. (with) The Monarchy of the Middle Classes. New York: 1836. V. 43

BULWER LYTTON, ROSINA, LADY

Cheveley; or, the Man of Honour. New York: 1839. V. 45

BUMSTEAD, FREEMAN

The Pathology and Treatment of Veneral Diseases: Including the Results of Recent Investigations Upon the Subject. Philadelphia: 1861. V. 42

BUNBURY, CHARLES J. F.

Journal of a Residence at the Cape of Good Hope; With Excursions into the Interior, and Notes on the Natural History and the Native Tribes. London: 1848. V. 38; 41

BUNBURY, E. H.

A History of Ancient Geography Under the Greks and Romans, fromt he earliest AGes Till the Fall of the Roman Empire. London: 1883. V. 45

BUNBURY, HENRY WILLIAM

An Academy for Grown Horsemen. London: 1787. V. 45

An Academy for Grown Horsemen . . . London: 1808. V. 45

Academy for Grown Horsemen: Annals of Horsemanship. London: 1812. V. 46

Academy for Grown Horsemen . . . London: 1825. V. 40

An Academy for Grown Horsemen . . . New York: 1929. V. 46

An Academy for Grown Horsemen. Philadelphia: 1813. V. 37

Annals of Horsemanship . . . London. V. 43

BUNBURY, HENRY WILLIAM continued

Annals of Horsemanship . . . Dublin: 1792. V. 45

Early Days in Western Australia Being the Letters & Journal of Lieut. H.W. Bunbury 21st Fusiliers. 1930. V. 37

BUNBURY, SELINA

Life in Sweden; with Excursions in Norway and Denmark. London: 1853. V. 40; 43

BUNBURY, WILLIAM

Reports of Cases in the Court of Exchequer, from the Beginning of the Reign of King George the First, until the Fourteenth Year of the Reign of King George the Second . . . In the Savoy: 1755. V. 45

BUNCE, DANIEL

Language of the Aborigines of the Colony of Victoria and Other Australian Districts. Geelong: 1859. V. 38

BUND, J. W. WILLIS

Salmon Problems. London: 1885. V. 39

BUNDGAARD, J. A.

The Excavation of the Athenian Acropolis 1882-1890. Copenhagen: 1974. V. 40; 44

BUNDY, HALLOCK C.

The Valdez-Fairbanks Trail. Seattle: 1910. V. 42

BUNIN, I. A.

The Gentleman from San Francisco and Other Stories. London: 1922. V. 45

The Gentleman from San Francisco and Other Stories. Richmond: 1922. V. 41; 44

BUNN, ALFRED

Old England and New England, in a Series of Views Taken On the Spot. London: 1853. V. 42; 43; 46

The Stage: Both Before and Behind the Curtain, from 'Observations Taken on the Spot.' London: 1840. V. 38; 44; 45; 46

The Stage: Both Before and Behind the Curtain, Taken from Observations on the Spot. London: 1840. V. 46

BUNN, MATTHEW

A Journal of the Adventures of Matthew Bunn . . . on an Expedition into the Western Country . . . Was Taken by the Savages, Escaped to Detroit. Litchfield: 1796. V. 38

BUNNELL, DAVID C.

The Travels and Adventures of David C. Bunnell, During Twenty-Three Years of Seafaring Life . . . Palmyra: 1831. V. 39

BUNNELL, LAFAYETTE HOUGHTON

Discovery of the Yosemite and the Indian War of 1851, Which Led to that Event. Chicago: 1880. V. 39; 42; 43; 45

Discovery of the Yosemite and the Indian War of 1851 Which Led to that Event. Los Angeles: 1911. V. 45

Winona and Its Environs on the Mississippi in Ancient and Modern Days. Winona: 1897. V. 37; 38; 44

BUNNELL, STERLING

Hand Surgery in World War II. Washington: 1955. V. 42

Surgery of the Hand. Philadelphia: 1944. V. 42

BUNNER, H. C.

A Woman of Honor. Boston: 1883. V. 43

BUNOARROTI, MICHEL ANGELO 1475-1564

Poesie. Montagnola: 1923. V. 46

BUNSEN, CHRISTIAN CHARLES JOSIAS, BARON VON 1791-.

Outline of the Philosophy of Universal History, Applied to Language and Religion. By Christian Charles Josias Bunsen, D.D., D.C.L., D. PH. London: 1854. V. 37

BUNSEN, FRANCES, BARONESS

A Memoir of Baron Bunsen. London: 1868. V. 40

BUNSEN, ROBERT

Gasometrische Methoden. Braunschweig: 1877. V. 46

Gasometry. London: 1857. V. 40

BUNT, C. G. E.

The Little Masters of English Landscape. Leigh-on-Sea: 1949. V. 39

BUNTING, BASIL

Briggflatts. 1966. V. 45

Collected Poems. London: 1968. V. 37; 38; 45; 46

Loquitur. London: 1965. V. 41; 42; 43; 46

Poems: 1950. Galveston: 1950. V. 38

Redimiculum Matellarum. Milan: 1930. V. 46

Redimiculum Materllarum: Poems. Milan: 1950. V. 43

The Spoils. 1965. V. 39

Two Poems. 1967. V. 46

Two Poems. 1967. V. 45

Two Poems. 1967. V. 43

What the Chairman Told Tom. 1967. V. 39

What the Chairman Told Tom. Cambridge: 1967. V. 44; 45

BUNTING, EDWARD

The Ancient Music of Ireland . . . a Dissertation on the Irish Harp and Harpers etc . . . Dublin: 1840. V. 37; 43

A General Collection of the Ancient Music of Ireland, Arranged for the Piano Forte . . . (with) A Historical and Critical Dissertation on the Egyptian, British and Irish Harp. London: 1809. V. 41; 43

BUNYAN, JOHN 1628-1688

The Acceptable Sacrifice; or the Excellency of a Broken Heart; Shewing the Nature, Signs and Proper Effects of a Contrite Spirit. London: 1691. V. 41

The Acceptable Sacrifice; or, the Excellency of a Broken Heart . . . London: 1698. V. 37; 40; 44

Bunyan's Pilgrim's Progress, Metrically Condensed. London: 1834. V. 42

The Christian Pilgrim . . . Montpelier: 1819. V. 45

The Christian Pilgrim. Salem: 1820. V. 38

The Entire Works of John Bunyan. New York: 1866. V. 39; 41; 43; 44

The Heliga Kriget Huru thet Blifwer Fordt af Christo Jesu . . . Stockholm: 1728. V. 43

The Jerusalem Sinner Saved. Amherst: 1798. V. 38

The Pilgrim's Progress. London. V. 39

The Pilgrim's Progress and Other Select Works. London. V. 44

The Pilgrim's Progress . . . London: 1678. V. 45

The Pilgrim's Progress. London: 1741. V. 40; 43

The Pilgrim's Progress from This World to That Which is to Come, Deliver'd Under the Similitude of a Dream . . . London: 1755. V. 44

The Pilgrim's Progress from This World to that Which Is To Come . . . London: 1760. V. 44

The Pilgrim's Progress From This World to That Which Is To Come. London: 1767, 1765. V. 40

The Pilgrim's Progress. London: 1775. V. 39

The Pilgrim's Progress from this World to that Which is to Come . . . London: 1797. V. 44

The Pilgrim's Progress from This World to that Which is to Come. Hartford: 1824. V. 44

The Pilgrim's Progress. London: 1830. V. 43; 45

The Pilgrim's Progress. Hartford: 1842. V. 40

The Pilgrim's Progress. London: 1844. V. 42

The Pilgrim's Progress. London: 1850. V. 45

The Pilgrim's Progress. London;: 1851. V. 39; 43

Pilgrim's Progress. London: 1860. V. 39

The Pilgrim's Progress from This World to that Which is to Come. London: 1861. V. 41

The Pilgrim's Progress. London: 1861. V. 46

The Pilgrim's Progress. London & New York: 1863. V. 40

Pilegrimsferd or denne Verdi til den Komande. Bergen: 1868. V. 43

The Pilgrim's Progress . . . London: 1876. V. 43

The Pilgrim's Progress . . . London: 1880. V. 43

The Pilgrim's Progress . . . London: 1881. V. 44

Uhambo Lo Mhambi, Owesuka Kweli Lizwe, Waye Esinga Kwelo Lizayo. (The Pilgrim's Progress). 1889. V. 39

The Pilgrim's Progress . . . London: 1898. V. 43

The Pilgrim's Progress. New York: 1898. V. 40; 44; 46

The Pilgrims Progress from this World to That Which is to come. Bow: 1899. V. 44

The Pilgrim's Progress. Bow: 1899. V. 43

The Pilgrims Progress from This World to that Which is to come. London: 1899. V. 44

Pilgrim's Progress. London: 1899. V. 37; 39; 40; 41; 42; 43; 44; 45; 46

The Pilgrim's Progress. London: 1901. V. 40; 41; 43; 45

The Pilgrim's Progress from This World to that Which is to Come. London: 1903. V. 45

The Pilgrim's Progress. London: 1906. V. 39

The Pilgrim's Progress. London: 1920. V. 43

The Pilgrim's Progress and The Life and Death of Mr. Badman. London: 1928. V. 45

The Pilgrim's Progress from This Wold to that Which is to Come. London: 1928. V. 41; 46

The Pilgrim's Progress. London: 1928. V. 41; 42; 44; 45

The Pilgrim's Progress. New York: 1941. V. 40; 42; 45

The Pilgrim's Progress from this World to that which is to come . . . Edited by George Godwin. With a Memoir of the Author and a Bibliographical Notice. London: 1844. V. 37

The Pilgrim's Progress . . . London: 1895. V. 37

BUNYAN, JOHN 1628-1688 continued

The Pilgrim's Progress from this world to that which is to come. With an Introduction by the Rev. H.R. Hawes. Embellished with over one hundred and twenty designes done by three brothers George Wolliscroft Rhead, Frederick Rhead . . . London: 1898. V. 37

The Pilgrims Progress from This World to that Which is to Come. 1899. V. 37

Pilgrim's Progress: Retold and Shortened for Modern Readers, by Mary Godulphin, 1884. New York: 1939. V. 37

A Relation of the Imprisonment of John Bunyan . . . Written by Himself . . . London: 1765. V. 38

Sighs from Hell or, Groans of a Damned Soul. Edinburgh: 1777. V. 42

Solomon's Temple Spiritualiz'd; or, Gospel-Light fetch'd out of the Temple at Jerusalem, to let us more easily unto the glory of New Testament Truths. Th eight edition. Dublin: 1754. V. 37

Solomon's Temple Spiritualiz'd Or Gospel-Light Fetcht Out of the Temple at Jerusalem. London: 1688. V. 37

Te Tere no te Tuitarere Mei Teianei ao Ki Te Ao A Muri Atuq; e Mea Akakiteia Mai, Mel te Mea e Moe. Rarotonga: 1846. V. 46

The Whole Selected Works of the Reverened Mr. John Buynan . . . With notes, explanatory, experimental, practical etc by William Mason. London: 1780. V. 37

The Works of that Eminent Servant of Christ Mr. John Bunyan. London: 1736-37. V. 41; 44

The Whole Selected Works of the Rev. Mr. John Bunyan . . . London: 1780. V. 39

Works. London: 1855-53. V. 41

The Works . . . London: 1860. V. 42

BUNZEL, RUTH

The Pueblo Potter: a Study in Creative Imagination in Primitive Art. New York: 1929. V. 38; 39

BUONAIUTI, M.

Italian Scenery. London: 1806. V. 39

BUONANNI, FILIPPO 1638-1725

Gabinetto Armonico Pieno d'Istromenti Sonori Indicati . . . Rome: 1722. V. 44; 45

Museum Kircherianum sive Musaeum A.P. Athanasio Kirchero in Collegio Romano Societatis Jesu iam Pridem Incoeptum Nuper Restitum, Auctum, Descriptum & Iconibus Illustratum . . . Rome: 1709. V. 46

Numismata Summorum Pontificum Templi Vaticani Fabricam Indicantia, Chronolgica Ejusdem Fabricae Narratione . . . Romae: 1715. V. 40

BUONAROTTI, MICHEL ANGELO

The Letters of Michelangelo. London: 1963. V. 38; 39

The Letters of Michelangelo. Stanford: 1963. V. 44

Poesie. 1923. V. 42

Poesie. 1923. V. 45

Poesie. Montagnola: 1923. V. 40; 42; 43; 44

Rime di Michelagnolo Buonarotti. Raccolte da Michelagnolo suo Nipote. Florence: 1623. V. 40

The Sonnets of . . . London: 1904. V. 44

The Sonnets. London: 1926. V. 40

BUONARROTI, PHILIPPE 1761-1837

Buonarroti's History of Babeuf's Conspiracy for Equality with the Author's Reflections on the Causes and Character of the French Revolution, and His Estimate of the Leading Men and Events of that Epcoh. London: 1836. V. 39

BUONI, THOMASSO

Problems of Beauty, Love and All Humane Affections. London: 1618. V. 44

BURBANK, LUTHER

His Methods and Discoveries and Their Practical Application. New York & London: 1914. V. 40

His Methods and Discoveries and Their Practical Application, Prepared from His Original Field Notes Covering More Than 100,000 experiments . . . New York: 1914. V. 37; 46

Luther Burbank, His Methods and Discoveries and Their Practical Application. New York: & London: 1914. V. 40; 45

Luther Burbank. His Methods and Discoveries and Their Practical Application. New York: & London: 1914-15. V. 43

Works. New York: & London: 1914. V. 46

BURBIDGE, F. W.

Cool Orchids and How to Grow Them. London: 1874. V. 40

The Narcissus: Its History and Culture with Coloured Plates and Descriptions of All Known Species and Principal Varieties . . . London: 1875. V. 39; 42

BURBURY, JOHN

A Relation of a Journey to the Right Honourable My Lord Henry Howard, from London to Vienna, and Thence to Constantinople . . . London: 1671. V. 38; 44

BURCE'S NEW YORK TYPE FOUNDRY

Specimens of Printing Types. New York: 1882. V. 44

BURCH, C. S.

Hand-Book of Fort Smith and Sebastian County, Arkansas. Chicago: 1887. V. 38; 39; 41

BURCH, EDWARD

A Catalogue of One Hundred Proofs from Gems, Engraved in England by E. Burch, R. A. Engraver to His Majesty, for Medals and Gems. London: 1795. V. 45; 46

BURCH, L. D.

Kansas As It Is. Chicago: 1878. V. 38; 42

BURCH, R. M.

Colour Printing and Colour Printers. New York: 1911. V. 38; 44

BURCHARDUS, BP. OF WORMS

Decretorum Libri XX.. Paris: 1550. V. 45

BURCHELL, WILLIAM J.

Travels in the Interior of Southern Africa. London: 1822-24. V. 42

Travels in the Interior of Southern Africa. London: 1953. V. 37; 38; 40

BURCHETT, JOSIAH

A Complete History of the Most Remarkable Transactions at Sea, From the Earliest Accounts of Time to the Conclusion of the Last War with France . . . London: 1720. V. 43; 44; 45

BURCHIELLO, DOMENICO 1403-1448

Rime. Venice: 1553. V. 39

BURCKART, AARON

Analysai Rollenhagianum. Magdeburg: 1609. V. 41

BURCKHARD VON PUERCKENSTEIN, ANTON ERNST

Mathematischen Wissenschafften. Augspurg: 1713. V. 38

BURCKHARDT, CARL J.

Hans Erni. Zurich: 1964. V. 43

Hans Erni. Zurich: 1967. V. 41

BURCKHARDT, JOHN LEWIS

Arabic Proverbs, or the Manners and Customs of the Modern Egyptians. London: 1830. V. 40

Arabic Proverbs; or the Manners and Customs of the Modern Egyptians . . . London: 1875. V. 42

Notes on the Bedouins and Wahabys, Collected During His Travels in the East. London: 1830. V. 40; 43

Notes on the Bedouins and Wahabys . . . London: 1831. V. 43

Travels in Nubia. London: 1819. V. 37; 38; 40; 42; 43; 45; 46

Travels in Nubia by the Late John Lewis Burckhardt. London: 1822. V. 38; 39; 45

Travels in Arabia, Comprehending an Account of Those Territories in Hedjaz Which the Mohammedans Regard as Sacred. London: 1829. V. 46

Travels in Arabia, Comprehending an Account of those Territories in Hedjaz which the Mohammendans Regard as Sacred. By John Lewis Burckhardt. London: 1829. V. 37; 43

BURDEKIN, RICHARD

Memoir of the Life and Character of Mr. Robert Spence of York. York: 1827. V. 44

BURDEN, MRS.

The Three Baskets of How Henry, Richard and Charles Were Occupied While Papa Was Away. London: 1845. V. 45

BURDER, GEORGE

The Closet-Companion; or an Help to Serious Persons, in the Important Duty of Self Examination. Providence: 1805. V. 45

BURDETT, C. D., MRS.

English Fasionables Abroad. London: 1827. V. 43

BURDETTE, ROBERT J.

Chimes from a Jesters Bells. Indianapolis and Kansas City: 1897. V. 38

BURDETTE, WILLIAM

Obi or Three Fingered Jack. New York: 1825. V. 38; 39; 40; 42

BURDICK, JOEL W.

Our World Tour. 1922-1923. In the First Passenger Ship to Circumnavigate the Globe. Pittsburgh: 1923. V. 41

BURDICK, WILLIAM

An Oration on the Nature and Effects of the Art aof Printing. Delivered in Franklin Hall, July 5, 1802, Before the Boston Franklin Association. Boston: 1802. V. 37; 39; 40; 41; 43; 44

BURDO, ADOLPHE

Les Belges dans l'Afrique Centrale. Brussels: 1886. V. 38

BURDON, WILLIAM

The Gentleman's Pocket-Farrier. London: 1730. V. 43

The Gentleman's Pocket-Farrier. London: 1737. V. 43

Life and Character of Bonaparte, From His Birth to the 15th of August, 1804. Newcastle-upon-Tyne: 1805. V. 42

BURDSALL, RICHARD L.

Men Against the Clouds. The Conquest of Minya Konka. New York: 1935. V. 44

BURET, EUGENE

De La Misere des Classes Laborieuses en Angleterre et en France... Paris: 1840. V. 38

BURFORD, J.

Description of a View of the City of Mexico, and Surrounding Country... London: 1826. V. 39

BURFORD, JOHN

An Argument to Prove that the XXXIXth Section of the ... Chapter of the Statutes Given by Queen Elizabeth to the University of Cambridge... London: 1727. V. 43

BURFORD, ROBERT

Description of the Panorama of the Superb City of Mexico, and the Surrounding Scenery, Painted on 2700 Square Feet of Canvas, by Robert Burford... New York: 1828. V. 42

Description of a View of Hobart Town, Van Dieman's Land and the Surrounding Country, Now Exhibiting at the Panorama, Strand. London: 1831. V. 46

BURGER, GOTTFRIED AUGUST

Lenore. London: 1900. V. 38; 41

Leonara. London: 1796. V. 45; 46

BURGER, GOTTFRIED AUGUSTUS

The Chase, and William and Helen. Edinburgh: 1796. V. 37

BURGERSDIJCK, FRANCO

Institutionum Metaphysicarum Lib. II. Opus Posthumum. Oxon: 1675. V. 42

BURGES, BARTHALOMEW

A Series of Indostan Letters by a Traveller, Containing a Striking Account of the Manners and Customs of the Gentoo Nations, and of the Moguls and Other Mahomedan Tribes in Indostan. New York: 1817. V. 37; 40; 43

BURGES, BARTHOLOMEW

A Series of Indostan Letters... Containing, A Striking Account of the Manners and Customs of the Gentoo Nations & of the Moguls and Other Mahomedan Tribes in Indostan... New York: 1790. V. 42

BURGES, GEORGE

Cato to Lord Byron on the Immorality of His Writings. London: 1824. V. 42

BURGES, JAMES BLAND

Riches; or the Wife and Brother: A Play, in Five Acts. New York: 1810. V. 37

BURGES, TRISTAM

Battle of Lake Erie with Notices of Commodore Elliot's Conduct in that Engagement. London: 1839. V. 42

Battle of Lake Erie with Notices of Commodore Elliot's Conduct in that Engagement. Philadelphia: 1839. V. 42; 45

Speech of Mr. Burges, of Rhode Island, in the Case of Samuel Houston, Charged with a Violation of the Rights and Powers of the Hosue, by Assaulting the Hon. William Stanberry, a member from Ohio... Washington: 1832. V. 39

BURGES, W.

Architectural Drawings. London: 1870. V. 38

BURGES, WILLIAM 1827-1881

Report to the Courts of Justice Competition by William Burges; Design for the New Law Courts Submitted by Geo. Gilbert Scott... London: 1867. V. 38

BURGESS, ANTHONY 1917-

The Age of the Grand Tour. London: 1967. V. 39

Beds in the East. London: 1959. V. 42

A Clockwork Orange. London: 1962. V. 39; 40; 41; 42

A Clockwork Orange. 1963. V. 45

A Clockwork Orange. New York: 1963. V. 38; 39; 41; 43

A Clockwork Orange. 1962. V. 37

Coaching Days of England. London: 1966. V. 39; 44; 45

The Doctor is Sick. London: 1960. V. 38

Enderby Outside. London: 1978. V. 46

Honey for the Bears. London: 1963. V. 38; 39

Inside Mr. Enderby. London: 1963. V. 41; 45

Language Made Plain. London: 1964. V. 38; 41; 42

Malayan Trilogy; Time for a Tiger; The Enemy in the Blanket; Beds in the East. London: 1956/58/59. V. 41

One Hand Clapping. London: 1961. V. 42; 46

Time for a Tiger. London: 1956. V. 37; 46

A Tremor of Intent. London: 1966. V. 43

A Tremor of Intent. 1966. V. 37

A Vision of Battlements. London: 1965. V. 46

The Wanting Seed. New York: 1963. V. 42

Will and Testament. Verona: 1977. V. 41; 42; 43; 44; 45

The Worm and the Ring. London: 1961. V. 45

BURGESS, C. M.

Cowries of the World. Cape Town: 1985. V. 37; 38

BURGESS, E. S.

Studies in the History and Variations of ASter. New York: 1902-06. V. 46

BURGESS, F. F. R.

Sporting Fire-Arms for Bush and Jungle. London: 1884. V. 39

BURGESS, GELETT FRANK 1866-1951

Bayside Bohemia: Fine de Siecle San Francisco & Its Little Magazine. San Francisco: 1954. V. 37

Behind the Scenes: Glimpses of Fin de Siecle. San Francisco: 1968. V. 37; 40; 46

Behind the Scenes. Glimpses of Fin De Siecle San Francisco. San Francisco: 1980. V. 44

Blue Goops and Red: a Manual of Polite Deportment for Children Who Would be Good Showing them How and How Not to Behave Everywhere. New York: 1909. V. 41

The Burgess Nonsense Book. New York: (1901). V. 37

Goop Tales Alphabetically Told. New York: 1904. V. 45

Goops and How to Be Them: A manual of Manners for Polite Infants... London: 1900. V. 45

Goops and How To Be Them. A Manual of Manners for Polite Infants Inculcating many Juvenile Virtues Both by Precept and Example With Ninety Drawings. New York: (1900). V. 37

The Purple Cow. San Francisco: 1895. V. 37; 38; 39; 41; 43

The Romance of the Commonplace. San Francisco: 1902. V. 37; 38

Vivette; or, the Memoirs of the Romance Association. Boston: 1897. V. 41

BURGESS, HENRY W.

Studies of Trees. London: 1828. V. 41; 45; 46

BURGESS, JOHN 1563-1635

An Answer Reioyned to that Much Applauded Pamphlet... a Reply to Dr. Mortons Generall Defence of Three Nocent Ceremonies. The Lawfulness of Kneeling in the Act of Receiving the Lord's Supper. London: 1631. V. 39

The Doctor is Sick. London: 1960. V. 40

BURGESS, N. G.

The Photograph and Ambrotype Manual... New York: 1861. V. 46

BURGESS, RICHARD

Greece and the Levant; or, Diary of a Summer's Excursion in 1834... London: 1835. V. 42

BURGESS, SAMUEL WALTER

Historical Illustrations of the Origin and Progress of the Passions, and Their Influence of the Conduct of Mankind... London: 1825. V. 42

BURGESS, THOMAS

The Arabic Alphabet, or an Easy Introduction to the Reading of Arabick. Newcastle: 1809. V. 38; 40

An Essay on the Study of Antiquities. Oxford: 1782. V. 42

The Samaritan and Syriack Alphabets, with Praxis to Each. London: 1814. V. 37

BURGESS, THOMAS H.

The Physiology or Mechanism of Blushing. London: 1839. V. 38; 45

BURGESS, THORNTON

Along the Laughing Brook; on the Green Meadows. Boston: 1954. V. 46

At Paddy the Beaver's Pond. Boston: 1950. V. 46

Aunt Sally's Friends in Fur. Boston: 1955. V. 46

The Feast of the Big Rock and Other Stories. New York: 1914. V. 38

BURGESS, THORNTON W.

The Burgess Animal Book for Children. Boston: 1937. V. 41

BURGESS, THORTON B.

The Bride's Primer. Text by Thorton B. Burgess and others. New York: (c. 1905). V. 37

BURGH, ALLATSON

Anecdotes of Music, Historic and Biographical; in a Series of Letters from a Gentleman to His Daughter. London: 1814. V. 40; 42; 43

BURGH, JAMES

The Art of Speaking. London: 1768. V. 46

The Art of Speaking. Dublin: 1784. V. 39

Britain's Remembrancer: or the Danger Not Over . . . London: 1746. V. 40

The Dignity of Human Nature. Or, a brief account of the certain and established means for attaining the true end of our existence. In four books . . . London: 1767. V. 37

BURGH, N. P.

A Treatise on Sugar Machinery . . . London: 1863. V. 45

BURGHARDT, G. M.

Iguanas of the World, Their Behavior, Ecology and Conservation. Park Ridge: 1982. V. 37; 38

BURGHERSH, LORD

Memoir of the Early Campaigns of the Duke of Wellington in Portugal and Spain. London: 1820. V. 38; 42

BURGHLEY, WILLIAM CECIL, BARON 1520-1598

A Description of Maps and Architectural Drawings in the Collection Made by William Cecil, First Baron Burghley, Now at Hatfield House. Oxford: 1971. V. 40

Precepts or Directions for the Well Ordering and Carriage of a Mans Life. London: 1636. V. 40

BURGIN, RICHARD

Conversations with Jorge Luis Borges. New York: 1969. V. 46

BURGIS, JOHN

Myrianthea, or Numberless Groups of Changeable Flowers, Intended to Teach . . . the ARt of Composing, Drawing and Colouring Groups of Flowers . . . to Which is added the Method of Imitating Bronze Vases, Shading and Varnishing Gold Ornaments . . . London: 1825. V. 46

BURGMAIR, HANS

Triumph of the Emperor Maximilian I, in a Sucession of a Hundred and Thirty Five Wood Engravings . . . . London: 1875. V. 40

BURGO, PETRO BATTISTA fl. 1531-53

De Bello Suecico . . . Liege: 1633. V. 40

BURGOYNE, JOHN 1722-1792

A Letter from Lieut. Gen. Burgoyne to His Constituents, Upon His Late Resignation; with the Correspondences . . . Relative to His Return to America. London: 1779. V. 38; 41; 43; 45; 46

A State of the Expedition from Canada as Laid Before the House of Commons. London: 1780. V. 38

The Substance of General Burgoyne's Speeches, on Mr. Vyner's Motion . . . and Upon Mr. Hartley's Motion . . . of May, 17778. London: 1778. V. 45

BURGOYNE, RODERICK HAMILTON

Historical Records of the 93rd Sutherland Highlanders, Now the 2nd Battalion Princess Louise's Argyll and Sutherland Highlanders. London: 1883. V. 40

BURGRESS, A.

Coaching Days of England. Containing An Account of whatever was most remarkable for Grandeur, Elegance and Curiosity in the time of the Coaches of England, comprehending the years 1750 until 1850. Together with an Historical Commentary by . . . London;: 1966. V. 37

BURGSDORFF, FRIEDRICH AUGUST LUDWIG VON

Versuch Einer Vollstandigen Geschichte Vorzuglicher Holzarten in Systematischen Abhandlungen zur Erweiterung der Naturkunde und Forsthaushaltungwissenschaft. Berlin: 1783-1800. V. 39

BURGUM, JESSAMINE S.

Zezula or Pioneer Days in the Smoky Water Country. Valley City: 1937. V. 43; 45

BURHANS, ROBERT D.

The First Special Service Force, a War History of the North Americans 1942-1944. Washington: 1947. V. 44

BURK, DALE A.

New Interpretations. N.P.: 1969. V. 38

New Interpretations. N.P.: 1969. V. 40

BURK, JOHN

Bunker-Hill; or, the Death of Warren. New York: 1817. V. 37

The History of Virgina, From Its First Settlement to the Present Day. Petersburg: 1804-05. V. 45

The History of Virginia, from Its First Settlement to the Present Day. Petersburg: 1804-5-16. V. 39; 42

BURKE, A. L.

The Mayberry Murder Mystery of Bonito City. Alamogordo. V. 43

BURKE, AEDANUS

Considerations on the Society or Order of Cincinnait . . . Hartford: 1784. V. 42

Considerations on the Society or Order of Cincinnati, Lately Instituted by the Major Generals, Brigadier Generals and Other Officers of the American Army. Newport: 1784. V. 46

BURKE, BERNARD

Burke's Landed Gentry. London: 1937. V. 43

A Genealogical and Heraldic History of the Landed Gentry of Ireland. London: 1904. V. 43

Landed Gentry of Ireland. London: 1958. V. 43

Peerage and Baronetage. London: 1930. V. 43

BURKE, CLIFFORD

A Chiroxylographic Book. Anacrotes: 1981. V. 40

A Chiroxylographic Book. N.P.. V. 38

BURKE, EDMUND 1729-1797

An Account of the European Settlements in America. London: 1760. V. 37; 40; 42; 45

An Account of the European Settlement in America. Dublin: 1762. V. 39; 41

An Account of the European Settlements in America. V. 39; 42

An Account of the European Settlements in America. London: 1765. V. 39; 42

An Account of the European Settlements in America. London: 1770. V. 44

An Account of the European Settlements in America. London: 1777. V. 41; 42; 44; 45

An Account of the European Settlements in America. London: 1757. V. 37

An Account of the European Settlements in America. A New Edition. London: 1808. V. 37

The Annual Register, or a View of the History, Politicks and Literature, for the Year 1758 (to the Year 1766). London: 1764-67. V. 39

The Annual Register of the History, Politics and Literature, for the Year 1774. London: 1775. V. 37; 42

An Appeal from the New to the Old Whigs, in Consequence of Some Late Discussions in Parliament, Relative to the Reflections on the French Revolution. Dublin: 1791. V. 41; 42

An Appeal from the New to the Old Whigs, In Consequence of Some Late Discussions in Parliament, Relative to the Reflections on the French Revolution. London: 1791. V. 39

An Authentic Copy of Mr. Pitt's Letter to His Royal Highness the Prince of Wales, with His Answer. London: 1789. V. 44

Beauties of the Right Hon. Edmund Burke . . . to Which is Sketched a Sketch of His Life. London: 1798. V. 39; 40; 43; 45

Correspondence of the Right Honourable Edmund Burke; Between the Year 1744, and the Period of His Decease in 1797. London: 1844. V. 37; 40; 41; 42; 45

A Letter from Edmund Burke, Esq . . . to John Farr and John Harris . . . on the Affairs of America. London: 1777. V. 37; 38; 42; 45

A Letter from Mr. Burke, to a Member of the National Assembly: In Answer to Some Objections to His Book of French Affairs. London: 1791. V. 39

A Letter . . . to a Member of the National Assembly . . . Paris: 1791. V. 43

A Letter from Mr. Burke, to a Member of the National Assembly; In Answer to Some Objections to His Book on French Affairs. Paris Printed: 1791. V. 39

A Letter . . . to a Noble Lord, on the Attacks Made Upon Him and His Pension, in The House of Lords, by the Duke of Bedford, and the Earl of Lauderdale, Early in the Present Sessions of Parliament. London: 1796. V. 40; 41

A Letter from the Right Honourable Edmund Burke to a Noble Lord, on the Attacks Made Upon Him and His Pension, in the House of Lords, by the Duke of Bedford and the Earl of Lauderdale. London: 1796. V. 40

A Letter from the Rt. Honourable Edmund Burke to His grace the Duke of Portland, on the Conduct of the Minority in Parliament. London: 1797. V. 40; 45; 46

A Letter . . . to His Grace the Duke of Portland, on the Conduct of the Minority in Parliament . . . London: 1797. V. 37; 38; 43

A Letter to a Noble Lord, on the Attacks made upon him and his Pension, in the House of Lords, by the Duke of Bedford and the Earl of Lauderdale, early in the presnet Sessions of Parliament. London: 1795. V. 37

A Letter . . . to John Farr and John Harris . . . on the Affairs of America. London: 1777. V. 37

Maxims, Opinions and Characters, Moral, Political and Economical, from the Works of the Right Hon . . . . London: 1811. V. 46

Mr. Edmund Burke's Speeches at his arrival at Bristol, and at the Conclusion of the Poll. London: 1774. V. 39

Mr. Burke's Speech on the Motion Made for Papers Relative to the Directions for Charing the Nabob of Arcot's Private Debts to Europeans . . . London: 1785. V. 42

Mr. Burke's Speech in Westminster Hall, On the 18th and 19th Feb. 1788, with Explanatory Notes. London: 1792. V. 39; 42

Mr. Burke's Speech on the Motion made for papers relative to the Directions for charging the Nabob of Arcot's Private Debt to Europeans, on the Revenues of the Carnatic. February 28th 1785. With an Appendix containing several documents. London: 1785. V. 37

BURKE, EDMUND 1729-1797 continued

Nouvelles Reflexions Sur la Revolution de France . . . Paris: 1791. V. 38

Observations on a Late State of the Nation. London: 1769. V. 42

On Conciliation With the Colonies and Other Papers on the American Revolution. Lunenberg: 1975. V. 40; 41

A Philosophical Enquiry into the Origin of Our Ideas of the Sublime and Beautiful. London: 1757. V. 37; 38; 39; 41; 43; 45

A Philosophical Enquiry Into the Origin of Our Ideas of the Sublime and Beautiful. London: 1759. V. 38; 39; 40; 44; 45

A Philosophical Enquiry into the Origin of Our Ideas of the Sublime and Beautiful. London: 1761. V. 39; 40

A Philosophical Enquiry into the Origin of Our Ideas of the Sublime and Beautiful. Dublin: 1766. V. 38

A Philosophical Enquiry into the Origin of Our Ideas of the Sublime and Beautiful. London: 1770. V. 39

A Philosophical Enquiry into the Origin of Our Ideas of the Sublime and Beautiful. Berwick: 1772. V. 46

A Philosophical Enquiry into the Origin of Our Ideas of the Sublime and Beautiful. London: 1776. V. 44

A Philosophical Enquiry into the Origin of Our Ideas of the Sublime and Beautiful. London: 1782. V. 38; 45

A Philosophical Enquiry Into the Origin of Our Ideas of the Sublime and Beautiful. London: 1787. V. 44

A Philosophical Enquiry into the Origin of Our Ideas of the Sublime and Beautiful. London: 1793. V. 41; 43

A Philosophical Enquiry into the Origin of Our Ideas of the Sublime and Beautiful. London: 1798. V. 43

A Philosophical Enquiry into the Origin of Our Ideas of the Sublime and Beautiful. London: 1803. V. 40; 41

A Philosophical Inquiry into the Origin of Our Ideas of the Sublime and Beautiful. Portland: 1806. V. 45

A Philosophical Enquiry Into the Origin of Our Ideas of the Sublime and Beautiful. London: 1807. V. 39; 41

A Philosophical Inquiry into the Origin of Our Ideas of the Sublime and Beautiful. London: 1810. V. 41

The Political Tracts and Speeches of Edmund Burke, Esq., Member of Parliament for the City of Bristol. Dublin: 1777. V. 37; 40; 41; 45; 46

Recherche Philosophique sur l'Origine de Nos Idees du Sublime et du Beau . . . Paris: 1803. V. 45

Reflections on the Revolution in France, and on the Proceedings in Certain Societies in London, Relative to that Event. Dublin: 1790. V. 37; 38; 39

Reflections of the Revolution in France, and on the Proceedings in Certain Societies in London Relative to that Event. London: 1790. V. 37; 38; 39; 40; 41; 42; 43; 44; 45; 46

Reflections on the Revolution in France. London: 1791. V. 38; 39; 41; 45

Reflections on the Revolution in France. Philadelphia: 1792. V. 45

Reflections on the Revolution in France and on the Proceedings in certain Societies in London relative of that event. Dublin: 1790. V. 37

A Reply to the Treasury Pamphlet, entitled 'The Proposed System of Trade with Ireland Explained'. London: 1785. V. 46

The Speech of Edmund Burke, Esq. on Moving His Resolutions for conciliation with the Colonies, March 22, 1775. Dublin: 1775. V. 45

Speech of . . . on American Taxation, April 19, 1774. London: 1775. V. 37; 39; 41; 42; 45

Speech . . . on Presenting to the House of Commons (on the 11th of Feburary, 1780), a plan for the better security of the independence of Parliament, and the Oeconomical Reformation of the Civil and Other Establishments. London: 1780. V. 43

Speech of Edmund Burke, Esq. London: 1780. V. 45

A Speech at the Guildhall, in Bristol, Previous to the Late Election in that City, Upon Certain Points Relative to His Parliamentary Conduct. London: 1780. V. 37

The Speeches of the Right Honourable Edmund Burke, in the House of Commons, and in Westminster-Hall. London: 1816. V. 38

Substance of the Speech of the Right Honourable Edmund Burke, in the Debate on the Army Estimates, in the House of Commons, on Tuesday, the 9th Day of February, 1790. London: 1790. V. 39

Thoughts on the Prospect of a Regicide Peace, in a Series of Letters. London. V. 44

Three Memorials on French Affairs, Written in the Years 1791, 1792 and 1793. London: 1797. V. 37; 38; 39; 40; 41

Two Letters Addressed to a Member of the Present Parliament on the Proposals for Peace with the Regicide Directory of France . . . London: 1796. V. 39; 40; 42; 44; 45; 46

Two Letters on the Conduct of Our Domestick Parties, with Regard to French Politicks . . . London: 1797. V. 38; 39; 40; 41; 43

A Vindication of Natural Society . . . London: 1756. V. 42

A Vindication of Natural Society . . . London: 1757. V. 45

The Works . . . Dublin: 1792-93. V. 42

The Works of the Right Honourable Edmund Burke. London: 1801. V. 46

Works. London: 1803. V. 38

The Works. London: 1808-13. V. 43

The Works of the Right Honourable Edmund Burke. London: 1823. V. 39; 46

The Works. London: 1826. V. 42; 46

The Works. London: 1826-27. V. 40

The Works of Edmund Burke. New York: 1837. V. 38; 41

The Works of . . . London: 1854. V. 42

The Works of . . . London: 1854-55-56-57. V. 43

The Works of the Right Honourable Edmund Burke. Boston: 1877. V. 41

The Works. London: 1887. V. 39; 40; 44

The Works of the Right Honourable . . . London: 1887. V. 38; 46

The Works. London: 1891. V. 37

Works. London: 1899. V. 41; 44

The Works of the Right Honourable . . . London: 1899. V. 37; 40; 42; 44

The Works. London: 1908. V. 39

The Works. London: 1975. V. 39

The Works of the Right Honourable Edmund Burke. London: 1826-27. V. 37

Writings and Speeches. Boston: 1901. V. 42

BURKE, EMILY P.

Reminiscences of Georgia. Oberlin: 1850. V. 41

BURKE, HENRY FARNHAM

Examples of Irish Bookplates from the Collections of Sir Bernard Burke. London: 1894. V. 44

BURKE, J.

The Royal Families of England, Scotland and Wales. London: 1848-51. V. 41

BURKE, J. BERNARD

Anecdotes of the Aristocracy. London: 1849. V. 42

Anecdotes of the Aristocracy and Episodes in Ancestral Story. First and Second Series. London: 1849/50. V. 42

The Historic Lands of England. London: 1849. V. 40; 41

A Visitation of the Seats and Arms of the Noblemen and Gentlemen of Great Britain. London: 1852-55. V. 38

BURKE, JACKSON

Prelum to Albion. San Francisco: 1940. V. 46

BURKE, JAMES LEE

Heaven's Prisoners. New York: 1988. V. 44

The Neon Rain. New York: 1987. V. 44

BURKE, JAMES LESTER

The Adventures of Martin Cash. Hobart Town: 1870. V. 40

BURKE, JOHN

A Genealogical and Heraldic History of the Commoners of Great Britain and Ireland . . . London: 1834-38. V. 42

A Genealogical and Heraldic Dictionary of the Landed Gentry of Great Britian and ireland. London: 1848/47. V. 39

A General and Heraldic Dictionary of the Peerage and Baronetage of the United Kingdom for MDCCCXXVI . . . with an Appendix. London: 1826. V. 38

A General Armory of England, Scotland and Ireland. London: 1842. V. 39; 40

BURKE, PETER

The Romance of the Forum, or Narratives, Scenes and Anecdotes from Courts of Justice. London: 1852. V. 39

BURKE, THOMAS

East of Mansion House. London: 1928. V. 40

Go, Lovely Rose. Brooklyn: 1931. V. 43

Limehouse Nights. 1917. V. 39

Limehouse Nights. New York: 1917. V. 45

The London Spy: a Book of Town Travels. London: 1922. V. 39

The Outer Circle. London: 1921. V. 43

Pavements and Pastures. N.P.: 1912. V. 43

The Pleasantries of Old Quong. London: 1931. V. 40; 44

Twinkletoes. London: 1917. V. 43

Whispering Windows. Tales of the Waterside. London: 1921. V. 43

Whispering Windows - Tales of the Waterside. London: 1921. V. 40; 43

Will Someone Lead Me To a Pub? London: 1936. V. 43

The Wind and the Rain: A Book of Confessions. London: 1924. V. 39

BURKE, WILLIAM

An Account of the European Settlements in America. London: 1757. V. 45

An Account of the European Settlements in America. London: 1760. V. 45

Memoirs of William Burke. Hartford: 1837. V. 42

The Mineral Springs of Western Virginia. New York: 1846. V. 41

The Rudiments of Latin Grammar, Founded on the Definitions and Rules of Thomas Ruddiman . . . Richmond: 1832. V. 43

BURKE, WILLIAM P.

The Irish Priests in the Penal Times 1660-1760, from the States Papers in H.M. Record Offices, The Bodleian Library, and the British Museum. Waterford: 1914. V. 38

BURKE, WILLIAM S.

Outline History of Council Bluffs, & Its Railroads: Showing the Commercial Advantages of the City, Its Rapid Progress in The Past & Its Prospects in the Future. Chicago: 1867. V. 37

BURKE'S Handbook to the Most Excellent Order of the British Empire, containing biographies, a full list of persons appointed to the Order, showing their relative precedence, and coloured plates of the Insignia. London: 1921. V. 37

BURKE'S Texas Almanac and Immigrant's Handbook for 1882. Houston: 1881. V. 42

BURKE'S Texas Almanac and Immigrant's Handbook for 1883. Houston: 1882. V. 40

BURKILL, H. M.

Useful Plants of West Tropical Africa. Volume I. Kew Gardens. V. 39

The Useful Plants of West Tropical Africa. Volume I: Familes A-D. London: 1984. V. 37; 38

BURKILL, ISAAC H.

A Dictionary of the Economic Products of the Malay Peninsula. London: 1935. V. 42; 43

BURKITT, F. CRAWFORD

The Hymn of Bardaisan. London: 1899. V. 46

BURKITT, LEMUEL

A Concise History of the Kehukee Baptist Assocation from Its Original Rise to the Present Time. Halifax: 1803. V. 45

BURKITT, WILLIAM

Expository Notes, with Practical Observations on the Four Holy Evangelists. London: 1700. V. 38

Expository Notes, with Practical Observations on the New Testament. New York: 1796. V. 46

BURKLEY, FRANK J.

The Faded Frontier. Omaha: 1935. V. 37; 42

BURLAGE, JOHN

Abstract of Land Claims Compiled from the Records of the General Land Office of the State of Texas . . . Galveston: 1852. V. 38; 40; 45

Abstract of Land Claims, Compiled from the Records of the General Land Office and Court of Claims. Austin: 1859. V. 37

BURLAMAQUI, JEAN JACQUES

The Principles of Natural Law. London: 1752. V. 42

The Principles of Natural and Politic Law. Dublin: 1776. V. 40

The Principles of Natural and Politic Law. London: 1784. V. 40; 43

The Principles of Natural and Politic Law. Oxford and London: 1817. V. 40

BURLAND, BRIAN

A Fall from Aloft. London: 1968. V. 41

A Fall from Aloft. New York: 1969. V. 41

St. Nicholas and the Tub. New York: 1964. V. 41

BURLEIGH, A. H.

John Adams. New Rochelle: 1969. V. 39

BURLEIGH, BENNET

Khartoum Campaign 1898 or the Re-conquest of the Soudan. London: 1899. V. 41

BURLEN, REBECCA

A True Picture of Emigration; or Fourteen Years in the Interior of North America. London: 1848. V. 37; 38; 41; 42; 43; 44; 45

BURLESON, GEORGIA J.

The Life and Writings of Rufus C Burleson. Waco: 1901. V. 37; 38

BURLEY, WALTER c. 1275- c. 1346

Ambrosius Batavus, O. F. M . . . . Sup(er) decem Libros Ethico(rum) Aristotelis . . . Venice: 1521. V. 40

Vitae Philosophorum et Poetarum cum Auctoritatibus et Sententiis Aureis Eorundem Annexis. Hagenau,: 1510. V. 39

BURLINGTON & MISSOURI RIVER RAILROAD CO.

Views & Descritpions of Burlington and Missouri River Railroad Lands . . . Burlington & Lincoln: 1872. V. 38

BURLINGTON, CEDAR RAPIDS AND NORTHERN RAILROAD

Business Directory of the Burlington, Cedar Rapids and Northern Railway. Chicago: 1882. V. 37

BURLINGTON FINE ARTS CLUB

Catalogue of a Collection of Early Drawings and Pictures of London, with Some Contemporary Furniture. London: 1920. V. 41; 42

Catalogue of an Exhibition of Ancient Egyptian Art. London: 1922/21. V. 44

Catalogue of a Collection of Counterfeits, Imitations and Copies of Works of Art. London: 1924. V. 44

Early Venetian Pictures and Other Works of Art. 1912. V. 44

Early Venetian Pictures and Other Works of Art. London: 1912. V. 42

Exhibition of English Embroidery, Executed Prior to the Middle of the XVI Century. London: 1905. V. 37; 39; 44

Exhibition of a Collection of Silversmiths' Work of European Origin. London: 1901. V. 37

The Venetian School: Pictures by Titian and His Contemporaries. 1915. V. 42

BURLIUK, D.

Trebnikh Troikh. (The Service Book of the Three). Moscow: 1913. V. 45

BURMAN, CHARLES

The Lives of Those Eminent Antiquaries Elias Ashmole, Esq. and Mr. William Lilly. London: 1774. V. 41

The Lives of Those Eminent Antiquaries Elias Ashmole, Esquire and Mr. William Lilly . . . with Several Occasional Letters. London: 1774-7. V. 46

BURMAN, JAMES

Statute Laws of the Isle of Man . . . Douglas: 1853. V. 40

Statute Laws of the Isle of Man. London: 1853. V. 40

BURMAN, PETER

Poetae Latinae Minores. Glasguae: 1752. V. 44

BURMANN, J.

Thesaurus Zeylanicus, Exhibens Plantas in Insula Zeylana Nascentes. Amsterdam: 1737. V. 39; 43

BURMANN, PIETER

Vectigalia Populi Romani . . . Leidae: 1734. V. 43

BURMANNUS, PETRUS

Poetae Latini Minores Sive Gratii Falisci Cynegeticon, M. Aurelii Olympii Nemesiani Cynegeticon, et Eiusdem Eclogae IV . . . . Leyden: 1731. V. 41; 46

BURMEISTER, H.

Vues Pittoresques de la Republique Argentine. Berlin: 1881. V. 39

BURMEISTER, HERMAN

The Black Man. New York: 1853. V. 42

BURN, A.

Geodosia Improved . . . London: 1775. V. 42

BURN, EDWARD

A Reply to Dr. Priestley's Appeal to the Public, on the Subject of the Late Riots in Birmingham, in Vindication of the Clery, and Other Respectable Inhabitants of the Town. Birmingham: 1792. V. 39

BURN, J. I.

Case of the Right Hon. Alexander, Earl of Stirling and Dovan, Respecting His Lordship's Title to Nova Scotia, and Other Territorial Possessions in North America . . . London: 1833. V. 43; 45

BURN, JACOB HENRY

A Descriptive Catalogue of the London-Traders, Tavern, and Coffee House Tokens Current in the Seventeenth Century . . . London: 1855. V. 41

BURN, JAMES DAWSON

Three Years Among the Working-Classes in the United States During the War. London: 1865. V. 45

BURN, JOHN

A New Law Dictionary for General Use as well as for Gentlemen of the Profession. Dublin: 1792. V. 37

BURN, JOHN S.

The Fleet Registers. Rivingtons: 1833. V. 44

BURN MURDOCH, WILLIAM GORDON 1862-

From Edinbrugh to the Antarctic. London: 1894. V. 45

From Edinburgh to the Antarctic. London: 1894. V. 41

BURN, RICHARD

Ecclesiastical Law. London: 1763. V. 38

Ecclesiastical Law. London: 1781. V. 45

Ecclesiastical Law. London: 1788. V. 38; 40

The Ecclesiastical Law. London: 1824. V. 40

The Justice of the Peace, and the Parish Officer. London: 1755. V. 37; 38; 44; 46

BURN, RICHARD continued

The Justice of the Peace, and Parish Officer. London: 176. V. 40

The Justice of the Peace and Parish Officer . . . London: 1793. V. 44

The Justice of the Peace, and Parish Officer. London: 1776. V. 37

BURN, ROBERT SCOTT

The New Guide to Masonry, Bricklaying and Plastering, Theoretical and Practical. London: 1868-72. V. 43

The Practical Directory for the Improvement of Landed Property Rural and Suburban and the Economic Cultivation of Its Farms. Edinburgh: 1862. V. 42

Working Drawings and Designs in Architecture and Building. Edinburgh: 1860. V. 37; 40; 44

BURNABY, ANDREW

Reisen Durch Die Mittlern Kolonien der Englander in Nord Amerika . . . Hamburg: 1776. V. 38

Travels through the Middle Settlements in North America, in the Years 1759 and 1760. With Observations Upon the State of the Colonies. Dublin: 1775. V. 43

Travels through the Middle Settlements in North America, in the Years 1759 and 1760. London: 1775. V. 37; 39; 40; 42; 45

Travels Through the Middle Settlements in North America, in the Years 1759 and 1760. London: 1798. V. 43

Travels Through the Middle Settlements in North America, In the Years 1759 and 1760 . . . London: 1798. V. 41

BURNABY, ANTHONY

Two Proposals Humbly Offer'd to the Honourable House of Commons . . . I. That a Duty be Laid on Malt, in the Stead of the Present Duty on Beer and Ale . . . II. That a Duty be Laid on Malt, and the Present Duty on Beer and Ale be Continued. London: 1696. V. 37; 38

BURNABY, FREDERICK GUSTAVUS

On Horseback through Asia Minor. London: 1877. V. 40

A Ride to Khiva. London: 1876. V. 43

A Ride to Khiva; travels and adventures in Central Asia. New York: 1877. V. 37

BURNABY, WILLIAM

The Ladies Visiting-Day. London: 1701. V. 45

The Ladies Visiting-Day. London;: 1701. V. 38; 39; 44; 45

The Reform'd Wife. London: 1700. V. 37

BURNAND, FRANCIS COWLEY

The 'A.D.C.' Being Personal Reminiscences of the University Amateur Dramatic Club, Cambridge. London: 1880. V. 43

Mo Keanna! A Treble Temptation . . . London: 1873. V. 42

The New History of Sandford and Merton. London: 1872. V. 42

BURNAP, GEORGE W.

The Sphere and Duties of Woman and Other Subjects. Baltimore: 1841. V. 45

The Sphere and Duties of Woman. Baltimore: 1848. V. 37

BURNAP, WILLARD A.

What Happened During One Man's Lifetime 1840-1920. Fergus Falls: 1923. V. 45

BURNBY, JOHN

An Historical Description of the Cathedral and Metropolitical Church of Christ, Canterbury. Canterbury: 1772. V. 41

An Historical Description of the Cathedral and Metropolitical Church of Christ, Canterbury: containing an accounts of its antiquities, and of its accidents and improvements, since the first establishment. Canterbury/Oxford: 1772. V. 37

BURNE-JONES, EDWARD 1833-1898

The Beginning of the World. London: 1903. V. 40; 42; 44

The Beginning of the World. Twenty-Five Pictures. Preface by Georgiana Burne-Jones. London: 1902. V. 37; 38; 39; 40; 42; 44

The Flower Book: Reproductions of Thirty Eight Water-Colour Designs by Edward Burne-Jones. London: 1905. V. 43; 44

The Flower Book. London: 1955. V. 38

In the Dawn of the World . . . Boston: 1903. V. 39; 42; 46

Letters to Katie. London: 1925. V. 42

Pictures on Romance and Wonder. New York: 1902. V. 42

The Works . . . London: 1902. V. 38

BURNE-JONES, GEORGINA

Memorials of Edward Burne-Jones. London. V. 46

Memorials of Edward Burne-Jones. London. V. 44

Memorials of Edward Burne-Jones. London: 1904. V. 38; 39

Memorials of Edward Burne-Jones. London: 1906. V. 37

BURNELL, ARTHUR COKE

Elements of South-Indian Palaeography from the Fourth to the Seventeenth Century a.d. Being an Introduction to the Study of South-Indian Inscriptions and Mss. London: 1878. V. 37

BURNES, ALEXANDER

Cabool: Being a Personal Narrative of a Journey to and Residence in that City, in the Years 1836, 7, and 8. London: 1842. V. 40

Cabool: a Personal Narrative of a Journey to and Residence in that City, in the Years 1836, 7 and 8. London: 1843. V. 44; 46

Travels into Bokhara; Being the Account of a Journey from India to Cabool, Tartary and Persia . . . London: 1834. V. 38; 41; 44

Travels into Bokhara. London: 1835. V. 38

BURNES, JAMES

A Sketch of the History of the Knights Templars. London: 1837. V. 38

BURNES, ROBERT

Poems, Chiefly in the Scottish Dialect. Edinburgh: 1787. V. 37

Poems Chiefly in the Scottish Dialect, by Robert Burns. Glasgow: (1900). V. 37

BURNESS, ALEXANDER

The Specific Action of Drugs on the Healthy System . . . London: 1874. V. 45

BURNESS, JOHN

The Comical Story of Thrummy Cap & the Ghaist; to Which is Added William and His Dog. Paisley: 1831. V. 37; 40

BURNET, BISHOP

History of His Own Time. London: 1753. V. 46

BURNET, DAVID G.

David G. Burnet Letters. LaGrange: (1937). V. 37

Government of the Republic of Texas Bond. Austin: 1841. V. 37

BURNET, FRANCES HODGSON

That Lass O' Lowries. New York: 1877. V. 46

BURNET, GILBERT, BP. OF SALISBURY 1643-1715

The Abridgment of the History of the Reformation of the Church of England. London: 1683. V. 39

Bishop Burnet's History of His Own Time. Oxford: 1823. V. 41; 42

The Conversion and Persecutions of Eve Cohan, Now Called Eliabeth Verboon, a Person of Quality of the Jewish Religion. London: 1680. V. 39

A Defence of Natural and Revealed Religion. London: 1737. V. 39

An Edict in the Roman Law: in the 25. Book of the Digests, Title 4. Section 10. As Concnering the Visiting of a Big-Bellied Woman, and the Looking After What May be Born by Her. London: 1688. V. 39

An Essay on the Memory of the Late Queen. London: 1695. V. 45

An Essay on the Memory of the Late Queen. London: 1696. V. 41; 42

An Exhortation to Peace and Union. A Sermon Preached at St. Lawrence-Jury, at the Election of the Lord-mayor of London, on the 29th of September, 1681. (with) A Sermon Preached at the Funeral of . . . John (Tillotson) . . . Lord Archbishop of Canterbury . . . London: 1681, 1694. V. 39

An Exposition of the Thirty-Nine Articles of The Church of England. London: 1705. V. 39

The History of the Reformation of the Church of England. London: 1679/81/1715. V. 38

The History of the Reformation of the Church of England. London: 1681. V. 39; 43

The History of the Reformation of the Church of England. (with) The Third Part, Being a Supplement. London: 1681-83/1715. V. 39; 40; 43

The History of the Reformation of the Church of England. London: 1715. V. 39

The History of the Reformation of the Church of England . . . London: 1715. V. 42

Bishop Burnet's History of His Own Time. London: 1724. V. 40

Bishop Burnet's History of His Own Time. London: 1724-34. V. 39; 40; 42; 44; 46

Bishop Burnet's History of His Own Time. London: 1766. V. 40; 44

History of His Own Time from the Restoration of King Charles II to the Conclusion of the Peace at Utrecht . . . London: 1809. V. 39; 40

Bishop Burnet's History of the Reformation of the Church of England. London: 1820. V. 38; 40

Bishop Burnet's History of His Own Time. Oxford: 1823. V. 42

Bishop Burnet's History of His Own Time. Oxford: 1969. V. 39

The History of the Reformation of the Church of England. Oxford: 1829. V. 46

The History of the Reformation of the Church of England. (with) The Second Part, Of the Progress Made In It Till the Settlement of It Is the Beginning Of Q. Elizabeth's Reign . . . London: 1681/81. V. 46

History of the Rights of Princes in the Disposing of Ecclesiastical Benefices and Churchlands. (with) A Collection of Letters and Instruments that Have Passed During the Late Contests in France Concerning that Regale. London: 1682/81. V. 45; 46

BURNET, GILBERT, BP. OF SALISBURY 1643-1715 continued

The Life and Death of Sir Matthew Hale, Kt. Sometimes Lord Chief Justice of His Majesties Court of Kings Bench. London: 1682. V. 37; 46

The Life of William Dedell, D.D. London: 1685. V. 42

The Life and Death of Sir Matthew Hale . . . London: 1705? V. 45

Life of William Bedell, D.D., Bishop of Kilmore in Ireland. Dublin: 1736. V. 43

The Memoires of the Lives and Actions of James and William Dukes of Hamilton and Castlehearld. London: 1677. V. 44; 45; 46

Reflections on Mr. Varillas's History of the Revolutions that Have Happened in Europe In Matter of Religion. Amsterdam: 1686. V. 42

Relfections on Mr. Varillas's History of the Revolutions that Have Happened in Europe . . . and More Particularly on His Ninth Book that Relates to England. London: 1686. V. 38; 39

A Sermon Preached . . . 1680 at St. Margaret's Westmisnter . . . London: 1681. V. 46

A Sermon Preached in the Chapel of St. James's, Before His Highness the Prince of Orange, the 23rd of December, 1688 . . . London: 1689. V. 41

A Sermon Preach'd at St. brides Before the Lord-Mayor and the Court of Aldermen . . . 1711. London: 1711. V. 40

A Sermon Preached at the Funeral of the Honourable Robert Boyle, at St. Martins in the Fields, January 7. 1691/2. London: 1692. V. 38

Some Passages of the Life and Death of the Right Honourable John Earl of Rochester . . . London: 1680. V. 43

Some Letters Containing, An Account of What Seemed Most Remarkable in Switzerland, Italy &c. Rotterdam: 1686. V. 38; 39; 42; 43

Some Letters Containing an Account of What Seemed Most Remarkable in Travelling through Switzerland, Italy, Some Parts of Germany &c. in the Years 1685 and 1686. London: 1689. V. 40

Some Letters, Containing an Account Of What Seem'd Most Remarkable in Travelling thro' Switzerland, Italy, Some Parts of Germany &c. London: 1729. V. 41

Some Passages in the Life and Death of John, Earl of Rochester, with a Sermon Preached on the Funeral of the Said Earl. London: 1787. V. 37; 39; 40; 41; 43; 46

Some Passages in the Life and Death of John, Earl of Rochester, with a Sermon Preached on the Funeral of the Said Earl. London: 1797. V. 45

Some Passages in the Life and Death of the Earl of Rochester. London: 1805. V. 42

Some Passages in the Life and Death of John Earl of Rochester. London: 1819. V. 41

Three Letters Concerning the Present State of Italy, Written in the Year 1687. London: 1688. V. 42; 44

BURNET, GILBERT, BP. OF SALISBURY 1643-1715

A Vindication of the Bishop of Salisbury and Passive Obedience, with Some Remarks Upon a Speech Goes Under His Lordship's Name, and a Postscript, in Answer to a Book, Just Published' Entitul'd, Some Considerations Humbly Offer'd to the Right Reverend the.. London: 1710. V. 44

BURNET, JACOB

Letters Relating to the Early Settlement of the Northwestern Territory - Contained in a Series Addressed to J. Delafield During the Years 1837-8. Cincinnati. V. 46

Notes on the Early Settlement of the North-Western Territory. Cincinnati: 1847. V. 42

BURNET, JOHN

A Practical Treatise on Painting. London: 1827. V. 45

A Practical Treatise on Painting in Three Parts Consisting of Composition, Chiaroscuro and Colouring. London: 1827. V. 37; 40

A Practical Treatise on Painting. London: 1827-45. V. 44

A Practical Treatise on Painting. London: 1828-1829. V. 41

A Practical Treatise on Painting. London: 1830. V. 44

Practical Hints on Composition in Painting. (with) Practical Hints on Light and Sahde in Painting. (with) Practical Hints on Colour in Painting. London: 1836/35/38/ V. 39

A Treatise on Painting. London: 1835-38. V. 39

A Treatise on Painting in Four Parts. London: 1837. V. 39

BURNET, THOMAS 1635-1715

Archaeologiae Philoshieae; sive Doctrina Antiqua de Rerum Originibus. 1692. V. 41

Archaeologiae Philosophicae . . . Londini: 1692. V. 39; 42

Archaeologiae Philosophicae: Sive Doctrina Antiqua de Rerum Originibus. 1692. V. 37

De Fide & Officiis Christianorum Liber. Londini: 1722. V. 43

Homerides: or a Letter to Mr. Pope, Occasion'd by His Intended Translation of Homer. London: 1715. V. 41; 45

The Sacred Theory of the Earth . . . London: 1726. V. 45

The Sacred Theory of the Earth. London: 1759. V. 40

A Second Tale of a Tub; or, the History of Robert Powell the Puppet Show Man. London: 1715. V. 38; 40; 42; 45

De Statu Mortuorum et Resurgentium Liber. Londini: 1723. V. 43

De Statu mortuorum et Resurgentium Tractatus. (with) De Fide & Officiis Christianorum. London: 1727. V. 38

De Statu Mortuorum et Resurgentium Tractatus. London: 1728. V. 41

Telluris Theoria Sacra: Orbis Nostri Originem & Mutationes Generales, Quas Aut jam subiit . . . 1689. V. 41

Telluris Theoria Sacra . . . Kettilby: 1689. V. 45

Telluris Theoria Sacra: Orbis Nostri Originem & Mutationes . . . Libri Duo Posteriores de Conflagratione Mundi, et de Futuro Rerum Statu. Londini: 1689. V. 40

The Theory of the Earth, Containing an Account of the Original of the Earth, and of all the General Changes Which It Hath Already Undergone . . . London: 1684. V. 43

The Theory of The Earth. (with) An Answer to the Late Exceptions Made by Mr. Erasmus Warren Against the Theory of the Earth. (with) A Review of the Theory of the Earth and of Its Proofs . . . London: 1684 & 1690. V. 40; 42

Thesaurus Medicinae Practicae, ex Prastantissimorum tum Vereum tum Recentiorum Medicorum Observationibus, Consultationibus, Consilius & Epistolis . . . London: 1673. V. 46

A Treatise Concerning the State of Departed Souls Before, and at, and After the Resurrection. London: 1730. V. 39

BURNETT, DAVID

The Heart's Undesign. Edinburgh: 1977. V. 44

The Heart's Undesign. London: 1977. V. 41

Root and Flower; Selected Poems. 1990. V. 45

BURNETT, FRANCES HODGSON 1849-1924

The Captain's Youngest, Piccino & Other Child Stories. London: 1894. V. 45

Haworth's: a Novel. London: 1879. V. 38

In the Closed Room. London: 1904. V. 46

In the Closed Room. New York: 1904. V. 43; 46

Little Lord Fauntleroy. New York: 1886. V. 37; 40; 41; 42; 43; 44

Little Lord Fauntleroy. Toronto: 1887. V. 39

A Little Princess. New York: 1905. V. 45

The One I Knew the Best of All. New York: 1893. V. 43

The Secret Garden. New York: 1911. V. 42; 43; 45

That Lass o'Lowrie. New York: 1877. V. 39

BURNETT, GEORGE

Specimens of the English-Prose Writers, from the Earliest Times to the Close of the Seventeenth Century . . . London: 1807. V. 44

BURNETT, H. C.

1889. New Mexico Winter Edition. New Mexico: 1889. V. 43

BURNETT, HELEN PURVINE

Mary B. Purvine: Pioneer Doctor. Santa Barbara: 1958. V. 42

BURNETT, PETER H.

Address to the Inhabitants of California and New Mexico. New York: 1849. V. 41

Recollections and Opinions of an Old Pioneer. New York: 1880. V. 37; 39; 40; 41; 42; 43; 45

BURNETT, W. R.

The Asphalt Jungle. New York: 1949. V. 41; 42; 44; 46

Badlands. Hollywood: 1961. V. 45

Good-Bye, Chicago. New York: 1981. V. 39

High Sierra. New York: 1940. V. 46

Iron Man. New York: 1930. V. 39; 40; 41; 42

Little Caesar. New York: 1929. V. 40; 44

Vanity Row. New York: 1952. V. 46

BURNEY, CHARLES 1726-1814

An Account of the Musical Performances in Westminster Abbey and the Pantheon . . . 1784. Dublin: 1784. V. 41; 43; 46

An Account of the Musical Performances in Westminster-Abbey, and the Pantheon, May 26th . . . 1784 . . . Dublin: 1785. V. 42; 46

An Account of the Musical Performances in Westminster Abbey, and the Pantheon, May 26th, 27th, 29th and June the 3d, and 5th, 1784. London: 1785. V. 37; 38; 42; 43

An Account of the Musical Performances in Westminster Abbey, and the Pantheon, May 27th . . . June the 3rd and 5th, 1784 . . . London: 1834. V. 42

Dr. Burney's Musical Tours in Europe. Volume I: An Eighteenth Century Musical Tour in France and Italy. Volume 2: An Eighteenth Century Musical Tour in Central Europe and the Netherlands. Edited by Percy Sholes. London: 1959. V. 37; 39

A General History of Music, From the Earliest Ages to the Present Period. London: 1776-89. V. 38; 40; 44; 46

A General History of Music from the Earliest Ages to the Present Period. To which is prefixed a Dissertation on the Musick of the Ancients. London: 1776-89. V. 37; 38

A General History of Music, from the Earliest Ages to the Present Period. London: 1789-82-89-89. V. 37; 39; 41; 42

A General History of Music. New York: 1935. V. 37

Memoirs of the Life and Writings of the Abate Metastasio, in Which are Incorporated Translations of His Principal Letters. London: 1796. V. 38

BURNEY, CHARLES 1726-1814 continued

The Present State of Music in France and Italy. The Present State of Music in Germany, the Netherlands and The United Provinces. London: 1771-1773. V. 37

Tentamen de Metris ab Aeschylo in Choricis Cantibus Adhibitis, In Latin and Greek. Cambridge: 1809. V. 39

BURNEY, FRANCES

Tragic Dramas. London: 1818. V. 38

BURNEY, GILBERT

History of His Own Time. Oxford: 1833. V. 37

BURNEY, JAMES

A Chronological History of the Discoveries in the South Sea or Pacific Ocean. London: 1803-07. V. 42

A Chronological History of the Discoveries in the South Sea or Pacific Ocean. London: 1803-17. V. 40; 45

History of the Buccaneers of America. London: 1816. V. 38; 39; 40; 41

BURNEY, SARAH HARRIET

Traits of Nature. London: 1812. V. 39; 40

Traits of Nature. London: 1813. V. 42

BURNEY, THOMAS

Brachygraphy; or an Easy and Compendious System of Short-Hand . . . London: 1817. V. 44

BURNEY, WILLIAM

The British Neptune; or, a History of the Achievements of the Royal Navy, from the Earliest Periods to the Present Time. London: 1807. V. 38; 42

The Naval Heroes of Great Britain. London: 1806. V. 38

BURNHAM, CARRIE

Woman Suffrage. The Argument of . . . Before Chief Justice Reed and Associate Justices . . . of the Supreme Court of Pennsylvania, in Banc, on the third and fourth of April 1873. Philadelphia: 1873. V. 37

BURNHAM, FREDERICK RUSSELL

Taking Chances. Los Angeles: 1944. V. 41

BURNHAM, JONATHAN

The Life of Col. Jonathan Burnham, Now Living in Salisbury, Mass. Portsmouth: 1814. V. 44

BURNLEY, CYNTHIA B.

'The Aspidistra.' V. 37

BURNLEY, JAMES

The History of Wool and Woolcombing. London: 1889. V. 40; 45

BURNQUIST, JOSEPH ALFRED ARNER

Minnesota and Its People. Chicago: 1924. V. 37; 38

BURNS, A.

Photographs of Edinburgh, with Descriptive Letterpress by R. M. Ballantyne. Glasgow: 1868. V. 41

BURNS, ALLAN 1781-1813

Observations on Some of the Most Frequent and Important Diseases of the Heart . . . Edinburgh: 1809. V. 37; 42

BURNS, BOB

Wyoming's Pioneer Ranches by Three Native Sons of the Laramie Plains. Laramie: 1955. V. 46

THE BURNS Club of St. Louis. St. Louis: 1937. V. 39

BURNS, JABEZ

A Retrospect of Forty Five Years' Christian Ministry: Public Work in Other Spheres of Benevolent Labors and Tours in Various Lands. London: 1875. V. 39

BURNS, JAMES DAWSON

Three Years Among the Working Classes in the United States During the War. London: 1865. V. 42

BURNS, JOHN

The Anatomy of the Gravid Uterus. Boston: 1808. V. 41

Burns' Obstetrical Works. New York: 1809. V. 37

An Historical and Chronological Remembrancer of all Remarkable Occurences from the Creation to His Present Year of Our Lord 1775. Dublin: 1775. V. 44

Observations on Abortion: Containing an Account of the Manner In Which It Takes Place . . . Troy: 1808. V. 43

Observations on Abortion. Springfield: 1809. V. 42

The Principles of Midwifery; Including the Diseases of Women and Children. Philadelphia: 1810. V. 43

BURNS, JOHN H.

Memoirs of a Cow Pony As Told by Himself. Boston: 1906. V. 41; 42

BURNS, ROBERT 1759-1796

An Address to the Devil. London: 1830. V. 41

Burn's Tam O'Shanter. London: 1902. V. 42

The Complete Works. London. V. 43

The Complete Works of . . . London: 1842. V. 41

The Complete Works. Edinburgh: 1883. V. 42

The Complete Works . . . Philadelphia: 1895. V. 46

The Complete Poetical Works of . . . New York: 1900. V. 44

The Complete Writings. Boston & New York: 1926. V. 38; 42

The Complete Writings of Robert Burns. Boston: 1926-27. V. 44

The Complete Poems of Robert Burns. London: 1927. V. 37

The Correspondence Between Burns and Clarinda. Edinburgh: 1843. V. 43; 45

Illustrated Songs. London: 1861. V. 39

The Jolly Beggars: a Cantata. Northampton: 1963. V. 40; 41; 42; 44; 45; 46

Letters Addressed to Clarinda, &C. Glasgow: 1802. V. 37; 40

The Life and Works. Edinburgh and London: 1856-57. V. 45

Not for maids, Ministers, or Striplings. The Merry Muses, a Choice Collection of Favourite Songs Gathered From many Sources . . . London: 1872? V. 43; 46

Poems, Chiefly in the Scottish Dialect. Edinburgh: 1787. V. 37; 38; 40; 41; 42; 43; 44; 46

Poems Chiefly in the Scottish Dialect. New York: 1788. V. 37; 40

Poems Chiefly in the Scottish Dialect. Philadelphia: 1788. V. 44

Poems, Chiefly in the Scottish Dialect. Dublin: 1790. V. 40

Poems, Chiefly in the Scottish Dialect. Edinburgh: 1793. V. 39; 41

Poems Chiefly in the Scottish Dialect. Edinburgh: 1794. V. 37; 42

Poems, Chiefly in the Scottish Dialect. Edinburgh: 1797. V. 45

Poems, Chiefly in the Scottish Dialect. Edinburgh: 1798. V. 41

Poems Chiefly in the Scottish Dialect. Edinburgh: 1800. V. 42

Poems Ascribed to Robert Burns, the Ayrshire Bard, Not Contained in Any Edition of His Works Hitherto Published. Glasgow: 1801. V. 38; 40

Poems, Chiefly in the Scottish Dialect. Cork: 1804. V. 41

Poems Chiefly in the Scottish Dialect. London: 1824. V. 42; 45

The Poems, Letters and Land of Robert Burns. London: 1840. V. 40

Poems and Songs. London: 1858. V. 43

Poems and Songs. Edinburgh: 1868. V. 39; 43

Poems. Boston: 1908. V. 40

Poems, Chiefly in the Scottish Dialect. London: 1909. V. 40

Poems Chiefly in the Scottish Dialect. London: 1927. V. 44

The Poems of Robert Burns. New York: 1965. V. 42

The Poems and Songs of Robert Bruns. London: 1968. V. 39

The Poems and Songs. Oxford: 1968. V. 40

Poems and Songs. Kilmarnock Complete Edition. London: 1869-70. V. 37

Poems Chiefly in the Scottish Dialect. Dublin: 1789. V. 37

Poems, chiefly in the Scottish Dialect. The Third edition. London/Edinburgh: 1787. V. 37

Poems, chiefly in the Scottish Dialect. In Two Volumes. A New edition, considerably enlarged. Edinburgh: 1794. V. 37

The Poems, Letters and Land of Robert Burns. London: 1840. V. 37

Poems. 'The Geddes Burns.: Boston: 1908. V. 37

The Poetical Works. London: 1804. V. 39

The Poetical Works. London: 1808? V. 40

Poetical Works of Robert Burns. Edinburgh: 1896. V. 41

Poetical Works. London. V. 37

The Poetical Works. London: 1839. V. 38

The Poetry. London. V. 38

Poetry. Boston/New York: 1896. V. 37

The Poetry of Robert Burns. Edinburgh: 1896. V. 41

The Poetry of Robert Burns. Edinburgh: 1896-97. V. 46

The Poetry. London: 1900. V. 38

The Prose Works, now first collected. Containing his letters and correspondence, literary and critical; extracts from his journal and commonplace book; and amatory epistles, including letters to Clarinda, &c. Newcastle Upon Tyne: 1816. V. 37

The Prose Works of Robert Burns; containing his Letters and Correspondence . . . and Amatory Epistles, including Letters to Calrinda, &c. &c . . . Newcastle-Upon-Tyne: 1819. V. 37

Reliques of Robert Burns; Consisting Chiefly of Original Letters, Poems and Critical Observations on Scottish Songs. London: 1808. V. 37; 39; 42

Scots Ballads. London: 1939. V. 38

Scots Ballads. London: 1940. V. 42

Sir Patrick Spens. London: 1930. V. 38

The Songs of Robert Burns. London: 1903. V. 41

Songs from Robert Burns. Berkshire: 1925. V. 46

BURNS, ROBERT 1759-1796 continued

Songs from Robert Burns. (London): 1925. V. 37

Songs from Robert Burns. Waltham St. Lawrence: 1925. V. 37; 40; 45

Tam O'Shanter. London: 1902. V. 38; 45

The Works . . . Liverpool: 1800. V. 42

The Works of Robert Burns. London: 1806. V. 38

The Works. Edinburgh: 1809. V. 39

The Works of Robert Burns: With an Account of His Life, and a Criticism on His Writings. London: 1820. V. 39

Works of . . . London: 1834. V. 40

The Works . . . London: 1834. V. 44

The Works . . . London: 1834. V. 46

The Works . . . with His Life, By Allan Cunningham. London: 1834-35. V. 39

The Works . . . London: 1834-35-36. V. 46

The Works. Edinburgh: 1877. V. 42; 44

Works. Edinburgh: 1877-79. V. 38

The Works. Edinburgh: 1878-79. V. 42

The Works. Edinburgh: 1891. V. 42; 44

BURNS, ROBERT HOMER

Wyoming Pioneer Ranches. Laramie: 1955. V. 43

BURNS, THOMAS

Old Scottish Communion Plate. Edinburgh: 1892. V. 37; 40

BURNSIDE, HELEN MARION

Buttercup Pictures. London & New York: 1880. V. 38

Dolly in the Country. London: 1896. V. 39

BURNSIDE, WESLEY M.

Maynard Dixon: Artist of the West. Provo: 1974. V. 39

BURNSIDE, WILLIAM

Theory of Groups of Finite Order. Cambridge: 1897. V. 37

BURNYEAT, JOHN

The Truth Exalted in the Writings of . . . John Burnyeat, Collected Into this Ensuing Volume as a Memorial to His Faithful Labours in and for the Truth. London: 1691. V. 38; 40; 41; 43; 44; 46

BURPEE, L. J.

Among the Canadian alps. London: 1915. V. 44

BURPEE, LAWRENCE J.

Among the Canadian Alps. New York: 1914. V. 46

Journals and Letters of Pierre Gaultier de Varennes de al Verendrye and His Sons. Toronto: 1927. V. 46

Journals and Lettes of La Verendrye and His Sons. Toronto: 1927. V. 45

Jungling in Jasper. Ottawa: 1929. V. 39

On the Old Athabaska Trail. Toronto: 1926. V. 40

The Search for the Western Sea. London: 1908. V. 40

the Search for a Western Sea: the Story of the Exploration of North Western America. Toronto: 1908. V. 45

The Search for the Western Sea. Toronto: 1935. V. 39; 46

BURR, AARON

The Examination of Col. Aaron Burr, Before the Chief Justice of the United States, Upon the Charges of a High Misdemeanor, and Of Treason Against the United States; Together with the Agruments of Counsel and Opinion of the Judge . . . Richmond: 1807. V. 42

An Examination of the Various Charges exhibited against Aaron Burr, Esq. Vice-President of the U.S.; and a Development of the Characters and Views of His Political Opponents. By Arstides. N.P.: 1804. V. 37

The Private Journal of . . . During His Residence of Four Years in Europe . . . New York: 1838. V. 42

BURR, HATTIE A.

The Woman Suffrage Cook Book . . . Contributed Especially for this Work. 1890. V. 45

BURR, JAMES D.

Three Years Among the Working-Classes in the United States During the War. London: 1865. V. 44

BURRARD, G.

Big Game Hunting in the Himalayas and Tibet. London: 1925. V. 39; 42

The Modern Shotgun. London: 1948-51. V. 40

The Modern Shotgun. London: 1951-52. V. 45

BURRARD, GERALD

The Modern Shotgun. London: 1931-32. V. 37

BURRELL, ANDREWES

A Briefe Relation Discovering Plainely the True Causes Why the Great Levell of Fenns in the Severall Counties of Norfolk, Suffolk, Cambridge, Huntington, Northmapton and Lincolne Shires . . . London: 1642. V. 39

BURRELL, JOHN PALFREY

Official Bulletins of the Battle of Waterloos in the Original Languages, with Translations into English. London: 1846. V. 41

BURRELL, MRS.

Thoughts for Enthusiasts at Bayreuth Collected in Memory of 1882 and 1883. London: 1888-89. V. 37

BURRELL, W. H.

Report on the Plauge of Malta in 1813. London: 1854. V. 43

BURRIDGE, BRAINERD MARC

Robert Browning as an Exponent of a Philosophy of Life. Cleveland: 1893. V. 43

BURRIDGE, RICHARD

Hell in an Uproar, Occasioned by a Scuffle that Happened Between the Lawyers and Physicians for Superiority. London: 1700. V. 38

The History of Schism in Europe, to the Great Scandal of the Christian Religion. London: 1714. V. 46

BURRINGTON, GEORGE

Seasonable Considerations of the Expediency of a War with France . . . London: 1743. V. 41; 46

BURRIS, ERNEST J.

Kino and the Cartography of Northwestern New Spain. Tucson: 1965. V. 38; 39

BURRISH, ONSLOW

Batavia Illustrata. London: 1731. V. 37

BURROUGH, EDWARD

A Declaration of the Present Sufferings of Above 140 Persons of the People of God (Who are Now in Prison), Called Quakers. London: 1659. V. 39

A Declaration of the Sad and Great Persecution and Martyrdom of the People of God, Called Quakers, in New England for the Worshipping of God, Wherof 22 Have Been Banished Upon Pain of Death, 03 Have been Martyred, 03 Have Had Their Right Ear Cut off . . . London: 1660. V. 39; 42; 43; 44; 45

The Memorable Works of a Son of Thunder and Consolation. London: 1672. V. 42

The Memorable Works of a Son of Thunder and Consolation . . . Who Died a Prisoner for the Word of God, in the City of London, the Fourteenth of the Twelfth Moneth, 1662. London: 1672. V. 44

BURROUGHS, ALTHEA LAW

For the Little Ones. Savannah: 1861. V. 44

BURROUGHS, CHARLES

A Discourse Delivered in the Chapel of the New Alms-House, in Portsmouth, N.H. Dec 15, 1834 on the Occasion of Its Being First Opened for Religious Services. Portsmouth: 1835. V. 38; 41

BURROUGHS, EDGAR RICE 1875-1950

At the Earth's Core. Chicago: 1922. V. 45

At the Earth's Core. 1968. V. 43

Back to the Stoneage. Tarzana: 1937. V. 37; 39; 46

Back to the Stone Age. Tarzana: 1938. V. 42

The Beasts of Tarzan. Chicago: 1916. V. 38; 44

The Beasts of Tarzan. Racine: 1937. V. 46

Carson of Venus. 1939. V. 43

Carson of Venus. 1939. V. 44

Carson of Venus. Tarzana: 1939. V. 38; 43; 46

The Deputy Sheriff of Comanche County. 1940. V. 37

The Deputy Sheriff of Comanche County. Tarzana: 1940. V. 46

Escape on Venus. Tarzana: 1946. V. 46

The Eternal Lover. Chicago: 1925. V. 43; 45

The Girl From Hollywood. New York: 1923. V. 37

The Gods of Mars. New York: 1920. V. 46

Jungle Tales of Tarzan. Chicago: 1919. V. 46

Jungle Girl. 1933. V. 43

Jungle Girl. London: 1933. V. 37; 45

The Lad and the Lion. 1938. V. 39

The Lad and the Lion. 1938. V. 37

The Lad and the Lion. Tarzana: 1938. V. 43; 46

Land of Terror. 1944. V. 43

Land of Terror. 1944. V. 44

Lallana of Gathol. Tarzana: 1948. V. 46

Llana of Gathol. Tarzana: 1948. V. 37; 41; 42; 43; 44; 45; 46

BURROUGHS, EDGAR RICE 1875-1950 continued

Llana of Gathol. Llana. Tarzana: 1948. V. 45

The Mucker. Chicago: 1921. V. 37

A Princess of Mars. 1917. V. 39

A Princess of Mars. 1917. V. 39

A Princess of Mars. Chicago: 1917. V. 37; 42

A Princess of Mars. Tarzana: 1939. V. 44

The Return of Tarzan. Chicago: 1915. V. 38; 42

The Return of Tarzan. New York: 1915. V. 46

The Son of Tarzan. Chicago: 1917. V. 38; 41; 45

The Son of Tarzan. Chicago: 1917. V. 45

Swords of Mars. 1936. V. 43

The Synthetic Men of Mars. 1940. V. 44

Synthetic Men of Mars. Tarzana: 1940. V. 38; 42; 46

Tarzan of the Apes. Chicago: 1914. V. 39

Tarzan and the Jewels of Opar. Chicago: 1918. V. 40; 42

Tarzan Triumphant. 1932. V. 39

Tarzan and the City of Gold. 1933. V. 43

Tarzan and the Golden Lion. Chicago: 1923. V. 43

Tarzan and the Invincible. Tarzana: 1931. V. 43

Tarzan and the Jewels of Opar. Chicago: 1918. V. 42; 43; 44; 46

Tarzan and the Last Empire. 1929. V. 39

Tarzan and the Leopard Man. 1935. V. 44

Tarzan and the Leopard Man. 1935. V. 43

Tarzan and the Lion Man. 1934. V. 43

Tarzan and the Lion Man. Tarzana: 1934. V. 46

Tarzan and the Lost Empire. 1929. V. 43

Tarzan and the Lost Empire. 1929. V. 37

Tarzan and the Lost Empire. New York: 1929. V. 37; 46

Tarzan and the Lost Empire. New York: (1929). V. 37

Tarzan at the Earth's Core. 1930. V. 43

Tarzan at the Earth's Core. 1930. V. 39

Tarzan of the Apes. 1914. V. 43

Tarzan of the Apes. New York: 1914. V. 44

Tarzan of the Apes. 1932. V. 45

Tarzan the Invincible. Tarzna: 1931. V. 45

Tarzan the Magnificent. Tarzana: 1939. V. 44

Tarzan the Terrible. 1921. V. 44

Tarzan the Terrible. Chicago: 1921. V. 46

Tarzan the Untamed. Chicago: 1920. V. 46

Tarzan Triumphant. Tarzana: 1932. V. 43; 45

Tarzan's Quest. Tarzana: 1936. V. 46

The War Chief. Chicago: 1927. V. 38; 42; 45

The Warlord of Mars. Chicago: 1919. V. 37; 38; 42; 43

BURROUGHS, J.

The Complete Writings. New York: 1924. V. 39

BURROUGHS, JOHN

Alaska. Harriman Alaska Expedition, with Cooperation of Washington Academy of Sciences. New York: 1901. V. 39; 42; 44

Bird and Bough. Boston: 1906. V. 45

Notes on Walt Whitman, as Poet and Person. New York: 1871. V. 41

Wake-Robin. New York: 1871. V. 39; 42; 43; 45

Writings of John Burroughs. 1895. V. 38

The Writings. Boston: 1904-13. V. 38

The Writings of John Burroughs. Boston: 1904-15. V. 44

The Writings of John Burroughs. Boston: 1904-16. V. 46

BURROUGHS, JOHN R.

Guardian of the Grasslands; The First Hundred Years of the Wyoming Stock Growers Assocition. Cheyenne: 1971. V. 38; 43; 46

BURROUGHS, SAMUEL

An Enquiry into the Customary-Estates and Tennant-Rights of Those Who Hold Lands of Church and Other Foundations, by the Tenure of Three Lives and Twenty-One Years. London: 1731. V. 39

BURROUGHS, STEPHEN

Memoirs of Stephen Burroughs. Boston: 1804. V. 41

Memoirs of Stephen Burroughs. Hanover: 1804. V. 37

Sketch of the Life of the Notorious Stephen Burroughs. Ostego: 1810. V. 40

Sketch of the Life . . . Brookfield: 1814. V. 43

BURROUGHS, WILLIAM

Mummies. Dusseldorf & New York: 1982. V. 38

The Streets of Chance. New York: 1981. V. 42

Time. New York: 1965. V. 41

BURROUGHS, WILLIAM S.

APO-33. San Francisco: 1967. V. 45

The Book of Breething. Berkeley: 1980. V. 45

The Cat Inside. 1986. V. 40

Cities of the Red Night. New York: 1981. V. 43

Cobble Stone Gardens. New York: 1976. V. 39; 45

Dead Fingers Talk. 1963. V. 45

Dead Fingers Talk. London: 1963. V. 43

The Dead Star. San Francisco: 1969. V. 46

Doctor Benway: A Passage from 'The Naked Lunch'. Santa Barbara: 1979. V. 37; 43; 44; 45

Early Routines. Santa Barbara: 1981. V. 45

The Exterminator. San Francisco: 1960. V. 45

Junkie. New York: 1953. V. 39; 42; 45

The Last Words of Dutch Schultz. London: 1970. V. 40; 43; 46

Let the Mice In. West Glover: 1973. V. 37

The Naked Lunch. Paris: 1959. V. 37; 39; 40; 42; 43; 45; 46

Naked Lunch. New York: 1962. V. 43; 45

The Naked Lunch. London: 1964. V. 45

Nova Express. London: 1966. V. 45

The Place of Dead Roads. New York: 1983. V. 43

The Place of Dead Roads. New York: 1984. V. 46

Roosevelt After Inauguration. New York: 1964. V. 45

Sidetripping. New York: 1975. V. 43

The Soft Machine. 1961. V. 43

The Soft Machine. Olympia: 1961. V. 42

The Soft Machine. Paris: 1961. V. 42; 45

The Ticket that Exploded. 1962. V. 40

The Ticket That Exploded. Paris: 1963. V. 42

The Ticket that Exploded. Paris: 1962. V. 37; 42; 43; 44; 45

Tornado Alley. Cherry Valley: 1989. V. 43

Where Naked Troubadours Shoot Snotty Baboons. Northridge: 1978. V. 46

White Subway. London: 1973. V. 45

BURROW, E. I.

The Elgin Marbles. London: 1837. V. 39

BURROW, J. C.

'Mongst Mines and Miners; or Underground Scenes by Flash-Light. London: 1893. V. 43; 45

BURROW, JAMES

Reports of Cases Argued and Adjudged in the Court of King's Bench, During the Time of Lord Mansfield Presiding in that Court . . . 1756 to 1772. Dublin: 1794. V. 39

BURROWES, THOMAS H.

Pennsylvania School Architecture . . . Harrisburg: 1855. V. 42; 45

BURROWS, E. I.

Elements of Conchology According to the Linnean System. London: 1844. V. 42; 43

BURROWS, GEORGE

On Disorders of the Cerebral Circulation; and on the Connection Between Affections of the Brain and Diseases of the Heart. Philadelphia: 1848. V. 42

BURROWS, GEORGE MAN

An Inquiry into Certain Errors Relative to Insanity; and Their Consequences; Physical, Moral and Civil. London: 1820. V. 38

BURROWS, GUY

The Curse of Central Africa With Which is Incorporated a Campaign Amongst the Cannibals. London: 1903. V. 40

The Land of the Pigmies. London: 1898. V. 45

BURROWS, JOHN LANSING

The Christian Scholar and Soldier. Raleigh: 1864. V. 44

BURROWS, JOHN M. D.

Fifty Years in Iowa; Being the Personal Reminiscences of J. M. D. Burrows, Concerning the Men and Events, Social Life, Industrial Interests, Physical Development . . . Davenport: 1888. V. 38

BURROWS, MONTAGU

The Family of Brocas of Beaurepaire and Roche Court . . . London: 1886. V. 39

BURROWS, RONALD M.

The Discoveries in Crete and Their Bearing on the History of Ancient Civilisation. London: 1907. V. 40

BURROWS, WILLIAM

Adventures of a Mounted Trooper in the Australian Constabulary . . .
London: 1859. V. 41

BURRUS, ERNEST J.

Kino and Cartography of Northwestern New Spain. 1965. V. 40
Kino and the Cartography of Northwestern New Spain. Tucson: 1965.
V. 38; 39; 40; 42; 43

BURSILL, HENRY

Hand Shadows to be Thrown Upon the Wall. London: 1859. V. 37; 38; 40
hand Shadows to be Thrown Upon the Wall . . . London: 1860. V. 45

BURSON, WILLIAM

A Race for Liberty; or, My Capture, Imprisonment and Escape . . .
Wellsville: 1867. V. 38; 39; 40

BURSTON, G. W.

*Round About the World on Bicycles. The Pleasure Tour of . . . For Private
Circulation Only.* Melbourne, Sydney: 1890. V. 37

BURT, EDWARD

*Letters from a Gentleman in the North of Scotland to His Friend in
London . . .* London: 1754. V. 43

BURT, J. W.

Life and Marvelous Adventures of Wild Bill, the Scout . . . Chicago: 1880.
V. 45

BURT, JOHN T.

*Results of the System of Separate Confinement, as Adminsitered at the
Pentonville Prison.* London: 1852. V. 39

BURT, KATHARINE NEWLIN

The Branding Iron. Boston: 1919. V. 39; 42
A Man's Own Country. Boston: 1931. V. 37; 42

BURT, STRUTHERS

When I Grew Up to Middle Age. New York: 1925. V. 42

BURTHOGGE, RICHARD 1638-1694?

An Essay Upon Reason and the Nature of Spirits. London: 1694. V. 37; 39

BURTIN, FRANCOIS XAVIER

Oryctographie de Bruxelles, ou Description des Fossiles, Tant Naturels . . .
Bruxelles: 1784. V. 42
Treatise on the Knowledge Necessary to Amateurs in Pictures. London:
1845. V. 38; 44; 45

BURTON-BROWN, T.

Excavations in Azarbaijan, 1948. London: 1951. V. 42; 44

BURTON, CHARLES PIERCE

The Bashful Man and Others. Chicago: 1902. V. 37; 41; 43

BURTON, EDWARD

*A Description of the Antiquities and Other Curiosities of Rome, from
Personal Observation During a Visit to Italy in the Years 1818-19.* London:
1828. V. 37; 40; 43

BURTON, FREDERICK R.

American Primitive Music. New York: 1909. V. 44

BURTON, HARLEY TRUE

A History of the J A Ranch. Austin: 1928. V. 37; 39; 42; 45

BURTON, HENRY

*Babel No Bethel. That Is, The Church of Rome No True Visible Church of
Christ.* London: 1629. V. 41; 44
*The Grand Impostor Unmasked, or, a Detection of the Notorious Hypocrisie,
and Desparate Impiety of the Late Archbishop (so styled) of
Canterbury . . .* London: 1644. V. 38
A Narration of the Life of Mr. Henry Burton. London: 1643. V. 40

BURTON, ISABEL

AEI: Arabia, Egypt, India. A Narrative of Travel. London: 1879. V. 37
*The Inner Life of Syria, Palestine and the Holy Land, from My Private
Journal.* London: 1875. V. 40
The Life of Capt. Sir Richard F. Burton. London: 1893. V. 37; 38; 39; 43;
44; 45; 46
The Life of Sir Richard F. Burton by His Wife. London: 1898. V. 43

BURTON, JOHN

*A Genuine and True Journal of the Most Miraculous Escape of the Young
Chevalier, from the Battle of Dulloden, to His Landing in France.* London:
1749. V. 38; 40; 41
Lectures on Female Education and Manners. New York: 1794. V. 44; 45
Lectures on Female Education and Manners. Dublin: 1794. V. 38; 42
Monasticon Eboracense. London: 1758. V. 38; 40

The Parish Priest. London: 1800. V. 40
Trackless Winds. San Francisco: 1930. V. 37

BURTON, JOHN HILL

The Book-Hunter, Etc. Edinburgh: 1862. V. 38; 39
The Book-Hunter. Edinburgh & London: 1862. V. 38
The Book Hunter. 1882. V. 43
The Book-Hunter, Etc. Edinburgh: 1882. V. 45
Life and Correspondence of David Hume. Edinburgh: 1846. V. 42
Life and Correspondence of David Hume. Edinburgh: 1846. V. 37; 41;
42; 45
Political and Social Economy . . . Edinburgh: 1848. V. 45
Political and Social Economy: its Practical Applications. Edinburgh: 1849.
V. 37; 42

BURTON, KATHERINE

The Idolatry of Books, a Collected Edition of the Bibliolatrous Series.
Norton: 1939. V. 37; 41

BURTON, LEWIS W.

*Annals of Henrico Parish, Diocese of Virginia and Especially of St. John's
Church (Richmond), from 1611 to 1884.* Richmond: 1904. V. 42

BURTON, MARIA AMPARO RUIZ

The Squatter and the Don. San Francisco: 1885. V. 44

BURTON, NATHANAEL

Narrative of a Voyage from Liverpool to Alexandria, Touching at Malta . . .
Dublin: 1838. V. 43

BURTON, P.

*Cases with Opinions of Eminent Counsel, In Matters of Law, Equity and
Conveyancing.* London: 1779. V. 40

BURTON, R.

Venus Oceanica. New York: 1935. V. 38

BURTON, R. G.

Sport and Wild Life in the Deccan. Seeley: 1928. V. 42

BURTON, RICHARD

A Christmas Story. London: 1965. V. 44
*Historical Remarks on the Ancient and Present State of the Cities of
London and Westminster.* Westminster: 1810. V. 37
The History of the Kingdom of Ireland. 1811. V. 46

BURTON, RICHARD FRANCIS 1821-1890

Abeokuta and the Camaroons Mountains. London: 1863. V. 37; 46
*Ananga-Ranga; (Stage of the Bodiless One) or, The Hindu Art of Love. (Ars
Amoris Indica.) Translated from the Sanskrit, and Annotated by A.F.F. &
B.F.R.* Cosmopoli: 1885. V. 37
The Book of the Sword. London: 1884. V. 37; 38
*The Book of the Thousand Nights and a Night With Introduction, Explantor
Notes on the Manners and Customs of Moslem Men, and a Terminal
Essay Upon the History of the Nights.* (London): n.d. V. 37
Camoens: His Life and His Lusiads. London: 1881. V. 41; 43
*The Captivity of Hans Stade of Hesse, in A.D. 1547-1555, Among the Wild
Tribes of Eastern Brazil. Translated by Albert Tootal, Esq., of Rio de
Janeiro, and Annotated by Richard F. Burton.* London: 1874. V. 37
*The Carmina of Caius Valerius Catullus Now First Completely Englished into
Verse and Prose, the Metrical Part by Capt. Sir. Richard F. Burton . . . and
the Prose Portion, Introduction, and Notes Explanatory and Illustrative by
Leonard C. Smithers.* London: 1894. V. 37
The City of the Saints and Across the Rocky Mountains to California.
London: 1861. V. 38; 41; 42; 45
The City of the Saints and Across the Rocky Mountains to California.
London: 1862. V. 37; 38; 40
The City of the Saints, and Across the Rocky Mountains to California. New
York: 1862. V. 38; 39; 42; 46
Etruscan Bologna: A Study. London: 1876. V. 37; 38; 39; 41; 43; 44
Explorations of the Highlands of the Brazil. London: 1869. V. 37; 38
Falconry in the Valley of the Indus. London: 1852. V. 37; 43
First Footsteps in East Africa, or, an Exploration of Harar. London: 1894.
V. 45
First Footsteps in East Africa; or, an Exploration of Harar. London: 1856.
V. 37; 38; 40; 41; 42; 43; 44; 46
A Glance at the Passion Play. London: 1881. V. 37
Goa, and the Blue Mountains; or, Six Months of Sick Leave. London: 1851.
V. 37; 43
*The Gold-Mines of Midian and the Ruined Midianite Cities. A Fortnight's
Tour in Norht-Western Arabia. Preface by Lady Burton.* London: 1878.
V. 37; 38; 41; 44
The Guide-Book. A Pictorial Pilgrimage to Mecca and Medina. London:
1865. V. 45; 46
The Gulistan or Rose Garden of Sa'di Faithfully Translated Into English.
Benares: 1888. V. 37
The Highlands of Brazil. London: 1869. V. 41

BURTON, RICHARD FRANCIS 1821-1890 continued

Il Pentamerone; or, the Tale of Tales. Being a Translation by the late Sir Richard Burton . . . of Giovanni Battista Basile, Count of Torone . . . London: 1893. V. 37; 46

The Jew, The Gypsy and El Islam. Edited with a Preface and Brief Notes by W.H. Wilkins. London: 1898. V. 37

The Journal of the Royal Geographical Society. London: 1879. V. 41

The Kasidah of Jahi Abu El-Yezdi: a Lay of the Higher Law. London: 1880. V. 46

The Hasidah of Haji Abdu El Yezdi. London: 1914. V. 42

The Kasidah of Haji Abdu El-Yezdi. San Francisco: 1919. V. 45

The Kasidah of Jahi Abdu El-Yezdi. New York: 1937. V. 46

The Kasidah of Haji Abdu El-Yezdi. Philadelphia: 1931. V. 37; 40

Lacerda's Journey to Cazembe in 1798; Also, Journeys of the Pombeiros P. J. Baptista and Amaro Jose . . . London: 1873. V. 41

The Lake Regions of Central Africa; A Picture of Exploration. London: 1860. V. 37; 38; 40; 41; 43; 44; 45; 46

The Lake Regions of Central Africa. A Picture of Exploration. New York: 1860. V. 37; 41; 43; 46

The Land of Midian (Revisited). London: 1879. V. 44

The Land of Midian (Revisited). London: 1879. V. 38

The Land of Midian (Revisited). London: 1879. V. 37; 38; 39; 41; 43; 44; 45; 46

The Lands of Cazembe. Lagerda's Journey to Cazembe in 1798. London: 1873. V. 41; 42

Letters from the Battlefields of Paraguay. London: 1870. V. 38

Letters from the Battlefields of Paraquay. London: 1879. V. 37

The Life of Sir Richard Burton. New York/London: 1906. V. 37

A Mission to Gelele, King of Dahome. With Notices of the So-Called 'Amazons,' the Grand Customs, the Yearly Customs, the Human Sacrifices, the Present State of the Slave Trade, and the Negro's Place in Nature. London: 1864. V. 37; 38; 40; 43; 46

Narrative of a Pilgrimage to Meccah and Medinah. London & Belfast: 1879. V. 42

Personal Narrative of a Pilgrimage to El-Medinah and Meccah. London: 1855. V. 43

Personal Narrative of a Pilgrimage to El-Medinah and Meccah. London: 1855-56. V. 40; 44

Personal Narrative to El-Medinah and Meccah. London: 1855, v.3 1856. V. 44

Personal Narrative of a Pilgrimage to El-Medinah and Meccah . . . New York: 1856. V. 40

Personal Narrative of a Pilgrimage to Mecca and Medina. Leipzig: 1874. V. 46

Personal Narrative of a Pilgrimage to Al-Madinah & Meccah . . . London: 1893. V. 38; 41; 45

Personal Narrative of a Pilgrimage to Al-Madinah and Meccah . . . London: 1898. V. 44

Personal Narrative of a Pilgrimage to El-Medinah and Meccah. London: 1857. V. 37

A Plain and Literal Translation of the Arabian Nights' Entertainments, Now Entitled the Book of The Thousand Nights an a Night. With Introduction, Explanatory Notes, and a Terminal Essay . . . by Capt. R.F. Burton. (London): 1910. V. 37

Priapeia or the Sportive Epigrams of divrs Poets on Priapus: the Latin Text now for the first time Englished in Verse and Prose (the Metrical Version by 'Outidanos') with Introduction, Notes Explantory and Illustrative, and . . . Cosmopoli: 1890. V. 37; 41

Scinde: or, The Unhappy Valley. London: 1851. V. 44; 45

Selected Papers on Anthropology, Travel & Exploration. London: 1924. V. 37; 38; 41; 44; 46

Selected Papers on Anthropology, Travel and Exploration. London: 1925. V. 39

Sind Revisited: With Notices of the Anglo-Indian Army . . . London: 1877. V. 38

To The Gold Coast for Gold. A Personal Narrative. London: 1883. V. 37

Two Trips to Gorilla Land and the Cataracts of the Congo. London: 1876. V. 37

Ultima Thule; or, A Summer in Iceland. London: 1875. V. 37; 38; 41; 42; 43; 44

Unexplored Syria: Visits to the Libanus, the Tulul et Safa, the Anti-Libanus, the Norther Libanus, and the 'Alah. London: 1872. V. 38; 39; 41; 42

Vakram and the Vampire; or, Tales of Hindu Devilry. Adapted by Richard F. Burton. London: 1870. V. 37

Vikram and the Vampire or Tales of Hindu Devilry adapted by . . . Edited by his Wife Isabel Burton. With 33 Illustrations by Ernest Griset and a New Photogravure Frontispiece by Albert Letchford. London: 1893. V. 37

Voyage Aux Grands Lacs de l'Afrique Orientale. Paris: 1862. V. 40

Wanderings in Three Continents. London: 1901. V. 41

Wanderings in West Africa from Liverpool to Fernando Po. By a F.R.G.S. London: 1863. V. 37; 38; 39; 40; 44

The Memorial edition of the Works of . . . . London: 1893-94. V. 45

Zanzibar; City, Island and Coast. London: 1872. V. 43; 46

BURTON, ROBERT 1577-1640

The Anatomy of Melancholy. Boston. V. 46

The Anatomy of Melancholy. Oxford: 1621. V. 38; 39; 40; 46

The Anatomy of Melancholy. Oxford: 1624. V. 38

The Anatomy of Melancholy. Oxford: 1628. V. 40; 46

The Anatomy of Melancholy. Oxford: 1632. V. 37; 39; 40; 41

The Anatomy of Melancholy. London: 1651. V. 40

The Anatomy of Melancholy. Oxford: 1651. V. 39

The Anatomy of Melancholy. London: 1652. V. 46

The Anatomy of Melancholy . . . London: 1660. V. 38

The Anatomy of Melancholy. London: 1676. V. 37; 38; 40; 41

The Anatomy of Melancholy . . . London: 1800. V. 46

The Anatomy of Melancholy . . . London: 1804. V. 42

The Anatomy of Melancholy. London: 1806. V. 40; 42; 43; 46

The Anatomy of Melancholy . . . London: 1854. V. 42

The Anatomy of Melancholy. London: 1883. V. 46

The Anatomy of Melancholy. London: 1893. V. 38; 40; 46

The Anatomy of Melancholy. London: 1923. V. 38

The Anatomy of Melancholy. London: 1925. V. 39; 40; 41; 44; 45

The Anatomy of Melancholy. London: 1935. V. 39

The Anatomy of Melancholy. 1989. V. 46

The Anatomy of Melancholy. Oxford: 1638. V. 37

The Anatomy of Melancholy. London: Prtd. for H. Cripps: 1660. V. 37

The Anatomy of Melancholy . . . London: 1660. V. 37

Melancholy; As It Proceeds from the Dispostion and Habit, the Passion of Love, and the Influence of Religion. London: 1801. V. 46

BURTON, W. K.

The Water Supply of Towns and the Construction of Waterworks, a Practical Treatise. London: 1928. V. 44

BURTON, WARREN

The District School As It Was, Scenery-Showing and Other Writings. Boston: 1852. V. 46

BURTON, WILLIAM 1609-1657

A Commentary on Antoninus His Itinerary, or Journies of the Romane Empire, So Far As It Concerneth Britain . . . L: 1658. V. 43

A Commentary on Antoninus His Itinerary or Journies of the Romane Empire, so Far As It Concerneth Britain. London: 1658. V. 39; 40; 45

Description of Leicestershire. London: 1622. V. 41; 44

The Description of Leicestershire. Lynn: 1777. V. 41

A General History of Porcelain. London: 1921. V. 42

A History and Description of English Earthenware and Stoneware to the Beginning of the 19th Century. London: 1904. V. 39

BURTON, WILLIAM E.

The Cyclopaedia of Wit and Humor. New York: 1867. V. 39

BURTON, WILLIAM WESTBROOKE

The State of Religion and Education in New South Wales. London: 1840. V. 46

BURWELL, LETITIA

Plantation Reminiscences. Richmond: 1878. V. 38

BURWELL, WILLIAM M.

Memoir Explantory of the Transunion and Tehuantepec Route Between Europe and Asia. Washington: 1851. V. 39; 43

BURY, ADRIAN

John Varley of the Old Society. Leigh-on-Sea: 1946. V. 38; 40; 42; 44

Richard Wilson, R.A. the Grand Classic. Leigh-on-Sea: 1947. V. 39

BURY, CHARLOTTE SUSAN MARIA 1775-1861

Conduct is Fate. Edinburgh: 1822. V. 44

The Exclusives. (with) A key to the Royal Novel the Exlusives!!! London: 1830. V. 46

Family Records; or, The Two Sisters. Paris: 1841. V. 46

The History of a Flirt. London: 1841. V. 44

The Roses. London: 1853. V. 42

The Separation. London: 1830. V. 37; 38

The Three Great Sanctuaries of Tuscany, Valombrosa, Camaldoli, Laverna. London: 1833. V. 38; 40

BURY, P. S.

Polycystins. London: 1869. V. 39

BURY, SAMUEL

An Account of the Ofe and Death of Mrs. Elizabeth Bury, Who Died, May the 11th, 1720, Aged 76. Boston: 1743. V. 43

BURY, THOMAS TALBOT 1811-1877

Coloured Views on the Liverpool and Manchester Railway, with Plates of the Coaches, Machines . . . London: 1831. V. 39

BURY, THOMAS TALBOT 1811-1877 continued

Coloured Views on the Liverpool and Manchester Railway . . . London: 1833. V. 39; 46

Coloured Views on the Liverpool and Manchester Railway. Oldham: 1977. V. 39

Remains of Ecclesiastical Woodwork. London: 1847. V. 38

Remains of Ecclesiastical Woodwork. London: 1847. V. 46

Six Coloured Views on the Liverpool and Manchester Railway with a Plate of the Coarches, Machines, etc. from Drawings Made on the Spot. London: 1831. V. 39; 44

BUSBECQ, OGIER GHISLAIN DE

Omnia Quae Extant; Quibus Accedit Epitome De Moribus Turcarum . . . London: 1660. V. 37

BUSBEQ, OGIER GISELIN

Itinera Constantinopolitanum et Amasianum . . . ad Sollimannum Turcarum Imperatorem. Antwerp: 1581. V. 41

BUSBY, ALLIE B.

Two Summers Among the Musquakies, Relating to the Early History of the Sac and Fox Tribe. Vinton: 1880. V. 37; 42; 45

BUSBY, CHARLES AUGUSTUS

An Essay on the Propulsion of Navigable Bodies. New York: 1818. V. 42

BUSBY, JAMES

Journal of a Recent Visit to the Principal Vineyards of Spain and France. New York: 1835. V. 39; 45

BUSBY, RICHARD

Graecae Grammatices Rudimenta in Usum Scolae Westmonsteriensis. London: 1671. V. 46

Graece Grammatices Rudimenta. London: 1693. V. 45

Rudimentum Anglo-Latinum Grammaticae Literalis & Numeralis . . . London: 1688. V. 39

BUSBY, T. L.

Costume of the Lower Orders of London. London: 1820. V. 43

The Fishing Costume and Local Scenery of Hartlepool, in the County of Durham. London: 1819. V. 42

BUSBY, THOMAS

A Complete Dictionary of Music. London: 1806. V. 44

A Complete Dictionary of Music. London: 1801. V. 37

A General History of Music, from the Earliest Times to the Present Condensed from the Works of Sir John Hawkins and Charles Burney . . . London: 1819. V. 37; 46

A Grammar of Music: To Which is Prefixed Obsergations Explanatory of the Properties and Powers of Music as a Science. London: 1818. V. 38; 39; 40; 41; 42

Rugantino, or the Bravo of Venice. London: 1805. V. 40

BUSCH, GEORG

Beschreibung von Zugehorigen Eigenschafften und Naturlicher Influentz des Grossen und Erschrecklichen Cometen Welcher in Diesem 1577. Erfurt: 1577. V. 38

BUSCH, J. G.

The Practical Correspondent for Merchants. Hamburg: 1800. V. 39; 41

BUSCH, MAX

Max and Moritz, a Story in Seven Tricks. Munich: 1874. V. 40

BUSCH, WILHELM

A Bushel of Merry-Thoughts. London: 1868. V. 37

Max and Maurice. Boston: 1899. V. 38

BUSCHMANN, J. C.

Das Apache als eine Athapaskische Sprache Erwiesen . . . (with) Die Verwandtschafts-Verhaltnisse der Athapskischen Sprachem . . . (and) Systematische Worttafel des Athapaskischen Sprachstmms . . . Berlin: 1860-63. V. 38

BUSH, BELLE

Voices of the Morning. Philadelphia: 1865. V. 38

BUSH, GEORGE

The Valley of Vision; or the Dry Bones of Israel Revived. New York: 1844. V. 43

BUSH, I. J.

Gringo Doctor. Caldwell: 1939. V. 46

BUSH, MARTIN H.

Ben Shahn: The Passion of Sacco and Vanzetti. 1968. V. 38

BUSH, RICHARD J.

Reindeer, Dogs and Snow-Shoes; a Journal of Siberian Travel and Explorations Made in the Years 1865, 1866 and 1867. New York: 1871. V. 41; 43

BUSHBY, HENRY JEFFREYS

A Month in the Camp Before Sebastopol. London: 1855. V. 45

BUSHBY, JAMES

Authentic Information Relative to New South Wales and New Zealand. London: 1832. V. 39

BUSHE, AMYAS

Socrates, a Dramatic Poem. London: 1758. V. 43

Socrates: a Dramatic Poem. London: 1768. V. 40

BUSHE, PETER KENDAL

Through the Troposcope. Paris and London: 1966. V. 46

BUSHELL, SETH

The Believers Groan for Heaven: in a Sermon at the Funeral of the Honorable Sir Richard Hoghton of Hoghton Baronet. London: 1678. V. 44

BUSHELL, STEPHEN W.

Chinese Art. London: 1904-10. V. 42

Chinese Art. London: 1905. V. 41

Chinese Art. London: 1905-06. V. 37; 41

BUSHNAN, JOHN STEVENSON

Hints on Certifying in Cases of Insanity. Salisbury: 1862. V. 46

BUSHNELL, HORACE

Barbarism the First Danger: a Discourse for Home Missions. New York: 1847. V. 46

BUSHNELL, WILLIAM P.

The Mexican Petroleum Company, Limited. N.P.: 1913. V. 46

A BUSINESS Outing in Texas. A Visit of the Commercial Club of Kansas City to Northern Texas, Indian Territory, Oklahoma and Kansas. Kansas City: (1891). V. 37; 43

BUSSAGLI, MARIO

5000 Years of the Art of India. New York. V. 38

5000 Years of the Art of India. New York. V. 41

BUSSATO, MARCO

Giardino D'Agricoltura Di . . . Da Ravenna, Nel Quale, Con Bellissimo Ordine . . . In Venetia: 1612. V. 38

BUSSY, ROGER DE RABUTIN, COMPTE DE 1618-1693

La France Galante ou Histoires moureuses de la Cour. Cologne: 1695. V. 38

BUSTAMANTE, CARLOS MARIA DE

El Gabinete Mexicano . . . Mexico: 1842. V. 38

BUSTAMENTE, CARLOS MARIA DE

Mananas De La Alameda de Mexico. Mexico City: 1835-36. V. 38

BUSTI, BERNARDINUS DE

Mariale. Milan: 1493. V. 37

Rosarium Sermoum (with Additions by Illuminatus Novariensis and Samuel Cassinensis). Hagenau. V. 45

Rosarium Sermonum (with additions by Illuminatus Novariensis and Samuel Cassinensis). Venice: 1498. V. 45

BUTCHER, DAVID

The Whittington Press: a Bibliography 1971-1981. 1982. V. 40

The Whittington Press. A Bibliography 1971-1981 . . . Andoversford: 1982. V. 45

The Whittington Press: A Bibliography, 1971-1981. Gloucestershire: 1982. V. 38

BUTCHER, E.

Sidmouth Scenery, or Views of the Principal Cottages and Residence of the Nobility and Gentry. Sidmouth: 1817. V. 46

BUTCHER, EDMUND

The Beauties of Sidmouth Displayed. Sidmouth: 1825. V. 39

BUTCHER, RICHARD

The Survey and Antiquity of the Towns of Stamford in the County of Lincoln and Tottenham-High-Cross in Middlesex. London: 1717. V. 38; 40; 43

BUTEL-DUMONT, GEORGES MARIE

Histoire et Commerce des Colonies Angloises, dans l'Amerique Septentrionale. London & Paris: 1755. V. 41; 45

BUTEL-DUMONT, GEORGES MARIE continued

Histoire et Commerce des Colonies Angloises, dan l'Amerique Septentrionale ou l'on Trouve l'Etat Actuel de Leur Population & des Details Curieux sur la Constitution de Leur Gouvernement, Principalement sur Celui de la Nouvelle-Angleterre . . . La Haye: 1755. V. 39

BUTEONIS, JOHANNES

Del Phinatici Opera Geometrica, Quorum Tituli Sequuntur. Colophon: 1554. V. 43; 45

BUTLER, A. G.

Foreign Finches in Captivity. London: 1899. V. 41

BUTLER, A. S. G.

The Architecture of Sir Edwin Lutyens. London: 1950. V. 38

BUTLER, ALBAN

Lives of the Fathers, Martyrs, and Other Principal Saints . . . etc. (By A. Butler). London: 1756-59. V. 37

BUTLER, ALFRED J.

The Ancient Coptic Churches of Egypt. Oxford: 1884. V. 42

BUTLER, ANNA B.

Centennial Records of the Women of Wisconsin. Madison: 1876. V. 37

BUTLER, ARTHUR GARDINER

Birds of Great Britain and Ireland. London: 1908. V. 42

Birds' Eggs of the British Isles. London: 1904. V. 43

Birds of Great Britain and Ireland. London: 1904-08. V. 43

British Birds with Their Nests and Eggs. London: 1896-98. V. 37; 38

British Birds, with Their Nests and Eggs. London: 1899. V. 46

Foreign Finches in Captivity. London: 1899. V. 39

Foreign Finches in Captivity. London: 1894. V. 38; 40

Foreign Finches in Captivity. London: 1894-96. V. 43; 44

Foreign Finches in Captivity. Hull and London: 1899. V. 46

Foreign Finches in Captivity. London: 1899. V. 37; 42; 43

BUTLER, ARTHUR GARDNER

Birds of Great Britain and Ireland, Order Passeres. London: 1907-08. V. 39

BUTLER, ARTHUR STANLEY GEORGE 1888-

The Architecture of Sir Edwin Lutyens. London: 1984. V. 40

The Work of Sir Edward Lutyens. 1984. V. 42

BUTLER, B. C.

Lake George and Lake Champlain, from Their First Discovery to 1759. Albany: 1868. V. 43; 46

BUTLER, BENJAMIN F.

Proclamation (Declaring a State of Martial Law). Headquarters Dept. of the Gulf. May 1, 1862. New Orleans: 1862. V. 41

BUTLER, BENJAMIN FRANKLIN

Private and Official Correspondence of Gen. Benjamin F. Butler, During the Period of the Civil War. Norwood: 1917. V. 37; 39

BUTLER, CHARLES

Reminiscences. London: 1822. V. 43

BUTLER, E. A.

A Catalogue of the Birds of Sind (etc.) Contributed to the Bombay Gazetteer. Bombay: 1879. V. 43

BUTLER, ELIZABETH BEARDSLEY

Women and the Trades. Pittsburgh, 1907-1908. New York: 1909. V. 40; 45

BUTLER, ELLIS PARKER

Philo Gubb. Correspondence School Detective. Boston & New York: 1918. V. 39

'Pigs Is Pigs.' Chicago-New York: 1905. V. 37

BUTLER, FRANCES ANNE KEMBLE 1809-1893

Journal. London: 1835. V. 37

Journal of a Residence on a Georgia Plantation in 1838-1839. London: 1863. V. 38

Journal of a Residence on a Georgian Plantation in 1838-1839. New York: 1863. V. 39

The Journal of . . . Philadelphia: 1835. V. 37

Records of a Girlhood. London: 1878. V. 37

BUTLER, FRANCIS GOULD

A History of Farmington, Franklin County, Maine, from the Earliest Explorations to the Present Time, 1776-1885. Farmington: 1885. V. 46

BUTLER, FREDERICK

The Farmer's Manual. Hartford: 1819. V. 41

The Farmer's Manual, Being a Plain Practical Treatise on the Art of Husbandry . . . Weathersfield: 1821. V. 39; 42

BUTLER, HENRY

South African Sketches. London: 1841. V. 45

BUTLER, HENRY D.

The Family Aquarium; or Acqua Vivarium. New York: 1858. V. 44

BUTLER, HERBERT J.

Motor Bodywork. London: 1924. V. 38

BUTLER, HILLARY

The Mayor of Wigan, a Tale. London: 1760. V. 38; 45

BUTLER, HOWARD CROSBY

Sardis: Volume I: The Excavations. Part I: 1910-1914. Leyden: 1922. V. 42

BUTLER, HUBERT

The Story of Tobit. 1970. V. 38

The Story of Tobit. London: 1970. V. 40

BUTLER, ISABEL

Our Lady's Tumbler: a Tale of Mediaeval France. Boston: 1898. V. 41

BUTLER, J.

The Most Sacred and Divine Science of Astrology. London: 1680. V. 37

BUTLER, JAMES

American Bravery Displayed, in the Capture of Fourteen Hundred Vessels of War and Commerce Since the Declaration War by the President. Carlisle: 1816. V. 39; 45

BUTLER, JAMES D.

Nebraska. Its Characteristics and Prospects. N.P.: 1873. V. 42

BUTLER, JOHN

A Consultation on the Subject of a Standing Army Held at the King's Arms Tavern on the Twenty-Eighth Day of February 1763. London: 1763? V. 37

A Sketch of Assam with Some Account of the Hill Tribes. London: 1847. V. 39

Some Account of the Character of the Late Right Honourable henry Bilson Legge. London: 1764. V. 45

Travels and Adventures in the Province of Assam, During a Residence of Fourteen Years. London: 1855. V. 39; 45

BUTLER, JOHN C.

Historical Record of Macon and Central Georgia, Containing Many Interesting and Valuable . . . Macon: 1879. V. 45

BUTLER, JOSEPH 1692-1752

The Analogy of Religion, Natural and Revealed, to the Constitution and Course of Nature. Dublin. V. 40

The Analogy of Religion. Dublin: 1736. V. 40

The Analogy of Religion, Natural and Revealed, to the Constitution and Course of Nature. London: 1736. V. 38; 39; 42; 45

The Analogy of Religion, Natural and Revealed . . . Boston: 1793. V. 40

Fifteen Sermons Preached at the Rolls Chapel. London: 1726. V. 40

The Works. Oxford: 1836. V. 38; 39

The Works of . . . Oxford: 1874. V. 38

BUTLER, JOSEPHINE E.

Government by Police. London: 1879. V. 42

The Salvation Army in Switzerland. London: 1883. V. 39

BUTLER, LEWIS

The Annals of the King's Royal Rifle Corps. London: 1913-71. V. 41

BUTLER, M. B.

My Story of the Civil War and the Underground Railroad. Huntington: 1914. V. 45

BUTLER, MANN

A History of the Commonwealth of Kentucky. Louisville: 1834. V. 37; 38; 39; 40; 44; 45; 46

BUTLER, PIERS EDMUND

Raymond, a Tale of the Nineteenth Century; and other Poems. Dublin: 1830. V. 37

BUTLER, RICHARD

An Essay Concerning Blood-Letting . . . London: 1734. V. 37

BUTLER, RUTH LAPHAM

A Bibliographical Check List of North and Middle American Indian Linguistics in the Edward E. Ayer Collection. Chicago: 1941. V. 43

A Bibliographical Check List of North and Middle American Indian Linguistics in the Edward E. Ayer Collection. Chicago: 1949. V. 41

BUTTERFIELD, CONSUL WILSHIRE continued

History of the Girtys. Cincinnati: 1890. V. 39

History of Brule's Discoveries and Explorations 1610-1626. Cleveland: 1893. V. 39

History of Brule's Discoveries and Explorations 1610-1626 . . . Cleveland: 1898. V. 46

The Washington-Crawford Letters. Cincinnati: 1877. V. 45

Washington-Irvine Correspondence. Madison: 1882. V. 39

Washington-Irvine Correspondence. Madison: 1882. V. 45

BUTTERFIELD, DANIEL

Camp and Outpost Duty for Infantry . . . New York: 1863. V. 40

THE BUTTERFLY. London: 1893. V. 40
THE BUTTERFLY. (London): (1899-1900). V. 37

BUTTERWORTH, ADELINE

William Blake, Mystic: a Study Together with Young's Night Thoughts: Nights I and II. London: 1911. V. 45

BUTTERWORTH, ADELINE M.

William Blake: a Study. London & Liverpool: 1911. V. 39

BUTTERWORTH, BENJAMIN

The Growth of Industrial Art . . . Washington: 1888. V. 39

The Growth of Industrial Art. Washington: 1892. V. 44

BUTTLES, JANET R.

The Queens of Egypt. London: 1908. V. 44

BUTTON, EDWARD

A New Translation of the Persian Tales, From an Original Version of the Indian Comedies of Mocles . . . London: 1754. V. 43

BUTTRE, J. C.

Catalogue of Engravings by J. C. Buttre, Publisher, Engraver and Plate Printer. New York: 1870. V. 44

BUTTRICK, DANIEL S.

Antiquities of the Cherokee Indians. Vinita: 1884. V. 43

BUTTRICK, TILLY

Voyages, Travels and Discoveries of . . . Boston: 1831. V. 37; 38; 40; 42; 45

BUTTS, MARY

Armed with Madness. London: 1928. V. 37; 39; 42; 45

Ashe of Rings. Paris: 1925. V. 37; 42

Ashe of Rings. 1933. V. 42

Ashe of Rings. London: 1933. V. 42

The Crystal Cabinet - My Childhood at Salterns. London: 1937. V. 37; 41; 42

iMAGINARY iETTERS. pARIS. V. 45

Imaginary Letters. Paris. V. 45

Imaginary Letters. Paris: 1929. V. 38

Imaginary Letters. With Engravings on Copper from the Original Drawings by Jean Cocteau. Paris: 1928. V. 37; 40; 42; 43

Last Stories. London: 1938. V. 37; 39

The Macedonian. London: 1933. V. 37; 42

Scenes from the Life of Cleopatra. London: 1935. V. 43; 45

Scenes from the Life of Cleopatra. London: 1937. V. 37; 42

Several Occasions. London: 1932. V. 42

Speed the Plough and Other Stories. London: 1923. V. 40; 41; 45

Traps for Unbelievers. London: 1932. V. 37; 40; 42

BUTTS, SARAH HARRIET

The Mothers of Some Distinguished Georgians of the Last Half of the Century. New York: 1902. V. 43; 46

BUXTOF, JOHANN 1564-1629

Lexicon Chaldaicum Talmudicum et Rabbinicum, In Quo Omnes Voces Chaldaicae . . . Basileae: 1639. V. 46

BUXTON, CHARLES

An Inaugural Dissertation on the Measles. New York: 1793. V. 42

Memoirs of Sir Thomas Fowell Buxton, Baronet. London: 1848. V. 42

BUXTON, EDWARD NORTH

Short STalks; or Hunting Camps, North, South, East and West. London: 1892. V. 44

Short Stalks; or, Hunting Camps North, South, East and West. London: 1892/98. V. 45

Short STalks or Hunting Camps North, South, East and West. London: 1893. V. 39; 42

Short Stalks; or, Hunting Camps North, South, East and West. London: 1893 & 1898. V. 39; 40; 43

Two African Trips with Notes and Suggestions on Big Game Preservation in Africa. London: 1902. V. 39; 43; 44

BUXTON, GEORGE

The Political Quixote; or, the Adventures of the Renowned Don Blackibo Dwarino, and His Trusty 'Squire Seditiono'. London: 1820. V. 37

BUXTON, GEORGE FREDERICK

Life in the Far West. Edinburgh and London: 1851. V. 45

BUXTON, THOMAS FOWELL 1786-1845

The African Slave Trade. London & New York: 1840. V. 40

The African Slave Trade. London: 1839. V. 37; 46

An Inquiary, Whether Crime and Misery are Produced or Prevented by Our Present System of Prison Discipline. London: 1818. V. 39; 42; 43

Memoirs of Sir Thomas Fowell Buxton. London: 1848. V. 39

Speech in the House of Commons, Wednesday, Mary 23rd, 1821. The Bill 'for Mitigating the Severity of Punishment in Certain Cases of Forgery, and the Crimes Connected Therewith.' London: 1821. V. 37; 39

BUXTORF, JOHANNIS

Grammaticae Chaldaicae et Syriacae. Libri III. Basle: 1615. V. 37

Thesaurus Grammaticus Linguae Sanctae Hebraeae, Duobus Libris Methodice Propositus . . . Basilea: 1629. V. 37

THE BUYER'S Manual and Business Guide; Being a Description of the Leading Business Houses, Manufactories, Inventions, etc. of the Pacific Coast, together with copious and Readable Selections, Chiefly from California Writers. San Francisco: 1872. V. 37; 38

BUYICK, T. LINDSAY

New Zealand's First War, or the Rebellion of Hone Heke. Wellington: 1926. V. 42

BUYS, PIETER

Authoritatum Sacrae Scripturae, et Sanctorum Patrum, Quae in Summa Doctrinae Christianae Doctoris Petri Canisii . . . Citanur. Venice: 1571. V. 37

BUZACOTT, AARON

E Aronga Imene: Koia Oki Te Tuatua Akameitaki I Te Atua. Raratonga: 1843. V. 40

BUZZELL, JOHN R.

Trial of John R. Buzzell, the Leader of the Convent Rioters, for Arson and Burglary. Boston: 1834. V. 44

BY-LAWS of the Blue Ledge Gold and Silver Quartz Mining Company. San Francisco: 1863. V. 37

BYAM, LYDIA

A Collection of Exotics, from the Island of Antigua. London: 1797. V. 38

A Collection of Fruits from the West Indies, Drawn and Coloured from Nature . . . London: 1800. V. 37; 42

BYAM, W.

The Practice of Medicine in the Tropics. London: 1921-23. V. 45

BYATT, A. S.

The Tame. London: 1967. V. 46

BYE, JOHN O.

Back Trailing in the Heart of the Short-Grass Country. Everett: 1956. V. 38; 43; 44

BYERS, CHESTER

Roping, Trick and Fancy Rope Spinning. New York: 1928. V. 39

BYERS, S. H. M.

What I Saw In Dixie . . . Dansville: 1868. V. 42

With Fire and Sword. New York: 1911. V. 44

BYERS, SAMUEL HAWKINS MARSHALL

Iowa. Read at the Semi-centennial Burlington. Des Moines. V. 38

BYERS, WILLIAM N.

Encyclopedia of Biography of Colorado: History of Colorado. Chicago: 1901. V. 37

BYFIELD, NATHANIEL

An Account of the Late Revolution in New-England. London: 1689. V. 39

BYFIELD, NICHOLAS

A Commentary Upon the Three First Chapters of the First Epistle Generall of St. Peter. London: 1637. V. 46

BYFIELD, TIMOTHY

Some Plain Directions for the Use of Our Sal Oleosum Volatile. London: 1710? V. 42

BYGOTT, JOHN

Two Soldier Brothers. 'Bert' (Lieut. Walter Bertram Wood, M.C. and Bar, Hampshire Regiment R.F.C.). 'Ted' (Second Lieut. Edwin Leonard Wood, 1st Royal Scots Fusiliers). London: 1920. V. 46

BYINGTON, MARGARET

Homestead, The Households of a Mill Town. New York. V. 37

BYINGTON, MARGARET F.

Homestead. The Households of a Mill Town. New York: 1910. V. 46

BYLES, JOHN BARNARD 1801-1884

Sophisms of Free-Trade and Popular Political Economy Examined. London: 1849. V. 43

BYLLESBY, LANGDON

Observations on the Sources and Effects of Unequal Wealth. New York: 1826. V. 39; 44

BYMES, THOMAS

Professional Criminals of America. New York: 1886. V. 39

BYNE, ARTHUR

Majorcan Houses and Gardens: a Spanish Island in the Mediterranean. 1928. V. 46

Majorcan Houses and Gardens. New York: 1928. V. 37

Provincial Houses in Spain. New York: 1925. V. 39; 46

Rejeria of the Spanish Renaissance. New York: 1914. V. 39; 43

BYNE, MILDRED STAPLEY

Important Mediaeval and Early Renaissance Works of Art from Spain. New York: 1927. V. 43

Spanish Gardens and Patios. Philadelphia: 1924. V. 38; 44; 46

Spanish Gardens and Patios. Philadelphia & London: 1924. V. 45

BYNG, GEORGE 1663-1733

An Account of the Expedition of the British Fleet to Sicily in the years 1718, 1719, and 1720. London: 1739. V. 37

BYNG, JOHN

A Candid Examination of the Resolutions and Sentence of the Court-Martial on the Trial of Admiral Byng, as Founded on the Principles of Law, Evidence and Discipline. London: 1757. V. 37; 41

A Letter to a Member of Parliament in the Country From His Friend in London, Relative to the Case of Admiral Byng with Some Original Papers and Letters Which Passed During the Expedition . . . London: 1756. V. 41

The Torrington Diaries. London: 1934-38. V. 46

The Trial of the Honourable Admiral Byng, at a Court Martial as Taken by Mr. Chrles Fearne, Judge Advocate of H.M. Fleet. London: 1757. V. 38; 42

The Trial of the Honourable Admiral John Byng. New York: 1757. V. 44

BYNNER, WITTER 1881-

Book of Lyrics. New York: 1955. V. 38

A Canticle of Praise. San Francisco: 1918. V. 38; 41

An Ode to Harvard and Other Poems. Boston: 1907. V. 37

the Persistence of Poetry. San Francisco: 1929. V. 46

Spectra: A Book of Poetic Experiments. New York: 1916. V. 37

Spectra - New Poems. New York: 1916. V. 38

Tiger. New York: 1913. V. 44

BYRD, CECIL KASH

Bibliography of Indiana Imprints 1804-1853. Indianapolis: 1955. V. 43

BYRD, RICHARD EVELYN

Discovery: the Story of the Second Byrd Antarctic Expedition. New York: 1935. V. 45

Discovery: The Story of the Second Byrd Antarctic Expedition. New York: 1935. V. 37; 43; 44; 45

Little America: Aerial Exploration in the Antarctic the Flight to the South Pole. New York: 1930. V. 40; 43; 46

Skyward. New York: 1928. V. 40; 43; 45

BYRD, WILLIAM

My Ladye Nevells Booke. London: 1926. V. 39

The Westover Manuscripts . . . Petersburg: 1841. V. 45

The Writings of 'Colonel William Byrd of Westover in Virginia Esqr.' New York: 1901. V. 38; 44

BYRN, MARCUS LAFAYETTE

The Life and Adventures of an Arkansaw Doctor. Washington: 1879. V. 38; 39

BYRNE, BERNARD J.

Frontier Army Surgeon: an Authentic Description of Colorado in the Eighties. Cranford: 1935. V. 37; 46

BYRNE, DONN

Brother Saul. New York: 1927. V. 42

Hangman's House. New York & London: 1926. V. 39

Stories Without Women (and a Few With Women). New York: 1915. V. 39; 43

BYRNE, EDWARD

The Dark Shore. Brockport: 1977. V. 39

BYRNE, JULIA CLARA BUSK 1819-1894

Curiosities of the Search Room. London: 1880. V. 37; 44

Gossip of the Century: Personal and Traditional Memories - Social, Literary, Artistic &c. London: 1892. V. 44

BYRNE, LAWRENCE J.

Visit of the Detached Squadron With Their Royal Highnesses Prince Edward and Prince George of Wales to Brisbane from 16th to 20th August 1881. Brisbane: 1881. V. 41

BYRNE, MATTHEW J.

Ireland Under Elizabeth. Dublin: 1903. V. 43

BYRNE, MURIEL ST. CLARE

The Lisle Letters. Chicago: 1981. V. 40

BYRNE, OLIVER

Euclid; The First Six Books of the Elements of Euclid. London: 1847. V. 37

The First Six Books of the Elements of Euclid in Which Colored Diagrams and Symbols are Used Instead of Letters for the Greater Ease of Learners. London: 1847. V. 37

The Handbook for the Artisan, Mechanic and Engineer. Philadelphia: 1853. V. 40

Spons' Dictionary of Engineering, Civil, Mechanical, Military and Naval, with Technical Terms in French, Mechanical, Military and Naval . . . London: 1869-74. V. 42; 44

BYRNES, THOMAS

Professional Criminals of America. New York: 1886. V. 38; 40

BYROM, JOHN

Miscellaneous Poems. Manchester: 1773. V. 37; 38; 40; 41; 43; 45; 46

Miscellaneous Poems. Leeds: 1814. V. 40

Miscellaneous Poems. Leeds: 1814. V. 37

The Universal English Short-Hand; or, The Way of Writing English, in the Most Easy, Concise, Regular and Beautiful Manner . . . Manchester: 1767. V. 39; 42

BYRON, GEORGE

The Works, Volume VIII. London: 1825. V. 37

BYRON, GEORGE ANSON

Voyage of the H.M.S. Blonde to the Sandwich Islands, in the Years 1824-1825. London: 1826. V. 38; 41; 46

BYRON, GEORGE GORDON NOEL 1788-1824

Conversations on Religion with Lord Byron and others, held in Cephalonia, a short time previous to His Lordship's Death. By the late James Kennedy, M.D. of H.M. Medical Staff. London;: 1830. V. 37

The Deformed Transformed: a Drama. London: 1824. V. 38

Letters and Journals . . . with Notices of His Life. By Thomas Moore. London: 1830. V. 41

Poems of Lord Byron. London: 1923. V. 41

The Vision of Judgement. A Vision of Judgement. Harrow Weald: 1932. V. 38

BYRON, GEORGE GORDON NOEL, 6TH BARON 1788-1824

The Age of Bronze; or Carmen Seculare et Annus Haud Mirabilis. London: 1823. V. 39; 40; 42; 44

The Age of Bronze. Paris: 1823. V. 39

Beppo, a Venetian Story. London: 1818. V. 37; 39; 43

The Bride of Abydos: a Turkish Tale. London: 1813. V. 39; 43; 44; 46

The Bride of Abydos, a Tragick Play, in three acts: as performed at the Theatre Royal, Drury-Lane. London: 1818. V. 37

The Byron Gallery. London: 1833. V. 45

Byron Kvaede. Fritt Umskrivne ved Edvard Alme. Bjorgvin, i.e. Bergen: 1920. V. 40

Byron: a Self-Portrait, Letters and Diaries 1798 to 1824. London: 1950. V. 45

A Byron Library. A Catalogue of Printed Books, Manuscripts and Autograph Letters . . . Collected by Thomas James Wise. London: 1928. V. 37

Cain: a Mystery. London: 1822. V. 42; 46

Cain. Paris: 1822. V. 41; 42

Child Harold's Pilgrimage. A Romaunt, in four cantos. In Two Volumes. London: 1819. V. 37

Childe Hrold's Pilgrimage. London: 1812. V. 44

Childe Harold's Pilgrimage. London: 1812. V. 44; 46

Childe Harold's Pilgrimage. Philadelphia: 1812. V. 37; 44

BYRON, GEORGE GORDON NOEL, 6TH BARON 1788-1824 continued

Childe Harold's Pilgrimage. London: 1812/16/18. V. 44

Childe Harold's Pilgrimage. London: 1814. V. 44

Childe Harold's Pilgrimage . . . London: 1815-18. V. 38

Childe Harold's Pilgrimage. Canto the Third. London: 1816. V. 37; 39; 42; 43

Childe Harold's Pilgrimage. Canto the Fourth. London: 1818. V. 39; 40; 41; 42; 43; 44

Childe Harold's Pilgrimage, Canto the Fourth. New York: 1818. V. 42

Childe Harold's Pilgrimage. London: 1825. V. 39

Childe Harold's Pilgrimage. A Romaunt. London: 1841. V. 39; 46

Childe Harold's Pilgrimage. London: 1859. V. 38

Childe Harold's Pilgrimage. 1931. V. 42

Childe Harold's Pilgrimage. 1931. V. 40

Childe Harold's Prilgrimage. 1931. V. 45

Childe Harold's Pilgrimage: a Romaunt . . . New York: 1931. V. 46

Childe Harold's Pilgramage: a Romaunt . . . New York: 1931. V. 46

Childe Harold's Pilgrimage. Paris: 1931. V. 37; 38; 46

Childe Haraold's pilgrimaage. London: 1841. V. 37

Complete Works, Including His Suppressed Poems. (with) Letters and Journals, with Notices of His Life by Thomas Moore. Paris: 1832-33. V. 38

Correspondence of Lord Byron, with a Friend, Including His Letters to His Mother. Paris: 1825. V. 40; 46

The Corsair. London: 1814. V. 39; 40; 44; 46

The Corsair, a Tale. London: 1815. V. 44

The Curse of Minerva. Philadelphia: 1815. V. 45

The Deformed Transformed, a Drama. London: 1824. V. 37; 38; 42

Don Juan. London: 1819. V. 44

Don Juan. (Cantos I & II). London: 1819. V. 42

Don Juan . . . London: 1819. V. 43

Don Juan (Cantos I & II). Cantos III, IV, & V); London: 1819-21. V. 42

Don Juan, Cantos I and II; Cantos III, IV and V; Cantos VI, VII and VIII; Cantos IX, X and XI; Cantos XII, XIII and XIV; Cantos XV and XVI. London: 1819-23. V. 38

Don Juan. London: 1819-24. V. 39; 41; 44

Don Juan. London: 1820. V. 39

Don Juan. Cantos 1 (-16). London: 1820-24. V. 42

Don Juan . . . London: 1821. V. 39; 44

Don Juan. Cantos III, IV and V; Cantos Vi, VII and VIII; Cantos IX, X and XI; Cantos XII, XIII and XIV; Cantos XV, and XVI. London: 1821-24. V. 39

Don Juan. London: 1822, 1824. V. 42

Don Juan. London: 1822-23-24. V. 46

Don Juan, Cantos VI-VII and VIII. London: 1823. V. 39

Don Juan. London: 1828. V. 42

Don Juan. Complete in Sixteen Cantos. London: 1836. V. 39

Don Juan. Stockholm: 1838. V. 46

Don Juan: in Sixteen Cantos. Halifax: 1857. V. 46

Don Juan, Oversat Paa Dansk af Holger Drachmann, Med Indledningsdigt af Oversatteren. Copenhagen: 1882/1902. V. 44

Don Juan. London: 1906. V. 46

Don Juan. Austin: 1957. V. 42

English Bards and Scotch Reviewers. London: 1809. V. 42; 44; 45; 46

English Bards and Scotch Reviewers, a Satire. London: 1809. V. 44

English Bards and Scotch Reviewers. London: 1810. V. 38; 40; 41; 43; 45; 46

English Bards and Scotch Reviewers: a Satire. London: 1810. V. 45

English Bards and Scotch Reviewers. London: 1810.18/22. V. 40

English Bards and Scotch Reviewers. Charleston: 1811. V. 41

English Bards and Scotch Reviewers. London: 1811. V. 44; 45

English Bards and Scotch Reviewers. Philadelphia: 1811. V. 38; 44

English Bards and Scotch Reviewers. London: 1812. V. 42

English Bards and Scotch Reviewers. London: 1818. V. 40

English Bards, and Scotch Reviewers; a Satire. Paris: 1818. V. 39

English Bards, and Scotch Reviewers. Forfar: 1825. V. 42

Fare Thee Well! London: 1816. V. 39; 40; 42; 43

Fare Thee Well! A Sketch &c. Napoelon's Farewell. On the Star of the Legion of Honour. And an Ode. Sherwood: 1816. V. 39

Fugitive Pieces. London: 1886. V. 39

The Genuine Rejected Addresses, Presented to the Committee of Management for Drury Lane Theatre . . . London: 1812. V. 44; 45

The Giaour, a Fragment of a Turkish Tale. London: 1813. V. 43; 44; 45

The Giaour, a Fragment of a Turkish Tale. London: 1814. V. 40; 44; 46

Hebrew Melodies. London: 1814. V. 40

Hebrew Melodies. London: 1815. V. 37; 38; 39; 40; 41; 42; 45; 46

Hours of Idleness, a Series of Poems, Original and Translated. Newark: 1807. V. 38; 39; 41; 42; 44

Hours of Idleness, a Series of Poems, Original and Translated. Paris: 1819. V. 44

Hours of Idleness. London: 1820. V. 39

Hours of Idleness. London: 1822. V. 39

Hours of Idleness; a Series of Poems, Original and Translated. Paris: 1822. V. 41

The Island, or Christian and His Comrades. London: 1823. V. 38; 39; 41; 42; 43; 44

Lara, a Tale. London: 1814. V. 38; 41; 42; 43; 44; 45

Letter to **** ****** (i.e. John Murray), on the Rev. W. L. Bowles's Strictures on the Life and Writings of Pope. London: 1821. V. 37; 39; 40; 43; 44

Letter to **** ****** (John Murray) on the Rev. W. L. Bowles' Strictures on the Life and Writings of Pope. (with) Two Letters to . . . Lord Byron in Answer to His Lordship's Letter . . . London: 1871. V. 40

Byron's Letters and Journals. Cambridge. V. 38

Letters and Journals of Lord Byron. London: 1830. V. 38; 40; 41; 42; 44; 46

Letters and Journals of Lord Byron, with Notices of His Life. Paris: 1833. V. 46

Letters and Journal of Lord Byron. Paris: 1833. V. 43

Letters and Journals of Lord Byron: With Notices of His Life. London: 1833, 1830. V. 39

Letters Written by Lord Byron During His Residence at Missolonghi Jan. to April 1824 to Mr. Samuel Barff at Zante. Naples: 1884. V. 42

Byron's Letters and Journals. London: 1974-82. V. 44

Letters and Journals. London: 1974-82. V. 46

Letters and Journals of Lord Byron: With Notices of His Life. New York: 1830. V. 37

Letters and Journals of Lord Byron: With Notices of His Life, By Thomas Moore. London: 1833. V. 37

The Liberal. Verse and Prose from the South. London: 1822-23. V. 42

Life, Letters and Journals of Lord Byron. London: 1838. V. 44

The Life of Lord Byron, with His Letters and Journals. London: 1847. V. 42

Lord Byron's Sammtliche Werke. Frankfurt am Main: 1830-31. V. 39

Manfred. London: 1817. V. 38; 39; 41; 42; 44; 46

Manfred: a Tragedy. 1929. V. 45

Manfred: a Tragedy. London: 1929. V. 41; 46

Marino Faliero. London: 1821. V. 37; 38; 39; 40; 41; 42; 43; 45; 46

Marino Faliero, Doge of Venice. Leipzig: 1922. V. 38; 40

Marino Faliero, Doge of Venice. Wien und Leipzig: 1922. V. 40

Mazeppa, a Poem. London: 1819. V. 44

Mazeppa. London: 1819. V. 37; 38; 40; 42; 44; 45; 46

Monody on the Death of the Right Honourable R. B. Sheridan, Written at the Request of a Friend, to be Spoken at Drury Lane Theatre. London: 1816. V. 37; 39; 44

The New Don Juan. London: 1880. V. 39

Ode to Napoleon Bonaparte. London: 1814. V. 38; 39; 44

The Parliamentary Speeches . . . London: 1824. V. 44; 45; 46

Poems Original and Translated. Newark: 1808. V. 40; 43; 44

Poems: Lara, a Tale; Jacqueline; a Tale. London: 1814. V. 43

Poems on His Domestic Circumstances. I. Fare Thee Well! II. A Sketch from Private Life . . . with Star of the Legion of Honour, and Other Poems. London: 1816. V. 39; 41

Poems. London: 1816. V. 38; 39; 40; 41; 42; 44

Poems on His Domestic Circumstances . . . London: 1823. V. 42

The Poems of Lord Byron. London: 1923. V. 46

The Poetical Works. London: 1839. V. 41

Poetical Works. London: 1904. V. 42

Poetical Works. London: 1855-56. V. 37

Poetical Works. London: 1879. V. 37

Poetry of Byron. London: 1881. V. 46

The Prisoner of Chillon and Other Poems. London: 1816. V. 37; 38; 39; 40; 43; 45; 46

The Prisoner of Chillon. Lausanne: 1818. V. 42

The Prisoner of Chillon. London: 1865. V. 43

The Prisoner of Chillon. London: 1865. V. 44

The Prisoner of Chillon. London: 1865. V. 39; 44

Sardanapal, Tragoedie af Lord Byron . . . Kiobenhaven: 1827. V. 44

Sardanapalus, a Tragedy. London: 1821. V. 38; 39; 40; 41; 42; 46

Sardanapalus, a Tragedy. The Two Foscari, a Tragedy. London: 1821-24. V. 42

The Siege of Corinth. London: 1816. V. 38; 39; 40; 42; 43; 46

Udvalgte Dramtiske Digte Og Fortaellinger. Copenhagen: 1873-76. V. 40

A Venetian Story. Kentfield: 1963. V. 37; 39; 42; 44

Waltz: an Apostrophic Hymn. London: 1821. V. 42; 44; 45; 46

Waltz: an Apostrophic Hymn. London: 1813. V. 41; 42; 43; 44

Werner, a Tragedy. London: 1822-23. V. 46

Werner, a Tragedy. London: 1823. V. 37; 38; 39; 40; 41; 42; 43; 44; 45

Works of . . . London. V. 46

Works of . . . London. V. 40

Works. London: 1814-18. V. 37

BYRON, GEORGE GORDON NOEL, 6TH BARON 1788-1824 continued

The Works of the Right Honourable Lord Byron . . . London: 1815.
V. 43; 44

The Works. London: 1815-17. V. 39

The Works of the Right Honorable Lord Byron. London: 1815-18. V. 39; 46

The Works of the Right Honorable Lord Byron. London: 1815-20. V. 45

The Works of the Right Honorable Lord Byron. London: 1815-20.
V. 45; 46

The Works. London: 1817. V. 42

The Works of the Right Honourable Lord Byron. London: 1818. V. 46

The Works of Lord Byron. London: 1819. V. 42; 44

The Works of the Right Honourable Lord Byron. Philadelphia: 1820. V. 40

The Works of Lord Byron. London: 1821. V. 40; 46

Lord Byron's Works. Paris: 1821-23. V. 44

The Works of Lord Byron. London: 1822-25. V. 44

Works. London: 1823-26. V. 40

The Works . . . London: 1824-1825. V. 40

The Works. London: 1824-25. V. 37

The Works. London: 1825. V. 42

The Works. Philadelphia: 1825. V. 41

The Works. London: 1826. V. 43

The Works. London: 1827. V. 38; 45

The Works of Lord Byron. London: 1828. V. 42

The Works. Paris: 1828. V. 39

The Works of Lord Byron Complete in One Volume. Francfort: 1829. V. 42

The Works. London: 1829. V. 39; 42

The Works. London: 1830-31. V. 39

Works. London: 1832. V. 42

The Works of Lord Bywon, with His Letters and Journals, and His Life, by Thomas Moore, Esq. London: 1832-3. V. 44

The Works. (with His Letters and Journals and His Life). London: 1832-33. V. 39; 45

Works. London: 1832-33. V. 39; 41; 42; 46

The Works of Lord Byron, with His Letters and Journals and His Life by Thomas Moore. London: 1832-37. V. 42

The Complete Works of Lord Byron. Paris: 1833. V. 44; 45

The Complete Works of Lord Byron, Reprinted from the Last London Edition. Paris: 1835. V. 44

The Complete Works of Lord Byron, From the Last London Edition. Paris: 1835. V. 44

The Works of Lord Byron, Complete in One Volume . . . London: 1837. V. 44

The Works of Lord Byron. London: 1837. V. 44

The Works of . . . Philadelphia: 1839. V. 41

The Works of Lord Byron. Leipzig: 1842. V. 44

The Works. London: 1847. V. 37

Oeuvres Completes de Lord Byron. Paris: 1851. V. 44

Works. London: 1898. V. 42

The Works of . . . London: 1898. V. 39

The Works of Lord Byron. London: 1898. V. 41

The Works of Lord Byron . . . London: 1898-1904. V. 39; 44

Works. London: 1898-1904. V. 46

The Works. London: 1898-1905. V. 43

The Works. Boston: 1900. V. 38; 42; 43; 44; 45

The Works of Lord Byron. London: 1902. V. 43

The Works of Lord Byron. London: 1902. V. 41

Works. London: 1905-22. V. 38

The Works. London: 1918. V. 38

Works. London: 1932-1833. V. 37

The Works of Lord Byron. London: 1932-4. V. 38

The Works, Volume VIII. London: 1825. V. 37

BYRON, JOHN

The Narrative of the Honourable John Byron (Commodore in a Late Expedition Round the World) Containing an Account of the Great Distresses Suffered by Himself and His Companions on the Coast of Patagonia, from the Year 1740, till Their Arrival in England . . . London: 1768. V. 37; 39; 40; 42; 44; 46

The Narrative of the Honourable John Byron, Commodore in a Late Expedition Round the World. Aberdeen: 1822. V. 45

The Universal English short hand; or, the way of writing English in the most easy, concise, regular, and beautiful manner . . . Manchester: 1767. V. 37

A Voyage Round the World, In His Majesty's Ship the Dolophin . . . London: 1767. V. 44

Voyage Autour du Monde, Fait en 1764 and 1765, sur le Vaisseau de Guerre Anglois le Dauphin . . . Paris: 1767. V. 42

Voyage of H. M. S. 'Blonde' to the Sandwich Islands in the Years 1824-25. London: 1826. V. 42

BYRON, MAY

Cat's Cradle: A Picture Book for Little Folk. London. V. 45

BYRON, MEDORA GORDON

Celia in Search of a Husband. London: 1809. V. 39; 44

Hours of Affluence, a nd days of Indigence. London: 1809. V. 39

BYRON, ROBERT

The Birth of Western Painting, a History of Colour, Form and Iconography, Illustrated from the Paintings of Mistra and Mount Athos of Giotto and Duccio and of El Greco. London: 1930. V. 42; 44; 45

The Byzantine Achievement: an Historical Perspective A.D. 330-1453. London: 1929. V. 41

An Essay on India. London: 1931. V. 38; 41; 44

Europe in the Looking Glass. London: 1926. V. 40

First Russia Then Tibet. London: 1933. V. 37

From Herat to Kabul - Notes on a Lecture. London: 1935. V. 44

How We Celebrate the Coronation Architectural Press. London: 1937. V. 40; 41; 46

Imperial Pilgrimage. London: 1937. V. 46

The Road to Oxiana. London: 1937. V. 38

The Station. London: 1928. V. 41

BYRRNE, E. FAIRFAX

The Heir Without a Heritage: a Novel. London: 1887. V. 44

BYSSHE, EDWARD

The Art of English Poetry. London: 1705. V. 41; 43

The Art of English Poetry . . . London: 1710. V. 45

The Art of English Poetry. London: 1737. V. 44

The British Parnassus; or, a Compleat Commonplace Book of English Poetry. London: 1714. V. 43

A Visitation of the County of Essex. London: 1888. V. 45

BYTHNER, VICTORINUS

Lyra Prophetica Davidis Regis. Sive Analysis Critico-Practica Psalmorum . . . Index Libri Psalmorum . . . Lingua Eruditorum, sive Institutio Methodica Lingue Saanctae . . . cui Addita est Introductio ad Linguam Chaldaeam Veteris Teatamenti . . . Zuerich: 1670. V. 38

BYWATER, INGRAM

Gnomologium Baroccianum. Oxonii: 1878. V. 45

BYWATER, JOHN

An Essay on the History, Practice and Theory, of Electricity. London: 1810. V. 42; 44; 45

C

C., A.

The Footstep to Mrs. Trimmer's Sacred History. London: 1795. V. 45

C., D. M.

A Sign of the Day of God: a Conversation. Battle Creek: 1870. V. 42

C., E.

A Faithful Account of the Present State of Affairs, in England, Scotland and Ireland. London: 1690. V. 42

C. H. ST. J. HORNBY. 25 June 1867 - 26 April 1956. An Anthology of Appreciations. London: 1946. V. 41

C, I. Y.

The Sketch Book of I. Y. C., Containing Tales, Anecdotes &c. Original and Select, Also a Voyage to Rio de Janeiro, the Capital of the Empire of Brazil. Leeds: 1829. V. 41

C., J.

Lettre a un Gentilhomme Allemand, Touchant le Gente & la Force de la Langue Angloise . . . London: 1708. V. 45

CAARR, JOHN

The Stranger in France . . . London: 1803. V. 37

CABALA Mysteries of Statae in Letters of the Great Minsters of K James and K Charales . . . Faithfully Collected by a Noble Hand. London: 1654. V. 37

CABALA, Mysteries of State, In Letters of the Great Ministers of K. James and K. Charles. Wherein Much of the Publique Manage of Affaires is Related. (with) Scrinia Sacra; Secrets of Empire, in Letters of Illustrious Persons. A Supplement of the Cabala. London: Ptd. for M.M.G.: 1654. V. 37

CABALA; Sive Scrinia Sacra. Mysteries of State & Government: in Letters of Illustrious Persons and Great Agents, in the Reigns of Henry the Eighth, Queen Elizabeth, K. James and the Late King Charls. London: 1654. V. 46

CABALA, Sive Scrinia Sacra, Mysteries of State and Government: In Letters of Illustrious Persons and Great Ministers of State. London: 1663. V. 45

CABALLERIA, JUAN

History of San Bernardino Valley from the Padres to the Pioneers. San Bernardino: 1902. V. 38

CABALLERIA Y COLLELL, JUAN

History of the City of Santa Barbara, California. From its Discovery to out Own Days. Santa Barbara: 1892. V. 37

CABANNE, PIERRE

The Brothers Duchamp: Jacques Villon, Rayomond Duchamp-Villon, Marcel Duchamp. Boston: 1976. V. 46

CABEEN, D. C.

Critical Bibliography of French Literture. 1952-62. V. 38

CABELL, JAMES BRANCH 1879-1958

Chivalry. New York: 1909. V. 44

The Cream of the Jest. New York: 1927. V. 45

The Eagle's Shadow. London: 1904. V. 46

The Eagle's Shadow. New York: 1904. V. 37; 39; 43; 46

The Eagle's Shadow. New York: 1940. V. 46

The First Gentleman of America. New York: 1942. V. 37; 40

From the Hidden Way . . . New York: 1916. V. 43

Gallantry: an Eighteenth Century Dizain in Ten Comedies with an Afterpiece. New York: 1907. V. 44; 46

The Judging of Jurgen. Chicago: 1920. V. 41; 43

Jurgen. New York: 1919. V. 39; 40; 43; 44

Jurgen and the Censor. New York: 1920. V. 43

Jurgen. London: 1921. V. 40

Jurgen. London: 1923. V. 45

Jurgen. 1940. V. 39

Jurgen. Waltham St. Lawrence: 1949. V. 44

Jurgen. A Comedy of Justice. By James Branch Cabell. Wood Engravings by John uckland Wright. London: 1949. V. 37; 40; 43

Ladies and Gentlemen: a Parcel of Reconsiderations. New York: 1934. V. 43; 45

The Line of Love. New York: 1905. V. 46

The Line of Love. New York: & London: 1905. V. 43

The Lineage of Lichfield: an Essay in Eugenics. New York: 1922. V. 38; 39; 46

The Music from Behind the Moon. New York: 1926. V. 37

Smirt: an Urban Nightmare. New York: 1934. V. 41; 44; 46

Smith. A Sylvan Interlude. New York: 1934. V. 43

Something About Eve. New York: 1927. V. 42

Sonnets from Antan. New York: 1929. V. 44; 46

The Soul of Melicent. New York: 1913. V. 38; 46

Straws and Prayer Books. New York: 1924. V. 38

Gallantry: an Eighteenth Century Dizain in Ten Comedies with an Afterpiece. New York: 1907. V. 44

These Restless Heads: a Trilogy of Romantics. New York: 1932. V. 39

The Way of Ecben: a Comedietta Involving a Gentleman. New York: 1929. V. 43; 46

The Works of James Branch Cabell. New York: 1927. V. 38; 39; 42

The Works of . . . New York: 1927-30. V. 46

CABEZA DA VACA, ALVAR NUNEZ

Relation . . . of What Befel the Armament in the Indias . . . San Francisco: 1929. V. 38

CABEZA DE VACA, ALVAR NUNEZ

Voyages, Relationes et Memoires Originaux pour Servir a l'Histoire de la Decouverte de l'Amerique . . . Relation et Naufragaes . . . (with) . . . Commentaires. Paris: 1837. V. 37

THE CABINET Makers' London Book of Prices, and designs of Cabinet Work . . . London: 1793. V. 38; 40; 44

THE CABINET of Curiosities; or Mirror of Entertainment. London: 1810. V. 46

THE CABINET of Momus. Philadelphia: 1809. V. 40

CABLE, BOYD

A Hundred Year History of the P. & O., Peninsular and Orient Company. London: 1937. V. 38

CABLE, GEORGE WASHINGTON 1844-1925

The Amateur Garden. New York: 1914. V. 40

Bonaventure. New York: 1899. V. 39; 41

The Cavalier. New York: 1901. V. 40

The Creoles of Louisiana. London: 1885. V. 38

Dr. Sevier. Boston: 1885. V. 40

Dr. Sevier. New York: 1901. V. 39

Famous Adventures and Prison Escapes of the Civil War. New York: 1893. V. 42

Gideon's Band. A Tale of the Mississippi. New York: 1914. V. 40

The Grandissimes. New York: 1880. V. 37; 40; 43; 45

The Grandissimes. New York: 1880. V. 37; 40; 43; 45; 46

The Grandissimes. New York: 1899. V. 39; 40; 41

The Negro Question. New York: 1888. V. 42

Old Creole Days. New York. V. 43

Old Creole Days. New York: 1879. V. 37; 38; 39; 40; 41; 42; 43; 46

Old Creole Days. New York: 1897. V. 38; 39; 40; 41; 42; 45

Old Creole Days. 1943. V. 39

Old Creole Days. 1943. V. 40

Posson Jone and Pere Raphael with a New Word Setting Forth How and Why the Two Tales are One. New York: 1909. V. 45

Strange True Stories of Louisiana. New York: 1889. V. 37; 39; 43

Strong Hearts. New York: 1899. V. 40

CABORNE, W. F.

Sons of Our Navy. London: 1917. V. 41

CABOT, WILLIAM BROOKS

Algonquian Proper Names. Boston: 1921. V. 42

In Northern Labrador. Boston: 1912. V. 43; 44

Labrador. Boston: 1920. V. 42; 43

CABRERA INFANTE, G.

View of the Dawn in the Tropics. New York: 1978. V. 44

CACOUAULT DE LA MIMARDIERE, ELIZABETH

The Young Ladies Mythology. London: 1783. V. 40

THE CACTUS Journal. London: 1898-1900. V. 37

CADBURY, RICHARD

Cocoa; All About It. London: 1892. V. 42

CADDY, FLORENCE

Through the Fields With Linnaus. London: 1887. V. 40

CADELL, F. C. B.

Jack and Tommy. London: 1916. V. 44

CADELL, WILLIAM ARCHIBALD

A Journey in Carniola, Italy and France in the Years 1817, 1818 . . . Edinburgh: 1820. V. 46

CADENA, MARIANO VELZQUEZ

A New Pronouncing Dictionary of the Spanish and English Languages. New York: 1900. V. 39; 46

CADLWELL, CHARLES

A Discourse on the Genius and Character of the Rev. Horace Holley, Late President of Transylvania University with an Appendix Containing Copious Notes, Biographical and Illustrative. Boston: 1828. V. 37

CADMUS, PAUL

Paul Cadmus: Prints and Drawings 1922-1967. New York: 1968. V. 46

CADOGAN, WILLIAM

A Dissertation on the Gout, and all Chronic Diseases, Jointly Considered, As Proceeding from the Same Causes . . . London: 1771. V. 37; 38; 41; 43; 45

CADOGAN, WILLIAM BROMLEY

The Life of the Rev. William Romaine, M.A. Late Rector of the United Parishes of St. Andrew by the Wardrobe, and St. Ann's, Blackfriars, and Lecturer of St. Dunstan's in the West. London: 1796. V. 38

CADOUX, CECIL JOHN

Ancient Smyrna: a History of the City from the Earliest Times to 324 A.D. Oxford: 1938. V. 40

CADWALADER, JOHN

A Reply to General Joseph Reed's Remarks, on a Late Publication in the Independent Gazetteer, with some Observations on his Address to the People of Pennsylvania. Philadelphia: 1783. V. 37

CADWELL, ERSKINE PRESTON 1903-

We Are the Living. New York: 1933. V. 39

CADY, ANNIE COLE

The American Continent And Its Inhabitants Before Its Discovery by Columbus. Philadelphia: 1893. V. 39

CADY, JOHN H.

Arizona's Yesterday: Being the Narrative of John H. Cady, Pioneer. Patagonia: 1916. V. 41; 44

CADY, JOHN HUTCHINS

The Civic and Architectural Development of Providence 1638-1950. Providence: 1957. V. 42

CAELIUS AURELIANUS

On Acute Diseases and on Chronic Diseases. Chicago: 1950. V. 38; 41

CAESAR, GAIUS JULIUS 100-44 BC

C. Julii Caesaris Omnia Quae Extant . . . Lugduni Batavorum: 1593. V. 43

C. Julii Caesaris Quae Extant. Leyden: 1635. V. 39; 42

Caii Julii Caesaris Quae Extant. London: 1744. V. 41

Caii Julii Caesaris: Invictissimi Imperatoris Commentaria. Venice: 1511. V. 45

I Commentari, con Le Figure in Rame . . . Fatte da Andrea Palladio. In Venetia: 1575. V. 44

Commentaria; Seculorum Iniuria Antea Difficilia & Valde Mendosa. Venice: 1511. V. 43; 44

Commentaria. Venice: 1517. V. 37

The Commentaries. Venetiis: 1519. V. 37

The Commentaries of C. Julius Caesar. London: 1655. V. 38

Caii Julii Caesaris et A. Hirtii de Rebus a Caesare Gestis Commentarii. Cum Fragmentis. Glasgow: 1750. V. 39

The Commentaries of Caesar. London: 1753. V. 44

Julius Caesar's Commentaries. 1951. V. 44

Commentarii, Novis Emendationibus Illustrati. Antwerp: 1570. V. 37

Commentarii. 1914. V. 39

Commentarii Rerum in Gallia Gestarum VII . . . London: 1914. V. 46

Commentariorum de Bello Gallico Libri VIII. Venice: 1513. V. 37

The Eyght Bookes of Caius Iulius Caesar Conteyning His Martial Exploytes in the Realme of Gallia and the Countries Bordering Vppon the Same . . . London: 1565. V. 38; 44

Gai Juli Caesaris Commentarii. 1914. V. 37

The Gallic Wars. New York: 1954. V. 41; 43

The Gallic Wars. Verona: 1954. V. 38; 42; 44; 45; 46

The Gallic Wars. By Julius Caesar. A New Translation by John Warrington with a preface by John Mason Brown & an introduction by the translator. Illustrated with engravings by Bruno Bramanti. 1954. V. 37

I Commentarii . . . da M. Francesco Baldelli Nuovamente di Lingua Latina Tradotti in Thoscana, con Figure. Venice: 1554. V. 40

Julii Caesaris Quae Extant. London: 1712. V. 38

(Opera) que Exstant. Amsterdam: 1675. V. 37

(Opera) et A. Hirtii De REbus A Caesare Gestis Commentari. Glasguae: 1750. V. 46

Cai Julii Caesaris Opera Omnia. Londini: 1790. V. 44

Quae Extant Ex Emendatione Jos. Scaligeri. Leiden: 1635. V. 42

Rerum ab se Gestarum Commentarii. Lyon: 1549. V. 41

Works. Bologna: 1504. V. 45; 46

CAESAR, GAOIS JULIUS 100-44 BC

Commentaries. London: 1951. V. 39; 40

CAESARII HEISTERBACHENSIS

Illustrium Miraculorum et Historiarum Memorabilium Libri XII. Cologne: 1591. V. 37; 41

CAFFIN, CHARLES H.

Photography as a fine Art . . . New York: 1901. V. 46

CAFFREY, A.

The Smallest Dragonboy. 1982. V. 44

CAFFYN, KATHLEEN MANNINGTON HUNT d. 1926

Anne Mauleverer. London: 1899. V. 44

CAFKY, MORRIS

Colorado Midland. Denver,: 1965. V. 37; 39; 43; 45

Rails Around Gold Hill. Denver: 1955. V. 38; 40

CAFMEYER, PIERRE DE

Venerable Histoire du Tres-Saint Sacrement de Miracle . . . Brussels: 1720-35. V. 46

CAGANNE, PIERRE

Edgar Degas. Paris & New York: 1958. V. 39

CAGE, JOHN

Silence. 1961. V. 44

Silence. 1961. V. 43

Silence. Middletown: 1961. V. 41

CAGNOLA, LUIGI

Le Solenni Esequie di Monsignor Filippo Visconti, Archivescovo di Milano . . . Milan: 1802. V. 46

CAGNOLO, F. C.

The Akikuyu. Their Customs, Traditions and Folklore. Kenya: 1933. V. 43; 44

The Akikuyu. Nyeri: 1933. V. 39; 42

CAHILL, HOLGER

George O. Hart 'Pop'. Twenty-Four Selections from His Work. New York: 1928. V. 46

Max Weber. By Holger Cahill. 32 Illustrations of Works by Weber, Including 1 Original Lithograph Signed by Weber as Frontispiece. New York: 1930. V. 37; 41; 44; 46

CAHOON, HERBERT

The Overbrook Press Bibliography, 1934-1959. Stamford: 1963. V. 38; 45

CAILHAVA DE L'ESTANDOUX, JEAN FRANCOIS 1731-1813

De L'Art de La Comedie. Paris: 1772. V. 46

CAILLIAUD, FREDERIC 1787-1869

Voyage a l'Oasis de Thebes et Dans les Deserts Situes a l'Orient at a l'Occident de la Thebiade, Fait Pendant les Annees 1815, 1816, 1817 et 1818 . . . Paris: 1821. V. 41; 43; 44

CAILLIE, RENE

Journal d'un Voyage a Temboctou et a Jenne Dans l'Afrique Centrale, precede d'Observations Faites chez les Maures Braknas . . . Paris: 1830. V. 46

CAILLIEAUX, HENRI 1794-1859

Manuel d'Hippiatrique a l'Usage de M. M. les Officiers de Cavalerie. Vendome: 1825. V. 38

CAIN, JAMES MALLAHAN 1892-

Cain X 3. New York: 1969. V. 43

Double Indemnity. New York: 1943. V. 42

Galatea. New York: 1953. V. 43; 44; 45

Jealous Woman. 1950. V. 39

Love's Lovely Counterfeit. 1942. V. 39

Love's Lovely Conterfeit. New York: 1942. V. 43; 45; 46

The Magician's Wife. New York: 1965. V. 45

CAIN, JAMES MALLAHAN 1892- continued

Mildred Pierce. New York: 1941. V. 37; 42; 43; 44; 45

The Moth. New York: 1948. V. 44

Our Government. New York: 1930. V. 37

Past All Dishonour. New York: 1946. V. 37; 45

The Postman Always Rings Twice. 1934. V. 39

The Postman Always Rings Twice. London: 1934. V. 42; 46

The Postman Always Rings Twice. New York: 1934. V. 37; 39; 42; 46

Rainbow's End. New York: 1975. V. 43; 45

Serenade. New York: 1937. V. 37; 43

Serenade. London: 1938. V. 45

Three of a Kind: Double Indemnity; Career in C. Major; The Embezzler. New York: 1943. V. 42; 45

CAIN, JOHN

The Officer's Guide and Farmer's Manual . . . Indianapolis: 1832. V. 42

CAIN, T. HALL

Cobwebs of Criticism: a Review of the First Reviewers of the Lake, Satanic and Cockney Schools. London: 1883. V. 44

CAINE, CAESAR

Cleator and Cleator Moor: Past and Present. Kendal: 1916. V. 38

CAINE, HALL

The Bondman. London: 1890. V. 42

The Deemster. A Romance. London;: 1887. V. 37; 40

King Albert's Book. London: 1914. V. 38

The Manxman. New York: 1895. V. 42

My Story. London: 1908. V. 41; 42

Pete: A Drama in Four Acts . . . London: 1908. V. 43

The Scapegoat a Romance. London: 1891. V. 43; 46

Sonnets of Three Centuries: A Selection Including Many Examples Hitherto Unpublished. London: 1882. V. 38

The Woman of Knockaloe. London: 1923. V. 43

CAINE, HENRY 1853-1931

Recollections of Dante Grabriel Rossetti. London: 1882. V. 42

CAINE, NATHANIEL

History of the Royal Rock Beagle Hunt. Liverpool: 1895. V. 37; 42

CAINE, W. S.

A Trip Round the World in 1887-88. London: 1892. V. 45

CAINES, GEORGE

Practical Forms of the Supreme Court, Taken from Tidd's Appendix of the Forms of the Court of King's Bench, in Personal Actions, and Adapted to the Supreme Court of the State of New York . . . New York: 1808. V. 40

Term Reports of Cases Argued and Determined in the Supreme Court of the State. New York: 1813. V. 39

CAIRD, EDWARD

A Critical Account of the Philosophy of Kant. Glasgow: 1877. V. 41

The Critical Philosophy of Immanuel Kant. Glasgow: 1889. V. 41

CAIRD, JAMES 1818-1892

English Agriculture in 1850-1. London: 1852. V. 37; 40; 42

Prairie Farming in America. With Notes by the Way on Canada and the United States . . . London: 1859. V. 37; 44

CAIRNCROSS, DAVID

The Origin of the Silver Eel, with Remarks on Bait and Fly Fishing. London: 1862. V. 39; 40

CAIRNES, JOHN ELLIOT 1823-1875

The Character and Logical Method of Political Economy . . . London: 1875. V. 38; 39; 40; 41; 42

The Character and Logical Method of Political Economy: Being a Course of Lectures Delivered in Hilary Term, 1857. London: 1857. V. 37

Essays in Political Economy. London: 1873. V. 39

Political Essays. London: 1873. V. 42

Some Leading Principles of Political Economy Newly Expounded. London: 1874. V. 38; 39; 40; 42

Some Leading Principles of Political Economy Newly Expounded. London: 1885. V. 41; 42

CAIRNIE, J.

Essay on Curling and Artificial Pond Making. Glasgow: 1833. V. 38

CAIRNS, JOHN

Unbelief in the Eighteenth Century as Contrasted with Its Earlier and Later History. Edinburgh: 1881. V. 41

CAIRNS, WILLIAM

A Treatise on Moral Freedom. London: 1844. V. 39; 40; 41

CAIUS, JOHN

De Canibus Britannicis, Liber Unus; De Rariorum Animalium & Stirpium Historia, Liber Unus . . . London: 1729. V. 41

CAIUS, PSEUD.

Letters of Caius Concerning the Times. In Which Various Characters are Exhibited. London: 1780. V. 38

CAIUS, THOMAS

Vindiciae Antiquitatis Academiae Oxoniensis Contra Joannem Caium, Cantabrigiensem. Oxonii: 1730. V. 38

CAJETAN, TOMMASO DE VIO

Opuscula Questiones & Quolibet Omnia . . . in Quattuor Tomos Distincta . . . Venice: 1531. V. 45

CALABRELLA, E. C. DE, BARONESS

Evenings at Haddon Hall. London: 1846. V. 40

The Prism of Imagination. London: 1844. V. 38; 41; 44

CALAMY, EDMUND

An Abridgement of Mr. Baxter's History of His Life and Times . . . London: 1702. V. 44

An Abridgment of Mr. Baxter's History of His Life and Times. London: 1713. V. 41

The Noblemans Patterne of True and Real Thankfulnesse. London: 1643. V. 46

The Nonconformist's Memorial . . . London: 1775. V. 42

CALANDRI, FILIPPO fl. 1491.

Pictagoras Arithmetrice Introductor. Florence: 1518. V. 44

CALAPAI, LETTERIO

25 Original Wood Engravings Inspired by Thomas Wolfe's 'Look Homeward Angel.' 1948. V. 41

25 Original Wood Engravings Inspired by Thomas Wolfe's 'Look Homeward Angel.' 1948. V. 39

CALASIO, MARIO DE c. 1550-1620

Concordantiae Sacrorum Bibliorum Hebraicorum. London: 1747-49. V. 39

CALCAGNINUS, CAELIUS 1479-1541

Opera Aliquot Extant. Basil: 1544. V. 38; 40; 42; 43

CALCOTT, JOHN W.

A Musical Grammar in Four Parts. Boston: 1810. V. 38

CALCOTT, WELLINS

A Candid Disquisition of the Principles and Practices of the Most Ancient and Honourable Society of Free and Accepted Masons . . . London: 1769. V. 42

A Candid Disquisition of the Principles and Practices of the Most Antient and Honourable Society of Free and Accepted Masons . . . London: 1772. V. 40; 44

CALCUTTA: a Poem. London: 1811. V. 40

CALCUTTA Journal of Natural History, and Miscellany of the Arts and Sciences of India, Conducted by J. McClelland et al. Dehra Dun: 1985. V. 37

CALDANI, LEOPOLDO MARCANTONIO

Institutiones Pathologicae . . . Padua: 1772. V. 45

Institutiones Physiologicae . . . Padua: 1773. V. 45

CALDAS BARBOSA, DOMINGOS

Descripcao da Grandiosa Quinta dos Senhores de Bellas, e Noticia do Seu Melhoramento . . . Lisbon: 1799. V. 45

Narracado dos Applausos Com que o Juiz do Povo e Casa dos Vinte-Quatro Festeja a Felicissima Inauguracao da Estatua Equestre onde Tambem se Expoem as Allegorias dos Carros, Figuras, e tudo o mais concernente as ditas Festas. Lisbon: 1775. V. 38

Recopilcaco dos Successos Principaes da Historia Sagrada em Verso . . . Lisbon: 1793. V. 39

CALDCLEUGH, ALEXANDER

Travels in South America, During the Years 1819-20-21; Containing an Account of the Present State of Brazil, Buenos Ayres and Chile. London: 1825. V. 38; 40; 44; 46

CALDECOTT, RANDOLPH

The Complete Collection of Pictures and Songs by Randolph Caldecott. London: 1887. V. 46

The Complete Collection of Randolph Caldecott's Contributions to the 'Graphic'. London: 1888. V. 40

Gleanings from the 'Graphic.' London: 1889. V. 42

'Graphic' Pictures. London: 1891. V. 46

CALDECOTT, RANDOLPH continued

Last Graphic Pictures. London: 1888. V. 40; 45

More Graphic Pictures. London: 1887. V. 45

R. Caldecott's Second Collection of Pictures and Songs . . . London. V. 40

A Sketch-Book of R. Caldecott's. London. V. 45

A Sketch-Book of R. Caldecott's. London: 1883. V. 46

CALDECOTT, THOMAS

Catalogue of the Exceedingly Curious Collection of Books, Illustrative of Early English Literature, Formed by the Late Thomas Caldecott . . . London: 1833. V. 41

CALDER, ALEXANDER

Animal Sketching. New York: 1926. V. 38; 39; 41; 42

Animal Sketching. Pelham: 1926. V. 40

A Bestiary. New York: 1955. V. 37; 41

Calder's Circus. New York: 1964. V. 41

Fables of Aesop according to Sir Roger L'Estrange. Paris: (1931). V. 37

Works. New York: 1971. V. 39

CALDER, J. A.

Some Phases of the Canada '49 Issue. Plymouth. V. 44

CALDER-MARSHALL, ARTHUR

A Crime Against Cania. Waltham St. Lawrence: 1934. V. 37; 41; 42; 44

A Crime Against Cania. London: 1934. V. 37

Occasion of Glory. London: 1955. V. 41

CALDER, W. M.

Anatolian Studies Presented to William Hepburn Buckler. Manchester: 1939. V. 44

Monumenta Asiae Minoris Antiqua. Manchester: 1928-62. V. 40

CALDERON DE LA BARCA, FRANCES ERSKINE INGLIS

Life in Mexico During a Residence of Two Years in taht Country by . . . . Boston: 1843. V. 39; 43

Life in Mexico During a Residence of Two Years in that Country. London: 1843. V. 38; 41; 42; 44; 46

CALDERON DE LA BARCA, PEDRO 1600-1681

Autos Sacramentales, Alegoricos, y Historiales . . . Obras Posthumas, que del Archivo de la Villa de Madrid Saca Originales a luz Don Pedro de Pando y Mier. Madrid: 1717. V. 40

Autos Sacramentales. Madrid: 1759-60. V. 40

Comedias . . . Que Nuevamente Corregidas Publica Don Iuan de Vera Tassis y Villaroel su Mayor Amigo. Madrid: 1682-91/1715. V. 40

La Vida es Sueno. Barcelona: (1933). V. 37

The Mighty Magician (and) Such Stuff as Dreams are Made of. London: 1865. V. 41

Six Dramas of Calderon. London: 1853. V. 41

CALDERONE, MARY STEICHEN

The First Picture Book: Everyday Things for Babies. New York: 1991. V. 46

CALDERWOOD, DAVID

The History of the Kirk of Scotland. Edinburgh: 1842. V. 37

CALDERWOOD, G. W.

Oakland 'Athens of the Pacific' . . . Also Facts and Figures of Alameda County. Oakland: 1896. V. 40

CALDERWOOD, W. L.

The Life of the Salmon, With Reference More Especially to the Fish in Scotland. London: 1907. V. 41

Salmon and Sea Trout, with Chapters on Hydro-electric Schemes, Fish Passes, &c. London: 1930. V. 41

CALDESI, GIOVANNI

Osservazioni intorno alle Tartarughe Marittime, d'Acqua dolce, e Terrestri, scritte in una Lettera all'illustriss. Florence: 1687. V. 37; 39; 41; 43

CALDICOTT, J. W.

Values of Old English Silver and Sheffield Plate, from the XVth to the XIXth Centuries. London: 1906. V. 38; 40

CALDWALL, THOMAS

A Collection of Epitaphs and Inscriptions . . . London: 1802. V. 38

CALDWELL, CHARLES

The Author Turned Critic; or the Reviewer Reviewed . . . Philadelphia: 1816. V. 41

An Elegaic Poem on the Death of General George Washington, Commander in the Chief of the Armies of the United States. Philadelphia: 1800. V. 45

Elements of Phrenology. Lexington: 1827. V. 41; 45

Essays on Malaria and Temperament. Lexington: 1831. V. 39; 42

Memoirs of the Life and Campaigns of the Hon. Nathaniel Greene. Philadelphia: 1819. V. 45

Phrenology Vindicated, and Antiphrenology Unmasked. New York: 1838. V. 37

Thoughts on the Original Unity of the Human Race. Cincinnati: 1852. V. 42

CALDWELL, ERSKINE PRESTON 1903-

All Night Long. New York: 1942. V. 43

All-Out on the Road to Smolensk. New York: 1942. V. 37; 38; 39; 40; 42

American Earth. New York: 1931. V. 42

The Bastard. New York: 1929. V. 44

God's Little Acre. New York: 1933. V. 39

God's Little Acre. 1979. V. 38

God's Little Acre. Franklin Center: 1979. V. 43

In Defense of Myself. Portland: 1929. V. 40

In Defense of Myself. 1982. V. 42

Jackpot. Short Stories of . . . New York: 1940. V. 39

Journeyman. New York: 1935. V. 38; 41; 42; 46

Kneel to the Rising Sun. New York: 1935. V. 37; 38; 39; 40; 42; 43; 45; 46

Mama's Little Girl. Mt. Mermon, (Maine): 1932. V. 37

A Message for Genevieve. Mount Vernon: 1933. V. 37; 43; 46

North of the Danube. New York: 1939. V. 39

Poor Fool. New York: 1930. V. 37; 39; 43

The Sacrilege of Alan Kent. Portland, Maine: 1936. V. 37; 39; 43

The Sacrilege of Alan Kent. Paris: 1976. V. 37; 39; 42

Say, Is This the U.S.A. New York: 1941. V. 46

Tenant Farmer. New York: 1935. V. 43; 46

Three by Caldwell. Tobacco Road. Georgia Boy. The Sure Hand of God. Boston: 1947. V. 43

Tobacco Road. New York. V. 42

Tobacco Road. New York. V. 41

Tobacco Road. New York: 1932. V. 40; 44; 45

Trouble in July. New York: 1940. V. 39

We are the Living. New York: 1933. V. 37; 39; 40; 42; 43; 44; 46

When You Think of Me. Boston: 1936. V. 43

You Have Seen Their Faces. New York: 1937. V. 42; 45

CALDWELL, H. R.

South China Bird Books. Shanghai: 1931. V. 37

CALDWELL, JAMES

Debates Relative to the Affairs to Ireland; in the Years 1763 and 1764. London: 1766. V. 42; 43

Debates Relative to the Affairs of Ireland: in the Years 1763 and 1764, Taken by a Military Officer . . . London: 1776. V. 39

CALDWELL, JAMES FITZ JAMES

The History of a Brigade of South Carolinians, Known First as 'Greggs' and Subsequently as 'McGowan's Brigade.' Philadelphia: 1866. V. 44

CALDWELL, JOHN EDWARDS

A Tour through Part of Virginia, in the Summer of 1808. New York: 1809. V. 38; 45

THE CALEDONIAN Bee; or, A Select Collection, of Interesting Extracts, from Modern Publications. Perth: 1795. V. 45

THE CALEDONIAN Muse: A Chronological Selection of Scottish Poetry from the Earliest Times. London: 1821. V. 41

THE CALEDONIAN Musical Repository. London: 1806. V. 37
THE CALEDONIAN Musical Repository. Edinburgh: 1811. V. 40

CALEF, ROBERT

More Wonders of the Invisible World; or, the Wonders of the Invisible World, Display'd in Five Parts. London: 1700. V. 42; 45

CALENDAR. A.D. 1936. Ditchling: 1935. V. 45

CALENDAR of Letters, Despatches and State Papers, Relative to the Negotiations Between England and Spain/English Affairs . . . London: 1866-1954. V. 46

CALENDAR of Plea and Memoranda Rolls Preserved Among the Archives of the Corporation of the City of London at the Guildhall Rolls . . . a.d. 1323-1364 1413-1437. Cambridge: 1926, 1943. V. 40

CALENDAR of the Stevens Family Papers, 1664-1777. Newark: 1940-41. V. 46

CALENDARIUM Generale. Nuremberg: 1530. V. 44

CALENDARIUM Inquisitiones Post Mortem. London: 1806-1831. V. 40

CALEPINO, AMBROGIO 1435-1511

Dictionarium. Venice: 1521. V. 38

CALEPINUS, AMBROSIUS

Ambrosius Calepinus Passeratii, Siue Linguarum Nouem Romanae, Graecae, Ebraicae, Gallicae, Italicae, Germanicae, Hispanicae, Anglicae, Belgicae Dictionarium. Lugdun. Bat.,: 1654. V. 37

CALFHILL, JAMES 1530-1570

An Aunswere to the Treatise of the Crosse; Wherein ye Shall see by the Plaine and Undoubted Word of God, the Vanities of Men Disproved. London: 1565. V. 38

CALHOUN, ARTHUR W.

Social History of the American Family from Colonial Times to the Present. Cleveland: 1917. V. 42; 43

A Social History of the American Family from Colonial Times to the Present. Cleveland: 1917-19. V. 38; 39; 40

CALHOUN, CHARLES M.

Liberty Dethroned, a Concise History of Some of the Most Startling Events Before, During, and Since the Civil War. Greenwood?: 1903. V. 42; 44; 46

CALHOUN, J. S.

Life and Confession of Mary Jane Gordon. Augusta: 1847. V. 45

CALHOUN, JAMES S.

Official Correspondence of James S. Calhoun While Indian Agent at Santa Fe and Superintendent of Indian Affairs in New Mexico. Washington: 1915. V. 45

CALHOUN, JOHN C.

Mr. Calhoun's Reply to Col. Benton. To the People of the Southern States. N.P.: 1848. V. 42; 45

Speech . . . On the Slavery Question. Washington: 1850. V. 42

To the People of the Southern States. Washington: 1849. V. 39

CALHOUN, JOHN CALDWELL 1782-1865

Correspondence Between Gen. Andrew Jackson and John C. Calhoun President and Vice-President of the United States, on the Subject of the Course of the Latter, in the Deliberations in the Seminole War. Washington: 1831. V. 46

Exposition and Protest, Reported by the Special Committee of the House of Representatives . . . Columbia: 1829. V. 46

The Papers of John C. Calhoun. Columbia: 1959. V. 46

The Works of . . . Columbia. V. 46

CALHOUN, WILLIAM LOWNDES

History of the 42nd Regiment. Georgia Volunteers, Confederate States Army. Infantry . . . Atlanta: 1900. V. 38; 39; 41; 42

CALICO MUSEUM OF TEXTILES, ALMEDABAD.

The Chintz Collection the Calico Museum of Textiles, India. Almedabad: 1983. V. 39

CALIFORNIA As It Is. San Francisco: 1881. V. 38

CALIFORNIA Claims . . . The Memorial of John Charles Fremont, Praying an Investigation of the Claims of Citizens of California Against the U.S. Washington: 1848. V. 45

CALIFORNIA Column. Its Campaigns and Services in New Mexico, Arizona and Texas, During the Civil War, with Sketches of Brigadier General James H. Carleton, Its Commander, and Other Officers and Soldiers. Santa Fe: 1908. V. 43

CALIFORNIA. CONSTITUTION - 1879

The Constitution of the State of California, Adopted in 1879. San Francisco: 1879. V. 37; 39

CALIFORNIA. CONSTITUTIONAL CONVENTION

Debates and Proceedings of the Constitutional Convention of he State of California, Convened at the City of Sacramento, Saturday, September 28, 1878. Sacramento: 1880-81. V. 39

CALIFORNIA Gold Regions, With a Full Account of Their Mineral Resources . . . New York: 1849. V. 38; 42; 45

A CALIFORNIA Gold Rush Miscellany. San Francisco: 1934. V. 42; 46

CALIFORNIA HISTORICAL SOCIETY

Papers of the California Historical Society. San Francisco: 1887. V. 44; 46

CALIFORNIA. LAWS, STATUTES, ETC.

The Practice Act of California, Entitled 'An Act to Regulate Proceedings in Civil Xases in the Courts of Justice in This State'. Sacramento: 1854. V. 43

The Statutes of California, Passed at the Fifth Session of the Legislature, January-May, 1854. Sacramento: 1854. V. 37; 42; 43

The Statutes of California, Passed at the Tenth Session of the Legislature. Sacramento: 1859. V. 43

CALIFORNIA. LAWS, STATUTES, ETC. - 1850

Statutes of California, Passed at the First Session of the Legislature. Begun the 15th Day of Dec. 1849 and ended the 22nd Day of April, 1850, at the City of Pueblo de San Jose. San Jose: 1850. V. 41; 43

CALIFORNIA. LAWS, STATUTES, ETC. - 1853

Compiled Laws of the State of California . . . With the Constitution of California. Benicia: 1853. V. 39

CALIFORNIA. LAWS, STATUTES, ETC. - 1854

The Practice Act of California, Entitled an Act to Regulate Proceedings in Civil Cases in the Courts of Justice of this State. Sacramento: 1854. V. 39

CALIFORNIA. LAWS, STATUTES, ETC. - 1857

The Statutes of California, Passed at the Eighth Session of the Legislature 1857. Sacramento: 1857. V. 41

CALIFORNIA. LEGISLATIVE - 1851

Journals of the Legislature of the State of California; at Its Second Session; Held at the City of San Jose, Commencing on the Sixth Day of Jan. & Ending on the First Day of May, 1851. San Jose: 1851. V. 44

CALIFORNIA MINERS' ASSOCIATION

California Mines and Minerals. San Francisco: 1899. V. 37; 40

CALIFORNIA. NATIONAL GUARD

Rules and Regulations of the First Cavalry Battalion Second Brigade. National Guard of California. Adopted October 25, 1878. San Francisco: 1878. V. 39

CALIFORNIA State Almanac and Annual Register for 1856. Sacramento: 1856. V. 45

CALIFORNIA. STATE EARTHQUAKE COMMISSION.

Atlas of Maps and Seismograms Accompanying the Report of the State Earthquake Investigation Commission Upon the California Earthquake of April 18, 1906. Washington: 1908. V. 39

CALIFORNIA. SUPREME COURT

In the Supreme Court of the State of California. A. W. Delane and Anton Reif, Copartners &c. Respondents vs. The Pacific Coast Land Bureau, Appellants. San Diego: 1890. V. 40

In the Supreme Court of the State of California: J.S. Polack, Et. Ux . . . Vs James Shafer, Et Als. San Francisco: 1870. V. 37

Reports of Cases Aruged and Determined in the Supreme Court of the State of California, in the year 1852. Philadelphia: 1854. V. 39

Reports of Cases Argued and Determined in the Supreme Court of the State of California, in the Year 1853. Philadelphia: 1855. V. 39

CALISHER, HORTENSE

In the Absence of Angels. London: 1953. V. 45

CALKINS, D.

Strange Adventures in the Spider Ship. 1935. V. 43

Strange Adventures in the Spider Ship. 1935. V. 43

CALKINS, N. A.

A Classified List of Object Teaching Aids for Home and School. New York: 1872. V. 37

CALL, I.

Scenes in Texas, Being a Recital of the Sufferings of a Lady in Her Escape from the Indians . . . Springfield: 1852. V. 41; 42

CALLAGHAN, E. B.

Documents Relative to the Colonial History of the State of New York. Albany: 1856-87. V. 42

CALLAGHAN, JEREMIAH 1780-1861

Usury; or, Lending at Interest, Also . . . The Payment of Certain Church-Fees . . . London: 1828. V. 41

CALLAGHAN, MORLEY EDWARD

A Broken Journey. New York: 1932. V. 41

It's Never Over. Toronto: 1930. V. 43

No Man's Meat. Paris: 1931. V. 37; 40; 41; 42; 43

Now That April's Here. New York: 1936. V. 41

Strange Fugitive. New York: 1928. V. 37; 43

That Summer in Paris. New York. V. 38

That Summer in Paris. New York. V. 37

CALLAHAN, HARRY

Color. Providence: 1980. V. 42

Harry Callahan: Photographs. Santa Barbara: 1964. V. 41; 46

CALLANDER, JOHN

A Critical Review of the Works of Dr. Samuel Johnson. London: 1783. V. 42

CALLAWAY, JOHN

A Vocabulary; with Useful Phrases, and Familiar Dialogues; in the English, Portuguese and Cingalese, Languages . . . Colombo: 1818. V. 41

CALLCOTT, JOHN WALL

A Musical Grammar, In Four Parts. Boston: (1810). V. 37

A Musical Grammar, in four parts: I. Notation, II. Melody, III. Harmony, IV. Rhythm. London: 1806. V. 37; 40; 42

CALLCOTT, MARIA DUNDAS GRAHAM

Voyage of H.M.S. Blonde to the Sandwich Islands, in the years 1824-1825. Captain the Right Hon. Lord Byron, Commander. London: 1826. V. 37

CALLCOTT, MARIA DUNDAS GRAHAM, LADY

Description of the Chapel of the Annunziata Dell' Arena. London: 1835. V. 44

CALLCOTT, WILFRID H.

Santa Anna: The Story of an Enigma Who Once was Mexico. Norman: 1936. V. 37; 45

CALLE, CALEB

On His Royal Highness's Miraculous Delivery and Happy Return. London: 1682. V. 41

CALLENBACH, ERNEST

Ecotopia. Berkeley: 195. V. 45

CALLENDER, GEORGE W.

Anatomy of the Parts Concerned in Femoral Rupture. London: 1863. V. 39

CALLENDER, JAMES T.

The American Annual Register; or, Historical Memoirs of the United States. Philadelphia: 1797. V. 46

The History of the United States for 1796, including a Variety of Interesting Particulars Relative to the Federal Government previous to that Period. Philadelphia: 1797. V. 37

Letters to Alexander Hamilton, King of the Feds . . . Being Intended as a Reply to a Scandalous Pamphlet Lately PUblished . . . by Tom Callender, Esq. New York: 1802. V. 41

The Political Progress of Britain . . . London: 1795. V. 42

Sketches of the History of America. Philadelphia: 1798. V. 42

CALLENDER, JAMES THOMPSON

Short History of the Nature and Consequences of Excise Laws . . . Philadelphia: 1795. V. 43

CALLENDER, JOHN

An Historical Discourse on the Civil and Religious Affairs of the Colony of Rhode-Island and Providence Plantations in New England in America, From the First Settlement 1638 to the End of the First Century. Boston: 1739. V. 39; 40; 42; 43

CALLENDER, M. H.

Roman Amphorae with Index of Stamps. London: 1970. V. 42

CALLICK Reports or an Historical Collection of Criminal Cases Adjudges in Supreme Courts of Judicataure in France . . . (with) a Copious Preface, in Relation to the Laws and Constitution of France . . . London: 1737. V. 38

CALLIERES, FRANCOIS DE

The Knowledge of the World and the Attainments Useful in the Conduct of Life. London: 1770. V. 44

CALLIMACHUS OF CYRENE

(Greek title) Epigrammata. Glasgow: 1755. V. 45

Hymni & Epigrammata, Eiusdem Poemtaium de Coma Berenices . . . Geneva: 1577. V. 44

Hymni (Cum Suis Scholiis Graecis), & Epigrammata. Geneva: 1577. V. 37; 38; 40; 41; 42; 46

Hymni Epigrammata et Fragmenta . . . Antwerp: 1584. V. 37; 43

The Hymns of Callimachus . . . to which are added, Select Epigrams, & the Coma Bernices of the Same Author, Six Hymns of Orpheus & The Encomium of Ptolemy by Theocritus. London: 1755. V. 38

The Hymns of Callimachus . . . Select Epigrams . . . Coma Berenices, Six Hymns of Orpheus and the Encomium of Ptolemy by Theodritus. V. 46

The Works. London: 1793. V. 38; 45

CALLIOPE or English Harmony. London: 1739. V. 40

CALLIOPE; or, the Musical Miscellany. Edinburgh: 1788. V. 42

CALLIS, JO ANNE

Objects of Reverie. Selected Photographs 1977-1989. Des Moines: 1989. V. 42; 44

CALLIS, ROBERT fl. 1634

The Reading of that Famous and Learned Gentleman, Robert Callis, Esq; Sergeant at Law Upon the Statute of 23 H.S. Cap. 5 of Sewers. London: 1647. V. 40

CALLISON, JOHN

Bill Jones of Paradise Valley Oklahoma. Chicago: 1914. V. 43

CALLISON, JOHN J.

Bill Jones of Pradise Valley Oklahoma. 1914. V. 44

CALLMANN, ELLEN

Apollonio di Giovanni. Oxford: 1974. V. 43; 45

CALLOT, JACQUES

Combat a la Barriere, Faict en Cour de Lorraine le 14. Febvrier . . . Representee par les Discours & Poesie du Sieur Henry Humbert . . . Nancy: 1627. V. 38

Exercises Militaires Fait par Noble I. Callot Mis en Lumiere par Israel son Amy . . . Paris: 1635. V. 42

CALLOW, EDWARD

From King Orry to Queen Victoria. A Short and Concise History of the Isle of Man. London: 1899. V. 39

CALMET, AUGUSTIN

A Dissertation Upon the High-Roads of the Duchy of Lorraine, As Well Ancient as Modern. London: 1729. V. 43

CALMET'S Great Dictionary of the Holy Bible; Historical, Critical, Geographical, and Etymological . . . London: 1797-1803. V. 40; 41

CALMO, ANDREA

Delle Lettere. Venice: 1580. V. 44

CALMOUR, ALFRED CECIL

Fact and Fiction About Shakespeare with Some Account of the Playhouses, Players and Playwrights of His Period. Stratford-upon-Avon: 1894. V. 40; 43

Rumbo Rhymes; or the Great Combine: a Satire. 1911. V. 41

Rumbo Rhymes of the Great Combine, a Satire. London: 1911. V. 37; 41; 46

CALONNE, CHARLES ALEXANDRE DE 1734-1802

A Catalogue of All That Noble and Superlatively Capital Assemblage of Valuable Pictures, Drawings, Miniatures, and Prints. London. V. 44

Museum Calonnianum. Specification of the Various Articles of Natural History Collected by M. de Calonne. London: 1797. V. 38

The Speech Delivered by the Order and in the Presence of the King in the Assembly of the Notables, Held at Versailles, on the 22nd of February 1787. (with) Appendix - A Memorial Upon the Land Tax . . . London: 1787. V. 39

CALOT, F.

Indispensable Orthopaedics. London: 1914. V. 42

CALTHROP, DION CLAYTON

English Costume. London: 1906. V. 46

CALTHROPE, CHARLES d. 1616

The Relation Betweene the Lord of a Manor and the Coppy-Holder His Tenant. London: 1635. V. 40

CALVERT, ALBERT F.

The Exploration of Australia. London: 1895. V. 46

Spain. An Historical and Descriptive Account of Its Architecture, Landscape and Arts. London: 1924. V. 38; 40

CALVERT, FREDERICK

The Isle of Wight Illustrated in a Series of Coloured Views . . . London: 1846. V. 41; 43

Picturesque Views, and Descriptions of Cities, Towns, Castles, Mansions and Other Objects of Interesting Features in Staffordshire and Shropshire . . . Birmingham: 1830-31. V. 39

Ruins, Illustrative of Ancient Splendor . . . London: 1821-24, 1825. V. 40

The Young Artist's Instructor. London: 1823. V. 44

CALVERT, FREDERICK, BARON BALTIMORE

Gli Abitatori del Cielo e Dell' Inferno . . . Venezia: 1771. V. 45

CALVERT, GEORGE CHAMBERS

A Defence of the Dilettante. N.P.: 1919. V. 46

A Defense of the Dilettante. 1919. V. 38

CALVERT, GEORGE H.

Correspondence Between Schiller and Goethe, from 1794 to 1805. New York: 1845. V. 39

CALVERT, HARRY

Regulations and instructions for the infantry sword exercise. Adjutant General's Office, Horse-Guards, 10th September, 1819. By Authority. London: (1819). V. 37

CALVERT, HENRY M.

Reminiscences of a Boy in Blue, 1862-1866. New York: 1920. V. 44

CALVERT, J.

The Gold rocks of Great Britain and Ireland, with a Treatise on the Geology of Gold. London: 1853. V. 44; 46

CALVI, DONATO

Scena Letteraria de gli Scrittori Bergamaschi. Bergamo: 1664. V. 41

CALVIN, JEAN 1509-1564

Commentarii in Isaiam Prophetam. Geneva: 1583. V. 40

Commentarius in Librum Psalmorum. Geneva: 1578. V. 41; 42

In Omnes Pauli Apostoli Epistolas, atque Etia in Epistolam ad Hebraeos . . . Commentarii.(with) Commentarii in Epistolas Canonicas . . . ad Edvardum VI. Angliae Regem . . . Geneva: 1557, 1554. V. 41

Institvtio Christianae Religionis . . . Genevae: 1568. V. 40

Two and Twentie Sermons of Maister Iohn Calvin, in Which Sermons Is Most Religiously Handled, the Hundredth and Nineteenth Psalme of Dauid, by Eight Verses Aparte According to the Hebrew Alphabet. London: 1850. V. 41

CALVIN, JOHN

A Commentarie of John Calvine, Upon the First Booke of Moses Called Genesis: Translated Out of Latine into English by Thomas Tymme, Minister. London: 1578. V. 38

The Commentaries of M. John Calvin Upon the Actes of the Apostles. Londini: 1585. V. 38

Commentarii in Quatuor Eungelistas Matthaeum, Marcum, Lucam & Joannem. Quorum Tres Priores in Formn Harmoniae sunt Digest . . . Nec non in Acta Apostlolrum . . . Amsterdam: 1667. V. 38

Commentarii in Omnes Epistolas S. Pauli Apostoli, et que etiam in Epistolam ad Hebraeos; nec non in Epistolas Canonicas . . . Amsterdam: 1667. V. 38

A Commentary Upon the Prophecie of Isaiah. London: 1609. V. 44

A Harmonie upon the three Euangelistes Mathewe, Marke, and Luke, with the Commentarie of M. John Caluine: Faithfully translated out ot Latine into English by E.P. Whereunto is also added a Commentarie upon the Euangelist S. John, by . . . London: 1610. V. 37

The Institution of the Christian Religion, in Four Books. Glasgow: 1762. V. 39

Institutionum Christianae Religionis Libri Quatuor. Amsterdam: 1667. V. 38

Praeclectiones in Librum Prophetiarum Danielis, Jonnis Budaei & Caroli Jonvillaei Labore & Industria Excerptae. Amsterdam: 1667. V. 38

Praelectiones Ioannis Calvini in Librum Prophetiarum Danielis, Ioannis Budei & Caroli Ionukllei Labore & Industria Exeptae. Lyon: 1571. V. 38

Preces et Soliloquia. Christliche, Ausserlesene Gebet und Heimliche Gesprech Beide mit Gott und Mit Ihm Selbst, in Allerley not und Anligen . . . Herborn: 1616. V. 38

CALVIN, ROSS

River of the Sun: Stories of the Storied Gila. Albuquerque: 1946. V. 41

THE CALVINISTIC Family Library, Devoted to the Republication of Standard Calvinistic Works. Cadiz: 1835-36. V. 41

CALVINO, ITALO

The Baron in the Trees. New York: 1959. V. 43; 46

Invisible Cities. 1974. V. 44

Invisible Cities. London: 1974. V. 40

invisible Cities. New York: 1974. V. 46

Italian Fables. New York: 1959. V. 46

The Nonexistent Knight and the Cloven Viscount. New York: 1962. V. 44; 46

Prima che tu Dicta 'Pronto'. Cottondale: 1985. V. 45

The Silent Mr. Palomar. 1981. V. 43

The Silent Mr. Palomar. New York: 1981. V. 46

Tarots. Parma: 1975. V. 43

Ti Con Zero. Torino: 1967. V. 44

Time and the Hunter. London: 1970. V. 45

CAMAC, C. N. B.

Counsels and Ideals from the Writings of Sir William Osler. Boston: 1905. V. 42

CAMAC, WILLIAM

Memoirs of the Camacs of County Down (Ireland), with some account of their predecessors, in one volume, to which is added brief sketches of some of the Families with whom they intermarried. Philadelphia: 1913. V. 37

CAMACHO, SIMON

Costas de los Estados Unidos por Nazareno. New York: 1864. V. 38

CAMARD, FLORENCE

Ruhlmann: Master of Art Deco. New York: 1984. V. 46

CAMBAGE, RICHARD HIND

Notes on the Botany of the Interior of New South Wales. 1900-03. V. 37

CAMBELL, KEN

In the Door Stands a Jar. 1987. V. 40

CAMBOUT DE PONT CHATEAU, S. J.

The Moral Practice of the Jesuites Demonstrated by Many Remarkable Histories of Their Actions in all Parts of the World . . . London: 1671. V. 39

CAMBPELL, ARCHIBALD

A Voyage Round the World, from 1806 to 1812 . . . Charaleston: 1822. V. 38

CAMBPELL, THOMAS

Life of Mrs. Siddons. London: 1834. V. 37

CAMBRELENG, CHURCHILL CALDOM

An Examination of the New Tariff Proposed by the Hon. Henry Baldwin, a Representative in Congress. New York: 1821. V. 37

Report of the Committee on the Commerce and Navigation of the United States. London: 1830. V. 39

CAMBRIDGE Ancient History. 1923-39. V. 45
CAMBRIDGE Ancient History. Cambridge: 1927-39. V. 44
CAMBRIDGE Ancient History. 1964-84. V. 45
CAMBRIDGE Ancient History. Cambridge: 1970-1977. V. 40

CAMBRIDGE Bibliography of English Literature. Cambridge: 1940-57. V. 37
CAMBRIDGE Bibliography of English Literature. Cambridge: 1941-57. V. 42

THE CAMBRIDGE Book of Poetry For Children. Cambridge: 1932. V. 46

CAMBRIDGE CAMDEN SOCIETY

Illustrations of Monumental Brasses. Cambridge: 1846. V. 37

Reports, 1841-46. Cambridge: 1841-46. V. 37

CAMBRIDGE History of English Literature. Cambridge: 1907-16. V. 46
CAMBRIDGE History of English Literature. 1907-16 & 1934. V. 46
THE CAMBRIDGE History of English Literature. Cambridge: 1933-53. V. 39

THE CAMBRIDGE Modern History. New York: 1902. V. 45
CAMBRIDGE Modern History. Cambridge: 1934. V. 37
CAMBRIDGE Modern History. Cambridge: 1957-59. V. 37

CAMBRIDGE Natural History. London: 1895-1909. V. 37; 40

CAMBRIDGE Poetry 1929. London: 1929. V. 39

CAMBRIDGE Poetry 1929 - Hogarth Living Poets No. 8. London: 1929. V. 40

CAMBRIDGE Poetry 1930 - Hogarth Living Poets No. 13. London: 1930. V. 40

THE CAMBRIDGE Review. Cambridge: 1932-36. V. 46

CAMBRIDGE, RICHARD

The Works. Including Several Pieces Never Before Published. London: 1803. V. 38; 43

CAMBRIDGE, RICHARD OWEN

An Account of the War in India Between the English and French, on the Coast of Coromandel. From the Year 1750 to the Year 1760. London: 1761. V. 41

The Fable of Jotham . . . London: 1754. V. 43

The Scribleriad: an Heroic Poem. In Six Books. London: 1751. V. 37; 40; 43

The Works, Including Several Pieces Never Before Published, with an Account of His Life and Character. London: 1803. V. 37; 39; 40; 45; 46

CAMBRIDGE SPINNING-HOUSE

Rules and Regulations. N.P.: 1854. V. 43

CAMBRIDGE UNIVERSITY. FITZWILLIAM MUSEUM

Catalogue of the Glaisher Collection of Pottery and Porcelain in the Fitzwilliam Museum, Cambridge. Cambridge: 1935. V. 45

The Fitzwilliam Music. London: 1827. V. 39

CAMBRIDGE UNIVERSITY. LIBRARY

A Catalogue of Persian Manuscripts in the Library of the University of Cambridge. Cambridge: 1896. V. 46

A Catalogue of the Fifteenth Century Printed Books in the University Library, Cambridge. Cambridge: 1954. V. 46

Early English Printed Books in the University Library Cambridge (1475-1640). Cambridge: 1900-07. V. 39

CAMBRIDGE. UNIVERSITY. LIBRARY. BRADSHAW IRISH COLLECTION

A Catalogue of the Bradshaw Collection of Irish Books in the University Library, Cambridge. Cambridge: 1916. V. 40; 43

CAMBRIDGE UNIVERSITY PRESS

Oriental Founts Available for Book Composition at the University Press. Cambridge: 1933. V. 45

THE CAMBRIDGE University Press Collection of Private Press Types: Kelmscott, Ashendene, Eragny, Cranach. Cambridge: 1951. V. 43; 45

THE CAMBRIDGESHIRE Tragedy, or Burwell in Tears Being a Sad But True Relation of that Dreadful Fire, Which Happened at a Poppet-Show Belonging to one Mr. Shepherd; at a place Call'd Brnwell (sic) in Cambridgeshire . . . London: 1730. V. 46

CAMBRILL, RICHARD V. N.

Sporting Stables and Kennels. London: 1936. V. 44

CAMDEN, Ouachita County, Arkansas. Resources and Advantages of Camden, with a Description of Soil Climate, Timber . . . for Those Seeking Homes in the Southwest. Little Rock: 1883. V. 44

CAMDEN, WILLIAM 1551-1623

Annales Rerum Anglicarum, et Hibernicarum . . . London: 1615. V. 40; 42; 43; 45

Annales Rerum Anglicarum et Hibernicarum, Regnante Elizabetha, ad Annum Salutis. London: 1616. V. 41

Annales Rerum Anglicarum et Hibernicarum, Regnante Elizabetha. Lug. Batavorum: 1625. V. 39

Britain, or, a Chorographical Description of the Most Flourishing Kingdomes, England, Scotland and Ireland . . . London: 1610. V. 41; 46

Britannia, Sive Florentissimo Regnorum Angliae, Scotiae, Hiberniae, et Insularum Adiacentium Ex Intima Antiquitate Chorographica Descriptione. London: 1594. V. 40; 43

Britannia Sive Florentissimorum Regnorum, Angliae, Scotiae, Hiberniae . . . London: 1600. V. 41

Britain, or a Chorographicall Description of the Most Flourishing Kingdomes, England, Scotland and Ireland and the Islands Adjoyning . . . London: 1637. V. 40

Britain, or, A Chorographicall Description of the Most Flourishing Kingdomes of England, Scotland and Ireland . . . London: 1695. V. 40

Britannia . . . London: 1695. V. 40; 42; 43

Britannia Abrig'd; with Improvements and Continuations . . . London: 1701. V. 39; 41

Britain, or, A Chorographicall Description of the Most Flourishing Kingdomes, England, Scotland, and Ireland . . . London: 1722. V. 40; 41; 42; 44

Britannia. London: 1772. V. 40; 42

Britannia; or a Chorographical Description of the Flourishing Kingdoms of England, Scotland and Ireland. London: 1806. V. 37; 39; 40; 41; 46

Britannia. London: 1974. V. 39

Britannia: or, a chorographical description of Great Britain and Ireland . . . (translated) . . . (and) revised by Edmund Gibson, the third edition . . . London: 1753. V. 37; 39

The History of the Most Renowned and Victorious Princess Elizabeth, Late Queen of England. London: 1675. V. 37; 38

The History of the Most Renowned and Victorious Princess Elizabeth, Late Queen of England . . . London: 1688. V. 37; 44; 45

Reges, Reginae, Nobiles, et Alii in Ecclesia Collegiata. London: 1600. V. 44

Remaines, Concerning Britaine: But Especially England and the Inhabitants Thereof . . . London: 1614. V. 41

Remaines concerning Britaine. The fifth Impression, with many rare Antiquities never before imprinted. By the industry and care of John Philipot, Somerset Herald. London: 1637. V. 37

Remains Concerning Britain: Their Languages, Names Surnames, Allusions, Anagrammes, Armories, Monies . . . London: 1636. V. 40; 43

Remains Concerning Britain: Their Languages, Names, Surnames, Allusions, Anagrammes, Armories, etc. London: 1657. V. 40; 41

Remains Concerning Britain. London: 1870. V. 41

Rerum Anglicarum et Libericarum Annales Regnante Elisabetha . . . Lugd. Batavorum: 1639. V. 41

CAMERA CLUB

Photographic Pictures of the Year. London: 1892. V. 46

A CAMERA in the Gold Rush. 1946. V. 44
A CAMERA in the Gold Rush. San Francisco: 1946. V. 41

CAMERARIUS, JOACHIM 1500-1574

Capita Pietatis Religionis Christianae . . . Liepzig: 1564. V. 38; 40; 46

Hortus Medicus et Philosophicus . . . Francofurti A. M.: 1588. V. 37

De Philippi Melanchthonis, ortu, Totius Vitae Curriculo et Morte, Implicata Rerum Memorabilium Temporis Illius Hominumque . . . Lipsiae: 1566. V. 38; 44

Symbolorum Emblematum ex re Herbaria Desumtorum Centuria Una Collecta . . . Nuremberg: 1590. V. 46

CAMERARIUS, PHILIP

The Living Librarie, or Meditations and Observations Historical, Natural, Moral, Political and Poetical. London: 1625. V. 45

Operae Horarvm Succisivarvm Sive Meditationes Historicae. Nuremberg: 1591. V. 39

CAMERON. A Novel. London: 1832. V. 39; 46

CAMERON, CHARLES A.

History of the Royal College of Surgeons in Ireland and of the Irish Schools of Medicine . . . Dublin: 1916. V. 40

CAMERON, CHARLES HAY

Two Essays. On the Sublime and the Beautiful, and on Duelling. London: 1835. V. 37

CAMERON, D.

Thaumaturgus; or, Wonders of the Magic Lantern. Glasgow: 1816-17. V. 38

CAMERON, DAVID YOUNG

D. Y. Cameron, an Illustrated Catalogue of His Etched Work. Glasgow: 1912. V. 45

The Etchings of D. Y. Cameron. London: 1924. V. 44

CAMERON, DUNCAN

Reports of Cases Ruled and Determined by the Court of Conference of North Carolina. Raleigh: 1805. V. 44

CAMERON, GEORGE G.

Persepolis Treasury Tablets. Chicago: 1948. V. 40; 42

CAMERON, GORDON RAY

Pathology of the Cell. Edinburgh and London: 1952. V. 45

CAMERON, ISABELLE DOROTHEA

The American Book of Beauty. New York: 1904. V. 37; 38

CAMERON, JOHN

The Messiah. Belfast: 1768. V. 41

Ordnance Survey. London: 1855. V. 44

Our Tropical Possessions in Maylayan India. London: 1865. V. 38; 42

CAMERON, JULIA MARGARET

Alfred Lord Tennyson, and His Friends. London: 1893. V. 37

Victorian Photographs of Famous Men and Fair women. London. V. 40

Victorian Photographs of Famous Men and Fair Women. London: 1926. V. 37; 38; 40; 41; 42; 45; 46

Victorian Photographs of Famous Men and Fair Women. New York: 1926. V. 37

CAMERON, KATHERINE

The Enchanted Land. London: 1906. V. 42; 43

Where the Bee Sucks - Book of Flowers. London: and Boston. V. 45

CAMERON, KENNETH NEILL

The Carl H. Pforzheimer Library - Shelley and His Circle 1773-1922. Cambridge: 1961. V. 44; 46

Shelley and His Circle, 1773-1822. Cambridge: 1961-73. V. 44

CAMERON, PETER

A Monograph of the British Phytophagous Hymenoptera. London: 1882-92. V. 43

A Monograph of the British Phytophagous Hymenoptera. London: 1882-93. V. 37

CAMERON, VERNEY LOVETT

Across Africa. London: 1865. V. 39

Across Africa. Dalby: 1877. V. 44

Across Africa. London: 1877. V. 38; 41; 42; 43; 44; 45; 46

In Savage Africa, or, the Adventures of Frank Baldwin from the Gold Coast to Zanzibar. London: 1887, 1886. V. 39

CAMERON, WILLIAM

Poems on Various Subjects. Edinburgh: 1780. V. 40

Poetical Dialogues (in Verse) on Religion in the Scots Dialect, Between Two Gentlemen and Two Ploughmen. Edinburgh: 1788. V. 40; 42

CAMILLI, CAMILLO

Imprese Illustri di Diversi . . . Parte Prima (-Terza). Venice: 1586. V. 37; 38; 39; 40

CAMILLO, GIULIO

Tutte l'Opere di M. Giulio Camillo Delminio, il Catalogo delle Quali s'ha Nella Seguente Facciata . . . Vinegia: 1568. V. 46

CAMINOS, RICARDO A.

Literary Fragments in the Hieratic Script. Oxford: 1956. V. 41

The New-Kingdom Temples of Buhen. London: 1974. V. 37; 40

CAMMACK, JOHN HENRY

Personal Recollections of Private John Henry Cammack, a Soldier of the Confederacy. Huntington: 1920. V. 43; 44

CAMMAERTS, EMILE

Rubens - Painter and Diplomat. London: 1932. V. 46

CAMMERMEIR, SIMON

Neues Zierathenbuch . . . Nuremberg: 1650. V. 44

CAMMIDGE, P. J.

The Insulin Treatment of Diabetes Mellitus. Edinburgh: 1924. V. 40

CAMOENS, LUIZ DE 1524?-1580

Love Poems. 1886. V. 38

The Lusiad; or, the Discovery of India, an Epic Poem. Oxford: 1778. V. 37; 46

Poems, from the Portuguese of Camoes: with Remarks on His Life and Writings. London: 1804. V. 46

Poems, from the Portuguese . . . with Remarks on His Life and Writings. London: 1895. V. 41

CAMOES, LUIZ DE 1524?-1580

The Lusiad or the Discovery of India, an Epic Poem. London: 1778. V. 39

The Lusiad; or, The Discovery of India, an Epic Poem. Oxford: 1778. V. 43

The Lusiad or the Discovery of India an Epic Poem . . . Oxford: 1778. V. 40

The Lusiad. Oxford: 1778. V. 45

The Lusiad, or the Discovery of India. London: 1807. V. 40

Camoens. The Lyricks . . . London: 1884. V. 43

The Lyrics. London: 1884. V. 45

Poems from the Portuguese. London: 1804. V. 45

CAMP, CHARLES L.

Essays for Henry R. Wagner. San Francisco: 1947. V. 37; 41

James Clyman, Frontiersman, 1792-1881. Edited by Charles L. Camp. Portland: (1960). V. 37; 46

Muggins the Cow Horse. Denver: 1928. V. 37

CAMP, DAVID N.

History of New Britain. New Britain: 1889. V. 40; 41; 42

CAMP FIRE GIRLS, INC.

The Book of the Camp Fire Girls. New York: 1936. V. 42

CAMP, L. SPRAGUE

The Dragon of the Ishtar Gate. New York: 1961. V. 45

Wall of Serpents. 1978. V. 45

CAMP Merryweather Songs. N.P.: 1930. V. 41

CAMP, WALTER

American Football. New York: 1891. V. 38

Drives and Puts. Boston: 1899. V. 38

CAMPAN, JEAN LOUISE HENRIETTE

Memoirs of the Private Life of Marie Antoinette . . . London: 1823. V. 39

CAMPAN, JEANNE LOUISE HENRIETTE

The Private Life of Marie Antoinette. New York: 1883. V. 38

CAMPANA, CESARE

Delle Historie del Mondo . . . Venetia: 1599-97. V. 37

CAMPANA, DINO

Episolario. Milan: 1985. V. 41; 44

CAMPANELLA, TOMMASO 1568-1639

Apologia pro Galileo, Mathematico Italiano. Francofurti: 1622. V. 40; 42

De Monarchia Hispanica: Discursus. Hardovici: (1640). V. 37

Medicinalium Juxta Propria Principia, Libri Septem. Lugduni: 1635. V. 40

Philosphiae Rationalis Partres Quinque . . . Grammatica, Dialectica, Rhetorica, Poetica, Historiographia, Iuxta Propria Principia. Paris: 1637-38. V. 37

De Sensu Rerum et Magia, Libri Quatuor. Frankfurt: 1620. V. 39; 46

CAMPANIUS HOLM, THOMAS 1811-1896

Kort Beskrifning Om Provincien Nya Swerige Uti America, som nu Fortjden af the Engelske Kallas Pensylvania . . . Stockholm: 1702. V. 37; 41; 43; 45

A Short Description of New Sweden, Now Called by the English, Pennsylvania . . . Philadelphia: 1834. V. 39; 41; 42; 43

CAMPBEL, WILFRED

Canada. London: 1907. V. 45

CAMPBELL, A. J.

Nests and Eggs of Australian Birds. Sheffield: 1901. V. 38

CAMPBELL, ALBERT H.

Pacific Wagon Roads. Letter from the Sec. of The Interior, Transmitting a Report Upon the Several Wagon Roads Constructed Under the Direction of the Interior Dept. Washington: 1859. V. 37; 40; 41; 42; 43; 45; 46

CAMPBELL, ALEXANDER 1764-1825

Christian Baptism: with Its Antecedents and Consequents. Bethany: 1853. V. 46

Debate on Christian Baptism, Between the Rev. W. I. Mac Calla, a Presbyterian Teacher, and Alexander Campbell . . . in Which Interspersed and to Which are Added Animadversions on Different Treatises on the Same Subject. Buffalo: 1824. V. 40; 42

A Debate on the Roman Catholic Religion; Held in the Sycamore Street Meeting House, Cincinnati, from the 13th to the 21st of January, 1837 . . . Cincinnati: 1837. V. 45

A Journey from Edinburgh Through Parts of North Britain. London: 1802. V. 38; 39; 46

Psalms, Hymns and Spiritual Songs, Original and Selected. Bethany: 1860. V. 46

A Short Treatise Upon the Improvement of Planted Timber Trees, and Natural Growing Woods Over Scotland at Large . . . London: 1799-1810. V. 43

A Voyage Round the World, from 1806 to 1812 . . . Edinburgh: 1816. V. 39

CAMPBELL, ALFRED W.

Histological Studies on the Localisation of Cerebral Function. Cambridge: 1905. V. 46

CAMPBELL & DAVISON

St. Paul City Directory for 1874, Comprising a Complete List of the Citizens of St. Paul . . . St. Paul: 1874. V. 42

CAMPBELL AND DUNN

The Child's First Book. Richmond: 1864. V. 38

CAMPBELL, ARCHIBALD 1726-1780

An Enquiry into the Original of Moral Virtue. London: 1734. V. 42

Lexiphanes. London: 1767. V. 43

Lexiphanes, a Dialogue . . . Dublin: 1774 (84?). V. 39; 41; 42; 43

Lexiphanes, a Dialogue. London: 1783. V. 38; 40; 41

Reports Upon the Survey of the Boundary Between the U.S. and the Possessions of Great Britain from Lake of the Woods to Rocky Mountains. Washington: 1878. V. 38; 39

A Voyage Around the World, from 1806 to 1812. Edinburgh: 1816. V. 38; 40; 43; 45; 46

A Voyage Around the World, from 1806 to 1812. New York: 1817. V. 40; 42; 45

A Voyage Round the World, from 1806 to 1812 . . . Roxbury: 1825. V. 38

CAMPBELL, CHARLES

History of the Colony and Ancient Dominion of Virginia. Philadelphia: 1860. V. 42

CAMPBELL, COLEN

Vitruvius Britannicus, or the British Architect . . . London. V. 38

Vitruvius Britannicus, or the British Architect. London: 1767, 1771. V. 40

Vitruvius Britannicus, or the British Architect . . . London: 1771. V. 38

Vitruvius Britannicus, or the British Architect. London: 1967. V. 40; 45

Vitruvius Britannicus, or, the British Archetect, containing the plans, elevations, and sections of the regular buildings, both publick and private in Great Britain. (London: 1765-1771). V. 37

CAMPBELL, COLIN

The Miraculous Birth. Edinburgh: 1912. V. 44

CAMPBELL, DONALD

Arabian Medicine and Its Influence on the Middle Ages. London: 1926. V. 37; 38; 43

CAMPBELL, DONALD A.

Narrative of the Extraordinary Adventures, and Sufferings by Shipwreck and Imprisonment, of Donald Campbell of Barbreck . . . London: 1797. V. 38; 41; 44

CAMPBELL, DOROTHEA PRIMROSE

Poems. London: 1816. V. 39; 43

CAMPBELL, DOUGLAS

The Puritan in Holland, England, and America. By Douglas Campbell. New York: 1892. V. 37

CAMPBELL, DUNCAN 1819?-1886

History of Prince Edward Island. Charlottetown: 1875. V. 38; 39; 42; 46

Secret Memoirs of the Late Mr. Duncan Campel, the Famous Deaf and Dumb Gentleman. London: 1732. V. 38; 42

CAMPBELL, ETHEL

The Life of Sam Campbell, Told in Verse and Lettered by His Daughter. Pietermaritzburg: 1938. V. 39

CAMPBELL, F. A.

A Year in the New Hebrides, Loyalty Islands, and New Caledonia. Melbourne: 1873. V. 41

CAMPBELL, F. R.

The Language of Medicine: a Manual Giving the Origin, Etymology, Pronunciation and Meaning of the Technical Terms Found in Medical Literature. New York: 1888. V. 45

CAMPBELL-FOSTER, THOMAS

Letters on the Condition of the People of Ireland. Reprinted by permission, with additions and copious notes from 'The Times' newspaper. London: 1846. V. 37

CAMPBELL, G. W.

Memorial of the Members of the bar of Nashville, in the State of Tennessee. Washington: 1825. V. 37

CAMPBELL, GEORGE

Dissertation sur les Miracles, Contenant l'Examen des Principes Poses par M. David Hume. Utrecht: 1765. V. 39

A Dissertation on Miracles . . . Edinburgh: 1812. V. 40; 42; 43; 45

The Philosophy of Rhetoric. London: 1776. V. 40; 46

The Philosophy of Rhetoric . . . Boston: 1818. V. 40

Poems on Several Occasions. Kilmarnock: 1787. V. 40; 42

White and Black: the Outcome of a Visit to the United States. London: 1879. V. 45

CAMPBELL, HARRIETTE

The Cardinal Virtues; or, Morals and Manners Connected. London: 1841. V. 44

CAMPBELL, HARRY

Headache and Other Morbid Cephalic Sensations. London: 1894. V. 45

CAMPBELL, ILAY 1734-1823

Memorial for Archibald Douglas of Douglas, Esq. and for Margaret Dutchess of Douglas, and Charles Duke of Queensberry and Dover, His Curators, Defenders . . . Edinburgh: 1766. V. 40

CAMPBELL, J.

The Black Star Passes. 1953. V. 44

The Moon is Hell. 1951. V. 43

Who Goes There? 1948. V. 43

Who Goest There? 1948. V. 44

CAMPBELL, J. B.

Campbell's Abstract of Seminole Indian Census Cards and Index. Muskogee: 1925. V. 41

CAMPBELL, J. F.

The Celtic Dragon Myth. Edinburgh: 1911. V. 41

Popular Tales of the West Highlands, Orally Collected. London: 1890-93. V. 43; 46

CAMPBELL, J. H.

History of the Friendly Sons of St. Patrick for the Relief of Emigrants from Ireland of Philadelphia, 1771-1892 (abridged) and 1892 to 1951. Philadelphia: 1952. V. 37

CAMPBELL, J. L.

The Great Agricultural and Mineral West . . . Chicago: 1866. V. 45

CAMPBELL, J. RAMSEY

The Inhabitant of the Lake and Less Welcome Tenants. Sauk City: 1964. V. 37

CAMPBELL, J. W.

A History of Virginia, From Its Discovery Till the Year 1781. Petersburg: 1813. V. 45

CAMPBELL, JAMES

Journal of James Campbell. San Antonio: 1955. V. 43

CAMPBELL, JAMES B.

Two Letters from the . . . U.S. Senator Elect From South Carolina, on Public Affairs, and Our Duties to the Colored Race . . . Charleston: 1868. V. 38

CAMPBELL, JOHN 1708-1775

An Account of the Spanish Settlements in America. Edinburgh: 1762. V. 45; 46

Biographia Nautica: or, Memoirs of these Illustrious Seamen, to whose Interepidity and Conduct the English are indebted, for the Victories of their Fleet, the Increase of their Dominions, the Extension of their Commerce, and their . . . Dublin: 1785. V. 37; 41

Candid and Impartial Considerations on the Nature of the Sugar Trade; the Comparative Importance of the British and French Islands in the West Indies . . . London: 1763. V. 45

The Case of the Opposition Impartially stated. London: 1739? V. 41

A Concise Account of the Spanish America. London: 1741. V. 39

An Exact and Authentic Account of the Greatest White-Herring-Fishery in Scotland, Carried on Yearly in the Island of Zetland, by the Dutch only. London: 1750. V. 40; 41; 45

Lives of the Admirals, and Other Eminent British Seamen. London: 1742-44. V. 38; 40

Lives of the Admirals and Other Eminent British Seamen. Dublin: 1748. V. 41; 43

Lives of the Admirals and Other British Seamen. (with) A Continuation Down to the Year 1779 . . . London: 1750/1781. V. 45

Lives of the Admirals and Other Eminent British Seamen. (with) A Continuation Down to the Year 1779, Including the Naval Transactions of the Late and Present War . . . London: 1750/1781. V. 41; 43

Lives of the British Admirals. London: 1779. V. 38

Lives of the British Admirals; Containing Also a New and Accurate Naval History from the Earliest Periods Continued to the Year 1779 . . . London: 1812. V. 41

Lives of the British Admirals: Containing also a New and Accurate Naval History, from the Earliest Periods . . . Continued to the Year 1779. London: 1812-17. V. 37

The Lives of the Chief Justices of England. Boston: 1873. V. 38

Maritime Discovery and Christian Missions. London: 1840. V. 37; 39

The Military History of the Late Prince Eugene of Savoy, and of the Late John Duke of Marlborough . . . London: 1736-37. V. 40

The Naval History of Great Britain, Commencing with the Earliest Period of History, and Continuing to the Expedition Against Algiers . . . in 1816. London: 1818. V. 46

A Personal Narrative of Thirteen Years Service Among the Wild Tribes of Khondistan. London: 1864. V. 43

A Political Survey of Britain: being a Series of Reflections on the Situation, Lands, Inhabitants, Revenues, Colonies, and Commerce of this Islands . . . London: 1774. V. 37; 38; 39; 40; 41; 43; 45

The Present State of Europe. London: 1750. V. 38

The Present State of Europe; Explaining the Interests, Connections, Political and Commercial Views of its Several Powers . . . London: 1757. V. 42

The Spanish Empire in America. London: 1747. V. 42; 43; 46

The Travels and Adventures of Edward Brown, Esq. Formerly a Merchant in London. London: 1739. V. 45; 46

Travels in South Africa, Undertaken at the Request of the Missionary Society. London: 1815. V. 39; 40

Travels in South Africa . . . London: 1822. V. 38; 40; 43; 44; 45; 46

Travels in South Africa . . . a Second Journey. London: 1822. V. 43

CAMPBELL, JOHN CAMPBELL, 1ST BARON 1779-1861

Lives of the Lord Chancellors and Keepers of the Great Seal of England from the Earliest Times Till the Reign of Queen Victoria. London: 1845-69. V. 39

The Lives of the Chief Justices of England. London: 1849. V. 40

The Lives of the Chief Justices of England from the Norman Conquest Till the Death of Lord Mansfield. (with) The Lives of the Chief Justices of England from the Norman Conquest Till the Death of Lord Tenterden. London: 1849/57. V. 44

The Lives of the Chief Justices of England. Boston: 1873. V. 39

The Lives of the Chief Justices of England. Boston: 1873, 1874. V. 40

Lives of the Lord Chancellors and Keepers of the Great Seal of England . . . London: 1856-57. V. 37

Shakespeare's Legal Acquirements Considered. In a Letter to J. Payne Collier. London: 1859. V. 39

CAMPBELL, JOHN FRANCIS

Leabhar na Feinne. Heroic Gaelic Ballads. London: 1872. V. 37

Popular Tales of the West Highlands orally collected. With a Translation. New Edition. London/Paisely: 1890-93. V. 37

A Short American Tramp in the Fall of 1864. Edinburgh: 1865. V. 40

CAMPBELL, JOHN H.

History of the Friendly Sons of St. Patrick, and of the Hibernian Society for the Relief of Emigrants from Ireland, 1771-1892. Philadelphia: 1892. V. 37; 38; 39

CAMPBELL, JOHN L.

The Great Agricultural and Mineral West . . . Chicago: 1866. V. 43

Idaho: Six Months in the New Gold Diggings. New York: 1864. V. 42; 43

CAMPBELL, JOHN LOGAN

Poenamo. Sketches of the Early Days of New Zealand. London & Edinburgh: 1881. V. 37

CAMPBELL, JOHN MENZIES

A Dental Bibliography, British and American 1682-1880 with an Index of Authors. London: 1949. V. 45

CAMPBELL, JOHN P.

An Essay. Negotiations for Peace at the Court of Heaven, The Only Way to Close the War Honorably to the South. Jackson: 1863. V. 44

CAMPBELL, JOHN W.

Who Goes There? Chicago: 1948. V. 39

CAMPBELL, JOHN WILSON

A History of Virginia. Petersburg: 1813. V. 43

CAMPBELL, JOHN WILSON continued

A History of Virginia, from Its Discovery Till the Year 1781 . . . Philadelphia: 1813. V. 38; 40; 43; 44; 45

CAMPBELL, JOSEPH

The Flight of the Wild Gander. New York: 1969. V. 45

The Masks of God. New York: 1959/62/64/67, V. 42

CAMPBELL, KEN

AbAb. Norwich: 1983-84. V. 37; 39

Broken Rules and Double Crosses. Norwich: 1983-84. V. 37; 39

Execution. 1990. V. 45

Father's Hook: Songs from a Living Son. 1978. V. 40

Father's Garden. 1989. V. 43

Father's Hook. Bath: 1978. V. 37

Horse. N.P.: 1985. V. 37; 39

In the Door Stands a Jar. 1987. V. 40

In the Door Stands a Jar. N.P.: 1987. V. 39

A Knife Romance. 1988. V. 40

A Knife Romance. 1988. V. 45

Martyrs. 1989. V. 43

Night Feet on Earth. N.P.: 1986. V. 39

Night Feet On Earth; a Poem. 1987. V. 45

Night Feet on Earth. N.P.: 1986. V. 37

Night Feet On Earth: a Poem. 1987. V. 40

Tilt: the Black flagged Streets. 1989. V. 40

Tilt: the Black Flagged Streets. 1988. V. 43

CAMPBELL, LEWIS

The Life of James Clerk Maxwell . . . London: 1882. V. 39

CAMPBELL, M. G. GUNNING

Delhi Hunt. Hints on Riding to Hounds. Simla: 1929. V. 43

CAMPBELL, MARGARET O.

A Memorial History of the Campbells of Melfort, Argyllshire Records of the different Highlands and other Families with whom they have Intermarried. 1882.-Supplement to a Memorial History of the Campbells of Melfort. London: 1882-94. V. 37

CAMPBELL, MARIA HULL

Revolutionary Services & Civil Life of General William Hull, Prepared from His Manuscripts by His Daughter. New York: 1848. V. 37; 38; 42

CAMPBELL, MARIE

Folks Do Get Born. New York: 1946. V. 45

CAMPBELL, MARIUS R.

Guidebook of the Western United States. Washington: 1916. V. 44

CAMPBELL, MARQUIS R.

Guidebook of the Western United States. Washington: 1915. V. 40

CAMPBELL, MUNGO

The Trial of Mungo Campbell, Before the High Court of Justiciary in Scotland, for the Muder of Alexander Earl of Eglintoun . . . London: 1770. V. 43

CAMPBELL, NEIL

Instructions for Light Infantry and Riflemen . . . London: 1813. V. 42

CAMPBELL, ORSON

Treatise on Carriage, Sign and Ornamental Painting, Containing Directions for Forming the Principal Colouring Substances, Composition of Colours . . . New York: 1841. V. 42

CAMPBELL, PATRICK

Travels in the Interior Inhabited Parts of North America. Edinburgh: 1793. V. 39

Travels in the Interior Inhabited Parts of North America in the Years 1791 and 1792. Toronto: 1937. V. 39; 42; 43; 45

CAMPBELL, R.

The London Tradesman. Being a compendious view of all the trades, professions, arts, both liberal and mechanic, now practised in the cities of London and Westminster . . . London: 1747. V. 37

CAMPBELL, R. BURLEIGH

A Night's Salmon Fishing on the Wye (Mon.). London: 1884. V. 42; 43

CAMPBELL, RACHEL

The Prodigal Daughter, or the Price of Virtue. Grass Valley: 1885. V. 43

CAMPBELL, RAMSEY J.

The Inhabitant of the Lake and Less Welcome Tennants. Sauk City: 1964. V. 42; 43; 45

CAMPBELL, REAU

Complete Guide and Descriptive Book of Mexico. Chicago: 1895. V. 39

CAMPBELL, ROBERT

The Life of . . . John, Duke of Argyle and Greenwich. London: 1745. V. 41

Paintings of Tom Roberts. Adelaide: 1963. V. 41

To the Honourable President and Members of the Senate of the State of Georgia. Savannah: 1829. V. 42

CAMPBELL, ROY 1901-1957

Adamastor. London: 1930. V. 38; 39; 41; 43; 45

Broken Record: Reminiscences. London: 1934. V. 38; 40; 41

Choosing a Mast. London: 1931. V. 39; 41

Choosing a Mast. London: 1951. V. 38

Collected Poems. London: 1949. V. 40

The FLaming Terapin. London: 1924. V. 38; 41; 42; 43; 44

The Flaming Terrapin. New York: 1924. V. 38; 44

Flowering Reeds. London: 1931. V. 38

Flowering Reeds; Poems. 1933. V. 46

Flowering Reeds. Poems. London: 1933. V. 38; 41; 42

The Georgiad. London: 1931. V. 37; 39; 41

The Gun Trees. London: 1930. V. 38

Poems. Paris: 1930. V. 37; 38; 40; 44

Pomegranates: a Poem. London: 1932. V. 38; 42

Selected Poems. Chicago: 1955. V. 38

Talking Bronco. London: 1946. V. 37; 41

CAMPBELL, RUTH

Small Fry and the Winged Horse. Joliet: 1927. V. 46

CAMPBELL, SAMUEL

Something New, in Eight Letters to Joseph Meeker Elizabeth-Town Occasioned by Reading miscellaneous Essays, by Joseph Lyon, Sen. of Lyon's Farms. (Elizabethtown): 1799. V. 37

CAMPBELL, THOMAS 1777-1844

Essay on English Poetry. London: 1819. V. 39

Gertrude of Wyoming: A Pennsylvanian Tale and other Poems. London: 1809. V. 37; 38; 39; 40; 41; 42; 44; 46

A Letter to His Grace the Duke of Portland, Lord Lieutenant of Ireland, touching Internal Regulation: with particular strictures upon the Linen Board, Excise Laws, &c. &c. Dublin: 1782. V. 39; 40

Letters from the South. London: 1837. V. 44; 45; 46

Life of Mrs. Siddons. London: 1834. V. 37; 38; 39

A Philosophical Survey of the South of Ireland, in a Series of Letters to Dr. John Watkinson. London: 1777. V. 43

A Philosophical Survey of the South of Ireland, in a Series of Letters to John Watkinson, M.D. Dublin: 1778. V. 42; 44

The Pleasures of Hope; with Other Poems. Edinburgh: 1799. V. 44

The Pleasures of Hope and Other Poems. London: 1819. V. 40

The Pleasures of Hope. London: 1825. V. 37

Poems, in Two Volumes. London: 1810. V. 39

Poetical Works. London: 1828. V. 39; 42; 46

The Poetical Works. London: 1837. V. 37; 42

The Poetical Works of Thomas Campbell. London: 1843. V. 46

The Poetical Works of . . . London: 1851. V. 46

The Poetical Works. London: 1854. V. 42; 43

Poetical Works. London: 1839. V. 37

Specimens of the British Poets. London: 1819. V. 37; 38; 40; 42; 46

Specimens of the British Poets. London: 1841. V. 39; 42

CAMPBELL, TONY

The Earliest Printed Maps 1472 - 1500 . . . 1987. V. 41

The Earliest Printed Maps 1472-1500. London: 1987. V. 42

Early Maps. New York: 1981. V. 43

CAMPBELL, W. G.

The New World; or, Recent Visit to America. Together with Observations for Tourists, and Four Appendices, Containing all Suitable Information for Tourists. London: 1871. V. 37; 38; 42

CAMPBELL, W. M.

St. Paul City Directory for 1875, Comprising a Complete List of the Citizens of St. Paul, with Place of Business and Residence . . . St. Paul: 1875. V. 42; 45

CAMPBELL, W. W.

East Africa by Motor Lorry. London: 1928. V. 41

CAMPBELL, WALTER

My Indian Journal. Edinburgh: 1864. V. 43; 45

The Old Forest Ranger . . . London: 1845. V. 45

CAMPBELL, WILFRED

A Poem. 1899. V. 43

CAMPBELL, WILLIAM

An Account of the Missionary Success in the Island of Formosa Published in the Year 1650 and Now Reprinted.. London: 1889. V. 45

Canada. London: 1907. V. 44; 46

The Crown Lands of Australia. Glasgow: 1855. V. 40

CAMPBELL, WILLIAM A.

The Child's First Book. By Campbell and Dunn. Richmond: 1864. V. 37; 38

CAMPBELL, WILLIAM J.

The Collection of Franklin Imprints in the Museum of the Curtis Publishing Company . . . Philadelphia: 1918. V. 45

CAMPBELL, WILLIAM W.

Annals of Tryon Country; or, the Border Warfare of New York, During the Revolution. New York: 1831. V. 41; 42; 43; 45

CAMPBENHAUSEN, BARON

Travels through Several Provinces of the Russian Empire. London: 1808. V. 40

CAMPDEN, JACOB VAN

Verscheide Nieue Festonnen. Amsterdam: 1650. V. 38

CAMPE, J. H.

Pizarro; or, the Conquest of Peru; As Related by a Father to His Children . . . London: 1799. V. 42; 46

CAMPE, JOHANN HEINRICH

The New Robinson Crusoe; an Instructive and Entertaining History, for the Use of Children of Both Sexes. London: 1789. V. 37

CAMPEAU, F. R. E.

Illustrated Guide to the House of Commons of Canada . . . Ottawa: 1875. V. 45

CAMPEGGI, CAMILLO

De Mundi Fallaciis et Ruina. Venice: 1562. V. 40

CAMPEN, JACOB VAN

Bouwschilder en Beeldhouw-Werk, van Het Stadhuis van Amsterdam. Amsterdam: 1747. V. 39

CAMPER, PETRI 1722-1789

Demonstrationum Anatomico-Pathologicarum Liber Primus (together with) (Liber Secundus). Amsteladami: 1760-62. V. 37; 38; 39; 40; 41; 43; 45

CAMPER, PETRUS 1722-1789

The Works of the Late Professor Camper, on the Connexion Between the Science of Anatomy and the Arts of Drawing, Painting, Statuary, &c. London: 1794. V. 39; 45

CAMPER, PIETER

The Works . . . on the Connexion Between the Science of Anatomy and the Arts of Drawing, Painting, Statuary, etc., etc. London: 1821. V. 38

CAMPIN, FRANCIS

On the Construction of Iron Roofs. New York: 1868. V. 44

CAMPION, EDMUND

Fifty Songs. Chelsea: 1896. V. 37

CAMPION, J. S.

On Foot in Spain. London: 1879. V. 43

On the Frontier: Reminiscences of Wild Sports, Personal Adventures and Strange Scenes. London: 1878. V. 37; 39; 40; 42; 44

CAMPION, P.

The Honourable Women of the Great War and the Women's (War) Who's Who. Bournemouth: 1919. V. 46

CAMPION, THOMAS

Fifty Songs by Thomas Campion. London: 1896. V. 38; 41; 42; 43

Selected Songs of Thomas Campion. Boston: 1973. V. 41; 43; 44; 46

Songs and Masques with Observations in the Art of English Poesy. London: 1903. V. 37

CAMPO, ANTONIO

Cremona Fedelissima Citta et Nobilissima Colonia de Romani Rappresentata in Disegno col suo Contado. Et Illustrata d'una Breve Historia della cose Piu Notabili Appartenti ad essa. Milan: 1645. V. 37

CAMPOMANES, PEDRO RODRIGUEZ CONDE DE

Discurso Sobre el Fomento de la Industria Popular. Madrid: 1774. V. 41; 45

CAMPOS, JULES

Josef de Creeft. New York: 1945. V. 39; 42; 43

CAMUS, A.

Les Chenes, Monographie du Genre Quercus. Paris: 1934-54. V. 38

CAMUS, A. G.

Notice d'un Livre Imprime a Bamberg en 1462. Paris: 1799. V. 38

CAMUS, ALBERT 1913-1960

Albert Camus September 15th 1937. Bronxville: 1963. V. 42; 46

La Chute; recit. Paris: 1956. V. 40

L'Etat de Siege: Spectacle en Trois Parties. Gallimard: 1949. V. 40

The Fall. Kentfield: 1960. V. 46

The Fall. Kentfield: 1966. V. 39; 46

L'Homme Revolte. Paris: 1951. V. 40

Le Minotaure ou La Halte d'Oran. N.P.: 1950. V. 38

Le Mythe de Sisyphe. Paris: 1945. V. 40

The Myth of Sisphus and Other Essays. New York: 1955. V. 44

September 15th, 1937. Bronxville: 1963. V. 46

The Stranger. New York: 1946. V. 40

CAMUS, E. G.

Iconographie d'Europe et du Bassin Mediterraneen. Paris: 1921-29. V. 46

CAMUS, JEAN PIERRE

Natures Paradox; or the Innocent Impostor. London: 1652. V. 39; 44; 46

The Triumphs of Love. Glasgow: 1784. V. 44

CAMUTIUS, ANDREAS ca. 1510-1578

De Amore Atque Felicitate. Vienna: 1574. V. 43

CANADA

Canada Waste Lands. Return to an Address to His Majesty . . . For, Copy of the Report of Mr. Richards to the Colonial Secretary, Respecting the Waste Lands in the Canadas, and Emigration . . . London: 1832. V. 37

CANADA. COMMISSIONERS FOR EXPLORING THE SAGUENAY

Report of the Commissioners for Exploring the Saguenay. Ordered by the Assembly, the Fourteenth January 1829, to be printed. Quebec: 1829. V. 37

CANADA. DEPARTMENT OF AGRICULTURE - 1876

Province of Manitoba: and North West Territory of the Dominion of Canada. Ottawa: 1876. V. 39

CANADA. DEPARTMENT OF INTERIOR

Atlas of Canada. 1906. V. 42

Atlas of Canada. 1906. V. 44

Atlas of Canada. Ottawa: 1915. V. 44

CANADA. DEPARTMENT OF INTERIOR - 1906

Atlas of Canada. 1906. V. 41

CANADA. DEPARTMENT OF MILITIA AND DEFENCE - 1901

Supplementary Report. Organization, Equipment, Despatch and Service of the Canadian Contingents During the War in South Africa, 1899-1900. Ottawa: 1901. V. 38

CANADA. DEPARTMENT OF THE SECRETARY OF STATE - 1885

Epitome of Parliamentary Documents in Connection with the North-West Rebellion, 1885. Ottawa: 1886. V. 37

CANADA. DEPT. OF INTERIOR - 1916

The Yukon Territory. Ottawa: 1916. V. 40

CANADA. DEPT. OF MARINE & FISHERIES - 1914

Port Directory of Principal Canadian Ports and Harbours and a large Number of Minor Ports, Wharves, Depth of Water, Facilities for Loading Etc. Ottawa: 1914. V. 40

CANADA. DEPT. OF THE INTERIOR - 1914

Description of Surveyed Lands in the Railway Belt of British Columbia. Ottawa: 1914. V. 40

CANADA. GEOLOGICAL SURVEY

Petroleum: Its Geological Relations Considered with Especial Reference to Its Occurence in Gaspe, Being a Report Addressed to the Hon. Commissioner of Crown Lands . . . Quebec: 1865. V. 39

Report of Progress for the Year 1847-48. Montreal: 1849. V. 40

CANADA. GEOLOGICAL SURVEY - 1853

Reports of Progress for the Years 1853-54-55-56. (with) Plans of Various Lakes and Rivers Between Lake Huron and The River Ontario, to Accompany the Geological Reports for 1853-54-55-56. Toronto: 1857. V. 37

CANADA. GEOLOGICAL SURVEY - 1857

Report of Progress for the Years 1853-54-55-65. Toronto: 1857. V. 37; 38

CANADA. GEOLOGICAL SURVEY - 1858

Report of Progress for the Year 1857. Toronto: 1858. V. 37

CANADA. GEOLOGICAL SURVEY - 1863

Report of Progress from 1863 to 1866. Ottawa: 1866. V. 37

CANADA in the Great World War; An Authentic Account of the Military History of Canada from the Earliest Days to the Close of the War of the Nations. Toronto: 1917-21. V. 46

CANADA. LEGISLATIVE ASSEMBLY

Report of the Committee Appointed to Receive and Collected Evidence as to the Rights of the Hudson's Bay Company Under Their Charter &c. Toronto: 1857. V. 42

CANADA. LEGISLATIVE ASSEMBLY - 1849

Report of the Select Committee of the Legislative Assembly, Appointed to Inquire into the Causes and Importance of the Emigration, Which Takes Place Annually, From Lower Canada to the United States. Montreal: 1849. V. 37

CANADA. MINISTER OF THE INTERIOR

The Yukon Territory. Ottawa: 1916. V. 42

CANADA. NORTH-WEST MOUNTED POLICE - 1897

Report of the Commissioner of the North-West Mounted Police, 1897. Ottawa: 1898. V. 40

CANADA. PARLIAMENT

Report of the Commissioners of the Intercolonial Railway. Ottawa: 1870. V. 45

CANADA. ROYAL NORTHWEST MOUNTED POLICE

Report of the North-West Mounted Police, 1899. Ottawa: 1900. V. 42

CANADA SOUTHERN RAILWAY

First Annual Report of the Canada Southern Railway Company and Its Extensions and Connections. New York: 1873. V. 45

CANADA SOUTHERN RAILWAY COMPANY

Prospectus, Reports and Other Documents. New York: 1872. V. 39

CANADA'S Royal Visitors. A Pictorial Souvenir of the Visit of the Duke and Duchess of Cornwall and York. Canada From Ocean to Ocean by Royal Train (cover title). Toronto: (1901?). V. 37

CANADIAN Affairs. Volume I, Number 14. November 15, 1943. Published for the Canadian Armed Forces by the Wartime Information Board. (London).. V. 37

THE CANADIAN Alpine Journal. Vancouver: 1928. V. 38
THE CANADIAN Alpine Journal. Montreal: 1929. V. 38
THE CANADIAN Alpine Journal. Montreal: 1930. V. 38
THE CANADIAN Alpine Journal. N.P.: 1932. V. 38
THE CANADIAN Alpine Journal. N.P.: 1933. V. 38
THE CANADIAN Alpine Journal. N.P.: 1934. V. 38
THE CANADIAN Alpine Journal. Winnipeg: 1936. V. 38

CANADIAN ARTILLERY ASSOCIATION

Officers Who Served Overseas in the Great War with the Canadian Artillery. 1914-1919. Ottawa: 1922. V. 37

THE CANADIAN Church Harmonist: a Collection of Sacred Music . . . Toronto: 1864. V. 44

THE CANADIAN Journal. Winnipeg: 1931. V. 38

THE CANADIAN Journal of Industry, Science, and Art: Conducted by the Editing Committee of the Canadian Institute. New Series. Totonto: 1856-62. V. 37

THE CANADIAN Naturalist and Geologist. Montreal: 1857-63. V. 44

THE CANADIAN North-West! Land of Opportunity! Ottawa: 1903. V. 42

CANADIAN PACIFIC RAILWAY

Canadian Pacific Railway Primers No. 3: Summer Tours by the Canadian Railway 1888. Montreal: 1888. V. 45

Description of the Country Between Lake Surperior and the Pacific Ocean, on the Line of the Candian Pacific Railway. Ottawa: 1876. V. 40

Manitoba - The Canadian North-West. Testimony of Actual Settlers. N.P.: 1886. V. 45

A Timetable with Notes of the Westbound Transcontinental Train, The Great Lakes Route, Toronto and Chicago Line. Montreal: 1887. V. 45

CANADIAN RAILWAY NEW CO.

All Round Route and Panoramic Guide of the St. Lawrence, Niagara Falls, Toronto, the Thousand Islands and the River St. Lawrence, Ottawa, Montreal, Quebec, The Lower St. Lawrence and Saguenay Rivers, The White Mountains and Adirondacks. Montreal: 1890's. V. 38

CANADIAN Scenery, Illustrated from Drawings by W.H. Bartlett. London: 1842. V. 37

CANADIAN Tour: A Reprint of Letters from the Special Correspondent of the Times. London: 1886. V. 38

CANADIAN WAR RECORDS OFFICE

Art and War Canadian War Memorials. London. V. 44

CANADIANS In Khaki. South Africa 1899-1900. Montreal: 1900. V. 44

CANANO, IOANNES BAPTISTA

Musculorum Humani Corporis Picturata Dissectio (Ferrara 1541?). Facsimile Edition annotated by Harvey Cushing and Edward C. Streeter. Florence: 1925. V. 37

CANBY, HENRY SEIDEL

Thoreau. Boston: 1939. V. 44

CANCELLIERE, VINCENZO

Copia di Vn Caso Notabile Interventvto a Vn Gran Gentil'hvomo Genovese; cosa Molto Vtile da Intender et di Gran Piacere . . . Venice: 1550. V. 43

A CANDID and Impartial Discussion of the False Reasonings, Gross Misrepresentations, and Studies Fallacies of Two late Pieces; the Former Written to Vilify the Inhabitants of One End of This Island; the Latter of the Other. London: 1747. V. 41

CANDID And Impartial Strictures on the Performers Belonging to Drury-Lane, Covent-Garden and the Haymarket Theatres. London: 1795. V. 40

A CANDID Appeal to the Publick, Concerning the Case of the Late Miss Mary Blandy: Wherein all the Ridiculous and False Assertions Contained in a Pamphlet, Entitled, Miss Mary Blandy's Own Account of the Affair Between Her and Mr. Cranstoun . . . London: 1752. V. 45

A CANDID Enquiry into the Present Ruined State of the French Monarchy. London: 1770. V. 38

CANDLER, ALLEN D.

The Confederate Records of the State of Georgia. Atlanta: 1909. V. 43

CANDLER, EDMUND

The Long Road to Bagdad. London: 1919. V. 43

CANDLER, ISAAC

A Summary View of America . . . Being the Result of Observations and Enquiries During a Journey in the United States. London: 1824. V. 41; 43

CANDLER, JOHN

Brief Notices of Hayti and Its Condition, Resources and Prospects. London: 1842. V. 45

West Indies. Extracts from the Journal of John Candler Whilst Travelling in Jamaica. London: 1840-41. V. 39

CANDLER, STEPHEN CURTIS

Theory of the Causation and Suggestions for the Prevention, of Dysentery: together with Hypotheses on the Causation, and Views as to the Prevention, of Typohid, Cholera, Yellow Fever, Remittent, Diphtheria, Typhys and other Zymotic . . . Melbourne: 1873. V. 37; 39

CANDOLLE, AUGUSTIN PYRAMUS DE

Vegetable Organography; or an Analytical Description of the Organs of Plants. London: 1841. V. 40

CANDOUR

The Pope and Turk. A Poem on the origin of James Crowley's thoughts on emancipatio nof Catholics. By Candour. Dublin. V. 37

CANE, CLAUDE

Summer and Fall in Western Alaska: the Record of a Trip to Cook's Inlet After Big Game. London: 1903. V. 39; 41; 42

CANEPARI, PIETRO MARIA

De Atramentis Cuiuscunque Generis . . . in Sex Descriptiones Digestum. London: 1660. V. 37

CANES, JOHN VINCENT

Fiat Lux. Douay: 1661. V. 42

CANESTRELLI, PHILIP

Catechism of Christian Doctrine Prepared and Enjoined by Order of the Third Plenary Council of Baltimore. Translated into Flathead by a Father of the Society of Jeses. Woodstock College, Md.: 1891. V. 37

CANESTRELLI, PHILIP S. J.

A Kootenai Grammar . . . Spokane: 1959. V. 43

CANETTI, ELIAS

Crowds and Power. New York: 1962. V. 42

CANFIELD, CHAUNCEY L.

The Diary of a Forty-Niner. New York: and San Francisco: 1906. V. 44
The Diary of a Forty-Niner. San Francisco: 1906. V. 44

CANFIELD, THOMAS HAWLEY

Life of Thomas Hawley Canfield . . . and His Connection with the Early History of the Northern Pacific Railroad. Burlington: 1889. V. 45

Northern Pacific Railroad . . . Report to the Board of Directors, of a Reconnaissance Made in the Summer of 1869 . . . For Private Circulation Only. New York: 1870. V. 37; 38; 39; 42; 45

CANFIELD, W. H.

Pen and Pencil Sketches of Devil's Lake Near Baraboo, Sauk County, Wisconsin. Madison: 1871. V. 41; 42

CANIFF, MILTON

Terry and the Pirates in Shipwrecked. The Illustrated Pop-Up Edition. Chicago: (1935). V. 37

CANIFF, WILLIAM

History of the Settlement of Upper Canada (Ontario) With Special Reference to the Bay of Quinte. Toronto: 1869. V. 44

CANINI, GIOVAN ANGELO

Iconografia. Cioe Disegni d'Imagini de Famosissimi Monarchi, Regi, Filosofi, Poeti ed Oratori dell'Antichita. Rome: 1669. V. 37; 45

CANISIUS, PETRUS, SAINT

(In Greek): Katechismos Eikonismenos. Augsburg: 1613. V. 40

CANISIUS, THEODOR

Abraham Lincoln. Historisches Charakterbild. Wien: 1867. V. 45

CANNAN, GILBERT

Mendel - a Story of Youth. London: 1916. V. 40

CANNECATTIM, BERNARDO MARIA DE

Colleccao de Observacoes Grammaticas Sobre a Lingua Bunda ou Angolense . . . Lisbon: 1805. V. 38

CANNER, THOMAS

Scheeps-Togt Van Martin Pringe, Gedaan in't Jaar 1603. Van Bristol Nat Noorder-Gedeelte Van Virginien . . . Leyden: 1706. V. 39

CANNIFF, WILLIAM

The Medical Profession in Upper Canada, 1783-1850. Toronto: 1894. V. 42

CANNING, GEORGE

Horace's First Satire Modernised and Addressed to Jacob Henriques. London: 1762. V. 42

A Letter to the Earl of Camden; Containing a Full, Correct, and Authentic Narrative of the Transactions Connected with the Late Duel (Between Canning and Lord Castlereagh). London: 1809. V. 42; 44

Poems. (with) A Translation of Anti-Lucretius. London: 1767, 1766. V. 37

Speeches of the Right Hon. George Canning Delivered on Public Occasions in Liverpool. Liverpool: 1825. V. 41

The Speeches . . . with a Memoir of His Life. London: 1828. V. 38; 41

CANNING, JOSIAH D.

Poems. Greenfield: 1838. V. 40

CANNING, S.

The Miniature by Solomon Gildrig of the College of Eton. London: 1806. V. 46

CANNING'S Magazine; or, A Review of the Whole Evidence That Has Been Hitherto Offered for, or Against Elizabeth Canning, and Mary Squires. London: 1753. V. 46

CANNON, CARL L.

American Book Collectors and Collecting from Colonial Times to the Present. New York: 1941. V. 37

CANNON, GEORGE Q.

The Delegate from Utah. Salt Lake City: 1882. V. 42

The History of the Mormons. Salt Lake City: 1891. V. 42

The Life of Joseph Smith the Prophet. Salt Lake City: 1888. V. 42

CANNON, JOHN

History of Grant's Campaign for the Capture of Richmond (1864-1865). London: 1869. V. 41

CANNON, MILES

Waiilatpu Its Rise and Fall. Boise: 1915. V. 41

CANNON, RICHARD

Historical Record of the Second, or Queen's Royal Regiment of Foot. London: 1837. V. 42

Historical Records of the British Army: the Fifth, or Princess Charlotte of Wales's Regiment of Dragoon Guards. London: 1839. V. 41

Historical Record of the Sixth Regiment of Dragoon Guards. London: 1839. V. 42

Historical Record of the Seventh or Princess Royal's Reiment of Dragoon Guards . . . London: 1839. V. 42

Historical Record of the Fourth, or Royal Irish Regiment of Dragoon Guards. London: 1839. V. 42

Historical Record of the Thirteenth Regiment of Light Dragoons . . . London: 1842. V. 42

Historical Records of the Sixteenth Regiment of Fott. London: 1848. V. 43

Historical Record of the Ninety-Second Regiment, Originally Termed 'The Gordon Highlanders' . . . London: 1851. V. 42

Historical Record of the Thirty-Sixth, or the Herefordshire Regiment of Foot . . . London: 1853. V. 41

Historical Record of the Twenty-First Regiment, or the Royal North British Fusiliers. Containing an account of the formation of the Regiment in 1678 and of ist subsequent services to 1849. London: 1849. V. 37

CANNON, WALTER BRADFORD 1871-1945

Bodily Changes in Pain, Hunger, Fear and Rage . . . New York: 1915. V. 45

The Mechanical Factors of Digestion. Mechanical. London: 1911. V. 45

CANNON, WILLIAM

To the Senate and House of Representatives of the State of Delaware, in General Assembly Met . . . Doer: 1865. V. 42

CANNON, Z. W.

San Antonio, Texas: The Commercial Hub of the Southwest. San Antonio: 1905. V. 46

CANO, MELCHIOR 1523-1560

De Locis Theologicis Libri Duodecim. Salamanca: 1563. V. 38

CANON Sacratissime Misse: Una Cum Expositione Eiusdem. Nuremberg: 1507. V. 40

CANONES et Decreta Sacrosancti . . . Concili Tridentini. Antwerp: 1565. V. 45

CANOVA, ANTONIO 1757-1822

The Works of Antonio Canova, in Sculpture and Modelling, Engraved in Outline by Henry Moses . . . London: 1849. V. 41

The Works of Antonio Canova in Sculpture and Modeling with Descriptions from the Italian of the Countess Albrizzi and a Biographical Memoir by Count Cigognara. Boston: 1876. V. 41

CANRIGHT, D. M.

Seventh-Day Adventism Renounced After an Experience of Twenty Eight Years by a Prominent Minister and Writer of that Faith . . . Kalamazoo: 1888. V. 43

CANT, ARENT

Impetus Primi Anatomici ex Lustratis Cadaveribus Natai. Lugduni Batavorum: 1721. V. 42

CANTEMIR, DEMETRIUS

The History of the Growth and Decay of the Othman Empire Containing the Grwoth of the Othman Empire, from the Reign of the Othman the Founder, to the Reign of Mahomet IV . . . London: 1734. V. 41

CANTERBURY, ENGLAND. (PROVINCE). ARCHBISHOP 1414-1443 HENRY CHICHELE

The Register of Henry Chichele, Archbishop of Canterbury, 1414-1443. Oxford: 1938-43-45-47. V. 44; 45

CANTI, EGNATIO 1536-1586

Dell'uso et Fabricia dell'Astrolabio et del Planisferio. Florence: 1578. V. 45

CANTICA Natalia. Viginti Hymni in Honorem Nativitatis Domini Nostri Jesu Christi. Ditchling: 1926. V. 39

THE CANTICLE of the Sun. New York: 1951. V. 45

CANTICUM Canticorum Salomonis, Quod Hebraice Dicitur Sir Hasirim. Leipzig: 1931. V. 41
CANTICUM Canticorum Salomonis Quod Hebraice Dicitur Sir Hasirim. Weimar: 1931. V. 44; 45

CANTILLON, RICHARD

Essai sur la Nature du Commerce en General. Londres. V. 38

Essai Sur la Nature du Commerce en General. London: 1755. V. 41; 45

LE CANTIQUE de Cantiques. Paris: 1914. V. 38

CANTON, GUSTAVUS

The Zoological Garden. Philadelphia: 1850. V. 40

CANTUS Sanctus. Santa Fe: 1982. V. 38

CANYONLANDS Country 1975. N.P.: 1975. V. 45

CAORSIN, GULIELMUS

Gulielmi Caorsin Rhodiorum Vicecancellarii . . . Venice: 1840. V. 45

CAPA, ROBERT

Images of War. New York: 1964. V. 44

CAPABLANCA, J. R.

Capablanca's Chess Fundamentals. New York: 1921. V. 44

CAPALLI, GIOVANNI BATTISTA

Epigrammata. Florence: 1684. V. 37

CAPART, JEAN

Thebes: the Glory of a Great Past. New York: 1926. V. 37; 42

CAPE, JONATHAN

American Tour . . . November 20-Dec. 11 1937. N.P.: 1938. V. 40

CAPE of Good Hope Government and Legislature Considered. London: 1851. V. 40

CAPEFIGUE, M.

A king's Mistress, or Charles VII and Agnes Sorel. Edinburgh: 1887. V. 45; 46

CAPEK, KAREL

The Absolute at Large. 1927. V. 43
The Absolute at Large. London: 1927. V. 43
Krakatit. New York: 1925. V. 38
The Makropoulous Secret. Boston: 1925. V. 37; 40; 42
R. U. R. A Play (Rossum's Universal Robots). Oxford: 1923. V. 37
War with the Newts. London: 1937. V. 46

CAPEL, ARTHUR, BARON

Excellent Contemplations, Divine and Moral. London: 1683. V. 40; 42; 44

CAPEL, ARTHUR, LORD HADHAM

Obsequies . . . London: 1649. V. 45

CAPELL, EDWARD

Prolusions: or, Select Pieces of Antient Poetry . . . London: 1760. V. 41; 42; 45

CAPELLA, GALEAZZO 1487-1537

Commentarii . . . delle Cose Fatte per la Restitutione di Francesco Sforza . . . Venice: 1539. V. 46

CAPELLA, MARTIANUS FELIX

Satyricon. Leyden: 1599. V. 40

CAPELLMANN, CARL

Pastoral Medicine. New York: 1879. V. 42

CAPELLO, H.

From Benguella to the Territory of the Yacca. Description of a Journey into Central and West Africa. London: 1882. V. 45

CAPEN, NAHUM

The Republic of the United States of America: Its Duties to Itself, and Its Responsible Relations . . . Embracing . . . A Review of the Late War. New York: 1848. V. 37

CAPERN, THOMAS

The Mighty Curative Powers of Mesmerism, Proved In Upwards of One Hundred and Fifty Cases of Various Disease. London: 1851. V. 41; 46

CAPERS, WALTER B.

The Soldier-Bishop: Ellison Capers. New York: 1912. V. 40; 42

CAPES, ALFRED

The Old and New Churches of London . . . London: 1880. V. 38

CAPES, BERNARD

The Romance of Lohengrin. London: 1903. V. 44

CAPITAL Punishment. A Tale of the Nineteenth Century. London: 1867. V. 37

CAPITULA sive Constitutiones Ecclesiasticae. London: 1597. V. 41

CAPOTE, TRUMAN 1924-1985

Answered Prayers. New York: 1986. V. 39
Breakfast at Tiffany's. London: 1958. V. 45
Breakfast at Tiffany's. New York: 1958. V. 37; 43; 45
A Christmas Memory. New York: 1966. V. 38; 39; 40; 42
The Grass Harp. New York: 1951. V. 42; 43; 44; 45; 46
The Grass Harp. London: 1952. V. 43
The Grass Harp. New York: 1952. V. 45
In Cold Blood. New York: 1965. V. 37; 40; 41; 43; 45
In Cold Blood. New York: 1966. V. 46
Local Color. New York: 1950. V. 39; 40; 41; 42; 44; 45
Local Color. N.P.: 1954. V. 44
Miriam. Mankato, Minn.: (1982). V. 37; 46

The Muses are Heard. New York: 1956. V. 39; 44; 45
Music for Cameleons. New York. V. 39
Music for Chameleons. New York: 1980. V. 37; 38; 39; 43; 45; 46
Music for Chameleons. New York: 1982. V. 45
Observations. New York: 1959. V. 37; 38; 39; 40; 41
One Christmas. New York: 1983. V. 39; 41; 43; 46
Other Voices, Other Poems. Franklin Center: 1979. V. 43
Other Voices, Other Rooms. New York: 1948. V. 37; 38; 39; 42; 43; 44; 46
Selected Writings of Truman Capote. New York: 1963. V. 46
The Thanksgiving Visitor. New York: 1967. V. 39; 43
A Tree of Night and Other Stories. New York: 1949. V. 39; 43; 44; 45; 46
A Tree of Night. New York: 1950. V. 37
A Tree of Night and Other Stories by Truman Capote. 1949. V. 37

CAPP, EDWARD H.

The Story of Baw-A-Ting Being the Annals of Sault Sainte Marie. Sault Sainte Marie: 1904. V. 39; 45

CAPPELLETTI, MAURO

Integration Through Law, Europe and the American Frederal Experience. Berlin: 1986. V. 44

CAPPER, BENJAMIN PITTS

A Compendious Geographical Dictionary. London: 1813. V. 38; 41; 43; 45

CAPPER, JAMES

Meteorological and Miscellaneous Tracts, Applicable to Navigation, Gardening and Farming . . . Cardiff: 1809. V. 43
Observations on the Passage to India, Through Egypt and Across the Great Desert. London: 1783. V. 40
Observations on the Winds and Monsoons. London: 1801. V. 37; 39; 42

CAPPER, JOHN

The Emigrant's Guide to Australia . . . Liverpool: 1853. V. 43
The Three Presidencies of India; a History of the Rise and Progress of the British Indian Possessions, From the Earliest Records to the Present Time. London: 1853. V. 43; 46

CAPPER, LOUISA

An Abridgment of Locke's Essay Concerning Human Understanding . . . London: 1811. V. 42; 43

CAPPER, W. BENTLY

Licensed Houses and Their management; the Trade Encyclopaedia. London: 1928. V. 46

CAPPIELLO, L.

Nos Actrices. Paris: 1899. V. 41

CAPPONI, LORENZO

Pianta, e Spaccato del Nuovo Teatro di Bologna. Venice: 1764. V. 37
Pianta e Spaccato del Nuovo Teatro di Bologna. Bologna: 1771. V. 37

CAPRA, ALESSANDRO

La Nuova Architettura Famigliare Di . . . Architetto, e Cittadino Cremonese Divisa in Cinque Libri Corrispondenti a'cinque Ordini . . . Bologna: 1678. V. 38; 40; 44
La Nuova Architettura Civile e Militare di Alessandro Capra . . . in Questa Nuova Impressione Diligentemente Corretta, ed Accresciuta. Cremona: 1717. V. 37

CAPRA, BALDASSAR

Consideratione Astronomica Circa la Nova & Portentosa Stelle Che Nell'anno 1604 . . . Padua: 1605. V. 38; 44

CAPRA, FRANK

The Name Above the Title: an Autobiography. New York: 1971. V. 45

CAPRIATA, PIETRO GIOVANNI

Dall'Historia . . . Ne'quali si Contengono Tutti i Movimenti d'Armee Successi in Italia dal MDCXIII fina al . . . Genova: 1638-63. V. 37; 44; 45

CAPRICORN, CORNELIUS

Speculations on the Comet. New York: 1832. V. 40

CAPRIOLO, ALIPRANDO

Ritratti et Elogi di Capitani Illustri . . . Rome: 1635. V. 37

CAPRON, ELISHA S.

History of California, From Its Discovery to the Present Time . . . Boston: 1854. V. 39; 41; 42
History of California, from its Discovery to the Present Time . . . with a Journal of the Voyage from New York, via Nicaragua to San Francisco and back, via Panama . . . Boston/Cleveland: 1854. V. 37

CAPS Well Fit; or, Select Epigrams, Serious & Comic. Newcastle: 1785. V. 40

CAPTAIN Jones Expedition. Successful Exploration of a New Route to the Wonders of Yellowstone. New York: 1873. V. 43

CAPUTO, PHILIP

A Rumour of War. New York: 1977. V. 44

CARACCIOLUS, ROBERTUS

Sermones de Timore Divinorum Judiciorum. Venetia: 1475. V. 38

CARACCIOLUS, ROBERTUS DE LICIO

Quadragesimale de Poenitentia. Strasbourg: 1473. V. 39

Sermones Quadragesimales de Poenitentia. Venice: 1472. V. 42; 43

Sermones de Timore Divionorum Judiciorum. Venice: 1475. V. 40; 42; 45

Sermones de Timore Divinorum Judiciorum. Venetia: 1475. V. 37

CARADOC OF LLANCARFAN

The Historie of Cambria, now Called Wales. London: 1584. V. 37

CARADOC PRESS

The Caradoc Kalendar 1902. Chiswick: 1902. V. 41

CARBONE, INC.

Catalogue (of) Italian ARts & Antiques. Potteries of Capri, Castelli . . . Quimper (French) . . . Venetian Glass, Carbone Studio Lamp Shades, Bronzes, Wrought Iron . . . 1925. V. 46

CARBURI DE CEFFALONIE, MARIN

Monument Eleve a la Gloire de Pierre-le Grand, ou Relation des Travaux et des Moyens Mechaniques qui ont ete Employee Pour Transporter a Petersbourg un Rocher de Trois Millions Pesant, Destine a Servir de Basse a la Statue Equestre de cet Empereur . . . Paris: 1777. V. 38; 42

CARBUTT, JOHN

Biographical Sketches of the Leading Men of Chicago. Chicago: 1868. V. 38; 39

CARCANI, GAETANO

Anthologias Diaphoron Epigrammation. Raccolta di Varii Epigrammi in Sette Libri. Napoli: 1788-1796. V. 40

CARCANO, MICHAEL DE

Sermoniaru de Comendatione Virtutu & Reprobatioe Vicio. Milan: 1495. V. 37

CARCO, FRANCIS

Perversity. Chicago: 1928. V. 38; 42

Rue Pigalle. Paris: 1927. V. 40

CARD, O. S.

Cardography. 1987. V. 39

Ender's Game. 1985. V. 39

The Folk of the Fringe. 1989. V. 43

CARDANO, GERONIMO

De Rerum Varietate Libri XVII. Basle: 1557. V. 41

CARDANO, GIROLAMO 1501-1576

Contradicentium Medicorum Liber Continens Contradictiones Centum Octo. Venetiis: 1545. V. 44

Contradicentium Medicorum Liber . . . Lyons: 1548. V. 45

Contradicentium Medicorum Libri Duo, Qorum Primus Centum & Octo, Alter Vero Totidem Disputationes Continet . . . aris: 1565. V. 40

De Subtilitate Libri XXI. Lyon: 1554. V. 37

In Hippocratis Coi Prognostica . . . Basel: 1568. V. 45

Opus Novum Cunctis de Sanitate Tuenda . . . Romae: 1580. V. 44

Proxeneta, seu De Prudentia Civili Liber. Leiden: 1627. V. 37

De Rervm Varietate Libri XVII. Basileae: 1557. V. 38; 45

Somniorum Synesiorum Omnis Generis Insomnia Explicantes . . . Basileae: 1585. V. 46

CARDANUS, HIERONYMUS

In Septem Aphorismorum Hippocratis Particulas Commentaria . . . (bound with) In Hippocratis Coi Prognostica . . . Basel: 1568. V. 38

Somnium Synesiorum Omnis Generis Insomnia Explicantes Libri IIII . . . De Libris Propriis . . . (and other works). Basle: 1562. V. 39

De Subtilitate Libri XXI. Basel: 1582. V. 39

CARDELL, WILLIAM SAMUEL

Essay on Language, as Connected with the Faculties of the Mind, and as Applied to Things in Nature and Art. New York: 1825. V. 39

CARDEN, ALEXANDER

The Missouri Harmony, or a Choice Collection of Psalm Tunes, Hymns and Anthems . . . Cincinnati: 1820. V. 40

CARDENAS, BERNARDINO DE

Coleccion General de Documentos, Tocantes a la Persecucion que los Regulares de la Compania . . . Madrid: 1768-70. V. 45

CARDIGAN, JAMES THOMAS BRUDENELL, 7TH EARL OF 1797-1868

The Cavalry Brigade Movements. London: 1861. V. 41

Eight Months on Active Service. London: 1856. V. 41

The Trial of James Thomas Earl of Cardigan Before the Right Honourable the House of Peers, in full Parliament for felony, on Tuesday, the 17th day of February, 1841. London: 1841. V. 41

CARDINELL, CHARLES

Adventures on the Plains. San Francisco: 1922. V. 37; 40; 43; 45

CARDINO, PEDRO

The New Guide of the Conversation in Portuguese and English. Boston: 1883. V. 37

THE CARDOC Kalendar MDCCCCI. Bedford Park: 1900. V. 46

CARDONNE, DENIS DOMINIQUE

A Miscellany of Eastern Learning. London: 1771. V. 38

CARDONNEL, ADAM DE

Picturesque Antiquities of Scotland. London: Printed for the: 1788. V. 37

Picturesque Antiquities of Scotland. London: 1788-93. V. 38

CARDOZA, JACOB N.

Reminiscences of Charleston. Charleston: 1866. V. 45

CARDOZO, BENJAMIN

In the Supreme Court of the United States . . . (Brief in Support of Petition) of the Leaf Tobacco Board of Trade of the City of New York . . . (in) the United Dstates of America, Complainant, Against the American Tobacco Company et als. New York: 1911. V. 45

What Medicine Can Do For Law. New York: 1930. V. 46

CARDOZO, BENJAMIN N.

The Nature of the Judicial Process. New Haven: 1925. V. 37

Paradoxes of Legal Science. New York: 1928. V. 42; 44

CARDOZO, JACOB NEWTON

Reminiscences of Charleston. Charleston: 1866. V. 37; 43

CARDULO, FULVIO

Sanctorum Martyrum Abundii Ppresbyteri Abundantii Diaconi, Maciani & Joannis Eius Filii, Passio es Tribus Vetustissimis . . . Rome: 1584. V. 45

CARDWELL, EDWARD

Synodalia: a Collection of Articles and Religion, Canons and Proceedings of Convocations in the Province of Canterbury from the Year 1547 to the Year 1717. Oxford: 1842. V. 40

CARDWELL, K. H.

Bernard Maybeck, Artisan, Architect, Artist. Santa Barbara: 1977. V. 46

CARE, HENRY

English Liberties or, the Free-Born Subject's Inheritance . . . London: 1680. V. 38; 40

English Liberties; or, the Free-Born Subject's Inheritance. London: 1700. V. 42

English Libert(ies) or the Free-Born Subject's Inheritance. London: 1706. V. 39

English Liberties or, the Free-Born Subject's Inheritance . . . London: 1719. V. 40

English Liberties, or the Freeborn Subject's Inheritance . . . Boston: 1721. V. 46

English Liberties, or the Free-Born Subject's Inheritance. Providence: 1774. V. 38; 41; 44

CARELESS, JOHN

The Old English 'Squire'. A Jovial Gay Fox Hunter, Bold, Frank and Free. London: 1821. V. 37; 46

CAREW, ELIZABETH

The Tragaedie of Miriam, The Faire Queene of Iewry. London: 1613. V. 37

CAREW, F. W.

No. 747: Being the Autobiography of a Gipsy. London: 1890. V. 42

CAREW, HAROLD

History of Pasadena and the San Gabriel Valley California. N.P.: 1930. V. 39

CAREW, HAROLD D.

History of Pasadena and the San Gabriel Valley. N.P.: 1930. V. 46

CAREW, RICHARD

Carew's Survey of Cornwall; to Which are Added Notes Illustrative of Its History and Antiquaries . . . London: 1811. V. 41

The Survey of Cornwall. London: 1602. V. 38; 39; 40; 43; 44

CAREW, THOMAS 1595-1639

Coelum Britanicum. London: 1634. V. 38

Poems. London: 1642. V. 37; 38; 39; 41; 43

A Rapture. By Thomas Carew. With engravings by J.E. Laboureur. Waltham Saint Lawrence: 1927. V. 37; 45

A Selection from the Poetical Works of Thomas Carew. London: 1810. V. 40; 46

The Works of Thomas Carew. Edinburgh: 1824. V. 38

The Works of Thomas Carew, Sewer in Ordinary to Charles the First. London: 1824. V. 40

CAREWE, NICHOLAS

The Voyage of Sir Nicholas Carewe to the Emperor Charles V in the Year 1529. Cambridge: 1959. V. 44

CAREY, BERTRAM

Gazeteer of the Chin Hills . . . Rangoon: 1896. V. 43

CAREY, DAVID

Beauties of the Modern Poets . . . London: 1826. V. 40

A Legend of Argyle; or 'Tis a Hundred Years Since. London: 1821. V. 40; 41; 42

Life in Paris; comprising the rambles, sprees, and amours, of Dick Wildfire, of Corinthian celebrity and his bang up companion, Squire Jenkins . . . London: 1822. V. 37; 38; 40; 41; 42

The Reign of Fancy, a Poem. London: 1804. V. 43; 45

CAREY, GEORGE C.

500 Useful and Amusing Experiments in the Arts and Manufactures; with Observations on the Properties of the Substances Employed . . . London: 1822. V. 42; 45

CAREY, GEORGE SAVILLE

The Balnea. London: 1801. V. 40

A Rural Ramble: to Which is Annexed a Poetical Tagg, or Brighthelmstone Guide. London: 1777. V. 40

CAREY, H. C.

The Geography, History and Statistics of America and the West Indies; a correct account of the discovery, settlement, and progress of the various kingdoms, states and provinces of the Western Hemisphere, to the Year 1822. With additions relative . . . London: 1823. V. 37

CAREY, HENRY

Blunderella; or, the Impertinent. London: 1730. V. 41

Cupid and Hymen: a Voyage to the Isles of Love and Matrimony . . . London: 1748. V. 46

The Dramtick Works of . . . London: 1742. V. 45

The Dramtick Works of . . . London: 1743. V. 38; 41; 45; 46

The Honest Yorskhire-Man: a Ballad Farce. London: 1736. V. 40; 42

Poems on Several Occasions. London: 1729. V. 38; 41; 45

Songs and Poems. Waltham St. Lawrence: 1924. V. 41; 43; 45

CAREY, HENRY C. 1547-1616

The Paper Question. Letters to the Hon. Schuyler Colfax. Philadelphia: 1865. V. 37

CAREY, JOHN

Cary's New and Correct English Atlas. London: 1793. V. 44

Vegetable Gardening; an Essay. 1989. V. 45

Vegetable Gardening. Cambridge: 1989. V. 43

CAREY, M.

Vindiciae Hibernicae or, Ireland Vindicated. Philadelphia: 1828. V. 46

CAREY, MARY

Meditations from the Note Book of Mary Carey 1649-1657. 1918. V. 40

CAREY, MATHEW 1760-1839

Addresses of the Philadelphia Society for the Promotion of National Industry . . . Philadelphia: 1819. V. 40; 41

The American Remembrancer. Philadelphia: 1795. V. 37

A Calm Address to the People of the Eastern States, on the Subject of the Representation of Slaves . . . Boston: 1814. V. 44

Carey's American Pocket Atlas: Containing Twenty Maps . . . Philadelphia: 1805. V. 41; 43; 45

Carey's American Pocket Atlas . . . Philadelphia: 1813. V. 42; 43

Carey's American Pocket Atlas. Philadelphia: 1814. V. 41

Carey's American Pocket Atlas . . . Philadelphia: 1814. V. 43; 45

Catalogue of Books, Pamphlets, Maps and Prints Published by Mathew Carey . . . Philadelphia: 1793. V. 45

The New Olive Branch. Philadelphia: 1820. V. 38

The Olive Branch. Philadelphia: 1814. V. 38

The Olive Branch; or, Faults on Both Sides, Federal and Democratic. Philadelphia: 1815. V. 42; 45

The Pamphlet is Dedicated with Due Respect, to Messrs. A. & A. Larence, Patrick Jackson, Tileston & Brown and Wm. Appleton of Boston, Mass. Philadelphia: 1833. V. 40

Philosophy of Common Sense. Philadelphia: 1838. V. 41

Railway. To Lay Before the Public Correct Information on the Subject of Railways. Philadelphia: 1825. V. 42

A Short Account of the Malignant Fever, Lately Prevalent in Philadelphia . . . Philadelphia: 1793. V. 38; 39; 42; 43; 45

A Short Account of the Plague, or Malignant Fever Lately Prevelant in Philadelphia . . . London: 1794. V. 38; 43

Treaty of Amity, Commerce, and Navigation Between His Britannic Majesty and the United States of America. Conditionally ratified by the Senate of the United States, at Philadelphia, June 24, 1795. To which is annexed, a Copious Appendix. Philadelphia: 1795. V. 37

Vindiciae Hibernicae: or, Ireland Vindicated. Philadelphia: 1819. V. 39; 44

CAREY, PATRICK

Trivial Poems and Triolets. London: 1820. V. 38; 39; 46

CAREY, PETER

Oscar and Lucinda. Queensland: 1988. V. 46

Oscar and Lucinda. St. Lucia: 1988. V. 44

CAREY, ROSA NOUCHETTE

Barbara Heathcote's Trial. London: 1871. V. 44

Heriot's Choice: a Tale. London: 1879. V. 44

Lover or Friend? London: 1890. V. 43

Nellie's Memories. 1868. V. 44

Wee Wifie. London: 1869. V. 44

CAREY, THOMAS

The History of the Pirates, Containing the Lives of Those Noted Pirate Captains . . . Norwich: 1814. V. 44

The History of the Pirates. Haverhill: 1825. V. 40; 43; 44; 45

The History of the Pirates . . . Hartford: 1829. V. 45

The History of the Lives and Bloody Exploits of the Most Noted Pirates, with the Late Piraces Committed in the West Indies. Hartford: 1835. V. 39

CAREY, WILLIAM

A Dictionary of the Bengalee Language . . . Calcutta: 1839-40. V. 41

The Stranger's Guide through London. London: 1808. V. 40

CARICATURES Pertaining to the Civil War; Reproduced from a Private Collection of Originals Designed for Currier & Ives. New York: 1892. V. 39

CARION, JOHANN 1499-1538

The Three Bokes of Cronicles, Whyche John Carion . . . Gathered wyth Great Diligence of the Beste Authours that Have Written in Hebrue, Greike or Latine. London: 1550. V. 45

CARISBRICK, EDWARD

The Life of the Lardy Warner of Parham in Suffolk. London: 1691. V. 40; 41; 43; 46

CARITAT, MARIE JEAN ANTOINE NICOLAS DE, MARQUIS DE CONDORCET

The Life of Voltaire by . . . London: 1790. V. 39

CARLEN, EMILIE

The Rose of Tistelon. London: 1844. V. 43

CARLETON, DON D.

Who Shot the Bear? J. Evetts Haley and the Eugene C. Barker Texas History Center. Austin: 1984. V. 40; 41; 46

CARLETON, GEORGE, BP. OF CHICHESTER

The Life of Bernard Gilpin, a Man Most Holy and Renowned Among the Northerne English . . . With His Sermon Preached Before King Edward the Sixth Anno 1552. London: 1636. V. 42; 44

CARLETON, GEORGE W.

The Memoirs of Cap. George CArleton, an English Officer . . . London: 1743. V. 43

Our Artist in Cuba. New York: 1865. V. 40

Our Artist in Peru. 1866. V. 45

Our Artist in Peru. New York: 1866. V. 40

CARLETON, J. HENRY

The Prairie Logbooks 1844-45. Chicago: 1943. V. 40; 43

CARLETON, J. W.

Hyde Marston; or, a Sportsman's Life. London: 1844. V. 43

The Sporting Sketch Book. London: 1842. V. 39; 40

CARLETON, JAMES HENRY

The Battle of Buena Vista With the Operations of the 'Army of Occupation' for One Month. New York: 1848. V. 37; 40; 42; 43; 45

CARLETON, JAMES HENRY continued

The Overland Route to California. Philadelphia: 1850. V. 42

CARLETON, JOHN WILLIAM

Recreations in Shooting. London: 1846. V. 40

CARLETON, WILLIAM 1794-1869

Alley Sheridan and Other Stories. Dublin: n.d. V. 37

Art Maguire or The Broken Pledge, a Narrative. Dublin: 1845. V. 37

The Clarionet, the Dead Boxer and Barney Branagan. London: 1850. V. 37; 43

Count Redmond O'Hanlon, the Irish Rapparee, an Historical Tale. Dublin: 1862. V. 37

The Emigrants of Ahadarra, a Tale of Irish Life. London: 1848. V. 37; 43; 44

Father Butler. The Lough Dearg Pilgrim. Dublin: 1829. V. 43

Father Butler. The Lough Dearg Pilgrim. Dublin: 1839. V. 46

The Life of William Carleton, Being His Autobiography and Letters. London: 1896. V. 43

The Squanders of Castle Squander. London: 1852. V. 37; 40; 43

Tales of Ireland. Dublin: 1834. V. 37

The Tithe Proctor. A Novel; being a Tale of the Tithe Rebellion in Ireland. London: 1849. V. 37

The Tithe Proctor. A Tale of the Tithe Rebellion in Ireland. London/Belfast: 1849. V. 37

Traits and Stories of the Irish Peasantry. Dublin: 1843. V. 38; 39

Traits and Stories of the Irish Peasantry. London: 1868. V. 38

Traits and Stories of the Irish Peasantry. London: 1877. V. 40

Traits and Stories of the Irish Peasantry. Dublin: 1833. V. 37

Traits and Stories of the Irish Peasantry, editor D.J. O'Donoghue. London: 1896. V. 37

Traits and Stories of the Irish Peasanty. Dublin: 1843-44. V. 39; 42

The Works of William Carleton. New York: 1900. V. 38

CARLETON, WILLIAM MCKENDREE

Poems. Chicago: 1871. V. 40

CARLETTI, FRANCESCO

Ragiomenti di Francesco Carletti Fiorentino Sopra le Cose da lui Vedute ne' Suoi Viaggi si dell'Indie Occidentali . . . Florence: 1701. V. 45

CARLETTI, NICCOLO 1723-1796

Istituzioni di Architettura Idraulica . . . Naples: 1780. V. 40

CARLI, ENZO

Italian Primitives: Panel Paintings of the Twelfth and Thirteenth Centuries. New York: 1965. V. 42

CARLI, GIAN-RINALDO

L'Uomo Libero Ossia Ragionamento Sulla Liberta Naturale e Civile dell' Uomo. Milan;: 1779. V. 39

CARLI, GIOVANNI FINALDO

Lettres Americaines, dans Laquelles on Examine l'Origine, l'Etat Civil, Politique, Militaire & Religieux, les Arts l'Industrie, les Sciences, les Moeurs . . . Boston: 1788. V. 44

CARLIER, AUGUSTE

Marriage in the United States. Boston & New York: 1867. V. 40

CARLILE, JAMES

The Fortune-Hunters: Or, Two Fools well Met. London: 1689. V. 37; 38; 39; 41; 44

Select Sacred Melodies for all the Metres in General Use . . . London: 1821. V. 45

CARLILE, RICHARD

The Character of the Jew Books: Being a Defence of the Natural Innocence of Man, Against Kints and Priests, or Tyrants and Imposters. London: 1821. V. 45

The Deist; or, Moral Philosopher . . . London: 1819-26 (but. V. 44

CARLISLE, ANTHONY

An Essay on the Disorders of Old Age and on the Means for Prolonging Human Life. London: 1817. V. 40

An Essay on the Disorders of Old Agae, and on the Means of Prolonging Human Life. Philadelphia: 1819. V. 37; 40; 45

The Hunterian Oration, Delivered Before the Royal College of Surgeons. London: 1820. V. 40

CARLISLE, ARTHUR DRUMMOND

Round the World in 1870. London: 1872. V. 44

CARLISLE, FREDERICK HOWARD, 5TH EARL OF

Poems. London: 1807. V. 38; 40; 45

Thoughts Upon the Present Condition of the Stage and Upon the Construction of a New Theatre. London: 1808. V. 45

The Tragedies and Poems. London: 1801. V. 37

CARLISLE, FREDERICK HOWARD, EARL OF

Thoughts Upon the Present Condition of the Stage, and Upon the Construction of a New Theatre. London: 1809. V. 41

CARLISLE, GEORGE WILLIAM FREDERICK HOWARD, 7TH EARL OF 1802-1864

The Last of the Greeks; or, the Fall of Constantinople. London: 1828. V. 39

Lines on Yorkshire, Written in 1832. London: 1860. V. 39

CARLISLE, ISABELLA BYRON HOWARD, COUNTESS

Thoughts in the Form of Maxims Addressed to Young Ladies on Their First Establishment in the World. London: 1789. V. 42

CARLISLE, JOHN G.

Mrs. John G. Carlisle's Kentucky Cook Book. Chicago: 1893. V. 45

CARLISLE, NICHOLAS

A Concise Description of the Endowed Grammar Schools in England and Wales. London: 1818. V. 40

Hints on Rural Residences. London: 1825. V. 44

CARLISLE, ROBERT J.

An Account of Bellevue Hospital with a Catalogue of the Medical and Surgical Staff from 1736 to 1894. New York: 1893. V. 38; 39; 40

CARLL, LEWIS BUFFETT

A Treatise on the Calculus of Variations. New York: 1881. V. 45

CARLOS II, KING OF SPAIN

El Rey. Por Quanto en Diez y Nueve de Julio Passado Deste ano Mande dar la Cedula del Tenor Siguiente por Quanto Por Parte del Prior, y Consules de la Universidad de los Cargadores a las Indias de la Ciudad de Sevilla . . . Madrid: 1677. V. 40

CARLOS III, KING OF SPAIN

Coleccion de las Reales Resoluciones de Su Magestad Relativas al Libre Comercio de las Islas de Barlovento, Provincias de Campeche, Santa Marta, rio del Hacha, y Buenos-Ayres . . . de America Meridional . . . Madrid: 1778. V. 40

CARLSON, NORMAN V.

Casanova and Boswell: an Encounter? Owl Hill: 1978. V. 46

CARLSTADT, ANDREAS RUDOLF BODENSTEIN VON

De Legis Litera Sive Carne & Spiritu. VVittembergae: 1521. V. 38

Verba Dei Quanto Candore & qz Syncere Predicari, Quantaqz Solicitudine Vnieursi Debeant Addiscere. Vuittenbergae: 1520. V. 38

CARLTON, A. B.

The Wonderlands of the Wild West, with Sketches of the Mormons. N.P.: 1891. V. 40

The Wonderlands of the Wild West, with Sketches of the Mormons. N.P.: 1891. V. 39

CARLYLE, ALEXANDER 1722-1805

Autobiography, Containing Memorials of the Men and Events of His Time. London: 1861. V. 41

The Question Relating to a Scots Militia Considered. Edinburgh: 1760. V. 42

CARLYLE, J. D.

Specimens of Arabian Poetry, from the Earliest Time to the Extinction of the Khaliphat, with Some Account of the Authors. London: 1810. V. 41

CARLYLE, JANE WELSH

Letters and Memorials of Jane Welsh Carlyle. London: 1883. V. 39; 42; 45; 46

CARLYLE, JOSEPH DACRE

Poems, Suggested Chiefly by Scenes in Asia-Minor, Syria and Greece . . . London: 1805. V. 43

CARLYLE, R.

Six Views of the Ruins of Furness Abbey . . . London: 1835. V. 40

CARLYLE, THOMAS 1795-1881

Chartism. London: 1840. V. 38; 39; 41; 43

Chartism. London: 1842. V. 38

The Correspondence of Thomas Carlyle and Ralph Waldo Emerson 1834-1872. Boston: 1883. V. 43

Critical and Miscellaneous Essays. Boston: 1838-9. V. 40; 41; 44; 46

Critical and Miscellaneous Essays . . . London: 1847. V. 39; 41

Critical and Miscellaneous Essays. London: 1904. V. 39

The French Revolution: a History. London: 1837. V. 38; 40; 43

The French Revolution: a History. London: 1842. V. 40

The French Revolution: a History. London: 1848. V. 39; 41

The French REvolution: a History in Three Parts. London: 1857. V. 44

CARLYLE, THOMAS 1795-1881 continued

The French Revolution. Mt. Vernon: 1956. V. 45

German Romance: Specimens of Its Chief Authors; with Biographical and Critical Notices. Edinburgh: 1827. V. 37; 40; 42; 44; 45

History of Friedrich II of Prussia, Called Frederick the Great. London: 1859-65. V. 39; 42

History of Friedrich II of Prussia, Called Frederick the Great. New York: 1900. V. 42

Inaugural Address at Edinburgh, April 1866, by . . . Edinburgh: 1866. V. 43

Last Words of Thomas Carlyle. Edinburgh: 1882. V. 39

Latter-Day Pamphlets. London: 1850. V. 38; 39; 40; 41; 42

Letters Addressed to Mrs. Basil Montagu and B. W. Procter by . . . London: 1881. V. 44

The Life of Friedrich Schiller. London: 1825. V. 37; 42

The Life of Friedrich Schiller . . . London: 1845. V. 43

Life of John Sterling. London: 1851. V. 38; 39

The Life of John Sterling. London: 1871. V. 38

Occasional Discourse on the Nigger Question. London: 1853. V. 39

Oliver Cromwell's Letters and Speeches: With Elucidations. London: 1845. V. 44

Oliver Cromwell's Letters and Speeches: with Elucidations. London: 1846. V. 44

On Heroes, Hero-Worship and the Heroic in History. London: 1841. V. 39; 44

Past and Present. London: 1843. V. 37; 40; 44

Past and Present. London: 1853. V. 39

Reminiscences of My Irish Journey in 1849. London: 1882. V. 38

Reminiscences. London: 1887. V. 43

Samuel Johnson. London: 1853. V. 42

Sartor Resartus (and) Lectures on Heroes. London. V. 46

Sartor Resartus. London: 1834. V. 42; 43; 46

Sartor Resartus. 1836. V. 43

Sartor Resartus. Boston: 1836. V. 40

Sartor Resartus. London: 1898. V. 43; 44; 46

Sartor Resartus. Hammersmith: 1907. V. 40; 41; 42; 43; 44; 45; 46

Sartor Resartus. London: 1907. V. 37; 38; 44; 45

Sartor Resartus. (with) Lectures on Heroes. London: 1868. V. 40

Shooting Niagra: and After? London: 1867. V. 38; 40

Thomas Carlyle's Counsels to a Literary Aspirant. Edinburgh: 1886. V. 43; 45

Wilhelm Meister's Apprenticeship and Travels. Philadelphia: 1840. V. 44

Wilhelm Meister's Apprenticeship. Edinburgh: 1824. V. 37

The Works of . . . London. V. 39

Works. Boston: 1884. V. 40; 45

Works. London: 1885. V. 42

Works. London: 1885-88. V. 37

The Works. London: 1896-99. V. 37

The Works. London: 1897-1902. V. 42

The Works. London: 1897-99. V. 38

Works. Boston: (ca. 1920). V. 37

CARMACK, GEORGE W.

My Early Experiences in the Yukon. Seattle: 1933. V. 43

CARMALT, WILLIAM

A Letter to the Rt. Hon. George Canning, on the Principle and the Administration of the English Poor Laws. London: 1823. V. 41

CARMAN, BLISS 1861-1929

Ballads of Lost Haven. Boston: 1897. V. 46

Ballads and Lyrics. Toronto: 1923. V. 38; 41

The Girl in the Poster; for a Design by Miss Ethel Reed. N.P.: 1897. V. 44

More Songs from Vagabondia. Boston: 1896. V. 37; 38; 41; 43

An Open Letter. Boston: 1920. V. 43

Poems. New York: 1904. V. 37; 38

Poems. Boston: 1905. V. 43

Songs from Vagabondia. Boston: 1894. V. 41; 42

CARMAN, EZRA A.

Special Report on the History and Present Condition of the Sheep Industry of the U. S. Washington: 1892. V. 45

CARMAN, W. Y.

Indian Army Uniforms Under the British from the 18th Century to 1947. Cavalry. London: 1961. V. 41

CARMER, CARL LAWSON

Deep South. New York: 1930. V. 39

French Town. 1928. V. 39

French Town. New Orleans: 1928. V. 37; 42; 46

CARMICHAEL, A. C., MRS.

Domestic Manners and Social Condition of the White, Coloured and Negro Population of the West Indies. London: 1833. V. 42

CARMICHAEL, ALEXANDER

Carmina Gadelica, Hymns and Incantations . . . Einburgh: 1927. V. 43

Carmina Gadelica; Hymns and Incantations. Edinburgh: 1928. V. 43

Carmina Gadelica. London: 1928-41. V. 38

Carmina Gadelica, Hymns and Incantations, with Illustrative Notes on Words, Rites and Customs, Dying and Obsolete. Edinburgh: 1954-78. V. 37; 42

Carmina Gadelica: Hymns and Incantations with illustrative notes . . . orally collected in the Higlands and Islands of Scotland, and translated into English . . . Edinburgh: 1900-54. V. 37

CARMICHAEL, ANDREW

A Memoir of the Life and Philosophy of Spurzheim. Dublin: 1833. V. 39

CARMICHAEL, ANDREW BLAIR

The Law Scrutiny; or, Attornies' Guide. Dublin: 1807. V. 38

The Metropolis. (with) Second Part of the Metropolis. Dublin: 1805, 1806. V. 38

CARMICHAEL, MARY D. I.

A New Dress for an Old Friend, Intended for the Amusement of Children, Being a Fable of Aesop in Rhyme. London: 1857. V. 38; 42

CARMICHAEL, MRS.

Domestic Manners and Social Conditions of the White, Colored & Negro Population of the West Indies. London: 1833. V. 45

CARMICHAEL, SARAH E.

Poems. San Francisco: 1866. V. 40; 45; 46

CARMICHAEL, THOMAS

The Autobiography of a Rejected MS. London: 1870. V. 40

CARMINA Quadragesimalia ab Aedis Christi Oxon. Alumnis Composita. Oxonii: 1723. V. 39

CARMINA Qvinqve Illvstrivm Poetarvm . . . Florence: 1552. V. 45

CARMODY, FRANCIS

Four Poems of the Occult, by Yvan Goll. Edited and with Introduction by Francis Carmody. Illustrations by Fernand Leger, Pablo Picasso, Yves Tanguy and Jean Arp. (Kentfield): 1962. V. 37

CARMONTELLE, LOUIS CARROGIS DE

Jardin de Monceau, Pres de Paris, Appartenant a Son Altesse Serenissime Monseigneur Le Duc de Chartres. Paris: 1779. V. 41

CARNARVON, EARL OF

Catalogue of Books Selected from the Library of an English Amateur. London: 1893-97. V. 45

CARNE, JOHN

Letters from the East. London: 1826. V. 39; 42

Syria, The Holy Land, Asia Minor, Etc. Illustrated In a Series of Views Drawn From Nature. London;: 1836. V. 39; 45

Syria, the Holy Land, Asia Minor &c. Illustrated in a Series of Views Drawn from Nature by W. H. Bartlett, William Purser, &c. London: 1836-38. V. 37; 40; 43; 45

Syria, The Holy Land, Asia Minor &c. London, Paris & America: 1836-38. V. 39

Syria, the Holy Land and Asia Minor Illustrated . . . London: 1842. V. 41; 42; 43

CARNEAL, GEORGETTE

A Conqueror of Space: An Authorized Biography of the Life and Work of Lee DeForest. New York: 1930. V. 39

CARNEAU, ETIENNE

La Piece Charmante de Cabinet Descouverte. Paris: 1649. V. 37

CARNEGIE, ANDREW

Our Coaching Trip. Brighton to Iverness. New York: 1882. V. 39; 46

Round the World: Notes of a Trip. New York: 1879. V. 39

CARNEGIE, DAVID

The History of Munitions Supply in Canada 1914-1918. London: 1925. V. 37

CARNEGIE, HELENA

Catalogue of the Collection of Antique Gems Formed by James Ninth Earl of Southkesk K.T. London: 1908. V. 44

CARNEGIE STEEL CO.

Pocket Companion Containing Useful Information and Tables, Appertaining to the Use of Steel, as Manufactured by Carnegie Steel Co., Pittsburgh, Pa. for Engineers, Architects and Builders. Pittsburgh: 1900. V. 44

CARNEVALI, EMANUEL

A Hurried Man. 1925. V. 41

A Hurried Man. Paris: 1925. V. 37; 42; 43

CARNOCHAN, JANET

History of Niagara. Toronto: 1914. V. 38

CARNOT, NICOLAS LEONARD SADI 1796-1832

Reflexions sur la Puissance Motrice de Feu et sur les machines Propres a Developper Cette Puissance. Paris: 1824. V. 42

CARO, ANNIBALE 1507-1566

Apologia de Gli Academici di Banchi di Roma, Contra M. Lodovico Castelvetro da Modena. Parma: 1558. V. 37; 38; 45

De le Lettere Familiari. Venice: 1610. V. 37

Rime. Venice: 1584. V. 37; 45

CARO DE TORRES, FRANCISCO

Historia de las Ordenes militares de Santiago, Calatrava y Alcantara Desde su Fundacion Hasta el Rey Felipe Segundo . . . Madrid: 1629. V. 38

CAROCHI, HORACIO

Compendio Del Arte de la Lengua Mexicana. Mexico City: 1759. V. 38

CAROL, MARK

Ancient Needs. Easthampton: 1989. V. 45

THE CAROLINA Housewife, or, House and Home. Charleston: 1851. V. 41

THE CAROLINA Low-Country. New York: 1931. V. 45

CAROLINE AMELIA ELIZABETH, QUEEN OF GREAT BRITAIN.

The Trial at Large of Her Majesty Caroline Amelia Elizabeth, Queen of Great Britain; in the House of Lords on Charges of Adulterous Intercourse . . . London: 1821. V. 46

CAROLINE, QUEEN OF GREAT BRITAIN

Fairburn, (Senior's) Edition of the Letter from Her Royal Highness the Princess of Wales to His Royal Highness the Prince Regent. Dated January 14, 1813 . . . London: 1813? V. 45

The Trial at Large of Her Majesty Caroline Amelia Elizabeth, Queen of Great Britain. London: 1821. V. 45

The Whole Proceedings on the trial of Her Majesty Caroline Amelia Elizabeth, Queen of England . . . London: 1802. V. 45

CAROLINO, PEDRO

English As She Is Spoke - the New Guide of the Conversation in Portuguese and English. London: 1960. V. 42

The New Guide of the Conversation in Portuguese and English in Two Parts. Peking, Paris: 1869. V. 41

The New Guide of the Conversation in Portuguese and English in Two Parts. Boston: 1883. V. 41; 42; 44

The New Guide of the Conversation in Portuguese and English in two parts. (Paris): 1869. V. 37

CARON, AUGUSTE

The Lady's Toilette. London: 1808. V. 41

CARON, FRANCOIS

A True Description of the Mighty Kingdoms of Japan and Siam . . . London: 1935. V. 41

CARON, JOHANNES

Carmina Tumultuaria. Paris: 1496/97. V. 40

CAROVE, FRIEDRICH WILHELM 1789-1852

The Story Without End. London: 1868. V. 42; 45

The Story Without an End. London: 1879. V. 46

The Story Without an End. London: 1909. V. 40

CAROVE, FRIEDRICK W.

Story Without End. Boston: 1836. V. 44

CARPENTER, ANDREW

Irish Writings from the Age of Swift. Dublin: 1972-79. V. 38; 39

CARPENTER, CHARLES H.

Gorham Silver, 1831-1981. New York: 1982. V. 40

CARPENTER, EDWARD

Democracy. Manchester: 1883. V. 38

Forecasts of the Coming Century, by a Decade of Writers . . . London: 1897. V. 42

Homogenic Love, and Its Place in a Free Society. Manchester: 1894. V. 37

Never Again! A Protest and a Warning Addressed to the Peoples of Europe. London: 1916. V. 43

CARPENTER, EDWIN H.

A Sixteenth Century Mexican Broadside from the Collection of Emilio Valton . . . Los Angeles: 1965. V. 38; 39; 42

CARPENTER, G. D. HALE

A Naturalist on Lake Victoria, with an Account of Sleeping Sickness and the Tse-Tse Fly. New York: 1920. V. 44; 45

A Naturalist in East Africa . . . Oxford: 1925. V. 44

CARPENTER, GEORGE N.

History of the Eighth Regiment Vermont Volunteers, 1861-1865. Boston: 1886. V. 38; 39; 42

CARPENTER, GEORGE W.

Essays on Some of the Most Important Articles of the Materia Medica . . . . Philadelphia: 1834. V. 44

CARPENTER, H. BARRETT

Colour. A Manual of Its Theory and Practice. London: 1933. V. 46

CARPENTER, JOHN

Liber Albus: The White Book of the City of London. London: 1861. V. 40

CARPENTER, L.

An Introduction to the Geography of the New Testament . . . Cambridge: 1811. V. 45

CARPENTER, MARY

Juvenile Delinquents, Their Condition and Treatment. London: 1853. V. 45

Our Convicts. London: 1864. V. 41; 42; 45

Reformatory Prison Discipline, as Developed by the Rt. Hon. Sir Walter Crofton, in the Irish Convict Prisons. London: 1872. V. 46

Six Months in India. London: 1868. V. 40; 45

CARPENTER, R. R. M.

Game Trails from Alaska to Africa. London: 1938. V. 39

CARPENTER, S. D.

Logic of History. Madison: 1864. V. 42

CARPENTER, SAMUEL WARNER

Law of Water for Irrigation in Colorado. Denver: 1886. V. 42

CARPENTER, THOMAS

American Senator, a Copious and Impartial Report of the Debates in the Congress of the United States, All Treaties, Addresses, Proclamations Which Occurred, 2nd of the 4th Congress. Philadelphia: 1796. V. 39

The American Senator. Philadelphia: 1796-97. V. 40

CARPENTER, W. M.

Kipling's College. Evanston: 1929. V. 46

CARPENTER, WESLEY M.

Proceedings at the Dinner Given by the Medical Profession of the City of New York, April 12, 1883 to Oliver Wendell Holmes. New York: 1883. V. 40

CARPENTER, WILLIAM

The Angler's Assistant. London: 1848. V. 39

The Political Text Book. London: 1833. V. 38

CARPENTER, WILLIAM B.

Introduction to the Study of Foraminifera. London: 1862. V. 43

The Microscope and Its Revelations. New York: 1883. V. 42

CARPENTER, WILLIAM HOOKMAN

Pictorial Notices, a memoir of Anthony Van Dyck, with a Descritpive Catalogue of the Etchings Executed by Him. London: 1844. V. 40

CARPENTER, WILLIAM W.

Travels and Adventures in Mexico: In the Course of Journeys of Upward of 2500 Miles, Performed on Foot. New York: 1851. V. 39; 42; 45

CARPENTIER, ALEJO

The Kingdom of this World. 1987. V. 42

The Kingdom of This World. New York: 1987. V. 40

CARPI, UGO DA

Thesauro de Scrittori. Roma: 1535. V. 45

CARPUE, JOSEPH CONSTANTINE 1764-1846

An Introduction to Electricity and Galvanism; with Cases, Shewing Their Effects in the Curse of Diseases. London: 1803. V. 37; 42

CARR, A.

Illustrated Hand-Book of California: Her Climate, Trade, Exports . . . London: 1870. V. 37

CARR, A. W.

Byzantine Illumination. 1150-1250: A Study of a Provincial Tradition. London: 1987. V. 39

CARR, ALICE VANSITTART STRETTELL 1850-

North Italian Folk. Sketches of Town and Country Life. New York: 1878. V. 41

CARR, COMYNS, MRS.

North Italian Folk. Sketches of Town and Country Life. London: 1878. V. 38; 43

North Italian Folk. Sketches of Town and Country Life. New York: 1878. V. 37

CARR, EMILY

The Heart of a Peacock. Toronto: 1953. V. 37

The House of All Sorts. Toronto: 1944. V. 41

Hundreds and Thousands: The Journals . . . Toronto: 1966. V. 37

Klee Wyck. Toronto: 1941. V. 41

CARR, FRANCIS

Brandon Tower. London: 1876. V. 37

Not Lancelot, Nor Another. London: 1875. V. 41

CARR, J. L.

A Day in Summer. London: 1963. V. 42

A Month in the Country . . . 1990. V. 45

A Season in Sinji. London: 1967. V. 38

What Hetty Did. London: 1988. V. 40

CARR, J. W. COMYNS

The Abbey Church of St. Albans. London: 1877. V. 39

CARR, J. WINGATE

Discriptive (sic) Catalogue of Fruit and Ornamental Trees, Shrubs, Roses, Vines &c. Cultivated and for Sale by J. Wingate Carr, North Nursery, Bangor, Me. Bangor: 1856. V. 45

CARR, JOHN 1772-1832

Analyses of New Works of Voyages and Travels Lately Published in London. London: 1806. V. 40

Caldedonian Sketches, or a Tour through Scotland in 1807 . . . London: 1809. V. 38; 39; 41; 44

Descriptive Travels in the Southern and Eastern Parts of Spain and the Balearic Isles in the Year 1809. London: 1811. V. 38; 42; 45

A Northern Summer; or Travels Round the Baltic, Through Denmark, Sweden, Russia, Prussia and Part of Germany, in the Year 1804. London: 1805. V. 37; 38; 40; 41; 44; 45

Pioneer Days in California . . . Historical and Personal Sketches. Eureka: 1891. V. 38; 40; 42; 43; 45; 46

The Stranger in France. London: 1803. V. 37; 38; 40

The Stranger in France; or a Tour from Devonshire to Paris. Hartford: 1804. V. 40

The Stranger in Ireland; or a Tour in the Southern and Western Parts of that Country in the Year 1805. London: 1806. V. 38; 39; 46

The Stranger in France . . . London: 1807. V. 39; 43

A Tour through Holland, Along the Right and Left Banks of the Rhine, to the South of Germany, in the Summer and Atumn of 1806. Philadelphia: 1807. V. 41

CARR, JOHN DICKSON

The Crooked Hinge. 1938. V. 39

Death Turns the Tables. New York & London: 1941. V. 37

The Department of Queer Complaints. 1940. V. 39

The Emperor's Snuff-Box. 1942. V. 39

The Four False Weapons. New York: 1937. V. 42

He Who Whispers. New York: 1946. V. 46

It Walks by Night. 1930. V. 39

The Judas Window. 1930. V. 39

The Life of Sir Arthur Conan Doyle. London: 1949. V. 39

The Man Who Could Not Shudder. New York: 1940. V. 39

The Murder of Sir Edmund Godfrey. 1936. V. 39

The Problem of the Green Capsule. New York: 1939. V. 45

Seeing is Believing. New York: 1941. V. 42

She Died a Lady. 1943. V. 39

CARR, LARRY

Four Fabulous Faces: The Evolution and Metamorphosis of Greta Garbo, Gloria Swanson, Joan Crawford and Marlene Dietrich by Larry Carr, with an Introduction by Adela Rogers St. John. 1970. V. 37

CARR, MARY FRANCIS

Shakers: A Correspondence Between Mary F. C. of Mt. Holly City and a Shaker Sister, Sarah L. of Union Village. Cincinnati: 1869. V. 37

CARR, RALPH

The Penalty of Death Retained for cruel Atrocities. Part the Firt. The Divine Sanction. London: 1841. V. 38

CARR, RICHARD

Epistolae Medicinales Variis Occasionibus Conscriptae. London: 1691. V. 38

CARR, WILLIAM

An Accurate Description of the United Netherlands, and of the Most Considerable Parts of Germany, Sweden and Denmark . . . London: 1691. V. 38; 40; 43; 44

The Dialect of Craven, in the West-Riding of the County of York, with a Copious Glossary . . . London: 1828. V. 45

Horae Momenta Cravenae; or, the Craven Dialect, Exemplified in Two Dialogues Between Farmer Giles and His Neighbour Bridget. London: 1824. V. 45

CARRACCIOLI, MARQUEZ

Os Caracteres da Amizde, Nova Ediccao. Lisbon: 1776. V. 38

CARRACIOLUS, ROBERTUS 1425-1495

Sermones per Adventum . . . With the Sermo de Conseptione Viginis Marie of Domenicus Bollanus. Strassburg: 1485. V. 40

CARRADORI, FRANCESCO 1747-1825

Istruzione Elementare per gli Studiosi della Scultura. Florence: 1802. V. 37; 42; 46

CARRANZA, ALONSO

El Aiustamiento i Proporcion de las Monedas de Oro, Plata i Cobre i La Reduccion Destos Metales a su Debida Estimacion . . . Madrid: 1629. V. 39

CARRANZA, BARTHOLOME DE, ABP. OF TOLEDO

Summa Conciliorum et Pontificum. Paris: 1550. V. 45; 46

CARRANZA, DOMINGO GONZALES

A Geographical Description of the Coasts, Harbours and Sea Ports of the Spanish West Indies . . . London: 1740. V. 40

CARRASCO DEL SAZ, FRANCISCO

Doctoris Francisci Del Saz . . . Opera. (with) Tractatus De Casibus Curiae. Madrid: 1648, 1630. V. 37

CARREL, ALEXIS

The Preservation of Tissues and Its Application in Surgery. 1912. V. 42

The Treatment of Infected Wounds. New York: 1917. V. 42

Uniterminal and Biterminal Venous Transplantations. 1906. V. 42

CARRELL, CHRISTOPHER

Beyond This Horizon - an Anthology of Science Fiction and Science Fact. Sunderland: 1973. V. 41

CARRER, LUIGI 1801-1850

Il Clotaldo, Poema. Padua: 1826. V. 38

CARRERE, LOUIS

Technique du Lancer Leger. Toulouse: 1947. V. 43

CARRIAGE BUILDERS' NATIONAL ASSOCIATION OF THE U.S.A.

Twenty-eighth through Thirty-third Annual Reports. Philadelphia: 1900-05. V. 43

CARRICK, JOHN DAVID

Whistle-Binkie: a Collection of Songs for the Social Circle. Glasgow: 1846. V. 39; 45

CARRICK, T. W.

The Story of Wigton (Cumberland) From Its Origin to the Close of the 19th Century. Carlisle: 1949. V. 44

CARRIER, A H.

Monument to the Memory of Henry Clay. Philadelphia: 1858. V. 39

Monument to the Memory of Henry Clay. Philadelphia: 1859. V. 39

CARRIER'S Message to the Patrons of the Ithaca Herald. January 1, 1837. ?Ithaca: 1837. V. 39

CARRIER'S New Year Address to the Patrons of the Erie Gazette. Jan. 1, 1851. Erie: 1851. V. 40

CARRILLO, ANTONIO

Exposition Addressed to the Chamber of Deputies of the Congress of the Union by Senor Don Carlos Antonio Carrillo . . . San Francisco: 1938. V. 43

CARRILLO Y ANCONA, CRESCENCIO

Compendio de la Historia de Yucatan Precedido del de su Geografia y Dispuesto en Forma de Lecciones Para Servir de Texto a la Ensenanza de Ambos Ramos en los Establecimientos de Instruccion primaria y Secundaria. Merida: 1871. V. 38

CARRINGTON, CHARLES

Untrodden Fields of Anthropology. Paris: 1898. V. 44

CARRINGTON, EDMUND FREDERICK JOHN

Confessions of an Old Bachelor. London: 1827. V. 43

CARRINGTON, F.

The Queen's Garland. London: 1900. V. 41

CARRINGTON, F. A.

Latest Information from the Settlement of New Plymouth on the Coast of Taranake, New Zealand . . . London: 1842. V. 40

CARRINGTON, FRANCES

Army Life on the Plains. Philadelphia: 1910. V. 37

CARRINGTON, HENRY B.

Ab-Sa-Ra-Ka, Land of Massacre. Philadelphia: 1879. V. 39

Battles of the American Revolution, 1775-1781. Historical and Military Criticism, with Topographical Illustrations. New York: 1888. V. 46

The Indian Question. Boston: 1884. V. 39; 43; 45

The Indian Question- An Adress. Boston: 1909. V. 39

Passing Shadows. (and) Heavenly Voices. N.P.: 1898. V. 45

Some Phases of the Indian Question. Boston: 1884. V. 41; 42

CARRINGTON, JOHN BODMAN

The Plate of the Worshipful Company of Goldsmiths. Oxford: 1926. V. 42

CARRINGTON, LEONORA

The Oval Lady. Santa Barbara: 1975. V. 39

The Oval Lady. Santa Barbara: 1978. V. 42

CARRINGTON, MARGARET

Ab-Sa-Ra-Ka Home of the Crows. Philadelphia: 1868. V. 45

Ab-Sa-Ra-Ka. Home of the Crow. New York: 1869. V. 45

CARRINGTON, NOEL

Carrington: Paintings, Drawings and Decorations. Oxford: 1978. V. 42

CARRINGTON, NOEL THOMAS

The Collected Poems of the Late N. T. Carrington. London: 1834. V. 40

CARRINGTON, RICHARD CHRISTOPHER

Observations of the Spots on the Sun From November 9, 1853 to March 24, 1861, Made at Redhill. London: 1863. V. 45

CARRION, LOUIS

Emendationvm Et Observationvm Liber Primvs (-Secundus). Paris: 1583. V. 39

CARROL, WILLIAM

An Account of the Later Emperor Napoleon the First, at St. Helena. St. Helena: 1875. V. 40

CARROLL, B. R.

A Sketch of the Agricultural History of SC: Being a Communcation Read before the Agricultural Society of St. John's Colleton. Charleston: 1837. V. 46

CARROLL, BARTHOLOMEW RIVERS

Historical Collections of South Carolina . . . New York: 1836. V. 45

CARROLL, CAMPBELL

Three Bar: The Story of Douglas Lake. Vancouver: 1958. V. 43

CARROLL, GEORGE D.

The Art of Correspondence and usages of Polite Society. New York: 1880. V. 37

Diamonds from Brilliant Minds. New York: 1881. V. 38

Out of the Ashes. New York: 1890. V. 44

CARROLL, H. BAILEY

Texas County Histories: A Bibliography. Austin: 1943. V. 37; 41

CARROLL, J. M.

Just Such a Time: Recollections of Childhood on the Texas Frontier, 1858-1867. By J.M. Carroll. With woodcuts by Barbara Whitehead. Austin, Texas: 1987. V. 37; 41; 42

CARROLL, JIM

Forced Entries. New York: 1987. V. 39

Living at the Movies. New York: 1973. V. 38

CARROLL, JOHN

An Address to the Roman Catholics of the United States of Ameraica. London: 1785. V. 37

CARROLL, JOHN M.

The Black Military Experience in the American West. New York: 1971. V. 46

4 on Custer by Carroll. New Brunswick: 1976. V. 45

I. Varnum. The Autobiographical Reminiscences of Custer's Chief of Scouts. Glendale: 1982. V. 45

The Unpublished Papers of the Order of Indian Wars Boook 1-10. New Brunswick. V. 45

CARROLL, JONATHAN

The Land of Laughs. New York: 1980. V. 45; 46

CARROLL, PATRICK

The Trial of Patrick Carrol with Particulars Relative to His Execution This Morning, In Front of the Jail at Maidstone, for the Wilful Murder of Mrs. Browning . . . London: 1835. V. 42

CARROLL, W.

The Angler's Vade Mecum, Containing a Descriptive Account of the Water Flies . . . Edinburgh: 1818. V. 39; 41

CARROLL, WESLEY P.

Moss Agates: to My Brother Members of the Wyoming Bar. Cheyenne: 1890. V. 37; 38

CARROLL, WILLIAMS

A Handbook of the Literature of the Rev. C.L. Dodgson (Lewis Carroll). London: 1931. V. 37

CARRON COMPANY

Architects' Catalogue. Stirlingshire: 1935. V. 44

General Ironfounders, Iron and Coal Masters, Engineers, Brass Founders, Galvanisers, Shipowners, Bonded Warehousemn. Rosk: Carron. Stirlinghsire. London: 1931. V. 37

CARRUTH, HAYDEN

Journey to a Known Place. Norfolk: 1961. V. 39; 45

North Winter. Iowa City: 1964. V. 44

The Return. Rome: 1949. V. 38

Track's End. New York: 1911. V. 37

CARRUTH, JANE

Horses and Pony Stories. London: 1978. V. 39

CARRUTHERS, DOUGLAS

Beyond the Caspian. Edinburgh: 1949. V. 39; 43

CARRUTHERS, GEORGE

Paper Making. Toronto: 1947. V. 42

CARRUTHERS, JOHN

Retrospect of Thirty-six Years' Residence in Canada West: Being a Christian Journal and Narrative. Hamilton: 1861. V. 37

CARRYL, GUY WETMORE

Fables for the Frivolous. New York: 1898. V. 44

Grimm Tales Made Easy. Boston: (1902). V. 37

Mother Goose for Grown Ups. New York: 1900. V. 43

Mother Goose for Grown-Ups. New York: and London: 1900. V. 46

CARSE, ROLAND

Monarchs of Merrie England. London. V. 42

The Monarchs of merry England. (with) More Monarchs of Merry England. London: 1908. V. 46

CARSON, HAMPTON L.

The Hampton L. Carson Collection of Engraved Portraits with Many Views, Letters and Historical Documents. Philadelphia: 1904. V. 39; 44

The History of the Supreme Court of the United States . . . Philadelphia: 1904. V. 43

History of the Celebration of the One Hundredth Anniversary of the Promulgation of the Constitution of the United States. Edited by . . . Philadelphia: 1889. V. 37

CARSON, JOSEPH

A History of the Medical Department of the University of Pennsylvania, From Its Foundation in 1765. Philadelphia: 1869. V. 42

Illustrations of Medical Botany . . . Philadelphia: 1847. V. 45; 46

THE CARSON Ladies' Domestic Guide. Carson City: 1874. V. 39

CARSON, RACHEL

The Sea Around Us. London: 1980. V. 43

The Sea Around Us. New York: 1980. V. 41; 45; 46

Silent Spring. Boston: 1962. V. 46

CARSON, THOMAS

Ranching, Sport and Travel. London: 1911. V. 39; 44

CARSON, THOMAS continued

Ranching, Sport and Travel. London & Leipzig: 1911. V. 41

CARSTAIRS, CARROLL

A Generation Missing. London: 1930. V. 46

CARSTAIRS, JOHN PADDY

Movie Merry Go-Round. London: 1937. V. 45

CARSTAIRS, JOSEPH

The Art of Writing, Shewing Several Methods of Acquiring Improvement in Business Hand Writing . . . London: 1837. V. 40

Lectures on the Art of Writing, Comprehending a Variety of Observations on the Impediments that Retard the Progress of the Learner. London: 1836. V. 43

CARSTAIRS, JOSPEH

Lectures on the Art of Writing. London: 1822. V. 40

CARSTARPHEN, JAMES

My Trip to California in '49. Louisiana: 1914. V. 43

My Trip to California in '49. Louisianna, Missouri: 1914. V. 41

CARSTENSEN, A. RISS

Two Summers in Greenland an Artist's Adventures Among Ice and Islands, in Fjords and Mountains. London: 1890. V. 38; 39; 40; 42

CARSWELL, CHRISTINE

The Savage Pilgrimage: a Narrative of D. H. Lawrence. London: 1932. V. 40

CARSWELL, JOHN

The American Churches and Other Buildings. Oxford: 1968. V. 46

Coptic Tattoo Designs. 1958. V. 41

Kutahya Tiles and Pottery from the Armenian Cathedral of St. James, Jerusalem. Oxford: 1972. V. 42

CARTARI, VINCENZO

Les Images des Dieux des Anciens, Contenans Les Idoles, Coustumes, Ceremonies & Autres Choses Appartenans a la Religion des Payens . . . Lyon: 1581. V. 38; 40

Imagines Deorum, qui ab Antiquis Colebantur. Lugduni: 1581. V. 37; 39

Le Imagini De gli dei de Gli Antichi. Venetia: 1624. V. 39

Le Imagini de Dei de Gli Antichi. Lyon: 1581. V. 37

Le Imagini de i Dei Degli Antichi. Padua: 1603. V. 37

CARTE, THOMAS 1686-1755

An Account of the Numbers of Men Able to Bear Arms in the Provinces and Towns of France, Taken by the King's Orders in 1743. And also of the King of France's Revenue and Expences in the Years 1741, and 1742. London: 1744. V. 41; 45

Catalogue des Roles Gascons, Normans et Francois Conserves dans les rchives de la Tour de Londres. London: 1743. V. 38; 40

A Full answer to the Letter from a Bystander, &c. Wherein His False Calculations, and Misrepresentation of Facts in the Time of King Charles II are Refuted . . . London: 1742. V. 41; 45

A Full and Clear Vindication to a Letter from a Bystander. London: 1743. V. 41

A General Account of the Necessary Materials for an History of England. London: 1738. V. 42

A General History of England Containing an Account of the First Inhabitants of the Country . . . London: 1747-50-52. V. 39

A General History of England. London: 1747-55. V. 37; 38

The History of James, Duke of Ormonde, from 1610 to 1688, wherein is contained an account of the most remarkable affairs of his time, and particularly of Ireland, under his Government, etc. etc. London: 1736. V. 37; 45

CARTER, A. M.

Texas Laws Relating to the Collection of Debts, Damages &c . . . Forth Worth: 1881. V. 42

CARTER, ANGELA

Heroes and Villains. London: 1969. V. 44

Love. London: 1971. V. 44

Several Perceptions. London: 1968. V. 43; 45

CARTER, CHARLES MORLAND

Shooting in the Early Days from 1863 to 1919. St. Joseph: 1919. V. 40; 43

CARTER, CLARENCE EDWIN 1881-

The Territorial Papers of the United States. Washington: 1934-75. V. 39; 40; 42; 44; 45

CARTER, DENNY

Henry Farney. New York: 1878. V. 42

CARTER, E. S.

The Life and Adventures of E. S. Carter Including a Trip Across the Plains and Mountains in 1852, Indian Wars in the Early Days of Oregon in the Years 1854-5-6 . . . St. Joseph: 1896. V. 41; 42; 45

CARTER, ELIZABETH

Letters from Mrs. Elizabeth Carter to Mrs. Montagu between the years 1755 to 1800, chiefly upon literary and moral subjects. London: 1817. V. 37; 39; 40

Memoirs of the Life . . . London: 1816. V. 38; 46

Poems on Several Occasions. London: 1762. V. 40; 41; 42; 43

Poems on Several Occasions. London: 1766. V. 42; 46

Poems on Several Occasions. Dublin: 1777. V. 43

A Series of Letters Between Mrs. Elizabeth Carter and Miss Catherine Talbot from the Year 1741 to 1770. London: 1808. V. 39

A Series of Letters Between Mrs. Elizabeth Carter and Miss Catherine Talbot, from the Year 1741 to 1770. London: 1809. V. 37; 43; 46

A Series of Letters Between Mrs. Elizabeth Carter and Miss Catherine Talbot from the Year 1741 to 1770. London: 1819. V. 40

CARTER, F.

Gold Like Glass. London: 1932. V. 44; 45

CARTER, FRANCIS

An Account of he Various Systems of Medicine, from the Days of Hippocrates to the Present Time . . . London: 1788. V. 42; 43

CARTER, FREDERICK

D. H. Lawrence and the Body Mystical. London: 1932. V. 43

CARTER, GEORGE

A Narrative of the Loss of the Grosvenor East Indiaman . . . London: 1791. V. 39; 40; 43

CARTER, GEORGE R.

The School Boy's Reverie. London: 1826. V. 40

CARTER, HARRY

The House of Enschede, 1703-1753. Haarlem: 1953. V. 45

CARTER, HENRY J.

Geological Papers on Western India, ... Bombay: 1857. V. 45

CARTER, HENRY ROSE

Yellow Fever, an Epidemiological and Historical Study of Its Place of Origin. Baltimore: 1931. V. 41

CARTER, HOWARD

The Tomb of Tut-Ankh-Amen. London: 1927-33. V. 38; 39

The Tomb of Tut-anhk-Amen, Discovered by the Late Earl of Carnarvon and Howard Carter. London, New York, etc.: 1923-27-33. V. 37

The Tomb of Tut-Ankh-Amen: Discovered by the Late Earl of Carnarvon and Howard Carter. London: 1923. V. 37

CARTER, HOWELL

A Cavalryman's Reminiscences of the Civil War. New Orleans: 1900. V. 43

CARTER, HUNTLY

The New Spirit in Drama and Art. London: 1912. V. 37

The New Spirit in the Russian Theatre 1917-1928. New York: 1929. V. 37

CARTER, J. SMYTH

The Story of Dundas: Being a History of the County of Dundas from 1784 to 1904. Iroquois: 1905. V. 42; 44

CARTER, JAMES EARL

Everything to Gain: Making the Most of the Rest of Your Life. New York: 1987. V. 39; 42; 43; 44; 46

Farewell Address. 1981. V. 42

Keeping Faith. New York: 1982. V. 43

Keeping Fath. Memoirs of a President. Toronto, New York: 1982. V. 39

An Outdoor Journal. New York: 1988. V. 43

An Outdoor Journal - Adventures and Reflections. Tornto: New York: London: 1988. V. 41; 42

CARTER, JIMMY

The Blood of Abraham. V. 39

CARTER, JOHN 1748-1817

The Ancient Architecture of England, in Two Parts. London: 1795/1807. V. 41

The Ancient Architecture of England, Including the Orders During the British, Roman, Saxon and Norman Eras . . . London: 1837. V. 45

The Ancient Architecture of England. London: 1845. V. 45

The Ancient Architecture of England. London: 1887. V. 42

The Ancient Architecture of England, in Two Parts. London: 1806/7. V. 37

CARTER, JOHN 1748-1817 continued

Binding Variants in English Publishing 1820-1900. London: 1932. V. 39; 43; 44

An Enquiry into the Nature of Certain Nineteenth Century Pamphlets. London: 1934. V. 37; 38; 39; 41; 43; 44; 45

An Enquiry into the Nature of Certain Nineteenth Century Pamphlets. London: & New York: 1934. V. 40; 43; 45; 46

An Enquiry into the Nature of Certain Nineteenth Century Pamphlets 1934; the Firm of Ottley, Landond & Co., Footnote to an Enquiry 1948. London: 1934-48. V. 39; 44

An Enquiry into the Nature of Certain 19th Century Pamphlets. (&) The Firm of Charles Ottley, Lndon & Co., Footnote to an Enquirer. London & New York: 1943-48. V. 38

An Enquiry into the Nature of Certain Nineteenth Century Pamphlets. With an Epilogue by John Carter and Graham Pollard. With a Sequel to an Enquiry into the Nature . . . The Forgeries of H. Buxton Forman and T. J. Wise Re-Examined . . . London: 1983. V. 41

New Paths in Book Collecting. London: 1934. V. 40; 42

Printing and the Mind of Man. Lon. V. 45

Printing and the Mind of Man. London: 1963. V. 39; 45

Printing and the Mind of Man. 1967. V. 39

Printing and the Mind of Man. London: 1967. V. 37; 38; 39; 40; 41; 42; 44; 46

Printing and the Mind of Man. London/New York: 1967. V. 45

Printing and the Mind of Man. New York: 1967. V. 38; 39; 40; 46

Printing and the Mind of Man. N.P.: 1967. V. 39

Printing and the Mind of Man. Munich: 1983. V. 38; 39; 40; 41; 42; 43; 44; 45; 46

The Progress of Architecture . . . Taken from Existing Remains in South Wales . . . London: 1830. V. 38; 40; 44

Some Account of the Abbey Church of Bath. London: 1798. V. 38

Some Account of the Abbey Church of St. Alban. London: 1813. V. 38

Specimens of the Ancient Sculpture and Painting Now Remaining in England . . . London: 1887. V. 42; 45

Specimens of the Ancient Scuplture and Painting now remaining in England . . . A New and Improved Edition. London: 1838. V. 37

Victorian Fiction. Cambridge: 1947. V. 43; 46

CARTER, LIONEL

The Masque. London: 1946-49. V. 41

CARTER, MATTHEW

Honor Redivivus or an Analysis of Honor and Armory. London: 1655. V. 42; 45

Honor Redivivus: or, the Analysis of Honor and Armory. London: 1673. V. 39; 43; 44

Aa Most Trve and Exact Relation of that as honourable as Unfortunate Expedition of Kent, Essex and Colchester. London: 1650. V. 38; 39; 40

CARTER, NATHANIEL H.

Reports of the Proceedings and Debates of the Convention of 1821, Assembled for the Purpose of Amending the Constitution of theat State of New York . . . Albany: 1821. V. 41

CARTER, R. R.

Pictures and Engravings at Haughton Hall, Tarporley . . . London: 1904. V. 44

CARTER, RICHARD

A Short Sketch of the Author's Life . . . Versailles: 1825. V. 45

CARTER, ROBERT 1819-1879

A Summer Cruise on the Coast of New England, a Leisure Fishing Cruise on a Thirty-Two Foot Sloop the 'Helen' from Boston to Cape Cod and then to Maine. Boston: 1888. V. 41

CARTER, ROBERT BRUDENELL

On the Pathology and Treatment of Hysteria. London: 1853. V. 37

CARTER, ROBERT G.

Four Brothers in Blue; or, Sunshine and Shadows of the War of the Rebellion. Washington: 1913. V. 38

CARTER, ROBERT GOLDTHWAITE

Massacre of Salt Creek Prairie and the Cow-Boy's Verdict. Washington: 1919. V. 37

The Old Sergeant's Story: Winning the West from the Indians and Bad men in 1870 to 1876. New York: 1926. V. 37

On the Border with MacKenzie, or Winning West Texas from the Comanches. Washington: 1935. V. 39; 46

On the Border with Mackenzie; or, Winning West Texas From the Comanchies. New York: 1961. V. 37; 41; 42

On the Trail of Deserters - a Phenomenal Capture. Washington: 1920. V. 37

CARTER, SAMUEL

Lex Custumaria; or, a Treatise of Copyhold Estates, in Respect of the Lord, Copyholder. (with) Precedents of Conveyances. London: 1701. V. 38

Reports of Sevral (sic) Special Cases Argued and Resolved in the Court of Common Pleas . . . London: 1688. V. 45

CARTER, SUSANNAH

The Frugal Housewife; or, Complete Woman Cook . . . Philadelphia: 1796. V. 39; 40

The Frugal Housewife; or Complete Woman Cook. Philadelphia: 1802. V. 40

CARTER, THOMAS

Historical Record of the Thirteenth, First Somersetshire, or Prince Albert's Regiment of Light Infantry. London: 1867. V. 42

Historical record of the Twenty-Sixth, or Cameronian Regiment. London: 1867. V. 37

Medals of the British Army, and How They Were Won. The Crimean Campaign; Egypt, Peninsula, Waterloo, and South Africa; India, China, etc. London: 1861. V. 37; 42; 43; 44; 45

Memoirs of a Working Man. London: 1845. V. 41

CARTER, THOMAS FORTESCUE

A Narrative of the Boer War: Its Causes and Results. South Africa and London: 1896. V. 41

CARTER, THOMAS FRANCIS

The Invention of Printing in China and Its Spread Westward. New York: 1925. V. 41

The Invention of Printing In China and Its Spread Westward. New York: 1931. V. 38; 41; 44

CARTER, W. A.

McCurtain County and Southeast Oklahoma, History, Biography, Statistics. Idabel: 1923. V. 43

CARTER, WILLIAM

The Disbanded Subaltern. a Poem. London: 1780? V. 40; 41; 42

CARTER, WILLIAM H.

From Yorktown to Santiago with the Sixth U.S. Cavalry . . . Baltimore: 1900. V. 42

Horses, Saddles and Bridles. Leavenworth: 1895. V. 37; 42

Horses Saddles and Bridles. Baltimore: 1906. V. 43

The Life of Lieutenant General Chafee. Chicago: 1917. V. 46

Old Army Sketches. Baltimore: 1906. V. 43

CARTER, WILLIAM RANDOLPH

History of the First Regiment of Tennessee Volunteer Cavlary in the Great War of the Rebellion, with the Armies of the Ohio and Cumberland . . . Knoxville: 1902. V. 45

CARTERET, JOHN DUNLOE

A Fortune Hunter; or, the Old Stone Corral. Cincinnati: 1888. V. 42

CARTHEW, THOMAS

Reports of Cases Adjudged in the Court of King's Bench (1687-1700) from the Third Year of King James the Second to the Twelfth Year of King William the Third . . . London: 1741. V. 38; 40

CARTIER-BRESSON, HENRI

The Decisive Moment. New York & Paris: 1952. V. 37; 41

The Descisive Moment. New York: 1952. V. 37; 38; 39; 41; 44

The Europeans. New York: 1955. V. 37; 41; 42; 45

From One China to the Other. New York: 1956. V. 41

Man and Machine. New York: 1970. V. 39

CARTIER-BRESSON, HENRY

The People of Moscow. New York: 1955. V. 37; 38; 39; 41; 45

CARTIER, JACQUES

Voyages de Decouverte au Canada, Entre les Annees 1534 et 1542, par Jacques Quartier (sic), le Sieur de Roberval, Jean Alphonse de Xanctoigne, &c . . . Quebec: 1843. V. 39

CARTLIDGE, BARBARA

Twentieth-Century Jewlery. New York: 1985. V. 41

CARTMELL, T. K.

Shenandoah Valley Pioneers and Their Descendants: a History of Frederick County, Virginia, from Its Formation in 1738 to 1908. Winchester: 1909. V. 37; 39

CARTOONS From 'Punch.' London: 1906. V. 38

CARTWIRGHT, H., MRS.

The Platonic Marriage. Dublin: 1787. V. 39

CARTWRIGHT, DAVID W.

Natural History of Western Wild Animals and Guide for Hunters, Trappers and Sportsmen . . . also Narratives of Personal Adventure. Toledo: 1875. V. 38; 39; 40; 43; 45

CARTWRIGHT, EDMUND

The Prince of Peace; and Other Poems. London: 1779. V. 39; 40

CARTWRIGHT, FAIRFAX L.

The Mystic Rose from the Garden of the King . . . London: 1898. V. 46

CARTWRIGHT, FREDERICK FOX

The English Pioneeers of Anaesthesia. Bristol: 1952. V. 45

CARTWRIGHT, GEORGE

A Journal of Transations and Events, During A Residence of Nearly Sixteen Years on the Coast of Labrador; containing many interesting Particulars, both of the Country and its Inhabitants, not Hitherto Known. Newark: 1792. V. 37; 38; 39; 43; 44

CARTWRIGHT, JOHN 1740-1824

An Appeal on the Subject of the English Constitution. Boston: 1797. V. 39; 42

England's Aegis: or, the Military Energies of the Empire. London: 1804. V. 46

Give Us Our Rights! London: 1782. V. 38

CARTWRIGHT, JULIA

Jean Francois Millet: His Life and Letters. London: 1896. V. 39

CARTWRIGHT, THOMAS

In Librum Saolominis . . . cum Metaphrasi, Homiliae (etc). London: 1604. V. 44

CARTWRIGHT, VICKERS VINCENT

The Google Book. London: 1931. V. 46

CARTWRIGHT, W. C.

Gustave Bergenroth: a Memorial Sketch. Edinburgh: 1870. V. 39; 42; 43

CARTWRIGHT, WILLIAM

Comedies, Tragi-Comedies . . . London: 1651. V. 45

Rambles and Recollections of a Fly-Fisher. London: 1854. V. 40

The Royall Slave. A Tragi-Comedy, Presented to the King and Queene by the Students of Christ-Church in Oxford, August 30, 1636. Presented since to both their Majesties at Hampton-Court by the Kings Servants. Oxford: 1640. V. 37

The Sledge; or, Love's Convert. London: 1651. V. 42; 43

CARUS, CARL GUSTAV

The King of Saxony's Journey through England and Scotland in the Year 1844. London: 1846. V. 39; 40

CARUTHERS, ABRAHAM

History of a Law Suit, in the Circuit Court of Tennessee. Nashville: 1856. V. 42

CARUTHERS, E. W.

A Sketch of the Life and Character of the Rev. David Caldweil, D.D . . . Greensborough: 1842. V. 45

CARUTHERS, WILLIAM ALEXANDER

The Cavaliers of Virginia, or the Recluse of Jamestown. New York: 1834. V. 43

The Cavaliers of Virginia, or the Recluse of Jamestown. New York: 1834-35. V. 45

The Kentuckian in New-York; or, the Adventures of Three Southerns. New York: 1834. V. 42; 43

CARVALHO DA COSTA, ANTONIO

Compendio Geographico Distribuido em Tres Tratados . . . Lisbon: 1686. V. 45

Corografia Portugueza e Descripcam Topografica do Famoso Reyno de Portugal, com as Noticias das Fundacoes das Cidades, Villas, & Lugares, que Contem . . . Lisbon: 1706-12. V. 38

CARVALHO E SAMPAYO, DIOGO DE

Dissertacao Sobre As Cores Primitivas: Com Hum Breve Tratado Da Composicao Artificial Das Cores. Lisbon: 1788. V. 39

CARVALHO, F. JORGE DE

Relacao Verdadeira Dos Sucessos Do Conde De Castelmelhor, Preso na Cidaded de Cartagena de Indias . . . Lisbon: 1642. V. 40

CARVALLO, S. N.

Incidents of Travel and Adventure in the Far West . . . New York: 1857. V. 37; 39; 40; 41; 42; 45; 46

CARVEL, JOHN L.

The Alloa Glass Work, an Account of Its Development Since 1750. Edinburgh: 1953. V. 40

THE CARVER and Gilder. London: 1870. V. 38

CARVER, ELIZABETH

The Old Woman. London: 1800. V. 39

CARVER, HARTWELL

A Memorial for a Private Charter. Washingtoan: 1849. V. 37

CARVER, JONATHAN 1710-1780

Carver's Travels in Wisconsin. New York: 1838. V. 43; 46

The New Universal Traveller. London: 1779. V. 41

Three Years Travels throughout the Interior Parts of North America, for More than Five Thousand Miles . . . Boston: 1797. V. 37; 39; 41; 42; 45

Three Years Travels through the Interior Parts of North America, for More than Five Thousand Miles . . . Edinburgh: 1798. V. 39

Three Years' Travels thoughout (sic) the Interior Parts of North America, for More than Five Thousand Miles . . . Walpole: 1813. V. 38; 45

Three Years Travels through the Interior Parts of North Ameraica for More than Five Thousand Miles. Philadelphia: 1796. V. 37

Travels through the Interior Parts of North America, in the Years 1766, 1767 and 1768. London: 1778. V. 37; 39; 43; 45

Travels Through the Interior Parts of North America in the Years 1766, 1767, and 1768. Dublin: 1779. V. 41; 42; 43; 45

Travels through the Interior Parts of North America, in the Years 1766, 1767 and 1768. London: 1779. V. 38; 39

Travels in the Interior Parts of North America for More than Five . . . Charlestown: 1802. V. 38

Travels through the Interior Parts of North America, in the Years 1766, 1767 and 1768. London: 1781. V. 37

Voyage Dans les Parties Inerieures de l'Amerique Septentrionale Pendant les Annees 1766, 1767 & 1768. Paris: 1784. V. 38; 43

CARVER, NORMAN F.

Form and Space of Japanese Architecture. Tokyo: 1955. V. 39

CARVER, RAYMOND

At Nignt the Salmon Move. Santa Barbara: 1976. V. 39; 42; 43

Batavia. Burlington: 1986. V. 45

Cathedral. New York: 1983. V. 44; 45; 46

Early for the Dance. Concord: 1986. V. 44

Elephant. Farifax: 1988. V. 41; 42

Elephant and Other Stories. London: 1988. V. 44

Fires: Essays, Poems, Stories. Santa Barbara: 1983. V. 42; 43

Fires. New York: 1984. V. 44

Furious Seasons. Santa Barbara: 1977. V. 42; 45

Glimpses. Northampton: 1985. V. 44; 45

His Bathrobe Pockets Stuffed with Notes. Elmwood: 1988. V. 42; 43

If It Please You. Northridge: 1984. V. 43

In a Marine Light - Selected Poems. London: 1987. V. 45

Music. Concord: 1987. V. 42; 44

My Crow. Concord: 1984. V. 45

My Father's Life. Derry: 1986. V. 44

Near Klamath. Sacramento: 1968. V. 43

A New Path to the Waterfall. London: 1989. V. 44

A New Path to the Waterfall. New York: 1989. V. 41; 42; 43; 45; 46

The Painter and the Fish. Concord: 1988. V. 42; 43; 44; 46

The Pheasant. Worcester, Mass.: 1982. V. 37; 42; 43; 44

Put Yourself in My Shoes. Santa Barbara: 1974. V. 43; 44; 45

Put Yourself in My Shoes. Santa Barbara: 1976. V. 42

The River. Concord: 1986. V. 42; 45; 46

Those Days. Elmwood: 1987. V. 39; 43

The Toes. Concord: 1988. V. 45

Two Poems. Salisbury: 1982. V. 45

Two Poems. Scarab: 1982. V. 39

Two Poems. Concord: 1986. V. 42

Ultramarine. New York: 1986. V. 39; 43

Vitamins. N.P.. V. 42

What We Talk About When We Talk About Love. New York: 1981. V. 42; 46

What Will We Talk About When We Talk About Love. New York: 1982. V. 44

Where I'm Calling From. Boston: 1988. V. 44

Where I'm Calling From. Boston: 1988. V. 46

Where I'm Calling From. Franklin Center: 1988. V. 44

Where I'm Calling From. Franklin Library,: 1988. V. 43

Where I'm Calling From: New and Selected Stories. New York: 1988. V. 39; 40; 42; 45; 46

Will You Please be Quiet, Please? New York: 1976. V. 42; 43; 44; 45

Winter Insomnia. 1970. V. 44

Winter Insomnia. Santa Cruz: 1970. V. 37; 41; 42; 43; 44

CARVER, WILLIAM

Practical Horse Farrier. Philadelphia: 1820. V. 37

CARY, ALICE

The Josephine Gallery. New York: 1859. V. 46

CARY, ELIZABETH LUTHER

The Novels of Henry James, A Study. New York: 1905. V. 43; 46

CARY, H. F.

The Poetical Works of John Milton, James Thomson and Eward Young. London: 1841. V. 46

CARY, JOHN

An Account of the Proceedings of the Coporation of Bristol, in Execution of the Act of Parliment for the Better Employing and Manufacturing the Poor of that City. London: 1700. V. 38

Cary's Actual Survey of The Country Fifteen Miles Round London . . . London: 1786. V. 40

Cary's Traveller's Companion, or, a Delineation of the Turnpike Roads of England and Wales . . . London: 1791. V. 43

Cary's New and Correct English Atlas. London: 1793. V. 40

Cary's New Map of England and Wales, with Part of Scotland. London: 1794. V. 39; 40

Cary's New Itinerary . . . London: 1798. V. 45

Cary's Traveller's Companion, or, a Delineation of the Turnpike Roads of England and Wales. London: 1806. V. 42

Cary's New English Atlas. London: 1809. V. 39

An Essay on the State of England, In Relation to Its Trade, Its Poor, and Its Taxes, For Carrying on the Present War Against France . . . Bristol: 1695. V. 39

New and Correct English Atlas . . . London: 1787. V. 42

New English Atlas; Being a Complete Set of County Maps, from Actual Surveys Corresponding in Size with His General Atlas . . . London: 1801. V. 41

New Itinerary; or, an Accurate Delineation of the Great Roads, Both Direct and Cross . . . London: 1806. V. 40; 42

Carey's Survey of the High Roads from London to Hampton Court Bagshot . . . Guildford, Richmond . . . London: 1790. V. 41

A Survey of the High Roads from London. London: 1799. V. 42

CARY, JOYCE 1888-1957

The African Witch. 1936. V. 43

The African Witch. London: 1936. V. 37; 42; 46

The African Witch. New York: 1936. V. 40; 41; 42; 43; 44; 45

The Case for African Freedom. London: 1941. V. 41

The Drunken Sailor - a Ballad Epic. London: 1947. V. 43

The Horse's Mouth. London: 1944. V. 40; 42; 43

The Horse's Mouth. London: 1957. V. 45

Illustrations by Joyce Cary for the Old Strife at Plant's. Oxford: 1956. V. 40

The Old Strife at Plant's . . . (with) Illustrations by Joyce Cary for the Old Strife at Plant's. Oxford: 1956. V. 38

CARY, LUCIUS

His Discourse of Infallibility, with an Answer to It . . . London: 1651. V. 38

CARY, MARY

The Daughter of the Stars. London: 1939. V. 46

CARY, THOMAS G.

Memoir of Thomas Handasyo Perkins . . . . Boston: 1856. V. 43

CARY, THOMAS GREAVES

Letter to a Lady in France on the Supposed Failure of a National Bank, the Supposed Delinquency of the National Government, the Debits of the Several States and Repudiation; with Answers to Enquiries Concerning the Books of Capt. Marryat & Mr. Dickens. Boston: 1844. V. 38

CARY, WILLIAM S.

Wrecked on the Feejees: Experiences of a Nantucket Man a Century Ago. Nantucket: 1922. V. 44

CARYL, CHARLES W.

New Era. Presenting the Plans for the New Era Union to Help Develop and Utilize the Best Resources of this Country. Denver: 1897. V. 38; 39

CARYL, JOSEPH

An Exposition with Practical Observations Continued Upon The Thirty Second, the Thirty Third and the Thirty Fourth Chapters of the Book of Job . . . London: 1661. V. 44

CARYLL, JOHN 1625-1711

Naboth's Vineyard; or, The Innocent Traytor. London: 1679. V. 40; 41; 43

Sir Salomon; or, the Cautious Coxcomb. London: 1671. V. 40

CARY'S Survey of the High Roads from London, to Hampton Court, Bagshot, Oakingham, Binfield, Windsor, Maidenhead, High Wycombe, Amersham . . . London: 1790. V. 44

CARY'S Traveller's Companion, or A Delineation of the Turnpike Roads of England and Wales . . . London: 1822. V. 40

CASA, GIOVANNI DELLA

La Galatee, Premierement Compose en Italien . . . & Depuis mis en Francois, Latin, Allemand & Espagnol. Geneva: 1609. V. 37

Il Galateo, o Vero Tratatto de' Costumi, e Modi che si Debbono Tenere, o Schifare Nella Commune Conuersatione . . . Florence: 1572. V. 45

Galateo of Manners and Behaviours, a Renaiisance Courtesy Book. London: 1914. V. 42

Prose et Rime . . . Paris: 1727. V. 40

Rime et Prose. Venice: 1558. V. 44

CASA, GIOVANNI J.

Casa His Galateus, or a Treatise of Manners. London: 1701. V. 39

CASA YRUJO, CARLOS MARTINEZ DE YRUJO Y TACON, MARQUES DE

Letters of Verus, addressed to the Native American. Philadelphia: 1797. V. 37

THE CASALE Pilgrim. London: 1929. V. 45

CASALIO, GIOVANNI BAPTISTA

De Veteribus Aegyptiorum Ritibus. Rome: 1644. V. 45

CASALIUS, JOHN BAPTIST

De Profanis et Sacris Veteribus Ritibus. Frankfurt & Hanover: 1861. V. 41

CASANOVA DE SEINGALT, GIACOMO GIROLAMO

The Memoirs of Giacomo Casanova di Seingalt. London: 1922. V. 38

CASANOVA DE SEINGALT, GIROLAMO 1725-1798

Memoires. Paris: 1922-25. V. 39; 42

Memoirs . . . N.P.: 1925. V. 42

The Memoirs of . . . London: New York: 1928. V. 44

The Memoirs of Jacques Casanova, an Autobiography. London: 1929. V. 43; 45; 46

The Memoirs of Jacques Casanova de Seingalt. Edinburgh: 1940. V. 42; 45

The Memoirs. New York: 1940's. V. 40

CASAS, BARTOLOME DE LAS

Conquista dell'Indie Occidentali. Venice: 1645. V. 39

Entre Lo Remedios Que do Fray Bartolome de Las Casas. Seville: 1552. V. 37

Il Supplice Schiavo Indiano. Venice: 1657. V. 39

Il Supplice Schiavo Indiano . . . Venice: 1636. V. 37; 38

Istoria o Brevissima Relatione Della Distruttione dell' Indie Occidentali . . . Venice: 1626. V. 39

Istoria, o Brevissima Relatione dell Distruttione dell'Indie Occidentali. Venice: 1643. V. 39

La Liberta Pretesa Sal Supplice Schiavo Indiano . . . Venice: 1640. V. 37

CASAS, CHRISTOVAL DE LAS d. 1576

Vocabulario de las dos Lenguas Toscana y Castellana . . . Venice: 1587. V. 37; 38

CASATI, MAJOR GAETANO

Ten Years in Equatoria and the Return with Emin Pasha. London: 1891. V. 39; 41

CASATI, PAOLO

Fabrica et Uso del Compasso di Proportione, dove Insegna a gli Artefici il Modo di Fare in Esso le Necessarie Divisioni, e con Varii Problemi Usuali Mostra l'Utilita di Questo Stromento . . . Bologna: 1664. V. 38

CASAUBON, MERIC

Of Credulity and Incredulity; In things Divine & Spiritual: Wherein, among other things, A true and faithful account is given of the Platonick Philosophy, As it hath reference to Christianity: As also the business of Witches and . . . London: 1670. V. 37; 40

Of Credulity and Incredulity, in Things Natural, Civil, and Divine . . . Among Other Things, the Sadducism of these times, in denying Spirits, Witches and Supernatural Operations . . . is fully confuted. London: 1668. V. 37; 38

CASCIATO, MARISTELLA

Il Problema Sociale Costruttivo ed Economico dell'Abitazione. Rome: 1984. V. 46

CASDORPH, PAUL

A History of the Republican Party in Texas, 1865-1965. Austin: 1965. V. 42

THE CASE and Claim of the American Loyalists Impartially Stated and Considered. London: 1783. V. 42

CASE, ARTHUR E.

A Bibliography of English Poetical Miscellanies 1521-1750. 1935. V. 39

A Bibliography of English Poetical Miscellanies 1521-1750. London: 1935. V. 40; 42

CASE, ARTHUR E. continued

A Bibliography of English Poetical Miscellanies: 1521-1750. Oxford: 1935. V. 42

A Bibliography of English Poetical Miscellanies 1521-1750. Oxford: 1935 for 1929. V. 44

CASE, BENJAMIN

History of Old Chester from 1719 to 1869. Auburn: 1869. V. 42

CASE, ECKSTEIN

Notes on the Origin and History of the 'Ark'. Cleveland: 1902. V. 41

CASE, JOHN d. 1600

Sphaera Civitatis; Hoc est; Reipublicae Recte ac Pie Secundum Leges Administrandae Ratio. Frankfurt am Main: 1593. V. 41

CASE, NELSON

History of Labette County, Kansas. Topeka: 1893. V. 43

THE CASE of Dominick Donnelly, Gentleman, Humbly Offer'd to the Consideration of the Honourable House of Commons. N.P.: 1716. V. 41

THE CASE of Elizabeth Canning Fairly Stated. London: 1753. V. 46

THE CASE of George Earl of Cromartie. London: 1746. V. 39

THE CASE of Hanover Forces in the Pay of Great-Britain, Impartially and Freely Examined. London: 1743. V. 38

THE CASE of James Butler, Esq. Late an Officer in His Majesty's Navy, Respecting His Connexions with the House of Ormond. London: 1780. V. 39

THE CASE of Messieurs Penn, and the People of Pensylvania, and the Three Lower Counties of Newcastle, Kent and Sussex, on Delaware, in Relation to a Series of Injuries and Hostilities Made Upon Them, for Several Years Past . . . London: 1737. V. 44

THE CASE of Miss Blandy Considered as a Daughter, as a Gentlewoman, and as a Christian with a Particular Refernece to Her Own Narrative. Oxford: 1752. V. 45

THE CASE of Richard Toler, Esq.; Late Surveyor, of the Cove of Cork, in Ireland. London: 1757. V. 41

THE CASE of Six Mutineers, Whose Conviction and Sentence Were Approved of by General Jackson, Fairly Stated: with a Refutation of Some of the Falsehoods Circulated on This Subject. Albany: 1828. V. 44

THE CASE of the Bankers in the Court of the Exchequer, and Afterwards in the Court of Exchequer-Chamber and Parliament: With the Arguments of Lord Chief Justice Treby, Lord Chief Justice Holt, and of the Lord Keeper Somers, June 23rd 1696. Dublin: 1791. V. 38

THE CASE of the Charter of London Stated. Shewing, I. What a Corporation is. II. Whether a Corporation may be forefeited. III. Whether the Mayor, Commonalty, and Citizens have done any Act in Their Common Council, Whereby to Forfeit Their Corporation . . . London: 1683. V. 38

THE CASE of the Hertfordshire Witchcraft Consider'd Being an Examination of a Book, Entitul'd a Full and Impartial Account of the Discovery of Sorcery and Witchcraft, Practis'd by Jane Wenham of Walkern, Upon the Bodies of Anne Thorne, Anne St., etc. London: 1712. V. 42; 45; 46

THE CASE of the Officers and Soldiers of the Late Garisons of London-Derry and Enniskilling in Ireland, Their Relicts and Representatives. London? Dublin?: 1712. V. 41

THE CASE of the People of Western Australia . . . The Secession Referendum Act, 1932, and The Secession Act, 1934. In the matter of the desire of the People of Western Australia to withdraw from the Commonwealth of Australia . . . Perth, Western Australia: 1934. V. 37

THE CASE of the Planters of Tobacco in Virginia, as Represented by Themselves, to which is added a vindication of the said representation. London: 1733. V. 37; 42; 46

CASE of the Rev. Thomas Jephson. N.P.: 1823. V. 39

CASE, ROBERT HOPE

A Theory of the Universe. New York: 1868. V. 38

CASE, THEODORE S.

History of Kansas City Missouri with Illustrations and Biographical Sketches of Some Prominent Men and Pioneers. Syracuse: 1888. V. 39

CASE, WALTER H.

History of Long Beach and Vicinity. Chicago: 1927. V. 40

History of Long Beach. Long Beach: 1935. V. 40

CASELIUS, JOHANNES 1533-1613

Memoriae V. Cl. D. Ioannis Placotomi Medici Illvstris. Carmina Amicorvm. Rostock: 1578. V. 39

CASELLA, LOUIS

An Illustrated Catalogue of Surveying, Philosophical, Mathematical, Optical, Photographic and Standard Meteorological Instruments. London: 1870. V. 40

An Illustrated and Descriptive Catalogue of Surveying, Philosophical, Mathematical, Optical, Photographic and Standard Meteorological Instruments. London: 1871. V. 42

CASH, J.

British Freshwater Rhizopod and Heliozoa. London: 1905-21. V. 38

CASH, W. J.

The Mind of the South. New York: 1941. V. 37; 39; 45

CASHEL, FRANCES SARAH HOEY

Falsely True. London: 1890. V. 41

CASHIN, HERSCHEL V.

Under Fire with the Tenth U.S. Cavalry . . . a PUrely Military History of the Negro . . . Chicago: 1902. V. 46

CASKEY, L. D.

Attic Vase Paintings in the Museum of Fine Arts, Boston. Boston: 1931. V. 44

Attic Vase Paintings in the Museum of Fine Arts, Boston. Boston: 1954. V. 42

Attic Vase Paintings in the Museum of Fine Arts, Boston. Boston: 1963. V. 42; 44

Catalogue of Greek and Roman Sculpture. Boston: 1925. V. 37; 40

CASLER, JOHN O.

Four Years in the Stonewall Brigade. Girard: 1906. V. 43

CASLEY, DAVID

A Catalogue of the Manuscripts of the King's Library, an Appendix to the Catalogue of the Cottonian Library . . . London: 1734. V. 38; 40; 43

CASLON & SONS

Caslon & Son's Specimen of Printing Types. London: 1848. V. 38

CASLON, H. W., & CO.

Specimens of Printing Types of the Caslon Letter Foundry. London: 1868. V. 41

Specimens of Types & Borders and Illustrated Catalogue of Printers' Joinery and Materials. London: 1919. V. 44

CASLON, WILLIAM

A Specimen of Printing Types, By William Caslon, Letter-Founder to His Majesty. N.P.: 1785. V. 41

A Specimen of Printing Types. N.P.: 1785. V. 41

CASONI, GIOVANNI AGOSTINO

Manuale Choricanum ab Utriusque Sexus Choricistis Concupitum, Clericis Omnibus Necessarium & Maxime Iuvenibus. Genoa: 1649. V. 38

CASONI, GUIDO

Della Magi d'Amore . . . Nella Quale si Dimostra Come Amore sia Metafisico, Fisico, strologo, Musico, Geometr, Aritmetico, Grammatico, Dialetico . . . Venetia: 1591. V. 38

CASOS Notables, Sucedidos en Las Costas de la Ciudad de Lima, en Las Indias, Y Como el Armada Olandesa Procuraua Coger el Armadilla Nuestra . . . Madrid: 1625. V. 40; 43

CASPAR, C. N.

Directory of the Antiquarian Booksellers and Dealers in Second-Hand Books of the United States . . . Milwaukee: 1885. V. 39

CASPER, JOHANN

A Handbook of the Practice of Forensic Medicine, Based Upon Personal Experience. London: 1861-65. V. 37; 41; 42; 45

CASS, LEWIS

France, Its King, Court and Government. New York: 1840. V. 46

Letter from the Secretary of War, Transmitting Documents in Relation to Hostilities of Creek Indians. Washington: 1836. V. 43; 44; 46

Substance of a Speech Delivered by Hon. Lewis Cass, of Michigan, in a Secret Session of the Senate . . . On the Ratification of the Oregon Treaty . . . Detroit: 1846. V. 42

Trade and Intercourse with the Indian Tribes. Washington: 1832. V. 38

CASSADORUS, GUILELMUS

Decisiones seu Conclusiones Aureae. Venice: 1590. V. 38

CASSADY, NEAL

The First Third. San Francisco: 1971/1981. V. 43

CASSAN, STEPHEN HYDE

The Lives of the Bishops of Winchester, from Birinus, First Bishop of the West Saxons to the Present Time. London: 1827. V. 39

CASSAS, L. F.

Travels in Istria and Dalmatia, Drawn Up from the Itinerary of L. F. Cassas . . . London: 1805. V. 40

CASSEBOHM, JOHANN FRIEDRICH

Tractatus Quatuor Anatomici de Aura Humana. Cui Accedit Tractatus Sextus Anatomicus de Aure Monstri Humana. Halae Magdeburgicae: 1734-35. V. 38

CASSEDAY, BEN

The History of Louisville, From Its Earliest Settlement Till the Year 1852. Louisville: 1852. V. 43

CASSEL, GUSTAV 1866-1944

The Nature and Necessity of Interest. London: 1903. V. 43

CASSELL, JOHN

John Cassell's Illustrated History of England. London: 1865-75. V. 38

CASSELLA, LEOPOLD & CO.

The Dyeing of Cotton and Other Vegetable Fibres with Dyestuffs of Leopold Cassell & Co. London: 1902. V. 38

CASSELL'S Book of Birds. London: 1869-73. V. 37; 38

CASSELL'S Cyclopaedia of Mechanics. London. V. 46

CASSELL'S Dictionary of Cookery, with Numerous Engravings and Full Page Colored Plates. Containing about Nine Thousand Recipes. London: (c. 1880). V. 37

CASSELL'S Gazetteer of Great Britain and Ireland, Being a Complete Topographical Dictionary of the United Kingdom. London: 1893. V. 39; 44

CASSELL'S Popular Natural History. London. V. 40

CASSELMAN, ALEXANDER CLARK

Richardson's War of 1812. Toronto: 1902. V. 42; 44

CASSERIO, GIULIO

De Vocis Auditusq Organis Historia Anatomica. Ferrara: 1600-01. V. 37

CASSERIO, GUILIO

De Vocis Auditusque Organis Historia Anatomica Singulari Fide Methodo ac Industria Concinnata Tractatibus Duobus Explicata ac Variis Iconibus . . . colophon: 1600-01. V. 46

CASSERUIS

Tabulae Anatomicae De Formato Foetu Tabulae. N.P.. V. 38

CASSIANUS, JOANNES

Opus Ioannis Eremitae; qui et Cassianus Dicitur. De Institutis Cenobiorum Origine, Causis et Remediis Vitiorum, Collationibusque Patrum. Bologna,: 1521. V. 37; 38

CASSIDY, PATRICK SARSFIELD

The Borrowed Bride. New York: 1892. V. 43

CASSIN, JOHN

Illustrations of the Birds of California, Texas, Oregon, British and Russian America. Philadelphia: 1856. V. 39; 46

Illustrations of the Birds of California, Texas, Oregon, British and Russian America. Philadelphia: 1862. V. 42; 45

Illustrations of the Birds of California, Texas, Oregon, British and Russian America. Philadelphia: 1865. V. 39; 45

Illustrations of the Birds of California, Texas, Oregon, British and Russian America. Austin: 1991. V. 45

CASSINI, GIAN DOMENICO

La Meridiana del Tempio di S. Petronio Tirata, e Preparata per le Osservazioni Astromomiche l'anno 1655. Rivista, e Restaurata l'anno 1695. Bologna: 1695. V. 37

CASSINI, GIOVANNI MARIA

Pitture Antiche Ritrovate nello Scavo Aperto di Ordine di Nostre Signore Pio Sesto . . . Rome: 1783. V. 44

CASSINI, JACQUES

Elements d'Astronomie. (with) Tables Astronomiques du Soleil, de la Lune, des Planetes, des Etoiles Fixes, et des Satellites de Jupiter et de Saturne . . . Paris: 1740. V. 38; 41

De la Grandeur et de la Figure de la Terre. Paris: 1720. V. 38

CASSINI, JEAN DOMINIQUE DE, COMTE

Voyage Fait par Ordre du Roi en 1768, Pour Eprouver les Montres Marines Inventees par M. le Roy . . . avec le Memoire sur la Meilleure Maniere de Mesurer le tems en Mer. Paris: 1770. V. 42

CASSINO, SAMUEL

The Naturalist's Directory 1884. Boston: 1884. V. 45

CASSIODORUS, FLAVIUS MAGNUS AURELIUS

Ecclesiastica et Tripartita Historia. Strassburg: 1500? V. 45

Expositio Psalterium. Basel: 1491. V. 38

Historia Tripertita de Regiminee Ecclesie Primitive. Lyon: 1534. V. 37

Opera Omnia Quae Exstant. Geneva: 1609. V. 38

Opera Omnia Quae Extant. Geneva: 1650. V. 41

Psalterii Davidici Expositio. Paris: 1519. V. 42

CASSIRER

An Essay on Man. 1944. V. 44

CASSIRER, ERNST

Language and Myth. New York: 1946. V. 46

CASSON, HUGH

Diary. London: 1981. V. 43

CASSOU, JEAN

Fernand Leger: Drawings and Gouaches. Greenwich: 1973. V. 39

CASTAGNO, GIO. PAOLO

Reggimento Contra Peste di Gio. Paolo Castagno, per Conservare i Sani, & Curare gli Infermi, Col Modo di Usare il Composito . . . Ferrara: 1572. V. 42

CASTAI, GAETANO

Ten Years in Equatoria and the Return with Emin Pasha. London: 1891. V. 38

CASTAING, JOHN

An Interest-Book at 4, 5, 6, 7, 8, per C. from 10001. to 11. for 1 Day to 92 Days, and for 3, 6, 9, 12 Months. London: 1724. V. 39; 40; 41

CASTANEDA, CARLOS

The Teachings of Don Juan. Berkeley: 1968. V. 43

The Teachings of Don Juan: a Yaqui Way of Knowledge. Berkeley/Los Angeles: 1968. V. 39

CASTANEDA, CARLOS EDUARDO 1896-1958

The Mexican Side of the Texas Revolution, 1836. Dallas: 1928. V. 37; 42; 44

Our Catholic Heritage in Texas 1519-1936. Austin: 1936. V. 42

Our Catholic Heritage in Texas, 1519-1936. New York: 1976. V. 38; 40

Our Catholic Heritage in Texas, 1519-1936. Austin: 1936-1950. V. 37

A Report on the Spanish Archives in San Antonio, Texas. San Antonio: 1937. V. 38; 42

CASTANEDA, PEDRO DE ca.1515-ca.1554

The Coronado Expedition. Washington: 1896. V. 39

THe Journey of Francisco Vazquez de Coronado, 1540-1542, as told by Castaneda, Coronado, and Others. San Francisco: 1933. V. 37; 38; 40

CASTANENDA, PEDRO ca.1515-ca.1554

Relation du Voyage de Cibola, Enterpris en 1540. Paris: 1838. V. 39

CASTANIS, CHRISTOPHER P.

The Greek Exile, or a Narrative of the Captivity and Escape of . . . Philadelphia: 1851. V. 45

CASTELDEN, GEORGE

Woburn Park; a Fragment, in Rural Rhyme. London: 1840. V. 37

CASTELFRANCO, GIORGIO

Donatello. New York: 1965. V. 41; 42; 43

CASTELL, EDMUND

Lexicon Heptaglotton. London: 1669. V. 45

CASTELL, ROBERT

The Villas of the Ancients Illustrated . . . London: 1728. V. 37; 45

CASTELLAMONTE, AMEDEO DI

Venaria Reale. Palazzo di Piacere, e di Caccia, Ideato dall' Altezza Reale di Carlo Emmanuel II. Turin: 1674. V. 37; 40

CASTELLAN, ANTOINE L.

Turkey. Being a Description of the Manners, Customs, Dresses and Other Peculiarities Characteristic of the Inhabitants of the Turkish Empire. Philadelhia: 1829. V. 40; 43

CASTELLANUS, PETRUS

Kreophagia (Greek) Sive de Esu Carnium. Antwerp: 1626. V. 37; 38

CASTELLENSIS, HADRIANUS, CARDINAL

De Vera Philosophia Libri IIII. ex Quattuor Ecclesiae Doctoribus Consipti, Varia Eruditione & Multa Pietate Referti, Suae Integritati, Qua Fieri Potuit Solertia, Nunc Primu Restituti. Coloniae: 1540. V. 46

CASTELLESI, ADRIANO

De Sermone Latino, et Modis Latine Loquendi. Rome: 1515. V. 40

CASTELLI, BARTOLOMMEO

Lexicon Medicum Graeco-Latinum ex Hippocrate, et Galeno Desumptum. Rotterdam: 1644. V. 41

Lexicon Medicum, Primum a Bartholomaeo Castello Messanensi Inchoatum . . . Norimbergae: 1688. V. 45; 46

CASTELLI, BENEDETTO

Della Misura dell'Acque Correnti. Rome: 1639. V. 38

Delle Misure dell'acque Correnti; Demostrazioni Geometriche Della Misura Dell-acque Correnti. Rome: 1628. V. 37; 42

CASTELLI, ONOFRIO

Distributione Universale dell'Archettura de Fiumi & Delle Altre Acque. Milan: 1631. V. 40; 44

CASTELLI, PIETRO

Exactissima Descriptio Quarundum Plantarum, Quae Continentur Rome in Horto Farnesiano: Tobia Aldino Cesenate . . . Rome: 1625. V. 37

CASTELLO, ALBERTO DA

Liber Sacerdotalis Nuperrime ex Libris Sancte Romane Ecclesie. Venice: 1537. V. 43

Rosario Della Gloriosa Virginia Maria. Venice: 1561. V. 38

CASTELLUM Huttonicum. Some Aacount of Sheriff-Hutton Castle, with Brief Notices of the Church of St. Helen, the Ancient Forest of Galtres, the Poet Gower of Stitenham. York: 1824. V. 45

CASTELNAU, MICHEL DE, SIEUR DE LA MAUVISSIERE 1520-1592

Memoirs of the Reigns of Francis II and Charles IX of France. London: 1724. V. 39; 45

CASTENEDA, PEDRO DE

The Journey of Francisco Vazquez de Coronado, 1540-1542. San Francisco: 1933. V. 42

CASTERA, J. 1749-1838

The Life of Catherine II. Empress of Russia. London: 1799. V. 38

CASTERA, JEAN HENRI

History of Catherine II, Empress of Russia. London: 1800. V. 45

CASTIGLIONE, BALDASSARE 1478-1529

Baltasaris Castilionis Comitis de Curiali Sive Aulico Libri Quatour . . . Londini: 1593. V. 46

The Book of the Courtier. New York: 1901. V. 38; 43

Il Cortegiano. Venice: 1544. V. 38

Il Cortegiano . . . Venice: 1574. V. 40

Il Cortegiano, or The Courtier . . . London: 1727. V. 40; 44; 45

The Courtier. London: 1724. V. 41

The Courtyer of . . . Mile End: 1900. V. 39

The Courtyer of Count Baldassar Castilio, Divided Into Foure Bookes. London: 1900. V. 37; 40; 41; 42; 43; 46

Il Libro del Cortegiano. Venice: 1528. V. 39

Il Libro Del Cortegiano del Conte Baldesar Castiglione, Novamente Revisto. Venice: 1538. V. 38

CASTIGLIONE, BALDESSARE 1478-1529

Il Cortegiano Del Conte Baldessar Castiglione . . . Lyon: 1562. V. 39

Libri IV De Curiali sive Aulico ex Italico Sermone in Latinum Conversi. Cambridge: 1713. V. 39

CASTIGLIONE, GIOVANNI ONORATO

Prospectvs, Pharmacevtici. Mediolani: 1698. V. 39

CASTIGLIONI, ARTURO

A History of Medicine. New York: 1941. V. 37; 38; 42; 45; 46

CASTILLEJO, CRISTOBAL DE

Dialogo Entre la Verdad y la Lisonja. Alcala: 1614. V. 38

CASTILLO DE VILLASANTE, DIEGO DEL

Tractatus de Duello. Turin: 1525. V. 43

CASTILLO SOLORZANO, ALONSO DEL

The Spanish Pole-Cat, or the Adventures of Seniora Rufina; in Four Books. London: 1717. V. 45

CASTLE, EGERTON

English Book-Plates. London: 1894. V. 44

CASTLE, HENRY ANSON

Minnesota, Its Story and Biography. Chicago & New York: 1915. V. 38; 46

THE CASTLE Howell School Record, Comprising a List of Pupils from the Beginning . . . Lancaster: 1888. V. 46

CASTLE, T. A., MRS.

A Warning to Colored Girls Against Vice. Bryan: 1900. V. 39

CASTLE, THOMAS

An Introduction to Medical Botany. London: 1829. V. 38; 42

A Manual of Surgery, Founded Upon the Principles and Practice Lately Taught by Sir Astley Cooper . . . Boston: 1839. V. 44

CASTLEDEN, GEORGE

Woburn Park; a Fragment in Rural Rhyme. London: 1840. V. 40

CASTLEHAVEN, EARL OF

Memoirs, of His Review of the Late Wars of Ireland. Waterford: 1753. V. 46

CASTLEHAVEN, JAMES TOUCHET, 3RD EARL OF 1617?-1684

Review, or His Memoirs of . . . the Irish Wars. Dublin: 1815. V. 40

CASTLEMAN, JOHN BRECKINRIDGE

Active Service. Louisville: 1917. V. 43

CASTLERAGH, VISCOUNT

A Journey to Damascus through Egypt, Nubia, Arabia Petraea, Palestine and Syria. London: 1847. V. 46

CASTRO ALVES, ANTONIO DE

Espumas Fluctuantes. Poesias. Bahia: 1870. V. 38

CASTRO, BERNARDO JOSE D'ABRANTES

Carta Do Conselheiro Abrantes a Sir William A'Court Sobre a Regencia de Portugal, e a Authoridade do Senhor Dom Pedro IV. 1827. V. 40

CASTRO, D. JOAO DE

Charts of the Rutters of India of Dom Joao de Castro. Lisbon: 1988. V. 46

CASTRO, JOAO DE

Discurso da Vida do Sempre bem Vindo, et Apparecido Rey Dom Sebastiam Nosso Senhor o Encuberto Desdo (sic) seu Nacimento tee (sic) o Presente . . . Paris: 1602. V. 41

CASTRO SARMENTO, JACOB DE

Materia Medica Physico-Historico-Mechanica, Reyno Mineral. London: 1735. V. 38

CASWALL, EDWARD

Sketches of Young Couples, Young Ladies, Young Gentlemen. London: 1869. V. 43

CASWALL, HENRY

The City of the Mormons; or, Three Days at Nauvoo in 1842. London: 1842. V. 38

CASWELL, HARRIET S.

Our Life Among the Iroquois Indians. Boston: 1892. V. 46

THE CAT and the Monkey. London: 1840. V. 44

CATALOGUE OF a Genuine and Extensive Collection of English Portraits, Consisting of the Royal Families, Peers, Gentry, Clergy, Lawyers, Military..Phenomena, Convicts, Monsters, &c from Egbert the Great to the Present Time . . . 1800. V. 39

A CATALOGUE Of a . . . Highly Valuable Collection of Pictures, Being the Greater Part of the Well-Known Collection of the Novellara, a Ducal Villa in the Neighbourhood of Modena, and Purchased from the French . . . London: 1804. V. 38; 40

CATALOGUE of Alpine and Herbaceous Plants 1926. Stevenage: 1926. V. 38

A CATALOGUE of an Extensive and Extraordinary Assemblage of the Productions of the Aldine Press, from Its First Establishment at Venice in 1494, Together with Lyonese and Venetian Counterfeits, the Giunta and Other Works, Illustrative of the Series. London: 1880. V. 39

A CATALOGUE of Birds, Insects, Etc. Now Exhibiting at Spring Gardens . . . 1765. London: 1765. V. 39

A CATALOGUE of Books, in the Various Branches of Literature, Which Lately Formed the Library of a Distinguished Collector, and were sold by Auction by Mr. Jeffery of Pall Mall, with Their Prices and Purchaser's Names. London: 1811. V. 46

A CATALOGUE of Books . . . to Begin Selling by Auction at Bate-Hall, on (blank), also Complete Sets of Letters for Marking Linen, Silk, Books &c. Macclesfield: 1780. V. 39

A CATALOGUE Of Drugs, Chymical and Galenical Medicines, Prepared and sold by (blank) Chymist and Druggist. London: 1796. V. 46

A CATALOGUE of Drugs, Chymical and Galenical Medicines Prepared and sold by (blank) Chymist U Druggist. London: 1799. V. 46

CATALOGUE of Five Hundred Celebrated Authors of Great Britain, Now Living . . . London: 1788. V. 42; 44; 46

A CATALOGUE of Modern Books in Divinity, History, Law, Philosophy, Mathematicks, Poetry, &c. London: 1722. V. 45; 46

CATALOGUE of Rare Florida Flowers and Fruits from Jessamine Gardens. 1892. V. 45

CATALOGUE of Short Horned Durham Cattle Devonshire Cattle, New Leicester or Bakewell Sheep and Horse. To be Sold at Greenbush, Opposite Albany, on Thursday, October 29, 1829, at Public Auction. Albany: 1829. V. 45

CATALOGUE of Some Five Hundred Examples of the Prining of Edwin and Robert Grabhorn, 1917-1960. San Francisco: 1961. V. 39

CATALOGUE Of Some five Hundred Examples of the Printing of Edwin and Robert Grabhorn, 1917-1960. 1961. V. 45

CATALOGUE of the Asiatic Library of Dr. G. E. Morrison. Tokyo: 1924. V. 44

CATALOGUE of the Collection of Indian Arms and Objects of Art Presented by the Princes and Nobles of India to H.R.H. the Prince of Wales, on Occasion of His Vivist to Indian in 1875-1876. Now in the Indian Room at Marlborough House. London: 1898. V. 41

CATALOGUE of the Special Loan Exhibition of Enamels on Metal Held at the South Kensington Museum in 1874. London: 1875. V. 37

CATALOGUE OF Typefounders' Specimens, Books Printed in Founts of Historical Importance, Works on Typefounding, Printing and Bibliography. London: 1928. V. 37

CATALOGUE with Purchasers' Name and Prices Realised of the Scarce and Curious Collection of Books, Silver Plates, Prints, Pictures, Wood Blocks, Copper Plates and Bewick Relics, etc., sold by Auction at Newcastle Upon Tyne . . . London: 1884. V. 40

CATALONIA, a Poem; with Notes Illustrative of the Present State of Affairs in the Peninsula. Edinburgh: 1811. V. 46

CATANEO, GIROLAMO

Dell'Arte Militare Libri Tre, Ne' Quali si Tratta il Modo di Fortificare, Offendere, Diffendere, & Fare gli Allogiamenti Campali, con l'Effami de Bombardieri & Formare le Battaglie . . . Terza Impressione, Ampliati e Corretti. Brescia: 1571. V. 39

Opera Nuova di Fortificare, Offendere et Difendere . . . Brescia: 1564. V. 38

Panegyricvs De Institutione Collegii Germanici et Vngarici. Italy: 1652. V. 39

Tavole Brevissime per Sapere con Prestezza Quante File Vanno a Formare una Giustissima Battaglia con li Suoi Armati de Corsaletti, da Cento fin' a Ventimilia Huomini. Brescia: 1567. V. 40

CATASTRO Delle Tenute dell'Agro Romano . . . . Rome: 1783. V. 43

THE CATECHISM of the French Constitution. London: 1791. V. 39

CATERINA DA SIENA, SAINT

Obra de las Epistolas y Oraciones. Alcala: 1512. V. 37

CATES, JAN

Spiegel Van den Ouden ende Nieuvven Tijdt, Bestaende ugt Spreeck-vvoorden ende Sinspreucken, Ontleent van de Voorige Ende Jegenvvoordige Eeuvre . . . In'Sgraven-Hague,: 1632. V. 43

CATESBY, MARK

The Natural History of Carolina, Florida, and the Bahama Islands . . . Revised by Mr. Edwards . . . London: 1771. V. 39; 40; 44; 46

The Natural History of Carolina, Florida and the Bahama Islands. Savannah: 1974. V. 43

Piscium Serpentum Insectorum Aliorumque Nonnullorum Animanlium Nec Non Plantarum Quarundam Imagines Quas Marcus Catesby . . . Nuremberg: 1750. V. 42; 44

CATHALAN, STEPHEN

Recueil de Pieces Relatives a la Frevre Jaune d'Amerique . . . Marseille: 1799. V. 45

CATHARINA DE SIENA, SAINT

Epistole Devotissime. Venice: 1500. V. 38; 40; 42

CATHCART, CHARLES

Johnstons' Students' Atlas of Bones and Ligaments. Edinburgh: 1885. V. 40

CATHCART, GEORGE

Correspondence of, Relative to His Military Operations in Kaffraria, Until the Termination of the Kaffir War, and of His Measures for the Future Maintenance of Peace on the Frontier, and the Protection and Welfare of the People of South Africa. London: 1856. V. 39

Correspondence of Lieut-General Sir George Cathcart, K.C.B., Relative to His Military Operations in Kaffraria, Until the Termination of the Kaffir War, and His Measures for the Future Maintenance of Peace on that Frontier . . . London: 1857. V. 39; 40

CATHCART, JOHN

A Letter to the Honourable Edward Vernon Esq. Vice Admiral of the Red. London: 1744. V. 37

CATHER, WILLA SIBERT 1873-1947

Alexander's Bridge. Boston: 1912. V. 42

Alexander's Bridge. Boston & New York: 1912. V. 39; 41; 43

April Twilights. Boston: 1903. V. 37; 39; 40; 41; 42; 43; 45; 46

April Twilights. New York: 1923. V. 40; 42; 43

Death Comes for the Archbishop. New York: 1927. V. 38; 39; 42; 43; 45

Death Comes for the Archbishop. New York: 1929. V. 37; 38

December Night. New York: 1933. V. 46

Father Junipero's Holy Family. Lexington: 1956. V. 40

A Lost Lady. 1983. V. 45

A Lost Lady. 1983. V. 42

A Lost Lady. New York: 1983. V. 38

A Lost Lady. New York: 1923. V. 37; 38; 41; 43; 44; 45

Lucy Gayheart. New York: 1935. V. 37; 38; 39; 40; 41; 43; 44; 45; 46

My Antonia. Boston: 1918. V. 38; 39; 42; 44

My Antonia. Boston: 1918. V. 38

My Antonia. Boston: 1918. V. 38

My Antonia. Boston/New York: 1918. V. 43

My Mortal Enemy. New York: 1921. V. 44; 45

My Antonia. Boston: 1924. V. 44

My Antonia. Boston and New York: 1926. V. 39

My Mortal Enemy. New York: 1926. V. 39; 43; 45

My Autobiography. By S.S. McClure. New York: (1914). V. 37; 38

Not Under Forty. New York: 1936. V. 39; 41; 42; 43; 44

The Novels and Stories of Willa Cather. Boston: 1937/38/41. V. 44

The Novels and Stories of Willa Cather. Boston: 1937-41. V. 43

O Pioneers! Boston: 1913. V. 38; 39; 43

Obscure Destinies. New York: 1932. V. 41; 43

One of Ours. New York: 1922. V. 41

The Professor's House. New York: 1925. V. 37; 38; 40; 41; 42; 43; 44; 45; 46

Sapphira and the Slave Girl. New York: 1940. V. 38; 39; 41; 42; 43; 46

Shadows on the Rock. New York: 1931. V. 37; 38; 39; 40; 41; 43; 45; 46

Shadows on the Rock. London: 1932. V. 40

Shadows on the Rock. 1931. V. 37

The Song of the Lark. Boston: 1915. V. 41; 42; 44

The Song of the Lark. Boston & New York: 1915. V. 39

The Troll Garden. New York: 1905. V. 39; 40; 41

The Unrelenting Struggle. London: 1942. V. 43

Willa Cather's Red Cloud. Salisbury: 1980. V. 41; 46

Youth & the Bright Medusa. London: 1920. V. 39

Youth and the Bright Medusa. New York: 1920. V. 38; 39; 42; 46

CATHERINE I, EMPRESS OF RUSSIA

The Northern Heroine. London: 1727. V. 40

CATHERINE II, EMPRESS OF RUSSIA

The Grand Instructions to the Commissioners Appointed to Frame a New Code of Laws for the Russian Empire. London: 1768. V. 46

CATHERINET DE VILLEMAREST, C. M.

The Hermit in Italy, or Observations on the Manners and Customs of Italy. London: 1825. V. 39

CATHERWOOD, FREDERICK

Views of Ancient Monuments in Central America Chiapas and Yucatan. London: 1844. V. 40

CATHOLIC Anthology 1914-1915. London: 1915. V. 37

CATHOLIC CHURCH

Acta Apostolicae Sedis. Commentarium Officiale. Rome: 1909-78. V. 39

Kalendarivm Gregorianvm Perpetvvm. Paris: 1583. V. 38

Catechismo, Cioe Istrvttione, Secondo il Decreto del Concilio di Trento . . . Venice: 1567. V. 45

Officium Hebdomadae Sanctae Iuxta Forman Missalis, & Breviarii Romani. Venice: 1658. V. 46

CATHOLIC CHURCH. CATECHISMUS ROMANUS

Catechismus ex Decreto Concilii Tridentini ad Parochos, ante Quidem Pii V. Pont. Max. Cologne: 1572. V. 43

Catechismus Romanus, ex Decreto Concilii Tridentiii, & Pii V. Pontificis Maximi Iussu Primum Editus. Antwerp: 1572. V. 37

CATHOLIC CHURCH. COUNCILS

Canones, et Decreta Sacrosancti Oecumenici et Generalis Concilii Tridentini sub Paulo III, Iulio III, Pio IIII Pontificibus Max. Romae: 1564. V. 37; 38

Concilorum Quatuor Generaliu Niceni, Constantinopolitani, Ephesini, & Calcedonesis. Paris: 1535. V. 37

CATHOLIC CHURCH. INDEX - 1582

INDEX Librorum Authorumque S. Sedis Apostolicae Sacrique Concilio Tridentino Authoritate Prohibitorum. Munich: 1582. V. 38

CATHOLIC CHURCH. INDEX - 1601

INDEX Librorum Expurgatorum. Saumur: 1601. V. 38

CATHOLIC CHURCH. INDEX - 1764

INDEX Librorum Prohibitorum. Rome: 1764. V. 38

CATHOLIC CHURCH. LITRUGY & RITUAL. HOURS

Hore Deipare Virginis Mariae Secundu Usum Romanum. Paris: 1519. V. 41

CATHOLIC CHURCH. LITURGY & RITUAL

Respo(n)soria Nouiter cu(m) Notis Impressa: de t(em)p(o)re & Sanctis Pertotum Annu(m); Regentibus & Scolaraibus Vtilissima. Nuremberg: 1509. V. 38

Ritual Rimski Istomaccen Slovinski. Rome: 1640. V. 46

CATHOLIC CHURCH. LITURGY & RITUAL. BREVIARY

Breviarium Romanum. Venice: 1478. V. 39

Breviarvm Romanum ex Sacra Potissimvm Scriptvra, Et Probatis Sanctoru Historijs Nuper Confectum, ac Denuo per Eundem Authorem Accuratius Recognitum . . . Lyon: 1543. V. 39

Use of Sarum. Portiforium seu Breuiarium ad Isignis Sarisburiesis Ecclesie Vsum. London: 1556. V. 37

CATHOLIC CHURCH. LITURGY & RITUAL. BREVIARY - 1740

Diurnal du Breviarire Romaine. Lyon: 1740. V. 40

CATHOLIC CHURCH. LITURGY & RITUAL. CAERMONIALE ROMANUM

Sacrarum Caeremoniarum. Sive Rituum Ecclesiasticorum S. Rom. Ecclesiae. Venice: 1582. V. 40

CATHOLIC CHURCH. LITURGY & RITUAL. CEREMONIAL BISHOPS

Caeremoniale Episcoporum Iussu Clementis VIII Pont, Max. Reformatum. Paris: 1633. V. 43

CATHOLIC CHURCH. LITURGY & RITUAL. CEREMONIAL OF BISHOPS

Caeremoniale Episcoporum Jussu Clementis VIII Pont. Max Reformatum . . . Paris: 1633. V. 41

Caeremoniale Episcoporum Clementis VIII Primum Nunc Denuo Innocentii Papae X Auctoritate Recognitum. Rome: 1651. V. 40; 43

CATHOLIC CHURCH. LITURGY & RITUAL. COMPAGNIA DEI BATTUTI

Libro da Compagnie: o Vero da Fraternite de Battuti; Nouame(n)te Stampato & Dilige(n)temente Corretto . . . Spoleto: 1544. V. 44

Libro da Compagnia Nuoamente Stampato . . . Florence: 1563. V. 40

CATHOLIC CHURCH. LITURGY & RITUAL. HOURS

Book of Hours, Latin, Use of Rome. Paris. V. 46

Horae B.V.M. as Usum Romanum cum Calendrio. Heures a Lusaige de Rome tout au Long sans Rien Requerir. Paris: 1517-27. V. 45; 46

Horae B. V. M. as Usum Romanum cum Calendario. Heures a Lusaige de Rome tout au Long Sans Rien Requerir. Paris: 1527. V. 44

Horae Beatae Marie Virginis Secunda Usum Romanarum . . . Paris: 1528-45. V. 44

Horae Beate Marie Virginis Secunda Usum Romanum. Paris: 1528-45. V. 45

Horae Beate Marie Virginis Secundum Usum Romanum . . . Paris: 1534. V. 46

Horae Beatae Virginis Mariae Juxta Ritum Sacri Ordinis Praedicatorum. Ditchling: 1923. V. 43

Livres d'Heures a l'Usage de Rome. Paris. V. 41

Horae B.M.V. in Latin, 2nd Use of Rome. Paris: 1511. V. 45

Ces Presentes Heures a Lusaige de Paris Toutes au Long Sans Riens Requerir . . . Paris: 1523? V. 39; 40; 41

Officium B. Mariae Virg. Nuper Reformatum & Pii V. Pont. Max. iussu Editum; Ad instar Breviarii Romani sub Urbano VIII recogniti. Antwerp: 1677. V. 37

Miniature Bookf of Hours. A Facsimile of Ms. Ross 94 in the Vatican Library. London: 1984. V. 39

Le Livre d'Heures de la Reine Anne de Bretagne. Paris: 1861. V. 43

Livre d'Heures. Paris: 1889. V. 44

Livre d'Heures. Satirique et Libertin du XIXme Siecle. Brussels: 1890. V. 44; 45

Officium Beatae Mariae Virginis. Paris: 1616. V. 45

CATHOLIC CHURCH. LITURGY & RITUAL. HOURS - 1730

Heures Nouvelles Our Prieres Choisies. Lyon: 1730. V. 40

CATHOLIC CHURCH. LITURGY & RITUAL. HOURS - 1749

Heures Nouvelles Dedie'es au Roy, Contenant L'Office de L'Eglise, Suivant les Nouveaux Breviarires et Missels de Paris et de Rome . . . Paris: 1749. V. 40

CATHOLIC CHURCH. LITURGY & RITUAL. HOURS - 1756

Officio della B. V. Maria. Rome: 1756. V. 40

CATHOLIC CHURCH. LITURGY & RITUAL. MISSAL

Missale Monasticum Secundum Consuetudinem Ordinia Vallisumbrosae. Venice: 1503. V. 38

Missale Romanum ad Longum Absque Ulla Requisitione . . . Paris: 1565. V. 38

Missale Romanum. Ex Decreto Sacrosancti Concili Tridentini Restitutum Pii V. Pont. Max. iussu editum. Paris: 1573. V. 37

Missale Monasticum Secundum Consuetudienm Ordinis Vallisumbrose. Venice: 1503. V. 45

Missale Secundum Ordinem Fratrum Predicatorum, Juxta Decreta Capituli Generalis, Salmantice, Anno d(omi)ni 1551 . . . Venice: 1575. V. 43

Missale Romanum ex Decreto Sacrosancti Concilii Tridentini Restitutum. Pii V. Pont. Max. Iussu Editum. Venice: 1576. V. 43

Missale Romanum Ex Decreto Sacrosancto Concilii Tridentini Restitutum . . . London: 1657. V. 46

Missale Romanum ad Usum Pontificum. Antwerp: 1846. V. 46

Missale Romanum. Turonibus: 1869. V. 43

Missel Romain. Paris: 1890's. V. 45

The Office of the Holy Week According to the Roman Missal and Breviary. London: 1688. V. 46

Vade Mecum. Missale Itinerantium seu Misse Peculiares Valde Devote. Nuremberg: 1510. V. 46

CATHOLIC CHURCH. LITURGY & RITUAL. MISSAL - 1512

Ordo Misse Secundario Diligenter Correctus cum Notabilibus & Glossiaribus Sacri Canonis Noviter Additis. Cracow: 1512. V. 40

CATHOLIC CHURCH. LITURGY & RITUAL. MISSAL - 1540

Misse Quadragesimales a Primo die Cinerum Usque ad Tertium Festum Resurrectionis. Venice: 1540. V. 40

CATHOLIC CHURCH. LITURGY & RITUAL. MISSAL - 1617

Missale Romanum ex Decr. Sancros. Conc. Trid. Restitutum, Pii V Pontificis Maximi Iussu Editum, at Clementis VIII Auctoritate Recognitum. Venice: 1617. V. 40

CATHOLIC CHURCH. LITURGY & RITUAL. OFFICE

The Office of the Holy Week, According to the Roman Missal and Breviary. Baltimore: 1810. V. 41

CATHOLIC CHURCH. LITURGY & RITUAL. PONTIFICAL

Pio V. Pont. Max Pontificale Romanum . . . in Tres Partes Distinctum. Venice: 1572. V. 43

CATHOLIC CHURCH. LITURGY & RITUAL. PSALTER

The Luttrell Psalter. London: 1932. V. 39

Psalterium Chorale Frautru. Venice: 1551. V. 39

Psalterium Hebreum, Grecum, Arabicum & Chaldeum, cum Tribus Latinis Inter-Pretationibus & Glossis. Genoa: 1516. V. 37

CATHOLIC CHURCH. LITURGY & RITUAL. RITUAL - 1841

Rituale Romanum. Daventriae: 1841. V. 40

CATHOLIC CHURCH. MISSALE

Missale monasticum secundum consuetudinem ordinis Vallisumbrosae. (Venice: 1503). V. 37

CATHOLIC CHURCH. ROTA ROMANA

Formularium Terminorum seu Registrorum. Rome: 1537. V. 37

CATHOLIC Miracles. London: 1825. V. 38

CATHOLIC PUBLICATION HOUSE

A Catalogue of American and English CAtholic Books for Sale, . . . New York: 1867. V. 44

CATHOLICUS, PSEUD.

The Apocalyptic Beasts, Seen in Vision by St. John, in His Holy Revelation. New York: 1843. V. 39

CATHRALL, WILLIAM

Wanderings in North Wales . . . London: 1851. V. 42

CATICH, EDWARD M.

Letters Redrawn from the Trajan Inscription in Rome. Davenport: 1961. V. 43; 44

The Origin of the Serif; Brush Writing and Roman Letters. Davenport: 1968. V. 39; 41; 42; 44

The Origin of the Serif. Iowa: 1968. V. 45

Pen and Brush Alphabets for Writing and Lettering. Davenport: 1972. V. 37; 42; 45; 46

CATICH, EDWARD M. continued

The Trajan Inscription, an Essay by Edward M. Catich, Together with an Original Rubbing from the Inscription. Boston: 1973. V. 37; 39; 41; 42

CATLIN, GEORGE 1796-1872

Adventures of the Ojibbeway and Ioway Indians in England, France and Belgium . . . London: 1852. V. 43; 45

The Breath of Life or Mal-Respiration (sic) and Its Effects Upon the Employments & Life of Man. London: 1862. V. 39

Buffalo Hunt, Chase. London: 1844. V. 41

Catalogue of Catlin's Indian Gallery of Portraits, Landscapes, Manners and Customs, Costumes, &c. &c. Collected During Seven Years' Travel Amongst Thirty-Eight Different Tribes, Speaking Different Languages. New York: 1838. V. 39; 42

Catalogue Raisonne e La Galerie Indienne d Mr. Catlin, Renfermant des Portraits, des Paysages, des Costumes, etc., et des Scenes de Moeurs et Coutumes des Indiens de l'Amerique du Nord . . . Paris: 1845. V. 39

Catalogue Descriptive and Instructive of Catlin's Indian Cartoons. New York: 1871. V. 37

Catalogue of Catlin's Indian Gallery of Portraits, Landscapes, Mannrs and Customs, Costumes, &c., &c. New York: 1838. V. 37

Catlin's North American Indian Portfolio. London: 1844. V. 43

Catlin's Notes of Eight Years' Travels and Residence in Europe with His North American Indian Collection. London: 1848. V. 38; 39

Catlin's North American Indian Portfolio. Chicago: 1970. V. 39; 42

A Descriptive Catalogue of Catlin's Indian Collection, Containing Portraits, Landscapes, Costumes &c., and Representations of the Manners and Customs of the North American Indians. London: 1848. V. 37; 39

A Descriptive Catalogue of Catlin's Indian Collection. London: 1848. V. 37

A Descriptive Catalogue of Catlin's Indian Gallery. London: 1842. V. 37

Drawings of the North American Indians. Garden City: 1984. V. 39

Folium Reservatum. London: 1867. V. 38

George Catlin Drawings of the North American Indians. Garden City: 1984. V. 42

Illustrations of the Manners, Customs, and Condition of the North American Indians. London: 1848. V. 38; 43; 44

Illustrations of the Manners, Customs and Condition of the North American Indians. London: 1851. V. 45

Illustrations of the Manners, Customs, and Condition of the North American Indians: In a Series of Letters and Notes. London: 1845. V. 37; 39; 41; 42; 43; 45

Illustrations of the Manners, Customs, and Condition of the North American Indians: With Letters and Notes. London: 1857. V. 37

Joc-o-sot, the Walking Bear, a Sauk Chief from the Upper Missouri. London: 1844. V. 41

Last Rambles Amongst the Indians of the Rocky Mountains and the Andes. London: 1868. V. 37; 38

Letters and Notes on the Manners, Customs, and Condition of the North American Indians. New York: 1841. V. 37; 38; 39; 41

Letters and Notes on the Manners, Customs and Condition of the North American Indians. London: 1842. V. 43

Letters and Notes on the Manners, Customs and Conditions of the North American Indians. Philadelphia: 1857. V. 45

Letters and Notes on the Manners, Customs and Condition of the North American Indians. London: 1892. V. 39

Letters and Notes on the Manners, Customs and Condition of the North American Indians. London: 1841. V. 37; 38; 39; 40; 41; 42; 43; 45

Life Amongst the Indians. London: 1861. V. 38; 45

The Manners, Customs and Condition of the North American Indians . . . London: 1892. V. 42; 45

The Manners, Customs and Condition of the North American Indians . . . London: published by: 1890's. V. 37

The Manners, Customs, and Conditions of the North American Indians Written During Eight Years Travel Amongst the Wildest Tribes of Indians in North America, 1832-39. V. 37

Nord-Amerikas Indianer. Stockholm: 1848. V. 40

North American Indians, Being Letters and Notes on Their Manners, Customs and Conditions . . . London: 1880. V. 45

North American Indians. Edinburgh: 1903. V. 39; 44; 46

The North American Indian, Being Letters and Notes on the Manners, Customs and Conditions, Written During Eight Years Travel Among the Wildest Tribe of Indians of North America 1832-29. Edinburgh: 1903. V. 39

The North American Indians. Philadelphia: 1913. V. 37; 38; 39; 41; 45

North American Indians, Being Letters and Notes on the Manners, Customs and Conditions Written During Eight Years' Travel Amongst the Wildest Tribes in North America, 1832-1839. Edinburgh: 1926. V. 37; 38; 39; 41

North American Indian Portfolio. Chicago: 1970. V. 38; 41

North American Indian Portfolio. New York: 1989. V. 41

North American Indian Portfolio. London: 1844. V. 37

Notes of Eight Years' Travels and Residence in Europe with his North American Indian Collection. London: 1848. V. 37

O-Kee-Pa: a Religious Ceremony: and Other Customs of the Mandans. Philadelphia: 1867. V. 37; 39; 40; 43; 45

O'Kee Pa: A Religious Ceremony; and Other Customs of the Mandrans. London: 1867. V. 37; 38; 42; 43; 45

Rambles Among the Indians of the Rocky Mountains and the Andes. London & Edinburgh: 1877. V. 40

Shut Your Mouth and Save Your Life. London: 1882. V. 43

CATLING, H. W.

Cypriot Bronzework in the Mycenaean World. Oxford: 1964. V. 40; 44

CATLOW, AGNES

Sketching Rambles; or Nature in the Alps and Appenines. London: 1861. V. 46

Sketching Rambles; or, Nature in the Alps and Apennines. London: 1862. V. 41; 46

CATLOW, JOSEPH PEEL

On the Principles of Aestethic Medicine . . . London: 1867. V. 43

CATNACH, JAMES

A Collection of the Books and Woodcuts of James Catnach. London: 1869. V. 40

CATO, DIONYSIUS

Cato's Moral Distichs. (San Francisco): 1939. V. 37

(Disticha de Moribus). Cato Cum Commento. Paris: 1485. V. 46

Disticha de Moribus ad Filium . . . Flosculis Poeticis . . . (with) Historica Critica Catoniana . . . Maximi Planudis Metaphrasis Graeca..Itemque Desiderii Eraasmi Expositio . . . Amsterdam: 1759. V. 38

CATO, MARCUS PORCIUS

De Re Rustica; Varro Marcus Terentius. De Re Rustica; Columella, Lucius Junius Moderatus. De Re Rustica, De Arboribus; Palladius, Rutilius Taurus Aemilianus. De Re Rustica. Venice: 1515. V. 37

Libri de Re Rustica. Venice: 1514. V. 38; 40

CATON, JOHN DEAN

The Antelope and Deer of America. New York: 1877. V. 39; 43; 44

CATON, T. M.

Practical Treatise on the Prevention and Cure of the Veneral Disease . . . London: 1809. V. 44

CATON-THOMPSON, GERTRUDE

The Desert Fayum. London: 1934. V. 40

Kharga Oasis in Prehistory. London: 1952. V. 40; 44

CATONIS DISTICHA

Catonis Libri Quinque Moralis Philosphiae, cum Scholiis Lucretiae Lucensis in Treis Primos & Andreae Lancianensis in Duos Posteriores. Lyon: 1548. V. 38

Cato's Moral Distichs. Los Angeles: 1939. V. 43

Distcha de Moribus ad Filium, cum Notis Integris Scaligeri, Barthii, Daumii . . . Amstelaedami: 1754. V. 43

Disticha de Moribus. Paris: 1541. V. 38

Les Mots et Sentences Dorees. Paris: 1540. V. 40

CATS, JACOB

Moral Emblems with Aphorisms, Adages and Proverbs of all Ages and Nations from . . . London: 1860. V. 45

Ouderdom, Buyten-Leven: En Hof-Gedachten. Amsterdam: 1678. V. 44

Silenus Alcibiadis, Sive Proteus . . . (with) Maechden-plicht ofte Ampt der Ionck-Vrouwen . . . (with) Self-Stryt . . . Middelburg: 1618-18-20. V. 39

Spiegel van den Ouden ende Nieuvven Tijdt. Graven-Hage: 1632. V. 41; 46

Spiegel van den Ouden ende Nieuvven Tijdt. Hague: 1632. V. 41

THE CATS Party. London: 1840. V. 39

CATTAN, CHRISTOPHER

The Geomancie. London: 1591. V. 38; 41

CATTELL, EDWARD JAMES

To the Healing of the Sea. London. V. 43

CATTERMOLE, RICHARD

The Great Civil War of the Times of Charles I and Cromwell. London: 1857. V. 42

CATTLE Brands Owned by members of the Wyoming Stock Grower's Association. Chicago: 1882. V. 42; 45

CATTON, CHARLES

Thirty-Six Animals, Drawn From Nature, and Engraved in Aquatint . . . New Haven: 1825. V. 40; 42; 45

CATULLUS, C. VALERIUS 84-54 BC

The Carmina of . . . London: 1894. V. 39; 44; 46

Catvlli, Tibvlli, Properti Carmina Quae extant Omnia Cura Robinson Ellis (and others) Londini: 1911. V. 38

Camina Quae Extant Omnia. London: 1911. V. 46

Carminia. Venice: 1496. V. 37

CATULLUS, C. VALERIUS 84-54 BC continued

Catulli, Tibulli, Properti, Nova Editio. Antwerp: 1582. V. 40

Catulli, Tibulli et Propertii. Opera. Brimingham: 1772. V. 39; 40; 41; 42; 43; 45

Catullus, Tibullus, Propertius, Iampridem Viri Docti Judicio Castigati. Leiden: 1592. V. 40

Catullus, Tibullus, Propertius. Opera. Parma: 1794. V. 41

Catvlli, Tibvlli, Propertii Nova Editio. Paris: 1577. V. 38

The Complete Poetry of Gaius Catullus. N.P.: 1926? V. 41

The Complete Poetry. London: 1929. V. 37; 39; 44

Catullus, Tibullus and Propertius. Opera. Paris: 1577. V. 45

Catulli, Tibulli, et Propertii Opera. Cambridge: 1702. V. 39

Catullus, Tibullus & Propertius Opera. Birmingham: 1772. V. 40

The Poetry of Catullus. Omaha: 1979. V. 40; 44; 45

Quae Extant Omnia. London: 1911. V. 45

A Selection from Catullus, by Donovan McCune. San Francisco: 1969. V. 38

Vernonensis Epithalmivm, seu Carmen Nuptiale. Lvtetiae: 1587. V. 38

CATULLUS, TIBULLUS & PROPERTIUS

Poemata. Venice: 1502. V. 37

CAUCHY, AUGUSTIN LOUIS

Cours d'Analyse de l'Ecole Royale Polytechnique . . . Paris: 1821. V. 38

CAUDWELL, CHRISTOPHER

Illusion and Reality - a Study of the Sources of Poetry. London: 1937. V. 40

Studies in a Dying Culture. London: 1938. V. 38

CAULFEILD, A. ST. G.

The Temple of the Kings at Abydos. London: 1902. V. 44

CAULFIELD, JAMES

Calcographiana; the Printsellers Chronicle and Collectors Guide to the Knowledge and Value of Engraved British Portraits. London: 1814. V. 38

Memoirs of the Celebrated Persons Compsoing the Kit-Cat Club. London: 1821. V. 39; 42

Portraits, Memoirs, and Characters of Remarkable Persons, from the Reign of Edward the Third to the Revolution. London: 1813, 1819-20. V. 40

Portraits, memoirs and Characters of Remarkable Persons from the Revolution in 1688 to the End of the Reign of George II. London: 1819. V. 38; 45

Portraits, Memoirs and Characters of Remarkable Persons from the Revolution . . . London: 1819-20. V. 37; 38; 46

Portraits, Memoirs and Character of Remarkable Persons, from the Reign of Edward the Third to the Revolution. London: 1813. V. 38

Portraits, Memoirs and Characters of Remarkable Persons, from the Reign of Edward the Third, to the Revolution. London: 1794. V. 37

CAULFIELD, S. F. A.

The Dictionary of Needlework, an Encyclopaedia of Artistic, Plain and Fancy Needlework . . . London: 1887. V. 39

The Dictionary of Needlework . . . dealing fully with the details of all the Stitches Employed, the Method of Working, the Materials used, the meaning of Techincal Terms . . . Plain Sewing, Textiles, Dressmaking, Appliances and Terms . . . London: (c. 1880). V. 37; 40

CAULKINS, DANIEL

Aerial Navigation. The Best Method. Toledo: 1895. V. 37

CAUNTER, HOBART

Caunter's and Daniell's Oriental Annual, 1839. Eastern Legends. London: 1838. V. 39

The Oriental Annual. London: 1834. V. 42

The Oriental Annual. London: 1835. V. 42

The Oriental Annual. London: 1836. V. 42

The Oriental Annual. London: 1837. V. 42

CAUS, ISAAC DE

Nouvelle Invention de Lever l'Eau plus Hault Que la Source avec Qualques Machines. 1644. V. 38

CAUSEY, ANDREW

Edward Burra. Complete Catalogue. London: 1985. V. 42

Paul Nash. Oxford: 1980. V. 42

CAUSLEY, CHARLES

Benedict - a Play in One Act. London: 1938. V. 44

Timothy Winters. London: 1970. V. 46

Twenty-One Poems. 1986. V. 41

Twenty-One Poems. London: 1986. V. 38

CAUSSIN, NICHOLAS

the Holy Court in Five Tomes . . . London: 1663. V. 45; 46

The Unfortunate Politique, First Written in French by C.N. Oxford: 1638. V. 46

CAUSTEN, JAMES H.

View of the Claims of American Citizens . . . Washington: 1829. V. 45

CAUTLEY, PROBY T.

Ganges Canal. London: 1864. V. 42

CAUTY, WILLIAM

Natura, Philosophia & Ars in Concordia. London: 1772. V. 46

CAUVET, GILLES-PAUL

Receuil d'Ornemens a l'Usage des Jeunes Artistes qui se Destinent a la Decoration des Batimens. Paris: 1777. V. 46

CAVAFY, C. P.

C. P. Cavafy: a Selection of Poems. London: 1985. V. 37; 39; 41

Fourteen Poems by C.P. Cavafy. Chosen and illustrated with twelve original etchings by David Hockney. Translated by Nikos Stangos and Stephen Spender. London: 1967. V. 37; 40

Morning Sea - A Poem. London: 1977. V. 37; 40

Poems (1905-1915). Alexandria: 1928 & 1930. V. 40

Works. Athens: 1982. V. 40

CAVALCA, DOMENICO

Libro Della Pazienza Chiamato Medicina di Cuore. Florence: 1490. V. 37

CAVALCANTI, GUIDO

The Sonnets and Ballate of Guido Cavalcanti. Boston: 1912. V. 37; 45

The Sonnets and Ballate of Guido Cavalcanti. London: 1912. V. 39

CAVALIERI, BONAVENTURA

Appendice Della Nuova Prattica Astrologica . . . Bologna: 1640. V. 45

CAVALIERI, GIOVANNI BATTISTA

Romanorum Imperatorum Effigies. Rome: 1583. V. 38

CAVALLIER, JEAN 1681-1740

Memoirs of the Wars of the Cevennes, Under Colonel Cavallier in Defence of the Protestants Persecuted in that Country. London: 1727. V. 38

CAVALLO, TIBERIUS

A Complete Treatise on Electricity, in Theory and Practice, with Original Experiments. London: 1782. V. 42; 45

A Complete Treatise of Electricty in Theory and Practice with Original Experiments. London: 1777. V. 37

The Elements of Natural or Experimental Philosophy. London: 1803. V. 40

The Elements of Natural or Experimental Philosophy. Philadelphia: 1819. V. 40

The History and Practice of Aerostation. London: 1785. V. 38

A Treatise on the nature and properties of air and other permanently elastic fluids, to which is prefixed, an introduction to chymistry. London: 1781. V. 37

CAVALRY ! Young Men and Middle Aged Men! Your Country Calls You! . . . Now is the Time to Manifest Your Patriotism! Unite Under the Head of Col. Zahm! of Monroeville (Ohio), to do Battle for Your Country . . . N.P.. V. 39

CAVAN, RICHARD LAMBART, 6TH EARL OF

A New System of Military Discipline, Founded Upon Principle. Philadelphia: 1776. V. 37

CAVANIS, PIERRE JEAN GEORGES

Rapports du Physique et du Moral de l'Homme. Paris: 1802. V. 45

CAVAZZI DA MONTECUCCOLO, GIOVANNI ANTONIO

Istorica Descrittione De' Tre Regni Congo, Matamba et Angola. Milan: 1690. V. 40

CAVE, F. O.

Birds of the Sudan. London: 1955. V. 39

CAVE, FRANCIS O.

Birds of the Sudan. Their Identification and Distribution. Edinburgh: 1955. V. 45

CAVE, HENRY

The Book of Ceylon. London: 1908. V. 38

CAVE, HENRY W.

Golden Tips. London: 1900. V. 38; 40; 44; 46

CAVE, JANE

Poems on Various Subjects, Entertaining, Elegiac and Religious. Winchester: 1783. V. 41; 42

CAVE, ROBERT

Typographia Naturalis. Wymondham: 1967. V. 44

CAVE, RODERICK

The Private Press: Five Hundred Years of the Amateur Printer. 1971. V. 39

The Private Papers. London: 1971. V. 39

Typographia Naturalis. 1967. V. 40

Typographia Naturalis. Wymondham: 1967. V. 37; 41; 43; 44; 45

CAVE, WILLIAM 1637-1713

Antiquitates Apostolicae; or, the History of the Lives, Acts and Martyrdoms of the Holy Apostles . . . London: 1677. V. 39; 46

Apostolici; or, the History of the Lives, Acts, Death and Martyrdoms of Those Who Were Contemporary With, or Immediately Succeeded the Apostles. London. V. 44

Apostolici; or, the History of the Lives, Acts, death and Martyrdoms of Those Who Were Contemporary with or Immeditely Succeeded the Apostles. London: 1682. V. 44

Apostolici: or the History of the Lives, Acts, Death and Martyrdoms of Those Who Were Contemporary With, or Immediately Succeeded the Apostles . . . London: 1687. V. 39; 40

Apostolici; or The History of the Lives, Acts, Death and Martyrdoms of Those Who Were Contemporary. (with) Ecclesiastici; or, the History of the Lives . . . of the Most Eminent Fathers of the Church that Flourisht in the Fourth Century. London: printed by B.W. for: 1687/83. V. 45

Apostolici: or the History of the Lives, Acts, Death and Martyrdoms of Those Who Were Contemporary With, or Immediately Succeeded the Apostles . . . London: 1716. V. 39

Ecclesiastici: or the History of the Lives, Acts, Death and Writing of the Most Eminent Fathers of the Church That Flourished in the Fourth Century. London: 1683, 1682. V. 40; 41; 43; 44

Primitive Christianity. London: 1673. V. 41

Scriptorum Ecclesiasticorum Historiae Literaria, a Christo Nato Usque ad Saeculum XIV Facili Methodo Digesta . . . London: 1688-89. V. 39

Scriptorum Ecclesiasticorum Historiae Literaria, a Christo Nato usque ad Saeculum XIV Facili Methodo Digesta . . . Oxford: 1740. V. 39

CAVELER, WILLIAM

Select Specimens of Gothic Architecture . . . London: 1839. V. 38

CAVENDISH

The Game of Lawn Tennis with the Laws of the Marylebone and All England Clubs. London: 1888. V. 40

CAVENDISH, GEORGE 1500-1561?

The Life of Thomas Wolsey, Cardinal Archbishop of York. V. 45

The Life of Cardinal Wolsey and Metrical Visions from the Original Autograph Manuscript. Chiswick: 1825. V. 39

The Life of Cardinal Wolsey and Metrical Visions from the Original Manuscript. London: 1825. V. 39

The Life of Cardinal Wolsey . . . London: 1827. V. 37; 39; 45

The Life of Thomas Wolsey, Cardinal Archbishop of York. 1893. V. 45

The Life of Cardinal Wolsey, Archbishop of York. Hammersmith: 1893. V. 39; 45; 46

The Life of Thomas Wolsey, Cardinal Archbishop of York. London: 1893. V. 42

Life and Death of Cardinal Wolsey. Boston: 1905. V. 39

The Negotiations of Thomas Woolsey, the Great Cardinall of England. London: 1641. V. 37

CAVENDISH, HENRY 1731-1810

The Electrical Researches . . . . Cambridge: 1879. V. 37; 42

CAVENDISH, THOMAS

Journalen Van Drie Voyagien. Te Weten: I. Van Mr. Thomas Candish (sic). Met Drie Schepen Door de Magallanensche Straet Rondom de Werelt, in Den Iare 1586, 1587, en 1588 . . . Amsterdam: 1643. V. 40; 43

CAVENDISH, WILLIAM

A New Method, and Extraordinary Invention, to Dress Horses and Work . . . London: 1667. V. 42

THE CAVERN of Death. London: 1794. V. 40

THE CAVERN of Death, a Moral tale. Baltimore: 1801? V. 40

THE CAVERN of Strozzi. a Novel. Boston?: 1812. V. 39; 44

CAVICEO, GIACOMO

Libro del Peregrino Novement Impresso e Redutto alla Sua Sincerita con la Vita Dello Auctore. Venice: 1520. V. 37

CAVICEO, JACOPO 1443-1511

Il Peregrino . . . Nuouamente con Somma Dilgenza Reuisto & Ristampato. Colophon: 1538. V. 43

Il Peregrino. N.P.: 1553. V. 40

CAVOS, ALBERT

Reconstruction du Grand Theatre de Moscou dit Petrovski. Paris: 1859. V. 37

Traite de la construction des Theatres. Paris: 1847. V. 37

CAW, JAMES L.

Scottish Portraits. With an Historical and Critical Introduction and Notes. Edinburgh: 1902-03. V. 39

Sir James Guthrie. London: 1932. V. 39; 40; 43

CAWCDREY, DANIEL

Superstitio Svperstes: or, the Reliques of Svperstition Newly Revived. London: 1641. V. 37

CAWDELL, JAMES

The Miscellaneous Poems of . . . Sunderland: 1785. V. 40

the Miscellaneous Poems of J. Cawdell, Comedian. London: 1785. V. 40

CAWEIN, MADISON

Moods and Memories. Poems. New York: 1892. V. 45; 46

Myth and Romance. New York & London: 1899. V. 40

The Shadow Garden (a Phantasy) and Other Plays. New York: 1910. V. 40

CAWEIN, MADISON J.

Blooms of the Berry. Louisville: 1887. V. 43

CAWSE, J.

Introduction to the Art of Painting in Oil Colours. London: 1829. V. 37

CAWTHORN, JAMES 1719-1761

Poems. London: 1771. V. 40

CAWTHORN, JOHN

Views in Yorkshire. London: 1800-08. V. 39; 44

CAWTHORNE, G. J.

Royal Ascot: Its History and Its Associations. London: 1900. V. 37; 42

CAXTON CLUB

Catalogue of an Exhibition of Nineteenth Century Bookbindings. Chicago: 1897. V. 41

CAXTON, WILLIAM

The Life of St. George. New Fairfield: 1957. V. 45; 46

The Mirrour of the World. Translated & Printed by William Caxton in 1481. (Kentfield: 1964). V. 37

The Noble Knight Paris & the Fair Vienne. (Translated from the French to English by William Caxton). With decorations in the margins of the text after wood engravings by Malette Dean, hand coloured by Dorothy Allen. (Kentfield, Calif.: 1956). V. 37

An Original Leaf from the Polycronicon printed by William Caxton at Westminster in the year 1482. The Life and Works of William Caxton, with an historical reminder of fifteenth century England by Benjamin P. Kurtz together . . . San Francisco: 1938. V. 37

CAY, HENRY BOULT

An Abridgment of the Publick Statutes Now in Force and of General Use from 11 Geo.2 to Geo.3 . . . N.P.: 1766. V. 40

CAYET, PIERRE VICTOR PALME

Chronologie Septenaire de l'Histoire de la Paix Entre les Roys de France et d'Espagne . . . Paris: 1605. V. 37; 38; 40; 41; 43; 44

Paradigmata de Quatuor Linguis Orientalibus. Paris: 1596. V. 44

CAYLEY, ARTHUR 1821-1895

The Collected Mathematical Papers. Cambridge: 1889-98. V. 37

An Elementary Treatise on Elliptic Functions. Cambridge: 1876. V. 40; 42

CAYLEY, CORNELIUS 1729-1780?

The Seraphical Young Shepherd. London: 1762. V. 41

CAYLEY-WEBSTER, H.

Through New Guinea and the Cannibal Countries. London: 1898. V. 39

CAYLUS, ANNE CLAUDE PHILIPPE, COMTE DE 1692-1765

Les Etrennes de la St. Jean. (with) Les Ecosseuses ou Les Oeufs de Pasques. Troyes: 1742, 1739. V. 38

Les Manteaux. Recueil. The Hague: 1746. V. 39

CAZENAVE, A.

A Practical Synopsis of Cutaneous Diseases, From the Most Celebrated Authors, and Particularly from Documents Afforded by the Clinical Lectures on Dr. Biettt . . . Philadelphia: 1832. V. 42

CAZENOVE, JOHN

Thoughts on a Few Subjects of Political Economy. London: 1859. V. 42

CAZNEAU, JANE MC MANUS STORMS

Eagle Pass: or, Life on the Border by Cora Montgomery. New York: 1852. V. 39; 43

CENDRARS, BLAISE continued

Little Black Stories For Little White Children. New York: 1929. V. 40; 41

Panama: or the Adventures of My Seven Uncles. New York: 1931. V. 39; 40; 41; 42; 45

Panama or the Adventures of My Seven Uncles. New York: & London: 1931. V. 43

La Prose du Transsiberien, et de La Petite Jehanne de France. Paris: 1913. V. 42

CENNINI, CENNINO

A Treatise on Painting . . . London: 1844. V. 41; 44

THE CENTAUR and the Bacchante. London: 1899. V. 37

THE CENTENARY of the Birth of Ralph Waldo Emerson as Observed in Concord May 25 1903. 1903. V. 45

THE CENTENNIAL History of Chautauqua County . . . Jamestown: 1904. V. 46

THE CENTENNIAL History of West Point 1802-1902. N.P.: 1904. V. 45

CENTENO, AMARO

Historia De Cosas Del Oriente Primera y Segunda Parte. Cordoba: 1595. V. 41

CENTLIVRE, SUSANNAH 1667-1723

The Dramatic Works of the Celebrated . . . with a New Account of Her Life. London: 1872. V. 46

The Gamester. London: 1705. V. 40

The Gamester . . . London: 1714. V. 44

Mar-lot; or the Second Part of the Busie-Body. London: 1711. V. 45

Works of . . . Edinburgh: 1760-61. V. 42; 46

Works of the Celebrated Mrs. Centlivre, with a New Account of Her Life. London: 1760-61. V. 37

The Works of the Celebrated Mrs. Centlivre. London: 1761. V. 38

CENTRAL NEW JERSEY BAPTIST ASSOCIATION

Minutes of the (33rd) through 94th Anniversary . . . 1861-1922. V. 41

CENTRAL PACIFIC RAILROAD

The Central Pacific Railroad: A Trip Across the North American Continent from Ogden to San Francisco. New York: 1870-71. V. 37

Information Concerning the Terminus of the Railroad System of the Pacific Coast. Oakland: 1871. V. 40

THE CENTRAL Pacific Railroad. A Trip Across the North American Continent from Ogden to San Francisco. New York: 1870's. V. 39

CENTRAL PACIFIC RAILROAD COMPANY

Lands of the Central Pacific Railroad Company in California, Nevada and Utah. 1877. V. 37

CENTRAL RAILROAD AND BANKING COMPANY OF GEORGIA

First through Eleventh Reports by the President and Engineer. Savannah: 1838-1845. V. 37; 38; 39; 42

CENTRAL SOUTHERN RAILROAD CO.

Sixth Annual Report of the Board of Directors of the Central Southern Railroad Company, to the Stockholders, 1861. Nashville: 1861. V. 44

THE CENTURY Atlas of the World. New York: 1897. V. 45
THE CENTURY Atlas of the World. New York: 1903. V. 45
THE CENTURY Atlas of the World. New York: 1906. V. 45

THE CENTURY Dictionary and Cyclopedia. New York: 1906. V. 45

CENTURY Dictionary and Cyclopedia with a New Atlas of the World. New York: 1911. V. 40

THE CENTURY Guild Hobby Horse. Volume I. (Edited by H.P. Horne). Title page design by Selwyn Image, initials and decorations by Image and Horne, illustrations by Madox Brown, William Strang, Image, Blake, and Rossetti. London: 1886. V. 37

A CENTURY of Detective Stories. London. V. 46

CEPEDA, FERNANDO DE

Con Orden Que He Tenido Del Marques de Cadereyta, Virrey Desta Nueua Espana, Para Hazer Esta Relacion a V. Magestad del Mas Feliz Sucesso, Que en Muchos Siglos ha Dado Dios Nuestro Senor a Esta Monarquia, en la Detencion de la Flota Deste Reyno . . . Mexico: 1638. V. 40

Relacion que Embio a Su Magestad el Marques de Cadereyta, Virrey de la Nueua Espana . . . Madrid: 1639. V. 40

CEPHALAS, CONSTANTINE

Anthologiae Graecae. Oxford: 1766. V. 40

CERATI, ANTONIO

I Sanvitali, Prose e Versi di Filandro Cretense. Parma: 1787. V. 41

CERCEAU, JACQUES ANDROUET DU

French Chateaux and Gardens in the XVIth Century. New York: 1909. V. 41

CEREDI, GIUSEPPE

The Discorsi Sopra Il Modo d'alzar Acque da'Luoghi Bassi. Parma: 1567. V. 39

Tre Discorsi Sopra Il Modo D'Allzar Acque Da' Luoghi Bassi. In Parma: 1567. V. 38

CEREMONIES Attending the Unveiling of the Equestrian Statue to Major General George Armstrong Custer by the State of Michigan. N.P.: 1910. V. 37

CEREMONIES Attending the Unveiling of the Equestrian Statute to Major General George Armstrong Custer by the State of Michigan, and Formally Dedicated at the City of Monroe, Michigan, June Fourth, Nineteen Hundred and Ten . . . Detroit: 1911. V. 39; 44

CERNY, JAROSLAV

Coptic Etymological Dictionary. Cambridge: 1976. V. 44

Hieratic Ostraka. Oxford: 1957. V. 40; 42; 44

CERRI, URBANO

Etat Present de l'Eglise Romaine dans Toute les Parties du Monde. Amsterdam: 1716. V. 39

CERTAIN Necessary Directions, As Well for the Cure of the Plague, As For Preventing the Infection. London: 1665. V. 40

CERTAIN Sermons or Homilies Appointed to be Read in Churches, in the Time of Queen Elizabeth of Famous Memory . . . London: 1673. V. 41; 42

CERTAINE Sermons or Homilies Appointed to be Read in Churches. London: 1623. V. 38; 40; 41

CERVANTES SAAVEDRA, MIGUEL DE

V. 44

The Dialogues of the Dogs. 1969. V. 44

The Dialogue of the Dogs. By Miguel de Cervantes. Translated by Walter Kelly. Ornaments & Initials in Red and Green Engraved by Mallette Dean. Kentfield, Calif.: 1969. V. 37; 38; 43; 44; 46

The History of Don Quixote. London. V. 39

The History of Don Quioxte. London. V. 45

El Ingenioso Hidalgo Don Quixote de la Mancha. Brussels: 1607. V. 40

El Ingenioso Hidalgo Don Quixote de la Mancha. Madrid: 1608/15. V. 46

L'Ingegnoso Cittadino Don Chisciotte Della Mancia . . . Venice: 1622. V. 40

The History of the Valorous and Witty Knight Errant, Don Quixote of the Mancha. London: 1675. V. 40; 44

The History of the Valorous and Witty Knight Errant Don Quixote of the Mancha . . . London: 1725. V. 44

The History of the Knight Errant Don Quixote of the Mancha. London: 1731. V. 46

Vida y Hechos del Ingenioso Hidalgo Don Quixote de La Mancha. London: 1738. V. 42

The Life and Exploits of the Ingenious Gentleman Don Quixote de la Mancha. London: 1742. V. 37; 38; 40

The Life and Exploits of the Ingenious Gnetleman Don Quixote De La Mancha. London: 1752. V. 40

The History and Adventures of the Renowned Don Quixote. London: 1755. V. 37; 38; 39

The History of the Renowned Don Quixote de la Mancha. London: 1774. V. 40

El Ingenioso Hidalgo Don Quixote de la Mancha. Madrid: 1780; V. 40; 43

El Ingenioso Hidalgo Don Quixte De La Mancha . . . Madrid: 1797. V. 42

Don Quixote De La Mancha. Madrid: 1797-98. V. 40

The Life and Exploits of the Ingenious Gentleman Don Quixote de La Mancha. London: 1801. V. 40; 46

The Life and Exploits of the Ingenious Gentleman Don Quixote de la Mancha. London: 1810. V. 45

Don Quixote de la Mancha. London: 1818. V. 37; 38; 39; 42

Don Quixote de la Mancha. London: 1819. V. 37; 43

El Ingenioso Hidalgo Don Quixote De la Mancha. Madrid: 1829. V. 46

The History of Don Quixote. London: 1867. V. 40

The History of Don Quixote. London: 1868. V. 45

The History of the Ingenious Gentleman Don Quixote of La Mancha. Edinburgh: 1879. V. 42; 43; 44

The History of the Ingenious Gentleman Don Quixote of La Mancha. London: 1892. V. 40

Don Quixote de la Mancha. London: 1898. V. 39

Don Quixote of the Mancha. London: 1900. V. 43

El Ingenioso Hidalgo Don Quijote de la Mancha. Madrid: 1901. V. 39

The History of the Ingenious Gentleman Don Quixote. Edinburgh: 1910. V. 38; 44

History of the Valorous and Wittie Knight Errant Don Quixote of the Mancha. Chelsea: 1927. V. 46

CERVANTES SAAVEDRA, MIGUEL DE continued

The Historie of Don Quixote of the Mancha. Chelsea: 1927-28. V. 39; 41; 44; 45

The First (and Second) part(s) of the History of the Valorious and Wittie Knight-Errant Don Quixote of the Mancha. London: 1927-28. V. 37; 40; 42; 44; 45; 46

Don Quioxte de la Mancha. London: 1930. V. 40; 45; 46

El Ingenioso Hidalgo Don Quixote de La Mancha . . . (with) The Visionary Gentleman Dox Quixote de la Mancha. New York: 1932. V. 42; 46

Don Quixote of La Mancha. Barcelona: 1933. V. 40

El Ingenioso Hidalgo Don Quixote de la Mancha. Madrid: 1947. V. 46

Don Quixote. Mexico City: 1950. V. 44

The Life and Exploits of the Ingenious Gentleman Don Quixote de La Mancha. Translated by Charles Jarvis. London: 1749. V. 37

The History of the Ingenious Gentleman, Don Quixote of La Mancha. Edinburgh: 1822. V. 37; 42

Adventures of Don Quixote de la Mancha. London: 1866. V. 38

The History of the Ingenious Gentleman, Don Quixote of la Mancha. Translated from the Spanish by P.A. Motteux. Edinburgh: 1906. V. 37; 38

The History of Don Quixote. The text edited by J.W. Clark and a biographical notice of Cervantes by T. Teignmouth Shore. London: (ca. 1864-67). V. 37

The History of the Valorous and Witty - Knight Errant, Don Quixote of the Mancha. London: 1652. V. 37; 41

The Life and Exploits of the Ingenious Gentleman Don Quixote De la Mancha. London: 1749. V. 41

Don Quixote. Edinburgh: 1879. V. 41

The History of Don Quixote of La Mancha. London: 1880. V. 38

The History of the Ingenious Gentleman Don Quixote of La Manacha. London: 1892. V. 38

The History of the Renowned Don Quixote de la Mancha. London: 1774. V. 38

The Ingenious Gentleman Don Quixote of the Mancha. Philadelphia. V. 38

The Life and Exploits of . . . Don Quixote de la Mancha. London: 1788. V. 43

Novelas Exemplares. Brussels: 1614. V. 44

Novelas Exemplares. Pamplona: 1614. V. 44

Novellas Exemplares; or, Exemplary Novels in Six Books. London: 1743. V. 46

Persiles and Sigismunda. London: 1741. V. 37; 39; 40; 42; 45

The Spanish Ladie and Two Other Stories from Cervantes. London: 1928. V. 44

CERVIO, VINCENZO

Il Trinciante Di . . . Ampliato et A Perfettione Ridotto dal Cavalier Reale Fusoritto da Narni, Gia Trinciante dell'Illustrissimo. Roma: 1593. V. 38

CESALPINO, ANDREA 1519-1603

De Metallicis Libri Tres. Rome: 1596. V. 43

CESARESCO, EVELYN M.

The Fairies' Fountain and Other Stories. London: 1908. V. 44

CESCINKSY, HERBERT

The Old English Master Clockmakers and Their Clocks, 1670-1820. New York: 1938. V. 39

CESCINSKY, HERBERT

Early English Furniture and Woodwork. London: 1922. V. 39; 41; 42; 44; 45; 46

English Domestic Clocks. London: 1914. V. 39; 44

English Domestic Clocks Illustrated from Drawings and Photographs by Author. London: 1913. V. 39

English Furniture of the Eighteenth Century. London. V. 40

English Furniture of the Eighteenth Century. London. V. 38

English Furniture of the Eighteenth Century. London: 1909-11. V. 39; 44

English Furniture of the Eighteenth Century. 1909-12. V. 42

English Furniture of the Eighteenth Century. London: 1910. V. 39; 40

The Old English Master Clockmakers and Their Clocks 1670-1820. New York: 1938. V. 39; 45

CESNOLA, LUIGI PALMA DI 1832-1904

Cyprus: Its Ancient Citites, Tombs and Temples. London: 1877. V. 46

Cyprus: Its Ancient Cities, Tombs and Temples. New York: 1878. V. 40; 44

CESSOLIS, JACOBUS DE

The Game of the Chesse. London: 1855. V. 41

The Game of the Chesse by . . . Reproduced in Facsimile from a Copy in the British Museum. London: 1860. V. 38

The Game and Playe of the Chesse, 1474. London: 1883. V. 38

The Game of Chess. London: 1921. V. 42

The Game of Chess. Wembley Hill, London: 1921. V. 42

CETECEA, The Great Whales. Easthampton. V. 39

CEULEN, LUDOLPH VAN

Vanden Circkel. Delft: 1596. V. 41

CEZANNE, PAUL

Cezanne. Paris: 1914. V. 41

Preface d'Octave Mirbeau. Paris: 1914. V. 39

CHABERT, JOSEPH BERNARD, MARQUIS DE

Voyage fait Par Ordre du Roi en 1750 et 1751, Dans l'Amerique Septentrionale, Pour Rectifier les Cartes des Cotes de l'Acadie, de l'Isle Royale et de l'Isle de Terre-Neuve . . . Paris: 1753. V. 38; 39; 43; 44; 45

CHABOT, F. C.

McFarland Journal. San Antonio: 1942. V. 38

CHABOT, FREDERICK C.

The Alamo, Altar of Texas Liberty. San Antonio: 1931. V. 44

Excerpts from the Memorirs for the History of the Province of Texas. San Antonio: 1922. V. 44

Pictorial Sketch of Mission San Jose de San Miguel de Aguayo on the San Antonio River . . . San Antonio: 1935. V. 40

Texas Letters. San Antonio. V. 44

Texas Letters. San Antonio. V. 45

Texas Letters. San Antonio: 1940. V. 46

CHABOUILLET, A.

Description des Antiquites et Objets d'Art Composant le Cabinet de M. Louis Fould. Paris: 1861. V. 45

CHABREE, DOMINIQUE

Stirpium Icones et Sciagraphia . . . Geneva: 1666. V. 37

CHACON, PETRUS

De Triclinio, Sive de Modo Convivandi Apud Priscos Romanos . . . Amsterdam: 1689. V. 37

CHAD, G. W.

A Narrative of the Late Revolution in Holland. London: 1814. V. 46

CHADWICK, ALBERT

Little Churches of France - Their Origin: Their Characteristics . . . New York: 1930. V. 43

CHADWICK, ALBERT A.

Little Churches of France Their Origin, Their Periods. New York: & London: 1930. V. 43

CHADWICK, EDWARD MARION

Ontario Families. Toronto: 1894. V. 43

CHADWICK, EDWIN

Poor Law Commissioners Report . . . on an Inquiry into the Sanitary Condition of the Labouring Population of Great Britain. London: 1842. V. 38

Report (and Supplementary Report on Internment in Towns, and Sanitary Inquiry: England (and Wales) and Sanitary Inquiry - Scotland) to Her Majesty's Principal Secretary of State of the Home Department, from the Poor Law Commissioners . . . London: 1842-43. V. 42

CHADWICK, FRENCH E.

The Relations of the United States and Spain: Diplomacy. New York: 1909. V. 42

The Relations of the United States and Spain; the Spanish American War. New York: 1911. V. 42

CHADWICK, H. MUNRO

The Growth of Literature. Cambridge: 1932-40. V. 42

The Growth of Literature. Cambridge: 1968. V. 39

CHADWICK, JAMES R.

The Study and Practice of Medicine by Women. New York: 1879. V. 37; 39; 41

CHADWICK, WILLIAM

The Life and Times of Daniel Defoe. London: 1859. V. 38

CHAFFERS, W.

Catalogue of the Works of Antiquity and Art Collected by the Lage William Henry Forman and Removed to Callally Castle, Northumberland by A. H. Browne. London: 1892. V. 44

CHAFFERS, WILLIAM

Gilda Aurifaborum: a History of English Goldsmiths & Plateworkers, and Their Marks Stamped on Plate. London: 1883. V. 41

Marks and Monograms on European and Oriental Pottery and Porcelain, with Historical Notices of Each Manufactory. London: 1932. V. 41

Marks and Monograms on European and Oriental Pottery and Porcelain. London: 1912. V. 38

CHAGALL, BELLA

Brenendicke Licht. New York: 1945. V. 42; 46

CHAGALL, MARC

The Biblical Message. New York: 1973. V. 39

The Ceramics and Sculptures of Chagall. Monaco: 1972. V. 40; 41

Chagall at the 'Met'. Text by Emily Genauer. New York: 1971. V. 37; 44

Le Cirque. Geneve: 1972. V. 42

Drawings for the Bible. New York: 1960. V. 46

Drawings and Water Colors for the Ballet. New York: (1969). V. 37

His Graphic Work. New York: 1957. V. 46

Illustrations for the Bible by Marc Chagall. New York: 1956. V. 41

The Jerusalem Windows. 1962. V. 44

The Jerusalem Windows. New York: 1962. V. 41; 43

The Jerusalem Windows. (1962). V. 37

The Lithographs of Chagall. Chagall. Lithographs 1957-1962. The Lithographs of Chagall 1962-1968. The Lithographs of Chagall 1969-1973; Chagall Lithographs 1974-1979. Monte Carlo: 1960. V. 41

The Lithographs . . . Sauret: 1960. V. 45

Lithographs. Monte Carlo: Paris: 1960-86. V. 44

The Story of Exodus. Paris-New York: 1966. V. 38

Vitreaux pour Jerusalem. Introduction and notes by Jean Leymarie. Monte Carlo: 1962. V. 37; 40

CHAIGNEAU, WILLIAM

The History of Jack Connor. London: 1752. V. 38

CHAILLOU, JACQUES

Recherches sur l'Origine et le Mouvement du Sang, du Coeur, et de ses Vaisseux; du Lait, des Fievres Intermittentes & des Humeurs. (bound with) Trait du Mouvement des Humeurs, dans les Plus Ordinaires Emotions des Hommes. Paris: 1677-1678. V. 38

CHAILLU, PAUL B. DU

A Journey to Ashango-Land; and Further Penetration into Equatorial Africa. London: 1867. V. 42

CHAILLY, M.

A Practical Treatise on Midwifery. New York: 1844. V. 42

CHAIN AND HARDY

Topographical & Township Map of the Territories of New Mexico & Arizona . . . Denver: 1881. V. 37

CHAISNEAU, CHARLES

Tableau Elementaire d'Histoire Naturelle, Contenant Les Trois Regnes De La Nature . . . Paris: 1806. V. 42

CHALES, CLAUDE FRANCOIS MILLIET DE

Traitte du Mouvement Local, et du Ressort. Dans Lequel, Leur Nature & Leurs Casses, Sont Curieusement Recherchees & ou les Loix qu'ils Observent dans l'Acceleration & les Pendules, & Encore Dans la Percussion & la Reflexion des Corps . . . London:yon: 1682. V. 41

CHALFANT, W. A.

The Story of Inyo. N.P.: 1922. V. 46

CHALIAPIN, FEODOR

Man and Mask - Forty Years in the Life of a Singer. London: 1932. V. 42

CHALICE, HARRIET

A Narrative of the Recent Inhuman Murder of an Infant, by Its Mother! London: 1834. V. 42

CHALIFOUR, J. E.

Atlas of Canada. Ottawa: 1915. V. 37

CHALKLEN, CHARLES WILLIAM

Babylon: a Poem. London: 1821. V. 39

CHALKLEY, LYMAN

Chronicles of the Scotch-irish Settlement in Virginia Extracted from the Original Court Records of Augusta County 1745-1800. Rosslyn: 1912. V. 46

CHALKLEY, THOMAS

A Collection of the Works of . . . Philadelphia: 1749. V. 43; 45

A Collection of the Works of that Ancient Faithful Servant of Jesus Christ . . . Who Departed This Life in the Island of Tortola . . . London: 1791. V. 44

CHALLE, CHARLES MICHEL ANGE

Description du Mausolee Erige . . . pour les Obseques de . . . Louis XV. (and) Description du Catafalque . . . (and) Description du Mausolee de Tres-Haute . . . Reine de France. (and) Oraison Funebre de Tres Haut . . . Paris: 1774-74-68-76. V. 38

CHALLICE, ANNIE EMMA

French Authors at Home. London: 1864. V. 45

CHALLONER, RICHARD

The Grounds of the Old Religion: or, Some General ARgument in Favour of the Catholick, Apostolick, Roman Communion . . . 1742. V. 45

The True Principles of a Catholic. Philadelphia: 1789. V. 46

CHALMERS, ALEXANDER

The British Essaysits; with Prefaces, Historical and Biographical. London: 1823. V. 38; 41; 44

The General Biographical Dictionary. London: 1812. V. 42

The General Biographical Dictionary . . . London: 1812-17. V. 38; 42

A History of the Colleges, Halls and Public Buildings, Attached to the University of Oxford, Including the Lives of the Founders. Oxford: 1810. V. 37; 41; 45

The Works of the English Poets from Chaucer to Cowper. London: 1969-70. V. 39

CHALMERS, CHARLES

Electro-Chemistry, with positive results; and Notes for Inquiry on the Sciences of Geology and Astronomy; with a Tract of Miscellanies. London: 1858. V. 37

Notes, Thoughts, and Inquiries. London: 1852. V. 37

CHALMERS, GEORGE 1742-1825

Caledonia; or, an Account Historical and Topographic of North Britain. London: 1807. V. 46

A Collection of Treaties Between Great Britain and Other Papers. London: 1790. V. 42

An Estimate of the Compartive Strength of Great Britain During the Present and Four Preceding Reigns, and of the Losses of Her Trade from Every War Since the Revolution. London: 1786. V. 38; 39; 41

An Estimate of the Comparative Strength of Great Britain During the Present and Four Preceding Reigns and of the Losses of Her Trade from Every War since the Revolution. London: 1794. V. 37; 40; 41; 43; 46

An Estimate of the Comparative Strength of Great Britain and of the Losses of Her Trade . . . London: 1804. V. 43

The Life of Thomas Paine, the Author of Rights of Man. London: 1791. V. 39; 42

The Life of Thomas Ruddiman. London: 1794. V. 37; 38; 41; 42; 45; 46

The Life of Mary, Queen of Scots; Drawn from the State Papers. With Six Subsidiary Memoirs. Illustrated with Ten Plates of Medals, Portraits and Prospects. London: 1818. V. 37; 38

Opinions on Interesting Subjects of Public Law and Commercial Policy Arising from American Independence. London: 1784; V. 37; 38; 41; 42

Opinions on Interesting Subjects of Public Law and Commercial Policy. London: 1785. V. 37; 38

Political Annals of the Present United Colonies, from the Settlement to the Peace of 1763. London: 1780. V. 38; 41

A Supplemental Apology for the Believers in the Shakespeare-Papers: Being a Reply to Mr. Malone's Answer, which was early announced but never published; with a dedication to George Steevens and a Postscript to J. Matthais . . . London: 1799. V. 37

CHALMERS, JAMES

The Channel Railway Connecting England and France. London: 1861. V. 38; 40

Pioneer Life and Work in New Guinea 1877-1894. London: 1895. V. 40

Plain Truth: Addressed to the Inhabitants of America. Dublin: 1776. V. 40

Plain Truth: Addressed to the Inhabitants of America. London: 1776. V. 41; 46

Strictures on a Pamphlet Written by Thomas Paine, on the English System of Finance. London: 1796. V. 39

CHALMERS, JOHN P.

A Bookbinders' Florilegium. Austin: 1988. V. 40; 43; 44

CHALMERS, LIONEL

An Account of the Weather and Diseases of South-Carolina. London: 1776. V. 38

CHALMERS, MARGARET

Poems. Newcastle: 1813. V. 39; 42

CHALMERS, PATRICK R.

Birds Ashore and Aforeshore. 1935. V. 46

Birds Ashore and Aforeshore. London: 1935. V. 39; 43; 44; 45; 46

A Dozen Dogs or So. London: 1928. V. 46

Gun-Dogs. London: 1931. V. 39

The History of Hunting. London: 1936. V. 39

Kenneth Grahame. Life, Letters and Unpublished Work. London: 1933. V. 41

CHALMERS, THOMAS 1780-1847

The Application of Christianity to the Commercial and Ordinary Affairs of Life . . . Glasgow: 1820. V. 39; 42

CHALMERS, THOMAS 1780-1847 continued

Letter to the Royal Commissioners for the Visitation of Colleges in Scotland. Glasgow: 1832. V. 46

Of the Power, Wisdom and Goodness of God as Manifested in the Adaption of External Nature to the Moral and Intellectual Constitution of Man. London: 1833. V. 37

On the Use and Abuse of Literary and Ecclesiastical Endowments. Glasgow: 1827. V. 45

On Political Economy, in Connexion with the Moral State and Moral Prospects of Society. Glasgow: 1832. V. 38; 42; 44; 46

On the Power Wisdom and Goodness of God as Manifested in the Adaptation of External Nature to the Moral and Intellectual Constitution of Man. London: 1834. V. 37; 40

On the Wisdom and Goodness of God as manifested in the Adaptation of External Nature to the Moral and Intellectual Constitution of Man. London: 1839. V. 42

Sermons, Preached in the Tron Church, Glasgow. Glasgow: 1819. V. 40; 43

Sketches of Moral and Mental Philosophy: Their Connexion With Each Other and Their Bearings on Doctrinal and Practical Christianity. Edinburgh: 1857. V. 43; 45

CHALON, JOHN JAMES

Twenty Four Subjects Exhibiting the Costume of Paris. London: 1820-22. V. 38

CHALONER & FLEMING, LIVERPOOL.

The Mahogany Tree. Liverpool: 1850. V. 40

CHALONER, EDWARD

The Mahogany Tree. Liverpool: 1850. V. 38

CHALONER SMITH, JOHN

British Mezzotint Portraits. London: 1884. V. 45

CHALONER, W. G.

Evolution and Environment in the Late Silurian and Early Devonian. London: 1986. V. 37

CHAMBAUD, LOUIS

Fables Choisies. Baltimore: 1810. V. 46

A Grammar of the French Tongue. London: 1787. V. 41

CHAMBERLAIN, ARTHUR B.

Hans Holbein the Younger. London: 1913. V. 37; 39; 40; 43

CHAMBERLAIN, BASIL HALL

Things Japanese Being Notes on Various Subjects Connected with Japan for the Use of Travellers and Others. Tokyo: 1902. V. 41

CHAMBERLAIN, BRENDA

Alun Lewis and the Making of the Caseg Broadsheets. London: 1970. V. 42

The Green Heart - Poems. London: 1958. V. 41

Poems with Drawings. London: 1969. V. 42

CHAMBERLAIN, FREDERICK

Lucretia; or, the Robbers of the Hyrcanean Forest: a Romance. London: 1810. V. 44

CHAMBERLAIN, GEORGE AGNEW

African Hunting Among the Thongas. New York: 1923. V. 43; 46

CHAMBERLAIN, JACOB CHESTER

A Bibliography of the First Editions . . . of Henry Wadsworth Longfellow. New York: 1908. V. 39

CHAMBERLAIN, JOSEPH EDGAR

The Listener in the Town, the Listener in the Country. Boston: 1896. V. 41

CHAMBERLAIN, NEWLL D.

The Call of Gold. Mariposa: 1936. V. 43

CHAMBERLAIN PRESS

Chamberlain Press, 1980-1985. Portland: 1986. V. 42

CHAMBERLAIN, R. S.

The Conquest and Colonization of Yucatan, 1517-1550. Washington: 1948. V. 37

CHAMBERLAIN, SAMUEL

Domestic Architecture in Rural France. New York: 1928. V. 42

France Will Live Again: the Portrait of a Peaceful Interlude 1919-1939. New York: 1940. V. 41

Tudor Homes of England . . . New York: 1929. V. 44; 46

CHAMBERLAIN, SARAH

Alphabetarium. 1982. V. 41

Alphabetarium. 1982. V. 43

CHAMBERLAINE, JOHN 1745-1812

Imitations of Original Drawings by Hans Holbein, in the Collection of His Majesty, for the Portraits of Nortorious Persons of the Court of Henry VIII. London: 1792-1800. V. 39

Original Designs of the Most Celebrated Masters of the Bolognese, Roman, florentine & Venetian Schools . . . In His Majesty's Collection. London: 1812. V. 39

CHAMBERLAINE, WILLIAM W.

Memoirs of the Civil War Between the Northern and Southern Sections of the United States of America, 1861 to 1865. Washington: 1912. V. 44

CHAMBERLAYNE, C. G.

Ham Chamberlayne, Virginian. Richmond: 1932. V. 37; 38

CHAMBERLAYNE, E. H.

War History and the Roll of the Richmond Fayette Artillery, 38th Virginia Battalion Artillery, Confederate States Army, 1861-65. Richmond: 1883. V. 44

CHAMBERLAYNE, EDWARD 1616-1703

Angliae Notitia. London: 1704. V. 40

Englands Wants: or, Several Proposals Probably Beneficial for England, Humbly Offered to the Consideration of all Good Patriots in Both Houses of Parliament. London: 1685. V. 39; 46

Magnae Britanniae Notitia: or, the Present State of Great Britain, with Divers Remarks Upon the Antient State Thereof. London: 1708. V. 46

The New State of England, Under Our Present Monarch K. William III. London: 1702. V. 46

The Present Warre Parallel'd. N.P.: 1647. V. 44

The Present Warre Parallel'd. N.P.: 1647. V. 39

CHAMBERLAYNE, ISRAEL

The Australian Captive; or, an Authentic Narrative of Fifteen Years in the Life of William Jackman. New York: 1859. V. 46

CHAMBERLAYNE, JOANNES

Oratio Dominica . . . Plus Centum Linguis Versionibus aut Characteribus Reddita et Expressa . . . (with) Dissertationes ex Occasione Sylloges Ortionum Dominicarum. Amsterdam: 1715. V. 38

CHAMBERLAYNE, JOHN

Magnae Britanniae Notitia. London: 1741. V. 39

Magnae Britanniae Notitia: or, the present state of Great Britain; with diverse remarks upon the ancient state thereof. The Thirty-Sixth edition of the South Part, called England, and the fifteenth of the North Part . . . London: 1745. V. 37

Memoirs of the Royal Academy of Sciences in Paris Epitomised. London: 1721. V. 45

Oratio Dominica in Diversas Omnium Fere Gentium Linguas Versa et Propriis Cujusque Linguae Characteribus Expressa, Una cum Dissertationibus Nonnullis de Linguarum Origine, Variisque Ipsarum Permutationibus . . . Amstelaedmai: 1715. V. 45

CHAMBERLAYNE, JOHN HAMPDEN

Ham Chamberlayne - Virginian: Letters and Papers of an Artillery Officer in the War for Southern Independence, 1861-1865. Richmond: 1932. V. 42

CHAMBERLEN, HUGH

A Few Proposals Humbly Recommending . . . the Establishing a Land-Credit in this Kingdom . . . Edinburgh. V. 38

A Fund for Supplying and Preserving Our Coin. Or, an Essay on the Project of New-Coining Our Silver. N.P.,: 1695. V. 38

CHAMBERLIN, A. N.

The Shorter Catechism with Proof Texts. 1892. V. 38

CHAMBERLIN, JOHN

Noticia de la Gran Bretana con Relacion a su Estado Antiguo y Presente. Madrid: 1767. V. 37

CHAMBERLIN, THOMAS

History of the 150 Pennsylvania Volunteers, Second Regiment, Bucktail Brigade. Philadelphia: 1905. V. 42

CHAMBERS, A. H. 1763-1853

Thoughts on the Resumption of Cash Payments by the Bank; and on the Corn Bill, as Connected with that Measure; in a Letter Addressed to the Right Hon. the Chancellor of the Exchequer. London: 1819. V. 38; 41

CHAMBERS, A. J.

Recollections . . . N.P.: 1948. V. 42

CHAMBERS, ABRAHAM HENRY

Observations on the Formation, State and Condition of Turnpike Roads, and Other Highways with Suggestions for Their Permanent Improvement on Scientific Principles by Means of Natural Materials . . . London: 1820. V. 39; 42

CHAMBERS, ALEX

A History of the University of Oxford, Including the Lives of the Founders. Oxford: 1810. V. 38

CHAMBERS, ANDREW JACKSON

Recollections by Andrew Jackson Chambers. N.P.: 1944. V. 39

Recollections. N.P.: 1947. V. 43

Recollections. N.P.: 1947. V. 42

Recollections by Andrew Jackson Chambers. N.P.: 1947. V. 40

Recollections by . . . N.P.: 1947. V. 38

Recollections of Andrew Jackson Chambers. N.P.: 1947. V. 43

Recollections by . . . (N.P.: ca. 1947). V. 37

CHAMBERS, C. E. S.

A Catalogue of Some of the Rarer Books, Also Manuscripts in the Collection of . . . Edinburgh: 1889. V. 45

CHAMBERS Cyclopaedia of English Literature. London: 1978. V. 46

CHAMBERS, D.

Cock-A-Hoop, A Sequel to Chanticleer, pertelote, and Cockalorum. Being a Bibliography of the Golden Cockerel Press 1949-1961. By D. Chambers & Christopher Sandford. London: (1959). V. 37

CHAMBERS, DAVID

Joan Hassall: Engravings and Drawings. 1985. V. 44

Joan Hassall: Engravings and Drawings. London: 1985. V. 37; 40; 41

Lucien Pissaro, Notes on a Selection of Wood-Blocks Held at the Ashmolean Museum, Oxford. Ilkley: 1980. V. 42

Notes on a Selection of Wood Blocks Held at the Ashmolean Museum, Oxford. Oxford: 1981. V. 44

CHAMBERS, DAVID, LORD ORMOND 1530?-1592

Histoire Abbrege de Tous les Roys de France, Angleterre et Ecosse, Mise en Ordre par Forme d'Harmonie . . . Paris: 1579. V. 43

CHAMBERS, E. J.

Canada's Fertile Northland. Ottawa: 1908. V. 43; 44

CHAMBERS, E. K.

The Elizabethan Stage. Oxford: 1923. V. 42

The Elizabethan Stage. 1974. V. 40

The Mediaeval Stage. Oxford: 1978. V. 42

William Shakespeare, a Study of Facts and Problems. Oxford: 1930. V. 42

William Shakespeare a Study of Facts and Problems. Oxford: 1963. V. 42

CHAMBER'S Encyclopeida. Philadelphia: 1870. V. 40

CHAMBERS, EPHRAIM

Cyclopaedia; or, an Universal Dictionary of Arts and Sciences . . . London: 1751-52. V. 39

Cyclopaedia; or, an Universal Dictionary of Arts and Sciences. London: 1784-89. V. 40

Cyclopaedia; or, an Universal Dictionary of Arts and Sciences . . . London: 1786. V. 37; 46

Cyclopaedia; or an Universal Dictionary of Arts and Sciences . . . (with) A Supplement to Mr. Chambers' Cyclopaedia. London: 1741, 1753. V. 37

Cyclopaedia: or, An Universal Dictionary of Arts and Sciences . . . (with) Supplement and Modern Improvements Incorporated in One Alphabet, by Abrham Rees. London: 1786-91. V. 37

Cyclopaedia: or, an universal dictionary of arts and sciences . . . with the supplement and modern improvements incorporated in one alphabet by Abraham Rees. In four volumes (& volume of plates). London: 1786-83. V. 37

CHAMBERS, ERNEST J.

Canada's Fertile Northland. (with) Portfolio of Maps to Accompany Report. Ottawa: 1908. V. 40

History of the 90th Regiment, Winnipeg Rifles. Winnipeg: 1906. V. 37

The Royal Grenadiers. Toronto: 1904. V. 40

CHAMBERS, GEORGE

A Tribute to the principles etc. of the Irish and Scotch Early Settlers of Pennsylvania. (By a descendant). Chambersburg, PA: 1871. V. 37

CHAMBERS, GEORGE W.

San Agustin: First Cathedral Church in Arizona. Tucson: 1974. V. 38

CHAMBERS, JAMES

The Poetical Works of James Chambers, Itinerant Poet, with the LIfe of the Author. Ipswich: 1820. V. 43

CHAMBERS, JOHN

A General History of Malvern. Worcester: 1817. V. 39; 44

A Pocket Herbal. Bury: 1800. V. 40; 46

CHAMBER'S Journal, 1865. London & Edinburgh: 1865. V. 38

CHAMBERS, JULIUS

The Mississippi River and Its Wonderful Valley, Twenty-Seven Hundred and Seventy-Five Miles from Source to Sea. New York: 1910. V. 37

CHAMBERS, PATRICK

A Dozen Dogs or So. London: 1928. V. 41

CHAMBERS, R.

The Book of Days. London & Edinburgh: 1888. V. 41

CHAMBERS, ROBERT

A Biographical Dictionary of Eminent Scotsmen. Glasgow: 1835. V. 44

Domestic Annals of Scotland from the Reformation to the Revolution. Edinburgh & London: 1869. V. 45

The Scottish Songs. London: 1829. V. 40

Tracings of Iceland and the Faroe Islands. London: 1856. V. 40

Vestiges of the Natural History of Creation. London: 1844. V. 37; 45; 46

Vestiges of the Natural History of Creation. (with) Explanations . . . New York: 1845 & 1846. V. 38

Vestiges of the Natural History of Creation. New York: 1846. V. 39; 45

Vestiges of the Natural History of Creation. London: 1860. V. 38; 45

Vestiges of the Natural History of Creation. London: and Edinburgh: 1884. V. 45

CHAMBERS, ROBERT W.

The King in Yellow. Chicago: 1895. V. 39

The King in Yellow. London: 1895. V. 39

CHAMBERS, THOMAS

Catalogue of . . . Library of Books. Sheffield: 1870. V. 45

CHAMBERS, THOMAS F.

The Early Germans of New Jersey Their History, Churches and Genealogies. Dover: 1895. V. 39; 41

CHAMBERS, WILLIAM

Atlas of Ancient and Modern Geography. Edinburgh: 1845. V. 41

Chamber's Atlas for the People, with Descriptive Introduction. London:/Edinburgh: 1855. V. 45

Designs of Chinese Buildings, Furniture, Dresses, Machines and Utensils. London: 1757. V. 37; 38; 39; 40; 42

A Dissertation on Oriental Gardening. London: 1772. V. 38; 39; 40; 41; 44

Exploits and Anecdotes of the Scottish Gypsies with Traits of Their Origin, Character and Manners. Edinburgh: 1886. V. 45

Memoir of Robert Chambers. Edinburgh: 1872. V. 44; 45

Plans . . . of the Gardens and Buildings at Kew in Surrey. London: 1966. V. 38

Things As They Are in America. London: & Edinburgh: 1854. V. 39; 43

Things as They Are in America. Philadelphia: 1854. V. 39

Traite des Edifices, Meubles, Habits, Machines et Utensils des Chinois . . . Paris: 1776. V. 41

A Treatise on Civil Architecture in Which the Principles of that Are are Laid Down. London: 1759. V. 37; 38

A Treatise on Civil Architecture. London: 1768. V. 38

A Treatise on the Decorative Part of Civil Architecture. London: 1791. V. 38; 41

A Treatise on the Decorative Part of Civil Architecture . . . London: 1825. V. 39

A Treatise on the Decorative Part of Civil Architecture. London: 1862. V. 46

A Treatise on the Decorative Part of Civil Architecture . . . London: 1862. V. 40

CHAMBLESS, E.

Roadtown. 1910. V. 44

CHAMBLISS, WILLIAM H.

Chambliss' Diary; or Society As It Really Is. New York: 1895. V. 39

CHAMBOUT DE PONT CHATEAU, S. J. DU

The Moral Practice of the Jesuites Demonstrated by Many Remarkable Histories of Their Actions in All Parts of the World. London: 1671. V. 45

THE CHAMELEON. London. V. 41

CHAMEROVZOW, LOUIS ALEXIS

The Chronicles of the Bastile. London: 1845. V. 40; 42

CHAMFORT

Maxims and Considerations of Chamfort. London: 1926. V. 44

CHAMFORT, SEBASTIAN ROCH NICHOLAS DE

Maxims and Considerations of Chamfort. Waltham St. Lawrence: 1926. V. 37

CHAMFORT, SEBASTIEN ROCH NICOLAS DE

Maxims and Considerations. Berkshire: 1926. V. 46

CHAMIER, FREDERICK

Ben Brace, the Last of Nelson's Agaemnons. London: 1836. V. 42

Ben Brace, the Last of Nelson's Agamemnons. London: 1850. V. 40

CHAMIER, FREDERICK continued

The Life of a Sailor, By a Captain in the Navy. London: 1832. V. 39; 42

The Life of a Sailor. London: 1833. V. 39

My Travels: or an Unsentimental Journey through France, Switzerland and Italy. London: 1855. V. 43

The Unfortunate Man. London: 1835. V. 45

CHAMISSO, ADALBERT VON 1781-1838

Peter Schlemihl's Wundersame Geschichte. The Wonderful History of Peter Schlemihl. London: 1843. V. 38

CHAMISSO, ADELBERT VON 1781-1838

Peter Schlemihl. London: 1824. V. 39; 40; 41; 43

Peter Schlemihl. London: 1861. V. 38

A Sojourn at San Francisco Bay 1816 By . . . Scientist of the Russian Exploring Ship Rurik Illustrated by a Series of Drawings First Published in 1822 by the Rurik's Artist Louis Choris. San Francisco: 1936. V. 41; 45

THE CHAMPAGNE Charlie and Coal Oil Tommy Songster. San Francisco: 1868. V. 46

CHAMPIER, SYMPHORIEN

Claudii Galeni Pergameni Historiales Campi . . . In Quatuor Libros Congesti & Commentarijs Non Poenitendis Illustrati. D. Symphoriani Campegii Clysteriorum Camporum Secundum Galeni Mentem Libellus Utilis . . . Basilae: 1532. V. 38; 42

CHAMPIER, V.

Exposition Universelle, 1900. The Chefs - D'Oeuvre. Philadelphia: 1900-02. V. 41

CHAMPION DE CRESPIGNY, MARY CLARKE, LADY d. 1812

Letters of Advice from a Mother to Her Son. London: 1803. V. 46

CHAMPION, JOSEPH

New and Complete Alphabets in All the Various Hands . . . London: 1770? V. 40

CHAMPION, RICHARD

Two Centuries of Ceramic Art in Bristol Being a History of the Manufacture of 'The True Porcelain' . . . London: 1873. V. 39

CHAMPION, THOMAS EDWARD

History of the 10th Royals and of the Royal Grenadiers from the Formation of the Regiment Until 1896. Toronto: 1896. V. 41

CHAMPLAIN, SAMUEL DE

Oeuvres de Champlain Publiees Sous Le Patronage de l'Universite Laval . . . Quebec: 1870. V. 42; 44

Les Voyages de la Nouvelle France Occidentale, Dicte Canada, Faits par le Sr. de Champlain . . . Paris: 1632. V. 38; 39; 40

Voyages of Samuel de Champlain. Boston: 1878-82. V. 38

Voyages of Samuel De Champlain. Boston: 1880-82. V. 37

The Works of Samuel de Champlain. Toronto: 1922-36. V. 45

The Works of Samuel de Champlain. Toronto: 1971. V. 38; 43; 44; 45; 46

CHAMPLIN, EDWIN R.

Lovers' Lyrics, and Other Songs. Philadelphia: 1888. V. 40

CHAMPLIN, JAMES

Early Biography, Travels and Adventures of Rev. James Champlin, who Was Born Blind. Columbus. V. 40

CHAMPLIN, JOHN D.

Hayti. New York: 1880. V. 41

CHAMPNEYS, AMIAN L.

Public Libraries. A Treatise on Their Design, Construction & Fittings. With a Chapter on the Principles of Planning & a Summary of the Law. With many illustrations of Modern Examples & Fittings from Photographs & Drawins. London: 1907. V. 37

CHAMPNEYS, ARTHUR C.

Irish Ecclesiastical Architecture with Some Notice of Similar or Related Works in England, Scotland, and Elsewhere. London: 1910. V. 42; 44

CHAMPOLLION, JEAN FRANCOIS

Dictionnaire Egyptien en Ecriture Hieroglyphique. 1841. V. 40

L'Egypte sous les Pharaons, ou Recherches sur la Geographie, la Religion, la Language, les Ecritures et l'Histoire de l'Egypte Avant l'Invasion de Chambyse. Paris: 1814. V. 40

CHAMPOMIER, P. A.

Statement of Sugar Made in Louisiana in 1844. New Orleans: 1845. V. 39; 44

A Statement of the Sugar Crop Made in Louisiana in 184-46. New Orleans: 1846. V. 42

Statement of the Sugar Crop Made in Louisian in 1850-51. New Orleans: 1851. V. 44

Statement of the Sugar Crop Made in Louisiana in 1851-52, with an Appendix. New Orleans: 1852. V. 37; 41

A Statement of the Sugar Crop of Louisiana, of 1859-60. New Orleans: 1860. V. 42; 46

Statement of the Sugar Crop of Louisiana of 1860-61. New Orleans: 1861. V. 42

Statement of the Sugar Crop, Made in Louisiana, in 1861-62 with an Appendix. New Orleans: 1862. V. 39; 42; 43

CHANCE, EDWARD J.

On the Nature, Causes, Variety and Treatment of Bodily Deformities . . . London: 1862. V. 43

CHANCELLOR, EDWIN BERESFORD

The Lives of the Rakes. London: 1924. V. 44

The Lives of the Rakes. London: 1924 & 1925. V. 37

CHANCELLOR, WILLIAM E.

Our Presidents and Their Office . . . New York: 1912. V. 42

CHANCERY Lane; or, The Glass Case. London: 1862. V. 39

CHANDLER, BRUCE

Lovejoy, Excerpts from a Memoir. Boston: 1988. V. 44

CHANDLER, C. H.

The History of New Ipswich, New Hampshire 1735-1914 with Genealogical Records of the Principal Families. Fitchburg: 1914. V. 39

CHANDLER, ELIZABETH MARGARET 1807-1834

The Poetical Works. (with) Essays, Philanthropic and Moral . . . Philadelphia: 1836. V. 43

CHANDLER, FRANCIS W.

Municipal Architecture in Boston, from Designs by Edmund M. Wheelwright, 1891-95. Boston: 1898. V. 44

CHANDLER, FRANK W.

The Literature of Roguery. Boston: 1907. V. 38

CHANDLER, GEORGE

A Treatise on the Diseases of the Eye, and Their Remedies, To Which is Prefixed, the Anatomy of the Eye . . . London: 1780. V. 45

CHANDLER, GOERGE

Four Centuries of Banking as Illustrated by the Bankers, Customers and Staff Associated with the Consituents Banks of Martins Bank Limited. London: 1964-68. V. 41

CHANDLER, HELEN

Illustration Portfolio No. 1 . . . Los Angeles: 1925. V. 44

CHANDLER, J G.

Remarkable Story of Chicken Little. Roxbury: 1842. V. 38

CHANDLER, JOHN

A Treatise of the Disease Called a Cold . . . London: 1761. V. 41

CHANDLER, JOSEPH EVERETT

the Colonial Architecture of Maryland, Pennsylvania and Virginia. Boston: 1900. V. 46

CHANDLER, MARY

A Description of Bath: a Poem. London: 1763. V. 40; 43

CHANDLER, MELBOURNE C.

Of Garrvowen in Glory. Annadales: 1960. V. 45

CHANDLER, MR.

In the Senate of the United States . . . from the Select Committee on Indian Traders. Washington: 1889. V. 43

CHANDLER, PELEG W.

American Criminal Trails. Boston: 1841. V. 37; 43; 45

CHANDLER, R.

Travels in Asia Minor. London: 1776, V. 40

CHANDLER, RAYMOND 1886-1959

Backfire. Santa Barbara: 1984. V. 45; 46

Before Marlowe. 1973. V. 42

The Big Sleep. 1939. V. 39

The Big Sleep. London: 1939. V. 45; 46

The Big Sleep. New York: 1939. V. 38; 39; 42; 44

The Big Sleep. London: 1945. V. 41; 42

The Big Sleep. San Francisco: 1986. V. 41; 42

Chandler Before Marlowe. 1973. V. 41

Farewell My Lovely. 1940. V. 39

CHANDLER, RAYMOND 1886-1959 continued

Farewell, My Lovely. New York: 1940. V. 37; 41; 42; 45; 46

The Finger Man and other Stories. 1946. V. 39

The Finger Man and Other Stories. 1946. V. 39

The Finger Man and Other Stories. New York: 1946. V. 46

Five Murderers. 1944. V. 39

Five Sinister Characters. 1945. V. 39

Five Sinister Characters. New York: 1945. V. 37; 41; 42

The High Window. New York: 1942. V. 37; 38; 39; 41; 45; 46

Killer in the Rain. 1964. V. 45

Killer in the Rain. 1964. V. 39

Killer in the Rain. London: 1964. V. 40; 43; 45; 46

The Lady in the Lake. 1943. V. 39

Lady in the Lake. London: 1945. V. 42

The Lady in the Lake. New York: 1943. V. 37; 39; 44; 45; 46

Letters. Santa Barbara: 1978. V. 39; 44

The Little Sister. 1949. V. 39

The Little Sister. Boston: 1949. V. 37; 38; 39; 41; 42; 43; 44; 45; 46

The Long Goodbye. 1953. V. 39

The Long Goodbye. London: 1953. V. 40; 42; 43; 45; 46

The Long Goodbye. Boston: 1954. V. 37; 42

Playback. 1958. V. 39

Playback. London: 1958. V. 39; 43; 45; 46

Poodle Springs. 1989. V. 45

The Raymond Chandler Omnibus. 1944. V. 43

The Raymond Chandler Omnibus. London: 1953. V. 46

Raymond Chandler Speaking. London: 1962. V. 46

Raymond Chandler's Unknown Thriller: the Screenplay of Playback. New York: 1985. V. 44

The Raymond Chandler Omnibus. 1944. V. 37

The Simple Art of Murder. Boston: 1950. V. 37; 39; 43; 45

CHANDLER, RICHARD

The History and Proceedings of the House of Commons (Relating to 1660 to 1743). London: 1742-44. V. 38; 45

Inscriptiones Antiquae, Pleraeque Nondum Editae. Oxford: 1774. V. 39

Ionian Antiquities, Published, with Persmission of the Society of Dilettanti, by . . . London: 1769. V. 39

Ionian Antiquities, Published, with Permission of the Society of Dilettanti . . . London: 1784. V. 45

The Life of William Waynflete, Bishop of Winchester, Lord High Chancellor of England in the Reign of Henry VI . . . London: 1811. V. 44; 46

The Life of William of Waynflete, Bishop of Winchester. London: 1840. V. 40

Travels in Asia Minor. Oxford: 1775. V. 42; 46

Travels in Asia Minor and Greece. Oxford: 1825. V. 42

Travels in Asia Minor; or An Account of a Tour Made at the Expense of the Socety of Dilettanti. London: 1776. V. 37; 39; 42; 46

Travels in Greece. London: 1776. V. 39

CHANDLER, THOMAS BRADBURY

The Appeal Farther Defended; in an Answer to the Farther Misrepresentations of Dr. Chauncy. 1771. V. 43

The Appeal Farther Defended, in Answer to the Farther Misrepresentation of Dr. Chauncy. New York: 1771. V. 39; 46

The Appeal Defended: or, The Proposed American Episcopate Vindicated, in Answer to the Objections and Misrepresentations of Dr. Chauncy and Others. New York: 1769. V. 37; 38

The life of Samuel Johnson, D.D. The First President of King's College in New York . . . New York: 1805. V. 37

CHANDLER, WILLIAM ASTOR

Through Jungle and Desert - Travels in Eastern Africa. London: 1896. V. 42

CHANDLESS, WILLIAM

A Visit to Salt Lake; Being a Journey Across the Plains and Residence in the Mormon Settlements at Utah. London: 1857. V. 38; 39; 43

A Visit to Salt Lake: Being a Journey Across the Plains and a Residence in the Mormon Settlements at Utah. London: 1857. V. 38; 41; 42; 43; 45

CHANDOS Herald. The Black Prince. An Historical Poem, Written in French . . . London: 1842. V. 43

CHANDOS OF SUDLEY, GREY BRYDGES, 5TH BARON d. 1601

Horae Subsecivae. Observations and Discussion. London: 1620. V. 40

THE CHANGED Cross. London: 1875. V. 40

CHANLER, WILLIAM A.

Through Jungle and Desert. New York: 1896. V. 38

CHANNING, HENRY

The Consideration of Divine Goodness an Argument for Religious Gratitude and Obedience. A Sermon Delivered at New London, November 27, 1794. New-London: 1794. V. 45

CHANNING, WALTER

A Treatise on Etherization in Childbirth. Boston: 1848. V. 39; 40

CHANNING, WILLIAM ELLERY 1780-1840

Carta al Honorable Henrique Clay Sobre la Agregacion de Tejas a los Estados-Unidos, por Guillermo E. Channing. Mexico: 1837. V. 42

Discourses, Reviews and Miscellanies. Boston: 1830. V. 39

Discourses, Reviews, and Miscellanies. Boston: 1830/34. V. 42

A Letter to the Hon. Henry Clay, on the Annexation of Texas to the United States. Boston: 1836. V. 39

A Letter to the Hon. Henry Clay, on the Annexation of Texas. Boston: 1837. V. 40; 45

Poems. Boston: 1843. V. 45; 46

Thoreau the Poet Naturalist with Memorial Verses. Boston: 1902. V. 42; 45

Thoughts on the Evils of a Spirit of Conquest, and on Slavery: A Letter on the Annexation of Texas to the United States. London: 1837. V. 37

The Woodman and Other Poems. Boston: 1849. V. 45

The Works. Glasgow: 1840. V. 43; 46

CHANSON DE ROLAND

The Song of Roland. Boston: 1906. V. 46

The Song of Roland. Cambridge: 1906. V. 45

The Song of Roland. London: 1919. V. 46

The Song of Roland, Done Into English in the Original Measure by Charles Scott Moncrieff. New York: 1938. V. 38; 39; 43; 45; 46

The Song of Roland. New York: 1938.5. V. 41

CHANTICLEER. A Bibliography of the Golden Cockerel Press, April 1921-1936 August. 1936. V. 45; 46

CHAPELLE, HOWARD I.

The Baltimore Clipper. Its Origin and Development. Salem: 1930. V. 39

CHAPIN, ANNA ALICE

The Everyday Fairy Book. New York: 1915. V. 42

The Everyday Fairy Book. London: 1917. V. 46

The Everyday Fairy Book. London: 1924. V. 46

The Everyday Fairy Book. London: 1930. V. 43

The Now-A-Days Fairy Book. New York: 1911. V. 37; 41; 44

CHAPIN, FREDERICK

Mountaineering in Colorado. Boston: 1889. V. 39

CHAPIN, GEORGE H.

Health Resorts of the South. Boston: 1888. V. 41; 44

CHAPIN, J. P.

The Birds of the Belgian Congo. New York: 1932-54. V. 43

CHAPIN, SAMUEL A.

Statement and Reports Concerning the Uncle Same Senior and Gold Canon Silver Lodes, in Nevada. Boston: 1865. V. 39; 41; 43

CHAPIN, WILLIAM

Complete Reference Gazetteer of the United States of North America . . . New York: 1844. V. 43

A Complete Reference Gazetteer of the United States of North America; Contining a General View of the United States, and of each State and Territory, and a Notice of the Various Canals, Railroads, and Internal Improvements . . . Al the Post . . . New York: 1839. V. 37

CHAPIN, WILLIS O.

The Masters and Masterpieces of Engraving. New York: 1894. V. 38; 40; 44

CHAPIUS, A.

Automata, a Historical and Technological Study. New York: 1958. V. 46

CHAPIUS, ALFRED

Technique and History of the Swiss Watch, from Its Beginnings to the Present Day . . . Olten: 1953. V. 43

CHAPLIN, CHARLES

My Life in Pictures. London: 1974. V. 46

CHAPMAN, ABEL

Bird-Life of the Borders. London: 1889. V. 44; 46

Bird-Life of the Borders on Moorland and Sea, with Faunal Notes Extending Over Forty Years. London: 1907. V. 42; 44

The Borders and Beyond. London: 1924. V. 37; 41; 44

First Lessons in the Art of Wildfowling. London: 1896. V. 39; 40; 44; 46

CHAPMAN, ABEL continued

Memories of Fourscore Years Less Two, 1851-1929. London: 1930.
V. 37; 40; 44

On Safari, Big Game Hunting in British East Africa. London: 1908.
V. 39; 42; 44

Retrospect. Reminiscences and Impressions of a Hunter-Naturalist in Three Continents 1851-1928. London: 1928. V. 44; 46

Savage Sudan, Its Wild Tribes, Big-Game and Bird-Life. London: 1921.
V. 38; 39; 40; 44; 45

Unexplored Spain. London: 1910. V. 38; 45; 46

Unexplored Spain. New York: 1910. V. 39

Unexplored Spain. London: 1919. V. 44

Wild Spain. London: 1893. V. 45

Wild Spain. London: 1893. V. 40

Wild Spain . . . Records of Sport with Rifle, Rod and Gun, Natural History and Exploration . . . London: 1893. V. 38; 40; 44; 46

Wild Norway; with Chapters on Spitsbergen, Denmark, etc. London: 1897.
V. 44

CHAPMAN, C. A.

Southwestern Minnesota: a Descriptive Sketch. N.P.: 1881. V. 44

CHAPMAN, C. E.

Catalogue of Materials in the Archivo General de Indias for the History of the Pacific Coast and the American Southwest. Berkeley: 1919. V. 38

CHAPMAN, CHARLES

All About Ships and the Way to Make Models of Them. London: 1873.
V. 41

The Ocean Waves: Travels by Land and Sea. London: 1875. V. 42; 45

CHAPMAN, F.

Reminiscences of the Wensleydale Hounds. 1775-1907. London: 1908.
V. 39

CHAPMAN, FRANK M.

The Warblers of North America. New York: 1907. V. 46

The Warblers of North America. New York: 1917. V. 37

CHAPMAN, FREDERICK HENRY DE

Traite de la Construction des Vaisseaux, avec une Explication ou l'on Demontre les Principes de l'Architecture Navale Marchande, & des Navires Arames en Course . . . Paris: 1779. V. 38

A Treatise Concerning the True Method of Finding the Proper Area of the Sails for Ships of the Line, and from Thence the Length of Masts and Yards. London: 1794. V. 40

A Treatise on Ship-Building, with Explanations and Demonstrations Respecting the Architectura Nvalis Mercatoria. Cambridge: 1820. V. 38; 40

CHAPMAN, FREDERICK SPENCER

Northern Lights: the Official Account of the British Arctic Air-Route Expedition 1930-1931. London: 1932. V. 38; 46

CHAPMAN, GEORGE

The Comedies and Tragedies. London: 1873. V. 40

A Treatise on Education. Edinburgh: 1773. V. 43; 46

A Treatise on Education in Two Parts with the Author's Method of Instruction While He Taught the School of Dumfires. London: 1790. V. 42

CHAPMAN, GEORGE THOMAS

Sermons, Upon the Ministry, Workshop, and Doctrines of the Protestant Episcopal Church, and Other Subjects. Lexington: 1828. V. 44

CHAPMAN, GUY

A Bibliography of William Beckford of Fonthill. 1930. V. 42

A Bibliography of William Beckford of Fonthill. London: 1930. V. 38; 40; 42

CHAPMAN, ISAAC A.

A Sketch of the History of Wyoming . . . to Which is Called an Appendix . . . Wilkesbarre: 1830. V. 41; 42; 43; 45

CHAPMAN, J. G.

The Picture of the Baptism of Pocahontas. Washington: 1840. V. 45

CHAPMAN, JOHN

Eusebius; or the Ture Christian's Defense Against a late book entitul'd the Moral Philosopher (by Thomas Morgan). Cambridge: 1739. V. 39; 40

CHAPMAN, JOHN GADEBY

The American Drawing-Book . . . New York: 1864. V. 42

The American Drawing Book. New York: 1847. V. 38; 40

CHAPMAN, JOHN KEMBLE

A Complete History of Theatrical Entertainments, Dramas, Masques, and Triumphs . . . London: 1849. V. 42

The Court Theatre, and Royal Dramatic Record . . . London: 1849? V. 38

CHAPMAN, JOHN RATCLIFFE

Instructions to Young Marksmen . . . New York: 1848. V. 44

CHAPMAN, KENNETH M.

Pottery of Santo Domingo Pueblo. A Detailed Study of Its Decoration. Santa Fe: 1936. V. 37; 39

Pueblo Indian Pottery. Nice: 1933 & 1936. V. 39

CHAPMAN, MARIA WESTON

the Eleventh Massachusetts Anti-Slavery Fair. Boston: 1844. V. 45

Liberty and Equality. Boston?: 1840-45. V. 44

Right and Wrong in Massachusetts. Boston: 1839. V. 42

Songs of the Free, and Hymns of Christian Freedom. Boston: 1836. V. 42

CHAPMAN, NATHENIAL

Dr. Chapman's Course of Lectures on Fevers. Philadelphia: 1835. V. 40

CHAPMAN, R. W.

Cancels. London: 1930. V. 42

Cancels. London: 1930. V. 37; 39; 40; 41; 42; 43; 46

The Portrait of a Scholar and Other Essays. London: 1922. V. 40

CHAPMAN, ROGER G.

Charles Darwin, 1809-1882. A Centennial Commemorative. Wellington: 1982.
V. 41; 42; 43; 46

CHAPMAN, SYDNEY J.

Work and Wages in Continuation of Lord Brassey's 'Work and Wages' and 'Foreign Work and English Wages'. London: 1904-08-14. V. 46

CHAPMAN, THOMAS

interesting and Most Severe Case of Mr. Thomas Chapman, who First Discovered the Means of making the Fur of the Seal Available. London: 1819. V. 37

CHAPMAN'S Magazine of Fiction. London: 1895. V. 40

CHAPOMIER, P. A.

Statement of the Sugar Crop Made in Louisiana in 1851-52. New Orleans: 1852. V. 44

CHAPONE, HESTER

Letters on the Improvement of the Mind Addressed to a Young Lady. Walpole: 1802. V. 39

Letters on the Improvement of the Mind. London: 1822. V. 38; 40; 42; 46

Miscellanies in Prose and Verse. London: 1755. V. 43

Miscellanies in Prose and Verse. London: 1789. V. 41

The Works . . . Dublin: 1786. V. 38

CHAPPE D'AUTEROCHE, JEAN 1728-1769

Voyage en Siberie Fait par Ordre Du Roi en 1761 . . . Paris: 1768. V. 43

A Voyage to California to Observe the Transit of Venus . . . with An Historical Description of the Author's Route through Mexico, and the Natural History of that Province. London: 1778. V. 38; 39; 42; 43

CHAPPEL, ALONZO

Lives and Portraits of the Presidents of the United States, From Washington to Johnson. New York: 1865. V. 46

CHAPPEL, WILLIAM

Fonteyn-Impressions of a Ballerina. London: 1951. V. 40

CHAPPELL, ABSALOM H.

Miscellanies of Georgia, Historical, Biographical, Descriptive &c. Columbus: 1874. V. 43

CHAPPELL, EDWARD

Narrative of a Voyage to Hudson's Bay in His Majesty's Ship Rosamond. London: 1817. V. 46

Voyage to His Majesty's Ship Rosamond to Newfoundland and the Southern Coast of Labrador of Which Countries No Account Has Been Published . . . London: 1818. V. 43; 44

CHAPPELL, GEORGE S.

A Basket of Poses. New York: 1924. V. 37; 39; 43

A Basket of Poses. New York: 1925. V. 41

CHAPPUIS, ADRIAN

The Drawings of Paul Cezanne. New York: 1973. V. 44

CHAPPUIS, ADRIEN

The Drawings of Paul Cezanne: a Catalogue Raisonne. London: 1973.
V. 42

The Drawings of Paul Cezanne: A Catalogue Raisonne. Greenwich: 1973.
V. 37; 40; 41; 43

CHAPTAL DE CHANTELOUP, JEAN ANTOINE 1756-1832

Elements of Chemistry. Philadelphia: 1796. V. 39

CHAPTAL DE CHANTELOUP, JEAN ANTOINE 1756-1832 continued

Elements of Chemistry. London: 1800. V. 39

CHAPTAL DE CHANTELOUP, JEAN ANTOINE CLAUDE, COMTE 1756-1832

Chimie Appliquee Aux Arts. Paris: 1807. V. 41; 45

De l'Industrie Francoise. Paris: 1819. V. 41; 45

CHAPTAL DE CHANTELOUP, JEAN ATOINE CLAUDE, COMTE 1756-1832

Elemens de Chimie. Montpellier: 1790. V. 38; 41; 45

CHAPTAL, J. A. C.

Elements of Chemistry. Translated from the French. Philadelphia: 1796. V. 37; 38; 41; 43; 45; 46

Elements of Chemistry. Translated from the French. The Third Edition. London: 1800. V. 37

CHAPTAL, M. I. A.

Elements of Chemistry. Boston: 1806. V. 38

Elements of Chemistry. Philadelphia: 1807. V. 38

A CHAPTER to the English Multitude by One of the People. London: 1798. V. 43

CHAPTERS on Writing and Printing. Lexington: 1963. V. 40

CHAPUIS, ALFRED

Automata: Historical and Technological Study. London: 1958. V. 42

Automata: a Historical and Technological Study. Neuchtel and London: 1958. V. 38

Histoire de la Pendulerie Neuchateloise. Paris et Neuchatel;: 1917. V. 41

Technique and History of the Swiss Watch, From Its Beginnings to the Present Day. Olten: 1953. V. 39; 42

CHAPWELL, FRED

It Is Time Lord. New York: 1963. V. 41

CHAR, RENE

Anthologie. Paris: 1960. V. 37

La Chien de Coeur. Paris: 1968. V. 40

Dent Prompte. Paris: 1969. V. 39

Poems. Rome: 1952. V. 37

Ralentir Travaux. Paris: 1930. V. 45

THE CHARACTER of Sultan Galga, the Present Cham of Tartary, Drawn by a Walachian, Who Had Seen His Favourite for Several Years. London: 1718. V. 45

A CHARACTER Of Don Sacheverellio, Knight of the Firebrand; in a Letter to Isaac Bickerstaff Esq. Censor of Great Britain. Dublin. V. 40

A CHARACTER of France. To Which is Added, Gallus Castratus. Or an Answer to a Late Slanderous Pamphlet Called the Character of England. London: 1659. V. 40

A CHARACTER of John Sheffield Late Duke of Buckinghamshire. London: 1729. V. 41

CHARACTERISTIC Sketches of Young Gentlemen. London: 1838. V. 40; 43

CHARAKA CLUB

The Proceedings of the Charaka Club. 1902-1941. V. 38

The Proceedings of the Charaka Club. 1902-1941. V. 42

The Proceedings of the Charaka Club. 1902-41. V. 41

The Proceedings of the Charaka Club. New York: 1910. V. 37; 38; 41; 42; 45; 46

The Proceedings of the Charaka Club. New York: 1916. V. 41; 42; 45; 46

The Proceedings of the Charaka Club. New York: 1919. V. 37; 38; 41; 42; 45

Proceedings of the Charaka Club. Volume 8. New York: 1935. V. 38; 41

Proceedings of the Charaka Club. Volume 9. New York: 1938. V. 38; 41

Proceedings of the Charaka Club. Volume 10. New York: 1941. V. 41

The Proceedings of the Charaka Club. Volumes 1-10. 1902-1941. V. 37

Proceedings of . . . Volume 1. New York: 1902. V. 38

Proceedings of . . . Volume 10. New York: 1941. V. 38

Proceedings of . . . Volume 2. New York: 1906. V. 38

Proceedings of . . . Volume 4. New York: 1906. V. 38

Proceedings of . . . Volume 6. New York: 1925. V. 38

CHARAS, M.

New Experiments Upon Vipers . . . London: 1670. V. 43

CHARAS, MOYSE

Pharmacopee Royale Galenique et Chimique. Paris: 1691. V. 40; 42

CHARBONNEAUX, JEAN

Archaic Greek Art (620-480 B.C.). London: 1971. V. 40; 42

Archaic Greek Art (620-480 B.C.). New York: (1971). V. 37

Classical Greek Art, 480-330 B.C. London: 1973. V. 42

Hellenistic Art (330-50 B.C.). London: (1973). V. 37; 42

CHARCOT, J. M.

Lectures on Bright's Disease of the Kidneys. Delivered at the School of Medicine of Paris. New York: 1878. V. 41

CHARCOT, JEAN

The Voyage of the 'Why Not?' in the Antarctic: the Journal of the Second French South Polar Expedition, 1908-10. London: 1911. V. 38; 40; 43; 44

CHARCOT, JEAN BAPTISTE AUGUST ETIENNE

Contribution a l'Etude de l'Atrophie Musculaire Progressive Type Duchenne-Aran. Paris: 1895. V. 37

CHARCOT, JEAN MARTIN 1825-1893

Clinical Lectures on Senile and Chronic Diseases. London: 1881. V. 39; 40; 45

Clinical Lectures on the Diseases of Old Age. New York: 1881. V. 42; 43

Lecons sur les Maladies du Systeme Nerveaux Faites a La Salpetriere. Paris: 1872-77. V. 43

Lectures on the Diseases of the Nervous System. London: 1877. V. 39

Lectures on Localization in Diseases of the Brain, Delivered at the Faculte de Medecine, Paris, 1875 . . . New York: 1878. V. 39

Lectures on the Diseases of the Nervous System. London: 1881. V. 38; 39; 42

Lectures on the Diseases of the Nervous System. London: 1883. V. 39; 40

Lectures on Localisation of Cerebral and Spinal Diseases. London: 1883. V. 42

Lectures on Diseases of the Nervous System . . . London: 1889. V. 39

Neue Vorlesungen Uber die Krankheiten des Nervensystems Insbesondere Uber Hysterie. Leipzig & Wien: 1886. V. 45

Oeuvres Completes . . . Paris: 1888-1894. V. 37

CHARDIN, JEAN 1643-1713

Le Chevalier Chardin, en Perse, et Autres Lieux de l'Orient. Amsterdam: 1711. V. 40; 42

Journal du Voyage du Chevalier Chardin en Perse & aux Indes Orientales . . . Londres: 1686. V. 43

CHARDIN, JOHN

Sir John Charin's Travels in Persia. 1927. V. 44

Sir John Chardin's Travels in Persia. London: 1927. V. 38

The Travels of Sir John Chardin into Persia and the East Indies. To Which is Added, The Coronation of This Present King of Persia, Solyman the Third. London: 1686. V. 39; 42

The Travels of Sir John Chardin into Persia and the East Indies, through the Black Sea, and the Country of Colchis. London: 1691. V. 41

Travels in Persia. London: 1927. V. 37; 39; 45

CHARDON, FRANCIS A.

Chardon's Journal at Fort Clark, 1834-1839. Pierre: 1932. V. 38; 40; 43; 45

CHARDON, P.

Exercises Upon the French Grammar, with the Rules Prefixed to Them. Chester: 1798. V. 41

THE CHARGE of J--- P---- to the Grand Jury of M-----x, on Saturday May 22, 1736. London: 1738. V. 43

CHARITABLE IRISH SOCIETY OF BOSTON

The Constitution and By-Laws of the Charitable Irish Society of Boston, inst. 1737, adopted 1876, with List of Officers and Members and many interesting extracts from the Records of the Society etc. etc. Boston: 1876. V. 37

CHARITON

Ton Peri Chairean Kai Kallirroen Erotikon Diegematon Logoi. Amsterdam: 1750. V. 38

CHARKE, CHARLOTTE

The Art of Management. London: 1735. V. 38

A Narrative of the Life of Mrs. Charlotte Charke . . . Written by Herself. London: 1755. V. 38

THE CHARLEMAGNE Tower Collection of American Colonial Laws. Philadelphia: 1890. V. 37; 40

CHARLES, C. J.

Elizabethan Interiors. London. V. 46

CHARLES, C. J. DUVEEN

Elizabethan Interiors. London & New York: 1917. V. 41

CHARLES Darwin 1809-1882: a Centennial Commemorative. Wellington: 1982. V. 45

THE CHARLES Dickens Dinner. An Authentic Record of the Public Banquet Given to Mr. Charles Dickens at the Freemasons' Hall, London, on Saturday, November 2, 1867, Prior to His Departure for the United States. London: 1867. V. 43; 46

CHARLES D'ORLEANS 1394-1465

Poemes. Paris: 1950. V. 38

CHARLES, ELIZABETH RUNDLE

Against the Stream. The Story of an heroic age of England. In Three Volumes. London: 1873. V. 37

CHARLES I, KING OF GREAT BRITAIN 1600-1649

Basilika The Works . . . with His Life and Martyrdom. London: 1687. V. 41

Bibliotheca Regia, or the Royal Library, Containing A Collection of Such of the Papers of his Late Majesty King Charls . . . as have Escaped the Wrack and Ruines of these Times. London: 1659. V. 39; 45; 46

By the King a Proclamation . . . Whereas the Safeguard and Protection We Owe to Such of Our Own Subjects. London: 1683/4. V. 40

A Collection of Declarations, Treaties and Other Principal Passages Concerning the Differences Between King Charles I, and His Two Houses of Parliament. London: 1662. V. 39

An Exact Collection of all Remonstrances, Declarations, Votes, Orders, Ordinances, Proclamations, Petitions, Messages, Answers and Other Remarkable Passages Betweene the Kings most Excellent Majesty . . . London: 1643. V. 43

His Maiesties Declaration to All His Louing Subjects, Of the Causes Which Moued Him to Dissoule the Last Parliament. London: 1628. V. 44

His Majesties Declaration; to All His Loving Subjects, Of the Causes Which Moved Him to Dissolve the Last Parliament. London: 1640. V. 40; 45

His Majesties Answer, to a Booke, Intituled, The Declaration, Remonstrance of the Lords and Commons of the 19 of may, 1642. Imprinted at Yorke and: 1642. V. 43

His Majesties Declaration Concerning Leavies. London: 1642. V. 39

His Majesties Declaration to All His Loving Subjects, Occasioned by a False and Scandalous Imputation Laid Upon His Majestie . . . London: 1642. V. 46

His Majesties Answer to the Declaration of Both Houses of Parliament. Yorke: 1642. V. 46

His Majesties Letter and Declaration to the Sheriffes and City of London, January 17, 1642. Oxford: 1642/3. V. 41

The Kings Cabinet Opened; or, Certain Packets of Secret Letters and Papers Written with the Kings Own Hand and Taken in His Cabinet at Nasby-Field, June 14, 1645 . . . London: 1645. V. 46

The Kings Declaration to all His Subjects, Of Whatsoever Nation, Quality or Condition. London: 1648. V. 45

The Kings Most Gracious Messages for Peace and a Personal Treaty. London: 1648. V. 38

The Kings Majesty's Declaration to His Subjects, Concerning Lawful Sports to be Used. London: 1716. V. 45

A large Declaration concerning the late Tumults in Scotland from Their first originals: together with a particular deduction Of the seditious Practices of the prime Leaders of the Covenanters: Collected out of their own foule Acts and Writings . . . London: 1639. V. 37

His Majesties Speech and Protestation, Made in the Head of His Armie, Between Stafford and Wellington, the 19th of September, 1642. London: 1642. V. 45

The Papers Which Passed at Newcastle Betwixt His Sacred Majestie and Mr. Al: Henderson . . . London: 1649. V. 37

Reliquiae Sacrae Carolinae, The Workes of that Great Monarch and Glorious Martyr King Charles the 1st Both Civil and Sacred, With a Short View of the Life and Reign of that Most Blessed Prince from His Birth to His Buriall. Hague: 1648. V. 41

Reliquiae Sacrae Carolinae, or the Works of that Great Monarch and Glorious Martyr King Charles the I. Hague: 1650. V. 45

Reliquiae Sacrae Carolinae. Hague: 1651. V. 44

Reliquiae Sacrae Caroline. Or the Works of the Great Monarch and Glorious Martyr . . . London: 1651. V. 46

The Royall Legacies of Charles the First . . . to His Persecutors and Murderers. London: 1649. V. 38; 41

The Workes of that Great Monarch and Glorious Martyr King Charles the 1st . . . (with) The Pourtraicture of His Sacred Majesty in His Solitudes and Sufferings. Hague: 1648/48. V. 46

The Works of King Charles the Martyr: With a Collection of Declarations, Treaties, and Other Papers Concerning the Differences Betwixt His Said Majesty and His Two Houses of Parliament. London: 1662. V. 39; 42; 44; 46

CHARLES II, KING OF GREAT BRITAIN

An Account of the Preservation of King Charles II. After the Battle of Worcester, Drawn Up By Himself. To Which are Added His Letters to Several Persons. Glasgow: 1766. V. 38

By the King. A Proclamation for Apprehension of Edward Whalley and William Goffe . . . London: 1660. V. 44

By the King. A Proclamation for Quieting Possessions. London: 1660. V. 42; 46

His Majesties Gracious Patent to the Goldsmiths, for Payment and Satisfaction of their Debt. London: 1677. V. 39

A Proclmation for Apprehension of Edward Whalley and William Goffe. London: 1660. V. 40

CHARLES II, KING OF GREAT BRITIAN

His Majesties Declaration . . . Concerning the Treasonable Conspiracy Against His Sacred Person and Government, Lately Discovered. London: 1683. V. 46

CHARLES III, KING OF SPAIN

Real Cedula de S.M. y Senores del Consejo. En que se manda Guardar el Reglamento Inserto, Formado Para el Exterminio de Lobos, Zorros, y Otros Animales Daninos, en la Conformidad que se Expresa. Pamplona: 1788. V. 45

CHARLES IV, KING OF SPAIN

Real Cedula de S.M. Y Senores del Consejo en Que se Manda Observar y Guardar el Tratado de Amistad, Limites de Navegacion Concluido Y Ratificado Entre su Real Persona Y Los Estados Unidos de America. Madrid: 1796. V. 40

CHARLES IX, KING OF FRANCE

Edict. und Erclerung, von der Koniglichen wurden in Frankreich, Carolo dem IX. Aussganagen, von Wegen der Friedtshandlung und Hinlegung der Entborungen, so in Gemeltem Konigreich Enstanden. N.P.: 1563. V. 37

CHARLES, NICHOLAS

A Topographical Dictionary of Scotland and of the Islands in the British Seas . . . London: 1813. V. 41

CHARLES, R.

A Roundabout Turn. London: 1930. V. 43; 44; 46

CHARLES, ROBERT

The Illustrious French Lovers. London: 1739. V. 38

CHARLES, ROLLO

Continental Porcelain of the Eighteenth Century. London: 1964. V. 41

CHARLES, TOM, MRS. 1887-

Tales of the Tularosa. Alamogordo: 1953. V. 44

CHARLES V,

Verschrybung und Verwilligung des Neuen Erwelten Roemischen Koenigs Karoli Gegen dem Heyligen Reych. Strasbourg: 1519. V. 40; 41

CHARLES V, HOLY ROMAN EMPEROR 1500-1558

Apologetici Libri Duo . . . Mainz: 1527. V. 46

CHARLES VII, EMPEROR

The Emperor's Plan for a Peace. With Remarks Upon It. London: 1743. V. 41

CHARLES VII, KING OF FRANCE

Pragmatica Sanctio, cum Glossis Cosme Guimier. Paris: 1546. V. 38

CHARLES Wain: a Miscellany of Short Stories. London: 1933. V. 39; 45; 46

CHARLES XII, King of Sweden, a Character and Two Poems. Brisbane: 1983. V. 39

CHARLES XII of Sweden: a Character and Two Poems. 1983. V. 40

CHARLESTON ORPHAN HOUSE

By-Laws of the Orphan House of Charleston, South Carolina. Charleston: 1861. V. 40

CHARLESTON, R. J.

English Porcelain, 1845-1850. London: 1965. V. 38

CHARLESTON, ROBERT J.

World Ceramics: an Illustrated History. London: 1968. V. 41

CHARLESWORTH, J. K.

The Quarternary Era. London: 1957. V. 37

CHARLETON, RICE

A Treatise on the Bath Waters; Wherein are Discover'd the Several Principles of Which They are Compos'd . . . Bath: 1724. V. 42

CHARLETON, WALTER

Chorea Gigantum; or, The Most Famous Antiquity of Great-Britain; Vulgarly called Stone-Henge, Standing on the Salisbury Plain, Restored to the Danes . . . London: 1663. V. 37

Spiritus Gorgonicus. Leyden: 1650. V. 38

CHARLEVOIX, PIERRE FRANCOIS XAVIER DE

Histoire de L'Isle Espanole ou de S. Domingue. Paris: 1730. V. 46

Histoire de l'Isle Espagnole ou de S. Domingue. Paris: 1730-31. V. 42

Histoire et Description Generale de la Nouvelle France, avec Le Journal Historique d'un Voyage Fait Par Ordre du Roi . . . Paris: 1744. V. 46

Histoire et Description Generale de la Nouvelle France, Avec Le Journal Historique d'un Voyage Fait par Ordre du Roi Dans l'Amerique Spetenrionale. Paris: 1744. V. 38

CHARLEVOIX, PIERRE FRANCOIS XAVIER DE continued

Histoire et Description Generale de la Nouvelle France, Avec le Journal Historique d'un Voyage Fait par Ordre du Roi Dans l'Amerique Septentrionale. Paris: 1744. V. 37; 38; 39; 42; 43; 44; 45; 46

Histoire et Description Generale de la Nouvelle France, avec Le Journal Historique d'un Voyage fait par parr. Paris: 1844. V. 42

The History of Paraguay. London: 1769. V. 41; 42

History and General Description of New France. New York: 1866-72. V. 37

Journal of a Voyage to North American. London: 1716. V. 45

Journal of a Voyage to North America. London: 1761. V. 37; 38; 41; 42; 43; 44; 45; 46

Journal of a Voyage to North America. Dublin: 1766. V. 38; 41; 42; 43; 44; 45

Journal of a Voyage to North America. Chicago: 1923. V. 39

CHARLEY Chalk; or, the Career of an Artist: Being Sketches from Real Life; Comprising a Narrative of His Extraordinary Adventures in Great Britain and Ireland, France and Greece. London: 1839. V. 37

CHARLIE Wyndham; or, the Adventures of Modern Midshipman. Hanley: 1887. V. 43; 45

CHARLOT, JEAN

Jean Charlot: Posada's Dance of Death. New York: 1964. V. 41

Picture Book (I). New York: 1933. V. 37; 41; 43; 46

Picture Book II. Los Angeles: 1973. V. 43

Portrait of Latin America as Seen by Her Print Makers. New York: 1946. V. 38

CHARLOTTE, ELIOT

Savonarola. A Dramtic Poem. London: 1926. V. 41

CHARLTON, JASPER

The Ladies Astronomy and Chronology, in Four Parts. London: 1735. V. 42

CHARLTON, JOHN

Twelve Pakcs of Hounds. London: 1891. V. 37

CHARLTON, LIONEL

The History of Whitby, and of Whitby Abbey, Collected from the Original Records of the Abbey . . . York: 1779. V. 37; 38; 45

CHARLTON, MARY

Phedora; or, the Forest of Minski. London: 1798. V. 39

CHARLTON, THOMAS U. P.

The Life of Major General James Jackson. Atlanta: 1898. V. 43; 44; 45

CHARLTON, W. A.

Hudson's Bay Railway Route, Via Missanabie and Valley of Moose River. Toronto: 1898. V. 42; 43

CHARLTON, W. H. BURGHLEY

The Life of William Cecil, Lord Burghley . . . a Description of Burghley House . . . and Brief Notice of the Family Monuments . . . Stamford: 1847. V. 38; 44

CHARMET, RAYMOND

French Paintings in Russian Museums. Geneva: 1970. V. 41

CHARMETON, GEORGES

Diverses Ornemens et Masque. (with) Ornemens de Plusieurs Sortes. Paris: 1676. V. 44

THE CHARMS of Liberty: a Poem. N.P.: 1709. V. 43

CHARNAY, DESIRE

Les Anciennes Villes du Nouveau Monde, Voyages d'Explorations au Mexique et Dans l'Amerique Centrale. Paris: 1885. V. 46

The Ancient Cities of the New World. London: 1887. V. 45; 46

The Ancient Cities of the New World, Being Voyages and Explorations in Mexico and Central America from 1857-1882. New York: 1887. V. 39; 42

CHARNLEY, JOHN

The Closed Treatment of Common Fractures. Edinburgh: 1950. V. 42

CHARNOCK, JOHN

Biographical Memoirs of Lord Viscount Nelson with Observations General & Explanatory. London: 1806. V. 42; 45

An History of Marine Architecture. London: 1800-1802. V. 41

CHARPENTIER DE COSSIGNY, JOSEPH FRANCOIS 1730-1809

Voyage a Canton, Cap-itale de La Province de ce Nom, a La Chine, par Goree, Le Cap de Bonne-Esperance, et Les Isles de France et de Reunion; Suive d'Observations sur le Voyage a La Chine de Lord MaCartney et du Citoyen Van-Braam, et d'une Esquisse . . . 1799. V. 39

CHARPENTIER, FRANCOIS 1620-1702

Les Voyages du Sieur du Loir . . . Contenus en Plusieurs Lettres Ecrites du Levant . . . Paris: 1654. V. 39

CHARPENTIER, JOHANN DE

Essai sur la Constitution Geognostique des Pyrenees. Paris: 1823. V. 46

CHARPY, EDMOND

Imperatorum XII . . . Effigies Resque Gestae Iconibus. Paris: 1610. V. 45

CHARRAS, MOSES

The Royal Pharmacopoea, Galenical and Chymical, according to the Practice of the most Eminent and Learned Physicians of France, and . . . London: 1678. V. 37; 38

CHARRON, PIERRE 1541-1603

De la Sagesse, Trois Livres. Leiden: 1656. V. 37

De La Sagesse, Trois Livres. Amsterdam: 1662. V. 42; 45

CHARSLEY, F. A.

The Wild Flowers Around Melbourne. London: 1867. V. 41

CHART, D. A.

The Drennan Letters . . . Corresondence Which Passed Between William Drennan, M.D. and Samuel and Martha McTier, during the Years 1776-1819. Belfast: 1931. V. 37; 43

A Preliminary Survey of the Ancient Monuments of Northern Ireland. Belfast: 1940. V. 37

THE CHARTERHOUSE with the Last Will and Testament of Thomas Sutton Esquire. London: 1614. V. 45

CHARTERIS, LESLIE

Meet the Tiger. London: 1928. V. 40

The Saint Sees Its Through. London: 1947. V. 42

THE CHARTERS of the British Colonies in America. London: 1774. V. 39; 44; 45

CHARTIER, ALAIN

Delectable Demaundes and Pleasant Questions, with Their Severall Answers in Matters of Love . . . London: 1596. V. 39

CHARTIER, JEAN

Joan the Maid of Orleans Being that Portion of the Chronicles of St. Denis Which Deals with Her Life and Times . . . San Francisco: 1938. V. 38

CHASE BROS. CO., NEW ENGLAND NURSERIES

With Camera and Brush. Rochester: 1908. V. 37

CHASE, C. THURSTON

A Manual of School-Houses and Cottages for the People of the South. Washington: 1868. V. 37; 40

CHASE, CHARLES M.

The Editor's Run in New Mexico and Colorado. Lyndon: 1882. V. 38; 45

The Editor's Run in New Mexico and Colorado: Embracing 28 Letters on Stock Raising, Agriculture, Territorial History. Lyndon: 1882. V. 38

The Editor's Run in New Mexico and Colorado. Montpelier: 1882. V. 37; 39; 42

CHASE, FRANCIS

Gathered Sketches from the Early History of New Hampshire and Vermont. Claremont: 1856. V. 41; 42

CHASE, GEORGE H.

Catalogue of American Pottery. Boston: 1916. V. 44

Catalogue of Arretine Pottery. Boston & New York: 1916. V. 37; 39

Greek and Roman Sculpture in American Collections. Cambridge: 1924. V. 37; 40

The Loeb Collection of Arretine Pottery. New York: 1908. V. 40; 42

CHASE, HEBER

The Final Report of the Committee of the Philadelphia Medical Society on the Construction of Instruments and Their Mode of Action in the Radical Cure of Hernia. Philadelphia: 1837. V. 40; 42

CHASE, J. SMEATON

California Caost Trails: a Horseback Ride from Mexico to Oregon. Boston & New York: 1913. V. 46

Yosemite Trails. Camp and Pack-Train in the Yosemite Region of the Sierra Nevada. Boston: 1911. V. 44; 46

CHASE, JOHN CARROLL

History of Chester, N. H. Including Auburn. Derry: 1926. V. 42

CHASE, JOHN CENTLIVRES

The Cape of Good Hope, and the Eastern Province of Algoa Bay, etc. with Statistics of the Colony. London: 1843. V. 39; 40

CHASE, JULIA A.

Mary A. Bickerdyke, 'Mother.' The Life Story of Army Nurse, Pension Agent, and City Missionary. Lawrence: 1896. V. 38; 41

CHASE, MARY

Harvey A Play. New York: 1953. V. 37

CHASE, OWEN

Narrative of the Most Extraordinary and Distressing Shipwreck of the Whale Ship Essex, of Nantucket . . . New York: 1821. V. 44

Narratives of the Wreck of the Whale Ship Essex of Natucket, Which was Destroyed by a Whale in the Pacific Ocean in the Year 1819 . . . London: 1935. V. 41; 44

CHASE, PHILANDER

A Plea for the West. Philadelphia: 1826. V. 42

CHASE, ROBERT

Atlas of Hand Surgery. Philadelphia: 1973. V. 42

CHASE, SAMUEL

To the Citizens of Baltimore-Town . . . Baltimore: 1794. V. 44

Trial of Samuel Chase, an Associate Justice of the Supreme Court of the United States, Impeached by the House of Representatives, for High Crimes and Misdemeanors, Before the Senate of the United States. Washington City: 1805. V. 43

CHASE, SAMUEL P.

The Answers and Pleas of Samuel Chase, One of the Associate Justices of the Supreme Court of the United States. Philadelphia: 1805. V. 42

Report of the Trial of the Hon. Samuel Chase, One of the Associate Justices of the Supreme Court of the U.S. Before the High Court of Impeachment . . . for High Crimes and Misdemeanors, Supposed to Have Been by him Committed . . . Baltimore: 1805. V. 40; 41; 42

CHASE, STUART

Rich Land - Poor Land. New York: 1936. V. 37; 40; 42

CHASE, WILL

Reminiscences of Captain Billie Moore. Kansas City: 1947. V. 39

CHASSEAUD, GEORGE WASHINGTON

The Druses of the Lebanon: Their Manners, Customs and History. London: 1855. V. 37; 45

CHASSENEUX, BARTHELEME DE 1480-1541

Catalogus Gloriae Mundi . . . Venice: 1571. V. 38

CHASSEPOL, FRANCOIS DE

The History of the Grand Viziers, Mahomet and Achmet Caprogli, of the Three Last Signiors, Their Sultana's and Chief Favourites . . . London: 1677. V. 37

CHAST, ROZ

Last Resorts. New York: 1979. V. 37

CHASTEL, ANDRE

The Myth of the Renaissance, 1420-1520. Geneva: 1969. V. 38

CHASTELET, PAUL HAY, MARQUIS DU

Traitte de la Politique de France. Cologne: 1669. V. 38

CHASTELLUX, FRANCOIS JEAN, MARQUIS DE 1734-1788

De la Felicite Publique. Ou Considerations sur le Sort des Hommes dans les Differentes Epoques de l'Histoire. Amsterdam: 1772. V. 38

Travels in North America in the Years 1789, 1781, and 1782 . . . Dublin: 1787. V. 38; 40; 45

Travels in North America, in the Years 1780, 1781 and 1782. London: 1787. V. 38; 39; 40; 42; 43; 44; 45

Travels in North America. New York: 1827. V. 45

Voyage de Mr. Le Chevalier de Chastellux en Amerique. Paris: 1785. V. 38

Voyages dans l'Amerique Septentrionale dans les Annees 1780, 1781, 1782. Paris: 1786. V. 37; 38; 42; 43; 45

CHATEAUBRIAND, FRANCOIS AUGUSTE RENE, VICOMTE DE 1768-1848

Atala. Bath: 1802. V. 40; 42

Atala: or the Amours of Two Indians, in the Wilds of America. London: 1802. V. 42

Atala. New York, London & Paris: 1884. V. 39; 40

Atala. Chicago & New York: 1886. V. 39

Atala. From the French . . . With explanatory notes. Bath/London: 1802. V. 37

The Loves of Eudorous and Cymodoce. London: 1813. V. 39; 42

The Natchez, an Indian Tale. London: 1827. V. 43

Recollections of Italy, England and America with Essays on Various Subjects. Philadelphia: 1816. V. 39; 46

Travels in Greece, Palestine, egypt and Barbary, During the Years 1806 and 1807. London: 1812. V. 41; 44

Travels in Greece, Palestine, Egypt and Barbary, During the Years 1806 and 1807. New York: 1814. V. 40

Travels in America and Italy. London: 1828. V. 37; 40; 42; 45

CHATEAUCLAIR, WILFRID

The Young Seigneur; or Nation-Making. Montreal: 1888. V. 44

CHATEAUNEUF, ALEXIS DE 1799-1853

The Country House (with Designs). London: 1843. V. 38

CHATELAIN, CLARA DE PONTIGNY DE

The Silver Swan. London: 1847. V. 46

CHATELAIN, JEAN

The Biblical Message of Marc Chagall. New York: 1973. V. 42; 44

Marc Chagall. London: 1964. V. 44

CHATELAIN, MADAME DE

Babyland. Pot Luck. Up Horsie! The Night Laundress. London: 1830. V. 39

CHATELAIN, VERNE E.

The Defenses of Spanish Florida, 1565 to 1763. Washington: 1941. V. 42

CHATELET, GABRIELE EMILE DE BRETEUIL, MARQUISE DU

Institutions de Physique. Paris: 1740. V. 38

CHATER, SIR CATHICK PAUL 1846-

The Chater Collection. London: 1924. V. 39; 43; 44

CHATFIELD, ROBERT

An Historical Review of the Commercial, Political and Moral State of Hindoostan, From the Earliest Period to the Present Time; the Rise and Progress of Christianity in the East . . . London: 1808. V. 39; 45

CHATHAM, RUSSELL

The Angler's Coast. Livingston: 1991. V. 46

CHATHAM, WILLIAM PITT, 1ST EARL OF 1708-1778

Anecdotes of the Life, and of the Principal Events of His Time, with His Speeches in Parlimaent from 1736 to 1778. London: 1792. V. 41; 43

Anecdotes of the Life of the Right Hounourable William Pitt, Earl of Chatham . . . London: 1796. V. 41; 43

Letters Written to His Nephew Thomas Pitt, Then at Cambridge. London: 1804. V. 38

Plan Offered by the Earl of Chatham to the House of Lords, Entitled, a Provisional Act, for Settling the Troubles in America, and for Asserting the Supreme Legislative Authority and Superintending Power of Great Britain Over the Colonies. London: 1775. V. 38

CHATTERTON, ALFRED

Experiments on the Strength of Building Materials Used in Southern India. Madras: 1900. V. 44

CHATTERTON, EDWARD KEBLE

Old Ship Prints. London: 1927. V. 38; 39; 40; 42; 46

Old Ship Prints. London: 1927. V. 46

Old Ship Prints. London & New York: 1927. V. 41

Old Sea Paintings. London: 1928. V. 39; 42; 45

Sailing Models, Ancient and Modern. London: 1934. V. 41

Ship-Models. London: 1932. V. 38

Ship Models. London: 1923. V. 37

Ships and Ways of Other Days . . . London: 1913. V. 39

Steamship Models. London: 1924. V. 38; 41; 42

CHATTERTON, G.

Rambles in the South of Ireland during the year 1838. London: 1839. V. 37

CHATTERTON, GEORGIANA

Leonore, a Tale: and Other Poems. London & Cambridge: 1864. V. 37

CHATTERTON, LADY

The Pyrenees with Excursions into Spain. London: 1843. V. 45

CHATTERTON, THOMAS 1752-1770

The Execution of Sir Charles Bawdin. London: 1772. V. 40

Miscellanies in Prose and Verse. London: 1778. V. 37; 38; 39; 41; 42; 43; 44; 45; 46

Poems, Supposed to Have Been Written at Bristol, by Thomas Rowley, and Others in the Fifteenth Century. London: 1777. V. 38; 39; 40; 41; 42; 43; 44; 46

Poems, Supposed to Have been Written at Bristol, By Thomas Rowley, and Others in the Fifteenth Century. London: 1778. V. 38; 41; 42

Poems, Supposed to Have Been Written at Bristol in the Fifteenth Century, by Thomas Rowley, Priest &c. London: 1782. V. 38; 45

Poems Supposed to Have Been Written at Bristol by Thomas Rowley and Others, in the Fifteenth Century. Cambridge: 1794. V. 38; 39; 41; 44

The Revenge, a Burletta; Acted At Marybone Gardens, MDCCLXX. London: 1795. V. 38

The Rowley Poems. London: 1898. V. 37; 44

The Works of . . . Containing His Life by G. Gregory. London: 1803. V. 38; 39; 40; 41

CHAUCER, GEOFFREY 1340-1400 continued

The Works. London: 1928. V. 45

The Works. Oxford: 1928. V. 45

The Works. 1928-29. V. 46

Works. 1928-29. V. 40

The Works of . . . Oxford: 1928-29. V. 43; 44

The Works. Stratford-upon-Avon: 1928-29. V. 37; 38; 41

The Works of Geoffrey Chaucer. Cleveland: 1958. V. 38; 39; 40; 43; 45

The Works of . . . London: 1974. V. 40; 42

The Works. 1975. V. 38

The Works of -. 1975. V. 37

The Works of . . . 1975. V. 45

The Works of Geoffrey Chaucer. (with) A Companion Volume to the Kelmscott chaucer. London: 1975. V. 41; 43

The Workes. London: 1976. V. 39

CHAUDHURI, K. N.

Sport in Jheel and Jungle. Calcutta: 1918. V. 42

CHAUDON, LOUIS MAIEUL

Historical and Critical Memoirs of the Life and Writings of M. De Voltaire. Interspersed with numerous anecdotes, poetical pieces, epigrams and bon mots . . . relative to the Literati of France . . . Dublin: 1786. V. 37

CHAUFFOURT, JACQUES DE

Instruction sur le Faict des Eaues et Forests. Rouen: 1618. V. 43

CHAUFFPIE, JAQUES GEORGE

The Life of Sevetus. London: 1771. V. 43

CHAULNES, MICHEL-FERDINAND D'ALBERT D'AILLY, DUC DE

Nouvelle Methode Pour Diviser les Instruments de Mathematique et d'Astronomie. (with) Description d'un Miscroscope et des Differents Micrometres Destines a Mesurer des Parties Circularies ou Droites . . . Paris: 1768. V. 44

CHAUMEAU, JEAN

Histoire de Berry, Contenant l'Origine, Antiquite, Gestes, Prouesees, Privileges & Libertes des Berruyrs. Lyons: 1566. V. 43

CHAUMETON, FRANCOIS PIERRE

Flore Medicale. Paris: 1814-20. V. 37; 41; 42

CHAUMETTE, ANTOINE

Enchiridion Chirurgicum, Extenorum Morborum Remedia tum Universalia tum Particularia . . . Paris: 1560. V. 45

CHAUMONT, JEAN DE 1583-ca. 1667

Discours de l'Accoustumance. Paris: 1613. V. 43

CHAUNCY, CHARLES 1705-1787

Breaking of Bread in Remembrance of the Dying Love of Christ, a Gospel Institution. Boston: 1772. V. 38

Enthusiasm Described and Caution'd Against . . . (with) A Letter to the Reverend Mr. James Davenport. Boston: 1742. V. 43; 44

Ministers Cautioned Against the Occasions of Contempot. A Sermon Preached Before the Ministers of the Province of the Massachusetts Bay in New England, at Their Annual Convention, In Boston, May 31, 1744. Boston: 1744. V. 43; 44

The Only Compulsion Proper to Be Made Use of in the Affairs of Conscience and Religion. Boston: 1739. V. 43

Seasonable Thouhts on the State of Rebellion in New-England, a Treatise in Five Parts. Boston: 1743. V. 38; 43; 44

Trust in God, the Duty of a People in a Day of Trouble. A Sermon Preached, May 30th, 1770 at the Request of a Great Number of Gentlemen, Friends to the Liberties of North America. Boston: 1770. V. 45

CHAUNCY, HENRY

The Historical Antiquities of Hertfordshire. 1826. V. 42

The Historical Antiquities of Hertfordshire. 1826. V. 39

CHAUNDLER, CHRISTINE

Arthur and His Knights. London. V. 46

Arthur and His Knights. London: 1920. V. 40; 42

CHAUT, CHRISTOPHER

The Cavendish Illustrated Encyclopedia of World War II. Edited by Christopher Chaut. 1972. V. 37

CHAUVENET, WILLIAM 1820-1870

A Manual of Spherical and Practical Astronomy. Philadelphia: 1876. V. 40

A Manual of Spherical and Practical Astronomy . . . Philadelphia: 1887. V. 42

CHAUVIN, ETIENNE

Lexicon Rationale sive Thesaurus Philosphicus Ordine Alphabetico Digestus . . . Rotterdam: 1692. V. 43; 46

CHAUVIN, JEAN

Ateliers. Montreal: 1928. V. 37

CHAVANNE, J.

The Literature on the Polar-Regions of the Earth. Vienna: 1878. V. 44

CHAVASSE, PYE H.

Advice to a Wife, and Advice to a Mother. London: 1854. V. 40

CHAVEZ, FRAY ANGELICO

Origins of New Mexico Families in the Spanish Colonial Period. Santa Fe: 1954. V. 43

CHAVLIER, M.

Briefe Uber Nord-Amerika Oder Schilderung der . . . Zustande der Vereinigten Staaten . . . Leipzig: 1837. V. 40

CHAYEFSKY, PADDY

Television Plays. New York: 1955. V. 39

CHAYT, STEVEN

Collotype, Being a History-Practicum-Bibliogtraphy. Winter Haven: 1983. V. 38; 39

A History Practicum Bibliography. Winter Haven: 1983. V. 44

A Ludlow Anthology, Compiled & Edited by Steven & Meryl Chayt. Winter Haven: 1986. V. 37; 38; 39; 40; 41; 42; 44

CHAZAL MALCY DE

The Medicinal Plants of Mauritius. London: 1989. V. 45

CHEADLE, W. B.

Cheadle's Journal of a Trip Across Canada, 1862-1863. Ottawa: 1931. V. 40; 42

CHEATHAM, KITTY

A Nursey Garland. New York: 1917. V. 46

CHEATLE, GEORGE

Tumors of the Breast. Philadelphia: 1931. V. 40; 42

CHECK List of Tennessee Imprints, 1841-1850. Nashville: 1941. V. 38

CHECKLEY, JOHN 1680-1754

The Speech of Mr. John Checkley Upon His Tryal, at Boston in New-England, for publishing The Short and Easy Method with the Deists . . . London: 1730. V. 38; 41; 45

CHEDWORTH, JOHN HOWE, BARON

Notes Upon Some of the Obscure Passages in Shakespeare's Plays. London: 1805. V. 45

A CHEERFUL Heart Has a Continual Feast. Hilversum: 1961. V. 45

CHEESEMAN, T. F.

Illustrations of the New Zealand Flora. Wellington: 1914. V. 37; 38

Manual of the New Zealand Flora. (with) Illustrations of the New Zealand Flora. London: 1906-14. V. 37; 38

CHEESMAN, R. E.

In Unknown Arabia. London: 1926. V. 39; 45

CHEETHAM, F. H.

The Church Bells of Lancashire. Manchester: 1915-30. V. 39

CHEETHAM, JAMES

An Answer to Alexander Hamilton's Letter, Concerning the Public Conduct and Character of John Adams . . . New York: 1800. V. 44; 45

A Letter to a Friend on the Conduct of the Adherents to Mr. Burr. New York: 1803. V. 45; 46

A Narrative of the Suppression by Col. Burr, or the History of the Adminstration of John Adams, Late President of the United States. New York: 1802. V. 41; 45

A Reply to Aristides. New York: 1804. V. 41; 44

A View of the Political Conduct of Arron Burr, Esq., Vice President of the United States. New York: 1802. V. 45

CHEEVER, GEORGE B.

The American Common-Place Book of Poetry, with Occasional Notes. Boston: 1831. V. 37; 39

Protest Against the Robbery of the Colored Race by the Proposed Amendment of the Constitution. New York: 1866. V. 42

Wanderings of a Pilgrim in the Shadow of Mont Blanc and the Jungfrau Alp. Glasgow. V. 39

Wanderings of a Pilgrim in the Shadow of Mont Blanc and the Jungfrau Alp. London. V. 41

Wanderings of a Pilgrim in the Shadow of Mont Blanc and the Jungfrau Alp. London. V. 46

Wanderings of a Pilgrim in the Shadow of Mont Blanc and the Jungfrau Alp. Aberdeen: 1848. V. 40

CHEEVER, GEORGE BARRELL

The Dream; or, the True History of Deacon Giles' Distillery and Deacon Jones' Brewery . . . New York: 1848. V. 43

The Dream; or the True History of Deacon Giles's Distillery. New York: 1859. V. 43

CHEEVER, HENRY T.

Life in the Sandwich Islands: or, the Heart of the Pacific, as It Was and Is. New York: 1851. V. 41

The Whale and His Captors; or, the Whaleman's Adventures, and the Whale's Biography, as Gathered on the Homeward Cruise of the 'Commodore Preble.' New York: 1850. V. 41; 42; 43

CHEEVER, JOHN 1912-1984

Atlantic Crossings: Excerpts from the author's Journals. Cottondale: 1986. V. 40; 45

Atlantic Crossing. Tuscaloosa: 1986. V. 39; 41; 42

The Brigadier and the Golf Widow. New York: 1964. V. 41; 42; 43; 44; 45; 46

Bullet Park. New York: 1969. V. 41; 42

The Day the Pig Fell Into the Well. Northridge: 1978. V. 43; 45; 46

The Enormous Radio. 1953. V. 43

The Enormous Radio and Other Stories. New York: 1953. V. 39; 40; 42; 44

Expelled. Los Angeles: 1988. V. 41

Expelled. N.P.: 1988. V. 42

Expelled. N.P.: 1988. V. 41

Falconer. New York: 1977. V. 39; 43

Homage to Shakespeare. Stevenson: 1968. V. 38; 39

The Housebreaker of Shady Hill and Other Stories. New York: 1958. V. 40; 42

Some People, Places and Things That Will Not Appear in My Next Novel. New York: 1961. V. 42

The Stories of John Cheever. New York: 1978. V. 39; 42; 46

The Uncollected Stories of John Cheever. Chicago: 1988. V. 46

The Wapshot Chronicle. New York: 1957. V. 41; 42

The Way Some People Live. New York: 1943. V. 39; 40; 42; 43

CHEFFONTAINES, CHRISTOPLE

Varii Tractatvs et Dispvtationes. Paris: 1586. V. 44

CHEFFONTAINES, F. CHRISTOPHE

Chrestienne Confvtation dv Poinct d'Honnevr, svr Leqvel la Noblesse Fonde Auiourd'huy ses Querelles & Monomachies. Paris: 1568. V. 44

CHEKE, JOHN

De Pronvntiatione Graecae Potissimum Linguae Disputationes cum Stephano Vuintoniensi Episcopo, Septem Contrarijs Epistolis Comprehensae, Magna Quadam & Elegantia & Eruditione Refertae. Basle: 1555. V. 37; 39; 40; 42

CHEKHOV, ANTON

The Note. V. 45

The Short Stories of Anton Chekhov. Avon: 1973. V. 46

That Worthless Fellow Platonov. New York: 1930. V. 46

Two Plays by Tchekhof: The Seagull, the Cherry Orchard. London: 1912. V. 42

CHELIUS, MAXIMILIAN JOSEPH

A System of Surgery. London: 1847. V. 38

A System of Surgery. Philadlephia: 1847. V. 43

CHELONIIDAE - Sea Turtles. Easthampton: 1987. V. 39

CHELSUM, JAMES

A History of the Art of Engraving in Mezzotinto, from It's Origin to the Present Times . . . Winchester: 1786. V. 40; 45

Remarks on the Last Two Chapters of Mr. Gibbon's History of the Decline and Fall of the Roman Empire, in a Letter to a Friend. London: 1776. V. 37; 39; 42; 43

CHELTAIN, AUGUSTUS LOUIS

Recollections of Seventy Years. Galena: 1899. V. 38

CHEMISTRY, Theoretical, Practical and Analytical, as applied to the Arts and Manufactues. By Writers of Eminence. London: (n.d.). V. 37

CHEMISTRY, Theoretical, Practical and Analytical, as Applied to the Arts and Manufactures. London: 1860. V. 40
CHEMISTRY, Theoretical, Practical and Analytical, As Applied to the Arts and Manufactures. London: 1882. V. 45; 46

CHEMITZ, MARTIN 1522-1586

Examen Concilii Tridentini, in III. partes diuisum, Praecipuorum Totius Doctrinae Pontificiae Capitum Firmam, Solidamque Refutationem Complectens . . . Francofurti ad Moenum: 1707. V. 38

CHEMNITZ, MARTIN 1522-1586

De Duabus Naturis in Christo. De Hypostatica Earum Unione. Lipsiae: 1578. V. 44

Examinis Concilii Tridentini, per Martinum Chemnicium Scripti, Opus Integrum: Quatuor Partes. Francoforti and Moenum: 1585. V. 43

CHENEVIX, RICHARD

Observations on Mineralogical Systems. London: 1811. V. 37

CHENEY, CHRISTOPHER R.

John Cheney and His Descendants. Banbury: 1936. V. 40

John Cheney and His Descendants. Banbury: 1936. V. 40

CHENEY, EDNAH

Louisa My Alcott, the Children's Friend. Boston: 1888. V. 41; 43

CHENEY, EMMA

Mistress Alice Jocelyn Letters, Etc. Chicago: 1903. V. 37

CHENEY, HARRIET VAUGHAN FOSTER

A Peep at the Pilgrims in Sixteen Hundred Thirty Six. London: 1825. V. 46

CHENEY, HARRIET VAUGHN FOSTER

A Peep at the Pilgrim in Sixteen Hundred Thirty-Six. Boston: 1824. V. 43

CHENEY, JOHN

John Cheney and His Descendants. Banbury: 1936. V. 46

CHENEY, JOHN VANCE

Inaugural Addresses of the Presidents of the United States from Johnson to Roosevelt. Chicago: 1950. V. 42

Out of Silence. Boston: 1897. V. 38

Queen Helen and Other Poems. Chicago: 1895. V. 38

CHENEY, SHELDON

Stage Decoration. London: 1928. V. 44

CHENEY, WARREN

Yosemite Illustrated in Colors. San Francisco: 1890. V. 46

CHENEY, WILLIAM M.

Fleecestreet's Improved Pig Latin Grammar for Modern Scholars. Los Angeles: 1963. V. 41

Type Specimen Book, Types in the Cases of William M. Cheney. Los Angeles: 1961. V. 41

CHENG, TSO-HSIN

A Synopsis of the Avifauna of China. Beijing: 1987. V. 38

CHENU, J. C.

Encyclopedie d'Histoire Naturelle . . . Paris: 1850-60. V. 39

CHEPHAN, ROBERT COTTMAN

The Defensive Armour and the Weapons and Engines of War of Mediaeval Times, and of the 'Renaissance'. London: 1900. V. 46

CHERBURY, EDWARD HERBERT, LORD

The Expedition to the Isle of Rhe. London: 1860. V. 38

The Life of Edward Lord Herbert of Cherbury, Written by Himself. Strawberry Hill,: 1764. V. 37

The Life written by himself. London: 1764. V. 37

CHEREAU, CLAUDE

Suite of Nudes. Paris: 1929. V. 41

CHERNIKOV, I.

Konstruktslia Arkhitekturnykh I Mashinykh Form. Leningrad: 1931. V. 38

CHERNIKOV, IA.

Konstrukstlia Architekturnykh i Mashinykh Form. 1931. V. 42

CHEROKEE NATION

The Act of Union Between the Eastern and Western Cherokees, the Constitution and Amendments and Laws of the Cherokee Nation, passed during the Session of 1868 and Subsequent Sessions. Tahlequah, Cherokee Nation: 1870. V. 37; 45

Communication of the Delegation of the Cherokee Nation to the President of the United States, Submitting the Memorial of Their National Council . . . Washington: 1866. V. 45

Constitution of the Cherokee Nation, Made and Established at a General Convention of Delegates . . . at New Echota, July 26, 1827. Milledgeville: 1827. V. 41

Constitution and Laws of the Cherokee Nation. St. Louis: 1875. V. 37; 39; 41; 42; 45

Constitution and Laws of the Cherokee Nation Published by an Act of the National Council. Parsons, Kansas: 1892. V. 37; 46

Laws of the Cherokee Nation; Adopted by the Council at Various Periods. (and) The Constitution and Laws of the Cherokee Nation, 1839-1851. Tahlequah: 1852-52. V. 44

CHEROKEE NATION continued

Memorial and Protest of the Cherokee Nation. Memorial of the Cherokee Representatives, Submitting the Protest of the Cherokee Nation Against Ratification . . . of the Treaty Negotiated at New Echota, in December 1835. Washington: 1836. V. 45

Memorial of John Ross Representative of the Cherokee Nation of Indians, on the Subject of the Existing Difficulties in that Nation and Their Relation with the United States. Washington: 1846. V. 39; 41; 44

Reply of the Delegates of the Cherokee Nation to the Demands of the Commissioner of Indian Affairs. Washington: 1866. V. 41

CHEROKEE NATION. CONSTITUTION

The Act of Union Between the Eastern and Western Cherokees, the Constitution and Amendments and Laws of the Cherokee Nation, Passed Upon the Session of 1868 and Subjsequent Sessions. Tahlequah, Cherokee Nation: 1870. V. 38

CHEROKEE NATION. CONVENTION - 1861

Proceedings of the Cherokee Convention. Talquah: 1861. V. 42

CHEROKEE NATION. LAWS, STATUTES, ETC. - 1893

Constitution and Laws of the Cherokee Nation. Parsons: 1893. V. 42

THE CHEROKEE Strip. The Mound City, Cherokee Strip Town Site and Land Company . . . St. Louis: 1892? V. 42

CHERRY-GARRARD, APSLEY

The Worst Journey in the World. 1923. V. 39

The Worst Journey in the World. Antarctic 1910-1913. London: & New York: 1923. V. 42

The Worst Journey in the World. London: 1929. V. 37

The Worst Journey in the World. Antarctic 1900-1913. London: 1922. V. 37; 43

CHERRY, J. L.

Life and Remains of John Clare. London: 1873. V. 42

CHERTABLON

La Maniere de se Bien Preparer a La Mort par des Considerations sur la Cene, la Passion, et la Mort de Jesus-Christ, avec des Tres Belles Estampes Emblematiques. Antwerp: 1700. V. 38

CHERUBIN D'ORLEANS, FRANCOIS LASSERE

La Dioptrique Oculaire, ou La Theorique, La Positive, et La Mechanique, de l'Oculaire Dioptrique en Toutes ses Especes. Paris: 1671. V. 38

CHERUBINI, LUIGI

A Course of Counterpoint and Fugue. London: 1837. V. 37

CHERUBINO DA SIENA

Regola De la Vita Spirituale. Florence: 1490. V. 40

CHESAPEAKE AND DELAWARE CANAL CO.

Laws of the Legislatures of Maryland, Delaware and Pennsylvania, Respecting the Chesapeake & Delaware Canal. Philadelphia: 1803. V. 39

CHESAPEAKE & OHIO CANAL CONVENTION

Proceedings of the . . . . Which Assembled in the Capitol of the United States, in the City of Washington. On the Sixth Day of November, 1823, and re-assembled in the same city on the Sixth Day of December, 1826. Washington City: 1827. V. 42

CHESELDEN, WILLIAM

The Anatomy of the Human Body. London: 1726. V. 46

The Anatomy of the Human Body. London: 1740. V. 41

The Anatomy of the Human Body. London: 1741. V. 41

The Anatomy of the Human Body. London: 1768. V. 43

The Anatomy of the Human Body. London: 1778. V. 46

The Anatomy of the Human Body. Boston: 1795. V. 45

The Anatomy of the Human Body. Boston: 1806. V. 40; 42

The Anatomy of the Human Body. London: 1868. V. 46

The Anatomy of the Human Body. London: 1756. V. 37

Cheselden's Plates of the Human Bones, correctly reduced from the original copy and improved with additional figures . . . Edinburgh: 1816. V. 37

Osteographia, or the Anatomy of the Bones. N.P.. V. 40

Osteographia, or, the Anatomy of the Bones. Philadelphia: 1968. V. 42

CHESHIRE, EDWARD

The Results of the Census of Great Britain in 1851 . . . London: 1853. V. 41

CHESHIRE, FRANK R.

Bees and Bee-keeping: Scientific and Practical. London: 1886-88. V. 40; 45

CHESHIRE, JOHN

A Treatise Upon the Rheumatism, with Observations Upon Some Causes that May Produce It. London: 1723. V. 41

CHESNEAU, AUGUSTIN

Emblemes Sacrez sur le Tres-Saint et Tres-Adorable Sacrement de l'Euchariste. Paris: 1667. V. 39

CHESNEY, A. G.

Historical Records of the Maltese Corps of the British Army. London: 1897. V. 42

CHESNEY, ALAN

The Johns Hopkins Hospital and the Johns Hopkins University School of Medicine, A Chronicle . . . Baltimore: 1943-1963. V. 37

CHESNEY, ALAN M.

The Johns Hopkins Hospital and Johns Hopkins University School of Medicine. A Chronicle. Baltimore: 1943. V. 40

The Johns Hopkins Hospital and the Johns Hopkins University School of Medicine, a Chronicle. Baltimore: 1943/58/63. V. 38; 40

CHESNEY, DORA GREENWELL

Miriam cromwell Royalist. Chicago: 1897. V. 38

CHESNEY, F. R.

Observations on the Past and Present State of Fire-Arms and on the Probable Effects in War of the New Musket. London: 1852. V. 46

CHESNEY, FRANCIS RAWDON

Narrative of the Euphrates Expedition carried on by Order of the British Government during the Years 1835, 1836 and 1837. London: 1868. V. 37; 40

Reports on the Navigation of the Euphrates. London: 1833. V. 40

CHESNEY, G. T.

The Battle of Dorking. Edinburgh: 1871. V. 38

CHESNUTT, CHARLES WADDELL

The Colonel's Dream. New York: 1905. V. 39; 41; 42; 44; 45; 46

The Conjure woman. Boston: 1899. V. 37; 38; 39; 44; 46

The House Behind the Cedars. Boston: 1900. V. 43; 44

The Marrow of Tradition. 1901. V. 44

The Marrow of Tradition. Boston: 1901. V. 45

The Wife of His Youth. 1899. V. 44

CHESS Made Easy. Philadelphia: 1802. V. 40

CHESSON, NORA

Selected Poems. London: 1906. V. 41

CHESTER, ALDEN

Courts and Lawyers of New York: a History 1609-1925. New York: 1925. V. 46

CHESTER & HOLYHEAD RAILWAY

Railway Companion from Chester to Holyhead and Guide to Dublin. Chester: 1849. V. 46

CHESTER, ANTHONY

Scheeps-Togt Van Anthony Chester, Na Virginia, Gedaan in Het Jaar 1620 . . . Leyden: 1707. V. 39; 41

CHESTER ARCHAEOLOGICAL SOCIETY

Journal. London: 1851-1970. V. 38

CHESTER, LEONARD

Federalism Triumphant in the Steady Habits of Connecticut Alone, or, the Turnpike Road to a Fortune. N.P.: Hartford?: 1802. V. 37

THE CHESTER Miscellany. Chester: 1750. V. 42

THE CHESTER Play of the Deluge. 1927. V. 38
THE CHESTER Play of the Deluge. Waltham St. Lawrence: 1927. V. 37; 42; 45
THE CHESTER Play of the Deluge. London: 1977. V. 37; 40; 41; 42; 45

CHESTER PLAYS

The Chester Plays: a Collection of Mysteries Founded Upon Scriptural Subjects . . . London: 1843/47. V. 44

The Chester Play of the Deluge. 1927. V. 40

The Chester Play of the Deluge. 1977. V. 42

The Chester Play of the Deluge. 1977. V. 42

CHESTER, SAMUEL HALL

Pioneer Days in Arkansas. Richmond: 1927. V. 42

CHESTERFIELD Burlesqued, or, School for Modern Manners. London: 1811. V. 38; 39

CHESTERFIELD, PHILIP DORMER STANHOPE, 4TH EARL OF 1694-1773

An Apology for a Late Resignation: in a Letter from an English Gentleman to His Friend at the Hague. London: 1748. V. 43

CHESTERFIELD, PHILIP DORMER STANHOPE, 4TH EARL OF 1694-1773 continued

The Case of the Hanover Forces in the Pay of Great Britain, Impartially and Freely Examined . . . London: 1743. V. 41; 45

Characters of Eminent Personages of His Own Time . . . London: 1777. V. 39; 45; 46

Correspondence with Various Ladies, among whom is notably Barbara Villiers . . . an Letters Exchanged with Sir Charles Sedley, Dryden, Charles Cotton, Mr. Bates, etc. London: (1930). V. 37; 42

Letter Written by the Late Right Honourable Philip Dormer Stanhope, Earl of Chesterfield, to His Son Philip Stanhope, Esq. London: 1774. V. 41

Letters Written by the Late Right Honourable Philip Dormer Stanhope, Earl of Chesterfield, to his son, Philip Stanhope. Dublin: 1774. V. 38; 41; 43; 44; 46

Letters Written by the Late Right Honorable Philip Dormer Stanhope, Earl of Chesterfield to His Son . . . London: 1774. V. 37; 38; 39; 40; 42; 43; 45; 46

Letters to His Son. London: 1774. V. 44

Letters to His Son, Philip Stanhope, Esq. London: 1774. V. 38; 46

Letters. (with) Miscellaneous Works. Dublin: 1775. V. 40

Letters . . . to His Son, Philip Stanhope, Esq. London: 1775. V. 40

Letters Written by the Late Right Honourable Philip Dormer Stanhope, Earl of Chesterfield to His Son Philip Stanhope . . . London: 1776. V. 46

Letters Written . . . To His Son . . . Together with Several Other Pieces on Various Subjects. London: 1792. V. 42

Letters Written . . . to His Son . . . Together with Several Other Pieces on Various Subjects. London: 1792. V. 46

Letters Written by the Late Right Hon. Philip Dormer Stanhope . . . London: 1803. V. 40

The Letters of . . . Including Numerous Letters Now First Published from the Original Manuscripts. London: 1845. V. 39; 43

Letters to His Godson and Successor. Oxford: 1890. V. 37; 43

Letters of Philip Dormer . . . to His Godson and Successor. Oxford: 1890. V. 41

Letters of . . . to His Son. London: 1901. V. 37; 44

Letters to His Son by the Earl of Chesterfield, on The Fine Art of Becoming a Man of the World and a Gentleman. London: 1926. V. 38; 45

The Letters . . . London: 1932. V. 46

The Letters of Philip Dormer Stanhope, 4th Earl of Chesterfield. London: 1932. V. 38; 39; 40; 42; 46

The Life of the Late Earl of Chesterfield: or the Man of the World. London: 1774. V. 37; 45

The Life of the Late Earl of Chesterfield; or, the Man of the World. Philadelphia: 1775. V. 44

Lord Chesterfield's Advice to His Son, on Men and manners . . . London: 1795. V. 41

Miscellaneous Works . . . Dublin: 1777. V. 41

Miscellaneous Works. London: 1777. V. 37; 39; 43; 44; 46

Miscellaneous Works . . . London: 1778. V. 38

Miscellaneous Works . . . London: 1779. V. 39; 41; 46

The Poetical Works. 1927. V. 39

The Poetical Works. 1927. V. 38

Poetical Works. London: 1927. V. 40; 45

CHESTERFIELD, RUTH

A New Version of Old Mother Hubbard. New York: 1866. V. 45

Old Mother Hubbard. A New Version. Boston: 1866. V. 41

CHESTERFIELD Travestie; or, School for Modern Manners. London: 1808. V. 38

CHESTERON, GEORGE LAVAL

A Narrative of Proceedings in Venezuela, in South America, in the Years 1819 and 18120. London: 1820. V. 43

CHESTERTON, GEORGE LAVAL

Peace, War and Adventure: an Autobiographical Memoir. London: 1853. V. 43; 45; 46

Revelations of Prison Life . . . London: 1856. V. 42

CHESTERTON, GILBERT KEITH 1874-1936

Autobiography. London: 1936. V. 39; 43

The Ball and the Cross. London: 1910. V. 41

The Ballad of the White Horse. London: 1911. V. 40; 41; 42

The Ballad of the White Horse. London: 1928. V. 45

Biography for Beginners; Being a Collection of Miscellaenous Examples for the Use of Upper Forms. London: 1905. V. 39

The Catholic Church and Conversion. New York: 1926. V. 41

Charles Dickens. London: 1906. V. 38; 40

The Club of Queer Trades. London: 1905. V. 40; 46

The Collected Poems. London: 1927. V. 41

The Coloured Lands. 1938. V. 43

The Coloured Lands. London: 1938. V. 43

The Coloured Lands. New York: 1938. V. 42

The Coloured Lands. 1938. V. 43

The Crimes of England. London: 1915. V. 38

The Defendant. London: 1901. V. 43

Divorce Verses Democracy. London: 1916. V. 38

Eugenics and Other Evils. London: 1922. V. 41

The Flying Inn. London: 1914. V. 38; 44

Gloria, In Profundis. (London: 1927). V. 37

Gloria in Profundis. New York: 1927. V. 37; 42; 43; 44

The Grave of Arthur. London: 1930. V. 43

Greybeards at Play Literature and Art for Old Gentlemen. London: 1900. V. 41; 42

A Half Century of Views. 1987. V. 40

The Incredulity of Father Brown. New York: 1926. V. 45

The Innocence of Father Brown. London: 1911. V. 38; 41; 42; 45

The Innocence of Father Brown. Illustrated by Will B. Foster. New York: 1911. V. 37

London. London: 1914. V. 37

Magic - a Fantastic Comedy. London: 1913. V. 43

The Man Who was Thursday. 1908. V. 39

The Man Who Knew Too Much. 1922. V. 37

The Man Who Knew Too Much. New York: 1922. V. 43; 46

Manalive. London: 1912. V. 37; 38; 40; 46

The Napoleon of Notting Hill. London: 1904. V. 38; 42; 44

Orthodoxy. New York: 1911. V. 45

The Poet and the Lunatics. New York: 1929. V. 41; 42; 43; 45

The Resurrection of Rome. London: 1934. V. 41; 42

The Return of Don Quioxte. 1927. V. 44

The Return of Don Quixote. 1927. V. 45

The Return of Don Quixote. London: 1927. V. 41; 42; 44; 46

Robert Louis Stevenson. London: 1927. V. 38

St. Francis of Assisi. London: 1926. V. 41

The Scandal of Father Brown. London: 1935. V. 43

The Sword of Wood. London: 1928. V. 38

The Sword of Wood. London. V. 37

Tales of the Long Bow. London: 1925. V. 45

The Thing - a Book of Essays. London: 1929. V. 40; 43

The Turkey and the Turk. N.P.: 1930. V. 46

What's Wrong With the World. London: 1910. V. 44

CHETHAM, HUMPHREY

The Last Will of Humphrey Chetham, of Clayton, in the County of Lancester, Esq. Dated December 16, 1651. Manchester: 18th century? V. 39

CHETHAM, JAMES

The Anglr's Vade-Mecum . . . London: 1689. V. 39; 40

The Anglers Vade Mecum; or, a Compendious yet Full Discourse of Angling. London: 1700. V. 43

CHETLAIN, AUGUSTUS L.

Recollections of Seventy Years. Galena: 1899. V. 37; 39

CHETWOOD, WILLIAM RUFUS d. 1766

A General History of the Stage, From its Origin in Greece Down to the Present Time. London: 1649. V. 42

A General History of the Stage, From Its Origin in Greece Down to the Present Time. London: 1749. V. 40

The Voyages, Dangerous, Adventures, and Imminent Escapes of Capt. Rich. Falconer. London: 1724. V. 43

Voyages and Adventures of Captain Robert Boyle, in Several Parts of the World. London: 1768. V. 40

The Voyages and Adventures of Captain Robert Boyle, in Several Parts of the World. London: 1781. V. 44

The Voyages and Adventures of Captain Robert Boyle, in Several Parts of the World. New York: 1805. V. 45

The Voyages and Adventures of Captain Robert Boyle, in Several Parts of the World . . . To Which is added, the Voyagae, Shipwreck and Miraculous Preservation of Richard Castaleman, Gent . . . London: 1726. V. 37

The Voyages, Dangerous Adventures and Imminent Escapes of Captain Richard Falconer. London: 1720. V. 37

CHETWYND, GEORGE

Racing Reminiscences and Experiences of the Turf. London: 1891. V. 43; 44

CHETWYND, JULIA BOSVILLE DAVIDSON

Neighbors and Friends. London: 1868. V. 40

CHETWYND, WILLIAM

The Trial of William Chetwynd, Gent. on Three Several Indictments, for the murder of Mr. Thomas Ricketts. Dublin: 1744. V. 37

CHEVALIER, FRANCOIS

America's Cup Yacht Designs 1851-1986. Paris: 1987. V. 41

CHEVALIER, GUILLAUME DE d. 1620

Le Decez ou Fin du Monde, Divise en Trois Visions. Paris: 1584. V. 39

CHEVALIER, JEAN BAPTISTE

Description of the Plain of Troy . . . Edinburgh: 1791. V. 40; 45

CHEVALIER, MICHEL

Briefe uber Nord-Amerika oder Schilderung der . . . Zustande der Vereinigten Staaten . . . Leipzig: 1837. V. 38

Cours d'Economie Politique Fait au College de France. Paris: 1855-58-66. V. 43

The Labour Question. London: 1848. V. 42

Lettres sur l'Amerique Du Nord. Paris: 1837. V. 43

Mexico, Ancient and Modern. London: 1864. V. 37

On the Probable Fall in Value of Gold. Manchester: 1859. V. 38

On the Probable Fall in the Value of Gold; The Commercial and Social Consequences Which May Ensue, and the Measures Which It Invites. Manchester/London/Edinburgh: 1859. V. 41

On the Probable Fall in the Value of Gold; the Commercial and Social Consequences Which May Ensure, and the Measures Which It Invites. New York: 1859. V. 41

On the Probable Fall in the Value of Gold: The Commerical and Social Consequences which may ensue, and the Measures which it invites. Translated from the French with preface by Richard Cobden. Machester/London: 1859. V. 37

Society, Manners and Politics in the United States: Being a SEries of Letters on North America. Boston: 1839. V. 38; 39; 40; 42; 43

CHEVALIER, NICHOLAS

Histoire de Guillaume III . . . Amsterdam: 1692. V. 44

CHEVREUIL, MICHEL EUGENE

The Prinipals of Harmony and Contrast of Colours and Their Applications to the Arts . . . London: 1855. V. 44

The Principles of Harmony and Contrast of Colours, and Their Applications to the Arts . . . London: 1890. V. 44

CHEVREUL

The Laws of Contrast of Colour: An Their Application to the Arts . . . London: (c. 1868). V. 37

CHEVREUL, MICHEL EUGENE

De la Loi du Contraste Simultane des Couleurs, et de l'Assortiment des Objets Colores. Paris: 1889. V. 46

The Laws and Contrast of Colour; and Their Application to the Arts of Painting, Decoration of Buildings, Mosaic Works, Tapestry and Carpet Weaving, Calico Printing, Dress, Paper Staining, Printing, Illumination . . . London: 1859. V. 41

The Laws of Contrast of Colour; and Their Application to the Arts. London: 1860. V. 38

The Laws of Contrast of Colour; and their Application to the Arts of Painting, Decoration of Buildigns, Mosaic Work . . . London: 1861. V. 42

The Laws of Contrast of Colour and their Application to the Arts of Paitning, Decoration of Buildings, Mosaic Work, Tapesty and Carpet Weaving, Calico Printing, Dress, Paper STaining, Printing, Military Clothing, Illumination . . . London: 1880. V. 46

The Laws of Contrast of Colour: and their Application to the Arts . . . London: 1858. V. 38

The Principles of Harmony and Contrast of Colours, and Their Applications to the Arts. London: 1855. V. 45

The Principles of Harmony, and Contrast of Colours, and Their Applications to the Arts. London: 1870. V. 42

The Principles of Harmony and Contrast of Colours, and Their Applications to the Arts. London: 1870. V. 38

CHEVRIER, ANTOINE FRANCOISE

Le Colporteur. Histoire Morale et Critique. London - Paris: ?1761. V. 39

CHEVRILLON, ANDRE

England and the War. New York: 1918. V. 41

CHEW, BEVERLY

Essays and Verses about Books. New York: 1926. V. 44

The Longfellow Collectors' Handbook: a Bibliography of First Editions. New York: 1885. V. 42; 46

CHEW, ROGER PRESTON

Stonewall Jackson. Lexington: 1912. V. 44

CHEW, SAMUEL

Lectures on Medical Education, Or On the Proper Method of Studying Medicine. Philadelphia: 1864. V. 42

CHEWETT, W. C.

W. C. Chewett and Co.'s Toronto City Directory, 1868-9. Toronto: 1868. V. 44

CHEYNE, GEORGE 1671-1743

Dr. Cheyne's Own Account of Himself and of His Writings. London: 1743. V. 41

The English Malady. London: 1733. V. 45

The English Malady; or, A Treatise of Nervous Diseases of All Kinds . . . London: 1734. V. 40; 41; 45

The English Malady: or, a Treatise of Nervous Diseases of all Kinds; as Spleen, Vapours, Lowness of Spirits, Hypochondriacal, and Hysterical Distempers, &c. London: 1735. V. 37; 42

An Essay on the Gout, with an Account of the Nature and Qualities of the Bath Waters. London: 1720. V. 42

An Essay on Health and Long Life. London: 1724. V. 37; 38; 39; 40; 41; 45; 46

An Essay on Health and Long Life. London: 1725. V. 40; 41; 42

An Essay on Regimen. Together With Five Discourses, Medical, Moral and Philosophical . . . London: 1740. V. 40; 42

An Essay of Health and Long Life. London: 1745. V. 44

An Essay of the True Nature and Due Method of Treating the Gout . . . London: 1724. V. 38; 39; 40

Essay on Health and Long Life. New York: 1813. V. 38

An Essay on the True Nature and Due Method of Treating the Gout . . . London: 1738. V. 38

The Natural Method of Cureing the Diseases of the Body and the Disorders of the Mind Depending on the Body . . . London: 1742. V. 38; 43

A New Theory of Acute and Slow Continu'd Fevers . . . London: 1702. V. 41

Philosophical Principles of Religion; Natural and Revealed, In Two Parts. London: 1715. V. 38

Philosophical Principles of Religion. Natural and Revealed. London: 1724. V. 41

CHEYNE, JOHN

An Essay on Cynanche Trachealis or Croup. Philadelphia: 1813. V. 37; 38

An Essay on the Bowel Complaints of Children . . . Philadelphia: 1813. V. 41

An Essay on Hydrocephalus Acutus. Philadelphia: 1814. V. 40

CHEYNE, W. WATSON

Recent Essays by Various Authors on Bacteria in Relation to Diesease. London: 1886. V. 45

CHI, LU

Wen Fu: The Art of Writing. British Columbia: 1986. V. 41

CHIAIE, S. DELLE

Hydrophytologiae Regni Neapolitani Icones. Naples: 1829. V. 40

CHIANG, MEI-LING SUNG 1897-

Sian: a Coup d'Etat. Shanghai: 1937. V. 42; 46

War Messages and Other Selections by May-Ling Soon Chiang (Madame Chiang Kai-Shek). N.P.: 1938. V. 39

CHIARAMONTI, SCIPION

De Sede Cometarum, et Novorum Phaenoemn. Forolivii: 1648. V. 38

CHIARI, JOSEPH

Collected Poems. London: 1978. V. 37

CHIARINI, MARCO

Claudio Lorenese Disegni. Florence: 1968. V. 43

CHIARTI, L'ABBATE

The Prize in the Lottery; or, the Adventures of a Young Lady. London: 1817. V. 41

CHICAGO AND NORTH WESTERN RAILWAY COMPANY

Sixth Annual Report of the Chicago and North Western Railway Company. New York: 1865. V. 37; 39; 42

CHICAGO and the World's Fair 1933. Chicago: 1933. V. 37

CHICAGO By Day and Night. Palmyra: 1892. V. 37

THE CHICAGO Chronicle's Unrivaled Atlas of the World. Chicago/New York: 1901. V. 45

CHICAGO Great Western Railroad's New Census Atlas of the United States, Canada and Mexico. Chicago: 1912. V. 41

CHICAGO. LINCOLN PARK COMMISSIONERS.

Report of the Commissioners and a History of Lincoln Park. Chicago: 1899. V. 39

THE CHICAGO Magazine. Chicago: 1857. V. 39

CHICAGO, MILWAUKEE & PUGET SOUND RAILWAY

Across the Continent. Seattle: 1911. V. 46

CHICAGO ROCK ISLAND AND PACIFIC RAILROAD

Great Overland Route! . . . for California, Oregon, Australia, China and Japan. Chicago: 1870's. V. 39

Take the . . . for Peoria, Des Moines, Council Bluffs, Omaha, Cheyenne, Denver, Salt Lake, Ogden . . . San Francisco, and all Points in the Territories . . . Chicago: 1870's. V. 39

CHICHELE, HENRY

The Register of Henry Chichele, Archbishop of Canterbury, 1414-1443. Oxford: 1938-43-45-47. V. 43

CHICHESTER, HENRY MANNERS

The Records and Badges of Every Regiment and Corps in the British Army. London: 1895. V. 40

The Records and Badges of Every Regiment and Corps in the British Army. Aldershot: 1899. V. 38

CHICKASAW NATION

Constitution, Laws and Traties of the Chickasaws. Tishomingo City: 1860. V. 45

CHICKASAW NATION. CONSTITUTION

Constitution, Treaties and Laws of the Chickasaw Nation. Atoka Indian Territory: 1890. V. 39

CHICKERING, FRANCES E.

Cloud Crystals. New York: 1883. V. 38

CHICKERING, FRANCIS E.

Cloud Crystals; a Snow Flake Album. New York: 1864/63. V. 44

CHICKERING, WILLIAM H.

Letters from the Pacific Written by . . . War Correspondent to His Family 1942-1944. San Francisco: 1946. V. 40

CHIDLAW, B. W.

Yr American, Yr Hwn Sydd Yn Cynnwys Nodau, at Daith O Ddyffryn Ohio I Gymru, Golwg Ar Dalaeth Ohio . . . Llanrwst: 1840. V. 45

CHIEFS of the Blackfeet Nation. N.P.. V. 41

LES CHIENS Le Gibier et ses Ennemis. Saint-Etienne: 1907. V. 41

CHIERA, EDWARD

Joint Expedition with the Iraq Museum at Nuzi. Paris: 1927-30. V. 42

Lists of Personal Names from the Temple School of Nippur. A syllabary of personal names. Philadelphia: 1916-1919. V. 37; 40; 42; 44

Sumerian Religious Texts. Upland: 1924. V. 40

Sumerian Epics and Myths. Chicago: (1934). V. 37

CHIEREGATUS, LEONELLO d. 1506

Oratio Habita Rome in Ecclesia Sancti Petri in Funere . . . Rome: 1492. V. 40

CHIEWITZ, ELIS

Svenska Teater-Galleriet. Stockholm: 1826. V. 38

CHIFFLET, JEAN JACQUES 1588-1660

De Linteis Sepulchralibus Christi Servatoris Crisi Historica. Antwerp: 1624. V. 45

CHIFFLET, JULES

Les Marques d'Honneur de la Maison de Tassis. Antwerp: 1645. V. 46

CHIFNEY, SAMUEL

Genius Genuine. London: Jan. 9, 1804. V. 43

CHIGNELL, ROBERT

The Life and Paintings of Vicat Cole, R.A. London: 1896. V. 38; 40

CHIKAMATSU

Masterpieces of Chikamatsu: the Japanese Shakespeare. London: 1926. V. 41

CHIKASHIGE, MASUMI

The Complete Distiller: Combining Theory and Practice; and Explaining the Mysteries and Most Recent Improvements of Distilling and Brewing . . . Edinburgh: 1793. V. 42

CHIKU, K. S.

The Complete Distiller. Edinburgh: 1793. V. 40

CHILCOTT, JOHN

Chilcott's New Guide to Bristol, Clifton and the Hotwells. Bristol: 1826. V. 40

THE CHILD Set in the Midst. London: 1892. V. 38

CHILD, ANDREW

Overland Route to California. Los Angeles: 1946. V. 40

CHILD, DAVID LEE

An Appeal from David L. Childs (sic) Editor of the Anti-Slavery Standard, to the Abolitionists. Albany: 1844. V. 39; 42

The Texan Revolution. Washington: 1843. V. 38; 39; 42; 45

CHILD, EDMUND B.

Child's Albany Directory and City Register. Albany: 1833. V. 46

CHILD, FRANCIS JAMES

The English and Scottish Popular Ballads. Boston: 1882. V. 41; 44

The English and Scottish Popular Ballads. Boston: 1882-98. V. 46

The English and Scottish Popular Ballads. Boston & New York: 1892-98. V. 42

English and Scottish Ballads. Boston: 1864. V. 37

Some British Ballads. New York: 1919. V. 46

CHILD, HAMILTON

Gazetteer of Grafton County, N.H. 1709-1886. Syracuse: 1886. V. 39

CHILD, JOHN

New-Englands Jonas Cast Up at London: or, A Relation of the Proceedings of the Court at Boston in New England . . . London: 1647. V. 42; 44

CHILD, JOSIAH 1630-1699

A New Discourse of Trade, Wherein is Recommended Several Weighty Points Relating to Companies of Merchants. London: 1693. V. 38; 42; 44; 46

A New Discourse of Trade, Wherein is Recommended Several Weighty Points Relating to Companies of Merchants. London: 1698. V. 38; 41; 45

A New Discourse of Trade . . . Relating to Companies of Merchants; the Act of Navigation, Nturalization of Strangers, and Our Woolen Manufactures. London: 1740? V. 38

A New Discourse of Trade . . . Glasgow: 1751. V. 39; 46

A New Discourse of Trade . . . relating to Companies of Merchants . . . Act of Navigation . . . Naturalization of Strangers . . . Woollen manufactures . . . Balance of Trade . . . Employment and Maintenance of the Poor . . . Reduction of Interest . . . London: (1700). V. 37

A Treatise Wherein Is Demonstrated, I. That the East-India Trade is the Most National of All Foreign Trades. II. That the Clamors, Aspersions, and Operations Made Against the Present East-India Co . . . IV. That the Trade of the East-Indies . . . London: 1681. V. 42; 44; 45

CHILD, LYDIA MARIA FRANCIS 1802-1880

The American Frugal Housewife. New York: 1842. V. 40

American Frugal Housewife, Dedicated to Those Who are Not Ashamed of Economy. Boston: 1836. V. 37; 45

Ann Greene Chapman of Boston. N.P.: 1837? V. 44

Anti-Slavery Catechism. Newburyport: 1836. V. 42

An Appeal in Favor of that Class of Americans Called Africans. Boston: 1833. V. 43; 44

An Appeal in Favor of That Class of Americans, Called Africans. New York: 1836. V. 42

Autumnal Leaves. Tales and Sketches in Prose and Rhyme. New York: 1857. V. 45

Frugal Housewife. Dedicated to Those Who Are Not Ashamed of Economy. Boston. V. 37

Hobomok, a Tale of Early Times. Boston: 1824. V. 46

Isaac T. Hopper: a True Life. Boston: 1853. V. 44

Letters from New York. New York: 1843. V. 43; 44

Letters from New York. (First Series). New York: & Boston: 1843. V. 44

Letters from New York. Second Series. New York: 1845. V. 44

Letters . . . Boston: 1883. V. 37; 39

Married Women: Biographies of Good Wives. New York: 1871. V. 44

The Mother's Book. Boston: 1831. V. 40

The Oasis. Boston: 1834. V. 43

The Progress of Religious Ideas, Through Successive Ages. New York: 1855. V. 45

CHILD, THEODORE

The Spanish American Republics. New York: 1891. V. 41

CHILD, WILLIAM H.

History of the Town of Cornish, New Hampshire with Genealogical Record 1763-1910. Concord: 1911. V. 42

CHILDBIRTH; Its Pains Greatly Lessened, Its Perils Entirely Obviated . . . New York: 1845. V. 45

CHILDE, V. GORDON

Prehistoric Migrations in Europe. Oslo: 1950. V. 41

Skara Brae. A Pictish Village in Orkney. London: 1931. V. 45

CHILDE, WILFRED ROLAND

Dream English, a Fantastical Romance. London: 1917. V. 40

CHILDERS, ERSKINE

Military Rule in Ireland . . . Dublin: 1920. V. 41

CHILDERS, ERSKINE continued

The Riddle of the Sands - a Record of Secret Service Recently Recieved. Barre: 1971. V. 44

CHILDERS, JAMES SAXON

The Bookshop Mystery. New York: 1930. V. 38

THE CHILDREN in the Wood. London: 1830. V. 39

THE CHILDREN of Apollo: a Poem. London: 1794? V. 41

THE CHILDREN of the Bible. London: 1850's. V. 38

THE CHILDREN'S Book of Pantomimes . . . London: 1930. V. 43

THE CHILDREN'S Christmas Treasury of Things New and Old. London: 1905. V. 45

THE CHILDREN'S Hour. Boston: 1907. V. 46

THE CHILDREN'S Miscellany. London: 1815. V. 45

A CHILDREN'S Sampler: Selections from Famous Children's Books. V.P.: 1950. V. 39

CHILDREN'S Songs for Town and Country Life. 1860. V. 45
CHILDREN'S Songs for Town and Country Life. London: 1860. V. 46

CHILDRESS, ALICE

Like One of the Family. Brooklyn: 1956. V. 45
Like One of the Family. Indepdence: 1956. V. 44

A CHILD'S Book of Stories. New York: 1911. V. 43

CHILDS, C. G.

No. 1. Views of Philadelphia. Philadelphia: 1827. V. 41; 45

THE CHILD'S First Book. Richmond: 1864. V. 43; 45

CHILDS, GEORGE

Childs' Drawing Book of Objects . . . Philadelphia: 1845. V. 44
Woodland Sketches, a Series of Characteristic Portraits of Trees . . . London: 1839. V. 46

THE CHILD'S Instructor or Picture Alphabet. Glasgow: 1815. V. 43

CHILDS, J. RIVES

An Annotated World Bibliography of Jacques Casanova de Seingalt and of Works Concerning Him. Vienna: 1956. V. 40

THE CHILD'S Picture Scrap Book . . . London: 1865. V. 45

CHILD'S Play. London: 1859. V. 44

A CHILD'S Rosary Book. Ditchling: 1924. V. 41

THE CHILD'S Treasury of Knowledge and Amusement; or, Reuben Ramble's Picture Lessons. London: 1842. V. 44

CHILE. CONSTITUTION - 1818

Proyecto de Constitucion Provisoria Para el estado de Chile. Santiago de Chile: 1818, V. 38

CHILLINGWORTH, WILLIAM 1602-1644

The Religion of Protestants a Safe Way to Salvation. London: 1638. V. 39
The Works. London: 1704. V. 39
The Works . . . London: 1742. V. 45

CHILTON, CHARLES

Journey Into Space. London: 1954. V. 42

CHILTON, F. B.

Unveiling and Dedication of Monument to Hood's Texas Brigade on the Capitol Grounds at Austin, Texas . . . Houston: 1911. V. 44

CHILVER, G. E. F.

Cisalpine Gaul: Social and Economic History from 49 BC to the Death of Trajan. Oxford: 1941. V. 42; 44

CHINA in Miniature. Boston: 1833. V. 39

CHINATOWN Declared a Nuisance! San Francisco,: 1880. V. 39

CHINESE Decorated Papers. 1987. V. 40
CHINESE Decorated Papers. 1987. V. 45
CHINESE Decorated Papers. Newtown: 1987. V. 38; 40; 45

CHINESE Immigration; Its Social, Moral and Political Effect. Sacramento: 1878. V. 40

THE CHINESE Junk 'keying'. Descriptive Particulars; with an Account of Her Voyage from China. London: 1848. V. 40

CHINESE Natural History Drawings, Selected from the Reeves Collection in the British Museum (Natural History). London: 1974. V. 37

THE CHINESE Traveller. London: 1772. V. 42; 44
THE CHINESE Traveller. London: 1775. V. 41

CHING, RAYMOND

The Bird Paintings. Watercolours and Pencil Drawings 1969-1975. London: 1978. V. 37

Studies and Sketches of a Bird Painter. Melbourne: 1981. V. 37; 40

CHIPMAN, DANIEL

An Essay on the Law of Contracts, for the Payment of Specifick articles. Middlebury: 1822. V. 38; 40

CHIPMAN, GEORGE

The American Moralist. Wrentham: 1801. V. 42

CHIPMAN, NATHANIEL

Principles of Government, a Treatise on Free Insitutitions, Including the Constitution of the United States. Burlington: 1833. V. 38; 43; 44
Reports and Dissertations, In Two Parts. Rutland: 1793. V. 40

CHIPPENDALE, THOMAS

The Gentleman and Cabinet-Maker's Director. London: 1754. V. 40; 44
The Gentleman and Cabinet-Maker's Director. London: 1755. V. 45
The Gentleman and Cabinet Maker's Director. London: 1762. V. 41
The Gentleman and Cabinet-Maker's Director. (with) Supplement. A Gallery of Chippendale Furniture and a Sketch of Chippendale's Life and Works by Walter Rendell Storey. New York: 1938. V. 39; 41
Le Guide du Tapissier de l'Ebeniste, et de Tous Ceux qui Travaillent en Meubles. London: 1762. V. 41

CHIRINO, JUAN

Sumario de las Persecuciones que a Tenido la Yglesia Desde su Principio. Granada: 1593. V. 37

CHIRONE, VANNA

The House of God through the Ages. Rome: 1960-61. V. 39

CHISELDEN, WILLIAM

Osteographia or the Anatomy of Bones. London: 1970's. V. 39

CHISHOLM, C. R.

Chisholm's All Round Route and Panoramic Guide of the St. Lawrence; The Hudson River; Trenton Falls, Niagara; Toronto, The Thousand Islands and the River St. Lawrence . . . . Montreal: 1872. V. 38; 40; 42; 43; 44
Chisholm's Stranger's Guide to Montreal. Montreal: 1871. V. 40

CHISHOLM, C. R., & BROS.

The International Railway and Steam Navigation Guide, No. 132, August, 1875. Montreal: 1875. V. 45
The International Railway and Steam Navigation Guide, No. 152, April, 1877. Montreal: 1877. V. 45

CHISHOLM, LOUEY

The Enchanted Land: Tales Told Again. London: 1906. V. 45; 46
In Fairyland. London: 1904. V. 37

CHISHOLM'S All Round Route and Panoramic Guide of the St. Lawrence. Montreal: 1874. V. 46

CHISHOLM'S All Round Route and Panoramic Guide of the St. Lawrence: the Hudson River; Saratoga; Trenton Falls; Niagara; Toronto; Thousand Islands and the River St. Lawrence; Ottawa; Montreal; Quebec; the Lower St. Lawrence and the Saguenay Rivers; the .. Montreal: 1877. V. 46

CHISOLM, J. JULIAN

A Manual of Military Surgery, for the Use of Surgeons in the Confederate States Army . . . Columbia: 1864. V. 45
A Manual of Military Surgery for the Use of Surgeons in the Confederate States Army . . . Richmond: 1862. V. 38

CHIT-CHAT; or, Natural Characters; and the Manners of Real Life, Represented in a Series of Interesting Adventures. London: 1755. V. 40

CHITTENDEN, FREDERICK JAMES

The Royal Horticultural Society Dictionary of Gardening. Oxford: 1951. V. 38; 40; 46
The Royal Horticultural Society Dictionary of Gardening . . . Oxford: 1956. V. 42
Royal Horticultural Society. Dictionary of Gardening. 1956-69. V. 39

CHITTENDEN, HIRAM MARTIN

The American Fur Trade of the Far West. New York: 1902. V. 37; 38; 39; 40; 41; 42; 43; 45; 46
The American Fur Trade of the Far West . . . New York: 1935. V. 39; 42; 45
The American Fur Trade of the Far West. New York: 1936. V. 39
History of Early Steamboat Navigation on the Missouri River. New York: 1903. V. 39; 40; 41; 43; 44; 45

CHITTENDEN, HIRAM MARTIN continued

Life, Letters and Travels of Father Pierre-Jean De Smet, S.J., 1801-1873. New York: 1905. V. 37; 42; 43; 44; 45

CHITTENDEN, RUSSELL

History of the Sheffield Scientific School of Yale University 1846-1922. New Haven: 1928. V. 42; 45

CHITTENDEN, RUSSELL HENRY 1856-1943

The Nutrition of Man. New York: 1907. V. 40; 45

Physical Economy in Nutrition. New York: 1904. V. 45

CHITTENDEN, WILLIAM LARRY

Ranch Verses. New York: 1893. V. 39; 46

CHITTENDEN, WILLIAM LAWRENCE

Ranch Verses. New York & London: 1893. V. 38

CHITTY, EDWARD

The Commercial and General Lawyer . . . with a Particular Consideration . . . Which Relates to Commerce, Trade and Manufacture. London: 1834-36. V. 38; 40

The Illustrated Fly-Fisher's Text Book. London: 1845. V. 39

CHITTY, JOSEPH 1776-1841

A Practical Treatise on the Law of Nations, Relative to the Legal Effect of War on the Commerce of Belligerents and Neutrals. London: 1812. V. 38; 40

Practical Treatise on Bills of Exchange, Promissory Notes, and Bankers' Checks. London: 1834. V. 38

Precedents in Pleading: With Copious Notes on Practice, Pleading and Evidence. Springfield: 1839. V. 39

A Treatise on the Game Laws and On Fisheries. London: 1812. V. 38; 40

CHIUSHINGURA

Chiushingura or the Loyal League, a Japanese Romance. Yokhoama: 1875. V. 40

Chiushingura, or the Loyal League. London: 1880. V. 40

CHIVERS, HERBERT C.

Artistic Homes. St. Louis: 1905. V. 44

CHIVERS, THOMAS HOLLEY

The Lost Pleiad; and Other Poems. New York: 1845. V. 38; 42

Nacoochee; or, the Beautiful Star. New York: 1837. V. 44; 45; 46

Nacoochee; or, The Beautiful Star, with Other Poems. New York: 1817. V. 38

Virginalia; or, Songs of My Summer Nights. Philadelphia: 1853. V. 42

CHLADNI, ERNST FLORENS FRIEDRICH 1756-1827

Die Akustik. Leipzig: 1802. V. 42

CHMURY, B.

Anatol Petrizky. Theater-Trachten. 1929. V. 41

CHOCHRANE, CHARLES STUART

Journal of a Residence and Travels in Colombia During the years 1823 and 1824. London: 1825. V. 39

CHOCTAW NATION

Acts and Resolutions of the General Council, of the Choctaw Nation. Passed, 1904. Hugo: 1904. V. 37

Constitution and Laws of the Choctaw Nation. Together with Treaties of 1855, 1865 and 1866. New York: 1869. V. 42

CHOCTAW NATION. LAWS, STATUTES, ETC. - 1894

Chahta Oklah I Nanvlhpisa Noshkobo Micha Nanvlhpisa. (Constitution and Laws of the Choctaw Nation.) Dallas: 1894. V. 37; 39

CHOICE Examples of Art Workmanship. Selected from the Exhibition of Ancient and Medieval Art at the Society of Arts. Drawn and engraved under the superintendence of Philip de la Motte. London: 1851. V. 37

CHOICE Iowa Farming Lands 1,000,000 Acres for Sale at Low Prices on Credit or for Cash by the Iowa Railraod Land Company in Tracts to Suit Purchasers. Cedar Rapids: 1870. V. 37

CHOICE Recipes of Georgia Housekeepers. New York: 1880. V. 37

CHOICE Receipts Selected from the Best Manuscript Authorities. Published Toward the Erection of a Girl's School at Walla-Walla. Hartford: 1873. V. 40

CHOISEUL, E. F.

Memoire Historique Sur la Negociation de La France & De L'Angleterre, Depuis Le 26 Mars 1761 Jusqu'au 20 Septembre de la meme Annee, Avec Les Pieces Justificatives. Paris: 1761. V. 46

CHOISEUL-STAINVILLE, ETIENNE FRANCOIS, DUC DE

Memoire Historique sur la Negociation de la France & de l'Angleterre, Depuis le 26 Mars 1761 Jusqu'au 20 Septembre de la Meme Anee, Avec les Pieces Justificatives. Paris: 1761. V. 39; 46

CHOLET DE JETPHORT, M.

Projet d'Organisation de l'Imprimerie-Librairie, et des Arts, Etats et Professions qui y sont Attaches . . . Paris: 1807. V. 38

CHOLMLEY, HUGH

Memoirs . . . Addressed to his Two Sons, in which he gives some Account of his Family and the Distresses they underwent in the Civil Wars. London: 1787. V. 37

CHOLMONDELEY, MARY

The Danvers Jewels. London: 1887. V. 44

A Devotee: an Episode in the Life of a Butterfly. London: 1897. V. 44

Moth and Rust, Together with Geoffrey's Wife and the Pitfall. London: 1902. V. 44

Prisoners (Fast Bound in Misery and Iron). London: 1906. V. 44

Prisoners: Fast Bound in Misery and Iron. New York: 1906. V. 44

Red Pottage. London: 1899. V. 44

The Romance of His Life and Other Romances. London: 1921. V. 44

Sir Charles Danvers. London: 1889. V. 44

Under One Roof: a Family Record. London: 1918. V. 44

CHOLMONDELLEY-PENNELL, H.

Puck on Pegasus. London: 1869. V. 39

CHOLNOKY, B. J.

Diatomaceae I and II. Lehre: 1966-70. V. 38

CHOMEL, NOEL

Dictionaire Oeconomique; or, the Family Dictionary . . . Dublin: 1727. V. 38; 39

Dictionnaire Oeconomique; or, the Family Dictionary . . . London: 1725. V. 38; 39; 40; 41

CHOPIN, KATE

Bayou Folk. Boston: 1894. V. 39; 41; 45; 46

Bayou Folk. Boston and New York: 1894. V. 46

A Night in Acadie. Chicago: 1897. V. 41; 42; 45

CHOQUET DE LINDU, ANTOINE

Description des Trois Formes du Port de Brest, Baties, Desinees et Gravees in 1757. Brest: 1757. V. 38

CHORIS, LOUIS

Voyage Pittoresque Autour du Monde, avec Des Portraits de Sauvages d'Amerique, d'Asie, d'Afrique, et des Iles du Grand Ocean . . . Paris: 1822. V. 37

CHORLEY, HENRY F.

The Authors of England. London: 1838. V. 41; 43

CHORLEY, HENRY FOTHERGILL

Modern German Music. London: 1854. V. 42

Music and Manners in France and Germany . . . London: 1841. V. 42

CHOROGRAPHICA Descriptio Provinciarum, et Conventum Fratrum, Minorum S. Francisci Capucinorum . . . Turin: 1649. V. 40

CHORON, ALEXANDRE

A Dictionary of Musicians, from the Earliest Ages to the Present Time. London: 1827. V. 42

CHOUKRI, MOHAMED

Tennessee Williams in Tangiers. Santa Barbara: 1979. V. 41; 42; 44

CHOULANT, LUDWIG

History and Bibliography of Anatomic Illustration In Its Relation to Anatomic Science and the Graphic Arts. Chicago: 1920. V. 41; 46

History and Bibliography of Anatomic Illustration. New York: 1945. V. 42

History and Bibliography of Anatomic Illustrations Translated and annotated by Motimer Frank . . . New York: 1962. V. 37

CHOULES, JOHN OVERTON

The Cruise of the Steam Yacht North Star. Boston: 1854. V. 43

CHREITZBERG, A. M.

Early Methodism in the Carolinas. Nashville: 1897. V. 42

CHRETIEN, CHARLES P.

An Essay on Logical Method. Oxford: 1848. V. 43

CHRETIEN, DOUGLAS

The Battle Book of the O'Donnells. Berkeley: 1935. V. 46

CHRIMHILDEN Rache und Die Klage. Zurich: 1757. V. 40

CHRIST-CHURCH, BELFAST

Catalogue of the Major and Minor Libraries of Christ-Church. Belfast: 1837. V. 38

CHRIST, JAY FINLEY

An Irregular Guide to Sherlock Holmes. 1947. V. 39

An Irregular Guide to Sherlock Holmes of Baker Street. 1947. V. 43

An Irregular Chronology of Sherlock Holmes of Baker Street. Chicago: 1947. V. 42

An Irregular Guide to Sherlock Holmes of Baker Street. New Jersey & New York: 1947. V. 42

An Irregular Guide to Sherlock Holmes of Baker Street. New York: 1947. V. 44

CHRISTESEN, C. B.

The Gallery on Eastern Hill: The Victorian Artists' Society Centenary. Melbourne: 1970. V. 41

THE CHRISTIAN Almanac for South Carolina . . . 135 . . . Charleston: 1834. V. 44

THE CHRISTIAN Almanac, for the Carolinas and Georgia . . . 1828. Charleston: 1827. V. 44

CHRISTIAN Doctrines: from the Words of Our Lord of the Apostles and the Prophets. 1850. V. 43
CHRISTIAN Doctrines: from the Words of Our Lord, of the Apostles and the PRophets. London: 1850. V. 37

CHRISTIAN, EDWARD, MRS.

Weimar's Trust. London: 1873. V. 40

CHRISTIAN F. W.

The Caroline Islands Travels in the Sea of the Little Lands. London: 1899. V. 43

CHRISTIAN, FLETCHER

The Letters of Fletcher Christian. Guildford: 1984. V. 41; 43

THE CHRISTIAN History, Containing Accounts of the Revival and Propagation of Religion in Great Britain and America. For the Year 1743. Boston: 1744. V. 43; 44

CHRISTIAN, JOACHIM

A Political Discourse Upon the Different Kinds of Militia, Whether, Mercenary or Auxiliary . . . London: 1757. V. 42

THE CHRISTIAN Keepsake and Missionary Annual, 1840. Philadelphia: 1839. V. 40; 43

CHRISTIAN Sentiments Proper for Sick and Infirm People . . . London: 1747. V. 42

THE CHRISTIAN Traveller. Western Africa, Being an Account of the Country and Its Products of the People and Their Condition . . . London: 1841. V. 44

CHRISTIAN WOMAN'S EXCHANGE OF NEW ORLEANS, LOUISIANA

The Creole Cookery Book. New Orleans: 1885. V. 43

CHRISTIANI, FRANCESCO

Rime di Diversi ecc. Autori, in Vita, e in Morte dell'ill. Rome: 1555. V. 40

CHRISTIANITY and Infidelity. Or a Discussion on the Doctrine of Materialism. North Wrentham: 1834. V. 40

CHRISTIANSEN, KEITH

Gentile de Fabriano. London: 1982. V. 44

CHRISTIE, A. G. I.

English Medieval Embroidery, a Brief Survey of English Embroidery Dating from the Beginning of the 10th Century until the End of the 14th . . . Oxford: 1938. V. 37

CHRISTIE, AGATHA 1891-1976

The Adventure of the Christmas Pudding. London: 1960. V. 45

And Then There Were None. New York: 1940. V. 39; 44

The Big Four. 1927. V. 37

The Body in the Library. New York: 1942. V. 43

Cards on the Table. London: 1936. V. 43

A Caribbean Mystery. New York: 1964. V. 46

Crooked House. London: 1949. V. 38; 46

Death on the Nile. London: 1937. V. 41

Death Comes as the End. 1945. V. 37

Death Comes as the End. London: 1945. V. 42; 43; 44; 45; 46

Elephants Can Remember. London: 1972. V. 40; 45

Endless Night. London: 1967. V. 43

Evil Under the Sun. London: 1941. V. 38

Evil Under the Sun. New York: 1941. V. 42

4.50 from Paddington. London: 1957. V. 42; 44; 46

Hercule Poirot Master Detective. New York: 1936. V. 39

The Hound of Death: and Other Stories. London: (1933). V. 37; 41; 42; 45; 46

The Labours of Hercule. London: 1947. V. 45

Mrs. McGinty's Dead. London: 1952. V. 42

The Moving Finger. London: 1943. V. 44; 45

The Moving Finger. New York: 1949. V. 42

The Murder of Roger Ackroyd. 1926. V. 45

The Murder of Roger Ackroyd. 1926. V. 39

The Murder of Roger Ackyroyd. London: 1926. V. 43; 46

The Murder at the Vicarage. London: 1930. V. 46

Murder in Three Acts. 1934. V. 39

A Murder is Announced. London: 1950. V. 43; 45

A Murder is Announced. New York: 1950. V. 43; 45

A Murder is Announced. N.P.: 1950. V. 44

The Mysterious Affair at Styles. London: 1921. V. 45

The Mysterious Affair at Styles. 1927. V. 39

The Mysterious Mr. Quinn. London: 1930. V. 38; 46

N or M? New York: 1941. V. 39

N or M? 1941. V. 37

Nemesis. London: 1971. V. 40

One Two Buckle My Shoe. London: 1940. V. 44

Ordeal in Innocence. London: 1958. V. 38

Partners in Crime. New York: 1929. V. 42

Passenger to Frankfurt. London: 1970. V. 40; 44

A Pocketful of Rye. London: 1953. V. 40; 43

Poirot Investigates. London: 1924. V. 42

Poirot Loses a Client. 1937. V. 39

Poirot and the Regatta Mystery. London: 1941-44? V. 41

Poirot and the Regatta Mystery. London: 1941? V. 42

Poirot and the Regatta Mystery. London: 1942. V. 45

Postern of Fate. London: 1973. V. 40

Sad Cypress. 1940. V. 39

The Seven Dials Mystery. London: 1929. V. 46

The Seven Dials Mystery. 1929. V. 37

Sleeping Murder - Miss Marples' Last Case. London: 1976. V. 45

Sparkling Cyanide. London: 1945. V. 45

Star Over Bethlehem and Other Stories. London: 1965. V. 41; 42; 43

Taken at the Flood. London: 1948. V. 38; 42

Ten Little Niggers. London: 1939. V. 41; 46

There is a Tide. New York: 1948. V. 41

Thirteen at Dinner. 1933. V. 39

13 at Dinner. New York: 1933. V. 43; 44

Towards Zero. 1940. V. 43

Towards Zero. London: 1944. V. 38

Unfinished Portrait. New York: 1934. V. 44

CHRISTIE, H. KENRICK

Techniques and Results of Grafting Skin. New York: 1932. V. 42

CHRISTIE, JAMES

A Catalogue of a Most Superb, Capital and Valuable Collection of Italian, french, Flemish and Dutch Pictures, the Property of a Gentleman . . . Brought from His Seat at Fonthill. 1802. V. 39

A Disquisition Upon Etruscan Vases. London: 1806. V. 38

Disquisitions Upon the Painted Greek Vases and . . . Connection With the Shows of the Eleusinian and Other Mysteries. London: 1825. V. 39

CHRISTIE, JOHN

Mirror Book. Guildford: 1985. V. 45

CHRISTIE-MILLER

Catalogue of the Library of . . . London: 1873-76. V. 46

CHRISTIE-MILLER, SYDNEY RICHARDSON 1874-1931

The Britwell Short-Title Catalogue of the Principal Volumes From the Time of Caxton to the Year 1800 Formerly in the Library of Britwell Court. London: 1933. V. 44

The Britwell Hand-List or Short-Title Catalogue of the Principal Volumes from the Time of Caxton to the Year 1800 Formerly in the Library of Britwell Court, Buckinghamshire. London: 1933. V. 39

CHRISTIE, O. F.

Johnson the Essayist, His Opinions on Men, Morals and Manners. London: 1924. V. 44

CHRISTIE, RICHARD COPLEY

Etienne Dolet, the Martyr of the Renaissance, a Biography. London: 1899. V. 43; 45

CHRISTIE, THOMAS

Letters on the Revolution of France, and on the New Constitution Established by the National Assembly . . . London: 1791. V. 39; 40

CHRISTINA; Or, Memoirs of a German Princess. By the Author of Caroline of Lichtfield. London: 1808. V. 37

CHRISTINE DE PISAN

The Epistle of Othea to Hector or the Boke of Knyghthode . . . London: 1904. V. 44; 46

CHRISTISON, ROBERT

The Life . . . Edited by His SOns. Edinburgh: 1885. V. 37; 45

On Granular Degeneration of the Kidnies, and Its Connexion with Dropsy, Inflammation and Other Diseases. Edinburgh: 1839. V. 38

A Treatise on Poisons, In Relation to Medical Jurisprudence, Physiology and the Practice of Physic. Edinburgh: 1829. V. 39

A Treatise on Poisons, in Relation to Medical Jurisprudence, Physiology and the Practice of Physic. Edinburgh: 1836. V. 42

A Treatise on Poisons in Relation to Medical Jurisprudence, Physiology and the Practice of Physic. Philadelphia: 1845. V. 40; 41

A Practical Treatise on Poisons, in Relation to Medical Jurisprudence, Physiology and the Practice of Physic. Edinburgh: 1846. V. 44

CHRISTMAS ABC. Boston: 1890. V. 45; 46

CHRISTMAS Carols. Evanston: 1966. V. 44

CHRISTMAS Eve with the Spirits; or, the Canon's Wanderings Through Ways Unknown. London: 1870. V. 40

CHRISTMAS, H.

The Shores and Islands of the Mediterranean, Including a Visit to the Seven Churches of Asia. London: 1851. V. 40

CHRISTMAS in Art and Song. New York: 1879. V. 40

CHRISTMAS Pictures by Children. London: 1922. V. 41

CHRISTMAS Poems and Pictures: a Collection of Songs, Carols and Descriptive Poems Relating to the Festival of Christmas. New York: 1864. V. 39

CHRISTMAS Tales of Flanders. London: 1917. V. 43

THE CHRISTMAS Treat; or Gay Companion. Dublin: 1767. V. 42; 46

THE CHRISTMAS Tree: a Present for Germany. London: 1844. V. 41

CHRISTMAS Tyde. London: 1849. V. 42

CHRISTMAS With the Poets. London: 1872. V. 38

CHRISTMAS With the Poets: A Collection of Songs, Carols and Descriptive Verses, Relating to the Festival of Christmas . . . London: 1851. V. 39; 46

CHRISTMAS With the Poets: a Collection of Songs, Carols and Descriptive Verses, Relating to the Festival of Christmas, from the Anglo-Norman Period to the Present Time. London: 1855. V. 45

CHRISTOPHER, A. B.

The Word Accompolished; Extracts. 1974. V. 45

The World Accomplished. By A.B. Christopher. With seventeen etchings by Natalie d'Arbeloff. London: 1974. V. 37; 39; 40; 41; 42; 44; 45; 46

CHRISTOPHER Columbus. Documents & Proofs of His Genoese Origin. Bergamo: MCMXXX. V. 40

CHRISTOPHERSEN, H. O.

A Bibliographical Introduction to the Study of John Locke. Oslo: 1930. V. 42

CHRISTY, CUTHBERT

Big Game Hunting and Pygmies: Experiences of a Naturalist in Central African Forests in Quest of the Okapi . . . London: 1924. V. 38; 39; 42

CHRISTY, DAVID

Cotton is King; or, The Culture of Cotton, and Its Relation to Commerce: The the Free Colored People: and to Those Who Hold that Slavery is in Itself Sinful. Cincinnati: 1855. V. 38; 43

CHRISTY, HOWARD CHANDLER

The American Girl. As Seen and Portrayed by H.C. Christy. New York: 1906. V. 37

The Christy Girl. Indianapolis: 1906. V. 41

Liberty Belles. Indianapolis: 1912. V. 38

CHRISTY, MILLER

The Silver Map of the World: A Contemporary Medallion Commemorative of Drake's Great Voyagae . . . London: 1900. V. 38; 42

The Voyages of Captain Luke Foxe of Hull, and Captain Thomas James of Bristol, in Search of a North-West Passage. London: 1894. V. 37; 43; 46

CHRISTYN, J. B.

Les Delices des Pais-Bas ou Description Generale. Brusselle: 1697. V. 45

THE CHROMOLITHOGRAPH. 1867-69. V. 41

THE CHRONICLE & Directory of China, Japan and the Philippines for the Year 1870. Hong Kong: 1870. V. 43

THE CHRONICLE of Charles, the Young Man. N.P.: 1745. V. 39
THE CHRONICLE of Charles, the Young Man. N.P.: 1745. V. 39

CHRONICLE OF ENGLAND

The St. Albans Chronicle, with The Descrypcyon of Englonde. London: 1515. V. 43

A CHRONICLE of London, from 1089 to 1483: Written in the Fifteenth Century, and for the First Time Printed from Mss. in the British Museum . . . London: 1827. V. 39

THE CHRONICLE of the Royal Highland Regiment. The Black Watch. Edinburgh: 1913. V. 42

CHRONICLES of London Bridge: by an Antiquary. London: 1827. V. 42

CHRONICLES of Oklahoma. Oklahoma City: 1921-79. V. 39; 40
CHRONICLES of Oklahoma. 1941-66. V. 39

CHRONICLES of the Reigns of Stephen, Henry II and Richard I . . . London: 1884-89. V. 44

CHRONICON Mirabile, or Extracts from Parish Registers Principally in the North of England. London: 1841. V. 37; 44

CHRONIQUES DE SAINT DENIS

Chroniques de France. Paris: 1493. V. 40

Joan the Maid of Orleans: Being that Portion of the Chronicles of St. Denis Which Deals with Her Life and Times from the Chronicques de France. San Francisco: 1938. V. 40; 41

LES CHRONIQUES et Annales de France des l'Origine des Francois, et Leur Venues ez Gaules. Paris: 1585. V. 39

CHRONISTER, E.

Reminiscences of Army Life: Four Years in My Country's Service. Eagle Grove: 1908. V. 45

A CHRONOLOGICAL Chart of the Visions of Daniel and John. Boston: 1843. V. 44

A CHRONOLOGICAL History of Lincoln, Containing an Account of Every Remarkable Occurrence that Has Happened Therein, from the Earliest Period to the Present Time, from authentic Sources. Lincoln: 1850. V. 46

CHRYSOLORAS

Erotemata. De Anomalis Verbis. Venice: 1517. V. 37

CHRYSOSTOM, JOANNES, ST. PATRIARCH OF CONSTANTINOPLE d. 407

Opera. Eton: 1613/12. V. 44

CHRYSOSTOMUS, JOANNES, ST. PATRIARCH OF CONSTANINOPLE d. 407

Homilae ad Populum Antiochenum. Londini: 1590. V. 37; 45

XXVI Homilies . . . 1621. V. 45

CHRYSOSTOMUS, JOANNES, ST. PATRIARCH OF CONSTANTINOPLE d. 407

Dialogus de Episcopatu & Sacerdotio, Germano Brixio Antissidorensi Interprete. Marburg: 1537. V. 37; 40

Homiliae Duae, Nunc Primum in Lucem Aeditae. London: 1543. V. 40

S. Ioannis Chrysostomi Opera Graece. Eton: 1610-13. V. 41

XXVI Homilies. Paris: 1621. V. 38

CHRYSOSTUM, JOANNES, ST. PATRIARCH OF CONSTANTINOPLE d. 407

Of the Priesthood. London: 1759. V. 37

CHRYSOTOMUS, JOANNES, ST. PATRIARCH OF CONSTANTINOPLE d. 407

XXVI Homilies. Paris: 1521. V. 37

CHUAN, SHUI HU

All Men are Brothers. V. 45

All Men are Brothers. New York: 1948. V. 44

CHUBB, CHARLES

The Birds of British Guiana. London: 1916-21. V. 37; 38; 39; 41

CHUBB, GEORGE HAYTER

Protection from Fire and Theives, Including the Construction of Locks, Safes, Strong Rooms, and Fireproof Buildings; Burglary, and the Means of Preventing it; Fire, its Detection, Prevention and Extinction, Etc . . . London: 1875. V. 37

CHUBB, RALPH

The Book of God's Madness. London: 1928. V. 45

A Fable of Love and War. London: 1925. V. 45

CHUBB, RALPH continued

Manhood. Curridge, Berkshire: 1924. V. 45

Songs Pastoral and Paradisal. Brockweir: 1935. V. 45

Songs Pastroal and Paradisal. Gloucestershire: 1935. V. 40

Woodcuts. London: 1928. V. 41; 42; 45

CHUBB, THOMAS

A Collection of Tracts, on Various Subjects. London: 1730. V. 39

The Ground and Foundation of Morality Considered. London: 1745. V. 38

The Printed Maps in the Atlases of Great Britain and Ireland: a Bibliography, 1579-1870. London: 1927. V. 39; 43

The Printed Maps in the Atlases of Great Britain and Ireland, a Bibliography, 1579-1870. London & Edinburgh: 1927. V. 46

The Printed Maps in the Atlases of Great Britain and Ireland: a Bibliography, 1579-1870. London: 1977. V. 39

CHUDLEIGH, MARY

Essays Upon Several Subjects in Prose and Verse . . . London: 1710. V. 41; 45

Poems on Several Occasions. Together with the Song of the Three Children Paraphras'd. London: 1703. V. 45

Poems on Several Occasions. Together with the Song of the Three Children Paraphras'd. London: 1713. V. 39

CHUIKEVICH, PETER A.

Reflections of the War of 1812. Boston: 1813. V. 43

CHUINARD, E. G.

Only One Man Died, The Medical Aspects of the Lewis and Clark Expedition. Glendale: 1979. V. 46

CHURCH, A. H.

Some Minor Acts as Practised in England. London: 1894. V. 38; 42; 43; 44

CHURCH, ALBERT COOK

Whale Ships and Whaling. New York: 1938. V. 41

CHURCH, ARCHIBALD

East Africa: a New Dominion. London: 1927. V. 43

CHURCH, ARTHUR H.

japanese Sword Guards. Reading: 1914. V. 42

CHURCH, BENJAMIN

The Choice; a Poem, After the Manner of Pomfret. Worcester: 1802. V. 39

The History of King Philip's War. Boston: 1865. V. 39

CHURCH Decoration. A Practical Manual of Appropriate Ornamentation. New York: 1876. V. 44

CHURCH, ELIHU DWIGHT 1835-1908

A Catalogue of Books Relating to the Discovery and Early History of North and South America Forming a Part of the Library of E. D. Church. New York: 1907. V. 42; 44

Catalogue of Books Relating to the Discovery and Early History of North and South America. Magnolia: 1951. V. 42

A Catalogue of Books Relating to the Discovery and Early History of North and South American . . . New York: 1951. V. 39; 40; 41; 45

Classical Bronzes. Providence: 1975. V. 40

The E. D. Church Library. A Catalogue of Books Relating to the Discovery and Early History of North and South America. New York: 1951. V. 46

CHURCH, FREDERIC EDWARD

Church's Painting of Nature's Grandest Scene. New York: 1857. V. 45

CHURCH, H. E.

Making a Start in Canada. Letters from Two Young Immigrants. London: 1889. V. 38; 39

CHURCH, J.

A Cabinet of Quadrupeds. London: 1805. V. 38

CHURCH, JOHN

The Divine Warrant of Infant-Baptism. London: 1652. V. 43

CHURCH, JOHN H. C.

Diary of a Trip through Mexico and California. Pittsfield: 1887. V. 40

CHURCH Music and Musical Life in Pennsylvania in the Eighteenth Century. Philadelphia: 1926/27/38/47. V. 41; 42

CHURCH OF ENGLAND.

Articles, Whereupon It Was Agreed . . . In the Conuocation Holden at London in . . . 1562 . . . for the Auoyding of the Diuersities of Opinions and for the Stablishing of Consent Touching True Religion. London: 1612. V. 45

The Booke of Common Prayer, and Administration of the Sacraments. (with) The Psalter, or, Psalmes of David. Edinburgh: 1637, 1636. V. 39

The Book of Common Prayer and Administration of the Sacraments . . . (with) The Whole Book of Psalms Collected into English Meeter . . . London: 1669. V. 39

The Book of Common Prayer, and Administration of the Sacraments and Other Rites of Ceremonies of the Church of England with the Psalter or Psalms of David. Oxford: 1683. V. 39

Book of Common Prayer. Oxford: 1701. V. 39

The Book of Common Prayer. London: 1716. V. 39

The Book of Common Prayer and Adiministration of the Sacraments and Other Rites and Ceremonies of the Church . . . Edinburgh: 1737. V. 39

The Book of Common Prayer, and Administration of the Sacraments, and Other Rities and Ceremonies of the Church According to the Use of the Church of England. Cambridge: 1761. V. 38; 39; 44; 46

The Book of Common Prayer, and Administration of the Sacraments, and Other Rities and Ceremonies . . . Philadelphia: 1786. V. 39

The Book of Common Prayer, and Administration of the Sacraments, and Other Rites and Ceremonies of the Church, According to the Use of the Protestant Episcopal Church in the United States of America. Philadelphia: 1790. V. 39

Book of Common Prayer. London: 1863. V. 39

The Book of Common Prayer. New York: 1893. V. 39

Te Deum Laudamus and Nunc Dimittis, from the Book of Common Prayer. Bognor Regis: 1929. V. 39

Liber Precum Publicarum. London: 1594. V. 38

Il Libro Delle Preghiere Publiche ed Amministrazione de'Sacramenti, ed Altri riti e Cerimonie della Chiesa, Secondo l'uso della Chiesa Anglicana . . . Londra: 1685. V. 38; 44

Il Libro delle Preghiere Publiche & Amministrazione de' Scraamenti . . . London: 1733. V. 38

Book of Common Prayer. Edinburgh: 1752. V. 38

Book of Common Prayer Together with the Psalter of Psalms of David. Cambridge: 1760. V. 37; 38; 44; 46

The Book of Common Prayer, and Administration of the Sacraments, and Other Rites and Ceremonies of the Church, According to the Use of the Church of England; together with the Pslater or Psalms of David. Oxford: 1793. V. 37

The Book of Common Prayer. Oxford: 1796. V. 38

Book of Common Prayer, Church of England. London: 1821. V. 37

The Book of Common Prayer . . . together with the Psalter . . . in Eight Languages, namely English, French, Italian, German, Spanish, Greek, Ancient and Modern Latin, to which are added, the Services of the Sea. London: 1821. V. 38

Book of Common Prayer. Philadelphia: 1831. V. 37

The Book of Common Prayer, According to the Use of the Church of England, Translated into the Mohawk Language, Compiled from Various Translations . . . (second title in Mohawk). Hamilton, Ontario: 1842. V. 37

Book of Common Prayer. 1844. V. 38

The Book of Common Prayer. London: 1845. V. 38; 44

Book of Common Prayer, printed from the Manuscript in the Rolls Office. Dublin/London: 1849. V. 37

The Book of Common Prayer. (For Ireland). London: 1849. V. 38

The Book of Common Prayer and Administration of the Sacraments. London: 1853. V. 38; 40

Book of Common Prayer. London: 1863. V. 37; 38

The Book of Common Prayer and Administration of the Sacraments and Other Rites and Ceremonies of the Church in the United States . . . Together with the Psalter or Pslams of David. New York: 1893. V. 37

The Book of Common Prayer and Administration of the Holy Communion According to the Use of the Church of England. Together with the Pslter or Psalms of David. London: 1900. V. 38

The Finger Prayer Book. Printed on the Oxford Indian Paper: The Book of Common Prayer . . . Church of England. Oxford/London: 1900. V. 37

The Book of Common Prayer and Administration of the Sacraments . . . together with the Psalter or Psalms of David. Begun at Essex House, Bow,: 1903. V. 37

THE PRAYER Book of King Edward VII. London: 1903. V. 37

*The Book of Common Prayer, and Administration of the Sacraments & Other Rites and Ceremonies of the Church, according to the Use of the Church of England . . . (Authorised American Edition of the Prayer-Book of Edward VII. The Design and . . . (New York: 1904). V. 37; 41

The Book of Common Prayer . . . According to the Use of the Church of England . . . With the Psalter. Norwood: 1904. V. 37

Te Deum Laudamus and Nunc Dimittis. From the Book of Common Prayer. Flansham: 1929. V. 38

Certaine Sermons or Homilies Appoynted to Be Read in Churches, In the Time of the Late Queene Elizabeth . . . (with) The Second Tome of Homilies . . . London: 1633. V. 39

Constitutions and Canons Ecclesiasticall: Treated Upon by the Archbishops of Canterbury and York . . . and the Rest of the Bishops and Clergie . . . and Agreed Upon with the Kings Majesties Licence in Their Several Synods Begun at London and York, 1640. London: 1640. V. 38

Constitutions and Canons Ecclesiasticall; Treated Upon by the Archbishops of Canterbury and York . . . and the Rest of the bishops and Clergie of Those Provinces . . . London: 1640. V. 40

Constitutions and Canons Ecclesiasticall . . . Agreed Upon . . . in . . . synods Begun at London and York 1640. London: 1640. V. 45

The English Liturgy. From the Book of Common Prayer, With Additional Collects, Epistles and Gospels. London: 1909. V. 37

CHURCH OF ENGLAND. continued

The Form and Manner of Consecrating and Administring the Holy Communion, According to the Liturgy of King Edward VI called The Book of Common Prayer . . . London: 1717. V. 39

Iniunctions Giuen by the Queenes Maiestie Anno Com. 1559. London: 1600. V. 45

Liturgia Inglesa. London: 1623. V. 45

The New Week's Preparation for a worthy receiving of the Lord's Supper as appointed by the Church of England, etc. Cork: 1801. V. 37

Visitation Articles. Articles to be Enquired of in the Visitation, in the First Yeere of the Raign of Our Most Dread Soueraign Ladie Elizabeth. London: 1600. V. 45

CHURCH OF ENGLAND. BOOK OF COMMON PRAYER

Biblos tas Demosias Euxas . . . Cantabrigia: 1665. V. 41

Book of Common Prayer and Administration of the Sacraments . . . V. 46

The Book of Common Prayer . . . London. V. 42

Book of Common Prayer, and Administration of the Sacraments and Other Rites and Ceremonies of the Church, According to the Use of the Church of England, Together With the Psalter or Psalms of David . . . London. V. 43

The Book of Common Prayer. Oxford. V. 41

The Book of Common Praier Noted. London: 1550. V. 40

Liber Precum Publicarum, seu Ministerii Ecclesiastice Administrationis Sacramentorum Aliorumque Rituum & Caeremoniarum, in Ecclesia Anglicana. Londini: 1574. V. 40

The Book of Common Prayer and Administration of the Sacraments, and Other Rites and Ceremonies of the Church of England. London: 1632. V. 40

The Book of Common Prayer. London: 1662. V. 46

The Book of Common Prayer, and Administration of the Sacraments and Other Rites and Ceremonies of the Church, According to the Use of the Church of England. In the Savoy: 1671. V. 40

The Book of Common Prayer and Administration of the Sacraments . . . Together with the Psalms of David. London: 1678. V. 41; 46

The Book of Common Prayer and Administration of the Sacraments, and Other Rites and Ceremonies of the Church, According to the Use of the Church of England . . . Cambridge: 1683. V. 42

The Book of Common Prayer, and Administration of the Sacraments, and Other Rites and Ceremonies of the Church . . . London: 1683. V. 46

The Book of Common Prayer and Administration of the Sacraments . . . Together with the Psalter of Psalms of David. London: 1702. V. 44

Book of Common Prayer. London: 1717. V. 45; 46

The Book of Common Prayer and Administration of the Sacraments and Other Rites and Ceremonies of the Church, According to the Use of the Church of England. London: 1724. V. 46

Book of Common Prayer, and Administration of the Sacraments, and Other Rites and Ceremonies of the Church, According to the Use of the Church of England. Together with the Psalter of Psalms of David. London: 1725. V. 41

Book of Common Prayer and Psalms. London: and Oxford: 1745. V. 46

Book of Common Prayer and Administration of the Sacraments and Other Rites and Ceremonies of the Church According to the Use of the Church of England, Together with the Psalter or Psalms of David . . . Oxford: 1745. V. 41

Book of Common Prayer, and Administration of the Sacraments, and Other Rites and Ceremonies of the Church According to the Use of the Church of England . . . Oxford: 1753. V. 41

Book of Common Prayer. London: 1756. V. 45

The Book of Common Prayer, and Administration of the Sacraments and Other Rites and Ceremonies of the Church . . . Birmingham: 1762. V. 42

The Book of Common Prayer . . . According to the Use of the Church of England; Together With the Psalter, or Psalms of David . . . Cambridge: 1762. V. 42; 44; 46

The Book of Common Prayer. Cambridge: 1762. V. 42; 45; 46

Book of Common Prayer. And Administration of the Sacraments . . . London: 1766. V. 46

The Book of Common Prayer and Administration of the Sacraments and other Rites and Ceremonies of the Church. Cambridge: 1767. V. 44

The Book of Common Prayer and Administration of the Sacraments and Other Rites and Ceremonies of the Church, According to the Use of the Church of England. Cambridge: 1767. V. 46

The Book of Common Prayer, and Administration of the Sacraments, and Other Rites and Ceremonies of the Church. Oxford: 1767. V. 40; 41

The Book of Common Prayer, and Administrations of the Sacraments, and Other Rites and Ceremonies of the Church, According to the Use of the Church of England . . . Oxford: 1781. V. 42

The Book of Common Prayer, and Administration of the Sacraments, and Other Rites and Ceremonies of the Church, According to the Use of the Church of England . . . Oxford: 1787. V. 44

The Book of Common Prayer, and Administration of the Sacraments, and Other Rites and Ceremonies of the Church, According to the Use of the Church of England . . . Oxford: 1790. V. 46

Book of Common Prayer, and Administration of the Sacrament, According to the Use of the Church of England; Together with the Psalter or Psalms of David . . . London: 1792. V. 46

The Book of Common Prayer, and Administration of the Sacraments, and Other Rites and Ceremonies of the Church . . . London: 1802. V. 44

The Book of Common Prayer, and Administration of the Sacraments and Other Rites and Ceremonies of the Church, According to the Use of the United Churches of England and Ireland. London: 1807. V. 42

Book of Common Prayer . . . Together with the Psalms of David. London: 1809. V. 40

The Book of Common Prayer . . . London: 1813. V. 43; 44; 45

The Book of Common Prayer . . . with the . . . Psalms . . . London: 1813. V. 43

The Book of Common Prayer, and Administration of the Sacraments . . . London: 1820. V. 43

The Book of Common Prayer . . . Together with the Psalter or Psalms of David . . . Oxford: 1823. V. 46

The Book of Common Prayer . . . Cambridge: 1830-29. V. 42

Book of Common Prayer. London: 1835. V. 40

The Book of Common Prayers, and Administration of the Sacraments, and Other Rites and Ceremonies of the Church . . . London and Paris: 1838. V. 40

The Book of Common Prayer According to the Use of the Church of England. Hamilton: 1842. V. 42

Book of Common Prayer. London: 1843/44. V. 44

The Book of Common Prayer, Together with the Psalms of David. London: 1848. V. 43

The Book of Common Prayer. London: 1853, 1855. V. 42

The Book of Common Prayer Ornamented With Wood Cuts From Designs of Albert Durer, Hans Holbein and Others. London: 1855. V. 42

Book of Common Prayer. London: 1856. V. 43

The Pictorial Edition of the Book of Common Prayer, According to the Use of the United Kingdom of England and Ireland. London: 1880. V. 41

Book of Common Prayer. London: 1880. V. 45

The Book of Common Prayer and Administration of the Sacraments . . . Cambridge: 1890. V. 40

The Book of Common Prayer, as Issued in the Year 1549 . . . 1896. V. 44

The Book of the Common Prayer, as issued in the Year 1549, in the Reign of King Edward the Sixth, Being the Original Edition of the Prayer Book. 1896. V. 44

The Book of Common Prayer, as issued in the year 1549 in the Reign of King Edward the Sixth . . . London: 1896. V. 46

The Book of Common Prayer. Camden: 1904. V. 44

The Psalter, or Psalms of David. Taken from the Book of Common Prayer. Waltham St. Lawrence: 1927. V. 40

The Form and Manner of Consecrating and Administring the Holy Communion According to the Liturgy of King Edward VI called The Book of Common Prayer . . . printed 1549. London: 1717. V. 41

Holy Communion from the Book of Common Prayer. Bedford: 1904. V. 46

Liber Precum Publicarum, Sev Ministerii Ecclesiasticae Administrationis Sacramentorum. Excusum Londini: 1594. V. 44

The Orthodox Communicant, by Way of Meditation on the Order for the Administration of the Lord's Supper, or Holy Communion; According to the Liturgy of the Church of England. London: 1721. V. 44

Queen Mary's Psalter. Miniatures and Drawings by an English Artist of the 14th Century Reprodcued from the Royal Ms. 2 B.VII in the British Museum. London: 1912. V. 40

CHURCH OF ENGLAND. HOMILIES

Certaine Sermons or Homilies Appoynted to be Read in Churches, in the Time of the Late Queene Elizabeth of Famous Memory, And Now Thought Fit to Be Reprinted by Authority from the Kings Most Excellent Maiesty. London: 1635. V. 43

CHURCH OF IRELAND

Report (and Appendix) of Her Majesty's Commissioners on the Revenues and Condition of the Established Church (Ireland). Dublin: 1868. V. 43

CHURCH OF IRELAND. BOOK OF COMMON PRAYER

The Book of Common Prayer, and Administration of the Sacraments and Other Rites and Ceremonies of the Church, According to the Use of the . . . Dublin: 1721. V. 40

The Book of Common Prayer. Dublin: 1772. V. 43

The Book . . . (Leabhar . . .) . . . . Dublin: 1832. V. 43

Book of Common Prayer, printed from the Manuscript in the Rolls Office, Dublin, by Archibald J. Stephens, B. Law. London: 1849. V. 43

CHURCH OF JESUS CHRIST OF LATTER DAY SAINTS

Book of Doctrine and Covenants of the Church of Jesus Christ of Latter Day Saints. Carefully Selected from the Revelations of God and Given in the Order of Their Dates. Cincinnati: 1864. V. 42; 45

A Circular of the High Council. To the Members of the Church of Jesus Christ of Latter Day Saints. Nauvoo: 1846. V. 40

CHURCH OF SCOTLAND. BOOK OF COMMON PRAYER

The Book of Common Prayer, and Administration of the Sacraments, and Other Parts of Divine Service for the Use of the Church of Scotland. Edinburgh: 1637. V. 42

CHURCH, RICHARD

Selected Poems from North of Rome. (Hove): (ca. 1980). V. 37

Small Moments. London: 1957. V. 41; 44

CHURCH, SAMUEL HARDEN

Oliver Cromwell: a History. New York: 1894. V. 38

CHURCH, THOMAS

The Entertaining History of King Philip's War, Which Began in the Month of June, 1675. As Also of Expeditions More Lately Made Against the Common Enemy, and all Indian Rebels, in the Eastern Parts of New England. Newport: 1772. V. 37

The History of Philip's War, Commonly Called the Great Indian War, of 1675 and 1676. Boston: 1827. V. 43

The History of the Philip's War, Commonly Called the Great Indian War, of 1675 and 1676. Exeter: 1829. V. 45; 46

The History of King Philip's War. By Benjamin Church. With an Introduction and Notes by Henry M. Dexter. Boston: 1865. V. 37

CHURCH, W. E.

W.M. Thackeray as an Artist and Art Critic: an essay. (London): (1880). V. 37; 40

CHURCH, WILLIAM HENRY

Description and Use of the Laryngoscope. New York: 1861. V. 42

THE CHURCH Yard: a Satirical Poem. London: 1739. V. 46

CHURCHEY, WALTER

An Essay on Man Upon Principles Opposite to Those of Lord Bolingbroke in four Epistles. London: 1804. V. 45

CHURCHILL, A.

A Collection of Voyages and Travels. 1704/1732. V. 41

CHURCHILL, CHARLES

The Candidate. London: 1764. V. 40

The Farewell. A Poem. London: 1764. V. 40

Poems. (with) The so-called Volume II, a Nonce Collection of Ten Independetly Printed Pieces. London. V. 45

Poems. London: 1763. V. 38; 40; 43

Poems. London: 1763-65. V. 38; 41; 43; 45

Poems. London: 1764-65. V. 43

Poems. London: 1766. V. 37; 38; 39; 43

The Prophecy of Famine. Dublin: 1763. V. 43

The Rosciad. London: 1761. V. 38

Sermons. Dublin: 1765. V. 40

The Times. London: 1764. V. 40

CHURCHILL, CLEMENTINE

My Visit to Russia. 1945. V. 43

CHURCHILL, FLEETWOOD 1808-1878

Essays on the Puerperal Fever and Other Diseases Peculiar to Women. London: 1849. V. 41

Observations on the Diseases Incident to Pregnancy and Childbed. Philadelphia: 1840. V. 41

On the Theory and Practice of Midwifery. Philadelphia: 1843. V. 43

CHURCHILL, FREDERICK

Face and Foot Deformities. Philadelphia: 1885. V. 42

CHURCHILL, RANDOLPH

Winston S. Churchill. (The definitive biography). Volume I to VI with Companion volumes I-III (in seven volumes). London: 1966-1983. V. 37

CHURCHILL, RANDOLPH S.

Men, Mines and Animals in South Africa. New York: 1892. V. 44

CHURCHILL, T. O.

The Life of Lord Viscount Nelson, Duke of Bronte, &c. London: 1808. V. 38

CHURCHILL, W. A.

Watermarks in Paper, in Holland, England, France, Etc. in the XVII and XVIII Centuries, and Their Interconnection. Amsterdam: 1965. V. 40

Watermarks in Paper in Holland, England, France, etc. in the XVII and XVIII Centuries and Their Interconnection. Nieuwkoop: 1985. V. 40; 45

CHURCHILL, WILLIAM

Dictionary of Samoan Speech. Samoa: 1903. V. 40

CHURCHILL, WINSTON 1871-1947

Coniston. New York: 1906. V. 42

Divi Britannici. London. V. 43

Divi Britannici. London: 1675. V. 40

CHURCHILL, WINSTON LEONARD SPENCER 1874-1965

V. 42

An Address Delivered Before Members of the Congress. December 26th, 1941. Stamford: 1942. V. 41; 42

Addresses Delivered in the Year Nineteen Hundred and Forty to the People of Great Britain, of France, and to the Members of the English Houe of Commons, by the Prime Minister. San Francisco: 1940. V. 38

The Aftermath. London: 1929. V. 46

The Aftermath, 1918-1928. New York: 1929. V. 44

The American Civil War. London: 1958. V. 43

The American Civil War. London: 1961. V. 41

Arms and the Covenant. London: 1938. V. 41; 43; 44; 45

Beating the Invader. A Message from the Prime Minister. London: 1941. V. 43

Blood Sweet and Tears. New York: 1941. V. 44; 45

Blood Sweat and Tears. Toronto: 1941. V. 40; 42

Charles IXth Duke of Marlborough, K.G. London: 1934. V. 41; 43; 44

The Chartered Surveyor. His Training and His Work. London: 1932. V. 41

Collected Works. London: 1973. V. 44; 45

The Collected Works of . . . London: 1973-76. V. 43; 45

The First Collected Works of Sir Winston Churchill. London: 1974. V. 46

The Collected Essays of . . . London: 1976. V. 46

Contemporaries. London: 1937. V. 40

Discours de Guerre 1940-1942. N.P.. V. 43

The Dream. 1987. V. 42

The Dream. 1987. V. 41

The End of the Beginning: The Third Volume of Winston Churchill's War Speeches. London: 1943. V. 39

The Great War. London: 1933. V. 43

The Great War. London: 1933-Oct. 1934. V. 41; 43; 44

The Great War. London: 1934. V. 46

Great Contemporaries. London: 1937. V. 41; 43; 44; 46

Great Destiny. New York: 1965. V. 41; 42

A History of the English Speaking Peoples. London: 1956. V. 39; 44

A History of the English-Speaking Peoples. London: 1956-57. V. 46

A History of the English Speaking Peoples. 1956-58. V. 45

A History of the English-Speaking Peoples. London: (1956-58). V. 37; 38; 40; 42; 43; 45; 46

Ian Hamilton's March. London: 1900. V. 39; 41; 44; 46

Ian Hamilton's March, Together, With London to Ladysmith Via Victoria. New York: 1900. V. 40; 45

India. Speeches and an Introduction. London: 1931. V. 41

Into Battle. London: 1941. V. 43

London to Ladymsith Via Pretoria. London: 1900. V. 37; 38; 39; 40; 42; 43; 44; 45; 46

Lodon to Ladysmith Via Pretoria. New York: 1900. V. 37; 39; 41; 45

London to Ladysmith Via Pretoria. Toronto: 1900. V. 39

Lord Randolph Churchill. London: 1906. V. 41; 44; 46

Lord Randolph Churchill. New York: 1906. V. 44

Marlborough. His Life and Times. London: 1933. V. 39; 40; 41; 44

Marlborough - His Life and Times. London: 1933-38. V. 41; 42; 43; 45; 46

Marlborough: His Life and Times. New York: 1933-38. V. 40; 45

Marlborough, His Life and Times. London: 1934-39. V. 43

Memoirs of the Second World War. Boston: 1959. V. 41; 42

Ministry of Foreign Affairs of the U.S.S.R. V. 46

Mr. Churchill in 1940. London: 1950. V. 41

My African Journey. London: 1908. V. 41; 42; 44; 45; 46

My Early Life. London: 1941. V. 44

My Early Life. London: 1948. V. 41

My Early Life. A Roving Commission. London: 1949. V. 45

My African Journey. London: 1908. V. 37

My Early Life: a Roving Commission. London: 1930. V. 38; 39; 40; 41; 43; 46

Proceedings of the Presentation of the Williamsburg Award by the Trustees of Colonial Williamsburg to the Rt. Hon. Sir Winston S. Churchill at Draper's Hall, London, Dec. 7, 1955. Williamsburg: 1957. V. 41

The River War. London: 1899. V. 38; 41; 42

The River War. London: 1900. V. 39; 44

Savrola. London: 1900. V. 45

Savrola. New York: 1900. V. 37; 39; 46

The Second World War. London: 1945-54. V. 42

The Second World War. London: 1948. V. 39; 41

The Second World War. London: Toronto: 1948. V. 42

The Second World War . . . Boston: 1948-53. V. 45; 46

The Second World War. London: 1948-54. V. 37; 38; 39; 40; 41; 43; 44; 45; 46

The Second World War. New York: 1959. V. 37

A Speech by the Prime Minister in the House of Commons August 20th 1940. V. 45

A Speech by the Prime Minster . . . In the House of Commons August 20th, 1940. 1940. V. 43

CHURCHILL, WINSTON LEONARD SPENCER 1874-1965 continued

A Speech in the House of Commons, 20 August 1940. In Parliamentary Debates. London: 1940. V. 43; 44; 45

Step by Step. 1936-1939. London: 1939. V. 40; 41; 46

Step by Step 1936-1939. New York: 1939. V. 46

The Story of the Malakand field Force. London: 1898. V. 44; 46

Thoughts and Adventures. London: 1932. V. 43

Thoughts and Adventures. London: 1932. V. 39

Through Terror to Triumph. Edinburgh: 1914. V. 43

The Unknown War. New York: 1931. V. 43

The Unrelenting Struggle. Boston: 1942. V. 43

War Speeches. London: 1941-46. V. 41; 43

War Speeches. London: 1941-48. V. 43

The War Speeches of the Rt. Hon. Winston S. Churchill . . . Boston: 1953. V. 39

Winston S. Churchill, His Memoirs and Speeches: from Armistice to Victory 1918 to 1945. New York: 1964. V. 39

The Collected Works of . . . (with) The Collected Essays of . . . London: 1973-76. V. 39; 46

The World Crisis 1911-1914. London: 1923. V. 41

The World Crisis. London: 1923-31. V. 41; 42; 43; 44

The World Crisis 1911-1918. London: 1931. V. 41

CHURCHMAN, JOHN 1705-1775

An Account of the Gospel Labours, and Christian Experiences of a Faithful Minister of Christ, John Churchman . . . Philadelphia: 1779. V. 44

An Account of the Gospel Labours, and Christian Experiences of . . . John Churchman. Philadelphia: 1780. V. 37; 39

An Account of the Gospel Labours, and Christian Experiences of a Faithful Minister of Christ, John Churchman, Late of Nottingham in Pennsylvania, Deceased. To which is added a Short Memorial of . . . Joseph White, Late . . . Philadelphia: 1799. V. 37

An Explanation of the Magnetic Atlas or Variation Chart . . . Philadelphia: 1790. V. 41; 43

THE CHURCHMAN'S Calendar . . . Designed to Exhibit and Actual View of the Holy Catholic and Apostolic Church . . . No. VIII. New York: 1868. V. 42

THE CHURCH'S Floral Kalandar. London: 1869. V. 39

CHURCHWARD, JAMES

The Children of Mu. New York: 1931. V. 41; 46

Cosmic Forces, as They Were Taught in Mu. Mt. Vernon: 1934. V. 42

The Lost Continent of Mu. New York: 1926. V. 39; 46

CHURCHYARD, THOMAS

Churchyard's Chips concerning Scotland: being a Collection of his Pieces relative to that Country; with Historical Notices, and a Life of the Author . . . by George Chalmers, with an engraved coat of arms, and a facsimile of . . . London: 1817. V. 37; 44

The Worthies of Wales. London: 1776. V. 38; 41

CHURI, JOSEPH H.

Sea Nile, The Desert, and Nigritia: Travels in Company with Captain Peel, R.N. 1851-52. London: 1853. V. 40

CHURTON, E.

The Handbook of Taste in Book-Binding. London: 1855. V. 41

CHURTON, EDWARD

the Railroad Book of England . . . London: 1851. V. 41

CHUTE, A. C.

The Religious Life of Acadia. Wolfville: 1933. V. 42

CHUTE, CAROLYN

The Beans of Egypt, Maine. 1985. V. 44

The Beans of Eygpt Maine. New York: 1985. V. 44; 46

CHUTE, CHALONER W.

A History of the Vyne. Winchester: and: 1888. V. 45

A History of the Vyne. Winchester & London: 1888. V. 37

CHUTE, FRANCIS

Beauty and Virtue. A Poem Sacred to the Memory of Anne, Late Countess of Sunderland. Humbly Inscrib'd to . . . The Duke of Marlborough. London: 1716. V. 37; 45

The Petticoat: an heroi-comical poem. In two books. By Mr. Gay (pseud.) London: 1716. V. 37; 45

CHYMIA: Annual Studies in the History of of Chemistry. Philadelphia: 1948-67. V. 46

CHYTRAEUS, DAVID 1530-1600.

Regulae vitae. Wittenberg: 1555. V. 37

CHYTRAEUS, NATHAN

Contra Pestem Epistola Satyrica. Rostock: 1577. V. 38

Epigrammata Qvaedam Non Illepida, in Aduentum Friderici I. Regis; Et Sophiae Reginae Danorvm et Norvegiorvm Feliciss. Et Potentiss &c. Collecta Studio. Rostochii (Rostock): 1576. V. 38

CIAMPINI, JOANNIS

De Sacris Aedificiis a Constantino Magno Constructis Synopsis Historica. Rome: 1693. V. 42

CIBA Symposia. 1939-51. V. 41

CIBBER, COLLEY 1671-1757

Another Occasional Letter from Mr. Cibber to Mr. Pope . . . London: 1744. V. 41

An Aplogy for the Life . . . London: 1756. V. 39; 46

An Aplogy for the Life of Mr. Colley Cibber. London: 1740. V. 37; 38; 40; 44; 45

An Apology for the Life of Mr. Colley Cibber, Comedian . . . . Dublin: 1740. V. 42

An Apology for the Life of Colley Cibber. London: 1750. V. 38

An Apology for the Life . . . London: 1889. V. 46

An Apology for the Life of Colley Cibber . . . London: 1925. V. 44; 46

An Apology for the Life of Colley Cibber, Comedian. Waltham St. Lawrence: 1925. V. 46

Caesar in Egypt. London: 1725. V. 38; 42

The Careless Husband. London: 1705. V. 39; 45

The Double-Gallant: or, the Sick Lady's Cure. London: 1707. V. 38; 40

The Dramatic Works of Colley Cibber, Esq. London: 1760. V. 38; 41; 43; 44

The Egotist; or, Colley Upon Cibber. London: 1743. V. 37; 38; 39; 40; 41

The Lady's Last Stake, or, the Wife's Resentment. London: 1707/08. V. 45

The Lady's Lecture, a Theatrical Dialogue, Between Sir Charles Easy and His Mariageable Daughter. London: 1748. V. 41

A Letter from Mr. Cibber to Mr. Pope, Inquiring Into the Motives That Might Induce Him In His Satyrical Works to be so Frequently Fond of Mr. Cibber's Name. London: 1742. V. 38; 40; 41; 42; 43; 46

A Letter from Mr. Cibber, to Mr. Pope, Inquiring into the Motives that Might Induce Him in His Satyrical Works . . . (with) Another Occasional Letter from Mr. Cibber to Pope. London: 1742, 1744. V. 38

Love Makes a Man; or, The Fop's Fortune. London: 1701. V. 38

Love in a Riddle. London: 1719. V. 38

Love's Last Shift; or, the Fool in Fashion. London: 1696. V. 38; 42

Love's Last Shift; or, the Fool in Fashion . . . London: 1606. V. 37

The Non Juror. London: 1718. V. 38; 39; 42

Perolla and Izadora. London: 1706. V. 38

Plays. London: 1721. V. 42; 44

Ximena; or, The Heroick Daughter. London: 1719. V. 42

CIBBER, THEOPHILUS

An Apology of Mr. The' Cibber, Comedian . . . Dublin: 1741. V. 42; 43

The Lives of the Poets of Great Britain and Ireland to the Time of Dean Swift. London: 1753. V. 43

The Lives of the Poets of Great Britain and Ireland . . . . London: 1753. V. 38; 41; 43; 45

The Tryal of a Cuase or Criminal Conversation, Between Theophilus Cibber, Gent. Plantiff and William Sloper, Esq., Defendant. London: 1739. V. 42; 45

CIBRARIO, LUIGI

Le Feste Torinesi dell' Aprile 1842. Turin: 1842. V. 46

CICCIO, PAULO

Dialogo Utile col Quale s'nstruiscono li Giovani Nelli Costumi Christiani. Cremona: 1580. V. 37

CICERI, EUGENE

Les Pyrenees Dessinees d'Apres Nature et Lithographiees par . . . Luchon: 1871. V. 40

CICERO, MARCUS TULLIUS 106-43 BC

V. 44

M. Tullii Ciceronis Academica. Cambridge: 1736. V. 38

Ad Q. Fratrem dialogi Di Dialogi Oratore. Paris: 1537. V. 40

The Booke of Freendeship of Marcus Tullie Cicero. Gloucestershire: 1904. V. 38

The Booke of Freendeship. Chipping Campden: 1904. V. 46

The Booke of Friendship. London: 1904. V. 46

Cato Major, or His Discourse of Old-Age. Philadelphia: 1744. V. 38; 40; 41; 43

Cato Major . . . Paris: 1758. V. 46

Cato, or an Essay on Old Age . . . Laelius, or an Essay on Friendship . . . London: 1773-77. V. 46

Cato, or an Essay on Old Age. (and) Laelius, or an Essay on Friendship. London: 1777. V. 44

CIRKER, HOWARD B.

Dictionary of American Portraits: 4045 Pictures of Important Americans from Earliest Times to the Beginning of the 20th Century. New York: 1967. V. 46

CISCAR, FRANCISCO

Reflexiones Sobre las Maquinas y Maniobras del Uso de a Bordo. Madrid: 1791. V. 45

CISNERO, HIERONYMO

La Mas Verdadera Relacion . . . de Los Prodigiosos y Venturosos Sucessos del . . . Juan Baptista Suarez Gallinato . . . Seville: 1604. V. 40

CISNERSO, JOSE

V. 44

CIST, CHARLES

Cincinnati in 1841: Its Early Annals and Future Prospects. Cincinnati: 1841. V. 37; 45; 46

The Cincinnati Miscellany, or Antiquities of the West; and Pioneer History and Local Statistics . . . Cincinnati: 1845. V. 42

The Cincinnati Miscellany, or Antiquities of the West, and Pioneer History and General and Local Statistics Compiled from the Western General Advertiser, From October 1st 1844 . . . (to April 1st 1846). Cincinnati: 1845-46. V. 42; 45

The Cincinnati Miscellany, or Antiquities of the West: and Pioneer History and General and Local Statistics. Cincinnati: 1846. V. 39

Sketches and Statistics of Cincinnati in 1851. Cincinnati: 1851. V. 46

CISTULA Entomologica, Sive Insectorum Novorum Diagnoses. London: 1869-85. V. 42

CITADEL. Cairo: 1942. V. 38

THE CITIES of the Bay Illustrated. N.P.: 1888. V. 46

CITINO, DAVID

A Letter to Columbus. 1989. V. 41

THE CITIZEN of the World: Letters from a Chinese Philosopher Residing in London to His Friends in the East. Dublin: 1769. V. 40

CITIZENS CONSTITUTIONAL ASSOCIATION OF DAKOTA

Proceedings of the Convention of the Citizens Constitutional Association of Dakota, Held at Canton, D.T. June 21st 1882. Yankton: 1882. V. 39; 43

CITRI DE LA GUIETTE, SAMUEL

The History of the Triumvirates. London: 1686. V. 45

The History of the Triumvirates. London: 1690. V. 45

LA CITTA di Roma Ovverso Breve Descrizione di Questa Superba citta, Diviso in Quattro Tomi. Roma: 1779. V. 37

THE CITY and County of El Paso, Texas, Containing Useful and Reliable Information Concerning the Future Great Metropolis of the Southwest. El Paso: 1886. V. 41

CITY Atlas of Orange and Township of West Orange, New Jersey. Philadelphia: 1878. V. 41

CITY Biography, Containing Anecdotes and memoirs of the Rise, Progress, Situation and Character of the Aldermen and Other Conspicuous Personages of the Corporation and City of London. London: 1800. V. 38

CITY Cries: or, a Peep at Scenes in Town by an Observer. Philadelphia: 1850. V. 44

CITY of Cairo. Philadelphia: 1839. V. 40

CITY OF GLASGOW BANK

Report of the Trial of the Directors of the City of Glasgow Bank Before the High Court of Justiciary, Edinburgh. Edinburgh: 1879. V. 37

CITY of London, Ontario, Canada. The Pioneer Period and The London of To-Day. London, Ontario: 1897. V. 45

THE CITY of Mitchell and the Country Tributary Thereto. Mitchell: 1887. V. 45

THE CITY of New Orleans. New Orleans: 1894. V. 45

THE CITY of Oxford. London: 1885. V. 38

THE CITY of Toronto: Illustrated with Oil-Colour Views Taken from Photographs. Toronto: 1860. V. 41

CITY Patriotism Displayed: a Poem. Addressed to Rt. Hon. Frederick Lord North. London: 1773. V. 45

THE CITY Remembrancer: Being Historical Narratives of the Great Plague at London, 1665; Great Fire, 1666; and great Storm, 1703. To Which are Added Observations and Reflections on the Plague in General . . . London: 1769. V. 40

THE CIVIL War and the Battles of Corinth and Shiloh. The Daily Corinthian Civil War Centennial Souvenir Edition. Corinth: 1961. V. 44; 45

CIVIL War Naval Chronology 1861-1865. Washington: 1971. V. 44

CIVIL War Papers . . . Massachusetts, Military Order of the Loyal Legion . . . Boston: 1900. V. 38

CIVIL War through the Camera, Hundreds of Vivid Photographs Actually Taken in Civil War Times. Together with Elson's New History. Springfield: 1912. V. 38

CIVILTA. Rivista Bimestrale Della Esposizione Universale di Roma. Milan: 1940-1942. V. 38

CIVINNI, GIOVANNI DOMENICO

Della Storia e Natura del Caffe Discorso Accademico. Florence: 1731. V. 42; 46

CLACY, HELEN

Aunt Dorothy's Will. London: 1860. V. 38

CLADEL, JUDITH

Rodin: the Man and His Art with leaves from His Notebook. New York: 1917. V. 40; 44

CLAFLIN, MARY B.

Personl Recollections of John G. Whittier. New York: 1893. V. 46

CLAFLIN, TENNIE C.

Constitutional Equality a Right of Woman, In Consideration of the Various Relations Which She Sustains as a Necessary Part of the Body of Society and Humanity . . . New York: 1871. V. 37

CLAGETT, MARSHALL

Archimedes in the Middle Ages. Madison: 1980. V. 37

CLAGETT, WILLIAM 1646-1688

An Abridgment of the Prerogatives of St. Ann . . . Done into English to Accompany The Contemplations on the Life and Glory of Holy Mary. London: 1688. V. 39

A Discourse Concerning the Operations of the Holy Spirt. London: 1678. V. 39

CLAIBORNE, JOHN FRANCIS HAMSTRANCK

Historical Account of the Hancocok County and the Sea Board of Mississippi. New Orleans: 1876. V. 44

Life and Times of Gen. Sam Dale, the Mississippi Partisan. New York: 1860. V. 41; 45; 46

Life and Times of Gen. Sam. Dale, the Mississippi Partisan. New York: 1860. V. 46

Mississippi, as a Province, Territory and State . . . Jackson: 1880. V. 45

CLAIBORNE, JOHN HERBERT

Personal Reminiscences of the 'Last Days of Lee and His Paladins'. Petersburg: 1890. V. 44

Seventy Five Years in Old Virginia. New York & Washington: 1904. V. 42

CLAIBORNE, NATHANIEL HERBERT

Notes on the War in the South . . . Richmond: 1819. V. 44; 45

CLAIMS in the Territory of New Mexico. Washington: 1858. V. 40; 46

CLAIMS of the Citizens of the Territory of Kansas. Report of H. J. Stryckler, Commissioner to Audit. Washington: 1859. V. 46

THE CLAIMS of the People of England, Essayed. In a Letter from the Country. London: 1701. V. 40; 45; 46

THE CLAIMS of Thomas Jefferson to the Presidency, Examined at the Bar of Christianity. Philadelphia: 1800. V. 45

CLAIRAC, CHEVALIER DE

The Field Engineer. London: 1773. V. 40

CLAIRMONT, CHRISTOPH W.

The Glass Vessels. New Haven: 1963. V. 40; 42; 44

CLAMPITT, AMY

A Homage to John Keats. (N.P.): (1984). V. 37

A Homage to John Keats. New York: 1985. V. 37; 46

Manhattan. An Elegy, and Other Poems by . . . . Iowa City: 1990. V. 45

Multitudes, Multitudes. New York: 1973. V. 41

Multitudes, Multitudes. New York City: (1937). V. 37

CLAMPITT, JOHN W.

Echoes from the Rocky Mountains. Chicago: 1888. V. 46

CLANCEY, P. A.

The Birds of Natal and Zululand. 1964. V. 46

The Birds of Natal and Zululand. 1964. V. 45

The Birds of Natal & Zululand. London: 1964. V. 37; 44

CLANCY, JAMES

An Essay on the Equitable Rights of Married Women, With Respect to their Separate Property, and Also on Their Claim to a Provision, Called the Wife's Equity. Dublin: 1819. V. 38

CLANCY, MICHAEL

Hermon Prince of Choreae, or, the Extravagant Zealot, a Tragedy. Dublin: 1746. V. 38

CLANCY, TOM

The Hunt for Red October. Annapolis. V. 42

The Hunt For Red October. 1984. V. 45

The Hunt for Red October. Annapolis: 1984. V. 41; 43

Patriot Games. New York: 1987. V. 43

Red Storm Rising. New York: 1986. V. 43

CLANNY, W. R.

New Researches on flame. Sunderland: 1834. V. 45

CLANNY, W. REID

Hyperanthraxis; or, the Cholera of Sunderland. London: 1832. V. 39

CLAP, ROGER

Memoirs of Captain Roger Clap Relating to Some of God's Remarkable Providences to Him. Boston: 1807. V. 45

CLAP, THOMAS

The Annals of History of Yale-College, in New Haven, in the Colony of Connecticut, From the First Founding Thereof, in . . . 1700 to . . . 1766 . . . New Haven: 1766. V. 39

The Religious Constitution of Colleges, Especially of Yale College in New Haven in the Colony of Connecticut. New London: 1754. V. 44

CLAPHAM, HENOCK

A Briefe of the Bibles History . . . London: 1639. V. 40

CLAPHAM, JOHN fl. 1566-1600

An Economic History of Modern Britain. Cambridge: 1926-38. V. 42

An Economic History of Modern Britian. Cambridge: 1939/37/38. V. 45

The Historie of Great Britannie Declaring the Successe of Times and Affaires in that Iland . . . London: 1606. V. 41; 43

A History of the Bank of England. Cambridge/New York: 1945. V. 41

CLAPP, FREDERICK MORTIMER

Jacopo Carucci da Pontormo: His Life and Work. New Haven: 1916. V. 40; 44

CLAPP, THEODORE

Autobiographical Sketches and Recollections, During a Thirty-Five Years' Residence in New Orleans. Boston: 1857. V. 38; 39; 42

CLAPP, WILLIAM W.

A Record of the Boston Stage. Boston and Cambridge: 1853. V. 43

CLAPPE, LOUISE AMELIA KNAPP SMITH 1819-1906

California in 1851 (and 1852). San Francisco: 1933. V. 38; 43; 45; 46

The Shirley Letters from California Mines in 1851-52. San Francisco: 1922. V. 38; 39; 43

The Shirley Letters. San Francisco: 1933. V. 38

CLAPPERTON, HUGH 1788-1827

Journal of a Second Expedition into the Interior of frica, from the Bight of Benin to Soccatoo. London: 1829. V. 38; 39; 41

CLAPPERTON, R. H.

Paper. An Historical Account of Its Making by Hand from Earliest Times Down to the Present Day. Oxford: 1924. V. 44

Paper, an Historical Account of Its Making by Hand from the Earliest Times Down to the Present Day. Oxford: 1934. V. 38

The Paper-Making Machine, Its Invention, Evolution and Development. Oxford: 1967. V. 38; 44

CLARA OF ASSISI, SAINT d. 1253

Vita di Santa Chiara Vergine Composta per Ugolino Verino Cittadino Fiorentino. Chelsea: 1921. V. 39

CLARA Woodward and Her Daydreams. London. V. 46

CLARE COLLEGE

Clare College 1326-1926. University Hall 1326-1346. Clare Hall 1346-1856. Cambridge: 1928-30. V. 37; 41

CLARE, JOHN 1793-1864

Birds Nesting. 1987. V. 40

Birds Nesting. 1987. V. 38

Birds Nesting. the Lost Manuscript. London: 1987. V. 39; 43

Birds Nesting, the Lost Manuscript. Market Drayton: 1987. V. 38; 39

Birds Nesting. By John Clare. The lost manuscript edited by Eric Robinson. Withe prints by Nicholas Parry. Shropshire: 1987. V. 37; 38; 40; 41; 43

The Early Poems. London: 1989. V. 46

Life and Remains of John Clare, the 'Northamptonshire Peasant Poet.' By J.L. Cherry. London/Northampton: 1873. V. 37

The Life of John Clare. By Frederick Martin. London: 1865. V. 37

Madrigals & Chronicles, Being Newly Found Poems. London: 1924. V. 37; 44

The Pimrose Bank. 1986. V. 38

Poems Descriptive of Rural Life and Scenery. London: 1820. V. 39; 40; 42; 45; 46

Poems Descriptive of Rural Life and Scenery. London: 1821. V. 43

Poems. Rugby: 1901. V. 38

The Primrose Bank. London: 1986. V. 43

The Primrose Bank. Market Drayton: 1986. V. 39

The Rural Muse, Poems. London: 1835. V. 37; 39; 42

The Shepherd's Calendar. London: 1978. V. 38; 39; 46

The Shepherd's Calendar. London: 1827. V. 37

Trees; Poems and Prose Extracts. 1989. V. 45

Trees 'The Spirit of the Woods.' 1989. V. 41

Trees 'the Spirit of the Woods.' 1989. V. 43

The Village Minstrel, and Other Poems. London: 1821. V. 37; 40; 41; 42; 43; 45

CLARE, JOHN FITZGIBBON, 1ST EARL OF 1749-1802

The Speech in the House of Lords of Ireland on a Motion Made by the Earl of Moira, Feb. 19, 1798. Dublin: 1798. V. 39; 41; 42

The Speech of the Right Honourable John Earl of Clare, Lord High Chancellor of Ireland, in the House of Lords of Ireland, Monday, February 19, 1798, On a Motion Made by the Earl of Moira . . . London: 1798. V. 39

CLARE, MARTIN

The Motion of Fluids, Natural and Artificial. London: 1737. V. 38

The Motion of Fluids, Natural and Artificial; in Particular that of the Air and Water, in a Familiar Manner, Proposed and Proved by Evident and Conclusive Experiments, with Useful Remarks . . . London: 1735. V. 37; 45

Youth's Introduction to Trade and Business. London: 1791. V. 46

CLARE, PETER

A Treatise on the Gonorrhoea: to Which is Added, a Critical Enquiry into the Different Methods of Administering Mercury. London: 1781. V. 44

CLAREMONT, L.

The Gem-Cutter's Craft. London: 1906. V. 45

CLARENDON, EDWARD, 1ST EARL OF 1609-1674

The History of the Rebellion and Civil Wars in England. Oxford: 1843. V. 46

CLARENDON, EDWARD HYDE, 1ST EARL OF 1609-1674

A Brief View and Survey of the Dangerous and Pernicious Errors to Church and State in Mr. Hobbe's Book, Entitled Leviathan. London: 1676. V. 38; 40

A Brief View and Survey of the Dangerous and Pernicious Errors to Church and State. Oxford: 1676. V. 38; 40; 41; 42; 43; 44

A Brief View and Survey of the Dangerous and Pernicious Errors to Church and State, in Mr. Hobbe's Book Entitled Leviathan. Oxon: 1676. V. 40

A Collection of Several Tracts . . . Published from His Lordship's Original Manuscripts. London: 1727. V. 41; 45

A Full Answer to an Infamous and Trayterous Pamphlet, Entituled, a Declaration of the Commons of England in Parliament Assembled, Expressing Their Reasons and Grounds of Passing the Late Resolutions Touching no Further Address or Application to be Made . . . London: 1648. V. 43

The History of the Rebellion and Civil Wars in England, Begun in the Year 1641. V. 39

The History of the Rebellion and Civil Wars in England, Begun in the Year 1641. Oxford: 1705-6. V. 40

The History of the Rebellion and Civil Wars in England, Begun in the Year 1641 . . . Oxford: 1707. V. 40

The History of the Rebellion and Civil Wars in England, Begun in the Year 1641 . . . Dublin: 1719. V. 40

The History of the Rebellion and Civil Wars in Ireland. London: 1720. V. 37; 43

The History of the Rebellion and Civil Wars in England, Begun in the Year 1641. Oxford: 1732. V. 38

The History of the Rebellion and Civil Wars in England. Oxford: 1807. V. 38; 46

CLARENDON, EDWARD HYDE, 1ST EARL OF 1609-1674 continued

History of the Rebellion and Civil Wars in England, Begun in the Year MDCXLI, to the Happy End of the King's Blessed Restoration and Return, 29th May MDCLX. No publisher or date: 1820. V. 44

The History of the Rebellion and Civil Wars in England. Oxford: 1826. V. 37; 39; 42; 45

The History of the Rebellion and Civil Wars in England, To Which is Added an Historical View of the Affairs of Ireland. Boston: 1827. V. 45

The History of the Rebellion and Civil Wars in England. 1849. V. 39

The History of the Rebellion and Civil Wars In England, Together with an Historical View of the Affairs of Ireland . . . Oxford: 1849. V. 39; 44

The Life of Edward Earl of Clarendon . . . (together with) The Continuation of the Life. Oxford: 1759. V. 40; 44; 46

The Life of . . . Containing I. An Account of the Chancellor's Life From His Birth to the Restoration in 1660. II. A Continuation of the Same, and of His History of the Grand Rebellion, From the Restoration to His Banishment in 1667 . . . Oxford: 1760. V. 41

Religion and Policy and the Countenance and Assistance Each Should Give to the Other, With a Survey of the Power and Jurisdiction of the Pope in the Dominions of Other Princes. Oxford: 1811. V. 41

State Letters of Henry Earl of Clarendon, Lord Lieutenant of Ireland, During the Reign of K. James the Second and His Lordship's Diary, 1687-90. Oxford: 1763. V. 39

CLARENDON, EDWARD HYDE, FIRST EARL OF

The History of the Rebellion and Civil Wars in England to which is added an Historical View of the Affairs of Scotland. (with) The Life of . . . Oxford: 1826-27. V. 37

The History of the Rebellion and Civil Wars in England, together with an Historical View of the Affairs of Ireland. Now for the First Time carefully printed from the Original MS. preserved in the Bodleian Library to which are . . . Oxford: 1849. V. 37

The History of the Rebellion and Civil Wars in England. (with) The Life . . . Oxford: 1760-1807. V. 37

The Life of Edward Earl of Clarendon, Lord High Chancellor of England . . . in which is included a Continuation of His History of the Grand Rebelion Written by Himself. Now for the First Time carefully printed from the Original MS. Preserved in . . . Oxford: 1857. V. 37

CLARENDON, R. V.

A Sketch of the Revenue and Finances of Ireland and of the Appropriated Funds, Loans and Debt of the Nation From Their Commencement . . . London: 1791. V. 43

CLARIDGE, JOHN

The Shepherd of Banbury's Rules to Judge of the Changes of the Weather, Grounded on Forty Years Experience. London: 1744. V. 43

The Shepherd of Banbury's Rules to Judge of the Changes of the Weather, Grounded on Forty Years Experience. London: 1748. V. 43

CLARIDGE, W. WALTON

A History of the Gold Coast and Ashanti from the Earliest Times to the Commencements of the Twentieth Century. London: 1915. V. 45

CLARK, A. H.

A Monograph of the Existing Crinoids. Washington: 1915-47. V. 43; 45

CLARK, AUSTIN S.

Reminiscences of Travel 1852-1865. Middletown: n.d. V. 37

CLARK, BARRETT H.

America's Lost Plays. Princeton: 1940-42. V. 46

CLARK, BETTY

Shall we Join the Ladies. Wood engravings by Women Artists of the Twentieth Century. With tail-piece and front cover engravings by Joan Hassall with an appreciation by George Mackley. Oxford: 1979. V. 37; 40

CLARK, BRACY

A Series of Experiments on the Foot of the Living Horse . . . London: 1809-11. V. 40

CLARK, C.

An Historical and Descriptive Account of the Town of Lancaster. Lancaster: 1807. V. 42

CLARK, CHARLES

Epsom Races: a Poem, Comic, Punning and Racy. Great Thotham, Essex: 1836. V. 45

John Noakes and Mary Styles . . . London: 1839. V. 43

Rates and Taxes and How They Were Collected. Groombridge: 1866. V. 40

Some Rejected Stanzas of 'Don Juan.' Great Thotham: 1845. V. 38

CLARK, CHARLES M.

A Trip to Pike's Peak and Notes by the Way . . . Chicago: 1861. V. 37; 38; 39; 40; 42; 43

CLARK, CLARENCE H.

A Descriptive Catalogue of the Book Forming the Library of Clarence H. Clark, Chestnut-Wold, Philadelphia. Philadelphia: 1888. V. 39

CLARK, DANIEL

Deposition of Daniel Clark, the Delegate in the House of Representatives . . . from the Territory of Orleans, in Relation to the Conduct of General James Wilkinson . . . Washington: 1808. V. 37; 45

Proofs of the Corruption of General James Wilkinson and of His Connexion with Aaron Burr. Philadelphia: 1809. V. 37; 38; 39; 40; 45

CLARK, DANIEL KINNEAR

Railway Machinery: a Treatise on the Mechanical Engineering of Railways . . . Glasgow: 1855/51-55. V. 42

Railway Machinery: A Treatise on the Mechanical Engineering of Railways: Embracing the Principles and Construction of Rolling and Fixed Plant; Illustrated by a Series of Plates on a Large Scale, and by . . . Glasgow/Edinburgh: 1855. V. 37

Tramways Their Construction and Working . . . With Special References to the Tramways of the United Kingdom. London: 1894. V. 40

Tramways. Their Construction and Working, Embracing a Comprehensive History of the System, with an Exhaustive Analysis the Various Modes of Traction . . . London: 1878. V. 38

CLARK, DONALD

Australian Mining and Metallurgy. Melbourne: 1904. V. 39

CLARK, E.

History of the Seventh Regiment of New York 1806-1889. New York: 1890. V. 38

CLARK, EDSON L.

The Races of European Turkey. New York: 1878. V. 45

CLARK, EDWARD

Catalogue of the Edward Clark Library. Edinburgh: 1976. V. 46

Proceedings of Two Meetings of Citizens of Philadelphia Respecting Col. Clark's Plan for Ascending Rapids in Rivers, and Thereby Improving the Navigation of the Delaware, Beyond Trenton . . . Philadelphia: 1824. V. 41

CLARK, EDWARD DANIEL

Greek Marbles Brought from the Shores of the Euxine, Archipelago and Mediterranean, and Deposited in the Vestibule of the Public Library of the University of Cambridge. Cambridge: 1809. V. 38

CLARK, EDWARD L.

Daleth, or the Homestead of the Nations. Boston: 1864. V. 42

CLARK, ELEANOR

Rome and a Villa. Garden City: 1952. V. 39; 46

CLARK, EWAN

Miscellaneous Poems. Whitehaven: 1779. V. 37; 40; 42; 43

CLARK, FRANCIS D. 1846-1882.

The First Regiment of New York Volunteers Commanded by Col. Jonathan D. Stevenson, in the Mexican War. Names of the Members of the Regiment During its Term of Service in Upper and Lower California, 1847-1848. New York: 1882. V. 37; 45

CLARK, GEORGE

Oxford History of England. 1937-87. V. 46

CLARK, GEORGE H.

Farm Weeds of Canada . . . Ottawa: 1906. V. 43

CLARK, GEORGE ROGERS

Colonel George Rogers Clark's Sketch of His Campaign in the Illinois in 1778-79. Cincinnati: 1869. V. 41

George Rogers Clark's Sketch of His Campaign in the Illinois in 1778-79. Cincinnati: 1869. V. 46

Sketch of His Campaign in the Illinois in 1778-9 . . . Cincinnati: 1869. V. 39

CLARK, GEORGE T.

Mediaeval Military Architecture in England. London: 1884. V. 38; 40

CLARK, GEORGE W.

The Liberty Minstrel. New York: 1844. V. 43

CLARK, GEORGINA C.

Servittes. Dinner Napkins and How to Fold Them. London: 1875. V. 42

CLARK, HAMLET

Letters Home from Spain, Algeria and Brazil, During Past Entomological Rambles. London: 1867. V. 46

CLARK, HARRY

The Year's at the Spring. An Anthology of Recent Poetry, compiled by L.D.'O. Walters. Introduction by Harold Monro. New York: (1920). V. 37

CLARK, HENRY G.

Ship Fever, so Called: Its History, Nature and Best Treatment. Boston: 1850. V. 41

CLARK, HIRAM C.

History of Chenango County, Containing the Divisions of the County and Sketches of the Towns . . . Norwich: 1850. V. 43

CLARK, HUGH

An Introduction to Heraldry. London: 1854. V. 40

CLARK, J.

Illustrations to Don Quixote. London: 1819. V. 39

A Treatise on the Prevention of Diseases Incidental to Horses. Edinburgh: 1788. V. 37

CLARK, J. COOPER

The Story of 'Eight Deer' in Codex Colombino. London: 1912. V. 37; 42

CLARK, J. F.

The Society in Search of Truth; or, Stock Gambling in San Francisco. Oakland: 1878. V. 43; 44; 46

CLARK, J. H.

Myiorama a Collection of Many Thousand Landscapes. London: 1824. V. 44

CLARK, JAMES

Historical Record and Regimental Memoir of the Royal Socts Fusiliers, Formerly Known as the 21st Royal North British Fusiliers. Edinburgh: 1885. V. 40; 46

The Influence of Climate in the Prevention and Cure of Chronic Diseases More Particularly of the Chest and Digestive Organs . . . London: 1830. V. 39; 44

Observations on the Shoeing of Horses. Edinburgh: 1783. V. 39

The Sanative Influence of Climate. Philadelphia: 1843. V. 42

The Sanative Influence of Climate. London: 1841. V. 38

A Treatise on the Prevention of Diseases Incidental to Horses, from Bad management in Regard to Stables, Food, Water, Air and Exercise. Philadelphia: 1791. V. 43; 45

CLARK, JAMES A.

Spindletop. New York: 1952. V. 37; 38; 39; 42

The Wyoming Valley, Upper Waters of the Susquehanna, and the Lackawanna Coal-Region, Including Views of the Natural Scenery of Northern Pennsylvania, from the Indian Occupancy to the Year 1875. Scranton: 1875. V. 39; 42

CLARK, JAMES MAXWELL

Colonial Days. Denver: 1902. V. 42; 45

CLARK, JOHN

The Amateur's Assistant. London: 1826. V. 38

Elements of Drawing and Painting in Water Colours. London: 1841. V. 44

Ill Newes From New England: or a Narative (sic) of New Englands Persecution. London: 1652. V. 45

Observations on the Diseases in Long Voyages to Hot Countries, and Particularly On Those Which Prevail in the East Indies. London: 1773. V. 42

Poems on Several Subjects, and Occasions, Both Moral and Entertaining.. Trowbridge: 1799. V. 40; 42; 45

CLARK, JOHN A.

Gleanings by the Way. Philadelphia: 1842. V. 45

CLARK, JOHN BATES

The Distribution of Wealth a Theory of Wages, Interest and Profits . . . New York: 1899. V. 37

CLARK, JOHN HEAVISIDE

A Practical Essay on the Art of Colouring and Painting Landscapes in Water Colours. London: 1812. V. 38; 45

CLARK, JOHN WILLIS

The Care of Books. Cambridge: 1901. V. 44

The Care of Books; an Essay on the Development of Libraries and Their Fittings . . . Cambridge: 1909. V. 39

The Life and Letters of the Reverend Adam Sedgwick. 1890. V. 44

The Life and Letters of the Rev. Adam Sedgwick. Cambridge: 1890. V. 44

CLARK, JOSEPH G.

Lights and Shadows of Sailor Life, as Exemplified in Fifteen Years' Experience, Including the More Thrilling Events of the U.S. Exploring Expedition . . . Boston: 1848. V. 41

CLARK, KENNETH

A Catalogue of the Drawings of Leonaro DaVinci, in the collections of His Majesty the King of Windsor Castle. London: 1935. V. 37

The Drawings of Leonardo Da Vinci in the Collection of Her Majesty the Queen at Windsor Castle. London: 1968-69. V. 37; 42; 44; 45

The Drawings by Sandro Botticelli for Dante's Divine Comedy after the Originals in the Berlin Museums and the Vatican. New York: 1976. V. 39

The Gothic Revival. London: 1928. V. 45

Henry Moore Drawings. New York: 1974. V. 43; 46

Piero Della Francesca. London: 1951. V. 44; 45

Sidney Nolan. London: 1961. V. 46

CLARK, LATIMER

General Description of the Britannia and Conway Tublar Bridges on the Chester and Holyhead Railway. London: 1849. V. 43

General Description of the Britannia and Conway Tubular Bridges on the Chester and Holyhead Railway. London: 1850. V. 42

CLARK, LEWIS GAYLORD

Knick-Knacks from an Editor's Table. New York: 1852. V. 45

CLARK, LEWIS J.

Wild Flowers of British Columbia. Sidney: 1973. V. 37; 41

CLARK, ORTON S.

Clay Allison of the Washita First a Cow Man and Then an Extinguisher of Bad Men. Attica: 1922. V. 45

CLARK, PETER 1693-1768

The Witness of the Spirit in the Hearts of Believers. Boston: 1744. V. 43

CLARK, R.

Pot Luck . . . West Hartford: 1945. V. 43

CLARK, R. INGHAM

Few Notes on Varnishes and Fossil Resins. London: 1891. V. 40

CLARK, RICHARD H.

Memoirs of Judge Richard H. Clark. Atlanta: 1898. V. 43

CLARK, ROBERT

Golf: a Royal and Ancient Game. London: 1893. V. 42

CLARK, ROBERT STERLING

Drawings from the Clark Art Institute: A Catalogue Raisonne of the Robert Sterling Clark Collection of European and American drawings . . . New Haven & London: 1964. V. 41

Through Shen-kan. The Account of the Clark Expedtion in North China 1908-09. London: 1912. V. 45

CLARK, ROLAND

Gunner's Down. New York: 1937. V. 39; 40; 43; 44

Roland Clark's Etchings. New York: 1938. V. 39; 42; 43

CLARK, RONALD

The Splendid Hills. The Life and Photographs of Vittorio Sella, 1859-1943. London: 1948. V. 44

CLARK, S. R.

S. R. Clark, Furrier and Fur Skin Dresser . . . Before Purchasing Your Wraps, &c, for the Coming Winter Read a Few Hints to the Unwary! Melbourne: 1887. V. 38

CLARK, SAMUEL

The British Gauger: or, Trader and Officer's Instructor, in the Royal Revenue of the Excise and Customs. Part I. Containing the necessary rules of vulgar and decimal arthimetic, and the whole art of practical guaging . . . Part II. An historical . . . London: 1765. V. 37; 41

England's Remembrancer, a True and Full Narrative of Those Two Never to Be Forgotten Deliverances . . . London: 1679. V. 46

CLARK, THOMAS BLAKE

Omai, First Polynesian Ambassador to England. San Francisco: 1940. V. 37; 44

Omai, First Polynesian Ambassador to England. London: 1941. V. 39; 40

CLARK, THOMAS D.

Travels in the New South . . . 1865 (through) 1955. Norman: 1962. V. 40

Travels in the Old South. Norman: 1969. V. 39; 40

CLARK, VICTOR S.

History of Manufactures in the United States (1607-1928). New York: 1929. V. 46

CLARK, W. A.

Historical Society of Montana. Helena: 1902. V. 46

CLARK, W. P.

The Indian Sign Language, With Brief Explanatory Notes of the Gestures Taught Deaf-Mutes In Our Institutions for Their Instruction . . . Philadelphia: 1885. V. 43; 45; 46

CLARK, WALTER

Histories of the Several Regiments and Battalions from North Carolina in the Great War 1861-65. Raleigh: 1901. V. 38

Histories of the Several Regiments and Battalions from North Carolina in the Great War. Raleigh & Goldsboro: 1901. V. 38

Histories of the Several Regiments and Battalions from North Carolina in the Great War. Wendell: 1982. V. 38

CLARK, WALTER VAN TILBURG

The City of Trembling Leaves. New York: 1945. V. 44; 46

The Ox Bow Incident. 1940. V. 43

The Watchful Gods. New York: 1950. V. 43

CLARK, WILLIAM

The Field Notes of Captain William Clark. New Haven: 1964. V. 37; 40; 42; 44

History of Hampton, Battery 'F', Indepdendent Pennsylvania Light Artillery. Pittsburgh: 1909. V. 42

CLARK, WILLIAM ANDREWS

The Library of William Andrews Clark, Jr.: Wilde and Wildeiana. San Francisco: 1922-31. V. 44

CLARK, WILLIAM BELL

Naval Documents of the American Revolution. Washington: 1964-70. V. 44

CLARK, WILLIAM P.

The Indian Sign Language, with Brief Explanatory Notes of the Gesturing Taught Deaf-Mutes . . . Philadelphia: 1885. V. 42; 46

CLARK, WILLIS GAYLORD

The Literary Remains of the Late Willis Gaylord Clark. New York: 1844. V. 45

CLARKE, A. B.

Travels in Mexico and California: Comprising a Journal of a Tour from Brazos Santiago . . . Boston: 1852. V. 42; 43

CLARKE, ADAM

An Account of the Infancy, Religious and Literary Life of Adam Clarke . . . London: 1833. V. 44

A Bibliographical Dictionary. Liverpool: 1802-04. V. 45

a Bibliographical Dictonary. (with) The Bibliographical Miscellany. Liverpool & London: 1802-04/1806. V. 46

The Bibliographical Miscellany . . . London: 1806. V. 38

CLARKE, ANTHONY M.

Pompeo Batoni Complete Catalogue. Oxford: 1985. V. 46

CLARKE, ARTHUR

A Code of Instructions for the Treatment of Sufferers from Railroad and Steam-Boat Accidents . . . Dublin: 1849. V. 41

An Essay on Warm, Cold and Vapour Bathing, with Practical Observations on Sea Bathing . . . Dublin: 1816. V. 37

Interplanetary Flight: An Introduction to Astronautics. New York: 1951. V. 40

CLARKE, ARTHUR C.

2061: Odyssey Three. 1988. V. 37

Across a Sea of Stars. New York: 1959. V. 37; 39; 42

Childhood's End. 1953. V. 43

Childhood's End. 1954. V. 44

The City and the Stars. New York: 1956. V. 45

A Code of Instructions for the Treatment of Suffers from Railroad to Steam Boat Accidents. Dublin: 1849. V. 40

Dolphin Island. 1963. V. 43

Earthlight. 1955. V. 43

Expedition to Earth. 1953. V. 39

The Exploration of Space. 1951. V. 39

A Fall of Moondust. New York: 1961. V. 39

Imperial Earth. London: 1975. V. 44

Interplantetary Flight: An Introduction to Astronautics. New York: 1951. V. 37; 43

Prelude to Mars. 1965. V. 44

Prelude to Space. New York. V. 37

Rama II. 1989. V. 43

Reach for Tomorrow. 1956. V. 43

Reach for Tomorrow. 1956. V. 39

Reach for Tomorrow. 1962. V. 39

Rendezvous with Rama. 1973. V. 43

Rendezvous With Rama. London: 1973. V. 44

The Sands of Mars. 1951. V. 39

Sands of Mars. New York: (1952). V. 37

The Songs of the Distant Earth. 1986. V. 39

The Songs of Distant Earth. 1986. V. 37

2001: a Space Odyssey. 1968. V. 44

2001: a Space Odyssey. 1968. V. 45

2001. New York: 1968. V. 42

2001: a Space Odyssey. New York: 1968. V. 44

2001: Odyssey Two. 1982. V. 39

2010: Odyssey Two. 1982. V. 43

2010: Odyssey Two. 1982. V. 45

2010: Odyssey Two. Huntington Woods: 1982. V. 37; 43; 45

2010: Odyssey Two. New York: 1982. V. 39; 42

2001: Odyssey Three. 1988. V. 44

2061: Odyssey Three. 1988. V. 43

2061: Odyssey Three. 1988. V. 39

CLARKE, ASA B.

Travels In Mexico and California: Comprising a Journal of a Tour from Brazos Santiago. Boston: 1852. V. 39; 40; 41; 42; 44; 45; 46

CLARKE, AUSTIN 1896-1974

The Cattledrive in Connaught and Other Poems. London: 1925. V. 38

Collected Poems. London: 1936. V. 41; 45

The Fires of Baal. Dublin and London: 1921. V. 38

First Visit to England and Other Memories. Dublin and London: 1945. V. 41

Forget-Me-Not. Dublin: 1962. V. 38; 41

Pilgrimage and Other Poems. London: 1929. V. 38

The Plot Succeeds. Dublin and London: 1950. V. 38

The Son of Learning - a Poetic Comedy in Three Acts. London: 1927. V. 38

The Sword of the West. Dublin and London: 1921. V. 38

The Vengeance of Fionn. Dublin and London: 1917. V. 38

The Vengeance of Fionn. London: 1917. V. 42

CLARKE, C. PURDON

Arms and Armour at Sandringham - The Indian Collection. London: 1910. V. 40

CLARKE, CHARLES

Architectura Ecclesiastica Londini. London: 1820. V. 40

Illustrations of the Cyperaceae. London: 1909. V. 43

CLARKE, CHARLES COWDEN

Adam, the Gardener. London: 1834. V. 45

CLARKE, CHARLES G.

The Men of the Lewis and Clark Expedition: a Biographical Roster of the Fifty-One Members and a Composite Diary of Their Activities from All Known Sources. Glendale: 1970. V. 46

CLARKE, D. L.

Beaker Pottery of Great Britain and Ireland. Cambridge: 1970. V. 42

CLARKE, E. G.

Compendium of the Practice of Physic. Philadelphia: 1818. V. 44

CLARKE, E. M.

A Litter of Letters; a Linocut Alphabet. 1987. V. 40

CLARKE, E. Y.

Atlanta Illustrated. Atlanta: 1881. V. 41

CLARKE, EDWARD DANIEL 1769-1822

Greek Marbles Brought from the Shores of the Euxine, Archipelago and Mediterranean, and Deposited in the Vestibule of the Public Library of the University of Cambridge. Cambridge: 1809. V. 45

Testimonies of Different Authors Respecting the Colossal Statue of Ceres . . . Cambridge: 1803. V. 38

The Tomb of Alexander . . . Cambridge: 1805. V. 43

A Tour through the South of England, Wales and Part of Ireland, Made During 1791. London: 1793. V. 39

Travels in Various Countries of Europe Asia and Africa . . . Part the First Russia Tartary and Turkey. London: 1810. V. 40

Travels in Various Countries of Europe, Asia and Africa. New York: 1813. V. 39

Travels in Various Countries of Europe, Asia and Africa. London: 1816-19. V. 42

Travels in Various Countries of Europe, Asia and Africa. London: 1817-24. V. 45

Travels in Various Countries of Scandinavia, Including Denmark, Sweden, Norway, Lapland and Finland. London: 1838. V. 39

CLARKE, EDWARD HAMMOND 1820-1877

Visions: a Study of False Sight. Boston: 1878. V. 43; 45

CLARKE, EDWIN

The Human Brain and Spinal Cord. Berkeley: 1968. V. 41

An Illustrated History of Brain Function. Oxford: 1972. V. 44

CLARKE, FRANCIS G.

The American Ship-Master's Guide, and Commercial Assistant . . . Boston: 1838. V. 40; 42

The Seaman's manual . . . Portland: 1830. V. 40; 41

CLARKE, G. S.

The Navy and the Nation or Naval Warfare and Imperial Defense. London: 1897. V. 38

CLARKE, GRAHAM

Balyn and Balan. Broughton Monchelsea: 1970. V. 37; 41; 45

CLARKE, H.

John Coney, Silversmith, 1655-1722. Boston: 1932. V. 37

CLARKE, H. C.

The Confederate States Almanac, and Repository of Useful Knowledge for the Year 1864 . . . Mobile: 1864. V. 41

CLARKE, H. G.

Baxter Colour Prints, Pictorially Represented. London: 1920-21. V. 38; 40

The Centenary Baxter Book Being an Appreciation of George Baxter (1804-1867) The Nineteenth Century Colour Picture Printer, Together with a Catalogue Resume of His Works. 1936. V. 46

CLARKE, HERMANN FREDERICK

John Coney, Silversmith 1655-1722. Boston: 1932. V. 38

John Coney, Silversmith. 1655-1722. Boston & New York: 1932. V. 42

John Hull a Builder of the Bay Colony. Portland: 1940. V. 37; 38

CLARKE, J. LOCKHARDT

On Certain Functions of the Spinal Chord, with Further Investigations Into its Structure. 1853. V. 41

CLARKE, J. O.

Ocala, Fla. A Sketch of Its History, Residences, Business Interests, etc. New York: 1891. V. 41

CLARKE, JAMES

Historical Record and Regimental Memoir of the Royal Scot Fusiliers Formrly Known as the 21st Royal North British Fusiliers. Edinburgh: 1885. V. 41

A Survey of the Lakes of Cumberland, Westmorland and Lancashire . . . London: 1787. V. 44; 46

CLARKE, JAMES F.

Some Remarks on the Proposal to Annex Texas to the United States. Louisville: 1837. V. 37; 39

CLARKE, JAMES FREEMAN

The Annexation of Texas. A Sermon Delivered in the Masonic Temple on Fast Day. Boston: 1844. V. 42

Eleven Weeks in Europe: and What May Be Seen in That Time. Boston: 1852. V. 45

CLARKE, JAMES STANIER

The Life of Admiral Nelson, K.B. from His Lordship's Manuscripts. London: 1809. V. 38; 41; 42

The Life and Services of Horatio Viscount Nelson, Duke of Bronte; Vice-Admiral of the White . . . London: 1880. V. 42

CLARKE, JOHN

The Architectural History of Gloucester from the Earliest Period to the Close of the Eighteenth Century. Gloucester: 1850. V. 41

Clarke's Bibliotheca Legum; or complete catalogue of the common and statute law-books of the United Kingdom, with an account of their dates and prices. Originally compiled by J. Worrall; now further improved, and arranged in a new . . . London: (1810). V. 37; 38; 40

Commentaries on Some of the Most Important Diseases of Children. London: 1815. V. 39

A Demonstration of Some of the Principal Sections of Sir Isaac Newton's Principles of Natural Philosophy. London: 1730. V. 39

An Essay Upon the Education of Youth in Grammar-Schools. London: 1720. V. 41; 45

An Essay Upon the Education of Youth in Grammar Schools. London: 1730. V. 38; 41; 42; 46

An Essay Upon Study. London: 1731. V. 39; 41; 42; 43

An Essay Upon Study. Wherein directions are given for the due conduct therof, and the collection of a library, proper for the purpose, consisting of the choicest Books in all the several parts of Learing. London: 1731. V. 37; 38

An Impartial and Authentic Account of the Battle Fought on the 17th June 1775 . . . on Bunker's Hilll, Near Charles Town, in New England. London: 1775. V. 40

Letters to a Student in the University of Cambridge, Massachusetts. Boston: 1796. V. 37; 39

A New Grammar of the Latin Tongue, Comprising All in the Art Necessary for Grammar Schools. London: 1754. V. 42

CLARKE, JOHN WILLIS

The Life and Letters of the Reverend Adam Sedwick . . . Woodwardian professor of Geology, 1818-1873. Cambridge: 1890. V. 37

CLARKE, JOSEPH CLAYTON

The Characters of Charles Dickens. Pourtrayed in a Series of Original Water Colour Sketches by 'Kyd'. London: 1889. V. 40

CLARKE, KIT

Where the Trout Hide. New York: 1889. V. 43

CLARKE, LEWIS

Narratives of the Sufferings of . . . Sons of a Soldier of the Revolution During a Captivity of More than Twenty Years Among the Slaveholders of Kentucky, One of the So Called Christian States of North America. Boston: 1846. V. 38; 42

CLARKE, LINDSAY

The Chymical Wedding. London: 1989. V. 45

CLARKE, M. ST. CLAIR

Legislative and Documentary History of the Bank of the United States. Washington: 1832. V. 39

CLARKE, MARCUS

For the Term of His Natural Life. Sydney: 1929. V. 43

CLARKE, MARY ANNE

The Authentic and Impartial Life of Mrs. Mary Anne Clarke . . . London: 1809. V. 46

The Rival Princes. London: 1810. V. 42

CLARKE, MARY COWDEN

idyl of London Streeters. Rome: 1875. V. 43

CLARKE, MARY WHATLEY

A Century of Cow Business: a History of the Texas and Southwestern Cattle Raisers Association. Forth Worth: 1976. V. 42

CLARKE, MATTHEW ST. CLAIR

Legislative and Documentary History of the Bank of the United States . . . Washington: 1832. V. 44

CLARKE, M'DONALD

The Gossip; or, a Laugh with the Ladies, a Grin at the Gentlemen, and Burlesques on Byron. New York: 1823. V. 42

Sketches. New York: 1826. V. 42

CLARKE, MRS. J. STIRLING

The Ladies' Equestrain Guide; or, The Habit & The Horse: A Treatise on Female Equitation. London: (1857). V. 37

CLARKE, PETER DOOYENTATE

Origin and Traditional History of the Wyandots and Sketches of the Other Indian Tribes of North America. Toronto: 1870. V. 39

CLARKE, S. A.

Pioneer Days of Oregon History. Cleveland: 1905. V. 38

CLARKE, S. J.

History of McDonough County, Illinois, Its Cities, Towns and Villages, with Early Reminiscences . . . Springfield: 1878. V. 46

CLARKE, SAMUEL 1626-1701

A Brief Concordance to the Holy Bible, of the Most Usual and Useful Places Which One May Have Occasion to Seek For. London: 1696. V. 39

A Collection of the Lives of Ten Eminent Divines, Famous in Their Generations for Learning, Prudence, Piety and Painfulness in the Work of the Ministry. London: 1662. V. 42

A Collection of Papers, Which Passed Between . . . Mr. Leibnitz, and Dr. Clarke in the Years 1715 and 1716, Related to the Principles of Natural Philosophy and Religion. London: 1717. V. 38; 39; 41; 42; 43; 44; 45; 46

A Discourse Concerning the Being and Attributes of God, the Obligations of Natural Religion, and the Truth and Certainty of the Christian Revelation. London: 1716. V. 39; 41

A Discourse Concerning the Being and Attributes of God, the Obligations of Natural Religion, and the Truth and Certainty of the Christian Revelation. London: 1719. V. 43

A Discourse Concerning the Being and Attributes of God, the Obligations of Natural Religion, and the Truth and Certainty of the Christian Revelation. London: 1732. V. 38; 41

A General Martyrologie, Containing a Collection of All the Greatest Persecutions Which Have Befallen the Church of Christ . . . London: 1660. V. 42

The Life and Death of Hannibal . . . as Also the Life and Death of Epaminondas the Great Captain of the Thebans . . . London: 1665. V. 45

The Life of Tamerlane the Great. London: 1664. V. 45

The Marrow of Ecclesiastical History . . . London: 1675. V. 45

A Mirrour or Looking-Glasse Both for Saints and Sinners, Held Forth in Some Thousands of Examples. London: 1657. V. 40; 43

A Mirrour or Looking Glasse Both for Saints and Sinners, Held Forth in Some Thousands of Examples . . . Mirrour: 1657. V. 40

A Paraphrase on the Four Evangelists; Wherein, for the Clearer Understanding of the Sacred History, the Whole Text . . . London: 1795. V. 39

CLARKE, SAMUEL 1626-1701 continued

A True and Faithful Account of the Four Chiefest Plantations of the English in America. London: 1670. V. 41

CLARKE, SEYMOUR

Cameron Highlanders. Officers Present at the Various Campaigns, Battles &c. in Which the Regiment Has Taken Part. Edinburgh: 1913. V. 41

CLARKE, SOMERS

Ancient Egyptian Masonry: the Building Craft. London: 1930. V. 40

CLARKE, STEPHEN

Hortus Anglicus, or the Modern English Garden . . . London: 1822. V. 40; 44

CLARKE, THOMAS BROOKE

An Historical and Political View of the Disorganisation of Europe; Wherein the Laws and Characters of Nations, and the Maritime and Commercial System of Great Britain and Other States, are Vindicated Against the Imputations and Revolutionary Proposals . . . London: 1803. V. 44

CLARKE, THOMAS COTTRELL

A Collection of Fugitive Poems. Philadelphia: 1824. V. 40

CLARKE, THOMAS D.

Travels in the Old South, a Bibliography. Norman: 1956. V. 40

CLARKE, WILLIAM

Every Night Book or, Life After Dark. London: 1827. V. 38

Three Courses and a Dessert. London: 1830. V. 46

The Undoubted Heir; and He Must Reign. London: 1714. V. 46

CLARKE, WILLIAM EAGLE

A Handbook of the Vertebrate Fauna of Yorkshire. London: 1881. V. 43

Studies in Bird Migration. 1912. V. 46

Studies in Bird Migration. London: 1912. V. 37; 43; 45

CLARKE, WILLIAM NELSON

Parochial Topography of the Hundred of Wanting, with Other Miscellaneous Records Relating to the County of Berks. Oxford: 1824. V. 42

CLARKE'S Confederate Household Almanac, for the Year 1863. Vicksburg: 1863. V. 44

CLARKE'S Confederate Household Almanac, for the Year of Our Lord 1864 . . . Mobile: 1863. V. 44

CLARKSON, CHARLES TEMPEST

Police! London: 1889. V. 37

CLARKSON, CHRISTOPHER

The History and Antiquities of Richmond, in the County of York. Richmond: 1821. V. 46

CLARKSON, DAVID

Diocesan Churches Not Yet Discovered in the Primitive Times. London: 1682. V. 42

A Discourse of the Saving Grace of God. London: 1688. V. 42

The Practical Divinity of the Papists Discovred to be Destructive of Christianity and Mens Souls. London: 1676. V. 44

CLARKSON, L.

Fly-Away Fairies, and Baby Blossoms. New York: 1882. V. 39; 45

Indian Summer; Autumn Poems and Sketches. New York: 1883. V. 39

Violet Among the Lilies. New York: 1885. V. 43

CLARKSON, LOUISE

The Gathering of the Lilies. Philadelphia: (1877). V. 37

CLARKSON, PAUL S.

Bibliography of William Sydney Porter. Caldwell: 1938. V. 43; 46

CLARKSON, THOMAS

An Essay on the Slavery and Commerce of the Human Species, Particularly the African. London: 1786. V. 37; 40; 45

An Essay on the Slavery and Commerce of the Human Species, Particularly the African. Philadelphia: 1787. V. 39

An Essay on the Impolicy of the African Slave Trade. London: 1788. V. 37; 39; 42; 45; 46

An Essay on the Slavery and Commerce of the Human Species . . . London: 1788. V. 37; 43

An Essay on the Slavery and Commerce of the Human Species, Particularly the African. Philadelphia: 1804. V. 37

An Essay on the Slavery and Commerce of the Human Species, Particularly the African. Georgetown: 1816. V. 45

The History of the Rise, Progress and Accomplishment of the Abolition of the African Slave-Trade by the British Parliament. London: 1808. V. 37; 38; 39; 40; 42; 43; 44

Memoirs of the Private and Public Life of William Penn. London: 1813. V. 37; 39; 40; 41; 44

Strictures on a Life of William Wilberforce by the Rev. W. Wilberforce and the Rev. S. Wilberforce . . . London: 1838. V. 43

Thoughts on the Necessity of Improving the Condition of the Slaves in the British Colonies, With a View to Their Ultimate Emancipation; and on the Probability, the Safety and the Advantages of the Latter Measurae. London: 1823. V. 37; 42

THE CLARKSONS of New York. A Sketch. New York: 1875-6. V. 37

CLARY, DEXTER

History of the Churches and Ministers Connected with the Presbyterian and Congregational Convention of Wisconsin, and of the Operations of the American Home Missionary Society in the State for the Past Ten Years.. Beloit: 1861. V. 43

CLARY, WILLIAM W.

B. Franklin: Printer and Publisher. Los Angeles: 1935. V. 41

History of the Law Firm of O'Melveny and Myers, 1885-1965. Los Angeles: 1966. V. 37; 38; 43

CLASS Poem. Cambridge: 1838. V. 43

CLASSICAL Selections, in Verse. Liverpool: 1808. V. 45; 46

CLATER, FRANCIS

Every Man His Own Cattle Doctor, or, a Practical Treatise on the Diseases of Horned Cattle . . . London: 1817. V. 41

CLATHROP, DION CLAYTON

The Guide to Fairyland. London: 1905. V. 42

CLAUDEL, PAUL

The Book of Christopher Columbus. 1930. V. 41

The Book of Christopher Columbus A Lyrical Drama in Two Parts. New Haven: 1930. V. 38; 42

CLAUDET, F. G.

Gold, Its Properties, Modes of Extractions, Valvue, Etc. Vancouver: 1958. V. 37; 39; 43; 45

CLAUDIANUS, CLAUDIUS

Cl. Claudiani Quae Exstant. Leyden: 1650. V. 45

Opera. Venice: 1500. V. 40; 46

CLAUDIN, A.

The First Paris Press. London: 1897. V. 38; 40

The First Paris Press. London: 1898 for 1897. V. 39

CLAUDINUS, JULIUS CAESAR d. 1618

Responsionum et Consultationum Medicinalium Tomus Unicus . . . Frankfort: 1607. V. 44

CLAUSIUS, RUDOLF

The Mechanical Theory of Heat, With Its Applications to the Steam Engine and to the Physical Properties of Bodies. London: 1867. V. 40

The Mechanical Theory of Heat. London: 1879. V. 40; 45

CLAVELL, JAMES

King Rat. Boston: 1962. V. 38; 39; 43

King Rat. Boston & Toronto: 1962. V. 43

King Rat. London: 1963. V. 39; 44; 45

Noble House: A Novel of Contemporary Hong Kong. New York: (1981). V. 37; 39; 43

Tai-Paon. New York: 1966. V. 41; 43

CLAVERING, HENRY

The New Complete Parish Officer. London: 1801. V. 40

CLAVERING, ROBERT

An Essay on the Construction and Building of Chimneys Including an Enquiry into the Common Causes of Their Moaking, and the Most Effectual Remedies for Removing so Intolerable a Nuisance . . . London: 1779. V. 37; 41; 43; 45

CLAVERING, VERE

Barcaldine. London: 1889. V. 41

Hugh Deyne of Plas-Idrys. London: 1893. V. 41

A Modern Delilah. London: 1888. V. 37

CLAVERS, MARY

A New Home - Who'll Follow? or Glimpses of Western Life. New York: 1839. V. 45

CLAVIERE, ETIENNE

Considerations on the Relative Situation of France and the United States of America: Shewing the Importance of the American Revolution to the Welfare of France . . . London: 1788. V. 39

CLAYTON, W. WOODFORD

History of Union and Middlesex Counties, New Jersey with Biographical Sketches of Many of Their Pioneers and Prominent Men. Philadelphia: 1882. V. 44

CLAYTON, WILLIAM

The Latter-Day Saints' Emigrants' Guide: Being a Table of Distances . . . Salt Lake City,: 1930? V. 39

William Clayton's Journal . . . Salt Lake City: 1921. V. 38; 39; 40; 42

CLEASBY, RICHARD

An Icelandic-English Dictionary . . . Oxford: 1874. V. 44

CLEAVELAND, AGNES MORLEY

No Life for a Lady. Boston: 1941. V. 40; 46

CLEAVELAND, CHARLES HARLEY

Galvanism; Its Application as a Remedial Agent. New York: 1853. V. 37

CLEAVELAND, GEORGE

American Landmarks, A Collection of Pictures of Our Country's Historic Shrines, with descriptive Text. Boston: 1893. V. 37

CLEAVELAND, PARKER 1780-1858

Results of Meteorological Observations Made at Brunswick, Maine, Between 1807 and 1859. Reduced and Discussed at the Expense of the Smithsonian Institution, by Charles A. Scott. Washington City: 1867. V. 37; 42

CLEAVER, ROBERT

A Briefe Explanation of the Whole Booke of the Proverbs of Salomon. London: 1615. V. 42

CLEEVE, BOUCHIER

A Scheme for Preventing a Further Increase of the National Debt and for Reducing the Same. London: 1756. V. 43

CLEGG, SAMUEL

Clegg's Patent Atmospheric Railway. London: 1839. V. 46

CLEGHORN, GEORGE

Observations on the Epidemical Diseases in Minorca. From the Year 1744 to 1749. To which is prefixed, a Short Account of the Climate, Productions, Inhabitants, and Enemial Distempers of the Island. London: 1751. V. 37

Observations on the Epidemical Diseases in Minorca. From the Year 1744 to 1749. To which is prefixed, a Short Account of the Climiate, Productions, Inhabitants and Enemial Distempers of that Islands. London: 1751. V. 37; 39; 42

CLELAND, HENRY WILSON

On the History and Properties Chemical and Medical of Tobacco . . . Glasgow: 1840. V. 42

CLELAND, JAMES

Description of the Banquet Given in Honour of the Right Hon. Sir Robert Peel, on His Election as Lord Rector of the University of Glasgow. Glasgow: 1837. V. 37; 38; 40

CLELAND, JOHN

Memoirs of a Woman of Pleasure. Keene: 1814. V. 39

Memoirs of a Woman of Pleasure . . . Worcester: 1814. V. 43

Memoirs of Fanny Hill . . . Paris: 1888. V. 42

Memoirs of Fanny Hill. Paris: 1890. V. 43

Memoirs of Fanny Hill. London: 1919. V. 42

CLELAND, ROBERT G.

The Cattle on a Thousand Hills. San Marino: 1941. V. 45

CLELAND, THOMAS MAITLAND 1880-1964

The Decorative Work of T. M. Clelland. New York: 1929. V. 41; 43; 44; 45

A Grammar of Color. Mitteague: 1921. V. 37; 40

Harsh Words. Newark: 1940. V. 42; 44

The Shrine of Death and the Shrine of Love, by Lady Dilke. Boston: 1901. V. 37

CLELAND, THOMAS MATILAND

'Progress' in the Graphic Arts. Stamford: 1950. V. 40

CLELLAN, ELISABETH

Historic Dress in America 1607-1800. Philadelphia: 1904-10. V. 38

CLELLAND, T. M.

The Decorative Work of T. M. Cleland. New York: 1929. V. 39

CLEM, CHARLOTTE

Experiences. Dallas: 1916. V. 37

CLEMENS ALEXANDRINUS ca. 150-215

Opera. Florence: 1550. V. 43

CLEMENS, CLARA

My Father Mark Twain. New York: 1931. V. 42; 43; 44

CLEMENS, CYRIL

Mark Twain and Mussolini. Webster Grove: 1934. V. 40

CLEMENS, JEREMIAH

Mustang Gray. Philadelphia: 1858. V. 38

CLEMENS, ORION

City of Keokuk in 1856; A View of the City, Embracing Its Commerce & Manufactures . . . Also, A Sketch of the Black Hawk War, & History of the Half Breed Tract. Keokuk, O.: 1856. V. 37

CLEMENS, SAMUEL LANGHORNE 1835-1910

Adventures of Huckleberry Finn. New York: 1885. V. 37; 38; 39; 40; 42; 43; 44; 45; 46

The Adventures of Huckleberry Finn. New York: 1933. V. 41; 44

The Adventures of Tom Sawyer. London: 1947. V. 38

Adventures of Huckleberry Finn. Northampton: 1984. V. 38

Adventures of Huckleberry Finn. Hatfield: 1985. V. 38

The Adventures of Huckleberry Finn. V. 42

Adventures of Huckleberry Finn. Northampton. V. 39

The Adventures of Huckleberry Finn (Tom Sawyer's Comrade). London: 1884. V. 37; 39; 41; 42; 43; 44; 45; 46

Adventures of Huckleberry Finn. 1885. V. 46

Huck Finns Haendelser. Copenhagen: 1885. V. 40

Adventures of Huckleberry Finn. Montreal: 1885. V. 46

Les Adventures de Huck Finn . . . Paris: 1886. V. 40

Adventures of Huckleberry Finn. New York: 1889. V. 40

The Adventures of Huckleberry Finn. New York: 1936. V. 41

Hucklebbery Finn. 1942. V. 39

Adventures of Huckleberry Finn. New York: 1942. V. 45

Huckleberry Finn. London: 1948. V. 41

Adventures of Huckleberry Finn. Detroit: 1983. V. 38

Adventures of Huckleberry Finn. By Mark Twain. Illustrated by Barry Moser. With a foreword by Henry Nash Smith. Northampton, Mass.. V. 37

Adventures of Huckleberry Finn. Illustrated with Forty-Nine Wood Engravings by Barry Moser. Foreword by Henry Nash Smith. West Hatfield: 1985. V. 37

The Adventures of Thomas Jefferson Snodgrass. Chicago: 1922. V. 45

The Adventures of Thomas Jefferson Snodgrass . . . Chicago: 1928. V. 38; 39; 43; 44

The Adventures of Tom Sawyer. Hartford: 1876. V. 38; 39; 40; 42; 44; 45; 46

The Adventures of Tom Sawyer. Hartford: Chicago &: 1876. V. 45

The Adventures of Tom Sawyer. New York: 1876. V. 37; 42

The Adventures of Tom Sawyer. Toronto: 1876. V. 39; 40; 44; 45

The Adventures of Tom Sawyer. Toronto: 1879. V. 39

The Adventures of Tom Sawyer. Hartford: 1901. V. 40

The Adventures of Tom Sawyer. New York: 1903. V. 46

The Adventures of Tom Sawyer. New York: 1936. V. 43

Tom Sawyer. 1939. V. 39

The Adventures of Tom Sawyer. Cambridge: 1939. V. 45

The Adventures of Tom Sawyer. New York: 1940. V. 41

The Adventures of Tom Sawyer. London: 1962. V. 39; 45

Ah Sin. A Dramatic Work. San Francisco. V. 40

'Ah Sin', a Dramatic Work . . . 1961. V. 42

Ah Sin. A Dramatic Work. San Francisco: 1961. V. 37; 38

The American Claimant. London: 1892. V. 43; 46

The American Claimant. New York: 1892. V. 37; 38; 40; 42; 43; 44; 45; 46

Autobiography and First Romance. New York: 1871. V. 37; 40; 42

A Boy's Adventure. N.P.: 1928. V. 45

A Boy's Adventure. N.P.: n.d.,: 1928. V. 42

A Boy's Adventure. N.P.: n.p., n.d.: 1928. V. 41

A Burlesque Autobiography and First Romance. New York: 1871. V. 40

Captain Stormfield's Visit to Heaven. New York: 1909. V. 37

The Celebrated Jumping Frog of Calaveras County. New York: 1867. V. 37; 38; 40; 43; 44; 45; 46

The Celebrated Jumping Frog of Calaveras County, and Other Sketches. New York: 1868. V. 39; 45

The Celebrated Jumping Frog of Calaveras County, and Other Sketches. New York: 1869. V. 43

The Celebrated Juming Frog of Calaveras County, and Other Sketches. New York: 1870. V. 40

The Jumping Frog. Easthampton: 1985. V. 39

The Jumping Frog. Williamsburg: 1986. V. 40

CLEMENS, SAMUEL LANGHORNE 1835-1910 continued

The Celebrated Jumping Frog of Calaveras County and Other Sketches. Toronto: 1870. V. 37

A Champagne Cocktail Party and a Catastrophe. New York: 1930. V. 42; 43; 44

A Champagne Cocktail and a Catastrophe. Westport: 1930. V. 43

Choice Bits from Mark Twain. London: 1885. V. 40

The Choice Humorous Works of Mark Twain. London: 1873. V. 37

Christian Science. New York: 1907. V. 37; 39; 40; 43; 44; 46

Christian Science. New York & London: 1907. V. 39; 42

Concerning Cats. Two Tales. San Francisco: 1959. V. 37; 38; 40; 46

A Connecticut Yankee in King Arthur's Court. New York: 1889. V. 37; 38; 39; 40; 41; 42; 43; 44; 45; 46

A Connecticut Yankee at King Arthur's Court. Toronto: 1889. V. 40

A Yankee at the Court of King Arthur. London: 1893. V. 40

Connecticut Yankee in King Arthur's Court. New York: 1949. V. 45

A Connecticut Yankee in King Arthur's Court. 1889. V. 37

Coyote. Hemet, CA: 1986. V. 37

A Curious Dream and Other Sketches. London: 1872. V. 42

The Curious Republic of Gondour. New York: 1919. V. 37; 40; 42; 43; 44

Death-Disk. New York: 1913. V. 44

Dog's Tale. London: 1904. V. 41; 43

A Dog's Tale. New York: 1904. V. 44

A Double Barrelled Detective Story. London: 1902. V. 38; 40

A Double Barrelled Detective Story. New York: 1902. V. 39; 40; 41; 42; 43; 44; 45; 46

A Double Barrelled Detective Story. New York & London: 1902. V. 37; 39; 46

Editorial Wild Oats. New York: 1905. V. 37; 40; 46

Editorial Wild Oats. New York & London: 1905. V. 39

English As She is Taught, Being Genuine Answers to Examination Questions In Our Public Schools Collected by Caroline B. Le Row . . . London: 1887. V. 41; 42; 44

English As She is Taught. Boston: 1900. V. 40; 44; 45

Europe and Elsewhere. New York: 1923. V. 45; 46

Europe and Elsewhere. New York: London: 1923. V. 43

Eve's Diary. New York: 1906. V. 43

Extract from Captain Stromfield's Visit to Heaven. New York: 1909. V. 43; 44; 45

Extract from Captain Stromfield's Visit to Heaven. New York & London: 1909. V. 43

Extracts from Adam's Diary. New York: 1904. V. 44

Extracts from Adam's Diary. New York & London: 1904. V. 43

Following the Equator. Hartford: 1897. V. 37; 38; 39; 40; 41; 42; 43; 44; 45; 46

Following the Equator. Hartford: & New York: 1897. V. 42; 43; 45

Following the Equator. New York: 1898. V. 39

Meine Reise Um Die Welt. Stuttgart: 1898. V. 40

The Gilded Age. Hartford: 1871. V. 44

The Gilded Age. Hartford: 1873. V. 39; 44

The Gilded Age. Hartford & Chicago: 1873. V. 46

The Gilded Age. Hartford: & Cincinnati: 1873. V. 43

The Gilded Age. Hartford: 1874. V. 37; 39; 40; 41; 42; 43; 44

The Gilded Age. London: 1883. V. 40

The Gilded Age. London: 1883. V. 39

The Gilded Age. Hartford: 1884. V. 41; 45

Horse-Cart Poetry. New York: 1876. V. 43

A Horse's Tale. New York: 1907. V. 44; 46

How to Tell a Story, and Other Essays. New York: 1897. V. 39; 40; 43; 44; 46

An Idle Excursion. Toronto: 1878. V. 40

Information Wanted and Other Sketches. London: 1876. V. 43

Innocence at Home . . . N.P.: 1929. V. 41

The Innocents Abroad. Hartford: 1869. V. 38; 39; 40; 41; 42; 43; 46

The Innocents Abroad. Hartford: 1871. V. 44

The Innocents Abroad. Melbourne: 1871. V. 40; 42

The Innocents At Home. London: 1872. V. 37; 42

The Innocents Abroad. London: 1882. V. 40

The Innocents Abroad. Leipzig: 1885. V. 44

The Innocents Abroad. Boston: 1895. V. 46

The Innocents Abroad or the New Pilgrim's Progress. Boston and Hartford: 1895. V. 44

The Innocents Abroad. Melbourne: 1895. V. 40

The Innocents Abroad. 1962. V. 39

The Innocents Abroad; or, the New Pilgrims' Progress. New York: 1962. V. 46

The Innocents Abroad; or, the New Pilgrims' Progress. New York: 1962. V. 44

Is Shakespeare Dead? New York: 1909. V. 41; 43; 44

Is Shakespeare Dead? New York & London: 1909. V. 37; 41

Is He Living or Is He Dead? by Samuel L. Clemens. (Worcester: 1984). V. 37

Joan of Arc. London: 1896. V. 43

The Jumping Frog in English and Then in French, Then Clawed Back Into a Civilized Language Once More. New York: 1903. V. 42; 44

The Jumping Frog. Easthampton: 1985. V. 46

King Leopold's Soliloquy. Boston: 1905. V. 46

Letters from Honolulu Written for the Sacramento Union. Honolulu: 1939. V. 44

Letters from the Sandwich Islands . . . San Francisco: 1937. V. 43; 44

Life on the Mississippi. Boston: 1883. V. 37; 38; 39; 40; 41; 42; 43; 44; 45; 46

Life on the Mississippi. London: 1883. V. 37; 38; 39; 40; 41; 42; 43; 44; 45; 46

Life on the Mississippi. London: 1883. V. 43

Life on the Mississippi. Montreal: 1883. V. 40

Life of the Mississippi. 1944. V. 39

Life on the Mississippi. New York: 1944. V. 38; 40; 45; 46

Lotos Leaves. Boston: 1875. V. 40; 43

The Love Letters of Mark Twain. New York: 1949. V. 38; 39; 45; 46

The Man that Corrupted Hadleyburg and Other Stories and Sketches. London: 1900. V. 44

The Man That Corrupted Hadleybrug and Other Stories and Essays. New York: 1900. V. 37; 39; 40; 43; 44; 46

The Man that Corrupted Hadleyburg and Other Stories and Essays. New York: & London: 1900. V. 46

Mark Twain's Patent Self-Pasting Scrap Book. New York: 1873. V. 40

Mark Twain: San Francisco Correspondent. Selections from His Letters to the Territorial Enterprise: 1865-1866. 1957. V. 38

Mark Twain: San Francisco Correspondent. Selections from His Letters to the Territorial Enterprise, 1865-1866. San Francisco: 1957. V. 37; 38; 41; 42

The Mark Twain Birthday Book. London: 1890? V. 40

Mark Twain Compliments the President's Wife. Boston: 1984. V. 39

Mark Twain-Howells Letters. Cambridge: 1960. V. 46

Mark Twain in Eruption. New York: 1940. V. 46

Mark Twain Library Auction. Tues. April 10th . . . 1951. V. 43

Mark Twain on Simplified Spelling. New York: 1906. V. 41; 46

Mark Twain: San Francisco Correspondent . . . Selections from His Letters to 'The Territorial Enterprise' 1865-1866. 1957. V. 39

Mark Twain: San Francisco Virginia City Territorial Enterprise Correspondent. San Francisco: 1957. V. 43; 44; 46

Mark Twain Sketches New and Old. Hartford: 1875. V. 39; 40

Mark Twain's Autobiography. New York: 1924. V. 37; 41; 44; 45; 46

Mark Twain's (Burlesque) Autobiography. New York: 1871. V. 37; 39; 40; 41; 43; 44; 45; 46

Mark Twain's (Burlesque) Autobiography and First Romance. London: 1871. V. 39; 40

Mark Twain's Letter to William Bowen Buffalo, February Sixth, 1870. San Francisco: 1938. V. 43

Mark Twain's Letters, Arranged with Comment by Albert Bigelow Paine. New York: 1917. V. 39; 43

Mark Twain's Letters Arranged With Comment by Albert Bigelow Paine. New York: & London: 1917. V. 43

Mark Twain's Library of Humor. New York: 1888. V. 38; 40; 43; 46

Mark Twain's Library of Humour. London: 1888. V. 42

Mark Twain's Memoranda. Toronto: 1871. V. 39

Mark Twain's Memory Builder. Hartford: 1891. V. 44

Mark Twain's Memory Builder. New York: 1891. V. 44

Mark Twain's Nicodemus Dodge. San Diego: 1989. V. 46

Mark Twain's Nightmare, a Story of Haunting Horror. London: 1878. V. 39; 40

Mark Twain's Notebook. New York: 1935. V. 39; 44

Mark Twain's Pleasure Trip ont he Continent. London: 1871. V. 46

Mark Twain's Scrapbook. New York: 1892. V. 42

Mark Twain's Sektches, New and Old. Hartford: 1875. V. 37; 40; 41; 42; 43; 44; 45; 46

Mark Twain's Sketches. London: 1872. V. 40; 44

Mark Twain's Sketches. New York: 1874. V. 40; 41; 43; 44

Sketches. Toronto: 1879. V. 40

Sketches. N.P.: Toronto: 1880. V. 40

Mark Twain's Sketches New and Old. Hartford: 1875. V. 42

Mark Twain's Speeches. New York: 1923. V. 45

Memoranda from The Galaxy. Toronto: 1871. V. 37

Merry Tales. New York: 1892. V. 37; 38; 43; 44; 45; 46

More Tramps Abroad. London: 1897. V. 37; 38; 39; 42; 44; 45; 46

More Maxims of Mark. N.P.: New York: 1927. V. 40

My First Publication. San Francisco: 1961. V. 37

CLEMENS, SAMUEL LANGHORNE 1835-1910 continued

The Mysterious Stranger; a Romance. New York: 1916. V. 40; 44

The Mysterious Stranger and Other Stories. London: 1922. V. 46

The Mysterious Stranger and Other Stories. New York: 1922. V. 43; 45

The New Pilgrim's Progress. London: 1870. V. 43

The New Pilgrim's Progress. London: 1872. V. 40

The New Guide of the Conversation in Portuguese and English. Boston: 1883. V. 37; 44

The New War Scare. Santa Barbara: 1981. V. 41; 42

The Niagara Book. Buffalo: 1893. V. 40

Old Times on the Mississippi. Toronto: 1876. V. 39; 40; 41; 44

The 1,000,000 Bank-Note and Other New Stories. London: 1893. V. 39; 40; 42; 44

The 1,000,000 Pound Bank Note and Other New Stories. New York: 1893. V. 39; 40; 42; 43; 44; 45; 46

An Open Letter to Commodore Vanderbilt. Boston: 1956. V. 39; 41

Personal Recollections of Joan of Arc. London: 1896. V. 42

Personal Recollections of Joan of Arc. London: 1896. V. 40; 43

Personal Recollections of Joan of Arc. New York: 1896. V. 37

Personal Recollections of Joan of Arc. New York: 1896. V. 44

Phunny Phellows . . . Chicago: 1885. V. 39

The Prince and the Pauper. London: 1881. V. 40; 41; 42; 43

The Prince and the Pauper. Montreal: 1881. V. 39; 40; 42

The Prince and the Pauper. 1882. V. 46

The Prince and the Pauper. Boston: 1882. V. 38; 39; 40; 41; 42; 43; 45; 46

The Prince and the Pauper. Toronto: 1882. V. 39; 40

Der Prinz und der Betteljunge (The Prince and the Pauper). Giessen: 1890. V. 40

The Prince and the Pauper. 1964. V. 40

The Prince and the Pauper. New York: 1964. V. 41; 46

The Prince and the Pauper. Westerham: 1964. V. 43

The Private Life of Adam and Eve . . . New York: 1931. V. 46

Publisher's Salesman's Dummy copy for Mar. V. 44

Pudd'n Head Wilson. London: 1894. V. 38; 39; 40; 42; 46

Pudd'nhead Wilson's Calendar for 1894. New York: 1893. V. 41

Pudd'nhead Wilson. Hartford: 1894. V. 38; 43; 44; 45

Pudd'nhead Wilson (with) Pudd'nhead Wilson's Calendar. Avon: 1974. V. 46

Punch, Brothers, Punch, and Other Sketches by . . . New York: 1878. V. 37; 38; 39; 40; 43; 44; 46

The Quaker City Holy Land Excursion. N.P.: New York: 1927. V. 40

Quaker City Holy land Excursion: An unfinished Play. 1927. V. 37

Queen Victoria's Jubilee. The Great Procession of June 22, 1897, in the Queen's Honor, Reported Both in the Ligh of History and as a Spectacle, by Mark Twain. N.P.,: 1910. V. 40

Queen Victoria's Jubilee, the Great Procession of June 22, 1897 in the Queen's Honor, Reported Both in the Light of History and as a Spectacle. V. 44

Rambling Notes of an Idle Excursion . . . Toronto: 1878. V. 39; 40; 43; 44

Roughin' It. Hartford: 1872. V. 39; 40; 41; 42; 43; 44; 45; 46

Roughing It. 1872. V. 46

Roughing It. Toronto: 1880. V. 40

Roughing it in California. Kentfield: 1953. V. 38; 43; 44; 45

Saint Joan of Arc. New York: 1919. V. 39; 40; 41; 42; 43; 44

Saint Joan of Arc. New York/London: (1919). V. 37

San Francisco Correspondent. 1957. V. 44

The Sandwich Islands. New York: 1920. V. 43; 46

Seventy-First Anniversary Celebration of the New-England Society in the City of New York at Delmonico's, Dec. 22, 1876. V. 37

1601. Conversation As It Was by the Social Fireside in the Time of the Tudors. N.P.: 1902. V. 43

'1601.' Or Conversation at the Social Fireside As It Was in the Time of the Tudors. New York: 1927. V. 40

'1601' or Conversation at the Social Fireside as It Was in the Time of the Tudors. Chicago: 1962. V. 46

1601. Hamburg: 1974. V. 38

1601. 1978. V. 40

Mark Twain's Sketches. New York: 1874. V. 38

Sketches . . . Toronto: 1879. V. 39

The Stolen White Elephant. Boston: 1882. V. 37; 39; 40; 41; 42; 43; 44; 46

The Stolen White Elephant. London: 1882. V. 39; 40; 42

A Tramp Abroad. Hartford: 1880. V. 44

Th: Nast's Illustrated Almanac for 1873. New York: 1872. V. 37

The $30,000 Bequest and Other Stories. New York: 1906. V. 39; 40; 41; 43; 44; 46

Three Aces: Jim Todd's Episode in Social Euchre, a Poem and a Denial. New York: 1929. V. 43; 44

Three Aces. Jim Todd's Episode in Social Euchre. Westport: 1929. V. 39

Three Aces. Jim Todd's Episode in Social Euchre. A Poem and a Denial. Westport: 1930. V. 40; 41; 43

To the Person Sitting in Darkness. New York: 1901. V. 40; 41; 43; 44; 46

To the Person Sitting in the Darkness and Concerning the Rev. Mr. Ament. N.P.: 1926. V. 43

Tom Sawyer Abroad. London: 1894. V. 40; 42

Tom Sawyer Abroad. New York: 1894. V. 40; 41; 42; 43; 44; 45; 46

Tom Sawyer Abroad, Tom Sawyer, Detective and Other Stories. New York: 1896. V. 40; 46

Tom Sawyer Abroad; Tom Sawyer Detective and Other Stories. New York: 1896. V. 40

Tom Sawyer Abroad, Tom Sawyer Detective & Other Stories. New York & London: 1896. V. 43

Tom Sawyer, Detective. 1897. V. 43

Tom Sawyer Detective. Leipzig: 1897. V. 39

Tom Sawyer, Detective . . . and Other Tales. London: 1897. V. 38; 41; 43

Tom Sawyer, Detective. 1897. V. 37

Tom Sawyer, Detective. London: 1897/98. V. 44

Tom Sawyer - Detective in Harpers for August and September, 1896. V. 37

The Tragedy of Puddinhead Wilson, and the Comedy Those Extraordinary Twins. Hartford: 1894. V. 37; 38; 39; 40; 41; 42; 43; 44; 45; 46

Pudd'nhead Wilson. Connecticut: 1974. V. 43

A Tramp Abroad. Hartford: 1879. V. 39; 44

A Tramp Abroad. Hartford: 1880. V. 37; 38; 39; 40; 41; 42; 43; 44; 45; 46

A Tramp Abroad. Hartford & London: 1880. V. 45

A Tramp Abroad. London: 1880. V. 38; 39; 40; 41; 42; 43; 45; 46

A Tramp Abroad. Toronto: 1880. V. 40; 43

A Tramp Abroad. Toronto & Montreal: 1880. V. 39

A Tramp Abroad. Hartford: 1880/1879. V. 44

A Tramp Abroad. London: 1882. V. 38

A Tramp Abroad. London: 1894. V. 40

A Tramp Abroad. 1966. V. 43

The War Prayer. New York: 1968. V. 37

The Washoe Giant in San Francisco, Being Heretofore Uncollected Sketches by Mark Twain. San Francisco: 1938. V. 37; 39

What Is man? London: 1910. V. 39; 40; 41; 43; 44

What is Man? And Other Essays. New York: 1917. V. 40; 43

The Complete Works. New York: 1922-23. V. 40

The Writings of Mark Twain . . . New York. V. 41

The Writings of Mark Twain. Hartford: 1899. V. 43

The Writings of Mark Twain. New York: & London: 1899. V. 46

The Writings . . . New York: 1907. V. 42

The Writings of . . . Hartford: 1908. V. 43

The Writings of Mark Twain. New York: 1923-25. V. 38

The Writings of Mark Twain. New York: 1925. V. 46

The Writings. New York: 1929. V. 42; 46

A Yankee at the Court of King Arthur. London: 1889. V. 42

A Yankee in King Arthur's Court. New York: 1889. V. 45

CLEMENS, WILL

Mark Twain, His Life and Work. San Francisco: 1892. V. 46

CLEMENS, WILL M.

A Ken of Kipling. New York: 1899. V. 38

CLEMENT, H.

Mission of Gravity. 1954. V. 39

CLEMENT I, SAINT

(Greek title) . . . Constitutiones Sanctorum Apostolorum Doctrina Catholica a Clemente Romano Episcopo & Cive Scripta Libris Octo. Venice: 1563. V. 46

CLEMENT-JANIN

Essai sur la Bibiliophille Contempraine de 1900 a 1928. Paris: 1932. V. 41

CLEMENT, JOHN

Sketches of the First Emigrant Settlers in Newton Township, Old Gloucester County, West New Jersey. Camden: 1877. V. 46

CLEMENT, LEWIS

Modern Wildfowling. London: 1880. V. 40

CLEMENT, NICOLAS DE TREILLE

Austrasiae Reges et Duces Epigrammatis. Cologne: 1591. V. 40

CLEMENT OF ALANDRIA, SAINT B. 150.

Omnia . . . Opera. Florence: (1551). V. 37

CLEMENT, SIMON

A Dialogue Between a Countrey Gentlemn and a Merchant, Concerning the Falling of Guinea's. London: 1696. V. 38

CLEMENT, SIMON continued

Faults on Both Sides; or an Essay Upon the Original Cause, Progress and Mischievous Consequences of the Faction in this Nation. London: 1710. V. 45

CLEMENT V, POPE

Constitutiones. Venice: 1489. V. 40

De Constitutionibus Apostolicis . . . Libri VIII . . . Io. Carolo Bovio, Episcopo Ostuniensi Interprete . . . Omnia Nunc Primum e Tenebris Eruta. Paris: 1564. V. 45

CLEMENT VII, POPE

Lamento di Fiorenzo qual Supplica la Santita del Papa Adunirsi con Essa Lei Con Invocatione di Tutte le Potentie Christianne con la Guerra & Quando si Rese con Patti & Conventione Fatti con la Sanita di Nostri Signore & Maesta Cesaria. Florence: 1530. V. 40

CLEMENT VIII, POPE

Ad Futuram Rei Memoriam. Suscepti Muneris Ratio Postulat, Ut Que a Romanis Pontificibus Praedecessoribus Nostris ad Animarum Salutem Pie ac Prudenter Statuta Fuerant. Spain: 1600. V. 40

CLEMENTINO, CLEMENTE

Lucubrationes, In Quibus Nihil est Quid Non Sit ex Usu Artis . . . Basel: 1535. V. 38; 41

CLEMENTS, F. E.

Rocky Mountain Flowers. New York: 1914. V. 40

CLEMENTS, L.

Shooting, Yachting and Sea-Fishing Trips. London: 1877. V. 39

CLEMENTS, WILLIAM L.

The William L. Clements Library of Americana at the University of Michigan. Ann Arbor: 1923. V. 40

CLEMONS, MRS.

The Manners and Customs of Society in India . . . London: 1841. V. 39

CLENARDUS, NICHOLAS

Institutiones Linquae Graecae. Venice: 1570. V. 37

CLENARDUS, NICOLAUS 1495-1542

Institutiones ac Meditationes in Graecam Linguam . . . Frankfurt: 1590-91. V. 40

Institutiones ac Meditationes in Graecam Linguam cum Scholiis & Praxi Antesignani . . . Genevae: 1580. V. 38

CLENDENEN, CLARENCE

United States and Pancho Villa, A Study in Unconventional Diplomacy. Ithaca: 1961. V. 42

CLEOMEDES

Kyklike Theoria Eis Biblia B. Nunc Primum Typis Excusa Prodit, Cum Regio Priuilegio in Quinquennium. Paris: 1539. V. 40

CLEPHAN, R. COLTMAN

The Tournament, Its Periods and Phases. London: 1919. V. 39

CLERC, JEAN LE

Negociations Secretes Touchant La Paix de Munster et D'Osnabrug . . . The Hague: 1725-26. V. 43

CLERCQ, LOUIS DE

Collection de Clerq; Catalogue Methodique et Raisonne Antiquites Assyriennes, Cylinders Orientaux . . . Paris: 1888. V. 44

CLERIDES, GLAFKOS

Cyprus: My Deposition. Nicosia: 1989-90. V. 45

CLERISSEAU, CHARLES LOUIS

Antiquites de al France, Tome Premier. Paris: 1804. V. 45

CLERK, ARCHIBALD

Memoir of Colonel John Cameron, Fassiefern, K.T.S., Lieutenant-Colonel of the Gordon Highlanders, or 92nd Regiment of Foot. Glasgow: 1859. V. 41

CLERK, H.

On the Application of Hydraulic Buffers, to Prevent the Destructive Effects of Railway Collisions. Woolwich: 1868. V. 46

CLERK, JOHN

Catalogue of the Library of the Late John Clerk of Eldin. (bound with) Catalogue of the Extensive, Genuine, and Highly Valuable Collection of Pictures, Late the Property of the Hon. John Clerk of Eldin. London: 1833. V. 38; 41

The Circumstances of Scotlnd Consider'd, With Respect to the Present Scarcity of Money. Edinburgh: 1705. V. 38

An Essay on Naval Tactics, Systematical and Historical. London: 1790-97. V. 46

An Essay on Naval Tactics Systematical and Historical with Explanatory Plates. Edinburgh: 1804. V. 41; 46

Memoirs, Extracted by Himself from His Own Journals 1676-1755. 1895. V. 45

CLERKE, BARTHOLOMEW

Fidelis Servi, Subdito Infideli Responsio Una cum Errorum & Calumniarum Quarundan Examaine Quae Continentur in Septimo Libro de Visibili Ecclesiae Monarchia a Nicholas Sardero Conscripta. London: 1573. V. 37; 39; 42

CLERKE, CHARLES

A Voyage Round the World, in His Majesty's Ship the Dolphin, Commaneded by the Hourable Commodore Byron. London: 1767. V. 38; 39

THE CLERK'S Instructor in Ecclesiastical Courts: Consisting of a Variety of the Best Precedents in English, Now Made Use of In the Practice of Civil Law. Dublin: 1766. V. 42

CLERMONT-GANNEAU, CHARLES

Archaeological Researches in Palestine During the Years 1873-1874. London: 1899-96. V. 40; 44

CLERY, J. B. C.

A Journal of Occurrences in the Tower of the Temple, During the Confinement of Louis XVI, King of France. Boston: 1799. V. 38; 40

CLERY, JEAN BAPTISTE CANT HANET

A Journal of Occurrences at the Temple During the Confinement of Louis XVI, King of France. London: 1798. V. 43

CLERY, LUGHAIDH

Beatha . . . the Life of Hugh Roe O'Donnell, Prince of Tirconnell (1586-1602). Dublin: 1893. V. 41

CLEVE-EULER, A.

Die Diatomeen von Schweden und Finnland. London: 1968. V. 38

CLEVELAND BRIDGE & ENGINEERING CO.

Bridges, Roofs and Constructional Work in Iron and Steel. Darlington: 1910. V. 44

CLEVELAND, CATHERINE LUCY WILHELMINA STANHOPE POWLETT 1819-1901

The Life and Letters of Lady Hester Stanhope. London: 1897. V. 42

CLEVELAND, EDMUND J.

The Genealogy of the Cleveland and Cleveland Families. Hartford, Conn.: 1899. V. 37

CLEVELAND, GEORGE

American Landmarks, a Collection of Pictures of Our Country's Historic Shrines, with Descriptive Text. Boston: 1893. V. 42

CLEVELAND, H. W. S.

Landscape Architecture, as Applied to the Wants of the West . . . Chicago: 1873. V. 44

Voyages of a Merchant Navigator of the Days That are Past. New York: 1886. V. 39

CLEVELAND, HENRY W.

Village and Farm Cottages . . . American Village Homes. New York: 1856. V. 42

CLEVELAND, HORACE G.

A Genealogy of Benjamin Cleveland. Chicago: 1879. V. 46

CLEVELAND, HORACE WILLIAM SHALER

Hints to Riflemen. New York: 1864. V. 42

CLEVELAND, JOHN

The Character of a London-Diurnall: with Several Select Poems: by the Same Author. London: 1647. V. 46

Clievelandi Vindiciae; or Cleveland's Genuine Poems, Orations, Epistles, etc. Purged from Many False and Spurrious Ones Which Had Usurped His Name and From Innumerable Errours and Corruptions . . . London: 1677. V. 37; 38; 40; 41; 42; 46

The Idol of the Clownes . . . London: 1654. V. 38; 40; 42; 44; 46

Poems by J. C. London: 1657. V. 46

The Works of Mr. John Cleveland. London: 1687. V. 38; 41; 45; 46

CLEVELAND. MUSEUM OF ART

Chinese Art Under the Mongols: The Yuan Dynasty (1279-1368). 1968. V. 41

CLEVELAND PUBLIC LIBRARY

Out-Of-Print Books from the John G. White Folklore Collection at the Cleveland Public Library. Cleveland: 1966. V. 43

CLEVELAND, RICHARD JEFFRY

A Narrative of Voyages and Commercial Enterprises. Cambridge: 1842. V. 46

A Narrative of Voyages and Commercial Enterprises . . . Cambridge: 1843. V. 38

A Narrative of Voyages and Commercial Enterprises. London: 1842. V. 37

Voyages, Maritime Adventures, and Commercial Enterprises, in all Parts of the World. London: 1842. V. 38

CLEVELAND TYPE FOUNDRY

Catalogue and Price List of Type and Material. Cleveland: 1890. V. 42

Catalogue and Price List of Type and Material. Cleveland: 1893. V. 46

CLEVELAND, W.

Extracts from a Journal Kept on Board the Ship 'Madagascar' on Her Passage from Calcutta to England. Deal: 1847. V. 45

CLEVENGER, S. V.

Spinal Concussion: Surgically Considered as a Cause of Spinal Injury and Neurologically Restricted to a Certain Symptom Group, For Which is Suggested the Designation Erichsen's Disease, As One Form of the Traumatic Neroses. Philadelphia: 1889. V. 40; 46

CLEVER, CHARLES P.

New Mexico: Her Resource: Her Necessities for Railroad Communication with the Atlantic and Pacific States; Her Great Future. Washington: 1868. V. 40

CLEVER Clarence and Other Funny Stories. London: 1865. V. 44

CLEVERDON, DOUGLAS

The Chester Play of the Deluge. London: 1977. V. 40

The Engravings of David Jones. London: 1981. V. 37; 45

Opera Omnia, ex Recensione Jo. Augusti ERnesti cum Ejusdem Notis. V. 43

Third List of Douglas Cleverdon. London: 1927. V. 46

CLIAS, P. H.

An Elementary Course of Gymnastic Exercises. London: 1825. V. 40

CLICHTHOVE, JOSSE 1472/3-1543

Termini . . . In Terminorum Cognitonem Introductio . . . De Artium Divisione Introductio . . . Paris: 1505. V. 43

CLIFFE, CHARLES FREDERICK

The Book of South Wales, the Bristol Channel, Monmouthshire and the Wye. London: 1847. V. 46

CLIFFE, JOHN HENRY

Notes and Recollections of an Angler. London: 1860. V. 39

CLIFFORD, ANNE

The Diary of Lady Anne Clifford. London: 1923. V. 38

CLIFFORD, CHARLES CAVENDISH

A Tour (To Iceland) Twenty Years Ago. Southampton: 1862. V. 38

A Tour Twenty Years Ago. London: 1863. V. 38; 40

CLIFFORD, ELIZABETH

Our Days on the Gold Coast, In Ashanti in the Northern Territories, and the British Sphere of Occupation in Togoland. Accra: 1918. V. 40

CLIFFORD, HENRY

His Letters and Sketches from the Crimea. London: 1956. V. 41

CLIFFORD, HUGH

A Free Lance of To-Day. London: 1903. V. 43

CLIFFORD, JAMES L.

Johnsonian Studies, Including a Bibliography of Johnsonian Studies 1950-1960. Cairo: 1962. V. 45

Samuel Johnson, a Survey and Bibliography of Critical Studies. 1970. V. 46

CLIFFORD, JERONIMY

The Case and Replication of the Legal Representatives of Jeronimy Clifford, a British Subject and Late Merchant and Planter of Surinam, Deceased; to the Information of the Directors of the Society of Surinam, Presented, on the 7th of October 1762 . . . London: 1763. V. 41

CLIFFORD, M. M.

Egypt: a Poem of that Country and Its Inhabitants. London: 1802. V. 43

CLIFFORD, MARTIN d. 1677

A Treatise on Humane Reason. London: 1675. V. 38; 41; 42

CLIFFORD, SIGERSON

Iascar Rock - a Ballad. Dublin: 1953. V. 44

CLIFFORD, THOMAS

A Topographical and Historical Description of the Parish of Tixall, in the County of Stafford. Paris: 1817. V. 42

CLIFT, WILLIAM

New Mexico. Portfolio of Eight Photographic Prints. Santa Fe: 1975. V. 37

CLIFTON, FRANCIS

The Story of Physick, Ancient and Modern, Briefly Consider'd. London: 1732. V. 39

The State of Physick Ancient and modern, Briefly considered: with a plan for the Improvement of it. London: 1832. V. 37

CLIFTON, LUCILLE

Good Times: Poems. New York. V. 46

CLINCH, BRYAN J.

California and Its Missions: Their History to the Treaty of Guadalupe Hidalgo. San Francisco: 1904. V. 40; 43

CLINCH, G.

English Hops. London: 1919. V. 45

CLINE, WALTER M.

The Muzzle-Loading Rifle Then and Now. West Virginia: 1942. V. 44

CLINTON-BAKER, H.

Illustrations of Conifers. London: 1909-13. V. 41; 42

Illustrations of Conifers. (with) Illustrations of New Conifers. London: 1910-13. 1935. V. 42

CLINTON, CHARLES A.

A Winter From Home. New York: 1852. V. 43

CLINTON, DE WITT

An Account of Abimelech Coody and Other Celebrated Writers of New York; in a Letter from a Traveller, to His Friend in South Carolina. N.P.: 1815. V. 40

Annual Report of the Canal COmmissioners, COmmunicated to the Legislature, February 18, 1820. Albany: 1820. V. 37

Correspondence on the Importance & Practicability of a Rail Road from New York to New Orleans. New York: 1830. V. 42

A Discourse Delivered at Schenectady . . . Before the New York Alpha of the Phi Beta Kappa. Albany: 1823. V. 40

An Introductory Discourse, Delivered Before the Literary and Philosophical Society of New York, on the Fourth of May, 1814. New York: 1815. V. 44

Letters on the Natural History and Internal Resources of the State of New York. New York: 1822. V. 39

CLINTON, GEORGE

Memoirs of the Life and Writings of Lord Byron. London: 1825. V. 39; 41; 44

Memoirs of the Life and Writings of Lord Byron. London: 1830. V. 37; 39

Public Papers of George Clinton, First Governor of New York, 1777-1904. V. 46

Public Papers of George Clinton, First Governor of New York, 1777-1795 - 1801-1804. New York & Albany: 1801-1804. V. 38

CLINTON, H. R.

From Crecy to Assye: Being Five Centuries of the Military History of England. London: 1881. V. 39

CLINTON, HENRY

Authentic Copies of Lettes Between Sir Henry Clinton, K.B. and the Commissioners for Auditing the Public Accounts. London: 1793. V. 38; 39; 40; 43; 44; 45

A Letter from Lieut. Gen. Henry Clinton, K.B. to the Commissioners of Public Accounts, Relative to Some Observations in Their Seventh Report . . . London: 1784. V. 37; 38; 39; 40; 41; 44; 45

Memorandums, &c. &c. Respecting the Unprecedented Treatment Which the Army Have Met With Respecting the Plunder Taken after a Siege, and of Which Plunder the Navy Serving with the Army Divided Their More than Ample Share . . . London: 1794. V. 40; 43; 44; 45

Narrative of . . . Relative to His Conduct During Part of His Command of the King's Troops in North America. London: 1783. V. 40; 44; 45

Observations of Mr. Stedman's History of the American War. London: 1794. V. 38; 40; 42; 44; 45

Observations of Earl Cornwallis's Answer. Philadelphia: 1896. V. 43

CLINTON, HENRY FYNES

Fasti Hellenici. The Civil and Literary Chronology of Greece from the LVth to the CXXIVth Olympiad. Oxford: 1824. V. 41

CLINTON-HOPE, FRANCIS FELHAM

The Hope Collection of Pictures of the Dutch and Flemish Schools. London: 1898. V. 40; 44

CLIO & Euterpe or British Harmony. A Collection of Celebrated Songs and Cantatas by the Most Approved Masters, Curiously Engraved with the Thorough Bass for the Harpsichord and Transposition for the German Flute. London: 1762. V. 38; 40; 44; 46

CLIVE, ROBERT 1725-1774

Lord Clive's Speech, in the House of Commons, 30th March 1772 on the Motion Made for Leave to Bring in a Bill. London: 1772. V. 37; 41

Lord Clive's Speech, in the House of Commons, on the Motion Made for an Inquiry into the Nature, State and Condition of the East India Company and of the British Affairs in the East Indies, in the Fifth Session of the Present Parliament. N.P.: 1772. V. 41

Lord Clive's Speech, in the House of Commons, on the Motion Made for an Inquiry into the Nature, State and Condition of the East India Company and of the British Affairs in the East Indies, in the Fifth Session of the Present Parliament, 1772. N.P.: 1772. V. 42

CLODE, CHARLES M.

The Early History of the Guild of Merchant Taylors of the Fraternity of St. John the Baptist. London: 1888. V. 41

CLOISTER PRESS

A Specimen Book of Types and Ornaments in Use at the Cloister Press. Manchester: 1935. V. 44

CLONARD, SERAFIN MARIA DE SOTO, CONDE DE

Album de la Infanteriaa Espanola Desde sus Primitivos Tiempos Hasta el Dia. Madrid: 1861. V. 38

CLONCURRY, VALENTINE

Personal Recollections of the Life and Times of, with Extracts from the Correspondence of Valentine Lord Cloncurry. Dublin: 1850. V. 38

CLONEY, THOMAS

A Personal Narrative of Those Transactions in the County Wexford in Which the Author was Engaged During the Awful Period of 1798. Dublin: 1832. V. 39; 46

CLOPET, LILIAN

Once Upon a Time. London: 1944. V. 44

CLOPPER, JONAS

Fragments of the History of Bawlfredonia. 1819. V. 38

Fragments of History of Bawlfredonia . . . N.P.: Baltimore?: 1819. V. 43

CLOPTON, A. G.

An Eulogy on the Life and Character of Dr. Ashbel Smith. Jefferson: 1886. V. 37; 39; 41; 42; 44; 45

CLOQUET, JULES

Anatomie de l'Homme. Paris: 1821-1831. V. 37

Recollections of the Private Life of General Lafayette. New York: 1836. V. 37; 38

CLOQUET, M. JULES

Recollections of the Private Life of General Lafayette. London: 1835. V. 41; 42

THE CLOTHIER'S Letter to the Inhabitants of the Liberties. Dublin: 1759. V. 40

CLOUD, C. CAREY

Puss in Boots. New York: (1934). V. 37

CLOUD, D. C.

Monopolies and the People. Davenport: 1873. V. 39

CLOUDS and Sunshine. London: 1829. V. 42

CLOUGH, A. BRYANT

The Contractor's Manual and Builder's Price-Book. Philadelphia: 1855. V. 44

CLOUGH, ARTHUR HUGH

Ambarvalia. London: 1849. V. 40; 46

The Bothie of Toper-na-fuosich. Oxford: 1848. V. 46

Letters and Remains of Arthur Hugh Clough, sometime Fellow of Oriel College, Oxford. London: 1865. V. 37; 46

Poems. Cambridge: 1862. V. 40

The Poems and Prose Remains . . . London: 1869. V. 46

CLOUGH, ROBERT T.

The Lead Smelting Mills of the Yorkshire Dales and Northern Pennies. London: 1980. V. 46

CLOUSTON, J. STORER

Carrington's Cases. London: 1920. V. 40; 41; 42; 43

The Lunatic at Large. Edinburgh: 1899. V. 42

Lunatic in Charge. London: 1926. V. 41

CLOUSTON, W. A.

The Book of Sinibad, or the Story of the King, His Son, the Damsel and the Seven Vazirs. 1884. V. 43

A Group of Eastern Romances and Stories from the Persian Tamil and urdu. Glasgow: 1889. V. 43

Hieroglyphic Bibles Their Origin and History and a New Hieroglyphic Bible told in Stories by Frederick A. Laing. Glasgow: 1894. V. 40; 46

CLOUZOT, HENRI

La Ferronnerie Moderne. 1, 2, 3 Serie. Paris: 1925-27. V. 38

Painted and Printed Fabrics. The History of the Manufactory at Jouy and Other Ateliers in France 1760-1815 . . . New York: 1927. V. 38; 44

CLOWES, G. S. LAIRD

Sailing Ships - Their History and Development as Illustrated by the Collection of Ship-Models in the Science Museum. London: 1931 & 1952. V. 39

CLOWES, JOHN

Dialogues on the Nature, Design, and Evidence of the Theological Writings of the Hon. Emanual Swedenborg, with a Brief Account of Some of His Philosophical Works. Boston: 1794. V. 37

CLOWES, WILLIAM

History of Scottish Medicine. London: 1932. V. 42

CLOWES, WILLIAM LAIRD

The Royal Navy: a History from the Earliest Times to the Present. London: 1897. V. 41

The Royal Navy. London: 1897-1903. V. 37; 39; 44; 45; 46

The Royal Navy: a History from the Earliest Times to the Present . . . London: 1898. V. 41

CLUBBE, JOHN

Byron's Natural Man, Daniel Boone & Kentucky. Lexington: 1980. V. 40

Miscellaneous Tracts. Ipswich: 1770? V. 41; 42

CLUBBE, WILLIAM

The Omnium; Containing the Journal of a Late Three Days Tour into France . . . Ipswich: 1798. V. 37; 42

Six Satiraes of Horace, in a style Between Free Imitation and Literal Version. Ipswich: 1795. V. 37

CLUBS and Yachts of the Great Lakes. Toronto: 1908? V. 40

CLUM, WOODWORTH

Apache Agent - the Story of John P. Clum. Boston: 1936. V. 39; 40

CLUNES, JOHN

Itinerary and Directory for Western India. Calcutta and Bombay: 1826-28. V. 40

CLUNY, ALEXANDER

The American Traveller; or, Observations on the Present State, Culture and Commerce of the British Colonies in America . . . London: 1769. V. 41

CLUSIUS, CAROLUS

Rariorum Aliquot Stirpium per Hispanias Observatarum Historia. Antwerp: 1576. V. 41

Rariorum Plantarum Historia. Antwerp: 1601. V. 41

CLUTE, EUGENE

The Treatment of Interiors. New York: 1926. V. 38

CLUTE, ROBERT F.

The Annals and Parish Register of St. Thomas and St. Denis Parish in South Carolina from 1680-1884. Charleston: 1884. V. 40; 42

CLUTTERBUCK, ROBERT

The History and Antiquities of the County of Hertford . . . London: 1815-27. V. 39; 40; 42; 43

CLUTTON, HENRY

Remarks, With Illustrations on the Domestic Architecture of France from the Accesssion of Charles Vi to the Demise of Louis XII. London: 1853. V. 37

CLUVERIUS, PHILIPPUS

Introductionis in Universam Geographiam . . . Amsterdam: 1637. V. 39

Introductionis in Universam Geograpahiam, tam Veterem Quam Novam. Venice: 1646. V. 37

Introductions in Universam Geographiam tam Veterem Quam Novam Libri VI. Amsterdam: 1672. V. 37

CLUVERIUS, THOMAS J.

Cluverius. My Life, Trial and Conviction. Richmond: 1887. V. 40

CLUYSENAAR, J. P.

Chemin de Fer Dendre-et-Waes et de Bruxelles Vers Gand par Alost, Batiments des Stations et Maisons de Garde. Brussels: 1855. V. 44

CLYDE, NORMAN

Norman Clyde of the Sierra Nevada. San Francisco: 1971. V. 44

CLYMAN, JAMES 1792-1881

James Clyman, American Frontiersman, 1792-1881. San Francisco: 1928. V. 41

James Clyman, Frontiersman (1772-1881). Portland: 1960. V. 37; 38; 39; 43

CLYMER, GEORGE

The Principles of Naval Staff Rank; and its History in the United States Navy for Over Half a Century. N.P.. V. 40

The Principles of Naval Staff Rank; and Its History in the United States Navy, for Over Half a Century. N.P.: 1869. V. 40

The Principles of Naval Staff Rank; and Its History in the United States Navy, for Over Half a Century. N.P.: 1869. V. 41

CLYMER, W. B. SHUBRICK

Robert Frost, a Bibliography. Amherst: 1937. V. 40; 43

CLYNE, GERALDINE

The Jolly Jump-Ups Journey Through Space. New York: 1952. V. 44

COADE, ELEANOR

A Descriptive catalogue of Coade's Artificial Stone Manufactory, at King's Arms Staris, Narrow-Wall, Lambeth . . . With prices affixed . . . London: 1784. V. 37

COAHUILA AND TEXAS. (STATE). LAWS, STATUTES, ETC. - 1839

Laws and Decrees of the State of Coahuila and Texas, in Spanish and English, to Which is Added the Constitution of Said State, Also the Colonization Law. Houston: 1839. V. 39; 42

COALE, WILLIAM EDWARD

A Practical Essay on Aneurism. Boston: 1861. V. 43

THE COALITION; or, An Essay on the Present State of Parties. London: 1783. V. 46

COAN, B.

The Red Web. 1925. V. 46

COAN, CHARLES F.

A History of New Mexico. Chicago: 1925. V. 46

COAST Castle, Its Environs, Its Inhabitants and Its Visitors. Belfast: 1864. V. 43

COATES, DANDESON

The New Zealanders and Their Lands. London: 1844. V. 42; 43

COATES, DORA MEESON

George Coates: His Art and His Life. London: 1937. V. 41

COATES, JOHN

A Collection of Original Miscellaneous Poems and Translations. London: 1770. V. 40; 43

COATES, ROBERT M.

All the Year Round - Stories. New York: 1943. V. 37; 40

The Eater of Darkness. (Paris: 1926). V. 37; 40

Yesterday's Burdens. New York: 1933. V. 37; 40

COATES, WILLIAM R.

History of Cuyahoga County and the City of Cleveland. Historical and Biographical. Chicago & New York: 1924. V. 42

COATSWORTH, ELIZABETH

The Cat Who Went to heaven. New York: 1930. V. 45

COATTS, MARGOT

Edible Architecture. By Margot Coatts. Drawings by Ian Beck. Wiltshire: 1987. V. 37

COBB, DANIEL J.

A Supplement to the Family Adviser: Containing Some Remarks on the Diseases of Women and Children. Westfield: 1831. V. 42

COBB, H.

Iron Mountain Region. St. Louis: 1855. V. 39

COBB, HOWELL

Speech of Mr. Cobb of Georgia on the Annexation of Texas. Washington: 1845. V. 39; 44

COBB, HUMPHREY

Paths of Glory. New York: 1935. V. 37; 41; 42

COBB, JAMES

The Cherokee: An Opera. London: 1795. V. 38

COBB, JONATHAN HOLMES

A Manual Containing Information Respecting the Growth of the Mulberry Tree . . . Boston: 1833. V. 37; 38; 39; 42; 45

A Manual containing information respecting the growth of the Mulberry Tree, with suitable directions for the culture of silk. Boston: 1831. V. 37; 43

COBB, JOSEPH B.

Leisure Labors, or Miscellanies Historical, Literary and Political. New York: 1858. V. 43

Mississippi Scenes, or, Sketches of Southern and Western Life and Adventure, Humourous, Satirical and Descriptive. Philadelphia: 1851. V. 37; 41

COBB, LYMAN

A Critical Review of the Orthography of Dr. Webster's Series of Books for Systematick Instruction in the English Language. New York: 1831. V. 38

The Reticule and Pocket Companion. New York: 1835. V. 40

COBB, MARY

Extracts from the Diary and Letters. London;: 1805. V. 37

COBB, SAMUEL

Clavis Virgiliana; or New Observations Upon the Works of Virgil. London: 1714. V. 39; 42

Poems on Several Occasions. With Imitaitions from Horace, Ovid, Martial, Theocritus, Bachylides, Anacreon, &c. To which is prefix'd a Discourse on Criticism and the Liberty of Writing . . . to which is added, poems on the Duke of Marlborough . . . London: 1710. V. 37

COBB, SYLVANS

The Gun Maker of Moscow, or Vladmir the Monk. New York: 1888. V. 46

COBB, SYLVANUS

Fernando: or, the Moor of Castile. Boston: 1853. V. 39

COBB, THOMAS R. R.

A Digest of the Statute Laws of the State of Georgia, with Notes. Athens: 1851. V. 37; 39; 42

An Inquiry Into the Law of Negro Slavery in the United States of America, To Which is Prefixed an Historical Sketch of Slavery. Philadelphia: 1858. V. 44

COBBAN, J. MACLAREN

The Burden of Isabel. London: 1893. V. 41

COBBE, FRANCES POWER

The Cities of the Past. London: 1864. V. 37

Religious Duty. Boston: 1883. V. 37; 44; 45

COBBET, THOMAS

The Civil Magistrates Power in Matters of Religion Modestly Debated, Impartially stated according to the Bounds and Grounds of Scripture . . . London: 1653. V. 45

A Practical Discourse of Prayer. London: 1654. V. 38; 42; 44

COBBETT, ANNE

The English housekeeper: or, manual of domestic management . . . for the use of young ladies who undertake the superintendence of their own housekeeping. London: (1835). V. 37

COBBETT, JAMES P.

Journal of a Tour in Italy, and Also in Part of France and Switzerland . . . from October 1828 to September 1829 . . . London: 1830. V. 43; 46

COBBETT, WALTER WILLSON

Cobbett's Cyclopedic Survey of Chamber Music. Oxford: 1963. V. 41

COBBETT, WILLIAM 1763-1835

V. 44

Advice to Young Men, and Incidentally to Young Women in the Middle and Higher Ranks of Life. London: 1830. V. 40

Advice to Young Men, and (Incidentally) to Young Women, in the Middle and Higher Ranks of Life. Andover: 1829. V. 37; 44

Advice to Young Men and (incidentally) to Young Women, in the Middle and Higher Ranks of Life. In a series of letters, addressed to a youth, a bachelor, a lover a husband, a father, a citizen or a subject. London: 1829. V. 37

The American Gardener; a Treatise on the Situation, Soil, Fencing and Laying-Out of Gardens . . . Concord: 1842. V. 45

A Bone to Gnaw, for the Democrats . . . Philadelphia: 1795. V. 38; 43

A Bone to Gnaw for the Democrats. London: 1797. V. 41; 43

Cobbett's Parliamentary History of England. London: 1806-14. V. 41

Cobbett's Parliamentary History of England. London: 1806-20. V. 43

Cobbett's Parliamentary History of England. London: 1806-20. V. 41

Cobbett's Oppression! London: 1809. V. 41; 42

Cobbett's Paper Against Gold. London: 1812-17. V. 41

Cobbett's Paper Against Gold. London: 1817. V. 40

COBBETT, WILLIAM 1763-1835 continued

Cobbett's Sermons on 1. Hyopocrisy and Cruelty. 2. Drunkenness. 3. Bribery. 4. Oppression. 5. Unjust Judges. 6. The Sluggard. 7. Murder. 8. Gaming. 9. PUblic Robbery. 10. The Unnatural Mother. 11. Forbidding Marriage. 12. Parsons & Tithes. London: 1822. V. 40

Cobbett's Plan of Parliamentary Reform; Addressed to the Young Men of England. London: 1830. V. 38

Cobbett's Manchester Lectures, in Support of His Fourteen Reform Propositions . . . London: 1832. V. 42

Cobbett's Tour in Scotland; and in the Four Northern Counties of England. London: 1833. V. 40; 46

Cobbett's Legacy to Labourers; or, What Is the Right Which the Lords, Baronets and Squires, Have to the Lands of England? London: 1835. V. 37; 42; 44; 45

Cobbett's Political Register. London: 1802-1812. V. 41

A Collection of Facts and Observations Relative to the Peace with Bonaparte, Chiefly Extracted from the Porcupine . . . Philadelphia: 1802. V. 39; 43

Cottage Economy . . . London: 1823. V. 45

Cottage Economy. London: 1828. V. 42

Cottage Economy. New York: 1833. V. 39

The Democratic Judge: or, the Equal Liberty of the Press, as Exhibited, Explained and Exposed, in the Prosecution of William Cobbett, for a Pretended Libel Against the King of Spain and His Embassador, Before Thomas M'Kean . . . Philadelphia: 1798. V. 38

Detection of a Conspiracy Formed by the United Irishmen; with the Evident Intention of Aiding the Tyrants of France in Subverting the Government of the United States of America. London: 1799. V. 39

The Emigrant's Guide. London: 1829. V. 43

The English Gardener. London: 1829. V. 39; 43

The English Gardener. London: 1833. V. 39; 42; 46

The English Gardener. London: 1835. V. 40

The English Gardener; or, a Treatise on the Situation, Soil, Enclosing and Laying-Out of Kitchen Gardens. London: 1838. V. 41

The English Gardener. London: 1845. V. 43; 44

A French Grammar, or Plain Instructions for the Learning of French. London: 1824. V. 38; 44; 46

A Full and Accurate Report of the Trial of William Cobbett, Esq . . . . on Thurs. July 7, 1831 in the Court of King's Bench, Guildhall. London: 1831. V. 43

A Grammar of the English Language, in a Series of Letters . . . London: 1819. V. 44; 45

A Grammar of the English Language, in a Series of Letters. London: 1819, 1818. V. 41

A Grammar of the English Language . . . London: 1824. V. 40

A History of the Protestant 'Reformation' in England and Ireland. London: 1824. V. 39; 45

A History of the Protestant Reformation in England and Ireland. London: 1829. V. 38; 40; 41; 42; 45

A History of the Reformation in England and Ireland, in a Series of Letters. Philadelphia:)1824-6). V. 37

Impeachment of Mr. Lafayette: Containing His Accusation. Philadelphia: 1793. V. 37

Important Considerations for the People of this Kingdom. London: 1803. V. 40

The Law of Turnpikes; or, an analytical arrangment of, and illustrative commentaries on, all the general Acts relative to the Turnpike roads of England. London: 1824. V. 37

Legacy to Labourers. London: 1834. V. 38

A Letter to the Infamous Tom Paine, in Answer to His Letter to General Washington. London: 1797. V. 39

Letters on the Late War Between the United States and Great Britain . . . New York: 1815. V. 39; 43; 45

The Life and Adventures of Peter Porcupine, With a Full and Fair Account of All His Authoring Transactions . . . Glasgow: 1798. V. 43

Life of Andrew Jackson. London: 1834. V. 39; 43

Life of Andrew Jackson. London: 1835. V. 43; 44; 45

Life and Adventures of Porcupine: With Other Records of His Early Career in England and America . . . London: 1927. V. 46

A Little Plain English . . . on the Treaty with His Britannic Majesty, and the Conduct of the President. Philadelphia: 1795. V. 39

Cobbett's Manchester Lectures, in Support of His Fourteen Reform Propositions. London: 1832. V. 39

Observations on the Emigration of Dr. Joseph Priestley and on the Several Addresses Delivered to Him, on His Arrival at New York. Philadelphia: 1796. V. 45

Observations on the Debates of the American Congress, on the Addresses Presented to General Washington, on His Resignation . . . London: 1797. V. 39

Observations on the Debates of the American Congress, on the Addresses Presented to General Washington on His Resignation . . . Philadelphia: 1797. V. 43

Observations on the Emigration of Dr. Joseph Priestley, and the Several Addresses Delivered to Him, On His Arrival in New York, with Additions . . . London: 1798. V. 39

Paper Against Gold, or, The History and Mystery of the Bank of England, of the Debt, of the Stocks, of the Sinking Fund, And Of All the Other Tricks and Contrivances . . . London: 1828. V. 41

Paper Against Gold; or the History and Mystery of the Bank of England . . . New York: 1834. V. 45

Paper against Gold: containing the History and Mystery of the Bank of England, the Funds, the Debt, the Sinking Fund, the Bank stoppage, the lowering and the raising of the value of Paper-money: and shewing, that . . . London: (1817). V. 37; 38; 39; 43

The Political Censor, or Monthly Review of the Most Interesting Political Occurrences, Relative to the United States of America. Philadelphia: 1797. V. 43

The Pride of Britannia Humbled. Philadelphia: 1815. V. 39

Proceedings of a General Court Martial held at the Horse-Guards on the 24th and 27th of march, 1792. London: 1809. V. 45

Proposals for Publishing by Subscription, a New, Entire and Neat Edition of Porcupine's Works. London: 1799. V. 39

Remarks on the Explanation, Lately Published by Dr. Priestley, Respecting the Intercepted Letters to His Friend and Discipline John H. Stone. London: 1799. V. 39

The Republican Judge; or the American Liberty of the Press, as Exhibited, Explained and Exposed in the Base and Partial Prosectuion of William Cobbett, for a Pretended Libel Against the King of Spain and His Ambassador . . . London: 1798. V. 38; 39

Rural Rides. London: 1853. V. 38; 46

Rural Rides. London: 1885. V. 39

Rural Rides in the Counties of Surrey, Kent, Sussex, Hants, Berks, Oxford, Bucks, Wilts, Somerset, Gloucester, Hereford, Salop, Worcester, Stafford, Leicester, Hertford, Essex, Suffolk, Norfolk, Cambridge, Huntingdon, Nottingham, Lincoln, York . . . London: 1893. V. 40

Rural Rides in the Counties of Surrey, Kent, Sussex . . . (Etc.) with Economical and Political Observations relative to matters applicable to and illustratec by, the state of those Counties respectively. London: 1830. V. 37; 38; 40; 41; 42; 43; 45; 46

Selections from Cobbett's Political Works. London: 1835-37. V. 39; 40

Selections from Cobbett's Political Works. London: 1838? V. 39

Cobbett's Sermons on 1. Hypocrisy and Cruelty. 2. Drunkenness. 3. Bribery. 4. Oppression. 5. Unjust Judges. 6. The Sluggard. 7. Murder. 8. Gaming. 9. Public Robbery. 10. The Unnatural Mother. 11. Forbidding Marriage. 12. Parsons & Tithes. London: 1822. V. 41

Tour in Scotland; and in the Four Northern Counties of England in the Autumn of the Year 1832. London: 1833. V. 38; 39; 40; 41; 42

A Treatise on Cobbetts Corn, Containing Instructions for Propagating and Cultivating the Plant and for Harvesting and Preserving the Crop and Also an Account of the Several Uses to Which the Produce is Applied . . . London: 1828. V. 45

The Woodlands; or, a Treatise on the Preparing of Ground for Planting . . . London: 1825. V. 39; 40; 43; 45; 46

The Woodlands; or a Treatise on the Preparing of Ground for Planting. London: 1825-1828. V. 40

The Woodlands; or, a Treatise on the Preparing of Ground For Planting . . . London: 1828. V. 43

The Woodlands: or, a Treatise on the Preparing of Ground for Planting. London: 1828. V. 38; 41

Porcupine's Works . . . London: 1801. V. 39; 40; 41

A Year's Residence, in the United States of America. London: 1818-19. V. 41

A Year's Residence in the United States of America. London: 1819. V. 39; 43

A Year's Residence in the United States of America. London: 1822. V. 45

A Year's Residence in the United States of America. Andover: 1828. V. 42

A Year's Residence in the United States of America, in Three Parts. London: 1828. V. 41

COBBETT'S Gridiron: Written to Warn Farmers of their Danger; and to Put Landholders . . . and Indeed all Classes of the Community on Their Guard. London: 1822. V. 39

COBBOLD, ELIZA KNIPE

The Mince Pye: an Heroic Epistle: Humble Addressed to the Soverign Dainty of a British Feast. London: 1800. V. 41; 42

Six Narrative Poems. London: 1787. V. 41; 42

COBBOLD, ELIZABETH

Poems . . . with a Memoir of the Author. Ipswick: 1825. V. 37

COBBOLD, RALPH P.

Innermost Asia. Travel and Sport in the Pamirs. London: 1900. V. 40

Innermost Asia. New York: 1900. V. 45

COBBOLD, RICHARD

The Character of Woman, a Lecture, Delivered in the hanover Square Rooms, April 13, 1848, for the Benefit of the Governesses Benevolently Institution. Diss: 1848. V. 37; 44; 45

Geoffery Gambardo; or, a Simple Remedy for Hypochondriacism and Melancholy Splenetic Humours. London: 1850. V. 45

Mary Anne Wellington, the Soldier's Daughter, Wife and Widow . . . London: 1846. V. 39; 45

Valentine Verses; or Lines of Truth, Love and Virtue. Ipswich: 1827. V. 38; 45

COBBOLD, T. SPENCER

Parasites; a Treatise on the Entozoa of Man and Animals . . . London: 1879. V. 37

COBDEN CLUB

Systems of Land Tenure in Various Countries. London: 1870. V. 39

COBDEN, EDWARD

Poems on Several Occasions. London: 1748. V. 42; 45

COBDEN, JOHN C.

The White Slaves of England. Auburn and Buffalo: 1854. V. 39

COBDEN, RICHARD

Cobden as a Citizen, a Chapter in Manchester History. London: 1907. V. 39

COBDEN-SANDERSON, THOMAS JAMES 1840-1922

Amantium Irae. Hammersmith: 1914. V. 37; 40; 41; 43; 46

Arts and Crafts Movement. Hammersmith: 1905. V. 37; 41

The Book Beautiful. San Francisco: 1930. V. 38

The Bookbindings of T. J. Cobden-Sanderson. London: 1984. V. 46

C-S the Master Craftsman. Harper Woods: 1969. V. 45

Catalogue Raisonne of Books Printed and Published by the Doves Press. Hammersmith: 1908. V. 41; 46

Catalogue Raisonne of Books Printed and Published at the Doves Press 1900-1911. Hammersmith: 1911. V. 46

Catalogue Raisonne of Books Printed & Published at the Doves Press, 1900-1915. Hammersmith: 1914. V. 46

Catalogue Raisonne of Books printed and Published at the Doves Press, 1900-1916. Hammersmith: 1916. V. 37

The City Planned. V. 44

The City. Hammersmith: 1910. V. 37; 46

Cosmic Vision. London: 1922. V. 42

Credo. Hammersmith: 1908. V. 42; 44

Credo. London: 1908. V. 37; 42; 43; 45

The Doves Press: Salve Aeternum Aeternumque Vale. Hammersmith: 1916. V. 46

Ecce Mundus: Industrial Ideas and the Beautiful. Hammersmith: 1902. V. 40; 46

Ecce Mundus. London: 1902. V. 41

Four Lectures. San Francisco: 1974. V. 37; 39; 41; 42; 43; 45; 46

The Ideal Book or Book Beautiful. London: 1900. V. 41

The Ideal Book or Book Beautiful. New York: 1900. V. 39

The Ideal Book or Book Beautiful. Hammersmith: 1900. V. 37; 45

The Jouranls 1879-1922. London: 1926. V. 39; 40; 43

The Journals of 1879-1922 . . . New York: 1926. V. 38; 40; 42; 43; 44

The Journals of Thomas James Cobden-Sanderson. London: 1922. V. 37

London. A Paper Read at a Meeting of the Art Workers Guild . . . March 6, 1891. Hammersmith: 1906. V. 42; 46

London. A Paper Read at Meeting of the Art Workers Guild, March 6, 1891. London: 1906. V. 38; 40; 42; 43; 44

The New Science Museum. Hammersmith: 1914. V. 46

Note On a Passage in Julius Caesar. Hammersmith: 1913. V. 46

Note on a Passage in Shelley's Ode to Liberty. Hammersmith: 1914. V. 46

Prospice. Hammersmith: 1913. V. 46

Shakespearian Punctuation. A Letter Addressed to the Editor of 'The Times', October 26, 1911. Hammersmith: 1912. V. 45; 46

Towards an Empire of Science. Hammersmith: 1916. V. 46

Wordsworth's Cosmic Poetry. Hammersmith: 1914. V. 37; 46

COBHAM, ALAN J.

My Flight to the Cape and Back. London: 1926. V. 45

Twenty Thousand Miles in a Flying Boat. London: 1930. V. 45

COBHAM, JOHN CAVENDISH LYTTELTON, 9TH VISCOUNT

The Yeomanry Cavalry of Worcestershire 1914-22. Stourbridge: 1926. V. 46

COBHAM, VISCOUNT

Report of the Committee on Leather for Bookbinding. London: 1905. V. 37; 38; 41

COBRES, JOSEPH PAUL VON

Deliciae Cobresianae. J. P. Cobres Buchersammlung zur Naturgeschichte. colphon: 1782. V. 46

COBURN, ALVIN LANGDON

The Book of Harlech: 20 Photographs. Harlech: 1920. V. 41

Cotton Waste. Manchester: 1920. V. 46

London. London: 1909. V. 39

Men of Mark. London: 1913. V. 39; 41

More Men of Mark. New York: 1922. V. 37; 41

New York. London & New York;: 1910. V. 37

Poor Mark Rickemansworth - a Series of Photographs. London: 1915. V. 45

A Portfolio of Sixteen Photographs by . . . New York: 1962. V. 42; 44

COBURN, WALLACE D.

Rhymes from a Round-Up Camp. Great Falls: 1899. V. 37

COBURN, WALLACE DAVID

The Battle of the Little Big Horn. N.P.: 1936. V. 37

COCCHI, ANTONIO

Graecorum Chirurgici Libri Sorani Unus de Fracturarum Signis, Oribasii Duo de Fractus et de Luxatis . . . Florence: 1754. V. 43

COCERELL, SIDNEY C.

Some German Woodcuts of the 15th Century. Hammersmith: 1897. V. 40

COCHIN, C. N.

Observations Upon the Antiquities of the Town of Herculaneum. London: 1753. V. 37

COCHINCHINA Relatione delle Missini de'Vescovi Vicarii Apostolici Mandati Dalla S. Sede Apostolica Alli Regni Di Siam, Cocincina, Camboia, E. Tunkino. Rome: 1677. V. 40

COCHLAEUS, JOHANNES

Antiqua Regum Italiae Gothicae Genus Rescripta, ex 12 Libris Epistolarum Cassiodori ad Ethuaricum. (with) Autenticae Justiniani Imperatoris Augusti De Rebus Sacris, per Compendium Commemoratae. Leipzig: 1529. V. 41

Historia. Martini Lutheri Das ist, Kurtze Beschreibung Seiner Handlungen und Geschrifften, der Zeit nach vom MDXVII bis suff das XLVI. Dilingen: 1622. V. 38

Septiceps Lutherus, Ubiqz Sibi, Suis Scriptis, Cottari, in Visittione Saxonica . . . Lypsiae: 1529. V. 38

Sermo D. Johannis Cochlei Alias Wendelstein, ad Exemplum pro Omnibus qui Contra Lutherum Volut Scrip Turas Magistraliter et for Maliter Tractare. 1530. V. 38

Vita Theodorici Regis . . . Ostrogothorum. Ingolstadt: 1544. V. 43

COCHRAN, JOHN

A Catalogue of Manuscripts . . . from the Twelth to the Eighteenth Century, Many of Them Upon Vellum and Adorned with Spendid Illuminations. London: 1829. V. 39; 44

COCHRAN, JOHN S.

Bonnie Belmont: a Historical Romance of the Days of Salvery and the Civil War. N.P.: 1907. V. 44

Bonnie Belmont: A Historial Romance of the Days of Slavery and The Civil War. N.P.: 1907. V. 37

COCHRAN-PATRICK, R. W.

Catalogue of the Medals of Scotland. Edinburgh: 1884. V. 46

Records of the Coinage of Scotland. Edinburgh: 1876. V. 46

COCHRAN, ROBERT

The Life of . . . London: 1734. V. 45

COCHRANE-BAILLIE, ALEXANDER

Young Italy. London: 1850. V. 37; 44

COCHRANE, BASIL

An Improvement in the Mode of Administering the Vapour Bath, and the Apparatus Connected With It.. London: 1809-1810. V. 38

COCHRANE, CHARLES STUART

Journal of a Residence and Travels in Colombia, During the Years 1823 and 1824. London: 1825. V. 37; 38; 39; 41; 42; 43; 46

COCHRANE, GEORGE

Wanderings in Greece. London: 1837. V. 37

COCHRANE, GEORGE E.

Regulations Applicable tot eh European Officer in India. London: 1865. V. 42

COCHRANE, GORDON S.

Baseball: The Fan's Game. New York: 1939. V. 42

COCHRANE, JOHN DUNDAS

Narrative of a Pedestrian Journey Through Russia and Siberian Tartary, from the Frontiers of China to the Frozen Sea and Kamtchatka; Performed During the Years 1820, 1821, 1822 and 1823. London: 1824. V. 38; 40; 41; 42; 43; 46

Narrative of a Pedestrian Journey through Russia and Siberian Tartary, from the Frontiers of China to the Frozen Sea and Kamtchatka. London: 1825. V. 45

COCK-A-HOOP: A Sequel to Chanticleer, Pertelote and Cockalorum. Middlesex: 1976. V. 46

COCK Robin Alive and Well Again Grandpapa Easy's New and Original Pictorial Books. London: 1840. V. 41

COCK, WILLIAM

Meteorologia; or, the True Way of Fore-Seeing and Judging the Inclination of the Air and Alteration of the Weather in Several Regions. London: 1703. V. 43

COCKALORUM: A Sequel to Chanticleer and Pertelote: Being a Bibiliography of the Golden Cockerel Press, June 1943-December 1948. Waltham St. Lawrence: 1948. V. 44

COCKALORUM: a Sequel to Chanticleer and Pertelote: Being a Bibiliography of the Golden Cockerell Press June 1943-December 1948. 1948. V. 42

COCKALORUM: A Sequel to Chanticleer and Pertelote: Being a Bibliography of the Golden cockerel Press, June 1943-December 1948. London: 1950. V. 46

COCKAYNE, ANDREAS EDWARD

Cockayne Memoranda; Collections towards a Historical Record of the Family of Cockayne. Congleton: 1869. V. 37

COCKBURN, CATHARINE

Remarks Upon the Principles and Reasonings of Dr. Rutherforth's Essay on the Nature and Obligations of Virtue. London: 1747. V. 38

COCKBURN, CATHERINE TROTTER

Agnes De Castro. London: 1696. V. 42

COCKBURN, GEORGE

Buonaparte's Voyage to St. Helena; Comprising the Diary of . . . Boston: 1833. V. 38

A Voyage to Cadiz and Gibraltar up the Mediteranean to Sicily and the Lipari Islands . . . London: 1815. V. 41; 44

COCKBURN, HENRY

Memorials of His Time. Edinburgh: 1856-74. V. 37

COCKBURN, JAMES

Swiss Scenery from Drawings . . . London: 1820. V. 41; 44

Views to Illustrate the Route of the Simlon, Drawn from Nature by Major Cockburn and on Stone by J. Harding. London: 1822. V. 38

COCKBURN, JOHN

The History of Duels. Edinburgh: 1888. V. 44

A Journey Over Land, from the Gulf of Honduras tot he Great South-Sea. London: 1735. V. 40

A Short History of the Revolution in Scotland. London: 1712. V. 39

COCKE, JOHN

Letter to the Honorable John H. Eaton. December 16, 1818. Knoxville: 1819. V. 42

COCKE, RICHARD

Veronese's Drawings. A Catalogue Raisonne. London: 1984. V. 39

COCKER, EDWARD

Cocker's Decimal Arithmetick. London: 1720. V. 42; 44

Cocker's Arithmetick . . . London: 1725. V. 41

The Young Clerks Tutor Enlarged. London: 1670. V. 38; 40; 42; 46

COCKERAM, HENRY fl. 1650

The English Dictionary of 1623. New York: 1930. V. 41; 43

COCKERELL, CHARLES ROBERT

Iconography of the West Front of Wells Cathedral . . . Oxford: 1841. V. 38

The Temples of Jupiter Panhellenius at Aegina, and of Apollo Epicurius at Bassae near Phigaleia in Arcadia. London: 1860. V. 40

COCKERELL, DOUGLAS

Bookbinding, and the Care of Books. London: 1901. V. 39; 40

Bookbining, and the Care of Books. New York: 1906. V. 45

Some Notes on Bookbinding. London: 1929. V. 39

COCKERELL, SIDNEY

A Psalter and Hours, Executed Before 1270 for Isabelle of France . . . Now in the Collection of Henry Yates Thompson. Described by S. C. Cockerell . . . London: 1905. V. 40

COCKERELL, SYDNEY

Some German Woodcuts of the Fifteenth Century. Edited by Sydney Cockerell. London: 1897. V. 37

COCKERELL, SYDNEY C.

Some German Woodcuts in the Fifteenth Century. Hammersmith: 1897. V. 38; 39; 42; 43

COCKIN, WILLIAM

The Rural Sabbatha, a Poem In Four Books; and Other Poems. London: 1805. V. 45

COCKINGS, GEORGE

War; an Heroic Poem, from the Taking of Minorca, by The French; to the Reduction of the Havannah, by the Earl of Albermare, Sir George Peacock, &c. The Second Edition (sic), To the Raising the Seige of Quebec: With Large Amendments, and . . . Boston: 1762. V. 37; 43

COCKLE, MARY

Important Studies for the Female Sex, in Reference to Modern Manners; Addressed to a Young Lady of Distinction. London: 1809. V. 42

COCKLE, MAURICE J. D.

A Bibliography of English Military Books Up to 1642 and of Contemporary Foreign Works. London: 1900. V. 37; 38; 39; 40; 41

COCKRUM, WILLIAM M.

History of the Underground Railroad As It Was Conducted by the Anti-Slavery League . . . Oakland City: 1915. V. 42

COCKS, ANNA SOMERS

The Thyssen-Bornemisza Collection: Renaissance Jewels, Gold Boxes and Objets de Vertu. New York: 1984. V. 43

The Thyssen-Bornemisza Collection: Renaissance Jewels, Gold Boxes and Objets de Vertu. New York: 1986. V. 41

COCKTON, HENRY

The Life and Adventures of Valentine Vox, the Ventriloquist. London: 1840. V. 38; 40; 41; 43

The Life and Adventures of George St. Julian, the Prince of Swindlers. London: 1844. V. 39; 46

Stanley Thorn. London: 1841. V. 41; 44

Stanley Thorn. Philadelphia: 1841. V. 42

The Steward: a Romance of Real Life. London: 1850. V. 40

COCTEAU, JEAN 1889-1963

Cock and Harlequin. London: 1921. V. 37

The Eagle Has Two Heads. London: 1948. V. 39; 45; 46

Le Grand Ecart. Paris: 1923. V. 41; 46

The Infernal Machine. London: 1936. V. 39

Jean Marais. Paris: 1951. V. 41

Le Livre Blanc. Paris: 1928. V. 46

Opium: the Diary of a Cure. New York: 1958. V. 40; 44

Picasso. London: 1923. V. 41

Picasso. Paris: 1923. V. 46

Picasso de 1916-1961. Monaco: 1962. V. 37; 38

Thomas L'Imposteur. Paris: 1923. V. 46

Vaslav Nijinsky. Paris: 1910. V. 46

CODDINGTON, HENRY

The Complete Distiller; Combining Theory and Practice; and Explaining the Mysteries and Most Recent Improvements of Distilling and Brewing . . . Edinburgh: 1793. V. 45

CODE Duello. Letters Concerning the Prentiss-Tucker Duel of 1842. Dallas: 1931. V. 42

A CODE of Gentoo Laws, or Ordinations of the Pundits. London: 1777. V. 46

A CODE of Gentoo Laws, or, Ordinations of the Pundits from a Persian Translation, Made from the Original . . . London: 1781. V. 43; 46

CODERIUS, MATURINI

School Colloquies, English and Latin. London: 1667. V. 40

CODMAN, E. A.

The Shoulder. Rupture of the supraspinatus tendon and other lesions in or about the subacromial bursa. Boston: 1934. V. 37; 38; 42; 43

A Study in Hospital Efficeny as demonstrated by the case report of the first five years of a private hospital. Boston: ca. 1917. V. 37

CODMAN, JOHN

Arnold's Expedition to Quebec. New York: 1903. V. 43

The Mormon Country. New York: 1874. V. 42

Sailors' Life and Sailors' Yarns. New York: 1847. V. 43; 44

Ten Months in Brazil; With Notes on the Paraguayan War. New York: 1872. V. 40

CODMAN, JOHN D.

American Natural History - Mastology engraved title, 40 copperplates. Philadelphia: 1826-28. V. 37

CODMAN, JOHN THOMAS

Brook Farm: Historical and Personal Memoirs by John Thomas Codman. Boston: 1894. V. 37; 41; 43; 44

CODRINGTON, ROBERT

The Life and Death of the Illvstrious Robert Earle of Essex, &c. London: 1646. V. 46

CODRONCHIUS, BAPTISTA

De Morbis Qui Imolae, et Alibi Communiter Hoc Anno MDCII, Vagati Sunt, Commentariolum, in Quo Potissimum de Lumbricis Tractatur, et de Morbo Novo Prolapsii Scilicet Mucronatae Cartilaginis Libellus. Bononiae: 1603. V. 40

CODY, HIRAM A.

An Apostle of the North: Memoirs of the Right Rev. William Carpenter Bompas, D.D. London: 1910. V. 43

CODY, WILLIAM F.

Buffalo Bill's Own Story of His Life and Deeds. N.P.: 1917. V. 45

A Peep at Buffalo Bill's Wild West. New York: 1887. V. 40

COE, MICHAEL D.

In the Land of the Olmec. Volume I - The Archaeology of San Lorenzo Tenochtitlan. Volume II - The People of the River. Austin and London: 1980. V. 38

The Maya Scribe and His World. New York: 1973. V. 39; 41; 42

COE, WILBUR

Ranch on the Rudioso: the Story of a Pioneer Family in New Mexico 1871-1968. New York: 1968. V. 42; 46

COE, WILLIAM

Travels Into Poland, Russia, Sweden and Denmark. London: 1785-90. V. 44

COELHO DE FREITAS, ANTONIO

Tratado da Vetteranda et Prodigiosa Imagem do Senhor de Boucas de Matozinhos, em Que se Contem o Manifesto da Procissao Solemne em que foi Levada a Citade do Porto Pella Necessidade des Doencas, em 2 de Abril do anno de 1696. Coimbra: 1699. V. 46

COELHO DE SEABRA, VICENTE

Elementos de Chimica Offerecidos a Sociedade Litteraria do Rio de Janeiro Para o Uso do Seu Curso de Chimica. (with) Dissertacao Sobre o Calor. Coimbra: 1788-90. V. 41

COETLOGAN, DENNIS DE

Natural Sagacity the Principal Secret, If Not the Whole in Phsysick. London: 1742. V. 41; 43

COETZEE, J. M.

Dusklands. Johannesburg: 1974. V. 42; 43; 44; 45; 46

Dusklands. London: 1982. V. 41

From the Heart of the Country. New York: 1977. V. 45

Life and Times of Michael K. New York: 1983. V. 45

White Writing. New Haven: 1988. V. 42

COFFEY, BRIAN

Death of Hektor. N.P.: 1979. V. 45

Death of Hektor. Poem by Brian Coffey. Guildford: (1979). V. 37; 40

COFFEY, CHARLES

The Devil to Pay; or, The Wives Metamorphos'd. London: 1732. V. 43

COFFEY, P.

Epistemology or the Theory of Knowledge. New York: 1938. V. 41

COFFEY, W. A.

Inside Out: or an Interior View of the New York State Prison, together with Biographical Sketches of the Lives of Several of the Convicts. New York: 1823. V. 38

COFFIELD, GLEN

The Night is Where You Fly. San Francisco: 1949. V. 44

COFFIN, A. I.

Botanic Guide to Health, and the Natural Pathology of Disease. London: 1852. V. 40

COFFIN, ADDISON

Life and Travels of Addison Coffin. Cleveland: 1897. V. 41

COFFIN, ALBERT ISAIAH

The Complete Distiller . . . Edinburgh: 1793. V. 43

A Treatise on Midwifery and the Diseases of Women and Children . . . Manchester: 1849. V. 39; 43

COFFIN, C. C.

The Seat of Empire. Boston: 1870. V. 43

COFFIN, CHARLES CARLETON 1823-1896

The Great Commercial Prize. Addressed to Every American Who Values the Prosperity of His Country. Boston: 1858. V. 37

The Seat of Empire. Boston: 1870. V. 37

COFFIN, GEORGE

A Pioneer Voyage to California and Round the World 1849-1852, in the Ship 'Alhambra', from a manuscript in the Possession of the author's Son Gordon B Coffin. Chicago: 1908. V. 39

COFFIN, JOSHUA

Sketch of the History of Newbury, Newburyport and West Newburyport. Boston: 1845. V. 39; 46

COFFIN, ROBERT S.

The Life of the Boston Bard, Written by Himself. Mount Pleasant: 1825. V. 41

COFFIN, ROBERT STEVENSON

The Printer, and Several Other Poems. Boston: 1817. V. 37

COFFIN, W.

Quirks of Diplomacy. Montreal: 1874. V. 43

COFFIN, WILLIAM

A Narrative of the Robbery of the Nantucket Bank. Nantucket: 1816. V. 42; 45

COFFINBERRY, ANDREW

Forest Rangers: Poetic Tale of the Western Wilderness in 1794. Columbus: 1842. V. 38; 40

COGAN, HENRY

The Court of Rome. London: 1654. V. 46

COGAN, T.

A Philosophical Treatise on the Passions. Bath: 1800. V. 37; 40

The Rhine, or a Journey from Utrecht to Francfort, Chiefly by the Borders of the Rhine, and the Passage Down the River from Metz to Bonn. London: 1794. V. 42

COGAN, THOMAS

Ethical Questions; or Speculations on the Principal Subjects of Controversy in Moral Philosophy. London: 1817. V. 40

The Haven of Health, Chiefly Made for the Comfort of Students . . . London: 1612. V. 41; 45

The Haven of Health. London: 1636. V. 44

COGGESHALL, GEORGE

History of the American Privateers, the Letters-of-Marque, During Our War with England in the Years 1812, '13, '14. New York: 1856. V. 39; 45

Voyages to Various Parts of the World, Made Between the Years 1799 and 1844. New York: 1851. V. 41; 42; 43

COGGESHALL, WILLIAM T.

The Protective Policy in Literature. Columbus: 1859. V. 46

COGHLAN, FRANCIS

The Iron Road Book and Railway Companion from London to Birmingham, Manchester and Liverpool . . . London: 1838. V. 46

COGHLAN, MARGARET MONCRIEFF

Memoirs of Mrs. Coghlan (Daughter of the Late Major Moncrieffe), Written by Herself . . . London: 1794. V. 46

COGHLAN, MARGARET MONCRIEFFE

Memoirs of Mrs. Coghlan, (Daughter of the Late Major Moncrieffe). New York: 1795. V. 37; 40; 41; 43; 44; 45

COGSWELL, JOSEPH GREEN

Life of Joseph Green Cogswell as Sketched in His Letters. New York: 1874. V. 41

COHAUSEN, JOHANN HEINRICH 1665-1750

Hermippus Redivivus: or the sage's triumph over old age and the grave. Wherein a method is laid down for prolonging the life and vigour of man . . . the whole interspersed with a great variety of remarkable and well attested relations . . . London: 1749. V. 37; 38; 40; 42; 43

Satyrische Gedanken von der Pica Nasi. Leipzig: 1720. V. 38

COHEN, ALLEN

The San Francisco Chronicle. Berkeley: 1990. V. 45

The San Francisco Oracle. Berkeley: 1990. V. 45

COHEN, ARTHUR A.

Herbert Bayer. The Complete Work. Cambridge: 1984. V. 39

Sonia Delaunay. New York: 1975. V. 39

COHEN, I. B.

Benjamin Franklin's Experiments. Cambridge: 1941. V. 41

COHEN, LEONARD

Beautiful Losers. Toronto: 1966. V. 43

The Favorite Game. New York: 1963. V. 43

COHEN, LEONARD continued

Let Us Compare Mythologies. Montreal: 1956. V. 43

The Spice-Box of Earth. New York: 1961. V. 45

The Spice-Box of Earth. Toronto: 1961. V. 43

COHEN, MEYER M.

Notices of Florida and the Campaigns. Charleston & New York: 1836. V. 41

Notices of Florida and the Campaigns. Charlestown: 1836. V. 37

COHEN, OCTAVIUS ROY

The Townsend Murdery Msytery. New York: 1933. V. 45

COHEN, S. I.

Elements of Jewish Faith. Philadelphia: 1823. V. 43

COHEN, SOL

Education in the United States: a Documentary History . . . New York: 1974. V. 40; 42

COHLIN, DIANE DE GRAZIA

Prints and Related Drawings by the Carracci Family. 1979. V. 44

COHN, ALBERT M.

A Bibliographical Catalogue of the Printed Works Illustrated by George Cruikshank. London: 1914. V. 42

A Bibliographical Catalogue of the Printed Works of George Cruikshank. New York: 1914. V. 38

George Cruikshank: A Catalogue Raisoone of the Work Executed During the Years 1806-1877 . . . London: 1971. V. 39

George Cruikshank: A Cataglogue Raisonne of the Work Executed during the Years 1806-1877. London: 1924. V. 37; 39; 41

COHN, ALFRED

The Function of the Sino-Auricular Node. 1911. V. 42

COHN, LOUIS HENRY

Bibliography of the Works of Ernest Hemingway. New York: 1931. V. 39; 43; 44; 46

COHNHEIM, JULIUS

Lectures on General Pathology . . . London: 1889-90. V. 41; 44

COIGNET, MATTHIEU

Politique Discovrses Vpon Trveth and Lying. An Instrvction to Pinces to Keepe. London: 1586. V. 37; 45

COIGNEY, RUDY

A Bibliography of Izaak Walton. New York: 1989. V. 43

COILLARD, FRANCOIS

On the Threshold of Central Africa. London: 1897. V. 44; 46

COIMBRA. UNIVERSIDADE DE

Estatutos da Universidade de Coimbra Compilados Debaixo da Immediata e Suprema Inspeccado de El-Rei D. Jose I . . . Lisbon: 1772. V. 45

COINTERAUX, FRANCOIS

Architecture Periodique, ou Notice des Travaux et Approvisionnemens que Chacun Peut Faire . . . Paris. V. 44

COIT, DANIEL WADSWORTH

An Artist in El Dorado. The Drawings and Letters of . . . San Francisco: 1937. V. 41

Digging for Gold Without a Shovel. Denver: 1967. V. 46

COKAYNE, GEORGE EDWARD

The Complete Peerage of England, Scotland, Ireland, Great Britain, and the United Kingdom, Extant, Extinct or Dormant. London: 1910-59. V. 41

The Complete Peerage of England, Scotland, Ireland, Great Britain and the United Kingdom . . . London: 1910-59-40. V. 42

Complete Peerage. London: 1887-96. V. 37

COKE, DANIEL PARKER

Coke and Birch. The Paper War Carried on at the Nottingham Election, 1803 . . . Nottingham: 1803. V. 41

COKE, EDWARD 1552-1634

Argumentum Anti-Anormanicum: or an Argument proving, from Ancient Histories and Records, that William Duke of Normandy, Made no absolute Conquest of England. London: 1682. V. 37

A Book of Entries: Containing of Presidents of Counts, Declarations, etc. London: 1671. V. 38; 40

The Compleat Copy-Holder . . . Learned Discourse . . . of Manors and Copy-Holds; Relation Between the Lord of a mannor and Copy-holder his Tenant. London: 1650. V. 38

The Complete Copy-Holder. Wherein is contained a Learned Discourse of the Antiquity and nature of Manors and Copy-Holds . . . London: 1641. V. 37

The Compleate Copy-Holder; Wherein Is Contained a Learned Discourse of the Antiquity and Nature of Manors and Copyholds . . . London: 1644. V. 40

The Complete Copy-Holder, Being a Learned Discourse of the Antiquity and Nature of Manors and Copy-Holds, with all Things Thereto Incident. London: 1673. V. 45; 46

The Fift Part of the Reports of Sr. Edward Coke Knight, the Kings Attorney General (etc.). London: 1624. V. 46

The Fifth Part of the Reports. (with) the Sixth Part of the Reports of Sir Edward Coke. Savoy: 1738. V. 39

The First Part of the Institutes of the Laws of England. London: 1628. V. 45

The First Part the Institutes of the Lawes of England . . . London: 1628/29. V. 46

The First Part of the Institutes of the Laws of England, or, a Commentarie Upon Littleton . . . (with) A Table to the First Part of the Institutes. London: 1628/30. V. 46

The First Part of the Institutes of the Lawes of England, or a Comentary Upon Littleton, not the Name of a Lawyer only, but of the Law Itself. London: 1633. V. 38

The First Part of the Institutes of the Laws of England. London: 1684. V. 46

The First Part of the Institutes of the Laws of England; or a Commentary Upon Littleton; Not the Name of the Author Only . . . London: 1794. V. 39; 45

The First Part of the Institutes of the Laws of England. London: 1719. V. 37

The First Part of the Institutes of the Laws of England or a Commentary on Littleton. London: 1788. V. 37

The First Part of the Institutes of the Laws of England or a Commentary Upon Littleton, also, Three Learned Tracts of the Same Author Entitled The Statute of Levying Fines - Of Ball and Main Prize - The Compleat Copyholder . . . London: 1738. V. 37

The Fourth Part of the Institutes of the Laws of England: Concerning the Jvrisdiction of Courts . . . London: 1644. V. 38; 40; 45

The Fourth Part of the Institutes of the Laws of England Concerning the Jurisdiction of Courts. London: 1648. V. 40

Haec Epitome Undecim Librorum Relationum . . . London: 1640. V. 44

The Lord Coke His Speech and Charge (Given at the Norwich Assizes). With a Discouverie of the Abuses and Corruption of Officers. London: 1607. V. 45; 46

Le Quart Part Des Reportes del Edward Coke Chiualier, L'Attorny General Le Roy (etc.). Londini: 1635. V. 46

Les Reports (Parts One through Six) D'Edward Coke L'Attorney Generall le Roigne (etc.). London: 1618-24. V. 46

Les Reports de Edward Coke L'Attorney Generall le Roigne (Part 1) (etc.). Londini: 1636. V. 46

The Reports of Sir Edward Coke Kt. Savoy: 1738. V. 39

The Reports of Sir Edward Coke, Kt. in Verse. London: 1742. V. 38

The Second Part of the Institutes of the Laws of England Containing the Exposition of Many Ancient and Other Statutes. London: 1671. V. 37; 38; 40

La Size Part des Reports . . . des Diuers Resolutions & Iudgements dones sur Solemne Arguments . . . London: 1607. V. 45

Synopsis or, an Exact Abridgement of the Lord Coke's Commentaries Upon Littleton. London: 1652. V. 40

The Third Part of the Reports of Edward Coke, Her Majesty's Attorney General, of Divers Resolutions and Judgements Given with Great Deliberation . . . . (with) the Fourth Part of the Reports . . . Savoy: 1738. V. 39

Les Tierece Part des Reportes del Edward Coke L'Attourney General Le Roigne (etc.). London: 1635. V. 46

The Twelfth Part of the Reports of . . . of Divers Resolutions and Judgements in Cases of Law. (with) Certain Select Cases in Law Reported by . . . London: 1677. V. 45

COKE, G.

In Search of James Giles (1718-1780). Wingham, Kent,: 1983. V. 37

COKE, HENRY JOHN

A Ride Over the Rocky Mountains to Oregon and California. With a Glance at some of the Tropical Islands, including the West Indies and the Sandwich Isles. London: 1852. V. 37; 38; 39; 43; 44

Tracks of a Rolling Stone . . . London: 1905. V. 40; 43

COKE, MARY

The Letters and Journals of Lady Mary Coke. Edinburgh: 1889-96. V. 45

COKE, ROGER

A Detection of the Court and State of England During the Four Last Reigns and the Inner-Regnum. London: 1696. V. 46

COKE, THOMAS

Extracts of the Journals of the Rev. Dr. Coke's Five Visits to America. London: 1793. V. 40

A History of the West Indies, Containing the Natural Civil and Ecclesiastical History of Each Island. Liverpool: 1808. V. 38

A History of the West Indies . . . Liverpool: 1808/10/11. V. 39; 40; 42

A History of the West Indies, Containing the natural, Civil and Ecclesiastical History of Each Island . . . Liverpool/London: 1808-11. V. 43

COKE, THOMAS continued

A History of the West Indies. Liverpool/London: 1808-11. V. 43

A History of the West Indies, Containing the Natural, Civil and Ecclesiastical History of Each Island. London: 1808-11. V. 41

A History of the West Indies, Containing the Natural, Civil and Ecclesiastical History of Each Island . . . Liverpool: 1810-11. V. 43

The Life of John Wesley including an Account of the Great Revival of Religion in Europe and America, Of Which He Was the First and Chief Instrument. London: 1792. V. 41

COKE, WILLIAM

Travel Into Poland, Russia, Sweden and Denmark. London: 1784-90. V. 45

COKER, JAMES LIDE

History of Company G, Ninth S.C. Regiment, Infantry, S.C. Army; and of Company E, Sixth S.C. Regiment, Infantry, S.C. Army. Charleston, SC: 1899. V. 37

COKER, JOHN

A Survey of Dorsetshire. London: 1732. V. 45

COLAHAN, COLIN

Max Meldrum: His Art and Views. Melbourne: 1920. V. 41

COLANGE, LEO DE

The Heart of Europe: from the Rhine to the Danube. Boston: 1883. V. 40; 41

COLARDEAU, CHARLES PIERRE 1732-1776

Oeuvres de Colardeau. Paris: 1779. V. 39; 42

COLAS, ACHILLE

The Authors of England, a Series of Medallion Portraits of Modern Library Characters . . . London: 1838. V. 41

COLBATCH, JOHN

An Account of the Court of Portugal. London: 1700. V. 41

A Dissertation Concerning Mistletoe . . . London: 1730. V. 45

The Generous Physician, or medicine made easy: containing plain and exact descriptions of the causes, symptoms, and method proper for cure of several distempers . . . with the best receipts in English, and directions how to use them . . . London: (1733). V. 37

COLBECK, NORMAN

A Bookman's Catalogue. The Norman Colbeck Collection of the Nineteenth Century and Edwardian Poetry and Belles Lettres in the Special Collections of the University of British Columbia. Vancouver: 1897. V. 38

COLBERT, E.

Chicago. Historical and Statistical Sketch of the Garden City . . . Chicago: 1868. V. 43

COLBERT, E. D.

Statement of the Choctaw Fredmen Setting Forth Their Wrongs, Grievences, Claims and Wants. Fort Smith: 1894. V. 45

COLBERT, JEAN BAPTISTE, MARRQUIS DE TORCY

Memoirs of the Marquis of Torcy, Secretary of State of Lewis XIV. London: 1757. V. 45

COLBORNE, J.

With Hicks Pasha in the Soudan. London: 1884. V. 40

COLBURN, ALVIN LANGDON

Men of Mark. (with) More Men of Mark. London: 1913/22. V. 43

COLBURN, FRONA EUNICE WAIT SMITH

Yermh the Dorado. San Francisco: 1897. V. 38

COLBURN, MARY J.

Minnesota as a Home for Immigrants. St. Paul: 1865. V. 38

COLBURN, WARREN

He Helunaau, He Mea e Maai'i Ke Kanaka, i ka Helu i na Mea a Pau ma Ka Noonoo Wale No. Oahu: 1843. V. 38

COLBURN, ZERAH

Locomotive Engineering and the Mechanism of Railways . . . London: 1871. V. 46

The Locomotive Engine. Philadelphia: 1853. V. 38

A Memoir, Written by Himself, Containing an Account of the First Discovery of His Remarkable Powers . . . Springfield: 1833. V. 39; 43; 46

The Permanent Way and Coal Burning Locomotive Boilers of European Railways . . . New York: 1858. V. 41

The Permanent Way and Coal-Burning Locomotive Boilers of European Railways; with a Comparison of the Working Economy of European and American Lines, and the Principles upon which Improvement must Proceed. New York: 1858. V. 37; 41; 42; 43

The Waterworks of London, Together with a Series of Articles on Various Waterworks. Philadelphia: 1868. V. 38

COLBY, CHARLES

The Diamond Atlas. New York: 1857. V. 45

Hand-Book of Illinois, Accompanying Morse's New Map of the State. New York: 1854. V. 40; 45

COLBY, THOMAS

Ordnance Survey of Ireland: Abstracts of Principal Lines of Spirit Levelling in Ireland carried on in the years 1839 to 1843, under the direction of Col. Colby. London: 1855. V. 37

Ordnance Survey of the County of Londonderry, Parish of Templemore. Dublin: 1837. V. 37; 43

COLCHESTER, ELIZABETH SUSAN, BARONESS, COLCHESTER

Giustina; a Spanish Tale of Real Life. (with) Miscellaneous Poems Dedicated to Joseph Jeckyll, Esq. London: 1833/32. V. 42

COLCORD, CHARLES FRANCIS

The Autobiography of Charles Francis Colcord 1859-1934. 1970. V. 44

COLDEN, CADWALLADER 1688-1776

The Conduct of Cadwallader Colden, Esquire, Late Lieutenant-Governor of New York . . . London: 1767. V. 46

the History of the Five Indian Nations of Canada, Which are the Barrier Between the English and French . . . London: 1750. V. 40; 43; 45; 46

The History of the Five Indian Nations of Canada. London: 1755. V. 45

The History of the Five Indian Nations of Canada Which are Dependent on the Province o New York, and are a Barrier Between the English and the French . . . New York: 1902. V. 38; 44; 45

The History of the Five Indian Nations of Canada, Which are Dependent on the Province of New York in America, and are the Barrier Between the English and French in that Part of the World. London: 1747. V. 37; 38; 39; 41; 43; 45; 46

COLDEN, CADWALLADER DAVID 1769-1834

The Life of Robert Fulton . . . New York: 1817. V. 38; 41; 42; 46

Memoir, Prepared at the Request of the Committee of the Common Council of the City of New York, and Presented to the Mayor of the City, at the Celebration of the Completion of the New York Canals. New York: 1825. V. 37; 43; 44; 45

Memoir Prepared at the Request of the Committee of the Common Council of the City of New York, and Presented to the Mayor the City . . . New York: 1825-26. V. 39; 42; 43; 45

A Vindication of the Steam Boat Right Granted by the State of New York. Albany: 1818. V. 38

COLDONI, CARLO

The Liar. London: 1922. V. 46

COLDSTREAM, J. N.

Kythera: excavations and studies conducted by the University of Pennsylvania Museum and The British School at Athens. London: (1972). V. 37; 42; 44

COLE

The Cole Library of Early Medicine and Zoology. Catalogue of Books and Pamphlets. Part I. 1472-1800. Part 2. 1800 to Present Day and Supplement to Part 1. Reading: 1969, 1975. V. 40

COLE, A. C.

Studies in Microscopical Science. London: 1883-86. V. 45

COLE, ALPHAEUS P.

Timothy Cole: Wood Engraver. New York: 1935. V. 39

COLE, CHARLES NALSON

A Collection of Laws which form the Constitution of the Bedford Level Corporation; together with an Introductory History therof. London: 1761. V. 37; 41; 42

COLE, CORNELIUS

Memoirs of Corenlius Cole, Ex-Senator of the United States from California. New York: 1908. V. 39

Memoirs of Cornelius Cole, Ex-Senator of the United States from California. New York: 1908. V. 39; 40; 43

COLE, EMMA, PSEUD.

The Life and Sufferings of Miss Emma Cole, Being a Narrative of Her Life. Boston: 1844. V. 37; 43

COLE, F. J.

The Cole Library of Early Medicine and Zoology. Catalogue of Books and Pamphlets. Part I, 1472-1800. Part 2. 1800 to Present Day and Supplement to Part 1. Reading: 1969/75. V. 44; 45; 46

COLE, G. D. H.

William Cobbett. 1925. V. 41

COLE, GEORGE WATSON

Catalogue of Books Relating to the Discovery and Early History of North and South America Forming a Part of the Library of E. D. Church. New York: 1951. V. 37; 40

COLERIDGE, SAMUEL TAYLOR 1772-1834 continued

I. On the Constitution of the Church and State, According to the Idea of Each. II. Lay Sermons. I. The Statesman's Manual. II. 'Blessed are ye that Sow Beside all Waters.' London: 1839. V. 41

Osorio: a Tragedy as Originally Written in 1797. London: 1873. V. 38; 39; 42

The Plot Discovered; or an Address to the People Against Ministerial Treason. Bristol: 1795. V. 39

Poems on Various Subjects. Bristol: 1796. V. 44

Poems on Various Subjects. London: 1796. V. 38; 39; 40; 41; 42; 43; 45

Poems on Various Subjects. London & Bristol: 1796. V. 38

Poems. 1797. V. 42

Poems. To Which are now Added Poems by Charles Lamb, and Charles Lloyd. Bristol: 1797. V. 39; 45

Poems By S. T. Coleridge, to Which are Now Added Poems by Charles Lambs and Charles Lloyd. Bristol: 1797. V. 41; 45

Poems. London: 1797. V. 46

Poems. To Which are Now Added Poems by Charles Lamb and Charles Lloyd. London: 1797. V. 42; 43

Poems. London: 1803. V. 40

The Poems of Samuel Taylor Coleridge. London: 1852. V. 38

Poems Chosen Out of the Works. 1896. V. 43

Poems Chosen Out of the Works of Samuel Taylor Coleridge. 1896. V. 45

Poems Chosen Out of (His) Works. Hammersmith: 1896. V. 43; 46

Poems Chosen Out of the Work of Robert Herrick. London: 1896. V. 40; 41

Poems Chosen Out of the Works of . . . Hammersmith: 1896. V. 37; 38

The Poetical Works . . . London: 1828. V. 42

The Poetical Works of . . . Including the Dramas of Wallenstein, Remorse and Zapolya. London: 1829. V. 41; 42

The Poetical Works of Coleridge, Shelley, and . . . Paris: 1829. V. 39; 42

The Poetical Works. London: 1834. V. 42

The Poetical and Dramatic Works. Boston: 1854. V. 39

The Poetical and Dramatic Works of . . . London: 1877. V. 46

The Complete Poetical Works . . . Oxford: 1912. V. 42

Remorse. London: 1813. V. 38; 41; 45

Remorse. New York: 1813. V. 42

The Rime of the Ancient Mariner. London. V. 38

The Rime of the Ancient Mariner in Seven Parts. London. V. 45

The Rime of the Ancient Mariner in Seven Parts. London. V. 41

The Rime of the Ancient Mariner. London. V. 40

The Rhyme of the Ancient Mariner. London: 1863. V. 40

Coleridge's Ancient Mariner. Boston: 1864. V. 42

The Rime of the Ancient Mariner . . . London: 1875. V. 45

The Rime of the Ancient Mariner. London: 1899. V. 38; 41; 42; 44

The Rime of the Ancient Mariner. 1903. V. 40

The Rime of the Ancient Mariner. 1903. V. 45

The Rime of the Ancient Mariner. Campden: 1903. V. 41

The Rhyme of the Ancient Mariner. London: 1910. V. 45

The Rime of the Ancient Mariner. London: 1910. V. 37; 41; 42; 44

The Rime of the Ancient Mariner, in Seven Parts. London: 1910. V. 46

The Rime of the Ancient Mariner. New York: 1910. V. 40

The Rime of the Ancient Mariner . . . New York: 1928? V. 42

The Rime of the Ancient Mariner. 1929. V. 38

The Rime of the Ancient Mariner. 1929. V. 40

The Rime of the Ancient Mariner. Bristol: 1929. V. 37; 38; 39; 40; 41; 42; 44

The Rime of the Ancient Mariner. London: 1930. V. 40

The Ancient Mariner. Oxford: 1930. V. 45

The Rime of the Ancient Mariner. Oxford: 1930. V. 38; 40; 42; 45

The Ancient Mariner. London: 1943. V. 40

The Rime of the Ancient Mariner. London: 1945. V. 38; 43

The Rime of Ancient Mariner. New York: 1945. V. 40

The Rime of the Ancient Mariner. New York: 1945. V. 44

The Rime of the Ancient Mariner. New York: 1946. V. 43

The Rime of the Ancient Mariner. London: 1972. V. 46

The Rime of the Ancient Mariner. New York: 1874. V. 37

The Rime of the Ancient Mariner. East Aurora: 1899. V. 37

The Rime of the Ancient Mariner. In Seven Parts. London: (n.d.). V. 37

Selected Poems. 1935. V. 43

Selected Poems. London: 1935. V. 37; 38; 44; 45; 46

Selected Poems. 1988. V. 45

Selected Poems. 1988. V. 40

Seven Lectures On Shakespeare and Milton. London: 1856. V. 39

Sibylline Leaves. London: 1817. V. 39; 40; 42; 43; 46

Specimens of the Table Talk of the Late . . . London: 1835. V. 38; 39; 42; 46

Specimens of the Table Talk of the Late Samuel Taylor Coleridge. New York: 1835. V. 44

Specimens of the Table Talk of Samuel Taylor Coleridge. London: 1836. V. 39; 40

The Statesman's Manual; or the Bible the Best Guide to Political Skills and Foresight. London: 1816. V. 38; 39; 42

The Statesman's Manual . . . V. 44

The Statesman's Manual . . . A Lay Sermon. Burlington: 1832. V. 38

The Complete Works. New York: 1856. V. 40

Zapolya: a Christmas Tale. London: 1817. V. 38; 39; 40; 45

COLERIDGE, SARA 1802-1852

Memoir and Letters. London: 1873. V. 39; 42

Phantasmion. London: 1837. V. 39; 42; 43; 44

Phantasmion: Prince of Palmland. New York: 1839. V. 40; 43

Phantasmion. A Fairy Tale. Boston: 1874. V. 41; 43; 45

Phantasmion. London: 1874. V. 39

The Right Joyous and Pleasant History of the Feats, Gests and Prowesses of the Chevalier Bayard. London: 1825. V. 38

COLERUS, JOHN

The Life of Benedict de Spinosa. London: 1706. V. 39

COLES, BENJAMIN

A Memoir on the Subject of the Wheat and Flour of the State of New York . . . New York: 1820. V. 45

COLES, C.

An English Dictionary . . . London: 1732. V. 40

Game Birds. London: 1981. V. 42; 43; 45

COLES, ELISHA

A Dictionary, English-Latin, Latin-English containing all things Necessary for the Translation of either Language into the Other, the eleventh edition corrected. London: 1727. V. 37

An English Dictionary . . . London: 1676. V. 43

An English Dictionary, Explaining the Difficult Terms That are Used . . . London: 1692. V. 41; 43

An English Dictionary . . . London: 1701. V. 43

An English Dictionary, Explaining the Difficult Terms . . . London: 1701. V. 41

An English Dictionary, Explaining the Difficult Terms that Are Used in Divinity, Husbandry, Physick, Philosophy, Law, Navigation, Mathematicks and Other Arts and Sciences. London: 1732. V. 42

A Practical Discourse of God's Sovereignty: With Other Material Points Dervied Thence . . . London: 1788. V. 37

COLES, JOHN

Summer Travelling in Iceland. London: 1882. V. 40

COLES, W.

Adam in Eden; or, Nature's Paradise. The History of Plants, Fruits, Herbs and Flowers . . . London: 1657. V. 37

COLETI, GIOVANNI DOMENICO

Dizionario Storico-Geografico dell'America Meridionale. Venice: 1771. V. 46

COLETTE, SIDONIE GABRIELLE 1873-1954

Barks and Purrs. New York: 1913. V. 40

Break of day. 1983. V. 40

Break of Day. New York: 1983. V. 38; 39; 41; 45

Dialogues de Betes. Paris: 1904. V. 39

L'Ingenue Libertine. Monte Carlo: 1947. V. 46

La Naissance du Jour. Paris: 1928. V. 45

Oeuvres Completes. Paris: 1948-50. V. 46

The Pure and the Impure. New York: 1933. V. 45

La Vagabonde. Paris: 1923. V. 37

COLETTI, SEBASTIANO

Catalogus Librorum . . . Catalogi di Libri Italiani . . . Catalogue des Livres Francois . . . Venice: 1783. V. 46

COLGAN, NATHANIEL

Flora of the County Dublin: Flowering Plants, Higher Cryptogams, and Characeae. (and) Supplement . . . Dublin: 1904/61. V. 39; 42; 43

COLGATE, WILLIAM

Horace Walpole on Milton. Toronto: 1953. V. 44

Horace Walpole on Milton. A Summary of His Annotations on the Work of Thomas Warton concerning the Poems of John Milton from the London edition of James Dodsley 1785. Toronto: 1953. V. 37; 44

COLGNEY, R. I.

Izaak Walton: a New Bibliography 1653-1987. New York: 1989. V. 45

COLIN, ALEXANDER

Historical Illustrations of Lord Byron's Works in a Series of Etchings by Reveil from Original Paintings by A. Colin. London: 1835. V. 41

COLLADO, FRAY DIEGO

Fray Diego Collado de la Orden de Santo Domingo, Procurador General Por la Provincia de Japon, Filipinas, y China . . . Madrid: 1629. V. 40

Fray Diego Collado de la Orden de Predicadores . . . Madrid: 1631. V. 40

COLLADO, LUIS

Platica Manual de Artilleria. Milan: 1592. V. 46

COLLAERT, ADRIEN

Icones Sanctae Clarae . . . Antwerp: 1600. V. 46

COLLAMORE, HARRY BACON

Edwin Arlington Robinson 1869-1935. A Collection of His Works from the Library of Bacon Collamore. Hartford: 1936. V. 41; 44

COLLARD, ALLAN OVENDEN

The Oyster Dredgers of Whitstable. London: 1902. V. 42

COLLECTANEA Chymica: a Collection of Ten several Treatises in Chymistry, concerning the Liquor Alkahest, the Mercury of Philosophers and Other Curiosities Worthy the Perusal. Philadelphia. V. 46

COLLECTEANA Adamantea XV; The Un-Natural History, or Myths of Ancient Science. Edinburgh;: 1886. V. 39

COLLECTIO Eorum Quae Secreto et Alias in Missae Sacrificio Fere Communiter Dicuntur. Rome: 1576. V. 38

COLLECTION Completes des Tableaux Historiques de la Revolution Francaise. Paris: 1804. V. 39; 40

COLLECTION de Peintures Antiques qui Ornoient les Palais Thermes, Mausolees . . . des Empereurs, tan a Rome qu'aux Environs. Rome: 1781. V. 44

A COLLECTION of Above Three Hundred Receipts in Cookery, Physick and Surgery. London: 1719. V. 40

A COLLECTION of Acts of Parliament, Relative to Those Protestant Dissenters Who are Usually Called by the Name of Quakers, from the Year 1688. London: 1757. V. 39; 44

A COLLECTION of all Such Statutes and Parts of Statutes as Any Way Relate to the Admiralty, Navy and Ships of War. London: 1742. V. 40

A COLLECTION of All Such Statutes, and Parts of Statutes, As Any Way Relate to the Admiralty, Navy and Ships of War, and Other Incidental Matters . . . London: 1755. V. 40

A COLLECTION Of All the Letters Which Have Appeared in the Newcastle Papers with Other Documents Relating to the Safety Lamps. Newcastle printed: 1817. V. 45

A COLLECTION of all the Publicke Orders Ordinances and Declarations of Both Houses of Parliament, from the Ninth of March 1642 Until December 1646. London: 1646. V. 43

A COLLECTION of all the Statues now in force, relating to the excise on beer, ale and other liquors; with an Abridgment of the siad Statues and a Table of the Tares upon the several Liquors . . . London: 1722-30. V. 37

A COLLECTION of all the Statutes Now in Force, Relating to the Excise Upon Beer, Ale, and Other Liquors . . . Edinburgh: 1704. V. 41

A COLLECTION of all The Treaties of Peace, Alliance, and Commerce Between Great-Britain and Other Powers, from the Treaty Signed at Munster in 1648, to the Treaties Signed at Paris in 1783. London: 1785. V. 44

A COLLECTION of Anthems, as The Same Are Now Performed in His Majesty's Chapels Royal . . . London: 1736. V. 44

A COLLECTION of Antique Prints in Europe: Sarasa & Paisley. Japan: 1970's. V. 43

A COLLECTION of Book Plate Designs by Louis Rhead. Boston: 1907. V. 37

A COLLECTION of Bookplates from the Libraries of Hugo, Rollins, Johnson, Anderson, Allen, Alcorn, Finch, Emery, Rudge. (Connecticut): 1938. V. 37

A COLLECTION of Cases and Other Discourses Lately Written to Recover Dissenters to the Communion of the Church of England. London: 1698. V. 39

A COLLECTION of Declarations, Proclamations and Other Valuable Papers. N.P.: 1746. V. 42

A COLLECTION of English Songs, with an Appendix of Original Pieces. London: 1796. V. 42; 45

COLLECTION of Epigrams. To which is Prefix'd, a Critical Dissertation on this Species of Poetry. London: 1727. V. 38

A COLLECTION of Famous Paintings of the Sung Dynasty Forerly Preserved by the Tien Lai Studio. (Shanghai): (ca. 1960). V. 37; 45

A COLLECTION of Hymns and Psalms . . . Selected and Prepared by Andrew Kippis (and others). London: 1825. V. 41

A COLLECTION of Hymns of the Children of God in All Ages. London: 1754. V. 37

A COLLECTION of Letters Relative to Foreign Missions . . . Andover: 1810. V. 45

A COLLECTION of Loyal Songs Written Against the Rump Parliament, Between the Years 1639 and 1661. London: 1731. V. 39; 43; 45

COLLECTION of Memoires et de Relations sur l'Histoire Ancienne du Canada, d'Apres des manuscrits Recemment Obtenus des Archives et Bureaux Publics en France. Quebec: 1840. V. 39

A COLLECTION of Memorials Concerning Divers Deceased Ministers and Others of the People Called Quakers, in Pennsylvania, New Jersey, and Parts Adjacent, From Nearly the First Settlement Thereof to the Year 1787 . . . Philadelphia: 1787. V. 41; 42; 44

A COLLECTION of Modern and Contemporary Voyages and Travels. London: 1805-10. V. 46

COLLECTION of Odes, Songs and Epigrams, Against the Whigs, Alias the Blue and Buff . . . London: 1790. V. 46

A COLLECTION of Papers Relative to Half-Pay, and the Commutation Thereof, Granted by Congress to the Officers of the Army. Together with a Circular Letter, from His Excellency General Washington . . . Boston: 1783. V. 39; 40; 44

COLLECTION of Poems Relating to State Affairs From Oliver Cromwell to this Present Time . . . London: 1705. V. 44

A COLLECTION of Poems: viz. The Temple of Death; by the Marquis of Normanby. An Epistle . . . by Charles Montagu . . . The Duel of Stags: by Sir Robert Howard. With Several Original Poems, Never Before Printed, by Roscommon, Rochester, Orrery . . . Dryden &c . . . London: 1701. V. 39

A COLLECTION of Poems: viz. The Temple of Death: by the Marquis of Normanby. An Epistle to the Earl of Dorset: by Charles Montague, Lord Halifax . . . With Several Original Poems, Never Before Printed, by the E. of Roscommon. The E. of Rochester . . . . London: 1701. V. 39; 41; 45

A COLLECTION Of Poems: viz. The Temple of Death (etc). London: 1702. V. 39

A COLLECTION of Poems, Written Upon Several Occasions. London: 1672. V. 39

A COLLECTION of Poetry, Scared and Moral, for the Use of Schools. Yarmouth: 1804. V. 39

A COLLECTION of Right Merrie Garlands . . . Newcastle: 1820-45. V. 37

A COLLECTION of Scarce and Valuable Tracts on the Most Interesting and Entertaining Subjects . . . from . . . the Royal, Cotton, Sion and Other Publick, as well as Private Libraries . . . London: 1748. V. 45

A COLLECTION of Scarce and Valuable Treatises Upon Metals, Mines and Minerals. London: 1738. V. 44

A COLLECTION of Scarce and Valuable Treatises Upon Metals, Mines and Minerals . . . London: 1740. V. 40; 42; 43; 45

A COLLECTION of Scarce, Curious and Valuable Pieces, Both in Verse and Prose . . . Edinburgh: 1773. V. 44

A COLLECTION of Select Moral Sentences; extracted from the Greatest Authors, Ancient and Modern: and Digested under proper Heads. London: 1776. V. 37

A COLLECTION Of Several Papers Relating to Elizabeth Canning. London: 1754. V. 46

A COLLECTION of Some Writings of the Most Noted of the People Called Quakers in Their Times. Philadelphia: 1767. V. 39; 41

A COLLECTION of Songs. Edinburgh: 1762. V. 41; 43

COLLECTION of Sundry Publications, and Other Documents, in Relation to the Attack Made During the Late War Upon the Private Armed Brig General Armstrong, of New York, Commanded by S. C. Reid, on the Night of the 26th of September, 1814, at the Island . . . New York: 1833. V. 42

A COLLECTION of the Laws Relating to the Ordnance. London: 1774. V. 40

A COLLECTION of the Several Statutes, and Parts of Statutes, Now in Force, Relating to High Treason, and Misprision of High Treason. London: 1709. V. 40; 46

A COLLECTION of the Statutes Relating to the Admiralty, Navy, Ships of War, and Incidental Matters; to the 8th Year of King George III. London: 1768. V. 40

A COLLECTION of Tracts, Concerning the Present State of Ireland, With Respect to Its Riches, Revenues, Trade and Manufacture. London: 1729. V. 41

A COLLECTION of Twenty-Eight Sermons and Two Related Works. London/Oxford: 1679-1693. V. 37

A COLLECTION of Voyages and Travels, Some Now First Printed from Original Manuscripts, Others Now First Published in English. London: 1732. V. 46

A COLLECTION Of Voyages Undertaken by the Dutch East India Company, for the Improvement of Trade and Navigation. London: 1703. V. 42

A COLLECTION of Welsh Tours; or, a Display of the Beauties of Wales. London: 1798. V. 44

A COLLECTIONS of Voyages and Travels, some Now Printed from the Original Manuscripts. London: 1704. V. 44

THE COLLECTS Proper to the Sundays and Holydays of the Christian Year . . . Rendered inot Latin Verses by Reginald Walter Macan. Oxford: 1928. V. 42

COLLEDGE, J. J.

Ships of the Royal Navy. London: 1987/89. V. 46

COLLEGIATE CHURCH OF ELY

The Statutes of the Collegiate Church of Ely . . . London: 1817. V. 44

COLLEGIO Sopra Boschi. Terminazione del Giorno 16. Decembre 1777. Per la Custodia, Disciplina, e Coltura Dei Boschi Della Provincia Dell'Istria. Venice: 1778. V. 39

COLLEN, GEORGE WILLIAM

Britannia Saxonica. London: 1833. V. 38

COLLENETTE, A.

An Illustrated Guide to the Flowers of Saudi AArabia. London: 1985. V. 38

COLLENUCCIO, PANDOLFO

Apologus: cui Titulus Agenoria . . . (with) Alithia. Leipzig: 1506. V. 38

COLLES, ABRAHAM

Selections from the Works of Abraham Colles . . . London: 1891. V. 38; 41; 42; 45

COLLES, CHRISTOPHER

An Account of the Astonishing Beauties and Operations of Nature, in the Minute Creation . . . New York: 1816. V. 41

COLLET, STEPHEN

Relics of Literature. London: 1823. V. 43

A COLLETION of the Most Remarkable and Interesting Trials. Particulary of those Persons who have Forfeited their Lives to the injured Laws of their Country. In which the most Remarkable of the State Trials will be Included . . . London: 1775-76. V. 37

COLLETTA, PIETRO

History of the Kingdom of Naples 1734-1825. Edinburgh: 1858. V. 41

COLLIADO, LUIGI

Prattica manuale Della' Artiglieria, Opera Historica, Politica, E Militare . . . Milano: 1641. V. 38

COLLIBER, SAMUEL

Columna Rostrata: or, A Critical History of the English Sea-Affairs. London: 1727. V. 38; 41

COLLIE, J. NORMAN

Climbing on the Himalaya and Other Mountain Ranges. Edinburgh: 1902. V. 42

COLLIER, J. D.

The Life of Abraham Newland, Late Principal Cashier at the Bank of England . . . London: 1808. V. 39

COLLIER, J. P.

The History of English Dramatic Poetry to the Time of Shakespeare and Annals of the Stage. London: 1831. V. 39

COLLIER, JANE

An Essay on the Art of Ingeniously Tormenting; with Proper Rules for the Exercise of the Pleasnant Art, Humbly addressed, in the First Part, to the Master, Husband, &c. In the Second Part, to the Wife, Friend, etc. With some General Instructions . . . London: 1753. V. 38; 40; 42; 43; 44; 45

An Essay on the Art of Ingeniously Tormenting . . . London: 1757. V. 42

An Essay on the Art of Ingeniously Tormenting. London: 1809. V. 37; 39

COLLIER, JEREMY 1650-1726

A Defence of the Reasons for Restoring Some Prayers and Directions of King Edward the Sixth's First Liturgy. London: 1718. V. 39

A Defense of the Short View of the Profaness and Immorality of the English State, etc. London: 1699. V. 37; 42; 43

An Ecclesiastical History of Great Britain Chiefly of England, from the First Planting of Christinaity to the End of the Reign of King Charles II, With a Brief Account of the Affairs of Religion in Ireland . . . London: 1708-14. V. 39

An Essay Upon Gaming.Times. London: 1713. V. 38

An Essay Upon Gaming in a Dialogue Between Callimachus and Dolomedes. Edinburgh: 1885. V. 39

Essays Upon Several Moral Subjects. London: 1698. V. 40; 43

Essays Upon Several Moral Subjects . . . London: 1700. V. 42; 44; 46

Essays Upon Several Moral Subjects. (with) Essays Upon Several Moral Subjects Part III. London: 1703, 1705. V. 39

Essays Upon Several Subjects. (with) Essays..Part III. London: 1703/02/05. V. 38

The Great Historical, Geographical, Genealogical and Poetical Dictionary . . . London: 1701/27/21. V. 39

Miscellanies: in Five Essays (with: Miscealnies upon Moral Subjects. the Second Part). London: 1694-95. V. 44; 46

Mr. Collier's Dissuasive from the Play House . . . London: 1704. V. 42

A Second Defence of the Short View of the Profaness and Immorality of the English Stage. London: 1700. V. 42; 43

A Short View of the Immorality, and Profaneness of the English Stage. (with) A Defence of the Short View . . . Being a Reply to Mr. Congreve's Amendments. (with) A Second Defence. London: 1698-1700. V. 38

A Short View of the Immorality and Profaneness of the English Stage . . . London: 1699. V. 42

A Short View of the Profaness and Immorality of the English Stage, etc. London: 1728. V. 42

A Short View of the Immorality and Profaneness of the English Stage: Together with the Sense of Antiquity upon this Argument. The Second Edition. London: 1698. V. 37; 38; 39; 41; 42; 45; 46

Some Thoughts Concerning the Stage in a Letter to a Lady. London: 1704. V. 37

A Supplement to the Great Historical, Geographical, Genealogical and Poetical Dictionary . . . London: 1727. V. 42

COLLIER, JOHN 1901-

Defy the Foul Fiend. London: 1934. V. 38

Defy the Fowl Fiend. New York: 1934. V. 42; 43; 45

The Devil and All. London: 1934. V. 42

Gemini. 1931. V. 37

Gemini. London: 1931. V. 42

Green Thoughts. 1932. V. 40; 42; 44

His Monkey Wife or, Married to a Chimp. London: 1920. V. 39

His Monkey Wife, or Married to a Chimp. London: 1930. V. 37; 42; 44

His Monkey Wife. 1931. V. 43

His Monkey Wife. 1931. V. 43

His Monkey Wife. New York: 1931. V. 37; 40; 45

His Monkey Wife or Married to a Chimp. London: 1969. V. 40

The Lancashire Dialect . . . London: 1785? V. 42

The Miscellaneous Works of Tim Bobbon Esq. Containing His View of the Lancashire Dialect . . . London: 1791. V. 39

No Traveller Returns. London: 1931. V. 44

Patterns and Ceremonials of the Indians of the Southwest. New York: 1949. V. 44

Presenting Moonshine. New York: 1941. V. 41

Presenting Moonshine - Stories. London: 1947. V. 45

Shadows Which Haunt the Sun Rain. New York: 1917? V. 39

Tim Bobbon's Lancashire Dialect; and Poems. London: 1828. V. 38; 40; 43

Tim Bobbon's Lancashire Dialect; and Poems. London: 1833. V. 40

Tom's A-Cold. London: 1933. V. 37; 38; 39

A View of the Lancashire Dialect; By Way of Dialogue; Between Tummus o'Williams, of Margit o'Dicks, o'Tummy o'Peggy's. London: 1775. V. 43

A View of the Lancashire Dialect . . . London: c. 1800? V. 41; 43

Witch's Money. New York: 1940. V. 39; 44

COLLIER, JOHN D.

The Life of Abraham Newland, Esq. London: 1808. V. 42

COLLIER, JOHN PAYNE

Criticisms on the Bar; Including Strictures on the Principal Counsel Practising in the Courts of King's Bench . . . London: 1819. V. 40; 43

The History of English Dramatic Poetry to the Time of Shakespeare and Annals of the Stage to the Restoration. London: 1831. V. 42; 43

The Poetical Decameron, or Ten Conversations on English Poets and Poetry. Edinburgh: 1820. V. 40; 43

Punch and Judy. London: 1828. V. 38; 42; 43

Punch and Judy. New York: 1937. V. 40; 44

COLLIER, JOHN PAYNE continued

Shakespeare's Library: a Collection of Romances, Novels and Histories, Used by Shakespeare as the Foundation of His Drama. London: 1840-41. V. 43

COLLIER, JON

Patterns and Ceremonials of the Indians of the Southwest. New York: 1949. V. 37

COLLIER, MARY

The Woman's Labour. London: 1739. V. 41

COLLIER, V. W. F.

Dogs of China and Japan in nature and Art. New York: 1921. V. 39

COLLIER, W. V. F.

Dogs of China and Japan in Nature and Art. New York: 1920. V. 38

COLLIER, WILLIAM FRANCIS

The International Atlas . . . New York: 1872. V. 45

COLLIGNON, CHARLES

The Miscellaneous Works of Charles Collignon, M.D. Cambridge: 1786. V. 38; 39; 40; 41; 45; 46

The Miscellaneous Works of Charles Collignon, M.D . . . Cambridge: 1786. V. 37

Moral and Medical Dialogues. Cambridge: 1769. V. 38

COLLIN, M.

A Short Treatise on the Different Methods of Investigating the Diseases of the Chest. Boston: 1829. V. 40

COLLIN, W. E.

Clockmaker of Souls. New York: 1933. V. 43

The White Savannahs. Toronto: 1936. V. 43

COLLING, JAMES KELLAWAY

Examples of English Mediaeval Foliage and Coloured Decoration, Taken from Buildings of the Twelfth to the Fifteenth Century, by James Kellaway Colling. London: 1874. V. 37; 39

COLLINGE, W. E.

The Food of Some British Wild Birds. London: 1913. V. 43

The Food of Some British Wild Birds. York: 1924-27. V. 38; 40

COLLINGS, ELLSWORTH

The 101 Ranch. Norman: 1937. V. 43; 46

COLLINGWOOD, CUTHBERT

Rambles of a Naturalist on the Shores and Waters of the China Sea. London: 1868. V. 37; 43; 45

COLLINGWOOD, CUTHBERT, LORD

A Selection from the Public and Private Correspondence of Vice-Admiral Lord Collingwood . . . London: 1837. V. 46

COLLINGWOOD, FRANCIS

The Universal Cook & City and Country Housekeeper. London: 1801. V. 37

COLLINGWOOD, G. L. NEWNHAM

A Selection from the Public and Private Correspondence of Vice-Admiral Lord Collingwood. London: 1828. V. 40

A Selection from the Public and Private Correspondence of Vice Admiral Lord Collingwood. New York: 1829. V. 40

COLLINGWOOD, STUART DODGSON

The Life and Letters of Lewis Carroll. London: 1898. V. 40

COLLINGWOOD, W. G.

The Life and Work of John Ruskin. London: 1893. V. 40

COLLINGWOOD, WILLIAM GERSHOLM

Northumbrian Crosses of the Pre-Norman Age. London: 1927. V. 38; 45; 46

A Pilgrimage to the Saga-Steads of Iceland. Ulverston: 1899. V. 38

COLLINS, A. FREDERICK

Experimental Television, a Series of Simple Experiments with Television Apparatus Also How to Make a Complete Home Television Transmitter and Television Receiver. Boston: 1932. V. 38

COLLINS, ALPHEUS R.

The Second Texas Bonanza Struck. Denison: 1875. V. 44; 45

COLLINS, ANGELINA MARIA LORRAINE

Mrs. Collins Table Receipts; Adpated to Western Housewifery. New Albnay: 1851. V. 45

COLLINS, ANTHONY 1676-1729

Discours sur la Liberte de Penser. Londres: 1714. V. 39; 45

A Discourse on Free-Thinking Occasion'd by the Rise and Growth of a Sect Call'd Ree-Thinkers. London: 1713. V. 37; 38; 39

A Discourse of the Grounds and Reasons of the Christian Religion. 1724. V. 42

The Independent Whig; or, a Defence of Primitive Christianity, and of Our Ecclesiastical Establishment, Against the Exorbitant Claims and Encroachments of Fanatical and Disaffected Clergymen. London: 1732. V. 41

The Life and Glorious Actions of Edward Prince of Wales . . . London: 1740. V. 39

A Philosophical Inquiry Concerning Human Liberty. London: 1717. V. 41; 42; 45

A Philosophical Inquiry Concerning Human Liberty. Birmingham: 1790. V. 42

COLLINS, ARTHUR

Historical Collections of the Noble Families of Cavendishe, Holles, Vere, Harley and Ogle with the Lives of the Most Remarkable Persons, Particularly of William Cavendishe, Duke of Newcastle. London: 1752. V. 45

The Life of the Great Statesman William Cecil, Lord Burghley, Secretary of State in the Reign of King Edward the Sixth and Lord High Treasurer of England in the Reign of Queen Elizabeth. London: 1732. V. 46

The Peerage of England. London: 1709. V. 40

The Peerage of England; or, an Historical and Genealogical Account of the Present Nobility. London: 1710-14. V. 43

The Peerage of England. (with) A Supplement to . . . London: 1735, 1760. V. 38

The Peerage of England, Containing a Genealogical and Historical Account of all the Peers of that Kingdom, Now Exisiting Either by Tenure, Summons, or Creation. London: 1779. V. 39

Proceedings, Precedents and Arguments, on Claims and Controversies, Concerning Baronies by Writ and Other Honours. London: 1734. V. 38; 40

COLLINS BAKER, C. H.

Lely & the Stuart Portrait Painters. A Study of English Portraiture Before and After Van Dyck. London: 1912. V. 39

COLLINS, CECIL

In the Solitude of This Land - Poems 1940-81. Ipswich: 1981. V. 41; 43

The Vision of the Fool. London: 1947. V. 40

COLLINS, CHARLES

Juvenile Blossoms. London: 1823. V. 37

COLLINS, CHARLES ALLSTON

A Cruise Upon Wheels: the Chronicle of Some Autumn Wanderings Among the Deserted Post-Roads of France. 1862. V. 40

A New Sentimental Journey. London: 1859. V. 44

COLLINS, CHARLES PALK

Notes on the Chase of the Wild Red Deer in Devon & Somerset. London: 1862. V. 37

COLLINS, DAVID

An Account of the English Colony, in New South Wales . . . London: 1798. V. 42

An Account of the English Colony in New South Wales . . . to Which are Added Some Particulars of New Zealand . . . London: 1804. V. 39

COLLINS, DENNIS

The Indians' Last Fight, Or, the Dull Knife Raid. Girard, Kansas: 1915. V. 37; 45

COLLINS, EDMUND

Annette, the Metis Spy; a Heroine of the N.W. Rebellion. Toronto: 1886. V. 44

COLLINS, FRANCIS

Voyages to Portugal, Spain Sicily, Malta, Asia-Minor, Egypt &c. Philadelphia: 1809. V. 40

COLLINS, GREENVILLE

Cartes et Plans de Plusieurs Parties des Cotes d'angleterre, D'Ecosse et D'irlande, Copiees sur celles du Pilote Cotier de la Grande-Bretagne, de Greenville-Collins. N.P.: 1757. V. 39

COLLINS, HILDA C.

My Guardian, a Novel. San Antonio: 1902. V. 38

COLLINS, HUBERT E.

Warpath and Cattle Trail. New York: 1928. V. 45

COLLINS, J. E.

The Story of Louis Riel the Rebel Chief. Whitby: 1885. V. 37; 42

COLLINS, JOHN

The City and Scenery of Newport, Rhode Island. Burlington: 1857. V. 39; 40

COLLINS, JOHN continued

Geometricall Dyalling: or, Dyalling performed by a Line of Chords only, or, by the Plain Scale . . . being a full Explication and Demonstration of divers difficulties in the Works of Learned Mr. Samuel Foster deceased . . . . London: 1659. V. 37

COLLINS, JOHN A.

The Anti-Slavery Picknick; a Collection of Speeches, Poems, Dialogues and Songs . . . Boston: 1842. V. 42

COLLINS, JOHN S.

Across the Plains in '64. Omaha: 1904. V. 41; 44; 45

Across the Plains in '64. Omaha: 1904, 1911. V. 37; 40; 41; 42

COLLINS, JOSEPH

The Genesis and Dissolution of the Faculty of Speech: A Clinical and Psychological Study of Aphasia. New York: 1898. V. 42

Neurological Clinics Exercise in the Diagnosis of Diseases of the Nervous System. New York: 1918. V. 40

COLLINS, MR.

The Chapter of Kings. London: 1818. V. 41

COLLINS, MORTIMER

Miranda: a Midsummer Madness. London: 1873. V. 41; 43

Pen Sketches, by a Vanished Hand: from the Papers of the Late Mortimer Collins. London: 1879. V. 46

Squire Silchester's Whim. London: 1873. V. 43; 45; 46

Sweet Anne Page. London: 1868. V. 41; 43

Thoughts in My Garden. London: 1880. V. 43

COLLINS, PERRY MCDONOUGH

A Voyage down the Amoor: with a Land Journey through Siberia, and incidental notices of Manchooria, Kamschatka, and Japan. New York: 1860. V. 37; 40; 41; 44

COLLINS, R. M.

Chapters from the Unwritten History of the War; or, the Incidents in the Life of a Confederate Soldier in Camp, on the March, in the Great Battles and in Prison. St. Louis: 1893. V. 46

COLLINS, SAMUEL

Paradise Retriev'd . . . London: 1717. V. 40; 41

COLLINS, THOMAS B.

With the 114th Machine Gun Battalion 1917-1919. Tennessee: 1931. V. 41

COLLINS, VICTOR

Attempt at a Catalogue of the Library of Prince Louis Lucien Bonaparte. London: 1894. V. 38; 40

COLLINS, W. J. T.

The Romance of the Echoing Wood. Newport: 1927. V. 40

The Romance of the Echoing Wood. Newport: 1937. V. 43

COLLINS, WILKIE 1824-1889

After Dark. London: 1856. V. 40

Antonina; or, the Fall of Rome. London: 1850. V. 43

Armadale. 1866. V. 39

Armadale. A Novel. New York: 1866. V. 44

Blind Love. London: 1890. V. 38

The Dead Secret. London: 1875. V. 40

The Frozen Deep. Boston: 1875. V. 46

The Frozen Deep and Other Tales. London: 1875. V. 39

The Frozen Deep. Boston: 1875, 1874. V. 40

The Frozen Deep and Other Stories. London: 1874. V. 37; 42; 45

The Haunted Hotel. Toronto: 1878. V. 39

The Haunted Hotel: a Mystery of Modern Venice . . . London: 1879 (1878). V. 46

Heart and Science. London: 1883. V. 38; 40; 43

The Law and the Lady. Toronto: 1875. V. 37; 39; 40; 42

Man and Wife. London: 1870. V. 46

Man and Wife. New York: 1870. V. 38; 40

Memoirs of His Father: Wilkie Collins' First Book. Memoirs of the Life of William Collins, Esq., R.A. with selections from his journals and correspondence. By his son. London: 1848. V. 37; 39; 43

Miss or Mrs.? A Christmas Story, in Twelve Scenes. London: 1871. V. 46

Mr. Wray's Cash Box. London: 1852. V. 38; 44; 46

The Moonstone. London: 1868. V. 39; 40; 42; 43

The Moonstone. New York: 1868. V. 44; 45

The Moonstone. London: 1871. V. 46

The Moonstone. London: 1894. V. 46

My Miscellanies. London: 1863. V. 40; 41

The New Magdalen. London: 1873. V. 40

No Name. London: 1862. V. 37; 38; 42; 44; 46

No Name. London: 1862. V. 46

No Name. Boston: 1863. V. 39; 43; 45; 46

No Name. London: 1863. V. 41

No Name. New York: 1863. V. 39; 40; 43; 45; 46

Poor Miss Finch. A Novel. London: 1872. V. 37

The Queen of Hearts. London: 1862. V. 46

Rambles Beyond Railways. London: 1851. V. 38; 45

Rambles Beyond Railways; or, Notes in Cornwall Taken A-Foot. London: 1852. V. 45

Rambles Beyond Railways; or, Notes in Cornwall Taken a-foot. London: 1861. V. 46

A Rogue's Life. London: 1879. V. 46

The Two Destinies. London: 1876. V. 38

The Two Destinies; a Romance. London: 1888. V. 40

The Woman in White. London: 1860. V. 37; 38; 39; 42; 43

The Woman in White. New York: 1860. V. 39; 42; 46

The Woman in White. London: 1861. V. 39; 43; 45

The Woman in White. New York: 1861. V. 43

The Works of Wilkie Collins. New York: 1890. V. 46

Works. London: 1890-1896. V. 37; 41; 42

The Works. New York: 1895. V. 42

COLLINS, WILLIAM 1721-1759

Odes on Several Descriptive and Allegoric Subjects. London: 1747. V. 45

Odes on Several Descriptive and Allegoric Subjects. London: 1747. V. 38

Odes on Several Descriptive and Allegoric Subjects. London: 1747. V. 40

Odes On Several Descriptive and Allegoric Subjects. London: 1747, 1746. V. 40

Persian Eclogues. London: 1742. V. 38

Persian Eclogues. London: 1742. V. 43

The Poems of William Collins. London: 1929. V. 37

The Poetical Works . . . with Memoirs of the Author; and Observations on His Genius and Writings. London: 1765. V. 41

The Poetical Works. Glasgow: 1787. V. 44

The Poetical Works of . . . London: 1798. V. 44

The Poetical Works of William Collins. London: 1827. V. 41

Poetical Works. London: 1853. V. 39

COLLINS, WILLIAM JOHN TOWNSEND 1868-

The Romance of the Echoing Wood. Newport: 1937. V. 39

COLLINSON, JOHN 1757?-1793

The Beauties of British Antiquity . . . London: 1779. V. 37; 43

The History and Antiquities of the County of Somerset. Bath: 1791. V. 38

The Life of Thuanus, with Some Account of His Writings. London: 1807. V. 39

COLLINSON, RICHARD

The China Pilot. London: 1855. V. 45

Journal of H.M.S. Enterprise, on the Expedition In Search of Sir John Franklin's Ships by Behring Strait, 1850-55, with a Memoir of His Other Services. London: 1889. V. 43; 46

COLLIS, EDGAR

The Health of the Industrial Worker. Philadelphia: 1921. V. 45

COLLIS, MAURICE

Quest for Sita of Ravana the Dark Angel and His Paradise at Lanka . . . London: 1946. V. 40; 43

COLLIS, SEPTIMA MARIA 1842-1917

A Woman's Trip to Alaska: Being an account of a voyage through the Inland Seas of the Sitkan Archipelago in 1890. New York: (1890). V. 37; 38; 43; 45

COLLISON, GEORGE

Cemetery Interment, containing . . . Descriptions of the English Metropolitan and Provincial Cemeteries, and More Particularly of the Abney Park Cemetery at Stoke Newington. London: 1840. V. 45

COLLISON-MORLEY, L.

Giuseppe Baretti. London: 1909. V. 39

COLLISON, W. H.

In the Wake of the War Canoe. Toronto: 1915. V. 37

A COLLLECTION of Poems: viz. The Temple of Death: by the Marquis of Normandy. An Epistle to the Earl of Dorset: By Charles Montague, Lord Halifax. The Duel of the Stags: by Sir Robert Howard. With Several Original Poems, Never Before Printed. London: 1701. V. 37

COLLMAN, H. L.

Ballads & broadsides chiefly of the Elizabethan Period and printed in black letter most of which were formerly in the Heber Collection and are now in the Library at Britwell Court Buckinghamshire. Oxford: 1912. V. 37

COLLMANN, HERBERT L.

Ballads and Broadsides Chiefly of the Elizabethan Period and Printed in Black-Letter Most of Which were Formerly in the Heber Collection and Are Now in the Library at Britwell Court, Bucks. Oxford: 1912. V. 38; 45

COLLON, DOMINIQUE

Catalogue of the Western Asiatic Seals in the British Museum: Cylinder Seals III. London: 1986. V. 42

COLLOQUIA et Distionariolum Octo Linguarum. Venice: 1656. V. 46

COLLUM, RICHARD S.

History of the United States Marine Corps. Philadelphia: 1890. V. 41; 42

COLLURAFFI, ANTONIO

Il Nobile Veneto. Venice: 1623. V. 43

COLLYER, JAMES N.

An Historical Record of the Light Horse Volunteers of London and Westminster . . . London: 1843. V. 38; 40

COLLYER, ROBERT

Ilkley: Ancient and Modern. Otley: 1885. V. 45

COLLYER, ROBERT H.

Lights and Shadows of American Life. Boston: 1843? V. 44

COLLYNS, CHARLES PALK

Notes on the Chase of the Wild Red Deer in the Counties of Devon and Somerset. With an Appendix Descriptive of Remarkable Runs and Incidents Connected with the Chase from the Year 1780 to the Year 1860. With numerous illustrations. London: 1862. V. 37; 39

COLMAN, BENJAMIN 1673-1747

A Humble Discourse of the Incomprehensivlness of God. Boston: 1740. V. 43; 44

Ossa Josephi. Or, the Bones of Joseph. Consider'd in a Sermon. Boston: 1720. V. 38

Practical Discourses on the Parable of the Ten Virgins. Boston: 1747. V. 44; 45

A Sermon Preached Before His Excellency the Governor, and Her Majesties Council, at Boston in New England on July 22d, 1708. Boston: 1708. V. 45

Souls Flying to Jesus Christ Pleasant and Admirable to Behold. Boston: printed,: 1741. V. 43

Souls Flying to Jesus Christ Pleasant and Admirable to Behold. A Sermon Preach'd to a Very Crowded Audience, at the Opening an Evening Lecture, in Brattle Street, Boston, Tuesday, October 21, 1740 . . . London: 1741. V. 44

Two Sermons Preached in Boston, March 5, 1723, on a Day of Prayer . . . To Ask the Effusion of the Spirit of Grace on Their Children, and on the Children of the Town . . . Boston: 1723. V. 37

COLMAN, GEORGE 1732-1794

The Clandestine Marriage, a Comedy. London: 1766. V. 39

The Dramatick Works. London: 1777. V. 45

The Dramatick Works. (together with) Peoms on Several Occasions. London: 1777, 1787. V. 38

Eccentricities For Edinburgh . . . Edinburgh. V. 42

Eccentricities for Edinburgh . . . Edinburgh: n.d. V. 37

The Jealous Wife. Newbery: 1761. V. 46

My Night Gown and Slippers; or Tales in Verse. London: 1797. V. 39; 42

Poetical Vagaries . . . London: 1814. V. 42

Some Particulars of the Life of the Late George Colman, Esq. London: 1795. V. 40

Some Particulars of the Life of the Late George Colman, Esq. London: 1795. V. 45

T. Harris Dissected. London: 1768. V. 38; 43

COLMAN, HENRY

The Agriculture and Rural Economy of France, Belgium, Holland and Switzerland . . . London: 1848. V. 42

European Life and Manners; in Familiar Letters to Friends. Boston and London: 1849. V. 40

COLMAN SMITH, PAMELA

The Golden Vanity and the Green Bed. London: 1903. V. 41

COLMAN, W. GOODING

Colman's Normandy, Picardy, etc., Picturesque Exteriors and Interiors of Cathedral Churches and Other Objects in Northern France. London: 1838. V. 41

COLNAGHI, P.

Persian and Mughal Art. Catalogue published to coincide with the exhibition at Colnaghi's, 7 April - 20 May, 1976. London: (1976). V. 37

COLNETT, JAMES

The Journal of Captain James COlnett Aboard the Arbonaut From April 26, 1789 to Nov. 3, 1791. Editor F.W. Howay. Toronto: 1940. V. 37; 42; 43; 45

A Voyage into the South Atlantic, and Round Cape Horn into the Pacific Ocean, for the Purpose of Extending the Spermaceti Whale Fisheries Attempting to Establish an English Fur-Trading Post at Nootka . . . London: 1798. V. 38; 40; 41; 42

A Voyage to the South Atlantic and Round Cape Horn into the Pacific Ocean . . . Amsterdam: 1968. V. 43

COLOMB, P. H.

Naval Warfare Its Ruling Principles and Practices Historically Treated. London: 1891. V. 46

Naval Warfare, Laws Governing the Conduct of Naval Engagements from 1512 - 1898 . . . London: 1899. V. 39

COLOMBIA. (REPUBLIC OF NEW GRANADA 1832-1858).

Contract Between the Republic of New Granada and the Panama Railroad Company. New York: 1856. V. 38

COLOMBO, CHRISTOFORO

Gleanings in Europe. England: By an American. Philadelphia: 1837. V. 43

Journals and Documents on the Life and Voyages of Christopher Columbus. New York: 1963. V. 40

The Letter In Spanish of Christopher Columbus Written on His Return from His First Voyage and Addressed to Luis De Sant angel, 15 Feb.-14 March, 1493. London: 1889. V. 41

Fac-Simile of the Spanish Quarto Letter of Columbus Giving an Account of His First Voyage from the Unique Example of Eight Pages Preserved in the Ambrosian Library at Milan. New York: & London: 1892. V. 46

Letter of Christopher Columbus to Rafael Sanchez. Chicago: 1893. V. 40

Letter of Christopher Columbus. Albany: 1900. V. 46

The Letter of Christopher Columbus Concerning His First Voyage to the New World. San Francisco: 1924. V. 39; 45

Personal Narrative of the First Voyage of Columbus to America. Boston: 1827. V. 41

The Voyages of . . . Being the Journals of His First and Third, and the Letters Concerning His First and Last Voyages to Which is Added the Account of His Second Voyage Written by Andres Bernaldez . . . London: 1930. V. 39; 42

COLOMBO, CRISTOFORO

Christopher Columbus. His Own Book of Privileges 1502. London: 1893. V. 39

COLOMBO, FERNANDO

Histoire del S. D. Fernando Colombo Nelle Quali s'hi Particolare & Vera Relatione Della Vita & de'Fatti dell'Ammiraglio D. Christoforo Colombo, Suo Padre . . . Venice: 1571. V. 46

Historie del Signor D. Fernando Colombo, Nelle Quali s'ha Particolare & Vera Relatione Della Vita e de'Fatti dell'Ammiraglio D. Christofor Colombo . . . Venice: 1685. V. 46

COLONEL Crockett's Exploits and Adventures in Texas; Wherein Is Contained a Full Account of His Journey from Tennessee to the Red River and Natchitoches, and Thence Across Texas to San Antonio . . . Philadelphia: 1837. V. 39

COL. Harneys' (sic) Charge on the Mexican Lancers' Commanded by General La Vega Near Vera Cruz. Philadelphia: 1847. V. 40

COLONEY, MYRON

Manomin: a Rhythmical Romance of Minnesota. The Great Rebellion and the Minnesots Massacres. St. Louis: 1866. V. 40; 42

COLONIAL Dames of America, Chapter I. Ancestral Records and Portraits. New York: 1910. V. 44

COLONIAL Law for the Danish Westindia Islands. Christianborg: 1863. V. 38

COLONNA, AEGIDIUS 1247-1297

Le Mirouer Exemplaire et tres Fructueuse Instruction . . . Du regime . . . Paris: 1517. V. 45

COLONNA, EGIDIO

Theoreumata de Esse et Essentia. Leipzig: 1495. V. 38

COLONNA, FABIO 1567-1650

Phytobasanos, Sive Plantarum Aliquot Historia. Neapoli: 1592. V. 37; 42

COLONNA, FRANCESCO

Hypnereotomachi Poliphili. London: 1904. V. 46

Hypnerotomachia Poliphili. London: 1963. V. 37

The Strife of Love in a Dream. London: 1890. V. 45

COLONNA, VITTORIA

Tvtte Le Rime. Venice: 1558. V. 37

COLONUS, PSEUD.

Does the Discovery of Gold in Victoria, Viewed in Relation to Its Moral and Social Effects, as Hitherto Developed, Deserve to Be Called a National Blessing or a National Curse? Melbourne: 1853. V. 41

COLONY, HORATIO

Free Forester. Boston: 1935. V. 38; 40; 42

Free Forester: a Novel of Pioneer Kentucky. V. 37

THE COLOPHON. New York: 1930-50. V. 38; 39; 41; 46

COLORADO and Asthma. Denver: 1874. V. 39

COLORADO as an Agricultural State: the Progress of Irrigation; Denver, the City of the Congress . . . Denver: 1894. V. 42

COLORADO. CONSTITUTION - 1876

Constitution of the State of Colorado, adopted in Convention, March 14, 1876; Also the Address of the Convention to the People of Colorado. Election, Saturday July 1, 1876. Denver: 1876. V. 37; 43

COLORADO. LAWS, STATUTES, ETC. - 1865

General Laws, and Joint Resolutions, Memorials and Private Acts, Passed at the Fourth Session of the Legislative Assembly of the Territory of Colorado. Denver: 1865. V. 37

COLORADO. LEGISLATIVE ASSEMBLY - 1862

Council Journal of the legislative Assembly of the Territory of Colorado First Session. Denver: 1862. V. 37

COLORADO. LEGISLATIVE ASSEMBLY - 1868

House Journal of the Legislative Assembly of the Territory of Colorado Seventh Aession. Central City: 1868. V. 37

COLORADO. LEGISTLATIVE ASSEMBLY - 1864

House Journal of the Legislative Assembly of the Territory of Colorado Third Session. Denver: 1864. V. 37

COLORADO: Some Answers to Questions Likely to be asked by the Members of the American Society of Civil Engineers During their Visit to Denver on the Occasion of their Annual Convention . . . Denver: 1886. V. 37

COLORADO Springs. Health Resort. County Seat of El Paso County. Elevation 5922 Feet. Colorado Springs: 1883. V. 46

COLORADO. (TERRITORY).

Council Journal of the Legislative Assembly of the Territory of Colorado. First Session. Denver: 1862. V. 43

Official Information. Colorado. A Statement of Facts Prepared and Published by Authority of the Territorial Board of Immigration. Denver: 1872. V. 37

COLORADO. (TERRITORY). BOARD OF IMMIGRATION

Official Information. Colorado. A Statement of Facts Prepared and Published by Authority of the Territorial Board of Immigration . . . Denver: 1872. V. 40; 46

Resources and Advantages of Colorado. Denver: 1873. V. 46

COLORADO. (TERRITORY). LEGISLATIVE ASSEMBLY - 1864

House Journal of the Legislative Assembly of the Territory of Colorado Third Session. Denver: 1864. V. 39

COLORADO. (TERRITORY). LEGISLATIVE ASSEMBLY - 1868

House Journal of the Legislative Assembly of the Territory of Colorado Seventh Session. Central City: 1868. V. 39

COLORADO Tourist and Illustrated Guide, to the Rocky Mountain Resorts, Via the Golden Belt. Kansas City: 1880. V. 39

COLPANI, GIUSEPPE

Il Gusto Poemetto. Premessovi un Ragionamento Filosofico sull' Istesso Argomento Estratto Dai Signori Montesquieu, E. Voltaire. Venice: 1767. V. 39

COLQUHOUN, ARCHIBALD ROSS

Across Chryse, Being the Narrative of a Journey of Exploration through the South Chhna Border Lands, from Canton to Mandalay. London: 1883. V. 44; 46

China in Transformation. London: 1898. V. 42

The Key to the Pacific. Westminster: 1895. V. 40; 43

The 'Overland' to China. London: 1900. V. 39; 41; 46

The Overland to China. London: New York: 1900. V. 43

COLQUHOUN, J. A. S.

With the Kurram Field Force, 1878-79. London: 1881. V. 41

COLQUHOUN, JOHN

The Moore and the Loch, Containing Minute Instructions in all Highland Sports. London: 1888. V. 37

Salmon-Casts and Stray Shots, Being Fly-Leaves from the Note Book of . . . London: 1858. V. 40

COLQUHOUN, JOHN CAMPBELL 1785-1854

An Isis Revelata: an Inquiry into the Origin, Progress and Present State of Animal Magnetism. Edinburgh: 1836. V. 46

Scattered Leaves of Biography. London: 1864. V. 37

COLQUHOUN, PATRICK 1745-1820

A Summary of the Roman Civil Law, Illustrations by Commentaries on and Parallels from the Mosaic, Canon, Mohammendan, English, and Foreign Law. London: 1849-54. V. 37

A Treatise on the Police of the Metropolis, Explaining the Various Crimes and Misdemeanors Which at Present are Felt as a Pressure Upon the Community. London: 1796. V. 37; 38; 39; 40; 41

A Treatise on the Police of the Metropolis . . . London: 1797. V. 42

A Treatise on the Police of the Metropolis . . . London: 1800. V. 42; 43; 44; 46

Treatise on the Police of the Metropolis . . . London: 1806. V. 38; 40; 42

A Treatise on the Wealth, Power and Resources of the British Empire . . . Including the East Indies. London: 1815. V. 37; 38; 41; 42

A Treatise on Indigence; Exhibiting a General View of the National Resources for Productive Labour. London: 1806. V. 37

A Treatise on the Police of London. Philadelphia: 1798. V. 39

A Treatise on the Wealth, Power and Resources of the British Empire, In Every Quarter of the World Including the East Indies. London: 1814. V. 39

COLQUITT, ANTHONY

Modern Reports or Select Cases Adjudged in the Courts of Kings Bench, Chancery, Common Pleas and Exchequer, Since the Restoration of His Majesty King Charles II. London: 1682. V. 45

COLSON, LANCELOT

Philosophia Maturata: an Exact Piece of Philosophy . . . London: 1668. V. 46

COLSON, NATHANIEL

The Mariners New Kalendar. London: 1724. V. 40

The Mariner's New Calendar. London: 1761. V. 46

The Mariner's Calendar. London: 1766. V. 40

COLT, ARMIDA MARIA-THERESA

Weeds and Wildflowers: Some Irreverent Words. London: 1965. V. 40; 41; 46

COLT, H. DUNSCOMBE

Excavations at Nessana (Auja Hafir, Palestine). London: 1962. V. 40; 42

COLT HOARE, RICHARD

A Tour through the Island of Elba. London: 1814. V. 39

COLT, MIRIAM DAVIS

Went to Kansas; Being a Thrilling Account of an Ill-Fated Expedition to that Fairy Land, and Its Sad Results. New York: 1862. V. 40

Went to Kansas; Being a Thrilling Account of an Ill-Fated Expedition to that Fairy-Land and Its Sad Results. Watertown: 1862. V. 37; 38; 39; 41; 42; 43; 44; 45; 46

Went to Kansas; Being a Thrilling Account of an Ill-Fated Expedition to that Fairy Land, and Its Sad Results, Together With a Sketch of the Life of the Author. Watertown: 1862. V. 41

COLT, SAMUEL

Samuel Colt's Own Record of Transactions with Capt. Samuel Walker and Eli Whitney, Jr. in 1847. Hartford: 1949. V. 37; 39; 40

COLTMAN, NATHANIEL

Laurie and Whittle's New Traveller's Companion. London: 1807. V. 46

COLTON, CALVIN

Abolition a Sedition. Philadelphia: 1839. V. 38; 43

Annexation of Texas, By Junius. New York: 1844. V. 37; 39; 40; 42

The Crisis of the Country. Philadelphia: 1840. V. 41

Tour of the American Lakes, and Among the Indians of the North-West Territory, in 1830: Disclosing the Character and Prospects of the Indian Race. London: 1833. V. 37

COLTON, CHARLES CALEB

Hypocrisy. A Satire, in three books. Book the First. Tiverton: 1812. V. 37; 38; 42; 43; 45

COLTON, GEORGE WOOLWORTH 1827-1901

Colton's General Atlas. New York: 1861. V. 42

Colton's Atlas of America . . . New York: 1855. V. 45

Colton's Atlas of the World. New York:/London: 1855-56. V. 45

Colton's General Atlas. New York:/London: 1857. V. 45

Colton's General Atlas . . . New York: 1859. V. 45

Colton's General Atlas of the World . . . New York: 1886. V. 45

COLTON, HAROLD SELLERS

The Sinagua: Summary of the Archaeology of the Region of Flagstaff, Arizona. Flagstaff: 1946. V. 44

COLTON, HENRY E.

Mountain Scenery. Raleigh: 1859. V. 39

COLTON, JOSEPH HUTCHINS

Colton's Traveler and Tourist's Guide-Book through the New England and Middle States and the Canadas. New York: 1852. V. 38

Colton's Traveler and Tourist's Guide-Book through the Western States and Territories . . . New York: 1856. V. 43

Illinois. New York: 1854. V. 46

Particulars of Routes, Distances, Fare, Etc. to Accompany Colton's Map of California and the Gold Region. New York: 1849. V. 40; 41; 43

The State of Indiana Delineated. New York: 1838. V. 38; 39; 45

The State of Indiana Delineated: Georgraphical, Historical, Statistical & Commercial, & A Brief View of the Internal Improvements, Geology, Education, Travelling Routes, &C. Prepared to accompany Colton's map. New York: 1838. V. 37

COLTON, ROBERT

Rambles in Sweden and Gottland . . . London: 1847. V. 43

COLTON, THOMAS

A Sermon Preached in the City of York December, 31st 1706. York: 1707. V. 45

COLTON, WALTER

Deck and Port; or, Incidents of a Cruise in the United States Frigate Congress to California. N: 1850. V. 40

Deck and Port. New York: 1850. V. 40; 41; 42; 44

Deck and Port; or Incidents of a Cruise in the United States Frigate Congress to California. With Sketches of Rio Janeiro, Valparaiso, Lima, Honolulu and San Francisco. New York/Cincinnati: 1850. V. 37

Land and Lee in the Bosphorus and Aegean; or Views of Athens and Constantinople. Cincinnati: 1851. V. 41

Three Years in California. New York: 1850. V. 37; 38; 39; 40; 42; 43; 44; 45; 46

COLUM, PADRAIC 1881-1972

A Boy in Eirinn. London: 1915. V. 43

Creatures. New York: 1927. V. 38; 46

Orpheus, Myths of the World. New York: 1930. V. 39; 46

COLUMBIA UNIVERSITY. LIBRARIES. AVERY ARCHITECTURAL LIBRARY

Catalogue of the Avery Architectural Library, a Memorial Library of Architecture, Archaeology and Decorative Art. New York: 1895. V. 41

THE COLUMBIAN *Atlas of the World We Live In.* New York: 1893. V. 45

THE COLUMBIAN *Muse: A Selection of American Poetry from Various Authors of Established Reputation.* New York: 1794. V. 37

THE COLUMBIAN *World's Fair Atlas.* Lousiville: 1892-93. V. 45

THE COLUMBUS *Business Directory, for 1843-4.* Columbus: 1843. V. 40

COLUMBUS, CHRISTOPHER

Journal and Other Documents on the Life and Voyages of . . . Hartford: 1963. V. 38

The Spanish Letter of Columbus. (with) The Latin Letter of Columbus. London: 1893. V. 44

Voyages of Christopher Columbus. London: 1930. V. 38

COLUMBUS, FERNANDO

Historie Del S.D. Fernando Colombo; Nelle Quali s'ha Particolare & Vera Relatione Della Vita & De Fatti Dell' Venice: 1571. V. 40

COLUMELLA, LUCIUS JUNIUS MODERATUS

De Culta Hortorum Carmen Liber Undecimus. Erfurt: 1510. V. 37

De Re Rustica Libri XII. Paris: 1543. V. 38

COLUMNA, F.

Minus Cognitarum Rariorumque Nostro Coelo Orientium Stirpium Ecphrasis . . . Purpura . . . Pars Altera . . . Rome: 1616. V. 39

COLUSA *County Annual.* Colusa: 1878. V. 37

COLVILE, EDEN

London Correspondence Inward from Eden Colvile, 1849-1852. London: 1956. V. 46

COLVILE, H. E.

The Work of the Ninth Division. London: 1901. V. 46

COLVILE, HENRY

The Land of the Nile Springs Being Chiefly an Account of How We Fought Kabarega. London: 1895. V. 46

COLVILL, HELEN HESTER

The Princess Royal. London: 1894. V. 40; 43

COLVILL, ROBERT

Britain, a Poem in Three Books. Edinburgh: 1757. V. 43

COLVILL, SAMUEL

The Grand Imposter Discovered; or, an Historical Dispute of the Papacy and Popish Religion . . . Edinburgh: 1673. V. 42; 45

COLVILLE, ARTHUR, MRS.

1,000 Miles in a Machilla: Travel and Sport in Nyasaland, Angoniland and Rhodesia. London: 1911. V. 46

COLVILLE, EDEN

London Correspondence Inward from Eden Colville 1849-1852. London: 1956. V. 43; 44

COLVILLE, ROBERT

The Feast of Holyrood. Edinburgh: 1768. V. 40; 41; 43

COLVIN, F. F.

Diary of the 9th (Q.R.) Lancers During the South African Campaign 1899 to 1902. London: 1904. V. 46

COLVIN, H. M.

The History of the King's Works. London: 1963. V. 37

COLVIN, HOWARD MONTAGU

Architectural Drawings in the Library of Elton Hall by Sir John Bnbrugh and Sir Edward Lovett Pearce. Oxford;: 1964. V. 38

COLVIN, SIDNEY

John Keats: His Life and Poetry, His Friends, Critics and Afterfame. London: 1917. V. 40; 45

Keats. London: 1887. V. 37

COLVOCORESSES, GEORGE M.

Four Years in a Government Exploring Expedition . . . New York: 1852. V. 38; 39; 41

COLWELL, STEPHEN

The Five Cotton States and New York; or Remarks Upon the Social and Economical Aspects of the Southern Political Crisis. Philadelphia: 1861. V. 42

The Ways and Means of Payment: a full analysis of the Credit System, with its various modes of adjustment. Philadelphia: 1859. V. 37

COLWEY, MALCOLM

Exile's Return. New York: 1981. V. 40

COLYAR, A. S.

Life and Times of Andrew Jackson: Soldier, Statesman, President. Nashville: 1904. V. 39; 42

COLYER, FRANK

Variations and Diseases of the Teeth of Animls. London: 1936. V. 38

COLYER, VINCENT

Brief Report of the Services Rendered by the Freed People to the United States Army in North Carolina, in the Spring of 1862, After the Battle of Newbern. New York: 1864. V. 42; 44

COMAN, KATHARINE

Economic Beginnings of the Far West: How We Won the Land Beyond the Mississippi. New York: 1912. V. 43

COMAZZI, JOHN BAPTISTA, COUNT

The Morals of Princes . . . London: 1729. V. 44

COMBE, ANDREW 1797-1847

Observations on Mental Derangement. Edinburgh: 1831. V. 39; 46

The Physiology of Digestion Considered With Relation to the Principles of Dietetics. Boston: 1836. V. 42

the Physiology of Digestion Considered with Relation tot he Principles of Dietetics. Edinburgh: 1841. V. 40

The Physiology of Digestion Considered with Relation to the Principles of Dietetics . . . Edinburgh & London: 1836. V. 37

The Physiology of Digestion Considered with Relation to the Principles of Dietetics . . . Boston & New York: 1837. V. 37

The Physiology of Digestion Considered with Relation to The Principles of Dietics. Edinburgh: 1836. V. 37; 41; 43; 46

COMBE, GEORGE

Essays on Phrenology. Edinburgh: 1819. V. 38

Moral Philosophy. Edinburgh: 1840. V. 40

COMENIUS, JOHANNES AMOS 1592-1671

Ianua Aurea Reserata Duarum Linguarum. Geneva: 1650. V. 38

Ianua Linguarum Reserata. London: 1650. V. 38

Ianua Linguarum Reserata. Amsterdam: 1649. V. 38

Janua Linguarum Reserata Aurea . . . Cologne: 1641. V. 41

Latinae Linguae Janua Reserata. London: 1656. V. 38

COMERFORD, JAMES

Catalogue of the Extensive and Very Valuable Library . . . London: 1881. V. 39

COMERFORD, M.

Collections Relating to the Diocese of Kildare and Leighlin. Dublin: 1883. V. 38

Collections relating to the Dioceses of Kildare and Leighlin. Dublin: (1883-1886). V. 37

COMERFORD, T.

The History of Ireland from the Earliest Account of Time to the Invasion of the English Under King Henry II. Dublin: 1790. V. 46

COMERTY, GEORGE, EARL OF

An Historical Account of the Conspiracies by the Earls of Gowry and Robert Logan of Restalrig Against James VI . . . Edinbrugh: 1713. V. 46

COMEZ DE LA SERNA, RAMON

Le Cirque. Paris: 1920. V. 38

COMFORT, ALEX

The Song of Lazarus. London: 1945. V. 41

THE COMIC Adventures of Old Dame Trot and Her Cat. London: 1824. V. 45

THE COMIC Adventures of Old Mother Hubbard and Her Dog. London: 1830. V. 42

COMIC Crumbs to Feed Little Ones. London: 1858. V. 39

THE COMIC Token for 1836, a Companion to the Comic Almanac. Boston: 1835. V. 39

THE COMICAL Jester. Charlestown: 1810. V. 40

COMIERS, CLAUDE

Traite de la Parole, Langues et Ecritures, Contenant la Steganographie Impenetrable, Avec Tout ce qui Concerne les Encres, Cachets et Cire a Cacheter. Liege: 1691. V. 37

COMINES, PHILIPPE DE, SIEUR D'ARGENTON 1445-1511

The Historie of Philip De Commines, Knight, Lord of Argenton. London: 1596. V. 39; 44; 45

The Historie of Philip De Commines Knight, Lord of Argenton. London: 1601. V. 40; 43; 45

The Historie of Philip De Commines Knight, Lord of Argenton. London: 1614. V. 42

The History of Philip de Commines, Knight, Lord of Argenton. London: 1674. V. 41

Les Memoires . . . sur les Faits & Gestes de Loys Onziesme & de Charles Huitiesme son Fils, Rois de France. Paris: 1577. V. 40

The Memoirs . . . London: 1823. V. 42

COMINI, ALESSANDRA

Egon Schiele's Portraits. 1974. V. 44

COMINI, ALESSANDRE

Egon Schiele's Portraits. 1974. V. 42

COMITIA Westmonasteriensium in Collegio Sti. Petri Habita Die Anniversario Fundatricis Suae Reginae Elizabethae Inagurarate Jan XV. Londini: 1728. V. 44

COMMANDINO, FEDERICO

Liber de Centro Gravitatis Solidorum. Bologna: 1565. V. 38

COMMANDMENTS to California Wives. San Francisco: 1855. V. 40

COMMELINUS, HIERONYMUS

Rerum Britannicarum, Id Est Angliae, Scotiae, Vicinarumque Insularum Ac Regionum. Heidelberg: 1587. V. 37

COMMEMNORATIVE Historical and Biographical Record of Wood County, Ohio; Its Past and Present, Early Settlement and Development. Chicago: 1897. V. 46

COMMEMORATIVE Biographical Record of Central Pennsylvania, Including the Counties of Centre, Clinton, Union and Snyder. Chicago: 1898. V. 41

COMMEMORATIVE Biographical Record of the Upper Lake Region, Containing Biographical Sketches of Prominent & Representative Citizens & many of the early Settled Families. Chicago: 1905. V. 37

COMMENORATIVE, Historical and Biographical Record of Wood County, Ohio: Its Past and Present. Chicago: 1897. V. 38; 42

A COMMENTARY, Mythological, Historical and Geographical on Pope's Homer and Dryden's Aeneid of Virgil, with a Copious Index. London: 1829. V. 43

THE COMMERCIAL Advertiser Directory for the City of Buffalo. Buffalo: 1855. V. 46

COMMERCIAL Directory; Containing A Topographical Description, Extent and Productions of Different Sections of the Union, Statistical Information Relative to Manufactures, Commercial and Port Regulations, etc. Philadelphia: 1823. V. 39; 43

THE COMMERCIAL Handbook of the Telephone Service. London: 1906. V. 40

COMMERCIAL Suggestions to the Citizens of Cleveland and Ohio City Concerning the Cleveland and St. Louis Rail Road. Cleveland: 8154. V. 37; 41

COMMERCIAL TRAVELERS' ASSOCIATION

Constitution and By-Laws of the Commercial Travelers' Association of the State of California. San Francisco: 1878. V. 44

COMMINES, PHILIP DE, SIEUR D'ARGENTON 1445-1511

The Memoirs of . . . . London: 1855. V. 46

COMMINES, PHILIPPE DE

Equitis, de Carolo Octavo, Galliae Rege, & Bello Neapolitano, Commentarii Ioanne Sleidano Interprete. Strasburg: 1548. V. 41

COMMITTEE OF ANCIENT NEAR EASTERN SEALS

Corpus of Ancient Near Eastern Seals in North American Collections. New York: 1948. V. 39

THE COMMON Carol Book. A Collection of Christmas and Easter Hymns. Ditchling, Sussex: 1926. V. 42; 45

COMMON-PLACE Arguments Against Administration with Obvious Answers (Intended for the Use of the new Parliament). London: 1780. V. 37

A COMMONPLACE Book, or In and Out of the Public Domain. San Francisco: 1956. V. 45; 46

A COMMONPLACE Book, Profound and Profane Thoughts and Observations Gathered, Set in Type and printed, with Embellishments by John Depol. Maple Shade: 1985. V. 41

COMMONPLACE Book Six. Aptos & Woodside: 1983. V. 42

COMMONPLACE Book Three. San Francisco: 1960. V. 41; 45

COMMONS, J. R.

A Documentary History of American Industrial Society. Cleveland: 1910-11. V. 38

THE COMMONS Petitjon (sic) to the King in Defence of Mr. Pym. Answering Those Seven Articles Whereof Hee Was Impeached. London: 1641. V. 40

COMMONWEALTH v. Gordo et al. The Opinion of Judge Bok, March Eighteenth 1949. San Francisco: 1949. V. 46

COMMUCK, THOMAS

Indian Melodies. New York: 1845. V. 40

COMMUNICATING Assistant; Containing Devotions to be Used in Church, Before at, and After Receiving the Blessed Sacrament of the Lord's Supper . . . London: 1753. V. 42

COMMUNICATION from the Commissioner of Indian Affairs and Other Documents, In Relation to the Indians in Texas. Washington: 1848. V. 37

COMMUNICATION of Property. Or, a Voluntary Contribution for Publick and Charitable Uses to Be Distributed by Lot. London: 1708. V. 43

A COMPANION to the Theatre; or, a View of Our Most Celebrated Dramatic Pieces: in Which the Plan, Characters and Incidents of Each are Particularly Explained. Dublin: 1751. V. 45

COMPANY OF CLOCKMAKERS, LONDON

The Charter and Bye Laws of the Company of Clockmakers, London. London: 1817? V. 37

COMPANY OF SCOTLAND

The Original Papers and Letters, Relating to the Scots Company, Trading to Africa and the Indies. N.P.: Edinburgh: 1770. V. 40

COMPANY OF SCOTLAND TRADING TO AFRICA AND THE INDIES

An Exact List of All the Men, Women and Boys that Died on Board the Indian and African Company's Fleet During Their Voyage from Scotland to America . . . Edinburgh: 1699. V. 43

COMPANY OF THE ROYAL FISHERY OF ENGLAND

A Discourse Concerning the Fishery Within the British Seas, and Other His Majesties Dominions, and More Especially, As it Relates to the Trade of the Company of the Royal Fishery of England. London: 1695. V. 39

COMPARATIVE Anatomy of the Heart. Madison: 1984. V. 45

COMPARATIVE View of the British and American Constitutions: With Observations on the Present State of the British Politics, and on the Probable Consequences of Introducing into Great Britain the Mode of Suffrage that Exists in the United States. Edinburgh: 1817. V. 41

A COMPARISON of the Spirit of the Whigs and Jacobites. Edinburgh: 1746. V. 39

A COMPASSIONATE Address to the Christian World. London. V. 38

A COMPEND of Certain Laws for the Organization and Government of the Militia of the United States; and of the District of Columbia. Washington: 1814. V. 37

COMPENDIO de Los Sucesos que Con Grande Gloria de Dios, Lustre, Y Honor de las Catholicas Reales Armas de S. M. en Defensa de Estas Christiandades, e Islas de Bisayas se Consiguieron Contra los Mahometanos Enemigos, por el Armamento Destacado . . . Manila: 1755. V. 40

A COMPENDIOUS Account of the Most Important Battles of the Late War, To Which is Added, the Curious Adventures of Corporal Samuel Stubbes . . . Boston: 1817. V. 42; 45

A COMPENDIOUS Geographical and Historical Grammar; Exhibiting a Brief Survey of the Terraqueous Globe. London: 1795. V. 38
A COMPENDIOUS Geographical and Historical Grammar. London: 1802. V. 38; 41

COMPENDIOUS Geographical Dictionary, Containing a Concise Description of the Most Remarkable Places, Ancient and Modern in Europe, Asia, Africa & America. London: 1795. V. 38; 42; 45

A COMPENDIOUS Geographical Dictionary, Containing a Concise Description of the Most Remarkable Places, Ancient and Modern in Europe. London: 1804. V. 38; 41

A COMPENDIOUS Library of the Law, Necessary for Persons of all Degrees and Professions. In the Savoy: 1740. V. 45

A COMPENDIOUS Library of the Law; Necessary for Persons of all Degrees and Professions . . . London: 1743. V. 40

A COMPENDIOUS View of the Grounds of the Teutonick Philosphy. London: 1770. V. 39; 40; 43

A COMPENDIOUS View of the Most Recent and Interesting Travels in Africa and America. London: 1831. V. 40

COMPENDIUM OF History and Biography of North Dakota, Containing a History of North Dakota, Early Exploration, Early Settlement, etc. Chicago: 1900. V. 38; 39

A COMPENDIUS Account of the Late War to Which is Added The Curious Adventures of Corporal Samuel Stubbs. New York: 1916. V. 42

COMPERTZ, M. L. A.

The Road to Lamaland. London: 1925. V. 45

A COMPILATION of all the Acts, Resolutions, Reports, and Other Documents, in Relation to the Bank of the State of South Carolina Affording Full Information Concerning that Institution. Columbia: 1848. V. 46

THE COMPLEAT Brewer; or, the Art and Mystery of Brewing Explained. London: 1760. V. 42

A COMPLEAT Catalogue of All the Plays That Were Ever Yet Printed in the English Language . . . . Continued to This Present Year 1726. London: 1726. V. 42; 43

THE COMPLEAT Clark, Containing the Best Forms of All Sorts of Presidents, For Conveyances and Assurances . . . London: 1683. V. 40; 46

THE COMPLEAT Clark, Containing the Best Forms of All Sorts of Presidents For Conveyances and Assurances, and Other Instruments Now in Use and Practice. London: 1671. V. 38; 40; 46

A COMPLEAT Collection of all the Verses, Essays, Letters and Advertisements, Which Have Been Occasioned by the Publication of Three Volumes of Miscellanies, by Pope and Company. London: 1728. V. 42

THE COMPLEAT Constable Directing all Constables, Headboroughs, Tithingmen, Churchwardens, Overseers of the Poor, Surveyors of the Highways . . . London: 1700. V. 40

THE COMPLEAT English and French Vermin-Killer. London: 1710. V. 40

THE COMPLEAT English and French Vermin-Killer . . . London: 1707. V. 40

THE COMPLEAT Florist. London: 1747. V. 39

THE COMPLEAT Herbal; or Family Physician. Manchester: 1787. V. 38

THE COMPLEAT History of Bob of Lyn. London: 1741. V. 38

THE COMPLEAT History of Thamas Kouli Kan, (at Present Called Schah Nadir) Sovereign of Persia. London: 1742. V. 41

THE COMPLEAT Jane Grabhorn. San Fransico: 1968. V. 41

THE COMPLEAT Justice: Being an Exact and Compendious Collection . . . Principally Out of Mr. Lambert, Mr. Crompton and Mr. Dalton . . . London: 1667. V. 40; 42

THE COMPLEAT Letter Writer; or, New and Polite English Secretary. London: 1756. V. 41; 43

THE COMPLEAT Marksman; or, The True Art of Shooting - Flying: a Poem. London: 1759. V. 40

THE COMPLEAT Planter & Cyderist: Or, Choice Collections and Observations for the Propagating All Manner of Fruit Trees, and the Most Approved Ways and Methods Yet Known for the Making and Ordering of Cyder and Other English Wines. London: 1685. V. 40; 42

THE COMPLEAT Sheriff Wherein is Set Forth His Office and Authority . . . (with) The Office and Duty of a Coroner . . . London: 1696. V. 40

A COMPLEAT Translation of the Whole Case of Mary Catherine Cadiere, Against the Jesuite Father John Baptist Girard, in a Memorial Presented to the Parliament of Aix, In Which the Jesuit is Accused of Seducing Her, by the Abominable Doctrines of Quietism . . . London: 1732. V. 38

A COMPLEAT View of the Present Politicks of Great-Britain. In a Letter from a GErman Nobleman, to His Friend at Vienna. Dublin: 1743. V. 39

A COMPLEAT View of the Present Politicks of Great Britian. London: 1743. V. 41; 43

A COMPLETE Account of the Ceremonies Observed in the Coronations of the Kings and Queens of England . . . London: 1727. V. 41; 42

A COMPLETE and Accurate Account of the Very Important Debate in the House of Commons, July 9, In Which the Cause of Mr. Fox's Resignation, and the Great Question of American Independence Came Under Consideration. London: 1782. V. 46

THE COMPLETE Art of Boxing, According to the Modern Method; Wherein the Whole of That Manly Accomplishment is Rendered So Easy and Intelligent that Any Person May be an Entire Master of the Science in a Few Days . . . London: 1788. V. 45

THE COMPLETE Assistant for the Landed Proprietor, Estate and House Agent, Land Steward, Proctor, Architect, Surveyor, Builder, Auctioneer, Appraiser, Upholsterer, Cabinet-Maker, etc . . . London: 1824. V. 39

THE COMPLETE Brewer, or the Art and Mystery of Brewing Explained . . . London: 1760. V. 40

A COMPLETE Collection of Protests from the Year MDCXLI to the Present Year MDCCXXVII. London: 1737. V. 40; 45; 46

A COMPLETE Collection of State Trials and Proceedings for High Treason and Other Crimes and Misdemeanours; from the Reign of King Richard II to the End of the Reign of King George I. (1407-1709). London: 1730. V. 40

A COMPLETE Collection of State Trials and Proceedings fro High-Treason and Other Crimes and Misdemeanours from the Reign of King Richard II . . . to the Reign of Queen Anne to the Present Time . . . London: 1742 & 1766. V. 40

A COMPLETE Collection of the Genuine Papers, Letters &c. in the Case of John Wilkes, Esq . . . Paris: 1767. V. 37; 39; 46

A COMPLETE Collection of the Genuine Papers, Letters, &c. in the Case of John Wilkes, Esq. Elected Knight of the Shire for the County of Middlesex March XXVIII, MDCCLXVIII. Berlin: 1769. V. 37; 38; 45

THE COMPLETE Confectioner, Pastry-Cook and Baker. Philadelphia: 1844. V. 43

A COMPLETE Dictionary of the Greek and Roman Antiquities. London: 1700. V. 38

A COMPLETE Dictionary of the Greek and Roman Antiquities . . . London: 1700. V. 43

THE COMPLETE Distilelr; Combining Theory and Practice; and Explaining the Mysteries and Most Recent Improvements of Distilling and Brewing, in a Most Simple, Easty and Familiar Manner. Edinburgh: 1793. V. 46

THE COMPLETE Family-Piece; and, Country Gentleman, and Farmer's Best Guide. London: 1736. V. 43

THE COMPLETE Family-Piece: and Country Gentleman, and Farmer's Best Guide. In Three Parts . . . The Fifth Edition, Improved. London/Dublin: 1749. V. 37

THE COMPLETE Farmer; or, a General Dictionary of Husbandry, In All Its Branches . . . London: 1793. V. 41; 42; 44

THE COMPLETE Farrier, or, Gentleman's Travelling Companion . . . Philadelphia: 1809. V. 43

THE COMPLETE Grazier: or, Gentleman and Farmers Directory. London: 1767. V. 37; 42; 43; 44

THE COMPLETE Grocer: Being a Series of Valuable Receipts, for Distilling and Mixing Cordials of all Kinds . . . New York: 1832. V. 39

A COMPLETE Guide to All Persons Who Have Any Trade or Concern with . . . London. London: 1765. V. 44

COMPLETE Hand Atlas of the World. New York/Buffalo: 1899. V. 45

A COMPLETE Historical, Chronological and Geographical Atlas . . . of North and South America, and The West Indies . . . Philadelphia: 1822. V. 40

COMPLETE History of the 46th Illinois Veteran Volunteer Infantry . . . Freeport: 1866. V. 45; 46

COMPLETE History of the Late Mexican War. New York: 1850. V. 42; 46

A COMPLETE History of the Late War, or Annual Register, of Its Rise, Progress and Events in Europe, Asia, Africa and America. Dublin: 1774. V. 39

A COMPLETE History of the Origin and Progress of the Late War, From Its Commencement to the Exchange of the Ratifications of Peace, Between Great Britain, France and Spain; on the 10th of Feburary 1763. London: 1764. V. 45

A COMPLETE History of the Present War, from Its Commencement in 1756 to the End of the Campaign 1760 . . . London: 1761. V. 44; 45

A COMPLETE Key to the Tale of a Tub; with Some Account of the Authors, The Ocasion and Design of Writing It, and Mr. Wooton's Remarks Examin'd. London: 1710. V. 38

A COMPLETE Roll of All Choctaw Claimants and Their Heirs Existing Under the Treaties Between the United States and the Choctaw Nation, as Far As Shown by the Records of The United States and of the Choctaw Nation. St. Louis: 1889. V. 44

A COMPLETE View of the Birth of the Pretender, As Collected from Our Histories, State Tracts, and Other Authorities; In Which All the Arguments for and Against that Intricate Birth are Impartially Stated. London: 1744. V. 41

THE COMPLETE Young Man's Companion; or, Self Instructor . . . Manchester: 1804. V. 45

A COMPREHENSIVE Study of the Traditional Architecture of the Greek Lands in All Its Extent, from the 15th to the 20th Century. Volume I: Eastern Aegean, Sporades, Ionian Islands; Volume II: Aegean, Cyclades. Athens: 1983. V. 37

COMPTON, ARTHUR HOLLY 1892-1962

   X-Rays and Electrons. New York: 1926. V. 42

COMPTON-BURNET, IVY 1892-1969

   Brothers and Sisters. New York: 1956. V. 37

COMPTON-BURNETT, IVY 1892-1969

   Brothers and Sisters. London: 1929. V. 42

   Daughters and Sons. London: 1937. V. 42

   Dolores. Edinburgh: 1911. V. 37

   A God and His Gifts. London: 1963. V. 41

   Men and Wives. London: 1931. V. 40; 41

   More Women than Men. London: 1933. V. 39; 41

   Mother and Son. London: 1955. V. 43

   Novels. London: 1972. V. 38

   Pastors and Masters. London: 1925. V. 37; 38; 39; 44; 45

   Pastors and Masters. London: 1925. V. 40

COMPTON, HENRY

   An Account of the Whole Proceedings Against . . . Henry, Lord Bishop of London, Before the Lord Chancellor, and Other Ecclesiastial Commissioners. London: 1688. V. 39

COMPTON, THOMAS

   The Northern Cambrian Moutains: or a Tour through North Wales, Describing the Scenery and General Characters of that Romantic Country. London: 1817. V. 39; 44

   The Northern Cambrian Mountains; or, a Tour through North Wales . . . London: 1820. V. 41

A COMPUTATION of the Increase of London, and Parts Adjacent, with Some Causes Thereof, and Remarks Thereon . . . London: 1719. V. 40; 41

COMPUTUS Nouus Adiecto Comentariolo Totius Fere Astronomie Fundamentu. Cologne: 1505. V. 40

COMRIE, JOHN D.

   History of Socttish Medicine to 1860. London: 1932. V. 38; 39; 40; 41; 42; 44; 45

COMSTOCK, FRANCIS

   The Work of Thomas W. Nason, N.A. Boston: 1977. V. 42

COMSTOCK, FRANCIS ADAMS

   A Gothic Vision: F. L. Griggs and His Work. 1978. V. 44

   A Gothic Vision: F. L. Griggs and His Work. Boston: 1978. V. 42

COMSTOCK, J. C.

   Principles of Physiology. New York & Hartford: 1851. V. 41

COMSTOCK, J. L.

   Elements of Chemistry in Which the Recent Discoveries in the Science are Included. Hartford: 1832. V. 38

COMSTOCK, JOHN A.

   Butterflies of California, a Popular Guide to a Knowledge of the Butterflies of California. London: 1927. V. 43

   Butterflies of California, a Popular Guide to a Knowledge of all the Butterflies of California, Embracing All the 477 Species and Varieites at Present Recorded for the State. Los Angeles: 1927. V. 37

COMSTOCK, JOHN T.

   Poems by . . . A Pioneer who Emigrated to the Western Wilds in 1834. Hudson, Mi.: 1874. V. 37

COMSTOCK, JOSEPH

   Remarks on Febrile Diseases, with a Definition of Fever. Providence: 1814. V. 42

   The Tongue of Time, and Star of the States . . . New York: 1838. V. 43

COMSTOCK, MARY

   Greek, Etruscan and Roman Bronzes in the Museum of fine Arts, Boston. Greenwich: 1971. V. 38

COMTE, A.

   The Book of Birds. London: 1841. V. 37; 41

COMTE, AUGUSTE 1798-1857

   Catechisme Positiviste, ou Sommaire Exposition de la Religion Universelle . . . Paris: 1852. V. 45

   The Cathechism of Positive Religion. London: 1858. V. 39; 40; 44

   A General View of Positivism. London: 1865. V. 43; 45

   The Positive Philosophy. London: 1853. V. 39; 40; 43

   The Positive Philosophy of Auguste Comte. New York: 1853. V. 42

   Seven Lectures on the Doctrine of Positivism, Delivered at the Positivist School, Chapel Street, Lamb's Conduit Street, in May, June and July 1879 by J. Kaines. London: 1880. V. 39

COMYNS, JOHN

   A Digest of the Laws of England. London: 1762-67. V. 46

   A Digest of the Laws of England. Dublin: 1793. V. 39

CONABERE, B.

   Wildflowers of South-Eastern Australia. London: 1974. V. 45

CONANT, A. J.

   Foot-Prints of Vanished Races in the Mississippi Valley; Being an Account of Some of the Monuments and Relics of Pre-Historic Races Scattered Over Its Surface, with Suggestions as to Their Origin and Uses. St. Louis: 1879. V. 39; 44

CONANT, CHARLES A.

   A History of Modern Banks of Issue with an Account of the Economic Crises of the Present Century. New York: 1897. V. 41

CONARD, HOWARD LOUIS

   Encyclopedia of the history of Missouri: A Compendium of History and Biography. New York: 1901. V. 37

   'Uncle Dick' Wootton, the Pioneer Frontiersman of the Rocky Mountain Region . . . Chicago: 1890. V. 37; 40; 44

CONAWAY, JAMES

   The Big Easy. Boston: 1970. V. 42

CONCANEN, MATTHEW

   The Flowerpiece. London: 1731. V. 38; 41

CONCEALMENT. a Novel. London: 1837. V. 39; 42; 46

CONCILIATORY Address to the People of Great Britain and of the Colonies, on the Present Important Crisis. London: 1775. V. 41; 42; 46

CONCIONES sive Orationes ex Graecis Latinisque Historicis Excerptae. Geneva: 1570. V. 43

A CONCISE Account, Historical and Descriptive, of Lambeth Palace. London;: 1806. V. 39

THE CONCISE English-Arabic Dictionary of Current Usage. 1982. V. 38

A CONCISE Historical and Topographical Sketch of Hastings, Winchelsea & Rye, Including Also Several Other Places in the Vicinity of those Ancient Towns . . . Hastings: 1820. V. 46

A CONCISE History of Printing. London?: 1774. V. 42

A CONCISE Introduction to the Knowledge of the Most Eminent Painters. London: 1778. V. 38; 44

CONCLIN, GEORGE

Conclins' New River Guide, or a Gazetteer of All the Towns of the Western Waters. Cincinnati: 1861. V. 46

CONCORAN, MATHEW

The Speculatist. London: 1730. V. 43

CONCORD Lectures on Philosophy. Cambridge: 1883. V. 41

CONCORDIA, y Reglamento Solemne, Celebrado Entre la Noble Villa de Bilbao, y Cofradia de San Gregorio Nacianzeno, de Heredros Proprietarios de su Distrito . . . N.P.: 1723. V. 45

CONCOREGIO, JOANNIS

Practica Nova Medicine. Venetiis: 1501. V. 44

CONDAMINE, CHARLES M. DE

Journal du Voyage Fait par Ordre du Roi, a l'Equateur, Servant d'Introduction Historique a la Mesure des Trois Premiers Degres du Meridien. Paris: 1751. V. 38

CONDER, CHARLES

The Life & Death of Conder. 1938. V. 37

CONDER, CLAUDE REIGNIER

Heth and Moab. Explorations in Syria in 1881 and 1882. London: 1883. V. 40; 44; 46

The Latin Kingdom of Jerusalem. 1029 to 1291. London: 1897. V. 44

Syrian Stone-Lore; or, The Monumental History of Palestine. London: 1886. V. 46

Tent Work in Palestine, a Record of Discovery and Adventure. London: 1878. V. 39

Tent Work in Palestine. New York: 1878. V. 42; 44

Tent Work in Palestine. London: 1879. V. 45

CONDER, F. R.

Personal Recollections of English engineers and of the Introduction of the Railway System into the United Kingdom. London: 1868. V. 46

CONDER, JOSIAH

The Associate Minstrels. London: 1810. V. 37; 44

The Flowers of Japan and the Art of Floral Arrangement . . . Tokio (sic): 1891. V. 42

Landscape Gardening in Japan. Tokyo: 1893. V. 39; 44

CONDIE, THOMAS

History of the Pestilence, Commonly Called Yellow Fever, Which Almost Desolated Philadelphia in the Months of August, September and October 1798. Philadelphia: 1799. V. 44

CONDILLAC, ESTIENNE BONNOT DE

Oeuvres Completes . . . Revues, Corrigees par l'Auteur, et Imprimees sur ses Manuscrits Autographes. Paris: 1803. V. 42

CONDILLAC, ETIENNE BONNOT DE

An Essay on the Origin of Human Knowledge. London: 1756. V. 38

La Logique, ou les Premiers Developpemens de l'Art Penser . . . Paris: 1780. V. 38

Traite des Sensations, a Madame la Comtesse de Vasse . . . London: and Paris: 1754. V. 45

Traite des Sensations, a Madame la Comtesse de Vasse. Londres & se vend a Paris: 1754. V. 42

CONDILLAC, ETIENNE BONNOT DE, ABBE

Le Commerce et Le Gouvernement, Consideres Relativement l'un a l'Autre: Ouvrage Elementaire . . . Premier Partie (Seconde Partie). Amsterdam and Paris: 1776. V. 41; 45

Traite des Sensations, a Madame la Comtesse de Vasse. Londres: 1754. V. 39; 41; 45

CONDIT, CHARLES L.

Painting and Painters' Materials. New York: 1883. V. 40

CONDON, RICHARD

The Manchurian Candidate. New York: 1959. V. 45

CONDON, THOMAS

The Two Islands and What Came of Them. Portland: 1902. V. 46

CONDORCET, MARIE JEAN ANTOINE NICOLAS DE CARITAT, MARQUIS DE 1743-1794

Eloges de M. Franklin Lu a la Senace Publique de l'Academie des Sciences le 13 Nov. 1790. Paris: 1791. V. 42

The Life of Voltaire. Philadelphia: 1792. V. 42

Outlines of an Historical View of the Progress of the Human Mind . . . London: 1795. V. 39; 43; 45

Outlines of an Historical View of the Progress of the Human Mind. Philadelphia: 1796. V. 38

Outlines of an Historical View of the Progress of the Human Mind. Philadelphia/New York: 1796. V. 39

Vie De Turgot. London: 1786. V. 45

Vie de Turgot. Berne: 1787. V. 38

Vie de Turgot. Londres: 1797. V. 41

CONDUCT. a Novel. London: 1814. V. 39; 42

THE CONDUCT of Cadwallader Colden, Esquire, Late Lieutenant-Governor of New York: Relating to the Judges Commissions, Appeals to the King, and the Stamp Duty. London: 1767. V. 37

THE CONDUCT of the Admiralty, in the Late Expedition of the Enemy to the Coast of Ireland. London: 1797. V. 41

THE CONDUCT of the East-India Company, with Respect to Their Wars, &c. London: 1767. V. 37

THE CONDUCT of the Two B----Rs Vindicated. London: 1749. V. 41

CONDUCTOR Generalis, or the Office, Duty and Authority of Justices of the Peace, High-Sheriffs, Under Sheriffs, Goalers, Coroners, Jury Men, Over-Seers of the Poor . . . Philadelphia: 1722. V. 40

CONDY, NICHOLAS

Cothele, on the Banks of the Tamar, the Ancient Seat of the Rt. Honble. the Earl of Mount Edgecumbe. London: 1839. V. 38

Cothele, on the Banks of the Tamar, the Ancient Seat of the Right Honourable Earl of Mount Edgecumbe. London: 1840. V. 38; 45

CONE, ANDREW

Petrolla: a Brief History of the Pennsylvania Petroleum Region, Its Development, Growth, Resources, etc. from 1859 to 1869. New York: 1870. V. 39; 41; 42

CONE, HELEN GRAY

Bonnie Little People. New York: 1890. V. 45

CONE, MARY

Two Years in Calfiornia. Chicago: 1876. V. 43

CONEL, J. LE ROY

The Postnatal Development of the Human Cerebral Cortex. Cambridge: 1939-47. V. 46

CONERLY, LUKE WARD

Pike County Mississippi 1798-1876 Pioneer Familes and Confederate Sildiers Reconstruction and Redemption. Nashville: 1909. V. 46

CONESTAGGIO, GIROLAMO FRANCHI DE

Dell' Unione del Regno di Portogallo. Alla Corona da Castiglia. Genoa: 1585. V. 40

Historien der Konigkreich Hispanien, Portugal und Aphrica . . . Munich: 1589. V. 45

CONESTAGGIO, GIROLAMO FRANCHI DI

Dell'Unione del Regno di Portogallo alla Corona di Castiglia. Genoa: 1589. V. 40; 45

The Historie of Uniting of the Kingdom of Portugal to the Crowne of Castill. London: 1600. V. 40; 45

CONEY, JOHN

Beauties of Continental Architecture in a Series of Views of Ancient Cathedrals and Other Remarkable Public Buildings . . . London: 1840. V. 37

Ecclesiastical Edifices of the Olden Time. London: 1842. V. 39

THE CONFEDERATE Soldier's Wife Parting From Her Husband! N.P.: 1861? V. 40

THE CONFEDERATE States Almanac 1862 . . . Nashville: 1862. V. 44

THE CONFEDERATE States Almanac 1865 . . . Macon: 1865. V. 44

THE CONFEDERATE States Almanac, and Repository of Useful Knowledge for 1862. Vicksburg: 1861. V. 40; 42

CONFEDERATE States Almanac for the Yer of Our Lord 1864 Being Bissextile, or Leap Year and the 4th Year of the Independence of the Confederate States of America . . . Macon: 1863. V. 41

CONFEDERATE STATES OF AMERICA

Army Regulations Adopted for the Use of the Army of the Confederate States . . . Articles of War. Richmond: 1861. V. 37

Army Regulations, Adopted for the Use of the Army of the Confederate States, in Accordance with Late Acts of Congress . . . to which is added, An Act for the Establishment and Organization of the Army of the Confederate States of America . . . Raleigh: 1861. V. 37

Official Reports of Battles. Richmond: 1864. V. 44

Regulations for the Army of the Confederate States. Richmond: 1862. V. 37

Regulations for the Government of the Ordnance Department of the Confederate States of America. Richmond: 1862. V. 37

Report from the Joint Select Committee, to Investigate the Management of the Navy Department. Richmond: 1864. V. 44

CONFEDERATE STATES OF AMERICA. ARMY

Army Regulations . . . of the Army of the Confederate States . . . (and) An Act for the Establishment and Organization of the Army of the Confederate States of America, Also, Articles of War for the Government . . . Raleigh: 1861. V. 44

General Orders. No. 6. Houston: 1865. V. 45

General Orders. No. 94. The Following regulations for the Subsistence Department. Are Published for the Information and Government of all Connected with the Forces. Tupelo: 1862. V. 45

Regulations for the Army of the Confederate States, 1862. Richmond: 1862. V. 44

Regulations for the Army of the Confederate States, 1863. Richmond: 1863. V. 44

Regulations for the Army of the Confederate States with a Full Index. Richmond: 1864. V. 44

CONFEDERATE STATES OF AMERICA. ARMY - 1864

Special Orders. No. 62. Head-Quarters Dist. Miss. and East. La. Jackson, Miss., Dec. 20, 1864. N.P.: 1864. V. 42

CONFEDERATE STATES OF AMERICA. ARMY - 1865

Head Quarters Trans Mississippi Department. Shreveport, La. April 1, 1865. General Orders. No. 31. Shreveport: 1865. V. 42

CONFEDERATE STATES OF AMERICA. ARMY. CAVALRY CORPS

General Orders No. 7. Head Quarters, Wheeler's Cavalry Corps, June 3rd, 1863. N.P.: 1863. V. 45

General Orders No. 2, 1. The Following Schools of Instruction Will be Established and Maintained at all Times, Except When on the March. N.P.: 1864. V. 45

CONFEDERATE STATES OF AMERICA. ARMY. CAVALRY CORPS - 1863

Head Quarters. Wheeler's Cavalry Corps. June 3rd. 1863. General Orders. N.P.: 1863. V. 42

CONFEDERATE STATES OF AMERICA. ARMY. DEPT. OF NORTHERN VA.

reports of the Operations of the Army of Northern Virginia, From June, 1862, to and Including the Battle of Fredericksburg Dec. 13, 1862. Richmond: 1864. V. 44

CONFEDERATE STATES OF AMERICA. ARMY. DEPT. OF TENNESSEE

Official Report of the Battle of Chickamauga. Richmond: 1864. V. 44

CONFEDERATE STATES OF AMERICA. CONGRESS

Address of the Congress to the People of the Confederate States. Richmond: 1864. V. 43

CONFEDERATE STATES OF AMERICA. CONGRESS - 1861

Journal of the Congress of the Confederate States of America, 1861-65. Washington: 1904. V. 42

Journals of the Congress of the Confederate States of America, 1861-1865. Washington: 1904-05. V. 42

CONFEDERATE STATES OF AMERICA. CONSTITUTION

Provisional and Permanent Constitutions of the Confederate States. Richmond: 1861. V. 42

State Convention. May 1861. Ordered to be Printed, Syme & Hall Printers to the Convention. Constitution of the Confederate States of America. Raleigh: 1861. V. 45

CONFEDERATE STATES OF AMERICA. CONSTITUTION - 1861

Constitution of the Confederate States of America. Adopted Unanimously by the Congress of the Confederate States of America (sic) March 11, 1861. Montgomery, Ala.: 1861. V. 37

CONFEDERATE STATES OF AMERICA. DEPARTMENT OF JUSTICE

Attorney General's Report. Richmond: 1862. V. 39

CONFEDERATE STATES OF AMERICA. JUSTICE DEPARTMENT - 1864

Report of the Attorney General . . . Department of Justice . . . to the President . . . Richmond: 1864. V. 39; 42

CONFEDERATE STATES OF AMERICA. LAWS, STATUTES, ETC.

By Authority of Congress. The Statutes At Large of the Provisional Government of the Confederate States of America . . . Richmond: 1864. V. 45

The Statutes at Large of the Provisional Government of the Confederate States of America . . . Feb. 8, 1861 to . . . February 18, 1862. Richmond: 1864. V. 43

CONFEDERATE STATES OF AMERICA. LAWS, STATUTES, ETC. - 1861

An Act to Amend an Act Entitled 'An Act Recognizing the Existence of War Between the United States and the Confederate States . . . . Montgomery: 1861. V. 40; 42

An Act to Amend an Act Entitled 'An Act Recognizing the Existence of War Between the United States and the Confederate States, and Concerning Letters of Marque, Prizes and Prize Goods. N.P.: 1861. V. 40

An Act to Perpetuate Testimony in Cases of Slaves Abducted or Harbored by the Enemy and Of Other Property Seized, Wasted, or Destroyed by them . . . Richmond: 1861. V. 39; 42

CONFEDERATE STATES OF AMERICA. LAWS, STATUTES, ETC. - 1864

A Bill to Be Entitled an Act to Provide for Organizing, Arming and Disciplining the Militia of the Confederate States . . . Richmond: 1864. V. 42

CONFEDERATE STATES OF AMERICA. LAWS, STATUTES, ETC. - 1865

A Bill to Increase the Efficiency of the Cavalry of the Confedrate States. Richmond: 1865. V. 42

CONFEDERATE STATES OF AMERICA. NAVY DEPARTMENT - 1862

Letter of the Secretary of Navy . . . March 11th 1862. Richmond: 1862. V. 39

CONFEDERATE STATES OF AMERICA. ORDNANCE DEPT. - 1862

Regulations for the Government of the Ordnance Department of the Confederate States of America. Richmond: 1862. V. 39; 42

CONFEDERATE STATES OF AMERICA. PRESIDENT - 1861

Message of the President. Richmond: 1861. V. 41

CONFEDERATE STATES OF AMERICA. PRESIDENT - 1862

Message of the President. Richmond: 1862. V. 41

CONFEDERATE STATES OF AMERICA. PRESIDENT - 1863

President's Message to the Senate and House of Representatives of the Confederate States. Richmond: 1863. V. 38; 39; 42; 43

CONFEDERATE STATES OF AMERICA. PRESIDENT - 1865

Message of the President to the Senate and House of Representatives of the Confederate States of America. Richmond: 1865. V. 42

CONFEDERATE STATES OF AMERICA. WAR DEPARTMENT - 1863

Correspondence Between the War Department and General Lovell, Relating to the Defences of New Orleans. Richmond: 1863. V. 38

CONFEDERATE STATES. WAR DEPARTMENT

Correspondence Between the War Department and General Lovell, Relating to the Defences of New Orleans. Richmond: 1863. V. 44

CONFEDERATE Victories in the Southwest: Prelude to Defeat. (and) Union Army Operations in the southwest: Final Victory. Albuquerque: 1961. V. 45

CONFEDERATE War Journal Illustrated . . . New York: and: 1893-March 1895. V. 44

A CONFERENCE Desired by the Lords and Had by a Committee of Both Houses, Concerning the Rights and Privileges of the Subjects . . . London: 1642. V. 38

A CONFESSION of Faith. New London: 1760. V. 39

CONFESSION of Faith of the Kirke of Scotland (thus titled on spine). Edinburgh: 1638. V. 37

A CONFESSION of Faith Owned and Consented to by the Elders and Messengers of the Churches in the Colony of Connecticut in New-England, Assembled by Delegation at Saybrook . . . New London: 1760. V. 37; 38; 44; 45

A CONFESSION of Faith, Put Forth by the Elders and Brethren of Many Congregations of Christians . . . to which are added. Two Articles viz. Of Imposition of Hands, and Singing of Psalms in Publick Worship. Also, A Short Treatise of Church Discipline. Philadelphia: 1743. V. 38

THE CONFESSIONS of a Gamester. London: 1824. V. 37

THE CONFESSIONS of a Lady's Maid; or, Boudoir Intrigue. London: 1860. V. 42

CONFESSIONS of a Medium. London: 1882. V. 37

CONFIDENTIAL Memorandum for the Use of the Commissioners of the Part of the United States in the American British Joint High Commission, Washington, 1871. Washington: 1871. V. 42

CONFUCIUS

The Analects of Confucius. Shanghai: 1933. V. 41; 42; 45; 46

The Analects of Confucius. 1970. V. 38

Confucius: The Unwobbling Pivot and the Great Digest. Norfolk: 1947. V. 46

The Morals of Confucius a Chinese Philosopher. London: 1691. V. 38; 41

The Works of Confucius. Serampore: 1809. V. 39; 41

CONGAR, STEPHEN

Herbert Wendall: a Tale of the Revolution. New York: 1835. V. 46

CONGDON, GEORGE EDWARD

Sugar Grove and the Class of 1886 . . . Hiawatha: 1911. V. 46

CONGLETON, HENRY BROOKE PARNELL, 1ST BARON 1713-1800

A Treatise on Roads. London: 1833. V. 38

A CONGRATULATORY Epistle from a Reformed Rake, to John F-----g, Esq. Upon the New Scheme of Reclaiming Prostitutes. London: 1758. V. 46

A CONGRATULATORY Poem on the Whigg's Entertainment. London: 1682. V. 40

CONGREGATIONAL CHURCHES OF MASSACHUSETTS

Proceedings of the Convention of Congregational Ministers . . . Boston: 1795. V. 40

THE CONGRESS. a Poem. London: 1714. V. 41

THE CONGRESS of the Beasts, Under the Meditation of the Goat, for Negociating a Peace Between the Fox, the Ass Wearing a Lion's Skin, the Horse, the Tigress and Other Quadrupeds at War . . . London: 1748. V. 41; 46

CONGREVE, W.

A Treatise on the General Principles, Powers and FAcility of Application of the Congreve Rocket System . . . London: 1827. V. 42

CONGREVE, WILLIAM

Amendments of Mr. Collier's False and Imperfect Citations &c. From the Old Batchelour, Double Dealer, Love for Love, Mourning Bride. By the Author of those Plays. London: 1698. V. 37; 38; 43

The Double-Dealer. London: 1694. V. 38; 41

The Double Dealer. London: 1777. V. 38; 42; 45

The Dramatick Works. London: 1773. V. 38

An Impossible Thing. London: 1720. V. 38

Love for Love: a Comedy. London: 1695. V. 38

The Mourning Muse of Alexis. London: 1695. V. 38

The Mourning Bride. London: 1697. V. 44

Plays . . . London: 1735. V. 45

Poems Upon Several Occasions. Glasgow: 1752. V. 44; 45

A Short Account of a Patent Lately Taken Out for a New Principle of Steam Engine . . . London: 1819. V. 39; 44; 45

The Way of the World. London: 1700. V. 38; 40

The Way of the World. London: 1790. V. 41

The Way of the World. London: 1928. V. 41

The Works of William Congreve. London: 1710. V. 38; 39; 41; 44; 46

The Works of . . . London: 1730. V. 46

The Works . . . Dublin: 1736. V. 41

The Works of . . . Birmingham: 1761. V. 46

The Works . . . Birmingham: 1761. V. 37; 38; 40; 42; 43; 45; 46

The Works. London: 1761. V. 41

Works . . . . London: 1774. V. 40

The Complete Works of William Cowper. London: 1923. V. 42; 46

The Complete Works of William Congreve. Soho: 1923. V. 41; 42

The Works in two volumes, consisting of his plays and poems. The third edition, revised by the author. London: 1719-20. V. 37

CONINGSBY, THOMAS, EARL OF

The Abstract of Earl Coningsby's Title to Royal Franchises within His Liberty of Leominster in the County of Hereford . . . N.P.? London: 1721. V. 39

CONKEY, HARRIET E.

Dakota War Whoop; or, Indian Massacres and War in Minnesota. St. Paul: 1863. V. 37

CONKLIN, EMMA B.

A Brief History of Logan County, Colorado with Reminiscences by Pioneers. Denver: 1928. V. 43

CONKLIN, EUGENE

Picturesque Arizona. New York: 1878. V. 37; 39; 42; 44; 46

CONKLING, EDGAR

Benton's Policy of Selling and Developing the Mineral Lands, and the Necessity of Furnishing Access to the Rocky Mountains by the Construction of the Northern and Central Pacific Railroads . . . Cincinnati: 1864. V. 39

CONKLING, HENRY

An Inside View of the Rebellion, and American Citizens' Text Book. Chicago: 1864. V. 44

CONKLING, HOWARD

Mexico and the Mexicans or, Notes of Travel in the Winter and Spring of 1883. New York: 1883. V. 40

CONKLING, ROSCOE P.

The Butterfield Overland Mail. Glendale: 1947. V. 37; 38; 46

CONLKING & JACKMAN

Steens Mountains in Oregon's High Desert Country. Caldwell: 1967. V. 43

CONNECTICUT

Journal fo the Constitutional Convention of Connecticut. Hartford: 1902. V. 37

CONNECTICUT ACADEMY OF ARTS AND SCIENCES

Memoirs of the Connecticut Academy of Arts and Sciences. New Haven: 1810. V. 40

Transactions. New Haven: 1949. V. 37

CONNECTICUT. (COLONY). LAWS, STATUTES, ETC.

Acts and Laws of His Majesty's English Colony of Connecticut in New-England in America . . . New-London: 1750. V. 45

CONNECTICUT. (COLONY). LAWS, STATUTES, ETC. - 1750

Acts and Laws of His Majesty's English Colony of Connecticut in New England in America. London: 1750. V. 42

CONNECTICUT. GENERAL ASSEMBLY

At a General Assembly of the Governor and Company of the State of Connecticut . . . on the 10th Day of January . . . 1782. Hartford: 1782. V. 46

CONNECTICUT. LAWS, STATUTES, ETC. - 1780

At a General Assembly of the Governor and Company of the State of Connecticut, Holden at Hartford, on the Second Thursday of October A.D. 1780. An Act of Filling Up and Compleating this State's Quota of the Continental Army. Hartford: 1780. V. 38; 44

CONNECTICUT. LAWS, STATUTES, ETC. - 1784

Acts and Laws of the State of Connectitcut in America. New London: 1784. V. 40; 46

THE CONNECTICUT River Banking Company. One Hundred Years of Service 1825-1925. Hartford: 1925. V. 41

CONNELL, E.

The Anatomy Lesson and Other Stories. New York: 1957. V. 37; 43; 45

CONNELL, EVAN S.

The Connoisseur. New York: 1974. V. 46

Mrs. Bridge. New York: 1959. V. 46

Son of the Morning Star. 1984. V. 44

Son of the Morning Star. San Francisco: 1984. V. 46

CONNELL, JOHN

A Treatise on the Law of Scotland Respecting Tithes. Edinburgh: 1830. V. 38

CONNELL, WILL

In Pictures, A Hollywood Satire. New York: 1937. V. 37; 41

CONNELLAN, OWEN

The Annals of Ireland. Dublin: 1846. V. 46

CONNELLEY, WILLIAM ELSEY

Doniphan's Expedition. Kansas City: 1907. V. 40; 42; 43; 44; 45

Doniphan's Expedition, Conquest of New Mexico and California. Topeka: 1907. V. 46

History of Kansas Newspapers. Topeka: 1916. V. 44

Quantrill and the Border Wars. Cedar Rapids: 1910. V. 38; 40; 42; 45; 46

Quantrill and the Border Wars. Cedar Rapids: 1909. V. 43

War with Mexico, 1846-1847. Doniphan's Expedition and the Conquest of New Mexico and California. Topeka: 1907. V. 39; 40

Wild Bill and His Era: the Life and Adventures of James Butler Hickock. New York: 1922. V. 40

Wild Bill and His Era: The Life and Adventures of James Butler Hickok. New York: 1933. V. 37; 40; 41; 45

CONNELLY, JAMES H.

A Storm Ashore. New York: 1890. V. 37

CONNELLY, MARC

The Green Pastures, a Fable. New York: 1929. V. 42

The Green Pastures. New York: 1930. V. 37; 46

CONNER, H.

Spearhead, 5th Marine Div. in WWII. Washington: 1950. V. 39

CONNER, JAMES

Letters of James Conner, C.S.A. Columbia: 1950. V. 44

CONNER, JAMES & SON

Abridged Specimens of Printing Types, Brass Rule, Electrotypes, and Revised Catalogue Printing Materials. New York: 1888. V. 38

Specimens of Printing Type and Ornaments Cast by James Conner & Son. New York: 1850. V. 38

CONNER, P. S. P.

The Home Squadron Under Commodore Conner in the War with Mexico, Being a Synopsis of Its Services . . . Philadelphia: 1896. V. 37

CONNER, PHILIP

Home Squadron Under Commodore Conner in the War with Mexico 1846-47. Philadelphia: 1896. V. 37

CONNES, G. A.

A Dictionary of Characters and Scenes in the Novels, Romances and Short Stories of H. G. Wells. Dijon: 1926. V. 42

CONNETT, EUGENE V.

American Big Game Fishing. New York: 1935. V. 43; 45

A Decade of American Sporting Books and Prints by the Derrydale Press, 1927-1937. New York: 1937. V. 38; 41

Duck Shooting Along the Atlantic Tidewater. Edited by Eugene V. Connett. Illustrated with 13 Mounted Color Plates by Edgar Burke & Lynn Bogue Hunt. New York: 1947. V. 37; 44

Feathered Game From a Sporting Journal. New York: 1929. V. 44

Fishing a Trout Stream. New York: 1934. V. 43; 44

Upland Game Bird Shooting in America. 1930. V. 38

Upland Game Bird Shooting in America. Introduction by Co. Lewis S. Thompson. Illustrations by Lynn Bogue Hunt, Edgar Burke, William J. Schaldach, Bert Cobb and others. New York: 1930. V. 37; 39; 40; 43; 44

Wind Shooting and Anglin. New York: 1922. V. 37

CONNICK, CHARLES J.

Adventures in Light and Color. London: 1937. V. 39

Adventures in Light and Color. New York: 1937. V. 37; 44; 46

CONNICK, GILES DE

Commentatiorum ac Disputationum in Universam Doctrinam D. Thomae Sacramentis et Censuris Tomi Duo. Antwerp: 1624. V. 37

CONNINGHAM, R. O.

Notes on the Natural History of the Straits of Magellan and West Coast of Patagonia Made During the Voyage of H.M.S. 'Nassau' 1866. Edinburgh,: 1871. V. 37

THE CONNOISSEUR. London: 1761. V. 43
THE CONNOISSEUR. London: 1793. V. 38

CONNOLLY BROS. LTD.

Nothing Like Leather. London: 1927. V. 38

CONNOLLY, CYRIL 1903-1974

Enemies of Promise. London: 1938. V. 37; 38; 42; 45

Enemies of Promise. Boston: 1939. V. 45

The Evening Colonnade. London: 1973. V. 40; 42; 45

The Modern Movement - 100 Key Books from England France and America 1880-1950. London: 1965. V. 41; 42; 45

Previous Convictions - Selected Writings of a Decade. London: 1963. V. 42

The Rock Pool. New York: 1936. V. 39; 43

The Rock Pool. Paris: 1936. V. 37; 38; 40; 41; 42; 44

Sarah: By Her Friends and For Them. (Cambridge): 1965. V. 37

The Ubu Plays. Being Ubu Rex, Ubu Cuckolded and Ubu Enchained. New York: 1969. V. 41

The Uniquiet Grave; A Word Cycle. New York: 1945. V. 37

The Unquiet Grave. London: 1944. V. 40; 42; 46

The Unquiet Grave. London: 1945. V. 43

CONNOLLY, JAMES

The Legacy and Songs of Freedom. Dublin. V. 43

CONNOLLY, T. W. J.

History of the Royal Sappers and Miners, from the Formation of the Corps in March 1772 to the Date When Its Designation Was Changed to that of Royal Engineers in Oct. 1856 . . . London: 1857. V. 43

History of the Royal Sappers and Miners from the Formation of the Corps in March 1772 to the date When Its Designation was Changed to that of Royal Engineers in October 1856. London: 1857. V. 46

History of the Royal Sappers and Miners, from the Formation of the Corps in March 1772, to the Date when its Designation was changed to that of Royal Engineers, in October 1856. London;: 1857. V. 37

CONNOLLY, THOMAS W. J.

The History of the Corps of Royal Sappers and Miners. London: 1855. V. 38

CONNOR, J. WALTER

Conner's Irish Song Book . . . San Francisco: 1868. V. 44

CONNOR, JACK

Game in the Desert. New York: 1939. V. 45

CONNOR, JEFF

Stephen King Goes to Hollywood. New York: 1987. V. 44

CONNOR, JOSEPH

The Trial, Sentence and Execution of Joseph Connor, Who Was Executed at the Old Bailey this Morning (Monday June 2, 1845, in ms.) for the Wilful Murder of Mary Brothers on Monday March 31st. London: 1845. V. 42

CONNOR, MARIE

Husband and Wife. London: 1888. V. 38

Sweet Magdelen. London: 1887. V. 38; 43

CONNOR, RALPH

Breaking the Record. New York: 1904. V. 43

The Doctor. A Tale of the Rockies. Toronto: 1906. V. 45

The Swan Creek Blizzard. New York: 1904? V. 43

CONNOR, SEYMOUR

The Peters Colony in Texas: a History . . . Austin: 1959. V. 42

CONNOR TYPE FOUNDRY

Compact Specimens of James Connor's Sons. New York: 1891. V. 42

CONOLD, ROBERT

The Notion of Schism Slated According to the Antients, and Considered with Reference to the Non-Conformists . . . London: 1677. V. 44

CONOLLY, ARTHUR

Journey to the North of Indian, Overland from England, through Russia, Persia, and Affghaunistan. London: 1834. V. 40

CONOLLY, JOHN 1794-1866

An Inquiry Concerning the Indications of Insanity with Suggestions for the Better Protection and Care of the Insane. London: 1830. V. 38; 43; 45

The Reports of Jon Conolly, M.D. The Resident Physician of the Country Lunatic Asylum, at Hanwell. London;: 1842. V. 37

The Treatment of the Insane Without Mechanical Restraints. London: 1856. V. 45

CONOR, WILLIAM

The Irish Scene. Belfast: 1944. V. 43

CONOVER, CHARLOTTE REEVE

Dayton and Montgomery County Resources and People. New York: 1932. V. 46

CONOVER, GEORGE W.

Sixty Years in Southwest Oklahoma or the Autobiography of George W. Conover with some Thrilling Incidents of Indian Life in Oklahoma and Texas. Anadarko: 1927. V. 37; 39; 42; 45

CONQUEST, ROBERT

The Egyptologists. London: 1965. V. 41

CONRAD, AUGUST

The Destruction of Columbia, S.C. Roanoke: 1902. V. 42

CONRAD, C. M.

Report . . . Communicating a Copy of W. H. Sidell's Survey of a Route for a Railroad from the Great Bend, on Red River, to Providence, on the Mississippi River. Washington: 1851. V. 39

Report . . . Communicating a Copy of W.H. Sidell's Survey of a Route for a Railroad from the Great Bend, on Red River, to Porvidence, on the Mississippi River. Washington: 1851. V. 37

CONRAD, HENRY C.

History of the State of Delaware. Wilmington: 1908. V. 46

CONRAD, HENRY S.

The Waterlilies. A Monograph of the Genus Hymphaea. 1905. V. 38

CONRAD HOLZINGER DE SAXONIA

Speculum Beatae Mariae Virginis. Augsburg: 1477. V. 37

CONRAD, JESSIE

A Handbook of Cookery for a Small House. Garden City: 1923.
V. 37; 39; 41

A Handbook of Cookery for a Small House. New York: 1923. V. 37; 43

A Handbook of Cookery for a Small House. London: 1923. V. 44; 45

Joseph Conrad and His Circle. London: 1935. V. 44

Personal Recollections of Joseph Conrad. London: 1924. V. 38; 39

CONRAD, JOSEPH 1857-1924

Admiralty Paper. New York: 1925. V. 39

Almayer's Folly. London: 1921. V. 46

Almayer's Folly. New York: 1895. V. 37; 42

Almayer's Folly: A Story of an Eastern River. London: 1895. V. 37; 38; 39; 40; 41; 42; 43; 44; 46

Arrow of Gold. Arrow. Garden City: 1919. V. 39; 43

The Arrow of Gold . . . London: 1919. V. 39; 40; 41; 42; 43; 44; 45

Catalogue of Books, Mss., Typescripts . . . London: 1925. V. 45

Chance. London: 1913. V. 40

Chance. London: 1914. V. 37; 38; 39; 41; 42; 43

The Children of the Sea. New York: 1897. V. 39; 41; 43; 45; 46

The Children of the Sea. New York: 1898. V. 38

The Children of the Sea. A Tale of the Forecastle. London: 1897. V. 37

Confidence. London: 1920. V. 41

The Dover Patrol. Canterbury: 1922. V. 40

The Dover Patrol: A Tribute. Canterbury: 1922. V. 37; 40; 41; 46

Falk. New York: 19-3. V. 37

Falk, Amy Foster, To-Morrow, Three Stories. New York: 1903. V. 38; 44; 46

Five Letters Written to Edward Noble in 1895. London: 1925. V. 38; 41; 43

Geography and Some Explorers. London: 1924. V. 44

Heart of Darkness. New York: 1969. V. 37

The Inheritors. London: 1901. V. 43; 46

John Galsworthy. An Appreciation. Canterbury: 1922. V. 37; 40

Joseph Conrad's Letters to His Wife. Boston: 1927. V. 41

Joseph Conrad on Stephen Crane. Ysleta: 1932. V. 39

Joseph Conrad's Command, Otago. San Francisco: 1980. V. 46

Joseph Conrad-Life and Letters. By G. Jean-Aubry. London: 1927. V. 37

Last Essays. London: 1926. V. 42

Laughing Anne: a Play. London: 1923. V. 38; 42; 43; 44

Laughing Anne and One Day More. London: 1924. V. 37; 39

The Lesson of the Collision. London: 1919. V. 40

A Letter to William Nicholson. London: 1985. V. 41

Letters to His Wife. London: 1927. V. 41; 42; 43; 44

Letters from Conrad 1895-1924. London: 1928. V. 39; 44; 45

Letters of Joseph Conrad to Richard Curle. New York: 1928. V. 39; 41; 43

Letters From . . . 1895-1924. Indianapolis: 1928. V. 43

Lord Jim. 1900. V. 43

Lord Jim, a Tale. Edinburgh: 1900. V. 42; 43; 44

Lord Jim, a Tale. Edinburgh & London: 1900. V. 39; 40; 41

Lord Jim. London: 1900. V. 39; 42

Lord Jim: a Romance. New York: 1900. V. 39; 40; 43; 44; 45; 46

Lord Jim. Garden City: 1922. V. 46

Lord Jim. New York: 1959. V. 45

Manifesto Preface to a Career. Northampton: 1966. V. 38

Manifesto: Preface to a Career. Philadelphia: 1966. V. 40

Manifesto Preface to a Career. Philadelphia & Northampton: 1966. V. 39

Marcel Proust, an English Tribute. London: 1923. V. 41

The Mirror of the Sea. New York: 1906. V. 41; 43; 44; 46

The Mirror of the Sea. London;: (1906). V. 37; 40; 43; 44

My Return to Cracow. London: 1919. V. 40

The Nature of a Crime. London: 1924. V. 39; 43

The Nigger of the 'Narcissus.' Preface. Hythe: 1902. V. 38

The Nigger of the 'Narcissus'. Los Angeles: 1965. V. 46

The Nigger of the 'Narcissus.' A Tale of the Sea. London: 1898. V. 37; 38; 39; 41; 42; 43; 45; 46

Nostromo: a Tale of the Seaboard. London: 1904. V. 38; 39; 41; 42; 43; 44

Nostromo: A Tale of the Seaboard. London & New York: 1904. V. 39

Nostromo, a Tale of the Seaboard. London & Toronto: 1904. V. 42

Nostromo: a Tale of the Seaboard. New York: 1904. V. 43; 44

Nostromo. New York & London: 1904. V. 43

Nostromo. London & Toronto: 1918. V. 42

Nostromo. New York: 1961. V. 39; 40; 41; 42

Nostromo: a Tale of the Seaboard. San Francisco: 1961. V. 43

Notes on My Books. Garden City: 1921. V. 40; 44

Notes on Life and Letters. Garden City & Toronto: 1921. V. 39

Notes on Life and Letters. London: 1921. V. 40; 42

Notes on My Books. New York: 1921. V. 43; 45

Notes on My Books. London: 1921. V. 37

Notes on My Books. New York & Toronto: 1921. V. 38; 41

One Day More. London: 1919. V. 40; 44

One Day More. New York: 1920. V. 38; 40; 42

One Day More. New York: 1923. V. 42

One Day More. Westmisnter: 1919. V. 38

One Day More. Garden City: 1920. V. 38; 44; 46

An Outcast of the Islands. New York: 1896. V. 39; 40; 42; 43

An Outcast of the Islands. London: 1896. V. 37; 39; 41; 42; 43; 44

A Personal Record. New York: 1912. V. 39; 40

A Personal Record. London: 1919. V. 37

The Point of Honour. New York: 1908. V. 38; 41; 42; 44; 46

The Point of Honor: A Military Tale. 1908. V. 37

The Rescue. Garden City: 1920. V. 39

The Rescue. London: 1920. V. 38; 39; 40; 41; 42; 44

The Rescue. New York: 1920. V. 44

The Rescue: A Romance of the Shallows. London/Toronto: 1920. V. 37; 38; 45

Romance. London: 1903. V. 37; 39; 42; 43

Romance, a Novel. New York: 1904. V. 38; 39; 40; 43

The Rover. Garden City: 1923. V. 39; 42; 45

The Rover. London: 1923. V. 37; 38; 39; 40; 41; 42; 43; 44; 45; 46

The Rover. New York: 1923. V. 41

The Secret Agent. London: 1907. V. 37; 39; 41; 42; 43; 46

The Secret Agent. New York: 1907. V. 38; 41; 42; 45; 46

The Secret Agent. Toronto: 1907. V. 39

The Secret Agent, a Drama in Three Acts. London: 1923. V. 38; 39; 40; 41; 42; 46

The Secret Sharer. New York: 1955. V. 38

The Secret Sharer. 1985. V. 44

The Secret Sharer. 1985. V. 40

The Secret Sharer: an Episode from the Coast. New York: 1985. V. 44; 45

The Secret Agent. 1907. V. 37

A Set of Six. London: 1908. V. 40; 43; 44

A Set of Six. London: 1920. V. 41

The Shadow Line. London: 1917. V. 39; 44

The Shadow-Line. London: & Toronto: 1917. V. 43; 44

The Shadow Line. New York: 1917. V. 41

The Shorter Tales. Garden City: 1924. V. 43

The Sisters. New York: 1928. V. 38; 42; 44

A Sketch of Joseph Conrad's Life, Written by Himself in 1900. N.P.: 1939. V. 39

Some Reminiscences. London: 1912. V. 39; 41; 42; 43; 44; 46

Suspense. London: 1925. V. 37; 39; 41; 42; 43; 44

Suspense. London: & Toronto: 1925. V. 43; 46

Suspense. New York: 1925. V. 46

Suspense a Napoleonic Novel. Garden City: 1925. V. 37; 39

Tales of Hearsay. London: 1925. V. 39; 40; 41; 42; 43; 44; 45

Tales of Hearsay. Garden City: 1925. V. 37

Tales of Hearsay. New York: 1925. V. 43

Tales of Unrest. London: 1898. V. 37

Tales of Unrest. London: 1898. V. 37; 38; 40; 41; 42; 43; 46

Tales of Unrest. New York: 1898. V. 37; 39; 43

To My Brethren of the Pen. London: 1927. V. 39

The Tremolino. New York: 1942. V. 45; 46

Twixt Land and Sea Tales. London: 1912. V. 37; 39

Typhoon. New York: 1902. V. 38

Typhoon and other Stories. London: 1903. V. 37; 38; 39; 40; 41; 42; 43; 44; 46

Under Western Skies. London: 1911. V. 39; 40; 41; 42; 43; 44; 46

Under Western Eyes. New York: 1911. V. 40

Victory. Garden City: 1915. V. 39

Victory: an Island Tale. London: 1915. V. 39; 41; 43; 44; 46

Victory. New York: 1915. V. 41

Victory. An Island Tale. Toronto: 1915. V. 39; 42

Within the Tides. London: 1915. V. 39

Collected Works of Joseph Conrad. V. 46

the Works of Joseph Conrad. London: 1921. V. 46

CONRAD, JOSEPH 1857-1924 continued

The Works of Joseph Conrad. London: 1921-26. V. 41

The Works. Edinburgh & London: 1921-27. V. 42

The Works. London: 1921-27. V. 37; 42

The Works. London: 1923. V. 42

Works. New York: 1924. V. 41

The Works. Edinburgh & London: 1925. V. 42

Works. Garden City: 1925. V. 44

The Works. London: 1925. V. 37; 39; 41; 42; 46

Collected Works. New York: 1925. V. 38; 46

The Complete Works. Garden City: 1928. V. 42

Works. New York: 1928. V. 43

Collected Edition of the Works of Joseph Conrad. London: 1961. V. 39

Youth. Edinburgh: 1902. V. 41; 42

Youth. London: 1902. V. 40; 44

Youth. 1903. V. 43

Youth and Two Other Stories. New York: 1923. V. 44; 45

Youth. Kentfield: 1959. V. 45; 46

Youth: A Narrative and Two Other Stories. Edinburgh/London: 1902. V. 37; 39; 42; 45; 46

Youth and Two Other Stories. New York: 1903. V. 37; 41; 42; 44; 46

CONRAD, T. A.

Monography of the family Unionidae, or Naiades of Lamarck, (Fresh Water Bivalve Shells) of North America. Philadelphia: 1836. V. 40

CONRADS, U.

The Architecture of Fantasy: Utopian Building and Planning in Modern Times. New York: 1966. V. 46

CONRADUS OF LICHTENAU

Chronicum . . . a Nino Assyriorum Rege ad Tempora Frederici II . . . Paraleipomena Rerum Memorabilium a Frederico II Usque Carolum V. Strassburg: 1538. V. 45

CONRAN, ANTHONY

Claim, Claim, Claim: a Book of Poems. Guildford: 1969. V. 41

Metamorphoses. (Market Drayton): 1979. V. 37

CONRINGIUS, H.

The Gentleman Angler. London: 1726. V. 41

CONRINGIUS, HERMANN

Dubravius, Varro, Pliny, etc. Helmstadt: 1657. V. 39; 41

CONROY, JACK

A World to Win. New York: 1935. V. 37

CONROY, JAMES

The Emigrant's Wife; or, One in Ten Thousand. London: 1871. V. 42

CONROY, JOHN C.

A History of Railways in Ireland. London: 1928. V. 39

CONROY, PAT

The Boo. Verona: 1970. V. 39; 44; 46

The Boo. Atlanta: 1988. V. 44; 45

The Boo. Atlanta: 1990. V. 44; 45

The Great Santini. Boston: 1976. V. 42; 45

The Great Santini. Boston: 1978. V. 42

The Lords of Discipline. Boston: 1980. V. 43

The Water is Wide. Boston: 1872. V. 44

The Water is Wide. Boston: 1972. V. 39; 41; 42; 43; 44; 45; 46

CONSAG, FERNANDO

Carta del P. Fernando Consag de la Companian de Jesus, Visitador de ls Missiones de Californias, a los Padres Superiores de Esta Provincia de Nueva-Espana. San Ignacio: 1748. V. 38

CONSEQUENCES - a Complete Story in the Manner of the Old Parlour Game in Nine Chapters Each by a Different Author. Waltham Saint Lawrence: 1932. V. 43

CONSETT, MATTHEW

A Tour through Sweden . . . London: 1789. V. 38; 40; 42; 43; 44; 45

A Tour through Sweden, Swedish-Lapland, Finland and Denmark, in a Series of Letters. Stockton: 1789. V. 38; 42; 45

CONSIDERATIONS Concerning the Expediency of a General Naturalization of Foreign Protestants and Others. London: 1747. V. 41

CONSIDERATIONS Concerning the Proper Method of Carrying on the South-Sea Company's Trade to Caraccas (with) Some Observations Humbly Offered in this Manner by Reason That the Gentlemen Who Applied in Favour of Antigua . . . London: 1730. V. 41

CONSIDERATIONS Humbly Offer'd to the Honourable House of Commons, by the Planters and Others. N.P.: 1709? V. 40

CONSIDERATIONS on Mr. Paine's Rights of Man. Edinburgh: 1791. V. 39

CONSIDERATIONS on the Advantages of Yielding Up to Spain the Un-Expired Term of the Assiento Contract for an Equivalent. London: 1748? V. 41; 45

CONSIDERATIONS on the American Trade, Before and Since the Establishment of the South-Sea Company. London: 1739. V. 39
CONSIDERATIONS on the American Trade, Before and Since the Establishment of the South-Sea Company. London: 1739. V. 43

CONSIDERATIONS on the Bill for the Better Government of the Navy. By a Sea Officer. London: 1749. V. 41; 46

CONSIDERATIONS on the Bill Now Depending in Parliament, Concerning the British Sugar Colonies in America. Wherein All the ARguments for the Support of the Said Bill Are Considered. In a Letter to a Member of Parliament. London: 1731. V. 39

CONSIDERATIONS on the Conduct of the Dutch; Containing a Candid Examination Whether There Was Any Just Reasons to Expect They Should Concurr With Us in Declaring War Against France, or Whether There be any Sufficient Cause to Warrant . . . London: 1745. V. 41

CONSIDERATIONS on the Definitive Treaty, Signed at Aix la Chapell, October 7/18th, 1748. London: 1748. V. 45

CONSIDERATIONS on the Dispute Now Depending Before the Honourable House of Commons, Between the British, Southern, and Northern Plantations in America. London: 1731. V. 37

CONSIDERATIONS On the Present State of Affairs in Europe, and Particularly with Regard to the Number of Forces in the Pay of Great Britain. London: 1730. V. 45

CONSIDERATIONS On the Present State of the Intercourse Between His Majesty's Sugar Colonies and the Dominions of the United States of America. London: 1784. V. 40

CONSIDERATIONS on the Present State of the Nation, as to Publick Credit, Stocks, the Landed and Trading Interests. London: 1720. V. 38

CONSIDERATIONS on Two Papers, Published at Antwerp, Respecting a Loan for 3,6000,000 Guilders, to the Subscribed at the Houses of Messieurs J.E. Werbouck and C. J. M. De Wolf, of that City. London: 1791. V. 46

CONSIDERATIONS Relating to a New Duty Upon Sugar. London: 1746. V. 41; 45

CONSIDERATIONS Relating to the Laying Any Additional Duty on Sugar from the British Plantations. London: 1747. V. 45

CONSIDERATIONS Upon the French and American War. London. V. 38

CONSIDERATIONS Upon the Intended Navigable Communication Between the Firth of Forth and Clyde. Edinburgh: 1767. V. 42

CONSILIORUM Theologicorum Decas I. & II. Tubingen: 1605. V. 38

A CONSOLATORY Ode. Inscribed to the Marquis de la Chetardie, on His Disgrace, and Return from the Russian Court: London: 1744. V. 40

CONSTABLE, FREDA

The England of Eric Ravilious. London: 1982. V. 41

CONSTABLE, HENRY

Dianna: The Sonnets and Other Poems of Henry Constable. London: 1859. V. 43

The Poems and Sonnets of Henry Constable. London: 1897. V. 38; 40; 43

CONSTABLE, JOHN

The Conversation of Gentlemen Considered in Most of the Ways, That Make Their Mutual Company Agreeable, or Disagreeable. London: 1738. V. 45

The Later Drawings and Paintings of John Constable. 1984. V. 39

Remarks Upon R. Le Courayer's Book in Defence of the English Ordinations. N.P.: 1727. V. 44

CONSTABLE, THOMAS

Archibald Constable and His Literary Correspondents: A Memorial by His Son. Edinburgh: 1873. V. 37

CONSTABLE, W. G.

Exhibition of British Primitive Paintings from the Twelfth to the Early Sixteenth Century with Some Related Illuminated Manuscripts, Figure Embroidery and Alabaster Carvings, Royal Academy of Arts, London, Oct. and Nov. 1923. 1924. V. 44

Exhibition of British Primitive Paintings from the Twelfth to the Early Sixteenth Century with Some Related Illuminated Manuscripts, Figure Embroidery and Alabaster Carvings. Oxford: 1924. V. 42

Giovanni Antonio Canal, 1697-1768. Life and Work: Catalogue Raisonne. Oxford: 1989. V. 44

CONSTABLE, W. G. continued

Richard Wilson. London: 1953. V. 44; 45

CONSTABLE with His Friends in 1806. London: 1981. V. 46

CONSTANT, BENJAMIN

On the Liberty of the Press. London: 1815. V. 41

CONSTANT, LOUIS CONSTANT WAIRY, known as b. 1778

Memoirs of Constant, the Emperor Napoleon's Head Valet. London: 1896. V. 39

THE CONSTANT Lovers Garland or the Yarmouth Tragedy Shewing How By The Cruelty of Their Parents Two Faithful Lovers Were Destroy'd. Coventry. V. 42

CONSTANT WAIRY, LOUIS

Memoirs of Constant. London: 1896. V. 42

CONSTANTIA, a Poem. Edinburgh: 1755. V. 40

CONSTANTINI, ANGELO

The Birth, Life and Death of Scaramouch. London: 1924. V. 40

CONSTANTINUS, ROBERTUS

Supplementum Linguae Latinae, seu Dictionarium Astrusorum Vocabulorum. Lyon: 1573. V. 37

A CONSTELLATION of Genius. New Haven: 1958. V. 41

THE CONSTITUTION Asserted and Vindicated. London: 1763. V. 42

THE CONSTITUTION of the Several Indepedent States of America; The Declaration of Independence; The Articles of Confedertion Between the Said States; The Treaties Between His Most Christian Majest and the United States of America. Philadelphia: 1781. V. 38; 46

CONSTITUTIONAL Considerations on the Power of Parliament to Levy Taxes on the North American Colonies. London: 1766. V. 42

THE CONSTITUTIONS and Standards of the Associate-Reformed Church in North-America. New York: 1799. V. 44

THE CONSTITUTIONS of the Several Independent Sttes of America; The Declaration of Independence; the Articles of Confederation Between the Said States; and the Treaties Between His Most Christian Majesty and the United States of America. Dublin: 1783. V. 38; 44

CONSTITUTIONS of the Society of Stewards and Subscribers for Maintaining and Educating Poor Orphans of the Clergy Till of an Age to be Put Apprentice. London: 1782. V. 40

CONSTOCK, F. A.

A Gothic Vision: F. L. Griggs and His Works. Boston: 1978. V. 39

THE CONSTRUCTION of Mill Dams: Comprising Also the Building of Race and Reservoir Embarkments and Head Gates ... Springfield: 1874. V. 38; 41

CONSTRUCTIVE Cover Designing, a Book of Seventy-Six Original Designs Reproduced in Color on Sunburst Cover Paper. Hampden: 1923. V. 38

CONSULTATION de Douze des Plus Celebres Avocats de Paris, Touchant les Droits de Propriete du Seminaire de Montreal en Canada. Paris: 1819. V. 39

CONTACT Collection of Contemporary Writers. Paris: 1925. V. 45

CONTANT, CLEMENT

Parallele des Principaux Theatres Modernes de l'Europe et des Machiens Theatrales Francaises, Allemande et Anglaises. Paris: 1842. V. 37; 38

Parallele des Principaux Theatres Modernes de l'Europe et des Machines Theatarales Francaises, Allemande et Anglaises. Paris: 1860. V. 37; 38; 42; 46

CONTEMPO. Chapel Hill: 1932. V. 38

CONTEMPORARY American etching. New York: 1930. V. 41; 42; 46

CONTEMPORARY American Prints: Etchings, Woodcuts and Lithographs. New York: 1931. V. 41

THE CONTEST. A Poem. London: 1764. V. 40; 42

CONTESTACIONES de los Gefes, Corporaciones y Vecinos de la Isla de Puerto-rico. Puerto Rico: 1830. V. 45

CONTI, ARMAND DE BOURBON, PRINCE DE 1629-1666

The Works of the Most Illustrious and Pious Armand de Bourbon Prince of Conti. London: 1711. V. 42; 43

CONTI, NATALE

Mythologiae, Sive Explicationum Fabularum Libri Decem. Venice: 1567. V. 38

CONTILE, LUCA

Ragionamento ... Sopra la Proprieta delle Imprese con le Particolari de gli Academici Affidati et con le Interpretationi et Croniche. Pavia: 1574. V. 40; 43

THE CONTINENTAL Tourist and Pictorial Companion.. London: 1850. V. 39

CONTINUATION of the Account of the Pennsylvania Hospital; From the First of May 1754 to the Fifth of May 1761 ... Philadelphia: 1761. V. 42

A CONTINUATION of the Plain Reasoner. London: 1745. V. 41

CONTOSTAVLOS, ALEXANDER

A Narrative of the Material Facts in Relation to the Building of the Two Greek Frigates. New York: 1826. V. 41; 45

CONTRIBUTIONS to Medical and Biological Research Dedicated to Sir William Oser In Honour of His Seventieth Birthday, July 12, 1919 By His Pupils and Co-Workers. New York: 1919. V. 39; 40; 41

CONTRIBUTIONS to Natural History, Chiefly in Relation to the Flood of the People. Edinburgh: 1865. V. 40

CONVENTION OF THE CITIZENS CONSTITUTIONAL ASSOC. OF DAKOTA

Proceedings of the Convention of the Citizens Constitutional Association of Dakota, Held at Canton D.T. June 21st 1882. Yankton: 1882. V. 40

CONVERSE, LORING

Notes of What I Saw and How I Saw It: a Tour Around the World, Including California ... Cuba and Mexico. Bucyrus: 1882. V. 39

IL CONVITO Amoroso! Or, a Serio-Comico-Philosophical Lecture, on the Causes, Nature and Effects of Love and Beauty, at the Diffferent Periods of Human Life ... London: 1782. V. 46

CONWAY, HERBERT

Plastic Surgery at the New York Hospital one Hundred Years ago with Biographical Notes on Gordon Buck. New York: 1953. V. 37

CONWAY, JAMES

The Big Easy. Boston: 1970. V. 43

Forays Among Salmon and Deer. London: 1861. V. 41; 43

CONWAY, MARTIN

Aconcagua and Tieraa Del Fuego. London: 1902. V. 46

The Bolivian Andes: A Record of Climbing & Exploration in the Cordillera Real in the Years 1898 and 1900. London & New York: 1901. V. 38

The Bolivian Andes: a Record of Climbing and Exploration in the Cordillera Real in the Years 1898 and 1900. New York: 1901. V. 40; 46

CONWAY, MONCURE DANIEL

The Life of Thomas Paine. New York: 1892. V. 39

CONWAY, PAT

The Great Santini. Boston: 1976. V. 43

CONWAY, R. S.

The Italic Dialects. Cambridge: 1897. V. 38

CONWAY, T. W.

Report on the Condition of the Freedman, of the Department of the Gulf, to Major General N. P. Banks ... New Orleans: 1864. V. 42

CONWAY, WILLIAM MARTIN

Aconcagua and Tierra del Fuego. A Book of Climbing and Travel Exploration. London: 1902. V. 39; 41

The Alps from End to End. London: 1895. V. 41; 43; 44

The Alps from End to End. Westminster: 1895. V. 40; 41

The Bolivian Andes. London: 1901. V. 41

Climbing and Exploration in the Kara-Koram Himalayas. London: 1894. V. 37; 39; 41; 43

The First Crossing of Spitsbergen. London: 1897. V. 40; 44

The Woodcutters of the Netherlands in the Fifteenth Century. Cambridge: 1884. V. 44

CONYBEARE, EDWARD

Highways and Byways to Cambridge and Ely. London: 1910. V. 41

CONYBEARE, JOHN JOSIAS

Illustrations of Anglo-Saxon Poetry. London: 1826. V. 40

CONYBEARE, W. D.

Outlines of the Geology of England and Wales, with an Introductory Compendium of the General Principles of that Science, and Comparative Views of the Structure of Foreign Countries. Part I. London: 1822. V. 37; 38

CONYBEARE, WILLIAM DANIEL 1787-1857

Ten Plates Comprising a Plan, Sections and Views Representing the Changes Produced on the Coast of East Devon, Between Axmouth and Lyme Regis by the Subsidence of the Land and Elevation of the Bottom of the Sea, Dec. 26th 1839 and Feb. 3rd 1840. London: 1840. V. 41

COOK, ANDREW GEORGE

The New Builder's Magazine and Complete Architectural Library . . . London: 1819. V. 38; 45

COOK, BENJAMIN F.

History of the Twelfth Massachusetts Volunteers (Webster Regiment). Boston: 1882. V. 37

COOK, C. H.

Among the Pimas; or, the Mission to the Pima and Maricopa Indians. Albany: 1893. V. 39; 44

COOK, C. K.

Fairy Flights in Cloudland. London: (1919). V. 37

COOK, CLARENCE

The House Beautiful. New York: 1878. V. 37; 38; 41; 43

What Shalll We Do With Our Walls. New York: 1881. V. 44

COOK, DAVID J.

Hands Up; or, Thirty Five Years of Detective Life in the Mountains and on the Plains. Reminiscences of John W. Cook, Chief of th Rocky Mountains Detective Association . . . A Condensed Criminal History of the Far West. Denver: 1897. V. 37; 38; 39; 43; 44; 45

COOK, DUTTON

A Book of the Play. London: 1876. V. 39; 41; 44

COOK, EDWARD

The Life of Florence Nightingale. New York: 1913. V. 42

COOK, EDWARD T.

Studies in Ruskin: Some Aspects of the Work and Teaching of John Ruskin. London: 1890. V. 41

COOK, ELIZA

Poems. London: 1860. V. 37

COOK, FREDERICK

Journals of the Military Expedition of major General Sullivan Against the Six nations of Indians in 1779. Auburn: 1887. V. 46

COOK, FREDERICK A.

My Attainment of the Pole. New York & London: 1913. V. 42

My Attainment of the Pole. New York: 1911. V. 37

Through the First Antarctic Night 1898-1899. London: 1900. V. 40; 41

Through the First Antarctic Night 1898-1899. New York: 1900. V. 38; 44; 46

Through The First Antarctic Night 1898-1899. A Narrative of the Voyage of the 'Belgica' Among Newly Discovered Lands & Over an Unknown Sea about the South Pole. New York: 1909. V. 37

COOK, GEORGE

History of the Reformation in Scotland. Edinburgh: 1819. V. 46

COOK, GEORGE CRAM

The Provincetown Plays. Cincinnati: 1921. V. 39

COOK, H. C. B.

The Battle of Honours of the British and Indian Armies 1662-1982. London: 1987. V. 46

COOK, HARVEY TOLIVER

Rambles in the Pee Dee Basin, South Carolina. Columbia: 1926. V. 40; 42

COOK, HENRY

Patent Artificial Slate Manufactory, Woodford Bridge, Essex, for Covering Roofs . . . N.P.: 1786. V. 38

COOK, J.

Captain Cook's Florilegium. London: 1973. V. 42

COOK, J. F.

Miscellaneous Poems; and thoughts on the bettering the condition of the Poor. London: 1833. V. 37

COOK, J. KINGSLEY

Aftermath. 1986. V. 38

COOK, JACQUES

Voyage dans L'Hemisphere Austral et Autour du Monde, Fait sur les Vaisseaux de Roi L'Aventure & La Resolution en 1772-1775. Paris: 1778. V. 46

COOK, JAMES 1728-1779

Capt. Cook's Third and Last Voyages to the Pacific Ocean in the Years 1776 . . . 1780. Philadelphia: 1796. V. 42

Captain Cook's Florilegium, a Selection of Engravings from the Drawings of Plants Collected by Joseph Banks and Daniel Solander on Captain Cook's first Voyage to the Islands of the Pacific with Accounts of the Voyage by W. Blunt . . . London: 1973-76. V. 37

The Charts and Coastal Views of Captain Cook's Voyages: The Voyage of the Endeavour, 1768-1771. London: 1988. V. 40; 43

The Charts and Coastal Views of Captain Cook's Voyages. London: 1989. V. 42; 43

The Exploration of Captain James Cook in the Pacific. Adelaide: 1957. V. 44

Explorations in the Pacific as told by Selections from His own Journals 1768-9. Adelaide: 1957. V. 37; 38; 42

James Cook, Surveyor of Newfoundland: Being a Collection of Charts of the Coasts of Newfoundland and Labradore (sic) . . . San Francisco: 1965. V. 40; 43

James Cook, Surveyor of Newfoundland> San Francisco: 1965. V. 39

The Journal of H.M.S. Resolution 1772-1775. Guildford: 1981. V. 41; 43; 46

The Journals (and Life). London: 1955-74. V. 42

The Journals of His Voyages of Discovery. Cambridge: 1967-1974. V. 40

Journals of Captain James Cook on His Voyages of Discovery. Cambridge: 1967-67. V. 44

The Journals of Captain James Cook on His Voyages of Discovery. Cambridge: 1967-68. V. 46

The Journals of Capt. James Cook on His Voyages of Discovery. Millwood: 1988. V. 46

New Discoveries Concerning the World . . . London: 1778. V. 45

A New, Authentic and Complete Collection of Voyages Around the World . . . London: 1785. V. 45

Observations Made by Appointment of the Royal Society at King George's Island in the South Sea . . . V. 40; 42

Observations Made by Appointment of the Royal Society at King George's Island in the South Sea . . . London: V. 45

Troisieme Voyage de Cook, ou Voyage a l'Ocean Pacifique . . . Paris: 1785. V. 38; 40; 44

Captain Cook's Third and Last Voyage to the Pacific Ocean . . . London: 1785? V. 44

The Three Voyages of Captain James Cook . . . London: 1773/84/85. V. 38

The Three Voyages of Captain James Cook Round the World. London: 1821. V. 38; 40; 41; 42; 45; 46

The Three Voyages of Captain James Cook. London: 1842. V. 42; 43

The Three Voyages of Captain James Cook Round the World. London: 1921. V. 42

A Voyage to the Pacific Ocean. London: 1784. V. 37; 38; 41; 42; 43; 46

A Voyage to the Pacific Ocean. London: 1785. V. 46

A Voyage Around the World with Captain James Cook in H.M.S. 'Resolution.' London: 1974. V. 45

A Voyage Towards the South Pole, and Round the World. London: 1777. V. 42; 45

The Voyages of Captain James Cook Round the World. London: 1809. V. 44

Voyages Round the World for Making Discoveries Towards the North and South Poles. Manchester: 1811. V. 46

Voyages Round the World, Performed by Captain James Cook . . . London: 1822. V. 44

Voyages Round the World, Comprehending a History of the South Sea Islands &c. London: 1836. V. 46

The Voyages of Captain James Cook. London: 1842. V. 38

The Voyages of Capt. James Cook Round the World. London: 1853. V. 40

COOK, JAMES H.

Fifty Years on the Old Frontier as Cowboy, Hunter, Guide, Scout and Ranchman. New Haven: 1923. V. 40; 41; 46

COOK, JANE E.

The Sculptor Caught Napping: a Book for the Children's Hour. London: 1911. V. 42

COOK, JOHN

The Border and the Buffalo: an Untold Story of the SW Plains. Topeka: 1907. V. 39; 40; 41; 42; 43; 45; 46

Cursory Remarks on the Subject of Wheel Carriages. London: 1817-18. V. 45

King Charles His Case; or, the Appeal to All Rational men Concerning His Tryal at the High Court of Justice . . . London: 1649. V. 45

Observations on Fox-Hunting, and the Mangement of Hounds in the Kennel and the Field. London: 1826. V. 37; 43; 44

Voyages and Travels Through the Russian Empire Tartary and Part of the Kingdom of Persia. Edinburgh: 1770. V. 43

COOK, JOHN A.

Pursuing the Whale. Boston & New York: 1926. V. 43

COOK, JOHN KINGSLEY

Aftermath: Seven Poems. 1986. V. 40

COOK, JOSEPH W.

Diary and Letters of the Reverend Joseph W. Cook, Missionary to the Cheyenne. Laramie: 1919. V. 37; 45

COOK, MADGE

Thoughts in the Half Light. (Stamford): 1936. V. 37; 42

COOK, MOSES

The Manner of Raising, Ordering and Improving Forest Trees. London: 1724. V. 38

The Manner of Raising, Ordering and Improving Forest and Fruit Trees. London: 1679. V. 38; 40; 42

COOK, OLIVE

The English House through Seven Centuries. London: 1968. V. 42

COOK, PEYTON E.

Military Policy of the United States, 1865-1898. Austin: 1963. V. 39

COOK, ROBERT M.

Greek and Roman Pottery. New York: 1979. V. 42; 44

COOK, ROBIN

The Crust on Its Uppers. London: 1962. V. 41

COOK, SAMUEL

The Jenolan Caves: an Excursion in Australian Wonderland. London: 1889. V. 45

COOK, TENNESSEE CELEST, LADY 1845-1923

Constitutional Equality a Right of Woman . . . New York: 1871. V. 43; 44

COOK, TENNESSEE CELESTE, LADY 1845-1923

Essays on Social Topics. Westminster: 188-? V. 44; 45

COOK, THEODORE ANDREA

Eclipse & O'Kelly: Being a Complete History . . . London: 1907. V. 46

Eclipse and O'Kelly. London: 1907. V. 37; 39; 42; 43

A History of the English Turf. London: 1901. V. 43

A History of the English Turf. London: 1901-04. V. 42

Twenty-Five Great Houses of France. London. V. 38; 40; 44; 46

Twenty-Five Great Hosues of France. London: 1916? V. 40

COOK, THOMAS

Letters from the Sea and From Foreign Lands, Descriptive of a Tour Round the World . . . New York: 1873. V. 43

The Universal Letter-Writer; or, New Art of Polite Correspondence . . . London: 1798. V. 41

COOK, THOMAS HAGUE

Lett's Game Book, in Which to Register the Number and Kind of Game Killed, by Whom, How Disposed of, &c. London: 1861-73. V. 39

COOK, W. PAUL

In Memoriam: Howard Philips Lovecraft, Recollections, Appreciations, Estimates. Montpelier: 1941. V. 38

In Memoriam: Howard Phillips Lovecraft: Recollections, Appreciations, Estimates. North Montpelier: 1941. V. 37

COOK, WILLIAM

The Beauties of Johnson, consisting of Maxims and Observations . . . to which are now added Biographical Anecdotes . . . selected from Mrs. Piozzi, Mr. Boswell and other Authentic Testimonies, also his Will and the Sermon he wrote for the late . . . London: 1787. V. 37

A Handbook of Family Medicine and Hygiene. Together With Descriptions of Remedies, Numerous Choice Formulas, Dietary for the Sick, Rules for Nursing, Etc. Cincinnati: 1890. V. 42

The Life of Samuel Johnson with Occasional Remarks on His Writings . . . Dublin: 1785. V. 39; 40

The Mormons, the Dream and the Reality. London: 1857. V. 38

COOKE, ALEXANDER

Pope Joan. London: 1625. V. 42; 44

COOKE, ANTHONY C.

Routes in Abyssinia. Presented to . . . Lords . . . November 26, 1867. London: 1867. V. 42

COOKE, BELLE W.

Tears and Victory, and Other Poems. Salem: 1871. V. 39

COOKE, CASSANDRA

Battlerigdge: an Historical Tale Founded on Facts. London: 1799. V. 41

COOKE, CHARLES

A Series of Proof Portraits and Embellishments, Executed by First-Rate Artists to Illustrate the Best English Novelists, Poets and Essayists. London: 1805. V. 40

COOKE, CHRISTOPHER

Curiosities of Occult Literature. London: (1863). V. 37

A Journey Due East, Being the Journal of a Five Months' Trip to Lower Egypt, Palestine and Turkey, in the Winter of 1862-3, Returning by Athens and Rome to London. London: 1864. V. 39

COOKE, E. W. 1811-1880

Fifty Plates of Shipping and Craft, Drawn and Etched by . . . London: 1829. V. 39; 41

Landscapes British and Foreign. London: 1874. V. 41

Sixty Five Plates of Shipping and Craft. London. V. 38; 42

COOKE, EDMUND VANCE

The Biography of Our Baby. New York: 1906. V. 37

COOKE, EDWARD

An Inquiry Into the State of the Law of Debtor and Creditor in England with Reference to the Expedience of Allowing Arrest for Debt, as Well Upon Mesne Process . . . London: 1829. V. 40

Love's Triumph, Or, The Royal Union. London: 1678. V. 37

A Voyage to the South, Sea, the Round the World, Perform'd in the Years 1708, 1709, 1710 and 1711. A Journal of all Memorable Transactions During the Said Voyage . . . London: 1712. V. 38; 41; 45; 46

COOKE, EDWARD WILLIAM

Views of the Old and New London Bridges Drawn and Etched, with Scientific and Historical Notices of the Two Bridges . . . London: 1833. V. 45

COOKE, GEORGE

Animals After the First Masters for Examples in Drawing. London: 1829. V. 44

Charts of Classic Art, Embracing Photographs and Descriptions of the Most Celebrated Works of Ancient Greek Sculpture and of the Modern Masters. Boston: 1872. V. 41

Rules, Orders and Notices in the Court of Common Pleas at Westminster: From the Thirty-fifth of King Henry VI (1457) to Trinity Term the Twenty-first of King George II 1747 Inclusive. London: In the Savoy: 1747. V. 37

The Vicinity of the River Rhone Displayed in a Series of Views from Original Drawings by P. Dewint . . . London: 1825. V. 45

COOKE, GEORGE ALEXANDER

Topographical and Statistical Description of the County of Nottingham. (with) A Copious Traveling Guide . . . London: 1803-1810? V. 40

COOKE, GEORGE PAUL

Moolelo o Molokai. A Ranch Story of Molokai. Honolulu: 1949. V. 40

COOKE, GEORGE WINGROVE 1814-1865

The History of the Party; from the Rise of the Whig and Tory Factions . . . to the Passing of the Reform Bill. London: 1936-7. V. 37

COOKE, HENRY T.

The Churches of Warwickshire. Warwick: 1847-58. V. 44

COOKE, JAMES

Mellificium Chirurgiae: or, the Marrow of Chirurgery. London: 1685. V. 39

Mellificium Chirurgiae: or, the Marrow of Chirurgery. London: 1693. V. 41

COOKE, JAY

New 7-30 Gold Loan of the Northern Pacific Railroad Co. Philadelphia: 1870. V. 39

COOKE, JOHN

A Concise Description of the Royal Hospital for Seamen at Greenwich. London: 1793. V. 45

An Historical Account of the Royal Hospital for Seamen at Greenwich. A copy of the King William's commission, 1695, a review of the buildings designed by Christopher Wren and details of art work. London;: 1789. V. 37; 45

A Treatise of Pathology and Therapeutics. Lexington: 1828. V. 42

COOKE, JOHN E.

An Essay on the Invalidity of Presbyterian Ordinanation. (with) Answer to the Review of An Essay on the Invaldity of Presbyterian Ordination . . . Lexington: 1829, 1830. V. 40

COOKE, JOHN ESTEN 1830-1886

An Essay on the Invalidity of Presbyterian Ordination. Lexington: 1829. V. 37; 39; 42; 44

Fairfax; or, The Master of Greenway Court. New York: 1868. V. 43

Hammer and Rapier. New York: 1870. V. 43

COOKE, JOHN ESTEN 1830-1886 continued

The Last of the Foresters; or, Humors on the Border. New York: 1856. V. 43

Leather Stocking and Silk: or, Hunter John Myers and His Times. New York: 1854. V. 41; 43

A Life of Gen. Robert E. Lee. New York: 1871. V. 42

Mohun. Or, The Last Days of Lee and His Paladins. New York: 1869. V. 42; 43

Stonewall Jackson: a Military Biography. New York: 1866. V. 38; 39; 42

Stonewall Jackson: a Military Biography. New York: 1876. V. 38; 45

Stonewall Jackson: a Military Biography. V. 39

Surry of Eagle's-Nest: or, the Memoirs of a Staff Officer Serving in Virginia. New York: 1866. V. 39; 41; 43

The Virginia Comedians... New York: 1854. V. 41; 43; 44

Wearing of the Gray... New York: 1867. V. 39; 42; 43

The Youth of Jefferson; or, a Chronicle of College Scrapes at Williamsburg, in Virginia A.D. 1764. New York: 1854. V. 43

COOKE, JOHN HENRY

A Narrative of Events in the South of France; and the Attack of New Orleans in 1814 and 1815. Washington: 1836. V. 39; 42

COOKE, JOSIAH P.

Elements of Chemical Physics. Boston: 1860. V. 40; 42

COOKE, M. C.

British Fresh-Water Algae, Exclusive of Desmidiae and Diatomaceae. London: 1882-84. V. 37; 38

Illustrations of British Fungi (Hymenomycetes). London: 1881-96. V. 37

Illustrations of the British Fungi (Hymenomycetes). London: 1881-91. V. 37; 41; 42; 43

A Plain and Easy Account of the British Fungi. London: 1871. V. 44

COOKE, MARY

The Picards or Pychards of Stradewy (now Tretower) Castle, and Scethrog, Brecknockshire, with some Account of the faimly of Sapy of Upper Sapey, Herefordshire. London: 1878. V. 37

COOKE, MR.

The Trial of Mr. Cooke, Malt Distiller, of Stratford, for the Crime of Adultery with Mrs. Walford, Wife of Mr. Walford of the same Place Before Lord Kenyon, and a Special Jury, Who Gave a Verdict for the Plaintiff Three Thousand Five Hundred Pounds Damages! London: 1789. V. 46

COOKE, NICHOLAS F.

Satan in Society. Cincinnati & New York: 1872. V. 41

COOKE, PARSONS

Female Preaching, Unlawful and Inexpedient... Lynn: 1837. V. 44

COOKE, PHILIP PENDLETON

Froissart Ballads and Other Poems. Philadelphia: 1847. V. 44

COOKE, PHILIP ST. GEORGE

The Conquest of New Mexico and California: an Historial and Personal Narrative... New York: 1878. V. 38; 42; 43

Report of the Secretary of War Communicating... the Official Journal of Lieutenant Col. Philip St. George Cooke, from Santa Fe to San Diego... Washington: 1849. V. 41; 45

Scenes and Adventures in the Army: Or Romance of Military Life. Philadelphia: 1857. V. 37; 41

COOKE, ROBERT 1550-1615

Censura Quorundam Scriptorum... London: 1623. V. 38

COOKE, ROSE TERRY

The Deacon's Week. Boston: 1886. V. 38

COOKE, TENNESSEE CELESTE

Constitutional Equality, A Right of Woman. New York: 1871. V. 39

COOKE, THOMAS

The Complete Distiller... London: 1757. V. 42

A Practical and Familiar View of the Science of Physiognomy... London: 1819. V. 42

Tales, Epistles, Odes, Fables, &c. London: 1729. V. 38

The Universal Letter-Writer; or, new Art of Polite Correspondence. London: 1771? V. 45

The Universal Letter-Writer... London: 1788. V. 43; 46

COOKE, THOMAS FOTHERGILL

Authorship of the Practical Electric Telegraph of Great Britain... Bath: 1868. V. 45

COOKE, THOMAS L.

The Picture of Parsonstown (Birr) in the King's County (Co. Offaly), Containing the History of That Town, from the Earliest Period to the King 1798; Together with Its Description at the Present Day. Dublin: 1826. V. 42

COOKE, W.

A New Picture of the Isle of Wight. Southampton: 1812. V. 44

COOKE, W. B.

The Fungi of Our Mouldy Earth (a compilation). 1986. V. 38

The Fungi of Our Mouldy Earth (a Compilation). London: 1986. V. 37

Rome and Its Surrounding Scenery... London. V. 42

Rome and Its Surrounding Scenery. London: 1840. V. 37

COOKE, WILLIAM

A Commentary of Medical and Moral Life; or Mind and the Emotions, Considered in Relation to Health, Disease and Religion. London: 1852. V. 43

The Conquest of Quebec: a Poem. London: 1769. V. 37

The Elements of Dramatic Criticism. London: 1775. V. 38; 43

The Life of Samuel Johnson, LL.D. Dublin: 1785. V. 38; 42; 46

The Life of Samuel Johnson, LL.D. (with) Johnsoniana. London: 1785. V. 39

The Medallic History of Imperial Rome. London: 1781. V. 40

Memoirs of Charles Macklin, Comedian... London: 1804. V. 42; 46

Memoirs of Samuel Foote, Esq. With a Collection of His Genuine Bon-Mots, Anecdotes, Opinions &c... London: 1805. V. 39; 42

A New Picture of the Isle of Wight. London: 1808. V. 37; 45

Poetical Essays on several Occasions. London: 1775. V. 40; 41

COOKE, WILLIAM BERNARD

Richmond. London: 1832. V. 44

The Thames; or, Graphic Illustrations of Seats, Villas, Public Buildings and Picturesque Scenery on the Banks of that Noble River... London: 1811. V. 41

THE COOK'S Own Book. Boston: 1832. V. 46

COOKSON, JAMES

A New Family Prayer-Book, Containing the Book of Common Prayer and Administration of the Sacraments... Winchester: 1789. V. 44

COOKSON, WILLIAM

Agenda - volume 2, number 1 - SEamus Heaney - Fiftieth Birthday Issue. London: 1989. V. 44

COOLBRITH, INA D.

A Perfect Day, and Other Poems. San Francisco: 1881. V. 39

Songs from the Golden Gate. Boston & New York: 1895. V. 39

COOLEY, ARNOLD J.

A Dictionary of the English Language Exhibiting the Orthography, Pronunciation and Definition of Words... London: 1861. V. 41

The Toliet and Cosmetic Arts in Ancient and Modern Times. London: 1866. V. 39

COOLEY, DEWITT CLINTON

Triennial Messsage of the Governor of the Sovereigns, of Minnesota. Delivered To Their Representatives Assembled in the Third House, Feb. 8th, 1860. St. Paul: 1860. V. 42

COOLEY, J. E.

Extracts from Humbugiana; or, the World's Convention. Gotham: 1847. V. 43

COOLEY, THOMAS M.

The American Railway: Its Construction, Development, Management and Appliances. New York: 1889. V. 43; 44

COOLEY, TIMOTHY MATHER

Sketches of the Life and Character of the Rev. Lemuel Haynes, for Many Years Pastor of a Church in Rutland, Vt., and Late in Granville, New York. New York: 1838. V. 45

COOLEY, WILLIAM DESBOROUGH

Inner Africa Laid Open, in an Attempt to Trace the Chief Lines of Communication Across that Continent South of the Equator. London: 1852. V. 39

The Negroland of the Arabs Examined and Explained. London: 1841. V. 40

COOLIDGE, BERTHA

A Catalogue of the Altschul Collection of George Meredith in the Yale University Library... Boston: 1931. V. 43

Some Unrecorded Letters of Caroline Norton in the Altschul Collection of Yale University. 1934. V. 38

COOLIDGE, CALVIN

The Autobiography of... New York: 1929. V. 40; 42; 45; 46

The Autobiography of Calvin Coolidge. Kingsport: 1930. V. 41

COOLIDGE, CALVIN continued

Have Faith in Massachusetts: Speeches and Addresses of . . . Boston: 1919. V. 39; 43

COOLIDGE, L. A.

Klondike and the Yukon Country. Philadelphia: 1897. V. 39; 42

COOLIDGE, MARY ROBERTS

Chinese Immigration. New York: 1909. V. 45

COOLIDGE, RICHARD H.

Statistical Report on the Sickness and Mortality in the Army of the United States . . . Washington: 1856. V. 42; 46

Statistical Report on the Sickness and Mortality in the Army of the United States. Washington: 1856, 1860. V. 41

Statistical Report on the Sickness and Mortality in the Army of the United States . . . Washington: 1858. V. 37; 38; 41

Statistical Report on the Sickness and Mortality in the Army of the United States. Washington: 1860. V. 37; 38; 39; 41; 42; 43; 44; 45

COOLING, EDWIN

The Domestic Gardener's Assistant . . . Derby: 1837. V. 45

COOMANS, J.

A True and Compendious French and English Grammar. Edinburgh: 1764. V. 41

COOMARASWAMY, ANANDA K.

History of Indian and Indonesian Art. New York: 1927. V. 42; 44

Mediaeval Sinhalese Art. New York: 1956. V. 41

Selected Examples of Indian Art. Campden: 1910. V. 43

COOMBE, FLORENCE

Islands of Enchantment . . . Melanesia. London: 1911. V. 43

COOMBE, THOMAS

The Peasant of Auburn; or, the Emigrant. London: 1783. V. 46

COOMBS, CAREY

Rheumatic Heart Disease. New York: 1924. V. 42

COOMBS, DAVID

Churchill, His Paintings. A Catalogue . . . London: 1967. V. 42

COONEY, SEAMUS

The Black Sparrow Press: a Checklist. V. 39

A Checklist of the First One Hundred Publications of the Black Sparrow Press. 1971. V. 38; 41; 44

A Checklist of the First One Hundred Publications of the Black Sparrow Press. Los Angeles: 1971. V. 39; 40

COONLEY, LYDIA AVERY

Under the Pines and Other Verses. Chicago: 1895. V. 38

COOP, J. O.

The Story of the 55th (West Lancashire) Division. Liverpool: 1919. V. 40

COOPER, A.

Impressions of a Series of Animals, Birds, &c. Illustrative of British Field Sports. London: 1821. V. 43

COOPER, ALONZO

In and Out of Rebel Prisons. Oswego: 1888. V. 42; 46

COOPER, AMBROSE

The Complete Distiller. London: 1797. V. 40

The Complete Distiller . . . to Which are Added Accurate Descriptions of the Several Drugs, Plants, Flowers, Fruits &c. Used by Distillers . . . for the Use Both of Distillers and Private Families. London: 1810. V. 42

The Complete Distiller. London: 1757. V. 38

The Complete Distiller . . . London: 1760. V. 37

COOPER, ASTLEY

The Anatomy and Surgical Treatment of Inguinal and Congenital Hernia. London: 1804. V. 44; 45; 46

The Anatomy and Surgical Treatment of Abdominal Hernia. Philadelphia: 1844. V. 40; 42

A Case of Aneurism of the Carotid Artery. 1806. V. 42

Lectures on the Principles and Practice of Surgery, As Delivered in the Theatre of St. Thomas's Hospital (Taken in Shorthand). London: 1829. V. 44; 45

The Lectures of Sir Astley Cooper on the Principles and Practice of Surgery, with Additional Notes and Cases. Philadelphia: 1835. V. 41

The Principles and Practice of Surgery. London: 1809-10. V. 45; 46

A Series of Lectures on the Most Approved Principles and Practice of Modern Surgery . . . Boston: 1823. V. 41

A Treatise on Dislocations and on Fractures of the Joints. London: 1824. V. 45

A Treatise on Dislocations and Fractures of the Joints. Philadelphia: 1851. V. 42

COOPER, BRANSBY B.

Surgical Essays: The Result of Clinical Observations Made at Guy's Hospital. London: 1843. V. 39; 41; 44; 45; 46

COOPER, C. S.

Trees and Shrubs of the British Isles. London & New York: 1909. V. 41

COOPER, CHARLES HENRY

Athenae Cantabrigienses. Cambridge: Deighton Bell &: 1858-61-1913. V. 41

Memorials of Cambridge. Cambridge: 1858-66. V. 44

Memorials of Cambridge. Cambridge: 1860. V. 41

Memorials of Cambridge. Cambridge: 1860/61/66. V. 41

COOPER, DIANA

Trumpets from the Steep. Venice: 1962. V. 44

COOPER, DOUGLAS

The Work of Graham Sutherland. London: 1962. V. 44

Pablo Picasso Les Dejeuners. New York: 1963. V. 46

Picasso Theatre. London: 1968. V. 37; 43; 46

The Work of Graham Sutherland. London: 1961. V. 40

The Work of Graham Sutherland. London: 1962. V. 42

COOPER, DUFF

The Toast of the Immortal Memory of Quintus Horatius Flaccus - Proposed at the Annual Banquet of the Horatian Society on 22nd Nov. 1937. London: 1937. V. 41

COOPER, ELIZABETH

The Muses Library; or a Series of English Poetry, From the Saxons to the Reign of King Charles II. London: 1741. V. 37; 41

COOPER ELLWOOD

Forest Culture and Eucalyptus Trees. San Francisco: 1876. V. 43

COOPER, FREDERIC TABER

An Argosy of Fables, a Representative Selection from the Fable Literature of Every Age and Land. New York: 1921. V. 42; 44; 46

COOPER, FREDERICK FOX

A Tale of Two Cities; or, The Incarcerated Victim of the Bastille. London: 1885. V. 43

COOPER, FREDERICK H.

The Crisis in the Punjab, from the 10th of May Until the Fall of Delhi . . . Lahore: 1858. V. 42

The Handbook for Delhi . . . Lahore: 1865. V. 42; 43

COOPER, GEORGE

A Treatise of Pleading on the Equity Side of the High Court of Chancery. New York: 1813. V. 38; 40

COOPER, H.

What the Fusiliers Did. An Account of the Part Taken by The 1st Battalion 5th Northumberland Fusiliers, in the Afghan Campaigns of 1878-79 and 1879-80. Lahore: 1880. V. 41

COOPER, H. M.

A Naval History of South Austalia and Other Historical Notes. Adelaide: 1950. V. 41

COOPER, H. STONEHEWER

Coral Lands. London: 1880. V. 37; 42; 43

COOPER, J. C.

Military History of Yamhill County. McMinnville: 1899. V. 39; 41; 42

COOPER, J. E.

Diseases of the Reptilia. London: 1982. V. 37

COOPER, J. W.

The Experienced Botanist or Indian Physician, Being a New System of Practice, Founded on Botany. Lancaster: 1840. V. 45

COOPER, JAMES F.

The Technique of Contraception: the Principles and Practice of Anti-Conceptional Methods. New York: 1928. V. 40

COOPER, JAMES FENIMORE 1789-1851

Afloat and Ashore. London: 1854. V. 40

Afloat and Ashore; or, the Adventures of Miles Wallingford. London: 1844. V. 37

The American Democrate, or Hints on the Social and Civic Relations of the United States of America. Cooperstown: 1838. V. 40; 44

The Borderers; a Tale. London: 1829. V. 37; 42; 43

The Borderers, or The Wept of Wish-ton-Wish. Paris: 1829. V. 37

COOPER, JAMES FENIMORE 1789-1851 continued

The Bravo. London: 1831. V. 37; 43

The Bravo. Philadelphia: 1831. V. 40; 42; 43

The Chain Bearer; or, the Littlepage Manuscripts. London: 1845. V. 37; 42; 43

The Chainbearer. New York: 1845. V. 43

The Chainbearer; or, The Littlepage Manuscripts. London: 1945. V. 37

Correspondence. New Haven: 1922. V. 37

The Deerslayer. Philadelphia: 1841. V. 37; 38; 40; 42; 43; 46

The Deerslayer. New York: 1925. V. 41

The Deerslayer . . . N.P.: 1961. V. 43

England. With Sketches of a Life in the Metropolis. London: 1837. V. 37

Eve Effingham. London: 1838. V. 37; 42; 43; 45

Excursions in Italy. London: 1838. V. 40

Excursions in Switzerland. London: 1836. V. 40

Gleanings in Europe, England; by an American. Philadelphia: 1837. V. 39; 40; 44

The Headsman. London: 1833. V. 37; 41; 42; 43; 45; 46

The Headsman; or, the Abbaye des Vigneerons. Philadelphia: 1833. V. 40

The Heidenmauer, or, the Benedictines. Philadelphia: 1832. V. 39; 40

The Heidenmauer; or the Benedictines. London: 1832. V. 37; 39; 41; 42; 43

History of the Navy of the United States of America. Philadelphia: 1840. V. 41

History of the Navy of the United States of America. Paris: 1839. V. 37

The History of the Navy of the United States of America. Philadelphia: 1839. V. 37; 44; 45

Home as Found. Philadelphia: 1838. V. 37; 40; 45; 46

The Jack O'Lantern. London: 1842. V. 41

The Jack O'Lantern. Leipzig: 1843. V. 41

The Last of the Mohicans. Paris: 1826. V. 42

The Last of the Mohicans. Philadelphia: 1826. V. 39; 40; 43; 44

The Last of the Mohicans; A Narrative of 1757. London: 1826. V. 37; 42; 44

The Last of the Mohicans; a Narrative of 1757. Zwickau: 1827. V. 37

A Letter to His Countrymen. New York: 1834. V. 38; 45

The Letters and Journals. Cambridge: 1960-68. V. 43

Lionel Lincoln. New York: 1825. V. 43; 45

Lionel Lincoln: or the Leaguer of Boston. Paris: 1825. V. 39; 42

Lionel Lincoln. London: 1825. V. 37; 39; 42; 45; 46

Lionel Lincoln or, the Leaguer of Boston. New York: 1824-25. V. 37; 40; 43; 45; 46

Lives of Distinguised American Naval Officers. Philadelphia: 1846. V. 40

Mark's Reef; or, The Crater. London: 1847. V. 37; 38

Mercedes of Castile. Philadelphia: 1840. V. 41; 46

Mercedes of the Castile. London: 1841. V. 43

Mercedes of Castile: A Romance of the Days of Columbus. Paris: 1841. V. 37

The Monikins. 1835. V. 39; 45

The Monikins. London: 1835. V. 37; 40

Naval History of the United States. Philadelphia: 1839. V. 42

Ned Myers; or, a Life Before the Mast. Philadelphia: 1843. V. 42

New York. Being an Introduction to an Unpublished Manuscript by the Author Entitled 'The Towns of Manhattan.' New York: 1930. V. 45

Notions of the Americans . . . London: 1828. V. 37; 38; 43; 45

Notions of the Americans. Philadelphia: 1828. V. 39; 40

Notions of the Americans: Picked Up by a Travelling Bachelor. Philadelphia: 1833. V. 46

Novels. New York: 1859-61. V. 38; 40

The Novels of . . . 23 Volumes. New York: 1892. V. 37

Oak Openings: or, the Bee Hunter. New York: 1848. V. 38

Pages and Pictures. New York: 1861. V. 42; 43

The Pathfinder. London: 1840. V. 37; 40; 41; 43; 45

The Pathfinder. Philadelphia: 1840. V. 43

The Pilot; a Tale of the Sea. London: 1826. V. 40; 43; 45

The Pilot. New York: 1925. V. 37

The Pioneers. London: 1823. V. 39; 44; 45

The Pioneers. New York: 1823. V. 45; 46

Le Sorgenti del Susquehanna Ossia i Coloni. Romanzo Storico Descrittivo Americano. Napoli: 1829-30. V. 39

The Prairie. London: 1827. V. 39; 40; 44

The Prairie. Paris: 1827. V. 37; 38; 39

The Prairie. Philadelphia: 1827. V. 40

The Prairie. Menasha: 1940. V. 41

Precaution, a Novel. New York: 1820. V. 43; 45

Ravensnest; or the Redskins. London: 1846. V. 39; 40; 43; 45

The Red Rover. London: 1827. V. 39; 43; 45

The Red Rover, a Tale. Paris: 1827. V. 42

The Red Rover. Philadelphia: 1828/1827. V. 44

The Red Rover. Philadelphia: 1832. V. 38; 45; 46

The Red Rover. London: 1828. V. 37

Satanstoe; or, The Family of Littlepage. London: 1845. V. 40

Satanstoe. New York: 1845. V. 43

Satanstoe: Or the Family of Littlepage: A Tale of the Colony. Paris: 1845. V. 37

The Sea Lions; or, the Lost Sealers. London: 1849. V. 37; 42

Sketches of Switzerland. By an American. Philadelphia: 1836. V. 37; 40; 45; 46

The Spy. London: 1822. V. 41; 43; 45

The Spy. London: 1823. V. 40

The Spy; a Tale of the Neutral Ground . . . Paris: 1825. V. 45

The Spy: A Tale of the Neutral Ground. New York: 1963. V. 43

The Two Admirals. London: 1842. V. 43

The Two Admirals. Philadelphia: 1842. V. 43

The Water Witch - or the Skimmer of the Seas. London: 1830. V. 37; 42; 43; 44; 45

The Water-Witch. Philadelphia: 1831. V. 39

The Ways of the Hour. London: 1850. V. 37; 42

The Wept of Wish Tom-Wish. Philadelphia: 1829. V. 39; 40

The Wing and Wing, or Le Feufollet; A Tale. Philadelphia: 1842. V. 37

The Works. New York. V. 38

Works. New York: 1852. V. 42; 45

Works. London: 1888-1895. V. 37; 39

Wyandotte; or, the Hutted Knoll. London: 1843. V. 37; 42; 43

Wyandotte; or, the Hutted Knoll. London: 1855. V. 40

Wyandotte, or the Huted Knoll. A Tale. Philadelphia: 1843. V. 37

COOPER, JAMES IRWIN

The History of the Montreal Hunt. Montreal: 1953. V. 38

COOPER, JOHN B.

The History of Prahran, From Its First Settlement to a City. Melbourne: 1924. V. 46

COOPER, JOHN G.

Letters Concerning Taste. London: 1755. V. 40; 44

COOPER, JOHN GILBERT

The Life of Socrates . . . London: 1749. V. 42

The Life of Socrates, Collected from the Memorabilia of Xenophon and the Dialogues of Plato . . . London: 1750. V. 42

Poems on Several Subjects. London: 1764. V. 38

The Power of Harmony. London: 1745. V. 40

COOPER, JOSEPH

The Lost Continent; or, Slavery and the Slave-Trade in Africa, 1875. London: 1875. V. 44

COOPER-KING, C.

The British Army and Auxillary Forces. London: 1893. V. 42

COOPER, MERIAN C.

The Sea Gypsy. New York: 1924. V. 39

COOPER, MYLES

National Humiliation and Repentence Recommended and the Causes of the Present Rebellion in America Assigned in a Sermon Preached Before the Unviersity of Oxford, on . . . December 13, 1776 . . . Oxford: 1777. V. 41

Patriots of North America; a Sketch with Explanatory Notes. New York: 1775. V. 37; 38; 42; 44

Poems on Several Occasions. Oxford: 1761. V. 43

COOPER, PHILIP

The Craft of Surgery. Boston: 1964. V. 41

COOPER, REV.

The History of South America, Containing the Discoveries of Columbus, the Conquest of Mexico and Peru and Other Transaction of the Spaniards in the New World. London: 1789. V. 46

COOPER, ROBERT

The Infidel's Text-Book, Being the Substance of Thirteen Lectures on the Bible. Hull: 1846. V. 43

COOPER, S.

Over Sea. Under Stone. The Dark is Rising. Greenwitch. They Grey King & Silver on the Tree. 1965-77. V. 43

COOPER, S. C.

Trees and Shrubs of the British Isles. London & New York: 1909. V. 40

COOPER, SAMUEL 1798-1876

A Concise System of Instructions and Regulations for the Militia and Volunteers of the United States . . . The Exercises and Movements of the . . . Philadelphia: 1836. V. 41; 42

A Dictionary of Practical Surgery, Exhibiting the Present State of the Principles, and Practice of Surgery. London: 1813. V. 38; 39

A Dictionary of Practical Surgery . . . Philadelphia: 1816. V. 42

A Dictionary of Practical Surgery. London: 1822. V. 38

A Dictionary of Practical Surgery . . . New York: 1823. V. 45

A Dictionary of Practical Surgery. New York: 1830. V. 41; 42

A Dictionary of Practical Surgery. New York: 1834. V. 38

A Dictionary of Practical Surgery. London: 1838. V. 38

An Epitome of Modern Surgery. London: 1813. V. 38; 39; 40

The First Lines of the Practice of Surgery . . . London: 1807. V. 45; 46

The First Lines of the Practice of Surgery. London: 1809. V. 38

The First Lines of the Theory and Practice of Surgery. New York: 1844. V. 38

A Sermon Preached Before . . . the Senate, and House of Representatives of the Commonwealth of Massachusetts, oct. 25, 1780. Boston: 1780. V. 39

COOPER, SUSAN

The Rhyme and Reason of Country Life. New York: 1855. V. 37

COOPER, SUSAN FENIMORE

Rural Hours. New York: 1850. V. 38
Rural Hours. New York: 1851. V. 46

COOPER, T.

The Men of Mark. A Gallery of Contemporary Portraits of Men Distinguished in the Senate, the Church, In Science, Literature and Art, The Army, Navy, Law, Medicine, etc. London: 1876-1880. V. 39

COOPER, T. T.

Travels of a Pioneer of Commerce in Pigtail and Petticoats . . . London: 1871. V. 42

COOPER, THOMAS 1759-1839

An Account of the Trial of Thomas Cooper, of Northumberland; on a Charge of Libel Against the President of the United States . . . Philadelphia: 1800. V. 42

The Baron's Yule Feast: a Christmas Rhyme. London: 1846. V. 39

On the Connection Between Geology and the Pentateuch, in a Letter to a Professor Silliman . . . Boston: 1837. V. 43

Extract of a Letter from a Gentleman in America to a Friend in England, on the Subject of Emigration. London: 1798. V. 46

The Fabrication of the Pentateuch Proved, by the Anachronisms Contained in Those Books. Granville: 1840. V. 38

Facts Illustrative of the condition of the Negro Slaves in Jamaica . . . London: 1824. V. 45

Introductory Lecture on Chemistry, Delivered at the College of South Carolina, in Columbia, Jan. 1820. Columbia: 1820. V. 44

Lectures on the Elements of Political Economy. Columia: 1829. V. 38

The Life of Thomas Cooper. London: 1877. V. 42

A Manual of Political Economy. Washington: 1834. V. 38

The Purgatory of Suicides. London: 1845. V. 43

The Purgatory of Suicides. London: 1847. V. 42

The Right of Free Discussion. New York: 1829. V. 43

The Sacred Mysterie of the Government of the Thoughts . . . London: 1619. V. 44

The Scripture Doctrine of Materialism. Philadelphia: 1823. V. 43

Some Information Respecting America, Collected by Thomas Cooper, Late of Manchester. London: 1794. V. 39; 40

Some Information Respecting America. London: 1795. V. 38; 39; 41; 42

Strictures Addressed to James Madison on the Celebrated Report of William H. Crawford, recommending the Inter-Marriage of Americans with the Indian Tribes. Philadelphia: 1824. V. 39

Thesaurus Linguae Romanae & Britannicae . . . 1573. V. 45

Thesaurus Linguae Romanae & Britannicae, tam Accurate Congestus, Vel Nihil Pene in Eo Desyderari Possit . . . London: 1578. V. 46

Thoughts on Emigration. In a Letter from a Gentleman in America to a Friend in England. London: 1794. V. 42

Tracts on Medical Jurisprudence. Philadelphia: 1819. V. 43; 45

A Treatise on the Law of Libel and the Liberty of the Press. New York: 1830. V. 38

Two Orations Against Takin Away Human Life, Under Any Circumstances . . . London: 1846. V. 43

A View of the Metaphysical and Physiological Arguments in Favor of Materialism. Philadelphia: 1824. V. 43

COOPER, W. HEATON

The Hills of Lakeland. London: 1938. V. 42; 46

Mountain Painter; an Autobiography. 1984. V. 39

COOPER, WILLIAM

A Catalogue of Chymical Books. London: 1675. V. 43

A Guide to the Wilderness; or, the History of the First Settlements in the Western Counties of New York . . . Dublin: 1810. V. 38

A Guide in the Wilderness or The History of the First Settlements in the Western Counties of New York . . . Rochester: 1897. V. 43

It Happened in Prk (sic). New York: 1934. V. 44

One Shall be Taken and Another Left. A Sermon Preach'd to the Old South Church in Boston, March 22, 1740-41. Boston: 1741. V. 43

Practical Remarks on Near Sight, Aged Sight and Impaired Vision: With Observations Upon the Use of Glasses and on Artificial Light. London: 1847. V. 42

Three Marriages. London: 1946. V. 45

COOPER, WILLIAM DURRANT

A Glossary of Provincialism in Use in the County of Sussex. London: 1853. V. 41

The Parliamentary History of the County of Sussex, and of the Several Boroughs and Cinque Ports Therein. Lewes: 1834. V. 42

COOTE, ROBERT

The Compleat Marksman; or, The True Art of Shooting-Flying. London: 1757. V. 42

COOVER, ROBERT

The Fallguy's Faith. Evanston: 1975. V. 46

The Origin of the Brunists. New York: 1966. V. 37; 39; 42; 44; 46

The Origin of the Brunists. London: 1967. V. 37; 45

Spanking the Maid. 1981. V. 45

Spanking the Maid. Bloomfield Hills &: 1981. V. 42; 46

The Universal Baseball Association, Inc. New York: 1968. V. 39; 46

The Water Pourer. Bloomfield Hills &: 1972. V. 41; 46

COPE, E. D.

The Vertebrata of the Tertiary Formations of the West. Washington: 1883. V. 41

COPE, GEORGE W.

The Iron and Steel Interests of Chicago. Chicago: 1890. V. 44

COPE, GILBERT

Historic Homes and Institutions and Genealogical and Personal Memoirs of Chester & Delaware Counties, Pa. New York: 1904. V. 41; 42

COPE, WENDY

Men and Their Boring Arguments. Winchester: 1988. V. 38

COPELAND, CHARLES HENRY

The Life and Singular Adventures of Charles Henry Copeland, Who Was, by Birth, Heir to an Immense Property . . . London: 1808. V. 44

COPELAND, PETER

America's Fighting Men: Twenty-Four Paintings in Full Color by . . . Greenwich: 1971. V. 46

COPELAND, THOMAS

Observations on Some of the Principal Diseases of the Rectum and Anus. Philadelphia: 1811. V. 40; 42

Observations on the Principal Diseases of the Rectum and Anus; particularly Stricture of the Rectum, th Haemorrhoidal Excrescence, and Fistula in Ano. London: 1824. V. 37

COPELAND, WALTER

Babes and Blossoms. Verses by Walter Copeland. London: (c. 1908). V. 37

COPEMAN, S. MONCKTON

Vaccination, Its Natural History and Pathology. London: 1899. V. 39; 42

COPEMAN, SYDNEY ARTHUR MONKTON 1862-1947

Reports concerning the Glycinerated Calf Lymph Establishment. London: 1895-1903. V. 37

COPEMAN, WILLIAM SYDNEY CHARLES

A Short History of the Gout and the Rheumatic Diseases. Berkeley: 1964. V. 45

COPERNICUS, NICOLAUS

Astronomia Insaturata, Libris Sex Comprehensa, qui de Revolutionibus Orbium Caelestium Inscribuntur. Amsterdam: 1617. V. 38

De Revolutionibus Orbium Coelestium, Libri VI. Nuremberg: 1543. V. 38

COPE'S Smoke Room Booklets. Numbers 1-14 Complete. Liverpool: 1889-93. V. 37

COPI, RIVING

Introduction to Logic. New York: 1953. V. 45

COPIES or Extracts of Correspondence Relative to the Discovery of Gold in the Fraser's River District, in British North America. Presented to Both Houses of Parliament by Commande of Her Majesty, July 2, 1858. London: 1858. V. 39; 40

COPINGER, W. A.

Facsimiles of the Incunabula Biblica. London: 1892/1898. V. 42

Facsimiles of the Incunabula Biblica. London: 1898. V. 46

History and Records of the Smith-Carington Family from the Conquest to the Present Time. London: 1907. V. 37; 42

COPINGER, WALTER ARTHUR

Incunabula Biblica, or the First Half Century of the Latin Bible. London: 1892. V. 46

COPLAND, ALEXANDER

The Existence of Other Worlds, People with Living and Intelligent Beings, Deduced from the Nature of the Universe. London: 1834. V. 45

COPLAND, SAMUEL

A History of the Island of Madagascar, Comprising a Political Account of the Island, the Religion, Manners and Customs of Its Inhabitants, and Its Natural Productions. London: 1822. V. 38; 41

COPLESTON, EDWARD

Advice to a Young Reviewer, with a Specimen of Art. Oxford: 1777. V. 38

Advice to a Young Reviewer, with a Specimen of the Art. Oxford: 1807. V. 37

A Letter to the Rt. Hon. Robert Peel . . . on the Pernicious Effects of a Variable Standard of Value. Oxford: 1819. V. 37

A Reply to the Calumnies of the Edinburgh Review Against Oxford . . . . (with) A Second Reply to the Edinburgh Review. Oxford: 1810. V. 42

A Second Letter to the Right Hon. Robert Peel . . . on the Causes of the Increase of Pauperism and on the Poor Laws. By One of his Constitutents. Oxford: 1819. V. 37

COPLEY, FREDERICK S.

A Set of Alphabets of all the Various Hands in Modern Use. New York: 1877. V. 42

COPLEY GALLERY, BEVERLY HILLS.

Max Ernst. At Eye Level/Paramyths. 30 Years of His Work. A Survey. January 10 - February 20, 1949. V. 39

COPLEY, H.

The East African Sportsman's Handbook. Nairobi: 1932. V. 41

COPLEY, JOHN M.

A Sketch of the Battle of Franklin, Tenn . . . . Austin: 1893. V. 46

COPPARD, ALFRED EDGAR 1878-1957

Adam and Eve and Pinch Me. Berkshire: 1921. V. 46

Adam & Eve & Pinch Me. Tales by A.E. Coppard. Watlham Saint Lawrence: 1921. V. 37

Cheefoo. Croton Falls: 1932. V. 45

Cherry Ripe: Poems. Chepstow: 1935. V. 45; 46

Cherry Ripe. Windham: 1935. V. 43; 46

Clorinda Walks in Heaven . . . 1922. V. 42

Clorinda Walks in Heaven: Tales of . . . Waltham St. Lawrence: 1923. V. 45

Collected Poems. London: 1928. V. 37; 41

Count Stefan. Waltham St. Lawrence: 1928. V. 37; 38; 39; 40; 41; 42; 45; 46

Crotty Whinkwin and The Beauty Spot. Waltham St. Lawrence. V. 43

Crotty Shinkwin (with) The Beauty Spot. Great Britain: 1932. V. 46

Crotty Shinkwin, a Tale of the Strange Adventure that Befell a Butcher of County Clare (and) The Beauty Spot . . . Waltham St. Lawrence: 1932. V. 38; 42; 45; 46

Fishmonger's Fiddle: Tales. London: 1925. V. 42

Hips & Haws. Poems. 1922. V. 39; 41; 42; 43

Hips and Haws: Poems. Waltham St. Lawrence: 1922. V. 39; 40; 42; 44; 46

The Hundredth Story of A. E. Coppard. London: 1930. V. 41

The Hundredth Story. Waltham St. Lawrence: 1930. V. 39

The Hundredth Story. Waltham: 1931. V. 38

The Hundredth Story. Waltham St. Lawrence: 1931. V. 37; 38; 39; 40; 41; 42; 44; 46

Pelagea and Other Poems. 1926. V. 42

Pelagea and Other Poems. Berkshire: 1926. V. 41

Pelagea and Other Poems. Waltham St. Lawrence: 1926. V. 37; 39; 42; 45

Pink Furniture. London: 1930. V. 39; 40; 41

Rummy, That Noble Game. Waltham St. Lawrence: 1932. V. 37; 41; 46

Tapster's Tapestry. London: 1938. V. 41

Yokohama Garland. Philadelphia: 1926. V. 37; 39; 43

COPPENS, CHARLES

Moral Principles and Medical Practice, the Basis of Medical Jurisprudence. Cincinnati: 1897. V. 42

COPPER & Gold Alaska and Idaho the Hartford Copper and Gold Mining Company. Boston: 1901. V. 42

COPPER, FREDERIC D. BREBANT

Wild Adventures in Australia and New South Wales, Beyond the Boundaries, with Sketches of Life at the Mining Districts. London: 1857. V. 39

COPPER, THOMAS

Strictures Addressed to James Madison on the Celebrated Report of William Crawford, Recommending the Intermarriage of Americans with the Indian Tribes. Philadelphia: 1824. V. 37

COPPING, H.

Character Sketches from Dickens. London: 1924. V. 44

COPPING, HAROLD

Candian Pictures. London: 1912. V. 44

COPPINGER, JOSEPH

The American Practical Brewer and Tanner . . . New York: 1815. V. 40; 42; 45

COPPINGER, R. W.

Cruise of the 'Albert' London: 1883. V. 40; 41; 42; 46

Cruise of the 'Alerte' Four Years in Patagonian, Polynesian and Mascarene Waters, 1878-82. London: 1885. V. 41

COPPINGER, WILLIAM

Roman Catholic Bishop of the Diocese of Cloyne and Ross. The Polemic Catechism of John James Scheffmacher. Cork: 1830. V. 46

COPTIC Studies in Honor of Walter Ewing Crum. Boston: 1950. V. 44

COPWAY, GEORGE

The Life, History and Travels of Kah-Ge-Ga-Gah-Bowh. Albany: 1847. V. 42

The Life, Letters and Speeches of Kah-Ge-Ga-Gah-Bowh. New York: 1850. V. 40

Organization of a New Indian Territory East of the Missouri River . . . New York: 1850. V. 37; 42

Running Sketches of men and Places in England, France, Germany, Belgium and Scotland. New York: 1851. V. 37; 40; 42

COQUIOT, G.

Poupees de Paris, Bibelots de Luxe. Paris: 1912. V. 38

CORAELLI, FILIPPO

Etruscan Cities. New York: 1975. V. 44

CORAM, ROBERT

Political Inquiries: to which is added, a Plan for the General Establishment of Schools Throughout the United States. Wilmington: 1791. V. 37

CORAND, JOSEPH

The Arrow of Gold: A Story Between Two Notes by Joseph Conrad. 1919. V. 37

CORBELLI, LUIGI

Intagli e Dichiarazioni di Apparati e di Carri Trionfali Fatti in Reggio nel Maggio dell'Anno 1842 per le Nozze Delle Altezze Reali L'Aracid. Reggio: 1842. V. 37

CORBESIER, A. J.

Theory of Fencing; with the Small Sword Exercise. Washington: 1873. V. 42

CORBET, RICHARD

Poems. London: 1672. V. 42

CORBETT, EDWARD

An Old Coachman's Chatter. London: 1890. V. 43

CORBETT, HOWE, & CO.

III Annual City Directory of the Inhabitants, Institutions, Incorporated Companies, Manufacturing Establishment, Business . . . in the City of Denver for 1875. Denver: 1875. V. 42

CORBETT, JULIAN

The Fall of Asgard. London: 1886. V. 43

CORBETT, JULIAN S.

Official History of the Great War Naval Operations, from the Battle of the Falklands, Dardenelles to Jutland, to the end of the war in November, 1918. London: 1920-31. V. 37

CORBETT, THOMAS

An Account of the Expedition of the British Fleet to Sicily. London: 1739. V. 41

CORBETT, THOMAS continued

An Account of the Expedition of the British Fleet to Sicily in 1718 and 1720. London: 1739. V. 41

CORBIN, JOHN

The Elizabethan Hamlet. London: 1895. V. 43

CORBIN, P.

Hardward. Illustrated and Descriptive Catalog and Price List. New Britain: 1885. V. 38

CORCORAN, MICHAEL

The Captivity of General Corcoran. Philadelphia: 1864. V. 39; 42

CORDASCO, FRANCESCO

American Medical Imprints, 1820-1910. London: 1985. V. 43

American Medical Imprints, 1820-1910. New Gersey: 1985. V. 40

American Medical Imprints 1820-1910. Totowa: 1985. V. 38; 39; 40; 41; 42; 44; 45; 46

American Medical Imprints. 1820-1910. V. 37

CORDEAUX, E. H.

A Bibliography of Printed Works Relating to the University of Oxford. Oxford: 1968. V. 42

CORDELL, EUGENE F.

The Medical Annals of Maryland, 1799-1899. Baltimore: 1903. V. 40

CORDEMOY, J. L. DE

Nouveau Traite de Toute l'Architecture ou l'Art de Bastir. Paris: 1714. V. 38

CORDEN, SETH K.

The Oklahoma Red Book. Oklahoma City: 1912. V. 37

CORDER, SUSANNA

Life of Elizabeth Fry. Philadelphia: 1853. V. 44

CORDIALE Quattuor Novissimorum. Paris: 1482-85. V. 45

CORDIER, ALBERT HAWES

A Wyoming Big Game Hunt. Kansas City: 1907. V. 38; 42

Some Big Game Hunts. Kansas City: 1911. V. 37; 42

CORDIER & EKSTROM GALLERY, NEW YORK.

Not Seen and /or Less Seen of/by Marcel Duchamp/Rrose Selavy 1904-64. The Mary Sister Collection. January 14-February 1965. V. 39

CORDIER, MATHURIN

Mat Corderii Colloquiorum Scholasticorum Libri iv. Diligenter Recogniti... 1679. V. 44

CORDINER, CHARLES

Antiquities and Scenery of the North of Scotland, in a Series of Letters to Thomas Pennant. London: 1780. V. 37; 38; 40; 42; 44

Antiquities and Scenery of the North of Scotland. London: 1780. V. 45

Remarkable Ruines, and Romantic Prospects of North Britain, with Ancient Monuments, and Singular Subjects of Natural History. London: 1788-95. V. 37

Remarkable Ruins, and Romantic Prospects of North Britain, with Ancient Monuments and Singular Subjects of Natural History. London: 1795. V. 37

CORDINER, JAMES

A Description of Ceylon, Containing an Account of the Country, Inhabitants, and Natural Productions... London: 1807. V. 38; 41

CORDION'S Song and Other Verses from Various Sources. London: 1894. V. 40; 44
CORDION'S Song and Other Verses from Various Sources. London: and New York: 1894. V. 45

CORDLEY, RICHARD

A History of Lawrence, Kansas from the First Settlement to the Close of the Rebellion. Lawrence: 1895. V. 46

CORDNER, JOHN

American Conflict: an Address Before the New England Society of Montreal, and a Public Audience, in Nordheimer's Hall... Montreal: 1865. V. 42

The Christian Idea of Sacrifice. A Discourse Preached at the Dedication of the Church of the Messiah... Montreal: 1858. V. 37

The Foundations of Nationality. A Discourse, Preached in the Unitarian Church, Montreal, on the Sunday After the Great Railway Celebration, November 1856. Montreal: 1856. V. 46

CORDOBA, ANTONIO DE

Relacion del Ultimo Viage al Estrecho de Magallanes de la Fragata de S. M. Santa Maria de la Cabeza en los anos de 1785 & 1786. Madrid: 1788-93. V. 38

CORDOVA, DIEGO DE

Vida, Virtudes, y Milagros del Apostol del Peru el Venerable Pe. fray Francisco Solano de la Seraafica Orden de los Menores... Madrid: 1643. V. 37

CORDUS, VALERIUS

De Halosantho Seu Spermate Ceti Vulgo Dicto, Liber, Nunc Primum in Lucem Aeditus. Tiguri: 1565. V. 42; 43; 45

COREAL, FRANCOIS

Voyages De... Aux Indes Occidentales... Amsterdam: 1722. V. 45

CORELLI, MARIE

Barabbas. London: 1893. V. 38; 41; 46

A Dream of the World's Tragedy. London: 1893. V. 43

Free Opinions, Freely Expressed. London: 1905. V. 37

The Murder of Delicia. London: 1896. V. 45

The Secret Power. Garden City: 1921. V. 37

COREY, ALLEN

Gazetteer of the County of Washington, New York. Schuylersville: 1849-50. V. 39

COREY, EDWARD

Bug Book. (1959). V. 37

CORFIELD, W. H.

Catalogue of the Collection of Books in Valuable Bindings of the Late Professor W. H. Corfield, M.D. London: 1904. V. 41

THE CORHNILL Gallery, Containing One Hundred Engravings from Drawings on Wood... London: 1865. V. 39

CORK AND ORRERY, JOHN BOYLE, 5TH EARL OF 1707-1762

English Adventures. London: 1676. V. 37

The First Ode of the First Book of Horace Imitated and Inscribed to the Earl of Chesterfield. London: 1741. V. 40; 42

Letters from Italy, in the Years 1754 and 1755... London: 1773. V. 41

A Poem, Sacred to the Memory of Edmund Sheffield, Duke of Buckingham. London: 1736. V. 42

Remarks on the Life and Writings of Dr. Jonathan Swift, Dean of St. Patrick's Dublin. Dublin: 1752. V. 38; 40

Remarks on the Life and Writings of Dr. Jonathan Swift. London: 1752. V. 37; 38; 41; 43; 46

CORK, IRELAND. CORPORATION

The Council Book of the Corporation of the City of Cork, from 1609 to 1643 and from 1690 to 1800. Guildford: 1876. V. 45

CORK, RICHARD

Vorticism and Abstract Art in the First Machine Age. Cambridge: 1975. V. 44

CORLE, EDWIN

Burro Alley. New York: 1938. V. 39

Death Valley and the Creek Called Furnace. Los Angeles: 1962. V. 37; 38; 41

Igor Stravinsky. New York: 1939. V. 45

CORMAC MAC CUILENNAIN, BP. OF CASHEL

Sanas Chormaic. Cormac's Glossary. Calcutta: 1868. V. 44

CORMACK, JOHN ROSE

Clinical Studies Illustrated by Cases Observed in Hospital and Private Practice. Philadelphia: 1876. V. 38

CORMAN, CID

Clocked Stone. Ashland: 1959. V. 37; 44; 46

Nonce. New Rochelle: 1965. V. 38

CORMICK, FRANKLIN X.

The Portfolio of Ecclesiastical Designs. Greenwich: 1954. V. 39

CORNARO, LEWIS 1475-1566

Discourses on a Sober and Temperate Life. London: 1768. V. 38

Discourses on a Sober and Temperate Life. London: 1776. V. 42

Discourses on a Sober and Temperate Life. New York: 1833. V. 41

The Immortal Mentor; or, Man's Unerring Guide to a Healthy, Wealthy and Happy Life. Trenton: 1810. V. 42

Sure and Certain Methods of Attaining a Long and Healthful Life: with Means of Correcting a Bad Constitution, &c... London: 1727. V. 37; 41

Sure and Certain Methods of Attaining a Long and Healthful Life. London: 1737. V. 39; 41; 42

The Temperate Man, or the Way of Preserving Life and Health. London: 1678. V. 40

CORNAZANO, ANTONIO

Cornazano De Re Militari Nuovamente Consomma Diligentia Impresso. colophon: In Vinegia: 1536. V. 45

CORNAZZANO, ANTONIO

De re Militari Novamenti Impresso. Venice: 1515. V. 44

De re Militari Nuovamente con Somma Diligentia Impresso. Colophon: Firenze: 1520. V. 40

Delle' Artae Militare Novamente Impresso. Venice: 1521. V. 37

De Re Militari Nvovamente con Somma Diligentia Impresso. Venetia: 1536. V. 42

CORNEILLE, PIERRE

Oeuvres . . . Avec les Commentaires de Voltaire. V. 46

Oeuvres. Paris: 1862. V. 46

Pompey the Great. London: 1664. V. 39; 45

Theatre de Pierre Corneille, Avec des Commentaires. Geneva: 1764. V. 41

Theatre de . . . Geneva: 1774. V. 40

CORNEILLE, THOMAS

A Collection of 6 plays. (?Amsterdam): 1690-91. V. 37

Poemes Dramatiques. Paris: 1692. V. 40

CORNELIUS, BROTHER

Keith. Old Master of California. New York: 1942. V. 42

Keith. Old Master of California. New York: 1942-56. V. 45

Keith, Old Master of California. New York: 1942/57. V. 44

Keith. Old Master of California. New York: 1942 & 1956. V. 37

CORNELIUS, CHARLES OVER

Furniture Masterpieces of Duncan Phyfe. Garden City: 1923. V. 39

CORNELIUS, MRS.

The Young Housekeeper's Friend. Boston: 1846. V. 38

CORNELIUS NEPOLS

Excellentium Imperatorum Vitae. Glasguae: 1761. V. 46

CORNELIUS NEPOS

De Vita Excellentium Imperatorum. Paris: 1745. V. 40

Vitae Excellentium Imperatorum. Parmae: 1799. V. 41; 43

CORNELL, E. C.

Tales of Marthas Vineyard, Cape Cod and All Along Shore. Boston: 1873. V. 41

CORNELL, JOSEPH

An Exhibition of Works by Joseph Cornell. V. 44; 46

CORNER, E. J. H.

Wayside Trees of Malaya. Singapore: 1952. V. 46

CORNER, JAMES M.

Examples of Domestic Colonial Architecture in New England. Boston: 1901. V. 46

CORNER, JULIA 1798-1875

The History of China and India, Pictorial and Descriptive. London: 1845. V. 39

The History of China and India. London: 1847. V. 41; 43

Scriptural Tales. London: 1863. V. 39

Spring Flowers; or, the Poetical Bouquet. London. V. 40; 45

CORNER, SIDNEY

Rural Churches. London: 1869. V. 38; 39; 40; 43; 44

CORNER, WILLIAM

San Antonio de Bexar. A Guide and History. San Antonio: 1890. V. 37; 41; 46

San Antonio de Bexar, a Guide and History: 1890. V. 42

CORNEY, BOLTON

Curiosities of Literature. Greenwich: 1837. V. 37; 44

Curiosities of Literature. London: 1838. V. 44

Researches and Conjectures on the Bayeux Tapestry. London. V. 44

CORNEY, BOLTON GLANVILL

Voyage of Captain Don Felipe Gonzalez in the Ship of the Line San Lorenzo, with the Frigate Santa Rosalia in Company, to Easter Island in 1770- I: Preceded by an Extract from Mynheer Jacob Roggeveen's Official Log of his Discovery . . . in 1772. Cambridge: 1908. V. 39

CORNEY, P.

Voyages in the Northern Pacific. Narrative of Several Trading Voyages from 1813 to 1818. Honolulu: 1896. V. 37

CORNEY, PETER

Voyages in the Northern Pacific. Honolulu: 1896. V. 37; 38; 39; 40; 41; 42; 43; 45; 46

CORNFIELD, JIM

Fat Tuesday. Los Angeles: 1976. V. 42; 44

CORNFORD, FRANCES

Autumn Midnight. London. V. 45

Autumn Midnight. London: 1923. V. 41; 42; 43; 45; 46

Death and the Princess: a Morality. Cambridge: 1912. V. 41; 43

Death and the Princess. London: 1912. V. 42; 46

Different Days. London: 1928. V. 41

Fifteen Poems from the French. Edinburgh: 1976. V. 41

Mountains and Molehills. Cambridge: 1934. V. 42

On a Calm Shore. Poems. Cambridge: 1960. V. 41

On a Calm Shore. London: 1960. V. 38

On a Calm Shore. Cambridge: 1966. V. 39

Poems. Hampstead: 1910. V. 37; 39; 41

Spring Morning. London: 1915. V. 38

Spring Morning. London: 1923. V. 43

CORNHILL Gallery. London: 1864. V. 39; 44

THE CORNHILL Magazine. London: 1860-75. V. 41

CORNIER, SIDNEY

Rural Churches, Their Histories, Architecture and Antiquities. London: 1869. V. 38

CORNING, J. LEONARD

Brain Exhaustion, with Some Preliminary Considerations on Cerebral Dynamics. New York: 1884. V. 39

A Treatise on Headache and Neuralgia, Including Spinal Irritation and A Disquisition on Normal and Morbid Sleep. New York: 1888. V. 41

CORNISH, HENRY

Under the Souther Cross. Madras: 1879. V. 39

Under the Southern Cross. Madras: 1880. V. 46

CORNISH, J.

A View of the Present State of the Salmon. London: 1824. V. 39; 41; 44

CORNISH, JAMES

Cornish's Grand Junction, and the Liverpool and Manchester Railway Companion . . . Birmingham: 1837. V. 46

CORNISH'S Grand Junction and the Liverpool and Manchester Railway Companion. Birmingham & London: 1837. V. 40

CORNISH'S Guide and Companion to the Grand Junction and the Liverpool and Manchester Railways. London: 1838. V. 38

CORNUTUS, J. P.

Canadensium Plantarum Historia . . . Paris: 1635. V. 38; 40

CORNWALL, BRUCE

Life Sketch of Pierre Barlow Cornwall. San Francisco: 1906. V. 39; 40; 42; 43; 45

CORNWALLIS, CAROLINE FRANCES

Pericles. London: 1846. V. 39

CORNWALLIS, CHARLES

An Answer to the Part of the Narrative of Lieutenant-General Sir Henry Clinton, K.B. London: 1783. V. 46

CORNWALLIS, CHARLES, 1ST EARL 1738-1805

An Answer to that Part of the Narrative of Lieut.-Gen. Sir Henry Clinton Which Relates to the Conduct of Lieut.-Gen. Cornwallis During the Campaign in North-America in the Year 1781. London: 1783. V. 38; 40; 42; 45

Answer to Sir Henry Clinton's Narrative of the Campaign in 1781 in North America. Philadelphia: 1866. V. 46

CORNWALLIS, FIENNES

Letters Written from the Crimea to Several Members of His Family. London: 1868. V. 41

CORNWALLIS, KINAHAN

The New Eldorado; or British Columbia. London: 1858. V. 45; 46

CORNWALLIS, WILLIAM

Essayes. London: 1632. V. 37; 45

The Miraculous and Happie Union of England and Scotland . . . London: 1604. V. 38

CORNWELL, BRUCE

Life Sketch of Pierre Barlow Cornwall. San Francisco: 1906. V. 37

CORONADO, FRANCISCO VAZQUEZ DE

The Journey of Francisco Vazquez de Coronado 1540-1542. San Francisco: 1933. V. 45

CORONADO, JUAN DE

Do. Ivan de Coronado Escrivano de Svs Magestades y Escrivano del Cabildo y Regimiento de Esta Ciudad de Seuilla (etc.) Seville: 1552. V. 44

CORONELLI, MARCO VINCENZO

Memoires Historiques & Geographiques du Royaume de la Moree, Negropong & des Places Maritimes, Jusques a Thessalonique. Amsterdam: i.e. Paris,: 1686. V. 37

CORONELLI, P. M.

An Historical and Geographical Account of the Morea, NEgropont, and the Maritime Places, as far as Thessalonica. London: 1687. V. 39

CORONELLI, VINCENZO MARIA 1650-1718

An Historical and Geographical Account of the Morea. London: 1687. V. 38

Ordinum Equestrium ac Militarum Brevis Narratio, Cum Imaginibus Exposita. Ap Coronelli Quamplurimis Additionibus Locupletatis Nempe Curiae Romanae, Hebrooerum, Graecorumves in Anterioribus Editionibus Ommissis. Venice: 1715. V. 41

COROVA, DON A. DE

A Voyage of Discovery to the Strait of Magellan . . . London: 1820. V. 41

CORP, HARRIET

An Antidote to the Miseries of Human Life, in the History of the Widow Placid and Her Daughter Racheal (sic) . . . (with) Sequel to an Antidote to the Miseries of Human Life . . . New York: 1808-10. V. 43

CORPUS Juris Civilis. Volumen Parvum & Institutiones. Volumen Legum quod Parvum Vocant (Comm. A. Leconte & D. Godefroy). Institutionum sive Primorum Totius Iurisprudentiae Elementorum Libri Quatuor. Lyon: 1604. V. 37

CORPUS Juris Civilis. Volumen Parvum. Imperatoris Iustiniani Volumen Legum, ut Peculiari Vocabulo Nuncupant. Paris: 1526. V. 37

CORRADO, SEBASTIANO

Commentarius in Quo M.T. Ciceronis de Claris Oratoribus Liber, Qui Dicitur Brutus, & Loci Pene Innumerabiles Quum Aliorum Scriptorum, tum Ciceronis Ipsius Explicantur. Florence: 1552. V. 37

CORRADUS, QUINTUS MARIUS 1508-1575

De Lingua Latina, ad Marcellum Fratrem Libri XIII. Bonn: 1575. V. 45

CORRARIO, GREGORIO 1411-1464

Progne Tragoedia Nunc Primum Edita. Venice: 1558. V. 45

CORRE, M. P.

Diccionario des ¢Plantas Uteis de Brasil e das Exoticas Cultivadas. Rio de Janiero: 1926-75. V. 38

CORREA DE MELLO, JOSE

Allegacaeo do Brigadeiro Jose Correa de Mello, Governador das Armas da Provincia de Pernambuco . . . Lisbon: 1822. V. 39

CORRECT Account of the Rise and Progress of the Recent Popular Movements in Lower Canada. Bungay: 1838. V. 45

A CORRECT copy of the Will of the Late Mr. William Moulton . . . Also Remarks Upon the Nature of the Will and the Law of Mortmain. Newcastle-upon-Tyne: 1829. V. 45

CORRECTIONAL ASSOCIATION OF NEW YORK

Twenty-Fourth Annual Report of the Executive Committee and Accompanying Documents for 1868. Albany: 1879. V. 40

CORREDOR-MATHEOS, J.

Miro's Poster. Barcelona: 1987. V. 45; 46

CORREIA, THOMAS

De Toto eo Poematis Genre, Qvod Epigramma Vvlgo Dicitvr. Venice: 1569. V. 38

CORRELL, CHARLES

All About Amos N' Andy and Their Creators. 1920. V. 43

Amos 'n' Andy. Chicago: 1929. V. 39

CORRELL, D. S.

Manual of the Vascular Plants of Texas. 1979. V. 45

CORRELL, DONOVAN S.

Aquatic and Wetland Plants of Southwestern United States. Stanford: 1972. V. 39

Flora of the Bahama Archipelago. 1982. V. 38; 39

CORRELL, J. LEE

Through White Men's Eyes: a Chronological Record of the Navajo People from Earliest Times to the Treaty of June 1, 1968. Window Rock: 1979. V. 41

CORRESPONDENCE Between the American and British Plenipotentiaries Relative to the Commercial Convention Concluded on the 3rd of July, 1815. Washington: 1816. V. 41

CORRESPONDENCE Relating to the Claim of the South African Republic for Damages on Account of Dr. Jameson's Raid. Presented to Both Houses of Parliament by Comman of Her Majesty June 1899. London: 1899. V. 39; 40; 45

CORRESPONDENCE Relative to Hostilities of the Arickaree Indians. Washington: 1823. V. 38

CORRESPONDENCE Relative to the Affairs of Hungary, 1847-1849. London: 1851. V. 45

CORRESPONDENCE Respecting the Bering Sea Seal Fisheries: 1886-1890. Presented to Parliament, August 1890. London: 1890. V. 39

CORRESPONDENCE Respecting the Proposed Channel Tunnel and Railway. Presented to Both Houses of Parliament by Command of Her Majesty. London: 1875. V. 43

THE CORRESPONDENTS. An Original Novel; in a Series of Letters. London: 1775. V. 39; 42; 45
THE CORRESPONDENTS, an Original Novel; in a Series of Letters. London: 1776. V. 38

CORREVON, HENRY

The Alpine Flora. London: 1911. V. 44

CORRIE, EDGAR

Letters on the Subject of the Duties on Coffee. London: 1808. V. 42; 43; 46

Letters on the Subject of Coffee (Letter Fifth. June 15th, 1808). London: 1808. V. 42

Letters on the Subject of the Scotch Distillery Laws. Liverpool: 1796. V. 43

CORRIGAN, DOUGLAS

That's My Story. New York: 1938. V. 41; 42

CORRO, J. J.

La Providencia, Cuyos Decretos son Inescrutables, ha Permitido Que Una Corta Parte de Nuestro Ejercito Sufriera en Tejas un Reves, Cuando el Resto de las Fuerzas Mexicanas . . . Puebla: 1836. V. 39; 40

CORROZET, GILLES

Epitome Des Histoires Dès Roys d'Espagne & Castille. Paris: 1553. V. 38

Hecatongraphie. C'est a dire Les Descriptions de Cent Figures & Hystoires Contenants Plusieurs Appophthegmes, Proverbes, Sentences & Dictz . . . Paris: 1543. V. 38

CORRY, J.

A History of Lancashire. London: 1825. V. 38

CORRY, JOHN

The Life of George Washington . . . Dublin: 1801. V. 42

Observations Upon the Windward Coast of Africa. London: 1807. V. 42

A Satirical View of London at the Commencement of the Nineteenth Century, by an Observer. London: 1801. V. 37; 40; 42

CORRY, JOHN P.

Indian Affairs in Georgia 1732-1756. Philadelphia: 1936. V. 42

CORSARO, FRANK

The Love for Three Oranges. New York: 1984. V. 37; 41; 42; 46

CORSER, H. P.

Seventy-Six History of Alaska. N.P.: 1927. V. 41

CORSER, THOMAS

Catalogue of the First (-Eighth) Portion of the Valuable and Extensive Library, Formed by the Rev. Thomas Corser, M.A., F.S.A., of Stand rEctory near Manchester . . . London: 1868-1873. V. 44

Collectanea Anglo-Poetica: or, a Bibliographical and Descriptive Catalogue of a Portion of a Collection of Early English Poetry. Manchester: 1860-83. V. 44

Collectanea Anglo-Poetica; or, a Bibliographical and Descritpive Catalogue of a Portion of a Collection of Early English Poetry, with Occasional Extracts and Remarks Biographical and Critical. London: 1860-73. V. 37

CORSO, GREGORY

Bomb. 1958. V. 45

Gasoline. San Francisco: 1958. V. 45

The Geometric Poem. Milan: 1966. V. 44; 46

Long Live Man. New York: 1962. V. 45

The Vestal Lady on Brattle, and Other Poems. Cambridge: 1955. V. 39

CORSO, RINALDO

Fondamenti del Parlar Thoscano. Venice: 1549. V. 45

CORSON, F. REID

The Atlantic Ferry in the 20th Century, the Advances in Trans-Atlantic Travel from 1900 to 1930. London: 1930. V. 42

CORSON, JULIET

Cooking School Text Book; and Housekeeper's Guide to Cookery and Kitchen Management. New York: 1879. V. 37

Family Living on $500 a Year. New York: 1888. V. 37

CORT, C. F.

A Tribute to Learning, Fame, Science and Genius. London: 1834. V. 37; 42

CORTAZAR, JULIO

The Winners. London: 1965. V. 38

CORTE REAL, JERONIMO

Naufragio e Lastimoso Sucesso da Perdicam de Manoel de Sousa de Sepulveda & Dona Lianor de Sa Sua Mulher, e Filhos, Vindo da India Para Este Reyno na Nao Chamada o Galiao Grande S. Jodo . . . Lisbon: 1594. V. 45

CORTES, HERNAN

Historia de Nueva-Espana. Mexico: 1770. V. 40

CORTES, HERNANDO 1485-1547

The Despatches of Hernando Cortes, the Conqueror of Mexico, Addressed to the Emperor Charles V . . . New York & London: 1843. V. 39; 45

CORTES OSSORIO, JUAN DE, S. J. 1623-1688.

Reparos historiales Apologeticos. Pamplona: 1677. V. 37

CORTESAO, A.

History of Portuguese Cartography. Coimbra: 1969. V. 40

The Nautical Chaart of 1424 and the Early Discovery and Crtographical Representation of America. Coimbra: 1954. V. 38; 41; 43; 44; 46

Portugaliae Monumenta Cartographica. Lisbon: 1960. V. 40; 41; 42; 43; 45

CORTESAO, ARMANDO

Cartografia e Cartografos Portugueses dos Seculos XV e XVI. Lisbon: 1935. V. 43

History of Portuguese Cartography. Coimbra: 1969-71. V. 39

CORTESE, JAMES

What the Owl Said. West Burke: 1979. V. 39; 42; 44

What the Owl Said. Vermont: 1979. V. 39

What the Owl Said. By James Cortese. Newark, Vermont: 1979. V. 37

CORTEZ SOLPOSTO, JOSE

Flores Celestes Colhidas Entre os Espinhos da Sagrada Coroa da Augusta, Veneravel, e Soberana Cabeca do Divino e Immortal Rei Dos Seculos, Jesu Christo . . . Lisbon: 1807. V. 39; 45

CORTI, E.

A History of Smoking. London: 1931. V. 43

CORTISSOZ, ROYAL

Augustus Saint-Gaudens. Boston: 1908. V. 41

Catalogue of the Etchings and Dry-Points of Childe Hassam. New York: 1925. V. 41

Monograph on the Work of Charles A. Platt. New York: 1913. V. 42; 44

CORTUSO, GIACOMO ANTONIO

L'Horto de i Semplici di Padova, ove si Vede Primieramente la Forma di Tutta la Pianta con le Sue Misure. Venetia: 1591. V. 39

CORVINUS, LAURENTIUS

Cosmographia dans Manductionem in Tabulas Ptholomei . . . Basle: 1497. V. 38

CORVISART, J. N.

Nouvelle Method Pour Reconnaitre les Maladies Internes de la Poitrine par la Percussion de Cette Cavite . . . Paris: 1808. V. 40; 41

A Treatise on the Diseases and Organic Lesions of the Heart and Great Vessels. London: 1813. V. 42

CORVISART, JEAN NICOLAS

Essai sur les Maladies et Les Lesions Organiques du Coeur et des Gros Vaisseaux. Paris: 1806. V. 38

CORVO, 1860-1960. A Collection of Essays by Various Hands to Commemorate the Centenary of the Birth of Fr. Rolfe, Baron Corvo. Aylesford: 1961. V. 40

CORWIN, BRUCE R.

A Trip to the Rockies. New York: 1889. V. 46

A Trip to the Rockies. By B.R.C. New York: 1890. V. 37

CORWIN, NORMAN

Prayer for the 70's. Los Angeles: 1972. V. 43; 46

CORWIN, THOMAS

Report of the Trade and Commerce of the British North American Colonies With the United States . . . Washington: 1851. V. 39; 42

CORY, C. B.

Birds of the Bahama Islands. Boston: 1880. V. 37; 42; 43

CORY, CHARLES B.

The Birds of Haiti and San Domingo. Boston: 1885. V. 44; 46

CORY, CHARLES BARNEY

A Naturalist in the Magdalen Islands. Boston: 1878. V. 37

CORY, ISAAC PRESTON

Ancient Fragments of the Phoenician, Chaldaean, Egyptian, Tyrian, Carthaginian, Indian, Persian and Other Writers . . . London: 1832. V. 38

CORY, JOHN

The Detector of Quackery; or, Analyser of Medical, Philosophical, Political, Dramatic and Literary Imposture . . . London: 1802. V. 38

CORY, ROBERT

A Narrative of the Grand Festival at Yarmouth, on Tuesday, the 19th of April, 1814. Yarmouth: 1814. V. 39

CORY, WILLIAM

Ionica. London: 1855, 1877. V. 37

Lucretilis. Cambridge: 1951. V. 40; 41

CORY, WILLIAM JOHNSON

Ionica. London: 1858. V. 38

Ionica II. London: 1877. V. 40

Lucretilis; Latin Poems. London: 1951. V. 45

CORYATE, THOMAS 1577?-1617

Coryat's Crudities Hastily Gobled Up in Five Months Travells in France, Savoy, Italy, Rhetia, Commonly Called the Grisons Country . . . London: 1611. V. 39; 41; 43

Coryat's Crudities . . . London: 1611. V. 43

Coryat's Crudities, Reprinted from the Edition of 1611. London: 1776. V. 37; 39; 40; 42

Coryat's Crudities. Glasgow: 1905. V. 41; 42

Traveller for the English Wits: Greeting. London. V. 43

CORYE, JOHN

A Cure for Jealousie, a Comedy. London: 1701. V. 44; 45

The Generous Enemies or the Ridiculous Lovers: A Comedy. London: 1672. V. 37

CORYNE, J. STIRLING

The Scenery and Antiquities of Ireland, Illustrated from Drawings by W. H. Bartlett. London: 1850. V. 43

COS, MARTIN PERFECTO

Correspondence del Supremo Gobierno Sobre los Departamentos de Tejas. Matamoros: 1835. V. 45

COSENS, JOHN

The Economy of Beauty. London: 1777. V. 38; 41

The Economy of Beauty; in a Series of Fables Addressed to the Ladies. London: 1777 & 1773. V. 38

COSENTINO, FRANK F.

Edward Marshall Boehm, 1913-1969. Chicago: 1969. V. 38

COSENTINO, GIOVANNI SAPPETTI 1692-1772

Elementi di Commerzio o Siano Regole Generali per Coltivarlo Appoggiate Alla Regione, Alla Practica Delle Nazioni, ed Alle Autorita de'Scrittori di Questa Materia. Genova: 1742. V. 39

COSGROVE, ART

A New History of Ireland. II: Medieval Ireland, 1169-1534. Oxford: 1987. V. 37

COSGROVE, RACHEL

Hidden Valley of Oz. 1951. V. 46

COSIN, RICHARD

An Apologie for Sundrie Proceedings by Jurisdiction Ecclesiasticall, of Late Times by Some Chalenged, and Also Diversly by Them Impugned. London: 1593. V. 40

COSMETICS for My Lady and Good Fare for My Lord. London: 1934. V. 42

COSMO III, GRAND DUKE OF TUSCANY 1642-1723

Travels of Cosmo the Third . . . Through England, During the Reign of King Charles the Second (1669). London: 1821. V. 39

COSNAHAN, MARK

Important Observations for the Benefit of Commerce and Navigation, with Salutary Remarks Upon Mariner's Lights in the Channel . . . Liverpool: 1823. V. 42

COSSA, LUIGI 1831-1896

Guide to the Study of Political Economy. London: 1880. V. 37

An Introduction to the Study of Political Economy. London: 1893. V. 42

COSSALI, PIETRO

Origine, Traporto in Italia, Primi Progressi in Essa dell'Algebra. Storia Critica di Nuove Disquisizioni Analithiche e Metafische Arricchita. Parma: 1797-99. V. 37

COSSIM, PSEUD.

Considerations on the Danger and Impolicy of Laying Open the Trade With India and China . . . London: 1813. V. 42

COSTA, CHRISTOVAM

Aromatum & Medicamentorum in Orientali India Nascentium Liber . . . Antverpiae: 1582. V. 45

COSTA, CLAUDIO MANOEL DA

Orbas (sic). Coimbra: 1768. V. 39

COSTA DE MACEDO, JOAQUIM JOSE DA

Memoria em Que se Pertende Provar que os Arabes nao Conhecerao as Canarias antes dos Portuguezes. Lisbon: 1844. V. 38

COSTA, JOAO SEVERIANO MACIEL DA

Memoria Sobre a Necessidade de Abolir a Introducao dos Escravos Africanos No Brasil. Coimbra: 1821. V. 37

COSTAIN, THOMAS B.

The White and the Gold. Garden City: 1954. V. 43

The White and the Gold. New York: 1954. V. 44

COSTAKIS, GEORGE

The George Costakis Collection of Russian Avant-Garde Art. New York: 1981. V. 39

COSTANSO, MIGUEL

The Spanish Occupation of California. San Francisco: 1934. V. 39; 41

COSTARD, GEORGE

The History of Astronomy, with Its Application to Geography, History and Chronology . . . . London: 1767. V. 42

COSTE, JEAN FRANCOIS

Oratio Habita in Capitolio Guliemopolitano in Comitiis Universitatis Virginiae die XII Junii MDCCLXXXII. Lugduni: 1783. V. 40

COSTE, PIERRE

The Life of Lewis Bourbon, Late Prince of conde. London: 1693. V. 45

COSTELLO, A. E.

History of the Police Department of Jersey City. Jersey City: 1891. V. 41

COSTELLO, AUGUSTINE E.

Our Fireman. A History of the New York Fire Departments, Volunteer and Paid. New York: 1887. V. 39

COSTELLO, DUDLEY

Holidays with Hobgoblins, and Talk of Strange Things. London: 1861. V. 38

COSTELLO, EDWARD

The Adventures of a Soldier, or Memoirs of Edward Costello, K.S.F . . . London: 1841. V. 43

COSTELLO, J. A.

The Siwash Their Life, Legends and Tales. Seattle: 1895. V. 44

COSTELLO, LOUISA STUART

The Rose Garden of Persia. London: 1845. V. 38; 39; 42; 43; 44

The Rose Garden of Persia. London: 1888. V. 42

Specimens of the Early Poetry of France. London: 1835. V. 37; 38; 41

A Summer Among the Bocages and the Vines. London: 1840. V. 39; 45

COSTER, J.

Manual of Surgical Operations: Containing the New Methods of Operating Devised by Lisfranc . . . Philadelphia: 1825. V. 37

COSTIGAN, ARTHUR WILLIAM

Sketches of Society and Manners in Portugal. London: 1787. V. 37; 39

Sketches of Society and manners in Portugal, in a series of Letters from Arthur W. Costigan, Late a Captain of the Irish Brigade in the Service of Spain, to his brother in London. (N.P.): 1787. V. 37

COSTS, ALICE

The Book of Flowers. New York: 1973. V. 37

THE COSTUME of the Russian Empire. London: 1803. V. 38; 42
THE COSTUME of the Russian Empire. London: 1804. V. 46

COSTUMES and Curtains from the Diaghilev and De Basil Ballets. New York: 1972. V. 41

COSTUMES Espagnols. New York: 1930. V. 44

COSTUMES of British Ladies from the Time of William the 1st to the Reign of Queen Victoria. London: 1840. V. 39; 41

COTELIER, JEAN BAPTISTE 1627-1686

SS. Patrum qui Temporibus Apostolicis Floruerunt, Barnabae, Clementis, Hermae, Ignatii, Polycarpi Opera Edita et Inedita, Vera & Supposititia . . . Amsterdam: 1724. V. 39

COTES, ROGER

Hydrostatical and Pneumatical Lectures. London: 1738. V. 41; 45

Hydrostatical and Pneumatical Lectures. London: 1775. V. 39

COTGRAVE, RANDAL

A Dictionarie of the French and English Tongues. London: 1611. V. 38; 43

COTHER, E.

A Serious Proposal for Promoting Lawful and Honourable Marriage. London: 1750. V. 43

COTMAN, J. S.

Excursions in the County or Essex . . . London: 1818. V. 45

COTMAN, JOHN SELL

Antiquities of Saint Mary's Chapel, at Stourbridge, Near Cambridge. London: 1819. V. 44

Antiquities of St. Mary's Chapel at Stowbridge Near Cambridge. Yarmouth: 1819. V. 37

Architectural Antiquities of Normandy, Accompanied by Historical and Descriptive Notices by Dawson Turner. London: 1822. V. 37; 39

Engravings of Sepulchural Brasses in Norfolk and Suffolk. London: 1839. V. 41

THE COTTAGE Minstrel; or, Verses on Various Subjects. Philadelphia: 1827. V. 41

COTTAGE Designs with Constructive Details. New York: 1897. V. 37

COTTART, PIERRE

Receuil des plus Beaux Portraits de Plusieurs Eglises de Paris. Antwerp: 1660. V. 38; 40; 44

COTTE, LOUIS

Traite de Meteorologie. Paris: 1774. V. 41; 45

COTTERELL, H. H.

Old Pewter, Its Makers and Mars in England, Scotland and IReland. London: 1929. V. 38; 46

COTTERELL, S.

A Handbook to Various Publications, Documents and Charts Connected with the Rise and Development of the Railway System . . . (with) Supplement to the Railway Handbook . . . Birmingham: 1893/95. V. 46

COTTERILL, H. B.

A History of Art. London: 1922. V. 41

COTTERILL, ROBERT S.

History of Pioneer Kentucky. Cincinnati: 1917. V. 42

COTTIER, LIZZIE D.

The Right Spirit. Buffalo: 1885. V. 42

COTTIN, SOPHIE RISTAUT DE 1773-1807

Elisabeth; or The Exiles of Siberia. A Tale Founded upon Facts. From the French. London: 1817. V. 37; 42

Elizabeth; or, the Exiles of Siberia: a Tale. London: 1818. V. 37

Mathilde, ou Memoires Tires de l'Histoire des Croisades. Londres: 1809. V. 37

COTTINGHAM, E. R.

Pedigree of Bowen of Court House. London: 1927. V. 43

COTTINGHAM, L. N.

Plans, Elevations, Sections and Details of King Henry the Seventh's Chapel at Westminster. London: 1822. V. 37

Working Drawings from Gothic Ornaments. London: 1824. V. 40

COTTLE, JOSEPH

Early Recollections Chiefly relating tot he Late Samuel Taylor Coleridge, During His residence in Bristol. 1837. V. 40

Early Recollections, Chiefly Relating to the Late Samuel Taylor Coleridge During His Long Residence in Bristol. London: 1837. V. 37; 41

Reminiscences of Samuel Taylor Coleridge and Robert Southey. London: 1848. V. 39; 42

COTTLE, LUIS

Traite de Meteorologie, Contenant. Paris: 1774. V. 44

COTTON, A. CALVELEY

The Planning of Modern Building. London: 1936. V. 38

COTTON, ALFRED

Cotton's Sketch-Book. Portland: 1874. V. 45

COTTON, CHARLES 1630-1687

The Genuine Works. London: 1715. V. 42; 45

The Planter's Manual. London: 1675. V. 38; 40; 41; 43

Poems from the Works of Charles Cotton. London. V. 41

Poems on Several Occasions. London: 1689. V. 38; 39; 42; 44; 46

Poems from the Works of Charles Cotton. New York: 1925. V. 39

Scarronides: or, Le Virgile Travesty. A Mock Poem. London: 1664. V. 39

Scarronnides (sic). London: 1667. V. 46

Scarronides or Virgil Travestie. Whitehaven: 1776. V. 38

Scarronnides, or Virgil Travestie . . . London: 1804. V. 38

Scarronnides, or Virgile Travestie. London: 1691. V. 38

Scarronnides, or Virgil Travestie. London: 1692. V. 38; 40; 42; 44

The Wonders of the Peake. London: 1681. V. 39; 40; 42; 44; 46

The Genuine Works. London: 1715. V. 38; 40; 46

COTTON, CLEMENT

The Christian's Concordance. London: 1622. V. 39

A Complete Concordance to the Bible of the Last Translation. London: 1631. V. 37; 46

A Complete Concordance to the Bible of the Last Translation . . . London: 1635. V. 39

COTTON, EDWARD

A Voice from Waterloo: a History of the Battle . . . with a Selection from the Wellington Dispatches, General Orders and Letters Relating to the Battle. London: 1849. V. 39

COTTON, HENRY

A List of Editions of the Bible and Parts Thereof in English from the Year MDV to MDCCCXX. Oxford: 1821. V. 42

A List of Editions of the Bible and Parts Thereof . . . 1852. V. 38

A Typograpahical Gazeteer. Oxford: 1825. V. 37; 40; 46

A Typographical Gazeteer, Attempted by the Rev. Henry Cotton, D.C.L. Late Sublibrarian of the Bodleian Library. Oxford: 1831. V. 38

COTTON, JOHN 1584-1652

An Abstract of the Lavves of Nevv England, as They Are Novv Established. London: 1641. V. 42; 44

An Abstract of Laws and Government. London: 1655. V. 40

The Churches Resurrection, or the Opening of the First and Sixth Verses of the 20th Capt. of the Revelation. London: 1642. V. 41

The Controversie Concerning Liberty of Conscience in matters of Religion. Truly stated, and distinctly and plainly handled. By way of answer to some Arguments to the contrary sent unto him. London: 1646. V. 37

An Exposition Upon the Thirteenth Chapter of the Revelation . . . London: 1655. V. 45

Gods Promise to His Plantation . . . as It Was Delivered in a Sermon. London: 1630. V. 42

Ministers of the Gospel Should Speak, Not as Pleasing Men, But God, Who Tries Their Hearts. Boston: 1734. V. 45

A Modest and Cleare Answer to Mr. Balls Discourse of set Formes of Prayer . . . London: 1642. V. 45

The Powring Out of the Seven Vials . . . London: 1642. V. 43

A Practical Commentary, or an Exposition With Observations, Reasons, and Vses Upon the First Epistle Generall of John. London: 1656. V. 37; 38; 39

Singing of Psalmes A Gospel-Ordinance, or a Treatise Wherein are Handled These Foure Particulars . . . London: 1647. V. 42; 44

Singing of Psalmes. London: 1650. V. 38

The Song Birds of Great Britain. London: 1836. V. 42

The Way of the Churches of Christ in New England. London: 1645. V. 42; 44

The Way of Congregational Churches Cleared: in Two Treatises. London: 1648. V. 44

COTTON, ROBERT 1571-1631

Cottoni Posthuma; Divers Choice Pieces of That Renowned Antiquary Sir Robert Cotton . . . London: 1672. V. 39; 42; 46

COTTON, ROBERT BRUCE 1571-1631

The Danger Wherein the Kingdome Now Standeth and the Remedie. London: 1628. V. 41

An Exact Abridgement of the Records in the Tower of London, from the Reign of King Edward II . . . Richard III . . . London: 1657. V. 40; 45

An Exact Abridgement of the Records in the Tower of London, From the Reign of King Edward II . . . Richard III . . . London: 1679. V. 38; 40

The Forme of Governement of the Kingdom of England. London: 1642. V. 38; 40

Seriovs Considerations for Repressing of the Increase of Jesvites, Priests and Papists, Without Shedding of Blood. London: 1641. V. 43

COTTON, WALTER

The Sea and the Sailor, Notes on France and Italy, and Other Literary remains . . . with a Memoir. New York: 1851. V. 40

COTTON, WILLIAM

Illustrations of Stone Circles, Cromlehs and Other Remains of the Aboriginal Britons, in the West of Cornwall: From Drawings Made on the spot, in 1826. London: 1827. V. 45

COTTON, WILLIAM CHARLES

My Bee Book. London: 1842. V. 44

COTTRELL, CHARLES HERBERT

Recollections of Siberia in the Years 1840 and 1841. London: 1842. V. 37; 38; 42

COTTU, CHARLES b. 1777

The Administration of the Criminal Code in England, and the Spirit of the English Government. London: 1820. V. 40

COTTU, M.

The Administration of the Criminal Code in England, and the Spirit of the English Government. London: 1820. V. 38

COUCH, JOHNATHAN

A History of the Fishes of the British Islands. London: 1862. V. 39

COUCH, JONATHAN

A History of the Fishes of the British Islands. London: 1862-67. V. 39

A History of the Fishes of the British Islands. London: 1864-65. V. 39; 44

A History of the Fishes of the British Islands. London: 1866-7. V. 41

A History of the Fishes of the British Islands. London: 1868/65-65. V. 43

A History of the Fishes of the British Islands. London: 1877. V. 38; 40; 42; 43

A History of the Fishes of the British Isles. London: 1879, (1877). V. 46

A History of the Fishes of the British Islands. London: 1864-67. V. 37

A History of the Fishes of the British Islands. London: 1868-1869. V. 37

Illustrations of Instinct Deduced from the Habits of British Animals. London: 1847. V. 40

COUCH, NEVADA

Pages From Cherokee Indian History, as Identified with Samuel Austin Worcester. St. Louis: 1885. V. 37; 45

COUCHE, CHARLES

Permanent Way, Rolling Stock, and Techinical Working of Railways . . . London/Paris: 1872-82. V. 37

THE COUCHER Book of Selby. London: 1891-93. V. 37

COUDRAIN, BRIGITTE

Liebesgarten; Mon Amour. Stuttgart: 1965. V. 40; 41; 44

COUES, ELLIOTT

The Expeditions of Zebulon Montgomery Pike, to Headwaters of the Mississippi River, Through Louisiana Territory and in New Spine, 1805-6-7. A New Edition from Original of 1811. New York: 1895. V. 37; 46

Forty Years a Fur Trader on the Upper Missouri. New York: 1898. V. 39; 43; 45

The Journal of Jacob Fowler from Arkansas through the Indian Territory . . . to the Sources of the Rio Grande del Norte 1821-22. New York: 1898. V. 37

New Light On the Early History of the Greater Northwest. New York: 1897. V. 37; 40; 43; 44

On the Trail of a Spanish Pioneer. New York: 1900. V. 37; 42; 45

COUGHLIN, JACK

Grotesques. Baltimore: (1970). V. 37

COULING, SAMUEL

The Encyclopaedia Sinica. London: 1917. V. 45

COULTER, EDITH M.

A Camera in the Gold Rush. San Francisco: 1946. V. 37; 43; 44; 46

COULTER, ELLIS MERTON

The Civil War and Readjustment in Kentucky. Chapel Hill: 1926. V. 37

COURTIN, PIERRE

Nouvelle Description de l'Univers, c'est a Dire des Cieux et des Elemens . . . Paris: 1667. V. 44

COURTIVRON, GASPARD LE COMPASSEUR DE CREQUY-MONTOFORD

Traite d'Optique ou l'on donne la Theorie de la Lumiere dans le Systeme Newtonien, aved de Nouvelles Solutions des Principaux Problemes de Dioptrique & de Catoptrique. Paris: 1752. V. 38

COURTNAY Earl of Devonshire: or, the Troubles of the Princess Elizabeth. London: 1705? V. 39

COURTNEY, ABRAM V.

Anecdotes of the Blin . . . Boston: 1835. V. 42

COURTNEY, W. L.

Constructive Ethics. London: 1856. V. 43

COURTNEY, W. P.

A Bibliography of Samuel Johnson. 1984. V. 45

COURTNEY, WILLIAM L.

The Feminine Note in Fiction. London: 1904. V. 39; 41

COURTNEY, WILLIAM PRIDEAUX

Dodsley's Collection of Poetry. London: 1910. V. 39; 42

COURTNEY, WILSHIRE S.

The Gold Fields of St. Domingo. New York: 1860. V. 39

COURTONNE, JEAN 1671-1739

Traite de la Perspective Pratique, avec des Remarques sur l'Architecture, Suivis de Quelques Edifices Considerables . . . Paris: 1725. V. 41; 44

COURVILLE, CYRIL

Injuries of the Skull and Brain as Described in the Myths, Legends and Folk-Tales of the Various Peoples of the World, with Some Comments on the Significance and Reliability of This Information in Evaluating Contemporary Concepts as To Their Nature . . . New York: 1967. V. 41

COURVILLE, CYRIL B.

Birth and Brain Damage. Pasadena: 1971. V. 42

COUSE, L. E.

Button Classics. Chicago: 1941. V. 37

COUSE, L. ERWINA

Button Classics. Chicago: 1942. V. 38

COUSIN, JACQUES ANTOINE JOSEPH 1739-1800

Introduction a l'Etude de l'stronomie Physique. Paris: 1787. V. 38

COUSIN, JEAN

Livre de Perspective. Paris: 1560. V. 38; 40; 44

COUSIN, VICTOR

Introduction to the History of Philosophy. Boston: 1832. V. 39

The Philosophy of Kant: Lectures by Victor Cousin. London: 1854. V. 39; 40; 41

COUSINS, SHEILA

To Beg I Am Ashamed. London: 1938. V. 41; 45

To Beg I Am Ashamed. New York: 1938. V. 41

COUSTAU, PIERRE

Pegma, Cum Narrationibus Philosophicis. Lyon: 1555. V. 37; 40

COUSTOS, JOHN

Horrid Tortures; or, the Unparalleled Sufferings of John Coustos; Who Nine Times Underwent the Most Cruel Tortures Ever Invented by Man, and Sentenced to the Gallies, for Years . . . Putney: 1798. V. 45

The Sufferings of John Coustos for Free-Masonry, and for His Refusing to Turn Roman Catholic, in the Inquisition at Lisbon. London: 1746. V. 39; 41

COUSTUMES et Usaiges de la Ville de Lille Confirmez et Approvez par s'Imperiale Majeste. Imprime en Anvers par: 1556. V. 38

COUTANT, C. G.

The History of Wyoming from the Earliest Known Discoveries. Laramie: 1899. V. 39; 41; 42; 43; 44; 45

COUTAUD, LUCIEN

Ma Civilisation. By Gilbert Lely. Paris: 1947. V. 37

COUTEREELS, JAN

t'Konstigh Cyffer-boek..Met volkomene Uytwerkingh aller Questien en Byvoegingh van veelerley andere soo noodige als Konstige Opgevingen. Utrecht: 1690. V. 38

COUTINHO, A. X. PEREIRA

Flora de Portugal. 1973. V. 39

COUTINHO, FRANCISCO DE SOUSA

Propositie Ghedaen ter Verga-Deringe Van Hare Hoogh Mog, D'Heeren Staten Generael der Vereenigde Nederlanded . . . The Hague: 1647. V. 37; 40

COUTO, ANTONIO DO

Gentilis Angollae Fidei Mysteriis Lusitano Olim Idiomate per . . . Rome: 1661. V. 38

COUTO, DIOGO DO

Decada Quinta da Asia . . . Lisbon: 1612. V. 41

COUTS, CAVE J.

From San Diego to the Colorado in 1849. Los Angeles: 1932. V. 43; 45

Journal and Maps . . . Los Angeles: 1933. V. 37; 41

COUTTS, FRANCIS

The Romance of King Arthur. London: 1907. V. 46

COUTTS, HENRY T.

Manual of Library Bookbinding, Practical and Historical. London: 1911. V. 41; 45

COVARRUBIAS, MIGUEL

The Eagle, the Jaguar, and the Serpent. New York: 1954. V. 38; 39; 40

Indian Art of Mexico and Central America. New York: 1957. V. 37; 44

Indian Art of Mexico and Central America. New York: 1971. V. 37

Island of bali. New York: 1942. V. 37

The Prince of Wales and Other Famous Americans. New York: 1925. V. 38

COVARRUBIAS, PEDRO DE

Remedio de Jugadores . . . Nueuamente Anadido y Emendado: Con Muchos Ausos y Sentencias que Hasta Aqui no se Auian Sacado a luz en Impression Ninguna. Salamanca: 1543. V. 39

THE COVENT Garden Repository or Ranger's Packet of Whim, Frolick and Amusement. Number III. London: 1788? V. 42

COVENTRY, FRANCIS

The History of Pompey the Little. Dublin: 1751. V. 46

The History of Pompey the Little. London: 1751. V. 37; 38; 40; 42; 44; 45; 46

The History of Pompey the Little. London: 1761. V. 39

The History of Pompey the Little or the Adventures of a Lap Dog. London: 1773. V. 40

The History of Pompey the Little. 1926. V. 40

The History of Pompey the Little, or, The History Life and Adventure of a Lap-Dog. Waltham St. Lawrence: 1926. V. 37; 40; 46

The History of Pompey the Little, or the Life . . . of a Lap Dog. (London): 1926. V. 37

COVENTRY, HENRY

Philemon to Hydaspes; Relating Several Conversations with Hortensius, Upon the Subject of False Religion. London: 1742. V. 39; 42; 43; 46

COVERDALE, MILES 1488-1568

Certain Most Godly, Fruitful, and Comfortable Letters of Such True Saintes and Holy Martyrs of God, as in the Late Bloodye Persecution Here within This Realme, Gaue Their Lyues. London: 1564. V. 37

COVERTE, ROBERT

A True and Almost Incredible Report of an Englishman that . . . Travelled to Land Thorow Many Unknowne Kingdomes and Great Cities. London: 1631. V. 41

COVES, ELLIOTT

Key to North American Birds. Boston: 1890. V. 42

COVILLE, F. V.

Botany of the Death Valley Expedition. Washington: 1893. V. 46

COVONI, MARCO

Regolamento del Regio Arcispedale di Santa Maria Nuova di Firenze. 1783. V. 44

Regolamento del Regio Arcispedale di Santa Maria Nuova di Firenze. Florence: 1783. V. 39

COW, JOHN

Remarks on the Manner of Fitting Boats for Ships of War and Transports: Addressed to Officers of the Royal Navy and Royal Artillery. London: 1843. V. 45

COWAN, ALEXANDER

Remains . . . Consisting of His Verses and Extracts from His Correspondence. Edinburgh: 1839. V. 42

COWAN, JAMES

Maori Biographies. Skethces of Old New Zealand. N.P.: 1901. V. 40

The New Zealand Wars. Wellington: 1922-23. V. 42

COWAN, JOHN F.

A New Invasion of the South: Being a Narrative of the Expedition of the Seventy-First Infantry, National Guard through the Southern States to New Orleans . . . 1881. New York: 1881. V. 38

COWAN, M. G.

The Door of Youth - a Selection of Poems from Edinburgh School Magazines. Edinburgh and: 1930. V. 43

COWAN, P. J.

The Welland Ship Canal Between Lake Ontario and Lake Erie, 1913-1932. London: 1935. V. 43

COWAN, R. M. W.

The Newspaper in Scotland. Glasgow: 1946. V. 44

COWAN, ROBERT ERNEST

A Bibliography of the History of California, 1510-1930. San Francisco. V. 38

A Bibliography of the History of California 1510-1930. San Francisco: 1933. V. 42; 43; 46

A Bibliography of the History of California 1510-1930. San Francisco: 1933-64. V. 37; 38; 44

A Bibliography of the History of California 1510-1930. San Francisco: 1933 & 1964. V. 39; 40

A Bibliography of the History of California and the Pacific West 1510-1596 . . . Columbus: 1952. V. 42; 44; 46

A Bibliography of the History of California 1510-1930. Los Angeles: 1964. V. 43

A Bibliography of the Spanish Press of California, 1833-1945. San Francisco: 1919. V. 42

Spanish Press of California 1833-1845. San Francisco: 1931. V. 38; 39; 40; 41; 42; 43; 44

COWAN, SAMUEL

The Lord Chancellors of Scotland from the Insitution of the Office to the Treaty of Union. Edinburgh/London: 1911. V. 40

COWANS, DAVID

Anecdotes of a Life on the Ocean. Montreal: 1871. V. 37

COWARD, HOWARD L.

'Uncle Dick' Wooton. Chicago,: 1890. V. 37

COWARD, NOEL 1899-1973

Bon Voyage and Other Stories. London: 1967. V. 41

Chelsea Buns: Poems. London: 1925. V. 43

The Collected Plays of Noel Coward. London: 1958. V. 38

The Collected Short Stories. London: 1962. V. 46

Fallen Angels. London: 1925. V. 38

The Lyrics of Noel Coward. London: 1965. V. 41

The Noel Coward Song Book. London: 1953. V. 40; 41

Not Yet the Dodo and Other Verses. London: 1967. V. 41

Not Yet Dodo and Other Verses. New York: 1968. V. 41

Play Parade. London: 1949/50/54. V. 43

Post-Mortem. Garden City: 1931. V. 37

Present Indicative. Garden City: 1937. V. 37; 39

Present Indicative. London: 1937. V. 45; 46

Present Indicative. New York: 1937. V. 40

Present Laughter. London: 1943. V. 45

Pretty Dolly Barlow and Other Stories. London: (1964). V. 37

Quadrille. London: 1952. V. 46

Relative Values. London: 1952. V. 38; 46

Sail Away. New York: 1961. V. 38

Star Quality. London: 1951. V. 42

Suite in Three Keys - Three Plays. London: 1966. V. 41

Terribly Intimate Portraits. New York: 1922. V. 46

This Was a Man - a Comedy in Three Acts. New York: 1926. V. 37

To Step Aside. New York: 1939. V. 46

Tonight at 8:30. Garden City: 1936. V. 37

The Vortex. London: 1925. V. 38

The Vortex. New York and London: 1925. V. 39

A Withered Nosegay. London: 1922. V. 41

COWARD, T. A.

The Vertebrate Fauna of Cheshire and Liverpool Bay. London: 1910. V. 37; 40; 41

COWBOY Artists of America - Tenth Annual Exhibition in 1975. Flagstaff: 1975. V. 39; 46

COWBOY Artists of America - Twelfth Annual Exhibition in 1977. Flagstaff: 1977. V. 46

COWBOY Artists of America - Fifteenth Annual Exhibition In 1980. Flagstaff: 1980. V. 46

COWBOY Artists of America - Seventeenth Annual Exhibition in 1982. Flagstaff: 1982. V. 46

COWBOY Artists of America - Twentieth Annual Exhibition in 1985. Flagstaff: 1985. V. 38; 40; 46

COWBOY Artists of America - Twenty-First Annual Exhibition in 1986. Flagstaff: 1986. V. 46

COWBOY Artists of America - Twenty-Second Annual Exhibition in 1987. Flagstaff: 1987. V. 46

COWBOY Artists of America - Twenty-Third Annual Exhibition In 1988. Flagstaff: 1988. V. 46

COWBOY Artists of America - Twenty-Fourth Annual Exhibition in in 1989. Flagstaff: 1989. V. 46

COWBOY Artists of America - Eighth Annual Exhibition in 1973. Flagstaff: 1973. V. 46

COWDEN-CLARKE, MARY

My Long Life: an Autobiographical Sketch. London: 1896. V. 44

COWDERY, OLIVER

Cowdery's Letters on Brining In of the New Dispensation. Burlington: 1899. V. 39; 42

COWDRY, E. V.

General Cytology. Chicago: 1924. V. 40; 42

Special Cytology: the Form and Functions of the Cell in Health and Disease. New York: 1932. V. 40

COWELL, JOHN

The Curious and Profitable Gardener . . . London: 1703. V. 41

The Curious and Profitable Gardener. London: 1730. V. 38; 39; 44

The Interpreter: or Booke Containing the Signification of Words . . . London: 1637. V. 37; 38; 40

The Interpreter, Containing the Genuine Signification of Such Obscure Words and Terms Used Either in the Common or Statute Laws of This Realm. London: 1672. V. 41; 42

A Law Dictionary. London: 1708. V. 40

COWEN, W.

Six Views of Woodsome Hall: Embellished with Costume Figures of the Olden Time. London: 1851. V. 38

COWHAM, HILDA

Fiddlesticks. London: 1902. V. 46

COWIE, G.

The Bookbinder's Manual. London: 1832. V. 41

Bookbinder's Manual. London: 1835. V. 40

COWLES, B. K.

Alaska, Interesting and Reliable Information. Madison: 1885. V. 41; 44; 45

COWLEY, ABRAHAM 1618-1667

Anacreon. Done into English out of the Original Greek by Abraham Cowley. Soho: (1923). V. 37

The English Writings. Cambridge: 1906. V. 44

Loves Riddle. London: 1638. V. 38; 44

The Mistress with Other Select Poems. London: 1926. V. 38

Poemata Latina. London: 1668. V. 39; 40; 43

Poemata Latina. London: 1678. V. 38

Poems. London: 1656. V. 38; 40; 41

Select Works. Dublin: 1772. V. 38

Select Works . . . London: 1772. V. 41; 44

Select Works. London: 1777. V. 39; 42

THe Third Part of the Works . . . Being His Six Book of Plants. Made English by several hands. London: 1708. V. 37

The Works . . . London: 1672. V. 37; 42; 43; 44

Works . . . London: 1674. V. 43

The Works Consisting of Those of Which were Formerly Printed and Those Which He designed for the Press . . . London: 1678. V. 38; 43

The Works . . . London: 1678. V. 38; 42

The Works of . . . London: 1680. V. 39; 42

Works . . . London: 1681. V. 38; 41; 44

The Works. London: 1700. V. 38

The Works. London: 1707-08. V. 38

The Works . . . in Two Volumes. (with) The Third and Last Volume of the Works. London: 1710/11. V. 42

COWLEY, ABRAHAM 1618-1667 continued

The Works. Consisting of those which were formerly printed: and those which he Design'd for the Press, Now Published out of the Authors Original Copies. London: 1668. V. 37

COWLEY, HANNAH 1743-1809

The Maid of Arragon. London: 1780. V. 40; 42

The Poetry of Anna Matilda . . . To which are added Recollections. London: 1788. V. 46

The Runaway, a Comedy. London: 1776. V. 42; 46

Who's the Dupe? London: 1779. V. 42

Who's the Dupe? London: 1780. V. 43

COWLEY, JOHN D.

A Bibliography of Abrigments, Digests, Dictionaries and Indexes of English Law to the Year 1800. London: 1932. V. 43

COWLEY, MALCOLM

Blue Juniata. New York: 1929. V. 37

The Dry Season. Norfolk: 1941. V. 46

Exile's Return. New York: 1981. V. 37; 39; 40; 41; 43; 44; 46

Exile's Return. New York: 1991. V. 44

Racine. Paris: 1923. V. 38

A Second Flowering. New York: 1973. V. 46

COWLEY, MATTHIAS F.

Wilford Woodruff Fourth President of the Church of Jesus Christ of Latter Day Saints History of His Life and Labors as Recorded in His Daily Journals. Salt Lake City: 1909. V. 42

COWPER, ASHLEY

Poems and Translations. London: 1769. V. 41

COWPER, BP. OF GALLOWAY 1568-1619

Anatomia Corporum Humanorum. Leyden: 1739. V. 40

COWPER, HENRY

Reports of Cases Adjudged in the Court of King's Bench: From Hilary Term, the 14th of George III, 1774 to Trinity Term, the 18th of George III, 1778 (both inclusive) . . . London: 1783. V. 45

COWPER, HENRY SWAINSON

Hawkshead: (the Northernmost Parish of Lancahsire) Its History, Archaeology, Industries, Folklore, Dialect, Etc. London: 1899. V. 38; 46

The Oldest Register Book of the Parish of Hawkshead in Lancashire 165-1704. London: 1897. V. 46

Through Turkish Arabia. London: 1894. V. 41; 43

COWPER, JOHN

An Essay Proving that Inclosing Commons, and Common-Fieldlands, is a Contrary to the Interest of the Nation . . . London: 1732. V. 39; 42

COWPER, L. I.

The King's Own. The Story of a Royal Regiment. Oxford: 1939. V. 37

COWPER, MARIA FRANCES CECILIA

Original Poems, on Various Occasions. London: 1792. V. 37; 42

COWPER, WILLIAM 1666-1709

Anatomia Corporum Humanorum. Leyden: 1739. V. 42; 44

The Anatomy of the Humane Bodies . . . London: 1698. V. 40

The Anatomy of Humane Bodies. Leyden: 1737. V. 37; 41; 43

The Anatomy of Humane Bones. Leyden: 1737. V. 40

The Diverting History of John Gilpin. London: 1828. V. 38

John Gilpin. 1952. V. 41

Johnny Gilpin's Journey to Ware. London: 1830. V. 39

Life and Posthumous Writings. Chichester: 1803-04. V. 43

The Life and Posthumous Writings of . . . Chichester: 1806. V. 45

The Life and Works. London: 1836. V. 39; 40

The Loved Haunts of Cowper. Olney: 1867. V. 38

Memoir of the Early Life of William Cowper. London: 1816. V. 39; 46

Myotomia Reformata: or an Antomical Treatise on the Muscles of the Human Body, illustrated with Figures after the Life. London: 1724. V. 37; 39

Olney Hymns. London: 1779. V. 40; 41; 44

Olney Hymns, in Three Books. London: 1810. V. 40

Poems. London: 1782. V. 38; 40

Poems. London: 1782-1785. V. 38; 40; 41; 45

Poems. London: 1782/85. V. 44; 45

Poems. Dublin: 1787. V. 37; 42

Poems. London: 1787. V. 41

Poems. London: 1788. V. 41

Poems. London: 1794. V. 37; 46

Poems. London: 1794/95. V. 45

Poems. London: 1798. V. 40

Poems. London: 1800. V. 39; 41

Poems. London: 1803. V. 43

Poems. Dublin: 1805. V. 40

Poems. London: 1808. V. 40; 42; 44; 46

Poems. London: 1811. V. 42

Poems. New York: 1811. V. 46

Poems. London: 1812. V. 41; 46

Poems . . . London: 1820. V. 40; 42; 46

The Poems. London: 1825. V. 37

Poems. London: 1843. V. 38

Poems. London: 1843. V. 42

Poetical Works. London: 1830. V. 43

Poetical Works. London: 1841. V. 38; 39

The Poetical Works. London: 1843. V. 46

The Poetical Works. London: 1846. V. 39; 43

The Poetical Works. London: 1850's. V. 39

The Poetical Works. London: 1853. V. 39

Poetical Works. London: 1860. V. 40; 41

Private Correspondence. London: 1824. V. 40; 42

Proposals for Printing by Subscription a New Translation of the Iliad and Odyssy of Homer, into Blank Verse. London: 1786. V. 43

The Rural Walks of Cowper; Displayed in a Series of Views Near Olney, Bucks; Representing the Scenery Exemplified in His Poems; with Descriptive Sketches, and a Memoir of the Poets's Life. London: 1835-37. V. 37

A Summary of the Life of St. Werburgh. Chester: 1749. V. 38

Table Talk and Other Poems. London: 1817. V. 41

Table Talk and Other Poems. London: 1825. V. 42

The Task, a Poem in Six Books. Phladelphia: 1787. V. 39

The Works. London: 1835. V. 41; 44

The Works of William Cowper.. London: 1835-37. V. 42

Works. London: 1836. V. 38

The Works . . . with a Life of the Author by the Editor, Robert Southey. London: 1853-55. V. 46

The Works of William Cowper. London: 1815. V. 43

COWPERTHWAIT & CO.

Description of the Republic of Mexico Including Its Physical and Moral Features, Geography . . . Philadlephia: 1846. V. 45

COWTAN, ROBERT

A Biographical Sketch of Sir Anthony Panizzi . . . Late Principal Librarian, British Museum. London & Berlin: 1873. V. 39

Memories of the British Museum. London: 1872. V. 40

COX, A. B.

The Merchant Prince or the Pioneers of Aristocracy . . . London: 1928. V. 44

COX, ANNA

A Pre-Raphaelite Aeneid of Virgil in the Collection of Mrs. Edward Laurence Doheny of Los Angeles, Being an Essay in Honor of the William Morris Centenary, 1934. Los Angeles: 1934. V. 38

COX, C. W. M.

Monumenta Asiae Minoris Antiqua. Manchester: 1937. V. 42; 44

COX, CHARLES

John Tobias Sportsman. New York: 1934. V. 44

COX, CHARLES J.

Notes on the Churches of Derbyshire. Chesterfield: 1875. V. 41

COX, CLIFFORD R.

Strathroy (Red Valley) 1834-1934. N.P.. V. 42

COX, DANIEL

An Appeal to the Public, in Behalf of Elizabeth Canning, in Which the Material fActs in Her Story are Fairly Stated and Shewn to be True, on the Foundation of Evidence. London: 1753. V. 46

COX, DAVID

Memoir of the Life of David Cox, Member of the Society of Painters in Water Colours, with Selections from His Correspondence, and Some Account of His Early Works. London: 1873. V. 40

A Series of Progressive Lessons, Intended to Elucidate the Art of Landscape Painting in Water Colours. London: 1812. V. 41

A Series of Progressive Lessons Intended to Elucidate the Art of Landscape Painting in Water Colours . . . London: 1828. V. 45

A Series of Progressive Lessons Intended to Elucidate the Art of Painting in Water Colours. London: 1839. V. 38

A Treatise on Landscape Painting and Effect in Water Colours . . . London: 1812. V. 44

COYNE, J. STIRLING

The Scenery and Antiquities of Ireland, Illustrated from Drawings by W. H. Bartlett. London: 1850. V. 40

COYNER, DAVID E.

The Lost Trappers: A Collection of Interesting Scenes and Events in the Rocky Mountains; Together with a Short Description of California: Also, some Account of the Fur Trade . . . Cincinnati: 1858. V. 37; 46

COYNER, DAVID H.

The Lost Trappers: a Collection of Interesting Scenes and Events in the Rocky Mountains. Cincinnati: 1847. V. 40; 45

The Lost Trappers; a Collection of Interesting Scenes and Events in the Rocky Mountains . . . Cincinnati: 1856. V. 40; 45

COYNER, J. M.

Hand Book on Mormonism. Salt Lake: Chicago &: 1882. V. 42

COYPEL, C.

Illustrations to Don Quixote. London. V. 40

COYPEL, CHARLES ANTOINE

Catalogue des Tableaux, Desseins, Marbres, Bronzes, Modeles, Estampes, et Planches Gravees . . . Paris: 1753. V. 44

COZINE, JOHN C.

The Day-Book Account of John C. Cozine: a Journey from Harrodsburg, Kentucky to New York and Return, September 10th through November 27th, 1828. Lexington: 1976. V. 45

COZZENS, FREDERIC S.

Acadia; or, a Month with the Blue Noses. New York: 1859. V. 38; 41; 46

COZZENS, FREDERICK S.

Father Tom and the Pope . . . Philadelphia: 1861. V. 43

Father Tom and the Pope, or a Night in the Vatican. New York: 1867. V. 43

The Sparrowgrass Papers: or Living in the Country. New York: 1856. V. 43; 45

COZZENS, ISSACHAR

A Geological History of Manhattan or New York Island. New York: 1843. V. 38; 40; 41

COZZENS, JAMES GOULD

Confusion. Boston: 1924. V. 45

Men and Brethren. London: 1936. V. 43

Michael Scarlett. New York: 1925. V. 45

A Rope for Doctor Webster. 1976. V. 45

The Son of Perdition. New York: 1929. V. 45

COZZENS, SAMUEL WOODWORTH

Marvellous Country; or, Three Years in Arizona and New Mexico, the Apaches' Home. Boston: 1873. V. 37; 38; 42

The Marvelous Country; or, Three Years in Arizona and New Mexico. London: 1875. V. 37

CRAAMER, JOHANN ANDREAS

Elements of the Art of Assaying Metals. London: 1764. V. 37

Elements of the Art of Assaying Metals. In Two Parts. The First containing the Theory, the Second the Practice of the said Art. The whole deduced from the true Properties and Nature of Fossils; confirmed by the most accurate and unquestionable . . . London: 1741. V. 37

CRAB, ROGER

The English Hermit. London: 1843. V. 39

CRABB, GEORGE 1778-1851

English Synonymes, with Copious Illustrations and Explanations . . . London: 1826. V. 42

A History of English Law; or an Attempt to Trace the Rise, Progress and Successive Changes of the Common Law; from the Earliest Period to the Present Time. Burlington: 1831. V. 39

Universal Technological Dictionary, or Familiar Explanation of the Terms Used in All Arts and Sciences . . . London: 1823. V. 46

CRABB, JAMES

The Gipsies Advocate or Observations on the Origin, Character, Manners and Habit of the English Gypsies. London: 1831. V. 39; 42

The Gipsies' Advocate; Or Observations on the Origin, Character, Manners and Habits of the English Gipsies. London: 1832. V. 39

CRABB, RICHARD

Empire on the Platte. Cleveland: 1967. V. 39; 42

Empire on the Platte. Cleveland and New York: 1967. V. 45

CRABBE, GEORGE 1754-1832

The Borough. London: 1810. V. 38; 40; 42; 43; 45; 46

The Borough; a Poem, in Twenty-Four Letters. London: 1812. V. 42

The Borough; Tales; Poems. London: 1812-13. V. 44; 46

The Borough: a Poem, in Twenty Four Letters. London: 1820. V. 46

A Discourse, Read in the Chapel at Belvoir Castle, After the Funeral of His Grace the Duke of Rutland. London: 1788. V. 41

The Library. London: 1781. V. 40

The News-Paper: a Poem. London: 1785. V. 38

Poems. London: 1807. V. 37; 38; 40; 41; 43

Poems. Cambridge: 1905. V. 42

The Poetical Works. London: 1834. V. 40; 46

Poetical Works . . . With His Letters and Journals, and His Life, by His Son. London: 1834. V. 38

The Poetical Works of . . . London: 1840-1851. V. 38; 40

The Complete Poetical Works. 1988. V. 44

The Complete Poetical Works. Oxford: 1988. V. 40

Poetical Works, with his Letters and Journals, and his Life, by his Son. London: 1835-36. V. 37

Readings in Crabbe. London: 1883. V. 44

Tales. London: 1812. V. 37; 41; 43; 44

Tales of the Hall. London: 1819. V. 37; 38; 39; 40; 41; 42; 43; 45

Universal Technological Dictionary or Familiar Explanation of the Terms Used in All Arts and Sciences, Containing Definitions Drawn from the Original Writers . . . London: 1823. V. 41

The Village. London: 1783. V. 38; 40; 41; 42; 43; 45; 46

Works. London: 1813-20. V. 37; 42

The Works. London: 1823. V. 38; 39; 40; 41; 44; 45; 46

The Works. London: 1823. V. 40

The Works of . . . London: 1823. V. 38

CRABBE, HARRIETTE

Edith VErnon; or, Contrasts of Character. London: 1855. V. 44

CRABTRE, A. D.

The Funny Side of Physic; or, the Mysteries of Medicine . . . an Expose of Medical Humbugs, Quacks and Charlatans in all Ages and All Countries. Hartford: 1872. V. 42

The Funny Side of Physic; or, the Mysteries of Medicine, Presenting the Honorous and Serious Sides of Medical Practice. Hartford: 1874. V. 45

The Funny Side of Physic; or, the Mysteries of Medicine, Presenting the Humorous and Serious Sides of Medical Practice. Hartford: 1880. V. 41

CRABTREE, ADAM

Animal Magnetism, Early Hypnotism and Physical Research, 1766-1925. Millwood: 1988. V. 43; 45; 46

CRABTREE, JOHN

A Concise History of the Parish and Vicarage of Halifax, in the County of York. Halifax: 1836. V. 41

A Concise History of the Parish and Vicarage of Halifax. Hartley & Walker,: 1836. V. 41

CRACE, JIM

Continent. London: 1986. V. 46

CRACKANTHORP, RICHARD

Logicae Libri Qvinque . . . London: 1677. V. 42

CRACKANTHORPE, HUBERT

Wreckage. Seven Studies. London: 1893. V. 38; 41; 43; 45

CRACKEL, THEODORE

Custer's Kentucky: General George Armstrong Custer and Elizabethtown, Kentucky, 1871-1873. New York: 1974. V. 45

CRADDOCK, H. C., MRS.

Josephine, John and the Puppu. London: 1940. V. 44

CRADDOCK, HARRY

The Savoy Cocktail Book. London: 1910. V. 43

The Savoy Cocktail Book. London: 1930. V. 37; 40

The Savoy Cocktail Book. New York;: 1930. V. 37; 39; 40

CRADOCK, H. C., MRS.

Josephine Goes Travelling. London: 1940. V. 46

CRADOCK, SAMUEL

The Harmony of the Four Evangelists, and Their Text Methodiz'd According to the Order and Series of Times, in Which the Several Things by Them Mentioned Were Transacted. London: 1668. V. 44

CRAFTON, WILLIAM BELL

A Short Sketch of the Evidence for the Abolition of the Slave Trade, Delivered Before a Committee of the House of Commons. London: 1792. V. 41

A Short Sketch of the Evidence for the Abolition of the Slave Trade.. Philadelphia: 1792. V. 42

CRAFTS, ELIZA PERIS RUSSELL ROBBINS b. 1825
Pioneer Days in the San Bernardino Valley. Redlands: 1906. V. 38; 43

CRAFTS, WILLIAM A.
History of the United States. Boston. V. 43

CRAFTSMAN, LONDON.
The Craftsman. London: 1731-7. V. 39

CRAFTSMEN'S GUILD
Traditional Works in Metal, Wood, Stone, Marble and the Precious Metals for the Adornmetn of the Sacred Edifice. London: 1935. V. 37

CRAG, J. B.
Advances in Ecological Research. London & New York: 1962-74. V. 38

CRAHAN, MARCUS ESKETH
Early American Inebriatatis. Los Angeles: 1964. V. 44

CRAIG, CLIFFORD
Old Tasmanian Prints Prepared in Great Britain, Europe and on the Mainland of Australia. Launceston: 1964. V. 41

CRAIG, COLIN
A Suitor from the Stars. Baltimore: 1928. V. 42

CRAIG, EDWARD 1872-1966
Edward Gordon Craig: the Last Eight Years 1958-1966 . . . Andoversford: 1983. V. 39
Edward Gordon Craig: the Last Eight Years 1958-1966. 1983. V. 39

CRAIG, EDWARD GORDON 1872-1966
Bethlehem. A Nativity Play. London: 1902. V. 38
The Black Figures of Edward Gordon Craig. Irchester: 1989. V. 44
The Black Figures of Edward Gordon Craig. Irchester: 1989. V. 45
The Black Figures of Edward Gordon Craig. Wellingborough: 1989. V. 43; 44
Books and Theatres. London: 1925. V. 38; 42; 45
Edward Gordon Craig: The Last Eight Years 1958-66. Andoversford: 1983. V. 37; 38
Ellen Terry and Her Secret Self. London. V. 39
Ellen Terry and Her Secret Self. London: 1931. V. 46
Fourteen Notes (i.e., 'On Eight Pages from the Story of the Theatre by Glenn Hughes with Some Fourteen Notes by Edward Gordon Craig'). Seattle: 1931. V. 37
Gordon Craig's Paris Diary 1932-1933. 1982. V. 40; 44; 45
Gordon Craig's Paris Diary, 1932-1933. North Hills: 1982. V. 37; 38; 39; 40; 41; 42; 43; 44; 46
Gordon Craig's Paris Diary 1932-1933. North Hills: 1982. V. 44
Henry Irving. Ellen Terry, Etc. A Book of Portraits. Chicago: 1899. V. 41
Henry Irving. London: 1930. V. 37; 38
Henry Irving. London: (1930). V. 37
Index to the Story of My Days: Some Memoirs . . . 1872-1907. London: 1957. V. 37
A Living Theatre: The Gordon Craig School, the Arena Goldoni, the Mask. V. 37
The Marionnette. Florence: 1918. V. 38
The Mask, a Journal of the Art of the Theatre. New York: 1966-68. V. 41
Nothing or the Bookplate. London: 1924. V. 41
Nothing or the Bookplate. London: 1925. V. 37; 46
On the Art of the Theatre. Chicago: 1911. V. 37; 38
On the Art of the Theatre. London: 1911. V. 37
Plays for an Irish Theatre, by W.B. Yeats. London: 1911. V. 37
A Production. Being Thirty-Two Collotype Plates of Designs Projected or Realized for The Pretenders of Henrik Ibsen and Produced at the Royal Theatre Copenhagen 1926 by Edward Gordon Craig. London: 1930. V. 37
Scene. London: 1923. V. 37; 42
Scene. Oxford: 1923. V. 41
'Souvenir: Acis and Galatea (Handel). Masque of Love (Henry Purcell).' By Martin Shaw (Musical Director) and Gordon Craig (Stage Director). London: 1902. V. 37
Towards a New Theatre. New York: 1913. V. 42
Woodcuts and Some Words. London: 1924. V. 37; 39; 40
Woodcuts and Some Words. Introduction by Campbell Dodgson. New York: (ca. 1923). V. 37
Woodcuts and Some Words . . . with an introduction by Campbell Dodgson. London: 1924. V. 37

CRAIG, ELLEN GORDON
Edward Gordon Craig: The Last Eight Years 1958-1966. Letters from Ellen Gordon Craig. Edited with an introduction by Edward Craig. 1983. V. 37

CRAIG, ERIC
New Zealand Ferns. Auckland: 1890. V. 41
New Zealand Ferns. Auckland: 1890. V. 39; 41

CRAIG, JAMES T. GIBSON
Catalogue of the Valuable and Very Extensive Library of the Late James T. Gibson Craig, Esq . . . London: 1887. V. 44

CRAIG, JOHANNE
Theologiae Christianae Principia Mathematica. London: 1699. V. 37

CRAIG, JOHN
De Calculo Fluentium Libri Duo. Quibus Subjunguntur Libri Due De Optica Analytica. London: 1718. V. 37
The Locks of the Oxford Canal. 1984. V. 44
Methodus Figurarum Lineis Rectis & Curvis Comprehensum Quadraturas Determinandi. London: 1685. V. 41
Tractatus Mathematicus de Figurarum Curvilinearum Quadraturis et Locis Geometricis. London: 1693. V. 41

CRAIG, JOHN R.
Ranching With Lords and Commons of Twenty Years on the Ranch. Toronto: 1903. V. 44; 46

CRAIG, M.
Irish Book Bindings, 1600-1800. London: 1954. V. 39

CRAIG, MARY ELIZABETH
The Scottish Periodical Press 1750-1789. Edinburgh: 1931. V. 40

CRAIG, MAURICE
Irish Bookbinding 1600-1800. London: 1954. V. 38; 39; 40; 41; 42; 44

CRAIG, NEVILLE B.
The History of Pittsburgh, with a Brief Notice of Its Facilities and Communication. Pittsburgh: 1851. V. 37
Memoirs of Major Robert Stobo of the Virginia Regiment. Pittsburgh: 1854. V. 37
The Olden Time . . . Cincinnati: 1876. V. 42
The Olden Time; a Monthly Publication Devoted to the Preservation of Documents . . . Pittsburgh: 1846-47. V. 37

CRAIG, ROBERT H.
Rules and Regulations for the Sword Exercise of the Cavalry. To which is added, the Rules for Drill, and the Evolutions of the Light Cavalry. Baltimore: 1812. V. 37

CRAIG, THOMAS 1548-1608
Scotlands Sovereignty Asserted Being a Dispute Concerning Homage, against Those Who Maintain that Scotland is a Feu, Or Fee-Liege of England . . . London: 1695. V. 40; 45

CRAIG, WILLIAM MARSHALL
Traders of London in Their Ordinary Costume . . . London: 1804. V. 43

CRAIGE, THOMAS
A Conversation Between a Lady and Her Horse. Philadelphia: 1851. V. 44; 45

CRAIGHEAD, FRANK
Hawks in the Hand. Boston: 1939. V. 39

CRAIGHEAD, MEINRAD
The Mother's Birds. Images for a Death and a Birth. Worcester: 1976. V. 39; 41; 45; 46

CRAIGIE, DOROTHY
Victorian Detective Fiction. London: 1966. V. 38; 39; 40; 41; 45; 46

CRAIGIE, PEARL MARY TERESA RICHARDS 1867-1906
The Dream and the Business. London: 1906. V. 44; 46

CRAIGIE, WILLIAM A.
A Dictionary of American English on Historical Principles. Chicago: 1938-44. V. 39
A Dictionary of American English On Historical Principles compiled at the University of Chicago . . . 4 Volumes. 1938-1944. V. 37

CRAIK, DINAH MARIA MULOCK 1826-1887
The Adventures of a Brownie as Told to My Child. New York: 1893. V. 46
The Adventures of a Brownie as told to My Child. London: 1872. V. 38
Christian's Mistake. London: 1865. V. 40
Godfrey Helstone. London: 1884. V. 43
The Head of the Family. London: 1852. V. 40
John Halifax, Gentleman. London: 1856. V. 37; 38; 40; 41; 43; 44; 45
A Legacy. London: 1878. V. 39; 46
A Life for a Life. London: 1859. V. 41
Studies from Life. London: 1861. V. 42
A Woman's Thoughts About Women. London: 1858. V. 41
The Woman's Kingdom. New York: 1868. V. 37; 41; 43
Young Mrs. Jardine. London: 1879. V. 40

CRAIK, GEORGE L.

The History of British Commerce, from the Earliest Times. London: 1844. V. 38

Sketches of the History of Literature and Learning in England ... With Specimens of the Principal Writers. London: 1844-1845. V. 37; 38

CRAIK, GEORGE LILLIE

The New Zealanders. London: 1830. V. 39

The New Zealanders ... London: 1847. V. 39

The Pursuit of Knowledge Under Difficulties. London: 1845. V. 40

CRAIK, GEORGIANA

Patience Holt. London: 1891. V. 41; 42

Leslie Tyrrell. London: 1867. V. 42

CRAIK, HELEN

Henry of Northumberland, of the Hermit's Cell. A Tale of the Fifteenth Century. Dublin: 1800. V. 37

CRAIS, ROBERT

The Monkey's Raincoat. New York: 1987. V. 43

CRAKANTHORP, RICHARD

logicae Libri Quinque: De Praedicabilibus, Praedicamentis Syllogismo ... London: 1641. V. 43; 45

CRAKES, SYLVESTER

Five Years a Captive Among the Black-Feet Indians. Columbus: 1858. V. 37; 39; 40

CRAM & FERGUSON

Work of Cram and Ferguson, Architects: Including Work by Cram, Goodhue and Ferguson. New York: 1929. V. 41

CRAM, GEORGE F.

The Columbian World's Fair Atlas ... Astabula: 1892. V. 45

Cram's Imperial Office Directory and Reference Atlas of the United States. Chicago: 1890. V. 45

Cram's Modern Atlas. Chicago/New York: 1903. V. 45

Cram's Quik Reference Atlas and Gazetteer of the World ... Chicago/New York: 1904. V. 45

Cram's Standard American Railway System Atlas of the World. Chicago/New York: 1896. V. 45

Cram's Superior Reference Atlas of Missouri and the World. Chicago: 1908. V. 45

Cram's Superior Reference Atlas to Texas. New York: 1915. V. 46

Cram's Township and Rail Road Map of Kansas. Chicago: 1880. V. 42

Cram's Universal Atlas. Chicago/New York: 1901. V. 45

Cram's Universal Atlas ... New York: 1888. V. 45

Cram's Universal Atlas, Geographical, Astronomical and Historical ... Chicago: 1894. V. 45

Cram's Unrivaled Atlas of the World. Chicago: 1887. V. 45

Cram's Unrivaled Atlas of the World. Cincinnati: 1887. V. 45

Cram's Unrivaled Atlas of the World. Chicago: 1888. V. 45

Cram's Unrivaled Atlas of the World. Chicago: 1889. V. 45

Cram's Unrivaled Atlas of the World. Kansas City: 1889. V. 45

Cram's Unrivaled Atlas of the World. New York: 1889. V. 45

Cram's Unrivaled Atlas of the World. Chicago: 1891. V. 45

Cram's Unrivaled Atlas of the World. Chicago/New York: 1891. V. 45

Cram's Unrivaled Family Atlas of the World. Chicago: 1883. V. 45

Cram's Unrivaled Family Atlas of the World. Cincinnati: 1886. V. 45

Cram's Unrivaled Family Atlas of the World. Chicago/Atlanta: 1887. V. 45

International Office and Family Atlas of the World. Chicago: 1891. V. 45

New Popular Atlas of the World ... Chicago: 1892. V. 45

The People's Atlas of the World. Philadelphia: 1901. V. 45

Pictorial Atlas Illustrating the Spanish American War. Chicago/New York: 1898. V. 45

Pictorial Atlas Illustrating the Spanish American War ... New York/Chicago: 1899. V. 45

The Twentieth Century Atlas of the World. Chicago: 1900. V. 45

CRAM, RALPH ADAMS

The Ruined Abbeys of Great Britain. Boston: 1927. V. 39

CRAM, THOMAS J.

Topographical Memoir of the Department of the Pacific ... the Topographical memoir and Report of Captain ... Relative to the Territories of ORegon and Washington ... Washington: 1859. V. 46

CRAMER, JOHN ANDREW

Elements of the Art of Assying Metals. London: 1741. V. 40; 41; 42; 43; 45

CRAMER, JOHN ANTONY

A Dissertation on the Passage of Hannibal Over the Alps. Oxford: 1820. V. 46

CRAMER, PATRICK

The Illustrated Books: Catalogue Raisonne. Geneva: 1989. V. 44

CRAMER, ZADOCK

The Navigator, Containing Directions for Navigating the Monongahela, Allegheny, Ohio and Mississippi Rivers ... Pittsburgh: 1818. V. 43

The Navigator, Containing Directions for Navigating the Ohio and Mississippi Rivers ... Pittsburgh: 1824. V. 44

CRAMER, ZADOK

Cramer's Pittsburgh Magazine Almanack for the Year of Our Lord 1809 ... Pittsburgh: 1808. V. 45

The Navigator. Pittsburgh: 1811. V. 42; 43

The Navigator. Pittsburgh: 1814. V. 39

CRAMP, S.

The Birds of the Western Palearctic. London: 1977-85. V. 37

The Birds of the Western Palearctic: Volume 4: Terns to Woodpeckers. London: 1985. V. 37

CRAMP, STANLEY

Handbook of the Birds of Europe, the Middle East and North Africa, Birds of the Western Palearctic, Volume 5: Tyrant Flycathers to Thrushes. V. 39

Handbook of the Birds of Europe, the Middle East and North Africa. Volume 1. Ostrich to Ducks. Oxford: 1978, 1977. V. 39

Handbook of the Brids of Europe, the Middle East and North Africa. Volume 2. Hawks to Bustards. Oxford: 1980. V. 39

Handbook of the Birds of Europe, the Middle East and North Africa. Volume 3. Waders to Gulls. Oxford: 1983. V. 39

Handbook of the Birds of Europe, the Middle East and North Africa. Volume 5. Tyrant Flycatchers to Thrushes. Oxford: 1985. V. 39

CRAMP, WILLIAM

Hints to Dairy Farmer; Being an Account of the Food, and Extraordinary Produce of a Cow. London: 1813. V. 39

CRANAGE, D. H. S.

An Architectural Account of the Churches of Shropshire. Wellington: 1901-12. V. 41

CRANBROOK PRESS

Cranbrook Papers, by the Cranbrook Society. Detroit: 1901. V. 44

CRANBROOK SOCIETY, DETROIT.

Cranbrook Papers, by the Cranbrook Society ... First Book. Detroit: 1901. V. 40

CRANDALL, MARJORIE LYLE

Confederate Imprints; a Checklist. Boston: 1955. V. 37; 38; 40; 42

CRANE, CHARLES JUDSON

The Experiences of a Colonel of Infantry. New York: 1923. V. 39; 45

CRANE, EDWARD

Examples of Colonial Architecture in South Carolina and Georgia. Berlin. V. 44

CRANE, GEORGE

Poems from the Novel. N.P.: 1976. V. 41

CRANE, HART 1899-1932

The Bridge, a Poem. 1930. V. 44

The Bridge. New York: 1930. V. 40

The Bridge. Paris: 1930. V. 40; 45

The Bridge. New York: 1981. V. 38; 39; 40; 41; 42; 43; 44

Collected Poems. New York: 1933. V. 37; 40; 41; 44

Voyages - Six Poems. New York: 1957. V. 37; 39; 46

Voyages. Northampton: 1957. V. 37; 40

White Buildings: Poems. London: 1926. V. 42

White Buildings. New York: 1926. V. 37; 39; 40

White Buildings. New York: 1929. V. 39; 42

White Buildings. New York: 1929. V. 42

CRANE, JAMES M.

The Past, the Present and the Future of the Pacific. San Francisco: 1856. V. 37; 46

CRANE, LOUISE

China in Sign and Symbol. Shanghai: 1926. V. 41; 43; 44

China in Sign and Symbol. Shanghai: 1926. V. 43

CRANMER, THOMAS

An Avnsvvere . . . vnto a Craftie and Sophisticall Cauillation, Deuised by Stephen Gardiner . . . London: 1580. V. 46

A Defence of the True and Ctholike Doctrine of the Sacrament of the Body and Blood of Our Saviour . . . London: 1550. V. 38

A Necessary Doctrine and Erudition for Any Christen Man, Sette Furthe by the Kynges Maiestie of England &c. Colophon: 1543. V. 44

Reformatio Legvm Ecclesiasticorum, ex Authoritate Primum Regis Henrici 8 Inchoata . . . Londini: 1641. V. 45

Reformation Legum Ecclesiasticarum Ex Authoritate Primum Regis Henrici & Inchoata . . . Londini: 1640. V. 44

CRANSTOUN, JOHN DALRYMPLE, 4TH BARONET

Essay Towards A General History of Feudal Property in Great Britain. London: 1759. V. 38

CRANTZ, DAVID

Historie Von Gronland Enthaltend die Beschreibung des Landes Und Der Einwohner U. Insbesondere die Geschichte der Dortigen Mission der Evangelischen Brueder zu Neu-Herrnhut und Lichtenfels. Barby: 1765. V. 41

The History of Greenland. London: 1767. V. 38; 39; 40; 42; 43

The History of Greenland . . . London: 1767. V. 37; 42; 43; 46

The History of Greenland. London: 1820. V. 39; 40; 41; 42; 44

CRANWELL, JOHN PHILLIPS

Notes on Figures of Earth. New York: 1929. V. 38; 39; 40

CRANWORTH, BERTRAM F. GURDON, BARON

A Colony in the Making, or Sport and Profit in British East Africa. London: 1912. V. 43

Profit and Sport in British East Africa. London: 1919. V. 43

CRAPO, THOMAS

Strange But True; Life and Adventures of Captain Thomas Crapo and Wife. New Bedford: 1893. V. 45

CRAPSEY, ADELAIDE

Verse. Rochester: 1915. V. 37; 38; 44; 46

CRAPSEY, EDWARD

The Nether Side of New York; or, the Vice, Crime and Poverty of the Great Metropolis. New York: 1872. V. 44

CRARY, L. P.

A Directory for the Village of Buffalo, Containing the Names and Residence of the Heads of Families and Householders, in Said Village . . . Buffao: 1828. V. 45

CRARY, MARY

The Daughters of the Stars. London: 1939. V. 37; 38; 39; 40; 41; 44

CRASHAW, RICHARD

Caritas Nimia. Worcester: 1963. V. 38

Musicks Duell. London: 1935. V. 43

Steps to the Temple. London: 1646. V. 43; 45

Steps to the Temple. London: 1670. V. 38; 41

CRASHAW, WILLIAM 1572-1624

Romish Forgeries and Falsifications. London: 1606. V. 38

CRASSUS, GIUNIO PAOLO

Medici Antiqui Graeci Aretaeus, Plladius, Ruffus, Theophilus; Physici & Chirurgi. Basle: 1581. V. 38; 40; 42

CRASTER, EDMUND

History of the Bodleian Library 1845-1945. Oxford: 1952. V. 46

CRASTER, J. E.

Pemba, the Spice Island of Zanzibar. London: 1913. V. 41

CRASTON, JEAN

Dictionarium Graecum . . . Venice: 1524. V. 38

CRASTONUS, JOHANNES

Dictionarium Graecum Copiosissimum Secundum Ordinem Alphabeti cum Interpretatione Latina . . . Venice: 1497. V. 46

CRASY, EDWARD SHEPHERD

The Fifteen Decisive Battles of the World, from Marathon to Waterloo. London: 1851. V. 37

CRATO VON KRAFTHEIM, JOHANNES

Consiliorum et Epistolarum Medicinalium Liber Primus (-Liber Septimus). Frankfurt: 1609-14-19. V. 42

CRAUFURD, ALEXANDER H.

General Craufurd and His Light Division. London: 1891. V. 41

CRAUFURD, DAVID

Courtship A-La-Mode. London: 1700. V. 38

CRAUFURD, GEORGE

The Doctrine of Equivalents . . . Rotterdam: 1803. V. 38; 41; 45

CRAUFURD, QUINTIN 1743-1819

Sketches Chiefly Relating to the History, Religion, Learning and Manners of the Hindoos. London: 1790. V. 43

Sketches Chiefly Relating to the History, Religion, Learning and manners of the Hindoos. London: 1792. V. 38

CRAUZAT, E. DE

La Reliure Francaise de 1900 a 1925. Paris: 1932. V. 40

CRAVEN, ELIZABETH, BARONESS, LATER MARGRAVINE OF ANSPACH 1750-1828

A Journey through the Crimea to Constantinople in a Series of Letters from the Right Honorable . . . to His Serene Highness . . . London: 1789. V. 37; 39; 45

Voyage a Constantinople par la Crimee en 1786 traduit de l'Anglois. Berlin?: 1789. V. 38

CRAVEN, ELIZABETH BERKELEY

Modern Anecdote of the Ancient Family of Kinkvervandotsdarsprakengotchderns: a Tale for Christmas 1779. London: 1779. V. 37

CRAVEN, ELIZABETH BERKELEY, BARONESS LATER MARGRAVINE OF 1750-1828

Voyage de Milady Craven a Constantinople, par la Crimee en 1786. N.P.: 1789. V. 43

CRAVEN, KEPPEL

Excursions in the Abruzzi & Northern Provinces of Naples. London: 1838. V. 37

CRAVEN, PAULINE

Fleurange. London: 1872. V. 41

CRAWFORD, ADAIR

An Experimental Enquiry into the Effects of Tonics. London: 1816. V. 38

Experiments and Observations on Animal Heat and the Inflmmation of Combustible Bodies. London: 1788. V. 38

CRAWFORD, ALEXANDER WILLIAM CRAWFORD LINDSAY, 25TH EARL OF 1812-1880

Address to Her Most Gracious Majesty the Queen. London: 1850. V. 42

Letters on Egypt, Edom and the Holy Land. London: 1847. V. 40

CRAWFORD AND BALCARRES, ALEXANDER WILLIAM LINDSAY, EARL OF

Sketches of the History of Chritisn Art. London: 1847. V. 39

CRAWFORD & BALCARRES, JAMES LUDOVIC LINDSAY, EARL OF

Catalogue of A Collection of English Ballads of the XVIIth and XVIIIth Centuries for the Most Part Printed in Black Letter. London: 1890. V. 44

CRAWFORD, CHARLES H.

Scenes of Earlier Days in Crossing the Plains to Oregon, and Experiences of Western Life. Petaluma: 1898. V. 37; 38; 39; 40; 42; 43; 45

CRAWFORD, D. G.

A History of the Indian Medical Service 1600-1913. London: 1914. V. 38

CRAWFORD, EVERETT LAKE

Let's Rude to Hounds. New York: 1929. V. 39

CRAWFORD, FRANCIS MARION 1854-1909

An American Politician. London: 1884. V. 43; 46

Corleone. London: 1897. V. 41; 46

Katharine Lauderdale. London: 1894. V. 42; 43

Marzio's Crucifix. London: 1887. V. 43

Pietro Ghisleri. London: 1893. V. 38

The Rulers of the South; Sicily, Calabria, Malta. London: 1900. V. 43

Saracinesca. Edinburgh: 1887. V. 41; 43; 46

Taquisara. New York: 1896. V. 41; 43

The Three Fates. London: 1892. V. 38

Works. London: 1890-1909. V. 37

The Complete Works. New York: 1914. V. 42

Works. New York: 1920. V. 43; 44

CRAWFORD, GEORGE

A Sketch of the Rise and Progress of the Trades' House of Glasgow, Its Constitution, Funds and Bye-Laws. Glasgow: 1851. V. 39

A Sketch of the Rise and Progress of the Trades' House of Glasgow, its Constitution, Funds and Bye-laws. Glasgow: 1858. V. 37

CRAWFORD, J. MARSHALL

Mosby-and His Men: a Record of the Adventures of that Renowned Ranger, John S. Mosby . . . New York: 1867. V. 44

CRAWFORD, JACK

What' the Hand O' God is Seen and Other Poems. New York: 1910. V. 41

CRAWFORD, JAMES COUTTS

Recollections of Travel in New Zealand and Australia. London: 1880. V. 43

CRAWFORD, JAMES LUDOVIC LINDSAY, EARL OF

Bibliotheca Lindesiana. London: 1890. V. 44; 45

CRAWFORD, JOHN LINSDAY, 19TH EARL OF

Information for the Earl of Crawfurd and the Earl Marischall; Against the Earl of Sutherland. Edinburgh: 1706. V. 45

CRAWFORD, JOHN M.

Chinese Calligraphy and Painting in the Collection of John M. Crawford. New York: 1926. V. 42

Chinese Calligraphy and Painting in the Collection of John M. Crawford, Jr. New York: 1962. V. 40

CRAWFORD, LEWIS F.

History of North Dakota. Chicago: 1931. V. 45

Rekindling Camp Fires. Bismark: 1926. V. 37; 38; 42; 45

CRAWFORD, LEWIS H.

Scenes of Earlier Days in Crossing the Plains to Oregon, and Experiences of Western Life. V. 45

CRAWFORD, MEDOREM 1819-1891

Letter of the Secretary of War Communicating . . . A Copy of the Report and Jouranl of Captain Medorem Crawford, Commanding the Emigrant Escort to Oregon and Washington Territory in the Year 1862. Washington: 1863. V. 39; 41; 46

CRAWFORD, MICHAEL H.

Roman Republican Coinage. Cambridge: 1974. V. 42

CRAWFORD, O. G. S.

Abu Geili and Saqadi & Darl el Mek. London: 1951. V. 40; 42

Aspects of Archaeology in Britain and Beyond. London: 1951. V. 45

The Long Barrows of the Cotswolds. Gloucester: 1925. V. 45

CRAWFORD, OSWALD

By Path and Trail. N.P.: 1908. V. 39; 44; 46

CRAWFORD, REBEKAH

Musicians in Rhyme for Childhood's Time. New York: 1890. V. 46

CRAWFORD, ROBERT

Reminiscences of Foreign Travel. London: 1888. V. 43

CRAWFORD, S. J.

Argument Before the Honorable Secretary of the Interior, On Appeal From the Decision of the Commissioner of the General Land Office, in the Maater of the Claim of the State of Kansas Relating to Agricultural College Lands. Topeka: 1881. V. 42

Before the Committee on Public Lands, House of Representatives-48th Congress. Topeka: 1884. V. 38

CRAWFORD, SOPHIA

The Double Marriage, a Novel. London: 1852. V. 44

CRAWFORD, THOMAS

The Life and Adventures of Thomas Crawford, a Native of England. Concord: 1849. V. 39

CRAWFORD, WILLIAM

A History of Ireland. Strabane: 1783. V. 37; 40; 42; 43

CRAWFORD, WILLIAM H.

Letter From . . . to the Chairman of the Committee on Public Lands. Transmitting Documents in Realtion to Land Claims in Florida. Washington: 1824. V. 38; 42

CRAWFURD, GEORGE d. 1748

A General Description of the Shire of Renfrew. (with) A Genealogical History of the Royal House of Stewart. 1818. V. 39

The Lives and Characters of the Officers of the Crown, and of the State in Scotland from King David I to the Union and the Two Kingdoms . . . Edinburgh: 1726. V. 38; 40

CRAWFURD, JOHN

History of the Indian Archipelago. Edinburgh: 1820. V. 38; 41

Journal of an Embassy from the Governor-General of India to the Courts of Siam and Cochin China . . . London: 1828. V. 43

CRAWHALL, JOSEPH

Chaplets from Croquet-Side. London: 1873. V. 40

Chorographia. Newcastle: 1884. V. 40; 46

A Collection of Right Merrie garlands for North Country Anglers. Newcastle-upon-Tyne: 1864. V. 37; 39; 40; 41; 44

The Compleatest Angling Book. Newcastle-upon-Tyne: 1881. V. 38; 39; 40; 43

Impresses Quaint. Newcastle: 1889. V. 40

A Jubilee Thought. Newcastle: 1887. V. 40

Olde Ffrendes with Newe Faces. London: 1883. V. 39; 41

Olde Tayles Newly Relayted. London: 1883. V. 38; 40; 44; 46

CRAWLEY-BOEVEY, ARTHUR W.

The 'Preverse Widow' Being Passages from the Life of Catharina. London: 1898. V. 38

CRAWLEY, CAPTAIN

The Billiard Book. London: 1866. V. 44

Billiards for Beginners. London: 1870. V. 38

CRAWLEY, ERNEST

The Mystic Rose: a Study of Primitive Marriage. London: 1902. V. 39

CRAWSHAY, RICHARD

The Birds of Tierra del Fuego. London: 1907. V. 37; 42

CREA, BENEDETTO ORIGO

Etruria Unveiled: The Drawings of Samuel James Ainsley in the British Museum. Roma: 1984. V. 37; 40

CREAKE, B.

A Compendious and Curious Miscellaneous History from the Creation to William the Conqueror. London: 1754. V. 42

CREALOCK, HENRY HOPE

Among the Red Deer. The Stalking Portfolios of . . . London: 1983. V. 38

CREASE, FRANCIS

Thirty-Four Decorative Designs. 1927. V. 41

Thirty-Four Decorative Designs. N.P.: 1927. V. 41

Thirty-Four Decorative Designs. N.P.: 1928. V. 38

CREASEY, JOHN

Safari with Fear. London: 1953. V. 42

CREASY, E. S.

History of the Ottoman Turks . . . London: 1856. V. 44

CREASY, EDWARD S.

Memoirs of Eminent Etonians; with Notices of the Early History of Eton College. London: 1850. V. 39; 43

CREASY, EDWARD SHEPHERD 1812-1878

Fifteen Decisive Battles of the World. London: 1851. V. 38; 44

CREBILLON, CLAUDE PROPSER JOLYOT DE

The Memoirs of Ninon de l'Enclos, with Her Letters to Monsr. de St. Evremond and to the Marquis de Sevigne. London: 1761. V. 42

CREBILLON, CLAUDE PROSPER JOYLET DE

The Memoirs of Ninon de l'Eclos . . . Dublin: 1762. V. 41

CREBILLON, PROSPER JOLYOT, SIEUR DE 1674-1762

Oeuvres Complettes . . . Paris: 1785. V. 45

CREECH, THOMAS

Library Sale Catalogue. Oxford: 1700. V. 38; 41

CREECH, WILLIAM

Edinburgh Fugitive Pieces. Edinburgh: 1791. V. 38; 39; 42

Edinburgh Fugitive Pieces. Edinburgh: 1791. V. 42

CREELEY, ROBERT

The Charm. 1967. V. 39

The Charm. Mt. Horeb: 1967. V. 38; 45

The Charm. 1969. V. 39

The Charm. San Francisco: 1969. V. 39; 40; 41; 42

The Complete Correspondence. 1980-83. V. 46

Desultory Days. 1978. V. 39

The Finger. Los Angeles: 1968. V. 40

5 Numbers. New York: 1968. V. 39

The Gold Diggers. Mallorca: 1954. V. 39

The Gold Diggers. N.P.: 1954. V. 43

The Immoral Proposition. Baden: 1953. V. 39

Le Fou. Columbus: 1952. V. 45

CREELEY, ROBERT continued

Mother's Voice. N.P.: 1981. V. 44

Myself. 1977. V. 39

Numbers. Stuttgart: 1968. V. 41

1 2 3 4 5 6 7 8 9 0. San Francisco/Berkeley: 1970. V. 45

Poems 1950-1965. London: 1946. V. 45

Poems 1950-1965. London: 1956. V. 38

Poems 1950-1965. London: 1966. V. 39; 46

Robert Creeley Reads. London: 1967. V. 39; 44

Robert Creeley and Charles Olson: The Complete Correspondence. Santa Barbara: 1980-87. V. 38

A Sight. London: 1987. V. 40

The Whip. Worcester: 1957. V. 39

CREENY, W. F.

Illustrations of Incised Slabs on the Continent of Europe from Rubbings and Tracings. London: 1901. V. 39

CREENY, WILLIAM F.

A Book of Fac-similes of Monumental Brasses on the Continent of Europe, with Brief Descriptive Notes. Norwich: 1884. V. 38; 41; 43; 46

Illustrations of Incised Slabs on the Continent of Europe from Rubbings and Tracings. Norwich: 1891. V. 37; 38; 40

CREEVEY, THOMAS 1768-1838

The Creevey Papers, a Selection from the Correspondence and Diaries of . . . London: 1903. V. 38; 39

CREGEEN, ARCHIBALD

A Dictionary of the Manks Language . . . Douglas;: 1835. V. 42; 46

CREIGH, ALFRED

History of Washington County fomr Its First Settlement to the Present . . . N.P.: 1870. V. 42

History of Washington County From Its First Settlement to the Present . . . Harrisburg: 1871. V. 41

CREIGHTON, CHARLES

Contributions to the Physiology and Pathology of the Breast and Its Lymphatics Glands. London: 1878. V. 45; 46

A History of Epidemics in Britain From A.D. 664 to the Extinction of Plague. Cambridge: 1891. V. 41

A History of Epidemics in Britain, from A.D. 664 to the Extinction of Plague . . . Cambridge: 1891, 1894. V. 37; 42

A History of Epidemics in Britain from A.D. 664 to the Present Time. Cambridge: 1891-94. V. 40; 41; 42

The Natural History of Cow-Pox and Vaccinal Syphilis. London: 1887. V. 42

CREIGHTON, D. B.

The Commercial Empire of the St. Lawrence, 1760-1805. Toronto: New Haven: 1937. V. 40; 44

CREIGHTON, HELEN

Songs and Ballads from Nova Scotia Collected by . . . London: 1932. V. 38

CREIGHTON, MANDELL

Queen Elizabeth. 1896. V. 46

Queen Elizabeth. London: 1896. V. 40; 42

Queen Elizabeth. Paris: 1896. V. 41

CRELLE, A. L.

Memoire sur les Differentes Manieres de se SErvir de l'Elasticite de l'air Atmospherique Comme Force Motrice sur les Chemins de fer. Berlin: 1846. V. 46

CREMER, W. H.

Easter Eggs: A Sketch of a Good Old Custom. Ipswich. V. 37

CREMER, WILLIAM HENRY

The Magician's Own Book. London: 1871. V. 44

Patience by Perseverance. London: 1860. V. 38

CREMONINUS, CAESAR

De Calido Innato, et Semine, pro Aristotele Adversus Galenum. Leiden: 1634. V. 42

CREMONY, JOHN C.

Life Among the Apaches. San Francisco: 1868. V. 37; 39; 40; 43; 45; 46

Life Among the Apaches. San Francisco: 1868. V. 42

THE CREOLE CASE, and Mr. Webster's Despatch; with the Comments of the New York American. New York: 1842. V. 42

CRESCENTIO, PIETRO

Opera di Agricoltura. Venegia: 1536. V. 39

CRESCENZI, PIETRO DE

De Agricultura Vulgare. Colophon: 1519. V. 37

Trattato dell' Agricultura. Florence: 1605. V. 37

CRESPEL, EMMANUEL

Voyages du R.P. Emanuel Crespel, Dans Le Canada et Son Naufrage en Revenant en France . . . Frankfurt: 1752. V. 40; 42; 44; 45

CRESPEL, R. P. EMMANUEL

Voiages du R. P. Emmanuel Crespel, dans le Canada et son Naufrage en Revenant en France. Francfort sur le Meyn: 1742. V. 39

CRESPELLE, JEAN PAUL

The Fauvres. Greenwich: 1962. V. 43; 46

CRESPIGNY, MARY CHAMPION

Letters of Advice from a Mother to Her Son. London: 1803. V. 37

CRESPIN, JEAN

Coprus Iuris Civilis. Institutiones. 1568. Institutionvm Libri III: Perpetuis Doctiss. Scriptoru Notis Illustrati . . . Appendicis Loco, Leges XII Tabvlarum, Explicatas. Geneva: 1568. V. 38

CRESSENER, DRUE

A Demonstration of the First Principles of the Protestant Apocalypse. London: 1690. V. 46

CRESSEWLL, BEATRICE F.

The Royal Progress of King Pepito. Illustrated by Kate Greenaway. Engraved and Printed by Edmund Evans. London: n.d. V. 37

CRESSON, JOSHUA

Meditations Written During the Prevalance of the Yellow Fever in the City of Philadelphia in the Year 1793. London: 1803. V. 43

CRESSWELL, BEATRICE F.

The Royal Progress of King Pepito. London: 1889. V. 39; 45

CRESSWELL, HENRY

Sliding Sands. London: 1890. V. 43

The Survivors. London: 1886. V. 43

CRESSWELL, S. GURNEY

A Series of Eight Sketches in Colour . . . of the Voyage of H.M.S. Investigator, Capt. M'Clure, During the Discovery of the North West Passage. London: 1854. V. 43

CRESSWELL, T. E.

A Narrative of the Affair Between Mr. Cresswell and Mis Sc--e, Addressed to G---v----e Sc----e, Esq. London: 1747. V. 45

CRESSWICK, MR.

The Lady's Preceptor; or, a Series of Instructive and Pleasing Exercises in Reading; for the Particular Use of Females. London: 1792. V. 41

CRESSY, EDWARD

Illustrations of Stone Church, Kent. London: 1840. V. 37

CRESSY, HUGH PAULIN

The Church History of Brittany from the Beginning of Christianity to the Norman Conquest . . . Rouen: 1688. V. 40; 46

Exomologensis, or a Faithfull Narration of the Occasion and Motives of the Conversion Unto Catholique Unity. 1647. V. 46

Roman-Catholick Doctrines No Novelties. N.P.: 1663. V. 40

CRESWEEL, SAMUEL GURNEY

A Series of Eight Sketches on Colour of the Voyage of H.M.S. Investigator. London: 1854. V. 41

CRESWELL, HENRY

Fair and Free. London: 1882. V. 42

CRESWELL, K. A. C.

Early Muslim Architecture. Part 1 only. Umayyads A. D. 622-750. Oxford: 1932. V. 37

The Muslim Architecture of Egypt. Volume 1 only. Ikhhshids and Fatimids, A.D. 939-1171. Oxford: 1952. V. 37

CRESWELL, KEPPEL ARCHIBALD CAMERON

Early Muslim Architecture Umayyards AD 622-750. 1969. V. 46

CRESWELL, THOMAS ESTCOURT

A Narrative of the Affair Between Mr. Creswell and Miss Scrope, Address'd to G(er)v(as)e Sc(rop)e. London: 1747. V. 44

CRESWICK, WILFRED

Essays on the Prevention of Explosions and Accidents in coal Mines. London: 1874. V. 45

CRESWICKE, LOUIS

South Africa and the Transvaal War. Edinburgh. V. 38; 39

South Africa and the Transvaal War. Edinburgh. V. 38

South Africa and the Transvaal War. Edinburgh: 1900. V. 38; 39

South Africa and the Transvaal War. Edinburgh: 1900-01. V. 42; 45; 46

CRESY, EDWARD

An Encyclopaedia of Civil Engineering, Historical, Theoretical and Practical. (with) Supplement . . . London: 1847/56. V. 43

Illustrations of Stone Church, Kent. London: 1840. V. 40

A Practical Treatise on Bridge-Building and on the Equilibrium of Vaults and Arches.. London: 1839. V. 44; 45

CREUZBAUR, ROBERT

Route from the Gulf of Mexico and the Lower Mississippi Valley to California and the Pacific Ocean. Austin & New York: 1849. V. 38; 39

CREUZE, AUGUSTIN F. B.

Treatise on the Theory and Practice of Naval Architecture . . . Edinburgh: 1840. V. 42

CREUZEVAULT, COLETTE

Henri Creuzevault, 1905-1971. Paris: 1987. V. 38; 39; 41; 42; 44

CREVECOEUR, MICHEL GUILLAUME ST. JEAN DE 1735-1813

Letters from an American Farmer . . . London: 1782. V. 39; 42; 43

Letters from an American Farmer . . . Conveying Some Idea of the Late and Present Interior Circumstances of the British Colonies in North America. Belfast: 1783. V. 38

Letters from an American Farmer . . . London: 1783. V. 38; 42; 43; 45

Sittliche Schilderungen von Amerika . . . Liegnitz/Leipzig: 1784. V. 38

Lettres d'un Cultivateur Americain . . . Depuis l'Annee 1770 Jusqu'en 1786. Paris: 1787. V. 38; 45

Letters from an American Farmer. V. 37

Lettres d'un Cultivateur Americain. Paris: 1784. V. 42

Voyage dans la Haute Pennsylvanie et dans L'Etat de New York . . . Paris: 1801. V. 41; 43; 45

Voyage dan la Haute Pensylvanie et dans l'Etat de New York. Paris: 1801. V. 44

CREVEL, RENE

La Clavecin de Diderot. Paris: 1932. V. 46

The Negress in the Brothel. London: 1989. V. 46

CREW, BARBARA

An Acrobatic Alphabet. Gloucestershire: 1986. V. 37; 38; 39; 40; 43; 45

CREWE, NATHANAEL

Catalogue of the Library at Bamburgh Castle. London: 1859. V. 40

CREWS, HARRY

Blood and Grits. New York: 1979. V. 44

The Body. New York: 1990. V. 45

Car. New York: 1972. V. 44; 45; 46

Car. London: 1973. V. 45; 46

A Childhood: The Biography of a Place. New York: 1978. V. 39; 42; 44; 45

A Feast of Snakes. New York: 1796. V. 44

A Feast of Snakes. New York: 1976. V. 44; 45

The Gospel Singer. 1968. V. 44

The Gospel Singer. New York: 1968. V. 44; 45

The Gypsy's Curse. New York: 1974. V. 44; 46

The Hawk is Dying. New York: 1973. V. 43; 44; 45; 46

Karate is a Thing of the Spirit. New York: 1971. V. 37; 42; 43; 44; 45; 46

The Knockout Artist. New York. V. 44

Naked in Garden Hills. New York: 1969. V. 39; 43; 44; 45; 46

This Thing Don't Lead to Heaven. 1970. V. 45

This Thing Don't Lead to Heaven. New York: 1970. V. 41; 42; 43; 45

2 by Crews. Northridge: 1984. V. 45

CRICHTON, A. W.

A Naturalist's Ramble to the Orcades. London: 1866. V. 43

CRICHTON, ARTHUR

The Festival of Flora. London: 1818. V. 38; 40; 42

CRICHTON, KYLE S.

Law and Order, Ltd. The Rousing Life of Elfego Baca of New Mexico. Santa Fe: 1928. V. 38; 43

The Marx Brothers. Garden City: 1950. V. 38

CRICHTON, M.

Jasper Johns. New York: 1977. V. 46

CRICHTON, PATRICK

Observations on a Machine for the Speedy Conveyance of Troops and Report of an Experiment for that Purpose . . . Edinburgh: 1804. V. 37; 42

CRICK, THOMAS

Sketches from the Diary of a Commercial Traveler. London: 1847. V. 43

CRICK, THORNE

Sketches from the Diary of a Commercial Traveller. London: 1847. V. 40

CRICK, THRONE

Sketches from the Diary of a Commercial Traveller. London: 1847. V. 39

CRICKET and How to Play It. London: 1869. V. 43; 46

THE CRIES of London. London: 1850. V. 42

THE CRIES of York. York: 1820. V. 39

CRIGHTON, ARCHIBALD WILLIAM

Dissertatio Medica Inauguralis, De Melancholia. Edinburgh: 1810. V. 45

CRILE, GEORGE

Anemia and Resucitation: an Experimental and Clinical Research. New York: 1914. V. 42

Blood Pressure in Surgery and Experimental and Clincal Research. Philadelphia: 1903. V. 42

An Experimental and Clinical Research into Certain Problems Relating to Surgical Operations . . . Philadelphia: 1901. V. 41

Hemorrhage and Transfusion: an Experimental and Clinical Research. New York: 1909. V. 41

CRILE, GEORGE WASHINGTON

Anoci-Association. Philadelphia & London: 1914. V. 43

THE CRIMINAL Recorder, or Biographical Sketches of the Notorious Characters. London: 1804. V. 38

CRIMINAL Trials, Illustrative of the Tale Entitled 'The Heart of Mid-Lothian.' . . . Edinburgh: 1818. V. 42; 44

CRIMMINS, JOHN D.

Irish American Historical Miscellany, Relating largely to New York and Vicinity, together with material relating to other parts of the Country. New York: 1905. V. 37

CRIMONT, RAPHAEL

Prayers in the Crow Indian Language Composed by the Missionaries of the Society of Jesus. 1891. V. 45

Prayers in the Crow Indian Language Composed by the Missionaries of the Society of Jesus. Idaho: 1891. V. 41; 42

Selecta Ex Historia Sacra. 1891. V. 45

CRINITUS, P. RICCIUS

(Opera) Honesta Disciplina, Lib. XXV. Poetis Latinis, Lib. V. Poemation Lib. II Cum Indicibus. Luguduni: 1543. V. 40

THE CRIPPLE Creek Gold Fields. Placer Lodes. N.P.: 1892. V. 41

CRIPPS, GEORGE R.

About Furs. Liverpool. V. 39

About Furs. Liverpool: n.d. V. 41

THE CRISIS: on the Origin and Consequences of Our Political Dissensions. Ablany: 1815. V. 42

THE CRISIS; or, a Letter to the Right Honourable the Chancellor of the Exchequer Stating the True Cause of the Present Alarming State of the Country . . . London: 1816. V. 43

CRISP, F. A.

Abstracts of Somersetshire Wills, etc. Copied from the Ms Collections of the Last Rev. F. Brown. London: 1887-90. V. 38

CRISP, FRANK

Mediaeval Gardens. London: 1924. V. 43

Mediaeval Gardens. New York: 1924. V. 39; 45

CRISP, FREDERICK ARTHUR

Alumni Carthusiani. London: 1913. V. 42

Armorial China. London: 1907. V. 42

Collections Relating to the Family of Crispe. London: 1882-1913. V. 42

Collections Relating to the Family of Crispe. London: 1882-4. V. 38

CRISP, JOHN

The Conveyancer's Guide; a poem in two books, describing estates as they relate to conveyances, and conveyances as the relate to estates. By a Gentleman of Gray's Inn. London: 1821. V. 37

CRISP, STEPHEN

A Memorable Account of the Christian Experiences, Gospel Labours, Travels and Sufferings of that Ancient Servant of Christ Stephen Crisp . . . London: 1694. V. 39; 42; 43; 44

CRISP, WILLIAM

The Printers' Business Guide and Ready-Reckoned General Price Lists, for Printing Cards, Circulars, Handbills, Memorandums, Posters, Cheque Books, Labels, Bill Heads, etc. To Which are Added Miscellaneous Receipts . . . London: 1869. V. 41

CRISPIN, EDMUND

Beware of the Trains. London: 1953. V. 46

Buried for Pleasure. London: 1948. V. 40

Frequent Hearses. London: 1950. V. 40; 41

Holy Disorders. London: 1945. V. 38

Holy Disorders. 1946. V. 39

Love Lies Bleeding. London: 1948. V. 41

The Moving Toyshop. 1946. V. 39

The Moving Toyshop. London: 1946. V. 38

CRISPOLTI, CESARE

Perugia Augusta Descritta. Perugia: 1648. V. 45

CRISSEY, FORREST

The Young Newspaper Scout. Chicago: 1897. V. 43

CRISTIANI, RICHARD S.

Perfumery and Kindred Arts. Philadelphia: 1877. V. 40

CRITCHELL, ROBERT S.

Recollections of a Fire Insurance Man . . . Chicago: 1909. V. 38

CRITCHLEY, MAC DONALD

The Parietal Lobes. London: 1953. V. 43

CRITE, ALLAN ROHAN

Three Spirituals from Earth to Heaven. Cambridge: 1948. V. 42

CRITES, ARTHUR S.

Pioneer Days in Kern County. Los Angeles: 1951. V. 46

A CRITICAL Analysis of Several Striking and Incongruous Passages in Madame de Stael's Work on Germany . . . . London: 1814. V. 39; 41; 43; 45

A CRITICAL, Expatiatory, and Interesting Address to a Certain Right Honourable Apostate, on His Present Unaccountable Conduct at Thus Critical Juncture; and On Several Other Important and National Affairs. London: 1747? V. 41; 42

CRITICAL Remarks on the Metaphysical Poets: an Interlude. Mt. Vernon: 1945. V. 46

A CRITICAL Review of the Liberties of British Subjects. London: 1750. V. 40; 41

A CRITICAL Review of the Publick Buildings, Statues and Ornaments In, and About London and Westminster. London: 1734. V. 38

CRITICISM On the Rolliad. Part I (part II) with Probationary Odes for the Laureatship . . . (with) Political Miscellanies. London: 1791/90/90. V. 41

A CRITQUE of the Poems of Robert Burns. Edinburgh: 1812. V. 39

CRITTENDEN, H. H.

The Crittenden Memoirs. New York: 1936. V. 39

CRITTENDEN, H. M.

The Crittenden Memoirs. New York: 1936. V. 44

CROAGAN, JOHN

Rambles in Mammoth Cave, During the Year 1844. Louisville: 1845. V. 39

CROASDAILE, HENRY E.

Scenes on Pacific Shores; with a Trip Across South America. London: 1873. V. 38; 40

CROCE, BENEDETTO 1866-1952

Historial Materialism and the Economics of Karl Marx. London: 1931. V. 43

The Philosophy of Giambattista Vico. London: 1913. V. 39

CROCE, GIOVANNI ANDREA DELLA

Cirugia Universale e Perfetta di Tutte le Parti Pertinenii All'Ottimo Chirurgo . . . Venetia: 1583. V. 41

CROCE, GIULIO CESARE

Bertolo con Bertoldino e Cacasenno, in Ottava Rima, con Argomenti e Figure in Rame. Bologna: 1736. V. 39

L'Dsgrazi D'Bertuldin Dalla Zena . . . Bologna: 1736. V. 45; 46

CROCHERON, AUGUSTA JOYCE

Representative Women of Deseret. Salt Lake City: 1884. V. 42

CROCKATT, GILBERT

The Scotch Presbyterian Eloquence. London: 1719. V. 38

CROCKER, A.

The Elements of Land Surveying, Designed Principally for the Use of Schools and Students. London: 1806. V. 40; 46

CROCKER, ALAN

Paper Mills of the Tillingbourne: a History of Paper Making in a Surrey Valley, 1704-1875. Surrey: 1988. V. 40; 41; 43; 45

CROCKER & BREWSTER

Fiftieth Anniversary of the CoPartnership of Crocker & Brewster. Boston: 1869. V. 40

CROCKER, H. S.

Railroad Gazetteer . . . Sacramento: 1870. V. 37

CROCKER, HENRY J.

Hawaiian Numerals. San Francisco: 1909. V. 38

CROCKER, JAMES F.

Gettysburg--Pickett's Charge and Other War Addresses. Portsmouth: 1915. V. 39

CROCKER, JOHN WILSON

An Answer to O'Meara's Napoleon in Exile; or, a Voice From St. Helena. New York: 1823. V. 42

Familiar Epistles to Frederick J---s, Esq. Dublin: 1804. V. 39

CROCKER-LANGLEY San Francisco Directory for Commencing April 1896. San Francisco: 1896. V. 41

CROCKER, ZEBULON

The Catastrophe of the Presbyterian Church in 1837, Including a Full View of the Recent Theological Controversies in New England. New Haven: 1838. V. 46

CROCKET, G. L.

Two Centuries in East Texas: A History of San Augustine Country and Surrounding Territory from 1685 to the Present Time. Dallas: 1932. V. 37; 38; 39

CROCKETT Almanac 1852. Boston: 1852. V. 45

CROCKETT Almanac Improved 1842. Boston: 1841. V. 39; 45

CROCKETT, DAVID

An Account of Col. Crockett's Tour to the North and Down East. Philadelphia: 1835. V. 37; 38; 39; 40; 45

Address of Mr. Crockett, to the Voters of the Ninth Congressional District of the State of Tennessee; Together with His Remarks in the House of Representatives, January 5, 1829. Washington: 1829. V. 46

Col. Crockett's Exploits and Adventures in Texas . . . Philadelphia: 1836. V. 38

'Go Ahead!' The Crockett Almanac 1804. Nashville: 1839. V. 46

The Life and Adventures of Colonel David Crockett, of West Tennessee. Cincinnati: 1833. V. 42; 45

The Life of Martin Van Buren . . . Philadelphia: 1835. V. 38; 39; 42; 44; 45

A Narrative of the Live of . . . of the State of Tennessee Written by Himself. Philadelphia: 1834. V. 37; 41; 42

Sketches and Eccentricities of Col. David Crockett. New York: 1833. V. 37

CROCKETT, GEORGE W.

Mustang Training; or, a Lesson Not Taught by Prof. Rarey: a Sketch of Prairie Life in the Southwest. Centreville: 1858. V. 39

CROCKETT, S. R.

Dulce Cor, Being the Poems of Ford Bereton. London: 1886. V. 43

Kit Kennedy, Country Boy. London: 1899. V. 43

Lad's Love. London: 1897. V. 39; 42; 46

A Romancer's Local Colour. London: 1900. V. 43

Sir Toady Crusoe. London: 1905. V. 43

CROFF, G. B.

Modern Suburban Architecture. New York: 1870. V. 45; 46

CROFFUTT, GEORGE A.

Great Trans-Continental Tourists' Guide Containing a full and Accurate Description of Over 500 Cities . . . New York: 1870. V. 42

CROFT, HEBERT

A Short Narrative of the Discovery of a College of Jesuits, at a Place Called the Come, in the County of Hereford . . . London: 1679. V. 43

CROFT, HERBERT

The Abbey of Kilhampton; or, Monumental Records for the Year 1980. London: 1780. V. 46

A Brother's Advice to His Sisters. London: 1775. V. 41

Love and Madness. London: 1780. V. 38

Love and Madness: In a Series of Letters, One of Which Contains the Original Account of Chatterton. London: 1786. V. 42

Some Animadversions Upon a Book Intituled, The Theory of the Earth. London: 1685. V. 37

CROFT, JOHN

A Treatise on the Wines of Portugal. York: 1788. V. 38

CROFT, PETER JOHN

Autograph Poetry in the English Language . . . London: 1973. V. 37; 39; 40; 43

Autograph Poetry in the English Language. New York: 1973. V. 44

CROFTON, HELEN A.

Records of the Slacke Family in Ireland. V. 38

CROFTS, FREEMAN WILLS

Death of a Train. London: 1946. V. 43; 45

Sir John Magill's Last Journey. New York: 1930. V. 44

CROFTS, THOMAS

Bibliotheca Croftsiana. London: 1783. V. 39

CROFUTT, GEORGE A.

Crofutt's Trans Continental Tourist's Guide . . . New York: 1871. V. 43

Crofutt's Trans-Continental Tourist's Guide . . . Chicago: 1872. V. 38

Crofutt's Western World. New York: 1873. V. 43

Crofutt's Trans-Continental Tourist's Guide . . . New York: and Chicago: 1873. V. 42

Crofutt's New Overland Tourist and Pacific Coast Guide . . . Chicago: 1879. V. 40

Crofutt's Grip-Sack Guide of Colorado. Omaha: 1881. V. 44

Crofutt's New Overland Tourist and Pacific Coast Guide . . . Chicago: 1882. V. 40

Crofutt's Overland Guide. Chicago: 1890. V. 37

Transcontinental Tourist Guide. New York: 1872. V. 38; 45; 46

CROGHAN, JOHN

Rambles in Mammoth Cave. During the Year 1844. London: 1845. V. 43

Rambles in Mammoth Cave, During the Year 1844. Louisville: 1845. V. 45

CROIL, JAMES

Steam Navigation and Its Relation to the Commerce of Canada and the United States. Montreal: 1898. V. 42

Steam Navigation and Its Relation to the Commerce of Canada and the United States. Toronto: 1898. V. 40

CROKATT, GILBERT, PSEUD. fl. 1692-1708

The Scotch Presbyterian Eloquence Display'd. London: 1738. V. 40

CROKE, ALEXANDER

An Essay on the Origin, Progress and Decline of Rhyming Latin Verse with Many Specimens. Oxford: 1828. V. 37

A Report of the Case of Horner Against Liddiard, Upon the Question of What Consent is Necessary to the Marriage of Illegitimate Minors . . . London: 1800. V. 40; 42; 46

CROKE, GEORGE 1560-1642

The First Part (The Second Part, & The Third Part) of the Reports of Sir George Croke. London: 1661-69-57. V. 39

Reports of Cases in King's Bench and Common Bench (1582-1641) Collected and Written in French . . . London: 1683. V. 40

Reports . . . of Such Select Cases as Were Adjudged in the Said Courts, from the 24th of the Late Queen Elizabeth. London;: 1683. V. 39

The Second Part of the Reports of Sir George Croke Kt . . . London: 1683. V. 45

The Third Part (though the First Publish't) of the Reports of Sir George Croke Kt . . . of Such Select Cases as Were Adjudged . . . During the First Sixteen Years Reign of King Charles the First. London: 1683. V. 45

CROKER, B. M.

Interference: a Novel. London: 1891. V. 43

Married or Single? London: 1895. V. 43

CROKER, JOHN WILSON

Familiar Epistles (in verse) to Frederick J(one)s Esq. on the Present State of the Irish Stage. Dublin: 1804. V. 39; 40; 46

Two Letters on Scottish Affairs, From Edward Bradwardine Waverley, Esq. to Malachi Malagrowther, Esq . . . London: 1826. V. 42

CROKER, RICHARD

Travels through Several Provinces of Spain and Portugal, etc. London: 1799. V. 38

CROKER, T. CROFTON

The Popular Songs of Ireland. London: 1839. V. 46

CROKER, TEMPLE HENRY

The Complete Dictionary of Arts and Sciences. London: 1764-73. V. 40; 42

CROKER, THOMAS CROFTON 1798-1854

Fairy Legends and Traditions of the South of Ireland. London: 1826. V. 43

Fairy Legends and Traditions of the South of Ireland. London: 1826-28. V. 42

Fairy Legends and Traditions of the South of Ireland. New Series. London: 1828. V. 43

Researches in the South of Ireland, Illustrative of the Scenery, Architectural Remains and the Manners and Superstitions of the Peasantry. London: 1824. V. 43

A Walk from London to Fulham. Revised and edited by his son T.F. Dillon Croker. London: 1860. V. 37; 44; 45

CROLIUS, TUCKER & ALLEN CO.

Illustrated Catalogue of Surgical Instruments, Galvanic and Faradic Batteries, Microscopes, Artificial Limbs, Deformity, Apparatus, Trusses, Supporters, etc., etc. Minneapolis: 1885. V. 41

Illustrated Catalogue of Surgical Instruments, Glavanic and Faradic Batteries, Microscopes, Artificial Limbs, Deformity Apparatus, Trusses, Supporters, etc. Minneapolis: 1892. V. 42

CROLL, OSWALD

Basilica Chymica Continens Philosophicam Propria Laborum Experimentia Confirmatam Descriptionem et Usum Remediorum Chymicorum Selectissimorum . . . Frankfurt: 1611. V. 40

Philosophicam Propria Laborum Experimentia Confirmatam Descriptionem et Usum Remediorum Chymicorum Selectissimorum . . . Frankfurt: 1611. V. 38

CROLY, DAVID G.

Miscegenation; The Theory of the Blending of the Races, Applied to the American White Man and Negro . . . London: 1864. V. 42

CROLY, DAVID GOODMAN

Miscegenation: the Theory of the Blending or the Races, Applied to the American White Man and Negro. New York: 1864. V. 37; 42

CROLY, GEORGE

The Angel of the World; an Arabian Tale; Sebastian; a Spanish Tale; with Other Poems. London: 1820. V. 39; 42

The Holy Land 1842. Holland. V. 43

The Holy Lnd: Idumea, Arabia, Egypt & Nubia. New York: 1855-56. V. 38

A Memoir of the Political Life of the Right Honourable Edmund Burke, with Extracts from His Writings. Edinburgh: 1840. V. 46

Paris in 1815. London: 1817. V. 42

Salathiel. London: 1828. V. 40

Salathiel. London: 1828. V. 45

Salathiel. A Story of the Past, The Present, and the Future. London: 1828. V. 41; 43

Salathiel. A Story of the Past, the Present and the Future. New York & Philadelphia: 1828. V. 46

Tales of the Great St. Bernard. London: 1828. V. 37; 42; 46

CROLY, JANE CUNNINGHAM 1829-1901

The History of the Woman's Club Movement in America. New York: 1898. V. 39

CROMARTY, GEORGE MAC KENZIE, 1ST EARL OF 1630-1714

A Vindication of Robert III. King of Scotland, From the Imputation of Bastardy, by the Clear Proof of Elizabeth Mure (Daughter of Sir Adam Mure of Rowallan) Her Being the First Lawful Wife of Robert II, Then Stewart of Scotland and Earl of Strathern.. Edinburgh: 1695. V. 45

CROMARTY, GEORGE MACKENZIE, 1ST EARL OF

Parainesis Pacifica. Edinburgh: 1702. V. 38

CROMBIE, ALEXANDER 1762-1840

An Essay on Philosphical Necessity. London: 1793. V. 42; 45

Natural Theology; or Essays on the Existence of Deity and of Providence on the Immateriality of the Soul . . . London: 1829. V. 42

CROMBIE, BENJAMIN W.

Modern Athenians. London: 1882. V. 38

CROMBIE, CHARLES

The Laws of Cricket. London: 1907. V. 42

CROMBIE, JOHN

Biobibliographique. 1986. V. 40; 45

Stitches in Time. 1985. V. 40; 45

CROMBIE, JOHN continued

Tutti Frutti. Paris: 1987. V. 46

CROME, JOHN

Etchings of Views in Norfolk, by the Late John Crome. Norwich: 1838. V. 44

CROME, ROBERT

The Fiddle New Model'd. London: 1765. V. 40

CROMER, MARTIN

De Origine et Rebus Gestis Polonorum Libri XXX. Basle: 1555. V. 37
De Origine et Rebus Gestis Polonorum Libri XXX. Basle: 1555. V. 37; 40

CROMIE, ROBERT

A Plunge into Space. London: 1890. V. 38

CROMMELIN, MAY

Joy or The Light of Cold-Home Ford. London: 1884. V. 44

CROMMELYNCK, ALDO

Picasso 347. New York: 1970. V. 43; 46

CROMPTON, D. W. T.

Biology of the Acanthocephala. Cambridge: 1985. V. 37; 38

CROMPTON, HENRY 1836-1904

Industrial Conciliation. London: 1876. V. 40; 43; 46

CROMPTON, RICHARD

L'Authorite et Jurisdiction des Courts de la Maiestie de la Roygne. London: 1637. V. 38
L' Avthoritie et Jurisdiction des Courts de la Majestie de la Roygne. London: 1594. V. 37
The Copie of a Letter to the . . . Earle of Leycester..with a Report of Certaine Petitions and Declaration Made to the Queen's Majestie (etc.). London: 1586. V. 37

CROMPTON, WILLIAM

Saint Austins Summes: or the Summe of Saint Austins Religion. London: 1625. V. 39

CROMWELL, OLIVER

A coppie of a Letter, to be Sent to Lieutenant Generall Crumwell From the Well-Affected Partie in the City. London: 1647. V. 40
A Declaration of His Highnes, by the Advice of His Council, Shewing the Reasons of Their Proceedings for Securing the Peace of the Commonwealth, Upon Occasion of the Late Insurrection and Rebellion. Wednesday Oct. 31, 1655. London: 1655. V. 40
A Declaration of His Highness the Lord Protector, Upon His Actual Dissolution of the Parliament of England, on Munday the 22th of January 1654. London: 1655. V. 40
His Highness Speech to the Parliament in the Printed Chamber, at Their Dissolution, Upon Monday the 22d of January 1654-(5). London: 1654. V. 43; 46
Irenodia Gratulatoria. Sive Illustrissimi Amplissimiq . . . London: 1652. V. 42

CROMWELL, RICHARD

The Speech of His Highness the Lord Protector, Made to Both Houses of Parliament at Their First Meeting, on Thursday the 27th of January 1658 . . . London: 1659. V. 46

CROMWELL, THOMAS

Excursions in the County of Sussex. London: 1822. V. 40
Excursions in the County of Kent: London: 1822. V. 40; 44
History and Description of the Ancient Town and Borough of Colchester, in Essex. London: 1825. V. 37; 39; 42; 44

CROMWELL, THOMAS KITSON

Excursions in the County of Essex. London: 1818-19. V. 40
Excursions through Suffolk. London: 1819. V. 40
The Essex Tourist, or Excursions in the County of Essex, Comprising Brief Historical and Topographical Delineations . . . London: 1819. V. 41

CRONE, RAINER

Andy Warhol. New York: Washington. V. 41

CRONIN, ARCHIBALD JOSEPH 1896-1981

Hatter's Castle. London: 1931. V. 37
Investigations in First-Aid Organization at Collieries in Great Britain. London: 1927. V. 37; 38; 41; 42; 44

CRONISE, TITUS FEY

The Natural Wealth of California . . . San Francisco: 1868. V. 37; 39; 41; 45; 46

CRONQUIST, A.

An Integrated System of Classification of Flowering Plants. New York: 1981. V. 37

CRONSTEDT, AXEL FREDRIK

An Essay Towards a System of Mineralogy . . . London: 1770. V. 38; 43
An Essay Towards a System of Mineralogy. London: 1788. V. 38

CROOK, GEORGE

Letter from Gen. Crook on Giving the Ballott to Indians. N.P.: 1885. V. 46

CROOK, J. MORDAUNT

Victorian Architecture. New York: 1971. V. 45

CROOK, WILLIAM

Ireland and the Centenary of American Methodism. Chapters on the Palatines, Philip Embury and Barbara Heck, and other Irish Emigrants who laid the foundation of the Methodist Church in the U.S.A., Canada and Eastern British America . . . London: 1866. V. 37

CROOKE, HELKIAH

Mikrokosmographia (in Greek). London: 1618. V. 38; 41; 45

CROOKE, JOHN

A Short History of the Life of John Crook. London. V. 44

CROOKE, WILLIAM

A Catalogue of Such Books that are Printed and Sold by . . . London: 1683. V. 40

CROOKS, JOHN J.

A History of the Colony of Sierra Leone, Western Africa. Dublin: 1903. V. 43; 46

CROOKS, WILLIAM

General Orders no. 55. Helena: 1864. V. 41

CROOKSHANK, C. DE W.

Prints of British Military Operations. A Catalogue Raisonne with Historical Descriptions Covering the Period from the Norman Conquest to the Campaign in Abyssinia. London: 1921. V. 46

CROOKSHANK, C. H.

History of Methodism in Ireland. Belfast: 1885. V. 38

CROOKSHANK, EDGAR MARCH

History and Pathology of Vaccination. London: 1889. V. 38; 41; 43; 44; 45
History and Pathology of Vaccination. Philadelphia: 1889. V. 37; 42; 45

CROOKSHANK, H.

History of Methodism in Ireland. Belfast: 1885. V. 43

CROON, PEETER

Moy-Al Oft Vermaeckelycke Bedenckingen Op Verscheyde Oeffeningen. Mechelen: 1666. V. 40

CROP, P. J.

Autograph Poetry in the English Language. London: 1973. V. 45

CROPPER, JAMES

Letters Addressed to William Wilberforce, M.P. Recommending the Encouraagement of the Cultivation of Sugar in Our Dominions in the East Indies, as the Natural and Certain Means of Effecting the General and Total Abolition of the Slave Trade. Liverpool: 1822. V. 38

CROS, CHARLES 1842-1888

Solution Generale du Probleme de la Photographie des Couleurs. Paris: 1869. V. 38

CROSBIE, EDWARD WILLIAM

An Accurate and Impartial Narrative of the Apprehension, Trial & Execution on the 5th of June, 1798, of Sir Edward William Crosbie, Bart. Dubling: 1802. V. 40

CROSBY, B.

The Irish Musical Repository. London: 1808. V. 43

CROSBY, CARESSE 1892-1970

Crosses of Gold. Paris: 1925. V. 38
Graven Images. Boston & New York: 1926. V. 46
Painted Shores. paris: 1927. V. 41
The Passionate Years. London: 1955. V. 37
Poems for Harry Crosby. Paris: 1931. V. 37

CROSBY, DIXI

Report of a Trial for Alleged Malpractice, Against Dixi Crosby, M.D. Verdict for the Defendant. Woodstock: 1854. V. 45

CROSBY, EVERETT U.

Nantucket in Print, Checklist of Writings from Gosnold 1602 to the Present Day, by Those 'off' Who Admired the Islanders and Their Successes at Sea. Nantucket: 1946. V. 38
Susan's Teeth and Much About Scrimshaw. Nantucket Island: 1955. V. 39; 44

CROSBY, FRANK

Das Leben Abraham Lincolns... Seine Fruhere Geschichte und Politische Laufbahn, Sowie Seine Reden Botschaften, Proklamationen und Andere Mit Seiner... Philadelphia: 1865. V. 42

CROSBY, HARRY

Devour the Fire. Berkeley. V. 44

Devour the Fire the Selected Poems of... Berkeley: (1983). V. 37; 44

Mad Queen: Tirades. Paris: 1929. V. 46

CROSBY, P. A.

Lovell's Gazetteer of British North America. Montreal: 1881. V. 38

CROSBY, PERCY

Sport Drawing. McLean: 1933. V. 39

CROSBY, SUMNER MCKNIGHT

The Abbey of St. Denis, 475-1122. New Haven: 1942. V. 45

CROSDALE, HENRY E.

Scenes on Pacific Shores. London: 1873. V. 38

CROSE, CORNELIA A. H.

Memorials, Scientific and Literary, of Andrew Crosse, the Electrician. London: 1857. V. 37

CROSIER, JOHN

Catalogue of the ... Furniture, Foreign Curiosities ... Library of Medical and Other Books. London: 1806. V. 40; 44

CROSKEY, JOHN W.

History of Blockley: A History of the Philadelphia General Hospital from Its Inception, 1731-1928. Philadelphia: 1929. V. 41; 42

CROSLAND, T. W.

The Coronation Dumpty Book. London. V. 46

CROSLAND, T. W. H.

The First Stone. On Reading the Unpublished Parts of 'De Profundis.' London: 1912. V. 40

Little People: An Alphabet. Pictures by Henry Mayer. London: 1901. V. 37

The Wild Irishman. London: 1905. V. 41

CROSLEGH, CHARLES

Descent and Alliances of Croslegh or Crossle, or Crossley, and Coddington, of Oldbridge, Co. Louth. London. V. 38

CROSS, AMANDA

In the last Analysis. New York: 1964. V. 37

CROSS, DOROTHY

Archaeology of New Jersey. Trenton: 1941. V. 41

Archaeology of New Jersey ... The Abbott Farm. Trenton: 1956. V. 41

CROSS, HENRY

An Answer to an Invidious Pamphlet, Intituled a Brief State of the Province of Pennsylvania. London: 1755. V. 38; 42

CROSS, IRA B.

Financing an Empire: History of Banking in California. Chicago: 1927. V. 37; 38; 40

CROSS, J. W.

George Eliot's Life as Related in Her Letters and Journals... Edinburgh: 1885. V. 44

George Eliot's Life as Related in Her Letters and Journals. Edinburgh and London: 1885. V. 41; 44; 46

George Eliot's Life as Related in Her Letters and Journals. New York: 1885. V. 44; 46

CROSS, JOE

Cattle Clatter. Kansas City: 1938. V. 42; 46

CROSS, ODO

The Snail that Climbed the Eiffel Tower. London: 1947. V. 40; 45

CROSS, OSBORN

A Report in the Form of a Journal to the Quartermaster General of the March of the Regiment of Mounted Riflemen to Oregon, from May 10 to October 5, 1849. V. 39

A Report, in the Form of a Journal, to the Quartermaster General, of the March of the Regiment of Mounted Riflemon to Oregon from May 10 to October 5, 1849 by Major O. Cross. Washington: 1850. V. 40; 45

A Report in the Form of a Journal to the Quartermaster General of the March of the Regiment of Mounted Riflemen to Oregon, From May 10 to Oct. 5, 1849. Washington: 1850-51. V. 46

CROSS, OSBORNE

A Report ... of the March of the Regiment of Mounted Riflemen to Oregon, from May 10 to October 5, 1849 ... Washington: 1851. V. 37

CROSS, R. W.

The True Masonic Chart, or Hieroglyphic Monitor. New York: 1845. V. 39

A CROSS Section: The Society of Wood Engravers in 1987. London: 1988. V. 44

A CROSS Section. The Society of Wood Engravers in 1988. Wakefield: 1988. V. 42

CROSS, THOMAS

The Autobiograpahy of a Stage Coachman. London: 1904. V. 37

The Autobiography of a Stage-Coahcman. London: 1861. V. 43

The Autobiography of a Stage Coachmen. London: 1904. V. 37; 42

CROSS, WILBUR L.

The Life and Times of Laurnece Sterne. New Haven: 1929. V. 40

CROSSE, JOHN GREEN

Cases in Midwifery by the Late John Green Crosse, M.D., F.R.S .... London: 1851. V. 43

CROSSEN, FOREST

The Switzerland Trail of America. Boulder: 1962. V. 40

CROSSLEY-HOLLAND, KEVIN

The Seafarer. 1988. V. 40

The Seafarer. 1988. V. 45

CROSSMAN, CARL L.

The China Trade: Export Paintings, Furniture, Silver & Other Objects. Princeton: 1973. V. 37; 38; 41

The China Trade, Export Paintings, Furniture, Silver and Objects. Princeton: 1972. V. 37

CROSSMAN, MARTIN L.

The Philosophy of Mesmerism, or Animal Magnetism ... Montreal: 1844. V. 43

CROSSMAN, SAMUEL

Journal accounts of blacksmith business at Sandyston, Sussex Coutn, february 1840 through June 1845. V. 37

CROSTHWAITE, PETER

Maps of the Lakes. London: 1809. V. 44

Maps of the Lakes. London and Keswick: 1809. V. 40

Seven Engraved Maps of the Lakes. Keswick: 1788. V. 44

CROSTON, JAMES

Chantrey's Peak Scenery or Views in Derbyshire. Derby: 1886. V. 45

A History of the Ancient Hall of Samlesbury. London: 1871. V. 37; 40

CROSWELL, ANDREW 1716-1757

The Heavenly Doctrine of Man's Justification Only by the Obedience of Jesus Christ, ... Boston: 1758. V. 43

Mr. Croswell's Reply to the Declaration of a Number of the Associated Ministers in Boston and Charlestown, With Regard to the Rev. Mr. James Davenport and His Conduct. Boston: 1742. V. 43; 44

CROTHERS, SAMUEL MC CHORD

The Children of Dickens. V. 45

The Children of Dickens. New York: 1925. V. 37; 41; 43

CROTTY, DANIEL G.

Four Years Campaigning in the Army of the Potomac. By Color Sergeant, D.G. Crotty, Third Michigan Volunteer Infantry. Grand Rapids: 1874. V. 37; 38

CROUCH, ARCHER P.

Captain Enderis, First West African Regiment. London: 1893. V. 38

CROUCH, EDMUND A.

An Illustrated Introduction to Lamrack's Conchology. London: 1826. V. 40

CROUCH, NATHANIEL 1632?-1725?

Admirable Curiosities Rarities and Wonders in England, Scotland and Ireland. London: 1684. V. 41; 42

Choice Emblems, Divine and Moral, Antient and Modern; or, Delights for the Ingenious in Above Fifty Select Emblems ... London: 1732. V. 41

The English Empire in America: or a Prospect of His Majesties Dominions ... London: 1685. V. 40

The English Acquisitions in Guinea and East India ... London: 1700. V. 39

The English Hero of Sir Francis Drake Reviv'd by R.B. London: 1710. V. 44

The General History of Earthquakes. London: 1734. V. 38

CROUCH, NATHANIEL 1632?-1725? continued

Historical Remarques, and Observations of the Ancient and Present State of London and Westminster. London: 1681. V. 38

The History of the House of Orange . . . together with the History of William and Mary. London: 1693. V. 41

The History of Oliver Cromwel, Lord Protector of the Commonwealth . . . London: 1698. V. 42

The Kingdom of Darkness: or the History of Daemons, Specters, Witches, Apparitions, Possessions, Disturbances, and Other Wonderful and Supernatural Delusions . . . London: 1688. V. 39

A New View and Observations..of London and Westminster. London: 1730. V. 45

Unparallel'd Varieties; or, the Matchless Actions and Passions of Mankind. London: 1699. V. 43

The Wars in England, Scotland and Ireland. London: 1681. V. 42; 45

The Wars in England, Scotland and Ireland . . . From the Beginning of the Reign of King Charles I . . . to the Restoration of King Charles II in 1660. Westmisnter: 1810. V. 41

CROUSE, RUSSEL

Mr. Currier and Mr. Ives, a Note on Their Lives and Times. Garden City: 1930. V. 42

Mr. Currier and Mr. Ives. Garden City: 1937. V. 44

Mr. Currier and Mr. Ives. A Note on Their Lives and Times. New York: 1936. V. 38

CROW, BARBARA

An Acrobatic Alphabet. 1986. V. 38

An Acrobatic Alphabet. Andoversford: 1986. V. 37; 39

CROW, FANNIE

Little Mama Sarah. V. 45

CROW, GERALD H.

William Morris Designer. London: 1934. V. 37; 38; 39; 42; 44

CROW, WILLIAM

Banks of the Hudson, a Poem, Descriptive of Rural Scenery, Manners and Customs in the United States of America. Leith: 1821. V. 40

CROWDER, HENRY

Henry-Music. Paris: 1930. V. 37; 38

CROWDER, JAMES H.

Before and After Vicksburg. Dayton: 1924. V. 45

CROWE, CATHERINE 1800-1876

Light and Darkness; or, Mysteries of Life. London: 1850. V. 45

CROWE, CATHERINE STEVENS 1800-1876

Light and Darkness; or, Mysteries of Life. London: 1850. V. 46

The Night Side of Nature; or, Ghosts and Ghost Seers. London: 1852. V. 40; 42

The Nightside of Nature; or, Ghosts and Ghost Seers. London: 1848. V. 37

CROWE, EYRE EVANS 1799-1868

The English in Italy. London: 1825. V. 42

The History of France. London: 1858-68. V. 42

With Thackeray in America. New York: 1893. V. 45

CROWE, GEORGE

The Commission of H.M.S. 'Terrible' 1898-1902. London: 1903. V. 46

CROWE, J. A.

A History of Painting in Italy, Umbria, Florence and Siena from the 2nd to the 16th Century. London: 1923/1908-14. V. 46

CROWE, PAT

Pat Crowe: His Story, Confession and Reformation. New York: 1906. V. 39

Spreading Evil, Pat Crowe's Autobiography. New York: 1927. V. 46

CROWE, WILLIAM 1745-1829

Lewesdon Hill. Oxford: 1788. V. 38; 41; 42; 44

Oratio ex Instituto Hon. Dom. Nathanielis Dom. Crew, Habita in Theatro Oxon. Oxonii: 1788. V. 41; 45

CROWFIELD, CHRISTOPHER

House and Home Papers. Boston: 1865. V. 42

CROWFOOT, J. W.

The Island of Meroe and Meroitic Inscriptions. London: 1911-12. V. 37; 40; 42; 44

CROWLEY, ALEISTER

Ahab and Other Poems. London: 1903. V. 40

The Book of Thoth. London: 1944. V. 40

Carmen Saeculare. London: 1903. V. 40

The City of God. A Rhapsody. London: 1943. V. 41

The Confessions of Aleister Crowley. London: 1969. V. 46

The Diary of a Drug Fiend. New York: (1923). V. 37

Eight Lectures on Yoga. London: 1939. V. 39

In Residence: The Don's Guide to Cambridge. Cambridge: 1904. V. 37; 40

Jephthath. London: 1899. V. 40

Jezebel. London: 1898. V. 40

Knox on Pax, Essays in Light. London: 1907. V. 39

Konx Om Pax. Essays in Light. Boleskine: 1907. V. 39

The Magical Record of the Beast 666. London: 1972. V. 39

Moonchild. London: 1929. V. 37; 38; 43

The Mother's Tragedy and other Poems. N.P.: 1901. V. 44

Olla. An Anthology of Sixty Years of Song. London: 1946. V. 43

Oracles. Inverness: 1905. V. 40

Orpheus: a Lyrical Legend. Inverness: 1905. V. 40

Songs of Spirit. London: 1898. V. 38; 39; 40

The Soul of Osiris. London: 1901. V. 40

The Star and the Garter. London: 1903. V. 40

The Tale of Archais a Romance in Verse. London: 1898. V. 37

Thumbs Up! California: 1941. V. 45

Thumbs Up! a Pentagram - a Pantacle to Win the War. Palomar Mountains: 1941. V. 44

White Stains: the Literary Remains of George Archibald Bishop . . . Amsterdam: 1898. V. 44

Why Jesus Wept - a Study of Society and the Grace of God. London: 1904. V. 38

The Works of Aleister Crowley. London: 1905. V. 46

CROWLEY, ALESITER

The Collected Works. 1905. V. 44

CROWLEY, D. O.

A Chaplet of Verse by California Catholic Writers . . . San Francisco: 1889. V. 46

CROWLEY, J.

Little Big. 1982. V. 43

CROWLEY, THOMAS

Letters and Dissertations, by the author of the Letter Analaysis A.P. On the Disputes Between Great Britain and America. London: 1782. V. 37; 46

CROWNE, JOHN

Caligula. London: 1698. V. 38

The Countrey Wit. London: 1675. V. 39

Darius King of Persia. London: 1688. V. 40

The Destruction of Jerusalem by Titus Vespasian. London: 1677. V. 37; 38

The Dramatic Works of John Crowne. Edinburgh & London: 1872-74. V. 42; 46

The Dramatic Works. Edinburgh: 1873. V. 42; 44

The History of Charles the Eighth of France. London: 1672. V. 38; 41

Juliana or the Princess of Poland. London: 1671. V. 40

The Misery of Civil War. London: 1680. V. 37

Thyestes, a Tragedy. London: 1681. V. 38

CROWNE, WILLIAM

A True Relation of all the Remarkable Places and Passages Observed in the Travels of the Right Honourable Thomas Lord Howard, Earle of Arundell. London: 1637. V. 44

CROWNINSHIELD, BENJAMIN W.

An Account of the Yacht Cleopatra's Barge, Built at Salem in 1816. Salem: 1889. V. 44

CROWNINSHIELD, FRANCES B.

The Story of George Crowninshield's Yacht Cleopatra's Barge on a Voyage of Pleasure to the Western Islands and the Mediterranean 1816-1817. Boston: 1913. V. 38; 39; 43

CROWSON, R. A.

The Biology of the Coleoptera. London: 1981. V. 37

CROWTHER, ALICE

Golden Thoughts from Great Authors. Selected by Alice Crowther. Glasgow: 1900. V. 37

CROWTHER, BOSLEY

The Lion's Share. New York: 1957. V. 45

CROWTHER, T. B.

Andereida; or, the Briton and the Saxon, A.D. CCCCXLI. London: 1875. V. 38; 40

CRUISE, WILLIAM

An Essay on the Nature and Operation of Fines and Recoveries. London: 1794. V. 38

A Treatise on the Origin and Nature of Dignities, or Titles of Honor. London: 1823. V. 38; 40

CRULL, JODOCUS

The Antiquities of St. Peter's, or the Abbey Church of Westminster. London: 1711. V. 40

CRUM, HOWARD A.

Mosses of Eastern North America. 1981. V. 39

CRUM, MARGARET

First Line Index of English Poetry 1500-1800 in Manuscripts of the Bodleian Library Oxford. Oxford: 1969. V. 42

CRUM, W. E.

Coptic Ostraca from the Collection of the Egypt Exploration Fund and the Cairo Museum and Others. London: 1902. V. 42; 44

A Coptic Dictionary. Oxford: 1939. V. 42

CRUM, WALTER

An Experimental Inquiry into the Number and Properties of the Primary Colours and the Source of Colour in the Prism. Glasgow: 1830. V. 38; 44

CRUMB, R.

Head Comix. New York: 1968. V. 44

Sketchbook 1966-67. Frankfurt: 1981. V. 45

CRUMLEY, JAMES

Dancing Bear. New York: 1982. V. 43

Dancing Bear. New York: 1983. V. 41

Muddy Fork and Other Things. Livingston: 1922. V. 46

The Muddy Fork. Northridge: 1984. V. 41; 42; 44

One to Count Cadence. New York: 1969. V. 37; 39; 41; 42; 43; 44; 45; 46

The Pigeon Shoot: a Screenplay. Santa Barbara: 1987. V. 42

The Wrong Case. New York: 1975. V. 37; 39; 42

CRUMMELL, ALEXANDER

The Relations and Duties of Free Colored Men in America to Africa. Hartford: 1861. V. 42; 43

CRUMMER, LEROY

A List of Old Medical Books, Books on the History of Medicine and Medical Bibliography and a List of Medical Portraits, in the Possession of Le Roy Crummer. Omaha, Nebraska. Together with some Bibliographical Notes . . . Omaha: 1925. V. 40; 41; 44

CRUMP, ARTHUR

The Theory of the Stock Exchange Speculation. London: 1874. V. 41

CRUMPE, SAMUEL 1766-1796

An Essay on the Best Means of Providing Employment for the People. London: 1793. V. 39

CRUMPTON, HEZEKIAH J.

The Adventures of Two Alabama Boys . . . Montgomery: 1912. V. 42; 45

CRUNDEN, JOHN

Convenient and Ornamental Architecture Consisting of Original Designs . . . London: 1785. V. 42; 44

Convenient and Ornamental Architecture, Consisting of Original Designs . . . London: 1791. V. 38

Convenient and Ornamental Architecture, Consisting of Original designs . . . London: 1804. V. 38

Convenient and Ornamental Architecture, Consisting of Original Designs. London: 1804. V. 38

Convenient and Ornamental Architecture, Consisting of Original Designs . . . London: 1805. V. 42

THE CRUSADE of Fidelis, a Knight of the Order of the Cross; Being the History of His Adventures, During His Pilgrimage to the Celestial City. Derby: 1828. V. 38

CRUSADERS

The Crusaders, of the Minstrels of Acre. A Poem. In Six Cantos. London: 1808. V. 37

CRUSE, THOMAS

Apache Days and After. Caldwell: 1941. V. 37; 39; 44

CRUSO, J.

Military Instructions for the Cavallrie . . . Cambridge: 1644. V. 44; 46

CRUTCHLEY, BROOKE

A Printer's Christmas Books. Cambridge: 1974. V. 39; 40; 41; 45

Two Men. Walter Lewis and Stanley Morison at Cambridge. Cambridge: 1968. V. 38; 39; 40; 41; 42; 45; 46

CRUTTWELL, CLEMENT

A Tour through the Whole Island of Great Britain. London: 1801. V. 38; 39

CRUVEILHIER, JEAN 1791-1874

The Anatomy of the Human Body. New York: 1844. V. 44

CRUZ, MARTIN DE LA

The De La Cruz - Badiano Aztec Herbal of 1552. Baltimore: 1939. V. 39; 42

THE CRYSTAL Palace that Fox Built. A Pyramid of Rhyme . . . London: 1851. V. 40

CUADWELL, CHRISTOPHER

Poems. London: 1939. V. 38

CUBA and the Winward Passages. New York: 1867. V. 42

CUBAS, A. C.

The Republic of Mexico in 1876. Mexico: 1876. V. 37

CUBERO SEBASTIAN, PEDRO

Breve Relacion de La Peregrinacion que Ha Hecho de la Mayor Parte del Mundo . . . Madrid: 1680. V. 41

CUBIERES, SIMON LOUIS PIERRE, MARQUIS DE

Histoire Abregee des Coquillages de Mer, de Leurs Moeurs, et de Leurs Amours. Versailles: 1799-1800. V. 46

CUDAHY PACKING CO.

From the Ranch to the Table. Omaha: 1893. V. 42

CUDLIP, PENDER, MRS.

Mrs. Cardigan? A Novel. London: 1879. V. 43

CUDWORTH, RALPH

A Treatise of Freewill. London: 1838. V. 38

The True Intellectual System of the Universe . . . London: 1678. V. 37; 38; 39; 45

The True Intellectual System of the Universe . . . London: 1743. V. 39; 41

CUDWORTH, WILLIAM

Historical Notes on the Bradford Corporation, with Records of the Lighting and Watching Commissioners and Board of Highway Surveyors. Bradford: 1881. V. 37

Histories of Bolton and Bowling. Bradford: 1891. V. 45

Life and Correspondence of Abraham Sharp, the Yorkshire Mathematician and Astronomer and Assistant of Flamsteed. London: 1889. V. 45

Manningham, Heaton and Allerton . . . Bradford: 1896. V. 45

CUFFE, PAUL

Narrative of the Life and Advenutes of Paul Cuffe, A Pequot Indian. Vernon: 1839. V. 37; 38; 41

CUFFEL, CHARLES A.

History of Durell's Battery in the Civil War. Philadelphia: 1903. V. 42; 44

CUITT, GEORGE

Six Etchings of Select Parts of Fountains Abbey, Yorkshire . . . London: 1822. V. 38

Six Etchings of Select Parts of Riveaux Abbey, Yorkshire. London: 1824. V. 38

Wanderings and Pencillings Amongst Ruins of the Olden Time . . . London: 1848. V. 39; 42

Wanderings and Pencillings Amongst Ruins of the Olden Time. London: 1855. V. 39; 44

CUJAS, JACQUES

(Greek Title) Epistolae Graecanicae Mvtvae, Anatiqvorvm Rhetorvm, Oratorum, Philosophorum, Medicorum, Theologorum, Regum, ac Imperatorum . . . Geneva: 1606. V. 37

Opera. Cologne: 1588. V. 40

. . . Opera, quae de Iure fecit, et edi volvit . . . Francofurti: 1595. V. 38

CUKOR, EVELYN VICTORIA

Fancies and Thoughts. Los Angeles: 1938. V. 39

CULBERT, DICK

A Climber's Guide to the Coastal Rangers of British Columbia (International Boundary to Nass River). N.P.: 1965. V. 44

CULBERTSON, THADDEUS A.

Journal of an Expediton to the Mauvaises Terres and the Upper Missouri in 1850. V. 40

CULIN, STEWART

Games of the North American Indians. Washington: 1907. V. 38

CULLAGH, W. TORRENS MC

The Industrial History of Free Nations. London: 1846. V. 38

CULLEN, COUNTEE

The Ballad of the Brown Girl. New York: 1927. V. 43

The Ballad of the Brown Girl. New York: London: 1927. V. 41; 42

The Black Christ and Other Poems. New York: 1929. V. 41; 43; 44

The Black Christ & Other Poems . . . New York & London: 1929. V. 39

Color. New York: 1925. V. 43; 44

Copper Sun. New York: 1927. V. 42; 44

Copper Sun. New York: & London: 1927. V. 45; 46

The Lost Zoo. New York: 1940. V. 41; 43

The Medea. New York: 1935. V. 44

CULLEN, FRANCIS GRANT

Sadducismus Debellatus: or, a True Narrative of the Sorceries and Witchcrafts Exercis'd by the Devil and His Instruments Upon Mrs. Christian Shaw . . . London: 1698. V. 38

CULLEN, J. B.

The Irish in Boston. The Story of the Irish in Boston, together with Biographical sketches of Representative Men and Women. Boston: 1889. V. 37

CULLEN, STEPHEN

The Castle of Inchvally; a Tale, Alas, Too True. London: 1802? V. 46

The Haunted Priory, or, the Fortunes of the House of Rayo. Dublin: 1794. V. 37; 40

CULLEN, THOMAS

Adenomyoma of the Uterus. Philadelphia: 1908. V. 38; 39; 40; 42

Cancer of the Uterus: Its Pathology, Symptomatology, Diagnosis, and Treatment Also the Pathology of Diseases of the Endometrium. New York: 1909. V. 42

CULLEN, THOMAS S.

The Collected Reprints of . . . Baltimore: 1925-1946. V. 39; 44; 45; 46

CULLEN, WILLIAM

First Lines of the Practice of Physic. Edinburgh: 1784. V. 39

First Lines of the Practice of Physic. Philadelphia: 1792. V. 40

First Lines of the Practice of Physic. New York: 1793. V. 40; 42

First Lines of the Practice of Physic. New York: 1805. V. 41; 42

Institutions of Medicine. Part I. Physiology . . . Boston: 1788. V. 37

Lectures on the Materia Medica. Philadelphia: 1775. V. 42

Lectures on the Materia Medica. Philadelphia: 1775. V. 37

A Letter to Lord Cathcart, President of the Board of Police in Scotland; concerning the Recovery of Persons drowned, and seemingly dead. London & Edinburgh: 1784. V. 39

New Edinburgh and London Practice of Physic: With Notes, Explanatory and Practical by a Licentiate of the Royal College of Physicians . . . London: 1817. V. 42

A Treatise of the Materia Medica. Dublin: 1789. V. 40; 44

CULLEY, JOHN H.

Cattle, Horses and Men of the Western Range. 1940. V. 42

Cattle, Horses and Men of the Western Range. Los Angeles: 1940. V. 43

CULLIMORE, CLARENCE

Santa Barbara Adobes. Santa Barbara: 1948. V. 44

CULLINGS from the Confederacy: Southern Poems Popular During the War 1861-1865. Washington: 1903. V. 44

CULLIS, CHARLES

Faith Cures; or, Answers to prayer in the Healing of the Sick. Boston: 1879. V. 45

CULLUM, GEORGE W.

Campaigns of the War of 1812-15, Against Great Britain, Sketched and Criticised . . . New York: 1879. V. 45

Register of the Officers and Graduates of the U.S. Military Academy, 1802-1850. New York: 1850. V. 37; 38; 39

CULLUM, JOHN

The History and Antiquities of Hawsted and Hardwick in the County of Suffolk. London: 1813. V. 39

CULLYER, JOHN

The Gentleman and Farmer's Assistant. Norwich: 1795. V. 38

The Gentleman's and Farmer's Assistant: containing first Tables for finding the Content of any Piece of Land, from dimensions taken in yards. Second, tables . . . showing width required . . . third. Tables . . . showing the number of . . . Norwich: 1805. V. 37

CULMAN, LEONHARD

Ein Unterrichtung Vo(n) der Eltern Kindern unnd Frembden Auch Eygenen Sunden . . . Nuremberg: 1550. V. 40

CULME, JOHN

The Directory of Gold and Silversmiths and Allied Traders 1838-1914. Woodbridge: 1987. V. 44

CULPEPER, NICHOLAS 1616-1654

The Complete Herbal . . . London: 1835. V. 41

Culpeper's School of Physick; or the Experimental Practice of the Whole Art. London: 1678. V. 42

Culpeper's Complete Herbal . . . London: 1824. V. 45; 46

The English Physician Enlarged. London: 1656. V. 38

The English Physician Enlarged with Three Hundred and Sixty Nine Medicines, Made of English Herbs. London: 1733. V. 42

The English Physician Enalarged with Three Hundred and Sixty Nine Medicines, Made for English Herbs . . . London: 1733. V. 45

The English Physician. London: 1752. V. 40

The English Physician Enlarged with Three Hundred and Sixty-Nine Medicines, Made of English Herbs . . . London: 1775. V. 40

the English Physician Enlarged . . . London: 1787. V. 44

The English Physician Enlarged. London: 1788. V. 42; 43; 45

Culpeper's English Physician and Complete Herbal. To Which are now added, Upwards of One Hundred Additional Herbs, with a Display of Their Medicinal and Occult Properties . . . London: 1790. V. 43

Culpeper's English Physician and Complete Herbal. London: 1793. V. 43

Culpeper's English Physician and Complete Herbal. London: 1799. V. 38

English Physician and Complete Herbal. London: 1810. V. 38

The English Physician. Taunton: 1826. V. 44

The English Physician. Taunton: 1826. V. 37

English Physician and Complete Herbal. London: 1800. V. 37

The Idea of Practical Physick in Twelve Books. Viz . . . These Twelve books are of excellent use for all young students in Physick. The contain the Marrow of all the works of Daniel Dennertus, and Fernelius, and . . . London: 1657. V. 37

Pharmacopoeia Londinensis; or the London Dispensatory Further Adorned by the Studies and Collections of the Fellows . . . London: 1653. V. 42; 46

Pharmacopoeia Londinensis. London: 1654. V. 38; 40; 42; 46

A Physicall Directory or a Translation of the London Dispensatory Made by the College of Physicians in London. London: 1649. V. 46

CULS de Lampe. 1968. V. 39

CULS de Lampe. Northampton: 1968. V. 46

CULS De Lampe. 19 Engraved Color Designs Intended for Book Decoration . . . etc. by Eminent Printers of the Past. Northampton: 1968. V. 39

CULVER, HENRY

Contemporary Scale Models of Vessels of the 17th Century . . . New York: 1926. V. 41

CULVER, HENRY B.

Forty Famous Ships Their Beginnings, Their Life Histories, Their Ultimate Fate, etc. New York: 1936. V. 39

CULVERWELL, NATHANIEL

An Elegant and Learned Discourse of the Light of Nature with Several Other Treatises. London: 1652. V. 37

CUMBERLAND, BARLOW

The Northern Lakes of Canada: The Niagara River and Toronto, the Lakes of Muskota. Toronto: 1886. V. 45

CUMBERLAND, DUKE OF

The Trial of His R. H. the D. of C. July 5, 1770. For Criminal Conversation with Lady Harriet G----r. London. V. 43

CUMBERLAND, GEORGE

Reliquiae Conservatae, From the Primitive Materials of Our Present Globe, with Popular Descriptions of the Prominent Characters of Some Remarkable Fossil Encrinites, and Their Connecting Links. Bristol: 1826. V. 37

CUMBERLAND, RICHARD 1732-1811

Anecdotes of Eminent Painters in Spain, During the Sixteenth and Seventeenth Centuries; with Cursory Remarks Upon the Present State of Arts in that Kingdom. London: 1782. V. 38; 40; 41

Arundel. London: 1789. V. 40

The British Drama, a Collection of the Most Esteemed Dramatic Productions . . . London: 1817. V. 38

Calvary; or The Death of Christ. London: 1800. V. 38

Calvary; or, the Death of Christ. London: 1803. V. 42; 46

De Legibus Naturae Disquisitio Philosophica, in qua Earum Forma, Summa Capita, Ordo, Promulgatio & Obligatio e Rerum Natura Investignatur . . . London: 1672. V. 37

An Essay Towards the Recovery of the Jewish Measures and Weights, Comprehending Their Monies . . . London: 1686. V. 43; 46

CUMBERLAND, RICHARD 1732-1811 continued

An Essay Towards the Recovery of the Jewish Measures and Weights, Comprehending Their Monies . . . London: 1699. V. 42

Henry. London: 1795. V. 39; 40; 42; 45

Henry. London: 1798. V. 40

De Legibus Naturae Disquisitio Philosophica in Qua Earum Forma, Summa Capita Ordo, Promulgatio & Obligatio e Rerum Natura Investigantur, Quinetiam elementa Philosophiae Hobbianae, cum Moralis Tum Civilis, Considerantur & Refutantur. London: 1672. V. 39; 41; 42

De Legibus Naturae Disquisitio Philosophica . . . Dublin: 1720. V. 45

A Letter to Richard (Watson) Lord Bishop of Landaff on the Subject of His Lordship's Letter to the Late Archbishop of Canterbury (Frederick Cornwallis). London: 1783. V. 40

Memoirs of Richard Cumberland. London: 1806. V. 37; 42; 43; 45

Memoirs. Written by Himself. London: 1806-07. V. 38; 41

Memoirs of . . . Written by Himself. London: 1807. V. 37; 39; 41; 45

The Note of Hand. London: 1774. V. 37

The Observer: a Collection of Moral, Literary and Familiar Essays. Dublin: 1791. V. 38; 41; 43; 46

The Observer: Being a Collection of Moral, Literary and Familiar Essays. London: 1791/88. V. 43

The Observer. London: 1798. V. 37

The Observer: being a collection of Moral, Literary and Familiary Essays. London: 1786-90-91. V. 37

Odes. Dublin: 1776. V. 40

Origines Gentium Antiquissimae; or Attempts for Discovering the Times of the First Planting of Nations. London: 1724. V. 38

A Philosophical Enquiry into the Laws of Nature . . . Dublin: 1750. V. 42; 44

The Posthumous Dramatick Works of the Late Richard Cumberland. London: 1813. V. 41; 43; 44; 46

CUMBERLAND VALLEY RAILROAD

Report on the Proposed Construction of a Rail Road from New York to the Cumberland Valley Rail Road. Baltimore: 1847. V. 38

CUMING, E. D.

British Sport Past and Present. London: 1909. V. 41; 45; 46

The Three Jovial Puppies. London: 1908. V. 46

CUMING, FORTESCUE

Sketches of a Tour to the Western Country, through the States of Ohio and Kentucky. Pittsburgh: 1810. V. 38

CUMINGS, SAMUEL

The Western Pilot, Containing Charts of the Ohio River and of the Mississippi from the Mouth of the Missouri to the Gulf of Mexico.. Cincinnati: 1829. V. 38

The Western Pilot. Cincinnati: 1832. V. 43

The Western Pilot, Containing Charts of the Ohio River, and of the Mississippi . . . Cincinnati: 1832. V. 37

CUMMING, ALEXANDER

The Elements of Clock and Watch-Work. London: 1766. V. 38; 39; 40; 43; 45

CUMMING, ALFRED

Indians on the Upper Missouri. Message from the President . . . Transmitting a Report in Regard to the Expedition Among The . . . Washington: 1856. V. 39; 41; 44

CUMMING, CONSTANCE FREDERICA GORDON

Fire Fountains. Edinburgh & London: 1883. V. 37; 38

Granite Crags. Edinburgh & London: 1884. V. 39; 40

Granite Crags of California. Edinburgh & London: 1886. V. 44

Two Happy Years in Ceylon. New York: 1892. V. 38

CUMMING, D.

Handbook of Lithography. London: 1904. V. 44

CUMMING, FORTESCUE

Sketches of a Tour to the Western Country. Pittsburgh: 1810. V. 39; 41; 42; 43

CUMMING, HIRAM

Secret History of the Perfidies, Intrigues and Corruptions of the Tyler Dynasty, with the Mysteries of Washington City. Washington: 1845. V. 39; 42

CUMMING, KATE

Gleanings from Southland Sketches of Life and Manners of the People of the South Before, During and After th War of Secession with Extracts from the Author's Journal and an Epitome of the New South. Birmingham: 1895. V. 38; 44; 46

A Journal of Hospital Life in the Confederate Army of Tennessee from the Battle of Shiloh to the End of the War. Louisville: 1866. V. 42

CUMMING, R. GORDON

Five Years of a Hunter's Life in the Far Interior of South Africa. London: 1850. V. 41; 44

Five Years of a Hunter's Life in the Far Interior of South Africa. New York: 1852. V. 42

Five Years of a Hunter's Life in the Far Interior of South Africa . . . London: 1864. V. 37; 38

A Hunter's Life Among Lions, Elephants and Other Wild Animals of South Africa. New York: 1857. V. 39

CUMMING, ROBERT

Poems on Several Occasions. Edinburgh: 1791. V. 39

CUMMING, T. G.

Description of the Iron Bridges of Supsension Now Erecting Over the Straight of Menai, at Bangor and Over the River Conway, in North Wales . . . London: 1824. V. 41

CUMMING, W. F.

Notes of a Wanderer, in Search of Health, through Italy, Egypt, Greece, Turkey, Up the Danube, and Down the Rhine. London: 1839. V. 37; 39

Notes of a Wanderer, In Search of Health, through Italy, Egypt, Greece, Turkey, Up the Danube, and down the Rhine. London: 1839. V. 37

Notes on Lunatic Asylums in Germany and other Parts of Europe. London;: 1852. V. 37

CUMMING, WILLIAM P.

The Southeast in Early Maps. Princeton: 1958. V. 37; 39; 45

The Southeast in Early Maps. Chapel Hill: 1962. V. 39; 40; 45

The Southeast in Early Maps. Chapel Hill: 1973. V. 40; 41; 45

CUMMINGHAM, HENRY STEWART

The Coeruleans. A Vacation Idyll. London: 1887. V. 37

CUMMINGHAM, PETER

The Story of Nell Gwynn: and the sayings of Charles the Second. London: 1862. V. 37

CUMMINGS, ALEXANDER

Governor's Message, Delivered to the Territorial Legislatur of the Territory of Colorado in Joint Convention, Friday, Jan. 5th, 1866. Denver: 1866. V. 37

CUMMINGS, ARIEL IVERS

The Factory Girl, or, Gardez la Coeur. Lowell: 1847. V. 43

CUMMINGS, D. C.

A Historical Survey of the Boiler Makers' and Iron and Steel Ship builders' Society From August 1834 to August 1904 . . . Newcastle-on-Tyne: 1905. V. 44

CUMMINGS, EDWARD ESTLIN 1894-1962

Christmas Tree. New York: 1928. V. 37; 39; 40

Christmas Tree. N.P.: 1960. V. 39; 41; 42; 43; 44

Complete Poems. 1968. V. 41

Complete Poems. London: 1968. V. 39; 45

Cummings: a Miscellany. New York: 1958. V. 37; 39; 42; 44; 46

Eimi. London: 1933. V. 42

Eimi. New York: 1933. V. 38; 39; 40; 41; 42; 43; 44; 45; 46

Eimi. New York: 1958. V. 39; 43

Eimi. New York: 1973. V. 39

The Enormous Room. New York: 1922. V. 37; 38; 39; 41; 42; 46

The Enormous Room. Introduction by Robert Graves. London: 1928. V. 37

50 Poems. New York: 1940. V. 38; 39

XLI Poems. New York: 1923. V. 38

XLI Poems. New York: 1925. V. 40; 42

Him. New York: 1927. V. 38; 39; 40; 43

Is 5. New York: 1926. V. 39; 43

95 Poems. New York: 1958. V. 39; 43; 46

No Thanks. New York: 1935. V. 39; 43

(No Title). New York: 1930. V. 42

1/20 - Poems by E. E. Cummings - a Selection Made by the Author. London: 1936. V. 37; 40; 46

One Times One. London: 1947. V. 37; 40

Poems 1905-1962. London: 1973. V. 39

The Red Front. By Louis Aragon. Chapel Hill: (1933). V. 37

Santa Claus. New York: 1946. V. 39

73 Poems. New York: 1963. V. 45

Six Nonlectures. Cambridge: 1953. V. 39; 43

Sketches and Watercolors of the Twenties and Forties. 9 March - 6 April, 1968. New York. V. 39

Tulips and Chimneys. New York: 1923. V. 39

Tulips and Chimneys. Mount Vernon: 1937. V. 39; 43

VV (Viva). New York: 1931. V. 37; 39

CUNNINGHAM, HENRY STEWART

The Heriots. London: 1890. V. 41

Lord Bowen, a Biographical Sketch. 1896. V. 43

CUNNINGHAM, IMOGEN

Imogen Cunningham: Photographs. Seattle: 1971. V. 37

Photographs. 1970. V. 39

CUNNINGHAM, J. V.

Doctor Drink. Cummington: 1950. V. 39; 41

Trivial, Vulgar and Exhalted: Epigrams. San Francisco: 1957. V. 44

12 Poems in a Yearbook of Stanford Writing. 1932. V. 46

CUNNINGHAM, J. W.

Cautions to Continental Travellers. London: 1818. V. 38

CUNNINGHAM, JOHN 1729-1773

The Contemplatist. London: 1762. V. 38; 41

Poems Chiefly Pastoral. Dublin: 1766. V. 38; 41

Poems Chiefly Pastoral. London: 1766. V. 38; 40; 43

Poems, Chiefly Pastoral. Newcastle: 1771. V. 38; 42; 43; 46

Suggestions on the Causes of the Present Scarcity of Money, and in Favor of Essential Reforms in Our Banking System. Charleston: 1854. V. 37

CUNNINGHAM, JOHN WILLIAM

De Rance. A Poem. London: 1815. V. 38

The Velvet Cushion. London: 1814. V. 43; 46

CUNNINGHAM, P.

Two Years in New South Wales . . . London: 1827. V. 44

Two Years in New South Wales; Comprising Sketches of the Actual State of Society in that Colony; or Its Peculiar Advantages to Emigrants, of Its Topography, Natural History &c. London: 1828. V. 39

CUNNINGHAM, PETER

Inigo Jones. A Life of the Architect. London: 1848. V. 38; 42

Saint Anne's Hill. A Poem. London: 1800. V. 39; 42

The Songs of England and Scotland. London: 1835. V. 37; 42; 46

The Story of Nell Gwyn: and the Sayings of Charles the Second. London: 1852. V. 45

CUNNINGHAM, ROBERT O.

Notes on the Natural History of the Strait of Magellan and West Coast of Patagonia. Edinburgh: 1871. V. 39

CUNNINGHAM, TIMOTHY

A Critical Review of the Liberties of British Subjects. With a Comparative View of the Proceedings of the H(ous)e of C(mmon)s of I(relan)d (etc.). London: 1750. V. 45

The Law of Bills of Exchange, Promissory Notes, Bank Notes and Insurances. London: 1766. V. 39

The Law of Simony. London: 1784. V. 40

CUNNINGHAME, PETER

Account of the Experiments Tried by the Board of Agriculture in the Composition of Various Sorts of Bread, Anno 1795. London: 1795. V. 39

CUNNINGTON, C. WILLETT

English Women's Clothing in the Present Century. London: 1962. V. 43

CUNO, JOHANN

Hoffarts Laster An Einem Wunderewechs/vor Soldwedel Gewachsen/Neben Desselben Histori vnd Draus Herruehdrenden Notwendigen Erinnerungen/Gewiesen. Wittenberg: 1590. V. 38

CUNYNGHAME, ARTHUR THURLOW

My Command in South Africa 1874-1878 . . . London: 1879. V. 38

My Command in South Africa 1874-78. London: 1880. V. 39; 40; 41; 42; 43

Travels in the Eastern Caucasus, on the Caspian and Black Seas, Especially Daghestan, and on the Frontiers of Persia and Turkey, during the Summer of 1871. London: 1872. V. 42; 43

CUNYNGHAME, HENRY H.

European Enamels. New York: 1906. V. 41

CUPID & PSYCHE

Les Amours de Psyche et de Cupidon, avec le Poeme d'Adonis. Paris: 1795. V. 44

De Cupidinis et Psyches Amoribus. London: 1901. V. 46

Cupid and Psyche. London: 1935. V. 46

The Story of Cupid and Psyche. 1974. V. 46

The Story of Cupid and Psyche. London: 1974. V. 39

The Story of Cupid and Psyche. London: and Cambridge: 1974. V. 44

CUPID'S Horn Book. Songs and Ballads of Marriage and Cuckoldry. Mt. Vernon: 1936. V. 37

THE CURATE, an Elegiac Poem. London: 1802. V. 38

CURDY, GEORGE GRANT MAC

A Study of Chiriquian Antiquities. New Haven: 1911. V. 38

CUREY, EDWIN A.

Nebraska: Its Advantages, Resources and Drawbacks. New York: 1875. V. 42

CURIDEMUS, VESPASIANUS, PSEUD.

Disputatio De Cornelio et Ejusdem Natura Ac Proprietate. Cujus Positiones Sub Praesidio Vesp. Curidemi. In Illustri Gaudecapensium Academia Publice Proponit Zachaeus Pertinax. Gremerstadt,: 1627. V. 39

CURIE, MARIE SKLODOWSKA 1867-1934

Pierre Curie. New York: 1923. V. 42; 46

Theses Presentees a la Faculte des Sciences de Paris pour Obtenir le Grade de Docteur es Sciences Physiques . . . Paris: 1903. V. 38

Traite de Radioactivite. Paris: 1910. V. 40

CURIE, PIERRE

Theses Presentees a la Faculte des Sciences de Paris pour Obtenir le Grade de Docteur es Sciences Physiques. 1re These-Proprietes Magnetiques des Corps a Diverses Temperatures, 2e These-Propositions Donees par la Faculte. Paris: 1895. V. 38

CURIO, CAELIUS

The Visions of Pasquin, or, a Character of the Roman Court, Religion and Practices . . . London: 1689. V. 45

CURIO, CAELIUS AUGUSTINUS

A Notable History of the Saracens, Briefly and Faithfully Descrybing the Originall Beginning . . . London: 1775. V. 43

CURIO, COELIUS AUGUSTINUS

Pasquine in a Traunce. London: 1584. V. 42

CURIONE, CELIO SECONDO

Francisci Spierae, Quiquod Susceptam Semel Eva(n)gelice(m) Veritatis Prosossione(m) Abnegasset, Damnasset q(ue) in Horrendam Incidit Desparationem, Historia . . . N.P.: 1550. V. 43

CURIOSA. A Modern Dissertation on a Certain Necessary Piece of Household Furniture. London: 1752. V. 40

THE CURIOSITIES Natural and Artificial of the Island of Great Britain. London. V. 39

CURIOSITIES of Street Literatue: Comprising 'Cocks', or 'Catchpennies' . . . Street Drolleries . . . In Prose and Verse. London: 1871. V. 37

CURIOUS Enquiries. Being Six Brief Discourses, viz. 1. Of the Longitude. II. The Tricks of Astrological Quacks. III. Of the Dept of the Sea. IV. Of Tabacco. V. Of Europes Being Too Full of People. VI. The Various Opinions Concerning the Time . . . London: 1688. V. 45

A CURIOUS Traveller. London: 1742. V. 46

CURLE, ALEXANDER

The Treasure of Traprain, a Scottish Hoard of Roman Silver Plate. Glasgow: 1923. V. 42

CURLE, JAMES

A Roman Frontier Post and Its People. Glasgow: 1911. V. 38; 39; 40

CURLE, RICHARD

Collecting American First Editions, Its Pitfalls and Its Pleasures. Indianapolis: 1930. V. 44

A Handlist of the Various Books, Pamphlets, Prefaces, Notes, Articles, Reviews and Letters Written About Joseph Conrad by Richard Curle. Pennsylvania: 1932. V. 43

Into the East; Notes on Burma and Malaya. London: 1923. V. 41; 42; 43; 44

Joseph Conrad, a Study. New York: 1914. V. 41; 43

CURLEY, EDWIN

Nebraska, Its Adventures, Resoures and Drawbacks. London: 1875. V. 43

CURLEY, EDWIN A.

Nebraska: Its Advantages, Resources and Drawbacks. New York. V. 39

Nebraska: Its Advantages, Resources and Drawbacks. New York: 1875. V. 40; 45

Nebraska: Its Advantages, Resources and Drawbacks . . . New York: 1976. V. 46

CURLING, HENRY

Geraldine Maynard; or, the Abduction. London: 1864. V. 41

Recollections of the Mess-Table and the Stage. London: 1855. V. 37

CURLING, T. B.

Observations on the Diseases of the Rectum. London: 1851. V. 42

CURLING, T. B. continued

A Practical Treatise on the Diseases of the Testes and of the Spermatic Cord and Scrotum. Philadelphia: 1843. V. 42; 43

CURLL, EDMUND

A Catalogue of Books. London: 1725. V. 46

Curlicism Display'd: or, an Appeal to the Church. London: 1718. V. 39

Curll Papers, Stray Notes on the Life and Publications of Edmund Curll. N.P.: 1879. V. 46

CURMER, L.

Oeuvre de Jehan Foucquet. Heures de Maistre Etienne Chevalier. Paris: 1866-67. V. 41

CURMER, LEON 1801-1870

Les Evangiles des Dimanches et Tetes de l'Annee. Paris: 1864. V. 43

CURR, EDWARD

An Account of the Colony of Van Dieman's Land . . . London: 1824. V. 43

CURR, JOHN

Railway Locomotion, and Steam Navigation: Their Principles and Practice. London: 1847. V. 39

CURRAN, C. P.

The Rotunda Hospital, Its Architects and Craftsmen. Dublin: 1946. V. 40

CURRAN, JAMES W.

Here Was Vinland. Sault Ste. Marie: 1939. V. 40; 43

Here Was Vinland. Sault Ste. Marie: 1939. V. 43

CURRAN, WILLIAM HENRY

The Life of the Right Honourable John Philpot Curran, Late Master of the Rolls in Ireland, by His Son. New York: 1820. V. 39

The Life of the Right Honourable John Philpot Curran, Late Master of the Rolls in Ireland. Edinburgh: 1822. V. 39

The Life of the Right Honourable John Philpot Curran. Redfield: 1855. V. 46

CURRELLY, CHARLES T.

Stone Implements. Le Caire: 1913. V. 42; 44

CURREY, RICHARD O.

A Sketch of the Geology of Tennessee. Knoxville: 1857. V. 37; 38

CURRIE, BARTON

Fishers of Books. Boston: 1931. V. 45

CURRIE, JAMES 1756-1805

A Letter, Commercial and Political, Addressed to the Rt. Honble. William Pitt . . . London: 1793. V. 37; 41; 42

Medical Reports, on the Effects of Water, Cold and Warm as a Remedy in Feber and Febrile Diseases . . . Liverpool: 1797. V. 43; 46

Medical Reports, on the Effects of Water, Cold and Warm, as a Remedy in Fever and Dibral Diseases, Whether Applied to the Surface of the Body or Used Internally. Volume 2. London: 1805. V. 42

Medical Reports, on the Effects of Water, Cold and Warm, as a Remedy in Fever and Other Diseases. Philadelphia: 1808. V. 40; 41; 42; 43

CURRIE, JOHN

A Full Vindication of the People's Right to Elect Their Own Pastors. Edinburgh: 1733. V. 43

CURRIE, MARY MONTGOMERIE LAMB SINGLETON, BARONNESS 1843-1905

Poems. London: 1892. V. 41

CURRIE, WILLIAM

A View of the Diseases Most Prevalent in the United States of America, At Different Seasons of the Year. Philadelphia: 1811. V. 42

CURRIER, E. M.

Marks of Early American Silversmiths. Portland: 1938. V. 37

CURRIER, JOHN J.

History of Newburyport, Massachusetts 1764-1909. Newburyport: 1906-09. V. 46

CURRIER, N.

Sporting Prints. New York: 1930. V. 45

CURRIER, THOMAS FRANKLIN

A Bibliography of Oliver Wendell Holmes. New York: 1953. V. 38

CURRY, E. S.

The No-Din: Romance, History & Science of the Pre-Historic Races of America & Other Lands. Christy, MO: 1899. V. 37

CURRY, J. G.

The Defence of Lucknow. London: 1858. V. 38

CURRY, JOHN

An Historical and Critical Review of the Civil Wars in Ireland, from the Reign of Queen Elizabeth, to the Settlement Under King William. Dublin: 1786. V. 42

An Historical and Critical Review of the Civil Wars in Ireland, from the Reign of Queen Elizabeth to the Settlement Under King Willim, with the State of the Irish Catholics, from the Settlement to the Year 1778. London: 1786. V. 38

An Historical and Critical Review of the Civil Wars in Ireland from the Reign of Queen Elizabeth to the Settlement Under King William. Dublin: 1793. V. 46

An Historical and Critical Review of the Civil Wars in Ireland, from the Reign of Queen Elizabeth to the Settlement Under King William, with the State of the Irish Catholics. Dublin: 1810. V. 37; 43

The History of Bristol, Civil and Ecclesiastaaical: Including Biographical Notices of Eminent and Distinguished Natives. Bristol: 1816. V. 37

CURRY-LINDAHL, K.

Bird Migration in Africa, Movements Between Six Continents. London: 1981. V. 38

CURRY, WILLIAM L.

Raid of the Confederate Cavalry through Central Tennessee in October, 1863, Commanded by General Joseph Wheeler. Cincinnati: 1908. V. 43

CURSITER, J.

List of Books and Pamphlets Relating to Orkney and Shetland, . . . Kirkwall: 1894. V. 44

CURSON, H. H.

Regimental Devices in South Africa 1783-1954. Pretoria: 1954. V. 41

CURTE, ROCHUS DE

Fertilissimus Consuetudinum Tractatus Pulchro Ordine Compositus Super Rubrica . . . Papie (Pavia): 1519. V. 37

CURTIN, L. S. M.

Healing Herbs of the Upper Rio Grande. New Mexico: 1947. V. 39

CURTIS, A.

Synopsis of a Course of Lectures on Medical Science, Delivered to the Students of the Botanico-Medical College of Ohio. Cincinnati: 1846. V. 38

CURTIS, ALVA

Lectures on Midwifery and the Forms of Disease Peculiar to Women and Children, Delivered to the Members of the Botanico-Medical School of Columbus, Ohio . . . Columbus: 1837. V. 45

CURTIS, ATHERTON

Catalogue de l'Oeuvre Lithographie et Grave de R. P. Bonington. Paris: 1939. V. 39

CURTIS-BENNETT, NOEL

The Food of the People. Being the History of Industrial Feeding. With a preface by the Rt. Hon. Lord Woolton. London: 1946. V. 37

CURTIS, CHARLES P.

Hunting in Africa East and West. Boston: 1925. V. 43

Hunting in Africa East and West. Cambridge: 1925. V. 43; 44

CURTIS, EDWARD

Indian Life and Indian Lore. In the Land of the Head Hunters. New York: 1915. V. 42

CURTIS, EDWARD S.

In the Land of the head-Hunters. Yonkers-on-Hudson: 1915. V. 44

Indian Days of the Long Ago. New York: 1915. V. 46

Indian Life and Indian Lore. In the Land of the Head-Hunters. New York: 1915. V. 37

Indian Life and Indian Lore. In the Land of the Head Hunters. (NW Coast): 1915. V. 37

The North American Indian . . . Volume Ten. (The Kwakiutl). N.P.: 1915. V. 39

The North American Indian. New York: 1924. V. 45

The North American Indian. Norwood: 1926. V. 38

The North American Indian, Being a Series of Volumes Picturing and Describing the Indians of the United Sttes and Alaska. Norwood: 1907-30. V. 37

The North American Indian. Volume 13: Hupa; York; Shasta; Klamath, etc. New York: 1924. V. 37

Portraits from North American Indian Life. New York: 1972. V. 39

CURTIS, GEORGE MUNSON

Early Silver of Connecticut and Its Makers. Meriden: 1913. V. 41

CURTIS, GEORGE T.

Letter to the Secretary of the Interior on the Affairs of Utah, Polygamy, 'Cohabitation' &c. Washington: 1886. V. 42

CURTIS, GEORGE TICKNOR

Life of Daniel Webster. New York: 1870. V. 44

CURTIS, GEORGE WILLIAM

Lotus-Eating: a Summer Book. New York: 1852. V. 39; 40; 43

Trumps. New York: 1861. V. 44

Washington Irving: a Sketch. New York: 1891. V. 39; 40; 42

Washington Irving: a Sketch. New York: 1901. V. 44

CURTIS, HENRY

Beauties of the Rose. Bristol: 1850-53. V. 41; 45

Beauties of the Rose . . . Bristol: 1850-53. V. 42

CURTIS, J.

An Authentic and Faithful History of the Mysterious Murder of Maria Marten, with a Full Development . . . London: 1828. V. 38; 40; 46

CURTIS, JOHN 1791-1862

British Entomology. London: 1823-40. V. 43; 45

British Entomology. London: 1824-30. V. 40; 42

British Entomology. London: 1823-40/62. V. 38

British Entomology: Coleoptera. London: 1862. V. 37

Farm Insects. London: 1857. V. 43

Farm Insects. Glasgow: 1860. V. 38

Farm Insects: Being the Natural History and Economy of the Insects Injurious to the Field Crops of Great Britain and Ireland . . . London: 1860. V. 44

Farm Insects. London: 1883. V. 37; 38

The Genera of British Lepidoptera. London: 1858. V. 38

Harvey's Views on the Use of the Circulation of the Blood. New York: 1915. V. 41

Shipwreck of the Stirling Castle . . . London: 1841. V. 38

CURTIS, JOHN HARRISON

A Treatise on the Physiology and Diseases of the Eye. London: 1833. V. 37; 38

A Treatise of the Physiology and Pathology of the Ear . . . Together with Remarks on the Deaf and Dumb. London: 1836. V. 38

CURTIS, NATALIE

The Indian's Book. New York: 1907. V. 41; 43

The Indians' Book. New York: & London: 1923. V. 44

The Indians' Book. London: 1935. V. 42

CURTIS, NEWTON M.

The Bride of the Northern Wilds. New York: 1843. V. 40

CURTIS, NEWTON MARTIN

From Bull Run to Chancellorsville: The Story of the Sixteenth New York Infantry Together with Personal Reminiscences. New York & London: 1906. V. 39

CURTIS, O. B.

History of the Twenty-Fourth Michigan of the Iron Brigade, Known as the Detroit and Wayne County Regiment. Detroit: 1891. V. 44

CURTIS, PAUL A.

Sportsmen All. New York: 1938. V. 39; 43

Sportsmen All. 1938. V. 38

CURTIS, SAMUEL

Curtis's Botanical Magazine. London: 1828-33. V. 41

Curtis's Botanical Magazine. London: 1835. V. 41

Curtis's Botanical Magazine. London: 1837. V. 41

Curtis's Botanical Magazine. London: 1865. V. 41

Curtis's Botanical Magazine. London: 1839-45. V. 41

A Valuable Collection of Recipes, Medical and Miscellaneous, Useful in Families, Valuable to Every Description of Persons. Amherst: 1819. V. 41

CURTIS, W.

Practical Observations on the British Grasses. London: 1805. V. 43

CURTIS, WILLIAM

Flora Londinensis . . . London: 1817-28. V. 46

Fundamenta Entomologiae. London: 1772. V. 38

Instructions for Collecting and Preserving Insects. London: 1771. V. 43

Instructions for Collecting and Preserving Insects; particularly Moths and Butterflies. Illustrated with a copper plate, on which the Nets, and other Apparatus necessary for that purpose are delineated. London: 1771. V. 37

Practical Directions for Laying Down or Improving Meadow and Pasture Land . . . London: 1834. V. 46

CURTIS, WILLIAM E.

The Capitals of Spanish America. New York: 1888. V. 40

A Summer Scamper Along the Old Santa Fe Trail and Through the Gorges of Colorado to Zion. Chicago: 1883. V. 37; 38

CURTISS AEROPLANE & MOTOR CORPORATION

Curtiss Aeroplanes. Garden City: 1919. V. 39

CURTIS'S Botanical Magazine. London: 1948-83. V. 40
CURTIS'S Botanical Magazine. London: 1948-84. V. 37

CURTISS, DANIEL S.

Western Portraiture. New York: 1852. V. 37; 39; 40; 41; 42; 43; 45

CURTISS, GEORGE B.

Industrial Development of Nations and a History of the Tariff Policies of the United States, and of Great Britain, Germany, France, Russia, and Other European Countries. Binghamton: 1912. V. 42

CURTISS, MARION FOSTER

P'sich. New York. V. 43

CURTIUS RUFUS, QUINTUS

Alexander Magnus . . . Commentarius Samuelis Pitisci . . . Amsterdam: 1673. V. 40

De Rebus Gestis Alexandri Magni Regis Macedonum Opus, Ita Demum Emendatum Atque Illustratum . . . Basiliae: 1545. V. 43

De Rebus Gestis Alexandri Magni. Venice: 1494. V. 37

Historiarum: Libri Accuratissime Editi. Amsterdam: 1670. V. 39

The Historie of . . . London: 1561. V. 42

The Hisorie (sic) of Quintus Curtius . . . London: 1602. V. 40

The History of Quintus Curtius. London: 1614. V. 38; 40; 44

The History of the Wars of Alexander the Great. London: 1747. V. 45

Opera. Venice: 1520. V. 37; 46

Quinto Curtio La Historia d'Alexandro Magno . . . Scripta da Quinto Curio Ruffo et Tradotta in Vulgare da P. Candido, Della Quale Questo e il Terzo Libro Perche il Primo e'l Secondo a Tempi Nostri Non Si Trovano. Florentia: 1530. V. 38

Q. Curtii . . . De Rebus Gestis Alexndri Magni Regis Macedonum Opus, Ita Demum Emendatum Atque Illustratum . . . Basileae: in officina: 1545. V. 38

De Rebus Gestis Alexandri Magni. Lyon: 1556. V. 46

CURWEN, HENRY

A History of Booksellers, the Old and the New. London: 1873. V. 41

CURWEN, JOHN C.

Observations on the State of Ireland, Principally Directed to Its Agriculture and Rural Population; in a Series of letters, Written on a Tour throught that country. London: 1818. V. 38; 41

CURWEN, JOHN CHRISTIAN

Hints on Agricultural Subjects, and on the Best Means of Improving the Condition of the Labouring Classes. London: 1809. V. 37; 39

Hints on the Economy of Feeding Stock, and Bettering the Condition of the Poor. London: 1808. V. 37; 46

CURWEN, JOHN F.

The Castles and Fortified Towers of Cumberland, Westmorland and Lancashire North-of-the-Sands . . . Kendal: 1913. V. 41

CURWEN PRESS

Catalogue Raisonne of Books Printed at the Curwen Press, 1920-1923. London: 1924. V. 45

The Curwen Press Almanack. London: 1926. V. 41

A New Specimen Book of Curwen Pattern Papers. Andoversford: 1987. V. 40

A Specimen Book of Types and Ornaments in Use at the Curwen Press. London: 1928. V. 40; 42; 43; 45

The Stencil Process at the Curwen Press (cover title). London: 1928. V. 37

CURWEN PRESS LTD.

Newsletter No. 5-12. Plaistow: 1933-36. V. 44

CURWOOD, JAMES OLIVER 1878-1927

The Alaskan: A Novel of the North. New York: 1923. V. 37

The Ancient Highway: A Novel of High Hearts and Open Roads. New York: 1925. V. 37

Baree: Son of Kazan. Garden City: 1917. V. 37

The Black Hunter: A Novel of Old Quebec. New York: 1926. V. 37

The Country Beyond: A Romance of the Wilderness. New York: 1922. V. 37

The Flaming Forest. New York: 1921. V. 37

God's Country: The Trail to Happiness. New York: 1921. V. 37

The Grizzly King: A Romance of the Wild. Garden City: 1916. V. 37

The Valley of Silent Men: A Story of the Three River Country. New York: (1920). V. 37

CURZON, G.

The Violinist of the Quartier Latin. London: 1884. V. 37

CURZON, GEORGE N.

Persia and the Persian Question. London: 1892. V. 39; 41

CURZON, GEORGE NATHANIEL, 1ST MARQUIS OF 1859-1925

British Government in India. London: 1925. V. 40

Russia in Central Asia in 1889 and the Anglo-Russian Question. London: 1889. V. 46

CURZON, ROBERT

Armenia: a Year at Erzeroom, and on the Frontiers of Russia, Turkey and Persia. London: 1854. V. 39

Armenia: a Year at Erzeroom, and on the Frontiers of Russia, Tukrey and Persia. New York: 1854. V. 39

Visits to Monasteries in the Levant. London: 1849. V. 38

CUSACK, M. E.

The Liberator: His Life and Times. V. 46

CUSACK, M. F.

The Life of. Apostle of Ireland. By M.F. Cusack. New York: 1870. V. 37

The Trias Thaumaturga, or Three Wonder-Working Saints of Ireland, St. Patrick, St. Bridget and St. Columba. London: 1870. V. 43

CUSHING, ABEL

Historical Letters on the First Chapter of Massachusetts Government. Boston: 1839. V. 46

CUSHING, CALEB 1800-1879

The History and Present State of the Town of Newburyport. Neburyport, (Mass.): 1826. V. 37; 43

Report (and Supplemental Report) on the Territory of Oregon Beyond the Rocky Mountains. Washington: 1839. V. 39; 40; 43; 45

Speech Delivered in Faneuil Hall, Boston, October 27, 1857. Also Speech Delivered in City Hall, Newburyport, October 31, 1857. Boston: 1857. V. 39

Territory of Oregon. Washington: 1839. V. 38; 40

Territory of Oregon . . . Washington: 1839. V. 38

Territory of Oregon: Supplemental Report. Washington: 1839. V. 40

The Treaty of Washington: Its Negotiation, Execution and the Discussions Relating Thereto. New York: 1873. V. 45

CUSHING, E. H.

From the West. Houston: 1863. V. 44

The New Texas Reader. Houston: 1864. V. 38; 39; 41; 42

CUSHING, ELIZABETH LANESFORD

Saratoga; a Tale of the Revolution. Boston: 1824. V. 37

CUSHING, FRANK HAMILTON

My Adventures in Zuni. Santa Fe: 1941. V. 37; 38; 44

Zuni Breadstuff. New York: 1920. V. 39; 42; 43

CUSHING, HARVEY

A Classification of the Tumors of the Glioma Group on a Histogenetic Basis with a Correlated Study of Prognosis. Philadelphia: 1928. V. 37

CUSHING, HARVEY WILLIAMS 1869-1939

Alterations of Intracranial Tension By Salt Solutions in the Alimentary Canal. 1920. V. 41

A Bio-Bibliography of Andreas Vesalius. New York: 1943. V. 41; 46

A Bio-Bibliography of Andreas Vesalius. Hamden: 1962. V. 46

A Bio-Bibliography of Andreas Vesalius. New York: 1962. V. 38

Classification of the Tumors Of the Glioma Group on a Histogenetic Basis with a Correlated Study of Prognosis. Philadelphia: 1926. V. 40; 46

Consecratio Medici and Other Papers. Boston: 1928. V. 41; 42; 45

Consecratio Medici and Other Papers. Boston: 1929. V. 38

The Doctor and His Books. Cleveland: 1926. V. 38

Electro-Surgery As an Aid to the Removal of Intracranial Tumors. 1928. V. 42

From a Surgeon's Journal. Boston: 1936. V. 42; 46

The Harvey Cushing Collection of Books and Manuscripts. New York: 1943. V. 41; 45

Intracranial Tumors. London: 1932. V. 44

Intracranial Tumors. Springfield: 1932. V. 39; 40; 41

Intracranial Tumours . . . Springfield & Baltimore: 1932. V. 44

A Large Epidermal Cholesteatoma of the Parieta-Temporal Region Deforming the Left Hemisphere Without Cerebral Symptons. 1922. V. 41

Life of Sir William Osler. London: 1925. V. 38

The Life of Sir William Osler. Oxford: 1925. V. 37; 38; 39; 40; 41; 42; 43; 44; 45; 46

The Life of Sir William Osler. Oxford: 1925. V. 41

The Life of Sir William Osler. Oxford: 1925. V. 45

Life of Sir William Osler. London: 1926. V. 38

The Life of Sir William Osler. Oxford: 1926. V. 37; 39; 40; 41; 42; 44; 45; 46

The Medical Career. Hanover: 1930. V. 42

The Meningiomas Arising from the Olfactory Groove and Their Removal by the Aid of Electro-Surgery. 1927. V. 42

The Meningiomas Arising From the Olfactory Groove and Their Removal by Aid of Electrosurgery. Glasgow: 1927. V. 39; 42

Meningiomas. Their Classification, Regional Behaviour, Life History & Surgical End Results. Springfield: 1938. V. 43; 44; 46

Meningiomas Their Classification, Regional Behaviour, Life History and Surgical End Results. New York: 1962. V. 40

Papers Relating to the Pituitary Body, Hypothalamus and Parasympathetic Nervous System. Philadelphia & London: 1912. V. 44

Papers Relating to the Pituitary Body, Hypothalamus and Parasympathetic Nervous System. Springfield: 1932. V. 37; 38; 39; 40; 42

Papers Relating to the Pituitary Body, Hypothalamus and Parasympathetic Nervous System. Springfield & Baltimore: 1932. V. 45

The Pathological Findings in Four Autopsied Cases of Acromegaly with a Discussion of Their Significance. New York: 1927. V. 44

The Pituitary Body and Its Disorders. Philadelphia & London: 1912. V. 45

The Pituitary Body and Its Disorders. Philladelphia: 1912. V. 39; 40; 42; 43; 44; 45; 46

The Pituitary Body and Its Disorders. Birmingham: 1979. V. 42

The Principles and Practice of Medicine. London: 1901. V. 46

Selected Papers on Neurosurgery. New Haven: 1969. V. 41

Special Field of Neurological Surgery After Another Interval. Columbus: 1921. V. 41

STudies in Intracranial Physiology and Surgery. Oxford: 1926. V. 44

Tumors of the Nervous Acusticus and the Sydrome of the Cerebellopontile Angle. Philadelphia: 1917. V. 38; 39; 42; 46

Tumors of the Nervous Acusticus and the Syndrome of the Cerebellopontile Angle. Philadelphia & London: 1917. V. 44

Tumors Arising from the Blood-Vessels of the Brain Angiomatous Malformations and Hemagioblastomas. Springfield & Baltimore: 1928. V. 44; 45

A Visit to Le Puy-En-Velay. Cleveland: 1944. V. 37; 46

Xanthochromia and Increased Protein In the Spinal Fluids Above Tumors of the Cauda Equina. Chicago: 1923. V. 41

CUSHING, HENRY

Meningiomas. Their Classification, Regional Behaviour, Life History and Surgical End Results. Springfield: 1938. V. 41

CUSHING, J.

The Exotic Gardener. London: 1814. V. 39; 40

CUSHING, JOHN

The Exotic Gardener . . . London: 1812. V. 42

The Exotic Gardener; in which the management of the hot-house, green-house and conservatory, is fully and clearly delineated according to moder practice; with an appendix containing observations on the soils suitable to tender exotics . . . Dublin: 1811. V. 37

CUSHING, LUTHER S.

Manual of Parliamentary Practice. Boston: 1845. V. 40

CUSHING, SAMUEL B.

Report of Samuel B. Cushing, Esq., Civil Engineer, Respecting the Harbor of Van Buren, on Lake Erie, in the County of Chautauque, and the State of New York. New York: 1836. V. 43

CUSHING, THOMAS

History of the Counties of Gloucester, Salem & Cumberland, New Jersey. Philadelphia: 1883. V. 38; 39; 41; 46

CUSHMAN, H. B.

Choctaw, Chickasaw, and Natachez Indians. Greenville: 1899. V. 39; 41; 42; 43; 45

CUSHWA, FRANK W.

M. Fred Loewenstein, 1910-1933. San Francisco: 1934. V. 38; 46

CUSICK, DAVID

David Cusick's Sketches of Ancient History of the Six Nations . . . Lockport: 1848. V. 37

CUSPINIAN, JOHANNES 1473-1529

De Caesaribus Atque Imperatoribus Romanis Opus. Strasbourg: 1540. V. 38; 41

CUSSANS, JOHN EDWIN

History of Hertfordshire . . . Hertford: 1870-81. V. 39

History of Hertfordshire. London: 1870-81. V. 39; 42; 44

History of Hertfordshire, Containing an Account of the Descents of the Various Manors. London: 1870-83. V. 41; 44

CUSSANS, JOHN EDWIN continued

History of Hertfordshire, Containing an account of the Descents of the Various Manors, Pedigrees of Families, Connected with the County, Antiquities, Local Customs . . . London & Hertford: 1880-81. V. 41

CUSSONS, MAY & CO.

Salesman's Sample Book. Richmond: 1880-1905. V. 44

CUST, C. LEOPOLD

Naval Battles from the Collection of Prints Formed and Owned by . . . . London: 1911. V. 46

CUST, HENRY

Occasional Poems by . . . . Jerusalem: 1918. V. 43

CUST, L.

Eton College Portraits. London: 1910. V. 45

CUST, LIONEL

Anthony Van Dyck: an Historical Study of His Life and Works. London: 1900. V. 40; 43

A Description of the Sketchbook by Sir Anthony Van Dyck Used by Him in Italy, 1621-1627, and Preserved in the Collection of the Duke of Devonshire, K. G. at Chatsworth. London: 1902. V. 40; 43

The National Portrait Gallery. London: 1901. V. 41

The Royal Collection of Paintings at Buckingham Palace and Windsor Castle. London: 1905-06. V. 40

CUST, R. N.

Linguistic and Oriental Essays. London: 1880-1904. V. 38

CUST, ROBERT

Pictures of Anglo-Indian Life, Sketched with the Pen. 1860. V. 41

CUSTANCE, HENRY 1842-1908

Riding Recollections and Turf Stories. London: 1894. V. 42; 46

CUSTER, ELIZABETH B. 1842-1933

Boots and Saddles. New York: 1885. V. 37, 39; 41

Following the Guidon. New York: 1890. V. 39

Tenting on the Plains; or General Custer in Kansas and Texas. New York: 1887. V. 37; 38; 39; 40; 42; 43; 45

Tenting on the Plains Or General Custer in Kansas and Texas. London: 1888. V. 41

Tenting on the Plains: or General Custer in Kansas and Texas. New York: 1944. V. 46

CUSTER, GEORGE

Life on the Plains; or Personal Experiences with Indians. New York: 1876. V. 45

My Life on the Plains. New York: 1874. V. 38; 41

CUSTINE, ADOLPHE, MARQUIS DE

The Empire of the Czar. London: 1843. V. 43

CUSTIS, G. W. PEAKE

Recollections and Private memoirs of Washington. Washington: 1859. V. 38

CUSTOMS and Privileges of the Manors of Stepney and Hackney . . . London: 1736. V. 46

CUSTOMS and Privileges of the manors of Stepney and hackney in the County of Middlesex. In the Savoy: 1736. V. 44

CUSTOS, DOMINICUS

Fuggerorum et Fuggerarum . . . Imagines. Augsburg: 1593. V. 38; 39

CUSTOT, PIERRE

Sturly. London: 1924. V. 40

CUTBUSH, JAMES

The American Aartist's Manual. Philadelphia: 1814. V. 38; 45

A System of Pyrotechny Comprehending the Theory and Practice . . . Philadelphia: 1825. V. 38; 42

CUTCHEON, BYRON M.

The Story of the Twentieth Michigan Infantry July 15th, 1862 to May 30th 1865. Lansing: 1904. V. 46

CUTCLIFFE, H. C.

The Art of Trout Fishing on Rapid Streams. South Molton: 1863. V. 40

The Art of Trout Fishing on the Rapid Streams. 1982. V. 43

The Art of Trout Fishing on the Rapid Streams. Tiverton, Devon: 1982. V. 39

The Art of Trout Fishing on Rapid Streams. (Tiverton): 1982. V. 37

CUTHBERTSON, CATHERINE

Forest of Montalbano. London: 1810. V. 37

CUTHBERTSON, GEORGE A.

Freshwater. A History and a Narrative of the Great Lakes. Toronto: 1931. V. 41; 44

CUTLER, CARL C.

Greyhounds of the Sea: The Story of the American Clipper Ship. New York: 1930. V. 41

The Story of the American Clipper Ship Greyhounds of the Sea. New York: 1930. V. 40

CUTLER, CONDICT W.

The Hand, Its Disabilities and Diseases. Philadelphia: 1942. V. 38; 42

CUTLER, ELLIOTT

A Journal of the Harvard Medical School Unit to American Ambulance Hospital in Paris, Spring of 1915. New York: 1920. V. 42

Surgery of the Heart and Pericardium. New York: 1927. V. 42

CUTLER, EPHRAIM

Life and Times of Ephraim Cutler Prepared from His Journals and Correspondence . . . Cincinnati: 1890. V. 45

CUTLER, JERVIS

A Topographical Description of the State of Ohio, Indiana Territory and Louisiana. Boston: 1812. V. 37; 38; 39; 41; 42; 43; 45

A Topographical Description of the State of Ohio, Indiana Territory and Louisiana. Boston: 1812. V. 41

A Topographical Description of the State of Ohio, Indiana Territory and Louisiana . . . to Which is Added an Interesting Journal of Mr. Chas. Le Raye . . . Boston: 1812. V. 45

CUTLER, JULIA P.

Life and Times of Ephriam Cutler Prepared From His Journal and Correspondence . . . Cincinnati: 1890. V. 43; 46

CUTLER, MANASSEH

An Explanation of the Map Which Delineates that Part of the Federal Lands, Comprehended Between Pennsylvania West Line, the Rivers Ohio and Sioto. Newport: 1788. V. 38; 40

CUTLER, MANESSEH

Life Journals and Correspondence of Rev. Manasseh Cutler . . . Cincinnati: 1888. V. 45

CUTLER, THOMAS W.

A Grammar of Japanese Ornament and Design. London: 1880. V. 38; 44

CUTLER, WILLIAM P.

Life, Journals and Correspondence of Manasseh Cutler. Cincinnati: 1888. V. 43

CUTTER, BLOODGOOD H.

The Long Island Farmer's Poems. New York: 1886. V. 40

CUTTER, CHARLES

Cutter's Guide to the Hot Springs of Arkansas. St. Louis: 1882. V. 37; 40

CUTTER, G. W.

Buena Vista and Other Poems. Cincinnati: 1848. V. 44

CUTTER, WILLIAM R.

New England Families. New York: 1913. V. 46

CUTTS, EDWARD L.

An Essay on Church Furniture and Decoration. London: 1854. V. 37; 40; 44

An Essay on the Christmas Decoration of Churches . . . London: 1863. V. 42

CUTTS, JAMES M.

The Conquest of California and New Mexico, by the Forces of the United States, in the Years 1846 and 1847. Philadelphia: 1847. V. 39

CUTTS, JOHN, BARON

Poetical Exercises Written Upon Several Occasions. London: 1687. V. 40

CUTTS, MISS

Almeria; or Parental Advice. London: 1785. V. 40; 42

CUTTS, SIMON

Pianostool Footnotes. Highlands: 1982. V. 44

CUVIER, GEORGES, BARON 1769-1832

The Animal Kingdom Arranged in Conformity with Its Organization. New York: 1831. V. 42

The Animal Kingdom Arranged in Conformity With Its Organization . . . New York: 1831. V. 42

The Animal Kingdom . . . London: 1833/34-37. V. 37; 41

The Animal Kingdom. 1834-36. V. 40

CUVIER, GEORGES, BARON 1769-1832 continued

The Animal Kingdom, Arranged According to Its Organization, Serving as a Foundation for the Natural History of Animals, and an Introduction to Comparative Anatomy. London: 1834-36. V. 39

The Animal Kingdom . . . London: 1834/7. V. 39

The Animal Kingdom. Class Mammalia. London: 1827. V. 37

Description geologique des Environs de paris. Paris: 1822. V. 39

Essai sur la Geographie Mineralogique des Environs de Paris, avec une Carte Geognostique, et des Coupes de Terrain. Paris: 1811. V. 45

Essay on the Theory of the Earth. Edinburgh: 1813. V. 43

Essay on the Theory of the Earth. Edinburgh: 1827. V. 38

Historical Eulogium on Joseph Priestley, Read at the Public Sitting of the National Insitute, in the Class of Mathematical and Physical Sciences, the 5th of Messidor, Year 13. Paris: 1807. V. 42

Le Regne Animal Distribue d'Apres son Organisation. Paris: 1817. V. 37; 39; 41; 42; 43

CUXSON, GERRARD & CO., BIRMINGHAM & OLBURY.

Price List of Antiseptic Surgical Dressings, Instruments and Appliances, Used in Hospital and Surgical Practice, &c . . . Birmingham: 1903. V. 43

CYCLIST COMPANY

The Story of the 60th (London) Divisional Cyclist Company. Including the History of the XVIII Corps Cyclist Batallion. 1935. V. 45

THE CYCLOPAEDIA of American Biography. New York: 1918. V. 46

CYCLOPAEDIA of Commercial and Business Anecdotes Comprising Interesting Reminiscences and Facts . . . New York: 1864. V. 38

CYCLOPEDIA of Eminent and Representative Men of the Carolinas of the Nineteenth Century. Madison: 1892. V. 40; 43; 45

CYNWAL, WILLIAM

In Defence of Women. London: 1960. V. 37; 41; 46

CYPRESS, J.

Sporting Scenes and Sunday Sketches. New York: 1842. V. 43

CYPRIAN

. . . *Opera.* Paris: 1726. V. 38

CYPRIAN, SAINT

St. Cyprian's Discourse to Donatus. London: 1716. V. 37

Sancti Caecilii Cypriani Opera . . . Oxford: 1682. V. 39

CYPRIANUS, SAINT, BP. OF CARTHAGE

Opera. Basle: 1520. V. 40

Opera Omnia. Paris: 1564. V. 40

St. Cyprian's Discourse to Donatus. London: 1716. V. 41; 42; 46

CYRANO DE BERGERAC, SAVINIEN

The Agreement. A Satyrical and Facetious Dream. N.P.: London:?: 1756. V. 45

The Comical History of the States and Empires of the Worlds of the Moon and Sun. London: 1687. V. 45

A Voyage to the Moon: With Some Account of the Solar World. Dublin: 1754. V. 45

CYRIL, SAINT, OF JERUSALEM c. 315-386

Opera, Quae Supersunt Omnia . . . Oxford: 1703. V. 39

CYRILLUS BEHNAM BENNI, ABP. OF MOSUL

The Traditions of the Syriac Church of Antioch, Concerning the Primacy and the Prerogatives of St. Peter, and of His Successors the Roman Pontiffs. London: 1871. V. 39

CZAPSKA, LA COMTESSE

The Romance of a German Court. A Translation of Ary Wclilaw's 'Le Roi de Thessalie'. London: 1886. V. 37

CZECHOSLOVAKIA: Romanesque and Gothic Illuminated Manuscripts. New York: 1959. V. 46

CZWIKLITZER, CHRISTOPHER

Picasso's Posters. New York: 1970/71. V. 45; 46

Picasso's Posters. New York: 1971. V. 39; 43

D

D., A. Y.

The Owls of Olynn Belfry. London: 1886. V. 37

D., G.

A Briefe Discoverie of Doctor Allens Seditious Drifts Contrived in a Pamphlet Written by Him, Concerning the Yeilding Up of the Town of Deuenter . . . London: 1588. V. 41

D., J.

An Humble Proposal to Prevent the Beginnings of Theft, viz . . . . N.P.. V. 43

An Humble Proposal to Prevent the Beginnings of Theft, viz. the Picking Pockets of Handerchiefs. London: 1720. V. 43

D., P.

A Candid Enquiry into the Principles and Practices of the Most Ancient and Honourable Society of Bucks Together with Some Thoughts on the Origin, Nature and Design of that Institution, Dedicated to the Brthren of the Order. London: 1770. V. 38

DABBS, EDITH M.

Face of an Island. Leigh Richmond Miner's Photographs of Saint Helena Island. New York: 1971. V. 41; 44

DABNEY, JOHN

An Address to Farmers . . . Salem: 1796. V. 37

DABNEY, OWEN P.

The Lost Shackle or Seven Years with the Indians. Salem: 1897. V. 42; 43

True Story of the Lost Shackle or Seven Years with the Indians. Salem: 1897. V. 37

DABNEY, ROBERT L.

Life of Lieut.-Gen. Thomas J. Jackson (Stonewall Jackson). London: 1864-66. V. 37

D'ABRERA, B.

Butterflies of the Australian Region. London: 1971. V. 38

Butterlies of the Neotropical Region Parts 1-3. London: 1981-87. V. 39

Butterflies of the Neotropical Region, Parts 1 to 4. London: 1981-88. V. 41

Butterflies of the Oriental Region. Melbourne: 1982-85. V. 37; 39; 41

Butterflies of the Afro-Tropical Region. Melbourne: 1980. V. 37

Butterflies of the Neotropical Region, Part 2: Danaidae, Ithomiidae, Heliconidae and Morphidae. Melbourne: 1984. V. 37

Butterflies of the Neotropical Region, Part I: Papilionidae and Pieridaeaa. Melbourne: 1981. V. 37

D'ACHE, CARAN

Marlborough. A Humorous Picture Book. London: 1897. V. 41

DACIER, ANDRE

The Life of Pythagoras, with His Symbols and Golden Verses. London: 1707. V. 38; 46

DA COSTA, ISAAC

Noble Families Among the Sephardic Jews . . . Oxford: 1936. V. 41

DACRE, BARBARINA BRAND, LADY

Dramas, Translations and Occasional Poems. London: 1821. V. 42

Recollections of a Caperon. London: 1833. V. 45

DACRE, CHARLOTTE ROSA MATILDA

Zofloya or the Moor. London: 1915. V. 44

D'ACRES, R.

The Art of Water Drawing. London: 1930. V. 40

DACUS, J. A.

Illustrated Lives and Adventures of Frank and Jesse James and the Younger Brothers, the Noted Western Outlaws. St. Louis: 1882. V. 42; 45

Life and Adventures of Frank and Jesse James, The Noted Western Outlaws. St. Louis: 1881. V. 43; 46

A Tour of St. Louis; or, the Inside Life of a Great City. St. Louis: 1878. V. 46

DADDOW, S. H.

Coal, Iron and Oil; or the Practical American Miner . . . Pottsville: 1866. V. 40

DADDY'S Little Rhyme Book. London. V. 43

DADDY'S Makings: Little Rhyming Undertakings, Very New and Very Funny. London. V. 40

DADE, ERNEST

Sail & Oar, A North Sea Sketch Book. London;: 1933. V. 37

DADE, WILLIAM

A New Alamancke, and Prognostication, with the Forraigne Computations. London: 1635. V. 39

DAELLI, G.

A Relic of the Italian Revolution of 1849. New Orleans: 1850. V. 39; 44

DAGGE, HENRY

Considerations on Criminal Law. London: 1772. V. 40; 45

DAGGETT, DAVID

Count the Cost. Hartford: 1804. V. 44

Mr. Daggett's Argument, Before the General Assembly of the State of Connecticut, October 1804, in the Case of Certain Justice of the Peace . . . New Haven: 1804. V. 45

Sun-Beams May Be Extracted from Cucumbers, But the Process Is Tedious. New Haven: 1799. V. 44

Three Letters to Abraham Bishop, Esquire, Containing Some Strictures on His Oration . . . Hartford: 1800. V. 45

DAGGS, RUEL

Fugitive Slave Case. District Court of the US. for the Southern Division of Iowa, Burlington, June Term, 1850. Daggs vs. Elihu Frazier, et als. Trespass on the case. Burlington: 1850. V. 38

DAGLEY, RICHARD

Death's Doings; Consisting of Numerous Original Compositions, in Prose and Verse, the Friendly Contributions of Various Writers. London: 1826. V. 37; 39; 40; 43

Death's Doings: Original Compositions in Prose and Verse, the Friendly Contributions of Various Writers. Boston: 1828. V. 41

Death's Doings . . . London: 1827. V. 37

Gems. Principally from the Antique. London: 1822. V. 39

Takings, or the Life of a Collegian. London: 1831. V. 40

Takings; or the Life of a Collegian. A Poem. Illustrated by Twenty six Etchings, from designs by R. Dagley. London: 1821. V. 37; 43; 44

DAGLISH, ERIC FITCH

The Birds of the British Ballads. London: 1948. V. 45

Birds of the British Isles. London: 1948. V. 38; 42; 43; 44

Woodcuts of British Birds. London: 1921. V. 46

Woodcuts of British Birds. London: 1925. V. 41

DAGONET, HENRI 1823-1902

Nouveau Traite Elementaire et Pratique des Maladies Mentales Suivi de Considerations Pratiques sur l'Administration des Asiles d'Alienes. Paris: 1876. V. 45

DAGUERRE, LOUIS

A Full Description of the Daguerreotype Process. New York: 1840. V. 46

DAHL, BASIL

To the Toilers and other Verses. By Basil Dahl. With an appreciation by Benjamin R. Tucker. Including translations from the Yiddish by Rose Freeman-Ishill. Berkeley Heights, N.J.: 1929. V. 37; 40

DAHL, JOHAN ANDREAS

Norwegian and Swedish Poems. Bergen: 1872. V. 44

DAHL, ROALD

The BFG. New York: 1982. V. 40; 41; 42; 45; 46

The Champion of the World. New York: 1975. V. 46

Charlie and the Chocolate Factory. New York: 1964. V. 42; 45

Charlie and the Great Glass Elevator. New York: 1972. V. 46

Dirty Beasts. London: 1983. V. 45

Englesh Skolegrammatikk. Oslo: 1953, V. 46

The Gremlins: A Royal Air Force Story. New York: 1943. V. 38; 46

Kiss Kiss. London: 1960. V. 37; 43

Kiss Kiss. New York: 1960. V. 42

Over to You. 1946. V. 45

Over to You - Ten Stories of Flyers and Flying. London: 1946. V. 38

Over to You. New York: 1946. V. 42; 46

Over to You: 10 Stories of Flyers and Flying. New York: 1946. V. 45

Some Time Never: a Fable for Supermen. New York: 1948. V. 42

Sometime Never. London: 1944. V. 43

Two Fables. London: 1986. V. 43

The Witches. New York: 1983. V. 42

DAHLBERG, EDWARD

Bottom Dogs. London. V. 44

Bottom Dogs. London: 1929. V. 39; 40; 41; 42; 43; 44

Bottom Dogs. 1930. V. 44

Bottom Dogs. Introduction by D.H. Lawrence. London. V. 37

The Confessions of Edward Dahlberg. New York: 1971. V. 39; 44; 46

Do These Bones Live. New York: 1941. V. 42; 44; 46

The Flea of Sodom. London: 1930. V. 39

From Flushing to Calvary. New York: 1932. V. 42

Kentucky Blue Grass, Henry Smith. Cleveland: 1932. V. 42

The Sorrows of Priapus. 1957. V. 40

The Sorrows of Priapus. Connecticut: 1957. V. 41

The Sorrows of Priapus. New York: 1957. V. 38; 41

The Sorrows of Priapus. Norfolk: 1957. V. 41; 44

DAHLGREN, JOHN ADOLPHUS BERNARD

Boat Armament of the U. S. Navy - Designed and Executed by the Author . . . Philadelphia: 1856. V. 37; 39; 42

Shells and Shell-Guns. Philadelphia: 1856. V. 37

DAHLGREN, MADELEINE VINTON

South Sea Sketches . . . Boston: 1881. V. 45

DAHLGREN, R. M. T.

The Families of the Monocotyledons: Structure and Evolution and Taxonomy. Berlin: 1985. V. 37

DAHN, FELIX

A Struggle for Rome. London: 1878. V. 40; 43

DAHURON, RENE

Nouveau Traite de la Taille des Arbres Fruitiers. Paris: 1740. V. 42

DAILEY, ABRAHAM H.

Mollie Fancher, the Brooklyn Enigma. Brooklyn: 1894. V. 43

DAILY Companion; or, A Little Pocket Manual. London: 1779. V. 44

THE DAILY Express ABC. London: 1940's. V. 46

DAILY Journal City Register and Directory for 1851-52; Together with the Advertisements of the Principal Business Men and an Alphabetical List of Streets and Public Squares of he City. Syracuse: 1851. V. 40; 43

DAILY Journal for 1904. (At head of title: Dominion Diary). Toronto. V. 37

THE DAILY Journal; or The Gentleman's and Tradesman's Complete Annual Accompt-book for the Pocket or Desk . . . London: 1759. V. 45

THE DAILY News' History of Buchanan County and St. Joseph, Missouri: from the Time of the Platte Purchase to the End of the Year 1898. St. Joseph: 1898. V. 38

DAILY News' History of Buchanan County and St. Joseph, Missouri. From the Time of the Platte Purchase to the End of the Year 1898 . . . 1898. V. 38; 46

THE DAILY News' History of Buchanan County and St. Joseph, Mo. Hardman: 1898. V. 38

DAINELLI, GIOTTO

Buddhists and Glaciers of Western Tibet. London: 1933. V. 37

DAISY Days. London. V. 46

DAIX, PIERRE

Picasso: the Blue and Rose Periods. A Catalogue Raisonne of the Paintings, 1900-1906. Greenwich: 1966. V. 39; 43

Picasso 1900-1906 (Blue Period). Paris: 1966. V. 46

Picasso: the Blue and Rose Periods. Greenwich: 1967. V. 45; 46

DAKIN, WILLIAM JOHN

Whalemen Adventurers: the Story of Whaling in Australian Waters and Other Southern Seas Related Thereto. Sydney: 1934. V. 41

DAKOTA CONSTITUTIONAL CONVENTION

Presentation of Dakota's Claims and Memorial Praying for Admission. The Constitution Adopted by the Convention Held at Sioux Falls, Dakota, September 1885. Sioux Falls: 1885. V. 43

Rules, Order of Business and Standing Committees, September, 1883. Sioux Falls: 1883. V. 40; 43

DAKOTA. CONSTITUTIONAL COVNENTION, SIOUX FALLS, 1883.

Rules, Order of Business and Standing Committees, September 1883. Sioux Falls: 1883. V. 39

DAKOTA CORP OF ENGINEERS

Annual Report of Lt. Edward Maguire Corps of Enginners for the Fiscal Year Ending June 30, 1877, Explorataions and Surveys in the Dept. of Dakota. St. Paul: 1877. V. 37

DAKOTA. LAWS, STATUES, ETC.

General Laws, Memorials, and Resolutions of the Territory of Dakota. Yankton: 1867. V. 37

DAKOTA LOAN AND TRUST CO.

Real Estate Mortgages. 7 Per Cent Semi-Annual Interest Guaranteed. Negotiated by Dakota Loan and Trust Company of Pierre, Dakota. N.P.: 1886. V. 45

DAKOTA: Proofs in Support of the Protest Against Admission as a State. Yankton: 1882? V. 40; 43

DAKOTA. (TERRITORY). GOVERNOR - 1865

Fifth Annual Session. Third Annual Message of Governor Newton Edmunds Delivered to the Legislative Assembly of the Territory of Dakota . . . Yankton: 1865. V. 39

DAKOTA. (TERRITORY). GOVERNOR - 1866

Sixth Annual Session. First Annual Message of Governor A. J. Faulk to the Legislative Assembly of the Territory of Dakota. Yankton;: 1866. V. 39

DAKOTA. (TERRITORY). GOVERNOR - 1868

Eighth Annual Session. Third Annual Message of Governor A. J. Faulk, to the Legislative Assembly of the Territory of Dakota. Yankton: 1868. V. 39

DAKOTA. (TERRITORY). GOVERNOR - 1881

Message of Nehemiah G. Ordway, Governor of Dakota Territory. Yankton: 1881. V. 39

DAKOTA. (TERRITORY). LAWS, STATUTES, ETC.

General and Private Laws and Memorials and Resolutions of the Territory of Dakota, Passed at the First Session of the Legislative Assembly . . . Yankton: 1862. V. 39; 42; 45

General Laws, Memorials and Resolutions of the Territory of Dakota Passted at the Ninth Session of the Legislative Assembly . . . Yankton: 1870-71. V. 46

DAKOTA. (TERRITORY). LAWS, STATUTES, ETC. - 1863

General Laws and Memorials and Resolutions of the Territory of Dakota Passed at the Second Session of the Legislative Assembly . . . January 9, 1863 . . . (with) Private Laws of the Territory of Dakota . . . Yankton: 1862-3. V. 39

DAKOTA. (TERRITORY). LAWS, STATUTES, ETC. - 1864

General and Private Laws and Memorials and Resolutions of the Territory of Dakota . . . Commenced at Yankton December 5, 1864 and Concluded January 13, 1865. Yankton: 1864-65. V. 39

DAKOTA. (TERRITORY). LAWS, STATUTES, ETC. - 1867

General Laws, Memorials and Resolutions of the Territory of Dakota. Yankton: 1867. V. 39

DAKYN, JOHANNEM

Statuta Eleemosynariae Sive Hospitalis Sancti Johannis Baptistae, in Kirkby-Ravenswath. York: 1786. V. 45

D'ALBARET

Differens Projets Relatif Au Climat et la Maniere La Plus Convenable De Batir Dans Les Pays Chaud, et Plus Particulierement Dans Les Indes Occidentales. Paris: 1776. V. 46

DALBERT, J. F. H. VON, BARON

Mehaled and Sedli; or, the History of a Druse Family . . . London: 1816. V. 43

DALBEY, E. F.

Pictorial History of the City of Richmond, Indiana. Richmond: 1896. V. 41; 46

DALBY, FRANCIS

Mr. Dalby's Case . . . London: 1756? V. 38

DALCHO, FREDERICK

An Historical Account of the Protestant Episcopal Church in South Carolina, from the First Settlement of the Province to the War of the Revolution . . . Charleston. V. 38

Historical Account of the Protestant Episcopal Church in South Carolina, from the First Settlement of the Province to the War of the Revolution . . . Charleston: 1820. V. 42; 43

DALE, ARCH

Five Years of R. B. Bennett with Arch Dale and the Winnipeg Free Press. Winnipeg. 1935. V. 44

DALE, EDWARD EVERETT

Cherokee Cavaliers. Norman: 1939. V. 44

DALE, EDWARD EVERETT continued

History of the Ranch Cattle Industry in Oklahoma: Cherokee Strip Live Stock Association; Old Navajoe and Cheyenne-Arapahoe Country. Washington: 1924-1946. V. 39

The Prairie Schooner and Other Poems. Guthrie: 1929. V. 39

The Range Cattle Industry. New York:orman: 1930. V. 45

The Range Cattle Industry. Norman: 1930. V. 37; 38; 39; 43; 44; 45; 46

DALE, G. E.

A Familiar Essay on Electricity, with an Arrangement of Experiments, Illustrative of the Phenomena of This Interesting Branch of natural Science. Liverpool: 1812. V. 41

DALE, HARRISON CLIFFORD

The Ashley-Smith Explorations and the Discovery of Central Route to the Pacific 1822-1829. Cleveland: 1918. V. 39; 41; 45; 46

The Ashley-Smith Explorations and the Discovery of a Central Route to the Pacific 1822-1829, with the Original Journals. Glendale: 1941. V. 37; 40; 42; 43; 44

DALE, SAMUEL 1659-1739

The History and Antiquites of Harwick and Dovercourt. London: 1730. V. 39; 41

Pharmacologia, seu Manuductio ad Materiam Medicam. Londini: 1693. V. 38; 42

Pharmacologia, Seu Manuductio Ad Materiam Medicam . . . London: 1737. V. 40; 41

DALE, T. F.

The History of the Belvoir Hunt. London: 1899. V. 37; 39; 42

DALE, THOMAS

The Widow of the City of Nain; and Other Poems by an Undergraduate of the University. London: 1819. V. 42

DALE, WILLIAM

The Unhappy Transport; or, the Sorrowful Sufferings of William Dale . . . London: 1825. V. 46

DALEY, C. F.

Sundials. New York: 1891. V. 41

DALI, SALVADOR

Babaouo. Paris: 1978. V. 38

Conquest of the Irrational. New York: 1935. V. 45

La Conquete de l'Irrationnel. 1935. V. 39

La Conquete de l'Irationnel. Paris: 1935. V. 42

Da Da Dali. Bremen: 1966. V. 44

Dali on Modern Art. New York: 1957. V. 44

Dali's Mustache; a Photographic Interview. New York: 1954. V. 46

50 Secrets of Magic Craftsmanship. New York: 1948. V. 39; 46

Hidden Faces. New York: 1944. V. 44

Hidden Faces. London: 1973. V. 43

Hidden Faces. London: 1974. V. 46

Metamorphosis of Narcissus. New York: 1937. V. 39

The Secret Life of Salvador Dali. New York: 1942. V. 41; 46

Dali: A Study of His Art In Jewels. Greenwich: 1959. V. 40

Dali: The Wines of Gala. New York: 1978. V. 45; 46

DALIE, SALVADOR

The Wines of Gala. 1978. V. 39

DALL, CAROLINE HEALEY

'Alongside' Being Notes Suggested by 'A New England Boyhood' of Doctor Everett Hale. Boston: 1900. V. 40; 45

The College, the Market and the Court . . . Boston: 1867. V. 37; 44; 45

My First Holiday; or Letters Home from Colorado, Utah and California. Boston: 1881. V. 37; 39; 42

My First Holiday; or, Letters Home from Colorado, Utah and California. Boston: 1886. V. 44

The Romance of the Association; or, One Last Glimpse of Charlotte Temple and Eliza Wharton. Cambridge: 1875. V. 44

Woman's Rights Under the Law: in Three Lectures, Delivered in Boston, January, 1861. Boston: 1861. V. 37

DALL, WILLIAM

Alaska and Its Resources. Boston: 1870. V. 39; 42; 43

DALL, WILLIAM H.

History of the Sixth Regiment, Indiana Volunteer Infantry in the Civil War. Columbus: 1903. V. 46

On Masks, Labrets and Certain Aboriginal Customs . . . Washington: 1884. V. 37

On the Remains of Later Pre-Historic Man, Obtained from Caves in the Catherina Archipelago, Alaska Territory, and Especially from Caves of the Aleutian Islands. Washington: 1878. V. 38; 39

Tribes of the Extreme Northwest. Part 1. Washington: 1876. V. 38; 39; 43; 46

DALLAS, ALEXANDER JAMES

An Exposition of the Causes and Character of the War Between the United States and Great Britain. Concord: 1815. V. 45

Features of Mr. Jay's Treaty, To Which is Annexed a View of the Commerce of the United States, As It Stands at Present, and As It Is Fixed by Mr. Jay's Treaty. Philadlephia: 1795. V. 42; 44

Reports of Cases Ruled and Adjudged in the Courts of Pennsylvania Before and Since the Revolution. Philadelphia: 1799-1807. V. 38; 39

DALLAS, ALEXANDER R. C.

Felix Alvarez; or, Manners in Spain . . . London: 1818. V. 46

DALLAS, ENEAS SWEETLAND

Poetics: an Essay on Poetry. London: 1852. V. 37

DALLAS, GEORGE

Speech of George Dallas, Esq. Member of the Committee Appointed by the British Inhabitants Residing in Bengal, for the Purpose of Preparing Petitions to His Majesty and Both Houses of Parliament . . . London: 1785. V. 42

DALLAS, ROBERT

Considerations Upon the American Enquiry. London: 1779. V. 41; 45

DALLAS, ROBERT CHARLES 1754-1824

Elements of Self-Knowledge . . . London: 1802. V. 43

The History of the Maroons, from Their Origin to the Establishment of Their Chief Tribe at Sierra Leone . . . London: 1803. V. 39; 40; 42; 46

Recollections of the Life of Lord Byron, from the Year 1808 to the End of 1814 . . . . London: 1824. V. 38; 39; 40; 44

Recollections of the Life of Lord Byron, from the Year 1808 to the End of 1814. Philadelphia: 1825. V. 37; 39; 45

DALLAS, SANDRA

Sacred Paint, ned jacob. Santa Fe: 1979. V. 46

DALLAS, WILLIAM S.

Birds. N.P.. V. 42

DALLAWAY, HARRIET

Etchings of views in the Vicarage of Leatherhead, Surrey. London: 1821. V. 38

A Manual of Heraldry for Amateurs. London: 1828. V. 39; 41

DALLAWAY, JAMES 1763-1834

Anecdotes of the Arts in England. London: 1800. V. 37; 38; 41; 43; 45; 46

Antiquities of Bristow in the Middle Centuries. Bristol: 1834. V. 39; 44

Constantinople Ancient and Modern, with Excursions to the Shores and Islands of the Archipelago and to the Troad. London: 1797. V. 37; 38; 41; 43

A History of the Western Division of the County of Sussex, Including the Rapes of Chichester, Arundel & Bramber, with the City and Diocese of Chichester. London: 1815 & 1819. V. 40

Inquiries into the Origin and Progress of the Science of Heraldry in England. Gloucester: 1793. V. 42; 45

Notes of Anicent Church Architecture, in the Fifteenth Century . . . Bristol: 1823. V. 37

Observations on English Architecture. London: 1806. V. 37

William Wyrcestre Redivivus, Notices of Ancient Church Architecture . . . Bristol: 1823. V. 37; 40

DALLAWAY, R. C.

Observations on the Most Important Subjects of Education. London: 1812. V. 37; 38; 43

DALLIBA, JAMES

A Narrative of the Battle of Brownstown, Which was Fought on the 9th of August 1812, During the Campaign of the North Western Army Under the Command of Brigadier General Hull. New York: 1816. V. 42

DALLIMORE, W.

Poisonous Plants; Deadly, Dangerous and Suspect. London: 1927. V. 45

DALLINGTON, ROBERT

Aphorismes, Civill and Militarie. London: 1613. V. 38; 40; 42; 43

A Survey of the Great Dukes State of Tuscany, in the Yeare of Our Lord 1596. London: 1605. V. 38

DALLY, JOSEPH W.

Woodbridge & Vicinity. New Brunswick: 1873. V. 39; 41

DALLY, NATE

Tracks and Trails of Incidents in the Life of a Minnesota Territorial Pioneer. Walker, Mn.: 1931. V. 37

D'ALMEIDA, WILLIAM BARRINGTON

Life in Java: With Sketches of the Javanese. London: 1864. V. 38

DALMON, C. W.

Song Favors. Chicago: 1895. V. 38

DALRYMPLE,

Plan for Promoting the Fur-Trade and Securing It to This Country. Montreal: 1975. V. 40

DALRYMPLE, ALEXANDER

A Collection of Charts and Memoirs. London: 1769-72. V. 42

An Historical Collection of the Several Voyages and Discoveries in the South Pacific Ocean. London: 1770, 1771. V. 39; 42; 44; 45

Memoir of a Chart of the Southern Ocean. London: 1769. V. 42

Roteiro do Neptuna Oriental Para Usa Das Cartas. Lisbon: 1783. V. 41

DALRYMPLE, CAMPBELL

Extracts from a Military Essay. Philadelphia: 1776. V. 37; 39; 40; 42

DALRYMPLE, DAVID 1665-ca. 1721

Annals of Scotland. Edinburgh: 1776-79. V. 41; 42

An Inquiry Into the Secondary Causes Which Mr. Gibbon Has Assigned for the Rapid Growth of Christianity. Edinburgh: 1786. V. 45

DALRYMPLE, DAVID, 3RD BARONET, LORD HAILES

Annals of Scotland from the Accession of Malcolm III in the Year MLVII to the Accession of the House of Stewart in the Year MCCCLXXI. Edinburgh: 1819. V. 38

Memorials and Letters Relating to the History of Britian in the Reign of James I. Glasgow: 1762. V. 38

Memorials and Letters Relating to the History of Britian in the Reign of James the First. Glasgow: 1766. V. 40

Tracts Relative to the History and Antiquities of Scotland. Edinburgh: 1800. V. 38

DALRYMPLE, HUGH

Rodondo: or the State Jugglers. Canto I, Canto II, Canto III. London: 1763, 1770. V. 38

Rodondo; or the State Jugglers. Cantos I-III. London: 1763-63-70. V. 42

Rondondo; or the State Jugglers. London: 1763. V. 40

DALRYMPLE, JAMES fl. 1714

Collections Concerning the Scottish History, Preceeding the Death of King David I in . . . 1153 . . . Edinburgh: 1705. V. 41

DALRYMPLE, JOHN

The Address of the People of Great Britain to the Inhabitants of America. London: 1775. V. 38; 40; 45; 46

The Question Considered, Whether Wool Should be Allowed to Be Exported, When the Price is Low at Home, on Paying a Duty to the Public? London: 1781. V. 40; 43

DALRYMPLE, JOHN, 4TH BARONET 1726-1810

Memoirs of Great Britain and Ireland from the Dissolution of the last Parliament of Charles II until the Sea-Battle of La Hogue. London: 1771-1788. V. 38

Memoirs of Great Britain and Ireland. London/Edinburgh: 1771/3. V. 37; 38

Memoirs of Great Britain and Ireland; from the Dissolution of the Last Parliament of Charles II. London: 1790. V. 41

DALTON, CHARLES

A Christmas Eve Family Story. Boston: 1904. V. 40

George the First's Army 1714-1727. London: 1910-12. V. 41

D'ALTON, E. A.

The History of Ireland from the Earliest Times to the Present Day. Dublin and Belfast. V. 40; 46

DALTON, EMMETT

When the Daltons Rode. New York: 1931. V. 42; 46

DALTON, HENRY G.

History of British Guiana. London: 1855. V. 39

DALTON, J.

The Gentleman in Black. London: 1831. V. 38

DALTON, JAMES

Chartley the Fatalist. London: 1831. V. 41

The Invisible Gentleman. London: 1833. V. 41

DALTON, JOHN

An Epistle to a Young Nobleman, from His Praeceptor. London: 1736. V. 37; 39; 40; 45

The History of the County of Dublin. Dublin: 1838. V. 37; 42; 44; 45

Illustrations, historical and genealogical, of King James's Irish Army List, (1689). Dublin: 1855. V. 37

Meteorological Observations and Essays. London: 1793. V. 38; 41; 42; 44; 45

Meterological Observations and Essays. Manchester: 1834. V. 40

A New System of Chemical Philosophy. Manchester: 1808. V. 37; 42

A New System of Chemical Philosophy. Parts I and II. Manchester: 1808-10. V. 38

A New System of Chemical Philosophy. Manchester: 1808-10-27. V. 42

Sequel to an Essay on the Constitution of the Atmosphere. London: 1837. V. 38; 40; 46

Two Epistles. The First, to a Young Nobleman from His Preceptor. Written in the year 1735-6. The second, to the Right Honourable the Countess of Harford, at Percy Lodge: in the Year 1744. London: 1745. V. 38

DALTON, JOHN CALL 1825-1889

Topogrpahical Anatomy of the Brain. Philadelphia: 1885. V. 41; 42; 45

A Treatise on Human Physiology. Philadelphia: 1859. V. 38

A Treatise on Human Physiology. Philadelphia: 1861. V. 42

DALTON, KIT

Under the Black Flag. Memphis: 1914. V. 39; 42

DALTON, MCIAHEL d. 1648

The Country Justice . . . In the Savoy: 1777. V. 45

DALTON, MICHAEL d. 1648

The Countrey Jusftice, Containing the Practice of the Juftices of the Peace Out of Their Session . . . London: 1661. V. 44

The Country Justice. London: 1727. V. 38; 40

Officium Vicecomitum. The Office and Authority of Sherifs . . . London: 1670. V. 38; 40

Officium Vicecomitum. London: 1623. V. 37

DALTON, O. M.

Byzantine Art and Archaeology. Oxford: 1911. V. 39; 43

Catalogue of the Engraved Gems of the Post-Classical Periods in the Department of British and Mediaeval Antiquities and Ethnography in the British Museum. London: 1915. V. 37

East Christian Art. A Survey of the Monuments. Oxford: 1925. V. 37

The Treasure of Oxus with Other Examples of Early Oriental Metal-Work. London: 1926. V. 44

The Treasure of the Oxus and Other Examples of Early Oriental Metal-Work. London: 1964. V. 37; 40; 42

DALTON, RICHARD

A Series of Views in Sicily, Greece, Turkey and Egypt. (and) Manners, Customs, &c. of the Present Inhabitants of Egypt. London: 1751-52. V. 37

DALTON, WILLIAM

Phaulcon the Adventurer; or, the Europeans in the East. London: 1862. V. 39; 43

DALVIMART, OCTAVIEN

The Costume of Turkey. London: 1802. V. 38

DALY, AUGUSTIN

Woffington: a Tribute to the Actress and the Woman. Philadelphia: 1888. V. 45

DALY, CESAR

L'Architecture Privee au XIXe Siecle, Nouvelles Maisons de parais et des Environs. Paris: 1870/72/77. V. 38

Decorations Interieures. Paris: 1877. V. 46

Historical Motifs of Architecture and Sculpture in France: Interior Work, Epochs Francis I-Louis XVI. New York: 1880. V. 39

Historical Motifs of Architecture and Sculpture in France: Interior Work, Epochs Francis I-Louis XVI. New York: 1880. V. 41

Historical Motifs of Architecture and Sculpture in France . . . New York: 1920. V. 46

DALY, JOHN CARROLL

Tainted Power. New York: 1931. V. 42

DALY, LOUISE HASKELL

Alexander Cheves Haskell: the Portrait of a Man. Norwood: 1934. V. 37; 45

DALY, MARY

Gyn/Ecology. Boston: 1979. V. 46

Pure Lust. 1984. V. 42

DALY, T. A.

Madrigali. Philadelphia: 1912. V. 43; 46

DALYELL, JOHN GRAHAM

The Darker Supersitions of Scotland. Edinburgh: 1834. V. 38

The Darker Superstitions of Scotland. Glasgow: 1835. V. 45

Fragments of Scotish (sic) History. Edinburgh: 1798. V. 38; 41

Shipwrecks and Disasters at Sea. Edinburgh: 1812. V. 45

DALZIEL, GEORGE

The Brothers Dalziel. London: 1901. V. 37; 38; 42; 44

DALZIEL, THE BROTHERS

Dalziels' Illustrated Arabian Nights' Entertainments. The text revised and emendated throughout H.W. Dulcken. With upwards of two hundred illustrations by eminent artists . . . London: (n.d.). V. 37

DALZIEL'S Bible Gallery. London: 1881. V. 39

DAMASCENE, JOHN 700-754

Theologia . . . quatuor libris explicata. Paris: 1512. V. 37

DAMASCINOS, Metropolitan of Switzerland, et al: The Oecumenical Patrilarchate. The Great Church of Christ. Athens: 1989. V. 45

DAMASE, JACQUES

Rhythms and Colours. London: 1972. V. 46

DAMBERGER, CHRISTIAN FREDERICK

Travels in the Interior of Africa, from the Cape of Good Hope to Morocco, 1781 to 1797, Through Caffraria, the Kingdoms of Mataman, Angola, etc . . . Likewise Across the Great Desert of Sahara and the Northern Parts of Barbay. London: 1801. V. 39; 45; 46

D'AMBROSIO, JOSEPH J.

Birds of Paradise (or) Life Upon a Japanese Screen. Sherman Oaks: 1985. V. 37; 38; 39

Nineteen Years and Counting; a Retrospective Bibliography 1969-1988. Los Angeles: 1989. V. 41

Nineteen Years and Counting: a Retrospective Bibliography 1969 to 1988. Sherman Oaks: 1989. V. 42

The Small Garden of Gloria Stuart. Sherman Oaks: 1986. V. 37; 40; 42

THE DAME and Her Donkeys Five. Deborah Dent and Her Donkey. Dame Wiggins of Lee. London: 1887-8. V. 38; 41

LES DAMES de Byron; or, Portraits of the Principal Female Characters in Lord Byron's Poems. London: 1836. V. 40

DAMI, LUIGI

The Intalian Garden. New York: 1925. V. 45

DAMON & PEETS

Specimen Book, Types and Borders, Ornaments and Brass Rules, Catalogue of Printing Machinery and Printers' Supplies. New York: 1906. V. 41

DAMON, ETHEL M.

Koamalu. A Story of Pioneers on Kauai and of What They Built in the Island Garden. Honolulu: 1931. V. 37; 42

DAMON, S. FOSTER

Note on the Discovery of a New Page of Poetry in William Blake's Milton. Boston: 1925. V. 42

William Blake: His Philosophy and Symbols. Boston: 1924. V. 44

DAMON, SAMUEL C.

The Friend . . . a Journal Devoted to Temperance, Seamen, Marine and General Intelligence. Honolulu: 1844-82. V. 42

A Journey to Lower Oregon and Upper California 1848-9. San Francisco: 1927. V. 37; 38

A Trip from the Sandwich Islands, to Lower Oregon and Upper California . . . Honolulu: 1849. V. 44

DAMON, WILLIAM E.

Ocean Wonder: a Companion for the Seaside . . . New York: 1879. V. 44

DAMPIER, WILLIAM 1652-1715

A Collection of Voyages. London: 1729. V. 45

A History of Science and Its Relations with Philosophy and Religion. Cambridge: 1942. V. 41

A New Voyage Round the World. (with) Voyages and Descriptions Volume Two, A Voyage To New Holland . . . A Continuation of a Voyage to New Holland. London: 1697/99/1703/09. V. 41

A New Voyage Round the World. London: 1699. V. 46

A New Voyage Round the World. (with) Voyages and Descriptions. London: 1699 & 1705. V. 38; 41

A New Voyage Round the World. (with) Voyages and Descriptions. (with) A Voyage to New Holland, &c . . . (with) A Continuation of a Voyage to New Holland, &c . . . London: 1717/05/09. V. 41

A New Voyage Round the World the 1679-91 . . . London: 1927. V. 39

A New Voyage Round the World. London: 1927. V. 37; 38; 39; 45; 46

A New Voyage Round the World. Illustrated with Particular Maps and Draughts. London: 1698. V. 37

A Voyage to New Holland. 1939. V. 39

A Voyage to New Holland. 1939. V. 37

Dampier's Voyages, Consisting of a New Voyage Round the World, A Supplement to othe Voyage Round the World. London: 1906. V. 38

Voyages and Discoveries. London: 1927. V. 42; 44; 46

Voyages and Discoveries. London: 1931. V. 38; 40; 45

DAMPIER, WILLIAM JAMES

A Memoir of John Carter. London: 1850. V. 40; 43; 44

A Memoir of John Carter. London: 1850. V. 40

DAN de Quille of the Big Bonanza. San Francisco: 1980. V. 46

DANA, C. W.

The Garden of the World, or the Great West. Boston: 1856. V. 40; 41; 43; 45

DANA, CHARLES A.

The United States Illustrated. New York: 1855. V. 37; 39; 42; 45

The United States Illustrated: In Views of City and Country. New York: 1865. V. 42

DANA, DANIEL

Memoirs of Eminently Pious Women, Who Were Ornaments to Their Sex . . . London: 1803. V. 45

DANA, EDMUND

Geographical Sketches on the Western Country, Designed for Emigrants and Settlers. Cincinnati: 1819. V. 38; 39; 41; 42; 43; 45

DANA, JAMES DWIGHT 1813-1895

Characteristics of Volcanoes with Contributions of Facts and Principles from the Hawaiian Islands. London: 1890. V. 37; 40

Corals and Coral Islands. London: 1872. V. 39; 42; 43

Corals and Coral Islands. New York: 1872. V. 37; 40; 43

Corals and Coral Islands. New York: 1879. V. 38; 41

Descriptive Mineralogy. London: 1883. V. 43

Descriptive Mineralogy. London: & New York: 1883. V. 42

The 'Examination of the Late Rev'd President Edwards's Enquiry on Freedom of Will,' Continued . . . to which are Subjoined, Strictures on the Rev'd Mr. West's 'Essay on Moral Agency.' New Haven: 1773. V. 39

United States Exploring Expedition . . . Atlas. Zoophytes. Philadelphia: 1859. V. 39; 40

DANA, JAMES F.

Outlines of the Mineralogy and Geology of Boston and Its Vicinity, with a Geological Map. Boston: 1818. V. 43

Report on a Disease Afflicting Neat Cattle, in Burton, N.H. Read Before the New Hampshire Medical Society . . . June 1822. Concord: 1822. V. 43

DANA, JAMES FREEMAN 1793-1827

An Epitome of Chymical Philosophy . . . Concord: 1825. V. 42

DANA, RICHARD HENRY 1815-1882

An Oration Delivered Before the Washington Benevolent Society at Cambridge, July 4, 1814. Cambridge: 1814. V. 39; 43

Richard Henry Dana Architect. New York: 1965. V. 46

The Seaman's Friend. Boston: 1841. V. 37; 38; 44

The Seaman's Friend. Boston: 1851. V. 39

The Seaman's Manual - A treatise on practical seamanship, rigging, making sail, and handling a full-rigged ship, with a dictionary of sea terms and plates on spars, rigging, sails and types of ships. London: 1846. V. 37

To Cuba and Back. Boston: 1859. V. 40

To Cuba and Back. London: 1859. V. 42

Two Years Before the Mast. London. V. 40

Two Years Before the Mast. New York: 1840. V. 37; 38; 39; 40; 41; 42; 43; 44; 45

Two Years Before the Mast. London: 1841. V. 37; 43; 44

Two Years Before the Mast. New York: 1841. V. 39

Two Years Before the Mast. Boston: 1869. V. 38; 39; 41; 45; 46

Two Years Before the Mast. Chicago: 1930. V. 37; 38; 39; 43; 45; 46

Two Years Before the Mast. New York: 1936. V. 42

Two Years Before the Mast . . . New York: 1957. V. 41

Two Years Before the Mast. Los Angeles: 1964. V. 39; 40; 43

William Beach Lawrence vs. Richard H. Dana . . . Brief for the Complainant. Boston: 1867. V. 41

DANA, SAMUEL L.

A Muck Manual for Farmers . . . Lowell: 1851. V. 40

DANA, SAMUEL W.

Yale-College Subject to the General Assembly. New Haven: 1784. V. 37; 38

DANBY, THOMAS OSBORNE, EARL OF

A Collection of Some Memorable and Weighty Transactions in Paliament, in the Year 1678 and Afterwards. London: 1695. V. 41

Copies & Extracts of Some Letters Written to and From the Earl of Danby . . . London: 1710. V. 46

Memoirs Relating to the Impeachment of Thomas, Earl of Danby, Now Duke of Leeds . . . London: 1710. V. 46

DANCE Book. French: 1840. V. 37

DANCE, CHARLES DANIEL

Recollections of Four Years in Venezuela. London: 1876. V. 40

DANCE, GEORGE 1741-1825

A Collection of Portraits Sketched from the Life Since the Year 1793. London: 1809, 1814. V. 39

The Representation of the Lease-Holders and Contractors Interested in the House and Buildings in Picket Street, Near Temple Bar . . . London: 1806. V. 37

DANCE OF DEATH

The Celebrated Hans Holbein's Alphabet of Death. Paris: 1856. V. 45

The Dance of Death. London: 1816. V. 41; 43

The Dance of Death of the Celebrated Hans Holbein; in a Series of Fifty-Two Engravings on Wood by Mr. Bewick. London: 1825. V. 43; 45

Holbein's Dance of Death. London: 1858. V. 41; 44

Dances of Death. London: 1803. V. 43

Death's Doings . . . Boston: 1828. V. 43

La Grande Danse Macabre des Hommes et des Femmes, Historiee & Renouvellee de Vieux Gaulois . . . Troyes: 1728. V. 44

Imagines Mortis. Coloniae: 1572. V. 44

THE DANCING Dolls. London: 1910. V. 46

DANCKERTS, CORNELIS

D'Volgende Deuren syn Geteekent op de Amsterdamse Voetmaet van 11 Duyn. Amsterdam. V. 38

DANDOLO, VINCENZO, CONTE 1758-1819

The Art of Rearing Silk-Worms. London: 1825. V. 39; 42

DANDY, WALTER EDWARD 1886-1946

Benign Tumors in the Third Ventricle of the Brain: Diagnosis and Treatment. Springfield: 1933. V. 37; 41; 42; 45

Benign Tumors in the Third Ventricle of the Brain: Diagnosis and Treatment. Springfield & Baltimore: 1933. V. 45

Intracranial Arterial Aneurysms. Ithaca: 1944. V. 42

Intercranial Arterial Aneurysms. Ithaca: 1945. V. 37; 45

Orbital Tumors. Results Following the Transcranial Operative Attack. New York: 1941. V. 38

Selected Writings of Walter E. Dandy. Springfield: 1957. V. 42; 45

Surgery of the Brain. Hagerstwon: 1945. V. 42

DANE, CLEMENCE

A Bill of Divorcement by Clemence Dane. London: (1930). V. 37

He Brings Great News by Clemence Dane. London: (1944). V. 37

Wild Decembers by Clemence Dane. Garden City: (1933). V. 37

DANE, EDMUND

British Campaigns in the Nearer East 1914-1918. London: 1919. V. 46

DANE, RICHARD

Sport in Asia and Africa. London: 1921. V. 42

DANE, SILAS

The Deane Papers 1774-1790. New York: 1887-1891. V. 44

DANEBURY; or the Power of Friendship, a Tale. Bristol: 1755? V. 40; 42

DANES, RICHARD

Cassell's History of the Boer War 1899-1902. London: 1903. V. 42

Cassel's History of the Boer War, 1899-1902. London: 1902. V. 39

DANET, GUILLAUME

L'Art des Armes. Paris: 1788. V. 37

DANET, PIERRE

A Complete Dictionary of the Greek and Roman Antiquities . . . London: 1700. V. 42

DANETT, THOMAS

A Continuation of the Historie of France, From the Death of Charles the Eighth . . . London: 1600. V. 45

The Historie of Philip De Commines Knight, Lord of Argenton. London: 1614. V. 37

DANFORTH, I. N.

The Life of Nathan Smith Davis. Chicago: 1907. V. 39

DANFORTH, JOSHUA N.

Faithful Elder: a Memoir of David M. Wilson . . . Philadelphia: 1860. V. 44

THE DANGER and Unreasonableness of a Toleration: in Reference to Some Late Papers Which Have Passed Concerning Liberty of Conscience. London: 1685. V. 42

DANGER, T. P.

The Art of Glass Blowing. 1831. V. 40

THE DANGEROUS Consequences of Parliamentary Divisions. Occasion'd by Refusal of the Place Bill, the Act of Indemnity, &c. London: 1742. V. 41

DANGEROUS Errors. London: 1822. V. 39; 42

THE DANGERS of Europe, from the Growing Power of France, with Some Free Thoughts on Remedies. London: 1702. V. 40; 46

DANICAN, FRANCOIS ANDRE

Chess Rendered Familiar by Tabular Demonstrations . . . London: 1819. V. 39

DANIEL CHARLES

Al. A Social Vision. Philadelphia: 1892. V. 41

DANIEL, DAVID

Axolotl. University of Massachusetts: 1975. V. 37

DANIEL, GABRIEL

A Voyage to the World of Cartesius. London: 1692. V. 37; 39; 46

A Voyage to the World of Cartesius. London: 1694. V. 40

DANIEL, GEORGE 1789-1864

Catalogue of the most valuable, interesting and Highly Important Library of the late George Daniel, Esq. of Canonbury, together with his collection of original Drawings and engraved Portraits of . . . London: (1864). V. 37; 38; 39; 41; 42

Democritus in London: with Mad Pranks and Comical Conceits of Motley and Robin Good-Fellow. London: 1852. V. 39

Love's Last Labour Not Lost. London: 1863. V. 38

Merrie England in the Olden Time. London: 1842. V. 43

The Modern Dunciad, Virgil in London, and Other Poems. London: 1835. V. 39

The Times; a Poem. London: 1810. V. 42

DANIEL, J. FREDERIC

An Introduction to the Study of Chemical Philosophy. London: 1839. V. 38

DANIEL, JOHN

The Life and Astonishing Adventures of John Daniel, a Smith at Royston in Hertfordshire . . . London: 1770. V. 42

DANIEL, MR.

A Bill Supplemental to the Act for the Admission of the States of Iowa and Florida Into the Union. Washington: 1845. V. 46

DANIEL PRESS

Pulls from Formes in the Clarendon Press. Oxford: 1923. V. 46

DANIEL, ROBERT MACKENZIE

The Poor Cousin. London: 1846. V. 41

DANIEL-ROPS, HENRI

History of the Church of Christ. London: 1963-67. V. 39

DANIEL, SAMUEL

A Panegyrike Congratulatorie Delivered to the Kings Most Excellent Maiestie at Burleigh Harrington in Rutlandshire . . . London: 1603. V. 43

The Vision of the 12 Goddesses . . . London: 1604. V. 45

The Works of Samuel Daniel Newly Augmented. London: 1601. V. 37

The Complete Works in Verse and Prose. London: 1885-1896. V. 43; 45

DANIEL, W. B.

Rural Sports. London: 1802-13. V. 45

DANIEL, WILLIAM B.

Rural Sports. London: 1801. V. 39; 46

Rural Sports. London: 1801-02-13. V. 46

Rural Spots. London: 1801-13. V. 40

Rural Sports. London: 1813. V. 40

Sketches Representing the Native Tribes, Animals and Scenery of Southern Africa . . . London: 1820. V. 40

DANIELL, J. FREDERIC

An Introduction to the Study of Chemical Philosophy. London: 1839. V. 38; 46

DANIELL, JOHN F.

Elements of Meteorology. London: 1845. V. 37; 39

DANIELL, L. E.

Personnel of the Texas State Government with Sketches of Distinguished Texans . . . Austin: 1887. V. 37

Types of Successful Men of Texas. Austin: 1890. V. 38

DANIELL, S.

African Scenery and Animals. London: 1804-05. V. 42

DANIELL, THOMAS

Oriental Scenery. London: 1812-16. V. 42

A Picturesque Voyage to India; by the Way of China. London: 1810. V. 43

DANIELL, WILLIAM

The Adventures of Hunch-back and the Stories Connected With It. London: 1814. V. 41

The Oriental Annual, or Scenes in India . . . London: 1835. V. 42

Six Views of London. London: 1804-05. V. 39

Sketches Representing the Native Tribes, Animals and Scenery of Southern Africa. London: 1820. V. 42

A Voyage Round Great Britain. Under-taken in the Summer of the Year 1813 and Commencing from the Land's End, Cornwall . . . London: 1814-25. V. 41

A Voyage Round Great Britain. London: 1814-26. V. 44

DANIELLE, T. G.

California, Its Products, Resources, Industries & Attractions. Sacramento: 1909. V. 38

DANIELSON, HENRY

Arthur Machen: a Bibliography. London: 1923. V. 42

The First Editions of the Writings of Thomas Hardy and Their Values. London: 1916. V. 38

DANISH 'Dana' Expeditions 1920-22 in the North Atlantic and the Gulf of Panama. Copenhagen: 1926-31. V. 37

THE DANISH Laws; or, the Code of Christian the Fifth. London: 1756. V. 41

DANKARS, JASPAR

Journal of a Voyage to New York and a Tour in Several of the American Colonies in 1679-80. Brooklyn: 1867. V. 45

DANNELEY, JOHN FELTHAM

An Encyclopaedia or Dictionary of Music . . . London: 1825. V. 43

DANNENBERG, JOSEPH

Film Year Book 1922-1923/1924. New York. V. 46

DANNESKIOLD, CHRISTIAN

Bibliotheca Daneschioldiana. (and) Verzeichniss Derer Sachen. Copenhagen: 1732-32-31. V. 38; 40

DANREITER, FRANZ ANTON

Vier and Zwantzig Garten-Grund-Risse. Salzburg: 1740. V. 40

DANTE and His Circle: With the Italian Poets Preceding Him (1100-1200-1300). London: 1874. V. 41; 46

DANTE, ALIBHIERI 1265-1321

Dante Petrarch Camoens CXXIV Sonnets. London & Boston: 1896. V. 40

DANTE, ALIGHIERI 1265-1321

La Comedia. Venice: 1497. V. 46

Comedia . . . con la Dotta . . . Venice: 1536. V. 42

La Comedia Con la Nova Expositione di Alessandro Velutello. Venice: 1544. V. 37

Comedia con l'Espositione de M. Bernardino Daniello da Lucca. Venice: 1568. V. 40

The Comedy of Dante Alighieri of Florence. San Francisco: 1929. V. 45

Dante, Con Lespositione di Christoforo Landino, et Di Alessandro Vellutello, Spora La Sua Comedia Dell'Inferno . . . Venice: 1564. V. 37

Con le Spositioni di Christophoro Landino, e d'Allesandro Vellutello, Sopra la Sua Commendia dell'Inferno, del Purgatorio e del Paradiso, con Tavole, Argomenti & Allegorie . . . Venetiis: 1578. V. 37

Il Dante, Con Argomenti & Dechiaratione ne de Molti Luoghi, Novamente Reuisto & Stampato. Lyon: 1547. V. 41

Dante Con l'Espositioni di Christoforo Landino et d'Alessandro Vellutello. Venetia: 1596. V. 38

La Divina Comedia . . . Venice: 1629. V. 39

La Divina Comedia di . . . Firenze: 1821. V. 39

La Divina Commedia . . . London: 1826-27. V. 40; 41

The Divine Comedy of . . . London: 1867. V. 39

La Divina Commedia. Munich: 1921. V. 44

The Comedy of Dante Alighieri. V. 45

La Commedia. Venice: 1484. V. 40

La Comedia. Brescia: 1487. V. 38

La Divina Commedia . . . Florence: 1595. V. 38

The Divini Commedia of . . . London: 1802. V. 38; 43

The Comedy of . . . London and Cambridge: 1865. V. 43

The Divine Comedy of Dante Alighieri. Boston: 1899. V. 41

The Divine Comedy. London: 1900. V. 46

La Divina Commedia. Chelsea: 1902-05. V. 45

(The Divine Comedy). The Vision of Purgatory and Paradise; The Vision of Hell. London: 1903. V. 46

The Divine Comedy. New York: 1906. V. 43

La Divina Comedia. Zurich: 1921. V. 45

La Divina Commedia, or the Divine Vision . . . London: 1928. V. 37; 38; 39; 40; 41; 42; 43; 45; 46

The Divine Comedy. 1929. V. 44

The Divine Comedy. New York: 1932. V. 37; 42

The Divine Comedy. New York: 1932. V. 44; 45; 46

The Divine Comedy. Verona: 1932. V. 44

The Divine Comedy. 1933. V. 40

The Divine Comedy of . . . New York: 1955. V. 39; 45; 46

The (Divine) Comedy. San Francisco: 1958. V. 38; 43; 46

The (Divine) Comedy. New York: 1969. V. 41; 43; 45

Divine Comedy, commentary by Christopher Landino. London. V. 37

The Dore Dante. London: 1904. V. 42

The Dore Dante. London: 1914. V. 38

A Translation of the Inferno . . . in English Verse. London: 1785. V. 40

The First Ten Cantos of the Inferno. Boston: 1843. V. 44

Lo Inferno. Chelsea: 1902. V. 41

The Inferno from La Divina Commedia of . . . New York: 1931. V. 41; 42; 45

The New Life. London: 1911. V. 43

The New Life. London: 1916. V. 44

(Opera) con l'Espositione di Christofor Landino et di Alessandro Vellutello, Sopra la Sua Comedia dell'Inferno, del Purgatorio . . . Venice: 1578. V. 40

Opere del Divino Poeta Danthe con Suoi Comenti: Recorrecti et Con Ogne Diligentia Novamente in Littera Cursiva Impresse. Venetia: 1512. V. 46

Opere. Venice: 1757-1758. V. 41; 42

Opere Del Divino Poeta Dante/ Venetia: 1520. V. 37

The Paradiso of Dante, Translated. London: 1840. V. 41

The Purgatorio of Dante. London: 1836. V. 43

Rime di Diversi Antichi Avtori Toscani in Dieci Libri Raccolte. Venice: 1532. V. 45

Sonetti e Canzoni di Diversi Antichi Autori Toscani . . . Florence: 1527. V. 40

The Stone Beloved: Six Poems. Austin: 1986. V. 37; 38; 39; 41; 44; 45

Le Terze Rime. Venice: 1502. V. 40; 41; 43

The Vision of Hell. London: 1866. V. 45

The Vision; or, Hell, Purgatory and Paradise. London: 1892. V. 37

La Vita Nuova (the New Life). London. V. 43

La Vita Nuova. 1895. V. 39

La Vita Nuova. Ashendene: 1895. V. 40

La Vita Nuova . . . Ashendene: 1895. V. 42; 43

La Vita Nuova. Firenze: 1910. V. 40

La Vita Nuova. London: 1916? V. 39; 41; 42

La Vita Nuova. London: 1916? V. 41

Vita Nuova di Dante. Montagnola: 1925. V. 38; 41; 44; 46

DANTE Gabriel Rossetti: An Illustrated Memorial of His Art and Life. London: 1899. V. 45

DANTI, IGNATIO 1536-1586

Dell'Uso et Fabricia dell'Astrolabio et Del Planisferio. Florence: 1578. V. 40

Trattato Dell' Uso et Della Fabbrica dell' Astrolabio . . . Florence: 1569. V. 45

D'ANVERS, CALEB

The Craftsman. London: 1731-37. V. 38

DANVERS, F. C.

The Portuguese in India Being a History of the Rise and Decline of Their Eastern Empire. London: 1894. V. 46

DANVERS, JOHN THIERRY

A Picture of a Republican Magistrate of the New School. New York: 1808. V. 44

D'ANVILLE, MONS.

A Complete Body of Ancient Geography . . . London: 1818. V. 38

DAPPER, OLFERT

Description Exacte des Isles de l'Archipel, et de Quelques Autres Adjacents . . . Amsterdam: 1703. V. 40

DAPPERT, OLFERT

Historische Beschrijving der Stadt. Amsterdam: 1663. V. 45

D'ARANDA, EMANUEL

The History of Algiers and Its Slavery. With Many Remarkable Particularities of Africk. London: 1666. V. 39

D'ARBELOFF, NATALIE

Philosophy. 1990. V. 45

DARBISHIRE, HELEN

Some Variants in Wordworth's Text in the Volumes of 1836-7 in the King's Library. Oxford: 1949. V. 40

D'ARBLAY, FRANCES BURNEY 1752-1840

Camilia. London: 1802. V. 37

Camilla or a Picture of Youth by the Author of Evelina and Cecilia. Dublin: 1796. V. 37

Camilla: or, a Picture of Youth. By the Author of Evelina and Cecilia. In Five Volumes. London: 1796. V. 37

Cecilia. London: 1782. V. 37

Cecilia or Memoirs of an Heiress by the Author of Evelina. London: 1783. V. 37

Diary and Letters. London: 1900. V. 37

Diary and Letters. London: 1904. V. 37

Diary and Letters of Madame D'Arblay. London: 1842-46. V. 37

Evelina. London: 1779. V. 37

Evelina; or, the History of a Young Lady's Entrance into the World. London: 1898. V. 37

DARBY, CHARLES

Bacchanalia; or a Description of a DRunken Club. London: 1680. V. 38; 41; 42; 45

DARBY, JOHN F.

Personal Recollections of many Prominent People Whom I Have Known and of Events . . . St. Louis: 1880. V. 40

DARBY, WILLIAM 1755-1854

Darby's Universal Gazetteer, or, a New Geographical Dictionary . . . Philadelphia: 1827. V. 45; 46

A Dictionary, Geographical, Historical and Statistical . . . Philadelphia: 1842. V. 45

The Emigrant's Guide to the Western and Southwestern States and Territories . . . New York: 1818. V. 42

Geographical Description of the State of Lousiana . . . Philadelphia: 1816. V. 39; 40; 43

A Geographical Description of the State of Louisiana. Philadelphia: 1816. V. 43

A Geographical Description of the State of Louisiana, the Southern Part of the State of Mississippi, and Territory of Alabama . . . New York: 1817. V. 38

Memoir on the Geography and Natural and Civil History of Florida . . . Philadelphia: 1821. V. 41

A New Gazetteer of the United States of America . . . Including, other Interesting and Valuable Geographical, historical, political, and Statistical Information; with the Population of 1830. Hartford: 1833. V. 37; 38; 40

A Tour From the City of New-York, To Detroit, in the Michigan Territory. New York: 1819. V. 37; 38; 39; 41; 42; 43; 45

View of the United States . . . Philadelphia: 1828. V. 42

DARBY, WILLIAM J.

Food: The Gift of Osiris. London: 1977. V. 37; 40

DARBYSHIRE, ALFRED

A Booke of Olde Manchester and Salford. Manchester: 1887. V. 38

DARCY, GEORGES

Idees 2. Paris: 1925. V. 38

Idees 2. Paris: 1925. V. 44

D'ARCY, HUGH ANTOINE

The Face Upon the Floor and Other Ballads. Brooklyn: 1912. V. 41

DARDE, JEAN

Histoire de ce qui s'est Passe au Royaume d'Ethiopie es Annees 1624, 1625 and 1626. Paris: 1629. V. 40; 45

DARE, JOSEPH

Counsellor Manners His Last Legacy to His Son . . . London: 1673. V. 38

DARELL, WILLIAM

The Gentleman Instructed, in the Conduct of a Virtuous and Happy Life. London: 1713. V. 43

DARIEN, PETER

Darien's World, a Compendium of Poems in Ten Slender Volumes. 1961. V. 46

Echo and Reflection. Berkeley Heights: 1935. V. 37; 40; 41

DARIOT, CLAUDE 1533-1594

Ad Astrorum Indicia Facilis Introductio . . . Eiusdem Tractatus . . . De Morbis & Diebus Criticis ex Astrorum Motu . . . Lyons: 1557. V. 42

DARIOTT, CLAUDIUS

Dariotus Redivivus; or a Briefe Introduction Conducing to the Judgement of the Stars. London: 1653. V. 45

DARIUS'S Feast; Or the Force of Truth . . . Addressed to . . . the Earl of Salisbury and Exeter. London: 1734. V. 37

DARJOU, A.

Le Caire et la haute Egypte. Paris: 1872. V. 45

DARKNESS at Noon; or, the Great Solar Eclipse of the 16th of June, 1806, Described and Represented in Every Particular. Boston: 1806. V. 39; 45
DARKNESS at Noon; or, the Great Solar Eclipse of the 16th of June, 1806, Described and Represented in Every Particular. New York: 1806. V. 45

DARLES DE LINIERE, M.

Pompes sans Cuirs. Paris: 1768. V. 42

DARLEY, ALEXANDER M.

The Passionists of the Southwest, or The Holy Brotherhood. Pueblo: 1893. V. 37; 40

DARLEY, FELIX 0CTAVIUS CARR 1822-1888

Pen and Pencil Sketches in Europe. Boston: 1890. V. 38

DARLEY, FELIX OCTAVIUS CARR 1822-1888

Character Sketches from Dickens. N.P.: 1888. V. 45

Character Sketches from Dickens. Boston: 1892. V. 40

Compositions in Outline from Judd's Margaret. New York: 1856. V. 40

Skethces Abroad with Pen and Pencil. New York: 1868. V. 40

DARLEY, GEORGE

The Labours of Idleness; or, Seven Nights' Entertainments. London: 1826. V. 46

The New Sketch Book; by G. Crayon, Jun. London: 1829. V. 37

Thomas a Becket. A Dramatic Chronicle. In Five Acts. London;: 1840. V. 37

D'ARLINCOURT, CHARLES VICTOR PREVOST

Ipsiboe. London: 1823. V. 42

D'ARLINCOURT, CHARLES VICTOR PREVOT

Charles the Bold; or, the Recluse of The Wild Mountain. London: 1821. V. 43

DARLING, CHARLES JOHN DARLING, 1ST BARON 1849-1936

On the Oxford Circuit and Other Verses. London: 1909. V. 40

DARLING, E. B.

The Great Dog Races of Nome. Held Under the Auspices of the Nome Kennel Club, Nome, Alaska. Nome: 1917. V. 44

DARLING, HENRY

Slavery and the War: an Historical Essay. Philadelphia: 1863. V. 45

DARLING, WILLIAM STEWART

A Presbyter of the Diocese of Toronto. London: 1849. V. 44

DARLINGTON, MARY C.

Fort Pitt and Letters from the Frontier. Pittsburgh: 1892. V. 42

DARLINGTON, WILLIAM

Flora Cestrica: an Attempt to Enumerate and Describe the Flowering and Filcoid Plants of Chester County, in the State of Pennsylvania. West Chester: 1837. V. 39; 41; 42

Flora Cestrica . . . Philadelphia: 1853. V. 42

Memorials of John Bartram and Humphry Marshall, with Notices of Their Botanical Contemporaries. Philadelphia: 1849. V. 37; 44

DARLY, MATTHEW

A Political and Satirical History of the Years 1756 and 1757. London: 1758. V. 38

DARNELL, A. W.

Hardy and Half Hardy Plants. London: 1930. V. 38; 43

DARNELL, ELIAS

A Journal Containing an Accurate and Interesting Account of the Hardships, Suffering, Battles, Defeat and Captivity of Those Heroic Kentucky Volunteers and Regulars. Philadelphia: 1854. V. 37; 38; 39; 42; 43; 45

D'ARNOUX, CHARLES ALBERT

The Communists of Paris 1871. London: 1874. V. 39; 44

The Communists of Paris 1871. Paris: London: 1874. V. 42

DARWIN, CHARLES ROBERT 1809-1882 continued

Journal of Researches . . . into the Natural History and Geology of the Countries Visited During the Voyage of H.M.S. Beagle . . . Cambridge: 1956. V. 46

The Voyage of HMS Beagle. New York: 1956. V. 44

The Journal of a Voyage in H.M.S. Beagle. Guildford: 1979. V. 39; 41

Journal of Researches into the Geology and Natural History of the Various Countries Visited by H. M. S. Beagle, Under the Command of Captain Fitzroy, R.N. from 1832-1836. London: 1840. V. 37

Journal of Researches into the Natural History and Geology of the Countries Visited During the Voyage of H.M.S. Beagle Round the World. London: 1869. V. 37

The Life and Letters of Charles Darwin. London: 1883. V. 40

Life and Letters. London: 1887. V. 37; 39; 40; 46

The Life and Letters of Charles Darwin . . . New York: 1887. V. 39; 40; 44

The Life and Letters of Charles Darwin. London: 1888. V. 37; 43; 45

The Life and Letters of Charles Darwin Including an Autobiographical Chapter. London: 1888-87. V. 45

A Monograph on the Fossil Lepadidae. London: 1851. V. 39

A Monograph on the Fossil Lepadidae, or, Pedunculated Cirripedes of Great Britain. (with) A Monograph on the Fossil Balanidae and Verrucidae of Great Britain. London: 1851, 1854. V. 37

A Monograph on the Sub-Class Cirripedia, with Figures of All the Species . . . London: 1851-54. V. 46

More Letters of Charles Darwin. London: 1903. V. 37; 40

The Movements and Habits of Climbing Plants. London: 1875. V. 42

The Movements and Habits of Climbing Plants. London: 1876. V. 40

Narrative of the Surveying Voyage of H. M. Ships Adventure and Beagle Between the Years 1826 and 1836. London: 1839. V. 37; 38; 39; 44; 45; 46

Narrative of the Surveying Voyages of H. M. Ships Adventure and Beagle Between the Years 1826 and 1836. London: 1839-40. V. 37; 38

On the Origin of Species by Means of Natural Selection . . . London: 1859. V. 37; 38; 41; 42; 43; 44; 46

On the Origin of the Species by Means of Natural Selection . . . 1860. V. 46

On the Origin of Species by Means of Natural Selection. London: 1860. V. 37; 42; 45

On the Origin of the Species by Means of natural selection, or the Preservation of Favoured Races in the Struggle for Life. New York: 1860. V. 39; 40; 41; 46

On the Origin of Species by Means of Natural Selection. London: 1866. V. 39; 45

The Origin of Species by Means of Natural Selection. London: 1875. V. 37; 38

The Origin of Species by Means of Natural Selection . . . London: 1880. V. 40

The Origin of the Species by Means of Natural Selection, or the Preservation of Favoured Races in the Struggle for Life. London: 1886. V. 43

On the Origin of Species. London: 1897. V. 40

On the Origin of Species by Means of Natural Selection . . . New York: 1963. V. 38; 41

On the Various Contrivances by Which British and Foreign Orchids are Fertilised by Insects . . . London: 1862. V. 37

On Various Contrivances by Which British and Foreign Orchids are Fertilised by Insects. London: 1862. V. 40

The Various Contrivances by Which Orchids are Fertilised by Insects. London: 1890. V. 40

The Power of Movement in Plants. London: 1880. V. 37; 42

Selected Works. New York. V. 45

The Structure and Distribution of Coral Reefs. London: 1889. V. 43

The Structure and Distribution of Coral Reefs. London: 1874. V. 37

The Variation of Animals and Plants Under Domestication. London: 1868. V. 37; 38; 39; 40; 42; 43; 44; 45; 46

The Variation of Animals and Plants Under Domestication. New York: 1868. V. 40

The Variation of Animals and Plants Under Domestication. Stuttgart: 1868. V. 40

The Variation of Animals and Plants Under Domestication. London: 1875. V. 38; 46

The Variation of Animals and Plants Under Domestication. New York: 1876. V. 42

The Variation of Animals and Plants Under Domestication. London: 1882. V. 39

The Variation of Animals and Plants Under Domestication. London: 1893. V. 37

The Variation of Animals and Plants Under Domestication. New York: 1968. V. 46

The Various Contrivances by Which Orchids are Fertilised by Insects. London: 1877. V. 38; 39; 42

The Various Contrivances by Which Orchids are Fertilised by Insects. London: 1882. V. 39

Voyage of a Naturalist. 1846. V. 43

Works. London: 1890-1900. V. 42

Zoology of the Voyage of H.M.S. Beagle, Part I, Fossil Mammlia. London: 1838-40. V. 38

The Zoology of the Voyage of H.M.S. Beagle, Under the Command of Capt. Fitzroy, 1832-36. Wellington: 1979. V. 39

DARWIN, EMMA

Emma Darwin, A Century of Family Letters 1792-1896. London: 1915. V. 39

DARWIN, ERASMUS 1731-1802

The Botanic Garden, a Poem. London: 1791. V. 37; 38; 43; 44

The Botanic Garden. & Part II. Containing the Loves of the Plants. London: 1791, 1789. V. 40

The Botanic Garden, a Poem in Two Parts. London: 1791-90. V. 40

The Botanic Garden. London: 1794-95. V. 44

The Botanic Garden. New York: 1798. V. 40; 41; 43

The Botanic Garden. London: 1791, 1794. V. 37

The Botanic Garden. New York: 1798. V. 37

The Botanic Garden, a Poem. London: 1799. V. 37; 46

Memoirs of the Life of Dr. Darwin, Chiefly During His Residence at Lichfield, with Anecdotes of His Friends, and Criticisms on His Writings. London: 1804. V. 46

O Jardim Botanico de Darwin. Lisbon: 1803-1804. V. 38

Phytologia; or the Philosophy of Agriculture and Gardening . . . London: 1800. V. 39; 40; 42; 44; 46

A Plan for the Conduct of Female Education in Boarding Schools. Derby: 1797. V. 39; 40; 41; 42; 43; 45

The Poetical works of Erasmus Darwin. London;: 1806. V. 37

The Temple of Nature; or, the Origin of Society. London: 1803. V. 38; 42

Zoonomia or, the Laws of Organic Life. Philadelphia: 1797. V. 39

Zoonomia; or, the Laws of Organic Life. London: 1801. V. 39; 40

Zoonomia; or, the Laws of Organic Life. Boston: 1803. V. 40; 42

DARWIN, FRANCIS 1848-1925

Life and Letters of Charles Darwin. London: 1887. V. 38

The Life and Letters of Charles Darwin. London: 1888. V. 38

DAS, KEDARNATH

Obsteric Forceps. Its history and evolution. Calcutta.. V. 37

DAS, SARAT CHANDRA

Journey to Lhasa and Central Tibet. London: 1902. V. 40; 45

DASENT, GEORGE WEBBE

Norse Fairy Tales. London: 1910. V. 45; 46

The Story of Burnt Nijal or, Life in Iceland at the End of the Tenth Century. Edinburgh: 1861. V. 37; 39; 40; 42; 46

The Vikings of the Baltic. London: 1875. V. 38; 39; 41; 43

DASGUPTA, SURENDRANATH

A History of Indian Philosophy. 1951-52. V. 45

DASHIELL, ALFRED

Editor's Choice. New York: 1934. V. 39

DASHWOOD, GEORGE HENRY

Siglia Antiqua, Engravings from Ancient Seals Attached to Deeds and Charters in the Muniment Room of Sir Thomas Hare, Baronet of Stowe-Bardolph. Stowe-Bardolph: 1847. V. 40; 44

DASHWOOD, R. L.

Chiploquorgan; or, Life by the Camp Fire. Dublin: 1871. V. 39; 43

DA SILVA, OWEN

Mission Music of California. Los Angeles: 1941. V. 39; 44; 46

DASSIE, F.

Le Routier des Indes Orientales et Occidentales: Traitant des Saisons Propres a y Faire Voyage. Paris: 1677. V. 38

D'ASSIGNY, MARIUS

The Art of Memory. London: 1699. V. 46

A Treatise Useful for Such as Are to Speak in Publick. London: 1697. V. 39

DATHE, A.

An Essay on the History of Hamburgh, from the Foundation of the City to the Convention Between the Senate and Burghers in the Year One Thousand Seven Hundred and Twelve. London: 1766. V. 41

DAUBENY, CHARLES

An Introduction to the Atomic theory . . . Oxford: 1831. V. 44

An Introduction to the Atomic Theory. Oxford: 1850. V. 45

Lectures on Roman Husbandry Delivered Before the University of Oxford. Oxford: 1857. V. 37

Miscellanies, Being a Collection of Memoirs and Essays on Scientific and Literary Subjects. London: 1867. V. 40

DAUBENY, CHARLES GILES BRIDLE

Journal of a Tour through the United States and in Canada, Made During the Years 1837-38. Oxford: 1843. V. 40; 45

DAUBICHON, J.

An English Exercise-Book, fro the Construction of the French Language . . . Dublin: 1776. V. 39

D'AUBIGNE, J. H. MERLE

History of the Reformation in the Sixteenth Century. London: 1842. V. 40

History of the Reformation in the Sixteenth Century. Glasgow: 1844. V. 39

The History of the Reformation of the Sixteenth Century. Edinburgh: 1853. V. 44

History of the Reformation in the Sixteenth Century ; . . . London: 1869. V. 46

History of the Reformation of the Sixteenth Century. (with) History of the Reformation in Europe in Time of Calvin. London: 1853-69. V. 37

DAUBOURG, E.

Interior Architecture. London: 1877. V. 41; 46

DAUDET, ALPHONSE

Lettres de Mon Moulin. Paris: 1938. V. 43

The Nabob. London: 1878. V. 42

Port Tarascon. London: 1891. V. 39; 44

Port Tarascon: the Last Adventures of the Illustrious Tartarin. New York: 1891. V. 39; 41; 44

The Works. Boston: 1899-1906. V. 38

DAUDET, LEON

Le Partage de l'Enfant. Paris: 1905. V. 38

DAUGHTERS OF THE AMERICAN REVOLUTION

History and Reminiscences of Doughery County Georgia. Albany: 1924. V. 45

DAULBY, DANIEL

A Descriptive Catalogue of the Works of Rembrandt and of His Scholars. Liverpool: 1796. V. 38

DAULTE, FRANCOIS

Alfred Sisley: Catalogue Raisonne de l'Oeuvre Peint. Lausanne: 1959. V. 41

DAUMAS, E.

The Horses of the Sahara, and the Manners of the Desert. London: 1863. V. 39; 42; 46

DAUMIER, HONORE

240 Lithographs. New York: 1946. V. 38; 39; 40

DAUNCEY, JOHN

A Compendious Chronicle of the Kingdom of Portugal, From Alfonso the First King to Alfonso the Sixth, Now Reigning. London: 1661. V. 41; 42

D'AUREVILLY, BARBEY

What Never Dies: a Romance. Paris: 1902. V. 44

DAUXION-LAVAYSSE, JEAN JOSEPH

A Statistical, Commercial and Political Description of Venezuela, Trinidad, Margarita and Tobago . . . London: 1820. V. 38; 40

Voyage Aux Iles de Trinidad, De Tabago, De La Marguerite, et dans Diverses Parties de Venezuela, Dans l'Amerique Meridionale. Paris: 1813. V. 39; 43

DAVANZATI, BERNARDO

Discourse on Coins Translated Out of the Italian by John Toland. London: 1696. V. 42; 45

Scism d'Inghilterra. Con altre Operette . . . Fiorenza: 1638. V. 38

DAVDISON, JOHN

Plays. London: 1894. V. 46

DAVELOURT, DANIEL

Briefe Instruction sur le Faict de l'Artillerie de France . . . Paris: 1610. V. 38

DAVENANT, CHARLES 1656-1714

Circe. London: 1703. V. 46

A Discourse Upon Grants and Resumptions. London: 1700. V. 37; 38; 39; 41; 45

Dr. D------nant's Prophecys. London: 1713. V. 46

An Essay Upon the Ways and Means of Supplying the War. London: 1695. V. 38; 43; 45; 46

Essays Upon I. The Balance of Power. II. The Right of Making War, Peace and Alliances. III. Universl Monarchy. London: 1701. V. 37; 38; 41; 45; 46

Essays Upon Peace at Home, and War Abroad. London: 1704. V. 41; 45

A Report to the Honourable the Commissioners for Putting In Execution the Act, Intitled, An Act for the Taking, Examining, and Stating the Publik Accounts of Kingdom. London: 1712. V. 43

Tom Double Return'd Out of the Country; or the True Picture of a Modern Whig, set Forth in a Second Dialogue Between Mr. Whiglove & Mr. Double, at the Rummer Tavern in Queen-Street. London: 1702. V. 37; 39; 42; 45

D'AVENANT, WILLIAM 1606-1668

The Cruell Brother. London: 1630. V. 38

The Dramatic Works. Edinburgh: 1872-4. V. 38

Gondibert. London: 1651. V. 37; 40; 43

Madagascar, With Other Poems. London: 1648. V. 37; 38; 42

The Platonick Lovers. London: 1636. V. 38

The VVitts. London: 1636. V. 37

The Works. London: 1673. V. 37; 40; 42; 43; 45

DAVENPORT, A.

Camp and Field Life of the 5th NY Volunteer Regt. (Duryee Zouaves). New York: 1879. V. 39

DAVENPORT, A. H.

A Narrative of the Cruise of the Yacht Maria Among the Feroe Islands in the Summer of 1854. London: 1855. V. 38; 40; 42; 43

DAVENPORT, BISHOP

A New Gazetteer, or Geographical Dictionary of North America and the West Indies . . . Baltimore: 1832. V. 45; 46

A New Gazetteer or Geographical Dictionary, of North America and the West Indies . . . Baltimore/Providence: 1832. V. 45

A New Gazetteer, or Geographical Dictionary of North American and the West Indies . . . Philadelphia: 1836. V. 45

A New Gazetteer, or Geographical Dictionary of North America and the West Indies. Philadelphia: 1838. V. 38

A Pocket Gazetteer, or Traveller's Guide through North America and the West Indies. Baltimore: 1834. V. 45

DAVENPORT, CYRIL

Cameo Book-Stamps, Figured and Described. London: 1911. V. 41; 42

English Embroidered Bookbindings. London: 1899. V. 37; 38; 39; 40; 41; 43; 44

English Heraldic Book Stamps. London: 1909. V. 39; 41; 42

The English Regalia. London: 1897. V. 38

Goldfinch Thistle Star. N.P.: 1968. V. 45

Mezzotints. New York: 1903. V. 40

Roger Payne, English Bookbinder of the Eighteenth century. Chicago: 1928. V. 38

Roger Payne. English Bookbinder of the Eighteenth Century. Chicago: 1929. V. 38; 41; 42; 45

Royal English Book Bindings. London: 1896. V. 37; 38; 39; 40; 41; 42; 44; 46

Samuel Mearne, Binder to King Charles II. Chicago: 1906. V. 42; 46

Thomas Berthelet, Royal Printer and Bookbinder to Henry VIII. Chicago: 1901. V. 37; 39; 41; 42

DAVENPORT, EDWARD ADOLPHOUS

History of the Ninth Regiment Illinois Cavalry Volunteers. Chicago: 1888. V. 43

DAVENPORT, GUY

Belinda's World Tour. New York: 1991. V. 45

The Bicycle Rider. New York: 1985. V. 42; 44

The Bowmen of Shu. New York: 1983. V. 37; 39; 41; 42

Father Louie. New York: 1991. V. 45

Flowers and Leaves. Highlands: 1966. V. 41; 46

Goldfinch Thistle Star. New York: 1983. V. 42; 44

Jonah: a Story. New York: 1986. V. 40; 41; 42; 46

Trois Caprices. Louisville: 1981. V. 39

Trois Caprices. N.P.: 1981. V. 40

DAVENPORT, HENRY

The Publican's Lawyer. London: 1795. V. 40

DAVENPORT, HERBERT JOSEPH 1861-1931

Value and Distribution. A Critical and Constructive Study. Chicago: 1908. V. 41

DAVENPORT, JAMES HENRY

Literary Doctors of Medicine. Providence: 1926. V. 38

DAVENPORT, JOHN

Aphrodisiacs and Anti-Aphrodisiacs. London: 1869. V. 42

Aphrodisiacs and Anti-Aphrodisiacs. (with) Curiositates Eroticae Physiologiae. London: 1869, 1875. V. 37; 38; 41; 45; 46

A New Dictionary of Italian and English Langauges, Based Upon that of Baretti. London: 1854. V. 40

The Power of the Congregational Churches, Asserted and Vindicated. In Answer to a Treatise of Mr. J. Paget . . . London: 1672. V. 41; 42

DAVENPORT, R. A.

The Life of Ali Pasha, of Tepeleni, Vizier of Epicurs: Surnamed Aslan, or the Lion. London: 1837. V. 45

New Elegant Extracts. Chiswick: 1827. V. 39

DAVENPORT, RICHARD

The Amateur's Perspective. London: 1828-29. V. 45

The Amateur's Perspective. London: 1828. V. 38

DAVENPORT, RICHARD ALFRED

The Poetical Register and Repository of Fugitive Poetry. London: 1803-15. V. 46

DAVENPORT, THOMAS

Electro-Maganetism. History of Davenport's Invention of the Application of Electro-Magnetism to Machinery . . . New York: 1837. V. 37

DAVENPORT, W.

Historical Portraiture of Leading Events in the Life of Ali Pacha, Vizier of Epirus, Surnamed the Lion . . . London: 1823. V. 45

DAVEY, HENRY

A Set of ETchings Illustrative of Beccles Church and Other Suffolk Antiquities . . . Norwich: 1818. V. 38

DAVEY, NORMAN

Poems. With a Prefixed Essay. London: 1914. V. 37

DAVEY, RICHARD

The Sultan and His Subjects. New York: 1897. V. 39

The Sultan and His Subjects. London: 1907. V. 45

DAVEY, SCOTT

A Guide to the Collector of Historical Documents, Literary Manuscripts and Autograph Letters. London: 1901. V. 38

DAVID, A.

Les Oiseaux de la Chine. Paris: 1877. V. 40

DAVID, DONALD

Three for Watermusic. (Hove): (ca. 1980). V. 37

DAVID, JAN

Occasio Arrepta. Neglecta. Hujus Commoda: Illius Incommoda. Antwerp: 1605. V. 39

DAVID, JOANNES

Veridicus Christianus. Antverpiae: 1606. V. 41

DAVID JOHN

Travels of Four Years and a Half in the United States of America; During 1798, 1799, 1800, 1801 and 1802. London: 1803. V. 38

DAVID, PERCIVAL

A Catalogue of Chinese Pottery and Porcelain in the Collection of Sir Percival David Bt., F.S.A. London: 1934. V. 42

DAVID, R. C.

Reminiscences of a Voyage Round the World. Ann Arbor: 1869. V. 44

DAVID, ROBERT B.

Finn Burnett, Frontiersman. Glendale: 1936. V. 38

Finn Burnett Frontiersman. The Life and Adventures of an Indian Fighter, Mail Coach Driver, Miner, Pioneer, Cattleman, Participant in the Powder River Expedition . . . Glendale: 1937. V. 39; 40; 42; 43

Malcolm Campbell, Sheriff. Casper: 1932. V. 41; 45

DAVID, VILLIERS

The Guardsman and Cupid's Daughter and Other Poems by Villiers David. London: 1930. V. 46

A Winter Firework. London: 1937. V. 45

A Winter Firework. Waltham St. Lawrence: 1937. V. 40; 45

DAVIDGE, WILLIAM

Footlight Flashes. New York: 1866. V. 40

DAVIDICO, LORENZO

Tractatvlvs Avrevs . . . de Laudabili Liberorum Instructione Humilique Eorum Erga Parentes . . . Padua: 1567. V. 42

DAVIDMAN, JAY

War Poems of the United Nations. New York: 1943. V. 37

DAVIDOFF, LEO

Brain Tumors. 1931. V. 44

DAVIDS, ARTHUR LUMLEY

Grammaire Turke. London: 1836. V. 37; 38; 40

DAVIDSON, ALFRED

A History of the Holtes of Aston. Birmingham: 1854. V. 37

DAVIDSON, ANDREW

Geographical Pathology. Edinburgh: 1892. V. 40; 42

DAVIDSON, BRUCE

East 100th Street. Cambridge: 1970. V. 37

DAVIDSON, C. J. C.

Diary of Travels and Adventures in Upper India . . . London: 1843. V. 40

DAVIDSON, DONALD

Joseph Conrad's Directed Indirections. 1929. V. 45

The Long Street. Nashville: 1961. V. 46

An Outland Piper. New York: 1924. V. 44

An Outland Piper. Boston: 1924. V. 37; 45

Poems 1922-1961. Minneapolis: 1966. V. 46

The Tall Men. Boston: 1927. V. 37

DAVIDSON, EDWARD

The Railways of India. London: 1868. V. 37; 42

DAVIDSON, ELLIS A.

A Practical Manual of House-Painting, Graining, Marbling and Sign-Writing. London: 1891. V. 38; 41

A Practical Manual of House-Painting, Graining, Marbling and Sign-Writing . . . London: 1896. V. 43; 44

DAVIDSON, FRANCIS

Unstable as Water. London: 1875. V. 37

DAVIDSON, GEORGE

The Alaska Boundary. San Francisco: 1903. V. 42; 43; 45

The Glaciers of Alaska. That are shown on Russian Charts or Mentioned in Older Narratives. San Francisco: (1904). V. 37

Pacific Coast. Coast Pilot of California, Oregon and Washington Territory. Washington: 1869. V. 42

Pacific Coast Pilot of Alaska, (First Part), From Southern Boundary to Cook's Inlet. Washington: 1869. V. 39; 44; 46

The Tracks and Landfalls of Bering and Chirikof on the Northwest Coast of America . . . 1741. San Francisco: 1902. V. 43

DAVIDSON, GORDON CHARLES

The North West Company. Berkeley: 1918. V. 42

DAVIDSON, GRACE G.

Early Records of Georgia: Wilkes County. Macon: 1932. V. 42

DAVIDSON, H. C.

King Diddle. London: 1860. V. 40

DAVIDSON, HAROLD G.

Edward Borein Cowboy Artist. Garden City: 1974. V. 41; 42; 46

The Lost Works of Edward Borein. Santa Barbara: 1978. V. 44

DAVIDSON, J.

An Investigation of the Native Rights of British Subjects. London: 1784. V. 40

DAVIDSON, J. D.

A Curiosity in Chancery, in the Circuit Court of Rockbridge, Before the Hon. Hugh W. Sheffey. Rockbridge?: 1868. V. 39

DAVIDSON, JAMES W.

The Florida of Today, a Guide for Tourists and Settlers. New York: 1889. V. 41; 43

DAVIDSON, JOHN

An Address on Embalming Generally, Delivered at the Royal Institution, on the Unrolling of a Mummy. London: 1833. V. 38; 45

Bruce. London: 1886. V. 43

Bruce. A Drama in Five Acts. Glasgow: 1886. V. 37

Conifers, Junipers and Yew. London: 1927. V. 37; 38; 41; 45

Diabolus Amans. Glasgow: 1885. V. 38

A Full and True Account of the Wonderful Mission of Earl Lavender Which Lasted One Day and One Night. London: 1895. V. 39; 41; 43

The Last Ballad and Other Poems. London: 1899. V. 39

New Ballads. London: 1897. V. 38

The North Wall. Glasgow: 1885. V. 43

Perfervid; the Career of Ninain Jamieson. With twenty-three illustrations by Harry Furniss. London;: 1890. V. 37

Plays. Greencok: 1889. V. 43

Plays. L: 1894. V. 37

Plays. London: 1894. V. 40; 41; 43

DAVILLIER, CHARLES continued

Spain. New York: 1876. V. 39; 41

DAVIN, NICHOLAS FLOOD

Homes for Millions, the Great Canadian NorthWest. Ottawa: 1891. V. 42

DAVINI, JOHANNES BAPTISTA

De Potu Vini Caldi. Dissertatio. Mutinae: 1725. V. 39

DAVIS, A. C.

A Hundred Years of Portland Cement. 1824-1924. London: 1924. V. 44

DAVIS, A. J.

History of Clarion County, Pennsylvania. New York: 1887. V. 41; 42

DAVIS, ANDREW F.

Colonial Currency Reprints, 1682-1751. Boston: 1910. V. 38

DAVIS, ANDREW JACKSON

The Magic Staff: an Autobiography of Andrew Jackson Davis. New York: 1857. V. 44

DAVIS, BRITTON

The Truth About Geronimo. New Haven: 1929. V. 44

DAVIS, C. H.

Narrative of the North Polar Expedition U.S. Ship Polaris. Washington, D.C.: 1876. V. 37; 39; 42

DAVIS, C. M.

Los Angeles Illustrated, Showing Homes, Public Buildings, Business Blocks, Parks and General Views. Los Angeles: 1899. V. 37

DAVIS, CARLYLE C.

Olden Times in Colorado. Los Angeles: 1916. V. 37; 38

DAVIS, CHARLES

A Description of the Works of Art Forming the Collection of Alfred de Rothschild. London: 1884. V. 40

DAVIS, CHARLES E.

Three years in the Army, the Story of the Thirteenth Massachusetts Volunteers. Boston: 1894. V. 37

DAVIS, CHARLES G.

The Conduct of the Law in the Bordern Case with Suggestions of Changes in Criminal Law and Practice. Boston: 1894. V. 46

Ship Models: How to Build Them, an important book by a foremost authority, supplies complete instructions & the progressive steps in the laying out and construction of the hull an fittings. Salem: 1925. V. 37

Shipping & Craft in Silhouette. Salem: 1929. V. 39

Ships of the Past. Salem: 1929. V. 37; 46

DAVIS, CHARLES H.

Report on Interoceanic Canals and Railroads Between the Atlantic and Pacific Oceans. Washington: 1867. V. 41

DAVIS, CHARLES H. S.

The Egyptian Book of the Dead. New York: 1894. V. 40

DAVIS, CHARLES W.

Report on Interoceanic Canals and Railroads Between the Atlantic and Pacific Oceans. Washington: 1867. V. 44

DAVIS, DAVID

Elements of Operative Midwifery; comprising a Description of Certain New and Improved Powers for assisting Difficult and Dangerous labours; Illustrated by Plates . . . London: 1825. V. 37

DAVIS, DAVID D. 1777-1841

Acute Hydrocephalus, or Water in the Head. Philadelphia: 1840. V. 44

DAVIS, E. A.

The Historical Encyclopedia of Texas. N.P.: 1940. V. 40

DAVIS, E. J.

Life in Asiatic Turkey. London: 1879. V. 37; 39

DAVIS, ELLIS A.

Davis' Commercial Encylcopedia of the Pacific Southwest. Berkeley: 1911. V. 39

The Historical Encyclopedia of Texas. Dallas: 1937. V. 37; 39

The New Encyclopedia of Texas. Dallas,: 1915. V. 37; 44

DAVIS, EMERSON

The Half Century: or, a History of the Changes that Have Taken Place, and Events that Have Transpired, Chiefly in the United States, Between 1800 and 1850. Boston: 1851. V. 43

DAVIS, F. A.

Facts and Suggestions for Persons Forced to Seek Permanent or Temporary Homes on the Pinellas Peninsula for Relief from Consumption, Chronic Bronchitis, Rheumatism, Gout, Neurasthenia, and Kindred Diseases. Philadelphia: 1896. V. 37

DAVIS, F. HADLAND

Myths and Legends of Japan. London: 1912. V. 39

DAVIS, FLOYD

Natural Gas. N.P.: 1887. V. 38

DAVIS, FRANK MARSHALL

Black Man's Verse. Chicago: 1961. V. 46

Black Man's Verse. Chicago and Skokie: 1961. V. 41

DAVIS, GEORGE

Recollections of a Sea Wanderer's Life: an Autobiography of an Old Time Seaman who has Sailed in . . . Nearly Every Quarter of the Globe . . . New York: 1887. V. 37; 38; 45

DAVIS, GEORGE W.

Sketches of Butte. Boston: 1921. V. 38

DAVIS, GHERADI

Alice and I at Larchmont. New York: 1915. V. 43

DAVIS, GHERARDI

Alice and I and Alice Q and her Rivals. New York: 1913. V. 43

the United States Navy and Merchant Marine from 1840 to 1880. New York: 1923. V. 39; 43; 46

DAVIS, GREGSON

Antigua Glack: Portrait of an Island People. San Francisco: 1973. V. 42

DAVIS, HENRY EDWARDS

An Examination of the Fifteenth and Sixteenth Chapters of Mr. Gibbon's . . . Decline and Fall . . . London: 1778. V. 45

DAVIS, HENRY T.

Solitary Places Made Glad. Cincinnati: 1890. V. 37; 39; 40; 42; 43; 45; 46

DAVIS, I. B.

The Ancient and Modern History of Nice. London: 1807. V. 38

DAVIS, J. B.

The Origin and Description of Bognor, or Hothamton. London: 1807. V. 38

Pottery Mechanics' Institution. Hanley: 1836. V. 43

DAVIS, J. C.

The History of the Late Expedition to Cuba. New Orleans: 1850. V. 41; 42; 45

DAVIS, J. C. B.

Treaties and Conventions Concluded Between the United States and Other Powers Since July 4, 1776. Washington: 1873. V. 37; 38

DAVIS, J. K.

The Sailor's Companion. New York: 1849. V. 37

DAVIS, JAMES

West Yorkshire . . . London: 1878. V. 42; 46

DAVIS, JAMES D.

History of Mepmphis. Memphis,: 1873. V. 45

DAVIS, JAMES EDWARD

Prize Essay on the Laws for the Protection of Women. London: 1854. V. 40

DAVIS, JAMES LUCIUS

The Trooper's Manual; or, Tactics for Light Dragoons and Mounted Riflemen. Richmond: 1862. V. 44

DAVIS, JEFFERSON 1808-1889

In the Senate of the United States. January 31, 1849 . . . Recommending the Survey of a Route and the Construction of a National Road to the Territory Recently Acquired from Mexico, and Suggesting as the Most Eligible Line of Location . . . Washington: 1849. V. 39

Inaugural Address of President Davis, Delivered at the Capitol. Montgomery, Ala.: 1861. V. 37

Jefferson Davis, Constitutionalist: His Letters, Papers and Speeches. Jackson: 1923. V. 41; 42

Message of the President. (Richmond: 1861). V. 37

President's Message, to the Senate and House of Representatives of the Confederate States. Richmond: 1863. V. 37

Relations of State. Speech . . . Delivered in the Senate . . . Baltimore: 1860. V. 42

DAVIS, T. E.

From New Jersey to California, '97: a History of the Journey of the New Jersey C. E. Special to the Sixteenth International C. E. Convention at San Francisco July 6-12, 1897. Somerville: 1897. V. 46

DAVIS, THEODORE M.

Excavations: Biban el Moluk. London: 1906-12. V. 46

Theodore M. Davis' Excavations: Biban el Moluk. The Tomb of Ioulya and Touiyou. London: 1907. V. 37; 40; 42

Theodore M. Davis' Excavations: Biban el Moluk. The Tomb of Hatshopsitu. London: 1906. V. 40

Theodore M. Davis' Excavations: Biban el Moluk. The Tomb of Siphtah; the Monkey Tomb and the Gold Tomb. London: 1908. V. 40

DAVIS, THOMAS

General View of the Agriculture of the County of Wilts, with Observations on the Means of Its Improvement. London: 1794. V. 41

General View of the Agriculture of Wiltshire Drawn Up and Published by Board of Agriculture. London: 1811. V. 37; 41

DAVIS, VARINA HOWELL

Jefferson Davis. Ex-President of the Confederate States of America. New York: 1890. V. 39; 45; 46

DAVIS, WALTER B.

An Illustrated History of Missouri, Comprising its Early Record and Civil, Political and Military History. St. Louis: 1876. V. 37

DAVIS, WILLIAM

An Essay and Comprehensive Description of the Terrestrial and Celestial Globes. London: 1795. V. 41

A Journey Round the Library of a Bibliomaniac, or Cento of Notes and Reminiscences Concerning Rare, Curious and Valuable Books. London: 1821. V. 38; 40

An Olio of Bibliographical and Literary Anecdotes. London: 1817. V. 38

DAVIS, WILLIAM C.

The Image of War: 1861-1865. Garden City: 1981. V. 42

DAVIS, WILLIAM HEATH 1822-1909

Seventy-Five Years in California. San Francisco. V. 45

Seventy Five Years in California: a History of Events and Life in California. San Francisco: 1899. V. 37; 39

Seventy Five Years in California . . . San Francisco: 1929. V. 38; 39; 41; 43; 44; 45

Sixty Years in California. San Francisco: 1889. V. 40; 42; 43; 44

DAVIS, WILLIAM M.

Nimrod of the Sea; or, The American Whaleman. New York: 1874. V. 38; 39

Nimrod of the Sea. Boston: 1926. V. 45

DAVIS, WILLIAM W.

History of Whiteside County, Illinois from Its Earliest Settlement to 1908. Chicago: 1908. V. 38

DAVIS, WILLIAM WATSON

The Civil War and Reconstruction in Florida. New York: 1913. V. 39; 44

DAVIS, WILLIAM WATTS HART 1820-1910

El Gringo; or, New Mexico and Her People. New York: 1857. V. 37; 40; 41; 45

El Gringo; or, New Mexico and Her People. Doylestown: 1869. V. 39

The Fries Rebellion, 1798-99: An Armed Resistance to the House Tax Law, Passed by Congress, July 9, 1798, in Bucks and Northampton Counties, Pennsylvannia. Doyleston: 1899. V. 37; 39

History of the 104th Pennsylvania Regiment, from April 22, 1861 to September 30th, 1864. Philadelphia: 1866. V. 42

The History of Bucks County, Pennsylvania, form the Discovery of the Delaware to the Present . . . Doylestown: 1876. V. 41; 42

History of Doylestown, Old and New. Doylestown: 1904. V. 42

History of Bucks County, Pennsylvania, from the Discovery of the Delaware to the Present . . . New York: 1905. V. 42

Spanish Conquest of New Mexico. Doylestown: 1869. V. 37; 40; 42; 43

DAVIS, WINFIELD J.

History of Political Conventions in California, 1849-1892. Sacramento: 1893. V. 39; 40; 44; 45

An Illustrated History of Sacramento County, California. Chicago: 1890. V. 44; 45

DAVISON, CHARLES

Autoplatic Bone Surgery. Philadelphia: 1916. V. 42

The Hereford Earthquake of December 17, 1896. Birmingham: 1899. V. 45

DAVISON, FRANCIS

The Poetical Rhapsody; ot which are added several other pieces . . . London: 1826. V. 38; 46

DAVISON, JOHN

Considerations on the Poor Laws. Oxford: 1817. V. 45

In a Music-Hall and other Poems. London: 1891. V. 37

A New System of Arithmetic. To which is added a Geographical Table. London: 1780. V. 37

DAVISON, R. H.

Reform in the Ottoman Empire 1856-1876. Princeton: 1963. V. 44

DAVISON, SIMPSON

The Gold Deposits in Australia . . . London: 1861. V. 40

DAVITT, MICHAEL 1846-1906

The Boer Fight for Freedom from the Beginning of the Hostilities to the Peace of Pretoria. New York: 1902. V. 38

The Fall of Feudalism in Ireland, or the Story of the Land League Revolution. London: 1904. V. 39; 46

Leaves from a Prison Diary; or, Lectures to a Solitary Audience. London: 1885. V. 38; 42

Leaves from a Prison Diary. London: 1885. V. 37

Within the Pale. The True Story of Anti-Semitic Persecutions in Russia. New York: 1903. V. 38

DAVY, C.

Architectural Precedents . . . London: 1841. V. 38

Architectural Precedents; with Notes and Observations. London: 1908. V. 38

DAVY, CHRISTOPHER

The Architect, Engineer and Operative Builder's Constructive Manual. London: 1839. V. 41; 45

DAVY Crockett's 1844 Almanac. Boston: 1843. V. 45

DAVY, EDWARD

An Experimental Guide to Chemistry. London: 1836. V. 37

DAVY, GYPSY

The Himalayan Letters of Gypsy Davy and Lady Ba. Cambridge: 1927. V. 44

DAVY, HENRY

A Series of Etchings Illustrative of the Architectural Antiquities of Suffolk, Accompanied by an Historical Index. Southwold: 1827. V. 41

Views of the Seats of the Noblemen and Gentlemen of Suffolk. Southwould: 1827. V. 39

DAVY, HUMPHRY 1778-1829

Consolations in Travel, or the Last Days of a Philosopher. London: 1830. V. 42

Elements of Chemical Philosophy. London: 1812. V. 40

Elements of Agricultural Chemistry, In a Course of Lectures for the Board of Agriculture. London: 1813. V. 37; 38; 39; 40; 41; 42; 44; 45; 46

Elements of Agricultural Chemistry, in a Course of Lectures for the Board of Agriculture. London: 1814. V. 42; 43; 44; 46

Elements of Agricultural Chemistry. London: 1821. V. 40; 42; 43

Elements of Agricultural Chemistry . . . Philadelphia: 1821. V. 43

Elements of Agricultural Chemistry, in a Course of Lectures for the Board of Agriculture. London: 18313. V. 38

Elements of Agricultural Chemistry. London: 1844. V. 37

A Lecture, on the Plan Which is Proposed to Adopt for Improving the Royal Institution and Rendering it Permanent. Delivered in the Theatre of the Royal Institution March 3rd 1810. London: 1810. V. 40

On the Fire-Damp of Coal Mines and on Methods of Lighting the Mines So as to Prevent Its Explosion. (and) An Account of an Invention for Giving Light in Explosive Mixtures of Fire-Damp in Coal Mines, by Consuming the Fire-Damp. London: 1816. V. 40; 42

On the Safety Lamp for Coal Miners; with some Researches on Flame. London: 1818. V. 41; 44

On the Safety Lamp for Preventing Explosions in Mines, Houses Lighted by Gas, Spirit Warehouses or Magazines in Ships . . . London: 1825. V. 38

The Papers . . . Communicated to the Royal Society on the Fire-Damp of Coal Mines . . . Newcastle: 1817. V. 45

Researches, Chemical and Philosophical. London: 1800. V. 38

Salmonia; or, Days of Fly Fishing. London: 1828. V. 39; 42; 46

Salmonia: or Days of Fly Fishing. London: 1829. V. 37; 38; 39

Salmonia; or Days of Fly Fishing . . . London: 1832. V. 39

Salmonia; or Days of Fly Fishing. London: 1832. V. 37

Six discourses delivered before the Royal Society at the anniversary meetings . . . preceded by an address to the Society on the progress and prospects of science. London: 1827. V. 37

DAVY, JOHN

The Angler in the Lake District, or Piscatory Colloquies and Fishing Excursions in Westmoreland and Cumberland . . . . London: 1857. V. 41

Memoirs of the Life of Sir Humphry Davy, Bart. London: 1836. V. 40; 42

Notes and Observations on the Ionian Islands and Malta with Some Remarks on Constantinople and Turkey . . . London: 1842. V. 37; 39; 45

DAVY, JOHN continued

On Some of the More Important Diseases of the Army. London: 1862. V. 43

DAVYDOV, GAVRIIL IVANOVICH

Reise der Russisch-Kaiserlichen Flott-Officiere Chwostow und Dawydow von St. Petersburg Durch Sibirien Nach Amerika und Zuruck in den Jahren 1802, 1803 and 1804. Berlin: 1816. V. 40

DAVYS, JOHN

An Essay on the Art of Decyphering. London: 1737. V. 42; 46

An Essay on the Art of Decyphering. London: 1773. V. 42

DAWE, EDWARD A.

Paper and Its Uses, a Treatise for Printers, Stationers and Other. London: 1929. V. 38

DAWE, GEORGE

The Life of George Morland, with Remarks on His Works. London: 1807. V. 38; 40; 44

The Life of George Morland . . . London: 1910. V. 39

DAWE, GROSVENOR

Melvil Dewey. Seer, Inspirer, Doer, 1851-1931. Essex County: 1932. V. 39

DAWES, HENRY L.

Address of the United States Commission to the Five Tribes. Muskogee: 1894. V. 40; 45

DAWES, MANASSEH

The Deformity of the Doctrine of the Libels, and Information Ex Officio, with a View of the Case of the Dean of Saint Asaph, and an Enquiry into the Rights of Jurymen, in a Letter to the Honourable Thomas Erskine. London: 1785. V. 38

England's Alarm! on the Prevailing Doctrine of Libels, as Laid Down by the Earl of Mansfield in a Letter to His Lordship by a Country Gentleman. London: 1785. V. 38

DAWES, RUFUS R.

Service With the Sixth Wisconsin Volunteers. Marietta: 1890. V. 39

DAWKINS, G. H.

Present Day Sires and the Figure System. London: 1897. V. 37

DAWKINS, R. M.

Modern Greek in Asia minor. Cambridge: 1916. V. 38

The Sanctuary of Artemis Orthia at Sparta Excavated and Described by Members of the British School of Athens 1906-1910. London: 1929. V. 42

DAWSON, CHARLES

Charles Dawson: His Book of Bookplates, Consisting of 24 Original Designs. Edinburgh: 1907. V. 40; 43

History of Hastings Castle. London: 1909. V. 42

History of Hastings Castle. N.P.: 1909. V. 46

Pioneer Tales of the Oregon Trail and of Jefferson Country. Topeka: 1912. V. 46

DAWSON, D.

Harry Clyde, or Only a Schoolmasater. Leeds: 1875. V. 38

DAWSON, EMMA FRANCES

A Gracious Visitation. San Francisco: 1921. V. 37; 38; 42

DAWSON, FIELDING

The Dream/Thunder Road. Santa Barbara: 1972. V. 37; 40; 42

The Greatest Story Every Told. Santa Barbara: 1973. V. 37; 40; 42

2 + 4 Poems. 1950. V. 46

Two Penny Lane. Santa Barbara: 1977. V. 37; 40; 42

DAWSON, FLORA

Princes, Public Men, and PRetty Women . . . London: 1864. V. 42

DAWSON, FRANCIS W.

Reminiscences of Confederate Service, 1861-1865. Charleston: 1882. V. 45

DAWSON, G. A. B.

Nilgiri Sporting Reminiscences. Madras: 1880. V. 46

DAWSON, G. M.

Report on an Exploration the Yukon district, N.W.T. and Adjacent Northern Portion of British Columbia, 1887. Montreal: 1888. V. 46

DAWSON, GEORGE

Origo Legum; or a Treatise on the Origin of Laws, and Their Obliging Power; also of Their Great Variety, and Why Some Laws are Immutable, and Some Not . . . in Seven Books. London: 1694. V. 40

The Pleasures of Angling with Rod and Reel for Trout and Salmon. New York: 1876. V. 39; 40

DAWSON, GEORGE PEARSON

A Nosological Practice of Physic, Embracing Physiology. London: 1824. V. 44

DAWSON, HENRY B.

The Gazette Series: 1. Papers Concerning the Capture and Detention of Major John Andre. 2. Papers Concerning the Town & Village of Yonkers Westchester County . . . 3. Papers Concerning the Boundary Between the States of New York & New Jersey. 4. Rambles in . . . Yonkers: 1866. V. 39; 43; 45

Westchester County, New York, During the American Revolution. New York: 1886. V. 44

DAWSON, J. W.

A Handbook of the Geography and Natural History of the Province of Nova Scotia. Pictou: 1851. V. 42

DAWSON, JAMES

Australian Aborigines. Melbourne, Sydney &: 1881. V. 38

DAWSON, JOHN

Lexicon Novi Testamenti Alphabeticum . . . Cambridge: 1706. V. 46

DAWSON, JOHN WILLIAM

Arcadian Geology. London: 1878. V. 40

DAWSON, LIONEL

Sport in War. London: 1936. V. 42

DAWSON, LUCY

Neighbours. London: 1946. V. 46

DAWSON, MOSES

A Historical Narrative of the Civil and Military Services of Major-General William H. Harrison . . . Cincinnati: 1824. V. 37

Sketches of the Life of Martin Van Buren, President of the United States. Cincinnati: 1840. V. 39

DAWSON, MUIR

History and Bibliography of Southern California Newspapers, 1851-1876. Los Angeles: 1950. V. 46

DAWSON, NELSON

Goldsmiths' and Silversmiths' Work. London: 1907. V. 38; 40

Goldsmiths' and Silversmith's Work. New York: 1907. V. 41

DAWSON, NICHOLAS

Narrative of Nicholas 'Cheyenne' Dawson (Overland to California in '41 and '49 and Texas in '51). San Francisco: 1933. V. 39; 41; 43; 45; 46

DAWSON, ROBERT

The Present State of Australia, a Description of the Country, Its Advantages and Prospects with Reference to Emigration and a Particular Account of the Manners, Customs and Condition of Aboriginal Inhabitants. London: 1830. V. 46

DAWSON, SAMUEL EDWARD

The Saint Lawrence Basin and its Border-Lands Being the Story of their Discovery, Exploration and Occupation. London: 1905. V. 46

The Voyages of the Cabots. Ottawa: 1897. V. 41

DAWSON, SARAH M.

A Confederate Girl's Diary. Boston: 1913. V. 45

DAWSON, SIMON JAMES

Rapport sur l'Exploration de la Contree Situee Entre le Lac Superieur et al Colonie de la Riviere Rouge. Toronto: 1859. V. 41

Report on the Exploration of the Country Between Lake Superior and the Red River Settlement, and Between the Latter Place and the Assiniboine and Saskatchewan. Toronto: 1859. V. 37; 41; 43; 45

Report on the Line of Route Between Lake Superior and the Red River Settlement. Ottawa: 1869. V. 40

DAWSON, THOMAS

Memoirs of St. George the English Patron; and of the Most Noble Order of the Garter . . . London: 1714. V. 39; 44; 46

DAWSON, THOMAS F.

The Ute War. Denver: 1879. V. 42

DAWSON, THOMAS FULTON

The Ute War. Denver: 1879. V. 37; 38; 41; 42; 44; 45; 46

DAWSON, W.

Ten Plates Comprising a Plan, Sections and Views, Representing the Changes Produced on the Coast of East Devon . . . London: 1840. V. 43

DAWSON, W. F.

Christmas: Its Origin and Associations. London: 1902. V. 43

DE LA BECHE, HENRY T. continued

Report on the Geology of Cornwall, Devon and West Somerset. London: 1839. V. 45

Researches in Theoretical Geology. London: 1834. V. 43

DE LA CAMPA, MIGUEL

A Journal of Explorations Northward Along the Coast from Monterey in the Year 1775. San Francisco: 1964. V. 46

DE LA COUR, JAMES

Poems. Cork: 1778. V. 42

DE LA CREQUINIERE,

The Agreement of the Customs of the East Indians, with Those of the Jews and Other Ancient People . . . London: 1705. V. 42

DE LA FAILLE, J. B.

Vincent Van Gogh. London: 1932. V. 40

DE LA MARE, A. C.

The Handwriting of Italian Humanists. London: 1973. V. 39

DE LA MARE, WALTER 1873-1956

Alone. New York: 1927. V. 37; 43; 44

At First Sight. New York: 1928. V. 43

Behold, This Dreamer - of Reverie, Night, Sleep, Dream, Love-Dreams, Nightmare, Death, the Unconscious, the Imagination, Divination, the Artist and Kindred Spirits. London: 1939. V. 38; 45

Bells and Grass. New York: 1942. V. 43

Broomsticks and Other Tales. London: 1925. V. 37; 42

The Burning-Glass, and Other Poems. London: 1945. V. 46

Come Hither. London: 1923. V. 37; 39; 42; 45

Come Hither: A Collection of Rhymes and Poems for the Young of all Ages. London: 1933. V. 37

The Connoisseur and Other Stories. London: 1926. V. 37; 40; 42; 43

Crossings. London: 1921. V. 39

Crossings: a Fairy Play. Westminster: 1921. V. 40

Desert Islands and Robinson Crusoe. London: 1930. V. 37; 39; 40; 41; 42; 43; 44; 46

Desert Islands and Robinson Crusoe. London & New York: 1930. V. 37; 39; 40; 41; 42; 43; 44

Ding Dong Bell. London: 1924. V. 38; 43; 45

Down-Adown-Derry. London: 1922. V. 37; 43

Early One Morning in the Spring: Chapters on Children and on Childhood. London: 1935. V. 37

The Fleeting and Other Poems. London: 1933. V. 37; 39

Flora a Book of Drawings . . . with Illustrative Poems. London: 1919. V. 42

Henry Brocken. London: 1904. V. 37

Lispet, Lispett and Vaine. London: 1923. V. 37; 42; 43

The Listeners and Other Poems. London: 1912. V. 41

The Lord Fish. London: 1933. V. 37; 41; 43; 44; 46

Love (an Anthology). London: 1943. V. 40

Memoirs of a Midget. London: 1921. V. 37; 39; 40; 41; 42; 46

Memoirs of a Midget. London: 1921. V. 46

O Lovely England and Other Poems. London: 1953. V. 40; 43

On the Edge, Short Stories. London: 1930. V. 43

Peacock Pie. London: 1913. V. 39

The Peacock Pie. London: 1915. V. 42

Peacock Pie. London: 1916. V. 41

Peacock Pie. London: 1924. V. 40; 45

Peacock Pie. New York: 1924. V. 41; 46

Peacock Pie - a Book of Rhymes. London: 1946. V. 42

Poems. London: 1906. V. 37; 44; 45

Poems 1901 to 1918. London: 1920. V. 38; 40; 45

Poems. London: 1927. V. 42

Poems from Children. London: 1930. V. 43

Poems for Children. New York: 1930. V. 41

Poems. London: 1937. V. 40

The Riddle and Other Stories. 1923. V. 37

Ruppert Brooke The Intellectual Imagination. London: 1919. V. 39

Seven Short Stories, Chosen from the Connoisseur and Other Stories, Broomsticks and Other Stories, The Riddle and Other Stories. London: 1931. V. 37; 41; 43

Seven Short Stories. London: 1937. V. 38

Songs of Childhood. London: 1902. V. 37; 39

Stuff and Nonsense, and So On. London: 1927. V. 37; 41; 43; 46

The Sunken Garden and Other Poems. Westminster: 1917. V. 39

This Year; Next Year. London: 1937. V. 40; 45

The Three Mulla-Mulgars. London: 1910. V. 37; 40; 41; 42; 43; 45

The Three Mullamulgars. New York: 1919. V. 43

Told Again. Oxford: 1927. V. 42

The Traveller. London: 1946. V. 41

Two Tales. London: 1925. V. 40; 41; 43; 45

The Wind Blows Over. London: 1936. V. 41

Winged Chariot. London: 1951. V. 40; 41

DE LA MOTTE, PHILIP

Choice Examples of Art Workmanship. London: 1851. V. 40

Choice Examples of Art Workmanship; London: 1851. V. 38

DE LA RAMEE, LOUISA

Folle-Farine. London: 1871. V. 38

DE LA RAMEE, LOUISE 1839-1908

Ariadne. London: 1877. V. 43; 44

A Dog of Flanders and Other Stories. 1872. V. 43

Folle Farine. London: 1871. V. 40; 41; 43

Friendship. A Story. London: 1878. V. 41; 43

Guilderoy. London: 1889. V. 43

Pascarel. London: 1873. V. 43; 45; 46

Princess Napraxine. London: 18814. V. 43

Syrlin. London: 1890. V. 43

The Tower of Taddeo. London: 1892. V. 43

Two Little Wooden Shoes, a Sketch. London: 1874. V. 39

A Village Commune. London: 1881. V. 39

DE LA REE, GARY

Space Travel - When and How? River Edge: 1953. V. 43

DE LA ROCHE, MICHAEL

New Memoirs of Literature, Containing an Account of New Books Printed Both at HOme and Abroad . . . London: 1725. V. 41

New Memoirs of Literature . . . London: 1725. V. 38

DE LA ROQUE, JEAN

Voyage dans la Palestine, Vers le Grand Emir, Chef des Princes Arabes du Desert, Connus Sous Le Nom de Bedouins. Amsterdeam: 1718. V. 39

Voyage de Syrie et du Mont Liban. Contenant la Description de Tout le Pays Compris Sous le nom de Liban et d'Antiliban, Kesroan etc . . . Amsterdam: 1723. V. 39

DE LA SERRE, ABBE

Le Livre de l'Euchariste. Paris: 1920. V. 41

DE LA TORRE, LILLIAN

Dr. Sam Johnson, Detector. New York: 1946. V. 42

Elizabeth is Missing . . . London: 1947. V. 43

DE L'ORME, PHILIBERT 1515?-1570

Architecture . . . Oeuvre Entiere Contenant Onze Livres, Augmentee de Deux . . . Paris: 1626. V. 39

L'Oeuvre de Philibert de L'Orme . . . Paris: 1894. V. 44

Tome de l'Architecture. Paris: 1568. V. 40

DEACON, AUGUSTUS OAKLEY

Manual of Elementary Practice in Drawing Real Objects . . . London: 1845. V. 38

DEACON, EDWARD E.

A Practical Treatise on the Game Law, as Amended by the New Act . . . London: 1831. V. 40

DEACON, THOMAS

A Compleat Collection of Devotions, Both Publick and Private . . . London: 1734. V. 42

DEACON, WILLIAM FREDERICK

Warreniana; with Notes, Critical and Explanatory . . . London: 1824. V. 39; 42

DEADLY Adulteration and Slow Poisoning. London: 1829. V. 42

DEADRICK, WILLIAM

The Endemic Diseases of the Southern States. Philadelphia: 1916. V. 40; 42

DEADWOOD GULCH HYDRAULIC MINING CO.

Prospectus of the Deadwood Gulch Hydraulic Mining Company of Deadwood Gulch, Lawrence County, Black Hills, of the Territory of Dakota. Deadwood: 1882. V. 39

DEAKIN, ANDREW

Musical Bibliography . . . Birmingham: 1892. V. 38; 40

DEAKIN, F. W.

The Case of Richard Sorge. London: 1966. V. 40

DEAKIN, RICHARD

Florigraphia Britannica; or, Engravings and Descriptions of the Flowering Plants and Ferns of Britian. London: 1841-47. V. 46

Florigraphia Britannica, or Engravings and Descriptions of the Flowering Plants and Ferns. London: 1841-48. V. 37; 42; 46

Florigraphia Britannica or Engravings and Descriptions of the Flowering Plants and Ferns of Britain. London: 1857. V. 37

DE ALARCON, PEDRO ANTONIO

The Three-Cornered Hat, by Pedro Antonio de Alarcon. New York: 1944. V. 37

DEALTRY, WILLIAM

The Principles of Fluxions: Designed for the Use of Students in the Universities. Cambridge: 1816. V. 44

DEAN, B.

A Bibliography of Fishes. New York: 1973. V. 37

DEAN, BASHFORD

Catalogue of European Daggers 1300-1800. Catalogue of European Court Swords and Hunting Swords. New York: 1929. V. 37; 45

DEAN, EZRA

Doctor Dean's Patent Vegetable Rheumatic Pills. Boston?: 1823? V. 44

DEAN, GEORGE ALFRED

Essays on the Construction of Farm Buildings and Labourers' Cottages. London: 1849. V. 38; 42

Essays on the Construction of Farm Buildings and Labourers' Cottages. Stratford, Essex: 1849. V. 39

The Land Steward. London: 1851. V. 37; 40; 46

A Series of Selected Designs for Country Residences, Entrance Lodges, Farm Offices, Cottages . . . Worthing, York & London: 1867. V. 40

DEAN, HARRY 1864-

The Pedro Gorino. Boston/New York: 1929. V. 37; 40; 42

DEAN, HENRY

Dean's Analytical Guide to the Art of Penmanship. New York: 1808. V. 38; 43

DEAN, JAMES

An Alphabetical Atlas, or, Gazetteer of Vermont . . . Montpelier: 1808. V. 37; 45

DEAN, JOHN

A True and Genuine Narrative of the Whole Affair Relating to the Ship Sussex, as Sent to the Directors of the Honourable East India Company . . . London: 1740. V. 45; 46

DEAN, JOHN WARD

Capt. John Mason, The Founder of New Hampshire. Boston: 1887. V. 38; 39

Memoir of Rev. Michael Wigglesworth, Author of Day of Doom by John Ward Dean. Albany, New York: 1871. V. 37

DEAN, WILLIAM

An Historical and Descriptive Account of Croome d'Abitot, the Seat of the Right Hon. the Earl of Coventry . . . Worcester: 1824. V. 46

DEANE, JOHN BATHURST

The Worship of the Serpent Traced Throughout the World; Attesting to the Temptation and Fall of Man by the Instrumentality of a Serpent Tempter. London: 1833. V. 45

DEANE, MARY

Kinsfolk. London: 1891. V. 43

DEANE, SAMUEL

The New-England Farmer . . . Worcester: 1790. V. 43

The New England Farmer. Worcester: 1797. V. 38; 39

The New England Farmer; or Georgical Dictionary . . . Boston: 1822. V. 41; 43

DEANE, SILAS 1737-1789

An Address to the Free and Independent Citizens of the United States of North-America. Hartford: 1784. V. 37; 38

An Address to the United States of America. London: 1784. V. 37; 38

Deane Papers 1777-1778. New York: 1897-91. V. 45

DEANE, WILLIAM

The Description of the Copernican System, with the Theory of the Planets . . . London: 1738. V. 45

DEANS, ARCHIBALD

An Account of the Last Words of Christian Kerr, who Died at Edinburgh, the 4th of Feb. 1702 in the 11th Year of Her Age. Glasgow: 1773. V. 42

DEAN'S New Book of Dissolving Views. London: 1860. V. 40

DEAR Alec . . . A Tribute for His Eightieth Birthday from Friends Known and Unknown. Worcester: 1972. V. 41; 45; 46

DEARBORN, F. M.

American Homeopathy in the World War. London: 1923. V. 46

DEARBORN, H. A. S.

Letters on the Internal Improvements and Commerce of the West. Boston: 1839. V. 39; 41

DEARBORN, HENRY

Defence of Gen. Henry Dearborn, Against the Attack of Gen. William Hull. Boston: 1824. V. 45

Revolutionary War Journals of . . . 1775-1783. Chicago: 1939. V. 42

DEARBORN, JOHN J.

The History of Salisbury, New Hampshire. Manchester: 1890. V. 42

DEARDEN, ROBERT R.

An Original Leaf from the Bible of the Revolution and an Essay Concerning It. San Francisco: 1930. V. 38; 39; 41; 45; 46

DEARING, J. S.

A Drummer's Experience. Colorado Springs: 1913. V. 44

DEARN, THOMAS DOWNES WILMOT

Designs for Lodges and Entraces to Parks, Paddocks, and Pleasure-Grounds, in the Gothic, Cottage and Fancy Styles . . . London: 1811. V. 38

Sketches In Architecture, Consisting of Original Designs for Public and Private Buildings. London: 1814. V. 45

DEARNESS Not Scarcity. Its Cause and Remedy. London: 1800. V. 39

DEAS, ALSTON

The Early Ironwork of Charleston. Columbia: 1941. V. 44

DEASE, E. F.

A Complete History of the Westmeath Hunt, From Its Foundation. Dublin: 1898. V. 42

DEASY, H. H. P.

In Tibet and Chinese Turkestan, being the Record of Three Years' Exploration. London: 1901. V. 40; 44

THE DEATH and Dissection, Funeral Procession and Will, of Mrs. Regency. London: 1789. V. 39

DEATH Blow to the Corrupt Doctrines A Plain Statement of Facts. Shanghai: 1870. V. 40

THE DEATH of Captain Cook; a Grand Serious-Pantomimic-Ballet, in Three Parts. As Now Exhibiting in Paris with Uncommon Applause with the Original French Music . . . London: 1789. V. 42

THE DEATH Valley Chuck-Walla. Los Angeles: 1990. V. 45

DEATHERAGE, CHARLES P.

Early History of Greater Kansas City, Missouri and Kansas. Kansas City: 1927. V. 38

DEATON, E. L.

Indian Fights on the Texas Frontier: a True Account of Exciting Encounters in Hamilton, Comanche, Brown, Erath and Adjoining Counties. Ft. Worth: 1927. V. 46

DEAVER, JOHN BLAIR

Surgical Anatomy. A Treatise on Human Anatomy in Its Application to the Practice of Medicine and Surgery. Philadelphia: 1899. V. 42

Surgical Anatomy. Philadelphia: 1899/1900/1902. V. 45

Surgical Anatomy of the Head and Neck. Philadelphia: 1910. V. 42

A Treatise on Appendicitis. Philadelphia: 1896. V. 42

DEAVILLE, A. S.

The Colonial Postal Systems and Postage Stamps of Vancouver Island and British Columbia, 1849-1871. Victoria: 1928. V. 43

DE BACA, MANUEL C.

Vicente Silva and His 40 Bandits. Washington: 1947. V. 44

DE BARRI, GIRALDUS

The Itinerary of Archbishop Baldwin through Wales, A.D. MCLXXXVIII. London: 1806. V. 39

DE BARROS, JOAO

Asia de Joam de Barros, dos Fectos que os Portugueses Fizeram no Descobrimento & Conquista dos Mares & Terras do Oriente. (with) Segunda Decada da Asia. Lisbon: 1552/53. V. 41

Decada Primeira da Asiade Ioao de Barros; Dos Feitos Qve Os Portvgveses Fezerano no Descobrimento . . . (with) Wuarta Decada de Asia de Ioao de Barros . . . Lisbon: 1628. V. 41; 43

DE BARTHE, JOE

The Life and Adventures of Frank Grouard. St. Joseph: 1894. V. 38; 39; 42; 45; 46

DE BARY, A.

Lectures on Bacteria. Oxford: 1887. V. 38

DEBAT, FRANCOIS

New York. Images Mouvantes. Paris: 1929. V. 41

THE DEBATE of a Motion for the Abolition of the Slave Trade, in the House of Commons, on Monday the Second of April, 1792 Reported in Detail. London: 1792. V. 42; 46

DE BAUSSET, M. L. F.

The Life of Fenelon, Archbishop of Cambrai. London: 1810. V. 46

DE BEAUCHAMP, ALFRED

The Life of Ali Pacha, of Jannina, Late Vizier of Epirus, Surnamed Aslan, or the Lion. London: 1823. V. 37

DE BEAUFORT, DANIEL

The History of the Marquisate of Veere and Flushing . . . London: 1747. V. 41

DE BEAUJOUR, LOUIS A. FELIX 1784-1857

Sketch of the United States . . . London: 1814. V. 43

DE BEAUMONT, GUSTAVE

Ireland, Social, Political an Religious. London: 1839. V. 37

DE BEAUVOIR, SIMONE

The Mandarins. Cleveland: 1956. V. 45

DE BEAUVOISIN, M. MARIOT

An Entirely Original System for Acquiring the French Language. London: 1852. V. 37

DE BECK, WILLIAM L.

Murder Will Out. The First Step in Crime Leads to the Gallows. The Horrors of the Queen City. Cincinnati: 1867. V. 37; 39; 43

DE BECKER, J. E.

The Nightless City. Yokohama etc.: 1905. V. 41; 46

The Sexual Life of Japan. ?Yokohama: 1905-10. V. 40

DE BEERSKI, P. JEANNERAT

Angkor Ruins in Cambodia. London: 1923. V. 37

DE BELLAIGUE, GEOFFREY

The Louis XVI Service. Cambridge: 1986. V. 41

DE BELLEMARE, LUIS

The Wood Rangers. London: 1860. V. 40

DE BENNEVILLE, JAMES SEGUIN

Saito Musashi-Bo Benkei. Yokohama: 19120. V. 42

DE BERNEAUD, ARSIENNE THIEBAUT

A Voyage to the Isle of Elba . . . London: 1814. V. 43

DEBERNY ET PEIGNOT

'Photo'. N.P., (Paris): (c. 1935). V. 37

DEBES, LUCAS JACOBSON

Faeroae & Faeroa Reserata: That Is a Description of the Islands and Inhabitants of Foeroe . . . London: 1676. V. 42; 43; 44

DE BETHUNE, MAXIMILIAN

Memoirs of Maximilian de Bethune, Duke of Sully, Prime Minister to Henry the Great . . . etc. To which is added The Tryal of Ravaillac for the Murder of Henry the Great. London: 1761. V. 37

DEBEVOISE, NEILSON C.

Parthian Pottery from Seleucia on the Tigris. Ann Arbor: 1934. V. 42; 44

DE BLANCOURT, FRANCOIS HAUDICQUER

The Art of Glass. London: 1699. V. 44

DEBO, ANGIE

The Cowman's Southwest. Glendale: 1953. V. 38; 43; 46

The Road to Disappearance. Norman: 1941. V. 46

DE BOURBON, ARMAND, PRINCE OF CONTI

The Works of the Most Illustrious and Pious Armand de Bourbon Prince of Conti. London: 1711. V. 40

DE BOURDEILLE, PIERRE

The Lives of Gallant Ladies. London: 1924. V. 38

The Lives of Gallant Ladies. N.P.: 1924. V. 46

The Lives of Gallant Ladies. Waltham St. Lawrence: 1924. V. 38; 44

DE BOW, J. D. B.

De Bow's Review. New Orleans: 1846-1870. V. 38; 39

DE BRACK, F.

Advance Posts of Light Cavalry. Recollections. Madras: 1850. V. 41

DE BRANTOME, PIERRE DE BOURDEILLE, ABBOT OF

The Lives of Gallant Ladies. London: 1924. V. 41

DEBRETT'S Correct Peerage of England, Scotland and Ireland with the Extinct and Forfeited Peerages of the Three Kingdoms. London: 1806. V. 40

DE BRITAINE, WILLIAM

The Interest of England in the Present War with Holland. London: 1672. V. 41

DE BROGLIE, DUC

The King's Secret: Being the Secret Correspondence of Louis XV, with His Diplomatic Agents from 1752 to 1774. London: 1870. V. 46

DE BRUNHOFF, JEAN

Babar and Father Christmas. New York: 1940. V. 39

Babar's Anniversary Album. New York: 1981. V. 39

Le Roi Babar. Paris: 1933. V. 45

The Travels of Babar. New York: 1934. V. 45

DE BRUNHOFF, LAURENT

Picnic at Babar's. London. V. 44

DE BRY, JOHAN

Petit Voyages - Part VI. Frankfurt: 1603. V. 38

DE BRY, JOHANN THEODORE

Florilegium Novum, hoc Est: Variorum Maximeque Rariorum Florum ac Plantarum Singularaium Una Cum Suis Radicibus & Cepis, Eicones Diligenter in Aere Sculptae & ad Vivum ut Plurimum Expressae. New Gewachs: 1611. V. 37

DEBS and the Poets. Pasadena: 1920. V. 42

DEBS, EUGENE VICTOR

Walls and Bars. Chicago: 1927. V. 41; 42

DE BUCK, ADRIAAN

The Egyptian Coffin Texts V: texts of Spells 355-471. Chicago: (1961). V. 37

The Egyptian Coffin Texts. III. Texts of Spells . . . Chicago: 1962. V. 41

DE BURE, GUILLAUME FRANCOIS

Bibliographie Instructive: ou Traite de La Connoissance des Livres Rares et Singuliers. Paris: 1763-68. V. 38; 46

DE BURGH, EMMA MARIA

The Voice of Many Waters. London: 1858. V. 40

DEBUS, ALLEN G.

The Chemical Philosophy. New York: 1977. V. 40

DE CAMP, L. SPRAGUE

Divide and Rule. 1948. V. 43; 44

The Dragon of the Ishtar Gate. New York: 1961. V. 39

A Gun for Dinosaur. 1963. V. 39

Land of Unreason. 1942. V. 39

Sprague DeCamp's New Anthology. 1953. V. 39

Wall of Serpents. HW: 1978. V. 37; 39; 42

DE CASTELLANE, COMTE

Souvenirs of Military Life in Algeria. London: 1886. V. 41

DECASTON, HERBERT

Peerless Prestidigitation. London: 1910. V. 46

DE CASTRO, ADOLPHE DANZIGER 1866-

In the Garden of Abdullah: and Other Poems. Los Angeles: 1916. V. 39

DE CAUS, SALOMON 1576-1626

Les Raisons des Forces Mouvantes, avec Diverses Machines Tant Utiles que Plaisantes . . . Paris: 1624. V. 39; 42

DECCAN, HILARY

Light in the Offing. London: 1892. V. 43

THE DECEITFUL Irishman, and Artful Cheat: Being the Whole Life and Remarkable Robberies and Forgeries Committed by William Smith, Who was Executed at Tyburn on Wednesday the 3d of October. London: 1750? V. 45

DECEMBRIO, P. C.

The Book of Animals. New York: 1986. V. 37; 38

DE CHAIR, SOMERSET STRUBEN

The First Crusade, the Deeds of the Franks and Other Jerusalemites, 'Gesta Francorum et Aliorum Hierolimitanorum'. London: 1945. V. 37; 39; 40

The First Crusade: the Deeds of the Franks and Other Jerusalemites. Waltham St. Lawrence: 1945. V. 40

The Golden Carpet. London: 1943. V. 38; 39; 40; 43; 44; 46

Julius Caesar's Commentaries. A Modern Rendering by Somerset de Chair. (Waltham St. Lawrence): 1951. V. 37

The Silver Crescent. London. V. 38

The Silver Crescent. London: 1943. V. 37; 39; 40; 44; 46

The Story of a Lifetime. N.P.: 1954. V. 37

The Story of a Lifetime. Waltham St. Lawrence: 1954. V. 44; 46

The Story of a Lifetime. London: 1954. V. 37

DE CHANTELOUP, JEAN ANTOINE CLAUDE, COMTE 1756-1832

Elements of Chemistry. Philadelphia: 1796. V. 40

DE CHASSEPOL, FRANCOIS DE

The History of the Grand Visiers, Mahomet, and Achmet Coprogli, of the Three Last Grand Signiors, Their Sultana's and Chief Favourites . . . London: 1677. V. 39

DE CHATEAUNEUF, ALEXIS 1799-1853

The Country House (With Designs). London: 1843. V. 38

DECHEVRENS, F. R. MARC

Zi-Ka-Wei Observatory Near Shanghai China. Zi-ka-wei: 1880. V. 42

DE CHIRICO, GIORGIO

Hebdomeros. Paris: 1920. V. 46

DECHY, EDOUARD

Voyage Irlande en 1846 et 1847. Paris: 1847. V. 38

DECISIONES Provinciales cum Notis Variorum et Fusty-Whyggii. Edinburgh?: 1771? V. 45

DECIUS, PHILIPPUS 1453-1535

De Regulis Iuris. Cologne: 1598. V. 44

Scripta Sive Lectura Super Titulo de Regulis Juris . . . Lyon: 1536. V. 40

DECKER, MATTHEW

An Essay on the Causes of the Decline of the Foreign Trade, Consequently of the Value of the Lands of Britain, and on the Means to Restore Both. London: 1750. V. 46

An Essay on the Causes of the Decline of the Foreign Trade, Consequently of the Value of the Lands of Britain and on the Means to Restore Both. Edinburgh: 1756. V. 43

Serious Considerations on the Several High Duties Which the Nation in General . . . London: 1743. V. 42

DECKER, P.

Gothic Architecture Decorated. London: 1759. V. 45

DECKER, PAUL

Fuerstlicher Bau - Meister/ Oder Architectura Civilis, Wie Grosser Fuersten und Herren Pallaeste/ mit Ihren Hoefen/ Lust=Haeusern/ Gaerten/ Grotten/ Orangieren/ und Anderen Darzu Gehoerigen Gebaueden Fueglich Anzulegen/ und Nach Heutiger Art Auszuzieren. Augsburg: 1711-13-16. V. 40

DECKER, PETER

A Descriptive Check List Together with a Short Title Index Describing Almost 7500 Items of Western Americana . . . New York: 1940-45. V. 46

A Descriptive Check List Together With Short Title Index Describing Almost 7500 Items of Western Americana . . . New York: 1960. V. 37; 39; 40

The Diaries of Peter Decker. Georgetown: 1966. V. 38; 40; 44

Peter Decker's Catalogues of Americana. Austin: 1979. V. 40; 42; 44

Peter Decker's Catalogues of Americana, 1944-1963. Austin: 1980. V. 37; 38; 39; 41; 42; 43; 44; 46

DECKER, THOMAS

The Gull's Hornbook. Bristol: 1812. V. 41

A **DECLARATION** and Remonstrance of the Distressed and Bleeding Frontier Inhabitants of the Province of Pennsylvania. Philadelphia: 1764. V. 41

A **DECLARATION** of the Causes Which Impel the State of Texas to Secede from the Federal Union. Austin: 1861. V. 39; 42

A **DECLARATION** of the Demeanor and Carriage of Sir Walter Raleigh, Knight, as Well in His Voyage, as In and Since His Return. London: 1618. V. 38; 40

A **DECLARATION** of the General Council of the Army: Agreed Upon at Wallingford-House, 27th October, 1659. London: 1659. V. 37

DECLARATION of the Immediate causes Which Induce and Justify the Secession of South Carolina From the Federal Union; and the Ordinance of Secession. Charleston: 1860. V. 42

DECLAUX, E.

Pasteur, the History of a Mind. Philadelphia: 1920. V. 39

DECLE, LIONEL

Three Years in Savage Africa. London: 1898. V. 40; 45

DE COETLOGON, CHARLES EDWARD

The Temple of Truth; or, the Best System of Reason, Philosophy, Virtue and Morals, Analytically Arranged. London: 1806. V. 44

The Temple of Truth . . . London: 1808. V. 42

DE COETLOGON, DENIS

Serious and Impartial Relfections on the Conduct of the Several Princes and States of Europe at This Present Conjuncture. London: 1743. V. 41

DECORATIVE Metalwork and Cotton Textiles: Third International Exhibition of Contemporary Industrial Art. N.P. (NY): 1930. V. 37

DE CORDOVA, DON A.

A Voyage of Discovery in the Strait of Magellan. London: 1820. V. 38; 40

DE CORDOVA, JACOB

Lecture on Texas Delivered by Mr. J. De Cordova, at Philadelphia, New York, Mount Holly, Brooklyn, and Newark, Also, a Paper Read by Him Before the New York Geographical Society, April 15th, 1858. Philadelphia: 1858. V. 40; 45

The Texas Immigrant and Traveller's Guide Book. Austin: 1856. V. 42; 45

Texas: Her Resources and Her Public men. Philadelphia: 1858. V. 38; 39; 42

DE COSSON, E. A.

The Cradle of the Blue Nile A Visit to the Court of King John of Ethiopia. London: 1877. V. 40

DE COUVRAY, J. B. L.

The Amours of the Chevalier de Fabulas. London: 1890. V. 38

A **DECREE** of Starre-Chamber: Concerning Inmates and Divided Tenements, in London or Three Miles About (Restricting Their Number and Requiring Provision for the Poor). London: 1636. V. 40

DE CREUX, FRANCOIS

History of Canada or New France. Toronto: 1951. V. 39

DEDEKIND, FRIEDRICH

Grobianus; or, the Compleat Booby. London: 1739. V. 40

Grobianvs. De Morvm Simplicitate, Libri duo. Frankfurt: 1150. V. 40

De Morvm Simplicitate, Libri Duo. In Gfatiam Omnium Rusticitatem Amantium Conscripti. Frankfurt a.M.: 1550. V. 39

DE DINO, DUCHESSE

Memoirs of the Duchesse De Dino: 1831-1835; 1836-1840. London: 1909-10. V. 38

DE DURFORT, CLAIRE

Ourika. Austin: 1977. V. 40; 44

DEE, ARTHUR

Fasciculus Chemicus: or Chymical Collections, Expressing the Ingres, Progress and Egress of the Secret Hermetick Science, Out of the Choicest and Most Famous Authors. London: 1650. V. 38

DEE, JOHN

The Private Diary of Dr. John Dee, and the Catalogue of His Library of Manuscripts. London: 1842. V. 45

DEEBLE, E. B.

Description of the Patent Metallic Caisson, for Constructing Piers, Harbors, Breakwaters, Basins, Locks, Quay, docks, Mill-Dams, Roads . . . London: 1828. V. 41

DEED and Ordinances of the Foundation Schools at Chigwell in Essex. N.P.: 1790. V. 45

DEEPING, WARWICK

Roper's Row. London: 1929. V. 41

DEER, W. A.

Rock-Forming Minerals. New York: 1962. V. 43

DEERING, CHARLES

Nottinghamia Vetus et Nova or an Account of the Ancient and Present State of the Town of Nottingham . . . Nottingham: 1751. V. 39

DEERING, JOHN R.

Lee and His Cause; or, the Why and the How of the War Between the States. New York: 1907. V. 46

DEFEBAUGH, JAMES E.

History of the Lumber Industry of America. Chicago: 1906-07. V. 46

DEFENCE of Col. Fremont & the Republican Party, Before the Young Men's Fremont and Dayton Central Union of New York . . . New York: 1856. V. 40

A DEFENCE of Natural and Revealed Religion: Being a Collection of the Sermons Preached at the Lecture Founded by the Honourable Boyle, Esq . . . London: 1739. V. 39

A DEFENCE of Roy's Hebrew Dictionary, Against a Review of It by Moses Stuart of Andover. N.P.: 1838? V. 43

A DEFENCE of Some Proceedings Lately Depending in Parliament, to Render More Effectual the Act for Quieting the Possession of the Subject, Commonly Called the Nullum Tempus Act. London: 1771. V. 38; 40

A DEFENCE of the Character of the Late Richard Archbold Esqr., Formerly a Jeusuit . . . in Confutation of . . . a Popish Pamphlet Entitled a Letter to the Rt. Revd. Lord Bishop of Down and Connor, with a Supplement . . . Belfast: 1769. V. 38

A DEFENCE Of the Examination of a Book, Entituled, A Brief Account of Many of the Prosecutions of the People Called Quakers &c. So Far as the Clergy of the Diocese of Lichfield and Coventry are Concerned in It. London: 1738. V. 38

DEFENCE Of the Honourable Andrew Cochrane Johnstone; Including a View of the Evidence Produced on His Trial; with the Sentence and Varied Commentaries Thereon by the Judge Advocate General; and with a Relative Series of Interesting Letters . . . London: 1805. V. 39

A DEFENCE of the Knights of the House of Austria, Against the Unjust Claims of the King of Prussia. London: 1741. V. 41

A DEFENCE of the People; or, Full Confutation of the Pretended Facts, Advanc'd in a Late Huge, Angry Pamphlet; Call'd Faction Detected . . . London: 1744. V. 41

DEFENCE Of the Perthshire Resolutions. In Answer to a Letter Upon the Distillery. Edinburgh: 1784. V. 42

A DEFENCE of the Roman Catholic Bill. London: 1780. V. 39

DEFENCE of the Working Classes, In Reply to an Article in 'Chamber's Edinburgh Journal' entitled 'Strikes - Their Statistics'. London: 1838. V. 40

THE DEFENCES of England. London: 1862. V. 40

THE DEFENSE Of Gracchus Babeuf Before the High Court of Vendom. Northampton: 1964. V. 37; 42; 43; 45

DEFER, JULES

souvenirs Pittoresques des Pyrenees. Paris: 1820. V. 46

DEFFRANS, CHRISTOFLE

Niort. Portau: 1595. V. 43

DE FILIPPI, FILIPPO

The Ascent of Mount St. Elias (Alaska) by H.R.H. Prince Luigi Amedeo Di Savoia Duke of the Abruzzi. London: 1900. V. 41

Karakoram and Western Himalaya 1909. London: 1912. V. 46

Karakoram and Western Himalaya 1909, an Account of the Expedition of H. R. H. Prince Luigi Amedeo of Savoy Duke of Abruzzi. New York: 1912. V. 40

Ruwenzori an Account of the Expedition of H.R.H. Prince Luigi Amedeo of Savoy . . . New York: 1908. V. 45

DEFINICOES, e Estatutos Cavalleiros, e Freires da Ordem de Nosso Senhor Jesus Christo, com a Historia da Origem, e Principio Della . . . Lisbon: 1746. V. 38

DE FLEURY, MARIA

Divine Poems and Essays on Various Subjects . . . London: 1791. V. 41; 42

DEFLORATIONES Patrum. Basle: 1494. V. 38

DEFLOT DE MOFRAS, EUGENE

Exploration du Territoire de l'Oregon, des Californies et de la Mer Vermeille, Executee Pendant les Annees 1840, 1841, et 1842. Paris: 1844. V. 39

DEFOE, DANIEL 1661?-1731

An Account of the Conduct of Robert Earl of Oxford. London: 1715. V. 42; 44

The Adventures of Robert Drury Druing Fifteen Years Captivity on the Island of Madagascar. London: 1807. V. 38

The Anatomy of Exchange-Alley; or, a System of Stock-Jobbing . . . London: 1719. V. 38

An Argument Proving that the design of Employing and Enobling Foreigners, Is a Treasonable Conspiracy Against the Constitution, Dangerous to the Kingdom, an Affront to the Nobility of Scotland . . . London: 1717. V. 37; 45

Caledonia, &c. A Poem in Honour of Scotland, and the Scots Nation. Edinburgh: 1706. V. 38

A Collection of the Most Remarkable Casualties and Disasters, Which Happen'd in the Late Dreadful Tempest . . . London. V. 43

A Collection of the Writings of the 'True-born Englishman'. London: 1703. V. 37; 38; 41

A Collection of the Writings of the Author of the True-Born Englishman. London: 1705. V. 43

The Complete English Tradesman. London: 1726. V. 45

The Complete English Tradesman . . . London: 1726-27. V. 45

Conjugal Lewdness; or Matrimonial Whoredom. London: 1727. V. 45

Conugal Lewdness; or Matrimonial Whoredom. I: 1728. V. 46

The Consolidator. London: 1705. V. 37; 40; 43; 46

The Dreadful Visitation, in a Short Account of the Progress and Effects of the Plague, the Last Time It Spread in the City of London, in the Year 1665. Philadelphia: 1774. V. 45

The Dyet of Poland, a Satyr. 1705. V. 43

Eleven Opinions About Mr. H(arle)y; with Observations. London: 1711. V. 42

An Essay Upon Publick Credit. London: 1710. V. 37

The Experiment; or, the Shortest Way with the Dissenters Exemplified. London: 1705. V. 38

The Farther Adventures of Robinson Crusoe. London: 1719. V. 39

The Fortunate Mistress. New York: 1924. V. 43

The Fortunes and Misfortunes of the Famous Moll Flanaders, &c. London: 1722. V. 37

The Four Years Voyages of Capt. George Roberts. London: 1726. V. 37; 38; 41; 46

A Fourth Essay, at Removing National Prejudices; with Some Reply to Mr. H--dges and Some Other Authors, Who Have Printed Their Objections Against an Union with England. Edinburgh: 1706. V. 42

A General History of the Robberies and Murders of the Most Notorious Pyrates. London: 1724. V. 37; 39; 40; 45

A General History of the Pyrates, from Their First Rise and Settlement in the Island of Providence, to the Present Time . . . London: 1726-28. V. 44

The History of the Kentish Petition. N.P.: 1701. V. 42

The History of the Union of Great Britain. Edinburgh: 1709. V. 37; 38; 43

The History of the Life and Adventures of Mr. Duncan Campbell. London: 1720. V. 37; 39; 41; 43; 45

The History and Remarkable Life of the Truely Honourable Colonel Jacque, Vulgarly call'd Colonel Jack, Who was Born a Gentleman . . . London: 1724. V. 46

The History of the Great Plague in London, in . . . 1665. London: 1754. V. 42; 43

The History of Mademoiselle de Beleau; or, the New Roxana, the Fortunate Mistress . . . London: 1775. V. 40; 46

The History of the Union Between England and Scotland . . . London: 1786. V. 37; 40; 45

The History of the Most Remarkable Life and Adventures of Colonel Jack . . . London: 1809. V. 46

The History of the Lives and Actions of the Most Famous Highwaymen, Street Robbers &c. Edinburgh: 1813. V. 45

The History and Remarkable Life of the Truely Honourable Col. Jaque, Vulgarly call'd Colonel Jack . . . London: 1724. V. 43

The History of the Devil, As Well Ancient as Modern. London: 1727. V. 45

The History of the Devil, Both Ancient and Modern. Philadelphia: 1809. V. 41

The History of the Wars . . . of Charles XII, King of Sweden . . . London: 1720. V. 38

A Hymn to the Pillory. London: 1703. V. 40

A Hymn to Victory. London: 1704. V. 39; 40

An Impartial History of the Life and Actions of Peter Alexowitz, the Present Czar of Muscovy . . . London: 1723. V. 38; 39; 43; 45

A Journal of the Earl of Marr's Proceedings, From His First Arrival in Scotland; to His Embarkation for France. London: 1716. V. 45

A Journal of the Plague Year. London: 1722. V. 41

A Journal of the Plague Year. London: 1935. V. 40

Jure Divino. London: 1706. V. 38; 39; 40; 41; 42; 44; 45; 46

The Justice and Necessity of a War with Holland, in Case the Dutch Do Not Come Into Her majesty's Measures, Stated and Examined. London: 1712. V. 42

The Layman's Vindication of the Church of England, As Well AGainst Mr. Howell's Charge of Schism, as Against Dr. Bennett's Pretended Answer to It. London: 1716. V. 44

Legion's New Paper: Being a Second Memorial to the Gentlemen of a Late House of Commons. London: 1702. V. 42; 45

A Letter Concerning Trade, from Several Scots-Gentlemen that are Merchants in England, To Their Countrymen that are Merchants in Scotland. Edinburgh: 1706. V. 41

DEFOE, DANIEL 1661?-1731 continued

The Pretences of the French Invasion Examined. For the Information of the People of England. London: 1692. V. 45

The Re-Representation; or, a Modest Search After the Great Plunderers of the Nation . . . London. V. 42

The Re-Representation; or, a Modest Search After the Great Plunderers of the Nation . . . London. V. 43

The Re-Presentation, or a Search for Plunderers of the Nation. London: 1711. V. 37

Reasons Against a War with France, or an Argument Showing that the French King's Owning the Prince of Wales as King of England, Scotland and Ireland, is No Sufficient Ground of a War. London: 1701. V. 38; 46

Reflections Upon the Late Great Revolution. London: 1689. V. 43

The Romances and Narratives. London: 1895. V. 37; 38

Romances and Narratives. London: 1895-1900. V. 37; 39

Roxana. Connecticut: 1976. V. 43

the Scotch Medal Decipher'd, and the New Hereditary Right Men Display'd . . . London: 1711. V. 42; 46

A Seasonable Warning or the Pope and King of France Unmasked. Edinburgh: 1706. V. 45

A Seasonable Warning and Caution Against the Insinuations of Papists and Jacobites in Favour of the Pretender. London: 1712. V. 40; 42

The Secret History of the October Club: From Its Original to this Time. (with) Part II. London: 1711. V. 37; 40

The Secret History of the White Staff, Being an Account of Affairs Under the Condut of Some Late Ministers and What Might Probably Have Happened If Her Majesty Had Not Died. London: 1714. V. 40; 45

Secret Memoirs of the Late Mr. Duncan Campbell. London: 1732. V. 45

The Secret History of State Intrigues in the Management of the Scepter, In the late Reign. London: 1715. V. 37

The Secrets of the Invisible World Disclos'd . . . London: 1725. V. 46

The Secrets of the Invisible World Disclos'd . . . London: 1735. V. 46

The Secrets of the Invisible World Disclos'd, or, an Universal History of Apparitions Sacred and Profane, Under all Denominations. London: 1738. V. 41; 44

Seldom Comes A Better. London: 1710. V. 39

The Shortest-Way with the Dissenters. London: 1702. V. 39

Some Reasons Offered by the Late Ministry in Defence of Their Administration. London: 1715. V. 37

A Speech Without Doors. London: 1710. V. 42

The Storm. London: 1704. V. 37; 38; 40; 41; 44; 45

The Storm; or, a Collection of the Most Remarkable Casulaties and Disasters Which Happen'd in the Late Dreadful Tempest . . . Sawbridge,: 1704. V. 46

The Storm; or a Collection of the Most Remarkable Casualties and Disasters Which Happened if Her Majesty Had Not Died. London: 1714. V. 45

Strike While the Iron's Hot, or, Now Is the Time to Be Happy. London: 1715. V. 40

A Supplement to the Faults of Both Sides. London: 1710. V. 38

A System of Magick; or, A History of the Black Art. London: 1727. V. 38; 42

A System of Magick or a History of the Black Art. London: 1728. V. 39

A System of Magic; or a History of the Black Art. Oxford: 1840. V. 37

A Tour Thro' the Whole Island of Great Britain. London: 1724. V. 44

A Tour Thro' the Whole Island of Great Britain . . . London: 1762. V. 38; 42

A Tour through the Whole Island of Great Britain. London: 1769. V. 37; 38; 44; 46

A Tour thro' the Whole Island of Great Britain, Divided into Circuits or Journies. London: 1927. V. 37; 41; 43

A Tour through the Whole Island of Great Britain. London: 1983. V. 46

A Treatise Concerning the Use and Abuse of the Marriage Bed . . . 1717. V. 37

A True Collection of the Writings of the Author of the True Born Englishman. London: 1703. V. 38; 39; 40; 43; 44; 45; 46

The True Brown Englishman. London: 1750. V. 43

The Works. London: 1840-43. V. 38

Works. New York: 1903. V. 41; 43

The Works. New York: 1905. V. 41

The Works of Daniel Defoe. New York: 1907. V. 39

Works. London: 1923-25. V. 37

Writings. New York: 1928. V. 38

Ye True-born Englishman Proceed. N.P.: 1701. V. 43

DE FONTAINE, F. G.

A Cyclopedia of the Best Thoughts of Charles Dickens. New York: 1873. V. 39; 44

DE FONTAINE, FELIX GREGORY 1832-1896

Marginalia; or, Gleanings from an Army Note-Book. Columbia: 1864. V. 43

DE FOREST, J. W.

Miss Ravenel's Conversion from Secession to Loyalty. New York: 1867. V. 39

DE FOREST, JOHN W.

History of the Indians of Connecticut from the Earliest Known Period to 1850. Hartford: 1851. V. 37; 43; 45

DE FOREST, JOHN WILLIAM

History of the Indians of Connecticut from the Earliest Known Period to 1850. El Paso: 1947. V. 44

Overland, a Novel. New York: 1871. V. 44

DE FOREST, L. EFFINGHAM

James Cox Brady and His Ancestry. New York: 1933. V. 46

Moore and Allied Families, The Ancestry of William Henry Moore. New York: 1938. V. 39

DE FOREST, LEE

Father of Radio: the Autobiography of. Chicago: 1950. V. 45

DE FOREST, LOCKWOOD 1850-1932

Indian Domestic Architecture. 1885. V. 38

A Wallon Family America, Lockwood de Forest and his Forbears, 1500-1848, by Mrs. Robert W. de Forest, Together with a Voyage to Fuiana being the Journal of Jesse de Forest and His Colonists 1623-1625. Boston: 1914. V. 37

DEFOURI, JAMES H.

Historical Sketch of the Catholic Church in New Mexico. San Francisco: 1887. V. 40; 42

DE FREES, MADELINE

Light Station on Tillamook Rocks. Lewisburgh: 1989. V. 43

DE FREVAL, J. B.

The History of the Heavens. London: 1752. V. 39

DEGARMO, MARIE E.

Pathfinders of Texas 1836-1846. Austin: 1951. V. 41

DEGAS, EDGAR

Works in Sculpture. New York: 1944. V. 46

DEGERANDO, M. LE BARON

Self-Education; or the Means and Art of Moral Progress. Boston: 1830. V. 45

The Visitor of the Poor. Boston: 1832. V. 41

DEGERING, HERMANN

Lettering, a Series of 240 Plates Illustrating Modes of Writing in Western Europe from Antiquity to the End of the 18th Century. London: 1929. V. 45

DEGGE, SIMON 1612-1704

The Parsons Councellor With the Law of Thithes of Rithing. London: 1681. V. 38; 40

DE GOLYER, E.

Across Aboriginal America. El Paso: 1947. V. 37; 38; 39; 40; 41; 42; 43; 45

The Journey of Three Englishmen Across Texas in 1568. El Paso: 1947. V. 44; 46

DE GONCOURT, EDMOND

Love in the Eighteenth Century. London: 1905. V. 42

DE GONTAUT, DUCHESSE

Memoirs. New York: 1894. V. 41

DE GOUY, LOUIS P.

Derrydale Cook Book of Fish and Game. New York: (1937). V. 37; 39

DE GRAAF, REGNER

De Virorum Organis Generationi Inservientibus, de Clisteribus et de Usu Siphonis in Anatomia . . . Leyden & Rotterdam: 1668. V. 41

DE GRAEVE, MARIE-CHRISTINE

The Ships of the ancient Near East (c. 2000-500 B.C.). Leuven: 1981. V. 37

DE GRAFF, SIMON

The Modern Geometrical Stair-Builder's Guide . . . New York: 1845. V. 40

DEGRAND, P. P. F.

An Address on the Advantages of Low Fares and Low Rates of Freight. Boston: 1840. V. 38; 39

Proceedings of the Friends of a Railroad to San Francisco. Boston: 1849. V. 41

DE GRAZIA, TED

Ah Ha Toro. De Grazia Paints and Sketches the Bullring. Flagstaff: 1967. V. 44

DE GRAZIA, TED continued

De Grazia Paints the Yaqui Easter: the Forty Days of Lent in Forty Painting with a Personal Commentary. Tucson: 1968. V. 39

Father Junipero Serra. Los Angeles: 1970. V. 42; 44

Padre Kino. Los Angeles: 1962. V. 44; 46

Padre Kino. A Portfolio Depicting Memorable Events in the Life and Times of the Immortal Priest, Colonizer of the Southwest, Depicted in Drawings. Tucson: 1962. V. 46

The Rose and the Robe: the Travels and Adventures of Fray Junipero Serra in California, 1769-1784. Los Angeles: 1968. V. 46

The Seri Indians. Flagstaff: 1970. V. 44

Troopers West: Military & Indian Affairs on the American Frontier. San Diego: 1970. V. 44

DEGREVANT

Sire Degrevaunt. Hammersmith: 1896. V. 42

DEGREVANT (ROMANCE)

The Romance of Sir Degrevant. Hammersmith: 1896. V. 40

Sire Degrevaunt. London: 1896. V. 41

DE GREY, THOMAS

The Compleat Horse-Man and Expert Farraier. London: 1670. V. 37

The Compleat Horseman and Expert Ferrier. London: 1651. V. 37

DE GRIJS, A.

Insulinde Twaalf Tafereelen uit Nederlandsch Indie Volgens Teekeneningen en Studien Naar de Natuur. Rotterdam: 1879-82. V. 45

DE GROOT, HENRY

Recollections of California Mining Life, Primitive Placers, Primitive Places and the First Important Discovery of Gold . . . San Francisco. V. 46

Recollections of California Mining Life . . . Primitive Placers and the First Important Discovery of Gold. San Francisco: 1884. V. 40; 45

DE GRUCHY, AUGUSTA

Under the Hawthorn and Other Verse. London: 1893. V. 38

DE GUERIN, MAURICE

The Centaur. Montague: 1915. V. 45

DE GUEVARA, ANTONIO

The Praise and Happinesse of the Countrie-Life. Newtown: 1938. V. 37

DE GUIGNES, JOSEPH 1721-1800

Histoire Generale des Huns, des Turcs, des Mogols, et des Autres Tartares . . . Paris: 1756-58. V. 40

DEGUILEVILLE, GUILLAUME DE

Le Pelerinage de Vie Humaine. London: 1893. V. 44

Le Pelerinage de l'Ame. London: 1895. V. 44

Le Pelerinage Jhesucrist. London: 1897. V. 44

The Pilgrimage of the Life of Man. London: 1905. V. 44

DE HAE, R.

Clar Litridheacht na Nua-Ghaedhilge. A Bibliography of Irish Literature and History 1850-1936. Dublin: 1938/40. V. 38

Clar Litridheacht na Nua-Ghaedhilge, 1850-1936. Dublin: 1940. V. 43

DE HAMEL, CHRISTOPHER

Glossed Books of the Bible and the Origins of the Paris Booktrade. 1984. V. 45

Glossed Books on the Bible and the Origins of the Paris Booktrade. London: 1984. V. 40

DE HART, WILLIAM CHETWOOD 1800-1848

Observations on Military Law, and the Constitution and Practice of Courts Martial, with a Summary of the Law of Evidence, as Applicable to Military Trials . . . New York: 1863, c. 1846. V. 42

DE HASS, WILLS

History of the Early Settlement and Indian Wars of Western Virginia . . . Wheeling: 1851. V. 37; 46

DE HAVILLAND, OLIVIA

Every Frenchman Has One. New York: 1962. V. 45

DE HELL, XAVIER HOMMAIRE

Travels in the Steppes of the Caspian Sea, the Crimea, the Caucasus &c. London: 1847. V. 37; 39; 45

DE HERIZ, PATRICK

La Belle O'Morphi, a Brief Biography . . . London. V. 43

DE HERRERA, ANTONIUS

Aankomst van Jean d'Ezquebel ter Bevolking van Jamaica, Door den Ammiraal Diego Kolumbus, van Hispaniola Derwaards Gezonden, In't Faar 1510 . . . Leyden: 1706. V. 38

DEIDIER, ANTOINE

An Historical Account of the Plague at Marseilles. London: 1722. V. 43

DEIDIER, L'ABBE

La Mechanique Generale, Contenant la Statique l'Airometrie, l'Hydrostatique, et l'Hydraulique . . . Paris: 1741. V. 45

DEIGHAN, P.

Philomath. A Complete Treatise of Arithmetic, Rational and Practical . . . Suited to the Man of Business and Those Desirous of Becoming Efficient in Accounts . . . Dublin: 1804. V. 38

DEIGHTON, LEN

Billion Dollar Brain. London: 1966. V. 44; 45; 46

Billion Dollar Brain. London: 1967. V. 44

Close-Up. London: 1972. V. 44; 45

Declarations of War. London: 1971. V. 44; 45

An Expensive Place to Die. London: 1957. V. 45

An Expensive Place to Die. New York: 1967. V. 39; 45

Funeral in Berlin. London: 1964. V. 45

Funeral in Berlin. London: 1965. V. 44; 45

Funeral in Berlin. New York: 1965. V. 45

Horse Under Water. London: 1963. V. 40; 44; 45

Horse Under Water. New York: 1966. V. 46

The Ipcress File. London: 1962. V. 41

The Ipcress File. New York: 1963. V. 37; 39; 42; 43; 44

The Ipcress File. 1962. V. 37

Only When I Larf. London: 1968. V. 44; 45

Only When I Laugh. New York: 1986. V. 42; 46

Ou est Le Garlic. New York: 1977. V. 44

SS-GB. London: 1976. V. 46

Twinkle, Twinkle, Little Spy. London: 1976. V. 44; 45

Yesterday's Spy. London: 1975. V. 44; 45

DEJERINE, J.

The Psychoneuroses and their treatment by Psychotherapy. Authorized translations by Smith E. Jelliffe, Second English edition. Philadelphia: 1915. V. 37

DEJERINE, JOSEPH

Anatomie Des Centres Nerveux. Paris: 1895. V. 42

DE JOHNSTONE, CHEVALIER

Memoirs of the Rebellion in 1745 and 1746. London: 1822. V. 42; 46

DEJONG, MEINDERT

The Little Cow and the Turtle. New York: 1955. V. 46

DE KAY, JAMES E.

Anniversary Address on the Progress of the Natural Sciences in the United States, Delivered Before the Lyceum of Natural History. New York: 1826. V. 40

Birds of New York: Part 2 of Zoology of New York or the New York Fauna. Albany: 1844. V. 39

Natural History of New York. Part One. Zoology. Mollusca & Crustacea. New York: 1843. V. 45; 46

Natural History of New York. Zoology. Par II: Birds. Albany: 1844. V. 37

Sketches of Turkey in 1831 and 1832. New York: 1833. V. 37

Zoology of New York, or the New York Fauna . . . Part II. Birds. Albany: 1844. V. 41

DE KIEWIET, C. W.

Dufferin-Carnarvon Correspondence, 1874-1878. Toronto: 1955. V. 45

DEKKER, THOMAS

The Batchelers Banqvet. London: 1630. V. 38; 44

The Dramatic Works . . . 1953-61. V. 40

The Gull's Hornbook . . . Bristol: 1812. V. 42

The Magnificent Entertainment: Given Unto King James, Queene Anne His Wife, and Henry Frederick the Prince . . . London: 1604. V. 43

The Seven Deadly Sins of London. London: 1905. V. 42

DE KOVEN, ANNA FARWELL 1860-

The Life and Letters of John Paul Jones. New York: 1913. V. 42

DE KROYFT, S. H., MRS.

A Place in the Memory. New York: 1854. V. 38

DEL Museo Capitolino. Rome: 1741-82. V. 41; 42

DE LA COUR, JAMES

Poems. Cork: 1778. V. 38

DE LA FAILLE, J. B.

The Works of Vincent Van Gogh by J.B. de la Faille. 1970. V. 37

DELABARRE, CHRISTOPHE FRANCOIS

Traite de la partie Mecanique de l'art du Chirurgien-Dentiste. Paris: 1820. V. 45

DE LABORDE, LEON

Journey from Arabia Petraea, to Mount Sinai and the Excavated City of Petra. London: 1836. V. 39

Journey Through Arabia Petraea, to Mount Sinai, and the Excavated City of Petra, the Edom of the Prophecies. London: 1838. V. 37

DELACOUR, JEAN

Pheasants of the World. London: 1951. V. 38; 46

The Pheasants of the World. London: 1951, 1964. V. 38

The Pheasants of the World. Salt Lake City: 1957. V. 39

The Waterfowl of the World. London: 1954. V. 38; 40

The Waterfowl of the World. London: 1954-64. V. 39; 46

The Waterfowl of the World. London: 1974. V. 40

Waterfowl of the World. 1975. V. 45; 46

DELACROIX, EUGENE

The Journal of Eugene Delacroix. London: 1938. V. 46

The Paintings. A Critical Catalogue 1832-1863; 1986. V. 40

DELACROIX, HENRY

Boutiques. Paris: 1930. V. 46

DELACROIX, JACQUES VINCENT

A Review of the Constitutions of the Principal States of Europe, and of the United States of America . . . . London: 1792. V. 43

DE LAET, JOHANNES

De Imperio Magni Mogolis Sive India Vera Commentarius E Varys Auctoribus Congestus. Ludguni Batavorum: 1631. V. 46

DELAFIELD, E. M.

Diary of a Provincial Lady. London: 1930. V. 37; 40; 45

DELAFIELD, FRANCIS

A Manual of Physical Diagnosis. New York: 1878. V. 40; 42; 45

DELAFIELD, JOHN

An Inquiry into the Origin of the Antiquities of America. Cincinnati: 1839. V. 37; 42

An Inquiry into the Origin of the Antiquities of America. New York: 1839. V. 42; 45

DELAFIELD, JOHN ROSS

Delafield. The Family History. 1945. V. 43

DELAFIELD, R.

Report on the Art of War in Europe in 1854, 1855 and 1856. Washington: 1861. V. 37; 44

DELAFOSSE, JEAN CHARLES

Receuil des Fontaines, Frontispieces, Pyramides, Cartouches, Dessus-de-Portres, Bordures, Medallions, Trophees, Vases.. Amsterdam: 1770. V. 38

DELAGARDETTE, C. M.

Les Ruines de Paestum ou Posidonia, Ancienne ville de la Grande Grece . . . Paris: 1799. V. 38

DE LAGUNA, FREDERICA

Under Mt. Saint Elias: The History and Culture of the Yakutat Tlingit. Washington: 1972. V. 37; 39; 43

DELAHAY, MARK

Circular Issued by the Surveyor General of Kansas and Nebraska, and Estimates for the Extension of Surveys Based Upon the Reports of His Deputies and Petitions From Settlers Residing on the Unsurveyed Lands in Kansas. Leavenworth: 1861. V. 41; 43

DE LAIRESSE, GERARD

The Principles of Drawing, Containing a Curious Collection of Examples . . . After the Designs of Albert Durer, Le Clerc, Hollar, and other Great Masters. London: 1748. V. 45

DE LAMA, GIOVANNI

Vita del Cavaliere Giambattista Bodoni Tipografo Italiano e Catalogo Cronologico Delle Sue Edizioni. Parma: 1816. V. 38; 41; 44

DE LAMARTINE, ALPHONSE

Souvenirs, Impressions, Pensees et Paysages, Pendant un Voyage en Orient 1832-33, ou Notes d'un Voyageur. Paris and Brussels: 1835. V. 46

DELAMAYNE, THOMAS HALLIE

The Patricians; or, a Candid Examination Into the Merits of the Principal Speakers of the House of Lords . . . London: 1773. V. 46

The Senators; or, A Candid Examination into the Merits of the Principal Performers of St. Stephen's Chapel. London: 1772. V. 41

DE LAMOTTE, FREEMAN GAGE 1814-1862

The Book of Ornamental Alphabets Ancient and Mediaeval, from the Eighth Century, with Numerals . . . London: 1860. V. 39; 40

Mediaeval Alphabets and Initials for Illuminators. London: 1861. V. 39; 45

Mediaeval Alphabet and Initials for Illuminators. London: 1864. V. 40

Primer of the Art of Illumination for the Use of Beginners . . . London: 1860. V. 43

DELAMOTTE, W. ALBERT

Illustrations of Viriginia Water and the Adjacent Scenery, Celebrated as the Favourite and Frequent Retreat of His Most Gracious Mystery, in a series of Views from Sketches Made on the Spot. London: 1828. V. 41

DELAND, MARGARET

The Awakening of Helena Richie. New York: 1906. V. 43

The Awakening of Helena Richie. New York: & London: 1906. V. 43

An Encore. New York & London: 1907. V. 39

Florida Days. Boston: 1889. V. 42

The Old Garden and Other Verse. Boston: 1886. V. 43

The Old Garden and Other Verses. London: 1893. V. 45; 46

The Old Garden and Other Verses. Boston: 1894. V. 39; 41

Old Chester Tales. New York: 1899. V. 43; 46

Old Chester Tales. New York: 1899, 1898. V. 42; 44

DELANEY, MATILDA, J. S.

A Survivor's Recollections of the Whitman Massacre . . . Spokane: 1920. V. 40; 43

DELANO, ALONZO

Across the Plains and Among the Diggings. New York: 1936. V. 42; 45

Life on the Plains and Among the Diggings. Auburn: 1854. V. 40; 44

Life on the Plains and Among the Diggings, Being Scenes and Adventures of an Overland Journey to California with Particular Incidents of the Route . . . Auburn and Buffalo: 1854. V. 45; 46

Life on the Plains, and Among the Diggings; Being Scenes and Adventures of an Overland Journey in California. New York: 1859. V. 40

A Live Woman in the Mines; or, Pike County Ahead! New York: 1857. V. 40

Pen-Knife Sketches or Chips of the Old Block. San Francisco: 1934. V. 41; 43; 45

DELANO, AMASA

Narrative of Voyagaes and Travels in Northern and Southern Hemispheres . . . Boston: 1817. V. 38; 39; 41; 42; 43; 45

A Narrative of Voyages & Travels, in the Northern & Southern Hemispheres. Boston: 1818. V. 39; 43; 45

DELANY, MARTIN

Principia of Ethnology; the Origin of Races and Color, with an Archeaological Compendium of Ethiopian and Egyptian Civilization. Philadelphia: 1879. V. 42

DELANY, MARTIN ROBINSON

Official Report of the Niger Valley Exploring Party. London: 1861. V. 37

DELANY, MARY GRANVILLE PENDARVES 1700-1788

The Autobiography and Correspondence of Mary Granville, Mrs. Delany. London: 1861. V. 43

DELANY, PATRICK

Longford's Glyn: a True History. London & Dublin: 1732. V. 40

Longford's-Glyn, or the Willow and the Brook. London: 1789. V. 40; 45

Observations Upon Lord Orrery's Remarks on the Life and Writings of Dr.. Jonathan Swift. London: 1754. V. 38; 40; 41; 42; 44

Reflections Upon Polygamy and the Encouragement Given to the Practice in the Scriptures of the Old Testament. London: 1739. V. 43

DELANY, SAMUEL R.

Babel-17. 1967. V. 39

Babel 17. London: 1967. V. 45

Dahlgren. Boston: 1977. V. 42

The Motion of Light in Water. New York: 1988. V. 42

Nova. Garden City: 1968. V. 46

DELAPLAINE, JOSEPH

Delaplaine's Repository of the Lives and Portraits of Distinguished American Characters. Philadelphia: 1815-18. V. 45

DE LATOCNYE, C.

A Frenchman's Walk Through Ireland. Belfast: 1917. V. 38

DE LAUNAY, ABBE

Les Evangiles. aris: 1864. V. 43

DELAUNAY, SONIA

Alphabet. New York: 1972. V. 45

DELAUNAY, SONIA continued

Sonia Delaunay: 27 Tableaux Vivants. Milano: 1969. V. 46

DE LAUTREAMONT, COMTE

The Lay of Maldoror, by the Comte de Lautreamont. Translated by John Rodker. London: 1924. V. 37

DELAVAL. New-bern: 1804. V. 40

DELAVIGNE, CASIMIR

Messenienne sur Lord Byron (in verse). Paris: 1824. V. 44

DELAWARE AND HUDSON CANAL CO.

The Summer Tourist: Descriptive of the Delaware and Hudson Canal Co.'s Railroads, and Their Summer Resorts! Season of 1880. Boston: 1880. V. 45

DELAWARE River Bridge Joint Commission OF THE STATES OF PENNSYLVANIA & NEW JERSEY The Quebec Bridge Over the St. Lawrence River, Report of the Government Board of Engineers. Quebec: 1919. V. 40

DELBRUCK, RICHARD

Antike Portraits. Bonn: 1912. V. 44

DELCROIX, JACQUES VINCENT

A Review of the Constitutions of the Principal States of Europe, and of the United States of America. London: 1792. V. 40

DE LEDREDE, RICHARD

A Contemporary Narrative of the Proceedings Against Dame Alice Kyteller, Prosecuted for Sorcery in 1324. London: 1843. V. 46

DELEGORGUE, ADOLPHE

Voyage dans l'Afrique Australe, Notamment dans le Territoire de Natal, dans Celui des Cafres Amazoulous et Makatisses . . . Paris: 1847. V. 38

DE LEON, PERRY M.

Navies in War and The Confederate Navy in the War Between the States. Washington: 1910. V. 44

DE LEON, THOMAS COOPER

Four Years in Rebel Capitols: an Inside View of Life in the Southern Confederacy, From Birth to Death. Mobile: 1890. V. 42; 43

Our Creole Carnivals: Their Origin, History, Progress and Results, with Sketches of Outside Carnivals. Mobile: 1890. V. 44

The Rock of the Rye. Mobile: 1888. V. 43

DELEPIERRE, OCTAVE

Album Pittoresque de Bruges, ou Collection des plus belles vues et des Principaux Monuments de cette Ville, dessines par A. Tessaro. Bruges: 1837. V. 39

DE LESSEPS, M. DE

The Voyage of La Perouse Round the World in the Years 1785, 1786, 1787 and 1788. London: 1798. V. 40

DELEUZE, JOSEPH PHILLIPPE FRANCOIS

Practical Instruction in Animal Magnetism . . . Providence: 1837. V. 40; 41

Practical Instruction in Animal Magnetism. New York: 1843. V. 46

Practical Instruction in Animal Magnetism. London: 1845. V. 46

DELGADO, JAMES P.

The Log of Apollo: Joseph Perkins Beach's Journal of the Voyage of the Ship Apollo from New York to San Francisco> San Francisco: 1986. V. 40; 44

LES DELICES de la Hollande, Contenant une Description fort Exacte de Son Pais, de Ses Villes & de la Condition des Hiabitans; avec un racourci de ce qui s'est passe depuis les temps qu'ils se sont mis en libete, jusqu'a lannee 1680. Amsterdam: 1685. V. 37

LES DELICES du Sentiment; or the Passionate Lovers; in a Series of Letters Which Have Recently Passed Between Two Celebrated Characters, Well Known in Polite Life for Their Virtues, Talents and Accomplishments. London: 1781. V. 39; 42; 44

DELICIARUM Hortensium, Das ist Kurze und Verstandlich Mitgetheilte Anleitung . . . Magdeburg: 1705. V. 38

DE LIEFDE, JOHN

The Romance of Charity. London: 1867. V. 43

DELILLE, JACQUES

The Garden; or, the Art of Laying Out Grounds. London: 1789. V. 42

The Gardens, a Poem. London: 1798. V. 38; 40; 44

Les Trois Regnes de la Nature. Paris: 1808. V. 39

DELILLIO, DON

Americana. New York: 1971. V. 45

DELILLO, DON

Americana. Boston: 1971. V. 41; 42; 44; 46

The Day Room. New York: 1987. V. 44

End Zone. Boston: 1972. V. 42; 45

Great Jones Street. Boston: 1973. V. 42; 46

The Names. New York: 1982. V. 45; 46

Ratner's Star. New York: 1976. V. 46

White Noise. New York: 1985. V. 44

DELKESKAMP, F. W.

Panorama of the Rhine and the adjacent country, from Cologne to Mayence; together with the Steamboat Companion. London: n.d. V. 37

DELL, BLOYD

Sweet and Twenty. Cincinnati: 1921. V. 46

DELL, ETHEL M.

The Way of an Eagle. London: 1916. V. 43

DELL, FLOYD

Moon-Calf: A Novel. New York: 1920. V. 37

This Mad Ideal. London: 1925. V. 43

Were You Ever a Child. New York: 1919. V. 39

Women as World Builders. Chicago: 1913. V. 41; 43

DELL, HENRY

the Booksellers. London: 1766. V. 46

DELL, J.

The West Australian Bird Folio. West Perth: 1982. V. 37; 38

DELL, JOHN

The West Australian Bird Folio. Perth: 1981. V. 39

DELL, WILLIAM

Christ's Spirit, a Christian's Strength. Germantown: 1760. V. 39; 44

The Doctrine of Baptisms, Reduced from Its Ancient and Modern Corruptions. Philadelphia: 1759. V. 39; 43

The Trial of the Spirits, Both in Teachers and In Hearers. Philadelphia: 1760. V. 39; 43

The Trial of Spirits, Both in Teachers and Hearers . . . London: 1770. V. 38; 39

DELLA BARBA, POMPEO

Spositione d'un Sonnetto Platonico Fatto Sopra il Primo Effecto (sic) d'Amore, che e il Separae l'Anima dal Corpo de l'Amante Secondo Aristotile e Secondo Platone. In Fiorenza: 1554. V. 38

DELLA Robbia Papers. Suggestions for Their Use Together with a Short Treatise on the Work of Della Robbia. Springfield: 1928. V. 41; 43; 45

DELLA VALLE, GUGLIEMO

Storia del Duomo di Orvieto. Rome: 1791. V. 37

DELLA CASA, GIOVANNI

Galateo of Manners and Behaviours, a Renaissance Courtesy Book. London: 1914. V. 41

DELLANAVE, ANTONIO VICENTE

Historia do Descobrimento, e Conquista do Imperio Mexicano. Rio de Janeiro: 1821, 1823. V. 39

DELLENBAUGH, FREDERICK S.

Bearing the Wilderness . . . New York: 1905. V. 42

Breaking the Wilderness. New York: 1905. V. 45

A Canyon Voyage: the Narrative of the Second Powell Expedtiion Down the Green - Colorado River from Wyoming . . . 1871-1872. New York: 1908. V. 43

Fremont and '49. New York: 1914. V. 44

The Romance of the Colorado River. New York: 1902. V. 38; 39; 40; 42

The Romance of the Colorado River. New York: and: 1904. V. 45

The Romance of Colorado River. New York: & London: 1904. V. 44

DELLON, CHARLES

The History of the Inquisition, as It Is Exercised at Goa. London: 1732. V. 43; 44; 45

DELLON, GABRIEL

The History of the Inquisition, as It Is Exercised at Goa . . . London: 1688. V. 40; 43

DEL MAR, ALEXANDER 1836-1926

History of Monetary Systems: Record of Actual Experiments in Money Made by Various States of the Ancient and Modern World as Drawn from their Statues . . . Chicago: 1895. V. 41

DE LOLME, JEAN LOUIS 1740-1806

The Constitution of England, or An Account of the English Government . . . London: 1775. V. 38; 40

The Constitution of England, or and Account of the English Government. London: 1789. V. 40

The History of the Flagellants, or the Advantaages of Discipline. London: 1777. V. 38; 41; 44

Memorials of Human Superstition. London: 1784. V. 38

DE LOLME, JOHN LOUIS

Constitution of England; or, an Account of the English Government, In Which it Is Compared with . . . Other Monarchies. London: 1810. V. 46

DE LOMENIE, LOUIS

Beaumarchais and His Times. London: 1856. V. 39

DELONEY, THOMAS

The Works. Oxford: 1912. V. 41

DE LONG, GEORGE WASHINGTON 1844-1881

The Voyage of the Jeannette. Boston: 1883. V. 37; 42; 45

The Voyage of the Jeanette. Boston & New York: 1883. V. 42

Voyage of the Jeannette. New York: 1883. V. 37

The Voyage of the Jeannette . . . Boston: 1884. V. 42

Voyage of the Jeannette. Boston: 1884. V. 43

Voyage of the Jeannette. New York: 1886. V. 37

DELORD, TAXILE

Les Fleurs Animees. Paris: 1847. V. 43

DELORME, PHILIBERT 1515?-1570

Le Premier tome d l'Architecture. Paris: 1568. V. 42; 46

DELOUGAZ, PINHAS

Private Houses and Graves in the Diyala Region. Chicago: 1967. V. 40

DELPAR, HELEN

The Discoverers. New York: 1980. V. 45

DELPINO, JOSEPH GIRAL

A Dictionary, Spanish and English, and English and Spanish . . . London: 1763. V. 37; 38; 42; 43

DEL REY, LESTER

And Some were Human. Philadelphia: 1948. V. 37

DEL RIO, MARTIN ANTOINE 1551-1608

Disquisitionum Magicarum Libri Sex, in Tres Tomos Partii. Louvain: 1599-1600. V. 40; 41; 43

Disquisitionum Magicarum. Lugduni: 1608. V. 42

DELTEIL, LOYS

Le Peintre-Graveur Illustre. Tome Dixieme (et) Tome Onzieme. H. de Toulouse-Laurtrec. Paris: 1920. V. 41

Le Peintre-Graveur Illustre. Tome Vingtieme (a) Tome Vingt-Neuvieme Bis. Honore Daumier. Paris: 1925-30. V. 41

DE LUC, J. A.

Geological Travels in Some Parts of France, Switzerland and Germany. London: 1813. V. 40

DE LUCCHI, M. R.

A Stereotaxic Atlas of the Chimpanzee Brain (Pan Satyrus). 1965. V. 37

THE DELUGE: or, Cautious Old Woman. London: 1723. V. 37; 38

DE LUGO, ANTHONY BENITEZ

A Summary of Surrey Cricket 1844-99. Madrid: 1900. V. 42

THE DELUSIONS of Hope, a Poem. London: 1806. V. 41

DEM Durchleutigsten Fursten und Herrn Ferdinand . . . Regiereren des Hausses Lobbowitz . . . Wird Deroselben . . . Residenz und Schloss Raudnitz . . . Augsburg. V. 40

DEMACHY, JACQUES FRANCOIS

L'Art du Distillateur, &c. Paris: 1773. V. 39

DE MADARIAGA, SALVADOR

Don Quixote, an Introductory Essay in Psychology. London: 1934. V. 40

DE MAGALHAES, PERO

The Histories of Brazil, with a Facsimile of the Portuguese Original, 1576. New York: 1922. V. 42

DE MAINTENON, MADAME

The Secret Correspondence of Madame de Maintenon, with the Princess Des Ursins. London: 1827. V. 42

DEMAISON, A.

Le Livre des Betes qu'on Appelle Sauvages. Paris: 1930. V. 38

DE MAISTRE, XAVIER

A Journey Round my Room. New York: 1871. V. 46

DE MAN, ALPHONSE

The De Man System of Fireproof Construction. New York: 1901. V. 43

DE MARBOT, BARON

The Memoirs of Baron de Marbot, Late Lieut. General in the French Army. London: 1892. V. 42; 46

DEMARGNE, PIERRE

The Birth of Greek Art. New York: 1964. V. 40; 42

DE MARIA, ROBERT

Johnson's Dictionary and the Language of Learning. Chapel Hill: 1986. V. 41

DE MARINIS, TAMMARO

Il Castello de Monselice. Raccolta Degli Antichi Libri Veniziani Figurati. Verona: 1941. V. 41

DE MARNE, LOUIS ANTOINE 1675-1755

Histoire Sacree de la Providence et de la Conduite de Dieu sur les Hommes . . . Paris: 1728-29. V. 45

DE MASSEY, ERNEST

A Frenchman in the Gold Rush. San Francisco: 1927. V. 40; 44; 45

DE MAY, R.

Narrative of the Sufferings and Adventures of Hendrick Portenger, a Private Soldier of the Late Swiss Regiment de Mueron . . . London: 1819. V. 37; 40

DE MENEVAL, CLAUDE FRANCOIS, BARON

Memoirs to Serve for the History of Napoleon I from 1802 to 1815. London: 1894. V. 41

DEMENTEV, GLADKOV

The Birds of the Soviet Union. London: 1966/69. V. 45

DE MEZIERES, ATHANASE

Anthanase De Mezieres and the Louisiana-Texas Frontier, 1768-1780. Edited and Annotated by Herbert E. Bolton. Cleveland: 1914. V. 37; 39

DE MICHELI, MARIO

Siqueiros. New York: 1968. V. 42; 46

DEMIDOFF, E.

After Wild Sheep in the Altai and Mongolia. London: 1900. V. 39

Hunting Trips in the Caucasus. London: 1898. V. 39

A Shooting Trip to Kamchatka. London: 1904. V. 39; 45

DEMIJOHN, THOM

Black Alice. Garden City: 1968. V. 42

DE MILLE, CECIL B.

Jeanne D'Arc edited by T. Douglas Murray. 1902. V. 37

DE MILLE, JAMES

A Strange Manuscript Found in a Copper Cylinder. London: 1888. V. 43

A Strange Manuscript Found in a Copper Cylinder. New York: 1888. V. 39

D'EMILLIAUME, GABRIEL

A Short History of Monastical Orders, in Which the Primitive Insitution of Monks, Their Tempers, Habits, Rules and the Condition They are in at Present . . . London: 1693. V. 41

DEMING, THERESE

Edwin Willard Deming. New York: 1925. V. 39

DEMING, THERESE O.

American Animal Life. New York: 1916. V. 42

DEMING, WILLIAM CHAPIN

Collected Writings & Addresses. Edited by Agnes Wright Spring. Privately printed in a limited edition. Glendale, CA: 1946. V. 37; 38

DEMIROVIC, HAMDIJA

Thirty-Five Poems. Richmond: 1980. V. 41

DEMMIN, AUGUSTE

An Illustrated History of Arms and Armour. From the Earliest Period to the Present Time. By . . . with nearly 2000 Illustrations. London: 1877. V. 37

DEMOCRATIC PARTY. NATIONAL CONVENTION

The Democratic National Convention, 1936. Philadelphia: 1936. V. 39

THE DEMOCRATIC Review. New York: 1841-42. V. 44

DE MOIVRE, ABRAHAM

Annuities Upon Lives. London: 1725. V. 38

The Doctrine of Chances: or, a Method of Calculating the Probabilities of Events in Play. London: 1738. V. 37; 38

DE MOLEVILLE, BERTRAND

The Costume of Hereditary States of the House of Austria Displayed in Fifty Coloured Engravings. London: 1822. V. 46

The Costume of the Hereditary States of the House of Austria. Displayed in Fifty Coloured Engravings; With Descriptions and An Introduction. Translated by R.C. Dallas. London: 1804. V. 37; 45

DE MOLINET, CLAUDE 1620-1687

Le Cabinet de la Bibliotheque de Sainte-Genevieve. Paris: 1692. V. 43

DE MONT, JEAN

A New Voyage to the Levant, Containing an Account of the Most Remarkable Curiosities in Germany, France, Italy, Malta & Turkey. London: 1696. V. 39

DE MONTESQUIEU, CHARLES LOUIS DE SECONDAT, BARON DE LA BREDE ET 1689-1755

The Complete Works. Translated from the French. Dublin: 1777. V. 37

Defense de l'Esprit des Loix, a Laquelle on a Joint Quelques Eclaircissemens. Geneva: 1750. V. 41

Miscellaneous Pieces. London: 1759. V. 38; 40; 42; 43; 46

Oeuvres de Montesquieu. Paris: 1796. V. 45

Persian Letters. London: 1722. V. 45; 46

Persian Letters. London: 1892. V. 43

Reflections on the Causes of the Grandeur and Declension of the Romans . . . Dublin: 1734. V. 38

Reflexions on the Causes of the Rise and Fall of the Roman Empire. London: 1759. V. 39

The Spirit of Laws. London: 1750. V. 43; 46

The Spirit of Laws . . . Aberdeen: 1756. V. 40

The Spirit of Laws. London: 1758. V. 43

The Spirit of Laws. London: 1766. V. 38; 40

The Spirit of Laws. Edinburgh: 1768. V. 42

The Spirit of Laws. Dublin: 1792. V. 46

The Spirit of Laws. Giasgow: 1793. V. 40

The Spirit of Laws. Worcester: 1802. V. 37; 40

Le Temple De Gnide. Paris: 1772. V. 38; 40

The Complete Works. Dublin: 1777. V. 38

The Complete Works of . . . London: 1777. V. 37; 46

The Works. London: 1800. V. 39

DEMOREST, W. J.

The Great Southern Liliputian Champion of All Musical Wonders, the Infant Drummer; America's Pride . . . New Orleans: 1853. V. 43

DE MORGAN, AUGUSTUS 1806-1871

Arithmetical Books from the Invention of Printing to the Present Time. London: 1847. V. 37; 42

A Budget of Paradoxes. London: 1872. V. 39; 42; 43; 45

A Budget of Paradoxes. Chicago: 1915. V. 42

The Differential and Inegral Calculus. London: 1842. V. 37; 39; 40; 42; 45

Elements of Algebra Preliminary to the Differential Calculus and Fit for the Higher Classes of Schools in Which the Principles of Arithmetic are Taught. London: 1837. V. 42

An Essay on Probabilities. London. V. 40

An Essay on Probabilities, and on Their Application to Life Contingencies and Insurance Offices. London: 1838. V. 41; 42

Essays on the Life and Work of Newton. Chicago & London: 1914. V. 39

An Explanation of the Gnomonic Projection of the Sphere. London: 1836. V. 40; 41

First Notions in Logic. London: 1839. V. 45

Formal Logic; or, the Calculus of Inference. London: 1847. V. 37; 38; 42; 43; 45

Newton: His Friend and His Neice. London: 1885. V. 38; 39

On Probability. London: 1831. V. 44

On the Symbols of Logic, the Theory of the Syllogism and in Particular of the Copula, and the Application of the Theory of Probabilities to Some Questions of Evidence. Cambridge: 1850. V. 43; 45

DE MORGAN, MARY

The Necklace of Princess Fiorimonde & Other Stories. London: 1880. V. 37; 40; 41; 42

DE MORGAN, WILLIAM

Joseph Vance. London: 1906. V. 40; 42; 43

DEMOSTHENES

Aischinou o Kata Ktesiphontos Kai Demosthenous o Peri Stephanou Logos. Dublin: 1769. V. 45

Demosthenis et Aeschinis Principum Oratorum Opera . . . Basilieae: 1572, 1571. V. 40

Orationes Duae & Sexaginta. Libanii Sophistae in Eas Ipsas Orationes Argumenta. Venetiis: 1504. V. 38

Orationes et Epistolae. Paris: 1570. V. 40

Several Orations of Demosthenes, to Encourage the Athenians to Oppose the Exorbitant Power of Philip of Macedon. London: 1702. V. 37

DEMPSEY, G. DRYSDALE

Atlas of the Engravings to Illustrate and Pictorially Explain the Locomotive Engine in All Its Phases. London: 1856. V. 40

Papers on the Mechanical and Engineering Operations and Structures Combined in the Making of a Railway. London: 1846. V. 38

The Practical Railway Engineer. London: 1855. V. 39; 42; 46

DEMPSEY, JACK

Round-by-Round. New York: 1940. V. 39

DEMPSTER, R.

Rambles in Palestine . . . 1879. V. 41

DEMPSTER, THOMAS

Apparatus ad Historiam Scoticam . . . Scriptorum Scotorum MDCIII Nomenclatura. Bologna: 1622. V. 38

De Etruria Regali Libri Septem. Opus Postumum. Florence: 1723-24. V. 37

Historia Ecclesiastica Gentis Scotorum: Sive de Scriptoribus Scotis Editio Altera. Edinburgh: 1829. V. 39

DEMUS, OTTO

Romanesque Mural Painting. London: 1970. V. 42; 44

Romanesque Mural Painting. New York: 1970. V. 38; 39; 42

DEMUTH, I.

A Feast of Cold Facts: A review for 1895-6 of the Commercial and Financial Resources: the Railroad interests and Transportation Facilities . . . of Pettis County and Sedalia, Mo . . . Sedalia: 1895. V. 37

DEN BOESTERD, MARIA H. P.

The Bronze Vessels in the Rijksmuseum G. M. Kam at Nijmegen. Nijmegen: 1956. V. 40; 44

DENDY, WALTER COOPER

On the Phenomena of Dreams, and Other Transient Illusions. London: 1832. V. 40; 42

The Philosophy of Mystery. London: 1841. V. 40

DENECK, M. M.

Indian Sculpture: Masterpieces of Indian, Khmer and Cham Art. London: 1963. V. 41

DE NEUVILLE, CHICANEAU

Dictionnaire Philosophique ou Introduction a la Connoissance de l'Homme. Londres: 1751. V. 44

DENHAM, DIXON

Narrative of Travels and Discoveries in Northern and Central Africa. Boston: 1826. V. 39; 42

Narrative of Travels and Discoveries in Northern and Central Africa, in the Years 1822, 1823 and 1824. London: 1826. V. 38; 40; 41; 44; 45

Narrative of Travels and Discoveries in Northern and Central Africa in the Years 1822, 1823 and 1824. London: 1828. V. 42

DENHAM, H. M.

Sailing Directions from Point Lynas to Liverpool, Under Sanction of the Rt. Hon. Lords Commissioners of the Admiralty. (with) Remarks and Sailing Directions for Approaching and Navigating the Sea-Reach of Wyre up to Port Fleetwood . . . Liverpool: 1840. V. 41; 43

denham, john

Cato Major, Of Old Age. In the Savoy: 1669. V. 46

Poems and Translations, with the Sophy. London: 1608. V. 42

Poems and Translations. London: 1668. V. 40; 41; 45; 46

Poems and Translations with Sophy. London: 1671. V. 41; 43; 45

Poems and Translations, with the Sophy. London: 1684. V. 37; 38

Poems and Translations with Sophy. The Second Impression. London: 1671. V. 37

Poems and Translations, with the Sophy, a Tragedy. The Seventh Edition. London: 1769. V. 37

DENHAM, MICHAEL AISLABIE

The Denham Tracts. London: 1892/95. V. 44

DENHOLM, JAMES

History of the City of Glasgow and Suburbs. Glasgow: 1804. V. 39

DENHOLM, JAMES continued

A Tour to the Principal Scotch and English Lakes. London: 1804. V. 42

DENHOLM-YOUNG, NOEL

Magna Carta and Other Charters of English Liberties. London: 1938. V. 39; 41; 42

DENINA, CARLO

Della Rivoluzioni d'Italia Libri Ventiquattro. Torino: 1769-70. V. 43

DENING, C. F. W.

The Eighteenth Century Architecture of Bristol. Bristol: 1923. V. 37; 40

DE NIORD, CHARD

Inferno. Putney: 1990. V. 44

River. Putney: 1991. V. 44

DENIS, CHARLES

Select Fables. London: 1754. V. 43

DENIS, JEAN BAPTISTE

Recueil des Memoires et Conferences qui ont Este Presentees a Monseigneur le Dauphin Pendant l'Annee MDCLXXII. Paris: 1672. V. 38

DENIS, MICHAEL

Die Merkwurdigkeiten der K. K. Garellischen Offentlichen. Vienna: 1780. V. 38; 40

Einleitung in Die Bucherkunde. Wien: 1777-78. V. 44; 45

Wiens Buchdruckergeschichte bis MDLX. Vienna: 1782. V. 38

DENIS, VALENTIN

The Adoration of the Mystic Lamb. Milan: 1964. V. 41; 46

DENISON, E. S.

E. S. Denison's Yosemite Views. San Francisco?: 1881. V. 45

DENISON, EDWARD

A Reivew of the State of the Question Respecting the Admission of Dissenters to the Universities. London: 1835. V. 40

DENISON, GEORGE T.

The Fenian Raid on Fort Erie with an Account of the Battle of Ridgeway, June, 1866. Toronto: 1866. V. 44

A History of Cavalry, from the Earliest Times. London: 1913. V. 38

Modern Cavalry: Its Organisation, Armament and Employment. London: 1868. V. 44

A Review of Militia Policy of the Present Administration. Hamilton: 1863. V. 39

DENMAN, JAMES L.

Vine and Its Fruit, more especially in relation to The Production of Wine: Embracing An Historical and Descriptive Account of the Grape . . . and incorporating A Brief Discourse on Wine. London: 1864. V. 39; 42

DENMAN, JOHN DOE

The Drama Vindicated, with Copious Notes. Cambridge: 1835. V. 41

DENMAN, THOMAS

Aphorisms on the Application and Use of the Forceps and Vectis . . . Philadelphia: 1803. V. 42

Every Man His Own Attorney. London: 1830? V. 37

An Introduction to the Practice of Midwifery. New York: 1821. V. 42

An Introduction to the Practice of Midwifery . . . New York: 1825. V. 38

A Letter to Dr. Richard Huck, on the Construction and Method of Using Vapour Baths. N.P.: 1768. V. 42

DENNETT, DANIEL

Louisiana as It Is: Its Topography and Material Resources . . . New Orleans: 1876. V. 38

DENNIE, W. H. O.

Personal Narrative of the Campaigns in Afghanistan, Sinde, Beloochistan, etc . . . . Dublin: 1843. V. 39

DENNIS, FREDERIC S.

System of Surgery. Philadelphia: 1894-96. V. 38

System of Surgery. Philadelphia: 1895. V. 44; 46

DENNIS, GEORGE

The Cities and Cemeteries of Etruria. London: 1848. V. 37; 39; 40; 42; 44

The Cities and Cemeteries of Etruria. London: 1878. V. 42; 45

The Cities and Cemeteries of Etruria. London: 1883. V. 38

The Cities and Cemeteries of Etruria. London: 1883. V. 40; 42; 45

DENNIS, H. J.

Third Grade Perspective, Comprising Angular and Oblique Perspective, Shadows and Reflections, Specially Prepared for the Use of Art Students. London: 1879. V. 40

DENNIS, J.

Subversion of Materialism, by Credible Attestation of Supernatural Occurrences . . . Bath: 1826. V. 42

DENNIS, JOHN

Appius and Virginia. London: 1709. V. 38; 46

The Comical Gallant . . . London: 1702. V. 43

English Lyrics from Spenser to Milton. London: 1898. V. 40; 43

An Essay on the Navy, or Englands Advantage and Safety, prov'd Dependant on a Formidable and well-Disciplined Navy . . . London: 1702. V. 43

Iphigenia. London: 1700. V. 46

Julius Caesar Acquitted, and His Murderers Condemn'd. London: 1722. V. 45; 46

Liberty Asserted. London: 1704. V. 38; 41

Miscellany Poems . . . With Select Translations of Horace, Juvenal, Mons, Boileau's Epistles, Satyrs, etc., and Aesop's Fablues, in Burlesque Verse. London: 1697. V. 39; 41

Original Letters, Familiar, Moral and Critical. London: 1721. V. 38

A Plot, and No Plot. London: 1697. V. 38; 46

A Proposal for Putting a Speedy End to the War, by Ruining the Commerce of the French and Spaniards, and Securing Our Own, Without Any Additional Expence to the Nation. London: 1703. V. 43; 45

Rinaldo and Armida. London: 1699. V. 40

The Select Works of Mr. John Dennis. London: 1718. V. 39; 40; 45

The Stage Defended, from Scripture, Reason, Experience, and the Common Sense of Mankind, for Two Thousand Years. London: 1726. V. 37; 38; 39

The Usefulness of the Stage, to the Happiness of Mankind. London: 1698. V. 38; 39; 40; 44; 45

DENNIS, JONAS

The Landscape Gardener; Comprising the History and Principles of Tasteful Horticulture. London: 1835. V. 41; 44

DENNIS, NIGEL

Cards of Identity. London: 1955. V. 45

DENNIS, R. W. G.

British Ascomycetes. Vaduz: 1981. V. 37

DENNIS, TRUMAN B.

The Two Roads With a Vivid Description of Sheridan's Ride, and the Battle of Cedar Creek. N.P.: 1889. V. 38

DENNISON, D.

Photographic Senatorial Album of the Empire State, 1860-1861. Albany: 1860. V. 40

DENNISON MANUFACTURING CO.

Stationers Catalogue, Tags and Specialties. South Framingham: 1910. V. 38; 41

DENNISON, WALTER

Studies in East Christian and Roman Art. New York: 1918. V. 40; 43; 46

DENNISTON, JAMES

The Battle of Craignilder, a Very Ancient Gallovidian Ballad . . . Edinburgh: 1832. V. 45; 46

DENNISTOUN, JAMES

Memoirs of the Dukes of Urbino, Illustrating the Arms, Arts and Literature of Italy, 1440-1630. London: 1851. V. 38; 39; 42

Memoirs of Sir Robert Strange, Engraver. London: 1855. V. 38; 39

Memoirs of the Dukes of Urbino, Illustrating the Arms, Arts and Literature of Italy 1440-1630. London: 1909. V. 42

DENNY, ARTHUR A.

Pioneer Days on Puget Sound. Seattle: 1888. V. 38; 39; 40; 42; 43; 45

Pioneer Days on Puget Sound. Seattle: 1908. V. 45

DENNY-BROWN, DEREK

Centennial Anniversary Volume of the American Neurological Association 1875-1975. New York: 1975. V. 42

DENNY, EMILY INEZ

Blazing the Way or True Stories, Songs and Sketches of Puget Sound and Other Pioneers. Seattle: 1909. V. 45

DENNY, HENRY

Monographia Anoplurorum Britanniae . . . London: 1842. V. 42; 43

DENNY, P.

The Ecology and Management of African Wetland Vegetation. London: 1985. V. 37; 38

The Ecology and Management of African Wetland Vegetation. The Hague: 1985. V. 37

DENNYS, JOHN

Bibliotheca Curiosa. Edinburgh: 1885. V. 45

The Secrets of Angling 1613. London: 1883. V. 40; 42; 46

DE NOLHAC, PIERRE

Marie Antoinette. London: 1905. V. 38

DENON, DOMINIQUE VIVANT, BARON

Travels in Sicily and Malta. London: 1789. V. 45

Travels in Upper and Lower Egypt, in Company with Several Divisions of the French Army . . . London: 1803. V. 38; 39; 41

Voyage dans la Basse et la Haute Egypte, Pendant les Campagnes du General Bonaparte. London: 1802. V. 39

Voyage dans la Basse et la Haute Egypte, Pendant Les Campaganes du General Bonaparte. Paris: 1802. V. 38

Voyages dans la Basse et la Haute Egypte, Pendant les Campagnes de Bonaparte, en 1798 et 1799. London: 1807. V. 42

Viaggio nel Basso ed Alto D'Egitto Illustrato Dietro alle Tracce e ai Disegni del Sig. Denon. Florence: 1808. V. 39

DENORES, JASON

Breve Trattato del Mondo e Delle sue Parti, Semplici e Miste . . . Venice: 1571. V. 38; 40; 42

THE DENS of London Exposed. London: 1835. V. 43

DENSLOW, W. W.

Billy Bounce. Chicago: 1917. V. 42

Denslow's Picture Books for Children. New York: 1902. V. 38

Through Foreign Lands with 'Sunny Jim'. Buffalo: 1910. V. 46

DENSMORE, G. B.

The Chinese in California. San Francisco: 1882. V. 43

DENT, EDWARD J.

A Treatise on the Aneroid. London: 1849. V. 40

DENT, EMMA

Annals of Winchcombe and Sudeley. London: 1877. V. 45

DENT, HERBERT C.

Old English Bronze Wool-Weights. Norwich: 1927. V. 37

DENT, JOHN

Catalogue of the Splendid, Curious and Extensive Library . . . (Parts I-II). London: 1827. V. 45

DENT, JOHN CHARLES

The Last Forty Years: Canada Since the Union of 1841. Toronto: 1881. V. 37; 38; 40; 42

The Story of the Upper Canadian Rebellion. Toronto: 1885. V. 46

DENT, ROBERT K.

The Making of Birmingham. Birmingham: 1894. V. 40

Old and New Birmingham. A History of the Town and Its People. Birmingham: 1880. V. 37

DENTON, SHERMAN FOOTE

Moths and Butterflies of the United States, East of the Rocky Mountains. Boston: 1900. V. 37; 40; 43

DENVER and Colorado Industrial Exposition 1887. Denver: 1887. V. 46

DENVER AND RIO GRANDE RAILROAD

First Annual Report of the Board of Directors . . . April 1st, 1873. Philadelphia: 1873. V. 41

DENVER MANUFACTURING CO.

Illustrated Catalogue No. 2. Denver Manufacturing Co. Denver: 1880's. V. 41

DENVER VILLA PARK ASSOCIATION

Articles of Incorporation and By Laws of the Denver Villa Park Association. Denver: 1872. V. 45

DENYS, NICHOLAS

The Description and Natural History of the Coasts of North America. Toronto: 1908. V. 37; 45

DE OCA, MONTES

Hummingbirds and Orchids of Mexico. Mexico: 1963. V. 40

DEODATUS, CLAUDIUS

Pantheum Hygiasticum Hippocraatico-Hermeticum, de Hominis Vita, ad Centum et Viginti Annos Salubriter Producenda . . . Pruntrut: 1628. V. 38

DE PALOL, PEDRO

Early Medieval Art in Spain. New York: 1966. V. 39; 46

Early Medieval Art in Spain. London: 1967. V. 42

DEPARCIEUX, ANTOINE 1703-1768

Essai sur les Probabilites de la Duree de la Vie Humaine . . . (with) Objections Faites A. M. Deparcieux . . . Paris: 1746 & 1847. V. 41

Nouveaux Traites de Trigonometric Rectiligne et Spherique. Paris: 1741. V. 38; 41; 44

DE PAUW, CORNEILLE

Philosophical Dissertations on the Egyptians and Chinese. London: 1795. V. 39

DEPDENDENCE. By the Author of Little Sophy . . . Derby: 1830. V. 46

DE PEYSTER, ARENT S.

Miscellanies by an Officer . . . New York: 1888. V. 43; 45

DE PILES, ROGER 1635-1709

The Art of Painting and the Lives of the Painters . . . to Which is added an Essay Towards an English School . . . London: 1706. V. 42

DE POL, JOHN

Ireland Remembered. Madison: 1982. V. 39

DEPONS, F.

Travels in Parts of South America, During the Years 1801, 1802, 1803 and 1804. London: 1806. V. 39; 40; 41

Travels in South America, During the Years 1801, 1802, 1803 and 1804. London: 1807. V. 37; 44; 45

A Voyage to the Eastern Part of Terra Firma. New York: 1806. V. 41; 42

DEPONS, F. A.

Voyage to the Eastern Part of Terra Firma, or the Spanish Main, in South-America, during the years 1801-4. Translated by An American Gentleman, (Washington Irving). New York: 1806. V. 37

DEPPING, GEORG BERNARD

La Suisse, ou Esquisse d'un Tableau Historique, Pittoresque et Moral des Cantons Helvetiques. Paris: 1824. V. 42

DEPREDATIONS and Massacre by the Snake River Indians . . . Report of the Commissioner of Indian Affairs Relative to the Indian Depredations Committed in the State of Oregon and Territory of Washington . . . Washington: 1861. V. 37

DE PUTEO, PARIS

Solemnis et utilis Tractatus de re militari . . . materia (m) duelli Singularisq(ue) Certaminis Egregie Contiens. Lyon: 1543. V. 38; 40

DEPUY, W. H.

The Universal Guide and Gazetteer to the Countries, Peoples and Governments of the World . . . New York: 1887. V. 45

DE QUERVAIN, F.

Goiter: a Contribution to the Study of the Pathology and Treatment of the Diseases of the Thyroid Gland. New York: 1924. V. 40

DE QUINCEY, THOMAS 1785-1859

V. 44

The Collected Writings. Edinburgh: 1889-90. V. 39; 40

The Collected Writings. London: 1889-90. V. 46

The Collected Writings. London: 1896. V. 38; 42

The Collected Writings. London: 1896-97. V. 37; 42

Confessions of an English Opium Eater. London: 1822. V. 37; 38; 39; 40; 43; 44

Confessions of an English Opium Eater. London: 1823. V. 37; 39; 40; 42

Confessions of an English Opium Eater. London: 1826. V. 39

Confessions of an English Opium-Eater. Boston: 1841. V. 44

Confessions of an Opium Eater. East Aurora: 1898. V. 46

The Confessions of an English Opium Eater and Other Essays. London: 1924. V. 42

Confessions of an English Opium Eater. 1930. V. 37; 43; 45

Confessions of an English Opium Eater. New York: 1930. V. 41; 43

Confessions of an English Opium Eater. Oxford: 1930. V. 38; 39; 40; 43; 45

The Confessions of an English Opium Eater. London: 1948. V. 41

Confessions of an English Opium Eater. London: 1828. V. 37

Confessions of an Opium-Eater. (East Aurora: 1898). V. 37

Klosterheim; or, The Masque. Edinburgh: 1832. V. 39; 40; 42

Literary Reminiscences: from the Autobiography of an English Opium Eater. Boston: 1851. V. 45

The Logic of Political Economy. Edinburgh and London: 1844. V. 39; 43

The Logic of Political Economy and Other Papers. Boston: 1859. V. 41

Revolt of the Tartars, or, Flight of Kalmuck Khan and His People from the Russian Territories to the Frontiers of China. London: 1948. V. 38; 43

Walladmor. London: 1825. V. 43

Works of Thomas De Quincey. Boston: 1851-53. V. 41; 44

The Works. Edinburgh: 1862-3. V. 39; 42

DE QUINCEY, THOMAS 1785-1859 continued

Works. Edinburgh: 1862-63. V. 37

Works. London: 1862-71. V. 42

Works. Edinburgh: 1863. V. 38

Works. Edinburgh: 1863-1878. V. 37; 39

The Works of . . . Edinburgh: 1867. V. 40; 46

The Works. Edinburgh: 1886. V. 38; 43

The Works of . . . Edinburgh: 1878. V. 37

Writings. Boston: 1866. V. 40

DER Blutige Schau-Platz Oder Mar-tyrer-Spiegel der Tauffs-Gesinnten oder Wehrlossen-Christen, die um des Zeugnuss Jesu Ihres Seligmachers Willen Gelitten Haben, und Seynd Getodtet Worden von Chrisit Zeit an bis auf das Jahr 1660. Ephrata: 1748. V. 39

DER Blutige Schau-Platz oder Mar-tyrer-Spiegel der Tauffs-Gesinnten oder Wehrlossen-Christen, die um des Zeugnuss Jesu ihres Seligmachers Willen Gelitten Haben, und seynd Getodtet Worden von Christi Zeit an bis auf das Jahr 1660. Ephrata: 1748. V. 41

DER PREDIGER zu Magdeburgk Ware Gegruendte Antwort Auff Das Rhuemen Ihrer Feinde Das Sie Auch Gottes Wort Reine Inhalts der Augspurgischen Confession so Wol Als Die Zu Magdeburgk Haben . . . Magdeburgk: 1551. V. 41

DERBY, CHARLES STANLEY, EARL OF

The Protestant Religion is a Sure Foundation and Principle of a True Christian . . . London: 1671. V. 43

DERBY, EDWARD HENRY STANLEY, 15TH EARL OF 1826-1893

A Catalogue of the Library at Knowsley Hall, Lancashire. London: 1893. V. 38

Farther Facts Connected with the West Indies. London: 1851. V. 40

DERBY, GEORGE HORATIO

Phoenixiana; or, Sketches and Burlesques. New York: 1856. V. 38; 46

Phoenixiana. Chicago: 1897. V. 40

Phoenixiana, A Collection of the Burlesques and Sketches of John Phoenix, Alias John P. Squibob, Who Was in Fact, Lieutenant George H. Derby, U.S.A. San Francisco: 1937. V. 40; 43; 46

DERBY, H. W.

Volumes to Be Sold at Panic Prices! New York: 1861. V. 43

DERBY, J. C.

Fifty Years Among Author, Books and Publishers. New York: 1884. V. 43

DERBY, W. L. A.

The Tall Ships Pass: The Story of the Last Years of Deepwater and Square-Rigged Sail . . . London: 1937. V. 39

DERCUM, FRANCIS

A Text-Book on Nervous Diseases by American Authors. Philadelphia: 1895. V. 46

DE RE, MARC ANTONIO

Villa di Delizia, o Siano Palagi Camparecci Nello Stato di Milano, Divise in Due Tomi. Milan: 1743. V. 37

DE REAUMUR, RENE ANTOINE FERCHAULT

The Art of Hatching and Brining of Domestick Fowls of all Kinds, at Any Time of the Year, Either by the Means of Hot-Beds, or That of Common-Fire. London: 1750. V. 39

DE RECY, GEORGES

The Decoration of Leather. London: 1905. V. 38

DE REGNIERS, BEATRICE SCHENK

What Can You Do with a Shoe? New York: 1955. V. 39

DE RENNE, WYMBERLY JONES

Books Relating to Georgia in the Library of . . . Savannah: 1905 & 1911. V. 43

DERENZY, MARGARET GRAVES

A Whisper to a Newly-Married Pair, From a Widowed Wife. Philadelphia: 1844. V. 39

DERHAM, WILLIAM 1657-1735

The Artificial Clock-Maker. London: 1696. V. 38; 45; 46

The Artifical Clock Maker. London: 1700. V. 39

Artificial Clock-Maker. London: 1714. V. 38

Astro-Theology: or a Demonstration of the Being and Attributes of God From a Survey of the Heavens. London: 1719. V. 39

Astro-Theology: or, A Demonstration of the Being and Attributes of God, from a Survey of the Heavens. London: 1750. V. 37

Physico-Theology. V. 41

Physico - Theology. London: 1714. V. 38; 40

Select Remains of the Learned John Ray, M.A. & F.R.S., with His Life, Written by . . . London: 1760. V. 38; 45

DE RIBERA, GIOVANNI

Lettera Annua Della Vice-Provincia Delle Filippine dal Giugno del 1602 al Sequente Giugno del 1603 al P. Claudio Acquaviva. Venice: 1605. V. 40

DE RINALDIS, ALDO

Neapolitan Painting of the Seicento. Paris: 1929. V. 45

DERING, EDWARD HENEAGE

The Chieftan's Daughter . . . London: 1870. V. 43

Freville Chase. London: 1880. V. 42

Sherborne; or, the House at the Four Ways. London: 1875. V. 37; 40

DERLETH, AUGUST WILLIAM 1909-

Arkham House - the First 20 Years. Sauk City: 1959. V. 44

The Arkham Collector. Sauk City: 1971. V. 45

The Casebook of Solar Pons. Sauk City: 1965. V. 41; 46

Dark of the Moon. 1947. V. 45

Dark of the Moon, Poems of Fantasy and Macabre. Sauk City: 1947. V. 45

Dark of the Moon. Sauk City: 1947. V. 39; 43; 44; 45; 46

Far Boundaries: Twenty Science-Fiction Stories. New York: 1951. V. 42; 43; 45

In Re: Sherlock Holmes. Sauk City: 1945. V. 38

It's A Boy's World. Sauk City: 1948. V. 42; 43; 45

Last Light. 1978. V. 39; 42; 45

Last Light. Mt. Horeb: 1978. V. 39; 42

Last-Light. Wisconsin: 1978. V. 41

The Mask of Cthulhu. 1958. V. 42

The Mask of Cthulhu. Sauk City: 1958. V. 45

The Memoirs of Solar Pons. Sauk City: 1951. V. 43; 45

The Narracong Riddle. New York: 1940. V. 37

The Night Side. Masterpieces of the strange and terrible. New York: (1947). V. 37

Not Long for This World. Sauk City: 1948. V. 45

Place of Hawks. New York: 1935. V. 43; 46

The Reminiscences of Solar Pons. Sauk City: 1961. V. 45

Restless in the River. New York: 1939. V. 43

The Return of Solar Pons. Sauk City: 1958. V. 39; 41; 43; 45

Sac Prairie People. Sauk City: 1948. V. 42; 43; 45

The Shield of the Valiant. New York: 1945. V. 37; 42; 43; 45

The Shuttered Room and Other Pieces. Sauk City: 1959. V. 39; 42

The Sleeping and the Dead: Thirty Uncanny Tales. Chicago: 1947. V. 39

Someone in the Dark. N.P.: 1941. V. 37; 39; 44

Someone in the Dark. Suak City: 1941. V. 43; 45

Something About Cats and Other Pieces. Sauk City: 1949. V. 45

Something Near. 1945. V. 45

Something Near. Sauk City: 1945. V. 39; 42; 43; 45

The Trail of Cthulhu. Sauk City: 1962. V. 42; 45

Wind Over Wisconsin. New York: 1938. V. 43

Wisconsin Country: a Sac Prairie Journal. New York: 1965. V. 42; 43; 45

DERMODY, THOMAS

The Harp of Erin, Containing the Poetical Works of the Late Thomas DErmody. London: 1807. V. 45

Peace. a Poem. London: 1801. V. 39

Poems, Moral and Descriptive. London: 1800. V. 42

DERMOTT, HUGH F.

Poems: Epic, Comic and Satiric . . . Dedicated to Free Lunchers and Noddle-Headed Scribblers. San Francisco: 1857. V. 40

DER NERSESSIAN, SIRAPIE

The Chester Beatty Library; a Catalogue of the Armenian Manuscripts. Dublin: 1958. V. 38

DERODON, DAVID d. 1664

The Funeral of the Mass. Dublin: 1726. V. 39

DE RONDE, LAMBERTUS

A System: Containing the Principles of the Christian Religion, Suitable to the Heidelberg Catechism. New York: 1763. V. 37

The True Spiritual Religion, or Delightful Service of the Lord . . . New York: 1767. V. 41

DE ROODE, KATE

An Ode to the Princess of Wales. N.P.: 1892. V. 38

DE ROQUEFORT, JEAN BAPTISTE

Vues Pittoresque et Perspectives des Salles du Musee des Monuments Francois et des principaux . . . Paris: 1816. V. 44

DE ROQUETTE, HENRI EMMANUEL

Oraison Funebre de Tres-Haut . . . Jacques II, Roy de la Grand Bretagne. Paris: 1702. V. 38

DE ROS, JOHN FREDERICK FITZGERALD 1804-1861

Personal Narrative of Travels in the United States and Canada in 1826 . . . With Remarks on the Present State of the American Navy. London: 1827. V. 37; 38; 39; 40; 42; 43; 44; 45; 46

DE ROSE, PETER

A Concordance to the Works of Jane Austen. London: 1982. V. 46

DEROZARIO, M.

The Complete Monumental Register. Calcutta: 1815. V. 39

DERRA DE MORODA, FRIDERICA

The Dance Library a Catalogue (of the) Derra de Moroda Dance Archives. Munich: 1982. V. 39

DERRA DE MORODA, FRIDERICA

The Dance Library a Catalogue of the Derra de Mororda Dance Archives. Munich: 1982. V. 40

DERRECAGAIN, VICTOR BERNARD

Modern War. Part II. Grand Tactics. Washington: 1890. V. 37

DERRICK, CHARLES

Memoirs of the Rise and Progress of the Royal Navy. London: 1806. V. 37; 38

DERRICK, SAMUEL

The Battle of Lora. London: 1762. V. 42

DERRICKE, JOHN

The Image of Irelande, with, A Discoverie of Woodkarne. 1985. V. 38

The Image of Ireland, with a Discoverie of Woodkarne. Belfast: 1985. V. 41; 42; 43

The Image of Irelande With a Discoverie of Woodkarne. London: 1986. V. 39

THE DERRICK'S Handbook of Petroleum: A Complete Chronological and Statistical Review of Petroleum Developments from 1859 to 1898 (. . . during 1898 and 1899). Oil City: 1898-1900. V. 37

DERRIEY, CHARLES

Specimen-Album. Paris: 1862. V. 38

DERRY, JOSEPH T.

Confederate Military History: Georgia. Atlanta: 1899. V. 46

Georgia: a Guide to Its Cities, Towns, Scenery and Resources. Philadelphia: 1878. V. 41; 44; 45

DERRYDALE PRESS

A Decade of American Sporting Books and Prints, 1927-1937. New York: 1937. V. 39; 41; 44

DERZHAVIN

A Poem on God by Derzhavin the Russian Poet. Glasgow: 1820. V. 44

DE SADE, DONATIEN ALPHONSE FRANCOIS, COMTE DE 1740-1814

The Life of Petrarch. Dublin: 1777. V. 38

DE SADE, JACQUES FRANCOIS PAUL ALONCE DE

The Life of Petrarch. London: 1775. V. 45

DESAGULIERS, JEAN THEOPHILE

A Course of Experimental Philosophy. London: 1763. V. 40; 41; 46

Fires Improved: Being a New Method of Building Chimneys So As To Prevent Their Smoaking . . . London: 1715. V. 41; 45

DESAINLIENS, CLAUDE

The French Schoole Maister. London: 1629. V. 46

DESAINT, A.

Ideas and Studies in Stencilling and Decorating. London: 1927. V. 44

DE SAINT-AMAND, IMBERT

Famous Women of the French Court. New York: 1893-1902. V. 39; 43

DE SAINT MARTHE, SCEVOLE

Paedotrophia, or the Art of Nursing and Rearing Children. London: 1797. V. 40

DE SANA, JIMMY

Submission. New York: 1979. V. 44

DE SAULCY, LOUIS FELICIEN JOSEPH CAIGNART

Narrative of a Journey Round the Dead Sea and In the Bible Lands in 1850 and 1851. London: 1853. V. 43

Narrative of a Journey Round the Dead Sea, and in the Bible Lands in 1850 and 1851. London: 1854. V. 39; 45

DESAULT, PIERRE J.

A Treatise on Fractures, Luxations and Other Affections of the Bones . . . Philadelphia: 1817. V. 41; 42

DE SAUVENIERE, ALFRED

Alfred Le Levrier et Son Sport. Paris: 1881. V. 38

DESBILLONS, FRANCOIS JOSEPH T. 1711-1789

Fabularum Aesopiarum Libri Quinque Priores, Diligenter Emendati, Editio Tertia, Quam Solam Auctor Agnoscit. Paris: 1759. V. 40

DESBOROUGH, V. R.

The Last Mycenaeans and Their Successors. An Archaeological Survey c. 1200-c. 100 BC. Oxford: 1964. V. 40; 42; 44; 46

Protogeometric Pottery. Oxford: 1952. V. 42

DESCALVES, ALONZO

New Travels to the Westward; or, Unknown Parts of Columbia. Being a Tour of almost Fourteen Months. Containing, an account of the Country, Upwards of Two Thousand Miles West of the Known parts of North-Columbia . . . Greenwich, Ma.: 1805. V. 37

DESCAMPS, JEAN BAPTISTE

La Vie des Peintres Flamands, Allemands et Hollandois, Avec des Portraits. Paris: 1753-63. V. 40

DESCARTES, RENE 1596-1650

Discours de la Methode Pour Bien Conduire sa Raison & Chercher la verite dans les Sciences. Leiden: 1637. V. 44

Discours de la Methode Pour Bien Conduire sa Raison & Chercher la Verite dans les Sciences. Paris: 1658. V. 40

Discours de la Methode Pour Bien Conduire sa Raison . . . plus la Dioptique et les Meteores, Qui Sont des Essais de Cette Methode . . . Paris: 1668. V. 42; 46

Epistolae, Partim ab Auctore Latino Sermone conscriptae Partim ex Gallico Translatae . . . London: 1668. V. 39; 45

Epistolae Partim ab Auctore Latino sermone conscriptae, partim ex Gallico translatae . . . Pars prima (et secunda). Amsterdam: 1668. V. 37

Geometria . . . Anno 1637 Gallice Edita . . . Leiden: 1649. V. 41

L'Homme de . . . et un Traitte de la Formation du Foetus du Mesme Autheur. Paris: 1664. V. 42; 46

L'Homme de Rene Descartes, et la Formation Du Foetus. Paris: 1677. V. 40

Meditationes de Prima Philosophia . . . (with) Appendix, Continens Objectiones Quintas, & Septimas (and with) Epistola Renati Descartes . . . Amsterdam: 1663. V. 40

Les Meditations Metaphysiques . . . Paris: 1673. V. 39

Passiones Animae. gallice ab Ipso Conscriptae, Nunc Autem in Exterorum Gartium Latina Civitate Donatae ab H.L.D.M. Amsterdam: 1651. V. 46

Les Principes de la Philosophie . . . Revue & Corrigee Fort Exactement par Monsieur CLR (i.e. Claude Clerselier). Paris: 1681. V. 42

Principia Philosophiae. Amsterdam: 1685. V. 43

Six Metaphysical Meditations. London: 1680. V. 41

Specimina Philosophiae: Seu Dissertatio de Methodo Recte Regendae Rationis & Veritatis in Scientiis Investigandae. Amsterdam: 1650. V. 45

Tractatus de Homine et de Formatione Foetus . . . Notis Perpetuis Ludovici de la Forge, M.D. Amsterdam: 1677. V. 37; 42

Oeuvres de Descartes. Publiees par Charles Adam & Paul Tannery sous les auspices du Ministere de l'Instruction Publique. V. 37

Opera Philosophica. Amstelodami: 1650. V. 42

(Opera Philosophica). Principia Philosophiae; Specimina Philosophiae; seu dissertatio de methodo . . . Dioptrice et Meteora; Passiones Animae. Amsterdam: 1656. V. 37

Opera Philosophia . . . (with) Appendix (with) Epistola. (with) Principia Philosophiae. (with) Specimina Philosophiae . . . (with) Passiones Animae. 1670-72. V. 43

Opera Philosohica Editio Quinta Nunc Demum hac Editione Diligenter Recognita & Mendis Expurgata. Amstelodami: 1672. V. 41

Opera Philosophica Editio Quinta, Nunc Demum hac Editione Diligenter Recognita & Mendis Expurgata. Amstelodami: 1672. V. 37

Opera Philosophica. Amsterdam: 1677. V. 40

Oeuvres de Descartes, Publiees par Victor Cousin. Paris: 1824-26. V. 39; 41; 45

Oeuvres de Descartes. Paris: 1897-1913. V. 42

DESCHARNES, ROBERT

The World of Salvador Dali. New York: 1968. V. 41; 42; 44

DE SCHAUENSEE, R. M.

The Birds of China. London: 1984. V. 45

The Birds of China. Washington: 1984. V. 46

The Birds of Columbia and Adjacent Areas of South and Central America. 1964. V. 46

DE SCHWEINITZ, EDMUND ALEXANDER

The Life and Times of David Zeisberger. Philadelphia: 1870. V. 44

DE SCHWEINITZ, EDMUND ALEXANDER continued

The Moravian Manual: Containing an Account of the Protestant Church of the Moravian United Brethren, or Unitas Fratrum. Philadelphia: 1859. V. 44

DESCLOZEAUX, ADRIEN

Gabrielle D'Estrees. London: 1907. V. 43

DESCOLE, H. R.

Genera et Species Plantarum Argentinarum. Buenos Aires: 1943-56. V. 42

DESCOURTILZ, J. T.

Pageantry of Tropical Birds. London: 1960. V. 39

DESCRIPCAO dos Embelmas Allegoricos, e Seus Epigramas, com Que se Adornou a Illuminacao que na Fachada das Cazas de Sua Residencia Appresentou ao Publico o Coronel Antonio Jose da Silva Braga na Noite de 6 de Fevereiro de 1818 . . . Rio de Janeiro: 1821. V. 45

DESCRIPTION Exacte de tout ce Qui Est Passe Dans les Guerres Entre le Roy d'Angleterre, le Roy de France et les Etats des Provinces-Unies dy Pays-Bas & l'Eveque de Muenster . . . Amsterdam: 1668. V. 40; 44; 46

DESCRIPTION of an Unimmergible Life. Boat. London: 1807. V. 41

DESCRIPTION of . . . . Ancient Terracottas in the British Museum: with Engravings. London: 1810. V. 37

THE DESCRIPTION of Corsica, with the Account of its Union to the Crown of Great Britain. London: 1795. V. 38

A DESCRIPTION of England and Wales. London: 1769-70. V. 38

A DESCRIPTION of Fonthill Abbey, Wiltshire. London: 1812. V. 40

A DESCRIPTION of Gibraltar, with an Account of the Blockade, Siege, the Attempt by Nine Sail of Fire-Ships . . . and Every Thing Remarkable or Worthy Notice that Has Occurred in That Place Since the Commencement of the Spanish War . . . London: 1782. V. 37

A DESCRIPTION of Holland: or, the Present State of the United Provinces . . . Account of the Hague . . . Principal Cities and Towns . . . Manners and Customs . . . Navigations, Commerce . . . Universities, Arts, Sciences, Men of Letters . . . London: 1743. V. 37; 46

A DESCRIPTION of Killarney. London: 1776. V. 38; 39; 42

A DESCRIPTION of Malta, With a Sketch of Its History and That of Its Fortifications . . . Malta: 1801. V. 40

A DESCRIPTION of that Barbarous Action of Monsieur Guiscard in the Stabbing of Mr. Harley at the Council Chamber March ye 8th 1711. London: 1711. V. 41

DESCRIPTION of the Coast of Northumberland, from Sunderland Point to Warnham Flats; with Sailing Directions for the Same. London: 1819. V. 46

DESCRIPTION of the Procession on the Coronation of His Majesty George the Fourth . . . New Represented and Exhibiting in the Great Rotunda of Henry Aston Barker's Panorama. London: 1823. V. 46

A DESCRIPTION of the Town of Ludlow, with an Historical Account of the Castle. Ludlow: 1811. V. 41

A DESCRIPTION of the United States Armory at Springfield, (Mass.) with a Statement Exhibiting the Number of ARms Manufactured and Repaired, and the Amoung of Expenditures Annually, from the Commencement of the Establishment in 1795, to the Close of . . . N.P.: 1818. V. 46

A DESCRIPTION of the Works of the Ingenious Delineator and Engraver Wenceslaus Hollar . . . London: 1745. V. 45

DESCRIPTION Of the Wrought-Iron Tubular Suspension Bridge on the South Wales Railway, Over the River Wye at Chepstow . . . London: 1856. V. 43

DESCRIPTIONS Pittoresques de Jardins du Gout le Plus Moderne. Leipzig: 1805. V. 40

DESCRIPTIONS Pittoresques de Jaardins du Gout le plus Moderne. Leipzig: 1802. V. 38; 40; 41

DESCRIPTIVE and Historical View of the Seven Mile Mirror of the Lakes, Niagara, St. Lawrence and Saguenay Rivers, Embracing the Entire Range of Border Scenery of the United States and Canadian Shroes . . . New York: 1854. V. 42; 43

DESCRIPTIVE Atlas of Western Canada Showing Maps of the Provinces of Ontario, Quebec, New Brunswick, Nova Scotia, Prince Edward Island, Manitoba, British Columbia and Districts of Assinoboia, Alberta, Saskatchewan and Athabasca. Ottawa: 1900. V. 38

A DESCRIPTIVE Catalogue of Catlin's Indian Gallery. London: 1840. V. 37

A DESCRIPTIVE Catalogue of the Marine Collection to Be Gound at India House. New York: 1935. V. 46

DESCRIPTIVE Dover, Containing a Concise Account of the Castle, Heights, Harbour and Town. Dover: 1817. V. 39

DESCRIPTIVE... Information Relative to the City of San Diego . . . San Diego: 1874. V. 37

DESCRIZIONE delle Feste Celebrate in Parma, l'anno 1769..i'Infante Don Ferdinando Calla Reale Archiduchesa Maria Amalia. Parma: 1769. V. 37

DE SCUDERY, GEORGES

Curia Politiae: or, the Apologies of Severall Princes: Justifying to the World Their Most Eminent Actions, by Strength of Reason, and the Most Exact Rules of Policie . . . London: 1654. V. 38

DE SEINGALT, GIROLAMO 1725-1798

The Memoirs of Jacques Casanova de Seingalt. Haarlem: 1972. V. 44

DESENFANS, NOEL JOSEPH

Letter from Monsieur Desenfans to Mrs. Montagu. London: 1777. V. 39

THE DESERET First Book. New York: 1836. V. 41

DE SEZE, J. B. A. M.

The English and French Interpreter, or, School and Countinghouse Companion . . . New York: 1813. V. 42

DES FONTAINES, PIERRE FRANCOIS GUYOT DE

The History of the Revolutions of Poland, From the Foundation of that Monarchy, to the Death of Augustus II. London: 1736. V. 45

DESGODETZ, ANTOINE

Les Edifices Antiques de Rome Dessines et Measures tres Exactement. Paris: 1682. V. 37; 38; 40; 42

Les Loix des Batimens Suivant la Coutume de Paris. Paris: 1748. V. 37

DESGRAND, LOUIS

Les Trois Missions de Stanley dans l'Afrique Equatoriale. Lyon: 1891. V. 39

DESHA, JOSEPH

Kentucky Gazette - Extra. Governor's Message, In Reply to the Resolutions Adopted in the House of Representatives on the Motion of Mr. Breckinridge. Lexington?: 1825. V. 41

DES HAYES, LOUIS, BARON DE COURMENIN

Les Voyages de Monsieur des Hayes, Baron de Courmesuin (sic) en Dannemarc. Paris: 1664. V. 44

DE SHIELDS, JAMES T.

Border Wars of Texas. Tioga: 1912. V. 37; 38; 39; 42; 43; 45

Cynthia Ann Parker: the Story of Her Capture at the Massacre of Parker's Fort, of Her Quarter Century Spent Among the Comanches . . . San Antonio: 1934. V. 46

DESIDERI, F. HYPOLITE

Lettres Edifiantes et Curieuses, Ecrites des Missions Etrangeres, par Quelques Missionaires de la Compagnie de Jesus. XV. Recueil. Paris: 1722. V. 45

DESILVER, ROBERT

Desilver's Philadelphia Directory and Strangers Guide for 1828. Philadelphia: 1828. V. 42; 44; 45

DESJARDINS, L. G.

Decisions of the Speakers of the Legislative Assembly of the Province of Quebec 1867-1901. Quebec: 1902. V. 44

DESJARDINS, MARIE CATHERINE HORTENSE d. 1683

Les Desordres De l'Amour. Paris: 1676. V. 39

The Unfotunate (sic) Heroes; or, the Adventures of Ten Famous Men, viz . . . In the Savoy: 1679. V. 42

DESLANDES, ANDRE F. B.

The Art of Being Easy at All Times and In All Places. London: 1724. V. 38

DES MAIZEAUX, PIERRE

An Historical and Critical Account of the Life and Writings of the Ever Memorable Mr. John Hales Fellow of Eton College . . . London: 1719. V. 38; 42; 43

DESMAREST, A. G.

Histoire Naturelle des Tangaras, des Manakins et des Todiers. Paris: 1805-07. V. 37; 38; 42

DESMARETS DE SAINT SORLIN, JEAN

Ariana. London: 1641. V. 42

L'Ariane. Paris: 1639. V. 45

DE SMET, PIERRE JEAN 1801-1873

Letter and Sketches: with a Narrative of a Year's Residence Among the Indian Tribes of the Rocky Mountains. Philadelphia: 1943. V. 37; 38; 39

Life, Letters and Travels of . . . 1801-1873. New York: 1905. V. 39

DESMONCEAUX, ABBE

Traite des Maladies des Yeux et des Oreilles, Considerees sous la Rapport des Quatre Parties ou Quatre Ages de la Vie de l'Homme . . . Paris: 1786. V. 43

DESMOND, WILLIAM

Directions for Tanning all Sorts of Hides and Skins According to the New Process Introduced by Mr. W. Desmond. London: 1801. V. 40

DE SOLIS, DON ANTONIO

The History of the Conquest of Mexico by the Spaniards. London: 1724. V. 38

The History of the Conquest of Mexico by the Spaniards. London: 1738. V. 42

DE SOMMIERES, L. C. VIALLA

Travels in montenegro. London: 1820. V. 37

DE SOTO, FERNANDO

True Relation of the Hardships Suffered by Governor . . . & Certain Portugese Gentlemen during the Discovery of the Province of Florida. Now Newly set forth by a Gentleman of Elvas. Deland: 1932. V. 37

DE SOULIGNE, M.

The Desolation of France Demonstrated. London: 1697. V. 41

DESPAUTERIUS, JOHANNES

Commentarii Grammatici. Paris: 1537. V. 40

DES PERIERS, JEAN BONAVENTURE

Cymbalum Mundi. Or, Saatyrical Dialogues Upon Several Subjects . . . London: 1712. V. 37

DESPORTES, PHILIPPE

Les CL Pseaumes . . . avec Quelques Cantiques . . . et Autres Oeuvres. Paris: 1604-3. V. 44

Les Premieres Oeuvres. Paris: 1600. V. 39

THE DESPOSITION and Examination of Mr. Edmund Everard. Concerning the Horrid Popish Plot against the life of his Sacred Majesty, the Government, and the Protestant Religion. London: 1679. V. 37

DES ROCHES, CATHERINE FREDONNOIT

La Puce de Madame Des Roches. Qui est un Recueil de Divers Poemes Grecs, Latins & Francois, Composez par Plusieurs Doctes Personnages aux Grans Iours Tenus a Poitiers l'an MDLXXIX. Paris: 1583. V. 37; 40; 43

DESRUELLES, H. M. J.

Memoir on the Treatment of Veneral Diseases Without Mercury, Employed at the Military Hospital of the Val-De-Grace . . . Philadelphia: 1830. V. 40; 41

DES RUES, FRANCOIS

Les Flevrs Dv Bien Dire. Langres: 1598. V. 40

DE STAEL DE LAUNAY, MADAME

Memoirs of . . . New York: 1892. V. 39

DE STUTT DE TRACY, ANTOINE LOUIS CLAUDE, COMTE 1754-1836

A Commentary and Review of Montesquieu's Spirit of Laws. Philadelphia: 1811. V. 37; 38; 42; 44

Translation of a Letter from Monsieur De Tracy, Member of the French National Assembly to Mr. Burke, In Answer to His Remarks on the French Revoluiton. London: 1790. V. 41

Treatise on Political Economy, To Which is Prefixed a Supplement to a Preceeding Work on the Understanding, or Elements of Ideology . . . Georgetown: 1818. V. 44

A Treatise on Political Economy. Georgetown: 1817. V. 37; 38

DESULTORY Observations on the Public Securities; and Hints on Taxation. By a Revenue Officer. London: 1806. V. 37

DE TABLEY, JOHN BYRNE LECIESTER WARREN, 3RD BARON 1835-1895

Poems, Dramatic and Lyrical. London: 1893. V. 39; 40; 42; 43; 46

DE TABLEY, JOHN BYRNE LEICESTER WARREN, 3RD BARON 1835-1895

Hence These Tears. London: 1872. V. 38; 40

Poems Dramtic and Lyrical. First Series. Second Series. London: 1893, 1895. V. 38; 40; 43

Poems Dramatic and Lyrical: Second Series. London: 1895. V. 40

DE TAVERA, T. H. PARDO

The Medicinal Plants of the Philippines. Philadelphia: 1901. V. 40

A DETECTION of the Considerations on the Navy Bill. London: 1749. V. 41

A DETECTION of the Proceedings and Practices of the Directors of the Royal African Company of England, from Their First Establishment by Charter in the Year 1672, to the Present Year 1748. London: 1749. V. 41

THE DETECTION Of the Views of Those Who Would, in Present Crisis, Engage an Incumber'd, Trading Nation, as Principals, in a Ruinous Expensive Land-War . . . London: 1746. V. 45

THE DETECTOR Detected; or, the Danger to Which Our Constitution Now Lies Exposed, Set in a True and Manifest Light. London: 1743. V. 41; 45

THE DETERIORATED Condition of Our Saddle-Horses: The Causes and the Remedy. London: 1853. V. 41

DETMOLD, CHARLES MAURICE

Pictures from Birdland. London: 1899. V. 40

DETMOLD, E. J.

Baby Birds and Beasts. Oxford: 1930. V. 41

The Book of Baby Pets. London: 1910. V. 46

Illustrations to Rudyard Kipling's Jungle Book. London: 1903. V. 44

Our Little Neighbours. London. V. 46

Twenty-Four Nature Pictures. London: 1920. V. 44

DETMOLD, EDWARD J.

Twenty-Four Nature Pictures. London: (1919). V. 37

DE TOLNAY, CHARLES

Hieronymus Bosch. London: 1966. V. 44

The Medici Chapel. Princeton: 1948. V. 44

The Sistine Ceiling. Princeton: 1949. V. 41

DE TOUSARD, LOUIS

American Artillerist's Companion, or Elements of Artillery, Treating of All Kinds of Firearms in Detail and of the Formation, Object and Service of the Flying or Horse ARtillery, Preceded by an Introductory Dissertation on Cannon. Philadelphia: 1809. V. 41

DE TRAFFORD, HUMPHREY F.

The Horses of the British Empire. London: 1907. V. 37

DETROIT. CITY PLAN COMMISSION

Detroit Master Plan. Detroit: 1951. V. 44

DEUCHAR, DAVID

A Collection of Etchings After the Most Eminent Masters of the Dutch and Flemish Schools . . . Edinburgh: 1803. V. 40

DEULIN, CHARLES

Johnny Nut and the Golden Goose . . . London: 1887. V. 46

DEUTSCH, FELIX

Heart and Athletics, Clinical Researches Upon the Influence of Athletics Upon the Heart. St. Louis: 1927. V. 42

DER DEUTSCHE Pionier. Eine Monatsschrift fur Erinnerungen aus dem Deutschen Pionier-Leben in den Vereinigten Staten. Cincinnati: 1869-70. V. 38

DEUX-PONTS, WILLIAM DE

My Campaigns in America: A Journal Kept by Count William De Deux-Pont, 178 0-1781. Boston: 1868. V. 37; 39; 42; 43

DEVA, S.

The Orchid Flora of North West Himalaya. 1986. V. 39

DE VALERA, R.

Survey of the Megalithic Tombs of Ireland. Dublin: 1961/72. V. 38

Survey of the Megalithic Tombs of Ireland. Dublin: 1961/82. V. 43

DEVAS, CHARLES STANTON 1848-1906

Groundwork of Economics. London: 1883. V. 43

DE VAUBAN

New Method of Fortification. London: 1748. V. 38

DEVAUCHELLE, R.

Le Reliure en France de ses Origines a Nos Jours. Paris: 1959-61. V. 44

DE VAUDONCOURT, GUILLAUME

Memoirs on the Ionian Islands, Considered in a Commercial, Political and Military Point of View. London: 1816. V. 37; 39

DE VEAUX, SAMUEL

The Falls of Niagara; or, Tourist's Guide to the Wonder of Nature . . . Buffalo: 1839. V. 44; 45

DE VEAUX, SAMUEL continued

Legend of the Whirlpool. Buffalo: 1840. V. 39

DE VEGA, LOPE

The Star of Seville . . . Newtown: 1935. V. 42

DEVEIL, THOMAS

Memoirs of the Life and Times of Sir Thomas Deveil, Knight One of His Majest's Justices of the Peace, for the Counties of Middlesex, Essex, Surrey and Hertfordshire, the City and Liberty of Westminster . . . London: 1748. V. 38; 41; 43; 44

Observations on the Practice of a Justice of the Peace . . . London: 1747. V. 42

DEVENISH, ROBERT J.

Historical and Genealogical Records of the Devenish Families of England and IReland . . . Chicago: 1948. V. 46

DEVENS, R. M.

Our First Century. Springfield: 1876. V. 46

DEVENS, SAMUEL ADAMS

Sketches of Martha's Vineyard and Other Reminiscences of Travel at Home . . . Boston: 1838. V. 42

DEVENTER, HENDRIK VAN

Observations Importantes sur le Manuel des Accouchemens . . . Paris: 1734. V. 41; 45

DE VERE, AUBREY

The Infant Bridal and Other Poems. London: 1864. V. 45

Medieval Records and Sonnets. London: 1893. V. 37

DEVEREUX, JOHN C.

The Most Material Parts Reduced to Questions and Answers. New York: 1891. V. 40

DEVEREUX, WALTER B.

Lives and Letters of the Devereux, Earls of Essex, in the Reigns of Elizabeth, James I and Charles I, 1540-1646. London: 1853. V. 39

DE VERVILLE, BEROALDE

Fantastic Tales; or, the Way to Attain. Carbonnek: 1890. V. 39

DEVEY, LOUISA

Life of Rosina, Lady Lytton, with Numerous Extracts from Her MS. Autobiography and other Original Documents . . . London: 1887. V. 46

DEVICES of Forty-Eight Famous Persons and Vices of Two Not So Famous. 1958. V. 46

DE VIGNY, ALFRED

Cinq-Mars; Or, A Conspiracy Under Louis XIII. Boston: 1888. V. 37

THE DEVIL and Doctor Faustus. Montpelier: 1807. V. 40

THE DEVIL In Search of a Wife. New York: 1908. V. 41; 44

DEVILLE, MR.

Catalogue of an Assemblage of . . . Bronzes, also some Antique Gems, Gold and Silver Coins . . . London: 1847. V. 40

A Catalogue of Antique, Ancient and Italian Works of Art in Bronze, on View and Sale at Mr. Deville's Rooms. London: 1834. V. 38; 40

DE VILLIERS, C. G.

Genealogies of Old South African Families. Completely revised edition augmented and rewritten by C. Parma. Cape Town/Amsterdam: 1966. V. 37

THE DEVIL'S Almanac . . . London: 1745. V. 43

DE VINNE PRESS

The Roman and Italic Printin Types in the Printing House of Theodore L. DeVinne & Co. New York: 1891. V. 38

Styles (Old and New) of Types for Books and Advertisements in the Use at the De Vinne Press. New York: 1905. V. 42

Types of the DeVinne Press, Specimens for the Use of Compositiors, Proofreaders and Publishers. New York: 1907. V. 38

DE VINNE, THEODORE LOW 1828-1914

Bruce's NY Type Foundry. Specimens of Printing Types. (&) First Supplement, 1883. (with Volume III) The Invention of Printing a Collection of Facts and Opinions . . . New York: 1878-83. V. 40

A Catalogue of Books in First Editions Selected to Illustrate the History of English Prose Fiction From 1485 to 1870. New York: 1917. V. 37

Christopher Plantin and the Plantin-Moretus Museum at Antwerp. New York: 1888. V. 38

The First Editor: Aldus Pius Manutius. New York: 1983. V. 38; 45; 46

Historic Printing Types. New York: 1886. V. 42

The Invention of Printing, a Collection of Facts and Opinions Descriptive of Early Prints and Playing Cards . . . New York: 1876. V. 40; 41; 43; 45

The Invention of Printing. New York: 1878. V. 37; 38; 40; 41; 42; 43; 44

Notable Printers of Italy During the Fifteenth Century. New York: 1910. V. 46

The Plantin-Moretus Museum. 1929. V. 37; 39

The Plantin-Moretus Museum. San Francisco: 1929. V. 38; 41; 45

The Practice of Typography. New York: 1900-04. V. 45

The Printers' Price List. New York: 1871. V. 44

Specimens of Printing Types Made at Bruce's New-York Type-Foundry, Established in 1813. (with) The Invention of Printing, a Colllection of Facts and Opinions . . . New York: 1882/1878. V. 44

Title-Pages as Seen by a Printer, with Numerous Illustrations in Facsimile and Some Observations on the Early and Recent Printing of Books. New York: 1901. V. 38

DEVIS, ELLIN

The Accidence; or First Rudiments of English Grammar. London: 1775. V. 44

DEVLIN & CO.

The Uniform of the United States Army and the National Guard. New York: 1875. V. 44

DEVLIN, DENIS

Inetercessons: Poems. London: 1937. V. 41; 42; 46

DEVOE, ALAN

The Portait of Mr. O. W. New York: 1930. V. 38; 40

DEVOL, GEORGE H.

Forty Years a Gambler on the Mississippi. New York: 1892. V. 45

DE VOLPI, CHARLES P.

The Eastern Townships. Montreal: 1962. V. 37

Montreal. Recueil Iconographique. A Pictorial Record. Montreal: 1963. V. 37

Toronto: a Pictorial Record. 1813-1882. Montreal: 1965. V. 42

DEVON BIRD-WATCHING AND PRESERVATION SOCIETY

Devon and Lundy Bird Reports, Bein Annual Reports of the . . . 1946-78. V. 38

DEVON CHAPPLE, WILLIAM

A Review of Part of Risdon's Survey of Devon, containing the General Description of that County; with Corrections, Annotations, and Additions. Exeter: 1785. V. 37

DEVON, FREDERICK

Issues of the Exchequer, Being Payments Made Out of His Majesty's Revenue During the Reign of James I. London: 1836. V. 39

DEVONSHIRE, GEORGIANA SPENCER CAVENDISH, DUCHESS OF 1757-1806

The Sylph; a Novel. London: 1779. V. 41; 43

DEVONSHIRE, SPENCER COMPTON CAVENDISH, 8TH DUKE OF 1833-1908

Reproductions of Drawings by Old Masters in the Collection of the Duke of Devonshire at Chatsworth. London: 1902. V. 39

DEVONTINAL Somnium; or, a Collection of Prayers and Exhortations, Uttered by Miss Rachel Baker, in the City of New York, in the Winter of 1815 During Her Abstracted and Unconscious State . . . New York: 1815. V. 39; 40; 41; 44; 46

DE VOTO, BERNARD

Across the Wide Missouri. Boston: 1947. V. 37; 40; 42; 43; 45

DEVOY, JOHN

Recollections of an Irish Rebel. New York: 1929. V. 41

DE VRIES, PETER

Angels Can't Do Better. New York: 1944. V. 43

No But I Saw the Movie. Boston: 1952. V. 45; 46

DEW, THOMAS RODERICK

Lectures on the Restrictive System Delivered to the Senior Political Class of William and Mary College. Richmond: 1829. V. 37; 38

DE WAAL, D. C.

With Rhodes in Mashonaland. Cape Town: 1896. V. 39

DE WAAL, RONALD BURT

The World Bibliography of Sherlock Holmes and Dr. Watson's Classified and Annotated List. Boston: 1974. V. 42

DE WALDEN, HOWARD

Some Feudal Lords and Their Seals MCCCI, with an Introduction. N.P.: 1904. V. 45

DEWAR, DANIEL

Elements of Moral Philosophy, and of Christian Ethics. London: 1826. V. 43

DEWAR, DANIEL continued

Observations on the Character, Customs and Superstitions of the Irish . . . London: 1812. V. 41; 42; 46

Observations on the Character, Customs, and Superstitions of the Irish; and on some of the causes which have retarded the Moral and Political Improvement of Ireland. Dublin: 1812. V. 37

DEWAR, DOUGLAS

Game Birds. London: 1928. V. 42; 44

DEWAR, GEORGE

Wild Life in Hampshire Highlands. London: 1899. V. 44

DEWAR, GEORGE A. B.

The South Country Trout Streams. London: 1899. V. 39

DEWAR, J. CUMMING

Voyage of the Nyanza R.N.Y.C. Edinburgh: 1892. V. 43

DEWAR, J. CUMMINGS

The Voyage of the 'Nyanza', a 3-Year Cruise in 100' Schooner Yacht in 1887 from Plymouth, England, Down the Atlantic, through the Straits of magellan, up the Coast of South America to the Pacific Isles and Japan, and Final Shipwreck on a Reef in Ponapi . . . London: 1892. V. 38

DE WAVRIN, JOHN

A Collection of the Chronicles and Ancient Histories of Great Britain, now Called England. London: 1864-91. V. 37

DEWDNEY, KEEWATIN

The Book of London. London: 1965. V. 42

DEWEES, F. P.

The Molly Maguires. Philadelphia: 1877. V. 42

DEWEES, JACOB

The Great Future of America and Africa. Philadelphia: 1854. V. 42

DEWEES, WILLIAM

A Compendious System of Midwifery. Philadelphia: 1828. V. 42

An Essay on the Means of Lessening Pain and Facilitating Certain Cases of Difficult Parturition. Philadelphia: 1819. V. 42

Essays on Various Subjects Connected with Midwifery. Philadelphia: 1823. V. 42

Letters from an Early Settler of Texas. Louisville: 1858. V. 38; 43; 44

A Practice of Physic, Comprising Most of the Diseases Not Treated of in 'Diseases of Females' and 'Diseases of Children.' Philadelphia: 1830. V. 45

A Practice of Physic . . . Philadelphia: 1833. V. 45

A Treatise on the Diseases of Females. Philadelphia: 1828. V. 45

A Treatise on the Diseases of Females. Philadelphia: 1847. V. 42

A Treatise on the Physical and Medical Treatment of Children. Philadelphia: 1825. V. 42

A Treatise on the Physical and Medical Treatment of Children. Philadelphia: 1826. V. 37

DEWELL, T.

The Philosophy of Physic, Founded on One General and Immutable Law of Nature . . . Marlborough: 1785. V. 46

DE WET, CHRISTIAAN RUDOLF

Three Years War (October 1899-June 1902). Westminster: 1902. V. 42

DEWEY, CHESTER

Reports on the Herbaceous Plants and on the Quadrupeds of Massachusetts. Cambridge: 1840. V. 40

DEWEY, J. L.

Dewey's County Directory . . . Galesburg, Ill.: 1868. V. 37

DEWEY, JOHN

Essays in Experimental Logic. Chicago: 1916. V. 45

Ethical Principles Underlying Education. Chicago: 1903. V. 46

The Influence of Darwin on Philosophy and Other Essays. New York: 1910. V. 45

Psychology. New York: 1887. V. 37; 42

The School and Society. Chicago: 1899. V. 46

DEWEY, MELVILLE

Decimal Classification and Realtiv Index for Arranging Cataloguing and Indexing Public and Private Libraries . . . Boston: 1885. V. 39

DEWEY, SQUIRE P.

The Bonanza Mines of Nevada. San Francisco: 1878. V. 41

DEWEY, THOMAS E.

Journey to the Far Pacific. Garden City: 1952. V. 44

DEWHURST, H. W.

The Natural History of the Order Cetacea, and the Oceanic Inhabitants of the Arctic Regions. London: 1834. V. 43

DEWHURST, WILLIAM W.

The History of Saint Augustine, Florida. New York: 1881. V. 41

DEWICK, E. S.

Facsimiles of Horae De Beata Maria Virgine From English Mss. of the 11th century. London: 1902. V. 40

DE WINDT, HARRY

From Paris to New York by Land. London: 1904. V. 40; 42

Through the Gold Fields of Alaska to Bering Straits. London: 1898. V. 40; 41; 42; 43; 46

DE WITT, DAVID MILLER

The Judicial Murder of Mary E. Surratt. Baltimore: 1895. V. 39; 44; 46

DE WOLFE, J. H.

Pawnee Bill, His Experiences and Adventures on the Western Plains. N.P.: 1902. V. 45

DEWSBURY, WILLIAM

The Faithful Testimony of that Antient Servant of the Lord and Minister of the Everlasting Gospel, William Dewsbury. London: 1689. V. 40

DEXTER, A. HERSEY

Early Days in California. Denver: 1886. V. 39

DEXTER, COLIN

The Dead of Jericho. London: 1981. V. 43

The Jewel That Was Ours. Bristol: 1991. V. 45

Last Bus to Woodstock. London: 1975. V. 42; 43

Last Seen Wearing. London: 1976. V. 38

The Silent World of Nicholas Quinn. London: 1977. V. 38

DEXTER, ELISHA

Narrative of the Loss of Whaling Brig William and Joseph, of Martha's Vineyard and the Sufferings of Her Crew for Seven Days, a Part of the Time on a Raft in the Atlantic Ocean . . . Boston: 1848. V. 44

DEXTER, PETE

God's Pocket. New York: 1983. V. 46

God's Pocket. New York: 1984. V. 44

DEXTER, PETER

Paris Trout. New York: 1988. V. 42

DE YOUNG, JOE

Friend Will. Santa Barbara: 1936. V. 44

DEZALLIER D'ARGENVILLE, ANTOINE JOSEPH 1680-1765

L'Histoire Naturelle Eclaircie dans Une de Ses Parties Principales, l'Oryctologie, Qui . . . Paris: 1755. V. 43

La Theorie et la Pratique du Jardinage. Paris: 1709. V. 41

La Theorie et la Practique du Jardinage . . . Paris: 1713. V. 39

The Theory and Practice of Gardening . . . London: 1712. V. 43; 46

The Theory and Practice of Gardening . . . London: 1728. V. 39; 45

DEZILIER D'ARGENVILLE, ANTOINE JOSEPH 1680-1765

La Theorie et la Practique du Jardinage . . . The Hague: 1715. V. 46

D'HARCOURT, RAOUL

Textiles of Ancient Peru and Their Techniques. Seattle: 1962. V. 40

DHLOMO, R. R. R.

An African Tragedy. N.P.: 1928. V. 38

D'HOMERGUE, JOHN

Silk Culturist's Manual; or, a Popular Treatise on the Planning and Cultivation of Mulberry Trees, the Rearing and Propagating of Silk Worms . . . Philadelphia: 1839. V. 46

D'HULST, R. A.

Jordaens Drawings. London: 1974. V. 42

A DIALOGUE Between a Member of Parliament a Divine, a Lawyer, A Freeholder, a Shopkeeper and a Country Farmer . . . London: 1703. V. 42

A DIALOGUE Between Death and a Lady. N.P.: 1790-1810. V. 45

A DIALOGUE Between Death and Doctor Robert Wyld, Who Dyed Lately of an Apoplexy. London: 1679. V. 41

A DIALOGUE on One Thousand Seven Hundred and Thirty-Eight: Together with a Prophetic Postscript as to One Thousand Seven Hundred and Thirty-Nine. London: 1738. V. 46

A DIALOGUE Which Lately Pass'd Between the Knight and His Man John. London: printed by W. Lloyd,: 1739. V. 45

DIALOGUES of Creatures Moralised. (Kentfiled: 1967). V. 37

DIALOGUS CREATURARUM

Ancient Fables, Curious to the Philoliger, Interesting to the Lover of Natural History, and Helpful to the Moralist. 1967. V. 44

The Dialogues of Creatures Moralised. London: 1816. V. 45

Dialogues of Creatures Moralised. Kentfield: 1967. V. 38; 41; 42; 44

Herball from the Dialogues of Creatures Moralised . . . Vermont: 1979. V. 41; 45

Herball. From the Dialogues of Creatures Moralised. West Burke: 1979. V. 40

DIALOGUS Linguae et Ventris. Paris: 1499-1500. V. 40

DIAMANT Classics. New York: 1944-53. V. 46

DIAMOND, A. W.

Studies of Mascarene Island Birds. Cambridge: 1987. V. 38; 39

THE DIAMOND Gazetteer of Great Britain and Ireland . . . London: 1833. V. 39

DIANNYERE, ANTOINE

Essais d'Arithmetique Politique. Paris: 1799. V. 45

DIARIO Ecclesiastico . . . Lisbon: 1791. V. 38

DIARIO Ecclesiastico Para o Reino de Portugal . . . Lisbon: 1805. V. 38

DIARY of a British Soldier May 5 1793-Mar 4 1795. San Francisco: 1941. V. 42

DIARY of a Nun. London: 1840. V. 39

A DIARY of the Wreck of His Majesty's Ship Challenger, on the Western Coast of South America in May, 1835. London: 1836. V. 40

DIARY: With Dominican Calendar and XII Wood Engravings. Ditchling: 1928. V. 46

DIAZ, ABBY MORTON

Domestic Problems: Work and Culture in the Household, and the Schoolmater's Trunk Containing Papers on Home Life in Tweenit. Boston: 1884. V. 37

The William Henry Letters. Boston: 1870. V. 42; 44

William Henry and His Friends. Boston: 1872/71. V. 42; 44

DIAZ DE GAMEZ, GUTIERRE

Croncia de Don Pedro Nino. Historia del Grand Tamorlan. Sumario de los Ryes de Espana por el Despensero Mayor de la Reyna Dona Leonor, Muger del Rey Don Juan I de Castilla. Madrid: 1782-82-81. V. 37

DIAZ DEL CASTILLO, BERNAL 1496-1584

The Discovery and Conquest of Mexico 1517-1521. Mexico City: 1942. V. 37; 39; 40; 44; 46

Histoire Verdique de la Conquete de la Nouvelle-Espagne. Paris: 1876. V. 41; 42

Historia Verdadera de la Conquista de la Nueva-Espana. Madrid: 1632. V. 43

The Memoirs of Conquistador Bernal Diaz Del Castillo . . . London: 1844. V. 38

The True History of the Conquest of Mexico. London: 1800. V. 38; 39; 42

DIAZ, F. PEDRO

Avisi Nuovi et Certezza Della Parte di Mezzo Giorno, Dove s'Intede tre Infideli Re Della Fede Mahomettana Convertiti, & Battezzati con Lisuoi Regni . . . Florence: 1571. V. 45

DIAZ, FERNANDO

La Vida y Excelentes Dichos Delos Mas Sabios Filosofos Que vo en Este Mundo. Sevilla: 1549. V. 38

DIAZ, JOSE DOMINGO

Manifestos de la Correspondencia que ha Mediado Entre los Generales conde de Cartagena y Don Miguel de la Torre, gefes del Ejercito de Costa-firme . . . Madrid: 1821. V. 38

Recuerdos Sobre la Rebelion de Caracas. Madrid: 1829. V. 39; 40

DIAZ PEREZ Y CALVILLO, JUAN BAUTISTA

Sermons Que en El Aniversario Solemne de Gracias a Maria Santisima de los Remedios, Celebrado en Esta Santa Iglesia Catedral el Dia 30 de Octubre de 1811, Por la Victoria del Monte de las Cruces . . . Mexico: 1811-12. V. 41

DIAZ PIMIENTA, FRANCISCO

Relacion Del Sucesso que Tuvo Francisco Diaz Pimienta, General de la Real Armada de las Indias, en las Isla de Santa Catalina. Madrid: 1642. V. 41

DIAZ VARA CALDERON, GABRIEL

Grandezas y Maravillas de la Inclyta y Sancta Cividad de Roma. Madrid: 1677. V. 45

DIAZ Y DIAZ, JESUS

Itinerario que Manifiesta Varios Puntos de la Republica Mexicana . . . Mexico: 1869. V. 38

DIBBLE, SHELDON

History and General Views of the Sandwich Islands' Mission. New York: 1839. V. 40; 41

History of the Sandwich Islands. Lahainaluna: 1843. V. 37; 38

DIBDIN, CHARLES 1745-1814

The Benevolent Tar; or, The Miller's Daughter . . . N.P.: 1785. V. 42

The Collection of Sons, Selected from the Works of Mr. Dibdin. London: 1790. V. 37

Hannah Hewit; or, The Female Crusoe. London: 1792. V. 40

Hannah Hewit; or, The Female Crusoe. London: 1796. V. 39

Hannah Hewit; or, the Female Crusoe, being the History of a Woman of uncommon, mental and personal accomplishemts; who after a variety of extraordinary and interesting adventures in almost every station of life, from splendid . . . London: (1792). V. 37

Henry Hooka. London: 1807. V. 38

The Lion and the Water Wagtail: a Mock Heroic Poem in Three Cantos. London: 1809. V. 39

The Lion and the Water-Wagtail. London: 1809. V. 38

The Musical Tour of Mr. Dibdin. Sheffield: 1788. V. 38; 43

Observations on a Tour through Almost the Whole of England and a Considerable Part of Scotland . . . London: 1801. V. 44

Observations on a Tour through Almost the Whole of England and a Considerable Part of Scotland, in a Series of Letters. London: 1801-02. V. 39; 43

Songs &c. in Heads or Tails. London: 1805. V. 42

Songs Naval and National, of the Late Charles Dibdin, with Memoir and Addenda. London: 1841. V. 38

The Yonger brother: A Novel, in two volumes. Dublin: 1793. V. 37

The Younger Brother; a Novel. London: 1793. V. 40

The Younger brother: A Novel, in three volumes. London: (1793). V. 37

DIBDIN, CHARLES ISAAC MUNGO

Young Arthur; or the Child of Mystery. London: 1819. V. 43

DIBDIN, T.

Songs of the Late Charles Dibdin: with a Memoir. London: 1849. V. 46

DIBDIN, THOMAS FROGNALL 1776-1847

Aedes Althorpianae . . . 1822. V. 45

Aedes Althorpianae. London: 1822. V. 37

A Bibliographical Antiquarian and Picturesque Tour in France and Germany. London: 1821. V. 38

A Bibliographical, Antiquarian and Picturesque Tour in France and Germany. London: 1829. V. 37; 39; 40; 42; 43; 45; 46

A Bibliographical, Antiquarian and Picturesque Tour in the Northern Counties of England and Scotland. London: 1838. V. 37; 39; 42; 43; 44; 45

A Bibliographical Antiquarian and Picturesque Tour in France and Germany. London: 1821. V. 37; 39; 40; 44; 46

The Bibliographical Decameron . . . London. V. 44

The Bibliographical Decameron. London: 1817. V. 37; 39; 40; 42; 44; 45; 46

The Bibliographical decameron; or, Ten Days Pleasant Discource upon illuminated manuscripts and subjects connected with early engraivngs, typography, and bibliography. 1817. V. 37

Bibliography: a Poem. London: 1812. V. 39; 40; 41; 42; 44; 46

Bibliography: A Poem. (London: 1812). V. 37

The Bibliomania; or Book Madness. London: 1809. V. 38; 39; 40

Bibliomania. London: 1811. V. 37; 40; 41; 42; 46

Bibliomania. London: 1842. V. 37; 38; 40; 41; 44; 45; 46

Bibliomania; or Book-Madness. London: 1876. V. 37; 38; 40; 45

The Bibliomania, or Book Madness. Boston: 1903. V. 39; 40; 45

Bibliophobia. London: 1832. V. 37; 38; 39; 40; 45; 46

Bibliotheca Spenceriana; or a Descriptive Catalogue of the Books Printed in the Fifteenth Century and of Many Valuable First Editions . . . London: 1814-15. V. 39; 45

Bibliotheca Spenceriana. (with) Aedes Althorpianae . . . London: 1814-15, 1821. V. 41

Cranmer; a Tale of Modern Times. London: 1841-43. V. 42

A Descriptive Catalogue of the Books Printed in the Fifteenth Century, Lately Forming Part of the Library of the Duke Di Cassano Serra, and now the Property of George John Earl Spencer, K.G. London: 1823. V. 38

The Fate of Calas. A Tragic Melodrame, in Three Acts. Altered from the French of M. Victor. London: 1820. V. 37

The History of Cheltenham and Its Environs . . . Cheltenham: 1803. V. 41

Holbein's Dance of Death. London: 1858. V. 37

DIBDIN, THOMAS FROGNALL 1776-1847 continued

Horae Bibliographicae Cantabrigienses: a Facsimile of Dibdin's Cambridge Notebook 1823. New Castle: 1989. V. 45

An Introduction to the Knowledge of Rare and Valuable Editions of the Greek and Roman Classics. Glocester: 1802. V. 45

An Introduction to the Knowledge of Rare and Valuable Editions of the Greek and Roman Classics. Gloucetser: 1802. V. 38; 45

An Introduction to the Knowledge of Rare and Valuable Editions of the Greek and Latin Classics, with Some Account of Polyglot Bibles and the Best Editions of the Greek Septuagint and Testament. London: 1804. V. 37; 40

An Introduction to The Knowledge of Greek and Latin Classics. London: 1827. V. 38; 39; 40; 41; 42; 43; 44; 45; 46

An Introduction to the Knowledge of Rare and Valuable Editions of the Greek and Roman Classics . . . Gloucester/London: 1802. V. 37

The Library Companion. London: 1824. V. 37; 38; 39; 40; 41; 42; 43; 45

Poems. London: 1797. V. 37; 39; 40

The Reminiscences of Thomas Dibdin, of the Theatres Royal, Covent Garden, Drury Lane, Haymarket &c. London: 1827. V. 41; 45

Reminiscences of a Literary Life. London: 1836. V. 37; 38; 39; 40; 41; 44; 45; 46

Typographical Antiquities; or The History of Printing in England, Scotland and Ireland. London: 1810-12-16-19. V. 41

Typographical antiquities, or the History of Printing in England, Scotland and Ireland . . . London: 1810/19. V. 45

DIBDIN, THOMAS JOHN 1771-1841

The Fate of Calas: A Tragic Melodrama in Three Acts. London: 1820. V. 41; 43

The Last Lays of the Last of the Three Dibdins . . . London: 1833. V. 38

The Reminiscences of Thomas Dibdin, of the Theatre Royal, Covent-Garden, Drury-Lane, Haymarket &c. London: 1827. V. 41

DI CESNOLA, A. P.

Salaminia (Cyprus). The History, Treasures and Antiquities of Salamis in the Island of Cyprus. London: 1884. V. 45

DICEY, EDWARD

Six Months in the Federal States. London. V. 43

Six Months in the Federal States. London: 1863. V. 37; 38

Six Months in the Federal States. London: and Cambridge: 1863. V. 39; 43

DICEY, THOMAS

An Historical Account of Guernsey, From Its Earliest Settlement Before the Norman Conquest to the Present Time. London: 1751. V. 39; 40; 46

An Historical Account of Guernsey, from its First Settlement Before the Norman Conquest to the Present Time . . . London: 1751. V. 46

DICK, EVERETT

Vanguards of the Frontier: a Social History of the Northern Plains and Rocky Mountains . . . New York:/London: 1941. V. 45

DICK, JACK R.

The Mr. and Mrs. Jack R. Dick Collection of English Sporting and Conversation Paintings . . . Sold at Auction by Sothebys. London: 1973-75. V. 41

DICK, JOHN

Report of Committee on Mines and mining Interests. Sacramento: 1856. V. 37

DICK, MAXWELL

Description of the Suspension Railway Invented by Maxwell Dick. Irvine: 1830. V. 46

DICK, PHILIP K.

Dr. Bloodmoney or How We Got Along After the Bomb. Boston: 1977. V. 42

The Game-Players of Titan. 1974. V. 44

A Handful of Darkness. 1955. V. 39

A Handful of Darkness. Boston: 1978. V. 42; 45

The Man in the High Castle. 1962. V. 39

The Man in the High Castle. 1962. V. 39

The Man in the High Castle. 1962. V. 37

Martian Time-Slip. 1976. V. 37

Solar Lottery. Boston: 1976. V. 42

The Three Stigmata of Palmer Eldritch. New York: 1965. V. 44

Time Out of Joint. 1959. V. 39

Ubik. Garden City: 1969. V. 42

DICK, R. A.

The Ghost and Mrs. Muir. Chicago: 1945. V. 39

DICK, STEWART

Arts and Crafts of Old Japan. London: 1914. V. 44; 46

The Cottage Homes of England. Painted by Helen Allingham, R.W.S., described by Stewart Dick. London: 1909. V. 37

DICK, WILLIAM BRISBANE

The American Hoyle. New York: 1864. V. 39

DICK, WILLIAM ROBERTSON

Inscriptions and Devices, in the Beauchamp Tower, Tower of London . . . London: 1853. V. 38

DICKENS, CHARLES 1812-1870

V. 46

Address Delivered at the Birmingham and Midland Institute, on the 27th September, 1869. Birmingham: 1869. V. 40

All the Year Round. New York: 1859-60. V. 43

All the Year Round. 1859-67. V. 40

All the Year Round. London: 1863-67. V. 40

American Notes. London. V. 40

American Notes for General Circulation. London: 1842. V. 41

American Notes. London: 1842. V. 37; 38; 39; 40; 41; 42; 43; 44; 45; 46

American Notes for General Circulation. New York: 1842. V. 37; 40; 43

American Notes for General Circulation. Paris: 1842. V. 44

American Notes for General Circulation. Philadelphia: 1842. V. 43

American Notes for General Circulation. London: 1850. V. 38; 44

American Notes for General Circulation. London: 1855. V. 43

American Notes for General Circularion. Boston: 1867. V. 40

American Notes for General Circulation. New York: 1868. V. 43

American Notes . . . and Pictures for Italy. London: 1875. V. 40

American Notes for General Circulation. London. V. 37

American Notes For General Circulation. London: 1847. V. 37

Barnaby Rudge. London: 1841. V. 40; 43

Barnaby Rudge. London: 1842. V. 43

Barnaby Rudge. Philadelphia: 1842. V. 43; 45; 46

Barnaby Rudge. London: 1849. V. 44

Barnaby Rudge. London: 1841. V. 37

The Battle of Life. Philadelphia: 1842. V. 45

The Battle of Life. London: 1846. V. 45

The Battle of Life. London: 1846. V. 37; 38; 39; 40; 41; 42; 43; 44; 45; 46

The Battle of Life. New York: 1847. V. 40

The Battle of Life. London: 1856. V. 46

Bleak House. London: 1852-1853. V. 37; 40; 41; 42; 43

Bleak House. London: 1852-Sept. 1853. V. 43; 45

Bleak House. London: 1853. V. 37; 38; 39; 40; 41; 42; 43; 44; 45; 46

Bleak House. New York: 1853. V. 38; 40; 41; 42; 43; 44; 45; 46

Bleak House. London: 1860. V. 43

Bleak House. London: 1875. V. 40

Captain Boldheart's Voyage - a Holiday Romance. Manchester: 1982. V. 45

Catalogue of the Beautiful Collection of Modern Pictures, Water-Colour Drawings and Objects of Art . . . Which . . . Will Be Sold by Auction by Messrs. Christie, Manson & Woods . . . on Saturday, July 9, 1870 . . . London: 1870. V. 40; 43

The Charles Dickens Birthday Book. London: 1882. V. 43; 44

Charles Dickens Rare Print Collection. Philadelphia: 1900. V. 43

Charles Dickens and Maria Beadnell - Private Correspondence. 1908. V. 43

Charles Dickens & Maria Beadnell: Private Correspondence. Boston: 1908. V. 38; 40; 43

Les Chefs-d'oeuvre . . . Paris: 1847. V. 45

The Child-Wife from the David Copperfield of Charles Dickens. New York: 1855. V. 46

The Children of Dickens. New York: 1925. V. 44

A Child's Dream of Star. Boston: 1871. V. 40

A Child's Dream of a Star. London: 1899. V. 43

Child's History of England. London: 1852. V. 45

A Child's History of England. London: 1852-4. V. 39; 41; 42; 43; 45

A Child's History of England. London: 1852/53/54. V. 43

A Child's History of England. New York: 1853-4. V. 41

The Child's History of England. London: 1853-54/52-53. V. 40

A Child's History of England. London: 1854-59. V. 40

A Child's History of England. London: 1854/59/59. V. 43

The Chimes. London: 1844. V. 45

The Chimes. Leipzig: 1845. V. 43

The Chimes. London: 1845. V. 37; 38; 39; 40; 41; 43; 44; 46

The Chimes. New York: 1845. V. 40; 43

The Chimes. Philadelphia: 1845. V. 40; 45

The Chimes. London: 1845, 1844. V. 40; 41; 44

The Chimes. London: 1858. V. 43

The Chimes. London: 1870. V. 40

The Chimes. London: 1905. V. 41

The Chimes. A Goblin Story. London: 1906. V. 37

The Chimes. London: 1913. V. 43

DICKENS, CHARLES 1812-1870 continued

The Chimes. 1931. V. 46

The Chimes. London: 1931. V. 37; 38; 39; 40; 41; 43; 44; 45; 46

The Chimes. New York: 1931. V. 40; 43

The Chimes. 1985. V. 40

The Chimes, or Some Bells Rang an Old Year Out and a New Year In. Mission: 1986. V. 38

The Christmas Books. London: 1845-48. V. 39

Christmas Books. London: 1852. V. 40; 43

Christmas Books. London: 1852. V. 40

Christmas Books. New York: 1861. V. 43

Christma. New York: 1861. V. 41

Christmas Books. London: 1875. V. 40

The Christmas Books. London: 1886-7. V. 43

A Christmas Carol in Prose Being a Ghost Story for Christmas. London. V. 44

A Christmas Carol. 1843. V. 37

A Christmas Carol. Leipzig: 1843. V. 40; 43

A Christmas Carol. London: 1843. V. 37; 38; 40; 41; 42; 43; 44; 45; 46

A Christmas Carol in Prose, The Chimes, The Cricket on the Hearth. Leipzig: 1843/45/46. V. 39

A Christmas Carol in Prose, The Chimes, The Cricket on the Hearth. Leipzig: 1843/45/46. V. 44

A Christmas Carol; The Chimes; The Cricket on the Hearth; The Battle of Life The Haunted Man. London: 1843/45/46/48. V. 37

A Christmas Carol. (with) The Chimes, The Cricket on the Hearth, The Battle of Life, and The Haunted Man. London: 1843-48. V. 39

A Christmas Carol, The Chimes, The Cricket on the Hearth, The Battle of Life, and the Haunted Man. London: 1843-48. V. 43

A Christmas Carol. London: 1844. V. 40; 43

A Christmas Carol in Prose. London: 1844. V. 40

A Christmas. London: 1844. V. 41

A Christmas Carol. In Prose. Being a ghost story of Christmas. Philadelphia: 1844. V. 37

A Christmas Carol. Philadelphia: 1844. V. 44; 45

A Christmas Carol. London: 1845. V. 43

A Christmas Carol. New York: 1845. V. 40; 43

A Christmas Carol. Leipzig: 1846. V. 43

A Christmas Carol in Prose. London: 1846. V. 44

A Christmas Carol. London: 1846. V. 43

The Christmas Papers of Charles Dickens. London: 1850-64. V. 45

A Christmas Carol. London: 1855. V. 43

A Christmas Carol in Prose. London: 1858. V. 40

A Christmas Carol. London: 1860. V. 40

Christmas Stories from 'All the Year Round.' London: 1863-67. V. 38

The Christmas Numbers of All the Year Round, Conducted by Charles Dickens. London: 1868. V. 38

A Christmas Carol, The Battle of Life, The Chimes, The Haunted Man, The Ghost's Bargain, The Cricket on the Hearth. London: 1886-88. V. 37

A Christmas Carol. London: 1890. V. 40

The Christmas Carol. A Facsimile Reproduction of the Author's Original MS. With an Introduction by F.G. Kitton. London: 1890. V. 37

A Christmas Carol. East Aurora: 1902. V. 40; 43

A Christmas Carol. London: 1911. V. 40

A Christmas Carol. London: 1915. V. 38; 42; 44; 46

A Christmas Carol. London & Philadelphia: 1915. V. 42

A Christmas Carol. Philadelphia: 1915. V. 38; 43

A Christmas Carol. Philadelphia/London: (1915). V. 37

De Weihnachtsabend. (Christmas Carol). Zurich & Leipzig: 1917. V. 40

A Christmas Carol. Mt. Vernon: 1930. V. 43

A Christmas Carol. In Prose. Being a Ghost Story of Christmas. New York: 1930. V. 37

A Christmas Carol in Prose. New York: 1930. V. 40

A Christmas Carol. New York: 1930. V. 44

A Christmas Carol. N.P.: 1930. V. 40

Christmas Tales. London: 1932. V. 45

A Christmas Carol. New York: 1932. V. 43

A Christmas Carol. Boston: 1934. V. 37; 39; 42; 43; 46

A Christmas Carol in Prose. Chicago: 1940. V. 40

A Christmas Carol in Prose. New York: 1940. V. 43

A Christmas Carol. New York: 1940. V. 40; 43

Cantique De Noel. Paris: 1946. V. 40

A Christmas Carol. London: 1948. V. 43

A Christmas Carol in Prose. London: 1950. V. 41

A Christmas. San Francisco: 1950. V. 41

A Christmas Carol. Being a ghost story of Christmas. San Francisco: 1950. V. 37

A Christmas Carol. San Francisco: 1950. V. 38; 44; 46

A Christmas Carol. London: 1958. V. 37

A Christmas Carol or, the Miser's Warning. Mission: 1984. V. 39

A Christmas Carol. Mission: 1984. V. 38

Christmas Stories. New York: 1864. V. 40

Christmas Stories from 'All the Year Round'. London: 1867. V. 40

Christmas Stories from 'All the Year Round.' London: 1868. V. 39

Christmas Stories from 'Household Words' and 'All the Year Round'. London: 1891. V. 40

Christmas Stories as follows: A Christmas Carol; The Chimes; The Battle of Life; The Cricket on the Hearth; The Haunted Man. Together 5 Volumes. London: 1906. V. 37

The Collected Works. London: 1873. V. 46

Les Contes . . . de l'Anglais . . . par Amedee Pichot. Premiere Serie. (Deuxieme Serie). Paris: 1847. V. 41

The Cricket on the Hearth. London: 1846. V. 37; 39; 40; 43; 44; 45; 46

The Cricket on the Hearth. New York: 1846. V. 46

The Cricket on the Hearth. London: 1846, 1845. V. 38; 40; 43

The Cricket on the Hearth. London: 1905. V. 41

The Cricket on the Hearth. London: 1927. V. 41

The Cricket on the Hearth. London: 1933. V. 41

The Cricket on the Hearth. A Fairy Tale with seven posthumous illustrations by Hugh Thomson. London: 1933. V. 37

The Cricket on the Hearth. New York: 1933. V. 43

The Cricket on the Hearth: A Fairy Tale of Home. (New York): 1933. V. 37

The Cruikshank Edition of Dickens's Works. Boston: (c. 1900). V. 37

A Curious Dance Round a Curious Tree. 1860. V. 43

A Curious Dance Round a Curious Tree. 1860. V. 43

A Curious Dance Round a Curious Tree. London: 1860. V. 44

A Curious Dance Round a Curious Tree. (London: 1860). V. 37

A Curious Dance Round a Curious Tree. N.P.: 1860. V. 43

Dombey and Son. London. V. 40

Dombey & Son. London: 1846-1848. V. 38

Dealings with the Firm of Dombey and Sons. London: 1846-48. V. 44; 45

Dombey & Son. London: 1846-48. V. 37; 38; 39; 41; 42; 46

Dombey and Son. New York: 1846-48. V. 43; 46

Dombey & Son. London: 1846-April 1848. V. 39; 43

Dealings with the Firm of Dombey and Son. New York: 1847. V. 44

Dealings with the Firm of Dombey and Son. Leipzig: 1847-48. V. 40

Dombey and Son. New York: 1847-48. V. 45

Dealings with the Firm of Dombey and Son. London: 1848. V. 37; 38; 39; 40; 41; 42; 43; 44; 45; 46

Dealings with the Firm of Dombey and Son. New York: 1848. V. 41

Dombey and Son. London: 1858. V. 41

Dombey and Son. London: 1875. V. 40; 43

Dombey and Son. Bloomsbury: 1937. V. 46

Dombey and Son. New York: 1957. V. 40

Dickens Memento . . . Catalogue with Purchasers' Names and Prices Realised of the Pictures, Drawings and Objects of Art of the Late Charles Dickens. Sold by Auction in London by Messrs. Christie, Manson & wood. London: 1870. V. 43

Dickens in Italy. A Letter to Thomas Mitton, Written in 1844 and Now Published for the First Time. New York: 1956. V. 42

Dickens' Short Stories. Philadelphia: 1859. V. 46

Dickens's Children. New York: 1912. V. 46

Dr. Marigold's Prescriptions. New York: 1866. V. 43

Dombey & Son. London: 1846-48. V. 39

Drawn from Life. New York: 1875. V. 43; 46

For These Times. London: 1854. V. 37

Great Expectations. Leipzig: 1861. V. 43

Great Expectations. London: 1861. V. 37; 38; 39; 40; 43; 46

Great Expectations. New York: 1861. V. 44

Great Expectations. Philadelphia: 1861. V. 43

Great Expectations. Leipzig: 1861, c. 1880. V. 40

Great Expectations. Boston: 1862. V. 40; 43

Great Expectations. London: 1862. V. 37

Great Expectations. London: 1864. V. 40; 43

Great Expectations. Edinburgh: 1937. V. 43; 45

Hard Times. London: 1854. V. 37; 38; 40; 41; 42; 43; 44; 45; 46

Hard Times. New York: 1854. V. 41; 44

The Haunted man. London: 1848. V. 37; 40; 43; 44

The Haunted Man and the Ghost's Bargain. V. 37

A Holiday Romance. London: 1868. V. 43

The Holly Tree. East Aurora: 1903. V. 43

Home Narratives: Or, Stories from Household Words. New York: 1852. V. 40

Home and Social Philosophy: Chapters on Everyday Topics. New York: 1854. V. 44

Household Words. London: 1850-59. V. 40; 41

DICKENS, CHARLES 1812-1870 continued

Household Words Christmas Stories 1851-1858. London: 1858. V. 44

The Humour of Dickens Chosen by R. J. Cruikshank. London: 1932. V. 37

Hunted Down: and Other Reprinted Pieces. Philadelphia: 1865. V. 44

Hunted Down. London: 1870. V. 39; 43

Is She His Wife? Or Something Singular. (with) The Lamplighter. London: 1883? V. 40

The Lamplighter. London: 1879. V. 37; 40; 43

The Lamplighter. N.P.: 1879. V. 40

The Lamplighter's Story; Hunted Down; The Detective Police; and other Novelettes. Philadelphia: 1861. V. 43; 46

The Lazy Tour of Two Idle Apprentices. No. Thoroughfare. The Perils of Certain English Prisoners. London: 1890. V. 38; 40; 43

The Letters of Charles Dickens. London: 1880. V. 40

The Letters. London: 1880-82. V. 40; 43; 44

The Earliest Letters of Charles Dickens (Written to His Friend Henry Kolle). Cambridge: 1910. V. 40

The Life of Our Lord. New York: 1934. V. 44

Martin Chuzzlewit in the U.S.A. V. 46

Leven en Lotgevallen van Maarten Chuzzlewit. Amsterdam: 1843-44. V. 40

Martin Chuzzlewit. London: 1843-44. V. 38; 42; 43; 44; 45; 46

The Life and Adventures of Martin Chuzzlewit, His Relatives, Friends, and Enemies . . . London: 1843-July 1844. V. 43

The Life and Adventures of Martin Chuzzlewit. London: 1843-June 1844. V. 43

The Life and Adventures of Martin Chuzzlewit. Leipzig: 1844. V. 45

The Life and Adventures of Martin Chuzzlewit. London: 1844. V. 37; 38; 39; 40; 41; 42; 43; 44; 45; 46

The Life and Adventures of Martin Chuzzlewit. Philadelphia: 1844. V. 40

The Life and Adventures of Martin Chuzzlewit. Philadelphia: 1844. V. 43

The Life and Adventures of Martin Chuzzlewit. London: 1875. V. 40

The Life and Adventures of Nicholas Nickleby. London: 1838-Oct. 1839. V. 43

The Life and Adventures of Nicholas Nickleby. London: 1839. V. 37; 38; 39; 41; 42; 43; 44; 45; 46

The Life and Adventures of Nicholas Nickleby. London: 1839. V. 38; 40; 44

The Life and Adventures of Nicholas Nickleby. New York: 1839. V. 43

The Life and Adventures of Nicholas Nickleby. Philadelphia: 1839. V. 44

The Life Adventures of Nicholas Nickleby. Philadelphia: 1839. V. 45

The Life and Adventures of Nicholas Nickleby. London: 1860. V. 43

The Life and Adventures of Nicholas Nickleby. London: 1863. V. 39; 42

The Life and Adventures of Nicholas Nickleby. London: 1875. V. 40

The Life and Adventures of Nicholas Nickleby. New York: 1939. V. 40

The Life and Adventures of Nicholas Nickleby. London: 1838-39. V. 40; 43

The Life and Adventures of Nicholas Nickleby. London: 1838-1839. V. 38; 40; 41; 42; 43; 44

The Life of Our Lord. London: 1934. V. 37; 40; 41; 43; 44; 46

The Life of Our Lord. New York: 1934. V. 37; 38; 41; 43; 44

Little Dorrit. London: 1857. V. 41; 46

Little Dorrit. London: 1855-1857. V. 37; 38; 40; 41; 43; 44; 45

Little Dorrit. London: 1855-June 1857. V. 43; 46

Little Dorrit. London: 1856. V. 41

Little Dorrit. Leipzig: 1856-57. V. 43

Little Dorrit. London: 1856-7. V. 41

Little Dorrit. London: 1857. V. 37; 38; 39; 40; 41; 42; 43; 44; 45; 46

Little Dorritt. Philadelphia: 1857. V. 45

Little Dorrit. London: 1861. V. 40; 44

Little Dorrit. London: 1865. V. 46

Little Dorrit. London: 1875. V. 40

Little Dorrit. London: 1855-56. V. 37

Little Paul. From the Dombey and Son of Charles Dickens. New York: 1855. V. 40

The Loving Ballad of Lord Bateman. London: 1839. V. 40; 43

Lord Bateman. London: 1841. V. 43

The Loving Ballad of Lord Bateman. London: 1841. V. 40

Master Humphrey's Clock. London: 1840. V. 37; 40; 41; 42; 43; 44

Master Humphrey's Clock. London: 1840-1. V. 37; 38; 39; 40; 41; 42; 43; 44; 45; 46

Master Humphreys Clock. Includes Old Curiosity Shop and Barnaby Rudge. London: 1840-41. V. 39

Master Humphrey's Clock. London: 1840/41/42. V. 43

Master Humphrey's Clock. London: 1840-Nov. 1841. V. 43

Master Humphrey's Clock. London: 1841. V. 39

Master Humphrey's Clock. New York: 1841. V. 43; 44

Master Humphrey's Clock. Paris: 1841. V. 40; 43

Master Humphrey's Clock. London: 1850. V. 43

Master Humphrey's Clock. 1940. V. 45

Memoirs of Joseph Grimaldi. London: 1838. V. 37; 38; 39; 40; 41; 45

Memoirs of Joseph Grimaldi. New York: 1838. V. 40

Memoirs of Joseph Grimaldi. London: 1846. V. 38

Mrs. Lirriper's Legacy. London: 1864. V. 44

Mr. Nightingale's Diary. Boston: 1877. V. 38; 43

Mr. Pickwick. London: 1910. V. 37; 40; 41

Mr. Pickwick. Paris: 1910. V. 43

Mr. Pickwick. London: 1912. V. 37

The Mudfog Papers. London: 1880. V. 40; 43; 45; 46

The Mudfog Papers. New York: 1880. V. 41

Mugby Junction. London: 1866. V. 44

The Mystery of Edwin Drood. London. V. 42

The Mystery of Edwin Drood, and Some Uncollected Pieces. Boston: 1870. V. 43

The Mystery of Edwin Drood. London: 1870. V. 37; 38; 39; 40; 41; 42; 43; 44; 45; 46

The Mystery of Edwin Drood. No. I (-VI). London: 1870. V. 40

The Mystery of Edwin Drood. New York: 1870. V. 43

The Mystery of Edwin Drood. London: 1870-Sept. 1870. V. 43

The Mystery of Edwin Drood (completed by the spirit-pen of Charles Dickens). Philadelphia: 1871. V. 42

The Mystery of Edwin Drood. Brattleboro: 1873. V. 39; 44

The Mystery of Edwin Drood. New York: 1941. V. 40; 41

A New Piljians Projiss. London: 1900? V. 40

Newgate. London: 1881. V. 45

Newsvendors Benevolent Institution Speeches . . . by the Late Charles Dickens, President. London: 1871. V. 39

No Thoroughfare. London: 1867. V. 40

No Thoroughfare. New York: 1867. V. 40; 43

The Nonesuch Dickens. Bloomsbury: 1937-38. V. 43; 46

The Nonesuch Dickens. London: 1937-38. V. 41

The Novels of Charles Dickens. London: 1981-87. V. 46

The Old Curiosity Shop. London: 1841. V. 38; 42; 43; 46

The Old Curiosity Shop. London: 1842. V. 43

The Old Curiosity Shop. London: 1845. V. 40; 43

The Old Curiosity Shop and Other Tales. Philadelphia: 1853. V. 40; 43

The Old Curiosity Shop. London: 1900's. V. 41

The Old Curiosity Shop. London: 1913. V. 40

The Old Curiosity Shop. London: 1913. V. 37; 38; 40; 41

Old Lamps for New Ones and Other Sketches and Essays, Hithero Uncollected. New York: 1897. V. 43

Oliver Twist. London: 1838. V. 37; 38; 39; 40; 41; 42; 43; 44; 45; 46

Oliver Twist. Cincinnati: 1839. V. 40

Oliver Twist. London: 1839. V. 40

Oliver Twist. New York: 1839. V. 43; 46

Oliver Twist. Paris: 1839. V. 37; 40

Oliver Twist. London: 1840. V. 38; 43

Oliver Twist. London: 1841. V. 37; 43

Oliver Twist. Philadelphia: 1843. V. 43

Oliver Twist. Philadelphia: 1845. V. 43

Oliver Twist. London: 1846. V. 43

The Adventures of Oliver Twist. London: 1846. V. 38; 40; 45

The Adventures of Oliver Twist. London: 1846. V. 37; 38; 46

Oliver Twist. London: 1860. V. 43

The Adventures of Oliver Twist. London: 1895. V. 43

The Adventures of Oliver Twist. London: 1903. V. 40; 43

The Adventures of Oliver Twist. London: 1939. V. 41

Our Mutual Friend. London: 1863-65. V. 39

Our Mutual Friend. London: 1864-1865. V. 37; 38; 40; 41; 42; 43; 45

Our Mutual Friend. London: 1864-Nov. 1865. V. 43

Our Mutual Friend. London: 1865. V. 37; 38; 39; 40; 41; 43; 44; 45; 46

Our Mutual Friend. London: 1865. V. 40

Our Mutual Friend. New York: 1865. V. 40; 43; 45; 46

Pearl-Fishing. Auburn: 1854. V. 43

Pearl-Fishing, First Series. New York: 1854. V. 44

The Personal History of David Copperfield. London. V. 43

The Personal History of David Copperfield. London. V. 41

The Personal History, Adventures, Experience and Observation of David Copperfield the Younger of Blunderstone Rookery . . . Copyright Edition. Leipzig: 1849. V. 37

The Personal History, Adventures, Experience and Observtion of David Copperfield. David: 1849, 1850. V. 38

The Peronsal History, Adventures, Exprience and Observations of David Copperfield. London: 1849-50. V. 38; 40; 42; 43; 44; 46

The Personal History and Experience of David Copperfield the Younger. New York: 1849-50. V. 43

The Personal History of David Copperfield. London: 1849-Nov. 1850. V. 43

David Copperfield. London: 1850. V. 40

DICKENS, CHARLES 1812-1870 continued

The Personal History of David Copperfield. London: 1850. V. 37; 38; 39; 40; 41; 43; 44; 45; 46

The Personal History and Experience of David Copperfield. New York: 1850. V. 40; 43; 46

The Personal History of David Copperfield. Paris: 1850. V. 40

The Personal History of Daivd Copperfield. Philadelphia: 1851. V. 45

The Personal History and Experience of David Copperfield, the Younger. New York: 1852. V. 40

The Personal History of David Copperfield. New York: 1852? V. 40

The Personal History of David Copperfield. New York: 1852? V. 43

The Personal History of David Copperfield. London: 1866. V. 40

The Personal History of David Copperfield. London: 1870. V. 43

The Personal History of David Copperfield. London: 1875. V. 40

The Personal History of David Copperfield. London: 1911. V. 40; 43

The Personal History of David Copperfield. London: 1920. V. 38

David Copperfield. A Reading in Five Chapters. London: 1921. V. 43

The Personal History of David Copperfield. London: 1921. V. 40

The Personal History of David Copperfield. London: 1930. V. 37

David Copperfield. Philadelphia, Toronto: 1948. V. 40

The Pic Nic Papers. London: 1841. V. 40; 43; 44; 46

The Pic Nic Papers. Paris: 1841. V. 41; 44; 45; 46

The Pic Nic Papers. Philadelphia: 1841. V. 40

The Pickwick Papers. London: 1837. V. 40; 43; 44

Pickwick Papers. London: 1838. V. 43

Pickwick Papers. New York: 1838. V. 43

Pickwick Papers. London: 1839. V. 43

Pickwick Papers. New York: 1842. V. 43

Pickwick Papers. Philadelphia: 1846. V. 43

Pickwick Papers . . . National Phonographic Library. London: 1891. V. 46

Pickwick Papers . . . National Phonographic Library. London: & Bath: 1891. V. 44; 45

The Pickwick Papers. New York: & London: 1910. V. 46

Pictures from Italy. Leipzig: 1846. V. 39

Pictures from Italy. London: 1846. V. 37; 38; 39; 40; 41; 42; 43; 44; 45; 46

Pictures from Italy. Genoa: Venice: Rome: 1982. V. 44

Pictures from Italy. Greembrae: 1982. V. 37; 39; 40; 42; 43; 45

Pictures from Italy. Greenbrae: 1982. V. 42

The Plays and Poems of . . . London: 1882. V. 45

Plays and Poems, with a few miscellanies in prose. Now first collected. Edted, prefaced and annotated by Richard Herne Shepherd. London: 1885. V. 37

The Poems and Verses. London: 1903. V. 40

The Poor Traveller; Boots at the Holly-Tree Inn; and Mrs. Gamp. London: 1858. V. 39; 40; 43; 44

The Posthumous Papers of the Pickwick Club. V. 37

The Posthumous Papers of the Pickwick Club. London. V. 44

The Posthumous Papers of the Pickwick Club. London. V. 37

The Posthumous Papers of the Pickwick Club. London. V. 40

The Posthumous Papers of the Pickwick Club . . . London: 1836. V. 41

The Posthumous Papers of the Pickwick Club. Edited by 'Boz'. Philadelphia: 1836-1837. V. 37

The Posthumous Papers of the Pickwick Club. London: 1836-37. V. 38; 40; 41; 43; 44; 46

Posthumous Papers of the Pickwick Club . . . London: 1836-37. V. 44

The Posthumous Papers of the Pickwick Club. Philadelphia: 1836-37. V. 38

The Posthumous Papers of the Pickwick Club. London: 1836-Nov. 1837. V. 40; 43

The Posthumous Papers of the Pickwick Club. London: 1837. V. 39

The Posthumous Papers of the Pickwick. London: 1837. V. 37; 38; 39; 40; 41; 42; 43; 44; 45; 46

The Posthumous Papers of the Pickwick Club. London: 1837, 1838. V. 40

The Posthumous Papers of the Pickwick Club. London: 1838. V. 45; 46

The Posthumous Papers of the Pickwick Club. New York: 1838. V. 40; 43

The Posthumous Papers of the Pickwick Club. Paris: 1838. V. 40

The Posthumous Papers of the Pickwick Club . . . Paris: 1838. V. 40

The Posthumous Papers of the Pickwick Club. Lanceston: 1838-39. V. 40

The Posthumous Papers of the Pickwick Club. Leipzig: 1839. V. 40

The Posthumous Papers of the Pickwick Club. London: 1839. V. 43

The Posthumous Papers of the Pickwick Club. Philadelphia: 1841. V. 37

The Posthumous Papers of the Pickwick Club. Leipzig: 1842. V. 40

The Posthumous Papers of the Pickwick Club. New York: 1842. V. 40

The Posthumous Papers of the Pickwick Club. Philadelphia: 1846. V. 40

The Posthumous Papers of the Pickwick Club. London: 1850. V. 41

The Posthumous Papers of the Pickwick Club. London: 1860. V. 40; 43

The Posthumous Papers of the Pickwick Club. London: 1875. V. 40

The Posthumous Papers of the Pickwick Club. London: 1880. V. 46

The Posthumous Papers of the Pickwick Club. London: 1887. V. 37; 40; 41; 44; 46

Posthumous Papers of the Pickwick Club. New York/London: 1902-3. V. 37

The Posthumous Papers of the Pickwick Club. London: 1910. V. 37; 39; 40; 41; 46

The Posthumous Papers of the Pickwick Club. London: 1930. V. 43

The Posthumous Ppaers of the Pickwick Club. London: 1931-2. V. 46

The Posthumous Papers of the Pickwick Club. London: 1931-32. V. 37; 40; 43; 45

The Posthumous Papers of the Pickwick Club. London: 1931-33. V. 42

The Posthumous Papers of the Pickwick Club. London: 1933. V. 44

The Posthumous Papers of the Pickwick Club. New York: 1933. V. 38; 41; 45

The Posthumous Papers of the Pickwick Club. Oxford: 1933. V. 37; 44; 46

The Posthumous Papers of the Pickwick Club. London: 1937. V. 37

The Posthumous Papers of the Pickwick Club. New York: 1945/1944. V. 43

A Pottery Story. Boston: 1878. V. 45

The Readings of Mr. Charles Dickens, as Condensed by Himself. Boston: 1868. V. 43

Readings from the Works of Charles Dickens and Irish and American Authors. Dublin: 1882. V. 40

(Wrapper title) The Readings of Mr. Charles Dickens, as Condensed by Himself. New York: 1868. V. 37

Reprinted Pieces. London: 1858. V. 39

Reprinted Pieces and the Lazy Tour of Two Idle Apprentices. New York: 1896. V. 46

Schools and School-Masters: from the Writings of Charles Dickens. New York & Chicago: 1871. V. 41; 42

Selections from Household Words, a Weekly Journal. New York: 1864. V. 45

Sikes and Nancy. London: 1921. V. 40; 43; 44

Sketches of Young Couples, Young Ladies, Young Gentlemen. London: 1869. V. 39; 44

Sketches by 'Boz' Illustrative of Every-Day Life and Every-Day People . . . London: 1836. V. 39

Sketches by Boz. London: 1836. V. 38

Sketches by Boz, Illustrative of Every-Day Life and Every-Day People. London: 1836. V. 40

Sketches by Boz. London: 1836. V. 40; 41; 43

Sketches by 'Boz.' First-Second Series. London: 1836, 1837. V. 40

Sketches by Boz. (with) Second Series. London: 1836, 1837. V. 38

Sketches by Boz . . . . (with) The Second Series. London: 1836, 1837. V. 40

Sketches by Boz. (with) Sketches by Boz, the Second Series. London: 1836-37. V. 39

Sketches by Box. With: The Second Series. London: 1836-37. V. 40

Sketches by 'Boz'. The Second Series. London: 1837. V. 45

Sketches by Boz. London: 1837. V. 43

Sketches by Box. London: 1837. V. 43

Sketches by Boz. Second Series. London: 1837. V. 40; 43; 45; 46

Sketches by Box. Philadelphia: 1837. V. 43

Sketches By Boz. Philadelphia: 1837. V. 40

Sketches by 'Boz'. (with) Sketches by 'Boz'. Second Series. London: 1837, ie. 1836. V. 45

Sketches by 'Boz.' London: 1837-June 1839. V. 45

Sketches by Boz. London: 1837-June 1839. V. 43

Sketches by Boz. Philadelphia: 1838. V. 43

Sketches by Boz Illustrative of Everday Life & Everyday People. London: 1839. V. 38

Sketches by Boz Illustrative of Every-Day Life and Every Day People. London: 1839. V. 38

Sketches by Boz. London: 1839. V. 37; 38; 39; 40; 41; 42; 43; 44; 45; 46

Sketches by Bos. London: 1839. V. 41

Sketches by Boz. Philadelphia: 1839. V. 40; 43

Sketches by Boz. Leipzig: 1843. V. 40

Sketches by Boz. London: 1850. V. 43

Sketches by Boz. London: 1850. V. 40

Sketches by Boz. London: 1856. V. 39; 42

Sketches by Boz. London: 1857. V. 46

Sketches by Boz. London: 1867. V. 40; 43

Sketches by Boz. London: 1839. V. 37

Sketches of Young Couples. London: 1840. V. 37; 38; 40; 43; 46

Sketches of Young Gentlemen. London: 1838. V. 43

Sketches of Young Gentlemen. London: 1838. V. 43

Sketches of Young Ladies, Young Gentlemen and Young Couples. London: 1843. V. 40

Speech of Charles Dickens, Esq., at the Anniversary Festival for the Hospital for Sick Children, 49, Great Ormond Street, on Tuesday, February the 9th, 1858. London: 1858. V. 45

Speech of Charles Dickens Delivered at Gore House. Boston: 1909. V. 45

The Speeches of Charles Dickens (1841-1870). London: 1884. V. 43

DICKENS, CHARLES 1812-1870 continued

The Speeches of Charles Dickens (1841-1870). London: 1884. V. 41

Station Mugby. Ene Kertsvertelling. Amsterdam: 1867. V. 41

The Story of Little Dombey. London: 1858. V. 40; 43; 44; 45; 46

The Strange Gentleman. London: 1837. V. 44

The Strange Gentleman; a Comic Burletta, in two Acts by Boz. First Performed at the St. James's Theatre, on Thursday, September 29, 1836. London: 1837. V. 46

The Strange Gentleman, a Comic Burletta. London: 1837 ca. 1871. V. 45

The Strange Gentleman. London: 1871. V. 40; 43; 46

The Strange Gentleman. 1928. V. 43

Sunday Under Three Heads. As It Is; As Sabbath Bills Would Make It; As It Might Be Made. London: 1836. V. 37; 43; 45

Sunday Under Three Heads. Manchester: 1884. V. 45

A Tale of Two Cities. Leipzig: 1859. V. 43

A Tale of Two Cities. London: 1859. V. 37; 38; 39; 40; 41; 43; 44; 45; 46

A Tale of Two Cities. London: 1859-Dec. 1859. V. 43

A Tale of Two Cities. London: 1860. V. 40; 43; 46

A Tale of Two Cities. London: 1861. V. 39

A Tale of Two Cities. London: 1864. V. 43

A Tale of Two Cities. London: 1875. V. 40

A Tale of Two Cities. London: 1896? V. 43

A Tale of Two Cities. Bloomsbury: 1937. V. 44

Tales for Pickwick with The Five Sisters of York . . . London: 1893. V. 39

Thackeray, the Humorist and the Man of Letters. New York: 1864. V. 41

To Be Read at Dusk. London: 1890. V. 40; 43

To Be Read at Dusk and Other Stories, Sketches and Essays. London: 1898. V. 40; 41

The Tuggs's at Ramsgate, by 'Box'. Together with Other Tales, by Distinguished Writers. Philadelphia: 1837. V. 43

The Uncommercial Traveller. London: 1860. V. 40; 44

The Uncommercial Traveller. London: 1861. V. 38; 39; 43; 45

The Uncommercial Traveller. London: 1866/65. V. 43

The Unpublished Letters of Charles Dickens to Mark Lemmon. London: 1927. V. 39; 41

The Village Coquettes. London: 1836. V. 38; 46

The Village Coquettes. London: 1878. V. 43

The Village Coquette. London: 1878-1900. V. 46

The Works. London. V. 38

The Works. London. V. 39

The Works. London. V. 42

The Works. London. V. 42

The Complete Works. London. V. 43

Works of . . . London. V. 39

Dickens' Works. Philadelphia. V. 43

Works. Philadelphia: 1850-70's. V. 42; 43

People's Edition. Philadelphia: 1860. V. 40

Works. New York: 1861. V. 42; 43

Works of Charles Dickens. New York: 1861-62. V. 44; 45; 46

Works. London: 1863-66. V. 40

Works. London: 1867-70. V. 40

Works of . . . Boston: 1871. V. 46

The Works. (with) The Life of Charles Dickens. London: 1871-1879. V. 43

The Works of Charles Dickens. London: 1871-Jan. 1880. V. 43

Works. Original Illustrations by Cattermole, Phiz (H.K. Brown), and George Cruikshank. London: 1873. V. 37

Complete Works. London: 1874. V. 37; 39

Works. New York: 1874. V. 42

Works. London: 1874-76. V. 40; 41; 42; 43

Works. London: 1875. V. 37

The Works. London: 1879-80. V. 43

The Works. London: 1880. V. 38

The Works of . . . London: 1881. V. 41

Works. London: 1887-88. V. 41

The Roxburgh Edition of Dickens's Works. Boston: 1892. V. 41

The Works. Boston & New York: 1894. V. 38; 42

The Writings. Boston & New York: 1894. V. 38

Works. London: 1897. V. 40

The Works of Charles Dickens. London: 1897-1908. V. 43

Works. London: 1897-1908. V. 46

The Works. London: 1897-99. V. 42

The Works of . . . London: 1899. V. 37

The Cruikshank Edition of Dickens' Works. Boston: 1900. V. 38; 41

Complete Works. Boston: 1900. V. 41

The Works. London: 1900. V. 40

The Complete Works. New York: 1900. V. 40

The Complete Works of Charles Dickens. London: 1901-02. V. 43

The Works of . . . London: 1901-03. V. 38

The Complete Works of Charles Dickens. New York: London: 1902. V. 45

The Biographical Edition of the Works of Charles Dickens. London: 1902-03. V. 43

The Biographical Edition of the Works. London: 1903. V. 37

The Fireside Edition (of the Works). London: 1903-07. V. 46

Works. London: 1906. V. 42

The Gadshill Edition. London: 1907-08. V. 38

Works. London: 1907-1923. V. 39

Works. London: 1910. V. 41; 44

Complete Works. London: 1910-11. V. 46

The Works. London: 1910-11. V. 43

Works. London: 1910-11. V. 37

The Centenary Edition of the Works of Charles Dickens. London: 1910-19. V. 42; 43

The Works. New York: 1911. V. 40; 45

The Works. London: 1912. V. 40; 46

Complete Works. London: 1929. V. 37

The Works. London: 1929. V. 42; 45

The Works. London: 1937. V. 42

The Nonesuch Dickens. Bloomsbury: 1937-38. V. 42

The Nonesuch Dickens. London: 1937-38. V. 37

Works of . . . 'The Author's Favourite Edition' In Facsimile. London: (n.d.). V. 37

Works. Forty volumes, extensively illustrated from the original plates with facsimiles of bindings, &c. London: 1906-8/ V. 37

Works. Library Edition. London: 1963-66. V. 37

The Wreck of the Golden Mary. Kentfield: 1956. V. 38; 41; 43; 45

The Writings. With Critical and Bibliographical Introductions and Notes by Edwin Percy Whipple and Others. Boston: 1894. V. 40

The Writings. With Critical and Bibliographical Introductions and Notes by Edwin Percy Whipple and Others. Boston: (1894). V. 37

The Writings. Boston & New York: 1894. V. 42

DICKENS, F. V.

Chiushingura; or, The Loyal League. A Japanese Romance translated by . . . with Notes and an Appendix containing a Metrical Version of the Ballad of Takasago, and a Specimen of the Original Text in the Japanese Character. New Edition. London: 1880. V. 37

DICKENS, HELEN

Wild Wood. London: 1872. V. 41

DICKENS, MARY

The Charles Dickens Birthday Book. London: 1882. V. 40

DICKENS, MARY ANGELA

Children's Stories from Dickens. London: 1915. V. 42

DICKENSON, JONATHAN

God's Protecting Providence, Man's Surest Help and Defence, in Difficulty, and Most Eminent Danger . . . London: 1720. V. 39; 43

God's Protecting Providence, Man's Surest Help and Defence in Times of Greatest Difficulty and Most Eminent Danger, Evidenced in the Remarkable Deliverance of Robert Barrow, with Divers Other Persons . . . London: 1790. V. 39; 40; 43

God's Protecting Providence . . . Evidenced in the Delivery of Robert Barrow . . . From the Cruel Devouring Jams of the Inhuman Cannibals of Florida. London: 1787. V. 37; 38

God's Protecting Providence, Man's Surest Help and Defense, in Times of Greatest Difficulty, and Most Eminent Danger, Evidenced in the Remarkable Deliverance of Robert Barrow, with Divers Other Persons, from the Devouring Waves of the Sea . . . London: 1759. V. 37

Narrative of a Shipwreck in the Gulph of Florida . . . Stanford. V. 45

Ongelukkige Schipbreuk en Yslyke Reystogt, Vn Etlyke Engelscen, in den Jaare 1696 Van Jamaika in West-Indien . . . Leyden: 1707. V. 38

DICKERSON, EDWARD N.

The Navy of the United States, an Exposure of Its Condition . . . (with) The Argument . . . New York: 1864-56. V. 42

DICKERSON, OLIVER MORTON

American Colonial Government 1696-1765. Cleveland: 1912. V. 45

DICKERSON, PHILIP

History of the Osage Nation, Its People, Resources and Prospects. N.P.: 1906. V. 44

History of the Osage Nation, Its People, Resources and Prospects. Pawhuska: 1906. V. 37; 38; 39; 41; 45; 46

DICKERSON, PHILIP J.

Truth is Stanger Than Fiction. Hobart: 1907. V. 39

DICKERT, D. AUGUSTUS

History of Hershaw's Brigade, with Complete Roll of Companies, Biographical Sketches, Incidents, Anecdotes, Etc. Newberry: 1899. V. 44

DICKES, WILLIAM

The Babes in the Wood. London: 1863. V. 43

DICKESON, M. W.

Monumental Grandeur of the Mississippi Valley! Newark: 1845-50. V. 45

DICKEY, JAMES 1923-

Buckdancer's Choice. London: 1979. V. 42
Deliverance. Boston: 1970. V. 43; 44; 45
Drowning with Others. Middletown: 1962. V. 39
The Enemy of Eden. Northridge: 1978. V. 42
The Eye-Beaters, Blood, Victory, Madness. New York: 1970. V. 39
In the Child's Night. 1981. V. 42
Into the Stone and Other Poems. New York: 1960. V. 39
Jericho: the South Beheld. Birmingham: 1974. V. 39
The Owl King; a Poem. New York: 1977. V. 40; 45
The Shark at the Window. 1979. V. 42
Two Poems of the Air. Portland: 1964. V. 39
Varmland: Poems Based on Poems. 1982. V. 42
Veteran Birth - the Gadfly Poems 1947-1949. 1978. V. 39
The Zodiac. Bloomfield Hills: 1976. V. 38; 39; 40

DICKEY, LUTHER S.

History of the 103rd Regiment Pennsylvania Veteran Volunteer Infantry 1861-1865. Chicago: 1910. V. 42
History of the 85th Regiment Pennsylvania Volunteer Infantry, 1861-1865. New York: 1915. V. 42

DICKEY, WILLIAM

The Sacrifice Consenting. San Francisco: 1981. V. 46

DICKINS, GUY

Catalogue of the Acropolis Museum. Cambridge: 1912-21. V. 37; 44

DICKINSON, EMILY ELIZABETH 1830-1886

Five Poems. 1989. V. 45
Further Poems. Boston: 1929. V. 37; 39; 41; 42; 43; 45
Letters. Boston: 1894. V. 37; 38; 39; 41; 42; 43; 45; 46
Letters of . . . Boston: 1894, c. 1899. V. 42
Letters of Emily Dickinson. Boston: 1899. V. 42
The Manuscript Books of Emily Dickinson. Cambridge & London: 1981. V. 45
A Masque of Poets. Boston: 1878. V. 41
Poems. Boston: 1890. V. 45
Poems. Boston: 1891. V. 42; 43
Poems. Second Series. Boston: 1891. V. 43
Poems. Second Series. Boston: 1891. V. 38; 44; 45
Poems. London: 1891. V. 46
Poems. Second Series. Boston: 1892. V. 39
Poems - Third Series. Boston: 1896. V. 39
Poems by Emily Dickinson. Boston: 1896. V. 45; 46
Poems, Third Series. Boston: 1896. V. 38; 41; 45; 46
The Poems of Emily Dickinson. Boston: 1930. V. 46
The Poems of Emily Dickinson. London: 1930. V. 41
Poems. New York: 1952. V. 46
Poems of Emily Dickinson. New York: 1952. V. 45
The Poems of Emily Dickinson Including Variant Readings . . . Cambridge: 1955. V. 45
Selected Poems of Emily Dickinson. London: 1924. V. 45
The Single Hound Poems of a Lifetime. Boston: 1914. V. 38; 39; 43; 45
The Single Hound Poems of a Lifetime. Boston: 1915. V. 45
Ten Poems. London. V. 46
Unpublished Poems. Boston: 1935. V. 41; 45

DICKINSON, ERIC

Kishangarh Painting. New Delhi: 1959. V. 41

DICKINSON, F. A.

Big Game Shooting on the Equator. London: 1908. V. 43
Lake Victoria to Khartoum with Rifle and Camera . . . London: 1910. V. 45

DICKINSON, G. LOWES

From King to King: The Tragedy of the Puritan Revolution. London: 1891. V. 37

DICKINSON, H. W.

James Watt and the Steam Engine. Oxford: 1927. V. 43

John Wilkinson, Ironmaster. Ulverston: 1914. V. 44

DICKINSON, JOHN

An Address on the Past, Present and Eventual Relations of the United States to France. New York: 1803. V. 45
The Declaration by the Representatives of the United Colonies of North America, Now Met in General Congress in Philadelphia . . . London: 1775. V. 45
Dhar Not Restored; in Spite of the House of Commons and of Public Opinion. London: 1864. V. 42
An Essay on the Constitutional Power of Great-Britain Over the Colonies in America; with the Resolves of the Committe for the Province of Pennsylvania, and Their Instructions to Their Representatives in Assembly. Philadelphia: 1774. V. 39
The Late Regulations, Respecting the British Colonies on the Continent of America Considered; In a Letter from a Gentleman in Philadelphia to His Friend in London. London: 1774. V. 44
Letters from a Farmer in Pennsylvania, to the Inhabitants of the British Colonies. Boston: 1768. V. 37; 38
Letters from a Farmer in Pennsylvania, To the Inhabitants of the British Colonies. London: 1768. V. 38; 45
Letters from a Farmer, in Pennsylvania to the Inhabitants of the British Colonies. London: 1774. V. 41; 45
Letters from a Farmer in Pennsylvania, To the Inhabitants of the British Colonies. Philadelphia: 1774. V. 45
Letters from a Farmer in Pennsylvania. New York: 1903. V. 39; 41; 42; 43
A New Essay (by the Pennsylvania Farmer) on the Constitutional Power of Great Britain Over the Colonies in America . . . London: 1774. V. 44
A New Essay (by the Pennsylvania Farmer) on the Constitutional Power of Great-Britain Over the Colonies in America . . . London: 1774. V. 42; 43; 45; 46
A New Essays (by The Pennsylvania Farmer) on the Constitutional Power of Great-Britain Over the Colonies In America. Philadelphia: 1774. V. 39
The Political Writings of . . . Late President of the State of Delaware and of the Commonwealth of Pennsylvania. Wilmington: 1801. V. 39

DICKINSON, JONATHAN

Familiar Letters to a Gentleman, Upon . . . Subjects in Religion. Boston: 1745. V. 41
Familiar Letters to a Gentleman Upon a Variety of Seasonable and Importrant Subjects in Religion. Edinburgh: 1757. V. 39
Familiar Lettes to a Gentleman Upon a Variety of Seasonable and Importat Subjects in Religion . . . Dundee: 1772. V. 45
Familiar Letters to a Gentleman, upon a Variety Of Seasonable and Important Subjects in Religion. Newark: 1797. V. 37
God's Protecting Providence, Man's Surest Help and Defence . . . London: 1772? V. 38

DICKINSON, JOSEPH

The Flora of Liverpool. London: 1851. V. 44

DICKINSON, RODOLPHUS

A Digest of the Common Law, the Statue Laws of Massachusetts, and of the U.S. . . . Relative to the Powers and Duties of Justices of the Peace. Deerfield: 1818. V. 38

DICKINSON, THOMAS

A Narrative of the Operations for the Recovery of the Public Stores and Treasure Sunk in H.M.S. Thetis, at Cape Frio on the Coast of Brazil, on the 5th Dec. 1830. London: 1830. V. 40
A Narrative of the Operations for the Recovery of the Public Stores and Treasure Sunk in H.M.S. Thetis at Cape Frio, on the Coast of Brazil, on the 5th December 1803. London: 1836. V. 40

DICKINSON TYPE FOUNDRY

A General Book of Specimens. Boston: 1876. V. 38

DICKINSON, W. H.

On Renal and Urinary Affections. New York: 1885. V. 42

DICKINSON, WILLIAM

A Practical Exposition of the Law Relative to the Office and Duties of a Justice of the Peace Continued to the End of Trinity Term 52 George III. London: 1813. V. 40

DICKISON, MARY ELIZABETH 1830-1886

Dickison and His Men: Reminiscenes of the War in Florida. Louisville: 1890. V. 37; 38; 39; 43

DICKS, JOHN

The Story of Valentine and Orson. London. V. 42; 43

DICKSON, A.

A Treatise of Agriculture. Edinburgh: 1762. V. 43
A Treatise of Agriculture. London: 1770. V. 46

DICKSON, ARTHUR JACKSON

Covered Wagon Days. Cleveland: 1929. V. 43; 44; 45; 46

DICKSON, CARTER

He Wouldn't Kill Patience. 1944. V. 45

The Red Widow Murders. New York: 1935. V. 45

DICKSON, DAVID

Therapeutica Sacra. Edinburgh: 1656. V. 37

DICKSON, H. R. P.

The Arab of the Desert. London: 1949. V. 46

The Arab of the Desert. London: 1951. V. 45

DICKSON, J. THOMPSON

The Science and Practice of Medicine in Relation to Mind . . . London: 1874. V. 43

DICKSON, JAMES H.

The Fibre Plants of India, Africa and Our Colonies. London: 1864. V. 45

DICKSON, JOHN

Speech . . . in the Case of Samuel Houston, Tried for a Breach of the Privileges of the House of Representatives of the United States. Washington: 1832. V. 37

DICKSON, R.

Annals of Scottish Printing From the Introduction of the Art in 1507 . . . Cambridge: 1890. V. 44

DICKSON, R. W.

The Farmer's Companion, Being a Complete System of Modern Husbandry . . . London: 1813. V. 39

An Improved System of Management of Live Stock and Cattle; or a Practical Guide to the Perfecting and Improvement of the Several Breeds and Varieites of Agricultural Stock and Domestic Animals. London: 1822-24. V. 46

Practical Agriculture . . . London: 1805. V. 44; 45

Practical agriculture; or, a complete system of modern husbandry. In Two Volumes. London: 1805. V. 37

Practical Architecture; or, A Complete System of Animal Husbandry . . . London: 1807. V. 37

DICKSON, ROBERT

Annals of Scottish Printing. Cambridge: 1890. V. 39; 44

Introduction of the Art of Printing Into Scotland. Aberdeen: 1885. V. 37; 40; 42; 45; 46

DICKSON, SAMUEL H.

Essays on Life, Sleep, Pain, Etc. Philadelphia: 1852. V. 40

DICKSON, SARAH

Poems on Several Occasions. Canterbury: 1790. V. 44

DICKSON, W. E. CARNEGIE

The Bone-Marrow, a Cytological Study Forming an Introduction to the Normal and Pathological Histology of the Tissue, More Especially with Regard to Blood Formation, Blood Destruction, Etc. London: 1908. V. 42

DICKSON, W. G.

Gleanings from Japan. Edinburgh: 1889. V. 46

DICKSON, W. K. L.

The Life and Inventions of Thomas Alva Edison. London: 1894. V. 37; 39

The Life and Inventions of Thomas Alva Edison. New York: 1894. V. 46

DICKSON, WALTER

Gleanings from Japan. Edinburgh: 1889. V. 40

Japan Being a Sketch of the History Government and Officers of the Empire. Edinburgh: 1869. V. 40

DICKSON, WILLIAM STEEL

A Narrative of the Confinement and Exile of William Steel Dickson, D.D. Dublin: 1812. V. 38

DICKSONS

A Catalogue of Fruit and Forest Trees, Herbaceous Plants . . . Garden Utensils, etc. Edinburgh: 1827. V. 37

THE DICTES and Sayings of the Philosophers. London: 1877. V. 38

DICTIONARY of American Biography. New York: 1957. V. 46
DICTIONARY of American Biography. New York: 1964. V. 39; 43
DICTIONARY of American Biography. New York: 1966. V. 42; 44

DICTIONARY of Daily Wants. London: 1860. V. 42

DICTIONARY of Gardening, Edited by Fred J. Chittenden. 1956-69. V. 37

DICTIONARY of National Biography. 1973. V. 40

DICTIONARY of National Biography, 1961-1970. Oxford: 1981. V. 39

DICTIONARY of National Biography, Founded in 1822 by George Smith. London: 1967-68, 1959. V. 40

DICTIONARY of National Biography, Founded in 1882 By George Smith. London: 1949-50. V. 39

DICTIONARY of National Biography. (with) The Twentieth Century. London: 1937-86. V. 37
DICTIONARY of National Biography. (with) The Twentieth Century. London: 1958-86. V. 37
DICTIONARY of National Biography. (with) The Twentieth Century. London: 1959-86. V. 37

A DICTIONARY of Natural History. London: 1818. V. 37

A DICTIONARY of Natural History, or Complete Summary of Zoology. London: 1815. V. 37; 38

DICTIONARY of Scientific Biography. New York: 1981. V. 46

A DICTIONARY of Slang Jargon and Cant Embracing English, American, Anglo-Indian, Pidgin-English, Tinker's Jargon & Other Irregular Phraseology. London: 1889. V. 44

A DICTIONARY of the English Language: In Which the Words Deduced From Their Originals, Explained in Their Different Meaning and Authorized by the Names of the Writers . . . London: 1773. V. 42

A DICTIONARY of the English Language. To Which are Added, An Alphabetical Account of the Heathen Deities . . . London: 1791. V. 41

A DICTIONARY of the English Language . . . To Which is Prefixed a Comprehensive View of English Grammar. London: 1794. V. 41

A DICTIONARY of the English Language, With an Alphabetical Account of the Heathen Deities . . . To Which is Prefixed a Comprehensive View of English Grammar. London: 1797. V. 41; 43

A DICTIONARY of the Scottish Language. Edinburgh: 1818. V. 38

DICTIONNAIRE Universelle d'Histoire Naturelle. Paris: 1849. V. 38

DICTYS, CRETENSIS

De Bello Troyano et Dares Phrygius de Excidio Troiae Cum Notis Ad Dictum. Amsterdam: 1631. V. 44

De Historia Belli Troiani et Historia Troiana. Venice: 1499. V. 44

DICTYS, OF CRETE, PSEUD.

Les Histoires de Dictis Cretensens, Traitant des Guerres de Troye, & du Retour des Grecz en Leurs Pais, Apres Ilion Ruine . . . Paris: 1556. V. 45

DIDAY, P.

A Treatise on Syphilis in New-Born Children and Infants at the Breast. New York: 1883. V. 42

DIDEROT, DENIS

Les Bijoux Indiscretes. Or, the Indiscreet Toys. Tobago: 1749. V. 43

Encyclopedie ou Dictionnaire Raisonne de Sciences, des Arts, et des Metiers . . . (with) Supplement Dictionnaire . . . (with) Recueil de Planches . . . Livourne: 1770-79. V. 39

Oeuvres Philosophiques. Amsteram: 1772. V. 38; 41; 45

Pensees Philosophiques. La Haye: 1746. V. 39

Rameau's Neffe . . . Aus dem Manuskript Ubersetzi und Mit Anmerkungen Begleitet von Goethe. Leipzig: 1805. V. 39

DIDION, JOAN

Salvador. New York: 1983. V. 40

DIDONATO, PIETRO

Christ in Concrete. Chicago: 1937. V. 46

DIDORUS SICULUS

The Historical Library of Diodorus the Sicilian. London: 1700. V. 38

DIDOT, PIERRE 1761-1853

Specimen des Nouveaux Caracteres de la Fonderie et de L'Imprimerie de P. Didot, L'aine . . . Paris: 1819. V. 38; 39; 45; 46

DIDUSCH, WILLIAM

A Collection of Urogenital Drawings. New York: 1942. V. 42

A Collection of Urogenital Drawings. New York: 1952. V. 40

DIDYMUS

(Title in Greek, then:) Didymi Antiquissimi Auctoris Interpretatio in Odisseam. Paris: 1530. V. 40

DIE Nurnbergischen Kunstler. Nurnberg: Schrag,: 1822-31. V. 45

DIE Spielende Magie. Erstes (-Funftes) Stuck(e). Berlin: 1790-93. V. 43

DIE Zwo Episteln Saint Peters. Augsburg: 1522. V. 40

DIEBERT, RALPH C.

A History of the Third United States Cavalry 1846-1937. Harrisburg. V. 45

DILKE, CHARLES WENTWORTH continued

Problems of Greater Britain. London: 1890. V. 38

DILKE, EMILIA

French Furniture and Decoration in the XVIIIth Century. London: 1901. V. 44

French Furniture and Decoration in the XVIIIth Century. London: 1911. V. 46

DILKE, EMILLA

French Engravers and Draughtsmen of the XVIIIth Century. London: 1902. V. 42

DILKE, O. A. W.

Roman Books and Their Impact. 1977. V. 40; 45

DILLARD, ANNIE

Encounters with Chinese Writers. Middletown: 1984. V. 40

Tickets for a Prayer Wheel. Columbia: 1974. V. 38; 44

The Weasel. Claremont: 1981. V. 46

DILLENIUS, JOHN JAMES

Historia Muscorum. Oxford: 1741. V. 43

Historia Muscorum: a General History of Land and Water & Mosses and Corals. London: 1768. V. 40

DILLEY, ARTHUR URBANE

Oriental Rugs and Carpets. New York: 1931. V. 44; 45

DILLON, ARTHUR

A Winter in Iceland and Lapland. London: 1840. V. 42

DILLON, EDWARD

Glass. New York: 1907. V. 40

Porcelain. London: 1904. V. 42

DILLON, GEORGE F.

The Virgin Mother of Good Counsel. Rome: 1884. V. 41

DILLON, GEORGE H.

The World Goes Turning. Chicago: 1925. V. 44

DILLON, JOHN B.

The History of Indiana, From Its Earaliest Exploration by Europeans to the Close of the Territorial Government, in 1816. Indianapolis: 1859. V. 37; 38; 39

DILLON, JOHN JOSEPH

A Memoir Concerning the Political State of Malta. London: 1807. V. 40; 43

DILLON-LEE, HENRY AUGUSTUS, VISCOUNT DILLON

The Life and Opinions of Sir Richard Maltravers, an English Gentleman of the Seventeenth Century. London: 1822. V. 39; 42; 46

DILLON, MALCOLM

The History and Development of Banking in Ireland from the Earliest Times to the Present Day. London: & Dublin: 1889. V. 43

The History and Development of Banking in Ireland from the Earliest Times to the Present Day (1889). London: 1889. V. 37; 38

DILLON, PETER

Narrative and Successful Result of a Voyage in the South Sea, Performed by Order of the Government of British India . . . London: 1829. V. 41; 46

DILLON, RICHARD

Images of Chinatown. Louis J. Stellman's Chinatown Photographs. San Francisco: 1976. V. 37

DILLON, RICHARD H.

Bully Waterman and the Voyage of the Clipper Challenge, New York to San Francisco 1851. San Francisco: 1956. V. 39; 44

Texas Argonauts. Isaac H. Duval and the California Gold Rush. San Francisco: 1987. V. 39; 42; 44; 46

DILLON, VISCOUNT

An Almain Armourer's Album, Selections from an Original Manuscript in the Victoria and Albert Museum. London: 1905. V. 37

DILLON, WILLIAM

Life of John Mitchel. London: 1888. V. 37

DILLS, R. S.

History of Fayette County, Together with Historic Notes on the Northwest, and the State of Ohio . . . Dayton: 1881. V. 42

DILLWYN, L. W.

British Confervae. London: 1802-09. V. 37

A Review of the References to the Hortus Malabaricus of Henry van Rheede van Draaakenstein. Swansea: 1839. V. 37

DILS, LENORE

Horny Toad Man, Bold and Vivid Tales of the Horny Toad Division. El Paso: 1966. V. 46

DILWORTH, THOMAS

A New Guide to the English Tongue: in Five Parts. Philadelphia: 1793. V. 44

The Schoolmasters Assistant: Being a Compendium of Arithmetic, Both Practical and Theoretical. London: 1744. V. 41

The Schoolmaster's Assistant. London: 1798. V. 43

The' Schoolmaster's Assistant. New York: 1806. V. 42

DILWORTH, W. H.

The Conquest of Peru, by Francis Pizarro . . . Together with the Voyages of the First Adventurers, Particularly Ferdinand de Soto, for the Discovery of Florida. London: 1759. V. 41

The Conquest of Peru, by Francis Pizarro . . . Together with the Voyages of the First Adventurers . . . London: 1759. V. 45

The Life and Heroic Actions of Frederick III King of Prussia. London: 1758. V. 46

The Life of Alexander Pope, Esq; with a View of His Writings and Many Curious Anecdotes of His Noble Patrons. London: 1758. V. 41

The Life of Dr. Jonathan Swift, Dean of Saint Patrick's, Dublin. London: 1758. V. 38

The Life of Alexander Pope, Esq. With a View of His Writings. London: 1759. V. 41

The Life of Alexander Pope, Esq . . . London: 1760. V. 42

The Royal Assasins . . . London: 1759. V. 46

DILWYN, L. W.

Memoranda Relating to Coleopterous Insects, found in the Neighborhood of Swansea. Swansea: 1829. V. 37

DIMAN, GEORGE WATERS

Autobiography and Sketches of My Travels by Sea and Land. Bristol: 1896. V. 40; 41

DIMAND, MAURICE S.

The Ballard Collection of Oriental Rugs in the City Art Museum of St. Louis. St. Louis: 1935. V. 39; 46

THE DIME Dialogues No. 10. New York: 1871. V. 43

DIME Novel Roundup, Official Organ of the Happy Hours Brotherhood. 1931-1973. V. 43

DIMENT, J. A.

Catalogue of the Natural History Drawings Commissioned by Joseph Banks on the Endeavour Voyage 1768-1771 . . . London: 1984-87. V. 38

DIMITRY, CHARLES

The House in Balfour Street. New York: 1868. V. 45

DIMMACK, MAX

Noel Counihan. Melbourne: 1974. V. 41

DIMOCK, J. F.

Illustrations of the Collegiate Church of Southwell, in a Series of Ten Views of the Exterior and Interior, in Tinted Lithography, from Drawings by E. H. Buckler. London: 1854. V. 41; 45

DIMOND, WILLIAM

Petrarchal Sonnets, and Miscellaneous Poems. Bath: 1800. V. 40

DIMSDALE, THOMAS

The Present Method of Inoculating for the Small-Pox. Dublin: 1767. V. 38; 40

DIMSDALE, THOMAS JOSIAH

The Vigilantes of Montana . . . Virginia City: 1882. V. 42; 45

DI NARDO, ANTONIO

Farm Houses, Small Chateux and Country Churches in France. Cleveland: 1924. V. 38

DINE, JIM

Diary of A Non Deflector, Selected Poems. San Francisco: 1987. V. 42

Diary of a Non-Deflector. Selected Poems. San Francisco: 1987. V. 39

Welcome Home Lovebirds. London: 1969. V. 39

LES DINERS de Gala. New York: 1973. V. 41

DINES, H. G.

The Metalliferous Mining Region of South-West England. London: 1956. V. 45

DINESEN, ISAK 1885-1962

Anecdotes of Destiny. London: 1958. V. 42; 46

Anecdotes of Destiny. New York: 1958. V. 39

DINESEN, ISAK 1885-1962 continued

The Angelic Avengers. New York: 1949. V. 45

Out of Africa. London: 1937. V. 39; 42; 45

Out of Africa. New York: 1938. V. 37; 38; 39; 41; 42; 43; 45; 46

Seven Gothic Tales. London: 1934. V. 37; 40; 43

Seven Gothic Tales. New York: 1934. V. 38; 39; 42; 44; 46

Winter's Tales. New York: 1942. V. 38

DINET, E.

The Life of Mohamad the Prophet of Allah. Paris: 1918. V. 46

DINGMAN, LARRY

Booksellers Marks. Minneapolis: 1986. V. 41; 42

DINGWELL, ERIC JOHN

Artificial Cranial Deformation: A Contribution to the Study of Ethic Mutilations. London: 1931. V. 41; 43; 45; 46

DINKINS, JAMES

The Balaclava of America. New Orleans: 1903. V. 44

1861 To 1865, by an Old Johnnie. Personal Recollections and Experiences in the Confederate Army. Cincinnati: 1897. V. 42

DINMORE, RICHARD

Select and Fugitive Poetry. Washington City: 1802. V. 44

DINNER and Dinner Parties. London: 1862. V. 42

DINNER Commemorative of Charles Sumner and Complimentary to Edward L. Pierce, Boston, December 29, 1894. Cambridge: 1895. V. 44

DINSDALE, A.

First Principles of Television. London: 1932. V. 45

DINSDALE, ALFRED 1880-1946

Television. London: 1926. V. 45

Television. London: 1928. V. 40; 42

DINSMOOR, ROBERT

Incidental Poems, Accompanied with Letters. Haverhill: 1828. V. 39; 41; 42; 46

DINSMOOR, WILLIAM BELL

The Athenian Archon List in the Light of Recent Discoveries. Morningside Heights: 1939. V. 40; 42; 44

DINSMORE, ISABELLA KIMBALL

Trips and Travel Letters to the Unitarian Alliance. Belfast: 1929. V. 40

DIO CASSIUS c. 150-235

(Greek title, then:) Dionis Romanorum Historiarium Libri. Paris: 1548. V. 45

Dionis Nicaei, Rerum Romanarum a Pompeio Magno, ad Alexandrum Mamaeae Filium Epitome . . . Paris: 1551. V. 45

Historico delle Guerre & Fatti de Romani. Venezia: 1533. V. 42

Rerum Romanarum a Pompeio Magno ad Alexandrum Mamaeae, Epitome Authore Ioanne Xiphilino. (with) Rerum Romanararum . . . Epitome, Ioanne Xiphilino Authore, Guilielmo Blanco Albiensi Interprete. Paris: 1551. V. 43

(Greek) Romanarum Historiarum Libri XXIII. Paris: 1548. V. 44

DIO CHRYSOSTOMUS

De Regno. Bologna: 1493. V. 44

De Troia Non Capta. Cremona: 1492. V. 46

DIO COCCEIANUS, CHRYSOSTOMUS, OF PRUSA

Oratio and Ilienses. Cremona: 1492. V. 40

De Troia non Capta. Cremona: 1492. V. 43

DIO CASSIUS

Fatti de Romani dalla Guerra di Candia, fino alla Morte di Claudio Imperatoore. Venice: 1567. V. 37

DIODATI, JOHN 1576-1649

Pious and Learned Annotations Upon the Holy Bible. London: 1648. V. 42

Pious and Learned Annotations Upon the Holy Bible. London: 1651. V. 39

DIODORUS SICULUS

Bibliotheca Historica; Tacitu. V. 45

Bibliotheca Historicae Libri Quindecim. Geneva: 1559. V. 44; 46

Bibliothecae Historicae Libri VI. Venice: 1481. V. 46

Bibliothecae Historicae Libri XV. Basle: 1578. V. 45

Bibliothekes Istorikes (Gr. letters). Diodori Siculi Bibliothecae Historicae Libri Quindecim de Quadraginta. Geneva: 1559. V. 45

Della Libraria Historica . . . Venice: 1574. V. 45

DIOGENES LAERTIUS

Diogenis Laertii de Vitis, Decretis & Responsis Celebrium Philosophorum . . . Basle: 1533. V. 45

Diogenis Laertii de Vita et Moribus Philosophorum Libri X. Lyon: 1559. V. 38; 41; 45

Diogenis Laertii Mamaeae, Dogmatis & Apophthegmatis Eorum qui in Philosophia Claruerunt, Libri X. Geneva: 1570. V. 38

The Lives, Opinions and Remarkable Sayings of the Most Ancient Philosophers. London: 1688/96. V. 43

De Uita & Moribus Philosophorum. Venice: 1490. V. 46

(Greek Title) De Uitis, Decretis & Responsis Celebrium Philosophorum. Basel: 1533. V. 40

De Utis, Decretis & Responsis Celebrium Philosophorum. Basel: 1533. V. 42

De Vita et Moribus Philosophorum. Venice: 1490. V. 40

Vitae et Sententiae Philosophorum. Venice: 1493. V. 40; 42

Vitae et Sententiae Eorum qui in Philosophia Probati Fuerunt. Venice: 1475. V. 37

De Vitis Dogm. & Apophth. Clarorum Philosophorum Libri X (etc.). Geneva: 1593. V. 44

DIOMEDES

De Arte Grammatica Opus. Venice: 1491. V. 43

DION CASSIUS

(Greek title) Dionis Nicaei Rervm Romanarum a Pompeio Magno ad Alexandrum Mamaeae, Epitome Authore Ioanne Xiphilino . . . (with) Dionis Nicaei, Reru Romanarvm . . . Lvtetiae (Paris): 1551. V. 41

DION CASSIUS, NICAEUS

Aelius Spartianus, Iulius Capitolinus, Aelius Lampridius, Vulcatius Gallicanus. Paris: 1544. V. 44

DION CHRYSTOSTOM

Orationes LXXX, cum Vetustis Codd. MSS. Reg. Bibliothecae Sedulo Collatae . . . Paris: 1604. V. 37

DIONIS DU SEJOUR, ACHILLE PIERRE

Essai sur les Phenomenes Relatifs aux Disparitions Periodiques de l'Anneau de Saturne. Paris: 1776. V. 37

DIONIS, PIERRE

The Anatomy of Humane Bodies Improv'd, According to the Circulation of the Blood and all the Modern Discoveries. London: 1703. V. 42

A Course of Chirurgical Operations, Demonstrated in the Royal Garden at Paris. London: 1733. V. 43

DIONYSIUS AREOPAGITICUS

D. Dionysii Areopagitae Scripta, cum D. Ignatii Martyris Epistolis: & aliis quae D. Dionysii Scriptis Annectuntur. Alcala de Henares: 1541. V. 38

Coelestis Haerarchia (and other works). Paris: 1515. V. 38

De Mystica Theologia . . . Augsburg: 1519. V. 44

Opera. Strassburg: 1503-02. V. 40

Opera Omnia. Venetiis: 1755-56. V. 44

DIONYSIUS HALICARNASEUS

Antiquatates Romanae. Treviso: 1480. V. 38

Delle Cose Antiche Della Citta di Roma. Venetia: 1545. V. 40; 42

DIONYSIUS HALICARNASSUS

Antiquatates Romanae. Treviso: 1480. V. 37

(Antiquitates Romanae.) Originvm Sive Antiqvitatvm Romanarvm. Treviso: 1480. V. 46

Antiqvitatvm Sive Originvm Romanarum Libri X. Basileae: 1549. V. 37; 38

Dionisio Halicarnaseo Cose Antiche Della Citta di Roma. V. 46

DIONYSIUS PERIEGETES

Cosmographia Sive De Situ Orbis. Venice: 1478. V. 40; 45

De Situ Orbis. Venice: 1478. V. 37; 40; 42; 43; 45

De Situ Orbis. Venice: 1478. V. 45

De Situ Orbis Libellus. Paris: 1547. V. 40

De Situ Orbis. Basel: 1556. V. 38

DIONYSIUS PERIGETES

De Situ Orbis. Venetiis: 1498. V. 38

DIOPHANTUS OF ALEXANDRIA

Arithmeticorum Libri Sex, et de Numeris Multangulis Liber Unus. Paris: 1621. V. 38

Arithmeticorum Libri Sex, et de Numeris Multangulis Liber Unus. Toulouse: 1670. V. 38

DIORAVANTI, LEONARDO

Del Compendio de' Secreti Rationali Libri Cinque, nel Primo de'Quale si Tratta de' Secreti Piu Importante Nella Professione Medicinale . . . Venice: 1675. V. 46

DIOSCORIDES

... *Pedacii Dioscoridis Anazarabaei Opera Qvae Extant Omnia.* 1598. V. 41

(Greek title) ... *Pedacii Dioscoridis Anazarabaei Opera Qvae Extant Omnia.* 1598. V. 45

(Title in Greek) Pedacii Dioscidis Anazarabaei Opera Qvae Extant Omnia. 1598. V. 40

Pedacii Dioscoridis Anazarabaet Opera Qvae Extant Omnia. Sumptivbus: 1598. V. 46

DIOSCORIDES, P.

Pedacii Dioscorideae Anazabei de Materia Medica Libri Sex. Florentiae: 1518. V. 37

DI PESO, CHARLES C.

Casas Grandes. A Fallen Trading Center of the Gran Chichimeca. Dragoon: 1974. V. 37; 42

Casas Grandes: A Fallen Trading Center of the Gran Chichimeca Flagstaff. (1974). V. 37

The Upper Pima of San Cayetano Del Tumacacori: an Archaeohistorical Reconstruction of the Ootam of Primeria Alta. Arizona: 1956. V. 44

DIPLOCK, JOSEPH BRAMAH

A New System of Heavy Goods Transport on Common Roads. London: 1902. V. 45

DI PRIMA, DIANE

Loba. New York: 1978. V. 39

DIPROSE, JOHN

Some Account of the Parish of Saint Clement Danes (Westminster) Past and Present. London: 1868-76. V. 40

DIRAC, PAUL ADRIEN MAURICE

The Principles of Quantum Mechanics. Oxford: 1930. V. 42

DIRCKS, HENRY

Inventors and Inventions, in Three Parts. London: 1867. V. 40

The Life, and Scientific Labours of the Second Marquis of Worcester ... London: 1865. V. 38; 40; 42

Perpetuum Mobile; or, Search for Self-Motive Power, During the 17th, 18th and 19th Centuries. London: 1861. V. 39

DIRECT Trade Between Great Britain and the Mississippi Valley. United States. London: 1874. V. 44

A DIRECTION for the English Traveller By Which He Shal be Inabled to Coast About all England and Wales. London: 1677. V. 39

THE DIRECTION of the Views of Those Who Would, in the Present Crisis Engage an Incumber'd, Trading Nation, as Principals, in a Ruinous Expensive Land War. London: 1746. V. 41

A DIRECTORY for the Publique Worship of God, Together with an Ordinance of Parliament for the Taking Away of the Book of Common Prayer ... London: 1644. V. 37

A DIRECTORY for the Village of Rochester, Containing the Names, Residence and Occupations of All Male Inhabitants Over Fifteen Years of Age, in Said Village, on the First of January, 1827 ... Rochester: 1827. V. 45

DIRECTORY of Newark, for 1835-6. Newark: 1835. V. 46

DIRECTORY of the Boroughs of Norristown & Bridgeport, Montgomery Co., Pa. for 1860-61 ... West Chester: 1860. V. 41; 42

DIRECTORY of the City of Rochester for 1838 ... Rochester: 1838. V. 43

DIRECTORY Of West Chester. For 1857 ... West Chester: 1857. V. 41

DIRINGER, DAVID

The Alphabet, a Key to the History of Mankind. New York: 1953. V. 41

The Alphabet, a Key to the History of Mankind. London: 1968. V. 37; 43

The Illuminated Book Its History and Production. London: 1958. V. 44

The Illuminated Book, Its History and Production. London: 1967. V. 41; 44

The Illuminated Book, Its History and Production. New York: 1967. V. 37

DIRLETON, JOHN NISBET, LORD 1609-1687

Some Doubts and Questions in the Law, Especially of Scotland, as also, Some Decisions of the Lords of Council and Session. Edinburgh: 1698. V. 40

DIROM, ALEXANDER

A Narrative of the Campaign in India Which TErminated the War with Tippoo Sultan in 1792 ... London: 1794. V. 43

DISBURY, DAVID G.

T. E. Lawrence of Arabia - a Collector's Booklist. Egham: 1972. V. 41

DISCH, THOMAS

Camp Concentration. 1968. V. 39

Echo Round His Bones. 1969. V. 43

334. London: 1972. V. 43

DISCH, THOMAS M.

Black Alice. Garden City: 1968. V. 43; 45

Camp Concentration. London: 1968. V. 45

DISCIPLINA et Institutio Puerorum: ex Politiano: Erasmo: Rodolpho Agricola & Aliis. Italy?: 1500-1520? V. 38

DISCORD. a Satire. London: 1773. V. 40; 42

DISCOURS Oupartydich, Opte Handelinge vande Indien. N.P.: 1608. V. 45

DISCOURS sur les Preparatifs et Magnificences Faictes Pour la Reception de sa majeste en sa Bonne Ville de Rouen. Paris: 1617. V. 41

THE DISCOVERY of Anaesthesia. The Medical and Dental Fraternities of Connecticut, and Others Who Respect the Memory of the Late Dr. Horace Wells, Respectfully Present an Application to the General Assembly for a Grant of a Few Thousand Dollars ... N.P.,: 1875. V. 39

THE DISCOVERY of Florida, Being a True Relation of the Vicissitudes that Attended the Governor Don Hernando De Soto and Some Nobles of Portugal in the Discovery of Florida. Now Just Given by a Fidalgo of Elvas. Translated by Buckingham Smith ... (San Francisco: 1946). V. 37; 43

A DISCUSSION of Lord Camden's Opinion and Decree in Allen and the Duke of Newcastle. London: 1774. V. 45

THE DISCUSSION; or the Character, Education, Prerogatives and Moral Influence of Woman. Boston: 1837. V. 37; 43

THE DISEASES of Bath. London: 1737. V. 41

DISNEY, ALFRED M.

Origin and Development of the Microscope as Illustrated by Catalogues of the Instruments and Accessories, in the Collections of the Royal Microscopical Society ... London: 1928. V. 44; 45

DISNEY, JOHN

Memoirs of Thomas Brand-Hollis, Esq. London: 1808. V. 41

Museum Disneianum, Being a Description of a Collection of Ancient Marbles, Specimens of Ancient Bronze and Various Ancient Fictile Vases ... at the Hyde, Near Ingatestone. London: 1848-1849. V. 40

A View of Ancient Laws, Against Immorality and Profaneness, Under the Following Heads, Lewdness; Profane Swearing ... Cambridge: 1729. V. 46

DISNEY, WALT

The Art of Walt Disney. By Robert D. Field. New York: 1942. V. 37

Book of Snow White and Seven Dwarfs. London: 1938. V. 46

Mickey Mouse Bedtime Stories. London: V. 45

Mickey Mouse (Goes Fishing). Racine: 1936. V. 42

The Mickey Mouse Fire Brigade. Racine: 1936. V. 45

Mickey Mouse Annual. London: 1940. V. 45

Mickey Mouse Annual. London: 1941. V. 45

Mickey Mouse Annual. London: 1946. V. 44

Mickey Mouse Book No. 4. Philadelphia: 1934. V. 46

Mickey Mouse in King Arthur's Court. London: 1934. V. 46

Mickey Mouse Waddle Book. New York: 1934. V. 46

Mickey Never Fails. Boston: 1939. V. 46

The 'Pop-Up' Silly Symphonies Containing Babes in the Woods and King Neptune. New York: 1933. V. 46

Snow White Magic Mirror Book and the Story of Snow White and the Seven Dwarfs. London: V. 45

Three Little Pigs. New York: 1933. V. 45; 46

Three Little Pigs. The Big Bad Wolf and Little Red Riding Hood. New York: 1933/34. V. 45

The Three Orphan Kittens. London: 1935. V. 44

The Tortoise and the Hare. 1935. V. 46

The Victory March. New York: 1942. V. 41

The Water Babies. London: 1936. V. 44; 45

The Wonderful Tar Baby. New York: 1946. V. 46

DISNEY (WALT) PRODUCTIONS

The Adventures of Mickey Mouse. 1931. V. 41; 43

DISNEY, WILLIAM

Nil Dictum Quod nom Dictum Prius. Or the Case of the Government of England Established by Law. London: 1681. V. 45

A DISPASSIOANTE Remonstrance of the Nature and Tendency of the Law Now In Force for the Reduction of Interest; and the Consequences That Must Inevitably Flow from them, if Continued in their Present Form. London: 1751. V. 41

THE DISPENSATORY of the Royal College of Physicians, London. London: 1760. V. 44

DISRAELI, BENJAMIN 1804-1881

Collection of Novels. London: 1894-1901. V. 46

Coningsby. London: 1844. V. 37; 38; 39; 40; 42; 45

Contarini Fleming. A Psychological Autobiography. London: 1832. V. 39; 45

The Dunciad of Today. London: 1928. V. 43

Endymion. London: 1880. V. 37; 38; 39; 40; 41; 43; 44; 46

Endymion. Montreal: 1880. V. 46

Endymion. Paris: 1881. V. 37

England and France; or, a Cure for the Ministerial Gallomania. London: 1932. V. 39

Henrietta Temple, a Love Story. London: 1837. V. 39; 45

Inaugural Address . . . Delivered on Wednesday, November 19, 1873, on the Occasion of His Installation as Lord Rector of the University of Glasgow. Glasgow: 1873. V. 45

Inaugural Address Delivered at the University of Glasgow November 19, 1873. London: 1873. V. 45

The Infernal Marriage. London: 1929. V. 45

The Letters of Runnymede. London: 1836. V. 39; 45

Lord George Bentinck: a Political Biography. London: 1842. V. 45

Lord George Bentinck: a Political Biography. London: 1852. V. 37; 38; 39; 42; 45

Lord Beaconsfield on the Constitution. London: 1884. V. 45

Lothair. 1870. V. 43

Lothair. London: 1870. V. 41; 43

The Ministerial Crisis. Westminster: 1873. V. 45

Novels and Tales. London: 1881. V. 37; 38; 42

Novels and Tales by the Earl of Beaconsfield. London: 1881. V. 39; 46

The Novels and Tales. London: 1882. V. 38; 39

Novels and Tales. London: 1900. V. 39; 40; 44

Novels and Tales. London: 1924. V. 42

The Novels and Tales. London: 1926. V. 38; 42; 43

The Bradenham Edition of the Novels and Tales of Benjamin Disraeli, 1st Earl of Beaconsfield. London: 1926. V. 41

The Novels and Tales. London: 1926-27. V. 38; 44; 46

The Bradenham Edition of the Novels and Tales. London: 1926-27. V. 38; 45

Novels and Tales. London: 1916. V. 37

The Revolutionary Epick. London: 1864. V. 42

The Speech . . . in the House of Commons, on Friday, 15th May, 1846. London: 1846. V. 38

Speech of the Right Hon. B. Disraeli, M.P. at the Free Trade Hall, Manchester, April 3, 1872. London: 1872. V. 38

Sybil; or, The Two Nations. London: 1845. V. 38

Sybil or, the Two Nations. Paris: 1845. V. 42

Tancred. London: 1847. V. 38; 39; 40; 42; 46

The Tragedy of Count Alarcos. London: 1839. V. 38; 45

Venetia. London: 1837. V. 38

Vindication of the English Constitution in a Letter to a Noble and Learned Lord. London: 1835. V. 39; 42; 45

Vivian Grey. London: 1826-27. V. 40; 46

Vivian Grey. London: 1827. V. 39; 45

Vivian Grey. London: 1847. V. 42

The Voyage of Captain Popanilla. London: 1828. V. 38; 39; 41; 44; 45; 46

The Voyage of Captain Popanilla. Philadelphia: 1828. V. 37

The Voyage of Captain Popanilla, to the Glorious Island of Vraibleusia, the Wonderful City of Hubbabub, and the Peaceable Isle of Blunderland. London: 1829. V. 37

The Wondrous Tale of Alroy. The Rise of Iskander. London: 1833. V. 37

The Wondrous Tale of Alroy. The Rise of Iskander. Philadelphia: 1833. V. 37

The Young Duke. London: 1831. V. 38; 39; 45

The Young Duke. New York: 1831. V. 46

D'ISRAELI, ISAAC 1776-1848

Amenities of Literature, Consisting of Sketches & Characters of English Literature. London: 1841. V. 39; 40; 44

Amenities of Literature. New York: 1841. V. 44; 45

Amenities of Literature. London: 1842. V. 38; 40

Calamities of Authors. London: 1812. V. 38; 40; 44

Calamities of Authors . . . New York: 1812. V. 44

Commentaries on the Life and Reign of Charles the First, King of England. London: 1851. V. 46

Curiosities of Literature. London: 1791. V. 44

Curiosities of Literature. London: 1793. V. 44

Curiosities of Literature. London: 1793-94. V. 43

Curiosities of Literature. London: 1794. V. 38

Curiosities of Literature. London: 1797. V. 44

Curiosities of Literature . . . London: 1807. V. 42

Curiosities of Literature . . . First and Second Series. London: 1807-17-23. V. 38; 40

Curiosities of Literature. London: 1817. V. 38

Curiosities of Literature. London: 1817-24. V. 38

Curiosities of Literature. London: 1823. V. 37; 42

Curiosities of Literature. Paris: 1835. V. 38; 44

Curiosities of Literature. Ninth Edition, Revised. London: 1834. V. 37

Despotism; or the Fall of the Jesuits. London: 1811. V. 44

A Dissertation on Anecdotes. London: 1793. V. 44

Domestic Anecdotes of the French Nation. London: 1794. V. 44; 45

Eliot, Hampden and Pym, or, a reply of 'The Author of a Book' Entitled 'Commentaries on the Life and Reign of Charles the First' . . . London: 1832. V. 44

An Essay on the Manners and Genius of the Literary Character. London: 1795. V. 37; 42; 43; 44

Flim-Flams! Or, the Life and Errors of My Uncle and the Amours of My Aunt. London: 1805. V. 38; 44; 46

The Illustrator Illustrated. London: 1838. V. 44

An Inquiry into the Literary and Political Character of James the First. London: 1816. V. 40

The Literary Character, Illustrated by the History of Men of Genius . . . London: 1818. V. 44

The Literary Character, Illustrated by the History of Men of Genius . . . New York: 1818. V. 44

The Literary Character; or, The History of men of Genius from Their Own Feelings and Confessions. London: 1828. V. 44; 45

Miscellanies or, Literary Recreations. London: 1796. V. 38; 41; 42; 44; 46

Literary Miscellanies . . . London: 1801. V. 44

Narrative Poems. London: 1803. V. 41; 44; 46

Quarrels of Authors . . . London: 1814. V. 37; 43; 44

Romances. London: 1799. V. 37; 39; 40; 42; 44; 46

Romances . . . London: 1801. V. 44

Romances; Consisting of a Persian, a Roman, and an Arcadian Romance. London: 1807. V. 37

A Second Series of Curiosities of Literature. London: 1823. V. 44

Vaurien; or, Sketches of the Times . . . London: 1797. V. 37; 44

Works of . . . London: 1838-59. V. 44

The Works. London: 1858-9. V. 44

Works. London: 1880. V. 46

DISSELHOFF, H. D.

The Art of Ancient America. Civilizations of Central and South America. New York: 1960. V. 45

A DISSERTATION on Comedy: In Which the Rise and Progress of that Species of the Drama is . . . Consider'd . . . from the Earliest to the Present Age. London: 1750. V. 39

A DISSERTATION on the Laws of Elections; Explaining Who Have a Right to Vote For, Or Be Elected, Members of Parliament for the Counties of Scotland. Glasgow: 1767. V. 43

DISSERTATION Sur le Commencement du Siecle prochain, Et La Solution Du Probleme, Scavoir laquelle des Deux Annees 1700 ou 1701 est la Premiere du Siecle. Paris: 1699. V. 40

A DISSERTATION Upon the Earthquakes, Their Causes and Consequences . . . London: 1750. V. 42

DISTANT, W. L.

The Fauna of British India Including Ceylon and Burma: Rhynchota. London: 1902-18. V. 38

A Naturalist in the Transvaal. London: 1892. V. 39; 41; 43; 44; 46

Rhopalocera Malayana: A Description of the Butterflies of the Malay Peninsula. London: 1882-86. V. 40

THE DISTILLER OF London. London: 1698. V. 39

DISTILLERS COMPANY

The Distiller of London. Compiled and Set Forth by the Special License and Command of the King's Most Excellent Majesty . . . London: 1698. V. 37; 38

A DISTINCT and Impartial History of the Conspiracies, Trials, Characters, Behaviour and Dying Speeches of All Those Who Have Suffered on Account of the House of Stewart, from the Revolution Down to the Commencement of the Late Rebellion. London: 1747. V. 37

A DISTINGUISHED Family of French Printers of the Sixteenth Century: Henri & Robert Estienne. New York: 1929. V. 38; 44

DISTON, JOHN

The Seaman's Guide, Chiefly the Experience of the Author. Liverpool: 1785? V. 42; 46

DISTURNELL, JOHN

The Emigrant's Guide to New Mexico, California and Oregon. New York: 1850. V. 37

The Great Lakes, or Inland Seas of America . . . New York: 1863. V. 43

The Great Lakes, Or Insland Seas of America . . . Together with a Guide to the Upper Mississippi River . . . Philadelphia: 1871. V. 38; 39

Great Lakes, or Inland Seas of America. Embracing a full description of Lakes Superior, Huron, Michigan, Erie & & Ontario; rivers St. Mary, St. Clair, Detroit, Niagara, & St. Lawrence . . . together with a Guide to the Upper Mississippi River . . . New York: 1868. V. 37

Influence of Climate in North and South America. New York: 1867. V. 42

United States Register, or Blue Book for 1862. New York: 1861. V. 38; 42

DISTURNELL, W. C.

Disturnell's Guide to San Francisco and Vicinity: A Complete and Reliable Book of Reference. San Francisco: 1883. V. 37

DIT Boecxken. A Literal Translation into English of the Earliest Known Book of Fowling and Fishing and Printed at Antwerp in the Year 1492. Twickenham: 1978. V. 39

DIT is die Afcomeste ende Genalogie der Hertogen ende Hertoginnen van Brabandt vande Welcke de Eerste was Saluius Brabon/met Zyn Huysvrouwe Swana. Antwerp: 1561. V. 46

DITCHFIELD, P. H.

The City Companies of London and Their Good Works. London: 1904. V. 39; 41

The Cottages and the Village Life of Rural England. London: 1912. V. 41

DITMAS, CHARLES ANDREW

Historic Homesteads of Kings County. Brooklyn: 1909. V. 39

DITSON, GEORGE LEIGHTON

Circassia; or, a Tour to the Caucasus. New York: 1850. V. 43; 46

The Para Papers on France, Egypt and Ethiopia. New York: 1858. V. 44

DITTON, HUMPHREY 1675-1715

A Discourse Concerning the Resurrection of Jesus Christ. London: 1712. V. 39

DITTON, HUMPHRY

The General Laws of Nature and Motion. London: 1709. V. 40

An Institution of Fluxions. London: 1726. V. 38; 40; 46

DIVES AND PAUPER

A Compeniouse Tretise Dyalogue of Dives and Pauper. London: 1493. V. 37

DIX, D. L.

Memorial to the Legislature of Massachusetts. Boston: 1843. V. 45

DIX, DOROTHEA LYNDE 1802-1887

Memorial. To the Legislature of Massachusetts. Boston: 1843. V. 38; 39

Memorial . . . to the Honorable the General Assembly in Behalf of the Insane of Maryland. Annapolis: 1852. V. 39

DIX, JOHN A.

Speech of Gen. Dix, President of the Mississippi and Missouri Railroad Company, at Iowa City on the Completion of the Road to that Point. New York: 1856. V. 39; 41; 42

DIX, JOHN ADAMS

Sketch of the Resources of the City of New York. New York: 1827. V. 39; 43

DIX, JOHN HOMER

Treatise on Strabismus, or Squinting, and the New Mode of Treatment. Boston: 1841. V. 41; 45

DIX, WILLIAM GILES

The Deck of the Crescent City. Boston & Cambridge: 1852. V. 40

DIXEY, ANNIE COATH

The Lion Dog of Peking . . . New York. V. 44

DIXIE, FLORENCE

Across Patagonia. London: 1880. V. 39; 44

DIXIE, FLORENCE, LADY

In the Land of Misfortune . . . London: 1882. V. 45

DIXIE, LADY FLORENCE

Redeemed in Blood. London: 1889. V. 43

DIXON, CHARLES

The Game Birds and Wild fowl of the British Islands: London: 1895. V. 42; 43; 44

The Game Birds and Wild Fowl of the British Islands. Sheffield: 1900. V. 37; 39; 40; 46

DIXON, ELIZABETH I. G.

Journal of a Voyage from Syndey to London in the Bark 'Standerings'. London: 1946. V. 40

DIXON, F.

The Geology and Fossils of the Tertiary and Cretaceous Formations of Sussex. London: 1850. V. 40

The Geology of Sussex. Brighton: 1878. V. 38; 40

DIXON, FRANKLIN W.

The Footprints Under the Window. 1939. V. 46

DIXON, FREDERIC

The Geology and Fossils of the Tertiary and Cretaceous Formations of Sussex. London: 1805. V. 41

The Geology and Fossils of the Tertiary and Cretaceous Formations of Sussex. London: 1850. V. 39; 42; 46

The Geology of Sussex. Brighton: 1878. V. 42

DIXON, G.

The Leaguer of Ladysmith. London: 1900. V. 42

DIXON, G. W.

The National Poem, Delivered in Washington City, At the Capitol, July the Fourth, 1833. Washington: 1833. V. 45

DIXON, GEORGE d. 1800

A Voyage Round the World. London: 1789. V. 37; 38; 39; 40; 41; 42; 44; 45; 46

Voyage Autour du Monde, et Principalement a La Cote Nord-Ouest de l'Amerique, Fait en 1785, 1786, 1787, et 1788 Abord Du King-George et de la Queen Charlotte . . . Paris: 1789. V. 39; 41; 45

A Voyage Round the World; but More Particularly to the North-West Coast of America, Peformed in 1785 . . . 1788. Amsterdam: 1968. V. 40

DIXON, HENRY

Moral Essays: or, the Wisdom of All Nations. London: 1760? V. 37; 39

DIXON, JAMES

Narrative of a Voyage to New South Wales and Van Dieman's Land in the Ship Skelton, During the years 1820. Edinburgh: 1822. V. 40

DIXON, JOSEPH K.

The Vanishing Race: the Last Great Indian Council. New York: 1914. V. 37; 45

The Vanishing Race. the Last Great Indian Council. Philadelphia: 1925. V. 45

The Vanishing Race: the Last Great Indian Council. Garden City: 1913. V. 37

DIXON, JOSHUA

The Literary Life of William Brownrigg . . . London: 1801. V. 38

DIXON, MAYNARD

Poems and Seven Drawings. San Francisco: 1923. V. 43

Rim-Rock and Sage. San Francisco: 1977. V. 44

DIXON, RICHARD WATSON

Mano. A Poetical History: of the Time of the Close of the Tenth Century . . . London: 1883. V. 38

DIXON, SAM HOUSTON

The Heroes of San Jacinto. Houston: 1923. V. 38

The Heroes of San Jacinto. Houston: 1932. V. 38

DIXON, SARAH

Poems on Several Occasions. Canterbury: 1740. V. 38

DIXON, SOPHIE

Castalian Hours. London: 1829. V. 43

DIXON, THOMAS

The Fall of a Nation. New York: 1916. V. 44; 46

The Leopard's Spots. New York: 1902. V. 40

DIXON, W. W.

Kings of the Hunting Field. London: 1899. V. 39

DIXON, W. WILLMOTT

Kings of the Turf. London: 1898. V. 42

DIXON, WILLIAM H.

White Conquest. London: 1876. V. 39

DIXON, WILLIAM HEPWORTH

Free Russia. London: 1870. V. 44

Her Majesty's Tower. London: 1865. V. 46

History of William Penn, Founder of Pennsylvania. London: 1872. V. 38; 40

DIXON, WILLIAM HEPWORTH continued

John Howard, and the Prison World of Europe . . . New York: 1849. V. 43
New America. London: 1867. V. 38; 42
Spiritual Wives. London: 1868. V. 45

DIXON, WILLIAM SCARTH

Annals of a Record Season: Being a Diary of the Meath Hounds During 1895-1896 . . . Dublin. V. 43
Hunting in the Olden Days. London: 1912. V. 41
Loose Reign by 'Wanderer.' London: 1887. V. 39

D'O WALTERS, L.RY

The Year's at the Spring. An Anthology of recent poetry compiled by L. d'O Walters . . . with an introduction by Harold Monro. London: 1920. V. 37

DOAK, SAMUEL

Lectures on Human Nature . . . To Which is Added an Essay on Life by Rev. John W. Doak. Jonesborough: 1845. V. 41

DOANE, A. SIDNEY

Surgery Illusrated. New York: 1836. V. 43

DOANE, GILBERT

About Collecting Bookplates. Madison: 1941. V. 43

DOANE, GUSTAVUS C.

Letter fromt he Secretary of War, Communicating the Report of . . . Upon the So-Called Yellowstone Expedition of 1870. Washington: 1871. V. 46
Report Upon the so-Called Yellowstone Expedition of 1870. Washington: 1871. V. 39

DOANE, WILLIAM CRESWELL

Sunshine and Play-Time. New York: 1893. V. 42

DOBB, MAURICE

Capitalist Enterprise and Social Progress. London: 1925. V. 43
Studies in the Development of Capitalism. London: 1946. V. 46

DOBBIN, M. D.

Memorial and Affidavits Showing Outrage's Perpetrated by the Apache Indians in the Territory of Arizona for the Years 1869 and 1870. San Francisco: 1871. V. 42

DOBBINS, FRANK S.

Error's Chains: How Forged and Broken. New York: 1883. V. 46

DOBBINS, M. D.

Memorial and Affidavits Showing Outrages Perpetrated by the Apache Indians, in the Territory of Arizona, During the Years 1869 and 1870. San Francisco: 1871. V. 39

DOBBS, ARTHUR

Reasons to Shew, That There Is a Great Probability of a Navigable Passage to the Western American Ocean, through Hudson's Streights, and Chesterfield Inlet. London: 1749. V. 41
Remarks Upon Captain Middleton's Defence: Wherein His Conduct During His Late Voyage for Discovering a Passage from Hudson's Bay to the South Sea is Impartially Examined . . . London: 1744. V. 43
A Reply to Capt. Middleton's Answer to the Remarks on His Vindication of His Conduct in a Late Voyage Made by Him the Furnace Sloop by Orders of the Late Commissioners . . . London: 1745. V. 43

DOBBS, FRANCIS

A Letter to the Rt. Hon, Lord North on his Propositions in favour in Ireland. Dublin: 1780. V. 37

DOBELL, BERTRAM

Rosemary and Pansies. N.P.: 1901. V. 43
Sidelights on Charles Lamb. London: 1903. V. 41

DOBELL, CLIFFORD

Antony Van Leeuwenhoek and His 'Little Animals' Being Some Account of the Father of Protozoology and Bacteriology . . . Amsterdam: 1932. V. 39
Antony van Leeuwenhoek and His 'Little Animals.' New York: 1932. V. 39; 40; 41; 44

DOBELL, JOHN

A New Selection of Seven Hundred Evangelical Hymns. Morristown: 1815. V. 39

DOBIE, BERTHA MC KEEE

Growing Up in Texas . . . Austin: 1972. V. 42

DOBIE, JAMES FRANK 1888-1964

The Alamo's Immortalization of Words. Austin: 1942. V. 39
Apache Gold and Yaqui Silver. Boston: 1939. V. 38; 39; 40; 43; 44; 46
As the Moving Finger Writ. Austin: 1955. V. 41
The Ben Lilly Legend. Boston: 1950. V. 37; 39; 42; 46

Bigfoot Wallace and the Hickory Nuts. Austin: 1936. V. 37; 42
Bob More, Man and Bird Man. Austin: 1941. V. 37; 38; 40
Bob More, Man and Bird Man. Austin: 1965. V. 45
Bob More: Man and Bird Man. Dallas: 1965. V. 44
Books and Christmas. Austin?: 1951. V. 42
Carl Sandburg & Saint Peter at the Gate. Austin: 1966. V. 38; 39; 40; 42; 44
Coronado's Children. Dallas: 1930. V. 37; 38; 42; 43; 45
Coronado's Children. Dallas: 1980. V. 37; 38; 39; 40; 42; 46
Cow People. Boston: 1964. V. 38
Coyote Wisdom. Austin: 1938. V. 37; 38; 40
The First Cattle in Texas and Southwest Progenitors of the Longhorns. Austin: 1939. V. 40
The Flavor of Texas. Dallas: 1936. V. 39; 45
Folk Lore of the Southwest. (Austin): 1924. V. 37
Forty-Four Range Country Books. Austin: 1941. V. 42
Frontier Tales of the White Mustang. Dallas: 1979. V. 41
The Ghost Bull of the Mvericks and Other Tales. Austin: 1961. V. 46
He Belongs to the Texas Folk-Lore Society. Austin: 1936. V. 43
His Looks and My Ways Would Hang Any Man. Austin: 1956. V. 41
I'll Tell You a Tale. Boston: 1960. V. 44
John C. Duval, First Texas Man of Letters: His Life and Some of His Unpublished Writings. Austin: 1939. V. 37; 46
John C. Duval, First Texas Man of Letters. His Life and Some of His Unpublished Writings. Dallas: 1939. V. 37; 38; 42; 45
Legends of Texas. Austin: 1924. V. 38; 39; 40; 41
The Longhorns. Boston: 1941. V. 38; 39; 44; 45
The Longhorns. Boston: 1947. V. 39
Mesquite. N.P.: 1938. V. 39
the Mezcla Man. El Paso: 1954. V. 46
Mustangs and Cow Horses. Austin: 1940. V. 46
The Mustangs. Boston: 1952. V. 37; 38; 39; 43; 44; 46
On the Open Range. Dallas: 1931. V. 42; 43
Picthing (sic) Horses and Panthers. Austin: 1940. V. 39
The Praire Dog Lawyer. Dallas: 1945. V. 37
Publications of the Texas Folklore Society. Austin: 1925. V. 38
A Schoolteacher in Alpine. Austin?: 1963. V. 42
The Seven Mustangs. Austin: 1948. V. 38
Snowdrift. N.P.: 1959. V. 37; 38; 40
Storytellers I Have Known. Austin: 1961. V. 39; 41
Tales of the Mustang. Dallas: 1936. V. 38; 39; 42; 44; 45; 46
Tales of Old Time Texas. Boston: 1952. V. 44
Tales of Old-Time Texas. Boston: 1955. V. 44
A Texan In England. Boston: 1944. V. 43
A Texan in England. Boston: 1945. V. 43
Tom Gilroy's Fiddler. Austin: 1958. V. 41
Tongues of the Monte. New York: 1935. V. 37; 38; 39; 40
Tongues of the Monte. Boston: 1955. V. 39
Tongues of the Monte. Boston: 1955 or later. V. 39
A Vaquero of the Brush Country. Dallas: 1929. V. 37; 38; 39; 40; 42; 43; 44; 46
A Vaquero of the Brush Country. Boston: 1943. V. 44
The Voice of the Coyote. Boston: 1949. V. 37; 38; 39; 41; 42; 43; 46
The Voice of the Coyote. Boston: 1950. V. 39
Wild and Wily: Range Animals. Flagstaff: 1980. V. 37; 39; 42; 43
The Writer and His Region. Austin?: 1951. V. 42

DOBLIN, ALFRED

Das Stiftsfraulein und der Tod. Berlin-Wilmersdorf: 1913. V. 41

DOBRIZHOFFER, MARTIN

An Account of the Abipones. London: 1822. V. 46

DOBRZENSKI, J. I. W.

Nova et Amaenior de Admirando Fontium Genio (ex Abditis Naturae Claustris, in Orbis Lucem Emanente) Philosophia . . . Ferrara: 1657-59. V. 46

DOBSON, ALBAN

Austin Dobson - Some Notes. London: 1928. V. 46
A Bibliography of the First Editions of Published and Privately printed Books and Pamphlets by Austin Dobson. London: 1925. V. 44

DOBSON, AUSTIN 1840-1921

At the Sign of the Lyre. London: 1885. V. 45
The Ballad of Beau Brocade and Other Poems of the XVIIIth Century. London: 1892. V. 41; 44; 46
Carmina Votiva and Other Occasional Verses. London: 1901. V. 44
Corridon's Songs. London: 1894. V. 42

DOBSON, AUSTIN 1840-1921 continued

Eighteenth Century Vignettes. London: 1892. V. 37; 45

Eighteenth Century Vignettes. First and Second Series. London: 1892-94. V. 43

Eighteenth Century Vignettes (First through Third Series). London: 1896. V. 38

Horace Walpole - a Memoir. London: 1893. V. 40; 43

Horace Walpole, a Memoir with an Appendix of Books Printed at the Strawberry Hill Press. New York. V. 37

A Paladin of Philanthropy and Other Papers. London: 1899. V. 45

Poems on Several Occasions. New York. V. 39

Poems on Several Occasions. New York. V. 41

Poems on Several Occasions. New York. V. 41

Poems in Several Occasions. 1895. V. 38

Poems on Several Occasions. London: 1895. V. 38; 40

Poems on Several Occasions. New York: 1895. V. 43

Poems on Several Occasions. New York. V. 38

Proverbs in Porcelain. London: 1893. V. 38; 41; 44

The Story of Rosina and Other Verses. London: 1895. V. 46

William Hogarth. London: 1891. V. 39; 45

William Hogarth. London: 1898. V. 39

William Hogarth. London: 1902. V. 46

DOBSON, EDWARD

A Rudimentary Treatise on Foundations and Concrete Works . . . London: 1850. V. 44

A Rudimentary Treatise on the Manufacture of Bricks and Tiles . . . London: 1866. V. 44

The Rudiments of Masonry and Stonecutting. London: 1878. V. 38

DOBSON, G.

Russia. London: 1913. V. 45

DOBSON, G. E.

Monograph of the Asiatic Chiroptera and Catalogue of the Species of Bats in the Indian Museum. Calcutta: 1876. V. 38

DOBSON, JOHN

A Sermon Preacht at the Funeral of the Honourable the Lady Mary Farmor, Relict of Sir William Farmor, Baronet. London: 1670. V. 40

DOBSON, JOSEPH B.

A Sermon on the Communion. Greenville: 1850. V. 44

DOBSON, MATTHEW

A Medical Commentary of Fixed Air . . . Second Edition. With an Appendix on the use of the solution of fixed alkaline salts saturated with fixible air, in the stone and gravel. By William Falconer. London: 1785. V. 37

DOBSON, SUSANNAH DAWSON

The Life of Petrarch. London: 1797. V. 45; 46

DOBSON, THOMAS

Encyclopaedia: or, a Dictionary of Arts, Sciences and Miscellaneous Literature. Volume III. Philadelphia: 1791. V. 45

Index to the Bible, In Which the Various Subjects Which Occur in the Scriptures are Alphabetically Arranged . . . Philadlephia: 1804. V. 44

DOBSON, WILLIAM

Kunopaedia. A Practical Essay on Braking or Training the English Spaniel or Pointer. London: 1814. V. 43

Kunopaedia. A Practical Essay on Breaking or Training the English Spaniel or Pointer. London: 1817. V. 43

Soloman De mundi vanitate. Poema Matthaei Prior Arm. Latine redditum, per Guil. Dobson, Nov. Coll. Oxon. Schol. Oxford: 1734. V. 39; 40

DOBYNS, W. S.

California Gardens. New York: 1931. V. 46

DOBZHANSKY, THEODOSIUS

Genetics and the Origin of Species. New York: 1937. V. 42

DOCK, GEORGE

The Audubon Folio. New York: 1964. V. 46

DOCKER, ALFRED

The Colour Prints of William Dickes. V. 38

The Colour Prints of William Dickes. London. V. 40

The Colour Prints of William Dickes. London: 1924. V. 39; 44

DOCKER, FRANCES

John Paas & James Cook, Provincial Bookbinding in the Eighteen Thirties. Leicestershire: 1978. V. 40

DOCKSTADER, FREDERICK J.

Indian Art in Middle America. Greenwich: 1964. V. 45

Indian Art in Middle America. New York: 1964. V. 38

DOCTOR Comicus; or The Frolics of Fortune. London: 1828. V. 43

THE DOCTOR Disected; or, Willy Cadogan in the Kitchen. Addressed to all Invalids, and Readers of a Late Dissertation on the Gout. London: 1771. V. 37; 40

DOCTOROW, E. L.

American Anthem. New York: 1982. V. 43

Bad Man from Bodie. London: 1961. V. 46

Big as Life. New York: 1966. V. 38; 39; 42; 44; 45; 46

Billy Bathgate. New York: 1989. V. 44

Lives of the Poets. New York: 1984. V. 45

Loon Lake. New York: 1980. V. 41; 46

Ragtime. New York: 1970. V. 45

Ragtime. New York: 1975. V. 45

Welcome to Hard Times. New York: 1960. V. 41; 42; 43; 45; 46

World's Fair. New York: 1985. V. 45

THE DOCTRINE of the Bible; or Rules of Discipline, Briefly Gathered Thorow the Whole Course of Scripture by Way of Questions and Answers. London: 1652. V. 42

DOCTRINES and Discipline of the Wesleyan Methodist Church in Canada. Toronto: 1859. V. 38; 42

DOCUMENTARY History of the Constitution of the United States of American, 1786-1870. Washington: 1894. V. 37

DOCUMENTARY History of the Constitution of the U.S. 1786-1870. Washington: 1894-1900. V. 46

DOCUMENTS and Brief Remarks, in Reply to the Pamphlet Written by General (Peter Buell) Porter and Published by Direction of the Black Rock Harbor Company, at Albany in Dec. 1822 and at Buffalo in Jan. 1823. Buffalo: 1823. V. 40

DOCUMENTS Lithographiques. Quarante Planches Comportant Plus de 300 Compositions Originales en Couleurs. Paris: 1900. V. 41; 45

DOCUMENTS Relating to the Organization of the Illinois Central Railroad. New York: 1852. V. 42

DOD, CHARLES EDWARD

An Autumn Near the Rhine; or, Sketches of Courts, Society, Scenery, &c. in Some of the German Sttes Bordering on the Rhine. London: 1818. V. 37

DOD, I. S.

A Satirical Lecture on Hearts; as It Has Been Performed, at Exeter Exchange on the Strand, Westminster, and also at Manchester, Liverpool, Chester and Other Places . . . London: 1790. V. 45

DOD, JOHN

Old Mr. Dod's Sayings. London: 1721. V. 41

Old Mr. Dod's Sayings (:On Matters of Religion). London: 1726. V. 43

DODART, DENIS

Memoires Pour Servir a l'Histoire des Plantes. Paris: 1675. V. 43

DODD, ALFRED

The Ballad of the Iron Cross. London: 1918. V. 43

DODD, C. T.

The Cricket Match, Tonbridge School. Tonbridge Wells. V. 43

DODD, CHARLES EDWARD

Doubtful Questions in the Law of Elections stated and Canvassed. London: 1826. V. 40

DODD, DAVID OWEN

Letters of David O. Dodd with a Biographical Sketch. N.P.: 1917. V. 43

DODD, EPHRAIM SHELBY

Diary of Ephraim Shelby Dodd, Member of Company D. Terry's Texas Rangers, 1862-1864. Austin: 1914. V. 38; 42; 44

DODD, ERICA CRUIKSHANK

Byzantine Silver Stamps. Washington: 1961. V. 44

DODD, GEORGE

British Manufactures. London: 1844/45/51. V. 40

The Curiosities of Industry and Applied Sciences. London: 1857. V. 38

The Curiosities of Industry and the Applied Sciences. London: 1852. V. 37

The Curiosities of Industry and the Applied Sciences. London: 1857. V. 37

Days at the Factories. London: 1843. V. 39

Pictorial History of the Russian War, 1854-5-6 . . . London: 1856. V. 46

DODD, JAMES SOLAS

An Essay Towards a Natural History of the Herring. London: 1752. V. 40; 41; 45

A Physical Account of the Case of Elizabeth Canning. London: 1753. V. 46

DODD, JAMES WILLIAM

Ballads of Archery, Sonnets, etc. London: 1818. V. 39; 43

DODD, JOHN

Journal of a Blockaded Resident in North Formosa, During the Franco-Chinese War, 1884-5. Hong Kong: 1888. V. 43

DODD, ROBERT

Part of the Crew of His Majesty's Ship Guardian Endeavouring to Escape in the Boats. London: 1790. V. 45

DODD, STEPHEN

The East-Haven Register. New Haven: 1824. V. 40; 43

DODD, WILLIAM

An Account of the Rise, Progress, and Present State of the Magdalen Charity . . . London: 1761. V. 38

An Account of the Rise, Progress and Present State of the Magdalen Charity. London: 1763. V. 38

An Account of the Rise, Progress and present State of the Magdalen Charity to which are Added the Rev. Dr. Dodd's Sermons Preached Before the President, Vice President's and Governors &c . . . London: 1766. V. 38

An Account of the Rise, Progress and Present State of the Magdalen Hospital, for the Reception of Penitent Prostitutes . . . London: 1770. V. 41

Authentic Memoirs of the life of William Dodd, LL.D . . . with the particulars of his trail and execution, and a review of the arguments, for and against his suffering the sentence of the law. To which is added a letter from Lady Huntington . . . Salisbury: (1777). V. 37

The Beauties of Shakespear. London: 1752. V. 40

The Beauties of History or Pictures of Virtue and Vice, Drawn from Examples of Men Eminent for Their Virtues or Infamous for Their Vices. London: 1796. V. 45; 46

A Day In Vacation at College. London: 1751. V. 41; 42

A Familiar Explanation of the Poetical Works of Milton. London: 1762. V. 38; 41

The Hymns of Callimachus . . . London: 1755. V. 43

A New Book of the Dunciad: Occasion'd by Mr. Warburton's New Edition of the Dunciad Complete. London: 1750. V. 38

An Oration Delivered at the Dedication of Free-Mason's Hall, Great Queen-Street, Lincoln's-Inn-Fields, On Thursday, May 23, 1776. London: 1776. V. 43; 46

Poems. London: 1767. V. 41; 42; 43

Reflections on Death. London: 1772. V. 38

Reflections on Death. London: 1777. V. 42

The Rules and Regulations of the Magadalen Charity with Instructions to the Women Who are Admitted and Prayers for Their Use. London: 1769. V. 38; 41

Sermons to Young Men. Dublin: 1771. V. 41

The Sisters; or, the History of Lucy and Caroline Sanson. London: 1791. V. 42; 43; 44

Thoughts in Prison: in Five Parts. To which are added, His Last Prayer Written the Night Before His Death . . . Boston: 1777. V. 38

Thoughts in Prison. London: 1777. V. 42; 43

Thoughts in Prison . . . To Which are Added, His Last Prayer . . . Dublin: 1778. V. 46

Thoughts in Prison. London: 1789. V. 38; 40; 41

Thoughts in Prison in Five Parts . . . London: 1809. V. 46

DODDRIDGE, JOHN 1555-1628

A Compleat Parson. London: 1630. V. 40; 46

The English Lawyer. London: 1631. V. 38; 40

The History of the Ancient and Modern Estate of the Principality of Wales, Duchy of Cornewall, and Earldome Chester. London: 1630. V. 38; 40; 44

Honors Pedigree, Or the Several Fountains of Gentry, Being A Treatise of the Distinct Degrees of the Nobilitie of this Kingdome . . . London: 1652. V. 45

DODDRIDGE, JOSEPH

Notes on the Settlement and Indian Wars of the Western Parts of Virginia and Pennsylvania, from the Year 1763 Until the Year 1783 Inclusive . . . Wellsburgh: 1824. V. 37; 38; 39; 42; 44; 45

DODDRIDGE, P.

The Rise and Progress of Religion in the Soul. London: 1822. V. 42

Some Remarkable Passages in the Life of the Honourable Col. James Gardiner Who Was Slain at the Battle of Preston-Pans, 21st September 1745. London: 1747. V. 40

DODDRIDGE, PHILIP

The Absurdity and Iniquity of Perecution for Conscience-sake, in all Its Kings and Degrees. Northampton: 1736. V. 44

A Brief and Easy System of Short Hand: First Invented by Mr. Jeremiah Rich and Improved. London: 1799. V. 40

A Course of Lectures on the Principal Subjects in Pneumatology, Ethics, and Divinity. London: 1776. V. 37; 40; 42

The Family Expositor. London: 1792. V. 39

Letters to and From the Rev. Philip Doddridge, D.D. Late of Northampton . . . Shrewsbury: 1790. V. 38; 41; 45

The Rise and Progress of Religion in the Soul, Illustrated in a Course of Serious and Practical Addresses. Paris: 1815. V. 43

The Rise and Progress of Religion in the Soul. London: 1822. V. 42

The Rise and Progress of Religion in the Soul. London: 1827. V. 43

Some Remarkable Passages in the Life of the Honourable Col. James Gardiner, Who Was Slain at the Battle of Preston-Pans, 21st September 1745 . . . Derby: 1745. V. 38

Some Remarkable Passages in the Life of the Honourable Col. James Gardiner who Was Salin at the Battle of Preston-Pans, 21st September 1745 . . . . London: 1747. V. 39; 43; 46

Some Remarkable Passages in the Life of the Honourable Col. James Gardiner, Who Was Slain at the Battle of Preston-Pans, September 21, 1745, to Which is Added the Sermon Occasioned by His Heroick Death. Boston: 1748. V. 38

Some Remarkable Passages in the Life of the Hon. Col. James Gardiner, Who Was Slain at the Battle of Preston-Pans, September 21st, 1745. Bungay: 1808. V. 39

DODD'S Church History of England from the Commencement of the Sixteenth Century to the Revolution in 1688 . . . London: 1839-43. V. 39

DODDS, E. KING

Every Man His Own Horse and Cattle Doctor. Toronto: 1886. V. 40

DODDS, G.

Pictorial History of the Russian War 1854-5-6. London: 1856. V. 41

DODDS, MADELEINE HOPE

A History of Northumberland. Volume XII. The Parishes of Heddon-on-the-Wall, Newburn, Long Benton and Wallsend . . . Newcastle-upon-Tyne: 1930. V. 45

DODDS, SUSANNA W.

Health in the Household . . . New York: 1884. V. 45

DODGE City Directory, 1915-1916. Witchia: 1916. V. 46

DODGE, G. M.

Biographical Sketch of James Bridger Mountaineer, Trapper and Guide. New York: 1905. V. 41

DODGE, GRENVILLE M.

General Doge's Report. Washington: 1868. V. 45

Romantic Realities: The Story of the Building of the Pacific Roads . . . Omaha: 1889. V. 42

DODGE, GRENVILLE MELLEN

Biographical Sketch of James Bridger, Mountaineer, Trapper and Guide. New York: 1905. V. 38

Paper Read Before the Society of the Army of the Tennessee at Its 21st Annual Reunion at Toledo, O., Sept. 15, 1888. New York: 1899. V. 38

Union Pacific Railfoad. Report of the Chief Engineer on Bridging the Missouri River. New York: 1867. V. 37

Union Pacific Railroad. Report of G.M. Dodge, Chief Engineer, to the Board of Directors, on a Branch Railroad Line from the Union Pacific Railroad to Idaho, Montana, Oregon & Puget's Sound. Washington: 1868. V. 37

DODGE, HENRY

Colonel Dodge's Journal. Report of the Secretary of War . . . Transmitting a Report of the Expedition of the Dragoons Under the Command of Colonel Henry Dodge, to the Rocky Mountains, During the Summer of 1835. Washington: 1836. V. 37

Report of the Expedition of the Dragoons, Under the Command of Colonel Henry Dodge, to the Rocky Mountains, During the Summer of 1853. Washington: 1836. V. 37

DODGE, J. R.

West Virginia: Its Farms and Forests, Mines and Oil Wells. Philadelphia: 1865. V. 37; 38; 39

DODGE, JOHN

Narrative of the Mr. John Dodge During His Captivity at Detroit Reproduced in Facsimile From the Second Edition of 1780 . . . Cedar Rapids: 1909. V. 42

DODGE, JONATHAN

A Complete System of Stenography, or Short Hand Writing . . . . New London: 1823. V. 43

DODGE, M. E.

Hans Brinker; or, the Silver Skates. New York: 1866. V. 46

DODGE, MARY ELIZABETH MAPES

Hans Brinker; or, the Silver Skates. New York: 1866. V. 42

DODGE, NANNIE O. SMITH

In Memory of Colonel D. C. Dodge. Denver: 1923. V. 39

DODGE, ORVIL

The Heroes of Battle Rock; Narrative of the Desperate Encounter of Nine White Men with Three Hundred Indians. N.P.: 1904. V. 42

Pioneer History of Coos and Curry Counties, or Heroic Deeds and Thrilling Adventures of the Early Settlers. Salem: 1898. V. 44

DODGE, RICHARD IRVING

The Black Hills. New York: 1876. V. 38; 39; 40; 41; 45

The Black Hills. New York: 1876. V. 38

The Black Hills. New York: 1876. V. 38

The Hunting Grounds of the Great West. London: 1877. V. 39; 42

Our Wild Indians: Thirty Three Years Personal Experience Among the Redmen of the Great West. Hartford: 1882. V. 37; 41; 44

Our Wild Indians: 39 Years Personal Experience Among the Redmen of the Great West . . . Washington: 1882. V. 46

Our Wild Indians. Hartford: 1882, 1883. V. 39

Our Wild Indians: Thirty-Three Years' Personal Experience Among the Red Men of the Great West. Hartford: 1883. V. 37; 39; 45

The Plains of the Great West and Their Inhabitants. New York: 1877. V. 37; 39; 41; 43; 45

DODGE, THEODORE

Riders of Many Lands. New York: 1894. V. 37

DODGE, THEODORE AYRAULT

A Bird's-Eye View of Our Civil War. Boston: 1883. V. 38

Riders of Many lands. New York: 1894. V. 46

DODGE, WILLIAM SUMNER

History of the Second Division. Chicago: 1864. V. 45

Oration . . . Delivered at Sitka, Alaska, Saturday July 4, 1868. San Francisco: 1868. V. 37; 42

DODGSON, CAMPBELL 1867-1948

Contemporary English Woodcuts. London: 1922. V. 39

The Etchings of James McNeill Whistler. London: 1922. V. 39; 40; 44; 46

An Iconography of the Engravings of Stephen Gooden. London: 1944. V. 37; 38; 39; 40; 41

Old French Colour-Prints. London: 1924. V. 38; 42; 44

The Weigel-Felix Biblia Pauperum. London: 1906. V. 44

DODGSON, CHARLES LUTWIDGE 1832-1898

Alice in Wonderland. V. 39

Alice in Wonderland. London. V. 38

Alice in Wonderland. Amsterdam: 1908. V. 38

Alice's Adventures in Wonderland. London. V. 41

Alice's Adventures in Wonderland. London. V. 41

Alice's Adventures in Wonderland. London. V. 38

Alice's Adventures in Wonderland. London. V. 45

Alice's Adventures in Wonderland. London. V. 45

Alice in Wonderland. London. V. 42

Alice's Adventures in Wonderland by Lewis Carroll. (with) Through the Looking Glass and What Alice Found There. London: 1866. V. 42

Alice's Adventures in Wonderland. New York: 1866. V. 40; 42; 44

Alice's Adventures in Wonderland and Through the Looking Glass and What Alice Found There. London: 1866/72. V. 45

Alice's Adventures in Wonderland. Boston: 1869. V. 39

Aventures d'Alice au Pays des Merveilles. London: 1869. V. 39; 42; 45

Alice's Adventures in Wonderland (with) Through the Looking Glass and What Alice Found There. London: 1870-72. V. 41; 44

Alice's Adventures in Wonderland. Boston: 1871. V. 39

Alice's Adventures in Wonderland. London: 1871. V. 40; 41; 45; 46

Le Aventure d'Alice Nel Paese Delle Meraviglie. London: 1872. V. 44

Alice in Wonderland. (and) Through the Looking Glass. London: 1872. V. 45

Alice's Adventures in Wonderland. (with) Through the Looking Glass and What Alice Found There. London: 1877-78. V. 39

Alice's Adventures Under Ground . . . London: 1886. V. 37; 39; 40; 41; 43; 44; 45; 46

Alice's Adventures Underground. London & New York: 1886. V. 38

Alice's Adventures in Wonderland. New York: 1899. V. 41

Alice's Adventures in Wonderland. New York: 1901. V. 45

Alice's Adventures in Wonderland. New York: 1907. V. 38

Alice's Adventures in Wonderland. London: 1910. V. 45

Alice's Adventures in Wonderland. London: 1914. V. 37; 41; 42; 46

Alice's Adventures in Wonderland. New York: 1914. V. 45

Alice's Adventures in Wonderland. London: 1922. V. 42

Alice's Adventures in Wonderland, and through the Looking Glass. London: 1927. V. 40

Alice's Adventures in Wonderland. New York: 1929. V. 40

Alice's Adventures in Wonderland. London: 1932. V. 41

Alice's Adventures in Wonderland. New York: 1932. V. 39; 40; 46

Alice in Wonderland. London: 1938. V. 45

Alice's Adventures in Wonderland. New York: 1941. V. 39

Alice's Adventures in Wonderland and Through the Looking Glass and What Alice Saw There. Paris: 1950. V. 38; 42; 43

Alice's Adventures in Wonderland and Through the Looking Glass. 1954. V. 40; 46

Alice's Adventures in Wonderland and Through the Looking Glass. London: 1954. V. 40; 42; 43; 45

Alice's Adeventures in Wonderland. London: 1958. V. 43

Alice im Wunderland. Berlin: 1967. V. 45

Alice's Adventures in Wonderland. New York: 1969. V. 39

Alice's Adventures in Wonderland. 1982. V. 38

Alice's Adventures in Wonderland. Berkeley: 1982. V. 39

Alice's Adventures in Wonderland. West Hatfield: 1982. V. 43; 45; 46

Alice's Adventures in Wonderland. London: 1866. V. 37; 38; 46

Alice's Adventures in Wonderland. London: 1867. V. 41; 46

Alice's Adventures in Wonderland. (with) Through the Looking Glass and What Alice Found There. London: 1867/72/71. V. 46

Alice's Adventures in Wonderland. (with) Through the Looking Glass. London: 1868, 1872. V. 37

Alice's Adventures in Wonderland. Boston: 1869. V. 37; 41; 43; 44; 45

Alice's Adventures in Wonderland. Boston: 1869. V. 44

Alice's Adventures in Wonderland. New York: 1900. V. 43

Alice's Adventures in Wonderland. London: 1907. V. 37; 38; 41; 42; 45; 46

Alice in Wonderland. Chicago: 1915. V. 46

Alice's Adventures in Wonderland. London: 1915. V. 46

Alice in Wonderland. London: 1916. V. 46

Alice in Wonderland. London: 1917. V. 46

Alice's Adventures in Wonderland. New York: 1917. V. 38

Alice's Adventures in Wonderland. London: 1920. V. 46

Alice's Adventures in Wonderland. London: 1922. V. 46

Alice's Adventures in Wonderland. New York: 1927. V. 44

Alice's Adventures in Wonderland. 1932. V. 44

Alice's Adventures in Wonderland: And, Through the Looking-Glass and what Alice found there. London: 1934. V. 37

Alice in Wonderland. London: 1940. V. 46

Alice's Adventures in Wonderland and Through the Looking Glass. Stockholm: 1946. V. 46

Alice's Adventures in Wonderland. By Lewis Carroll. New York: 1969. V. 37; 46

Alice's Adventures in Wonderland & Through the Looking Glass. London: 1931, 1929. V. 44

Alice's Adventures in Wonderland. (with) Through the Looking Glass and What Alice Found There. London: 1955-59. V. 46

Alice's Adventures Under Ground. London: 1885. V. 44

The Collected Verse of . . . New York: 1933. V. 46

Curiosa Mathematica. London: 1888. V. 40

Curiosa Mathematica. Pt. III: Pillow Problems. London: 1893. V. 44; 45

The Diaries of Lewis Caroll. New York: 1954. V. 40

Doublets. A Word Puzzle. London: 1880. V. 40

An Easter Greeting to Every Child Who Loves 'Alice'. Oxford: 1876. V. 46

Eight or Nine Wise Words About Letter-Writing. Oxford: 1907. V. 46

Eight of Nine Wise Words About Letter-Writing. Oxford: 1910. V. 43

An Elementary Treatise on Determinants with Their Application to Simultaneous Linear Equations and Algebraical Geometry. London: 1867. V. 39

Feeding the Mind. London: 1907. V. 39; 41; 43; 46

For the Train. Five Poems and a Tale. London: 1932. V. 38

Formulae. Group C. N.P.. V. 41

The Formulae of Plane Trigonometry, Printed with Symbols (instead of words) to Express the 'Goniometrical Ratios.' Oxford: 1861. V. 37

Further Nonsense. New York: 1926. V. 43

Further Nonsense Verse and Prose. London: (1926). V. 37

The Game of Logic. London: 1886. V. 46

The Game of Logic. London: 1887. V. 43; 45

The Hunting of the Snark. London: 1876. V. 37; 39; 41; 42; 43; 44; 45; 46

The Hunting of the Snark. New York: 1903. V. 41; 43; 46

The Hunting of the Snark, an Agony in Eight Fits. London: 1931. V. 43

The Hunting of the Snark. London: 1974. V. 40

The Hunting of the Snark. London: 1975. V. 42

The Hunting of the Snark. Los Altos: 1981. V. 37; 42; 45

The Hunting of the Snark, an Agony. 1983. V. 44

The Hunting of the Snark: An Agony in Eight Fits, by Lewis Carroll. Stuttgart: 1968. V. 37

Jabberwocky. Berkeley: 1987. V. 38

The Letters to Marion from Lewis Carroll. Bristol: 1932. V. 39

DODGSON, CHARLES LUTWIDGE 1832-1898 continued

Lewis Carroll Picture Book. London: 1899. V. 44; 45

Logical Nonsense: The Works of Lewis Caroll. New York: 1934. V. 41

The New Belfry of Christ Church, Oxford. (with) *The Blank Cheque, a Fable.* (and) *The Vision of the Three T's.* Oxford: 1873. V. 40

The Nursery 'Alice.' London: 1890. V. 37; 39; 45; 46

The Nursery Alice. London: 1896. V. 44

The Nursery Alice. London: 1897. V. 45

The Nursery Alice containing twenty coloured enlargments from Tenniel's illustrations . . . the cover designed and coloured by E. Gertrude Thomson. London: 1889. V. 37

Phantasmagoria and Other Poems. London: 1869. V. 37; 38; 39; 42; 43; 44

The Principles of Parliamentary Representation. (with) *Supplement to the Principles of Parliamentary Representation.* London: 1844. V. 41

The Rectory Umbrella and Mischmasch. London: 1932. V. 39

Rhyme and Reason? London: 1883. V. 37; 38; 39; 40; 42; 43; 44; 45; 46

Songs from Alice in Wonderland and Through Looking Glass. London: 1921. V. 45; 46

Sylvia and Bruno. London: and New York: 1890. V. 42

Sylvia and Bruno and Sylvia and Bruno Concluded. London: 1889, 1893. V. 37; 38; 39; 40; 41; 44

Sylvie and Bruno. & Sylvie and Bruno Concluded. London: 1889-93. V. 37; 38; 39; 40; 41; 43; 44

Sylvie and Bruno Concluded. London: 1893. V. 38; 39; 40; 41; 43; 45

Sylvie and Bruno Concluded. New York: 1894. V. 44; 46

Sylvie and Bruno. London: 1889. V. 37

Symbolic Logic. London: 1896. V. 39; 43; 46

A Tangled Tale. London: 1885. V. 37; 39; 42; 44; 46

365 Minus 1 Equals 364, or Chapter VI Humpty Dumpty from Through the Looking Glass. London: 1971. V. 39

Through the Looking Glass and What Alice Found There. 1872. V. 46

Through the Looking Glass and What Alice Found There. London: 1872. V. 37; 38; 39; 40; 41; 42; 44; 46

Through the Looking Glass. London: 1898. V. 38

Through the Looking-Glass; and What Alice Found There. New York: 1902. V. 39

Through the Looking Glass and What Alice Found There. New York: 1909. V. 46

Through the Looking Glass and What Alice Found There. New York: 1931. V. 41; 44

Through the Looking Glass and What Alice Found There. London: 1972. V. 44

Through the Looking Glass and What Alice Found there. West Hatfield: 1982. V. 38; 42; 45

Through the Looking-Glass, and What Alice Found There. London: 1872 (1871). V. 37

Through the Looking Glass. London: 1898. V. 37

Through the Looking Glass and what Alice Found There. New York: 1931. V. 37

Through the Looking Glass and What Alice Found There. New York: 1935. V. 37; 46

Through the Looking-Glass, and What Alice Found There. New York: & London: 1872. V. 45

The Wonderland Postage Stampe Case. Oxford: 1890. V. 45

The 'Wonderland' Postage Stamp Case. (and) *Eight or Nine Wise Words about Letter Writing.* Oxford: 1890-1910. V. 37

Wonderland. London: 1940. V. 45

The 'Wonderland' Postage Stamp Case. (with) *Eight or Nine Words About Letter-Writing by Lewis Carroll.* Oxford: 1890. V. 37

DODGSON, GEORGE HAYDOCK

Illustrations of the Scenery on the Line of the Whitby and Pickering Railway, in the North Eastern Part of Yorkshire. London: 1836. V. 46

DODGSON, J.

The Places Names of Cheshire. Cambridge: 1970-81. V. 41

DODINGTON, GEORGE BUBB 1691-1762

The Diary of the Late George Bubb Dodington, Baron of Melcombe Regis: from March 8, 1749 to February 6, 1761. Salisbury: 1748. V. 41

The Diary of the Late George Bubb Dodington, Baron of Melcombe Regis, from March 8, 1748-9 to February 6, 1761. London: 1784. V. 38; 43; 45

The Diary of the Late George Bubb Dodington, Baron of melcombe Regis, from March 8, 1748-49 to February 6, 716. Salisbury: 1784. V. 37; 41; 43; 46

An Epistle from John More, Apothecary of Abchurch-Lane, to L-- C-----, Upon His Treatise of Worms. London: 1743. V. 41

DODOENS, R.

A Herball, or Historie of Plantes. London: 1586. V. 37

A Niewe Herball or Historie of Plantes . . . London: 1578. V. 41

DODOENS, REMBERT

Cruydt-Boeck . . . Volghens Signe Laetste Verbeteringhe . . . Antwerp: 1644. V. 37; 42

Historia Frumentorum, Leguminum, Palustrium et Aquatilium Herabarum, ac Eorum quae eo Pertinent . . . Antwerp: 1569. V. 37; 42

Historia Vitis Viniqve: Et Stirpivm Nonvallarum Aliarum. Cologne: 1580. V. 39

Medicinalium Observationum Exempla Rara. Harderwijck: 1621. V. 37

A New Herball, or Historie of Plants. London: 1586. V. 37; 38; 44

A New Herbal, or Historie of Plants. London: 1619. V. 37

A New Herball, or Historie of Plants . . . not only of those which are here growing in this our Countrie of England, but of al others also of foraine Realms commonly used in Physicke. First set foorth in the Dutch or Almaigne toong . . . London: 1595. V. 37

A Niewe Herball, or Historie of Plantes . . . London: 1578. V. 39; 43; 46

A Nievve Herball, or Historie of Plantes . . . Imprinted at Antwerpe: by me: 1578. V. 44

A Niewe Herball, or Historie of Plantes. colophon: Imprinted at: 1578. V. 45

Stirpium Historiae Pemptades Sex, Sive Libri . . . Antwerp: 1616. V. 43

Trium Priorum De Stirpium Historia Commentariorum Imagines ad Vivum Expressae . . . (with) *Posteriorum Trium . . .* Antwerp: 1553-54. V. 42; 45

DODONAEUS, REMBART

Historia Vitis Vinique et Stirpium Aliarum. Item Medicinalium Observationum Exempla. Cologne: 1580. V. 38

DODRIDGE, JOHN

An Historical Account of the Ancient and Modern State of the Principality of Wales, Dutch of Cornwal (sic) and Earldom of Chester. London: 1714. V. 42

The History of the Ancient and Modern Estate of the Principality of Wales, Dutch of Cornewall and Earldome of Chester, etc. London: 1630. V. 44

DODS, ANDREW

Pathological Observations on the Rotated or Contorted Spine, Commonly Called Lateral Curvature . . . London: 1824. V. 38

DODS, MATILDA LEES

Handbook of Practical Cookery. London: 1906. V. 38

DODSLEY, ROBERT 1703-1764

The Art of Preaching. London: 1738. V. 37; 38; 40; 41; 45

The Art of Preaching. London: 1738. V. 38

A Collection of Poems, by Several Hands. London: 1748. V. 38

A Collection of Poems. London: 1748-55-58. V. 38; 41; 45

A Collection of Poems. London: 1748-58. V. 38; 40

A Collection of Poems. London: 1748/66. V. 45

A Collection of Poems in Six Volumes. London: 1765. V. 37; 42

A Collection of Poems in Six Volumes. London: 1766. V. 39; 41

A Collection of Poems in Six Volumes by Several Hands. (with) *A Collection of Poems in Two Volumes. By Several Hands.* London: 1766, 1768. V. 39

A Collection of Poems in Six Volumes. By Several Hands. London: 1775. V. 39

A Collection of Poems. London: 1775. V. 38

A Collection of Poems in Six Volumes by Several Hands, with Notes. London: 1782. V. 38

A Collection of Poems by Several Hands. London: 1782. V. 39; 45; 46

A Collection of Poems by Several Hands. London;: 1763/66. V. 37

The Economy of Human Life. London: 1805. V. 42

Fugitive Pieces on Various Subjects. London: 1761. V. 37; 43; 46

Fugitive Pieces, on Various Subjects. London: 1765. V. 42; 46

Fugitive Pieces on Various Subjects by Several Authors. London: 1771. V. 37; 39

The King and the Miller of Mansfield. London: 1737. V. 41; 42; 43; 45

Miscellanies. London: 1777? V. 41

The Modern Reasoners; an Epistle to a Friend. London: 1734. V. 42; 43; 45

The Oeconomy of Human Life. London: 1751. V. 38; 39; 42; 46

The Oeconomy of Human Life. New York: 1793. V. 43

The Oeconomy of Human Life. London: 1795. V. 38; 39

The Preceptor. Dublin: 1749. V. 44

The Preceptor. London: 1775. V. 41; 43

Public Virtue: a Poem. London: 1753. V. 38; 41; 45; 46

A Select Collection of Old Plays. London: 1744. V. 38; 42; 45

Select Fables of Esop and Other Fabulists. Birmingham: 1761. V. 42

Select Fables of Esop and Other Fabulists. Birmingham: 1764. V. 43

A Select Collection of Old Plays. London: 1780. V. 42; 44

A Select Collection of Old Plays. London: 1825-27. V. 42

A Select Collection of Old English Plays. London: 1874-76. V. 44

Sir John Cockle at Court. London: 1738. V. 41

Trifles. London: 1745. V. 37; 38; 40; 41; 44; 45

DODSON, JAMES 1710-1757

The Mathematical Repository, Containing Analytical Solutions of Five Hundred Questions, Mostly Selected from Scarce & Valuable Authors . . . London: 1748-55. V. 37; 38

DODSWORTH, WILLIAM

An Historical Account of the Episcopal See, and Cathedral Church of Sarum, or Salisbury . . . London: 1814. V. 45

An Historical Account of the Episcopal See, and Cathedral Church of Sarum, or Salisbury . . . Salisbury: 1814. V. 45

DODWELL, EDWARD

Views in Greece, from Drawings by Edward Dodwell, Esq. London: 1821. V. 37; 45

DODWELL, HENRY

An Epistolary Discourse Proving from the First Fathers that the Soul is a Principle Naturally Mortal but Immortalised Actually by the Pleasure o od to Punishment . . . London: 1706. V. 38; 40; 41

Henrici Dodwell De Parma Esquestri Woodwardiana Dissertatio. Oxonii: 1723. V. 44

DODWELL, WILLIAM

The Sick Man's Companion; or the Clergyman's Assistant in Visiting the Sick. London: 1768. V. 44

DOE, JANET

A Bibliography of the Works of Ambroise Pare. Chicago: 1937. V. 38; 39; 40; 41

DOEBEREINER, PHILLIP, VON TUERSCHENREUT

Sendtschreiben und Warhaffte Zeytungen. N.P.: 1571. V. 38

DOEGEN, MATTHIAS

L'Architecture Militaire Moderne, ou Fortification. Amsterdam: 1648. V. 45

DOEHRING, KARL SIEGFRIED

Art and Art Industry in Siam. Berlin: 191-? V. 41

DOERFLINGER, CHARLES H.

Me-Le-O-Ki. Novelle Aus Dem Urwald, Und Culturhistorische Skizze Amerikanischer Stadte-Entwicklung. Milwaukee: 1894. V. 40

DOERR, HARRIET

Stones for Ibarra. New York: 1984. V. 39; 46

DOGEN, MATTHIAS

L'Architecture Militaire Moderne, ou Fortification. Amsterdam: 1648. V. 38

DOGGET, THOMAS

The Country-Wake. London: 1696. V. 37; 38; 39; 42

D'OGLIO, PELLEGRINO

D.O.M. Constitvtioni Del Seminario Della Parocchiale Chiesa Della B. V. M. Dolorosa E Di S Celestino PP. I. Delle Ca'Del Bosco Di Sopra Fatti, e dati in adi 6 Aprile 1679. Reggio: 1805. V. 42

THE DOG'S Grand Dinner Party. London: 1855. V. 41

DOHAN, EDITH HALL

Italic Tomb-Groups in the University Museum. Philadelphia: 1942. V. 42; 44

DOHENY, ESTELLE

Catalogue of Books and Manuscripts in the Estelle Doheny Collection. Los Angeles: 1940. V. 39

A Catalogue of Books and Manuscripts in the Collection of Estelle Doheny. Los Angeles: 1940/46/55. V. 46

Catalogue of Books. V. 39

The Estelle Doheny Collection. New York: 1987-89. V. 46

The Estelle Doheny Collection, Part I-VII. New York: 1987-89. V. 46

The Estelle Doheny Collection from the Edward Lawrence Doheny Memorial Library St. John's Seminary, Camarillo, California. New York: 1987-89. V. 45

The Estelle Doheny Collection of Books and Manuscripts. 1988-89. V. 45

DOIG, IVAN

This House of Sky. New York: 1978. V. 42; 45

Winter Brothers. New York: 1980. V. 46

DOINGS in London; or, Day and Night Scenes of the Frauds, Frolics, Manners and Depravities of the Metropolis. London: 1827. V. 40

DOKE, CLEMENT M.

The Lambas of Northern Rhodesia. London: 1931. V. 41

DOLAUS, JOHANNES

Encyclopaedia Chirurgica Rationalis. Venetiis: 1695. V. 40; 41; 45; 46

DOLBEAR, A. E.

The Art of Projecting. Boston: 1877. V. 46

The Telephone; an Account of the Phenomena of Electricity, Magnetism, and Sound, as Involved in Its Action. Boston: 1877. V. 38; 40; 42; 45

The Telephone: an Account of the Phenomena of Electricity, Magnetism and Sound . . . Boston & New York: 1877. V. 40

The Telephone: an Account of Electricity, Magnetism and Sound, as Involved in Its Action. London: 1878. V. 39

DOLBEN, DIGBY MACKWORTH

The Poems of . . . London: 1911. V. 43

Poems. Oxford: 1911. V. 38

DOLBY, A.

Church Vestments: Their Origin, Use and Ornament Practically Illustrated. London: 1868. V. 38

DOLBY, GEORGE

Charles Dickens As I Knew Him. London: 1885. V. 43

DOLBY, RICHARD

The Cook's Dictionary and Housekepper's Directory. London: 1833. V. 40

DOLBY, THOMAS

Floreston; or, the New Lord of the Manor. London: 1839. V. 43; 46

The Shakespearian Dictionary . . . London: 1832. V. 42

DOLCATER, MAX W.

3d Infantry Division in Korea. Tokyo: 1953. V. 45

DOLCE, LODOVICO

Aretin: a Dialogue on Painting. London: 1770. V. 44

Dialogo Nel Quale si Ragiona Del Modo Di Accrescere e Conservar La Memoria. Venice: 1562. V. 40

Dialogo . . . nel Quale si Ragiona del Mondo di Accrescere, & Conseruar la Memoria. Venice: 1586. V. 37

Giornale delle Historie del Mondo, Delle Cose Degne di Memoria . . . dal Principio del Mondo Sino a' Suoi Tempi . . . Venice: 1571. V. 41

I Quattro Libri delle Osservationi . . . Ricorrette & Ampliate, e con le Postille. Venice: 1563. V. 43

DOLE, NATHAN HASKELL

America in Spitsbergen: The Romance of an Arctic Coal-Mine . . . Boston: 1922. V. 37

The Pilgrims and Other Poems. Boston: 1907. V. 46

DOLGE, ALFRED

Pianos and Their Makers. Covina: 1911. V. 45; 46

DOLINS, DANIEL

The Charge of Sir Daniel Dolins, Kt. to the Grand Jury, and Other Jurie of the County of Middlesex; 7th October 1725 at Westminster Hall. (with) The Second Charge . . . 18th April 1726 . . . (with) the Third Charge . . . 6th October 1726. London: 1725, 1726. V. 38

DOLL, JOSEPH

Leichter Unterricht in der Vocal Musik Enthaltened eine Sammlung Geistreicher Gesange. Harrisburg: 1815. V. 44

DOLLAR, ROBERT

Memoirs of Robert Dollar. San Francisco: 1927. V. 42

Memoirs of Robert Dollar. San Francisco: 1927/22/28. V. 41

DOLLARD, ROBERT

Recollections of the Civil War and Going West to Grow Up with the Country. Scotland: 1906. V. 37; 39

DOLLMAN, F. T.

An Analysis of Ancient Domestic Architecture, Exhibiting the Best Examples in Great Britain. London: 1861-63. V. 44

DOLLOND, G.

The Atmospheric Recorder or Self-Registering Apparatus for the Various Changes of the Barometer, Thermometer, Hygrometer . . . London: 1851. V. 40

DOLLOND, P.

Description of the Two Feet and Half Achromatic Telescope, Made by P. and J. Dollond, in St. Paul's Churchyard. London: 1770. V. 42

DOLLOND, PETER

A Catalogue of Optical, Mathematical and Philsophical Instruments, Made by P. and G. Dollond, Opticians to His Majesty. London: 1800. V. 42

A Catalogue of Optical, Mathematical and Philosophical Instruments . . . London: 1812-19. V. 42

THE DOLL'S House. London: 1896. V. 42

DOLLY Dubbings' Diary. Cheltenham: 1829. V. 39

DOLLY'S Mansion. London: 1880. V. 43

DOLMETSCH, H.

Ornamental Treasures. London. V. 38

DOLMETSCH, HEINRICH

The Historic Styles of Ornament. London: 1912. V. 39

DOLMETSCH, MABEL

Dances of England and France from 1450 to 1600. London: 1949. V. 46

Dances of Spain and Italy, from 1400 to 1600. London: 1954. V. 46

THE DOLPHIN. New York: 1933/35/38. V. 40
THE DOLPHIN. New York: 1933-38. V. 39
THE DOLPHIN. New York: 1933-41. V. 37; 41; 45

DOMAGE, CECIL G.

Astronomy of To-day: a Populara Introduction in Non-Technical Language. London: 1909. V. 37

DOMAN, HENRY

Songs of Lymington. London: 1867. V. 40

THE DOME. London: 1897-98. V. 37; 40; 41; 42; 44
THE DOME. London: 1897-98. V. 41
THE DOME: a Quarterly Containing Examples of All the Arts. London: 1897-98. V. 41

THE DOME: An Illustrated Magazine and Review of Literature, Music, Architecture and the Graphic Arts. London: 1898-1900. V. 46

DOMENECH, EMMANUEL HENRI D.

Journal d'un Missionnaire au Texas et au Mexique . . . 1846-52. Paris: 1857. V. 43

DOMENECH, EMMANUEL HENRI DIEUDONNE

Missionary Adventures in Texas and Mexico. London: 1858. V. 37; 38; 39; 40; 42; 43; 45

Seven Years' Residence in the Great Deserts of North America. London: 1860. V. 37; 38; 39; 41; 43; 45; 46

Voyage Pittoresque dans les Grands Deserts du Nouveau Monde. Paris: 1862. V. 42

DOMENECH, FRANCISCO

Pro Lege Divina Prohibente Clericis Mercaturam Apologia. Florence: 1616. V. 45

DOMENICHI, LODOVICO

Dailoghi. In Vinegia: 1562. V. 44

Facetie Motti, et Burle, di Diversi Signori . . . Con una Nuova Aggiunta di Motti Raccolti de M. Tomaso Poracchi. Venice: 1599. V. 37

Rime Diverse di Molti Eccellentiss. Auttori Nuovamente Raccolte. Venice: 1549. V. 46

DOMENICHINO

Picturae Dominici Zampierii Vulgo Domenichino, Nunc Primum Tabulis Aeneis Incisae . . . Rome: 1762. V. 45

DOMENY DE RIENZI, GREGOIRE LOUIS

Oceanie ou Cinquieme Partie du Monde. Paris: 1836, 43, 45. V. 38

DOMESDAY BOOK

The Domesday Book: seu Liber Censualis Wilkhelmi Primi Regis Angliae, Inter Archivos Regni in Domo Capitulari Westmonasterii Asservatus. London: 1783. V. 38

THE DOMESTIC History of the Learned Seals, 'Ned' and 'Fanny' at the Boston Aquarial Gardens . . . New York: 1860. V. 45

THE DOMESTIC Manners of the Americans; or, Sketches of the People of the United States. N.P.: 1835. V. 40; 46

DOMETT, HENRY W.

The Bank of New York: A History 1784-1884. New York: 1884. V. 41

DOMINCETI, BARTHOLOMEW DE

An Address from Dr. Dominceti, of Chelsea. London: 1782. V. 38; 42

DOMINGUEZ, FRANCISCO ATANASIO

The Missions of New Mexico, 1776: A Description by Fray Francisco Atanasio Dominguez. Albuquerque: 1956, 1975. V. 39

DOMINICUS DE FLANDRIA

Questionum Super XII Libros Metaphisice. Venice: 1499. V. 37; 44

DOMINICUS DE SANCTO GEMINIANO

Prima Pars Lecture (Secunda Pars) Super Sexto Decretalium. (Lectures on the Decretals of Boniface VIII). Venetiis: 1502. V. 40

DOMINION of Canada Guide Book Containing Information for Intending Settlers. Ottawa: 1886. V. 44

DOMINIS, MARCO ANTONIO DE

A Manifestation of the Motives, Whereupon the Most Reuerend Father, Marcus Antonius de Dominis, Archbishop of Splatato . . . London: 1616. V. 39

A Sermon Preached in Italian . . . the First Sunday in Advent Anno 1617. London: 1617. V. 40

DOMINQUIN, LUIS MIGEL

Pablo Picasso. Toros y Toreros, et une Etude de Georges Boudaille. New York: 1961. V. 45

DOMVILLE-FIFE, C. W.

Square-Rigger Days - Autobiography of Sail Experiences of 38 Years Aloft of the Deep Sea Sailor . . . London: 1938. V. 41

DON, GEORGE

A General System of Gardening and Botany. London: 1831-37. V. 46

DON John Further Display'd: Being a Supplement to Considerations on the American Trade. London: 1740. V. 43

DON John, or Don Juan Unmasked. London: 1819. V. 42

DON Juan. Canto the Third. London: 1821. V. 42

DON Tomazo, or the Juvenile Rambles of Thomas Dangerfield. London: 1680. V. 39; 45

DONAGH, THOMAS

Last and Inspiring Address of Thomas MacDonagh. Dublin: 1916. V. 44

DONAGHEY, GEORGE W.

Autobiographical Sketch of George H. Donaghey. Little Rock. V. 43

DONAGHY, JOHN

Army Experience of Capt. John Donaghy 103rd Penn'a Vols. 1861-1864. Deland: 1926. V. 42

DONAGHY, LYLE

Into the Light, and Other Poems. Dublin: 1934. V. 39

DONAHEY, MARY DICKERSON

Peter and Paul, the Tale of the Runaways. Chicago: 1924. V. 42

DONAHOE, JAMES

Prince Edward Island Priests Who Have Laboured or are Labouring in the Sacred Ministry, Outside the Diocese of Charlottetown. St. Paul: 1912. V. 40

DONAHUE, H. E. F.

Conversations with Nelson Algren. New York: 1964. V. 43

DONALD, GEORGE

The Princess and Curdie. London: 1900. V. 43

DONALD, JAY

Outlaws of the Border a Complete and Authentic History of the Lives of Frank and Jesse James. Chicago: 1882. V. 44

Outlaws of the Border. Cincinnati: 1882. V. 39; 45

DONALDSON, ALFRED L.

A History of the Adirondacks. New York: 1921. V. 39; 43

DONALDSON, ASA

Conversations on Christian Baptism, Showing the Abrahamic Covenant to be a Gospel Covenant. Chicago: 1853. V. 40

DONALDSON, D.

Epic Fantasy in the Modern World. 1986. V. 44

DONALDSON, DIXON

Historical, Traditional and Descriptive Account of Islandmagee (Co. Antrim). Belfast;: 1927. V. 37

DONALDSON, FLORENCE

Lepcha Land or Six Weeks in the Sikhim Himalayas. London: 1900. V. 43; 44

DONALDSON, JAMES

Certain and Infallible Measures Laid Down Whereby the Whole Begging-Poor of the Kingdom May be Alimented at Much Less Charge than They are at Present. Edinburgh: 1701. V. 42

Modern Agriculture. Edinburgh: 1795-96. V. 38

DONALDSON, PETER

A Review of the Present Systems of Medicine and Chirurgery of Europe and America . . . New York: 1821. V. 37; 45

A Review of the Present Systems of Medicine and chirurgery of Europe and America . . . Viewed in Connexion with the most Refined Principles and Demonstrations of Anatomy, Physiology, pathology, Nosology, pharmacy, chemistry . . . New York: 1821. V. 37

DONALDSON SMITH, A.

Through Unknown African Countries. London: 1897. V. 41

DONALDSON, STEPHEN R.

The Chronicles of Thomas Covenant the Unbeliever. New York: 1977. V. 39; 42

DONALDSON, THOMAS

Extra Census Bulletin. Indians. Eastern Band of Cherokees of North Carolina. Washington: 1892. V. 41

The George Catlin Indian Gallery in the U.S. National Museum. Washington: 1886. V. 38

The George Catlin Indian Gallery in the U.S. National Museum (Smithsonian Institution) with Memoir and Statistics. Washington: 1887. V. 37; 39; 45

The Public Domain, Its History with Statistics, to June 30 and December 1, 1883. Washington: 1884. V. 41; 45

Report on Indians Taxed and Indians Not Taxed in the United States (Except Alaska) at the Eleventh Census. Washington: 1894. V. 37; 39

DONALDSON, THOMAS LEVERTON

Architectural Maxims and Theorems . . . and Lecture on the Education and Character of the Architect. London: 1847. V. 40

A Collection of the Most Approved Examples of Doorways from Ancient Buildings in Greece and Italy. London: 1833. V. 40; 44

DONALDSON, WILLIAM

North America, a Descriptive Poem. London: 1757. V. 40; 43

DONAN, P.

The Heart of the Continent: an Historical and Descriptive Treatise for Business Men, Home Sekkers and Tourists, of the Advantages, 'Resources and Scenery of the Great West. Chicago: 1882. V. 39

The Land of Golden Grain: North Dakota. Chicago: 1883. V. 43

DONATI, PAOLO

Theoriche Overo Speculationi Intorno Alli Moti Celesti. Venice: 1575. V. 46

DONATO D'EREMITA

Dell' Elixir Vitae Libri Quattro. Naples: 1624. V. 46

DONATUS, MARCELLUS

De Medicina Historia Mirabili Libri Sex Nunc Primum in Lucem Editi. Venetiis: 1588. V. 37

DONDERS, F. C.

New Researches on the Systems of Colour-Sense. Utrecht: 1882. V. 44

On the Anomalies of Accommodation and Refraction of the Eye. London: 1864. V. 42

DONDINI, GUGLIELMO

Carmina. Rome: 1653. V. 39

DONDIUS, HENRICUS

Grondige Onderrichtinge in de Optica, ofte Perspective Konste. Amsterdam: 1730. V. 43

DONI, ANTONIO FRANCESCO 1513-1574

Disegno, Partito in Piu Ragionamenti, ne Quali si Tratta della Scoltura et Pittura . . . Venice: 1549. V. 37; 38; 39

La Librari(a). (with) La Seconda Libraria. Venice: 1550-51. V. 41; 46

La Libreria, Divisa in Tre Trattati. Venice: 1558. V. 46

La Seconda Libraria . . . Ristampata Novamente con Giunta da Molti Libri. Viengia: 1555. V. 37; 46

La Zucca . . . Divisa in Cinque Libri di Gran Valore. Venice: 1589. V. 43

DONKIN, JOHN G.

Trooper and Redskin in the Far North-West. London: 1889. V. 41

DONKIN, ROBERT

Military Collections and Remarks. New York: 1777. V. 37; 38; 39; 40; 43

DONLEAVY, J. P.

The Destines of Darcy Dancer, Gentleman. 1977. V. 41

The Ginger Man. Paris. V. 42

The Ginger Man. Paris: 1955. V. 38; 39; 42; 43; 45; 46

The Ginger man. Paris: 1955. V. 42

The Ginger Man. London: 1956. V. 37; 42

The Ginger Man. New York: 1958. V. 42; 44

The Ginger Man. Paris: 1958. V. 41; 46

The Giner Man. Los Angeles: 1965. V. 44; 45

DONLEVY, ANDREW

The Catechism. Paris: 1742. V. 43

DONN, BENJAMIN

A Map of the County of Devon. London: 1765. V. 44

DONN, JAMES

Hortus Cantabrigiensis or an accented Catalogue of Indigenous and Exotic Plants Cultivated in the Cambridge Botanic Garden . . . London: 1845. V. 39

Hortus Cantabrigiensis . . . London: 1826. V. 43

DONNADIEU, A.

Catalogue of Highly Interesting and Valuable Autograph Letters and Historical Manuscripts Being the Well Known Collection of Monsr. A. Donnadieu. London: 1851. V. 39

DONNAN, ELIZABETH

Documents Illustrative of the History of the Slave Trade to America. Washington: 1930. V. 44

DONNANT, D. F.

Statistical Account of the United States of America . . . London: 1805. V. 45

DONNE, JOHN 1571-1631

An Anatomy of the World. Cambridge: 1951. V. 44

Biaeanatoe. A Declaration of that Paradoxe, or Thesis, that Self-Homicide is not so Naturally Sinne, that It May Never be Otherwise. London: 1646 or 1647. V. 45

Bianthantos. (In Greek Characters) a Declaration of that Paradox. London: 1648. V. 46

(Biathanatos, in Greek letters) A Declaration of that Paradox, or Thesis, That Self-Homicide is Not so Naturally Sin, That It May Never be Otherwise. London: 1700. V. 42

Complete Poetry and Selected Prose. London: 1929. V. 37; 39; 40; 45

Deaths Duell: a Sermon. Boston: 1973. V. 37; 46

A Declaration of the Paradoxe, or Thesis, that Selfe-Homicide is Not So Naturally Sinne, That It May Never Be Otherwise. London: 1644. V. 46

A Declaration of That Paradoxe, Or Thesis, That Self-Homicide is Not so Naturally Sin, That it May Never be Otherwise. London: 1648. V. 37

A Defence of Women for Their Inconstancy and Their Paintings. London: 1925. V. 41

Devotions Upon Emergent Occasions, and Several Steps in My Sickness. London: 1626. V. 39

Donne's Sermon of Valediction At His Going into Germany Preached at Lincoln's Inn April 18, 1619. London: 1932. V. 43; 46

Essayes in Divinity . . . London: 1651. V. 45

The Holy Sonnets of John Donne. London: 1938. V. 37; 41; 42; 43; 46

Holy Sonnets. Winchester: 1986. V. 46

Ignatius His Conclave; or, His Inthronation in a Late Election in Hell . . . London: 1634. V. 43; 45

Letters to Several Persons of Honour. London: 1651. V. 38; 43; 46

Letters to Severall Persons of Honour . . . London: 1654. V. 46

The Love Poems of John Donne. Boston: 1905. V. 45

The Love Poems . . . Boston: 1905. V. 39

The Love Poems of John Donne, with Some Account of His Life Taken from Writings in 1639 of Izaak Walton. London: 1923. V. 43

Love Poems of . . . Soho: 1923. V. 45

Paradoxes and Problems by John Donne With Two Characters and an Essay of Valour. London: 1923. V. 43

Paradoxes and Problems. Soho: 1923. V. 41; 46

Poems by J.D. with Elegies on the Authors Death. London: 1633. V. 38; 40; 43

Poems. London: 1635. V. 43; 46

Poems by J.D. With Elegies on the Authors Death. London: 1639. V. 39; 43; 45

Poems, by J.D. With Elegies on the Author's Death. London: 1650. V. 45

Poems, &c. With Elegies on the Authors Death. In the Savoy: 1669. V. 44

Poems &c. by John Donne . . . London: 1669. V. 39; 42; 43

Poems on Several Occasions; with Elegies on the Author's Death. (and) Some Account of the Life of the Author. London: 1719. V. 37; 41

Poems of John Donne, Selected From His Songs, Sonnets, Elegies, Letters, Satires and Divine Poems. New York: 1905. V. 40; 44

The Poems of John Donne. Cambridge: 1968. V. 45

The Poems. New York: 1968. V. 38

A Sermon, Preached to the Kings Mtie. at Whitehall, 24 Feb. 1625. London: 1626. V. 43

A Sermon Upon the Ninth Verse of the Thirty-Eighth Psalm. London: 1921. V. 41

The Sermons. 1953-62. V. 46

Six Sermons Upon Severall Occasions, Preached Before the King, and Elsewhere. Cambridge: 1634. V. 42

Six Poems from the Songs and Sonnets of John Donne. Austin: 1986. V. 37; 41

Songs and Sonets (sic). Paris: 1969. V. 41

X Sermons Preached by the late Learned and Rev. Divine John Donne. London: 1923. V. 37; 38; 39; 43; 46

The Works . . . with a Memoir of His Life. London: 1839. V. 46

DONNE, T. E.

The Game Animals of New Zealand. London: 1934. V. 43

DONNELL, A. J.

Cyclorama of Gen. Custer's Last Fight Against the Sioux Indians, or the Battle of the Little Big Horn. (Boston: 1889). V. 37

DONNELLAN, JOHN

The Life of Captain John Donnellan, Late Master of the Ceremonies at the Pantheon, Convicted of the Murder of Sir Theod. London: 1781. V. 42; 46

DONNELLE, A. J.

Cyclorama of Custer's Last Battle or the Battle of the Little Big Horn. Boston: 1889. V. 37

DONNELLY, EDWARD

The Manly Art of Self Defence. New York: 1886. V. 43
Ned Donnelly's Art of Boxing. New York: 1910. V. 43
Unparalleled Murder! N.P.: 1808. V. 45

DONNELLY, I.

Caesar's Column - a Story of the Twentieth Century. London: 1890. V. 44

DONNELLY, NED

The Art of Boxing . . . London: 1879. V. 46

DONNELY, IVON A.

Chinese Junks and Other Native Craft. Shanghai: 1924. V. 39

DONNER Miscellany. 41 Diaries and Documents. San Francisco: 1947. V. 46

DONNYBROOK Fair. Belfast: 1830. V. 46

DONOGHUE, STEPHEN

Donoghue Up! London: 1938. V. 42
Just My Story. London: 1923. V. 37

DONOHO, MILFORD H.

Circle-Dot: a True Story of Cowboy Life Forty Years Ago. Topeka: 1907. V. 42

DONOSO, JOSE

Charleston. 1977. V. 43
Charleston & Other Stories. Boston: 1977. V. 41; 42; 43; 44

DONOVAN, E.

Instructions for Collecting and Preserving Various Subjects of Natural History . . . London: 1794. V. 43; 45
The Natural History of British Fishes. London: 1802-8. V. 44
The Natural History of British Quadrupeds. London: 1820. V. 42
The Natural History of British Birds. London: 1820. V. 44

DONOVAN, EDWARD

Descriptive Excursions through South Wales and Monmouthshire, in the Year 1804, and the Four Preceding Summers. London: 1805. V. 41
An Epitome of the Insects of Asia. London: 1798-1805. V. 40
An Epitome of the Natural History of the Insects of China. London: 1798-1799. V. 37
Instructions for Collecting and Preserving Various Subjects of Natural History. London: 1794. V. 37; 40
The Natural History of the Nests and Eggs of British Birds. London: 1826. V. 38; 40
Natural History of the Insects of India. London: 1842. V. 38
The Natural History of British Birds. London: 1794-1819. V. 37; 39
The Natural History of British Birds. London: 1799. V. 41
The Natural History of British Fishes. London: 1802-08. V. 39; 41
The Natural History of British Fishes. London: 1806. V. 39
The Natural History of British Insects. London: 1792-1813. V. 39; 41
The Natural History of British Quadrupeds. London: 1820. V. 39; 41
Natural History of the Insects of India. London: 1842. V. 37; 39

DONOVAN, MICHAEL

Domestic Economy. London. V. 44; 46
Domestic Economy. London: 1830-37. V. 40

DONOVAN, MIKE

The Science of Boxing. New York: 1893. V. 43

DONTOPPIDAN, E.

The Natural History of Norway. London: 1755. V. 37

DONZELLINI, GIROLAMO d. 1588

Remedium Ferendarum Iniuriarum, Sive De Compescenda Ira . . . Venice: 1586. V. 40

DOOLITTLE, HILDA

Choruses from Iphigeneia in Aulis. London: 1916. V. 37
Collected Poems. New York: 1925. V. 37; 39; 40; 42
The Hedgehog. London: 1936. V. 37; 38
Hedylus. Boston: 1928. V. 37
Hedylus. Boston & New York: 1928. V. 40; 41; 42
Hippolytus Temporizes: a Play in Three Acts. Boston: 1927. V. 46
Hyman. New York: 1921. V. 37; 38; 39; 42
Palimpsest. Boston: 1926. V. 42
Palimpsest: by H. D. London: 1926. V. 40
Palimpsest. Paris: 1926. V. 37; 39; 42; 43
Red Roses for Bronze. Boston: 1931. V. 37
Red Roses for Bronze. London: 1931. V. 37
Sea Garden. London: 1916. V. 37; 38; 40; 42
Sea Garden: Imagist Poems. Boston/New York: 1917. V. 37
Temple of the Sun. N.P.: 1972. V. 39
The Walls do Not Fall, The Tribute to the Angels and The Flowering of the Rod. London: 1944. V. 37
The Walls Do Not Fall, Tribute to the Angels, and the Flowering of the Rod. London: 1944-46. V. 38; 41

DOOLITTLE, J. R.

Condition of the Indian Tribes. Washington: 1867. V. 41
Letter Printed from J. R. Doolittle: Sir. Racine: 1865. V. 41

DOOLITTLE, JAMES R.

Argument of the Hon. James R. Doolittle Upon the Validity of the Choctaw Claim, Submitted by Him as Counsel for the Choctaw Nation, to the Senate Committee on Indian Affairs, April, 1869. Washington: 1869. V. 43

DOOLITTLE, JUSTUS

Social Life of the Chinese; with Some Account of Their Religious, Governmental, Educational and Business Customs and Opinions. New York: 1865. V. 41; 42
Social Life of the Chinese . . . Regigious, Governmental, Educational and Business Customs and Opinions. London: 1866. V. 39

DOOLITTLE, LAURA SEYMOUR

Reflections and Memories. New Haven: 1949. V. 38; 41

DOORLY, ELEANOR

The Insect Man. London: 1936. V. 45

DOPPELMAYR, JOHANN GABRIEL

Historische Nachricht von den Nurnbergischen Mathematicis und Kunstlern . . . Nuremberg: 1730. V. 38; 44; 46

DOR DE LA SOUCHERE, ROMAULD

Picasso in Antibes. New York: 1960. V. 40

DORAN, DR.

Annals of the English Stage from Thomas Betterton to Edmund Kean. London: 1888. V. 40; 41

DORAN, JOHN

Habits and Men. London: 1855. V. 46
The History of Court Fools. London: 1858. V. 42; 44
In and About Drury Lane, and Other Papers, Reprinted from the Page of the 'Temple Bar Magazine. London: 1881. V. 42
'The Majesties' Servants' Annals of the English Stage from Thomas Betterton to Edmund Kean. London: 1888. V. 46
Table Traits with Something On Them. Boston. V. 44
Their Majesties Servants. London: 1864. V. 38; 39; 45
Their Majesties Servants. London: 1888. V. 37; 42; 43; 46
'Their Majesties' Servants.' Annals of the English Stage, from Thomas Betterton to Edmund Kean. London: W. H. Allen & Co.,: 1887. V. 37

DORAT, C. J.

Fables Nouvelles. Paris and the Hague: 1773. V. 38; 39; 40; 41

DORAT, CLAUDE JOSEPH

Les Baisers, Precedes du Mois de Mai, Poeme. La Haye & Paris: 1770. V. 41

DORBIN, SANFORD

A Bibliography of Charles Bukowski. 1969. V. 42

DORBRIZHOFFER, MARTIN

An Account of the Abipones, an Equestrian People of Paraguay. London: 1822. V. 42

DORE, GUSTAVE

The Bible Gallery. London: 1880. V. 43
The Dore Gallery of Scripture Illustrations. London: 1875. V. 46
London. New York: 1890. V. 46

DORE, GUSTAVE continued

Two Hundred Sketches, Humorous and Grotesque. London: 1867. V. 43

DORE, HENRI

Researches into Chinese Superstitions. Shanghai: 1914-22. V. 44; 45

DORE, J. R.

Old Bibles. London: 1888. V. 38; 40

DORE, PIERRE d. 1569

Le Pasturage de la Brebis Humaine . . . Paris: 1554. V. 38; 40

DOREY, JACQUES

Legendary Stories of Old Brittany, Normandy and Provence. New York: 1929. V. 41

DORING, ERNEST N.

The Guadagnini Family of Violin Makers. Chicago: 1949. V. 37
How Many Strads? Chicago: 1945. V. 38

DORLANDUS, PETRUS

Dialogus de Hominis Natura Seu Viola Animae: inter Raymundum Sebundium: Artium, Medicinae & Sacrae Theologiae Professorem Eximium, et Dominum Dominicum seminiverbium. Cologne: 1499. V. 37; 38; 40

D'ORLEANS, CHARLES

Poemes. Paris: 1950. V. 38

DORMAN, LONG & CO.

Steel Sections, Manufactured by Dorman, Long and Co., Limited, Middlesbrough, England. London: 1895. V. 44

DORMAN, MARCUS R. P.

A Tour in the Congo Free State. Brussels and London: 1905. V. 39; 45

DORMAN, WILLIAM HENRY

Results of a Series of Experiments on the Comparative Strength of Marriott & Atkinson's Boiler Plate Cast Steel, Lowmoor Iron and Puddled Steel, When Exposed to Tensile Transverse . . . London: 1862. V. 44

DORN, EDWARD

From Gloucester Out. London: 1964. V. 38; 39; 41
Gunslinger Book I & II. Los Angeles: 1968/69. V. 39; 41
The Gunslinger Book I & II. Los Angeles: 1968 & 1969. V. 41
Gunslinger Book I & II. Los Angeles: 1968, 1969. V. 37; 38
Hello, La Jolla. Berkeley: 1978. V. 39; 41
Hello, La Jolla. Berkeley: 1978. V. 38
Manchester Square. London: 1975. V. 39
The Shoshoneans, the People of the Basin-Plateau. New York: 1966. V. 46
Slinger. Berkeley: 1975. V. 38
What I See in the Maximus Poems. Ventura: 1960. V. 42
Yellow Lola. Santa Barbara: 1981. V. 38; 39; 41

DORN, GERHARD

Clavis Totius Philsophiae Chymisticae . . . Heborn: 1594. V. 46
Congeries Paracelsicae Chemiae de Transmutationibus Metallorum, Ex Omnibus Quae de his Ab Ipso Scripta Reperire Licuit Hactenus . . . Frankfurt: 1581. V. 46

DORNAU, CASPAR

Vlysses Scholasticvs, Hoc est, de Erroribvs, Qvi in Scholis Quas Appellant, Triuialibus, Admitturntur, Dissertatio Dvplex. Hanau: 1620. V. 42

DORNER, ALEXANDER

The Way Beyond 'Art'. The Work of Herbert Bayer. New York: 1947. V. 39

DORNFORD, JOSIAH

The Motives and Consequences of the Present War Impartially Considered. London: 1792. V. 39
Seven Letter to the Lords and Commons of Great Britain, Upon the Impolicy, Inhumanity, and Injustice of Our Present Mode of Arresting the Bodies of Debtors . . . London: 1786. V. 41
Seven Letters to the Lords and Commons of Great Britain. London: 1787. V. 40

DOROTHY, TERENCE

The Anatomical Works of George Stubbs. London: 1974. V. 46

DORR, NELL

In a Blue Moon. New York: 1939. V. 45

DORRINGTON, THEOPHILUS d. 1715

Observations Concerning the Present State of Religion, in the Romish Church, with Some Reflections Upon Them. London: 1699. V. 39

D'ORS, EUGENIO

Pablo Picasso. Paris & New York: 1930. V. 41; 46

DORSET, CAHTERINE ANN

The Peacock at Home. The Butterfly's Ball; and the Fancy Fair. London: 1840. V. 39

DORSET, CATHERINE ANN

The Peacock at Home and Other Poems. London: 1809. V. 42
The Peacocks 'At Home' & The Butterfly's Ball. London: 1834. V. 46
The Peacock 'At Home', The Butterfly's Ball & the Fancy Fair. London: 1845. V. 46
The Peacock at Home. London;: 1851. V. 37
Think Before You Speak, or the Three Wishes. Londn: 1823. V. 39

DORSEY, GEORGE

The Arapaho Sun Dance: The Ceremony of the Offerings Lodge. Chicago: 1903. V. 38; 39

DORSEY, GEORGE A.

The Cheyenne. Part I. The Sun Dance, Part II. Ceremonial Organization. Chicago: 1905. V. 45

DORSEY, HUGH M.

Argument of Hugh M. Dorsey, Solicitor-General, Atlanta Judicial Circuit, at the Trial of Leo M. Frank . . . Murder of Mary Phagan. Atlanta: 1914. V. 44

DORSEY, JOHN SYNG

Elements of Surgery: for the Use of Students: With Plates. Philadelphia: 1818. V. 42

DORSEY, SARAH ANNE

Recollections of Henry Watkins Allen, Brigadier-General Confederate States Army, Ex-Governor of Louisiana. New York: 1866. V. 45

DORST, J.

The Life of Birds. New York: 1981, 1971. V. 39

DORSTEN, THEODRICH

Botanicon. Frankfurt: 1540. V. 37

DORTU, M. G.

Toulouse-Lautrec et son Oeuvre. V. 44
Toulouse-Lautrec et son Oeuvre. New York: 1971. V. 41

DOS PASSOS, JOHN RODERIGO

Adventures of a Young Man. 1939. V. 37
Airways, Inc. New York: 1928. V. 38; 41; 42
The Big Money. London: 1936. V. 41; 42
The Big Money. New York: 1936. V. 37; 41
The Big Money. New York: 1960. V. 43
Chosen Country. London: 1952. V. 43
Facing the Chair. Boston: 1927. V. 38; 39; 41; 42
The 42nd Parallel. New York: 1930. V. 39; 42; 46
The Head and the Heart of Thomas Jefferson. New York: 1954. V. 38; 39
Manhattan Transfer. New York: 1925. V. 45
Mid-Century. Boston: 1961. V. 45
Most Likely to Succeed. New York: 1954. V. 41; 42
1919. New York: 1932. V. 37; 38; 39; 41; 45
One Man's Initiation - 1917. London: 1920. V. 44; 46
Orient Express. London: 1928. V. 38
Panama or the Adventures of My Seven Uncles. New York: 1931. V. 39
A Pushcart at the Curb. New York: 1922. V. 43
Three Soldier's. New York: 1921. V. 37; 38; 39; 42
Tour of Duty. Boston: 1946. V. 38; 39
The U.S.A. Trilogy . . . 1946. V. 45
U.S.A. The 42nd Parallel, Nineteen Nineteen, The Big Money. Boston: 1946. V. 37; 43
The Villages Are the Heart of Spain. Chicago: 1937. V. 43

DOSSIE, R.

The Handmaid to the Arts. London: 1764. V. 37

DOSSIE, ROBERT

The Elaboratory Laid Open, or, the Secrets of Modern Chemistry and Pharmacy Revealed . . . London: 1758. V. 42; 45
The Handmaiden to the Arts. London: 1758. V. 38; 41

DOSTOEVSKII, FEDOR MIKHAILOVICH 1821-1881

The Brothers Karmazov. New York: 1933. V. 41
The Brothers Karmazov. Brattleboro: 1949. V. 44
The Brothers Karamazov. New York: 1949. V. 45
Buried Alive or Ten Years of Penal Servitude in Siberia. New York: 1881. V. 38; 40; 45
Prestupleniye I Nakazaniye . . . (Crime and Punishment). Petersburg: 1867. V. 42

DOSTOEVSKII, FEDOR MIKHAILOVICH 1821-1881 continued

Crime and Punishment. Brattleboro: 1948. V. 44

Crime and Punishment. New York: 1948. V. 40; 45

A Gentle Spirit. 1931. V. 40

The Grand Inquisitor. London: 1930. V. 42

The House of the Dead. New York: 1982. V. 43

The Idiot. New York: 1956. V. 43; 44

Besy. (The Possessed) St. Petersburg: 1873. V. 42

The Possessed. New York: 1959. V. 43

A Raw Youth. Verona: 1974. V. 45

Stavrogin's Confession and The Plan of the Life of a Great Sinner. Richmond: 1922. V. 40

DOSTOEVSKII, FEODOR MIKHAILOVICH 1821-1881

A Gentle Spirit: a Fantastic Story. New York: 1931. V. 46

A Gentle Spirit: A Fantistic Story. Paris: 1931. V. 46

DOSTOEVSKY, FYODOR

A Gentle Spirit. 1931. V. 37

The Grand Inquisitor. London: 1930. V. 39

The House of the Dead. 1982. V. 38

A Raw Youth. New York: 1974. V. 38; 46

Stavrogin's Confession and the Plan of the Life of a Great Sinner. London: 1922. V. 38

DOSTOYEVSKY, FYODOR

Buried Alive. London: 1881. V. 38

DOSWETT, J. MOREWOOD

Big Game and Big Life. London: 1925. V. 42; 45

DOTHAN, TRUDE

The Philistines and Their Material Culture. New Haven: 1982. V. 40; 42

DOTTER, CHARLES

Angiocardiography. New York: 1952. V. 42

DOTTERER, HENRY S.

The Perklomen Region, Past and Present. Philadelphia: 1895-1900. V. 42

DOTY, ROBERT

Photo Secession. Photography as a Fine ARt. Rochester: 1960. V. 46

DOUAT, DOMINIQUE

Methode Pour Faire une Infinite de Desseins. Paris: 1722. V. 40; 44

DOUBLEDAY, ARTHUR

Victoria History of the County of Hampshire and Isle of Wight. London: 1900-14. V. 37

DOUBLEDAY, RHODA VAN BIBBER TANNER

Journals of the Late Brevet Major Philip Norbourne Barbour and His Wife Martha Isabella Hopkins Barbour. New York: 1936. V. 42

DOUBLEDAY, THOMAS 1790-1870

A Financial, Monetary and Statistical History of England from the Revolution of 1688 to the Present Time. London: 1847. V. 38; 39; 43

A Financial, Monetary and Statistical History of England. London: 1858. V. 42

Matter for Materialists: a Series of Letters in Vindication and Extension of the Principles Regarding the Nature of Existence of the Right Rev. Dr. Berkeley. London: 1870. V. 41; 43

DOUCE, FRANCIS

The Dance of Death Exhibited in Elegant Engravings on Wood. London: 1833. V. 38; 42; 43

Illustrations of Shakespare, and of Ancient Manners . . . London: 1807. V. 43

Illustrations of Shakespeare, and of Ancient Manners . . . London: 1839. V. 43

DOUCET, JEROME

Contes de Haute-Lisse. N.P.: 1899. V. 44

La Grande Douleur des Sept Artistes. Paris: 1923. V. 46

Six Belles Histoires de Chasse. Paris: 1907. V. 41

DOUDNEY, SARAH

The Missing Rubies: a Novel. London: 1887. V. 44

Thistle-Down. London. V. 40

DOUGAL, J. D.

Shooting Simplified. Concise Treatise on Guns and Shooting. London: 1865. V. 37

DOUGALL, JOHN

The Modern Preceptor; or, a General Course of Education . . . Manchester: 1810. V. 42

DOUGHARTY, JOHN

The General Gauger; or, the Principles and Practice of Gauging Beer, Wine and Malt . . . London: 1727. V. 44

The General Gauger: or, the Principles and Practice of Gauging Beer, Wine and Malt. London: 1750. V. 37; 39

DOUGHTY, A.

The Siege of Quebec and the Battle of the Plains of Abraham. Quebec: 1901. V. 44

DOUGHTY, ARTHUR

Notes on the History of Canada Prepared for the Visit of His Royal Highness The Prince of Wales Under the Direction of the Public Archives, Ottawa. Ottawa: 1919. V. 40

DOUGHTY, ARTHUR G.

The Elgin-Grey Papers. Ottawa: 1937. V. 45

Helen and Aphrodite. Done Into Blank Verse from the Greek Books. Montreal: 1894. V. 37

Under the Lily and the Rose. Toronto & London: 1931. V. 43

DOUGHTY, CHARLES M.

The Dawn in Britain. London: 1906. V. 40

DOUGHTY, CHARLES MONTAGU 1843-1926

Adam Cast Forth. London: 1908. V. 41

Arabia Deserta. Baltimore: 1953. V. 45

Arabia Deserta. 2 Volumes. Introduction by T.E. Lawrence. New York: 1937. V. 37

The Clouds. London: 1912. V. 45

The Dawn in Britain. London: 1906. V. 44; 45; 46

Mansoul or the Riddle of the World. London: 1923. V. 40; 44; 45

The Titans. London: 1916. V. 44

Travels in Arabia Deserta. New York. V. 43

Travels in Arabia Deserta. Cambridge: 1888. V. 38; 40; 43

Travels in Arabia Deserta. London: 1923. V. 46

Travels in Arabia Deserta. London: 1936. V. 40; 41

Travels in Arabia Deserta. London: 1943. V. 42; 44; 46

Travels in Arabia Deserta. New York: 1953. V. 44; 45

Travels in Arabia Deserta. By Charles M. Doughty. New York: 1937. V. 37

Wanderings in Arabia. London: 1908. V. 41

DOUGHTY, CHARLES MONTAGUE 1843-1926

Mansoul, or the Riddle of the World. London: 1920. V. 39

Travels in Arabia Deserta. London: 1921. V. 39; 43

Travels in Arabia Deserta. London: 1928. V. 39

Travels in Arabia Deserta. London: 1928, 1921. V. 38

Travels in Arabia Derserta. London: 1936, 1943. V. 39

Travels in Arabia Deserta. London: 1949. V. 38; 42

DOUGHTY, J.

Some Early American Hunters, Being Stories from the Cabinet of Natural History and American Rural Sports . . . New York: 1928. V. 46

DOUGHTY, JOHN

The Cabinet of Natural History and American Rural Sports. Philadelphia: 1830-32. V. 42; 43

DOUGHTY, LUCY E.

Pioneers Across the Continent of Our Ancestors & Their Descendants. Bay City: 1935. V. 38

Pioneers Across the Continent or Out Ancestors & Their Descendants. Bay City, OR: (1935). V. 37

DOUGHTY, MARION

Afoot Through the Kashmir Valleys. London: 1902. V. 40; 42; 46

DOUGLAS, A.

Cumberland, Westmorland, Gloucestershire. London: 1986. V. 39

DOUGLAS, ALFRED

City of the Soul. London: 1899. V. 37; 38; 42; 43

The Collected Poems of Lord Alfred Douglas. London: 1919. V. 46

The Collected Satires. London: 1926. V. 42

In Excelsis. London: 1924. V. 41; 46

Lyrics. London: 1935. V. 44

The Murder of Lord Kitchener and the Truth About the Battle of Jutland and the Jews . . . Galashiels: 1923. V. 46

My Friendship with Oscar Wilde. New York: 1932. V. 38

Poems. (Poemes.) Paris: 1896. V. 42

DOUGLAS, ROBERT kENNAWAY

The Language and Literature of China. London: 1875. V. 37; 43

Society in China. London: 1894. V. 43

DOUGLAS, ROBERT THOMAS

Jerubaal; or, a Vindication of the Sober Testimony Against Sinful Complyance, from the Exceptions of Mr. Tombs . . . London: 1668. V. 44

DOUGLAS, STEPHEN

A Bill for the Admission of the STate of Iowa Into the Union. Washington: 1846. V. 46

A Bill to Define the Boundaries of the States of Iowa. Washington: 1846. V. 46

DOUGLAS, STEPHEN A.

Remarks Of the Hon. . . . On Kansas, Utah, and the Dred Scott Decision, Delivered at Springfield Illinois, June 12th, 1857. Chicago: 1857. V. 42

DOUGLAS, STUART

A Military Dissertation, Containing a Plan for Recruiting the British Army, and Improvings Its Establishment . . . London: 1781. V. 42

DOUGLAS, SYLVESTER

Reports of Cases Argued and Determined in the Court of King's Bench, in the 19th, 20th and 21st Years of the Reign of George III. Philadelphia: 1807. V. 39

DOUGLAS, WALTER B.

Manuel Lisa. St. Louis: 1964. V. 44

DOUGLAS, WILLIAM

Duelling Days in the Army. London: 1887. V. 43

A Summary, Historical and Political, of the First Planting, Progressive Improvements, and Present State of the British Settlements in North-America. London: 1760. V. 37

DOUGLAS, WILLIAM FETTES

Catalogue of the Valuable Library in Antiquarian, Art and Scottish Literature. Edinburgh: 1891. V. 45

DOUGLASS, FREDERIC

National Convention of Colored Men at Louisville, Ky., September 25, 1883. Louisville: 1883. V. 45

DOUGLASS, FREDERICK

Life and Times of Frederick Douglass from 1817 to 1882. London: 1882. V. 41

My Bondage and My Freedom. New York: 1855. V. 43

My Bondage and My Freedom. New York: & Auburn: 1855. V. 44

Narrative of the Life of Frederick Douglasss, an American Slave. Boston: 1845. V. 39; 40; 41

Narrative of the Life of Frederick Douglass, an American Slave. Boston: 1849. V. 41

Oration Delivered in Corinthian Hall, Rochester, By Frederick Douglasss. Rochester: 1852. V. 41

Speeches of Hon. Frederick Douglass, and Robert G. Ingersoll. Washington: 1883. V. 41

DOUGLASS, MARGARET

Educational Laws of Virginia. Boston & Cleveland: 1854. V. 42

DOUGLASS, WILLIAM 1691-1752

A Discourse Concerning the Currencies of the British Plantations in America. London: 1741. V. 41

Discourse Concerning the Currencies of the British Plantations in America. London: 1741? V. 41

A Summary, Historical and Political of the First Planting, Progressive Improvements and Present State of the British Settlements in North America. Boston: 1752. V. 40

A Summary, Historical and Political, of the First Planting, Progressive Improvements, and Present State of the British Settlements in North America. London: 1755. V. 39; 43

A Summary, Historical and Political, of the First Planting, Progressive Improvements and Present State of the British Settlements in North America. London: 1760. V. 38; 41; 42; 44; 45

DOUMAS, C.

Thera and the Aegean World: Papers Presented at the Second International Scientific Congress, Santorini, Greece, August 1978. London: 1980. V. 42; 44

DOURNOVO, LYDIA A.

Armenian Miniatures. New York: 1961. V. 38; 41

DOUSA, JAN VAN d. 1571

Bataviae Hollandiaeque Annales. Antwerp: 1601. V. 40

DOUTHIT, MARY OSBORN

The Souvenir of Western Women. Portland: 1905. V. 38; 43

DOUXMENIL d. 1778?

The Memoirs of Ninon DE L'Enclos, with Her Letters to Monsr. de ST. Evremond and to Marquis de Sevigne. London: 1761. V. 42; 45

The Memoirs of Ninon de l'Enclos, with her Letters to Monsr. de St. Evremond and to the Marquis de Sevigne. Dublin: 1762. V. 45; 46

The Memoirs of Ninon De L'Enclos, with Her Letters to Monsr. de ST. Evremont and . . . Marquis de Sevigne. London: 1776. V. 45

The Memoirs of Ninon de l'Enclos: with Her Letters to Mons. de St. Evremond, and to the Marquis de Sevigne. Dublin: 1778. V. 41; 42

The Memoirs of Ninon de l'Enclos. Dublin: 1778. V. 38

The Memoirs of Ninon de l'Enclos: with Her Letters to Mons De St. Evermond, and to the Marquis de Sevigne. Dublin: 1788. V. 38

DOVAR, THOMAS

The Ancient Physician's Legacy to His Country. London: 1733. V. 40; 44

DOVASTON, JOHN

The Harp of the Beech Woods. Montrose: 1822. V. 39; 46

DOVASTON, JOHN F. M.

Poems, Legendary, Incidental and Humorous. Shrewsbury: 1825. V. 40

DOVASTON, JOHN FREEMAN MILWARD

Floribelle; or, the Tale of the Foreste, a Balla: in Four Parts. Oxford: 1803. V. 45

DOVE at the Windows: Last Letters of Four Quaker Martyrs. Lincoln: 1973. V. 38

DOVE, H. W.

The Distribution of Heat Over the Surface of the Globe. London: 1853. V. 40; 45

The Law of Storms. London: 1862. V. 40

DOVE, P. EDWARD

Domesday Commemoration 1086 A.D. - 1886 A.D. London: 1888-91. V. 43

DOVER, THOMAS

The Ancient Physician's Legacy to His Country, Being What He Has Collected in Forty-Nine Years Practice . . . V. 42

The Ancient Physician's Legacy to His Country. London: 1733. V. 39

DOVES PRESS

Catalogue Raisonne of Books Printed and Published at the Doves Press, 1900-1911. Hammersmith: 1911. V. 39

Catalogue Raisonne of Books Printed and Published at the Doves Press No. 1. The Terrace Hammersmith. Hammersmith: 1908. V. 37; 38; 39; 41

Catalogue Raisonne of Books Printed & Published at the Doves Press No 1. the Terrace Hammersmith. London: 1908. V. 37; 43; 44

Catalogue Raisonee of Books Printed and Projected at the Doves Press 1900-1913. London: 1913. V. 43

Catalogue Raisonne of Books Printed and Published at the Doves Press, 1900-1916. Hammersmith: 1916. V. 37

Catalogue Raisonne of Books Printed & Published at the Doves Press 1900-1916. London: 1916. V. 37

DOVIE, JAMES FRANK

Bigfoot Wallace and the Hickory Nuts. V. 46

DOW, ALEXANDER

The History of Hindostan; from the Earliest Account of Time, to the Death of Akabar . . . . London: 178. V. 38

DOW, DANIEL

A Dissertation, on the Sinaitic and Abrahamic Covenants . . . Hartford: 1811. V. 43

DOW, GEORGE FFRANCIS

Slave Ships and Slaving, an Account of the Adventure of the Blackest Page in the Chronicles of the Sea, the Trade as Conducted by America and the Principle Maritime Nations at Different Periods. Salem: 1927. V. 41

DOW, GEORGE FRANCIS

The Arts and Crafts of New England 1704-1775, Gleanings from Boston Newspapers Relating to Painting, Engraving, Silversmiths, Pewterers, Clockmakers, Furniture, Pottery . . . Topsfield, Ma.: 1927. V. 37

Essex County Massachusetts. Topsfield: 1921. V. 46

The Pirates of the New England Coast 1630-1730. Salem: 1923. V. 37; 39

Slave Ships and Slaving. Salem: 1927. V. 37; 39; 43; 44; 45

Whale Ships and Whaling: a Pictorial History of Whaling During Three Centuries. Salem: 1925. V. 37; 39; 41; 44; 45

DOW, JOSEPH

History of the Town of Hampton, New Hampshire. V. 44

DOW, LORENZO

All the Polemical Works of Lorenzo (and) History of Cosmopolite; or the Four Volumes of Lorenzo's Journal. New York: 1814. V. 40

DOWSON, ERNEST continued

Dilemmas - Stories and Studies in Sentiment. London: 1895. V. 40; 43

New Letters. (Andoversford): (1984). V. 37

The Pierrot of the Minute. London: 1897. V. 37; 40; 43

The Pierrot of the Minute. New York: 1923. V. 37; 40; 45

The Poems of Ernest Dowson. London: 1905. V. 37; 46

DOWSON, ERNEST CHRISTOPHER

The Poetical Works of Ernest Christopher Dowson. London: 1934. V. 41

DOWSON, ROSINA

Three Japanese Plays for Children. Oxford: 1897. V. 46

DOWTY, AGLEN A.

The Coming K---. N.P.: 1873. V. 45

DOYLE, ADRIAN CONAN

Sir Arthur Conan Doyle Centenary 1859-1959. London: 1959. V. 38

DOYLE, ARTHUR CONAN 1859-1930

The Adventure of Charles Augustus Milverton. Chicago: 1911. V. 46

Adventures of Gerard. London. V. 40

The Adventures of Sherlock Holmes. London: 1892. V. 37; 38; 40; 41; 43; 44; 45; 46

The Adventures of Sherlock Holmes. London: 1892. V. 46

Adventures of Sherlock Holmes. New York: 1892. V. 39; 46

The Adventures of Sherlock Holmes. (with) The Memoirs of Sherlock Holmes. London: 1892, 1894. V. 40; 41

The Adventures of Sherlock Holmes. The Memoirs of Sherlock Holmes. London: 1892/94. V. 44; 45

The Adventures of Sherlock Holmes. (with) Memoirs of Sherlock Holmes. London: 1892-94. V. 37; 42; 43; 44

Adventures of Sherlock Holmes (with) Memoirs of Sherlock Holmes. London: 1892/94. V. 45

The Adventures of Sherlock Holmes. London: 1894. V. 42

Adventures of Sherlock Holmes. London: 1903. V. 46

The Adventures of Sherlock Holme. The Adventures of the Blue Carbuncle . . . New York: 1948. V. 39

The Adventures of Sherlock Holmes. New York: 1950. V. 38

The Adventures (Later Adventures . . . Final Adventures) . . . of Sherlock Holmes . . . New York: 1950-52. V. 42

The Adventures of Sherlock Holmes. The Later Adventures of Sherlock Holmes. The Final Adventures of Sherlock Holmes. New York: 1950-52. V. 38; 44

The Adventures of Sherlock Holmes/ The Later Adventures of Sherlock Holmes/ The Final Adventures of Sherlock Holmes. Verona: 1950-53. V. 44

The Adventures of Sherlock Holmes and the Memoirs of Sherlock Holmes. Tokyo: 1986. V. 39; 40

The Annotated Sherlock Holmes. The Four Novels and Fifty-Six Short Stories Complete. New York: 1967. V. 37; 38

The Annotated Sherlock Holmes: The Four Novels and the Fifty-Six Short Stories, Complete, by Sir Arthur Conan Doyle. Edited with an Introduction, Notes and a Bibliography by William Baring-Gould. 1967. V. 37

The British Campaign in France and Flanders. Maps. London: 1914-18/1916-20. V. 46

The British Campaign in France and Flanders. London: 1916-20. V. 42; 45; 46

The Captain of the Polestar. London: 1890. V. 39; 41; 42; 46

The Case of Oscar Slater. New York: 1912. V. 40

The Case-Book of Sherlock Holmes. London: 1927. V. 39; 40; 42; 43

The Coming of the Fairies. New York: 1922. V. 39

The Coming of the Fairies. 1928. V. 43

The Complete Sherlock Holmes. Garden City: 1953. V. 43

The Complete Sherlock Holmes. New York: 1956. V. 46

The Complete Sherlock Holmes Long Stories. London: (1977). V. 37

The Croxley Master. New York: 1907. V. 46

Danger! And Other Stories. 1919. V. 37

The Doings of Raffles Haw. Chicago: 1891. V. 39

The Doings of Raffles Haw (and) a Study in Scarlet. New York: 1891. V. 41

The Doings of Raffles Haw. London: Paris &: 1892. V. 44

Dreamland and Ghostland; an Original Collection of Tales and Warnings from the Borderland . . . London: 1887. V. 42

A Duet with an Occasional Chorus. Toronto: 1899. V. 45

The Edge of the Unknown. London: 1930. V. 46

The Edge of the Unknown. New York: and London: 1930. V. 43

English Traits. Boston: 1856. V. 42

The Exploits of Brigadier Gerard. London: 1896. V. 45; 46

The Field Bazaar. New Jersey: 1947. V. 43

The Final Adventures of Sherlock Holmes. New York: 1952. V. 45

The Firm of Girdlestone. New York: 1889. V. 41

The Firm of Girdlestone. London: 1890. V. 43

The Four Quartets. New York: 1943. V. 37

The Great Shadow and Beyond the City. London: 1892/3. V. 41

The Great Shadow and Beyond the City. Bristol: 1893. V. 43; 46

The Great Boer War. New York: 1900. V. 42

The Great Boer War. London: 1902. V. 41; 42

Great Britain and the Next War. Boston: 1914. V. 42

The Great Shadow & Beyong the City. Bristol: (1893). V. 37

The Green Flag and Other Stories of War and Sport. London: 1900. V. 39; 41; 42; 43

The Guards Came Through and Other Poems. London: 1919. V. 43

The Gully of Bluemansdyke, and Other Stories. London: 1894. V. 42

His Last Bow: Some Reminiscences of Sherlock Holmes. 1917. V. 39

His Last Bow. London: 1917. V. 37; 39; 40; 42; 44; 45; 46

His Last Bow. New York: 1917. V. 42

The History of Spiritualism. London: 1926. V. 38; 43; 45

The History of Spiritualism. London: etc.,: 1926. V. 39

The History of Spiritualism. New York: 1926. V. 40

The History of Spiritualism. London: (1926). V. 37

The Hound of the Baskervilles. 1902. V. 39; 45

The Hound of the Baskervilles. London: 1902. V. 39

The Hound of the Baskervilles. London: 1902. V. 37; 39; 40; 42; 43; 44; 45

The Hound of the Baskervilles. New York: 1902. V. 39; 42; 46

The Hound of the Baskervilles. Toronto: 1902. V. 39

The Hound of the Baskervilles. 1985. V. 42; 45

The Hound of Baskervilles. San Francisco: 1985. V. 44

The Hound of the Baskervilles. San Francisco: 1985. V. 37; 38; 39; 40; 41; 42; 44

The Last of the Legions and Other Tales of Long Ago. New York: 1922. V. 41; 42

The Later Adventures of Sherlock Holmes. New York: 1952. V. 45

The Lost World. London: 1912. V. 40; 42; 43; 44; 45; 46

The Lost World. New York: 1912. V. 46

The Lost World. 1912. V. 37; 39

The Maracot Deep. Garden City: 1929. V. 46

The Maracot Deep, and Other Stories. London: 1929. V. 42

The Memoirs of Sherlock Holmes. Leipzig: 1894. V. 46

Memoirs of Sherlock Holmes. London: 1894. V. 37; 38; 39; 41; 42; 43; 45; 46

Memoirs of Sherlock Holmes. New York: 1894. V. 41; 42; 45; 46

Memoirs of Sherlock Holmes. New York: 1894/1893. V. 44

The Memoirs of Sherlock Holmes. London: 1894 (1893). V. 37

The Memoirs of Sherlock Holmes. (with) The Adventures of Sherlock Holmes. London: 1893-94. V. 37

Memories and Adventures. Boston: 1924. V. 41; 42; 43

Memories and Adventures. London: (1924). V. 37

Micah Clarke. London: 1889. V. 42; 43

Micah Clarke. New York: 1894. V. 41

My Friend the Murder and Other Mysteries and Adventures. New York: 1893. V. 39; 41

The New Revelation. New York: 1918. V. 43

The New Revelation. 1918. V. 37

Our American Adventure. New York: 1923. V. 46

Our African Winter. Toronto: 1929. V. 38

The Parasite. London: 1894. V. 39; 42

The Parasite. Westminster: 1894. V. 38; 40

The Parasite. London: 1897. V. 40

The Parasite. Westminsnter: 1897. V. 39

The Poison Belt. 1912. V. 44; 45

The Poison Belt. London: 1913. V. 37

The Return of Sherlock Holmes. London: 1905. V. 42; 44

The Return of Sherlock Holmes. New York: 1905. V. 39; 41; 42

Rodney Stone. London: 1896. V. 43

Round the Red Lamp. London: 1894. V. 37; 39; 42; 44

Round the Fire Stories. London: 1908. V. 43

The Complete Sherlock Holmes. New York: 1950-52. V. 39

The Complete Sherlock Holmes. London: 1953. V. 42

The Sherlock Holmes Collected Edition. London: 1974. V. 42

Sherlock Holmes. The Complete Short Stories. London: 1980. V. 44

Sherlock Holmes . . . The Complete Short Novels. London: (1980). V. 37

The Sign of Four. London: 1890. V. 41

The Sign of the Four. London: 1892. V. 42

The Sign of the Four. New York: 1894. V. 41; 46

Sir Arthur Conan Doyle Centenarry 1859-1959. Garden City: 1959. V. 46

The Stark Munro Letters. 1895. V. 39

The Stark Munro Letters. London: 1895. V. 37; 38; 39; 40; 41; 43; 44; 46

DOYLE, ARTHUR CONAN 1859-1930 continued

The Story of British Prisoners. London: 1915. V. 46

A Study in Scarlet. London: 1888. V. 40; 42

A Study in Scarlet. London: 1891. V. 42

A Study in Scarlet. New York: 1893. V. 42

A Study in Scarlet. London: 1987. V. 43

Tales of Sherlock Holmes. New York: 1906. V. 44

Three of Them: a Reminiscence. London: 1923. V. 43

Through the Magic Door. New York: 1908. V. 43

The Tragedy of Korosko. London: 1898. V. 38; 39; 40; 43; 45

Uncle Bernac. London: 1897. V. 37; 39; 40; 41; 43

The Valley of Fear. 1914. V. 39

The Valley of Fear. New York: 1914. V. 39; 45

The Valley of Fear. London: 1915. V. 37; 39; 41; 42; 43; 44; 45

The Valley of Fear. New York: 1916. V. 42

A Vist to Heaven. 1899. V. 43

The Wanderings of a Spiritualist. New York: 1921. V. 46

The White Company. London. V. 40

The White Company. London: 1891. V. 38; 40; 41; 43; 44

The White Company. New York: 1891. V. 41

The White Company. New York: 1922. V. 37; 38; 45

The Works. London: 1903. V. 44; 46

The Crowborough Edition of the Works of Arthur Conan Doyle. Garden City: 1930. V. 46

The Crowborough Edition of the Works. New York: 1930. V. 42

The Works. New York: 1930. V. 42

DOYLE, BERNARD W.

Comb Making in America. Boston: 1925. V. 40

DOYLE, FRANCIS HASTINGS

The Two Destinies. London: 1844. V. 43

DOYLE, J. B.

Tours in Ulster. Dublin: 1854. V. 46

DOYLE, JAMES

Letters on the State of Education in Ireland, and on Bible Societies, Addressed to a Friend in England. Dublin: 1824. V. 41

DOYLE, JAMES E.

A Chronicle of England B.C. 55 A.D. 1485. London: 1864. V. 37; 38; 39; 41; 42; 43; 44; 46

The Official Baronage of England, Showing the Succession, Dignities, and Offices of Every Peer from 1066 to 1885. London: 1886. V. 41

DOYLE, JAMES WARREN

Letter on the State of Ireland Addressed by J. K. L. to a friend in England. Dublin: 1825. V. 46

DOYLE, JOHN

Political Sketches &c. London: 1831. V. 40; 46

DOYLE, JOHN A.

The English in America. The Puritan Colonies. London: 1887. V. 45

The Middle Colonies. (with) The Colonies Under the House of Hanover. London: 1907. V. 45

DOYLE, JOSEPH B.

Frederick William Von Steuben and the American Revolution, Aide to Washington and Inspector General of the Army. Steubenville: 1913. V. 46

DOYLE, MARTIN

An Address to the Landlords of Ireland, on Subjects Connected with the Melioration of the Lower Classes. Dublin: 1831. V. 39

Hints Originally Intended for the Small Farmers of the County of Wexford . . . Dublin: 1832. V. 45

DOYLE, PATRICK

A Contribution to Burman Mineralogy. Calcutta: 1879. V. 41

Papermaking in India. Lucknow: 1885. V. 38

Petroleum: Its History, Origin and Use . . . Brisbane: 1880. V. 41

DOYLE, RICHARD

Fairyland Pictures from the Elf World. London: 1875. V. 41

Fairyland, a Series of Pictures from the Elf-World. London: 1975. V. 45

The Foreign Tour of Messrs. Brown, Jones and Robinson, Being the History of What They Saw, and Did, in Belgium, Germany, Switzerland, and Italy. London: 1854. V. 39; 41

In Fairyland. London: 1875. V. 38

Jack the Giant-Killer. London: 1880. V. 42; 46

Jack the Giant Killer. London. V. 37

Jack the Giant Killer. London: (1888). V. 37

Manner and Customs of ye Englyshe. London: 1850. V. 42

Manners and Customs of ye Englyshe. London: 1849. V. 38; 45

Manners and Customs of Ye Englyshe Drawn from Ye Quick by Richard Doyle. London: 1849-50. V. 37; 40; 43

Richard Doyle's Pictures of Extra Articles and Visitors to the Exhibition. London: 1851? V. 38

Scenes from English History. London: 1866. V. 39

The Story of Jack and the Giants. London: 1851. V. 45

DOYLEY, CHARLES

The European in India. London: 1813. V. 38

D'OYLY, CHARLES

Tom Raw. The Griffin. London: 1828. V. 43; 44

DOYNE, PHILIP

Irene, a Canto, on the Peace . . . Dublin: 1763. V. 38

Irene, a Canto, on the Peace; Written in the Stanza of Spencer. Dublin: 1763. V. 40; 42

The Triumph of Parnassus, a Poem. Dublin: 1763. V. 38; 40; 42

DOZIER, HOWARD

A History of the Atlantic Coast Line Railroad. Boston: 1920. V. 45

DRABBLE, MARGARET

The Garrick Year. London: 1964. V. 46

A Summer Bird-Cage. London: 1962. V. 45

Virginia Woolf: a Personal Debt. New York: 1973. V. 46

The Waterfall. London: 1969. V. 39; 41

DRACHMANN, HOLGER

Paul and Virgina of a Northern Zone. Chicago: 1895. V. 38; 41

DRACO, JOHANN JACOB

De Origine et Ivre Patriciorvm, Libri Tres, Ex Continva Romanorvm, Graecorvm, & Ermanorvm, Aliarum Item Gentium Civitatum Historia. Basle: 1627. V. 40

DRACOPOLI, I. N.

Through Jubaland to the Lorian Swamp. London: 1914. V. 39

DRAGE, THEODORE

An Account of a Voyage for the Discovery of a North-West Passage by Hudson's Streights, to the Western and Southern Ocean of America, Performed in the Years 1746 nd 1747, in the Ship California . . . London: 1748. V. 37; 38

DRAGE, THEODORE SWAINE

An Account of a Voyage for the Discovery of a North West Passage by Hudson's Streights, to the Western and Southern Ocean of America. London: 1748-49. V. 43

DRAGO, HARRY SINCLAIR

Outlaws on Horseback: The History of the Organized Bands of Bank & Train Robbers Who Terrorized the Prairie Towns of Missouri, Kansas . . . New York: 1964. V. 38; 39; 40

Wild, Woolly and Wicked: the History of the Kansas Cow Towns and the Texas Cattle Trade. New York: 1960. V. 40

DRAKE, BENJAMIN

Cincinnati in 1826. Cincinnati: 1827. V. 37; 38; 43; 45

Life of Tecumseh, and of His Brother the Prophet; With a Historical Sketch of the Shawanoe Indians. Cincinnati: 1841. V. 37

Life of Tecumseh, and His Brother the Prophet. Cincinnati: 1855. V. 37

DRAKE-BROCKMAN, R. E.

British Somaliland. London: 1912. V. 45

DRAKE, BURGESS

Poems and Drawings. London: 1965. V. 45

DRAKE, DANIEL

Natural and Statistical View, or Picture of Cincinnati in the Miami Country. Cincinnati: 1815. V. 37; 40; 43; 45

Pioneer Life in Kentucky, etc. Cincinnati: 1870. V. 41

Practical Essays on Medical Education and the Medical Profession in the United States. Cincinnati: 1832. V. 40; 41

A Systematic Treatise, Historical, Etiological and Practical On the Principle Diseases of the Interior Valley of North America. Cincinnati: 1850. V. 41; 43; 45

A Systematic Treatise, Historical, Etological and Practical, On the Principle Diseases of the Interior Valley of North America. Philadelphia: 1854. V. 41; 43

DRAKE, EDWIN L.

Chronological Summary of Battles and Engagements of the Western Armies of the Confederate States, Including Summary of Lt. Joseph Wheeler's Cavalry Engagements. Nashville: 1879. V. 44

DRAKE, FRANCIS

Eboracum; or the History and Antiquities of the City of New York, from Its Original to the Present Times. London: 1736. V. 44

The World Encompassed by Sir Francis Drake. Cleveland: 1966. V. 41

The World Encompassed . . . Concerning Circumnavigation of the World with Appreciation of the Achievement by R. C. Temple from Eleven Selections of Analogous Documents of Contemporary Date. London: 1926. V. 38

DRAKE, FRANCIS S.

The Indian Tribes of the United States, Their History, Antiquities, Customs, Religion, Arts, Langauge, Traditions, Oral Legends and Myths. Philadelphia: 1884. V. 45

DRAKE, FRANICS

Eboracum: or the History and Antiquities of the City of York, from Its Original to the Present Times. Together with the History of the Cathedral Church, and the Lives of the Archbishops of that See . . . Collected from Authentick Manuscripts . . . London: 1736. V. 37

DRAKE, J. MADISON

The History of the Ninth New Jersey Veteran Vols . . . Sept. 13th, 1861 to July 12th, 1865, with a Complete Official Roster and Sketches of Prominent Members . . . New York: 1889. V. 39

DRAKE, JAMES

Anthropologia Nova; or a New System of Anatomy. London: 1707. V. 46

Anthropologia Nova; or, a New System of Anatomy. London: 1727. V. 41; 45

Anthropologia Nova; or, a New System of Anatomy . . . London: 1727-28. V. 42; 45; 46

The Antient and Modern Stages Survey'd. London: 1699. V. 40

Historia Anglo-Scotica; or an Impartial History of All that Happen'd Between the Kings and Kingdoms of England and Scotland . . . London: 1703. V. 43

DRAKE, JOSEPH RODMAN

The Croakers. New York: 1860. V. 38; 41; 46

The Culprit Fay and Other Poems. New York: 1835. V. 44; 46

DRAKE, LEAH BODINE

A Hornbook for Witches. Sauk City: 1950. V. 45

DRAKE, MAURICE

A History of English Glass Painting. London: 1912. V. 38; 40; 42

A History of English Glass painting. New York: 1913. V. 45

Saints and Their Emblems. London: 1916. V. 38; 40

DRAKE, NATHAN

Essays, Biographical, Critical and Historical Illustrative of the Rambler, Adventuer and Idler, and of the Various Periodical Publications Which in Imitation of the Writings of Steele and Addison . . . Buckingham: 1809-10. V. 38; 41; 43

The Gleaner. London: 1811. V. 38

Literary Hours, or Sketches Critical and Narrative. Sudbury: 1798. V. 42

Literary Hours or Sketches Critical and Narrative. Sudbury: 1800. V. 44

Literary Hours; or Sketches Critical, Narrtive, and Poetical. London: 1804. V. 38; 46

Shakespeare and His Times. London: 1817. V. 40

DRAKE, PETER

The Memoirs of Captain Peter Drake, Containing an Account of Many Strange and Surprising Events, Which Happened to Him through a Series of Sixty Years, and Upwards . . . Dublin: 1755. V. 38

DRAKE, ST. CLAIRE

Black Metropolis. New York: 1945. V. 43

DRAKE, SAMUEL A.

Catalogue of Useful, Curious and Rare Books, Tracts &c. in American Literature, Chiefly Historical, on Sale at the Prices Annexed . . . Boston: 1866. V. 40

The Heart of the White Moutains (:New Hampshire): their Legend and Scenery. London: 1882. V. 46

DRAKE, SAMUEL G.

Annals of Witchcraft in New England, and Elsewhere in the United States, from their First Settlement. Boston: 1869. V. 38

Early History of Georgia, Embracing the Embassy of Sir Alexander Cuming to the Country of the Cherokees, in the Year 1730, with a Map. Boston: 1872. V. 43

Early History of New England; Being a Relation of Hostile Passages Between the Indians and European Voyagers and First Settlers . . . to the Close of the War with the Pequots, in the year 1637. Boston: 1864. V. 37

Indian Biography, Containing the Lives of More Than Two Hundred Indian Chiefs . . . Boston: 1832. V. 45

The Old Indian Chronicle: Being a Collection of Exceeding Rare Tracts Written and Published in the Time of King Philip's War . . . Boston: 1836. V. 37; 45

The Old Indian Chronicle . . . Boston: 1867. V. 38; 39; 45

A Particular History of the Five Years French and Indian War in New England and Parts Adjacent, From . . . 1744 to . . . 1749. Boston: 1870. V. 39

Result of the Researches Among the British ARchives for Information Relative to the Founders of New England: Made in the Years, 1858, 1859 and 1860 . . . Boston: 1860. V. 39

The Witchcraft Delusion in New England . . . Rosbury: 1866. V. 43

DRAKE, WILLIAM

The First Battle of Bull Run. N.P.: 1967. V. 40

DRAKE, WILLIAM RICHARD

Notes, Geneaogical, Historical and Heraldic, of the Family of Chichester of Devon. London: 1886. V. 38

DRAKENBORCH, A.

Maps and Plans Illustrative of Livy . . . Oxford. V. 40

DRAKE'S Plate of Brass. Evidence of His Visit to California in 1579. San Francisco: 1937. V. 39

DRAKE'S Road Book of the Grand Junction Railway from Birmingham to Liverpool and Manchester . . . London: 1838/9. V. 40

THE DRAMA; or, Theatrical Pocket Magazine. London: 1821-24. V. 42

THE DRAMATICK Miscellany: Consisting of the New Plays, Both Tragedies and Comedies, Which Have Been Written in the Years 1718, 1719 and 1720. London: 1721. V. 45

DRANE, FRANCIS S.

Life and Correspondence of Henry Knox, Major-General in the American Revolutionary Army. Boston: 1873. V. 46

DRANE, ROBERT BRENT

A Sketch of the Life of Tristrim Lowther Skinner, Major of First Regiment, North Carolina Bolunteers, Confederate States Army. (Edenton, NC: 1931). V. 37

DRANNAN, WILLIAM F.

Capt. W. F. Drannan, Chief of Scouts, as Pilot to Emigrants and Government Trains, Across the Plains of the Wild West of Fifty Years Ago. Chicago: 1910. V. 39

Thirty One Years on the Plains and in the Mountains, or the Last Voice from the Plains . . . San Francisco: 1893. V. 40

Thirty-One Years on the Plains and in the Mountains or the Last Voice from the Plains. Chicago: 1899. V. 39

DRAPER, JOHN

The Young Student's Pocket Companion, or Arithmetic, Geometry, Trigonometry and mensuration, Calculated for the Improvement of Youth at School, and for the Benefit of Such as have not the Opportunity of a Tutor. Whitehaven: 1772. V. 38

DRAPER, JOHN W. 1893-

A Century of Broadside Elegies Being Ninety English and Ten Scotch Broadsides . . . London: 1928. V. 42; 43

DRAPER, JOHN WILLIAM

A History of the Intellectual Development of Europe. New York: 1863. V. 40

History of the Intellectual Development of Europe. London: 1864. V. 42

History of the Conflict Between Religion and Science. New York: 1912. V. 42

History of the Intellectural Development of Europe. By John William Draper, M.D., LL.D . . . London: 1863. V. 37

Scientific Memoirs . . . New York: 1878. V. 40

A Treatise on the Forces Which Produce the Organization of Plants. New York: 1844. V. 42; 45

DRAPER, JOSEPH

The Vermont Asylum for the Insane. Brattleboro: 1887. V. 45

DRAPER, LYMAN C.

King's Mountain and Its Heroes. Cincinnati: 1881. V. 40; 45

Madison, the Capital of Wisconsin Its Growth, Progress, Condition, Wants and Capabilities. Madison: 1857. V. 40; 43

DRAPER, MATTHEW

The Spend-Thrift. London: 1731. V. 42

DRAPER, WILLIAM

A Plain Narrative of the Reduction of Manila and the Philippine Islands. N.P., London?: 1764? V. 37

A Treatise on the Forces Which Produce the Organization of Plants. New York: 1845. V. 40

THE DRAPER'S Host's Answer to the Clothier's Letter. Dublin: 1760. V. 40

DRESSER, H. E. continued

A Manual of Palaearctic Birds. London: 1902-03. V. 40

A Monograph of the Coraciidae, or Family of the Rollers. London: 1893. V. 37; 38; 39; 41; 42

DRESSER, HENRY EELES

A History of the Birds of Europe. London: 1871-96. V. 37

A Monograph of the Meropidae, or Family of the Bee Eaters. London: 1884-86. V. 37

DRESSER, MATTHAEUS

De Partibus Corporis Humani et de Anima, Eiusque Potentiis, Libri Duo. Witebergae: 1581. V. 37

De Partibus Corporis Humani et de Anima, Eiusdem Potentijfs, Libri Duo. Wittenberg: 1581. V. 46

Rhetorica Inventionis Et Dispositionis, Illustrata & Locupletata Quam Plurimis Exemplis. Basle: 1567. V. 40

DREVON, I. F. HENRY

A Journey through Sweden Containing a Detailed Account of Its Population, Agriculture, Commerce, nd Finances . . . London: 1790. V. 38; 40; 42

DREW, CHARLES

An Authentick Account of the Life of Mr. Charles Drew. London: 1740. V. 37; 41

DREW, CHARLES S.

Communication from C. S. Drew . . . Giving an Account of the Origin and Early Prosecution of the Indian War in Oregon . . . Washington: 1860. V. 37; 38; 42; 45

DREW, H. T. B.

The Official History of Australia in the War 1914-1918. Volume IV. The War Effort of New Zealand. Auckland: 1923. V. 45

The War Effor of New Zealand. Auckland: 1923. V. 44

DREW, SAMUEL

An Essay on the Immateriality and Immortality of the Human Soul, Founded Soley on Physical and Rational Principles. St. Austell: 1802. V. 40

An Essay on the Identity and General Resurrection of the Human Body in Which the Evidences in Favour of These Important Subjects are Considered in Relation Both to Philosophy and Scripture. Brooklyn: 1811. V. 40

The Life of the Rev. Thomas Coke, LL.D. London: 1817. V. 37; 38

DREW, WILLIAM A.

Original Sermons on Various Subjects by Living Universalist Ministers. Gardiner: 1831-32. V. 45

DREXEL, HIEREMIAS

Tobias, Morali Doctrina Illustratus. Antwerp: 1642. V. 38

DREXEL, JEREMIAH 1581-1638

Opera, cum Indice Quadruplici & Symbolis Aeneis, Coniunctim Edita. Munich: 1628. V. 45

DREXEL, JEREMIAS

Aloe, Amari Sed Salubris Succi Jejunium. N.P.: 1637. V. 44

The Considerations of Drexelius Upon Eternity. London: 1684. V. 44

DREXELIO, HIERONYMO

Gymnasium Patientale. Cologne: 1634. V. 39

DREY Hundert Auserlesene Amerikanische Gewaechse Nach Linnaeischer Ordnung. Nuernberg: 1789/86/87/88. V. 40

DREYFUS, JOHN

Aspects of French 18th Century Typography. Cambridge: 1982, 1983. V. 38

Aspects of French Eighteenth Century Typography, a Study of Type Specimens in the Broxbourne Collection at Cambridge University Library. Cambridge: 1982. V. 37; 44

Bruce Rogers and American Typography. A paper read to the Double Crown Club by John Dreyfus. Printed to celebrate the tenth anniversary of the foundation of the American Branch of Cambridge University Press. New York: 1959. V. 37; 46

Four Lectures by T. J. Cobden-Sanderson. San Francisco: 1974. V. 46

Giovanni Mardersteig. An Account of His Work. Verona: 1966. V. 41; 42; 43

A History of the Nonesuch Press. London: 1981. V. 39; 40; 41; 42; 45; 46

A History of the Nonesuch Press with introduction by G. Keynes & a descriptive catalogue by D. McKitterick, S. Rendall & J. Dreyfus. 1981. V. 37

Italic Quartet. Cambridge: 1966. V. 38; 40; 45; 46

The Survival of Baskerville Punches. Cambridge: 1949. V. 40; 41; 45; 46

Type Specimen Facsimiles. London: 1963. V. 38

Typographical Partnership; Ten Letters Between Bruce Rogers and Emery Walker, 1907-1931. Cambridge: 1971. V. 41

A Typographical Masterpiece. San Francisco: 1990. V. 45

Typographical Partnership: Ten Letters Between Bruce Rogers and Emery Walker, 1907-31, Together with an Unpublished Fragment of Bruce Rogers' 'Bye Ways of Bookmaking.' New York: 1971. V. 38

The Work of Jan van Krimpen: a Record in Honour of His Sixtieth Birthday. Haarlem: 1952. V. 45

The Work of Jan Van Krimpen, a Record in Honour of His Sixtieth Birthday. London: 1952. V. 44

DRIAULT, EDOUARD

Pictorial History of Napoleon. 1930. V. 46

DRIESCH, HANS A. E.

The Science and Philosophy of the Organism. London: 1908. V. 43

DRIFTWOOD Flames. Nashville: 1923. V. 39; 42
DRIFTWOOD Flames. Nashville: 1923. V. 44

DRIGGS, B. W.

History of Teton Valley Idaho. Caldwell: 1926. V. 37; 42

DRIGGS, HOWARD R.

Westward America. New York: 1942. V. 40; 44; 46

DRING, THOMAS

A Catalogue of the Lords, Knights and Gentlemen that Have Compounded for Their Estates. London: 1655. V. 39

DRINKER, H.

Tunneling, Explosive Compounds, & Rock Drills . . . 1878. V. 37

DRINKER, HENRY S.

Tunneling, Explosive Compounds and Rock Drills . . . New York: 1878. V. 40; 41

THE DRINKER'S Farm Tragedy. Richmond: 1868. V. 45

DRINKWATER, JOHN 1882-1937

Abraham Lincoln. London: 1918. V. 37; 43

All About Me: Poems for a Child. London: 1928. V. 44

Claud Lovat Fraser. London: 1923. V. 39; 41; 42; 44

Collected Poems 1908-1922. London: 1923. V. 37

Cotswold Characters. New Haven: 1921. V. 41; 43

Cotswold Characters. New Haven & London: 1921. V. 44

A History of the Late Siege of Gibraltar. London: 1785. V. 38; 39; 43; 46

Loyalties. A Book of Poems. London: 1918. V. 40

Olton Pools. London: 1916. V. 44

Persephone. New York: 1926. V. 39; 43; 44; 45

Poems of Love and Earth. London: 1912. V. 46

The Poet and Communication. London: 1923. V. 43

Tides: a Book of Poems. 1917. V. 45

Tides. A Book of Poems. London: 1917. V. 42; 43

DRISCOLL, CLARA

In the Shadow of the Alamo. New York & London: 1906. V. 41

DRIVER, HENRY AUSTEN

The Arabs, a Tale in Four Cantos. London: 1825. V. 42

DROBNA, ZOROSLAVA

Medieval Costume, Armour and Weapons (1350-1450). London: 1960. V. 41

DROGHEDA, ANNE, COUNTESS OF

History of the Moore Family . . . Belfast: 1902. V. 38

DROMGOOLE, WILL ALLEN

The Sunny Side of the Cumberland. Philadelphia: 1886. V. 40

DROWER, E. S.

The Thousand and Twelve Questions. (Alf Trisar Suialia). A Mandaean Text. Berlin: 1960. V. 37

DROWN, WILLIAM

Compendium of Agriculture, or the Farmer's Guide, in the Most Essential Parts of Husbadnry and Gardening . . . Providence: 1824. V. 41

DRUCE, G.

The Flora of Oxfordshire. Oxford: 1927. V. 37

DRUE, THOMAS

The Life of the Dvtches of Svffolke. London: 1631. V. 37

DRUERY, JOHN HENRY

Historical and Topographical Notices of Great Yarmouth, in Norfolk, and Its Environs . . . London: 1826. V. 40

DRUITT, ROBERT

The Principles and Practice of Modern Surgery . . . with Notes and Comments by Joshua B. Flint. Philadelphia: 1844. V. 41; 44

DRUITT, ROBERT continued

Report on the Cheap Wines from France, Germany, Italy, Austria, Greece, Hungary and Australia. London: 1873. V. 38

DRUMHELLER, DAN

Uncle Dan Tells Thrills of Western Tales in 1854. Spokane: 1925. V. 38; 39; 42; 43; 46

DRUMMON, HENRY

the Monkey That Would Not Kill.. London: 1898. V. 46

DRUMMON, J. L.

Thoughts on the Study of Natural History and on the Importance of Attaching Museums . . . to National Seminaries of Education; addressed to the Proprietors of the Belfast Institution. Belfast: 1820. V. 37

DRUMMON, JAMES

Scottish Market-Crosses. Edinburgh: 1861. V. 45

DRUMMON, WILLIAM

A Cypress Grove. Introduction and Notes by Samuel Clegg. London: 1919. V. 37

DRUMMOND, ALEXANDER

Travels Through Different Cities of Germany, Italy, Greece and Several Parts of Asia . . . London: 1754. V. 40; 43; 46

DRUMMOND DE MELFORT, LOUIS HECTOR COMTE DE

Traite sur la Cavalerie. Paris: 1776. V. 42

DRUMMOND, HENRY

The Greatest Thing in the World. New York: (1890). V. 37

Principles of Ecclesiastical Buildings and Ornaments. London: 1851. V. 38

DRUMMOND, JAMES

Ancient Scottish Weapons. London: 1881. V. 41; 44; 46

Ancient Scottish Weapons by the Late James Drummond, R.S.A. Edinburgh: 1881. V. 37

Philo Judaeus; or, the Jewish-Alexandrian Philosophy and Its Development and Completion. London & Edinburgh: 1888. V. 39

Scottish Market-Crosses. Edinburgh: 1861. V. 46

DRUMMOND, JOHN

Evening Reverie. Cairo: 1945. V. 41

DRUMMOND, THOMAS

Botanical Miscellany; Containing Figures and Descriptions of Such Plants as Recommend Themselves by Their Novelty, Rarity, or History . . . London: 1830-33. V. 37

Poems Sacred to Religion and Virtue. London: 1756. V. 38; 40; 42

DRUMMOND, WILLIAM

A Cyprus Grove. London: 1919. V. 46

Memoir on the Antiquity of the Zodiacs of Esneh and Dendera. London: 1821. V. 45

The Oedipus Judaicus. London: 1811. V. 38

The Poetical Works; with 'A Cypresse Grove'. Manchester: 1913. V. 46

A Review of the Governments of Sparta and Athens. London: 1794. V. 37

The Works of William Drummond, of Hawthornden. Edinburgh: 1711. V. 38; 39; 40; 45

DRUMMOND, WILLIAM HAMILTON

The Battle of Trafalgar. Belfast: 1806. V. 42

Bruce's Invasion of Ireland; A Poem. Dublin: 1826. V. 37

The Giant's Causeway - a Poem. Belfast: 1811. V. 38

DRUMMOND, WILLIAM HENRY

Johnnie Courteau and Other Poems. New York: 1901. V. 44

The Large Game and Natural History of South and South-East Africa. Edinburgh: 1875. V. 38; 39

The Large Game and Natural History of South and South-East Africa. London: 1972. V. 38

Philo-Rum's Canoe and Madeleine Vercheres. New York: 1898. V. 42

The Voyageur and Other Poems. New York: 1905. V. 43

DRURY, ANNA HARRIET

The Brothers. London: 1865. V. 38

DRURY, CLIFFORD

First White Women Over the Rockies, Diaries, Letters and Biographical Sketches of the Six Women of the Oregon Mission Who Made th Overland Journey in 1836 and 1838. Glendale: 1963-66. V. 38

DRURY, CLIFFORD MERRILL

Henry Harmon Spalding: Pioneer of Old Oregon. Caldwell: 1936. V. 40; 44

Marcus and Narcissa Whitman and the Opening of Old Oregon. Glendale: 1973. V. 40; 44

DRURY, DRU

Illustrations of Natural History. London: 1770-82. V. 42

Illustrations to Exotic Entomology . . . London: 1837. V. 37; 41; 42

Illustrations of Exotic Entomology . . . London: 1837-1838. V. 38

DRURY, H.

Hand-book of the Indian Flora. Madras: 1864-69. V. 37; 38

DRURY, ROBERT

The Mad Captain, an Opera. London: 1733. V. 39

The Pleasant and Surprizing Adventures of Mr. Robert Drury, During His Fifteen Years Captivity on the Island of Madagascar . . . London: 1750. V. 41

DRURY, VICTOR

History of Rome and of the Roman People from Its Origin to the Invasion of the Barbarians. Boston: 1894. V. 37

DRURY, W. D.

British Dogs: Their Points, Selection and Show Preparation. London: 1903. V. 39

DRURY, W. P.

The Preadventures of Private Pagett. London: 1904. V. 41

DRUTEN, JOHN VAN

I Remember Mama. New York: 1945. V. 44

DRUTHMAR, CHRISTIAN

Christiani Druthmari Gramatici. Expositio in Matheu Evangelistam Familiaris Luculenta; Lectu Iucunda Epithomatib in Lucam Joanne. Colophon: Excursum: 1514. V. 41

DRYBROUGH, T. B.

Polo. London: 1906. V. 43

DRYDEN, ALICE

The Art of Hunting or Three Hunting MSS. Northampton: 1908. V. 46

DRYDEN, CHARLES

War in the Midst of America from a New Point of View. London: 1864. V. 39

DRYDEN, JOHN 1631-1700

Absalom and Achitophel. London: 1681. V. 38; 42; 45

Absalom and Achitophel. London: 1682. V. 38; 40; 41

Absalon et Achitophel. Poema Latino Carmine Donatum. Oxon: 1682. V. 45

The Address of John Dryden, Laureat, to His Highness the Prince of Orange. London: 1689. V. 41; 46

Alexander's Feast; an Ode for St. Cecilia's Day. 1697. V. 45

Alexander's Feast; or the Power of Music. 1904. V. 45

Alexander's Feast; or the Power of Music. Campden: 1904. V. 38; 40

Alexander's Feast; or, the Power of Music. Campden, Gloucestershire,: 1904. V. 38

Alexander's Feast. Glouscestershire: 1904. V. 38

Alexander's Feat: or the Power of Music. London: 1904. V. 46

Alexander's Feast. London: 1904. V. 40; 43

Alexander's Feast: An Ode for St. Cecilia's Day 1697. 1985. V. 40

All for Love. V. 44

All For Love; or, The World Well Lost. San Francisco. V. 39

All for Love; or, The World Well Lost. London: 1678. V. 40; 45

All for Love. San Francisco: 1929. V. 37; 38; 40; 43; 44; 45; 46

All for Love or the World Well Lost. Westminster: 1931. V. 41

All for Love, or the World Well Lost. London: 1931, 1932. .V. 40; 43; 46

All For Love. Kentfield: 1976. V. 42; 46

All for the Love. Anthony and Cleopatra. A Romatic Tragedy. (Kentfield, Calif.): 1976. V. 37

Amboyna. London: 1673. V. 38; 45

Amboyna: a Tragedy. London: 1691. V. 39; 45

Amphiryon. London: 1690, 1691. V. 37

Amphitryon. London: 1706. V. 38

Annus Mirabilis. London: 1667. V. 38; 40; 46

The Assignation: or, Love in a Nunnery. London: 1678. V. 38

Aureng-Zebe: a Tragedy. London: 1676. V. 38; 46

Britannia Redivia: a Poem on the Birth of the Prince. London: 1688. V. 38; 40; 41; 44; 45; 46

A Choice of Dryden's Verse. London: 1973. V. 38

A Choice of Dryden's Verse. London: 1973. V. 40

Cleomenes, the Spartan Hero. London: 1692. V. 37; 38; 40; 42; 43; 45; 46

The Conquest of Granada by the Spaniards. London: 1672. V. 40

The Critical and Miscellaneous Works . . . London: 1800. V. 37; 42

Don Sebastian, King of Portugal . . . London: 1681. V. 45

Don Sebastian, King of Portugal. London: 1692. V. 37; 42

DRYDEN, JOHN 1631-1700 continued

The Dramatick Works. London: 1725. V. 41

The Dramatic Works. London: 1931. V. 38; 40; 41; 42

The Dramatic Works. London: 1931-32. V. 37; 42; 43; 44; 45; 46

The Dramatick Works. London: 1735-53. V. 42; 43

The Dramatick Works of . . . London: 1762. V. 42; 46

The Duke of Guise. London: 1683. V. 38

The Duke of Guise. London: 1687. V. 40

Eleonora. London: 1692. V. 37; 38; 40; 44; 46

An Evening's Love, or the Mock Astrologer. London: 1671. V. 38; 40; 42; 44; 45

Examen Poeticum: Being the Third Part of Miscellany Poems. London: 1693. V. 46

Fables Ancient and Modern. London: 1700. V. 37; 39; 40

Fables Ancient and Modern. London: 1713. V. 39; 43

Fables Ancient and Modern. Glasgow: 1752. V. 41

The Fables. London: 1797. V. 40; 41; 43; 44; 46

The Fables of John Dryden . . . London: 1797. V. 37; 38; 42

The Fables of . . . London: 1798. V. 43

The Fables. London: 1979. V. 43

The Hind and the Panther. London: 1687. V. 37; 39; 40; 41; 44

His Majesties Declaration Defended; In a Letter to a Friend. London: 1681. V. 41

The Kind Keeper. London: 1680. V. 37; 38; 40; 42

The Kind Keeper; or, Mr. Limberham . . . London: 1690. V. 37; 40; 42

King Arthur: or, the British Worthy. London: 1691. V. 38

King Arthur: or, the British Worthy. London: 1695. V. 39

Love Triumphant. London: 1694. V. 38; 39; 42

Macflecknoe: a Poem . . . London: 1709. V. 41

Marriage A-La-Mode. London: 1673. V. 38; 40; 43

The Medall. A Satyre Against Sedition. London: 1682. V. 41

The Miscellaneous Works. London: 1760. V. 40; 42

The Miscellaneous Works . . . London: 1767. V. 40

A Complete Set of Dryden's Miscellanies. London: 1684-1709. V. 38

Miscellany Poems. London: 1684. V. 38

The First (-Sixth) Part of Miscellany Poems. London: 1716. V. 40

Miscellany Poems. London: 1702-1709. V. 38

The Mistaken Husband. London: 1675. V. 38

Oedipus: a Tragedy. London: 1696. V. 39

Oedipus: a Tragedy. London: 1687. V. 45

Of Dramtic Poesie, an Essay. London: 1668. V. 40

Of Dramatic Poesie. London: 1928. V. 38; 45; 46

Original Poems and Translations. London. V. 38

Original Poems. Glasgow: 1756. V. 40; 41

Original Poems. Glasgow: 1770. V. 39; 40; 41

Original poems and translations, now first collected and published together, in two volumes. London: 1743. V. 37

A Poem Upon the Death of His Late Highness Oliver, Lord Protector of England, Scotland and Ireland. London: 1659, i.e. 1691. V. 44

A Poem Upon the Death of His Late Highness Oliver, Lord Protector of England, Scotland and Ireland. London: 1691. V. 40; 46

Poems and Fables. Dublin: 1753. V. 43

The Poems. 1970. V. 46

The Poetical Works. London: 1811. V. 38

The Poetical Works . . . London: 1811. V. 42

The Poetical Works. London: 1832-33. V. 44; 46

The Poetical Works. London: 1843. V. 42

The Poetical Works of . . . London: 1852. V. 41

Religio Laici, or a Laymans Faith. London: 1682. V. 40; 42; 45

Religio Laici or a Laymans Faith. London: 1682. V. 44

Religio Laici or a Laymans Faith. London: 1683. V. 38; 40; 45

The Rival Ladies. London: 1675. V. 45

St. Martin Mar-all, or, the Feign'd Innocence. London: 1678. V. 38

The Satires of Decimus Junius Juvenalis. Translated into English Verse, by Mr. Dryden and Several other Eminent Hands. Together with The Satires of Aulus Persius Falccus. Made English by Mr. Dryden. With Explanatory Notes (and) . . . London: 1693. V. 37

The Second Part of Absalom and Achitophel. London: 1682. V. 38; 42

Secret Love, or the Maiden Queen. London: 1669. V. 40

Secret-Love: or, the Maiden-Queen. London: 1691. V. 37; 42

Songs and Poems Chosen and Introduced by Gwyn Jones. 1957. V. 43

Songs and Poems of John Dryden. London: 1957. V. 37; 41

Songs and Poems. London: 1957. V. 40; 41; 46

Songs and Poems of John Dryden. Waltham St. Lawrence: 1957. V. 44; 45

The Spanish Fryar; or the Double Discovery . . . London: 1681. V. 42; 45

The Spanish Fryar, or, the Double Discovery. London: 1690. V. 37; 38; 40; 41

The Spanish Fryar, or, the Double Discovery. London: 1695. V. 37; 42

Sr. Martin Marr-all; or, the Feign'd Innocence. London: 1691. V. 45

The State of Innocence, and Fall of Man. London: 1678. V. 38

Sylvae; or, the Second Part of Poetical Miscellanies. London: 1685. V. 46

The Tempest, or the Enchanted Island. London: 1676. V. 38

The Tempest, of the Enchanted Island. London: 1690. V. 46

Threnodia Augustalis: A Funeral Pindarique Poem Sacred to the Happy Memory of King Charles II. London: 1685. V. 38; 40; 41; 44; 46

Troilus and Cressida, or Truth Found Too Late. London: 1679. V. 37; 38; 41

Tyrannick Love or The Royal Martyr. London: 1686. V. 41

Tyrannick Love. London: 1702. V. 38

The Vindication. London: 1683. V. 37; 38; 40; 43; 44; 46

The Wild Gallant: A Comedy. London: 1669. V. 38

The Wild Gallant: a Comedy. London: 1684. V. 45; 46

Works. London: 1808. V. 38; 40

Works, with Notes, Historical, Critical and Explanatory and a Life of the Author by Sir Walter Scott. London: 1808. V. 37

The Works. Edinburgh: 1821. V. 40

DRYDEN, JONATHAN

Observations on the Construction of Railways and Upon Mechanics. London: 1829. V. 46

DRYGALSKI, ERICH VON

Zum Kontinent des Eisigen Suedens. Deutsche Suedpolarexpedition . . . Berlin: 1904. V. 46

DRYHOUT, J. H.

The Work of Augustus Saint-Gaudens. Hanover, London: 1892. V. 39

DRYSDALE, RUSSELL

The Paintings of Russell Drysdale. Sydney. V. 41

DU FAY, CHARLES JEROME DE CISTERNAY 1662-1723

Bibliotheca Fayana seu Catalogus Librorum Bibliothecae. Paris: 1725. V. 40

DU PUY DU GREZ, BERNARD 1640-1720

Traite sur la Peinture . . . Toulouse: 1699. V. 40

DUANE, WILLIAM

The American Military Library; or, Compenium of the Modern Tactic. Philadelphia: 1809. V. 37

A Hand Book for Infantry: Containing the First Principles of Military Discipline . . . Philadelphia: 1814. V. 38; 39; 40; 43

A Hand Book for Infantry: Containing the First Principles of Military Discipline, . . . for the Use of The Military Force of the United States. Philadelphia: 1812. V. 37

Ligan: A Collection of Tales and Essays. Philadelphia: 1857. V. 46

The London Catalogue of Books, Selected from the General Catalogue Published in 1786 . . . London: 1791. V. 44

The Mississippi Question. Philadelphia: 1803. V. 42

The Mississippi Question. Debate in the Senate on the Violation of the Right of Deposit on the Island of New Orleans. Philadelphia: 1803. V. 38; 39

Passages from the Diary of Christopher Marshall, Kept in Philadelphia and Lancaster During the American Revolution. Volume I 1774-1777. (all published). Philadelphia: 1839-1849. V. 38

Report of a Debate, in the United States Senate. N.P.: 1804. V. 44

The System of Infantry Discipline: According to the Regulation Established for the Army of the United States, 19 March, 1813. Philadelphia?: 1814. V. 37

Truth Will Out! The Foul Charges of the Tories Against the Editor of the Aurora Repelled by Positve Proof and Plain Truth and His Base Caluminators Put to Shame. Philadelphia: 1798. V. 44

DUANE, WILLIAM J.

Letters, Addressed to the People of Pennsylvania, Respecting Internal Improvement, of the Commonwealth by Means of Roads and Canals. Philadelphia: 1811. V. 37

DUARTE, KING OF PORTUGAL 1433-1438

Leal Conselheiro o Qual fez Dom Duarte . . . Seguido do Livro da Ensinanca de Bem Cavalgar Toda Sella, Que Fez o Mesmo Rei . . . Paris: 1842. V. 41

DU BAIL, LOUIS MOREAU, SIEUR

The Famous Chinois; or the Loves of Several of the French Nobility, Under Borrowed Names. London: 1669. V. 44

DUBAL, JOHN C.

The Adventures of Big-Foot Wallace, the Texas Ranger and Hunter. Philadelphia: 1885. V. 37

DU BARRY, MARIE JEANNE, COUNTESS

Letters to and From the Countess Du Barry . . . Dublin: 1780. V. 41

DUBUS, ANDRE continued

The Lieutenant. New York: 1967. V. 46

DUBUT, L. A.

Architecture Civile. Paris: 1803. V. 38; 42; 46

DU CANE, ELLA

The Flowers and Gardens of Japan. London: 1908. V. 46

DU CANGE, CHARLES DUFRESNE 1610-1688

Glossarium ad Scriptores Mediae & Infimae Graecitatis. Lyon: 1688. V. 39

DUCAREL, ANDREW COLTEE

Anglo-Norman Antiquities Considered in a Tour through Part of Normandy. London: 1767. V. 38; 45

DUCAREL, P. J.

Poems. London: 1805. V. 40

DUCAS, THEODORE

Travels of, in VArious Countries in Europe, at the REvival of Letters and Art. London: 1822. V. 44

DUCATIUS, LUCIUS FRANCIS

Praeludiorum Libri III. Paris: 1554. V. 39

DUCCI, LORENZO

De Inventione Medii Liber Unus. Lucca: 1550. V. 43

DU CERCEAU, JEAN ANTOINE

The Compleat Hisotry of Thomas Kouli Kan, (at present called Schah Nadir) Sovereign of Persia. London: 1742. V. 41

DU CHAILLU, PAUL

A Journey to Ashango-Land, and Further Penetration into Equatorial Africa. New York: 1867. V. 46

DU CHAILLU, PAUL B.

Explorations and Adventures in Equatorial Africa. London: 1861. V. 40

A Journey to Ashango-Land, and Futher Penetration into Equatorial Africa. London: 1867. V. 40

The Land of the Midnight Sun. New York: 1881. V. 44

The Land of the Midnight Sun: Summer and Winter Journeys through Sweden, Norway, Lapland and Northern Finland. New York: 1881-82. V. 40

The Land of the Midnight Sun Summer and Winter Journeys through Sweden, Norway, Lapland and Northern Finland. New York: 1882. V. 37; 38; 40; 42; 43

The Land of the Midnight Sun.. New York: 1889. V. 44

The Land of the Midnight Sun. London: 1899. V. 40

The Land of the Midnight Sun. London: 1882. V. 37

The Viking Age. London: 1889. V. 39; 40; 41

DU CHAILLU, PAUL BELLONI

Explorations and Adventures in Equatorial Africa. New York: 1861. V. 38

The Land of the Midnight Sun. London: 1881. V. 43; 45

The Land of the Midnight Sun. London: 1899. V. 38

The Viking Age. New York: 1889. V. 42; 43; 45

DU CHAILLU, PAUL BELLOW

Adventures in Equatorial Africa. London: 1861. V. 39

Explorations and Adventures in Equatorial Africa. London: 1861. V. 39

A Journey to Ashango-Land, and Further Penetration into Equatorial Africa. London: 1867. V. 39

DUCHAMP, MARCEL

Notes and Projects for the Large Glass. London: 1969. V. 42

Notes and Projects for the Large Glass. New York: 1969? V. 41

DUCHARME, LEANDRE

Journal d'un Exile Politique aux Terres Australes. Montreal: 1845. V. 38; 42; 43

DUCHARTRE, PIERRE L.

The Italian Comedy. London: 1929. V. 41

DUCHARTRE, PIERRE LOUIS

The Italian Comedy. New York: 1929. V. 37

DU CHASTEL, HONORE

Oratio Lutetia Habitae, qua Futuro Medico Necessaria Explicantur. Paris: 1555. V. 37

DUCHATEL, E.

Manuel de Lithographie Artistique pour l'Artiste et l'Imprimeur. Paris: 1907. V. 41

DUCHAUSSOIS, P.

Mid Snow and Ice. London: 1923. V. 40

DUCHE, JACOB

Caspipina's Letters; Containing Observations Upon a Variety of Subjects, Literary, Moral and Religious. Bath: 1777. V. 43; 46

The Duty of Standing Fast in Our Spiritual and Temporal Liberties. A Sermon . . . Philadelphia: 1775. V. 39; 44

The Duty of Standing Fast in our Spiritual and Temporal Liberites, a Sermon, preached . . . before the First Battalion of the City and Liberties of Philadelphia. Philadelphia/London: 1775. V. 37

Observations on a Variety of Subjects, Literary, Moral and Religious. Philadelphia: 1774. V. 37; 42; 43

DUCHENNE DE BOULOGNE, GUILLAUME BENJAMIN AMAND

Selections from the Clinical Works of . . . London: 1883. V. 37

DUCHENNE, GUILLAUME B. A.

Physiology of Motion Demonstrated by Means of Electrical Stimulation and Clinical Observation and Applied to the Study of Paralysis and Deformities . . . Philadelphia: 1949. V. 38; 41

DUCHENNE, GUILLAUME BENJAMIN

De l'Electrisation Localisee et de Son Application a la Physiologie, a la Pathologie et a la Therapeutique . . . Paris: 1855. V. 45

Physiology of Motion Demonstrated by Means of Electrical Stimulation and Clincal Observation . . . Philadelphia: 1949. V. 45

DU CHESNE, ANDRE 1584-1640

Bibliotheque des Autheurs . . . de la France. Paris: 1627. V. 40

Bibliotheque des Autheurs . . . de la France. Paris: 1618. V. 41

Historiae Normannorum Scriptores Antiqui . . . Paris: 1619. V. 39

DU CHESNE, JOSEPH

Recueil des Plus Curieux et Rares Secrets Touchant la Medecine Metallique & Minerale Tirez des Manuscrits. Paris: 1648. V. 46

DUCHOCHOIS, P. C.

Industrial Photography: Being a Description of the Various Processes of Producing Indestructible Photographic Images of Glass, Porcelain, Metal and Many Other Substances. New York: 1901/1891. V. 44

Photographic Reproduction Processes. New York: 1891. V. 46

Photographic Reproduction Processes: a Practical Treatise of the Photo-IMpressions without Silver Salts. London: 1897. V. 38; 40

DU CHOUL, GUILLAUME

Discorso Sopra La Castramentatione & Disciplina Militare de Rom . . . Venice: 1557. V. 40

DUCHOW, CHARLES

The Duchow Journal. Fairfax: 1959. V. 42; 43; 44

DUCHOW, JOHN CHARLES

The Duchow Journal. A Voyage from Boston to California 1852. 1959. V. 38

The Duchow Journal. A Voyage from Boston to California 1852. Kentfield: 1959. V. 41

THE DUCHOW Journal. A Voyage from Boston to California 1852. N.P.: 1959. V. 46

DUCK, STEPHEN

Poems on Several Subjects Written by Stephen Duck, Lately a Poor Thresher in a Barn in the County of Wiltshire, at the Wages of four Shillings Per Week . . . London: 1730. V. 40; 42; 45

Poems on Several Occasions. London: 1736. V. 38; 40; 41; 42; 45

The Vision. London: 1737. V. 43

DUCKS and Green Peas; or, The Newcastle Rider. Alnwick: 1827. V. 38

DUCKWORTH, ELEANOR

Poems and Sketches. Cincinnati: 1857. V. 40

DUCLOS, CHARLES PINOT

Discours sur l'Origine et les Revolutions des Langues Celtique et Francoise. Paris: 1780. V. 39

DUCOMPEX, ETIENNE ANATOLE

Portefeuille du Peintre en Batimens. Paris: 1885. V. 40; 44

DUCOUDRAY-HOLSTEIN, H. L. V.

Memoirs of Simon Bolivar, President Liberator of the Republic of Colombia . . . Boston: 1829. V. 37

DU COURET, LOUIS

Life in the Desert; or, Recollections of Travel in Asia and Africa. New York: 1860. V. 41

DUCRAY-DUMINIL, FRANCOIS

Ambrose and Eleanor . . . Philadelphia: 1799. V. 43

DU CREUX, FRANCOIS

The History of Canada or New France. Toronto: 1951-52. V. 37; 45

DUDDEN, F. HOMES

The Life and Times of St. Ambrose. 1935. V. 39

DUDEK, LOUIS

Cerberus. Toronto: 1952. V. 38

DUDIN, M.

The Art of the Bookbinder and Gilder (1772). 1977. V. 45

The Art of the Bookbinder and Gilder. Leeds: 1977. V. 40; 41

DUDLEY, DONALD R.

Urbs Roma: a Source Book of Classical Texts on the City and Its Monuments. London: 1967. V. 40; 42

Urbs Roma: a source book of classical texts on the city & its monuments. London: (1967). V. 37

DUDLEY, HOWARD

The History and Antiquities of Horsham. London: 1836. V. 37

DUDLEY, J. M.

Words of Command for the Sword Exercise, for Artillery; as Practised by the First Regiment, First Brigade, Third Division, of the massachusetts Milita. Concord: 1820. V. 37

DUDLEY, JOHN WILLIAM WARD, 1ST EARL OF 1781-1833

The Law of a Justice of Peace and Parish Officer. London: 1769. V. 40

DUDLEY, ROBERT ?1532-1588

The Perfect Picture of a Favourite; or, Secret Memoirs of . . . London: 1708. V. 43

DUDLEY, WILLIAM L.

City of Grand Forks Illustrated. 1897. Grand Forks: 1897. V. 42

DUER, WILLIAM A.

A Letter Addressed to Cadwallader D. Colden in Answer to the Strictures Contained In His 'Life of Robert Fulton' . . . Albany: 1817. V. 45

Reminiscences of an Old Yorker. New York: 1867. V. 39

DUERER, ALBRCHT 1471-1528

Della Simmetria Dei Corpi Humani, Libri IV. Venice: 1591. V. 44

DUERER, ALBRECHT 1471-1528

Albert Durer's Designs of the Prayer Book. London: 1817. V. 38

Albrecht Durers Christlichmythologische Handzeichnungen. Munich: 1808. V. 39

The Construction of Roman Letters. Cambridge: 1924. V. 45; 46

Della Simmetria dei Corpi Humani, Libri Quattro. Venice: 1585. V. 41

Della Simmetria del Corpi Humani, Libri Quattro. Venetia: 1591. V. 40

Designs of the Prayer Book. London. V. 41

The Great Procession. New York: 1919. V. 44

The Little Passion. London: 1894. V. 38; 41; 43

The Little Passion. Verona: 1971. V. 38; 45

Of the Just Shaping of Letters. New York: 1917. V. 41; 43; 44; 45

De Symmetria Partium in Rectis Formis Humanorum Corporum. Nuremberg: 1532. V. 41

DU FAUR, FREDA

The Conquest of Mount Cook and Other Climbs. London: 1915. V. 38

DUFEIF, N. G.

Nature Displayed in Her Mode of Teaching Language to Man. Philadelphia: 1810. V. 40

DUFF, E. GORDON

Early English Printing. London: 1896. V. 40

William Caxton. Chicago: 1905. V. 39

DUFF, EDWARD GORDON

Catalogue of the Library of the Late Edward Gordon. London: 1925. V. 41

Early Printed Books. London: 1893. V. 41

Fifteenth Century English Books. London: 1917. V. 38

William Caxton. Chicago: 1905. V. 38

DUFF, H. L.

Nyasaland Under the Foreign Office. London: 1906. V. 46

DUFF, JAMES GRANT

A History of the Mahrattas. London: 1826. V. 41; 43

DUFF, PATRICK

Sketch of the Geology of Moray. Elgin: 1842. V. 39; 43

Sketch of the Geology of Moray. London: 1842. V. 44

DUFF, WILLIAM ALEXANDER

History of North Central Ohio, Embracing Richland, Ashland, Wyane, Medina, Lorain, Huron & Knox Counties. Topeka-Indianapolis: 1931. V. 39

DUFFERIN & AVA, MARCHIONESS OF

My Canadian Journal 1872-8. London: 1891. V. 46

DUFFERIN & AVA, MARQUESS

Catalogue of the Helen's Tower Library, Belonging to the Marquess of Dufferin and Ava. Belfast: 1901. V. 43

DUFFERIN, LORD

Irish Emigration and the Tenure of Land in Ireland. London: 1867. V. 37

Letters from High Latitudes; Being Some Account of a Voyage. London: 1857. V. 38; 39

DUFFIELD, A. J.

Recollections of Travels Abroad. London: 1889. V. 39

DUFFIELD, GEORGE

A Sermon on American Slavery: Its Nature and the Duties of Christians in Relation To It. Detroit: 1840. V. 40; 44

DUFFY, CHARLES GAVAN 1816-1903

Conversations with Carlyle. London: 1892. V. 38

My Life in Two Hemispheres. London: 1898. V. 38

Young Ireland, a Fragment of Irish History, 1840-1850. (with) Four Years of Irish History, 1845 to 1849, A Sequel to Young Ireland. London: 1880/1883. V. 43

DUFFY, EDWARD

History of the 159th Regiment N.Y.S.V. New York: 1890. V. 43; 46

DUFFY'S Hibernian Magazine. Dublin: 1860. V. 39
DUFFY'S Hibernian Magazine. Dublin: 1862-June 1864. V. 39

DUFFY'S Irish Catholic Magazine. Dublin: 1848. V. 39

DUFIEF, N. G.

In the Press of R. and G. Palmer, and Speedily Will Be Published, an Extensive Work, Entitled, a New Universal and Pronouncing Dictionary of the French and English Languages. Philadelphia: 1810. V. 39

Nature Displayed in Her Mode of Teaching Language to Man. Philadelphia: 1806. V. 40

Nature Displayed in Her Mode of Teaching Language to Man. Philadelphia: 1821. V. 40

Nature Displayed in Her Mode of Teaching Language to Man. Philadelphia: 1810. V. 37

Nature Displayed in Her Mode of Teaching Language to Man. London: 1822. V. 37; 40; 41

Nature Displayed in Her Mode of Teaching Language to Man. New York: 1825. V. 37; 40

A New Universal Pronouncing Dictionary of the French and English Languages. Philadelphia: 1810. V. 37; 39

DUFLOT DE MOFRAS, EUGENE

Travels on the Pacific Coast. Santa Ana: 1937. V. 37; 38

DUFORT, GIAMBATTISTA

Trattato del Ballo Nobile. Naples: 1728. V. 39

DU FOUILLOX, JACQUES

La Venerie et Fauconnerie de Iaques Du Fouilloux, Iean de Franchieres, et Autres Autheurs . . . Paris: 1585. V. 39

DU FOUR DE LA CRESPELIERE, JACQUES

Commentaire sur l'Ecole de Salerne . . . Paris: 1672. V. 41

DUFOUR, JOHN JAMES

The American Vine-Dresser's Guide Being a Treatise on the Cultivation of the Vine and the Process of Wine Making, Adapted to the Soil and Climate of the United States. Cincinnati: 1826. V. 40

DUFOUR, PHILIPPE SYLVESTRE

Drey Neue Curieuse Tractaetgen von Dem Tranct Cafe, Sinesischen the, Und Chocolata. Budissin: 1701. V. 38

Moral Instructions of a Father to his Son, ready to unertake a long voyage . . . . To which is added, a collection of moral instructions in prose and verse, from the best authors. Edinburgh: 1775. V. 37; 41

Novi Tractatus de Potu Caphe; de Chinensium the; et de chocolata . . . Geneva: 1699. V. 37

Traitez Nouveaux & Curieux de Cafe, du The et du Chocolate. Lyon: 1685. V. 42

DUFRENE, MAURICE

Les Bijoux. Paris: 1901-06. V. 43

Ensemble Mobiliers: Exposition Internationale 1925. Paris: 1926. V. 40

DUFRENOY, A.

Traite de Mineralogie. Paris: 1844-47. V. 38

DUFRENOY, M.

On the Use of Air in the Iron Works of England and Scotland. London: 1836. V. 44; 45

DUFRESNE, FRANK

Alaska's Animals and Fishes. Hartford: 1946. V. 44; 46

Alaska's Animals and Fishes. West Hartford: 1946. V. 39; 46

DU FRESNOY, CHARLES ALPHONSE 1611-1665

L'Art de Peinture. Paris: 1668. V. 41; 45

The Art of Painting . . . London: 1695. V. 39

The Art of Painting . . . with Remarks. London: 1716. V. 38; 39; 41; 44

The Art of Painting. London: 1750. V. 42

The Art of Painting. York: 1783. V. 39; 41; 43; 45

De Arte Graphica. The Art of Painting, with Remarks. London: 1695. V. 46

DUFREY, THOMAS

A Commonwealth of Women. London: 1686. V. 43

DUFT, JOHANNES

Irish Miniatures in the Abbey Library of St. Gall. Berne:P: 1954. V. 38

DUFTON, HENRY

Narrative of a Journey through Abyssinia in 1862-3. London: 1867. V. 40

DUFTON, WILLIAM

The Nature and Treatment of Deafness and Diseases of the Ear; and the Treatment of the Deaf and Dumb. Philadelphia: 1848. V. 43

DUGAN, HUGH G.

Village on the Country Line: a History of Hinsdale, Illinois. Chicago: 1949. V. 44

DUGANNE, A. J. H.

Camps and Prisons: Twenty Months in the Department of the Gulf. New York: 1865. V. 42

The Tenant-House; or Embers from Poverty's Hearthstone. New York: 1857. V. 41

DUGANNE, AUGUSTINE

Camps and Prisons: Twenty Months in the Department of the Gulf. New York: 1865. V. 39; 41

DUGANNE, AUGUSTINE J. H.

Bianca. New York: 1854? V. 43

DUGDALE, FLORENCE E.

The Book of Baby Birds. London: 1912. V. 40

DUGDALE, MICHAEL

An Omelette of Vultures Eggs - Poems 1935-1945. London: 1982. V. 42; 44

DUGDALE, THOMAS

Curiosities of Great Britain. London: 1845. V. 45

DUGDALE, WILLIAM 1605-1686

The Antient Usage in Bearing Such Ensigns of Honour as Are Commonly Call'd Arms . . . Oxford: 1682. V. 43

The Antiquities of Warwickshire Illustrated. London: 1656. V. 45

The Baronage of England. London: 1675-76. V. 38; 39

The Baronage of England, or, an Historical Account of Our English Nobility. London: 1977. V. 39

The History of St. Paul's Cathedral in London, from Its Foundation . . . Lackington,: 1658. V. 44

The History of St. Paul's Cathedral in London. London: 1658. V. 37; 38; 41; 44

The History of Imbanking and Drayning of Divers Fenns and Marshes, Both in Foreign Parts and in This Kingdom; and of the Improvements Thereby. London: 1662. V. 39

The History of St. Paul's Cathedral in London . . . London: 1716. V. 42

The History of Saint Paul's Cathedral, in London . . . London: 1818. V. 38; 39; 44

The History of Imbanking and Draining of Divers Pens and Marshes both in Foreign Parts and in this Kingdom, and of the Improvements Thereby. London: printed by W.: 1772. V. 37

Kenilworth Illustrated; or, the History of the Castle, Priory and Church of Kenilworth. Chiswick: 1821. V. 41

Monasticon Anglicanum. London: 1655/61/73. V. 39

Monasticon Anglicanum, sive Pandectae Coenobiorum Benedictionorum, Cluniacensium, Cisterciensium . . . London: 1655-61-73. V. 39

Monasticon Anglicanum. London: 1655/73/73. V. 44

Monasticon Anglicanum . . . London: 1693. V. 37; 39; 43

Monasticon Anglicanum . . . . London: 1718. V. 41

Monasticon Anglicanum, or the History of the Ancient Abbies, Monasteries, Hospitals, Cathedrals and Collegiate Churches in England. London: 1718, 1722-3. V. 38

Monasticon Anglicanum. London: 1817. V. 40

Monasticon Anglicanum. London: 1846. V. 37

Origines Juridiciales, or Historical Memorials of the English Laws, Courts of Justice, Forms of Tryal, Punishment in Cases Criminal, Law-Writers, Law-Books . . . London: 1671. V. 43

A Perfect Copy of all Summons of the Nobility to the Great Councils and Parliaments of this Realm. London: 1685. V. 40

The Restoration of the Beauchamp Chapel at St. Mary's Collegiate Church Warwick 1674-1742. Oxford: 1956. V. 44

A Short View of the Late Troubles in England . . . Oxford: 1681. V. 37; 38; 39; 41; 43; 46

DUGGER, SHEPHERD M.

The War Trails of the Blue Ridge. Banner Elk: 1932. V. 44

The War Trails of the Blue Ridge. Banner Elk, NC: 1932. V. 37

DUGGER, SHEPHERD MONROE

The Balsam Groves of the Grandfather Mountain. Banner Elk: 1892. V. 40

The War Trail of the Blue Ridge Containing an Authentic Description of the Battle of Kings Mountain. Banner Elk: 1932. V. 46

DUGGES, DUDLEY

A Discourse of Sea-Ports, Principally of the Port and Haven of Dover . . . London: 1700. V. 41; 45

DUGLISON, ROBLEY

Medical and Surgical Monographs by Andral, Babbington, Beck, Bright, Brody, Burne, Carmichael, Clutterbuck, Cormack, Dubois, Farr, Itard, Louis, Manoir and Taylor . . . Philadelphia: 1838. V. 42

DUGMORE, A. A. RADCLYFFE

The Romance of the Newfoundland Caribou. London: 1913. V. 42; 43

DUGMORE, A. RADCLYFFE

The Wonderland of Big Game. London: 1925. V. 39

DU HALDE, J. B.

Description Georgaphique, Historique, Chronologique, Politique, et Physique de l'Empire de la Chine et de la Tartarie Chinoise . . . The Hague: 1736. V. 45

DU HALDE, JEAN BAPTISTE

A Description of the Empire of China and Chinese Tartary, Together with the Kingdoms of Korea and Tibet. London: 1738-1741. V. 41

DU HALDE, P.

The General History of China. London: 1736. V. 44

DUHAMEL DU MONCEAU, H.

Traite des Arbres Fruitiers . . . Paris: 1768. V. 42

DUHAMEL DU MONCEAU, HENRI LOUIS 1700-1781

Anweisung, Wie Die Verschiedenen Seltenheiten der Nturgeschichte zu Sammeln Zuzubereiten Zu Erhalten und Zu Verschicken Sind. Nuremberg: 1761. V. 38

De L'Exploitation des Bois ou Moyens de Tirer un Parti Avantageux des Taillis, Demi-Taillis, Demi-Futaies et Hautes-Futaies, et d'en Faire une Juste Estimation . . . Paris: 1764. V. 45

Du Transport, de la Conservation et de la Force des Bois . . . Paris: 1767. V. 44

The Elements of Agriculture. London: 1764. V. 38; 40

The Elements of Agriculture. Translated from the original French, and revised by Philip Miller. Dublin: 1767. V. 37

Elems de l'Architecture navale on Traite Practique de la Construction des Vaisseaux. Paris: 1752. V. 41

De L Exploitation des Bois ou Moyens de Tirer un Parti Avantageux des Taillis, Demi-Futales et Hautes-Futalies, et d'en Faire une Juste Estimation . . . Paris: 1764. V. 46

A Practical Treaise of Husbandry . . . London: 1762. V. 37; 46

A Practical Treatise of Husbandry. London: 1759. V. 37

Traite des Arbres et Arbustes qui se Cultivent en France en Pleine Terre . . . Pairs: 1755. V. 41; 43; 44; 45

Traite des Arbres Fruitiers. Paris: 1768. V. 40; 43; 44

Traite General des Pesches, et Histoire des Poissons qu'elles Fournissent, tant pour la Subsistance des Hommes, que Pour Plusieurs Autres Usages qui ont Rapport aux arts et au Commerce. Paris: 1769-82. V. 39

DUHAMEL, JEAN BAPTISTE

Regiae Scientiarum Academiae Historia . . . Paris: 1701. V. 38; 41

DU HAUSSET, NICOLLE

The Private Memoirs of Madame Du Hausset, Lady's Maid to Madame de Pompadour. London: 1825. V. 37; 41

DUHAUT-CILLY, AUGUSTE

Viaggio Intorno al Globo Principalmente Alla California ed Alle Isole Sandwich negli Anni 1826, 1827, 1828 e 1829. Torino: 1841. V. 39; 40; 45

DUHEM, PIERRE MAURICE MARIE 1861-1916

Hydrodynamique Elasticite, Acoustique. Paris: 1891. V. 40

DUHIGG, BARTHOLOMEW THOMAS

History of the King's Inns; or, an Account of the Legal Body in Ireland, From Its Connexion with England. Dublin: 1806. V. 44; 46

Observations on the Operation of Insolvent Laws, and Imprisonment for Debt. Dublin?: 1797? V. 46

Observations on the Operation of Insolvent Laws, and Imprisonment for Debt. Dublin?: 1797? V. 45

DUHRING, HENRY

The Art of Living. London: 1843. V. 42; 45

Remarks on the United States of America, with Regard to the Actual State of Europe. London: 1833. V. 39

DUHRING, LOUIS

A Atlas of Skin Diseases. Philadelphia: 1876. V. 38; 44; 45; 46

DUIGENAN, PATRICK 1735-1816

An Address to the Nobility and Gentry of the Church of Reland, Explaining the Real Causes of the Commotions and Insurrections in the Southern Parts of this Kingdom Respecting Tithes. Dublin: 1786. V. 39

A Fair Representation of the Present Political State of Ireland . . . Dublin: 1800. V. 44

DUIS, E.

The Good Old Times in McLean County, Illinois . . . Bloomington: 1874. V. 37; 46

DU JARRIC, PIERRE

Thesavrvs Rervm Indicarvm. In Quo Christianae ac Catholicae Religionis tam in India Orientali Quam Aliis Regionibus Lusitanorum . . . Cologne: 1615. V. 45

DU JON, FRANCOIS

The Painting of the Ancients, in Three Bookes. London: 1638. V. 45

DUKE, BASIL W.

History of Morgan's Cavalry. Cincinnati: 1867. V. 41; 43; 45

DUKE, CHARLES L.

The Story of Sioux County. Orange City: 1942. V. 46

DUKE, DANIEL HACK

Chapters in the History of the Insane in the British Isles. London: 1882. V. 45

DUKE, G.

The Law of Charitable Uses Revised and Much Enlarged, with Many Cases in Law Both Antient and Modern, Whereunto is now added the Learned Reading of Sir Francis Moor in Middle Temple Hall Upon the Statute 43 Eliz. Concerning Charitable Uses . . . London: 1676. V. 37

DUKE, J. A.

Handbook of Medicinal Herbs. Boca Raton: 1985. V. 37; 38

Medicinal Plants of China. Algonac: 1985. V. 38

DUKE, JANE TAYLOR

Kenmore and the Lewises. New York: 1949. V. 41

DUKE, JOSHUA

Recollections of the Kabul Campaign, 1879 and 1880. London: 1883. V. 41

DUKE, WILLIAM

Allergy: Asthma, Hayfever, Urticaria and Allied Manifestations of Reaction. St. Louis: 1925. V. 42

DUKES, THOMAS FARMER

Antiquities of Shropshire from an old Manuscript of Edward Lloyd, Esq. of Drenwydd. Shrewsbury: 1844. V. 41

DULAC, EDMUND

Edmund Dulac's Picture Book for the French Red Cross. London: 1915. V. 41; 45

Edmund Dulac's Fairy Book. London: 1916. V. 40; 42; 46

Edmund Dulac's Fairy-book. London. V. 45

Edmund Dulac's Fairy-Book. London/New York: (n.d.). V. 37

Edmund Dulac's Picture-Book for the French Red Cross. London: (1915). V. 37

Edmund Dulac's Picture Book for the French Red Cross. London: (c. 1915). V. 37

A Fairy Garland Being Fairy Tales from the Old French. London: 1928. V. 37; 40; 45

A Fairy Garland. London: 1929. V. 46

A Fairy Garland. New York: 1929. V. 39

Fairy-Book. Fairy Tales of the Allied Nations. London: 1916. V. 37

A Fairy Garland. London: (1928). V. 37

Lyrics Pathetic and Humorous from A to Z. London: 1908. V. 44; 45

Picture Book. London. V. 39

Princess Badoura. Retold by Laurence Housman. London: (n.d.). V. 37

Rubaiyat de Omar Khayyam. Paris: (c. 1910). V. 37

The Sleeping Beauty and other Fairy Tales, from the Old French. London: 1911. V. 37

Stories from the Arabian Nights. Retold by Laurence Housman. London: (1907). V. 37

DULANEY, DANIEL

Considerations on the Propriety of Imposing Taxes in the British Colonies, for the Purpose of Raising a Revenue, an Act of Parliament. Boston: 1766. V. 41; 42

Considerations on the Property of Imposing Taxes in the British Colonies, For the Purpose of Raising a Revenue, By Act of Parliament. North America: 1766. V. 45

Considerations on the Propriety of Imposing Taxes in the British Colonies, for the Purpose of Raising a Revenue, by Act of Parliament. North America: i.e.: 1766. V. 44

DULANY, DANIEL

Considerations on the Propriety of Imposing Taxes in the British Colonies, for the Purpose of Raising a Revenue by Act of Parliament. London: 1766. V. 37; 38; 39

DULANY, PATRICK

Considerations on the Propriety of Imposing Taxes in the British Colonies, for the Purpose of Raising a Revenue, by Act of Parliament. London: 1766. V. 44; 45

DU LAURENS, ANDRE

Historia Anatomica Humani Corporis. Paris: 1600. V. 38

DULCKEN, H. W.

Domestic Animals, Familiar Birds, &c. London: 1870. V. 39

DULLAERT, JOHANNES 1470-1530

Questiones Super Duos Libros Peri Hermenias Aristotelis. Salamanca: 1517. V. 40

DU LOIR, SIEUR

Les Voyages du . . . Contenus en Plusieurs Lettres Ecrites du Levant, avec Plusieurs Partaiculaaritez qui n'ont Point Encore Este Remarquees Touchant la Grece & la Domination du Grand Seigneur, la Religion & les Moeurs de ses Sujets. Paris: 1654. V. 37

DULUTH'S Relations to the Northwest. N.P.: 1888. V. 40; 42

DU MARTRE, A. P.

The Elements of Heraldry. London: 1765. V. 39

DUMAS, ALEXANDER

The Romances. London: 1891-99. V. 46

DUMAS, ALEXANDRE 1825-1895

Camille. 1937. V. 39; 40; 41

Camille. London: 1937. V. 38; 41; 42; 43; 44; 45

Celebrated Crimes. London: 1895. V. 40

The Count of Monte Cristo. Mt. Vernon: 1941. V. 41; 43

The Count of Monte Cristo. New York: 1941. V. 41

A Gil Blas in California. Los Angeles: 1933. V. 37; 39; 40

Historical Romaces. Frontispiece Illustrations. Boston: 1888-1890. V. 37

Impressions of Travel, in Egypt and Arabia Petraea. New York: 1839. V. 40

La Dame Aux Camelias. Paris: 1897. V. 44

Romances. Boston: 1900. V. 40

The Three Musketeers. V. 44

Les Trois Mousquetaires. Paris: 1844. V. 42

Les Trois Mousquetaires, Avec une Lettre d'Alexandre Dumas Fils. Paris: 1894. V. 40; 41; 44

The Three Musketeers. New York: 1932. V. 41

Three Musketeers. New York: 1953. V. 45

Three Musketeers. Translated by William Robson. Illustrations by Pierre Falke. Holland: 1932. V. 37

The Works. Boston: 1900. V. 42; 44

DUMAS, CHARLES LOUIS 1765-1813

Principes de Physiologie, ou Introduction a la Science Experimentale . . . Paris: 1806. V. 43

DUMAS, CHARLES ROBERT

Contes Roses de Ma Mere-Grand. Paris: 1932. V. 45

DUMAS, F. G.

Modern Artists. London: 1882/3. V. 39; 43

DUMAS, GUILLAUME MATHIEU 1753-1837

Precis des Evenements Millitaires. Campagnes de 1799 a 1807. V. 40

DUMAS, MATHIEU

Memoirs of His Own Time . . . London: 1839. V. 42

DU MAURIER, DAPHNE

Classics of the Macabre. London: 1987. V. 44

Daphne Du Maurier's Classics of the Macabre. London: 1987. V. 43

Frenchman's Creek. London: 1941. V. 41; 43

I'll Never Be Young Again. London: 1932. V. 46

Jamaica Inn. London: 1936. V. 42

My Cousin Rachel. Garden City: 1952. V. 37; 42

Rebecca. London: 1938. V. 40; 41; 42; 46

The Winding Stair - Francis Bacon, His Rise and Fall. London: 1976. V. 42

DU MAURIER, GEORGE

V. 46

English Society at Home. London: 1880. V. 39

A Legend of Camelot, Pictures and Poems, Etc. New York: 1898. V. 46

The Martian. New York: 1897. V. 38; 39; 40; 41; 42; 43; 45

The Martian; A Novel. London/New York: 1898. V. 37

Peter Ibbetson. London: 1892. V. 39; 46

Trilby . . . London: 1894. V. 37; 39; 40; 43; 46

Trilby. London: 1895. V. 39; 40; 41

DU MAURIER, GEORGE LOUIS PAMELLA BUSSON 1834-1896

A Legend of Camelot, Pictures and Poems. New York: 1898. V. 40

Peter Ibbetson. London: 1892. V. 38; 40; 43

Trilby. New York: 1895. V. 42; 43

DUMENIL, P.

Nouvelle Bibliotheque des Voyages Ancien et Modernes . . . Paris: 1840. V. 39

DUMMER, JEREMIAH 1681-1739

A Defence of the New-England Charters. London: 1721. V. 39; 44; 45

A Defence of the New England Charters. London: 1765. V. 38; 39; 41; 45; 46

A Defence of the New England Charters. London: 1765. V. 45

A Defence of the New-England Charters. London: (1765). V. 37

DU MONCEL, T. DE

The Telephone the Microphone & the Phonograph. Authorised Translation with Additions and Corrections by the Author. London: 1879. V. 37

DUMONT D'URVILLE, JULES SEBASTIEN CESAR

Voyage au Pole Sud et dans l'Oceanie sur les Corvettes l'Astrolabe et la Zelee . . . Paris: 1841-1854. V. 42

DUMONT D'URVILLE, M. J.

Voyage de la Corvette L'Astrolabe Execute par Ordre du Roi, Pendant les Annees 1826-27-28-29. Paris: 1830-33. V. 40

DU MONT, E. R.

The People's Natural History by E. R. DuMont. 1902. V. 37

DUMONT, ETIENNE

Recollections of Mirabeau, and of the Two First Legislative Assemblies of France. London: 1832. V. 39

DUMONT, GABRIEL MARTIN

Details des Plus Interessantes Parties d'Archiecture de la Basilique de St. Pierre de Rome. Paris: 1763. V. 38

DUMONT, H. J.

Tropical Zooplankton. The Hague: 1984. V. 38

DU MONT, JEAN

A New Voyage to the Levant, Containing an Account of the Most Remarkable Curisoities in Germany, France, Italy, Malta and Turkey. London: 1696. V. 37

DUMONT, JEAN, BARON DE CARLSCROON d. 1726

Voyages de Mr. DuMont, en France, en Italie, en Allemagne a Malthe, et en Turquie . . . The Hague: 1699. V. 38

DU MONT, JOHN S.

Custer Battle Guns. Ft. Collins: 1974. V. 45

DUMONT, P. J.

Narrative of Thirty-Four Years Slavery and Travels in Africa. London: 1819. V. 40; 46

DU MOULIN, PETER

The Elements of Logick . . . Oxford: 1647. V. 37

DU MOULIN, PIERRE

A Treatise on Peace of Soul and Content of Mind . . . Salisbury: 1765. V. 39

DUMOURIER, C. F. D.

Memoirs of General Dumourier. Philadelphia: 1794. V. 41; 43

DUNAHM, SAMUEL CLARKE

The Alaskan Gold Fields and the Opportunities They Offer for Capital and Labor. (&) Supplement. Washington: 1898. V. 45

DUNANT, J. HENRY

A Memory of Solferino. Washington: 1939. V. 39; 41; 44

DUNBABIN, KATHERINE M. D.

The Mosaics of Roman North Africa. Oxford: 1978. V. 40

DUNBABIN, T. J.

Perachora II: The Sanctuaries of hera Akraia and Limenia. Excavations of the British School of Archaeology at Athens 1930-1933. Oxford: 1962. V. 37; 40

DUNBAR, ALICE

The Goodness of Saint Rocque. New York: 1899. V. 44

DUNBAR & TRIMBLE

History of 93rd Regt. Illinois Vol. Inf. from Organization to Muster Out. Chicago: 1898. V. 39

DUNBAR BRANDER, A. A.

Wild Animals in Central India. London: 1927. V. 42

DUNBAR-BRUNTON, J.

Big Game Hunting in Central Africa. London: 1912. V. 45

DUNBAR, EDWARD E.

The Romance of the Age; or, the Discovery of Gold in California. New York: 1867. V. 40

DUNBAR, EDWARD ELY

American Pioneering, an Address Before the Travellers' Club. Jersey City: 1863. V. 42

DUNBAR, PAUL L.

Howdy Honey-Howdy. New York: 1905. V. 42

DUNBAR, PAUL LARUENCE

Candle Lightin' Time . . . New York: 1901. V. 39; 46

DUNBAR, PAUL LAURENCE

Candle-Lightin' Time. New York: 1902. V. 40

Chris'mus is a Comin' and Other Poems. New York: 1907. V. 39

The Complete Poems. New York: 1913. V. 45

Folks from Dixie. New York: 1898. V. 37; 39; 41

Howdy Honey Howdy. Toronto: 1905. V. 37

Joggin' Erlong. New York: 1906. V. 39

The Love of Laundry. New York: 1900. V. 39

Lyrics of Lowly Life. New York: 1896. V. 43

Lyrics of Lowly Life. New York: 1898. V. 39

Lyrics of Hearthside. New York: 1899. V. 39

Lyrics of Love and Laughter. New York: 1903. V. 42; 46

Lyrics of Sunshine and Shadow. New York: 1905. V. 41

Poems of Cabin and Field. New York: 1899. V. 37; 39; 45; 46

Poems of Cabin and Field. New York: 1901. V. 39

The Strength of Gideon and Other Stories. New York: 1900. V. 46

The Uncalled . . . New York: 1898. V. 39

When Malindy Sings. New York: 1903. V. 39; 41

DUNBAR, PAUL LAWRENCE

Poems of Cabin and Field. New York: 1899. V. 43

DUNBAR, SEYMOUR

A History of Travel in America. Indianapolis: 1915. V. 38; 39; 40; 42; 43; 44; 45

A History of Travel in America. Indianpolis: 1915. V. 45

A History of Travel in America . . . Indianapolis: (1915). V. 37

DUNBAR, WILLIAM

The Poems of William Dunbar, Now First Collected. Edinburgh: 1834. V. 38

DUNBOW, S. M.

History of the Jews in Russia and Poland. Philadelphia: 1916. V. 46

DUNCAN, ALEXANDER

Alphabetical Catalogue of the Library of the Faculty of Physicians and Surgeons of Glasgow. Glasgow: 1885-1901. V. 44

DUNCAN, ALEXANDER continued

Miscellaneous Essays, Naval, Moral, Political and Divine. London: 1799. V. 41

DUNCAN, ALEXANDER G.

The Long Bridge of Bideford and Bideford Under the Restored Monarchy. Bideford: 1930. V. 43

DUNCAN, ANDREW 1744-1828

An Account of the Life, Writings, and Character of the Late John Hope . . . Edinburgh: 1789. V. 44

The Edinburgh New Dispensatory. Worcester: 1805. V. 37; 45

Heads of Lectures on the Theory and Practice of Medicine. Edinburgh: 1776. V. 43

Medical Cases, Selected from the Records of the Public Dispensary at Edinburgh . . . Edinburgh: 1781. V. 45; 46

Observations on the Distinguishing Symptoms of Three Different Species of Pulmonary Consumption, The Catarrhal, The Apostematous and the Tuberculous . . . Edinburgh: 1816. V. 42

Observations On the Distinguishing Symptoms of Three Different Species of Pulmonary Consumption. Philadelphia: 1819. V. 38; 42

DUNCAN, ARCHIBALD

The British Trident: or Register of Naval Actions Including Authentic Accounts of all the Most Remarkable Engagements at Sea. British Naval action from Drake, 1588 to Nelson, 1804. London: 1809. V. 37

The Life of the Late Most Noble Lord Horatio Nelson . . . A Correct Narrative of the Funeral of Horatio Lord Viscount Nelson. London: 1806. V. 42

Mariner's Chronicle: Being a Collection of Narratives of Shipwrecks, Fires . . . Calamities . . . of Maritime Enterprises . . . Including the accounts of the Survivors. (1755-1801). London;: 1804. V. 37

DUNCAN, DANIEL

Explication Nouvelle et Mechanique des Actions Animales. Paris: 1678. V. 38; 42

DUNCAN, DAVID DOUGLAS

Great Treasures of the Kremlin. New York: 1968. V. 40

Picasso's Picassos. The Treasures of La Californie. London: 1961. V. 46

Picasso's Picassos. New York: 1961. V. 41; 45

Picasso's Piccaos. New York & Evanston: 1961. V. 40

This Is War! A Photo-Narrative in Three Parts. New York: 1951. V. 37; 44

War Without Heroes. New York: 1970. V. 37; 44

Yankee Nomad. New York: 1966. V. 41; 45

DUNCAN, ERIC

From Shetland to Vancouver Island. Edinburgh: 1939. V. 46

DUNCAN, FRANCIS

Our Garrisons in the West:, or, Sketches in British North America. London: 1864. V. 43

DUNCAN, GEORGE J. C., MRS.

Pre-adamite Man or, The Story of Our Old Planet and Its Inhabitants. London: 1860. V. 41

DUNCAN, H. O.

The World on Wheels. Paris: 1926. V. 37; 42

DUNCAN, HARRY

Doors of Perception. Austin: 1983. V. 37; 38; 39; 40; 44; 45

Doors of Perception: Essays in Book Typography. Austin, Texas: 1983. V. 37

The Technology of Hand Printing: A Burdern for Craftsmen as Delivered Last Sprint at West Chester State College and to the Colophon Club. Omaha: 1980. V. 45

DUNCAN, ISADORA

The Art of the Dance. New York: 1928. V. 45; 46

My Life. New York: 1927. V. 40

DUNCAN, JAMES

The Modern Traveller. A popular Description Geographical, Historical and topographical, of the various countries of the globe, Brazil and Buenos Ayers. London: 1825. V. 37

DUNCAN, JOHN

Dissertatio Medica. Edinburgh: 1785. V. 39

Practical and Descriptive Essays on the Art Of Weaving. Glasgow: 1808. V. 37

Travels in Western AFrica In 1845 and 1846. London: 1847. V. 43

DUNCAN, JOHN M.

Travels Through Part of the United States and Canada in 1818 and 1819. Glasgow: 1823. V. 39; 41; 43; 44

DUNCAN, JOHN SHUTE

Hints to the Bearers of Walking Sticks and Umbrellas. London: 1809. V. 43

DUNCAN, LOUIS C.

The Medical Department of the United States Army in the Civil War. N.P.: 1914. V. 42

Medical Men in the American Revolution, 1775-1783. Carlisle Barracks;: 1931. V. 39

DUNCAN Macdonald of the Shire of Caithness Gent. The Celebrated Scotish Equilibrist. London: 1753. V. 39

DUNCAN, NORMAN

The Way of the Sea. London: 1904. V. 43

DUNCAN, P. M.

A Manual for the Classification, Training and Education of the Feeble-Minded. London: 1866. V. 37

A monograph of the British Fossil Corals. London: 1866-72. V. 37; 38

DUNCAN, RICHARD

Notices and Documents Illustrative of the Literary History of Glasgow. Glasgow: 1831. V. 38; 40

DUNCAN, ROBERT

Bending the Bow. 1968. V. 44

Boob One and Boob Two. San Francisco: 1952. V. 45

A Book of Resemblances. New Haven: 1966. V. 39; 40; 41; 42; 44

Caesar's Gate: Poems 1949-1950. Majorca: 1955. V. 44

The Cat and the Blackbird as Told by Robert Duncan. San Francisco: 1967. V. 46

Derivations: Selected Poems 1950-1956. London: 1968. V. 42

The First Decade: Selected Poems 1940-1950. London: 1968. V. 45

The First Decade. (with) Derivations. London: 1969. V. 37

The Five Songs. La Jolla: 1981. V. 46

Heavenly City, Earthly City. Berkley: 1947. V. 42; 44

Heavenly City, Earthly City. New York: 1947. V. 44

Letters. Highlands: 1958. V. 37; 46

Letters. Highlands: 1958. V. 37

Medieval Scenes. San Francisco: 1950. V. 44

Names of People. Los Angeles: 1968. V. 44

Of the War: Passages 22-27. Berkeley: 1966. V. 40

A Paris Visit. New York: 1985? V. 42

A Paris Visit. Illustrated by R.B. Kitaj. (New York): (1985). V. 37

Poems 1948-49. Berkeley: 1949. V. 37

Roots and Branches: Poems. New York: 1964. V. 44

Selected Poems. San Francisco: 1959. V. 37

A Selection of 65 Drawings - From One Drawing-Book 1952-1956. 1925. V. 39

A Selection of 65 Drawings. 1970. V. 38; 42; 43; 44

A Selection of 65 Drawings from One Drawing Book 1952-1956. Los Angeles: 1970. V. 37; 39

A Selection of 65 Drawings. Santa Barbara: 1970. V. 39; 40

Song of the Border Guard. Black Mountain: 1952. V. 39

Tribunals. Passages 31-35. Los Angeles: 1970. V. 44; 46

Tribunals. Passages 31-35. Santa Barbara: 1970. V. 42

The Truth & Life of Myth: an Essay in Essential Autobiography. New York: 1968. V. 37; 39; 40; 41; 42; 45; 46

The Truth and Life of Myth. New York: 1968. V. 42

The Years as Catches. Berkeley: 1966. V. 39; 42; 46

DUNCAN, RONALD

Tale of Tails. Cornwall: 1975. V. 41

DUNCAN, SARA JEANETTE

An American Girl in London. New York: 1891. V. 43

DUNCAN, SARA JEANNETTE

Cousin Cinderella. Toronto: 1908. V. 43

A Daughter of To-Day. Toronto: 1894. V. 43

The Path of a Star. Toronto: 1899. V. 43

The Pool in the Desert. New York: 1903. V. 43

The Simple Adventures of a Memsahib. New York: 1893. V. 43

A Social Departure. New York: 1890. V. 43

A Voyage of Consolation. New York: 1898. V. 43

DUNCAN, STANLEY

The Complete Wildfowler. London: 1911. V. 45; 46

DUNCAN, THOMAS D.

Recollections of Thomas D. Duncan, a Confederate Soldier. Nashville: 1922. V. 45

DUNCAN, WILLIAM

The Elements of Logick. London: 1748. V. 38; 40; 42; 43; 45

DUNCAN, WILLIAM continued

The Elements of Logick. London: 1748. V. 42

The Elements of Logick. London: 1759. V. 42; 43; 45

The Elements of Logick. London: 1759. V. 45

The Elements of Logick. London: 1764. V. 42; 45

The Elements of Logick. Edinburgh: 1780. V. 43; 45

The Elements of Logick. London: 1787. V. 45

The Elements of Logic. Albany: 1811. V. 39

DUNCAN, WILLIAM JAMES

Notices and Documents Illustrative of the Literary History of Glasgow, During the Greater Part of the Last Century. Glasgow: 1831. V. 45

DUNCKER, MAXIMILIAN WOLFGANG 1812-1886.

The V. 45

DUNCKLEY, HENRY

The Charter of the Nations; or, Free Trade and Its Results . . . London: 1854. V. 42; 43; 46

DUNCOMB, GILES

Trials Per Pais: or, the Law of England Concerning Juries by Nisi Prius, &c. London: 1766. V. 39

DUNCOMBE, CHARLES

Duncombe's Free Banking: An Essay on Banking, Currency, Finance, Exchanges and Political Economy. Cleveland, Ohio: 1841. V. 37

Report Upon the Subject of Education, Made to the Parliament of Upper Canada, 25th February, 1836. Toronto: 1836. V. 44; 45

DUNCOMBE, JOHN

An Evening Contemplation in a College. London: 1753. V. 37; 38; 44

The Feminead: or, Female Genius. A Poem. And An Evening Contemplation in a College; Being a Parody on 'Elegy in a Country Church-Yard.' London: 1757. V. 37

A Select Collection of Letters: Written by the Most Eminent Persons, on Various Entertaining Subjects, and on Many Important Occasions; from the Reign of Henry the Eighth to the Present Time. London: 1755. V. 39

DUNCOMBE, WILLIAM

Athaliah. London: 1722. V. 42

DUNCUMB, JOHN

Collections Towards the History and Antiquities of the County of Hereford. Hereford: 1804. V. 39; 40

Collections Towards the History and Antiquities of the County of Hereford. Hereford: 1804-12. V. 39

General View of the Agriculture of the County of Hereford. London: 1805. V. 46

DUNDAS, HENRY

Scots Guards. A Memoir. London: 1921. V. 46

DUNDAS, JOHN

The Method of Procedure by Presbyteries in Settling of Schools in Every Parish . . . Edinburgh: 1709. V. 46

DUNDAS, L. M.

A Big Game Pocket-Book for Kenya Colony. London: 1927. V. 42

DUNDERBERG MINING COMPANY

Prospectus of the Dunderberg Mining Company. New York: 1872. V. 37

DUNDONALD, ARCHIBALD COCHRANE, 9TH EARL OF 1749?-1831

The Present State of the Manufacture of Salt, Explained . . . London: 1785. V. 42

A Treatise, Shewing the Intimate Connection that Subsists Between Agriculture and Chemistry . . . London: 1795. V. 45

DUNDONALD, THOMAS COCHRANE, 10TH EARL OF 1775-1860

The Autobiography of a Seaman. London: 1860. V. 41

Narrative of Services in the Liberation of Chili, Peru and Brazil, etc. London: 1859. V. 41; 43

Notes on Mineralogy, Government and Condition of the British West India Islands and North American Maritime Colonies; with a Statistical Chart of Newfoundland, Contrasting the Circumstances of the French and British Fisheries. London: 1851. V. 39

The Trial of Lord Cochrane . . . for an Escape . . . London: 1816. V. 38

DUNGLISON, ROBLE

On the Influence of Atmosphere and Locality; Change of Air and Climate; Seasons . . . on Human Health . . . Philadelphia: 1835. V. 40

DUNGLISON, ROBLEY

History of Medicine From the Earliest Ages to the Commencement of the Nineteenth Century. Philadelphia: 1872. V. 38; 41; 42; 45

The Medical Student . . . Philadelphia: 1837. V. 45

Medical and Surgical Monographs. Philadelphia: 1838. V. 45; 46

Medical Lexicon. Philadelphia: 1865. V. 40; 41

Medical and Surgical Monographs by Andral, Babbington, Beck, Bright, Brody, Burne, Carmichael, Clutterbuck, Cormack, Dubois, Farr, Itard, Louis, Manoir and Taylor with Occasional Comments by the Editor. Philadelphia: 1838. V. 37; 38

Medical Lexicon. A Dictionary of Medical Science . . . Philadelphia: 1874. V. 37

DUNHAM, DOWS

The Barkal Temples Excavated by George Andrew Reisner. Boston: 1970. V. 40; 42

Decorated Chapels of the Meroitic Pyramids at Meroe and Barkal by Suzanne E. Chapman. The Royal Cemeteries of Kush, volume 3. Boston: 1952. V. 37

The oyal Cemeteries of Kush. Volume IV. Royal Tombs at Meroe and Barkal. Boston: 1957. V. 41

Second Cataract Forts. Boston: 1960-67. V. 40; 42

The West and South Cemeteries at Meroe Excavated by the Late George Andrew Reisner. Boston: 1963. V. 42

DUNHAM, JACOB

Journal of Voyages: Containing an Account of the Author's Being Twice Captured by the English, and Once by Gibbs the Pirate. New York: 1850. V. 37; 40; 43

Journal of Voyages . . . New York: 1851. V. 42; 43; 45

Journal of Voyages; Containing an Account of the Author's Being Twice Captured by the English and Once by Gibbs the Pirate . . . New York: 1859. V. 41

DUNHAM, JOHN MOSELEY

The Vocal Companion, and Masonic Register. Boston: 1802. V. 40

DUNHAM, N. J.

History of Jerauld County, South Dakota. Washington Springs: 1910. V. 38; 39; 41; 43; 45

DUNHILL, ALFRED

The Pipe Book. London: 1924. V. 40

The Pipe Book. New York: 1924. V. 40

DUNIWAY, ABIGAIL J.

Captain Gray's Company; or, Crossing the Plains and Living in Oregon. Portland: 1859. V. 45

DUNIWAY, ABIGAIL SCOTT

David and Anna Matson. New York: 1876. V. 42; 44; 45

DUNKIE, JOHN J.

Prison Life During the Rebellion. Singer's Glen: 1869. V. 43; 46

DUNKIN, ROBERT

The Roe Deer. 1987. V. 46

The Roe Deer. London: 1987. V. 45

DUNKLE, JOHN J.

Prison Life During the Rebellion. Singer's Glen: 1869. V. 38; 39; 41; 42; 44

DUNLAP, JACK

American, British and Continental Pepperbox Firearms. California: 1964. V. 44

DUNLAP, W. W.

Charter and Digest of Ordinances of the City of San Antonio, Approved July 18, 1857. San Antonio: 1857. V. 37

DUNLAP, WILLIAM

Andre: a Tragedy. London: 1799. V. 37; 43

Fonteville Abbey, a Tragedy. New York: 1807. V. 37

A History of the American Theatre. New York: 1832. V. 40; 41; 43

History of the Rise and Progress of the Arts of Design in the United States. New York: 1834. V. 39; 40; 41; 44

A History of New York, for Schools. New York: 1837. V. 45

History of the New Netherlands, Province of New York, and State of New York, to the Adoption of the Federal Constitution. New York: 1839-40. V. 43

A History of the Rise and Progress of the Arts of Design in the United States. Boston: 1918. V. 37; 38; 43

A History of the American Theatre. New York: 1832. V. 37

The Italian Father. New York: 1810. V. 40

The Life of Charles Brockden Brown; Together with Selections from the Rarest of his Printed Works, from His Original Letters . . . Philadelphia: 1815. V. 42

Memoirs of George Fred. Cooke, Edq. Late of the Theatre Royal, Covent Garden . . . London: 1813. V. 39; 42

Memoirs of the Life of George Frederick Cooke, Esquire, Late of the Theatre Royal, Covent Garden. New York: 1813. V. 38

Peter the Great; or, the Russian Mother. New York: 1814. V. 44

DUNLAP, WILLIAM continued

Thirty Years Ago; or the Memoirs of a Water Drinker. New York: 1836. V. 43

DUNLAVY, JOHN

Manifesto; or, a Declaration of the Doctrine and Practice of the Church of Christ. New York: 1847. V. 39; 42; 43

DUNLOP, ALEXANDER 1798-1870

A Treatise on the Law of Scotland Relative to the Poor. Edinburgh: 1825. V. 38

DUNLOP, DURHAM

A Memoir of the Professional Life of William J. Barre, R.I.A.I., with photographic illustrations. Belfast: 1868. V. 37

DUNLOP, FRANCES

Our Forest Home: Being Extracts from the Correspondence of the Late Frances Stewart. Montreal: 1902. V. 44

DUNLOP, JOHN

The History of Fiction; Being a Critical Account of the Most Celebrated Prose Works of Fiction . . . Edinburgh: 1816. V. 42; 43

History of Roman Literature, From Its Earliest Period to the Augustan Age. London: 1823. V. 43

History of Roman Literature, from Its Earliest Period to the Augustan Age. (with) History of Roman Literature, During the Augustan Age. London: 1823-28. V. 45

The History of Fiction: Being a Critical Account of the most Celebrated Prose Works of Fiction, from the Earliest Greek Romances to the Novels of the Present Age . . . London: 1814. V. 37

DUNLOP, R. G.

Travels in Central America . . . London: 1847. V. 45

DUNLOP, R. H. W.

Hunting in the Himalaya. London: 1860. V. 39

DUNLOP, ROBERT HENRY WALLACE

Service and Adventure with the Khakee Reassalah; or, meerut Volunteer Horse, during the Mutinies of 1857-58. London: 1858. V. 37

DUNLOP, W. S.

Lee's Sharpshooters; or, The Forefront of Battle. Little Rock: 1899. V. 39; 43

DUNN,

A Description of Killarney. London: 1776. V. 41; 43

A Description of Kilarney; London: 1786. V. 39

DUNN, DOROTHY

American Indian Painting of the Southwest and Plains Areas. Albuquerque: 1968. V. 37; 40

DUNN, DOUGLAS

Europa's Lover. Newcastle-upon-Tyne: 1982. V. 43

DUNN, E. J.

Geology of Gold (South Africa, Australia, New Zealand). London: 1929. V. 38

DUNN, HENRY

Popular Education or, the Normal School Manual . . . London: 1837. V. 43

DUNN, J. B.

Perilous Trails of Texas. Dallas: 1932. V. 43

DUNN, J. E.

Indian Territory a Pre Commonwealth. Indianapolis: 1904. V. 38; 44

DUNN, J. P.

Massacres of the Mountains. New York: 1886. V. 37; 43; 45

DUNN, JACOB P.

Massacres of the Mountains: a History of the Indian Wars of the Far West. New York: 1806. V. 42

DUNN, JACOB PIATT

Greater Indianapolis: The History, the Industries, the Institutions and the People. Chicago: 1910. V. 37

DUNN, JOHN

The Oregon Territory, and the British North American Fur Trade. Philadelphia: 1845. V. 39; 43; 45

DUNN, KATHERINE

Geek Love. New York: 1989. V. 44; 45

3 Day Fox: a Tattoo. N.P.: 1979. V. 43; 44

Truck. New York: 1971. V. 44; 46

DUNN, MATTHIAS

An Historical, Geological and Descriptive View of the Coal Trade of the North of England. Newcastle-upon-Tyne: 1844. V. 37; 40; 43

An Historical, Geological and Descriptive View of the Coal Trade of the North of England . . . Newcastle-upon-Tyne: 1844. V. 43

A Treatise on the Winning and Working of Collieries. Newcastle-upon-Tyne: 1848. V. 40; 41

DUNN, MUSA

Sideways and Backward. Waxahachie: 1900. V. 41

DUNN, NATHAN

. . . A Descriptive Catalogue of the Chinese Collection in Philadelphia. With Miscellaneous Remarks Upon the Manners, Customs, Trade and Government of the Celestial Empire. Philadelphia: 1839. V. 41

DUNN, R. I.

A Condensed Military Pocket Manual, for Volunteer and Militia Officers, Non-Commissioned Officers and Privates . . . Lexington: 1841. V. 44

Military Pocket Manual, for Militia Officers . . . with a Short Treatise on the Cavalry and Infantry Swords . . . Cincinnati: 1831. V. 41

DUNN, SAMUEL

Scientia Terrarum et Coelorum or, the Heavens and Earth Astronomically and Geographically Delineated and Displayed . . . London. V. 43

DUNN, THOMAS

A Discourse Delivered in the New Dutch Church, Nassau Street, on Tuesday, the 21st of October, 1794, Before the New York Society for the Information and Assistance of Persons Emigrating from Foreign Countries. New York: 1794. V. 37

DUNNE, CHARLES

The Academicians of 1823 . . . London: 1823. V. 43

DUNNE, JOHN GREGORY

Delano: The Story of the California Grape Strike. New York: 1967. V. 44

DUNNE, P. C.

The Young Married Lady's Private Medical Guide. N.P.: 1854. V. 44

DUNNICLIFFE, HENRY

Selections from the Autobiography of Wilhelmina Waggles. London: 1863. V. 43

DUNNING, RALPH CHEEVER

Rococo. Paris: 1926. V. 40; 42; 43

DUNNY, SEYMOUR

Golf Fundamentals. Lake Placid: 1930. V. 37

DUNOYER, CHARLES

De La Liberte Du Travail, ou Simple Expose des Conditions dans Lesquelles les Forces Humaines . . . Paris: 1845. V. 41; 45

DUNPAR, PAUL LAURENCE

Lyrics of Lowly Life. New York: 1898. V. 37

DUNRAVEN, W. T. WINDHAM-QUIN, 4TH EARL OF

The Great Divide. Travels in the Upper Yellowstone in the Summer of 1874. London: 1876. V. 37; 45

DUNS, J.

Memoir of Sir James Y. Simpson, Bart. Edinburgh: 1873. V. 46

DUNS, JOANNES SCOTUS 1265-1308

In IIII Libros Sententiarum & Quodlibetales. Venetiis: 1617. V. 42

Quaestiones in Quattuor Libros Sententiarum. Venice: 1481. V. 43; 46

Quodlibeta. Venice: 1477. V. 40

DUNSANDY, EDWARD JOHN MORETON DRAX PLUNKETT 1878-1957

The Compromise of the King of the Golden Isles. New York: 1924. V. 43

DUNSANY, EDWARD JOHN MORETON DRAX PLUNKETT

Alexander and Three Small Plays. London: 1925. V. 42

The Book of Wonder. London: 1912. V. 39; 40

The Book of Wonder. London: 1912. V. 37

The Chronicles of Rodriguez. 1922. V. 44

The Chronicles of Rodriguez. London: 1922. V. 39; 40; 41; 43; 45; 46

The Chronicles of Rodriguez. London & New York: 1922. V. 43

The Chronicles of Rodriguez. London & New York: 1922. V. 39

The Chronicles of Rodriguez. London/New York: (1922). V. 37

The Compromise of the King of the Golden Isles. New York: 1924. V. 39; 40

The Curse of the Wise Woman. New York: 1933. V. 40; 42

A Dreamer's Tales. London: 1910. V. 41

A Dreamer's Tales. London: 1910. V. 41

DUNSANY, EDWARD JOHN MORETON DRAX PLUNKETT continued

A Dreamer's Tales and Other Stories. New York: 1919. V. 44

Fifty-One Tales by Lord Dunsany. London: 1915. V. 44

The Gods of Pegana. Boston. V. 46

The Golds of Pegana. London: 1905. V. 41

The King of Elfland's Daughter. London: 1924. V. 40; 41; 42; 43

The King of Elfland's Daughter. London: & New York: 1924. V. 45

The Last Revolution. London: 1951. V. 42

Lord Adrian - a Play. Waltham St. Lawrence: 1933. V. 42; 43

A Night at an Inn. New York: 1916. V. 41

The Old Folk of the Centuries. London: 1930. V. 43

Patches of Sunlight. London: 1938. V. 40

Selections from the Writings of Lord Dunsany. Churchtown: 1912. V. 41; 42

Selections from the Writings of Lord Dunsany. Churchtown, Dundrum: 1912. V. 37

The Sword of Welleran and Other Stories. London: 1908. V. 37; 40; 41

Tales of Wonder. London: 1916. V. 40; 41

Tales of War. Dublin: 1918. V. 39

Tales of Three Hemispheres. London: 1920. V. 38

Time and the Gods. London: 1906. V. 37; 39; 40; 41

Time and the Gods. London: 1922. V. 46

To Awaken Pegasus; and Other Poems. Oxford: 1949. V. 40

The Travel Tales of Joseph Jorkens. London: 1931. V. 42

The Tree of Idleness. London: 1955. V. 45

The Year. London: 1946. V. 41

DUNSANY, EDWARD PLUNKETT

The Compromise of the King of the Golden Isles. New York: 1924. V. 45

DUNSAY, EDWARD JOHN MORETON DRAX PLUNKETT

The Year. London: (1946). V. 37

DUNS SCOTUS

Questiones Quodlibetales ex Quatuor Sententiarum Voluminibus. Lyon: 1530. V. 37

Scriptum Joannis Duns Scoti . . . Super Quarto Sententiarum. Lyon: 1530. V. 37

DUNS SCOTUS, JOHANNES 1264-1308

Quaestiones Quas Reportationes Vocant, in Quatuor Libros Sententiarum Petri Lombardi. Venetiis: 1597. V. 39

Questiones Quolibetales. Colophon: Impresse Venetus..: 1497. V. 39

Summa Theologica ex Universis Operibus Ejus Concinnata, Juxta Ordinem & Dispositionem Summae Angelici Doctoris S. Thomae Aquinatis. Rome: 1739-27-38. V. 39

DUNSTAR, SAMUEL

Anglia Rediva. London: 1699. V. 38

DUNSTER, CHARLES

Considerations on Milton's Early Reading, and the Prima Stamina of His Paradise Lost. London: 1800. V. 38

DUNSTERVILLE, G. C. K.

Venezuelan Orchids Illustrated. London: 1959. V. 38; 46

DUNSTEVILLE, G. C. K.

Venezuelan Orchids Illustrated. London: 1959-76. V. 46

DUNTHORNE, GORDON

Flower and Fruit Prints of the 18th and Early 19th Centuries. Washington: 1938. V. 37; 39; 41; 42; 43; 45; 46

Flower and Fruit Prints of the 18th and Early 19th Centuries. Washington, DC: 1938. V. 37; 38

DUNTON, JOHN 1659-1733

The Athenian Oracle. London: 1703. V. 38

Athenian Sport. London: 1707. V. 37; 38; 43

Dunton's Whipping-Post: or, a Satyr Upon Every Body. (and) The Living Elegy: or, Dunton's Letter to His Few Creditors . . . London: 1706. V. 39

An Essay Proving We Shall Know Our Friends. London: 1698. V. 46

The Hazard of a Death-Bed Repetence, Fairly Argued, From the Late Remorse of W---- late D---- of D----. London: 1708. V. 38

Letters Written from New England, A.D., 1686 In Which are Described His Voyages by Sea, His Travels on Land and the Characters of His Friends and Acquaintances. Boston: 1867. V. 39

The Life and Errors of John Dunton, Late Citizen of London. London: 1705. V. 39; 44

The Life and Errors of John Dunton. London: 1818. V. 40; 41; 43; 44

The Life and Errors of John Dunton, Citizen of London. London: 1818. V. 40

The Merciful Assizes; or, a Panegyric of the Late Lord Jeffreys Hanging So Many in the West. London: 1701. V. 42

Neck or Nothing: in a Letter to the Right Honourable the Lord ----- Being a Supplement tot he Short History of the Parliament. London: 1713. V. 41

The Phenix: or a Revival of Scarce and Valuable Pieces From the Remotest Antiquity Down to the Present Times. London: 1707-8. V. 38; 46

The Tribute of a London Publisher to His Printers, John Dunton's Sketches of Printers, Stationers, Binders and Engravers of the City of London, 1689-1705. Cambridge: 1930. V. 39

A True Journall of the Sally Fleet, with the Proceedings of the Voyage. London: 1637. V. 41

The Visions of the Soul, Before It Comes Into the Body. London: 1692. V. 44

The Young Student's Library. London: 1692. V. 42

DUNVILLE, ROBERT GRIMSHAW

North Sea Bubbles. Belfast: 1890. V. 43; 44

DU PAGE DU PRATZ, ANTOINE

Histoire de la Louisiane . . . Paris: 1758. V. 38

DUPARCQUE, F.

A Treatise on the Functional and Orangic Diseases of the Uterus from the French of F. Duparcque. Philadelphia: 1837. V. 41; 44

DUPATY, CHARLES MARGUERITE JEAN BAPTISTE

Travels through Italy, in a Series of Letters, Written in the Year 1785, by President Dupaty. London: 1788. V. 38; 40; 44

DUPAU, J. AMEDEE

Lettres Physiologique et Morale sur le Magnetisme Animal, Contenant l'Expose Critique des Experiences les Plus Reccentes . . . Paris: 1826. V. 43

DU PERAC, ETIENNE

I Vestigi dell'Antichita di Roma. Rome: 1575. V. 41

DU PETIT-THOUARS, ABEL

Voyage Autour du Monde sur la Fregate la Venus Pendant Les Annees 1836-39 . . . Paris: 1841. V. 40

DUPIN, CHARLES

Narratives of Two Excursions to the Ports of England, Scotland and Ireland in 1816, 1817 and 1818. London: 1819. V. 40

Two Excursions to the Ports of England, Scotland and Ireland in 1816, 1817 and 1818.. London: 1819. V. 41; 43

DUPIN, CHARLES, BARON

Memoires sur la Marine et les Ponts et Chaussees de France et d'Angleterre Contenant Deux Relations de Voyaages faits par l'Auteur dans les Ports d'Angleterre . . . Paris: 1818. V. 38

DUPIN, JACQUES

Fits and Starts: Selected Poems. Weston. V. 41

Fits and Starts. Salisbury: 1974. V. 38; 40; 41

Joan Miro Life and Work. New York. V. 46

Miro. Paris: 1961. V. 46

Miro. New York: 1962. V. 46

DU PIN, LEWIS ELLIES

A New History of Ecclesiastical Writers. London: 1693-1706. V. 44

DU PIN, LOUIS ELLIES

Liber Psalmorum Cum Notis Quibus Eorum Sensus Litteralis Exponitur. Parisiis: 1691. V. 42

A New Ecclesiastical History of the Sixteenth Century . . . London: 1703-06. V. 46

A New History of Ecclesiastical Writers: Containing an Account of the Authors of the several Books of the Old and New Testament: and the Lives and Writings of the primitive Fathers; an Abridgment and . . . London: 1697. V. 37

A New History of Ecclesiastical Writers, Containing an Account of the Authors of the Several Books of the Old and New Testament, of the Lives and Writings of the Primitve Fathers . . . Together with a Judgement Upon Their Style and Doctrine. London: Printed for Abel: 1693. V. 37

DU PINET, ANTOINE

Historia Plantarum. Lyon: 1561. V. 42

DUPLAIX, GEORGES

Animal Stories. New York: 1944. V. 45

DUPLEIX, SCIPION

L'Ethique ou Philosophie Morale. Paris: 1610. V. 41

DU PLESSIS

Memoirs; or, Variety of Adventures Interspersed with Characters and Reflections Moral, Satorical, Instructie and Humorous. Dublin: 1757. V. 46

DU PONCEAU, P. S.

Opinion of the Case of the Alluvion Land or Batture Near New Orleans. New Orleans: 1808. V. 41

DU PONCEAU, P. S. continued

A Review of the Case of the New Orleans Batture and the Discussions That Have Taken Place Respecting . . . Philadelphia: 1809. V. 41

DU PONCEAU, PETER S.

A Dissertation on the Nature and Extent of the Jurisdiction of the Courts of the United States. Philadlephia: 1824. V. 43

A Review of the Cause of the New Orleans Batture and of the Discussions that Have Taken Place Respecting It . . . Philadelphia: 1809. V. 45

DUPONT, ALBERT

La Societe Paradisiaque ou Le Reve Helateur d'un Hypergraphe Sensible. 1989. V. 44

DUPONT-AUBERVILLE, M.

Ornamental Textile Fabrics of all Ages and Nations: a Practical Collection of Specimens. London: 1877. V. 42

DU PONT, BESSIE GARDNER

E. L. Du Pont de Nemours and Company, A History 1802-1902. Boston/New York: 1920. V. 39

DUPONT DE NEMOURS, PIERRE SAMUEL

Examen du Livre des M. Malthus sur le Principe de Population; Auquel on a Joint Traduction de Quatre Chaptres de ce Livre Supremes dans l'Edition Francais; et Une Lettre a M. Say sur son Traite d'Economie Politique. Philadelphia: 1817. V. 40

Memoires sur la Vie et les Ouvrages de M. Turgot, Ministre d'etat. Philadelphia (i.e. Paris): 1782. V. 38

Memoires sur la Vie et les Ouvrages . . . Philadelphie: 1782. V. 41; 45

DUPONT, GAETAN PIERRE MARIE

Anser to the Reflections of the Right Hon. Edmund Burke. London: 1791. V. 39

DUPONT, PAUL

Essais Pratiques d'Imprimerie Precedes d'une Notice Historique. Typographie, Lithographie. Paris: 1849. V. 39

DU PONT, SAMUEL F.

Official Dispatches and Letters of Rear Admiral Du Pont, U.S. Navy 1846-48. 1861-63. Wilmington: 1883. V. 43

DUPORT, JAMES 1606-1679

(Greek Title) Sive Metaphrasis Libri Psalmorum Graecis Versibus Contexta. Cambridge: 1666. V. 39

(Greek Title), Sive Liber Job Graeco Carmine Redditus. Cambridge: 1637. V. 37

DUPPA, R.

The Classes and Orders of the Linnaean System of Botany. London: 1816. V. 38; 39; 41

DUPPA, RICHARD

A Brief Account of the Subversion of the Papal Government, 1798. London: 1806. V. 43; 46

The Classes and Orders of the Linnaean System of Botany. London: 1816. V. 39

A Journal of the Remarkable Occurrences that Took Place in Rome, Upon the Subversion of the Ecclesiastical Government, in 1798. London: 1799. V. 39

The Life of Michel Angelo Buonarroti, With His Poetry and Letters. London: 1807. V. 40

The Life of Raffaello Sanzio da Urbino. London: 1816. V. 40

Miscellaneous Observations and Opinions on the Continent. London: 1825. V. 38; 40

Travels on the Continent, Sicily and the Lipari Isles. London: 1829. V. 39

DUPRE, L. J.

Austin and Travis County, Texas. Charms of the Capital City and Its Environs. Austin: 1876. V. 37

DU PREAU, GABRIEL 1511-1588

Nostrorum Temporum Calamitus. Paris: 1560. V. 38

DUPUIS, JOSEPH

Jouranl of a Residence in Ashantee. London: 1824. V. 37; 41

DUPUIT, ARSENE JULES E. J.

La Liberte Commerciale son Principe et ses Consequences. Paris: 1861. V. 38

DU PUY DU GREZ, BERNHARD 1640-1720.

Traite sur la peinture . . . Toulouse: 1699. V. 37

DUPUYTREN, BARON

Lectures on Clinical Surgery Delivered in the Hotel-Dieu of Paris. Washington: 1835. V. 38

DUPUYTREN, GUILLAUME

On Lesions of the Vascular System, Diseases of the Rectum and Other Surgical Complaints. London: 1854. V. 42

DURAND, CHARLES

Reminiscences of Charles Durand of Toronto. Barrister: 1897. V. 43

DURAND, DAVID

The Life of Lucilio (alias Julius Caesar) Vanini, burnt for Atheism at Thoulouse. London: 1730. V. 37

DURAND, GARBIZZA & MOPILLE

Vues des Plus Beaux Edifices Publics et Particuliers de la Ville de Paris. Paris: 1810. V. 39

DURAND, H. MORTIMER

The Thirteenth Hussars, in the Great War. London: 1921. V. 37; 46

DURAND, J. N. L.

Raccolta e Paralello delle Fabbriche Classiche di Tutti Tempi . . . Venice: 1833. V. 38; 42

Recueil et Parallele des Edifices de Tout Genre, Anciens et Modernes, Remarquables par Leur Beaute . . . Paris: 1801. V. 38; 42

Recueil et Parallele des Edifices de Tout Genre . . . Liege: 1841. V. 38

DURAND, J. P. L.

A Voyage to Senegal; or, Historical, Philosophical and Political Memoirs, Relative to the Discoveries, Establishments and Commerce of Europeans in the Atlantic Ocean, from Cape Blanco to the River of Sierra Leone. London: 1806. V. 38; 40; 41

DURAND, JEAN NICOLAS LOUIS 1760-1834

Precis des Lecons d'Architecture Donnees a l'Ecole Polytechnique . . . Paris: 1802-05. V. 40

DURANDUS

Rationale Divinorum Officiorum. Mainz: 1459. V. 37; 38; 39

DURANDUS, WILLIAM

Rationale Divinorum Officiorum . . . Venetiis: 1581. V. 43

DURANT, JACQUES

Variarvm Libri Dvo. In Qvibvs Praeter Veterum Ritus, Varij Auctores, vel Emendantur, vel Illustrantur. Paris: 1582. V. 39

DURANT, THOMAS

Union Pacific Railroad Report of Thomas C. Durant . . . In Relation to the Surveys Made Up to the Close of the Year 1864. New York: 1866. V. 41

DURANT, THOMAS J.

To the Hon. Henry Winter Davis, House of Representatives, Washington, D.C. New Orleans: 1864. V. 39

DURANT, WILL

The Story of Civilization by Will and Ariel Durant. V. 37

Transition. New York: 1927. V. 46

DURANTE, C.

Herbario Nuovo, Con Figure che Rappresentano le Vive Piante, Che Nascono in Tutta Europa & nell'Indie Orientali & Occidentali. Rome: 1585. V. 41

DURANTE, CASTAORE

Herbario Nuovo Medico & Cittadino Romano, Con Figure, Che Rappresentano le Viue Piante, Che Nascono in Tutta Europa, & Nell Indie Orientali & Occidentali. Venetia: 1684. V. 37; 38; 40

DURANTE, CASTORE

Herbario Nuovo Medico & Cittadino Romno, Configure, Che Rappresentano Le Viue Piante, Che Nscono in Tutta Europa & Nell Indie Orientali & Occidentali. Venetia: 1684. V. 38

DURANTI, GUILLELEMUS

Rationale Divionorum Officiorum. Mainz: 1459. V. 45

DURANTIS, GULIELMUS, BP. OF MENDE

Breuiarium Aurem Specula Totius . . . ad Oms . . . Delitescentes Materias . . . Paris: 1519. V. 40

DURAZZO, IPPOLITO

Elogi Storici di Cristoforo Colombo e di Andrea Doria. Parma: 1781. V. 40

D'URBAN, W. S. M.

The Birds of Devon. London: 1892. V. 39; 40; 43

The Birds of Devon. London: 1895. V. 37; 42; 43; 44

DURBIN, HENRY

A Narrative of Some Extraordinary Things that Happened to Mr. Richard Giles's Children, at the Lamb, Without Lawford's-Gate, Bristol . . . Bristol: 1800. V. 45

DURBIN, JOHN P.

Observations in the East, Chiefly in Egypt, Palestine, Syria and Asia Minor. New York: 1847. V. 37; 39; 45

Observations in the East. New York: 1854. V. 39; 42; 45

DU REFUGE, EUSTACHE

Arcana Aulica; or Walsingham's Manual of Prudential Maxims for the States-Man and Courtier. London: 1694. V. 43

DUREL, JOHN

A V. 45

DURENCEAU, ANDRE

Inspirations. Woodstock, New York: (1928). V. 37

DURET, C.

Historie Admirable des Plantes et Herbes Esmerveillables et Miraculeuses en Nature. Paris: 1605. V. 39

DURET, CLAUDE d. 1611

Thresor de l'Histoire des Langues de cest Univers, Contenant les Origines Beautez, Perfections, decadences, Mutations, Changements, Conversions & Rines des Langues. Yverdon: 1619. V. 43

DURET, JEAN 1540-1620

L'Harmonie et Conference des Magistrats Romains avec les Officiers Francois... Lyon: 1574. V. 46

DURET, THEODORE

Renoir. Paris: 1924. V. 38; 40; 41

Vincent Van Gogh. Paris: 1919. V. 37; 44

DURFEE, JOB

Whatcheer, or Roger Williams in Banishment. Providence: 1832. V. 43

D'URFEY, THOMAS 1653-1723

Butler's Ghost. London: 1682. V. 38; 39; 40; 44; 45

Collin's Walk through London and Westminster. London: 1690. V. 37; 41

The Fool Turn'd Critick... London: 1678. V. 37; 42

The Malecontent. London: 1684. V. 39; 44

A New Opera, Call'd Cinthia and Endimion, or, the Loves of the Deities. London: 1697. V. 38; 41

New Opera's With Comical Stories. London: 1721. V. 38; 39; 40; 41; 45

New Opera's, with Comical Stories and Poems on Several Occasions... London: 1721. V. 41

A Pill to Purge State-Melancholy. London: 1715. V. 39

The Progress of Honesty. London: 1681. V. 39; 40; 43; 44; 45

Squire Oldsapp; or, the Night Adventurers. London: 1679. V. 40

Stories, Moral and Comical. London: 1707? V. 38; 41

Wit and Mirth; or, Pills to Purge Melancholy. London: 1719-20. V. 37; 38; 39

DURFORT, CLAIR DE

Ourika. Austin: 1977. V. 37; 39; 41; 42; 43; 45; 46

Ourika. Austin: 1977. V. 39

DURFORT, CLAIRE DE

Ourika. Austin: 1977; V. 42

Ourika. Texas: 1977. V. 45

DURFORT, CLAIRE ROSE LOUISE BONNE DE, DUCHESS

Ourika. London: 1824. V. 46

DURHAM, EARL OF

The Report and Despatches of the Earl of Durham, Her Majesty's High Commissioner and Governor-General of British North America. London: 1839. V. 37; 42

DURHAM, JAMES

Clavis Cantici. Glasgow: 1767. V. 38

The Dying Man's Testament to the Church of Scotland. Edinburgh: 1659. V. 37

DURHAM, JOHN GEORGE LAMBERTON, 1ST EARL OF 1792-1840.

Report on the Affairs of British North AMerica... London: 1839. V. 39; 41

DURHAM, JOSEPH Z.

Ladies' Physo Medical Companion, Containing the Causes and Preventatives of a Premature Decline, with Review of the Various Changes and Derangments of the Female Constitution... Canton: 1850. V. 40

DURHAM, LUCAS

Lord Durham's Report on the Affairs of British North America. Oxford: 1912. V. 40

DURHAM, NELSON W.

History of the City of Spokane and Spokane County, Washington. Spokane: 1921. V. 37; 43

DURIEN, PAUL

Chinook Bible History. Kamloops: 1899. V. 45

DU RIETZ, R.

Bibliotheca Polynesiana. A Catalogue of Some of the Books in the Polynesiana Collection Formed by the Late Bjarne Kroepelien and Now in the Oslo University Library. Oslo: 1969. V. 39; 41; 42

DURIVAGE, FRANCIS A.

The Two Avengers. New York: 1875. V. 38

DURIVAGE, FRANCIS ALEXANDER

Edith Vernon; or, Crime and Retribution. Boston: 1845. V. 43

DURLACHER, LEWIS

A Treatise on Corns, Bunions, the Diseases of Nails, and the General Management of the Feet... Philadelphia: 1845. V. 37

DURLING, RICHARD

A Catalogue of Sixteenth Century Printed Books in the National Library of Medicine. Bethesda: 1967. V. 42; 45; 46

DU ROZOIR, CHARLES

Relation... du Voyage de S. M. charles X dans le Deparement du Nord..... Paris: 1827. V. 46

DURRANT, VALENTINE

The Cheveley Novels. Saul Weir. Edinburgh & London: 1878. V. 38

DURRELL, EDWARD H.

New Orleans as I Found It. New York: 1845. V. 39

DURRELL, LAWRENCE

The Alexandria Quartet: Justine, Balthazar, Mountolive, Clea. New York: (1962). V. 37

The Black Book, an Agon. Paris: 1938. V. 41

The Black Book. New York: 1960. V. 37

The Black Book, an Agon. Paris: 1938. V. 37

Cities, Plains and Peoples. London: 1946. V. 39; 41

Clea. London: 1959. V. 37

The Dark Labyrinth. London;: 1961. V. 37

La Descente du Styx. Montpelier: 1964. V. 37

Down the Styx. Santa Barbara: 1971. V. 39

Lifelines. Edinburgh: 1974. V. 37

Nothing is Lost, Sweet Self. London: 1967. V. 37

Panic Spring. New York: 1937. V. 37

Three Poems of Cavafy. Edinburgh: 1980. V. 37

The Tree of Idleness. London: 1955. V. 37

Tunc. New York: 1968. V. 37

Zero and Asylum in the Snow. Rhodes: 1946. V. 37

DURRELL, LAWRENCE GEORGE 1912-1990

The Alexander Quartet. London: 1962. V. 37; 38; 39; 40; 41; 42; 43; 44; 45

The Alexandria Quartet. Justine. Balthazar. Mountolive. Clea. London: 1957/58/58/60. V. 38

The Alexandria Quartet. London: 1957-60. V. 40

The Alexandria Quartet: Justine. Balthazar. Mountolive. Clea. London: 1957-60. V. 46

The Alexandria Quartet. New York: 1962. V. 40; 42

The Alexandria Quartet. Justine; Balthazar; Mountolive; Clea. London: 1957-60. V. 45

Beccafico. 1963. V. 46

Beccafico. Montpellier: 1963. V. 43

Bitter Lemons. New York: 1957. V. 46

The Black Book, an Agon. Paris: 1938. V. 38; 39; 41; 44

The Black Book. New York: 1960. V. 40; 42

The Black Book. London: 1973. V. 43

The Black Book. Paris: 1st edition; V. 43

Blue Thirst. Santa Barbara: 1975. V. 43

Cefalu. London: 1947. V. 38; 40

Cities, Plains and People. London: 1945. V. 40

Cities, Plains, and People. London: 1946. V. 38; 39; 41; 43

Collected Poems. London: 1960. V. 43

La Descente du Styx. Montpelier: 1946. V. 46

La Descente Du Styx. France: 1964. V. 43

La Descente du Styx. Lamurene: 1964. V. 41

Deus Loci. Ischia: 1950. V. 39; 43

Down the Styx. 1971. V. 39

Down the Styx. Santa Barbara: 1971. V. 39; 40; 41; 42; 43; 45; 46

Henri Michaux: the Poet of Supreme Solipsism. 1990. V. 43

Henri Michaux: The Poet of Supreme Solipsism. Birmingham: 1990. V. 45

DURRELL, LAWRENCE GEORGE 1912-1990 continued

In Arcadia. London: 1968. V. 38

An Irish Faustus. Birmingham: 1987. V. 38; 44

Justine. London: 1957. V. 40

Justine. Balthazar. Mountolive. Clea. 1957-60. V. 41

Lifelines - Four Poems. Edinburgh: 1974. V. 42

Monsieur or the Prince of Darkness. London: 1974. V. 45

Mountolive. London: 1958. V. 45

Mountolive. London: 1959. V. 41

Nothing Is Lost, Sweet Self. London: 1967. V. 38; 39; 43; 46

On Seeming to Presume. Poems . . . London: 1948. V. 43

On the Suchness of the Old Boy. 1972. V. 39

On the Suchness of the Old Boy. London: 1972. V. 41; 44; 45; 46

Panic Spring. London: 1937. V. 41

The Poet of Supreme Solipism. Birmingham: 1990. V. 43

A Private Country: Poems. London: 1943. V. 43

Proems. London: 1938. V. 46

The Red Limbo Lingo. New York: 1971. V. 46

Reflections on a Marine Venus - a Companion to the Landscape of Rhodes. London: 1953. V. 43

Ten Poems. London: 1932. V. 44

Transition: Poems. London: 1934. V. 44

The Tree of Idleness. London: 1955. V. 38; 43; 45

Tunc. London: 1968. V. 46

Tunc. New York: 1968. V. 38; 39

Two Excursions into Reality. Berkeley: 1947. V. 42; 43

DURRENMATT, FRIEDRICH

Oedipus. 1989. V. 42; 45

Oedipus. New York: 1989. V. 44

DU RU, PAUL

Journal of Paul Du Ru. Chicago: 1934. V. 46

DURUY, JEAN VICTOR

History of Greece and the Greek People, from the Earliest Times to the Roman Conquest. Boston: 1890. V. 45

DURUY, VICTOR

History of Rome, and of the Roman People, From Its Origin to the Establishment of the Christian Empire. Boston: 1884. V. 40

History of Rome, and of the Roman People, From Its Origin to the Invasion of the Barbarians and fall of the Empire. Boston: 1884-7. V. 42

History of Greece and of the Greek People. London: 1898. V. 37; 44; 45

D'URVILLE, M. DUMONT

Voyage Pittoresque Autour du monde, Resume General des Voyages de Decouvertes de Magellan . . . Paris: 1834-5. V. 38

DURWARD, B. I.

Poems. Milwaukee: 1882. V. 40

DURY, ANDREW

A New General and Universal Atlas. London: 1761. V. 45

A New, general, and universal atlas. Containing forty five maps . . . London: 1760. V. 37

DU SAIX, ANTOINE 1505-1579

Lesperon de Discipline Pour Inciter les Humains aux Bones Lettres. Geneva? or Lyon?: 1532. V. 37; 40

DUSART, CORNELIS

Renversement de la Morale Chretienne par les Ordres du Monachisme. Netherlands, probably: 1693. V. 40

DUSENBERY, B. M.

Monument to the Memory of General Andrew Jackson . . . Nashua: 1846. V. 43

DUSIMITIER, PIERRE EUGENE

Portraits of the Generals, Ministers, Magistrates, Members of Congress and Others, Who Have Rendered Themselves Illustrious in the Revolution of the United States of North America. London: 1783. V. 41

THE DUSKY Night, Together with Banish Sorrow. And an Ode Sung On Bunker's Hill. Boston: 1785? V. 46

DUSSAUCE, H.

A New and Complete Treatise on the Arts of Tanning, Currying and Leather Dressing . . . Philadelphia: 1867. V. 44

A New and Complete Treatise on the Arts of Tanning, Currying and Leather Dressing. Philadelphia: 1865. V. 38

DUSSEAU, MICHEL

Enchiridion ou Manipul des Miropoles Exactement Traduit. Lyon: 1655. V. 38

DUSTIN, FRED

The Custer Fight. Hollywood: 1936. V. 45

The Custer Tragedy. Ann Arbor: 1939. V. 45

Echoes from the Little Big Horn Fight, Reno's Positions in the Valley. Saginaw: 1953. V. 44

Echoes from the Little Big Horn. Reno's Positions in the Valley. Sginaw: 1953. V. 45

THE DUTCH Remonstrance Concerning the Proceedings and Practices of John De Witt Pensionary, and Ruwaert Van Putten his Brother, with Others of that Faction. London: 1672. V. 37; 43

THE DUTCH Remonstrance Concerning the Proceedings and Practices of John de Witt Pensionary, and Ruwaert van Putten his Brother, With Others of that Faction. London: 1672. V. 41

DUTENS, LOUIS

Correspondance Interceptee (Between the Chevalier De B** and the Marquis De L***). Paris: 1788. V. 46

An Inquiry into the Origins and Discoveries Attributed to the Mdoerns. London: 1769. V. 40

Memoirs of a Traveller, Now In Retirement. London: 1806. V. 46

DU TERTRE, MARGUERITE

Instruction Familiere et Tres Facile, Faite par Questions & Reponses Touchant Toutes les Choses Principales qu'une Sage-femme doit Scavoir pour l'Exercise de son Art. Paris: 1677. V. 40

THE DUTIES of a Lady's Maid; With Directions for Conduct, and Numerous Receipts for the Toilette. London: 1825. V. 41

DUTIES Payable by Law on All Goods, Wares and Merchandise, Imported Into the United States of America, After the Last Day of June, 1812. Washington?: 1812. V. 45

DU TILLET, JEAN

Libelli seu Decreta a Clodoveo, et Childeberto 7 Clothario Prius Aedita, ac Postremum a Carolo Lucide Emendata. Paris: 1550. V. 37

DU TILLIOT, J. BEN LUCOTTE

Memoires Pour Survir a l'Histoire de la Fete des Foux qui se Faisoit Autrefoix dands Plusieurs Eglises. Lausanne/Geneva: 1741. V. 38

DUTOT

Reflexions Politiques sur Les Finances et le Commerce. The Hague: 1738. V. 41; 45

DUTOURD, JEAN

'Papa' Hemingway. Liege: 1961. V. 46

Papa Hemingway. London: 1961. V. 40

DUTTON, BERTHA P.

Excavations at Tajumulco, Guatemala. Santa Fe: 1934. V. 44

Excavations at Tajumuleo, Guatemala. Santa Fe: 1943. V. 42

DUTTON, C. E.

Atlas of the District of the High Plateaus of Utah. Washington: 1879. V. 41

Report on the Geology of the High Plateaus of Utah. Washington: 1880. V. 39; 41; 46

DUTTON, CLARENCE EDWARD

The Physical Geology of the Grand Canon District. Washington: 1882. V. 41

Tertiary History of the Grand Canon District, with Atlas. Washington: 1882. V. 41

DUTTON, E. A. T.

Kenya Mountain. London: 1930. V. 44

DUTTON, F.

South Australia and Its Mines, with an Historical Sketch of the Colony, Under Its Several Administrations to the Period of Captain Grey's Departure. London: 1846. V. 41; 44; 45

DUTTON, GEOFFREY

Paintings of S. T. Gill. Adelaide: 1962. V. 41

DUTTON, HELY

A Statistical and Agricultural Survey of the County of Galway. Dublin: 1824. V. 38; 43

DUTTON, W. H.

The Boots and Shoes of Our Ancestors, As Exhibited by the Worshipful Company of Cordwainers . . . London: 1898. V. 43

DUTTON, WARREN

The Present State of Literature, a Poem Delivered in New Haven at the Public Commencement of Yale College, September 10, 1800. Hartford: 1800. V. 38; 41; 44

THE DUTY Of a Freeman Addressed to the Electors of Great Britain. London: 1780. V. 38

the DUTY of a Freeman, aDDRESSED TO THE eLECTORS OF gREAT bRITAIN. London: 1780? V. 46

DU VAIR, GUILLAUME

The Morall Philosophy of the Stoicks. London: 1671. V. 41; 44

DU VAL, CHALRES

With a Show through Southern Africa and Personal Reminiscences of the Transvaal War. London: 1882. V. 44

DU VAL, CHARLES

With a Show Through Southern Africa, and Personal Reminiscences of the Transvaal War. London: 1884. V. 42; 45

DU VAL, CLAUDE

A Geographical Dictionary, In Which are Described the Most Eminent Contreys, Towns, Ports, Seas . . . London: 1678. V. 42

DUVAL, E. W.

A Bibliography by E. W. Duval. New York: (1938). V. 37

DUVAL, ELIZABETH W.

T. E. Lawrence, a Bibliography. New York: 1938. V. 43; 45

DUVAL, I. H.

Texas Argonauts: Isaac H. Duval and the California Gold Rush. San Francisco: 1988. V. 41; 42; 45

DUVAL, ISAAC H.

Texas Argonauts. I.H.D. and the California Gold Rush. 1937. V. 44

Texas Argonauts: Issac H. Duval and the California Gold Rush. San Francisco: 1987. V. 39; 40; 46

DUVAL, JOHN C.

The Adventures of Big Foot Wallace, the Texas Ranger and Hunter. Philadelphia: 1871. V. 38; 39; 45

Adventures of Big Foot Wallace, the Texas Ranger and Hunter. Philadelphia: 1872. V. 42

The Adventures of Big-Foot Wallace, the Texas Ranger and Hunter. Philadelphia: 1885. V. 39; 42; 44

Early Times in Texas. Austin: 1892. V. 37; 38; 42; 45

DU VAL, MICHAEL

Rosa Hispani-Angelica. Seu Malum Punicum Angl'hispanicum. London: 1623. V. 39

DUVAL, PAUL

A. J. Casson, a Tribute. Toronto: 1980. V. 39

Canadian Drawings and Prints. Toronto: 1952. V. 41; 44

Canadian Water Colour Painting. Toronto: 1954. V. 41

DUVAL, PIERRE 1618-1683

Diverses Cartes et Tables Pour la Geographie Ancienne, Pour la Chronologie et Pour les Itineraires et Voyages Modernes. Paris: 1666. V. 39

A Geographical Dictionary . . . London: 1678. V. 42

La Geographie Francoise Contenant Les Descriptions, les Cartes, et le Blason des Prouinces de France. Paris: 1659. V. 39

DUVEEN BROTHERS

Duveen Pictures in Public Collections of America . . . (and) Duveen Sculptures in Public Collections of America . . . New York: 1944. V. 41

DUVEEN, DENIS

Bibliotheca Alchemica & Chemica. An Annotated Catalogue of Printed Books on Alchemy, Chemistry, Cognate Subjects. New York. V. 39

DUVEEN, DENIS I.

Benjamin Franklin . . . and Antoine Laurent Lavoisier . . . . Parts I, II, III. 1955/55/57. V. 46

A Bibliography of the Works of Antoine Laurent Lavoisier, 1743-1794. London: 1954. V. 40; 46

A Bibliography of the Works of Antoine Laurent Lavoisier 1743-1794. (and) Supplement. London: 1954-65. V. 37; 38; 40; 42

Bibliotheca Alchemica et Chemica. London: 1949. V. 42; 46

DUVEEN, DENIS L.

Bibliotheca Alchemica et Chemica. London: 1949. V. 43

DU VERDIER, CLAUDE

Abrege de l'Histoire de France. Tome Preimer (of 2). Paris: 1652. V. 37

DU VERGIER DE HAURANNE, JEAN

Theologi Opera . . . Complectens Assertionem Eipstolae . . . Quae Libros Nicolae Smithaei & Danielis a Isu Damnarunt. Paris: 1642. V. 39

DUVERNEY, GUICHARD JOSEPH

Observations sur la circulation du sang dans la foetus: et description du coeur de la tortue et de quelques autre animaus. Paris: 1699. V. 37

DUVERNEY, JOSEPH 1648-1730

Traite de l'Organe de l'Ouie . . . Paris: 1683. V. 42

DUVERNEY, M.

Anatomie de la Tete en Tableaux Imprimes. Paris: 1748. V. 41; 43; 45

DUVET, JOHN

The Apocalypse. London: 1962. V. 46

THE DUWAMISH Diary. 1849-1949. Seattle: 1949. V. 45

DUYCKINCK, EVERT

Cyclopaedia of American Literature. New York: 1855. V. 38

National Portrait Gallery of Eminent Americans. New York: 1862. V. 38; 42

DUYCKINCK, EVERT A.

History of the War for the Union: Civil, Military and Naval. New York: 1862. V. 44

National Portrait Gallery of Eminent Americans: Orators, Statesmen, Naval & Military Heroes, Jurists, Authors, etc. New York: 1862-63. V. 46

Nationale Geschichte des Krieges fur Die Union, Politische und Militarische. New York: 1865. V. 39; 42

DUYCKINCK, EVERT AUGUSTUS 1816-1878

National Portrait Gallery of Eminent Americans. New York: 1861. V. 41

DWARRIS, FORTUNATUS

A General Treatise on Statutes: Their Rules of Construction and the Proper Boundaries of Legislation and of Judicial Interpretation. Albany: 1885. V. 43

DWIGGINS, W. A.

Athalinthia III. The Glistening Hill. Puterschein-Hingham: 1950. V. 41

Form Letters: Illustrator to Author. New York: 1930. V. 40

The Glistening Hill, Athalinthia III. N.P.: 1950. V. 41

The Glistening Hill (Athalinthia III'). N.P. (Hingham, MA.): 1950. V. 37

Paraphs. New York: 1928. V. 37; 40

Prelude to Eden: a Drama for Marionettes. Hingham: 1956. V. 40

Towards a Reform of the Paper Currency. New York: 1932. V. 37; 40; 43; 44; 45; 46

Twenty-Two Printers' Marks and Seals Designed or Redrawn by W. A. Dwiggins. New York: 1929. V. 41; 42

The War Against Waak: Bellona. N.P. (Hingham, MA.): 1948. V. 37

DWIGGINS, WILLIAM ADDISON 1880-1956

Towards a Reform of the Paper Currency. New York: 1932. V. 38; 39

WAD to RR: A Letter About Designing Type. 1940. V. 37; 39

DWIGHT, CHARLES STEVENS

A South Carolina Rebel's Recollections. Columbia: 1917. V. 44

DWIGHT, EDWIN W.

Ka Moolelo o Heneri Opukahaia, Va Hanavia Ma Hawaii, M.H. 1787. A Va Make Ma Amerika, Febervari 17, 1818. New York: 1867. V. 42

Memoirs of Henry Obookiah, a Native of Owhyhee. New Haven: 1818. V. 37

DWIGHT, H. G. O.

Christianity in Turkey: a Narrative of the Protestant Reformation in the Armenian Church. London: 1854. V. 45

Christianity Revived in the East . . . New York: 1850. V. 45

DWIGHT, HARRY GRISWOLD

Constantinople Old and New. New York: 1915. V. 44

DWIGHT, JAMES

Lawn-Tennis by James Dwight. Boston/London: (1886). V. 37

DWIGHT, NATHANIEL

A Short But Comprehensive System of the Geography of the World . . . Hartford: 1795. V. 43

A Short But Comprehensive System of the Geography of the World . . . Albany: 1796. V. 42

DWIGHT, SERENO E.

Memoirs of the Rev. David Brainerd . . . Taken from His Own Diaray. New Haven: 1822. V. 37

DWIGHT, SERENO EDWARDS

The Greek Revolution. Boston: 1824. V. 40

The Greek Revolution, an Address Delivered in Park Street Church, Boston, on Thursday April 1, and Repeated at the Request of the Greek Committee, in the Old South Church. Boston: 1824. V. 39; 40; 45

The Hebrew Wife; or the Law of Marriage, Examined in Relation to the Lawfulness of Polygamy . . . Glasgow: 1837. V. 44; 45

DWIGHT, THEODORE

The Character of Thomas Jefferson, as Exhibited in His Own Writings. Boston: 1839. V. 40

History of the Hartford Convention: With a Review of the Policy of the United States Government, Which Led to the War of 1812. New York: 1833. V. 40; 44

The Northern Traveller, and Northern Tour with Routes to Springs, Niagara and Quebec, and the Coal Mines of Pennsylvania, also 'Tour of New England'. New York: 1831. V. 38

The Northern Traveller, and Northern Tour with Routes to Springs, Niagara, and Quebec, and the Coal Mines of Pennsylvania, also 'Tour of New England.' New York: 1834. V. 38

Things as They Are; or Notes of a Traveller Through Some of the Middle and Northern States. New York: 1834. V. 45

DWIGHT, THEODORE F.

Campaigns in Virginia 1861-1862. Massachusetts: 1895. V. 41

DWIGHT, THOMAS

Clinical Atlas: Variations of the Bones of the Hands and Feet. Philledelphia: 1907. V. 38

Frozen Secitions of a Child. New York: 1881. V. 37; 39; 42

Variations of the Bones of the Hands and Feet. Philadelphia: 1907. V. 42

Variations of the Bones of the Hands and Feet. Philadelphia: (1907. V. 37

DWIGHT, TIMOTHY

The Conquest of Canaan: a Poem, in Eleven Books. Hartford: 1785. V. 45

An Essay on the Stage . . . London: 1824. V. 42

Greenfield Hill: a Poem in Seven Parts. New York: 1794. V. 38; 40; 43

Greenfield Hill. (with) The Triumph of Infidelity. New York: 1788. V. 37

Statistical Account of the Towns and Parishes in the State of Connecticut. New Haven: 1811. V. 45

Travels: in New England and New York: by . . . Late President of Yale College. New Haven: 1821. V. 37; 39

Travels in New England and New York. New Haven: 1821-22. V. 37; 38; 41

Travels in New England and New York. London: 1823. V. 38; 39; 46

Travels in New England and New York. New York: London: 1823. V. 43

The Triumph of Infidelity; a Poem. 1788. V. 37; 40

DWINELLE, JOHN W.

American Opinions on the 'Alabama' and Other Political Questions. London: 1870. V. 46

The Colonial History of the City of San Francisco . . . San Francisco: 1866. V. 45; 46

The Colonial History of the City of San Francisco. San Diego: 1924. V. 39

The Colonial History of San Francisco. San Francisco: 1863. V. 37; 39

The Mayor, etc., of San Jose Against John Trimble. San Francisco: 1871. V. 46

D'WOLF, JOHN

A Voyage to the North Pacific and a Journey through Siberia More than a Century Ago. Bristol: 1983. V. 38; 40

DWORACZYK, EDWARD J.

The First Polish Colonies of America in Texas. 1936. V. 42; 44

DWYER, CHARLES P.

The Economic Cottage Building; or, Cottages for Men of Small Means. Buffalo: 1856. V. 39; 41; 44

DWYER, EUGENE J.

Pompeian Domestic Sculpture. Roma: 1982. V. 37; 40; 42

DWYER, J. P.

Traditional Art of AFrica, Oceania and the Americas. 1973. V. 46

DWYER, PHILIP

The Diocese of Killaloe, from the Reformation to the Close of the Eighteenth Century. Dublin: 1878. V. 38; 43

DYCE, ALEXANDER

Recollections of the Table Talk of Samuel Rogers. To Which is Added Porsoniana. New Southgate: 1887. V. 42

DYCHE, THOMAS

A New General English Dictionary Designed for the Use of Grammar Schools and Private Education. London: 1737. V. 39; 40

A New General English Dictionary . . . London: 1740. V. 41; 43

A New General English Dictionary. London: 1744. V. 41

A New General English Dictionary . . . London: 1765. V. 41

A New General Dictionary . . . . London: 1771. V. 40; 41

A New General English Dictionary; Peculiarly Calculated for the Use and Improvement of Such as Are Unacquainted with the Learned Languages . . . London: 1794. V. 41

A New General English Dictionary peculiarly calcuated for the Use and Improvement of such are unacquainted with the learned languages . . . to which is prefixed a Compendious English Grammar. Together with a Supplement . . . originally begun by the . . . London: 1744. V. 37

DYCKMAN, JACOB

An Inaugural Dissertation on the Pathology of the Human Fluids. New York: 1814. V. 44; 45; 46

DYDE, W.

The History and Antiquities of Tewkesbury. Tewkesbury: 1798. V. 37; 38; 40; 42; 43

DYE, EVA EMERY

McLoughlin and Old Oregon a Chronicle. Chicago: 1900. V. 42

DYE, JOHN SMITH

The Adder's Den; or Secrets of the Great Conspiracy to Overthrow Liberty in America. New York: 1864. V. 42

THE DYEING of Wool Including Wool-Printing with the Dyestuffs of Leopold Cassella & Co. Frankfort. American Branch: Cassella Color Company . . . New York. Frankfort: 1905. V. 37

DYER, D. B.

Fort Reno or Piecturesque 'Cheyenne and Arapahoe Army Life,' before the Opening of Oklahoma. New York: 1896. V. 37

DYER, DAVID P.

Autobiography and Reminiscences. St. Louis: 1922. V. 40; 46

DYER, E. E.

The History of the Volunteers of Clackmannan and Kinross. Alva: 1907. V. 38

DYER, F. L.

Edison, His Life and Inventions. New York & London: 1910. V. 39

DYER, G.

History of the University and Colleges of Cambridge. London: 1814. V. 39

Restoration of the Ancient Modes of Bestowing Names on the Rivers, Hills, Vallies, Plains and Settlements of Britain, Recorded by No Ancient, nor Explored by any Modern Author. Exeter: 1805. V. 41

DYER, GEORGE

A Dissertation on the Theory and Practice of Benevolence. London: 1795. V. 37; 40

History of the University and Colleges of Cambridge . . . London: 1814. V. 45

Poetics; or, a Series of Poems and Disquisitions on Poetry. London: 1812. V. 43

DYER, GILBERT

A Restoration of the Ancient Modes of Bestowing Names on the Rivers, Hills, Vaillies, Plains and Settlements of Britain. Exeter: 1805. V. 38

DYER, JAMES 1512-1582

Les Reports des Divers Select Matters & Resolutions des Reverend Judges & Sages del Ley. London: 1688. V. 39; 46

DYER, JOHN

The Fleece: a Poem in Four Books. London: 1757. V. 45

Grongar Hill . . . London: 1982. V. 42

Poems. London: 1761. V. 38; 40; 41; 43; 45; 46

The Ruins of Rome. London: 1740. V. 40; 45

DYER, JOHN L.

The Snow-Shoe Itinerant. Cincinnati: 1890. V. 37; 40; 42

DYER, JOSEPH

A Compendious Narrative, Elucidating the Character, Disposition and Conduct of Mary Dyer, from the Time of Her Marriage in 1799, Till She Left the Society Called Shakers in 1815 . . . Concord: 1819. V. 41

DYER, R. E. H.

The Raiders of the Sarhad, Being an Account of a Campaign of Arms and Bluff Against the Brigands of the Persian Baluchi Border Druing the Great War. London: 1921. V. 46

DYER, ROBERT

Nine Years of an Actor's Life. London: 1833. V. 42

DYER, THOMAS FIRMINGER THISTLETON

The Ghost World. London: 1893. V. 46

DYER, THOMAS H.

The Ruins of Pompeii . . . with an Account . . . London: 1867. V. 38; 44

DYER, THOMAS HENRY

The History of Modern Europe. London: 1861-64. V. 37; 40

DYHRENFURTH, G. O.

To the Third Pole: The History of the High Himalaya. London: 1955. V. 44

DYK, WALTER

Son of Old Man Hat. New York: 1938. V. 45

DYKE, DANIEL

The Mystery of Self-Deceiving. London: 1634. V. 46

DYKE, THOMAS

All Round Sport with Fish, Fur, Feather, also Adventures on the Road . . . London: 1887. V. 43

DYKES, H. P.

Notes on Tulip Species. London: 1930. V. 43

DYKES, JEFF

Fifty Great Western Illustrators, a Bibliographic Checklist. 1975. V. 38

Fifty Great Western Illustrations: a Bibliographic Checklist. Flagstaff: 1975. V. 41; 46

DYKES, JEFF C.

Billy the Kid, the Bibliography of a Legend. 1952. V. 42

DYKES, K. E.

Notes on Tulip Species. London: 1930. V. 37

DYKES, OSWALD

English Proverbs with Moral Reflexions . . . London: 1709. V. 40

The Royal Marriage. King Lemuel's Lesson of 1. Chastity, 2. Temperance, 3. Charity, 4. Justice, 5. Education, 6. Industry, 7. Frugality, 8. Religion, 9 Marriage &c. London: 1722. V. 37; 38; 41; 42

DYKES, W.

The Genus Iris. Cambridge: 1913. V. 37; 38; 40; 41; 42; 43; 46

DYKES, W. R.

Notes on Tulip Species. London: 1930. V. 37; 38; 42; 45

DYMOCK, WILLIAM

Pharmacographia Indica . . . London: Bombay: &: 1889-93. V. 45

DYMOND, JONATHAN

Essays on the Principles of Morality and on the Private and Political Rights and Obligations of Mankind. New York: 1834. V. 40

DYMOTT, G. M.

Silent Highways of the Jungle: Being the Records of an Adventurous Journey Across Peru to the Amazon. London: 1922. V. 39

DYOS, H. J.

The Victorian City: Images and Realities. London: 1973. V. 44

DYRENFORTH, JAMES

Adolf in Blunderland. London: 1939. V. 45

DYSON, ANTHONY

Pictures to Print. London: 1984. V. 40; 41; 42; 43; 44

Pictures to Print: the Nineteenth Century Engraving Trade. London: 1984. V. 40

E

E--L of CH----M's Apology, a Poem. London: 1766. V. 40; 42

E. W. Dennison, a Memorial. Boston: 1909. V. 41

E-YEH-SHURE

I Am a Pueblo Indian Girl. New York: 1939. V. 45

EACHARD, JOHN

Mr. Hobb's State of Nature Considered; in a Dialogue Between Philautus and Timothy. London: 1672. V. 37; 41

Some Opinions of Mr. Hobbs Considered in a Second Dialogue Between Philautus and Timothy. London: 1673. V. 38; 43

A Vindication of the Clery, from the Contempt Imposed Upon Them by the Author of the Contempt of the Clergy and Religion. London: 1672. V. 44

EACHARD, LAWRENCE

The Gazetteer's, or Newsman's Interpreter. London: 1704. V. 41

The Gazetteer's; or, Newsman's Interpreter. (with) . . . the Second Part. London: 1724. V. 43

EACKER, GEORGE I.

Observations on the National Character of the Americans; an Oration Delivered Before the Tammany Society, on the 12th of May 1798. New York: 1798. V. 45

EADMER

Eadmeri Monachi Cantuariensis Historiae Novorum Sive Sui Saeculi Libri IV . . . London: 1623. V. 38; 40; 41; 45

EADON, JOHN

The Aritmetician's Guide . . . Sheffield: 1766. V. 46

EADS, JAMES B.

Letters from Leading Engineers and Naval Architects as to the Practicability of Constructing and Operating a Ship Railway. St. Louis: 1882. V. 41; 42

THE EAGLE and Harp; a Collection of Patriotic and Humorous Songs and Odes. Baltimore: 1812. V. 40

THE EAGLE and the Fox. London: 1949. V. 46

EAGLES, JOHN

The Bristol Riots, Their Causes, Progress and Consequences. Bristol: 1832. V. 46

The Journal of Llewllin Penrose, a Seaman. London: 1815. V. 37

The Sketcher. Edinburgh & London: 1856. V. 39

EAKINS, THOMAS

The Photographs of Thomas Eakins. New York: 1972. V. 38

EALES, MARY

The Compleat Confectioner. London: 1733. V. 39

EALES, NELLIE

The Cole Library of Early Medicine and Zoology. Reading: 1969/75. V. 42; 45

EAMES, WILBERFORCE

Adventures in Americana 1492-1897 . . . New York: 1928-38. V. 42

Adventures in Americana 1492-1897 . . . Being a Selection of Books from the Library of Herschel V. Jones. New York: 1925-38. V. 40

Adventures in Americana 1492-1897 . . . Being a Selection of Books from the Library of Herschel V. Jones. New York: 1964. V. 40

Bibliographic Notes on Eliot's Indian Bible, and on His Other Translations and Works in the Indian Language of Massachusetts. Washington. V. 46

Bibliographic Notes on Eliot's Indian Bible, and On His Other Translations and Works in the Indian Language of Massachusetts. Washington: 1890. V. 43

John Eliot and the Indians 1652-1657. New York: 1915. V. 37; 38; 39

EARDLEY-WILMOT, JOHN

Reminiscences of the Late Thomas Assheton Smith, Esq . . . London: 1860. V. 43

A Short Defence of the Opposition; in Answer to a Pamphlet Intitled 'A Short History of the Opposoition.' London: 1779. V. 37; 41

EARDLEY-WILMOT, S.

Our Journal in the Pacific. London: 1873. V. 39; 45

EARHART, AMELIA

The Fun Of It. New York: 1932. V. 41; 43; 44

Last Flight. New York: 1937. V. 41

EARHART, JOHN F.

The Color Printer. Cincinnati: 1892. V. 37; 38; 39; 41; 43; 44

EARL, GEORGE WINDSOR

The Eastern Seas, or Voyages and Adventures in the Archipelago, in 1832-33-34 . . . London: 1837. V. 42; 43; 46

The Ethnographical Library. Volume I. The Native Races of the Indian Archipelago. London: 1853. V. 45

The Native Races of the Indian Archipelago. London: 1853. V. 38; 45

EARL OF SUFFOLK AND BERKSHIRE

The Encyclopaedia of Sport. Edited by the Earl of Suffold and Berkshire, Hedley Peek & F.G. Aflalo. Illustrations with hundreds of photos and drawings. New York/London: 1898. V. 37

EARLAND, ADA

John Opie and His Circle. London: 1911. V. 39

EARLE, ALICE MORSE

Child-Life in Colonial Days. New York: 1899. V. 40

In Old Narragansett, Romances and Realities. New York: 1898. V. 42; 43

Sun-Dials and Roses of Yesterday. New York: 1902. V. 37

EARLE, AUGUSTUS

A Narrative of a Nine Month's Residence in New Zealand, in 1827. London: 1832. V. 38; 41

EARLE, CYRIL

The Earle Collection of Early Staffordshire Pottery. London: 1915. V. 40

EARLE, FERDINAND

The Lyric Year. New York: 1912. V. 43

EARLE, HENRY 1789-1838

Practical Observations in Surgery. London: 1823. V. 42

EARLE, JAMES WILLIAM

A New Exposition of the Functions of Nerves. London: 1833. V. 39

A New Exposition of the Functions of the Nerves. London: 1883. V. 38

EARLE, JOHN

Micro-cosmographie or a Piece of the World Discovered. Waltham St. Lawrence: 1928. V. 44

Microcosmography; or a Piece of the World Discovered. London: 1811. V. 39

Microscosmography; or, a Piece of the World Discover'd in Essays and Characters. London: 1732. V. 46

EARLE, PLINY 1809-1892

Institutions for the Insane in Prussia, Austria and Germany. Utica: 1853. V. 45

EARLE, SWEPSON

The Chesapeake Bay Country. Baltimore: 1923. V. 43

The Chesapeake Bay Country. Baltimore: 1929. V. 37

Maryland's Colonial Eastern Shore. Baltimore: 1916. V. 39; 43; 45

EARLE, T. ALGERNON

List of Officers Who Have Served in the Lancashire Hussars, Yeomanary Cavalry . . . Liverpool: 1889. V. 42

EARLE, THOMAS

The Life, Travels and Opinions of Benjamin Lundy. Philadelphia: 1847. V. 38; 39; 42; 45

EARLE, WELBY T.

The Victorian Romantics 1850-1870. The Early Work of Dante Gabriel Rossetti, William Morris, Burne-Jones, Swinburne, Simeon Solomon and Their Associates. London: 1920. V. 41

EARLE, WILLIAM

Welsh Legends. London: 1802. V. 43

EARLY Books on Medicine, Natural Sciences and Alchemy. Zurich: 1930. V. 41

EARLY English Recipes. Cambridge: 1937. V. 40; 41

EARLY Guide; or Instructive Stories, for Young Children. New Haven: 1835. V. 45

EARLY, JUBAL ANDERSON

A Correspondence Between Generals Early and Mahone in Regard to a Military Memoir of the Latter. Lynchburg: 1871. V. 37; 43

EARLY, JUBAL ANDERSON continued

Lieutenant General Jubal Anderson Early, C.S.A. Autobiographical Sketch and Narrative of the War Between the Sates. Philadelphia: 1912. V. 37; 39

A Memoir of the Last Year of the War for Independence. Toronto: 1866. V. 37; 41

A Memoir of the Last Year of the War for Independence in the Confederate States of America, Containing an Account of the Operations of His Commands in . . . 1864 and 1865. Lynchburg: 1867. V. 37; 39

A Memoir of the Last Year of the War for Independence in the Confederate States of America . . . Lynchburg: 1867. V. 40; 42

A Memoir of the Last Year of the War . . . in Confederate States . . . New Orleans: 1867. V. 43

EARLY, RUTH R.

Water in a Thirsty Land. N.P.: 1955. V. 43

EARLY Travels in the Tennessee Country 1549-1800. Johnson City: 1928. V. 42

EARLY Western Travels, 1748-1846. New York: 1966. V. 38

EARNEST Expostulation in the Name of the Great and Glorious God with the Inhabitants of the Land, Especially the Rising Generation. Boston: 1739. V. 45

EARNEST-PENNIES: an Anthology of Prayers and Meditations on the Holy Eucharist. London: and Oxford: 1973. V. 46

EARNSHAW, CHRISTOPHER

Orthoepy Simplified: Being a New and Comprehensive Explanatory Pronouncing Dictionary of the English Language. Leeds: 1816? V. 41

EARNSHAW, JOHN

Early Sydney Cabinetmakers, 1804-1870. A Directory with an Introductory Survey. Surry Hills: (1971). V. 37

EARP, G. BUTLER

The Gold Colonies of Australia. London: 1852. 40; 41; 43

EARWAKER, J. P.

East Cheshire: Past and Present. London: 1877. V. 38; 40; 46

East Cheshire Past and Present . . . London: 1877-80. V. 39; 44

The History of the Ancient Parish of Sandbach Co. Chester . . . London: 1890. V. 38

Local Gleanings Relating to Lancashire and Cheshire. Manchester: 1875-80. V. 39

EASBY, ELIZABETH KENNEDY

Before Cortes; Sculpture of Middle America. New York: 1970. V. 42

EASDALE, JOAN ADENEY

Amber Innocent. London: 1939. V. 46

EASEL, THEODORE

Desultory Sketches and Tales of Barbados. London: 1840. V. 39

EASSIE, WILLIAM

Healthy Houses. A Handbook to the History, Defects and Remedies of Drainage, Ventilation, Warmin and Kindred Subjects. London: 1874. V. 38

EAST, EDWARD HYDE

A Treatise of the Pleas of the Crown. Philadelphia: 1806. V. 38; 40

EAST INDIA COMPANY

Chartered Rights. London: 1784. V. 41

An Infallible Remedy for the High Prices of Provisions. London: 1768. V. 41

A List of the Company's Civil Servants, at Their Settlements in the East Indies, the Island St. Helena and China. London: 1790. V. 41

EAST, ROBERT

Extracts from Records in the Possession of the Municipal Corporation of the Borough of Portsmouth, and from Other Documents. Portsmouth: 1891. V. 42

EAST TENNESSEE, VIRGINIA AND GEORGIA RAILROAD

Guide to the Summer Resorts and Water Places of East Tennessee. Memphis: 1879. V. 45

EASTCOTT, RICHARD 1740-1828

Sketches of the Origin, Progress and Effects of Music, with an Account of the Ancient Bards and Minstrels. Bath: 1793. V. 40; 42; 45; 46

EASTER, J.

Letters, on a Disputed Claim to John Mytton, Esquire, of Halston, Oswestry, Salop, Late of the Seventh Regiment . . . London: 1823. V. 37; 42

EASTERBY, J. H.

The Colonial Records of South Carolina. Series I: The Journal of the Commons House of Assembly, 1736-1750. Columbia: 1951-1962. V. 40

EASTERN Colorado: a Brief Description of the New Lands Now Being Opened Up. Lincoln: 1887. V. 39; 46

THE EASTERN Counties Railway. London: 1851. V. 45

EASTLAKE, CHARLES L.

Hints on Household Taste in Furniture, Upholstery and Other Details. London: 1868. V. 37; 38

Hints on Household taste in Furniture, Upholstery and Other Details. London: 1869. V. 40

Hints on Household Taste in Furniture, Upholstery and Other Details. London: 1878. V. 44

A History of the Gothic Revival. London: 1872. V. 37; 39; 40; 42; 46

EASTLAKE, CHARLES LOCK

Contributions to the Literature of Fine Arts. London: 1848. V. 44

EASTLAKE, ELIZABETH RIGBY

The Jewess; a Tale from the Shores of the Baltic. London: 1843. V. 42

EASTLAKE, WILLIAM

The Bronc People. New York: 1958. V. 39; 44

Go in Beauty. New York: 1956. V. 38; 41; 42; 43; 44; 46

Jack Armstrong in Tangier. Flint: 1984. V. 43; 45

The Long Naked Descent Into Boston. New York: 1977. V. 46

Portrait of an Artist with 26 Horses. New York: 1963. V. 44

EASTMAN, EDWIN

Seven and Nine Years Among the Camanches and Apaches. An Autobiography. Jersey City, N.J.: 1874. V. 37

EASTMAN, FRANK M.

Courts and Lawyers of Pennsylvania. A History 1623-1923. New York: 1922. V. 41; 42

EASTMAN, G.

Chronicle of an African Trip. London: 1927. V. 38

EASTMAN, MARY HENDERSON

The American Aboriginal Portfolio. Philadelphia: 1853. V. 37; 41; 42; 46

The American Annual: Illustrative of the Early History of North America. Philadelphia: 1854. V. 37; 44

Chicora and Other Regions of the Conquerors and the Conquered. Philadelphia: 1854. V. 37; 38; 39; 40; 41; 42; 43; 45

Dahcotah; or, Life and Legends of the Sioux Around Fort Snelling. New York: 1849. V. 37; 40; 41; 43

The Romance of Indian Life, With Other Tales. Philadelphia: 1853. V. 39

EASTMAN, MAX

Venture. New York: 1927. V. 37

EASTMAN, SETH

Treatise on Topographical Drawing. New York: 1837. V. 39; 43

EASTMEAD, WILLIAM

Historia Rievallensis. London: 1824. V. 38; 39

Historia Rievallensis . . . Thirsk: 1824. V. 44

EASTON, AUGUSTUS B.

History of the St. Croix Valley. Chicago: 1909. V. 39

EASTON, JAMES

Human Longevity. Salisbury: 1799. V. 38; 40; 41; 42; 45

EASTON, JOHN

A Narrative of the Causes Which Led to Philip's Indian War, of 1675 and 1676. Albany: 1858. V. 39; 43; 45

An Unfrequented Highway through Sikkim and Tibet. London: 1928. V. 40

EASTON, PHOEBE JANE

Marbling, a History and a Bibliography. Los Angeles: 1983. V. 37; 38; 39; 40; 41; 44

EASTWOOD, BENJAMIN

Sudd and Lilies. A Journey Round Lakes Kioga and Kwania and Neighbouring Waters Made in the Month of May (1916). Namasagali: 1916. V. 43

AN EASY and Comprehensive English Grammar, on a New Plan. Dublin, London: 1751. V. 41

EASY Catechism for Free Home-Seekers in Dakota. Milwaukee: 1885. V. 44

AN EASY Introduction to the Game of Chess . . . Philadelphia: 1817. V. 45

EASY Lessons for Young Beginners. London: 1830. V. 46

EAT Book. London: 1990. V. 46

EATES, MARGOT

Paul Nash. The Master of the Image 1889-1946. London. V. 42

Paul Nash: The Master of the Image, 1889-1946. London: 1973. V. 42; 43

EATON, A. E.

A Revisonal Monograph of Recent Ephemeridae or Mayflies. London: 1883-88. V. 37

EATON, ALLAN H.

Handicrafts of the Southern Highlands. New York: 1937. V. 37; 45

EATON, ANNA RUTH WEBSTER

The Origin of Mormonism. New York: 1881. V. 40

EATON, CHARLOTTE

Rome in the Nineteenth Century. Edinburgh: 1826. V. 37

Rome in the Nineteenth Century . . . Edinburgh: 1822. V. 45

EATON, CHARLOTTE ANNE

Continental Adventures. London: 1826. V. 44

Continental Adventures. London: 1827. V. 38

THE EATON Chronicle; or, the Salt Box. Chester: 1789. V. 40

EATON, DANIEL CODY

The Ferns of North America. Salem: 1879. V. 39

The Ferns of North America. Salem and Boston: 1879 & 1880. V. 41

The Ferns of North America. Salem: 1880. V. 46

EATON, E. H.

The Birds of New York. New York: 1910-14. V. 37

EATON, EDWARD BAILEY

Original Photographs Taken on the Battlefields During the Civil War of the United States by Mathew B. Brady and Alexander Gardner . . . Now the Private Collection of Edward Bailey Eaton . . . Hartford: 1907. V. 44

EATON, ELON HOWARD

Birds of New York. Albany: 1910. V. 41

Birds of New York. New York: 1910. V. 38; 40

Birds of New York. Albany: 1910-14. V. 39

Birds of New York. Albany: 1910-14. V. 39; 44

Birds of New York. 1910, 1914. V. 39

EATON, JOHANN HEINRICH

Leben des General Majors Andreas Jackson. Reading: 1831. V. 40

EATON, JOHN H.

Candid Appeal to the American Public. Washington: 1831. V. 37; 38

EATON, JOHN MATTHEWS

A Treatise on the Art of Breeding and Managing Tame, Domestic, Foreign and Fancy Pigeons. London: 1858. V. 37

EATON, L. K.

Landscape Artist in America: Life and Work of Jens Jensen. Chicago: 1964. V. 46

EATON, MARY

The Cook an Housekeeper's Complete and Universal Dictionary; Including A System of modern Cookery . . . Also a Variety of Original and Valuable Information Relative to Baking, Brewing, Carving, Cleaning, Collaring . . . Bungay: 1823. V. 37

EATON, MOSES

Five Years on the Erie Canal . . . Utica: 1845. V. 45

EATON, RICHARD

A Book of Rates, Inwards and Outwards . . . Dublin: 1767. V. 42

EATON, SEYMOUR

Charles Dickens Rare Print Collection. Philadelphia: 1900. V. 43

More About Teddy B and Teddy G the Roosevelt Bears, Depicting their Further Travel and Adventure. Philadelphia: 1907. V. 46

The Roosevelt Bears; Their Travels and Adventures. Philadelphia: 1906. V. 42; 45

Shakespeare Rare Print Collection. Philadelphia: 1900. V. 39

EATON, STEPHEN

An Exact Narrative of the Bloody Murder, and Robbery Committed by Stephen Eaton, Sarah Swift, George Rhodes and Henry Prichard, Upon the Person of Mr. John Talbot, Minister. London: 1669. V. 38

EATON, THEOPHILUS

Review of New York, or Rambles through the City. New York: 1814. V. 40

EATON, W. P.

Newark, a Series of Engravings on Wood. Newark: 1917. V. 37

EATON, WALTER PRICHARD

The Theatre Guild. New York: 1929. V. 38

EATON, WILLIAM

Interesting Detail of the Operations of the American Fleet in the Mediterranean. Springfield: 1805. V. 39; 43

EAVENSON, HOWARD N.

Map Maker and Indian Traders: an Account of John Patten Trader, Arctic Explorer and Map Maker . . . Pittsburgh: 1949. V. 39; 43

EAVES, LUCILE

A History of California Labor Legislation, with an Introductory Sketch of San Francisco Labor Movement. Berkeley: 1910. V. 45; 46

EBAN, ABBA

My People: The Story of the Jews by Abba Eban. New York: (1968). V. 37

EBBUTT, PERCY G.

Emigrant Life in Kansas. London: 1886. V. 43; 46

EBELING, KLAUS

Ragamala Painting. Basle: 1973. V. 39

EBELL, ADRIAN JOHN

Structure and Classification of Insects. New York: 1872. V. 39

EBER, PAUL

Calendarian Historicum, Conscriptum a P. Ebero . . . Basel: 1550. V. 42

EBERHARDT, FRITZ

A Babylonian Anthology. North Hills: 1966. V. 45

EBERHART, RICHARD

A Bravery of Earth. New York: 1930. V. 46

A Bravery of Earth. New York & London: 1930. V. 39

A Bravery of Earth. London: 1930. V. 37; 41; 45

Burr Oaks. London: 1947. V. 45

Collected Verse Plays. Chapel Hill: 1962. V. 41; 44; 46

Fields of Grace. New York: 1972. V. 46

An Herb Basket. 1950. V. 46

Reading the Spirit. London: 1936. V. 37; 39

Reading the Spirit. New York: 1937. V. 37

Selected Poems. New York: 1951. V. 44; 46

Song and Idea: Poems. London: 1940. V. 41

Ten Poems. 1984. V. 42

Thirty One Sonnets. New York: 1967. V. 45; 46

Undercliff: Poems 1946-1953. New York: 1953. V. 41

EBERLE, JOHN

Notes of Lectures on the Theory and Practice of Medicine, Delivered in the Jefferson Medical College at Philadelphia. Cincinnati: 1834. V. 42

EBERLEIN, HAROLD DONALDSON

Portrait of a Colonial City. Philadelphia: 1939. V. 42

Villas of Florence and Tuscany. Philadelphia: 1922. V. 45

EBERMAIER, JOHANN ERDWIN CHRISTOPH

Taschenbuch der Geburtshulfe fur Angehende Geburtshelfer . . . Leipzig: 1805-07. V. 45

EBERS, GEORG

Arachne. London: 1898. V. 45

Egypt: Descriptive, Historical and Picturesque. London: 1880. V. 41; 42; 44

Egypt: Descriptive, Historical and Picturesque. New York: 1880. V. 43

Egypt: Descriptive, Historical and Picturesque. New York: 1880/83. V. 46

Egypt: Descriptive, Historical, and Picturesque. London: 1887. V. 37

In the Fire of the Forge. London: 1895. V. 43

Papyros Ebers. Das Hermetische Buch Uber die Arzeneimittel der Alten Agypter in Hieratischer Schrift. Leipzig: 1875. V. 40; 42

Per Aspera. (A Thorny Path). London. V. 37

EBERS, JOHN

Seven Years of the King's Theatre. London: 1828. V. 42

EBERSTADT & SONS

The Annotated Eberstadt Catalogs of Americana in Four Volumes Including Index. New York: 1965. V. 39

EBERSTADT, CHARLES

Lincoln's Emancipation Proclamation. New York: 1950. V. 37; 40; 45

EBERSTADT, CHARLES E.

An Abbreviated Title Preliminary Check List in Preparation for a Bibliography of 'Modern' Narratives of the Plains and Rockies. New York: 1938. V. 39

EDGEWORTH, MARIA 1768-1849 continued

The Novels. London: 1893. V. 41; 42; 43; 44

Orlandino. Edinburgh: 1848. V. 43

The Parents' Assistant; or, Stories for Children. London: 1800. V. 39

Patronage. London: 1814. V. 38; 40; 41; 42; 46

Practical Education. London: 1801. V. 37; 38; 45

Practical Education . . . New York: 1801. V. 40

Practical Education. Boston: 1815. V. 38

Practical Education. London: 1815. V. 45

Practical Education. Providence & Boston: 1815. V. 43

Tales and Miscellaneous Pieces. London: 1825. V. 40; 42

Tales and Novels. London: 1823-3. V. 39

Tales and Novels. London: 1832-33. V. 42

Tales and Novels. London: 1832-33. V. 37; 38; 39; 40; 42; 44; 45

Tales and Novels. New York: 1832-46. V. 40

Tales and Novels. London: 1848. V. 37; 39; 42

Tales and Novels. London: 1857. V. 44

Tales and Novels. New York: 1860-65. V. 40

Tales and Novels. London: 1870? V. 44

Tales From . . . New York: 1903. V. 42; 44

Tales of Fashionable Life. London: 1809. V. 46

Tales of Fashionable Life. London: 1809-12. V. 41; 44

Tales of Fashionable Life. 1813. V. 40

Tales of Fashionable Life. London: 1831-33. V. 46

Tales of Fashionable Life. London: 1832-33. V. 37; 41; 43; 44

EDGEWORTH, MRS.

The Ballad Singer . . . London: 1814. V. 45; 46

EDGEWORTH, RICHARD LOVELL 1744-1817

Essay on Irish Bulls. London: 1802. V. 37; 38; 40; 42; 44; 46

Essay on Irish Bulls. London: 1803. V. 37; 38; 41; 42

An Essay on the Construction of Roads and Carriages. London: 1813. V. 37; 40

Essays on Professional Education. London: 1809. V. 37

Memoirs of Richard Lovell Edgeworth. London: 1820. V. 39; 42; 43; 45

EDGEWORTH, THEODORE

The Shipwreck; or, Memoirs of an Irish Officer and His Family. London: 1811. V. 38

EDIE, GEORGE

The Art of English Shooting. London: 1780. V. 45

A Treatise on English Shooting . . . London: 1773. V. 42

EDIE, JAMES M.

Russian Philosophy. Chicago: 1965. V. 37; 42

EDINBURGH.

Contract of Agreement, for Building an Exchange, in the City of Edinburgh, Between the Magistrates and Town-Council, and the Tradesmen. Edinburgh: 1754. V. 38

EDINBURGH & GLASGOW & LEITH RAILWAY

Reports by Messrs Grainger & Miller of Edinburgh and Mr. George Stephenson of Liverpool, Civil Engineers. Edinburgh: 1831. V. 46

EDINBURGH & GLASGOW RAILWAY

Remarks on the Reports of the Committee to the Subscribers for a Survey and Plan of a Railway from Edinburgh and Leith to Glasgow . . . Edinburgh: 1830. V. 46

EDINBURGH. FACULTY OF ADVOCATES. LIBRARY

Catalogue of the Printed Books in the Library of the Faculty of Advocates. London: 1867-79. V. 40

EDINBURGH in the Olden Time Displayed in a Series of Sixty-Three Original Views Between the Years 1717 and 1828, Reproduced in facsimile from the Original Drawings. Edinburgh: 1880. V. 38

EDINBURGH. MERCHANT COMPANY INSTITUTIONS

Landed Estates . . . Edinburgh: 1891. V. 38

THE EDINBURGH Philosophical Journal Exhibiting a View of the Progress of Discovery in Natural Philosophy, Natural History, Practical Mechanics . . . . Edinburgh: 1819-26. V. 45

THE EDINBURGH Review, or Critical Journal. Edinburgh: 1802-40. V. 38

THE EDINBURGH Review, or Critical Journal; for Oct. 1802 to Jan. 1824. Edinburgh: 1805-24. V. 41; 45

EDINBURGH UNIVERSITY

Catalogue of the Printed Books in the Library of the University of Edinburgh. Edinburgh: 1918-23. V. 39

EDINGTON, ROBERT

A Descriptive Plan for Erecting a Penitentiary House, For the Employment of Convicts . . . London: 1803. V. 39; 42

A Treatise on the Abuses of the Coal Trade . . . London: 1817. V. 42

EDIS, ROBERT W.

Decoration and Furniture of Town Houses. London: 1881. V. 38

EDKINS, JOSHUA

A Collection of Poems, Mostly Original, by Several Hands. Dublin: 1789. V. 39

A Collection of Poems, Mostly Original, By Several Hands. Dublin: 1789-90. V. 37

EDLIN, A.

A Treatise on the Art of Bread-Making . . . London: 1805. V. 37

EDMEADES, J. F.

Some Historical Records of the West Kent, (Q.O.) Yoemanry, 1704-1909. London: 1909. V. 38

EDMOND, J. P.

Catalogue of Early Printed Books in the Library . . . Edinburgh: 1906. V. 45

EDMOND, JOHN P.

Catalogue of English Broadsides 1505-1897. New York: 1968. V. 39

EDMOND, JOHN PHILIP

The Aberdeen Printers. Edward Raban to James Nicol. 1620-1736. Aberdeen: 1884-86. V. 44

EDMONDES, CLEMENT 1564?-1622

Observations upon Caesars Commentaries setting forth the Practise of ye Art militarie in the time of the Romaine Empire for the better directions of our moderne Warrs. London: 1604. V. 37

EDMONDES, THOMAS

The Edmondes Papers, a Selection from the Correspondence of . . . 1913. V. 38

A Selection from the Correspondence of . . . London: 1913. V. 44

EDMONDS, CHARLES

Poetry of the Anti-Jacobin. London: 1890. V. 46

EDMONDS, EMMA

Nurse and Spy in the Union Army . . . Hartford: 1865. V. 40; 42; 45

EDMONDS, H. H.

Brook and River Trouting. Bradford: 1916. V. 40; 46

Brook and River Trouting. A Manual of Modern North Country Methods. Yorks.: 1916. V. 40

EDMONDS, HARFIELD

Brook and River Trouting, a Manual of Modern North Country Methods. London: 1916. V. 40

EDMONDS, J. M.

Sappho Revocata: Being an Emended Text with an English Translation. London: 1928. V. 44

Some Greek Love-Poems Gathered and Translated with a Brief Account of Greek Love Poetry. London: 1929. V. 45

Twelve War Epitaphs. Chelsea: 1916 & 1918. V. 46

EDMONDS, JAMES E.

France and Belgium (1914-26th September 1918). London: 1922-48. V. 46

Italy: 1915-1919. London: 1949. V. 46

EDMONDS, JOHN MAXWELL

Some Greek Love-Poems Gathered and Translated with a Brief Account of Greek Love Poetry. London: 1929. V. 40

EDMONDS, RICHARD

The Land's End District; Its Antiquities, Natural History, Natural Phenomena and Scenery . . . London: 1862. V. 41; 46

EDMONDS, WALTER DUMAUX 1903-

The Big Barn. Boston: 1930. V. 37

Drums Along the Mohawk. Boston: 1936. V. 37

EDMONDSON, CHARLES H.

Reef and Shore Fauna of Hawaii. Honolulu: 1933. V. 38

EDMONDSON, JOSEPH

A Complete Body of Heraldry . . . London: 1780. V. 45

An Historical and Genealogical Account of the Noble Family of Greville. London: 1766. V. 37; 38; 45

Precedency. London: 1780? V. 42

EDWARDS, EDWARD, Captain, R.N.

Voyage of H.M.S. 'Pandora' Despatched to Arrest the Mutineers of the 'Bounty' in the South Seas, 1790-91. London: 1915. V. 39

EDWARDS, EDWIN

Old Inns. First Division - Eastern England. London: 1873. V. 46

EDWARDS, EUGENE

Jack Pots Stories of the Great American Game. Chicago: 1900. V. 45

EDWARDS, FRANCIS

Report on the Collections Made by the British Ornithologists' Union Expedition & The Wollaston Expedition in Dutch New Guinea 1910-13. V. 37

EDWARDS, FRANK S.

A Campaign in New Mexico with Colonel Doniphan. Philadelphia: 1847. V. 37; 38; 43; 46

A Campaign in New Mexico with Colonel Doniphan . . . London: 1848. V. 37; 38

EDWARDS, FREDERICK

Our Domestic Fire-Places. London: 1865. V. 37; 40

EDWARDS, GAWEIN

The Earth-Tube. New York: 1929. V. 46

EDWARDS, GEORGE 1752-1823

A Discourse on the Emigration of British Birds; or, This Question at Last Solv'd . . . London. V. 43

A Discourse on the Emigration of British Birds. London: 1781. V. 42

Essays Upon Natural History. London: 1770. V. 43

The Five Practical Plans, Whereby Wer Are Able Effectually to Meet and Remedy Our Present Distressed and Dangerous Situation and Carry All Our Civil, Agricultural . . . Barnard Castle: 1820. V. 38; 41

A Natural History of Uncommon Birds . . . (with) Gleanings of Natural History . . . London: 1743-64. V. 39; 43

A Natural History of Birds. London: 1802-06. V. 39

Reasons Why a True or Genuine System of Public and Private Welfare Adapted to the Present Crisis, and Drawn Up After Great Labour and Reflection, Should be Laid Before Parliament. London: 1803. V. 40; 43

The True Original Scheme of Human Economy, Applied to the Completion of the Different Interests and Preservation, of the British Empire . . . Newcastle-upon-Tyne: 1808. V. 38

EDWARDS, GEORGE C.

A Treatise on the Powers and Duties of Justices of the Peace and Town Officers, in the State of New York, Under the Revised Statutes with Practical Forms. Bath: 1830. V. 37

EDWARDS, GEORGE WHARTON

Thus Think and Smoke Tobacco. New York: 1890. V. 45

EDWARDS, H. SUTHERLAND

Idols of the French Stage. London: 1889. V. 44

The Missing Man. London: 1885. V. 43

EDWARDS, HARRY STILLWELL

Eneas Africanus. Dallas: 1930. V. 38; 39; 40; 42; 43; 44

EDWARDS, HUGH

All Night at Mr. Stanhurst's. London: 1963. V. 44

Surrealism and Its Affinities. A Bibliography of the Mary Reynolds Collection. Chicago: 1956. V. 39

EDWARDS, J. B.

Early. Abilene: 1946. V. 43

EDWARDS, JAMES

Catalogue of the Valuable Library. London: 1815. V. 46

The Hemiptera-Hemoptera (Cicadina and Psyllina) of the British Islands . . . London: 1896. V. 43

EDWARDS, JENNIE

John N. Edwards Biography, Memoirs, Reminiscences and Recollections . . . Kansas City: 1889. V. 43

EDWARDS, JOHN b. 1742

The British Herbal. London: 1769-70. V. 45

An Enquiry into Four Remarkable Texts of the New Testament . . . (with) A Farther Enquiry into Several Remarkable Texts of the Old and New Testament. London: 1692, 1694. V. 41

Some Thoughts Concerning the Several Causes and Occasions of Atheism, Especially in the Present Age. London: 1695. V. 45

EDWARDS, JOHN N.

John N. Edwards: Biography, Memoirs, Reminiscences and Recollections . . . Kansas City: 1889. V. 45

Noted Guerrillas or, the Warfare of the Border, Being a History of John Edwards, Bill Anderson, George Todd, Dave Poole . . . the James Boys, the Younger Brothers nd Others. St. Louis: 1877. V. 38

Shelby and His Men: or, The War in the West. Cincinnati: 1867. V. 41

EDWARDS, JONATHAN

Academiae Oxoniensis Gratulatio Pro Exoptato Serenissimi Regis Guilelmi ex Hibernia Reditu. Oxoniae: 1690. V. 40; 46

An Account of the Life of the Late Reverend David Brainerd. Boston: 1749. V. 38; 39; 45

An Account of the Life of the Late Reverend Mr. David Brainerd, Minister of the Gospel, Missionary to the Indians. Edinburgh: 1765. V. 37; 39; 43

An Account of the Life of the Reverend David Brainerd, Minister of the Gospel. Worcester: 1793. V. 39; 45

An Account of the Life of the Rev. David Brainerd . . . Missionary to the Indians . . . and Pastor of a Church of Christian Indians in New Jersey . . . To which are added, extracts from Mr. Brainerd's Journal . . . Newark: 1811. V. 37

A Careful and Strict Enqiury Into the Modern Prevailing Notions of that Freedom of Will, Which is Supposed to be Essential to Moral Agency, Vertue and Vice . . . Boston: 1754. V. 38; 39; 42; 45

A Careful and Strict Enquiry into the Modern Prevailing Notions of that Freedom of Will, Which is Supposed to Be Essential to Moral Agency. London: 1790. V. 40; 41; 42; 45

A Careful and Strict Inquiry into the Modern Prevailing Notions of that Freedom of Will . . . Wilmington: 1790. V. 38

Discourses on Various Important Subjects, Nearly concerning the Great Affair of the Soul's Eternal Salvation. Boston: 1738. V. 43

The Duty and Interest of a People, Among Who Religion Has Been Planted, to Continue Stedfast and Sincere in the Profession and Practice of It . . . Boston: 1736. V. 43

The Excellency of Christ. Boston: 1780. V. 38

A Faithful Narrative of the Surprising Work of God in the Conversion of Many Hundred Souls in Northampton, and the Neighbouring Towns and Villages of New Hampshire in New England. Edinburgh: 1737. V. 39

The Great Christian Doctrine of Original Sin Defended; Evidences of it's Truth Produced, and Arguments to the Contrary Answered. Boston: 1758. V. 38; 44

The Great Christian Doctrine of Original Sin, Defended; Evidences of Its Truth Produced, and Arguments to the Contrary Answered. Glasgow: 1819. V. 39

History of Redemption, or a Plan Entirely Original . . . New York: 1793. V. 39; 43; 44

An Humble Inquiry into the Rules of the Word of God Concerning the Qualifications Requisite to a Compleat Standing and Full Communion in the Visible Christian Chruch. Boston: 1749. V. 39

Indian-Missionaren David Brainerds Leswerne . . . Stockholm: 1862. V. 44

Memoirs of the Rev. David Brainerd; Missionary to the Indians on the Borders of New York, New Jersey, and Pennsylvania: Chiefly taken from his Own Diary . . . Including his Journal, now for the . . . New Haven: 1822. V. 37

Observations on the Language of the Muhhekaneew Indians . . . New Haven: 1789. V. 45

Remarks Upon a Book Lately Published by Dr. Will. Sherlock Dean of St. Pauls &c . . . Oxford: 1695. V. 45

The Salvation of All Men Strickly Examined. New Haven: 1790. V. 39; 45

A Treatise Concerning Religious Affections. New York: 1768. V. 39

A Treatise Concerning Religious Affections. Edinburgh: 1772. V. 42; 43; 45

A Treatise Concerning Religious Affections. Elizabeth-Town: 1787. V. 42

EDWARDS, LIONEL

Beasts o the Chase. London: 1950. V. 37

Famous Foxhunters. London: 1932. V. 39; 42

Forrard-On. London: 1930. V. 42

Hunting and Stalking the Deer. London: 1927. V. 37; 43

Huntsman Past and Present. London: 1929. V. 39; 44

Huntsmen Past and Present. London: 1939. V. 39

A Leicestershire Sketch Book. London: 1935. V. 37; 39

More Shires & Provinces. London: 1928l. V. 37

My Hunting Sketch Book. London: 1928. V. 37; 42

My Hunting Sketch Book. London: 1928-30. V. 37; 42

My Scottish Sketch Book. London: 1929. V. 37

The Passing Seasons. London: 1929. V. 37

Sketches in Stable and Kennel. London: 1933. V. 37

Sketches in Stable and Kennel. London: 1949. V. 37

The Wiles of the Fox. London: 1932. V. 39

EDWARDS, M. BETHAM

Little Bird Red and Little Bird Blue. London: 1861. V. 38

Through Spain to the Sahara. London: 1868. V. 45

EDWARDS, N. P.

Scenes and Life in the Transvaal . . . 1897. V. 44

EDWARDS, NEVILLE

The Transvaal in War and Peace. London: 1900. V. 45

EGE, OTTO F.

Original Leaves from Famous Bibles. Nine Centuries 1121-1935 A.D. Cleveland: 1936. V. 41

EGEDE, HANS

A Description of Greenland. London: 1745. V. 37; 43

A Description of Greenland. London: 1818. V. 37; 40; 42; 43

EGENOLPH, CHRISTIAN

Flores Hesperidum, Pulcherrimae Plerorumque Graeciae Comicorum Sententiae, cum Duplici Eorum Versione Latina . . . Frankfurt: 1574. V. 38

EGERER, J. W.

A Bibliography of Robert Burns. Edinburgh & London: 1964. V. 44

A Bibliography of Robert Burns. London: 1965. V. 42

EGERTON, DANIEL THOMAS

Fashionable Bores; or Coolers in High Life. London: 1824. V. 42

EGERTON, FRANCIS

Journal of a Tour in the Holy Land in May and June 1840. London: 1841. V. 37; 41; 45

EGERTON, GEORGE

Keynotes. London: 1893. V. 37; 38; 41; 43; 46

EGERTON, JUDY

The Paul Mellon Collection: British Sporting and Animal Drawings c. 1500-1850 (and) British Sporting and Animal Paintings 1655-1867. London: 1978. V. 42

EGERTON, M.

A Day's Journal of a Sponge. London: 1824. V. 37

EGERTON, T.

General Regulations and Instructions for the Ten Troops of Wiltshire Yeomanry. Whitehall: 1798. V. 37

EGERTON, THOMAS

Egerton's Theatrical Remembrancer. London: 1788. V. 38

The Speech of the Lord Chancellor of England, in the Eschequer Chamber, Touching the Post-Nati. London: 1609. V. 38; 40

EGERTON, W., 2ND BARON

A Description of Indian and Oriental Armour. London: 1896. V. 42

EGERTON-WARBURTON, R. E.

hunting Songs, Together with a Short Account of the Taporley Hunt Club, from Its Foundation in 1762 to 1869. Liverpool: 1912. V. 39

EGERTON, WILLIAM

Faithful Memoirs of the Life, Amours and Performances of that Justly Celebrated and Most Emminent Actress of Her Time, Mrs. Anne Oldfield. London: 1731. V. 40

EGGENHOFER, NICK

Eggenhofer: the Pulp Years. Fort Collins: 1975. V. 46

Horses, Horses, Always Horses. Cody: 1981. V. 43

Wagons, Mules and Men. New York: 1961. V. 44; 45; 46

EGGER, H. F. A.

St. Croix's Flora. Copenhagen: 1876. V. 38

EGGLESTON, BENJAMIN

The Wars of America; or a General History of All the Important Tragic Events that Have Occurred in the United States of North America . . . Baltimore: 1839. V. 45

EGGLESTON, EDWARD 1837-1902

The Hoosier School Boy. Toronto: 1883. V. 39

The Hoosier School-Master. New York: 1871. V. 38; 40; 42; 43

The Hossier School-Boy. New York: 1883. V. 43

The Manual: a Practical Guide to the Sunday School Work. Chicago: 1869. V. 42

Roxy. New York: 1878. V. 41; 44

EGGLESTON, GEORGE CARY

The History of the Confederate War: Its Causes and Its Conduct: a Narrative and Critical History. New York: 1910. V. 38; 39

EGGLESTON, WILFRID

The Queen's Choice. A Story of Canadas Capital. Ottawa: 1961. V. 37

EGLE, WILLIAM HENRY

Illustrated History of the Commonwealth of Pennsylvania, Civil, Political & Military, From its Earliest Settlement to the Present Time, Including Historical Descriptions of Each County in the State, Their Towns, & Industrial . . . Harrisburg: 1876. V. 37

Notes and Queries Historical and Genealogical Chiefly Relating to Interior Pennsylvania. Harrisburg: 1894-1899. V. 41

EGLESTON, NATHANIEL HILLYER

Villages and Village Life with Hints for Their Improvement. New York: 1878. V. 42

EGLINGTON, JOHN

Some Essays and Passages by . . . 1905. V. 42

EGMONT, J. AEGIDIUS VAN

Travels through Part of Europe, Asia Minor . . . Syria, Egypt, Palestine, Mount Sinai &c. London: 1759. V. 45; 46

EGMONT, JOHN PERCEVAL, 1ST EARL OF 1683-1748

Faction Detected, by the Evidence of facts. London: 1743. V. 46

A Journal of the Transactions of the Trustees for Establishing the Colony of Georgia in America. Wormsloe: 1886. V. 43

EGMONT, JOHN PERCEVAL, 2ND EARL OF 1711-1770

An Examination of the Principles, and an Enquiry Into the Conduct of the Two B*****rs; in Regard to the Establishment of Their Power, and Their Prosecution of the War. London: 1749. V. 41

Faction Detected by the Evidence of Facts . . . London: 1743. V. 41

Faction Detected, by the Evidence of Facts. London: 1744. V. 41

An Occasional Letter from a Gentleman in the Country, to His Friend in Town. London: 1749. V. 41

A Proposal for selling Part of the Forest Lands and Chaces, and disposing of the produce towards the discharge of that part of the National Debt, dut to the Bank of England; and for the establishment of a National Bank. London: 1763. V. 37

A Second Series of Facts and Arguments: Tending to Prove, That the Abilities of the Two B-----rs, are Not More Extraordinary than Their Virtues. London: 1749. V. 41

EGNATIUS, IOANNES BAPTISTA

De Caesaribus Libri III (Historiae Augustae Scriptores). Florence: 1519. V. 37

EHRENBERG,

Mikrogeologie: Das Erden und Felsen Schaffende Wirken des Unsichtbar Kleinen Selbstandigen Lebens auf der Erde. Leipzig: 1854-56. V. 45

Symbolae Physicae seu Icones et Descriptiones Corporum Naturalium Novorum aut Minus Cognitorum Quae ex Itineribus per Libyam Aegyptum Nubiam Dongalam Syriam Arabiam et Habessiniam . . . Berlin: 1828. V. 43

EHRENBERG, C. G.

Die Infusionsthierchen als Vollkommene Organismen. Leipzig: 1838. V. 41

Symbolae Physicae Seu Icones et Descriptiones Avium Quae ex Itinere per Africam Borealem . . . Berlin: 1828, 1829. V. 42

EHRENBERG, HERMANN

A Campaign in Texas. New York: 1846. V. 38

Fahrten und Schicksale eines Deutchen in Texas. Leipzig: 1845. V. 37

With Milam and Fannin: Adventures of a German Boy in Texas' Revolution. Dallas: 1935. V. 37

EHRENBERG, RICHARD

Das Zeitalter der Fugger. Jena: 1896. V. 38

EHRET, GEORGE

Twenty-Five Years of Brewing. New York: 1891. V. 46

EICHENBERG, FRITZ

Pigs and Eagles. North Brookfield: 1978. V. 46

The Wood and the Graver, the Work of Fritz Eichenberg. Barre: 1977. V. 39

EICHENDORF, JOSEPH VON

Memoirs of a Good-for-Nothing. 1866. V. 44

EICKEMEYER, CARL

Among the Pueblo Indians. New York: 1895. V. 46

Over the Great Navajo Trail. New York: 1900. V. 37; 44

EICKEMEYER, RUDOLF

Letters from the South-West. New York: 1894. V. 44

Winter. New York: 1903. V. 42

EIFFEL, ALEXANDER GUSTAVE

La Resistance de l'Air et l'Aviation. Paris: 1910. V. 38

EIFFEL, ALEXANDRE GUSTAVE

Nouvelles Recherches sur la Resistance de l'Air et l'Aviation faites au Laboratoire d'Auteuil. Paris: 1914. V. 38; 41; 44

EIGENMANN, C. H.

The Fishes of Western South America. Part 1, The Fresh-water Fishes of Northwestern South America (Panama to Peru). Pittsburgh: 1922. V. 37

The Freshwater Fishes of British Guiana. Pittsburgh: 1912. V. 37

EIGER, LARRY

Look at the Park. N.P.: 1958. V. 39

EIGHT Letters Between the People Called Buchanites, and a Teacher Near Edinburgh. Edinburgh: 1785. V. 45

EIGHT Speeches Made in Parliament, on Several Important Occasions. London: 1733. V. 41

1897 History of the Savannah Police Department. Savannah: 1897. V. 38

THE EIGHTH and Ninth Articles fo the Treaty of Commerce, with Relation to the Trade of Scotland, with France, Considered with a Postscript, showing the Falsities of a Letter Publish'd in the Mercator. Edinburgh: 1713. V. 43

EIGHTIETH Birthday Tribute to Sir Winston Churchill. Hampshire: 1955. V. 46

EIGHTY-NINE Fugitive Fables, in Verse; Moral, Prudential and Allegorical. London: 1792. V. 43

EIGNER, LARRY

Another Time in Fragments. London: 1967. V. 41

From the Sustaining Air. Palma de Mallorca: 1953. V. 37

The - I/Towards Autumn. San Francisco: 1967. V. 46

Waters/Places/A Time. Santa Barbara: 1983. V. 40; 42

The World and Its Streets, People. Santa Barbara: 1977. V. 40

The World and Its Streets, Places. Santa Barbara: 1977. V. 42

Eikon Basilike. London: 1648. V. 38; 43
ELKON Basilike. N.P.: 1648. V. 38
EIKON Basilike. Hague: 1649. V. 41
EIKON Basilike. London: 1649. V. 38
EIKON Basilike or the King's Book. London: 1903. V. 46

EIKON Basilike. 1649. V. 37

EINEDER, GEORG

The Ancient Papermills of the Former Austro-Hungarian Empire and Their Watermarks. Hilversum: 1960. V. 41

EINSTEIN, ALBERT 1879-1955

Die Grundlage der Allgemeinen Relativitats Theorie. Leipzig: 1916. V. 40; 42; 45

The Evolution of Physics. New York: 1938. V. 43

The Evolution of Physics. New York: 1942. V. 37

Investigations on The Theory of the Brownian Movement. London: 1926. V. 40

The Meaning of Relativty. London: 1922. V. 40; 44

On the Meaning of Relativity. Princeton: 1923. V. 42

The Meaning of Relativity. Princeton: 1945. V. 46

Relativity: The Special and the General Theory. London: 1920. V. 40

Relativity. New York: 1920. V. 41; 43; 44

Sidelights and Relativity. New York: 1922. V. 38; 40

EISELEY, LOREN

All The Strange Hours. New York: 1975. V. 46

The Brown Wasps. Mt. Horeb: 1969. V. 42; 44

Darwin's Century: Evolution and the Man Who Discovered It. Garden City: 1958. V. 39

EISEN, GUSTAVUS A.

Glass. Its Orgin, History, Chronology, Technic and Classification to the Sixteenth Century. New York: 1927. V. 37; 38

The Great Chalice of Antioch on Which are Depicted in Sculpture the Earliest Known Portraits of Christ, Apostles and Evangelists. New York: 1923. V. 37

Portraits of Washington. New York: 1932. V. 40

EISENBERG, BARON D'EISENBERG

Description du Manege Moderne dans sa Perfection. London: & Amsterdam: 1727. V. 44

EISENHART, WILLY

The World of Donald Evans. New York: 1980. V. 44

EISENHOWER, DWIGHT DAVID 1890-1969

Crusade in Europe. Garden City: 1948. V. 39

D-Day Order of the Day and the Guild Hall Speech. V. 43

The Inaugural Address of . . . Worcester: 1954. V. 38

Waging Peace, The White House Years 1956-1961. Garden City: 1965. V. 38; 44; 46

The White House Years: Mandate for Change 1953-1956. (with) The White House Years: Waging War, 1956-1967. Garden City: 1963. V. 38; 45

The White House Years: Mandate for a Change: 1953-1956. New York: 1963. V. 39

The White House Years. Garden City: 1963/65. V. 43

EISENLOHR, LOUIS H.

Memories from Philadelphia to Charlestown, Maryland via Nome, Alaska. Philadelphia: 1918. V. 40

EISENSCHIML, OTTO

The Civil War in Miniature. Chicago and Skokie: 1962. V. 41

EISENSCHMID, JOANN C. 1656-1712

De Ponderibus et Mensuris Veterum Romanorum, Graecorum, Hebraeorum; Nec Non de Valore Pecuniae Veteris . . . Argentorati: 1708. V. 38

EISENSTAEDT, ALFRED

People. Photographs. New York: 1973. V. 39

Witness to Our Time. New York: 1966. V. 37

EITNER, LORENZ

Gericault's Raft of the Medusa. London: 1972. V. 40; 43

EKELOF, ADOLF

Ett ar i Stilla Hafvet. Reseminnen Fran Patagonien, Chili, Peru, Californien, Britiska Columbia och Oceanien. Stockholm: 1872. V. 38

EKINS, JEFFREY

Poems. London: 1810. V. 42

EKKEHARD OF AURA

Conradi a Liechtenau Abbatis Urspergensis Chronicum Absolutissimum a Nino Assyriorum Rege Usque ad Tempora Frederici III. Paraleipomena Usque ad Carolum V. Basle: 1569. V. 37

EL- KHOULI, ALI

Egyptian Stone Vessels: Predynastic Period to Dynasty III. Typology and Analysis. Mainz: 1978. V. 37; 40; 42

ELA; or the Delusions of the Heart. Dublin: 1788. V. 44

ELAM, CHARLES

On Cerebria and Other Diseases of the Brain. London: 1872. V. 41; 44

Winds of Doctrine; Being an Examination of Modern Theories of Automatism and Evolution. London: 1876. V. 43; 46

ELBERTUS, FRA

Old John Burroughs. East Aurora: 1901. V. 41

ELBORN, GEOFFREY

Hand and Eye - an Anthology for Sacheverell Sitwell. Edinburgh: 1977. V. 38; 42; 44

Hand and Eye - an Anthology for Sacheverell Sitwell. London: 1977. V. 38

ELCHIES, PATRICK GRANT, LORD 1690-1754

A Letter from a Gentlemen at Edinburgh, to a Minister in the Country, Containing An Account of the Substance of the Late Conferences of Ministers at Edinburgh . . . Edinburgh: 1737. V. 43

ELD, S.

Six Views of the Ancient Gates of Coventry. Coventry: 1840. V. 38

ELDER, GEORGE

Das Guldene Fluss Christlicher Gemain und Gesellschafft . . . Ingolstadt: 1580. V. 40

ELDER, PAUL

California the Beautiful. San Francisco: 1911. V. 37; 38

The Old Spanish Missions of California. San Francisco: 1913. V. 37; 43

ELDER, WILLIAM

Aphasia and the Cerebral Speech Mechanism. London: 1897. V. 46

Biography of Elisha Kent Kane. Philadelphia: 1858. V. 43

ELDERKIN, JAMES D.

Biographical Sketches and Anecdotes of a Soldier of Three Wars . . . Detroit: 1899. V. 44

ELDREDGE, ZOETH SKINNER

The Beginnings of San Francisco from the Expedition of Anza, 1774 to the City Charter of April 15, 1850. San Francisco: 1912. V. 40; 44; 46

The Beginnings of San Francisco from the Expediton of Anza, 1774, to the City Charter of April 15, 1850. San Francisco: 1912. V. 40

History of California. New York. V. 38

History of California. New York: 1915. V. 37

ELDRIDGE, BENJAMIN P.

Our Rival the Rascal. Boston: 1897. V. 45

ELDRIDGE, ELLEANOR

Memoirs of . . . Providence: 1840. V. 39; 42

Memoirs of . . . Providence: 1843. V. 43

Memoirs of . . . Providence: 1846. V. 39

Memoirs of. Providence: 1847. V. 46

ELDRIDGE, F. B.

A History of the Royal Australian Navy College. Melbourne: 1949. V. 41

ELDRIDGE, GEORGE

Eldridge's Coast Pilot No. 4, From New York to Boston. Boston: 1893. V. 42

ELDRIDGE, GEORGE W.

George W. Eldridge's Book of Harbor Charts New York to Boston. Boston: 1902. V. 38

George W. Eldridge's Harbor Chart-Book Boston to Bar Harbor. Boston: 1929. V. 38

ELDRIDGE, LEMUEL B.

The Torrent; or an Account of a Deluge Occasioned by an Unparalleled Rise of the New Haven River in Which Nineteen Persons Were Swept Away, Five of Whom Only Escaped, July 26, 1830. Middlebury: 1831. V. 45

ELDRIDGE, WILLIAM HENRY

Henry Genealogy. Boston: 1915. V. 46

ELEANORA: London: 1785. V. 37
ELEANORA. London: 1787. V. 38

ELECTORAL Atlas of the Dominion of Canada As Divided for the Revision of the Voters' Lists Made in the Year 1894. Ottawa: 1895. V. 37

THE ELECTOR'S Guide; or the Parliamentary Reform Act of Scotland. Edinburgh: 1832. V. 43

ELECTRONICS: a New Science for a New World (cover title). N.P.: 1946. V. 37

ELEGANT Extracts from the Most Eminent Prose-Writers . . . London. V. 38

ELEGANT Extracts; or Useful and Entertaining Pieces of Poetry, Selected for the Improvement of Youth. Dublin: 1789. V. 43

ELEGANT, ROBERT SIMPSON

The Seeking. New York: 1969. V. 39

AN ELEGIE Upon Mr. Thomas Hobbes of Malmesbury, Lately Deceased . . . London: 1679. V. 39

AN ELEGY on the Much Lamented Death of Her Royal Highness the Princess Dowager of Wales, Who Departed This Life in Saturday Feb. 8, 1772, in the 54th Year of Her Age. London: 1772. V. 42

AN ELEGY Written at a Carthusian Monastery in the Austrian Netherlands. London: 1775. V. 43

ELEMENTARY Tables & Lessons, in the Siamese Language, prepared by Mrs. E. R. Bradley, revised and enalrged by D. B. Bradley. Bangkok: 1860. V. 37

ELEMENTS of Natural Philosophy . . . and the Human Understanding. Belfast: 1812. V. 45

ELEUSIS a Poem. Stroud. V. 39

ELFIE in Sicily. London: 1860. V. 39

ELGAR, FRANCIS

The Royal Navy; Lithographed in Colours, in a Series of Illustrations from Original Drawings. London & Portsmouth: 1875. V. 38

ELGEE, FRANK

Early Man in North-East Yorkshire. Gloucester: 1930. V. 45

ELGIN, THOMAS BRUCE, 7TH EARL OF

Memorandum on the Subject of the Earl of Elgin's Pursuits in Greece. Edinburgh: 1811. V. 46

ELGOOD, CYRIL

A Medical History of Persia and the Eastern Caliphate. Cambridge: 1951. V. 37; 39

ELGOOD, GEORGE

Some English Gardens. London: 1904. V. 45

ELGOOD, GEORGE S.

Some English Gardens. London: 1933. V. 38

ELIANA. London: 1661. V. 40

ELIAS BEN ASHER

Opus de Prosodia Hebraeorum. Paris: 1545. V. 46

ELIAS LEVITA

Accentum Hebraicorum Liber unus. Basel: 1539. V. 46

ELIE DE BEAUMONT, ANNE LOUISE

The History of a Young Lady of Distinction. London: 1754. V. 38

ELIO, FRANCISCO XAVIER

El Virrey de las Provincias del Rio de la Plata a los Habitantes de Esta Ciudad. Montevideo: 1811. V. 40

ELIOT, CHARLES

Japanese Buddhism. London: 1935. V. 39

ELIOT, CHARLOTTE

Savonarola. a Dramatic Poem. London: 1926. V. 38; 42

ELIOT, DANIEL GIRAUD

A Monograph of the Pittidae, or Family of Ant Thrushes. New York: 1863. V. 39

ELIOT, GEORGE 1819-1880

Adam Bede. Edinburgh: 1859. V. 38; 41; 42; 44

Adam Bede. New York: 1859. V. 38; 40; 43

Adam Bede. London: 1910. V. 43

Adam Bede. Edinburgh & London: 1859. V. 37; 43; 44; 45

Agatha. London: 1890. V. 41

Animula. London: 1929. V. 43

Complete Poems. Boston: 1890-1900. V. 42

Daniel Deronda. Edinburgh: 1876. V. 38; 40; 42; 44; 45

Daniel Deronda. Edinburgh & London: 1876. V. 37; 38; 39; 41; 42; 43; 44; 45; 46

Daniel Deronda. London: 1876. V. 37; 38; 40; 43

Daniel Deronda. Montreal: 1876. V. 39

Daniel Deronda. New York: 1876. V. 41

Daniel Deronda. New York: 1877. V. 43

Daniel Deronda. Edinburgh & London: 1878. V. 43

Early Essays. 1919. V. 37; 39; 43; 45

Early Essays. London: 1919. V. 40

Essays. Edinburgh: 1884. V. 38; 39; 42; 43

Essays and Leaves from a Notebook. Edinburgh & London: 1884. V. 37; 40; 41; 45; 46

Felix Holt. Edinburgh: 1866. V. 37; 38; 39; 40; 41; 42; 44

Felix Holt, the Radical. Edinburgh & London: 1866. V. 37; 38; 39; 41; 44

Felix Holt. London: 1866. V. 38; 45

George Eliot's Life as Related in Her Letters and Journals, Arranged and Edited by Her Husband, J.W. Cross. London: 1855. V. 39

George Eliot's Life as Related in Her Letters and Journals. Edinburgh & London: 1885. V. 41

How Lisa Loved the King. Boston: 1869. V. 38; 39; 40; 41

Impressions of Theophrastus Such. Edinburgh London: 1870. V. 37; 42

Impressions of Theophrastus Such. Edinburgh: 1879. V. 38; 39; 42; 43; 44

Impressions of Theophastrus Such. Edinburgh & London: 1879. V. 37; 40; 44

Impressions of Theophrastus Such. London: 1879. V. 40

Impressions of Theophrastus Such. London: 1879. V. 41

Impressions of Theophrastus Such. New York: 1879. V. 43

The Legend of Jubal; and Other Poems. Boston: 1874. V. 42; 44

The Legend of Jubal and Other Poems. London: 1874. V. 40; 45

The Legend of Jubal and Other Poems. Edinburgh & London: 1875. V. 46

The Legend of Jubal and Other Poems. Edinburgh & London: 1874. V. 37; 44

Life, as Related in Her Letters and Journals. Edinburgh: 1885. V. 42

Middlemarch. Edinburgh & London: 1871-1872. V. 37; 38; 41

Middlemarch. Edinburgh: 1871. V. 38; 39; 44; 45

Middlemarch. Edinburgh & London: 1871. V. 40; 44

Middlemarch. Edinburgh and London: 1871. V. 44

Middlemarch. London: 1871. V. 39

Middlemarch: a study of provincial life. Edinburgh: 1871-2. V. 37

Middlemarch: a Study of Provincial Life. Berlin: 1872. V. 44

Middlemarch: a Study of Provincial Life. Edinburgh: 1873. V. 41; 43; 45

Middlemarch. Edinburgh: 1873. V. 41; 42

The Mill on the Floss. Edinburgh & London: 1840. V. 38

The Mill on the Floss. Edinburgh: 1860. V. 37; 38; 40; 42; 44

The Mill on the Floss. Edinburgh and London: 1860. V. 37; 38; 44; 45; 46

The Mill on the Floss. New York: 1860. V. 39; 45; 46

The Mill on the Floss. Edinburgh: 1880. V. 46

The Mill on the Floss. London: 1860. V. 37; 40; 41; 43

ELIOT, THOMAS STEARNS 1888-1965 continued

Religious Drama: Mediaeval and Modern. New York: 1954. V. 40; 42

Reunion by Destruction - Reflections on a Scheme for Church Union in South India: Addressed to the Laity. London: 1943. V. 41

The Rock. London: 1934. V. 38; 39; 40; 44; 45

The Sacred Wood. London: 1920. V. 37; 38; 40; 45; 46

Selected Essays 1917-1932. London: 1932. V. 37; 44

Selected Essays 1917-1932. New York: 1932. V. 46

A Song for Simeon. London: 1928. V. 39; 41; 44; 45; 46

A Song for Simeon. 1928. V. 37

Sweeney Agonistes. London: 1932. V. 39; 42; 44; 46

Thoughts after Lambeth. London: 1931. V. 41; 43

Tierra Baldia. Barcelona: 1930. V. 40

Triumphal March. London: 1931. V. 43

T.S. Eliot: A Symposium for His Seventieth Birthday. London: 1958. V. 37

Undergaduate Poems of T. S. Eliot. Cambridge: 1949. V. 37; 39; 40; 46

The Undergraduate. Cambridge: 1948. V. 45

The Use of Poetry and the Use of Criticism. Cambridge: 1933. V. 44

The Use of Poetry and the Use of Criticism. London: 1933. V. 45; 46

What is A Classic? London: 1944. V. 40

The Waste Land. New York: 1922. V. 38; 39; 40; 41; 44; 45; 46

The Waste Land. London: 1923. V. 40

The Waste Land. Richmond: 1923. V. 38; 41; 44; 45

Braakland. Amsterdam: 1949. V. 44

The Waste Land. 1961. V. 38

The Waste Land. London: 1961. V. 41; 42; 43; 44

The Waste Land. London: 1971. V. 37; 40; 43

The Waste Land. A Facsimile and Transcript of the Original Drafts Including the Annotations of Ezra Pound. London: 1971. V. 40

ELIOT, WILLIAM GRANVILLE

A Treatise on the Defence of Portugal, with a Military Map of the Country . . . London: 1811. V. 42

ELIOT, WILLIAM H.

Catalogue of the Library of the Late William H. Eliot, Esq. Boston: 1832. V. 40

ELIOTT, DANIEL GIRAUD

The Birds of Daniel Giraud Elliott . . . London: 1979. V. 42

ELISOFON, ELIOT

The Sculpture of Africa. London: 1958. V. 46

The Sculpture of Africa. New York: 1958. V. 37; 44; 46

ELISON, THOMAS

Decorations for Parks and Gardens. London: 1800. V. 40

ELISSEEFF, DANIELLE

New Discoveries in China: Encountering History Through Archeology. Secaucus: 1983. V. 41

ELIZABETH Canning Drawn from the Life, as She Stood at the Bar to Receive Her Sentence, in the Session's-House in the Old Bailey. London: 1754. V. 46

ELIZABETH, CHARLOTTE

The Christian Lady's Magazine. London: 1834-1840. V. 40; 46

ELIZABETH II, QUEEN OF GREAT BRITAIN

The Address of Her Majesty, Delivered at Westminster Hall and Guildhall on the Occasion of Her Silver Jubilee 1952-1977. Worcester: 1977. V. 46

ELIZABETH, PRINCESS OF ENGLAND

Cupid Turned Volunteer: In a Series of Prints Designed by . . . London: 1804. V. 45

ELIZABETH, QUEEN CONSORT OF CHARLES I, KING OF RUMANIA 1843-1916

Edleen Vaughan; or, Paths of Peril. London: 1892. V. 38; 39; 42

How I Spent My Sixtieth Birthday. Guildford: 1904. V. 42

ELKIN, R. H.

The Children's Corner. London. V. 45

The Children's Corner. London: 1914. V. 46

The Children's Corner. 1918. V. 41

The Children's Corner. London: 1925. V. 44

Little People. Philadelphia. V. 40; 46

Little People. Philadelphia & London. V. 41

Little People. London: 1925. V. 44

Old Dutch Nursery Rhymes. London: 1917. V. 37; 43

ELKIN, STANLEY

A Bad Man. New York: 1967. V. 40

Boswell. New York: 1964. V. 37; 38; 42

The Coffee Room. Louisville: 1987. V. 43; 45

ELKINS, JOHN M.

Indian Fighting on the Texas Frontier. Amarillo: 1929. V. 46

ELKUS, RICHARD J.

Alamos, a Philosophy in Living. 1965. V. 39

Alamos, A Philosophy in Living. San Francisco: 1965. V. 37; 38; 45; 46

ELLACOMBE, H. N.

Shakespeare as an Angler. London: 1883. V. 39; 40

ELLARD, HARRY

Base Ball in Cincinnati. A History. Cincinnati: 1908. V. 39

Ranch Tales of The Rockies. Canon City: 1899. V. 41; 43

ELLEN Le Clair; or, the Mysterious Minstrel. London: 1810. V. 44

ELLENBECKER, JOHN G.

The Jayhawkers of Death Valley. Marysville: 1938. V. 40; 45

ELLENPORT, S.

An Essay on the Development and Usage of Brass Plate Dyes. Boston: 1980. V. 41

ELLER, IRVIN

The History of Belvoir Castle. London: 1841. V. 37; 38; 40; 44

ELLERMAN, ANNIE WINIFRED 'BRYHER'

Two Selves. Paris: 1923. V. 37

ELLERMAN, J. R.

The Families and Genera of Living Rodents. London: 1940-41. V. 42

The Families and Genera of Living Rodents. London: 1940-49. V. 37

ELLERMAN, JOHN

Why Do They Like It. Dijon: 1927. V. 37; 41

ELLERMAN, WINIFRED

Film Problems of Soviet Russia. Territet: 1929. V. 46

The Lighthearted Student. Territet: 1930. V. 46

ELLESMERE, FRANCES EGERTON, EARL OF

Guide to Northern Archaeology . . . London: 1848. V. 43

ELLET, CHARLES

The Mississippi and Ohio Rivers . . . Philadelphia: 1853. V. 46

The Position and Prospects of the Schuylkill Navigation Co. Philadelphia: 1845. V. 46

ELLET, ELIZABETH E.

Poems. Philadelphia: 1835. V. 37; 42

ELLET, ELIZABETH F.

The Women of the American Revolution. New York: 1848. V. 45

ELLET, ELIZABETH FRIES LUMMIS 1818-1877

The Court Circles of the Republic, or the Beauties and Celebrities of the Nation. Hartford: 1869. V. 38; 44

ELLICOTT, ANDREW

The Journal of Andrew Ellicott . . . Philadelphia: 1803. V. 37; 38; 39; 40; 41; 43; 45

The Journal of Andrew Ellicott, 1796-1800, For Determining the Boundary Between the U. S. and the Possessions of His Catholic Majesty. Philadelphia: 1814. V. 42; 43

ELLIGEN, J.

The Terrible Deeds of George L. Shaftesbury, Who Killed His Own Mother and Sister, Fled from Justice by Leaping from the Palisades, Swimming the Hudson River, and Taking Refuge in New York City, Where He Was Jointed by the Female Murderer! Marie Lavine . . . St. Louis: 1851. V. 37; 39; 44

ELLIN, STANLEY

Dreadful Summit. 1948. V. 39

Mystery Stories. New York: 1956. V. 46

ELLING, CHRISTIAN

Monumenta Architecturae Danicae. Danish Architectural Drawings, 1660-1920. Copenhagen: 1961. V. 41

ELLINGTON, CHARLES G.

Trial of U.S. Grant; the Pacific Coast Years 1852-1854. Glendale: 1987. V. 38

ELLIOT, ANNE

An Old Man's Favour. London: 1887. V. 41

ELLIOT, DANIEL GIRAUD

The Birds of Daniel Giraud Elliott . . . London: 1979. V. 44; 45; 46

The Life and Habits of Wild Animals Illustrated with Designs by Joseph Wolf. London: 1874. V. 42

A Monograph of the Phasianidae or Family of the Pheasants. New York: 1872. V. 42

A Monograph of the Paradiseidae of Birds of Paradise. London: 1873. V. 37; 45

A Monograph of the Bucerodtidae or Family of the Hornbills. London: 1877-1882. V. 38; 42

A Monograph of the Paradiseidae or Birds of Paradise. New York & Amsterdam: 1977. V. 38

A Review of the Primates. New York: 1912. V. 46

A Review of the Primates. New York: 1912/13. V. 42

The Wild Fowl of the United States and British Possessions. London: 1898. V. 37

ELLIOT, DANIEL GIROUD

A Monograph of the Bucerotidae, or Family of the Hornbills. London: 1877-1882. V. 40

Review of the Ibidinae, or Subfamily of the Ibises. 1877. V. 43

A Review of the Primates. New York: 1912. V. 40

A Review of the Primates. New York: 1912-13. V. 37; 43

ELLIOT, GEORGE H.

The Presidio of San Francisco. Washington: 1874. V. 45

ELLIOT, H.

Seal Islands of Alaska, a Monograph of the Pribylov Group, the Fur Seal Islands . . . Washington: 1881-84. V. 38

ELLIOT, HENRY W.

Profiles, Sections and Other Illustrations, Designed to Accompany the Final Report of the Chief Geologist of the Survey . . . New York: 1872. V. 40

Report Upon the Fur Seal Rookeries of the Pribilov Islands of Alaska. Washington: 1896. V. 37

ELLIOT, JAMES

The Poetical and Miscellaneous Works of James Elliot, Citizen of Guilford, Vermont and Late a Noncommissioned Officer in the Legion of the United States. Greenfield: 1798. V. 40; 43

ELLIOT, JOHN

An Account of the Nature and Medicinal Virtues of the Principal Mineral Waters of Great Britain and Ireland and those Most in Repute on the Continent. London: 1789. V. 40

ELLIOT, JONATHAN

The Debates in the Several State Conventions on the Adoption of the Federal Constitution . . . Washington, DC: 1836. V. 37

ELLIOT, MARY

Gems in the Mine. London: 1824. V. 45

Rustic Excursions to Aid Tarry-at-Home Travellers. Together with More Rustic Excursions. London: 1825/1827. V. 45; 46

ELLIOT, MISS

Fancy's Wreath. London: 1812. V. 42

ELLIOT, ROBERT

Views in the East; comprising Indian, Canton and the Shores of the Red Sea. Drawn by T. Boys, G. Cattermole, D. Cox, J.S. Cotman, F. Finch, W. Purser, S. Prout, C. Stanfeld &c &c. From Original Sketches . . . London: 1832. V. 37

Views in the East. London: 1833. V. 39; 42

Views in India, China and the Shores of the Red Sea, with descriptions by Emma Roberts. London: 1835. V. 37

ELLIOT, ROBERT H.

Gold, Sport and Coffee. London: 1894. V. 39; 46

Gold, Sport and Coffee. Westmisnter: 1894. V. 46

Written on Their Foreheads. London: 1879. V. 41; 43

ELLIOT, STEPHEN

Address of the Rt. Rev. Stephen Elliott, D.D., to the Thirty-Ninth Annual Convention of the Protestant Episcopal Church, in the Diocese of Georgia. Savannah: 1861. V. 44

God's Presence With Our Army at Manassas! A Sermon Preached in Christ Church, Savannah, on Sunday July 28th . . . Savannah: 1861. V. 44

Vain Is the Help of Man. A Sermon Preached in Christ Church, Savannah . . . September 15, 1864. Macon: 1864. V. 44

ELLIOT, W. J.

The Spurs. Spur: 1936. V. 42

The Spurs. Spur: 1939. V. 39

ELLIOT, W. R.

Encyclopaedia of Australian Plants Suitable for Cultivation. Melbourne: 1980-81-84. V. 37; 38

ELLIOT, WILLIAM

The Patentee's Manual; Containing a List of Patents Granted by the United States for the Encouragement of Arts and Sciences, Alphabetically Arranged, from 1790 to 1830 . . . Washington: 1830. V. 39

Remarks on the Proposed Railway from Hanover and Brunsiwck to Hamburg. Hamburg: 1835. V. 46

ELLIOTT, CHARLES

Life of Rev. Robert R. Roberts, One of the Bishops of the Methodist Episcopal Church. Cincinnati: 1844. V. 37; 42

ELLIOTT, CHARLES BOILEAU

Letters from the North of Europe. London: 1832. V. 43

Travels in the Three Great Empires of Austria, Russia and Turkey. London: 1838. V. 45

ELLIOTT, CLAUDE

Leathercoat. The Life History of a Texas Patriot. San Antonio: 1938. V. 44

ELLIOTT, DAVID

The Life of the Rev. Elisha Macurdy. Allegheny: 1848. V. 42

The Life of the Rev. Elisha Macurdy. Allegheny: 1848. V. 41

ELLIOTT, E. B.

On the Military Statistics of the United States of America. Berlin: 1863. V. 44

ELLIOTT, E. N.

Cotton is King, and Pro-Slavery Arguments. Augusta: 1860. V. 39

ELLIOTT, EBENEZER

More Verse and Prose by the Corn Law Rhymer. London: 1850. V. 39

The Splendid Village: Corn Law Rhymes; and Other Poems. London: 1834-1835. V. 39

ELLIOTT, F. R.

Hand-Book of Practical Landscape Gardening . . . Rochester: 1877. V. 37

Handbook of Practical Landscape Gardening Designed for City and Suburban Residences and Country School Houses . . . Rochester: 1881. V. 39

Handbook of Practical Landscape Gardening Designed for City and Subur ban Residences and Country School Houses. New York: 1885. V. 38; 39; 40

Handbook of Practical Landscape Gardening Designed for City and Suburban Residences . . . Rochester: 1885. V. 39

ELLIOTT, HENRY W.

An Arctic Province. Alaska and the Seal Islands. London: 1883. V. 39

A Monograph of the Pribilov Group, or the Seal-Islands of Alaska. Washington: 1896. V. 37

Our Arctic Province Alaska and the Seal Islands. New York: 1886. V. 42; 43; 46

Report on the Seal Islands of Alaska. Washington: 1880. V. 44

The Report of . . . on the Condition of the Fur-Seal Fisheries of Alaska. Together with all Maps and Illustrations . . . Letter from the Secretary of the Treasury. Washington: 1896. V. 37; 39

ELLIOTT, ISAAC H.

Record of the Services of Illinois Soldiers in the Black Hawk War, 1831-32, and in the Mexican War, 1846-8. Springfield: 1882. V. 40

ELLIOTT, JESSE D.

Correspondence in Relation to the Capture of the British Brigs Detroit and Caledonia, on the Night of October 8, 1812. Philadelphia: 1843. V. 45

Speech of Jesse Duncan Elliott, U.S.N. Delivered in Hagerstown, Md. on 14th November 1843. Philadelphia: 1844. V. 38; 40

ELLIOTT, JOHN

A Selected, Pronouncing and Accented Dictionary. Suffield: 1800. V. 40

ELLIOTT, JOHN MALSBURY KIRBY

Fifty Years' Fox-Hunting with the Grafton and Other Packs of Hounds. London: 1900. V. 43

ELLIOTT, M. A.

The Garden of Memory Stories of the Civil War as Told By Veterans and Daughters of the Confederacy . . . Camden: 1911. V. 43

ELLIOTT, MARY

Early Seeds to Produce Spring Flowers. London: 1824. V. 39

ELLIOTT, MARY BELSON

Beauty But Skin Deep. New York: 1864-70. V. 44

ELLIOTT, MAUD HOWE

Art and Handicraft in the Woman's Building. (Columbian Exposition 1893 Chicago). Paris & New York: 1893. V. 39

Art and Handicraft in the Woman's Building of the World's Columbian Exposition. Chicago: 1894. V. 45

Art and Handicraft in the Woman's Building of the World's Columbian Exposition, Chicago, 1893. New York: 1894. V. 40

Lord Byron's Helmet. Boston: 1927. V. 41

ELLIOTT, MISS

The Masqued Weddings. Dublin: 1781. V. 38

ELLIOTT, RICHARD S.

Notes Taken in Sixty Years . . . St. Louis: 1883. V. 40

Notes Taken in Sixty Years . . . St. Louis: 1883. V. 37; 38; 39; 40; 42; 43; 45

ELLIOTT, ROBERT

Views in India, China and on the Shores of the Red Sea. London. V. 38

Views in India, China and on the Shores of the Red Sea. London: 1835. V. 38

ELLIOTT, SIMON G.

Report on the Preliminary Survey of the California and Oregon Railroad. Boston: 1865. V. 42

ELLIOTT, STEPHEN

Ezra's Dilema: a Sermon Preached in Christ Church, Savannah, on Friday, August 21st 1863 . . . Savannah: 1863. V. 46

A Reply to a Resolution of the Georgia Historical Society Read Before the Society at Its Anniversary Meeting, February 12th, 1866. Savannah: 1866. V. 41

A Sketch of the Botany of South Carolina and Georgia. Charleston: 1821-24. V. 39

The Southern Review. Charleston: 1828-32. V. 40

ELLIOTT, STERLING

True Inwardness. Boston: 1888. V. 39

ELLIOTT, WILLIAM

Carolina Sports, By Land and Water, Including Incidents of Devil-Fishing, &c. New York: 1846. V. 41

Carolina Sports by Land and Water. New York: 1859. V. 37; 38; 40; 43; 44; 45

The Patentee's Manual . . . Washington: 1830. V. 42

ELLIS, A. B.

The Yoruba-Speaking Peoples of the Slave Coast of West Africa Their Religion, Manners, Customs, Laws, Langauge, etc. London: 1894. V. 40

ELLIS, A. H.

The Oklahoma Territory Pioneer. N.P.: 1926. V. 39

ELLIS, A. J.

English Dialects, Their Sounds and Homes. London: 1890. V. 40

ELLIS, ALEXANDER J.

On Early English Pronunciation, with Especial Reference to Shakespeare and Chaucer. London: 1869. V. 42

ELLIS, ASA

The Country Dyer's Assistant. Brookfield: 1798. V. 39; 40

ELLIS, AYTOUN

Three Hundred Years on London River -. . . London: 1952. V. 42

ELLIS, CHARLES

Richmond; and Other Poems. London: 1845. V. 40

ELLIS, CHARLES MAYO

An Essay on Transcendentalism. Boston: 1842. V. 43

ELLIS, CHARLES THOMAS

Practical Remarks, and Precedents of Proceedings in Parliament . . . London: 1802. V. 40

ELLIS, CLEMENT

The Gentile Sinner, or, England's Brave Gentleman. Oxford: 1660. V. 37

The Gentile Sinner, or England's Brave Gentleman Character'd in a Letter to a Friend. London: 1679. V. 40; 44; 46

The Vanity of Scoffing; or A Letter to a Witty Gentleman . . . London: 1674. V. 42

ELLIS, DANIEL

Memoir of the Life and Writings of John Gordon . . . Late Lecturer on Anatomy and Physiology in Edinburgh. Edinburgh: 1823. V. 43

Thrilling Adventures of Daniel Ellis, The Great Union Guide of East Tennessee for a Period of Nearly Four Years During the Great Southern Rebellion. New York: 1867. V. 42; 45

ELLIS, EDITH M. O.

Seaweed: a Cornish Idyll. London: 1898. V. 44

ELLIS, EDWARD

A Practical Manual of the Diseases of Children . . . New York: 1882. V. 45

ELLIS, EDWARD S.

History of the German People from the First Authentic Annals to the Present Time. New York: 1916. V. 40

The Life and Times of Christopher Carson, the Rocky Mountain Scout and Guide, with Reminiscences of Fremont's Exploring Expeditions, and Notes of Life in New Mexico. New York & London: 1861. V. 39

ELLIS, EDWIN JOHN

The Works of William Blake: Poetic, Symbolic and Critical. London: 1893. V. 41

ELLIS, EDWINA

The Maxims. 1986. V. 40

ELLIS, F. S.

The History of Reynard the Foxe, with Some Account of His Friends and Enemies. London: 1897. V. 41

ELLIS, FRANKLIN

History of Lancaster County, Pennsylvania. Philadelphia: 1883. V. 41; 42

ELLIS, G. A.

New Britain. A Narrative of a Journey . . . in the Vast Plain of the Missouri. London: 1820. V. 39

ELLIS, GEORGE

Bath: Its Beauties and Amusements. Bath: 1777. V. 40; 43

History of the late Revolution in the Dutch Republic. London: 1789. V. 37

Specimens of the Early English Poets. London: 1790. V. 41; 42; 45

Specimens of the Early English Poets, to Which is Prefixed An Historical Sketch of the Rise and Progress of English Poetry and Language. London: 1801. V. 40; 42; 45; 46

Specimens of the Early English Poets, to Which is Prefixed an Historical Sketch of the Rise and Progress of the English Poetry and Language . . . London: 1803. V. 39

ELLIS, GEORGE AGAR

Historical Inquiries Respecting the Character of Edward Hyde, Earl of Clarendon, Lord Chancellor of England. London: 1827. V. 46

The True History of the State Prisoner, Commonly Called the Iron Mask, Extracted from Documents in the French Archives. London: 1826. V. 41

ELLIS, GEORGE JAMES WELBORE AGAR

Characters of the Court. Oxford?: 1818? V. 42

ELLIS, GEORGE VINER

Illustrations of Dissections in a Series of Original Coloured Plates the Size of Life Representing the Dissection of the Human Body. London: 1867. V. 40; 41; 44; 45; 46

Illustrations of Dissections in a Series of Original Colored Plates the Size of Life Representing the Dissection of the Human Body. New York: 1882. V. 42; 45

ELLIS, HAVELOCK

An Australian Idyll. Berkeley Heights: 1938. V. 43

Kanga Creek: an Australian Idyll. Waltham St. Lawrence: 1922. V. 44; 45

Marriage Today and Tomorrow. San Francisco: 1929. V. 39

The Revaluation of Obscenity. Paris: 1931. V. 45

Sonnets with Folk Songs from the Spanish. Waltham St. Lawrence: 1925. V. 41

Studies in Psychology. Philadelphia: 1904-28. V. 44

Studies in the Psychology of Sex. New York: 1936. V. 44

The Unpublished Letters of Havelock Ellis to Joseph Ishill. Berkeley Heights: 1954. V. 41

ELLIS, HENRY

Doomsday Book. London: 1783. V. 40

Journal of the Proceedings of the Late Embassy to China. London: 1817. V. 39; 40; 41

Journal of the Proceedings of the Late Embassy to China. London: 1818. V. 40

Original Letters, Illustrative of English History. London: 1824. V. 40

Original Letters, Illustrative of English History. London: 1827, 1846. V. 40; 41; 43; 44; 46

Original Letters, Illustrative of English History. London: 1827, 1847. V. 41

Reise nach Hudsons Meerbusen, Welche . . . in den Jahren 1746 und 1747 Wegen Entdeckung Einer Nordwestlichen Durchfahrt in die Sud-See Verrichtet Worden. Gottingen: 1750. V. 38

A Voyage to Hudson's Bay, by the Dobbs Galley and California, in the Year 1746 and 1747, for Discovering a North West Passage . . . London. V. 42

A Voyage to Hudson's Bay, by the 'Dobbs Galley' and 'California', in the Years 1746 and 1747. London: 1748. V. 37; 39; 40; 43

ELLIS, HENRY continued

Voyage a la Baye de Hudson Fait en 1746 & 1747, Pour la Decouverte du Passage de Nord-Quest, Contenant une Description Exacte des Cotes & l'Histoire Naturelle du Pays . . . Paris: 1749. V. 39

ELLIS, HENRY HAVELOCK 1859-1939

Chapman. London: 1934. V. 40

Concerning Jude the Obscure. London: 1931. V. 37

George Chapman: With Illustrative Passages. Bloomsbury: 1934. V. 43; 44

Kanga Creek. Waltham St. Lawrence: 1922. V. 45

Kanga Creek and Australian Idyll. N.P.: 1935. V. 44

Kanga Creek. London: 1922. V. 38

A Note on the Bedborough Trial. Watford: 1898. V. 39

Psychology of Sex. London: 1933. V. 40

Sonnets with Folk Songs from the Spanish. (Walthan St. Lawrence): 1925. V. 37

Studies in the Psychology of Sex. New York: 1936. V. 37

The Unpublished Letters of Havelock Ellis to Joseph Ishill. Berkeley Heights: 1954. V. 37; 40

ELLIS, HENRY T.

Hong Kong to Manila and the Lakes of Luzon, in the Philippine Isles in the Year 1856. V. 46

ELLIS, J.

An Essay Towards a natural History of the Corallines. London: 1755. V. 37; 41; 42; 43

The Natural History of Many Curious and Uncommon Zeeophytes. London: 1786. V. 37

ELLIS, JOHN

The Ellis Correspondence. London: 1829. V. 43

An Essay Towards a Natural History of the Corallines. London: 1755. V. 38

An Historical Account of Coffee, With an Engraving, and Botanical Description of the Tree, To Which are Added Sundry Papers Relative to Its Culture and Use . . . London: 1774. V. 39

The Knowledge of Divine Things from Revelation, Not from Reason or Nature . . . (bound with) Some Brief Considerations Upon Mr. Locke's Hypothesis . . . London: 1743. V. 43

The Natural History of Many Curious and Uncommon Zoophytes, Collected from Various Parts of the Globe . . . London: 1784. V. 46

The Surprize; or, the Gentleman Turn'd Apothecary. London: 1739. V. 43

ELLIS, JOHN B.

Free Love and Its Votaries; or, American Socialism Unmasked. New York: 1870. V. 40; 42; 44

ELLIS, LEONARD BOLLES

History of New Bedford and Its Vicinity 1602-1892. Syracuse: 1892. V. 38; 40

ELLIS, OLIN O.

Life in UValde Texas 1882 to 1903. Baltimore: 1963. V. 44

ELLIS, RICHARD S.

A Bibliography of Mesopotamian Archaeological Sites. Wiesbaden: 1972. V. 40

ELLIS, S. M.

William Harrison Ainsworth and His Friends. London: 1911. V. 38; 41; 46

ELLIS, SARAH

Family Secrets, or Hints to Those Who Would Make Home Happy. London: 1841. V. 42

ELLIS, SARAH STICKNEY 1810-1872

The Daughters of England: Their Position in Society, Character & Responsibilities. London & Paris: 1842. V. 37; 41; 43; 45

Family Secrets, or Hints to Those Who Make a Home Happy. London: 1841. V. 37; 39; 43

Family Secrets. London: 1843. V. 44; 46

Family Secrets, or Hints to Those Who Make Home Happy. London & Paris: 1843. V. 38

My Brother; or, the Man of Many Friends. London: 1855. V. 43

Pictures of Private Life. London: 1833-34. V. 44

Social Distinction; or Hearts and Homes. London: 1848-49. V. 37; 41

Summer and Winter in the Pyrenees. London: 1847. V. 46

ELLIS, T.

Leaves from the Diary of an Army Surgeon . . . New York: 1863. V. 39

ELLIS, T. M.

Tales of the Klondike. London: 1898. V. 43

ELLIS, TRISTRAM J.

On a Raft, and Through the Desert. London: 1881. V. 37

ELLIS, W.

History of Madagascar . . . Progres of Christian Mission Established in 1818 . . . London: 1838. V. 37

ELLIS, W. MORRIS

Progressive West Denver . . . Denver: 1900. V. 37; 42

ELLIS, W. S.

The Parks and Forests of Sussex, Ancient and Modern, Historical, Antiquarian and Descriptive, with Biographical Notices of Some of the Former Owners. Lewes: 1885. V. 39

ELLIS, W. T.

Memories: My Seventy-Two Years in the Romantic County of Yuba, California. Eugene: 1939. V. 42

ELLIS, WILLIAM 1794-1872

An Authentic Narrative of a Voyage Performed by Captain Cook and Captain Clerke in His Majesty's Ship Resolution and Discovery, During the Years 1776-1780 . . . London: 1783. V. 38; 41

Chiltern and Vale Farming Explained, According to the Lastest Improvements. London: 1733. V. 39; 45

History of Madagascar. London: 1838. V. 38; 41; 45

A Journal of a Tour Around Hawaii, the Largest of the Sandwich Islands. Boston: 1825. V. 38; 39; 41

Lessons on the Phenomena of Industrial Life, and the Conditions of Industrial Success. London: 1854. V. 43

The London and Country Brewer. London: 1734. V. 42

The London and Country Brewer. London: 1744. V. 44

The London and Country Brewer. London: 1750. V. 46

Madagascar Revisited Describing the Events of a New Reign and the Revolution Which Followed . . . London: 1867. V. 44

The Modern Husbandman, or the Practice of Farming. (with) The Timber Tree Improv'd. (with) The Agriculture for May and June. (with) The Agriculture for July and August. (with) Chiltern and Vale Farming Explained. London: 1744-47. V. 39

Narrative of a Tour through Hawaii, or Owhyee . . . London: 1826. V. 37; 41; 45

Narrative of a Tour Through Hawaii, or Owyhee . . . London: 1827. V. 38

New Experiments in Husbandry, for the Month of April. London: 1736. V. 42

Polynesian Researches, During a Residence of Nearly Eight Years in the South Sea Islands . . . London: 1829. V. 37; 38; 41; 45; 46

Polynesian Researches, During a Residence of Nearly Six years in the South Sea Islands . . . London: 1830. V. 38

Polynesian Researches During a Residence of Nearly Eight Years in the Society & Sandwich Islands. New York: 1833. V. 38; 46

The Practical Farmer; or, the Hertfordshire Husbandman. London: 1732. V. 39; 42; 44

Reminiscences and Reflections of an Old Operative. London: 1852. V. 43; 46

Three Visits to Madagascar During the Years 1853-1854-1856. London: 1858. V. 39; 40; 42; 45; 46

Three Visits to Madagascar During the Years 1853, 1854, 1856. London: 1859. V. 38

Three Visits to Madagascar During the Years 1853-1854-1856. New York: 1859. V. 42

ELLIS, WILLIAM TURNER

Memories: My Seventy-Two Years in the Romantic County of Yuba, California. Eugene: 1939. V. 38

ELLISON, CUTHBERT

A Most Pleasant Description of Benwel Village, in the County of Northumberland. Newcastle-upon-Tyne: 1726. V. 41; 44

ELLISON, HARLAN

Again, Dangerous Visions. Garden City: 1971. V. 42

Again, Dangerous Visions. New York: 1972. V. 37; 43

Dangerous Visions. 1967. V. 39

Dangerous Visions: 33 Original Stories. Garden City: 1967. V. 46

Dangerous Visions. New York: 1967. V. 37

The Juvies. New York: 1961. V. 37

Love Ain't Nothing but Sex Misspelled. 1968. V. 39

Love Ain't Nothing but Sex Misspelled. New York: 1968. V. 42

Medea: Harlan's World. 1985. V. 37; 39

Stalking the Nightmare. 1982. V. 43

ELLISON, HENRY

Madmoments; or First Verseattempts. London: 1839. V. 41

ELLISON, RALPH

Invisible Man. 1952. V. 45

Invisible Man. New York: 1952. V. 37; 39

ELLISON, THOMAS

Slavery and Secession in America, Historical, Economical. London: 1861. V. 46

ELLISON, W. G. H.

The Settlers of Vancouver Island: a Tale for Emigrants. London: 1908. V. 43

ELLMANN, RICHARD

The Limits of Joyce's Naturalism. London: 1955. V. 44

ELLSWORTH, HENRY WILLIAM

Valley of the Upper Wabash. New York: 1838. V. 39; 43; 45

ELLSWORTH, R. H.

Chinese Furniture. New York: 1970. V. 37

ELLSWORTH, ROBERT HATFIELD

Chinese Furniture: Hardwood Examples of the Ming and Early Ch'ing Dynasties. New York: 1971. V. 39

ELLSWORTH, SPENCER

Records of the Olden Time, or Fifty Years on the Prairies. Lacon: 1880. V. 37; 38

ELLSWORTH, WILLIAM W.

Speech in the Case of Samuel Houston, Charged with a Contempot and Breach of the Privileges of the House by Assaulting Wm. Stanbery. Washington: 1832. V. 39

ELLWANGER, GEORGE H.

The Pleasures of the Table: an Account of Gastronomy from Ancient Days to Present Times. London: 1903. V. 42

ELLWANGER, W. D.

The Oriental Rug. New York: 1903. V. 45

ELLWOOD, THOMAS

The Foundation of Tythes Shaken. London: 1678. V. 46

ELLYS, ANTHONY 1690-1761

Tracts on the Liberty, Spiritual and Temporal, of Protestants in England. London: 1767. V. 39

ELMAN, ROBERT

The Great American Shooting Prints. New York: 1972. V. 37

ELMER, J.

Tables of Weights and Prices, On a New Plan; by Which the Value of Any Quantity of Goods, Sold by Avoirdupois Weight, from a Single Pound to Five Tuns, and from two Shillings to Ten Pounds in Ten Shillings Per Hundred . . . London: 1758. V. 38

ELMES, JAMES

A General and Bebliographical Dictionary of the Fine Arts . . . Principal Terms Used . . . Historical Sketches of . . . Different Schools . . . Accounts of the best Books and Treatises (etc). London: 1826. V. 37

Memoirs of the Life and Works of Sir Christopher Wren . . . London: 1823. V. 39

Memoirs of the Life and Works of Sir Christopher Wren. London: 1852. V. 37; 40

A Practical Treatise on Ecclesiastical and Civil Dilapidations . . . London: 1829. V. 38

ELMHIRST, PHILIP J.

Occurrences During a Six Months' Residence in the Province of Calabria Ulteriore, in the Kingdom of Naples, in the Years 1809, 1810 . . . London: 1819. V. 44

ELMHURST, PENNELL

Fox-Hound, Forest and Prairie. London: 1892. V. 38

ELMSLIE, KENWARD

Pavilions. New York: 1961. V. 44

ELOGIO Historico de Luiz do Rego Barreto por G.X.S. Coimbra: 1822. V. 38

ELOGIOS Funebres con que la Santa Igelsia Catedral de Guadalaxara ha Celebrado la Buena Memoria de su Prelado et Illmo y Rmo. Senor Mtro. D. Fr. Antonio Alcalde . . . Guadalajara: 1793. V. 41

THE ELOGY of Nothing, Dedicated to Nobody; with a Postface. London: 1742. V. 46

ELPHIN Lloyd Jones. Newtown: 1929. V. 45

THE ELPHIN Lloyd Jones Memorial Fund. Newtown: 1930. V. 46

ELPHIN Loyd Jones. 1929. V. 38

ELPHINSTON, JAMES

Education, in Four Books. London: 1763. V. 45

ELPHINSTONE, H. W.

Patterns for Turning. London: 1872. V. 40

ELPHINSTONE, MOUNTSTUART 1779-1859

An Account of Caubul, and Its Dependencies in Persia, Tartary and India. London: 1815. V. 43

An Account of the Kingdom of Caubul, and Its Dependencies, in Persia, Tartary and India. London: 1842. V. 39

ELREE, WILMER W.

Along the Western Brandywine. West Chester: 1909. V. 42

ELSAM, RICHARD

An Essay on Rural Architecture. London: 1803. V. 38; 39; 45

An Essay on Rural Architecture, Illustrated with Original and Oenconomical Designs . . . London: 1805. V. 39

Hints for Improving the Condition of Peasanty in All Parts of the United Kingdom . . . London: 1816. V. 39; 41; 42; 46

ELSBERG, CHARLES

Surgical Diseases of the Spinal Cord, Membranes and Nerve Roots. New York: 1941. V. 42

Tumors of the Spinal Cord and the Symptoms of Irritation and Compression of the Spinal Cord and Nerve Roots. New York: 1925. V. 42

ELSEN, ALBERT

Paul Jenkins. New York. V. 46

The Sculpture of Henri Matisse. New York. V. 46

Seymour Lipton. New York. V. 43; 46

ELSENSOHN, M. AFLREDA

Pioneer Days in Idaho County. Caldwell: 1947-51. V. 43

ELSENSOHN, M. ALFREDA

Pioneer Days in Idaho Country. Volume I and II. Caldwell: 1947. V. 46

Pioneer Days in Idaho County. Caxton: 1947, 1951. V. 39

ELSHOLTZ, JOHANN SIGISMUND

The Curious Distillery; or the Art of Distilling Coloured Liquors, Spirits, Oyls &c . . . London: 1677. V. 37; 39

ELSKAMP, MAX

Salutations, Dont D'Angeliques. Brussels: 1893. V. 44; 46

ELSTOB, ELIZABETH 1683-1756

An Anglo-Saxon Homily . . . London: 1709. V. 38

An English Saxon Homily on the Birthday of St. Gregory. London: 1709. V. 38; 41; 42; 44

The Rudiments of Grammar for the English-Saxon Tongue, First Given in English . . . London: 1715. V. 38; 43

ELSTOBB, WILLIAM

A Book of References to the Map of Sutton and Mepall Levels, Done from a Survey Taken in 1750 . . . Cambridge. V. 38

ELSTON PRESS

The Tale of Gamelyn. (New Rochell: 1901). V. 37

ELSUM, JOHN

The Art of Painting After the Italian Summer. London: 1703. V. 37

Epigrams Upon the Paintings of the Most Eminent Masters. London: 1700. V. 38; 45

ELSYNGE, HENRY 1598-1654

The Ancient Method and Manner of Holding Parliaments in England. London: 1675. V. 39; 41; 42; 43; 45; 46

The Manner of Holding Parliaments in England . . . London: 1768. V. 40

ELTING, VICTOR

A Canadian Expedition. N.P.: 1933. V. 43

ELTON, CHARLES

The Great Book Collectors. London: 1893. V. 37; 41

ELTON, CHARLES A.

Tales of Romance, with Other Poems, Including Specimens from Propertius. London: 1810. V. 43

ELTON, J. F.

Travels and Researches Among the Lakes and Mountains of Eastern and Central Africa. London: 1878. V. 40

ELTON, JAMES FREDERIC

Travels and Researches Among the Lakes and Mountains Of Eastern and Central Africa . . . London: 1879. V. 45

ELTON'S Comic All-My-Nack. New York: 1843. V. 39

ELTRINGHM, H.

African Mimetic Butterflies. Oxford: 1910. V. 38

ELUARD, PAUL

Au Rendez-Vous Allemand. Paris: 1945. V. 38

Le Dur Desir de Durer. London: 1950. V. 37; 41

Le Meilleur Chix de Poemes. Paris: 1947. V. 38

Pablo Picasso. Paris: 1944. V. 42

Thorns of Thunder - Selected Poems. London: 1936. V. 38

AN ELUCIDATION of Several Parts of His Majesty's Regulations for the Formations and Movements of Cavalry. 1808. V. 37

ELVIN, CHARLES N.

A Hand-Book of the Orders of Chivalry, War Medals and Crosses with Their Clasps and Ribbons and Other Decorations. London: 1892. V. 42

A Hand-Book of Orders of Chivalry, War Medals and Crosses with Their Clasps and Ribbons and Other Decorations. London: 1893. V. 44; 45

ELWELL, JAMES

The Medical Companion: Treating the Diseases Common to Warm Climates on Ship Board . . . Philadelphia: 1817. V. 39

ELWES, ALFRED

Jaufry the Knight and the Fair Brumissende a Tale of the Times of King Arthur. Translated from the French version of Mary-Lafon. New York: 1857. V. 37

ELWES, D. G. C.

A History of the Castles, Mansions and Manors of Western Sussex . . . Lewes: 1876. V. 38

ELWES, DUDLEY G. CARY

A History of the Castles, Mansions and Manors of Western Sussex. London: 1876. V. 39

ELWES, H. J.

A Monograph of the Genus Lilium - Supplement. London: 1933-40. V. 41

The Trees of Great Britain and Ireland. Edinburgh: 1906-13. V. 37; 42; 45

The Trees of Great Britain and Ireland. London: 1969-72. V. 43

The Trees of Great Britain and Ireland. Edinburgh: 1906-10/71-72. V. 37

ELWES, ROBERT

A Sketcher's Tour Round the World. London: 1854. V. 39; 46

ELWOOD, ANNE KATHARINE

Narrative of a Journey Overland from England, by the Continent of Europe, Egypt and the Red Sea to India . . . London: 1830. V. 39; 43; 45

ELWOOD, JOHN W.

Elwood's Stories of the Old Ringgold Cavalry, 1847-1865. Coal Center: 1914. V. 43

ELWOOD, LOUIE B.

Queen Calafia's Land: an Historical Sketch of California. San Francisco: 1940. V. 39; 44

ELWOOD, P. H.

American Landscape Architecture. New York: 1924. V. 37; 41; 44; 45

ELWORTHY, FREDERICK THOMAS

The Evil Eye: an Account of This Ancient and Widesperead Superstition. London: 1895. V. 46

An Outline of the Grammar of the Dialect of West Somerset. London: 1877. V. 43

ELWYN, HERMAN

Diseases of the Retina. Philadelphia: 1947. V. 42

ELY, ALFRED

North American Big Game. New York: 1939. V. 39; 43

ELY, EZRA STILES

Visits of Mercy; Being the Journal of the Stated Preacher to the Hospital and Almshouse of the City of New York, 1811. New York: 1813. V. 37

ELY, TIMOTHY C.

Approach to the Site. New York: 1986. V. 37; 39; 40

Axis 7. 1986. V. 37

On Telepathy. 1984. V. 37

ELY, WILLIAM

The Big Sandy Valley. Catlettsburg: 1887. V. 42; 45

ELYOT, THOMAS

The Boke Named the Govenour. London: 1553. V. 45

The Boke, Named the Governour. London: 1580. V. 38

The Castel of Helth Corrected and In Some Places Augmented. London: 1541. V. 43

The Case of Health, Corrected and in Some Places Augmented. London: 1547. V. 45

The Castel of Helth. London: 1560? V. 38

The Castel of Helth. New York: 1940. V. 42; 45

The Image of Governaunce Compiled of the Actes and Sentences Notable, of the Most Noble Emperour Alexander Seuerus . . . London: 1549. V. 37; 40

ELZE, KARL

A Biography with a Critical Essay on His Place in Literature. London: 1872. V. 44

EMANUEL, HARRY

Diamonds and Precious Stones . . . London: 1865. V. 45

EMANUEL, SOLOMON

An Historical Sketch of the Georgetown Rifle Guards and As So. A Of the Tenth Regiment, So. Ca. Volunteers, in the Army of the Confederate States. N.P.: 1909. V. 44

EMANUEL, WALTER

The Dog Who Wasn't What He Thought He Was. London. V. 41

The Snob. London: 1904. V. 43

EMBALMER'S Anatomical Aid. New York: 1921. V. 43

LES EMBLEMES d'Amour Divin et Humain . . . Paris: 1631. V. 39

EMBLEMS for the Improvement and Entertainment of Youth, Containing Emblematical Hieroglyphs and Aenigmatical Devices, Relating to Al Parts and Stations of Life. London: 1750. V. 40

EMBODEN, WILLIAM

Jean Cocteau and the Illustrated Book. Northridge: 1960. V. 44

Jean Cocteau and the Illustrated Book. Northridge: 1990. V. 45

EMBREE, EDWIN R.

Brown America: the Story of a New Race. New York: 1931. V. 46

EMBURY, EMMA C.

Nature's Gems. New York & Philadelphia: 1845. V. 39

The Poems of . . . New York: 1869. V. 41

EMERSON, AMELIA FORBES

Early History of Naushon Island. Boston: 1935. V. 38

EMERSON, B. A. C., MRS.

Historic Southern Monuments: Representative Memorials of the Heroic Dead of the Southern Confederacy. New York: 1911. V. 41

EMERSON, BENJAMIN KENDALL

The Ipswich Emersons, A.D. 1636-1900. Boston: 1900. V. 46

EMERSON, CHARLES L.

Rise and Progress of Minnesota Territory. St. Paul: 1855. V. 37; 38; 42; 45

EMERSON, E. S.

Santa Claus and a Sun Dial: An Australian Christmas Fantasy. Melbourne: 1909. V. 41

EMERSON, EDWARD WALDO

Emerson in Concord. Boston & New York: 1889. V. 46

EMERSON, ELLEN RUSSELL

Indian Myths, or Legends, Traditions and Symbols of the Aborigenes of America. London: 1884. V. 37

EMERSON, G. B.

A Report on the Trees and Shrubs Growing Naturally in the Forests of Massachusetts. Boston: 1846. V. 46

A Report on the Trees and Shrubs Growing Naturally in the Forests of Massachusetts. Boston: 1875. V. 37; 42

A Report on the Trees and Shrubs Growing Naturally in the Forests of Massachsetts. Boston: 1878. V. 40

EMERSON, GOUVERNEUR

Medical Statistics; Consisting of Estimates Relating to the Population of Philadelphia, with the Changes as Influenced by the Deaths and Births, During Ten Years, viz from 1821 to 1830. Philadlephia: 1831. V. 42; 43

EMERSON, JAMES

Letters from the Aegean. London: 1829. V. 40; 45

EMERSON, JOSEPH

A Thanksgiving-Sermon Preach'd at Pepperell, July 24th, 1766. Boston: 1766. V. 40

EMERSON, P. H.

Wild Life on a Tidal Wataer. The Adventures of a House-Boat and Her Crew. London: 1890. V. 37; 38

EMERSON, RALPH WALDO 1803-1882

An Address Delivered in the Court-House in Concord, Massachusetts, on 1s Aug. 1844 on the Anniversary of the Emancipation of the Negroes in the British West Indies. Boston: 1844. V. 39; 40; 42; 43; 46

An Address Delivered Before the Senior Class in Divinity College, Cambridge, Sunday Evening, 15 July, 1838. Boston: 1838. V. 39; 43

The American Scholar. Ithaca: 1955. V. 41

Books, Art, Eloquence. Boston: 1877. V. 43

Borrowings. San Francisco: 1889. V. 45

Compensation. East Aurora: 1904. V. 38

The Conduct of Life. Boston: 1860. V. 37; 39; 40; 42

The Correspondence of Thomas Carlyle and Ralph Waldo Emerson. 1834-1872. Boston: 1883. V. 41; 44

English Traits. Boston: 1856. V. 37; 38; 39; 40; 43; 46

Essays. Boston: 1841. V. 39; 40; 41; 43; 45

Essays. Boston: 1841, 1844. V. 40

Essays. (and) Essays: Second Series. Boston: 1841, 1844. V. 37; 38; 39; 40; 45

Essays. (with) Essays: Second Series. London: 1841/45. V. 41

Essays: Second Series. Boston: 1844. V. 41; 42; 43; 44; 45; 46

Essays. (with) Essays. Second Series. London: 1845. V. 43

Essays. First Series. Boston: 1847. V. 45; 46

Essays. Hammersmith: 1906. V. 37; 41; 42; 43; 45

Essays. London: 1906. V. 37; 40; 43; 44; 46

The Essays. New York: 1934. V. 38

The Essays of Ralph Waldo Emerson. San Francisco: 1934. V. 40; 45

The Essays of . . . First Series 1841 and The Second Series 1844. San Francisco: 1934. V. 37; 38

Fortune of the Republic. Boston: 1878. V. 41; 43; 46

A Historical Discourse, Delivered Before the Citizens of Concord, 12th September 1835. Concord: 1835. V. 43

A Historical Discourse. Boston: 1875. V. 41

Journals of Ralph Waldo Emerson. Cambridge: 1909-14. V. 39; 41; 44; 46

Journals of Ralph Waldo Emerson, with Annotations. Boston: 1910. V. 43; 46

Letters and Social Aims. Boston: 1876. V. 39; 42; 43; 46

Letters and Social Aims. London: 1876. V. 44

May Day; and Other Pieces. Boston: 1867. V. 38; 39; 42; 46

May-Day and Other Pieces. London: 1867. V. 43; 45; 46

The Method of Nature. Boston: 1841. V. 43

Miscellanies, Embracing Nature, Addresses and Lectures. Boston: 1856. V. 39; 42

Nature. V. 39; 41; 43; 44

Nature. Boston: 1836. V. 40; 45

Nature: Addresses, and Lectures. Boston: 1849. V. 41

Nature: Addresses and Lectures. Boston and Cambridge: 1849. V. 39

Nature. Munich: 1929. V. 37; 38; 40

Nature. New York: 1929. V. 41; 43; 45

Nature. Croton Falls: 1932. V. 45

Nature. New York: 1949. V. 43; 45

An Oration Delivered Before the Literary Societies of Dartmouth College, July 24, 1838. V. 39

An Oration Delivered Before the Phi Beta Kappa Society at Cambridge, August 31, 1837. Boston: 1837. V. 44

An Oration Delivered Before the Literary Socieites of Dartmouth College, July 24, 1838. Boston: 1838. V. 38; 43; 45; 46

Paranassus. Boston: 1875. V. 40

Poems. Boston: 1847. V. 37; 39; 41; 43

Poems. London: 1847. V. 37

Poems. London: 1850. V. 40

Poems. Boston: 1876. V. 44

Poems. London: 1914. V. 37

The Preacher. Boston: 1880. V. 39; 44

The Prose Works of Ralph Waldo Emerson. Boston: 1870. V. 46

Representative Men. Boston: 1850. V. 39; 40; 41; 45; 46

Representaive Men. London: 1850. V. 38; 39; 42

Self-Reliance. East Aurora: 1902. V. 41

Society and Solitude. Boston: 1870. V. 38; 39; 40; 42; 43; 44; 46

A Western Journey with Mr. Emerson. Boston: 1884. V. 46

Complete Works. Cambridge: 1883. V. 37

Complete Works. London: 1883-84. V. 39

Complete Works. Boston: 1899. V. 46

The Complete Works. Boston: 1903. V. 42

The Complete Works. Boston and New York: 1903. V. 45

The Complete Works. Cambridge: 1903. V. 42

Works. London: 1903. V. 37

Works. 1903-04. V. 44

The Complete Works. Cambridge: 1903-04. V. 37; 40; 42

The Complete Works. (with) The Journals . . . Boston: 1903-14. V. 43

The Complete Works. (with) The Journals, 1820-1872. Cambridge: 1903-14. V. 38

Works of . . . Philadelphia: 1906. V. 40

EMERSON, W. A.

A System of Astronomy, Containing the Investigation and Demonstration of the Elements of Science. London: 1769. V. 38; 40

EMERSON, WILLIAM 1701-1782

The Art of Surveying, or Measuring Land. London: 1770. V. 39

Calculation, Libration and Mensuration. London: 1770. V. 39

The Doctrine of Fluxions. London: 1757. V. 37; 41

The Elements of Optics. London. V. 42

The Elements of Optics. London: 1768. V. 37; 40; 41; 44; 45

The Elements of Geometry, in Which the Principal Propositions of Euclid, Archimedes and Others are Demonstrated After the Most Easy Manner. London: 1794. V. 39; 43

The Elements of Trigonometry. Containing the Properties, Relations, and Calculations of Sines, Tangents, Secants &c. The Doctrine of Spheres, and the Principles of Plain and Spherical Geometry . . . London: 1749. V. 37

The Mathematical Principles of Geography. London: 1770. V. 43

The Method of Increments. London: 1763. V. 38

Navigation; or, the Art of Sailing Upon the Sea. London: 1755. V. 42

Old Bridges of France. New York: 1925. V. 39; 41

The Principles of Mechanics. London: 1758. V. 37; 41

The Principles of Mechanics. London: 1794. V. 40

The Principles of Mechanics. London: 1836. V. 38

The Projection of the Sphere, Orthographic, Stereographic and Gnomical. London: 1749. V. 37; 41; 43

EMERSON, WILLIS GEORGE

The Smoky God, or a Voyage to the Inner World. Chicago: 1908. V. 46

EMERY, ANTOINE JOSEPH D'

Nouveau Recueil de Secrets et Curiositez . . . Huitieme Edition. (Recueil des Plus Beaux Secrets de Medecine Pour la Guerison de Toutes les Maladies . . .). Amsterdam: 1709. V. 46

EMERY, HENRY CROSBY

Speculation on the Stock and Produce Exchanges of The United States. New York: 1896. V. 41

EMERY, JACK

The Putney Debates. 1983. V. 38; 44

EMERY, WALKER B.

The Excavations and Survey Between Wadi Es-Sebua and Adindan 1929-1932. Cairo: 1935. V. 37; 40

EMERY, WALTER B.

Great Tombs of the First Dynasty II. London: 1954. V. 40

Great Tombs of the First Dynasty III. London: 1958. V. 40

Hor-Aha Excavations at Saqqara 1937-1938. Cairo: 1939. V. 40

EMES, THOMAS

A Dialogue Between Alkali and Acid Containing Divers Philosophical and medicinal Considerations . . . London: 1699. V. 46

EMETT, ROWLAND

Buffer's End. London: 1949. V. 41

New World for Nellie. New York: 1952. V. 40

THE EMIGRANT'S Guide, or Pocket Geography of the Western States and Territories . . . Cincinnati: 1818. V. 45

EMILI, PAOLO

De Rebvs Gestis Francorvm. Libri III (-IX). Paris: 1520. V. 40

EMILIANE, GABRIEL D'

Observations on the Journy (sic) to Naples. London: 1691. V. 43

EMILIO, LUIS FENALLOSA

The Assault on Fort Wagner, July 18, 1863. The Memorable Charge of the Fifty-Fourth Regiment of Massachusetts Volunteers. Boston: 1887. V. 43

EMILIO, PAOLO

Pauli Aemylii Veronensis Historici Clarissimi, De Rebus Gestis Francorum Libri X. Paris: 1555. V. 45

EMMA: Or, the Child of Sorrow. Dublin: 1776. V. 38

EMMANUEL, HARRY

Diamonds and Precious Stones. London: 1865. V. 38

EMMART, EMILY WALCOTT

The Badianus Manuscript. Baltimore: 1940. V. 46

EMMET, JOHN PATTEN

An Essay on the Chemistry of Animated Matter. New York: 1822. V. 41

EMMET, THOMAS ADDIS

Incidents of My Life . . . with Services in the Cause of Ireland. New York: 1911. V. 38

Ireland Inder English Rule, or A Pleas for the Plaintiff. New York: 1903. V. 37

The Principles and Practice of Gynaecology. Philadelphia: 1880. V. 40; 42

Vesico-Vaginal Fistula from Parturition and Other Causes; with Cases of Recto-Vaginal Fistula. New York: 1868. V. 39; 40; 41

EMMETT, CHRIS

The General and the Poet. San Antonio: 1937. V. 40; 42

Shanghai Pierce, a Fair Likeness. Norman: 1953. V. 42

Texas Camel Tales. San Antonio: 1932. V. 37; 42

EMMETT, WILLIAM TEMPLE

Good Hunting! New York: 1901. V. 43

EMMONS, E.

Agriculture of New York.. Albany: 1843-49-51. V. 46

EMMONS, EBENEZER 1799-1863

Manual of Mineralogy and Geology . . . Albany: 1826. V. 42

EMMONS, GEORGE

Navy of the United States from . . . 1775 to 1853 . . . History of Fate of Each Vessel. Washington: 1853. V. 38

EMMONS, GEORGE T.

Jade in British Columbia and Its Use by the Natives. New York: 1923. V. 38

EMMONS, NATHANIEL

The Dignity of Man. New York: 1798. V. 40

EMMONS, RICHARD

The Fredoniad: or, Independence Preserved. Boston: 1827. V. 39; 44

EMMONS, STANLEY F.

Map of Alaska Showing Known Gold-Bearing Rocks with Descriptive text containing Sketches of the Geography, Geology and Gold Deposits and Routes to the Gold Fields. Washington: 1898. V. 37

EMMONS, WILLIAM

Authentic Biography of Col. Richard M. Johnson, of Kentucky. Boston: 1834. V. 42

EMORY, W. H.

Proclamation. Opelousas: 1863. V. 39

EMORY, WILLIAM HEMSLEY 1811-1887

Notes of a Military Reconnaissance from Fort Leavenworth, in Missouri, to San Diego, in California Including Part of the Arkansas, Del Norte, and Gila Rivers. 1848. V. 41

Notes of a Military Reconnoissance, from Fort Leavenworth in Missouri, to San Diego in California . . . New York: 1848. V. 42

Notes of a Military Reconnaissance from Fort Leavenworth, in Missouri to San Diego in California. Washington: 1848. V. 37; 38; 39; 40; 41; 42; 43; 45; 46

Observations, Astronomical, Magnetic, and Meterological, Made at Chagres and Gorgona, Isthmus of Darien, and at the City of Panama, New Grenada. Cambridge: 1850. V. 37

Proclamation. It Having Come to the Knowledge of the General . . . That Unauthorized Persons Banded Together and Committing Plunder . . . Opelousas: 1863. V. 45

Report of the United States and Mexican Boundary Survey . . . Washington: 1857. V. 40

United States and Mexican Boundary Survey. Report of William H. Emory, Major First Cavalry and U.S. Commissioner. Washington: 1857. V. 42

Report on the United States and Mexican Boundary Survey. Washington: 1857-59. V. 39; 40; 41; 45

Report on the United States and Mexican Boundary Survey. Austin: 1987. V. 38; 39; 40

Report on the United States and Mexican Boundary Survey. College Station: 1987. V. 38

EMPERAN, MADIE BROWN

The Vallejos of California. San Francisco: 1968. V. 37; 38; 40

EMPEROR COUSTANS

A Tale of The Emperor Coustans and of Over the Sea. Hammersmith: 1894. V. 43; 44

THE EMPEROR'S Plan for a Peace. With Remarks Upon It. London: 1743. V. 43

THE EMPIRE of Brazil at the Universal Exhibition of 1876 in Philadelphia. Rio de Janeiro: 1876. V. 44

EMPRIELLA, DON MANUAL ALVAREZ

Letters from England. London: 1808. V. 45

EMPSON, CHARLES

The Cowthorpe Oak. London: 1842. V. 44

Narratives of South America. London: 1836. V. 41; 44

EMPSON, WILLIAM

The Gathering Storm - Poems. London: 1940. V. 43

Poems. Kinuta-Mura: 1934. V. 40

Poems. London: 1935. V. 37; 38; 41

Seven Types of Ambiguity. London: 1930. V. 40; 42; 45

The Structure of Complex Words. London: 1951. V. 45

EMRE, KUTLU

A Hittite Cemetery Near Afton. Ankara: 1978. V. 40

EMSON, FRANK T.

Bumble's Courtship. London: 1873? V. 40

EMY

L'Art de Bien Faire les Glaces d'Office; ou Les Vrais Principes Pour Congeler tous les Refraichissemens. Paris: 1768. V. 39

EMY, A. R.

Traite de l'Art de la Charpenterie. Paris: 1837. V. 44

ENAULT, LOUIS

L'Amerique Centrale et Meridionale. Paris: 1867. V. 38

Londres, par Louis Enault, illustre par Gustave Dore. Paris: 1876. V. 39

ENBEL, JEAN JACQUES

Lettere Intorno alla Mimica. Milan: 1820. V. 37

ENCARNACAO, ANTONIO

Relacoes Summarias de Alguns Servicos que Fizeram a Deos, e a Estes Reynos, Os Religiosos Dominicos, nas Partes da India Oriental Nestes Annos Proximos Passados. Lisbon: 1635. V. 41

ENCICLOPEDIA Dello Spettacolo. Rome: 1954-62. V. 37
ENCICLOPEDIA Dello Spettacolo. Roma: 1954-66. V. 42

ENCYCLOPEDIA Britannica. N.P.. V. 38
ENCYCLOPEDIA Britannica. Edinburgh: 1842. V. 38
ENCYCLOPEDIA Britannica . . . New York: 1910. V. 40
THE ENCYCLOPEDIA Britannica. New York: 1910. V. 38
ENCYCLOPAEDIA Britannica. New York: 1910-11. V. 41
ENCYCLOPAEDIA Britannica. London: 1910-22. V. 42; 43
ENCYCLOPAEDIA Britannica. London: 1938. V. 39

ENCYCLOPAEDIA Britannica. A Dictionary of Arts, Sciences, Literature and General Information. London & New York: 1926. V. 40

ENCYCLOPAEDIA Britannica: or a Dictionary of Arts and Sciences . . . 1966. V. 44
ENCYCLOPAEDIA Britannica; or, a Dictionary of Arts and Sciences . . . Edinburgh: 1966. V. 46

ENCYCLOPAEDIA Britannica; or, A Dictionary of Arts, Sciences and Miscellaneous Literature. Edinburgh: 1797/1801. V. 41

ENCYCLOPAEDIA Britannica; or, a Dictionary of Arts, Sciences and Miscellaneous Literature . . . together with Sections on Agriculture and Horticulture from the 1824 edition. Edinburgh: 1797-1824. V. 45

THE ENCYCLOPAEDIA Britannica or Dictionary of Arts, Sciences and General Literature. Edinburgh: 1842. V. 39

ENCYCLOPAEDIA Londinensis. London: 1810-29. V. 40

AN ENCYCLOPAEDIA of Gardening . . . London: 1834. V. 41

THE ENCYCLOPAEDIA of Sports. London: 1897. V. 39

ENCYCLOPEDIA Americana - A Popular Dictionary of Arts, Sciences, Literature, History, Politics and Biography . . . Philadelphia: 1829. V. 37

ENCYCLOPEDIA Britannica. Edinburgh: 1810. V. 42
THE ENCYCLOPEDIA Britannica. London: & New York: 1926. V. 44
ENCYCLOPEDIA Britannica. London: 1938. V. 38

ENCYCLOPEDIA Britannica or a Dictionary of Arts and Sciences. V. 37

ENCYCLOPEDIA Methodique. Mathematiques. Paris: 1784-89. V. 44

THE ENCYCLOPEDIA of Wit. London: 1803. V. 46

ENCYCLOPEDIA of World Art. New York, Toronto, London: 1959-68. V. 41; 45

ENCYCLOPEDIE des Arts Decoratifs et Industriels Modernes au XXME Siecle. Paris: 1925. V. 44

ENCYCLOPEDIE Methodique: our Par Ordre de Matieres par une Societe de Gens de Lettres, etc. Recueil de Planches de l'Encyclopedie; Planches des Peches. Paris: 1793. V. 45

THE ENCYLOPEDIA Britannica, A Dictionary of Arts, Scienes, Literature and General Information. New York: 1910-22. V. 45

ENDERBY, CHARLES 1798-1876

Metallic Currency. London: 1839. V. 38; 41

ENDLESS Amusement, Containing Nearly Four Hundred Interesting Experiments, in Various Branches of Science . . . New York: 1831. V. 44

THE ENEMIES of the Constitution Discovered or an Inquiry into the Origin and Tendency of Popular Violence . . . Together with a Concise Treatise on the Practice of the Court of Judge Lynch. New York: 1835. V. 40

ENFIELD, WILLIAM

Exercises in Elocution. Warrington: 1780. V. 40

The History of Philosophy, from the Earliest Periods; Drawn Up from Brucker's Historia Critica Philosophiae. London: 1837. V. 41; 43

Institutes of Natural Philosophy, Theoretical and Experimental. London: 1785. V. 39

Institutes of Natural Philosophy, Theoretical and Experimental. London: 1799. V. 40

Institutes of Natural Philosophy, Theortetical and Experimental . . . London: 1799. V. 46

Institutes of Natural Philosophy, Theoretical and Practical. Boston: 1802. V. 45

The Speaker . . . Derby: 1816. V. 46

ENGEL, CARL

Musical Instruments. Victoria and Albert Museum. London: 1908. V. 37

ENGEL, HEINRICH

The Japanese House. London: 1970. V. 40; 41

ENGEL, SAMUEL

Essai sur cette Question: Quand et Comment lAmerique a-t-elle ete Peuplee d'Hommes et d'Animaux? Amsterdam: 1767. V. 38

Memoires et Observations Geographiques et Critiques sur la Situation des Pays Septentrionaux de l'Asie et de l'Amerique, D'Apres les Relations les Plus Recentes . . . Lausanne: 1765. V. 43

ENGELBACH, LEWIS

Naples and the Campagna Felice: in a Series of Letters. London: 1815. V. 42

Naples and the Campagna Felice In a Series of Letters Addressed to a Friend in England in 1802. London: 1815. V. 40

ENGELBACH, R.

Harageh. Inscriptions by Battiscombe Gunn. London: 1923. V. 37

ENGELHARDT, F. ZEPHYRIN 1851-1934

The Franciscans in California. Harbor Springs: 1897. V. 38; 43

The Franciscans in Arizona. Harbor Springs: 1899. V. 37; 38; 39; 41; 43; 44

Mission Dolores. San Francisco: 1928. V. 37; 39

The Missions and Missionaries of California. San Francisco: 1908-15. V. 40

The Missions and Missionaries of California. San Francisco: 1908-16. V. 44

ENGELHARDT, GEORGE W.

Philadelphia, Pa. The Book of Its Bourse and Co-Operating Public Bodies. Philadelphia: 1898-99. V. 41

ENGELMANN, C.

Paroissien Romain. Paris: 1858. V. 43

ENGELMANN, G.

Cactaceae of the Boundary. 1986. V. 37

ENGELMANN, GEORGE J.

Labor Among Primitive Peoples Showing the Development of the Obstetric Science of Today . . . St. Louis: 1884. V. 43

ENGELS, FREDERICK 1820-1895

The Condition of the Working Class in England in 1844. New York: 1887. V. 44

Feuerbach. The Roots of the Socialist Philosophy. Chicago: 1903. V. 39; 41

The Housing Question. New York. V. 41

ENGELS, FRIEDRICH

In Sachen Brentano Contra Marx Wegen ngeblicher Citatsfalschung. Hamburg: 1891. V. 38

ENGERRAN, GEORGE C.

The So-Called Wends of Germany and Their Colonies in Texas and in Australia. Austin: 1934. V. 37; 38

THE ENGINEER and Machinist's Drawing-Book; A Complete Course of Instruction for the Practical Engineer: Comprising Linear Drawing; Projections; Eccentric Curves; the Various Forms of Gearing; Reciprocating Machiner; Sketching and . . . Glasgow, London: 1860. V. 37

ENGINEERING RESEARCH ASSOCIATES

High Speed Computing Devices. New York: 1950. V. 45; 46

ENGLAND, G. A.

The Alibi. 1916. V. 44

ENGLAND, GEORGE

An Enquiry into the Morals of the Ancients. London: 1737. V. 40; 43

ENGLAND, GEORGE ALLAN

Darkness and Dawn. Boston: 1914. V. 37

ENGLAND, JOHN

A Brief Account of the Introduction of the Catholic Religion into the States of North Carolina, South Carolina and Georgia, U.S.A. Dublin: 1832. V. 41; 43

The Works of the Rt. Reverend John England . . . First Bishop of Charleston. Cleveland: 1908. V. 43; 44; 45

ENGLAND, RICHARD

The Life of Dick En-l-d, Alias Captain En-l-d; of Turf Memory. London: 1792. V. 40

ENGLAND, ROBERT

The Colonization of Western Canada . . . London: 1936. V. 45

ENGLAND'S Genius; or, Wit Triumphant. London: 1734. V. 45

ENGLANDS Golden Treasury; or, the True Vade Mecum. London: 1700. V. 39

ENGLAND'S Helicon. London: 1925. V. 46

ENGLANDS Petition to Their King. N.P.: 1643. V. 43

ENGLAND'S Remembrancer: Setting Forth the Beginning of Papal Tyrannies, Bloody Persecutions, Plots and Inhuman Butcheries . . . London: 1682. V. 42

ENGLE, PAUL

American Song: A Book of Poems. Garden City: 1934. V. 37

Break the Heart's Anger. Garden City: 1936. V. 37

Corn: A Book of Poems. New York: 1939. V. 37

West of Midnight. New York: (1941). V. 37

Worn Earth. New Haven: 1932. V. 39

ENGLEBACH, L.

Naples and the Campagna Felice. In a Series of Letters, Addressed to a Friend in England in 1802. London: 1815. V. 39

ENGLEFIELD, HENRY

Ancient Vases: From the Collection of Sir Henry Englefield. London: 1848. V. 38

ENGLEFIELD, HENRY C.

A Description of the Principal Picturesque Beauties of the Antiquities and Geological Phenomena of the Isle of Wight. London: 1816. V. 39; 42

Vases from the Collection of Sir Henry Englefield, Bart. London: 1819. V. 45

A Walk through Southampton. Southampton: 1801. V. 39; 40; 41

ENGLEMANN, GEORGE

The Botanical Works of the Late . . . Cambridge: 1887. V. 40

ENGLEMANN, WILHELM

Bibliotheca Medico-Chirurgica et Anatomico-Physiologica. Hildesheim: 1965. V. 37; 42

ENGLISH and Dakota Service Book: Being the Parts of the Book of Common Prayer Set Forth for Use in the Missionary Jurisdiction of Niobrara. New York: 1881. V. 37

ENGLISH Battledore. Alnwick: 1820. V. 39

THE ENGLISH Empire in America: or a Prospect of His Majesties Dominions . . . London: 1685. V. 38

THE ENGLISH Encyclopaedia: Being a Collection of Treatises . . . Illustrative of the Arts and Sciences . . . London: 1802. V. 37

ENGLISH Forests and Forest Trees, Historical, Legendary, and Descriptive. London: 1853. V. 41

AN ENGLISH Garner. London: 1903-04. V. 37

ENGLISH, GEORGE BETHUNE

A Narrative of the Expedition to Dongola and Sennaar. London: 1822. V. 46

ENGLISH, HARRIET

Conversations and Amusing Tales. London: 1799. V. 46

ENGLISH, HENRY 1803-1855

A Complete View of the Joint Stock Companies, Formed During the Years 1824 and 1825. London: 1827. V. 43

ENGLISH Hexameter Translations from Schiller, Goethe, Homer, Callinus and Meleager. London: 1847. V. 42

ENGLISH Lake Scenery. London: 1880. V. 44

THE ENGLISH Lakes in the Neighbourhood of Ambleside. London: 1870. V. 44

ENGLISH Liberty in Some Cases Worse Than French Slavery; Exemplified by Animadversions Upon the Tyrannical and Anti-Constitutional Power of the Justices of the Peace, Commissioners of Excise, Customs and Land-Tax &c . . . London: 1748. V. 41

ENGLISH Lyrics from Spenser to Milton. London: 1898. V. 38

ENGLISH Military Discipline, or, the Way and Method of Exercising Horse and Foot . . . London: 1680. V. 42

ENGLISH Minstrelsy. London: 1860. V. 44
ENGLISH Minstrelsy. London: 1870. V. 43

THE ENGLISH Musical Repository. Edinburgh: 1811. V. 39; 42

THE ENGLISH Pilot. London: 1752. V. 40

ENGLISH PLACE NAME SOCIETY

Publications. Cambridge: 1924-61. V. 46
Publications. Cambridge, etc.: 1924-89. V. 46

THE ENGLISH Pleader. Dublin: 1783. V. 46

ENGLISH Poetical Autographs. London: Toronto: etc.,: 1938. V. 44

ENGLISH, ROBERT

An Elegy on the Death of Sir Charles Saunders. London: 1777. V. 40

ENGLISH Rustic Pictures. London: 1882. V. 39

THE ENGLISH Struwwelpeter. London: 1880. V. 45

ENGLISH, THOMAS H.

A Memoir of the Yorkshire Esk Fishery Association. Whitby: 1925. V. 39

ENGLISH, WILLIAM HAYDEN

Conquest of the Country Northwest of the River Ohio 1778-1783 and Life of Gen. George Rogers Clark. Indianapolis: 1896. V. 37; 45

THE ENGLISHMAN: Being the Sequel to the Guardian. London: 1713-1714. V. 43

AN ENGLISHMAN'S Advice to His Countrymen, on the Present State of Their General Interest and Prosperity Under the Good Old Constitution. London: 1798. V. 39

THE ENGLISHMAN'S Mentor. The Picture of the Palais Royal . . . London: 1819. V. 42

ENLART, CAMILLE

Gothic Art and the Renaissance in Cyprus. London: 1987. V. 45

ENNEMOSER, F. J.

Eine Reise vom Mittelrhein (Mainz) uber Coln, Paris und Havre nach den Nordamerikanischen Freistaten, Beziehungsweise Nach New-Orleans. Kaiserslutern: 1867. V. 38

ENNETT, JOHN WHITCHURCH

A Selection from the Most Remarkable and Interesting Fishes Found on the Coast of Ceylon. London: 1830. V. 37

THE ENORMOUS Abomination of the Hoop-Petticoat, as the Fashion Now Is, and Has Been for About These Two Years Fully Display'd . . . London: 1745. V. 40; 42; 46

AN ENQUIRY into the Causes of the Miscarriage of the Scots Colony at Darien. Glasgow: 1700. V. 38

AN ENQUIRY into the Conduct of a Late Right Honourable Commoner. London. V. 39

AN ENQUIRY into the Life and Writings of Homer. London: 1735. V. 37

AN ENQUIRY Into the Merits of the Supposed Preliminaries of Peace, Signed on the 3d Instant. London: 1762. V. 42; 43

AN ENQUIRY Into the Practice and Legality of a Pressing by the King's Commission: Founded on a Consideration of the Methods in Use to Supply the Fleets and Armies of England. London: 1772. V. 39; 42

AN ENQUIRY into the State of the Farm. N.P.: 1808. V. 45

AN ENQUIRY Relative to the Highways in the Shire of Berwick. Submitted to the Consideration of the Heretors and Tenants in the Shire. N.P.: 1760? V. 38

ENRIGHT, D. J.

Season Ticket - Poems. Alexandria: 1948. V. 44
The Year of the Monkey. Kobe: 1956. V. 40; 44

ENRIQUEZ DE VILLEGAS, DIEGO

Leer sin Libro, Direcciones Acertadas Para el Govierno Ethico, Economico y Politico. Lisbon: 1672. V. 41

ENS, GASPAR

Indiae Occidentalis Historia. Cologne: 1612. V. 38; 40; 41

ENSCHEDE, CHARLES

Typefoundries in the Netherlands from the Fifteenth to the Nineteenth Century. Haarlem: 1978. V. 45

ENSKO, STEPHEN G. C.

American Silversmiths and Their Marks III. New York: 1948. V. 37; 40
American Silversmiths and Their Marks. New York: 1927/1937/1948. V. 37

ENSLIN, THEODORE

The Work Proposed. Ashland: 1958. V. 37; 40; 42

ENSOR, F. SIDNEY

Incidents of a Journey through Nubia to Darfoor. London: 1881. V. 40; 46

ENSOR, GEORGE

The Independent Man; or, an Essay on the Formation and Development of Those Principles and Faculties of the Human Mind Which Constitute Moral and Intellectual Excellence. London: 1806. V. 45

THE ENTERTAINER; Containing Remarks Upon Men, Manners, Religion and Policy. London: 1718. V. 46

AN ENTERTAINING Account of all the Countries of the Known World Describing the Different Religions, Habits, Tempers, Customs, Traffick and Manufactures . . . Sherborne: 1752. V. 44

THE ENTHUSIASTIC Patriot, or, Cobler of Messina. New York: 1769. V. 45

ENTICK, JOHN

Entick's New Spelling Dictionary . . . London: 1800. V. 41
Entick's New Spelling Dictionary, Comprehending a Copious and Accented Vocabulary of the English Language. London: 1791. V. 45; 46
Entick's New Spelling Dictionary, Teaching to Write and Pronounce the English Tongue with Ease and Propriety . . . London: 1788. V. 41; 43
The General History of the Late War. London: 1763-4. V. 37; 39; 43; 46
Tyronis Thesaurus of Entick's New Latin-English Dictionary Designed for the Use of Grammar Schools and Private Education . . . London: 1804. V. 40

THE ENTOMOLOGIST. London: 1882-90. V. 40

THE ENTOMOLOGIST'S Annual 1855-1874. London: 1855-74. V. 43

ENTZELT, CHRISTOPHER

De re Metallica . . . Metallicorum, Lapidum, Genmarum . . . ad Medicinae Usum Deservientium. Frankfurt: 1557. V. 42

ENUMERATION of the Contribtutions, Confiscations and Requisitions of the French Nation; with An Account of the Countries Revolutionized Since the Commencement of the Present War. London: 1798. V. 39

ENYEART, JAMES L.

Edward Weston's California Landscapes. Boston: 1984. V. 41

ENYS, JOHN S.

Remarks on the Duty of the Steam Engines Employed in the Mines of Cornwall at Different Periods. London: 1840. V. 38

EOBANUS, HESSUS

De Tuenda Bona Valetudine, Libellus Eobani Hessi, Commentariis Doctissimis a Ioanne Placotomo, Professore Medico Quondam in Academia Regiomontana Illustratus. Franc: 1564. V. 39

EPAMINONDAS AMERICANO, PSEUD.

Projectos do Novo Codigo Civil e Criminal do Imperio do Brasil . . . Maranhao: 1825. V. 45

EPHRAEM THE SYRIAN, ST. c. 306-373

Opera Omnia Quae Exstant, Graece, Syriace, Latine . . . Ad MSS. Codices Vaticanos Aliosque Castigata. Rome: 1732-46. V. 39

EPHRAIM THE SYRIAN, ST. c. 306-73

Divins Opuscules . . . Maintenant Mis en Notre Langue Francoise, Avec un Excelleni Sermon de S. Cyril Alexandrin . . . Paris: 1602. V. 44

EPHREM DIACONUS

Sermones Secundum Traditonem Venerabilis Patris Ambrosii Camaldolensis. Florence: 1481. V. 38

THE EPIC of Hades in Three Books . . . London: 1879. V. 44

EPICEDIA Academiae Oxoniensis, in Obitum Celesisimi Principis Henrici Ducis Glocestrensis. Oxoniae: 1660. V. 38; 41; 43

EPICTETUS

The Discourses. London: 1902. V. 39

The Discourses of Epictetus. Translated by E.P. Matheson. Berne: 1966. V. 37; 38

Enchiridion. Louvain: 1550. V. 40

Epicteti Enchiridion . . . Basle: 1563. V. 42; 45

Enchiridion, et Cebetis Tabula, Graece & Latine. Leyden: 1651. V. 39

(Greek title) Epicteti Enchiridion, Cebetis Thebani Tabula; et Theophrasti Characters Ethici. Oxonii: 1670. V. 42

Enchiridion Made English, in a Poetical Paraphrase by Ellis Walker of London-Derry. London: 1692. V. 40

Enchiridion. Glasgow: 1751. V. 45

Enchiridion. New York: 1989. V. 41; 45

Epictetus His Morals, with Simplicius His Comment. London: 1694. V. 40; 41; 46

Epictetus His Morals. London: 1702. V. 41

His Morals, with Simplicius His Commment Made English from the Greek, by George Stanhope. London: 1704. V. 43

Epictetus: a Poem, Containing the Maxims of that Celebrated Philosopher, for the Government of the Passions in the Conduct of Life. London: 1709. V. 37; 41

Epictetus Manuall Cebes Tables Theophrastus Characters. London: 1616. V. 38

The Life and Philosophy, of Epictetus. London: 1670. V. 40

All the Works of Epictetus Which are Now Extant . . . London: 1758. V. 38; 39; 40; 41; 43; 44; 45; 46

All the Works of Epictetus, which are now Extant; Consisting of His Discourses, preserved by Arrian, in Four Books, the Enchiridion, and Fragments. Translated from the Original Greek. By Elizabeth Carter. With an introduction . . . London: 1759. V. 37; 42

All the Works of Epictetus. London: 1768. V. 38; 40

EPICURUS

Epicurus: The Extant Remains of the Greek Text. New York: 1944. V. 44

Epicurus, the Extant Remains of the Greek Text. New York: 1947. V. 39; 40; 41; 45; 46

The Epicurus. Extant Remains of the Greek Text Translated by Cyril Bailey. New York: 1957. V. 42

Epicurus's Morals Collected Partly Out of His Owne Greek Text . . . London: 1656. V. 37; 38; 45

The Extant Works of Epicurus. New York: 1947. V. 44; 46

EPIGRAMMATA et Poematia Vetera. Parisiis: 1590. V. 44

EPIGRAMMATA Graeca Veterum Elegantissima, Eademque Latine Versa . . . Cologne: 1548. V. 38

EPIGRAMMATUM Graecorum Libri VII. Basle: 1549. V. 38; 40; 45
EPIGRAMMATUM Graecorum Libri VII. Frankfurt: 1600. V. 41

EPIGRAMS in Distich. London: 1740. V. 38; 41

EPIPHANIUS

Divi Epiphanii Episcopi Constantiae Cypri, Contra Octoginta Haereses Opus, Panarium. V. 44

EPIPHANIUS OF CONSTANTINOPLE

Contra Octoaginta Haereses Opus. Paris: 1564. V. 45

AN EPISTLE from a N--ble L--d to Mr. P---y. London: 1740. V. 38

EPISTLE from the Marquis de La Fayette to General Washington. Edinburgh: 1800. V. 46

AN EPISTLE to a Lady. London: 1808? V. 39

AN EPISTLE to a Member of the General Court of Massachusetts, for 1809. N.P.: 1809. V. 42

AN EPISTLE to the Fair-Sex, on the Subject of Drinking. Dublin: 1744. V. 41; 42; 46

AN EPISTLE to the Right Honourable Sir Robert Walpole (in verse). London: 1739. V. 41

EPISTOLAE Diversorum Philosophorum. Venice: 1499. V. 37; 38; 40; 45

EPISTOLAE Obscurorum Virorum ad Dn. M. Ortuinum Gratium. Francofurti ad Moenum,: 1643. V. 38; 43

EPITHALAMIA Exoticis Linguis Reddita. Parma: 1775. V. 41

EPITHALAMIA Oxoniensia. Oxonii: 1734. V. 42; 44

EPITHALAMIA Oxoniensia sive Gratulationes in Augustissimi Regis Georgii III et Illustrissimae Principissa Sophiae Charlottae Nupitas Auspicatissimas. Oxonii: 1761. V. 44

EPITOME Chronicorum Regum Galliae a Pharamundo ad Carolum Eius Nominis Nonum. Paris: 1566. V. 45

EPITOME of the Cruise of The United States Steam Frigate Niagara, on Special Service to Japan, and the Flag Ship of Gulf Blockading Squadron, During the Years 1860, 1861 and 1862. Boston: 1862. V. 40

EPITOMES des Roys de France en Latin & en Francoys auec Leur Vrayes Figures. Lyon: 1546. V. 39

EPITRES et Evangiles Pour Tous Les Dimanches et Fetes de L'Annee . . . Detroit: 1812. V. 42

AN EPSITLE from Mr. Bank's, Voyager, Monster-Hunter and Amoroso, to Obeara, Queen of Otaheite. Batavia: 1774. V. 42

EPSTEIN, CLAIRE

Palestinian Bichrome Ware. Leiden: 1966. V. 37; 40

EPSTEIN, JACOB

Epstein, Seventy-Five Drawings. London: 1929. V. 38; 41; 44; 46

Epstein. An Autobiography. London: 1955. V. 41

EQUESTRIAN Statue of George Armstrong Custer Unveiling Ceremonies. Monroe: 1910. V. 45

EQUIANO, OLAUDAH

The Interesting Narrative of the Life of Olaudah Equiano, or Gustavus Vassa, the African. Written by himself. London: 1793. V. 37

ERASMUS, DESIDERIUS 1466-1536

Adagiorum Opus. Basiliae: 1526. V. 42

Adagiorum Chiliades . . . Basileae: 1546. V. 44; 45

Adagiorum Chiliades Tres, ac Centuriae Fere Totidem. Venice: 1508. V. 40

Adagiorum Epitome. Amsterdam: 1650. V. 37

Apologia Adversus Rhapsodias Calumniosarum Querimoniarum Alberti Pii. Basel: 1531. V. 45

Apophthegmatum ex Optimis Utriusque Linguae Scriptorib(us) Libri Octo. Lyon: 1555. V. 37

Apophthegmatum Opus. Paris: 1534. V. 39

Auctarium Selectarum Aliquot Epistolarum Erasmi Roterodami as Eruditos, et Horum ad Illum. Basle: 1519. V. 37; 45

Brevissima Maximeque Compendiaria Conficiendarum Epistolarum Formula. Basle: 1521. V. 43

Christiani Matrimonii Institutio . . . Basle: 1526. V. 40

Colloquia, Nunc Emendatiora. Leyden: 1636. V. 38

All the Familiar Colloquies of Desiderius Erasmus, of Rotterdam, Concerning Men, Manners and Things. London: 1725. V. 38

The Colloquies, or Familiar Discourses Rendered into English . . . London: 1671. V. 37

Colloquiorum Desiderii Erasmi Roterodami Familiarium Opus Aureum . . . London: 1760. V. 40

De Conscribendis Epistolis Opus. Lugduni: 1556. V. 44

Consultatio de Bello Turcis Inferendo (1530). Leiden: 1643. V. 38

De Duplici Copia Verborum ac Rerum, Commentarii Duo. Lyon: 1541. V. 37

Desid. Erasmi Roterodami Coloquia Familiaria, Notis Novis Illustrata. Dublin: 1712. V. 37

Enchiridion. London: 1576. V. 41; 45

Encomium Matrimonii . . . Encomium Artis Medici. Basle: 1518. V. 43

Encomium Moriae i. e. Stultitiae Laus (In Praise of Folly). Basel: 1931. V. 42; 46

Epistola Apologetica de Interdictu Esu Carnium Deque Similibus Hominum Constitutionibus, cum aliis Nonnullis Novis. Strasbourg: 1522. V. 40

(Greek Title) id Est Stultitiae Laus. Mainz: 1522. V. 37

In Novum Testamentum ab Eodem Tertio Recognitum, Annotationes item ab Ipso Recognitae & Auctario Neutique Poenitendo Locupletatae. Basle: 1522. V. 40

In Acta Apostolorum Paraphrasis Erasmi Roterodami . . . Basel: 1524. V. 37

In Praise of Folly. New York: and Baltimore: 1972. V. 44

Lingua per ERasmum Roterodamum Conscripta . . . Basle: 1547. V. 44

Lingua, Sive de Linguae Usu, Atque Abusa. Leyden: 1624. V. 39

Io. Frobenius Lectori S. D. Habes Iterum Moriae Encomium, Pro Castigatissimo Castigatius Una cum Listrii Commentariis, & Aliis Complusculis Libellis . . . Basle: 1519. V. 40

Moriae Encomium, cum Gerardi Listrii Commentariis, Epistolae Aliquot in Fine Additae. Oxoniae: 1663. V. 39

Moriae Encomium, or the Praise of Folly. London: 1668. V. 38; 40

ERASMUS, DESIDERIUS 1466-1536 continued

Moriae Ercomium. Basel: 1676. V. 38; 42; 44

Moriae Encomium . . . London: 1709. V. 43

Moriae Encomium, or the Praise of Folly. London: 1724. V. 38

Moriae Encomium; or, the Praise of Folly. London: 1746. V. 41

Lingua . . . Opus Novum & Hisce Temporibus Aptissimum. Basileae: 1525. V. 40

Opus Familiarium Colloquiorum Des Erasmi Roterodami, ut Postremum a Frobenio est Editu . . . Cologne: 1568. V. 40

Opus Epistolarum des Erasmi Roterodami . . . Oxford: 1906-58. V. 46

Paraphraseon in Nouum Testamentum, Uidelicet in Quatour Euangelia (Matthiae), (secundum Joannem). Basle: 1524. V. 43

Paraphrases Erasmi Roterodami in Aliquot Pauli Apostoli Epistolas. Basileae: 1523. V. 40; 42

Paraphrases Erasmi Rotterdami in Aliquot Pauli Apostoliepistolas. Basileae: 1523. V. 38

Paraphrasis, sue Potius Epitome Inscripta . . . in Elegantiarum Libros Laurentii Vallae . . . Paris: 1548. V. 37

The Plea of Reason, Religion and Humanity, Against War. New York: 1813. V. 43

The Praise of Folie. London: 1557? V. 38; 40; 42

The Praise of Folly. London: 1740. V. 40

The Praise of Folie. London: 1901. V. 40; 43; 44; 46

The Praise of Folie. London: 1903. V. 41

Proverbiorum Chilias Prima. (Secunda, Tertia, Quarta). Ferrara: 1514. V. 40

De Recta Latini Graeciq(ue) Sermonis Pronu(n)tatione . . . Dialogus. (with) Aplolgia Aduersus Articulos Aliquot per Monachos Quosdam in Hispaniis . . . Basel: 1528. V. 44

Seutonius Tranquillus. Dion Cassius Nicaeus . . . (Historiae Augustae Scriptores) . . . Ex Recognitione Des. Erasmi Roterdami. Basle: 1518. V. 43

Twenty Two Select Colloquies out of Erasmus Roterodamus . . . London: 1689. V. 45

Twenty Select Colloquies Out of Erasmus Roterdomaus. London: 1699. V. 43

Witt Against Wisdom. Oxford: 1683. V. 46

ERASMUS, JOHANN GEORG

Kurtzer Doch Grundrichtig und Deutlicher Beircht von Denen Funff Seulen. (with) Anhang zum Seullen Buch. Nuremberg. V. 38

ERASTUS, THOMAS 1523-1583

Disputatio de Auro Potabili, in Qua Accurate Admodum Disquiritur, Num ex Metallis, Opera Chemiae, Concinnata Pharamaca Tute Utiliterque Bibi Possint. Basle: 1578. V. 41

ERB, WILHELM

Diseases of the Spinal Cord, and Medulla Oblongata. New York: 1878. V. 42

Handbook of Electrotherapeutics. New York: 1883. V. 40; 42

ERBSTEIN, C.

The Show Up. 1926. V. 45

ERCILLA Y ZUNIGA, ALONSO DE 1533-1594

La Araucana. Madrid: 1776. V. 45

Primera Y Segunda Parte de la Araucana. Madrid: 1578. V. 42

ERCKER, LAZARUS

Fleta Minor; Fleta Minor, Spagyrick Laws . . . London: 1683/83. V. 42

ERCKMANN, E.

The Outbreak of the Great French Revolution Related by a Peasant of Lorraine. London: 1871. V. 42

ERCOLANI, GIOVANNI BATTISTA

The Utricular Glands of the Uterus, and the Glandular Orang of New Formation Which is Developed During Pregnancy in the Uterus of the Mammalia. Boston: 1880. V. 45

ERDBERG, ELEANOR VON

Chinese Influence on European Garden Structures. 1936. V. 37

ERDRICH, LOUISE

Jacklight. New York: 1984. V. 42; 44

Love Medicine. New York: 1984. V. 42; 43; 44; 45

ERENBERG, SAM

The Spirit Tower. San Francisco: 1989. V. 44

ERICHSEN, HUGO

Medical Rhymes. Chicago: 1884. V. 41

ERICHSEN, JOHN

Observations on Aneurism Selected from the Works of the Principal Writers on that Disease from the Earliest Periods to the Close of the Last Century. London: 1844. V. 38; 40; 41; 42; 45; 46

Observations on Observations Selected from the Works of the Principal Writers on that Disease from the Earliest Periods to the Close of the Last Century. London: 1844. V. 37; 39; 40

The Science and Art of Surgery. Philadelphia: 1860. V. 42

ERICHSEN, JOHN ERIC

On Railway and Other Injuries of the Nervous System. London: 1866. V. 46

ERICKSON, ARTHUR

The Architecture . . . Montreal: 1975. V. 46

ERICKSON, JOHN R.

Ace Reid, Cowpoke. Perryton: 1984. V. 42

ERICKSON, MILTON H. 1901-1980

Collected Papers of Milton H. Erickson on Hypnosis. New York: 1980. V. 46

ERICUS, JOHANNES PETRUS

Renatum E Mysterio Principum Philologicum, in Quo Vocum, Signorum er Punctorum, Tum & Literarum Maxime ac Nuremorum Origo . . . Patavii: 1686. V. 46

ERIGENA, JOHANNES SCOTUS

De Divisione Naturae. Oxonii: 1681. V. 39

ERIKSEN, SVEND

Early Neo-Classicism in France. London: 1974. V. 42; 46

Serves Porcelain: Vincennes and Serves. London: 1987. V. 41

ERIKSSON, RUBEN

Andreas Vesalius' First Public Anatomy at Bologna, 1540, an Eyewitness Report by Baldasar Heseler, Medicinae Scolaris Together with His Notes on Mattheaus Curtius' Lectures on Anatomia Mundini. Stockholm: 1959. V. 41

ERIZZO, SEBASTIANO

Discorso Sopra le Medgaglie Antiche . . . Venice: 1559. V. 40

Discorso Sopra le Medaglie de Gli Antichi. Vinegia: 1571. V. 38

ERMAN, ADOLF

Life in Ancient Egypt. London: 1894. V. 42; 44

ERMAN, ADOLPH

Reise um Die Erde Durch Nord-Asien und die Beiden Oceane, in den Jahren 1828, 1829 und 1830 . . . Berlin: 1835. V. 42; 43

Travels in Siberia . . . London: 1848. V. 42; 43; 44

ERNEST *Gimson His Life and Work.* Stratford-upon-Avon: 1924. V. 42

ERNESTI, J. H. G.

Die Wol-Eingerichtete Buchdruckery . . . Nurenberg: 1721. V. 42; 46

ERNESTI, JOHANN HEINRICH

Adonis Curtianus Honoribus Renunicatorum Solenniter Philosophiae & Bonarum Artium Magistrorum. Leipzig: 1697. V. 45

Die Wol-eingerichtete Buchdruckery, mit Hundert und Achtzehen Teutsch-Lateinisch-Griechisch . . . Nuremberg: 1733. V. 38

ERNOUF, ALFRED AUGUSTE, BARON 1817-1889

L'Art des Jardins, Parcs-Jardins-Promenades. Paris: 1880. V. 38

ERNST, MAX

Beyond Painting. New York: 1948. V. 39

Cap Capricorne. Paris: 1964. V. 38

Les Chiens ont Soif. Paris: 1964. V. 41

La Femme 100 Tetes. Paris: 1929. V. 42

The Hunting of the Snark: An Agony in Eight Fits, by Lewis Carroll. Stuttgart: 1968. V. 37

Les Malheurs des Immortels. Paris: 1945. V. 43

Misfortunes of the Immortals. New York: 1943. V. 45

Misfortunes of the Immortals. N.P.: 1943. V. 46

Reves d'une Petite Fille qui Voulut Entrer au Carmel. 1930. V. 42; 44

Une Semaine de Bonte. Paris: 1934. V. 39; 42

ERRARD, IEAN

La Fortification Demontree et Reduicte en Art. Paris: 17th century. V. 39

ERREDGE, J. A.

History of Brighthelmston or Brighton as I View It and Others Knew It . . . Brighton: 1862. V. 46

ERRINGTON, HARRIET

The Trial of Mrs. Harriet Errington . . . for Committing Adultery with Augustus Murray Smith, Esquire, an Officer in a Corps of Marines; Captain Buckley, of the Guards, Captain Southby; the Reverend Thomas Walker, and Many Others (etc). London: 1785. V. 45

ERRO Y AZPIROZ, JUAN BAUTISTA

The Alphabet of the Primitive Language of Spain and Philosophical Examiniation of the Antiquity and Civilization of the Basque People. Boston: 1829. V. 38

ERROLL, HENRY

An Ugly Duckling. London: 1887. V. 43

ERSKINE, BEATRICE

Lady Diana Beauclerk. Her Life and Work. London: 1903. V. 39; 40; 41; 43

ERSKINE, GLADYS SHAW

Broncho Charlie A Saga of the Saddle. The Life Story of Broncho Charlie Miller, The Last of the Pony Express Riders. New York: (1934). V. 37

ERSKINE, JOHN 1695-1768

An Institute of the Law of Scotland. Edinburgh: 1773. V. 38; 40

The Philharmonic Symphony Society of New York. New York: 1943. V. 39

Uncle Sam in the Eyes of His Family. Indianapolis: 1930. V. 41; 43

ERSKINE, JOHN ELPHINSTONE

Journal of a Cruise Among the Islands of the Western Pacific. London: 1853. V. 38; 41; 42; 43

ERSKINE, MICHAEL

The Diary of Michael Erskine Describing His Cattle Drive From Texas to California, with Correspondence from the Gold Fields, 1854-1859. Austin: 1979. V. 39; 40; 46

ERSKINE, PAYNE

The Harper and the King's Horse. Chicago: 1905. V. 38; 41

A Tale. The Harper and King's Horse. Chicago: 1905. V. 41; 46

ERSKINE, THOMAS

An Essay on Faith. Edinburgh: 1829. V. 39

A Letter to the Earl of Liverpool, on the Subject of the Greeks. London: 1822. V. 37; 39

Letters. New York: 1877. V. 41

Letters. N.P.: 1877. V. 45

Observations on the Prevailing Abuses in the British Army, Arising from the Corruption of Civil Government. London: 1775. V. 41

Proceedings . . . in the Action Against . . . John Watson . . . brought by . . . William Hurry, for Malicious Prosecution . . . Norwich: 1787? V. 37

The Speech of the Hon. Thomas Erskine, at a Meeting of the Friends to the Liberty of the Press, at a Free-Mason's Tavern, Dec. 22, 1792. London: 1792. V. 39

The Speeches of the Hon. Thomas Erskine, (Now Lord Erskine), When at the Bar, on Subjects Connected with the Liberty of the Press . . . New York: 1813. V. 45

The Trial of Thomas Paine, from the Speeches of the Hon. Thomas Erskine (Now Lord Erskine), When at the Bar on Subjects Connected with the Liberty of the Press . . . London: 1813. V. 45

ERTE

At Ninety, the Complete Graphics. New York: 1982. V. 39

Erte at Ninety-Five. The Complete New Graphics. London: 1987. V. 39

Erte at Ninety-Five. The New Complete Graphics. New York: 1987. V. 38

ERWIN, ALLEN A.

The Southwest of John Horton Slaughter, Cattleman, Sheriff, 1841-1944. Glendale: 1965. V. 46

ESAREY, LOGAN

The Indiana Home. Bloomington: 1953. V. 41

ESBACH, LLOYD ARTHUR

Tyrant of Time. Reading: (1955). V. 37

ESCAPE from France. A Narrative of the Hardships and Sufferings of Several British Subjects Who Effected Their Escape from Verdun. London: 1811. V. 41

ESCHENBACH, WOLFRAM VON

The Romance of Parzival and the Holy Grail. 1990. V. 44; 45

The Romance of Parzival and the Holy Grail. Newtown: 1990. V. 45

ESCHRICHT, DANIEL FREDERIK

Recent Memoirs on the Cetacea by Professors Eschricht, Reinhardt and Lilljeborg. Edited by William Henry Flower. London: 1866. V. 37

ESCHSCHOLTZ, JOHANN FRIEDRICH

Zoologischer Atlas, Enthaltend Abbildungen und Beschreibungen Neuer Thierarten Wahrend des Flottcapitains Von Kotzebue Zweiter Reise Um Die Welt. Berlin: 1829-33. V. 41

ESCHUID, JOHANNES

Summa Astrologiae Judicialis. Venice: 1489. V. 40

ESCOFFIER, A.

A Guide to Modern Cookery. New York: 1907. V. 40

ESCOTT, T. H. S.

Anthony Trollope, His Public Services, Private Friends and Literary Originals. New York: 1967. V. 40

ESCUDERO, J. A. DE

Noticias Historicas y Estadisticas de la Antigua Provincia del Nuevo Mexico . . . Mexico: 1849. V. 42

ESDAILE, ARUNDELL

A List of English Tales and Prose Romances Printed Before 1740. London: 1912. V. 39; 42; 44

ESDAILE, JAMES

Mesmerism in India, and Its Practical Application in Surgery and Medicine. Hartford: 1847. V. 45

Natural and Mesmeric Clairoyance, with the Practical Application of Mesmerism in Surgery and Medicine. London: 1852. V. 46

ESEMPLARI per Li Principianti del Dissegno et Arte della Pittura. Roma: 1636. V. 44

ESHBACH, LLOYD ARTHUR

Of Worlds Beyond. Reading: 1947. V. 46

ESHLEMAN, CLAYTON

Altars. Santa Barbara: 1971. V. 40; 42

Coils. Santa Barbara: 1973. V. 40; 42

The Gull Wall. Santa Barbara: 1975. V. 40; 42

Human Wedding. Santa Barbara: 1973. V. 40; 42

Our Lady of the Three Pronged Devil. New York: 1981. V. 42; 44

ESHLEMAN, H. FRANK

Lancaster County Indians. Lancaster: 1908. V. 41; 42

ESKANDER BEG MONSHI

History of Shah 'Abbas the Great. Translation M. Savory. 1978. V. 37

ESKIMO Point, Northwest Territories. Eskimo Point Resident's: 1970. V. 42

ESMARCH, FRIEDRICH

The Surgeon's Handbook on the Treatment of Wounded in War. Hanover: 1878. V. 42; 45

ESMERIAN, RAPHAEL

Bibliotheque . . . Manuscrits a peintures, Livres du XVe et XVIe Siecles; Reliures de Quelques Ateliers du XVIIe Siecle, Livres en Divers Genres des XVIIe et XVIIIe Siecles . . . Paris: 1792-94. V. 39

Catalogue. Paris: 1972-74. V. 38; 40

ESPEJO, ANTHONY

Espejo's Journey to New Mexico in 1583. Lancaster: 1928. V. 46

ESPERANZA; or the Land of Hope. New York: 1864. V. 42

ESPIARD DE LA BORDE, FRANCOIS IGNACE

The Spirit of Nations. London: 1753. V. 43

ESPIE, FELIX FRANCOIS, COMTE D'

The manner of Securing all Sorts of Buildings from Fire, or a Treatise Upon the Construction of Arches. London: 1760. V. 37

ESPINASSE, ISAAC 1758-1834

A Digest of the Law of Actions at Nisi Prius. Dublin: 1790. V. 40

A Digest of the Law of Actions and Trials at Nisi Prius. Walpole: 1801. V. 39

A Digest of the Law of Actions and Trials at Nisi Prius (covering the period of 1793-1807). New York: 1820. V. 38

Reports of Cases Argued and Ruled at Nisi Prius, in the Courts of King's Bench and Common Pleas, (1793-1803). Hartford: 1808. V. 39

ESPINOSA, CARMEN

Shawls, Crinolines, Filigree . . . The Dress and Adornment of the Women of New Mexico 1739 to 1900. El Paso: 1970. V. 40

ESPINOSA, I. F. DE

Chronica Apostolica . . . Mexico: 1746. V. 38

Cronica de los Colegios de Propaganda Fide de la Nueva Espana . . . Washington: 1964. V. 42

El Peregrino Septentrional Atlante: Delineado en la Exemplarissima Vida del Venerable Padre Fr. Antonio Margil de Jesus . . . En Valencia: 1742. V. 37

Nuevas Empressas del Peregrino Americano Septentrional Atlante . . . Mexico: 1747. V. 40; 42; 45

El Peregrino Septentrional Atlante . . . Vida del Venerable Padre Fr. Antonio Margil de Jesus. Mexico: 1737. V. 39; 40; 42

ESPINOSA, I. F. DE continued

El Peregrino Septentrional Atlante . . . Vida del Venerable Padre Fr. Antonio Margil de Jesus . . . Valencia: 1742. V. 38

ESPINOSA, J. MANUEL

First Expedition of Vargas into New Mexico, 1692. Albuquerque: 1940. V. 39

ESPINOSA Y TELLO, JOSE

A Spanish Voyage to Vancouver and the North-West Coast of America Being the Narrative of the Voyage Made in the Year 1792 . . . London: 1930. V. 38; 39; 45

ESPOSITO, VINCENT J.

The West Point Atlas of American Wars. New York: 1959. V. 45
The West Point Atlas of American Wars. New York: 1978. V. 43

ESPRIELLA, DON MANUEL ALVAREZ

Letters from England. London: 1807. V. 43
Letters from England. London: 1814. V. 43

ESPY, JAMES P.

The Philosophy of Storms. Boston: 1841. V. 46

ESQUEMELING, ALEXANDER

Piratas De la America, Y Luz a La Defensa de Las Costas de Indias Occidentales. Cologne: 1681. V. 37

ESQUIROL, JEAN ETIENNE

Mental Maladies. A Treatise on Insanity. Philadelphia: 1845. V. 37; 42

ESQUIROL, JEAN ETIENNE DOMINIQUE

Des Maladies Mentales Considerees Sous les Raports Medical, Hygienique et Medico Legal. Paris: 1838. V. 40; 45; 46

ESQUIROS, ALPHONSE

The Dutch at Home. London: 1861. V. 42

AN ESSAY Concerning the Infinite Wisdom of God, Manifested in the Contrivance and Structure of the Skin of Human Bodies. London: 1724. V. 41

AN ESSAY for the Construction of Roads on Mechanical and Physical Principles. London: 1774. V. 45; 46

AN ESSAY in Praise of Knavery. Whether it be in C----ers, Politicians, or Lawyers . . . London: 1723. V. 38

AN ESSAY on Currency; Being a Serious Research Into the Various Bearings and Morbid Views of the Subject. London: 1829. V. 39; 43

AN ESSAY on Dancing, in a Series of Letters to a Lady, Where the Inconsistence of that Amusement with the True Spirit of Christianity is Demonstrated. Philadelphia: 1810. V. 43

AN ESSAY on Hunting. London: 1733. V. 37; 38; 42; 43

AN ESSAY on Marriage; or the Lawfullness of Divorce, in Certain Cases, Considered. Philadelphia: 1788. V. 39

ESSAY on Modern Martyrs: with a Letter to General Burgoyne. London: 1780. V. 45

AN ESSAY on Naturalization and Allegiance. Washington City: 1816. V. 45

ESSAY on Political Lying. London: 1757. V. 45

ESSAY on Political Society. Philadelphia: 1800. V. 41

AN ESSAY on Sugar, Proving It the Most Pleasant, Salubrious and Useful Vegetable; Especially as Refin'd and Brought to Its Present Pefection in England. London: 1752. V. 45

AN ESSAY on the Antiquity of the Irish Language. Dublin: 1772. V. 39; 42

ESSAY on the Arat of War: In Which the General Principles of all the Operations of War in the Field are Fully Explained. London: 1761. V. 37

ESSAY on the Corn Laws; to Evince, on the Most Indubitable Ground, in Opposition to the Inflammatory Memorial for the Merchants, Traders, and Manufacturers of Glasgow, the Equity and Expediency of Prohibiting the Importation of Oats or Oat-Meal . . . Edinburgh: 1777. V. 42; 44

AN ESSAY on the Effect of the Inequitable Modes of Pursuing Trade with Analogous Remedies: Comprising a Dissertation Upon the Diminution and Remuneration of Labour. London: 1813-1814. V. 38

AN ESSAY on the Evils of Scandal, Slander and Misrepresentation. London: 1821. V. 38

AN ESSAY on the Increase and Decline of Trade in London and the Outports; Wherein is Shown, That Monopolies Have Been the Ruin of Several Branches of the London Commerce . . . London: 1749. V. 41

AN ESSAY On the Life of David Gregory, D.D. Late Dean of Christ-Church Oxford. London: 1769. V. 41

AN ESSAY on the Most Rational Means of Preserving Health, and of Attaining an Advanced Age. London: 1799. V. 42

AN ESSAY on the Objects of Taste. Glasgow;: 1823. V. 40

AN ESSAY on the Present State of Our Public Roads . . . London: 1756. V. 43

AN ESSAY on the Ways and Means for Improving the Inland Navigation and Increasing the Number of Sailors in Great Britain. London: 1741. V. 42

AN ESSAY Upon Immorality. London: 1760. V. 40; 42

AN ESSAY Upon the Principles of Political Economy; Designed as a Manual for Practical Men. New York: 1837. V. 42

ESSAYS and Letters on the Most Important and Interesting Subjects. Dublin: 1783. V. 38

ESSAYS and Reviews. London: 1860. V. 41; 43

ESSAYS, Historical, Political and Moral: Being a Proper Supplement to Baratariana. Dublin: 1774? V. 46

ESSAYS Honoring Lawrence C. Wroth. Portland: 1951. V. 37; 43

ESSAYS in Defence of Women. London: 1868. V. 39; 40

ESSAYS in Honour of Victor Scholderer. Mainz: 1970. V. 42

ESSAYS in Tribute by Eugene Louis Julien, Jacques Madaule, Henry Miller, Henry de Montherplant, Fr. Brocard Sewell and F. J. Temple. London: 1962. V. 40; 41

ESSAYS on Gothic Architecture. London: 1800. V. 37
ESSAYS on Gothic Architecture. London: 1802. V. 38
ESSAYS on Gothic Architecture. London: 1803. V. 39
ESSAYS on Gothic Architecture. London: 1808. V. 45

ESSAYS on Reform. London: 1867. V. 42

ESSAYS on Several Subjects, viz Religious, Moral and Political, Chiefly Published in the York Protestant Courant, Now Reprinted . . . London: 1748. V. 41

ESSAYS on Slavery; Republished from the Boston Recorder and Telegraph for 1825. Amherst: 1826. V. 42

ESSAYS on the Eighteenth Century, Presented to David Nichol Smith, in Honour of His Seventieth Birthday. Oxford: 1945. V. 39

ESSAYS on the Principles of Charitable Institutions: Being an Attempt to Ascertain What Are the Plans Best Adapted to Improve the Physical and Moral Condition of the Lower Orders in England. London: 1836. V. 41

ESSAYS on the Repeal of the Union to Which the Association Prizes were Awarded, with a Supplemental Essay Recommended by the Judges. Dublin: 1845. V. 39

ESSAYS On the Spirit of Legislation, in the Encouragement of Agriculture, Population, Manufactures and Commerce. Newark: 1800. V. 43

ESSAYS on Various Subjects. As They Were Publish'd in the Weekly Essay, or Middlesex Journal . . . London: 1738. V. 38

ESSAYS Presented to Charles Williams. London: 1947. V. 39

ESSER, HERMANN

Draughtsman's Alphabets. New York & Chicago: 1877. V. 38

ESSER, K.

Cryptogams: Cyanobacteria, Algae, Fungi, Lichens. Cambridge: 1981. V. 39

ESSEX, ARTHUR CAPEL, EARL OF

Letters Written by . . . Arthur Capel, Earl of Essex, Lord Lieutenant of Ireland, in the Year 1675. Dublin: 1770. V. 42; 43

ESSEX County, Standard History: Embracing a History of the County from its First Settlement to the Present Time, with a History and Description of its Towns and Cities. Boston: 1878. V. 37; 42

ESSEX HOUSE PRESS

A Bibliography of the Essex House Press with Notes on the Designs, Blocks, Cuts, Bindings, etc., from the Year 1898 to 1904. (Cover title). (Campden: 1904). V. 37

THE ESSEX House Song Book. London: 1903-05. V. 46

ESSEX, JOHN

The Young Ladies Condcut; or, Rules for Education, Under Several Heads . . . London: 1722. V. 39

THE ESSEX Review. Chelmsford: 1892-1956. V. 41

ESSEX, W. H.

A Short Account of Ye Organ in Ye Church of St. Mary of Woolnoth, Lombard Street, in ye Citie of London. London: 1881. V. 38

ESSICK, ROBERT N.

William Blake's Relief Inventions. Los Angeles: 1978. V. 37; 40

ESSIS-MOR MORNAY, PHILIPPE DE, SEIGNEUR DU PLESSIS-MARLY, CALLED DU PL NAY 1549-1623

Fowre Bookes, of . . . the Holy Sacrament of the Eucharist in the Old Church. London: 1600. V. 37

A Woorke Concerning the Trewness of Christian Religion, Written in French. London: 1587. V. 38; 39; 42

ESSIS-MOR MORNAY, PHILIPPE DE, SIEGNEUR DU PLESSIS-MARLY, CALLED DU PL NAY 1549-1623

De L'Institution, Usage et Doctrine du sainct Sacrement de l'Eucharistie, en L'Eglise Ancienne. Geneva: 1599. V. 45

ESSLING, VICTOR MASSENA, PRINCE D'

Catalogue de Livres Rares et Precieux. Paris: 1845. V. 38

ESSWEIN, HERMANN

Aubrey Beardsley. Munchen: 1912. V. 43

ESTACO, AQUILES 1524-1581

Inlustrium Vivor(um) ut Exstant in Urbe Expressi Vultus. Rome: 1569. V. 40

ESTADO Actual de la Isla de Cuba, y Medios que Deben Adoptarse Parafomentarsu Prosperidad con Utilidad de la Madre Patria. Madrid: 1838. V. 45

ESTAING, CHARLES HENRI

Extrait du Journal d'un Officier de La Marine de L'Escadre de M. De Comte D'Estaing. Paris: 1782. V. 40; 44; 45

THE ESTATE & House Agents' Complete Assistant. London: 1824. V. 45

ESTATUTOS Para Os Estudos da Provincia de N. Sra. da Conceicao do Rio de Janeiro, Ordenados Segundo as Disposicoes dos Estatutos da Nova Universidade. Lisbon: 1776. V. 41

ESTCOURT, RICHARD

The Fair Example or the Modish Citizens. London: 1706. V. 38

ESTE, C.

A Journey in the Year 1793, through Flanders, Brabant and Germany to Switzerland. London: 1795. V. 44

ESTE, CHARLES

Carmina Quadragesimalia ab Aedis Christi Oxon. Oxford: 1723-48. V. 41

A Journey in the Year 1793 through Flanders, Brabant and Germany to Switzerland . . . London: 1795. V. 42

ESTE, WILLIAM

The Scourge of Securitie, or the Expulsion and Returne of the Uncleane Spirit. London: 1609. V. 44

ESTEMPLARI per li Principianti del Diseggno et Arte della Pittura. Novamente dati en Luce ad Instanza di Gio. Battista de Rossi. Rome: 1636. V. 42

ESTENS, JOHN LOCKE

The Paraclete and Mahdi or The Exact Testimony to Revelation and Exposition of the Most Ancient Mysteries and Cults. Sydney: 1912. V. 41

ESTERNOD, CLAUDE D'

L'Espadon Satyrique. Reveu & Augmente de Nouveau. Cologne: 1680. V. 38

ESTES, GEORGE

The Rawhide Railroad. Canby: 1916. V. 42

ESTEVAO DE SANTA ANNA, F.

Sermao do Acto da Fee, Que se Celebrou na Cidade de Coimbra, na Segunda Dominga da Quaresma. Anno de 1612. Coimbra: 1612. V. 41

ESTIENNE, CHARLES 1504-1564

De Dissectione Partium Corporis Humani Libri Tres . . . Paris: 1545. V. 37

De Re Hortensi Libellus, Vulgaria Herbarum, Florum, ac Fruticum, qui in Hortis Conseri Solent, Nomina Latinis Vocibus Efferre Docens ex Probatis Autoribus. Lyon: 1536. V. 45

De Re Hortensi Libellus, Vulgaria Herbarum Florum, ac Fruticum, qui in Hortis Conseri Solent Nomina Latinis Vocibus Efferre Docens ex Probatis Authoribus. Paris: 1536. V. 37

De Re Hortensi Libellus, Vulgaria Herbarum, Florum, ac Fruticum, qui in Hortis . . . Paris: 1545. V. 37

Dictionarium Historicum, Geographicum, Poeticum . . . Oxonii: 1671. V. 45

La Dissection des Parties du Corps. Paris: 1546. V. 46

Maison Rustique, or, The Country Farme. London: 1606. V. 39

Paradoxes . . . Pour Exerciter les Jeunes Esprits en Causes Difficiles. Paris: 1554. V. 40; 45

Praedivm Rvsticvm . . . Paris: 1554. V. 44

Seminarium, et Plantarium Fructiferarum. Paris: 1540. V. 37

ESTIENNE, HENRI 1528-1598

The Art of Making Devises; Treating of Hieroglyphicks, Symboles, Emblemes, Aenigmas . . . London: 1646. V. 39

Concoines sive Orationes ex Graecis Latinisque Historicis Excerpta. Geneva: 1570. V. 39; 41

Conciones sive Orationes ex Graecis Latinisque historicis excerptae. Quae ex Graecis excerptae sunt, interpretationem Latinam adjunctiam habent. N.P.: 1570. V. 37

Concordantiae Graecolantinae Testamenti Novi, Nunc Primum Plenae Editae. Geneva: 1600. V. 39

Deux Dialogues du Nouveau Langage Francois, Italianize 7 Autrement Desguize Principalement entre les Courtisans de Temps. Antwerp: 1579. V. 37

Epigrammata Graeca, Selecta ex Anthologia. Geneva?: 1570. V. 44

Epistolia, Dialogi Breves, Oratiunculae, Poematia, ex Variis Utriusque Linguae Scriptoribus. Geneva: 1577. V. 37

Fragmenta Poetarum. Geneva: 1564. V. 44

The Frankfort Book Fair . . . Chicago: 1911. V. 44

L'Introduction au Traite de la Conformite des Merveilles Anciennes avec les Modernes. Geneva?: 1579. V. 37

De Latinitate Falso Suspecta . . . Eivsdem de Plavti Latinitate Dissertatio, & ad Lectionem Illius Progymnasma. Geneva: 1576. V. 39

Parodiae Morales, in Poetarum Vet. Sententias Celebriores Totide(m) Versibus Gr. ab Eo Redditas. Geneva: 1575. V. 44

Thesaurus Graecae Linguae. Genevae: 1752-73. V. 46

Traite de la Conformite du Langage Francaois avec de Grec. Paris: 1569. V. 44

A World of Wonders. Edenburgh: 1608. V. 39

ESTIENNE, ROBERT

Dictionarium Propriorum Nominorum Virorum, Mulierum, Populorum. Paris: 1541. V. 44

Fragmenta Poetarum Veterum Laintorum, Quorum Opera Non Extant. Geneva: 1564. V. 38; 44

Hebraea, Chaldaea, Gracea et Latina Nomina Virorum, Mulierum, Populorum (etc.). Paris: 1537. V. 41

Thesaurus Linguae Latinae. London: 1734. V. 45

ESTIUS, WILLIAM 1542-1613

Absolutissima in Omnes Beati Pauli et Septem Catholicas Apostolorum Epistolas Commentaria Tribus Tomis Distincta. Coloniae Aggripinae: 1631. V. 39

ESTLIN, JOHN PRIOR

Familiar Lectures on Moral Philosophy. London: 1818. V. 40; 41; 42; 45

ESTRADA, A.

Frugivores and Seed Dispersal. London: 1986. V. 37

Frugivores and Seed Dispersal. The Hague: 1986. V. 37

ESTRID; An Account of a Swedish Maid, Who Hath Lived Six Years Without Food, and Hath Had, of God During that Time, Strange and Secret Communications. London: 1711. V. 38; 40

ESTRIDGE, H. W.

Six Years in the Seychelles. 1885. V. 43

ESTVAN, B.

War Pictures from the South. New York: 1863. V. 44

ESTVAN, BELA

War Pictures from the South. London: 1863. V. 43

ESTWICK, SAMUEL

A Letter to the Reverend Josiah Tucker in Which the Present War Against America is Shewn to Be the Effect, Not of the Causes Assigned by Him and Others But of a Fixed Plan of Administration. London: 1776. V. 38; 40; 45

ETCHECOPAR, R. D.

The Birds of North Africa. 1967. V. 46

The Birds of North Africa, from the Canary Islands to the Red Sea. Edinburgh: 1967. V. 43

Birds of North Africa. London: 1967. V. 37; 38; 40

ETCHELL, MABEL

Ten Years in a Lunatic Asylum. London: 1868. V. 39

THE ETCHER. Thirty Seven Examples of the Original Etched Work of Modern Artists. London: 1880. V. 42

ETCHINGS of Antiquities in Newcastle Upon Tyne. Newcastle: 1827. V. 39; 44

ETHEL Woodville; or, a Woman's Ministry; a Tale for the Times . . . London: 1859. V. 41

ETHELL, HENRY C.
The Rise and Progress of Civilization in the Hairy Nation. Bloomfield: 1883. V. 43; 45

ETHEREGE, GEORGE
The Comical Revenge; or, Love in a Tub. London: 1664. V. 41
The Comical Revenge; or, Love in a Tub. London: 1689. V. 45
The Man of Mode; or, Sr. Fopling Flutter. London: 1676. V. 45
The Man of Mode; or, Sr. Fopling Flutter. London: 1693. V. 39; 44
She Wou'd If She Cou'd. London: 1693. V. 39; 45
She Wou'd if She Cou'd. London: 1668. V. 37
Three Plays: The Comical Revenge, or Love in a Tub; She Would If She Could; The Man of Mode, or Sir Fopling Flutter . . . London: 1723. V. 44
The Works of Sir George Etherege. London: 1704. V. 38; 39; 40; 42; 44; 45
The Works . . . London: 1888. V. 40

ETHERIDGE, ROBERT
Fossils of the British Islands Stratigraphically and Zoologically Arranged. Oxford: 1888. V. 37; 42

ETHERIDGE, SAMUEL
Tables for the Use of Bankers, Merchants, Tradesmen and Others. London: 1773. V. 37

ETHERTON, P. T.
Across the Roof of the World. New York: 1911. V. 45

ETHICAL Travels: with Christian Experience. New England: 1790. V. 40

ETHISON, DENNIS
Lord John Ten, a Celebration. Northridge: 1988. V. 46

ETIENNE, H. J.
The Chisel in Greek Sculpture. Leiden: 1968. V. 40

ETIQUETTE at Washington; Together With the Customs Adopted by Polite Society in the Other Cities of the United States. Baltimore & Washington: 1850. V. 43

ETLTON, ARTHUR HALLAM
Below the Surface. London: 1857. V. 39

ETON, W.
A Survey of the Turkish Empire . . . Its Government, Finances, Military and Naval Force . . . London: 1789. V. 44

THE ETONIAN. London: 1822. V. 37

ETOWAH Papers. New Haven: 1932. V. 44

ETRENNES Interessantes des Quatre Parties du Monde (etc.). Paris: 1797-98. V. 39
ETRENNES Interessantes des Quatre Parties du Monde: Contenant la Population de l'Universe, les Ephemerides, les Puissances de l'Europe, et Toutes les Autorites Civiles et Militaires de l'Empire Francais. Paris: 1804-05. V. 39

ETRENNES de France Our l'Annee 1815; Contenant les Principales Puissances de l'Europe, les Colonels - Generaux, les Marechaux de France, les Ministres, les Maisons du Roi . . . Paris: 1815. V. 39

ETRENNES Militaires, Particulieres et Universelles. Paris: 1848. V. 39

ETTINGER, LEOPOLD L.
Antonio and Pero Pollaiuolo. London: 1978. V. 44

ETTINGHAUSEN, C. F. VON
Physiotypia Plantarum Austriacarum. Der Naturselbstdruck in Seiner Anwendung auf die Gefasspflanzen des Osterreichischen Kaiserataates. Vienna: 1855-56. V. 39

ETTINGHAUSEN, R.
Persian Miniatures in the Bernard Berenson Collection. Milan: 1961. V. 44

ETTMUELLER, MICHAEL
Opera Medica Theoretico-Practica . . . Frankfurt am Main: 1697. V. 46

ETTMULLER, MICHEL
Etmullerus Abridg'd; or a Compleat System of the Theory and Practice of Physic. London: 1703. V. 44
Pratique de Medecine Speciale. Lyon: 1581. V. 41; 44

ETTRICK, WILLIAM
A Fragment of the History of John Bull. London: 1820. V. 38

ETZLER, J. A.
The New World or Mecanichal System, To Perform the Labours of Man and Beast by Inanimate Powers, That Cost Nothing for Producing and Preparing the Substances of Life, with Plates. Philadelphia: 1841. V. 41

EUBULUS
Eubulus Oxoniensis Discipulis Suis. London: 1720. V. 38; 40; 42

EUCHARD, LAURENCE 1670-1730
A General Ecclesiastical History, from the Nativity . . . to the Emperor Constantine the Great. London: 1719. V. 39

EUCHARISTICA: Meditations and Prayers on the Most Holy Ucharist . . . London: 1856. V. 44

EUCLIDES
Elementa. Venice: 1482. V. 39; 40
Elementorum Geometricorum Libri XV (etc.). Basle: 1546. V. 44
Elementorum Libri Priores Sex. Item Undecimus & Dudodecimus. Oxford: 1747. V. 40
Elementorum Libri Priores Sex, item Undecimus & Duodecimus. Glasguae: 1756. V. 41
Elementorum Libri XV. Paris: 1573. V. 41; 45
Elementorum Libri XV. Parisiis: 1598. V. 43; 46
Elementorum Libri XV . . . Commentariorum Procli Libri IV. Basle: 1533. V. 40
Elementorum Libri XV. Una cum Scholiis Antiquis. Pesaro: 1572. V. 37; 44; 46
Elementa. Venice: 1482. V. 38
Elementorum Libri XV. Graece & Latine . . . Paris: 1573. V. 45
De Gli Elementi d'Euclid Libri Quindici con glit Scholii Antichi. Urbino: 1575. V. 45
Elementorum Euclidis Libri Tredecim. London: 1620. V. 38
Euclide's Elements . . . . London: 1722. V. 45
The Elements of Euclid Explain'd in a New, but Most Easie Method. London: 1726. V. 40
The Elements of Euclid; with Select Theorems out of Archimedes. London: 1727. V. 45
Euclide's Elements. London: 1732. V. 40
Euclides' Elements . . . London: 1751. V. 38
The Elements of Euclid; with Select Thorems out of Archimedes by the Learned Andrew Tacquet . . . Dublin: 1753. V. 38
The Elements of Euclid. Dublin: 1753. V. 40
Euclid's Elements . . . London: 1772. V. 42; 44
The Elements of Euclid. Edinburgh: 1775. V. 38; 40
The Elements of Euclid, With Dissertations . . . Oxford: 1781-88. V. 42
The Elements of Euclid. Edinburgh: 1787. V. 40
The Elements of Euclid. Edinburgh: 1793. V. 38; 40
The Elements of . . . London: 1836. V. 45
Euclid: The First-Six Books of the Elements of Euclid. London: 1847. V. 38; 40
The First Six Books of the Elements of Euclid. London: 1847. V. 38; 39
The Elements: with the Select Theorems Out of Archimedes. Dublin: 1953. V. 46
The Elements of Geometrie of the Most Ancient Philosopher Euclide . . . London: 1570. V. 43
The English Euclide Being the First Six Elements of Geometry. Oxford: 1705. V. 37
Euclid's Elements of Geometry, from the Latin Translation of Commandine. London: 1733. V. 40
Euclid's Elements of Geometry. London: 1762. V. 46
Elements of Geometry, Book I. New York: 1944. V. 40; 45
Elements of Geometry, Book One. New York: 1944. V. 42
Euclides Elementorum Libri XV Breivider Demonstrati . . . London: 1687. V. 41
Euclidis Quae Supersunt Omnia. Ex Recensione Davidis Gregorii. Oxoniae: 1703. V. 45
Gli Elementi di Euclide . . . Torino: 1753. V. 44
I Quindici Libri Degli Elementi . . . Rome: 1545. V. 44
Euclide Megarense Acutissimo Philosopho Solo Introduttore delle Scientie Mathematice . . . Venetia: 1586. V. 45
Orontii Finaei in Sex Priores Libros Geometricorum Elementorum Euclidis . . . Demonstrationes. Paris: 1544. V. 41
Euclid Posteriores Libri sex a x. ad xv. Rome: 1574. V. 40
Praeclarissimis Liber Elementorum . . . In Artem Geometrie. Venice: 1482. V. 38
Solo Introduttore delle Scientie Mathematice: Diligentemente Reassettato, et alla Integrita Ridotto per il Degno Professor di tal Scientie Nicolo Tartalea . . . Venice: 1543. V. 46

EUDORA Welty: a Tribute. 1984. V. 40; 41; 42

EUER, SAMPSON

Doctrina Placitandi, ou l'Art et Science de Bon Pleading. London: 1677. V. 40

EUGIPPIUS

Historia . . . Qua Tempora Quae Attilae Mortem Consequuta sunt, Occasione Vitae S. Severini Illustrantur. Augsburg: 1595. V. 40

EULENSPIEGEL

Noctvae Specvlvm. Omnes Res Memorabiles, Variasqve et Admirabiles, Tylis Saxonici Machinationes Complectens . . . Frankfurt am Main: 1567. V. 42

EULER, LEONHARD 1707-1783

A Complete Theory of the Construction and Properties of Vessels. London: 1790. V. 40

Constructio Lentium Objectivarum ex Duplici Vitro Quae Neque Confusionem a Figura Sphaerica Oriundam . . . St. Petersburg: 1762. V. 38; 41; 45

Elements of Algebra. London: 1810. V. 38

Institutiones Calculi Differentialis cum Eius usu in Analysi Finitorum ac Doctrina Serierum. St. Petersburg: 1755. V. 38

Introductio in Analysin Infinitorum. Lausanne: 1748. V. 38

Lettres a une Princesse d'Allemagne, Sur Divers Sujets de Physique et de Philosophie. Paris: 1812. V. 40

Mechanica Sive Motus Scientia Analytice Exposita. St. Petersburg: 1736. V. 40

Methodus Inveniendi Lineas Curvas Maximi Minimive Proprietate Gaudentes, Sive Solutio Problematis Isoperimetrici Latissimo Sensu Accepti. Lausanne & Geneva: 1744. V. 39; 40

Opuscula Varii Argumenti . . . Berlin: 1746. V. 42

Scienta Navalis seu Tractatus de Construendis ac Dirigendis Navibus. Petropoli: 1749. V. 39

Tentamen Novae Theoriae Musicae ex Certissimis Harmoniae Principiis Dilucide Expositae. St. Petersburg: 1739. V. 40

Theoria Mortium Planetarum et Cometarum.. Berlin: 1744. V. 40

Theorie der Planeten und Cometen von Johann Freyherrn von Paccassi Ubersetzt, und mit Einem Anhange und Tafeln Vermehrt. Vienna: 1781. V. 45

Vollstandige Anleitung zur Algebra . . . St. Petersburg: 1770. V. 38

EUNAPIUS SARDIANUS

Evnapivs Sardianvs, De Vitis Philosopharvm et Sophistarvm: Nunc Primum Graece & Latine editus . . . Antwerp: 1568. V. 46

De Vitis Philosophphorvm et Sophistarvm. Heidelberg: 1596. V. 44

EURIPIDES

The Bacchae, Dionysus, the God by Euripides. Kentfield: 1972. V. 38; 40

Choruses from the Iphigeneia in Aulis and the Hippolytus of Euripides. London: 1919. V. 39

Cyclops. Cum Duplici Versione Latina. Strassburg: 1582. V. 37

Euripides Quae Extant Omnia . . . Opera & studio Josuae Barnes. Hayes: 1694. V. 45

(Greek title) Evripidis Tragoediae XIX. In Qvibvs Praeter Infinita Menda Svblata, Carminum Omnium Ratio Hactenus Ignorata Nunc Primum Proditur . . . Antvverpiae: 1571. V. 41

(Greek) Tragoediae XIX. Antwerp: 1571. V. 38

Hippolytos. Northampton: 1969. V. 37; 41; 42; 43; 45

Ippolytos Stephanephoros cum Scholiis, Versione Latina, Variis Lectionibus, Valckenari Notis Integris, ac Selectis Aliorum Vv. Oxford: 1796. V. 45

Medea; Hippolytus; The Bacchae. 1967. V. 40

Medea. Hippolytus. The Bacchae. London: 1967. V. 41

Medea. Hippolytus. The Bacchae. New York: 1967. V. 38

The Nineteen Tragedies and Fragments. London: 1809. V. 38

(Opera) Euripides Que Extant Omnia . . . Oxford: 1778. V. 46

Opera Omnia. Glasguae: 1821. V. 39

The Plays of Euripides. 1931. V. 43

The Plays of Euripides. London: 1931. V. 40

The Plays of . . . Montgomeryshire: 1931. V. 40; 43

The Plays. Newtown: 1931. V. 37; 40; 41; 44; 46

Quae Extant Omnia. Tragoediae XX . . . (Greek and Latin title) Epistolae. Cambridge: 1694. V. 38; 43

The Tragedies. London: 1781. V. 43; 46

The Tragedies of Euripides. London: 1781-83. V. 43

Tragicoru Princeps in Latinum Sermonem Conuersus . . . Basil: 1562-63. V. 38

Tragoedia Hippolytus . . . Leiden: 1768. V. 42

Tragoediae Octodecim. Basileae: 1537. V. 44

Tragoediae Quae Supersunt, Ex Recensione Samuelis Musgravii. Glasgow: 1797. V. 45

Tragoediae Quattuor. Florence: 1495. V. 40

Tragoediae Viginti, Cum Variis Lectionibus. Oxonii: 1811-12. V. 45

Tragoedie Septendecim, ex Quib. Quaedam Habent Commentaria. Venice: 1503. V. 43

EUROPE AND AMERICA IN 1821. London: 1822. V. 39; 40

EUROPE Informed. An Exhibition of Early Books Which Acquainted Europe with the East. Cambridge: 1966. V. 42

EUROPEAN AND NORTH AMERICAN RAILWAY COMPANY

Acts Incorporating the European and North American Railway Company, and Facilitating the Construction of the Road, Passed 15th and 28th March 1851. Fredericton: 1851. V. 39

THE EUROPEAN Delineator. Leeds: 1815. V. 42

EUROPEAN MUSEUM

The Plan and New Descriptive Catalogue of the European Museum, King Street, St. James's Square; Instituted the 23d April, 1789 for the Promotion of the Fine Arts . . . London: 1808. V. 43

EUROPEAN Scenery . . . London: 1820-23. V. 46

EUSEBIUS

Chronicon. Venice: 1483. V. 38; 39; 46

Eusebii Pamphili, Ruffini, Socratis, Theodoriti, Sozomeni, Theodori, Evangrii, et Dorothei Ecclesiastica Historia . . . Basle: 1587. V. 39

The History of the Church From Our Lord's Incarnation to the Twelfth Year of the Emperour Mauricius Tiberius or the Year of Christ 594 . . . Cambridge: 1692. V. 39

The History of the Church . . . London: 1709. V. 39

EUSEBIUS, PAMPHILI

The Avncient Ecclesiasticall Histories of the First Six Hvndred Yeares After Christ, Wrytten in the Greek Tongue. London: 1577-76. V. 37

Eusebii Caesaris Episcopi Chronico: Quod Hieronymus Presbyter Diuino Eius in Genio Latinum . . . Paris: 1518. V. 37

Historia Ecclesiastica. Rome: 1476. V. 38; 39; 40; 41

Hystoria Ecclesiastica. Parisius: 1515. V. 37; 38; 40; 42

Historia Ecclesiastica . . . Lyon: 1533. V. 37

Ecclesiasticae Historia. Lutetiae Parisiorum: 1544. V. 38

Ecclesiasticae Historiae (and other works). Paris: 1544. V. 37; 45

EUSEBIUS PAMPHILI, BP. OF CAESAREA

The Auncient Ecclesiasticall Histories of the First Six Hundred Years After Christ. London: 1585. V. 42

The Ancient Ecclesiasticall Histories . . . London: 1619. V. 45

The Ancient Ecclesiasticall Histories of the First Six Hundred Years After Christ. London: 1650. V. 39

Chronicon . . . Complura Quae ad Haec Usque Tempora Subsecuta Sunt Adiecere . . . Paris: 1512. V. 38; 40; 42; 43

Chronicon Bipartitum. Venetiis: 1818. V. 42

De Evangelica Preparatione. Hagenau: 1522. V. 41

Historia Ecclesiastica. Mantua: 1479. V. 40

Chronica Das ist: Warhafftige Beschreibunge aller Alten Christlichen Kirchen. Frankfurt: 1565. V. 46

EUSTACE, JOHN CHETWODE

A Classical Tour through Italy, 1802. London: 1821. V. 37; 39; 44

A Classical Tour Through Italy. An. MDCCCII. London: 1819. V. 37

An Elegy To the Memory of the Right Honourable Edmund Burke. London: 1798. V. 43

A Tour Through Italy, Exhibiting a View of Its Scenery, Its Antiquities and Its Monuments . . . London: 1813. V. 42; 45

EUSTACE, P. BERYL

Registry of Deeds, Dublin. Abstracts of Wills, 1708-1832. Dublin: 1956-84. V. 37; 43

EUSTACHIUS, BARTHOLOMAEUS

Tabulae Anatomicae . . . Quas e Tenebris Tandem Vindicatas . . . Praefatione, Notisque Illustravit . . . Rome: 1714. V. 46

Tabulae Anatomocarum Clarissimi Viri Bartholomaei Eustachaet . . . Coloniae Allobrogum: 1716. V. 46

Tabulae Anatomicae. Amsterdam: 1722. V. 40; 42; 43; 44

EUSTAPHIEVE, ALEXIS

Reflections, Notes, and Original Anecdotes, Illustrating the Character of Peter the Great, To Which is Added . . . Boston: 1814. V. 40

The Resources of Russia, in the Event of a War With France . . . Boston: 1813. V. 42

EUSTATHIUS

Des Isemniae et Ismenes Amoribus. Paris: 1618. V. 37

EUSTIS, CELESTINE

Cooking in Old Creole Days. La Cuisine Creole a l'Usage des Petits Menages. New York: 1903. V. 43

Cooking in Old Creole Days. New York: 1904. V. 37; 45

EUSTOCHIUS, LAURENTIUS

Dialogus qui Inscribitur Studiosus. Brescia: 1488. V. 37

EUSTRATIUS, BP. OF NICAEA c. 1050- c. 1120

Commentaria in Secundum Librum Posteriorum Resolutiovorum Aristotelis. V. 40

EUTHELIUS

Religion Represented in a True Light. Oxford: 1761. V. 38

EUTROPIUS

De Inclytis Totius Italice Provincie, ac Romanorum Gestis Libri xxviii. Paris: 1512. V. 38; 46

THE EVANGELICAL Lutheran Preacher, and Pastoral Messenger . . . Winchester: 1833-1835. V. 41

EVANGELIUM Infantiae. Vel Liber Apocryphus de Infantia Servatoris. Utrecht: 1697. V. 37

LES EVANGILES des Dimanches et Fetes de L'Annee Suivis de Prieres a la Sainte Vierge et Aux Saints. Paris: 1864. V. 44

EVANS, A. H.

A Vertebrate Fauna of the Shetland Islands. Edinburgh: 1899. V. 40; 45

EVANS, ABEL

The Apparition. London: 1710. V. 44

The Apparition. Oxford: 1710. V. 37; 40

Vertumnus. Oxford: 1713. V. 40; 42; 45

EVANS, ARTHUR

The Palace of Minos at Knossos. London: 1921. V. 40

The Palace of Minos. London: 1921-30. V. 41

The Palace of Minos. A Comparative Account of the Successive Stages of the Early Cretan Civilization as Illustrated by the Discoveries at Knossos. London: 1921-36. V. 37

The Palace of Minos At Knossos. London: 1928. V. 40

The Palace of Minos at Knossos. London: 1930. V. 40

The Palace of Minos at Knossos. London: 1935, 1964. V. 40

The Prehistoric Tombs of Knossos. I: The Cemenrary of Zafer Papoura. II: The Royal Tomb of Isopata. London: 1906. V. 37

Scripta Minoa. Oxford: 1909. V. 40

The Shaft Graves and Bee-Hive Tombs of Mycenae and Their Interrelation. London: 1929. V. 42

EVANS, ARTHUR BENONI

Fungusiana; or the Opinions, and Table Talk of the Late Barnaby Fungus, Esq . . . London: 1809. V. 42

EVANS, ARTHUR J.

Through Bosnia and the Herzegovina on Foot During the Insurrection, Aug. and Sept. 1875. London: 1876. V. 43

EVANS, BESSIE

American Indian Dance Steps. New York: 1931. V. 42

American Indian Dance Steps. V. 37

EVANS, C. S.

Cinderella. London: 1919. V. 37; 38; 44

The Sleeping Beauty. London. V. 42; 44

The Sleeping Beauty. London: 1920. V. 38; 39; 40; 41; 42; 46

The Sleeping Beauty. Philadelphia: 1920. V. 41

EVANS, CALEB

Political Sophistry Detected, or Brief Remarks on the Rev. Mr. Fletcher's Late Tract, Entitled 'American Patriotism'. Brisol: 1776. V. 37; 39

EVANS, CHARLES

American Bibliography. Chicago: 1903-34. V. 43

American Bibliography 1639-1729. Boston: 1943. V. 37; 44; 45; 46

EVANS, CHARLES SEDDON

The Sleeping Beauty. Philadelphia: 1920. V. 45

EVANS, D.

The Birds of Prey of the British Islands. Kingston Deverill,: 1980. V. 38

The Birds of Prey of the British Islands. 1980. V. 37

EVANS, DAVID

The Birds of Prey of the British Islands. Wiltshire: 1980. V. 44

EVANS, DAVID MORIER

The City; or, the Physiology of London Business, with Sketches on Change and at the Coffee Houses. London: 1845. V. 37; 45

The Commercial Crisis, 1847-1848 . . . London: 1849. V. 43

The History of the Commerical Crisis, 1857-8 and the Stock Exchange Panic of 1859. London: 1859. V. 37

EVANS, DONALD

Discords. Philadelphia: 1912. V. 37

Nine Poems from a Valetudinarium. Philadelphia: 1916. V. 37; 40; 41; 42; 44

Sonnets From the Patgonian. The Street of Little Hotels. New York: 1914. V. 37

EVANS, E. EVERETT

Alien Minds. Reading: 1955. V. 37

The Man of Many Minds. Reading: 1953. V. 37

EVANS, E. M., MRS.

Living for Jesus; Or a Sketch of My City Mission Work in Atlanta, Georgia. Atlanta: 1910. V. 44; 45

EVANS, E. T.

Records of the Third Middlesex Rifle Volunteers and of the Various Corps Which Formed the Second and Sixth Middlesex Administrative Battalions, to which is Prefixed a General Account of the Volunteer Forces of the United Kingdom . . . London: 1885. V. 38

EVANS, EDMUND

The Illuminated Scripture Text Book. London: 1880. V. 38

The Reminiscences of Edmund Evans. London: 1967. V. 41

EVANS, EDWARD

British Polar Explorers. London: 1946. V. 40

EVANS, ELWOOD

History of the Pacific Northwest, Oregon and Washington. Portland: 1889. V. 39; 45

Oration. Portland: 1865. V. 42

Puyallup Indian Reservation Address Delivered Before the Tacoman Chamber of Commerce. Tacoma: 1892. V. 37

The State of Washington. Washington: 1893. V. 45

Washington Territory: Her Past, Her Present and the Elements of Wealth Which Ensure Her Future . . . Olympia: 1877. V. 37

EVANS, ERNESTINE

The Frescoes of Diego Rivera. New York: 1929. V. 41; 45

EVANS, ESTWICK

A Pedestrious Tour, of Four Thousand Miles, through the Western States and Territories, During the Winter and Spring of 1818. Concord: 1819. V. 37; 38; 39; 42; 45

EVANS, EVAN

Some Specimens of the Poetry of the Antient Welsh Bards. London: 1764. V. 37; 40; 42; 43; 45

EVANS, F. W.

Shakers. Compendium of the Origin, History, Principles, Rules and Regulations, Government and Doctrines of the United Society of Believers in Christ's Second Appearing . . . New York: 1859. V. 42

A Short Treatise on the Second Appearing of Christ, in and Through the Order of the Female. Boston: 1853. V. 44; 45

EVANS, FREDERIC WILLIAM

Autobiography of a Shaker, and Revelation of the Apocalypse. New York: 1869. V. 38

EVANS, G.

Sundry Resolutions and Proceedings in Cases Before the Board of Commissioners on the 6th Article of the Treaty . . . With Britain. Philadelhia: 1799. V. 37

EVANS, G. P.

Big Game Shooting in Upper Burma. London: 1912. V. 39; 42; 45

EVANS, G. W. D.

The Classic and Connoisseur in Italy and Sicily. London: 1835. V. 39

EVANS, GEORGE G.

Illustrated History of the United States Mint . . . Philadelphia: 1893. V. 41

Illustrated History of the United States Mint . . . Philadelphia: 1894. V. 38; 39; 41

EVANS, GRIFFITH CONRAD

Mathematical Introduction to Economics. New York: 1930. V. 45

EVANS, H. B.

Our West Indian Colonies, Jamaica a Source of National Wealth and Honour. London: 1855. V. 40

EVANS, HENRY

First Duet. San Francisco: 1950. V. 38

Western Bibliographies. San Francisco: 1951. V. 37

EVELYN, JOHN 1620-1706 continued

Memoirs of John Evelyn.. London: 1827. V. 40; 41; 42; 43; 44; 46

The Miscellaneous Writings. London: 1825. V. 37; 40; 42; 45; 46

Navigation and Commerce, Their Origin and Progress. London: 1674. V. 38; 40; 42; 44

A Philosophical Discourse of Earth, Relating to the Culture and Improvement of It for Vegetation. London: 1676. V. 41; 42

Publick Employment an Active Life Prefer'd to Solitude, and All Its Appanges, Such as Fame, Command, Riches, Conversation &c. London: 1667. V. 45

Sculptura; or the History, and Art of Chalcography and Engraving in Copper. London: 1662. V. 41; 45

Sculptura. London: 1755. V. 37; 38; 39; 41; 42; 44; 45; 46

Sculptura; or, the History and Art of Chalcography, and Engraving in Copper. London: 1769. V. 37; 40; 41; 44

Sculptura Historico-Technica. London: 1770. V. 38; 40; 43; 46

Sylva, or a Discourse of Forest Trees . . . London. V. 43

Sylva. London: 1664. V. 38; 39; 41; 43; 46

Sylva, or a Discourse of Forest Trees. London: 1670. V. 37; 41; 42

Sylva, or a Discourse of Forest Trees and the Propagation of Timber . . . London: 1679. V. 39

Silva, or a Discourse of Forest Trees . . . London: 1706. V. 37; 41; 42

Silva . . . (with) An Historical Account of the Sacredness and Use of Standing Groves; Terra, a Philosophical Essay of Earth . . . Pomona . . . Acetaria . . . London: 1729. V. 38

Silva. London: 1776. V. 40; 42; 43; 45

Silva. York: 1776. V. 37; 38; 45; 46

Silva. York: 1786. V. 37; 39; 43; 44

Silva. York: 1812. V. 42

The State of France, as it stood in the IXthe yer of this present Monarch, Lewsi XIII. Written to a Friend. London: 1652. V. 37

Terra: A Philosophical Discourse of Earth. York: 1787. V. 38; 40

Terra: a Philosophical Discourse of Earth. York: 1778. V. 37

EVELYN, JOHN, JR.

To the King: a Congratulatory Poem. London: 1685. V. 41

EVELYN, MARY

Mundus Muliebris. London: 1690. V. 40

EVELYN, W. GLANVILLE

Memoir and Letters of Captain W. Glanville Evelyn, of the 4th Regiment ('King's Own') from North America, 1774-1776. Oxford: 1870. V. 43

Memoir and Letters of Captain W. Glanville Evelyn, of the 4th Regiment from North America, 1774-1776. Oxford: 1879. V. 39

EVERAERTS, ANTHONY

Cosmpolitae Historia Naturalis, Comprehendens Humani Corporis Atomiam & Anatomicam Delineationem . . . Leiden: 1686. V. 43

EVERAERTS, NICOLAS

. . . Topicoru(m) Seu de Locis Legalibus Liber. Venundantur Louanii in Aedibus Theodorici Martini Alustensis Eregione Scholae Iuris Civilis, qui Exacte, & Exquisitis Characteribus Excudit . . . 1516. V. 38

Topicorum seu de Locis Legalibus. Louvain: 1516. V. 40

EVERARD, ANNE

Flowers from Nature, with the Botanical Name, Class and Order . . . London: 1835. V. 41; 43

EVERARD, EDWARD

A Bristol Printing House. London: 1903. V. 44

The Depositions and Examination of Mr. Edward Everard Concerning the Horrid Popish Plot Against the Life of His Sacred Majesty and the Protestant Religion. London: 1679. V. 41

EVERARD, GILLES

De Herba Panacea, Quam Alii Tabacum, Alii Petum, De Commodis et Incoloarum Ritibus Virginae. Frankfurt: 1590. V. 44

De Herba Panacea, Quam Alii Tabacum, Alii Petum, Avt Nicotianam Vocant, Breuis Commentariolus. Antwerp: 1587. V. 37; 38; 40

Panacea: or The Universal Medicine, Being a Discovery of the Wonderful Vertues of Tobacco Taken in a Pipe, with Its Operation and Use both in Physick and Chyrurgery. London: 1659. V. 40; 42

EVERARD, H. S. C.

Golf in Theory and Practice. London: 1898. V. 39; 43

EVEREST, ROBERT

A Journey through Norway, Lapland and Part of Sweden. London: 1829. V. 40; 43

EVEREST, THOMAS

A Popular View of Homoeopathy, with Annotations and a Brief Survey of the Progress and Homoeopathia in Europe . . . New York: 1842. V. 41; 42

EVERETT, ALEXANDER H.

Address: Delivered at Jefferson College St. James's Parrish, ;a. June 30, 1841, on Assuming the Functions of President of that Institution. New Orleans: 1841. V. 37

The Conduct of the Administration. Boston: 1832. V. 39

EVERETT, ALEXANDER HILL

America O Examine General De la Situacion Politica de las Differentes Potencias Del Continente Occidental . . . Northampton: 1828. V. 43

America; or A General Survey of the Political Situation of the Several Powers of the Western Continent. Philadelphia: 1827. V. 43

Europe: or a General Survey of the Present Situation of the Principal Powers . . . Boston: 1822. V. 41

New Ideas on Population: With Remarks on the Theories of Malthus and Godwin. Boston: 1823. V. 45

EVERETT, EDWARD

An Address Delivered at the Erection of a Monument to John Harvard Sept. 26, 1828. Boston: 1828. V. 44

Address of Hon. Edward Everett, at the Consecration of the National Cemetery at Gettysburg, 19th Nov. 1863 . . . Boston: 1864. V. 37; 43; 45

A Lecture on the Workingmen's Party. Boston: 1830. V. 40

The Mount Vernon Papers. New York: 1860. V. 43

An Oration Delivered on the Battlefield of Gettysburg, (November 19, 1863) at the Consecration of the Cemetery . . . To Which is Added Interesting Reports of the Dedicatory Ceremonies . . . New York: 1863. V. 45

The Uses of Astronomy. Boston: 1856. V. 40

EVERETT, HENRY

The History of the Somerset Light Infantry (Prince Albert's) 1685-1914 (and) 1914-1919. London: 1927-34. V. 46

The History of the Somerset Light Infantry (Prince Albert's) 1685-1914. London: 1934. V. 37

EVERETT, HORACE

Regulating the Indian Department. Washington: 1834. V. 37; 40; 41; 43; 45

Regulating the Indian Department . . . Mr. H. Everett, from the Committee on Indian Affairs, Made the Following Report . . . Washington: 1834. V. 41

EVERETT, L. S.

An Exposure of the Principles of the 'Free Inquirers.' Boston: 1831. V. 42

EVERETT, MARSHALL

Wreck and Sinking of the Titanic. N.P.: 1925. V. 42

EVERETT, T. H.

Encyclopedia of Horticulture. New York: 1980-82. V. 45

The New Illustrated Encylopedia of Gardening. New York: 1972-73. V. 45

EVERGREEN Review. New York: 1957. V. 40
EVERGREEN Review. 1957-63. V. 42

THE EVERGREEN State Souvenir Containing A Review of the Resources, Wealth, Varied, Industries and Commercial Advantages of the State of Washington. Tacoma and Seattle: 1893. V. 45

EVERHART, EDGAR

Petroleum of Texas. Austin: (1887). V. 37

EVERITT, C. R.

Westward - 1920. Huntington: 1921. V. 39

EVERITT, E. B.

Tour of St. Elmo's From the Nutmeg State to the Golden Gate. 1883. N.P.: 1883. V. 44

EVERITT, FRED

Fun with Game Birds. Harrisburg: 1950. V. 39

EVERITT, GRAHAM

English Caricaturists and Graphic Humorists of the Nineteenth Century: How They Interpreted Their Times. London: 1886. V. 37; 39

EVERLEIN, HAROLD D.

Portrait of a Colonial City. Philadelphia: 1939. V. 41

EVERLINE, FLORENCE MIRIAM

From a Pepper Bough: Brown Twigs. Los Angeles: 1941. V. 37

EVERMANN, WARREN

Investigations in Porto Rico of the United States Fish Commission Steamer Fish Hawk in 1899. 1899. V. 41

EVERSON, WILLIAM

Blame It On the Jet Stream! Santa Cruz: 1978. V. 38

Granite & Cypress, by Robinson Jeffers. Rubbins from the Rock Poems Gathered from His Stonemason Years when Submission to the Spirit of Granite in the Building of House & Tower & Wall Focused his Imagination & Gave Massive Permanence . . . Santa Cruz: 1975. V. 37

EVERSON, WILLIAM continued

In Medias Res. Canto One of an Autobiographical Epic: Dust Shall be the Serpent's Food. San Francisco: 1985. V. 38

The Masks of Drought. Santa Barbara: 1980. V. 37

San Joaquin. Los Angeles: 1939. V. 38

Tendril in the Mesh. San Francisco: 1973. V. 38

Who is she that Looketh Forth as the morning. By Brother Antoninus. Santa Barbara: 1972. V. 37

EVERSTADT, CHARLES

Lincoln's Emancipation Proclamation. New York: 1959. V. 43

EVERTS, L. H., & CO.

Illustrated Historical Atlas of Delaware County, Ohio. Philadelphia: 1875. V. 46

EVERTS, LOUIS H.

Combination Atlas Map of Portage County, Ohio. Chicago: 1874. V. 42

EVERTS, ORPHEUS

O-na-we-quah; and Other Poems. La Porte: 1856. V. 44

EVERY Day Occurrences. London: 1825. V. 37; 39; 42

EVERY Man His Own printer; or, Lithography Made Easy. London: 1854. V. 38

EVERYMAN. London: 1911. V. 46

EVERYMAN: a Morality Play. London: 1911. V. 38

EVERYMAN, BARTON W.

Aquatic Resources and Fisheries of Puerto Rico. Washington: 1900. V. 38; 40

EVERYMAN'S History of the English Church. London: 1914. V. 46

THE EVIAD: a Burlesque Poem. London: 1781. V. 38

EWALD, C. A.

The Diseases of the Stomach. New York: 1892. V. 42

EWALD, CARL

The Queen Bee and Other Nature Stories. London, Edinburgh, Dublin: 1907. V. 45

EWALD, G. H. A.

A Grammar of Hebrew Language of the Old Testament . . . London & Edinburgh: 1836. V. 38

EWALD, HENRY AUGUSTUS

A Grammar of the Hebrew Language of the Old Testament. London: 1836. V. 45

EWALD, HERMAN FREDERICK

The Story of Waldemar Krone's Youth. Edinburgh: 1867. V. 42

EWALD, JOHANNES

The Death of Balder. London: 1892. V. 38

EWAN, J.

William Bartram. Botanical and Zoological Drawings, 1756-1788. Philadelphia: 1968. V. 39

EWART, ALFRED

The Flora of the Northern Territory. Melbourne: 1917. V. 41

EWART, DAVID

A Scriptural View of the Moral Relations of African Slavery. Charleston: 1859. V. 42

EWART, GAVIN

Poems and Songs. London: 1939. V. 37; 44

EWART, J. S.

The Kingdom of Canada, the Imperial Federation, the Colonial Conference, the Alaska Boundary and Other Essays. Toronto: 1908. V. 44

EWBANK, J. W.

Picturesque Views of Edinburgh. Edinburgh: 1825. V. 41

EWBANK, THOMAS

Life in Brazil; or a Journal of a Visit to the Land of the Cocoa and the Palm. New York: 1856. V. 41; 45

The Spoon. London: 1845. V. 39

EWELL, JAMES

The Planter's and Mariner's Medical Companion. Philadelphia: 1807. V. 41; 44

EWELL, R. S.

The First Manassas. Correspondence Between General R. S. Ewell and G. T. Beauregard . . . Nashville: 1885. V. 37

The Making of a Soldier - Letters of General R. S. Ewell. Richmond: 1935. V. 44

EWELL, THOMAS

Plain Discourses on the Laws of Properties of Matter . . . New York: 1806. V. 39; 44

Statement of Improvements in the Theory and Practice of the Science of Medicine. Philadelphia: 1819. V. 44

EWEN, WILLIAM

Pyogenic Infective Diseases of the Brain and Spinal Cord. Glasgow: 1893. V. 46

EWICH, JOHANN 1525-1588

De Officio Fidelis et Prudentis Magistratus Tempore Pestilentiae . . . Naples: 1582. V. 40

EWING, ALEXANDER

Practical Astronomy. Edinburgh: 1797. V. 40

Practical Astronomy: Containing, A Description of the Solar System; the Doctrine of the Sphere; the Principal Problems in Astronomy, Illustrated with many Examples. Together with Astronomical Tables of the Sun, Moon . . . Burlington: 1812. V. 37

EWING, DOUGLAS C.

Pleasing the Spirits: A Catalogue of American Indian Art. With essays by C. Bates & T. Brasser. New York: 1982. V. 37

EWING, GREVILLE 1767-1841

Essays Addressed to Jews, on the Authority, the Scope and the Consummation, of the Law and Prophets. London: 1809-10. V. 37; 38

EWING, J. H.

Old Fashioned Fairy Tales. London: 1910. V. 46

EWING, JAMES

Neoplastic Diseases. Philadelphia: 1919. V. 40; 42

A Treatise on the Office and Duty of a Justice of the Peace, Sheriff, Coroner, Constable . . . the Rules for Conducting an Action in the Court for the Trial of Small Causes . . . a Digest of laws . . . a Variety of Approved Forms . . . Trenton: 1805. V. 37

A Treatise on the Office and Duty of a Justice of the Peace, Sheriff, Coroner, Constable and of Executors, Administrators and Guardians. Trenton: 1832. V. 37

EWING, JOHN

The Royal Scots 1914-1919. With a foreword by Lord Salvesen. London;: 1925. V. 37

EWING, JULIA HORATIO

A Week Spent in a Glass Pond, by the Great Water Bettle. London: 1882. V. 40

EWING, JULIANA HORATIA

Jackanapes. New York: 1948. V. 46

EWING, T.

Report of the Secretary of the Interior . . . (regarding) Information in Relation to the Operations of the Commission Appointed to Run and Mark the Boundary Between the United States and Mexico. Washington: 1850. V. 37; 43

EWING, THOMAS

Ewing's New General Atlas . . . Edinburgh: 1821. V. 45

Ewing's New General Atlas . . . Edinburgh: 1835. V. 45

Ewing's New General Atlas. Edinburgh: 1846? V. 43

EWING, WILLIAM

Arab and Druze at Home. London: 1907. V. 41

EX-LIBRIS SOCIETY

Journal of the Ex-Libris Society. London: 1892-97. V. 39

AN EXACT Account of the Ceremonies Observed at the Marriage of His Most Christian Majesty Lewis XV. London: 1726. V. 42

AN EXACT Account of the Manner of the Execution of Algernon Sidney Esq; On Tower-Hill, for High-Treason, With His Behaviour on the Scaffold. London: 1683. V. 38

AN EXACT and Circumstanial History of the Battle of Flodden in Verse Written About the Time of Queen Elizabeth in Which are Related Many Particular Facts Not to be Found in the English History. Berwick upon Tweed: 1774. V. 38

AN EXACT and Particular Narrative of a Cruel and Inhumane Murder Attempted on the Body of Edward Crispe, Esq. London: 1722. V. 42

AN EXACT and Perfect Relation of the Arrival of the Ship the James and May Captain Phipps (sic) Commander, 2000000 Pounds in Gold and Silver, Taken Up in Nine Fathom Water from the Bottom of the Sea . . . London: 1687. V. 44

AN EXACT and True Relation of the Dangerous and Bloudy Fight Betweene His Majesties Armie and the Parliaments Forces . . . London: 1642. V. 46

AN EXACT Collection of all Remonstrances, Declarations, Votes, Orders, Ordinances, Proclamations, Petitions, Messages, Answers and other Remarkable Passages Betweene the Kings Most Excellent Majesty and His Hight Court of Parliament . . . London: 1643. V. 46

AN EXACT Journal of the Victorious Expedition of the Confederate Fleet, the Last Year, Under the Command of the Right Honourable Admiral Russel . . . London: 1695. V. 43

AN EXACT List of the Lords Spiritual and Temporal . . . London: 1732. V. 45
AN EXACT List of the Lords Spiritual and Temporal; Distinguished by the Following Marks . . . London: 1734. V. 46

AN EXACT List of all the Fairs in England and Wales in Three Parts. London: 1752. V. 41

AN EXACT Relation of the Several Engagements and Actions of His Majesties Fleet Under the Command of His Highnesse Prince Rupert. London: 1673. V. 42

AN EXAGMINATION of James Joyce. Norfolk. V. 44

EXAMINATION and Refutation of a Late Pamphlet, Intitled, Considerations on the Navy Bill. Wherein the Present Power of the Lords Commissioners of the Admiralty Over Half-Pay Officers, Is Shewn to be Fully Sufficient . . . London: 1749. V. 41

AN EXAMINATION Into the Conduct of the Present Administration, from the Year 1774 to the Year 1778. London: 1778. V. 40; 42; 43

AN EXAMINATION of and Some Answer to a Pamphlet, intitled, A Narrative and Defence of the Proceedings of Ministers of Hampshire, Who Disapproved of Mr. Breck's Settlement at Springfield. Boston: 1736. V. 44

AN EXAMINE of the Expediency of Bringing Over Immediately the Body of Hanoverian Troops Taken Into Our Pay, in Exchange for the Like Number of English t be Sent to Flanders, In Order to a Total Suppression of the Rebellion, the Security of the . . . London: 1746. V. 41

EXAMPLES of Modern Bookbinding, Designed and Executed by Robt. Riviere & Son. London: 1919. V. 37

AN EXAPLANATION of the Nature of Equation of Time, and of the Use of the Equation Table for Adjusting Watches and Clocks to the Motion of the Sun. London: 1731. V. 41

THE EXCELLENCY of the Pen and Pencil . . . London: 1668. V. 39; 41

AN EXCELLENT New Ballad. To the Tune of Chivy Chace. N.P. DATIMP: n.d.: 1718? V. 40

AN EXCELLENT New Ballad. To the Tune of Chivy Chase. London?: 1718? V. 40

AN EXCELLENT New Ballad, to the Tune of, The Bonny Black Ladie. N.P.: 1745. V. 39

EXCURSIONS in County of Sussex, Comprising Brief Historical and Topographical Delineations . . . London: 1882. V. 44

EXCURSIONS in the County of Essex. London: 1818. V. 40; 41

EXCURSIONS in the County of Kent: Comprising Brief Historical and Topographical Delineations . . . London: 1822. V. 41

EXCURSIONS in the County of Norfolk . . . Historical and Topographical Description of Every Town and Village . . . London: 1819. V. 41

EXCURSIONS in the County of Suffolk . . . London: 1818. V. 40

EXELL, A. W.
Flora Zambesiaca. London: 1960-87. V. 38

EXEMPLORUM Memorabilium. Parisiis: 1575. V. 40

EXERCICIO Quotidano, Para os Treze Dias do Glorioso Portuguez, e Mosse Cidadao, o Senhor S. Antonio . . . Lisboa Occidental: 1739. V. 45

EXERCISES in Colouring. Russian Costumes and Habits. London: 1860. V. 41

EXERCISES, Instructive and Entertaining, in False English. Leeds: 1811. V. 39; 41; 44

EXERCISES, Instructive and Entertaining, In False English . . . Leeds: 1797. V. 46

EXERCISES to the Accidence; or, an Exemplification of the Several Moods and Tenses and of the Principal Rules of Construction; Consisting Chiefly of Moral Sentences Collected Out of the Best Roman Authors. London: 1707. V. 44

EXLEY, FREDERICK
A Fan's Notes. New York: 1968. V. 39; 40; 41; 42; 43; 44; 45; 46

EXLEY, THOMAS
Physical Optics. London: 1834. V. 38

EXNER, A. H.
Japan As I Saw It. London: 1930. V. 46

EXPANDED METAL AND CORRUGATED BAR CO.
Corrugated Bars for Reinforced Concrete. St. Louis: 1906. V. 44

EXPANDED METAL CO.
Some Particulars Concerning 'Expanded Metal', Its Production and Uses in Fire-Proof and Other Building Constructions. London: 1897. V. 44

AN EXPERIENCE by a Green Mountain Girl, To Which Is Added the Experience of Another . . . Hanover: 1821. V. 43

EXPERIENCED American Housekeeper, or Domestic Cookery: Formed on Principles of Economy for the Use of Private Families. New York: 1823. V. 37

EXPERIENCES and Observations of an American Consular Officer During the Recent Mexican Revolutions . . . as Mainly Told in a Series of Letters Written by the Author to His Daughter. Chula Vista: 1920. V. 44

EXPERIMENTS Lately Made by Several Eminent Physicians, on the Surprising and Terrible Effects of Almond Water and Black Cherry Water. London: 1741. V. 41

THE EXPERT Gardener; or, a Treatise Containing Certaine Necessary, Secret and Ordinary Knowledges in Grafting and Gardening. London: 1654. V. 37; 40

AN EXPLANATION of the Works of the Tunnel Under the Thames from Rothehithe to Wapping. London: 1837. V. 38; 45

AN EXPLANATION of the Works of the Tunnel Under the Thames from Rotherhithe to Wapping. London: 1839. V. 45
AN EXPLANATION of the Works of the Tunnel Under the Thames from Rotherhithe to Wapping. London: 1840. V. 41; 45; 46

EXPLANATORY Remarks Upon the Life and Opinions of Tristram Shandy. London: 1760. V. 37

AN EXPOSE of the Treaty of Paucarpata, in Peru and the Events Connected With It. Andover: 1838. V. 40

EXPOSITIO Pulcherrima Hymnorum per Annum Secuncum Curiam non Amplius Impressa. Venice: 1515. V. 40

EXPOSITIO Sequentiarum. Paris: 1519. V. 37

EXPOSITION and Protest, Reported by the Special Committee of the House of Representations on the Tariff. Read and Ordered to be Printed Dec. 19th, 1828. Columbia: 1829. V. 44

AN EXPOSITION of the Book of Common Prayer, And Administration of the Sacraments..Together with the Psalter . . . Sheffield: 1764. V. 44

AN EXPOSTULARY Letter to a Certain Right Honourable Person, (i.e. Earl of Chesterfield) Upon His Promotion. London: 1757. V. 41; 46

EXQUEMELIN, ALEXANDRE OLIVIER
Bucaniers of America. London: 1684. V. 38; 40; 46
Bucaniers of America . . . London: 1684-5. V. 39; 42; 44; 45
The History of the Bucaniers of America. London: 1774. V. 44
The History of the Bucaniers of America. London: 1810. V. 39
Histoire des Avanturiers Qui se Sont Signalez Dans Les Indes, Contenant ce Qu'Ils on Fait de Plus Remarquable Depuis Vingt Anees Avec La Vie . . . Paris: 1688. V. 41
Histoire der Boecaniers, of Vry-Buyters Van America . . . Amsterdam: 1700. V. 40; 43
Piratas de la America, Y Luz a La Defensa de Las Costas de Indias Occidentales. Cologne: 1681. V. 40
Piratas De La America. Y Luz a la Defensa de las Costas des Indias Occidentales Dedicado Al Muy Noble Senor Don Ricardo Whyte . . . Cologne: 1682. V. 39

EXSAMPLES of Railway Making. London: 1843. V. 37

EXSTEENS, MAURICE
L'Oeuvre Grave et Lithographie de Felicien Rops. Paris: 1928. V. 41

EXTEMPORE Lines on the Death of the Rev. Mr. John Wesley, By a Friend. N.P.: 1791. V. 46

EXTRA Census Bulletin. The Five Civilized Tribes in Indian Territory. The Cherokee, Chickasaw, Choctaw, Creek and Seminole Nations. Washington: 1894. V. 37

EXTRACT of a Letter from the House of Representatives of the Massachusetts-Bay, to Their Agent Dennys de Berdt, Esq. With some Remarks. London: 1770. V. 38

EXTRACTS from Some of the Communistic Inflammatory and Treasonable Documents Circulated by the National Greenback Party. Chicago: 1878. V. 43

EXTRACTS from the Italian Prose Writers. London: 1828. V. 45; 46

EXTRACTS from the Proceedings of the Convention at Concord, and of the Town of Boston; Containing the Regulation of the Prices of Merchandize, Provisions, &c. Boston: 1779. V. 37

EXTRAIT d'une Gazette Etrangere Faite a Schaffouse. Lyon?: 1762. V. 46

THE EXTRAORDINARY Account and Wonderful Preservation of Captain Bligh, and Eighteen Seamen, Who, Upon a Mutiny in the South Sea, Were Exposed in an Open Boat, with Only Five Days Provision; and After a Voyage of 3618 Miles, Performed in 44 Days . . . London: 1804. V. 40

THE EXTRAORDINARY Black Book, Comprising an Exposition of the United Church of England and Ireland . . . London: 1831. V. 38

EXTRAORDINARY Gazette. London: 1837. V. 43

THE EXTRAORDINARY Life, and Singular Adventures of Wolfe: Who Was Thiry Years a Notorious Robber, Murderer and Captain of a Gang of Fifty-three Thieves. London: 1825? V. 45

EXTRAORDINARY Trial. Achilli Versus Newman. A Full Verbatim Report of this Celebrated Trial, Before the Lord Chief Justice Campbell . . . London: 1852. V. 37

EYB, ALBERTUS DE

Margarita Poetica. Basel: 1495. V. 45

EYB, ALBRECHT VON 1420-1475

Spiegel der Sitten . . . Von Guten und Busen Sitten. Von Sunden und Tugenden Dargegen. Augsburg: 1511. V. 44

EYCLESHYMER, ALBERT

Anatomical Names Especially the Basle Nomina Anatomica with Biographical Sketches by Roy Lee Moodie. New York: 1917. V. 38

A Cross-Section Anatomy. New York: 1911. V. 42

EYLAND, EDWARD S.

Working Drawings and Designs in Architecture and Building. Edinburgh: 1863. V. 39

EYLAND, LIGHTBODY AND BURN

Working Drawings and Designs in Architecture and Building; with Essays on Various Subjects . . . London: 1863. V. 44

EYLES, DESMOND

Royal Doulton 1815-1965, the Rise and Expansion of the Royal Doulton Potteries. London: 1965. V. 37

EYRE, EDMUND JOHN

Observations Made at Paris During the Peace; and Remarks in a Tour . . . Bath: 1803. V. 42

EYRE, EDWARD

European Civilization: Its Origin and Development. Oxford: 1935-39. V. 42; 46

EYRE, FRANCIS

Few Remarks on the Hiistory of the Decline and Fall of the Roman Empire. London: 1778. V. 39

EYRE, JOHN

Christian Spectator: Being a Journey from England to Ohio. Albany: 1838. V. 41; 44

The European Stranger in America. New York: 1839. V. 44

EYRE-TODD, GEORGE

Ancient Scots Ballads, With the Traditional Airs to Which They Were Wont to be Sung. London: 1800. V. 41

The Book of Glasgow Cathedral. Glasgow: 1898. V. 39; 40

EYRE, VINCENT

The Military Operations at Cabul, Which Ended in the Retreat and Destruction of the British Army. London: 1843. V. 37; 38; 39; 41; 42; 44; 46

EYSTON, BERNARD

The Christian Duty. 1684. V. 44

EYTELWEIN, J. U.

Beschreibung der Erbauung und Einrichtung Einer Vereinigten Brauerei und Branntweinbrennerei . . . Berlin: 1802. V. 38

EYTELWEIN, JOHANN ALBERT

Praktische Anweisung zur Konstrutzion der Faschinenwerke und de Dazu . . . Berlin: 1800. V. 41; 45

EYTON, R. W.

Antiquities of Shropshire. London: 1854-60. V. 38; 40; 43

EYTON, ROBERT WILLIAM

Antiquities of Shropshire. London: 1854-60. V. 41

EYTON, T. C.

A History of the Rare British Birds. (with) A Catalogue of British Birds. London: 1836. V. 45

Osteologia Avium. London: 1867-75. V. 43

EYTZINGER, MICHAEL VON

Pentapulus Regnorum Mundi. Antwerp: 1579. V. 40; 45

F

F., A.

The Ladies' Pocket Book of Etiquette. Waltham St. Lawrence: 1928. V. 41

F., E.

A Letter from a Gentleman of Quality in the Country, to His Friend. Upon being Chosen a Member to serve in the Approaching Parliament, and Desiring his Advice. Being an argument relating to the point of . . . (London): 1679. V. 37

F., G.

The Compleat Conveyancer. London: 1701. V. 41

F., J.

The Golden Fleece: or, Old England Restored to Its Old Honest Vocation. London: 1679. V. 38

The Golden Fleece Revived &c. London: 1689. V. 38

Miscellaneous Pieces Including the Winchester Bushel. London: 1798. V. 39

F., J. S.

The Citizen's Pocket Chronicle . . . London: 1827. V. 45

FAAS, EKBERT

Towards a New American Poetics . . . Santa Barbara: 1978. V. 43

FABENS, JOSEPH WARREN

Life in Santo Domingo. New York: 1873. V. 42; 44

FABER, FELIX

Eigentlich Beschreibung der Hin Unnd Wider Farth Zu Dem Heyligen Landt Gen Jerusalem/und Furter Durch die Grosse Wuesten zum dem Heiligen Berge Horeb und Sinay . . . 1557. V. 40

FABER, G. L.

The Fisheries of the Adriatic and Fish Thereof. London: 1883. V. 39

FABER, GEORGE STANLEY 1773-1854

The Origin of Pagan Idolatry Ascertained from Historical Testimony and Cricumstantial Evidence. London: 1816. V. 38

FABER, H.

Caius Gabriel Cibber 1630-1700. His Life and Work. Oxford: 1926. V. 39

FABER, REGINALD STANLEY

Bibliotheque de la Providence. Catalogue of the Library of the French Protestant Hospital, Victoria Park Road, London . . . London: 1887. V. 45

FABER, THEODOR VON

Bagatelles. Promenades d'un Deoeuvre dans la Ville de St. Petersbourg. St. Petersbourg: 1811. V. 43

FABES, GILBERT H.

Modern First Editions: Points and Values. London: 1929, 1931. V. 40

Modern First Editions: Points & Values. London: 1929-32. V. 37; 39; 40; 41; 43

Modern First Editions: Points and Values: First, Second and Third Series. London: 1929-32. V. 39

FABIAN, ROBERT

The Chronicle of Fabian . . . London: 1559. V. 38

FABIAN SOCIETY

Fabian Tracts. London: 1884-1937. V. 37; 38

FABIAN SOCIETY, LONDON.

Fabian Tracts Nos. 1 to 231. London. V. 41

FABILLI, MARY

Saints. San Francisco: 1960. V. 45

FABLE, LIONEL

The Children at the Pole. London: 1914. V. 42

FABLES and Pictures for the Nursery, Fireside and School/ London: 1855. V. 46

FABRE, ANTOINE FRANCOIS HIPPOLYTE

Nemesis Medicale Illustree. Paris: 1840. V. 42

FABRE D'OLIVET, ANTOINE

Azalais et Le Gentil Aimar Histoire Provencale, Traduite d'un Ancien Manuscrit Provencal. Paris: 1799. V. 39

FABRE DU BOSQUET

Mes Idees sur la Nature et les Causes de l'Air Dephlogistique: d'Apres les Effets qu'il Produit sur les Animaux, en Prolongeant leur Force & Leur Vie. Londres: 1785. V. 39

FABRE, J. A.

Essai sur la Maniere la Plus Avantageuse de Construire les Machines Hydrauliques, et en Particulier les Moulins a Bled. Paris: 1783. V. 39; 40; 44

FABRE, J. H.

Fabre's Book of Insects. London. V. 46

Fabre's Book of Insects. London: 1920. V. 46

Fabre's Book of Insects. London: 1921. V. 43; 46

Fabre's Book of Insects . . . New York: 1936. V. 42

Fabre's Book of Insects. New York: 1939. V. 43

FABRE, JEAN ANTOINE 1749-1834.

Essai sur La Theorie des Torrens et des Rivieres. Paris: 1797. V. 43

FABRE'S Book of Insects. London. V. 41
FABRE'S Book of Insects. London: 1921. V. 44
FABRE'S Book of Insects. New York: 1935. V. 45
FABRE'S Book of Insects. New York: 1939. V. 40; 41

FABRETTI, RAFFAELE

De Columna Trajani Syntagma Accesserunt. Explicatio Veteris Tabellae Ana Glyphae Homeri Iliadem Atque ex Steschoro Arctino et Lesche Ilii Excidium Continentis. Rome: 1683. V. 37

FABRETTI, RAPHAEL

De Aquis et Aquaeductibus Veteris Romae Dissertationes Tres. Rome: 1680. V. 44

FABRETTI, RAPHAELIS

De Columna Trajani Syntagma Accesserunt. Rome: 1683. V. 42

FABRI, HONORATUS

Dialogi Physici in Quibus de Motu Terrae Disputatur, Marini Aestus Nova Causa Proponitur, Necnon Aquarum & Mercurij Supra Libellam Elevatio Examinatur. Lugduni: 1665. V. 42

FABRI, IOANNES

Moscovitarum Iuxta Mare Glaciale Religio. Basle: 1526. V. 37

FABRIC Design in Bookbinding (cover title). London: c. 1965-1970. V. 37

FABRICI, GIROLAMO

Fabricius ab Aquapendente Opera Chirurgica. Lugdvni Batavorum: 1723. V. 40

FABRICIUS AB AQUAPENDENTE

Opera Chirurgica. Quorum pars Prior Pentateuchum Chirurgicum Posterior Operationes Chirurgicase . . . Lugdvni Batavorum: 1723. V. 46

FABRICIUS AB AQUAPENDENTE, HIERONYMUS

The Embryological Treatises of . . . Ithaca: 1942. V. 38

Oevvres Chirvrgicales de Hierosme Fabrice d'Aqvapendente . . . Lyon: 1649. V. 37; 43

FABRICIUS, FREDERICK ERNEST

The Genuine Letters . . . London: 1761. V. 41

FABRICIUS, FRIEDRICH ERNST VON

The Genuine Letter of Baron Fabricius . . . to Charles XII of Sweden . . . London: 1761. V. 38; 40; 45

FABRICIUS, GEORG

De Metallicis Rebus Ac Nominibus Observationes Variae & Eruditae. Zurich: 1565. V. 38

FABRICIUS, GEORGIUS

De Re Poetica Libri IIII. Lyons: 1583. V. 37

FABRICIUS, HIERONYMOUS

The Embryological Treatise of Hieronymous Fabricius of Aquapendente . . . Ithaca: 1942. V. 45

FABRICIUS, J. C.

Species Insectorum Exhibentes Eorum Differentias Specificas etc. Hamburg: 1781. V. 42

FABRICIUS, JOHANNES ALBERTUS

Bibliotheca Latina sive Notitia Autorum Veterum Latinorum Quorumcunque Scripta ad nos Pervenerunt. Londini: 1703. V. 38

FABRICZY, CORNELIUS VON

Italian Medals. London: 1904. V. 44

FABRY VON HILDEN, WILHELM

Opera Quae Extant Omnia . . . Frankfurt: 1646. V. 45

THE FABULIST, Number Three. Boston: 1921. V. 44

FABYAN, ROBERT d. 1513

Fabyans Cronycle Newly Prynted wyth the Cronycle, Actes and Dedes Done in the Tyme of the Reygne of the Most Excellent Prynce Kynge Henry the VII. 1533. V. 39

The New Chronicles of England and France . . . London: 1811. V. 42; 44

THE FACE of New York: The City as It Was and as It Is. New York: 1954. V. 39

FACE to Face: Twelve Contemporary American Artists Interpret Themselves . . . 1985. V. 41; 42; 44

FACETS: an Anthonology of Verse. Nashville: 1928. V. 45; 46

FACTS About Cuba. Published Under the Authority of the New York Cuban junta. New York: 1870. V. 39

FACTS and Arguments in Favour of Adopting Railways in Preference to Canals, in the State of Pennsylvania. Philadelphia: 1825. V. 39; 41

FACTS and Arguments on the Transmission of Intellectual and Moral Qualities from Parent to Offspring. New York: 1843. V. 38

FACTS and Observations Relative to the Nature and Origin of the Pestilential Fever, Which Prevailed in This City, in 1793, 1797 and 798. Philadelphia: 1798. V. 41

FACTS: or, Plain and Explicit Narrative of the Case of Mrs. Rudd. London: 1775. V. 45

THE FACTS Respecting Indian Administration in the North-west. Ottawa: 1886. V. 45

FADIMAN, CLIFTON

The Joys of Wine. New York: 1975. V. 46

FADS & Fancies of Representative Americans at the Beginning of the Twentieth Century: a Portrayal of Their Tastes, Diversions & Achievements. New York: 1905. V. 46

FAENSEN, HUBERT d. 1561

Early Russian Architecture. New York: 1975. V. 38; 42

FAERNO, GABRIELLO d. 1561

Fables in English and French Verse. London: 1741. V. 42; 43

Fabulae Centum (Cest Fables Choisies des Anciens Auteurs). London: 1743. V. 38; 40; 42

Fabulae Centum ex Antiquis Auctoribus Delectae . . . et Carmina Varia. Parma: 1793. V. 38

FAERNUS, GABRIELIS

Fabulae Centum ex Antiquis Auctoribus Delectae . . . Parma: 1793. V. 39

FAGAN, DAVID D.

History of Benton County, Oregon. Portland: 1885. V. 38

FAGAN, LOUIS

The Reform Club: Its Founders and Architect. London: 1887. V. 38

FAGEL, GASPAR

A Letter Writ by Mijn Heer Fagel, Pensioner of Holland, to Mr. James Stewart, Advocate; giving an account of the Prince and Princess of Orange's Thoughts Concerning the Repeal of the Test, and the Penal Laws. Amsterdam: 1688. V. 38

FAGES, DON PEDRO

Letters of Captain Don Pedro Fages & The Reverend President Fr. Junipero Serra at San Diego, California, in October 1772. San Francisco: 1936. V. 38

FAGG, H.

Adventures in America 1492-1897. New York: 1964. V. 45

FAGG, WILLIAM

Nigeria: 2000 Jahre Plastik. Munich: 1962. V. 38
Nigerian Images. New York: 1963. V. 38
The Sculpture of Africa. London: 1965. V. 37
Tribes and Forms in African Art. New York: 1965. V. 37; 38; 46

FAHEY, HERBERT

Early Printing in California. San Francisco: 1956. V. 38; 40; 41; 42; 44; 46

FAHLE, J. J.

Galileo, His Life and Work. London: 1903. V. 39

FAIJA, HENRY

Portland Cement for Users. London: 1881. V. 44

FAILLE, J. B. DE LA

The Works of Vincent Van Gogh: His Paintings and Drawings. New York: 1970. V. 37; 40; 43; 45

FAINLIGHT, RUTH

Poems. 1971. V. 44

THE FAIR Carew; or, Husbands and Wives. London: 1851. V. 37

A FAIR Representation of His Majesty's Right to Nova-Scotia or Acadie. London: 1756. V. 40; 42

A FAIR Representation of His Majesty's Right to Nova Scotia or Arcadie. London: 1756. V. 43

THE FAIR Triumvirate at War. London: 1742. V. 38; 43

FAIRBAIRN, JAMES

Fairbairn's Crests of the Families of Great Britain and Ireland. Edinburgh: 1860. V. 38; 46

Fairbairn's Book of Crests of the Families of Great Britain and Ireland. Edinburgh: 1892. V. 44

Fairbairn's Book of Crests of the Families of Great Britain and Ireland. London: 1915. V. 39

FAIRBAIRN, WILLIAM

An Account of the Construction of the Britannia and Conway Tubular Bridges, with a Complete History of their Progress . . . London: 1849. V. 43

An Experimental Inquiry into the Strength of Wrought-Iron Plates and Their Riveted Joint as Appled to Ship Building and Vessels Exposed to Severe Strains. London. V. 44

An Experimental Inquiry Into the Strength, Elasticity, Ductility and Other Properties of Steel Manufactured by the Barrow Haematite Steel Company, Lancashire, England. London: 1869. V. 44

Iron, Its History, Properties and Processes of Manufacture. Edinburgh: 1861. V. 44

Iron, Its History, Properties & Processes of Manufacture. Edinburgh: 1865. V. 39; 44

On the Application of Cast and Wrought Iron to Building Purposes. London: 1857-58. V. 39

On the Application of Cast and Wrought Iron to Building Purposes. London: 1870. V. 45

On the Application of Cast and Wrought Iron to Building Purposes. London: 1864. V. 38

Report by Mr. Fairbairn to the Board of Trade of His Experiments for Ascertaining the Strength of Iron Structures. London: 1864. V. 44

Treatise on Iron Shipbuilding Its History and Progress . . . V. 41

Treatise on Mills and Millwork. London: 1861-63. V. 39

Treatise on Iron Ship Building . . . London: 1865. V. 44

Useful Information for Engineers . . . London: 1856. V. 44

Useful Information for Engineers. (First Series). London: 1860. V. 44

Useful Information for Engineers. (Second Series). London: 1860. V. 44

Useful Information for Engineers. (Third Series). London: 1874. V. 44

FAIRBANKS, ARTHUR

Athenian Lekythoi. New York: 1907-14. V. 39; 44

FAIRBANKS, GEORGE R.

The History and Antiquities of the City of St. Augustine, Florida. New York: 1858. V. 37; 40; 43; 45

History of Florida from Its Discovery . . . in 1512 to the Close of the Florida War in 1842. Philadelphia: 1871. V. 43

Spaniards in Florida, Comprising the Notable Settlement of the Huguenots in 1564 and the History and Antiquities of St. Augustine, Founded A. D. 1565. Jacksonville: 1868. V. 44

FAIRBANKS' Pocket Atlas of the United States and a Minature Railway Guide . . . New York: 1859. V. 45

FAIRBRIDGE, CHARLES

Catalogue of Books Relating to South Africa. Cape Town: 1886. V. 44

FAIRBRIDGE, DOROTHEA

Historic Farms of South Africa . . . 1931. V. 44
Historic Farms of South Africa . . . Oxford: 1931. V. 42

FAIRBRIDGE, R. W.

The Encyclopaedia of Climatology. London: 1986. V. 38

FAIRCHILD, G. M.

A Short Account of Ye Quebec Winter Carnival, Holden in 1894. Quebec: 1894. V. 43

FAIRCHILD, LUCIUS

Water Communication Between the Mississippi and the Lakes. Madison: 1870. V. 42; 44

FAIRCHILD, T.

The City Gardener . . . Ever-Greens, Fruit-Trees, Flowering Shrubs, Flowers . . . London: 1722. V. 43

FAIRFAX-BLAKEBOROUGH, J.

Northern Turf History. London: 1948-73. V. 42

FAIRFAX MURRAY, CHARLES

Catalogue of a Collection of Early French Books. London: 1961. V. 45

FAIRFAX, NATHANIEL

A Treatise on the Bulk and Slevedge of the World. Wherein the Greatness, Littleness and Lastingness of Bodies is freely Handled. With an Answer to the Tentamine de Deo of Samuel Parker. London: 1674. V. 37

FAIRFAX, THOMAS

The Complete Sportsman: or, Country Gentleman's Recreation. London: 1760. V. 39; 43

The Complete Sporstman. London: 1760. V. 39

The Complete Sportsman. London: 1760? V. 44

The Complete Sportsman; or Country Gentleman's Recreation . . . London: 1765. V. 43

A Declaration or Representation from His Excellency Sir Thomas Fairfax, and the Army Under His Command . . . London: 1647. V. 40

The Fairfax Correspondence: Memoirs of the Reign of Charles the First. London: 1848. V. 46

A Manifesto From His Excellency Sir Thomas Fairfax, and the Army Under His Command . . . Cambridge: 1647. V. 43

The New Complete Sportsman; or, The Town and Country Gentleman's Recreation. London. V. 45

A Petition from His Excellency Sir Thomas Fairfax, and the General Council of the Officers of the Army . . . Concerning the Draught of an Agreement of the People For a Secure and Present Peace, by them Framed and Prepared . . . London: 1649. V. 40

A Remonstrance of His Excellency Thomas Lord Fairfax, Lord Generall of the Parliaments Forces, ad of the General Councell of Officers Held at St. Albans the 16 of November, 1648. London: 1648. V. 40

FAIRFIELD, ASA MERRILL

Fairfield's Pioneer History of Lassen County, California. San Francisco: 1916. V. 38; 40

FAIRFIELD, SUMNER L. 1803-1844

Lays of Melpomene. Portland: 1824. V. 41

FAIRFIELD, SUMNER LINCOLN 1803-1844

The Last Night of Pompeii: a Poem; and Lays and Legends. New York: 1832. V. 42; 45

The Passage of the Sea; a Poem. New York: 1826. V. 45

FAIRHOLME, GEORGE

New and Conclusive Demonstrations Both of the Fact and Period of the Mosaic Deluge. London: 1837. V. 38

FAIRHOLT, F. W.

Gog and Magog. London: 1859. V. 39

Tobacco: Its History and Associations. London: 1876. V. 39

FAIRHOLT, FREDERICK W.

Miscellanea Graphica . . . London: 1857. V. 44

FAIRLESS, MICHAEL

An Excerpt from the Roadmender. Chicago: 1933. V. 43

The Gathering of Brother Hilarius. London: 1913. V. 42

The Gathering of Brother Hilarius. 1913. V. 37

FAIRLEY, W.

Glossary of Terms Used in the Coal-Mining Districts of (First) South Wales (Second) Bristol and Somersetshire. London: 1868. V. 40

FAIRLIE, ROBERT F.

Railways or No Railways. London: 1872. V. 37; 40

FAIRMAN, CHARLES E.

Art and Artists of the Capitol of the United States of America. Washington: 1927. V. 42; 46

FAIRMAN, E. JOHN

Trattato Sulle Zone Petroleifere d'Italia. Bologna: 1876. V. 43

FAIRMAN, HENRY CLAY

The Third World. New York & London: 1896. V. 38

FAIRMAN, WILLIAM

An Account of the Public Funds Transferable at the Bank of England, and of the Stocks of some of the Principal Public Companies in London. London: 1824. V. 38

The Stocks Examined and Compared. London: 1802. V. 37; 38; 46

The Stocks Examined and Compared . . . London: 1808. V. 41

THE FAIRY Family. London: 1857. V. 39

A FAIRY Garland. London: 1928. V. 38; 40; 43

FAIRY Garland, Being Fairy Tales from the Old French. New York. V. 41

A FAIRY Garland: Being Fairy Tales from the Old French. New York: 1928. V. 39

A FAIRY Garland, Being Fairy Tales From the Old French. London: 1929. V. 40

FAIRY Tales of the Allied Nations. London: 1915. V. 40

FAIRY Tales with Fairy Pictures. Snowy White and Rosy Red. London: 1881. V. 42

THE FAIRY'S Revel, or, Puck's Trip Thro' London by Moon Light. London: 1770. V. 40

A FAITHFUL Account of Catherine Mewis of Barton-under-Needwood, Staffordshire, Aged Seven Years, who for More than Twelve Months, Has and Still Continues, to be Deprived of Her Eye Signt, Six Days Out of Seven . . . London: 1810. V. 39

A FAITHFUL and Authentic Accout of the Siege and Surrender of St. Philip's Fort, in the Island of Minorca. Containing every particular occurence and remarkable incident during the defence of that important fortress . . . Drawn up from . . . London: 1757. V. 37

FAITHFUL, EMILY

Three Visits to America. New York: 1884. V. 37

FAITHFUL Friends: Pictures and Stories for Little Folk. New York: 1913. V. 40

FAITHFUL Narrative of the Proceedings in a Late Affair Between the Rev. Mr. John Swinton and Mr. George Baker, both of Wardham College, Oxford; Wherein the Reasons that Induced Mr. Baker to Acuse Mr. Swintopn of Sondomitical Practices . . . London: 1739. V. 38

A FAITHFUL Picture of the Political Situation of New Orleans, at the Close of the Last and the Beginning of the Present Year 1807. Boston: 1808. V. 42

A FAITHFUL Relation of the Most Remarkable Transactions Which Have Happened at Tangjier; Since the Moors Have Lately Made Their Attacques Upon the Forts and Fortifications of that Famous Garrison. London?: 1681. V. 42

THE FAITHFUL, Yet Imperfect Character of a Glorious King, King Charles I. His Country's & Religion's Martyr. London: 1660. V. 40

FAITHFULL, EMILY 1835-1895

Three Visits to America. Edinburgh: 1884. V. 39; 42

Three Visits to America. New York: 1884. V. 38; 43; 46

FAITHORN, JOHN

Facts and Observations on Liver Complaints, and Bilious Disorders in General. Philadelphia: 1822. V. 40

FAITHORNE, WILLIAM

The Art of Graveing and Etching . . . London: 1662. V. 38

FAKHRY, AHMED

The Egyptian Deserts. Cairo: 1942-50. V. 44

The Egyptian Deserts. The Necropolis of El-Bagawat in Kharga Oasis. Cairo: 1951. V. 44

The Monuments of Sneferu at Dahshur. Cairo: 1959-61. V. 42

The Monuments of Sneferu at Dahsher. Cairo: 1961. V. 44

Siwa Oasis, Its History and Antiquities. Cairo: 1944. V. 37; 40; 42

FALCKE, DAVID

Catalogue of the Magnificent Collection of Works of Art and Vertu, Formed by Mr. David Falcke, of New Bond Street . . . Sold by Auction by Messrs. Christie and Manson at their Great Room 8 King St. St. James's Sq. on Mon. April 19. V. 44

Catalogue of the Magnificent Collection of Works of Arat and Vertu . . . London: 1858. V. 38; 43

FALCONAR, WILLIAM

A Journey from Joppa to Jerusalem in May 1751. London: 1753. V. 41

FALCONBRIDGE, ANNA MARIA

Two Voyages to Sierra Leone, During the Years 1791-2-3. London: 1794. V. 43

FALCONER, J.

Cryptomenysis Patefacta; or the Art of Secret Information Disclosed Without a Key. London: 1685. V. 41; 43

FALCONER, RICHARD

The Voyages, Dangerous Adventures and Imminent Escapes of Captain Richard Falconer . . . London: 1710. V. 46

FALCONER, THOMAS 1805-1882

Letters and Notes on the Texan Santa Fe Expedition 1841-1842. New York: 1930. V. 37; 38; 39; 40; 42; 43; 44

Notes of a Journey through Texas and New Mexico in the Years 1841 and 1842. London: 1843. V. 44

I. On the Nomination of Agents Fromerly Appointed to Act in England for the Colonies of North America. II. A Brief Statement of the Dispute Between C. Metcalf and the House of Assembly of the Province of Canada. 1844. London: 1844. V. 39

The Oregon Question, or a Statement of the British Claims to the Oregon Territory. London: 1845. V. 39; 41

Texan Santa Fe Expedition, 1841-2. New York: 1930. V. 46

FALCONER, WILLIAM

A Dissertation on the Influence of the Passions Upon Disorders of the Body . . . London: 1788. V. 38; 40; 45

A Dissertation on the Influence of the Passions Upon Disorders of the Body. London: 1791. V. 42

The Mariner's New and Complete Naval Dictionary in Two Parts . . . London: 1804. V. 40

A New Universal Dictionary of the Marine. London: 1815. V. 41

Observations on Dr. Cadogan's Dissertation on the Gout and All Chronic Diseases. Bath. V. 38

Observations Respecting the Pulse . . . London: 1796. V. 42; 46

The Poetical Works. London: 1836. V. 45

A Practical Dissertation on the Medicinal Effects of the Bath Waters.. Bath: 1807. V. 37

Remarks on the Influence of Climate, Situtation, Nature of Country, Population, Nature of Food, and Way of Life on the Disposition and Temper, Manners and Behaviour . . . London: 1781. V. 40

The Ship Wreck. London: 1785. V. 38; 40

The Shipwreck. London: 1804. V. 37; 38; 40; 43; 45

The Shipwreck. London: 1811. V. 37; 38; 41; 45

The Shipwreck: A Poem. With a Life of the Author by J.S. Clarke. London: 1811. V. 37

An Universal Dictionary of the Marine. London: 1769. V. 38; 39; 42

An Universal Dictionary of the Marine . . . London: 1776. V. 38; 41; 42

An Universal Dictionary of the Marine . . . London: 1784. V. 38; 42

FALCOX, AYMAR

De Tvta Fidelivm Navigatione Inter Varias Peregrinoru Dogmatu nec Non Claudicantiu Opinioum Fluctuationes Dialogi. X. Lyon: 1536. V. 38

FALDA, GIOVANNI BATTISTA

Li Giardini di Roma con Le Loro Piante Alzate e Vedute in Prospettiva Disignate ed Intagliate da Gio. Battista Falda. Rome: 1683? V. 38

Il Nuovo Teatro Delle Fabriche et Edificii in Prospettiva di Roma Moderna, Sotto il Felice Pontificato di N. S. Papa Alessandro VII. Rome: 1665-1739. V. 37

Il Nuovo Teatro delle Fabriche et Edificii in Prospettiva di Roma Moderna, Sotto il Felice Pontificato di N. S. Papa Alessandro VII. Rome: G.G. de Rossi (Books 1: 1665/nd/99/1739. V. 41

FALILEI, GALILEO

Discorso al Serenissimo Don Cosimo II. Gran Duca di Toscana Intorno alle Cose, Che Stanno in su l'Acqua . . . Firenze: 1612. V. 38

FALK, BERNARD

Thomas Rowlandson: His Life and Art. London: 1949. V. 42

Thomas Rowlandson: His Life and Art. 1950. V. 39

Thomas Rowlandson, His Life and Art. New York: 1952. V. 37; 40; 46

FALKE, JACOB VON

Art in the House. Boston: 1879. V. 39; 41; 42; 46

FALKE, OTTON VON

Decorative Silks. New York: 1936. V. 43

FALKENER, EDWARD

Daedalus. London: 1860. V. 37; 39

Ephesus, and the Temple of Diana. London: 1862. V. 37; 39; 40; 42; 43; 44; 45

FALKLAND, AMELIA

Chow-Chow. London: 1930. V. 45

FALKLAND, HENRY CARY, 1ST VISCOUNT d. 1633

The History of the Most Unfortunate Prince King Edward II. London: 1680. V. 45

FALKLAND, LUCIUS CARY, VISCOUNT d. 1633

Sir Lucius Cary, Late Lord Viscount of Falkland, His Discourse of Infallibility, with an Answer to It and His Lordships Reply. London: 1651. V. 40

FALKNER, J. MEADE

The Lost Stradivarius. London: 1895. V. 43

FALKNER, THOMAS

An Historical and Topographical Description of Chelsea and Its Environs . . . London: 1829. V. 37

FALL, BERNARD

Hell in a Very Small Place. Philadelphia: 1966. V. 44

FALL, BERNARD B.

Hell in a Very Small Place. Philadelphia: 1967. V. 45

FALL, MARCUS RICHARD DOWLING

London Town: Sketches of London Life and Chracter. London: 1880. V. 40

THE FALL of the Niebelungers: Otherwise the Book of the Kriemhild. Translated by William Nanson Lettsom. London: 1850. V. 37

FALL, THOMAS

The Surveyor's Guide; Or, Every Man His Own Road Maker. Retford: (1827). V. 37

FALLA, R. A.

Birds (of the B.A.N.Z. Antarctic Research Expedition 1929-31 Under the Command of Sir Douglas Mawson. Adelaide: 1937. V. 43

FALLE, PHILIP

An Account of the Isle of Jersey, the Greatest of Those Island that are Now the Only Remainder of the English Dominons in France. London: 1694. V. 45

An Account of the Island of Jersey, with an Appendix of Records . . . Jersey: 1837. V. 43

Caesarea; or, An Account of Jersey, the Greatest of the Islands Remaining to the Crown of England of the Ancient Dutchy of Normandy . . . London: 1734. V. 9

FALLOON, E. L., MRS.

Wild Flowers from the Glens, by E. L. L. London: 1840. V. 43

FALLOPIO, GABRIELE

Secreti Diuersi e Miracolosi. Raccolti Dal Faloppia & Approbati da Altri Medici di Gran Sama . . . Venice: 1578. V. 41

FALLOPPIO, GABRIELE

De Medicatis Aquis, Atque de Fossilibus Tractatus Pulcherrimus, ac Maxime utilis . . . Venetiis: 1564. V. 38

De Medicatis Aquis, Atque de Fossilibus . . . Venice: 1564. V. 43

FALLOUT Protection; What to Know and What to Do About Nuclear Attack. Washington: 1961. V. 46

FALLS, DE WITT C.

The Comic Military Alphabet. New York: 1894. V. 44

FALSEHOOD and Forgery Detected and Exposed, or the Conduct of Thomas Jefferson, James Madison, James Monroe, Albert Gallatin, Levin Lincoln, John Gailliard, Wm. H. Crawford, Samuel M'Clay, Gen. Samuel Smith, Andrew Gregg and Other . . . Philadelphia: 1823. V. 42

FALSTAFF, JOHN

Original Letters, &c. of Sir John Falstaff, Selected from Genuine Manuscripts Which Have Been in the Possession of Dame Quickly and Her Descendants Near Four Hundred Years . . . Philadelphia: 1813. V. 37

THE FAMER'S Lawyer: Being a Manual of the Law of Scotland in Relation to Agricultural Subjects. Edinburgh: 1841. V. 45

FAME'S Trumpet, Twenty Rhymes. Brisbane: 1982. V. 39

FAME'S Trumpet: Twenty Traditional Nursery Rhymes. 1982. V. 40

A FAMILIAR Epistle from a Student of the Middle Temple. Dublin: 1771. V. 40

FAMILIAR Letters from a Gentleman at Damascus to His Sister in London. London: 1750. V. 46

THE FAMILY and Guest (in the United States), by the Father. New York: 1850. V. 43

THE FAMILY Guide to Health; or, a General Practice of Physic. London: 1767. V. 46

FAMILY-PRAYERS, and Moral Essays, in Prose and Verse. London: 1769. V. 45

THE FAMOUS History of Fryer Bacon: Containing the Wonderful Things That He Did in His Life . . . London: 1766. V. 41

FAMOUS Men of the United States. Philadelphia: 1848. V. 44
FAMOUS Men of the United States. Philadelphia: 1855. V. 39

FAMUEL, M.

La Logistique. Ou Arithmetique Francois . . . a Laquelle il ajoute le Toise des Bois & l'Arithmetique Decimale . . . A Metz: 1690. V. 37

THE FAN. Norwich: 1749. V. 40; 46

FANCOURT, CHARLES ST. JOHN

The History of Yucatan From Its Discovery to the Close of the Seventeenth Century. London: 1854. V. 37

FANE, J. H. C.

Tannhauser, or the Battle of the Bards. Mobile: 1863. V. 37

FANE, JULIAN H. C.

Tannhauser; or, the Battle of the Bards. Mobile: 1863. V. 39; 46

FANEY, HERBERT

Early Printing in California, from Its Beginning in the Mexican Territory to Statehood, September 9, 1850. San Francisco: 1956. V. 38

FANFARE; a Musical Causerie. London: 1921-22. V. 40

FANFARE PRESS

A Book of Fanfare Ornaments. 1938. V. 40

FANNIN & CO., DUBLIN

Fannin & Co., Illustrated Catalogue and Price List of Surgical Instruments and Medical Appliances. Dublin: 1908. V. 43

FANNING, EDMUND

Voyages Round the World . . . New York: 1833. V. 37; 41; 42

Voyages and Discoveries in the South Seas 1792-1832. Salem: 1924. V. 41

FANNING, NATHANIEL

Fanning's Narrative: Being the Memoirs of . . . New York: 1912. V. 42

Fanning's Narrative: the Memoirs of Nathaniel Fanning, an Officer of the American Navy, 1778-1783. New York: 1913. V. 46

FANNING, PETER

Great Crimes of the West. San Francisco: 1929. V. 39

FANSHAWE, ANNE

Memoirs of Lady Fanshawe, Wife of the Right Hon. Sir Richard Fanshawe . . . London: 1829. V. 42

FANSHAWE, E. L.

Liquor Legislation in the United States and Canada . . . London: 1892. V. 46

FANSHAWE, RICHARD

Original Letters . . . During His Embassies in Spain and Portugal . . . London: 1701. V. 38

Original Letters and Negotiations of His Excellency, Sir Richard Fanshawe, the Earl of Sandwich, the Earl of Sunderland, and Sir William Godolphin . . . London: 1724. V. 39

Il Pastor Fido. The Faithfull Shepherd. London: 1648. V. 38

FANTASTIC Adventures. Chicago: 1939-42. V. 37

FANTASY in Wood-Block, 'Or What Occurred When John James Audubon, the Naturalist Visited with Thomas Bewick, the Wood Engraver, in the Year 1827.' Chicago: 1972. V. 41

FANTE, JOHN

Ask the Dust. New York: 1939. V. 45

Dago Red. New York: 1940. V. 43

Full of Life. Boston: 1952. V. 44

Prologue to 'Ask the Dust'. 1990. V. 45

Wait Until Spring, Bandini. New York: 1938. V. 37

FANTI, VINCENZIO

Descrizzione Completa di Galleria di Pittura e Scultura di Sua Altezza Giuseppe Wenceslao . . . Della Casa di Lichtenstein. Vienna: 1767. V. 40

FANTI, VINZENZ ANTON JOSEPH 1719-1776

Descrizzione Completa di Galleria di Pittura e Scultura di . . . Casa di Liechtenstein. Vienna: 1767. V. 40

FANTUZZI, GIOVANNI

Universi Orbis Structura, et Partium Eius Principum Motus, et Quies Peripateticis Principiis Constabilita. Bologna: 1637. V. 38

FAR, ISABELLA

Giorgio de Chirico. New York: 1968. V. 46

FARADAY, MICAHEL 1791-1867

Experimental Researches in Chemistry and Physics. London: 1859. V. 45

FARADAY, MICHAEL 1791-1867

Chemical Manipulation: . . . . London: 1827. V. 44

Chemical Manipulation. Philadelphia: 1831. V. 40

A Course of Six Lectures on the Chemical Composition of a Candle . . . London: 1861. V. 38; 40; 42; 43; 45; 46

A Course of Six Lectures on the Chemical History of a Candle. New York: 1861. V. 38; 41

A Course of Six Lectures on the Chemical History of a Candle, To Which is Added a Lecture on Platinum . . . London: 1865. V. 40

Experimental Researches in Electricity. London: 1831-1855. V. 41

Experimental Researches in Electricity. London: 1839/44/55. V. 42

Experimental Researches in Chemistry & Physics. London: 1859. V. 38; 41; 42; 43

Experimental Researches in Electricity. London: 1878. V. 40

Experimental Researches in Electricity. London: 1880. V. 38; 40

Faraday's Diary. London: 1932-36. V. 37; 39

The Life and Letters. London: 1870. V. 45

Literature der medicin seit der Mitte des Achtzehnten Jahrhunderts bis auf die Neueste Zeit. London: 1862. V. 38

The Subject Matter of a Course of Six Lectures on the Non-Metallic Elements . . . London: 1853. V. 38; 40

FARCY, LOUIS DE

La Broderie Dux Xle Siecle Jusqu'a Nos Jours d'Apres des Specimens Authentiques et Les Anciens Inventaires. Angers: 1890. V. 43

FAREBROTHER, A.

Wages. A Story. London: 1873. V. 41

FAREHAM, ARTHUR LEE, VISCOUNT OF

A Good Innings and a Great Friendship Being the Life Story of Arthur and Ruth Lee. Woodchester: 1939-40. V. 39

FAREWELL Addresses, Presented to His Excellency, Sir Charles T Metcalfe, on the Occasion of His Resignation..and Departure from this Island, with His Excellency's Replies. Kingston: 1842. V. 38

FAREWELL Dinner to H. M. Tomlinson. New York: 1927. V. 38

FAREWELL to Washington of J. W. Forney, the Dinner to Him By His Contemporary Journalists of All Parties, His Hospitalities in Response, The Good-Bye of His Republican Associates. Philadelphia: 1871. V. 45

FAREWELLS. Long Crendon: 1927. V. 46

FAREY, JOHN

General View of the Agriculture and Minerals of Derbyshire. London: 1811-13. V. 40

FARGUS, FREDERICK JOHN

Living or Dead. London: 1886. V. 38

FARHNAM, ELIZA WOODSON

My Early Days. New York: 1859. V. 42

FARIA, FRANCISCO XAVIER DE

Vida Y Heroycas Virtudes del Vble. Padre Pedro de Velasco, Provincial que de la Compania de Jesus de Nueva Espana. Mexico: 1753. V. 39; 40; 42

FARIA Y SOUSA, MANUEL DE

Africa Portuguesa . . . Lisbon: 1681. V. 40

FARINA, RICHARD

Been Down So Long It Looks Like Up to Me. New York: 1966. V. 42

FARINGTON, J.

Britannia Depicta. London: 1816. V. 41

Magna Britannia. London: 1816. V. 42

FARINGTON, JOSEPH 1747-1821

The Diary of Joseph Farington. New Haven & London: 1978-84. V. 39

The Farington Diary. London: 1793-1821. V. 39

The Farington Diary 1793-1821. London: 1922-28. V. 41

The Farington Diary. London: 1923-8. V. 39

The Farington Diary. London: 1922-28. V. 37; 46

The Farington Diary. Edited by James Greig. London: 1922-1928. V. 37

The Lakes of Lancashire, Westmorland and Cumberland . . . London: 1816. V. 39; 44

Memoirs of the Life of Sir Joshua Reynolds . . . London: 1819. V. 46

FARINI, LUIGI CARLO

The Roman State from 1815 to 1850. London: 1851. V. 41; 43; 44; 46

FARISH, T. E.

History of Arizona. Phoenix: 1915-16. V. 37

FARISH, THOMAS E.

History of Arizona. Phoenix: 1915-18. V. 42

FARISH, THOMAS EDWIN

History of Arizona. Phoenix: 1915-16. V. 43

History of Arizona. Phoenix: 1915-20. V. 39

FARISH, WILLIAM

A Plan of a Course of Lectures on Arts and Manufactures, More Particularly Such as Relate to Chemistry. Cambridge: 1813. V. 37; 40

FARJEON, B. L.

The Mystery of M. Felix. London: 1890. V. 38

The Sacred Nugget. London: 1885. V. 41

FARJEON, BENJAMIN LEOPOLD

Grif, a Story of Australian Life. London: 1870. V. 37

FARJEON, ELEANOR

The Cock. London: 1923-1931. V. 41

The Country Child's Alphabet. London: 1924. V. 40

Elizabeth Myers. Aylesford: 1957. V. 37; 40; 42

Magic Casements. London: 1941. V. 38

Tomfooleries: Verses. London: 1920. V. 40

FARLEIGH, JOHN

Graven Image. London: 1940. V. 45

FARLEY, J. LEWIS

The Resources of Turkey Considered with Special Reference to the Profitable Investment of Capital in the Ottoman Empire. London: 1863. V. 43

FARLEY, JOHN

The London Art of Cookery. London: 1783. V. 42

London Art of Cookery and Housekeeper's Complete Assistant. London: 1783. V. 39

London Art of Cookery, and Housekeeper's Complete Assistant. London: 1800. V. 39

FARLOW, C., & CO., LTD.

C. Farlow & Co. Ltd., Fishing Tackle Manufactures. Croydon: 1919. V. 46

FARLOW, WILLIAM GILSON

Icones Farlowlanae. Cambridge: 1929. V. 44; 46

FARMAN, D.

Auto-Cars: Cars, Tramcars and Small Cars. London: 1896. V. 40; 46

FARMAN, DICK

The Aviator's Companion. London: 1910. V. 45

FARMBOROW, NICHOLAS

Fundamenta Grammatices; or, the Foundation of the Latin Tongue. London: 1679. V. 40

THE FARMER and Gardener's Directory . . . for Foretelling the Changes, Which Take Place in the Weather . . . Norwich. V. 39

FARMER, E. J.

The Resources of the Rocky Mountains . . . Cleveland: 1883. V. 39; 44

FARMER Hodge, or The Ludicrous, Serious, Droll and Descriptive Account of a Country Club. Halesworth: 1805. V. 42

FARMER, J. B.

An Essay on Liberty, and Other Poems. London: 1824. V. 42

FARMER, J. S.

Vocabularia Amatoria: A French English Glossary of words, phrases and allusions occurring in the works of Rabelais, Voltaire, Moliere, Rousseay, Beranger, Zola, and others, with English equivalents and synonyms. London: 1896. V. 37

FARMER, JOHN

The Concord (N.H.) Directory, Containing the Names of the Legal Votes and Householders . . . with Their Occupations (and) Places of Business . . . Concord: 1830. V. 37

The History of the Ancient Town, and Once Famous Abbey of Waltham. London: 1735. V. 45

Memorials of the Graduates of Harvard University in Cambridge, Massachusetts, Commencing with the First Class, 1642. Concord: 1833. V. 44

The New Military Guide . . . Organization of the Militia of New Hampshire . . . Duty of Officers . . . Concord: 1822. V. 41; 42

FARMER, JOHN S.

Americanisms - Old & New. London: 1889. V. 46

Merry Songs and Ballads. London: 1897. V. 40; 43

National Ballad and Song. Merry Songs and Ballads Prior to the Year 1800. London: 1897. V. 37; 38

'Twixt Two Worlds. London: 1866. V. 38

'Twixt Two Worlds. London: 1886. V. 40

Twixt Two Worlds. London: 1890. V. 39

Vocabula Amatoria. London: 1896. V. 40

FARMER, P.

Flesh. 1968. V. 43

FARMER, P., MRS.

The Captives and Other Poems. Laporte: 1856. V. 44

FARMER, PHILIP JOSE

The Fabulous Riverboat. 1971. V. 39

The Fabulous Riverboat. New York: 1971. V. 38

Flesh. Garden City: 1968. V. 37

The Green Odyssey. New York: 1957. V. 41; 42

Lord Tyger. Garden City: 1970. V. 42

Lord Tyger. New York: 1970. V. 37

The World of Tiers Comprising The Maker of Universes, The Gates of Creation, A Private Cosmos, Behind the Walls of Terra and the Lavalite World. 1980-83. V. 39

FARMER, RICHARD

Bibliotheca Farmeriana. A Catalogue of the Curious, Valuable and Extensive Library, in Print & Mss., of the Late Revd. Richard Farmer . . . . 1798. V. 38

Bibliotheca Farmeriana. A Catalogue of the Curious, Valuable and Extensive Library . . . of the Late Revd. Richard Farmer . . . London: 1798. V. 39; 41

An Essay on the Learning of Shakespeare. Cambridge: 1767. V. 39; 41; 42; 45; 46

FARMER, SILAS

The History of Detroit and Michigan: A Chronological Cyclopedia of the Past and Present. Detroit: 1884. V. 37

THE FARMER'S Lawyer; or Every Country Gentleman His Own Counsellor. London: 1774. V. 41

FARMILOE, EDITH

Piccalilli. London: 1900. V. 46

FARNABY, THOMAS

Index Rhetoricus et Oratius, Scholis & Institutioni Teneerioris Aetatis Accommodatus. London: 1713. V. 46

FARNBOROUGH, CHARLES LONG, BARON

A Temperate Discussion of the Causes Which Have Led to the Present High Price of Bread. London: 1800. V. 39

FARNEWORTH, ELLIS

The Life of Pope Sixtus the Fifth. London: 1754. V. 43

FARNHAM, ELIZA W. 1815-1864

California, In Doors and Out; or, How We Farm, Mine and Live Generally in the Golden State. New York: 1856. V. 37; 45

Life in Prairie Land. New York: 1846. V. 43

Life in Prairie Land. New York: 1847. V. 37

FARNHAM, ELIZA WOODSON 1815-1864

My Early Days. New York: 1859. V. 44

Woman and Her Era. New York: 1865. V. 44

FARNHAM, HENRY

Circular Statement of the Mississippi and Missouri Railroad Company, Embracing the Report of . . . New York: 1854. V. 37; 39

FARNHAM, J. E. C.

Providence to Dallas: a Brief Trip to the Southwest. Providence: 1897. V. 46

FARNHAM, THOMAS J.

Life, Adventures and Travels in California, To Which are Added the Conquest of California and Travels in Oregon. New York: 1849. V. 41; 42

Travels in the Great Western Prairies, the Anahuac and Rocky Moutains and in the Oregon Territory. Poughkeepsie: 1841. V. 37; 38; 39; 40; 43; 45

Travels in the Great Western Prairies, the Anahauc and Rocky Mountains and in the Oregon Territory. New York: 1843. V. 37; 42; 45

FARNHAM, THOMAS JEFFERSON

The Early Days of California: Embracing What I Saw and Heard There, with Scenes in the Pacific. Philadelphia: 1860. V. 45

History of the Oregon Territory . . . New York: 1844. V. 37; 39

Travels in the Great Western Priaires, the Anahuac and Rocky Mountains, and in the Oregon Territory. Ploughkeepsie (sic): 1843. V. 37; 39

Travels in the Californias and Scenes in the Pacific Ocean. New York: 1844. V. 45

FARNOL, JEFFREY

The Amateur Gentleman. London: 1916. V. 43

The Broad Highway. London: 1912. V. 43

FARNSWORTH, FREDERIC

The Man of the Mountain. Boston: 1818. V. 40

FARNSWORTH, R. W. C.

A Southern California Paradise. Pasadena: 1883. V. 40

FARQUARSON, ROBERT STUART

Reminiscences of Crimean Campaigning and Russian Imprisonment. London: 1883. V. 41

FARQUHAR, FERDINAND

The Relicks of a Saint. London: 1816. V. 46

FARQUHAR, FERDINAND, PSEUD.

The Relicks of a Saint. London: 1816. V. 39

FARQUHAR, FRANCIS P.

The Books of the Colorado River and the Grand Canyon: a Selective Bibliography. Los Angeles: 1953. V. 41; 43; 46
The Grizzley Bear Hunter of California. San Francisco: 1948. V. 37
History of the Sierra Nevada. Berkeley: 1965. V. 41
History of the Sierra Nevada. Berkeley and Los Angeles: 1965. V. 44
Mount Olympus. San Francisco: 1929. V. 41
Place Names of the High Sierra. San Francisco: 1926. V. 37; 44
Yosemite the Big Trees and High Sierra. Berkeley: 1948. V. 44; 46
Yosemite, the Big Trees and the High Sierra. Berkeley and Los Angeles: 1948. V. 40; 41; 43; 44
Yosemite, the Big Trees, and the High Sierra. Los Angeles: 1948. V. 46

FARQUHAR, FREDERICK

The Reclicks of a Saint. London: 1816. V. 39; 42; 45

FARQUHAR, GEORGE

The Beaux Strategem. Bristol: 1929. V. 42
Sir Harry Wildair; Being the Sequel to the Trip to Jubilee. London: 1701. V. 45
The Inconstant; or, the Way to Win Him. London: 1728. V. 42
The Plays of . . . London: 1735-36. V. 39
The Recruiting Officer: a Comedy . . . London: 1771. V. 45
The Recruiting Officer: a Comedy. London: 1926. V. 46
Sir Harry Wildair. London: 1701. V. 38
The Twin Rivals. Dublin: 1726. V. 42
The Works of the Late Ingenious Mr. George Farquhar. London: 1711. V. 38
The Works. Dublin: 1755. V. 38
The Works of the Late Ingenious Mr. George Farquhar. London: 1760. V. 40
The Works of the late Ingenious Mr. George Farquhar . . . London: 1772. V. 43
The Works . . . London: 1772. V. 43; 45
The Complete Works. Bloomsbury: 1930. V. 40; 41; 43; 46
The Complete Works. London: 1930. V. 42; 45; 46
The Works. London: 1987. V. 46

FARQUHAR, ROBERT TOWNSEND

Suggestions Arising from the Abolition of the African Slave Trade . . . London: 1807. V. 42

FARQUHAR, WILLIAM

Poems on Several Occasions, Consisting of Elegies and Epistles, Miscellanies and Scottish Pieces. Edinburgh: 1794. V. 43

FARQUHARSON, GEORGE

In the King's Bench. Manchester: 1822. V. 42; 46

FARR, DENNIS

William Etty. London: 1958. V. 39; 43
Wlliam Etty. English Master Painters Series. London: 1958. V. 37; 46

FARR, MICHAEL

Design in British Industry, A Mid-Century Sruvey. Cambridge: 1955. V. 44

FARRAGUT, D. G.

General Orders 10 through 13. Mobile Bay: 1864. V. 40

FARRAGUT, DAVID GLASGOW

Regulations for the Government of Commanders and Pursuers of the Vessels of the united States, and Recruiting Officers. Washington: 1838. V. 37

FARRAND, MAX

The Records of the Federal Convention of 1787. New Haven: 1911. V. 37

FARRAR, ELIZA WARE ROTCH

The Young Lady's Friend. Boston: 1836. V. 44

FARRAR, FERDINANDO RICHARD

Johnny Reb, the Confederate: and Rip Van Winkle, or the Virginian That Slept Ten Years . . . Richmond: 1869. V. 44

FARRAR, FREDERICK W.

Eric, or Little by Little. Edinburgh: 1858. V. 40

FARRAR, FREDERICK WILLIAM

The Life of Christ. London, Paris & New York: 1894. V. 42

FARRAR, JOHN 1779-1853

Elements of Electricity, Magnetism and Electro-Magnetism . . . Cambridge: 1826. V. 40
An Experimental Treatise on Optics, Comprehending the Leading Principles of Science, etc. Cambridge: 1826. V. 42

FARRAR, SAMUEL C.

The 22nd Pennsylvania Cavalry and the Ringgold Battalion 1861-1865. Pittsburgh: 1911. V. 42

FARRAR, TIMOTHY

Report of the Case of the Trustees of Dartmouth College Against William H. Woodward . . . Portsmouth: 1819. V. 39; 44

FARRE, H.

Sky Fighters of France. Boston: 1919. V. 38

FARRE, HENRY 1871-1934

Sky Fighters of France - Aerial Warfare, 1914-1918. Boston & New York: 1919. V. 46

FARRELL, F. A.

The 51st (Highland) Division War Sketches. Edinburgh: 1920. V. 44

FARRELL, FRED A.

The 51st (Highland) Division War Sketches. Edinburgh: 1920. V. 43

FARRELL, J. G.

A Girl in the Head. London: 1967. V. 38; 46

FARRELL, JAMES

The Lung. London: 1965. V. 40

FARRELL, JAMES T.

An American Dream Girl. New York: 1950. V. 41; 42
Calico Shoes and Other Stories. New York: 1934. V. 37
Ellen Rogers. New York: 1941. V. 39
Ellen Rogers. New York: 1951. V. 37
Gas-House McGinty. New York: 1933. V. 37; 45
It Has Come to Pass. New York: 1958. V. 39
Judgement Day. New York: 1935. V. 37; 41
Judgment Day. New York: 1936. V. 39
The League of Frightened Philistines. New York: 1945. V. 37
A Misunderstanding. New York: 1949. V. 42; 45; 46
$1,000 a Week and Other Stories. New York: 1942. V. 45
Reflections at Fifty and Other Essays. New York: 1954. V. 40; 46
This Man and This Woman. New York: 1951. V. 40
Tommy Gallagher's Crusade. New York: 1939. V. 37
Yet Other Waters. New York: 1952. V. 41; 42
Young Lonigan. New York: 1932. V. 42

FARRER, EDMUND

Portraits in Suffolk Houses (West). London: 1908. V. 44

FARRER, JAMES

Notice of Runic Inscriptions Discovered During Excavations in the Orkneys . . . London: 1862. V. 45
Notices of Runic Inscriptions Discovered . . . in the Orkneys. Edinburgh: 1862. V. 38; 40

FARRER, R.

Among the Hills. A Book of Joy in High Places. 1911. V. 46
The English Rock-Garden. London: 1938. V. 45

FARRER, REGINALD

The English Rock-Garden. London: 1925. V. 40
The English Rock-Garden. London: 1948. V. 44
The English Rock Garden. London: 1928. V. 37
On the Eaves of the World. London: 1917. V. 44; 46
On the Eaves of the World. London: 1917, 1926. V. 38
On the Eaves of the World. London: 1926. V. 44
The Plant Introductions of Reginald Farrer. London: 1930. V. 38
The Rainbow Bridge. London: 1921. V. 40

FARRER, RICHARD H.

A Tour in Greece 1880. Edinburgh: 1882. V. 37

FARRER, RICHARD RIDLEY

A Tour in Greece 1880. Edinburgh: 1882. V. 37

FARRER, WILLIAM

A History of the Parish of North Meols, in the Hundred of West Derby and County of Lancaster; with Historical and Descriptive Notices of Birkdale and Martin Mere. Liverpool: 1903. V. 39

FARRINGTON, JOSEPH

Memoirs of the Life of Sir Joshua Reynolds, with Some Observations on His Talents and Character. London: 1819. V. 42

FARRINGTON, OLIVE CUMMINGS

Gems and Minerals. Chicago: 1903. V. 38

FARRINGTON, S. KIP

Atlantic Game Fishing. New York: 1937. V. 45; 46

FARRIS, JOHN

Harrison High. New York: 1959. V. 44
King Windom. New York: 1967. V. 44; 45

FARROW, EDWARD S.

Mountain Scouting. A Hand-Book for Officers and Soldiers on the Frontiers. New York: 1881. V. 37; 45

FARROW, G. E.

Absurd Ditties. London: 1903. V. 41

FARROW, JOHN

Damien the Leper. New York: 1937. V. 45
Laughter Ends. New York: 1933. V. 44; 45
Seven Poems in Pattern. Cambridge: 1955. V. 41; 42

FARTHING Giles: A Poem Dedicated to Mrs. Wallis, of Seaham. Newcastle: 1784. V. 37

FARWELL, BYRON

Burton. A Biography of Sir Richard Francis Burton. London: 1963. V. 40

FARWELL, W. B.

Misrpresentation of Early California History Corrected. San Francisco: 1894. V. 40

FASSAM, THOMAS

An Herbarium for the Fair. Ditchling: 1949. V. 39
An Herbarium for the Fair. London: 1949. V. 40

FASSBENDER, ADOLF

Pictorial Artistry. New York: 1937. V. 39

FASSETT, F. G.

The Shipbuilding Business in the United States of America. New York: 1948. V. 41

FAST, HOWARD

Spartacus. New York: 1951. V. 46

THE FATAL Consequences To Be Feared (If not Speedily Prevented) by Our Assisting the Queen of Hungary, and the King of Sardinia in the Mediterranean, and on the Coasts of Italy, and From the Treaty We Entered into with Them at Worms in Sept. 1743 . . . London: 1744. V. 38; 41; 43

THE FATAL Effects of Gambling Exemplified in the Murder of Wm. Weare, and the Trial and Fate of John Thurtell, the Murderer, and His Accomplices . . . London: 1829. V. 42

FATE of the Steam-Ship President, Which Sailed from New-York, March 11th, 1841, Bound for Liverpool. Boston: 1845. V. 37; 40

FATHERLESS Fanny, or a Young Lady's First Entrance into Life, Being the Memoirs of a Little Mendicant and Her Benefactors. London: & Bristol: 1819. V. 42

THE FATHERS Legacy: or Councels to His Children. London: 1678. V. 38

FATIO DE DUILLIER, N.

Fruit Walls Improved, by Inclining Them to the Horizon. London: 1699. V. 37; 40

FATIO, GIULIO

De Mortificatione Nostrarum Passionum Pravorumque Affectuum. Ingolstadt: 1598. V. 37

FAUCHER, LEON

Manchester in 1844; Its Present Condition and Future Prospects . . . London: 1844. V. 42

FAUCHET, CLAUDE

Recueil des Antiquitez Gauloises et Francoises. Paris: 1579. V. 43

FAUCHET, JOSEPH

A Sketch of the Present State of Our Political Relations with the United States of North-America. Philadelphia: 1797. V. 37

FAUDEL, HENRY

A Few Words on the Jewish Disabilities. London: 1848. V. 45

FAUGERES, MARGARETTA V.

The Posthumous Works of Ann Eliza Bleecker in Prose and Verse to which is added, a collection of Essays, Prose and Poetical by Margaretta V. Faugeres. New York: 1793. V. 37

FAUJAS DE SAINT-FOND, BARTHELEMY

Description des Experiences de la Machine Aerostatique de MM. De Montgolfier. Paris: 1783. V. 40

Travels in England, Scotland, and the Hebrides . . . London: 1799. V. 39

Voyage en Angleterre, en Ecosse et aux Iles Hebrides; ayant Pour Object les Sciences, les Arts, l'Histore Naturelle et les Moeurs . . . Paris: 1797. V. 38

FAUJAS DE SAINT FOND, BARTHOLEMY

A Journey through England and Scotland to the Hebrides in 1784. Glasgow: 1907. V. 44

FAULDS, HENRY

Nine Years in Nipon Sketches of Japanese Life and Manners. London: 1887. V. 40

FAULK, A.

Eighth Annual Session. Third Annual Message of Governor A.J. Faulk, to the Legislative Assembly of the Territory of Dakota. Yankton, Dakota Territory: 1868. V. 37

FAULK, A. J.

Eighth Annual Session. Third Annual Message of Governor . . . to the Legislative Assembly of the Territory of Dakota. Yankton: 1868-69. V. 45

Sixth Annual Session. First Annual Message of Governor . . . to the Legislative Assembly of the Territory of Dakota. Yankton: 1866. V. 45

FAULKNER, ALEXANDER

The Orientalist's Grammatical Vade-Mecum . . . Bombay: 1853. V. 44

FAULKNER, CHARLES JAMES

The Speech of Charles Jas. Faulkner (of Berkeley) . . . on the Policy of the State with Respect to Her Slave Population . . . Richmond: 1832. V. 40

FAULKNER, FRITZ

Windless Sky. London: 1936. V. 40

FAULKNER, H. W. WALDRON

Measured Drawings of Woodwork. New York: 1925. V. 44

FAULKNER, HENRY

Elephant Haunts, Being a Sportman's Narrative of the Search for Doctor Livingstone . . . London: 1868. V. 43

FAULKNER, JOHN

Men Working. New York: 1941. V. 45

FAULKNER, JOSEPH P.

Eighteen Months on a Greeland Whaler. New York: 1878. V. 37; 39; 41; 43; 44; 45

FAULKNER, R. O.

The Ancient Egyptian Coffin Texts. Warminster: 1977-78. V. 40
The Ancient Egyptian Pyramid Texts. Oxford: 1969. V. 40

FAULKNER, RAYMOND O.

The Ancient Egyptian Coffin Texts. Oxford: 1969-70. V. 42

FAULKNER Studies. Denver & Minneapolis: 1952-54. V. 40

FAULKNER, THOMAS

The History and Antiquities of Brentford, Ealing & Chiswick. London: 1845. V. 39

FAULKNER, WILLIAM 1897-1962

Jealousy and Episode: Two Stories. Minneapolis: 1955. V. 46
Light in August. New York: 1932. V. 46
The Speech of Acceptance Upon the Award of the Nobel Prize . . . Stockholm 1950. New York. V. 44
William Faulkner Reads From His Works. New York: 1954. V. 44

FAULKNER, WILLIAM CUTHBERT 1897-1962

Absalom, Absalom! New York: 1936. V. 37
As I Lay Dying. New York: 1930. V. 37
Collected Stories. London: 1951. V. 37
Doctor Martino and Other Stories. New York: 1934. V. 37
Early Prose and Poetry. London: 1963. V. 37
Elmer. Northport: 1983. V. 37
A Fable. New York: (1954). V. 37
Father Abraham. New York: 1983. V. 37
Faulkner on Love: a Letter to Marjorie Lyons. Fargo: 1974. V. 37
Flags in the Dust. New York: 1973. V. 37
Go Down, Moses. London: 1942. V. 37
Go Down, Moses and Other Stories. New York: 1942. V. 37
A Green Bough. New York: 1933. V. 37
The Hamlet. 1940. V. 37
The Hamlet. New York: 1940. V. 37
Idyll in the Desert. New York: 1931. V. 37
Intruder in the Dust. New York: 1948. V. 37
Jealousy and Episode. Minneapolis: 1955. V. 37
Knight's Gambit. New York: 1949. V. 37
Light in August. New York: 1932. V. 37
Light in August. London: 1933. V. 37
The Mansion. New York: 1959. V. 37
The Marble Faun. Boston: 1924. V. 37
Marionettes: a Play in One Act. Oxford: 1975. V. 37
Mirrors of Chartres Street. Introduction by William Van O'Connor. Illustrated by Mary Demopoulos. Minneapolis: (1953). V. 37
Mississippi Poems. Oxford: 1979. V. 37
Mosquitoes. New York: 1927. V. 37
New Orleans Sketches. Tokyo: 1955. V. 37
The Nobel Prize Speech. New York: 1951. V. 37
Notes on a Horse Thief. Greenville: 1950. V. 37
Pylon. New York: 1935. V. 37
The Reivers. New York: 1962. V. 37
The Reivers, A Reminiscence. New York: (1962). V. 37
Requiem for A Nun. New York: 1951. V. 37
Salmagundi. Milwaukee: 1932. V. 37
Salmagundi. And a Poem by Ernest Hemingway. Milwaukee: 1932. V. 37
Sanctuary. London: 1931. V. 37
Sanctuary. New York: 1931. V. 37
Sartoris. New York: 1929. V. 37
Soldier's Pay. New York. V. 37
Soldier's Pay. New York: 1926. V. 37
Soldiers' Pay. London: 1930. V. 37
The Sound and the Fury. New York: (1929). V. 37
These 13. New York: 1931. V. 37
These Thirteen. London: 1933. V. 37
This Earth. New York: 1932. V. 37
The Town. New York: 1957. V. 37
The Unvanquished. New York: 1938. V. 37
Vision in Spring. Austin: 1984. V. 37
The Wild Palms. New York: 1939. V. 37
William Faulkner's Letters to Malcolm Franklin. Irvin: 1976. V. 37
The Wishing Tree. New York: 1967. V. 37
The Wishing Tree. New York: 1967, c. 1964. V. 37

FAULKNER, WILLIAM HARRISON 1897-1962

Absalom, Absalom. London: 1935. V. 44
Abaslom, Absalom! New York: 1936. V. 38; 39; 42; 43; 46
Absalom, Absalom! New York: 1986. V. 39
As I Lay Dying. London: 1930. V. 40; 43
As I Lay Daying. New York: 1930. V. 38; 39; 41; 42; 43; 44; 45; 46
As I Lay Dying. New York: 1933. V. 41
Mientras Agonizo. Madrid: 1957. V. 40
The Bear. Paderborn: 1958. V. 44
Big Woods. New York: 1955. V. 42; 43
Big Woods: The Hunting Stories. New York: 1955. V. 46
Collected Stories of William Faulkner. New York: 1943. V. 42; 44
The Collected Stories of William Faulkner. 1950. V. 45
Collected Stories. New York: 1950. V. 43; 45; 46
Collected Stories of William Faulkner. New York: 1950. V. 39; 41; 42
Collected Stories of . . . London: 1951. V. 43
Doctor Martino. New York: 1934. V. 38; 39; 42; 43
Doctor Martino and Other Stories. New York: 1934. V. 38; 39; 41; 43; 46
Elmer. Northport: 1983. V. 45

A Fable. New York: 1954. V. 39; 41; 42; 43; 44; 45; 46
A Fable. New York: 1954. V. 39
A Fable. London: 1955. V. 46
Father Abraham. New York: 1983. V. 38; 42; 44; 45
Father Abraham. New York: 1983. V. 45
Faulkner at Nagano. Tokyo: 1956. V. 40; 44; 45
Faulkner's County: Tales of Yoknapatawpha County, Chosen by the Author. London: 1955. V. 44
Go Down Moses, and Other Stories. London: 1942. V. 46
Go Down, Moses and Other Stories. New York: 1942. V. 39; 41; 42; 43; 44; 45; 46
Go Down Moses. New York: 1942. V. 38; 40; 43; 45; 46
Go Down, Moses. London: 1943. V. 38
A Green Bough. New York: 1933. V. 39; 42; 43; 44; 45; 46
A Green Bough. New York: 1938. V. 41
The Hamlet. New York: 1940. V. 38; 39; 41; 42; 43; 44; 45; 46
Le Hameau. Paris: 1959. V. 39
Helen: a Courtship. 1981. V. 39
Helen: A Courtship. Oxford: 1981. V. 45
Hunting Stories. New York: 1988. V. 40; 41; 42; 46
Idyll in the Desert. New York: 1931. V. 38; 39; 40; 41; 42; 43; 45; 46
Intruder in the Dust. New York: 1940. V. 42
Intruder in the Dust. 1948. V. 45
Intruder in the Dust. New York: 1948. V. 38; 39; 43; 46
Intruder in the Dust. London: 1949. V. 40; 45
Jealousy and Episode: Two Stories. Minneapolis: 1955. V. 39; 46
Knight's Gambit. New York: 1949. V. 43
Knight's Gambit. New York: 1949. V. 38; 41
Knight's Gambit: Stories. London: 1951. V. 43
Light in August. New York: 1932. V. 38; 39; 40; 41; 42; 43; 44; 45; 46
Light in August. Rahway: 1932. V. 46
Light in August. London: 1933. V. 43; 44
The Mansion. New York: 1959. V. 39; 41; 42; 43; 44; 45
The Marble Faun. Boston: 1924. V. 43; 45; 46
The Marionettes. Charlottesville: 1975. V. 46
Marionettes. Oxford: 1975. V. 45
The Marionettes. Virginia: 1975. V. 46
Mayday. 1798. V. 42
Mirrors of Chartres Street. Minneapolis: 1953. V. 38; 39; 45
Miss Zilphia Gant. Dallas: 1932. V. 42; 45; 46
Mississippi Poems. 1979. V. 39
Mississippi Poems. Oxford: 1979. V. 45
Mosquitoes. New York: 1927. V. 38; 39; 41; 42; 43; 45
New Orleans Sketches. Tokyo: 1955. V. 45; 46
New Orleans Sketches. New Brunswick: 1958. V. 39
The Nobel Prize Speech. New York: 1951. V. 39
Notes on a Horse Thief. Greenville: 1950. V. 38; 39; 40; 41; 42; 43; 44; 45; 46
Our Town. London: 1957. V. 43
Pylon. New York: 1935. V. 38; 39; 41; 42; 43; 45; 46
Pylon. 1935. V. 45
Pylon. London: 1935. V. 42
The Reivers. New York: 1962. V. 39; 42; 43; 46
Requiem for a Nun. New York: 1951. V. 38; 39; 40; 41; 42; 43; 44; 45; 46
Requiem for a Nun. New York: 1959. V. 39; 45
A Rose for Emily and Other Stories. New York: 1945. V. 45
Salmagundi. Milwaukee: 1932. V. 38; 40; 44; 45; 46
Salmagundi and a Poem by Ernest Hemingway. Milwaukee: 1932. V. 39
Salmagundi. (with) A Poem by Ernest Hemingway. Milwaukee: 1932. V. 46
Salmagundi By William Faulkner and a Poem by Ernest M. Hemingway. Milwaukee: 1932. V. 41
Sanctuary. 1931. V. 39
Sanctuary. London: 1931. V. 39; 43
Sanctuary. New York: 1931. V. 38; 39; 40; 43; 46
Sartoris. New York: 1929. V. 38; 42; 44; 45
Sartoris. London: 1932. V. 43
Soldier's Pay. New York: 1926. V. 38; 39; 40; 43; 45; 46
Soldier's Pay. London: 1930. V. 39; 40; 42; 44; 45; 46
A Sorority Pledge. Northport: 1983. V. 45
The Sound and the Fury. New York: 1929. V. 38; 39; 41; 43; 46
The Sound and the Fury. London: 1931. V. 41; 43; 44
These 13. New York: 1931. V. 38; 39; 40; 41; 42; 43; 44; 45; 46
These Thirteen. London: 1933. V. 42
This Earth. Equinox: 1932. V. 43
This Earth - a Poem. New York: 1932. V. 40; 41; 42; 43; 44

FAULKNER, WILLIAM HARRISON 1897-1962 continued

This Earth. New York: 1932. V. 39; 41; 46

Three Views of the Segregation Decisions. Atlanta: 1956. V. 41; 46

To the Voters of Oxford. Oxford: 1950. V. 39; 40; 43

The Town. New York: 1957. V. 39; 40; 41; 43; 44; 45; 46

The Unvanquished. New York: 1938. V. 38; 39; 41; 42; 44; 45; 46

Vision in Spring. Austin: 1984. V. 38; 39

the Wild Palms. London: 1939. V. 43

The Wild Palms. New York: 1939. V. 38; 39; 40; 41; 42; 43; 44; 45; 46

William Faulkner's Letters to Malcolm Franklin. Irving: 1976. V. 45

The Wishing Tree. New York: 1964. V. 45

The Wishing Tree. New York: 1967. V. 39; 44

FAUNA of Saudi Arabia. Basel: 1985. V. 37

FAUNTLEROY, JOSEPH

John Henry Nash Printer, by Joseph Fauntleroy. Oakland: 1948. V. 37; 39

FAUQUIER, FRANCIS

An Essay on Ways and Means for Raising Money for the Support of the Present War. London: 1756. V. 40; 41; 43

FAURE-FAVIER, LOUISE

Ces Choses qui Seront Vieilles. Paris: 1919. V. 38

FAURE, G.

The Gardens of Rome. New York: 1926. V. 45

FAUROT, C. S.

Resources, Wealth and Industrial Development of Colorado. N.P.: 1893. V. 44

FAUSSET, BRYANT

Inventorium Sepulchrate: an Account of Some Antiquites Dug Up at Gilton, Kingston, Sibertswold, Barfriston, Beakesborune, Chartham and Crundale, in the County of Kent from A.D. 1757 to A.D. 1773. London: 1856. V. 41

FAUST, ALBERT B.

Charles Sealsfield, (Carl Post) der Dichter Beider Hemispharen. Sein Leben und Seine Werke. Weimar. V. 39

Swiss Emigrants in the Eighteenth Century to the American Colonies. Washington: 1920-25. V. 42

FAUST, FREDERICK

Gunman's Gold. New York: 1939. V. 37

Silvertip Chase. New York: 1944. V. 37

Wine on the Desert. New York: 1940. V. 37

FAUTEUX, AEGIDIUS

The Introduction of Printing into Canada, a Brief History. Montreal: 1930. V. 39

The Introduction of Printing Into Canada. Montreal: 1957. V. 44

FAUVEL-GOURAUD, FRANCIS

Practical Cosmophonography. New York: 1850. V. 40

FAUVEL-GOURAUD, JEAN BAPTISTE FRANCOIS

Phrenomnemotechnic Dictionary . . . Part First (all published). New York: 1844. V. 38

FAUX, WILLIAM

Memorable Days in America. London: 1823. V. 38; 39; 45

FAVART, CHARLES SIMON

The Reapers: or the Englishman Out of Paris. London: 1770. V. 38

FAVENC, ERNEST

The History of Australian Exploration from 1788 to 1888 . . . London: 1888. V. 43

The History of Australian Exploration from 1788 to 1888. Sydney: 1888. V. 39

FAVENTIES, VALERIUS

De Montium Origine, Dialogus. Venice: 1561. V. 40

FAVISI, JEAN TEXIER DE

Officinae. Tomvs I. - Officinae . . . Seunda pars . . . -Cornucopiae, quo Continetur Loca Diuersis Rebus per Orbem Abundantia Secundum Literarum Ordienm Quam Antea Reposita. Lvgdvni: 1537. V. 39

FAVORITE Authors, a Companion Book of Prose and Poetry. Boston: 1861. V. 44
FAVORITE Authors, a Companion Book of Prose and Poetry. Boston: 1863. V. 43

FAVORITE Fairy Tales: The Childhood Choice of Representative Men and Women. New York: 1907. V. 37

FAVRE, ANTOINE 1557-1624

Codex Fabrianus Definitionum Forensium, et Rerum in Sacro Sabaudiae Senatu Tractatarum, ad Ordinem Titulorum Codicis Iustinianei. Lyon: 1661. V. 40

FAWCETT, BENJAMIN

Observations on the Nature, Causes and Cure of Melancholy . . . Shrewsbury: 1780. V. 37; 39; 42; 45; 46

FAWCETT, F. BURLINGTON

Broadside Ballads of the Restoration Period from the Jersey Collection Known as the Osterley Park Ballads . . . London: 1930. V. 43

FAWCETT, GRAHAM

Poems for Shakespeare 2. London: 1973. V. 38; 41

FAWCETT, H. W.

The Fighting at Jutland, Personal Experiences of 45 Officers and Men of the British Fleet on the Scene . . . London: 1917. V. 42

FAWCETT, HENRY 1833-1884

The Economic Position of the British Labourer. Cambridge and London: 1865. V. 39

FAWCETT, JOHN

An Essay on Anger. Leeds: 1788. V. 45

An Essay on Propagation of the Christian Religion. Cambridge: 1791. V. 39

Hymns Adapted to the Circumstances of Public Worship and Private Devotion. Leeds: 1782. V. 40

FAWCETT, W.

Rules and Regulations for the Sword Exercise of the Cavalry. Dublin: 1797. V. 38

FAWCETT, WILLIAM

Rules and Regulations for the Formations, Field Exercise and Movements of His Majesty's Forces. London: 1795. V. 42

Rules and Regulations for the Sword Exercise of the Cavalry. London: 1796. V. 37; 41; 46

FAWKES, FRANCIS

Original Poems and Translations. London: 1761. V. 42; 43; 45; 46

Original Poems. London: 1761. V. 40

FAWKES, ULLA S.

The Journal of Walter Griffith Pigman. New Mexico: 1942. V. 37

FAWKES, WALTER

The Chronology of the History of Modern Europe . . . York: 1810. V. 38; 40; 46

FAWTIER, ROBERT

Hand-List of Charters, Deeds and Similar Documents in the Possession of the John Rylands Library. Manchester: 1935. V. 42

FAXON, W.

Reports of Exploration off the West Coasts of Mexico, Central and South America and Off the Galapagos Islands by the 'Albatross' 1891, XV, The Stalk-Eyed Crutacea. Cambridge: 1895. V. 38

FAY, BERNARD

Notes on the American Press at the End of the 18th Century. New York: 1927. V. 37; 38; 39

FAY, GERDA

Poetry for Play Hours. London: 1860. V. 44

FAY, HERMAN A.

Collection of the Official Accounts, in Detail, of All the Battles Fought by Sea and Land, Between the Navy and Army of the United States, and the Navy and Army of Great Britain, During the Years 1812, 13, 14, and 15. New York: 1817. V. 45

FAY, SAM

A Royal Road: Being the History of the London & South Western Railway, from 1825 to the Present Time. London: 1883. V. 43

A Royal Road: Being the History of London and South Western Railway, from 1825 to the Present Time. Kingston-on-Thames: 1883. V. 38

FAY, THEODORE S.

The Countess Ida. New York: 1840. V. 39; 46

Hoboken: a Romance of New York. New York: 1843. V. 43; 45

Views in New-York and Its Environs, from Accurate, Characteristic and Picturesque Drawings, Taken on the Spot . . . New York: 1831-32? V. 39

Views in New York and Its Environs, from Accurate, Chracteristic & Picturesque Drawings . . . New York: 1831-34. V. 40

FAY, THEODORE SEDGWICK

Norman Leslie, a Tale of the Present Times. New York: 1835. V. 38

FAY, THEODORE SEDGWICK continued

Sketch of the Life of John Howard Payne, as Published in the Boston Evening Gazette . . . Boston: 1833. V. 43

Sydney Clifton; or, Vicissitudes in Both Hemispheres. New York: 1839. V. 45; 46

FAYLE, E.

Seaborne Trade, Official History of the Great War, 1914-1918, the Cruiser and Submarine Campaigns. London: 1920. V. 39

FAYRER, J.

H.R.H. The Duke of Edinburgh in India. Calcutta: 1870. V. 43

The Thanatophidia of India . . . the Venomous Snakes of the Indian Peninsula. London: 1872. V. 43

FEA, JAMES

Considerations on the Fisheries in the Scotch Islands: to which is prefixed a General Account elucidating the History, Soil, Productions, Curiosities, &c. of the same, the Manners of the Inhabitants, &c. Dover: 1787. V. 39

FEAR Itself: the Horror Fiction of Stephen King. 1982. V. 45

FEARING, F.

Reflex Action: a Study in the History of Physiological Psychology. Baltimore: 1930. V. 45

FEARING, KENNETH

Angel Arms. New York: 1929. V. 37; 39

FEARMAN, WILLIAM

Tales of My Landlord, New Series. London: 1820. V. 43

FEARNE, C.

An Essay on the Learning of Contingent Remainders and Executory Devises. London: 1809. V. 37

FEARNE, CHARLES 1742-1794

An Essay on the Learning of Contingent Remainders and Executory Devises. London: 1824. V. 40

FEARNSIDE, HENRY GRAY

Picturesque Beauties of the Rhine, Displayed in a Series of Eighty Splendid Views . . . London: 1840. V. 42

FEARNSIDE, W. G.

Eighty Picturesque Views on the Thames and Medway, Engraved on Steel by the First Artists. London: 1834. V. 46

FEARNSIDE, WILLIAM G.

The Thames and Medway. London: 1834. V. 40

FEARNSIDE, WILLIAM GRAY

The Great Metropolis; or, views and history of London in the nineteenth century . . . illustrated with splendid steel engravings. London: (c. 1860). V. 37

FEARON, HENRY B.

Sketches of America . . . London: 1819. V. 38; 39; 42; 45

FEARON, HENRY BRADSHAW

Sketches of America. London: 1818. V. 45

Sketches of America. London: 1818. V. 38; 39; 45

FEASEY, HENRY JOHN

Westminster Abbey. London: 1899. V. 40

FEASEY, J. EATON

Robin Hood and Other Stories of Yorkshire. London: 1913. V. 44

FEATHER, JOHN

English Book Prospectuses, an Illustrated History. Newtown: 1902. V. 41

English Book Prospectuses, an Illustrated History. Newtown: 1984. V. 37; 38; 39; 40; 41; 43; 46

English Book Prospectuses an Illustrated History. Newtown and Minneapolis: 1984. V. 39; 45

FEATHER, LEONARD

Inside Be-Bop. New York: 1949. V. 38; 39; 40; 42

THE FEATHERS, a Tale or, Venus Surpassed by a Beauty in Grosvenor Square. London: 1775. V. 40

FEATHERSTONAUGH, G. W.

A Canoe Voyage Up the Minnay Sotor; with an Account of the Lead and Copper Deposits in Wisconsin . . . London: 1847. V. 45

FEATHERSTONAUGH, GEORGE WILLIAM

Excursion through the Slave States, from Washington on the Potomac to the Frontier of New Mexico. London: 1844. V. 38

FEATHERSTONE, B. K.

An Unexplored Pass. London: 1926. V. 38

FEATHERSTONHAUGH, G. W.

A Canoe Voyage Up the Minnay Sotor. London: 1847. V. 41; 44

Geological Report of an Examination Made in 1834 of the Elevated Country Between the Missouri and Red Rivers. Washington: 1835. V. 42

Report of a Geological Reconnaissance Made in 1835, from the Seat of Government, By the Way of Green Bay and Wisconsin Territory to the Coteau De Prairie. 1836. V. 41

FEATHERSTONHAUGH, GEORGE W.

A Canoe Voyage Up the Minnay Sotor. London: 1847. V. 37

Geological Report of an Examination Made in 1834, of the Elevated Country Between the Missouri and Red Rivers. Washington: 1835. V. 37; 39; 42; 43; 46

FEATLEY, DANIEL

Clavis Mystica: a Key Oepning Divers Difficult and Mysterious Texts of Holy Scripture . . . London: 1636. V. 44

The Dippers Dipt, or, the Anabaptists Duck'd and Plung'd Over Head and Eares at a Disputation in Southwark. London: 1646. V. 39

Katabpostali Kataptustoi (in Greek). The Dippers Dept. or, The Anabaptists Duck'd and Plung'd Over Head and Eares . . . London: 1645. V. 46

Transubstantiation Exploded: or an Encounter with Richard the Titularie Bishop of Chacedon . . . . London: 1638. V. 45

FEATLY, DANIEL

Ancilla Pietatis. London: 1626-25. V. 38

FEATON, E. H.

The Art Album of New Zealand Flora. Wellington: 1889. V. 41; 46

FEAVER, WILLIAM

The Art of John Martin. Oxford: 1975. V. 39

FECHTER, PAUL

Das Graphische Werk Max Pechsteins. Berlin: 1921. V. 42

FEDDEN, ROBIN

Walter Smart by some of His Friends. London: 1963. V. 44

FEDER, JOHANN GEORG HEINRICH

Philosophische Bibliothek. Gottingen: 1788-91. V. 41

FEDER, NORMAN

American Indian Art. New York. V. 42

FEDERAL REPUBLIC OF CENTRAL AMERICA. CONSTITUTION

Constitucion Republicana Federal de Centro-America Dada por las Asamblea Nacional Constituyente en 22 de Noviembre de 1824. Guatemala: 1825. V. 40; 41

THE FEDERALIST. New York: 1788. V. 37
THE FEDERALIST. New York: 1802. V. 37
THE FEDERALIST. Philadelphia: 1826. V. 38
THE FEDERALIST. Hallowell: 1837. V. 38; 40
THE FEDERALIST: A Collection of Essays. Morrisania,: 1864. V. 43
THE FEDERALIST. New York: 1945. V. 43; 44

THE FEDERALIST: a Collection of Essays. New York: 1788. V. 44

THE FEDERALIST, On the New Constitution. New York: 1802. V. 40; 46
THE FEDERALIST, on the New Constitution. Hallowell: 1826. V. 46
THE FEDERALIST, on the New Constitution. Hallowell: 1842. V. 40

THE FEDERALIST, On the New Constitution . . . Philadelphia: 1818. V. 44

LE FEDERALISTE, ou Collection de Quelques Ecrits en Faveur de la Constitution Proposee Aux Etats-Unis de l'Amerique . . . Paris: 1795. V. 40; 46

FEDERER, CHARLES A.

Yorkshire Chap-Books. London: 1889. V. 43

FEDOROV

Collection des Uniformes de l'Armee Imperiale Russe Sous Nicolas. St. Petersburg: 1837. V. 39

FEDOROV, A.

Chromosome Numbers of Flowering Plants. London: 1974. V. 37

FEIBLEMAN, JAMES

Death of God in Mexico. New York: 1931. V. 41

FEIBLEMAN, JAMES KERN

Death of the God in New Mexico. New York: (1931). V. 37

FEIJOO Y MONTEGRO, BENITO JERONIMO 1676-1764

Theatro Critico Universl o Discursos Varios en Todo Genero de Materias, Para Desengano de Errores Communes . . . Madrid: 1781. V. 40; 45

FEIJOO Y MONTENEGRO, BENITO GERONIMO

Rules for Preserving Health, Particularly With Regard to Studious Persons. London: 1800. V. 42

FEILD, ROBERT

The Art of Walt Disney. New York: 1942. V. 45

FEILDS, ANNIE

The Singing Sheperd and Other Poems. Boston: 1895. V. 46

FEINAIGLE, GREGOR VON

The New Art of Memory, Founded Upon the Principles Taught by . . . London: 1813. V. 42; 43; 46

FEINT, ADRIAN

Adrian Feint, Flower Paintings. Sydney: 1948. V. 42

Flower Paintings. Sydney: 1948. V. 41

FEIST, CHARLES

Poetical Effusions; Comprising Poems, Ballads and Songs. London: 1813. V. 43

FEKULA, PAUL M.

The Paul M. Fekula Collection: a Catalogue. New York: 1988. V. 46

FELD, CHARLES

Picasso and His Recent Drawings 1966-1968. London: 1969. V. 46

FELDBORG, ANDREAS A.

Denmark Delineated . . . Edinburgh: 1824. V. 37; 43; 44; 45

FELDEN, BERNARD M.

Conservation of Historic Buildings. London: 1982. V. 39

FELGER, F. S.

People of the Desert and Sea. Ethnobotany of the Seri Indians. London: 1984. V. 37

FELIBIAN, ANDRE, SIEUR DES AVAUX ET DE JAVERCY 1619-1695

Des Principes de l'Architecture, de la Sculpture, De la Peinture. Paris: 1676. V. 44

FELIBIEN, JEAN FRANCOIS, SIEUR DES AVAUX 1658?-1723

Recueil Historique de la Vie et des Ouvrages des Plus Celebres Architectes. Paris: 1687. V. 44

FELICIANO, FELICE

Alphabetum Romanum. Verona: 1960. V. 37; 40; 41; 42; 44

Ippolito E Lionora, From a Manuscript of Felice Feliciano in the Harvard College Library. Cambridge: 1970. V. 41; 46

Ippolito e Lionora, from a Manuscript of Felice Feliciano in the Harvard College Library. Verona: 1970. V. 40

A FELICITY of Carols. West Burke: 1970. V. 39

FELIG, ARTHUR

Naked City. New York: 1945. V. 45

FELIPE II, KING OF SPAIN

Prematica, en Que se da la Orden Y Forma Que Se Ha De Tenner, Y Guardar, en Los Tratamientos y Cortesias de Palabras Y por Escrito: Y en Traer Coroneles, Y Ponellos en Qualesquier Partes Y Lugares. Mexico: 1600. V. 37

FELISSA; or the Life and Opinions of a Kitten of Sentiment. London: 1811. V. 46

FELKIN, WILLIAM

A History of the Machine-Wrought Hosiery and Lace Manufactures. London: 1867. V. 37; 42

A History of the Machine-Wrought Hoisery and Lace Manufactures. Cambridge: 1867. V. 37

FELL, ALFRED

The Early Iron Industry or Furness and District . . . Ulverston: 1908. V. 44

A Furness Manor: Pennington and Its Church. Ulverston: 1929. V. 44

A Furness Military Chronicle. Ulverston: 1937. V. 38; 44

FELL AND ROCK CLIMBING CLUB OF THE ENGLISH LAKE DISTRICT

Journal. London: 1907-21. V. 44

FELL, H. GRANVILLE

The Art of H. Davis Richter. Benfleet, Essex: 1935. V. 38

FELL, JOHN

Daemoniacs. An Enquiry Into the Heathen and the Scripture Doctrine of Daemons. London: 1779. V. 44

The Life of the Most Learned Reverend and Pious Dr. H. Hmmond. London: 1661. V. 38

A Specimen of the Several Sorts of Letter Given to the University by Dr. John Fell, Oxford, 1693. London: 1928. V. 38

Specimens of Books Printed at Oxford with the Types Given to the University by John Fell. Oxford: 1925. V. 44

FELL, MARGARET

A Brief Collection of Remarkable Passages and Occurrences . . . London: 1710. V. 45

FELL, R.

A Tour through the Batavian Republic During the Latter Part of the Year 1800. London: 1801. V. 38; 40

FELL, THOMAS

The Life of That Reverend Divine, and Learned Historian, Dr. Thomas Fuller. London: 1661. V. 38

FELLIG, ARTHUR

Naked Hollywood. New York: 1953. V. 37

FELLOW, JOHN

The Triumphs of the Cross, or Penitent of Egypt . . . Birmingham: 1776. V. 45

FELLOWES, EDMUND H.

The Tenbury Letters. London: 1942. V. 38

The Tenbury Letters. London: 1943. V. 43

FELLOWES, W. D.

Historical Sketches of Charles the First, Cromwell, Charles the Second and the Principal Personages of that Period Including the King's Trial and Execution . . . London: 1828. V. 37

A Visit to the Monastery of La Trappe in 1817. London: 1818. V. 40

A Visit to the Monastery of La Trappe in 1817. London: 1820. V. 40

A Visit to the Monastery of La Trappe in 1817. London: 1823. V. 37; 40; 44

FELLOWES, WILLIAM DORSET

A Narrative of the Loss of His Majesty's Packet the Lady Hobart, on an Island of Ice in the Atlantic Ocean, 28th of June, 1803 . . . London: 1803. V. 38

Narratives of Shipwrecks. Loss of the Lady Hobart Packet, of the Hon. East India Company's Ship Cabalva and of the Centaur and Litchfield Men-of-War. London: 1824. V. 46

A Visit to the Monastery fo La Trappe in 1817. London: 1818. V. 38; 39; 41; 46

A Visit to the Monastery of La Trappe in 1817, with Notes Taken During a Tour through Le Perche, Normandby, Bretagne, Poitou, Anjou, Le Bocage, Touraine, Orleanois,a nd the Environs of Paris. London: 1818. V. 39

A Visit to the Monastery of La Trappe in 1817. London: 1820. V. 38

A Visit to the Monastery of La Trappe in 1817. London: 1823. V. 38; 39; 46

FELLOWS, CHARLES

An Account of Discoveries in Lycia, Being a Journal Kept During a Second Excursion in Asia Minor. London: 1841. V. 37; 39; 42; 45

A Journal Written During an Excursion in Asia Minor. London: 1839. V. 39; 40; 42; 43; 45

FELLOWS, GEORGE

Historical Records of the South Nottinghamshire Hussars Yeomanry, 1794 to 1924. Aldershot: 1928. V. 38

History of the South Notts. Yeomanry Cavalry, 1794 to 1894. Nottingham: 1895. V. 38

FELLOWS, JOHN

An Elegiac Poem in Blank Verse on the Death of the Rev. Mr. A. M. Toplady. London: 1778. V. 42

FELLOWS, WILLIAM

Four Aquatint Sketches. London: 1804. V. 38; 40

FELLTHAM, OWEN

Resolves, a Duple Century. London: 1631. V. 43

FELT, JOSEPH B. 1789-1869

An Historical Account of Massachusetts Currency. Boston: 1839. V. 39

FELTHAM, JOHN

A Guide to All the Watering and Sea-Bathing Places . . . London: 1803. V. 45

A Guide to all the Watering and Sea Bathing Places. Description of the Lakes. Tour in Wales, &c, &c. London: 1825 or 1825. V. 37

A Tour Through the Isle of Mann, in 1797 and 1798 . . . Bath: 1798. V. 44; 45

FELTHAM, OWEN

A Brief Narrative of the Low Countries Under the States. London: 1660. V. 42

Resolues. A Duple Century. London: 1636. V. 41

Resolves. A Duple Century. London: 1634. V. 41

Resolves: Divine, Moral and Political. London: 1670. V. 42

Resolves: Divine, Moral, Political . . . London: 1677. V. 46

FELTON, HENRY

A Dissertation on Reading the Classics, and Forming a Just Style. London: 1713. V. 39; 41; 44

FELTON, J. B.

Oration Delivered at the Fouth Anniversary of the College of California . . . and the Addresses at the Festival in the College Grove. San Francisco: 1858. V. 37; 39

FELTON, MRS.

Life in America. A Narrative of Two Years City & Country Residence in the United States. Hull: 1838. V. 38

FELTON, MRS., PSEUD.

American Life. London: 1842. V. 46

FELTON, REBECCA L.

My Memoirs of Georgia Politics. Atlanta: 1911. V. 43

THE FEMALE Congress; or, The Temple of Cotytto. London: 1779. V. 37; 43

THE FEMALE Faction: or, the Gay Subscribers. London: 1729. V. 44; 45

THE FEMALE Instructor; or Young Woman's Guide to Domestic Happiness . . . London: 1822. V. 43

THE FEMALE Mentor; or, Select Conversations. Dublin: 1793. V. 46
THE FEMALE Mentor: or, Select Conversations. Philadelphia: 1802. V. 37

THE FEMALE Rambler. London: 1754. V. 40

FEN and Marshland churches: a Series of Photographs with Short Historical and Archietectural Descriptive Notes. Wisbech and London: 1867-69. V. 44

FENAROLO, LODOVICO

Il Sergio. Venice: 1568. V. 37

FENBY, J. BEVERLEY

Report on the Swinburn Breech-Loading Rifle. Birmingham: n.d.: 1873. V. 41

FENDALL, PERCY

Spiders and Flies. London: 1886. V. 39

FENELON, FRANCOIS

Part of the Spiritual Works of the Celebrated Francis Fenelon, Archbishop of Cambray . . . Dublin: 1771. V. 46

FENELON, FRANCOIS DE SALIGNAC DE LA MOTHE 1651-1715

The Adventures of Telemachus . . . London: 1742. V. 39

The Adventures of Telemachus the Son of Ulysses. Written in French. Translated from the last Paris Edition, which is the only genuine, and agreeable to the Author's Manuscript; and dedicated to the King of France. Done into English by . . . London: 1719. V. 37

Ethic Amusements by Mr. Bellamy, Formerly of St. John's College, Oxford. 1770. V. 37

Extracts from the Writings of Francis Fenelon. London: 1797. V. 39

Letters to the Duke of Burgundy. Dublin: 1758. V. 38

Pious Reflections for Every Day in the Month. London: 1800. V. 39

FENELON, FRANCOIS DE SALIGNAC DE LA MOTHE, ABP. 1651-1715

Aventures de Telemaque, fils d'Ulysse. London: 1810. V. 44

Instructions for the Education of a Daughter. London: 1707. V. 45

FENELON, FRANCOIS SALIGNAC DE LA MOTHE, ABP. 1651-1715

The Adventures of Telemachus, the Son of Ulysses. London: 1768. V. 40

Les Adventures de Telemaque fil d'Ulysse . . . Paris: 1784. V. 40

The Adventures of Telemachus. London: 1792-94. V. 40; 42

The Adventures of Telemachus, the Son of Ulysses. London: 1795. V. 38; 40; 46

Instructions for the Education of Machiavel's Prince. V. 45

Les Aventures de Telemaque, Fils d'Ulysse. Paris: 1795. V. 44

Aventures de Telemaque. Tours: 1873. V. 43

Dialogues Concerning Eloquence in General . . . London: 1722. V. 46

Dialogues on Eloquence; Wherein is Clearly Demonstrated, That Which is Best Adapted to the Pulpit . . . Leeds: 1806. V. 46

Education des Filles . . . Paris: 1687. V. 38; 39; 41

Education des Filles. Paris: 1696. V. 42

Fenelon's Treatise on the Education of Daughters. Cheltenham: 1805. V. 41

Fenelon's Treatise on the Education of Daughters. Albany: 1806. V. 39; 40; 42; 46

Instructions for the Education of a Daughter . . . Edinburgh: 1750. V. 42; 46

The Lives and Most Remarkable Maxims of the Antient Philosophers. London: 1726. V. 40; 43

A Patern of Christian Education. Germantown: 1756. V. 43

Tales and Fables in French and English . . . London: 1789. V. 38; 41

Twenty Seven Moral Tales and Fables, French and English. London: 1729. V. 44

FENESTELLA, LUCIUS

De Romanorum Magistratibus. N. P.: 1487. V. 40

FENLEY, FLORENCE

Old Timers of South West Texas. Uvalde: 1957. V. 42; 46

Oldtimers, Their Own Stories. 1939. V. 42

Oldtimers: Their Own Stories. Uvalde: 1939. V. 37; 38; 41; 44; 46

FENN, E.

The Juvenile Tatler. London: 1789. V. 45

Sketches of Little Boys. London: 1845. V. 45

FENN, ELEANOR

The Art of Teaching in Sport. London: 1785. V. 38

Juvenile Correspondence; or, Letters Suited to Children, From Four to Above Ten Years of Age. London: 1783. V. 40

Juvenile Correspondence; or, Letters Suited to Children, From Four to Above Ten Years of Age. London: 1790. V. 46

School Occurrences Supposed to Have Arisen Among a Set of Young Ladies Under Tuition of Mrs. Teachwell and to Be Recorded by One of Them. London: 1782. V. 40

School Occurrences: Supposed to Have Arisen Among a Set of Young Ladies, Under the Tuition of Mrs. Teachwell and to be Recorded by One of Them. London: 1782? V. 37

Sketches of Little Girls. London: 1845. V. 40

FENN, ELEANOR F.

Cobwebs to Catch Flies; or, Dialogues in Short Sentences, Adapted to Children from the Age of Three to Eight Yeras. London: 1837. V. 39

FENN, G. MANVILLE

Double Cunning. London: 1886. V. 42

FENN, GEORGE MANVILLE

George Alfred Henty: the Story of an Active Life. London: 1907. V. 40; 46

FENN, JOHN

Original Letters Written During the Reigns of Henry VI, Edward IV and Richard III. London: 1787. V. 39

Original Letters, Written During the Reigns of Henry VI, Edward IV and Richard III by Various Persons of Rank of Consequence. London: 1787-89. V. 38

The Paston Letters. Original Letters, Written During the Reigns of Henry VI, Edward VI, and Richard III. London: 1787-1823. V. 38

FENN, WILLIAM PURVIANCE

Ah Sin and His Brethren in American Literature. Peiping: 1933. V. 46

FENNEL, JAMES H.

A Natural History of British and Foreign Quadrupeds. 1843. V. 45; 46

FENNELL, JAMES

An Apology for the Life of James Fennell. Written by Himself. Philadelphia: 1814. V. 39

Lindor and Clara; or, the British Officer. London: 1791. V. 37

A Review of the Proceedings at Paris During the Last Summer . . . London: 1792. V. 43

FENNER, BALL

Raising the Veil; or, Scenes in the Courts. Boston: 1856. V. 45

FENNER, DUDLEY

The Whole Doctrine of the Sacraments, Plainlie and Fullie set Downe and Declared out of the Word of God. Middleburgh: 1588. V. 44

FENNER, REST

Rest Fenner's Pocket Atlas, of Modern and Ancient Geography. 1830. V. 42

FENNER, THOMAS

Religious Folk Songs of the Negro as Sung on the Plantations. Hamtpon: 1909. V. 40

FENNESSEY, RENA

Birds of the African Bush. London: 1975. V. 40

FENNING, DANIEL

The British Youth's Instructor . . . London: 1775. V. 43

The New Royal English Dictionary. London: 1763. V. 40; 45; 46

A New and Easy Guide to the Use of the Globes . . . London: 1770. V. 43

The Ready Reckoner, or the Trader's Sure Guide, Adapted to the Use of All Who Deal by Wholesale or Retail . . . Reading: 1789. V. 37

The Royal English Dictionary . . . London. V. 42

The Royal English Dictionary; or a Treasury of the English Language. London: 1761. V. 42

The Royal English Dictionary . . . London: 1763. V. 37; 39

The Royal English Dictionary. London: 1768. V. 41

The Royal English Dictionary. London: 1771. V. 41; 43

The Universal Spelling-Book; or, a New and Easy Guide to the English Language. London: 1776. V. 43

The Universal Spelling-Book; or a New and Easy Guide to the English Language. London: 1790? V. 45

FENNOR, WILLIAM

Vvat Nieus Boven Nieux/by Wilm Vener Engelshman/tot . . . Prins . . . Mauritius van Nassau . . . Item Hier is noch by Bhevoecht een Liedeken van het Bestandt. Rotterdam: 1609. V. 45

FENOLLOSA, ERNEST

Certain Noble Plays of Japan. Churchtown: 1916. V. 40; 41; 43; 45

The Chinese Written Character as a Medium for Poetry. New York: 1936. V. 43

The Chinese Written Character as a Medium for Poetry. Washington: 1951. V. 45

The Chinese Written Character as a Medium for Poetry. London: 1936. V. 37; 39; 40

Epochs of Chinese and Japanese Art. London: 1912. V. 39

Epochs of Chinese and Japanese Art: An Outline History of East Asiatic Design. London: 1921. V. 41; 42

Epochs of Chinese & Japanese Art; An Outline History of East Asiatic Design. London: (1921). V. 37

FENTON, ELIJAH 1683-1730

An Epistle to Mr. Southerne, from Mr. El. Fenton. London: 1711. V. 38

Poems on Several Occasions. London: 1717. V. 37; 38; 39; 40; 41; 42; 43; 44; 45; 46

FENTON, GEOFFREY

A Forme of Christian Pollicie. London: 1574. V. 41

FENTON, I. D.

Adventures of Mrs. Colonel Somerset in Caffraria During the War. London: 1858. V. 39; 40; 42; 43

FENTON, JAMES

Children in Exile. Edinburgh: 1983. V. 40

Children in Exile. London: 1983. V. 45

A German Requiem. Edinburgh: 1981. V. 37; 41; 45

A History of Tasmania from Its Discovery in 1642 to the Present Time. Hobart: 1884. V. 46

The Memory of War - Poems 1968-1982. Edinburgh: 1982. V. 40; 45

Our Western Furniture. Oxford: 1968. V. 38; 40; 41; 42; 45

Terminal Moraine. London: 1972. V. 38; 45

FENTON, RICHARD

A Historical Tour Through Pembrokeshire. London: 1811. V. 46

Memoirs of an Old Wig. London: 1815. V. 43; 46

Poems. London: 1790. V. 42

FENWICK, E. HURRY

The Electric Illumination of the Bladder and Urethra as a Means of Diagnosis of Obscure Vesico-Urethral Diseases. London: 1888. V. 42

FENWICK, JOHN

The Proceedings Against Sir John Fenwick, Bar., Upon a Bill of Attainder for High Treason. London: 1698. V. 37; 39; 41; 42; 43

The Proceedings Against Sir John Fenwick, Bar. Upon a Bill of Attainder for High Treason. Together with a copy of a Letter Sent by Sir John Fenwick to His Lady, Upon His Being Taken in Kent . . . London: 1702. V. 41

FENWICK, ROBERT ORME

The Goblin Groom: a Tale of Dunse. Edinburgh: 1809. V. 46

FENWICK, THOMAS

Four Essays on Practical Mechanics. Newcastle-upon-Tyne: 1802. V. 42; 44

FENWICK, THOMAS FITZROY

A Short Catalogue of some of Sir Thomas Phillips' Privately Printed Works. London: 1886. V. 40

FENWICK, THOMAS FITZROY PHILLIPPS

Catalogue of Drawings in the Collection Formed by Sir Thomas Phillipps. London: 1935. V. 44

FER DE LA NOUERRE, FRANCOIS DE d. ca. 1790

De La Possibilite de Faciliter l'Etablissement General de la Navigation Interieure du Royaume, de Supprimer l'Economie que l'on Desire. Paris: 1786. V. 39

FER, NICOLAS DE 1646-1720

A Short and Easy Method to Understand Geography. London: 1710. V. 39

FERBER, EDNA

American Beauty. Garden City: 1931. V. 40; 41

Cimarron. Garden City: 1930. V. 42

Cimarron. New York: 1930. V. 46

Giant. New York: 1952. V. 45

A Peculiar Treasure. 1939. V. 37; 42; 43; 44

A Peculiar Treasure. London: 1939. V. 41

A Peculiar Treasure. New York: 1939. V. 37; 43

Saratoga Trunk. Garden City: 1941. V. 39; 43

Show Boat. Garden City: 1926. V. 43

FERDINAND Franck; an auto-biographical sketch of the youthful days of a musical student. London: 1825. V. 37

FERDINAND I, ARCHDUKE OF AUSTRIA

Bergk Ordnung der Niderosterreichischen Lannde. Vienna: 1553. V. 40

FERENS, WILLIAM HENRY

Once Round the Globe. Durham: 1884. V. 43

FERENTILLI, AGOSTINO

Discorso Vniversale . . . nel Qvale Discorrendo si per le Sei Eta & le Quattro Monarchie; si Raccontano Tutte l'Historie, & l'Origine di Tutti gl'Impril, Regni & Nationi, Cominciando dal Principio del Mondo . . . Vinetia: 1572. V. 41

FERGUSON, ADAM

An Essay on the History of Civil Society. Dublin: 1767. V. 38

An Essay on the History of Civil Society. Edinburgh: 1767. V. 37; 39; 41; 45

An Essay on the History of Civil Society. Edinburgh: 1768. V. 40; 43

An Essay on the History of Civil Society. London: 1773. V. 37; 39

An Essay on the History of Civil Society. London: 1782. V. 40; 41; 42

An Essay on the History of Civil Society. Basle: 1789. V. 42; 43; 45

The History of the Proceedings in the Case of Margaret, Commonly Called Peg, Only Lawful Sister to John Bull, Esq. London: 1761. V. 42

The History of the Progress and Termination of the Roman Republic . . . London: & Edinburgh: 1783. V. 45

The History of the Progress and Termination of the Roman Republic. Edinburgh: 1813. V. 45

The History and Progress and Termination of the Roman Republic. Edinburgh: 1828. V. 40; 43

The History of the Progress and Termination of the Roman Republic. Edinburgh: 1828. V. 40; 41; 42

Institutes of Moral Philosophy. Edinburgh: 1769. V. 39

The Morality of Stage-Plays Seriously Considered. Edinburgh: 1757. V. 42

Principles of Moral and Political Science . . . Edinburgh: 1792. V. 42

Principles of Moral and Political Science. London: 1792. V. 41

FERGUSON, ALBERT

Orthopedic Surgery In Infancy and Childhood. Baltimore: 1957. V. 42

FERGUSON, CHARLES D.

The Experiences of a Forty Niner. Cleveland: 1888. V. 39; 40; 42; 43; 44; 45

FERGUSON, HENRY

Journal of . . . January to August 1866. Hartford: 1942. V. 39

FERGUSON, HENRY L.

Fisher Island 1614-1925 - the Admiral adrian Block Discovery, Early Settlers, Whalers Since 1647, Colonial Times, the Revolutionary Days, the War of 1812. New York: 1925. V. 39

FERGUSON, HENRY LEE

The English Springer Spaniel in America. New York: 1932. V. 40; 41

FERGUSON, J. A.

Bibliography of Australia 1784-(1900). London: 1941-86. V. 44

Bibliography of Australia . . . 1784 (through) 1850. Canberra: 1975. V. 40

Bibliography of Australia. Canberra: 1975-86. V. 46

FERGUSON, JAMES 1710-1776

Analysis of a Course of Lectures on Mechanics, Hydrostatics, Hydraulics, Pneumatics, Electricity and Astronomy. London: 1771. V. 41

The Art of Drawing in Perspective Made Easy to Those Who Have No Previous Knowledge of the Mathematics. London: 1775. V. 37; 38; 42; 44; 45

Astronomy Explained Upon Sir Isaac Newton's Principles and Made Easy to Those Who Have Not Studied Mathematics. London: 1756. V. 46

Astronomy Explained Upon Sir Isaac Newton's Principles and Made Easy to Those Who Have Not Studied Mathematics. London: 1757. V. 38; 45

Astronomy Explained Upon Sir Isacc Newton's Principles . . . London: 1773. V. 40

Astronomy Explained Upon Sir Isaac Newton's Principles and Made Easy to Those Who Have Not Studied Mathematics. London: 1778. V. 37; 42; 44

Astronomy Explained Upon Sir Isaac Newton's Principles . . . London: 1803. V. 41

Astronomy Explained Upon Sir Isaac Newton's Principles, and Made Easy to Those Who Have Not Studied Mathematics . . . Philadelphia: 1806. V. 43

An Easy Introduction to Astronomy, for Young Gentlemen and Ladies. London: 1779. V. 38

An Easy Introduction to Astronomy, for Young Gentlemen and Ladies: describing the Figure, Motions, and Dimensions of the Earth; the different Seasons; Gravity and Light; the Solar System; the Transit of Venus, and its Use in . . . London: 1769. V. 37

History of Architecture in all Countries. London: 1873-1876. V. 44

History of Indian and Eastern Architecture. London: 1910. V. 46

Introduction to Electricity . . . London: 1770. V. 40

An Introduction to Electricity. London: 1775. V. 41

Lectures on Select Subjects in Mechanics, Hydrostaticks, Penumaticks and Optics. London: 1760. V. 40

Lectures on Select Subjects in Mechanics, Hydrostatics, Pneumatics and Optics. London: 1764. V. 38; 45; 46

Lectures on Select Subjects in Mechanics, Pneumatics, Hydrostatics and Optics. (with) A Supplement to Mr. Ferguson's Book of Lectures. London: 1764, 1767. V. 38; 41; 44; 45; 46

Lectures on Select Subjects in Mechanics, Hydrostatics, Pneumatics & Optics. London: 1770. V. 37; 38; 39; 41

Lectures on Select Subjects in Mechanics, Hydrostatics, Hydraulics, Pneumatics, and Optics. London: 1790. V. 39

Lectures on Select Subjects in Mechanics, Hydrostatics, Hydraulics, Pneumatics and Optics . . . London: 1799. V. 45

Lectures on Select Subjects . . . Edinburgh: 1806. V. 40

Lectures on select Subjects in Mechanics, Hydrostatics, Pneumatics, Optics and Astronomy. London: 1843. V. 40

Select Mechanical Exercises. London: 1733. V. 40

Select Mechanical Exercises . . . London: 1778. V. 37; 46

Tables and Tracts, Relative to Several Arts and Sciences. London: 1767. V. 37; 38; 39; 41

Two Scottish Soldiers: a Soldier of 1688 and Blenheim A Soldier of the American Revolution. Aberdeen: 1888. V. 42; 46

The Young Gentleman and Lady's Astronomy, Familiarly Explained in Ten Dialogues Between Neander and Eudosia. Dublin: 1778. V. 38; 40

FERGUSON, JOHN

Bibliographical Notes on Histories of Inventions and Books of Secrets. London. V. 44

Bibliographical Notes on Histories of Inventions and Books of Secrets. London: 1959. V. 42; 46

Bibliotheca Chemica, a Bibliography of Books on Alchemy, Chemistry, and Pharmaceutics. London: 1954. V. 37; 38

Bibliotheca Chemica. London: 1954. V. 38

Bibliotheca Chemica, a Catalogue of the Alchemical, Chemical and Phaaremaceutical Books in the Collection of . . . James Young. London: 1954. V. 37

FERGUSON, JOHN A.

Bibliography of Australia. Canberra: 1980. V. 43

FERGUSON, JOHN C.

Chinese Painting. Chicago: 1927. V. 38; 41

Survey of Chinese Art. Shanghai: 1939. V. 38

FERGUSON, MUNGO

Printed Books in the Library of the Hunterian Museum in the University of Glasgow. Glasgow: 1930. V. 41; 42; 45

FERGUSON, ROBERT

A Brief Account of Some of the Late Incroachments and Depredations of the Dutch Upon the English . . . London?: 1695. V. 41

An Enquiry Into and Detection of the Barbarous Murther of the Late Earl of Essex; or, a Vindication of That Noble Person . . . . London. V. 37; 41; 43

An Enquiry Into and Detection of the Barbarous Murther of the Late Earl of Essex. Holland?: 1684. V. 45

A Just and Modest Vindication of the Scots Design, for Their Having Established a Colony at Darien. Edinburgh?: 1699. V. 38

A Just and Modest Vindication of the Scots Design, for the Having Established a Colony at Darien. London: 1699. V. 39

A Just and Modest Vindication of the Scots Design, for the Establishing a Colony at Darien. N.P.: Edinburgh?: 1699. V. 40

A Just and Modest Vindication of the Proceedings of the Two Late Parliaments. London: 1682. V. 38

FERGUSON, SAMUEL

Astronomy Explained Upon Sir Isaac Newton's Principles . . . Philadelphia: 1806. V. 37

The Cromlech on Howth, a Poem. London: 1861. V. 44

Father Tom and the Pope, or a Night in the Vatican. New York: 1867. V. 46

Father Tom and The Pope: Or a Night At the Vatican. Philadelphia: 1861. V. 37

Poems. Dublin: 1880. V. 37

FERGUSON, W.

List of Writers on Ceylon. 1885-86. V. 44

FERGUSON, WILLIAM DWYER

The Tenure and Improvement of Land in Ireland, Considered with Reference to the Relation of Landlord and Tenant. Dublin: 1851. V. 42

FERGUSSON, ADAM 1723-1816

An Essay on the History of Civil Society. London: 1782. V. 37

FERGUSSON, D.

Letter of the Secretary of War Communicating . . . A Copy of the Report of Major D. Fergusson on the Country, Its Resources, and the Route Between Tucson and Lobos Bay. Washington: 1863. V. 45

FERGUSSON, DAVID

. . . . Report of Major D. Fergusson on the Country, Its Resources and Route Between Tucson and Lobos Bay. Washington: 1863. V. 37; 39; 40; 41; 43

FERGUSSON, ERNA

Murder & Mystery in New Mexico. Santa Fe: 1991. V. 46

FERGUSSON, HARVEY

Wolf Song. New York: 1927. V. 38

FERGUSSON, JAMES

History of the Modern Styles of Architecture. London: 1873. V. 45

A History of Architecture in all Countries . . . London: 1873-74. V. 45; 46

Rude Stone Monuments in all Countries, Their Age and Ues. London: 1872. V. 45

FERGUSSON, PETER

Architecture of Solitude. Princeton: 1984. V. 38

FERGUSSON, R. MENZIES

Logie, A Parish History. Paisley: 1905. V. 38

FERGUSSON, ROBERT

The Poems. Edinburgh: 1821. V. 42

The Poetical Works . . . With Life of the Author by David Irving. Glasgow: 1800. V. 42

The Poetical Works . . . with His Life. Alnwick: 1814. V. 45

The Proposed Reform of the Counties of Scotland impartially examined: with observations on the Conduct of the Delegates. Edinburgh: 1792. V. 37

FERGUSSON, W. N.

Adventure, Sport and Travel on the Tibetan Steppes. London: 1911. V. 39; 40; 42; 45; 46

FERISHTA OF DELHI, MAHUMMUD CASIM

The History of Hindostan from the Earliest Account of Time, to the Death of Akbar. London: 1768-72. V. 44

FERLAND, J. B. A.

La France dans l'Amerique du Nord. Montreal: 1929-1930. V. 39

FERLINGHETTI, LAWRENCE

Pictures of the Gone World. San Francisco: 1955. V. 37

The Sea and Ourselves at Cape Ann. Madison: 1979. V. 42; 44

The Secret Meaning of Things. New York: 1969. V. 46

FERMI, ENRICO

Thermodynamics. New York: 1937. V. 42

FERMOR, PATRICK LEIGH

Between the Woods and the Water - On Foot to Constantinople from the Hook of Holland: The Middle Danube tot he Iron Gates. 1986. V. 37

Mani - Travels in the Southern Peloponnese. London: 1958. V. 46

Roumell - Travels in Northern Greece. London: 1966. V. 46

A Time to Keep Silence. London: 1953. V. 39; 44; 45

A Time of Gifts. London: 1977. V. 41; 43; 46

FERMOR, PATRICK LEIGH continued

The Traveller's Tree - a Journey through the Caribbean Islands. London: 1950. V. 40; 41; 43

Travels in Northern Greece. London: 1966. V. 41

The Violins of Saint-Jacques - a Tale of the Antilles. London: 1953. V. 43

FERN, ALAN

The Complete Prints of Leonard Baskin. Boston: 1984. V. 42

Notes on the Eragny Press, and a Letter to J. B. Manson. 1957. V. 39

FERNAN GONZALEZ

La Historia del Noble Cavallero, el Conde Fernan Gonzalez, con la Muerte de los Siete Infantes de Lara. Madrid: 1690. V. 37

FERNANDES, ANTONIO

Copia de Una (Carta) del Padre Antonio Fernandes Superior de las Casas que la Compania de Jesus Tiene en el Imperio de Etiopia . . . Madrid: 1627. V. 41

FERNANDEZ DE ANGULOA Y SANDOVAL, SANCHO

Relacion de Servicios del Comissario General de la Cavalleria Don Sancho Fernandez de Angulo y Sandoval . . . Madrid: 1682. V. 40

FERNANDEZ DE AVELLANEDA, ALONSO

The Life and Exploits, of the Ingenious Gentleman, Don Quixote, de la Mancha. Swaffham: 1805. V. 40

FERNANDEZ DE NAVARRETE, PEDRO

Discursos Politicos. Barcelona: 1621. V. 38

FERNANDEZ DE SAN SALVADOR, AGUSTIN

Los Jesuitas Quitados y Restituidos al Mundo. Historia de la Antigua California. Mexico: 1816. V. 40

FERNANDEZ, JOHN

An Address to His Majesty's Ministers, Recommending Efficacious Means for the Most Speedy Termination of African Slavery. London: 1827. V. 43

FERNANDEZ, JUSTINO

Danzas de los Concheros en Sam Miguel de Allende. Mexico: 1941. V. 42

FERNANDEZ PIEDRAHITA, LUCAS

Historia General de las Conquistas del Nuevo Reyno de Granada. Amberes: 1688. V. 39

Historia General de Las Conqvistas Del Nvevo Reyno de Granada . . . Antwerp: 1688. V. 41

FERNE, JOHN c. 1550-1610

The Blazon of Gentrie . . . London: 1586. V. 37; 39; 40; 43; 46

FERNEL, JEAN

. . . Universa Medicina, Primum Studio & DilIgentia Gulielmi Plantii . . . Coloniae Allobrogum: 1679. V. 45

Ambiani, Vniuersa Medicina, Tribvs et Viginti Libris Absolvta . . . Livtetiae Parisiorvm: 1567. V. 37; 39

Monalosphaerium, Partibus Constans Quatuor. Paris: 1526/27. V. 44

Universa Medicina . . . Lyon: 1581. V. 38

FERNIE, W. T.

Animal Simples Approved for Modern Uses of Cure. Bristol: 1899. V. 42

FERNINGHAM, EDWARD

The Old Bard's Farewell: a Poem. London: 1811. V. 43

FERNOW, BERTHOLD

The Ohio Valley in Colonial days. Albany: 1890. V. 41; 43

FERNYHOUGH, THOMAS

Military Memoirs of Four Brothers, Engaged in the Service of Their Country . . . London: 1829. V. 42

FERRALL, SIMON A.

A Ramble of Six Thousand Miles through the United States of America. London: 1832. V. 38

FERRAND, ANTOINE

L'Esprit de l'Histoire, ou Lettres Politiques et Morales. Paris: 1802. V. 38; 40

FERRAND, J.

Constructions en Fer et en Bois. Paris: 1860. V. 38

FERRAR, JOHN

An History of the City of Limerick . . . Limerick: 1767. V. 38

The History of Limerick, Ecclesiastical, Civil and Military, from the Earliest Records to the Year 1787. Limerick: 1787. V. 40

FERRARI, GIOVANNI BATTISTA 1584-1655

Flora Overo Cultura di Fiori . . . Rome: 1638. V. 37; 43

De Florum Cultura Libri IV. Rome: 1633. V. 38

Hesperides Sive de Malorum Aureorum Cultura et Usu Libri Quatuor. Rome: 1646. V. 37; 46

Libri Quattro: de' Quali si Tratta Delle Razze, Delle Disciplina Del Cavalcare, e di Molte altre Cose Appertinenti a si Fatto Essercitio. Campania: 1570. V. 37

(Syriac:) Nomenclator Syriacus. Rome: 1622. V. 40

FERRARI, OCTAVIO

Octavii Ferrarii: de Re Vestiaria. Patavii: 1642. V. 41

FERRARIS, LUCA

Promta Bibliotheca. Madrid: 1795. V. 38

FERREE, B.

American Estates and Gardens. New York: 1904. V. 37; 45

FERREE, J. W.

The Falls of Niagara and Scenes Around Them. New York: 1876. V. 43

FERREIRA BORGES, JOSE

Institucioes de Medicina Forense. Paris: 1832. V. 38

FERREIRA, CHRISTOVAM

Narratio Persecutionis Adversus Christianos . . . in Iaponiae. Antwerp: 1635. V. 41

FERREIRA DA GRACA, FRANCISCO

Estatutos Literarios dos Religiosos . . . Lisbon;: 1776. V. 38; 40

FERREIRA DE ARAUJO GUIMARAES, MANUEL

Hum Cidadao do Rio de Janeiro a Divisao Auxiliadora do Exercito de Portugal. Rio de Janeiro: 1822. V. 39

FERREIRA DE FREITAS, JOAQUIM

Memoria Sobre a Conspiracao de 1817, Vulgarmente Chamada a Conspiracao de Gomes Freire . . . London: 1822. V. 45

FERREIRA DRUMMON, FRANCISCO

Annaes da Ilha Terceira. Angra do Heroismo: 1850-64. V. 41

FERREIRA LEONARDO, MANUEL

Noticia Verdadeyra do Terrivel Contagio, Que Desde Outubro de 1748. Lisbon: 1749. V. 39

FERRELL, ROBERT N.

Journal of . . . of Greenbush, New York, 1849. N.P.: 1849? V. 41

FERRER DE VALDECEBRO, FR. ANDRES

Govierno General Moral, y Politico, Ballado en las Fieras y Animales Sylvestres. Barcelona: 1696. V. 39; 45

FERRER MALDONADO, LAURENT

Voyage de la Mer Atlantique a L'Ocean Pacifique Nord-Ouest Dans La Mer Glaciale par le Captaine . . . Plaisance: 1812. V. 40

ferrerio, pietro

Palazzi di Roma de'piu Celebri Architectti Disegnati da Pietro Ferrerio Pittore et Architetto. Rome: 1655, 1670. V. 37

FERRERIUS, VINCENTIUS

Sermones de Sanctis. Milan: 1488. V. 42

FERRERIUS, VINCENTIUS, SAINT

Sermones. Lyon: 1497. V. 43

FERRERS, THOMAS JOHN

The Book of Prayers for Morning and Evening Devotion. London: 1860. V. 40

FERRERY, BENJAMIN

The Antiquities of the Priory of Christ-Church, Hants . . . London: 1834. V. 39

FERRETTI, FRANCESCO

Diporti Notturni per Modo di Dialoghi Familiari. Ancona: 1579. V. 45

FERRETTI, GIULIO 1480-1547

De Re et Disciplina Militari Aureus Tractatus . . . Venice: 1575. V. 40

FERREY, BENJAMIN

The Antiquities of the Priory of Christ Church, Hants. London: 1834. V. 37; 39; 42

The Antiquities of the Priory of Christ-Church, Hampshire . . . London: 1841. V. 44

Recollections of A. N. Welby Pugin, and His Father Augustus Pugin . . . London: 1861. V. 38; 39

A Series of Ornmanetal Timber Gables, from Existing Examples in England and France, of the Sixteenth Century. London: 1831. V. 38

FERRI, ALFONSO

Alfonsi Ferri De Ligni Sancti multiplici medicina, & vini exhibitione, libri quatour. Hieronymi Franactorii Syphilis, sive Morbus Gallicus. Lyon: 1547. V. 37

De Ligni Sancti Multiplici Medicina and Vini Exhibitione, Libri IV. Lyon: 1547. V. 40; 42

De Sclopetorum sive Archibusorum Vulneribus. Romae: 1552. V. 42

FERRIAR, JOHN

An Essay Towards a Theory of Apparitions. London: 1813. V. 37; 38; 43

Illustrations of Sterne: With Other Essays and Verses. London. V. 40

Illustrations of Sterne; and Other Essays and Verses. Manchester: 1798. V. 41

Illustrations of Sterne; with other Essays and Verses. London: 1812. V. 39; 43; 44

FERRIER, AUGER

A Learned Astronomical Discourse of the Judgement of Nativities. London: 1593. V. 38; 44

FERRIER, DAVID

The Croonian Lecutre. Experiments on the Brain of Monkeys. Second Series. London: 1876. V. 40; 41

The Functions of the Brain. London: 1876. V. 40

The Functions of the Brain. New York: 1876. V. 42

The Functions of the Brain. London: 1886. V. 42; 43; 45

The Localisation of Cerebral Disease Being the Gulstonian Lectures. New York: 1879. V. 38; 39

FERRIER, FRANCOIS LOUIS AUGUSTE

Du Gouvernement Considere dans ses Rapports avec le Commerce. Paris: 1805. V. 38

FERRIER, J. P.

Caravan Journeys and Wanderings in Persia. London: 1856. V. 45

History of the Afghans . . . London: 1858. V. 45

FERRIER, JAMES

Institutes of Metaphysic. The Theory of Knowing and Being. Edinburgh and London: 1854. V. 40; 41

FERRIER, SUSAN EDMONDSTONE 1782-1854

Destiny. Edinburgh: 1831. V. 38; 41; 42; 43; 44; 45; 46

Destiny; or The Chief's Daughter. Edinburgh: 1831. V. 45

Destiny; or the Chief's Daughter. Edinburgh: 1831. V. 46

Destiny; or the Chief's Daughter. Edinburgh: 1831. V. 41

Destiny; or the Chief's Daughter. Edinburgh: 1831. V. 43

Destiny; or, the Chief's Daughter. Philadelphia: 1831. V. 46

The Inheritance. Edinburgh: 1824. V. 40; 42; 44

The Inheritance. Edinburgh & London: 1824. V. 43; 44

The Inheritance. Edinburgh: 1825. V. 40; 45

Marriage. Edinburgh & London: 1818. V. 42; 46

Marriage. Edinburgh: 1819. V. 40

FERRIER, SUSAN EDMONSTONE 1782-1854

Destiny. Edinburgh: 1831. V. 37; 38; 39; 41

The Inheritance. Edinburgh: 1824. V. 37

The Inheritance. Edinburgh/London: 1824. V. 37; 41

The Inheritance. By the Author of Marriage. In Three Volumes. London: 1824. V. 37

Marriage. Edinburgh: 1818. V. 37; 43

Marriage. Edinburgh & London: 1818. V. 37; 41

Marriage. Edinburgh: 1819. V. 37

Marriage (The Inheritance; Destiny.) London: 1881-82. V. 38

The Novels of . . . London: 1894. V. 37; 39

FERRIS, BENJAMIN

A History of the Original Settlements on the Delaware, From Its Discovery by Hudson to the Colonization by William Penn . . . Wilmington: 1846. V. 39; 41; 43

FERRIS, BENJAMIN G.

Utah and the Mormons. New York: 1854. V. 42; 43; 45

FERRIS, BENJAMIN, MRS.

The Mormons at Home; with Some Incidents of Travel from Missouri to California, 1852-3 . . . New York: 1856. V. 42

FERRIS, CORNELIA

The Mormons at Home. New York: 1856. V. 40; 41

FERRIS, HUGH

The Metropolis of Tomorrow. New York: 1929. V. 45

FERRIS, JACOB

The States and Territories of the Great West . . . New York: 1856. V. 45

States and Territories of the Great West. New York & Auburn: 1856. V. 37; 38

FERRIS, SAMUEL

A Dissertation on Milk. London: 1785. V. 45

A General View of the Establishment of Physic as a Science in England, by the Incorporation of the College of Physicians, London . . . London: 1795. V. 42

FERRIS, W. A.

Life in the Rocky Mountains. Denver: 1940. V. 42; 43; 46

FERRIS, WARREN ANGUS

Life in the Rocky Mountains, 1830-1835. Salt Lake City: 1940. V. 37; 39; 40; 41; 44; 45

FERRIS, WILLIAM H.

The African Abroad; or, His Evolution in Western Civilization Tracing His Development Under Caucasian Milieu. New Haven: 1913. V. 38

FERRISS, HUGH

The Metropolis of Tromorrow. New York: 1929. V. 41; 45

The Metropolis of Tomorrow. Washburn: 1929. V. 46

Power in Building: an Artist's View of Contemporary Architecture. New York: 1953. V. 46

FERRY, BENJAMIN

Recollections of A. N. W. Pugin and His Father, Augustus Pugin: With Notices of Their Works. London: 1861. V. 37

FERRY, DAVID

A Letter and Some Photographs. Seattle: 1981. V. 39; 42; 44

FERUSSAC, JEAN BAPTISTE LOUIS D'AUDEBARD DE

Histoire Naturelle Generale et Particuliere des Mollusques Terrestres et Fluviatiles . . . Paris: 1820-51. V. 43

FESSENDEN, THOMAS GREEN 1771-1837

Democracy Unveiled; or, Tyranny Stripped of the Garb of Patriotism. Boston: 1805. V. 39; 43

An Essay on the Law of Patents for New Inventions. Boston: 1810. V. 43

The Ladies' Monitor, a Poem. Bellows Falls: 1818. V. 37; 44

The Register of Arts, or a Compendious View of Some of the Most Useful Modern Discoveries and Inventions. Philadelphia: 1808. V. 44

Terrible Tractoration!! London: 1803. V. 43

Terrible Tractoration!! New York: 1804. V. 39; 43

The Weekly Inspector. New York: 1806-1807. V. 37

THE FESTIVAL of Wit; or, The Small Talker. London: 1782. V. 45

FESTIVAL of Song: a Series of Evenings with The Poets. New York: 1866. V. 46

FESTIVAL of the Sons of New Hampshire. Boston: 1850. V. 44

THE FESTIVAL of Wit, or the Small Talker. London: 1788. V. 45

THE FESTOON: a Collection of Epigrams, Ancient and Modern. London: 1766. V. 39; 45

FESTSCHRIFT for Marianne Moore's Seventy Seventh Birthday. New York: 1964. V. 39

FESTSCHRIFT in Honor of Abraham Jacobi to Commemorate the Seventeith Anniversary of His Birth, May Sixth, 1900. New York: 1900. V. 39; 40; 41

FETE Donnee par le Cercle Aristique sous Le Patronage du Roi. Brussels: 1849. V. 38

FETHERSTONHAUGH, MARIA GEORGIANA

Robin Adiar. London: 1879. V. 44

FETHERSTONHAUGH, R. C.

The Royal Candian Regiment, 1883-1933. Montreal: 1936. V. 39

The Royal Montreal Regiment 1925-1945. Westmount: 1949. V. 45

The 13th Battalion, Royal Highlanders of Canada, 1914-1919. Toronto: 1925. V. 39

FETRIDGE, W. PEMBROKE

Harper's Hand-Book for Travelers in Europe and the East. New York: 1862. V. 45

THE FETTER Lane Loyalist of a Description of a True Sonne of Rome. London: 1680? V. 41

FEUCHTERSLEBEN, ERNST

The Principles of Medical Psychology. London: 1847. V. 41; 45

FEUCHTWANGER, LION

Jew Suss, a Historical Romance. London: 1926. V. 39

Jew Suss: a Historical Romance. London: 1926, 1925. V. 39; 44; 45

FEUERBACH, ANSELM VON

Caspar Hauser. London: 1834. V. 42

FEUERBACH, LUDWIG

Das Wesen des Christenthums. Leipzig: 1841. V. 45

Sammtliche Werke. Leipzig: 1846-66. V. 38

FEUERBACH, LUDWIG ANDREAS

The Essence of Christianity. London: 1854. V. 43; 45

FEUILLEE, LUDWIG

Beschreibung Zur Arznei Dienlicher Pflanzen. Nuremberg: 1756. V. 38; 40; 42; 44

FEUILLET

Orchesography, or, the Art of Dancing, by Characters and Demonstrative Figures. London: 1706. V. 38

FEULNER, ADOLF

Historic Interiors in Colour. New York: 1929. V. 46

FEURBACH, ANSELM VON

Caspar Hauser. An Account of an Individual Kept in a Dungeon Separated from All Communication with the World from an Early Childhood to About the Age of Seventeen. London: 1834. V. 46

FEVAL, PAUL HENRI

Thrice Dead. London: 1869. V. 41

FEW, CHARLES

A Parody Upon the Poem of Alonzo the Brave and the Fair Imogene. London: 1799. V. 44

A FEW Days in Paris: Remarks Characteristic of Several Distinguished Persoanges. London: 1802. V. 37; 39

A FEW Examples of the Work of Carlton Illustrators Together with a Note on Modern Bookmaking. London: 1890. V. 46

A FEW Examples of the Work of Carlton Illustrators Together with a Note on Modern Bookmaking. (n.d.). V. 37

A FEW General Observations on the Principal Railways Executed in Progress & Projected, in the Midland Counties and North of England, with the Author's Opinion Upon them as Investments. London: 1838. V. 38; 46

A FEW Hours with Scott: Being Sketches in the Way of Supplement to the Two Poems of 'The Lord of the Isles' and of 'Rokeby' . . . By One of His Old Readers. Edinburgh: 1856. V. 39

A FEW Short Observations on the Currency by an Old Merchant. London: 1840. V. 38; 39

A FEW Words to Church Builders Published by the Cambridge Camden Society. Cambridge: 1841. V. 37; 40

FEWKES, FRANCIS

A Description of May. London: 1752. V. 37

FEWKES, J. WALTER

Few Summer Cremonials at Zuni Pueblo. Boston. V. 46

FEWKES, JESSE W.

Hopi Katchinas Drawn by Native Artists. Washington: 1904. V. 39

FEYDEL, GABRIEL

Remarques Morales, Philosophiques et Grammaticales sur le Dictionnaire de l'Academie. Paris: 1807. V. 38

FFLOYD, THOMAS

Bibliotheca Biographica . . . London: 1760. V. 42

FFOULKE, C. M.

The Ffoulke Collection of Tapestries. New York: 1913. V. 37; 38; 40; 42; 46

FFOULKES, CHARLES

The Armourer and His Craft from the XIth to the XVIth Century. London: 1912. V. 44; 46

The Gun Founders of England, with a List of English and Continental Gun Founders, from the XIV to the XIX Centuries. Cambridge: 1937. V. 37; 42

Inventory and Survey of the Armouries of the Tower of London. London: 1916. V. 44; 46

FIALA, ANTHONY

Fighting the Polar Ice. New York: 1907. V. 37; 43; 46

FIAMELLI, G. FRANCESCO 1565-1613

I Qvesiti Militari. Roma: 1606. V. 42

FICHTE, IMMANUEL HERMANN

Contributions to mental Philosophy . . . London: 1860. V. 41

FICHTE, JOHANN GOTTLIEB

Die Grundzuge des Gegenwartigen Zeitalters . . . Berlin: 1806. V. 38; 41

Das System der Sittenlehre nach de Principien der Wissenschatslehre. Jean ʌnd Leipzig: 1798. V. 38

FICINO, M. MARSILIO

Il Consiglio di M. Mansilio Ficino, Fiorentino, Contro la Pestilentia. In Venetia: 1556. V. 37

FICINO, MARSILIO

Il Comento di Marsilio Ficino Sopra il Convito di Platone et Esso Convito Tradotti in Lingua Toscana per Hercole Barbarasa da Terni. Venice: 1544. V. 43

De Vita, Libri Tres . . . Primus, de Studiosorum Sanitate Tuenda, Secundus, de Vita producenda, Tertius, de Vita Coelitus Comparanda . . . Venice: 1548. V. 38

Della Religione Christiana . . . del'Autore istesso Tradotta in Lingua Toscana. Florence: 1568. V. 37

Sopra lo Amore o ver' Convito di Platone. Florence: 1544. V. 38

De Vita Libri tres, Recens Iam a mendis Situq; Unidicati Qvorvm . . . Basileae: 1532. V. 41

FICKE, ARTHUR DAVIDSON 1883-1945

Christ in China. N.P.. V. 40

Selected Poems. New York: 1926. V. 46

Spectra. New York: 1916. V. 39; 41; 43; 45; 46

Spectra - New Poems. New York: 1916. V. 40

FICKE, ARTHUR DAVISON

Twelve Japanese Painters. Chicago: 1913. V. 37

FICORINI, FRANCESCO DE

La Vestigia e Rarita de Roma Antica . . . Libro Primo (Le Singolarita de Roma Moderna, Libro Seconda). Rome: 1744. V. 38

FICORONI, FRANCESCO DE 1646-1747

Le Maschere Sceniche e le Figure Comiche d'Antichi Romani. Rome: 1736. V. 40

Le Vestigia, e Rarita di Roma Antica . . . Roma: 1744. V. 46

FICOWSKI, J.

Lettre a Marc Chagall. V. 38

FIDDES, RICHARD

The Life of Cardinal Wolsey. London: 1724. V. 38; 39; 45

FIDFADDY, FREDERICK AUGUSTUS, PSEUD.

The Adventures of Uncle Sam, In Search After His Lost Honor. Middletown: 1816. V. 43

FIDLER, ISAAC

Observations on Professions, Literature, Manners and Emigration, in the United States and Canada, Made During a Residence There in 1832. London: 1833. V. 38; 39; 43

FIEDER, HERMANN

Atlas of Urinary Sediments; with Special Reference to Their Clinical Significance. London: 1899. V. 45

FIEDLER, CONRAD

Three Fragments from the Posthumous Papers of Conrad Fiedler, MDCCCXLI-MDCCCXCV. Lexington: 1951. V. 37; 40; 41; 44

Three Fragments from the Posthumous Papers of . . . Printed in Lexington. V. 37

FIELD, A. E.

Peaks, Passes and Glaciers by Members of the Alpine Club. Third Series. London: 1932. V. 40

FIELD, ANNIE

Authors and Friends. Boston: 1897. V. 38

FIELD, BARRON

An Analysis of Blackstone's Commentaries on the Laws of England, in a Series of Questions. London: 1817. V. 38; 40

FIELD, CHARLES D.

Three Years in the Saddle from 1861 to 1865. (Goldfield, Ia?): 1898. V. 37

FIELD, CHARLES VENTRIS

Narrative of the Case of Sir Charles Ventris Field, Knt. and John Williams Willaume, Esq. London: 1783. V. 38

FIELD, CYRIL

Britain's Sea Soldiers. Liverpool and Devonport: 1924/27. V. 41

FIELD, CYRUS W.

The Atlantic Telegraph: Proceedings of a Banquet Given to Mr. Cyrus W. Field by the Chamber of Commerce of New York. New York: 1866. V. 38

THE FIELD Day Anthology of Irish Writing. 550-1990. New York: 1991. V. 46

FIELD, EDWARD

State of Rhode Island and Providence Plantations, a History. Boston: 1902. V. 37; 38

FIELD, EUGENE

An Auto-Analysis. Chicago: 1896. V. 42

Christmas Tales and Christmas Verse. New York: 1924. V. 46

The Complete Writings in Prose and Verse. New York: 1896. V. 42

Echoes from the Sabine Farm. Chicago: 1893/1891. V. 44

Florence Bardsley's Story. Chicago: 1897. V. 41; 43

The Holy Cross; and Other Tales. Cambridge: 1893. V. 39

The Immortal Little Willie. San Francisco: 1929. V. 41; 46

In Imitation of Robert Herrick. N.P.: n.d. V. 44

A Little Book of Profitable Tales. Chicago: 1889. V. 43

A Little Book of Western Verse. Chicago: 1889. V. 42

The Lullaby Book of Poems. Evanston: 1963. V. 38

The Model Primer. Brooklyn: (1882). V. 37

My Book. N.P.: 1905. V. 46

My Book. St. Louis: 1905. V. 39

Poems of Childhood. New York: 1904. V. 39

Some Love Letters of Eugene Field. Buffalo: 1927. V. 44

The Symbol and the Saint. New York: 1924. V. 41; 44

The Tribune Primer. Chicago: 1916. V. 44

Verse and Prose. St. Louis: 1917. V. 39

With Trumpet and Drum. New York: 1892. V. 41; 46

The Writings in Prose and Verse of Eugene Field. New York: 1896. V. 46

FIELD, GEORGE

Chromatics, or, An Essay on the Analogy and Harmony of Colours. London: 1817. V. 42

Chromatography; or, a Treatise on Colours and Pigments, and of the Powers in Painting &c. London: 1835. V. 41; 46

Chromatography. A Treatise on Colours and Pigments for the Use of Artists, Modernized by J. Scott Taylor. London: 1885. V. 38

Field's Chromatography. London: 1885. V. 41; 46

Outlines of Analogical Philosophy . . . London: 1839. V. 45

Rudiments of the Painter's Art, or a Grammar of Colouring. London: 1850. V. 38; 40

A Treatise on Colours and Pigments for the Use of Artists. London: 1885. V. 42

FIELD, HENRIETTA DEXTER

The Muses Up to Date. Chicago: 1897. V. 38

FIELD, HENRY

Arabs of Central Iraq: Their History, Ethnology and Physical Characters. Chicago: 1935. V. 46

FIELD, HENRY M.

Blood is Thicker than Water: a Few Days Among Our Southern Brethren. New York: 1886. V. 41; 42; 43

The Irish Confederates and the Rebellion of 1798. New york: 1851. V. 37

Our Western Archipelago. Chicago: 1895. V. 41

Our Western Archipelago. New York: 1895. V. 37

FIELD, JULIAN OSGOOD

Little Hand and Muckle Gold. Edinburgh & London: 1889. V. 42

FIELD, LOUISE FRANCIS

The Child and His Book. London: 1891. V. 42

The Way Thither. London: 1882. V. 42

FIELD, LUCY

The Twin Sisters. London: 1853. V. 45

FIELD, MICHAEL

Canute the Great: the Cup of Water. London: 1887. V. 43

Fair Rosamund. London: 1897. V. 38; 41; 43

Fair Rosamaun. London: 1897. V. 38

The Father's Tragedy, William Rufus, Loyalty or Love. London. V. 43

Julia Domna. London: 1903. V. 39; 41; 43

A Question of Memory. London: 1893. V. 43

The Race of Leaves. London: 1901. V. 43

Sight and Songs. London: 1892. V. 41

Sight and Sound. London: 1892. V. 43

Stephania: a Trialogue. London: 1892. V. 38; 41; 43

The Tragic Mary. London: 1890. V. 43

The Tragic May. Cover design by Selwyn Image. London: 1890. V. 37

Wild Honey - From Various Thyme. 1908. V. 37

Works and Days from the Journal of Michale Field. Edited by T. & D. C. Sturge Moore. (Introduction by William Rothenstein). London: 1933. V. 37

FIELD, MICHAEL, PSEUD.

Callirrhoe: Fair Rosamund. London: 1884. V. 46

Canute the Great: the Cup of Water. London: 1882. V. 46

Fair Rosamund. London: 1897. V. 46

The Father's Tragedy, William Rufus, Loyalty or Love. London. V. 46

Julia Domna. London: 1903. V. 46

A Question of Memory. London: 1893. V. 44

The Race of Leaves. London: 1901. V. 42; 44

Sight and Song. London: 1892. V. 44

Stephania a Trialogue. London: 1892. V. 44; 46

The Tragic Mary. London: 1890. V. 44; 46

THE FIELD of Mars - An Alphabetical Digestion of the Principal Naval and military Engagements in Europe, Asia & America . . . from the Ninth Century to 1801. London;: 1801. V. 37

FIELD, OSGOOD

The Fields of Sowerby, Near Halifax, England, and of Flushing, New York. London: 1895. V. 38

FIELD, R.

All This and Heaven Too. 1938. V. 43

FIELD, RACHEL

Branches in Green. New York: 1934. V. 43

Hitty, Her First Hundred Years. New York: 1929. V. 43

FIELD, RACHEL LYMAN 1894-1942

Hitty: Her First Hundred Years. 1929. V. 37

Of the Church, Fiue Bookes. London: 1606. V. 37

FIELD, RICHARD

Alice's Adventures in Atomland in the Plastic Age. South Duxbury: 1949. V. 41

FIELD, RICHARD S.

Jasper Johns: Prints, 1960-1970. New York: 1970. V. 41

FIELD, ROBERT D.

The Art of Walt Disney. 1942. V. 46

FIELD, ROSWELL

The Bondage of Ballinger. Chicago: 1903. V. 42

Madeline. Chicago: 1906. V. 37

FIELD, SARA BARD

To a Poet Born on the Edge of Spring. San Francisco: 1925. V. 39

FIELD, SAUL

Bloomsday. Greenwich: 1972. V. 37; 40

FIELD, STEPHEN J.

Personal Reminiscences of Early Days in California with Other Sketches. San Francisco: 1880. V. 37; 39; 42

Personal Reminiscences of Early Days in California, with Other Sketches . . . N.P.: 1893. V. 45

Personal Reminiscences of Early Days in California with Other Sketches By . . . Washington: 1893. V. 37; 39; 41; 45

FIELD, THOMAS W.

The Battle of Long Island with Preceding and Subsequent Events. Brooklyn: 1869. V. 43

Catalogue of the Library Belonging to Mr. Thomas W. Field . . . New York: 1875. V. 39; 40

An Essay Towards an Indian Bibliography. Columbus: 1951. V. 39; 40; 42

FIELD, W. B. OSGOOD

Edward Lear on My Shelves. London: 1933. V. 46

FIELD, W. OSGOOD

Leech on My Shelves. N.P.: 1930. V. 40

FIELD, WILLIAM

An Historical and Descriptive Account of the town and Castle of Warwick . . . Warwick: 1815. V. 41

Memoirs of the Life, Writings and Opinions of The Rev. Samuel Parr, LL.D. London: 1828. V. 39

FIELD, WILLIAM B. OSGOOD

Edward Lear on My Shelves. 1933. V. 41; 44

Edward Lear on My Shelves. Zurich: 1933. V. 41

Edward Lear on My Shelves. Munich: 1933. V. 37

John Leech on My Shelves. Munich: 1930. V. 37; 44

John Leech on My Shelves. N.P.: 1930. V. 43

Leech On My Shelves. Munich: 1930. V. 41

FIELDE, JOHN

A Caveat for Parsons Howlet. London: 1581. V. 37; 38; 40; 42

FIELDER, CONRAD

Three Fragments from the Posthumous Papers of Conrad Fiedler . . . Printed at Lexington. V. 37; 45

FIELDING-HALL, H.

Margaret's Book. London: 1913. V. 46

FIELDING, HARRY 1707-1754

A True State of the Case of Bosavern Penlez, who suffered on Account of the late Riot in the Strand. In which the Law regarding these Offences, and the Statute of George the First, commonly called the Riot Act, are fully considered. London: 1749. V. 37

FIELDING, HENRY 1707-1754

Amelia. London: 1751. V. 46

Amelia. London: 1752. V. 37; 38; 41; 42; 43; 44; 45; 46

Amelia. London: 1752, 1751. V. 40

Amelie, Roman de Mr. Fiedling (sic). Paris: 1762. V. 46

Amelia. London: 1776. V. 40

An Apology for the Life of Mr. T . . . C . . . , Comedian. London: 1740. V. 37; 38; 40; 42; 46

An Apology for the Life of Mrs. Shamela Andrews. London: 1741. V. 46

An Apology for the Life of Mrs. Shamela Andrews. London: 1925. V. 46

An Apology for the Life of Mrs. Shamela Andrews. Berkshire: 1926. V. 40; 42; 44

An Attempt Towards a Natural History of the Hanover Rat. London: 1744. V. 46

The Author's Farce; and the Pleasures of the Town. London: 1730. V. 46

The Author's Frace; with a Puppet-Show, Call'd the Pleasures of the Town. London: 1750. V. 46

The Beauties of Fielding; Carefully Selected from the Whole Works of that Eminent Writer . . . London: 1782. V. 46

The Charge to the Jury; or, the Sum of the Evidence, on the Trial of A.B.C.D. and E.F., all M.D. for the Death of One Robert at Orfud . . . London: 1745. V. 46

The Champion . . . London: 1741. V. 46

A Charge Delivered to the Grand Jury, at the Sessions of the Peace Held for the City and Liberty of Westmisnter, &C. On Thursday the 29th of June, 1749. London: 1749. V. 46

Cheap Repository. Murders. True Examples of the Interposition of Providence, in the Discovery and Punishment of Murder. London: 1795. V. 46

A Clear State of the Case of Elizabeth Canning . . . Dublin: 1753. V. 45; 46

A Clear State of the Case of Elizabeth Canning . . . London: 1753. V. 45; 46

A Compleat and Authentick History fo the Rise, Progress and Extinction of the Late Rebellion, and of the Proceedings Against the Principal Persons Concerned Therin. Dublin: 1747. V. 46

A Complete and Authentick History of the Rise, Progress and Extinction of the Late Rebellion, and of the Proceedings Against the Principal Persons Concerned Therein . . . London: 1747. V. 45

The Covent-Garden Tragedy. London: 1732. V. 46

The Covent-Garden Journal and a Plan of the Universal Register-Office. Oxford: 1988. V. 44

The Crisis: a Sermon, on Revel. XIV.9, 10, 11. London: 1741. V. 46

A Dialogue Between a Gentleman of London, Agent for Two Court Candidates and an Honest Alderman of the Country Party. London: 1747. V. 43; 46

A Dialogue Between the Devil, the Pope, and the Pretender. London: 1745. V. 40; 46

Don Quixote in England. London: 1734. V. 38; 46

An Enquiry into the Causes of the Late Increae of Robbers, &c. London: 1751. V. 37; 38; 40; 41; 42; 43; 45; 46

Examples of the Interposition of Providence in the Detection and Punishment of Murder. Dublin: 1752. V. 46

Examples of the Interposition of Providence in the Detection and Punishment of Murder. London: 1752. V. 46

The Fathers. London: 1778. V. 38; 44; 46

A Full Vindication of the Dowager of Marlborough; Both with Regard to the Account Lately Published by Her Grace, and to Her Character in General. London: 1742. V. 46

The Genuine Grub-Street Opera. London: 1731. V. 46

The Grub-Street Opera. London: 1755. V. 46

Histoire de Jonathan Wild le Grand. Londres et se trouve a: 1763. V. 46

The History of the Adventures of Joseph Andrews, and His Friend Mr. Abraham Adams. London: 1768. V. 40

The History of the Adventures of Joseph Andrews, and His Friend Mr. Abraham Adams. London: 1781. V. 43

The Historical Register, for the Year 1736 . . . London: 1736. V. 38; 40

The Historical Register for the Year 1736. Dublin: 1737. V. 38; 46

The Historical Register, for the Year 1736. London: 1737. V. 44; 46

The Historical Register, for the Year 1736 (altered in ink to 1746). London: 1737. V. 41; 45

The History of the Adventures of Joseph Andrews, and His Friend Mr. Abraham Adams. London: 1742. V. 38; 39; 41; 42; 45; 46

The History of the Adventures of Joseph Andrews. London: 1743. V. 42; 44; 46

Avantures de Joseph Andrews, et de son Ami Abraham Adams. Amsterdam: 1744. V. 46

De Historie of Gevallen van Joseph Andriessen, Broeder van Pamela, en zyn Vriend de Heer Abraham Adams. Amsterdam: 1744. V. 46

The History of the Adventures of Joseph Andrews and His Friend Mr. Abraham Adams Written in Imitation of the Manner of Cervantes . . . London: 1751. V. 38; 41

Avventure di Gioseffo Andrews Fratello di Pamela, e del Dottor' Adami suo amico. Venice: 1752-53. V. 46

The History of the Adventures of Joseph Andrews, and His Friend Mr. Abraham Adams. London: 1762. V. 46

Joseph Andrews Och Hans Wan Abrahams Adams Handelser, Forfattade af Herr Fielding. Stockholm: 1779. V. 46

The History of the Adventures of Joseph Andrews, and His Friend Mr. Abraham Adams. London: 1781. V. 46

The Adventures of Joseph Andrews, and His Friend Mr. Abraham Adams. London & Edinburgh: 1792. V. 46

The History of the Adventures of Joseph Andrews, and His Friend Mr. Abraham Adams. Paris: 1794. V. 44

The History of the Adventures of Joseph Andrews and His Friend Mr. Abraham Adams. Philadelphia &: 1801. V. 46

Geschichte Tom Jones. Leipzig: 1826. V. 41

The History and Adventures of Joseph Andrews and His Friend Mr. Abraham Adams. London: 1749. V. 38

The Adventures of Joseph Andrews. London: 1832. V. 38

The History of the Adventures of Joseph Andrews, and His Friend Mr. Abraham Adams. London: 1794. V. 42

The History of the Present Rebellion in Scotland. London: 1745. V. 46

The History of the Adventures of Joseph Andrews, and His Friend Mr. Abraham Adams. London: 1768. V. 41

The History of Tom Jones. London: 1749. V. 37; 38; 40; 41; 42; 43; 44; 45; 46

The History of Tom Jones, a Foundling. London: 1749. V. 38

The History of Tom Jones, a Foundling. (with) The History of Tom Jones the Foundling in His Married State. London: 1749, 1750. V. 40; 41

The History of Tom Jones. London: 1750. V. 38

Histoire de Tom Jones . . . Londre (sic): 1750. V. 45

The History of Tom Jones, a Foundling. London: 1773. V. 40

The History of Tom Jones, a Foundling. Dresden: 1774. V. 39; 42

The History of Tom Jones a Foundling. Paris: 1780. V. 38; 40; 45; 46

The History of Tom Jones, a Foundling. London: 1782. V. 42; 43

The History of Tom Jones. London: 1792. V. 37; 38; 40; 44

Geschichte Tom Jones, Eines Findlings. Leipzig: 1826. V. 45

The History of Tom Jones, a Foundling. London: 1930. V. 39

Histoire de Tom Jones, ou l'enfant Trouve . . . Amsterdam: 1750. V. 46

Historie de Tom Jones, ou l'Enfant Trouve . . . Dresden: 1750. V. 46

Histoire de Tom Jones, ou l'Enfant Trouve. Londres: 1764. V. 46

The History of Tom Jones, a Foundling. Edinburgh: 1771. V. 46

The History of Tom Jones, a Foundling. London: 1780. V. 46

Tom Jones, ou l'Enfant Trouve . . . Paris: 1784. V. 46

The History of Tom Jones, a Foundling. London: 1795. V. 46

Tom Jones, au Histoire d'un Enfant Trouve. Paris: 1804. V. 46

The History of Tom Jones. New York: 1836. V. 41

Tom Jones, The History of a Foundling. New York: 1931. V. 42

The History of Tom Jones, a Foundling. London: 1749. V. 44

The History of Tom Jones, a Foundling. New York: 1952. V. 44

The Intriguing Chambermaid. London: 1734. V. 46

The Journal of a Voyage to Lisbon . . . London: 1755. V. 37; 38; 40; 41; 42; 43; 45; 46

The Journal of a Voyage to Lisbon. Cambridge: 1902. V. 43

A Journey from This World to the Next. Waltham St. Lawrence: 1930. V. 44

Julien l'Apostat, ou Voyage dans l'Autre Monde. Geneva: 1782. V. 39

The Letter-Writers; or, a New Way to Keep a Wife at Home. London: 1731. V. 44; 46

The Lottery. London: 1732. V. 46

The Lottery. London: 1733. V. 46

The Lottery. London: 1748. V. 46

Love in Several Masques. Dublin: 1728. V. 46

FIELDING, HENRY 1707-1754 continued

Love in Several Masques. London: 1728. V. 38; 44; 46

Miscellanies. London: 1743. V. 38; 41; 45; 46

The Miser. London: 1732. V. 45

The Miser. London: 1733. V. 37; 38; 46

The Miser. London: 1744. V. 46

The Miser. Glasgow: 1755. V. 46

The Miser. London: 1761. V. 46

The Miser. Dublin: 1762. V. 46

The Miser. London: 1773. V. 44

The Miser. London: 1788. V. 46

The Mock Doctor; or, the Dumb Lady Cur'd. London: 1734. V. 46

The Mock-Doctor; or, the Dumb Lady Cur'd. London: 1753. V. 46

The Modern Husband. London: 1732. V. 37; 38; 40; 42; 44; 46

The Novels. London: 1884. V. 43; 46

The Novels. New York: 1926. V. 43

Novels. Oxford: 1926. V. 37; 38; 39; 42; 44; 46

The Shakespeare Head Edition of Fielding's Novels. Oxford: 1926. V. 37; 41; 46

The Novels. Stratford-upon-Avon: 1926. V. 38; 42

Of True Greatness. London: 1741. V. 46

The Old Debauchees. London: 1732. V. 46

An Old Man Taught Wisdom; or, the Virgin Unmask'd. London: 1735. V. 46

Ovid's Art of Love Paraphrased and Adpated to the Present Time. London: 1747. V. 46

Pasquin. Dublin: 1736. V. 46

Pasquin. London: 1736. V. 37; 38; 39; 40; 41; 44; 46

The Plain Truth: a Dailogue Between Sir Courtly Lobber, Candidate for the Borough of Guzzledown and Tom Telltruth, School Master and Freeman in the Said Borough. London: 1741. V. 46

A Plan of the Universal Register Office, Opposite Cecil-Street in the Strand. London: 1751. V. 40; 46

A Plan of the Universal Register Office, Opposite Cecil-Street in the Strand, and of that in Bishopsgate-Street, the Corner of Cornhill. London: 1752. V. 46

A Proper Answer to a Late Scurrilous Libel, Entitled, An Apology for the Conduct of a Late Celebrated Second Rate Minsiter. London: 1747. V. 46

A Proposal for Making Effectual Provision for the Poor, Amending Their Morals, and for Rendering Them Useful Members of Society. Dublin: 1753. V. 46

A Proposal for Making an Effectual Provision for the Poor, for Amending Their Morals and for Tendering Them Useful Members of the Society. London: 1753. V. 46

Rape Upon Rape; or, the Justice Caught In his Own Trap. London: 1730. V. 46

Select Works of Henry Fielding, Esq. V. 43

Select Works of Henry Fielding. Edinburgh: 1812. V. 37; 40; 41; 44; 46

Select Works, to which is prefixed an original account of the life and writings of the author by William Watson. London: 1818. V. 37

A Serious Address to the People of Great Britain. London: 1745. V. 40; 46

Some Papers Proper to Be Read Before the R---l Society, Concerning the Terrestrial Chrysipus, Golden Foot or Guinea . . . London: 1743. V. 46

The Temple Beau. London: 1730. V. 38; 44; 46

Tom Thumb. London: 1730. V. 46

Tom Jones ou l'Enfant Trouve. Londres: 1767. V. 42

Tom Jones, ou l'Enfant Trouve. Paris: 1767. V. 42

Tom Jones. Paris: 1952. V. 45

The Tragedy of Tragedies; or the Life and Death of Tom Thumb the Great. London: 1731. V. 46

The Tragedy of Tragedies; or the Life and Death of Tom Thumb the Great. London: 1737. V. 46

The Tragedy of Tragedies. Narberth: 1932. V. 44

A True State of the Case of Bosavern Penlez, Who Suffered on Account of the Late Riot in the Strand. London: 1749. V. 45; 46

Tumble-Down Dick. London: 1744. V. 40; 42; 44; 46

Tumble-Down Dick, or Phaeton in the Suds. Boston: 1808. V. 46

The Universal Gallant; or, the Different Husbands. London: 1735. V. 46

The Wedding-Day. London: 1743. V. 44; 46

Der Hochzeitstag. (Wedding-Day). Mannheim: 1781. V. 46

The Welsh Opera; or, The Grey Mare the Better Horse. London: 1731. V. 46

Works. London. V. 38

The Works of Henry Field, Esq. London: 1762. V. 46

The Works of Henry Fielding, Esq. London: 1762. V. 38; 45

The Works . . . with the Life of the Author. London: 1762. V. 37; 46

The Works of Henry Fielding, Esq. Edinburgh: 1767. V. 37; 46

The Works. London: 1771. V. 39; 42; 43; 46

The Works. With the Life of the Author. London: 1771. V. 38; 43

The Works of Henry Fielding, Esq. London: 1775. V. 46

The Works of . . . London: 1783. V. 46

The Works. London: 1808. V. 38; 39; 46

Works. London: 1821. V. 38; 40

The Works. London: 1871. V. 45

Works. London: 1871-72. V. 38

The Works. London: 1882. V. 39

The Works. London: 1893. V. 39

The Works. London: 1898. V. 37

The Works. London: 1898-99. V. 39; 42

The Works of . . . Westminster: 1898-99. V. 46

The Works of . . . London: 1902-03. V. 38; 46

Works. London: 1903. V. 46

The Works. New York: 1903. V. 39; 42; 43; 46

FIELDING, JOHN

An Account of the Origin and Effects of a Police Set on Foot by His Grace the Duke of Newscastle, in the Year 1753, Upon a Plan Presented to His Grace by the Late Henry Fielding, Esq. London: 1751. V. 46

A Brief Description of the Cities of London and Westminster, the Public Buildings, Palaces, Gardens, Squares, etc. London: 1776. V. 41

Extracts from Such of the Penal Laws, as Particularly Relate to the Peace and Good Order of this Metropolis . . . London: 1761. V. 46

Extracts from Such of the Penal Laws, as Particularly Relate to the Peace and Good Order of This Metropolis . . . London: 1762. V. 46

A Plan for Preventing Robberies Within Twenty Miles of London. London: 1755. V. 46

The Universal Mentor . . . London: 1763. V. 46

The Universal Mentor; or Entertaining Instructor. London: 1777. V. 46

FIELDING, MANTLE

Dictionary of American Painters, Sculptors, and Engravers. Philadelphia. V. 42; 44

Gilbert Stuart's Portraits of Washington. Philadelphia: 1923. V. 38; 46

FIELDING, SARAH

The Adventures of David Simple. London: 1744. V. 37; 40; 41; 42; 46

The Adventures of David Simple . . . London: 1744/53. V. 46

The Adventures of David Simple . . . London: 1774. V. 42

The Cry. London: 1754. V. 40; 46

Familiar Letters Between the Principal Characters in David Simple and Some Others. London: 1747. V. 46

Familiar Letters Between the Principal Characters in 'David Simple,' and Some Others. Dublin: 1747. V. 38; 42

The Governess. London: 1749. V. 41; 43

The Governess; or, the Little Female Academy. London: 1765. V. 41

The Governess: or, the Little Female Academy. London: 1768. V. 46

The Governess; or, Little Female Academy. London: 1770? V. 45

The Governess; or, The Little Female Academy. London: 1781. V. 43

The History of Charlotte Summers, the Fortunate Parish Girl. London: 1750? V. 46

The History of the Countess of Dellwyn . . . London: 1759. V. 46

The History of Ophelia. London: 1760. V. 46

The Lives of Cleopatra and Octavi. London: 1757. V. 40; 46

The Lives of Cleopatra and Octavia. London: 1758. V. 46

FIELDING, T. H.

The Art of Engraving, with the Various Modes of Operation . . . London: 1841. V. 43

The Art of Engraving. London: 1844. V. 44

On Painting in Oil and Watercolours for Landscape and Portraits: Including the Preparation of Colours, Vehicles, Oils, etc. London: 1839. V. 46

On the Theory and Practice of Painting in Oil and Water Colours for Landscape and Portraits. London: 1846. V. 43

On Painting in Oil and Water Colours, for Landscape and Portraits . . . London: 1839. V. 43; 44

On the Theory of Painting . . . London: 1842. V. 44

On the Theory and Practice of Painting in Oil and Watercolours for Landscape and Portraits Including the Preparation of Colours, Vehicles, Varnishes, etc. with a Manual of Lithography. London: 1846. V. 46

A Picturesque Tour of the English Lakes . . . London: 1821. V. 46

Synopsis of Practical Perspective, Linear and Aerial, with Remarks on Sketching from Nature. London: 1843. V. 44

FIELDING, THEODORE HENRY

A Picturesque Tour of the English lakes, containing a description of the most romantic scenery of Cumberland, Westmoreland, and Lancashire, with the accounts of antient and moder manners and customs, and elucidation of the History and . . . London: 1821. V. 37

FIELDING, THEODORE HENRY ADOLPHUS

The Art of Engraving, With the Various Modes of Operation . . . London: 1841. V. 41

British Castles. London: 1825. V. 39; 41; 45

FIELDING, THEODORE HENRY ADOLPHUS continued

Cumberland, Westmoreland and Lancashire Illustrated in a Series of Forty-Four Engravings Exhibiting the Scenery of the Lakes, Antiquities and Other Picturesque Objects. London: 1822. V. 38; 39; 41

The Knowledge and Restoration of Old Paintings. London: 1847. V. 38

On Painting in Oil and Watercolours for Landscape and Portraits . . . London: 1839. V. 39

A Picturesque Tour of the English Lakes, Containing a Description of the Most Romantic Scenery of Cumberland . . . London: 1821. V. 41; 45

FIELDS, ANNIE

Authors and Friends. Boston: 1897. V. 41

FIELDS, JAMES T.

Anniversary Poem. Delivered Before the Mercantile Library Association of Boston, September 13, 1838. Boston: 1838. V. 43

Poems. 1849. V. 44

Poems. Boston: 1849. V. 40

The Token and Alantic Souvenir. Boston: 1840. V. 46

Yesterdays with Authors. Boston: 1886. V. 38

Yesterdays with Authors. Boston: 1900. V. 40

FIELDS, JOSEPH

My Sister Eileen. New York: 1941. V. 43

The Ponder Heart. New York: 1956. V. 39

FIELDS, JOSEPH A.

Wonderful Town: a New Musical Comedy. New York: 1953. V. 37; 45

FIELDS, WILLIAM

The Literary and Miscellaneous Scrap Book. Knoxville: 1833. V. 43

FIENNES, NATHANIEL

A Relation Made in the House of Commons . . . London: 1643. V. 39; 44

FIERRABRAS

Eyn Schoene Kurzweilige Histori von eym Machtige Riesen auss Hispanie/Fierrabras Gnant der Eyn Heyd Gewest/ und Bei Zeiten des Durchleuchtigsten Grossen Keyser Karls Gelebt . . . Simmern: 1533. V. 40

FIEVEE, JOSEPH

The Pope's Journey to the Other Worlds, to Seek Advice and Assistance Against the national Assembly of France. London: 1791. V. 37

FIFIELD, LIONEL

Infections of the Hand. London: 1926. V. 42

FIFOOT, RICHARD

A Bibliography of Edith Osbert and Sacheverell Sitwell. London: 1963. V. 39

FIFTH Annual Review of the Commerce, Manufactures, and the Public and Private Improvements of Chicago, for the Year 1856; with a Full Statement of Her System of Railroads, and a General Synopsis of the Business of the City. Chicago: 1857. V. 39

FIFTY Years of American Poetry: a Tribute to Marie Bullock 11 April 1984. 1984. V. 44

FIGG, ROYALL W.

'Where Men Only Dare to Go!' Richmond: 1885. V. 38; 39; 44

FIGGESS, FUJIO KOYAMA JOHN

Two Thousand Years of Oriental Ceramics. London: 1961. V. 42

FIGGINS, VINCENT

The Game of the Chesse. London: 1860. V. 46

FIGGIS, DARRELL

The Paintings of William Blake. London: 1925. V. 37; 39; 40; 42; 43

The Paintings of William Blake. New York: 1925. V. 40

FIGLIUCCI, FELICE

De La Politica, Overo Scienza Civile Secondo La Dottrina d'Aristotile. Venice: 1583. V. 41

FIGUEROA, JOSE

Manifesto a la Republica Mejicana . . . Monterrey: 1835. V. 38; 39

The Manifesto, Which the General of Brigade . . . Makes to the Mexican Republic, in Regarad to His Condut and that of the Snrs. D. Jose Maria de Hijars and D. Jose Maria Padres, as Directors of Colonization in 1833 and 1834. San Francisco: 1855. V. 37; 38; 40

FIGURE Prints of Old Japan. A Pictorial Pageant of Actors & Courtesans of the Eighteenth Century, . . . San Francisco: 1959. V. 46

FILARETTE, ANTONIO AVERLINO

Filarete's Treatise on Architecture Being the Treatise by Antonio de Piero Averlino, Known as Filarete. London: & New York: 1965. V. 46

FILCHER, J. A.

Untold Tales of California. N.P.: 1903. V. 40

FILCHNER, WILHELM

Das Ratsel des Matschu Meine Tibet-Expedition. Berlin: 1907. V. 43

FILELFO, FRANCESCO 1398-1481

Orationes (cum Quibusdam Aliis Eiusdem Operibus). Venice: 1491. V. 46

FILES, FRYE W.

Thirty Years in Topeka . . . Topeka: 1886. V. 37

FILIPPI, FILIPPO DE

Ruwenzori An Account of the Expedition of H.R.H. Prince Luigi Amedeo of Savoy Duke of the Abruzzi. New York: 1908. V. 40

An Account of the Expedition of H.R.H. Prince Luigi Amedeo fo Savoy, Duke of Abruzzi. With a Preface by H.R.H. the Duke of Abruzzi. London: 1908. V. 37

The Ascent of Mount St. Elias. Westminster: 1900. V. 43; 44

Ruwenzori. An Account of the Expedition of H.R.H. Prince Luigi Amadeo of Savoy. London: 1909. V. 38

FILIPPI, JOSEPH DE

Parallele des Principaux Theatres Modernes de l'Europe et des Machines Theatrales Francaises, Allemandes, et Anglaises. Paris: 1860. V. 46

FILISOLA, DON VICENTE

Memorias Para La Historia de La Guerra De Tejas . . . Mexico City: 1848-49. V. 38; 42

FILISOLA, VICENTE

Mejicanos. Habiendose Manifestado al Publico por Media del Diario del Supremo Gobierno 15 del Procsimo Pasado Junio Varios Documentos Relativos a los Ultimos Acontecimientos de Tejas. 1836. V. 40

Representacion en Defensa de Su Honor Y Aclaracion de Sus Operaciones Como General en Gefe del Ejercito Sobre Tejas. Mexico: 1836. V. 39

Representacion Dirigida al Supremo Gobierno . . . Mexico City: 1836. V. 39; 40

Representacion Dirigida al Supremo Govierno . . . en Defensa de su Honor y Aclaracion de sus Operaciones Como General en Gefe del Ejercito Sobre Tejas. Mexico City: 1836. V. 40; 41

FILLEY, WILLIAM

Life and Adventures of . . . Who Was Stolen from His Home in Jackson, Mich., by the Indians, August 3d, 1837, and His Safe Return from Captivity, Oct. 19, 1866. Chicago: 1867. V. 37; 39; 44

FILLMORE SILVER MINING CO.

Report and By-Laws of the Fillmore Silver Mining Co. Near Fort Fillmore, in the Organ Range of Mountains, in the Territory of New Mexico . . . New York: 1858. V. 40

FILMER, ROBERT

The Freeholders Grand Inquest, Touching Our Sovereign Lord the King and His Parliament. London: 1679. V. 46

Patriarcha; or the Natural Power of Kings. London: 1680. V. 37; 39

Patriarcha; or the Natural Power of Kings. London: 1685. V. 39; 46

FILOW, BOGDAN D.

Early Bulgarian Art. Berne: 1919. V. 38; 42

FILSON, JOHN

The Discovery, Settlement and Present State of Kentucky. London: 1793. V. 39; 42

Histoire de Kentucke, Nouvelle Colonie a L'Ouest de la Virginie . . . Paris: 1785. V. 38; 40; 45

FINAL Drafts of the Madates for Mesopotamia and Palestine Presented to Parliament by Command of His Majesty, August 1921. London: 1921. V. 38

THE FINAL Rolls of Citizens and Freedmen of the Five Civilized Tribes in Indian Territory. (and) Index to the Final Rolls of Citizens and Freedmen of the Five Civilized Tribes. Muskogee: 1907. V. 39

FINAUGHTY, WILLIAM

The Recollections of (an) Elephant Hunter, 1864-1875. Philadelphia: 1916. V. 39

FINBERG, ALEXANDER J.

The History of Turner's Liber Studiorum. V. 39

J.M.W. Turner's Liber Studiorum with a Catalogue Raisonne. San Francisco: 1988. V. 40

FINCH, ANNE

Miscellany Poems, on Several Occasions. London: 1713. V. 37

FINCH, C.

The Gamut and Time-Table, in Verse. For the Instruction of Children. Embellished with twelve illustrative coloured engravings. London: (ca. 1825). V. 37

FINCH, CHRISTOPHER

The Art of Walt Disney. New York: 1973. V. 40; 41

FINCH-DAVIES, C. G.

The Birds of Southern Africa. Johannesburg: 1982. V. 37

FINCH-DAVIS, C. G.

The Bird Paintings of C. G. Finch-Davis. Johannesburg: 1984. V. 45

FINCH, E.

Wilfrid Scawen Blunt 1840-1922. London: 1938. V. 44

FINCH, EDWIN WARD

The Frontier, Army and Professional Life of Edwin W. Finch, with Thoughts from His Own Personal Experiences in the Treatment of Pneumonia, Etc. New Rochelle: 1909. V. 44

FINCH, JOHN

To South Africa and Back. London: 1890. V. 40

Travels in the United States of America and Canada . . . London: 1833. V. 38; 39; 43

FINCH, MARGARET

The Original Norwood Gipsey. Derby: 1830. V. 38; 42

FINCHAM, JOHN

An Outline of Ship Building. London: 1852. V. 41

A Treatise on Masting Ships and Mast Makings, principles, practical operations, mode of forming and combining mast. London;: 1829. V. 37

FINCK, HENRY T.

The Pacific Coast Scenic Tour from Southern California to Alaska, the Canadian Pacific Railway, Yellowstone Park and the Grand Canyon . . . V. 42

FINDEN, EDWARD

The Ports, Harbours, Watering Places and Coast Scenery of Great Britain. London: 1844. V. 42

FINDEN, W.

Finden's Illustrations of the Life and Works of Lord Byron. London: 1833-34. V. 40

Landscape Illustrations of the Bible . . . London: 1836. V. 40; 46

Ports, Harbours, Watering-Places and Picturesque Scenery of Great Britain. London: 1840. V. 46

FINDEN, WILLIAM

Finden's Landscape Illustrations to Mr. Murray's First Complete and Uniform Edition of the Life and Works of Lord Byron. London: 1832-34. V. 42

The Ports, Harbours and Watering Places and the Coast Scenery of Great Britain . . . London: 1844. V. 42; 43

FINDLATER, CHARLES

General View of the Agriculture of the County of Peebles, with Various Suggestions as the the means of Both of the Local and General Improvement of Architecture. Edinburgh: 1802. V. 38

FINDLAY, ALEXANDER G.

The Sailing Directory for the Caribbee or West India Islands, from Porto Rico to Trinidad. london: 1863. V. 37

FINDLAY, ALEXANDER GEORGE

Directory for the Navigation of the North Pacific Ocean, With Descriptions of Its Coasts, Islands, etc . . . London: 1886. V. 40

FINDLAY, F. R. N.

Big Game Shooting and Travel in South East Africa. London: 1903. V. 38; 41

FINDLAY, FREDERICK RODERICK NOBLE

Big Game Shooting and Travel in South-East Africa. London: 1903. V. 37

FINDLAY, G. R.

A Directory for the Navigation of the Indian Archipelago, China and Japan, from the Straits of Malacca and Sunda, and the Passages East of Java, Canton, Shaghai, the Yellow Sea and Japan. London: 1878. V. 40

FINDLAY, J. M.

With the 8th Scottish Rifles. 1914-1919. London: 1926. V. 46

FINDLAY, RICHARD

Honour. London: 1936. V. 40; 42; 43

FINDLEY, PALMER

The Story of Childbirth. Garden City: 1934. V. 45

FINDLEY, RICHARD

Honour. N.P.: 1936. V. 38

FINDLEY, WILLIAM

Observations on 'The Two Sons of Oil' . . . Pittsburgh: 1812. V. 37; 39; 42; 43

THE FINE Art Collection of Glasgow. Glasgow: 1906. V. 40

THE FINE Book: a Symposium. Pittsburgh: 1934. V. 43

FINE, GEORGE W.

Beyond the West: Two Years' Travel in . . . The Rocky Mountains, and Picturesque Parks of Colorado . . . Utica: 1870. V. 43

FINE, ORONCE

Arithmetica Practica. Paris: 1542. V. 41

De Mundi Sphaera, sive Cosmographia, Primave Astronomiae Parte Lib V. Paris: 1542. V. 41

Quadrans Astrolabicus. Paris: 1534. V. 41

Quadratura Circula. Paris: 1554. V. 40; 41; 45

De Rectis in Circuli Quadrante Subtensis . . . Paris: 1550. V. 45

De Solaribus Horologiis & Quadrantibus Libri Quatuor. Paris: 1560. V. 41

La Theorique des Cielz, Mouvemens et Termes Pratiques des Sept Planetes, Nouvellement et Tresclerement Redigee en Langaige Francois. Paris: 1528. V. 38

FINE, RUTH E.

Claire Van Vliet - Landscape Paperworks. Philadelphia: 1984. V. 44

Printer's Choice. A Selection of American Press Books 1968-1974. Austin: 1983. V. 37; 40

A Selection of American Press Books, 1968-1978. Printer's Choice; A Catalogue of an Exhibition Held at the Grolier Club, New York, December 19, 1978-February 3, 1979. Austin: 1983. V. 39; 41

FINELLA, FILIPPO

De Quatuor Signis, Quae Apparent in Unguibus Manuum. Naples: 1649. V. 45

FINERTY, JOHN F.

War-Path and Bivouac of the Conquest. Chicago: 1890. V. 45

FINETT, JOHN

Finetti Philoxenis; Some Choice Observations of Sr. John Finett Knight, and Master of the Ceremonies to the Two Last Kings . . . London: 1656. V. 37; 40; 42

FINGER, F. L.

Catalogue of the Incunabula in the Elmer Belt Library of Vinciana. Los Angeles: 1971. V. 46

FINISHERS' FRIENDLY ASSOCIATION

The Book-Finishers' Friendly Circular. London: 1845-50. V. 41

THE FINISHING Stroke. Being a Supplement to the Queries to the People of Ireland. Dublin: 1754. V. 41

FINLASON, WILLIAM FRANCIS 1818-1895

Commentaries Upon Martial Law, with Special Reference to Its Regulation and Restaraint. London: 1867. V. 38; 40

A Report of the Case of the Queen v. Gurney and Others in the Court of Queen's Bench. London: 1870. V. 40

FINLAY, GEORGE

Greece Under the Romans. Edinburgh: 1854. V. 37; 39

The History of Greece from Its Conquest by the Crusaders to Its Conquest by the Turks, and of the Empire of Trebizond 1204-1461. Edinburgh: 1851. V. 37; 39

A History of Greece from Its Conquest by the Romans to the Present Time, BC 46 to AD 1864. Oxford: 1877. V. 37; 39

The History of Greece Under Othoman and Venetian Dimination. Edinburgh: 1856. V. 37; 39

History of the Greek Revolution. London: 1861. V. 37

FINLAY, IAN

Scottish Crafts. London: 1948. V. 41

FINLAY, IAN HAMILTON

Three Sundials. Exeter: 1974. V. 43

FINLAY, KIRKMAN

Letter to the Right Hon. Lord Ashlay, on the Cotton Factory System and the Ten Hours' Factory Bill. Glasgow: 1833. V. 42

FINLAYSON, ARCHIBALD W.

A Trip to America: A Lecture, Delivered by . . . in the Public Hall of the Johnstone Working Men's Institute . . . Glasgow: 1879. V. 38

FINLAYSON, DUNCAN

Traits of American-Indian Life and Character. V. 42

Traits of American Indian Life and Character. London: 1853. V. 37; 40

Traits of American-Indian Life and Character by a Fur Trader. San Francisco: 1933. V. 37

FINLAYSON, GEORGE

The Mission to Siam and Hue the Capital of Cochin China in the Years 1821-22. London: 1826. V. 43

FINLAYSON, ROBERT

Essay . . . to Captains of Royal Navy . . . and Merchant Service . . . London: 1824. V. 41

FINLEY, ANTHONY

A New General Atlas, Comprising a Complete Set of Maps, Representing the Grand Divisions of the Globe, Together with the Several Empires, Kingdoms and States in the World. Philadelphia: 1824. V. 41

FINLEY, CHARLES

The Circus of Dr. Lao. West Burke: 1984. V. 38

FINLEY, FLORENCE

Grandad and I - A Story of a Grand Old Man and Other Pioneers in Texas and the Dakotas as told by John Leaky. Leaky: 1951. V. 38

FINLEY, I. J.

Pioneer Record and Reminiscences of the Early Settlers of Ross County, Ohio. Cincinnati: 1871. V. 45

FINLEY, J. B.

History of the Wyanodtt Mission, at Upper Sandusky, Ohio. Cincinnati: 1840. V. 37; 38; 41

FINLEY, JAMES B.

Autobiography of Rev. James B. Finley; or Pioneer Life in the West. Cincinnati: 1853. V. 37; 40

FINN, EDMUND

The Chronicles of Early Melbourne. Melbourne: 1888. V. 41
The Cyclorama of Early Melbourne: an Historical Sketch. Melbourne: 1887. V. 41

FINN, F.

Indian Sporting Birds . . . Calcutta: 1915. V. 43
Indian Sporting Birds. London: 1915. V. 37; 38; 42

FINN, FRANK

Birds of Our Country: Their Eggs, Nests, Life Haunts and Identification. London: 1920. V. 40

FINN, HENRY J.

American Comic Annual. Boston: 1831. V. 39

FINN, JAMES

The Jews in China. London: 1843. V. 37; 43

FINNEY, CHARLES G.

The Circus of Doctor Lao. 1982. V. 38
The Circus of Doctor Lao. New York: 1982. V. 39; 40; 41; 42; 43; 44; 45
The Circus of Dr. Lao. Vermont: 1983. V. 41
The Circus of Doctor Lao. Newark: 1984. V. 38; 39
The Circus of Dr. Lao. Vermont: 1984. V. 39
The Circus of Doctor Lao. By Charles G. Finney. Newark, Vermont: 1984. V. 37
Justification by Faith. New York: 1837. V. 43
Lectures on Revivals of Religion. New York: 1835. V. 40
Past the End of the Pavement. New York: 1939. V. 46

FINNEY, JACK

The Body Snatchers. London: 1955. V. 41
I Love Galesburg in the Springtime. New York: 1963. V. 44
The Third Level. New York: 1957. V. 44
Time and Again. New York: 1970. V. 37; 39; 42; 44; 46

FIONN, MAC CUMHAILL

Fingal, a Fine-Erin; A Poem in Six Cantos. London: 1813. V. 43

FIORAVANTI, LEONARDO

Three Exact Pieces . . . viz. London: 1652. V. 46

FIORENTINO, UGOLINO VERINO CITTADINO

Vita di Santa Chiara Vergine Composta per . . . Chelsea: 1921. V. 40

FIRBANK, ARTHUR ANNESLEY RONALD 1886-1926

The Collected Works of Ronald Firbank. London: 1929. V. 45
The Flower Beneath the Foot. New York: 1924. V. 45
Odette D'Antrevernes and a Study in Temperament. London: 1905. V. 40; 42; 45
The Princess Zoubaroff: a Comedy. London: 1st edition; V. 45
Santal. New York: 1955. V. 45
Vainglory. New York: 1925. V. 45

Valmouth. London: 1919. V. 45

FIRBANK, RONALD 1886-1926

Concerning the Eccentricities of Cardinal Pirelli. London: 1926. V. 46
The Flower Beneath the Foot. New York: 1924. V. 39
The Flower Beneath the Foot Being a Record of the Early Life of St. Laura de Nazianzi and the Times In Which She Lived. London: 1923. V. 38; 40
Inclinations. London: 1916. V. 38
A Letter from Arthur Ronald Firbank to Madame Albani. London: 1934. V. 46
Odette d'Antrevernes. London: 1905. V. 39
Odette. London: 1916. V. 38; 41; 46
Prancing Nigger. New York: 1924. V. 39; 42; 46
The Princess Zoubaroff. London: 1920. V. 46
Santal. London: 1921. V. 37; 43
Sorrow in Sunlight. London: 1925. V. 46
Vainglory. London: 1915. V. 46
Valmouth. London: 1919. V. 38; 46
The Works. London: 1928. V. 46
The Works of Ronald Firbank. London: 1929. V. 39

FIREBAUGH, ELLEN

The Physician's Wife and the Things that Pertain to Her Life. Philadelphia: 1894. V. 41; 42; 45

FIREBAUGH, W. C.

The Inns of Greece and Rome. Chicago: 1928. V. 46

FIRENZUOLA, AGNOLO 1493-1543

Prose. Florence: 1552. V. 40
La Trinutia. Florence: 1551. V. 40

FIRISHTAH, MUHAMMAD QASIM HINDU SHAH ASTARABADI

The History of Hindostan. Dublin: 1792. V. 39

FIRMICIUS MATERNUS

Astronomicorum Libri Octo Integri (and Other Anatomical Works). Venice: 1499. V. 43

FIRMICUS MATERNUS, JULIUS

De Nativitatibus (and Other Works). Venice: 1499. V. 42

FIRMIN, GILES

Stablishing Against Shaking: or, A Discovery of the Prince of Darknesse (scarcely) Transformed into an Angel of Light. London: 1656. V. 37

FIRMIN, THOMAS

Some Proposals for the Imployment of the Poor, and for the Preservation of Idleness and the Consequence Therof, Begging. London: 1681. V. 38

FIRMINGER, THOMAS

A Manual of Gardening for Bengal and Upper India. Calcutta: 1874. V. 45

FIRRUFINE, JULIO CESAR

Ell Perfeto Artillero: Theorica y Pratica. Colophon: 1648. V. 37

THE FIRST and Large Petition of the City of London and of Other Inhabitants Thereabouts: for a Reformation in Church-Government, As Also for the Abolishment of Episcopacy. N.P.: 1641. V. 41

THE FIRST Book of the Parish Registers of Madron, in the County of Cornwall. Penzance: 1877. V. 40

THE FIRST Book of the 'Washington Benevolents;' Otherwise Called the Book of Knaves. Boston: 1813. V. 40

THE FIRST Chapter of Tear-em the Son of Gore'am, in the Apocripha. London: 1750. V. 38

FIRST Chess Tourney of 'The Danites.' Commencing November 13th, 1879. N.P.: 1879. V. 40

FIRST Congressional District of New Jersey. Biographical, Genealogical and Descriptive History. V. 41

THE FIRST Crusade. The Deeds of the Franks and Other Jerusalemites. London: 1945. V. 37; 44

FIRST EDITION CLUB

A Bibliographical Catalogue of the First Loan Exhibition of Books and Manuscripts. 1922. V. 44; 45
Bibliographical Catalogue of First Editions Proof Copies of Manuscripts of Books by Lord Byron. Exhibited at the Fourth Exhibition Held by the First Edition Club January 1925. London: 1925. V. 37

THE FIRST Five Years of my Married Life. Newcastle: 1853. V. 38

FIRST On the Moon: a Voyage With Neil Armstrong, Michael Collins, Edwin E. Aldrin Jr. Boston: 1970. V. 46

FIRST Papers of Surrealism. New York: 1942. V. 45

FIRST Reader in the English and Blackfoot Languages, with Pictures and Workds . . . for Use . . . Among the Blackfoot Tribes in the North West Territories. Montreal: 1886. V. 37

THE FIRST Settlers of Virginia. New York: 1806. V. 43

FIRST Steamship Pioneers. San Francisco: 1874. V. 37

THE FIRST Three Years: a Pictorial History of the 173D Airborne Brigade (Seperate). Tokyo. V. 39

THE FIRST Time. New York: 1975. V. 46

FIRTH, C. M.

The Archaeological Survey of Hubia. Report for 1908-1909. Cairo: 1912. V. 40; 42

FIRTH, EDITH G.

The Town of York 1793-1815. (with) The Town of York 1815-1834. 1962-66. V. 43

FIRTH, FRANK RUSSEL

Memoirs of Frank Russel Firth. Boston: 1873. V. 39

FIRTH, WILLIAM

The Lord Thanet's Case Considered, as to the Question Whether the Judgment be Specific or Arbitrary? London: 1799. V. 38; 42; 46

FIRTH, WILLIAM POWELL

John Leech. His Life and Work. London: 1891. V. 40

FISCH, M. H.

Nicolaus Pol Doctor 1494 (a Biography, With a Complete List of the Books He Owned). New York: 1947. V. 39

FISCHBACK, FRIEDRICH

The Principal Weaving Ornaments Up to the 19th Century. 1902-11? V. 38

FISCHEL, OSKAR

Modes and Manners of the Nineteenth Century as Represented in the Pictures and Engravings of the Time. London: 1927. V. 37; 38

Modes and Manners of the 19th Century, as Represented in the Pictures and Engravings of the Time. London & New York: 1927. V. 41

Raphael. London: 1948. V. 43

FISCHER, CHRISTIAN AUGUSTUS

A Picture of Madrid; Taken on the Spot. London: 1808. V. 41

FISCHER, E. S.

Elements of Natural Philosophy. Boston: 1827. V. 38

FISCHER, GOTTHELF

Essai sur les Monumens Typographiques de Jean Gutenberg. Mayence: 1802. V. 38

FISCHER, HENRY GEORGE

Dendera in the Third Millenium B.C. Down to the Theban Domination of Upper Egypt. Locust Valley: 1968. V. 44

FISCHER, JOSEPH

The Discoveries of the Norsemen in America . . . London: 1903. V. 44

FISCHER VON ERLACH, JOHAN BERNARD

Entwurff Einer Historischen Architecture, in Abbildungg Unterschiedener Beruhmten Gebaude. Leipzig: 1725. V. 42

FISH, DANIEL

Lincoln Bibliography, a List of Books and Pamphlets Relating to Abraham Lincoln. New York: 1906. V. 42

A Reprint of the List of Books and Pamphlets Relating to Abraham Lincoln. Rock Island: 1926. V. 39

FISH, DANIEL W.

Robinson's Progressive Intellectual Arithmetic . . . New York & Chicago: 1874. V. 39

FISH, DONALD

Airline Detective. London: 1962. V. 46

FISH, FRANKLIN W.

The Heart's Musings. New York: 1850. V. 44

FISH, JOSEPH

Christ Jesus the Physician and His Blood The Balm, Recommended for the Healing of Diseased People. New London: 1760. V. 38; 39; 40; 41

FISH, ROBERT L.

The Incredible Schlock Homes. New York: 1966. V. 42

FISH, SIMON d. 1531

Klagbrieff Oder Supplication der Armen Dursstigen in Engenlandt. Nuremberg: 1529. V. 44

FISH, THEOPHILUS

Labor the Only True Source of Wealth. Charleston: 1837. V. 37

FISHBEIN, I. LEO

The Gentle Art of Equanimity. The Making of Character. Enthusiasm - an Essential to Greatness. 1963. V. 46

FISHER, A. HUGH

Callisto. Chicago: 1934. V. 41

FISHER, A. K.

The Hawks and Owls of the United States in Their Relation to Agriculture. Washington: 1893. V. 42

Hawks and Owls of the United States in Their Relation to Agriculture. 1893. V. 38

FISHER, ABBY

What Mrs. Fisher Knows About Old Southern Cooking. San Francisco: 1881. V. 44

FISHER, ALEXANDER

Journal of a Voyage of Discovery to the Artic Regions. London: 1819. V. 39; 43

A Journal of a Voyage of Discovery to the Arctic Regions, In His Majesty's Ships Hecla and Griper, in the Years 1819 and 1820. London: 1821. V. 42; 43; 46

FISHER, ALFRED YOUNG

The Ghost in the Underblows. Los Angeles: 1940. V. 37; 42

FISHER & SON

Historic Illustrations of the Bible. London: 1840. V. 40

FISHER, ANN

A Practical New Grammar, with Exercises of Bad English . . . London: 1789. V. 46

FISHER, ANNE

The Pleasing Instructor or Entertaining Moralist Consisting of Select Essays, Relations, Visions, and Allegories Collected from the Most Eminent English Authors to Which are Prefixed New Thoughts on Education. 1777. V. 41

FISHER, BUD

Mutt and Jeff Big Book. New York: 1926. V. 45

FISHER, CHARLES

Some Unaccountable Exploits of Sherlock Holmes. Philadelphia: 1956. V. 43

FISHER, CHARLES HAWKINS

Reminiscences of a Falconer. London: 1901. V. 39; 43

FISHER, CLARENCE S.

The Minor Cemetery at Giza. Philadelphia: 1924. V. 40; 42; 44

FISHER, DANIEL

A System of Military Tactics, Containing the Principles of Discipline and Movements, Chiefly Applied to Infantry . . . New York: 1805. V. 39

FISHER, EDWARD

The Marrow of Modern Divinity . . . Boston: 1743. V. 43

FISHER, ELLWOOD

Lecture on the North and South, Delivered Before the Young Men's Mercantile Library Association, of Cincinnati, Ohio, January 16, 1849. Cincinnati?: 1849. V. 45

FISHER, FRED H.

Cyprus. Our New Colony and What We Know About It. London: 1878. V. 37

FISHER, G. P.

Life of Benjamin Silliman, M.D. New York: 1866. V. 46

FISHER, GEORGE

The Instructor; or, Young Man's Best Companion. London: 1751. V. 41; 42

The Instructor; or, Young Man's Best Companion. London: 1755. V. 41

The Instructor; or, American Young Man's Best Companion. Walpole: 1794. V. 46

The Instructor, or American Young Man's Best Companion . . . Philadelphia: 1801. V. 42

The Instructor, or, Young Man's Best Companion. London: 1788. V. 38

The Instructor: or, Young Man's Best Companion Containing Spelling, Reading, Writing and Arithmetick . . . Burlington, NJ: 1775. V. 37

FISHER, GEORGE A.

The Yankee Conscript; or, Eighteen Months in Dixie. Philadelphia: 1864. V. 37

FISHER, HARRIET WHITE

A Woman's World Tour in a Motor. Philadelphia: 1911. V. 38

A Woman's World-Tour in a Motor. Philadelphia & London: 1911. V. 41

FISHER, HARRISON

American Beauties. 1909. V. 38

Bachelor Belles. New York: 1908. V. 39

Bachelor Belles. New York: 1908. V. 40

Maidens Fair. New York: 1912. V. 37

FISHER, IRVING 1867-1947

The Making of Index Numbers. Boston/New York: 1922. V. 41

The Making of Index Numbers. New York: 1922. V. 41

The Purchasing Power of Money Its Determination and Relation to Credit Interest and Crises. New York: 1920. V. 41

Stabilizing the Dollar. New York: 1920. V. 39; 41

The Theory of Interest, as Determined by Impatience to Spend Income and Opportunity to Invest It. New York: 1930. V. 38; 41

FISHER, J.

The Fulmar. London: 1952. V. 37; 38

Sea Birds. London: 1954. V. 37; 38

FISHER, J. A.

Some Notes by Lord Fisher for His Friends. London: 1919. V. 39

FISHER, J. B.

Poetical Rhapsodies. London: 1818. V. 37

FISHER, J. R.

Camping in the Rocky Mountains. New York: 1880. V. 42

FISHER, JAMES

Sea-Birds. London: 1954. V. 40

The World of Birds. London: 1964. V. 45

FISHER, JOHN

Assertionis Lutheranae Confutatio per Reverendum Patrem Ioannem Roffensem Episcopum. Antwerp: 1523. V. 37

Burgess and Maclean. A New Look at the Foreign Office Spies. London: 1977. V. 40

The History and Antiquities of Masham and Mashamshire . . . London: 1865. V. 45; 46

An Illustrated Record of the Retrospective Exhibition Held at South Kensington 1896. London: 1897. V. 37

A Mornyng Remembraunce. London: 1906. V. 43

National Competitions 1896-97: An Illustrated Record of National Gold, Silver and Bronze Medal Designs, Models, Drawings, Etc. London: 1899. V. 37

Notable Women of the Southwest . . . Dallas: 1938. V. 38

Reisdence. London: 1821. V. 42

FISHER, JOHN, BP. OF ROCHESTER

De Veritate Corporis & Sanguinis Christi in Eucharistia . . . Cologne: 1527. V. 40; 44

FISHER, JOHN DIX

Description of the Distinct, Confluent and Inoculated Small Pox, Varioloid Disease, Cow Pox and Chicken Pox. Boston: 1829. V. 39; 40; 41; 45

Description of the Distinct, Confluent, and Inoculated Small Pox, Varioloid Disease, Cow Pox, and Chicken Pox. Boston: 1834. V. 40

FISHER, JOSEPH

Seventy Etched Facsimiles, on a Reduced Scale, After the Original Studies by Michael Angelo and Raffaelle in the University Galleries, Oxford. Oxford: 1852. V. 40

Seventy Etched Facsimiles . . . After the Original Studies by Michael Angelo and Raffaelle in the Unversity Galleries. Oxford: 1852. V. 40

FISHER, JOSHUA BRIDGES

Poetical Rhapsodies. London: 1818. V. 42

FISHER, KATHERINE

Romance of Watermarks. Cincinatti: 1939. V. 45

FISHER, LILLIAN ESTELLE

The Intendant System in Spanish America. Berkeley: 1929. V. 46

FISHER, M. F. K.

An Alphabet for Gourmets. New York: 1949. V. 44

Consider the Oyster. New York: 1941. V. 43; 46

The Gastronomical Me. New York: (1943). V. 37

Not Now But Now. New York: 1947. V. 45

Spirits of the Valley. New York: 1985. V. 43; 46

The Standing and the Waiting. Fallbrook: 1985. V. 37; 40

FISHER, NORMAN

The Last Assignment. New York: 1973. V. 38

FISHER, P.

The Anglers Souvenir. London: 1886. V. 38

The Anglers Souvenir. London: c. 1870. V. 37

The Angler's Souvenir by P. Fisher. London: 1935. V. 37

FISHER, PAYNE

Irenodia Gratulatoria, Sive Illustrissimi Amplissimiq; Viri Oliveri Cromwelli &c. London: 1652. V. 45

Marston Moor; Sive de Obsidione Praelioque Eboracensi Carmen . . . London: 1650. V. 46

Piscatoria Poemata: vel Panegyricum Carmen In Diem Inaugurationis Olivari . . . London: 1656-55. V. 43

A Synopsis of Heraldry, or, the Most Plain, Short and Easie Way for the Perfect Attaining of that Art. London: 1682. V. 45

FISHER, RAYMOND H.

The Russian Fur Trade, 1550-1700. Berkeley & Los Angeles: 1943. V. 44

FISHER, RICHARD

Catalogue of a Collection of Engravings, and Woodcuts. N.P.: 1879. V. 37; 41

Catalogue of a Collection of Engravings, Etchings and Woodcuts. Midhurst: 1879. V. 37

FISHER, RICHARD BARNARD

A Practical Treatise on Copyhold Tenure, with the Methods of Holding Courts Leet, Court Baron, and Other Courts and an Appendix . . . London: 1794. V. 40

A Practical Treatise on Copyhold Tenure, With Methods of Holding Courts-Leet, Court-Baron and Other Courts; and an Appendix. London: 1803. V. 38

FISHER, RICHARD S.

A Chronological History of the Civil War in America. New York: 1863. V. 38; 42; 44; 45

FISHER, ROBERT A.

Officers of the United States Army and Navy, Prisoners of War. Cincinnati: 1864. V. 44

FISHER, ROGER

Heart of Oak, the British Bulwark. London: 1764. V. 40

FISHER, RONALD AYLMER

The Genetical Theory of Natural Selection. Oxford: 1930. V. 37

FISHER, ROY

The Left-Handed Punch. By Roy Fisher and Ronald King. Surrey: 1986. V. 37

FISHER, RUTH B.

On the Borders of Pigmy Land. London: 1905. V. 39; 40

FISHER, S. W.

English Blue and White Porcelain of the 18th Century. London: 1947. V. 40

FISHER, ST. JOHN

Sermon Against Luther. 1935. V. 43

This Treatyse Concernynge the Fruytfull Sayenges of Dauyd the Kynge and Prophete in the Seuen Penytencyall Psalmes. London: 1525. V. 40

FISHER, SAMUEL 1605-1665

The Testimony of Truth Exalted, by the Collected Labours of that Worthy Man. London: 1679. V. 43; 46

FISHER, SIDNEY GEORGE

The Law of the Territories. Philadelphia: 1859. V. 42; 45

FISHER, THOMAS

The Negro's Memorial, or Abolitionst's Catechism. London: 1825. V. 40

FISHER, VARDIS

April, a Fable of Love. Caldwell: 1937. V. 38

Children of God. New York & London: 1939. V. 45

City of Illusion. Caldwell: 1941. V. 38

Forgive Us Our Virtues. Caldwell: 1938. V. 42

The Idaho Encyclopedia. Caldwell: 1938. V. 39; 44

Idaho Lore. Caldwell: 1939. V. 46

Neurotic Nightingale. USA: 1935. V. 46

Odyssey Of a Hero. Philadelphia: 1937. V. 41

Toilers of the Hills. Boston: 1928. V. 37

FISHER, W. K.

Asteroids of the North Pacific and Adjacent Waters. Washington: 1911-30. V. 43; 45

FISHER, WALTER M.

The Californians. London: 1876. V. 38; 44

FISHER, WILLIAM

An Interesting Account of the Voyages and Travels of Captains Lewis and Clark. Baltimore: 1813. V. 44

FISHING. Manor House Hotel, Moreton: 1957. V. 44

FISHING at Home and Abroad. London: 1913. V. 42

FISK, JAMES L.

Expedition of Captain Fisk to the Rocky Mountains. Washington: 1864. V. 40; 44; 45

FISK, JAMES LIBERTY

Expedition from Fort Abercrombie to Fort Benton. Letter from the Secretary of War. Washington: 1863. V. 39; 41; 42

Expedition of Captain Fisk to the Rocky Mountains. Washington: 1864. V. 41; 42

FISK, THEOPHILUS

Labor the Only True Source of Wealth. Charleston: 1837. V. 44

FISKAA, H. M.

Paper and Watermarks in Norway and Denmark. Amsterdam: 1978. V. 38

FISKE, FRANK

The Taming of the Sioux. Bismark: 1917. V. 37; 43; 45

FISKE, FRANK B.

Life and Death of Sitting Bull. Fort Yates: 1933. V. 45

FISKE, GERTRUDE HORSFORD

Studies in the Bi-Literal Cipher of Francis Bacon. London: 1913. V. 40

FISKE, JOHN

American Revolution. Cambridge: 1896. V. 38

Darwinism and Other Essays. London: 1879. V. 42

The Dutch and Quaker Colonies in America. Cambridge: 1903. V. 37; 38; 41

New France and New England. Cambridge: 1904. V. 38

Writings of . . . Cambridge: 1902. V. 40; 42

The Writings of . . . Boston: 1902. V. 38

FISKE, M.

A Visit to Texas: Being the Journal of a Traveller Through Those Parts Most Interesting to American Settlers . . . New York: 1834. V. 43

A Visit to Texas . . . with an Appendix . . . Mobile: 1836. V. 43

A Visit to Texas . . . with an Appendix, Containing a Sketch of the Late War. New York: 1836. V. 40

FISKE, NATHAN

The Moral Monitor. Worcester. V. 40

The Moral Monitor, or a Collection of Essays on Various Subjects . . . Worcester: 1801. V. 41

FISKE, WILLARD

Chess in Iceland and in Icelandic Literature. Florence: 1905. V. 38; 42

FISTER, R.

Golden Book of the Osages. Cleveland: 1950. V. 40; 42; 44; 45

FISTER, R. G.

Golden Books of the Osages. Cleveland: 1960. V. 46

FITCH, ELIJAH

The Beauties of Religion. Providence: 1789. V. 41

FITCH, FRANKLIN Y.

The Life, Travels and Adventures of an American Wanderer. New York: 1883. V. 38; 42

FITCH, JOHN

Annals of the Army of the Cumberland . . . Philadelphia: 1863. V. 39

FITCH, SAMUEL

A System of Dental Surgery. New York: 1829. V. 42

FITCH, THOMAS

Reasons Why the British Colonies in America, Should Not be Charged with Internal Taxes by Authority of Parliament . . . New Haven: 1764. V. 38

FITCH, WILLIAM EDWARDS

Some Neglected History of North Carolina. New York: 1905. V. 43

FITE, EMERSON D.

A Book of Old Maps Delineating American History from the Earliest Days Down to the Close of the Revolutionary War. Cambridge: 1926. V. 37; 43; 44

A Book of Old Maps, Delineating American History from the Earliest Days Down to the Revolutionary War. New York: 1969. V. 37

FITHIAN, PHILIP VICKERS

Philip Vickers Fithian Journal and Letters, 1767-1774, Student at Princeton College, 1770-72, Tutor at Nomini Hall in Virginia 1773-74. Princeton: 1900. V. 41

FITTLER, JAMES

Scotia Depicta. London: 1804. V. 38; 39; 40

FITTON, ELIZABETH

Conversations on Botany. London: 1823. V. 40

FITTON, SARAH MARY

Conversations on Botany. London: 1820. V. 40

FITTON, W. H.

Observations on Some of the Strata Between the Chalk and Oxford Oolite, in the South-East of England. London: 1836. V. 46

FITTON, WILLIAM HENRY

An Account of Some Geological Specimens from the Coasts of Australia. London: 1826. V. 38

Geological Sketch of the Vicinity of Hastings. London: 1833. V. 38

Observations on Some of the Strata Between the Chalk and Oxford Oolite, in the South-East of England. London: 1836. V. 39

FITZ-ADAM, ADAM

The World. Edinburgh: 1776. V. 38

The World. London: 1782 & 1789. V. 39; 40

FITZ-GEFFREY, CHARLES

The Curse of Corne-Horders. London: 1631. V. 39; 40

FITZ GERALD, E. A.

The Highest Andes. New York: 1899. V. 42

FITZ MAURICE, F. M., MRS.

Recollections of a Rifleman's Wife, at Home and Abroad. London: 1851. V. 45

FITZ-STEPHEN, WILLIAM

Fitz-Stephen's Descritpion of the City of London. London: 1772. V. 39

FITZCLARENCE, GEORGE A.

Journal of a Route Across India, through Egypt, to England, in the Latter End of the Year 1817, and the Beginning of 1818. London: 1819. V. 38; 41

FITZENMEYR, FRIEDA

Once Upon a Time: Book One. Easthampton: 1984. V. 45

FITZERALD, EDWARD

Euphranor. A Dialogue on Youth. London: 1851. V. 41

FITZGERALD, DAVID

A Narrative of the Irish Popish Plot for the Betraying the Kingdom into the Hands of the French, Massacring all English Protestants, etc. etc. London: 1680. V. 37

FITZGERALD, EDWARD

Agamemnon. N.P.: 1869. V. 46

Agamemnon. A Tragedy. Taken From Aeschylus. London: 1876. V. 37

The Downfall and Death of King Oedipus. N.P.: Guilford: 1880-18. V. 41

Euphranor. London: 1851. V. 38; 39; 41; 42; 46

Euphranor, a May-Day Conversation at Cambridge . . . Guildford: 1882. V. 41

Letters of Edward Fitzgerald (and) More Letters of Edward Fitzgerald. London: 1894, 1902. V. 41

Letters and Literary Remains. London: 1902. V. 37; 42; 44; 46

Letters and Literary Remains. London: 1902-03. V. 37; 40

The Letters from Edward Fitzgerald to Bernard Quaritch 1853 to 1883. London: 1926. V. 40; 41

Polonius. London: 1852. V. 37; 38; 44

Readings in Crabbe's 'Tales of the Hall.' N.P.: Guildford: 1879. V. 39

Readings in Crabbe. London: 1883. V. 37

Rubaigat of Omar Khayyam. V. 37

Rubaiyat of Omar Khayyam. London: 1922. V. 37

FITZHUGH, GEORGE

Cannibals All or, Slaves Without Masters. Richmond: 1857. V. 42

Sociology for the South, or the Failure of Free Society. Richmond: 1854. V. 37

FITZMAURICE-KELLY, J.

The Life of Miguel de Cervantes Saavedra. London: 1892. V. 40

FITZMAURICE, W. E.

A Cruise to Egypt, Palestine and Greece, During Five Months Leave of Absence. London: 1834. V. 40; 43

FITZOSBORNE, THOMAS

The Letters of Sir Thomas Fitzosborne, on Several Subjects . . . London: 1763. V. 45

FITZPATRICK, JOHN C.

Calendar of the Correspondence of George Washington . . . Washington: 1915. V. 44

FITZPATRICK, JOHN W.

The Friends, Foes and Adventures of Lady Morgan. Dublin: 1859. V. 40; 42

FITZPATRICK, PERCY

Jock of the Bushveld. London: 1907. V. 43

FITZPATRICK, ROBERT

The Bard's Museum; or, Rational Recreation. Dublin: 1809. V. 38; 42

FITZPATRICK, T. J.

Rafinesque. A Sketch of His Life With a Bibliography. Des Moines: 1911. V. 42

FITZPATRICK, THOMAS

Report of . . . Agent for the Indians On and Between the Upper Arkansas and Nebraska Rivers, Embracing Sioux, Cheyennes, Arapahoes and Other Wandering Tribes. Washington: 1848. V. 39; 41

FITZPATRICK, W. J.

Secret Service Under Pitt. London: 1892. V. 43

FITZPATRICK, W. S.

Treaties and Laws of the Osage Nation, as Passed, to November 26, 1890. Cedar Vale, Kansas: 1895. V. 37

FITZPATRICK, WILLIAM J.

The Sham Squire and the Informers of 1798 with a View of Their Contemporaries To Which is Added in the Form of an Appendix Jottings About Ireland Seventy Years Ago. Dublin: 1866. V. 46

FITZPATRICK, WILLIAM JOHN

The Friends, Foes, and Adventures of Lady Morgan. Dublin: 1859. V. 38; 42

FITZRALPH, RICHARD, ABP. OF ARMAGH

Summa in Questionibus Armenorum Nouiter Impressa Et Correcta a Magistro Nostro Johanne Sudoris Cum Aliquibus Sermonibus. Paris: 1512. V. 43

FITZROY, ROBERT 1805-1865

Narrative of the Surveying Voyages of His Majesty's Ships Adventure and Beagle, Between the Years 1826 and 1836 . . . London: 1839. V. 39; 40; 41; 42; 45

The Weather Book: a Manual of Practical Meteorology. London: 1863. V. 46

FITZSIMMONDS, JOSHUA

Free and Candid Disquisitions, on the Nature and Execution of the Laws of England. London: 1751. V. 41

FITZSIMMONS, CORTLAND

Death Rings a Bell. Philadelphia: 1942. V. 39; 42; 46

FITZSIMMONS, THOMAS

A Brief Statement of Opinions, Given in the Board of Commissioners, Under the Sixth Article of the Treaty of Amity, Commerce and Navigation with Great Britain . . . Philadelphia: 1800. V. 42; 43; 45

FITZSIMON, F. HENRY S. J.

Works of Comfort to Persecuted Catholics, Written in Exile, anno 1607. Dublin: 1881. V. 39

FITZSIMONS, F. W.

The Natural History of South Africa: Mammals (and) Birds. London: 1919-20/1923. V. 39; 45

The Snakes of South Africa. London: 1912. V. 39; 40

FITZURSE, R.

It Was Not Jones. London: 1928. V. 44

FITZWILLIAM, WILLIAM WENTWORTH

Protest of Earl Fitzwilliam in the House of Lords. London: 1795. V. 41; 42

FIVE Ballads about Robin Hood. Birmingham: 1899. V. 37

FIVE Canadian Poets in Greece. Athens: 1974. V. 41; 42

FIVE Chromo-Lithographc Drawings, Representing Irish Ecclesiastical Bell . . . Belfast: 1850. V. 44

FIVE Cummington Poems. Cummington: 1939. V. 39

FIVE Cummington Poems, 1939. Northampton. V. 39
FIVE Cummington Poems - 1939. 1939. V. 39

FIVE Discourses by the Author of the Snake in the Grass. London: 1700. V. 42

FIVE Extraordinary Letters Suppos'd to be Writ to Dr. B-----y, Upon His Edition of Horace, and Some Other Matters of Great Importance. London: 1712. V. 41

FIVE on Paper, a Collection of Five Essays on Papermaking, Books and Relevant Matters. North Hills: 1963. V. 39; 40

FIVE Young American Poets. Norfolk: 1940. V. 46
FIVE Young American Poets. Norfolk: 1944. V. 41; 44

FIZES, NICOLAS

Elemens D'Astronomie, Ou sont Expliques les Cercles de la Sphere, les Noms & les Mouvemens des Astres . . . Montpellier: 1689. V. 40

FIZTGERALD, P.

The History, Topography and Antiquities of the County and City of Limerick. Dublin: 1827. V. 46

FLACIUS ILLYRICUS, MATTHIAS

Varia Doctoru(m) Piorumque Virorum, De Corrupto Ecclesiae Statu, Poemata . . . Basle: 1557. V. 40

FLACIUS, MATTHIAS 1520-1575

Clavis Scripture S. seu de Sermone Sacrarum Literarum . . . Basileae: 1567. V. 44

Clavis Scripturae S. seu de Sermone Sacarum Literarum. Basileae: 1570/71. V. 44

FLADER, LOUIS

Achievement in Photo-Engraving and Letter-Press printing. Chicago: 1927. V. 38; 43

THE FLAG. The Book of the Union Jack Club. London: 1908. V. 46

FLAGG, E.

The Far West: or, a Tour Beyond the Mountains. New York: 1838. V. 37; 38; 39; 42; 43; 45

FLAGG, ERNEST

Genealogical Notes on the Founding of New England. Hartford: 1926. V. 42

FLAGG, J. FOSTER

Plastics and Plastic Filling; as Pertaining to the Filling of All Cavities of Decay in Teeth Below the Medium in Structure . . . Philadelphia: 1883. V. 38; 43

FLAGG, JAMES MONTGOMERY

Roses and Buckshot. New York: 1946. V. 43; 45

Why They Married. Text and Illustrations by Flagg. New York: 1906. V. 37

FLAGG, JARED B.

The Life and Letters of Washington Allston. London: 1893. V. 40

FLAGG, WILSON

The Woods and By-Ways of New England. Boston: 1872. V. 38

FLAGS of the Army of the United States Carried During the War of the Rebellion. Philadelphia: 1887. V. 37

FLAHERTY, LIAM

Thy Neighbor's Wife. London: 1923. V. 37

FLAHERTY, ROBERT

The Captain's Chair . . . New York: 1938. V. 42

FLAHERTY, ROBERT J.

My Eskimo Friends: 'Nanook of the North'. New York: 1924. V. 46

FLAMEN, ALBERT

Figures de Plusieurs Sortes de Poissons Tant de la Mer, que de L'Eau Douce. Paris: 1664. V. 37

Livre d'Oiseaux. Paris: 1650. V. 42; 46

FLAMENT, ALBERT

Personnages de Comedie. Paris: 1922. V. 38

FLAMINIO, MARCO ANTONIO 1498-1550

Fifty Select Poems of Marc-Antonio Flaminio, Imitated by the Late Rev. Edw. Will Barnard M.A. of Trinity College, Cambridge . . . Chester: 1829. V. 40

De Rebvs Divinis Carmina, Ad Margaritam Henrici Gallorum Regis Sororem. Paris: 1550. V. 43

FLAMINIUS, MARCUS ANTONIUS

Carmina. Padua: 1743. V. 37

FLAMMARION, CAMILLE

The Atmosphere. New York: 1873. V. 46

The Atmosphere. New York: 1874. V. 46

FLAMSTEED, JOHN

Atlas Coelestis. London: 1781. V. 38

Atlas Celeste de Flamsteed Publie en 1776, par J. Fortin, Ingenieur-Mecanicien Pour les Globes et Spheres. Paris: 1795. V. 41

A Letter Concerning Earthquakes, Written in the Year 1693 . . . London: 1750. V. 38

FLANAGAN, RODERICK

The History of New South Wales . . . London: 1862. V. 43

FLANAGAN, SUE

Trailing the Longhorns, a Century Later. Austin: 1974. V. 37; 41

FLANDERS Delineated; or, a View of the Austrian and French Netherlands . . . London: 1745. V. 39

FLANDERS, HENRY

The Lives and Times of the Chief Justices of the Supreme Court of the United States. First Series. London: 1855. V. 38

The Lives and Times of the Chief Justices of the Supreme Court of the United States. Philadelphia: 1885. V. 40

FLANIGAN, J. H.

Mormonism Triumphanti! Liverpool: 1849. V. 45

Mormonism Triumphant! London: 1849. V. 42

FLANNER, JANET

London Was Yesterday 1934-1939. New York: 1975. V. 45

FLANNERY, L. G.

John Hunton's Diary. Lingle & Glendale: 1956-70. V. 45

FLASHMAN, J. FROUDE

Reports from the Pathological Laboratory of the Lunacy Department of New South Wales. Volume I. Sidney: 1908. V. 43

THE FLATEY Book and Recently Discovered Vatican Manuscripts Concerning America . . . London: 1906. V. 43; 44

FLATLEY, P. J.

Ireland and the Land League. Boston: 1881. V. 39

FLATMAN, THOMAS

On the Death of Our Late Sovereign Lord King Charles II of Blessed Memory. London: 1685. V. 40

Poems and Songs. The Third Edition, with Additions and Amendments. London: 1682. V. 37

FLATT, W. D.

The Trail of Love. Toronto: 1916. V. 37

FLAUBERT, GUSTAVE

Bouvard and Pecuchet. London: 1896. V. 39; 42

The First Temptation of Saint Anthony. London: 1924. V. 41

Herodias. London: 1901. V. 43; 44; 46

La Legende de Saint Julien l'Hospitalier. London: 1900. V. 46

La Legende de Saint Julien l'Hospitalier. London: 1909. V. 46

Madame Bovary. Paris: 1857. V. 39

Madame Bovary. Paris: 1871. V. 46

Madame Bovary . . . With a Critical Introduction by Henry James. London: 1904. V. 45

Madame Bovary. London: 1928. V. 41

Madame Bovary. New York: 1950. V. 40; 44; 46

Salambo. New York: 1930. V. 46

Salambo. 1931. V. 39; 45

Salambo. Berkshire: 1931. V. 41

Salambo. New York: 1960. V. 44; 46

Salambo. By Gustave Flaubert. Translated by E. Powys Mathers. Engravings by Robert Gibbings. Berkshire: (1931). V. 37

Salammbo. London: 1886. V. 38; 40; 43

Salammbo. London & New York: 1886. V. 40

Salammbo. London: 1930. V. 38; 40

Salammbo. 1960. V. 40; 45

The Temptation of Saint Anthony. Kentfield: 1974. V. 38; 39; 41; 42; 43; 44; 45; 46

The Temptation of Saint Antony. London: 1895. V. 40

The Temptation of St. Anthony. New York: 1943. V. 44; 46

The Temptation of Saint Anthony. 1974. V. 39; 40; 41; 44

The Temptation of St. Anthony. New York/Seattle: 1910. V. 37

Three Tales. New York: 1978. V. 43

Un Coeur Simple. 1901. V. 38

Un Coeur Simple. London: 1901. V. 46

The Complete Works. New York: 1904. V. 42

FLAVEL, JOHN

Navigation Spiritualized; or a New Compass for Sea-Men. Newburyport: 1796. V. 40; 41; 43

FLAVELL, JOHN

The Fountain of Life Opened. London: 1698. V. 37

Husbandry Spiritualized; or, the Hevenly Use of Earthly Things. London: 1669. V. 46

Navigation Spirtualiz'd; or, a New Compass for Seamen . . . London: 1698. V. 46

A Saint Indeed; or, the Great Work of a Christian pen'd and Press'd from Prov. IV.23. London: 1698. V. 40

The Whole Works . . . London: 1820. V. 37; 40

FLAVIN, MARTIN

The Criminal Code. New York: 1930/1929. V. 44; 45

FLAXMAN, JOHN

Anatomical Studies of the Bones & Muscles for the Use of Artists. London: 1833. V. 37; 38; 42; 45

Compositions from the Tragedies of Aeschylus. London: 1795. V. 41

Compositions from the Divine Poems of Dante. London: 1807. V. 44

Compositions . . . from the Divine Poem of Dante Alighieri . . . London: 1807. V. 40

Compositions from the Tragedies of Aeschylus. London: 1831. V. 45

Illustrations to the Iliad of Homer and The Odyssey of Homer. London: 1805. V. 42

Lectures on Sculpture . . . London: 1838. V. 37; 38; 40; 42; 44

FLAXMEN, JOHN

Lectures on Sculpture. London: 1829. V. 44

FLECKER, JAMES E.

Letters of . . . to F. Savery. Westminster: 1926. V. 39; 40; 41; 42

FLECKER, JAMES ELROY

The Bridge of Fire. London: 1907. V. 38; 40

Hassan. The Story of Hassan of Bagdad and How He Came to Make the Golden Journey to Samarkand. London: 1924. V. 46

The Letters of J. E. Flecker to Frank Savery. London: 1926. V. 44

Some Letters from Abroad. London: 1930. V. 46

FLECKNOE, RICHARD

The Diarium, or Journall . . . London: 1656. V. 43; 45

FLECTHER, BANISTER F.

Andrea Palladio: His Life and Works. London: 1902. V. 37

FLEET, JOHN

A Discourse Relative to the Subject of Animation . . . Boston: 1797. V. 37

FLEET, THOMAS

A Pocket Almanac for the Year of Our Lord 1796 . . . to which is Annexed The Massachusetts Register . . . Boston: 1796. V. 45

FLEETWOOD, JOHN

The Life of Our Lord and Saviour Jesus Christ. Philadelphia: 1858. V. 39

FLEETWOOD, WILLIAM 1656-1723

Chronicon Preciosum; or, an Account of English Money, the Price of Corn and Other Commodities for the Last 600 Years. London: 1707. V. 37; 38; 41; 43

Chronicon Preciosum; or, an Account of English, Gold and Silver Money . . . London: 1745. V. 37; 38; 40; 41; 43; 46

An Essay Upon Miracles. London: 1701. V. 38

FLEG, EDMOND

The Wall of Weeping. London: 1929. V. 42

FLEHARTY, S. F.

Our Regiment. A History of the 102d Illinois Volunteers with Sketches of the Atlanta Campaign, the Georgia Raid, and the Campaign of the Carolinas. Chicago: 1865. V. 37

FLEISCHER, MAX

Noah's Shoes. Detroit: 1944. V. 44; 45

FLEISCHER, NAT

Gene Tunney, the Enigma of the Ring. New York: 1931. V. 41

The Ring Record Book. New York: 1952. V. 38

FLEMING, ALEXANDER

The Nobel Lecture on Penicillin. Les Prix Nobel en 1945. Stockholm: 1947. V. 41

On the Antibacterial Action of Cultures of a Pencilillium, with Special Reference to Their Use in the Isolation of B. Influenzae. London: 1944. V. 37.

Penicillin: Its Practical Application. London: 1946. V. 37; 42

FLEMING, ARNOLD

Scottish and Jacobite Glass. Glasgow: 1938. V. 40

FLEMING, FRANCIS PHILLIP

Memoir of Capt. C. Seton Fleming, of the Second Florida Infantry, C.S.A. Jacksonville: 1881. V. 44

FLEMING, G. A.

California. Its Past History: Its Present Position . . . London: 1850. V. 37; 40; 44

FLEMING, GEORGE

Horse-Shoes and Horse-Shoeing: Their Origin, History, Uses and Abuses. London: 1869. V. 37; 42

FLEMING, IAN LANCASTER 1908-1964

Casino Royale. London: 1953. V. 37; 39; 40; 41; 42; 45

Casino Royale. New York: 1954. V. 41; 42; 45

Chitty Chitty Bang Bang . . . London: 1964. V. 45

The Diamond Smugglers. London: 1957. V. 39; 41; 43; 45; 46

The Diamond Smugglers. New York: 1958. V. 42

The Diamond Smugglers. London: 1957. V. 45

Diamonds are Forever. 1956. V. 39

Diamonds are Forever. London: 1956. V. 41; 42; 45

Diamonds are Forever. New York: 1956. V. 41; 43

Dr. No. London: 1958. V. 39; 42; 44; 45; 46

For Your Eyes Only. London: 1960. V. 37; 45; 46

For Your Eyes Only. New York: 1960. V. 46

From Russia With Love. London: 1957. V. 41; 42; 43

From Russia with Love. New York: 1957. V. 46

Goldfinger. London: 1959. V. 39; 40; 41; 43; 45

Goldfinger. New York: 1959. V. 43; 46

Live and Let Die. London: 1954. V. 37; 39; 41; 42; 44; 45

Live and Let Die. New York: 1955. V. 41

The Man with the Golden Gun. London: 1965. V. 45; 46

Moonraker. 1955. V. 39

Moonraker. London: 1955. V. 39; 42; 43; 45; 46

Octopussy and the Living Daylights. London: 1966. V. 43; 44

On Her Majesty's Secret Service. London: 1936. V. 42

On Her Majesty's Secret Service. London: 1962. V. 39

On Her Majesty's Secret Service. London: 1963. V. 39; 42; 43; 44; 46

The Spy Who Loved Me. London: 1962. V. 37; 38; 39; 43; 46

The Spy Who Loved Me. London: 1962. V. 43

Thrilling Cities. London: 1963. V. 42

Thunderball. 1961. V. 39

Thunderball. London: 1961. V. 37; 39; 40; 41; 42; 43; 45

Thunderball. London: 1961. V. 39

Thunderball. London: 1961. V. 44

You Only Live Twice. London: 1964. V. 37; 42; 46

FLEMING, JOHN

A Short Sermon: Also Hymns, in the Muskokee or Creek Langauge. Boston: 1835. V. 37; 42; 45

FLEMING, JOHN F.

Virginia's Role in America's History. New York: 1958. V. 40

FLEMING, K.

Can Such Things Be? 1890. V. 44

FLEMING, MARY AGNES

The Queen of the Isle. New York: 1886. V. 43

FLEMING, PATRICIA LOCKHART

Upper Canadian Imprints 1801-1841. Toronto: 1987. V. 42

Upper Canadian Imprints 1801-1841: a Bibliography. Toronto: 1988. V. 40; 41; 42; 43

FLEMING, PETER

Geometrical Solutions of the Quadrature of the Circle. Montreal: 1850. V. 37

One's Company - a Journey to China. London: 1934. V. 46

FLEMING, ROBERT

The Mirrour of Divine Love Unvail'd, in a Poetical Paraphrase of the High Mysterious Song of Solomon. London: 1691. V. 41

FLEMING, SANDFORD

The Intercolonial. Montreal: 1876. V. 41; 45; 46

Report of Progress on the Explorations and Surveys Up to January 1874. Ottawa: 1874. V. 37; 43

Report of Progress on the Explorations and Surveys Up to January 1874. Ottawa: 1877. V. 42

Report on Surveys and Preliminary Operations on the Canadian Pacific Railway Up to January 1877. Ottawa: 1877. V. 38; 43

Report and Docments in Reference to the Canadian Pacific Railway: 1880. Ottawa: 1880. V. 37

Reports and Documents in Reference to the Location of the Line and Western Terminal Harbour, 1878. Ottawa: 1878. V. 42

FLEMING, VIVIAN MINOR

Campaigns of the Army of Northern Virginia Including the Jackson Valley Campaign 1861-1865. Richmond: 1928. V. 42

FLEMING, WALTER L.

Documentary History of Reconstruction: Political, Military, Social, Religious, Educational and Industrial. Cleveland: 1906. V. 37; 38; 42; 45

Documentary History of Reconstruction Political, Military, Social, Religious, Educational & Industrial 1865 to the Present. Cleveland: 1906-07. V. 39

Documentary History of Reconstruction Political, Military, Social Religious, Education and Industrial 1865 to the Present. Cleveland: 1906-07. V. 43

General W. T. Sherman as College President. Cleveland: 1912. V. 39

FLEMING, WILLIAM

A Manual of Moral Philosophy with Quotations and References for the Use of Students. Glasgow: 1860. V. 42

FLEMING, WILLIAM F.

The Keebles: a Half Century of Southern Family Life. Austin. V. 39

FLEMING, WILLIAM P.

Crisp County, Georgia: Historical Sketches. Volume I. Cordele: 1932. V. 44

FLEMMING, ERNST

Encyclopaedia of Textiles. London: 1958. V. 42

FLEMMING, HANNS THEODOR

Das Pompose Zeitalter . . . Berlin: 1915/26/28. V. 42

FLEMYNG, MALCOLM

An Introduction to Physiology, Being a Course of Lectures Upon the Most Important Parts of the Animal Oeconomy. London: 1759. V. 40

FLENTJE, E. L.

Government Publications on Western Exploration Etc. Arranged . . . Chicago: 1949. V. 40

FLERIEU, LE COMTE DE

Discoveries of the French in 1768 and 1769, to the South-East of New Guinea, with the Subsequent Visits to the Same Lands by English Navigators, Who Gave Them New Names. London: 1791. V. 45

FLETA Seu Commentarius Juris Anglicani, Accedit Tractatulus Vetus de Agendi Excipiendique Formulis Gallicanus. London: 1647. V. 40

FLETCHER, A.

The Universal Measurer. London: 1752/53. V. 44

FLETCHER, ALEXANDER

Trial of the Rev. Alexander Fletcher . . . before the Chief Justice of the Court of Common Sense and a Special Jury. London: 1825. V. 38; 43

FLETCHER, ALICE C.

Indian Education and Civilization. A Report Prepared in Answer to Senate Resolution of February 23, 1885. Washington: 1888. V. 38

FLETCHER, ANDREW

A Defense of the Scots Settlement at Darien. Edinburgh: 1699. V. 39; 42

The Poetical Works. Glasgow: 1749. V. 43

The Poetical Works. London: 1737. V. 37

Scotland's Interest: or, the Great Benefit and Necessity of a Communication of Trade with England. Edinburgh?: 1704. V. 38

A Speech Upon the State of the Nation. N.P.: 1701. V. 40; 43

Two Discourses Concerning the Affairs of Scotland; Written in the Year 1698. Edinburgh: 1698. V. 42; 43

FLETCHER, BANISTER

Light and Air, a Text-Book for Architects and Surveyors. London: 1879. V. 40

FLETCHER, BANISTER F.

Andrea Palladio: His Life and Works. London: 1902. V. 42

FLETCHER, C. R. L.

Collectanea. First-Fourth Series. London: 1885-90-96-1906. V. 40

Collectanea. First - Fourth Series. 4 Volumes. London;: 1885-1906. V. 37

FLETCHER, CHARLES

A Maritime State Considered, As to the Health of Seamen. Dublin: 1786. V. 44

FLETCHER, CORA C.

The Emperor's Lion. Verona: 1976. V. 45

FLETCHER, DANIEL COOLEDGE

Reminiscences of California and the Civil War. Ayer, Mass.: 1894. V. 37; 39; 40; 43; 44; 45

FLETCHER, F. N.

Early Nevada: The Period of Exploration, 1776-1848. Reno: 1929. V. 37

FLETCHER, FRANK MORLEY

Wood-Block Printing. London: 1916. V. 44

FLETCHER, G. A.

California, Its Past History, Its Present Position . . . London: 1850. V. 42

FLETCHER, HENRY

The Perfect Politician: or, A Full View of the Life and Actions (Miliatary and Vil) of O. Cromwel. London: 1660. V. 40

FLETCHER, JAMES GOULD

Branches of Adam. London: 1926. V. 45

FLETCHER, JOHN

The Chances. London: 1682. V. 39

The Elder Brother. London: 1637. V. 37

La Fida Pastora. Londini: 1658. V. 39

Monsieur Thomas. London: 1639. V. 40

Rvle a Wife and Have a Wife. Oxford: 1640. V. 42

Valentinian; a Tragedy. London: 1685. V. 42

The Wild Goose Chase. London: 1652. V. 38; 42

FLETCHER, JOHN GOULD

The Book of Nature 1910-1912. London: 1913. V. 37

The Burning Mountain. New York: 1946. V. 40

Fire and Wine. London: 1915. V. 42

Fire and Wine. London: 1913. V. 37

Japanese Prints. Boston: 1928. V. 37

Japanese Prints . . . With Illustrations by Dorothy Pulis Lathrop. Boston: 1918. V. 37

FLETCHER, JOHN WILLIAM

American Patriotism Farther Confronted with Reason, Scripture and the Constitution. Shrewsbury: 1776. V. 44

American Patriotism Farther Confronted with Reason, Scripture and the Constitution . . . London: 1777. V. 44; 45

An Answer to the Rev. Mr. Toplady's 'Vindication of the Decrees' . . . London: 1776. V. 44

The Bible and the Sword; or, the Appointment of the General Fast Vindicated . . . London: 1776. V. 44

The Doctrines of Grace and Justice Equally Essential to the Pure Gospel. London: 1787. V. 42

Logica Genevensis Continued. Bristol: 1774. V. 44

Reply to the Principal Arguments by Which the Calvinists and the Fatalists Support the Doctrine of Absolute Necessity . . . London: 1777. V. 44

A Second Check to Antinomianism; Occassioned by a Late Narrative, in three Letters, to the Hon. and Rev. Author. London: 1771. V. 42

A Third Check to Antinomianism; in a Letter to the author of Pieta Oxoniensis . . . Bristol: 1772. V. 42

A Vindication of the Rev. Mr. Wesley's Last Minutes . . . Bristol: 1771. V. 42

A Vindication of the Rev. Mr. Wesley's 'Calm Address to Our American Colonies' . . . London: 1776. V. 42; 45

FLETCHER, JOSEPH S.

The Wonderful City. London: 1894. V. 42

FLETCHER, PHINEAS

The Locusts, or Apollyonists. V. 45

Picatory Eclogues, With Other Miscellanies. Edinburgh: 1771. V. 41

Picatory Eclogues, with other Poetical Miscellanies. Illustrated with Notes Critical and Explantory (by A.F. Tytler, Lord Woodhouselee). Edinburgh/London: 1771. V. 37

Piscatory Eclogues. Edinburgh: 1771. V. 38; 40; 41; 43

The Purple Island Or the Isle of Man.. 1633. V. 45

The Purple Island, or The Isle of Man; Together with Piscatory Eclogs and Other Poetical Miscellanies. Cambridge: 1633. V. 42; 46

The Purple Island, or The Isle of Man . . . London: 1633. V. 37; 43

The Purple Island, or the Isle of Man. Cambridge: 1663. V. 40

FLETCHER, RALPH 1781-1851

Sketches from the Case Book, to Illustrate the Influence of the Mind on the Body, with the Treatment of Some of the More Important Brain and Nervous Disbturbances with Arise from This Influence. London: 1833. V. 45

FLETCHER, ROBERT H.

Free Grass to Fences. New York: 1960. V. 40; 45; 46

FLETCHER, SAMUEL

Emblematical Devices with Appropriate Mottos Collected by Samuel Fletcher Seal Engraver. London: 1810. V. 42

FLETCHER, W.

Bookbinding in France; Royal English Bookbindings. London: 1894/96. V. 41

FLETCHER, W. Y.

Bookbinding in France. London: 1894. V. 40

English Bookbindings in the British Museum. London: 1895. V. 37; 38; 39; 41; 44; 45; 46

Foreign Bookbindings in the British Museum. London: 1896. V. 37

FLETCHER, WILLIAM

The History and Development of Steam Locomotion on Common Roads. By William Fletcher, Mechanical Engineer. London: 1891. V. 37

FLETCHER, WILLIAM A.

Rebel Private, Front and Rear: Experiences and Observations from the Early Fifties and Through the Civil War. Austin: 1954. V. 46

FLETCHER, WILLIAM ANDREW

Rebel Private Front and Rear: Experiences and Observations from the Early Fifties through the Civil War. Beaumont: 1908. V. 42

FLETCHER, WILLIAM YOUNGER

Foreign Bookbindings in the British Museum. London: 1896. V. 45

FLETHCER, SAMUEL H.

History of Company A, Second Illinois Cavalry. Chicago: 1912. V. 38

FLETT, JOHN SMITH

The First Hundred Years of the Geological Survey of Great Britain. London: 1937. V. 45

FLEURETTE, MARIE

Words of Ugo Betti. Los Angeles: 1965. V. 46

FLEURIEU, CHARLES PIERRE 1738-1810

Voyage Autour du Monde, Pendant les Annees 1790, 1791, et 1792, Par Etienne Marchand . . . Paris: 1798-1800. V. 38

FLEURIEU, CHARLES PIERRE CLARET, COMTE DE 1738-1810

A Voyage Round the World . . . 1790-92. London: 1801. V. 43; 45

FLEURIEU, CHARLES PIERRE CLARET DE, COMTE 1738-1810

A Voyage Round the World . . . 1790-92, by Etienne Marchand . . . London: 1801. V. 39

THE FLEURON. London: 1923. V. 45
THE FLEURON. London: 1923-30. V. 37; 39; 40; 45; 46
THE FLEURON. London: 1924. V. 45; 46

THE FLEURON: a Journal of Typography. London, Cambridge & New York: 1923-30. V. 38

THE FLEURON: a Journal of Typography. No. 5. Cambridge: 1926. V. 45

THE FLEURON: a Journal of Typography. No. 6. Cambridge: 1928. V. 45

FLEURY, CLAUDE

Histoire Ecclesiastique. Paris: 1844. V. 39

The History, Choice and Method of Studies. London: 1695. V. 40; 42

FLEXNER, ABRAHAM

Medical Education: a Comparative Study. New York: 1925. V. 41

Medical Education in the United States and Canada. New York: 1910. V. 37

FLEXNER, JAMES THOMAS

Doctors of Horseback: Pioneers of American Medicine. New York: 1937. V. 37

John Singleton Copley. Boston: 1948. V. 40

Washington: The Indispensable Man. London: 1975. V. 46

FLICKER, KARL

The Antarctic Regions. London: 1900. V. 44

FLICKINGER, D. K.

Off Hand Sketches of Men and Things in Western Africa. Dayton: 1857. V. 42

FLICKINGER, ROBERT ELLIOTT

The Choctaw Fredmen and the Story of Oak Hill Industrial Academy, Valliant, McCurtain County, Oklahoma Now Called the Alice Lee Elliott Memorial. Pittsburg: 1914. V. 45

FLIESSBACH, FERDINAND

Neueste Munzkunde, Abbildung und Beschreibung der jezt Coursirenden Gold- und Silbermunzen . . . Leipzig: 1853. V. 40; 44

THE FLIGHT of the Pretender, with Advice to the Poets. London: 1708. V. 40; 42

FLINDERS, MATTHEW 1774-1814

Matthew Flinders' Narrative of His Voyage in the Schooner Francis, 1798. Waltham St. Lawrence: 1946. V. 46

Matthew Flinder's Narrataive of the Voyage of the Schooner Francis. London: 1946. V. 37

Narrative of His Voyage in the Schooner Francis: 1798 . . . London: 1946. V. 41; 44

Narrative of the Voyage of the Schooner Francis 1798. London: 1946. V. 41

A Voyage to Terra Australis; Undertaken for the Purpose of Completing the Discovery of that Vast Country, and Prosecuted in the Years 1801, 1802, and 1803, in His Majesty's Ship the Investigator, and Subsequently . . . London: 1814. V. 45

FLINN, FRANK M.

Campaigning with Banks in Louisiana '63 and '64 and with Sheridan in the Shenandoah Valley in '64 and '65. Lynn: 1887. V. 38

FLINT, AUSTIN 1812-1886

Clinical Medicine: A Systematic Treatise of the Diagnosis and Treatment of Diseases. Philadelphia: 1879. V. 42

Handbook of Physiology for Students and Practitioners of Medicine. New York: 1905. V. 46

A Manual of Auscultation and Percussion. Philadelphia: 1885. V. 45

On the Source of Muscular Power. New York: 1878. V. 39

Physical Exploration and Diagnosis of Diseases Affecting the Repiratory Organs. Philadelphia: 1856. V. 42

A Practical Treatise on the Diagnosis, Pathology and Treatment of the Heart. Philadelphia: 1859. V. 42

FLINT, F. S.

Cadences. London: 1915. V. 37

FLINT, GEORGE

Robin's Last Shift; or, Weekly Remarks and Political Reflections Upon the Most Material News Foreign and Domestick. London: 1717. V. 37; 42

FLINT, TIMOTHY

Arguments, Natural, Moral and Religious, for the Immortality of the Soul. Worcester: 1805. V. 39

Francis Berrian, or the Mexican Patriot. Boston: 1826. V. 37

George Mason, the Young Backwoodsman. Boston: 1829. V. 37; 40; 43

The History and Geography of the Mississippi Valley to Which is Appended a Condensed Physical Geography of the Atlantic United States and the Whole American Continent. (bound with) The United States and the Other Divisions of the American Continent . . . Vol. II. Cincinnati: 1832. V. 43

The History and Geography of the Mississippi Valley. (and) The United States and the Other Divisions of the American Continent. Cincinnati: 1832. V. 40

The History and Geography of the Mississippi Valley. Cincinnati: 1832. V. 37; 39; 41; 45

The History and Geography of the Mississippi Valley. Boston: 1833. V. 42

Indian Wars of the West. Cincinnati: 1833. V. 37; 45

Indian Wars of the West; Containing Biographical Sketches of Those Pioneers Who Headed the Western Settlers in Repelling the Attacks of the Savages, Together with a View of the Character, Manners, Monuments, and Antiquities of the Western Indians. Cincinnati: 1833. V. 37

Lectures on Natural History, Geology, Chemistry and the Application of Steam. Boston: 1833. V. 38; 39

FLINT, V. E.

A Field Guide to Birds of the USSR, Including Eastern Europe and Central Asia. Princeton: 1984. V. 40

FLINT, WILLIAM RUSSELL

Breakfast in Perigord. London: 1968. V. 39; 42; 44

Drawings. London: 1950. V. 37; 38; 39; 40; 41

Exhibition of Works by Sir William Russell Flint. London: 1962. V. 45

The Lisping Goddess. Worcester: 1968. V. 38

Minxes Admonished, or Beauty Reproved. London: 1955. V. 46

Minxes Admonished . . . London: 1955. V. 41; 45

Minxes Admonished or Beauty Reproved. Waltham St. Lawrence: 1955. V. 41; 42; 44

Models of Propriety. London: 1951. V. 41; 43; 44

Shadows in Arcady. London: 1965. V. 37; 40; 41; 46

FLINTOFT, J.

Collection of Mosses and Specimens of British Mosses. Keswick: 1860. V. 46

FLIPPER, HENRY O.

The Colored Cadet at West Point. New York: 1878. V. 40

FLITCH, J. E. CRAWFORD

Modern Dancing and Dancers. Philadelphia: 1912. V. 43

FLITNER, JOHANN

Nebulo Nebulonum: Hoc est, Locoseria Modernae Nequitiae Censura. Fancofurti: 1620. V. 38

FLLOYD, THOMAS

Bibliotheca Biographica: a Synopsis of Universal Biography, Ancient and Modern. London: 1760. V. 45

FLOCCUS, ANDREAS DOMINICUS d. 1452

De Magistratibus, Sacerdotiisque Romanorum. Pomponius Laetus Itidem . . . Paris: 1549. V. 40

FLOIRE ET JEANNE

The Tale of King Florus and the Fair Jehane. London: 1893. V. 41

The Tale of King Florus and the Fair Jehane. 1893. V. 39

FLOOD, H.

Baratariana, a Select Collection of Fugitive Political Pieces. Dublin: 1777. V. 37

FLOOD Views of San Antonio, Texas. Sept. 9th-10th, 1921. San Antonio: 1921. V. 45

FLORA Europaea. Cambridge: 1964-83. V. 37

FLORA Europea. Cambridge: 1964-80. V. 37

FLORA Malesiana. Being an Illustrated Systematic Account of the Malaysian Flora. Series I: Spermatophyta. Volume I. Malaysian Plant Collectors and Collections . . . 1985. V. 39

FLORAL FORMS in Historic Design. London: 1922. V. 37

THE FLORAL GIFT. London: 1863. V. 38

THE FLORAL Offering. London: 1870. V. 44; 46

FLORENCE GOLD MINING CO.

Florence Gold Mining Co. Portland. V. 39; 42

FLORENCE, OF WORCESTER

Chronicon Ex Chronicis, ab Initio Mundi Usque ad Annum Domini 1118 Deductum . . . London: 1592. V. 45

FLORENCE. PALAZZO PITTI

Pitture Del Salone Imperiale Del Palazzo Di Firenze si Aggiungono Le Pittvre Del Salone E Cortile Delle Imperiali Ville Della Petraia E Del Poggio A Caiano Opere Di Vari Celebri Pittori Fiorentini in Tavole XXVI. Florence: 1751. V. 39

FLORENCE, W. J.

The Gentleman's Hand-Book on Poker . . . New York: 1892. V. 44

FLORENCE, WILLIAM JAMES

The Handbook of Poker. London: 1892. V. 38

FLORENCIA, FRANCISCO DE

Narracion de la Marabillosa Aparicion, que Hizo el Archangel San Miguel a Diego Lazaro de San Francisco, Indio Feligres del Pueblo de S. Bernardo . . . Seville: 1692. V. 41

FLORES, ANGEL

Franz Kafka. A Chronology and Bibliography. Houlton: 1944. V. 42

FLORES, JUAN DE

L'Histoire d'Avrelio et Isabelle en Italien et Francoys . . . Lyon: 1582. V. 38; 42

FLORES, JUAN DE continued

Histoire de Aurelio, et Isabelle, fille du roy d'Escoce, Nouvellement Tradauict en Quatre Langues, Italien, Espaignol, Francois & Anglois . . . Brussels: 1608. V. 37

Historia di Avrelio et Isabella, Nell Aqvale si Disputa . . . In Vinegia: 1548. V. 40

FLOREZ, F. ENRIQUE

Clave Historial con que se Abra la Puerta a la Historia . . . Madrid: 1790. V. 38

FLORIAN, JEAN PEIRRE CLARIS DE 1755-1794

Gonsalva of Cordova; or, Granada Reconquered. Now first translated from the French . . . London: 1793. V. 37

FLORIAN, JEAN PIERRE CLARIS DE 1755-1794

The Adventures of Numa Pompilius, Second King of Rome. London: 1787. V. 38; 41; 43; 46

Fables. Paris: 1842. V. 40

Les Fables. Paris: 1899. V. 43

Galatea. Dublin: 1791. V. 45

Galatea; a Pastoral Romance. London: 1804. V. 42

Galatee, Roman Pastoral; Imite de Cervantes . . . Paris: 1793. V. 38; 40

Gonazlva. London: 1793. V. 39; 40; 42; 45

New Tales. Dublin: 1793. V. 38

William Tell: or, Switzerland Delivered . . . Concord: 1831. V. 39; 45

William Tell . . . . to which is prefixed a Life of the Author, by Jauffret. Concord: 1831. V. 37

FLORIDA. GENERAL ASSEMBLY. HOUSE OF REPRESENTATIVES

House Journal - 11th Sess. A Journal of the Proceedings of the House of Representatives of the General Assembly of the State of Florida . . . November 18, 1861. Tallahassee: 1861. V. 41

FLORIDA: Its Climate, Soil and Productions, with a Sketch of Its History . . . New York: 1869. V. 41

FLORIDA: Its Climate, Soil and Productions, with a Sketch of Its History, Natural Features and Social Condition. Jacksonville: 1869. V. 45

THE FLORIDA Pirate, or, an Account of a Cruise in the Schooner Esparanza(!) With A Sketch of the Life of Her Commander . . . New York: 1823. V. 42

THE FLORIDA Railway and Navigation Company. The Key Line Comprising the Gulf Coast Route from the Sea to the Gulf. New York: 1885. V. 41

FLORIDA: The American Riviera; St. Augustine. The Winter Newport: The Ponce de Leon. The Alcazar; the Casa Monica. New York: 1887. V. 42

FLORIDA, The Land of Oranges, Tropical Scenery, Health and Sunshine. New York;: 1885. V. 39

FLORILEGIUM Diversorum Epigrammatum Veterum, in Septem Libros Divisum. Geneva: 1566. V. 38

FLORIO, JOHN

Vocabulario Italiano & Inglese: A Dictionary of Italian and English. London: 1688. V. 42

Florios Second Frutes, to Be Gathered of Twelve Trees of Divers but Delightsome Tates to the Tongues of Italians and Englismen. London: 1591. V. 42

Queen Anna's New World of Words. Menston: 1968. V. 38; 42

Vocabolaro Italiano & Inglese, a Dictionary, Italian & English . . . London: 1659. V. 40

A Worlde of Wordes, Or Most Copious and Exact Dictionaire in Italian and English. London: 1598. V. 40

FLORIO, MICHELANGELO

Historia de la Vita de la Morte de l'Illustriss. Middleburg: 1607. V. 42

THE FLORIST'S Journal and Gardener's Record. London: V. 46

FLORUS, LUCIUS ANNAEUS

L. Annei Flori Rerum Romanorum Epitome. London: 1692. V. 44

FLORUS, LUCIUS JULIUS

The Roman Histories . . . London: 1636. V. 39; 42

FLORY, H. C.

An Essay on the Causes of the Indifference to the Study of Modern Languages and Literature in This Town and Vicinity. Sheffield: 1834. V. 45

FLORY, M. A.

A Book About Fans The History of Fans and Fan Painting . . . New York: 1895. V. 44

FLORY, S. P.

Fragments of Family History. London: 1896. V. 38; 40; 46

FLOSCULI Sententarium. Printers Flowers Moralized. 1967. V. 39

FLOSCULI Sententiarum. Printers Flowers Moralised. Northampton: 1959. V. 43

FLOSCULI Sententiarum. Printers Flowers Moralised. Northampton: 1967. V. 37; 38; 40; 41; 42

THE FLOURE of the Commaundementes of God with Many Examples and Auctorytees Extracte and Drawen as Well of Holy Scryptures as Other Doctours and Good Auncyente Faders . . . London: 1521. V. 38; 40

FLOURENS, MARIE JEAN PIERRE

Recherches Experimentales sur les Proprietes et les Fonctions du Systeme Nerveux dans les Animaux Vertebres. Paris: 1824. V. 40

FLOURENS, PIERRE

Recherches Experimentales sur Les Proprietes et Les Fonctions Du Systeme Nerveus dan Les Animaux Vertebre. Paris: 1824. V. 41; 44; 45; 46

FLOURNOY, THEODORE

From India to the Planet Mars. New York: 1900. V. 45

FLOWER ASSOCIATON OF JAPAN

Manual of Japanese Flowering Cherries. Tokyo: 1983. V. 37

FLOWER, GEORGE

History of the English Settlement in Edwards County Illinois, Founded in 1817 and 1818 by Morris Birkbeck and George Flower. Chicago: 1882. V. 37

FLOWER, J.

Views of Ancient Buildings in the Town and County of Leicester. London: 1973. V. 44

FLOWER, JOHN 1795-1861

Views of Ancient Buildings in the Town and Country of Leicester. Leicester: 1830. V. 37; 39

FLOWER, JOHN LARNOROCK

Historical Record of the 3rd Royal Surrey Regiment of Militia, No. 118, Raised in 1798 - Revived in 1853 . . . London: 1869. V. 38

FLOWER, NORMAN

The History of the Great War. London: V. 44; 45; 46

The History of the Great War. London: 1915-21. V. 43; 44; 45

FLOWER, P. W.

A History of the Trade in Tin: a Short Description of Tin Mining and Metallurgy. London: 1880. V. 37

THE FLOWER Piece: a Collection of Miscellany Poems. London: 1731. V. 42

THE FLOWER-PIECE: a Collection of Miscellany Poems. London: 1731. V. 39; 45

FLOWER, RICHARD

Letters from the Illinois, 1820, 1821. London: 1822. V. 39; 40; 45

FLOWER, ROBIN

Love's Bitter-Sweet. Dublin: 1925. V. 39

FLOWER, WILLIAM HENRY

Diagrams of the Nerves of the Human Body. London: 1861. V. 44

Recent Memoirs on the Cetacea . . . London: 1866. V. 43

FLOWERDEW, A.

Poems, on Moral and Religious Subjects. London: 1803. V. 37; 40

FLOWERDEW, ALICE

Poems on Moral and Religious Subjects. London: 1804. V. 43; 45

FLOWERING Plants: with Instructions How to Cultivate and Rear Them from Seeds, Cuttings and Layers . . . London: 1870. V. 40

FLOWERS of Loveliness: Forty Groups of Female Figures, Emblematic of Flowers, Designed by the First Artists, Expressly for this Work. 1850's. V. 39

FLOWERS, R. W.

From Ocean to Ocean, Being a Diary of a Three Months' Expedition from Liverpool to California and Back. London: 1871. V. 38; 45

FLOYD, GRACE C.

Puss in Boots. London: 1910. V. 39

FLOYD, JOHN 1572-1649

A Paire of Spectacles for Sir Humphrey Linde to see His Way Withall. N.P.: 1631. V. 38

FLOYD, JOHN B.

Protection of the Frontier of Texas. Washington: 1859. V. 38

FLOYD, N. J.

Thorns in the Flesh. Charleston: 1884. V. 39

Thorns in the Flesh. Lynchburg: 1884. V. 39

FLOYER, ERNEST AYSCOGHE

Unexplored Baluchistan. London: 1882. V. 43

FLOYER, JOHN

The History of Cold-Bathing . . . London: 1732. V. 45

The History of Cold Bathing: Both Ancient and Modern. London: 1706. V. 37

Medicina Gerocomica: or the Galenic Art of Preserving Old Men's Healths Explain'd . . . to which is added, a Letter to the Honble. Mr. Ch-- St.-- Concerning the Regimen of the Health of the Younger Years and Adults as Galen had Described Them. London: 1725. V. 38

Psychrolousia (Graece): or, The History of Cold Bathing . . . London: 1709. V. 45

The Sibylline Oracles. London: 1713. V. 42

FLOYER, PHILIP

The Proctor's Practice in the Ecclesiastical Courts . . . In the Savoy: 1746. V. 42

FLUCKIGER, F.

Pharmacographia. London: 1879. V. 38; 41; 42; 45

FLUCKIGER, FRIEDRICH

Pharmacographia. London: 1874. V. 44

FLUGGE, C.

Micro-Organisms with Special Reference to the Etiology of the Infective Diseases. London: 1890. V. 42

FLUNKEYISM, or Our Domestics in the Year of Grace 1859. London: 1864. V. 41

LE FLUX Dissenterique des Bourses Financieres, ou la Dissenterie des Financiers. N.P.: 1624. V. 45

THE FLY Maker's Handbook. Liverpool: 1887. V. 40

FLYNN, PAUL J.

The Book of the Galtees and the Golden Vein. Dublin: 1926. V. 42

FLYNT, HENRY

Twenty Sermons on Various Subjects. Boston: 1739. V. 40

FOA, EDOUARD

After Big Game in Central Africa. London: 1899. V. 37; 44; 45; 46

FOAN, GILBERT A.

The Art and Craft of Hairdressing. London: 1950. V. 40

FOCHER, JUAN

Itinerarium Catholicum Profiscentium, ad Infideles Convertendos . . . Seville: 1574. V. 38

FOCILLON, HENRI

Giovanni-Battista Piranesi 1720-1778. Paris: 1918. V. 39

FOCUS. London: 1938-39. V. 45

FOERSTE, A. F.

An Introduction to the Geology of Dayton and Vicinity . . . Dayton: 1915. V. 45

FOERSTER, E.

Schiller-Gallery From the Original Drawings of William Kaulbach and Others. London: 1880. V. 38

FOES, ANUCE 1528-1595

Oeconomia Hippocratis . . . Frankfurt: 1588. V. 42; 44

FOGAZZARO, ANTONIO

Eden Anto. San Francisco: 1930. V. 38; 45; 46

FOGERTY, J.

Robert Leeman's Daughters. London: 1889. V. 43

FOGG MUSEUM

Collection of Mediaeval and Renaissance Paintings. Cambridge: 1927. V. 44

FOGHT, H. W.

The Trail of the Loup; Being a History of the Loup River Region with Some Chapters on the State. N.P.: 1906. V. 37; 45

FOGHT, HAROLD WALDSTEIN

The Trail of the Loup, Being a History of the Loup River Region with Some Chapters on the State. Ord: 1906. V. 39

FOGLIETTA, UBERTO

Della Repvblica di Genova. Libri II. Rome: 1559. V. 42

FOKKER, ANTHONY H. G.

Flying Dutchman, the Life of Fokker. New York: 1931. V. 39

FOKKER, T. H.

Roman Baroque Art, The History of a Style. 1938. V. 44

Roman Baroque Art. London: 1938. V. 46

Roman Baroque Art, The History of a Style. Oxford: 1938. V. 37; 42

FOLCO, GUILIO

Effetti Mirabili de la Limosinia et Sentenze Degne di Memoria Appertenenti ad Essa. Rome: 1586. V. 40

A FOLDING Screen. Gloucestershire: 1974. V. 41

FOLENGO, TEOFILO 1496-1544

Opus Merlini Cocaii Poetae Mantuani Macaronicorum. Venetiis: 1581. V. 40

Opus Merlini Cocaii Poetae Mantuani Macaronicorum.. Venetiis: 1585. V. 38

Opus Macaronicorum. Venetiis: 1585. V. 37; 38

FOLEY, EDWIN

The Book of Decorative Furniture: Its Form, Colour and History. London. V. 38; 42

The Book of Decorative Furniture, Its Form, Colour and History. London: 1910. V. 41

The Book of Decorative Furniture. New York: 1911. V. 42

The Book of Decorative Furniture - Its Form, Colour and History. London: 1920. V. 38; 40

FOLEY, HENRY

Records of the English Province of the Society of Jesus. London: 1877-83. V. 46

FOLIO, FRED, PSEUD.

A Book for the Times. Lucy Boston; or Woman's Rights and Spiritualism . . . Auburn & Rochester: 1855. V. 44

FOLIO SOCIETY

Folio 21. A Bibliography of the Folio Society, 1947-1967. London: 1968. V. 38

Folio 25, a Bibliography of the Folio Society 1947-1971. London: 1972. V. 39; 40

FOLK Tales of Flanders. New York: 1918. V. 39

FOLKARD, ARTHUR CROUCH

A Monograph of the Family of Folkard of Suffolk. London: 1892-97. V. 42

FOLKARD, CHARLES

Jolly Calle & Other Swedish Fairy Tales. London: (ca. 1912). V. 37

Sing-A-Song-of-Sixpence. V. 46

FOLKARD, H. COLEMAN

The Wild-Fowler: a Treatise on Ancient and Modern Wild-Fowling, Historical and Practical. London: 1864. V. 37; 39; 42; 46

FOLKARD, HENRY COLEMAN

The Sailing Boat, a Treatise on Sailing Boats and Small Yachts. London: 1901. V. 46

The Sailing Boat. London: 1906. V. 42

The Wild-Fowler: a Treatise on Ancient and Modern Wild-Fowling, Historical and Practical. 1859. V. 44

FOLKES, MARTIN

A Table of English Silver Coins from the Norman Conquest to the Present Time . . . . (with) A Table of English Coins from the Eighteenth Year of King Edward the Third . . . London: 1745. V. 42; 43

FOLKHARD, H. C.

The Wildfowler. London: 1859. V. 45

The Wildfowler. London: 1864. V. 45

FOLKLORE SOCIETY

The Folklore Journal. London: 1883-85. V. 37

THE FOLLIES and Fashions of Our Grandfathers. London: 1886. V. 38

FOLLIES of the Year. London. V. 44

THE FOLLOWING Calculations of the Reductions of English Weights and Measures to Those of France, and Vice Versa Have Been Made by an Officer of the Army of Occupation . . . Paris: 1817. V. 40

THE FOLLY of Priest-Craft. London: 1690. V. 42

FOLMER, HENRY

Franco-Spanish Rivalry in North America, 1524-1763. Glendale: 1953. V. 38

FOLSOM, DAVID E.

Folsom-Cook Exploration of the Upper Yellowstone in the Year 1869. St. Paul: 1894. V. 37; 38

FOLSOM, G. F.

Mexico in 1842 . . . to Which is Added an Account of Texas and Yucatan and of the Santa Fe Expedition. New York: 1842. V. 37; 38; 39; 40; 41; 42; 43; 45

FOLSOM, GEORGE

History of Saco and Biddeford, with Notices of Other Early Settlements and of the Proprietary Governments, in Maine, Including the Provinces of New Somersetshire and Lygonia. Saco: 1830. V. 39

FOLSOM, JAMES

The Mariner's Medical Guide. Boston: 1876. V. 42

FOLSOM, W. H. C.

Fifty Years in the Northwest. St. Paul: 1888. V. 42; 43

FOLTZ, JONATHAN MESSERSMITH

The Endemic Influence of Evil Government, Illustrated in a View of the Climate, Topography and Diseases of the Island of Minorca, with Medical Statistics of a Voyage of Circumnavigation of the Globe. New York: 1843. V. 42

FOLWELL, WILLIAM WATTS

History of Minnesota. St. Paul: 1921-30. V. 37; 42

A History of Minnesota. Saint Paul: 1922. V. 44

A History of Minnesota. St. Paul: 1921. V. 37

FOMENT, E.

The Story of a Round Loaf. London: 1868. V. 46

FONBLANQUE, JOHN DE GRENIER

Thoughts on the Canada Bill, Now Depending in Parliament. London: 1791. V. 43

FONDO Editorial de la Plastica Mexicana: Mural Painting of the Mexican Revolution 1921-1960. Haarlem: 1960. V. 39

FONER, PHILIP S.

The Black Worker: A Documentary History from Colonial Times to the Present. Philadelphia: 1980. V. 42

FONERDEN, CLARENCE ALBERT

A Brief History of the Military Career of Carpenter's Battery. New Market: 1911. V. 46

FONESCA CHRISTOVAL DE

Devovt Contemplations Expressed in Two and Fortie Sermons Vpon all ye Quadragesimall Gospells . . . London: 1629. V. 43

FONESCA, CRISTOBAL DE

Tratado del Amor de Dios. Lisbon: 1603. V. 41

FONG, WEN

The Great Bronze Age of China. New York: 1980. V. 41

FONSANCII, F.

Carta Familiar de un Sacerdote, Resputesta a un Colegial Amigo Suyo, en Que le da Cuenta de la Admirable Conquista Espiritual del Vasto Imperio del Gran Thibet, y la Mission que los Padres Capuchinos Trienen Alli . . . Impressa en Mexico: 1765. V. 45

FONSECA, CHRISTOPHER DE

(Greek Title). A Discourse of Holy Love, by Which the Soul is United Unto God. London: 1652. V. 37; 41

FONSECA, CHRISTOVAL DE

Devout Contemplations Expressed in Two and Fortie Sermons Upon all ye Quadrages in all Gospels. London: 1629. V. 38

FONSECA, FRANCISCO DA

Embayxada do Conde de Villarmayor Fernando Telles de Sylva de Lisboa a Corte de Vienna . . . Vienna: 1717. V. 38

FONSTAD, KAREN WYNN

Atlas of Middle Earth. Boston: 1981. V. 46

FONT, PEDRO d. 1781

Font's Complete Diary. Berkeley: 1931. V. 40

San Francisco Bay and California in 1776. Providence. V. 38

FONTAINE, F. G.

Marginalia; or, Gleanings from an Army Note-Book. Columbia: 1864. V. 40; 41; 45

FONTAINE, JAMES

Memoirs of a Huguenot Family. New York: 1853. V. 40; 43

A Tale of the Huguenots, or Memoirs of a French Refugee Family. New York: 1838. V. 38

FONTAINE, JOHN BAPTIST DE LA

The French Spy; or, the Memoirs of John Baptist de la Fontaine . . . Containing many Secret Transactions relating to both England and France . . . from the French Original. London: 1700. V. 37

FONTAINE, NICOLAS 1625-1709

L'Histoire du Vieux et du Nouveau Testament . . . Paris: 1670. V. 40

The History of the Old Testament . . . London: 1688-90. V. 42

FONTAINES, U.

Wedgwood Fairyland Lustre. The Work of Daisy Makeig-Jones, 1975. 1975. V. 43

FONTANA, CARLO

L'Anfiteatro Flavio. The Hague: 1725. V. 37; 42

Il Tempio Vaticano a Suae Origine. Con gl'edifitii Piu Cospicui Antichi, e Moderni Fatti Dentro, e Fuori di Esso. Rome: 1694. V. 37

Utilissimo Trattato dell'Acque Correnti. Rome: 1696. V. 37

FONTANA, DOMENICO

Della Trasportatione dell' Obelisco Vaticano et delle Fabriche di Nostra Signore Papa Sisto V fatte dal Cavalier Domenico Fontana, Architteto di Sua Santita. Rome: 1590. V. 37

FONTANA, FELICE

Opuscoli Scientifici. Florence: 1783. V. 39

Traite sur le Venin de la Vipere sur les Poisons Americains sur le Laurier-Cersie et sur Quelques Autres Poisons Vegetaux. Florence and Paris: 1781. V. 45

Traite sur le Venin de la Vipere . . . Florence: 1781. V. 37

FONTANA, GIACOMO

Raccolta Delle Migliori Chiese di Roma e Surburgane Espresse in Tavole Disegnate ad Incise. Rome: 1838. V. 37; 42

FONTANON, DENIS

De Morborum Internorum Curatione Libri IIII . . . Venetiis: 1553. V. 37

FONTANON, DENYS

De Morborum Internorum Curatione Libri Qutuor. Lyon: 1550. V. 38

De Morborum Internorum Curatione Libri IIII . . . Adiectis ab Ioanne Raenerio Medico in Singulis Capitum Initiis Morborum Causis . . . Venetiis: 1553. V. 42

FONTENAY, GUY DE

Tu Iuuenibus Tu Artis & Poetice et Oratorie de Gustoribus Quibusvis Coducibiliu Apprime Synonimoru . . . Paris: 1510. V. 43

FONTENELLE, BERNARD LE BOVIER DE 1657-1757

Conversations on the Plurality of Worlds. Dublin: 1761. V. 38; 43

Conversations with a Lady of the Plurality of Worlds. London: 1719. V. 37

Dialgoues de Fontenelle. London: 1917. V. 45

Elements de la Geometrie de l'Infini. Paris: 1727. V. 38; 41; 45

Entretiens sur la Pluralite des Mondes. Paris: 1686. V. 37; 46

The History of Oracles, and the Cheats of the Pagan Priests. London: 1688. V. 38; 42; 46

A Plurality of Worlds. N.P.: 1929. V. 44

A Plurality of Worlds. London: 1702. V. 39

A Plurality of Worlds. London: 1929. V. 38; 41; 44; 46

A Plurality of Worlds. London: 1688. V. 38

FOOD For Poets. A Poem. London: 1775. V. 37

FOORD, ARTHUR H.

Monograph of the Carboniferous Cephalopoda of Ireland. London: 1897-1903. V. 39

FOORD, J.

Decorative Plant and Flower Studies. London: 1906. V. 42

FOOT, JESSE

The Life of John Hunter. London: 1794. V. 41; 42; 46

The Life of Arthur Murphy, Esq. London: 1811. V. 46

The Lives of Andrew Robinson Bowes, Esq. and the Countess of Strathmore, written from thirty-three years professional attendance, from letters and other well authenticated documents. London: (1812?). V. 37

FOOT, MIRJAM M.

The Henry Davis Gift. A Collection of Bookbindings. London: 1978. V. 39; 40; 41

The Henry Davis Gift. London: 1978-82. V. 41

The Henry Davis Gift. A Collection of Bookbindigs. Volume 1. Studies in the History of Bookbinding. London: 1982. V. 40; 42

The Henry Davis Gift. A Collection of Bookbindings, Volume 2, a Catalogue of North-European Bindings. London: 1983. V. 37; 39; 40; 42; 46

FOOT, MIRJAM M. continued

The Henry Davis Gift. A Collection of Bookbinding. London: 1978, 1983. V. 38

FOOT, PETER

General View of the Agriculture of the County of Middlesex. London: 1794. V. 41

FOOTE, A. H.

The African Squadron: Ashburton Treaty: Consular Sea Letters . . . Philadelphia: 1855. V. 42

FOOTE, ANDREW H.

Proclamation! To the Inhabitants of Clarksville, Tenn. Clarksville: 1862. V. 39

FOOTE, EDWARD JAMES

Captain Foote's Vindication of His Conduct, When Captain of H.M.S. Seahorse, and Senior Officer in the Bay of Naples. London: 1810. V. 38

FOOTE, HENRY S.

Casket of Reminiscences. Washington: 1874. V. 45

Texas and Texans. Philadelphia: 1841. V. 37; 38; 39; 40; 42

FOOTE, HENRY STUART

The Bench and Bar of the South and Southwest. St. Louis: 1876. V. 38

Texas and the Texans; or, Advance of the Anglo-mericans to the South-West. 1935. V. 38

FOOTE, SAMUEL

Bon-Mots. London: 1894. V. 46

The Comic Theatre. London: 1762. V. 42

The Dramatic Works. London: 1786. V. 38

The Dramatic Works. London: 1788. V. 38

The Dramatic Works of Samuel Foote. London: 1788. V. 40; 41; 43; 44

The Dramatic Works, To Which is Prefixed a Life of the Author. London: 1797? V. 41; 44

The Lame Lover, a Comedy in Three Acts. London: 1770. V. 45

FOOTE, SHELBY

The Civil War. New York: 1958/62/74. V. 39; 41; 45; 46

The Civil War. New York: 1958-74. V. 46

Follow Me Down. New York: 1950. V. 39

Jordan County. New York: 1954. V. 41; 46

Love in a Dry Season. New York: 1951. V. 39; 41; 46

September, September. New York: 1977. V. 44

Tournament. New York: 1949. V. 44

FOOTE, WILLIAM HENRY

Sketches of North Carolina. New York: 1846. V. 43

FOR Aaron Copland. 1978. V. 42; 44

FOR Aaron Copland on the Occasion of His Seventy-Eighth Birthday, 14 November 1978. Winston Salem: 1978. V. 39

FOR Doc Leslie's One Hundredth Birthday. New York: 1985. V. 40

FOR Our Darling. N.P.: 1890. V. 40

FOR Reynolds Price. Winston-Salem: 1983. V. 46

FOR Robert Penn Warren. V. 42
FOR Robert Penn Warren. 1980. V. 44

FORBERG, F. C.

The Manual of Classical Erotology. London: V. 41

The Manual of Classical Erotology. London: 1887. V. 39

FORBES, A. C.

English Estate Forestry. London: 1904. V. 44

FORBES, A. HOLLAND

Architectural Gardens of Italy. New York: 1902. V. 39

FORBES, ALEXANDER 1778-1864

California; a History of Upper and Lower California from Their First Discovery to the Present Time . . . London: 1839. V. 39; 40; 41; 42; 43; 44; 45

California. A History of Upper and Lower California from Their Discovery to the Present Time . . . San Francisco: 1919. V. 37; 39

California, A History of Upper and Lower California. San Francisco: 1937. V. 38; 39; 41; 43; 45

FORBES, ALEXANDER C. 1778-1864

California. A History of Upper & Lower California from Their First Discovery to the Present Time . . . San Francisco: 1919. V. 37

A Trip to Mexico or Recollections of a Ten Months' Ramble in 1849-50. By a Barrister. London: 1851. V. 37

FORBES, ALLAN

Special Exhibiton of Whaling Pictures From the Collection of Alban Forbes . . . Salem: 1919. V. 42

Yankee Ship Sailing Cards. (with) Other Yankee Ship Sailing Cards. (with) Yankee Ship Sailing Cards III. Boston: 1948-52. V. 45

FORBES, BRYAN

Truth Lies Sleeping. London: (1950). V. 37

FORBES, CHARLES

Prize Essay. Vancouver Island: Its Resources and Capabilities as a Colony. Victoria: 1862. V. 43

FORBES, CHARLES S.

Iceland: Its Volcanoes, Geysers and Glaciers. London: 1860. V. 42; 43; 45

FORBES, DAVID

On the Aymara Indians of Bolivia and Peru. London: 1870. V. 45

FORBES, DUNCAN

A Letter to a Bishop, Concerning Some Important Discoveries in Philosophy and Theology. London: 1732. V. 37; 42

Reflexions on the Sources of Incredulity. Edinburgh: 1750. V. 41; 42; 43; 44

The Whole Works of the Right Honourable Duncan Forbes . . . Edinburgh: 1750-55. V. 42

FORBES, E.

A History of British Mollusca and Their Shells. London: 1848-53. V. 37; 38

On the Tertiary Fluvio-Marine Formation of the Isle of Wight. London: 1856. V. 42

FORBES, EDWARD

A Monograph of the British Naked Eyed Medusae, with Figures of all the Species. London: 1848. V. 43

FORBES, EDWIN

Life Studies of the Great Army. New York: 1876. V. 39

Thirty Years After: An Artist's Story of the Great War. New York: 1880. V. 38

FORBES, ESTHER

A Mirror for Witches. London: 1928. V. 45

FORBES, F. B.

An Enumeration of all Plants Known from China Proper, Formosa, etc . . . Together with Their Distribution and Synonymy. 1866-1905. V. 38

An Enumeration of all the Plants Known from China Proper, Formosa, Hainan, Corea, the Luchu Archipelago and the Island of Hongkong Together with Their Distribution and Synonymy. London: 1886-1905. V. 37

FORBES, F. E.

Five Years in China: from 1842 to 1847. London: 1848. V. 38

FORBES, FRANCIS

Eloge de la Ville d'Edinbourg. Edinburgh: 1752. V. 41

FORBES, FREDERICK

Dahomey and the Dahomans. London: 1851. V. 41; 43; 44

FORBES, FREDRICH E.

Five Years in China; from 1842 to 1847. London: 1848. V. 43

FORBES, H. A. CROSBY

Chinese Export Silver 1785 to 1885. Milton: 1975. V. 44

FORBES, HENRY O.

A Handbook of the Primates. London: 1896. V. 38

The Natural History of Sokotra and Abd-el-Kuri. Liverpool: 1903. V. 45

FORBES, JAMES

Illustrations to Oriental Memoirs. London: 1835. V. 38

Letters from France, Written in the Years 1803 and 1804. London: 1806. V. 42

Oriental Memoirs . . . London: 1813. V. 42

FORBES, JAMES D.

Norway and Its Glaciers Visited in 1851. Edinburgh: 1853. V. 37; 38; 40; 41; 42; 43; 44; 45; 46

Occasional Papers on the Theory of Glaciers. Edinburgh: 1859. V. 45

FORBES, JAMES DAVID

Occasional Papers on the Theory of Glaciers. Edinburgh: 1859. V. 40

Travels through the Alps of Savoy and Other Parts of the Pennine Chain. Edinburgh: 1843. V. 41; 43; 44

Travels through the Alps of Savoy and Other Parts of the Pennine Chain with Observations on the Phenomena of the Glaciers. Edinburgh: 1845. V. 43

FORBES, JAMES DAVID continued

Travels through the Alps of Savoy and Other Parts of the Pennine Chain with Observations on the Phenomena of Glaciers. Edinburgh: 1865. V. 46

Travels through the Alps. London: 1900. V. 43

FORBES, JAMES GRANT

Sketches, Historical and Topographical of the Floridas . . . New York: 1821. V. 40; 41; 43

FORBES, JOHN

The Cyclopaedia of Practical Medicine; comprising treatises on the nature and treatment of diseases, materia media and therapeutics, medical jurisprudence, &c. &c. London: 1833. V. 37

A Manual of Select Medical Bibliography, In Which the Books are Arranged Chronologically According to the Subjects . . . London: 1835. V. 37

Memoirs of the Earls of Granard. London: 1860. V. 39

Memorandums Made in Ireland In the Autumn of 1852. V. 46

Sketch of the Medical Topography of the Hundred of Penwith, Comprising the District of the Landsend in Cornwall. Worcester. V. 38

The Theory of Differential and Integral Calculus. Glasgow: 1837. V. 40; 41

FORBES, JOHN MURRAY

Personal Reminiscences. Boston: 1882. V. 37

FORBES, KATHRYN

Transfer Point. New York: 1947. V. 42; 45

FORBES, MANFIELD D.

Clare College 1326-1926. Cambridge: 1928-30. V. 45

FORBES, MANSFIELD D.

Clare College 1326-1926. London: 1928-30. V. 42

FORBES, MURRAY

A Treatise upon Gravel and upon Gout, in which the sources of each are investigated, and effectual means of preventing, or of removing these diseases recommended. London: 1787. V. 37

FORBES, P. J.

Alphabetical and Analytical catalogue of the New York Society Library: with a Brief Historical Notice of the Institution. New York: 1838. V. 39

FORBES, PETER

Poems, Chiefly in the Scottish Dialect. Edinburgh: 1812. V. 40; 46

FORBES, R. B.

Rigs of Vessels. Boston: 1883. V. 46

Shipwreck by Lightning, Papers Relative to Harris's Lightning Condutors . . . Boston: 1853. V. 41

FORBES, R. J.

Studies in Ancient Technology. Leiden: 1955-58. V. 42; 45

FORBES, R. N.

Six Months' Service in the African Blockade, from April to October, 1848, in Command of HMS Bonetta. London: 1849. V. 39

FORBES, ROBERT

Ajax His Speech to the Gecian Knabbs. Edinburgh: 1748. V. 45

FORBES, ROBERT B.

Personal Reminiscences. Boston: 1882. V. 40

FORBES, W. A.

The Collected Scientific Papers of . . . London: 1885. V. 37; 38

FORBES, WILLIAM 1739-1806

An Account of the Life and Writings of James Beattie, LL.D., Late Professor of Moral Philosophy and Logic in the Marischal College and University of Aberdeen. Edinburgh: 1806. V. 46

An Account of the Life and Writings of James Beattie, LL.D. New York & Philadelphia: 1806. V. 40; 41; 42

Coutts Bank: Memoirs of a Banking-House by the Late . . . London: 1860. V. 41

Coutts Banks: Memoirs of a Banking House by the Late . . . London: & Edinburgh: 1860. V. 41

The Duty and Powers of Justices of Peace in This Part of Great Britain Called Scotland. Edinburgh: 1707. V. 43

A Methodical Treatise Concerning Bills of Exchange . . . Edinburgh: 1718. V. 37; 38; 40

FORBURY Hill; a Poem. Inscribed to the Memory of the Late Francis Annesley, Esq. London: 1813. V. 43

FORBUSH, EDWARD H.

Birds of Massachusetts and Other New England States. N.P.: 1927-29. V. 39; 43

FORBUSH, EDWARD HOWE

Birds of Massachusetts and Other New England States. Norwood: 1925-27-29. V. 39

FORBUSH, T. B.

Florida: the Advantages and Inducements Which It Offers to Immigrants. Boston: 1867? V. 41

FORBY, ROBERT 1759-1825

Pursuits of Agriculture, a Satirical Poem. London: 1808. V. 42

FORCADEL, ETIENNE

Cupido Iurisperitus . . . Eiusdem et Calumniatores Epistola. Lyons: 1553. V. 40

Promethevs Sive, de Raptu Animorum. Paris: 1578. V. 40

THE FORCE of Example; or, the History of Henry and Caroline . . . London: 1797. V. 37; 42

FORCE, PETER

American Archives. Washington: 1837-53. V. 39; 41; 42; 45; 46

The Declaration of Independence, or Notes on Lord Mahon's History of the American Declaration of Independence. London: 1855. V. 46

Tracts and Other Papers, Relating Principally to the Origin, Settlement and Progress of the Colonies in North America, from the Discovery of the Country to the Year 1776. Washington: 1836-46. V. 39; 41

FORCHE, CAROLYN

The Country Between Us. Port Townsend: 1981. V. 39; 40

Gathering the Tribes. New Haven: 1976. V. 39

FORD, ALICE

Edward Hicks: Painter of the Peaceable Kingdom. Philadelphia: 1952. V. 41

FORD, ANDREW E.

The Story of the Fifteenth Regiment Massachusetts Volunteer Infantry in the Civil War 1861-64. Clinton: 1898. V. 46

FORD, ARTHUR P.

Life in the Confederate Army. New York: 1905. V. 39

FORD, CHARLES HENRI

ABC's. Prairie City: 1940. V. 39; 40; 42

Emblems of Arachne. New York: 1986. V. 37

Poems from Painters. New York: 1945. V. 38; 41

Secret Haiku. New York: 1982. V. 42

Silver Flower Coo. New York: 1968. V. 39

Spare Parts. Greece: 1966. V. 39

The Young and Evil. Paris: 1933. V. 39

FORD, CHARLES HENRY

The Overturned Lake. Cincinnati: 1941. V. 37

FORD, DOUGLAS MOREY

Kate Savage; a Novel. London: 1873. V. 37

FORD, F. M.

A Man Could Stand Up. 1926. V. 43

FORD, FORD MADOX 1873-1939

The Benefactor: A Tale of a Small Circle. London: 1905. V. 44

The Brown Owl. London: 1891. V. 42

The Brown Owl. London: 1892. V. 37; 40; 42

Brown Owl: A Fairy Story. London: 1891. V. 38

Buckshee. Cambridge: 1956. V. 42

Buckshee. 1966. V. 37; 40; 41; 42; 44

Buckshee (Last Poems). Cambridge: 1966. V. 39

Catalogue of an Exhibition of Collected Works. 1909. V. 46

The Cinque Ports, a Historic and Descriptive Record. London: 1900. V. 44

Collected Poems of Ford Madox Ford. New York: 1936. V. 44

The English Novel. Philadelphia: 1929. V. 37

The Feather. London: 1892. V. 39; 46

The Fifth Queen: and How She Came to Court. (with) The Fifth Queen Crowned. London: 1906-08. V. 46

Ford Madox Brown. A Record of His Life and Work. London: 1896. V. 39; 42; 45; 46

The Good Soldier. New York: 1927. V. 38; 39

Great Trade Route. London: 1937. V. 39; 43; 44

Great Trade Route. New York: 1937. V. 38; 40

The Half Moon. London: 1909. V. 37; 40; 41; 42; 43; 44

The Heart of the Country. London: 1906. V. 39

Henry for Hugh. Philadelphia: 1934. V. 44

High Germany. London: 1911. V. 46

A House. London: 1921. V. 37; 38; 39; 41; 46

FORD, FORD MADOX 1873-1939 continued

It Was the Nightingale. Philadelphia: 1933. V. 43

It Was the Nightingale. Philadelphia and London: 1933. V. 46

Joseph Conrad: a Personal Remembrance. V. 44

Joseph Conrad - a Personal Remembrance. London: 1924. V. 40; 46

Ladies Whose Bright Eyes. London: 1911. V. 42

Last Post. London: 1928. V. 39; 40; 41; 43; 44

The Last Post. New York: 1928. V. 38

A Little Less than Gods. London: 1928. V. 37; 40; 41; 42; 43; 44

A Man Could Stand Up. London: 1926. V. 40; 42; 44

The March of Literature. London: 1939. V. 37

The Marsden Case. London: 1923. V. 39

Mightier than the Sword: Memories and Criticisms. London: 1938. V. 39

Mr. Apollo: a Just Possible Story. London: 1908. V. 44

Mister Bosphorus and the Muses. London: 1923. V. 37; 41; 42; 45

New York Is Not America. London: 1927. V. 40; 43; 44

New York Essays. New York: 1927. V. 39; 43; 44

New York: Essays. New York: 1927. V. 37; 45

No More Parades. London: 1925. V. 37; 42; 46

On Heaven and Poems Written on Active Service. London: 1918. V. 37; 39; 41; 42

On Heaven and Other Poems Written on Active Service. London: 1918. V. 43; 46

Poems from Pictures and for Notes of Music. London: 1900. V. 46

Portraits from Life: Memoirs and Criticisms. Boston: 1937. V. 37

Portraits from Life. Boston: 1938. V. 39

Provence - from Minstrels to the Machine. London: 1938. V. 41

The Rash Act. London: 1933. V. 46

The Rash Act. New York: 1933. V. 43; 44

Ring for Nancy. Indianapolis: 1913. V. 39

Rock Springs: Stories. New York: 1987. V. 46

Rossetti: a Critical Essay on His Art. London. V. 46

Rossetti: a Critical Essay on His Art. London: 1902. V. 39

Selected Poems. Boston: 1971. V. 39

Sleected Poems. Cambridge: 1971. V. 44

The Shifting of the Fire. London: 1892. V. 37; 41

Some Do Not . . . London: 1924. V. 44

Songs from London. London: 1910. V. 42

The Soul of London: a Survey of a Modern City. London: 1905. V. 44

Vive Le Roy. London: (1937). V. 37

When Blood is Their Argument. London: 1915. V. 38; 42

When Blood is their Argument. New York & London: 1915. V. 37; 40; 41

When the Wicked Man. New York: 1931. V. 37; 40; 44

Wildlife. New York: 1990. V. 46

Women & Men. Paris: 1923. V. 38; 39

The Young Lovell, Romance. London: 1913. V. 38; 44

Zeppelin Nights. London: 1916. V. 37; 40; 44

FORD, FRANK

Diseases of the Nervous System in Infancy, Childhood and Adolescence. Springfield: 1937. V. 40

FORD, G. H.

Illustrations of Dissections in a Series of Original Coloured Plates, the Size of Life Representing the Dissection of the Human Body . . . London: 1867. V. 37; 38; 39

FORD, GERALD

Churchill Lecture. An Address by Gerald R. Ford at the English Speaking Union, London, England. November 30, 1983. Northridge: 1984. V. 45

FORD, GERALD R.

A Time to Heal. New York: 1979. V. 38; 39; 46

A Vision for America. Northridge: 1980. V. 45

FORD, GUS L.

Texas Cattle Brands. Dallas: 1936. V. 42; 44

FORD, H. J.

The Red Fairy Book. London: 1890. V. 38

FORD, H. L.

Shakespeare 1700-1740, a Collation of the Editions and Separate Plays with Some Account of T. Johnson and R. Walker. Oxford: 1935. V. 39

FORD, H. W.

A Collation of Words Common to the French and English Languages. Jackson: 1893. V. 43

FORD, HELEN C.

Notes of a Tour in India and Ceylon During the Winter of 1888-89. London: 1889. V. 44

FORD, HENRY CHAPMAN

An Artist Records the California Missions. San Francisco: 1989. V. 43; 44; 46

Etchings of the Franciscan Missions of California. New York: 1883. V. 46

FORD, HENRY J.

The Green Fairy Book. London: 1892. V. 46

The Red Book of Romance. London: 1905. V. 45

FORD, HORACE A.

Archery: Its Theory and Practice. London: 1856. V. 46

Archery: Its Theory and Practice. London: 1859. V. 39

Archery: its Theory and Practice. Toledo: 1880. V. 41

FORD, J. D. M.

Letters of John III King of Portugal 1521-1557. Cambridge: 1931. V. 42

FORD, JOHN

The Dramatic Works. Edinburgh: 1811. V. 46

The Dramatic Works of John Ford. Edinburgh: 1811. V. 39; 45

The Works . . . London: 1869. V. 44

The Works of . . . London: 1865. V. 38

FORD, JOHN S.

Protection of the Frontier of Texas. Washington: 1859. V. 38

FORD, JOHN SALMON

Rip Ford's Texas. Austin: 1963. V. 42; 44

FORD, JOHN W.

Some Correspondence Between the Governors and Treasurers of the New England Company in London and the Commissioners of the United Colonies in America. London: 1896. V. 43

FORD, JULIA E.

Simeon Solomon. An Appreciation. New York: 1908. V. 42

FORD, JULIA ELLSWORTH

Imagina. New York: 1914. V. 37; 39; 40

Imagina. New York: 1923. V. 44; 45; 46

Snickerty Nick. New York: 1919. V. 38; 46

Snickerty Nick and the Giant. Los Angeles: 1933. V. 45

Snickerty Nick and the Giant. Los Angeles: 1935. V. 40

FORD, LAETITIA

The Butterfly Collector's Vade Mecum. Ipswich: 1824. V. 43

The Butterfly Collector's Vade Mecum. Ipswich: 1827. V. 43

FORD, LEMUEL

March of the First Dragoons to the Rocky Mountains in 1835. Denver: 1957. V. 38

FORD, MARGARET L.

Christ, Plato, Hermes Trismegistus. The Dawn of Printing: Catalogue of Incunabula in the Bibliotheca Philosophica Hermetica. Amsterdam: 1990. V. 46

FORD, PAUL LEICESTER 1865-1902

Franklin Bibliography. Brooklyn: 1889. V. 37; 39; 42; 43; 44; 45

The Honorable Peter Stirling and What People Thought of Him. New York: 1894. V. 43

The Journals of Hugh Gaine, Printer . . . Biography, and Bibliography. New York: 1902. V. 45

The New England Primer. New York: 1897. V. 42; 44

Webster Geneology. Brooklyn: 1876. V. 38; 41; 46

Webster Genealogy. New Haven: 1836. V. 37

Western Geneology. Brooklyn: 1876. V. 39

FORD, RANDOLPH

Christianae Religionis, Sive Ecclesiae Anglicanae Articuli XXXIX. London: 1720. V. 38

FORD, RICHARD

Communist. Derry: 1987. V. 39; 44

Gatherings from Spain. London: 1846. V. 37

A Hand-Book for Travellers in Spain, and Readers at Home . . . London: 1845. V. 37

Juke Joint. Jackson: 1940. V. 45

Juke Joint. Jackson: 1990. V. 43; 45; 46

My Mother, in Memory. Elmwood: 1988. V. 38; 39; 42; 44

A Piece of My Heart. New York: 1976. V. 42; 43; 44; 45; 46

FORD, RICHARD continued

Rock Springs. New York: 1987. V. 42

The Sportswriter. New York: 1986. V. 45; 46

Twelve Etchings After Drawings and Engravings by Parmigianino and Andrea Meldolla. London: 1822. V. 40

The Ultimate Good Luck. 1981. V. 43

The Ultimate Good Luck. Boston: 1981. V. 42; 44

The Ultimate Good Luck. London: 1989. V. 43

Wildlife. New York: 1990. V. 43; 44; 45; 46

FORD, SALLY ROCHESTER

Raids and Romance of Morgan and His men. New York: 1864. V. 45

FORD, SIMON

The Conflagration of London; Poetically Delineated. London: 1667. V. 40

Londini quod Reliquum. Or, London's Remains: in Latin and English. London: 1667. V. 45

Londons Resurrection, Poetically represented. London: 1669. V. 37

Original Poems and Translations: Consisting of the Microscope, Piscatio or Angling, the Beau and Academic. London: 1733. V. 39

FORD, THOMAS

A History of Illinois. Chicago: 1854. V. 39; 40; 42; 45

FORD, WILLIAM

A Description of Scenery in the Lake District . . . London: 1852. V. 44

FORD, WORTHINGTON CHAUNCEY

Boston Book Market, 1679-1700. Boston: 1917. V. 39

Defences of Philadelphia in 1777. Brooklyn: 1897. V. 42; 43

FORD, WORTHINGTON CHAUNCY

The Beacon Biographies of Eminent Americans; George Washington. Boston: 1910. V. 37; 45

The Isle of Pines, 1688. Boston: 1920. V. 39

FORDE, GERTRUDE

In the Old Palazzo. London: 1885. V. 41

FORDE, H. A.

The Fruit of the Spirit. London: 1919. V. 46

FORDHAM, ELIAS P.

Personal Narrative of Travels in Virginia, Maryland, Pennsylvania, Ohio, Indiana, Kentucky . . . . Cleveland: 1906. V. 37; 38; 39; 42; 43

FORDHAM, HERBERT GEORGE, BART b. 1854

Hertfordshire Maps: A Descriptive Catalogue of the Maps of the County 1579-1900. London: 1901-07. V. 39

The Road Books and Itineraries of Great Britain 1570 to 1850. Cambridge: 1924. V. 39

FORDHAM, MARY WESTON

Magnolia Leaves. Poems. 1897. V. 37

FORDYCE, DAVID

Dialogues Concerning Education. London: 1745-48. V. 41; 43

Dialogues Concerning Education. London: 1754-8. V. 41

FORDYCE, GEORGE

Five Dissertations on Fever. Boston: 1823. V. 37

FORDYCE, JAMES

Addresses to Young Men. London: 1777. V. 46

Addresses to the Deity. Dublin: 1785. V. 38

A Collection of Hymns and Sacred Poems. Edinburgh: 1788. V. 39; 40; 42

Poems. London: 1786. V. 41; 42

Sermons to a Young Women in Two Volumes. London: 1766. V. 43

FORDYCE, WILLIAM

The Great Importance and Proper Method of Cultivating and Curing Rhubarb in Britain, for Medical Uses. London: 1792. V. 38

the History and Antiquities of the County Palatine of Durham . . . Newcastle: 1857. V. 41; 46

The History and Antiquities of the County Palatine of Durham. Newcastle, London &: 1857. V. 38; 43

FOREEST, PIETER VAN 1522-1597

Observationum et Curationum Medicinalium . . . De Ventriculi Affectibus, In Quo Eorum Caussae, Signa Prognoses, Curatio Graphice Depinguntur. Raphelengius: 1606. V. 42

Observationum Curationrum Medicinalium ac Chirurgicarum Opera Omnia Quatuor Tomis Digesta. Rouen: 1653. V. 42

FOREIGN Essays on Agriculture and the Arts. London: 1766. V. 40

FOREIGN Field Sports, Fisheries, Sporting Anecdotes . . . London: 1819. V. 42; 46

FOREIGN Field Sports, Fisheries, Sporting Anecdotes &c, &c. London. V. 45

FOREIGN Field Sports, Fisheries, Sporting Anecdotes, &c. &c. With a Supplement of New South Wales. London: 1813. V. 37; 38

FOREIRO, FRANCISCO

Iesaiae Prophetae Vetus & Nova ex Hebraico Uersio, Cum Commentario . . . Venice: 1563. V. 41

FOREL, AUGUST

Hypnotism or Suggestion and Psychotherapy. New York: 1907. V. 44

FOREL, AUGUSTE 1848-1931

The Social World of the Ants Compared with That of Man. New York: 1929. V. 43

FOREL, AUGUSTE HENRI 1848-1931

Hygiene of Nerves and Mind in Health and Disease. New York: 1907. V. 45

FOREMAN, CHARLES

A Letter to the Right Honourable Sir Robert Walpole . . . London: 1732. V. 39; 43; 46

FOREMAN, GRANT

Advancing the Frontier 1830-1860. Norman: 1933. V. 37

The Adventures of James Collier. Chicago: 1937. V. 37; 38; 40

The Five Civilized Tribes. Norman: 1934. V. 41

Indians and Pioneers: the Story of the American Southwest Before 1830. New Haven: 1930. V. 46

Indians and Pioneers: The Story of the American Southwest Before 1830 by Grant Foreman. 1930. V. 37

Pioneer Days in the Early Southwest. Cleveland: 1920. V. 43

Pioneer Days in the Early Southwest. Cleveland: 1926. V. 39; 43; 46

The Story of the American Southwest Before 1830. New Haven: 1930. V. 46

FOREMAN, JOHN

The Philippine Islands. New York: 1906. V. 46

FOREMAN, PAUL

Quanah, the Serpent Eagle. Flagstaff: 1983. V. 37

FORE'S Sporting Notes and Sketches, A Quarterly Magazine Descriptive of British and Foreign Sport. London: 1885-1907. V. 39

FOREST, EARLE R.

Missions and Pueblos of the Old Southwest: Their Myths, Legends, Fiestas, and Ceremonies . . . Cleveland: 1929. V. 38

FOREST, JACOPO FILIPPO, DA BERGAMO 1434-1520

Supplementum Chronicorum . . . Cui Insuper Addita est Nostrorum Temporum . . . Paris: 1535. V. 39

FOREST, JOHN

The Piper of the Stars. A Story for Children, by John Forest. London: 1986. V. 37

FOREST, PIETER

Observations et Histories Chyrvrgigves Tirees des Oeuvres De Quatre Excellens Medecins . . . Geneve: 1669. V. 45

FORESTA, M. A.

George Tooker. N.P.: 1983. V. 46

FORESTER, CECIL SCOTT 1899-1966

The Age of Fighting Sail. Garden City: 1956. V. 38

The 'Annie Marble' in Germany. London: 1930. V. 41

The Barbary Pirates. London: 1956. V. 41

Beat to Quarters. Boston: 1937. V. 43

The Bedchamber Mystery. Toronto: 1944. V. 38; 43; 44; 46

Brown on Resolution. London: 1929. V. 37; 38; 43

Captain Horatio Hornblower. I. Beat to Quarters. II. Ship of the Line. III. Flying Colours. Boston: 1939. V. 38

The Captain from Connecticut. London: 1941. V. 40

Commodore Hornblower. 1945. V. 45

Commodore Hornblower. Boston: 1945. V. 38; 43

The Earthly Paradise. London: 1940. V. 40; 46

The Good Shepherd. Boston: 1955. V. 38

The Gun. Boston: 1933. V. 37

The Gun. London: 1933. V. 46

The Happy Return. London: 1937. V. 43

The Happy Return. 1937. V. 37

Hornblower and the Atropos. London: 1953. V. 38

FORREST, EARL R.

Missions & Pueblos of the Old Southwest; Their Myths, Legends, Fiestas, & Ceremonies, with Some Account of the Indian Tribes & Their Dances; & of the Penitentes. Cleveland: 1929. V. 37

FORREST, EARLE R.

Arizona's Dark and Bloody Ground. Caldwell: 1936. V. 40; 45; 46

Arizona's Dark and Bloody Ground. Caxton: 1936. V. 43

Lone War Trail of Apache Kid. Pasadena: 1947. V. 39; 44

Missions and Pueblos of the Old Southwest. Cleveland: 1929. V. 37; 38; 39; 43

FORREST, EBENEZER fl. 1779

An Account of What Seemed Most Remarkable in the Five Days Peregrination of the Five Following Persons, viz. Messieurs Tothall, Scott, Hogarth, Thornhill and Forrest. London: 1782. V. 39; 40; 45

Momus Turn'd Fabulist; or, Vulcan's Wedding. London: 1729. V. 38

FORREST, G. W.

A History of the Indian Mutiny Reviewed and Illustrated with Maps, Plans and Portraits. Edinburgh: 1904. V. 41

Selections from the State Papers of the Governors-General of India. London: 1910. V. 41

FORREST, H. E.

The Vertebrate Fauna of North Wales. 1907. V. 46

The Vertebrate Fauna of North Wales. London: 1907. V. 42; 43; 46

FORREST, JOHN

Explorations in Australia. London: 1875. V. 39

FORREST, LT. COL.

A Picturesque Tour Along the River Ganges and Jumna, in India. London: 1824. V. 40

FORREST, MARY

Women of the South Distinguished in Literature. New York: 1861. V. 37; 39; 41; 43

FORREST, NATHAN BEDFORD

Gen. Forrest to His Troops. V. 42

Maj. Gen. N. B. Forrest's Address to His Command. Tupelo: 1864. V. 39

FORREST, THOMAS

A Voyage to New Guinea, and the Moluccas, from Balambangan. Dublin: 1779. V. 37; 39; 43

A Voyage to New Guinea and the Moluccas, from Balambangan . . . London: 1779. V. 37; 46

A Voyage to New Guinea and the Moluccas, from Balmabangan . . . London: 1780. V. 41

A Voyage from Calcutta to the Mergui Archipelago . . . London: 1792. V. 45

FORREST, WILLIAM HUTTON

Report, Chemical and Medical, of the Airthrey Mineral Springs and a List of Phaenogamous Plants Collected In Their Vicinity. Stirling: 1831. V. 46

FORRESTER, ALFRED HENRY 1804-1872

Absurdities in Prose and Verse. London: 1827. V. 40

Alfred Crowquill's Comic History of the Kings and Queens of England from William the Conqueror to the Present Time. London: 1850. V. 41

Alfred Crowquill's Fairy Tales; Patty and Her Pitcher or Kindness of Heart. London: 1857. V. 41

Alfred Crowquill's Fairy Tales: Tiny and Her Vanity or Self-Opinion. London: 1857. V. 41

A Bundle of Crowquills Dropped by Alfred Crowquill, in His Eccentric Fights Over the Fields of Literature. London: 1854. V. 41

Comic History of the Kings and Queens of England from William the Conqueror to the Present Time. London: 1860. V. 38

A Few Words about Pipes, Smoking and Tobacco. New York: 1947. V. 46

Funny Leaves for Younger Branches. London: 1850. V. 45

A Good Natured Hint About California by Alfred Crowquill. London: 1849. V. 39

How He Reigned and How He Mizzled: a Railway Raillery. London: 1849. V. 45; 46

It: a Comic Perennial, in Prose and Verse. London: 1835. V. 39

Leaves from the Memorandum Book of Alfred Crowquill. London: 1834/March 1835. V. 42

Phantasmagoria of Fun. London: 1843. V. 38; 39; 40

Picture Fables. London: 1850. V. 39

Pictures Picked from the Pickwick Papers by Alfred Crowquill. London. V. 40

Pictures Picked from the Pickwick Papers. London: 1837. V. 40; 43

Strange Surprising Adventures of the Venerable Goodroo Simple. London: 1861. V. 39; 40; 43

Tales for Children. London: 1864. V. 45

What Uncle Told Us About I. London. V. 40

FORRESTER, ANDREW

Outside the Law . . . Glasgow: 1868. V. 42

Secret Service or Recollections of a City Detective. London: 1864. V. 39; 42

FORRESTER, JAMES

Dialogues on the Passions, Habits and Affections Peculiar to Children . . . London: 1748. V. 46

FORRESTER, MRS.

My Lord and My Lady. London: 1882. V. 41

FORRESTER, THOMAS

Norway in 1848 and 1849. London: 1850. V. 41

FORROW, ALEXANDER

The Thames and Its Docks. A Lecture. London: 1877. V. 38

FORRY, SAMUEL

The Climate of the United States and Its Endemic Infuences. New York: 1842. V. 38

FORSELL, CHRISTIAN

Une Annee en Suede. Ou Tableaux des Costumes, Moeurs et Usages des Paysans de la Suede, Suivis desSites et Monumens Historiques les Plus Remarquables. Stockholm: 1836. V. 40

FORSGREN, LYDIA WALKER

History of Box Elder County. N.P.: 1937. V. 42

FORSHAW, J.

Parrots of the World. Melbourne: 1973. V. 37; 38

Parrots of the World. London: 1973. V. 37

FORSHAW, J. M.

Australian Parrots. Melbourne: 1969. V. 38

The Birds of Paradise and Bower Birds. Sydney: 1977. V. 39; 42; 45

Kingfishers and Related Birds, Part I, Alcedinidae. Melbourne: 1983-85. V. 37; 38; 39; 42

Kingfishers and Related Birds, Part I. Alcedinidae. Melbourne: 1983-85. V. 42

Kingfishers and Related Birds, Part 2, Vol. I, Todidae, Momotidae and Meropidae. Melbourne: 1987. V. 39; 42

Kingfishers and Related Birds, Part Two, Volume I: Todiae & Momotidae. Lansdowne: 1988. V. 39

Parrots of the World. Melbourne: 1973. V. 38; 42

Parrots of the World. New York: 1973. V. 43

FORSHAW, JOSEPH M.

Kingfishers and Related Birds. Part 2. Volume 1: Todidae, Momotidae and Meropidae. Melbourne: 1987. V. 40

Kingfishers and Related Birds. Part I, Volume 1 & 2: Kingfishers Alcedinidae. V. 40

Parrots of the World. Melbourne: 1973. V. 40

FORSSELL, CHRISTIAN

Album Pittoresque du Nord. Tableaux des Costumes. Londres & Berlin: 1838. V. 38

FORSTER, C.

The One Primeval Language Traced Experimentally through Ancient Inscriptions in Alphabetic Characters of Lost Powers from the Four Continents . . . London: 1852-54. V. 38

FORSTER, CHARLES

The Historical Geography of Arabia . . . London: 1844. V. 39

The Monuments of Assyria, Babylonia and Persia. London: 1859. V. 46

The One Primeval Language Traced Experimentally Through Ancient Inscriptions in Alphabetic Characters of Lost Powers from the Four Continents . . . London: 1852. V. 37

FORSTER, CHARLES FFRENCH BLAKE

The Irish Chieftains; or, a Struggle for the Crown, with Numerous Notes and a Copious Appendix. Dublin: 1872. V. 41

FORSTER, EDWARD

The British Gallery of Engravings, from Pictures of the Italian, Flemish, Dutch and English Schools, Now in the Possession of the King, and Several Noblemen and Gentlemen of the United Kingdom. London: 1807. V. 40

Observations on the Evidence Relating to the Russia Trade; as Delivered at the Bar of the Honourable the House of Commons, on the 5th of May, 1774. London: 1774. V. 43; 46

FORSTER, EDWARD MORGAN 1879-1970

Abinger Harvest, London: 1936. V. 45; 46

Alexandria: A History and a Guide. Alexandria: 1922. V. 38; 39

Alexandria: A History and a Guide. Alexandria: 1938. V. 38; 45

FORSYTH, JOSEPH BELL

A Few Months in the East; or a Glimpse of the Red, the Dead and the Black Seas. Quebec: 1861. V. 45

A Few Months in the East; or a Glimpse of the Red, the Dead and the Black Seas. Quebec & London: 1861. V. 37; 40; 42; 43

FORSYTH, ROBERT

The Beauties of Scotland . . . London: 1805-08. V. 44; 46

FORSYTH, T. D.

Report of a Mission to Yarkund in 1873, Under the Command of Sir T. D. Forsyth with Historical and Geographical Information Regarding the Possessions of the Ameer of Yarkund. Calcutta: 1875. V. 40

FORSYTH, W.

A Treatise on the Culture and Management of Fruit Trees. London: 1803. V. 44

FORSYTH, WILLIAM

An Epitome of Mr. Forsyth's Treatise on the Culture and Management of Fruit-Trees. Philadelphia: 1804. V. 40

An Epitome of Mr. Forsyth's Treatise on the Culture and Management of Fruit Trees. Philadelphia: 1800. V. 37

Essays Critical and Narrative. London: 1874. V. 45

History of Captivity of Napoleon at St. Helena . . . London: 1853. V. 46

A Treatise on the Culture and Management of Fruit-Trees. London: 1802. V. 37; 42; 44; 46

A Treatise on the Culture and Management of Fruit Trees. Philadelphia: 1802. V. 42; 43

A Treatise on the Culture and Management of Fruit Trees . . . Albany: 1803. V. 45

A Treatise on the Culture and Management of Fruit Trees. London: 1803. V. 37; 38; 39; 40; 42; 43; 46

FORSYTHE, JAMES

The Sporting Rifle and Its Projectiles. London: 1858. V. 37

FORSYTHE, ROBERT

The Principles and Practice of Agriculture. Edinburgh: 1804. V. 37

FORT, C.

Lo! 1931. V. 43; 45

FORT, CHARLES

The Outcast Manufacturers. New York: 1909. V. 37; 43

THE FORT Collins Express. Fort Collins: 1894. V. 42

The Fort Collins Express Columbian Industrial Edition. Fort Collins: 1894. V. 37

FORT, G.

Coos-Coo-Soo; or Letters from Tangier, in Africa. Philadelphia: 1859. V. 42

FORT, PAUL

Les Ballades Francaises: Montagne, Foret, Plaine, Mer. Lyon: 1927. V. 45

FORT WILLIAM COLLEGE

The College of Fort William in Bengal. London: 1805. V. 37

FORTESCUE, J. W.

A History of the 17th Lancers (Duke of Cambridge's Own). London: 1895. V. 41

The Story of a Red Deer. Newtown: 1935. V. 37; 43; 44

FORTESCUE, JOHN

De Laudibus Legum Angliae. Hereunto is added the two sums of Sir Ralph de Hengham with Notes Both on Fortescue and Hengham by the Famous and Learned Antiquarie John Selden Esq. London: 1660. V. 37

De Laudibus Legum Angliae . . . Hereto are Added the Two Sums of Sir Ralph de Hengham . . . hengham Magna and Hengham Parva. London: 1660. V. 46

De Laudibus Legum Angliae . . . Hereto are Added the Two Sums of Sir Ralph de Hengham . . . London: 1672. V. 44

De Laudibus Legum Angliae. London: 1737. V. 38; 40

De Laudibus Legum Angliae. London: 1741. V. 40

A Learned Commendation of the Politique Lawes of England . . . London: 1573. V. 45

Reports of Select Cases in all the Courts of Westminster-Hall. In the Savoy: 1748. V. 45

The Royal Army service Corps: a History of Transport and Supply in the British Army. Cambridge: 1930-31. V. 46

FORTESCUE, JOHN WILLIAM

The Story of a Red-Deer. Newtown: 1936. V. 39

THE FORTH Bridge In Its Various Stages of Construction and Compared with the Most Notable Bridges of the World. Edinburgh: 1890. V. 37

FORTHCOMING, PSEUD.

President Holley - Not the Transylvania University, in a Letter to William Gibbes Hunt, Esq. in Consequence of the Attacks Made by Him in His 'Appeal' . . . Lexington: 1824. V. 44

FORTHINGHAM, N. L.

Gold: a Sermon. Boston: 1849. V. 43

FORTIER, ALCEE

A History of Louisiana. New York: 1904. V. 38; 43; 44

A History of Louisiana. Paris: 1904. V. 39; 40; 42

FORTIS, ALBERTO

Travels into Dalmatia. London: 1778. V. 40; 41; 45

THE FORTSAS Catalogue: a Facsimile . . . North Hills: 1970. V. 37; 39; 44; 45

THE FORTSAS Catalogue: a Facsimile with An Introduction by Lessing J. Rosenwald. Philadelphia: 1970. V. 43

THE FORTUNATE Youth; or, Chippenham Croesus . . . London: 1818. V. 43

THE FORTUNE Anthology. Stories, Criticism and Poems. London: (1942). V. 37

FORTUNE, J. I.

Fugitives the Story of Clyde Barrow and Bonnie Parker. Dallas: 1934. V. 46

THE FORTUNE of France, from the Prophetical Predictions of Mr. Truswell, the Recorder of Lincoln and Michael Nostradamus. London: 1678. V. 43

FORTUNE, ROBERT

A Journey to the Tea Countries of China . . . London: 1852. V. 45

A Residence Among the Chinese. London: 1857. V. 38; 41

Three Years' Wanderings in the Northern Provinces of China. London: 1847. V. 43; 46

Yedo and Peking. London: 1863. V. 44

FORTUNE'S Football. London: 1806. V. 46

45 Wood Engravers. 1982. V. 41

FORTY-FOUR Turkish Fairy Tales. London. V. 45

FORWOOD, GWENDOLEN

Filida and Corydon, with Other Stories. London: 1902. V. 42

FORY, WILLIAM

Art and Ingenuity Made Easy. London: 1729. V. 41

FOSBROKE, THOMAS DUDLEY

Abstracts of Records and Manuscripts Repsecting the County of Gloucester, Formed into a History . . . Glocester: 1807. V. 46

The Economy of Monastic Life . . . Gloucester: 1795. V. 42; 44

Encyclopaedia of Antiquities and Elements of Archaeology, Classical and Mediaeval. London: 1825. V. 39; 46

An Original History of the City of Gloucester, Almost Wholly Compiled from the New Materials . . . London: 1819. V. 46

Raglan Tour. A Picturesque and Topographical Account of Raglan Castle, with Cursory Sketches of Abergavenny and Crickhowell. Monmouth: 1831. V. 46

The Tourist's Grammar, or Rules Relating to the Scenery and Antiquities Incident to Travellers . . . London: 1826. V. 37

FOSBROOKE, THOMAS DUDLEY

British Monachism; or the Manners and Customs of the Monks and Nuns of England. London: 1802. V. 37; 40

British Monachism. London: 1843. V. 40

foscolo, ugo

Essays on Petratch. London: 1823. V. 40

FOSKETT, DAPHNE

A Dictionary of British Miniature Painters. London: 1972. V. 37; 38; 42

FOSS, EDWARD 1787-1870

Biographia Juridica. London: 1870. V. 38; 40

A Biographical Dictionary of the Judges of England 1066-1870. London: 1870. V. 38

The Judges of England. London: 1848-64. V. 38; 42

FOSS, SAM WATER

Dreams in Homespun. Boston: 1898. V. 46

FOSSATI, GIORGIO

Raccolta di Varie Favole, Delineate, ed Incise in Rame. Venice: 1744. V. 45; 46

FOSSE, CHARLES LOUIS FRANCOIS

Idees d'un Militaire Pour la Disposition des Troupes. Paris: 1783. V. 39; 44

FOSSETT, FRANK

Colorado: a Historical, Descriptive and Statistical Work on the Rocky Mountain Gold and Silver Mining Region. Denver: 1876. V. 41; 46

Colorado: Its Gold and Silver Mines, Farms and Stock Ranges and Its Health and Pleasure Resorts. New York: 1879. V. 44; 46

FOSSING, POUL

Catalogue of the Antique Engraved Gems and Cameos. Copenhagen: 1929. V. 44

Glass Vessels before Glass-Blowing. Copenhagen: 1940. V. 40

FOSTER, ALAN DEAN

Alien. New York: 1979. V. 46

FOSTER, B. F.

Foster's System of Penmanship; or, the Art of Rapid Writing Illustrated and Explained. Boston: 1835. V. 43

Practical Penmanship, Being a Development of the Carstairian System . . . Albany: 1832. V. 45

FOSTER, BIRKET

Brittany. London: 1878. V. 43

In the Sweet Summertime. London: 1885. V. 42

Pictures of English Landscape. London: 1863. V. 39

Pictures of English Landscape. London: 1864. V. 39

Pictures of English Landscape . . . London: 1881. V. 42; 43

24 Rustic Scenes. London: 1884. V. 43

FOSTER, CHARLES WILMER

History of the Wilmer Family, Together with Some Account of Its Descendants. Leeds: 1888. V. 37; 39; 42

FOSTER, E. M., MRS.

The Corinna of England, and the Heroine in the Shade . . . London: 1809. V. 45

FOSTER, EDITH FRANCIS

Puss in the Corner. Boston: 1904. V. 45

FOSTER, G. G.

New York by Gas-Light; With Here and There a Streak of Sunshine. New York: 1850. V. 43

FOSTER, GEORGE E.

Literature of the Cherokees; also Bibliography and the Story of Their Genesis. Ithaca: 1889. V. 42

Se-Quo-Yah. The American Cadmus and Modern Moses. Philadelphia: 1885. V. 41

FOSTER, GEORGE G.

The Gold Regions of California: Being a Succinct Description of the Geography, History, Trypography, and General Features of California: Including GOld Regions of that Fortunate Country . . . New York: 1848. V. 37

FOSTER, HANNAH

The Coquette; or History of Eliza Wharton. Charlestown: 1802. V. 44

FOSTER, HANNAH WEBSTER

The Coquette; or, the History of Eliza Sharton. Boston: 1797. V. 43

FOSTER, J.

A New System of Wooden Railways. Montreal: 1869. V. 45

FOSTER, J. J.

British Miniature Painters and Their Works. London: 1898. V. 40

Concerning the True Portraiture of Mary, Queen of Scots. London: 1904. V. 38

French Art from Watteau to Prud'hon Together with an Introduction and Some Studies in the Social History of the Period by Various Authors . . . London: 1905-06. V. 41

Miniature Painters. London: 1903. V. 39; 44; 45

FOSTER, J. W.

The Annexation of Hawaii. An Address Delivered Before the National Geographic Society . . . March 26, 1897. Washington: 1897. V. 42

The Mississippi Valley: Its Physical Geography, Including Sketches of the Topography, Botany, Climate and Mineral Resources . . . Chicago: 1869. V. 37; 39; 42; 43; 45

The Necessity of a Ship Canal Between the East and West . . . . Chicago: 1863. V. 42

Report on the Geology and Topography of a Portion of Lake Superior Land District, in the State of Michigan. Washington: 1850. V. 38

Report on the Lead Deposits of the New Diggings and Shullsburg Mining Company, in the County of Lafayette and State of Wisconsin. Chicago: 1864. V. 39; 45

Report on the Geology and Topography of a Portion of the Lake Superior Land District, in the State of Michigan. Part I. Copper Lands. Washington: 1850. V. 37

FOSTER, JAMES

An Account of the Behaviour of the Late Earl of Kilmarnock, After His Sentence, and on the Day of His Execution. Dublin: 1745. V. 41

Discourses on all the Principal Branches of Natural Religion and Social Virtue. London: 1749. V. 45

FOSTER, JEREMIAH J.

An Authentic Report on the Testimony in a Cause at Issue in the Court of Chancery of the State of New Jersey Between Thomas L. Shotwell, Complainant and Joseph Hendrickson and Stacy Decow, Defendants. Philadelphia: 1831. V. 43

FOSTER, JOHN

An Essay on the Different Nature of Accent and Quantity with Their Use and Application in the English, Latin and Greek Languages . . . Eton: 1763. V. 41; 42

An Essay on the Evils of Popular Ignorance. Edinburgh: Glasgow: 1820. V. 41

An Essay on the Evils of Popular Ignorance; and a Discourse on the Communication of Christianity to the People of Hindoostan. London: 1821. V. 38; 43

An Essay on the Different Nature of Account and Quantity with Their Use and Application in the English, Latin and Greek Languages. Eton: 1763. V. 43

The Life of Charles Dickens. London: 1872. V. 41; 42

Poems, Chiefly on Religious Subjects. London: 1797. V. 41

Sketch of the Tour of General Lafayette, on His Last Visit to the United States, 1824 . . . . Portland: 1824. V. 41

Collected Works. Edinburgh: 1834-47. V. 38

FOSTER, JOSEPH

Penningtonia. Pedigree of Sir Josslyn Pennington, 5th Baron Muncaster of Muncaster, & 9th Baronet. London: 1878. V. 38

The Royal Lineage of Our Noble and Gentle Families, Together With Their Paternal Ancestry. London: 1883-4. V. 41

FOSTER, LILLIAN

Way-Side Glimpses. North and South. New York: 1860. V. 40; 42

FOSTER, LOVELACE S.

History of the Columbus Baptist Association from 1840 to 1880. Starkville: 1881. V. 44

FOSTER, M.

A Report of Some Proceedings on the Commission for the Trial of the Rebels in the Year 1746 in the County of Surrey: and of Other Crown Cases: to which are added Discourses Upon a Few Branches of the Crown Law. Dublin: 1791. V. 37

FOSTER, M. E.

South and Southeast Texas: A Work for Newspaper and Library Reference. N.P.: 1928. V. 37; 38; 39; 42

FOSTER, MICHAEL

The Case of the King Against Alexander Broadfoot, at the Sessions of Oyer and Terminer and Gaol Delivery Held for the City of Bristol and County of the Same City, on the 30th of August 1743. Oxford: 1758. V. 38; 43; 46

Lectures On the History of Physiology. Cambridge: 1901. V. 41; 43

A Report of Some Proceedings on the Commission of Oyer and Terminer and Goal (sic) Delivery for the Trial of the Rebels in the Year 1746 in the County of Surry, and Of Other Crown Cases. Dublin: 1762. V. 42

A Report of Some Proceedings . . . for the Trial of the Rebels in the Year 1746 . . . and of Other Crown Cases. Oxford: 1762. V. 43

A Text Book of Physiology with Illustrations. London: 1890-95. V. 39

A Text Book of Physiology. New York: 1893. V. 41; 44; 45; 46

FOSTER, MYLES B.

A Day in a Child's Life. London: 1881. V. 37; 38; 46

FOSTER, MYLES BIRKET

Britanny. A Series of Thirty-Five Sketches. Surrey: 1878. V. 42

FOSTER, R. C., MRS.

The Foster Family. Santa Barbara: 1925. V. 43

FOSTER, ROBERT

The North American Indian Doctor, or Nature's Method of Curing and Preventing Disease According to the Indians . . . Canton: 1838. V. 37

FOSTER, ROXANNA C.

The Foster Family. California Pioneers. Santa Barbara: 1925. V. 37; 40; 42

FOSTER, STEPHEN C.

Jeannie With the Long Brown Hair. Foster's Melodies No. 26. New York: 185(4?). V. 44

FOSTER, STEPHEN COLLINS 1826-1864

Jeannie With the Light Brown Hair. Foster's Melodies No. 26. New York: 1854? V. 37

FOSTER, STEPHEN S.

The Brotherhood of Thieves, or a True Picture of the American Church and Clergy. New London: 1843. V. 42; 44

FOSTER, THOMAS C.

Letters on the Condition of the People of Ireland. London: 1846. V. 41; 42; 43; 46

FOSTER, VERE

Painting for Beginners. London. V. 39

FOSTER, WILLIAM C.

Poetry on Different Subjects, Written Under the Signature of Timothy Spectacles. Salem: 1805. V. 40

FOSTER, WILLIAM D.

Cottages, Manors and Other Minor Buildings of Normandby and Brittany. New York: 1926. V. 41; 44

FOTESCUE DUGUID, A.

Official History of the Canadian Forces in the Great War 1914-1918. London: 1938. V. 37

FOTHERGILL, EDWARD

Five Years in the Sudan. London: 1910. V. 43

FOTHERGILL, GEORGE

George A. Fothergill's Sketchbook. Darlington: 1903-07. V. 44; 46

FOTHERGILL, GEORGE A.

Hunting Racing Coaching and Boxing Ballads. London: 1926. V. 41; 44
The National Stud: a Gift to the State. A Memorial of It. Edinburgh: 1916. V. 39
The National Stud. London: 1916. V. 37; 38; 42
Notes from the Diary of a Doctor, Sketch Artist and Sportsman. York: 1900. V. 38

FOTHERGILL, JESSIE

Peril. London: 1884. V. 41; 43

FOTHERGILL, JOHN 1712-1780

An Account of the Life and Travels in the Work of the Ministry, of John Fothergill. London: 1753. V. 45
A Complete Collection of the Medical and Philosophical Works. London: 1781. V. 40; 43
Considerations Relative to the North American Colonies. London: 1765. V. 38
The Fothergill Omnibus . . . London: 1931. V. 43
An Innkeeper's Diary: Being the Spread Eagle Section of 'My Three Inns.' Oxford: 1987. V. 40
A Letter to a Friend in the Country, Relative to the Intended School, at Ackworth, in Yorkshire. London: 1779. V. 43; 45

THE FOTHERGILL Omnibus - for Which Seventeen Eminent Authors Have Written Short Stories Upon One and the Same Plot. London: 1931. V. 42

FOTOPOULOS, D.

Stage Settings in the Greek Theatre. Athens: 1987. V. 45

FOUCAULT, LEON

Recueil des Travaux Scientifiques . . . Paris: 1878. V. 38; 45

FOUCHE, JOSEPH 1760-1820

Memoirs. London: 1825. V. 39; 41; 44

FOUCHET, MAX-POL

Johnny Friedlaender: Oeuvre 1961-1965. New York. V. 46
Wifredo Lam. New York: 1976. V. 45; 46
Wifredo Lam. New York: 1976. V. 46

FOUCQUET, JEHAN 1415-1485

Oeuvre de Jehan Foucquet - Heures de Maistre Estienne Chevalier. Paris: 1866-67. V. 46

FOULERTON, ROBERT

A Letter to the Lords of the Admiralty on the Ship Manoeuvrer . . . London: 1846. V. 38; 41

FOULIS, JOHN

The Account of Book of Sir John Foulis of Ravelston 1671-1707. Edinburgh: 1894. V. 42

FOULIS, ROBERT

Books Printed By Robert and Andrew Foulis. Glasgow: 1775. V. 40

FOULKE, WILLIAM PARKER

Remarks on Cellular Separation. Philadelphia: 1861. V. 45

FOULKES, CHARLES

The Gun-Founders of England. With a List of English and Continental Gun-Founders from the 14th. to the 19th. Centuries. Cambridge: 1937. V. 37

FOULLON, ABEL c. 1513-1563

Descrittione, et Uso dell'Holometro . . . Venice: 1564. V. 42
De Holometri Fabrica et Uso Instrumento Geometrico (with) De Aestu Maris De Motu Octavae Sphaerae. Basel: 1577. V. 38

FOULSTON, JOHN

The Public Buildings, Erected in the West of England, as Designed by John Foulston . . . London: 1838. V. 38

THE FOUNDLING Hospital for Wit. London;: 1743-49. V. 39
THE FOUNDLING Hospital for Wit. London: 1746-64. V. 42
THE FOUNDLING Hospital for Wit. London: ptd. for G. Lion: 1746-7-8-9. V. 45
THE FOUNDLING Hospital for Wit. London: 1749-63. V. 37; 38; 39; 42

THE FOUNDLING Hospital for Wit . . . London: 1763. V. 39

FOUNTAIN & CHRISTIAN

Street Railway Guide to the City of New Orleans and Its Suburbs. New Orleans: 1884. V. 39

FOUNTAIN, PAUL

The Great North-West and the Great Lake Region of North America. London: 1904. V. 44
The River Amazon from Its Sources to the Sea. London: 1914. V. 38

FOUQUET, JEAN

The Hours of Etienne Chevalier. 1972. V. 39

FOUQUIER, MARCEL

De l'Art des Jardins. Paris: 1911. V. 37

THE FOUR Elements. Cheltenham: 1959. V. 45

FOUR Fictions. V. 41
FOUR Fictions. Kentfield: 1973. V. 40; 41; 42; 44

THE FOUR Gospels. Verona: 1962. V. 37
The FOUR Gospels. 1988. V. 44

FOUR Letters Publish'd in Old England; or, the Constitutional Journal. London: 1743. V. 41; 43

FOUR Negro Poets. New York: 1927. V. 41

FOURCADE, M.

Plantes des Pyrenees. V. 46

FOURCROY, ANTOINE FRANCOIS

Elements of Chemistry, and Natural History . . . London: & Edinburgh: 1796. V. 42

FOURCROY, ANTOINE FRANCOIS, COMTE DE

Elements of Natural History and Chemistry . . . London: 1790. V. 39

FOURGEAUD, VICTOR H.

The First Californiac. San Francisco: 1942. V. 39; 40; 46

FOURIER, JOSEPH

The Analytical Theory of Heat. Cambridge: 1878. V. 37; 38; 45

FOURMONT, ETIENNE 1683-1745

Linguae Sinarum Mandarinicae Hieroglyphicae Grammatica Duplex. Paris: 1742. V. 40

FOURNEL, H.

Les Berbers. - Etude sur la Conquete de l'Afrique par les Arabes, d'Apres les Textes Arabes Imprimes . . . Paris: 1875-81. V. 44

FOURNEL, VICTOR 1829-1894

Paris et Ses Ruines en Mai 1871 Precede d'Un Coup d'Oeil sur Paris, 1860-1870. Paris: 1872. V. 38

FOURNIER, ALAIN 1886-1914

The Wanderer. London: 1947. V. 45

FOURNIER, DENIS

L'Anatomie Pacifique Nouvelle et Curieuse. Paris: 1678. V. 42

FOURNIER, PIERRE SIMON

Des Caracters de L'Imprimerie, et Des Austres Choses Necessaires Audit Art. London: 1965. V. 39
Fournier on Typefounding. London: 1930. V. 38; 42; 44
Manuel Typographique, Utile Aux Gens de Lettres . . . Paris: 1764. V. 38

FOURNIER, PIERRE SIMON continued

Manuel Typographique. Paris: 1764-66. V. 37; 38

FOURNIVAL, RICHARD DE

Master Richard's Bestiary of Love, and Response. Northampton: 1985. V. 37

FOURTH Annual Review of the Commerce Railroads and Manufactures of Chicago for the Year 1855. Chicago: 1856. V. 45

A FOURTH Book of Things. Ditchling. V. 43

FOURTH March. On That Day We Will Rejoice, Because the Election of President Jefferson Put an End to the Aristocratic Influence of the Advocates of a Funding System and a British Treaty, and Scattered the Combined Forces of the Enemies of Our Revolution. N.P.: 1801. V. 40

FOVARGUE, STEPEHN

A New Catalogue of Vulgar Errors. Cambridge/Oxford: 1767. V. 37

FOVARGUE, STEPHEN

A New Catalogue of Vulgar Errors. Cambridge: 1767. V. 40; 46

FOWERS, W. R.

A Manual of Diseases of the Nervous System. Darien: 1970. V. 42

FOWKE, FRANK

The Bayeux Tapestry a History and Description. London: 1898. V. 46

FOWKE, GERARD

Archaeological History of Ohio. Columbus: 1902. V. 42; 44

FOWKE, MARTHA

The Epistles of Clio and Strephon, Being a Collection of Letters that Passed Between an English Lady, and an English Gentleman in France, Who Took an Affection to Each Other . . . London: 1720. V. 39; 42

FOWLER, ALFRED

The Woodcut Annual for 1925. Kansas City: 1925. V. 46

FOWLER AND FRY

List of Agricultural Implements . . . Bristol: 1851. V. 37; 40

FOWLER, EDWARD

A Discourse of the Great Disingenuity & Unreasonableness of Repining at Afflicting Providences . . . London: 1695. V. 45

FOWLER, FRANK A.

The Eye of the North-West. Milwaukee: 1890. V. 43

FOWLER, GENE

Father Goose: The Story of Mack Sennett. New York: (1934). V. 37; 45

Illusion in Java. New York: 1939. V. 39

In Pictures. New York: 1937. V. 37

Myron Selznick. Los Angeles: 1944. V. 37; 45

A Solo in Tom-Toms. New York: 1946. V. 44

FOWLER, GEORGE

A Treatise on Appendicitis. Philadelphia: 1894. V. 42

FOWLER, H. ALFRED

Gothic Book-Plates Being Certain Passages From the Nature of Gothic by John Ruskin & Certain Book-Plates by Bertha Gorst. Kansas City: 1912. V. 46

FOWLER, H. W.

A Dictionary of Modern English Usage. Oxford: 1926. V. 43

A Dictionary of Modern English Usage. Oxford & London: 1926. V. 44

Fishes of the Philippine and Adjacent Seas. Washington: 1928-43. V. 39

The Fishes of Oceania. Honolulu: 1928-49, 1968. V. 37; 38

FOWLER, JACOB

The Journal of Jacob Fowler. New York: 1898. V. 38; 41; 45

FOWLER, JAMES

The Diseases of the Lungs. London: 1898. V. 40; 42

On Mediaeval Representations of the Months and Seasons. London: 1873. V. 44

FOWLER, JOHN

Journal of a Tour in the State of New York, in the year 1830, with remarks on Agriculture in the parts most Eligible for Settlers a return to England by the Western Island, in consequence of shipwreck in the Robert Fulton. London: 1831. V. 37

FOWLER, LAURENCE HALL

The Fowler Architectural Collection of the John Hopkins University . . . San Francisco: 1991. V. 46

FOWLER, M. E.

Zoo and Wild Animal Medicine. London: 1986. V. 37

FOWLER, O. S.

Fowler's Works on Education and Self Improvement . . . New York: 1844. V. 40

Fowler's Practical Phrenology . . . New York: 1849. V. 45

A Home For All or the Gravel Wall and Octagon Mode of Building. New York: 1854. V. 37; 44; 45

Synopsis of Phrenology; and the Phrenological Developments Together with the Character and Talents of (in ink) Ann B. Kimball, Newbury Port, as Given by L.N. Flower, June 20th, 1844. New York: 1838. V. 44

FOWLER, ORSON SQUIRE

Fowler's Practical Phrenology. Philadelphia: 1840. V. 46

FOWLER, R. S.

The Operating Room and the Patient. Philadelphia: 1910. V. 40; 41

FOWLER, RICHARD

Experiments and Observations relative to the Influence lately discovered by M. Galvani, and commonly called Animal Electricity. Edinburgh: 1793. V. 37

FOWLER, ROBERT

A Complete History of the Case of the Welsh Fasting-Girl (Sarah Jacob) With Comments Thereon . . . London: 1871. V. 39

FOWLER, RUSSELL

The Operating Room and the Patient. Philadelphia: 1906. V. 38

FOWLER, SAMUEL P.

Salem Witchcraft: Comprising More Wonders of the Invisible World . . . Boston: 1865. V. 45

FOWLER, W. W.

The Coleoptera of the British Islands. (with) supplement. London: 1887-1913. V. 40

FOWLER, WILLIAM 1761-1832

Engravings of the Principal Mosaic Pavements, Which Have Been Discovered . . . in Various Parts of Great Britain . . . Winterton: 1796-1804. V. 46

FOWLER, WILLIAM WORTHINGTON

Ten Years in Wall Street. Hartford: 1870. V. 42

FOWLER, WRIGHT S.

Hampshire Poetry. London: 1928. V. 40

FOWLERS and Wells' Water-Cure Library. New York: 1855. V. 40

FOWLES, JOHN 1926-

The Aristos. 1964. V. 40

The Aristos. Boston: 1964. V. 37; 39; 40; 41; 42; 43; 44; 46

The Aristos. London: 1965. V. 46

Cinderella. London: 1974. V. 43

The Collector. Boston: 1963. V. 37; 38; 39; 40; 41; 42; 43; 44; 45; 46

The Collector. Boston & Toronto: 1963. V. 39; 40; 41; 42; 45

The Collector. London: 1963. V. 39

The Collector. 1982. V. 43

Conditional. Northridge: 1979. V. 45

Daniel Martin. London: 1977. V. 38; 39; 40; 41; 42; 43

The Ebony Tower. London: 1974. V. 39; 43; 45; 46

The Enigma of Stonehenge. London: 1980. V. 37; 40; 44

The Falklands, and a Death Foretold. N.P.: 1982. V. 40; 45

The French Lieutenant's Woman. London: 1969. V. 37; 38; 39; 40; 41; 42; 43; 46

Introduction: Remembering Cruikshank. Princeton: 1964. V. 45

Introduction: Remembering Cruikshank. Princeton. V. 45

A Maggot. Boston: 1985. V. 37; 40; 42; 43

A Maggot. London: 1985. V. 39; 40; 43; 44; 46

The Magus. Boston: 1965. V. 37; 39; 42; 43

The Magus. London: 1965. V. 38

The Magus. London: 1966. V. 37; 39; 40; 41; 44; 45; 46

Mantissa. Boston: 1982. V. 37; 39; 40; 41; 42; 43; 46

Mantissa. London: 1982. V. 43

My Recollections of Kafka. Manitoba. V. 45

My Recollections of Kafka. Manitoba: 1970. V. 44; 46

Of Memoirs and Magpies. Austin: 1983. V. 46

On Being English but not British. N.P.: 1964. V. 45

Poems. New York: 1973. V. 46

FOWLES, JOSEPH

Sydney in 1848. Sydney: 1848. V. 39

FOX, ALEY

Art Pictures from the Old Testament. London: 1894. V. 42

FOX, CARL

The Doll. New York: 1977. V. 40

FOX, CAROLINE

Memories of Old Friends. London: 1882. V. 40

FOX, CHARLES

The Adventures of Ebenezer Fox in the Revolutionary War. Boston: 1838. V. 46

Chronicles of Tonedale. Taunton: 1879. V. 40

A Series of Poems Containing the Plaints, Consolations and Delights of Achmed Ardebeili a Persian Exile. Bristol: 1797. V. 37

FOX, CHARLES H.

Chronicles of Tonedale. Taunton;: 1879. V. 38

FOX, CHARLES JAMES

A History of the Early Part of the Reign of James II. London: 1808. V. 37; 38; 40; 44; 45

A Letter to the Right Honourable Charles James Fox, Occasioned by His Speech at the Shakespeare Tavern, on the 10th of October, 1797, From a Yeoman of England. London: 1797. V. 39

The Speeches of the Right Honourable Charles James Fox, in the House of Commons. London: 1815. V. 40; 43

FOX, CYRIL

Monmouthshire Houses. Cardiff: 1951-54. V. 45

FOX, D.

The Bannatyne Manuscript: National Library of Scotland Advocates MS. 1.1.6. (Medieval Manuscripts in Facsimile Series). London: 1980. V. 39

FOX-DAVIES, A. C.

The Finances of Sir John Kynnersley. 1908. V. 39

FOX-DAVIES, ARTHR C.

The Art of Heraldry. London: 1904. V. 43

FOX-DAVIES, ARTHUR CHARLES

Armorial Families. Edinburgh: 1895. V. 37; 39; 41; 46

Armorial Families. London: 1895. V. 38; 40

Armorial Families. Edinburgh: 1897. V. 41

Armorial Families. Edinburgh: 1899. V. 41

Armorial Families. Edinburgh: 1902. V. 41

Armorial Families. London: 1902. V. 44; 46

Armorial Families. London: 1910. V. 41

Armorial Families. London: 1929. V. 41

The Art of Heraldry. London: 1904. V. 46

The Art of Heraldry. New York: 1976. V. 39

Fairbairn's Book of Crests of the Families of Great Britain and Ireland. Edinburgh: 1892. V. 38

FOX, EBENEZER

Revolutionary Adventures of . . . of Roxbury, Mass. Boston: 1838. V. 38

FOX, EDGAR B.

History and Directory of Green Lake and Waushara Counties, and the City of Ripon. Berlin: 1869. V. 41

FOX, FRANCIS

An Introduction to Spelling and Reading . . . London: 1799. V. 41

FOX, FRANK

Australia. London: 1910. V. 45

The Royal Inniskilling Fusiliers in the World War. London: 1928. V. 41

FOX, GEORGE 1624-1691

A Battle-Door for Teachers & Professors to Learn Singular and Plural. 1660. V. 40

A Battle-Door for Teachers and Professors to Learn Singular & Plural . . . London: 1660. V. 37; 39; 44

Canons and Institutions Drawn Up and Agreed Upon by the General Assembly or Meeting of the Heads of the Quakers. London: 1669. V. 44

A Collection of Many Select and Christian Epistles, Letters and Testimonies. London: 1698. V. 37; 43; 44; 46

An Epistle to be Read in all the Assemblies of the Righteous. London: 1666. V. 42; 45

Gospel Truth Demonstrated, in a Collection of Doctrinal Books . . . London: 1706. V. 37; 38; 39; 40; 41; 43; 46

Gospel Truth Demonstrated, in a Collection of Doctrinal Books . . . London: 1796. V. 46

The Great Mistery of the Great Whore Unfolded. London: 1659. V. 39; 40; 44; 46

Instructions for Right Spelling, and Plain Directions for Reading and Writing True English. Newport: 1769. V. 37

A Journal or Historical Account of the Life, Travels, Sufferings, Christian Experiences and Labour of Love . . . London: 1765. V. 38; 44; 45

A Journal or Historical account of the Life, Travels, Sufferings, Christian Experiences and Labour of Love in the Work of the Ministry . . . Leeds: 1836. V. 44

FOX, GEORGE HENRY

Photographic Atlas of the Diseases of the Skin. Philadelphia: 1900. V. 37

Photographic Atlas of the Diseases of the Skin. Philadelphia: 1902-1900. V. 42

Photographic Atlas of the Diseases of the Skin. New York: 1905. V. 40

Photographic Atlas of the Diseases of the Skin. Philadelphia: 1905. V. 39

Photographic Illustrations of Skin Diseases. New York: 1881. V. 40; 42

Photographic Illustrations of Skin Diseases. Second Series. New York: 1887. V. 42; 44

FOX, GUSTAVUS VASA

Confidential Correspondence of Gustavus Vasa Fox . . . New York: 1918-19. V. 44; 46

FOX, H. M.

Patio Gardens. New York: 1929. V. 46

FOX, HENRY

A New Dictionary, in French and English. London: 1769. V. 41; 42

FOX, JOHN

Blue-Grass and Rhododendron. New York: 1901. V. 38; 40

The Book of Martyrs or the Acts and Monuments of the Christian Church. London: 1811. V. 46

A Cumberland Vendetta. New York: 1896. V. 37; 41; 42; 43; 44

The Little Shepherd of Kingdom Come. New York: 1931. V. 37; 40

A Mountain Europa. New York: 1899. V. 43

The Trail of the Lonesome Pine. New York: 1908. V. 42

FOX, JOHN D.

A Mountain Europa. New York: 1899. V. 42

FOX, JOSEPH

The Natural History and Diseases of the Human Teeth. London: 1833. V. 41

The Natural History and Diseases of the Human Teeth . . . Philadelphia: 1846. V. 37; 39

The Natural History of the Human Teeth . . . ; The History and Treatment of the Diseases of the Teeth. London: 1803, 1806. V. 37

FOX, MARY

The Country House (with Designs). London: 1843. V. 42

FOX, MARY ANNA

George Allen, the Only Son. Boston: 1835. V. 44

FOX, PETER

Treasures of the Library of Trinity College, Dublin. Dublin: 1986. V. 43

FOX, R. FORTESCUE

Physical Remedies for Disabled Soldiers. New York: 1917. V. 42

FOX, RALPH

Storming Heaven. London: 1928. V. 40

FOX, RICHARD KYLE

Prize Ring Heroes. New York: 1889. V. 39

FOX, ROBERT WERE

Description of Some Improvements in the Dipping Needle Deflector . . . Falmouth: 1835. V. 37; 39; 42; 43

FOX, TILBURY

Atlas of Skin Diseases, Consisting of Seventy-Two Full Page Colored Illustrations, with Descriptive Text and Notes Upon Treatment. Philadelphia: 1877. V. 42

On Certain Endemic Skin and Other Diseases of India and Hot Climates Generally . . . London: 1876. V. 45

FOX, TRUMAN B.

History of the Saginaw Valley. East Saginaw: 1868. V. 46

FOX, W. J.

Finsbury Lectures. London: 1835-36. V. 42; 45

FOX, WELLS B.

What I Remember of the Great Rebellion. Lansing: 1892. V. 42; 46

FOX, WILLIAM

A Brief History of the Wesleyan Missions on the Western Coast of Africa. London: 1851. V. 42

Regimental Losses in the American Civil War 1861-1865. Albany: 1898. V. 38

FOX, WILSON

An Atlas of Pathological Anatomy of the Lungs. London: 1888. V. 37

The Diseases of the Stomach. London: 1872. V. 42

FOXCROFT, THOMAS

Observations Historical and Practical, on the Rise and Primitive State of New England. Boston: 1730. V. 38

The Pleas of Gospel-Impenitents Examin'd and Refuted. Boston: 1730. V. 43

FOXE, JOHN 1516-1587

Actes and Monuments of Matters Most Speciall and Memorable, Happening in the Church . . . London: 1610. V. 43

Acts and Monuments (Booke of Martyrs) of Matters Most Special and Memorable, Happening in the Church . . . London: 1684. V. 44

De Christo Gratis Iustificante. Contra Osorianam Iustitiam. Londini: 1583. V. 38; 44

The (First-) Second Volume of the Ecclesiastical History, Conteyining the Actes & Monumentes of Martyrs . . . London: 1576. V. 46

The New and Complete Book of Martyrs; or, an Universal History of Martyrdom . . . New York: 1794. V. 46

FOXON, D. F.

English Verse 1701-1750. Cambridge: 1975. V. 37; 38; 42; 44; 46

English Verse 1701-1750. London: 1975. V. 38; 42

FOXTON, THOMAS

Serino; or, the Character of a Fine Gentleman; with Reference to Religion . . . London: 1721? V. 43

FOYER, ARCHIBALD

A Defence of the Scots Settlement at Darien. Edinburgh: 1699. V. 40; 45

FRACASTORIUS, GIROLAMO FRACASTORO

Contagion, Contagious Diseases and Their Treatment. New York: 1930. V. 45

Heronymi Fracastorii Veronensis Opera Omnia Quorum Normina Sequens Pagina Plenius Indicat . . . Venetiis: 1584. V. 45

Syphilis Sive Morbus Gallicus. Verona: 1530. V. 45

FRACASTORIUS, HIERONYMUS

Homocentrica: Eiusdem De Causis Criticorum Dierum per ea Quae in Nobis sunt. Venetiis: 1538. V. 38

Syphilis Sive Morbus Gallicus. Verona: 1530. V. 38

Syphilis Sive Morbus Gallicus. Verona: 1530. V. 42

FRACASTORO, GIROLAMO

De Sympathia et Antipathia Rerum Liber Unus. De Contagione et Morbis et Curatione, Libri III. Venice: 1546. V. 37

Opera Omnia. Venetiis: 1584. V. 43

. . . Opera Omnia . . . Venetiis: 1574. V. 37

The Sinister Shepherd. Los Angeles: 1934. V. 39

Veronensis Opera Omnia. Venice: 1584. V. 44

FRACASTORO, GIROLAMO FRACASTORO

Fracastor. Syphilis or the French Disease. With a Translation . . . London: 1935. V. 45

FRACKELTON, S. S.

Tried by Fire. A Work on China Painting. New York: 1886. V. 42

FRACKENBERGER, ANDREAS

Institutionum Antiquitatis et Historiarum. Wittebergae: 1586. V. 46

FRACKER, GEORGE

A Voyage to South America, with an Account of a Shipwreck in the River La Plata, in the Year 1817. Boston: 1826. V. 39

FRAENKEL, MICHAEL

Bastard Death. Paris and New York: 1946. V. 38; 42

Death is Not Enough. London: 1939. V. 43

Werther's Younger Brother. The Story of an Attitude. New York: 1931. V. 39

A FRAGMENT From the Fine Art Folies of Frogmore; or, the Belgian Mystery Unveiled. London: 1869. V. 46

FRAIN DU TREMBLAY, JEAN

A Treatise of Languages. London: 1725. V. 42

FRAME, RICHARD

A Poem by Richard Frame from a Short Description on Pennsilvania. Easthampton: 1976. V. 39

FRANAU, JULIA

John Raphael Smith: His Life and Works. London: 1902. V. 42

FRANCA MIRANDA, FRANCISCO DA

Dispertador Brasiliense. Rio de Janeiro: 1821. V. 39

LES FRANCAIS Prints par Euxmemes Encyclopedie Morale de Dix-Neuvieme Siecle. Paris: 1841-42. V. 43

FRANCANCIANUS, ANTONIUS

De Morbo Gallico . . . Padua: 1564. V. 37

FRANCASTEL, PIERRE

Esteve. Paris: 1956. V. 44

FRANCATELLI, CHARLES ELME

The Modern Cook . . . Philadelphia: 1860. V. 45

The Modern Cook: A Practical Guide to the Culinary Art In all Its Branches . . . London: 1877. V. 38

The Modern Cook. London: 1883. V. 46

The Royal English and Foreign Confectioner. London: 1862. V. 42

FRANCE, ANATOLE

L'Affaire Crainquebille. Stamford: 1937. V. 39

Amycus et Celestin. New York: 1916. V. 38; 39; 41; 42

At the Sign of the Queen Pedauque. New York: 1933. V. 41

Balthasar et la Reine Balkis. Paris: 1900. V. 46

Clio. Paris: 1900. V. 37

The Crime of Sylvestre Bonnard by Anatole France. Translation and introduciton by Lafcadio Hearn. New York: 1890. V. 37

Honey-Bee. London: 1911. V. 39

Oeuvres. Paris: 1920's-30's. V. 46

Pierre Noziere. Paris: 1925. V. 39

Les Sept Femmes de La Barbe-Bleue et Autres Contes Merveilleux. Paris: 1909. V. 45

The Works. New York: 1924. V. 40; 42; 45

FRANCE, ANTATOLE

The Crime of Sylvestre Bonnard . . . New York: 1890. V. 43

FRANCE. CONSTITUTION - 1791

La Constitution Francaise, Decretee par l'Assemblee Nationale Constituante, aux Annees 1789, 1790 et 1791; Acceptee par le Roi le 14 Septembre 1791. Paris: 1792-1791. V. 39

FRANCE, GEORGE W.

The Struggles for Life and Home in the North West. New York: 1890. V. 44; 45

FRANCE, HECTOR

Musk Hashish and Blood. Paris: 1899. V. 37

FRANCE. LAWS, STATUTES, ETC. - 1561

Ordonnance Dv Roy, Contenant le Pois & Pris des Especes d'Or & d'Argent . . . Paris: 1561. V. 40

FRANCE. LAWS, STATUTES, ETC. - 1723

Arrest Du Conseil d'Estat du Roy, Pour La Prise de Possession du Privilege de la Vente Exclusive du Tabac Pour La Compagnie des Indes . . . Paris: 1723. V. 40

FRANCE. LAWS, STATUTES, ETC. - 1811

The Code Napoleon. (with) an Introductory Discourse, Containing a Succinct Account of the Civil Regulations, Comprised in the Jewish Law, the Ordinances of Menu . . . London: 1811. V. 38

THE Code Napoleon, Verbally Translated from the French (with) an Introductory Discourse, Containing a Succinct Account of the Civil Regulations . . . London: 1811. V. 40

FRANCE, LEWIS B.

Mountain Trails and Parks in Colorado. Denver: 1887. V. 37

FRANCE. SOVEREIGNS, ETC.

Ordonnances et Privileges Des Fores de Lyon; Et Leur Antiquite: Auec celles de Brie & Champaigne, et les Confirmations d'Icelles . . . Lyon: 1560. V. 40

FRANCE. SOVEREIGNS, ETC., 1715-1774 (LOUIS XV)

Edit du Roy, Donne a Paris au Mois d'Avril, 1717, Portant Reglement General Pour Le Commerce Des Indes et de l'Amerique . . . Grenoble: 1717. V. 42

FRANCES, LEWIS B.

With the Rod and Line in Colorado Waters. Denver: 1884. V. 37

FRANCES, MAY

Beyond the Argentine: or Letters from Brazil. London: 1890. V. 37

FRANCESCO D' ASSISI, SAINT 1182-1226

The Little Flowers of Saint Francis of Assisi. 1931. V. 40

FRANCESCO D'ASSISI, SAINT 1182-1226

I Fiorentti del Glorioso Povrello di Cristo. Chelsea: 1922. V. 40; 41; 43; 44; 45

I Fioretti del Glorioso Poverello di Cirsto. Colophon: 1922. V. 46

I Fioretti del Glorioso Pove Rello di Cristo . . . London: 1922. V. 45

Laudes Creaturarum. Hammersmith: 1910. V. 37; 44; 46

Laudes Creaturarum. London: 1911. V. 37; 40

The Litte Flowers of S. Francis of Assisi. 1909. V. 46

The Little Flowers . . . London: 1909. V. 46

The Little Flowers. New York: 1930. V. 38; 45

The Little Flowers of Saint Francis of Assisi. 1931. V. 46

Selections from the Life and Writings of Saint Francis of Assisi. Cleveland: 1953. V. 39; 43; 45

Un Mazetto Scelto di Certi Fioretti del Glorioso Poverello di Cristo. 1904. V. 39; 40; 41

Un Mazzetto Scelto di Certi Fioretti del Glorioso Poverello Cristo San Francesco di Assisi Insieme Col Cantico al sole del Medesimo. Chelsea: 1904. V. 40; 46

Un Mazzetto Scelto del Fiorettidel Glorioso Poverello di Cristo. London: 1904. V. 38

FRANCESCO D'ASSISSI, SAINT 1182-1226

I Fioretti del Glorioso Poverello di Christo S. Francisco di Assisi. Chelsea: 1922. V. 43

FRANCESCONI, DANIELE

Illustrazione di un Urnetta Lavorata d'Oro e di Vari Altri Metalli All Agemina Coll' Iscrizione Paulus Ageminius Faciebat. Venice: 1800. V. 44

FRANCESO D'ASSISI, SAINT 1182-1226

The Little Flowers of St. Francis . . . London: 1909. V. 46

FRANCH, JOSE A.

Pre-Columbia Art. New York: 1983. V. 40

FRANCH, JOSE ALCINA

Pre-Columbian Art. New York: 1983. V. 38; 42; 44

FRANCHERE, GABRIEL

The Journal of Gabriel Franchere, 1811-14. Toronto: 1969. V. 45

Journal of a Voyage on the North West Coast of North America During the Years 1811, 1812, 1813 adn 1814. Toronto: 1969. V. 39; 42; 44

Narrative of a Voyage to the Northwest Coast of America in the Years 1811, 1812, 1813 and 1814. New York: 1854. V. 37; 38; 39; 40; 41; 42; 44; 45

FRANCIA, LOUIS

Progressive Lessons Tending to Elucidate the Character of Trees . . . London: 1835. V. 44

A Series of Progressive Lessons, Intended to Elucidate the Art of Flower Painting in Water Colours. London: 1815. V. 41; 46

FRANCILLON, ROBERT EDWARD

Jack Doyle's Daughter. London: 1849. V. 41

FRANCINE, ALEXANDRE

Livre d'Architecture Contenant Plusieurs Portiques de Differents Inventions sur les Cinq Ordres de Colomnes. Paris: 1631. V. 46

FRANCINI, ALESSANDRO

Live d'Architectvre Contenant Plvsievs Portiqves de Differentes Inventions Sur les Cinq Ordres de Colomnes. Paris: 1640. V. 37

FRANCINI, HORACE DE

Hippiatrique. Ou est Traicte des Causes des Maladies du Cheval Tant Interieures qu'exterieures: le Moyen de la Guarir d'icelles. Paris: 1607. V. 37

FRANCIS, A. M.

Catskill Rivers. Birthplace of American Fly Fishing. New York: 1983. V. 38

FRANCIS, ANNE

Miscellaneous Poems. London: 1790. V. 42

FRANCIS, AUSTIN M.

Catskill Rivers: Birthplace of American Fly Fishing. New York: 1984. V. 39

FRANCIS, BRUCE

The Book Sail: 16th Anniversary Catalogue. Orange: 1984. V. 42; 45

FRANCIS, CLAUDE DE LA ROCHE

London Historic and Social. Philadelphia: 1902. V. 46

FRANCIS, DICK 1920-

Blood Sport. London: 1967. V. 38; 39; 41; 42; 45

Blood Sport. 1967. V. 37

Bonecrack. 1971. V. 39

Dead Cert. London: 1962. V. 40

Dead Cert. New York: 1962. V. 42

Enquiry. 1969. V. 39

Enquiry. London: 1969. V. 40; 46

Flying Finish. London: 1966. V. 38; 39; 40; 42; 46

Flying Finish. New York: 1967. V. 46

For Kicks. 1965. V. 39

For Kicks. London: 1965. V. 42; 46

For Kicks. New York: 1965. V. 42

Forfeit. London: 1968. V. 45

Four Kicks. New York: 1965. V. 40

Nerve. London: 1964. V. 42; 45

Nerve. New York: 1964. V. 39; 40; 42

Odds Against. 1965. V. 39

Odds Against. London: 1965. V. 37; 38; 40; 42; 46

Odds Against. New York: 1965. V. 42; 45

Odds Against. New York: 1966. V. 38; 39; 40

Rat Race. London: 1970. V. 40; 42

Slay-Ride. London: 1973. V. 43

Smokescreen. 1972. V. 39

The Sport of Queens. New York: 1969. V. 45

The Sport of Kings. London: 1957. V. 37

Trial Run. London: 1978. V. 46

FRANCIS, E. S.

The Rival Roses; or Wars of York and Lancaster. London: 1813. V. 43

FRANCIS, FRANCIS

A Book of Angling . . . London: 1867. V. 42; 46

A Book of Angling Being a Complete Treatise on the Art of Angling in Every Branch with Explanatory Plates, Etc. London: 1872. V. 39

A Book on Angling. London: 1880. V. 38

A Book of Angling, Being a Complete Treatise on the Art of Angling in Every Branch with Explanatory Plates, Etc. London: 1885. V. 39

Newton Dogvane. A Story of English Country Life. London: 1859. V. 38

FRANCIS, G.

The Dictionary of the Arts, Sciences and Manufactures. London: 1842. V. 38; 44

FRANCIS, G. R.

Old English Drinking Glasses. London: 1926. V. 37; 38; 39; 40

FRANCIS, HARRIET E.

Across the Meridians and Fragmentary Letters. N.P.: 1887. V. 44; 45

FRANCIS, JOHN

Annals, Anecdotes and Legends . . . London: 1853. V. 43

A History of the English Railway. London: 1851. V. 37

FRANCIS, JOHN W.

New York During the Last Half Century: A Discourse in Commemoration of the Fifty-Third Anniversary of the New York Historical Society, and of the Dedication of Their New Edifice. (November 17, 1857). New York: 1857. V. 45

FRANCIS, MISS

Santa Maura: Marion; and other Poems. London: 1821. V. 40

FRANCIS OF SALES, SAINT

A Treatise of the Love of God. Doway: 1630. V. 44

FRANCIS, PHILIP

Constantin: A Tragedy. London: 1754. V. 37

A Letter to (i.e. from) a Right Honourable Person (William Pitt, Earl of Chatham). London: 1761. V. 40

FRANCIS, PHILLIP

Constantine, a Tragedy . . . London: 1754. V. 40

FRANCIS, ROBERT

Six Poems. Montagaue: 1970. V. 37

The Trouble with God. West Hatfield: 1984. V. 37; 39

FRANCIS, SAINT, OF ASSISI

The Little Flowers. With 8 Illustrations by Paul Woodroffe. London: 1899. V. 37

FRANCIS, WILLIAM

The Gentleman's, Farmer's and Husbandman's Most Useful Assistant . . . Maidenhead: 1806. V. 43

Gwennap: a Descriptive Poem. Redruth: 1845. V. 40

FRANCISCI, ERASMUS

Das Eroffnete Lust-Haus der Ober-und Nieder-Welt; bey Mehrmaliger Unterredung vor Dissmal so wol von der Natur . . . Nurnberg: 1676. V. 38

FRANCISCUS Dracus Redivivus. Das ist, Kurtze Beschreibung aller Vornehmbsten Reysen, Schiffarten unnd Wasserschlachten, so der Weitberumbte Englische Admiral, Franciscus Dracus, Wlecher Inn Zwey Jahren und Zehen Monaten Orbem Mundi Beschiffet . . . Cologne?: 1596. V. 45

FRANCISCUS DE MAYRONIS

Sermones Ab Adventu cum Quadragesimall. Venice: 1491-92. V. 37

FRANCISCUS DE TOLEDO 1423-1479

V. 40

Oratio in Funere Leonardi de Robere. Rome: 1481-87. V. 40; 41

FRANCK, RICHARD

Northern Memoirs, Calculated fro the Meridian of Scotland. Edinburgh: 1821. V. 38; 39; 45

FRANCK, SEBASTIAN

Die Gulden Arch Darein der Kern und di Besten Hauptspruech der Heiligen Schrifft, Alten Lehrer und Vaetter der Kirchen, auch der Heyden und Philosophen . . . Bern: 1557. V. 38

Weltbuch. Tuebingen: 1534. V. 40; 41

FRANCKE, AUGUST H.

Faith's Work Perfected; or, Francke's Orphan House at Halle. London: 1867. V. 39

FRANCKLIN, THOMAS

An Authentic Narrative of the Late Extraordinary Proceedings at Cambridge Against the W-------r Club. London: 1751. V. 37

Sermons on the Relative Duties. London: 1765. V. 43

Translation: a Poem. London: 1753. V. 45

FRANCKLIN, WILLIAM

Inquiry Concerning the Site of Ancient Palibothra. Parts I and II. London: 1815-17. V. 37; 44

FRANCKLYN, G.

An Answer to the Rev. Mr. Clarkson's Essay on the Slavery and Commerce of the Human Species, particularly the African; in a series of Letters from a Gentleman in Jamaica, to his friend in London: . . . States and Conditions of Mankind. London: 1789. V. 39

FRANCO BARRETO, JOAO

Puras Verdades da Musa Portugueza, Compostas por Hum Curioso Portugues. Lisbon: 1641. V. 45

FRANCO, NICOLO

Dix Plaisans Dialogues. Lyon: 1579. V. 40

FRANCQUART, J.

Pompe Funebre du Tres-Pieux et Tres-Puissant Prince Albert . . . Representee au naturel en Tailles Douces . . . Brussels: 1729. V. 40

FRANCQUART, JACQUES

Pompa Funebris . . . Alberti Pii Archiducis Austriae . . . Brussels: 1623. V. 46

FRANGEPAN, FRANCISCUS

Eyn Oration unnd Rede des . . . Herren Franciscen Grafen von Frangepan . . . Ingolstadt: 1541. V. 44

FRANGIPANI, OCTAVIO MIRTO

Directorium Ecclesiasticae Disciplinae, Coloniensi Praesertim Ecclesiae Accommodatum. Birckmannica: 1597. V. 45

FRANK, ANNE

Anne Frank: The Diary of a Young Girl. Garden City: 1952. V. 41

Anne Frank: the Diary of a Young Girl. New York: 1952. V. 46

Diary of a Young Girl. West Hartfield: 1985. V. 44

Diary of a Young Girl. Massachusetts: 1985. V. 37

FRANK, AUGUST HERMANN

The Prayer of Faith Answered. Plymouth-Dock: 1794. V. 39

FRANK, ELIZABETH

Memoirs of the Life and Writings of Lindley Murray: In a Series of Letters Written by Himself. York: 1826. V. 38

FRANK Feingwell's Attempts to Amuse His Friends, Exhibited in a Series of Characters. London: 1811. V. 46

FRANK, GEORGE

Ryedale and North Yorkshire Antiquities. York & London: 1888. V. 39

FRANK, GEROULD

The Boston Strangler. New York: 1966. V. 40

France of the Past and France of Today. V. 40

FRANK, LEONARD

Beautiful Scenes of Alberni District Vancouver Island. Alberni: 1920's. V. 42

FRANK, LEONHARD

Brother and Sister. London: 1930. V. 43

FRANK Leslie's Historical Register of the United States Centennial Exposition 1876. New York: 1877. V. 37

FRANK, LOUIS F.

Pionierjahre der Deutsch-Americanischen Familien . . . Milwaukee: 1911. V. 44

FRANK, PAT

Alas, Babylon. Philadelphia: 1959. V. 42; 45

THE FRANK Reynolds Golf Book, Drawings From 'Punch'. London: 1932. V. 46

FRANK, RICHARD

Northern Memoirs, Calculated for the Meridian of Scotland . . . Edinburgh: 1821. V. 43

FRANK, ROBERT

The Americans. New York: 1959. V. 41

From Incas to Indios. Paris & New York: 1956. V. 41

The Lines of My Hand. New York: 1972. V. 45

FRANK, WALDO

America and Alfred Stieglitz. A Collective Portrait. Garden City: 1934. V. 37

City Block. Darien. V. 42; 43; 44

City Block. Darien: 1922. V. 42; 46

New Year's Eve, a Play. New York: 1929. V. 46

The Unwelcome Man. Boston: 1917. V. 41

FRANKAU, GILBERT

One of Us. London: 1917. V. 40; 44; 46

The Poetical Works of Gilbert Frankau. London: 1923. V. 40

FRANKAU, PAMELA

A Letter from R*b*cc* W*st. Edinburgh: 1986. V. 46

FRANKENSTEIN, ALFRED

After the Hunt: William Harnett and Other American Still-Life Painters, 1870-1900. Berkeley: 1969. V. 44; 45

FRANKFORT, H.

The Mural Painting of El'Amameh. 1929. V. 45

FRANKFORT, HENRI

The Cenotaph of Seti I at Abydos. London: 1933. V. 44

The City of Akhenaten, Part II (only): The North Suburb and the Desert Altars: the Excavations at Tell El Amarna During the Seasons 1926-1932. London: 1933. V. 42

Cylinder Seals: a Documentary Essay on the Art and Religion of the Ancient Near East. London: 1939. V. 44

Cylinder Seals: a Documentary Essay on the Art and Religion of the Ancient Near East. London: 1965. V. 40

The Mural Painting of El-'Amarneh. London: 1929. V. 40

Sculpture of the Third Millennium B.C. from Tell Asmar and Khafajan. Chicago: 1939. V. 44

Stratified Cylinder Seals from the Diyala Region. Chicago: 1955. V. 44

Studies in Early Poettery of the Near East. London: 1924-27. V. 44

FRANKIN, F. HARRISON

The White Man's Grave: a Visit to Sierra Leone in 1834. London: 1836. V. 44

FRANKL, PAUL T.

New Dimensions. New York: 1928. V. 44; 45

FRANKLAND, THOMAS

The Annals of King James and King Charles the First . . . . London: 1681. V. 46

Cautions to Young Sportsmen. London: 1801. V. 46

Cautions to Young Sportsmen. London: 1801. V. 43

FRANKLIN, AUGUSTUS

The American Farrier . . . Strasburg: 1803. V. 37; 45

FRANKLIN, B. J.

Report of the Governor of Arizona. Phoenix: 1896. V. 37; 39

FRANKLIN, BENJAMIN 1706-1790

The Almanacs for the Years 1733-1758. New York: 1964. V. 44; 46

The Autobiography of Benjamin Franklin. Chicago: 1903. V. 44

The Autobiography of Benjamin Franklin. New York: 1931. V. 41

The Autobiography. San Francisco: 1931. V. 43; 46

Benjamin Franklin's Jugendjahre, von Ihm Selbst fur Seinen Sohn Beschreiben. Berlin: 1792. V. 39

The Collection of Franklin Imprints in the Museum of the Curtis Publishing Co. Philadelpia: 1918. V. 40

Continuation of the Account of the Pennsylvania Hospital; from the First of May 1754 to the 5th of May 1761 . . . Philadelphia: 1761. V. 43

Cool Thoughts on the Present Situtation of Our Public Affairs. Philadelphia: 1764. V. 46

Correspondance Choisie de Benjamin Franklin, Paris: 1817. V. 41; 45

Correspondence Inedite et Secrete . . . Depuis l'Annee 1753 jusqu'en 1790 . . . Paris: 1817. V. 39

Electrical Experiments, Made in Pursuance of Those by Mr. Canton, dated Dec. 3, 1753 (and) Extract of a Letter Concerning Electricity from Mr. B. Franklin to Mons Delibard . . . London. V. 40

Experiences et Observations sur l'Electricite Faites a Philadelphie en Amerique . . . & Communiquees dans Plusieurs Lettres a M.P. Collinson de la Societe Royale de Londres. Paris: 1752. V. 38

Experiments and Observations in Electricity. London: 1769. V. 42; 45; 46

Experiments and Observations on Electricity Made at Philadelphia in America . . . London: 1774. V. 42; 44

Familiar Letters and Miscellaneous Papers . . . London: 1833. V. 40; 44

An Historical Review of the Constitution and Government of Pennsylvania, From Its Origin. London: 1759. V. 43

An Historical Review of Pennsylvania, From Its Origin, Embracing, Among Other Subjects, the Various Points of Controversy, Which Have Arisen, From Time to Time, Between the Several Governors and the Assemblies. Philadelphia: 1812. V. 41

The Interest of Great Britain Considered with Regard to Her Colonies and the Acquisitions of Canada and Guadaloupe, to Which are added Observations Concerning the Increase of Mankind, Peopling Countries &c. Boston: 1760. V. 44

Jugendjahre, von ihm Selbst sur Seinen Sohn Beschrieben und Ubersetzi von Gottfried August Burger. Berlin: 1792. V. 46

Letters to Benjamin Franklin from His Family and Friends 1751-1790. New York: 1859. V. 45

Vie de Benjamin Franklin. Paris: 1798. V. 41

Vita di Beniamino Franklin Scritta da Lui Medesimo. Bergamo: 1830. V. 45

The Life of Benjamin Franklin, Written by Himself. Now first editied from Original Manuscripts and from his Printed Correspondence and other Writings, by John Bigelow. Philadelphia: 1874. V. 37

Memoires de la Vie Privee de Benjamin Franklin. Paris: 1791. V. 38; 40; 43; 45; 46

Memoirs of the Life and Writings of Benjamin Franklin . . . by His Grandson. London: 1818. V. 37; 38

Memoirs of the Life and Writings of Benjamin Franklin. London: 1818/17. V. 37; 41; 43

Memoirs of the Life and Writings . . . London: 1833. V. 37; 42; 45

Memoirs of . . . Philadelphia: 1852. V. 42

Memoirs of Benjamin Franklin. New York: 1859. V. 45

Benjamin Franklin's Memoirs. Berkeley: 1949. V. 45

A Narrative of the Late Massacres, in Lancaster County, of a Number of Indians, Friends of This Province, by Persons Unknown. Philadelphia: 1764. V. 42

New Experiments and Observations on Electricity. London: 1760/62/54. V. 40

Observations on Smoky Chimneys, Their Causes and Cure, with Considerations on Fuel and Stoves. London: 1793. V. 42; 43

Oeuvres. Paris: 1773. V. 39

Opere Politiche de Beniamino Franklin . . . Padova: 1783. V. 39

Philosophical and Miscellaneous Papers. London: 1787. V. 39

Philosophical and Miscellaneous Papers. London: 1797. V. 46

Political, Miscellaneous and Philosophical Pieces. London: 1779. V. 37; 38; 39; 40; 42; 43

Poor Richard Improved. Philadelphia: 1754. V. 40

Poor Richard: The Almanacs for the Years 1733-1758. 1964. V. 40

Poor Richard. The Almanacks for the Years 1733-1758. Philadelphia: 1964. V. 37; 40; 41

The Private Life of the Late Benjamin Franklin . . . London: 1793. V. 40; 45

Rapport des Commissaires Charges par Le Roi, de l'Examen du Magnetisme Animal. Paris: 1784. V. 46

Recueil des Lois Constitutives des Colonies Angloises, Confderees Sous La Denomination D'Etats-Unis de l'Amerique Septentrionale . . . . Paris. V. 43

The Sayings of Poor Richard. Brooklyn: 1890. V. 42; 44

Some Account of the Pennsylvania Hospital; From Its First Rise, to the Beginning of the Fifth Month, Called May, 1754. (with) A Continuation of the Account of the Pennsylvania Hospital. From the First of May 1754 to the Fifth of May 1761 . . . Philadelphia: 1754, 1761. V. 39

Two Tracts: Information to Those Who Would Removed to America, and Remarks Concerning the Savages of North America. London: 1784. V. 46

La Science du Bonhomme Richard, ou Moyen Facile de Paper les Impots. Paris: 1777. V. 39

The Way to Wealth . . . New York: 1930. V. 46

The Way to Wealth, or Poor Richard Improved. Paris: 1795. V. 37

Oeuvres. Paris: 1773. V. 38; 39; 40; 42; 46

Works. London: 1793. V. 40; 43

Works of the Late Doctor Benjamin Franklin.. London: 1794. V. 42

The Complete Works in Philosophy, Politics, and Morals . . . London: 1806. V. 37; 38; 41

The Works of Benjamin Franklin. Boston: 1840. V. 39

The Complete Works. New York: 1887-88. V. 42

The Writings of Benjamin Franklin. New York: 1905-07. V. 39; 40; 42

FRANKLIN, C.

Catalogues 1-8. London: 1971-75. V. 39

FRANKLIN, COLIN

The Ashendene Press. 1986. V. 37; 39; 43

The Ashendene Press. Dallas: 1986. V. 37; 39; 40; 45; 46

Doves Press: The Start of a Worry. Dallas: 1983. V. 43

Emery Walker. Cambridge: 1973. V. 37; 38; 41; 46

Poets of the Daniel Press. Cambridge: 1988. V. 42; 46

Printing and the Mind of Morris: Three Paths to the Kelmscott Press. Cambridge: 1986. V. 46

Printing and the Mind of Morris: Three Paths to the Kelmscott Press. London: 1986. V. 44

Themes in Aquatint. San Francisco: 1978. V. 38; 39; 40; 41; 45; 46

FRANKLIN, EDWARD

The Life and Adventures of Obadiah Benj. Franklin Bloomfield, M.D . . . Philadelphia: 1818. V. 38

FRANKLIN, JAMES

The Philosophical and Political History of the Thirteen United States of America . . . London: 1784. V. 42; 45

FRANKLIN, JIM

Dillo Toons. Austin: 1969. V. 39

FRANKLIN, JOHN

Journey to the Shores of the Polar Sea, in 1819-20-21-22 . . . London: 1829. V. 44

Journey to the Shores of the Polar Sea in 1819, 20, 21, 22 with a Brief Acc't of the Second Journey in 1825-26-27. London: 1929. V. 44

Narrative of a Journey to the Shores of the Polar Sea, in the Years 1819, 20, 21, and 22. London: 1823. V. 37; 38; 39; 41; 42; 44; 46

Narrative of a Journey to the Shores of the Polar Sea, in the Years 1819, 20, 21, and 22. Philadelphia: 1824. V. 37; 38; 41; 42

Narrative of a Second Expedition to the Shores of the Polar Sea, 1825-1827. London: 1828. V. 37; 38; 39; 40; 41

Narrative of a Second Expedition to the Shores of the Polar Sea, in the Years 1825, 1826 and 1827. Philadelphia: 1828. V. 37; 38; 40

Narrative of a Second Expedition to the Shores of the Polar Sea in the Years 1825, 1826 and 1827. Edmonton: 1971. V. 45

Narrative of a Journey to the Shores of the Polar Sea, in the Years 1819-20-21-22. London: 1824. V. 37

Narrative of a Journey to the Shores of the Polar Sea in the Years 1819-20-21-22. With an Appendix on Various Subjects Relating to Science and Natural History. London: 1819, 20, 21. V. 37

Parables of Our Lord. London: 1851. V. 37; 39

Thirty Years in the Arctic Regions: A Narrative of the Expolorations . . . Philadelphia: 1859. V. 37

FRANKLIN, MALCOLM

Bitterweeds. Irving: 1977. V. 37; 42

FRANKLIN, MATTHEW

Address of the American Convention for Promoting the Abolition of Slavery and Improving the Condition of the African Race, Assembled at Philadelphia, in January 1804, to the People of the United States. Philadelphia: 1804. V. 41

FRANKLIN, S. R.

Memories of a Rear Admiral . . . New York: 1898. V. 39

FRANKLIN, THOMAS

The Greek Tragic Theatre. London: 1777. V. 40; 46

FRANKLIN, WILLIAM TEMPLE

Memoirs of the Life and Writings of Benjamin Franklin . . . by His Grandson. London: 1818. V. 38

FRANKS, DAVID

The New-York Directory . . . New York: 1786. V. 44; 45

THE FRAUDS and Abuses of Coal-Dealers Detected and Exposed; in a Letter to an Alderman of London. London: 1747. V. 41; 42

FRAUENTHAL, A. W.

Humpty Dumpty. The Great Trick Book. New York: 1869. V. 41

FRAWEN Beichlin zu rum und Breyse Allen Tugentsamen Auch Erberen Weybern . . . Augsburg: 1522/23. V. 43

FRAXI, P.

Bibliography of Prohibited Books . . . Bio-Biblio-Icono-graphical and Critical Notes on Curious, Uncommon and Erotic Books. London: 1962. V. 38

FRAY, CAROLINE

Death and Other Poems. London: 1823. V. 42

FRAY, EDWARD F.

Shingu. New York. V. 39

FRAY, ROGER

A Sampler of Castille. London: 1923. V. 43

FRAZAR, THOMAS

Oregon, Its Resources, Soil, Climate and Productions . . . Portland: 1869. V. 37; 43

FRAZER, AUGUSTUS SIMON

Letters of Colonel Sir Augustus Simon, K.C.B. London: 1859. V. 42

FRAZER, EDWARD

The War Drama of the Eagles. London: 1912. V. 41

FRAZER, JAMES GEORGE 1854-1921

Anthologia Anthroplogica. London: 1938-39. V. 42

Anthologia Anthropologica. London: 1938. V. 38

Antologia Anthropologia. The Native Races of America. 1939. V. 37

Folk-Lore in the Old Testament. Studies in Compartive Religion, Legend and Law. London;: 1919. V. 37

The Golden Bough. London: 1890. V. 38; 40; 43

The Golden Bough. London: 1922. V. 40

The Golden Bough: a Study in Magic and Religion. London: 1954. V. 37; 46

The Golden Bough. London: 1951. V. 37

The Golden Bough. New York: 1970. V. 37

The Golden Bough: A Study of Magic and Religion. New York: 1935. V. 37

The Native Races of Africa and Madagascar. London: 1938. V. 45

Totemism. Edinburgh: 1887. V. 38

Works of . . . New York: 1935/1919. V. 46

FRAZER, MRS.

The Practice of Cookery, Pastry and Confectionary. Edinburgh: 1804. V. 45; 46

FRAZETTA, F.

Golden Girl. 1970. V. 43; 45

FRAZIER, CHARLES

Surgery of the Spine and Spinal Cord. New York: 1918. V. 42; 46

FREAM, WILLIAM

Across Canada: a Report on Its Agricultural Resources. Ottawa: 1886. V. 46

FREAR, MARY DILLINGHAM

Flowers of Hawaii. New York: 1938. V. 38

FREART DE CHAMBRAY, ROLAND

Parallele de l'Architecture Antique et de la Moderne avec un Recueil des Dix Principaux Auteurs qui ont Ecrit des Cinq Ordres (etc.). Paris: 1650. V. 38

Parallele de l'Architecture Antique et de la Moderne, Avec un Recueil des Dix Principaux Auteurs qui ont Ecrit des Cinq Ordres (etc.). Paris: 1702. V. 39

FREART, ROLAND

An Idea of the Perfection of Painting . . . In the Savoy: 1668. V. 40

An Idea of the Perfection of Painting . . . London: 1668. V. 37; 38; 44

A Parallel of the Ancient Architecture with the Modern. London: 1664. V. 37; 42

A Parallel of the Ancient Architecture with the Modern. London: 1707-06. V. 37; 40

A Parallel of the Ancient Architecture with the Modern. London: 1723. V. 40

Parallele de l'Architecture Antique et de la Moderne . . . Paris: 1650. V. 45

Parallele de l'Architecture Antique et de la Moderne . . . Paris: 1689. V. 44

FREDEMAN, WILLIAM E.

Pre-Raphaelitism. A Bibliocritical Study. Cambridge: 1965. V. 42

FREDERAL WRITER'S PROJECT. IDAHO

Idaho, a Guide in Word and Picture. Prepared by the Federal Writer's Projects of the Works Progress Administration. Caldwell: 1937. V. 38

FREDERIC, H.

The Damnation of Theron Ware. 1836. V. 43

The Damnation of Theron Ware. 1896. V. 45

FREDERIC, HAROLD

The Damnation of Theron Ware. Chicago: 1895. V. 46

Seth's Younger Brother. New York: 1887. V. 37

FREDERIC II, KING OF PRUSSIA

Oeuvres Posthumes. Berlin: 1689. V. 38

FREDERIC, LOUIS

The Art of India: Temples and Sculpture. New York. V. 38; 41

Japan: Art and Civilization. New York: 1969. V. 38; 41

FREDERICK, CHARLES

Foxhunting. London: 1930. V. 39

FREDERICK II, ROMAN EMPEROR

Reliqua Librorum Frederici II. Imperatoris, De Arte Venandi cum Avibus, cum Manfredi Regis Additionibus. Augsburg: 1596. V. 37

FREDERICK, J. V.

Ben Holladay The Stagecoach King. Glendale: 1940. V. 37; 38; 42; 43

FREDERICKS, J. W.

Dutch Silver. Volume I. Embossed Plaquettes Tazze and Dishes . . . Volume II. Wrought Plate of North and South Holland . . . Volume III. Wrought Plate of the Central, Northern & Southern Provinces . . . Volume IV. Embossed Ecclesiastical & Secular Plate . . . The Hague: 1952-61. V. 39

FREDERICKSON, A. D.

Ad Orientem. London: 1889. V. 41; 45; 46

THE FREE and Voluntary Confession and Narrative of . . . (Addressed to His Majesty) . . . London: 1684. V. 37

FREE, B. D.

Ethicks; or, the Doctrine of Moral Agency, as Described by the Philosophers. London: 1782. V. 37

Rhetorick; or, the Art of Persuasion. London: 1782. V. 37

A FREE Comment on the Late Mr. W-G-N's (Winnington's) Apology for His Conduct . . . London: 1748. V. 40

A FREE Conference Touching the Present State of England Both at Home and Abroad: In Order to the Designs of France. London: 1668. V. 45

A FREE Examination of a Modern Romance, Intitled Memoirs of the Life of Lord Lovat. London: 1746. V. 39

FREE, JOHN

Advice to the Fair Sex. London: 1736. V. 42

THE FREE Mason's Health. London: 1725? V. 46

FREE RELIGIOUS ASSOCIATION

Proceedings at the Fifth (-Tenth) Annual Meeting of . . . Boston: 1872-77. V. 37

FREE Thoughts on the Late Treaty of Alliance Concluded at Worms. London: 1744. V. 41

FREEBAIRN, R.

Six Select Views in Italy. London: 1806. V. 40; 46

FREEDBERG, S. J.

Painting of the High Renaissance in Rome and Florence. Cambridge: 1961. V. 43

FREEDLEY, EDWIN T.

Leading Pursuits and Leading Men. Philadelphia: 1854. V. 37; 44

Philadelphia and Its Manufactures. Philadelphia: 1858. V. 41; 42

Philadelphia and Its Manufactures: a Hand-Book. Philadelphia: 1859. V. 38; 42

Philadelphia and Its manufactures . . . in 1867. Philadelphia: 1867. V. 38

A Practical Treatise on Business. Philadelphia: 1852. V. 39

FREEDLEY, GEORGE

Theatrical Designs from the Baroque Through Neoclassicism. New York: 1940. V. 37

FREEDMAN, BARNETT

The Post Office - a Review of the Activities of the Post Office; 1934. V. 37

FREEDMAN, BARNETT continued

Real Farmhouse Cheese. London: 1939. V. 40

A Series of Twenty-Two Original Sketches in Pencil and Wash for Walter De La Mare's Anthology 'Love.' London: 1943. V. 40

FREEDMAN, BENEDICT

Mrs. Mike: The Story of Katherine Marty Flannigan. New York: 1947. V. 45

FREEDMAN, EDWARD A.

The History of the Norman Conquest of England Its Causes and Results. Oxford: 1869-76. V. 40

FREELING, ARTHUR

Freeling's Grand Junction Railway Companion to Liverpool, Manchester and Birmingham and Liverpool, Manchester & Birmingham Guide . . . London: 1838. V. 46

The Grand Junction Railway Company to Liverpool, Manchester and Birmingham. Liverpool: 1837. V. 39

The Grand Junction Railway Companion to Liverpool, Manchester, and Birmingham; and Liverpool, Manchester, and Birmingham Guide: Containing an Account of Every Thing Worthy the Attention of the Traveller upon the Line; Including a Complete . . . Liverpool/London: 1837. V. 37

The London and Birmingham Railway Companion. London: 1836. V. 46

The London and Birmingham Railway Companion . . . London: 1838. V. 46

FREELING, NICOLAS

Valparaiso. New York: 1964. V. 40

FREEMAN, ALBERT C.

Crematoria in Great Britain and Abroad. London: 1928. V. 40

FREEMAN & O'NEIL

1876 Illustrated Catalogue and Price List of STair Builders' Supplies Manufactured by Freeman & O'Neil. Claremont: 1876. V. 41

FREEMAN, BENSON

The Yeomanry of Devon, 1794-1927. London: 1927. V. 38

FREEMAN, CHARLES

The New Lover's Instructor; or, Whole Art of Courtship. London: 1778? V. 41

FREEMAN, DOUGLAS C.

A Calendar of Confederate Papers. Richmond: 1908. V. 44

FREEMAN, DOUGLAS S.

R. E. Lee. A Biography. New York: 1944-45. V. 39

FREEMAN, DOUGLAS SOUTHALL

A Calendar of Confederate Papers. Richmond: 1908. V. 42

George Washington: A Biography. New York: 1948-54. V. 41

Lee's Lieutenants. 1942-44. V. 45

Lee's Lieutenants. New York: 1942-44. V. 37; 43; 45

Lee's Lieutenants. New York: 1946. V. 45

R. E. Lee. A Biography. New York: 1934-35. V. 38; 46

FREEMAN, E. A.

The History of the Norman Conquest of England, Its Causes and Its Results. Oxford: 1877-70-79. V. 38; 40

FREEMAN, EDWARD A.

An Essay on the Origin and Development of Window Tracery in England. Oxford & London: 1851. V. 39

The History of the Norman Conquest of England, Its Causes and Its Results. 1870-79. V. 39; 42

The History of the Conquests of the Saracens: Six Lectures Delivered Before the Edinburgh Philosophical Institution. London: 1876. V. 46

The History of Sicily, From the Earliest Times (to the Death of Agathokles). 1891-94. V. 39

The History of Sicily from the Earliest Times. Oxford: 1891-94. V. 42

The History of the Norman Conquest of England, Its Causes and Results. Oxford: 1870-76. V. 37

The Reign of William Rufus and Accession of Henry the First. Oxford: 1882. V. 42

FREEMAN, EDWIN A.

The Historical Geography of Europe, traces territorial changes around the Mediterranean dut to ancient Greek and Roman expansion and decline, as affecting boundaries of medieval & modern Europe . . . London: 1903. V. 37

FREEMAN, G. D.

Midnight and Noonday: or the Incidental History of Southern Kansas and the Indian Territory. 1892. V. 42

Midnight and Noonday or the Incidental History of Southern Kansas and the Indian Territory. Caldwell: 1892. V. 39; 46

FREEMAN, G. E.

Practical Falconry; to which is added, How I Became a Falconer. London: 1869. V. 37

FREEMAN, GAGE EARL

Falconry: Its Claim, History and Practice. London: 1859. V. 39

FREEMAN, GEORGE D.

Midnight and Noonday or Dark Deeds Unraveled. Caldwell: 1890. V. 42; 45

FREEMAN, HARRY C.

A Brief History of Butte, Montana. The World's Greatest Mining Camp. Chicago: 1900. V. 37; 39; 42; 46

FREEMAN, HILDREBRAND

Memoirs of Hildebrand Freeman, Esq. Or a Sketch of 'The Rights of Man.' London: 1792. V. 39

FREEMAN-ISHILL, ROSE

Havelock Ellis. And a Letter by Havelock Ellis. 1958. V. 46

O'tin-San from 'Rain Among the Bamboos'. 1958. V. 46

Seer in Darkness (a Group of Three Poems). London: 1964. V. 46

To the Unknown Martyrs. 1958. V. 46

Wellspring and Later Poems. 1965. V. 46

FREEMAN, J. J.

A Narrative of the Perscutions of the Christians in Madagascar . . . London: 1840. V. 39

FREEMAN, JAMES W.

Prose and Poetry of the Live Stock Industry of the United States. New York: 1959. V. 38; 39; 43

FREEMAN, JOHN

The Comforter or a Comfortable Treatise. London: 1614. V. 37

The Grove and Other Poems. London: 1924. V. 46

FREEMAN, JOHN RIPLEY

Earthquake Damage and Earthquake Insurance. New York: 1932. V. 40

On the Proposed Use of a Portion of the Hetch Hetchy, Eleanor and Cherry Valleys Within and Near to the Boundaries of the Stanislaus U.S. National Forest Reserve and Yosemite National Park as Reservoirs for Impouncing Tuolumne River Flood Waters and . . . San Francisco: 1912. V. 46

FREEMAN, LEWIS R.

On the Roof of the Rockies. New York: 1925. V. 37; 44

FREEMAN, MARY E. WILKINS

Giles Gorey, Yeoman. New York: 1893. V. 42

FREEMAN, R.

Kentish Poets. Canterbury: 1821. V. 44; 46

FREEMAN, R. AUSTIN

The Case of Oscar Brodski. New York: 1923. V. 41; 42; 43; 45

The Cat's Eye. London: 1923. V. 38

The Cat's Eye. London: 1938. V. 38

The Dr. Thorndyke Omnibus. 1938. V. 39

Helen Vardon's Confession. 1922. V. 39

The Red Thumb Mark. 1911. V. 39

The Singing Bone. 1912. V. 39

FREEMAN, RICHARD 1646-1710

Reports of Cases in Law and Equity: From 1670 to 1706. London: 1742. V. 40

FREEMAN, RICHARD AUSTIN

Travel and Life in Ashanti and Jaman. London: 1898. V. 44

FREEMAN, SAMUEL

The Massachuetts Justice. Boston: 1795. V. 38; 44; 45

The Probate Auxiliary. Portland: 1793. V. 38; 45

FREEMAN, STRICKLAND

Observations on the Mechanism of the Horse's Foot . . . London: 1796. V. 42; 46

FREEMAN, WALTER JACKSON 1895-1972

Psychosurgery. Intelligence, Emotion and Social Behaviour Following Prefrontal Labotomy for Mental Disorders. Springfield: 1942. V. 43

Psychosurgery: Intelligence, Emotion and Social Behavior Following Prefrontal Lobotomy for Mental Disorder. Springfield: 1950. V. 43

FREEMAN'S Address to the North Americans; Proving that Their Present Embarrassments Are Owing to Their Federal Union, Their Sovereign States, Their Constitutions and Their Statements and Containing Some Propositions for Relief. N.P.: 1846? V. 46

FREEMANTLE, BRIAN

Goodbye to an Old Friend. London: 1973. V. 45

FREEMASONS.

By-Laws of the Cyrus Chapter No. 2, of Royal Arch Masons . . . Held at Silver City, Owyhee County, Idaho Territory . . . Adopted February 13th 1872 . . . Silver City: 1872. V. 39

Constitution of the General Convention of State Grand Chapters in the United States of America. Windsor: 1829. V. 45

Constitutions of the Ancient Fraternity of Free and Accepted Masons. London: 1784. V. 40

FREEMASONS. KENTUCKY. GRAND LODGE

Proceedings of the Grand Lodge of Kentucky: Begun and Held at Mason's Hall in the Town of Lexington . . . A.L. 5822. A.D. 1822. Lexington: 1822. V. 44

FREEMASONS. NORTH CAROLINA. GRAND LODGE

Proceedings of the Grand Lodge of Free and Accepted Masons of North Carolina. Raleigh: 1865. V. 44; 45

FREEMASONS. OREGON. GRAND LODGE

Proceedings of the M. W. Grand Lodge of Ancient Free and Accepted masons of the Territory of Oregon, at its Eighth Annual Communication, Held at Astoria, O.T. Portland: 1858. V. 39

FREEMASONS. RICHMOND RANDOLPH LODGE

By-Laws and List of Members of Richmond Randolph Lodge No. XIX, Ancient York Masons. Richmond: 1864. V. 45

FREEMASONS. STEILACOOM, WASHINGTON LODGE NO. 8

The By-Laws of Steilacoom Lodge, No. 8 of Ancient, Free and Accepted Masons, Adopted June A.D. 1855. Steilacoom: 1855. V. 39

THE FREEMASON'S Vocal Assistant, and Register of the Lodges of Masons in South Carolina and Georgia. Charleston: 1807. V. 38

FREEMASONS. WISCONSIN. GRAND LODGE.

Proceedings of a Grand Annual Communication of the Grand Lodge of Wisconsin Begun and Held at Madison, W. T . . . Madison: 1846. V. 39

Proccedings of a Grand Annual Communication of the Grand Lodge of Wisconsin Holden at Madison, W.T . . . Platteville: 1847. V. 39

FREER GALLERY, WASHINGTON.

A Descriptive and Illustrative Catalogue of Chinese Bronzes Acquired During the Adiministration of John Ellerton Lodge. Washington: 1946. V. 42; 44

Oriental Ceramics. Tokyo: 1981. V. 42

FREGE, LUDWIG GOTLOB

Die Grundlagen der Arithmetik. Breslau: 1884. V. 38; 45

FREGOSO, ANTONIO

Opera Nova . . . Intitula Cerva Biancha. Venice: 1525. V. 40; 45

FREGOSO, ANTONIO PHILEREMO

Opera Nova . . . la Qual Tratta de Doi Philosophi, Cioe de Democrito Che Rideva de la Pacie de Questo Mondo & Heraclyto che Piangeva delle Miserie Humane. Venice: 1539. V. 39

FREHER, PAULUS

Theatrum Virorum Eruditione Clarorum in Quo Vitae & Scripta Theologorum, Jureconsultorum, Medicorum & Philosophorum, tam in Germania . . . Nuremberg: 1688. V. 39

FREILIGRATH, FERDINAND

The Rose, Thistle and Shamrock. Stuttgart: 1853. V. 38

FREILIGRATH-KROEKER, KATE

Alice. V. 44

FREIND, J.

History of Physick from the Time of Galen, to the Beginning of the Sixteenth Century. London: 1725. V. 41

FREIND, JOHN 1675-1728

Emmenologia. London: 1729. V. 38; 39; 40; 44

Emmenologia. London: 1752. V. 40

The History of Physick from the Time of Galen, to the Beginning of the Sixteenth Century. London: 1726. V. 40

Opera Omnia. Leyden: 1734. V. 42

FREIRE DE ANDRADA, JACINTO

The Life of Dom John de Castro, the Fourth Vice-Roy of India. London: 1664. V. 39

Vida de Dom Joao de Castro, Quarto Viso-rey da India. Lisbon: 1651. V. 38

FREIRE DE MONTERROYO MASCARENHAS, JOSE

Os Orizes Conquistados, ou Noticia da Conversam dos Indomitos Orizes Procazes, Povos Habitantes 7 Guerreyros do Certao do Brasil . . . Lisbon: 1716. V. 45

FREIRE MONTERROYO MASCARENAS, JOSE

Novo Triunfo da Religiam Serafica, ou Noticia Summaria de Martyrio e Morte que Padeceram em Odio de Nossa Santa . . . Lisbon: 1718. V. 41

FREJUS, ROLAND

The Relation of a Voyage Made Into Mauritania, in Africk, by the Sieur Roland Frejus of Marseilles, by the French King's Order, in the Year 1666. London: 1671. V. 46

FREKE, WILLIAM

Select Essays Tending to the Universal Reformation of Learning . . . London: 1693. V. 42; 43

FRELINGHUYSEN, THEODORE

Speech of Mr. Frelinghuysen, of New Jersey, Delivered in the Senate of the United States, April 6, 1830, On the Bill for an Exchange of Lands with the Indians Residing In Any of the States or Territories and for Their Removal West of the Mississippi. Washington: 1830. V. 44

FREMANTLE

Three Months in the Southern States, April-June 1863. Edinburgh/London: 1863. V. 37

FREMANTLE, ARTHUR J.

Three Months in the Southern States, April - June 1863. Mobile: 1864. V. 40; 42; 45

Three Months in the Southern States. New York: 1864. V. 38; 39; 45

FREMANTLE, E. R. 1836-1929

The Navy As I Have Known It, 1849-1899. London: 1904. V. 46

FREMANTLE, RICHARD

Florentine Gothic Painters from Giotto to Masaccio: A Guide to Painting in and Near Florence, 1300 to 1450. London: 1975. V. 42

FREMANTLE, T. F.

The Book of the Rifle. London: 1901. V. 38

FREMINVILLE, CHEVALIER DE LA POIX DE

Voyage to the North Pole, In the Frigate the Syrene; Including a Physical and Geographical Notice to the Island Of Iceland. London: 1819. V. 42

FREMONT, JESSIE B.

Memoirs of My Life. Chicago & New York: 1887. V. 40

FREMONT, JESSIE BENTON

The Story of the Guard: A Chronicle of the War. Boston: 1863. V. 37

The Will and the Way Stories. Boston: 1891. V. 38

FREMONT, JOHN CHARLES 1813-1890

Defense of Lieut. Colonel Fremont, Before the Court Martial. N.P.: 1848. V. 40; 43

The Expeditions of John Charles Fremont. Urbana: 1970. V. 38

Exploring Expedition to the Rocky Mountains in the Year 1842 and to Oregon and North California in the Years 1843-44. Washington: 1845. V. 37

The Exploring Expedition to the Rocky Mountains, Oregon and California. New York: 1855. V. 38

Geographical Memoir Upon Upper California in Illustration of His Map of Oregon and California. 1848. V. 41

Geographical Memoir Upon Upper California. Washington: 1848. V. 38; 39; 40; 41; 42; 43; 45

Geographical Memoir Upon Upper California, in Illustration of His Map of Oregon and California. Washington: 1849. V. 37; 40

Letter of J.C. Fremont to the Editors of the National Intelligencer, Communicating some General Results of a Recent Winter Expedition across the Rocky Mountains, from the Survey of a Route for a Railroad to the Pacific. (Washington: 1854). V. 37

The Life, Explorations and Public Services of John Charles Fremont. New York: 1856. V. 44

The Mariposa Company. New York: 1863. V. 38

Memoirs of My Life. Chicago: 1886-87. V. 40

Memoirs of My Life. Chicago: 1887. V. 38; 39; 40

Memoirs of My Life. Chicago and New York: 1887. V. 37; 39; 40; 42

Narrataive of the Exploring Expedition to the Rocky Mountains in the Yeara 1842; and to Oregon and North California, in the Years 1843-4. New York: 1846. V. 37; 45

Narrative of the Exploring Expeditions to the Rocky Mountains in the Year 1842 and to Oregon and North California in the Years 1843-44. Washington: 1845. V. 41

Narrative of the Exploring Expedition to the Rocky Mountains, in 1842, and to Oregon and North Carolina, in 1843-44. London: 1846. V. 37; 38; 39; 41; 42; 44

Narrative of an Exploring Expedition to the Rocky Mountains in the Years 1842, and to Oregon and North California in the Years 1843-44. London: 1848. V. 41

Narrative of the Exploring Expedition to the Rocky Mountains . . . and to Oregon and North California. Syracuse: 1846. V. 37

Notes of Travel in California. Dublin: 1849. V. 40

FREMONT, JOHN CHARLES 1813-1890 continued

Notes of Travel in California: Comprising Geographical, Agricultural, Geological, and Mineralogical Features of the Country . . . New York: 1849. V. 46

Notes of Travel in California . . . Also, the Route from Fort Leavenworth, in Missouri, to San Diego, in California . . . with: Narrative of the Exploring Expedition . . . 1843-4. New York: 1849. V. 37

A Report of an Exploration of the Country Lying Between the Missouri River and the Rocky Mountains on the Line of the Kansas and Great Platte Rivers. Washington: 1843. V. 41

Report of the Exploring Expedition to Rocky Mountains in the Year 1842, and to Oregon and North California in the Years 1843-44. Washington: 1845. V. 37; 38; 39; 40; 41; 42; 43; 44; 45; 46

Report of the Exploring Expedition to the Rocky Mountains in the Year 1842 and to Oregon and North California in the Years 1843-44. Washington: 1846. V. 45

Report from the Secretary of War, Communicating, in Compliance with a Resolution of the Senate, a Copy of Lieut. Fremont's Report of his Exploring Expedition tot eh Rocky Mountains. A Report on an Exploration of the Country . . . Washington: 1843. V. 37

FRENCH, ALICE 1850-1934

A Book of True Lovers. Chicago: 1897. V. 46

FRENCH, ALLEN

The Junior Cup. New York: 1901. V. 37; 40; 41; 43; 44

THE FRENCH 'Anas'. London: 1805. V. 46
THE FRENCH Anas. London: 1805. V. 41; 46

FRENCH, B. F.

Historical Collections of Louisiana. New York: 1846. V. 45

Historical Collections of Louisiana, Embracing Many Rare and Valuable Documents . . . New York: 1846-50. V. 43

Historical Collections of Louisiana, Embracing Many Rare and Valuable Documents Relating to the Natural Civil and Political History of that State. New York: 1846-53. V. 45

Historical Collections of Louisiana and Florida, Including Translations of Original Manuscripts Relating to Their Discovery and Settlement, with Numerous Historical and Biographical Notes. New York: 1869. V. 39

FRENCH, BENJAMIN F.

Biographia Americana: or, a Historical and Critical Account of the Lives, Actions, and Writings of the Most Distinguished Persons in North America . . . New York: 1825. V. 41

FRENCH, C.

A Handbook of the Destrucitve Insects of Victoria, with Notes on the Methods to be Adopted to Check and Exirpate Them. Melbourne: 1891-1911. V. 38

FRENCH, CECIL

Between Sun and Moon. London: 1922. V. 41

FRENCH, DOUGLAS S.

Lee's Lieutenants: a Study in Command. New York: 1942-44. V. 37

FRENCH, EDWIN DAVIS

A List of Book-Plates Engraved on Copper by Mr. Edwin Davis French. Cleveland: 1899. V. 40

FRENCH, ELIZABETH J.

A New manual of Electro-Therapeutics and a Brief Treatise on Anatomy and Physiology. Chicago: 1875. V. 37

THE FRENCH Expedition into Syria, Comprising General Buonaparte's Lettes, with Gen. Berthier's Narrative and Sir Wm. Sidney Smith's Letters from the London Gazette. London: 1799. V. 42

FRENCH Fraternity and French Protection, as Promised to Ireland and as Experienced by Other Nations. Dublin: 1798. V. 42; 46

FRENCH, FREDERICK W.

Catalogue of the Valuable Private Library of the Late Frederick W. French. Boston: 1901. V. 40; 44

FRENCH, GEORGE

The History of Col. Parke's Administration Whilst He Was Captain-General and Chief Governor of the Leeward Islands . . . London: 1717. V. 40; 44

FRENCH, GEORGE RUSSELL

The Palace, the National Gallery, and the Royal Academy. London: 1846. V. 38

FRENCH, GILBERT J. 1804-1866

Catalogue of Books on Heraldry, Archaeology, Mediaeval Art, and Miscellaneous Literature. Bolton: 1864. V. 38

The Life and Times of Samuel Crompton . . . London: 1859. V. 40; 46

Remarks on the Mechanical Structure of Cotton Fibre. Manchester: 1857. V. 42

FRENCH, H.

Jacob Hurd and His Sons Nathaniel and Benjamin, Silversmiths 1702-1781. Cambridge: 1939. V. 37

FRENCH Influence Upon English Counsels Demonstrated from an Impartial Examination of Our Measures for Twenty Years Past. London: 1740. V. 41

FRENCH, J. H.

Gazetteer of the State of New York. Syracuse: 1860. V. 40

FRENCH, J. STRANGE

Elkswatawa; or, the Prophet of the West. New York: 1836. V. 38

FRENCH, JACOB

Harmony of Harmony. Northampton: 1802. V. 37

The Psalmodist's Companion, in Four Parts . . . Worcester: 1793. V. 39

FRENCH, JAMES S.

Sketches and Eccentricities of Col. David Crockett of West Tennessee. London: 1834. V. 37; 38; 39; 40

FRENCH, JAMES STRANGE

Elkswatawa; or, the Prophet of the West. New York: 1836. V. 43; 44

FRENCH, JAMES WEIR

Machine Tools Commonly Empolyed in Modern Engineering Workshops. Together with a Series of Sectional Models Illustrating the Arrangment of the Parts and the Details of Some Typical Tools. With a Foreword by John Dewar Cormack . . . London: 1911. V. 37

Modern Power Generators. London: 1890. V. 46

Modern Power Generators: Steam, Electric and Internal-Combustion and their Application to Present-Day Requirements. 1908. V. 46

Modern Power Generators. London: 1908. V. 40; 45

FRENCH, JOHN

The Art of Distillation, or a Treatise of the Choisest Spagyricall Preparations Performed by Way of Distillation . . . London: 1651. V. 46

The Art of Distillation . . . London: 1667. V. 42

The York-shire Spaw, or a Treatise of Four Famous Medicinal Wells . . . London: 1652. V. 38; 40; 41; 42

FRENCH, LEIGH

The Smaller Houses and Gardens of Versailles 1680-1815. New York: 1926. V. 44

FRENCH, LEONARD

The Campion Paintings: Introduction and Annotation of Plates by Vincent Buckley. Melbourne: 1962. V. 41

FRENCH Master Goldsmiths and Silversmiths from the Seventeenth to the Nineteenth Century. New York: 1966. V. 44

FRENCH, ROBERT

The Constitution of Ireland, and Poyning's Laws Explained. Dublin: 1770. V. 42

FRENCH, S. G.

Two Wars: an Autobiography; Mexican War, War Between the States Diary . . . Nashville: 1901. V. 38

FRENCH, SAMUEL G.

Two Wars: an Autobiography of Gen. Samuel G. French. Nashville: 1901. V. 37

FRENCH-SHELDON, M. BEBE BWANA

Adventures in East Africa; or Sultan to Sultan. Boston: 1892. V. 40

FRENCH, W. J.

Wild Jim the Texas Cowboy and Saddle King. Antioch: 1890. V. 37; 39

FRENCH, WILLIAM

Instruction for Field Artillery. Philadelphia: 1860. V. 46

Some Recollections of a Western Ranchman, New Mexico, 1883-1889. London: 1927. V. 38; 42; 43; 45; 46

Some Recollections of a Western Ranchman: New Mexico 1883-1899. New York: 1928. V. 44; 45

Some Recollections of a Western Ranchman New Mexico 1883-1889. (with) Further Recollections of a Western Ranchman . . . New York: 1965. V. 37; 43; 45

FRENCH, WILLIAM H.

Instruction for Field Artillery. Philadelphia: 1860. V. 42

FRENCH, WILLIAM J.

Wild Jim the Texas Cowboy and Saddle King. Antioch: 1890. V. 40; 45

FRENEAU, PHILIP

Letters on Various Intersting and Important Subjects; Many of Which Have Appeared in the Aurora. Philadelphia: 1799. V. 46

FRENEAU, PHILIP continued

Poems on Various Subjects, But Chiefly Illustrative of the Events and Actors in the American War of Independence. London: 1861. V. 40

Poems Written Between the Years 1768 & 1794. Monmouth: 1795. V. 39; 40; 41; 42; 43; 44; 45

Poems Written and Published During the American Revolutionary War and Now Republished from the Original Manuscripts . . . Philadelphia: 1809. V. 40; 41

The Travels of the Imagination; A True Journey from Newcastle to London. Philadelphia: 1778. V. 37

FRENEAU, PHILIP MORIN 1752-1832

Poems Written Between the Years 1768 and 1795. Monmouth: 1795. V. 38

FRERE, ALICE M.

The Antipodes and Round the World. London: 1870. V. 39; 45

FRERE, BENJAMIN

The Adventures of a Dramatist . . . London: 1813. V. 40; 46

FRERE, GEORGES

A Short History of Barbados, From Its Discovery and Settlement, to the End of the Year 1767. London: 1768. V. 42

FRERE, JOHN HOOKHAM

Prospectus and Specimens of an Intended National Work, by William & Robert Whistlecraft, of Stow-marker in Suffolk, Harness and Collar-Makers. London: 1818. V. 45

Prospectus and Specimen of an Intended National Work, by William and Robert Whistlecraft, of Stow-Market in Suffolk, Harness and Collar-Makers. Bath: 1842. V. 40

Theognis Restiutus. Malta: 1842. V. 37

The Works . . . in Verse and Prose. London: 1872. V. 40; 42; 43

The Works . . . in Verse and Prose. London: 1874. V. 39; 42

FRERICHS, F. T.

A Clinical Treatise on the Diseases of the Liver. New York: 1879. V. 39; 42

FRESCHEUR, FRANCISCUS DAVID

Exercitatio Physica, de Artifico Navigandi per ARem. Rinteln: 1676. V. 42

FRESHFIELD, DOUGLAS

The Exploration of the Caucasus. London & New York: 1896. V. 39; 41

FRESHFIELD, DOUGLAS W.

The Exploration of the Caucasus. London: 1896. V. 37; 43; 45

Round Kanchenjunga. London: 1903. V. 46

Travels in the Central Caucasus and Bashan, Including Visits to Ararat and Tabrez, and Ascents of Kazbek and Elburuz. London: 1869. V. 37; 39; 42

FRESHFIELD, JANE QUENTIN CRAWFORD d. 1901

Alpine Byways or Light Leaves Gathered in 1859 and 1860 by a Lady. London: 1861. V. 45

FRESHMAN, CHARLES

The Autobiography of the Rev. Charles Freshman. Toronto: 1868. V. 43

FRESHWATER Fishes of Europe. Volume 1, part 1, Petromyzontiformes. Wiesbaden: 1986. V. 37

FRESNOY, CHARLES ALPHONSE

The Art of Painting. London: 1716. V. 38

FRESSMARKLE, HERCULES SAMSON, PSEUD.

Cupid Abroad. Philadelphia: 1846. V. 40

FRETZ, A. J.

A Genealogical Record of the Descendants of Christian and Hans Meyer and Other Pioneers. Harleysville: 1896. V. 46

FREUD, ANNA

The Writings of Anna Freud. New York: 1968-74. V. 39

FREUD, SIGMUND

An Autobiographical Study. London: 1935. V. 40

Bemerkungen Uber Cocainsucht und Cocainfurcht . . . Berlin: 1887. V. 41

Beyond the Pleasure Principle. London: 1922. V. 40

Beyond the Pleasure Principle. New York: 1922. V. 43

Civilization and its Discontents. New York: 1930. V. 39

Collected Papers. New York: 1924-25. V. 44

Collected Papers. London: 1949. V. 38

Collected Papers. London: 1950. V. 46

Collected Papers. London: 1953-56. V. 44

Collected Papers. New York: 1959. V. 45; 46

Standard Edition of the Complete Psychological Works of Sigmund Freud. London: 1989. V. 45

Das Ich und das Es. Leipzig, Vienna, Zurich: 1923. V. 37

Die Traumdeutung. V. 45

Die Traumdeutung. Leipzig: 1900. V. 44; 45; 46

Die Traumdeutung. Leipzig und Wien: 1900. V. 45

Die Traumdeutung . . . mit Beitragen von Dr. Otto Rank. Leipzig & Vienna: 1921. V. 41

The Ego and the Id. London: 1927. V. 43; 46

Ein Teufelsneurose Im 17. Jahrhundert. Wien: 1928. V. 46

The Future of Illusion. London: 1928. V. 40

A General Introduction to Psychoanalysis. New York: 1920. V. 43; 45

Group Psychology and the Analysis of the Ego. London: 1922. V. 40

The History of the Psychoanalytic Movement. New York: 1916. V. 38

Inhibitions, Symptoms and And Anxiety. 1936. V. 38; 39

Inhibitions, Symptoms and Anxiety. London: 1936. V. 40

Das Interesse an Der Psychoanalyse. Bologna: 1913. V. 41

The Interpretation of Dreams. New York: 1913. V. 41; 43; 45

The Interpretation of Dreams. London: 1954. V. 43

The Interpretation of Dreams. New York: 1955. V. 45

Introductory Lectures on Psycho-Analysis. London: 1922. V. 45

Moses and Monotheism. New York: 1939. V. 37

An Outline of Psycho-Analysis. London: 1949. V. 41

Psychoanalytische Bemerkungen Uber Einen Autobiographisch Beschriebenen Fall Von Paranoria. 1911. V. 45

The Standard Edition of the Complete Psychological Works of Sigmund Freud . . . London: 1966-74. V. 46

Reflections on War and Death. New York: 1918. V. 44

Studien Uber Hysterie. Leipzig & Vienna: 1895. V. 37

Studies in Hysteria. New York: 1936. V. 37; 40

Totem and Taboo. London: 1919. V. 42

Ueber Frauenemancipation. Plato. Arbeiterfrage. Sozialismus. John Von John Stuart Mill. Uebersezt von Siegmnund Freud. John Stuart Mill's Gesammelte Werke. Autorisierte Uebersetzung unter . . . Leipzig: 1880. V. 37

Wit and the Unconscious. 1916. V. 43

Wit and Its Relation to the Unconscious. London: 1916. V. 37

Wit and Its Relation to the Unconscious. Authorized English Edition with Introduction by A. A. Brill, Ph.B., M.D. New York: 1916. V. 37

Zur Aetiologie der Hysterie. Wein: 1896. V. 41

Zur Technik der Psychoanalyse und Zur Metapsychologie. Leipzig: 1924. V. 37

FREUNDLICH, AUGUST L.

William Gropper: Retorspective. Los Angeles: 1968. V. 40; 41; 45; 46

FREWEN, MORETON

Melton Mowbray and Other Memories. London: 1924. V. 46

FREY, JOSEPH SAMUEL

A Hebrew, Latin and English Dictionary. London: 1815. V. 40

FREY, JOSEPH SAMUEL CHRISTIAN FREDERICK

Essays on Christian Baptism . . . Newark: 1830. V. 41

A Hebrew Grammar, in the English Langauge . . . London: 1823. V. 41

FREY, SAMUEL C. F.

The Converted Jew; or Memoirs of the Life . . . Boston: 1815. V. 45

FREYCINET, LOUIS DE

Report Fait a l'Academie Royale Des Sciences de l'Institut dans la Seance du Decembre 1820. Paris: 1820. V. 41

FREYCINET, ROSE DE

Journal de Madame Rose de Saulces de Freycinet. Paris: 1927. V. 45

FREYGANG, FREDERICA

Letters from the Caucasus and Georgia. London: 1823. V. 37; 39; 40; 43

FREYLINGHAUSEN, JOHN A.

An Abstract of the Whole Doctrine of the Christian Religion. London: 1804. V. 38

FREYTAG, GUSTAV

Our Forefathers. London: 1873. V. 41

FREYTAS, NICHOLAS DE

The Expedition of Don Diego Dionisio de Penalosa, Governor of New Mexico, from Santa Fe to the River Mischip and Quivira in 1662 as Described by . . . New York: 1882. V. 37

FREZIER, AMADEE FRANCOIS 1682-1773

Relation du Voyage de la Mer du Sud aux Cortes de Chily et du Perou, Fait Pendant les Annees 1712, 1713, 1714 . . . Paris: 1716. V. 38

La Theorie et la Pratique de la Coupe des Pierres et des Bois, Pour la Construction des Voutes et Autres Parties des Batimens Civils & Militaires, Ou Traite de Stereotomie . . . Paris: 1754. V. 38

FREZIER, AMEDEE FRANCOIS

A Voyage to the South Sea . . . London: 1717. V. 39; 40; 42; 43; 45; 46

FREZIER, M.

La Theorie et la Pratique de la Coupe des Pierres et des Bois, Pour la Construction des Voutes et Autres Parties des Taimens Civils and Militaires, ou Tratie de Sterotomie a l'Usage de l'Architecture. Strasbourg: 1737/38/39. V. 44

FRIAS, PEDRO DE

Relacion del Martirio de Treinta y un Martires, Religiosos, Y Terceros, Hijos de Nuestro Padre San Francisco Los Veinte y Nueve en el Japon, Y Los Dos en Las Indias del Nuevo-Mexico. Madrid: 1633. V. 39

FRICK, CHARLES

Renal Affections: Their Diagnosis and Pathology. Philadelphia: 1850. V. 40

FRICKER, KARL

Antarctic Regions. London: 1804. V. 45

The Antarctic Regions. London: 1900. V. 43

The Antarctic Regions. London: New York: 1900. V. 42

FRIDGE, IKE

History of the Chisum War; or, Life of Ike Fridge. Electra: 1927. V. 37; 42

FRIED, MICHAEL

Morris Louis. New York. V. 39; 42; 46

FRIEDAN, BETTY

The Feminine Mystique. New York: 1963. V. 43

FRIEDENWALD, HARRY

Life, Letters and Addresses of Aaron Friedenwald. Baltimore: 1906. V. 38

FRIEDERICH II, EMPEROR OF GERMANY 1194-1250

The Art of Falconry. Stanford: 1961. V. 45

The Art of Falconry. 1969. V. 46

FRIEDLAENDER, JOHNNY

Friedlaender Etchings, Eaux-Fortes, Radierungen. Greenwich: 1972. V. 41

Johnny Friedlaender: Oeuvre, 1961-1965. New York. V. 43

FRIEDLAENDER, WALTER

Caravaggio Studies. Princeton: 1955. V. 37; 40

FRIEDLANDER, LEE

The American Monument. New York: 1976. V. 41; 44

FRIEDLANDER, MAX

The Paintings of Lucas Cranach. Ithaca: 1978. V. 46

FRIEDLANDER, WALTER

Caravaggio Studies. Prineton: 1955. V. 46

FRIEDMAN, B. H.

Almost a Life. New York: 1975. V. 44

FRIEDMAN, BRUCE JAY

Scuba Duba. New York. V. 46

Stern. New York: 1962. V. 46

FRIEDMAN, CHARLES

Charles Sheeler. New York: 1975. V. 46

FRIEDMAN, HERBERT

Birds Collected by the Childs Frick Expedition to Ethiopia and Kenya Colony. Washington: 1930-37. V. 40

FRIEDMAN, I. K.

The Lucky Number. Chicago: 1896. V. 38; 46

FRIEDMAN, M.

Charles Sheeler: Paintings, Drawings, Photographs. New York: 1975. V. 46

FRIEDMAN, MORRIS

The Pinkerton Labor Spy. New York: 1907. V. 42

FRIEDMANN, HERBERT

Birds Collected by the Childs Frick Expedition to Ethiopia and Kenya Colony. Part I: Non-Passeres; Part II: Passeres. Washington: 1930-37. V. 46

FRIEDRICH II, DER GROSE, KING OF PRUSSIA 1712-1786

Memoirs of the House of Brandenburg. London: 1748. V. 41

FRIEDRICH II, DER GROSSE, KING OF PRUSSIA 1712-1786

Anti-Machiavel; or, an Examination of Machiavel's Prince. London: 1741. V. 39; 42; 45

Familiar and friendly Correspondence of Frederick the Second, King of Prussia. London: 1787. V. 40

Epitre au Marquis d'Argens du 23 Septembre 1757. Montagnola: 1924. V. 45

L'Esprit du Chev. Folard tire de Ses Commentaires sur l'Histoire de Polybe pour l'Usage d'un Officier de Main de Mattre. Paris: 1760. V. 42

Instructions Militaires du Roi de Prusse Pour Ses Generaux. London: 1762. V. 42

Memoirs of the House of Brandenburg from the Earliest Accounts, to the Death of Frederick I. A Supplement to the Memoirs of the House of Brandenburg . . . London: 1751-68. V. 39

FRIEDRICH II, EMPEROR OF GERMANY 1194-1250

The Art of Falconry. Stanford: 1943. V. 39; 40

The Art of Falconry. Oxford: 1955. V. 39; 41

The Art of Falconry. Stanford: 1961. V. 40

The Art of Falconry. USA: 1969. V. 45

Qvermonia Friderici II. Imp. Qva Se A Romano Pontifice, & Cardinalibus Immerito Persecutum & Imperio Deiectum Esse, Ostendit . . . Hagenau: 1529. V. 40

FRIEDRICH WILHELM II, KING OF PRUSSIA

Memoirs of the House of Brandenburg from the Earliest Accounts, to the Death of Frederic I King of Prussia. London: 1758. V. 39

THE FRIEND. Honolulu: 1852. V. 41

FRIEND, DONALD

An Alphabet of Owls et cetera. South Melbourne: 1981. V. 41

FRIEND, H. KREBS

The Heardboy. Paris: 1926. V. 44

FRIEND, HERVE

Picturesque Los Angeles County, California. Chicago: 1887. V. 41

FRIEND, J.

The History of Physick from the Time of Galen to the Beginning of the Sixteenth Century. London: 1726-27. V. 37

THE FRIEND of Virtue. London: 1789. V. 37

A FRIENDLY Conference Concerning the New Oath of Allegiance to K. William and Q. Mary. London: 1689. V. 40

FRIENDS OF A RAILROAD TO SAN FRANCISCO

Preceedings of the Friends of a Rail-Road to San Francisco, at their Public Meeting, held at the U.S. Hotel in Boston, April 19, 1849 . . . Boston: 1849. V. 37

FRIENDS OF PHOTOGRAPHY

Untitled. Carmel and San Francisco: 1972-88. V. 41

FRIENDS, SOCIETY OF

A Brief Account of the Proceedings of the Committe, Appointed by the Yearly Meeting of Friends, Held in Baltimore for Promoting the Improvement and Civilization of the Indian Natives. Baltimore: 1806. V. 38

A Collection of Memorials Concerning Divers Deceased Ministers and Others of the People Called Quakers. Philadelphia: 1787. V. 42

Two Epistles, Taken Out of G. Fox's Collection of Epistles. Philadelphia: 1716? V. 40; 42

FRIENDS, SOCIETY OF. LONDON YEARLY MEETING.

Some Account of the Conduct of the Religious Society of Friends Towards the Indian Tribes in the Settlement of the Colonies of East and West Jersey and Pennsylvania. London: 1844. V. 40

FRIENDSHIP and Love from the Philosophers. London: 1909. V. 40

THE FRIENDSHIP of Amis and Amile. Hammersmith: 1894. V. 37

FRIENDSHIP, Progress, Civilization - Three Wartime Speeches to the Anglo-Swedish Society. London: 1943. V. 45

FRIENDSHIP'S Offering; and Winter's Wealth: a Christmas and New Year's Present, for MDCCCXXXVIII. London: 1838. V. 46

FRIERMAN, JAY D.

The Natalie Wood Collection of Pre-Columbian Ceramics from Chupicuaro, Guanajuato, Mexico, at UCLA. Los Angeles: 1969. V. 37; 38

FRIES, LORENZ

Spiegel der Artzney. Strassburg: 1529. V. 42; 44

FRIESNER, ISIDORE

Cerebellar Abscess, Its Etiology, Pathology, Diagnosis and Treatment, Including Anatomy and Physiology of the Crebellum. New York: 1916. V. 42

FRIGERIO, BARTOLOMEO d. 1636

L'Economo Prudente. Rome: 1629. V. 43

FRIGGE, KARLI

Marbled Landscapes. Buren: 1988. V. 42

Marbled Paper. Buren: 1985. V. 40

Marbled Paper. By Karli Frigge. (Translated by Tanya and Hans Schmoller). Netherlands: 1985. V. 37

Marbled Plants. Buren: 1988. V. 42; 43

FRILINGHUISEN, THEODORUS JACOBUS

Klagte van Eenige Leeden der Nederduytse Hervormde Kerk, Woonende of Raretans &c . . . New York: 1725. V. 42

FRINK, ELIZABETH

Elizabeth Frink's Etchings Illustrating Chaucer's Canterbury Tales. London: 1972. V. 37

FRINK, MARGARET A.

Journal of the Adventures of a Party of California Gold-Seekers Under the Guidance of Mr. Ledyard Frink During a Journey Across the Plains from Martinsville, Indiana, to Sacramento, California. Oakland: 1897. V. 37; 40; 42; 46

FRISBIE, LEVI

An Oration on Account of the Happy Restoration of Peace Between Great Britain and the United States. Boston: 1783. V. 39; 43

FRISCHLIN, NICODEMUS

Hebraeis. Strassburg: 1599. V. 38

Operum Poeticarum Pars Scenica, in qua sunt Comoediae Sex . . . Tragoediae Duo . . . In the end: Phasma. Strasbourg: 1598, 1595. V. 39

FRISIUS, ERNESTUS EREMUNDUS

Origo & Historia Belgicorvm Tvmvltvvm Immanissimaeque Crudelitatis per Cliviam & Westphaliam Patratae Fidelissime Conscripta & Tabellis Aeneis Repraesentata. Leiden: 1619. V. 40

FRISTOE, WILLIAM

A Concise History of the Ketocton Baptist Association. Staunton: 1808. V. 45

FRISTRUP, BORGE

The Greenland Ice Cap. 1966. V. 37

FRISWELL, J. HAIN

Varia: Readings from Rare Books. London: 1866. V. 40

FRISWOLD, CARROLL

The Killing of Chief Crazy Horse. Glendale: 1976. V. 45

FRITH, DAVID

Pageant of Cricket. London: 1987. V. 44

FRITH, FRANCIS

Egypt and Palestine. London: 1858-59. V. 44

Frith's Photo Pictures. Ambleside: 1870. V. 38

The Gossiping Photographer on the Rhine. Reigate (Surrey): 1864. V. 38; 45

The Gossipping Photographer on the Rhine. Frith: 1864. V. 43

Lower Egypt, Thebes, and the Pyramids. London: (1862?). V. 37

Sinai and Palestine; Upper Egypt and Ethiopia; Egypt, Sinai and Palestine; Lower Egypt and Thebes. London: 1862. V. 42

Upper Egypt and Nubia. London: (1862?). V. 37

FRITH, JOHN

A Boke Made by John Fryth Prysoner in the Tower of London Answerynge unto M. Mores letter . . . Newly Corrected. Antwerp: 1548. V. 41

A Boke Made by John Fryth Prysoner in the Tower of London, Answerynge into M. Mores Letter . . . London: 1548. V. 46

FRITH, W. P.

My Autobiography and Reminiscences. London: 1888. V. 39

FRITH, WILLIAM POWELL

John Leech, His Life and Work. London: 1891. V. 37; 38; 40

FRITSCH, A.

Birds of Europe. London: 1877. V. 37

FRITSCHE, MARCUS fl. 1555-1563

Meteorovm, hoc est, Impressionum Aerearum et Mirabilium Naturae Operum . . . Nuremberg: 1555. V. 43; 44

FRIZZELL, LODISA

Across the Plains to California in 1852. New York: 1915. V. 39; 40; 46

FROBENIUS, LEO

The Voice of Africa. London: 1913. V. 40

FROBESE, F. E.

The Origin and Meaning of the Totem Poles in South Eastern Alaska. Sitka: 1897. V. 39

FRODIN, D. G.

Guide to Standard Floras of the World. Cambridge: 1984. V. 37; 38

FRODIN, OTTO

Asine: Results of the Swedish Excavations 1922-1930. Stockholm: 1938. V. 40

FROEBEL, FRIEDRICH

The Education of man. New York: 1885. V. 41; 43

Mother Play and Nursery Songs. Boston: 1878. V. 40

FROEBEL, JULIUS

Seven Years' Travel in Central American, Northern Mexico and the Far West of the United States. London: 1859. V. 37; 39; 40

FROGER, F.

Relation d'un Voyage de la Mer Du Sud. Detroit de Magellan Bresil, Cayenne et les Iles Antilles . . . Amsterdam: 1715. V. 43

FROGER, FRANCOIS

A Relation of a Voyage Made in the Years 1695, 1696, 1697 on the Coasts of Africa. London: 1698. V. 45; 46

FROGGATT, W. W.

Some Useful Australian Birds. Sydney: 1921. V. 40

FROHAWK, F. W.

Natural History of British Butterflies. London: 1914. V. 37

Natural History of British Butterflies. London: 1925. V. 37

FROHLICH-BUME, L.

Ingres His Life and Art. London: 1926. V. 40; 42; 43; 44

FROISSANT, JEAN

The Chronicle. London: 1525. V. 37; 38; 40

FROISSART, JEAN

The Cronycles of Englande. London: 1523-25. V. 44

The Cronycles of England, France, Spain . . . etc. London: 1523-25. V. 46

(Chronicles) Here Begynneth the First Volum of Syr Johan Froyssart . . . London: 1525. V. 41

(Chronicles) Here Begynneth the First Volum of Syr Johan Froyssart . . . London: 1535/42 & 1525. V. 45

Histoire et Chronique Memorable de Messire Iehan Froissart. Paris: 1574. V. 40

Chronicles of England, France, Spain and the Adjoining Countries . . . London: 1805-06. V. 42

Chronicles of England, France, Spain and the Adjoining Countries . . . London: 1806. V. 45

Chronicles of England, France, Spain . . . London: 1812. V. 39

Chronicles of England, France, Spain and the Adjoining Countries from the Latter Part of the Reign of Edward II, to the Coronation of Henry IV. London: 1839. V. 46

Chronicles of England, France, Spain and the Adjoining Countries . . . London: 1839. V. 38; 45

The Chronicles of Sir John Froissart. London: 1842-44. V. 44

Chronicles of England, France, Spain and the Adjoining Countries . . . (with) Illuminated Illustrations of Froissart Selected from the MS. in the British Museum and in the Bibliotheque Royale. London: 1844. V. 41

Chronicles of England, France, Spain and the Adjoining Countries from the Latter Part of the Reign of Edward Ii to the Coronation of henry IV. London: 1857. V. 46

Chronicles of England, France, Spain and the Adjoining Countries From the Latter Part of the Reign of Edward II to the Coronation of Henry IV. London: 1874. V. 40

The Chronicles. Hammersmith: 1896. V. 46

The Chronicle of Froissart. London: 1901-03. V. 46

The Chronicles. New York: 1920. V. 46

Froissarts Chronycles. London: 1927. V. 43; 45

Cronycles. Oxford: 1927. V. 38

Froissart's Croncyles. Oxford: 1927. V. 38

Froissarts Cronycles. Stratford-upon-Avon: 1927. V. 39; 41; 42

Froissart's Chronycles. Oxford: 1927-28. V. 39; 46

Froissart's Chronycles of Englande, France, Spayne, Portynglae, Sctolande, Bretayne, Flaunders . . . Stratford-on-Avon: 1927-28. V. 38; 41; 42; 44; 46

The Chronicles of England, France, Spain and Other Places. New York: 1959. V. 40; 44

Of the Batayle of Cre-cy Bytwene the King of England & the French King from the Chronicles of Froissart. Shropshire: 1986. V. 40

Chronicles of England, France, Spain and the Adjoining Countries, from the Latter Part of the Reign of Edward II, to the Cornoation of Henry IV. London: 1844. V. 37

FROISSART, JEAN continued

Chronicles of England, France, Spain and the Adjoining Countries, from the Latter Part of the Reign of Edward II to the Coronation of Henry IV . . . London: 1852. V. 37

Chronicles of England, France, Spain & the adjoining Countries . . . Transalted from the French Editions . . . by Thomas Johnes, Esq. To which are prefixed, a Life of the Author, an Essay on His Works, & A Criticism On His History. In Two Volumes. London: 1844. V. 37

Historiarum Opus Omne. Paris: 1537. V. 41; 44

Le Premier (-Quart) Volume de Froissart. Des Cronicques de France . . . et Lieux Circonvoisins. Paris: 1518. V. 37

Sir John Froissart's Chronicles of England, France, Spain, Portugal, Scotland, Brittany, Flanders and Adjoining Countries. London: 1812. V. 37

Stories from Froissart. London: 1832. V. 43

FROISSART, JOHN

Chronicles of England, France, Spain and the Adjoining . . . London: 1839. V. 46

FROLICH, LORENZ

The Little Darling at the Sea Side. London: 1880. V. 46

FROM Manifesto to Trial. A Full History of the Jameson Raid and the Trial of the Members of the Reform Committe and of Dr. Jameson and His Staff. Johannesburg: 1896. V. 39

FROM the Land of the Rising Sun. London: 1890. V. 39

FROMBERG, EMANUEL OTTO

An Essay on the Art of Painting on Glass. London: 1851. V. 44

FRONTIER and Overseas Expeditions from India. Volume VI. Expeditions Overseas. Calcutta: 1911. V. 40

FRONTIER Crossings (The 45th World Science Fiction Convention Book). Brighton: 1987. V. 39

FRONTINUS, SEXTUS J.

Stratagemi Militari, Tradotti in Lingva Italiana, et Novamente Mandati in Lvce de Marc'Antonio Gandino. Venetia: 1574. V. 42

FRORIEP, AUGUST

Zur Kenntniss der Lagebeziehungen Zwischen Grosshirn und Schadeldach bein Menschen Verschiedener Kopfform. Leipzig: 1897. V. 45

FRORIEP, ROBERT

Chirurgische Anatomie der Ligaturstellen am Menschlichen Korper. Weimar: 1830. V. 42

FROSSARD, E.

Vues Prises Dans les Pyrenees Francaises . . . Paris: 1829. V. 39

FROST, ARTHUR BURDETT

A Portfolio of Twelve Original Illustrations . . . to Illustrate the Pickwick Papers. London: 1908. V. 40

FROST, CHARLES

An Address Delivered to the Literary and Philosophical Society at Kingston-upon-Hull . . . on Friday November 5th, 1830. Hull: 1831. V. 45

Notices Relative to the Early History of the Town and Port of Hull. (with) Select Views Illustrative of the History and Antiquites of the Town of Kingston-upon-Hull. Hull. V. 39

Notices Relative to the Early History of the Town and Port of Hull. London: 1827. V. 38; 39; 43; 45

FROST, DONALD M.

Notes on General Ashley the Overland Trail and South Pass. Worcester: 1945. V. 37; 40; 41; 43; 46

FROST, H. GORDON

I'm Frank Hammer: the Life of a Texas Peace Officer. Austin: 1968. V. 42

FROST, J.

The Mexican War and its Warriors . . . New Haven: 1849. V. 39; 45

FROST, JAMES

The History and Topography of the County of Clare, from the Earliest Times to the Beginning of the 18th Century. Dublin: 1978. V. 43

FROST, JENNETT BLAKESLEE

California's Greatest Curse. San Francisco: 1879. V. 38

FROST, JOHN

American Naval Biography . . . Philadelphia: 1844. V. 42

The Art of Swimming; a Series of Practical Instructions . . . New York: 1818. V. 45

The Book of the Navy. New York: 1842. V. 41

The Book of the Army . . . New York: 1846. V. 41; 42

The Class Book of American Literature . . . . Boston: 1826. V. 43

History of the State of California: From the Period of the Conquest by Spain, to Her Occupation by the United States of America. Containing an Account of the Discovery of the Immense Gold Mines and Placers . . . Auburn, N.Y.: 1850. V. 37

The Mexican War and Its Warriors . . . New Haven: 1849. V. 42

Pictorial History of Mexico and the Mexican War. Philadelphia: 1849. V. 42

FROST, LAWRENCE A.

Custer's 7th Cavalry and the Campaign of 1873. El Segundo,: 1986. V. 45

Some Observations on the Yellowstone Expedition of 1873. Glendale: 1981. V. 45

FROST, MAX

New Mexico Its Resources Climate Geography . . . Santa Fe: 1890. V. 42

FROST, ROBERT 1874-1963

Aforesaid. New York: 1951. V. 39

A Boy's Will. London: 1913. V. 39; 40; 41; 42; 43; 45; 46

A Boy's Will. New York: 1935. V. 39

A Boy's Will. New York: 1915. V. 37; 41; 42; 43; 45

A Cabin in the Clearing. New York: 1951. V. 39

Collected Poems. New York: 1939. V. 39; 45; 46

Collected Poems. New York: 1940. V. 40

Collected Poems of Robert Frost 1939. New York: 1945. V. 43

Collected Poems. New York: 1930. V. 37; 41; 43; 45

Come in and Other Poems. New York: 1943. V. 44

Complete Poems. V. 39

Complete Poems of Robert Frost. New York: 1948. V. 44

Complete Poems. New York: 1949. V. 39

The Complete Poems. New York: 1950. V. 37; 39; 40; 41; 46

Complete Poems. London: 1951. V. 41; 43

A Considerable Speck. N.P.: 1939. V. 37

Dedication and the Gift Outright. New York: 1961. V. 45

Education by Poetry - A Meditative Monologue. Amherst: 1931. V. 37

The Falls. Los Angeles: 1947. V. 37

Fifty Years of Robert Frost. Hanover: 1944. V. 37; 40; 42; 46

The Four Beliefs. 1944. V. 37

From a Milkwood Pod. New York: 1954. V. 39

From Snow to Snow. New York: (1936). V. 37; 44

A Further Range. New York: 1936. V. 39; 40; 43; 45; 46

The Gold Hesperidee. Cortland: 1935. V. 39

Greece. Chicago: 1948. V. 46

The Guardeen. Los Angeles: 1943. V. 37

Hard Not to Be King. New York: 1951. V. 42

In the Clearing. 1962. V. 39

In the Clearing. New York: 1962. V. 39; 40; 41; 42; 43; 44; 46

The Lone Striker. New York: 1933. V. 39

The Lovely Shall Be Choosers. New York: 1929. V. 43

A Masque of Mercy. New York: 1947. V. 37; 38; 39; 40; 41; 43; 44; 45; 46

A Masque of Reason. New York: 1945. V. 37; 38; 39; 40; 41; 44

Mountain Interval. New York: 1924. V. 39

Mountain Interval. New York: 1916. V. 37; 46

Neither Out Far Nor in Deep. New York: 1935. V. 40

New Hampshire, a Poem . . . New York: 1923. V. 38; 39; 41; 42

New Hampshire; a Poem. 1955. V. 40

New Hampshire. Hanover: 1955. V. 39

North of Boston. London: 1914. V. 37; 38; 39; 40; 41; 42; 45; 46

North of Boston. New York: 1915. V. 39

North of Boston. New York: 1917. V. 39

North of Boston. New York: 1919. V. 46

North of Boston. New York: 1926. V. 39

On the Inflation of the Currency: 1919. Los Angeles: 1948. V. 44

On a Tree Fallen Across the Road. New York: 1949. V. 38; 41

Percy MacKay. A Symposium on His Fiftieth Birthday 1925. Foreword by Amy Lowell. Hanover, NH: 1928. V. 37; 42

Selected Poems. New York: 1923. V. 40; 41; 42; 44

Selected Poems. New York: (1938). V. 37

Collected Poems, 1939. New York: (1939). V. 37

The Poetry of Amy Lowell. Boston: 1925. V. 39

The Poetry of Amy Lowell. V. 44

Several Short Poems. New York: 1924. V. 44; 46

Steeple Bush. New York: 1947. V. 37; 38; 39; 40; 41; 43; 46

To a Young Wretch. Amherst: 1937. V. 37

Triple Plate. London: 1939. V. 40

Triple Plate. New York: 1939. V. 45

An Unstamped Letter in Our Rural Mailbox. New York: 1944. V. 40; 42

FROST, ROBERT 1874-1963 continued

Watch the Northwind Rise. New York: 1949. V. 43

A Way Out. New York: 1929. V. 37; 39; 41; 42; 46

West Running Brook. New York: 1928. V. 37; 39; 40; 41; 42; 43; 44; 46

What Became Of New England? V. 41; 42

What Became of New England? 1937. V. 42

What Bcame of New England? Oberlin: 1938. V. 37; 40; 42; 46

Wilfred Davison Memorial Library. 1930. V. 37

A Witness Tree. New York: 1942. V. 39; 41; 42; 43; 46

FROST, W. ADAMS

The Fundus Oculi With an Ophthalmoscopic Atlas Illustrating Its Physiological and Pathological Conditions. Edinburgh: 1896. V. 40; 42

The Fundus Oculi, with An Ophthalmoscopic Atlas, Illustrating Its Physiological and Pathological Conditions. Edinburgh & London: 1896. V. 41

FROTHINGHAM, OCTAVIUS BROOKS

Gerrit Smith, a Biography. New York: 1878. V. 45; 46

FROTHINGHAM, RICHARD

History of the Siege of Boston and of the Battles of Lexington, Concord, and Bunker Hill. Boston: 1849. V. 38

FROUDE, J. A.

The English in the West Indies. London: 1888. V. 43

FROUDE, JAMES ANTHONY

The Book of Job. London: 1854. V. 37

The English in Ireland in the Eighteenth Century. London: 1872. V. 46

The English in Ireland in the 18th Century. London: 1872-74. V. 40

The English in the West Indies or the Bow of Ulysses. London: 1888. V. 38

Historical Works . . . London: 1856-96. V. 40

The History of England . . . London: 1862. V. 42

History of England, from the Fall of Wolsey to the Defeat of the Spanish Armada. London: 1870-75. V. 39

History of England. New York: 1875. V. 39; 40

History of England from the Fall of Wolsey to the Defeat of the Spanish Armada. London: 1880. V. 39; 42; 46

The Influence of the Science of Political Economy on the Moral and Social Welfare of a Nation. Oxford: 1842. V. 37

The Nemesis of Faith. London: 1849. V. 37

Shadows of the Clouds. London: 1847. V. 40; 42

Short Studies on Great Subjects. London: 1892. V. 39

Short Studies in Great Subjects. London: 1909. V. 38

The Spanish Story of the Armada, and Other Essays. London: 1892. V. 38

Two Lectures on South Africa. Delivered Before the Philosophical Institute Edinburgh, Jan. 6 & 9, 1880. 1880. V. 39

FROWHAWK, F. W.

Natural History of British Butterflies. London: 1914. V. 38

Natural History of British Butterflies. London: 1924. V. 38

FRY, C. B.

The Book of Cricket. London: 1899. V. 42

FRY, CAROLINE

The Assistant of Education: Religious and Literary. London: 1823-27. V. 40

A Word to Women, the Love of the Wold, and Other Gatherings: Being a Collection of Short Stories. Philadelphia: 1840. V. 37

FRY, CHARLES BURGESS

The Book of Cricket. London: 1899. V. 44

FRY, CHRISTOPHER

The Boy With a Cart -Cuthman, Saint of Sussex, a Play. London: 1939. V. 38; 43

Root and Sky. 1975. V. 38

Root and Sky. 1975. V. 40; 45

Root & Sky. Boston: 1975. V. 39

Root & Sky. Cambridge: 1975. V. 37; 39; 46

Root & Sky. Boston: 1976. V. 38; 44

FRY, EDMUND 1754-1835

Pantographia. London: 1799. V. 38; 40; 41; 42; 46

Specimen of Printing Types by Edmund Fry, Letter Founder to the King and Prince Regent . . . London: 1816. V. 41

FRY, ELIZABETH

Prison Discipline. Manchester: 1848. V. 42

FRY, ELIZABETH GURNEY 1780-1845

Memoir of the Life and Extracts from Her Journal and Letters. London: 1847. V. 37; 38; 39; 41

FRY, F.

Fry's Traveller's Guide. Cincinnati: 1865. V. 38

FRY, FRANCIS

The Bible by Coverdale, MDXXXV. Remarks on the Titles; the Year of Publication; the Preliminary; the Water-marks, &c., with Fac-similes. Bristol: Lasbury,: 1867. V. 37

A Proper Dyaloge Betwene a Gentillman and a Husbandman Eche Complaynynge to Other Their Miserable Calamite through the Ambicion of Clergye. Brisol: 1863. V. 40

The Souldiers Pocket Bible. London: 1862. V. 38

FRY, FREDERICK

Fry's Traveler's Guide, and Descriptive Journal of the Great North-Western Territories. Cincinnatii: 1865. V. 37; 39; 40; 41; 43; 45

FRY, HENRY

The History of North Atlantic Steam Navigation. London: 1896. V. 39

FRY, HENRY PHIBBS

The Scriptural Evidence of the Apostolic Ministry and Tradition of the Catholic Church. Hobart Town: 1843. V. 39

FRY, J.

Bibliographical Memoranda, in Illustration of Early English Literature. Bristol: 1816. V. 45

FRY, J. REESE

A Life of Zachary Taylor . . . Philadelphia: 1847. V. 46

FRY, JAMES B.

Army Sacrifices; or, Briefs from Official Piegeon Holes. New York: 1879. V. 37; 38; 39; 42; 44; 45

FRY, JOHN

The Legend of Mary, Queen of Scots and Other Ancient Poems . . . London: 1810. V. 38; 41

Select Poems, Containing Religious Epistles &c. To Which is Now Added, The History of Elijah and Elisha. Philadelphia: 1787. V. 39

FRY, JOHN STORRS

An Essay on the Construction of Wheel-Carriages, ad they Affect both the Roads and the Horses; with Suggestions Relating to the principles on whicl Tolls ought to be Imposed, and a Few Remarks on the Formation of Roads. Bristol/London: 1820. V. 37

FRY, JOSEPH

A Specimen of Printing by Joseph Fry and Son, Letter-Founders. London: 1785. V. 43

FRY, JOSEPH, & SONS

A Specimen of Printing Types, by Joseph Fry and Sons, Letter Founders, Worship Street, Moorfields, London, 1785. London: 1785. V. 40

A Specimen of Printing Types by Joseph Fry and Sons, Letter-Founders to the Prince of Wales. London: 1786. V. 45

FRY, JOSEPH STORRS

An Essay on the Construction of Wheel-Carriages As They Affect Both the Roads and the Horses. London: 1820. V. 38; 40

FRY, KATHARINE

History of the Parishes of East and West Ham . . . London: 1888. V. 45

FRY, ROGER

The Artist and Psychoanalysis. London: 1924. V. 41

The Artist and Psycho - Analysis. 1924. V. 37

Cezanne. London: 1927. V. 42

Last Lectures. Cambridge: 1939. V. 40

Polyphemus and Other Poems. London: 1901. V. 46

A Sampler of Castille. London: 1923. V. 41

A Sampler of Castile. Richmond: 1923. V. 45; 46

Ten Architectural Lithographs. London: 1930. V. 44

Transformations. New York: 1926. V. 41; 43; 44; 45; 46

Twelve Original Woodcuts by Roger Fry. Richmond: 1921. V. 41

Twelve Original Woodcuts. London: 1922. V. 38

FRY, ROGER ELIOT 1866-1934

Georgian Art (1760-1820) an Introductory Review of English Painting, Architecture, Sculpture, Ceramic, Glass, Metalwork, Furniture, Textiles and Other Arts During the Reign of George III. London: 1929. V. 39

FRYE, JAMES ALBERT

From Headquarters: odd Tales Picked Up in the Volunteer Service. Boston: 1893. V. 38; 39; 40; 42

FRYE, ROLAND MUSHAT

Milton's Imagery and the Visual Arts. Princeton: 1978. V. 46

FRYER, JANE EAYRE

Mary Frances Cook Book or Adventures Among the Kitchen People. Philadelphia: 1912. V. 37; 45

The Mary Frances Garden Book. Philadelphia: 1916. V. 45

The Mary Frances Sewing Book or Adventures Among the Thimble People. Philadelphia: 1913. V. 45

FRYER, JOHN

A New Account of East-India and Persia, in Eight Letters Being Nine Years Travels, Begun 1672. London: 1698. V. 41; 45

FRYER, MARY ANN

John Fryer of the Bounty. Waltham St. Lawrence: 1939. V. 46

FRYXELL, FRITIOF

William H. Jackson, Photographer, Artist, Explorer. V. 44; 46

FU, MARILYN

Studies in Connoisseurship: Chinese Paintings from the Arthur M. Sackler Collection in New York and Princeton. Princeton: 1973. V. 41

FUCHS, EDUARD

Die Grosen Mesiter der Erotik: Ein Beitrag zum Problem des Schopferischen in der Kunst, Mlerei und Plastik. Munich: 1928. V. 38

FUCHS, LEONARD 1501-1566

Hippocratis Cot Medicorvm Omnivm Sine Controuersia Principis Aphorismoru Sectiones Septem . . . Parisiis: 1545. V. 44; 45

FUCHS, LEONHARD

De Curandi Ratione Libri Octo. Venice: 1556. V. 42

De Historia Stirpium Commentarii Insignes. Basel: 1542. V. 42; 44

De Historia Stirpium Commentarii . . . Basel: 1542. V. 41; 45

Plantarum Effigies . . . ac Quinque Diversis Linguis Redditae . . . Lyon: 1549. V. 42; 45

FUCHS, LEONHART

De Curandi Ratione Libri Octo, Causarum Signorumque Catalogum Breviter Continentes . . . Lugduni: 1552. V. 43

Hippocratis Coi Medicorvm Omnivm Sine Controuersia Principis Aphorismoru Sectiones Septem, Recense, graeco in Latinum Sermonem . . . Parisiis: 1545. V. 46

Plantarum Effigies . . . ac Quinque Diversis Linguis Redditae. Lyon: 1549. V. 46

FUENTES, CARLOS

Chistopher Unborn. New York: 1989. V. 44; 45

The Good Conscience. New York: 1961. V. 44

FUENTES, MANUEL A.

Lima, Sketches of the Capital of Peru, Historical, Statistical, Administrative, Commercial and Moral. Paris: 1886. V. 39; 40; 45

FUERST, JULIUS

Librorum Sacrorum Veteris Testamenti Concordantiae Hebraicae Atque Chaldaicae. Leipzig: 1840. V. 39

FUERST, WALTER RENE

XXth Century Stage Decoration. London: 1928. V. 37; 39

FUGARD, ATHOL

The Blood Knot. Johannesburg: 1963. V. 45

FUGATE, FRANCIS

Spanish Heritage of the Southwest. El Paso: 1952. V. 37; 44; 45

FUGGER, MARCUS

Von der Gestuterey, Das ist Ein Grundtliche Beschreibung wie unnd wa Man ein Gestut von Guten Edlen Kriegrossen Auffirichten . . . Frankfurt am Mayn: 1584. V. 38; 39; 40

FUGGER, MARCUS, BARON 1529-1597

Von der Gestuterey, Das ist Ein Grundtliche Beschreibung Wie unnd wa Man ein Gestut von Guten Edlen Kriegrossen Auffrichten . . . Frankfurt: 1584. V. 42

Von der Gestuterey, Das ist Ein Grundtliche Beschreibung Wie unnd Wa Man Ein Gestut von Guten Edlen Kriegsrossen Auffrichten . . . Mayn: 1584. V. 41

FUGGER, WOLFGANG

Ein Nutzlich und Wolgerundt Formular/Mancherley Schoner Schriefften/als Teutscher, Lateinischer Griechischer, und Hebrayscher Buchstaben . . . Nuernberg: 1597-1605. V. 39

FUGITIVE Pieces, on Various Subjects. London: 1771. V. 43

FUGITIVES: an Anthology of Verse. New York: 1928. V. 38; 41; 42; 44

FUHRMANN, OTTO W.

Gutenberg and the Strasbourg Documents of 1439: an Inerpretation. New York: 1940. V. 38; 40; 44

FUJIWARA, KANESUKE

The Lady Who Loved Insects. 1929. V. 43; 45

The Lady Who Loved Insects. London: 1929. V. 40; 41; 45

FULBECKE, WILLIAM

A Direction or Preparative to the Dusty of the Law (etc.). London: 1620. V. 46

FULD, JAMES J.

A Pictorial Bibliography of the First Editions of Stephen C. Foster. Philadelphia: 1957. V. 41; 46

FULGOSUS, BAPTISTA

De Dictis Factisque Memorabilius Collectanea . . . Milan: 1509. V. 45

FULKE, WILLIAM

Meteors; or, a Plain Description of all Kind of Meteors, As Well Fiery and Ayrie, as Watry and Earthy . . . London: 1655. V. 38; 40; 43

A Most Pleasant Prospect Into the Garden of Natural Contemplation, to Behold the Natural Causes of All Kinde of Meteors . . . London: 1634. V. 40; 41; 44

A Most Pleasant Prospect into the Garden of Natural Contemplation, to Behold the Naturall Causes of all Kinde of Meteors. London: 1640. V. 37; 40

A Retentive to Stay Good Christians, in True Faith and Religion, Against the Motives of Richard Bristow. London: 1580. V. 44

A Sermon Preached at Hampton Court, on Sonday being the 12 Day of November in the Year of Our Lord 1570. London: 1579. V. 44

Two Treatises Written Against the Papistes, the One being an Answere of the Christian Protestant to the Proud Challenge of a Popish Catholicke . . . London: 1577. V. 40; 42; 44

FULKERSON, H. S.

A Civilian's Recollections of the War Between the States. Baton Rouge: 1939. V. 43

Random Recollections of Early Days in Mississippi. Vicksburg: 1885. V. 37; 45

A FULL Account of the Actions of the Late Famous Pyrate, Capt. Kidd, With the Proceedings Against Him, and a Vindiction of the Right Honourable Richard Earl of Bellomont, Lord Coloony, Late Governor of New England . . . Dublin: 1701. V. 40

A FULL Account of the Late Dreadful Earthquake At Port Royal in Jamaica, Written in Two Letters from the Minister at that Place . . . London: 1692. V. 40

A FULL and Complete Account of the Late and Awful Riots in Philadelphia. Philadelphia: 1848. V. 42

A FULL and Impartial Account of the Company of Mississippi, Otherwise Call'd the French East-India-Company, Projected and Settled by Mr. Law. London: 1720. V. 38; 40

A FULL and Impartial Account of the Robberies Committed by John Hawkins, George Sympson (Lately Executed for Robbing the Bristol Mails) and Their Companions. London: 1722? V. 37

A FULL and Particular Account of the Whole Distress and Misfortunes of Nelly Watson, Who Was Hired Servant to Mr. Cox, Vintner, in Chester of the Street Near Durham . . . Edinburgh? London?: 1730-40? V. 42

A FULL And True Account of the Strange and Wonderful Apparitions Which Were Seen Last Night in the Sky, All England Over, to the Great Amazement of the Whole Kingdom. London: 1716. V. 45

A FULL Collection of all Poems Upon Charles, Prince of Wales . . . N.P.: Edinburgh: 1745. V. 40

A FULL Collection of all Poems Upon Charles, Prince of Wales . . . Published Since His Arrival in Edinburgh the 17th Day of September, till the 1st of November 1745. N.P.: 1745. V. 39; 41; 45

A FULL Collection of all Poems Upon Charles, Prince of Wales, Regent of the Kingdoms of Scotland, England, France and Ireland, and Dominons Thereunto Belonging. Edinburgh: 1745. V. 38; 40

A FULL Collection of All Poems Upon Charles, Prince of Wales, Regent of the Kingdoms of Scotland, England, France and Ireland, and the Dominions Thereunto Belonging, Published Since His Arrival in Edinburgh the 17th Day of Sept. till the 1st Nov. 1745. V. 42

A FULL Report of All the Proceedings on the Trial of The Rev. William Jackson, at the Bar of His Majesty's Court of King's Bench, Ireland, on an Indictment for High Treason. Dublin: 1795. V. 45

FULL, THOMAS

The Church-History of Britian; from the Birth of Jesus Christ Until the Year MDCXLVIII. London: 1656, 1655. V. 38

Moral Tales in Verse, Founded on Real Events. London: 1797. V. 43

FULLAM, GEORGE TOWNLEY

The Journal of George Townley Fullam, Boarding Officer of the Confederate Sea Raider Alabama. Birmingham?: 1973. V. 44

FULLARTON, JOHN

On the Regulation of Currencies: Being n Examination of the Principles, on Which it is Proposed to Restrict, Within Certain Fixed Limits, the Future Issues on Credit of the Bank of England. London: 1844. V. 38

FULLARTON, WILLIAM

A Letter, Addressed to the Right Hon. Lord Carrington, President of the Board of Agriculture. London: 1801. V. 39

FULLER, ALVARADO M.

A.D. 2000. Chicago: 1890. V. 38; 46

FULLER, ANDREW S.

The Grape Culturist: a Treatise on the Cultivation of the Native Grape. New York: 1864. V. 38; 40

The Grape Culturist. New York: 1867. V. 38; 40

FULLER, ANNE

The Son of Ethelwolf. London: 1789. V. 38

FULLER, BUCKMINSTER

A Critical Path. New York: 1981. V. 41

FULLER, CLAUD

Breech Loader in the Service 1816-1917. Topeka: 1933. V. 37; 38

FULLER, DANIEL

The Diary of the Revd. Daniel Fuller with His Account of His Family and Other Matters. New York: 1894. V. 44

FULLER, EDGAR

The Visible of the Invisible Empire. Denver: 1925. V. 46

FULLER, EMELINE L.

Left by The Indians. Story of My Life. Mt. Vernon: 1892. V. 37; 41

FULLER, FRANCIS 1670-1706

Medicina Gymnastic. London: 1705. V. 39; 42; 44; 45

Medicina Gymnastica. London: 1728. V. 40; 42

Medicina Gymastica. London: 1718. V. 38

FULLER, GEORGE W.

A Bibliogrpahy of Bookplate Literature. Spokane: 1926. V. 41; 43

A History of the Pacific Northwest. New York: 1931. V. 41

FULLER, HENRY

On Rheumatism, Rheumatic Gout and Sciatica. New York: 1854. V. 42

FULLER, HENRY CLAY

A Texas Sheriff; A Vivid and Accurate Account of Some of the Most Nototious Murder Cases and Feuds in the History of East Texas . . . Nacogdoches: 1931. V. 37

FULLER, HENRY WILLIAM

On Rheumatism Rheumatic Gout and Sciatica, Their Pathology, Symptoms and Treatment. Philadelphia: 1864. V. 45

FULLER, HIRAM

Belle Brittan on a Tour, at Newport, and Here and There. New York: 1858. V. 46

FULLER, HUBERT B.

The Purchase of Florida Its History and Diplomacy. Cleveland: 1906. V. 38; 41; 43

FULLER, J. F. C.

The Star in the West. London: 1907. V. 40; 44

FULLER, JOHN

The History of Berwick upon Tweed, Including a Short Account of the Villages of Tweedmouth and Spittal, etc. Edinburgh: 1799. V. 38; 39; 41

FULLER, JOHN E.

Telegraphic Computer, a Most Wonderful and Extraordinary Instrument, By Which Business Questions of Every Possible Variety are Instantly Performed. Boston & New York: 1868. V. 41

FULLER, MARGARET

At Home and Abroad, or Things and Thoughts in America and Europe. Boston: 1856. V. 41

The Liberty Bell. Boston: 1846. V. 44

FULLER, PETER

Robert Nakian. New York: 1966. V. 42

Robert Natkin. New York: 1981. V. 39

FULLER, R. BUCKMINSTER

Nine Chains to the Moon. Phialdelphia, New York,: 1938. V. 39

Nine Chains to the Moon. Philadelphia: 1938. V. 39; 42; 45

FULLER, ROY

The Other Planet - Four Fables. Richmond: 1979. V. 38

Poems. London: 1939. V. 39; 46

FULLER, SAMUEL

Practical Astronomy, in the Description and Use of Both Globes, Orrery and Telescopes . . . Dublin: 1732. V. 38; 40; 42; 43

A Serious Reply to the Twelve Sections of Abusive Inquiries Proposed to the Consideration of the People Called Quakers . . . Dublin: 1728. V. 44

FULLER, SARAH M.

Summer on the Lake in 1843. Boston: 1844. V. 40

FULLER, SARAH MARGARET

Papers on Literature and Art. London: 1846. V. 37

FULLER, STEPHEN

Report, Resolutions and Remonstrance, of the Honourable the Council and Assembly of Jamaica, at a Joint Committee on the Subject of the Slave-Trade, In a Session Which Began the 20th of October 1789. London: 1790. V. 37

FULLER, THOMAS

Abel Redivivus; or, The Dead Yet Speaking. London: 1651. V. 41; 45

The Church History of Britain, from the Birth of Jesus Christ, Until the Year 1648. London: 1655. V. 41; 42; 46

The Church History of Britain; from the Birth of Jesus Christ Until the Year 1648. Oxford: 1845. V. 37; 39

Collected Works. London: 1840-42. V. 46

A Comment on Ruth; Together with Two Sermons; the One, Teaching How to Live Well, The Other, Minding How to Dye Well. London: 1654. V. 40

Directions Councels and Cautions, Tending to Prudent Management of Affairs in Common Life. London: 1725. V. 39

Exanthematologia . . . London: 1730-29. V. 43; 46

Gnomologia; Adages and Proverbs; Wise Sentences and Witty Sayings, Ancient and Modern, Foreign and British. London: 1732. V. 37; 41

Good Thoughts in Bad Times, Good Thoughts in Worse Times, Mixt Contemplations in Better Times, etc. London: 1841. V. 37; 41

A Happy Handful, or Green Hopes in the Blade, in Order to a Harvest of the Several Shires, Humblin Petitioning, or Heartily Declaring for Peace. London: 1660. V. 45

The Historie of the Holy Warre. Cambridge: 1647. V. 41; 43; 46

The Historie of the Holy Warre. (with) The Holy State. (with) The Profane State. Cambridge: 1640-42. V. 41

The Historie of the Holy Warre . . . Cambridge: 1651. V. 37; 40

The Historie of the Holy Warre. London: 1651. V. 39

The History of the Worthies of England. London: 1662. V. 37; 38; 45

The History of the Worthies of England. London: 1811. V. 38; 39; 40; 41

The Holy State. Cambridge: 1642. V. 43

The Holy State . . . (The Profane State). Cambridge: 1648. V. 38

Introduction ad Prudentiam; or Directions, Counsels and Cautions, Tending to Prudent Management of the Affairs in Common Life . . . London: 1726/27. V. 42; 45

Introduction ad Prudentiam; or Directions, Counsels and Cautions, Tending to Prudent Management of Affairs in Common Life. London: 1727. V. 41

Medicina Gymnastica: or, a Treatise Concerning the Power of Exercise, with Respect to the Animal Oeconomy . . . London: 1705. V. 38

Mixt Contemplations in Better Times. London: 1660. V. 40

Pharmacopoeia Extemporanea, Sive Praescriptorum Chilias, Etc. Amsterdam: 1717. V. 41

Pharmacopoeia Extemporanea Sive Praescriptorum Chilias. Venetiis: 1783. V. 42

A Pisagh-Sight of Palestine and the Confines Thereof, with the History of the Old and New Testament Acted Thereon. London: 1650. V. 41; 43

Collected Works. London: 1840-42. V. 38

FULLER, WILLIAM

Architecture of the Brain. Grand Rapids: 1896. V. 43

A Plain Proof of the True Father and Mother of the Pretended Prince of Wales by Several Letters Written by the Late Queen in France . . . London: 1700. V. 45

The Whole Life of Mr. William Fuller, Being an Impartial Account of His Birth, Education, Relations . . . London: 1703. V. 44; 45

FULLER, WILLIAM HENRY

H.M.S. 'Parliament', or the Lady Who Loved a Government Clerk. Ottawa: 1880. V. 40

FULLER, WILLIAM O.

A Night With Sherlock Holmes. 1929. V. 37

FULLER'S Telegraphic Computer . . . by Which Business Questions, of Every Possible Variety are Instantly Performed . . . New York: 1862. V. 42

FULLERTON, GEORGIANA

Ellen Middleton. London: 1844. V. 37; 38; 39; 41; 43; 45

Grantley Manor. London: 1847. V. 44

Grantley Manor. Paris: 1847. V. 42

Lady-Bird. London: 1852. V. 44

Too Strange Not to Be True. London: 1864. V. 38; 44

FULLMER, JOHN

Assassination of Joseph and Hyrum Smith. Liverpool: 1855. V. 42; 43; 45

FULLOM, S. W.

The Life of Sir Howard Douglas, Bart., from His Notes, Conversations, and Correspondence. London: 1863. V. 41

FULLWOOD, FRANCIS

Obedience Due to the Present King, Notwithstanding Our Oaths to the Former. London: 1689. V. 45

FULLYLOVE, JOHN

The Holy Land. London: 1902. V. 38

FULMAN, WILLIAM

Rerum Anglicrum Scriptorum Veterum. Oxford: 1684-91. V. 38

FULMORE, Z. T.

The History and Geography of Texas as Told in County Names. Austin: 1915. V. 38; 43; 45

FULOP-MILLER, RENE

The Mind and Face of Bolshevism . . . London: 1927. V. 45

The Russian Theatre its Character and History with Especial Reference to the Revolutionary Period. London: 1930. V. 37; 40; 41

FULTON, ALEXANDER R.

Red men of Iowa. Des Moines: 1882. V. 38

FULTON, AMBROSE C.

A Life's Voyage a Diary of a Sailor on Sea and Land, Jotted Down During a Seventy-Years' Voyage . . . New York: 1898. V. 39; 41; 42; 45

FULTON, FRANCES I. S.

To and Through Nebraska. Lincoln: 1884. V. 42; 43

FULTON, J. F.

A Bibliography of the Honourable Robert Boyle . . . (with) Addenda to a Bibliography of the Hon. Robert Boyle. 1932. V. 43

A Bibliography fo the Honourable Robert Boyle. (with) Addenda to the Bibliography . . . London: 1932. V. 44

A Bibliography of the Honourable Robert Boyle. plus Addenda to the Bibliography . . . Oxford: 1932. V. 40

A Bibliography of . . . Robert Boyle. Oxford: 1961. V. 43

Harvey Cushing. A Biography. Springfield: 1946. V. 40

Sir Kenelm Digby, Writer, Bibliophile. Writer, Bibliophile and Protagonist of William Harvey. New York: 1937. V. 40

FULTON, JOHN

Section of Primate Physiology: Laboratory of Physiology. Yale School of Medicine. Collected Papers. Volumes 1, 3-13. 1930-1948. V. 37

Selected Readings in the History of Physiology. Springfield: 1930. V. 42

Selected Readings in the History of Physiology. Springfield: 1966. V. 38

FULTON, JOHN F.

A Bibliography of the Honourable Robert Boyle. Oxford: 1932. V. 41; 46

A Bibliography of the Honourable Robert Boyle . . . (with) Addenda to A Bibliography of the Honourable Robert Boyle. Oxford: 1932-33. V. 41; 42

A Bibliography of the Honourable Robert Boyle, Fellow of the Royal Society. Oxford: 1961. V. 39; 42

The Centennial of Surgical Anesthesia. New York: 1946. V. 46

The Great Medical Bibliographers. Philadelphia: 1951. V. 45; 46

Harvey Cushing. A Bibliography. Springfield: 1946. V. 38

Harvey Cushing: a Biography. Springfield: 1946. V. 39; 41; 42

Michael Servetus, Humanist and Martyr, with a Bibliography of His Works and Census of Known Copies. New York: 1953. V. 39

Muscular Contraction and the Reflex Control of Movement. Baltimore: 1926. V. 42

Physiology of the Nervous System. London: 1938. V. 46

Physiology of the Nervous System. New York: 1938. V. 37

Selected Readings in the History of Physiology. Springfield: 1966. V. 45

The Sign of Babinski. A Study of the Evolution of Cortical Dominance in Primates. Springfield: 1932. V. 46

Sir Kenelm Digby, Writer, Bibliophile and Protagonist of William Harvey. New York: 1937. V. 39; 41; 46

FULTON, MAURICE

Maurice Fulton's History of the Lincoln County War. Tucson: 1968. V. 46

New Mexico's Own Chronicle. Three Races in The Writings of Four Hundred Years. Dallas: 1937. V. 46

FULTON, R.

The Illustrated Book of Pigeons. London: 1885-88. V. 43

FULTON, ROBERT

The Illustrated Book of Pigeons. London: 1889. V. 39; 42

Report of the Proposed Canal Between the Rivers Heyl and Helford. N.P.: 1796? V. 41; 42

Torpedo War, and Submarine Explosions. New York: 1810. V. 42; 45

A Treatise on the Improvement of Canal Navigation . . . V. 40

A Treatise on the Improvement of Canal Navigation . . . London: 1796. V. 42; 44

FULTON, ROBERT L.

Epic of the Overland. San Francisco: 1924. V. 39; 44

FULTON, STEPHEN W.

Poor-Law Rhymes; or, Anti-Marcus. London: 1839. V. 39

FULVIO, ANDREA

Illustrium Imagines. Paris: 1537. V. 45

FULVIO, PIETRO

Compendio del Celeste et Divino Tesoro Dell' Indulgenze, Induli, Gratie, Favori . . . Naples: 1595. V. 38

FUMEE, ANTOINE

Tractatus Tres. De eo Quod Interest., De Substitutionibus, De Coniunctionibus. Toulouse: 1546. V. 37

FUN for Little Folks. London: 1850. V. 39; 45

FUNCK, HENRY

Eine Restitution, Oder Eine Erklarung . . . Philadelphia: 1762. V. 44

FUND FOR PROMOTING FEMALE EMIGRATION

First Report of the Committee. London: 1851. V. 38

FUNDAMENTAL Law the True Security of Sov'reign Dignity and the People's Liberty. London: 1683. V. 41

A FUNERAL Discourse, Occasioned by the Much Lamented Death of Mr. Yorick, Prebendary of Y--k and Author of the Much Admired Life and Opinions of Tristram Shandy, Preached Before a Very Mixed Society of Jemmies, Jessamies, Methodists & Christians . . . London: 1761. V. 43; 45

FUNERAL Obsequies. Octobert 15, 1870. Order of Procession . . . N.P.: 1870. V. 39; 41

FUNERALI per Carlo III. Palermo: 1789. V. 46

FUNK, I. K.

A Standard Dictionary of the English Language. New York & London: 1900. V. 38

FUNNELL, WILLIAM

A Voyage Round the World. London: 1729. V. 41

FUNNY Physic to Cure Bad Habits. London: 1858. V. 44

FUR, Fin and Feather: a Compilation of the Game Laws of the Principal States and Provinces of the United States and Canada; Together with a List of Hunting and Fishing Localities and Other Useful Information for Gunners and Anglers. New York: 1870. V. 46

FURBANK, P. N.

E. M. Forster: a Life. London: 1977. V. 40

FURBER, R.

The Flower Garden Displayed . . . London: 1734. V. 38

FURETIERE, ANTOINE

Dictionnaire Universel, Contenant Generalement Tous les Mots Francois Tan Viewux Que Modernes & Les Termes de Toutes les Sciences et des Arts . . . La Haye & Rotterdam: 1690. V. 46

FURLEY, JOHN

Struggles and Experiences of a Neutral Volunteer. London: 1877. V. 46

FURLEY, ROBERT

A History of the Weald of Kent, with an Outline of the Early History of the County. Ashford: 1871-1874. V. 39

A History of the Weald of Kent, with an Outline of the Early History of the County. Ashford, Igglesden &: 1871-74. V. 42

FURLONG, LAWRENCE

The American Coast Pilot . . . Newburyport: 1800. V. 40; 45

The American Coast Pilot . . . New York: 1812. V. 45

The American Coast Pilot . . . New York: 1817. V. 45

FURMAN, A.

Atahualpa - the Last of the Incas. 1930. V. 43; 45

FURMAN, GABRIEL

Antiquities of Long Island . . . To Which is Added a Bibliography . . . New York: 1874. V. 45

FURMAN, GERRITT

Redfield: a Long Island Tale of the Seventeenth Century. New York: 1825. V. 39; 40; 43

FURMAN, JAMES CLEMENT

Sermon on the Death of Rev. James M. Chiles. Preached at Horeb Church, Abbeville District, S.C. On Sunday 29th of March, 1863. Greenville: 1863. V. 43

FURNAS, ROBERT W.

Nebraska. Her Resources and Advantages, Advancement and Promises. Lincoln: 1885. V. 39; 42

FURNEAUX, WILLIAM SAMUEL

Philip's Popular Mannikin or Model of the Human Body. London: 1902. V. 41

FURNESS, CHARLES E.

Facts About Minnesota. St. Paul: 1881. V. 39; 42

FURNEY, E. E.

Culture, a Modern Method. 1891. V. 43

FURNISS, DOROTHY

Sky-High, a Flight of Fancy for Children. London. V. 42

FURNISS, HARRY

The Confessions of a Caricaturist. London: 1901. V. 43; 45

The Confessions of a Caricaturist. New York: 1902. V. 38

FURNIVAL, W. J.

Leadless Decorative Tiles, Faience, and Mosaic. London: 1904. V. 38; 39

FURNIVAL, WILLIAM

Leadless Decorative Tiles. Faience and Mosaic. Staffordshire: 1904. V. 40; 42

FURNIVAL, WILLIAM JAMES

Leadless Decorative Tiles, Faience and Mosaic. London: 1904. V. 40

FURNIVALL, FREDERICK J.

Early English Meals and Manners. London: 1904. V. 44

FURSE, GEORGE ARMAND

Military Expeditions Beyond the Seas. London: 1897. V. 46

FURST, HERBERT

The Decorative Art of Frank Brangwyn. London: 1916. V. 46

The Decorative Art of Frank Brangwyn. London: 1924. V. 37; 38; 39; 40; 41; 42; 44

Leonard Campbell Taylor, R.A. His Place in Art. Leigh-on-Sea: 1946. V. 40

The Modern Woodcut. London: 1924. V. 37; 38; 39; 40; 46

The Woodcut - an Annual - Number 3, 1929. V. 44

The Woodcut: An Annual. Nos. 1-4. London: 1927. V. 44

The Woodcut. London: 1927-30. V. 39

FURST, PAUL

Das Neue Modelbuch von Schonen Nadereyen Laden Gewurck und Paterleinsarbeit. Nuremberg: 1666. V. 41

FURTENBACH, JOSEPH

Architectura Civilis, Das ist Eigentliche Beschreibung Wie Man Nach Bester Form und Gerechter Regel . . . Ulm: 1628. V. 45

FURTHER Adventures of Old Dame Trot and Her Comical Cat. London: 1830. V. 39

FURTHER and Still More Important Suppressed Documents. Boston: 1808. V. 44

FURTHER Information Respecting the Aborigines, Containing Extracts from the Proccedings of the Meeting for Sufferings in London, and of the Committees on Indian Affairs . . . London: 1839. V. 45

FURTHER Papers Relative to the Recent Arctic Expeditions in Searaach of Sir John Franklin and the Crews of H.M.S. 'Erebus' and 'Terror.' London: 1855. V. 38; 45

FURTHER Papers Relative to the Union of British Columbia and Vancouver Island. London: 1867. V. 46

A FURTHER Report From the Committee of Secrecy, Appointed to Enquire Into the Conduct of Robert, Earl of Orford; During the Last Ten Years of His Being First Commissioner of the Treasury and Chancellor and Under Treasurer of His Majesty's . . . London: 1742. V. 41; 45

A FURTHER Warning and Exhortation of a Member of the Reverend Commission of the General Assembly of the Church of Scotland to all Worthy and Sincere Christians of Their Communion. Edinburgh?: 1746. V. 39

FURTWANGLER, ADOLF

Aegina, das Heiligtum der Aphaia Unter Mitwirkung von Ernest R. Fiechter und Hermann Thiersch. Munchen: 1906. V. 40

FURUMARK, ARNE

Mycenaean Pottery. Stockholm: 1972. V. 37

FUSS, NICOLAI IVANOVICH

Instruction Detaillee Pour Porter Les Lunettes de Toutes les Differentes Especes au Plus Haut Degre de Perfection Dont Elles Sont Susceptibles. St. Petersburg: 1774. V. 38; 44

FUSSELL, G. E.

The Old English Farming Books. (with) More Old English Farming Books. London: 1947/50. V. 42

FUTHEY, J. S.

History of Chester County, Pennsylvania . . . Philadelphia: 1881. V. 41; 42

FUTRELLE, JACQUES

The Chase of the Golden Plate. 1906. V. 39

The Thinking Machine. 1907. V. 39

FYFE, ANDREW

A System of Anatomy and Physiology, with the Comparative Anatomy of Animals. Edinburgh: 1791. V. 40; 42

A System of the Anatomy of the Human Body . . . Edinburgh: 1806. V. 41

FYFE, HERBERT C.

Submarine Warfare, the development of the submersible as an engine of war, history, design, etc. Discussions of submarines used during the American Civil War. London/New York: 1902/1907. V. 37

FYLEMAN, ROSE

Fifty-One New Nursery Rhymes. London: 1931. V. 46

The Rose Fyleman Fairy book. London: 1923. V. 45; 46

FYSHER, JOHAN

A Mornynge Rembraunce . . . London: 1906. V. 44; 46

FYSON, P. F.

The Flora of the South Indian Hill Stations. Madras: 1932. V. 38

G

G----E and D----y; or, the Injur'd Ghost. A True Tale. In Imitation of William and Margaret. London: 1743. V. 40

G., W.

A Rich Store-House, or Treasury of the Diseases . . . London: 1650. V. 41

GABB, THOMAS

Finis Pyramidis; or Disquisitions on the Antiquity and Scientific End of the Great Pyramid of Giza. London: 1805. V. 45

GABBETT, JOSEPH

A Digested Abridgment and Comparative View of the Statute Law of England and Ireland, to 1811. Dublin: 1812. V. 40

GABELKHOVER, OSWALD

Artzneybuch, Darinnen . . . fast fur Alle fess Menschlichen Leibs Anligen und Gebrechen, Ausserlesene und Bewehrte Artzneyen, Gemeinem Vatterland Teutscher Nation zu Gutem, Auss Vielen Hohen und Niders Stands Personen . . . Frankfort: 1610. V. 45; 46

GABIN, D. ANTONIO

A Master-key to Popery: In Five Parts. Newport: 1773. V. 42

GABO, NAUM

Of Divers Arts. The A. W. Mellon Lectures in the Fine Arts. 1959. New York: 1962. V. 42

GABORGY, G.

La Cassette de Plomb . . . Ornee de Deux Gravures Originales et Inedites par Andre Derain. Paris: 1920. V. 38

GABRIELI, VITTORIO

A New Digby Letter Book: In praise of Venetia. 1955. V. 44

GABUCINO, GIROLAMO

De Lumbricis Alvvm Occupantibus, ac de Ratione Curandi eos, Qui ab Illis Infestantur. Venice: 1547. V. 42

GADBURY, JOHN

A Ballad Upon the Popish Plot. N.P.: 1679. V. 44; 46

Ephemerides of the Celestial Motions for X. Years . . . London: 1672. V. 42

Genethlialogia, or, the Doctrine of Nativities . . . London: 1658. V. 38

(Greek Title) Genethlialogia, or, the Doctrine of Nativities, Constaining the Whole Art of Directions and Annual Revolutions . . . (with) Collectio Genituraraum; or, a Collection of Nativities in CL Genitures . . . London: 1660, 1662. V. 38

GADD, C. J.

The Stones of Assyria. London: 1936. V. 37; 39; 42; 44; 46

GADDIS, MAXWELL P.

Foot-Prints of an Itinerant. Cincinnati: 1855. V. 42

Foot-Prints of an Itinerant. Cincinnati: 1856. V. 40

GADDIS, WILLIAM

Carpenter's Gothic. New York: 1985. V. 39; 43; 46

J.R. New York: 1975. V. 39; 40; 41; 42; 43; 44; 45; 46

The Recognitions. London: 1955. V. 41; 45

The Recognitions. New York: 1955. V. 37; 39; 40; 41; 42; 43; 44; 45; 46

GADESBY, RICHARD

A Treatise of Decimal Arithmetic; or, Decimals Applied to the Common Rules of Arithmetic . . . London: 1757. V. 38; 42

GADOW, HANS

In Northern Spain. London: 1897. V. 46

GADROIS, CLAUDE

Le Systeme du Monde, Selon Les Trois Hypotheses Ou Conformement aux Loix de la Mecahnique . . . Paris: 1675. V. 44

GADROYS, CLAUDE

Le Systeme du Monde, Selon les Trois Hypotheses . . . Paris: 1675. V. 38

GADSDEN, CHRISTOPHER E.

A Discourse Preached and Published by Request of the Vestry and Wardens of St. Michael's Church, and Also of the Protestant Episcopal Society for the Advancement of Christianity in South Carolina . . . Charleston: 1817. V. 41; 44

GAELIC SOCIETY OF DUBLIN

Transactions. Dublin: 1808. V. 44

GAERTNER, JOSEPH

De Fructibus et Seminibus Plantarum. Stuttgart. V. 42; 43

GAFFAREL, JACQUES

Curiositez Inouyes, sur la Sculpture Talismanique des Persans, Horoscope des Patriarches, et Lecture des Estoilles. Paris?: 1650. V. 46

Unheard-of Curiosities. London: 1650. V. 39

GAFFEY, LAURIE

A Free Lance Angler in Ireland. Dublin: 1930. V. 40

GAG, WANDA

Millions of Cats. New York: 1928. V. 46

GAGE, JOHN

The History and Antiquities of Hengrave in Suffolk. London: 1822. V. 44

The History and Antiquities of Suffolk. Thingoe Hundred. London: 1838. V. 41; 44; 45

GAGE, MATILDA JOSLYN

History of Women's Suffrage. New York: 1881-1922. V. 45

Woman, Church and State: An Historical Account of the Status of Woman through the Christian Ages . . . Chicago: 1893. V. 45

GAGE, THOMAS 1603?-1656

The English-American His Travail by Sea and Land. London: 1648. V. 38; 39; 40; 41; 42; 44; 45; 46

Historia Que Contem a Nova Relacao que o Padre M. Fr. Thomas Gage, R. Dominco, Fez a Nova Hespanha ou America Hespanhola . . . V. 40; 43

A New Survey of the West-Indias; or the English American His Travail by Sea and Land . . . London: 1655. V. 41

A New Survey of the West-Indies . . . 1677. V. 42

A New Survey of the West-Indies or the English American His Travel by Sea and Land. London: 1677. V. 45

A New Survey of the West-Indies . . . London: 1699. V. 41; 42

The Tyranny of Satan. London: 1642. V. 45

GAGUIN, ROBERT 1433-1501

Compendium Super Francorum Gestis. Paris: 1511. V. 40

De Origine & Gestis Francorum . . . Compendium. Paris: 1497-98. V. 40

GAHEIS, FR. V. P.

Burgerfeyer am 30. October 1804, bey der Einsetzung des Wohlgeboren Heern Stephan Edlen v. Wohlleben . . . in die Wurde Eines Burgermeisters der k. k. Haupt-und-Residenzstadt Wein. Vienna: 1804. V. 41

GAIGE, CROSBY

Dining with My Friends. New York: 1949. V. 38

GAILHABAUD, JULES

Monuments Anciens et Modernes. Collection Formants Une Histoire de l'Architecture des Differents Peuples a Toutes les Epoques. Paris. V. 38

GAILLOT, BERNARD 1780-1847

Les Metiers et Les Arts et Metiers. Paris: 1819-1826. V. 46

GAINE, HUGH

The Journals of Hugh Gaine, Printer. New York: 1902. V. 39; 41; 43; 44; 45

GAINES, CHARLES KELSEY

Echoes of Many Moods. 1926. V. 40

GAINES, EDMUND PENDLETON

Memorial of . . . to the Senate and House of Representatives of the United States in Congress Assembled. Memphis: 1840. V. 39

Memorial of Edmund P. Gaines, Proposing a System of National Defense, and Prayings Its Adoption by Congress. Washington: 1840. V. 44

A Plan for the Defence of the Western Frontier . . . . February 28, 1838 . . . Washington: 1838. V. 38; 40; 41; 46

GAINES, ERNEST J.

The Autobiography of Miss Jane Pittman. New York: 1971. V. 44

Catherine Carmier. New York: 1964. V. 42; 44

GAINES, MARY LOUISE

I Heah de Voices Callin'. Atlanta: 1916. V. 43

GAINSBOROUGH, THOMAS

A Collection of Prints Illustrative of English Scenery, from the Drawings and Sketches of Thos. Gainsborough, R.A . . . . London: 1819. V. 38; 39

The Letters of Thomas Gainsborough. London: 1961. V. 39

GAINSFORD, W. D.

Annals of the House of Gainsford, of Surrey, Oxon, Monmouth, Lincoln & Kent: 1331 to 1909. Horncastle: 1909. V. 38

GAIRDNER, JAMES

Lollardy and the Reformation of England . . . London: 1908-13. V. 42

GAIUS HUGINUS

The Poeticon Astonomicon. 1985. V. 45

GALAPAGOS the Flow of Wilderness. San Francisco, New York: 1968. V. 40

GALAVARIS, GEORGE

Illustrations of the Liturgical Homilies of Gregory Nazianzenus. Princeton: 1969. V. 42

GALE, GEORGE

Upper Mississippi; or, Historical Sketches of the Mound-Builders, the Indian Tribes and the Progress of Civilization in the North West . . . Chicago: 1867. V. 37; 38; 43; 45

GALE, JOHN

Gale's Cabinet of Knowlege; or, Miscellaneous Recreations . . . London: 1808. V. 43

GALE, NORMAN

A Book of Quatrains. Old Bilton, Rugby: 1909. V. 38

Orchard Songs, by Norman Gale. London: 1893. V. 37

Songs for Little People. London: 1896. V. 41

GALE, NORMAN ROWLAND

Thistledown: a Set of Six Essays . . . Rugby: 1890. V. 44

GALE, R.

Registrum Honoris de Richmond Exhibens Terrarum & Villarum Quae Quodam Fuerunt Edwini Comitis Infra Richmundshire Descriptionem . . . London: 1722. V. 39; 41; 44

GALE, T.

Electricity, or Ethereal Fire, Considered. Troy: 1802. V. 40

GALE, THEOPHILUS

The Court of the Gentiles . . . Oxford. V. 46

GALE, THOMAS

An Antidotarie Conteyning Hidde and Secrete Medicines Simple and Compounde, As Also All Suche as Are Required in Chirurgerie. London: 1563. V. 41; 44

Historiae Britannicae, Saxonicae, Anglo-Danicae. Oxford: 1691. V. 38

Opuscula Mythologica, Ethica, et Physica. Cambridge: 1671. V. 40; 42; 44; 45

GALE, ZONA

Miss Lulu Bett. New York: 1920. V. 42

GALEF, ROBERT

More Wonders of the Invisible World, or Wonders of the Invisible World Displayed. Salem: 1823. V. 38

GALEN

Liber De Facvltatvm Natvralivm Substantia . . . Paris: 1540. V. 46

GALEN, CHRISTOPH BERNARD VON 1605-1678

The Life and Actions of the Late Renowned Prelate and Souldier Christopher Bernard Von Gale, Bishop of Munster. London: 1680. V. 39

GALEN OF PERGAMON

Opvs Medicvm Practicv, Varivm, Vere Avrevm, et Postremae Lectionis Clavdii Galeni . . . Iani Cornarii Medici . . . Commentariorvm . . . Basilae: 1537. V. 38

GALENUS 130-200

De L'Usage des Parties du Corps Humain, Livres XVII. Lyon: 1566. V. 45

Epitome Galeni Pergame Ni Operum, in Quatuor Partes . . . Basileae: 1551. V. 44; 46

Epitomes Omnium Galeni Pergameni, Etc. Lugduni (Lyons): 1553. V. 41

Galen on the Usefulness of the Parts of the Body. Ithaca: 1968. V. 38; 41; 42; 44; 45

Galeni in Primvm Librvm Hippocratis De Morbis VVL Garibvs. Commentarivs Primvs, Hermanno Crvserio Campensi Interp. Venetiis: 1545. V. 44; 45; 46

Galen's Method of Physick . . . Edinburgh: 1656. V. 44; 45; 46

Liber de Plenitudine. Polybus. De Salubri Victus . . . Apuleius Platonicus de Herbarum Virtutibus. Antonio Benivieni Libellus de Abiditis Nonnullis. Paris: 1528. V. 37; 42

Methodi Medendi, id est, de Morbis Curandis Libri Quatuordecim, Denuo Magna Diligentia Martini Gregorii Recogniti, Thoma Linacro Anglo Interprete . . . Paris: 1538. V. 45

Methodi Medendi, vel De Morbis vrandis Libri XIIII, Postrema hac Editione ad Cuiuscunque Varietatis . . . Lvgdvni: 1580. V. 46

Methodus Medeni, vel de Morbis Cordanis. Paris: 1519. V. 38

Certaine Workes of Galens, Called Methodus Medendi . . . London: 1586. V. 40

Opus Medicvm Practicv, Varivm Vere Avrevm, et Postreamae Lectionis Claudii Galeni . . . Basilae: 1537. V. 39; 40; 41

De Sanitate Tuenda . . . Venice: 1523. V. 42

De l'Usage des Parties du Corps Humain, Livres XVII. Lyon: 1566. V. 44; 46

The Works. (Omnia Quae Extant Opera in Latinum Sermonem Conversa. Juntarum Quarta Editio.) Venetiis: 1565. V. 37

GALES, WINIFRED MARSHALL

Matilda Berkely, or, Family Anecdotes. Raleigh: 1804. V. 37; 40

GALET, JULES

Le Corps de l'Homme: Traite Complet d'Anatomie et de Physiologie Humaines, Contenant Pres de 200 Planches . . . Paris: 1844. V. 42

GALHEGOS, MANOEL DA

Templo da Memoria. Poema Epithalamico, nas Felicissimas Bodas do Excellentissimo Senhor Duque de Barganca (sic) . . . Lisbon: 1635. V. 45

GALIBERT, LEON

L'Algeria Antica e Moderna, dai Primi Ordini de'Cartginesi inso Alla Presa della Smala d'Abd-el-Kader. Napoli: 1846. V. 38

GALIGNANI & CO.

Galignani's New Paris Guide. Paris: 1844. V. 40

GALILEI, GALILEO 1564-1642

Dialogo de Galileo Galilei Linceo Matematico Sopraordinario Dello Studio di Pis E. Filosofo, E. Matematico Primario Del Serenissimo Gr. Duca Ditoscana. Fiorenza. V. 46

Dialogo . . . Sopra I Due Massimi Sistemi del Mondo Tolemaico, e Copernicano. Florence: 1632. V. 40; 42; 46

Dialogo . . . Sopra i Due Massimi Sistemi del Mondo Tolemaico, e Copernicano . . . Florence: 1710. V. 46

Discorsi e Dimostrazioni Matematiche, Intorno a Due Nuove Scienze Attenenti Alla Mecanica & i Movimenti Locali . . . Leyden: 1638. V. 37; 40

Discorso al Serenissimo Don Cosimo II. Gran Duca di Toscana Intorno alle Cose . . . Firenze: 1612. V. 38; 42

Istori E Dimostrazioni Intorno Alle Macchie Solari e Loro Accidenti. Rome: 1613. V. 38

Le Operazioni del Compasso geometrico et Militare. Padua: 1649. V. 46

Opere . . . Bologna: 1655-56. V. 46

Opere . . . coll' Aggiunta di VAri Trattai dell' Istesso Autore non Piu Dati Alle Stampe. Florence: 1718. V. 42; 44

Opere. Padova: 1744. V. 38; 43

Il Saggiatore nel Quale con Bilancia Esquisita e Giusta si Ponderano le Cose Contenute Nella Libra Astronomica e Filosofica di Lotario Sarsi Sigensano Scritto in Forma di Lettera. Rome: 1623. V. 40

Systema Cosmicum. Leiden: 1699-1700. V. 44

Systemata Cosmicum. In Quo Dialogis IV. de Duobus Maximis Mundi Systematibus.,, (with) Discursus et Demonstrationes Mathematicae, Circa Duas Novas Scientias . . . Leiden: 1699. V. 46

GALINDO, CATHERINE

Mrs. Galindo's Leeter to Mrs. Siddons: Being a Circumstantial Detail of Mrs. Siddon's Life for the Last Seven Years. London: 1809. V. 39

GALITZIN, PRINCE

Catalogue of the Secret Cabinet. London: 1975. V. 45

GALL, FRANCOIS JOSEPH

On the Origin of the Moral Qualities and Intellectual Faculties of Man. Boston: 1835. V. 39

GALL, FRANZ JOSEPH

Anatomie et Physiologie du Systeme Nerveux en General et du Cerveau en Particulier, avec des Observations sur la Possibilite de Reconnoitre Plusieurs Dispositions et Morales de l'Homme et des Animaux, par la Configuration de Leurs Tetes. Paris: 1810-19. V. 45

On the Functions of the Cerebellum. Edinburgh: 1838. V. 38

Sur les Fonctions du Cverveau et sur Celles de Chacune de ses Parties. Paris: 1825. V. 41

GALL, JAMES

A Historical Sketch of the Origin and Progress of Literature for the Blind; and Practical Hints and Recommendations as to Their Education. Edinburgh: 1834. V. 40

GALLACINI, TEOFILO 1564-1641

Trattato Sopra gli Errori Degli Architetti. Venice: 1767. V. 40; 41; 46

GALLAEUS, THEODORUS

Illustrium Imagines, Ex Antiquis Marmoribus, Nomismatibus, et Gemmis Expressae: Quae Exstant Romae, Maior Pars Apud Fulvium Ursinum . . . Antwerp: 1606. V. 45

GALLAGHER, MICHAEL

The Birds of Oman. 1980. V. 46

The Birds of Oman. London: 1980. V. 37; 38; 42; 43; 45

GALLAGHER, TESS

Under Stars: Poems by Tess Gallabher. Port Townsend: 1978. V. 46

GALLAHER, JAMES

The Western Sketch-Book. Boston: 1852. V. 39

GALLAND, PIERRE

De Agrorum Conditionibus . . . Paris: 1554. V. 43

Petri Castellani Magni Franciae Eleemosynarii Vita . . . Paris: 1674. V. 40

GALLANTRY, Crueltry and 500. The Interesting Trial Against E. L. Charlton, Esq. for Seducing (in the Company with Captain S(eymou)R, of the Guards), Hannah and Charlotte Gibberson . . . Whom . . . They conveyed to a Common Bagnio (etc.). London: 1816? V. 45

GALLATIN, ALBERT EUGENE 1761-1849

A. E. G. Modern Art at Venice and Other Notes. New York: 1910. V. 46

American Water-Colourists. New York: 1922. V. 46

Art and the Great War. New York: 1919. V. 37; 46

Aubrey Beardsley's Drawings. A Catalogue and a List of Criticisms. New York: 1903. V. 43

Aubrey Beardsley. Catalogue of Drawings and Bibliography. New York: 1945. V. 40

A Bibliography of the Works of Max Beerbohm. Cambridge: 1952. V. 40

Gaston Lachaise . . . New York: 1924. V. 44

Letter . . . Relative to the Expences Incurred by the U.S. In the Exercise of the Jurisdiction Over the Territory of Columbia. Washington: 1802. V. 39

Letters of Albert Gallatin on the Oregon Question. Washington: 1846. V. 37; 40

A Memoir on the North Eastern Boundary: In Connexion with Mr. Jay's Map . . . New York: 1843. V. 46

Notes on Some Rare Portraits of Whistler. New York: & London: 1916. V. 44

The Oregon Question. New York: 1846. V. 38; 39; 44

Peace with Mexico. New York: 1847. V. 46

The Portraits and Caricatures of James McNeill Whistler. London: 1913. V. 43

Report of . . . on the Subject of Public Roads and Canals . . . Washington: 1816. V. 37

The Right of the United States of America to the North-Eastern Boundary Claimed by Them. New York: 1840. V. 43

The Speech of Albert Gallatin . . . on the Important Question Touching the Validity of the Elections Held in the Four Western Counties of the State, on the 14th Day of October, 1794. Philadelphia: 1795. V. 39

The Speech of . . . Delivered in the House of Representatives of the United States on the First of March 1798, Upon the Foreign Intercourse Bill. Philadelphia: 1798. V. 38

A Synopsis of the Indian Tribes Within the United States East of the Rocky Mountains, and in the British and Russian Possesions in North America. Cambridge;: 1836. V. 41

Views of the Public Debt, Receipts & Expenditures of the United States. New York: 1800. V. 43; 45

Views of the Public Debt, Receipts and Expenditures of the United States. Philadelphia: 1801. V. 38; 39; 42; 45

Whistler. Notes and Footnotes and Other Memoranda. New York: 1907. V. 42; 46

Writings. New York: 1960. V. 37; 40; 42; 44

GALLATIN, EDWARD L.

What Life Has Taught Me. Denver: 1900. V. 40

GALLAUDET, THOMAS H.

Discourses on Various Points of Christian Faith and Practice; Most of Which were Delivered in the Chapel of the Oratoire, in Paris in the Spring of 1816. New York: 1818. V. 43

GALLAUDET, THOMAS HOPKINS

Hoike Akua. He Palapala ia e Hoike Ana Ma Na Mea I Hanaia, Aia no He Akua, He Mana Loa Knoa a Me La Ike Kupanaha . . . Lahainaluna: 1842. V. 40

GALLEGO, JULIAN

Zurbaran. London: 1955. V. 44

Zurbaran, 1598-1654. New York: 1977. V. 37; 40; 45

GALLENGA, ANTONIO

History of Piedmont. London: 1855. V. 44

Italy, Present and Future. London: 1887. V. 44

THE GALLERY of Modern British Artists Consisting of a Series of Engravings from the Works of the Most Eminent Artists of the Day . . . London: 1880. V. 39

THE GALLERY of Portraits: With Memoirs . . . London: 1833. V. 45

GALLERY of the Celebrated Landscapes of Switzerland. Zurich & Leeds: 1884. V. 41

GALLESIO, GIORGIO

Pomona Italiana Ossia Trattato Degli Alberti Fruttiferi. Pisa: 1817-39. V. 39

GALLICO, PAUL

Adventures of Hiram Holliday. New York: 1939. V. 41; 42

Confessions of a Story-Teller. London: 1961. V. 43

The Snow Goose. London: 1920. V. 42

The Snow Goose. London: 1946. V. 37; 39; 42; 43

GALLIENNE, RICHARD

Robert Louis Stevenson, an Elegy: and Other Poems. London: 1895. V. 44

GALLIER, JAMES

The American Builder's General Price Book and Estimator. Boston: 1836. V. 41

GALLINI, GIOVANNI ANDREA 1728-1805

Critical Observations on the Art of Dancing. London: 1770. V. 38; 39

GALLIPILLEE, MR.

A Letter from Mr. Gallipillee &c. N.P.. V. 43

A Letter from Mr. Gallipillee, &c. N.P.: 1740. V. 41

GALLO, AGOSTINO

Le Vinti Giornate dell'Agricoltvra, et de'Piaceri Della Villa. Venetia: 1573. V. 39

Le Vinti Giornate dell'Agricoltvra. Venetia: 1628. V. 39

GALLO, LEONORA

Peasant Art in Italy. Florence: 1929. V. 43

GALLO, MIGUEL MUJICA

The Gold of Peru: Masterpieces of Goldsmith's Work of Pre-Incan and Incan Time and the Colonial Period. Recklinghausen: 1959. V. 44; 45

GALLON, M. JEAN GAFON

Machines et Inventions Approuvees par l'Academie Royale des Sciences . . . Paris: 1735. V. 42

GALLOTTI, JEAN

Moorish Houses and Gardens of Morocco. New York: 1925. V. 37; 45

GALLOWAY, C. F. J.

The Call of the West: Letters from British Columbia. London: 1917. V. 45

GALLOWAY, CHARLES J.

Catalogue of Paintings and Drawings at Thorneyholme. Manchester: 1892. V. 44

GALLOWAY, ELIJAH

History and Progress of the Steam Engine. London: 1830. V. 39; 44

History and Progress of the Steam Engine. London: 1835. V. 38

GALLOWAY, F. C.

Objects in the Museum of the Bronte Society at Haworth. London: 1896. V. 41

GALLOWAY, H.

Ancient Egyptian Metallurgy. London: 1881. V. 42

GALLOWAY, JOSEPH

A Candid Examination of the Mutual Claims of Great-Britain and the Colonies . . . New York: 1775. V. 44; 45

Considerations Upon the American Enquiry. London: 1779. V. 39; 42; 44

Letters to a Nobleman, on the Conduct of the War in the Middle Colonies. London: 1779. V. 38; 39; 42

Letters to a Nobleman, on the Conduct of the War in the Middle Colonies. London: 1780. V. 40

Observations on the Fifth Article of the Treaty with America . . . London: 1783. V. 41; 42

Reflections on the Rise and Progress of the American Revolution. London: 1780. V. 37

A Reply to the Observations of Lt. Gen. Sir William Howe, on a Pamphlet Entitled Letters to a Nobleman. London: 1780. V. 41; 42; 43

A Reply to the observations of Lieut. Gen. Sir William Howe, on a Pamphlet, entitled His Letters to a Nobleman: in which His Misrepresentations are detached, and those Letters are supported by a Variety of New Matter and Argument . . . The Second edition. London: 1781. V. 37

A True and Impartial State of the Province of Pennsylvania. Philadelphia: 1769. V. 45

GALLOWAY, R. L.

Annals of Coal Mining and the Coal Trade. London: 1898-1904. V. 37; 42

GALLOWAY, VINCENT

The Oils and Murals of Sir Frank Brangwyn R.A. 1867-1956. Leigh-on-Sea: 1962. V. 40; 44

GALLUCCI, GIOVANNI PAOLO

De Fabrica, et Usu Cuisdam Instrumenti ad Omnia Horarum Genera Describenda, ad Omnem Latitudinem Peropportuni... Venice: 1592. V. 44

Theatro y Descricipcion Universal de Mundo... Granada: 1617. V. 45

Theatrum Mundi et Temporis, in Quo non Solum Precipuae Horum Partes Describuntur, & Ratio Metiendi eas Traditur... Venetiis: 1588. V. 38

GALLUZZI, RIGUCCIO

Istoria del Granducato Do Toscana Sotto Il Governo dell Casa Medici. Capolago: 1841-42. V. 38

GALLY, HENRY

A Dissertation Against Pronouncing the Greek Language According to Accents. (with) A Second Dissertation Against Pronouncing the Greek Language According to Accents. London: 1754/763. V. 45

GALPIN, FRANCIS W.

The Music of the Sumerians and Their Immediate Successors the Babylonians and Assyrians, Described and Illustrated From Original Sources. Cambridge: 1938. V. 44

GALSWORTHY-DAVIE, W.

Architectural Studies in France. London: 1877. V. 41

GALSWORTHY, JOHN 1867-1933

Author and Critic. New York: 1933. V. 42

Carmen: an Opera in Four Acts. London: 1932. V. 42

Castles in Spain and Other Screeds. London: 1927. V. 41

A Commentary. London: 1908. V. 46

The Creation of Character in Literature. Oxford: 1931. V. 43

The Forsyte Saga. London: 1922. V. 38; 39; 40

Four Forstye Stories. New York: 1929. V. 39

From the Four Winds. London: 1897. V. 37; 38; 39; 41; 44

International Thought. Cambridge: 1923. V. 42

Island Pharisees. London: 1904. V. 37

Jocelyn. London: 1898. V. 38; 39; 40

Loyalties. London: 1930. V. 38; 41

Maid in Waiting. London: 1931. V. 41

A Man of Devon. Edinburgh: 1901. V. 38; 40

The Man of Property. London: 1906. V. 39; 41; 45; 46

A Modern Comedy. London: 1929. V. 39; 44

A Modern Comedy. New York: 1930. V. 39

Novels, Tales and Plays. New York: 1926. V. 45

The Novels, Tales and Plays. New York: 1926-29. V. 42

The Plays. London: 1929. V. 39; 41; 43

The Silver Spoon. London: 1926. V. 38

Soames and the Flag. London: 1930. V. 41; 44

Swan Song. London: 1928. V. 41; 42

Swan Song. New York: 1928. V. 39

Two Essays on Conrad. Freelands: 1930. V. 41

Villa Rubein. London: 1900. V. 38

Villa Rubein. Edinburgh: 1901. V. 40

The Works. New York: 1922. V. 42

The Works of... New York: 1922-23. V. 38

Works. New York: 1922-36. V. 43

The Works. London: 1923. V. 38

Works of... London: 1923-29. V. 37

The Works. London: 1923-35. V. 37

The Works of John Galsworthy. New York: 1927-28. V. 40; 41

The Works of John Galsworthy. New York: 1927-33. V. 40

The Works of John Galsworthy. New York: 1929. V. 46

GALT, A. T.

Report of the Minister of Finance on the Reciprocity Treaty with the United States; Also the Memorial of the Chamber of Commerce of St. Paul, Minnesota, and report of Congress. Quebec: 1862. V. 39; 46

GALT, JAMES

The Ayrshire Legatees; or, the Pringle Family. Edinburgh: 1821. V. 43

Sir Andrew Wylie, of that Ilk. Edinburgh: 1822. V. 43

GALT, JOHN 1779-1839

Annals of the Parish; or the Chronicle of Dalmailing. Edinburgh: 1821. V. 40

The Ayrshire Legatees; or the Pringle Family. Edinburgh: 1821. V. 37; 39; 45

The Bachelor's Wife... Edinburgh: 1824. V. 45

Eben Erskine. London: 1833. V. 39

The Entail; or the Lairds of Grippy. Edinburgh. V. 42

The Entail; or the Lairds of Grippy. Edinburgh: 1823. V. 37; 40; 43; 46

The Entail; or The Lairds of Grippy. Edinburgh & London: 1823. V. 40

The Life and Studies of Benjamin West, Esq... Prior to His Arrival in England. Philadelphia: 1816. V. 38

The Lives of the Players. London: 1831. V. 39; 40

The Member: an Autobiography. London: 1832. V. 43

The New British Theatre. London: 1814-15. V. 38

Pictures Historical and Biographical, Drawn from English, Scottish and Irish History. London: 1821. V. 46

Ringan Gilhaize; or the Covenanters. Edinburgh: 1823. V. 37

Sir Andrew Wylie, of that Ilk. Edinburgh: 1822. V. 37; 45

The Works... Edinburgh: 1895. V. 38; 39; 41

Works. Edinburgh & London: 1895-1936. V. 37

The Works. Edinburgh: 1936. V. 37; 40; 41; 46

GALT, JOHN M.

Essays on Asylums for Persons of Unsound Mind. (with) Essays on Asylums... Second Series. Richmond: 1750/53. V. 43

Insanity in Italy. Utica: 1854. V. 43

GALT, P. H.

Infantry Tactis; or, Rules for the Exercises and manoeuvres of the Infantry of the U.S. Army. Washington: 1825. V. 38

GALTON, DOUGLAS

Healthy Hospitals. Oxford: 1893. V. 38

Observations on the Construction of Healthy Dwellings, Namely Houses, Hospitals, Barracks, Asylums, etc. Oxford: 1880. V. 37; 38; 39

GALTON, FRANCIS 1822-1911

The Art of Travel... London: 1855. V. 45

The Art of Travel; or Shifts and Contrivances Available in Wild Countries. London: 1860. V. 41

Finger Prints. London: 1892. V. 37; 41; 42; 43; 45

Finger Prints. London: 1892. V. 43

Finger Prints. London, New York: 1892. V. 40

Finger Prints. (with) Supplementary Chapter to 'Finger Prints'. (with) Fingerprint Directories. London: 1892/93/95. V. 41

Hereditary Genius; an Inquiry into Its Laws and Consequences. London: 1869. V. 37; 39; 42; 45

Hereditary Genius. New York: 1870. V. 38; 39; 40; 41

Hereditary Genius: an Inquiry Into Its Laws and Consequences. London: 1892. V. 45

Inquiries into Human Faculty and Its Development. London: 1883. V. 37; 40; 41; 42

Inquiries Into Human Faculty and Its Development. New York: 1883. V. 37; 42

Memories of My Life. London: 1908. V. 41

Natural Inheritance. London: 1889. V. 42; 45; 46

Vacation Tourists and Notes of Travel in 1860. London: 1861. V. 40

Vacation Tourists and Notes of Travel in 1860. (and) in 1861. (and) in 1862-63. Cambridge: 1861-64. V. 44

Vacation Tourists and Notes of Travels in 1861. Cambridge: 1862. V. 41

Vacation Tourists and Notes of Travel in 1862-63. London: 1864. V. 45

GALTON, GWENDOLEN DOUGLAS

A Step Aside. London: 1893. V. 39

GALTON, SAMUEL J.

The Natural History of Birds... Intended for the Amusement and Instruction of Children. London: 1791. V. 43

GALTREY, SIDNEY

Memoirs of a Racing Journalist. London: 1924. V. 42

Memoirs of a Racing Journalist. London: 1934. V. 37

GALTRUCHIO, PETRO

Philosophiae Ac Mathematicae (Plus): Physica Vniversalis (and:) Metaphysica (and): Vniversa Philosophia. 1666. V. 46

GALUCCI, GIOVANNI PAOLO

Della Fabricia et Uso di Diversi Stromenti di Astronomia et Cosmografia. Venice: 1598. V. 40; 45

GALVAN, MANUEL DE JESUS

The Cross and the Sword. London: 1956. V. 40

GALVAO, ANTONIO

Tratado dos Descobrimentos Aantigos, e Modernos, Feitos ate a Era de 1550, com os Nomes Particulares das Pessoas que os Fizerao.. Lisboa Occidental: 1731. V. 38

GALVESTON BAY & TEXAS LAND CO.

This Certifies That the Subscribers as the Trustees and Attorneys of Lorenzo de Zavala, Joseph Vehlein and David G. Burnet, Have Given and do Hereby Give to (William G. Buckner - in holograph) . . . New York: 1830. V. 39

GALVESTON BUILDING ASSOCIATION

Charter and By-Laws of the Galveston Building Association, of Galveston. Galveston: 1871. V. 41

GALVESTON GARTEN VEREIN

List of Members of the Galveston Garten Verein. Galveston: 1882. V. 45

GALVESTON, TEXAS. CHARTER

Charter and Revised Ordinances of the City of Galveston . . . and Catalogue of the City Government from 1839 to 1879 Inclusive. Galveston: 1880. V. 38

GALVESTON WHARF COMPANY

Charter and By-Laws of the Galveston Wharf Company. Galveston: 1879. V. 38

GALVEZ, BERNARDO DE

Instructions for Governing the Interior Provinces of New Spain, 1786. Berkeley: 1951. V. 39; 41

GALVIN, JOHN

The Coming of Justice to California. San Francisco: 1963. V. 37

The Etchings of Edward Borein. San Francisco: 1971. V. 37; 38; 44; 46

GAMA, JOSE BASILIO DA

Quitubia. Lisbon: 1791. V. 38

GAMALIEL

Gamaliel Nuevamente Traduzido en Lengua Castellana. Seville: 1534. V. 40

GAMBA, PIETRO

Lord Byron, als Mensch en Als Dichter; Benevens (Uit Het Dagverhaal van Graaf Pietro Gamba Getrokken) . . . Delft: 1825. V. 38

A Narrative of Lord Byron's Last Journey to Greece. London: 1825. V. 40; 42; 44; 46

GAMBADO, GEOFFERY

An Academy for Grown Horsemen. (with) Annals of Horsemanship. London: 1808. V. 38

GAMBADO, GEOFFREY

Annals of Horsemanship: Containing Accounts of Accidental Experiments, and Experimental Accidents, both Successful and Unsuccessful. Dublin: 1792. V. 37

GAMBARA, LORENZO 1506-1596

De Navigatione Christiphori Columbi Libri Qvatvor. Rome: 1535. V. 40; 42

Rervm Sacrarvm Liber. Antverpiae: 1577. V. 38

GAMBEE, ARTHUR

A Text-Book of the Physiological Chemistry of the Animal Body . . . London: 1880-93. V. 38

GAMBLE, G.

The 'Halls'. London: 1899. V. 46

GAMBLE, J. S.

Flora of the Presidency of Madras. 1979-80. V. 39

GAMBLE, JOHN

Sarsfield; or Wanderings of Youth. London: 1814. V. 38

Sketches of History, Politics and Manners in Dublin, and the North of Ireland in 1816. London: 1826. V. 42

Views of the Society and Manners in the North of Ireland . . . London: 1819. V. 38; 43

GAMBOA, FRANCISCO XAVIER DE

Commentaries on the Mining Ordinances of Spain: Dedicated to His Catholic Majesty, Charles III. London: 1830. V. 41; 46

GAMBOLD, JOHN

A Collection of Hymns of the Children of God in all Ages, From the Beginning Till Now. London: 1754. V. 45

GAMBRILL, RICHARD V. N.

Sporting Stables and Kennels . . . London. V. 43

Sporting Stables and Kennels. London: 1935. V. 42

Sporting Stables and Kennels. New York: 1935. V. 39

Sporting Stables and Kennels. London: 1936. V. 43; 45

GAME Animals. Easthampton: 1981. V. 39

THE GAME of Cricket Illustrated by a Series of Pictures in the Museum of the Marylebone Cricket Club . . . London: 1955. V. 42

THE GAMEKEEPER: a Journal Devoted to the Interests of Game Preservers. London: 1897-1914. V. 39; 40

GAMEL, THOMAS W.

Life of Thomas W. Gamel. N.P.: 1932. V. 43

THE GAMESTER, a True Story; on Which the Tragedy of that Name, Now Acting at the Theatre Royal in Drury-Lane, is Founded. London: 1753. V. 45

GAMGEE, ARTHUR

A Text-Book of the Physiological Chemistry of the Animal Body, Including an Account of the Chemical Changes Occurring in Disease. London: 1880-93. V. 46

GAMGEE, JOSEPH SAMPSON

Medical Reform a Social Question, Comprehensively Studied with the Light of Philosophy, History and Common Sense. London: 1857. V. 38

GAMMEL, H. P. N.

The Laws of Texas 1822-1897. Austin: 1898. 1906. V. 40

The Laws of Texas, 1822-1897. Austin: 1898. V. 37; 38

GAMUCCI, BERNARDO

Libri Qvattro dell'Antichita Della Citta di Roma. 1565. V. 42

GAN, ALEXIS

Konstruktivizm. Tver: 1922. V. 38

GANDEE, B. F.

The Artist, or, Young Ladies' Instructor in Ornamental Painting. London: 1835. V. 39; 44

GANDHI, M. K.

Satyagraha. Ahmedabad: 1951. V. 45

Songs from Prison. London: 1934. V. 43

GANDHI, MAHATMA

A Guide to Health. Triplicane: 1928. V. 46

GANDHI, MOHANDUS K.

The Story of My Experiments with Truth. N.P.: India: 1927-28. V. 38

GANDY, JOSEPH

Designs for Cottages, Cottage Farms and Other Buildings. London: 1805. V. 38; 40; 42

The Rural Architect; Consisting of Various Designs for Country Buildings; (with) Designs for Cottages, Cottage Farms and Rural Buildings. London: 1806-05. V. 37; 38; 40; 44

GANE BROTHERS & CO.

Ooze Sheep. Chicago, St. Louis &: 1911. V. 41

GANF, R. W.

Marsupials of Australia. Volume 2. Carnivorous Marsupials and Bandicoots. Melbourne: 1988. V. 40

GANILH, ANTHONY

Ambrosio de Letinez; or, the First Texian Novel Embracing a Description . . . New York: 1842. V. 38; 40; 42

GANILH, CHARLES BOILEAU

An Enquiry into the Various Systems of Political Economy. New York: 1812. V. 38; 42

GANNET, DEBORAH

An Adrss (sic) Delivered with Applause, at the Federal Street Theatre, Boston, Four Successive Nights of the Different Plays, Beginning March, 22, 1802 . . . Dedham: 1802. V. 43; 45

GANNETT, HENRY

Statistical Atlas of the United States . . . Washington: 1898. V. 41

GANS, C.

Biology of the Reptilia. Volumes 1-4, Morphology. London: 1969-73. V. 37

GANT, ROLAND

Mountains in the Mind. Gloucestershire: 1987. V. 37; 41

GANTILLON, SIMON

Maya. A Play. 1930. V. 38

Mayo. Waltham St. Lawrence: 1930. V. 38; 44

GANTT, E. W.

Address to the People of Arkansas. Philadelphia: 1863. V. 41

GANZ, PAUL

The Paintings of Hans Holbein. London: 1956. V. 43; 45

The Paintings of Hans Holbein. Complete Edition. London: 1950. V. 37; 43

GANZL, KURT

    The British Musical Theatre. 1865-1984. London: 1986. V. 37

THE GAPING, Wide-Mouthed, Waddling Frog. London: 1822. V. 46

GARBIT, F. J.

    The Phonograph and Its Inventor, Thomas Alvah Edison. Boston: 1878. V. 39

GARBUTT, GEORGE

    A Historical and Descriptive View of the Parishes of Monwearmouth and the Port and Borough of Sunderland. Sunderland: 1819. V. 41

GARCAEUS, JOHANN

    Tractatus Brevis et Utilis, de Erigendis Figuris Coeli, Vertificationibus, Revolutionibus et Directionibus . . . Wittenberg: 1556. V. 38

GARCES, FRANCISCO TOMAS HERMENEGILDO 1738-1781

    On the Trail of a Spanish Pioneeer: the Diary of . . . New York: 1900. V. 37; 38; 39; 41; 44

GARCIA CUBAS, ANTONIO

    Memoria Para Servir a la Carta General de la Republica Mexicana . . . Mexico: 1861. V. 38

    The Republic of Mexico in 1876. Mexico: 1876. V. 38; 44

GARCIA DE ZURITA, ANDRES

    Por la Iglesia Metropolitana de Los Reyes en El Peru. Madrid?: 1638. V. 40

GARCIA DEL RIO, JUAN

    Biografia. El Jeneral San Martin. London: 1823. V. 41

GARCIA, FRANCISCO

    Trattato di Tutti i Contratti che nei Negotii, et Commenertii Humani Sogliono Occorrere . . . In Brescia: 1589. V. 38

    Vida, y Martyrio de el Venerable Padre Diego Luis de Sanvitores, de la Compania de Iesus, Primer Apostol de las Islas Marianas . . . Madrid: 1683. V. 41

GARCIA, GENARO

    Documentos Historicos Mexicanos, Obra Commemorativa del Primer Centenario de la Independencia de Mexico. Mexico: 1910. V. 41; 42

GARCIA, GREGORIO

    Origen de Los Indios del Nuevo Mundo & Indias Occidentales, Averiguado con Discurso de Opiniones . . . Madrid: 1729. V. 42; 45

GARCIA MARQUEZ, GABRIEL 1928-

    The Autumn of the Patriarch. New York: 1976. V. 46

    A Chronicle of a Death Foretold. London: 1982. V. 42; 44

    Chronicle of a Death Foretold. New York: 1982. V. 46

    Collected Stories. New York: 1984. V. 42; 43; 46

    Collected Novellas. New York: 1990. V. 44

    The Doom of Damocles. Costa Rica: 1986. V. 46

    El Olor de la Guayaba. Bogata: 1982. V. 46

    El Colonel no Tiene Quien Le Escriba. (No One Writes to the Colonel). Medellin: 1961. V. 44

    The General in His Labyrinth. New York: 1990. V. 43; 44; 45; 46

    La Increible Y Triste Historia de la Candida Erendira Y De Su Abuela Desalmada. Barcelona: 1972. V. 45

    Innocent Erendiva and Other Stories. New York: 1978. V. 46

    Innocent Erendira and Other Stories. London: 1979. V. 45

    Leaf Storm and Other Stories. 1972. V. 46

    Leaf Storm and Other Stories. London: 1972. V. 42; 45

    Leaf Storm. New York: 1972. V. 44

    El Amor en los Tiempos del Colera. Bogota: 1985. V. 46

    Love in the Time of Cholera. London: 1988. V. 42

    Love in the Time of Cholera. New York: 1988. V. 39; 41; 42; 43; 44; 45; 46

    No One Writes to the Colonel. 1968. V. 46

    No One Writes to the Colonel. New York: 1968. V. 37; 43; 45; 46

    No One Writes to the Colonel. London: 1971. V. 40; 42

    No One Writes to the Colonel and Other Stories. Evanston & London: 1968. V. 46

    One Hundred Years of Solitude. 1970. V. 46

    One Hundred Years of Solitude. London: 1970. V. 39; 40; 46

    One Hundred Years of Solitude. New York: 1970. V. 37; 40; 41; 42; 43; 44; 45; 46

    One Hundred Years of Solitude. Lunenburg: 1982. V. 44; 46

    One Hundred Years of Solitude. New York: 1982. V. 39; 43

    One Hundred Years of Solitude. N.P.: 1982. V. 41

    One Hundred Years of Solitude. 1983. V. 39

GARCILASO DE LA VEGA, EL INCA 1539-1616

    First Part of the Royal Commentaries of the Yncas. London: 1869-71. V. 42

    La Florida del Ynca. Lisbona: 1605. V. 42

    La Florida Del Inca. Historia Del Adelantado Hernando De Soto . . . Madrid: 1723. V. 39; 40; 42

    Geschichte der Eroberung von Florida. Zelle, Franckfurt, und: 1753. V. 42

    Histoire de la Conquete de la Florida, ou Relation de ce Que s'Est Passe dans la Decouverte de ce pays Par Ferdinand De Soto. Paris: 1709-11. V. 39

    Histoire des Yncas Rois du Perou, Depuis le Premier Ynca Manco Capac . . . Amsterdam: 1737. V. 44

    Odes and Sonnets. London: 1930. V. 44

    The Royal Commentaries of Peru, in Two Parts. London: 1688. V. 38; 39; 40; 41; 42

    The Works of Garcilasso de la Vega . . . London: 1823. V. 40

GARD, ANSON

    Pioneers of the Upper Ottawa, and Humours of the Valley. Ottawa: 1907. V. 38

GARD, T.

    A Guide to the Turf. London: 1786. V. 38

    The Odds and Chances of Cocking and Other Games, Algebraically and Arithmetically Investigated. London: 1760. V. 40

GARD, WAYNE

    The Chisholm Trail. Norman: 1954. V. 37; 39; 44; 45

    Sam Bass. Boston: 1936. V. 38; 42

GARDEN, ALEXANDER

    Anecdotes of the Revolutionary War in America . . . Charleston. V. 43

    Anecdotes of the Revolutionary War in America. Charleston: 1822. V. 39

    Anecdotes of the American Revolution, Illustrative of the Talents and Virtues of the Heroes and Patriots, Who Acted the Most Conspicuous Parts Therein. Charleston: 1828. V. 38; 41; 45

    Eulogy on Gen. Chs. Cotesworth Pinckney . . . Charleston: 1825. V. 45

    The Genius of Erin, Columbia's Freedom, Flights of Fancy, Lucinda, &c. Charleston: 1836. V. 37; 46

GARDEN Beauties. London: 1860. V. 44; 46

THE GARDEN of Caresses. London: 1934. V. 41
THE GARDEN of Caresses. N.P.: 1934. V. 45
THE GARDEN of Caresses. Waltham St. Lawrence: 1934. V. 40

THE GARDEN of Kama and Other Love Lyrics from India. London: 1903. V. 37

GARDEN Suburbs: Town Planning and Modern Architecture. London: 1910. V. 38

GARDENER, RICHARD

    Memoirs of the Life and Writings (Prose and Verse) of . . . London: 1782. V. 43

GARDENIER, ANDREW A.

    Hand-Book of Ready Reference. Springfield: 1897. V. 41; 43

    The Successful Stockman and Manual of Husbandry. Springfield: 1901. V. 42

GARDENS Old and New. The Country House and Its Garden Environment. London: 1900. V. 44

GARDENSTONE, FRANCIS GARDEN, LORD 1721-1793

    Letter to the People of Lawrencekirk on the Occasion of Presenting the King's Charter . . . Edinburgh: 1823. V. 38; 40; 44

    Travelling Memorandums, Made in a Tour Upon the Continent of Europe, in the Years 1786, 87 & 88 . . . Edinburgh: 1781. V. 38

    Travelling Memorandums, Made in a Tour Upon the Continent of Europe, in the Years 1786, 87 and 88. Edinburgh: 1791. V. 38

GARDER, JOHN

    Vlemk. The Box Painter. Northridge: 1979. V. 39

GARDI, R.

    Indigenous African Architecture. New York: 1974. V. 46

GARDINER, ALAN H.

    The Admonitions of an Egyptian Sage from a Hieratic Papyrus in Leiden. Leipzig: 1909. V. 44

    Ancient Egyptian Onomastica. London: 1947. V. 44

    Egyptian Grammar. Oxford: 1927. V. 38; 42

    Egyptian Letters to the Dead, Mainly from the Old and Middle Kingdoms . . . London: 1928. V. 40; 42; 44

    Egyptian Letters to the Dead . . . London: 1975. V. 44

    Egyptian Grammar: Being an Introduction to the Study of Hieroglyphs. Oxford: 1973. V. 40

    The Royal Canon of Turin. Oxford: 1959. V. 40

    The Tomb of Amenemhet (No. 82) Copied in Line and Colour by Nina de GAris Davies. London: 1915. V. 40

GARDINER, ALAN H. continued

A Topographical Catalogue of the Private Tombs of Thebes. London: 1913. V. 40

The Wilbour Papyrus. Oxford: 1941-52. V. 40; 42

GARDINER, ALLEN

Narrative of a Journey to the Zoolu Country in South Africa. London: 1836. V. 38; 39; 40; 41; 44; 45

GARDINER, E. NORMAN

Olympia: Its History and Remains. Oxford: 1925. V. 42

GARDINER, G. A.

A Brief and Correct Account of an Earthquake Which Happened in South America, by Which some Eighty Thousand Persons Perished . . . Poughkeepsie: 1820. V. 40

GARDINER, HOWARD CALHOUN

In Pursuit of the Golden Dream: Reminiscences of San Francisco and the Northern and Southern Mines, 1849-1857. Stoughton: 1970. V. 37; 38; 41; 44; 45; 46

GARDINER, J. STANLEY

Fauna and Geography of the Maldive and Laccadive Archipelagoes. Cambridge: 1901-06. V. 38

The Fauna and Geography of the Maldive and Laccadive Archipelagoes, Being the Account of an Expedition 1899-1900. Cambridge: 1903. V. 38

The Fauna and Geography of the Maldive and Laccadive Archipelagoes. Cambridge: 1903-06. V. 45

GARDINER, JAMES

Lollardy and the Reformation in England. London: 1908-13. V. 38

GARDINER, JOHN

An Inquiry into the Nature, Cause and Cure of the Gout, and Of Some of the Diseases With Which It is Connected. Philadelphia: 1793. V. 41

GARDINER, JOHN B. S.

Local Notes on Science and Agriculture. Nassau: 1886. V. 40

GARDINER, JOHN SMALLMAN

The Art and Pleasures of Hare-Hunting. London: 1750. V. 45

GARDINER, JOHN SYLVESTER

An Epistle to Zenas. Boston: 1786. V. 40

GARDINER, RALPH

England Grievance Discovered, in Relation to the Coal Trade. Newcastle: 1796. V. 37; 38; 39; 43; 46

GARDINER, RICHARD

A Letter to the Honourable George Townsend, Esq . . . London: 1754. V. 42

GARDINER, SAMUEL R.

History of England from the Accession of James I to the Outbreak of the Civil War, 1603-1642. London: 1887. V. 46

Oliver Cromwell. London: 1899. V. 46

GARDINER, SILVESTER

A Full Answer to the Pamphlet Intitled 'A Short Vindication of the Conduct of the Referees, in the Case of Gardiner Versus Flagg,' etc. Boston: 1767. V. 37

GARDINER, STEPHEN

A Detection of the Devils Sophistrie, Wherwith He Robbeth the Unlearned People, Of the True Byleaf, in the Most Blessed Sacrament of the Aulter. Colophon: 1546. V. 40; 43

A Detection of the Devils Sophistrie . . . N.P.: 1546. V. 45

GARDINER, W. H.

Circular . . . Claimants Under the Award of the King of the Belgians Against Chile . . . N.P.: 1864. V. 39; 41

GARDINER, W. N.

Cupid Turned Volunteer. London: 1804. V. 39

GARDINER, WILLIAM

The Adventures of Congo in Search of His Master. London: 1823. V. 46

The Music of Nature. London: 1832. V. 39

The Music of Nature; or, an Attempt to Prove That What Is Passionate and Pleasing in the Art of Singing, Speaking and Performing Upon Musical Instruments, Is Derived from the Sounds of the Animated World. Boston: 1837. V. 46

GARDNER, A. B.

Dane Data. Hollywood: 1936. V. 45

GARDNER, ALBERT EN EYCK

Winslow Homer, American Artist: His World and His Work. New York: 1961. V. 39

GARDNER, ARTHUR

Alabaster Tombs of the Pre-Reformation Period in England. 1940. V. 46

English Medieval Sculpture. 1951. V. 44

GARDNER, AUGUSTUS K.

Causes and Curative Treatment of Sterility, With a Preliminary Statement of the Physiology of Generation. New York: 1856. V. 41; 42

GARDNER, BRIAN

The Terrible Rain. The War Poets 1939-1945. London: 1966. V. 41

GARDNER, CHARLES

Gardner's New Orleans Directory for 1861, Including Jefferson City, Gretna, Carrollton, Algiers and McDonogh . . . New Orleans: 1861. V. 38

GARDNER, CHARLES K.

Court Martial. Proceedings of a General Court Martial, Held at Fort Independence, (Boston Harbor), For the Trial of Major Charles K. Gardner, of the Third Regiment Infantry, Upon Charges of Misbehavior, Cowardice in the Face of the Enemy . . . Boston: 1816. V. 44

GARDNER, COLONEL

Rules and Regulations for the Field Exercise and Maneuvers of Infantry . . . To Which is added the Best System Extant for Light Infantry and Riflemen. New York: 1820. V. 38

GARDNER, DORSEY

Quatre Bras, Ligny and Waterloo. London: 1882. V. 46

GARDNER, E. C.

Home Interiors. Boston: 1878. V. 42

Homes, & How to Make Them. Boston: 1874. V. 46

The House That Jill Built. After Jack's Had Proved a Failure. New York: 1882. V. 42

GARDNER, ERLE STANLEY

Bats Fly at Dusk. 1942. V. 39

The Case of the Caretaker's Cat. New York: 1935. V. 41; 42

The Case of the Substitute Face. New York: 1938. V. 44

The Case of the Silent Partner. 1940. V. 39

Gold Comes in Bricks. 1940. V. 39

Gold Comes in Bricks. New York: 1940. V. 39; 42

Neighborhood Frontiers. New York: 1954. V. 38; 44

Neighborhood Frontiers. N.P.: 1954. V. 46

GARDNER, ERNEST ARTHUR

A Catalogue of the Greek Vases in the Fitzwilliam Museum, Cambridge. Cambridge: 1897. V. 44

Excavations a Megalogpolis, 1890-1891. London: 1892. V. 40

GARDNER, F. LEIGH

A Catalogue Raisonne of Works on the Occult Sciences. London: 1903-11. V. 42

A Catalogue Raisonne of Works on the Occult Sciences. Volume I. Rosicrucian Books. With an Introduction by Dr. William Wynn Westcott. London;: 1903. V. 37

GARDNER, GEORGE

Travels in the Interior of Brazil, Principally Through the Northern Provinces, and the Gold and Diamond Districts, During the Years 1836-1841. London: 1849. V. 39; 41

GARDNER, GEORGE PEABODY

Chiefly the Orient an Undigested Journal Kept by . . . 27 July 1910 - 10 June 1911. Norwood: 1912. V. 40

GARDNER, HENRY A.

Physical and Chemical Examination of Paints, Varnishes and Colors. Washington: 1925. V. 38

GARDNER, ISABELLA STEWART

A Choice of Manuscripts and Book-bindings from the Library. Boston: 1922. V. 46

GARDNER, J. S.

A Monograph of the British Eocene Flora. London: 1879-86. V. 38

GARDNER, JAMES

The Student's Guide to the Inner Temple. London: 1819. V. 40; 42

GARDNER, JAMES T.

Special Report of New York State Survey on the Preservation of the Scenery of Niagara Falls. Albany: 1880. V. 41; 43

GARDNER, JOHN

The Alliterative Morte Arthur. Carbondale: 1971. V. 44

Art and Tradition in Sir Gawain and the Green Night. N.P.: 1966. V. 45

The Art of Living. New York: 1981. V. 42

The Canon's Yeoman's Prologue and Tale: an Interpretation. N.P.: 1967. V. 45

The Case of the Troubled Trustee, a Perry Mason Mystery. New York: 1965. V. 38

The Forms of Fiction. 1962. V. 45

Forms of Fiction. New York: 1962. V. 37; 45

Freddy's Book. New York: 1980. V. 44

Grendel. New York: 1971. V. 37; 39; 40; 41; 42; 43; 44; 45; 46

Grendel. London: 1972. V. 37; 43; 44

Grendel. New York: 1980. V. 39

Gudgekin the Thistle Girl and Other Tales. New York: 1976. V. 42

An Invective Against Mere Fiction. N.P.: 1967. V. 43

Jason and Medeia. New York: 1973. V. 44

The King of the Hummingbirds and Other Tales. New York: 1977. V. 42

The King's Indian. New York: 1974. V. 44

Mickelsson's Ghosts. New York: 1982. V. 41; 42

The Miller's Mule and Six Other Tales. N.P.: 1965. V. 45

Nicholas Vergette 1923-1974. Northridge: 1978. V. 44

Nickel Mountain. New York: 1973. V. 44

October Light. New York: 1976. V. 46

On Moral Fiction. New York: 1978. V. 44

On Books. N.P.: 1981. V. 44

On Becoming a Novelist. New York: 1983. V. 42

The Poetry of Chaucer. Carbondale: 1977. V. 44

The Resurrection. 1966. V. 39

Resurrection. New York: 1966. V. 37; 44; 45

The Suicide Mountains. New York: 1977. V. 44

The Sunlight Dialogues. New York: 1972. V. 37; 41; 44

The Temptation Game. N.P.: 1980. V. 46

The Three Temptations: Medieval Man in Search of the World. N.P.: 1967. V. 45

Vlemk the Box-Painter. Northridge: 1979. V. 37

The Wreckage of the Agathon. New York: 1980. V. 41

The Wreckage of Agathon. New York: 1970. V. 39; 44; 46

The Wreckage of Agathon by John Gardner. 1970. V. 37

GARDNER, JOHN DUNN

Catalogue of the Principal Portion of the Valuable Library of . . . London: 1854. V. 39

GARDNER, KEITH S.

Sir William Russell Flint 1880-1969. Bristol: 1986. V. 39; 44; 46

A Comparative Review of the Artist's Signed Limited Edition Prints. London: 1986. V. 45

Sir William Russell Flint 1880-1969, a Comparative Review of the Artist's Signed Limited Edition Prints. Wrington: 1986. V. 39

GARDNER, MATTHEW

Autobiography of Elder Matthew Gardner, a Minister in the Christian Church Sixty Three Years. Dayton: 1874. V. 43

GARDNER, PERCY

Sculptured Tombs of Hellas. London: 1896. V. 37; 39

The Types of Greek Coins. Cambridge: 1883. V. 46

GARDNER, RICHARD

Memoirs of the Life & Writings (Prose and Verse) of R-ch-d G-rd-n-r, Esq. London: 1782. V. 38

GARDNER, ROBERT G.

A Human Document. Northampton: 1964. V. 37; 38

GARDNER, ROBERT W.

The Parthenon: Its Science of Forms. New York: 1925. V. 44

GARDNER-SHARP, ABBIE

History of the Spirit Lake Massacre and Captivity of Miss Abbie Gardner. Des Moines: 1885. V. 40

GARDNER, WASHINGTON

Michigan Legislative Manual and Official Directory for the Years 1897-1898. Lansing: 1897. V. 37

GARDNER'S New Orleans Directory for 1869, Including Jefferson City, Gretna, Carrollton, Algiers and McDonogh, with a Street and Levee Guide and Business Directory. New Orleans: 1868. V. 37

GARDNIER, ALLEN E.

Narrative of a Journey to the Zoolu Country in South Africa. London: 1836. V. 43

GARDNOR, J.

Hints of Occurrences on a Tour to Mayence, Aix-la-Chapelle, Brussels with Explanations of Views Taken on and Near the Rhine . . . London: 1791. V. 37

THE GARDYNERS Passetaunce. London: 1985. V. 45; 46

GARENGEOT, RENE JACQUES CROISSANT DE

Nouveau Traite des Instruments de Chirurgie les Plus Utiles, et de Plusieurs Machines Propres Pour les Maladies . . . Paris: 1728. V. 40

GARESCHE, LOUIS

Biography of Lieut. Col. Julius P. Garesche, Assistant Adjutant General U.S. Army. Philadelphia: 1887. V. 37; 39; 45

GARFIELDE, S.

Compiled Laws of the State of California . . . with the Constitution of California. Benicia: 1853. V. 37

GARGANO, GIOVAN BATTISTA

Fiori di Recami. Naples: 1613. V. 40

GARGAZ, PIERRE ANDRE

A Project of Universal and Perpetual Peace. New York: 1922. V. 45

GARGETT, VALERIE

The Black Eagle. V. 45

GARIBALDI, GIUSEPPE 1807-1882

An Autobiography. London: 1860. V. 37

GARIEL & GARNIER

Dessins et Notices Relatifs a Diverses Constructions en Ciment de l'Exploitation de Vassy-Les-Avallon (Yonne) appartenant a M. Gariel, Successeur de Gariel et Garnier. Paris: 1853. V. 44

GARIMBERTO, GIROLAMO

Concetti Divinissimi . . . Raccolti . . . per Scrivere & Ragionar Familiarmente. Venice: 1551. V. 43

De Regimenti Publici De La Citta. Venice: 1544. V. 37

Della Fortuna Libri Sei. Venice: 1547. V. 37

GARIMBERTO, HIERONIMO

Concetti . . . et Altri Degni Auttori. Venice: 1575. V. 40

GARIOT, JEAN BAPTISTE

Traite des Maladies de la Bouche, d'Apres letat Actuel des Connoissances en Medecine et en Chirurgie, Qui Comprend la Structure et les Fonctions de la Bouche . . . Paris: 1805. V. 41; 45

GARISENDI, ANTENOR

Torneo Fatto Sotto il Castello d'Argio. Bologna: 1578. V. 40

A GARLAND for Jake Zeitlin. Los Angeles: 1967. V. 38

A GARLAND for Stephen Spender. Edinburgh: 1991. V. 45

A GARLAND for the Laureate. Stratford-upon-Avon: 1981. V. 41; 45

GARLAND, H.

Ancient Egyptian Metallurgy. London: 1927. V. 44

GARLAND, HAMLIN

Back-Trailers from the Middle Border. New York: 1928. V. 37

The Book of the American Indian. New York: 1923. V. 38; 39; 42; 44; 45; 46

The Book of the American Indian. London: 1933. V. 40

Crumbling Idols. Chicago: 1894. V. 38

A Little Norsk, or Ol'Pap's Flaxen. New York: 1892. V. 39

Main-Traveled Roads, Being Six Stories of the Mississippi Valley. Chicago: 1893. V. 44; 46

A Member of the Third House. Chicago: 1892. V. 40; 43

The Mystery of the Buried Crosses: a Narrative of Psyhic Exploration. V. 39

A Pioneer Mother. Chicago: 1922. V. 41

Prairie Folks. Chicago: 1893. V. 41; 45

A Son of the Middle Border. New York: 1919. V. 41

The Spirit of Sweetwater. Philadelphia: 1898. V. 43

Studies in Literature and Expressive Art. Boston: 1888. V. 45

GARLAND, HUGH A.

The Life of John Randolph. New York: 1850. V. 46

Supreme Court of Missouri. John Perry vs. T. and J. O'Hanlon. Argument for Plantiff. St. Louis: 1847. V. 40

GARLAND, JAMES A.

The Private Stable Its Establishment, Management and Appointments . . . Boston: 1899. V. 43

GARLAND, LAWRENCE

The Affair of the Unprincipled Publisher. New Castle: 1983. V. 40; 41

GARLAND, N. SURREY

Garland's Banks, Bankers and Banking and Financial Directory of Canada . . . Ottawa: 1895. V. 44

A GARLAND of New Songs. Crockery's Lamentation. Death of Abercrombie. The Soldier's Funeral. The Wounded Hussar. The Banks of the Dee. The Blind Boy. Poor Mad Margery. Newcastle-upon-Tyne: 1805-10. V. 38

A GARLAND Of New Songs. The Battle of the Nile. Tom Starboard. The Sailor's Adieu. Tom Bowling. True Courage. The Sea Boy. Newcastle upon Tyne: 1810. V. 38

GARLICK, KENNETH

Sir Thomas Lawrence. London: 1954. V. 39

GARLICK, THEODATUS

A Treatise on the Artificial Propagation of Certain Kinds of Fish, with the Description and Habits . . . Cleveland: 1857. V. 44

GARNEAU, FRANCOIS XAVIER

History of Canada, from the Time of Its Discovery Till the Union Year (1840-41). Montreal: 1860. V. 38

GARNEAU, HECTOR DE SAINT-DENYS

Nine Poems from 'Poesias Completes' . . . Iroquois Falls: 1955. V. 43

GARNER, ALAN

Elidor. London: 1965. V. 38

The Owl Service. London: 1967. V. 46

The Weirdstone of Brisingamen - a Tale of Alderley. London: 1960. V. 38; 41

GARNER, JAMES W.

Reconstruction in Mississippi. New York: 1901. V. 44; 45

GARNER, R.

The Natural History of the County of Stafford . . . London: 1844-60. V. 42

The Natural History of the County of Stafford. London: 1844. V. 37

GARNER, R. L.

Gorillas and Chimpanzees. London: 1896. V. 41

GARNER, THOMAS

The Domestic Architecture of England During the Tudor Period Illustrated in a Series of Photographs and Measured Drawings of County Mansions, Manor Houses and Smaller Buildings. London: 1911. V. 41

GARNETT, ALGERNON S.

A Treatise on the Hot Springs of Arkansas. St. Louis: 1874. V. 37; 39; 43

GARNETT, DAVID 1892-1981

Aspects of Love. London: 1955. V. 42; 46

Beany-Eye. London: 1935. V. 42

The Golden Echo. The Flowers of the Forest. The Familiar Faces. London: 1953-62. V. 46

A Man in the Zoo. London: 1924. V. 41; 44; 46

No Love. London: 1929. V. 38; 41; 46

The Old Dovecote. London: 1928. V. 38

Purl and Plain and Other Stories. London: 1973. V. 41

The Sailor's Return. London: 1925. V. 41

GARNETT, EDWARD

The Paradox Club. London: 1888. V. 38

GARNETT, FRANK W.

Westmorland Agriculture 1800-1900. Kendal: 1912. V. 44

GARNETT, HENRY 1555-1606

A True and Perfect Relation of the Whole Proceedings Against the Late Most Barbarous Traitors, Garnet, a Iesuite and His Confederats. London: 1606. V. 40; 42

GARNETT, JAMES M.

Lectures on Female Education, Comprising the First and Second Series of a Course Delivered to Mrs. Garnett's Pupils, at Elm-Wood, Essex County, Virginia. Richmond: 1825. V. 44; 45

GARNETT, LOUIS AYRES

Creature Songs. Boston: 1912. V. 37

GARNETT, LUCY M.

Ottoman Wonder Tales. London: 1915. V. 44

GARNETT, LUCY M. J.

Greek Folk-Songs from the Turkish Provinces of Greece. London: 1885. V. 39

Greek Folk Posey: Annotated Translations, from the Whole Cycle of Romantic Folk-Verse and Folk-Prose. Guildford: 1896. V. 45

The Women of Turkey and Their Folk-Lore. London: 1893. V. 37

GARNETT, PORTER

A Documentary Account of the Beginnings of the laboratory Press, Carnegie Institute of Technology. Pittsburgh: 1927. V. 43

GARNETT, R. A.

Lady into Fox. London: 1923. V. 41

GARNETT, RANDALL

Too Many Magicians. Garden City: 1967. V. 39

GARNETT, RICHARD

English Literature An Illustrated Record in Four Volumes. London: 1903. V. 39

English Literature, an Illustrated Record. New York: 1905/04/03/05. V. 43

Three Hundred Notable Books: Added to the Library of the British Museum . . . 1890-1899. London: 1899. V. 46

The Twilight of the Gods and Other Tales. London: 1888. V. 46

The Twilight of the Gods. London: 1903. V. 41; 42; 43; 44

The Twilight of the Gods. London: 1924. V. 40; 41; 42; 45

GARNETT, T.

Observations On a Tour through the Highlands and Part of the Western Isles of Scotland; Particularly Staffa and Icolmkill . . . London: 1811. V. 41

GARNETT, THEODORE STANFORD

J. E. B. Stuart (Major-General). Commander of the Cavalry Corps, Army of Northern Virginia. C.S.A. New York: & Washington: 1907. V. 45

GARNETT, THOMAS

Experiments and Observations on the Horley Green Spaw, Near Halifax. Bradford: 1790. V. 42

A Lecture on the Preservation of Health. London: 1800. V. 41; 42

Observations on a Tour Through the Highlands and Part of the Western Isles of Scotland, Particularly Staffa and Icolmkill . . . London: 1800. V. 37; 42; 43

Popular Lectures on Zoonomia, or the Laws of Animal Life in Health and Disease. London: 1804. V. 41; 44

A Treatise on the Mineral Waters of Harrowgate . . . Leeds: 1794. V. 37

GARNEYS, CHARLES

Catalogue of the Collection of . . . Curiosities . . . Norwich: 1809. V. 44

GARNIER, ALBERT

Scientific Billiards. New York: 1880. V. 40; 42

GARNIER, CHARLES

Le Nouvel Opera de Paris. Paris: 1878-81. V. 37; 38

GARNIER, EDOUARD

The Soft Porcelain of Sevres. London: 1892. V. 41

GARNIER, JEAN LOUIS CHARLES

Restaurations des Monuments Antiques par les Architectes Pensionnaires de l'Academie de France a Rome . . . Paris: 1884. V. 45

GARNIER, JOSEPH

Du Principe de Population. Paris: 1857. V. 43

GARNIER, P. M.

Dialogues en Quatre Langues, Francoise, Espagnole, Italienne & Allemande. Gemein Gesprach in vier Spraachen, Frantzosisch, Spanisch, Italianisch, und Hoochdeutsch. Amsterdam: 1656. V. 37

GARNIER, RUSSELL M.

History of the English Landed Interest, Its Customs, Laws and Agriculture. London: 1892. V. 37

GARNIER, TONY

Les Grands Travaux de la ville de Lyon, Etudes, Projets et Tavaux Executes. Paris: 1920. V. 38

Une Cite Industrielle Etude Pour la Construction des Villes. Paris: 1932. V. 41; 45

GAROSI, ALCIDE

Siena Nella Storia Della Medicina. Florence: 1958. V. 46

GARRAGHAN, GIBLERT J.

The Jesuits of the Middle United States. New York: 1938. V. 44

GARRAN, ANDREW

Picturesque Atlas of Australasia. Sydney: 1886. V. 39

GARRAN, ANDREWS

Picturesque Atlas of Australasia. London: 1886. V. 38

GARRARD, LEWIS H.

Chambersburg in the Colony and the Revolution. Philadelhia: 1856. V. 37; 39; 43

Memoir of Charlotte Chambers. Philadelphia: 1856. V. 37; 45

Wah-To-Yah, and the Taos Trail. Cincinnati: 1850. V. 37; 39; 40; 42; 43; 45; 46

Wah-To-Yah & The Taos Trail. San Francisco: 1936. V. 37; 38; 40; 43; 45

Wah-to-Yah and the Taos Trail. Glendale: 1938. V. 40; 45

GARRATT, ALFRED

Electro-Physiology and Electro-Therapeutics: Showing the Best Method For the Medical Uses of Electricity. Boston: 1861. V. 42

GARRED, ARCHIBALD

The Inborn Factors in Disease, an Essay. Oxford: 1931. V. 40

GARREN, A.

Brand Book of Oregon Bands Published by A. Garren, Union, Oregon, 1899. Cheyenne: 1889. V. 41; 42

GARRET, DANIEL

Designs and Estimates of Arm Houses &c. for the County of York, Northumberland, Cumberland, Westmoreland, and Bishoprick of Durham. London: 1747. V. 39; 40

GARRETSON, JAMES E.

A System of Oral Surgery. Philadelphia: 1881. V. 42

GARRETT, CAROLINE

In-Whan and the Peachtree. Illustrated by Naoko Matsubara. Columbus: 1985. V. 37

GARRETT, EDMUND HENRY 1853-1929

Elizabethan Songs 'In Honour of Love and Beautie.' London: 1891. V. 42

Elizabethan Songs 'In Honour of Love and Beautie.' Boston: 1895. V. 40

GARRETT, JULIA K.

Green Flag Over Texas, A Story of the Last Years of Spain in Texas. New York: 1939. V. 44

Green Flag Over Texas: A Story of the Last Years of Spain in Texas. New York/Dallas: 1939. V. 37

GARRETT, PAT F.

The Authentic Life of Billy the Kid. New York: 1927. V. 46

GARRETT, RANDALL

Too Many Magicians. New York: 1967. V. 37

GARRETT, WILLIAM

Reminiscences of Public Men in Alabama, for Thirty Years. Atlanta: 1872. V. 42

GARRICK CLUB

A Catalogue of the Pictures in the Garrick Club. London: 1936. V. 45

GARRICK, DAVID 1717-1779

Catalogue of the Library, Splendid Books of Prints, Poetical and Historical Tracts . . . London: 1823. V. 40

A Catalogue of a Valuable and Highly Interesting Collection of Engravings, Consisting Chiefly of English and Foreign Portraits . . . London: 1825. V. 40; 42

The Dramatic Works, to Which is Prefixed a Life of the Author. Dublin: 1780. V. 43

The Dramatic Works, to Which is Prefixed a Life of the author. London: 1798. V. 42; 45

The Fribbleriad. London: 1761. V. 40; 45

The Guardian. London: 1759. V. 38

Lethe. London: 1749. V. 37; 38; 39; 40; 43; 45; 46

Letters of David Garrick and Georgina Countess Spencer 1759-79. Cambridge: 1960. V. 38; 44

The Letters of David Garrick. London: 1963. V. 42

Lilliput. London: 1757. V. 39

A New Dramatic Entertainment, Called a Christmas Tale . . . London: 1774. V. 39

An Ode on the Death of Mr. Pelham. London: 1754. V. 42; 43

An Ode Upon Dedicating a Building and Erecting a Statue, to Shakespeare. London: 1769. V. 38; 41

A Peep Behind the Curtain; or, the New Rehearsal. London: 1767. V. 37

The Poetical Works . . . London: 1785. V. 41; 42

The Private Correspondence of David Garrick with the Most Celebrated Persons of His Time. London: 1835. V. 38

The Sick Money, a Fable. London: 1765. V. 40; 42

Some Unpublished Correspondence of . . . Boston: 1907. V. 45

GARRICK, GEORGE

The Letters of George Garrick. Oxford: 1963. V. 45

GARRICK'S Vagary: or, England Run Mad. London: 1769. V. 37

GARRISON, EDWARD

Early Italian Painting. London: 1984. V. 44

GARRISON, EDWARD B.

Italian Romanesque Panel Painting. Florence: 1949. V. 46

GARRISON, EVERETT

A Master's Guide to Building a Bamboo Fly Rod. Katonah: 1977. V. 39

GARRISON, F. G.

Notes on the History of Military Medicine. London: 1921-22. V. 40

GARRISON, FIELDING H.

An Introduction to the History of Medicine. Philadelphia: 1914. V. 42; 45

An Introduction to the History of Medicine. Philadelphia: 1929. V. 37; 39; 43

Notes on the History of Military Medicine. Washington: 1922. V. 41

Principles of Anatomical Illustration before Vesalius: An Inquiry into the Rationale of Artistic Anatomy. New York: 1926. V. 37

GARRISON, GEORGE P.

Diplomatic Correspondence of the Republic of Texas. Washington: 1908. V. 37; 38; 43; 44; 45

Diplomatic Correspondence of the Republic of Texas. Washington: 1908-11. V. 38; 40; 42; 44

GARRISON, LLOYD MC KIM

An Illustrated History of the Hasty Pudding Club Theatricals. Cambridge: 1897. V. 44

GARRISON, WENDELL PHILLIPS

The New Gulliver. Jamaica: 1898. V. 46

William Lord Garrison, 1805-1879 . . . New York: 1885/89. V. 46

GARRISON, WILLIAM LLOYD

An Address Delivered Before the Old Colony Anti-Slavery Society, at South Scituate, Massachusetts, July 4, 1839. Boston: 1839. V. 42

The Attorney General, by Information, vs. William L. Garrison, et als., Trustees. Report, &c. Suffolk County. Boston: 1868. V. 40

A Brief Sketch of the Trial of William Lloyd Garrison, for an Alleged Libel on Francis Todd, of Newburyport, Massachusetts. Boston: 1834. V. 42

Sonnets and Other Poems. Boston: 1843. V. 37; 42; 46

Southern Hatred of the American Government, the People of the North and Free Insitutions. Boston: 1862. V. 42

The Spirit of the South Towards Northern Freemen and Soldiers Defending the American Flag Against Traitors of the Deepest Dye. Boston: 1861. V. 42

Thoughts on African Colonization; or, an Impartial Exhibition of the Doctrines, Principles and Purposes of the American Colonization Society. Boston: 1823. V. 44

Thoughts on African Colonization . . . Boston: 1832. V. 45

GARROD, ALFRED B.

A Treatise on Gout and Rheumatic Gout. London: 1876. V. 40

GARROD, D. A. E.

The Stone Age of Mount Carmel. Oxford: 1937-39. V. 40; 42

GARROW, D. W.

The History and Antiquities of Croydon, with a Variety of Other Interesting Matter . . . Croydon: 1818. V. 39

GARSAULT, A. DE

Le Nouveau Parfait Marechal. (with) Traite des Voitures. Paris: 1756. V. 44

GARSAULT, FRANCOIS ALEXANDRE DE

L'Art de La Lingerie. Paris: 1771. V. 41

GARSHIN, VSEVOLD MIKHAILOVICH

The Red Flower. Northampton: 1961. V. 39

GARSTANG, JOHN

The Burial Customs of Ancient Egypt as Illustrated by Tombs of the Middle Kingdom . . . London: 1907. V. 44

El Arabah: a Cemetery of the Middle Kingdom; Survey of the Old Kingdom Temenos . . . London: 1901. V. 44

Explorations in Cilicia. The Neilson Expedition . . . Liverpool: 1939. V. 44

The Geography of the Hittite Empire. London: 1959. V. 40

The Land of the Hitties. London: 1910. V. 40

Mahasna and Bet Khallaf. London: 1902. V. 44

GARSTANG, JOHN continued

Meroe, the City of the Ethiopians. Oxford: 1911. V. 40

Prehistoric Mersin: Humuk Tepe in Southern Turkey. Oxford: 1953. V. 37; 40; 42; 44

Tombs of the Third Egyptian Dynasty at Reqaqnah and Bet Khallaf. Westminster: 1904. V. 42; 44

GARSTIN, CROSBIE

Samuel Kelly, an Eighteenth Century Seaman, Whose Days Have Been Few and Evil, to Whom is Added Remarks, Etc. on Places He Visited During His Pilgrimage in this Wildneress. New York: 1925. V. 39

GARSTIN NORMAN

The Suitors of Aprille. London: 1900. V. 46

GARSTON, EDGAR

Greece Revisited and Sketches in Lower Egypt in 1840, with Thirty-Six Hours of a Campaign in Greece in 1825. London: 1842. V. 39

GARTH, SAMUEL

Claremont. London: 1715. V. 38; 41

The Dispensary: a Poem. London: 1699. V. 38; 41; 46

The Dispensary. London: 1706. V. 45

The Dispensary. A Poem. (with) A Complete Key to the Seventh Edition of the Dispensary. London: 1714. V. 41

The Dispensary. A Poem on Six Cantos. The Tenth Edition. London : 1741. V. 37

The Works of Sir Samuel Garth, Knight. Dublin: 1769. V. 38

GARTHWAIT, HENRY

The Evangelicall Harmonie, Reducing the Foure Evangelists Into One Continued Context . . . Cambridge: 1634. V. 45

GARVEY, ELEANOR

The Artist and the Book, 1860-1960. Boston: 1861. V. 42; 43; 44

GARY, ROMAIN

Lady L. New York: 1959. V. 45

GARZA, JOSE

Troubles in Texas, 1832: A Tejano Viewpoint from San Antonio. Austin: 1983. V. 37

GARZONI, TOMASO 1549-1589

L'Hospidale de'Pazzi, Incurabili, Nuovamente Ristampato & Posto in Luce. Venetia: 1594. V. 40; 44

L'Hospital des Fols Incurables . . . Paris: 1620. V. 43; 45

THE GAS-LIGHTER'S Poem, Addressed to His Worthy Masters and Mistresses. Hancock: 1830? V. 46

GASC, F. E. A.

The Smallest French and English Dictionary in the World. By F.E.A. Gasc. Glasgow/London: 1898. V. 37

GASCOIGNE, GEORGE

A Hundredth Sundrie Flowers. London: 1926. V. 46

The Queen's Majesty's Entertainment at Woodstock, 1575 . . . Oxford: 1903 & 1910. V. 39

GASCOIGNE, TRENCH, MRS.

The Handbook of Turning. London: 1846. V. 38

The Handbook of Turning. London: 1852. V. 38

GASCOYNE, CRISP

An Address to the Liverymen of the City of London, from Sir Crisp Gascoyne, Knt. Late Lord-Mayor, Relating to His Conduct in the Cases of Eliz. Canning and Mary Squires. London: 1754. V. 46

GASCOYNE, DAVID

Collected Poems. London: 1965. V. 40; 43

Holderlin's Madness. London: 1938. V. 44

Man's Life Is This Meat. 1936. V. 42

Man's Life is This Meat. London: 1936. V. 38; 43

Roman Balcony and Other Poems. London: 1932. V. 38

The Sune at Midnight. London: 1970. V. 37

Three Poems. Edinburgh: 1976. V. 42

Three Poems. London: 1976. V. 38; 42

A Vagrant. London: 1950. V. 40; 42

GASH, JONATHAN

Gold from Gemini. London: 1978. V. 45

GASK, NORMAN

Old Silver Spoons of England. London: 1962. V. 38

GASKELL, C. A.

The C. A. Gaskell Family and Business Atlas of the World. Chicago: 1895. V. 45

GASKELL, ELIZABETH CLEGHORN 1810-1865

Cranford. London: 1853. V. 38; 39

Cranford. London: 1891. V. 41; 42

Cranford. London: 1904. V. 41; 43; 45

Cranford. London: 1920. V. 38

Cranford. London: 1923. V. 45

Cranford. London: 1940. V. 38; 40; 46

The Life of Charlotte Bronte. London: 1857. V. 37; 38; 39; 41; 43; 44; 45

The Life of Charlotte Bronte. New York: 1857. V. 41; 44; 46

The Life of Charlotte Bronte. London: 1858. V. 41; 43

The Life of Charlotte Bronte. London: 1860. V. 44; 45

The Life of Charlotte Bronte. New York & London: 1900. V. 42

Mary Barton: a Tale of Manchester Life. London: 1848. V. 37; 43; 44; 45; 46

Mary Barton. London: 1849. V. 44

The Moorland Cottage. London: 1850. V. 40

My Lady Ludlow and Other Tales . . . London: 1861. V. 44

North and South. London: 1855. V. 37; 38; 44; 45; 46

North and South. London: 1900. V. 43; 45

Novels and Tales. London: 1889-95. V. 39

Round the Sofa. London: 1859. V. 44

Ruth. London: 1853. V. 44; 45; 46

Wives and Daughters. London: 1866. V. 44; 45

Wives and Daughters. New York: 1866. V. 37; 39; 43

The Works of Mrs. Gaskell. V. 37

The Works. London: 1890's. V. 41; 43; 45

The Works. New York: 1906. V. 42

The Works. London: 1974. V. 39

GASKELL, ERNEST

Ulster Leaders. Social and Political. London. V. 43

GASKELL, JANE

The Atlan Saga. New York: 1977-79. V. 37

GASKELL, PHILIP

John Baskerville. A Bibliography. Cambridge: 1959. V. 44

GASKILL, PETER

Old Bachelors; Their Varieties, Characters and Condtions. London: 1835. V. 40

GASKIN, ARTHUR, MRS.

ABC an Alphabet. London: 1895. V. 43

The Travellers and Other Tales. London: 1898. V. 42; 44

GASKIN, L. J. P.

A Bibliography of African Art. London: 1965. V. 38

GASPAR DA MADRE DE DEOS, F.

Memorias Para a Historia da Capitania de S. Vicente, Hoje Chamada de S. Paulo do Estado do Brasil . . . Lisbon: 1797. V. 45

GASPARI Colonii Castellonii, Magni Quondam Franciae Amirali, Vita. N.P.: 1575. V. 38

GASPEY, THOMAS

Takings, Or, The Life of a Collegian. London: 1821. V. 37; 38; 39; 40; 41; 42; 43; 45

GASPEY, WILLIAM

Tallis's Illustrated London, in Commemoration of the Great Exhibitions of All Nations in 1851. London & New York: 1851-52. V. 43; 45

GASQUET, ABBOT

The Greater Abbeys of England. London: 1908. V. 44

GASQUET, CARDINAL

Religio Religiosi. 1916. V. 41

GASS, JACOB

Chronicon Ephratense: a History of the Community of Seventh Day Baptists at Ephrata, Lancaster County . . . Lancaster: 1889. V. 39; 42

GASS, PATRICK 1771-1870

Gass's Journal of the Lewis and Clark Expedition . . . Chicago: 1904. V. 38; 39; 44

A Journal of the Voyages and Travels of a Corps of Discovery, Under the Command of Capt. Lewis and Capt. Clarke (sic) . . . Pittsburgh: 1804/05/06. V. 45

GASS, PATRICK 1771-1870 continued

A Journal of the Voyages and Travels of a Corps of Discovery, Under the Command of Capt. Lewis and Capt. Clark. Pittsburgh: 1807. V. 37; 41; 42; 43; 45

A Journal of the Voyages and Travels . . . Under the Command of Capt. Lewis and Capt. Clark. London: 1808. V. 38; 39

A Journal of the Voyages and Travels of a Corps of Discovery Under the Command of Captain Lewis and Captain Clarke (sic). Pittsburgh: 1808. V. 45

Journal of the Voyages and Travels of a Corps of Discovery, Under the Command of Capt. Lewis and Capt Clarke (sic). Philadelphia: 1811. V. 42; 45

Journal of the Voyages and Travels of a Corps of Discovery, Under the Command of Capt. Lewis and Capt. Clarke (sic) . . . From the Mouth of the River Missouri through the Interior Parts of North America to the Pacific Ocean . . . Philadelphia: 1812. V. 38; 40

Lewis & Clark's Journal to the Rocky Mountains in the Years 1804-5-6. Dayton: 1847. V. 40

Voyages des Capitaines Lewis et Clark, Depuis l'Embouchure du Missouri, jusqu'a lEntree de l'Ocean Pacifique; fait dans les annees 1804, 1805 et 1806, part Ordre du Gouvernement des Etats-Unis. Paris: 1810. V. 37

GASS, WILLIAM H.

The First Winter of My Married Life. Northridge: 1979. V. 45

In the Heart of the Heart of the Country. New York: 1968. V. 45

Omensetter's Luck. 1966. V. 42

Omensetter's Luck. New York: 1966. V. 37; 38; 39; 40; 42; 44; 45; 46

Omensetter's Luck. London: 1967. V. 37; 43; 45

On Being Blue. London. V. 42

On Being Blue. Boston: 1975. V. 42

On Being Blue. Boston: 1976. V. 46

Willie Masters' Lonesome Wife. Evanston: 1968. V. 46

Willie Masters' Lonesome Wife. N.P.: 1968. V. 39

GASSENDI, PIERRE

The Mirrour of the Nobility and Gentility. London: 1657. V. 39; 42; 44

GASSENDI, PIETRO

Viri Illustris Nicolai Clavdii Fabricii de Peiresc . . . Vita. The Hague: 1651. V. 37

GASSER, ACHILLES P.

Historiarum et Chronicorum Mundi Epitomes Libellus, Velut Index Accuratius Recens Recognitus, Emasculatus, Auctus & Locupletutus. Venice: 1533. V. 39

GASSER, ACHILLES PERMIN

Historiarum et Chronicorum Mundi Epitome Velut Index. N.P.: 1533. V. 46

GASSER, ACHILLES PIRMINIUS

Brief Recueil de Toutes Chroniques et Hystoriques Jusques 1534. Antwerp: 1534. V. 41

GASSIER, PIERRE

The Drawings of Goya: The Sketches, Studies and Individual Drawings. New York: 1975. V. 40; 43

The Life and Complete Work of Francisco Goya with a Catalogue Raisonne of the Paintings, Drawings and Engravings. New York: 1971. V. 37; 40; 43; 45

GASSNER, JOHN

Best American Plays 1918-1973. New York: 1939-73. V. 46

GAST, JOHANN

Scholae Christinae Epigrammatvm Libri Dvo, ex Uarijs Christinais Poetis Decerpti, in Usum Adolescentulorum. Basle: 1539. V. 42

GASTER, M.

The Titled Bible. A Model Codex of the Pentateuch Reproduced in Facsimile from Ms no. 85 of the Gaster Collection Now in the British Museum with a Dissertation on the History of the Titles . . . London: 1929. V. 44

GASTER, MOSES

Studies and Texts in Folklore, Magic, Medieval Romance, Hebrew Apocrypha and Samaritan Archaeology. London: 1925-28. V. 42

GASTINEAU, HENRY

South Wales Illustrated in A Series of Views . . . London: 1830. V. 39; 40; 42; 44; 46

South Wales Illustrated, In a Series of Views Comprising the Picturesque Scenery, Towns, Castles, Seats of Nobility and Gentry, Antiquities . . . London: 1832. V. 40

Wales Illustrated . . . Northern Series. London: 1840. V. 38

GASTONE, GIAN

The Last of the Medici. Florence: 1930. V. 43

GASTRELL, FRANCIS

The Bishop of Chester's Case with Relation to the Wardenship of Manchester in Which It is Shewn . . . Cambridge: 1731. V. 42

GATACRE, ALICE

The Keeshond. London: 1938. V. 40; 46

GATE, ETHEL MAY

Tales from the Enchanted Isles. New Haven: 1926. V. 43

GATENBY, GREG

52 Pickup 76. Toronto: 1977. V. 39

GATES, SUSA YOUNG

History of the Young Ladies' Mutual Improvement Association of the Church of Jesus Christ of Latter-Day Saints. From November 1869 to June 1910. Salt Lake City: 1911. V. 44

The Young Woman's Journal. Salt Lake City: 1889-1892. V. 42

GATES, THEODORE B.

The 'Ulster Guard' (20th New York State Militia) and the War of the Rebellion. New York: 1879. V. 43

GATES, THEOPHILUS R.

The Trials, Experience, Exercises of Mind and First Travels, of Theophilus R. Gates. Poughkeepsie: 1810. V. 40

GATES, WILLIAM

The Dresden Codex. Baltimore: 1932. V. 45

Recollections of Life in Van Dieman's Land; By . . . One of The Canadian Patriots. Lockport: 1850. V. 37

GATES, WILLIAM G.

City of Portsmouth: Records of the Corporation 1835-1927, (1928-1930) 1931, 1935). Portsmouth: 1928-36. V. 39; 42

Illustrated History of Portsmouth. Portsmouth: 1900. V. 39

GATHERINGS from the Wine-Lands. London: 1855. V. 45

GATHORNE-HARDY, ROBERT

A Month of Years. London: 1956. V. 45

Recollections of Logan Pearsaqll Smith - the Story of a Friendship. London: 1949. V. 38

GATKE, HEINRICH

Heligoland as an Ornithological Observatory. Edinburgh: 1895. V. 40

GATSCHET, ALBERT S.

The Klamath Indians of Southwestern Oregon. Washington: 1890. V. 37; 39; 44

A Migration Legend of the Creek Indians . . . Philadelphia: 1884. V. 45

GATTEY, HORATIA

K.F. Juliana Horatia Ewing and Her Books. London: 1887. V. 37

GATTY, ALFRED, MRS.

The Book of Sundials. London: 1900. V. 38

GATTY, C.

Catalogue of the Engraved Gems and Rings in the Collection of Joseph Mayer F.S.A. London: 1879. V. 37

GATTY, MARGARET SCOTT 1809-1873

Aunt Judy's Tales. London: 1859/58. V. 44

The Book of Sun-Dials. London: 1872. V. 44

British Sea-Weeds. London: 1872. V. 37; 38; 40; 42; 46

British Sea-Weeds . . . London: 1874. V. 42

The Old Folks Home. London: 1861. V. 39

Parables from Nature. London: 1865. V. 39

Recollections of the Life of the Rev. A. J. Scott. London: 1842. V. 39

GAUBIUS, HIERONYMUS DAVID 1705-1780

Institutiones Pathologiae Medicinalis. Leidae Batavorum: 1763. V. 44

GAUCI, W.

Windsor and Eton. London: 1828. V. 41

GAUDEN, JOHN 1605-1662

A Discourse of Artificial Beauty, in Point of Conscience Between Two Ladies. London: 1662. V. 42; 44; 45

A Discourse of Artificial Beauty, In Point of Conscience Between Two Ladies. London: 1692. V. 38; 45

Hieraspistes: a Defense by Way of Apology for the Ministry and Ministers of the Church of England . . . London: 1653. V. 42

GAUDIER-BRZESKA, H.

Twenty Drawings from the Notebooks of H. Gaudier-Brzeska. London: 1916. V. 38

GAUDIN, S. D.

Forty-Four Years with the Northern Crees. Toronto: 1942. V. 43

GAUGER, NICHOLAS

Fires Improv'd. London: 1715. V. 38; 39; 45

GAUGER, NICOLAS

La Mechanique du Feu, ou 'Art de'en Augmenter les Effets, et d'en Diminuer la Depense. Paris: 1749. V. 42

GAUGH, HARRY F.

De Kooning. New York: 1983. V. 43

GAUGIN, PAUL

Paul Gaugin Letters to Amborse Vollard & Andre Fontainas. Edited by John Rewald. San Francisco: 1943. V. 37

GAUGIN, ROBERT

Ars Versificatoria. Paris: 1505. V. 42

De Francorum Regum Gestis . . . Annales. Lyons: 1524. V. 42

GAUGUIN, PAUL

Intimate Journals. New York: 1921. V. 41

Noa Noa. New York. V. 45; 46

Noa Noa. 1919. V. 45

Noa-Noa. Paris: 1954. V. 44

GAUKES, YVO 1660-1738

Dissertatio de Medicina ad Certitudinem Mathematicam Evehenda . . . Amsterdam: 1712. V. 43

GAULDI, ABBOT

The Life of Donna Olimpia maldachini. Who governed the Church during the time of Innocent the X. Which was from the year 1644 to the Year 1655. London: 1667. V. 37

GAULE, JOHN

Practique Theories. London: 1629. V. 38

GAULTIER, ABBE

A Complete Course of Geography by Means of Instructive Games . . . London: 1808. V. 37

GAULTIER, ALOISIUS EDWARD CAMILE

Amusing and Instructive Conversations for Children of Five Years. Tewkesbury: 1800. V. 43

GAULTIER, RON

the Book of Ballads. Edinburgh & London: 1866. V. 45

The Book of Ballads. London: 1889. V. 44

The Book of Ballads. Edited by Ron Gaultier and illustrated by Doyle, Leech, and Crowquill. Edinburgh/London: 1877. V. 37

GAUNS-RUEDIN, E.

Caucasian Carpets. New York: 1986. V. 40

GAUNT, W.

The Etchings of Frank Bragwyn, R.A. A Catalogue Raisonne. London: 1926. V. 39; 44

GAURICO, LUCA 1476-1558

Pronosticon . . . Verona: 1518. V. 46

GAUSE, HARRY T.

A Detailed Description of the Scenes and Incidents Connected with a Trip Through the Mountains and Parks of Colorado. (Wilmington, Del.: 1871). V. 37

GAUSS, KARL FRIEDRICH

Disquisitiones Arthmeticae. Leipzig: 1801. V. 37

Theoria Motus Corporoum Coelestium in Sectionibus Conicis Solem Ambientium. Hamburg: 1809. V. 38; 40; 41; 42; 45

GAUTHERN, WILLIAM

The Tanner's Ass. Banbury: 1813. V. 39

GAUTHEY, E. M.

Dissertation sur les Degradations Survenues aux Pilliers du Dome du Pantheon Francois et sur les Moyens d'y Remedier. Paris: 1798. V. 39

GAUTIER D'AGOTY, JACQUES FABIAN

Anatomie Des Parties De La Generation De l'Homme et de la Femme, Representees Avec Leurs Couleurs Naturelles, Se Lon Le Nouvel Art, Jointe A L'Angelogoie de Tout Le Corps Humanin et a Ce Qui Conceren La Grossesse et Les Accouchemens. Paris: 1773. V. 41; 44

GAUTIER, HUBERT DE NISMES

L'Art de Laver ou Nouvelle Maniere de Peindre sur le Papier, Suivant le Coloris des Desseins qu'on Envoye a la Cour. Lyon: 1687. V. 40

GAUTIER, JUDITH

Album de Poemes Tires du Livre de Jade. Hammersmith: 1911. V. 39

The Book of Jade. New York: 1901. V. 42

The Usurper. London: 1884. V. 42

GAUTIER, JUDTIH

Album de Poemes Tires du Livre de Jade. 1911. V. 46

GAUTIER, THEOPHILE 1811-1872

Clarimonde. New York: 1899. V. 46

Mademoiselle de Maupin, Double Amour. Paris: 1883. V. 46

Mademoiselle de Maupin. London: 1938. V. 37; 38; 41; 42; 44

Mademoiselle de Maupoin. Waltham St. Lawrence: 1938. V. 37; 46

Wanderings in Spain. London: 1853. V. 42

Works of . . . New York: 1902. V. 40; 41; 46

The Works. Cambridge: 1906. V. 37

GAUTRUCHE, PIERRE

Philosophiae, Ac Mathematicae Totivs Institvtio . . . Vienna: 1661. V. 40

The Poetical History: Being a Compleat Collection of All the Stories Necessary for a Perfect Understanding. London: 1678. V. 46

GAVARNI, GUILLAUME SULPICE CHEVALIER 1804-1866

Gavarni in London: Sketches of Life and Character . . . London: 1849. V. 43

GAVARRI, JOSE

Instrucciones Predicables, y Morales, no Comunes que Deven Saber los Padres Predicadores y Confessores Principiantes, y en Especial los Misioneros Apostolicos . . . Malaga: 1674. V. 45

GAVILA, ONOFRE

Copia de Carta, que Escrivio el Assessor del Governador de Denia al Excelentisimo Senor Conde de Paredes, Virrey, y Capitan General del Reino de Valencia, Dandole Quenta Como Diez y Nueve Cautivos Que se Escaparon de la Ciudad de Argel . . . Madrid: 1673. V. 45

GAVIN, ANTONIO fl. 1726

A Master-Key to Popery: In Five Parts. Hagerstown: 1822. V. 44

GAVIN, C. M.

Royal Yachts. London: 1932. V. 46

GAVIN, D. ANTONIO

A Master-Key to Popery . . . Dublin: 1724. V. 43

A Master-Key to Popery: In Five Parts . . . Newport: 1773. V. 41

GAVITT, ELNATHAN C.

Crumbs from My Saddle Bags. Toledo: 1884. V. 42

GAWAIN AND THE GREEN KNIGHT

Sir Gawain and the Green Knight. London: 1952. V. 39; 42; 43; 44; 46

Sir Gawain and the Green Knight. London: 1971. V. 46

GAWAIN AND THE GRENE KNIGHT

Sir Gawain and the Greene Knight. Oxford: 1925. V. 39; 41

Sir Gawain and the Green Knight. Waltham St. Lawrence: 1952. V. 41

GAWAIN AND THE GRENE NIGHT

Sir Gawain and the Green Knight. 1956. V. 42

GAWDY, PHILIP

Letters of Philip Gawdy of West Harling, Norfolk, and of London to Various Members of His Family 1579-1616. 1906. V. 38

GAWLER, J. C.

Sikhim. With Hints on Mountain and Jungle Warfare. London: 1873. V. 40

GAWSWORTH, JOHN

Above the River. London: 1931. V. 45; 46

Annotations of Some Minor Writings of 'T. E. Lawrence.' London: 1935. V. 38; 44

Backwaters. Excursions in the Shades. London: 1932. V. 38

Collected Poems. London: 1948. V. 40

Known Signatures. London: 1932. V. 40

Legacy to Love - Selected Poems 1931-1941. London: 1943. V. 40

Mishka and Madelcinc. A Pocm Scqucncc for Marcia. London: 1932. V. 37

Poems. London: 1938. V. 38

Snow and Sand - Poems from the Mediterranean 1942-1944. Calcutta: 1945. V. 37

GAY, CLAUDIO

Historia Fisica y Politica de Chile, segun Documentos Abquiridos en Esta Republica Durante doce Anos de Residencia en Ella . . . Paris: 1844-71. V. 38

GAY, FREDERICK A.

Sketches of California. New York: 1848. V. 39; 43; 45

GAY, GEORGE

The Chinese as They Are: Their Moral, Society and Literary Character . . . London: 1841. V. 45

GAY, JOHN 1685-1732

Achilles. London: 1733. V. 37; 38; 39; 40; 41; 43; 44; 45; 46

Achilles. An Opera. (bound with) The Beggar's Opera. London: 1733, 1742. V. 37

The Beggar's Opera. London: 1728. V. 37; 39; 40; 41; 42; 45

The Beggar's Opera. London: 1735. V. 42

The Beggar's Opera. London: 1765. V. 40

The Beggar's Opera. London: 1922. V. 39

The Beggar's Opera. Paris: 1937. V. 40; 43; 45

The Beggar's Opera. London: 1921. V. 38; 42

The Captives. London: 1724. V. 37; 40; 42; 44

Dione, a Pastoral Tragedy. Glasgow: 1752. V. 42

Fables . . . London: 1703. V. 46

Fables by Mr. Gay. (with) Fables, by the Late Mr. Gay: Volume the Second. London: 1727/28. V. 46

Fables. London: 1729/1747. V. 41

Fables. London: 1733. V. 41

Fables. London: 1737/38. V. 41

Fables. London: 1746. V. 38

Fables. London: 1747. V. 39

Fables. London: 1753. V. 38

Fables. Second Series. London: 1761. V. 43; 46

Fables in two Parts. Newcastle-upon-Tyne: 1765. V. 41

Fables by the Late Mr. Gay. London: 1767. V. 40; 41

Fables of Mr. John Gay. London: 1773. V. 45

Fables by the Late Mr. Gay. London: 1775. V. 39; 42

Fables. London: 1778. V. 42

Fables. London: 1788. V. 44

Fables. London: 1793. V. 37; 39; 40; 41; 42; 43; 44; 45; 46

Fables by John Gay and by Edward Moore. Paris: 1802. V. 44

Gay's Fables. Philadelphia: 1808. V. 39; 43

Fables. Havant: 1816. V. 39

Fables by John Gay - With the Life of the Author. London: 1816. V. 44

Fables. In Two Volumes. London: 1757. V. 37; 38

Fabulae Selectae . . . London: 1777. V. 41

The Fan. A Poem. In Three Books. London: 1714. V. 37

The Female Faction. London: 1729. V. 40

The Fryar and the Nun. London: 1710-15. V. 45

A Letter to a Lady, Occasion'd by the Arrival of Her Royal Highness the Princess of Wales. London: 1714. V. 37; 40

A New Song of Old Similies to Ye Tune of Chevy Chace by Dean Swift (i.e. John Gay). London: 1728-29. V. 45

Plays Written by Mr. John Gay. London: 1760. V. 46

Plays . . . London: 1772. V. 41; 42

Poems on Several Occasions. London: 1720. V. 38; 39; 42; 44; 45; 46

Poems on Several Occasions. London: 1731. V. 43

Poems on Several Occasions. London: 1737. V. 45

Poems on Several Occasions. Glasgow: 1770. V. 38

Poems on Several Occasions. London: 1775. V. 37; 42

The Poems. Chiswick: 1820. V. 46

Poems on Several Occasions. Glasgow: 1776. V. 37

The Poetical Works of John Gay. Edinburgh: 1784. V. 39; 42

Polly. London: 1729. V. 37; 39; 40; 42; 44; 45; 46

Polly. London: 1923. V. 38; 39; 43

Rural Sports. New York: 1930. V. 39; 43

Rural Sports. London: 1950. V. 43

A Selection of Fables by . . . Huntingdon: 1823. V. 40

The Shepherd's Week. London: 1714. V. 40; 42

The Shepherd's Week. London: 1716? V. 41

The Shepherd's Week. London: 1721. V. 45

Three Hours After Marriage. London: 1717. V. 38; 40; 41

Trivia. London: 1716. V. 37; 38; 40; 41; 43; 44; 45; 46

Trivia, or, the Art of Walking the Streets of London. London: 1922. V. 38; 45

Two Epistles; one to the Right Honourable Richard Earl of Burlington; the other, to a Lady. London: 1717. V. 40; 44

The What D'Ye Call It . . . London: 1715. V. 38; 44

The What D'Ye Call It. London: 1716. V. 41; 45

The What d'ye Call It: a Tragi-Comi-Pastoral Farce. London: 1736. V. 37; 39

GAY, JULES

Bibliographie des Principaux Ouvragaes Relatifs a l'Amour, aux Femmes, au Mariage. Paris: 1861. V. 39

GAY, MARTIN

A Statement of the Claims of Charles T. Jackson, M.D. to the Discovery of the Applicability of Sulphuric Ether to the Prevention of Pain in Surgical Operations. Boston: 1847. V. 42

GAY, MARY ANN HARRIS

Life in Dixie During the War 1861-65. Atlanta: 1894. V. 42

Life in Dixie During the War, 1861-65. Atlanta: 1897. V. 37

GAY, THERESSA

James W. Marshall, the Discoverer of California Gold: a Biography. Georgetown: 1967. V. 40; 44

GAY, WALTER

Memoirs of Walter Gay. New York: 1930. V. 39

GAYA, LOUIS DE

The Art of War, and the Way That It Is at Present Practised in France. A Treatise of the Arms and Engines of War, of Fire-works, Ensigns and Military Instruments Both Ancient and Modern. London: 1678. V. 41

GAYAM, JOHN

G----e and D----y; or the Injur'd Ghost. London: 1743. V. 45

Marlborough Still Conquers; or, Union Has Got the Day. London: 1708. V. 45

GAYARRE, CHARLES

Histoire de la Louisiane. New Orleans: 1846-47. V. 40

History of Louisiana. The Spanish Domination. Redfield: 1854. V. 40; 44

History of Louisiana. New Orleans,: 1903. V. 42

Romance of the History of Louisiana. New York: 1848. V. 42; 43; 45

School for Politics: a Dramatic Novel. New York: 1877. V. 38; 39; 40; 42

GAYER, ARTHUR EDWARD

The Catholic Layman. Dublin: 1852-58-62. V. 42; 45

GAYLORD, REUBEN

An Address Delivered on the Occasion of Laying the Foundation of the Building For the Preparatory Department of Nebraska University, at Fontenelle, N.T . . . July 27, 1858. Omaha City: 1858. V. 44; 45

GAYNAM, JOHN

Marlborough Still Conquers; or, Union Has Got the Day. London: 1708. V. 40

GAYTON, EDMUND

Festivious Notes on the History and Adventures of the Renowned Don Quixote. London: 1768. V. 38

Festivious Notes on the History and Adventures of the Renowned Don Quixote. London: 1771. V. 38

Pleasant Notes Upon Don Quixote. London: 1654. V. 40

GAZA, THEODORUS 1400-1478

Grammaticae Introductionis Libri IIII. Paris: 1520. V. 37

Institutiones a Grammaticae Libri Quatuor, Addita Versione Latina . . . Paris: 1531-1540. V. 37

Introductionis Grammaticae, Libri Quator: Graece Simul cum Interpretatione Latina. Basileae: 1529. V. 41

Introductionis Grammaticae Libri Quatuor, Una cum Interpretatione Latina. Basel: 1523. V. 37

Introductivae Lib. IV Grammatices Libri Quatuor. Venice: 1495. V. 43

GAZAEUS, ANGELINUS

Pia Hilaria (in verse). Londini: 1657. V. 44

GAZE, HAROLD

Coppertop, the Queer Adventures of a Quaint Child. London: 1924. V. 43

Coppertop, The Queer Adventures of a Quaint Child. New York: 1924. V. 37

The Goblin's Glen, A Story of Childhood's Wonderland. Boston: 1924. V. 42

The Merry Piper, or the Magical Trip of the Sugar Bowl Ship. Boston: 1925. V. 38

LA GAZETTE Illustree des Amateurs de Jardins. Paris: 1913/40/20-39. V. 39

A GAZETTEER of the State of New Hampshire, in Three Parts. Exeter: 1817. V. 40

A GAZETTEER of the World, or Dictionary of Geographical Knowledge . . . Edinburgh: 1856. V. 39

GAZIUS, ANTONIO

Corona Florida Medicinae. Venice: 1491. V. 38

IL GAZZETIERE Americano. Livorno: 1763. V. 39; 41; 44

GEARY, EDWARD R.

Depredations and Massacre by the Snake River Indians. Letter of . . . Transmitting a Report of . . . the Indian Depredations . . . in the State of Oregon and Territory of Washington, and the Massacre of Emigrants. Washington: 1861. V. 41

GEARY, JOHN W.

A Sketch fo the Early Life and of the Civil and Military Services of maj. Gen. John W. Geary, Candidate of the National Union Party for Governor of Pennsylvania. Philadelphia: 1866. V. 46

GEBOW, JOSEPH

A Vocabulary of the Snake or Shoshone Dialect. G.S.L. City: 1859. V. 43

GEDDES, ALEXANDER

L'Avocat du Diable: the Devil's Advocate; or, Satan Versus Pictor. London: 1792. V. 45

GEDDES, JAMES

An Essay on the Compostion and Manner of Writing of the Antients, particularly Plato. Glasgow: 1748. V. 37

GEDDES, MICHAEL

The Church-History of Ethiopia. London: 1696. V. 45

The Council of Trent No Free Assembly: More Fully Discovered by A Collection of Letters and Papers of the Learned Dr. Vargas and Other Great Ministers . . . London: 1697. V. 39

GEDDES, NORMAN BEL

Horizons - a Glimpse into the Not Far-Distant Future. Boston: 1932. V. 45

GEDDES, PATRICK

Cities in Evolution. London: 1915. V. 42

City Development. A Study of Parks, Gardens and Culture Institutions. A Report to the Carnegie Dunfermline Trust. Edinburgh: 1904. V. 41

GEDDIE, JOHN

Beyond the Himalayas. London: 1884. V. 41

Missionary Life Among the Cannibals. Toronto: 1882. V. 40; 42

GEE, EDWARD

The Divine Right and Original of the Civill Magistrate from God . . . London: 1658. V. 42

A Plea for Non-(sub)scribers. London: 1650. V. 42

GEE, ERNEST

Early American Sporting Books. 1734 to 1844. New York: 1928. V. 37; 39; 42; 45; 46

Ernest Gee's Hunting Diary. New York: 1937. V. 43

GEE, JOSHUA fl. 1725-1750

The Trade and Navigation of Great-Britain Considered . . . London: 1731. V. 39

The Trade and Navigation of Great Britain Considered. Glasgow: 1760. V. 37; 38; 39; 41

GEELHAER, CHRISTIAN

Paul Klee and the Bauhaus. Greenwich: 1973. V. 43; 46

GEERLINGS, GERALD K.

Metal Crafts in Architecture. New York: 1929. V. 44

GEFFROY, GUSTAVE

Charles Meryon. Paris: 1926. V. 45

Charles Meryon. Paris: 1926; 1925. V. 44

La Vie Artistique. Paris: 1892-1908. V. 38

GEGOROVIUS, FERDINAND

History of the City of Rome in the Middle Ages. London: 1909-02. V. 39

GEHENNA PRESS

A List of Gehenna Press Books. 1967. V. 37

GEIGER, MAYNARD J.

The Life and Times of Fray Junipero Serra, O. F. M., or The Man Who Never Turned Back. Washington: 1959. V. 40; 45

GEIKIE, ARCHIBALD

The Ancient Volcanes of Great Britain. London: 1897. V. 45; 46

Annals of the Royal Society Dining Club. London: 1917. V. 38; 40

Life of Sir Roderick I. Murchison . . . London: 1875. V. 42

Memoirs of the Geologicl Survey of Scotland. Glasgow: 1900. V. 38

The Story of a Boulder or Gleanings from the Note-Book of a Field Geologist. London: 1858. V. 40

Text-Book of Geology. London: 1903. V. 45

GEIKIE, JAMES

Prehistoric Europe. London: 1881. V. 45

GEILER VON KEISERBERG, JOHANNES

Das Buch Granatapfel, im Latin Genant Malogranatus, Helt in Ym gar Vil und Manig Haylsam und Suesser Underweysung und Leer . . . Augsburg: 1510. V. 37; 38

GEISEL, THEODOR SEUSS 1904-

And to Think That I Saw It on Mulberry Street/ New York: 1937. V. 42

Boners. New York: 1931. V. 46

The 500 Hats of Bartholomew Cubbins. New York: 1938. V. 40; 42; 44

If I Ran the Zoo. New York: 1950. V. 42

McElligot's Pool. New York: 1947. V. 42

The Seven Lady Godivas. New York: 1939. V. 42

GEISELER, KAPITANLIEUTENANT

Die Oster-Insel. Eine Statte Prahistorischer Kultur in der Sudsee. Berlin: 1883. V. 46

GEISER, BERNHARD

Picasso, Peintre-Graveur: Catalogue Illustre de l'Oeuvre Grave et Lithographie 1899-1931. Berne: 1968. V. 41

GEISER, SAMUEL W.

Naturalists of the Frontier. Dallas: 1937. V. 38

GEISSLER, J. F. W.

Anleitung dem Dresdner Cantzley-Ductu . . . Dresden: 1720. V. 38; 40

GEISSLER, L. A.

Looking Beyond, a Sequel to 'Looking Backward' by Edward Bellamny, and an Answer to 'Looking Further Forward' by Richard Michaelis. London: 1891. V. 39; 40; 41

GEISSLER, P.

Index Hepaticarum. Volume 10: Lembidium to Mytilopsis. 1985. V. 39

GEISTREICHE Gesaenge und Lieder Ueber Sonn-und Festtags-Episteln und Evangelia, Welche in dem VI-XI Theiles des Christlichen Jahres . . . Schweidnitz: 1725-26. V. 38

GEKLE, WILLIAM FRANCIS

Arthur Machen: Weaver of Dreams. Millbrook: 1949. V. 46

GELB, IGNACE J.

Hittite Hieroglyphic Monuments. Chicago: (1939). V. 37

Inscriptions from Alishar and Vicinity. Chicago: 1935. V. 40

GELDARD, JAMES

Hand-Book on Cotton Manufacture . . . New York: 1867. V. 42

GELEE, CLAUD, CALLED CLAUDE LORRAIN 1600-1682

Liber Veritatis; or a Collection of Prints After the Original Designs of Claude Le Lorraine . . . London: 1777-1819. V. 42

GELEE, CLAUDE, CALLED CLAUDE LORRAIN 1600-1682

Liber Veritatis, or a Collection of Two Hundred Prints After the Original Designs Executed by Richard Earlom, in the Manner and Taste of the Drawings. London: 1777. V. 46

GELETT, CHARLES WETHERBY

A Life on the Ocean: Autobiography of Captain Charles Wetherby Gelett a Retired Sea Captain. Honolulu: 1917. V. 39

GELL, WILLIAM 1777-1836

The Geography and Antiquities of Ithaca . . . London: 1807. V. 38

Narrative of a Journey in the Morea. London: 1823. V. 37; 40

Pompeiana: The Topography Edifices, and Ornaments of Pompeii. London: 1817-19. V. 37; 40; 43; 46

Pompeiana. London: 1817-19, 1832. V. 38

Pompeiana: the Topography, Edifices, and Ornaments of Pompeii. London: 1824. V. 45

Pompeiana: The Topography, Edifices and Ornaments of Pompeii, the Result of Excavations Since 1819. London: 1832. V. 37; 38; 39; 40; 42; 44

Pompeiana: The Topography, Edifices and Ornaments of Pompeii, the Result of Excavations Since 1819. London: 1835. V. 46

Pompeiana. The Topography, Edifices and Ornaments of Pompeii. London: 1852. V. 41; 43

Pompeii, Its Destruction and Rediscovery . . . New York: 1880. V. 45

The Topography of Troy, and Its Vicinity . . . London: 1804. V. 42; 45

The Topography of Rome and Its Vicinity. London: 1834. V. 38

The Topography of Rome and Its Vicinity. London: 1846. V. 40; 42; 44

GELLERT, CHRISTIAN F. 1715-1769

Briefe . . . von dem Guten Geschmacke. Leipzig: 1751. V. 43

GELLERT, HUGO

Capital in Lithographs. New York: 1934. V. 45

GELLI, GIOVANNI BATISTA

La Circe Di Giovan-Batista Gelli. Firenze: 1549. V. 38; 44

Circes of Iohn Baptista Gello, Florentine. London: 1557. V. 38

La Circe. Venice: 1595. V. 40

The Circe . . . Done out of Italian. London: 1702. V. 38

Circe. London: 1744. V. 44

Circe. London: 1745. V. 38

GELLIUS, AULUS 130-80 BC

The Attic Nights. Amsterdam: 1665. V. 44

Attic Nights . . . London: 1795. V. 38; 40

Auli Gellii Noctium Atticarum Libri Undeuiginti. Colophon: 1515. V. 37

Noctes Atticae. Venetiis: 1515. V. 37; 38; 40; 42

Noctes Atticae. Cologne: 1526. V. 37

Noctivm Atticarvm Libri Undeviginti. Venice: 1515. V. 40; 43

GELVES, MARQUES DE

Memorial de lo Sucedido en la Ciudad de Mexico, Desde el Dia Primero de Noviembre, de 1623 Hasta Quinze de Enero de 1624. Mexico: 1624. V. 40

THE GEM. Troy. V. 41

THE GEM, a Literary Annual. London: 1831. V. 38

THE GEM of the Rockies! Manitou Springs, Colorado. Manitou Springs: 1885. V. 40

GEMELLI CARERI, JOHN FRANCIS

A Voyage Round the World . . . London: 1732. V. 40; 41

GEMINUS, THOMAS

Compendiosa Totius Anatomie Delineatio. London: 1959. V. 37; 38; 39; 40; 41; 44; 46

GEMMA, CORNELIUS

De Arte Cyclognomica Tomi III. Doctrinam Ordinum Universam . . . Antwerp: 1569. V. 43

GEMMA FRISIUS, REINER

De Principiis Astronomiae & Cosmographiae Deque usu Globi ab Eodem Editi. Antwerp: 1553. V. 41

GEMMILL, JOHN ALEXANDER

The Practice of the Parliament of Canada Upon Bills of Divorce Including an Historical Sketch of Parliamentary Divorce and Summaries of all the Bills of Divorce Presented to Parliament from 1867 to 1888 . . . Toronto: 1889. V. 44

GEMS For You: From New Hampshire Authors. Manchester: 1850. V. 46

GEMS from Shelley Illustrated. An Ode to the Wild West and The Question. London: 1850. V. 43

GEMS From the British Poets, American Poets and Shakespeare. London: 1838. V. 42

GEMS from the Poets. London. V. 43
GEMS from the Poets. London: 1860. V. 38; 40

GEMS of English Art. London: and New York: 1869. V. 44

GEMS of Nature and Art . . . London: 1869. V. 38

GENARD, FRANCOIS

The School of Man. London: 1753. V. 39; 41; 43; 44

GENAUER, EMILY

Chagall at the 'Met'. New York: 1971. V. 46

Rufino Tamayo. New York. V. 39; 46

THE GENEALOGICAL Advertiser. Cambridge: 1898-1901. V. 39

GENEALOGICAL and Family History of Southern New York and the Hudson River Valley. New York: 1913. V. 44

GENEALOGICAL and Family History of the Wyoming and Lackawanna Valleys Pennsylvania. New York: 1906. V. 41

GENEALOGICAL, Chronological, Historical and Geographical Atlas, Exhibiting All the Royal Families in Europe, Their Origin, Decendency, Marriages &c. of Each Kingdom. London: 1801. V. 45

GENEALOGICAL CO-OP SEARCH CLUB

Exchequer Deponents. The Names of 127,628 Deponents in the Exchequer Depositions from 1559-1695, Arranged in Geographical Groups . . . London: 1916/18. V. 43

A GENERAL Abridgment of Cases in Equity . . . High Court of Chancery . . . . London: 1739. V. 40

A GENERAL Abridgment of Cases in Equity . . . High Court of Chancery . . . Notes and References . . . London: 1756. V. 38; 40

GENERAL Address to the Freemen of New Hampshire; or, the General Government and the Leaders of New England Opposition Contrasted. N.P.: 1816. V. 45

GENERAL Atlas of the World Containing Large Scale Maps of Every State, Territory and Country in the World . . . Chicago: 1887. V. 45

THE GENERAL Biographical Dictionary: Containing the Lives and Writings of the Most Emient Persons in Every Nation. London: 1812-17. V. 46

GENERAL Collection of Treatys, Declarations of War, Manifestos and Other Public Papers, Relating to Peace and War Among the Potentates of Europe from 1648 to the Present Time . . . London: 1710. V. 41; 42; 45

A GENERAL Collection of Treatys, Declarations of War Manifestos and Other Publick Papers, Relating to Peace and War. London: 1732. V. 44

GENERAL Dictionary of Husbandry. Bath: 1779. V. 37

A GENERAL History of the Turks. London: 1730-29. V. 38

GENERAL Instructions for the Guidance of the Master Sailmakers &c of Her Majesty's Dockyards. 1867. London: 1867. V. 37

GENERAL Observations on the State of Affairs in Ireland, and its Defence Against Invasion. Dublin: 1797. V. 39

GENERAL Official Atlas of Wayne County, Michigan. Detroit: 1893. V. 39

GENERAL Regulations and an Explanation of the Principal Words of Command for the Use of the Light Horse Volunteers of the Cities of London & Westminster. London: 1795. V. 41

THE GENERAL Repository and Review. Cambridge: 1812-13. V. 38; 40

GENERAL Rules of the United Societies of the Methodist Episcopal Church. Translated into the Chahta language. Mehlotist Iksa . . . Park Hill: 1841. V. 37

THE GENERAL Stud-Book. London: 1803. V. 42

THE GENERAL Stud Book of South Africa. Volume I-V. Johannesburg: 1906-18. V. 43

A GENERAL Survey of that Part of the Island of St. Christophers, Which Formerly Belonged to France; and Was Yielded Up to Great Britain for Ever, by the Late Treaty of Utrecht . . . London: 1722. V. 38; 40; 44

GENERAL Taylor and His Staff; Comprising Memoirs of Generals Taylor, Worth, Wool and Butler . . . Philadelphia: 1848. V. 40

GENERAL Taylor's Calendar for 1849. Philadelphia: 1848. V. 42

A GENERAL Treatise of Naval Trade and Commerce. Founded on the Laws and Statutes of this Realm. London: 1753. V. 41

GENERAL View of the Agriculture of the County of Suffolk. London: 1804. V. 46

A GENERAL View of the Rise, Progress and Brilliant Achievements of the American Navy, Down to the Present Time . . . Brooklyn: 1828. V. 41; 42; 44

THE GENERIC Names of Moths of the World. London: 1975-87. V. 37; 38

GENEST, JOHN 1764-1839

Some Account of the English Stage from the Restoration in 1660 to 1830. Bath: 1832. V. 41; 42; 44

GENET, EDMOND CHARLES 1763-1834

Memorial on the Upward Forces of Fluids, and Their Applicability to Several Arts, Sciences and Public Improvements. Albany: 1825. V. 37; 40; 42; 45; 46

Memorial on the Upward Forces of Fluids, and Their Applicability to Several Arts, Sciences and Public Improvements . . . New York: 1825. V. 44

GENET, EDMOND CHARLES CLINTON

War Letters of Edmond Genet. New York: 1918. V. 42

GENET, EDMUND

Communications on the Next Election for President and on the Late Measures of the Federal Administration, with Notes, Illustrations and Documents. New York: 1808. V. 45

GENET, JEAN

The Balcony. New York: 1958. V. 37; 41; 46

Our Lady of the Flowers. Paris: 1949. V. 45

GENET, JEAN continued

Poemes. Lyon: 1948. V. 44

GENETHLIACUM Illustrissimorum Principum Caroli & Mariae a Musis Cantabrigiensibus Celebratum. Cantabrigiae: 1631. V. 44

GENGA, BERNARDINO

Anatomia Chirurgica Cioe Istoria Anatomica Dell'Ossa, e Muscoli del Corpo Humano con la Descrittione de Vasi Piu Riguardevoli Che Scorrono . . . Rome: 1672. V. 44

Anatomia per uso et Intelligenza del Disegno . . . Rome: 1691. V. 37

Anatomy Improv'd and Illustrated . . . N.P.. V. 42

Anatomy Improv'd and Illustrated with Regard to the Uses Thereof in Designing . . . London: 1723. V. 38

GENIN, J. N.

An Illustrated History of the Hat, from the Earliest Ages to the Present Time. New York: 1850. V. 39; 44

GENIN, THOMAS H.

The Napolead, in Twelve Books. St. Clairsville: 1833. V. 38; 39; 40

GENINI, RONALD

A California in Two Eras. San Francisco: 1985. V. 37

GENLIS, STEPHANIE FELICITE DUCREST DE ST. AUBIN, COMTESSE DE 1746-1830

Adelaide and Theodore; or, Letters on Education. London: 1784. V. 43

The Knights of the Swan . . . Dublin: 1797. V. 44

Memoirs of the Countess de Genlis, Illustrative of the Eighteenth and Nineteenth Centuries. London: 1825-6. V. 41

Nouvelle Methode d'Enseignement, Pour La Premiere Enfance. Besancon: 1800. V. 42

Short Account of the Conduct of Madame de Genlis, Since the Revolution. Perth: 1796. V. 45

Tales of the Castle . . . London: 1806. V. 42

Tales of the Castle. London: 1785. V. 37

Theatre of Education. London: 1781. V. 46

The Theatre of Education. London: 1787. V. 46

GENLIS, STEPHANIE FELICITE DUREST DE ST. AUBIN, COMTESSE DE 1746-1830

The Duchess of La Valliere. London: 1804. V. 41

GENSSANE, DE

La Geometrie Souterraine, ou Traite de Geometrie-Pratique . . . Montpellier: 1776. V. 45

GENT, THOMAS

The Ancient and Modern History of the Loyal Town of Rippon. York: 1733. V. 39; 41; 45

Annales Regioduni Hullini: or the History of Kingston-Upon-Hull . . . London: 1735. V. 39

Annales Regioduni Hullini: or, the History of the Royal and Beautiful Town of Kingston-upon-Hull. York: 1735. V. 45

The Antient and Modern History of the Famous City of York. York: 1703. V. 40

The Antient and Modern History of the Famous City of York . . . London: 1730. V. 40; 45

Divine Justice and Mercy Displayed. York: 1772. V. 41

The Life of Mr. Thomas Gent, Printer of York. Written by Himself. London: 1832. V. 37; 38; 39; 46

Poems. London: 1829. V. 46

GENTHE, ARNOLD

As I Remember: The Autobiography of . . . New York: 1936. V. 37

The Book of the Dance. New York: 1916. V. 37

Impressions of Old New Orleans. New York: 1926. V. 37; 46

Isadora Duncan. New York: 1929. V. 37; 38; 44; 46

Isadora Duncan. Twenty-Four Studies. New York & London: 1929. V. 37; 39; 46

Isadora Duncan, Twenty-Four Studies. New York: (1929). V. 37

Old Chinatown: a Book of Pictures. London: 1913. V. 40

Old Chinatown. New York: 1913. V. 37; 38; 44; 45

Pictures of Old Chinatown. New York: 1908. V. 41; 45

GENTIL, FRANCIS

Le Jardinier Solitiare, the Solitary or Carthusian Gard'ner . . . London: 1706. V. 37; 40

GENTILI, ALBERICO 1551-1611?

De Legationibus Libri Tres. New York: 1924. V. 40

GENTILI, GINO VINICIO

Mosaics of Piazza Armerina: the Hunting Scenes. Milano: 1964. V. 41

GENTILIS, ALBERICUS

De Legationibus Libri Tres. London: 1585. V. 37; 38

GENTILLET, INNOCENT

Le Bvreav dv Concile de Trente (etc.); Geneva?: 1586. V. 45

THE GENTLE Art: A Collection of Books and Wood Engravings by Lucien Pissarro. Zurich: 1974. V. 46

THE GENTLEMAN and Lady's Key, to Polite-Literature. London: 1790. V. 39

THE GENTLEMAN Angler. London: 1726. V. 39; 40; 41; 43; 45
THE GENTLEMAN Angler. London: 1736. V. 40; 43

GENTLEMAN, DAVID

Bridges on the Backs. Cambridge: 1961. V. 41; 44; 45

THE GENTLEMAN Farmer's Pocket Companion. London: 1788. V. 39; 41; 46

GENTLEMAN, FRANCIS

The Dramatic Censor . . . London: 1770. V. 42

The History of the Robinhood Society. London: 1764. V. 46

Royal Fables. London: 1766. V. 40; 42

GENTLEMAN OF ELVAS

Histoire de la Conquest de la Floride, Par les Espagnols, Sous Ferdinand de Soto . . . Paris: 1685. V. 38; 40; 44

The Discovery of Florida Being a True Relation of the Vicissitudes that Attended the Governor Don Hernando De Soto . . . San Francisco: 1946. V. 40

True Relation of the Hardships Suffered by Governor Fernando de Soto & Certain Portuguese Gentlemen During the Discovery of the Province of Florida. Deland: 1932. V. 40

GENTLEMAN, TOBIAS

Englands Way to Win Wealth, and to Employ ships and Mariners . . . London: 1614. V. 41

THE GENTLEMAN, Tradesman and Traveller's Pocket Library. London: 1753. V. 41

THE GENTLEMAN Turn's Water-Carrier. London: 1725. V. 37

THE GENTLEMAN'S Library, Containing Rules for Conduct in All Parts of Life. London: 1715. V. 43

GENTLEMANS Magazine Library: English Topography. London: 1891-1905. V. 39

THE GENTLEMAN'S Pocket Magazine and Album. London: 1830. V. 43

THE GENTLEMEN and Lady's Key to Polite Literature; or a Compendious Dictionary of Fabulous History . . . London: 1761 or earlier. V. 41

THE GENTLEMEN Angler Containing, Short, Plain and Easy Instructions Whereby the Most Ignorant Beginner May, in a Short Time Become a Perfect Artist in Angling for Salmon . . . London: 1736. V. 38

GENTLES, MARGARET O.

Japanese Prints: the Clarence Buckingham Collection, Harunobu, Koryusai, Shigemasa, Their Followers and Contemporaries. Chicago: 1965. V. 42

GENTLING, SCOTT

Of Birds and Texas. Fort Worth: 1986. V. 42

GENTRY, THOMAS G.

Nests and Eggs of Birds in the U.S. Philadelphia: 1882. V. 39

GENTZ, FRIEDRICH VON 1764-1832

On the State of Europe Before and After the French Revolution. London: 1802. V. 38; 40; 41

A GENUINE Account of the Lives, Behaviour, Confession, and Dyring Words of the Five Rebels . . . Executed at Kennington-Common, for High-Treason. London: 1746. V. 37

THE GENUINE Account of the Trial of Eugene Aram, for the murder of Daniel Clark, late of Knaresborough . . . To which are added, the remarkable defence he made on his trial: - his own accout of himself, written after his condemnation: . . . York: 1759. V. 37

GENUINE and Impartial Memoirs of Elizabeth Canning, Containing a Complete History of that Unfortunate Girl, from Her Birth to the Present Time, and Particularly Every Remarkable Occurence from the Day of Her Absence, January 1, 1753, to the Day . . . London: 1754. V. 46

GENUINE Memoirs of John Murray, Esq.; Late Secretary to the Young Pretender. Together with Remarks on the Same, in a Letter to a Friend. London: 1747. V. 45

THE GENUINE Memoirs of Miss Faulkner, Otherwise Mrs. D***l**n; or, Countess of H*****x, in Expectancy. London: 1770. V. 45

THE GENUINE Principles of the Ancient Saxon, or English Constitution. Carefully Collected from the Best Authorities. Philadelphia: 1776. V. 37

THE GENUINE Rejected Addresses, Presented to the Committee of Management for Drury-Lane Theatre; Preceded by that Written by Lord Byron, and Adopted by the Committee. London: 1812. V. 43

THE GENUINE Trial of John B. Gawler, Esq. For Ciminal Conversation with the Right Hon. Lady Valentia. London: 1795. V. 46

GENUINUS, HIERONYMUS

Metamorphoses Nominum, sive Metatheses Litterarum sive Anagrammata, in Quinque Libros Diversa . . . 1636. V. 46

GEOFFREY Langdon Keynes, Margaret Elizabeth Darwin, 1917-1967: to Celebrate Their Golden Wedding. Cambridge: 1967. V. 40

GEOFFREY, OF MONMOUTH

Britanniae Utriusque Regum et Principum Origo et Gesta Insignia . . . Paris: 1508. V. 40

The British History. London: 1718. V. 39

GEOGRAPHICA Anglicana Nova: or, A Dictionary Interpreting Such Hard Words of Whatever Language, As Are Present Used in the English Tongue . . . London: 1707. V. 41

THE GEOGRAPHICAL Annual for 1834. Philadelphia: 1834. V. 45

THE GEOGRAPHICAL Guide; a Poetical Naturical Trip Round the Island of Great Britain. London: 1805. V. 37; 38; 40

A GEOGRAPHICAL History of Nova Scotia. London: 1749. V. 41; 43

GEOGRAPHICAL Statistical and Public Amusement: by Which May Be Obtained a General and Particular Knowledge of the United States. Philadelphia: 1806. V. 46

A GEOGRAPHICAL Table Shewing All the Intermediate and Respective Distances Between the Principal Towns in France, Holland, Flanders, on the Rhine, in Switzerland, and Savoy . . . Dublin: 1780. V. 46

THE GEOGRAPHY and History of England: Done in the Manner of Gordon's and Salmon's Geographical and Historical Grammars, in Two Parts. London: 1765. V. 46

GEOGRAPHY for Children or a Short and Easy Method of Teaching and Learning Geography. London: 1787. V. 45

GEOGRAPHY Reformed. A New System of General Geography, According to an Accurate Analysis of the Science, Augmented with Several Necessary Branches Omitted by Former Authors . . . London: 1749. V. 39; 46

GEOLOGICAL SOCIETY OF LONDON

Correlation of Rocks in the British Isles. London: 1971-80. V. 44

GEOLOGICAL SURVEY OF ENGLAND AND WALES

Memoirs in Explnation of the New Series One Inch Maps. London: 1897-1972. V. 38

GEOLOGY of the European Centuries. London: 1982. V. 37; 38

GEORGE, ALEX

The Banksias. London: 1981. V. 41; 44

The Banksias. London: 1982. V. 37

GEORGE Bancroft, Secretary of the Navy, the Traducer and Eulogist of General Andrew Jackson. Washington: 1846. V. 46

GEORGE Bayntun Incorporating Robert Riviere & Son Bookbinder. (on leather label on front cover); Bath: 1935. V. 37

GEORGE, ERNEST

Etchings in Belgium with descriptive letterpress. Second Edition. London: 1883. V. 37

Etchings of Venice. London: 1888. V. 37; 42

Etchings on the Loire and in the South of France. London: 1875. V. 37

GEORGE Grosz Twelve Reproductions from His Original Lithographs. Chicago: 1921. V. 46

GEORGE, HENRY

The Condition of Labor. New York: 1891. V. 46

History of the 3rd, 7th, 8th and 12th Kentucky CSA. Louisville: 1911. V. 37

The Orthodox: an Examination of Mr. George's Position as a Systematic Economist. London: 1885. V. 39

Our Land and Land Policy, National and State. San Francisco: 1871. V. 40

A Preplexed Philosopher. New York: 1892. V. 40

Progress and Poverty: an Inquiry into the Cause of Industrial Depressions, and of Increase of Want, with Increase of Wealth. The Remedy. (with) The Irish Land Question . . . an Appeal to the Land Leagues. New York: 1883. V. 38; 39

Protection of Free Trade . . . New York: 1886. V. 39

Protection of Free Trade? An Examiniation of the Tarriff Question with Especial Regard to the Interests of Labor. New York: 1891. V. 38; 40

The Complete Works of . . . New York: 1904. V. 39

GEORGE, HEREFORD BROOKE

The Oberland and Its Glaciers. London: 1865. V. 40

The Oberland and Its Glaciers: Explored and Illustrated . . . London: 1866. V. 43

The Oberland and Its Glaciers . . . London: 1866. V. 37; 41; 43

GEORGE III: His Court and Family. London: 1821. V. 38

GEORGE III, KING OF GREAT BRITAIN

An Act for Enabling the . . . Universities . . . to Hold in Perpetuity Their Copy Right in Books, Given or Bequeathed to the Said Universities. London: 1775. V. 38

The Later Correspondence of George III. Cambridge: 1966-70. V. 41; 42

A Selection of the Papers of, at Windsor Castle. 1927. V. 45

A Selection from the Papers of King George III Preserved in the Royal Archives at Windsor Castle. Cambridge: 1927. V. 38

A Selection from the Papers of King George III Preserved in the Royal Archives at Windsor Castle. London: 1927. V. 38

GEORGE IV, KING OF GREAT BRITAIN

Memoirs of His Royal Highness the Prince of Wales. London: 1808. V. 42

GEORGE, J. N.

English Guns and Rifles, Being an Account of the Development, Design and Usage of English Sporting Rifles and Shotguns . . . Plantersville: 1947. V. 38

GEORGE, JAMES

A Brief Enquiry Into the Causes of the Poetic Element in the Scottish Mind; Being a Lecture Delivered Before the Christian Young Men's Association of the City of Kingston. Kingston: 1857. V. 45

GEORGE, W. L.

A Novelist on Novels. London: 1918. V. 38

GEORGE, WALDEMAR

Chirico. Paris: 1928. V. 46

Henri-Matisse. Dessins. Paris: 1926. V. 42

GEORGE, WALDMAR

Aristide Maillol. Greenwich. V. 43

GEORGE, WILLIAM

An Essay on Angling by a Member of the Worcester Anglers' Society. Worcester: 1840. V. 40; 43

GEORGI, JOHANN GOTTLIEB

Versuch einer Beschreibung der Russisch Kayserlichen Residentzstadt St. Petersburg, Under Merkwurdigkeiten der Gegend. St. Petersburg: 1790. V. 38

GEORGIA

Journal of the Proceedings of the Convention of the People of Georgia Together with the Ordinances and Resolutions Adopted. Milledgeville: 1865. V. 37

GEORGIA AIR LINE RAILROAD

Georgia Air Line Rail Road: Charter, Action at Madison Springs, Table of Distances, Engineer's Report, Speeches, Letters &c. Relating to the Same. Atlanta: 1857. V. 37

GEORGIA. (COLONY). LAWS, STATUTES, ETC.

Acts Passed by the General Assembly of the Colony of Georgia 1755 to 1774. Wormsloe: 1881. V. 45

GEORGIA. CONSTITUTION

Constitution of the State of Georgia as Passed by the Constitutional Convention Assembled at Atlanta, Ga. March 11th, 1868. Augusta: 1868. V. 44

GEORGIA. CONSTITUTION - 1868

Journal of the Proceedings of the Constitutional Convention of the People of Georgia . . . and Ordinances and Resolutions Adopted. Augusta, Ga.: 1868. V. 37

GEORGIA. CONVENTION - 1861

Journal of the Public and Secret Proceedings of the Convention . . . held in Milledgeville, and Savannah . . . With the Ordinances Adopted . . . Milledgeville, Ga.: 1861. V. 37

GEORGIA. CONVENTION. 1865

Journal of the Proceedings of the Convention of the People of Georgia Together with Ordinances and Resolutions Adopted. Milledgeville: 1865. V. 39

GEORGIA. GENERAL ASSEMBLY

Papers Relative to the Mission of Hon. T. Butler King, to Europe. Milledgeville: 1863. V. 43

Resolved by the General Assembly of Georgia, That the Governor Is Hereby Authorized to Take a Portion of the Money . . . for the Support of the Indigent Families of the Soldiers of This State, to Purchase Spun Yarn from the Different Factories of the State.. Milledgeville: 1863. V. 41

GEORGIA. GENERAL ASSEMBLY - 1862

Acts of the General Assembly of the State of Georgia passed at Milledgeville in 1862; Also, Extra Session of 1864. Milledgeville: 1864. V. 37

GEORGIA HISTORICAL SOCIETY

Collections of the Georgia Historical Society, Volume III. Part I. New York: 1848. V. 46

Collections of the Georgia Historical Society. Savannah: 1848. V. 37

Constitution, By-Laws, and List of Members of the Georgia Historical Society. Savannah: 1871. V. 41

GEORGIA. LAWS, STATUTES, ETC. - 1861

Acts of the General Assembly of the State of Georgia Passed in Milledgeville, at an Annual Session in November and December 1860. Milledgeville: 1861. V. 39; 42

GEORGIA. LAWS, STATUTES, ETC. - 1862

Acts of the General Assembly of the State of Georgia Passed at Milledgeville in 1862; Also Extra Session of 1864. Milledgeville: 1864. V. 39

GEORGIA. LEGISLATURE

Report and Resolutions of the Legislature of Georgia. Washington: 1827. V. 45

GEORGIA O'Keefe. New York: 1976. V. 44

GEORGIA RELIEF & HOSPITAL ASSOCIATION

Report of the Executive Committee of the Georgia Relief and Hospital Association to the Board of Superintendents . . . Augusta: 1862. V. 43

GEORGIA. STATE SANITARIUM. MILLEDGEVILLE

First Published Annual Report of the Resident Physician of the Lunatic, Idiot and Epiletpic Asylum of the State of Georgia . . . Milledgeville: 1845. V. 44

GEORGIAN Love Songs. Hertfordshire: 1949. V. 42

GEORGIAN Poetry 1920-1922. V. 41

GEORGIAN SOCIETY

The Records of Eighteenth-Century Domestic Architecture and Decoration in Dublin. Dublin: 1909-13. V. 39

Records of Eighteenth Century Domestic Architecture and Decoration in Dublin. Dublin: 1911. V. 41

Records of Eighteenth Century Domestic Architecture and Decoration in Dublin. Dublin: 1912. V. 41

Records of Eighteenth Century Domestic Architecture and Decoration in Dublin. Dublin: 1913. V. 41

Records of eighteenth-century domestic architecture and decoration in Dublin. Dublin: 1909-1915. V. 37

GEORGIAN Stories, 1926. London: 1926. V. 40

GEORGINA, Or, Memoirs of the Bellmour Family. London: 1787. V. 40

GEORGIRENES, JOSEPH

A Description of the Present State of Samos, Nicaria, Patmos and Mount Athos. London: 1678. V. 43; 46

GEORGIUS DE HUNGARIA

Tractatus de Moribus, Conditionibus et Nequicia Turcorum. Urach: 1481. V. 38

GEORGIUS TRAPEZUNTIUS 1395-1472

Commentarii in Philippicas Ciceronis. Venice: 1475. V. 43

GEORGYEVSKY, G.

Old Russian Miniatures (from Mss. in the Lenin Library, Moscow). Moscow: 1934. V. 39

GEPHART, RONALD M.

Revolutionary America 1763-1789. Washington: 1984. V. 40

GERANDO, JOSEPH MARIE

De La Bienfaisance Publique. Bruxelles: 1839. V. 38

GERARD, ALEXANDER 1792-1839

Account of Koonawur, in the Himalaya, etc. etc. London: 1841. V. 43

The Influence of Piety on the Public Good. Edinburgh: 1761. V. 45

GERARD DE NERVAL, GERARD LABRUNIE, Known as 1808-1855

Dreams and Life: Le Reve et la Vie. Devon: 1933. V. 40

GERARD, DOROTHEA

The Wrong Man. Edinburgh & London: 1895. V. 40

GERARD, EBENEZER

Letters in Rhume, to and From E. Gerard, Portrait Painter. Liverpool: 1825. V. 43

GERARD, EMILY

Beggar My Neighbour . . . Edinburgh: 1882. V. 44

GERARD, JEAN-IGNACE-JULIEN

Les Fleurs Animees. Text by Taxile Delord. Paris: 1847. V. 37

GERARD, JOHN 1545-1612

The Herbal or Genrallo Historie of Plantes . . . Very Much Enlarged and Amended by Thomas Johnson. London: 1636. V. 37; 38; 39; 40; 41; 42; 43; 44; 45; 46

The Herball. London: 1597. V. 42

The Herball or General Historie of Plants. London: 1633. V. 37; 38; 39; 41; 42; 43; 46

GERARD, M. G.

Report on the Proceedings of the Pamir Boundary Commission 1896. Calcutta: 1897. V. 45

GERARD Manley Hopkins. Norfolk: 1945. V. 37

GERARD, MAX

Dali de Draeger. Paris: 1968. V. 44; 46

GERARD, MONTAGU GILBERT

Leaves from the Diaries of a Soldier and Sporstman During Twenty Years' Service in India Afghanistan Egypt and Other Countries 1865-1885. London: 1903. V. 42

GERARDE, JOHN 1545-1612

The Herball or Generall Historie of Plants. London: 1597. V. 37; 38; 40

Gerard's Herball, the Essence therof distilled by Marcus Woodward from the Edition of Th. Johnson, 1636. London: 1927. V. 37

The Herball or Generall Historie. Amsterdam: 1975. V. 37; 38

GERARDIN, S.

Tableau Elementaire d'Ornithologie ou Histoire Naturelle des Oiseaux que l'on Recontre Communement en France. Paris: 1806. V. 43

GERAULDY, FRANCOIS

L'Art de Conserver Les Dents. Paris: 1737. V. 41

GERBERT, MARTIN

Iter Alemannicum, Accedit Italicum & Gallicum. St. Blasien: 1773. V. 40

GERBIER, BALTHAZAR

A Brief Discourse Concerning the Three Chief Principles of Magnificent Building. London: 1662. V. 37

Counsel and Advise to all Builders, for the Choice of their Surveyours, Clarks of their Works, Bricklayers, Masons, Carpenters, and Other Workmen therein concerned, as also in respect of their Works, Materials and Rates thereof. London: 1663. V. 37

GERDTS, WILLIAM H.

American Still-Life Painting. New York: 1971. V. 45; 46

American Impressionism. New York: 1984. V. 41

GERE, CHARLOTTE

American & European Jewelry 1830-1914. New York: 1975. V. 40; 46

Victorian Jewellery Design. Chicago: 1972. V. 45

GERHARD, FRED

Illinois as It Is. Chicago: 1857. V. 38

GERHARD, W. W.

Lectures on Diagnosis, Pathology and Treatment of the Diseases of the Chest. Philadelphia: 1842. V. 40; 42

On the Typhus Fever, Which Occurred at Philadelphia In the Spring and Summer of 1836 . . . (with) On the Typhus Fever Which Occurred at Philadelphia in the Spring and Summer of 1836. Part Second. Philadelphia. V. 42

GERHARDI, M. J.

Meditationes Sacra. Leyden: 1629. V. 39

GERHARDI, WILLIAM

Futility, a Novel on Russian Themes. London: 1922. V. 38

Memoirs of a Polyglot. London: 1931. V. 37; 40

The Memoirs of Satan. London: 1932. V. 40

Pending Heaven. London: 1930. V. 40

Resurrection. London: 1934. V. 40

The Romanovs - Evocation of the Past as a Mirror for the Present. London: 1940. V. 40; 41

GERHARDT, CHARLES FREDERIC

   Traite de Chimie Organique. Paris: 1853-56. V. 45

GERICKE, J. F. C.

   Eerste Gronden der Javaansche Taal . . . Batavia: 1831. V. 38

GERLACH, WALTER

   Matter, Electricity, Energy. New York: 1928. V. 42

GERLI, AGOSTINO

   Opuscoli. Parma: 1785. V. 39; 42; 44

THE GERM. London: 1850. V. 38; 46

THE GERM: Thoughts Toward Nature in Poetry, Literature and Art. Portland: 1898. V. 45

GERMAIN, PIERRE

   Elements d'Orfevrerie Divises. Paris: 1748. V. 38

GERMAINS, E. A.

   Left to Starve and no one Wants the Blame. New York: 1878. V. 37

GERMAN Aviation Medicine, World War II. Washington: 1950. V. 41; 42; 45

THE GERMAN Classics: Masterpieces of German Literature. New York: 1913. V. 40

GERMAN FRIENDLY SOCIETY

   Rules of the German Friendly Society, Founded on the Fifteenth of January 1766 at Charleston, South Carolina, and Incorporated on the 20th Dec. 1791. Charleston: 1828. V. 44

GERMAN-REED, T.

   Bibliographical Notes on T. E. Lawrence's Seven Pillars of Wisdom and Revolt in the Desert. London: 1928. V. 38; 41

GERMAN SOCIETY OF NEW YORK

   Rules and Orders of..in the State of New York; Established the 9th of October, in the Year 1784. New York: 1799. V. 45

GERMAN Songs in English Rhyme. Hartford: 1871. V. 45

THE GERMAN Theatre. London: 1801. V. 40; 45

GERMANICARUM Rerum Quatuor Celebriores Vetustioresque Chronographi ab Orbe Condito ad Tempora Henrici IV Imperatoris, ed. Simon Schard . . . Frankfurt: 1566. V. 41

GERMANO, GIOVANNI

   Additione Apologetico-Istorica alle Predittioni Circa i Somi Pontefici Romani del Glorioso Padre S. Malachia Metropolitano Primario dell'Ibernia. Naples: 1675-76. V. 45

GERNIER, ROBERT

   La Vie et l'Oeuvre de Gustave Courbet. Lausanne-Paris: 1977/78. V. 46

GERNING, J. J. VON

   A Picturesque Tour Along the Rhine, from Mentz to Cologne . . . London: 1820. V. 39; 41; 45

GERNSBACK, HUGO

   Ralph 124c 41 +. a Romance of the Year 2660. Boston: 1925. V. 39; 45

GERNSHEIM, HELMUT

   Creative Photography: Aesthetic trends 1839-1960. London: 1962. V. 41
   The History of Photography, From the Earliest Use of the Camera Obscura in the Eleventh Century Up to 1914. 1955. V. 45
   The History of Photography from the Earliest Use of the Camera Obscura in the Eleventh Century up to 1914. London: 1955. V. 39
   The History of Photography from the Camera Obscura to the Beginning of the Modern Era. London or New York: 1969. V. 42
   The History of Photography from the Camera Obscura to the Beginning of the Modern Era. New York: 1969. V. 37
   Julia Margaret Cameron - Pioneer of Photography. London: 1948. V. 41; 44
   Julia Margaret Cameron: Pioneer of Photography. London: 1949? V. 40; 42
   L. J. M. Daguerre, The History of the Diorama and the Daguerrotype. London: 1956. V. 39; 41
   Lewis Carroll: Photographer. New York: 1950. V. 39
   Lewis Carroll, Photographer. London: 1949. V. 37
   Those Impossible English. London: 1952. V. 41

GERRALD, JOSEPH

   Joseph Gerrald, Delegate from the London Corresponding Society, to the British Convention Before the High Court of Justiciary, at Edinburgh, 3rd-14, March 1794 for Sedition. Edinburgh: 1794. V. 38

GERRARD, FRANK

   The Book of the Meat Trade. London: 1949. V. 39

GERRARE, WIRT

   A Bibliography of Guns and Shooting. London: 1894. V. 39

GERRING, CHARLES

   Notes on Book Binding. Nottingham: 1899. V. 41; 43; 45
   Notes on Printers and Booksellers with a Chapter on Chap Books. London: 1900. V. 39; 41; 44

GERRISH, ANDREW

   A Synopsis on the Prevention and Cure of Disease. Boston: 1841. V. 43

GERRISH, THEODORE

   Life in the World's Wonderland. Biddeford: 1847. V. 40; 46

GERSDORFF, HANS VON

   Feldbuch der Wundtartzney. Strasburg: 1517. V. 46
   Feldt und Stattbuch Bewerter Wundt Artzney, Burch den Bolerfahrnen und Lang. Franckfurt A.M.: 1606. V. 46

GERSH, S.

   Middle platonism and neoplationism. The Latin Tradition. 1986. V. 37

GERSHEIM, H.

   Julia Margaret Cameron: Her Life and Photographic Work. London: 1948. V. 46

GERSHEVITCH, I.

   The Median and Archaemenian Periods. Editor I. Gershevitch. 1985. V. 37

GERSHWIN, GEORGE 1898-1937

   George Gershwin's Song Book. New York: 1932. V. 42; 45
   George Gershwin's Song Book. New York: 1941. V. 45
   Porgy & Bess: an Opera in Three Acts. New York: 1935. V. 37; 39; 41; 44; 46

GERSHWIN, IRA

   Lyrics on Several Occasions . . . New York: 1959. V. 41

GERSON, HORST

   Rembrandt Paintings. Amsterdam: 1968. V. 46

GERSON, JEAN

   De Meditatione Cordis: de Oratione et Valore Eius: Expositio Super Psalmos Poenitentiales. Cologne: 1470. V. 42; 45

GERSTAECKER, FREIDRICH WILHELM CHRISTIAN 1816-1872

   Gerstacker's Travels. London: 1854. V. 37; 39; 41; 45

GERSTAECKER, FRIEDRICH WILHELM CHRISTIAN 1816-1872

   Narrative of a Journey Round the World, Comprising a Winter Passage Across the Andes to Chile, with a Visit to the Gold Regions of California and Australia, the South Sea Islands, Java, &c. London: 1853. V. 38
   Narrative of a Journey Round the World. Comprising a Winter Passage across the Andes to Chili; with a Visit to the Gold Regions of California and Australia, the South Sea Islands, Java &c. New York: 1854. V. 37
   Reisen . . . Californien. Stuttgart & Tubingen: 1853. V. 38
   Scenes de la Vie Californienne. Geneva: 1859. V. 37; 39
   Scenes of Life in California. San Francisco: 1942. V. 45
   Travels Rio De Janeiro - Buenos Ayres - Ride Through the Pampas - Winter Journey Across the Cordilleras - Chili - Valparaiso - California and the Gold Fields. London: 1854. V. 41; 45
   Western Lands and Western Waters. London: 1864. V. 37; 38; 39
   Wild Sports in the Far West. London: 1854. V. 37; 40
   Wild Sports in the Far West. Boston: 1859. V. 39; 42

GERSTLE, SARA

   Three Houses. San Francisco: 1952. V. 37; 38; 42

GERSTMANN, ROBERT

   Chile: 280 Grabados en Cobre. Paris: 1932. V. 39

GERVAISE, NICOLAS

   An Historical Description of the Kingdom of Macasar in the East Indies . . . London: 1701. V. 39

GESCHICKTER, CHARLES F.

   Tumors of the Bone. New York: 1931. V. 42
   Tumors of Bone (Including the Jaws and Joints). New York: 1936. V. 42

GESELL, SILVIO 1862-1930

   The Natural Economic Order. 1929. V. 41
   The Natural Economic Order. Berlin-Frohnau: 1929. V. 39

GESENIUS, WILHELM 1786-1842

   Scripturae Linguaeque Phoenicae Monumenta. Leipzig: 1837. V. 43

GESENIUS, WILLIAM

A Hebrew and English Lexicon of the Old Testament. Boston: 1836. V. 43

A Hebrew and English Lexicon of the Old Testament . . . Boston: 1844. V. 37

GESNER, ABRAHAM

The Industrial Resources of Nova Scotia. Halifax: 1849. V. 40

A Practical Treatise on Coal, Petroleum and Other Distilled Oils. New York: 1856. V. 43

A Practical Treatise on Coal, Petroleum, and Other Distilled Oils. New York: 1861. V. 38; 45

A Practical Treatise on Coal, Petroleum, and Other Distilled Oils. New York: 1865. V. 43

GESNER, C.

Historiae Animalium Lib. I de Quadrupedibus Viviparis. Zurich: 1551. V. 41

GESNER, CONRAD 1516-1565

Bibliotheca Instituta et Collecta, Postremo Recognita & in Duplum Post Priores Editiones Aucta. Zuerich: 1574. V. 37

Bibliotheca Instituta et Collecta, Primum a Conrado Gesnero, Deinde in Epitomen Redacta . . . Zurich: 1583. V. 37

Epitome Bibliothecae Conscripta Primum a Conrado Lycosthene . . . Zurich: 1555. V. 38

Historiae Animalium Liber II, Qui Est de Quadrupedibus Oviparius (with) Historiae Animalium Liber III, Qui Est de Avium Natura. Frankfurt: 1586-85. V. 44

Historiae Animalium Liber III, qui est de Auium Natura. Francofurdi: 1585. V. 37

Mithridates, Exprimens Differentias Linguarum, Tum Veterum, tum Quae Hodie, per Totum Terrarum Orbem, is Usus Sunt. Zurich: 1610. V. 40

The Newe Iewell of Health, Wherein is Contayned the Most Excellent Sceretes of Phisicke and Philosophie. London: 1576. V. 37

Physicarum Meditationum. Zurich: 1586. V. 42; 44

The Practise of the New and Old Phisicke, Where is Contained the Most Excellent Secrets of Phisicke and Philosophie . . . London: 1599. V. 37

Quatre Livres des Secrets de Medecine, et de la Philosophie Chimique. Paris: 1579. V. 40

The Treasure of Euonymous, Conteyninge the Wonderfull Hid Secretes of Nature . . . London: 1559. V. 46

GESSI, ROMOLO

Seven Years in the Soudan: Being a Record of Explorations, Adventures, and Campaigns Against the Arab Slave Hunters. London: 1892. V. 38

GESSNER, CHRISTIAN FRIEDRICH

Der in der Buchdruckerei wohl Unterrichtete Lehr-Junge oder . . . Leipzig: 1743. V. 42

Die So Nothig Als Nutzliche Buchdrukerkunst und Schrift-Giesserey. Leipzig: 1740-41. V. 40; 44

GESSNER, S.

Idyls, or Pastoral Poems; to Which is Annexed a Letter to M. Fuesslin, on Landscape Painting. Edinburgh: 1798. V. 46

GESSNER, SALOMON

Chef d-Oeuvres de . . . Contenant la Mort d'Abel. Paris: 1820. V. 39

The Death of Abel. London: 1797. V. 37; 38

Mort d'Abel, Poeme . . . Paris: 1793. V. 40; 45

The Works . . . Liverpool: 1802. V. 40; 43; 46

GESSNER, SOLOMON

New Idylles. London: 1776. V. 44

GESTA FRANCORUM ET ALIORUM HIEROSOLYMITANORUM

The First Crusades, The Deeds of the Franks and Other Jerusalemites . . . Waltham St. Lawrence: 1943. V. 44

The First Crusade; The Deeds of the Franks and Other Jerusalemites. Waltham St. Lawrence: 1945. V. 41

GESTA Romanorum. Strasbourg: 1484. V. 38; 40
GESTA Romanorum. London: 1824. V. 38
GESTA Romanorum. London: 1871. V. 38

GESVRES, FRANCOIS JOACHIM BERNARD POTIER, DUC DE 1692-1757

The Case of Impotency Debated, in the Late Famous Tryal at Paris, Between the Marquis de Gesvres . . . . and Mademoiselle de Mascranny, His Lady . . . London: 1714. V. 43; 46

GETCHELL, FRANK H.

An Illustrated Encyclopedia of the Science and Practice of Obstetrics. Philadelphia: 1885. V. 41

An Illustrated Enclopedia of the Science and Practice of Obstetrics. Philadelphia: 1890. V. 45

GETLEIN, FRANK

Chaim Gross. New York: 1974. V. 39; 42; 45

Chaim Gross: Watercolors and Drawings. New York: 1979. V. 43; 46

Jack Levine. New York. V. 39; 42; 46
Jack Levine. New York: 1966. V. 45

GETTY, ALICE

The Gods of Northern Buddhism . . . Oxford: 1928. V. 46

GETTY, EDMUND

Notices of Chinese Seals Found in Ireland: Read Before the Belfast Literary Society6th May 1850. Dublin & Belfast: 1850. V. 46

GEVARTIUS, CASPAR

Pompa Introitus Honori Serenissimi Principis Ferdinandi Austriaci Hispaniarum Infantis S. R. E. card . . . Antwerp: 1642. V. 37; 46

GEVERS, ABRAHAM

Musaeum Geversianum . . . The Hague: 1787. V. 40; 46

GEYER, HENRY S.

A Digest of the Laws of Missouri Territory . . . to Which are Added, a Variety of Forms, Useful to Magistrates. St. Louis: 1818. V. 40

GEYMULLER, HENRY DE

Les Du Cerceau. Paris & London: 1887. V. 39

GHEVARA, FRANCISCUS DE

Speculum Ustorium Verae ac Primigeniae Suae Formae Restitutum. Romae: 1613. V. 37

GHILINI, GIROLAMO

Teatro d'Huomini Litterati. Milan: 1638. V. 41

Teatro d'Huomini Letterati. Milano: 1635. V. 37

GHIRARDI, BONETO

La Leonida Comedia. Venice: 1585. V. 37

GHIRSHMAN, ROMAN

Persian Art: The Parthian and Sassanian Dynasties. New York: 1962. V. 40

GHLISLANDIS, ANTONIUS DE

Opus Aureum Ornatum Omni Lapide Precioso Singulare Novissime Editum Super Evangeliis Totius Anni. Lyon: 1508. V. 37

GHOSE, SUDHIN N.

Folk Tales and Fairy Stories from India. London: 1961. V. 38; 39; 43; 44; 46

Folk Tales and Fairy Stories from India. Waltham St. Lawrence: 1961. V. 46

THE GHOST, or a Minute Account of the Appearance of the Ghost of John Croxford, Executed at Northampton, August the 4th, for the Murder of a Stranger. N.P.: Northampton?: 1764. V. 37

GHOST Stories: Collected with a Particular View to Counteract the Vulgar Belief in Ghosts and Apparitions, and Promote a Rational Estimate of the Nature of Phenomena Commonly considered as Supernatural. London: 1823. V. 41

GHURYE, G. S.

Indian Costume. Bombay: 1951. V. 37

GIACOMETTI, ALBERTO

Drawings. London: 1971. V. 44

GIACOMINI TEBALDUCCI MALESPINI, LORENZO

Oratione e Discorsi. Florence: 1597. V. 40; 45

GIAFERRI, PAUL LOUIS DE

The History of the Feminine Costume of the World. Paris: 1925. V. 38

GIAFFERRI, PAUL LOUIS DE

The History of the Feminine Costume of the World from the Year 5318 BC to Our Own Century. New York: 1927. V. 41

GIANI, GIAMPIERO

Catalogo delle utentiche Edizioni Bodonianae . . . Conchiglia: 1948. V. 38

GIANNONE, PIETRO

Civil History of the Kingdom of Naples. London: 1729-31. V. 41

GIBB, GEORGE DUNCAN

On Diseases of the Throat, Epiglottis and Windpipe. London: 1860. V. 39

GIBB, WILLIAM

The Royal House of Stuart. London: 1890. V. 40

The Royal House of Stuart. London & New York: 1890. V. 39

The Royal House of Stuart . . . Drawn From Relics of the Stuarts by William Gibb. N.P.: 1890. V. 42

GIBBENS, NICHOLAS

Questions and Disputations Concerning the Holy Scripture. London: 1601. V. 38

GIBBES, JAMES G.

Who Burn Columbia? Newberry: 1902. V. 40; 42

GIBBES, PHEBE

The Niece; or, The History of Sukey Thornby. London: 1788. V. 41

GIBBES, R. W.

Cuba for Invalids. New York: 1860. V. 40

THE GIBBET of Regina. The Truth About Riel. Sir John A. Macdonald and His Cabinet Before Opinion by one who Knows. New York: 1886. V. 37

GIBBINGS, ROBERT

Coconut Island or the Adventures of Two Children in the South Seas. London: 1936. V. 43

Coming Down the Seine. London: 1953. V. 37; 39; 43; 44; 45; 46

Engraved by Robert Gibbings: A Portrait of Lady Hester. Wiltshire: 1987. V. 41

Fourteen Wood Engravings . . . From Drawings Made on Orient Line Cruises. London: 1932. V. 41

Fourteen Wood Engravings by Robert Gibbings. London: 1922. V. 37

Iorana! Boston & New York: 1932. V. 38; 41; 44

John Graham (Convict). London: 1937. V. 43

Over the Reef. London: 1948. V. 38; 40; 41; 42

A Portrait of Lady Hester Stanhope from Alexander William Kinglake's Eothen. 1987. V. 38

The 7th Man. London: 1930. V. 38

The 7th Man. Waltham St. Lawrence: 1930. V. 37; 44

A True Tale of Love in Tonga Told in 23 Engravings and 333 Words. London: 1935. V. 38

Twelve Wood Engravings. London: 1921. V. 40

The Wood Engravings, with Some Recollections by the Artist. Chicago: 1959. V. 39

The Wood Engravings. London: 1959. V. 37; 39; 40; 41; 42; 45; 46

GIBBON, CHARLES

By Mead and Stream. London: 1884. V. 41

Heart's Delight. London: 1885. V. 46

GIBBON, EDWARD 1737-1794

Critical Observations on the Sixth Book of the Aeneid. London: 1770. V. 38

Essai sur l'Etude de la Litterature. London: 1761. V. 46

Essai sur l'Etude de la Litterature. Londres: 1762. V. 40

Essai sur l'Etude de la Litterature. Dublin: 1777. V. 41

An Essay on the Study of Literature. London: 1764. V. 37; 38; 42

Gibbon's Journey from Geneva to Rome. London: 1961. V. 45

Gibbon's Journal from Geneva to Rome: His Journal from 20 April to 2 October, 1764. London: (1962). V. 37

An Historical View of Christianity . . . London: 1806. V. 41

The History of the Decline and Fall of the Roman Empire. London. V. 40

The History of the Decline and Fall of the Roman Empire. Dublin: 1776-81. V. 38; 41; 45

The History of the Decline and Fall of the Roman Empire. London: 1776-88. V. 37; 40; 42; 43; 46

The History of the Decline and Fall of the Roman Empire. London: 1776-89. V. 37

The History of the Decline and Fall of the Roman Empire. London: 1777/81/88. V. 39; 40

The History of the Decline and Fall of the Roman Empire. London: 1777-88. V. 38; 39; 41; 45

The History of the Decline and Fall of the Roman Empire. London: 1777-89. V. 42

The History of the Decline and Fall of the Roman Empire. London: 1781-1788. V. 42

The History of the Decline and Fall of the Roman Empire. London: 1782-88. V. 37; 41

The History of the Decline and Fall of the Roman Empire. London: 1788-90. V. 37

The History of the Decline and Fall of the Roman Empire. Dublin: 1789. V. 37

Gibbon's History of the Decline and Fall of the Roman Empire. London: 1789. V. 38

The History of the Decline and Fall of The Roman Empire. London: 1789-88. V. 37; 44

The History of the Decline and Fall of the Roman Empire. (with) Miscellaneous Works. London: 1789-88-96. V. 38; 39; 45

The History of the Decline and Fall of the Roman Empire. London: 1791-92. V. 42

The History of the Decline and Fall of the Roman Empire. London: 1797. V. 39

The History of the Decline and Fall of the Roman Empire. Philadelphia: 1804-5. V. 37

The History of the Decline and Fall of the Roman Empire. London: 1807. V. 40; 44

The History of the Decline and Fall of The Roman Empire. London: 1820. V. 40; 46

History of the Decline and Fall of the Roman Empire. London: 1821. V. 40

The History of the Decline and Fall of The Roman Empire. London: 1823. V. 42; 43

The History of the Decline and Fall of the Roman Empire. Oxford: 1827. V. 41

The History of the Decline and Fall of the Roman Empire. Oxford: 1827-28. V. 37

The History of the Decline and Fall of the Roman Empire. Edinburgh: 1832. V. 43

The History of the Decline and Fall of the Roman Empire. London: 1846. V. 38; 39

The History of the Decline and Fall of the Roman Empire. London: 1854-55. V. 44

The History of the Decline and Fall of the Roman Empire. New York: 1858-59. V. 40

The History of the Decline and Fall of the Roman Empire. London: 1862. V. 37; 45

The History of the Decline and Fall of the Roman Empire . . . Philadelphia: 1872. V. 40

The History of the Decline and Fall of the Roman Empire. London: 1881. V. 43

The History of the Decline and Fall of the Roman Empire. London: 1887. V. 37; 41

The History of the Decline and Fall of the Roman Empire. London: 1896. V. 44; 46

The Decline and Fall of the Roman Empire. London: 1897. V. 38

The History of the Decline and Fall of the Roman Empire. London: 1900. V. 37; 46

The History of the Decline and Fall of the Roman Empire. London: 1903-1925. V. 38; 40

The History of the Decline and Fall of the Roman Empire. London: 1908. V. 38; 39

The History of the Decline and Fall of the Roman Empire. London: 1909. V. 37; 38; 39

The Decline and Fall of the Roman Empire. New York: 1910. V. 42

The Decline and Fall of the Roman Empire. New York: 1946. V. 38

An Inquiry into the Causes of the Progress and Establishment of the Christian Religion. London: 1820. V. 37; 41

Memoires de Gibbon. Paris: 1797. V. 40

Miscellaneous Works. Dublin: 1796. V. 38; 40; 41; 42; 43; 45; 46

Miscellaneous Works. London: 1796. V. 37; 38; 42; 43; 46

Miscellaneous Works. London: 1796-1815. V. 38; 39; 45

The Miscellaneous Works . . . London: 1814. V. 38; 41

Miscellaneous Works. London: 1976. V. 38; 41

Miscellaneous Works with Memoirs of his Life and Writings, composed by himself, illustrated from his Letters, with occasional notes and narrative by John Lord Sheffield. London: 1796/1815. V. 37

Miscellaneous Works. With Memoirs of the Life & Writins Composed by Himself: Illustrated from His Letters, with Occasional Notes & Narrative, by Lord John SHeffeild. London: 1776. V. 37

Private Letters of . . . (1753-1794). London: 1897. V. 38

A Vindication of Some Passages in the Fifteenth and Sixteenth Chapters of the History of the Decline and Fall of the Roman Empire. London: 1779. V. 39

The Works. London: 1814-1820. V. 40

GIBBON, FREDERICK P.

The 42nd (East Lancashire) Division 1914-1918. London: 1920. V. 44

GIBBON, J. M.

The True Annals of Fairyland. London: 1901. V. 44

GIBBON, JOHN

Introductio ad Latinam Blasoniam. London: 1682. V. 38

Journal of the Military Service Institution of the U.S. - Our Indian Question. New York: 1881. V. 37

GIBBON, MONK

The Branch of Hawthorn Tree. London: 1927. V. 44

GIBBONS, A. H.

Africa from South to North. Through Marotseland. London: 1904. V. 37

GIBBONS, A. ST. H.

Exploring and Hunting in Central Africa. London: 1898. V. 38

GIBBONS, C.

The Bat Woman. 1938. V. 39

GIBBONS, DAVID

A Treatise on the Law of Dilapidations and Nuisances. London: 1849. V. 38; 40

GIBBONS, F.

The Napoleon. 1929. V. 39

GIBBONS, F. continued

The Red Napoleon. 1929. V. 37; 43

GIBBONS, FELTON

Dosso and Battista Dossi, Court Painters at Ferrara. Princeton: 1968. V. 44; 45

GIBBONS, J. J.

In the San Juan, Colorado Sketches. N.P.: 1898. V. 43

GIBBONS, JAMES

A Short Appeal to Abolitionists by One of Their Number. N.P.: 1844? V. 42

GIBBONS, JAMES S.

The Banks of New York, Their Dealers, the Clearing House and the Panic of 1857. New York: 1873. V. 41

GIBBONS, STELLA

Cold Comfort Farm. London: 1932. V. 38; 42; 45

GIBBONS, THOMAS

An Elegy on the Death of the Reverend Mr. Peter Goodwin, Who Departed This Life November 27, 1747 in the LXIVth Year of His AGe. London: 1748. V. 40; 42

Memoirs of Eminently Pious Women. London: 1777. V. 38; 40

Memoirs of the Rev. Isaac Watts. London: 1780. V. 42; 44

Rhetoric; or a View of Its Principal Tropes and Figures. London: 1767. V. 44; 46

Tales That Were Told: Passages from the Journals of a Sea-Farer. New York: 1892. V. 40

GIBBONS, WILLIAM

An Exposition of Modern Scepticism. In a Letter, Addressed to the Editors of the Free Enquirer. Wilmington: 1829. V. 41; 44

A Reply to Sir Lucius O'Brien, Bart. Bristol: 1785. V. 43

GIBBS, BARBARA

The Meeting Place of the Colors: Poems. West Branch: 1972. V. 37; 42

GIBBS, FREDERICK T. M.

The Illustrated Guide to the Royal Navy and Foreign Navies; also Mercantile Marine Steamers Available as Armed Cruisers and Transports, &c, &c. Compiled and edted by Frederick T.M. Gibbs. London: 1896. V. 37

GIBBS, GEORGE

Alphabetical Vocabulary of the Chinook Language. New York: 1863. V. 40

A Dictionary of the Chinook Jargon, or Trade Language of Oregon. New York: 1863. V. 37; 38; 39; 40; 41; 42; 43; 44

A Dictionary of the Chinook Jargon, or Trade Language of Oregon. Washington: 1863. V. 46

The Judicial Chronicle, Being a Lit of the Judges of the Courts of Common Law and Chancery in England and America, and of the Contemporary Reports. Cambridge: 1834. V. 38

GIBBS, H. R. K.

Historical Record of the 6th Gurkha Rifles. Volume II. Aldershot: 1955. V. 42

GIBBS, HENRY HUCKS

A Collooquy on Currency . . . London: 1893. V. 37

GIBBS, J. F.

Lights and Shadows of Mormonism. Salt Lake City,: 1909. V. 39

GIBBS, J. WILLARD

The Collected Works. New York: 1928. V. 38

The Collected Works. New York: 1931. V. 45

The Collected Works. New Haven: 1948. V. 40; 46

The Scientific Papers. London: 1906. V. 46

GIBBS, JAMES

Bibliotheca Radcliffiana. Oxford: 1737. V. 38

Bibliotheca Radcliviana. London: 1747. V. 39; 40; 41; 43; 45

A Book of Architecture Containing Designs of Buildings and Ornaments. London: 1728. V. 44

A Book of Architecture, Containing Designs of Buildings and Ornaments. London: 1739. V. 38

Rules for Drawing the Several Parts of Architecture . . . London: 1732. V. 37

GIBBS, JAMES M.

History of the First Battalion Pennsylvania. Harrisburg: 1905. V. 39; 42

GIBBS, JOHN

English Gothic Architecture. Manchester: 1855. V. 38

Studies in Architecture and Ornament. Oxford: 1860. V. 38

GIBBS, JOHN A.

The History of Antony and Dorothea Gibbs and of their contemporary relatives, including the history of the orgin and early years of the house of Antony Gibbs and Sons. London: 1922. V. 37

GIBBS, JOSEPH

Report of Mr. Gibbs, Civil Engineer, Upon the Several Proposed Lines for a Brighton Railway. London: (1835?). V. 37

GIBBS, JOSIAH

The Mountain Meadows Massacre. Salt Lake City: 1910. V. 38

GIBBS, MAY

Little Ragged Blossom and More about Smugglepot and Cuddlepie. London: 1920. V. 46

GIBERT DE MONTREUIL

Roman de la Violette, ou de Gerard de Nevers, en vers du XIIIe Siecle . . . d'Apres Deux Manuscrits de la Bibliotheque Royale . . . Paris: 1834. V. 46

GIBNEY, JOHN

Practical Observations on the Use and Abuse of Cold and Warm Sea-Bathing, in Various Diseases . . . London: 1814. V. 44

GIBNEY, V. P.

The Hip and its Diseases. New York: 1884. V. 39; 40

GIBRALTER Directory and Guide Book, for 1917. Gibralter: 1917. V. 39

GIBRAN, KAHLIL

The Prophet. New York: 1927. V. 39; 40

Twenty Drawings. New York: 1919. V. 44

GIBSON, A. L.

Another Alice Book, Please! London: 1924. V. 46

GIBSON, ARTHUR HOPKIN

Robert Hopkin, Master marine and Landscape Painter. Detroit: 1962. V. 45

GIBSON, CHARLES

By Mead and Stream. London: 1884. V. 42

GIBSON, CHARLES B.

The History of the County and City of Cork. London: 1861. V. 37

GIBSON, CHARLES DANA 1867-1945

Americans. New York: 1900. V. 37

Drawings. New York & London: 1901. V. 39

Eighty Drawings Including the Weaker Sex. New York: 1903. V. 37

Everyday People. New York: 1904. V. 37

People of Dickens. New York: 1897. V. 40

The Social Ladder. New York: 1902. V. 37

A Widow and Her Friends. New York: 1901. V. 42

GIBSON CRAIG, JAMES T.

Catalogue of the Valuable and Very Extensive Lbrary of the Late James T. Gibson Craig, Esq., Which Will be Sold by Auction by Messers. Sotheby, Wilkinson and Hodge . . . on Monday, the 27th day of June, 1887 and Nine Following Days. London: 1887. V. 39

GIBSON, EDMUND 1669-1748

The Bishop of London's Pastoral Letter to the People of His Diocese; Especially Those of the Two Great Cities of London and Westminster. London: 1739. V. 43; 44

The Causes of the Discontents in Relation to the Plague, and the Provisions Against it Fairly Stated and Consider'd. London: 1721. V. 45; 46

Chronicon Saxonicum. Oxford: 1692. V. 46

Codex Juris Ecclesiastici Anglicani: or the Statutes, Constitutions, Canons, Rubrick and Articles of the Church of England. Oxford: 1761. V. 39

GIBSON, FRANK

The Art of Henri Fantin-Latour: His Life and Works. London. V. 44

The Art of Henri Fantin-Latour: His Life and Works. London: 1910. V. 43

Charles Conder - His Life and Work. London: 1914. V. 40

GIBSON, G. F.

The Story of the Imperial Light Horse in the South African War 1899-1902. London: 1937. V. 37

GIBSON, GEORGE ALEXANDER

Life of Sir William Tennant Gairdner, with a Selection of Papers on General and Medical Subjects. Glasgow: 1912. V. 39

GIBSON, GEORGE RUTLEDGE

Journal of a Soldier Under Kearny and Doniphan 1846-1847. Glendale: 1935. V. 39; 41; 43

GIBSON, GEORGE RUTLEDGE continued

Journal of a Soldier Under Kearny and Doniphan 1846-1847. Glendale: 1936. V. 45

GIBSON, J. M.

Memoirs of J. M. Gibson: Terrors of the Civil War and Reconstruction days. Houston?: 1966. V. 42

GIBSON, J. T.

History of the Seventy-Eighth Pennsylvania Volunteer Infantry. Pittsburgh: 1905. V. 39; 42

GIBSON, JAMES

A Journal of the Late Siege by the Troops from North America, Against the French at Cape Breton; the City of Louisbourg, and the Territories Thereunto Belonging. London: 1745. V. 41

A Journal of the Late Siege by the Troops from North America, Against the French at Cape Breton. London: 1747. V. 40; 42; 44; 45

A Journal of the Late Siege by the Troops from North America, against the French at Cape Breton . . . London: 1747. V. 42

Memoirs of the Brave: a Brief Account of the Battles of the Alma, Balaklava, and Inkerman, with Biographies. London: 1855. V. 42

GIBSON, JOHN

Atlas Minimus, or a New Set of Pocket Maps of Several Empires, Kingdoms and States of the Known World. London: 1758. V. 39; 41; 42

The Fruit-Gardener, Containing the Method of Raising Stocks, for Multiplying of Fruit-Trees, by Budding, Grafting, etc. London: 1768. V. 41

The History of Glasgow, from the Earliest Accounts to the Present Time . . . Glasgow: 1777. V. 42; 45

History of York County, Pennsylvania. Chicago: 1886. V. 39

Reminiscences of Sir Walter Scott. Edinburgh: 1871. V. 44

GIBSON, JOHN MASON

A Condensation of Matter Upon Anatomy, Surgical Observations and Treatment of Diseases of the Eye Together with Remarks. Baltimore: 1832. V. 43

GIBSON, MC GUIRE

Seals and Sealing in the Ancient Near East. Malibu: 1977. V. 44

GIBSON, R. W.

Francis Bacon. A Bibliography of His Works and of Baconiana to the Year 1750. Oxford: 1950. V. 42; 44; 46

St. Thomas More: a Preliminary Bibliography of His Works and of Moreana to the Year 1750. New Haven: 1961. V. 42; 46

St. Thomas More: a Preliminary Bibliography of His Works and of Oreana to the Year 1750. New Haven and London: 1961. V. 46

GIBSON, ROBERT

A Treatise of Practical Surveying. New York: 1798. V. 44

GIBSON, S.

Abstracts from the Wills and Testamentary Documents of Binders, Printers and Stationers of Oxford, from 1493 to 1638. London: 1907. V. 41

Early Oxford Bindings. Oxford: 1903. V. 41

GIBSON, SAMUEL O.

My Travels in the Eastern Hemisphere, or, Four Years' Commission in H.M.S. 'Thetis'. London: 1886. V. 43

GIBSON, THOMAS

The Anatomy of Human Bodies. London: 1688. V. 43

The Anatomy of Humane Bodies Epitomized. London: 1694. V. 42

The Anatomy of Human Bodies Epitomized. London: 1703. V. 39; 40

The Anatomy of Human Bodies Epitomized. London: 1684. V. 38; 46

The Birth of Christ, an Irregular Ode. Cambridge: 1765. V. 46

Syntaxis Mathematica; or, a Construction of the Harder Problems of Geometry . . . London: 1655. V. 42

GIBSON, W.

Mona Lisa Overdrive. London: 1988. V. 44

Neuromancer. 1984. V. 43

GIBSON, WILFIRD WILSON

The Web of Life, A Book of Poems. London: 1908. V. 40

GIBSON, WILFRID

The Young Whistler. New York: 1927. V. 39

GIBSON, WILFRID WILSON

Home: A Book of Poems, by W. W. Gibson. (Westminster: 1920). V. 37

Urlyn the Haroer and Other Song. London: 1902. V. 37

The Web of Life. London: 1908. V. 38

GIBSON, WILLIAM

The Farrier's Dispensatory. London: 1734. V. 38; 40; 41; 44

The Farrier's New Guide. London: 1720. V. 38

The Farrier's New Guide. London: 1738. V. 38

The Institutes and Practice of Surgery. Philadelphia: 1824-25. V. 38

The Institutes and Practice of Suergery . . . Philadelphia: 1832. V. 41; 44

The Institutes and Practice of Surgery; Being the Outlines of a Course of Lectures. Philadelphia: 1835. V. 44

The Institutes and Practice of Surgery. Philadelphia: 1838. V. 38

The Institutes and Practice of Surgery. Philadelphia: 1841. V. 40

Neuromancer. London: 1984. V. 46

A New Treatise on the Diseases of Horses . . . London: 1751. V. 37; 42; 43

GIBSON, WILLIAM HAMILTON

Happy Hunting Grounds. London: 1888. V. 43

GIBSON, WILLIAM SIDNEY

The History of the Monastery Founded at Tynemouth in the Diocese of Durham. London: 1846. V. 38; 41

GIDDINGS, FRANKLIN HENRY

The Principles of Sociology. An Analysis of the Phenomena of Association and of Social Organization . . . New York: 1896. V. 37

GIDDINGS, JOSHUA REED 1795-1864

The Exiles of Flordia . . . Columbus: 1858. V. 40; 41; 42

A Letter . . . Upon the Duty of Anti-Slavery Men in the Present Crisis. N.P.: 1844. V. 42

Pacificus: the Rights and Privileges of the Several States in Regard to Slavery . . . Warren: 1843? V. 42

GIDDINGS, LUTHER

Sketches of the Campaign in Northern Mexico. V. 43

Sketches of the Campaign in Northern Mexico in Eighteen Hundred Forty Six and Seven. New York: 1853. V. 38; 39; 45

GIDDY, DAVIES

A Plain Statement of the Bullion Question in a Letter to a Friend. London: 1811. V. 38; 39

GIDE, ANDRE 1869-1951

If It die . . . New York: 1935. V. 39; 46

If It Die. New York: (1935). V. 37

Montaigne. 1929. V. 42

Montaigne. London: 1929. V. 43

Montaigne, an Essay in Two Parts. London & New York: 1929. V. 39

Montaigne. An Essay in Two Parts. New York: 1929. V. 38

Les Nourritures Terrestres & Les Nouvelles Nourritures. 1950. V. 46

Oscar Wilde a Study. Oxford: 1905. V. 37; 41; 42

Paludes. Maestricht: 1930. V. 42

Prometheus Illbound. London: 1919. V. 37; 41; 42; 44; 46

Theseus. 1949. V. 44

Theseus. Norfolk: 1949. V. 39

Theseus. Verona: 1949. V. 37; 45; 46

Voyage au Congo; Suivi du Retour du Tchad. Paris: 1929. V. 46

GIDEON, D. C.

Indian Territory Descriptive Biographical and Genealogical Including the Landed Estates, County Seats. New York and Chicago: 1901. V. 42

GIEDION-WEICKER, CAROLA

Contemporary Sculpture: an Evolution in Volume and Space. New York: 1960. V. 46

GIEDION-WELCKER, C.

In Memorian James Joyce. Zurich: 1941. V. 41

GIEDION-WELCKER, CAROLA

Constantin Brancusi. New York: 1959. V. 39; 46

Contemporary Sculpture: an Evolution in Volume and Space. New York: 1960. V. 39

Jean Arp. New York: 1957. V. 45; 46

GIEGER, MAYNARD J.

The Life and Times of Fray Junipero Serra, O.F. M. or the Man Who Never Turned Back. Washington: 1959. V. 45

GIELGUD, JOHN

Early Stages. London: 1939. V. 45

GIELGUD, LEWIS

The Vigil of Venus. London;: (ca. 1930). V. 37

GIES, WILLIAM J.

Dental Education in the United States and Canada A Report to the Carnegie Foundation for the Advancement of Teaching. New York: 1926. V. 38

GIEURE, MAURICE

G. Braque. Paris: 1956. V. 46

G. Braque. Paris and New York: 1956. V. 41

GIFFARD, EDWARD

A Short Visit to the Ionian Islands, AThens, and the Morea. London: 1837. V. 37

GIFFARD, HENRY

Pamela. London: 1742, 1741. V. 39

GIFFEN, FANNIE REED

Oo-mah-ha Ta-wa-tha (Omaha City). Lincoln: 1898. V. 38

GIFFEN, ROBERT 1837-1910

The Growth of Capital. London: 1889. V. 40

Statistics. Written About the Year 1898-1900. London: 1913. V. 41

GIFFORD, EDWARD W.

California Indian Nights Entertainments. Glendale: 1930. V. 38

GIFFORD, HUMFREY

A Posie of Gilloflowers . . . London: 1933. V. 46

GIFFORD, ISABELLA

The Marine Botanist; an Introduction to the Study of Algology, Containing Description of the Commonest British Sea-Weeds, and the Best Method of Preserving Them, with Figures of the most Remarkable Species. London;: 1848. V. 37

GIFFORD, J.

The Complete English Lawyer, or, Every Man His Own Lawyer . . . London: 1820. V. 38

GIFFORD, JOHN

History of the Political Life of the Right Honourable William Pitt; Including Some Account of the Times in Which He Lived. London: 1809. V. 42; 45; 46

GIFFORD, THOMAS

Historical Description of the Zetland Islands in the Year 1733. Edinburgh: 1879. V. 43

GIFFORD, WILLIAM

The Baeviad, and Maeviad. London: 1811. V. 38

The Baviad, a Paraphrastic Imitation of the First Satire of Persius. London: 1791. V. 39; 45

THE GIFT. Philadelphia: 1844. V. 45; 46

THE GIFT: a Christmas and New Year's Gift for 1842. Philadelphia: 1841. V. 37; 38; 40; 41

THE GIFT: a Christmas and New Year's Present. Philadelphia: 1843. V. 44

THE GIFT: a Christmas and New Year's Present for 1836. Philadelphia: 1835. V. 38

THE GIFT: a Christmas and New Year's Present for 1842. Philadelphia: 1841. V. 40

THE GIFT: a Christmas and New Year's Present (for 1843). Philadlephia: 1842. V. 46

THE GIFT: a Christmas, New Year and Birthday Present. MDCCXLV. Philadelphia: 1845(44). V. 37; 42

THE GIFT: a Christmas, New Year and Birthday Present, MXCCCXLV. Philadelphia: 1845. V. 38; 44; 45

THE GIFT... for 1840. Philadelphia: 1839. V. 41

GIFT, GEORGE W.

Settler's Guide, Containing All the Circulars and Laws Relating to Pre-Emption Claims in California. Benicia: 1854. V. 44

Settler's Guide Containing the Pre-Emption Laws and Laws of Congress in Relation to Locating School and Warrants . . . Stockton: 1857. V. 46

GIGAS, HIERONYMOUS

Tractatus de Pensionibus Ecclesiasticis. Lyon: 1548. V. 40

GIL, MANUEL

Relacion de la Proclamacion del Rey Nuestro Senor Don Carlos IV. Madrid: 1790. V. 46

GILBART, JAMES WILLIAM 1794-1863

The History of Banking in America With an Inquiry How Far the Banking Institutions of America are Adapted to this Country; and a Review of the Causes of the Recent Pressure on the Money Market. London: 1837. V. 38

The History of Banking in Ireland. London: 1836. V. 37

An Inquiry into the Causes of the Pressure on the Money Market during the year 1839. London: 1840. V. 37

The Logic of Banking . . . London: 1859. V. 43; 45

A Practical Treatise on Banking. London: 1836. V. 40

A Practical Treatise on Banking. London: 1865. V. 43

GILBERT

The Railways of England . . . London: 1839. V. 46

GILBERT, B.

A Leaf from the Letters of St. Jerome First Printed by Sixtus Reissinger, Rome, c. 1466-67. Los Angeles: 1981. V. 39

GILBERT, BENJAMIN

A Narrative of the Captivity and Sufferings of Benjamin Gilbert and His Family . . . London: 1790. V. 43

GILBERT, BENNETT

A Leaf from the Letters of St. Jerome, First Printed by Sixtus Reissinger, Rome c. 1466-67. London: 1981. V. 45

GILBERT, BURNETT

The Life and Death of Sir Matthew Hale, Kt. London: 1682. V. 37

GILBERT, C.

The Life and Works of Thomas Chippendale. London: 1978. V. 37

GILBERT, C. S.

An Historical Survey of the County of Cornwall: to Which is added a Complete Heraldry of the Same. Plymouth-Dock: 1817-20. V. 41; 46

GILBERT, CHRISTOPHER

Furniture at Temple Newsam House and Lotherton Hall. London and Bradford. V. 42

Furniture of Temple Newsam House and Lotherton Hall. A Catalogue of the Leeds Collection. N.P.: 1978. V. 41

The Life and Work of Christopher Chippendale. London: 1978. V. 39

The Life and Works of Thomas Chippendale. London: 1979. V. 39; 42

GILBERT, FRANK T.

Historic Sketches of Walla Walla, Whitman, Columbia and Garfield Counties, Washignton Territory and Umatilla County, Oregon. Portland: 1882. V. 45

GILBERT, G. 1674-1726

The Law and Practice of Ejectments. London: 1741. V. 40

The Law of Distresses and Replevins, Delineated. London: 1758. V. 40

The Law of Distresses and Replevins, Delineated. London: 1758. V. 38; 40

The Law of Distresses and Replevins, Delineated. Dublin: 1792. V. 40

Reports of Cases in Equity, in the Courts of Chancery and Exchequer, (1705-1726) and the Court at Exchequer in Ireland. London: 1742. V. 38; 40

Reports of Cases in Equity in the Courts of Chancery and Exchequer (1705-1726) and in the Court of Exchequer in Ireland. London: 1742. V. 38

GILBERT, G. K.

Report on the Geology of the Henry Mountains. Washington: 1877. V. 41

GILBERT, GEOFFREY

The Law of Devises, Revocations and Last Wills. London: 1756. V. 46

The Law of Evidence. London: 1777. V. 41

GILBERT, HENRY

Robin Hood and the Men of Greenwood. London: 1912. V. 45; 46

GILBERT, HUMPHREY

The Voyages and Colonising Enterprises of Sir Humphrey Gilbert. London: 1940. V. 43

GILBERT, J. T.

Historic and Municipal Documents of Ireland, A.D. 1172-1320. London: 1870. V. 38

GILBERT, JAMES W.

The Logic of Banking: A familiar exposition of the principles of reasoning, and their application to the art and science of banking. London: 1859. V. 37

GILBERT, JAMES WILLIAM

Logic for the Million. London: 1851. V. 40

GILBERT, JEFFREY

Cases in Law and Equity . . . With Two Treatises, the One on the Action of Debt, the Other on the Constitution of England. Savoy: 1760. V. 39

The History and Practice of Civil Actions, Particularly in the Court of Common Pleas, Being an Historical account of the Parts and Order of Judicial Proceedings . . . London: 1761. V. 39

GILBERT, JEFFREY continued

The Law and Practice of Ejectments: Being a Compendious Treatise of the Common and Statute Law Relating Thereto: to Whcih are Added Select Precedents of Pleas, Special Verdicts, Judgments, Executions and Proceedings in Error . . . Savoy: 1741. V. 39

The Law of Evidence. London: 1769. V. 39

A Treatise of Tenures, in Two Parts. Savoy: 1757. V. 39

A Treatise on Rents. London: 1758. V. 41; 43

GILBERT, JOHN

An Answer to the Bishop of Condom (Now of Meaux) (i.e. J.B. Bossuet) His Exposition of the Catholic Faith, etc. London: 1686. V. 39

GILBERT, JOHN T.

The History, Position and Treatment of the Public Records of Ireland. London: 1864. V. 43

A History of the City of Dublin. Dublin: 1859. V. 37

A Jacobite Narrative of the War in Ireland, 1688-91, with cont. letters and papers now first published. Dublin: 1892. V. 37

GILBERT, JOSEPH HENRY

Agricultural Investigations at Rothamsted, England During a Period of Fifty Years. Washington: 1895. V. 45

GILBERT, JOSIAH

The Dolomite Mountains. London: 1864. V. 40; 42; 43

GILBERT, LINNE

Russia: An Historical and Descriptive Account of that Immense Empire . . . London: 1840. V. 39

GILBERT, LINNEY

India Illustrated. London. V. 40

Russia Illustrated: a Historical and Descriptive Account of the Immense Empire, Particularly as Regards St. Petersburgh and Moscow. London: 1844. V. 45

Russia Illustrated . . . London: 1844. V. 42; 45

GILBERT, MELVIN BALLOU

Round Dancing. Portland: 1890. V. 45

GILBERT, MICHAEL

Close Quarters. London: 1947. V. 42

GILBERT, OLIVE

Narrative of Sojourner Truth, a Northern Slave, Emancipated from Bodily Servitude by the State of New York, in 1828. Boston: 1850. V. 37

GILBERT, PAUL

Chicago and Its Makers: a Narrative of Events from the Day of the First White Man to the Inception of the Second World's Fair. Chicago: 1929. V. 42

GILBERT, ROSA MULHOLLAND, LADY

Life of Sir John T. Gilbert, Irish Historian and Archivist . . . London: 1905. V. 43

GILBERT, THOMAS 1720-1798

Considerations on the Bills for the Better Relief and Empolyment of the Poor, etc. intended to be offered to Parliament this Session. London: 1787. V. 37

A Scheme for the Better Relief and Employment of the Poor; humbly submitted . . . London: 1764. V. 37

A View of the Town (in verse): in an Epistle to a Friend in the Country. London: 1735. V. 45

A View of the Town (in Verse): in an Epistle to a Friend in the Country. London: piracy, 1735. V. 41

Voyage from New South Wales to Canton in the Year 1788, With Views of the Islands Discovered. London: 1789. V. 40; 41; 44

GILBERT, WILLIAM

De Magnete, Magneticisque Corporibus et de Magno Magnete Tellure. London: 1600. V. 37; 38; 40; 42; 45

The Inquisitor; or, The Struggle in Ferrara. London: 1870. V. 41

De Mundo Nostro Sublunari Philosophia Nova. Amsterdam: 1651. V. 41; 45

Tractatus, Sive Physiologia Nova de Magnete . . . Stettin: 1633. V. 37; 42

William Gilbert of Colchester, Physician of London, on the Loadstone and Magnetic Bodies and On the Great Magnet the Earth. London: 1893. V. 45

GILBERT, WILLIAM SCHENCK 1836-1911

The Bab Ballads. London: 1869. V. 38; 40

GILBERT, WILLIAM SCHWENCK 1836-1911

Bab Ballads With: More Bab Ballads. London: 1869. V. 38; 39; 41

Bab Ballads; Much Sound and Little Sense. (with) More Bab Ballads. London: 1869-70. V. 42

The 'Bab' Ballads and More 'Bab' Ballads. London: 1869/73. V. 41; 44; 46

The Bab Ballads With Which are Included Songs of A Savoyard. London: 1960. V. 44

The Bab Ballads. Much Sound and Little Sense. (and) More 'Bab' Ballads. London: 1869/(1873). V. 37

The Bab Ballads: with which are added and included Songs of a Savoyard. London: 1898. V. 37

An Entirely New and Original Drama, in Four Acts Entitled Brantingame Hall. London: 1888. V. 38

The First Night Gilbert & Sullivan. Containing Complete Librettos of the Fourteen Operas, Together with Facsimiles of the First-Night Programs. New York: 1958. V. 37

Foggerty's Fairy and Other Tales. London: 1890. V. 42

Gretchen. London: 1879. V. 46

H.M.S. Pinafore: or the Lass that Loved a Sailor. San Francisco: 1879. V. 44

Iolanthe and Other Operas. London: 1910. V. 37

Original Plays. London: 1876. V. 41

Original Plays. New York: 1876. V. 39

Original Plays. First, Second and Third Series. London: 1894-86-95. V. 45

Patience, or Bunthorne's Bridge. New York: 1902. V. 42

The Pinafore Picture Book. London: 1908. V. 40

Ruddigore; or, the Witche's Curse! London: 1887. V. 44

Savoy Operas. London: 1909. V. 39

The Savoy Operas. London: 1932. V. 40

Songs of a Savoyard. London: 1890. V. 41; 43; 45

The Story of the Mikado. 1921. V. 43

The Story of the Mikado. London: 1921. V. 43

The Wicked World. London: 1873. V. 46

GILBERTI, MATURINO

Arte de la Legua de Michuaca Copilada por el muy Reveredo Padre Fray Maturino Gylberti, de la Orden del Seraphico Padre Sant Francisco, de Regular Observacia. Mexico: 1558. V. 45

GILBERTSON, R. L.

North American Polypores. 1988. V. 39

GILBERTSON, RICHARD

The Manuscript Series. Crediton: 1969. V. 41

GILBERTUS DE HOYLANDIA

Sermones Super Cantica Canticorum. Florence: 1485. V. 37

GILBEY, WALTER

Animal Painters of England, from the Year 1650. London: 1900-11. V. 39

Animal Painters of England from the Year 1650. A Brief History of their Lives nd Works. London: 1900. V. 37

George Morland: His Life and Works. London: 1907. V. 37; 39; 42; 46

Modern Carriages. London: 1905. V. 40

GILCHREST, HELEN IVES

Catalogue of the Severance Collection of Arms and Armor in the Cleveland Museum of Art 1924. Cleveland: 1924. V. 45

GILCHRIST, ALEXANDER

Life of William Etty. London: 1855. V. 39; 43; 45

Life of William Blake. London: 1863. V. 43

Life of William Blake, 'Pictor Ignotus'. London: 1863. V. 37; 38; 39; 41; 42; 43

Life of William Blake. London: 1880. V. 37; 38; 39; 41; 42; 43; 44

Life of William Blake, 'Pictor Ignotus.' London & Cambridge: 1863. V. 37; 38

GILCHRIST, EBENEZER

The Use of Sea Voyages in Medicine, and Particularly in a Consumption; with Observations on that Disease. London: 1771. V. 46

Utilite des Voyages sur Mer, Pour la Cure de Differentes Maladies et Notamment de la Consomption . . . London: 1770. V. 39

GILCHRIST, ELLEN

The Annunciation. Boston: 1983. V. 41; 45

The Annunciation. 1983. V. 37

In the Land of Dreamy Dreams. Fayetteville: 1981. V. 39; 45

In the Land of Dreamy Dreams. London: 1982. V. 45; 46

In the land of Dreamy Dreams. Fayetteville, Ark: 1981. V. 37

The Land Surveyor's Daughter. Fayetteville: 1979. V. 45

The Land Surveyor's Daughter. Faytteville, Ark.: 1979. V. 37

GILCHRIST, JOHN BORTHWICK

Dialogues English and Hindoostanee . . . to Promote the Colloquial Intercourse of Europeans, On the Most Indispensable and Familiar Subjects . . . London: 1820. V. 38; 40

Dialogues, English and Hindoostanee . . . London: 1826. V. 38; 42

GILCHRIST, JOHN D. F.

Marine Investigations in South Africa. Cape Town: 1902/04/05/08. V. 38

GILDAS

The Epistle of Gildas, the Most Ancient British Author . . . London: 1638. V. 37; 40; 41; 42

GILDEMEISTER, E.

The Volatile Oils. Milwaukee: 1900. V. 40

GILDER, RICHARD WATSON

John Wesley. Middletown: 1903. V. 42

GILDER, WILLIAM H.

Schwatka's Search. London: 1881. V. 42

Schwatka's Search - Sledging in the Arctic in Quest of Franklin's . . . New York: 1881. V. 37

GILDON, CHARLES

Cato Examin'd; or, Animadversions on the Fable or Plot, Manners, Sentiments, and Diction of the New Tragedy of Cato. London: 1713. V. 39

The Complete Art of Poetry. London: 1718. V. 39; 43

The Golden Spy. London: 1709. V. 43; 46

The Life of Mr. Thomas Betterton, the Late Eminent Tragedian. London: 1710. V. 42

Love's Victim: or, The Queen of Wales. London: 1710. V. 38

Miscellaneous Letters and Essays on Several Subjects. London: 1694. V. 41; 45

The Patriot, or the Italian Conspiracy. London: 1703. V. 44; 46

The Post Man Robb'd of His Mail. London: 1719. V. 38; 41

GILES, ALFRED E.

Marriage Monogamy and Polygamy on the Basis of Divine Law, or Natural Law . . . Boston: 1882. V. 42

GILES, DAPHNE S.

A Collection of Scriptural and Miscellaneous Poems. Ann Arbor: 1845. V. 44

GILES, EDWARD B.

The West-End System: a Scientific and Practical Method of Cutting All Kinds of Garments . . . London: 1890. V. 37; 45

GILES, ERNEST

Geographic Travels in Central America From 1872 to 1874. Melbourne: 1875. V. 38; 40

GILES, FRYE W.

Thirty Years in Topeka . . . Topeka: 1886. V. 38

GILES, JAMES WILLIAM

Scottish Scenery. Aberdeen: 1820. V. 39

GILES, JOSEPH

Miscellaneous Poems; on Various Subjects and Occasions. London: 1771. V. 43

GILES, LEONIDAS B.

Terry's Texas Rangers. Austin: 1911. V. 37; 38; 39

Terry's Texas Rangers. (Austin: 1911). V. 37

GILES, T.

Scottish Scenery. Aberdeen. V. 38

GILES, WILLIAM B.

Political Miscellanies. Richmond: 1829. V. 38; 41; 44

GILFILLAN, GEORGE

Life of Sir Walter Scott, Baronet. Edinburgh: 1870. V. 37

GILFILLAN, ROBERT

Poems and Songs. Edinburgh: 1839. V. 39

GILFORD, HASTINGS

The Disorers of Post-Natal Growth and Development. London: 1911. V. 38

Tumors and Cancers, a Biological Study. London: 1925. V. 38

GILHAM, WILLIAM

Manual of Instruction for the Volunteers and Militia of the Confederate States. Richmond: 1862. V. 39; 42

Manual of Instruction for the Volunteers and Militia of the Confederate States. Richmond: 1861. V. 37

Manual of Instruction for the Volunteers and Militia of the United States. Philadelphia: 1861. V. 37; 38

GILHESPY, F. BRAYSHAW

Crown Derby Porcelain. Leigh-on-Sea: 1951. V. 38

GILHOOLEY, LORD

Son! Of the Wisdom of 'Uncle Eph' the Modern Yutzo. New York: (1902). V. 37

GILKERSON, WILLIAM

American Whalers in the Western Arctic . . . Fairhaven: 1983. V. 38

American Whalers in the Western Arctic. Fairhaven: 1988. V. 42

GILKES, ERWIN

Of Poetry and Power: Poems Occasioned by the Presidency and the Death of John F. Kennedy. New York: (1964). V. 37

GILKIE, JAMES

Every Man His Own Procurator. Edinburgh: 1778. V. 37

GILKIN, IWAN

Tenebres. Brussels: 1892. V. 37

GILL, BRENDAN

Happy Times. New York: 1973. V. 45

Wooings. Verona: 1980. V. 39; 40; 42; 45; 46

GILL, CONRAD

History of Birmingham. 1952. V. 43

History of Birmingham. London: 1952. V. 37

GILL, EMLYN M.

Practical Dry-Fly Fishing. New York: 1912. V. 44

GILL, ERIC 1882-1940

Ad Imaginem Dei Creavit Illum. Though Masterting Me God, Giver of Breath and Bread World's Strand Sway of the Sea Lord of Living and Dead Over Again I Feel Thy Finger and Find Thee. N.P.: 1938. V. 46

Architecture and Sculpture: a Lecture . . . Delivered at The University of Manchester on Feb. 16th, 1927. 1927. V. 43

Art and Love. Bristol: 1927. V. 37; 43; 45

Art and Prudence. London: 1928. V. 38

Art and Prudence. Waltham St. Lawrence: 1928. V. 37; 39; 40; 41; 42; 43

Art & Prudence. Waltham St. Lawrence: 1928. V. 45

Art Nonsense and Other Essays. London: 1929. V. 37; 38; 40; 42; 43; 44; 46

Art and Manufacture. London: 1929. V. 37

Art & Prudence, an Essay. (Waltham Saint Laurence): 1928. V. 37

Autobiography. London: 1940. V. 42

Beauty Looks After Herself. London: 1933. V. 42

Beauty Looks After Herself Essays. London: & New York: 1933. V. 42

A Book of Alphabets for Douglas Cleverdon Drawn by Eric Gill. Wellingborough: 1987. V. 40; 42; 43; 45

Catalogue of Drawings and Engravings by Eric Gill. Alpine Club Gallery, 5th to 14th May A.D. 1918. Ditchling: 1918. V. 40

Christianity and Art. Abergavenny: 1927. V. 37; 42; 43

Christianity and Art: an Essay. Capel-y-ffin: 1927. V. 40

Christianity and the Machine Age. London: 1940. V. 46

Clothes. London: 1931. V. 37; 38; 39; 40; 42; 43; 44; 45

Clothing Without Cloth: An Essay on the Nude. London: 1921. V. 38

Clothing Without Cloth. London: 1931. V. 39

Clothing without Cloth: an Essay on the Nude. Waltham St. Lawrence: 1931. V. 37; 42; 45

Drawings from Life. London: 1940. V. 42

Engravings by Eric Gill . . . Bristol: 1929. V. 37; 44; 45

Engravings 1928-1933. London: 1934. V. 44

The Engravings. 1983. V. 38

The Engravings of Eric Gill. London: 1983. V. 40

The Engravings of . . . Wellingborough: 1983. V. 45

The Engravings of Eric Gill. Wellingborough: 1983. V. 37; 39; 40; 42; 45

An Essay on Typography. London: 1931. V. 46

An Essay on Typography. London: 1931. V. 46

An Essay Upon the Nature and Significance of the Natural and Artificial Integuments Worn by Men and Women. London: 1931. V. 38

An Essay on Typography . . . London: 1936. V. 39

First Nudes. London: 1954. V. 40

From the Jerusalem Diary of Eric Gill. Jerusalem: 1953. V. 43

From the Jerusalem Diary of Eric Gill. London: 1953. V. 39; 42; 43; 46

From the Palestine Diary of Eric Gill. London: 1949. V. 40; 42

The Future of Sculpture. London: 1928. V. 38; 46

Gloria in Profundis. London: 1927. V. 42

Id Quod Visum Placet - a Practical Test of the Beautiful. Waltham Saint Lawrence: 1926. V. 40

Initial Letters, Etc. Engraved by Eric Gill. Cambridge: 1929. V. 46

Letters of Eric Gill. London: 1947. V. 40

The Lord's Song. London: 1934. V. 37; 38; 41; 42; 43

GILL, ERIC 1882-1940 continued

The Lord's Song. Waltham St. Lawrence: 1934. V. 37; 39; 40; 42; 45

The Lord's Song. (London): 1934. V. 37

The Murder of the Innocents. Belgium 1914. Catalogue of an Exhibition of Paintings and Sculptures Held at Ditchling, January 1914, in aid of the Belgian Refugees. Ditchling: Sussex: 1914. V. 46

No Hands Wanted. Ditchling. V. 43

Nonsense and Other Essays. London: 1929. V. 45

Passio Domini Nostri Jesu Christi. Waltham St. Lawrence: 1926. V. 41

The Passion of Our Lord Jesus Christ, According to the Four Evangelists. London: 1934. V. 46

Sacred and Secular in Art and Industry. A Lecture Given Before the Royal Insitutition London, Feb. 1939. Newport: 1939. V. 38

Sacred and Secular. London: 1940. V. 40

Sculpture. Ditchling, Sussex: 1918. V. 41

Sculpture: An Essay on Stone Cutting. Ditchling: 1923. V. 42

Sculpture: an Essay on Stone-Cutting. Ditchling: 1923 or 1924. V. 39

Sculpture: an Essay on Stone-cutting. 1924. V. 45

Sculpture: an Essay on Stone-Cutting. Ditchling: 1924. V. 37; 42; 43; 45; 46

Sculpture and the Living Model. London: 1932. V. 44

Sculpture; An Essay on Stone-cutting with a Preface about God. Ditchling, Sussex: (1924). V. 37

A Selection of Engravings on Wood and Metal Representative of His Work to the En of the Year 1927 . . . Bristol: 1929. V. 39

Social Justice and the Stations of the Cross. London: 1929. V. 46

Social Justice & The Stations of the Cross. London: 1939. V. 37

Songs Without Clothes. 1921. V. 39; 45

Songs Without Clothes. Ditchling: 1921. V. 39; 42; 45

Songs Without Clothes. Ditchling, Sussex: 1921. V. 38

Twenty-Five Nudes. London: 1933. V. 44

Unemployment. London: 1933. V. 37; 38

War Memorial. Ditchling: 1923. V. 38

The Way of the Cross. Ditchling, Sussex: 1917. V. 46

The Way of the Cross. New York: 1927. V. 42

Welfare Handbooks. Ditchling, Sussex: 1919-23. V. 46

Wood Engravings. Ditchling: 1924. V. 37; 41; 43; 44

Work and Leisure. London: 1935. V. 38; 40

GILL, EVAN R.

Bibliography of Eric Gill. London: 1973. V. 41

Eric Gill: a Bibliography. London: 1991. V. 45

GILL, G. HERMON

Royal Australian Navy. The Official History of the RAN in the War of 1939-1945. 1957 & 1968. V. 39

GILL, JOHN

Levi's Urim and Thummin Found with Christ. London: 1725. V. 39

Reminiscences of Four Years as a Private Soldier in the Confederate Army 1861-1865. Baltimore: 1904. V. 38

GILL, N. J.

The Aerial Arm. Its Functions and Development. London: 1919. V. 44

GILL, S. T.

14 Views of Old Adelaide from Sketches in 1840-1849. London. V. 43

GILL, SAMUEL THOMAS

The Australian Sketchbook by S. T. G. Melbourne: 1865. V. 40

GILL, THOMAS

Selections from the Court Reports Originally Published in the Morning Post. Boston: 1837. V. 39

GILL, W. B.

The Comic History of Victoria . . . Melbourne: 1880's. V. 41

GILL, WILLIAM

California Letters of William Gill Written in 1850 to His Wife Harriet Tarleton in Kentucky. New York: 1922. V. 37; 40; 42

Gems from the Coral Islands, or Incidents of Contrast Between Savage and Christian Life of the South Sea Islanders . . . Philadelphia: 1855. V. 40; 43

Gems from the Coral Islands; or, Incidents of Contrast Between Savage and Christian Life of the South Sea Islanders. London: 1856. V. 38; 39; 43; 45

GILL, WILLIAM F.

The Life of Edgar Allan Poe. New York: 1877. V. 41; 46

The Life of Edgar Allan Poe. New York: 1878. V. 37; 38; 40; 42

The Life of Edgar Allan Poe. London: 1878. V. 38

GILL, WILLIAM P. 1844-1917

The Life of Edgar Allan Poe. New York: 1878. V. 42

GILLELAND, J. C.

The Counting-House Assistant or a Brief Digest of American Mercantile Law. Pittsburgh: 1818. V. 38

The Ohio and Mississippi Pilot . . . Pittsburgh: 1820. V. 41

The Ohio and Mississippi Pilot. Pittsburgh: 1826. V. 42

GILLES, PIERRE 1490-1555

The Antiquities of Constantinople. London: 1729. V. 40

De Topographia Constantinopoleos, et de Illius Antiquitatibus Libri Quattuor. Lyon: 1562. V. 45

GILLESPIE, ALEXANDER

Gleanings and Remarks. Leeds: 1818. V. 38; 40

Gleanings and Remarks: Collected During Many Months Residence at Buenos Ayres . . . Leeds: 1818. V. 40

An Historical Review of the Royal Marine Corps from Its Original Institution Down to the Present Era in 1803. Birmingham: 1803. V. 38

An Historical Review of the Royal Marine Corps, From Its Original Institution Down to the Present Era, 1803. Birmingham: 1803. V. 38; 42

GILLESPIE, EDWARD T. W.

Picturesque Stamford: 1641-1892. Stamford: 1883. V. 44

GILLESPIE, GEORGE 1613-1648

A Dispute Against the English-Popish Ceremonies, Obtruded Upon the Church of Scotland. Leyden: 1637. V. 39

GILLESPIE, WILLIAM

Consolation, with Other Poems. Edinburgh: 1815. V. 42; 44

The Progress of Refinement, an Allegorical Poem with Other Poems. Edinburgh: 1805. V. 42

GILLET, R.

The Pleasures of Reasons; or the Hundred Thoughts of a Sensible Young Lady . . . London: 1798. V. 44; 45

GILLETT, CHARLES R.

Catalogue of the McAlpin Collection of British History and Theology. New York: 1927-30. V. 37

GILLETT, CHARLES RIPLEY

Burned Books, Neglected Chapters in British History and Literature. New York: 1932. V. 45

Catalogue of the McAlpin Collection of British History and Theology. New York: 1927-30. V. 43

The Union Theological Seminary in the City of New York. Catalogue of the McAlpin Collection of British History and Theology. New York: 1927-30. V. 42

GILLETT, JAMES B.

Six Years with the Texas Rangers, 1875 to 1881. Austin: 1921. V. 37; 38; 39; 43; 44; 45

GILLETT, R.

The Pleasures of Reason . . . London: 1798. V. 42

GILLETTE, JAMES B.

Six Years with the Texas Rangers. Austin: 1935. V. 43

GILLFRAY, JAMES

The Genuine Works. London: 1850. V. 39

GILLIAM, A. M.

Travels Over the Table Lands and Cordilleras of Mexico During the Years 1843 and 1844. Philadelphia: 1846. V. 42

GILLIAM, ALBERT M.

Travels Over the Table Lands and Cordilleras of Mexico. Philadelphia: 1846. V. 38; 41; 43

Travels Over the Table Lands and Cordilleras of Mexico 1843-44. Philadelphia: 1846. V. 39

Travels in Mexico, During the Years 1843 and 44 . . . Aberdeen: 1847. V. 38

Travels Over the Table Lands and Cordilleras of Mexico. Philadelphia: 1816. V. 38

GILLIES, H. D.

Plastic Surgery of the Face Based on Selected Cases of War Injuries of the Face Including Burns . . . London: 1920. V. 42; 44; 45

GILLIES, HAROLD

Plastic Surgery of the Face Based on Selected Cases of War Inuuries of the Face Including Burns, with Original Illustrations. London: 1983. V. 41

GILLIES, JOHN

The History of the World from the Reign of Alexander . . . to that of Augustus. London: 1807. V. 39

The History of Ancient Greece, Its Colonies and Conquests; from the Earliest Accounts, Till the Division of the Macedonian Empire in the East. Dublin: 1786. V. 38

GILLIES, JOHN continued

Memoirs of the Life of the Reverend George Whitefield, M.A. Late Chaplain tot he Right Honourable the Countess of Huntingdon . . . London: 1772. V. 44

GILLIES, ROBERT PEARSE

German Stories. Edinburgh & London: 1826. V. 38

Tales of a Voyager to the Arctic Ocean. London: 1826. V. 38; 41; 43; 44

GILLIGAN, OSCAR

The Birmingham Six - an Appalling Vista. Dublin: 1990. V. 44

GILLILAN, STRICKLAND W.

Including Finnigin - a Book of Gillilan Verse. Philadelphia: 1908. V. 40; 42

GILLILAND, THOMAS

The Dramatic Mirror . . . London: 1808. V. 45

Elbow Room, a Pamphlet . . . London: 1804. V. 37; 43

GILLINGHAM, HAROLD E.

Marine Insurance in Philadelphia 1721-1800. Philadelphia: 1933. V. 39

GILLINGHAM, ROBERT CAMERON

The Rancho San Pedro; The Story of a Famous Rancho in Los Angeles County and Of Its Owners, the Dominguez Family. Los Angeles: 1961. V. 38; 40; 46

GILLINGWATER, EDMUND

An Historical and Descriptive Account of St. Edmund's Bury, in the County of Suffolk . . . Saint Edmund's Bury: 1804. V. 39

GILLIS, CHARLES J.

A Summer Vacation in Iceland, Norway, Sweden and Russia. N.P.: 1898. V. 43

GILLIS, JAMES D.

Sailing Directions for the Pepper Ports of the West Coast of Sumatra . . . Salem: 1834. V. 37

GILLISPIE, CHARLES

Dictionary of Scientific Biography. New York: 1970-80. V. 41; 42; 45

GILLISS, J. M.

The U. S. Naval Astronomical Expedition to the Southern Hemisphere During 1849-52. Washington: 1855. V. 38

GILLISS, JAMES M.

Astronomical Observations Made at the Naval Observatory, Washington, Under Orders of the Honorable Secretary of War. Washington: 1846. V. 39

GILLISS, WALTER

The Story of a Motto and a Mark. Being a Brief Sketch of a Few Printers' 'Marks' and Containing the Facts Concerning the Mark of the Gilliss Press, by Walter Gilliss. New York: 1902. V. 37

GILLMAN, ALEXANDER W.

The Gillman's of Highgate with Letters from Samuel Taylor Coleridge. London: 1895. V. 42

GILLMAN, JAMES

The Life of Samuel Taylor Coleridge. London: 1838. V. 43

The Life of Samuel Taylor Coleridge. London: 1838/34. V. 42

GILLMAN, JMAES

The Life of Samuel Taylor Coleridge. London: 1838/1834. V. 39

GILLMORE, PARKER

Accessible Field Sports: The Experiences of a Sportsman in North America. London: 1869. V. 39

Adventures Afloat and Ashore. London: 1873. V. 39

The Great Thirst Land. London: 1878. V. 43

A Hunter's Adventures in the Great West. London: 1871. V. 39; 40

The Hunter's Arcadia. London: 1886. V. 40; 42

Lone Life: a Year in the Wildneress. London: 1875. V. 45

Prairie Farms and Prairie Folk. London: 1872. V. 37; 41; 43; 45

Prairie and Forest: a Descritpion of the game of North America, with Peronsla Adventures in Their Pursuit. London: 1874. V. 41

Prairie and Forest: a Guide to the Field Sports of North America. London: 1881. V. 45

Through Casa Land and the Scene of the Portuguese Aggression. London: 1890. V. 38; 40

Through Gasa Land and the Scene of the Portuguese Aggression. The Journey of a Hunter in Search of Gold and Ivory. London: 1890. V. 39

Travel, War and Shipwreck. London: 1880. V. 37

GILLMORE, Q. A.

Official Report to the United States Engineer Department of the Siege and Reduction of Fort Pulaski, Georgia, Feb., March and April, 1862. New York: 1862. V. 44

A Practical Treatise on Coignet-Beton and Other Artificial Stone. New York: 1871. V. 44

GILLMORE, QUINCY ADAMS

Engineer and Artillery Operations Against the Defences of Charleston Harbor in 1863. New York: 1868. V. 37

Engineer and Artillery Operations Against the Defences of Charleston Harbor in 1863; Comprising the Descent Upon Morris Island, the Demolition of Fort Sumter, the Reduction of Forts Wagner and Gregg . . . New York: 1865. V. 37

GILLRAY, JAMES

The Genuine Works . . . Engraved by Himself. London: 1830. V. 37

The Works of James Gillray, Caricaturist. London. V. 38

GILLUM, WILLIAM

Miscellaneous Poems . . . to Which is Added a Farce, Called What Will the World Say? London: 1787. V. 43

GILLY, DAVID 1748-1808

Handbuch der Land-Bau-Kunst. and Anweisung Zur Landwirthschaftlichen Baukunst. Braunschweig: 1811. V. 46

GILLY, NICOLAAS DE KONING

Tilly Harlemensis. Pouer an Working of the Medicammentum Gratia Probatum. This Remedy Cureth Without Dainger . . . Amsterdam: 1723. V. 46

GILLY, W. S.

The Peasantry of the Border; an Appeal in Their Behalf. Berwick-upon-Tweed: 1841. V. 43

GILLY, WILLIAM

Narrative of an Excursion to the Mountains of Piemont, in the Year MDCCCXXIII. London: 1826. V. 38; 43

GILLY, WILLIAM STEPHEN

Narrative of an Excursion to the Mountains of Piedmont, and Researches Among the Vaudois or Waldenses, Protestant Inhabitants of the Cottian Alps . . . London: 1824. V. 40; 41

Narrative of an Excursion to the Mountains of Piemont, in the Year MDCCCXXIII. London: 1827. V. 38; 39; 41

Waldensian Researches During a Second Visit to the Vaudois of Piedmont. London: 1831. V. 41

GILMAN, CAROLINE

Recollections of a Southern Matron. New York: 1838. V. 37; 38

GILMAN, CAROLINE HOWARD 1794-1888

The Lady's Annual Register and Housewife's Memorandum-Book for 1838. Philadelphia: 1837. V. 43

Recollections of a Housekeeper. New York: 1834. V. 43

Recollections of a Southern Matron. New York: 1838. V. 46

GILMAN, CHANDLER ROBBINS

Legends of a Log Cabin. New York: 1835. V. 40; 43

Life on the Lakes: Being Tales and Sketches Collected During a Trip to the Pictured Rocks of Lake Superior. New York: 1836. V. 43

GILMAN, CHARLOTTE PERKINS

Concerning Children. Boston: 1901. V. 44

The Crux. New York: 1911. V. 40; 44

The Crux. New York: 1911. V. 40

His Religion and Hers. New York: 1923. V. 44

Moving the Mountain. New York: 1911. V. 42

GILMAN, CHARLOTTE PERKINS STETSON 1860-1935

In This Our World. Oakland: 1893. V. 45; 46

The Living of Charlotte Perkins Gilman. New York: 1935. V. 45

The Living of . . . an Autobiography. New York: 1935. V. 45

The Man Made World. New York: 1911. V. 46

Women and Economics. Boston: 1898. V. 41

Women and Economics. Boston: 1898. V. 43; 45

The Yellow Wall Paper. Boston: 1899. V. 41

GILMAN, M. D.

Bibliography of Vermont or a List of Books and Pamphlets Relating in Any Way to the State. Burlington: 1897. V. 37; 38

GILMAN, S. C.

The Conquest of the Sioux. Indianapolis: 1897. V. 40

GILMER, FRANCIS WALKER

Sketches of American Orators. Baltimore: 1816. V. 37; 43

GILMER, JOHN H.

Letter Addressed to Hon. Wm. C. Rives, by John H. Gilmer, on the Existing Status of the Revolution &c. Richmond?: 1864. V. 38; 44

GILMOR, HARRY

Four Years in the Saddle. London: 1866. V. 37

GILMORE, F. GRANT

The Problem: A Military Novel. (Rochester: 1915). V. 37

GILMORE, JAMES ROBERTS 1822-1903

The Rear-Guard of the Revolution. New York: 1886. V. 42

GILMORE, PARKER

Adventures Afloat and Ashore. London: 1873. V. 38

GILPIN, JOHN

THe Diverting History of John Gilpin: showing how he went farther than he intended, and came safe home again. London: 1828. V. 37

GILPIN, LAURA

The Enduring Navaho. Austin: 1968. V. 41

The Pueblos, a Camera Chronicle. New York: 1941. V. 43

The Rio Grande, River of Destiny. New York: 1949. V. 37; 42; 43; 46

Temples in Yucatan, a Camera Chronicle of Chicken Itza. New York: 1948. V. 45; 46

Temples in Yucatan: a Camera Chronicle of Chichen Itza. New York: 1948. V. 46

Temples in Yucatan: a Camera Chronicle of Chichenitza. New York: 1948. V. 45

The Will Rogers Shrine of the Sun. Colorado Springs: 1937. V. 46

GILPIN, SIDNEY

The Songs and Ballads of Cumberland, to Which are Added Dialect and Other Poems. London: 1866. V. 45

GILPIN, THOMAS

Exiles in Virginia: With Observations on the Conduct of the Society of Friends During the Revolutionary War . . . . 1777-1778. Philadelphia: 1848. V. 39; 43

GILPIN, W. S.

Practical Hints Upon Landscape Gardening: With Some Remarks on Domestic Architecture as Connected with Scenery. London: 1832. V. 37

GILPIN, WILLIAM 1813-1894

The Central Gold Region, the Grain, Pastoral and Gold Regions of North America. Philadelphia: 1860. V. 37; 40; 42; 43; 45

The Central Gold Region. The Grain, Pastoral and Gold Regions of North America. Philadelphia: 1860. V. 41

A Dialogue Upon the Gardens of the Right Honourable the Lord Viscount Cobham, at Stow in Buckinghamshire. London: 1748. V. 41

An Essay Upon Prints. London: 1768. V. 38; 44

An Essay of Prints. London: 1781. V. 42

An Essay on Prints. London: 1792. V. 39; 41; 45

An Essay on Prints. London: 1802. V. 46

An Exposition of the New Testament . . . London: 1811. V. 46

The Last Work Published of the Rev. William Gilpin, M.A. London: 1801/11. V. 44

The Last Work Published of the Rev. William Gilpin, M.A. London: 1810. V. 44

The Last Work . . . Representing the Effect of a Morning, a Noon Tide, and an Evening Sun. London: 1810. V. 39

The Life of Thomas Cranmer, Archbishop of Canterbury. London: 1784. V. 37; 38; 42

The Life of Thomas Cranmer, Archbishop of Canterbury. London: 1784. V. 38

Memoirs of Josias Rogers, Esq. Commander of His Majesty's Ship Quebec. London: 1808. V. 45

Mission of the North American People Geographical, Social and Political. Philadelphia: 1873. V. 38; 39; 40; 43; 45

Notes on Colorado; and Its Inscription in the Physical Geography of the North American Continent. Liverpool: 1870. V. 42; 45

Observations on the River Wye and Other Parts of South Wales . . . London: 1782. V. 38; 45; 46

Observations on the Mountains and Lakes of Cumberland and Westmorland. London: 1786. V. 38

Observations Relative Chiefly to Picturesque Beauty, Made in the Year 1772, on Several Parts of England Particularly the Mountains and Lakes of Cumberland and Westmoreland. London: 1786. V. 40; 44; 46

Observations Relative Chiefly to Picturesque Beauty, Made in the Year 1776 . . . London: 1792. V. 40; 46

Observations on the Western Parts of England, Relative Chiefly to Picturesque Beauty. London: 1798. V. 38; 39; 40; 41; 42; 43; 44

Observations on Several Parts of Great Britain, Particularly the High-lands of Scotland . . . London: 1808. V. 39

Observations on several parts of the counties of Cambridge, Norfolk, Suffolk, and Essex. Also on several parts of North Wales . . . in two tours (in 1769 & 1773) . . . Published by his Trustees for the benefit of his school at Boldre. London: 1809. V. 37

Observations on the Coasts of Hampshire, Sussex and Kent, Relative Chiefly to Picturesque Beauty; Made in the Summer of the Year 1774. London: 1804. V. 39; 44

Observations on the River Wye, and Several parts of South Wales &c. London: 1789. V. 41; 44

Observations on the River Wye, and Several Parts of South Wales . . . London: 1792. V. 44

Observations on the Western Parts of England, Relative Chiefly to Picturesque Beauty. London: 1808. V. 41; 44

Observations on the Western Parts of England, Relative Chiefly to Picturesque Beauty. To which are Added a Few Remarks on the Picturesque Beauties of the Isle of Wight. (with) Observations on the Coasts of Hampshire, Sussex and Kent. London: 1798-1804. V. 41

Observations Relative Chiefly to Picturesque Beauty, Made in the Year 1776 . . . London: 1789. V. 39; 40; 44

Observations Relative Chiefly to Picturesque Beauty, Made in the Year 1776 . . . London: 1792. V. 39; 44

Observations Relative Chiefly to Picturesque Beauty, Made in the Year 1772, on Several Parts of England . . . London: 1788. V. 41; 45

Observations, relative chiefly to picturesque beauty, made in the year 1776, on several parts of Great Britain; particularly the High Lands of Scotland. 1789. V. 37

The Parks of Colorado. San Luis de Calebra Co.: 1866? V. 46

Practical Hints Upon Landscape Gardening . . . London: 1835. V. 44

Remarks on Forest Scenery, and Other Woodland Views (Relative Chiefly to Picturesque Beauty) Illustrated by the Scenes of New-Forest in Hampshire. London: 1791. V. 39; 43; 44

Remarks on Forest Scenery, and Other Woodland Views (Relative Chiefly to Picturesque Beauty) Illustrated by the Scenes of the New-Forest in Hampshire. London: 1794. V. 38; 39; 41; 44

Remarks on Forest Scenery and Other Woodland Views . . . London: 1808. V. 44; 46

Remarks on Forest Scenery, and Other Woodland Views. Edited by Sir Thomas Dick Lauder, Bart. Edinburgh: 1834. V. 37; 44

Sermons Preached to a County Congregation . . . Lymington: 1799-1805. V. 46

Six Landscapes from Drawings by the Reverend Mr. Gilpin, Engraved by S. Alken. London: 1794. V. 43

Spoken at the 'British Association of Science', Liverpool, Septr. 26th, 1870. Notes on Colorado. London: 1871. V. 38; 41

Three Essays: on Picturesque Beauty; on Picturesque Travel and on Sketching Landscape . . . London: 1792. V. 37; 38; 45

Three Essays: On Picturesque Beauty; On Picturesque Travel; and On Sketching Landscape. London: 1794. V. 38; 39; 40; 41; 44

Three Dialogues on the Amusements of Clergymen. London: 1796. V. 45

Three Dialogues on the Amusements of Clergymen. London: 1797. V. 39; 42

Three Essayes: on Picturesque Beauty; on Picturesque Travel; and on Sketching Landscape: with a Poem on Landscape Painting. To which are now added Two Essays . . . London: 1808. V. 38; 39; 42

Two Essays: One, on the Author's Mode of Executing Rough Sketches; the Other, on the Principles on Which They are Composed. (with) Observations on the Coasts of Hampshire, Sussex and Kent, Relative Chiefly to Picturesque Beauty . . . London: 1804. V. 46

GILPIN, WILLIAM S.

Practical Hints on Landscape Gardening . . . London: 1832. V. 39; 44

GILROY, C. T.

The Art of Weaving by Hand and by Power. New York: 1844. V. 37; 39; 42

The History of Silk, Cotton, Linen, Wool and Other Fibrous Substances. New York: 1845. V. 37; 42

GILROY, N.

Rough Notes on Wildlife. London: 1900-09. V. 37

GILROY, NORMAN

Norman Gilroy's Journal, Being an Account of Field Work in the Breeding Season . . . 1901-1908. London: V. 38

GILSON, J. P.

Lives of Lady Anne Clifford and of Her Parents. London: 1916. V. 38

GIMLETTE, T. P.

The History of the Huguenot Settlers in Ireland. Dunmore East: 1888. V. 43

GINGELEN, JACQUES VAN

Collection de 25 Planches . . . ?Brussels: 1841-43. V. 45

GINGER Beer; a Grand Pindaric, in Honour of the Radicals and Whigs; Humbly Dedicated to Those Great Northern Allies. Leeds: 1819. V. 46

GINGLE, JOSEPH

The Oxford Sermon Versified . . . London: 1730. V. 40

GINGOLD, HELEN A.

Steyneville; or Fated Fortunes. London: 1855. V. 41

GINN & Heath's Classical Atlas. Boston/New York/Chicago: 1880. V. 45

GINN, JOHN L.

Mormon and Indian Wars. V. 46

GINSBERG, ALLEN

Ankor-Wat. London: 1968. V. 43; 46

Bixby Canyon Ocean Path Word Breeze. New York: 1972. V. 39; 45; 46

Careless Love. Madison: 1978. V. 42; 44

First Blues. Rags, Ballads and Harmonium Songs 1971-74. New York: 1975. V. 46

The Gates of Wrath: Rhymed Poems 1948-1952. Bolinas: 1972. V. 39; 40; 41

Howl. San Francisco: 1971. V. 39; 43; 44

Howl. New York: 1986. V. 43

Indian Journals - March 1962- May 1963. 1970. V. 39

Mind Breaths - Poems 1972-1977. 1977. V. 39

The Moments Return. San Francisco: 1970. V. 45; 46

New Year Blues. New York: 1972. V. 46

Planet News 1961-1967. San Francisco: 1968. V. 46

Reality Sandwiches 1953-1960. San Francisco: 1963. V. 37

Scenes Along the Road. New York: 1970. V. 46

T.V. Baby Poems. London: 1967. V. 39

Wales - a Visitation, July 29th 1967. London: 1968. V. 45

White Shroud. New York: 1986. V. 43

GINTY, JOHN

Perfection Block and Street Guide of the City and County of San Francisco Containing a Complete Directory of all Streets, Avenues, Alleys, Courts and Terraces . . . San Francisco: 1914. V. 41; 46

GIOGRI, FELICE

Descrizione Istorica del Teatro di Tor di Nona. Rome: 1795. V. 43

GIOIA, DANA

Journeys in Sunlight. Cottondale: 1986. V. 39; 42

GIONO, JEAN

From Blue Boy. Ann Arbor: 1989. V. 44

Hill of Destiny. New York: 1929. V. 43

Presentation de Pan. Paris: 1930. V. 46

GIORDA, JOSEPH

A Dictionary of the Kalispel or Flat-Head Indian Language. St. Ignatius: 1877-8-9. V. 40; 42; 44; 45; 46

Lu Tel Kaimintis Kolinzuten Kuitlt Smimii. St. Ignatius: 1879. V. 39

GIORDANI, VITALE

De Componendis Gravium Momentis Dissertatio. (with) Fundamentum Doctrinae Motus Gravium . . . Rome: 1687, 1689. V. 38

GIORGIO, FRANCESCO

De Harmonia Mundi Totius Cantica Tria. Venice: 1525. V. 41

GIOVANELLI, PIETRO

Altvs Novi Thesavri Mvsici Liber Primus (-Secvndvs, Tertivs, Qvartvs, Qvintvs). Venice: 1568. V. 44

GIOVANPAOLO DA COMO, FATHER

Jesus Maria. Bellissimo, et Devotissimo Dialogo Overo Interrogatorio. Venetia: 1585. V. 40

GIOVIO, PAOLO

Commenario de le Cose de Turchi, et del S. Georgio Scanderbeg. Venice: 1541. V. 44

Descriptio Britanniae, Scotiae, Hyberniae, et Orchardum. Venice: 1548. V. 38

Dialogo Dell' Imprese Militari et Amorose. Lyone: 1574. V. 37; 38

Dialogo Dell'Imprese Militari et Amorose. Lyon: 1559. V. 37

Dialogue Des Devises d'Armes et d'Amour . . . . (with) Les Devises Heroques 7 Morales du Seigneur Gabriel Symeon. Lyon: 1561. V. 38

Elogia Doctorum Virorum. Basle: 1556. V. 37

Elogia Virorum Bellica Virtute Illustrium . . . et nunc ex Ejusdem Usaeo ad Vivum Expressis Imaginibus Exornata. Basel: 1575. V. 38

Le Iscrittioni Poste Sotto le Vere Imagini de Gli Huomini Famosi . . . Fiorenza: 1551. V. 38

Le Senteniose Imprese . . . Ridotte in Rima per il Detto Symeoni . . . Lyon: 1562. V. 38; 39

GIOVIO, PAOLO, BP. OF NOCERA 1483-1552

Anadido con Doze Libros Que Hasta Agora Faltavan . . . Granada: 1566. V. 46

Dialogo Dell'Imprese Militari et Amorose . . . Vencie: 1556. V. 39; 40

Dialogo dell'Imprese Militari et Amorose . . . Con un Ragionamento di K Lodofico Domenichi, nel Medesimo Soggeto. Lyon: 1574. V. 40

Edogia Virorum Bellica Virtute Illustrium . . . (with) Elogia Doctorvm Virorvm ab Arorvm Memoria Publicatis Ingeni Monumentis Illustrivm. Basileae: 1556? V. 46

Elogia Virorum Bellica Virtute Illustrium Veris Imaginibus Supposita. Florence: 1551. V. 41; 42

Histoires . . . sur les Choses Faictes et Avenues de son Temps en Toutes les Parties du Monde. Lyon: 1552-5. V. 40

Illustrium Virorum Vitae. (with) De Vita Leonis Decimi Pont. Max . . . Hadriani Sexti . . . et Pompeii Columnae Cardinalis Vitae . . . Florentiae: 1549. V. 38; 41

Illustrium Virorum Vitae. Florentiae: 1551. V. 39

Le Iscrittione Poste Sotte le Vere Imagini de gli Huomini Famosi. Florence: 1552, 1552. V. 41

Le Iscrittioni Poste Sotto le Vere Imagini de Gli Huomini Famosi. Florence: 1552. V. 40

Le Iscrittioni Poste Sotto Le Vere Imagini De Gli Hvomini Famosi; Le Quali a Como Nel Museo del Giovio si Veggiono. Florence: 1552. V. 43

Libro di Mons. Paolo Giovio de' Pesci Romani, Tradotto in Volgare da Carlo Zancaruolo. Venetia: 1560. V. 39

Pauli Iovii Descriptio Larii Lacus. Venetiis: 1559. V. 43

Pavli Iovii Novocomensis Episcopi Nucerini Descriptiones, Quotquot Extant, Regionum Atque Locorum. Basileae: 1571. V. 39

Ragionamento di Mons . . . Sopra I Motti & Disegni d'arme & d'amore, che Communemente Chiamano Imprese . . . Venice: 1556. V. 37; 39

Vitae Duodecim Vicecomitum Mediolani Principum. Paris: 1549. V. 38; 39

THE GIPSIES: Dedicated, by Permission, to James Crabb, The Gipsies' Friend. London: 1842. V. 39

GIRAFFI, ALESSANDRO

An Exact History of the Late Revolutions in Naples . . . London: 1664. V. 40

GIRALDI CINTHIO, GIOVANNI BATTISTA

De Gli Hecatommithi . . . Parte Prima (La Seconda Parte). Nel Monte Regale: 1565. V. 43

GIRALDI, LILIO GREGORIO 1479-1552

Historiae Poetarvm Tam Graecorvm Qvam Latinorvm Dialogi Decem, Quibus Scripta & Uitae Eorum sic Exprimuntur. Basle: 1545. V. 37; 43

Liber adversus ingratos. Florence: 1548. V. 37

GIRALDI, LILIUS GREGORIUS

De Annis Et Mensibvs, Caeterisqve Temporum Partibus, Difficili Hactenus & Impedita Materia, Dissertatio Facilis & Expedita, Eivsdem Calendarium & Romanum Graecum, Gentis Utriusq Solennia . . . Basle: 1541. V. 40

GIRALDO CINTHIO, GIOVANNI BATTISTA

Epitia. Venice: 1583. V. 40

Euphimia. Venice: 1583. V. 40

GIRALDUS CAMBRENSIS 1146?-1220?

Giraldus Cambrensis: Itinerary through Wales. Newton: 1989. V. 41

Itinerarium Cambriae seu Laboriosae Baldvini Cantuariensis Archiepiscopi per Walliam Legationis Accurata Descriptio . . . Londini: 1806. V. 39

Itinerary through Wales. 1989. V. 44; 45

GIRARD, CHARLES

Bibliographia Americana-Historico-Naturalis, or Bibliography of American Natural History for the Year 1851. Washington: 1852. V. 41

GIRARD, GUILLAUME

The History of the Life of the Duke of Espernon, the Great Favourite of France. London: 1670. V. 39

GIRARD, L'ABBE

Synonymes Francois. Paris: 1769. V. 40

GIRARD, P. S.

Traite Analytique de la Resistance des Solides, et des Solides d'egale Resistance. Paris: 1798. V. 44

GIRARDIN

An Essay on Landscape. London: 1783. V. 38; 40; 46

GIRAUD, J. P.

The Birds of Long Island. New York: 1844. V. 45

GIRAUD, JANE ELIZABETH

The Flowers of Shakespeare. London: 1846. V. 41

GIRAUD, S. LOUIS

Animal Life in the Fact, Fancy and Fun. London: 1930's. V. 45

GIRAUDOUX, JEAN

Amica America. Paris: 1928. V. 45

GIRAVA, GERONIMO

La Cosmographia, Y Geographia, en la Qual se Contiene La Descripcion de Todo el Mundo, Y de Sus Partes, Y Particularmente de las Indias Y Tierra Nueva. Venice: 1570. V. 40

GIRDLESTONE, A. G.

The High Alps Without Guides . . . London: 1870. V. 43

GIRDLESTONE, THOMAS

Facts Tending to Prove that General Lee . . . Was the Author of Junius. London: 1813. V. 38; 41; 44

THE GIRL in the Apple: from a Tuscan Folk Tale. 1984. V. 45

GIRLDLESTONE, A. G.

The High Alps Without Guides . . . London: 1870. V. 43

GIROD-CHANTRANS, JUSTIN

Voyage d'un Suisse dans Differentes Colonies d'Amerique Pendant La Derniere Guerre, Avec une Table d'Observations Meterorlogiques Faites a Saint-Domingue. Neuchatel: 1785. V. 38

GIROUARD, DESIRE

Supplement to 'Lake St. Louis' &c &c. Montreal: 1903. V. 40

GIROUARD, MARK

The Victorian Country House. New Haven: 1979. V. 38

GIRTIN, JAMES

Seventy-Five Portraits of Celebrated Painters, From Authentic Originals. London: 1817. V. 38

GIRTIN, THOMAS

The Art of Thomas Girtin. London: 1954. V. 39

Liber Naturae or a Collection of Prints from the Drawings of Thomas Girtin. Haddington: 1883. V. 39

GIRTY, GEORGE H.

The Carboniferous Formations and Faunas of Colorado. Washington: 1903. V. 43

GIRVIN, BRENDA

Round Fairyland with Alice and the White Rabbit. London: 1916. V. 42; 46

GISBERT, BLAISE

Christian Eloquence in Theory and Practice. London: 1718. V. 46

GISBORNE, LIONEL

Darien Ship Navigation. Engineer's Report. London: 1852. V. 38

The Isthumus of Darien in 1582. London: 1853. V. 40; 45

GISBORNE, THOMAS

An Enquiry into the Duties of Men in the Higher and Middle Classes of Society in Great Britain, Resulting from Their Respective Stations, Professions and Employments. London: 1794. V. 39; 45; 46

An Enquiry into the Duties of Men, in the Higher and Middle Classes of Society in Great Britain, Resulting from Their Respective Stations, Professions and Employments. Dublin: 1795. V. 42; 43

An Enquiry Into the Duties of Men in the Higher and Middle Classes of Society in Great Britain . . . London: 1797. V. 42

An Enquiry into the Duties of the Female Sex. London: 1797. V. 45

An Enquiry into the Duties of the Female Sex. London: 1797. V. 37; 38; 39; 41; 43; 45

An Enquiry into the Duties of the Female Sex. London: 1797. V. 39

An Enquiry Into the Duties of the Female Sex . . . London: 1798. V. 42

An Enquiry into the Duties of the Female Sex. London: 1799. V. 44

An Enquiry into the Duties of the Female Sex. London: 1801. V. 38

Poems, Sacred and Moral. London: 1798. V. 43

The Principles of Moral Philosophy Investigated, and Briefly Applied to the Constitution of Civil society. London: 1795. V. 42; 46

Walks in a Forest . . . London: 1796. V. 42

GISH, LILLIAN

Dorothy and Lillian Gish. New York: 1973. V. 45

GISLAIN, VICTOR

Epitomes Adagiorvm Omnivm, Qvae Hodie Ab Erasmo, Ivnio, et Aliis Collecta Exstant. Antwerp: 1566. V. 40

GISSING, ALGERNON

At Society's Expense. London: 1894. V. 41

A Vagabond in Arts. London: 1894. V. 41

A Village Hampden. London: 1890. V. 43

GISSING, GEORGE 1857-1903

Books and the Quiet Life, Being Some Pages from the Private Papers of Henry Ryecroft by George Gissing Chosen by W.R.B. Portland: 1914. V. 41; 46

Born in Exile. London: 1892. V. 40; 45

Born in Exile. London: & Edinburgh: 1892. V. 41; 43

By the Ionian Sea; Notes of a Ramble in Southern Italy. London: 1901. V. 40; 43

Charles Dickens: a Critical Study. London: 1898. V. 39; 40; 45

Demos. A Story of English Socialism. London: 1886. V. 39; 41; 43; 45

Demos; a Story of English Socialism. London: 1888. V. 46

Denzil Quarrier. London: 1892. V. 41

The Emancipated. London: 1890. V. 40; 42; 43; 45; 46

An Heiress on Condition. Philadlephia: 1923. V. 40; 45

The Immortal Dickens, Being Critical Studies of the Works of Charles Dickens. London: 1925. V. 40

In the Year of Jubilee. New York: 1895. V. 46

A Life's Morning. London: 1888. V. 39; 46

The Nether World. London: 1889. V. 38; 46

New Grub Street. London: 1891. V. 46

New Grub Street, a Novel. London: 1891. V. 38; 40; 41; 43; 45; 46

Our Friend the Charlatan. London: 1901. V. 39

The Paying Guest. London: 1895. V. 46

The Private Papers of Henry Ryecroft. London: 1903. V. 46

The Private Papers of Henry Ryecroft. Westminster: 1903. V. 39; 40; 41; 42

Selections: Autobiographical and Imaginative. London: 1929. V. 37; 40; 42; 44

The Sins of the Fathers. Chicago: 1924. V. 39

Veranilda. London: 1904. V. 39; 43; 45

The Whirlpool. New York: 1897. V. 44

Will Warburton. London: 1905. V. 39; 44; 46

Workers in the Dawn. London: 1880. V. 40; 44

GISSING, GEORGE ROBERT 1857-1903

Born in Exile. London: 1892. V. 38

The Town Traveller. London: 1898. V. 38; 39

The Town Traveller. New York: 1898. V. 38

The Unclassed. London: 1884. V. 38

The Whirlpool. London: 1897. V. 38; 46

GIUNTINI, FRANCESCO 1523?-1590

Tractatus Iudicandi Reuolutiones natiuitatum. Lugduni: 1570. V. 46

GIUSTINIANI, AGOSTINO

Castigatissimi Annali . . . Della . . . Republi Di Genoa. Genoa: 1537. V. 41

GIUSTINIANI, BERNARDO

Historia Cronologiche Della Vera Origine Di Tutti Gl'Ordini Equestri, e Religioni Cavalleresche, Consacrate Alla Sacra Maesta Cattolica Di D. Carlo II Monarca Delle Spagane. Venetia: 1672. V. 38

GIUSTINIANO, AGOSTINO

Castigatissimi Annali con la Loro Copiosa Tavola Della Eccelsa & Illustrissima Republi. di Genoa da Fiedeli & Approvati Scitori . . . Genoa: 1573. V. 45

GIVEON, RAPHAEL

Egyptian Scarabs from Western Asia from the Collection of the British Museum. Freiburg: 1985. V. 40; 44

GIVOIRA, G. T.

Moslem Architecture, Its Origins and Development. Oxford: 1918. V. 42

GJERSET, KUNT

History of Iceland. New York: 1925. V. 38

GJERSTAD, EINAR

Early Rome. Volume IV: 1 and 2 (only). Lund: 1966. V. 44

The Swedish Cyprus Expedition. Volume IV. Part 2: The Cypro-Geometric, Cypro-Archaic and Cypro-Classical Periods. Stockholm: 1948. V. 44

GLADKY, SERGE

Fleurs. Texte et Vingt-Six Planches en Couleurs. Paris: 1929. V. 46

GLADSTONE, H. S.

The Birds of Dumfriesshire. London: 1910. V. 37

GLADSTONE, T. H.

Englishman in Kansas; or, Squatter Life and Border Warfare . . . New York: 1857. V. 46

GLADSTONE, THOMAS H.

Kansas; or, Squatter Life and Border Warfare in the Far West. London: 1857. V. 39; 43; 45

Kansas: or Squatter Life and Border Warfare in the Far West. London: 1857. V. 45

GLADSTONE, W. E.

The State in Its Relations with the Church. London: 1841. V. 39

GLADSTONE, WILLIAM E.

Studies on Homer and the Homeric Age. Oxford: 1858. V. 41; 44

GLADSTONE, WILLIAM EWART

Address on the Place of Ancient Greece in the Providential Order of the World. London: 1865. V. 38

The Eton Miscellany. Eton: 1827. V. 43

Remarks Upon Recent Commercial Legislation Suggested by the Expository Statement of the Revenue from Customs, and Other Papers Lately Submitted to Parliament. London: 1845. V. 37

The State in its Relations with the Church. London: 1838. V. 37

Studies of Homer and the Homeric Age. 1858. V. 37; 43

GLADWIN, FRANCIS

A Compendium System of Bengal Revenue Accounts. Calcutta: 1790. V. 42

Dissertations on the Rhetoric, Prosody and Rhyme of the persians. London: 1801. V. 38

The Persian Moonshee. Calcutta: 1801. V. 42

GLADWIN, HAROLD

Excavations at Snaketown. Material Culture and Comparisions and Theories. Globe: 1937. V. 46

GLAISHER, ERNEST H.

A Journey on the Berbice River and Wieroonie Creek. Georgetown Demerara: 1885. V. 40

GLAISTER, G. A. 1917-

Glossary of the Book. Terms used in paper making, printing, bookbinding and publishing with notes on illuminated manuscripts, bibliophiles, private presses and printing societies. Including illustrations and translated extracts . . . (1960). V. 37

GLAISTER, GEOFFREY ASHALL 1917-

An Encyclopedia of the Book, Terms Used in Paper Making, Printing, Bookbinding and Publishing With Notes on Illuminated Manuscripts . . . Cleveland: 1960. V. 43

Glossary of the Book. London: 1960. V. 38; 45

GLANCES from the Moon; or, Lucubrations, Gathered from the Miscellany of One Unknown. Cheltenham: 1824. V. 43

GLANVIL, JOSEPH 1636-1680

Sadducismus Triumphatus; or, a Full and Plain Evidence, Concerning Witches and Apparitions. London. V. 43

Saducismus Triumphatus: or, full and plain evidence Concerning Witches and Apparitions. In Two Parts. The First treating of their Possiblility; The Second of their Real Existence . . . The Third Edition . . . London: 1689. V. 37; 38; 46

GLANVILL, E. d. 1190

Tractatus de Legibus & Consuetudinibus Regni Angliae, Tempore regis Henrici Secundi Compositus. London: 1673. V. 40

GLANVILL, JOSEPH 1636-1680

Essays on Several Important Subjects in Philosophy and Religion . . . London: 1676. V. 42

Lux Orientalis, or an Enquiry into the Opinion of the Eastern Sages, Concerning the Praexistence of Souls . . . London: 1662. V. 46

Philosophia Pia; or, a Discourse of the Religious Temper and Tendencies of the Experimental Philosophy . . . to which is annext A Recommendation, and Defence of Reason in the Affairs of Religion. London: 1671. V. 46

Philosohia Pia . . . . to which is Annext A Recommendation, and Defence of Reason in the Affairs of Religion. London: 1671/1670. V. 43

Sadducimus Triumphatus. London: 1726. V. 37; 38; 39; 40; 42; 43

Sadducismus Triumphatus. London: 1681. V. 38

Saducismus Triumphatus. London: 1681. V. 37; 41

Saducismus Triumphatus. London: 1681. V. 37

Scepsis Scientifica; or Confest Ignorance, the Way to Science . . . London: 1665. V. 39; 40; 46

Some Discourses, Sermons and Remains of the Reverend Mr. Jos. Glanvil . . . Collected into One Volume . . . London: 1681. V. 40; 46

Two Choice and Useful Treatises . . . London: 1682. V. 44

The Vanity of Dogmatizing. London: 1661. V. 41; 45

GLANVILLE, RANULPHUS DE

Tractatus de Legibus & Consuetudinibus Regni Angliae . . . London: 1604. V. 46

GLANVILLE, S. R. K.

Catalogue of Demotic Papyri in the British Museum. London: 1939. V. 42; 44

The Instructions of 'Onchsheshoqy (British Museum Papyrus 10508). London: 1955. V. 40

GLANVILLE WILLS, W.

There and Back Again: an Account of a Short Visit to Australia. Sheffield: 1871. V. 39

GLAPTHORNE, HENRY

The Hollander. London: 1640. V. 38

The Plays and Poems of Henry Glapthorne. London: 1874. V. 40; 42

The Plays and Poems . . . London: 1874. V. 40

GLAREAN, HEINRICH

Dodecachordon. 1965. V. 39

GLAREAN, HENRICUS

De Geographia Liber Unus. Freiburg: 1536. V. 44

GLAREANUS, HENRICUS

De Geographia Liber Unus. Basle: 1527. V. 40

GLAS, GEORGE

The History of Discovery and Conquest of the Canary Islands. London: 1764. V. 45; 46

The History of the Discovery and Conquest of the Canary Islands. London: 1764. V. 45

GLASCOCK, WILLIAM NUGENT 1787-1847

Naval Sketch Book: or the Service Afloat and Ashore, with Characteristic Reminiscences, etc., by an Officer of the Rank. One of the best accounts of life in the British Navy with chapters on corporal punishment . . . London;: 1826. V. 37

Sailors and Saints; or, Matrimonial Manoeuvres. London: 1829. V. 39

GLASCOCK, WILLIAN NUGENT 1787-1847

Land Sharks and Sea Gulls. London: 1838. V. 37

GLASER, CHRISTOPHER

Traite de la Chymie Enseignant par une Brieve et Facile Methode Toutes ses Plus Necessaires Preparations. Paris: 1663. V. 38

GLASER, CURT

Die Graphik der Neuzeit. Berlin: 1922. V. 45

GLASER, LYNN

Engraved America: Iconography of America through 1800. Philadlephia: 1970. V. 44; 46

GLASGOW ART CLUB

Album Songs by Members of the Glasgow Society of Musicians, Illustrated by Members of the Glasgow Art Club. Glasgow: 1892? V. 42

GLASGOW ART UNION OF GLASGOW

Fourth List of Paintings Bought . . . Glasgow: 1855. V. 40

GLASGOW BIBLIOGRAPHICAL SOCIETY

Catalogue of the Foulis Exhibition Held in the University of Glasgow. Glasgow: 1913. V. 40

GLASGOW, CAROLINE

The Romantic Comedians. Garden City: 1926. V. 39

GLASGOW, ELLEN 1874-1945

Barren Ground. Garden City: 1925. V. 39

The Descendant. New York: 1897. V. 37; 38; 39; 41; 42; 43; 45; 46

The Romantic Comedians. Garden City: 1926. V. 42; 44

The Sheltered Life. Garden City: 1932. V. 39; 41

Vein of Iron. New York: 1935. V. 38; 39

The Voice of the People. New York: 1900. V. 43

The Works. New York: 1938. V. 37; 39; 42

GLASGOW. FACULTY OF PROCURATORS

Catalogue of the Books in the Library of the Faculty of Procurators in Glasgow. Glasgow: 1903. 1923. V. 40

THE GLASGOW Geography, Containing a Physical, Political and Statistical View of the Various Empires, Kingdoms, States &c. Glasgow: 1825. V. 40

GLASGOW LUNATIC ASYLUM

A Selection of Sacred Poetry &c. with Specimens of Music, Used in Teaching the Blind at the Asylum. Glasgow: printed in the: 1840? V. 38

GLASGOW MECAHNIC'S INSTITUTION

Catalogue of the Library. Catalogue of the Library. Constitution, Rules and Regulations. Glasgow: 1823-27. V. 38

GLASGOW. ROYAL COLLEGE OF SCIENCE & TECH. ANDERSONIAN LIB.

Bibliotheca Chemica. 1954. V. 39; 42

GLASGOW. ROYAL COLLEGE OF SCIENCE & TECH. ANDERSONIAN LIB. continued

Bibliotheca Chemica: a Catalogue of the Alchemical, Chemical and Pharmaceutical Books in the Collection of the Late James Young. London: 1954. V. 39; 40; 42; 43; 45; 46

GLASGOW. ROYAL COLLEGE OF SCIENCE & TECHNOLOGY

Bibliotheca Chemica, a Catalogue of the Alchemical, Chemical and Pharmaceutical Books in the Collection of . . . James Young . . . Glasgow: 1906,: 1954. V. 46

Bibliotheca Chemica. London. V. 45

GLASGOW. Royal College of Science & TECHNOLOGY. ANDERSONIAN LIBRARY Bibliotheca Chemica. Glasgow: 1906. V. 42

GLASS, E. L. N.

The History of the Tenth Cavalry 1866-1921. Tucson: 1921. V. 45

The Punitive Expedition. Tucson: 1921. V. 39

GLASS, JOHN W.

The California Sacrifice. Cincinnati: 1860. V. 40

GLASS, MARK

Ancient Song. New York: 1980. V. 42

GLASS, SALOMON

Philologiae Sacrae . . . Libri Duo. Jenae: 1623. V. 44

GLASS, SAMUEL

Advice from a Lady of Quality to Her Children, in the Last State of a Lingering Illness. Boston: 1796. V. 41

An Essay on Magnesia Alba. Oxford: 1764. V. 37; 43; 46

GLASS, THOMAS

Twelve Commentaries on Fevers. London: 1752. V. 40

GLASSCO, JOHN

Fetish Girl. New York: 1972. V. 43

GLASSE, HANNAH

The Art of Cooking Made Plain and Easy. London: 1760. V. 38

The Art of cookery Made Plain and Easy . . . London: 1747. V. 42; 44

The Art of Cookery Made Plain and Easy . . . London: 1770. V. 44

The Art of Cookery, Made Plain and Easy . . . London: 1778. V. 46

The Art of Cookery Made Plain and Easy. Edinburgh: 1786. V. 45

The Art of Cookery, Made Plain and Easy . . . London: 1796. V. 38; 39

The Art of Cookery Made Plain and Easy . . . . Alexandria: 1805. V. 38; 40; 42

The Art of Cookery Made Plain and Easy. London: 1748. V. 37

The Complete Confectioner; or, the Whole Art of Confectionary Made Plain and Easy. London: 1765. V. 42

GLASSE, SAMUEL 1735-1812

The Magistrate's Assistant; or, a Summary of Those Laws Which Immediately Respect the Conduct of a Justice of the Peace . . . to July 12, 1788. Glocester: 1788. V. 45

The Magistrate's Assistant; or, a Summary of Those Laws Which Immediately Respect the Conduct of a Justice of the Peace. Glocester: 1794. V. 38; 40; 43; 46

GLASSER, OTTO

Wilhelm Conrad Roentgen and the Early History of the Roentgen Rays. Springfield: 1934. V. 45; 46

GLASSGOLD, PETER

Hwaet!: 4 Contemoprary American Poets Backstranslated into the Old English. 1987. V. 40

GLASSPOOLE, RICHARD

Mr. Glasspoole and the Chinese Pirates. Waltham St. Lawrence: 1935. V. 37; 41

GLAUBER, JOHANN RUDOLF

Furni Novi Philosophici Sive Descriptio Artis Destillatoriae Novae . . . Amsterodami: 1651. V. 37

GLAUBER, JOHANN RUDOLPH 1604-1670

Apologia Contra Mendaces Christophori Fameri Calumnias. Amsterdam: 1655. V. 42

De Auri Tinctura Sive Auro Potabili Vero. Amsterdam: 1651. V. 40

A Description of New Philosophical Furnacies, or a New Art of Distilling . . . London: 1651. V. 46

Operis Mineralis . . . . Amsterdam: 1651-52. V. 38

GLAZEBROOK, GEORGE DE T.

The Hargrave Correspondence, 1821-1843. Toronto: 1938. V. 37; 45

GLAZEBROOK, R.

A Dictionary of Applied Physics. London: 1922-23. V. 37

GLEADALL, ELIZA EVE

The Beauties of Flora, with Botanic and Poetic Illustrations. 1834. V. 37

THE GLEANER: a Selection from Modern Writers, in Prose and Verse. Perth: 1796. V. 46

GLEANINGS from Books, on Agriculture and Gardening. London: ptd. by W. Smith,: 1802. V. 45

GLEASON, DUNCAN

Islands of California: Their History, Romance and Physical Characteristics. Los Angeles: 1951. V. 39

GLEASON, WILLIAM J.

Historical Sketch of the 150th Regiment Ohio Volunteer Infantry . . . Delivered at the 5th Annual Reunion, Scenic Park, Rocky River, July 12th, 1899. N.P.: 1899. V. 46

GLEED, CHARLES S.

From River to Sea: A Tourist's and Miners' Guide from the Missouri River to the Pacific Ocean. Chicago: 1882. V. 41

GLEESON, JAMES

William Dobell. London: 1964. V. 39; 41; 43; 46

GLEESON, JOHN

Cashel of the Kings. A History of the Ancient Capital of Munster, from its Foundation to the Present Day; including Historical Notices of the Kings of Cashel etc. etc. Dublin: 1927. V. 37

GLEESON, WILLIAM

History of the Catholic Church in California. San Francisco: 1872. V. 46

GLEICHEN-RUSSWORM, WILHELM FRIEDRICH 1717-1783

Dissertation sur la Generation les Animalcules Spermatiques, et Ceux d'Infusions, avec des Observations Microscopiques sur la Sperme, et sur Differntes Infusions. Paris: 1798-99. V. 42

GLEICHEN-RUSSWORM, WILHELM FRIEDRICH VON

Auserlesene Mikroskopische Entdeckungen bey Den Pflanzen, Blumen und Bluthen, Insecten und Andern Merkwurdigkeiten . . . Nuremberg: 1777. V. 39

Das Neueste aus dem Reiche der Pflanzen, oder Mikroskopische Untersuchungen und Beobachtungen der Geheimen Zeugungstheile der Pflanzen in Ihren Bluten, und der in Denselben Befindlichen Insekten . . . Nurnberg: 1764. V. 38

GLEIG, G. R.

Essays Biographical, Historical and Miscellaneous Contributed Chiefly to the Edinburgh Reviews. London: 1858. V. 38; 42; 46

The Life of Major General Sir Thomas Munro, Bart. and K.C.B. London: 1830. V. 42

GLEIG, GEORGE

Chelsea Hospital and Its Traditions. London: 1838. V. 45

A Narrative of the Campaigns of the British Army at Washington and New Orleans . . . London: 1826. V. 45

GLEIG, GEORGE ROBERT

The Campaigns of the British Army at Washington and New Orleans in the Years 1814-1815. London: 1836. V. 41

Chelsea Hospital and Its Traditions. London: 1838. V. 37; 38; 41

The History of the British Empire in India. London: 1830-35. V. 39

The Hussar. London: 1837. V. 41

Memoirs of the Life of Warren Hastings . . . London: 1841. V. 39

A Narrative of the Campaigns of the British Army at Washington and New Orleans. London: 1821. V. 39; 41

The Subaltern. Edinburgh: 1825. V. 43

GLEIZES, A.

Du Cubisme. Paris: 1947. V. 45

GLEN, JAMES

A Description of South Carolina . . . . London: 1761. V. 39; 41; 44; 45

GLENCAIRN, ISABELLA CUNNINGHAM, COUNTESS OF

A Letter to the Right Hon. Spencer Percival, Chancellor of the Exchequer . . . Brisol: 1812. V. 37; 38

GLENFIN, PSEUD.

The Fishing Rod and How to Use It. London: 1860. V. 39; 40; 43

GLENIE, JAMES

A Short Essay on the Modes of Defence Best Adapted to the Situation and Circumstances of This Island. London: 1785. V. 38

GLENN, JAMES E.

Moral Truth, Fairly Stated in Reply to the Rev. Alexander Porter's check to Methodism. Augusta: 1815. V. 45

GLENN, MABELLE

The World of Music. Boston: 1937 & 1938. V. 37

GLENN, THOMAS

Merion in the Welsh Tracts. Norristown: 1896. V. 41

GLENNY, GEORGE

Glenny's Manual of Practical Gardening. London: 1850. V. 40

GLI Eroi Morosini Per le Faustissime Nozze del N. U. Francesco Morosini . . . colla N. D. Loredana Grimani. Rovigo: 1772. V. 45

GLICK, ALLEN

Winter's Coming, Winters Gone. Austin: 1984. V. 44

GLIES, JOSEPH

Miscellaneous Poems: on Various Subjects, and Occasions. London: 1771. V. 38

GLIKES, ERWIN

Of Poetry and Power: Poems Occasioned by the Presidency and the Death of John F. Kennedy. New York: 1964. V. 45

GLIMCHER, ARNOLD B.

Louise Nevelson. New York: 1972. V. 45

GLIMPSES of Life in Victoria. Edinburgh: 1872. V. 37

GLIMPSES of the Monastery: a Brief Sketch of the History of the Ursulines of Quebec During the Lifetime of Venerable Mother Mary of the Incarnation. Quebec: 1872. V. 43

GLIMPSES of the Nations' Struggle. St. Paul: 1887. V. 46

GLISAN, RODNEY

Journal of Army Life. San Francisco: 1874. V. 42; 44; 45

GLISSON, FRANCIS

De Rachitide sive Morbo Puerili, qui Vulgo The Rickets Dicitur . . . London: 1600. V. 41

De Rachitide, sive Morbo Puerili, Qui Vulgo. London: 1660. V. 43

GLOAG, JOHN

A History of Cast Iron in Architecture. London: 1948. V. 44

GLOBE GOLD AND SILVER MINING CO.

Some Facts About Gold and Silver Mines and Mining in California and Nevada. New York: 1868. V. 40

GLORIAE Theatrum . . . - Teatro della Gloria Consagrato all'Eccellent-issima Signora D. Felice Sandoval Enriquez, Duchessa d'Uceda, Defonta, dall-Eccellentissimo Signore D. Gaspar Tellez Giron, Duca d'Ossuna.. Milan: 1671. V. 38

A GLOSSARY of Terms Used in Grecian, Roman, Italian, and Gothic Architecture. Oxford: 1850. V. 37; 44

GLOSSOGRAPHIA Anglicana Nova, or a Dictionary Interpreting Such Harad Words of Whatever Language as are at Present Used in the English Tongue etc. London: 1707. V. 37

GLOSSOP, B. R. M.

Sporting Trips of a Subaltern. London: 1906. V. 41

GLOVE, MARY

Lectures To Women On Anatomy and Physiology. New York: 1846. V. 42

GLOVER, ALAN

Gloriana's Glass. London. V. 40

GLOVER, D. L.

The Heroines of Shakespeare: Comprising the Principal Female Characters in the Plays of the Great Poet by D. L. Glover. 1880. V. 37

GLOVER, DOROTHY

Victorian Detective Fiction. London: 1966. V. 46

GLOVER, E. S.

Bird's Eye View of Victoria, Vancouver Island, B.C. 1878. Victoria. V. 44

GLOVER, H. C.

The Rights and Wrongs of Woman. New York: 1873. V. 41

GLOVER, JOHN

Mr. Glover's Exhibition of Oil and Water-Colour Paintings, at the Great Rooms, No. 16, Old Bond Street . . . London: 1823. V. 40; 44

GLOVER, RICHARD

Admiral Hosier's Ghost. London: 1740. V. 41; 45

Leonidas; a Poem. Dublin: 1737. V. 39; 41

Leonidas. London: 1737. V. 37; 38; 39; 40; 42; 43; 45

London; or, the Progress of Commerce. London: 1739. V. 40; 42

Medea. London: 1761. V. 37; 38; 40; 42; 46

A Short Account of the Late Application to Parliament Made by the Merchants of London Upon the Neglect of Their Trade: With the Substance of the Evidence Thereupon; as sum'd up by Mr. Glover. London: 1742. V. 37

GLOVER, ROBERT

Nobilitas Politica vel Civilis. London: 1608. V. 43

GLOVER, STEPHEN

The History of the County of Derby. Derby: 1829. V. 41

The History, Gazetteer, and Directory of the County of Derby . . . 1829-33. V. 39; 42

The History and Gazetteer of the County of Derby: Drawn from Observation, and from the Best Authorities . . . London: 1831-33. V. 39

The Peak Guide, Containing the Topographical, Statistical and General History of Buxton, Chatsworth, Edensor, Castlteon, Bakewell, Haddon, Matlock and Cromford . . . Derby: 1830. V. 39; 40

GLOVER, THOMAS

An Account of Virginia, Its Scituation, Temperature, Productions, Inhabitants and their Manner of Planting and Ordering Tobacco. Oxford: 1904. V. 45

GLOVER, WILLIAM

The Mormons in California. Los Angeles: 1954. V. 38

GLUBB, J. B.

Handbook of the Nomad, Semi-Nomad, Semi-Sedentary and Sedentary Tribes of Syria. V. 45

GLUCK, LOUISE

Firstborn. New York: 1968. V. 37

Firstborn. Middlesex: 1969. V. 37; 40; 42

Firstborn. Northwood, Middlesex: 1969. V. 37

GLUE and Lacquer. London: 1941. V. 38; 46

GLUECK, NELSON

Explorations in Eastern Palestine I-IV. New Haven: 1934-51. V. 40; 42; 44

Explorations in Eastern Palestine I-IV. New Haven: 1934-51. V. 40

GLYN, RICHARD H.

Bull Terriers and How to Breed Them. Oxford: 1950. V. 40; 43

GLYNN, JOSEPH

Report on the Turbine on Horizontal Water-Wheel of France and Germany. London: 1848. V. 43

Rudimentary Treatise on the Construction of Cranes and Machinery for Raising Heavy Bodies, for the Erection of Buildings and for Hositing Goods. London: 1849. V. 43

GMELIN, J. G.

Flora Siberica. St. Petersburgh: 1747-69. V. 43

GMELIN, JOHANN GEORG

Voyage en Sibirie; Contenant la Description des Moeurs & Usages des Peuples de ce Pays . . . Paris: 1767. V. 38

GMELIN, LEOPOLD

Hand-Book of Chemistry. London: 1848-61. V. 46

GNUDI, MARTHA T.

The Life and Times of Gaspare Tagliacozzi, Surgeon of Bologna, 1545-1599. Los Angeles: 1976. V. 37; 39; 42

GNUDI, MARTHA TEACH

The Life and Times of Gaspare Tagliacozzi, Surgeon of Bologna 1545-1599. New York. V. 40

The Life and Times of Gaspare Tagliacozzi. New York: 1950. V. 39; 41; 42; 44; 45; 46

The Life and Times of Gaspare Tagliacozzi. New York: 1953. V. 40; 41; 44; 45; 46

The Life and Times of Gaspare Tagliacozzi, Surgeon of Bologna. Los Angeles: 1976. V. 42

The Life and Times of Gaspare Tagliacozzi . . . 1545-99. Bologna: 1950. V. 37

GO Ahead. Davy Crockett's Almanack of Wild Sports in the West and Life in the Backwoods. Nashville: 1835. V. 39; 40

GO Ahead! Davy Crockett's 1837 Almanack, of Wild Sports in the West, Life in the Backwoods & Sketches of Texas. Nashville: 1836. V. 39

GO Ahead! Davy Crockett's Almanack, 1838 of Wild Sports in the West, Life in the Backwoods, Sketches of Texas and Rows on the Mississippi. Nashville: 1837. V. 42; 45

GO Ahead!!! The Crockett Almanac 1839. Nashville: 1838. V. 45

GOAD, CHARLES EDWARD

The Mapping of Victorian Toronto: the 1884 and 1890 Atlases of Toronto in Comparative Rendition. Sutton West & Santa Barbara: 1984. V. 45

GOAD, JOHN

Astro-Meteorologica, or aphorism's and discourses of the bodies coelestial, their natures and influences. Discovered from the variety of the alterations of the air, temperate, or intemperate, as to heat or colf . . . London : 1686. V. 37

GOADBY, ROBERT

The Life, Voyages and Adventures of Bampfylde-Moore Carew . . . London: 1790. V. 46

GOBEL, GERT

Langer Als Ein Menschenleben in Missouri. St. Louis: 1877. V. 39

GOBET, NICHOLAS

Les Anciens Mineralogistes du Royaume de France. Paris: 1779. V. 40

GOBIEN, CHARLES LE

Histoire des Isles Marianes. Paris: 1700. V. 43

GOBINEAU, JOSEPH ARTHUR, COMTE DE

Essai sur l'Inegalite des Races Humaines. Paris: 1853-55. V. 43; 45

GOBIUS, JOHANNES

Scala Coeli. Ulm: 1480. V. 44

GOBLE, WARWICK

The Book of Fairy Poetry. Edited by Dora Owen. London: 1920. V. 37

GOCHAROV, IVAN

Oblomov. New York: 1915. V. 39

GOCHER, W. H.

Trotalong: Pacealong: Racealong. Hartford: 1928-30. V. 39

GOCK, CARL

Die Vertheidigung der Freyen Kirche von Nord-Amerika. Reading: 1822. V. 40

Die Vertheidigung der Freyen Kirche von Nord Amerika. Reading: 1822. V. 42

GODAN, D.

Pest Slugs and Snails. Berlin: 1983. V. 37

GODCHARLES, FREDERIC A.

Chronicles of Central Pennsylvania. New York: 1944. V. 39; 41; 42

GODDARD, F. B.

Where to Emigrate and Why. Homes and Fortunes in the Boundless West and the Sunny South. Philadelphia: 1869. V. 38; 39; 42

GODDARD, FREDERICK B.

Where to Emigrate and Why, Homes and Fortunes in the Boundless West and the Sunny South . . . Philadelphia: Cincinnati. V. 42

GODDARD, G. H.

Report of a Survey of a Portion of the Eastern Boundary of California and of a Reconnaissance of the Old Carson and Johnson Immigrant Roads over the Sierra Nevada. Sacramento: 1856. V. 37; 40

GODDARD, PAUL BECK

Plates of the Arteries, with References; for the Use of Medical Students. Philadelphia: 1839. V. 40

GODDARD, ROBERT H.

A Method of Searching Extreme Altitudes. Washington: 1919. V. 42

A Method of Reaching Extreme Altitudes. Washington: 1919. V. 37

GODDARD, T.

The Military Costume of Europe: Exhibited in a Series of Highly Finished Military Figures, in the Uniform of Their Several Corps . . . London: 1812-22. V. 39

GODDARD, THOMAS H.

A General History of the Most Prominent Banks in Europe. New York: 831. V. 39

A General History of the Most prominent Banks in Europe: particularly the Banks of England and France: the rise and progress of the Bank of North America; a full history of the late and present Bank of the United States, statistical . . . New York: 1831. V. 37

GODDEN, RUMER

Chinese Puzzle. London: 1936. V. 37; 40; 42

GODDISON, J. W.

Reynolds Stone, His Early Development as an Engraver on Wood. Cambridge: 1947. V. 41

GODDWIN, FRANCIS

Cottage Architecture: Being a Supplement to the First Series of Goodwin's Rural Architecture. (with) Cottage Architecture; Being a Supplement to the Second Series of Goodwin's Rural Architecture. London: 1835. V. 38

GODEFROID DE BUILLON 1058?-1100

The History of Godfrey of Boloyne and of the Conquest of Iherusalem. London: 1893. V. 41

Les Passages de Oultre Mer. Du Noble Godefroy Buillon, qui fut roy de Hierusalem. Paris: 1505. V. 40

GODEFROY, DENIS 1549-1621

Corpus Juris Civilis. Geneva: 1606. V. 40

Corpus Juris Civilis Pandectis Ac Florentinum Archetypum Expressis . . . Amsterdam: 1663. V. 40

GODEFROY, JACQUES

The History of the United Provinces of Achaia. London: 1673. V. 39

GODEY'S Lady Book. 1842. V. 45

GODFERY, M. J.

Monograph and Iconograph of Native British Orchidaceae. Cambridge: 1933. V. 38

GODFREY, JOHN THOMAS

The History of the Parish and Priory of Lenton in the County of Nottingham. London: 1884. V. 39; 40

GODFREY, M. J.

Monograph and Iconograph of Native British Orchidaceae. Cambridge: 1933. V. 37; 38; 39; 42

GODFREY, MRS.

On the Prevention and Cure of Spinal Curvatures and Deformities of the Chest and Limbs: Being the Result of Many Years Experience. London: 1851. V. 42

GODFREY of Bulliogne: or the Recovery of Jersualem, together with a Life of Godfrey. London: 1687. V. 37; 38

GODFREY, R. L.

Aquatic and Wetland Plants of Southeastern United States. London: 1979. V. 37

GODFREY, THOMAS

Juvenile Poems on Various Subjects. Philadelphia: 1765. V. 42

GODFREY, WILLIAM C.

Godfrey's Narrative of the Last Grinnell Arctic Exploring Expedition, in Search of Sir John Franklin, 1853-4-5. Philadelphia: 1857. V. 39

GODINE, DAVID R.

Lyric Verse, a Printer's Choice. Boston: 1966. V. 41

Lyric Verse: a Printer's Choice. Lunenburg: 1966. V. 40; 42; 44

Lyric Verse. A Printer's Choice. N.P.: 1966. V. 41

GODINHO, MANOEL 1645-1712

Relacap do novo caminho que fex por terra, e mar, vindo da India . . . Lisbon: 1665. V. 37; 39; 41; 43

GODKIN, G. S.

The Monastery of San Marco. Florence: 1890. V. 43

GODLEE, R. J.

An Atlas of Human Anatomy. London: 1880. V. 43

Lord Lister. Oxford: 1924. V. 39

GODLEE, RICKMAN, JOHN

An Atlas of Human Anatomy Illustrating Most of the Ordinary Dissections and Many Not Usually Practised by the Student . . . London: 1880. V. 46

GODLEY, ELIZABETH

Green Outside. London: 1931. V. 43

GODLEY, JOHN ROBERT

Letters from America. London: 1844. V. 42; 43; 46

GODMAN, ERNEST

Mediaeval Architecture in Essex. Campden: 1905. V. 40

Norman Architecture in Essex. London: 1905. V. 41; 44

GODMAN, F. DU CANE

A Monograph of the Petrels (Order Tubinares). London: 1907. V. 42

A Monograph of the Petrels (Order Tubinares). London: 1907-10. V. 37; 39; 41

GODWYN, THOMAS

Civil and Ecclesiastical Bites Used by the Ancient Hebrewes. London: 1655. V. 39

Moses and Aaron: Civil and Ecclesiastical Rites, Used by the Ancient Hebrewe . . . London: 1672. V. 43

Romanae Historiae Anthologia . . . London: 1674. V. 43

GOEBEL, FRIEDEMANN

Reise in die Steppen des Sudlichen Russlands . . . in Begleitung der Herren Dr. C. Claus and A. Bergmann. Dorpat: 1838. V. 40

GOEBEL, K.

Organography of Plants, Especially of the Archegoniatae and Spermophyta. Oxford: 1900-05. V. 37

GOEDE, C. A. G.

A Foreigner's Opinion of England, Englishmen, Englishwomen . . . London: 1821. V. 45

The Stranger in England; or, Travels in Great Britain. Containing Remarks on the Politics, Laws, Manners, Customs . . . and Chiefly its Metropolis. With Criticisms on the Stage . . . London: 1807. V. 37

GOEPPER, ROGER

The Essence of Chinese Painting. Boston: 1963. V. 41

GOERTZ, MAX

Gedichte. Leipzig: 1922. V. 38

GOES, DAMIANO DE 1501-1573

Damiani Goes . . . De Bello Cambaico Ultimo Commentarii Tres. Louvain: 1549. V. 40

GOES, DAMIAO

De Bello Cambaico Ultimo Commentarii Tres. Louvain: 1549. V. 45

GOES, DAMIAO DE

Damiani Goes . . . De Bello Cambaico Ultimo Commentarii Tres. Louvain: 1549. V. 45

GOES, WILLEM VAN DER 1611-1686

Rei Agrariae Auctores Legesque Variae. Amsterdam: 1674. V. 43

GOETGHEBUER, PIERRE JACQUES

Choix des Monumens, Edifices et Maisons les Plus Remarquables du Royaume des Pays-Bas. Ghent: 1827. V. 44

GOETHE: Auserlesene Lieder, Gedichte und Balladen. Ein Strauss. Hammersmith: 1916. V. 45

GOETHE, JOHANN WOLFGANG VON 1749-1832

Das Romische Carneval. Offenbach am Main: 1984. V. 39

Faust. Lowell and New York: 1840. V. 37

Faust. Boston and New York: 1906. V. 37

Faust. Hammersmith: 1906 & 1911. V. 37

Faust. A Tragedy. New York: (1930). V. 37

Faust. A Tragedy. Both parts translated by Bayard Taylor. Boston/New York: 1906. V. 37

Faust. With Illustrations by Harry Clarke. New York: (ca. 1925). V. 37

Faust. London. V. 39

Faust. New York. V. 39; 40; 46

Faust, Eine Tragodie (Part 1) and Faust (Part II). Tubingen & Stuttgart &: 1808, 1833. V. 40

Faust, a Drama. London: 1823. V. 38; 39

Faustus. London: 1824. V. 40

Faustus. London: 1835. V. 40

Faust. Boston: 1871. V. 41

Faust. Boston: 1906. V. 42; 43

Faust, eine Tragedie. Part One. London: 1906. V. 40

Faust. Hammersmith: 1906-10. V. 43; 45

Faust. Hammersmith: 1906/10. V. 46

Faust. London: 1908. V. 38; 41; 44

Faust. London: 1912? V. 42

Faust I - II. Frankfurt: 1922-23. V. 38

Faust. 1925. V. 37; 39

Faust. London: 1925. V. 37; 44; 45; 46

Faust. New York: 1925. V. 41; 42; 45

Faust, a Tragedy. New York: 1930. V. 40; 45

Faust. Paris: 1938. V. 43

Goethes Werke. Stuttgart u. Tuebingen: 1815-19. V. 45

Goethe's Correspondence with a Child. Lowell: 1841. V. 38

Goethe's Elective Affinities. Boston: 1872. V. 37

Goetz of Berlichingen, with the Iron Hand. London: 1799. V. 38

Gortz of Berlingen, With the Iron Hand. Liverpool: 1799. V. 38

Hermann und Dorothea. Munich: 1922. V. 45

Iphigenie auf Tauris: Ein Schauspiel. Hammersmith: 1912. V. 45

Iphigenie auf Tauris. Munich: 1922. V. 45

Italian Journey. 1962. V. 45

Orphisch: Five Poems. 1982. V. 40

Reineke Fuchs. Munchen: 1846. V. 45

Reynard the Fox, After the German Version of Goethe. London: 1853. V. 38; 46

Reynard the Fox. London: 1860. V. 39

Reynard the Fox after the German of . . . Boston: 1887. V. 41

The Story of Reynard the Fox. New York: 1954. V. 39

Das Romische Carneval. Offenbach am Main: 1984. V. 42

Samtliche Werke. Cotta: 1902-12. V. 41

The Sorrows of Werter. London: 1784. V. 37; 39; 40; 42; 45

The Sorrows of Werter. London: 1785. V. 45

The Sorrows of Werter. London: 1802. V. 40

Urworte, Orphisch, Five Poems by. London: 1982. V. 39

Versuch dei Metamorphose der Pflanzen zu Erklaren. Gotha: 1790. V. 39; 41; 43

West-Ostlicher Divan. Northampton: 1970. V. 38; 39

West-oestlicher Diwan. Stuggart: 1819. V. 44

Wilhelm Meister's Apprenticeship. Edinburgh: 1824. V. 39; 40

Goethe Werke. Stuttgart: 1815-19. V. 42

Samtliche Werke. Stuttgart: 1902-12. V. 41

Zur Farbenlehre. Vienna: 1812. V. 38

GOETZ, ANGELINA

Catalogue of the Angeina Goetz Library, Presented to the Royal Academy of Music. London: 1904. V. 38

GOETZ, GEORG FRIEDRICH

Naturgeschichte Einiger Vogel. Dresden: 1782. V. 43

GOETZ, HERMANN

The Art and Architecture of Bikaner State. Oxford: 1950. V. 38

GOETZINGER, CLARA PALMER

Smoldering Flames. Adventures and Emotions of a Flapper. Chicago: 1928. V. 39

GOETZMAN, H. J.

Souvenir of the Klondike. Dawson: 1901. V. 37

GOETZMANN, WILLIAM H.

Army Exploration in the American West 1803-1863. New Haven: 1959. V. 42

GOFARTH, WILLIAM 1697-1764

Hogarth's Graphic Works. New Haven & London: 1965. V. 39

GOFF, BEATRICE LAURA

Symbols of Prehistoric Mesopotamia. New Haven: 1963. V. 42

GOFF, BRUCE

Architecture: 30 Plates. Billings: 1978. V. 46

GOFF, FREDERICK R.

Incunabula in American Libraries. New York: 1964. V. 42; 44

Incunabula in American Libraries. A Third Census of Fifteenth-Century Books Recorded in North American Collections. 1973. V. 45; 46

A Third Census of Fifteenth Century Books Recorded in North American Collections. New York: 1964. V. 45

GOFF, FREDERICK RICHMOND

Incunabula in American Libraries. Millwood: 1973. V. 46

GOFFE, THOMAS

The Couragious Turke, or Amurath the First. London: 1632. V. 40

GOFFROES, GUILHERME

Relacam de hum Grandissimo Animal, de Cuja Incomparavel Fereza El Rey de Nauvu seu Senhor se Valeu nas Partes do Japano Para Alcancar . . . Lisbon: 1742. V. 43

GOFLIETTA, UBERTO

Clarorum Ligurum Elogia. Genoa: 1588. V. 41

GOGARTHY, OLIVER ST. JOHN 1878-1957

Wild Apples. Dublin: 1930. V. 38; 39; 42; 45

GOGARTY, OLIVER ST. JOHN 1878-1957

Blight The Tragedy of Dublin. Dublin: 1917. V. 38

Collected Poems. New York: 1954. V. 42

Elbow Room. 1939. V. 38

Elbow Room. Dublin: 1939. V. 40

GOGARTY, OLIVER ST. JOHN 1878-1957 continued

Elbow Room. Dublin: 1939. V. 37

Map Grandeur. A Novel. Philadelphia: 1941. V. 38

An Offering of Swans. Dublin: 1923. V. 38

Selected Poems. New York: 1933. V. 46

GOGH, VINCENT VAN 1853-1890

Letters to an Artist, from Vincent Van Gogh to Anton Ridder Van Rappard, 1881-1885. New York: 1936. V. 46

The Complete Letters. Greenwich: 1959. V. 39

GOGOL, NICOLAI

Dead Souls. New York: 1923. V. 44

GOGOL, NIKOLAI

Cossack Tales. London: 1860. V. 38

Dead Souls, Chichikov's Journeys; or, Home Life in Old Russia. New York: 1944. V. 41

The Diary of a Madman. London: 1929. V. 37; 38

The Overcoat and Other Stories. New York: 1923. V. 45

The Overcoat. 1975. V. 44

The Overcoat. Verona: 1975. V. 37; 38; 40; 41; 42; 44; 45; 46

The Overcoat and The Government Inspector. Connecticut: 1976. V. 43

Taras Bulba. New York: 1866. V. 43

GOGOL, NIKOLAI V.

The Gamblers and Marriage. New York: 1927. V. 39; 43

GOGUET, A. YVES DE

The Origin of Laws, Arats, and Sciences, and Their Progress Among the Most Ancient Nations. Edinburgh: 1761. V. 37

GOINES, DAVID LANCE

A Constructed Roman Alphabet. Boston: 1982. V. 41; 46

GOINS, JOSHUA VAN BUREN

Life and Work of Rev. Joshua Van Buren Goins, D.D., M.D. Austin?: 1913. V. 39

GOLD and Silver Mining in Sonora, Mexico. Cincinnati: 1867. V. 39; 44

GOLD Fields of the Klondike. Douglas: 1899. V. 39

GOLD HILL, NEVADA. FIRE DEPARTMENT

Constitution And By-Laws of the Fire Department of Gold Hill, Nevada, Organized May 22d, 1867. San Francisco: 1878. V. 38; 43

GOLD SEPARATOR AND SLUCING CO.

Gold Separator and Slucing Co. Irrigation and Mining. New York: 1894. V. 42

GOLDAMMER, HERMANN

The Kindergarten. Berlin: 1882. V. 45

GOLDAST AB HAIMINSFELD, MELCHIOR

Suevicarum Rerum Scriptores Aliquot Veteres. Frankfurt: 1605. V. 41

GOLDAST, MELCHIOR

Haiminsfeldius. Collectio Constitutionum Imperialium . . . Francofurti: 1713. V. 39

Haiminsfeldus. Monarchia S. Romani Imperii, Sive Tractatus de Jurisdictione Imperiali Seu Regia & Pontificia Seu Sacerdotali . . . Hanoviae: 1614, 1613. V. 39

GOLDBACH, CHRISTIAN FRIEDRICH

Neuster Himmels-Atlas zum Gebrauch fur Schul- und Akademischen Unterricht, Nach Flamsteed, Bradley, Tob. Mayer, De La Caille, Le Francais de la Lande und v. Zach . . . Weimar: 1799. V. 44

GOLDBERG, ISAAC

The Theatre World of George Jean Nathan. New York: 1926. V. 44

GOLDBERG, RUBE

Is There A Doctor In The House? New York: 1929. V. 42

GOLDEN A. B. C. London: 1856? V. 44

THE GOLDEN Book of Songs and Ballads. London: 1920. V. 41

THE GOLDEN Cabinet, Being the Laboratory or Handmaid of the Arts. Dublin: 1790. V. 38

THE GOLDEN Calendar. London: 1864. V. 44

THE GOLDEN Cockerel. New York: 1950. V. 41

THE GOLDEN Cockerel Greek Anthology. Waltham St. Lawrence: 1937. V. 37

GOLDEN COCKEREL PRESS

Cock-A-Hoop: a Sequel to Chanticleer, Pertelote and Cockalorum Being a Bibliography of the Golden Cockerel Press from September 1949-December 1961. Middlesex: 1976. V. 40

Cockalorum, a Sequel to Chanticleer and Pertelote. London. V. 40

The Illustrators of the Golden Cockerel Press; an Introduction to the Exhibition at the Mayor's Parlour Gallery, Hereford. Waltham St. Lawrence: 1980. V. 40

Pertelote, a Sequel to Chanticleer, being a Bibliography of the Golden Cockerel Press, October 1936-1943 April. London: 1943. V. 37

Pertelote. A Sequel to Chanticleer, Being a Bibliography of The Golden Cockerel Press, October 1936 - 1943 April. Foreword and notes by the Partners. (London: 1943). V. 37

THE GOLDEN Fleece Gazette. Madras: 1864. V. 38

THE GOLDEN Hind. London: 1922, 1924. V. 37

THE GOLDEN Moth - a Musical Play of Adventure. London: 1921. V. 41

GOLDEN, R. L.

Sir William Osler - an Annotated Bibliography with Illustrations. San Francisco: 1988. V. 39; 40; 41; 42; 43; 45; 46

Sir William Osler. An Annotated Bibliography with Illustrations. San Francisco: 1988. V. 41

GOLDEN, RICHARD

Sir William Osler: an Annotated Bibliography with Illustrations. San Francisco: 1988. V. 45

GOLDEN thoughts from Golden Fountains. London: 1867. V. 38

THE GOLDEN Treasury of Songs and Lyrics. New York: 1911. V. 44

GOLDEN Verses from the New Testament. London: 1868. V. 43

GOLDEN Verses from the New Testament, with Illuminations and Miniatures from Celebrated Missals and Books of the XIV and XV Centuries. London: 1868. V. 39

GOLDENBERG, ISAAC

Tin Pan Alley: A Chronicle of the American Popular Music Racket. New York: 1930. V. 45

GOLDER, F. A.

Russian Expansion on the Pacific 1641-1850. Cleveland: 1914. V. 38

GOLDER, FRANK A.

The March of the Mormon Battalion from Council Bluffs to California. New York: 1928. V. 37; 42

GOLDER, FRANK ALFRED

Bering's Voyages . . . . New York: 1922. V. 42

John Paul Jones in Russia. New York: 1927. V. 42

GOLDFINGER, M.

Villages in the Sun: Mediterranean Community Archiecture. New York: 1969. V. 46

GOLDING, BENJAMIN

Historical Account of the Origin and Progress of St. Thomas's Hospital, Southwark. London: 1819. V. 42; 43

GOLDING, HARRY

War in Dollyland. London: 1915. V. 46

GOLDING, LOUIS

The Song of Songs Rendered as a Masque. London: 1937. V. 46

Sorrow of War: Poems. London: 1919. V. 46

Terrace in Capri: an Imaginary Conversation with Norman Douglas. 1934. V. 45

GOLDING, WILLIAM 1911-

Boys and Girls Together. New York: 1964. V. 46

The Brass Butterfly. London: 1958. V. 45

The Brass Butterfly. London: 1958. V. 40; 43; 45

Close Quarters. London: 1987. V. 43

Darkness Visible. London: 1979. V. 38

Fire Down Below. London: 1989. V. 43; 45

Free Fall. London: 1959. V. 37; 43; 44; 46

The Hot Gates. London: 1965. V. 39; 43; 44

The Inheritors. London: 1955. V. 39; 40; 41; 42; 43; 46

The Ladder and the Tree Hand. London: 1961. V. 46

The Ladder and the Tree. Marlborough: 1961. V. 38

Lord of the Flies. London: 1954. V. 37; 39; 43; 44; 45

Lord of the Flies. London: 1955. V. 42

Lord of the Flies. New York: 1955. V. 37; 39

Nobel Prize Speech. Nobel. Leamington Spa: 1983. V. 44

GOLDING, WILLIAM 1911- continued

Nobel Lecture. Leamington Spa: 1984. V. 38

Nobel Lecture. London: 1984. V. 37; 39

The Paper Men. London: 1984. V. 41

Pincher Martin. London. V. 40

Pincher Martin. London: 1956. V. 39

Pincher Martin. London: 1956. V. 38; 39; 43; 45; 46

Pincher Martin. London: 1965. V. 40; 41

The Pyramid. London: 1967. V. 37; 40; 43; 45

Rites of Passage. London: 1980. V. 38; 43

Rites of Passage. New York: 1980. V. 37

The Scorpion God. London: 1971. V. 40; 43

Sometime Never. London: 1956. V. 40

The Sphire. London: 1964. V. 39; 40; 41; 43; 45

The Spire. New York: 1964. V. 45

GOLDMAN, EMMA

Anarchism and Other Essays . . . New York: 1910. V. 38

living My Life. New York: 1931. V. 42; 44

My Disillusionment with Russia. London: 1925. V. 43

GOLDMAN, HETTY

Excavations at Eutresis in Boestia. Cambridge: 1931. V. 44

Excavations at Gozlu Kule, Tarsus. Princeton: 1950. V. 42

GOLDMAN, WILLIAM

The Princess Bride. New York: 1973. V. 44; 46

The Temple of Gold. New York: 1957. V. 37; 41; 42; 43; 44; 45

Wigger. New York: 1974. V. 44; 45

GOLDMANN, CHARLES SYDNEY

With General French and the Cavalry in South Africa. London: 1902. V. 41

GOLDONI, CARLO

The Liar: a Comedy in Three Acts. London: 1922. V. 38; 41

GOLDSBOROUGH, CHARLES W.

The United States Naval Chronicle . . . Washington: 1824. V. 42

GOLDSCHMIDT, ADOLPH

An Early Manuscript of the Aesop Fables of Avianus and Related Manuscripts. Princeton: 1947. V. 38

German Illumination. Paris: 1928. V. 39

GOLDSCHMIDT, E. P.

The First Cambridge Press in Its European Setting. London: 1955. V. 39

Gothic and Renaissance Bookbindings. London: 1928. V. 41

Gothic and Renaissance Bookbindings, Exemplified and Illustrated from the Author's Collection. Niewkoop;;: 1962. V. 41

Gothic and Renaissance Bookbindings. Amsterdam: 1967. V. 39

The Printed Book of the Renaissance, Three Lectures on Type, Illustration and Ornament. Cambridge: 1950. V. 44

GOLDSCHMIDT, E. P. &, & CO., LTD.

Old Books on Various Subjects: Many Illustrated with Woodcuts and Engravings, Navigation and Maritime Law. London: 1939. V. 46

GOLDSCHMIDT, ERNST PHILIP 1887-1954

Gothic and Renaissance Bookbinding. London: 1928. V. 38

GOLDSCHMIDT, LUCIEN

The Truthful Lens. New York: 1980. V. 37; 39; 41; 42; 46

The Truthful Lens. New York: 1980. V. 42

GOLDSCHMIDT, RICHARD

The Mechanism and Physiology of Sex Determination. London: 1923. V. 42

Physiological Genetics. New York: 1938. V. 42

GOLDSMID, E.

Un-Natural History, or Myths of Ancient Science. Edinburgh: 1886. V. 37

GOLDSMID, EDMUND

Bibliotheca Curiosa. The Trial of Rancis Ravaillac for the Murder of King Henry the Great, Together with an Account of His Torture and Execution. Edinburgh: 1885. V. 45

Explanatory Notes of a Pack of Cavalier Playing Cards Temp. Charles II, Forming a Complete Political Satire of the Commonwealth. Edinburgh: 1886. V. 44

GOLDSMID, F. J.

Eastern Persia, an Account of the Journeys of the Persian Boundary Commission. London: 1876. V. 37; 38; 39

GOLDSMID, FRANCIS HENRY

Reply to the Arguments Advanced Against the Removal of the Remaining Disabilities of the Jews. London: 1848. V. 45

GOLDSMITH, JOHN

Almanack for the Yer . . . 1782. London: 1781. V. 38

GOLDSMITH, LEWIS

Statistics of France. London: 1832. V. 45

GOLDSMITH, OLIVER 1730-1774

The Beauties of English Poesy. London: 1767. V. 37; 38; 41; 45

The Beauties of Goldsmith. Dublin: 1790. V. 38

The Bee, a Select Collection of Essays on the Most Interesting and Entertaining Subjects. London. V. 39

The Citizen of the World. London: 1762. V. 37; 38; 41; 43; 44; 45

The Citizen of the World . . . London: 1774. V. 46

The Citizen of the World. Dublin: 1775. V. 40

The Citizen of the World; or, Letters from a Chinese Philosopher, Residing in London, to His Friends in the East. London: 1809. V. 46

The Collected Letters of Oliver Goldsmith. London: 1928. V. 41; 46

The Collected Letters of Olvier Goldsmith. London: 1928. V. 46

Collected Works of Oliver Goldsmith. Oxford: 1966. V. 38

Dalziel's Illustrated Goldsmith. London: 1865. V. 38

The Deserted Village. London: 1770. V. 38

The Deserted Village, a Poem. London: 1770. V. 40; 43

The Deserted Village. Philadelphia: 1888. V. 42

The Deserted Village. East Aurora: 1898. V. 44

The Deserted Village. London: 1899. V. 38; 44

The Deserted Village. 1904. V. 43

The Deserted Village. Campden: 1904. V. 38; 40; 44

The Deserted Village. London: 1904. V. 37; 40; 41; 46

The Deserted Village. London: 1904. V. 40

The Deserted Village. Boston: 1912. V. 41; 46

The Deserted Village. London: 1921. V. 44; 46

The Deserted Village. San Francisco: 1926. V. 38; 40; 41; 43; 45; 46

The Deserted Village. Springfield: 1783. V. 37

The Deserted Village. London/Glasgow: 1907. V. 37

An Enquiry into the Present State of Polite Learning in Europe. London: 1774. V. 42

An Enquiry into the Present State of Polite Learning in Europe. London: 1759. V. 37

Essays. Boston. V. 38

Essays. London: 1765. V. 37; 38; 41; 42; 43; 45

Essays. London: 1765. V. 45

Essays and Criticisms by Dr. Goldsmith with an Account of the Author. London: 1798. V. 40; 41; 46

Essays. Boston: 1928. V. 39

Essays. Boston: (n.d). V. 37

The Good Natur'd Man. London: 1768. V. 37; 38; 40; 41; 43; 45

Goldsmith & Parnell. Poems. London: 1795. V. 45

Goody Two Shoes: A Facsimile Reproduction of the Edition of 1766. London: 1882. V. 37

The Grecian History, from the Earliest State to the Death of Alexander the Great. London: 1774. V. 41

The Haunch of Venison. London: 1776. V. 43

The History of Rome, from the Foundation of the City of Rome, to the Destruction of the Western Empire. London: 1820. V. 42

A History of the Earth and Animated Nature . . . London. V. 40

An History of the Earth and Animated Nature. London: 1774. V. 37; 39; 40; 43; 44

An History of the Earth, and Animated Nature. Dublin: 1776. V. 38

An History of the Earth and Animated nature. Dublin: 1777. V. 43

The History of the Earth, and Animated Nature. Dublin: 1777-76. V. 42

A History of England in a Series of Letters from a Nobleman to His Son. London: 1787. V. 45; 46

An History of the Earth and Animated Nature. London: 1790. V. 45

History of the Earth and animated Nature . . . London: 1807. V. 45

A History of England in a Series of Letters . . . London: 1812. V. 46

A History of the Earth and Animated Nature. London: 1822. V. 39

A History of the Earth, and Animated Nature. Philadelhia: 1830. V. 45

A History of the Earth and Animated Nature. Edinburgh & London: 1850. V. 44

A History of the Earth and Animated Nature. Glasgow: 1853. V. 39

A History of the Earth and Animated Nature. London: 1855. V. 39

A History of the Earth and Animated Nature. London: 1855. V. 42

A History of the Earth and Animated nature. Edinburgh: 1870. V. 38

A History of the Earth and Animated Nature. Glasgow. V. 46

A History of the Earth and Animated Nature. Dublin: 1812-14. V. 46

GOLDSMITH, OLIVER 1730-1774 continued

The History of Little Goody Twoshoes; Otherwise Called Mrs. Margery Twoshoes. Worcester: 1787. V. 43

A History of the Earth and Aminated Nature . . . Together with the Elements of Botany, and an Account of the Most Rare and Curious Foreign Plants, the whole forming a Complete Panorama of Nature, by G.F. Shaw. London: 1817. V. 37; 40

A History of the Earth and animated nature. In Four Volumes. A New Edition, Improved. Liverpool: 1810. V. 37; 38

A History of the Earth and Animated Nature, with numerous notes, from the works of most distinguished British and Foreign naturalists. Glasgow: 1852. V. 37

A History of the earth and animated nature. With numerous notes . . . illustrated by upwards of two thousand figures. Glasgow: 1852. V. 37

The Life of Richard Nash of Bath . . . Bath: 1762. V. 39; 45; 46

The Life of Richard Nash, of Bath. London: 1762. V. 37; 38; 39; 40; 43; 45; 46

Life and Adventures. A Biography in four books, by John Forster. London: 1848. V. 37

The Life of Richard Nash, of Bath, Esq. 1762. V. 38

The Life of Richard Nash, of Bath, Esq. London: 1762. V. 37

The Miscellaneous Works. London: 1780. V. 39

The Miscellaneous Works . . . Perth: 1792. V. 43

Miscellaneous Works. London: 1801. V. 40

The Miscellaneous Works of . . . London: 1801. V. 40; 42

The Miscellaneous Works of Oliver Goldsmith. New York: 1805. V. 43

The Miscellaneous Works. London: 1812. V. 38; 43

The Miscellaneous Works . . . with Memoirs of His Life and Writings. Glasgow: 1816. V. 39; 40

Miscellaneous Works. London: 1820. V. 38

The Miscellaneous Works of Oliver Goldsmith. New York: 1850. V. 41; 44

The Miscellaneous Works of Oliver Goldsmith. With an account of his life and writings. Paris: 1825. V. 37

The Miscellaneous Works . . . . (with) The Life of Oliver Goldsmith, M.B., from a Variety of Original Sources, by James Prior. London: 1837. V. 37

Natural History, Abridged, for the Use of Schools, by Mrs. Pilkington. London: 1803. V. 38

Novellettes, selected for the Use of Young Ladies and Gentlemen . . . London: 1780. V. 41

Overland in Forty-Nine. Detroit: 1896. V. 45

Poems for Young Ladies. London: 1767. V. 42; 45

Poems and Plays. Dublin: 1777. V. 37; 40; 44

Poems and Plays . . . To Which is Prefixed the Life of the Author. London: 1780. V. 38

Poems Upon Young Ladies, in Three Parts. London: 1785. V. 42

Poems by Goldsmith and Parnell. London: 1795. V. 38; 42; 44; 45

The Poems of . . . London: 1800. V. 38; 39; 40; 45

Poems. London: 1804. V. 40; 42

The Poems of Oliver Goldsmith. London: 1859. V. 37; 40; 41; 44

The Poems of . . . London: 1860. V. 38; 44

Poems. London: 1877. V. 37

Poems by Goldsmith and Parnell. Bulmer: 1795. V. 37

The Poetical and Dramatic Works of Oliver Goldsmith, M.B. London: 1780. V. 38; 41; 43

The Poetical and Dramtic Works. London: 1786. V. 38

The Poetical Works of Oliver Goldsmith. Hereford: 1794. V. 38

The Poetical Works. London: 1811. V. 38; 42; 43

The Poetical Works . . . London: 1845. V. 45

The Poetical Works. London: 1845. V. 37; 38; 40

The Poetical Works. London: 1846. V. 42

The Poetical and Prose Works. Edinburgh: 1865. V. 46

The Poetical Works of . . . London: 1888. V. 39; 43

The Poetical and Dramatic Works . . . Now First Collected. London: 1780. V. 37

The Present State of the British Empire in Europe, America, Africa and Asia. London: 1768. V. 39

The Traveller, or a Prospect of Society. London: 1765. V. 41

The Renowned History of Goody Two-Shoes. London: 1881. V. 39

Retalliation. Westport: 1929. V. 41

The Roman History, From the Foundation of the City of Rome, to the Destruction of the Western Empire. London: 1769. V. 42

The Roman History, From the Foundation of the City of Rome, to the destruction of the Western Empire. Dublin: 1771. V. 40

She Stoops to Conqueor. London: V. 40

She Stoops to Conquer. London: 1749-1780. V. 44

She Stoops to Conquer. London: 1773. V. 38; 40; 41; 43; 45

She Stoops to Conquer. New York: 1887. V. 43

She Stoops to Conquer. London: 1912. V. 40; 41; 42; 43; 45; 46

She Stoops to Conquer, or, the Mistakes of a Night. London: New York: Toronto: 1912. V. 45

She Stoops to Conquer. New York: 1912. V. 37; 38

She Stoops to Conquer, or The Mistakes of a Night. By Oliver Goldsmith. London: (1912). V. 37

A Survey of Experimental Philosophy. London: 1776. V. 37; 38

The Traveller, or a Prospect of Society. London: 1765. V. 38; 41; 45; 46

The Traveller. London: 1770. V. 43

The Traveller. London: 1858. V. 37

The Traveller and the Deserted Village. Chelsea: 1929. V. 37

Versuche aus dem Englischen. Basle: 1780. V. 38

The Vicar of Wakefield. Philadelphia. V. 39; 41

The Vicar of Wakefield. Salisbury: 1756. V. 42

The Vicar of Wakefield. Dublin: 1766. V. 40

The Vicar of Wakefield. London: 1766. V. 37; 39; 40; 41; 42; 45; 46

The Vicar of Wakefield. London: 1766. V. 45

The Vicar of Wakefield. Salisbury: 1766. V. 38; 41; 43; 45; 46

Le Ministre de Wakefield. Londres: 1767. V. 38; 40

Le Minstre De Wakefield . . . Paris: 1767. V. 41; 45

The Vicar of Wakefield. London: 1770. V. 38; 41

The Vicar of Wakefield: a Tale Supposed to Be Written by Himself. Philadelphia: 1772. V. 43

The Vicar of Wakefield. London: 1773. V. 42

The Vicar of Wakefield. London: 1776. V. 38; 41

Landsbypraesten af Wakefield. Copenhagen: 1779. V. 40

The Vicar of Wakefield. London: 1781. V. 40

The Vicar of Wakefield, a Tale. London: 1781. V. 45

Land-Prastens I Wakefield Lefwerne. Stockholm: 1782. V. 40

The Vicar of Wakefield, a Tale. London: 1792. V. 38; 43

The Vicar of Wakefield. Berlin: 1794. V. 38

Le Cure de Wakefield. Dublin: 1797. V. 42

The Vicar of Wakefield, a Tale. London & Paris: 1815. V. 43

The Vicar of Wakefield. London: 1817. V. 40

The Vicar of Wakefield. London: 1818. V. 41

The Vicar of Wakefield; a Tale. Knoxville: 1831. V. 43

The Vicar of Wakefield. London: 1843. V. 39

Vicar of Wakefield . . . London: 1843. V. 38; 39; 45

The Vicar of Wakefield. London: 1855. V. 39; 41

The Vicar of Wakefield. London: 1889. V. 40

The Vicar of Wakefield. London: 1890. V. 37; 38; 40; 41; 42

The Vicar of Wakefield. Chiswick: 1903. V. 37; 38; 41; 45

The Vicar of Wakefield. London: 1903. V. 42; 46

The Vicar of Wakefield. London: 1904. V. 45

The Vicar of Wakefield. London: 1914. V. 39; 40; 44; 45; 46

The Vicar of Wakefield. London: 1924. V. 44

The Vicar of Wakefield. London: 1929. V. 37; 38; 39; 40; 41; 42; 43; 44; 45; 46

The Vicar of Wakefield. Philadelphia: 1929. V. 40; 41; 45; 46

The Vicar of Wakefield. Oxford: 1950. V. 44

The Vicar of Wakefield; A Tale. London: 1817. V. 37

The Vicar of Wakefield. Bedford Park, Chiswick: 1903. V. 37

The Vicar of Wakefield. Philadelphia: (1920). V. 37

The Vicar of Wakefield. London: (1929). V. 37

The Vicar of Wakefield. London: (1929). V. 37

The Works. Boston. V. 42

Oliver Goldsmith's Works: Poems, Comedies, Essays . . . London. V. 43; 44

The Works. London: 1845. V. 42

The Works. London: 1854. V. 38; 39; 41; 42; 45; 46

The Works of Oliver Goldsmith. New York: 1900. V. 39; 41; 44; 46

The Works. New York: 1908. V. 38; 41; 42

The Works. New York: & London: 1908. V. 40; 46

GOLDSMITH, OLIVR 1730-1774

The Traveller. London: 1765. V. 41

GOLDSTEIN, RUBY

Third Man in the Ring as Told to Frank Graham. New York: 1959. V. 38

GOLDSTEIN, SIDNEY M.

Pre-Roman and Early Roman Glass in the Corning Museum of Glass. Corning: 1979. V. 44

GOLDSTONE, ADRIAN

A Bibliography of Arthur Machen. 1965. V. 46

A Bibliography of Arthur Machen. Austin: 1965. V. 42

GOLDSTONE, ADRIAN H.

John Steinbeck, a Bibliographical Catalogue of the Adrian H. Goldstone Collection. Austin: 1974. V. 39; 40

GOLDWATER, ROBERT

Bambara Sculpture from the Western Sudan. New York: 1960. V. 37

Rufino Tamayo. New York: 1947. V. 38; 41; 43; 46

GOLDZIHER, I.

Muslim Studies. Chicago: 1971. V. 39

GOLF. Athletics. Tennis. Hockey and Other Ball Games, Winter Sports. London: 1937. V. 38

THE GOLFER'S Calendar. 1911. London: 1910. V. 38

GOLFFING, FRANCIS

Poems, 1943-49. Cummington: 1949. V. 46

GOLIKOVA, G. V.

DMT 42. New York: 1969. V. 46

DMT 42. Stuttgart & New York: 1969. V. 46

GOLL, CLAIRE

Diary of a Horse. Brooklyn: 1946. V. 43

Love Poems. New York. V. 41

GOLL, YVAN

Jean Sans Terre / Landless John. San Francisco: 1944. V. 37; 38; 46

GOLLANCZ, ISRAEL

A Book of Homage to Shakespeare (to Commemorate the Three Hundredth Anniversary of Shakespeare's Death 1916). Oxford: 1916. V. 40

The Caedmon Manuscript of Anglo-Saxon Biblical Poetry. Junius XI in the Bodleian Library. 1927. V. 38

GOLLES, ADRIAN

Abrege de l'Oeconomie du Grand et Petit Monde, Divise en Trois Parties. Rouen: 1670. V. 37

GOLOVIN, IVAN

The Caucasus. London: 1854. V. 46

GOLOWNIN, VASILI

Memoirs of a Captivity in Japan, During the Years 1811, 1812 and 1813. London: 1824. V. 45

GOLOWNIN, VASILI M.

Description of Remarkable Shipwrecks that Transpired in Various Times. (with DEscription of Remarkable Shipwrecks Suffered in VArious Times by Russian Seamen . . . St. Petersburg: 1853. V. 45

GOLTZ, FRIEDRICH L.

Beitrage zur Lehre von den Funktionen des Nervencentren des Frosches. Berlin: 1869. V. 46

GOLTZ, HUBERT

Caesar Augustus sive Historiae Imperatorum Caesarumque ex Antiquis Numismatibus Restitutae. Bruges: 1574. V. 41

GOLTZ, HUBERTO

C. Julius Caesar Sive Historiae Imperatorum Caesarumque Romanorum ex Antiquis Numismatibus Restitutae. Bruges & Flanders: 1653. V. 46

GOLTZIUS, HUBERT

Les Images Presque de Tous les Empereurs Depuis C. Iulius Caesar Iusques a Charles V et Ferdinand son Frere . . . 1561. V. 41

GOLTZIUS, HUBERTUS

Fasti Magistratuum et Triumphorum Romanorum ab Urbe Condita ad Augusti Obitum ex Antiquis tam Numismatum Quam Marmorum Monumentis. Antwerp: 1644. V. 40

Opera Omnia. Romanae et Graecae Antiquitatis Monumenta e Priscis Numismatibus Eruta. Antwerp: 1644-45. V. 40

GOMARA, FRANCISCO LOPEZ DE 1510-1560?

La Terza Parte delle Historie dell'Indie . . . Venice: 1566. V. 42

GOMBAULD, JEAN OGIER DE

Endimion. London: 1639. V. 46

GOMBAULT, JEAN OGIER DE

L'Endymion. Paris: 1624. V. 38

GOMES DA SILVA, FRANCISCO

Memorias Offerecidas a Nacao Brasileira. London: 1831. V. 39

GOMES DE BRITO, BERNARDO

Historia Tragico-Martima em Que Se Escrevem Chronolgicamente os Naufragios Que Tiverao os Naos de Portugal, Depois Que Se Poz em Exercicio A Navegasao da India. Lisbon: 1735-36. V. 40; 43

GOMES LOUREIRO, ANTONIO JOSE

Defeza do Tenente Coronel Antonio Jose Gomes Loureiro, Sobre a Sua Conducta, Desde o Dia 11 de Outubro de 1821, Que Foi Servir em Seu Regimento por Ordem de S. A. R. ate 11 de Maio de 1823 . . . Lisbon: 1825. V. 39

GOMEZ CARNEIRO, DIOGO

Oracao Apodixica aos Scismaticos da Partia. Lisbon: 1641. V. 45

GOMEZ, CRISTOBAL

Elogia Societatis Jesu Sive Propugnaculum Pontificum Conciliorum, Cardinalium, Antistitum, nec non Imperatorum, Regum, Principum . . . Antwerp: 1677. V. 45

GOMEZ, FRANCISCO d. 1671

Santo Domingo de Soriano Milagroso, y Aplaudido. Valladolid: 1640. V. 40

GOMEZ, ISAAC

Selections of a Father for the Use of His Children. New York: 1820. V. 43

GOMEZ, MADELEINE ANGELIQUE POISSON DE

Persian Anecdotes. London: 1730. V. 38

GOMEZ PEREYRA, JUAN

Antoniana Margarita. Medina del Campo: 1554. V. 38

GOMME, G. L.

Chap-Books and Folk-Lore Tracts. London: 1885. V. 39

GOMME, GEORGE LAURENCE

Romano-British Remains. London: 1887. V. 45

GOMPERTZ, EPHRAIM

A Theoretic Discourse on the Nature and Property of Money, Canvassing, Particularly, the Notion Respecting Mr. Pensey on the Precious Metals . . . London: 1820. V. 38

GOMPERZ, THEODOR

Greek Thinkers. A History of Ancient Philsophy. London: 1906/12. V. 39

GOMRINGER, EUGEN

Josef Albers. His work as Contribution to Visual Articulation in the Twentieth Century. New York: 1967. V. 44

Josep Albers, His Work as Contributed to Visual Articulation in the Twentieth Century. New York: 1968. V. 44

GOMRINGER, EUGENE

Josef Albers: His Work as Contribution to Visual Articulation in the Twentieth Century. New York. V. 42; 43

GONCALEZ DAVILA, GIL

Entrada que Hizo en la Corte del Rey de las Espanas Don felipe Quatro el Serenissimo Don Carlos Principe de Gales. Madrid: 1623. V. 41

GONCALVES, JOAQUIM

Arte China Constante de Alphabeto e Grammatica Comprehendendo Modelos das Differentes Composicoens. Macaeo: 1829. V. 41

GONCOURT, EDMOND DE

La Fille Elisa. Paris: 1931. V. 43

GONEIM, M. ZAKARIA

Horus Sekhem-Khet: The Unfinished Step Pyramid at Saqqara. Le Caire: 1957. V. 42

GONGORA, LUIS DE

Obras. Brussels: 1659. V. 37

GONGORA Y ARGOTE, LUIS DE 1561-1627

Soledades . . . Comentadas por D. Garcia de Salzedo Coronel . . . Madrid: 1636. V. 40

GONNE, MAUD

Celtic Wonder-Tales. Dublin: 1910. V. 40

GONNER, E. C. K. 1805-1875

The Social Philosophy of Rodbertus. London: 1899. V. 43

GONZAGA, TOMAS ANTONIO

Marilia de Dirceu. Lisbon: 1792. V. 39

GONZALES, AMBROSE ELLIOT

With Aesop Along the Black Border. Columbia: 1924. V. 44

GONZALES DE MENDOZA, GIOVANNI

Del 'Historia Della China. Venice: 1590. V. 38

GONZALES, ORTEGA JESUS

The Presidency of Mexico . . . New York: 1866. V. 38

GONZALEZ DE AGUEROS, PEDRO

Descripcion Historial de la Provincia y Archipielago de Chiloe, en el Reyno de Chile . . . Madrid: 1791. V. 46

GONZALEZ DE HOLGUIN, DIEGO

Vocabulario de la Lengua General de Todo el Peru Llamada Lengua Qquichua O Del Inca. Ciudad de los Reyes: 1608. V. 37; 40

GONZALEZ DE MENDOZA, JUAN

Dell'Historia Della China . . . Rome: 1586. V. 38; 40

Dell'Historia della China, Descritta nell Lingua Spagnuola . . . Venice: 1586. V. 38; 40; 42

Dell'Historia della China. Venice: 1588. V. 44

Historia de las Cosas mas Notables, Ritos y Costumbres, del Gran Reyno Dela China, Sabidas Assi Por Los Libros de Los Mesmos Chinas . . . Rome: 1585. V. 41

Historia de las Cosas mas Notables, Ritos y Costumbres del Gran Reyno de la China . . . 1586. V. 45

Historia de las Cosas Mas Notables, Ritos y Costubres del Gra Reyno dela China . . . Con un Itinerario del Nuevo Mondo. Medina del Campo: 1595. V. 40

Itinerario y Compendio de los Cosas Notables que ay Desde Espana, Hasta el Reyno de la China . . . Lisbon: 1586. V. 38

GONZALEZ DE MONTES, REINALDO

Sanctae Inquisitionis Hispanicae Artes Aliquot Detectae . . . Heidelburg: 1567. V. 38

GONZALEZ GARCIA, A.

Ensayo, Para la Historia General de la Florida . . . Madrid: 1723. V. 38

GONZALEZ, JOSE MARIA ELIAS

Viva la Independencia . . . Chihuahua: 1841. V. 40

GONZALEZ, RAFAEL

Nota Estadistica Remitida Por El Gobierno Supremo del Estado de Coahuila y Tejas. Mexico: 1826. V. 38

GOOCH, BERNARD

The Strange World of Nature. London: 1950. V. 40

GOOCH, ELIZABETH SARAH

The Life of Mrs. Gooch. London: 1792. V. 45

GOOCH, F. P.

British Documents on the Origins of the War 1898-1914. London: 1927-38. V. 45

GOOCH, FANNY CHAMBERS

Face to Face with the Mexicans . . . New York: 1887. V. 37; 42

GOOCH, G. P.

British Documents on the Origins of the War 1898-1914. Volume XI, The Outbreak of War. London: 1926. V. 41

GOOCH, RICHARD

Nuts to Crack, or Quips, Quirks, Anecdotes, and Facetiae of Oxford and Cambridge Scholars. London: 1835. V. 39

GOOCH, RICHARD HEATHCOTE

An Old Man-of-War's Man's Yarn, Dedicated (By Kind Permission) to Charles Dickens. London: 1870. V. 40; 41

GOOCH, T. C.

Texans and Their State. Fort Worth: 1919. V. 43

Texans and Their State. Fort Worth: (1919). V. 37

THE GOOD Child; or, Sweet Home. London: 1830. V. 46

GOOD Company for Every Day of the Year. Boston: 1866. V. 43; 44

GOOD, EDWARD

The Book of Affinity. London: 1933. V. 38

GOOD, FRANK MASON

Holy Land Pictures. London: 1870. V. 38

GOOD Health: 1870. A Popular Annual on the Laws of Correct Living, As Developed by Medical Science, Etc. Boston: 1870. V. 42; 45

GOOD, J.

Measuring Made Easy, or the Description and Use of Coggeshall's Sliding Rule. London: 1760. V. 40

GOOD, J. M.

Pantalogia . . . London: 1813. V. 42

GOOD, JOHN

The Art of Shadows; or, Universal Dialling; with Tables Exactly Calculated for the Lat. of 51 deg. 30 min. London: 1721. V. 44

Measuring Made Easy; or, the Description and Use of Coggeshall's Sliding-Rule. London: 1736. V. 44

GOOD, JOHN BOOTH

A Vocabulary and Outlines of Grammar of the Nitlakapamuk, or Thompson Tongue . . . Victoria: 1980. V. 44

GOOD, JOHN MASON

Dissertation on the Best Means of Maintaining and Employing the Poor in Parish Work-Houses. London: 1798. V. 42

GOOD King Wenceslas. Montreal: 1934. V. 44

GOOD, MILT

Twelve Years in a Texas Prison by Milt Good . . . Amarillo: 1935. V. 43

GOOD Nature. A Poem. London: 1744. V. 41
GOOD-NATURE. A Poem. London: 1744. V. 42

THE GOOD Old Cause Explained, Revived & Asserted. N.P. London: 1659. V. 43

GOOD, P. P.

A Materia Medica Animalia. Cambridge: 1853. V. 39

THE GOOD Sayings of Good Men. London: 1848. V. 44

THE GOOD Shunammite. London: 1847. V. 38; 41

GOOD Things from Good Cooks. Santa Barbara: 1909. V. 38

GOODALE, S. L.

The Principles of Breeding: or, Glimpses at the Physiological Laws Involved in the Reproduction and Improvement of Dometic Animals. Boston: 1861. V. 38

GOODALL, CHARLES

The Royal College of Physicians of London Founded and Established by Law . . . London: 1684. V. 46

GOODALL, E. M.

The Raid of 96. Boston?: 1896. V. 39

GOODALL, ELIZABETH

Prehistoric Rock Art of the Federation of Rhodesia & Nyasaland. Rhodesia & Nyasaland,: 1959. V. 40

GOODCHILD, CECIL WRAY

California Milestones. Los Angeles: 1931. V. 46

GOODCHILD, LAWRENCE

Warkworth, a Romance of the Fourteenth Century. London: 1874. V. 41

GOODE, ALEXANDER

A Brief Account of the Mechitaristican Society Founded on the Island of St. Lazaro. Venice: 1835. V. 41

GOODE, D.

Cycads of Africa. Cape Town: 1989. V. 46

GOODE, G. B.

Oceanic Ichthyology, a Treatise on the Deep-Sea and Pelagic Fishes of the World . . . Washington: 1895, 1896. V. 38

GOODE, GEORGE BROWN

The Fisheries and Fishery Industries of the United States. Section I Natural History of Useful Aquatic Animals. Washington: 1884. V. 41

The Fisheries and Fishery Industries of the United States. Section V History and Methods of Fisheries. Washington: 1887. V. 41

A Memorial of George Brown Goode, together with a Selection of His Papers on Museums and on the History of Science in America. Washington: 1901. V. 40; 42; 45

Oceanic Ichthyology, a Treatise on the Deep-Sea and Pelagic Fishes of the World, Based Chiefly Upon the Collections Made by the Steamers Blake, Albatross & Fish Hawk in the Northwestern Atlantic . . . Washington: 1895. V. 39; 43

GOODE, W. A. M.

With Sampson through the War - Being an Account of the naval Operations of the North Atlantic Squadron During the Spanish American War of 1898 . . . London: 1899. V. 41

GOODE, WILLIAM H.

Outposts of Zion. Cincinnati: 1864. V. 39; 46

GOODE, WILLIAM HENRY

Outposts of Zion, with Limnings of Mission Life. Cincinnati: 1863. V. 37

GOODELL, WILLIAM

Come-Outerism. The Duty of Secession from a Corrupt Church. New York: 1845. V. 42

GOODELL, WILLIAM continued

The Old and the New; or the Changes of Thirty Years in the East, With Some Alusions to Oriental Customs as Elucidating Scripture. New York: 1853. V. 44

GOODEN, MONA

The Poet's Cat. London: 1946. V. 37; 38; 40

GOODEN, STEPHEN

An Iconography of the Engravings of Stephen Gooden. London: 1944. V. 41

GOODENOUGH, ERWIN R.

Jewish Symbols in the Greco-Roman Period. New York: 1953-68. V. 42

Jewish Symbols in the Greco-Roman Period: Symbolism in the Dura Synagogue. New York: 1964. V. 41

GOODENOUGH, JAMES G.

Journal of Commodore Goodenough, on the Australian Station, 1873-75 . . . London: 1876. V. 39; 41

GOODERS, J.

Birds of the World. London: 1969-71. V. 38

GOODFELLOW, ROBIN

The Fairy Annual. London: 1838. V. 45

GOODHALL, WALTER

The Sportsman's Pocket Companion . . . London: 1809? V. 42

GOODHART, BRISCOE

History of the Independent Loudoun Virginia Rangers, U.S. Vol. Cav. (Scouts), 1862-65. Wasahington: 1896. V. 37

GOODHART, WILLIAM

Generation. Garden City: 1966. V. 39; 45

GOODHUE, BERTRAM GROSVENER

Book Decorations. New York: 1931. V. 40; 41; 44

GOODHUE, BERTRAM GROSVENOR

A Book of Architectural and Decorative Drawings. New York: 1924. V. 44; 46

Book Decorations. 1931. V. 37; 39; 40; 45

Book Decorations. New York: 1931. V. 37

GOODHUGH, WILLIAM

The English Gentleman's Library Manual. London: 1827. V. 38; 42; 45

GOODISON, J. W.

Reynolds Stone - His Early Development as an Engraver on Wood. Cambridge: 1947. V. 42; 43; 44

GOODISON, NICHOLAS

Ormolu: the Work of Matthew Boulton. London: 1974. V. 39

GOODISSON, WILLIAM

A Historical and Topographical Essay Upon the Islands of Corfu, Leucadia, Cephalonia, Ithaca and Zante . . . London: 1822. V. 42

GOODKIND, HERBERT K.

Violin Iconography of Antonio Stradivari. Larchmont: 1972. V. 38

GOODLAKE, THOMAS

The Courser's Manual or Stud-Book. Liverpool: 1828. V. 37; 42; 45; 46

GOODLANDER, C. W.

Memoirs and Recollections of . . . of the Early Days of Fort Scott from April 29, 1858 to January 1, 1870 . . . Fort Scott: 1900. V. 39

GOODLOE, ALBERT

Some Rebel Relics from the Seat of War. Nashville: 1893. V. 38

GOODMAN, FREDERICK DUCANE

A Monograph of the Petrels (Order Tubinares). London: 1907-10. V. 39

GOODMAN, JOHN

The Penitent Pardoned . . . London: 1679. V. 43

A Winter-Evening Conference Between Neighbours. London: 1684. V. 44; 46

GOODMAN, KENNETH SAWYER

The Wonder Hat: and Other One Act Plays. New York: 1935. V. 45

GOODMAN, RICHARD

The Face in Genetic Disorders. St. Louis: 1970. V. 40

GOODNIGHT, CHARLES

The Loving Brand Book. Austin: 1965. V. 43

Pioneer Days in the Southwest from 1850 to 1879 . . . Guthrie: 1909. V. 44

GOODNOW, FRANK J.

Comparative Administrative Law, an Analysis of the Administrative Systems National and Local . . . New York: 1893. V. 43

GOODRICH, CHARLES A.

Lives of the Signers of the Declaration of Independence. Hartford: 1842. V. 38

Stories on the History of Connecticut, Designed for the Instruction and Amusement of Young Persons. Hartford: 1829. V. 43; 44

GOODRICH, FRANCES LOUISA

Mountain Homespun. New Haven: 1931. V. 45

GOODRICH, FRANK B.

The Court of Napoleon; or, Society Under the First Empire. Philadelphia: 1864. V. 42

GOODRICH, LLOYD

Edward Hopper. New York. V. 39; 42; 43

Edward Hopper. New York: 1971. V. 41; 46

Edward Hopper. New York: 1978. V. 45

Edward Hopper. New York: 1978. V. 45

Georgia O'Keefe. New York: 1970. V. 38

Max Weber. New York: 1949. V. 40; 41; 46

Max Weber. New York: 1949. V. 41

Raphael Soyer. New York. V. 43; 46

Raphael Soyer. New York, Washington,: 1967. V. 46

Raphael Soyer. New York: Washington &: 1967. V. 44

Reginald Marsh. New York. V. 39; 42; 46

Thomas Eakins His Life and Work. New York: 1933. V. 39; 42; 43; 45

GOODRICH, PHINEAS G.

History of Wayne County, Pennsylvania. Honesdale: 1880. V. 41; 42

GOODRICH, S. G.

Enterprise, Industry and Art of Man, as Displayed in Fishing, Hunting, Commerce, Navigation, Mining, Agriculture and Manufactures. Boston: 1845. V. 40

Peter Parley's Method of Telling about Geography to Children. Boston: 1830. V. 39

The Token. Boston: 1830. V. 43

The World As It Is, and As It Has Been; or a Comprehensive Geography and History Ancient and Modern. New York: 1855. V. 39

GOODRICH, SAMUEL GRISWOLD 1793-1860

A History of All Nations . . . New York: Auburn: 1856. V. 45

Parley's Visit to London, During the Coronation of Queen Victoria. London: 1838. V. 46

Peter Parley's Method of Telling About Geography to Children. Boston: 1830. V. 44

Peter Parley's Universal History on the Basis of Geography. New York: 1856. V. 42

Peter Parley's Universal History on the Basis of Geography. New York: 1859. V. 42

Recollections of a Lifetime, or Men and Things I Have Seen. New York: & Auburn: 1857. V. 46

Tales About Europe, Asia, Africa and America. London: 1837. V. 44

GOODRICK, ALFRED T. S.

Edward Randolph; Including His Letters and Official Papers from the New England, Middle and Southern Colonies in America, and West Indies. Boston: 1909. V. 39; 42

GOODRIDGE, CHARLES MEDYETT

Narrative of a Voyage to the South Seas, and Shipwreck of the Princess of Wales Cutter with an Account of a Two Years Residence on an Uninhabited Island by . . . Exeter: 1839. V. 40

Narrative of a Voyage to the South Seas, and the Shipwreck of the Princess of Wales Cutter, With an Account of Two Years Residence on an Uninhabited Island. Exeter: 1841. V. 40; 41; 42

GOODRIDGE, JOHN

The Phoenix, an Essay. London: 1781. V. 42; 45

GOODSIR, JOHN

The Anatomical Memoirs. Edinburgh: 1868. V. 38; 41

GOODSIR, ROBERT ANSTRUTHER

An Arctic Voyage to Baffin's Bay and Lancaster Sound, in Search of Friends with Sir John Franklin. London: 1850. V. 40; 42

GOODSPEED, CHARLES E.

Angling in America: Its Early History and Literature. Boston: 1939. V. 39

Yankee Bookseller, Being the Reminiscences of . . . Boston: 1937. V. 41

GOODSPEED, E. J.

History of the Great Fires in Chicago and the West. New York: 1871. V. 41

GOODSPEED, W. A.

Counties of Porter and Lake, Indiana: Historical and Biographical. Chicago: 1882. V. 39

GOODSPEED, WESTON ARTHUR

History of Cook County, Illinois . . . Chicago: 1909. V. 46

GOODWIN, C. C.

As I Remember Them. Salt Lake City: 1913. V. 42

The Wedge of Gold. Salt Lake City: 1893. V. 38

GOODWIN, CARDINAL 1880-

The Trans-Mississippi West (1803-1853). New York: 1922. V. 37; 39; 42; 43

GOODWIN, F. A.

A Brief Description of California from the Time of its First Occupation by the United States and Subsequent Growth . . . New York: 1855. V. 37

GOODWIN, FRANCIS

Cottage Architecture: Being a Supplement to the First Series of Goodwin's Rural Architecture; with Cottage Architecture: Being a supplement to the Second Series of Goodwin's Rural Architecture. London: 1835. V. 38

Domestic Architecture. London: 1833. V. 37; 39; 41

Domestic Architecture . . . London: 1833. V. 39

Domestic Architecture . . . London: 1850. V. 42

GOODWIN, GEORGE

Rising Castle, with other Poems. Lynn/London: 1798. V. 37

GOODWIN, GODFREY

A History of Ottoman Architecture. London: 1971. V. 46

GOODWIN, GORDON

British Mezzotinters, Thomas Watson and Elizabeth Judkins. London: 1904. V. 46

GOODWIN, GRENVILLE

The Social Organization of the Western Apache. Chicago: 1942. V. 45

GOODWIN, H. M.

The Suggestive Method. Chicago: 1850. V. 43; 44

GOODWIN, HARRY

Through the Wordsworth Country. London: 1887. V. 44

Through the Wordsworth Country. London: 1906. V. 46

GOODWIN, HARVEY

Memoir of Bishop Mackenzie. Cambridge: 1865. V. 40

GOODWIN, HENRY L.

Memorial of the Penny Post Company of California . . . Washington: 1856. V. 37

GOODWIN, JOHN 1594-1665

(Greek) or Dis-Satisfaction Satisfied..Proposed by F. G. London: 1654. V. 41

Imputatio Fidei. Or a Treatise on Justification . . . London: 1642. V. 42

GOODWIN, RUTHERFORD

The William Parks Paper Mill at Williamsburg. Lexington, VA: 1939. V. 37

GOODWIN-SMITH, R.

English Domestic Metalwork. Essex: 1937. V. 38

English Domestic Metalwork. Leigh-on-Sea: 1937. V. 38; 42

GOODWIN, THOMAS

The History of the Reign of henry the Fifth, King of England . . . London: 1704. V. 45

GOODWIN, WILLIAM

Essays on Sepulchres. London: 1809. V. 37

GOODWYN, ALBERT TAYLOR

Memorial Address by General A. T. Goodwyn, Commander First Brigade, United Confederate Veterans. Montgomery: 1926. V. 44

GOODY Two-Shoes. London. V. 43

GOODY Two Shoes: A Facsimile Reproduction of the Edition of 1766. London: 1882. V. 39

GOODYEAR, W. A.

The Coal Mines of the Western Coast of the United States. San Francisco: 1877. V. 37; 38; 39; 40; 41; 42; 43; 44

GOODYEAR, WILLIAM HENRY

Greek Refinements: Studies in Temepremental Architecture. London: 1912. V. 44

GOOKIN, DANIEL

An Historical Account of the Doings and Sufferings of the Christian Indians in New England in the years 1675, 1676, 1677 . . . Cambridge: 1836. V. 37

GOOKIN, F. W.

Daniel Gookin, 1612-1687. Assistant and Major General of the Massachusetts Bay Colony. His Life and Letters and Some Account of His Ancestry. Chicago: 1912. V. 38; 39; 43; 45

GOOLD, THOMAS

A Vindication of the Right Hon. Edmund Burke's Reflections on the Revolution in France in Answer to All His Opponents. Dublin: 1791. V. 43

GOOLD WALKER, G.

The Honourable Artillery Company 1537-1926. London: 1926. V. 41

THE GOOSE Dinner Party and Death of Mrs. Duck. Boston: 1850. V. 41

THE GOPHER Calendar for 1900. Minneapolis: 1899. V. 46

GORDIMER, NADINE

Face to Face. Johannesburg: 1949. V. 37; 38; 40; 42; 44; 46

A Guest of Honor. London: 1971. V. 43

Livingstone's Companion. London: 1972. V. 46

The Lying Days. London: 1953. V. 46

Six Feet of Country. New York: 1956. V. 44

The Soft Voice of the Serpent. New York: 1952. V. 44; 45; 46

GORDON, A. C.

Befo' de War. New York: 1888. V. 44

GORDON, A. R.

Report of the Hudson's Bay Expedition of 1886. Ottawa: 1887. V. 42; 43

GORDON, ADAM LINDSAY

Poems. London: 1898. V. 40

GORDON-ALEXANDER, W.

Recollections of a Highland Subaltern During the Campaigns of the 93rd Highlanders in India, Under Colin Campbell, Lord Clyde in 1857, 1858 and 1859. London: 1898. V. 39; 42; 46

GORDON, ALVIN J.

Of Vines and Missions. Flagstaff: 1971. V. 44

GORDON, ANTOINETTE K.

The Iconography of Tibetan Lamaism. Rutland: 1959. V. 38

GORDON, ARTHUR H.

Letters and Notes Written During the Disturbances in Highlands of Viti Levu, Fiji 1876. Edinburgh: 1879. V. 41; 45

GORDON, BENJAMIN

Medicine Throughout Antiquity. Philadelphia: 1949. V. 45

Medieval and Renaissance Medicine. New York: 1959. V. 37; 38

GORDON, C.

The Women on the Porch. 1944. V. 37

GORDON, CAROLINE

Aleck Maur, Sportsman. New York: 1934. V. 39; 41; 44; 46

The Collected Stories of Caroline Gordon. New York: 1981. V. 46

The Forest of the South. New York: 1945. V. 39; 41; 46

The Garden of Adonis. New York: 1937. V. 39; 41; 43; 45; 46

The Glory of Hera. Garden City: 1972. V. 44

Green Centuries. New York: 1941. V. 39; 44

How to Read a Novel. New York: 1957. V. 39; 44; 45

How to Read a Novel. New York: 1957. V. 45

The Malefactors. New York: 1956. V. 45; 46

None Shall Look Back. New York: 1937. V. 39

Old Red and Other Stories. New York: 1963. V. 42

Penhally. New York: 1931. V. 39; 44; 45; 46

The Strange Children. London: 1951. V. 42

The Strange Children. New York: 1951. V. 38; 39; 40; 42

The Strange Children. New York: 1951. V. 39

The Women of the Porch. New York: 1937. V. 39

The Women on the Porch. New York: 1944. V. 39; 40; 43; 45

GORDON, CHARLES

Experiences of an Army Surgeon in India. London: 1872. V. 41

GORDON, CHARLES GEORGE

Colonel Gordon in Central Africa, 1874-1879 . . . London: 1881. V. 38

GORDON-CUMMING, CONSTANCE FREDERICA 1837-1924

Fire Fountains. The Kingdom of Hawaii, its Volcanoes, and the History of Its Missions. Edinburgh & London: 1883. V. 45

The Inventor of the Numeral-Type for China By the Use of Which Illiterate Chinese Both Blind and Sighted Can Very Quickly be Taught to Read and Write Fluently. London: 1899. V. 46

Two Happy Years in Ceylon. New York: 1892. V. 46

GORDON-CUMMING, CONSTANCE FREDERICA 1837-1924

In the Himalayas and On the Indian Plains. London: 1884. V. 45

GORDON-CUMMING, ROUALEYN GEORGE 1820-1866

Five Years of a Hunter's Life in the Far Interior of South Africa. New York: 1850. V. 46

GORDON, CYRUS H.

Ugaritic Handbook. Roma: 1947. V. 37; 40

GORDON, DANIEL M.

Mountain and Prairie: a Journey from Victoria to Winnipeg, Via Peace River Pass. Montreal: 1880. V. 37; 38; 42

GORDON, DONALD E.

Ernst Ludwig Kirchner. Cambridge: 1968. V. 39; 45; 46

GORDON, ELIZABETH

Bird Children. The Little Playmates of Flower Children. Joliet: 1912. V. 43

Flower Children. The Little Cousins of the Field and Garden. Chicago: 1910. V. 43

The Tale of Johnny Mouse. 1920. V. 46

The Turned-Into's. 1920. V. 46

GORDON, G. B.

Examples of Maya Pottery in the Museum and Other Collections. Philadelphia: 1925, 1928. V. 39

THE GORDON Garland. New York: 1965. V. 39

GORDON, GEORGE

An Introduction to Geography, Astronomy and Dialling. London: 1726. V. 41; 42

An Introduction to Geography, Astronomy and Dialling, Containing the Most Useful Elements of Said Sciences . . . London: 1729. V. 46

The Proceedings at large on the Trial of George Gordon, Esquire, Commonly Called Lord George Gordon, for High Treason, in the Court of the King's Bench, Westminster . . . on Monday and Tuesday, February the 5th and 6th, 1781. London: 1781. V. 39

GORDON, GEORGE BYRON

Examples of Maya Pottery in the Museum and Other Collections. Philadelphia: 1925-1943. V. 42

GORDON, GEORGE WILLIAM

Lecture on Lotteries. Boston: 1833. V. 41

GORDON, J. W.

Military Transactions of the British Empire; from the Commencement of the Year 1803, to the Termination of the year 1807. London: 1808. V. 38

GORDON, JAMES

History of the Rebellion in Ireland in the Year 1798 . . . London: 1803. V. 37; 43

GORDON, JAMES DOUGLAS

The Last Martyrs of Eromanga. Halifax: 1863. V. 39

GORDON, JOHN

Memoirs of the Life of John Gordon of Glencat, in the County of Aberdeen in Scotland, who was Thirteen Years in the Scots College in Paris. London: 1734. V. 43

Observations on the Structure of the Brain . . . Edinburgh: 1817. V. 44; 45

Poems. Edinburgh: 1807. V. 42

GORDON, JOHN B.

Reminiscences of the Civil War. New York: 1903. V. 44; 45

GORDON, JULIEN

Painted Tapesty and Its Application to Interior Decoration. London: 1879. V. 38

GORDON, LAURA DE FORCE

The Great Geysers of California and How to Reach Them. San Francisco: 1877. V. 37; 41

GORDON, MARTHA HUNTLY

Christopher North: a Memoir of John Wilson, compiled from family papers and other sources by his daughter Mrs. Gordon. Edinburgh: 1862. V. 37

GORDON, PAT

Geography Anatomiz'd; or, The Geographical Grammar. London: 1725. V. 39

GORDON, PATRICK

By the Honorable Patrick Gordon, Esq. Lieut. Governour of the Province of Pennsilvania . . . Philadelphia: 1729. V. 40; 44

Geography Anatomiz'd; or, the Geographical Grammar, Being a Short and Exact Analysis of the Whole Body of Modern Geography . . . London: 1740. V. 45

The History of the War in America, Between Great Britain and Her Colonies. Dublin: 1779-85. V. 44

GORDON, PRYSE LOCKHART

Belgium and Holland: with A Sketch of the Revolution in the Year 1830. London: 1834. V. 39; 46

GORDON, ROBERT

A Catalogue of the Singular and Curious Library . . . London: 1816. V. 45

A Genealogical History of the Earldom of Sutherland (the Gordon Family), From Its Origin to the Year 1630 with a Continuation to the Year 1651. Edinburgh: 1813. V. 38

GORDON, RUTH

The Leading Lady. New York: 1949. V. 45

Over Twenty-One. New York: 1944. V. 45

GORDON, S.

Recollections of Old Miletown. Miles City: 1918. V. 42; 43

GORDON, SETON

Amid Snowy Wastes. London: 1922. V. 40

Amid Snowy Wastes. New York, Toronto, &: 1922. V. 40; 42

GORDON, TAYLOR

Born to Be. New York: 1929. V. 39

GORDON, THOMAS

An Appeal to the Unprejudiced, Concerning the Present Discontents Occasioned by the Late Convention with Spain. London: 1739. V. 41; 45; 46

The Conspirators; or, the Case of Catiline . . . London: 1721. V. 45

General Remarks on the British Fisheries. London: 1784. V. 43

History of the Greek Revolution, and of the Wars and Campaigns Arising from the Struggles of the Greek Patriots in Emancipating Their Country from the Turkish Yoke. Edinburgh: 1844. V. 37

The Humourist: Being Essays on Several Subjects viz. News Writers, Enthusiasms . . . London: 1724/25. V. 42

The Humourist: Being Essays on Several Subjects. London: 1724/25. V. 42; 44

The Independent Whig. Philadelphia: 1724. V. 38

A Learned Dissertation upon Old Women, male and female, spiritual and temporal, in all ages; whether in church, state, or Exchange-Alley . . . To which is added, an essay upon the present union of the Whig-chiefs. London: 1720. V. 37

Principals of Naval Architecture. London: 1784. V. 41

GORDON, THOMAS EDWARD 1832-1914

A Varied Life, a Record of Military and Civil Service of Sport and of Travel in India, Central Asia and Persia, 1849-1902. London: 1906. V. 46

GORDON, THOMAS F.

A Gazetteer of the State of Pennsylvania. Philadelphia: 1832. V. 37

GORDON, W. J.

Bands of the British Army. London: 1921. V. 42

GORDON, WILLIAM

The History of the Rise, Progress and Establishment of the Independence of the United States of America . . . London: 1788. V. 41; 43

The History of the Rise, Progress and Establishment of the Independence of the United States of America. New York: 1794. V. 42

The History of the Rise, Progress, and Establishment of the Independence of the United States of America: Including an Account of the late war; and of the Thirteen Colonies, from their Origin to that period. New York: 1789. V. 37; 39

A New Geographical Grammar, and Complete Gazetteer. Edinburgh: 1789. V. 42

The Separation of the Jewish Tribes after the Death of Solomon, Accounted for, and Applied to the present day in a Sermon . . . July the 4th, 1777 being the Anniversary of the Declaration of Independency. Boston: 1777. V. 37; 39

A Sermon Preached Before the Honorable House of Representatives on the Day Intended for the Choice of Counsellors, Agreeable to the Advice of the Continental Congress. Watertown: 1775. V. 37; 38; 40; 43; 45

GORDON, WILLIAM ALEXANDER

The Killing of Adam Caperton by Indians, At 'Estill's Defeat' Near Mt. Sterling, Kentucky, 22 March 1782. Louisville: 1918. V. 44

GORE-BOOTH, EVA

The Death of Fionavar, from the Triumph of Maeve, by . . . London: 1916. V. 43

GORE, CATHERINE

Cecil, a Peer. London: 1841. V. 38

The Snow Storm, A Christmas Story. New Year's Day, A Winter's Tale. The Inundation; or Pardon and Peace. A Christmas Story. London: (1845-46-47). V. 37

Stokeshill Place. London: 1837. V. 38

GORE, CATHERINE GRACE FRANCES

The Diamond and the Pearl. London: 1849. V. 40

The Inundation: or, Pardon and Peace. A Christmas Story. Boston: 1840. V. 46

The Inundation; or, Peace and Pardon . . . London: 1847. V. 42

Memoirs of a Peeress, Or the Days of Fox. Edited by Lady Charlotte Bury. London: 1837. V. 37

New Year's Day, a Winter's Tale. London: 1846. V. 42

GORE, CATHERINE GRACE FRANCES MOODY 1800-1861

Hungarian Tales. London: 1829. V. 43; 45

GORE, CATHERINE MOODY 1799-1861

Agathonia. London: 1844. V. 39; 44; 46

Mrs. Armytage; or, Female Domination. London: 1836. V. 44

Mothers and Daughters. London: 1831. V. 44

The Tuileries. London: 1831. V. 44

GORE, CHRISTOPHER

Manlius: With Notes and References. Boston: 1794. V. 38; 45

GORE, THOMAS

Nomenclator Geographicus Latino-Anglicus & Anglico-Latinus . . . Oxoniae: 1667. V. 44

GORER, EDGAR

Chinese Porcelain and Hard Stones. London: 1911. V. 37; 39; 41; 42; 45

GORES, JOE

A Time of Predators. New York: 1969. V. 43

GOREY, E

The Vinegar Works Being the Insect God, the Gashlycrumb Tinies and the West Wing. 1963. V. 43

GOREY, EDWARD

Amphigorey Also. New York: 1983. V. 41

The Black Doll. New York: 1973. V. 39

The Bug Book. New York: (1959). V. 37

Category. (1973). V. 37

The Doubtful Guest. New York: 1957. V. 40

A Dwindling Party. New York: 1982. V. 41

F.M.R.A. New York: 1980. V. 41

The Gilded Bat. New York: 1966. V. 46

The Glorious Nosebleed. Fifth Alphabet. New York: 1974. V. 37; 46

Irene, Good-Night, by D. R. Bensen. New York: 1982. V. 37

The Listing Attic. Boston & New York: 1954. V. 41

Listing Attic. New York: 1954. V. 38; 39; 42; 45; 46

The Listing Attic. New York: & Boston: 1954. V. 39

The Lising Attic. New York: Boston: 1954. V. 38

The Listing Attic. New York/Boston: (1954). V. 37

The Unstrung Harp. Boston & New York: 1953. V. 39; 42

The Unstrung Harp; or, Mr. Earbrass Writes a Novel. New York: 1953. V. 41; 42; 45

The Unstrung Harp. Boston/New York: (1953). V. 37

The Unstrung Harp. New York/Boston: 1953. V. 37

Les Urnes Utiles. Cambridge: 1980. V. 41

The Vinegar Works. New York: 1963. V. 41; 44

The Vinegar Works. Zurich: 1972. V. 41

GORGES, FERDINANDO

America Painted to the Life. London: 1659. V. 40

GORHAM CO.

Famous Small Bronzes: a Representative Exhibit Selected from the Works of Noted Contemporary Sculptors. New York: 1928. V. 46

GORHAM, GEORGE CORNELIUS

The History and Antiquities of Eynesbury and St. Neot's, in Huntingdonshire . . . London: 1820/24. V. 42; 43

GORHAM, JOHN

The Rotation of Coloured Discs Applied to Facilitate the Study of the Laws of Harmonious Colouring by the Multiplication of Images of Objects into Kaleidoscopic Combinations. London: 1861. V. 40

GORI, ANTONIO FRANCESCO

Dactyliotheca Smithiana. Venice: 1767. V. 38; 44

GORING, HENRY

A Letter from H--- G----g, Esq: One of the Gentlemen of the Bed-Chamber to the Young Chevalier, and the Only Person of His Own Retinue that Attended from Avignon, in His Late Journey Through Germany, and Elsewhere. London: 1750. V. 39; 42

The Young Chevalier; or, A Genuine Narrative of All that Befell that Unofortunate Adventurer . . . London: 1746. V. 42

The Young Chevalier: or, A Geniune Narrative of all that Befell that Unfortunate Adventurer . . . London;: (c. 1746). V. 37

GORKI, MAXIM

Reminiscences of Leonid Andreyev. New York: 1928. V. 39; 40

GORKY, MAXIM

Reminiscnces of Tolstoy, Chekhov and Andreev. London: 1934. V. 45

GORMAN, JOHN C.

Lee's Last Campaign, with an Accurate History of Stonewall Jackson's Last Wound. Raleigh: 1866. V. 42; 45

GORMAN, R. C.

The Posters. Flagstaff: 1980. V. 39

GORMAN, T. M.

Christian Psychology: The Soul and the Body in Their Correlation and Contrast. London: 1875. V. 39

GOROSPE YRALA, FR. DIEGO DE

Oracion Funebre, que Predi. V. 45

GOROSTIZA, M. E.

Correspondencia Que ha Mediado Entre la Legacion Extraordinario de Mexico y el Departamento de Estado de Los Estado-Unidos, Sobre el Paso del Sabina por las Tropas Que Mandaba el General Gaines. Mexico: 1837. V. 42

Gorostiz Pamphlet . . . A Copy and Translation. Washington: 1838. V. 38; 45

GORRINGE, HENRY H.

Egyptian Obelisks. New York: 1882. V. 37; 39; 40; 42; 45

GORTON, SAMUEL

Simplicities Defense Against Seven-Headed Policy, or Innocency Vindicated, Being Unjustly Accused and Sorely Censured, by the Seven Headed Church Government in New England. London: 1646. V. 40; 43; 44

Simplicities Defence Against Seven Headed Policy, or Innocency Vindicated . . . London: 1846. V. 42

GOSCHEN, G. J. 1831-1907.

The Theory of the Foreign Exchanges. London: 1864. V. 37

GOSCHEN, GEORG JOACHIM 1752-1828

The Life and Times of Georg Joachim Goschen. London: 1903. V. 38; 40

GOSDEN, THOMAS

An Essay on Hunting. London: 1733. V. 46

Impressions of a Series of Animals, Birds &c. London: 1821. V. 39; 40; 43

GOSELINI, GIULIANO

Vita del Prencipe Don Fernando Gozaga. Milan: 1574, 1575. V. 40

GOSLING, JANE

Moral Essays and Reflections. Sheffield: 1789. V. 39; 41; 42; 44; 46

GOSLING, W. G.

Labrador: Its Discovery, Exploration and Development. Toronto: 1910. V. 44

GOSNELL, HARPUR A.

Before the Mast in the Clippers. New York: 1937. V. 39; 43; 45

GOSNELL, R.

A History of British Columbia. N.P.: 1906. V. 43

THE GOSPEL According to Thomas. New York: 1986. V. 40

GOSS, ELBRIDGE, H.

The Life of Colonel Paul Revere . . . Boston: 1891. V. 41

GOSS, F.

Memories of a Stag Harbourer. London: 1931. V. 37

GOSS, PROTHESIA S.

The Philanthropist; or Selfishness and Benevolence Illustrated . . . London: 1836. V. 44

GOSSE, EDMUND 1849-1928

The Allies Fairy Book. London: 1916. V. 39

The Allies Fairy Book. With an Introduction by Edmund Gosse and illustrations by Arthur Rackham. London: (1916). V. 37

The Augustan Books of Modern Poetry. London: 1926? V. 41

British Portrait Painters and Engravers of the Eighteenth Century. Paris: 1906. V. 46

Father and Son. London: 1907. V. 40; 42; 46

Father and Son. London: 1913. V. 38

Firdansi in Exile and Other Poems. London: 1886. V. 41

Firdausi in Exile. London: 1876. V. 40; 41

French Profiles. London: 1905. V. 37

A History of Eighteenth Century Literature. London: 1889. V. 43

In Russet and Silver. Chicago: 1894. V. 38

Letters to the Press. London: 1912. V. 46

Memoir of Thomas Lodge. London: 1882. V. 46

On Viol and Flute - Selected Poems. New York: 1883. V. 44

The Secret of Narcisse. London: 1892. V. 44; 46

Seventeenth Century Studies. New York: 1897. V. 40

Swinburne. Personal Recollections. London: 1909. V. 46

GOSSE, EDMUND WILLIAM

A Critical Essay on the Life and Works of George Tinworth. London: 1883. V. 42

GOSSE, IRENE

A Florilege. Chelsea: 1931. V. 37

A Florilege Chosen from the Old Herbals. London: 1981. V. 44

GOSSE, PHILIP

My Pirate Library. London: 1926. V. 38; 39; 40; 43

GOSSE, PHILIP HENRY

Actinologia Britannica. London: 1860. V. 37; 38

The Birds of Jamaica. London: 1847. V. 37; 38

The Birds of Jamaica. Illustrations of the Birds of Jamaica. London: 1847-49. V. 37

The Canadian Naturalist. London: 1840. V. 37; 38; 40; 44

Letters from Alabma, (U.S.) Chiefly Relating to Natural History. London: 1855. V. 38; 42

A Manual of Marine Zoology for the British Isles. London: 1855-56. V. 39; 40

A Naturalist's Rambles on the Devonshire Coast. London: 1853. V. 42; 43

A Naturalist's Sojourn in Jamaica. London: 1851. V. 37

Popular British Ornithology. London: 1849. V. 39

Tenby: a Sea Side Holiday. London: 1856. V. 42; 43; 44

A Year at the Shore. London: 1865. V. 41

GOSSI, GIOVANNI GIACOPO

Effigies, Nomina et Cognomina S.D.N. Alexandri Papae VII et Card, Nunc Viventium. Rome: 1674. V. 45

GOSTLING, WILLIAM

A Walk in and About the City of Canterbury, with Many Observations Not to Be Found in Any Description hitherto Pubished. Canterbury: 1777. V. 38

A Walk In and About the City of Canterbury, with Many Observations Not to be Found in Any Description Hitherto Published. London: 1777. V. 41; 45

GOTCH, FRANCIS

Croonian Lecture. On the Mammalian Nervous System, Its Functions and Their Localisation Determined by an Electrical Method. London. V. 42

GOTCH, J. ALFRED

Architecture of the Renaissance in England. Batsford: 1891. V. 39

Architecture of the Renaissance in England . . . London: 1891-94. V. 38

Architecture of the Renaissance in England. London: 1894. V. 40; 41; 46

GOTCH, PHYLLIS

The Romance of a Boo-Bird Chick. London: 1903. V. 44

GOTHEIN, M. L.

A History of Garden Art. New York: 1979. V. 37

GOTHEIN, MARIE LOUISE

A History of Garden Art. London: 1928. V. 38; 41; 43; 45

GOTHEIN, MARIE LUISE

A History of Garden Art. London & Toronto: 1928. V. 43

A History of Garden Art. New York: 1979. V. 37; 38

GOTHER, JOHN d. 1704

A Practical Catechism; In Fifty Two Lessons . . . London: 1701. V. 39

The Spiritual Works. Newcastle: 1780. V. 39

GOTO, SEIKICHIRO

Japanese Hand-Made Paper. V. 43; 45

Japanese Hand-Made Ppaer. Tokyo: 1958/60. V. 45

Japanese Hand-made Paper. Japanese Paper and Papermaking. Volume I: Northeastern Japan. Volume II: Western Japan. Tokyo: 1958 & 60. V. 43

GOTTFREDSON, PETER

History of Indian Depredations in Utah. Salt Lake City: 1919. V. 40; 42

GOTTFRIED, JOHAN LODEWYK

De Aanmerkenswaardigste en Alomberoemde Zeeen Landreizen der Portugeezen, Spanjaarden, Engelsen, en Allerhande Natien. Leyden: 1727. V. 45

GOTTHEIL, WILLIAM

Illustrated Skin Diseases. New York: 1902. V. 42

GOTTIGNIES, GILLES FRANCOIS

Logistica Universalis, . . . Amplectens Arithmeticae, Geometriae . . . Naples: 1687. V. 45

GOTTSCHALK, LAURA RIDING

The Close Chaplet. New York: (1926). V. 37

GOTTSCHALK, PAUL

The Earliest Diplomataic Documents on America. The Papal Bulls of 1493 and the Treaty of Tordesillas. Berlin: 1927. V. 37; 38; 40; 42

GOUAN, ANTOINE

Hortus Regius Monspeliensis. Lyons: 1762. V. 39

GOUBAUD, MME.

Pillow Lace Patterns, and Instructions in Honiton Lace Making. London: 1871. V. 38

GOUCH, HUBERT

The Fifth Army. London: 1931. V. 44

GOUDELIN, PIERRE 1579-1649

Las Obras. Amsterdam: 1700. V. 38

Las Obros, Augmentados Noubelomen de Forco Pessos, Ambe le Dictiounari sur la Lengo Moundino. Toulouse: 1713. V. 37

Le Ramelet Moundi de Tres Flouretos. Toulouse: 1638. V. 43

GOUDY, FREDERIC W.

The Alphabet and Elements of Lettering. Berkeley & Los Angeles: 1942. V. 39

The Capitals from the Trajan Column at Rome. New York: 1936. V. 40

Typologia: Studies in Type Design and Type Making. Berkeley & Los Angeles: 1940. V. 45

GOUDY, FREDERIC WILLIAM 1865-1947

The Alphabet Interpretative Designs Drawn and Arranged with Explanatory Text and Illustrations. New York: 1918. V. 41; 46

The Alphabet. New York: 1922. V. 46

Ands and Ampersands from the First Century B.C. to the Twentieth A.D. New York: 1936. V. 43

Design and Beauty in Printing. New York: 1934. V. 38

Half Century of Type Design and Typography, 1895-1945. New York: 1945. V. 42

A Half Century of Type Design. New York: 1946. V. 41

Typologia. Studies in Type Design & Type Making, with Comments on the Invention of Typography . . . Berkeley: 1940. V. 38; 44

GOUDY, FREDERICK W.

'A Speciman of Types Designed and Engraved at the Village Press Since 1932'. Marlborough, NY: 1938. V. 37

The Story of the Village Type, by its designer. New York: 1933. V. 37

GOUDY, FREDERICK WILLIAM 1865-1947

The Alphabet and Elements of Lettering. Berkeley: 1942. V. 38

GOUDY Gaudeamus: in Celebration of the Dinner Given Frederic W. Goudy on His 74th Birthday, March Eighth, 1939. V.P.: 1939. V. 45

GOUDY Gaudeamus. In Celebration of the Dinner Given Frederic W. Goudy on His 74th Brithday. N.P.: 1939. V. 45

GOUDY Greek. Easthampton: 1976. V. 38

GOUGE DE CESSIERRES, FRANCOIS ETIENNE

Les Jardins d'Ornamens, ou les Georgiques Francaises, Nouveau Poeme en Quatre Chants. Paris: 1758. V. 38

GOUGE, WILLIAM M. 1796-1863

The Curse of Paper-Money and Banking. London: 1833. V. 38; 39

The Fiscal History of Texas. Philadelphia: 1852. V. 37; 38; 39; 42

A Short History of Paper Money and Banking in the United States . . . Philadelphia: 1833. V. 43

GOUGER, ROBERT

A Letter from Sydney, the Principal Town of Australasia. London: 1829. V. 42

South Australia in 1837, in a Series of Letters . . . London: 1838. V. 46

GOUGH, HENRY

Scotland in 1298. London: 1888. V. 38

GOUGH, HUBERT

The Fifth Army. London: 1931. V. 45; 46

GOUGH, JOHN

The Stange Discovery. London: 1640. V. 38; 40

GOUGH, JOHN B.

Autobiography and Personal Recollections of John B. Gough. Chicago: 1870. V. 38

GOUGH, RICHARD 1735-1809

Anecdotes of British Topography. London: 1768. V. 39

A Catalogue of the Books, Relating to British Topography and Saxon and Northern Literature . . . Oxford: 1814. V. 46

The History and Antiquities of Plehy in the County of Essex. London: 1803. V. 38

Human Nature Displayed in the History of Myddle. London: 1834. V. 37

GOUGH, WILLIAM

Londinium Triumphans. London: 1682. V. 39; 44

GOUGH, WILLIAM M. 1796-1863

The Curse of Paper-Money and Banking; or, a short History of Banking in the United States of America . . . with an introduction by William Cobbett. London: 1833. V. 37

A Short History of Paper Money and Banking in the United States, Including an Account of Provincial and Continental paper money . . . Philadelphia: 1833. V. 37

GOULARD, THOMAS

A Treatise on the Effects and Various Preparations of Lead . . . London: 1769. V. 41; 45

A Treatise on the Effects and Various Preparations of Lead . . . London: 1769. V. 41

A Treatise on the Effects and Various Preparations of Lead, Particularly of the Extract of Saturn for Different Chirurgical Disorders. London: 1773. V. 40; 43; 44

A Treatise on the Effects and Various Preparations of Lead, Particualry of the Extract of Saturn . . . Dublin: 1777. V. 44

GOULBURN, EDWARD

The Blueviad, a Satyrical Poem. London: 1805. V. 45

GOULBURN, EDWARD MEYRICK

The Ancient Sculptures in the Roof on Norwich Cathedral. London: & Norwich: 1876. V. 44

GOULD, A. C.

Modern American Pistols and Revolvers. Boston: 1894. V. 45

Modern American Rifles. Boston: 1892. V. 45

GOULD & CURRY SILVER MINING COMPANY

Views of the Works. San Francisco: 1863. V. 46

GOULD, AUGUSTUS

A Report on the Invertebrata of Massachusetts Comprising the Mollusca, Crustacea, Annelida and Radiata. Cambridge: 1841. V. 39; 40

GOULD, BANKS & CO.

Catalogue of Ancient and Modern Law Books, for Sale by Gould, Banks & Co., Law Booksellers, Publishers and Importers . . . New York: 1842. V. 39

GOULD, CHARLES

Travels through Oklahoma. Oklahoma Ckity: 1928. V. 42

GOULD, CHARLES L.

A Nation United. (Baltimore): 1940). V. 37

GOULD, CHESTER

Dick Tracy: the Capture of Boris Arson. Chicago: 1935. V. 45

GOULD, E. W.

Fifty Years on the Mississippi; or, Gould's History of River Navigation. St. Louis: 1889. V. 39; 42; 43; 44

GOULD, EDWARD SHERMAN

The Sleep-Rider; or, the Old Boy in the Omnibus. New York: 1843. V. 40

GOULD, F. CARRUTHERS

Froissart's Modern Chronicles 1903-6. London: 1908. V. 38

Political Caricatures 1904. London: 1904. V. 46

The Struwwelpter Alphabet. London: 1900. V. 37; 45

GOULD, FLORENCE J.

Paintings and Drawings from the Estate of Florence J. Gould. New York: 1985. V. 41

GOULD, GEORGE

Anomalies and Curiosities of Medicine. New York: 1937. V. 41; 43

GOULD, GEORGE M.

Anomalies and Curiosities of Medicine. Philadelphia: 1897. V. 41

Anomalies and Curiosities of Medicine. Philadelphia & London: 1901. V. 41

Concerning Lafcadio Hearn . . . Philadelphia: 1908. V. 43; 46

GOULD, GEORGE MILBRY 1847-1922

An Illustrated Dictionary of Medicine, Biology and Allied Sciences . . . Philadelphia: 1904. V. 45

GOULD, HANNAH

Gathered Leaves, or Miscellaneous Papers. Boston: 1846. V. 41; 46

GOULD, HANNAH FLAGG

Poems. Boston: 1832. V. 44

GOULD, JAY

History of Delaware County, and Border Wars of New York, Containing a Sketch of the Early Settlements in the County, and A History of the Late Anti-Rent Difficulties in Delaware . . . etc. By Jay Gould. Roxbury: 1856. V. 37; 45

GOULD, JOHN 1804-1881

The Birds of Great Britain. London: 1862-73. V. 39; 42

Birds of Australia. London: 1967. V. 41

Birds of South America. London: 1972. V. 45

The Birds of Great Britain. London: 1980. V. 46

The Birds of Great Britain. London: 1980. V. 44; 46

Birds of Australia. Volume 1. Melbourne: 1972. V. 39

Birds of Australia. Volume 2. Melbourne: 1972. V. 39

Birds of Australia. Volume 4. Melbourne: 1974. V. 39

Birds of Europe. Birds of Australia. Birds of Asia. Birds of New Guinea. Birds of South America. London: 1966-72. V. 37

A Century of Birds from the Himalaya Mountains. London: 1831-32. V. 42

Handbook to the Birds of Australia. London: 1865. V. 37; 39

An Introduction to the Birds of Australia. London: 1848. V. 43

An Introduction to the Birds of Great Britain. London: 1873. V. 43

John Gould's Birds of Paradise. Volume I: Birds of New Guinea. London: 1988. V. 40; 41; 42

The Mammals of Australia. London: 1845-63. V. 37

Mr. Gould's Tropical Birds Comprising Twenty Four Plates Selected from John Gould's Folios . . . London: 1955. V. 39

A Monograph of the Odontophorinae or Partridges of America. London: 1850. V. 37; 38; 40; 42

Monograph of the Toucans. London: 1854. V. 40

Monograph of the Toucans. London: 1989. V. 41

Monograph of the Pittidae. London: 1880-81. V. 38

A Monograph of the Trogonidae or Family of Trogons. London: 1835-38. V. 38

A Monograph of the Trogonidae, or Family of Trogons. London: 1858-1875. V. 37; 42

Synopsis of the Birds of Australia and the Adjacent Islands. London: 1837. V. 39

GOULD, JOSEPH

The Story of the Forty-Eighth. The Record of the Campaigns of the 48th Regiment, Pennsylvania Veteran Volunteer Infantry. Philadelphia: 1908. V. 42

GOULD, M. T. C.

Report on the Trial of Friends, in the City of Philadelphia, June, 1828, Before the Honourable Edward King, Esq. Philadelphia: 1828. V. 45

GOULD, MARCUS T. C.

Report on the Trial of Friends, at Steubenville, Ohio, from the 15th to the 26th of October, 1828. Philadelphia: 1829. V. 44

GOULD, NATHANIEL DUREN

Old Hundred Collection of Sacred Music . . . Boston: 1824. V. 40

GOULD, R. F.

The History of Freemasonry, Its Antiquities, Symbols, Constitutions, Customs, Etc. London: 1898. V. 45

GOULD, ROBERT

Love Given Over; or, a Satyr Against the Pride, Lust and Inconstancy &c of Woman. London: 1690. V. 45

Poems, Chiefly Consisting of Satyrs and Satyrical Epistles. London: 1689. V. 40; 43

GOULD, ROBERT FREKE

The History of Freemasonry. London: 1882. V. 40; 46

The History of Freemasonry. London: 1882-87. V. 43

The History of Freemasonry. London: 1886. V. 38

The History of Freemasonry. Edinburgh: 1887. V. 37; 38

The History of Freemasonry: Its Antiquities, Symbols, Constitutions, Customs, etc. Edinburgh: 1890. V. 46

The History of Freemasonry. Its Antiquities, Symbols, Constitutions, Customes, etc. New York: 1887. V. 37

GOULD, THOMAS R.

The Tragedian; an Essay on the Histrionic Genius of Junius Brutus Booth. New York: 1868. V. 40

GOULD, WILLIAM

An Account of English Ants . . . London: 1747. V. 38; 46

GOULDER, W. A.

Reminiscences. Incidents in the Life of a Pioneer in Oregon and Idaho. Boise: 1909. V. 38; 42; 45

GOULDER, WILLIAM A.

Reminiscences, Incidents in the Life of a Pioneer in Oregon and Idaho . . . Boise, Idaho: 1909. V. 37

GOULD'S History of Freemasonry throughout the World. New York: 1936. V. 40

GOURLIER, CHARLES PIERRE 1786-1857

Chois d'Edifices Publics Projetes et Construits en France Depuis le Commencement du XIXeme Siecle. Paris: 1825-50. V. 38

GOURMELEN, ETIENNE

Advertissement Et Conseil Donne a Messieurs de Paris & Autres Villes de ce Royaume, Tant Pour se Preseruer de la Peste, Comme Aussi Pour Nettoyer Toutes Villes & Les Maisons qui Seront Infectees de Ladicte Maladie. Troyes: 1581. V. 39

GOURMONT, REMY DE 1858-1915

Litanie de la rose. Paris: 1919. V. 46

The Natural Philosophy of Love. London: 1926. V. 37; 40; 42; 43; 45; 46

The Natural Philosophy of Love By . . . London: 1926. V. 45

A Virgin Heart. Toronto: 1925. V. 41

GOUSTE, CLAUDE

Traicte de la Puissance et Authorite des Rois. Paris: 1561. V. 43

GOUVEA, ANTONIO DE

Relacam em que se Tratam as Guerras e Grandes Victorias que Alcancou o Grande Rey de Persia Xz Abbas do Grao Turco Mahometto . . . Lisbon: 1611. V. 41

GOUVEA, FR. ANTONIO

Historia de la Vida, Muerte Y Milagros del Glorioso Patriarca y Padre de los Pobres S. Juan de Dios, Fundador de la Orden de la Hospitalidad. Lisbon: 1659. V. 45

GOUVEIA PINTO, ANTONIO JOAQUIM DE

Manual de Appellacoes, e Aggravso, ou Deduccao Systematica dos Principios Mais Solidos, e Neccarios, Relativos a Sua Materia . . . Bahia: 1816. V. 39; 45

GOVE, JESS A.

The Utah Expedition 1857-1858: Letters fo Capt. Jess. A. Gove. Concord: 1928. V. 41; 42; 44; 45; 46

GOVENIUS, LARS JOHAN

Lithografiska Skizzer Fran Fregatten Norrkopings Expedition Till Amerika Och Westindien 1861-1862. Stockholm: 1863. V. 38

Lithographiska Skizzer Fran Fregatten Norrkopings Expedition Till Amerika Och Westindien, 1861-1862. Colophon: Stockholm: 1863. V. 38

THE GOVERNESS; or, Evening Amusements at a Boarding School. London: 1800. V. 40

GOVINDJEE, J. AMESZ

Light Emission by Plants and Bacteria. London: 1986. V. 37

GOW, A. S. F.

Letters from Cambridge 1939-1944. London: 1945. V. 42

GOW, LEONARD

Catalogue of the Leonard Gow Collection of Chinese Porcelain. London: 1931. V. 42

GOWAN, WILLIAM

The Phenix; a Collection of Old and Rare Fragments . . . New York: 1835. V. 41

GOWANLOCK, THERESA

Two Months in the Camp of Big Bear. The Life and Adventures of Theresa Gowanlock and Theresa Delaney. Parkdale: 1885. V. 37; 42; 45

GOWANS, ALAN

Building Canada. Toronto: 1966. V. 38; 43

GOWANS, WILLIAM

Catalogue of the Books Belonging to the Estate of the Late Mr. William Gowans, Bookseller of No. 115 Nassau Street, New York . . . New York: 1871-72. V. 37

GOWEN, HERBER H.

Church Work in British Columbia: Being a Memoir of the Episcopate of Action Windeyer Silliote. London: 1899. V. 43; 45

GOWER, FRANCIS LEVESON

The Mill. A Moravian Tale. London: 1826. V. 42

GOWER, JOHN

De Confession Amantis. London: 1532. V. 45

Confessio Amantis. London: 1857. V. 37

De Confessione Amantis. London: 1554. V. 46

Jo. Gower de Confessione Amantis. (The Confessions of a Lover). London in Flete-Strete by: 1554. V. 43

Jo. Gower de Confessione Amantis. London: 1554. V. 38; 41

Poema Quod Dicitur Von Clamantis, Necnon Chronica Tripartita . . . London: 1850. V. 40

Poema Quod Dicitur Von Clamantis. London: 1850. V. 40

The Complete Works of John Gower. Oxford: 1968. V. 39

GOWER, RICHARD HALL 1767-1833

A Narrative of a Mode Pursued by the British Government to Effect Improvements in Naval Architecture. London: 1811. V. 42

GOWER, RONALD SUTHERLAND

George Romney. London: 1904. V. 44

Sir Thomas Lawrence. London: 1900. V. 39; 46

GOWERS, W. R.

The Diagnosis of Diseases of the Spinal Cord. London: 1881. V. 39; 40; 41; 42

The Diagnosis of Diseases of the Spinal Cord. London: 1881. V. 39

The Diagnosis of Diseases of the Spinal Cord. London: 1884. V. 38; 39

Diagnosis of Diseases of the Brain and the Spinal Cord. New York: 1885. V. 41

Diagnosis of Dieasess of the Brain and the Spinal Cord. New York: 1885. V. 37

Epilepsy and Other Chronic Convulsive Diseases. New York: 1885. V. 37; 42; 44

Epilepsy and Other Chronic Convulsive Diseases. New York: 1885. V. 37

A Manual of Diseases of the Nervous System. Philadelphia: 1900. V. 41

Subjective Sensations of Sight and Sound, Abiotrophy, and Other Lectures. Philadelphia: 1904. V. 40

Subjective Sensations of Sight and Sound. Philadelphia: 1904. V. 40; 41

GOWERS, WILLIAM R.

Diagnosis of Diseases of the Brain and Spinal Cord. New York: 1885. V. 42

Epilepsy and Other Chronic Convulsive Diseases: Their Causes, Symptoms and Treatment. London: 1901. V. 42

The Influence of Heredity on Disease, With Special Reference to Tuberculosis, Center and Diseases of the Nervous System . . . London: 1909. V. 42

Lectures on the Diagnosis of Diseases of the Brain. Philadelphia: 1885. V. 42

GOWLAND, JOHN STAFFORD

War Is Like That. London: 1933. V. 46

GOWLANLOCK, THERESA

Two Months in the Camp of Big Bear. Parkdale: 1885. V. 45

GOYDER, DAVID GEORGE

My Battle for Life. London: 1857. V. 45

GOYEN, WILLIAM

A Book of Jesus. Garden City: 1973. V. 46

The House of Breath. New York: 1950. V. 45; 46

GOYEN, WILLIAM continued

The House of Breath. London: 1951. V. 38

Precious Door. New York: 1981. V. 42

GOYTISOLO, JUAN

Island of Women. New York: 1962. V. 44

GOZMANY, L.

Septemlingual Dictionary of the Names of European Animals. Budapest: 1979. V. 43

GOZZI, CARLO

Memoirs. London: 1890. V. 38; 39; 43

GRAAF, REGINER DE

Tractatus Anatomico-Medicus de Succi Pancreatici Natura & Usu. Lugd. Bat.: 1671. V. 38

GRAAF, REGNER DE

Opera Omnia. Leyden: 1678. V. 39; 43

Opera Omnia. Lyons: 1678. V. 41

GRAAF, REGNIER DE

De Mulierum Organis Generationi Inservientibus Tractatus Novus. Lugduni Batav.: 1672. V. 37

Opera Omnia. Lugd. Batav.: 1677. V. 46

Tractatus Anatomico-Medicus De Succi Pancreatici Natura & Usu. Lugd. Bat.: 1671. V. 39

Tractatus Anatomico-Medicus de Succi Pancreatici Natura et Usu. Leiden: 1671. V. 37

GRAAF, REINIER DE

Opera Omnia. Leiden: 1678. V. 46

De Virorum Organis Genertioni Inservientibus, de Clysteribus et de Usu Syphonis in Anatomia. Leiden: 1668. V. 45

De Virorum Organis Generationi Inservientibus, de Clisteribus et de Usu Siphonis in Anatomia . . . Leiden and Rotterdam: 1668. V. 45

GRAAH, WILHELM A.

Narrative of an Expedition to the East Coast of Greenland . . . In Search of the Lost Colonies . . . London: 1837. V. 37; 38; 39; 40; 42

A GRAB Horn Bag: Original Pages Found by Excavators at 642 Commercial S treet, San Francisco. San Francisco: 1941. V. 46

GRAB HORN Bag, Pages from Various Books Printed at the Grahorn Press, San Francisco, 1928-1940. San Francisco: 1941. V. 37

GRABAR, ANDRE

Early Christian Art, from the Rise of Christianity to the Death of Thodosius. New York: 1968. V. 46

The Golden Age of Justinian. New York: 1967. V. 38; 46

GRABBAR, IGOR EMMANUILOVITCH

Istorya Russkago Iskusstsva. (History of Russian Art). Moscow: 1910-15. V. 40; 46

GRABER, H. W.

The Life Record of a Terry Texas Ranger, 1861-1865. Dallas: 1916. V. 38; 39; 44

The Life Record of a Terry Texas Ranger, 1861-1865. Sixty-Two Years in Texas. (Dallas): 1916. V. 37

GRABER, HENRY WILLIAM

Life Record of H. W. Graber, a Terry Texas Ranger 1861-1865. Dallas?: 1916. V. 45

GRABHORN, EDWIN

The Fine Art of Printing. An Address by . . . Before the Roxburghe Club of San Francisco at Its Meeting in the Allied Arts Guild, Menlo Park, California, May 15, 1933. San Francisco: 1933. V. 38

The Fine Art of Printing. An address by Edwin Grabhorn before the Roxgurghe Club of San Francisco at its meeting in the Allied Arts Guild, Menlo Park, California, May 15, 1933. V. 37

GRABHORN, JANE

The Compleat Jane Grabhorn. San Francisco: 1968. V. 40; 41; 42; 45

The Compleat Jane Grabhorn: a Hodge-Podge of Typographic Ephemera, Three Complete Books, Broadsides, Invitations; Greetings, Place Cards &c. San Francisco: 1968. V. 37; 39; 41; 45

A Treatise and Some Letters. San Francisco. V. 44

GRABHORN, JANE B.

A California Gold Rush Miscellany . . . San Francisco: 1934. V. 45

GRABHORN, MARJORIE

Figure Prints of Old Japan. San Francisco: 1959. V. 38

GRABHORN PRESS

Bibliography of the Grabhorn Press, 1915-1940. Bibliography of the Grabhorn Press 1940-1956. San Francisco: 1975. V. 40

Bibliography of the Grabhorn Press 1957-1966 & Grabhorn-Hoyem, 1966-1973 . . . San Francisco: 1977. V. 45

Nineteenth Century Type Displayed in 18 Fonts: Cast By United States Founders, Now in the Cases of the Grabhorn Press. San Francisco: 1959. V. 42

GRABHORN PRESS, SAN FRANCISCO.

A Grab (Horn) Bag. San Francisco: 1941. V. 41

A Grab(horn) Bag Original Pages Found by Excavators of 642 Commercial Street San Francisco. San Francisco: 1941. V. 41

Nineteenth Century Type Displayed in 18 Fonts. San Francisco: 1959. V. 37; 41

GRABHORN, ROBERT

A Commonplace Book of Cookery. A Collection of Proverbs, Anecdotes, Opinion and Obscure Facts on Food, Drink, Cooks, Cooking, Dining, Diners and Dieters. San Francisco: 1975. V. 41

A Short Account of the Life and Work of Wynkyn de Worde. San Francisco: 1949. V. 37; 38; 44; 46

GRABO, CARL H.

Peter and the Princess. Chicago: 1920. V. 42; 46

GRACE, HENRY

The History of the Life and Sufferings of Henry Grace, of Basingstoke in the County of Southampton. Reading: 1764. V. 39; 40; 43; 45

GRACE, SHEFFIELD

An Ancient Feudal War-Song, Entitled Grasagh Aboe . . . London: 1839. V. 40

Bibliotheca Graceiana. Dublin: 1841. V. 43

A Descriptive and Architectural Sketch of the Grace-Mausoleum in the Queens County. (and) Survey of Tullaroan. Dublin: 1819. V. 45

Memoirs of the Family of Grace. London: 1823. V. 37; 42; 43

GRACE, W. G.

Cricket. Bristol: 1891. V. 42

Cricket. London: 1891. V. 37

THE GRACES: a Poetical Epistle from a Gentleman to his Son. London: 1774. V. 37; 42

THE GRACES; a Poetical Epistle from a Gentleman to His Son. London: 1774. V. 40

THE GRACES; a Poetical Epistle from a Gentleman to His Son. London: 1775. V. 40

GRACIAN, BALTASAR

The Compleat Gentleman; or a Description of the Several Qualificiations Both Natural and Acquired . . . London: 1730. V. 46

GRACIAN DE ANTISCO, LUCAS

Narcissus, or the Young Man's Entertaining Mirror. London: 1778. V. 40

GRACIAN Y MORALES, BALTASAR

The ARt of Prudence: or, A Companion for a Man of Sense. London: 1702. V. 42

The Courtier's Oracle . . . London: 1694. V. 41; 42

The Hero From the Spanish of Baltasar . . . ; with Remarks Moral, Political and Historical of the Learned Father J. de Courbeville. London: 1726. V. 43

GRADLE, H.

Bacteria and the Germ Theory of Disease. Chicago: 1883. V. 38

GRADUS ad Cantabrigiam; or New University Guide to Academical Customs, and Colloquial or Cant Terms Peculiar to the University of Cambridge. London: 1824. V. 43

GRADUS ad Parnassum: sive, Novus Synonymorum, Epithetorum, Phrasium Poeticarum, ac Versuum Thesaurus . . . Londini: 1687. V. 42

GRAEB, C.

Erinnerung an Sanssouci. Berlin: 1855-1859. V. 38; 40

GRAECAE Grammaticae Rudimenta. In Usum Regiae Scholae Etonensis. Etonae: 1772. V. 41

GRAEF, BOTHO

Die Antiken Vasen von der Akropolis zu Athen. Berlin: 1909-14. V. 42

GRAEME, JAMES

Poems on Several Occasions. Edinburgh: 1773. V. 43

GRAETER, FRANCIS

Hydriatics; or Manual of the Water Cure, Especially as Practised by Vincent Priessnitz in Graefenberg. New York: 1844. V. 40

GRAETZ, H.

History of the Jews. Philadelphia: 1891-92. V. 40; 42; 44

GRAETZ, HEINRICH

History of the Jews. New York: 1933. V. 40; 42

GRAF, A. B.

Exotica. 1963. V. 45

Tropica. East Rutherford: 1978. V. 45

Tropica, Color Encylopaedia of Exotic Plants and Trees from the Tropics and Subtropics for Warm-Region Horticulture, in Cool Climate the Sheltered Indoors. Rutherford: 1980. V. 37

GRAFF, JOHN FRANKLIN

'Graybeard's' Colorado; or, Notes on the Centennial State. Philadelphia: 1882. V. 43

Graybeard's Colorado; or, Notes on the Centennial State. Philadelphia: 1882. V. 37; 45

GRAFF, REGINER DE

Tractatus Anatomico-Medicus De Succi Pancretici Natura & Usu. 1671. V. 37

GRAFF, REGNER DE

De Virorum Organis Generataioni Inservientibus, de Clysteribus et de Usu Siphonis in Anatomia. Lugd.: 1668. V. 37

GRAFFE, W.

Poster Design. London: 1929. V. 43; 45

GRAFFIGNY, FRANCOIS DE 1695-1758

Lettres d'une Peruvienne. Paris: 1797. V. 45

GRAFFMAN, CARL SAMUEL

Skottska Vuer Tecknade after Naturen Under en Resa i Skottland ar 1830. Stockholm: 1831-33. V. 38

GRAFIGNY, FRANCOISE P. HUGUET DE

Letters Written by a Peruvian Princess. Dublin: 1774. V. 43

GRAFTON, RICHARD

A Chronicle at Large and Meere History of the Affayres of Englande and Kinges of the Same . . . London: 1569-8. V. 38

GRAFTON-SMITH, ADELE

A Railway Foundling. London: 1890. V. 44

GRAFTON, SUE

'C' is for Corpse. New York: 1986. V. 43

Keziah Dane. London: 1967. V. 43

Keziah Dane. New York: 1967. V. 45; 46

Mark, I Love You. Los Angeles: 1980. V. 44

Sex and the Single Parent. Studio City: 1979. V. 44

GRAGLIA, JOSEPH ANTONY

Albion Restituta: or, a Plan for the Periodical Abolition of all Taxes, raised by Means of Collectors. London: 1796. V. 39

GRAH, DOUGAL

The Witty and Entertaining Exploits of George Buchanan Commonly Called the King's Fool. Stirling. V. 45

GRAHAM, A. A.

History of Richland County, Ohio . . . Mansfield: 1880. V. 46

GRAHAM, ANDERSON PROBST & WHITE, CHICAGO

The Architectural Work of . . . and Their Predecessors D. H. Burnham & Co. and Graham, Burham & Co. London: 1933. V. 39; 41

GRAHAM, CLEMENTIA STIRLING

Mystifications. Edinburgh: 1859. V. 44

GRAHAM, CLIVE

The Grand National. London: 1972. V. 37

GRAHAM, DAVID

The Pioneer. Pittsburgh: 1812. V. 42

GRAHAM, DOUGLAS

The Merry and Entertaining Jokes of George Buchanan; Who Was Servant and Teacher to King James VIth as His Private Counsellor . . . (with) The Second Book of the Witty and Entertaining Exploits of George Bruchanan . . . Newcastle. V. 45

A Practical Treatise on Massage: Its History, Mode of Application and Effects, Indications and Contra-Indications with Results in Over Fourteen Hundred Cases. New York: 1884. V. 45

GRAHAM, E.

Aunt Liza's 'Praisin' Gate'. 1916. V. 45

GRAHAM, ELIZABETH S.

Voyage to Locuta; a Fragment with Etchings and Notes of Illustration. London: 1818. V. 37

GRAHAM, EVARTS AMBROSE 1883-1957

Some Fundamental Considerations in the Treatment of Empyema Thoracis. St. Louis: 1925. V. 45

GRAHAM, G. S.

The Walker Expedition to Quebec, 1711. Toronto: 1953. V. 45

GRAHAM, GEORGE

Letter from the Acting Secretary of War, Transmitting a Statement Showing the Expenditure of the Moneys Appropriated for the Contingent Expenses of the Military Establishment, for the Year 1816. Washington: 1817. V. 46

GRAHAM, GEORGE FARQUHAR

An Essay on the Theory and Practice of Musical Composition. Edinburgh: 1838. V. 38

General Observations Upon Music, and Remarks on Mr. Logier's System of Musical Education; with an Appendix . . . Edinburgh: 1817. V. 38

GRAHAM, GEORGE W.

The Mecklenburg Declaration of Independence, May 20, 1775 and Lives of Its Signers. New York: 1905. V. 42

The Mecklenburg Declaration of Independence May 20, 1775 and the Lives of its Signers. New York: & Washington: 1905. V. 46

GRAHAM, J. A.

A Descriptive Sketch of the Present State of Vermont, one of the United States of America. London: 1797. V. 38; 39; 40

GRAHAM, JAMES

Corn and Currency; in an Address to the Land Owners . . . London: 1827. V. 42

GRAHAM, JAMES D.

Annual Report of Bvt. Lt. Col. J. D. Graham . . . on the Improvement of the Harbors. Washington: 1859. V. 39

On the Latitude and Longitude of Milwaukee, Prairie Du Chien, Racine and Madison, Wisconsin. Milwaukee: 1859. V. 41; 42

. . . Report of Lieutenant Colonel Graham on the Subject of the Boundary Line Between the United States and Mexico. Washington: 1852. V. 38; 45

Report of Lieutenant Colonel Graham on the Subject of the Boundary Line Between the United States and Mexico. 1852. V. 44; 45

Report of Lieutenant Colonel Graham on the Subject of the Boundary Line Between the United States and Mexico. Washington: 1852. V. 37; 41; 43

GRAHAM, JAMES DUNCAN

The Report of Lieutenant Colonel Graham on the Subject of the Boundary Line Between the United States and Mexico . . . Washington: 1852. V. 43

GRAHAM, JERRY BENEDICT

Handset Reminiscences, Recollections of an Old-Time Printer and Journalist. Salt Lake City: 1915. V. 38

GRAHAM, JOHN

A Diary of the Siege of Londonderry and Defence of Enniskillen in 1688 and 1689. Londonderry. V. 43

GRAHAM, JOHN A.

A Descriptive Sketch of the Present State of Vermont. London: 1797. V. 43

GRAHAM, JOHN ANDREW 1764-1841

Memoirs of John Horne Tooke . . . New York: 1828. V. 43

Speeches Delivered at the City-Hall of the City of New York in the Courts of Oyer and Terminer, Common Pleas and General Sessions of the Peace. New York: 1812. V. 45

GRAHAM, JOSEPH A.

The Sporting Dog. New York: 1904. V. 37

GRAHAM, KENNETH

The Wind in the Willows. London: 1931. V. 42

GRAHAM, MARIA

Journal of a Residence in India. Edinburgh: 1813. V. 41

Journal of a Residence in India. Edinburgh: 1812. V. 37

Letters on India. London: 1814. V. 43

Three Months Passed in the Mountains East of Rome During the Year 1819. London: 1820. V. 39; 45; 46

Voyage of H. M. S. Blonde to the Sandwich Islands, in the Years 1824, 1825. London: 1826. V. 42; 45

GRAHAM, PATRICK

Sketches Descriptive of Picturesque Scenery, on the Southern Confines of Perthshire . . . Edinburgh: 1806. V. 44

GRAHAM, PETER

A Topographical Dictionary of Palestine or the Holy Land . . . London: 1836. V. 38

GRAHAM, R.

A Picture Book of the Life of Saint Anthony and the Abbot Reproduced from a Manuscript of the Year 1426 in the Malta Public Library at Valetta . . . 1937. V. 40

A Picture Book of the Life of Saint Anthony the Abbot. London: 1937. V. 44

GRAHAM, RIGBY

Christmas/New Years Cards: a Series of the Monographs of Irish Monastic Sites. Coalville. V. 46

Enigma. Leicester: 1969-71. V. 39

John Minton - a Commemorative Exhibition. Aylestone: 1967. V. 40

The Paper Makers Craft, verse by - illustrations by R. Graham. Printed by Will Carter at Cambridge for the Twelve by Eight Press. Leicester: 1965. V. 37

Patterned Papers. Wymondham: 1977. V. 38; 41

Sketchbook Drawing. Oxford: 1989. V. 43; 45

GRAHAM, ROBERT BONTINE CUNNINGHAME 1852-1936

Aurora La Cujini. A Realistic Sketch in Seville. London: 1898. V. 43

Bibi. London: 1929. V. 40

The District of Monteith. Stirling: 1930. V. 46

The Horses of the Conquest. Norman: 1949. V. 40; 42

Notes on the District of Mentieth for Tourists and Others. London: 1895. V. 37; 40; 42

Redeemed. London: 1927. V. 40; 44

GRAHAM ROBERTSON, W.

The Baby's Day Book - Songs of the Dy the Dusk and the Dark. London: 1908. V. 38

GRAHAM, SHIRLEY

Paul Robeson: Citizen of the World. New York: 1946. V. 39

GRAHAM, SYLVESTER

A Lecture to Young Men, on Chastity. Boston: 1841. V. 45

GRAHAM, THOMAS

Chemical and Physical Researches, Collected and Printed for Presentation Only. Edinburgh: 1876. V. 40

Chemical Reports and Memoirs, on Atomic Volume; Isomorphism; Endosmosis; the Simultaneous Contrast of Colours; the Latent Heat of Steam at Different Pressures; the Artificial Formation of Alkaloids; and Volcanic Phenomena. London: 1848. V. 40

A Treatise on Indigestion, with Observations on Some Painful Complaints Originating in Indigestion . . . Philadelphia: 1831. V. 40

GRAHAM, THOMAS JOHN

A Treatise on Indigestion. London: 1838. V. 38

GRAHAM, W. A.

Abstract of the Official Record of Proceedings of the Reno Court of Inquiry Convened at Chicago, Illinois 13, Jan. 1879 by the President of the United States Upon the Request of Major Marcaus A. Reno . . . Harrisburg: 1954. V. 43; 45

The Custer Myth . . . Harrisburg: 1953. V. 45

Major Reno Vindicated. Hollywood: 1935. V. 41

The Official Record of a Court of Inquiry . . . Convened at Chicago, Illinois, Jan. 13, 1879 Upon the Request of Major Marcus A. Reno, 7th Cavalry to Investigate His Conduct. Pacific Palisades: 1951. V. 45

GRAHAM, W. S.

Cage Without Grievance - Poems. Glasgow: 1942. V. 38

The Night Fishing. London: 1955. V. 40

The Nightfishing. Rome: 1951. V. 38

Second Poems. London: 1945. V. 46

The White Threshold - Poems. London: 1949. V. 44

GRAHAM, WILLIAM

The Art of Making Wines from Fruits, Flowers and Herbs, All Native Growth of Great Britain . . . London: 1760. V. 40; 42

The Art of Making Wines from Fruits, Flowers and Herbs, All the Native Growth of Great Britain. London: 1783. V. 40; 43

The Art of Making Wines from Fruits, Flowers, and Herbs all the Native Growth of Great Britain. Particulary of Grapes, Gooseberies, Currants, Rasberries, Mulberries . . . Apples, Pears, Cherries, Peaches, Apricots, Quinces, Plumbs . . . London: (c. 1760). V. 37

Idealism: an Essay, Metaphysical and Critical. London: 1872. V. 43

The Social Problem In Its Economical, Moral and Political Aspects. London: 1886. V. 39

GRAHAM, WILLIAM A.

Papers (1825-1868). Raleigh: 1957-84. V. 37; 40; 42

GRAHAME, JAMES

The Birds of Scotland, with Other Poems. Edinburgh: 1806. V. 39; 42

GRAHAME, KENENTH

Dream Days. London: 1899. V. 40; 42; 43

Dream Days. London: 1920. V. 43

GRAHAME, KENNETH 1859-1932

Dream Days. New York: 1898. V. 46

Dream Days. New York: & London: 1899. V. 46

Dream Days. London & New York: 1902. V. 40; 42; 45

Dream Days. London: 1922. V. 46

Dream Days. London: 1930. V. 40

Dream Days. New York: 1899. V. 37; 45

First Whisper of 'The Wind in the Willows'. London: 1944. V. 39

The Golden Age. London: 1895. V. 37; 40; 42; 44; 45; 46

The Golden Age. London: 1900. V. 43; 46

The Golden Age. London: & New York: 1900. V. 41; 42

The Golden Age. London: 1928. V. 38; 40; 42; 45

The Golden Age. Dream Days. London: 1928, 1930. V. 39

The Headswoman. London: 1898. V. 41

The Headswoman. London: & New York: 1898. V. 46

The Headswoman. London & New York: 1898. V. 42

The Headswoman. New York: 1898. V. 40

The Headswoman. London: 1921. V. 39; 40; 43; 46

Pagan Papers. London: 1894. V. 37; 38; 46

Pagan Papers. London & Chicago: 1894. V. 40; 42

Pagan Papers. London: 1894/1893. V. 43

The Piper at the Gates of Dawn. Kensington. V. 45

The Wind in the Willows. London: 1908. V. 37; 38; 39; 40; 41; 42; 43; 44

The Wind in the Willows. London: 1913. V. 42

The Wind in the Willows. London: 1931. V. 37; 46

The Wind in the Willow. New York: 1940. V. 45

The Wind in the Willows. New York: 1940. V. 37; 38; 39; 40; 41; 42; 45; 46

The Wind in the Willows. London: 1950. V. 40

The Wind in the Willows. London: 1951. V. 41

The Wind in the Willows. London: 1960. V. 44; 46

The Wind in the Willows. London: 1971. V. 38; 41

Wind in the Willows. London: 1984. V. 46

The Wind in the Willows. London: 1986. V. 44; 46

The Wind in the Willows. London: (1908). V. 37

The Wind In the Willows with Arthur Rackham plates. (1975). V. 37

GRAHAME, SIMION

The Anatomie of Humors, and the Passionate Sparke of a Relenting Minde. Edinburgh: 1830. V. 38; 40

The Anatomie of Humors, and the Passionate Sparke of a Relenting Minde. Edinburgh: 1830. V. 40

GRAHAME, THOMAS

A Letter Addressed to Nicholas Wood, Esq. on that Portion of Chapter IX of His Treatise on Railroads . . . Glasgow: 1831. V. 45

A Letter Addressed to Nicholas Wood, Esq. on that Portion of Chapter IX of His Treatise on Railroads, Entitled 'Comparative Performances of Motive Power on Canals and Railroads.' Glasgow/Edinburgh: 1831. V. 37

A Treatise on Internal Intercourse and Communication in Civilised States, and Particularly in Great Britain. London: 1834. V. 42

GRAILHE, ALEXANDER

Supreme Court. The States of Louisiana & Maryland Vs. The Executors of John McDonogh and the Cities of New Orleans and Baltimore, Argument for the Cities, by Alex. Grailhe . . . New Orleans: 1852. V. 37

GRAINGE, WILLIAM

Nidderdale; or, an Historical, Topographical and Descriptive Sketch of the Valley of the Nidd . . . Pateley Bridge: 1863. V. 45

GRAINGER, JAMES 1721-1766

The Sugar-Cane; a Poem. London: 1764. V. 40; 43

GRAINGER, THOMAS

Observations on the Formation of a Railway Communication Between the Cities of Edinburgh & Glasgow, with Branches to the Firth of Forth at Leith and the River Cyde at Glasgow. Edinburgh: 1830. V. 46

A GRAMMAR and Vocabulary of the Susoo Langauge. Edinburgh: 1802. V. 40

GRAMMATICA Latina In Usum Scholae Bremensis. Bremen: 1617. V. 39

GRAMMONT, JUSTIN

The League of the Merrimack. Manchester: 1848. V. 44

GRAMMONT, SIEUR DE

Heartsease and Honesty; the Pastimes . . . Waltham St. Lawrence: 1935. V. 40

GRAMP, WILLIAM EDGAR 1840-

The Journal of a Grandfather. St. Louis: 1912. V. 39; 41

GRANA, DAMIANUS

Vita B. Philippi Benicii Floren. Ord. Servorv. Rome: 1591. V. 37

GRANADA, LUIS DE

Conciones Quae de Praecipuis Sanctorum Festis in Ecclesia Habentur . . . Antwerp: 1593. V. 39

Flores Ex Omnibus Spiritualibus Eius Opusculis. Cologne: 1585. V. 37

GRANADOS Y GALVEZ, J. J.

Tardes Americanas . . . Mexico: 1778. V. 43

GRANBERG, P. A.

English and Swedish Pocket-Dictionary. Stockholm: 1807. V. 38

GRANCSAY, STEPHEN V.

Master French Gunsmith's Designs of the Mid-Seventeenth Century. New York: 1950. V. 39

GRAND, ANTHONY

An Entire Body of Philosophy, According to the Principles of the Famous Renate Des Cartes. London: 1694. V. 42

THE GRAND Canyon of Arizona. N.P.: 1906. V. 39

LE GRAND Coustumier du Pays Duche de Normendie. Rouen: 1539. V. 40

A GRAND Eastern Puzzle: The Following Chineze Puzzle Is Recommended to the Nobility, Gentry and Others . . . London: 1815. V. 40

GRAND, GORDON

The Banshee Shadow Flies. Toronto. V. 44

A Horse for Christmas Morning. New York: 1939. V. 43

Redmond C. Stewart: Foxhunter and Gentleman of Maryland. New York: 1938. V. 46

The Silver Horn, and Other Sporting Tales of John Weatherford. New York: 1932. V. 37; 39; 40; 42

The Silver Horn . . . Garden City: 1937. V. 43

LE GRAND Herbier en Francoys: Contenant les Qualitez/ Vertus et Proprietez des Herbes/ Arbres/ Gommes/ Semences/ Huyles/ et Pierres Precieuses. Paris: 1535. V. 42

THE GRAND International Centennial Chess Congress, Held in Philadelphia, in August, 1876, Being the Celebration of the American Centennial. Philadelphia: 1876. V. 40

THE GRAND Question Concerning the Judicature of the House of Peers Stated and Argued; with the Case of Thomas Skinner, Merchant, Complaining of the East India Company. London: 1669. V. 40

GRAND, SARAH, PSEUD.

A Domestic Experiment. Edinburgh: 1891. V. 44

The Heavenly Twins. London: 1893. V. 38; 44

THE GRAND Secret of Precipitating the Preliminaries Brought to Light; or, a View of the Motives That Induced the Courts of L----n and the Hague to Overlook the Visible Advantages of Continuing the War . . . London: 1748. V. 41

GRAND TRUNK PACIFIC

Canada's National Transcontinental Railway - The Only All Canadian Route. Montreal: 1912. V. 45

GRAND TRUNK RAILWAY CO.

Correspondence Between the Hon. William Napier, on Behalf of the English Shareholders of the Grand Trunk Railroad Company and the Honble. Wm. Cayley (Inspector General). Toronto: 1856. V. 45

Official Time Table: The Great International Route Between the East & West . . . Toronto: 1885. V. 45

Report of the Special Committee Appointed to Enquire and Report as to the Condition, Management and Prospects of the Grand Trunk Railway Co. Toronto: 1857. V. 45

Statements, Reports and Accounts of the Grand Trunk Railway Company of Canada. Toronto: 1857. V. 45

GRAND, W. JOSEPH

Illustrated History of the Union Stockyards. Chicago: 1896. V. 42; 46

Illustrated History of the Union Stockyards. Sketch-Book of Familiar Faces and Places at the Yards. Chicago: 1901. V. 43; 46

LA GRANDE Bible des Noels, sur la Nativite de Notre Seigneur Jesus Christ. Anger: 1750. V. 38

GRANDE Enciclopedia Portuguesa e Brasileira. Lisbon. V. 46

GRANDI, GUIDO

Flores Geometrici ex Rhodonearum, et Cloeliarum Curvarum Descriptione Resultantes . . . Florence: 1728. V. 43

GRANDI, LAZZARO

Alfabeti di Secreti Medicinali . . . Milan: 1670. V. 46

GRANDIDIER, A.

Histoire Physique, Naturelle et Politique de Madagascar: Mammiferes, Text. Paris: 1875-97. V. 40

Histoire Physique, Naturelle et Politique de Madagascar: Atlas des Plantes Phanerogames. Paris: 1886-1903. V. 40

GRANDIDIER, ALFRED

Histoire Physique, Naturelle et Politique de Madagascar . . . Volumes XII-XV. (with) Supplement par L. Lavauden. Paris: 1876-85, 1937. V. 42

GRANDIN, EGBERT

Obstetric Surgery. Philadelphia: 1895. V. 42

GRANDIN, EGBERT H.

Pregnancy, Labor and Puerperal State. Philadelphia: 1895. V. 43

GRANDJEAN DE MONTIGNY, A.

Architecture Toscane, ou Palais, Maisons, et Autres Edifices de la Toscane. Paris: 1837. V. 40

GRANDJEAN, SERGE

Gold Boxes and Miniatures of the Eighteenth Century. Fribourg: 1975. V. 42

GRANDMOTHER'S Stories for Little Children. Boston: 1854. V. 37

GRANDPRE, J.

The Traveller's Interpreter in Four Languages . . . London: 1728. V. 45

GRANDPRE, L. DE

A Voyage in the Indian Ocean and to Bengal, Undertaken in the Year 1790. Brattleborough: 1814. V. 40

GRANDVILLE, JEAN IGNACE ISIDORE GERARD 1803-1847

Les Fleurs Animees. Paris: 1847. V. 38

The Flowers Personified . . . New York: 1847. V. 44

Scenes de la Vie Privee et Publique des Animaux. Paris: 1842. V. 40

GRANELL, E. F.

Isla Cofre Mitico. Puerto Rico: 1951. V. 46

GRANET, JEAN JOSEPH

Histoire de l'Hotel Royal des Invalides. Paris: 1736. V. 44

GRANGE, HERBERT

An English Farmer in Canada, and a Visit to the States . . . London: 1904. V. 45

THE GRANGE. What It Has Accomplished . . . Is Laboring to Accomplish . . . Purposes . . . Membership . . . How to Organize a Subordiante Grange. Mechanicsburg: 1873. V. 39

THE GRANGE What It Has Accomplished . . . Is Laboring to Accomplish . . . Purposes . . . Membership . . . How to Organize a Subordinate Grange. Mechanicsburg: 1873. V. 42
THE GRANGE. What it has Accomplished . . . Is Laboring to Accomplish . . . Purposes . . . Membership . . . How to Organize a Subordinate Grange. Mechanicsburg, Pa.: ca. 1873. V. 37

GRANGER, B.

Address to the Public Relative to Some Supposed Failures of the Cow-Pox, at Repton and Its Neighborhood with Observations on the Efficacy and General Expediency of Vaccination, and on the Injurious Consequences of Inoculation for the Small Pox. Burton-upon-Trent: 1821. V. 41; 42

GRANGER, J. T.

Brief Biographical Sketch of the Life of Major-General Grenville M. Dodge, Compiled from Official Records. New York: 1893. V. 38

GRANGER, JAMES 1723-1776

A Biographical History of England, from Robert the Great to the Revolution. London: 1769, 1774. V. 39

A Biographical History of England from Egbert the Great to the Revolution Consisting of Characters Disposed in Different Classes and Adapted to a Methodical Catalogue of Engraved British Heads. London: 1769-74. V. 38

A Biographical History of England from Egbert the Great to the Revolution. London: 1775. V. 39

A Biographical History of England, from Egbert the Great to the Revolution. London: 1775-79. V. 46

A Biographical History of England, from Egbert the Great to the Revolution. London: 1779. V. 38; 45

A Biographical History of England, from Egbert the Great to the Revolution . . . London: 1804. V. 46

GRANGER, JAMES 1723-1776 continued

Letters Between the Rev. James Granger . . . and Many of the Most Eminent Literary Men of His Time . . . London: 1805. V. 37; 38; 41; 43; 46

GRANGIER, JEAN

Oratio Habita IV. Kal. Decmbr. Pro Restaurandis Scholis. Paris: 1619. V. 39

GRANIER DE CASSAGNAC, BERNARD ADOLPHE 1806-1880

History of the Working and Burgher Classes. Philadelphia: 1871. V. 41

GRANISS, RUTH

A Garland of Poppies, Gathered By . . . V. 46

GRANISS, RUTH S.

A Garaland of Poppies Gathered By . . . New York: 1905. V. 37; 42

A Garland of Poppies Gathered By . . . London: 1905. V. 40

GRANIT, RAGNAR

Sensory Mechanisms of the Retina . . . London: 1947. V. 44

GRANJON, ROBERT

Robert Granjon: Sixteenth Century Type Founder and Printer. Brooklyn: 1931. V. 37

GRANNISS, RUTH S.

A Descriptive Catalogue of the First Editions in Book Form of the Writings of Percy Bysshe Shelley; Based on a Memorial Exhibition Held at the Grolier Club from April 20 to May 20, 1922. New York: 1923. V. 42

GRANT, ALEXANDER CHARLES

Bush-Life in Queensland, or John West's Colonial Experience. Edinburgh: 1881. V. 38

Bush-Life in Queensland, or John West's Colonial Experiences. Edinburgh and London: 1881. V. 40

Bush-Life in Queensland or, John West's Colonial Experiences. In Two Volumes. Edinburgh/London: 1881. V. 37

GRANT, ANNE 1775-1838

Essays on the Superstitions of the Highlanders of Scotland . . . London: 1811. V. 44

Letters from the Mountains. London: 1806. V. 41

Memoirs of an American Lady . . . Boston: 1809. V. 44

Memoirs of an American Lady; with Sketches of Manners and Scenery in America . . . New York: 1809. V. 41; 45

Memoirs of an American Lady. London: 1811. V. 44

Memoirs and Correspondence of Mrs. Grant of Laggan. London: 1844. V. 44

Poems on Various Subjects. Edinburgh: 1803. V. 39; 42; 43

GRANT, ANNE MAC VICAR 1755-1838

Artiste. London: 1871. V. 46

Essays on the Superstitions of the Highlanders of Scotland. London: 1811. V. 45

Letters from the Moutains, Being the Real Correspondence of a Lady, Between the Years 1773 and 1803. London: 1806. V. 38

Letters from the Mountains . . . Ban: 1809. V. 45; 46

Letters from the Mountains; Being the Real Correspondence of a Lady, Between the Years 1773 and 1807. London: 1813. V. 38

Memoir and Correspondence of Mrs. Grant of Laggan. London: 1844. V. 38

Memoir and Correspondence of Mrs. Grant of Laggan . . . Edited by her son, J.P. Grant. 1844. V. 37

Memoirs of an American Lady. London: 1808. V. 37; 38; 40; 42; 46

Memoirs of an American Lady. New York: 1809. V. 38

Memoirs of an American Lady, with Sketches of Manners and Scenery in America as They Existed Previous to the Revolution. New York: 1846. V. 40

Memoirs of an American Lady. New York: 1901. V. 42

Memoirs of an American Lady with Sketches of Manners and Scenes in America as They existed Previous to the Revolution. New York: 1901. V. 38

Poems on Various Subjects. Edinburgh: 1803. V. 37; 42

GRANT, B.

The Orchids of Burma. Rangoon: 1895. V. 46

GRANT, BLANCHE C.

When Old Trails Were New: The Story of Two. New York: 1934. V. 43

GRANT, CHARLES

The History of Mauritius, or the Isla of France and the Neighboring Islands from Their First Discovery tot he Present Time . . . From the Papers and Memoirs of Baron Grant . . . London: 1801. V. 38; 41

GRANT, CHARLES, VISCOUNT DE VAUX

Appendix to the State of the Case of . . . Relative to His Origin from Great Britain, His Civil and Military Life, in France and in England, His Literary, Geographical and Astronomical Work . . . London: 1807? V. 37

The Means of Finding the Longitude at Sea, Gradually Developed, Discovered and Demonstrated in Four Astronomical, Geographical, Nautical, Historical, Mathematical and Mechanical Dissertations. London: 1808. V. 40

GRANT, COLESWORTHY

An Anglo-Indian Domestic Sketch. A Letter from an Artisan in India to His Mother in England. Calcutta: 1849. V. 39

Rural Life in Bengal. London: 1860. V. 39

GRANT, DUNCAN

Grant Duncan. London: 1923. V. 37

Living Painters. London: 1930. V. 40

GRANT, ELIHU

Beth Shemesh (Palestine): Progress of the Haverford Archaeological Expedition. Haverford: (1929). V. 37

GRANT, FRANCIS

A Letter to a Member of Parliament, Concerning the Free British Fisheries. London: 1750. V. 40; 41; 45

GRANT, FREDERIC JAMES

History of Seattle. New York: 1891. V. 46

GRANT, GEORGE

Ocean to Ocean. Toronto and London: 1873. V. 45

GRANT, GEORGE M.

Ocean to Ocean, Sandford Fleming's Expedtion through Canada in 1872. Canada & London: 1873. V. 42

GRANT, GEORGE MUNRO

Ocean to Ocean Sandford Fleming's Expedition through Canada in 1872. Canada & London: 1873. V. 37; 38; 39; 42

Ocean to Ocean. Toronto: 1873. V. 42; 43

Picturesque Canada: the Country as It Was and Is. London: 1882-85. V. 46

Picturesque Canada. Toronto: 189? V. 43

Picturesque Canada: The Country As It Was and Is. Toronto: 1882. V. 37; 41

GRANT, GORDON b. 1875

Sail Ho! Windjammer Sketches Alow and Aloft. New York: 1931. V. 39

GRANT, H. HORACE

A Text-Book of Surgical Principles and Surgical Diseases of the Face, Mouth and Jaws for Dental Students. Philadelphia: 1902. V. 42

GRANT, HENRY

Marquita. London: 1863. V. 38

GRANT, IAN

Great Interiors. London: 1967. V. 39

GRANT, JAMES

Bothwell: or, the Days of Mary Queen of Scots. London: 1851. V. 37

Cassell's Old and New Edinburgh. London: 1880-83. V. 42

History of the Newspaper Press: Its Origin - Progress - and Present Position. London: 1871-72. V. 42

History of the Burgh Schools of Scotland. London: 1878. V. 45

The Old Scots Navy 1689-1710, the Acts, Commissions, Directions, Letters and Warrants, from the 1689 Revolution to Its Absorption by the British Admiralty in 1710. London: 1912. V. 39

Sketches in London. London: 1838. V. 37; 40; 43

Sketches of London. Philadelphia: 1839. V. 46

Sketches in London. London: 1840. V. 40; 42; 43

Thoughts on the Origin and Descent of the Gael: with an account of the Picts. Caledonians, and Scots; and Observations relative to the authenticity of the poems of Ossian. Edinburgh: 1814. V. 37

Travels in Town (London). London: 1839. V. 42

Vere of Ours, the Eighth of King's. A Novel. London: 1878. V. 41

GRANT, JAMES AUGUSTUS

A Walk Across Africa or Domestic Scenes from My Nile Journal. Edinburgh: 1864. V. 40

A Walk Across Africa, or Domestic Scenes from my Nile Journal. London: 1864. V. 39

GRANT, JOEL

Why Christians Die. Sandwich: 1859. V. 39

GRANT, JOHN

Experiments of the Strength of Cement, Chiefly in Reference to the Portland Cement Used in Southern Main Drainage Works. London: 1875. V. 44

A Survey of the Province of Moray . . . Aberdeen: 1798. V. 44; 46

GRANT, JOHN CAMERON

The Ethiopian: a Narrative of the Society of Human Leopards. Paris: 1900. V. 39

GRANT, K. A.

Hummingbirds and Their Flowers. V. 45
Hummingbirds and Their Flowers. 1968. V. 46

GRANT, MARY ANN

Sketches of Life and Manners, with Deliniation of Scenery in England, Scotland, and Ireland. London: 1810. V. 38

GRANT, MAURICE HAROLD

A Chronological History of the Old English Landscape Painters (In Oil) From the XVIth Century to the XIXth Century. London. V. 38; 40; 46
Chronological History of the Old English Landscape Painters (in Oil) from the XVIth Century to the XIXth Century . . . London. V. 46
A Chronological History of the Old English Landscape Painters (in Oil) from the XVIth Century to the XIXth Century. London: 1940-47. V. 46
Chronological History of the Old English Landscape Painters (in Oil), from the XVIth Century to the XIXth Century . . . Leigh-on-Sea: 1957-61. V. 46
A Chronological History of the Old English Landscape Painters (in Oil) from the XVIth Century to the XIXth Century. Leight on Sea: 1973/74. V. 46
The Makers of Black Basaltes . . . Edinburgh and London: 1910. V. 45

GRANT, MAXWELL

The Living Shadow. New York: 1931. V. 37

GRANT, ROBERT 1779-1838

The Expediency Maintained by Continuing the System by Which the Trade and Government of India Are Now Regulated. London: 1813. V. 39; 40; 41; 43; 45
A History of Physical Astronomy from the Earliest Ages to the Middle of the 19th Century. London: 1852. V. 38; 40

GRANT, ULYSSES S. 1822-1885

Personal Memoirs of U. S. Grant. New York: 1885. V. 42; 43; 46
Report of Lieut. General U. S. Grant of the Armies of the United States, 1864-65. Washington: 1865. V. 42
Young John Russell. Around the World with General Grant . . . New York: 1879. V. 44

GRANT, ULYSSES SIMPSON 1822-1885

Personal Memoirs of U. S. Grant. New York: 1885-86. V. 37; 39
Report of Lieut. General U.S. Grant, of the Armies of the United States, 1864-65. Washington: 1865. V. 39

GRANT DUFF, MOUNTSTUART E.

Notes on an Indian Journey. London: 1876. V. 40

GRANTHAM, JOHN

Iron as a Material for Ship-Building; Being a Communication to the Polytechnic Society of Liverpool. London: 1842. V. 44
On Iron Shipbuilding with Practical Examples and Details in Twenty-Four Plates. London: 1864. V. 38

GRANTHAM, THOMAS

An Historical Account of Some Memorable Actions, Particularly in Virginia. Richmond: 1882. V. 39; 43; 45

GRANTS of Land to the Minnesota and Pacific R.R. Co. and Others Together with the Acts of Congress in Relation to the Same. St. Paul: 1857. V. 37

GRANUTIUS, PAULUS

Thorematum. Venice: 1581. V. 43

GRANVILLE, A. B.

Graphic Illustrations of Abortion and the Diseases of Mensturation. London: 1834. V. 42; 44
St. Petersburgh. London: 1829. V. 42
The Spas of England, and Principal Sea-Bathing Places. London: 1841. V. 38; 41; 45
The Spas of Germany. London: 1837. V. 45

GRANVILLE, AUGUSTUS BOZZI

The Spas of Germany. London: 1838. V. 37

GRANVILLE, GEORGE

The Genuine Works in Verse and Prose. London: 1732. V. 38

GRANVILLE, JOHN CARTERET, EARL OF

The State of the Nation for the Year 1747, and Respecting 1748 . . . London: 1748. V. 41; 45

GRANVILLE, ROGER

The History of the Granville Family. Exeter: 1895. V. 38

GRAPALDI, FRANCESCO MARIA ca. 1465-1515

De Partibus Aedium. Parmae: 1516. V. 39
De Partibvs Aedivm Libellvs Cvm Additamentis Emendatissimvs. Parma: 1501. V. 39

GRAPALDUS, F. M.

Lexicon de Partibus Aedium. Lyon: 1535. V. 37; 38

GRAPALDUS, FRANCISCUS MARIUS

De Partibus Aedium. Addita Modo Verborum Explicatione. Venice: 1517. V. 37
De Partibus Aedium. Parma: 1516. V. 46

GRAPES and Grape Vines of California. V. 46
GRAPES and Grape Vines of California. San Francisco: 1980. V. 38; 39

GRAPHAEUS, CORNELIUS

De Seer Wonderlijcke Schoone Triumpheliicke Incompst, van Den Hooghmogenden Prince Philips, Prince van Spaignen, Caroli des Vifdan, Keysers sone. Antwerp: 1550. V. 37

GRAPHEUS, CORNELIUS

Spectaculorum in Susceptione Philippi Hisp. prin. Divi Caroli V Caes. F. An. MDXLIX . . . Antwerp: 1550. V. 37; 46

GRAPHEUS, CORNELIUS SCRIBONIUS

Pacis Inter Carolum V Imp. Caes. Aug. & Franciscum I Galliarum Regem . . . Antwerp: 1540. V. 39

GRAPHIC Delineations of the Most Prominent Objects in the Isle of Wight. London: 1855. V. 37

GRAPPA, PSEUD.

Cicalamenti del Grappa Intorno al Sonetto . . . Mantua: 1545. V. 44

THE GRASIER'S Complaint and Petition for Redress; or, the Necessity of Restraining Irish Wool and Yarn; and of Raising the Supporting the Price of Wool of the Growth of Great-Britain, Consider'd. London: 1726. V. 46

GRASS, BARTH & CO.

Typen-Muster-Karte der Buchdruckerei von Grass, Barth & Co. in Breslau. V. 46

GRASS, GUNTER 1927-

The Flounder. 1985. V. 42
The Flounder. New York: 1985. V. 38; 39; 40; 42; 44; 45
The Tin Drum. London: 1962. V. 38; 39; 40; 42; 45

GRASS, GUNTHER

The Tin Drum. New York: 1962. V. 45; 46

GRASS VALLEY GOLD MINING CO.

Charter of the Grass Valley Gold Mining Company, Organized July 25, 1851, Under the General Incorporation Act of California. New York: 1852. V. 40

GRASSE, FRANCOIS J. P., COMTE DE

The Operations of the French Fleet Under the Count De Grasse in 1781-82. New York: 1864. V. 45

GRASSET, EUGENE

Les Mois, Douze Compositions, Gravees sur Bois & Imprimees en Chromotypographie. Paris: 1913. V. 39

GRASSI, BENEVENUTO

De Oculis Eroumque Egritudinibus et Curis. Stanford: 1929. V. 41

GRASSI, BENVENUTO

De Oculis Eorumque Egritudinibus et Curis. 1929. V. 41

GRASSI, GIUNIO PAOLO d. 1574

Medici Antiqui Graeci: Aretaeus, Palladius, Ruffus, Theophilus . . . Basilaeae: 1581. V. 44; 46

GRASSI, ORZIO

Libra Astronomica ac Philosophica Qua Galilaei Galilaei Opiniones de Cometis a Mario Guiducio in Florentina Academia Expositae, Atque in Lucem Nuper Editae . . . Perugia: 1619. V. 43

GRASTORF, DENNIS J.

Wood-type of the Angelica Press. New York: 1975. V. 39

GRASTORPF, DENNIS

Woodtype of the Angelica Press. Brooklyn. V. 42

GRASTY, JOHN S.

Memoir of Rev. Samuel B. McPheeters . . . St. Louis: 1871. V. 38

GRASWINCKEL, THEODORE 1600-1666

Dissertatio de Jure Praecedentiae Inter Serenissiman Venetam Rempubl. & Sereniss. Leyden: 1644. V. 40

GRATACAP, L. P.

The Certainty of a Future Life in Mars. N.P.: 1903. V. 39

GRATARALO, GUGLIELMO

Alchemiae, Quam Vocant, Artisque Metallicae, Doctrina, Certusque Modus . . . Basle: 1572. V. 46

GRATAROLI, GUGLIELMO

De Arte Peregrinandi Libri II. Noribergae: 1591. V. 37; 42; 44

Alchemiae Quam Vocant Artisque Metallicae Doctrina. Basilea: 1572. V. 44

GRATIA DEI, JOHANNES BAPTISTA

De Confutatione Hebraicae Sectae. Rome: 1500. V. 40

GRATIAN, BONONIENSIS

Decretum Gratiani iam Recens Innumeris Pene Mendis . . . Paris: 1538. V. 40

GRATIANUS, ANT. MARIA

De Vita Joannis Francisci Commendoni Cardinalis, Libri Quatuor. Paris: 1669. V. 37

GRATIUS FALISCUS

Cynegeticon. Or, A Poem on Hunting. London: 1654. V. 37; 38

Cynegetion, cum Poematio Cognomine M.A. Olympii Nemesiani . . . Londini: 1699. V. 44

Fati Falisci Cynegeticon. Or, A Poem of Hunting by Gratius . . . London: 1654. V. 42

GRATIUS FALSICUS

Cynegeticon: or, a Poem on Hunting. London: 1654. V. 37

GRATTAN, HENRY

Memoirs of the Life and Times of the Rt. Hon. Henry Grattan. London: 1839. V. 37; 38; 39; 43

Memoirs of the Life and Times of the Rt. Hon Henry Grattan. London: 1839. V. 43

Memoirs of the Life and Times of the Rt. Hon. Henry Grattan by His Son. London: 1839-46. V. 37

The Speeches of henry Grattan in the Irish and Imperial Parliament. V. 39

GRATTAN, THOMAS COLLEY

Beaten Paths; and Those Who Trod Them. London: 1865. V. 45

Civilized America. London: 1859. V. 42

The Heiress of Bruges. London: 1830. V. 39

Jacqueline of Holland. London: 1831. V. 37; 39

GRATTON, JOHN

A Journal of the Life of that Ancient Servant of Christ, John Gratton, etc. London: 1720. V. 44

GRATTON, T. C.

High Ways and By Ways, or Tales of the Roadside . . . London: 1825. V. 42

CAMBRIDGE Gratulatio Academiae Cantabrigiensis Natales Auspicatissimos Georgii Walliae Principis Augustissimi Georgi III Magnae Britanniae Regis et Serenissimae Charlottae Reginae Filii Celebrantis. Cantabrigiae: 1762. V. 41

GRATULATIO Academiae Cantabrigiensis Auspicatissimas Georgii III Magana Britannia Regis, et Serenissimae Charlottae Principis de Mecklenburgh-Strelitz Nuptias Celebrantis. Cantabrigiae: 1761. V. 44

GRATULATIO Academiae Cantabrigiensis De Pace Serenissimae Reginae Annae Auspiciis Feliciter Constiuta Anno 1713. Cantabrigiae: 1713. V. 44

GRATULATIO Academiae Cantabrigiensis in Pacem Augustissimi Principis Georgii III Magniae Britanniae Regis Auspiciis Europae Feliciter Restitutam Anno MDCCLXIII. Cantabrigiae: 1763. V. 44

GRATULATIO Academiae Cantabrigiensis Natales Aspicatissimos Georgii Walliae Principis Augustissimi Georgii III Magniae Britanniae Regis et Serenissimae Charlottae Reginae Filii Celebrantis. Cantabrigiae: 1762. V. 44

GRATULATIO Solennis Universitatis Oxoniensis ob Celsissimum Georgium Fred. Aug. Walliae Principem Georgio II et Charlottae Reginae Auspicatissime Natum. Oxonii: 1762. V. 44

GRATULATIONES Juventutis Academiae Dubliniensis in Serensis. Regis et Reginae Nuptialis. Dublin: 1761. V. 40

GRAU, SHIRLEY ANN

The Black Prince. New York: 1955. V. 37; 39; 42

Evidence of Love. Franklin Center: 1977. V. 46

GRAUX, LUCIEN

Le Tapis des Prieres. Paris: 1938. V. 38

GRAVELL, THOMAS L.

A Catalogue of American Watermarks, 1690-1835. New York & London: 1979. V. 42

GRAVELOT, HUBERT FRANCOIS BOURGUIGNON, CALLED

Iconologie par Figures, ou Traite Complete des Allegories, Emblemes, &c. Ouvrage Utile aux Artistes, aux Amateurs, et Pouvant Servir . . . A Paris: 1791. V. 44

GRAVES, ALFRED PERCEVAL

Welsh Poetry Old and New. London: 1912. V. 38

GRAVES, ALGERNON

The Society of Artists of Great Britain 1760-1791 The Free Society of Artists 1761-1783. London: 1907. V. 39

GRAVES, G.

Hortus Medicus. Edinburgh: 1844. V. 37

GRAVES, GEORGE

British Ornithology: Being the History with a Colored Representation of Every Known Species of British Birds. London: 1811-13. V. 39

British Ornithology. London: 1821. V. 39

The Naturalist's Pocket-Book or Tourist's Companion. London: 1818. V. 43

Ovarium Britannicum. London: 1816. V. 39

GRAVES, IDA

Epithalamion, a Poem. 1934. V. 45

Epithalamion. Colchester: 1934. V. 39; 41; 42

Epithalamion; a Poem by Ida Graves . . . 1980. V. 44

Epithalamion. Higham: 1980. V. 41; 43

Epithalamion. Higham, Colchester: 1980. V. 40

Epithalamion. London: 1980. V. 39

A Poem by Ida Graves with associate wood-engravings by Blair Hughes-Stanton. Colchester: 1934. V. 37

GRAVES, JAMES

A Roll of the Proceedings of the King's Council in Ireland, A.D. 1392-3. London: 1877. V. 38

GRAVES, JOHN

Goodbye to a River. London: 1961. V. 38; 40

Goodbye to a River. Austin: 1988. V. 39; 41; 42

Goodbye to a River. Austin: 1989. V. 45

The History of Cleveland. 1808. V. 38

The Last Running. Austin: 1974. V. 44

A Memorial; or, A Short Account of the Baham Islands; of Their Situation, Product Conveniency of Trading with the Spaniards; The Benefit that Ariseth by the Great Quantities of Salt that is Made by the Sun. London: 1706/07. V. 46

A Memorial; or, A Short Account of the Bahama-Islands . . . London: 1706-07. V. 42

GRAVES, R. P.

Life of Sir William Rowan Hamilton. Dublin: 1882-89. V. 38

GRAVES, RICHARD

Columella; or, the Distressed Anchoret. London: 1779. V. 38; 41; 42; 45; 46

Euphrosyne: or, Amusements on the Road of Life. London: 1776. V. 38

Euphrosyne: or, Amusements on the Road of Life. London: 1783. V. 39

The Festoon: a Collection of Epigrams, Ancient and Modern. London: 1766. V. 40

The Festoon: a Collection of Epigrams, Ancient and Modern. London: 1766, 1765. V. 42

The Festoon. London: 1767. V. 38; 43

The Rout; or a Sketch of Modern Life. London: 1789. V. 42

The Spiritual Quixote. London. V. 38

The Spiritual Quixote. London: 1773. V. 40; 44

The Spiritual Quixote; or, the Summer's Ramble of Mr. Geoffrey Wildgoose. London: 1774. V. 45

The Spiritual Quixote; or, the Summer's Ramble of Mr. Geoffrey Wildgoose. London: 1783. V. 37; 43; 46

The Spiritual Quixote. London: 1792. V. 40

GRAVES, RICHARD S.

Oklahoma Outlaws. Oklahoma City: 1915. V. 40; 43; 46

GRAVES, ROBERT 1895-1985

Adam's Rib. London: 1955. V. 40; 41

Advice from a Mother. London: 1970. V. 45

The Anger of Achilles. London: 1960. V. 40

GRAVES, ROBERT 1895-1985 continued

Ann at Highwood Hall - Poems for Children. London: 1964. V. 41

Another Future of Poetry. London: 1926. V. 41

Antigua, Penny, Puce. Deya: 1936. V. 43

Antigua Penny Puce. Deya, Majorca & London: 1936. V. 38

'Antigua, Penny, Puce'. Deya, Majoria: 1936. V. 46

Antigua, Penny, Puce. London: 1936. V. 44; 46

Antigua Penny Puce. Majorca: 1936. V. 38

Antigua, Penny, Puce. Toronto: 1936. V. 39

The Antigua Stamp. New York: 1937. V. 37; 38; 40; 42

At the Gate. London: 1974. V. 40; 41; 46

At the Gate. (London): 1974. V. 37

Beyond Giving, Poems. London: 1969. V. 38; 40; 43; 46

Beyond Giving: Poems. Hatfield: 1969. V. 37

But It Still Goes On. London: 1930. V. 39; 40; 42; 44; 46

But It Still Goes On. London: 1930. V. 39

But It Still Goes On: an Accumulation. London: 1932. V. 44

Claudius the God. London: 1934. V. 38; 39; 40; 41

Collected Poems. New York: 1938. V. 43

Collected Short Stories. New York: 1964. V. 40

Colophon to Love Respelt. 1967. V. 40; 42

Colophon to Love Respelt: Poems. London: 1967. V. 45

Colophon to Love Respelt. N.P.: 1967. V. 46

Contemporary Techniques of Poetry. London: 1925. V. 41

Count Belisarius. London: 1938. V. 41

Count Belisarius. New York: 1938. V. 42

Country Sentiment. London: 1920. V. 38; 43

Country Setiment. New York: 1920. V. 40

Eleven Songs. Majorca: 1983. V. 42

Eleven Songs. Mallorca: 1983. V. 39

Eleven Songs. (Mallorca: 1983). V. 37

The English Ballad. London: 1927. V. 38; 41

Fairies and Fusiliers. London: 1917. V. 37; 38; 40; 41; 42

The Feather Bed. London: 1923. V. 40; 44

George Sand in Majorca. 1986. V. 40

Goliath and David. N.P.: 1917. V. 44

Good-By to All Tht. London: 1929. V. 38; 39; 40; 41; 42; 43; 44; 45; 46

Good-Bye to All That: an Autobiography. New York: 1930. V. 45; 46

The Greek Myths. New York: 1957. V. 40

The Green Sailed Vessel Poems. Hatfield: 1971. V. 37; 40; 42

The Green Sailed Vessel. London: 1971. V. 40

Hebrew Myths - the Book of Genesis. London: 1964. V. 40

I, Claudius. 1934. V. 45

I, Claudius. London: 1934. V. 38; 39; 40; 43; 44

Impenetrability; or, The Proper Habit of English. London: 1926. V. 40

John Kemp's Wager. Oxford: 1925. V. 40; 42; 46

Lars Porsena. London. V. 40

Lars Porsena. London: 1927. V. 46

Lars Porsena. New York: 1927. V. 39

Lars Porsena. London: 1972. V. 38; 40; 41; 42; 43

Lawrence and the Arabs. London: 1927. V. 38; 39; 40; 42

Love Respelt. London: 1965. V. 40; 41

Man Does, Woman is. London: 1964. V. 38; 40; 42

The Marmosite's Miscellany. British Columbia: 1975. V. 46

Mock Beggar Hall. London: 1924. V. 42

Mock Beggar Hall. London: 1924. V. 40

Mock Beggar Hall. London: 1924. V. 38; 39; 40; 42; 43; 45

Mock Beggar Hall. London: 1924. V. 38

The More Deserving Cases. 1962. V. 40; 42; 45

The More Deserving Cases. Marlborogh College Press,: 1962. V. 37; 45

The More Deserving Cases. Marlborough College,: 1962. V. 37

My Head! My Head! London: 1925. V. 44

The Nazarene Gospel Restored. London: 1953. V. 45

The Nazarene Gospel Restored. New York: 1954. V. 43

No More Ghosts: Selected Poems. London: 1940. V. 37; 44

Ogham: a Calendar of Seasonal Bardic Lore Based on an Interpretation by Robert Graves of the Cyphers Used in the Book of Ballymote. 1978. V. 45

Ogham. An Interpretation of the Cyphers Used in the Book of Ballymote. London: 1978. V. 38

On English Poetry. London: 1922. V. 37; 38; 40; 41; 43

On English Poetry . . . New York: 1922. V. 37; 42

Oratio Creweiana. London: 1964. V. 40

Over the Brazier. London: 1916. V. 37; 41; 42; 44

Over the Brazier. London: 1920. V. 45

Oxford Addresses on Poetry. London: 1962. V. 38; 39; 40; 42

The Penny Fiddle - Poems for Children. London: 1960. V. 41

Pharsalia. London: 1957. V. 45

The Pier-Glass. London: 1921. V. 41

Poems. London: 1927. V. 40

Poems (1914-1926). London: 1927. V. 38; 39; 40; 42; 43; 46

Poems 1914-26. London: 1927. V. 40

Poems 1929. London: 1929. V. 39; 40; 41; 43

Poems (1926-1930). London: 1931. V. 38; 39; 40; 42; 44; 46

Poems for Children. London: 1964. V. 41

Poems. Lunenburg: 1980. V. 40

Poems of Robert Graves. New York: 1980. V. 40; 42

Poems. New York: 1980. V. 39; 40; 41; 45; 46

Poetic Unreason. London: 1925. V. 40; 41; 42

Proceed, Sergeant Lamb. London: 1941. V. 46

Proceed, Sergeant Lamb. New York: 1941. V. 40; 42

The Real David Copperfield. London: 1933. V. 37; 38; 39; 41; 43; 46

Sergeant Lamb of the Ninth. London: 1940. V. 40; 42; 45

Sergeant Lamb's America. New York: 1940. V. 40; 42; 44

Seventeen Poems Missing from Love Respelt. 1966. V. 40; 42

Seventeen Poems Missing from Love Respelt. London: 1966. V. 41

Seventeen Poems Missing from Love Respelt. Barnet,: 1966. V. 37

The Shout. London: 1929. V. 37; 38; 39; 40; 42; 43; 44; 46

The Siege and Fall of Troy - Retold for Young People. London: 1962. V. 43

Steps. London: 1958. V. 38; 43

Suite Sand/Graves: George Sand in Majorca. Deya, Majorca: 1896. V. 42

A Survey of Modernist Poetry. London: 1927. V. 37; 41; 45

Ten Poems More. Paris: 1930. V. 37; 39; 43; 46

Timeless Meeting - Poems. London: 1973. V. 40; 41; 43; 44; 46

To Whom Else. Deya, Majorca: 1931. V. 37; 38; 40

To Whom Else ? Poems. Majorca: 1931. V. 41; 42

To Whom Else. Majorca and London: 1931. V. 38

To Whom Else? Mallorca: 1931. V. 46

To Whom Else? Deya, Majorca: 1931. V. 37

Watch the Northwind Rise. New York: 1949. V. 38; 39; 40; 41; 42; 45

Welchman's Hose. London: 1925. V. 38; 39; 40; 42

Whipperginny. London: 1923. V. 38; 39; 40; 42

The White Goddess. New York: 1948. V. 40; 42

Winter In Majorca. London: 1956. V. 42

GRAVES, ROBERT J.

Clinical Lectures on the Practice of Medicine. Dublin: 1848. V. 41

Clinical Lectures on the Practice of Medicine. London: 1848. V. 39

GRAVES, ROBERT JAMES 1796-1853

Clinical Lectures on the Practice of Medicine. Dublin: 1864. V. 40

GRAVES, S. H.

On the 'White Pass' Payroll. Chicago: 1908. V. 37

GRAVES, SAMUEL ROBERT

A Yachting Cruise in the Baltic. London: 1863. V. 40

GRAVESANDE, WILLEM JACOB S'

Introduction a la Philosophie . . . Leyden: 1737. V. 38

GRAVESANDE, WILLEM JACOB VAN S' 1688-1742

Elemens de Physique, ou Introduction a la Philosophie de Newton. Paris: 1747. V. 41; 45

Mathematical Elements of Natural Philosophy. London: 1747. V. 40

Physices Elementa Mathematica, Experimentis Confirmata. Lugduni Batavorum: 1725, 1721. V. 40

GRAVIER, R. P. JACQUES

Relation ou Journal du Voyage en 1700 depuis le Pays des Illinois Jusqu'a l'Embouchure du Mississipi (sic). Manate: 1859. V. 39

GRAVIERE, E. JURIEN DE LA

Sketches of the Last Naval War. London: 1848. V. 42

GRAVINA, GIOVANNI VINCENZO 1664-1718

Originum Juris Civilis Libri Tres. Naples: 1713. V. 40

GRAY, ALASDAIR

Lanark. Edinburgh: 1981. V. 40

Unlikely Stories, Mostly. Edinburgh: 1983. V. 38

GRAY, ALISDAIR

Lanark. New York: 1985. V. 46

GRAY, THOMAS 1716-1771 continued

Designs by Mr. R. Bentley for Six Poems. London: 1753. V. 37; 38; 40; 42; 43; 45; 46

Designs by Mr. R. Bentley, for Six Poems by Mr. T. Gray. London: 1753. V. 37

Elegy Written in a Country Churchyard. London. V. 40; 46

An Elegy Written in A Country Church Yard. London: 1751. V. 37; 38; 40; 41; 43; 45

Elegia Scripta in Coemeterio Rustico Latine Reddita. Cantabrigae: 1762. V. 41

An Elegy Written in a Country Church Yard. London: 1763. V. 46

Elegi Inglese Sopra Un Cimitero Campestre. Parma: 1793. V. 38; 44

An Elegy Written by a Country Churchyard . . . Philadelphia: 1806. V. 39

Elegy Written in a Country-Church Yard. London: 1839. V. 41

Elegy. London: 1846. V. 39

Gray's Elegy. London: 1846. V. 37; 38; 42; 43; 44

Elegy. London: 1846. V. 39; 41

Elegy. London: & New York: 1846. V. 44

An Elegy Written in a Country Churchyard. London: 1855. V. 44

Gray's Elegy. London: 1860. V. 41

An Elegy Written in a Country Churchyard. London: 1861. V. 42; 44

An Elegy Written in a Country Churchyard. London: 1869. V. 39; 42; 43

Elegy Written in a Country Churchyard. London: 1899. V. 44

Elegy Written in a Country Churchyard. London: 1900. V. 37; 40; 43

Gray's Elegy in a Country Churchyard. London: 1901. V. 43

Elegy Written in a Country Churchyard. London: 1901. V. 39

An Elegy Written in A Country Churchyard. Blackheath: 1902. V. 40

Gray's Elegy: a Lyric Poem. East Aurora: 1903. V. 39

Elegy in a Country Churchyard and Other Poems. Glasgow: 1904. V. 44

Gray's Elegy. Boston: 1912. V. 41

An Elegy Written in a Country Church-Yard. San Francisco: 1925. V. 40; 43; 44

Elegy Writtein in a Country Church-Yard. London: 1938. V. 41; 43; 44; 46

Elegy Written in a Country Church-Yard. New York: 1938. V. 44

Elegy Written in a Country Church Yard. London: 1946. V. 44

Elegy Written in a Country Church-Yard. Waltham St. Lawrence: 1946. V. 46

Gray's Elegy Written in a Country Churchyard. London: 1956. V. 38

Elegy Written in a Country Churchyard. Worcester: 1960. V. 45

Elegy Written in a Country Churchyard. Mindelheim: 1965. V. 39

Elegy Written in a Country Church-Yard; Ode on the Spring; and Ode on a Distant Prospect of Eton College. London/New York: 1905. V. 37

An Elegy Written In a Country Churchyard. Philadelphia: (1883). V. 37

Poems. London: 1768. V. 41

Gray's Elegy: Written in a Country Churchyard. With a foreword by Christopher Sandford and eight engravings by Gwenda Morgan. London: 1946. V. 37

Observations on a General Iron Rail-way. London: 1822. V. 39; 45; 46

Observations of a General Iron Railway . . . London: 1823. V. 44

Observations on a General Iron Rail-Way, or Land Steam-Conveyance. London: 1825. V. 38; 46

Ode Performed in the Senate-House at Cambridge July 1, 1769, at the Installation of His Grace Augustus-Henry Fitzroy, Duke of Grafton . . . Cambridge: 1769. V. 37; 38

Ode on the Pleasure Arising from Vicissitude. San Francisco: 1933. V. 40; 43

Odes by Mr. Gray. 1757. V. 37; 40; 41

Odes by Mr. Gray. London: 1757. V. 37; 40; 43

Odes. Strawberry Hill: 1757. V. 37; 43; 44; 45; 46

Poems. Dublin: 1768. V. 38; 40

Poems. Glasgow: 1768. V. 38; 40; 41; 45

Poems. London: 1768. V. 37; 43; 45

Poems. Dublin: 1775. V. 37; 38; 42; 45

The Poems of Mr. Gray. To Which are Prefixed Memoirs of His Life and Writings. London: 1775. V. 40; 41

The Poems of Mr. Gray. York: 1775. V. 38; 41; 46

The Poems of Mr. Gray. To Which are Added Memoirs of His Life and Writings. York: 1778. V. 42

The Poems of Mr. Gray. York: 1778. V. 38; 40; 42; 43

Poems. London: 1786. V. 44

Poems by Mr. Gray. Parma: 1793. V. 39; 42

The Poems. London: 1800. V. 38; 39

The Poems of Thomas Gray. London: 1814. V. 41

The Poems and Letters . . . With Memories of His Life and Writings by William Mason. London: 1820. V. 43

Poems and Letters. London: 1867. V. 37; 38; 40; 44

Poems and Letters. London: 1874. V. 44

Poems and Letters. 1879. V. 38

Poems and Letters of Thomas Gray. London: 1879. V. 37; 43

Poems. Eton: 1894. V. 37

Poems. Eton: 1894. V. 37; 46

Poems. Eton: 1902. V. 39

Poems. London: 1928. V. 44

The Poetical Works . . . London: 1797. V. 45

Poetical Works. London: 1799. V. 45

A Supplement to the Tour through Great-Britain, Containing a Catalogue of the Antiquities, Houses, Parks, Plantations, Scenes and Situation, in England and Wales . . . London: 1787. V. 38

The Works. London: 1807. V. 38; 43

The Works of . . . London: 1825. V. 39; 44

The Works of Gray. London: 1836. V. 39

GRAY, THOMAS, of Nottingham

Observations of a General Iron Railway. London: 1823. V. 38

GRAY, W. H.

A History of Oregon, 1792-1849, Drawn from Personal Observation and Authentic Information. Portland: 1870. V. 40

GRAY, WILLIAM

Chorographia, or a Survey of Newcstle-upon-Tyne. Newcastle: 1884. V. 38

Travels in Western Africa, in the Years 1818, 19, 20, and 21 from the River Gambia, through Wooli, Bondoo, Galam, Kasson, Kaarta and Foolidoo, to the River Niger. London: 1825. V. 41; 42; 43

GRAY, WILLIAM FAIRFAX

From Virginia to Texas, 1835-1837. Houston: 1909. V. 37

GRAY, ZANE

The Hash Knife Outfit. London: 1933. V. 37

GRAYDON, ALEX

Memoirs of a Life, Chiefly Passed in Pennsylvania . . . Edinburgh: 1822. V. 44

GRAYDON, ALEXANDER

Memoirs of a Life, Chiefly Passed in Pennsylvania Within the Last Sixty Years. Harrisburg: 1811. V. 38; 39; 41; 42

GRAYSON, A. J.

Birds of the Pacific Slope. San Francisco: 1986. V. 37

GRAYSON, DAVID

Adventures in Contentment. New York: 1907. V. 37

GRAYSON, WILLIAM J.

The Hireling and Slave. Charleston: 1854. V. 41

The Hireling and the Slave Chicora, and Other Poems. Charleston: 1856. V. 37; 41

GRAZEBROOK, H. SYDNEY

The Heraldry of Worcestershire . . . London: 1873. V. 41

GRAZEBROOK, O. F.

Studies in Sherlock Holmes. V. 43

Oxford or Cambridge - Studies in Sherlock Holmes. London. V. 41

GRAZIA, VINCENZO

Considerazioni . . . Sopra'l Discorso di Galileo Galileo Intorno alle Cose Che Stanno su l'Acqua, e che in quella si Muouono . . . Florence: 1613. V. 38

GRAZIANI, GIROLAMO

Il Cromvele Tragedia. Bologna: 1671. V. 42

GRAZZINI, ANTONIO FRANCESCO

La Gelosia Comedia Nuovamente Ristampata & Aggiuntovi glIntermedi. Venice: 1582. V. 37

La Pinzochera Comedia. Venice: 1582. V. 37

La Sibilla Comedia. Venice: 1582. V. 37

GRAZZINI, ANTONIO FRANCESCO, CALLED IL LASCA 1503-1584

La Spiritata. Venice: 1582. V. 40

Lasca's Story of Doctor Manente. Florence: 1929. V. 39

The Story of Doctor Manente. Florence: 1929. V. 37; 38; 39; 40; 41

GREACEN, ROBERT

The Art of Noel Coward. Aldington: 1953. V. 41

GREARD, VALLERY, C. O.

Meissonier: His Life and Art. London: 1897. V. 40; 44

Meissonier: His Life and His Art. New York: 1897. V. 40

GREARY, EDWARD R.

Depredations and Massacre by the Snake River Indians . . . Washington: 1861. V. 42

THE GREAT Bastard, Protector of the Little One. Colognne: 1689. V. 45

THE GREAT Bastard, Protector of the Little One. London: 1702. V. 40

GREAT Books of the Western World. Chicago: 1977. V. 42

GREAT BRITAIN

Report to the Secretary of State for the Home Department, from the Poor Law Commissioners, on the Training of Pauper Children . . . London: 1841. V. 46

GREAT BRITAIN. ADJUTANT GENERAL'S OFFICE - 1796

Rules and Regulations for the Sword Exercise of the Cavalry. London: 1796. V. 46

GREAT BRITAIN. ARMY - 1704

Dress Regulations for the Officers of the Army (Including the Militia). 1904. London: 1904. V. 38

GREAT BRITAIN. ARMY - 1800

Regulations Relative to the Clothing and Half-Mounting of the Infantry, and the Inspection of Clothing of the Army in General. London: 1800. V. 38

GREAT BRITAIN. ARMY - 1822

Regulations for the Dress of General Staff, and Regimental Officers, 1822. Revised and Corrected 25th December 1826. London: 1826. V. 38

GREAT BRITAIN. ARMY - 1831

Regulations for the Dress of General, Staff, and Regimental Officers of the Army, 1831. London: 1831. V. 38

GREAT BRITAIN. ARMY - 1834

Regulations for the Dress of the General, Staff and Regimental Officers of the Army, 1834. London: 1834. V. 38

GREAT BRITAIN. ARMY - 1864

Regulations for the Dress of General, Staff and Regimental Officers of the Army, 1864. London: 1864. V. 38

GREAT BRITAIN. BOARD OF AGRICULTURE

Communications to the Board of Agriculture on Subjects Relative to the Husbandy and Internal Improvement of the Country. London: 1797-1805. V. 39

General View of the Agriculture in the County of Perth. Perth: 1799. V. 39

GREAT BRITAIN. CENSUS - 1801

Abstract of the Answers and Returns Made Pursuant to . . . 'An act for Taking an Account of the Population of Great Britian and the Increase or Diminution Thereof'. 1801-02. V. 45

GREAT BRITAIN. CENSUS OFFICE

Abstract of the Answers and Returns Made Pursuant to an Act, Passed in the 11th Year of the reign of His Majesty King George IV, Intituled 'An Act for Taking an Account of the Population of Great Britain . . . London: 1833. V. 41

Census of England and Wales 1871. London: 1871-72-73. V. 42; 43

GREAT BRITAIN. COLONIAL OFFICE - 1847

Papers Relative to Emigration to the British Provinces in North America and to the Australian Colonies. London: 1847. V. 40

GREAT BRITAIN. COLONIAL OFFICE - 1859

Papers Relative to the Exploration of the Country Between Lake Superior and the Red River Settlement. London: 1859. V. 40

GREAT BRITAIN. COLONIAL OFFICE. DISCOVERY COMMITTEE - 1929

Discovery Reports Issued by the Discovery Committee . . . on Behalf of the Government of the Dependcies of the Falkland Islands. Cambridge: 1929. V. 41

GREAT BRITAIN. COMM. NOMINATED TO TREAT A UNION BETWEEN THE KINGDOMS OF ENGLAND & SCOTLAND

Articles of Union, agreed on the Two and Twentieth Day of July, in the Fifth Year of the Reign of Her Most Excellant Majesty, Queen Anne, ... And also the Minutes of the Proceeding of the Commissioners of both Kingdoms, ... London: 1706. V. 39

GREAT BRITAIN. COMMISSION OF HISTORICAL MONUMENTS

An Inventory of the Ancient and Historical Monuments of Roxburghshire . . . with the Fourteenth report of the Commission. Edinburgh: 1956. V. 37

GREAT BRITAIN. COMMISSION ON HISTORICAL MONUMENTS

Royal Commission on the Ancient and Historical Monuments . . . of Scotland. Fifth report and inventory of monuments and constructions in Galloway. Edinburgh: 1914. V. 37

GREAT Britain. COMMISSION ON THE ANCIENT & HISTORICAL MONUMENTS & CONSTRTIONS OF ENGLAND (Royal) Hertfordshire. London: 1912. V. 39

GREAT BRITAIN. COMMISSIONERS OF LONGITUDE - 1772

Tables for Correcting the Apparent Distance of the Moon and a Star from the Effects of Refraction and Parallax . . . Cambridge: 1772. V. 43

GREAT BRITAIN. COURT OF STAR CHAMBER

A Decree of Starre-Chamber, Concerning Printing. London: 1637. V. 41

A Decree of Star Chamber Concerning Printing, Made the Eleventh Day of July 1637. New York: 1884. V. 45

GREAT BRITAIN. COURT OF STAR CHAMBER - 1633

A Decree Lately Made in the High Court of Starre-Chamber . . . (13th November 1633, Concerning Grain, Bread Prices, etc . . . And also a Confirmation of that Decree by His Sacred Maiestie . . . London: 1633. V. 45

GREAT BRITAIN. COURT OF STAR CHAMBER - 1636

A Decree of Starre-Chamber: Concerning Inmates, and Divided Tenements, in London or Three Miles About . . . London: 1636. V. 45

GREAT BRITAIN. COURT OF STAR CHAMBER - 1637

A Decree of Starre-Chamber, Concerning Printing . . . London: 1637. V. 44

GREAT BRITAIN. ECCLESIASTICAL COURTS COMMISSION

Report of the Commissioners Appointed to Inquire Into the Constitution and Working of the Ecclesiastical Courts. London: 1883. V. 39

GREAT BRITAIN. FOREIGN OFFICE

Correspondence Respecting the Proposed Channel Tunnel and Railway. Presented to Both Houses of Parliament by Command of Her Majesty. London: 1875. V. 39

GREAT BRITAIN. FOREIGN OFFICE - 1809

Papers Relating to America. Presented to the House of Commons, 1809. London: 1810. V. 40

GREAT BRITAIN. GEOLOGICAL SURVEY

Memoirs of the . . . of Great Britain and of the Museum of Economic Geology in London. London: 1846-48. V. 38

GREAT BRITAIN. IRISH RAILWAY COMMISSION - 1838

Second Report of the Commissioners Appointed to Consider and Recommend a General System of Railways for Ireland. Dublin: 1838. V. 42

GREAT BRITAIN. LAWS, STATUTES, ETC. - 1562

Anno XXVI Henrici Octavi. Actes Made in the Session of This Present Parliament. London: 1562? V. 40

GREAT BRITAIN. LAWS, STATUTES, ETC. - 1575

Anno xviii REgine Elizabethae. At This Present Session of Parliament . . . Holden the VIII Day of Feb . . . . & there Continued Intyle the XV Day of Arch Follwying. London: 1575. V. 44

GREAT BRITAIN. LAWS, STATUTES, ETC. - 1576

Magna Charta, cum Statutis, Tum Antiquis, Tum Recentibus, Maxim Opere, Animo Tenendis Nunc Demum ad Vnum Tipis Aedita per Richardum Tottell. London: 1576. V. 39

GREAT BRITAIN. LAWS, STATUTES, ETC. - 1587

Whole Volume of Statutes at Large, Which at Anie Time Heretofore Have Been Extant in Print, Since Magna Charta, Until XXIX Elizabeth. London: 1587. V. 40

GREAT BRITAIN. LAWS, STATUTES, ETC. - 1604

An. Reg. Iacobi . . . Primo . . . At the Parliament Begun and Holden at Westminster the XIX. Day of March, in the FIrst Yeere of the Raigne . . . And there Continued vntil the Seuenth Day of Iuly 1604 . . . London: 1604. V. 45

GREAT BRITAIN. LAWS, STATUTES, ETC. - 1606

An. Regni Iacobi, Regis Angl. Scotiae, Franc. & Hybern . . . at the Second Session of Parliament Begun and Holden . . . at Westminster the Fifth Day of Nouember, in the Third Yeere of the Raigne . . . and . . . Continued vntil the 27 of May . . . London: 1606. V. 45

GREAT BRITAIN. LAWS, STATUTES, ETC. - 1608

Magna Charta cum Statutis, tum Antiquis, rum Recentibus, Maximopere Animo Tenendis . . . London: 1608. V. 38; 40

GREAT BRITAIN. LAWS, STATUTES, ETC. - 1625

Anno Regni Caroli . . . Primo. At the Parliament Begun at Westminster the Eighteenth Day of Iune . . . 1625 . . . and There Continued vntil the 11, Day of Iuly . . . and the Adiourned vntill the 1. day of August . . . vnto Oxford . . . London: 1625. V. 45

GREAT BRITAIN. LAWS, STATUTES, ETC. - 1643

An Ordinance . . . in Parliament, for the Preservation and Keeping Together . . . Such Books, Evidences . . . Sequestered, as are fit to be so Preserved. London: 1643. V. 41; 46

An Ordinance of the Lords and Commons . . . Showing, that all His Majesties, the Queens, and Princes Honours . . . London: 1643. V. 43

An Ordinance of the Lords and Commons . . . for the Cutting and Selling of Wood Within Threescore Miles of London . . . London: 1643. V. 38

Two Ordinances of the Lords and Commons Assembled in Parliament. London: 1643. V. 40

GREAT BRITAIN. LAWS, STATUTES, ETC. - 1647

An Ordinance of the Lords and Commons . . . for the Raising of Moneys to be Imployed Towards the Maintenance of Forces . . . London: 1647. V. 43

An Ordinance of the Lords and Commons . . . for Raising of Twenty Thousand Pounds a Month for the Relief of Ireland. London: 1647. V. 43

GREAT BRITAIN. LAWS, STATUTES, ETC. - 1648

An Act Prohibiting the Proclaiming of Any Person to be King of England or Ireland. London: 1648. V. 40

Ordinance of the Lords and Commons . . . for, the Constituting and Setling of the Committee of the Militia of the City of London . . . London: 1648. V. 43

GREAT BRITAIN. LAWS, STATUTES, ETC. - 1649

An Act Against Unlicensed and Scandalous Books and Pamphlets, and for the Regulating of Printing. London: 1649. V. 38; 40

An Act of the Commons of England In Parliament Assembled, For the Abolishing of Deans, Deans and Chapters, Canons, Prebends and Other Offices and Titles, of Or Belonging to Any Cathedral, or Collegiate Church or Chappel within England and Wales. London: 1649. V. 45

GREAT BRITAIN. LAWS, STATUTES, ETC. - 1650

An Act Prohibiting Trade with the Barbada's Virginia, Bermuda's and Antego. London: 1650. V. 40; 45

GREAT BRITAIN. LAWS, STATUTES, ETC. - 1651

An Act of General Pardon and Oblivion, Tuesday the 24th of February 1651. London: 1651. V. 40

GREAT BRITAIN. LAWS, STATUTES, ETC. - 1653

An Ordinance Impowering Commissioners to Put in Execution an Act of Parliament, Intituled, an Act Prohibting the Planting of Tobacco in England. London: 1653. V. 41

GREAT BRITAIN. LAWS, STATUTES, ETC. - 1657

An Additional Act for the Better Improvement and Advancing the Receipts of the Excise and New-Impost. At the Parliament Begun at Westmisnter the 17 day of September, An. Dom. 1657. London: 1657. V. 37

GREAT BRITAIN. LAWS, STATUTES, ETC. - 1658

A Collection of Acts and Ordinances of General Use . . . Made in the Parliament 1640 to 1656. London: 1658-57. V. 40

GREAT BRITAIN. LAWS, STATUTES, ETC. - 1662

Anno Regni Caroli II. Regis . . . decimo Quarto. At the Parliament Begun at Westminster the Eighth Day of May, Anno Dom. 1661 . . . And there Continued Till the Nineteenth of May . . . & Thence Prorogued to the 18th of Feb. then Next Following. London: 1662. V. 44

GREAT BRITAIN. LAWS, STATUTES, ETC. - 1709

Anno Regni Annae Reginae Magnae Britanniae, Franciae & Hiberniae. London: 1709-11. V. 46

GREAT BRITAIN. LAWS, STATUTES, ETC. - 1711

An Act for Establishing a General Post-Office for all her Majesties Dominions, and for Settling a Weekly Sum out of the Revenues thereof, for the Service of the War and other Her Majesties Occasions. London: 1711. V. 37

Anno Regni Annae Reginae . . . An Act for Making Good Deficiencies, and Satisfying the Publick Debts; and for Erecting a Corporation to Carry on a Trade with the South Seas. London: 1711. V. 38

GREAT BRITAIN. LAWS, STATUTES, ETC. - 1721

Anno Regni Georgii Regis Magnae Britanniae, Francia, & Hiberniae, Septimo . . . An Act for Making Several Provisions to Restore the Publick Credit, Which Suffers by the Frauds and Mismanagements of the Late Directors of the South-Sea Co . . . . London: 1721. V. 41

GREAT BRITAIN. LAWS, STATUTES, ETC. - 1726

Acts of Tonnage and Poundage. Rates of Merchandize . . . Duties Rleating to H.M. Customs . . . Imported or Exported . . . London: 1726. V. 40

GREAT BRITAIN. LAWS, STATUTES, ETC. - 1729

An Act for Better Preservation of His Majesty's Woods in America, and for the Encouragement of the Importation of Naval Stores from Thence. London: 1729. V. 40

GREAT BRITAIN. LAWS, STATUTES, ETC. - 1730

Anno Regni Georgii II. Regis Magnae Britanniae Franciae & Hiberniae Tertio, an Act for Granting Liberty to Cary Rice . . . . London: 1730. V. 41

GREAT BRITAIN. LAWS, STATUTES, ETC. - 1744

Anno Regni Georgii II. An Act for Giving a Public Reward to Such Persons or Persons, His Majesty's Subject or Subjects, as Shall Discover a North West Passage through Hudson's Streights, to the Western and Southern Ocean of America. London: 1744. V. 39

GREAT BRITAIN. LAWS, STATUTES, ETC. - 1745

Anno Regno Georgii II. Regis . . . At the Parliament Begun and Holden at Westminster the First Day of December, Anno Dom 1741..An Act for Giving a Publick Reward to Such Person or Persons . . . As Shall Discover a North West Passage through Hudson's Streights . . . London: 1745. V. 39

GREAT BRITAIN. LAWS, STATUTES, ETC. - 1753

An Act for Vesting the Parts or Shares Late Belonging to Benjamin Brain, Merchant, Deceased, of and in One Twenty-Fourth Part of the Eastern Division of the Province of New Jersey in America, in Trustees, to be sold for the Purposes therein mentioned. London: 1753. V. 37

A Bill, with the Amendments, for the Amendment and Preservation of Public Roads of This Kingdom and for the More Effecual Execution of the Laws Relating Thereto. London: 1753. V. 43

GREAT BRITAIN. LAWS, STATUTES, ETC. - 1759

An Act to Enable the Most Noble Francis Duke of Bridgewater to Make Navigable Cut or Canal from or Near Worsley Mill, Over the River Irwell to the Town of Manchester in the County Palatine of Lancaster and to Or Near Longford Bridge . . . London: 1759. V. 45

GREAT BRITAIN. LAWS, STATUTES, ETC. - 1760

The Act of Permitting the Free Importation of Cattle from Ireland, Considered With a View to the Interests of Both Kingdoms. London: 1760. V. 41

GREAT BRITAIN. LAWS, STATUTES, ETC. - 1766

Anno Regni Georgii III (An Act for the Better Securing the Dependency of His Majety's Dominions in America Upon the Crown and Parliament of Great Britain. London: 1766. V. 38; 44

GREAT BRITAIN. LAWS, STATUTES, ETC. - 1767

Anno Regni Georgi III. Regis . . . An Act for Restraining and Prohibiting the Governor Council and House of Representatives, of the Province of New York, Until Provision Shall Have Been Made for Furnishing the King's Troops . . . London: 1767. V. 44

GREAT BRITAIN. LAWS, STATUTES, ETC. - 1772

A Collection of all the Treaties of Peace, Alliance and Commerce Between Great Britain and Other Powers from 1688. London: 1781. V. 40

GREAT BRITAIN. LAWS, STATUTES, ETC. - 1774

Anno Regni Georgii III. Cap. LXXXIII. An Act for Making More Effectual Provision for the Government of Quebec in North America. London: 1774. V. 39

Anno Regni Georgii III (An Act for the Better Regulating the Government of the Province of Massachusetts Bay, in New England). London: 1774. V. 38; 44

GREAT BRITAIN. LAWS, STATUTES, ETC. - 1775

An Act for Enabling the Universities . . . to Hold in Perpetuity Their Copy Right in Books, Given or Bequeathed tot he Said Universities. London: 1775. V. 41

Anno Regni Georgi III . . . An Act to Restrain the Trade and Commerce of the Colonies of New Jersey, Pennsylvania, Maryland, Virginia, and South Carolina, to Great Britain, Ireland, and the British Islands in the West Indies . . . London: 1775. V. 37; 38

GREAT BRITAIN. LAWS, STATUTES, ETC. - 1778

An Act to Enable His Majesty to Appoint Commissioners with Sufficient Powers to Treat, Consult and Agree Upon the Means of Quieting the Disorders Now Subsisting in Certain of the Colonies, Plantations, and Provinces of North America. London: 1778. V. 37

GREAT BRITAIN. LAWS, STATUTES, ETC. - 1782

An Act to Enable His Majesty to Conclude a Peace or Truce with Certain Colonies in North America Therein Mentioned. London: 1782. V. 37

GREAT BRITAIN. LAWS, STATUTES, ETC. - 1785

A Bill for Confining, for a Time to Be Limited, the Trade Between the Ports of the United States of America and His Majesty's Subjects in the Island of Newfoundland, to Bread, Flour and Live Stock, to be Imported in None But British-Built Ships . . . London: 1785. V. 46

GREAT BRITAIN. LAWS, STATUTES, ETC. - 1788

A Bill for Regulating the Trade Between the Subjects of His Majesty's Colonies, and Plantations in North America and in the West India Islands, and the Countries Belonging to the United States of America . . . London: 1788. V. 40

GREAT BRITAIN. LAWS, STATUTES, ETC. - 1791

A Bill (with the Amendments) for Establishing a Court of Civil Jurisdiction in the Island of Newfoundland. London: 1791. V. 46

GREAT BRITAIN. LAWS, STATUTES, ETC. - 1792

A Bill for Establishing Courts of Juricature in the Island of Newfoundland, and the Islands Adjacent. London: 1792. V. 46

GREAT BRITAIN. LAWS, STATUTES, ETC. - 1797

Anno Regni Georgii Regis. Tricesimo Septimo. An Act for Carrying into Execution the Treaty of Amity, Commerce and Navigation, Concluded Between His Majesty and the United States of America. (4 July 1797). London: 1797. V. 39

GREAT BRITAIN. LAWS, STATUTES, ETC. - 1803

Copies of the Several Acts of Parliament, Passed for Making and Repairing the Roads, Belonging to Sarum and Ealing Turnpike. Salisbury: 1803. V. 42

GREAT BRITAIN. LAWS, STATUTES, ETC. - 1810

Fairburn's Edition of Magna Charta, or the Great Charter of Liberties, Publicly Signed by King John . . . with the Petition of Right . . . also the Bill of Rights, of the People of England. London: 1810? V. 45

The Statutes of the Realm. London: 1810-28. V. 37

GREAT BRITAIN. LAWS, STATUTES, ETC. - 1816

Magna Carta Regis Johannis, X Die Junii Anno Regni XVIII A.D. London: 1816. V. 40

GREAT BRITAIN. LAWS, STATUTES, ETC. - 1824

Laws of the Stannaries of Cornwall, Made at the Convocation or Parliament of Tinners, at Truro, Sept. 13, Anno 27°Geo. II in Which the Laws Made: 22° Jac. I-12° Car. I.-4° Jac. II. are recited and confirmed. 1824. V. 40

GREAT BRITAIN. LAWS, STATUTES, ETC. - 1832

An Act for Regulating Schools of Anatomy. London: 1832. V. 40

GREAT BRITAIN. LAWS, STATUTES, ETC. - 1833

Anno Tertio & Quarto Gulielmi IV. Regis. Cap. LXXXII. An Act for Carrying Into Effect Two Conventions with the King of the French for Supressing the Slave Trade. London: 1833. V. 40

GREAT BRITAIN. LAWS, STATUTES, ETC. - 1838

Acts of Parliament Relating to the Post Office from 9 Anne to 1 Victoria. London: 1838. V. 40; 43

GREAT BRITAIN. LAWS, STATUTES, ETC. - 1839

An Act for Extending and Altering the Line of the Manchester and Leeds Railway. London: 1839. V. 40

GREAT BRITAIN. LAWS, STATUTES, ETC. - 1843

A Bill for Carrying into Effect the Treat Between Her Majesty and the Mexican Republic, for the Abolition of the Traffic in Slaves. London: 1843. V. 39

GREAT BRITAIN. LAWS, STATUTES, ETC. - 1859

Anno Vicesimo Secundo & Vicesimo Tertio Victoriae Reginae . . . an Act to Make Furthur Provision for the Regulation of the Trade with the Indians, and for the Administration of Justice in the North-Western Territories of America. London: 1859. V. 42

GREAT BRITAIN. NAVAL INTELLIGENCE DIVISION

French West Africa. Volume 1: The Federation. Volume II: The Colonies. London: 1943-44. V. 39

Western Arabia and the Red Sea. London: 1946. V. 39

GREAT BRITAIN. NAVY - 1746

Regulations and Instructions Relating to His Majesty's Service at Sea. London: 1746. V. 40

GREAT BRITAIN. OXFORD UNIVERSITY COMMISSION

Report of H. M. Commissioners Appointed to Inquire into the State, Discipline, Studies and revenues of the University and Colleges of Oxford. London: 1852. V. 39

GREAT BRITAIN. PARLIAMENT -

Report from the Joint Select Committee of the House of Lords and the House of Commons on the Stage Plays. London. V. 45

GREAT BRITAIN. PARLIAMENT - 1610

At the Fourth Session of Parliament Begun and Holden by Prorogation at Westminster . . . in the Seventh Yeere of the Reigne of Our Most Gracious Sovereign Lord James. London: 1610. V. 46

GREAT BRITAIN. PARLIAMENT - 1624

At the Parliament Begun and Holden at Westmisnter, the 19 Day of November in the 21, Yeere of the Reigne of Our Most Gracious Souveraigne Lord, James etc. London: 1624. V. 46

GREAT BRITAIN. PARLIAMENT - 1637

A Decree of Starre-Chamber, Concerning Printing, Made the Eleuenth Day of July Last Pasat. 1637. 1637. V. 37

GREAT BRITAIN. PARLIAMENT - 1641

The Diurnall Occurrences or Dayly Proceedings of Both Houses, in This Great and Happy Parliament, from the Third of Nov. 1640 to the Third of Nov. 1641, With a Continuation of all the Speeches from June last to the third of Nov. 1641. London: 1641. V. 42

GREAT BRITAIN. PARLIAMENT - 1643

An Ordinance by the Lords and Commons Assembled in Parliament, for the Preservation and Keeping Together for Publique Use Such Books, Evidences, Records and Writings Sequestered or Taken by Distresse or otherwise, as are fit to be so preserved. London: 1643. V. 37

GREAT BRITAIN. PARLIAMENT - 1647

Severall Orders and Votes of Both Houses of Parliament: Made on Friday and Saturday Last, for the Bringing of the Kings Majesty to Some of His Houses Neer London . . . 1647. V. 40

GREAT BRITAIN. PARLIAMENT - 1648

A Declaration of the Parliament of England, Expressing the Grounds of Their Late Proceedings and of Setling the Present Government in the Way of a Free State. London: 1648. V. 43

GREAT BRITAIN. PARLIAMENT - 1649

A Declartion of the Lords and Commons Assembled in Parliament, Concerning the Tryall of the King. London: 1649. V. 40

GREAT BRITAIN. PARLIAMENT - 1653

A Declaration of the Parliament of the Commonwealth of England, for a Time of Publique Thanksgiving, Upon the Five and Twentieth of this Instant August for the Great Victory Lately, Vouchsafed to Their Fleet at Sea. London: 1653. V. 40

GREAT BRITAIN. PARLIAMENT - 1695

Collection of the Debates and Proceedings in Parliament . . . Upon the Inquiry into the Late Briberies and Corrupt Practices. London: 1695. V. 41

GREAT BRITAIN. PARLIAMENT - 1698

The Report of the Committee of the House of Commons, to Whom the Petition of the Royal Lustring Company of England, Was Referred. London: 1698. V. 38

GREAT BRITAIN. PARLIAMENT - 1740

The Lords Protest, February 3, 1740-1. London: 1741. V. 45

GREAT BRITAIN. PARLIAMENT - 1746

The Lords Protest. Die Veneris 2do Maii, 1746. London: 1746. V. 45

GREAT BRITAIN. PARLIAMENT - 1751

The Parliamentary or Constitutional History of England; being a Faithful Account of All the Most Remarkable Transactions in Parliament. London: 1751-63. V. 44

GREAT BRITAIN. PARLIAMENT - 1802

Report from the Committe on Dr. Jenner's Petition, Respecting His Discovery of Vaccine Inoculation. London: 1802. V. 37; 38

GREAT BRITAIN. PARLIAMENT - 1811

Report from the Committee on the Highways and Turnpike Roads in England and Wales. London: 1811. V. 45

GREAT BRITAIN. PARLIAMENT - 1816

Minutes of Evidence Taken a Select Committee, Appointed by the House of Commons to Inquire into the State of the Police of the Metropolis. With Notes, Observations, and a Preface by a Magistrate of the . . . London: 1816. V. 37

GREAT BRITAIN. PARLIAMENT - 1817

Report from the Committe on Employment of Boys in Sweeping of Chimneys. London: 1817. V. 38

Report from the Committee on Employment of Boys in Sweeping of Chimneys: together with the minutes of the evidence taken before the committee and an appendix. Ordered by the House of Commons. (London): 1817. V. 37

GREAT BRITAIN. PARLIAMENT - 1820

Report of the Proceedings in the House of Lords on the Bill of Pains and Penalties Against the Queen. Edinburgh: 1820. V. 38

GREAT BRITAIN. PARLIAMENT - 1823

Report from the Select Committee on Mr. McAdam's Petition Relating to His Improved System of Construction and Repairing the Public Roads of the Kingdom. London: 1823. V. 45

GREAT BRITAIN. PARLIAMENT - 1829

Copy of the Evidence Taken Before a Committe of the House of Commons on the Newcastle & Carlisle Railway Bill. To which is added the Report of Mr. Leather, on the Projected Line of Railway. Newcastle upon Tyne: 1829. V. 46

GREAT BRITAIN. PARLIAMENT - 1840

Report from the Select Committee of the House of Lords Appointed to Consider of the Petition of the East India Company for Relief . . . with Minutes of Evidence. London: 1840. V. 38

GREAT BRITAIN. PARLIAMENT - 1845

Report from the Select Committee on Atmospheric Railways; Together with the Minutes of Evidence, Appendix and Index . . . London: 1845. V. 46

GREAT BRITAIN. PARLIAMENT - 1852

Report to the Lords of the Committee of Privy Council for Trade and Foreign Plantations, of the Proceedings of the Department Relating to Railways from the Year 1851. London: 1852. V. 38

GREAT BRITAIN. PARLIAMENT - 1854

Report of the Proceedings in Both Houses of Parliament on the Jarrow Dock Bill . . . Gateshead: 1854. V. 44

GREAT BRITAIN. PARLIAMENT - 1901

Report from the Joint Select Committee of the House of Lords and the House of Commons on London Underground Railways. London: 1901. V. 46

GREAT BRITAIN. PARLIAMENT. HOUSE OF COMMONS - 1642

A Declaration of the House of Commons, Touching a Late Breach of Their Priviledges; and for the Vindication Thereof, and of Divers Members of the Said House. London: 1642. V. 39

GREAT BRITAIN. PARLIAMENT. HOUSE OF COMMONS - 1648

A Declaration of the House of Commons in Parliament Assembled. Declaring 1. That the People are Under God the Originall of all Just power. 2. That the Commons of England in Parliament Assembled Being Chosen by, and Representing the People . . . London: 1648. V. 43

GREAT BRITAIN. PARLIAMENT. HOUSE OF COMMONS - 1689

An Exact Collection of the Debates of the House of Commons, Held at Westminster, Oct. 21, 1680. Prorogued the Tenth, and Dissolved the Eighteenth of Jan. following. With Debates of the House of Commons at Oxford, assembled March 21, 1680 . . . London: 1689. V. 44

GREAT BRITAIN. PARLIAMENT. HOUSE OF COMMONS - 1698

The Report of the Committee of the House of Commons, to Whom the Peition of the Royal Lustring-Company of England was Referred. Together with the Papers, Letters and Writings Relating to the Smuggling Trade. London: 1698. V. 39; 40

GREAT BRITAIN. PARLIAMENT. HOUSE OF COMMONS - 1741

Minutes of Several Resolutions of the Honourable House of Commons, in the Fifth, Sixth and Seventh Sessions of the Eighth Parliament of Great Britain. London: 1741. V. 41

GREAT BRITAIN. PARLIAMENT. HOUSE OF COMMONS - 1747

Standing Orders, and Resoltuions of the Honourable House of Commons, Relating to Their Form of Proceeding, Privileges &c. London: 1747? V. 41

GREAT BRITAIN. PARLIAMENT. HOUSE OF COMMONS - 1816

Report from the Select Committee of the House of Commons Appointed to Inquire into the Education of the Lower Orders in the Metropolis . . . London: 1816. V. 43

GREAT BRITAIN. PARLIAMENT. HOUSE OF COMMONS - 1839

Report from the Select Committee on Lighting the House; Together with the Minutes of Evidence. London: 1839. V. 39

GREAT BRITAIN. PARLIAMENT. HOUSE OF COMMONS - 1857

Copies or Extracts of any Despatches that Have Been Recieved by Her Majesty's Secretary of State on the Subject of the Establishment of a Representative Assembly at Vancouver's Island. London: 1857. V. 39

GREAT BRITAIN. PARLIAMENT. HOUSE OF COMMONS - 1863

Copies or Extracts of Any Correspondence Between Mr. Langford and the Colonial Department Relative to the Alleged Abuses in the Government of Vancouver's Island . . . 24th July 1863. London: 1863. V. 39

GREAT BRITAIN. PARLIAMENT. HOUSE OF COMMONS - 1869

Papers on the Union of British Columbia and the Dominion of Canada. London: 1869. V. 39

GREAT BRITAIN. PARLIAMENT. HOUSE OF COMMONS - 1873

Maps Annexed to the Case of Her Britannic Majesty . . . London: 1873. V. 39

GREAT BRITAIN. PARLIAMENT. HOUSE OF LORDS - 1660

Upon Complaint This Day Made by the Commons in Parliament, It Is Ordered by the Lords in the Parliament Assembled, That All These Persons . . . London: 1660. V. 40

GREAT BRITAIN. PARLIAMENT. HOUSE OF LORDS - 1835

First (and second) Report from the Select Committee of the House of Lords Appointed to Inquire into the Present State of the Several Gaols and Houses of Correction in England and Wales . . . London: 1835. V. 42; 43

GREAT BRITAIN. PATENT OFFICE - 1857

Catalogue of the Library of the great Seal Patent Office. London: 1857-58. V. 40

GREAT BRITAIN. POOR LAW COMM., SANITARY INQUIRY: SCOTLAND

Reports on the Sanitary Condition of the Labouring Population of Scotland, in Consequence of an Inquiry Directed to be made by the Poor Law Commissioners. London: 1842. V. 38

GREAT BRITAIN. POOR LAW COMMISSION

Reports . . . from the Poor Law Commissioners, on an inquiry into the sanitary condition of the labouring population of Great Britain. (with) Local reports on the sanitary condition of the labouring population of England . . . London: 1842-43. V. 37

GREAT BRITAIN. POOR LAW CONMMISSION

Report from His Majesty's Commissioners for Inquiring into the Adminstrataion and Practical Operation of the Poor Laws. London: 1834. V. 37

GREAT BRITAIN. POST OFFICE - 1855

First (second and third) Report of the Postmaster General on the Post Office . . . 1855-56-57. London: 1855-56-57. V. 43

GREAT BRITAIN. PRIVY COUNCIL

Orders and Directions, Together with a Commission for the Better Administration of Justice, and More Perfect Information of His Majestie . . . London: 1630. V. 38

GREAT BRITAIN. PRIVY COUNCIL - 1688

At the Council Chamber in Whitehall, Monday the 22 of October, 1688. This day an Extraordinary Council Met . . . London: 1688. V. 40

GREAT BRITAIN. ROYAL COMMISION

Reports from the Commissioners Appointed by His Majesty to Execute the Measures Recommended By a Select Committee of the House of Commons Respecting the Public Records of the Kingdom. London: 1819. V. 41

GREAT BRITAIN. ROYAL COMMISSION, CHICAGO EXHIBITION, 1893.

Official Catalogue of the British Section. London: 1893. V. 42

GREAT BRITAIN. ROYAL COMMISSION ON ALIEN IMMIGRATION

Report, Minutes of Evidence and Appendix. London: 1903. V. 42

GREAT BRITAIN. ROYAL COMMISSION ON HISTORICAL MONUMENTS, ENGLAND.

An Inventory of the Historical Monuments in London. London: 1924-30. V. 44

An Inventory of the Historical Monuments in Westmorland. London: 1936. V. 44

GREAT BRITAIN. ROYAL COMMISSION ON TAXATION - 1899

Memoranda Chiefly Relating to the Classification and Incidence of Imperial and Local Taxes. London: 1899. V. 43

GREAT Britain. Royal Commission on THE ANCIENT & HISTORICAL MONUMENTS & CONSTRUCTIONS OF ENGLAND An Inventory of the Historical Monuments in Buckinghamshire. Volume I South. (Volume II North). London: 1912-13. V. 41

GREAT BRITAIN. SOVEREIGNS, ETC.

His Majesties Declaration, to All His Loving Subjects. London: 1641. V. 43

GREAT BRITAIN. SOVEREIGNS, ETC. 1625-1649 (CHARLES I).

His Majesties Declaration to all His Subjects. The Reasons of His Proceedings in This His Present State and Condition, Mentioned in Severall Letters. London: 1647. V. 39

GREAT BRITAIN. SOVEREIGNS, ETC. 1660-1685 (CHARLES II)

Notes Which Passed at Meetings of the Privy Council Between Charles II and the Earl of Clarendon, 1660-1667, Together with a Few Letters, Reproduced in Facsimile from the Originals at the Bodleian Library. London: 1896. V. 40

GREAT BRITAIN. SURVEYOR-GENERAL OF PRISONS

Report of the Surveyor-General of Prisons on the Construction, Ventilation and Details of Pentonville Prison, 1844. London: 1844. V. 43

GREAT BRITAIN. TREATIES, ETC. - 1630

Articles of Peace, Intercourse and Commerce, Concluded in the Names of . . . Charles by the Grace of God King of Britaine . . . and Philip the Fourth King of Spain &c. in a Treaty at Madrit (sic) . . . London: 1630. V. 45

GREAT BRITAIN. TREATIES, ETC. - 1685

Several Treaties of Peace and Commerce Concluded Between the Late King (Charles II) and Other Princes and States. London: 1685. V. 40; 43

Treaty of Whitehall: Treaty of Peace, Good Correspondence and Neutrality in America. Between the Most Serene and Mighty Prince James II . . . London: 1685. V. 44

GREAT BRITAIN. TREATIES, ETC. - 1686

Treaty of Peace, Good Correspondence and Neutrality in America, Between the Most Serene and Mighty Prince James II . . . and Lewis XIV, the Most Christian King . . . In the Savoy. 1686. V. 41

Treaty of Peace, Good Correspondence and Neutrality in America, Between the Most Serene and Mightly Prince James II. By the Grace of God, King of Great Britian, France and Ireland . . . and the Might Prince Lewis XIV . . . London: 1686. V. 38; 41

GREAT BRITAIN. TREATIES, ETC. - 1702

Articles of Alliance Between the King of England, the Emperor of Germany and States-General, Against France and Spain. As Also Between the King of England, States of Holland and King of Sweden &c . . . Colophon: 1702. V. 40

GREAT BRITAIN. TREATIES, ETC. - 1706

Articles of Union, Agreed on the Two and Twentieth Day of July, in the Fifth Year of the Reign of Her Most Excellent Majesty, Queen Anne, by the Commissioners Nominated on the Behalf of the Kingdom of England . . . London: 1706. V. 40

GREAT BRITAIN. TREATIES, ETC. - 1707

The Articles of the Treaty for a Union Between England and Scotland, Agreed on by the Commissioners of Both Kingdoms . . . 1706. London: 1707. V. 40

GREAT BRITAIN. TREATIES, ETC. - 1713

Tractatus Pacis & Amcitiae . . . Treaty of Peace and Friendship Between the Most Serene and Most Potent Princess Anne, by the Grace of God, Queen of Great Britain, France and Ireland and the Most Serene and Most Potent Prince Lewis the XIVth . . . London: 1713. V. 39

Treaty of Peace and Friendship Between Queen Anne and Lewis the XIVth, King of France, Concluded at Utrecht, Together with the Treaty of Navigation and Commerce Between Queen Anne and Louis the XIVth, Concluded at Utrecht. London: 1713. V. 38; 40; 41

GREAT BRITAIN. TREATIES, ETC. - 1732

A General Collection of Treatys, Declarations of War, Manifestos, and Other Publick Papers, Relating to Peace and War (from 1495 to 1731); London: 1732. V. 40

GREAT BRITAIN. TREATIES, ETC. - 1739

The Convention Between the Crowns of Great Britain and Spain. Concluded at the Pardo on the 14th of Jan. 1739, N.S. The King of Great Brtain's Full Power. The King of Spain's Full Ratification of the Convention . . . London: 1739. V. 39; 43

GREAT BRITAIN. TREATIES, ETC. - 1758

Extracts, from Several Treaties Subsisting Between Great Britain and Other Kingdsoms and States, of Such Articles and Clauses, as Relate to the Duty and Conduct of the Commanders of His Majesty's Ships of War . . . London: 1758. V. 40; 46

GREAT BRITAIN. TREATIES, ETC. - 1762

Preliminary Articles of Peace, Between His Britannick Majesty, the Most Christian King, and the Catholick King. London: 1762. V. 44

GREAT BRITAIN. TREATIES, ETC. - 1790

A Collection of Treaties Between G. B. and Other Poers. London: 1790. V. 40

GREAT BRITAIN. TREATIES, ETC. - 1797

Anno Regni George III Regis Magnae Britanniae, Franciae & Hiberniae . . . The First Session of the Eighteenth Parliament of Great Britain. London: 1797. V. 40

Treaties of Amity and Commerce and of Alliance Eventual and Defensive Between His Most Christian Majesty and the Thirteen United States of America. Boston: 1797. V. 38

GREAT BRITAIN. TREATIES, ETC. - 1825

Treaty of Amity, Commerce and Navigation Between His Majesty and the State of Colombia, Together with an Additional Article Thereunto Annexed. London: 1825. V. 40

GREAT BRITAIN. TREATIES, ETC. - 1842

Convention Between Her Majesty and the Republic of Texas, Containing Arrangements Relative to Publick Debt. Signed at London, November 14, 1840. Presented to Both Houses of Parliament, by Command of Her Majesty, 1842. London: 1842. V. 42

GREAT BRITAIN. WAR OFFICE

Dress Regulations for the Officers of the Army. London: 1904. V. 39

A List of all the Officers of the Army and Royal marines On Full and Half Pay; with an Index; and a Succession of Colonels. London: 1811. V. 39

GREAT BRITAIN. WAR OFFICE - 1798

An Elucidation of Several Parts of His Majesty's Regulations for Formations and Movements of Cavalry. London: 1798. V. 37

GREAT BRITAIN. WAR OFFICE - 1844

The Queens Regulations and Orders for the Army. London: 1844. V. 37

GREAT BRITAIN. WAR OFFICE - 1900

Dress Regulations for the Officers of the Army, (Including the Militia). 1900. London: 1900. V. 41

GREAT BRITAIN. WAR OFFICE - 1904

Dress Regulations for the Officers of the Army. (Including the Militia). 1904. London: 1904. V. 37; 41

GREAT Britain's Memorial (with) The Second Part, Containing a Collection of the Instructions, Representations &c &c of the Freeholders and Other Electors of Great Britain to Their Representatives in Parliament, for these Two Years Past . . . London: 1741-42. V. 41

GREAT BRITIAN. LAWS, STATUTES, ETC. - 1774

An Act for Making More Effectual Provision for the Government of the Province of Quebec in North America. London: 1774. V. 42

GREAT BRITIAN. PARLIAMENT. HOUSE OF COMMONS - 1796

The First Report from the Select Committee of the Honourable House of Commons, Appointed to Take into Consideration the Means of Promoting and Cultivation and Improvement of the Waste, Uninclosed, and Unproductive Lands . . . London: 1796. V. 46

GREAT BRITIAN. PARLIAMENT. HOUSE OF COMMONS - 1844

First (-Sixth) Report from the Select Committe on Railways. London: July, 1844. V. 46

GREAT BRITIAN. TREATIES, ETC. - 1750

A Treaty Concluded and Signed at Madrid, on the 5th of October N.S. 1750. Between the Ministers Plenipotentiaries of Their Britannick and Catholick Majesties. London: 1750. V. 46

GREAT BRTIAN. PARLIAMENT - 1607

At the Parliament Begun and Holden at Westminster by Prorogation, the 18 Day of November, in the Fourth Yeere of the Raigne of Our Most Gracious Souveraigne. London: 1607. V. 46

GREAT CENTRAL RAILWAY

Per Rail. N.P.: 1913. V. 38

THE GREAT Charter of the Liberties of the City of Waterford, with Explanatory Notes. Kilkenny: 1840. V. 43

THE GREAT Company (1667-1871) Being a History of the Honorable Company of Merchants-Adventurers Trading Into Hudson's Bay. London: 1990. V. 42

THE GREAT Cronin Mystery, or, the Irish Patriot's Fate. V. 39

THE GREAT Evil of Health-Drinking: a Discourse Wherein the Original, Evil, and Mischief of Drinking of Healths are Discovered and Detected. London: 1684. V. 40

GREAT Georgian Houses of America. New York: 1933 & 1937. V. 41

THE GREAT Importance of Cape Breton, Demonstrated and Exemplified, by Extracts from the Best Writers, French and English, Who Have Treated of That Colony. London: 1746. V. 41; 43

GREAT Masters of Decorative Art. London: 1900. V. 44

THE GREAT Metropolis. London: 1836/37. V. 42

THE GREAT Metropolis . . . 1st and 2nd Series. London: 1836-37. V. 38

THE GREAT Northwest A Guide-Book and Itinerary for the Use of Tourist and Travelers over the Lines of the Northern Pacific Railraod. St. Paul: 1889. V. 40; 45

GREAT Register of the County of Placer. Auburn: 1876. V. 39

THE GREAT Revelation of 1891 of English Male and Female Mahatmas, Spiritism, Hypnotism, Sorcery and Witchcraft, by One Who Has Been Persecuted by Them for 10 Years. London: 1891. V. 39

GREAT Short Stories of the War: England, France, Germany, America. London: 1930. V. 40

GREAT Southern Railway. A Trunk Line, Between the North and the Tropics, to Within Ninety Miles of Havana . . . New York: 1878. V. 42

THE GREAT Storm of October 1987 and Its Aftermath. 1989. V. 45

GREAT Trans-Continental Tourist's Guide . . . New York: 1870. V. 42

THE GREAT War . . . 'I Was There!' Undying Memories of 1914-1918. London: 1938-39. V. 46

THE GREAT Western Railway. Fullerton: 1984. V. 38

GREAT WESTERN RAILWAY CO.

An Account of the Proceedings of the Great Western Railway Company, with Extracts from the Evidence Given in Support of the Bill, Before the Committee of the House of Commons, in the Session of 1834. London: 1834. V. 40

GREAT WESTERN TYPE FOUNDRY

Pony Specimen Book and Price List from Barnhart Bros. & Spindler . . . Chicago: 1893. V. 45

GREATHEAD, BERTIE

The Regent: a Tragedy. London: 1788. V. 39

GREATOREX, ELIZA

Summer Etchings in Colorado. New York: 1873. V. 38

GREATOREX, GRACE

Summer Etchings in Colorado. New York: 1873. V. 37; 38; 39

GREAVES, JOHN 1602-1652

Miscellaneous Works of Mr. John Greaves . . . London: 1737. V. 43

The Origin and Antiquity of Our English Weights and Measures Discover'd. London: 1745. V. 40

Pyramidographia; or a Description of the Pyramids in Aegypt. London: 1646. V. 42; 45

GREAVES, Whistler & Chelsea. Chelsea: 1911. V. 46

GREBAN, SIMON

Mystere des Actes des Apostres. (with) L'Apocalypse Sainct Jehan Zebedee. Paris: 1541. V. 38

GREBNER, PAUL

A Brief Description of the Future History of Europe . . . London: 1650. V. 42

GREBORIUS NAZIANZENUS

De Pauperibus Amandis et Benignitate Complectendis Oratio. Venice: 1547. V. 38

GRECO, GIOACHINO

The Royall Game of Chesse-Play. London: 1656. V. 45

GRECO, JOSEPH 1843-1908

A History of Parliamentary Elections and Electioneering in the Old Days. London: 1886. V. 42

GREE, ERNEST R.

Early American Sporting Books 1734 to 1844 A few Brief Notes. New York: 1928. V. 44

GREEFF, RICHARD

Atlas of External Diseases of the Eye. New York: 1914. V. 44

THE GREEK Heroes. Stories Translated from Niebuhr with Additions. London: 1910. V. 41

GREEK Merchant Marine, 1453-1850. Athens: 1972. V. 37

GREELEY, ANDREW

The Making of the Popes 1978. Kansas City: 1979. V. 46

GREELEY, HORACE

The American Conflict: A History of the Great Rebellion in the United States of America . . . Hartford: 1864-66. V. 39

Essays Designed to Elucidate the Science of Political Economy. Boston: 1870. V. 44

The History of the Struggle for Slavery Extension or Restriction in the United States . . . New York: 1856. V. 44

An Overland Journey, from New York to San Francisco, in the Summer of 1859. New York: 1860. V. 37; 42

An Overland Journey, from New York to San Francisco, in the Summer of 1859. New York/San Francisco: 1860. V. 37

GREELY, ADOLPHUS W.

International Polar Expedtiion . . . Washington: 1888. V. 41

Report on the Proceedings of the United States Expedition to Lady Franklin Bay. Washington: 1888. V. 37; 39; 43

Three Years of Arctic Service. London: 1886. V. 46

Three Years of Arctic Service. New York: 1886. V. 37; 39; 40; 42; 43; 44; 45

Three Years of Arctic Service. New York: 1886. V. 40

GREELY, ADOLPHUS WASHINGTON

International Polar Expedition. Report on the Proceedings of the United States Expedition to Lady Franklin Bay, G. V. 44

GREEN, A. C.

The Fifty Best Books on Texas. Dallas: 1981. V. 37

GREEN, A. ROMNEY

A Strange Visit. Flansham: 1930. V. 41

GREEN, ALBERT G.

Old Grimes. Providence: 1867. V. 40

GREEN, ANNA KATHARINE

The Circular Study. New York: 1900. V. 38; 42; 43; 45

Doctor Izard. New York: 1895. V. 43; 45

The Filigree Ball. Indianapolis: 1903. V. 43; 45; 46

Hand and Ring. New York: 1883. V. 43; 45; 46

The Leavenworth Case. New York: 1878. V. 43

Lost Man's Lane. New York: 1898. V. 43; 45

The Mayor's Wife. Indianapolis: 1907. V. 43

That Affair Next Door. New York: 1897. V. 39

The Woman in the Alcove. Indianapolis: 1906. V. 46

GREEN, ANNA KATHERINE

Marked 'Personal'. New York: 1893. V. 41

GREEN, B. R.

The Grammar of Form. London: 1840. V. 44

GREEN, B. W.

Word-Book of Virginia Folk speech. Richmond: 1912. V. 41

GREEN, BEN K.

Back to Back. Austin: 1970. V. 38; 40; 45

Ben Green Tales. I. When I was just a Colt. Illustrated by William Moyers. II. Up Fool's Hill Ahorseback. Illustrated by Joe Beeler. IV. How Come I Wrote a Book. Illustrated by James Boren. Flagstaff, Arizona: (1974). V. 37

The Color of Horses; the Scientific and Authoriative Identification of the Color of the Horse. 1974. V. 42; 44

The Color of Horses. The Scientific and Authoritative Identification of the Color of the Horse. With Paintings by Darol Dickinson. N.P.: (1974). V. 37

Horse Conformation, As to Soundness, Peformance, Ability. N.P.: 1963. V. 42

Horse Tradin'. New York: 1967. V. 42

Horse Conformation. Cumby: 1969. V. 38

The Last Trail Drive through Downtown Dallas. Flagstaff: 1971. V. 46

The Shield Mares. Austin. V. 42

The Shield Mares. Austin: 1967. V. 37; 38; 39; 40; 42; 45; 46

The Shield Mares. Austin: 1967. V. 42

Some More Horse Tradin'. New York: 1972. V. 37; 39

The Village Horse Doctor West of the Pecos. New York: 1971. V. 37; 42

Wild Cow Tales. New York: 1969. V. 37; 42

GREEN, BENJAMIN

The True Believer's Vademecum, or Shakerism Exposed . . . Concord: 1831. V. 42

GREEN, BERIAH

Four Sermons, Preached in the Chapel of the Western Reserve College . . . Cleveland: 1833. V. 44

Things for Northern Men to Do; a Discourse . . . July 17, 1836 . . . New York: 1836. V. 42

GREEN, C. R.

Patriotic Lyndon: History of Many Leading Organizations, Lyndon, Kansas. Lyndon: 1896. V. 39

Patriotic Lyndon: History of Many Leading Organizations, Lyndon, Kansas. Lyndon: 1897. V. 37; 39; 42

GREEN, CHARLES W.

A Sketch of Kingston and its Surroundings. The Mining Center of the Famous Percha District, New Mexico. Its Resources . . . Kingston: 1883. V. 37

GREEN, DAVID

Blenheim Palace. London: 1951. V. 38

Gardener to Queen Anne: Henry Wise 1653-1758 and the Formal Garden. 1956. V. 38

GREEN, DONALD EDWARD

Irrigation Frontier on the Texas High Plains: 1910-1960. Norman. V. 45

GREEN, DUFF

Facts and Suggestions Relative to Finance and Currently Addressed to the President of the Confederate States. Augusta: 1864. V. 44

The Register of Debates, Being a Report of the Speeches in the Two Houses of Congress, Reported for the United States Telegraph. Washington: 1834. V. 37

GREEN, E. L.

Landmarks of Botanical History. Stanford: 1983. V. 45; 46

GREEN, E. R. R.

The Industrial Archaeology of County Down. Belfast: 1963. V. 38

GREEN, FLORIDA

Some Personal Recollections of Lillie Hitchcock Coit - S. San Francisco: 1935. V. 37; 38; 44

GREEN, FRANCIS VINTON

The Russian Army and Its Campaign in Turkey in 1877-78. New York: 1879. V. 40

GREEN, GEORGE

An Original Journal from London to St. Petersburg by Way of Sweden; and, Proceeding from Thence, o Moscow, Riga, Mittau and Berlin . . . London: 1813. V. 37

GREEN, GEORGE H.

Index to the Marriage Licence Bonds of the Diocese of Cloyne, Ireland, from 1630 to 1800. Cork: 1899/1900. V. 38

GREEN, GUY W.

Fun and Frolic with an Indian Ball Team. Lincoln: 1907. V. 39

GREEN, H.

Andreae Alciati Emblematum Fontes Quator; Namely an Account of the Original Collection Made at Milan, 1522 and Photofacsimiles of the editions, Augsburg 1531, Paris, 1534 and Venice 1546. Manchester & London: 1870. V. 38

GREEN, HENRY 1905-1973

Back. London: 1946. V. 38; 41; 43; 46

GREEN, HENRY 1905-1973 continued

Blindness. London: 1926. V. 38; 40; 44; 45

Caught. London: 1943. V. 40

Caught. London: 1943. V. 38; 40; 41

Caught. New York: 1950. V. 41; 42

Concluding. London: 1948. V. 40; 46

CONCLuding. New York: 1950. V. 41; 42

Doting. London: 1952. V. 37; 41

The Four Fountains of the Emblems of Alciat. London: 1870. V. 40

Living. New York: 1929. V. 43

Nothing. London: 1950. V. 37; 40; 41

Pack My Bag - a Self-Portrait. London: 1940. V. 38; 40; 41

Party Going. London: 1939. V. 40; 46

GREEN, HENRY CLINTON

The Pioneer Mothers of America. New York: 1912. V. 42

GREEN, HORACE

Report on the Use and Effect of Applications of Nitrate of Silver to the Throat, Either in Local or General Disease. 1855. V. 42

Selections from Favorite Prescriptions of Living American Practitioners. New York: 1860. V. 42

A Treatise on the Diseases of the Air Passages . . . New York: 1846. V. 42

A Treatise on the Diseases of the Air Passages; Comprising an Inquiry Into the History, Pathology, Causes, and Treatment, of Those Affections of the Throat Called Bronchitis, Chronic Laryngitis, Clergyman's Sore Throat, etc. New York: 1852. V. 39

A Treatise on the Diseases of the Air Passages . . . New York: 1855. V. 40

GREEN-HOUSE Companion. London: 1832. V. 40

GREEN, J.

Ka Mooolelo No Ka Ekalesia O Iesu Kristo (History of the Church of Jesus Christ). Nu Ioka: 1863. V. 40

Ka Mooolelo No Ka Ekalesia o Iesu Kristo (History of the Church of Jesus Christ). Nu Ioka: (New York),: 1863. V. 38

GREEN, J. BARCHAM

Notes on the Manufacture of Hand Made Paper. London: 1936. V. 41

GREEN, J. F.

Ocean Birds. London: 1887. V. 37; 38; 39; 44

GREEN, J. H.

A Catalogue and Description of the Whole of the Works of the Celebrated Jacques Callot . . . London: 1804. V. 38; 40

An Exposure of the Arts and Miseries of Gambling; Designed Especially as a Warning to the Youthful and Inexperienced Against the Evils of that Odious and Destructive Vice. Philadelphia: 1847. V. 37; 40

Gambling Unmasked! Philadelphia: 1847. V. 37

GREEN, J. R. MRS.

Town Life in the Fifteenth Century. London: 1894. V. 37

GREEN, JACOB

Astronomical Recreations; or Sketches of the Relative Position and Mythological History of the Constellations. Philadelphia: 1824. V. 44

A Small Help Offered to Heads of Families, for Instructing Children and Servants. Morris-Town: 1814. V. 44

GREEN, JOHN

The New General Collection of Voyages and Travels. London: 1745-47. V. 39

The Privileges of the Lord Mayor and Aldermen of the City (London) with Several Acts of Parliament of Common Councils and Other Matters. London: 1722. V. 38

GREEN, JOHN PUGH

The Tour of the 'Gentlemen of Philadelphia' in Great Britain in 1884. Philadelphia: 1897. V. 43

GREEN, JOHN RICHARD

History of the English People. London: 1895. V. 38

History of the English People. London: 1895-96. V. 42

History of the English People. London: 1913. V. 41; 42

A Short History of the English People. London: 1878. V. 43

A Short History of the English People. London: 1902. V. 40; 42; 43

A Short History of the English People. London: 1892-93. V. 37

GREEN, JOHN RICHARDS 1758-1818

A History of the Political Life of the Right Honourable William Pitt. London: 1809. V. 39

A Short History of the English People. London: 1892. V. 39

GREEN, JONATHAN

Camera Work: a Critical Anthology. Millerton: 1973. V. 45

An Improved Mode of Successfully Treating Many Obstinate Diseases Through the Agency of Fumigating, Warm-Air and Vapour Baths. London: 1830. V. 43

GREEN, JONATHAN S.

Notices of Bartimeus and Hawaii, two Christian Sandwich Islanders. Boston: 1845. V. 38

GREEN, JOSEPH HENRY 1791-1863

Mental Dynamics or Groundwork of a Professional Education. London: 1847. V. 43

GREEN, JULIAN

The Pilgrim on the Earth. London: 1929. V. 41; 42; 43; 44

GREEN, JULIEN

The Pilgrim on the Earth. 1929. V. 45

GREEN, KEN K.

The Shield Mares. Introduction by A.C. Greene. Austin, Texas: 1967. V. 37

GREEN, LOUIS MEIGS

Brother of the Birds. Philadelphia: 1929. V. 46

GREEN, MATHEW

The Spleen. London: 1738. V. 39

GREEN, MATTHEW 1696-1737

The Spleen. London: 1737. V. 41; 45

The Spleen, and Other Poems. London: 1796. V. 38; 45

GREEN, PAUL

In the Valley and Other Carolina Plays. New York: 1928. V. 37

Song in the Wilderness: Cantata for Chorus and Orchestra, with Baritone Solo. Chapel Hill: 1947. V. 46

GREEN, PHILIP

What I Have Seen While Fishing and How I Have Caught My Fish. Friars Stile Lodge,: 1905. V. 43

GREEN, RALEIGH TRAVERS

Genealogical and Hsitorical Notes on Culpeper County, Virginia. Culpeper: 1900. V. 45

GREEN, RALPH

The Iron Hand Press in America. Rowayton: 1948. V. 42

GREEN, RICHARD

The Works of John and Charles Wesley. A Bibliography . . . London: 1896. V. 42

GREEN, ROBERT

Pandosto, or the Historie of Dorastus and Fawina. New Rochelle. V. 43

Pandosto, or the Historie of Dorastus and Fawnia. New Rochelle: 1902. V. 42

GREEN, ROBERT M.

History of the One Hundred and Twenty-Fourth Regiment Pennsylvania Volunteers in the War of the Rebellion - 1862-1863. Philadelphia: 1907. V. 42

GREEN, SARAH

The Fugitive, or Family Incidents. London: 1814. V. 38

GREEN, SARAH PRATT MAC LEAN

Cape Cod Folks. Boston: 1881. V. 46

GREEN, STANLEY

Starring Fred Astaire. New York: 1973. V. 46

GREEN, T. M.

The Spanish Conspiracy. Cincinnati: 1891. V. 38

GREEN, THOMAS

An Address to the Members of the Society of Friends . . . Called Quakers . . . Dublin: 1821. V. 43

Extracts from the Diary of a Lover of Literature. Ipswich: 1810. V. 38; 41; 42

Journal of the Texian Expedition Against Mier . . . New York: 1845. V. 41

The Tryal of Capt. Thomas Green and his Crew, before the Judge of the High Court of the Admirality of Scotland; . . . . Faithfully extracted from the Records . . . Edinburgh: 1705. V. 39

The Universal Herbal; or, Botanical, Medical and Agricultural Dictionary. Liverpool: 1816-20. V. 42

The Universal Herbal; or, Botanical, Medical and Agricultural Dictionary. London: 1824. V. 43; 46

GREEN, THOMAS continued

The Universal Herbal; or, Botanical, Medical and Agricultural Dictionary. London: 1824. V. 46

The Universal Herbal; or Botanical, Medical, and Agricultural Dictionary Containing an Account of All the Known Plants in the World . . . etc. By Thomas Green. Liverpool: (1820). V. 37

GREEN, THOMAS HILL

Works. London: 1885. V. 42; 43; 46

Works of Thomas Hill Green. London: 1893-1906. V. 38; 39

GREEN, THOMAS J.

Journal of the Texan Expedition Against Mier . . . New York: 1845. V. 37; 38; 39; 40; 42; 43; 46

Reply . . . to the Speech of General Sam Houston. Washington: 1855. V. 39; 40

GREEN, THOMAS M.

Spanish Conspiracy . . . Containing Proofs of the Intrigues of James Wilkinson . . . Cincinnati: 1891. V. 37; 39; 42; 43; 45

GREEN, THOMAS MARSHALL

Historic Families of Kentucky. Cincinnati: 1889. V. 42

GREEN, VALENTINE

The History and Antiquities of the City and Suburbs of Worcester. London: 1796. V. 41

A Survey of the City of Worcester, Containing Eccleasistical and Civil Government . . . Worcester: 1764. V. 40; 43; 45

GREEN, W. S.

Among the Selkirk Glaciers Being the Account of a Rough Survey in the Rocky Mountain Regions of British Columbia. London: 1890. V. 44; 46

Among the Selkirk Glaciers Being the Account of a Rough Survey in the Rocky Mountain Regions of British Columbia. London: 1890. V. 44

GREEN, WHARTON J.

Recollections and Reflections: an Auto of Half a Century and More. 1906. V. 38; 39; 42

Recollections and Reflections: an Auto of Half a Century and More. London: 1906. V. 42

Recollections and Reflections: an Auto of Half a Century and More. N.P.: 1906. V. 39

Recollections and Reflections: an Autobiography of a Half Century and More. Raleigh: 1906. V. 44

GREEN, WILLIAM

The Art of Living in Lond: a Poem. London. V. 39

Poetical Parts of the Old Testament. Cambridge: 1781. V. 39; 40; 45

The Song of Deborah, Reduced to Metre. Cambridge: 1753. V. 39

The Tourist's New Guide, Containing A Description of the Lakes, Mountains, and Scenery in Cumberland, Westmorland and Lancashire. Kendal: 1819. V. 40

GREEN, WILLIAM M.

Life and Papers of A. L. P. Green, D.D. Nashville: 1877. V. 44

GREEN, WILLIAM SPOTTISWOOD

Among the Selkirk Glaciers. London: 1890. V. 43

The High Alps of New Zealand or a Trip to the Glaciers of the Antipodes with an Ascent of Mount Cook. London: 1883. V. 43

GREENACRE, JAMES

Awful Confession of Greenacre to the Murder of Hannah Brown. London: 1837. V. 42

GREENAN, EDITH

Of Una Jeffers. 1939. V. 39

GREENAWAY, A. J.

The Life and Work of Professor William Henry Perkin. London: 1932. V. 40; 42

GREENAWAY, KATE 1846-1901

Almanac for 1890. London. V. 46

Almanack for 1884. London: 1883. V. 38

Almanac for 1891. London. V. 46

Almanac for 1929. London. V. 46

Kate Greenaway's Almanack, 1884. V. 39

Almanack for 1924. London. V. 44

Almanack for 1885. London. V. 41; 45

Almanack for 1883. London. V. 39; 41

Almanack for 1884. London. V. 41; 45

Almanack for 1883. London & New York. V. 41

Almanack for 1884. London: 1884. V. 39; 41

The Almanack for 1885. London: 1884. V. 41

Almanack for 1885. London: 1885. V. 39; 44

The Almanack for 1886. London: 1885. V. 41

Almanack for 1886. London: 1886. V. 41; 44

The Almanack for 1887. London: 1887. V. 39; 41

Almanack for 1888. London: 1887. V. 41

The Almanck for 1889. London: 1888. V. 37; 41

Almanack for 1890. London: 1890. V. 39; 44

Almanack for 1892. London: 1891. V. 41

Almanack for 1894. London: 1894. V. 41

Kate Greenaway's Alamanc for 1895. London: 1895. V. 39

Almanack and Diary for 1897. London: 1896. V. 41

Almanack for 1883-1895, 1897. London: 1897. V. 43

The Almanack for 1924. London: 1923. V. 41

Almanack for 1924. London: 1924. V. 41; 45

Almanack for 1926. London: 1926. V. 41

Almanack 1886. V. 45

Almanack 1888. London: 1888. V. 44

Almanack 1889. London: 1889. V. 44

Almanack 1890. London: 1890. V. 44

Almanack 1891. London: 1891. V. 44

Almanack 1892. London: 1892. V. 44

Almanack 1893. London: 1893. V. 44

Almanack 1894. London. V. 44

Almanack 1895. London. V. 44

Almanack for 1883. London: 1883. V. 45

Almanack for 1883. By Kate Greenaway. New York/London: n.d. V. 37

Almanack for 1885. London. V. 45

Almanack for 1885. Printed by Edmund Evans. London: (c. 1884). V. 37

Almanack for 1887. (c. 1887). V. 37

Almanack for 1890. V. 45

Almanack for 1891. V. 45

Almanack for 1894. V. 45

The Almanacks. London: 1884/83-97. V. 41

The Almanacs 1883-1895, 1897. London: 1883-95/97. V. 44

Alphabet. London: 1885. V. 37; 41; 43; 44

A Apple Pie. London: 1886. V. 43

An Apple Pie. London & New York: 1886. V. 41

A Apple Pie. Engraved and Printed by Edmund Evans. New York/London: n.d. V. 37

Book of Games. London: 1886. V. 44

Kate Greenaway's Book of Games. London: 1889. V. 38; 43; 44

A Day in a Child's Life. London. V. 41; 45; 46

A Day in a Child's Life. London: 1881. V. 37; 45

The English Spelling-Book. Printed by Edmund Evans. London: 1885. V. 37

Every Girl's Annual. London: 1882. V. 44

Kate Greenaway's Almanac for 1895. London: 1895. V. 46

Kate Greenaway Pictures. London: 1921. V. 37; 39; 40; 41; 42; 45; 46

Kate Greenaway's Alphabet. London: (1885?). V. 37

Kate Greenaway's Birthday Book for Children. With 382 Illustrations, Drawn by kate Greenaway, Printed by Edmund Evans. Verses by Mrs. Sale Barker. London/New York: n.d. V. 37

Language of Flowers. London. V. 40

Language of Flowers. London: 1884. V. 37; 44; 46

Language of Flowers. London. V. 37

The Little Folks Painting Book. New York: 1880's? V. 44

The Little Folks Painting Book. A Series of Outline Engravings for Water-Colour Painting. London: (1879). V. 37

Marigold Garden. London: 1885. V. 38; 40; 41; 43; 44; 46

The Marigold Painting Book. London & New York: 1911-1920. V. 38

Marigold Garden. Pictures and Rhymes by Kate Greenaway. Printed in Colours by Edmund Evans. London: (1885). V. 37

Mother Goose. New York: 1872. V. 38

A Painting Book. London: 1884. V. 39

Pictures from Originals Presented by her to John Ruskin and Other Personal Friends (hitherto unpublished). London & New York: 1921. V. 39

Printed Kate Greenaway. A Catalogue Raisonne. London: 1986. V. 39

Under the Window. London. V. 41; 45

Under the Window, Pictures and Rhymes for Children. London: & New York. V. 45

Under the Window. New York. V. 43

Under the Window. London: 1879. V. 41; 46

Under the Window. London: 1900. V. 41

Under the Window. London: 1st edition; V. 40

Under the Window. New York: (c. 1878). V. 37

Under The Window. Pictures & Rhymes for Children. Engraved and Printed by Edmund Evans. London/New York: (1878). V. 37

GREENBERG, CLEMENT

Joan Miro. New York: 1948. V. 46

GREENE, A. C.

The Fifty Best Books on Texas. Dallas: 1981. V. 37; 40

GREENE, ALBERT C.

The Last Captive. Austin: 1972. V. 37; 44; 45

GREENE, ALBERT G.

Catalogue of the Private Library of the Late Hon. Albert G. Greene. New York: 1869. V. 38; 42; 44

Old Grimes. Providence: 1867. V. 44

GREENE, ASA

The Life and Adventures of Dr. Dodimus Duckworth. New York: 1833. V. 40; 43

The Perils of Pearl Street, Including a Taste of the Dangers of Wall Street, by a Late Merchant. New York: 1834. V. 40

Travels in America. New York: 1833. V. 43; 45

GREENE, CHARLES W.

Sketch of Kingston and Its Surroudnings. Kingston: 1883. V. 37; 38; 45

GREENE, DR.

Catalogue of a Part of the . . . Museum of Natural and Artificial Curiosities . . . London: 1803. V. 40; 44

GREENE, E. L.

Landmarks of Botanical History. Stanford: 1983. V. 37

GREENE, EDWARD BURNABY

The Works of Anacreon and Sappho, with pieces from ancient authors; and occasional essays; illustrated by observations on their lives and writings, explanatory notes from established commentators, and additional remarks by the editor; with . . . London: 1768. V. 37

GREENE, EDWARD L.

Illustrations of West American Oaks. San Francisco: 1889. V. 38

GREENE, GEORGE d. 1813

A Relation of Several Circumstances Which Occured in the Province of Lower Normandy, During the Revolution, and Under the Governments of Robespierre and the Directory . . . London: 1802. V. 38; 41

GREENE, GRAHAM

Another Mexico. New York: 1939. V. 37

Babbling April. Oxford: 1925. V. 43

Basement Room. London: 1935. V. 40; 42

The Bear Feel Free. London: 1935. V. 38

Brighton Rock. Sydney. V. 45

Brighton Rock. London: 1938. V. 40; 43; 45

Brighton Rock. New York: 1938. V. 37; 40; 41

Brighton Rock. London: 1947. V. 40

Brighton Rock. London: 1959. V. 45

British Dramatists. London: 1942. V. 42

A Burnt-Out Case. London: 1961. V. 40; 41; 42; 45; 46

The Captain and the Enemy. Canada: 1988. V. 43

The Captain and the Enemy. Toronto: 1988. V. 42

Carving a Statue. London: 1964. V. 45

Carving a Statue a Play. London: 1964. V. 41

Collected Essays. London: 1969. V. 40; 42

The Comedians. London. V. 46

The Comedians. New York: 1965. V. 37; 38; 40; 41; 42; 43

The Comedians. London: 1966. V. 42; 46

The Comedians. New York: 1966. V. 42; 43; 45; 46

The Comedians. London: 1976. V. 45

The Complaisant Lover: a Play. London: 1959. V. 46

The Confidential Agent. London: 1939. V. 43

The Confidential Agent. New York: 1939. V. 37; 39; 41

L'Agent Secret. Paris: 1948. V. 42; 44; 45; 46

Confidential Agent. London: 1952. V. 40

The Confidential Agent. London: 1960. V. 45

Doctor Fischer of Geneva or the Bomb Party. New York: 1980. V. 37; 39; 40; 41; 42; 43; 44; 45; 46

Dear David, Dear Graham. London: 1989. V. 41

Dear David, Dear Graham, a Bibliophile Correspon-dence. Oxford: 1989. V. 46

Doctor Fisher of Geneva or the Bomb party. New York: (1980). V. 37

The End of the Affair. London: 1951. V. 40; 41; 45; 46

The End of the Affair. London: 1959. V. 45

England Made Me. Garden City: 1935. V. 39

England Made Me. New York: 1938. V. 40

Mere Angleterre. Paris: 1948. V. 46

England Made Me. London: 1951. V. 40

England Made Me. London: 1960. V. 45

The Great Jowett. London: 1981. V. 40; 45

The Great Jowett. London: 1981. V. 40

Tueur a Gage. Paris: 1947. V. 40; 44; 45

Gun for Sale. London: 1950. V. 40

A Gun for Sale. London: 1959. V. 45

The Heart of the Matter. London: 1948. V. 42; 43; 46

Heart of the Matter. London: 1951. V. 40

The Honorary Consul. London: 1973. V. 37; 39; 46

The Honorary Consul. London: 1980. V. 45

How Father Quixote Became a Monsignor. California: 1980. V. 37; 40; 42; 43; 45; 46

How Father Quixote Became a Monsignor. London: 1980. V. 46

How Father Quioxte Became a Monsignor. Los Angeles: 1980. V. 45

The Human Factor. London: 1978. V. 46

An Impossible Woman. New York: 1976. V. 40

In Search of a Character. London: 1961. V. 40

In Search of a Character. New York: 1961. V. 45

In Search of a Character: Two African Journals. New York: 1961. V. 41; 42; 43; 45

In Search of a Character. New York: 1962. V. 40; 42; 43; 44; 46

In Search of A Character: Two African Journals. New York: (1962). V. 37

Introductions to Three Novels. Stockholm: 1962. V. 38; 40; 46

It's a Battlefield. London: 1934. V. 41; 46

It's a Battlefield. London: 1950. V. 40

It's a Battlefield. London: 1959. V. 45

Journey Without Maps. Garden City: 1936. V. 37; 39; 44

Journey Without Maps. London: 1936. V. 40

Journey Without Maps. New York: 1936. V. 40; 41; 42; 44

Journey Without Maps. London: 1950. V. 40

The Labyrinthine Ways. New York: 1940. V. 41; 43; 46

THe Labyrinthine Ways. New York: (1940). V. 37

The Lawless Road. London: 1939. V. 38; 40; 43; 46

Lawless Roads. London: 1955. V. 40

The Lawless Roads. London: 1960. V. 45

The Little Fire Engine. V. 42

The Little Fire Engine. London: 1950. V. 38; 39; 40

The Little Horse Bus. London: 1952. V. 38; 41; 44

The Little Steamroller. London: 1953. V. 38; 44

The Little Steamroller. Garden City: 1974. V. 45

The Little Train. London. V. 37

The Living Room. London: 1953. V. 42; 43

Loser Takes All. London: 1955. V. 38; 39; 40; 43

The Lost Childhood. London: 1951. V. 40; 41; 42

The Man Within. Garden City: 1929. V. 44; 46

The Man Within. London: 1929. V. 37; 38; 40; 41; 44

Man Within. London: 1952. V. 40

The Man Within. London: 1959. V. 45

The Man Within. London: (1929). V. 37

May We Borrow Your Husband and Other Comies of the Sexual Life. London: 1967. V. 37; 38; 39; 40; 41; 42; 43; 45; 46

The Ministry of Fear. London: 1943. V. 41

The Ministry of Fear - an Entertainment. London: 1943. V. 40; 42

Ministry of Fear. London: 1950. V. 40; 45

The Ministry of Fear. London: 1960. V. 45

Mr. Visconti. London: 1969. V. 46

Monsigor Quixote. London: 1982. V. 46

Monsignor Quixote. New York: 1982. V. 43

The Name of Action. London: 1930. V. 43

The Name of Action. London: 1930. V. 37; 40; 41; 43; 46

The Name of Action. 1931. V. 45

19 Stories. London: 1947. V. 41; 46

19 Stories. New York: 1949. V. 43; 46

Orient Express. Garden City: 1933. V. 43

Our Man in Havana. London: 1958. V. 38; 41; 45

Our Man in Havanna. London: 1958. V. 41

Our Man in Havana. London, Melbourne, Toronto,: 1958. V. 39; 40

The Potting Shed. London: 1957. V. 38

The Potting Shed. London: 1958. V. 46

The Power and the Glory. London: 1940. V. 40; 46

La Puissance et la Gloire. Paris: 1948. V. 44; 45

Power and the Glory. London: 1951. V. 40

A Quick Look Behind. Los Angeles: 1983. V. 40; 43; 46

GREENE, GRAHAM continued

The Quiet American. London. V. 44

The Quiet American. London: 1955. V. 42; 46

The Quiet American. London: 1956. V. 40

The Quiet American. London: 1956 (sic). V. 44

The Quiet American. London: 1960. V. 45

Reflections on Travels with My Aunt. New York: 1989. V. 41; 42; 43; 44; 45; 46

Reflections on Travels with My Aunt. New York: 1989. V. 45

The Return of A. J. Raffles. London: 1975. V. 40; 45; 46

The Revenge. 1963. V. 46

The Revenge. London. V. 40

The Revenge. London: 1963. V. 40; 46

Romans. Rocher de Brighton/La Puissance de La Gloire/Le Fond du Probleme/La Fin d'une Liasion Avec trente-deux Aquarelles par Bernardette Kelly, Candido Portinari, Frans Masereel, Lucien Fleury. Paris: 1960. V. 46

Rumour at Nightfall. 1932. V. 45

A Sense of Reality. London: 1963. V. 40; 41; 46

Shakespeare-Preise 1968 und 1969. Hamburg: 1969. V. 46

A Sort of Life. London: 1971. V. 40; 46

Stamboul Train. London: 1932. V. 40; 42; 46

Stamboul Train. London: 1951. V. 40

Stamboul Train. London: 1959. V. 45

The Tenth Man. London: 1985. V. 40; 41

The Tenth Man. New York: 1985. V. 43

The Third Man and The Fallen Idol. London: 1950. V. 38; 40; 41; 44

The Third Man. New York: 1950. V. 37; 40

The Third Man. Helsinki: 1988. V. 45; 46

Travels with My Aunt. London. V. 46

Travels with My Aunt. London: 1969. V. 42; 46

Travels with My Aunt. New York: 1970/1969. V. 44; 45

Travels with My Aunt. London: 1980. V. 45

Twenty One Stories. London: 1954. V. 40

Victorian Detective Fiction a Catalogue of the Collection Made by Dorothy Glover and Graham Gren Bibliographically Arranged by Eric Osborne and Introduced by John Carter with a preface by Graham Greene. London: (1966). V. 37

The Virtue of Disloyalty. London. V. 46

The Virtue of Disloyalty. Hartford: 1972. V. 41; 46

The Virtue of Disloyalty. London: 1972. V. 40; 46

The Virtue of Disloyalty. London: 1972. V. 40

A Visit to Morin. London: 1959. V. 38; 41; 42; 45; 46

Ways of Escape. Canada: 1980. V. 41

A Wedding Among the Owls. London: 1977. V. 46

A Weed Among the Flowers. Los Angeles: 1990. V. 46

A Weed Among the Flowers. Los Angeles: 1990. V. 45

Why the Epigraph? London: 1989. V. 43; 44; 45; 46

Yes and No and For Whom the Bell Chimes. London. V. 45

Yes and No, a Play in One Act. Helsinki: 1983. V. 45; 46

Yes and No and For Whom the Bell Chimes. London: 1983. V. 38; 40; 41; 43; 44; 46

GREENE, HARRY PLUNKET

Where the Bright Waters Meet. London: 1924. V. 40

GREENE, HARVEY B.

Wild Flowers from Palestine. Lowell: 1895. V. 46

GREENE, HENRY COPLEY

Theophile a Miracle Play. Boston: 1898. V. 37

GREENE, JOHN P.

Facts Relative to the Expulsion of the Mormons, or Latter Day Saints, from the State of Missouri . . . Cincinnati: 1839. V. 44

GREENE, JOHN W.

Camp Ford Prison; and How I Escaped. An Incident of the Civil War. Toledo: 1893. V. 43

GREENE, MAX

The Kansas Region: Incidents of Travel on the Western Plains and in the Rocky Mountains . . . New York: 1856. V. 37; 40; 43

The Kanzas Region. New York: 1856. V. 37; 38; 39; 41; 42; 45

GREENE, MRS.

The Grey House on the Hill. London: 1903. V. 40

GREENE, RHODOM A.

The Georgia Justice: Being a Convenient Directory fo the Justices of Peace, and Various Other Civil Officers Known to the Laws of the State of Georgia. Milledgeville: 1835. V. 46

GREENE, ROBERT

Ciceronis Amore, Tvllies Love. London: 1628. V. 40; 42; 45

The Dramatic Works. London: 1831. V. 37; 38; 40; 42

Pandosto (or the Historie of Dorastus and Fawina). New York: 1902. V. 43

Pandosto, or Dorastus and Fawnia, Being the Original of Shakespeare's Winter's Tale. London: 1920's. V. 41

GREENE, TALBOT

American Nights' Entertainments . . . Jonesborough: 1860. V. 44

GREENE, W. HOWE

The Wooden Walls Among the Ice Floes. London: 1933. V. 41

GREENE, W. T.

Parrots in Captivity. London: 1848-87. V. 37; 45; 46

GREENE, WILLIAM

Some of the Difficulties in the Administration of a Free Government: a Discourse. Providence: 1851. V. 42

GREENE, WILLIAM THOMAS

Parrots in Captivity . . . London: 1884-7. V. 41

GREENER, W. W.

The Breech Loader, and How to Use It. London, Paris & Melborune: 1892. V. 41

The Breech-Loader and How to Use It. New York: 1892. V. 40

The Gun and Its Development. London, New York & Melbourne: 1888. V. 40

The Gun and Its Development. London: 1896. V. 39; 40; 45

The Gun and Its Development. London: 1899. V. 45

The Gun and Its Development. London: 1967. V. 40

The Gun and Its Development; with Notes on Shooting. London: (1881). V. 37

Modern Shot-Guns. London: 1888. V. 40

Modern Breech-Loaders Sporting and Military. London: (c. 1860). V. 37

GREENER, WILLIAM

The Science of Gunnery as Applied to the Use and Construction of Fire Arms. London: 1841. V. 43

GREENER, WILLIAM WELLINGTON

Choke-Bore Guns, and How to Load for All Kinds of Game. London: 1876. V. 39

The Gun and Its Development; with Notes on Shooting. London: 1881. V. 39

The Gun. London: 1885. V. 38

The Gun and Its Development: with Notes on Shooting. London: 1888. V. 39

The Science of Gunnery as Applied to the Military and Sporting Arms of England, France, Belgium, Austria, Prussia, Russia and America. London: 1846. V. 38

GREENEWALT, C. H.

Humming Birds. New York: 1960. V. 37; 39; 40; 41; 42; 44

GREENEWALT, CRAWFORD

Humming Birds. 1960. V. 39; 46

GREENEWALT, CRAWFORD H.

Hummingbirds. Garden City: 1960. V. 38; 39; 43

GREENEWALT, MARY HALLOCK

Nourathar. The Fine Art of Light Color Playing. Philadelphia: 1946. V. 42

GREENFIELD, J. GODWIN

The Cerebro-Spinal Fluid in Clinical Diagnosis. London: 1925. V. 42

GREENHAM, EDITH

Of Una Jeffers. Los Angeles: 1939. V. 39

GREENHAM, RICHARD

The Works. London: 1599. V. 44

GREENHILL, C.

The Life of a Regiment. The History of the Gordon Highlanders from its Formation in 1794 to 1816 to 1898. Edinburgh: 1901-1903. V. 37

GREENHILL, ELIZABETH

Elizabeth Greenhill, Bookbinder. A Catalogue Raisonne. Frenich, Foss: 1986. V. 39; 42

Elizabeth Greenhill, Bookbinder. A Catalogue Raisonne. London: 1986. V. 39

Elizabeth Greenhill, Bookbinder: a Catalogue Raisonne. Perthshire: 1986. V. 37; 40; 43

GREENHILL, F. A.

Incised Effigial Slabs. A Study of Engraved Stone Memorials in Latin Christendom, c. 1000 to c. 17600. London: 1976. V. 40

GREENHILL, RALPH

Early Photography in Canada. Toronto: 1965. V. 37

GREENHILL, THOMAS

Nekrokedeia; or, the Art of Embalming . . . London: 1705. V. 42

GREENHOW, EDWARD

On Addison's Disease, Being the Croonian Lectures for 1875. Philadelphia: 1875. V. 42

GREENHOW, EDWARD H.

On Diptheria. London: 1860. V. 43

GREENHOW, EDWARD HEADLAM

The Results of an Inquiry into the different Proportions of Death produced by certain Diseases in different Districts of Enlgnad . . . with an Introductory Report, by the Medical Officer of the Board (John Simon), on the . . . London: 1858. V. 37; 39

GREENHOW, ROBERT

The History of Oregon and California, and the Other Territories of the Northwest Coast of North America, Accompanied by a Geographical View and Map of Those Countries . . . Boston: 1844. V. 37; 38; 45

The History of Oregon and California, and Other Territories on the North-West Coast of North America. London: 1844. V. 41; 42; 43; 45

The History of Oregon and California and Other Territories on the North West Coast of North America. Boston: 1845. V. 38; 39; 42; 43; 45; 46

The History of Oregon and California, and the Other Territories . . . New York: 1845. V. 45

The History of Oregon & California & the Other Territories on the Northwest Coast of No. America, etc. Boston: 1847. V. 39

The History of Oregon and California, and the Other Territories on the Northwest Coast of North America. Boston: 1847. V. 39

Memoir, Historical and Political, of the Northwest Coast of North America, and the Adjacent Territories . . . Washington: 1840. V. 45

Memoir, Historical and Political, on the Northwest Coast of North America . . . Washington: 1840. V. 42; 43; 45

GREENHOW, THOMAS MICHAEL

Cholera, As It Has Recently Appered in the Towns of Nebraska and Gateshead . . . London: 1832. V. 45

GREENLAND. Copenhagen: 1928-29. V. 42

GREENLEAF, ELIZABETH B.

Ballads and Sea Songs of Newfoundland. Cabridge: 1933. V. 38

GREENLEAF, J.

The Family Gazetteer, Containing, At One View . . . Boston: 1844. V. 42; 45

GREENLEAF, JONATHAN

Sketches of the Ecclesiastica History of the State of Maine, From the Earliest Settlement to the Present Time. Portsmouth: 1821. V. 39

GREENLEAF, MOSES

A Statistical View of the District of Maine; More Especially with Reference o the Value and Importance of Its Interior.. Boston: 1816. V. 39; 43

GREENLY, A. H.

Bibliography of Father Richard's Press in Detroit. Ann Arbor: 1955. V. 41

GREENLY, ALBERT HARRY

A Selective Bibliography of Important Books, Pamphlets and Broadsides Relating to Michigan History. London:unenburg: 1958. V. 42

A Selective Bibliography of Important Books, Pamphlets and Broadsides Relating to Michigan History. Lunenburg: 1958. V. 42

GREENMAN, FREDERICK F.

Wire-Tapping: Its Relation to Civil Liberties. Stamford: 1938. V. 39; 46

GREENOUGH, CHESTER NOYES

A Bibliography of the Theophrastan Character in English . . . 1947. V. 42

GREENOUGH, G. B.

General Sketch of the Physical and Geological Features of British India. London: 1855. V. 42

GREENVILLE AND COLUMBIA RAILROAD CO.

Annual Report of the Greenville and Columbia Railroad Co. Exhibiting Its Condition and Prospects. Columbia: 1855. V. 44

GREENWALT, CRAWFORD H.

Humming Birds. London: 1960. V. 45

Hummingbirds. New York: 1960. V. 45

Hummingbirds. USA: 1960. V. 38; 45

GREENWELL, DORA

On the Education of the Imbecile . . . London: 1869. V. 46

GREENWELL, G. C.

A Practical Treatise on Mine Engineering. London: 1855. V. 45

A Practical Treatise on Mine Engineering. Newcastle-Upon-Tyne: 1855. V. 37

GREENWICH, ENGLAND. NATIONAL MARITIME MUSEUM

British and Foreign Medals. London: 1950. V. 39

GREENWOOD, C.

Atlas of the Counties of England, from Actual Surveys Made from the Years 1817 to 1833. London: 1834. V. 46

GREENWOOD, GEORGE

The Tree-Lifter. London: 1844. V. 40

GREENWOOD, ISAAC 1702-1745

A Philosophical Discourse Concerning the Mutability and Changes of the Material World; Read to the Students of Harvard College April 7, 1731. Upon the News of the Death of Thomas Hollis . . . Boston: 1731. V. 38; 39; 40

GREENWOOD, JAMES

Curiosities of Savage Life. London: 1863. V. 41

An Essay Towards a Practical English Grammar. London: 1711. V. 41

An Essay Towards a Practical English Grammar, Describing the Genius and Nature of the English Tongue . . . London: 1722. V. 41; 43

An Essay Towards a Practical English Grammar, Describing the Genius and Nature of the English Tongue. London: 1729. V. 39

Glad News for Shady-Land. London: 1870? V. 40

The Hatchet Throwers. London: 1866. V. 41

In Strange Company; Being the Experiences of a Roving Correspondent. London: 1883. V. 40

Legends of Savage Life. London: 1867. V. 46

The London Vocabulary English and Latin. London: 1752. V. 40

The London Vocabulary, English and Latin. London;: 1797. V. 39

The London Vocabulary. London: 1785. V. 37

The London Vocabulary English and Latin. London: 1752. V. 38

A Night in the Workhouse. London: 1866. V. 40

The Purgatory of Peter the Cruel. London: 1868. V. 46

The Seven Curses of London. London: 1869? V. 42

Silas the Conjuror; His Travels and Perils. London: 1866. V. 41

The Virgin Muse. London: 1717. V. 43

GREENWOOD, JEREMY

The Wood-Engravings of John Nash . . . Liverpool: 1987. V. 44

GREENWOOD, JOHN

Revolutionary Services of . . . of Boston & New York 1775-1783. New York: 1922. V. 39

GREENWOOD, JONATHAN

The Sailing and Fighting Instructions of Signals as They are Observed in the Royal Navy of Great Britain. London: 1715. V. 39; 42

GREENWOOD, ROBERT

The California Outlaw, Tiburcio Vasquez. Los Gatos: 1960. V. 46

California Imprints, 1883-1862. Los Altos: 1961. V. 42

California Imprints 1833-1862. Los Gatos: 1961. V. 38; 44; 45

GREENWOOD, THOMAS

A Tour in the States and Canada: Out and Home in Six Weeks. London: 1883. V. 37; 41

GREENWOOD, W. E.

The Villa Madama, Rome. London: 1928. V. 37; 40; 42; 44; 45

The Villa Madama, Rome, A Reconstruction. New York: 1928. V. 37; 44

GREENWOOD, WILLIAM

The Vale of Apperley and Its Vicinity. V. 46

The Vale of Apperley and Other Poems. Malton;: 1822. V. 41

GREENWOOD'S Picture of Hull. Hull & London: 1835. V. 39
GREENWOOD'S Picture of Hull. London: 1835. V. 37

GREENWORD, GEORGE

The Tree-Lifter. London: 1844. V. 39

GREER, GEORGEANNA H.

The Meyer Family: Master Potters of Texas. 1971. V. 45

GREER, JAMES

Colonel Jack Hays, Texas Frontier Leader and California Builder. New York: 1952. V. 46

The Windings of the Moy, with Skreen and Tireragh. Dublin: 1925. V. 38

GREER, JAMES K.

Bois d'Arc to Barb'd Wire, Ken Cary; Southwestern Frontier Born. Dallas: 1936. V. 39; 42; 43

Colonel Jack Hays: Texas Frontier Leader and California Builder. New York: 1952. V. 41; 44

Grand Prairie. Dallas: 1935. V. 38

GREET, DORA VICTOIRE

Story of the Golden Owl. London: 1892-93. V. 42

GREEY, WILLIAM

The Toronto Mill Furnishing Works. Toronto: 1901. V. 44

GREFRIER, LE SIEUR

Les Satyres de Perse Fidellement Traduites en Nostre Langue . . . Avec Deux Tables l'une Latine et l'Autre Francoise Pour Faciliter Ceux qui n'ont pas l'Usage de la Lngue Latine. Paris: 1658. V. 38

GREG, RICHARD

Memoria Technica; or, a New Method of Artificial Memory Applied to and Exemplified . . . London: 1730. V. 43; 44

GREG, WALTER WILSON 1875-

Bibliography of the English Printed Drama to the Restoration. London: 1939-51. V. 38

a Bibliography of the English Printed Drama to the Restoration. London: 1939-59. V. 39; 42

GREG, WILLIAM RATHBONE 1809-1881

An Enquiry into the State of the Manufacturing Population and the Causes and Cures of the Evils Therein Existing. London: 1831. V. 38; 39

Essays on Political and Social Science, Contributed Chiefly to the Edinburgh Review. London: 1853. V. 41

Sketches in Greece and Turkey: With the Present Condition and Future Prospects of the Turkish Empire. London: 1833. V. 37

GREGER, DEBORA

Blank County: Twenty Poems. 1985. V. 40

Blank Country. Sn Francisco: 1985. V. 38

GREGG, ALEXANDER

History of the Old Cheraws, Containing an Account of the Aborigines of the Pedee, the First White Settlements. Columbia: 1925. V. 39; 40; 42

History of the Old Cheraws: Containing an Account of the Aborigines of the Pedee, the First White Settlements . . . Extending About A.D. 1730 to 1810. New York: 1867. V. 37; 42

History of the Old Cheraws, Containing an Account of the Aborignies of the Pedee, the First White Settlements . . . 1730 to 1810. Columbia, S.C.: 1925. V. 37

GREGG, ASA

Personal Recollections of the Early Settlement of Wapsinonoc Township and the Murder of Atwood by the Indians. West Liberty: 1876. V. 39

GREGG, FRANK M.

The Founding of a Nation. Cleveland: 1915. V. 43

GREGG, JOSIAH

Commerce of the Prairies; or, the Journal of a Santa Fe Trader, During Eight Expeditions Across the Great Western Prairie. New York: 1844. V. 37; 38; 39; 40; 41; 42; 43; 45

Commerce of the Prairies; or, The Journal of a Santa Fe Trader, During Eight Expeditions Across the Great Western Prairie. New York: 1844. V. 42

Commerce of the Prairies. New York: 1845. V. 40

Commerce of the Prairies, or the Journal of a Santa Fe Trader, During Eight Expeditions Across the Great Western Prairies, and a Residence of Nearly Nine Years in Northern Mexico. New York: 1845. V. 37; 38; 39; 40; 41; 42; 43; 45

Commerce of the Prairies of the Journal of a Santa Fe Trader, During Eight Expeditions Across the Great Western Prairies, and a Residence of Nearly Nine Years in Northern Mexico. Philadelphia: 1851. V. 41

Diary and Letters of Josiah Gregg. Norman: 1941, 1944. V. 39

Diary and Letters of Josiah Gregg. Norman: 1941/44. V. 42

Diary and Letters of Josiah Gregg. Southwestern Enterprises, 1840-1850. Edited by Maurice Garland Fulton. Introduction by Paul Horgan. Norman, Oklahoma: 1941-1944. V. 37

GREGG, W. W.

English Literary Autographs 1550-1650; Supplement; Scholars & Archaeologists. Oxford: 1925-32. V. 39

GREGG, WILLIAM

Essay on Plank Roads. Charleston: 1851. V. 44

GREGO, JOSEPH

Pictorial Pickwickiana: Charles Dickens and his illustrators. London: 1899. V. 37

Rowlandson the Caricaturist. London: 1880. V. 37; 38; 41

Rowlandson the Caricaturist. A selection from his works with anecdotal descriptions of his caricatures and A sketch of His Life, Times and Contemporaries . . . with about 400 illustrations. 1880. V. 37

GREGOIRE, HENRI

An Enquiry Concerning the Intellectual and Moral Faculties, and Literature of Negroes and Mulattoes. Brooklyn: 1810. V. 40

GREGOIRE, PIERRE 1540-1597

De Republica Tomus Alter XIII. Alios Libros Continens . . . Pont a Mousson: 1596. V. 40

GREGOR, FRANCIS 1760-1815

The Works. Exeter: 1816. V. 37; 39; 42

GREGOR, JOSEPH

Masks of the World. London: 1936-37. V. 46

Masks of the World. London: 1936-7. V. 43

GREGORIETTI, GUIDO

Italian Gold, Silver and Jewelry: Their History and Centres. Milan: 1971. V. 46

GREGORIUS, BP. OF TOURS 538-594

Historiae Francorum Libri Decem . . . Adonis Viennensis Chronica. Paris: 1561. V. 40

GREGORIUS I, POPE

Pastorale, sive Regula Pastoralis. Cologne: 1482. V. 37

GREGORIUS NAZIANZENUS, SAINT

Opera. Paris: 1609-11. V. 38

Orationes Trigintaocto. Tractatus, Sermones & Libri Aliquot. Paris: 1532. V. 37

GREGORIUS, PETRUS

Syntaxes Artis Mirabilis, in Libros Septem Digestae . . . Venice: 1586. V. 40; 42; 43

GREGORIUS THAUMATURGUS, SAINT

Macarii Aegyptii, et Basilii Seleuciae . . . Opera Omnia. Paris: 1622. V. 38

GREGOROVIUS, FERDINAND

Wanderings in Corsica. Edinburgh: 1855. V. 42; 44; 46

GREGORSON, EDITH RAY

Timothy Tramcar. London. V. 45

GREGORY, A.

Hester Craddock. London: 1931. V. 41

Wheels on Gravel. London: 1938. V. 41

GREGORY, ALYSE

King Log and Lady Lea. London: 1929. V. 40

GREGORY, DAVID

Astronomiae Physicae & Geometricae Elementa . . . Acceserunt Praefatio Editoris . . . Geneva: 1726. V. 44

The Elements of Astronomy, Physical and Geometrical . . . London: 1715. V. 44

The Elements of Physical and Geometrical Astronomy . . . . London: 1726. V. 44

GREGORY, DICKSON

Australian Steamships, Past and Present. With a Foreword by Brig.-Gen. Sir Granville Ryrie, K.C.M.G., High Commissioner for Australia. London: 1928. V. 37

GREGORY, G.

A Dictionary of arts and sciences. In Two Volumes. London: 1806. V. 37

GREGORY, GEORGE

The Economy of Nature Explained and Illustrated on the Principles of Modern Philosophy . . . London: 1796. V. 42

The Economy of Nature Explained and Illustrated on the Principles of Modern Philosophy. London: 1798. V. 42; 43

The Life of Thomas Chatterton, with Criticism on His Genius and Writings and Concise View of the Controversy Concerning Rowley's Poems. London: 1789. V. 37; 38; 39; 41; 42; 45; 46

Treatise on the Theory and Practice of Physic. Philadelphia: 1836. V. 40; 41

GREGORY, HORACE

Chelsea Blooming House. New York: 1930. V. 40; 42

Chorus for Survival. New York: 1935. V. 37

D. H. Lawrence, Pilgrim of the Apocalypse, a Critical Study. New York: 1957. V. 44

GREGORY, I. B.

Gregorii Magni Episcopi Romani, De Cura Pastorali . . . London: 1629. V. 44

GREGORY I, POPE

Dialogi. Vita. Venice: 1487. V. 40; 45

GREGORY I, SAINT

Liber Moraliu in Beatu Job. Basel: 1514. V. 44

GREGORY, ISABELLA AUGUSTA PERSE 1859-1932

A Book of Saints and Wonders. Dundrum: 1906. V. 43

Coole. 1931. V. 42

Ideals in Ireland. London: 1901. V. 45

The Image, a Play in Three Acts. Dublin: 1910. V. 40

The Kiltartan Wonder Book. Dublin: 1910. V. 44

The Kiltartan Poetry Book Prose Translations from the Irish. Churchtown: 1918. V. 39

Kincora; a Drama in Three Acts. New York: 1905. V. 40

Spreading the News. The Rising of the Moon and the Poor-House. Dublin: 1906. V. 43

The White Cockade: a Comedy and The Travelling Man. New York: 1905. V. 44

GREGORY, ISABELLA AUGUSTA PERSSE 1859-1932

The Kiltartan Poetry Book. Dublin: 1918. V. 38

The Kiltartan History Book. London: 1909. V. 37

GREGORY, ISABELLA AUGUSTUA PERSE 1859-1932

Coole. Dublin: 1931. V. 39; 46

Our Irish Theatre. New York: 1913. V. 41

GREGORY IX, POPE

Decretales . . . Paris: 1516. V. 45

Decretales Epistolae Svmmorvm Collectae. Paris: 1550. V. 40

GREGORY, JACKSON

The Emerald Murder Trap. New York: 1934. V. 42

GREGORY, JAMES

Cases Treated by Dr. Gregory in the Clinical Ward. Edinburgh: 1783. V. 40

Dissertatio Medica Inauguralis, De Morbis Coeli Mutatione Medendis . . . Edinburgh: 1774. V. 37; 39; 41; 44; 46

The Great and New Art of Weighing Vanity . . . Glasgow: 1672. V. 42

Optica Promota, Seu Abdita Radiorum Reflexorum & Refractorum Mysteria . . . Londini: 1663. V. 42

GREGORY, JOHN

A Comparative View of the State and Faculties of man With Those of the Animal World. London: 1765. V. 42

A Comparative View of the State and Faculties of Man and Those of the Animal World. London: 1766. V. 42; 43; 45

A Comparative View of the State and Faculties of Man With Those of the Animal World. London: 1774. V. 42; 45

A Father's Legacy to His Daughter. London: 1793. V. 40

A Father's Legacy to His Daughters. London: 1795. V. 43

Gregorii Posthuma; or, Certain Learned Tracts . . . London: 1650. V. 45

The Works . . . London: 1671. V. 38

The Works. London: 1684. V. 39; 44

GREGORY, JOHN G.

History of Milwaukee, Wisconsin. Chicago: 1931. V. 37; 43

Southwestern Wisconsin: A History of Old Crawford County. Chicago: 1932. V. 46

GREGORY, JOHN WALTER

Australasia. London: 1907-08. V. 45

The Great Rift Valley, Being the Narrative of a Journey to Mount Kenya and Lake Baringo . . . London: 1806. V. 42

GREGORY NAZIANENSIS, SAINT

Sententia Tetrastichis Iambis Comprehensae. Paris: 1575. V. 40

GREGORY, OLINTHUS

Memoirs of the Life, Writings and Character, Literary, Professional and Religious, of the Late John Mason Good, M.D. London: 1828. V. 39; 40; 41

GREGORY THE GREAT, SAINT

Libri Dialogorum. Basle: 1496. V. 41

GREGORY, THOMAS JEFFERSON

History of Solano and Napa Counties, California. Los Angeles: 1912. V. 41

GREGORY, W.

The Beckford Family. Bath: 1887. V. 39

The Beckford Family. London: 1898. V. 39

GREGORY, W. H.

Egypt in 1855 and 1856; Tunis in 1857 and 1858. London: 1859. V. 40

GREGORY, WILLIAM 1803-1858

Letters to a Candid Inquirer on Animal Magnetism. London: 1851. V. 43; 46

Our Face From Fish to Man: A Portrait Gallery of Our Ancient Ancestors and Kinsfolk Together with a Concise History of Our Best Features. New York: 1929. V. 42

The Picture of Dublin; Being a Description of the City, and a Correct Guide to All Public Establisments . . . Dublin: 1815. V. 46

GREGORY, WINIFRED

American Newspapers 1821-1936, a Union List of Files Available in the United States and Canada. New York: 1967. V. 39

Union List of Serials in Libraries of the U.S. & Canada. New York: 1927. V. 38

Union List of Serials in Libraries of the United States and Canada. New York: 1943. V. 42

GREGORY XIV

Literae Facultatum et Privilegium . . . Capellanorum. Rome: 1592. V. 44

GREGORY XIV, POPE

Breve . . . Confirmationis, Extensionis, ac Communicationis Privilegiorum Cisterciensis Ordinis, & Eius Congregationum. Rome: 1591. V. 41

GREGSON, JOHN STANLEY

The Comical Budget of Fun and Frolic . . . Derby: 1830. V. 46

GREGSON, MATTHEW

History of Lancashire. Liverpool: 1817-24. V. 42; 46

Portfolio of Fragments, Relative to the History and Antiquities of the County Palatine and Duchy of Lancaster. Liverpool: 1817. V. 39

Portfolio. Liverpool: 1824. V. 42; 46

Portfolio of Fragments Relative to the History and Antiquities, Topography and Genealogies of the County Palatine and Duchy of Lancaster. London: 1869. V. 38

GREIG, JOHN

The Flower-Growers' Instructor; or, the Temple of Flora . . . London: 1840. V. 41; 46

GREIVE, CHRISTOPHER MURRAY

O Wha's Been Here Afore Me, Lass. London: 1931. V. 43

GRELLMANN, HEINRICH MORITZ GOTTLIEB

Dissertation on the Gipsies . . . London: 1787. V. 42

Dissertation on the Gipseys . . . London: 1807. V. 42

GRELOT, WILLIAM J.

A Late Voyage to Constantinople. London: 1683. V. 39; 45

GRELOT, WILLIAM JOSEPH

A Late Voyage to Constantinople . . . London: 1683. V. 45

GREMBS, FRANZ OSWALD

V. 45

Arbor Integra et Ruinosa Hominis, id est: Tractatus Medicus Theorico Practicus in Tres Libros Divisus . . . Frankfurt: 1657. V. 45

GRENARD, FERNAND

Tibet the Country and Its Inhabitants. London: 1905. V. 40

GRENFELL, ANNE

Le Petit Nord: Annals of a Labrador Harbour. London: 1920. V. 44

GRENFELL, PASCOE 1761-1838

The Speech of Pascoe Grenfell, Esq., in the House of Commons, on Tuesday, the 13th of Feb. 1816 on Certain Transactions Subsisting Between the Public and the Bank of England. London: 1816. V. 41

GRENFELL, PRICE A.

The Winning of Australian Antarctica. Mawson's Banzare Voyages 1929-31. 1962. V. 37

GRENFELL, WILFRED T.

Vikings of Today. London: 1895. V. 44

GRENFELL, WILFRED THOMASON

Labrador Days - Tales of Sea Toilers . . . Boston: 1905. V. 39

GRENVILLE, CAPTAIN

Great-Britain's Coasting Pilot. London: 1742. V. 38

GRENVILLE, GEORGE

An Ode Upon the Present Period of Time; with a Letter to the Right Honourable Grenville. London: 1769. V. 40; 42

The Regulations Lately Made Concerning the Colonies and the Taxes Imposed Upon Them Considered. London: 1765. V. 43

GRENVILLE, GEORGE continued

The Speech of a Right Honourable Gentleman, on the Motion for Expelling Mr. Wilkes, Friday Feb. 3, 1769. London: 1769. V. 39; 43

The Speech of a Right Honourable Gentleman, on the Motion for Expelling Mr. Wilkes, Friday, February 3, 1769. London: 1767. V. 37

GRENVILLE-TEMPLE, RICHARD

The Principles of the Late Changes Impartially Examined. London: 1765. V. 37; 38

GRENVILLE, WILLIAM WYNDHAM

Nugae Metricae. N.P.: 1824. V. 46

GREPPO, J. G. H.

Essay on the Hieroglyphic System of M. Champollion, Jun. Boston: 1830. V. 40; 42; 44

GRESLEY, ROGER

Sir Philip Gasteneys; a Minor. London: 1829. V. 43

GRESSET, J. B. L. 1709-1777

Vert-Vert. London: 1840. V. 44; 46

GRESSIT, J. L.

Biogeography and Ecology of New Guinea. London: 1981. V. 37

GRESWELL, RICHARD

On Education in the Principles of Art . . . Oxford: 1844. V. 38

GRESWELL, WILLIAM

Our South African Empire. London: 1885. V. 41

GRESWELL, WILLIAM PARR

Annals of Parisian Typography. London: 1818. V. 37; 38; 39; 40; 41; 43; 44; 45; 46

Annals of Parisian Typography. London: 1818. V. 40

Annals of Parisian Typography, containing as account of the earliest typographical establishments of Paris, and notices and illustrations of the most remarkable productions of the Parisian Gothic Press: compiled principally to shew its . . . 1818. V. 37

The Monastery of Saint Werburgh: a Poem . . . Manchester: 1823. V. 44

A View of the Early Parisian Greek Press. Oxford: 1833. V. 38

GRETSER, JACOB

Institvtionvm Lingvae Graecae Liber Primus. De Octo Partibvs Orationis. Rome: 1618/1618/1610. V. 42

GRETTIS SAGA

The Story of Grettir the Strong. London: 1901. V. 41

GRETTON, G. LE M.

The Campaigns and History of the Royal Irish Regiment from 1684 to 1902. London: 1911. V. 42

The Campaigns and History of the Roayl Irish Regiment from 1684 to 1922. London: 1911/1927. V. 37

GREVILLE, CHARLES C. F.

The Greville Memoirs. London: 1874-85-87. V. 39; 42; 43

Past and Present Policy of England Towards Ireland. London: 1845. V. 41

GREVILLE, CHARLES CAVENDISH FULKE 1794-1865

The Greville Memoirs. London: 1874/75/87. V. 39

The Greville Memoirs . . . (and) A Journal of the Reign of Queen Victoria. London: 1874-87. V. 37; 45

The Greville Memoirs: A Journal of the Reigns of King George IV, King William IV, and Queen Victoria (1837-1860). By Charles Greville. London: 1874. V. 37

Memoirs. A Journal of the Reigns of King George IV to King William IV . . . London: 1875-87. V. 37; 38

GREVILLE, F.

The Rail and the Rod; or, Tourist Angler's Guide to Waters and Quarters Thirty Miles Around London. London: 1867. V. 40

GREVILLE, FULKE

The Life of the Renowned Sir Philip Sidney. London: 1552. V. 44

Maxims, Characters and Reflections, Critical, Satyrical and Moral. London: 1756. V. 42

Maxims, Characters and Reflections, Critical, Satyrical and Moral. London: 1757. V. 44

GREVILLE, GEORGE

Caelica. Newtown: 1936. V. 40

GREVILLE, R. K.

Scottish Crylogamic Flora, or Coloured Figures and Descriptions of Cryptomagic Plants . . . Edinburgh: 1822-28. V. 42

Scottish Cryptogamic Flora, or Coloured Figures and Descriptions of Cryptogamic Plants Belonging Chiefly to the Order Fungi . . . Edinburgh: 1823-28. V. 42; 43; 45

Scottish Cryptogramic Flora, or Coloured Figures and Descriptions of Cryptogamic Plants Belonging Chiefly to the ORder Fungi . . . Edinburgh: 1823-28. V. 45

GREVIN-GEMINUS

Les Portraicts Anatomiqves de Tovtes les Parties du Corps Humain Gravez en Taille Douce . . . Paris: 1569. V. 46

GREW, J. C.

Sport and Travel in the Far East. Boston: 1910. V. 42

Sport and Travel in the Far East. London: 1910. V. 45

GREW, NEHEMIAH 1641-1712

Anatomie des Plantes qui Contient unde Descriptions Exacte de Leurs Parties 7 de Leurs Usages . . . Paris: 1675. V. 37

The Anatomy of Plants. London: 1682. V. 37; 38; 43; 45; 46

The Anatomy of Vegetables Begun. London: 1672. V. 37; 41; 45

Experiments in Consort of the Luctation Arising from the Affusions of Several Menstruums Upon all Sorts of Bodies, Exhibited to the Royal Society April 13 and June 1, 1676. London: 1678. V. 37; 38

An Idea of a Philosophical History of Plants. Read Before the Royal Society, January 8 and January 15, 1672. London: 1682. V. 39

Musaeum Regalis Societatis . . . London: 1681. V. 37; 38; 39; 40; 42; 43; 45; 46

Musaeum Regalis Societatis or a Catalogue and Description of the Natural and Artifical Rarities belonging to the Royal Society Preserved at Gresham College. Whereunto is subjoyned the Comparative Anatomy of Stomachs and Guts. London: (1681). V. 37

Tractatus de Salis Cathartici Amari in Aquis Ebeshamensibus, et Hujusmodi Aliis Contenti Natura & Usu. London: 1695. V. 46

tRACTATUS DE sALIS cATHARTICI aMARI IN aQUIS eBESHAMENSIBUS ET hUJUSMODI aLIIS cONTENTI nATURA & uSU. V. 46

GREY, ANDREW BELCHER 1820-1862

Report of the Secretary of Interior Communicating a Report and Map of A. B. Gray Relative to the Mexican Boundary. Washington: 1855. V. 42

GREY, BEN E.

House of Representatives . . . To My Constituents of the Second Congressional District . . . Washington: 1854. V. 45

GREY, C. H.

Hardy Bulbs, Including Half Hardy Bulbs and Tuberous and Fibrous Rooted Plants. London: 1937. V. 37; 38; 40

Hardy Bulbs. London: 1937-38. V. 37; 38

Hardy Bulbs. Volume 2, Amaryllidaceae, Commelinaceae, Haemodoraceae, Orchidaceae, Setamineae. London: 1938. V. 37

GREY, EDWARD

Fly Fishing. London: 1899. V. 40; 42; 46

GREY, EDWARD GREY, 1ST VISCOUNT 1862-1933

The Charm of Birds. London: 1927. V. 37; 41; 44

Fallodon Papers. London: 1926. V. 41; 46

Fly Fishing. London: 1930. V. 39; 44

Twenty-Five Years 1892-1916. London: 1925. V. 38

GREY, ELIZABETH CAROLINE

De Lisle; or, the Distrustful Man. London: 1828. V. 40

Good Society; or, Contrasts of Character. London: 1863. V. 44

One of the Family; or, the Ladies. London: 1861. V. 44

The Way of the World. London: 1831. V. 44

GREY, FREDERICK W.

Seeking Fortune in America. London: 1912. V. 43

GREY, GEORGE

Journals of Two Expeditions of Discovery in North-West & Western Australia During the Years 1837, 8 & 9 . . . Describing Newly Discovered Important & Fertile Districts with Observations on the Moral & Physical Condition of the Aboriginal Inhabitants. London: 1841. V. 37; 46

GREY, HENRY GEORGE, 3RD EARL OF 1802-1894

The Colonial Policy of Lord John Russell's Administration. London: 1853. V. 39

GREY, JAMES T.

Handbook for the Margaree. Yardley: 1976. V. 43

GREY, PAMELA

The Vein in the Marble. London: 1925. V. 43

GREY, R. C.

Adventures of a Deep-Sea Angler. New York: 1930. V. 37

GREY, ZANE 1872-1939 continued

Tappan's Burro and Other Stories. New York: (1923). V. 37
Tappan's Burro and Other Stories. New York: (1923). V. 37
30,000 on the Hoof. New York: 1940. V. 39; 41; 46
30,000 on the Hoof. London: (1940). V. 37
Thunder Mountain. New York: 1935. V. 37
The Thundering Herd. New York: 1925. V. 37; 43; 44
The Thundering Herd. New York & London: 1925. V. 39; 41; 42
Thundering Herd. New York: (ca. 1926). V. 37
To Last Man. New York: 1921. V. 39
To the Last Man. New York: and London: 1921. V. 45
To the Last Man. New York: (1921). V. 37
The Trail Driver. New York: 1936. V. 37
Twin Sombreros. London: (1941). V. 37
The U.P. Trail. New York: 1918. V. 39; 44
Under the Tonto Rim. Toronto: 1926. V. 39
Under the Tonto Rim. New York: 1926. V. 37; 44
The U.P. Trail. New York: (1918). V. 37
Valley of Wild Horses. New York: (1947). V. 37
The Vanishing American. New York: 1925. V. 37; 39; 40; 45; 46
The Vanishing Indian. London: (ca. 1925). V. 37
Wanderer of the Wasteland. London. V. 45
The Wanderer of the Wasteland. Toronto: 1923. V. 39
Wanderer of the Wasteland. New York: 1923. V. 37
West of the Pecos. New York: 1937. V. 44
West of the Pecos. Toronto: 1938. V. 39
West of the Pecos. New York: 1937. V. 37
Western Union. London: 1939. V. 44
Western Union. Toronto: 1941. V. 39
The Western Motion Picture. Los Angeles: 1984. V. 45
The Western Motion-Picture. Los Angeles: 1984. V. 37
Western Union. New York: 1939. V. 37
Wild Horse Mesa. London: 1928. V. 44
Wild Horse Mesa. New York: 1928. V. 37
Wildfire. New York: (ca. 1920). V. 37
The Wolf-Tracker. New York: 1930. V. 44
The Young Forester. New York: 1910. V. 39
The Young Forester. London: 1922, 1910. V. 44
The Young Lion Hunter. New York: 1941. V. 44
The Young Lion Hunter. London: (ca. 1919). V. 37
The Young Pitcher. New York: (1913, 1911). V. 37
Zane Grey's Book of Camps and Trails. New York: 1931. V. 39
Zane Grey's King of the Royal Mounted in Arctic Law. Racine: 1937. V. 39
Zane Grey: The Man and His Work. An Autobiographical Sketch, Critical Appreciations and Bibliography. New York: 1928. V. 37; 38
Zane Grey's Adventures in Fishing. New York: (1952). V. 37
Zane Grey's Book of Camp and Trails. New York: 1931. V. 37

GRHAME, JAMES

British Georgics. Edinburgh: 1809. V. 39

GRIBBLE, FRANCIS

Madame de Stael and Her Lovers. London: 1907. V. 38

GRIEKEN, T. M. M. VAN

De Plant in Hare Ornamentale Behandeling, Met Eene Inleiding Over de Zinnebeeldige Voorstelling. Groningen: 1888. V. 41
De Plant in Hare Ornamentale Behandeling, Met Eene Inleiding Over de Zinnebeeldige Voorstelling. London: 1888. V. 46

GRIER, RICHARD

An Answer to Ward's Errata of the Protestant Bible. London: 1812. V. 40

GRIER'S Southern Almanac for the States of Georgia, South Carolina, Alabama and Tennesse for the Year of Our Lord 1862. Augusta: 1861. V. 44

GRIER'S Southern Almanac for the States of Georgia, South Carolina, Mississippi, Louisiana, Alabama, Tennessee for the Year of Our Lord 1863. Augusta: 1862. V. 44

GRIERSON, B. H.

Annual Report of . . . Commanding Department of Arizona, 1889. N.P.: 1889. V. 37; 42

GRIERSON, FIONA

Haunting Edinburgh. Edinburgh: 1929. V. 38

GRIERSON, FLORA

Haunting Edinburgh. London: 1929. V. 44

GRIERSON, J. M.

Records of the Scottish Volunteer Force 1859-1908. Edinburgh: 1909. V. 37

GRIERSON, M.

An English Florilegium, Flowers, Trees, Shrubs, Fruits, Herbs, the Tradescant Legacy. London: 1987. V. 38

GRIESBACH, A. H. R.

Flora of the British West Indian Islands. London: 1864. V. 37

GRIESINGER, WILHELM

Mental Pathology and Therapeutics. New York: 1882. V. 38; 44; 45

GRIEVE, CHRISTOPHER MURRARY 1892-

A Drunk Man Looks at the Thistle. Verona: 1969. V. 40

GRIEVE, CHRISTOPHER MURRAY

The Blaward and the Skelly. N.P.: 1962. V. 39
The Burning Passion. Glasgow: 1965. V. 39
Complete Poems 1920-1976. London: 1978. V. 45
Direadh I, II and III. Frenich: 1974. V. 39; 46
Direadh I, II and III. Frenich Foss: 1974. V. 41
Direadh I, II and III. 1974. V. 42
Direadh I, II and III. Frenich, Foss: 1974. V. 37
A Drunk Man Looks at the Thistle. Edinburgh: 1926. V. 46
A Drunk man Looks at the Thistle. London: 1926. V. 46
A Drunk Man Looks at the Thistle. Falkland: 1969. V. 40; 42; 43; 45
A Drunk Man Looks at the Thistle. Verona: 1969. V. 44
Early Lyrics. 1968. V. 39
The Fire and the Spirit - Two Poems. Glasgwo: 1965. V. 39
First Hymn to Lenin and Other Poems. London: 1931. V. 44
The Kind of Poetry I Want. 1961. V. 44
The Kind of Poetry I Want. Edinburgh: 1961. V. 39; 40; 45
The Ministry of Water. Glasgow: 1964. V. 39
Northern Numbers Being Representative Selections from Certain Living Scottish Poets. (with) Northern Numbers . . . Second Series. Edinburgh: 1920-21. V. 38
O Wha's Been Her Afore Me, Lass. 1931. V. 45
O Wha's Been Here Afore Me, Lass. N.P.: 1931. V. 39
Penny Wheep. Edinburgh & London;: 1926. V. 39
Penny Wheep. Edinburgh: 1926. V. 37
Sangschaw. Edinburgh: 1925. V. 40; 42
Sangschaw. Edinburgh & London: 1925. V. 37
Sangschaw. London: 1925. V. 42
Scottish Eccentrics. London: 1936. V. 40
Selected Lyrics. 1977. V. 40; 44
Selected Lyrics. Foss: 1977. V. 45
Selected Lyrics. French Foss: 1977. V. 37
Sydney Goodsir Smith. Dublin: 1963. V. 39
To Circumjack Cencrastus, or The Curly Snake. Edinburgh & London: 1930. V. 39
To Circumjack Cencrastus or the Curly Snake. London: 1930. V. 41
To Circumjack Cencrastus or the Curly Snake. Edinburgh: 1930. V. 37
When the Rat-Race Is Over-Essay for John Gawsworth. London: 1962. V. 39

GRIEVE, JAMES

The History of Kamtschatka and the Kurilski Islands, with Countries Adjacent. Gloucester: 1765. V. 40

GRIEVE, MAUD

A Modern Herbal. London: 1931. V. 40; 42

GRIEVE, S.

The Great Auk. London: 1885. V. 38; 39; 40

GRIFFIN, A. P. C.

Bibliography of the Philippine Islands. Washington: 1903. V. 40; 42
Bibliography of the Philippine Islands. Washington: 1903. V. 44
A Catalogue of the Washington Collection in the Boston Athenaeum. Boston: 1897. V. 38; 40; 44; 46

GRIFFIN, EDWARD D.

A Plea for Africa. A Sermon Preached October 26, 1817 . . . before the Synod of New York and New Jersey, at the Request of the Board of Directors of the African School Established by the Synod. New York: 1817. V. 37

GRIFFIN, ELDON

Clippers and Consuls. American Consular and Commercial Relations with Eastern Asia. Ann Arbor: 1938. V. 38

GRIFFIN, GERALD

The Collected Works of Gerald Griffin. New York: c. 1860. V. 37

The Collegians. London: 1829. V. 37; 38; 40

Holland-Tide; or, Munster Popular Tales. London: 1827. V. 42

GRIFFIN, H. HEWITT

Cycles and Cycling. With a Chapter for Ladies, by Miss. L.C. Davidson. London: 1892. V. 37

GRIFFIN, JAMES BENNETT

The Fort Ancient Aspect, Its Cultural and Chronolgical Position in Mississippi Valley Archaeology. Ann Arbor: 1943. V. 37; 42; 44

GRIFFIN, JOHN

Memoirs of Captain James Wilson, Containing an Account of His Enterprises and Sufferings in India ... Boston: 1822. V. 45

GRIFFIN, JOHN HOWARD

Twelve Photographic Portraits. Greensboro: 1973. V. 39

GRIFFIN, JOHN JOSEPH

Chemical Handicraft. London: 1877. V. 38; 46

A System of Crystallography, with Its Application to Mineralogy. Glasgow: 1841. V. 38

GRIFFIN, JONATHAN

Paul Gauguin Noa Noa, Voyage to Tahiti. London: 1961. V. 42

GRIFFIN, MARCUS

Wise Guy James J. Johnston: a Rhapsody in Fistics. New York: 1933. V. 39

GRIFFIN, MARTIN I. J.

Stephen Moylan ... Aide de Camp to Washington. Philadelphia: 1909. V. 38

GRIFFIN, MR.

Juvenile Poems on Several Occasions. Oxford: 1764. V. 41; 42

GRIFFIN, SAMUEL STUART

Disputatio Physica Inaguralis de Terra Natorum Vegetatione ... Edinburgh: 1805. V. 40

GRIFFIS, W. E.

The Mikado's Empire ... New York: 1894. V. 40

GRIFFITH, A. F.

Bibliotheca Anglo-Poetica; or, a Descriptive Catalogue of a Rare and Rich Collection of Early Poetry ... London: 1815. V. 40

GRIFFITH, ELIZABETH

The Double Mistake. London: 1766. V. 37

The Morality of Shakespeare's Drama Illustrated. London: 1775. V. 37; 38; 40; 41; 42; 46

The Times, a Comedy. London: 1780. V. 42

GRIFFITH, F.

Stories of the High Priests of Memphis, the Sethon of Herodotus and the Demotic Tales of Khamuas. Atlas only. Oxford: 1900. V. 37

GRIFFITH, F. L.

Archaeological report. Comprising the recent work of the Egypt exploration fund and the progress of Egyptology. London: 1892-1912. V. 37

Beni Hasan, Part III. London: 1896. V. 40

A Collection of Hieroglyphs: a Contribution to the History of Egyptian Writing. London: 1898. V. 40; 42; 44

Stories of the High Priests of Memphis, the Sethon of Herodotus and the Demotic Tales of Khamuas. Oxford: 1900. V. 40

GRIFFITH, FREDERIC

Instruments of the Production of Abortion Sold in the Market Places of Paris. New York: 1904. V. 39

GRIFFITH, G. W.

The Micrographic Dictionary a Guide to the Examination and Investigation of the Structure and Nature of Microscopic Objects. London: 1875. V. 38

The Micrographic Dictionary. London: 1883. V. 38; 39

GRIFFITH, G. W. E.

My 96 Years in the Great West: Indiana, Kansas and California. Los Angeles: 1929. V. 39

GRIFFITH, GEORGE

The Life and Adventures of George Wilson, a Foundation Scholar. London: 1854. V. 43; 45

The Outlaws of the Air. London: 1897. V. 46

GRIFFITH, J. P. CROZER

The Care of the Baby. Philadelphia: 1900. V. 41

GRIFFITH, JOHN

A Journal of the Life, Travels and Labours in the Work of the Ministry, of John Griffith. Philadelphia: 1780. V. 42; 46

A Journal of the Life, Travels and Labours in the Work of the Ministry of ... (with) Some Brief Remarks ... Philadelphia: 1780, 1781. V. 39

GRIFFITH, LLEWELYN WYN

Up to Mametz. London: 1931. V. 38

GRIFFITH, MARY

Our Neighbourhood, or Letters on Horticulture and Natural Phenomena ... New York: 1831. V. 42

GRIFFITH, MATTHEW

A Pathetical Preswasion to Pray for Publick Peace. London: 1642. V. 40

GRIFFITH, MOSES

Practical Observations on the Cure of Hectic and Slow Fevers, and the Pulmonary Consumption ... London: 1776. V. 38

GRIFFITH, R. EGLESFELD

Medical Botany; or Descriptions of the Most Important Plants Used in Medicine. Philadelphia: 1847. V. 42

GRIFFITH, R. H.

A Descriptive Catalogue of an Exhibition of Manuscripts and First Editions of Lord Byron. Austin: 1924. V. 43

GRIFFITH, RICHARD

The Posthumous Works of a Late Celebrated Genius, Deceased. London: 1770. V. 41; 44

The Posthumous Works of the Celebrated Dr. Sterne, Deceased. London: 1775. V. 41; 42

GRIFFITH, ROBERT

Charity the Only Certain Infallible Note of a True Church. London: 1721. V. 42

GRIFFITH, THOMAS W.

Annals of Baltimore. Baltimore: 1833. V. 46

Sketches of the Early History of Maryland. (bound as issued with) Annals of Baltimore. Baltimore: 1821, 1833. V. 40

GRIFFITH, WILLIAM

The Scrivener's Guide. Newark;: 1797. V. 40

A Treatise on the Jurisdiction and Proceedings of the Justices of the Peace in Civil Suits, with an Appendix ... Burlington: 1796. V. 37

GRIFFITH, WILLIAM PETIT 1805-1884

Ancient Gothic Churches, their proportions and chromatics. London: 1848, 1852. V. 37

GRIFFITH, WILLIAM PETTIT

Ancient Gothic Churches. London: 1847/48/52. V. 42

GRIFFITHS, A. F.

Bibliotheca Anglo-Poetica. London: 1815. V. 38; 41; 45

Bibliotheca Anglo-Poetica ... London: 1815. V. 45

GRIFFITHS, ANSELM JOHN

Observations on Some Points of Seamanship, with Practical Hints on Naval Oeconomy, etc., etc. Cheltenham: 1824. V. 38

GRIFFITHS, ARTHUR

Memorials of Millbank, and Chapters in Prison History. London: 1875. V. 38; 40; 42

Mysteries of Police and Crime. London. V. 43; 46

Mysteries of Police and Crime: a General Survey of Wrongdoing and Its Pursuit. London: 1899. V. 46

Mysteries of Police and Crime. London: 1902. V. 42

Secrets of the Prison House or Gaol Studies & Sketches. London: 1894. V. 42

GRIFFITHS, BILL

The Rune Poem. 1989. V. 41

GRIFFITHS, F. A.

The Artillerist's Manual, and British Soldier's Compendium. London: 1868. V. 41

GRIFFITHS, J.

Travels in Europe, Asia Minor and Arabia. London: 1805. V. 39; 45

GRIFFITHS, JOHN W.

Treatise on Marine and Naval Architecture, or Theory and Practice Blended in Ship Building. London: 1853. V. 38

GRIFFITHS, RALPH

Ascanius: or the Young Adventurer. London: 1747. V. 46

GRIFFITHS, S. Y.

New Historical Description of Cheltenham and Its Vicinity. Cheltenham: 1826. V. 41

GRIFFITHS, SAMUEL

Griffith's Guide to the Iron Trade of Great Britian. London: 1873. V. 42

GRIFFITHS, WILLIAM

A Practical Treatise on Farriery; deduced from the experience of above forty years . . . Wrexham: (n.d. 1784). V. 37

GRIFFITHS, WILLIAM H.

The Story of American Bank Note Company. New York: 1959. V. 40

GRIFFITS, THOMAS E.

Colour Printing. London: 1948. V. 41

GRIGGS, F. L.

Campden XXIV Engravings After Pen Drawings. Oxford: 1940. V. 41

The Engraved Work of F. L. Griggs: Etchings & Drypoints, 1912-1928. Stratford-upon-Avon: 1928. V. 41

GRIGGS, GEORGE

History of Mesilla Valley, or the Gadsden Purchase Known in Mexico as the Treaty of Mesilla. Los Cruces: 1930. V. 43

GRIGGS, NATHAN KIRK

Lyrics of the Lariat. Poems with Notes. New York: 1893. V. 44

GRIGGS, ROBERT P.

The Valley of Ten Thousand Smokes. Washington: 1922. V. 37; 43

GRIGGS, W.

147 Examples of Armorial Book Plates (Second Series). London: 1892. V. 42; 44

GRIGGS, WILLIAM 1832-1911

India, Photographs and Drawings of Historical Buildings . . . from the Collection in the Late Office of the Curator of Ancient Monuments in India. London: 1896. V. 40

GRIGSBY, MELVIN

The Smoked Yank. Sioux Falls: 1888. V. 38; 39; 43

The Smoked Yank. Sioux Falls: 1888. V. 38

GRIGSON, GEOFFREY

The Englishman's Flora. London: 1960. V. 39

Samuel Palmer The Visionary Years. London: 1947. V. 39; 44

Several Observations - Thirty Five Poems. London: 1939. V. 38; 42

GRILDRIG, SOLOMON

The Miniature by Solomon Grildrig of the College of Eton . . . London: 1806. V. 40

GRILLI, ELISE

The Art of the Japanese Screen. New York: and Tokyo: 1970. V. 45

GRIMALDI, FRANCESCO MARIA

Physico-Mathesis de Lumine, Coloribus, et Iride, Aliisque Adnexis Libri Duo . . . Bologna: 1665. V. 38

GRIMALDI, JOSEPH 1779-1837

Memoirs of Joseph Grimaldi. London: 1838. V. 43

The Memoirs of Joseph Grimaldi. London: 1838. V. 43

Memoirs of Joseph Grimaldi. London: 1838. V. 43

Memoirs of Joseph Grimaldi. New York: 1838. V. 43

Memoirs of Joseph Grimaldi. London: 1846. V. 46

GRIMALDI, STACEY

A Suit of Armour for Youth. London: 1824. V. 39; 43

GRIMALKIN, or, The Rebel-Cat: a Novell. London: 1681. V. 37

GRIMAUDET, FRANCOIS

Des Monnoyes, Augment et Diminution du pris d'Icelles, Livre Unique. Paris: 1586. V. 37

Les Oeuvres . . . Paris: 1623. V. 38; 41; 45

GRIMBLE, A.

Deer-Stalking. London: 1888. V. 39

The Deer Forests of Scotland. London: 1896. V. 39

The Salmon Rivers of Scotland. London: 1902. V. 39

Shooting and Salmon Fishing. Hints and Recollections. London: 1892. V. 38; 39; 40; 41; 42; 43

Shooting and Salmon Fishing and Highland Sport. London: 1902. V. 39

GRIMBLE, AUGUSTUS

Highland Sport. London: 1894. V. 39; 40; 43

Leaves from a Game Book. London: 1898. V. 46

The Salmon Rivers of Scotland. Volume IV: Southern Scotland. London: 1900. V. 40

The Salmon Rivers of Ireland. London: 1903. V. 44; 46

The Salmon and Sea Trout Rivers of England and Wales. London: 1904. V. 43; 44; 45; 46

GRIME, J. P.

Comparative Plant Ecology, a Functional Approach to Common British Plants and Communities. London: 1986. V. 37; 38

GRIMES, J.

House Ghosts. 1924. V. 37; 43

GRIMES, MARTHA

The Anodyne Necklace. Boston: 1983. V. 43

The Man with a Load of Mischief. Boston: 1981. V. 43

GRIMES, ROY

300 Years in Victoria County. 1968. V. 42; 44

GRIMKE, ANGELINA EMILY

Letters to Catherine E. Beecher in Reply to an Essay on Slavery and Abolitonism. Boston: 1838. V. 42; 46

GRIMKE, FREDERICK

Considerations Upon the Nature and Tendency of Free Insitutions. Cincinnati: 1848. V. 40

GRIMKE, JOHN FAUCHERAUD

The Duty of Executors and Administrators: Pointing Out, in a Plain and Familiar Manner, How Executors are to Proceed with Full and Clear Directions to a Man's Relation . . . New York: 1797. V. 39

GRIMKE, THOMAS S.

Address on the . . . Principles of Peace and on the Unchristian Character and Influence of War and the Warrior. Hartford: 1832. V. 41; 42

Correspondence on the Principles of Peace, Manual Labor, Schools &c. Charleston: 1833. V. 38

An Oration on the Practicability and Expediency of Reducing the Whole Body of the Law to the Simplicity and Order of a Code. Charleston: 1827. V. 40

Oration on the Duties of Youth to Instructors and Themselves: on the Importance of the Art of Speaking and of Debating Societies. Charleston: 1832. V. 44

GRIMM, JACOB

Grimm's Other Tales. (London): 1956. V. 37

Teutonic Mythology. London: 1882. V. 37

GRIMM, THE BROTHERS

The Bremen Town Musicians. 1978. V. 41

Grimm's Fairy Tales for Children and the Household. London. V. 44

Fairy Tales of the Brothers Grimm. London: 1907. V. 46

The Fairy Tales. London: 1909. V. 40; 42; 44; 45; 46

The Fairy Tales of the Brothers Grimm. New York: 1909. V. 38; 42

Grimm's Fairy Tales. London: 1911. V. 43; 46

Grimm's Fairy Tales. London: 1913. V. 42

Grimm's Fairy Tales. London: 1920. V. 46

Fairy Tales. New York: 1931. V. 38; 39; 41; 44

Fairy Tales by the Brothers Grimm. Offenbach A/M: 1931. V. 44

German Popular Stories. London: 1823-26. V. 39; 45; 46

German Popular Stories. London: 1823/26. V. 42

German Popular Stories. London: 1824. V. 39

German Popular Stories. London: 1826. V. 40; 46

German Popular Stories. London: 1868. V. 40

German Popular Stories with illustrations after the Original Designs of George Cruikshank. With an introduction by John Ruskin. London: (1868). V. 37

Grimm's Fairy Tales. London: 1860. V. 45

Grimm's Fairy Tales. London: 1900. V. 45

Grimm's Other Tales. 1956. V. 41; 44; 45; 46

Grimm's Other Tales, a New Selection by Wilhelm Hansen. London: 1956. V. 37

Hansel and Gretel. Mainz: 1915. V. 38

Hansel and Gretel and Other Tales . . . London: 1920. V. 40

Hansel and Gretal and Other Tales by the Brothers Grimm. New York: 1920. V. 42

Hansel and Gretel. London: 1925. V. 40

Hansel and Gretal and Other Stories . . . New York: 1925. V. 41

Hansel and Gretel. London: (1925). V. 37

Grimm's Household Stories. London: 1882. V. 40

GRIMM, THE BROTHERS continued

Household Stories. London: 1882. V. 37; 38; 40; 41; 43

Household Tales. London: 1946. V. 38; 39; 44

Household Tales by . . . London: 1946. V. 39

Household Tales. 1946. V. 37

The Juniper Tree and Other Tales from Grimm. New York: 1973. V. 41

Little Brother and Little Sister. London: 1917. V. 37; 40; 41; 44; 46

Little Brother and Little Sister. London: 1917. V. 46

Little Brother and Little Sister and Other Tales. London: 1917. V. 41

Little Brother and Little Sister and Other Tales by Brothers Grimm. New York: 1917. V. 42

Little Brother and Little Sister and Other Tales. London: (1917). V. 37

Snowdrop and Other Tales. London: 1920. V. 44; 46

Snowdrop and Other Tales. New York: 1920. V. 42; 46

Three Gay Tales from Grimm. New York: 1943. V. 46

GRIMMELSHAUSEN, JOHANN JAKOB CHRISTOFFEL VON

The Adventures of Simplicissimus. New York: 1981. V. 38; 41; 43

GRIMSDELL, SAMUEL

Rules and Regulations Unanimously Adopted at a Meeting, Held by the Tradesmen, in the Employ of Mr. Samuel Grimsdell, on Wednesday, February the 4th, 135. London: 1842. V. 40

GRIMSHAW, ANNE

The Horse: a Bibliography of British Books 1851-1976 . . . London: 1982. V. 42

GRIMSHAW, ROBERT

Saws: the History, Development, Action, Classification and Comparison of Saws of all Kinds. Philadelphia: 1880. V. 38

GRIMSHAW, WILLIAM

Memoirs of the Life of the Late Rev. William Grimshaw, A.B., Minister of Haworth. London: 1799. V. 43

GRIMSTON, CHARLOTTE

The History of Gorhambury. London: 1821. V. 39

GRIMSTON, WILLIAM

The Lawyer's Fortune, or, Love in a Hollow Tree. London: 1705. V. 38

GRIMWADE, A. G.

London Goldsmiths 1697-1837. Their Marks and Lives. London: 1976. V. 37

GRIMWOOD, DANIEL

A Catalogue of Greenhouse Plants . . . London: 1783. V. 38; 41

GRIMWOOD, ETHEL ST. CLAIR

My Three Years in Manipur and Escape from the Recent Mutiny. London: 1891. V. 38

GRINDEA, MIRON

Adam - Number 446-448. London: 1984. V. 46

GRINDLAY, ROBERT MELVILLE

Scenery Costumes and Architecture, Chiefly on the Western Side of India. London: 1826. V. 42

Scenery, Costumes and Architecture Chiefly on the Western Side of India. London: 1830. V. 40

GRINDROD, RALPH BARNES

The Wrongs of Our Youth; an Essay on the Evils of the Late-Hour System (Third Thousand). London: 1843. V. 38

GRINLING, CHARLES H.

The History of the Great Northern Railway. 1845-1902. London: 1905. V. 41

GRINNELL, GEORGE B.

The Cheyenne Indians, Their History and Ways of Live. New Haven: 1924. V. 45

GRINNELL, GEORGE BIRD

American Duck Shooting. New York: 1901. V. 39

American Big Game In Its Haunts. New York: 1904. V. 37; 43

American Duck Shooting. New York: 1901. V. 37; 43

Bent's Old Fort and Its Builders. Topeka: 1923. V. 39

Blackfoot Lodge Tales. New York: 1908. V. 42

The Cheyenne Indians Their History and Ways of Life. New Haven: 1923. V. 37; 39; 43

The Fighting Cheyennes. New York: 1915. V. 45; 46

Hunting and Conservation. New Haven: 1925. V. 45

Hunting Trails of Three Continents. New York: 1933. V. 43; 44; 45

The Indians of Today. Chicago: 1900. V. 45

The North American Indians of To-day. London: 1900. V. 37; 44; 46

The North American Indians of Today. London: 1900. V. 37

Pawnee Hero Stories and Folk-Tales with Notes on the Origin, Customs and Character of the Pawnee People. New York: 1889. V. 44

Story of the Indian. New York: 1895. V. 42

Trails of the Pathfinders. New York: 1911. V. 42

Two Great Scouts and Their Pawnee Battalion. Cleveland: 1928. V. 37; 41; 42; 45

Wolf Hunters: a Story of the Buffalo Plains. New York: 1914. V. 42

GRINNELL, JOSEPH

Animal Life in the Yosemite. Berkeley: 1924. V. 38; 41; 44

Fur Bearing Mammals of California: Their Natural History, Systematic Status and Relations to Man. Berkeley: 1937. V. 38; 46

Gold Hunting in Alaska as Told by . . . Chicago: 1901. V. 37; 39; 42

GRINNELL, JOSEPH B.

Sketches of the West, or the Home Of the Badgers. New York: 1847. V. 40

GRINNELL, JOSIAH B.

Sketches of the West, or, the Home of the Badgers. Milwaukie: 1847. V. 37; 39; 43

Sketches of the West; or, the Home of the Badgers: Comprising an Early History of Wisconsin, with a Series of Familiar Letters and Remarks on Territorial Character . . . Milwaukee: 1847. V. 37

GRINNING Made More Easy. Oswestry: 1810. V. 43

GRINSELL, LESLIE

Egyptian Pyramids.to. Gloucester: 1947. V. 40

GRINSTEAD, J. E.

Southwest Texas: from the Mountains to the Sea. Kerrville: 1904. V. 45

GRINSTEIN, ALEXANDER

The Index of Psychoanalytic Writings. New York: 1956. V. 37; 42; 45

GRISAR, HARTMANN

History of Rome and the Popes in the Middle Ages. London: 1911-12. V. 39; 42

GRISCOM, JOHN H.

The Sanitary Condition of the Laboring Population of New York. New York: 1845. V. 41

GRISEBACH, A. H. R.

Flora of the British West Indian Islands. London: 1864. V. 38

Flora of the British West Indian Islands. 1963. V. 39

GRISET, ERNEST

Griset's Grotesques. London: 1867. V. 38; 39

GRISWOLD, B. J.

Fort Wayne, Gateway of the West 1802-1813. Garrison Orderly Books. Indian Agency Account Book. Indianapolis: 1927. V. 38

GRISWOLD, FRANK GRAY

After Thoughts. Recollections of . . . N.P.: 1936. V. 43

Big and Little Fishes. N.P.: 1927. V. 39; 43

The Cascapedia Club. N.P.: 1920. V. 43

Clipper Ships and Yachts. New York: 1927. V. 42

Fish Facts and Fancies (& Fish Facts and Fancies Volume II). N.P.: 1923/25. V. 43

The Gourmet. New York: 1933. V. 41

Observations on a Salmon River. New York: 1923. V. 43

Salmo Salar. London: 1929. V. 45

Salmo Salar. N.P.: 1929. V. 44

GRISWOLD, N. W.

Beauties of California . . . Views and Descriptions of Yosemite Valley, Big Trees, Geyers, Lake Tahoe, Donner Lake, San Francisco, '49 and '83, Los Angles and Towns Orange Groves and Vineyards of Southern California. San Francisco: 1884. V. 37

GRISWOLD, RUFUS

The Poets and Poetry of America. Philadelphia: 1852. V. 40

GRISWOLD, RUFUS W.

The Poets and Poetry of America. Philadelphia: 1842. V. 45

GRISWOLD, WAYNE

Kansas Her Resources and Developments. Cincinnati: 1871. V. 38

Kansas her Resources and Developments. Cincinnati: 1871. V. 38; 39; 43

GRITSCH, JOHANNES

Quadragesimale. Nuremberg: 1481. V. 44

GRIZMEK, B.

Grizmeks Animal Life Encyclopedia. New York: 1972-75. V. 37

THE GROANS of B----n; or, A Pathetical Display of the Many Hardships, Miseries and Oppressions to which this distressed Nation is Become Subjected . . . London: 1747? V. 39

GROBER, KARL

Children's Toys of Bygone Days. A History of Playthings of All Peoples from Prehistoric Times to the XIXth Century. London: 1928. V. 40; 45

Children's Toys of Bygone Days. New York: 1928. V. 42

Picturesque Palestine, Arabia and Syria. New York: 1925. V. 39

THE GROCER'S Guide; Being a Directory for Making and Managin All Kinds of Foreign Liquors and Domestic Compounds . . . New York: 1820. V. 43

GROCOTT and Sherry's Album of Grahamstown. Grahamstown: 1898. V. 45

GRODDECK, GEORGE

The Book of It. 1950. V. 43

The Book of the It. London: 1950. V. 43

GROEBEN, OTTO FRIEDRICH VON DER

Orientalische Reisebeschreibung des Brandenburgischen Adelichen Pilgers Nebst der Brandenburgischen Schiffahrt nach Guinea und der Verrichtung zu Morea, unter Ihrem Titel. Marienwerder: 1694. V. 46

GROEDEL, FRANZ M.

Die Magenbewegungen. Hamburg: 1912. V. 44

GROENEVELT, JOHANNES

De Tuto Cantharidum in Medicina Usu Interno. London: 1698. V. 37

GROENEWEGEN SIMONE

Tractatus de Legibus Abrogatis et Insitatis in Hollandia Vicinisque Regionibus . . . Noviomagi: 1664. V. 44

GROENVELDT, JOHANNES

A Treatise of the Safe, Internal Use of Cantharides in the Practice of Physick. London: 1706. V. 37; 38

GROGAN, EWART S.

From the Cape to Cairo. The First Traverse of Africa from South to North. London: 1900. V. 38; 40

GROHMAN, WILL

Paul Klee. New York: 1954-55? V. 45

GROHMANN, WILL

The Art of Henry Moore. New York. V. 46

The Art of Henry Moore. London: 1966. V. 46

E. L. Kirchner. New York: 1961. V. 41

Kandinsky. Anvers: 1933. V. 39

Paul Klee. New York. V. 44; 46

Paul Klee. New York: 1965. V. 44

Wassily Kandinsky: Life and Work. New York. V. 39; 43; 46

Wassily Kandinsky: Life and Work by . . . New York: 1958. V. 44

Willi Baumeister: Life and Work. New York. V. 39; 43; 45; 46

Willi Baumeister. Leben und Werk. Koln: 1963. V. 42

GROHMANN, WILLI

Paul Klee. Paris: 1929. V. 37; 39

GROLIER CLUB

Catalogue of the Works of the De Vinne Press Exhibited at the Grolier Club on the Occasion of the One Hundredth Anniversary of the Birth of Theodore Low de Vinne, December 25, 1828. With addresses by Ira Hutchinson Brainerd and John Clyde Oswald. New York: 1929. V. 37

A Catalogue of Books in First Editions, Selected to Illustrate the History of English Prose from 1485 to 1870. New York: 1917. V. 38

Catalogue of Original and Early Editions of Some of the Poetical Prose Works of English Writers from Langland to Prior. London: 1964. V. 38

Catalogue of Early Printed Books Relating to America. New York: 1888. V. 37

Description of the Early Printed Books Owned by the Grolier Club, with a Brief Account of Their Printers & the History of Typography in the 15th C. New York: 1895. V. 38

The Grolier Club, 1884-1984: Its Library, Exhibitions & Publications. New York: 1984. V. 37

GROLIER CLUB, NEW YORK.

Catalogue of Original and Early Editions of Some of the Poetical and Prose Works of English Writers from Langland to Wither. New York: 1893. V. 43

Catalogue of an Exhibition Commemorative of the Bicentenary of the Birth of Samuel Johnson, 1709-1909. Held at the Grolier Club, New York: Nov. - Dec. 1909. New York: 1909. V. 41

Catalogue of an Exhibition of the Works of Charles Dickens. New York: 1913. V. 43; 44

Catalogue of an Exhibition Illustrative of the Text of Shakespeare's Plays . . . New York: 1916. V. 41; 44

Catalogue of the Works of Rudyard Kipling. New York: 1930. V. 39

Catalogue of Original and Early Editions of Some of the Poetical Works of English Writers from Langland to Wither. One Volume and From Wither to Prior, 3 volumes. New York: 1963. V. 39; 46

Catalogue of an Exhibition of the Private Papers . . . from Malahide Castle. New York: 1930. V. 40

Catalogue of an Exhibition of the Works of Charles Dickens . . . New York: 1913. V. 40; 42

Catalogue of Etchings and Drypoints by Rembrandt Selected for Exhibition at the Grolier Club April-May 1900. New York: 1900. V. 40

Catalogue of Original and Early Editions of Some of the Poetical and Prose Works of English Writers From Langland to Prior. London: 1964. V. 40

Fifty-Five Books Printed Before 1525, Representing the Works of England's First Printers. An Exhibition from the Collection of Paul Mellon, January 17-March 3, 1968. New York: 1968. V. 41; 44

Grolier 75: a Bibliographical Retrospective to Celebrate the Seventy-Fifth Anniversary of the Grolier Club. New York: 1959. V. 38; 41; 46

The Grolier Club, 1884-1984: Its Library, Exhibitions & Publications. New York: 1984. V. 40

One Hundred Influential American Books. New York: 1947. V. 38; 39; 42; 43; 45; 46

Printer's Choice: a Selection of American Press Books, 1968-1978. Catalogue of an Exhibition Held at the Grolier Club, New York, December 19, 1978 - February 3, 1979. Austin: 1983. V. 38; 40; 42; 45

A Summary of the Work of Rudyard Kipling Including Items Ascribed to Him. (with) Catalogue of the Works of Rudyard Kipling Exhibited at the Grolier Club from February 21 to March 30, 1929. New York: 1930. V. 46

GROLLIER DE SERVIERE, GASPARD

Recueil d'Ouvrages et de Mechanique, ou Description du Cabinet de M. Grollier de Serviere. Lyons: 1719. V. 38

Recueil d'ouvrages Curieux de Mathematique et Mechanique ou Description du Cabient de Monsieur Grollier de Serviere . . . Paris: 1751. V. 44

GROLLMAN, ARTHUR

The Cardiac Output of Man In Health and Disease. Springfield: 1932. V. 42

GRONNIOSAW, JAMES ALBERT UKAWSAW

A Narrative of the Most Remarkable Particulars in the Life of James Albert, Akawsaw, Granwasa, as Dictated by Himself. Catskill: 1810. V. 40

GRONOVIUS, J. F.

Flora Viginica Exhibens Plantas Quas . . . J. Claytonus..In Virginia . . . Leyden: 1762. V. 39; 41; 42

GRONOVIUS, JACOB

Geographica Antiqua, hoc est: Scylacis Periplus Maris Mediterranei. Leyden: 1700. V. 39

GRONOVIUS, J.F.

Flora Virginica . . . Leyden: 1762. V. 44

GRONOVIUS, LAURENTIUS THEODORUS

Bibliotheca Regni Animalis Atque Lapidei, Seu Recensio Auctorum et Librorum, Qui de Regno Animali et Lapideo Methodice, Physice, Medice, Chemice, Philologice, vel Theologice Tractant . . . Leiden: 1760. V. 43

Museum Ichthyologicum, Sistens Piscium Indigenorum & Quorundam Exoticorum, Qui in Museo Laurentii Theodori Gronovii Adservantur . . . Leiden: 1754-56. V. 43

GRONOW, J.

A Review of England and Wales. London: 1849. V. 38

GRONOW, REES HOWELL 1794-1865

Reminiscences. London: 1862-66. V. 40; 41; 43

The Reminiscences and Recollections . . . London: 1889. V. 39

The Reminiscences and Recollections of Caption Gronow Being Anecdotes of the Camp, Court, Clubs and Society 1810-1860. London: 1889. V. 38; 44

The Reminiscences and Recollections. London: 1892. V. 42; 44

GROOMBRIDGE, R.

A Hand-book for Travellers Along the London and Birmingham Railway . . . London: 1839. V. 46

GROOME, FRANCIS HINDES

In Gipsy Tents. London: 1880. V. 42

GROOME, SAMUEL

A Glass for the People of New England, In Which They May See Themselves . . . London: 1676. V. 42; 44; 45

GROOT, WILLEM 1596-1662

De Principiis Juris Naturalis Enchiridion . . . Cantabridae: 1673. V. 43

HET GROOTE Tafereel der Dwaasheid, Vertoonende de Opkomst, Voortgang en Ondergang der Actie, Bubbel en Windnegotie, in Vrankryk, Engeland, en de Nederlanden, Gepleegt in de Jaare MDCCXX. Amsterdam: 1720. V. 45

GROPIUS, WALTER

Ausstellung Karlsruhe. Dammerstocksiedlung. Die Gebrauchswohnung. Karlsruhe: 1929. V. 39

Idee und Aufbau des Staatlichen Bauhauses Weimar. Munich: 1923. V. 39

The New Architecture and the Bauhaus. London: 1935. V. 41; 42

Town Plan for the Town of Selb. Cambridge: 1969. V. 46

GROS DE BESPLAS, JOSEPH MARIE ANNE, L'ABBE DE 1734-1783

Des Causes du Bonheur Public. Paris: 1768. V. 45

GROS, JOHAN DANIEL

Natural Principles of Rectitude, . . . in a Systematic Treatise on Moral Philosophy. New York: 1795. V. 37

GROSE, FRANCIS

Advice to the Officers of the British Army. London: 1783. V. 40; 43

The Antiquarian Repertory. London: 1775-79. V. 38

The Antiquarian Repertory. London: 1807. V. 38

The Antiquarian Repertory; a Miscellaneous Assemblage of Topography, History, Biography, Customs and Manners . . . London: 1807-09. V. 41

The Antiquities of England and Wales. London: 1773-87. V. 37; 38; 46

The Antiquities of England and Wales. London: 1781-87. V. 41

The Antiquities of Ireland. London: 1797. V. 38; 40

The Antiquities of England & Wales. London: 1773-1787. V. 37

The Antiquities of England and Wales. (and) The Antiquities of Scotland. (and) The Antiquities of Ireland. London: 1783-95. V. 37

Capricci Fatti Por . . . London: 1790. V. 45

A Classical Dictionary of the Vulgar Tongue. London: 1785. V. 39; 44

A Classical Dictionary of the Vulgar Tongue. London: 1788. V. 37; 38; 39

A Glossary of Provincial and Local Words Used in England. London: 1839. V. 41

Grose's Classical Dictionary of the Vulgar Tongue, Revised and Corrected, with the Addition of Numerous Slang Phrases . . . London: 1823. V. 41

Lexicon Balatronicum. London: 1811. V. 42; 43

Lexicon Balatronicum. London: 1811. V. 43

Military Antiquities Respecting a History of the English Army, from the Conquest to the Present Time. (with) A Treatise on Ancient Armour and Weapons. London: 1801. V. 39; 41; 46

Military Antiquities Respecting a History of the English Army, from the Conquest to the Present Time . . . (with) A Treatise on Ancient Armour and Weapons. (with) A Supplement to a Treatise . . . London: 1812. V. 41; 44; 46

The Olio; Being a Collection of Essays, Dialogues, Letters, Biographical Sketches, Anecdotes, Pieces of Poetry, Parodies, Bon Mots, Epigrams, Epitaphs &c . . . London: 1792. V. 38; 45

The Olio; Being a Collection of Essays, Dialogues, Letters, Biographical Sketcches, Anecdotes, Pieces of Poetry, Parodies, Bon Mots, Epigrams, Epitaphs &c. London: 1796. V. 41

A Provincial Glossary . . . London: 1811. V. 44

A Provincial Glossary, with a Collection of Local Proverbs and Popular Superstitions. London: 1787. V. 41; 43

A Provincial Glossary. London: 1790. V. 39; 41; 42; 44; 45

A Provincial Glossary. London: 1811. V. 38; 41; 42

Rules for Drawing Caricaturas: with an Essay on Comic Painting. London: 1791. V. 41

GROSE, JOHN HENRY

A Voyage to the East Indies, with Observations on Various Parts There. London: 1757. V. 40; 41

GROSETT, EMILIA

Nettlestead Abbey, or the Fair Maid of Suffolk. London: 1820. V. 44

GROSJEAN, GEORGES

Mapamundi: The Catalan Atlas of the Year 1375. Dietikon-Zurich: 1978. V. 43

GROSLEY, PIERRE JEAN

Londres. Lausanne: Paris: 1774. V. 39

New Observations on Italy and Its Inhabitants. London: 1769. V. 37; 40

Nouveaux Memoires, ou Observations sur l'Italie et sur les Italiens . . . Londres: 1764. V. 39

A Tour of London; or, New Observations on England and Its Inhabitants. London: 1772. V. 38

GROSS, ANTHONY

The Very Rich Hours of Le Boulve. London: 1980. V. 39

GROSS, CHAIM

Fantasy Drawings. New York: 1956. V. 39

The Gates of Prayer 1845-1960: Congreagation Shaaray Tefila. New York: 1960. V. 39

GROSS, IRA B.

Frank Roney, Irish Rebel and California Labor Leader, an Autobiography. Berkeley: 1931. V. 38

GROSS, LOUIS

The Blood Supply to the Heart in Its Anatomical and Clinical Aspects. New York: 1921. V. 42

GROSS, MILT

Dunt Esk!! New York: 1927. V. 43

He Done Her Wrong. New York: 1930. V. 38

GROSS, S. D.

Elements of Pathological Anatomy . . . Philadelphia: 1845. V. 40

A System of Surgery. Philadelphia: 1872. V. 39; 40; 41

GROSS, SAMUEL D.

Autobiography of Samuel D. Gross, M.D. with Sketches of His Contemporaries. Philadelphia: 1887. V. 38; 42; 46

Elements of Pathological Anatomy. Philadelphia: 1857. V. 42; 44

Elements of Pathological Anatomy. Illustrated by Colored engravings and 250 woodcuts. Second edition . . . greatly enlarged. Philadelphia: 1845. V. 37

A Practical Treatise on the Diseases and Injuries of the Urinary Bladder, the Prostrate Gland and the Urethra. Philadelphia: 1851. V. 42

A Practical Treatise on Foreign Bodies in the Air-Passages. Philadelphia: 1854. V. 42

A System of Surgery; Pathological, Diagnostic, Therapeutic and Operative. Philadelphia: 1859. V. 41; 43; 45

A System of Surgery; Pathological, Diagnostic, Therapeutic and Operative. Philadelphia: 1882. V. 42

GROSS, SAMUEL EBERLY

The Merchant Prince of Cornville. Cambridge: 1896. V. 38

GROSS, SAMUEL W.

A Practical Treatise on Tumors of the Mammary Gland: Embracing Their Histology, Pathology, Diagnosis and Treatment. New York: 1880. V. 44

GROSSE, KARL FRIEDRICH AUGUST 1768-1847

Horrid Mysteries; a Story. London: 1927. V. 40

GROSSMITH, GEORGE

The Diary of a Nobody. London. V. 40

The Diary of a Nobody. Bristol: 1892. V. 39; 42; 43; 46

The Diary of a Nobody. London: 1892. V. 42; 43

A Society of Clown. Reminiscences. Bristol: 1888. V. 37

GROSSMITH, WILLIAM ROBERT

The Life and Theatrical Excursions of William Robert Grossmith, the Juvenile Actor, Not Yet Nine Years of Age. Reading: 1827. V. 39

GROSVENOR, BENJAMIN

Health. An Essay On Its Nature, Value, Uncertainty, Preservation and Best Improvement. London: 1716. V. 41

Health, an Essay on Its Nature, Value, Uncertainty, Preservation and Best Improvement. London: 1748. V. 42; 43

Health, an Essay on Its Nature, Value, Uncertainty, Preservation and the Best Improvement. London: 1748. V. 46

GROSVENOR, E. M.

Narrative of a Yacht Voyage in the Mediterranean During the Years 1840-41. London: 1842. V. 39; 40

GROSZ, GEORGE

Das Neue Gesicht der Herrschenden Klasse. Berlin: 1930. V. 44

Drawings. New York: 1944. V. 39

Ecce Homo. New York: 1965. V. 41

George Grosz: Twelve Reproductions from His Original Lithographs. Chicago: 1921. V. 41

GROTE, GEORGE

Aristotle. London: 1872. V. 42

History of Greece. London: 1854. V. 43

History of Greece. New York: 1856. V. 44

A History of Greece, From the Earliest Period to the Close of the Generation Contemporary with Alexander the Great. London: 1869. V. 40; 44; 46

The Minor Works of George Grote. With Critical Remarks on His Intellectual Character, Writings and Speeches. London: 1873. V. 41

Plato, and Other Companions of Socrates. London: 1885. V. 38

Seven Letters on the recent Politics of Switzerland. London: 1847. V. 37

GROTE-HANSENBALG, WERNER

Masterpieces of Oriental Rugs. Berlin. V. 39

GROTE, HARRIET

Collected Papers, (Original and Reprinted), in Prose and Verse. London: 1862. V. 37; 45

GROTE-HASENBALG, WERNER

Masterpieces of Oriental Rugs. Berlin: 1925. V. 40

GROTE, JOHN

Exploratio Philosophica. Cambridge: 1900. V. 40; 42

GROTH, JOHN

John Groth's World of Sport. New York: 1970. V. 46

Studio: Asia. Cleveland: 1952. V. 46

GROTIUS, HUGO 1583-1645

Annales et Historiae de Rebus Belgicis. Amsterdam: 1657. V. 40

Bibliotheca Curiosa. On the Origin of the Native Races of America. Edinburgh: 1884. V. 40

De Jure Belli ac Pacis Libri Tres. Amsterdam: 1642. V. 37

His Discoures, of I. of God and His Providence. II. Of Christ, His Miracles and Doctrine . . . London: 1652. V. 43

De Jure Belli ac Pacis Libri Tres. Amsterdam: 1631. V. 40

Of The Rights of War and Peace. London: 1715. V. 43

Poemata Collecta Olim a Fratre Ejus Guil. Grotio . . . London: 1639. V. 45

De Principiis Juris Naturalis Enchiridion. Cantabrigiae: 1673. V. 45

The Truth of Christian Religion: In Six Books. London: 1680. V. 44

The Truth of Christian Religion: In Six Books . . . Now Translated into English with the Addition of a Seventh Book, by Simon Patrick, Dean of Peterburgh and Chaplain in Oridinay to His Majesty . . . London: 1680. V. 37

Two Discourses. 1. Of God, and His Providence. II. Of Christ His Miracles and Doctrine . . . With Annotations . . . London: 1653. V. 39

GROTO, LUIGI

La Emilia Comedia Nova. Venice: 1579. V. 37

GROU, JEAN N.

The Characters of Real Devotion. Dublin: 1795. V. 43; 44; 45

GROU, JEAN NICOLAS 1731-1803

Morality, Extracted from the Confessions of Saint Austin. London: 1791. V. 39

GROUCHY, NICOLAS DE 1520-1572

De Comitiis Romanorum Libri Tres. Venice: 1559. V. 40

GROUP of Valuable Silver Mines at Austin, Reese River, Lander County, State of Nevada. New York?: 1865. V. 42

GROUSSET, RENE

The Rise and Splendour of the Chinese Empire. London: 1952. V. 40

GROUT, LEWIS

A Reply to Bishop Colenso's 'Remarks on the Proper Treatment of Polygamy, as Found Already Existing in Conversts from Heathenism.' Natal: 1855. V. 40

GROUX, DANIEL E.

Prospectus on an Important Work in Three Volumes, to Be Called Numismatical History of the United States, Comprising a Full Description of Its Medals and Coins. Boston: 1856. V. 45

GROUX, EUGENE

Fissura Sterni Congenita: New Observations and Experiments in Amerika and Great Brtain . . . Hamburg: 1859. V. 44

GROVE, GEORGE

Dictionaray of Music and Musicians. London: 1954. V. 37

Grove's Dictionary of Music and Musicians. London: 1954-61. V. 42

The New Grove Dictionary of Music and Muscians. London: 1980. V. 37

GROVE, HENRY

The Regulation of Diversions. London: 1708. V. 45

GROVE, JOSEPH d. 1764

The History of the Life and Times of Cardinal Wolsey, Prime Minister to King Henry VIII. London: 1748. V. 39

GROVE, MARY

The Bard. London: 1844. V. 39

THE GROVE; or, a Collection of Original Poems, Translations, &c . . . . London: 1721. V. 37; 38; 39; 42

GROVE, W. R.

On the Gas Voltaic Battery. London: 1843. V. 40

GROVE, WILLIAM ROBERT 1811-1896

On the Correlation of Physical Forces: Being the Substance of a Course of Lectures Delivered in the London Institution in the Year 1843. London: 1846. V. 45

GROVER, EUALLIE OSGOOD

The Sunbonnet Babies' Primer. Chicago: 1902. V. 42; 44

GROVER, FRANK REED

Brief Early History of Les Cheneaux Islands, Some New Chapters of Mackinac History. Evanston: 1911. V. 43

GROVER, RAY

Art Glass Nouveau. Rutland: 1968. V. 40; 41

GROVER, SHERWOOD

A Commonplace Book for Typophiles. San Francisco: 1961. V. 45

A Commonplace Book With Something for Everybody. Aptos: 1989. V. 37; 42

Introduction to the Grabhorn/Hoyem Bibliography. San Francisco: 1977. V. 46

GROVER, TREVOR M.

The Career of John Silverthorne Banker. Toronto: 1914. V. 44

GROVE'S Dictionary of Music and Musicians. London: 1922. V. 40

GROVES, GEORGE

British Ornithology. London: 1821. V. 44

GROVES, J. PERCY

On Service at Home and Abroad. London: 1890. V. 42

GROVES, JONAS

A Tale of Other Times: the History of the Captivity of . . . With the Indians. The Murder of His Companions. His Adoption into the Indian Tribe. His Sufferings, and His Final Release . . . New York: 1938. V. 37

GROVES, NAOMI JACKSON

A. Y.'s Canada. Toronto & Vancouver: 1968. V. 42

A. Y.'s Canada. Toronto: 1968. V. 38

GROVES, SYLVIA

The History of Needlework Tools and Accessories. London: 1968. V. 41

GROWOLL, ADOLPH

Book Trade Bibliography in the United States. New York: 1939. V. 40; 42

The Profession of Bookselling . . . New York: 1893-1913. V. 40

GRUBB, DAVID

Eight Villiage Peoms. By David Grubbs. With pen drawings by Nicholas Parry. Shropshire: 1986. V. 37

GRUBB, DAVIS

Ancient Lights. New York: 1982. V. 46

The Night of the Hunter. New York: 1953. V. 41

GRUBB, SARAH

Some Account of the Life and Religious Labours of Sarah Grubb with An Appendix Containing an Account of ackworth Schook, Observations on Christian Discipline . . . Dublin: 1792. V. 39

GRUBE, HERMANN

De Arcanis Medicorum non Arcanis Commentatio ex Inventis Haravejanis, Bartholinianis, Sylvianis, Willisianis & Ceteris in Grataiam Tyronum Breviter Concinnata, Observationibus Nonnullis Illustrata . . . Hafniae: 1673. V. 37

GRUBER, FRANK

The Outlaw. New York: (1941). V. 37

The Talking Clock. New York: (1941). V. 37

GRUBER, IRA DEMPSEY

Admiral Lord Howe and the War for American Independence. Durham. V. 44

Admiral, Lord Howe and the War for American Independence. Durham: 1961. V. 43

GRUCHY, AUGUSTA DE

Under the Hawthorn and Other Verse. London: 1893. V. 43

GRUEL, L.

Manuel Historique et Bibliographique de l'Amateur de Reliures. London: 1887-95. V. 39

GRUEL, LEON

Manuel Historique et Bibliographique de l'Amateur de Reliures. Paris: 1887/1905. V. 43

GRUELINGIUS, PHILIPPUS

Florilegium Chymicum . . . Leipzig: 1631. V. 38

GRUELL, R. B.

Notes: Critical and Biographical. Indianapolis: 1895. V. 46

GRUELLE, JOHNNY

Beloved Belindy. Chicago: 1926. V. 45

Friendly Fairies. New York: 1919. V. 45

Little Sunny Stories: The Singing Thread, The Way to Fairyland, Mrs. Goodluck Cricket. Chicago: 1919. V. 42

The Magical Land of Noom with Sundry and Mondry. Chicago: 1922. V. 46

My Own Set of Sunny Books: The Cheery Scarecrow, Eddie Elephant, the Litee Brown Bear and Raggedy Ann's Alphabet Book. Chicago: 1930's. V. 45

GRUELLE, R. B.

Notes: Critical and Biographical. Collection of W. T. Walters. 1895. V. 46

Notes: Critical & Biographical. Indianapolis: 1895. V. 39; 41; 43; 44

GRUENPECK, JOHANN

Prognosticon . . . N.P.: 1532. V. 44

GRUFFYDD, W. G.

Caniadau. Newtown: 1932. V. 45; 46

GRUMBACH, DORIS

The Spoil of Flowers. 1962. V. 44

The Spoil of the Flowers. Garden City: 1962. V. 37; 38; 43

The Spoil of the Flowers. Garden City: 1962. V. 37

GRUND, F. J.

Handbuch und Wegweiser fur Auswanderer nach dem Vereinigten Staaten von Nordamerika und Texas. Stuttgart & Tubingen: 1846. V. 37

GRUND, FRANCIS J.

The Americans in Their Moral, Social and Political Relations. London: 1837. V. 41; 43

Aristocracy in America. London: 1839. V. 39

GRUND, JOHANN GOTTFRIED

Afbildning af Normanads-Dalen, i den Kongelige Lyst-Hauge ved Fredensborg . . . Copenahgen: 1773. V. 45

GRUNDTLICHER und Wahrhafter Bericht, von Eroberung der Statt S. Quintin . . . 1557. V. 42

GRUNER, ELIOTH

Elioth Gruner: Twenty-four Reproductions in Colour from Original Oil Paintings. Sydney: 1947. V. 41

GRUNER, LEWIS

Fresco Decorations and Stuccoes of Chruches and Palaces in Italy During the Fifteenth and Sixteenth Centuries. London: 1854. V. 38; 40

Fresco Decorations and Stuccoes of Churches and Palaces, in Italy, During the 15th and 16th Centuries . . . London: 1844. V. 37

Specimens of Ornamental Art Selected from the Best Models of the Classical Epochs. London: 1850. V. 46

The Terra-Cotta Architecture of North Italy. London: 1867. V. 38; 40

GRUNER, O. CAMERON

Treatise On the Canon of Medicine of Avicenna, Incorporating a Translation of the First Book. London: 1930. V. 42

GRUNERT, GEORGE

Report of the Army Pearl Harbor Board. N.P.: 1944. V. 42

GRUSHKIN, P. D.

The Art of Rock: Posters from Presley to Punk. New York: 1987. V. 46

GRUSKIN, ALAN D.

The Water Colors of Dong Kingman: and How the Artist Works. New York: 1958. V. 44

GRUYTRODE, JACOBUS DE

Lavacrum Conscientie. N.P.: 1505? V. 40; 45

GRYLLUS, LAURENTIUS

De Sapore Dulci & Amaro Libri Duo. Pragae: 1566. V. 37

GRYNAEUS, SIMON

Novis Orbis id est, Navigationes Primae in Americam . . . Roterodami: 1616. V. 45

Novus Orbus Regionum ac Insularum Veteribus Incognitarum . . . Paris: 1532. V. 41

Novus Orbis Regionum A Insularum Veteribus Incognitarum Una Cum Tabula Cosmographica & Aliquot Alijs Consimlis Argumenti Libellis . . . Basel: 1555. V. 40; 46

GRYPHIUS, CHRISTIAN 1649-1706

Kurtzer Entwurf Der Geist-und Weltlichen Ritterorden. Leipzig: 1697. V. 41

Poetische Waelder. Frankfurt/Leipzig: 1698. V. 41

GRZIMEK, B.

Grzimek's Animal Life Encyclopaedia. New York: 1972-75. V. 37; 38

Grzimek's Animal Life Encyclopedia. Volumes 7-9: Birds. London: 1972-73. V. 37

GSELL-FELS, THEODOR

Switzerland: Its Scenery and People. London: 1881. V. 43; 45

GUAINERIUS, ANTONIUS

Practica . . . et Omnia Opera. (De Egritudibus Capitis. De Pleuresi. De Passionibus Stomachi. Venice: 1500. V. 42

GUALDO PRIORATO, GALEAZZO

The History of the Managements of Cardinal Julio Mazarine . . . London: 1671-2. V. 38

The History of the Managements of Cardinal Julio Mazarine, Chief Minister of State of the Crown of France. London: 1671-72. V. 41

GUALTERUS AB CASTELLIONE

Elexandreidos Libri decem. Ingolstadt: 1541. V. 37

GUALTERUZZI, CARLO

Libro di Novelle, et di Bel Parlar Gentile. In Fiorenza: 1572. V. 45

GUALTHERI, GIORGIO

Siciliae Antiquae Tabulae Collectae. Messina: 1642. V. 40

GUALTIERI, GUIDO

Relationi Della Venuta Degli Ambasciatori Giaponesi a Roma Sino Alla Partita di Lisbona. Rome: 1586. V. 45

GUALTIERI, NICHOLAI

Index Testarum Conchyliorum Quae Adservantur in Museo. Florence: 1742. V. 44

GUANO: Its Analysis and Effects: Illustrated by the Latest Experiments. London: 1843. V. 39

THE GUARDIAN. London: 1714. V. 41; 43
THE GUARDIAN. London: 1767. V. 39

THE GUARDS. London: 1827. V. 38; 39; 41; 43

GUARINI, D. GUARINO

Caelestis Mathematicae . . . Milan: 1683. V. 40

GUARINI, GIOVANNI BATTISTA 1538-1612

Il Pastor Fido Tragicomedia Pastorale . . . In Venetia: 1590. V. 45

Il Pastor Fido . . . London: 1676. V. 46

Il Pastor Fido. Glasgow: 1763. V. 40

Il Pastor Fido, Tragicommedia Pastorale. Glasgua: 1763. V. 44

Il Pastor Fido. Glasguae: 1763. V. 46

Il Pastor Fido. Parigi: 1782. V. 40

Il Pastor Fido. Leyden: 1659. V. 40

Il Pastor Fido Tragicomedia. Londra: 1718. V. 44

Rime (sonetti di Diversi all'Autore, e Madrigali). Venice: 1598. V. 40

GUARINI, GUARINO

Architettura Civile. Milan: 1968. V. 46

Architettura Civile . . . Opera Postuma. Turin: 1737. V. 37

GUARINO DA VERONA

Lodovici Presbyteri de Pvppio in Differentias Gvarini Veronensis Interpretatio. Parma: 1492. V. 38

GUARINO OF FAVERA

Lexicon Barinoy Phaborinoy (Gr. letters). Dictionarium Varini Phavorini Camertis, Nucerini Episcopi, Magnum illud ac Pervtile Multis Verissque en Avtoribus Collectum, Totius Linguae Graecae Commentarius. Basiliae: 1538. V. 45

GUARINO OF FAVERA, BP. OF NOCERA

Mega Kai Pany Ophelimon Lexikon. Magnum ac Perutile Dictionarium. Rome: 1523. V. 37

GUARMANI, CARLO

Northern Najd a Journey from Jerusalem to Anaiza in Qasim. London: 1938. V. 43

GUARNELLO, ALESSANDRO

Canzone Nella Felicissima Vittoria Christiana Contra Infideli. Venice: 1571. V. 37

GUATTINI, MICHAEL ANGELO DE

Viaggio del Padre Michael Angelo Guattini da Reggio. Bologna: 1674. V. 44

GUAZZO, FRANCESCO MARIA

Compendium Maleficarum . . . London: 1929. V. 44; 46

GUAZZO, M. STEEVEN

The Civille Conversation. London: 1925. V. 41; 42

GUAZZO, STEAFNO

La Civil Conversatione. Venice: 1581. V. 46

GUAZZO, STEFANO 1530-1593

La Civil Conversatione . . . Divisa in Quattro Libri. Venice: 1588. V. 40

GUAZZO, STEPHEN

The Civile Conversation. London: 1586. V. 42

GUBB, ALFRED S.

Algiers s a Winter Resort and Its Therapeutical Indications. London: 1908. V. 38

GUBBINS, MARTIN RICHARD

An Account of the Mutinies in Oudh, and of the Siege of the Lucknow Residency; with Some Observations on the Condition of the Province of Oudh, and on the Causes of the Mutiny of the Bengal Army. London: 1858. V. 41

GUBERNATIS, ANGELO DE, COUNT

Zoological Mythology or the Legends of Animals. London: 1872. V. 42

GUDGEON, THOMAS W.

Reminiscences of the War in New Zealand. London: 1879. V. 42

GUDGEON, THOMAS WAYTH

The Defenders of New Zealand Being a Short Biography of Colonists Who Distinguished Themselves in Upholding Her Majesty's Supremacy in These Islands. Auckland: 1887. V. 39

GUDIOL, JOSE

Goya. New York: 1964. V. 40

Goya. 1746-1828: Biography; Analytical Study and Catalogue of Paintings. Barcelona: 1985. V. 39

Velazquez 1599-1660. London: 1974. V. 42

Velazquez 1599-1660. New York: 1974. V. 37; 40

GUE, BENJAMIN F.

History of Iowa From the Earliest Times to the Beginning of the Twentieth Century. New York: 1903. V. 37; 39

GUEDALLA, ROGER

Basil Bunting: a Bibliography of Works and Criticism. Norwood: 1973. V. 45

GUEDY, HENRY

Decorations Peintes Pour Devantures et Interieurs de Magasins. Dourdan: 1905. V. 40

GUELLETTE, THOMAS SIMON

Tartarian Tales; or a Thousand and One Quarter of Hours. London: 1759. V. 41

GUELLEUETTE, T. S.

Peruvian Tales Related in One Thousand and One Hours by One of the Select Virgins of Cusco to the Ynca of Peru. London: 1817. V. 40

GUENEE, ANTOINE

Letters of Certain Jews to Monsieur Voltaire. Philadelphia: 1795. V. 42

GUENTHER, CONRAD

Darwinism and the Problems of Life. London: 1906. V. 40

GUENTHER, GEORG CHRISTOPH

Praktische Anweisung zur Pastellmahlerey. Nuremberg: 1762. V. 45

GUENTHER, JOHANN CHRISTIAN 1695-1723

Sammlung von Bis An Hero Herausgegebenen Redichten auf Das Neue Uebersehen . . . Nachlese. Weitere Gedichte. Breslau & Leipzig: 1742. V. 39

GUERBER, H. A.

The Book of the Epic. London: 1916. V. 42

The Myths of Greece and Rome. London: 1913. V. 43

GUERICKE, OTTO VON

Experimenta Nova (Ut Vocantur) Magdeburgica de Vacuo Spatio. Amsterdam: 1672. V. 38; 43

GUERIN, JULES

A Collection of Color Prints. New York: 1920. V. 41

GUERIN, MARCEL

L'Oeuvre Grave de Manet, avec un Supplement Nouvellement Ajoute. New York: 1969. V. 41

GUERIN, MAURICE DE 1810-1839

The Centaur. Montague: 1915. V. 40

Le Centaure. Berkeley: 1985. V. 41; 42; 44

GUERINE, VINCENZO

A History of Dentistry from the Most Ancient Times Until the End of the Eighteenth Century. Philadelphia: 1909. V. 37; 38; 40; 41

GUERNSEY, ALFRED H.

Harper's Pictorial History of the Civil War. Chicago: 1866. V. 44

Harper's Pictorial History of the Civil War. Chicago: 1894. V. 46

GUERNSEY, CHARLES A.

Wyoming Cowboy Days. New York: 1936. V. 37

GUERNSEY, COUNTESS

Most Important and Interesting Pamphlet Being a New and Genuine Edition of the Death Bed Confessions of the Late Countess of Guernsey . . . London: 1822. V. 45

GUEROUT

Catalogue des Livres Nouveaux . . . Paris: 1670. V. 46

GUERRA, FRANCISCO b. 1916

American Medical Bibliography, 1639-1783. New York: 1962. V. 43

American Medical Bibliography 1639-1783. New York: 1962. V. 37; 38; 39; 40; 42; 43; 44; 45; 46

Iconographia Medica Mexicana. Mexico: 1955. V. 43

GUERREIRO CAMACHO DE ABOIM, DIOGO

Opusculum de Privilegijs Familiarium Officialium que Sanctae Inquisitionis Desideratissimum Nunc Primum in Lucem Editum . . . Coimbra: 1699. V. 41

GUESS If You Can, a Collection of Original Enigmas and Charades in Verse, Together with Fifty in the French Language. London: 1851. V. 45

GUEST, CHARLOTTE

The Mabinogion, from the Welsh of the Llyfr Coch O Hergest (The Red Book of Hergest), in the Library of Jesus College, Oxford. London: 1877. V. 37

GUEST, GRACE DUNHAM

Shiraz Painting in the Sixteenth Century. Washington: 1949. V. 42; 44

GUEST, JOHN

Historic Notices of Rotherham, Ecclesiastical, Collegiate and Civil. 1879. V. 45

Relics and Records of Men and Manufactures at Or in the Neighborhood of Rotherham, in the County of York. Rotherham: 1866. V. 44

GUEST, MOSES

Poems on Several Occasions . . . Cincinnati: 1823. V. 45

GUEULLETTE, THOMAS SIMON

Mogul Tales, or, the Dreams of Men Awake. London: 1736. V. 45

Tartarian Tales . . . London: 1739. V. 45

Tartarian Tales. London: 1759. V. 39; 40; 42; 45; 46

GUEVARA, ANTONIO

L'Horloge des Princes, avec le Tres Renomme Livre de Marc Avrele . . . Paris: 1578. V. 42

GUEVARA, ANTONIO DE

Archontorologion, or The Dial of Princes . . . London: 1619. V. 42

The Dial of Princes. London: 1568. V. 40; 44

The Dial of Princes. London: 1582. V. 37; 40; 42

The Familiar Epistles of Sir Anthonie of Guevara. London: 1577. V. 38; 41

Libro di Marco Aurelio con l'Horologio de' Principi . . . con la Giunta del Quarto Libro Novamente Tradotto di Lingua Spagnuola. Venice: 1571. V. 40

The Mount of Calvarie; and, Mount Calvarie, the Second Part. London: 1597. V. 40

The Mount of Calvarie. (and) Mount Calvarie, the second part. London: 1618, 1597. V. 38

The Praise and Happinesse of the Countrie-Life. Newtown: 1938. V. 37

Spanish Letters: Historical, Satyrical, and Moral . . . by way of Essay on different Subjects . . . . intermixt with both Raillerie and Gallantry. London: n.d. V. 37

GUEVARA, CHE

Guerilla Warfare. New York: 1961. V. 45

GUEVARA, DON ANTONIO DE

The Movnt of Caluarie . . . (with) Mount Caluarie. The Second Part. London: Printed by Edw.: 1618/1597. V. 41; 44; 45; 46

The Praise and Happiness of the Countrie-Life. Newtown: 1938. V. 46

GUEX, JEAN LOUIS

Letters of Mounseur (sic) de Balzac. Translated into English by Sir Richard Balser & Others. London: 1655. V. 37

GUGGENHEIM, PEGGY

Art of this Century. New York: 1942. V. 39

Out of this Century. New York: 1946. V. 39

GUGLIELMINI, DOMENICO

Della Nautra de'Fiumi. Bologna: 1697. V. 39

Riflessioni Filosofiche Detotte dalle Figure de'Sali . . . Padua: 1706. V. 46

De Sanguinis Natura & Constitutione Exercitatio Physico-Medica. Venice: 1701. V. 40

GUIA de Forasteros en Las Islas Filipinas, Para el Ano de 1842. Manila: 1844. V. 46

GUIBE, ROBERTUS

Oratio ad Innocentium VIII in obedientia Praestanda. Rome: 1485. V. 44

GUIBELET, JOURDAIN

Trois Discours Philosophiques. Evereux: 1603. V. 42

GUIBERT, JACQUES ANTOINE HIPPOLYTE, COMTE DE

Observations on the Military Establishment and Discipline of His Majesty the King of Prussia . . . London: 1780. V. 44

GUICCIARDINI, FRANCESCO

Detti et Fatti Piacevoli et Gravi dei Diversi Principi, Filosofi, et Cortigiani. Venice: 1566. V. 37

La Historia di Italia di M. Francesco Guicciardini Gentil'Huomo Florentino. Florence: 1561. V. 41; 45

L'Historia d'Italia. I Quattro Ultimi Libri. Venice: 1568. V. 39

The History of Guicciardin, Conteining the Warres of italie and Other Partes, Continued for Many Years Under Sundry Kings and Princes, Together with the Variations and Accidents of the Same. London: 1579. V. 38; 39

Histoire des Guerres d'Italie. Geneva: 1593. V. 39

The Historie of Guicciardin. London: 1618. V. 37; 39; 45

The Historie . . . Containing the Warres of Italie and Other Parts, Continued for Manie Yeares Under Sundrie Kings and Princes . . . London: 1618. V. 39

The Historie of Guicciardin. London: 1599. V. 37; 38

I Quattro Ultimi Libri dellHistorie d'Italia. Parma: 1564. V. 38

The History of Italy, from the Year 1490 to 1532 . . . London: 1753-56. V. 38

The Maxims. London: 1845. V. 38

GUICCIARDINI, LODOVICO 1521-1589

Commentarii Delle cose piu Memorabili Seguite in Europa . . . Venetia: 1566. V. 43

The Description of the Low Countreys and of the Provinces Thereof, Gathered into an Eptiome Out of the Historie of Lodouico Guicchardini. London: 1593. V. 45

GUICCIARDINI, LUDOVICO 1523-1589

Description de Touts les Pais-Bas. Anvers: 1582. V. 38

GUICHARD, CLAUDE

Funerailles & Diverses Manieres d'Enseuelir des Rommains, Grecs & Autres Nations. Lyon: 1581. V. 42; 44

GUICHARD, K. M.

British Etchers 1850-1940. London: 1977. V. 39

GUIDE Book to Lake Mohonk. Providence: 1875. V. 39

A GUIDE Book to West Point and Vicinity . . . New York: 1844. V. 42; 46

A GUIDE for the Use of the Managers of W. H. Smith & Son's Bookshops. London: 1908. V. 41; 46

A GUIDE Into the Knowledge of Publick Affairs, Both Foreign and Domestick . . . London: 1728. V. 43

A GUIDE to English Juries Setting Forth Their Antiquity, Power and Duty, from the Common Law, and Statutes. London: 1682. V. 38

A GUIDE to Hong Kong With a Short Account of Canton and Macao. Hong Kong: 1892. V. 41

GUIDE to Philadelphia: Its Public Buildings, Places of Amusement, Churches, Hotels &c. Philadelphia: 1866. V. 41

A GUIDE to the City of Chicago. Chicago: 1868. V. 39; 40; 42; 44; 45

GUIDE To the City of New York, with Views of the Most Interesting Points of the City, (Printed in Oil Colors) and a Map of Manhattan Island and the Central Park. New York: 1859. V. 41

GUIDE to the Glasgow and Ayrshire Railway, with Descriptions, of the Glasgow and Edinburgh, and Glasgow and Greenock Railways: to Ayr and Its Environs, and to the Land of Burns. Ayr and Glasgow: 1841. V. 38

A GUIDE to the Great Exhibition: Containing a Description of Every Principal Object of Interest. London: 1851. V. 38

A GUIDE to the Illinois Central Railroad Lands. Chicago: 1859. V. 44; 45
A GUIDE to the Illinois Central Railroad Lands. Chicago: 1860. V. 42

GUIDE to the Lands of the Northern Pacific Railroad in Minnesota. New York: 1872. V. 42
GUIDE to the Lands of the Northern Pacific Railroad in Minnesota. New York: 1872. V. 37; 38; 39

A GUIDE to the Lions of Philadelphia; Comprising a Description of the Places of Amusement, Exhibitions, Public Buildings, Public Squares, &c. in the City . . . Philadelphia: 1837. V. 41; 42

GUIDE to the Province of British Columbia for 1877-78. 1877. V. 43

GUIDE to the Province of British Columbia, for 1877-8. Victoria: 1877. V. 37

GUIDE to the Route Map of the Mormon Pioneers from Nauvoo to Great Salt Lake, 1846-1847. Salt Lake City: 1899? V. 40

GUIDETTI, GIOVANNI

Directorium Chori Ad Usum Ecclesiarum, tam Cathedralium, Quam Collegiatarum . . . Romae: 1589. V. 40

GUIDO DE COLONNA

Historia Destructionis Troiae. Strasbourg: 1486. V. 37; 38

GUIDO DE MONTE ROCHEN

Manipulis Curatorum. Strassburg: 1487. V. 42

Manipulus Curatorum. Strassburg: 1490. V. 44

GUIDO DE MONTE ROCHERII 14th century

Manipulus Curatorum, Qui Summopere . . . Venice: 1538. V. 45

GUIDOL, JOSE

Velazquez, 1599-1660. New York: 1974. V. 44

GUIDOT, THOMAS

Thomas Guidotti Anglo-Britanni de Thermis Britannicis Tractatas Accesserunt Observationes Hydrostaticae, Chromaticae & Miscellaneae . . . Londini: 1691. V. 39

GUIDOTT, THOMAS

Anglo-Britanni, De Thermis Britannicis Tractatus Accesserunt Observtiones . . . London: 1691. V. 38

A Collection of Treatises Relating to the City and Waters of Bath. London: 1725. V. 38

A Discourse of Bathe, and the Hot Waters There. London: 1675/76/77. V. 40

A Discourse of Bathe, and the Hot Springs there. Also some enquiries into the nature of the Water of St. Vincent's Rock, near Bristol; and that of Castle Cary. To which is added a Century of Observations, more fully declaring the . . . London: 1676. V. 37; 44

De Thermis Britannicis Tractatus. London: 1691. V. 40

GUIGARD, J.

Nouvelle Armorial du Bibliophile. Paris: 1890. V. 41

GUIGNES, CHRISTIAN DE

Voyages a Peking, Manille et l'Ile de France . . . Paris: 1808. V. 45

GUIGUES DU CHASTEL 1083-1137

On the Solitary Life. Pawlet: 1977. V. 40

THE GUILD of the Holy Cross; an Organization of the Laity, for the Defence of the Faith. New York: 1864. V. 44

GUILD AND SCHOOL OF HANDCRAFT

Transactions of the . . . London: 1890. V. 46

GUILD, GEORGE B.

A Brief Narrative of the Fourth Tennessee Cavalry Regiment Wheeler's Corps, Army of Tennessee. Nashville: 1931. V. 37; 38; 39

GUILD, HENRY ELIOT

Letters and Verses of . . . Boston: 1890. V. 37

GUILD, J. C.

Old Times in Tennessee, With Historical, Personal and Political Scraps and Sketches. Nashville: 1878. V. 39; 43

GUILD OF HANDICRAFT. LONDON.

Transactions of the Guild and School of Handicraft. London: 1890. V. 38

GUILD OF SAINT GEORGE

The Guild of St. George: Master's Report, 1884. V. 37

GUILD, REUBEN A.

The Librarian's Manual: a Treatise on Bibliography, Comprising a Select and Descriptive List of Bibliographical Works . . . New York: 1858. V. 38; 46

GUILELMUS DE GOUDA

Expositio Mysteriorn Misse. Denventer: 1946. V. 43
Expositio Misteriorum Misse. Cologne: 1506. V. 37

GUILEVILLE, GUILLAUME DE

A Modern Prose Translation of the Ancient Poem of Guillaume de Guileville, entitled the Pylgrymage of Man. London: 1859. V. 38

GUILFORD, FRANCIS NORTH, BARON 1637-1685

The Lord Keeper's Speech to Mr. Serjeant Saunders, at the Time He Was Sworn Lord Chief Justice of His Majestie's Court of Kings-Bench, Tuesday the 23d. January 1682. London: 1682. V. 40

GUILHOU, E.

Catalogue of a Collection of Ancient Rings Formed by the Late . . . Somerset: 1970. V. 40

GUILLAIN, M.

Voyage a la Cote Orientale d'Afrique. Album. Paris: 1856-57. V. 43

GUILLAIN, SIMONE

Vita de San Diego, Dipinta Nella Capella di Giacomo de Spagnuoli in Roma da Anibale Caracci . . . Rome: 1646. V. 46

GUILLAUME, HERBERT

The Amazon Provinces of Peru. London: 1888. V. 43

GUILLAUME, P.

Primitive Negro Sculpture. New York: 1926. V. 44; 46

GUILLAUMOT, AUGUSTE ETIENNE 1864-1890

Costumes of the Time of the French Revolution 1790-1793 Together with English Costumes During the Years 1795-1806. New York: 1889. V. 38

GUILLEBON, REGINE DE PLINVAL DE

Paris Porcelain 1770-1850. London: 1972. V. 37

GUILLEM DE POITOU

His Eleven Extant Poems. Mt. Horeb: 1976. V. 46

GUILLEMARD, F. H. H.

The Cruise of the Marchesa to Kamschatka and New Guinea with Notices of Formosa, Liu-Kiu and Various Islands of the Malay Archipelago. London: 1886. V. 38; 40; 45
The Cruise of the Marchesa to Kamchatka and New Guinea with Notices of Formosa, Liu-Kiu and Various Islands of the Malay Archipelago. London: 1889. V. 41

GUILLEMEAU, JACQUES

Child-Birth, or the Happy Deliverie of Women. Wherein is set downe the Government of Women. In the time of their breeding Childe. Or their Travaile, both Naturall and contrary to Nature: and of their . . . London: 1612. V. 37

GUILLEMIN, A.

The Applications of Physical Forces. London: 1877. V. 38; 40
The Applications of Physical Forces. London: 1877. V. 38

GUILLEN, GIOVANNI FRANCESCO

Ristretto Dello Stato Della Diocesi di Canaria. Lanzarote Island: 1700's. V. 43

GUILLERMUS ALTISSIODORENSIS

Summa Aurea in IV Libros Sententiarum. Paris: 1500/01. V. 42; 44

GUILLERMUS, EPISCOPUS PARISIENSIS

Rhetorica Divina. Basel: 1942. V. 44

GUILLET DE ST. GEORGE, GEORGES 1625?-1705

An Account of a Late Voyage to Athens . . . London: 1676. V. 39; 44
The Gentleman's Dictionary. London: 1705. V. 43

GUILLET DE ST. GEORGES, GEORGE

Athens Ancienne et Nouvelle et l'Estat Present de lEmpire des Turcs, Contenant la Vie du Sultan Mahomet IV. Paris: 1675. V. 37

Lettres Ecrites sur Une Dissertation d'un Voyage de Grece Publie par Mr. Spon, Medecin Antiquaire. Paris: 1679. V. 37

GUILLET, EDWIN C.

Early Life in Upper Canada. Toronto: 1933. V. 38; 45
Toronto from Trading Post to Great City by . . . Toronto: 1934. V. 38

GUILLET, PETER

Timber Merchant's Guide. Baltimore: 1823. V. 37; 45

GUILLIE, SEBASTIEN

Essai sur l'Instruction des Aveugles, ou Expose Analytique des Procedes Employes Pour les Instruire. Paris: 1817. V. 38

GUILLIM, JOHN 1565-1621

A Display of Heraldrie. London: 1632. V. 39; 41; 46
A Display of Heraldrie. London: 1632. V. 41
A Display of Heraldrie . . . London: 1638. V. 45
A Display of Heraldrie . . . London: 1660. V. 44
A Display of Heraldry. London: 1724. V. 37; 40; 46

GUILLON, RENE

De Generibvx Carminvm Graecorvm. Pari: 1548. V. 38
Gnomon. Paris: 1548. V. 37

GUILLONIUS, RENATUS

De Generibus Carminvm Graecorvm. Paris: 1560. V. 37

THE GUINESS Alice. Dublin: 1933. V. 41

GUINESS, BRYAN

Under the Eyelid. London: (ca. 1935). V. 37

GUINEY, LOUISE IMOGEN

Nine Sonnets Written at Oxford. Boston: 1895. V. 37

GUINN, JAMES MILLER

Historial and Biographical Record of Southern California. Containing a History of Southern California from its Earliest Settlement to the Opening Year of the Twentieth Century. Also Containing Biographies of . . . Chicago: 1902. V. 37; 39
History of the State of California and Biographical Records of the San Joaquin Valley California. Chicago: 1905. V. 38
History of the State of California and Biographical Record of Oakland and Environs . . . Los Angeles: 1907. V. 40

GUINNESS, BRYAN

Collected Poems 1927-1955. London: 1956. V. 40
Landscape with Figures. London: 1934. V. 41
Twenty-Three Poems. London: 1931. V. 40

GUINOT, M. EUGENE

A Summer at Baden-Baden. London. V. 38

GUINTER, JOANNES

Gynaeciorum Commentarius, de Gravidarum, Parturentium, Puerperarum & Infanitum, Cura. Argentorati: 1606. V. 37

GUION, LADY

The Exemplary Life of the Pious . . . Translated from Her Own Account in the Original French. Philadelphia: 1804. V. 45

GUISE, HENRY, DUC DE

Memoires of Henry Duke of Guise . . . London: 1669. V. 46

GUITEAU, CHARLES

The Truth, and the Removal. Washington: 1882. V. 41

GUIZOT, FRANCOIS PIERRE GUILLAUME

The Fine Arts, Their Nature and Relations. London: 1853. V. 38

GUIZOT, M.

The History of France from the Earliest Times to the Year 1789. London: 1872. V. 41; 42

GULDIN, PAUL

De Centro Gravitatis Trium Specierum Quantitatis Continuae. Vienna: 1635. V. 45

GULIK, ROBERT HANS VAN

Sexual Life in Ancient China. Leiden: 1961. V. 40

GULL, WILLIAM WITHEY

A Collection of the Published Writings of William Withy Gull. London: 1894. V. 37

GULLAND, W. G.

Chinese Porcelain. London: 1898-1902. V. 42

GULLAND, W. G. continued

Chinese Porcelain. London: 1928-29. V. 41

GULLIVER, PSEUD.

Amateur Etchings of Texas Characters and Else. Greenvill: 1888. V. 44

GULLIVERIANA: or, a Fourth Volume of Miscellanies. London: 1728. V. 45

GULLY, JAMES MANBY

The Water Cure in Chronic Diseases. New York: 1846. V. 42

GULLY, JOHN

New Zealand Scenery Chromolithographed after Original Water Color Drawings by John Gully. London: 1877. V. 40

GULLYER, JOHN

The Gentleman's & Farmer's Assistant. Norwich: 1805. V. 39

GULSTON, JOSEPH HEATH

Young Singleton. London: 1856. V. 41

GULZARA, Princess of Persia; or, the Virgin Queen. London: 1816. V. 40

GUMBLE, THOMAS

The Life of General Monck, Duke of Albemarle &c . . . London: 1671. V. 46

GUMMOW, JAMES REYNOLDS

Hints on House Building to Proprietors, Occupiers of Houses and Artisan Builders. Wrexham: 1874. V. 45

THE GUN at Home and Abroad. London: 1912. V. 39; 42
THE GUN at Home and Abroad. London: 1912-15. V. 39; 42; 46

GUNDRY, RICHARD

Report on Insanity. Columbus: 1860. V. 43

GUNN, ALEXANDER

The Hermitage Zoar Note-Book and Journal of Travel. (with) Letters. New York: 1902. V. 44

Memoirs of the Rev. John H. Livingston . . . New York: 1829. V. 46

GUNN, DOUGLAS

Picturesque San Diego, with Historical and Descriptive Notes. Chicago: 1887. V. 37; 39; 41; 45

GUNN, J. A.

Memorial Sketches of Doctor Moses Gunn by His Wife. Chicago: 1889. V. 43; 45

GUNN, JOHN

An Historical Enquiry Respecting the Performance on the Harp in the Highlands of Scotland . . . Edinburgh: 1807. V. 43

GUNN, JOHN C.

Gunn's Domestic Medicine, or Poor Man's Friend, Shewing the Diseases of Men, Women and Children, and Expressly Intended for the Benefit of Families. Knoxville: 1833. V. 41

Gunn's Domestic Medicine, or Poor Man's Friend. Madisonville: 1834. V. 45

Gunn's Domestic Medicine, or Poor Man's Friend, in the Hours of Affliction, Pain and Sickness. Madisonville: 1835. V. 44

Gunn's Domestic Medicine, or Poor Man's Friend . . . The Diseases of men, Women and Children . . . Madisonville: 1837. V. 43

Gunn's Domestic Medicine, or Poor Man's Friend in the Hours of Afflication, Pain and Sickness. . . New York: 1842. V. 42; 45

Gunn's New Domestic Physician. Cincinnati,: 1862. V. 38

Gunn's Dometic Medicine, or Poor Man's Friend . . . Louisville: 1842. V. 37

GUNN, JOHN MALCOLM

Schat-Chen: History, Traditions, and Narratives of the Queres Indians of Laguna and Acoma. Albuquerque: 1917. V. 40

GUNN, LEWIS

Records of a California Family. Journal and Letters. San Diego: 1928. V. 40

GUNN, MAURICE JAMES

Print Restoration and Picture Cleaning. London: 1911. V. 41

GUNN, THOM

At the Barriers. 1989. V. 42

At the Barriers: Poems. Nadja: 1989. V. 43

At the Barriers. New York: 1989. V. 41; 46

The Explorers. Bow, Crediton, Devon: 1969. V. 39

The Garden of the Gods. 1968. V. 40; 41; 42; 43; 44

Jack Straw's Castle. New York: 1975. V. 39

Lament. Champaign: 1985. V. 39; 42

Mandrakes. London: 1973. V. 39; 45

Mandrakes. N.P.: 1973. V. 46

The Missed Beat. 1976. V. 39

My Sad Captains and Other Poems. London: 1961. V. 43

Poem After Chaucer. N.P.: 1971. V. 40

Poetry from Cambridge. London: 1952. V. 42; 46

Poetry From Cambridge 1952-4. 1955. V. 37

Songbook. New York: 1973. V. 39

Sunlight: Poems. New York: 1969. V. 43

Touch. London: 1967. V. 38; 40

GUNN, THOMAS

Lament; a Poem. 1985. V. 41

The Sense of Movement. Chicago: 1957. V. 43

GUNNING, GEORGE

Documents of the Gunning Family. Cheltenham: 1834. V. 37

GUNNING, SUSANNAH MINIFIE

Memoirs of Mary, a Novel. London: 1793. V. 40

GUNNISON, J. W.

The Mormons, or, Latter Day Saints, in the Valley of the Great Salt Lake; A History of Their Rise and Progress, Peculiar Doctrines, Present Condition and Prospects . . . Philadelphia: 1852. V. 38; 39; 40; 41; 42; 45; 46

The Mormons, or, Latter-Day Saints in the Valley of the Great Salt Lake; a History of Their Rise and Progress . . . Philadelphia: 1856. V. 39; 40; 41; 45; 46

GUNNISON, JOHN W.

The Mormons; or Latter-Day Saints in the Valley of Great Salt Lake: a History of Their Rise, Progress, Condition and Prospects. Philadelphia: 1853. V. 38; 39

GUNN'S Domestic Medicine, or Poor Man's Friend. Knoxville, TN.: 1833. V. 37

GUNSAULUS, HELEN

Japanese Textiles. New York: 1941. V. 38; 44

GUNTER, A. C.

Mr. Potter of Texas. London: 1891. V. 41

GUNTER, EDMOND

The Works of Edmund Gunter, edited by William Leybourne 1626-1700. Containing the Description and use of the Sector, Cross-staff, Bow, Quadrant, and other Instuments . . . the practice of . . . Astronomy, Navigation, Dialling . . . the fifth edition. London;: 1673. V. 37; 45

GUNTHART, LOTTE

The Glory of the Rose. London: 1965. V. 45

Linger Golden Light. Catalogue and Exhibition of Water Colours by . . . Nov. 1984-Feb. 1985. Pittsburgh: 1984. V. 37

GUNTHER, A.

Catalogue of the Fishes in the British Museum. London: 1859-70. V. 37; 38

The Reptiles of British India. London: 1864. V. 37

GUNTHER, ALBERT

Catalogue of the Acanthopterygian Fishes (and) of the Physostomi in the Collection of the British Museum. London: 1937. V. 39

The Reptiles of British India. London: 1864. V. 43

GUNTHER, EDMUND

The Works of Edmund Gunther. 1673. V. 38

GUNTHER, R. T.

The Architecture of Sir Roger Pratt. Oxford: 1928. V. 38

Early British Botanists and Their Gardens. Oxford: 1922. V. 37; 38

The Herbal of Apuleius Barbarus from the Early 12th Century Manuscript Formerly in the Abbey of Bury St. Edmunds . . . Oxford: 1925. V. 38

GUOYNNEAU DE PAMBOUR, FRANCOIS MARIE, COMTE b. 1795

A Practical Treatise on Locomotive Engines Upon Railways . . . Philadelpia: 1836. V. 42

GUPPY, H. B.

Observations of a Naturalist in the Pacific Between 1896 and 1899. London: 1903-06. V. 40

The Solomon Islands. London: 1887. V. 38; 41; 43; 44

GUPPY, HENRY BROUGHAM

Observations of a Naturalist in the Pacific Between 1896 and 1899. London: 1903. V. 45; 46

GUPPY, SAMUEL

Mary Jane; or Spiritualism Chemically Explained with Spirit Drawings. London: 1863. V. 39

GUPTILL, A. B.

All About Yellowstone Park: a Practical Guide. St. Paul: 1882. V. 41

GUPTILL, ARTHUR L.

Norman Rockwell, Illustrator. New York: 1946. V. 39; 41

GURDON, THORNHAGH 1663-1733

The History of the High Court of Parliament, Its Antiquity, Pre-Eminence and Authority . . . London: 1731. V. 40; 41

GURGANUS, ALLAN

Oldest Living Confederate Widow Tells All. New York: 1989. V. 45; 46

GURLEY, L. B.

Memoir of Rev. William Gurley, Late of Milan, Ohio, a Local Minister of the Methodist Episcopal Church . . . Cincinnati: 1852. V. 38

GURLEY, ROYAL

Paper Trade Sale. New York: 1833. V. 40

GURNALL, WILLIAM

The Christian in Complete Armour, or, a Treaties of the Saints War Against the Devil. London: 1658/62. V. 42

GURNEY, IVOR

Severn and Somme. London: 1917. V. 38; 41

War's Embers and Other Verses. London: 1919. V. 37

GURNEY, J.

The St.-Memin Collection of Portraits. New York: 1862. V. 37

GURNEY, J. H.

The Gannet, a Bird with a History. London: 1913. V. 37; 38

GURNEY, JOSEPH

John Stockdale (1749?-1814) for a Libel . . . 9th December 1789 Before Chief Justic Lloyd Lord Kenyon. Dublin: 1790. V. 38

GURNEY, JOSEPH JOHN

Familiar Sketch of the Late William Wilberforce. Norwich: 1838. V. 45

Familiar Letters to Henry Clay of Kentucky, Describing a Winter in the West Indies. New York: 1840. V. 38; 40; 43

A Few Select Extracts from the Journal of Joseph John Gurney. (N.P.: ca. 1851). V. 37

Notes on a Visit Made to Some of the Prisons in Scotland and the North of England, in Company with Elizabeth Fry. London: 1819. V. 41; 42; 46

Observations on the Religious Peculiarities of the Society of Friends. London: 1824. V. 44

A Winter in the West Indies, Described in Familiar Letters to Henry Clay of Kentucky. London: 1840. V. 38; 39; 42; 46

A Winter in the West Indies . . . In Letters to Henry Clay of Kentucky, the voyage of the 'Camilla;' treatment of slaves in the 7 main islands of W.I.; anti-slavery interest from Santa Cruz to Cuba. London: 1840/41. V. 37

GURNEY, O. R.

The Sutantepe Tablest, I-II. London: 1957-1964. V. 37

GURNEY, SAMUEL

Address Delivered . . . . at the Meeting of Friends, Held in the Committee Room, Devonshire House, 11th Month 9th, 1832. V. 42

London and Its Environs Described . . . London: 1761. V. 46

GURNEY, THOMAS

Brachygraphy: or an Easy an Compendious System of Short Hand . . . London. V. 46

Brachygraphy: or an Easy and Compendious System of Shorthand, Adapted to the Various Arts, Sciences and Professions. London: 1778. V. 38

Brachygraphy: or an Easy and Compendious System of Short-Hand, Adapted to Various Arts, Sciences and Professions . . . London: 1785. V. 41; 43

Brachygraphy . . . London: 1835. V. 44

GURO, ELENA

Nebesnye Verblyuzhata. St. Petersburg: 1914. V. 42

GUSMAO, P. ALEXANDRE DE

Historia do Predestinado Peregrino, seu Irmao Precito . . . Evora: 1685. V. 45

GUSSOW, H. T.

Mushrooms and Toadstools. An Account of the More Common Edible and Poisonous Fungi of Canada. Ottawa: 1927. V. 37; 39; 46

GUSTAFSON, EVELINA

Ghost Towns 'Neath Quabbin Reservoir. Boston & Norwood: 1940. V. 44

GUTCH, JOHN

Collectanea Curiosa; or Miscellaneous Tracts, Relating to the History and Antiquities of England and Ireland . . . Oxford: 1781. V. 41; 42

GUTCHEN, SYLVIA

The Vertues of Salad. Kingston: 1979. V. 42

GUTEBERLETH, HEINRICH 1572-1635

Chronologia. Ante Obitum Auctoris Absoluta,. & Nunc Primum Edita. Amsterdam;: 1639. V. 39

GUTHRIE, A. B.

The Big Sky. New York: 1947. V. 46

These Thousand Hills. Boston: 1956. V. 44; 45

These Thousand Hills. Boston: 1956. V. 44

GUTHRIE, ALFRED BERTRAM 1901-

The Big Sky. New York: (1947). V. 37

GUTHRIE, GEORGE

Commentaries on the Surgery of the War in Portugal, Spain, France and the Netherlands . . . Philadelphia: 1862. V. 42

GUTHRIE, GEORGE J.

Lectures on the Operative Surgery of the Eye . . . London: 1827. V. 42

GUTHRIE, JAMES

An Account of the Aims and Intentions of His Press, with a List of Books. Harting: 1905. V. 41; 45

An Album of Drawings. London: 1900. V. 41

An Album of Drawings. White Cottage, Shorne,: 1900. V. 41

The Elf, A Sequence of the Seasons. London: 1902-04. V. 38; 41; 45; 46

The Elf, a Sequence of the Seasons. London: 1902-04. V. 45

The Elf. A Sequence of the Seasons. Flansham: 1902 to 1904. V. 37

James Guthrie His Book of Bookplates, Consisting of 24 Original Designs. Edinburgh: 1907. V. 40; 45

Last Bookplates - Being a Collection of Designs. Flansham: 1929. V. 43

A Little Anthology of Hitherto Uncollected Poems by Modern Writers. 1922. V. 45

A Little Anthology of Hitherto Uncollected Poems by Modern Writers. Bognor: 1922. V. 40

A Little Rosary. Sussex: 1930. V. 40; 41

A Little Rosary. Sussex: 1930. V. 41

A Second Book of Drawings. Edinburgh: 1907. V. 40; 41; 45

To the Memory of Edward Thomas. Flansham: 1937. V. 37; 45

To the Memory of Edward Thomas. Sussex: 1939. V. 40

The Wild Garden. Verses for Children. London: 1922. V. 46

GUTHRIE, JOHN

First Designs fro the Theatre. Flansham: 1923. V. 45

GUTHRIE, K. S.

A Romance of Two Centuries. 1919. V. 44

GUTHRIE, KATHARINE

Life in Western India. London: 1881. V. 45

GUTHRIE, MARIA

A Tour Performed in the Years 1795-6 through the Taurida or Crimea. London: 1802. V. 41; 42; 44; 45; 46

GUTHRIE, RAMON

Trobar Clus. Northampton: 1923. V. 44

GUTHRIE, STUART

A Little Anthology of Hitherto Uncollected Poems by Modern Writers. Bognor: 1922. V. 41

GUTHRIE, THOMAS 1803-1873

Seed-Time and Harvest of Ragged Schools or a Third Plea with New Editions of the First and Second Pleas. Edinburgh: 1860. V. 37; 42; 45

GUTHRIE, THOMAS ANSTEY

The Brass Bottle. London: 1900. V. 46

Vice Versa or a Lesson to Fathers. London: 1882. V. 38; 46

GUTHRIE, W.

The Christians Great Interest. London: 1679. V. 38

GUTHRIE, WILLIAM

The Christian's Great Interest, In Two Parts . . . South Hanover: 1834. V. 41

An Essay upon English Tragedy. With Remarks upon the Abbe de Blanc's Observations on the English Stage. London: 1757. V. 39

A New Geographical, Historical and Commercial Grammar, and Present State of the Several Kingdoms of the World. London: 1788. V. 39; 42; 43

A New Geographical, Historical and Commercial Grammar . . . London: 1790. V. 44

GUTHRIE, WILLIAM continued

A New Geographical, Historical, and Commercial Grammar: and present state of the several Kingdoms of the World. A voluminous encyclopedia. London: 1770. V. 37

A New Geographical, Historical and Commerical Grammar; and Present State of the Several Kingdoms of the World . . . Illustrated with a Correct Set of Maps, Engraved by Mr. Kitchin, Geographer. The Eighth Edition, with Great Additions . . . London: 1783. V. 37

GUTHRIE, WOODY

Bound for Glory. New York: 1943. V. 43

GUTHRY, HENRY

The Memoirs . . . Glasgow: 1748. V. 46

GUTIERREZ DE GUALBA, JEAN

Arte Breve Y provechoso de Cuenta Castellana y Arithmetica Donde se Muestran los Cinco Reglas de Guarismo por la Cuenta Castellana y Reglas de Memoria. Saragossa: 1555. V. 44

GUTKIND, ERICH

The Absolute Collective. London: 1937. V. 44

GUTMAN, RICHARD

American Diner. New York: 1979. V. 46

GUTS MUTHS, JOHANN C. F.

Gymnastics for Youth; or a Practical Guide to healthful and Amusing Exercises for the Use of Schools. Philadlephia: 1802. V. 45

GUTTA PERCHA COMPANY

Pattern Book of Ornament for the Use of the Trade. London: 1850. V. 40

GUTTIEREZ, VALENTIN LLANOS

Don Esteban; or Memoirs of a Spaniard. London: 1825. V. 39; 46

GUTWEIN, NICOLAUS ANTONIUS

Neu-Eroffnetes Theatrum. Augsburg: 1729. V. 40

GUTZLAFF, CHARLES KARL

A Sketch of Chinese History, Anicent and Modern . . . New York: 1834. V. 43

GUY DE CHAULIAC

Cyrugia Guidonis de Cauliaco et Cyrvrgia Brunai Teodorici Rolandi Lanfranci, Rogerii, Berttapafiae. Rolliter. Venice: 1519. V. 41

Inventario: over Collectorio Universalissimo de Tutte le Cose Notabele Delli Antiquissimi Medici Hebrei Greci, Latini & Arabi . . . Venice: 1521. V. 38

GUY, ROSA

A Measure of Time. New York: 1983. V. 46

GUY, THOMAS

A Copy of the Last Will and Testament of Thomas Guy, Esq. London: 1815. V. 38; 39

A True Copy of the Last Will and Testament of Thomas Guy, Esq . . . London: 1725. V. 42

GUY, W. H.

Abbe Fores; or the Unfortunate Family. Boston: 1846. V. 43

GUY, WILLIAM

Principles of Forensic Medicine. New York: 1845. V. 40; 42

GUY, WILLIAM AUGUSTUS 1810-1885

The Case of the Journeymen Bakers; Being a Lecture on the Evils of Night Work. London: 1848. V. 42

GUYE, SAMUEL

Time and Space: Measuring Instruments from the 15th to the 19th Century. New York: 1971. V. 38; 42

Time and Space. Washington: 1971. V. 42

GUYER, I. D.

History of Chicago; Its Commercial and Manufacturing Interests and Industry . . . Chicago: 1852. V. 45

History of Chicago . . . Chicago: 1862. V. 42; 45

GUYMIER, COSMAS d. 1503

Pragmatica Sanctio. Paris: 1514. V. 40

GUYON, JEANNE MARIE

Poems, Translated from the French of madame de la Mothe Guion, by the late William Cowper, Esq . . . To which are added some original Poems of Mr. Cowper, not Inserted in his Works. Burlington: 1815. V. 37

GUYON, LOUIS, SIEUR DE LA NAUCHE

Les Diverses Lecons . . . Divisees En Cinq Livres. Lyon: 1604. V. 39

GUYONNEAU DE PAMBOUR, FRANCOIS MARIE, COMTE d. 1795

A Practical Treatise on Locomotive Engines Upon Railways . . . Philadelphia: 1836. V. 46

GUYOT, ARNAUD

The Earth and Man . . . Boston: 1849. V. 45

GUYOT DESFONTAINES, PIERRE FRANCOIS

The Travels of Mr. John Gulliver, Son To Capt. Lemuel Gulliver. London: 1731. V. 38; 41; 45

GUY'S HOSPITAL

Guy's Hospital Reports. No. 1, January 1836. London: 1836. V. 37

GUYS, PIERRE AUGUSTIN

A Sentimental Journey through Greece, in a Series of Letters, Written from Constantinople . . . to M. Bourlate de Montredon, at Paris. London: 1772. V. 37; 38; 39

GUYSE, JACQUES DE

Illustrations de la Gaulle Belgique. Paris: 1531-32. V. 45; 46

GUYTON DE MORVEAU, LOUIS BERNARD

Elemens de Chymie, Theorique et Pratique. Dijon: 1777. V. 38

Memoire Sur l'Education Publique, Avec le Prospectus d'Un College, Suivant les Principes de cet Ouvrage. Dijon?: 1764. V. 39

Methode de Nomenclature Chimique . . . Paris: 1787. V. 42; 45

GUYTON, J. D.

Photo Records of the Guyton and Harrington Mule Company Properties. Kansas City: 1915. V. 42

GUZMAN, FRANCISCUS

Officivm Sacrorum Christi Iesu Seruatoris Nostri Vvulnerum Ex Sacrarum Scripturarum Monumentis, Tata & Eruditione & Pietate Selectum . . . Valencia: 1567. V. 39

GUZMAN, FRAY JOSE MARIA

Breve Noticia del Actual Estado Del Territorio De La Alta California, Y Medios Que Propone Para La Illustracion Y comercio en Aguel Pais. Mexico: 1833. V. 45

GWILLIM, HENRY

A Collection of Acts and Recods of Parliament with Reports of Cases, Argued and Determined in the Courts of Law and Equity, Respecting Tithes. London: 1801. V. 38

GWILT, JOSEPH

An Encyclopaedia of Architecture. London: 1842. V. 38

An Encyclopedia of Architecture Historical, Theoretical and Practical. London: 1888. V. 37; 42

GWIN, LAURA MC CLANAHAN

Miscellaneous Poems. Greenville: 1860. V. 46

GWINETT, AMBROSE

The Life, Strange Voyages and Uncommon Adventures of Ambrose Gwinett. London: 1785. V. 43

GWINNETT, RICHARD

Pylades and Corinna. London: 1731. V. 38

GWYN, NELL

The Story of Nell Gwyn, and the Sayings of Charles II. London: 1892. V. 41

GWYNN, AUBREY

Medieval Studies, Presented to Aubrey Gwynn. Dublin: 1962. V. 38

GWYNN, JOHN

An Essay on Design, Including Proposals for Erecting a Public Academy to be Supported by Voluntary Subscription . . . London: 1749. V. 39; 40; 41; 44

London and Westminster Improved, Illustrated by Plans. London: 1766. V. 38; 45

GWYNN, STEPHEN

River to River. London: 1937. V. 43; 45

GYLLENBORG, GUSTAF ADOLPH

The Natural and Chemical Elements of Agriculture. London: 1770. V. 38

GYLLENBORG, KARL

Letters Which Passed Between Count Gyllenborg, the Barons Gortz, Sparre and Others Relative to the Design of Raising a Rebellion in His Majesty's Dominions, to be Supported by a Force from Sweden. Edinburgh: 1717. V. 40

GYLLIUS, P.

De Constantinopoleos; Topographia Lib. V. Leyden: 1632. V. 39

GYMNASTIQUE des Jeunes Gens. Paris: 1828. V. 46

GYRON LE COURTOYS

Auecques la Deuise des Armes de Tous les Cheualiers de la Table Ronde Nouuellement Imprime. Paris: 1519. V. 40

GYSIN, BRION

Let the Mice In. West Glover: 1973. V. 38

The Process. New York: 1969. V. 37; 41; 46

The Process. New York: 1969. V. 41

To Master, a Long Goodnight. New York: 1946. V. 37

GYSIUS, JOHANNES

Origo & Historia Belgicorum Tumultuum, Immanissimaeque Crudelitatis per Cliviam & Westphaliam Patratae . . . Leiden: 1619. V. 37

H

H. & S.

Brass, Iron and Composite Bedsteads, Cots &c. Birmingham: 1895. V. 41

Brass, Iron and Composite Bedsteads, Cots, etc. Birmingham: 1985. V. 44

H., B.

The Children's Garden, a Memory of the Old Porch House. Chelsea: 1913. V. 45

H., C. A.

Letters on the Past and Present Foxhounds at Devonshire. Exeter: 1861. V. 39

H., D.

Choruses from Iphigeneia in Aulis. (1916). V. 37

H., E.

The History of the Imperial and Royal Families of Austria and Bourbon, Trac'd Down Their Original to This Present Time. London: 1708. V. 39

H., J.

Descriptive Excursionists and Pictorial Handbook, Season 1894-5. Melbourne: 1894. V. 38

H., J. B.

The 'Mohicans' in Iceland. Glasgow: 1887. V. 43

H., L.

Children's Songs for Town and Country Life. London: 1860. V. 39

H., M. S.

H.M.S. 'PARLIMENT,' or, The Lady who Loved a Government Clerk. Ottawa: 1880. V. 37

H., N.

The Pleasant Art of Money Catching . . . London: 1684. V. 45

H., R.

The Angler's Sure Guide; or, Angling Improved, and Methodically Digest. London: 1706. V. 39

H. R. - L. E. R. 1871-1921. N.P.: 1921. V. 44

H. R. - L. E. R. 1871-1921. N.P.: 1921. V. 40

HAAFNER, J.

Travels on Foot through the Island of Ceylon. London: 1821. V. 38

HAAGENSEN, C. D.

Diseases of the Breast. Philadelphia: 1956. V. 40; 42

HAAGNER, ALWIN

Sketches of South African Birds Life. Cape Town: 1914. V. 39; 40; 42

HAAK, B.

Rembrandt, His Life, His Work, His Time. New York: 1969. V. 37; 46

Rembrandt: His Life, His Work, His Time. 1969. V. 39

HAANEL, EUGENE

The Location and Examination of Magnetic Ore Deposits by Magnetometric Measurements. Ottawa: 1904. V. 45

HAARDT, GEORGES MARIE

La Croisiere Noire - Expedition Citroen Centre-Afrique. Paris: 1927. V. 42

HAARER, A. E.

Modern Coffee Production. London: 1856. V. 46

HAAS, ELISE

Letters from Mexico. San Francisco: 1937. V. 40

HAAST, JULIUS VON

Geology of the Provinces of Canterbury and Westland, New Zealand. Christchurch: 1879. V. 40

Report of a Topographical and Geographical Exploration of the Western Districts of the Nelson Province, New Zealand. Nelson: 1861. V. 39

HABBERTON, JOHN

Helen's Babies. Boston: 1876. V. 42; 43; 46

HABEL, S.

The Sculptures of Santa Lucia Cosumalwhuapa in Guatemala, with an Account of Travels in Central America and on the Western Coast of South America. Washington: 1878. V. 38

HABER, FRITZ 1863-1934

Thermodynamics of Technical Gas Reactions. London: 1908. V. 42

HABERLY, LOYD

Again, and Other Poems. 1953. V. 40

Almost a Minister . . . St. Louis: 1942. V. 44

An American Bookbuilder in England and Wales, Reminiscences of the Seven Acres and Gregynog Press. London: 1979. V. 43

Anne Boleyn and Other Poems. London: 1934. V. 40

Anne Boleyn and Other Poems. Newtown: 1934. V. 37; 40; 42; 43; 44; 45; 46

The Antiquary: a Poem Written in Waterperry Church and Decorated with Designs . . . Long Crendon: 1933. V. 46

Boy and the Bird, an Oregon Idyll. Long Crendon: 1932. V. 45; 46

The Clipper Coloured Cupid or the Cutting of the Cake the Second Book of Oregon's Orpheus: Twelve Poems Made to Match as Many Months . . . Long Crendon: 1931. V. 44

The Crowning Year and Other Poems. Dorset: 1937. V. 37; 42

Cymberina an Unnatural History in Woodcuts and Verse. Long Crendon: 1926. V. 44

Daneway, a Fairy Play for Emery Walker. Long Crendon: 1929. V. 40; 43

Echo and Other Poems. Long Crendon: 1935. V. 46

Farewells. Long Crendon: 1927. V. 44

The Fourth of July: or, An ORegon Orator. St. Louis: 1942. V. 46

John Apostate an Idyl of the Quays. Long Crendon: 1927. V. 46

Keeper of the Doves. Long Crendon: 1933. V. 37; 43; 45; 46

Mediaeval English Pavingtiles. Oxford: 1937. V. 39; 45

A Merry Christmas. N.P.. V. 46

Poems. Long Crendon: 1930. V. 37; 43; 45

Poems. London: 1931. V. 44

The Sacrifice of Spring: a Masque of Queens. 1927. V. 45

The Sacrifice of Spring, a Masque of Queens. Long Credon: 1927. V. 37; 39; 41

When Cupid Wins None Lose, or a True Report of Fairy Sport on the Lawns of a Manor House When the Master & Mistress First Came Home. Long Crendon, Bucks: 1927. V. 39; 42

HABERMANN, JOHANN

The Enemie of Security or a Daily Exercise of Godlie Meditations, Drawne Out of the Pure Fountains of the Holie Scriptures.. London: 1586. V. 39

HABERSHAM, A. W.

The North Pacific Surveying and Exploring Expedition; or, My Last Cruise. Philadelphia: 1857. V. 37; 38; 39; 40; 41

HABESCI, ELIAS

The Present State of the Ottoman Empire. London: 1784. V. 37

HABINGTON, WILLIAM

The Historie of Edward the Fourth, King of England. London: 1640. V. 40; 43; 45

The Queene of Arragon. A Tragi-Comedie. London: 1640. V. 37

HABIRSHAW, R.

Catalogue of the Diatomaceae. New York: 1877. V. 38

HABRECHT, ISAAC

Planiglobium Coeleste et Terrestre. Nurnberg: 1666. V. 45; 46

HACHISUKA, M.

The Birds of the Philippine Islands . . . London: 1931-35. V. 43

The Dodo and Kindred Birds, or the Extinct Birds of the Mascarene Islands. London: 1953. V. 38

HACK, MARIA

Stories for Animals Intended for Children Between Five and Seven Years Old. London: 1822. V. 45

Winter Evenings. London: 1819-20. V. 39

HACKENBROCH, YVONNE

Chelsea and Other English Porcelain, Pottery and Enamel. London: 1957. V. 46

Chelsea and Other English Porcelain Pottery and Enamel in the Irwin Untermyer Collection. Cambridge: 1957. V. 37

English Furniture with Some Furniture of Other Countries in the Irwin Untermeyer Collection. Cambridge: 1958. V. 37

Meissen and Other Continental Porcelain Faience and Enamel . . . Cambridge: 1956. V. 37; 42

Renaissance Jewellery. London: 1979. V. 42

HACKER, LILLIAN PRICE

Susan. London: 1912. V. 46

HACKET, CHARLES WILSON

Revolt of the Pueblo Indians of New Mexico and Otermin's Attempted Reconquest 1680-1682. Albuquerque: 1942. V. 39

HACKET, JOHN

Loiola. Scena est Amsterodami: a Vespera ad Vesperam Peraguntur Omnia. Londini: 1648. V. 40

Scrinia Reserata: a Memorial Offer'd to the Great Deservings of John Williams, D.D. Who Some Time Held the Places of Ld Keeper of the Great Seal of England, Ld Bishop of Lincoln, and Ld Archbishop of York. In the Savoy: 1693. V. 38

HACKETT, A. V.

Catalogue of Books and Bound Mss. of the Irish Historical, Arch. and Antiq. Library of Francis Joseph Bigger. Belfast: 1930. V. 43

HACKETT, CHARLES WILSON

Revolt of the Pueblo Indians of New Mexico and Otermin's Attempted Reconquest 1680-1682. Albuquerque: 1942. V. 43; 45

HACKETT, FRANK W.

Memoir of William H. Y. Hackett. Portsmouth: 1879. V. 44

HACKETT, JAMES

Narrative of the Expedition Which Sailed from England in 1817 to Join the South America Patriots . . . London: 1818. V. 39

HACKETT, JOHN

Select and Remarkable Epigraphs on Illustrious and Other Persons, in Several Parts of Europe. London: 1757. V. 37; 39; 43; 46

HACKLE, PALMER

Hints on Angling . . . In France and Belgium . . . English, Scottish, and Irish Waters. London: 1846. V. 37

HACKLEY, RICHARD S.

Petition and Protest of . . . A Citizen of the United States, Owner of Certain Lands in Florida. Baltimore: 1842. V. 41

HACKLEY, WOODFORD B.

The Little Fork Rangers. Richmond: 1927. V. 46

HACKMAN, JAMES

The Distracted Lover, a Poem . . . London: 1779. V. 44

HACKNEY FURNISHING CO.

Some Beautiful Furniture. London: 1910. V. 44

HACKNEY, JOHN

No Want of Meat, Sir! London. V. 40

HACKNEY, LOUIS WALLACE

A Study of Chinese Paintings in the Collection of Ada Small Moore. London: 1940. V. 38; 41

HACKSTAFF, G. H.

New Guide Book of Niagara Falls from Strangers. Niagara Falls: 1851. V. 37

HADDEN, JAMES

A History of Uniontown, Pa. N.P.: 1913. V. 39; 41

A History of Uniontown, Pennsylvania. N.P.: 1913. V. 42

HADDEN, JAMES M.

Hadden's Journal and Orderly Books: a Journal Kept in Canada and Upon Burgoyne's Campaign in 1776 and 1777. Albany: 1884. V. 41

HADDINGTON, EARL OF

Poems. N.P.. V. 45

HADDINGTON, THOMAS HAMILTON, 6TH EARL OF

Forty Select Poems on Several Occasions. London: 1769. V. 37; 38; 42

Select Poems on Several Occasions. London: 1824. V. 37

HADDOCK, J. A.

Mr. Haddock's Narrative of His Hazardous and Exciting Voyage in the Balloon Atlantic, with Prof. Jno. LaMountain. Philadelphia: 1872. V. 43

HADDON, A. C.

Canoes of oceania. Honolulu: 1936-38. V. 39

Reports of the Cambridge Anthropological Expedition to Torres Straits. Cambridge: 1901-35. V. 40

HADDON, A. L.

What Ails the House? London: 1893. V. 41

THE HADDON Hall Library. London: 1899-1903. V. 46

HADDON, WALTER

Lucubrationes. London: 1567. V. 37; 44

HADELN, DETLEV VON

The Drawings of Antonio Canal Called Canaletto. London: 1929. V. 37; 40; 43

HADEN, SEYMOUR

About Etching. London: 1879. V. 38; 39; 42; 46

HADER, BERTA

The Friendly Phoebe. New York: 1953. V. 46

Jamaica Johnny. New York: 1935. V. 37

HADFIELD, JAMES

Attempt on the Life of the King. The Trial of James Hadfield, for High Treason . . . June 26 . . . London: 1800. V. 38

HADFIELD, JOHN

Elizabethan Love Songs. London: 1955. V. 44

Georgian Love Songs. Hertfordshire: 1949. V. 41

Georgian Love Songs. Hitchin: 1949. V. 40

Restoration Love Songs. Hitchin: 1950. V. 37

HADFIELD, WILLIAM

Brazil, the River Plate, and the Falkland Islands. London: 1854. V. 37; 38; 41

Brazil and the River Plate in 1868. London: 1869. V. 40; 41; 42

HADIDI, ADNAN

Studies in the History and Archaeology of Jordan. Amman: 1985. V. 40; 42

HADLAM, CECIL

Oxford and Its Story. London: 1904. V. 41

HADLEY, GEORGE

Introductory Grammatical Remarks on the Persian Language. Bath: 1776. V. 42; 46

HAEBLER, KONRAD

The Early Printers of Spain and Portugal. London: 1897. V. 37; 45

Der Italienische Wiegendruck in Original Typenbeispielen. Munich: 1927. V. 38

West-European Incunabula. 60 Original Leaves from the Presses of the Netherlands, France, Iberia and Great Britain. Munich: 1928. V. 45

Der West-Europaeische Wiegendruck in Original Typenbeispielen. Munich: 1928. V. 38

HAECKEL, ERNST

Arabische Korallen. Berlin: 1876. V. 40

Kunstformen der Natur. Leipzig: 1904. V. 40

Wanderbilder. Nach Eigenen Aquarellen und Oelgemaelden. Die Naturwunder der Tropenwelt. Ceylon und Insulinde. Gera: 1905-06. V. 40

HAEGDOORN, C. W.

Eyquan, of Groote Mogol. Amsterdam: 1671. V. 46

HAENSEL, JOHN GOTTFRIED

Letters on the Nicobar Islands, Their Natural Productions and the Manners, Customs and Superstitions of the Natives . . . London: 1812. V. 45

HAESAERTS, PAUL

Ensor. London: 1957. V. 44; 46

Ensor: James Ensor. New York: 1959. V. 39; 43; 44; 45

HAFEN, LEROY R.

Handcarts to Zion, 1856-1860. Glendale: 1960. V. 46

The Overland Mail 1849-1869. Cleveland: 1926. V. 40; 43; 44; 46

The Overland Mail 1849-1869 Promoter of Settlement Percursor of Railroads. Cleveland: 1926. V. 46

Overland Routes to the Gold Fields, 1859. Glendale: 1942. V. 40

Pike's Gold Rush Guide Books of 1859. Glendale: 1941. V. 40; 45

HAFEN, LEROY REUBEN

Broken Hand - The Life Story of Thomas Fitzpatrick. Denver: 1931. V. 38; 39; 42; 43; 45; 46

Broken Hand. The Life of Thomas Fitzpatrick: Mountain Men, Guide and Indian Agent. Denver: 1973. V. 37; 44

Colorado and Its People, a Narrative and Topical History of the Centennial State. New York: 1948. V. 37; 38; 39; 46

The Far West and the Rockies 1820-1875. Glendale: 1954-61. V. 39; 46

The Far West and the Rockies, 1820-1875. Glendale: 1954-62. V. 40

Fort Laramie and the Pageant of the West, 1834-1890. Glendale: 1938. V. 39; 43; 44

The Life of Thomas Fitzpatrick: Mountain Man, Guide and Indian Agent. Denve: 1973. V. 39

HAFEN, LEROY REUBEN continued

The Mountain Men and the Fur Trade of the Far West. Glendale: 1965-1972. V. 39; 40; 42; 43

The Overland Mail 1849-1869. Cleveland: 1926. V. 38; 39; 40; 43; 45; 46

HAFEN, MARY ANN

Recollections of a Handcart Pionner of 1860. Denver: 1938. V. 37; 39; 40; 42; 45

HAFERKORN, HENRY E.

The War With Mexico, 1848-1848. Washington: 1914. V. 46

HAFIZ, 14th Century

Odes from the Divan of Hafiz, Freely Rendered from Literal Translations. New York: 1903. V. 39

HAFIZ, SHEMS-ED-DIN MUHAMMED

A Specimen of Persian Poetry . . . London: 1774. V. 41

HAFTMANN, WERNER

Emil Nolde. New York: 1959. V. 43; 46

Emil Nolde: Unpainted Pictures. New York & Washington: 1965. V. 40

Marino Marini. New York: 1968. V. 45

Painting in the Twentieth Century. New York: 1960. V. 39

HAGAN, VICTOR W. VON

The Aztec and Maya Papermakers. New York: 1944. V. 37

HAGEDORN, HERMAN

Roosevelt in the Badlands. Boston: 1921. V. 42

HAGEDORN, HERMANN

Theodore Roosevelt. New York: 1919. V. 46

HAGEMAN, JOHN F.

History of Princeton and Its Institutions. Philadelphia: 1879. V. 38; 41; 46

HAGEN, J. L. VON

Disputatio Theologica De Triplica Coena: Calvinistica, Lutherana, Catholica, Moguntiae Proposita . . . Mayence: 1608. V. 37

HAGEN, VICTOR WOLFGANG

The Aztec and Maya Papermakers. New York: 1944. V. 38

HAGENBECK, CARL

Beasts and Men: Being Carl Hagenbeck's Experiences for Half a Century Among Wild Animals. New York: 1909. V. 46

HAGER, GIUSEPPE

An Explanation of the Elementary Characters of the Chinese, with an Analysis of Their Ancient Symbols and Hieroglyphics. London: 1801. V. 41

HAGER, JOSEPH

The Elementary Characters of the Chinese. London: 1801. V. 46

Monument de Yu. Paris: 1802. V. 45

HAGERTY, FRANK H.

1889. The State of South Dakota: The Statistical, Historical and Political Abstract. Agricultural, Mineral, Commercial, Manufacturing, Educational, Social and General Statements. Aberdeen: 1889. V. 39

A Dictionary of Dakota, Conveniently Arranging a Multitude of Facts About the Resources and Capabilities of the Great Territory Soon to Become Two States. Aberdeen: 1888. V. 40

HAGGADAH

The Haggadah. Jerusalem: 1956. V. 39

HAGGARD, ELLA

Life and Its Author. An Essay in Verse. London: 1890. V. 41

HAGGARD, HENRY RIDER 1856-1925

The After-War Settlement & Employment of Ex-Service Men in the Oversea Dominions. London: 1916. V. 43

Allan Quartermain. London: 1887. V. 38; 39; 40; 41; 42

Allan the Hunter. 1898. V. 37; 39; 43

Allan's Wife, and Other Tales. London: 1889. V. 40

Ayesha. The Return of She. London: 1905. V. 37; 41

Belshazzar. 1930. V. 43

Benita. London: 1906. V. 41

Black Heart and White Heart. London: 1900. V. 39; 41

The Brethren. London: 1904. V. 40; 41

Cetawayo and His White Neighbours. London: 1882. V. 37; 38; 39; 40; 41; 42; 43; 44; 46

Child of Storm. London: 1913. V. 41; 42

Cleopatra. London: 1889. V. 38; 40; 42; 46

Colonel Quaritch, V. C. London: 1888. V. 37; 38; 39; 40; 46

Colonel Quaritch, V.C. Toronto: 1888. V. 39

The Days of My Life: an Autobiography. London: 1926. V. 43; 46

Doctor Therne. London: 1898. V. 39

Fair Margaret. London: 1907. V. 41

A Farmer's Year, Being His Commonplace Book for 1898. London: 1899. V. 39

The Holy Flower. London: 1915. V. 41; 42

The Ivory Child. London: 1916. V. 39; 41

Jess. London: 1887. V. 42

Joan Haste. London: 1895. V. 39

Joan Haste. London: New York: 1895. V. 41; 42

King Solomon's Mines. 1970. V. 37

The Lady of Blossholme. London: 1909. V. 41; 42

The Last Boer War. London: 1899. V. 45

Love Eternal. 1918. V. 43

Lysbeth. 1901. V. 44

Lysbeth. London: 1901. V. 40; 41

The Mahatma and the Hare. London: 1911. V. 39; 41

Maiwa's Revenge. London: 1888. V. 39; 40; 45

Marie. London: 1912. V. 41

Mr. Meeson's Will. 1888. V. 43; 45

Mr. Meeson's Will. London: 1888. V. 39; 45

Montezuma's Daughter. London: 1893. V. 40

Moon of Israel. London: 1918. V. 41

Morning Star. London: 1910. V. 41

Nada the Lily. London: 1982. V. 39

Pearl Maiden. London: 1903. V. 41

The People of the Mist. London: 1894. V. 39

The Poor and the Land. London & New York: 1905. V. 41; 42

Queen Sheba's Ring. London: 1910. V. 41

Queen of the Dawn - a Love Tale of Old Egypt. London: 1925. V. 40

Red Eve. London: 1911. V. 41

Regeneration. London: 1910. V. 43

Report on the Salvation Army Colonies in the United States and at Hadleigh, England, with Scheme of National Land Settlement. London: 1905. V. 45

Rural England Being an Account of Agricultural and Social Researches Carried Out in the Years 1901 and 1902. London: 1902. V. 41

She. 1887. V. 37; 39; 43

She. London: 1887. V. 37; 39; 41; 42; 44

She and Allan. London: 1921. V. 41

Stella Fregelius. London: 1904. V. 41

Swallow. A Tale of the Great Trek. London: 1899. V. 39

The Wanderer's Necklace. London: 1914. V. 41

When the World Shook. London: 1919. V. 41

The Witch's Head. London: 1885. V. 38

The Wizard. Bristol: 1896. V. 39

The Wizard. London: Bombay: 1896. V. 41; 42

The Wizard. New York: 1896. V. 41

The Works. New York: 1909. V. 42

HAGGARD, LILIAS RIDER

I Walked By Night. London: 1981. V. 45

HAGGART, DAVID

The Life of David Haggart, Alias John Wilson, Alias John Morison, Alias Barney M'Coul, Alias John M'Colgan, Alias Daniel O'Brien, Alias The Switcher. Edinburgh: 1821. V. 38

HAGHE, LOUIS

Haghe's Portfolio of Sketches. Belgium, Germany. London: 1850. V. 46

HAGOOD, JOHNSON

Memoirs of the War of Secession. New York: 1894. V. 42

Memoirs of the War of Secession, from the Original Manuscripts of Johnson Hapgood, Brigadier-General, C.S.A. Columbia: 1910. V. 43

The Services of Supply: a Memoir of the Great War. Boston: 1927. V. 44

HAGREEN, PHILIP

The Artist and His Work. Milford: 1975. V. 37

The Bookplates of Philip Hagreen. 1982. V. 41

The Bookplates of Philip Hagreen. Nappanee: 1982. V. 44

HAGUE, ARNOLD

Atlas . . . Geology of the Yellowstone National Park. Washington: 1904. V. 38; 40

HAGUE, ELEANOR

Latin American Music. Santa Ana: 1934. V. 43

HAHN, EMILY

Seductio Ad Absurdum. The Principles and Practices of Seduction. New York: 1930. V. 40

HAHN-HAHN, IDA, COUNTESS

Letters of a German Countess, Written During Her Travels in Turkey, Egypt, the Holy Land, Syria, Nubia, etc. in 1843-44. London: 1845. V. 41; 45

HAHNEMANN, SAMUEL 1755-1843

Apothekerlexikon. Leipzig: 1793-99. V. 42

The Chronic Diseases: Their Specific Nature and Homeopathic Treatment . . . New York: 1845-46. V. 45

The Lesser Writings of Samuel Hahnemann. New York: 1852. V. 38; 42

Organon of Homoeopathic Medicine. New York: 1843. V. 40; 44

Organon of Homoeopathic Medicine. New York: 1849. V. 42

Organon of Medicine. London: 1849. V. 37

HAIG-BROWN, RODERICK

Come Wade the River. The Photography of Ralph Wahl with Excerpts from 'A River Never Sleeps'. Seattle: 1971. V. 37

The Living Land: An Account of the Natural Resources of British Columbia. Toronto: 1961. V. 37

Panther. London: 1946. V. 44

The Salmon. Ottawa: 1974. V. 37

HAIG-BROWN, RODERICK L.

Alison's Fishing Birds. Vancouver: 1980. V. 39

Ki-Yu. A Story of Panthers. Boston: 1934. V. 39

A Primer of Fly Fishing. Toronto: 1964. V. 42

Return to the River; a Story of the Chinook Run. New York: 1941. V. 39

A River Never Sleeps. Toronto: 1946. V. 42

Silver, the Life Story of an Atlantic Salmon. London: 1931. V. 39

The Western Angler. New York: 1939. V. 39; 44

HAIG, DOUGLAS

Sir Douglas Haig's Desptaches (December 1915-April 1919). London: 1919. V. 38

The Western Front. London: 1917. V. 40

The Western Front. New York: 1917. V. 39

HAIGH, A. E.

The Attic Theatre. London: 1889. V. 40

HAIGH, JAMES

The Dier's Assistant in . . . the Art of Dying Wool and Woolen Goods . . . New York: 1813. V. 44

HAIGH, SAMUEL

Sketches of Buenos Ayres and Chile. London: 1829. V. 38

HAIGH, WALTER E.

A New Glossary of the Dialect of the Huddersfield District. 1928. V. 37

HAIGHT, SARAH R.

Letters of the Old World, by a Lady of New York. New York: 1840. V. 39

HAILE, BERARD

Emergence Myth. Santa Fe: 1949. V. 39

An Ethnological Dictionary of the Navaho Language. St. Michaels: 1910. V. 37

Learning Navaho. St. Michael's: 1941. V. 42

A Manual of Navaho Grammar. St. Michaels: 1926. V. 37

HAILES, DAVID DALRYMPLE, LORD 1726-1792

Ancient Scottish Poems. Edinburgh: 1770. V. 38

Annals of Scotland, From the Accession of Malcolm III . . . to the Accession of the House of Stewart . . . Edinburgh: 1819. V. 40

A Catalogue of the Lords of Sessions, from the Institution of the College of Justice, in the Year 1532. Edinburgh: 1767. V. 37

Memorials and Letters Relating to the History of Britain, in the Reign of James I. Glasgow: 1762. V. 40

Memorials and Letters Relating to the History of Britain in the Reign of James the First. London: 1762. V. 39

Tracts Relative to the History and Antiquities of Scotland. Edinburgh: 1800. V. 40

HAILES, W. L.

War Service of the 9th Jut Regiment. London: 1938. V. 46

HAILEY, CLARENCE

Stallions (Illustrated). London: 1910. V. 37; 42

HAILEY, JOHN

The History of Idaho. Boise: 1910. V. 38

HAILEY, WILLIAM MALCOLM HAILEY, BARON 1872-

An African Survey. A Study of Problems Arising in Africa South of the Sahara. 1938. V. 39

HAIMAN, GYORGY

Nicholas Kis, a Hungarian Punch-Cutter and Printer, 1602-1702. San Francisco: 1983. V. 44

HAINES, ALICE CAHOUN

Girls and Boys. New York: 1905. V. 37; 41

HAINES, ALICE CALHOUN

Boys. New York: 1905. V. 41

HAINES, CHARLES G.

An Appeal to the People of the State of New York on the Expediency of Abolishing the Councl of Appointment. New York: 1819. V. 41

Considerations on the Great Western Canal, from the Hudson to Lake Erie: with a View of Its Expense, Advantages and Progress. Brooklyn: 1818. V. 39

Public Documents, Relating to the New York Canals, Which Are to Connect the Western and Northern Lakes, with the Atlantic Ocean. New York: 1821. V. 38

HAINES, CHARLES R.

A Complete Memoir of Richard Haines (1633-85), a forgotten Sussex Worthy with a full account of his ancestry and posterity. London: 1899. V. 37

HAINES, ELIJAH M.

The American Indian. Chicago. V. 38

HAINES, FLORA E.

A Keramic Study. A Chapter in the History of Half a Dozen Dinner Plates. Bangor: 1895. V. 38

HAINES, FRANCIS

The Nez Perces Tribesmen of the Columbia Plateau. Norman: 1955. V. 42

HAINES, HERBERT

A Manual of Monumental Brasses. Oxford: 1861. V. 42; 44

A Manual of Monumental Brasses . . . Oxford & London: 1861. V. 39; 45

HAINES, JENNIE DAY

Weather Opinions: a Book of Quotations with Interleaves on Weather Subjects. San Francisco: 1907. V. 42

HAINES, MARY R.

Clovercroft Chronicles 1314-11893. Philadelphia: 1893. V. 46

HAINES, RICHARD

A Method of Government for Such Publick Working Alms-House as May Be Erected in Every Country for Bringing All Idle Hands to Industry. London: 1679. V. 45

Proposals for Building in Every County a Working-Alms-House or Hospital . . . London: 1677. V. 41

HAINES, WILLIAM P.

History of the Men of Co. F. with Description of the Marches and Battles of the 12th New Jersey Vols. Mickleton: 1897. V. 44

HAINES, ZENAS T.

Letters from the Forty-Fourth Regiment, N.V.M. Boston: 1863. V. 38; 43

HAINING, PETER

Movable Books, an Illustrated History. London: 1979. V. 41; 45

HAIR, T. H.

A Series of Views of the Collieries in the Counties of Northumberland and Durham, by T. H. Hair. London: 1844. V. 46

HAKE, ALFRED EGMONT

The New Dance of Death. London: 1884. V. 38

HAKE, LUCY

Something New on Men and Manners . . . Hallsham: 1828. V. 42; 45

HAKE, THOMAS GORDON

Parables and Tales. London: 1872. V. 37; 44

HAKEWEIL, GEORGE

An Answere to a Treatise Written by Dr. Carter. London: 1616. V. 46

HAKEWEL, W. 1574-1655

Modus Tenendi Parliamentum: or, the Old Manner of Holding Parliaments in England. London: 1671. V. 39; 40; 44

HAKEWIL, WILLIAM

The Manner How Statutes are Enacted in Parliament by Passing of Bills. London: 1641. V. 45

HAKEWILL, GEORGE

An Apologie or Declaration of the Power and Providence of God in the Government of the World. London: 1635. V. 39

An Apologie or Declaration of the Power and Providence of God in the Government of the World. Oxford: 1635. V. 40

HAKEWILL, JAMES

The History of Windsor and Its Neighbourhood. London: 1813. V. 39

A Picturesque Tour of Italy from Drawings Made in 1816-17. London: 1820. V. 38

A Series of Views of the Neighborhood of Windsor, Including the Seats of Several of the Nobility and Gentry. London: 1829. V. 37; 40

HAKEWILL, WILLIAM

The Libertie of the Subject; Against the Pretended Power of Impositions. London: 1641. V. 43

The Order and Course of Passing Bills in Parliament. London: 1641. V. 38; 45

HAKLUYT, RICHARD 1552-1616

Collection of the Early Voyages, Travels and Discoveries of the English nation. London: 1809-12. V. 37; 38; 41

Hakluyt's Collection of the Early Voyages, Travels, and Discoveries of the English Nation. New Edition with Additions. London: 1809-12. V. 37

The Principal Navigations, Voiages, Traffiques and Discoveries of the English nationa, Made by Sea or Over-land, to the Remote and Farthest Distant Corners of the Earth, at Any Time Within the Compasse of These 1500 Yeeres . . . Imprinted at London: 1598. V. 45

The Principal Navigations, Voiages, Traffiques and Discoveries of the English Language. London: 1598-1600. V. 37; 38; 40; 42; 45

The Principal Navigations, Voyages, Traffiques and Discoveries of the English Nation, Made by Sea or Overland to the Remote and Farthest Distant Quarters of the Earth . . . London: 1599. V. 39

The Principal Navigations, Voyages, Traffiques, and Discoveries of the English Nation . . . London: 1809-12. V. 42; 43

The Principal Navigations Voyages Traffiques & Discoveries of the English Nation. Glasgow: 1903. V. 38; 41; 42; 46

The Principal Navigations Voyages Traffiques & Discoveries of the English Nation Made by Sea or Over-land to the Remote and Farthest Distant Quarters of the Earth at Any Time Within the Compasse of These 1600 Yeeres. Glasgow: 1903-04. V. 46

The Principal Navigations, Voyages, Traffiques and Discoveries of the English Nation . . . London: 1927. V. 37; 42

The Principal Navigations, Voyages, Traffiques and Discoveries of the English Nation . . . London: 1927-28. V. 39

The Principall Navigations, Voiages and Discoveries of the English Nation. Cambridge: 1965. V. 39

The Principall Navigations. London: 1965. V. 42

The Principal Navi-gations, Voyages, Traffiques and Discove-ries . . . These 1600 Yeres . . . Worth Discoveries. London: 1599-1600. V. 38

The Principall navigations, Voyages, Traffiques and Discoveries of the English Nation. Glasgow: 1903-05. V. 38

The Principall Navigations, Voiages and Discoveries of the English Nation Made by Sea or Over Land . . . London: 1589. V. 41

The Principall Navigations, Voiages and Discoveries of the English Nation. Cambridge: 1965. V. 44

HALASZ, GYULA

Camera in Paris. London: 1949. V. 41

HALBERT, HENRY S.

The Creek War of 1813 and 1814. Chicago: 1895. V. 42; 45

HALDANE, AYLMER

How We Escaped from Pretoria. London: 1901. V. 39

HALDANE, JOHN

The Players Scourge, or a Detection of the Horrid Prophanity and Impiety of Stage-Plays and Their Wicked Supporters. Edinburgh: 1757. V. 43

HALDANE, JOHN SCOTT

Respiration. New Haven: 1922. V. 38; 42

HALE, ALBERT

Old Newburyport Houses. Boston: 1912. V. 41; 44

HALE, EDWARD EVERETT

The Fortunes of Rachel. New York: & London: 1884. V. 46

Kansas & Nebraska: The History, Geographical and Physical Characteristics and Political Position of Those Territories. Boston: 1854. V. 40; 41; 45

Kansas and Nebraska: The History, Geographical and Physical Characteristics, an Political Postion of those Territories; and Account of the Emigrants Aid Companies, and Directions to Emigrants. With an Original Map from the Latest Authorities. Boston/New York: 1854. V. 37; 41

The Man Without a Country. New York: 1940. V. 40

The Man Without a Country. Boston: 1856. V. 37

The Man Without a Country. Boston: 1865. V. 37

The Man Without a Country. New York: 1902. V. 37; 41; 44

Philip Nolan's Friends. New York: 1877. V. 40

Silhouettes and Songs, Illustrative of the Months. Boston: 1876. V. 37; 43

Six of One Half a Dozen of the Other. Boston: 1872. V. 46

A Tract for the Day, How to Conquer Texas, Before Texas Conquers Us. Boston: 1845. V. 43

HALE, EDWIN M.

A Systematic Treatise on Abortion. Chicago: 1866. V. 38

HALE, EDWIN MOSES

A Systematic Treatise on Abortion. Chicago: 1806. V. 42

HALE, ENOCH

History and Description of an Epidemic Fever, Commonly Called Spotted Fever, Which Prevailed at Gardiner, Maine in the Spring o 1814. Boston: 1818. V. 46

A Spelling Book; or the First Part of a Grammar of the English Language as Written and Spoken in the United States. Northampton: 1799. V. 41

HALE, HORATIO

An International Idiom. London: 1890. V. 44

An International Idiom. A Manual of the Oregon Trade Language or 'Chinook Jargon'. London: 1893. V. 43

The Iroquois Book of Rites. Philadelphia: 1883. V. 39

HALE, J. H.

How to Tie Salmon Flies. London: 1892. V. 37; 39

How to Tie Salmon Flies. London: 1930. V. 40; 43

HALE, JOHN

California as It Is. San Francisco: 1954. V. 46

A Compendious or Briefe Examination of Certayne Ordinary Complaints of Diuers of Our Countrymen in These Dayes . . . London: 1751. V. 41

HALE, JOHN PETER

Trans-Allegheny Pioneers. Historical Sketches of the First White Settlements West of the Alleghenies 1748 & After. Cincinnati: 1886. V. 37; 38; 39; 43; 46

HALE, KATHLEEN

Orlando (the Marmalade Cat) Keeps a Dog. London: 1949. V. 46

Orlando (The Marmalade Cat) A Seaside Holiday. London: 1952. V. 46

HALE, LINDA

Vancouver Centennial Bibliography. Vancouver: 1986. V. 43

HALE, LUCRETIA P.

The Last of the Peterkins, with Others of Their Kin. Boston: 1886. V. 43

The Peterkin Papers. Boston: 1880. V. 43

HALE, MATTHEW 1609-1676

The Analysis of the Law. (with) The History of the Common Law of England. London: 1713. V. 38; 45

The Analysis of the Law. London: 1716. V. 40

The Analysis of the Law. London: 1739. V. 37

Collection of Modern Relations of Matter of Fact Concerning Witches and Witchcraft . . . London: 1693. V. 46

Difficiles Nugae: or, Observations Touching the Torricellian Experiment and the Various Solutions of the Same, Especially Touching the Weight and Elasticity of Air. London: 1674. V. 39

A Discourse of the Knowledge of Gold, and of Out Selves. London: 1688. V. 40

Pleas of the Crown. London: 1682. V. 38

The Primitive Origination of Mankind, Considered and Examined According to the Light of Nature. London: 1677. V. 39; 43

HALE, NATHANIEL C.

Roots in Virginia: an Account of Thomas Hale, Virginia Frontiersman. Philadelphia: 1948. V. 42

HALE, PHILIP L.

Vermeer. Boston: 1937. V. 44; 45

HALE, SARAH J. 1788-1879

The Genius of Oblivion and Other Original Poems . . . Concord: 1823. V. 37; 40; 44

The Ladies' Wreath: a Selection from the Female Poetic Writers of England and America. Boston: 1837. V. 44

Manners or Happy Homes and Good Society All the Year Round. Boston: 1868. V. 45

Mary's Lamb. Worcester: 1937. V. 38

Northwood: a Tale of New England. Boston: 1827. V. 44

Northwood; or, Life North and South: Showing the True Character of Both. New York: 1852. V. 45

HALE-WHITE, W.

Bacon, Gilbert and Harvey . . . Harveian Oration. London: 1927. V. 45; 46

HALE, WILLIAM

Howard Blackburn: Hero and Fisherman . . . Gloucester: 1895. V. 41

HALEN, DON JUAN VAN

Narrative of Don Juan van Halen's Imprisonment in the Dungeons of the Inquisition at Madrid, and His Escape in 1817 and 1818. London: 1827. V. 37; 38; 41; 42

HALEOLE, S. N.

Ke Kaao Laieikawai: Ka Hiwahiwa o Oaliuli, Kawahneokaliula . . . Honolulu: 1863. V. 39; 44

HALES, CHARLES

The Theory of electic repulsion examined, in a series of experiments on certain properties attributable to the elements which constitute electric excitation, adduced principally to show the non-existence of . . . London: (1837). V. 37

HALES, J. H. M.

The Astrologer; or the Eve of San Sebastian. London: 1820. V. 45

HALES, JOHN

A Compendious or Briefe Examination of Certayne Ordinary Complaints of Diuers of Our Countrymen in These Our Dayes. London: 1751. V. 45

Golden Remains of the Ever Memorable Mr. Iohn Hales of Eton College . . . London: 1659. V. 38; 43

Golden Remains, of the Ever Memorable, Mr. John Hales . . . London: 1673. V. 37; 39; 46

Golden Remains of . . . London: 1688. V. 38

The Works of the Ever Memorable Mr. John Hales of Eaton. Glasgow: 1765. V. 42; 44

HALES, STEPHEN

Philosophical Experiments. London: 1739. V. 37; 39; 40; 42; 46

Some Considerations on the Causes of Earthquakes Which Were Read Before the Royal Society, April 5, 1750. London: 1750. V. 42

Statical Essays: Containing Vegetable Staticks: or, an Account of Some Statical Experiments on the Sap of Vegetables . . . (with) *Statical Essays: Containing Haemastaticks* . . . London: 1731, 1733. V. 39

Statical Essays: Containing Vegetable Staticks . . . London: 1731-33. V. 43

Statical Essays. London: 1738-40. V. 38

Statical Essays. London: 1740. V. 40

Statical Essays: Containing Vegetable Statics . . . . London: 1769. V. 39; 42

La Statique des Vegetaux, et l'Analyse de l'Air. Paris: 1735. V. 43

Vegetable Staticks. London: 1727. V. 39; 40

HALES, WILLIAM

Analysis Fluxionum. (with) Corrigenda et addenda ad Analysin Fluxionum. London: 1800. V. 43

Irish Pursuits of Literature in A.D. 1798 and 1799. Dublin: 1799. V. 41

HALEVY, LUDOVIC

The Cardinal Family. London: 1901. V. 42

Karikari. Paris: 1888. V. 40

HALEY, ALEX

The Autobiography of Malcolm X. New York: (1965). V. 37

Roots. Garden City: 1976. V. 41

Roots. Garden City: 1976. V. 37; 39; 40; 41; 43; 46

Roots. New York: 1976. V. 38; 39; 41

HALEY, JAMES EVETTS 1901-

The Alamo Mission Bell. Austin: 1974. V. 37; 38; 41; 42

Charles Goodnight, Cowman and Plainsman. Boston: 1936. V. 43

Charles Goodnight, Cowman & Plainsman. Boston & New York: 1936. V. 37; 38; 46

Charles Goodnight Cowman and Plainsman. Cambridge: 1936. V. 46

Charles Goodnight. Norman: 1936. V. 39

Charles Goodnight: Cowman and Plainsman. Boston: 1938. V. 42

Charles Schreiner, General Merchandise, the Story of a Country Store. Illustrations by H.D. Bugbee. Austin: 1944. V. 37; 38; 42; 44; 45; 46

A Day with Dan Casement. Canyon: 1939

Earl Vandale on the Trail of Texas Books. Canyon: 1965. V. 42; 45

The Flamboyant Judge: James D. Hamlin. Canyon: 1972. V. 37

Fort Concho and the Texas Frontier. El Paso: 1952. V. 42

Fort Concho and the Texas Frontier. San Angelo: 1952. V. 37; 38; 39; 40; 42; 44

George W. Littlefield: Texan. Norman: 1943. V. 37; 41; 45

Heraldry of the Range. Some Southwestern Brands. Canyon: 1949. V. 39; 44; 45

Jeff Milton a Good Man with a Gun. Norman: 1948. V. 39; 41; 42

Life on the Texas Range. Austin: 1952. V. 42

A Log of the Montana Trail - as Kept by Ealy Moore. N.P.: 1932. V. 37

Men of Fiber. El Paso: 1963. V. 37; 38

Ode to Nita. Canyon: 1959. V. 44

Robbing Banks Was My Business . . . Canyon: 1973. V. 42

Rough Times - Tough Fiber: a Fragmentary Family Chronicle. Canyon: 1976. V. 42

Some Southwestern Trails. El Paso: 1948. V. 39; 44; 45

The XIT Ranch of Texas and the Early Days of the Llano Estacado. Chicago: 1929. V. 37; 38; 39; 42; 43; 45; 46

HALEY, JAMES L.

Most Excellent Sir. Letters Received by Sam Houston, President of the Republic of Texas, Columbia 1836-1837. 1987. V. 45

HALEY, WILLIAM

Epistle to a Friend on the Death of John Thornton, Esq . . . London: 1780. V. 38

A Philosophical, Historical and Moral Essay on Old Maids by a Friend to the Sisterhood. Dublin: 1786. V. 38

The Triumphs of Temper. Chinchester: 1803. V. 37

HALF Hours in the Wide West: Over Mountains, Rivers and Prairies. London: 1878. V. 38

HALFER, JOSEF

The Progress of the Marbling Art From Technical Scientific Principles with a Supplement on the Decoration of Book Edges. Buffalo: 1893. V. 42

HALFORD, FREDERIC M.

An Angler's Autobiography. London: 1903. V. 39

Dry-Fly Fishing in Theory and Practice. London: 1889. V. 40; 43

Dry Fly Entomology. London: 1897. V. 39

The Dry-Fly Man's Handbook. London: 1913. V. 39

Dry Fly Entomology. London: 1902. V. 37; 40; 46

Floating Flies and How to Dress Them. London: 1886. V. 39; 46

Making a Fishery. London: 1895. V. 40; 43

Modern Development of the Dry Fly. London: 1910. V. 43

Modern Development of the Dry Fly. London: 1923. V. 43

HALFORD, HENRY

Essays and Orations, Read and Delivered at the Royal College of Physicians . . . London: 1831. V. 37; 43; 44

HALFPENNY, JOSEPH

Fragmenta Vetusta or the Remains of Ancient Buildings in York Drawn and Etched. York: 1807. V. 37

A Selection of Gothic Ornaments in the Cathedral Church of York . . . York: 1831. V. 37; 40

HALFPENNY, WILLIAM

The Art of Sound Building, Demonstrated in Geometrical Problems. London: 1725. V. 39

Chinese and Gothic Architecture. London: 1752. V. 46

The Country Gentleman's Pocket Companion and Builder's Assistant, for Rural Decorative Architecture. London: 1756. V. 37

Aa New and Compleat System of Architecture Delineated, In a Variety of Plans and Elevations of Designs for Convenient and Decorated Houses . . . London: 1749. V. 37; 39; 44; 46

Practical Architecture of a Sure Guide to the True Working According tot he Rules of that Science. London: 1724. V. 37; 42; 46

Rural Architecture in the Gothick Taste. London: 1752. V. 37; 46

Rural Architecture in the Chinese Taste . . . London: 1755. V. 39

Rural Architecture in the Gothick Taste . . . London: 1752. V. 37

Useful Architecture in Twenty-Five New Designs for Erecting Parsonage-Houses, Farm-Houses, and Inns. London: 1755. V. 37

HALHED, NATHANIEL B.

A Code of Gentoo Laws, or, Ordintions of the Pundits, from a Persian Translation. London: 1776. V. 38

HALHED, NATHANIEL BRASSEY

A Code of Gentoo Laws, or, Ordinations of the Pundists, from a Persian Translation. London: 1776. V. 38; 40

A Code of Gentoo Laws. London;: 1781. V. 39

A Code of Gentoo Laws, Or Ordinations of the Pundits. From a Persian Translation made from the Original, Written in the Shanscrit Language. London: 1781. V. 37; 39

Imitations of Some of the Epigrams of Martial. London: 1793-94. V. 46

Testimony of the Authenticity of the Prophecies of Richard Brothers, and of His Mission to Recall the Jews. London: 1795. V. 39

HALIBURTON, R. G.

The Effects of Our Commercial Policy on West Indian Labour. N.P.. V. 45

HALIBURTON, THOMAS CHANDLER 1796-1865

The Attache; or, Sam Slick in England. London: 1843. V. 41; 43

The Bubbles of Canada. London: 1839. V. 37; 41; 42

The Bubbles of Canada. London: 1829. V. 37

HALIBURTON, THOMAS CHANDLER 1796-1865 continued

The Clockmaker. New York: 1840. V. 44

The English in America. London: 1851. V. 38

An Historical and Statistical Account of Nova Scotia. Halifax: 1829. V. 39; 40

The Letter-Bag of the Great Western. Philadelphia: 1840. V. 39

The Letter Bag of the 'Great Western', or, Life in a Steamer . . . London: 1865. V. 42

Nature and Human Nature. London: 1855. V. 41

The Old Judge; or Life in a Colony. London: 1849. V. 41

Sam Slick's Wise Saws and Modern Instances; or What He Said, Did, or Invented. London: 1853. V. 41

Sam Slick's Wise Saws and Modern Instances; or, What He Said, Did or Invented. Philadelphia: 1953. V. 43

Yankee Notions, or, the American Joe Miller. London: 1839. V. 38

HALIBURTON, THOMAS CHARLES 1796-1865

The Old Judge; or, Life in a Colony. London: 1849. V. 38

HALIDAY, CHARLES

An Inquiry into the Excessive Use of Spirituous Liquors in Producing Crime, Disease and Poverty in Ireland . . . Dublin: 1830. V. 38

The Scandinavian Kingdom of Dublin. Dublin: 1882. V. 43

HALIFAX, CHARLES MONTAGU, 1ST EARL OF

The Works and Life of the Right Honourable . . . London: 1715. V. 38; 41; 42; 44

The Works and Life of the Right Honourable Charles, Late Earl of Halifax. London: 1715. V. 44

HALIFAX, GEORGE SAVILE, 1ST MARQUIS OF 1633-1695

A Character of King Charles the Second. London: 1750. V. 40

The Lady's New year's Gift or Advice to a Daughter. London: 1688. V. 46

Miscellanies Historical and Philological . . . London: 1703. V. 45

Miscellanies . . . London: 1704. V. 40; 42

Miscellanies . . . viz. I. Advice to a Daughter. II. Character of a Trimmer. . . . VI. A Rough Draught of a New Model at Sea. VII. Maxims of State, Uc. London: 1704. V. 45

Miscellanies. Viz. I. Advice to a Daughter. II. The Character of a Trimmer. III. The Anatomy of an Equivalent. IV. A Letter to a Dissenter. V. Cautions for Choice of Parliament Men. VI. A Rough Draught of a New Model at Sea. VII. Maxims of State . . . London: 1700. V. 37; 38

Some Cautions Offered to the Consideration of Those Who Are About to Chuse Members to Serve in the Ensuing Parliament. London: 1695. V. 42

HALIFAX, VISCOUNT

T. E. Lawrence - an Address. London: 1936. V. 45

HALIFAX, WILLIAM SAVILE, MARQUIS OF

The Character of a Trimmer. London: 1689. V. 38

HALKERSTON, PETER d. 1833

A Translation and Explanation of the Principal Terms and Phrases Used in Mr. Erskine's Institute of the Law of Scotland . . . Edinburgh: 1820. V. 40

HALKET, ANNA MURRAY, LADY

Meditations on the Twenty-Fifth Psalm. Also Meditations and Prayers Upon the First Week. Edinburgh: 1778. V. 46

HALKETT, JOHN

Historical Notes Respecting Indians of North America. London: 1825. V. 37; 38; 39; 40; 42; 45; 46

Statement Respecting the Earl of Selkirk's Settlement of Kildonan, Upon the Red River, in North America. London: 1817. V. 37; 38; 39; 40; 41; 42; 43

HALKETT, SAMUEL 1814-1871

Dictionary of Anonymous and Pseudonymous English Literature. London: 1926-1962. V. 38

Dictionary of Anonymous and Pseudonymous English Literature, 1926-1934. Edinburgh & London: 1926-34. V. 45

Dictionary of Anonymous and Pseudonymous English Literature. Edinburgh: 1926-62. V. 43

A Dictionary of Anonymous and Pseudonymous Publications in the English Language. London: 1980. V. 45

Dictionary of Anonymous and Pseudonymous English Literature. Edinburgh: 1926-32. V. 37

Dictionary of Anonymous and Pseudonymous English Literature. New York: 1971. V. 37

HALL, A. DANIEL

The Genus Tulipa. London: 1940. V. 37; 38; 39

HALL, A. J.

The Bushveld Igneous Complex of the Central Transvaal. Pretoria: 1932. V. 43

HALL, ADELAIDE S.

A Glossary of Important Symbols in Their Hebrew, Pagan and Christian Forms. Boston: 1912. V. 42

HALL, ALEXANDER

Universalism Against Itself . . . ST. Clairsville: 1846. V. 46

HALL, ALLEN

Observations on the Weather. Lincoln: 1788. V. 39

HALL, ANNA MARIA FIELDING 1800-1881

The Book of Royalty. London: 1939. V. 38; 39; 43

Chronicles of a School Room. Boston: 1830. V. 46

Lights and Shadows of Irish Life. London: 1838. V. 43

Midsummer Eve: a Fairy Tale of Love. London: 1848. V. 44

The Prince of the Fair Family. London: 1867. V. 38

Sketches of Irish Character. New York: 1829. V. 46

Stories of a Governess. London: 1852. V. 43; 44

The Whiteboy: a Story of Ireland, in 1822. London: 1845. V. 38; 40

HALL, ARTHUR VINE

Poems of a South African. London: 1931. V. 39; 46

Rainbow Houses for Boys and Girls Built by A. Vine Hall. London: 1923. V. 46

HALL, B. M.

The Life of Rev. John Clark . . . New York: 1856. V. 45

HALL, BASIL 1788-1844

Account of a Voyage of Discovery to the West Coast of Corea, and the Great Loo-Choo Island. London: 1818. V. 37; 38; 39; 42; 43; 44

Extracts from a Journal Written on the Coasts of Chili, Peru and Mexico in the Years 1820, 1821, 1822. Edinburgh: 1825. V. 38; 42

Extracts from a Journal Written on the Coasts of Chili, Peru and Mexico in the Years 1820, 1821, 1822. Edinburgh: 1824. V. 37; 41; 42; 43; 44; 45; 46

Forty Etchings, from Sketches Made with the Camera Lucida, in North America in 1827 and 1828. Edinburgh: 1829. V. 46

Forty Etchings, From Sketches Made with the Camera Lucida, in North America in 1827 and 1828. Edinburgh & London: 1829. V. 37; 38; 39; 43

Forty Etchings, from Sketches Made with the Camera Lucida, in North America, in 1827 and 1828. London: 1829. V. 37; 39; 41

Forty Etchings from Sketches Made with the Camera Lucida, in North America in 1827 and 1828. London: 1830. V. 42; 46

Forty Etchings, from Sketkches Made with the Camera Lucida, in North America, in 1827 and 1828. Edinburgh: 1830. V. 37; 42

Fragments of Voyages and Travels, Including Anecdotes of a Naval Life . . . Edinburgh: 1831. V. 41; 46

Fragments of Voyages and Travels, Including Anecdotes of a Naval Life, Chiefly for the Use of Young Persons. First (Second) Series. London: 1831-32. V. 38

Fragments of Voyages and Travels, Including Anecdotes of a Naval Life. Edinburgh & London: 1831-33. V. 39

Fragments of Voyages and Travels, Including Anecdotes of a Naval Life . . . Edinburgh: 1831-34. V. 42; 46

Fragments of Voyages and Travels, Including Anecdotes of a Naval Life. London: 1832-32. V. 41

The Great Polyglot Bibles. Including a Leaf from the Complutensian of Acala, 1514-17. San Francisco: 1966. V. 37; 38; 39; 40; 41; 42; 44; 46

Napoleon in Council, or the Opinions Delivered by Bonaparte in the Council of State. Edinburgh: 1837. V. 42

Patchwork. London: 1841. V. 39

Travels in North American, in the Years 1827 and 1828. Edinburgh: 1829. V. 38; 39; 40; 43; 46

Voyage to Corea and the Island of Loo-Choo. London: 1820. V. 37; 39

HALL, BAYNARD RUSH

The New Purchase; or, Seven and a Half Years in the Far West. New York: 1843. V. 39; 40; 42; 43; 45

HALL, BENJAMIN HOMER

A Collection of College Words and Customs. Cambridge: 1851. V. 41

HALL, CARROLL DOUGLAS

Bierce and the Poe Hoax. San Francisco: 1934. V. 37

Donner Miscellany. 41 Diaries and Documents. 1947. V. 38

Donner Miscellany: 41 Diaries and Documents. San Francisco: 1947. V. 37; 41; 46

Heraldry of New Helvetia . . . San Francisco: 1945. V. 39; 46

Journal of a Voyage from Boston to San Francisco in 1849. Redwood City, Calif.: 1933. V. 37

The Terry-Broderick Duel. San Francisco: 1939. V. 37; 42

HALL, CECIL GEORGINA CAROLINE

A Lady's Life on a Farm in Mainitoba. London: 1884. V. 46

HALL, CHARLES

Nukahiwa-English . . . English-Nukahiwa Vocabulary. Boston: 1848. V. 37

HALL, CHARLES B.

Military Records of General Officers of the Confederate States of America . . . New York: 1898. V. 42

HALL, CHARLES FRANCIS 1821-1871

Arctic Researches and Life Among the Esquimaux. New York: 1865. V. 37; 38; 39; 42; 43; 46

Arctic Researches and Life Among the Esquimaux. New York: 1866. V. 40; 42

Life with the Esquimaux, the Narrative of Capt. Hall of the Whaling Barque 'George Henry', from 29th May 1860 to 13th Sept. 1862. London: 1864. V. 46

Narrative of the North Polar Expedition: U.S. Ship Plaris, Captain Charles Francis Hall Commanding . . . Washington: 1876. V. 38; 45

Narrative of the Second Arctic Expedition Made by Charles F. Hall . . . Washington: 1879. V. 37; 38; 41; 42; 45

HALL, CHARLES HENRY

Memoirs of the Life of Andrew Hofer. London: 1820. V. 38

HALL, CHRISTOPHER NEWMAN

From Liverpool to St. Louis. London, New York: 1870. V. 42

HALL, DANIEL WESTON

Arctic Rovings; or the Adventures of a New Bedford Boy on Sea and Land. Boston: 1861. V. 41

HALL, DAVID

A Mite into the Treasury; or, Some Serious Remarks on the Solemn and Indispensable Duty of Duly Attending Assemblies for Divine Worship . . . Philadelphia: 1758. V. 43

HALL, DONALD

As the Eye Moves . . . a Sculpture by Henry Moore. New York. V. 39; 43; 46

Contemporary American Poetry. Harmondsworth: 1962. V. 45

Exile. Oxford: 1952. V. 39; 41

Exile. Swinford: 1952. V. 38; 45

Exile. Swinford, Eynsham: 1952. V. 41

Exile. The Newdigate Prize Poem, 1952. V. 37

Exiles and Marriages. New York: 1955. V. 39

The Fantasy Poets Number 4. Swinford: 1952. V. 38

To the Loud Wind and Other Poems. Cambridge: 1955. V. 37; 40

HALL, E. R.

Mammals of North America. 1971. V. 38

The Mammals of North America. New York: 1981. V. 37

HALL, E. RAYMOND

The Mammals of North America. New York: 1959. V. 40

HALL, EDWARD

Appleton's Hand Book of American Travel. New York: 1867. V. 39

HALL, EDWARD HEPPLE

The Great West: Travellers', Miners' and Emigrants' Guide and Hand-Book to the Western North-Western and Pacific States and Territories . . . New York: 1865. V. 37; 40; 41; 43

The Great West: Railroad, Steamboat and Stage Guide and Hand-book, for Travellers, Miners and Emigrants to the Western, Northwestern and Pacific States and Territories. New York: 1866. V. 40

The Great West: A Guide for Emigrants, Travellers, and Miners to the Western States and Territories of the American Union. London: 1870. V. 38; 41

HALL, EDWIN

An Examination of the Latest Defences of Dr. Hickok's Rational Psychology. New York: 1863. V. 39

HALL, ELIZA CALVERT

A Book of Hand-Woven Coverlets. Boston: 1912. V. 37

HALL, EMMA SWAN

Mendes I-II. Cairo: 1980-76. V. 40; 44

HALL, FAYRER

The Importance of the British Plantations in America to This Kingdom; With the State of Their Trade, and Methods for Improving It . . . London: 1731. V. 39

HALL, FITZEDWARD

Catalogue of the Valuable Library of . . . Albany: 1867. V. 39; 42

HALL, FRANCES

Narrative of the Capture and Providential Escape of Misses Frances and Almira Hall . . . N.P.: 1832. V. 37; 46

HALL, FRANCIS

Travels in Canada, and the United States, in 1816 and 1817. Boston: 1818. V. 39; 43; 44; 46

Travels in Canada and the United States in 1816 and 1817. London: 1819. V. 39; 43

HALL, FRANK

History of the State of Colorado. Chicago: 1889-95. V. 38; 39; 46

HALL, FREDERIC

The History of San Jose and Surroundings with Biographical Sketches of Early Settlers. San Francisco: 1871. V. 40

HALL, FREDERICK

Letters from the East and From the West. Washington: 1840. V. 39

HALL, FREDERICK G.

The Bank of Ireland, 1783-1946. Dublin: 1949. V. 46

HALL, FREDERICK GARRISON

Bookplates by . . . . Boston: 1905. V. 38; 43

HALL, GEORGE

The History of Chesterfield . . . Descriptive Accounts of Chatsworth, Hardwick and Bolsover Castle. Chesterfield & London: 1839. V. 37

HALL, GEORGE ELI

A Balloon Ascension At Midnight with Silhouettes by Gordon Ross. San Francisco: 1902. V. 38; 40

HALL, GERTRUDE

Poems of Paul Verlaine. Chicago: 1895. V. 46

HALL, H. R.

Babylonian and Assyrian Sculpture in the British Museum. Paris 7 Brussels: 1928. V. 40

Catalogue of Egyptian Scarabs, etc. in the British Museum. London: 1913. V. 44

Ur Excavations. London & New York: 1927-76. V. 42

HALL, HAL

Cinematographic Annual 1930. Volume One. Hollywood: 1930. V. 37

HALL, HARRISON

Hall's Distiller, Containing . . . Full and Particular Directions for Mashing and Distilling all Kinds of Grain, and Imitating Holland Gin and Irish Whisky . . . Philadelphia: 1813. V. 45

HALL, HENRY

Report on the Ship-Building Industry of the United States. Washington: 1884. V. 37; 40

The Tribune Book of Open-Air Sports. New York: 1887. V. 37; 38; 44

HALL, HERBERT BYNG

Highland Sports, and Highland Quarters. London: 1847. V. 45

HALL, J. K.

One Hundred Years of American Psychiatry. New York: 1944. V. 45

HALL, J. SPARKES

The Book of the Feet; a History of Boots and Shoes . . . New York: 1847. V. 41

The Book of the Feet, a History of Boots and Shoes, with Illustrations of the Fashions of the Egyptians, Hebrews, Persians, Greeks, and Romans, and the Prevailing Style throughout Europe During the Middle Ages down to the Present Period . . . London: 1846. V. 38

HALL, JAMES

Account of a Series of Experiments Shewing the Effects of Compression in Modifying the Action of Heat. 1805. V. 38

Eight Engravings of the Ruins Occasioned by the Great Fires in Edinburgh, on the 15th, 16th and 17th Novr. 1824. Edinburgh: 1825. V. 39; 44

Essay on the Origin, History and Principles of Gothic Architecture. London: 1813. V. 38

Essay on the Origin and Principles of Gothic Architecture. Edinburgh: 1797. V. 41

Faery Lands of the South Seas. New York & London: 1921. V. 41

Legends of the West. Philadelphia: 1833. V. 39

Letters from the West. London: 1828. V. 37; 40; 44

A Memoir of the Public Services of William Henry Harrison of Ohio. Philadelphia: 1836. V. 46

Notes on the Western States; Containing Descriptive Sketches of their Soil, Climate, Resources and Scenery. Philadelphia: 1838. V. 39; 42; 45; 46

Palaeontology of New-York. Albany: 1847. V. 37

Report of the Committee Appointed by the Citizens of Cincinnati, April 26, 1838, to Enquire into the Causes of the Explosion of the Moselle, and to Suggest Such Preventive Measures as May be Best Calculated to Guard Hereafter Against Such Occurrences. Cincinnati: 1838. V. 44

HALL, JAMES continued

Sketches of History, Life and Manners, in the West. Philadelphia: 1835. V. 39

Sketches of History, Life, and Manners in the West. Cincinnati: 1834. V. 37

The Soldier's Bride, and Other Tales. Philadelphia: 1833. V. 40; 43

Tour through Ireland, Particularly the Interior and Least Known Parts, Containing an Accurate View of the Parties, Politics and Improvements in the Different Provinces . . . London: 1813. V. 43

Travels in Scotland, by an Unusual Route: with a Trip to the Orkneys and Hebrides. London: 1807. V. 46

The War of Life: a Series of Poems. Aberdeen: 1860. V. 45

The West: Its Commerce & Navigation. Cincinnati: 1848. V. 39

The Wilderness and the War Path. New York: 1846. V. 37; 38; 43

Winter Evenings. A Series of American Tales. Philadelphia: 1829. V. 43

HALL, JAMES NORMAN 1887-

The Friends. Muscatine: 1939. V. 46

High Adventure: A Narrative of Air Fighting in France. Boston: 1918. V. 37

The Lafayette Flying Corps. Boston and New York: 1920. V. 38

The Tale of a Shipwreck. Boston: 1934. V. 41; 42

HALL, JOHN

The History of the Civil War in America. London: 1780. V. 41; 43

A Letter to the Hon. Thos. Spring Rice, Chancellor of Her Majesty's Exchequer . . . London: 1837. V. 38; 39

Memoirs of Matthew Clarkson of Philadelphia, 1735-1800. Philadelphia: 1890. V. 46

William Penn's Treaty with the Indians, When He Founded the Province of Pensylvania (!) In North America 1681. London. V. 43

HALL, JOHN E.

The Practice and Jurisdiction of the Court of Admiralty. Baltimore: 1809. V. 38; 40

HALL, JOHN LINVILLE

Around the Horn in '49. The Journal of the Hartford Union Mining and Trading Company Dec. 1848 to Sept. 1849. San Francisco: 1928. V. 38

HALL, JOSEPH

Characters of Vertues and Vices. London: 1608. V. 39; 43

Characters of Vertues and Vices. London: 1680. V. 45

Christ Mysticall: also, an Holy Rapture; also, The Christian laid Forth in His Whole Disposition and Carriage. London: 1647. V. 39

Epistles, The First (Second) Volume: Containing two Decades. London: 1608. V. 37

The Iron Question: Considered in Connection with Theory, Practice and Experience with Special References to 'The Bessmer Proces'. London: 1857. V. 44

Meditations and Vowes, Divine and Morall: Serving for Direction in Christian and Civil Practice. London: 1616. V. 45

Meditations and Vows, Divine and Morall. London: 1621. V. 41

A Recollection of Such Treatises as Have Been Heretofore Severally Published and Are Now Revised, Corrected, Augmented. London: 1615. V. 39

Satires . . . With the Illustrations of the late Rev. Thomas Warton. And Additional Notes by Samuel Singer. Chiswick: 1824. V. 37

HALL, JOSEPH, BP. OF NORWICH 1574-1656

The Kings Prophecie; or Weeping Joy. London: 1882. V. 40

Virgidemiarum. Oxford: 1753. V. 38; 40; 42; 44

HALL, LINVILLE, JOHN

Around the Horn in '89. Wethersfield: 1898. V. 42

HALL, LOUISA JANE PARK

Alfred. Boston: 1836. V. 43

Joanna of Naples, by the Author of 'Miriam'. Boston: 1838. V. 43

Miriam: a Dramatic Poem. Boston: 1837. V. 39

HALL, MADELINE

Miss Browne, the Story of a Superior Mouse. London: 1900. V. 43

HALL, MANLY P.

An Encyclopedic Outline of Masonic Hermetic, Qabbalistic and Rosicrucian Symbolical Philosophy. San Francisco: 1928. V. 44; 45; 46

HALL, MARSHALL

Cases of Serious Morbid Affection, Chiefly Occurring after Delivery, Miscarriage, etc. London: 1820. V. 38

Commentaries Principally on Some Diseases of Females Which are in Their Nature and Origin Consitutional. London: 1830. V. 38; 39; 43

A Critical and Experimental Essay on the Circulation of the Blood. Philadelphia. V. 41

A Critical and Experimental Essay on the Ciruclation of the Blood. (with) Reseraches Principally Relative to the Morbid and Curative Effects of Loss of Blood. Philadelphia: 1835. V. 45

A Descriptive, Diagnostic and Practical Essay on Disorders of the Digestive Organs and General Health. London: 1820. V. 38; 40

A Descriptive, Diagnostic and Practical Essay on Disorders of the Digestive Organs and General Health. Kenne: 1823. V. 40; 41; 44; 45

The Gulstonian Lectures for MDCCCXLII On the Mutual Relations Between Anatomy, Physiology, Pathology, and Therapeutics and the Practice of Medicine. London: 1842. V. 38

Lectures on the Nervous System and Its Diseases. Philadelphia: 1836. V. 40

Principles of the Theory and Practice of Medicine Including a Third Edition of the Author's Work Upon Diagnosis. London: 1837. V. 38

Principles of the Theory and Practice of medicine. Boston: 1839. V. 40; 41; 46

Researches Principally Relative to the Moribd and Curative Effects of Loss of Blood. London: 1830. V. 38

Synopsis of the Diastaltic Nervous System. London: 1850. V. 42

HALL, MARSHALL, MRS.

Memoirs of Marshall Hall, M.D., F.R.S . . . . by His Widow. London: 1861. V. 44

HALL, NEVIL

The Red Wing; or Belmont the Buccaneer of the Bay. Boston: 1846. V. 39

HALL, P. G.

The Bank of Ireland 1783-1946. Dublin/Oxford: 1949. V. 41

HALL, RACHEL

Narrative of the Capture and Providential Escape of Misses Frances and Almira Hall . . . N.P.: 1832. V. 45

HALL, RADCLYFFE

The Forgotten Island. London: 1915. V. 41

The Master of the House. London: 1932. V. 42; 43

Miss Ogilvy Finds Herself. London: 1934. V. 42

Poems of the Past and Present. London: 1910. V. 41

A Sheaf of Verses. London: 1908. V. 41

The Sixth Beatitude. London: 1936. V. 41

Songs of Three Counties and Other Poems. London: 1913. V. 41

The Well of Loneliness. London: 1928. V. 39; 40; 41

The Well of Loneliness. New York: 1928. V. 42; 44

The Well of Loneliness. New York: 1929. V. 43

HALL, RICHARD

The Life and Death of that Renowned John Fisher. London: 1655. V. 37; 42; 44; 45

HALL, ROBERT

An Apology for the Freedom of the Press, and for General Liberty. London: 1793. V. 39

A Reply to the Principal Objections Advanced by Cobbett and Others Against the Framework-Knitters' Friendly Relief Society. Leicester: 1821. V. 37

HALL, SAMUEL

Samuel Hall's Improvements in Steam Engines . . . Nottingham: 1838. V. 43

HALL, SAMUEL CARTER 1800-1889

The Baronial Halls, Picturesque Edifices, and Ancient Churches of England. London: 1843. V. 41

The Baronial Halls and Picturesque Edifices of England. London: 1848. V. 39; 45

The Baronial Halls and Ancient Picturesque Edifices of England. London: 1881. V. 44; 46

The Book of Gems. London: 1836-7-8. V. 45

The Book of British Ballads, First and Second Series. London: 1842-4. V. 39

The Book of British Ballads. First and Second Series. London: 1849. V. 39

The Book of British Ballads. London: 1853. V. 38

The Book of British Ballads. London: 1853. V. 38

The Book of the Thames, From Its Rise to Its Fall. London: 1859. V. 37; 45

The Book of Gems. From the Poets and Artists of Great Britain. London: 1871. V. 38; 41

A Book of Memories of Great men and Women of the Age from Personal Acquaintance. London: 1877. V. 38; 40

The Illustrated Catalogue of the Universal Exhibition. London: 1868. V. 46

Ireland: Its Scenery, Character &c. London: 1841. V. 43

Ireland, Its Scenery, Character, etc. London: 1841/43. V. 38

Ireland: Its Scenery, Character, &c. London: 1850. V. 37; 39; 40

The Poets and Artists of Great Britain. London: 1848. V. 41

The Sculpture Gallery. London: 1849-54. V. 46

HALL, SAMUEL READ 1795-1877

The Child's Assistant to a Knowledge of the Geography and History of Vermont. Montpelier: 1827. V. 46

HALL, SAMUEL READ 1795-1877 continued

Lectures on School-Keeping. Boston: 1829. V. 38

HALL, SHARLOT M.

Cactus and Pine: Songs of the Southwest. Boston: 1911. V. 39

HALL, SIDNEY

A Central Atlas, with the Divisions and Boundaries, Carefully Coloured . . . London: 1830. V. 41

HALL, SPARKES

The Book of the Feet. London: 1846. V. 42

HALL-STEVENSON, JOHN

Lyric Consolations with the Speech of Alderman W---Delivered in a Dram at the King's Bench Prison the Evening of His Inauguration. London: 1769. V. 38

Makarony Fables; with the New Fable of the Bees. London: 1768. V. 40

HALL, SYDNEY

Black's Generla Atlas: A Series of Fifty-Four Maps . . . Edinburgh: 1840. V. 39

HALL, SYDNEY PRIOR

Sketches from an Artist's Portfolio. London: 1875. V. 44

HALL, T. H.

Some Printers and Publishers of Conjuring Books and Other Ephemera 1800-1850. London: 1976. V. 44

HALL, T. Y.

On the Safety Lamp for the Use of Coal Mines. London: 1853. V. 45

HALL, THOMAS

The Fortunes and Adventures of Raby Rattler and His Man Floss. London: 1846. V. 40

National Brutality. Manchester: 1819. V. 42

HALL, TOM

The Fun and Fighting of the Rough Riders. New York: 1899. V. 42

HALL, TREVOR H.

A Bibliography of Books on Conjuring in English from 1580 to 1850. Minneapolis: 1957. V. 42

Some Printers & Publishers of Conjuring Books and Other Ephemera 1800-1850. 1976. V. 40

Some Printers and Publishers of Conjuring Books and Other Ephemera 1800-1850. Leeds: 1976. V. 43

HALL, W.

A Biography of David Cox with Remarks on His Works and Genius. London: 1881. V. 39

HALL, WALTER

Spider Poems. Madison: 1967. V. 39; 42; 44

HALL, WILLIAM

The Chief of St. Athans; and Words to Welsh Melodies, with Other Poems. London: 1822. V. 42

The Nemesis in China, Comprising a History of the Late War in that Country. London: 1846. V. 39; 42

HALL, WILLIAM A.

The Historic Significance of the Southern Revolution. Petersburg: 1864. V. 37

HALL, WILLIAM HENRY

The New Royal Encyclopaedia; or, Complete Modern Universal Dictionary of Arts and Sciences . . . London: 1788. V. 42

HALL, WILLIAM M.

Speech of . . . In Favor of a National Railroad to the Pacific, at the Great Chicago Convention. New York: 1853. V. 37; 39; 42

HALLADE, MADELEINE

Gandharan Art of North India and the Graeco-Buddhist Tradition in India, Persia and Central Asia. New York: 1968. V. 41

Gandharan Art of North India and the Graeco-Buddhist Tradition in India, Persia and Central Asia. New York: 1968. V. 38; 41

HALLAM, ARTHUR HENRY

Remains in Verse and Prose. London: 1863. V. 46

HALLAM, HENRY

The Constitutional History of England from the Accession of Henry VII to the Death of George II. View of the State of Europe During the Middle Ages. London: 1832, 1837. V. 42

The Constitutional History of England from the Accession of Henry VII to the Death of George II. London: 1827. V. 41

The Constitutional History of England from the Accession of Henry VII. London: 1850. V. 46

Histories: Including the Constitutional History of England, View of the State of Europe During the Middle Ages, and the Introduction to the Literature of Europe. London: 1846. V. 40

Introduction to the Literature of Europe in the Fifteenth, Sixteenth and Seventeenth Centuries. London: 1837-39. V. 39

Introduction to the Literture of Europe in the Fifteenth, Sixteenth and Seventeenth Centuries. London: 1843. V. 39

Introduction to the Literature of Europe in the Fifteenth, Sixttenth, and Seventeenth Centuries. London: 1855. V. 46

View of the State of Europe During the Middle Ages. London: 1847. V. 39

View of the State of Europe During the Middle Ages. London: 1853. V. 37; 39; 46

HALLAM, ISAAC

The Cocker: a Poem. Stamford: 1742. V. 38; 43

HALLE, EDWARD

The Union of the Two Noble and Illustre Famelies of Lancaster and Yorke. London: 1550. V. 41

HALLE, JOHN

An Historiall Expostulation . . . London: 1844. V. 42

HALLECK, FITZ-GREENE

Alnwick Castle, with Other Poems. New York: 1836. V. 38; 45

Fanny. New York: 1819. V. 40; 45

Fanny: a Poem. New York: 1866. V. 40

The Poetical Writings of Fitz-Greene Halleck. New York: 1869. V. 38; 41; 43; 44; 46

HALLECK, HENRY WAGER 1815-1872

Elements of Military Art and Science; or, Course of Instruction in Strategy, Fortification, Tactics of Battles &c . . . New York: 1846. V. 37

HALLENBECK, CLEVE

Alvar Nunez Cabeza de Vaca. The Journey and Route of the First European to Cross the Continent of North America, 1534-1536. Glendale: 1940. V. 44; 45

Alvar Nunez Cabeza de Vaca: the Journey and Route of the First European to Cross the Continent of North America 1534-1536. Glendale: 1940. V. 45

Journey of Fray Marcos de Niza. Dallas: 1949. V. 37; 38; 39; 40; 42; 44; 45

Legends of the Spanish Southwest. 1938. V. 42

Legends of the Spanish Southwest. Glendale: 1938. V. 44

Spanish Missions of the Old Southwest. Garden City: 1926. V. 38; 43; 44; 45

HALLER, ALBERTUS 1708-1777

First Lines of Physiology. Edinburgh: 1786. V. 46

HALLER, ALBRECHT VON

Academia Naturae Curiosorum Historia Morborum qui annis MDCXCIX, MDCCC, MDCCI, MDCCII. Lausanne & Geneva: 1746. V. 38

Allgemeine Historie der Natur. Hamburg & Leipzig: 1750-54. V. 38

Deux memoires sur le mouvement du sang, et sure les effets de la saignee. Lausanne: 1756. V. 37

Elementa Physiologiae Corporis Humani. Lausanne: 1757-1778. V. 41

Elementa Physiologiae Corporis Humani . . . Lausannae,: 1757-58. V. 37

First Lines of Physiology. Edinburgh: 1786. V. 38

Hermanni Boerhaave Methodus Studii Medici Emaculata & Accessionibus Locupletata ab Alberto ab Haller. Amsterdam: 1751. V. 38

Icones Anatomica Quibus Praecipuae Aliquae Partes Corporis Humani . . . Gottingen: 1743-56. V. 39; 40; 41

Icones Anatomica Quibus Praecipuae Aliquae Partes Corporis Humani . . . Gottingen: 1745-56. V. 44

Memoires sur la Nature Sensible et Irritible des Parties du Corps Animal . . . Lausanne: 1756-60. V. 38

Opuscula Pathologica Partim Recusa Partim Inedita. Lausanne: 1755. V. 38

Primae Lineae Physiologiae in Usum Praelectionum Academicarum. Gottingen: 1751. V. 38

Primae Lineae Physiologiae in Usum Praelectionum Academicarum nunc Quarto Conscriptae Emendatae et Pluribus Animadversionibus. Goettingae: 1780. V. 44

Primae Lineae Physiologiae in usum Praelectionum . . . editionem tertio actam & Emendatam . . . Edinburgh: 1767. V. 37

Usong. An Oriental History in Four Books. Translated from the German. London: 1773. V. 37

HALLER, ALBRECHT, VON, BARON

Letters to His Daughter on the Truths of the Christian Religion. London: 1780. V. 41

Usong. An Eastern Narrative. London: 1772. V. 43

HALLERSTEIN, AUGUSTIN

Observationes Astronomicae ab Anno 1717 ad Annum 1752 a Patribus Societatis Jesu Pekini Sinarum Factae . . . Vienna: 1768. V. 44

HALLES, STEPHEN

Philosophical Experiments. London: 1739. V. 38

HALLETT, JOSEPH

The Immorality of the Moral Philosopher . . . London: 1737. V. 41

HALLEY, EDMOND

Miscellanea Curiosa. London: 1723-27. V. 40

HALLEY, EDMUND

Astronomical Tables with Precepts Both in English and Latin for Computing the Places of the Sun, Moon, Planets and Comets. London: 1752. V. 37

Tabulae Astronomicae. (second part) Astronomical Tables with Percepts both in English and Latin . . . London: 1749. V. 46

HALLEY, JOHN

The History of Idaho. Boise: 1910. V. 42

HALLEY, ROBERT

Lancashire: Its Puritanism and Nonconformity. Manchester: 1869. V. 46

HALLEY, WILLIAM

Centennial Year Book of Alameda County, California . . . Oakland: 1876. V. 38

HALLIBURTON, RICHARD 1900-1939

New Worlds to Conquer. Indianpolis: (1929). V. 37; 45

The Royal Road to Romance. Indianapolis: (1925). V. 37

HALLIDAY, ANDREW

A General View of the Present State of Lunatics and Lunatic Asylums in Great Britain and Ireland and in some other Kingdoms. London: 1828. V. 37

The West Indies: the Natural and Physical History of the Windward and Leeward Colonies . . . London: 1837. V. 42

HALLIDAY, JOHN

The New London Method of Arithmetick. London: 1749. V. 42

HALLIDAY, W. M.

Potlatch and Totem and the Recollections of an Indian Agent. London: 1935. V. 39

Potlatch and Totem and the Recollections of an Indian Agent. London: & Toronto: 1935. V. 44

Williams' British Columbia Directory, 1891. Victoria: 1890. V. 41

HALLIWELL-PHILLIPPS, JAMES ORCHARD 1820-1889

A Brief Hand-List of the Records Belonging to the Borough of Stratford-on-Avon. London: 1862. V. 43

Catalogue of Proclamations, Broadsides, Ballads and Poems, Presented to the Chetham Library. London: 1851. V. 40; 44

A Dictionary of Archaic and Provincial Words, Obsolete Phrases, Proverbs and Ancient Customs, from the Fourteenth Century. London: 1847. V. 40

A Dictionary of Archaic and Provincial Words, Obsolete Phrases, Proverbs and Ancient Customs, from the Fourteenth Century. London: 1850. V. 42

A Dictionary of Archaic and Provincial Words . . . from the Fourteenth Century. London: 1874. V. 40

A List of Works Illustrative of the Life and Writings of Shakespeare. London: 1867. V. 40; 45

The Manuscript Rarities of the University of Cambridge. 1841. V. 46

The Manuscript Rarities of the University of Cambridge. London: 1841. V. 44

Nugae Poeticae. London: 1844. V. 44

The Nursery Rhymes and Nursery Tales of England. London. V. 40

Palatine Anthology: a Collection of Ancient Poems and Ballads, Relating to Lancashire and Cheshire. London: 1850. V. 42

Popular Rhymes and Nursery Tales. London: 1849. V. 44

Two Treatises on English Chap-Books. London: 1848-49. V. 46

HALLIWELL - PHILLIPS, JAMES ORCHARD 1820-1889

A Dictionary of Archaic and Provincial Words, Obsolete Phrases, Proverbs and Ancient Customs. London: 1852. V. 39

The Nursery Rhymes of England, Obtained Principally from Oral Tradition. London: 1843. V. 41

Outlines of the Life of Shakespeare. London: 1882. V. 43

Some Account of a Collection of Several Thousand Bills, Accounts and Inventories, Illustrating the History of Prices Between the Years 1650 and 1750. London: 1852. V. 38

HALLOCK, CHARLES

A Complete Biographical Sketch of 'Stonewall' Jackson . . . Augusta: 1863. V. 44

Our New Alaska: or the Seward Purchase Vindicated. New York: 1894. V. 38

The Salmon Fisher. New York: 1890. V. 39

HALLOCK, WILLIAM

Outlines of the Evolution of Weights and Measures and the Metric System. New York: 1906. V. 40

HALLOWELL, JOHN K.

Geological Monography. Denver: 1882. V. 42

Gunnison, Colorado's Bonanza Co . . . Denver, Co.: 1883. V. 37

HALLS, J. J.

The Life and Correspondence of Henry Salt, Esq. F.R.S. etc. London: 1834. V. 38; 39; 40

HALLS of the Montezumas; or Mexico in Ancient and Modern Times. New York: 1848. V. 43

HALLUM, JOHN

Address to the Jury, by Col. John Hallum, in Self Defense, in the Case of the state of Texas Against Him . . . for Shooting a Minister . . . Cleveland: 1900. V. 46

Biographical and Pictorial History of Arkansas. Albany: 1887. V. 40; 43

The Diary of an Old Lawyer: Scenes Behind the Curtain. Nashville: 1895. V. 40

The Diary of an Old Lawyer: Scenes Behind the Curtain. Nashville: 1895. V. 44

HALPER, ALBERT

Chicago Side-Show. N.P.: 1932. V. 38

Union Square. New York: 1933. V. 39; 40; 41

HALPERN, SAMUEL E.

West Pac '64. Boston: 1975. V. 44

HALPIN, T. M.

Halpin's City Directory Memphis, 1867-8. Memphis: 1867. V. 39

HALPIN, WARREN T.

Hoofbeats, Drawings and Comments by . . . Philadelphia: 1938. V. 39; 43; 46

HALSE, GEORGE F.

Fir Guy De Guy: a Stirring Romaunt. London: 1864. V. 44

HALSELL, H. H.

Cowboys and Cattleland. Nashville: 1937. V. 37; 39

My Autobiography . . . The Early Days of Texas When It Was a Primitive Wilderness. Dallas: 1948. V. 46

HALSEY, ALAN

Auto Dada Cafe: Poems. 1987. V. 40

HALSEY, FRANCIS W.

Authors of Our Day in Their Homes. New York: 1902. V. 46

The Pioneers of Unadilla Village, 1784-1804 . . . (and) Reminiscences of Village Life and of Panama and California from 1840 to 1850. Unadilla: 1902. V. 38; 41

HALSEY, FRANCIS WHITING

The Old New York Frontier: Its Wars with Indians and Tories, Its Missionary Schools, Pioneers and Land Titles 1614-1800. New York: 1901. V. 42

HALSEY, HARLAN PAGE

Macon Moore, the Southern Detective. New York: 1881. V. 43; 44

Phil Scott, the Indian Detective. New York: 1882. V. 41

The Ubiquitous Yank; or the Weird Narrative of a Lost Man. New York: 1886. V. 43

HALSEY, J. L.

Thomas Halsey of Hertfordshire, England and Southampton, Long Island, 1591-1679, with His American Descendants to the Eight and Ninth Generations. By J.L. Halsey and E. D. Halsey. Morristown, NJ: 1895. V. 37

HALSEY, JOSEPH

The Life and Dying Words of Capt. Joseph Halsey, Who was Executed at Execution-Dock, on Wednesday the Fourteenth of March, 1759. For the Murder of Daniel Davidson. On the High Seas. London: 1759. V. 37

HALSEY, RICHARD T. H.

The Boston Port Bill as Pictured by a Contemporary London Cartoonist. New York: 1904. V. 37; 38; 39; 43

Pictures of Early New York on Dark Blue Staffordshire Pottery. New York: 1899. V. 39

HALSMAN, PHILLIPPE

Marilyn, A Portfolio of Ten Photographs by Philippe Halsman. 1981. V. 46

HALSTEAD, BRUCE W.

Poisonous and Venomous Marine Animals of the World. Washington: 1965-70. V. 39

Poisonous and Venomous Marine Animals of the World. Washington: 1967. V. 41

HALSTEAD, ROBERT

Succinct Genealogical Proofs of the House of Greene that Were Lords of Drayton. 1896. V. 37; 42

HALSTED, CAROLINE

Investigation; or Travels in the Boudoir. London: 1837. V. 37

HALSTED, CAROLINE A.

Life of Margaret Beaufort, Countess of Richmond and Derby, Mother of King Henry the Seventh. London: 1839. V. 44

HALSTED, E. P.

The Screw Fleet of the Navy, the Forty Ship Fleet of the British Navy from 1839 to 1850, the Advantage of the Screw Propeller over the Paddle Wheel in Terms of Protection. London: 1850. V. 38

HALSTED, WILLIAM

The Employment of Fine Silk. Boston: 1939. V. 37; 41; 42

HALSTED, WILLIAM STEWART

Circular Suture of the Intestine: an Experimental Study. 1887. V. 42

The Effect of Ligation of the Common Iliac Artery of the Circulation of the Lower Extremity. 1912. V. 42

Ligations of the Left Subclavian Artery in its First Portion. (Baltimore: 1921). V. 37

Ligations of the Left Sublcavian Artery In Its First Portion. Ligations: 1920. V. 42

Surgical Papers. Baltimore: 1924. V. 38; 42; 45

Surgical Papers. Baltimore: 1952. V. 41; 44

The Training of the Surgeon. Londo. V. 41

HALVELY, LUDOVIC

L'Abbe Constantin. Paris: 1887. V. 46

HALYBURTON, THOMAS 1674-1712

Natural Religion Insufficient and Revealed Necessary to Man's Happiness in His Present State, Or, a Rational Inquiry into the Principles of Modern Deists . . . Albany: 1812. V. 41

HAMADY, WALTER

For the Hundredth Time Gabberjabb Number Five. Mt. Horeb: 1981. V. 44

For the Hundreth Time: Gaebboer Jabb Nubmer Five 19 & 17 November 1980. By Walter Hamady. Wisconsin: 1981. V. 37

Hand Papermaking. Mt. Horeb: 1982. V. 38; 42

Hand Papermaking. Perry: 1982. V. 38

Neopostmodernism. 1988. V. 40

Papermaking by Hand: a Book of Suspicions. Mt. Horeb: 1982. V. 42; 46

Papermaking by Hand. Wisconsin: 1982. V. 45

Plum-Foot Poems. Madison: 1967. V. 39

Plumfoot Poems. Wisconsin: 1967. V. 45

Seeds and Chairs. Mt. Horeb: 1979. V. 44

HAMANS, FELICIA

Poems. With Illustrated notes and selected contemporary criticisms. Edinburgh: 1854. V. 37

HAMBERG, GUSTAF

Studies in Roman Imperial Art with Special Reference to the State Reliefs of the Second Century. Uppsala: 1945. V. 44

HAMBLETON, CHALKLEY J.

A Gold Hunter's Experience . . . Chicago: 1898. V. 39; 41; 43; 45

HAMBLETON, RONALD

Unit of Five. Toronto: 1944. V. 38; 42

HAMBLETT, CHARLES

Call Wind to Witness . . . London: 1942. V. 42

HAMBLIN, P. R.

United States Criminal History . . . Fayetteville: 1836. V. 45

HAMBURGER, MICHAEL

In Suffolk. Hereford: 1982. V. 44

Trees: Thirteen Poems. Llangynog: 1988. V. 39

Tress: Poems. 1988. V. 40

HAMBURGISCHE Gesellschaft zur Beforderung der Kunste und Nutzlichen Gewerbe. Verzeichniss der . . . Vierten Ausstellung von Kunstwerken, Arbeiten und Nuetzlichen Erfindungen. Hamburg: 1794. V. 39

HAMEL, MAURICE

Corot and His Work. Glasglow: 1905. V. 44

HAMELLIUS, PASCASIUS

Perspectiva. Paris: 1556. V. 46

HAMELMAN, WILLIAM E.

Of Red Eagles and Royal Crowns. A Modern Translation of the Statutes of the Prussian Red Eagle Order and the Royal Crown Order. Texas: 1978. V. 37

HAMELMANN, HERMANN 1526-1595

Brevis Commentariolus, de Vero Vsv Monasteriorvm et Collegiorvm. In Qvo Perspicve Demonstratur..Nihil Aliud Olim Fuisse Quam Phrontisteria & Scholas, &c . . . Marburg: 1569. V. 39

HAMER, F.

Orchids of Nicaragua. Sarasota: 1983-84. V. 37

HAMER, J.

The Smoker's Text Book. London: 1874. V. 44

HAMER-JACKSON, CELESTA

The Story of Western Canada. V. 44

HAMER, S. H.

Cheepy the Chicken, Being a True and Particular Account of His Most Wonderful Adventures. London: 1904. V. 45

The Transformation of the Truefitts. London: 1908. V. 44

HAMERSLY, LEWIS R.

A Naval Encyclopedia. Philadelphia: 1884. V. 40; 41

The Records of Living Officers of the U. S. Navy and marine Corps; with a History of Naval Operations During the Rebellion of 1861-5, and a List of the Ships and Officers Participating in the Great Battles. Philadelphia: 1870. V. 41

HAMERTON, EUGENIE GINDRIEZ

Philip Gilbert Hamilton: Autobiography 1834-1858, and a Memoir by His Wife 1858-1894. London: 1897. V. 39

HAMERTON, P. G.

The Unknown River. London: 1861. V. 37

HAMERTON, PHILIP GILBERT 1834-1894

Chapters on Animals. Boston: 1874. V. 46

Contemporary French Painters: an Essay. 1868. V. 41

Drawing and Engraving a Brief Expostion of Technical Principles and Practice. London: 1892. V. 44

The Etcher's Handbook. London: 1881. V. 42

Etching and Etchers. London: 1868. V. 39

Etching and Etchers. London: 1880. V. 39

Etching and Etchers. London: 1968. V. 38

The Graphic Arts. London: 1882. V. 38; 39; 41; 45

The Intellectual Life. East Aurora: 1899. V. 41

Landscape. London: 1885. V. 39; 42; 44

A Painter's Camp in the Highlands, and Thoughts about Art. Cambridge: 1862. V. 39; 45

Painting in France After the Decline of Clasicism. London: 1869. V. 44

Paris In Old and Present Times with Especial Reference to Changes In Its Architecture and Topography. London: 1885. V. 39

The Portfolio: an Artistic Periodical. London: 1881-93. V. 46

The Portfolio, an Artistic Periodical. London: 1893. V. 41

The Sylvan Year: Leaves from the Note-Book of Raoul Dubois . . . London: 1876. V. 41

HAMES, MARQUIS

The Raven, a Biography of Sam Houston. Indianpolis: 1929. V. 44

HAMILL, ALFRED E.

The Decorative Work of T. M. Cleland. New York: 1929. V. 40

HAMILL, CLARICE

Mexican Bouquet. Chicago: 1946. V. 45

HAMILL, WILLIAM

A Memorial by William Hamill Gent. Agent and Trustee for the Officers and Soldiers of the two late Garrisons of London-derry and Enniskilling in Ireland, their relicts and representatives. London. V. 37

A View of the Danger and Folly of Being Public-Spirited, and Sincerley Loving One's Country . . . London: 1721. V. 40

HAMILTON, A. J.

Address of A. J. Hamilton, Military Governor, to the People of Texas. New Orleans: 1864. V. 45

Letter of Gen. A. J. Hamilton, of Texas to the President of the United States. New York: 1863. V. 39

HAMILTON, ADRIAN

The Infamous Essay on Woman, or, John Wilkes Seated between Vice and Virtue. London: 1972. V. 45; 46

HAMILTON, ALEXANDER 1712-1756

Hamilton's Itinerarium. St. Louis: 1744. V. 43

Hamilton's Intinerarium . . . St. Louis: 1907. V. 38; 39; 40; 41

The Illinois Form Book and Practical Guide . . . St. Louis: 1835. V. 46

A Letter from Phocion to the Considerate Citizens of New York, on the Politics of the Day. Boston: 1784. V. 42

A New Account of the East Indies. London: 1930. V. 46

Observations on Certain Documents Contained in No. V & Vi of 'The History of the United States for the Year 1796' In Which the Charges of Speculation Against Alexander Hamilton . . . is fully Refuted . . . Philadelphia: 1797. V. 39

Observations on Certain Documents Contained in . . . 'The History of the U.S. for the Year 1796,' in Which the Charge of Speculation Against Alexander Hamilton . . . Is Fully Refuted. Philadelphia: 1800. V. 39; 42

Observations on Certain Documents in 'The History of the United States for the Year 1796.' New York: 1865. V. 42

Outlines of the Theory and Practice of Midwifery. Northampton: 1797. V. 39; 40; 41

Outlines of the Theory and Practice of Midwifery. Philadelphia: 1797. V. 41

The Papers of Alexander Hamilton: 1768-1795. New York: 1961-73. V. 44

Report Relative to Appropriations of Money. Philadelphia: 1791. V. 39

Report on the Subject of Manufactures. Philadelphia: 1792. V. 38

Report Relative to a Provision for the Support of the Public Credit of the United States. New York: 1790. V. 37

Reports of Alexander Hamilton, Esq. London: 1795. V. 46

Sundry Statements Respecting the Several Foreign Loans Made Under the Authority of the United States. Philadelphia: 1793. V. 39

The Works. New York: 1810. V. 44; 45

The Works of . . . New York: 1885. V. 42

The Works of Alexander Hamilton. New York: 1885-86. V. 44

The Works. New York: 1900. V. 42

Works. New York: & London: 1903. V. 46

HAMILTON, ALEXANDER HAMILTON DOUGLAS, 10TH DUKE OF 1767-1852

Catalogue of the Collection of Pictures, Works of Art and Decorative Objects, the Property of His Grace the Duke of Hamilton, L.T . . . . London: 1882. V. 40

HAMILTON, ALICE

Manitoba Stained Glass. Winnipeg: 1970. V. 43

HAMILTON, ALLAN

Nervous Diseases: Their Description and Treatment. Philadelphia: 1878. V. 42

Railway and Other Accidents with relation to Injury and Diseases of the Nervous System. New York: 1904. V. 37

HAMILTON, ANDREW

The Actions of the Enniskillen - Men From Their Taking Up of Arms in 1688 in Defence of the Protestant Religion . . . London: printed,: 1813. V. 46

HAMILTON, ANTHONY 1646-1720

Memoires du Comte de Grammont . . . 1772. V. 46

Memoirs of the Life of Count de Grammont. London: 1714. V. 37; 38; 39; 43

Memoirs of the Count Grammont . . . London: 1793. V. 42; 46

Memoires du Comte de Grammont. Londres: 1793. V. 39

Memoirs of Count Grammont. London: 1794. V. 38; 41; 45

Memoirs of Count Grammont. London: 1809. V. 40

Memoirs of Count Grammont. London: 1811. V. 37; 38; 39; 40; 41; 42; 44

Memoirs of Count Grammont. London: 1828. V. 38

Memoirs of Count Grammont. London: 1860. V. 39

Memoirs of Count Grammont (sic). London: 1876. V. 38

Memoirs of Count rammont. London: 1889. V. 37; 38; 45

Memoirs of Count Grammont. Philadelphia: 1836. V. 37

HAMILTON, AUGUSTA

Marriage Rites, Customs and Ceremonies of All Nations of the Universe. London: 1822. V. 38; 43; 45

Marriage Rites, Customs and Ceremonies of the Nations of the Universe. London: 1824. V. 38; 42

HAMILTON, AUGUSTUS

The Art Workmanship of the Moori Race in New Zealand. Dunedin: 1896. V. 42

In Abor Jungles: Being an Account of the Abor Expedition, the Mishmi Mission and the Miri Mission. London: 1912. V. 42

HAMILTON-BROWNE, G.

With the Lost Legion in New Zealand. London: 1911. V. 46

HAMILTON, C. P.

Travels through the Interior Provinces of Columbia. London: 1827. V. 46

HAMILTON, CHARLES

Sketches of Life and Sport in South-Eastern Africa. London: 1870. V. 43

HAMILTON, COSPATRICK B., MRS.

A Series of Twelve Views in the Mediterranean, Grecian Archipelago, Bosphorus, and the Black Sea. London: 1857. V. 37

HAMILTON, DOUGLAS

Records of Sport in Southern India, Chiefly on the Annamullay, Nielgherry and Pulney Mountains. London: 1892. V. 39

HAMILTON, E.

A Catalogue Raissone of the Engraved Works of Sir Joshua Reynolds from 1755 to 1820. London: 1874. V. 39

The Metal Giants. 1932. V. 43

HAMILTON, EDITH

The Great Age of Greek Literature. New York: 1942. V. 46

HAMILTON, EDWARD

Recollections of Fly Fishing for Salmon, Trout and Grayling. London: 1884. V. 38; 41; 45

Recollections of Fly Fishings for Salmon, Trout and Grayling with Notes on Their Haunts, Habits and History. London: 1884. V. 38

The Star Kings. New York: 1949. V. 45

The Wild Cat of Europe. London: 1896. V. 37; 38

HAMILTON, ELIZABETH

The Cottagers of Glenburnie, a Tale for the Farmer's Ingle-Nook. Edinburgh: 1808. V. 37; 42; 46

Letters, addressed to the Daughter of a Nobleman, on the Formation of Religious and Moral Principle. London: 1806. V. 40; 46

Letters on the Elementary Principles of Education. London: 1818. V. 41

Letters Addressed to the Daughter of a Nobleman, on the Formation of Religious and Moral Principle. Salem: 1821. V. 37; 45

Memoirs of Modern Philosophers. Dublin: 1800. V. 41; 42; 44; 46

Memoirs of Modern Philosophers. Bath: 1804. V. 40

Memoirs of the Life of Agrippina, the Wife of Germanicus. Bath: 1804. V. 42

A Series of Popular Essays, Illustrative of Principles Essentially Connected With the Improvement of the Understanding, the Imagination and the Heart. Edinburgh: 1813. V. 39; 42; 43; 46

Translation of the Letters of a Hindoo Rajah . . . London: 1801. V. 45

HAMILTON, EMMA

Memoirs of Lady Hamilton. London: 1815. V. 39

HAMILTON, F. BUCHANAN

An Account of the Fishes Found in the River Ganges and Its Branches. Edinburgh: 1822. V. 37

HAMILTON, F. W.

The Origin and History of the First or Grenadier Guards; from Documents in the State Paper Office, War Office, Horse Guards, Contemporary History, Regimental Records, etc. London: 1874. V. 38

HAMILTON, FRANK HASTINGS

A Treatise on Military Surgery and Hygiene. New York: 1865. V. 45

HAMILTON, G. ROSTREVOR

The Latin Portrait, an Anthology. London: 1929. V. 41; 44; 46

HAMILTON, GAVIN

Schola Italica Picturae Sive Selectae Quaedam Summorum e Schola Italica Pictorum Tabulae. Rome: 1773. V. 37

HAMILTON, GEORGE

An Appeal for the Horse. Adelaide: 1866. V. 42; 46

The Elements of Drawing in Its Various Branches. London: 1812. V. 42; 43; 44; 45

The Elements of Drawing, In Its Various Branches, for the Use of Students . . . London: 1827. V. 44

The Telegraph; a Consolatory Epistle (in verse) from Thomas Muir, Esq. of Botany Bay, to the Hon. Henry ERskine . . . Edinburgh: 1796. V. 42

A Voyage Round the World in His Majesty's Frigate Pandora. Berwick: 1793. V. 41

HAMILTON, GRAY, MRS.

Tour to the Sepulchres of Etruria, in 1839. London: 1841. V. 45

HAMILTON, H. B.

Historical Record of the 14th (King's) Hussars from A.D. 1715 to A.D. 1900. London: 1901. V. 37

HAMILTON, H. W.

Rural Sketches of Minnesota, the El Dorado of the Northwest. Milan: 1850. V. 39; 45

HAMILTON, HENRY S.

Reminiscences of a Veteran. Concord: 1897. V. 37; 38

HAMILTON, HUGH

Philosophical Essays on the Following Subjects: I. On the Ascent of Vapours, the Formation of Clouds, Rain and Dew . . . II. Observations & Conjectures on the Nature of the Aurora Borealis . . . III. On the Principles of Mechanicks. London: 1767. V. 37

HAMILTON, HUGO

De Sectionibus Conicis. London: 1758. V. 45

HAMILTON, IAIN

Variations on an Original Theme for String. London: 1953. V. 45

HAMILTON, IAN

J. D. Salinger - a Writing Life. 1986. V. 45

J.D. Salinger: a Writing Life. New York: 1986. V. 40

HAMILTON, J. P.

Reminiscences of an Old Sportsman. London: 1860. V. 39

HAMILTON, JAMES

The Gospel of St. John Adapted to the Hamiltonian System, by an Analytical and Interlineary Translation. London: 1824. V. 45

The Hamilton Manuscripts, Containing Some Account of the Settlement of the Territories of Upper Clandeboye, Great Ardes and Dufferin, in the County of Down. Belfast: 1867. V. 37; 38; 40; 43

The History, Principles, Practice and Results of the Hamiltonian System, for the Last Twelve Years . . . Manchester: 1829. V. 45

A Letter to Sir William Garrow, His Majesty's Attorney General, on the Proposed Bill for Regulating the Practice of Surgery Throughout the United Kingdom of Great Britain and Ireland. Edinburgh: 1817. V. 38; 42

Life of Rear Admiral John Paul Jones . . . Philadelphia: 1846. V. 42

Observations on the Utility and the Administration of Purgative Medicines in Several Diseases. Philadelphia: 1809. V. 40; 42

Outlines of Midwifery for the Use of Students. Edinburgh: 1826. V. 41

Reminiscences of . . . or, Men and Events, at Home and Abroad. New York: 1869. V. 39

Wanderings in North Africa. London: 1856. V. 45

HAMILTON, JEFF

'My Master' the Inside Story of Sam Houston and His Times. Dallas: 1940. V. 37; 41; 42

HAMILTON, JOHANN GEORG 1730-1788

Kreuzzuge des Philologen. Kinigsberg: 1762. V. 44

HAMILTON, JOHN

The Case of John Hamilton, Against Joseph Hickey, Attorney. London: 1751. V. 38; 43

The Catechisme. St. Andrews: 1552. V. 40

Stereography, or a Compleat Body of Perspective, In All Its Branches. London: 1738. V. 38; 41

HAMILTON, JOHN P.

Travels through the Interior Provinces of Columbia. London: 1827. V. 38; 41

HAMILTON, JOHN R.

New Brunswick and Its Scenery. Saint John: 1874. V. 39

HAMILTON, JOSEPH

The Only Approved Guide through all the Stages of a Quarrel Containing the Royal Code of Honor . . . London: 1820. V. 43; 46

HAMILTON, MYRA

Kingdoms Curious. London: 1905. V. 37; 43

HAMILTON, PATRICK

Craven House. London: 1926. V. 38

Hangover Square. London: 1941. V. 44

Impromptu in Moribundia. London: 1939. V. 40

The Midnight Bell - a Love Story. London: 1929. V. 38

Mr. Stimpson and Mr. Gorse. London: 1953. V. 41

Money with Menaces and to the Public Danger - Two Radio Plays. London: 1939. V. 40

The Resources of Arizona: Its Mineral, Farming and Grazing Lands . . . Prescott: 1881. V. 39; 46

The Resources of Arizona. San Francisco: 1883. V. 37; 39; 46

The Resources of Arizona. San Francisco: 1884. V. 38; 39; 41; 42; 44

The Slaves of Solitude. London: 1947. V. 40

Twopence Coloured. London: 1928. V. 38

Unknown Assailant. London: 1955. V. 41

The West Pier. London: 1951. V. 41

HAMILTON, R.

Q.V.O. Madras Sappers and Miners in France and Iraq, 1914-1920. Bangalore: 1922. V. 42

HAMILTON, RICHARD WINTER

The Institutions of Popular Education. London: 1845. V. 43

The Institutions of Popular Education. Leeds: 1846. V. 41

HAMILTON, ROBERT

Letters on the Cause and Treatment of the Gout. London: 1806. V. 43

Mammalia. Amphibious Carnivora. Edinburgh: 1843. V. 41

Whales, the Natural History of the Ordinary Cetacea. (with) Walrus, Seals & Cetacea. Edinburgh: 1837, 1839. V. 38

HAMILTON, ROWAN

Betwixt Two Lovers. London: 1891. V. 38

HAMILTON, SCHUYLER

The History of the National Flag of the United States of America. Philadelphia: 1852. V. 38

HAMILTON, SINCLAIR

Early American Book Illustrators and Wood Engravers 1679-1870. Princeton: 1968. V. 40

Early American Book Illustrators and Wood Engravers 1679-1870. Princeton: 1970/1968. V. 43

HAMILTON, TERRICK

Antar, Roman Bedouin. Paris: 1819. V. 38

HAMILTON, THOMAS

Men and Manners in America. Philadelphia: 1832. V. 39; 42

Men and Manners in America. Edinburgh: 1833. V. 38; 42; 45

Men and Manners in America. Edinburgh & London: 1833. V. 42; 46

Men and Manners in America. London: 1833. V. 40

Men and Manners in America. Philadelphia: 1833. V. 38; 43

Men and Manners in America . . . Edinburgh: 1834. V. 38

Remarks on the Forms and Properties of Ships. London: 1793. V. 37

*Select Poems on Several Occasions. By the Right Hon. The Earl of H*******'n. To which are added, the Duke of Argyll's levee, and some ballads. By the late Lord Binning.* London: 1824. V. 37

The Youth and Manhood of Cyril Thornton. Boston: 1827. V. 46

The Youth and Manhood of Cyril Thornton. Edinburgh: 1827. V. 37

HAMILTON, VEREKER M.

Scenes in Ceylon. Colombo: (1881). V. 37

HAMILTON, W.

Memorandum on the Subject of the Earl of Elgin's Pursuits in Greece. London: 1811. V. 39

HAMILTON, WALTER

The Aesthetic Movement in England. London: 1882. V. 41

Dated Book Plates (Ex-Libris), with a Treatise on Their Origin and Development. London: 1895. V. 39; 42

The East-India Gazetteer. London: 1828. V. 38

The East-India Gazetteer. London: 1828. V. 38; 39

French Book-Plates. London: 1896. V. 38; 39; 40

A Geographical, Statistical and Historical Description of Hindostan and the Adjacent Countries. London: 1820. V. 39

HAMILTON, WILLIAM 1730-1803

Campi Phlegraei. Observations on the Volcanos of the Two Sicilies. (with) Supplement to the Campi Phlegraei Being an Account of the Eruption of Mount Vesuvius in the Month of August 1779. Naples: 1776, 1779. V. 39

Campi Phlaegri. (with) Supplement. Naples: 1776-79. V. 43; 46

Campi Phlegraei Osservazioni sui Vulcani del Regno delle Due Sicilie Communicate Alla Societa Reale di Londra. (and) Supplement to the Camp Phelgraei . . . Naples: 1985. V. 45

Collection of Engravings From Ancient Vases Mostly of Pure Greek Workmanship Discovered in Sepulchres in the Kingdom of the Two Sicilies But Chiefly in the Neighbourhood of Naples During the Course of the Years MDCCLXXXIX & MDCCLXXXX. Naples: 1791-95. V. 39

Descriptions of the Scheriffdoms of Lanark and Renfrew, compiled about M.DCC.X . . . with illustrative Notes and Appendices. Glasgow: 1831. V. 37

Discussions on Philosophy and Literature, Education and University Reform. London: 1852. V. 42; 43

Discussions on Philosophy and Literature, Education and University Reform. London: 1853. V. 38; 40; 41

Discussions on Philosophy and Literature, Education and University Reform. Edinburgh & London: 1866. V. 43; 45

HAMILTON, WILLIAM 1730-1803 continued

The History of medicine, surgery and anatomy, form the creation of the world, to the commencement of the nineteenth century. London: 1831. V. 37

Lectures on Metaphysics and Logic. Boston: 1860. V. 42; 43; 45

Lectures on Metaphysics and Logic. Edinburgh & London: 1865/66. V. 42

Letters Concerning the Northern Coast of the County of Antrim. Dublin: 1790. V. 38; 43

Letters concerning the Northern Coast of the County of Antrim . . . with a plain and impartial view of the Volcanic Theory of the Basaltes. London: 1786. V. 37

A New Edition of the Life and Heroick Actions of the Renoun'd Sir William Wallace, General and Governor of Scotland . . . Glasgow: 1722. V. 41; 42

The Life and Surprising Adventures and Heroic Actions of Sir William Wallace, General and Governor of Scotland. Aberdeen: 1774. V. 41

Observations on Mount Vesuvius, Mount Etna and Other Volcanos . . . V. 43

Observations on Mount Vesuvius, Mount Etna, and Other Volcanoes. London: 1772. V. 38; 39

Observations on Mount Vesuvius, Mount Etna, and Other Volcanos . . . London: 1773. V. 37; 44; 45

Observations on Mount Vesuvius, Mount Etna and Other Volcanoes. London: 1774. V. 39

Observations on Mount Vesuvius, Mount Etna and Other Volcanoes. London: 1783. V. 42

Outlines from the Figures and Compositions Upon the Greek, Roman, and Etruscan Vases of the Late Sir William Hamilton. London: 1804. V. 40

Outlines from the Figures and Compositions Upon the Greek, Roman and Etruscan vases of the Late . . . London: 1814. V. 38

Poems On Several Occasions. Edinburgh: 1760. V. 40; 41; 42; 44

Remarks on Several Parts of Turkey. London: 1809. V. 41

HAMILTON, WILLIAM D.

Recollections of a Cavlaryman of the Civil War After Fity Years 1861-1865. Columbus: 1915. V. 39

HAMILTON, WILLIAM GERARD 1729-1796

Parliamentary Logick; to Which are Subjoined Two Speeches Delivered in the House of Commons of Ireland, and Other Pieces. London: 1808. V. 38; 41; 42

HAMILTON, WILLIAM J.

Researches in Asia Minor, Pontus and Armenia with Some Account of Their Antiquities and Geology. London: 1842. V. 39; 45

HAMILTON, WILLIAM, M.B., of Plymouth

The History of Medicine, Surgery and Anatomy, From the Creation of the World to the Commencement of the Nineteenth Century. London: 1831. V. 39

HAMILTON, WILLIAM RICHARD

Memorandum on the Subject of the Earl of Elgin's Pursuits in Greece. Edinburgh: 1811. V. 43

HAMILTON, WILLIAM ROWAN 1805-1865

Elements of Quaternions. London: 1899. V. 38; 40

Lectures on Quaternions. Dublin: 1853. V. 40

HAMILTON, WILLIAM T.

Lecture on Millerism. Mobile: 1843. V. 40

My Sixty Years on the Plains. New York: 1905. V. 38; 39; 40; 41; 42; 45; 46

HAMLET, JAMES

The Fugitive Slave Bill: Its History and Unconstitutionality; with an Account of the Seizure and Enslavement of James Hamlet and His Subsequent Restoration to Liberty. New York: 1850. V. 45

HAMLEY, E. BRUCE

The Story of the Campaign of Sebastopol Written in the Camp. London: 1855. V. 42

HAMLEY, EDWARD

The War in Crimea. London: 1891. V. 41

The War in the Crimea. London: 1896. V. 44

HAMLIN, AUGUSTUS CHOATE

The Battle of Chancellorsville: the Attack of Stonewall Jackson and His Army Upon the Right Flank of the Army of the Potomac. Bangor: 1896. V. 41; 42; 44

HAMLIN, CHARLES E.

The Life and Times of Hannibal Hamlin. Cambridge: 1899. V. 46

HAMLIN, TALBOT

Forms and Functions of Twentieth Century Architecture. New York: 1952. V. 39

HAMMA, WALTER

Violin Makers of the German School from the 17th to the 19th Century. Tutzing: 1986. V. 38

HAMMACHER, A. M.

The Evolution of Modern Sculpture: Tradition and Innovation. New York. V. 39; 43; 46

Marino Marini: Sculpture, Painting, Drawing. New York. V. 46

HAMMAND, I. B.

Reminiscences of Frontier Life. Portland: 1904. V. 45

HAMMER, CAROLYN READING

Notes on the Two-Color Initials of Victor Hammer. Lexington: 1966. V. 38

Ravens Creek. Lexington: 1949. V. 40

Victor Hammer, Artist and Printer. Lexington: 1981. V. 40

HAMMER, JOSEPH VON

The History of Assassins. London: 1835. V. 41

HAMMER, KENNETH

Men With Custer. Ft. Collins: 1972. V. 44

HAMMER-PURGSTALL, JOSEPH VON

The History of the Assassins. London: 1835. V. 38

Mahmud Schebisteri's Rosenflor des Geheimnisses . . . Pest & Leipzig: 1838. V. 38; 40

HAMMER, U. T.

Saline Lake Ecosystems of the World. Dordrecht: 1986. V. 37; 38

HAMMER, VICTOR

Chapters on Writing and Printing. Lexington: 1963. V. 45

Concern for the Art of Civilized Man. Lexington: 1963. V. 37; 41; 44

A Dialogue on the Uncial Between a Paleographer and a Printer. Aurora: 1945. V. 37; 46

A Dialogue on the Uncial Between a Paleographer and a Printer. Wells: 1946. V. 41; 43

A Dialogue on the Uncial Between a Paleographer and a Printer. Faithfully recorded as it was heard . . . on a December evening in 1943. (Aurora: 1946). V. 37

Engravings on Woodcuts. Lexington: 1979. V. 45

Manifesto. Maple Shade: 1987. V. 38; 40; 41; 42; 44

Memory and Her Nine Daughters / The Muses / A Pretext for Printing / Cast Into the Mould of a Dialogue in Four Chapters. New York: 1957. V. 37

Some Fragments for C. R. H. Lexington: 1967. V. 40

A Theory of Architecture. Lexington: 1952. V. 38; 44

A Theory of Architecture. New York: 1952. V. 38; 41

Those Visible Marks . . . Lexington: 1988. V. 41; 44; 45

Victor Hammer's Engravings and Woodcuts. Lexington: 1979. V. 41; 45

Victor Hammer: Artist and Printer. Lexington: 1981. V. 44; 46

Victor Hammer, an Artist's Testament. Lexington: 1988. V. 44

HAMMER, VICTOR KARL 1882-

A Theory of Architecture, the Second Chapter from a Platonic Dialog. New York: 1952. V. 39

HAMMER, WILLIAM J.

Radium, and other Radio-Active Substances, Polonium, Actinium, and Thorium. New York: 1903. V. 37; 40; 42; 43; 45

HAMMERLE, ALBERT

Bunt-Papier . . . Munchen: 1961. V. 38

HAMMERSTEIN, OSCAR

Lyrics. New York: 1949. V. 37

Viennese Nights. N.P.: 1930. V. 46

HAMMERTON, JOHN

The Great War . . . I Was There! Undying Memories of 1914-1918. London: 1938-39. V. 44; 45; 46

The War Illustrated: a Pictorial Record of the Conflict of the Nations. London: 1919. V. 46

HAMMETT, DASHIELL

The Adventures of Sam Spade and Other Stories. 1944. V. 39

The Battle of the Eleutians . . . a Graphic History 1942-1943. Adak: 1943. V. 39

The Battle of the Aleutians. 1944. V. 45

The Big Knockover. New York: 1966. V. 41

The Continental Op. New York: 1974. V. 41

The Continental Op. New York: 1975. V. 37; 38; 40

The Crusader. 1980. V. 39

The Dain Curse. 1929. V. 39

HAMMETT, DASHIELL continued

The Dain Curse. New York: 1929. V. 39; 40; 45; 46

The Dashiell Hammett Omnibus. London: 1950. V. 44; 45

Dead Yellow Women. 1947. V. 39

The Glass Key. New York: 1931. V. 45; 46

The Maltese Falcon. 1930. V. 39

The Maltese Falcon. New York: 1930. V. 37; 39; 45; 46

The Maltese Falcon. San Francisco: 1983. V. 40; 41; 46

The Maltese Falcon. San Francisco: 1984. V. 39

Modern Tales of Horror. London: 1932. V. 46

$106,000 Blood Money. New York: 1943. V. 42; 45

Red Harvest. 1929. V. 39

Red Harvest. New York: 1929. V. 37; 41; 42; 43; 44; 45

Red Harvest. New York & London: 1929. V. 39; 40; 41

Secret Agent X-9. 1934. V. 45

The Thin Man. New York: 1934. V. 37; 39; 40; 41; 43; 45; 46

Woman in the Dark. 1951. V. 39

HAMMETT, MARY JANE

The Crusader. Sherman Oaks: 1980. V. 44

HAMMETT, SAMUEL

Piney Woods Tavern; or Sam Slick in Texas. Philadelphia: 1858. V. 41

HAMMETT, SAMUEL A.

A Stray Yankee in Texas. Redfield: 1853. V. 37; 38; 39; 40

A Stray Yankee in Texas. New York: 1853. V. 39; 45

HAMMOND, A. EDWARD

Men's Wear Display. London: 1930's. V. 41

HAMMOND, GEORGE P.

Campaigns in the West 1856-1861. The Journal of John Van Deusen DuBois. Tucson: 1949. V. 46

Captain Charles M. Weber: Pioneer of the San Joaquin and Founder of Stockton, California. Berkeley: 1966. V. 40

Don Juan de Onate, Colonizer of New Mexico, 1595-1628. Albuquerque: 1953. V. 39; 42

Narratives of the Coronado Expedition, 1540-1542. Albuquerque: 1940. V. 39; 42

New Spain and the Anglo-American West. Lancaster: 1932. V. 37; 38

The Rediscovery of New Mexico, 1580-1594: The Explorations of Chamuscado, Espejo, Castano de Sosa, Morlete and Leyva de Bonilla and Humana. Albuquerque: 1966. V. 41

A Scientist on the Trail. Berkeley: 1949. V. 38

The Treaty of Guadaloupe Hidalgo, February Second, 1848. Berkeley: 1949. V. 42

HAMMOND, GEORGE PETER

Coronado Cuarto Centennial Publications, 1540-1940. Albuquerque: 1940-66. V. 43

HAMMOND, HENRY

The Christians Obligations to Peace and Charity. London: 1649. V. 46

A Collection of Several Replies and Vindications Published of Late, Most of Them in Defence of the Church of England . . . London: 1657. V. 45

A Paraphrase and Annotations Upon all the Books of the New Testament. London: 1702. V. 39

A Paraphrase and Annotations Upon the Books of Pslams, Breifly Explaining the Difficulties Thereof. London: 1659. V. 44

A Practical Catechism. The Thirteenth Edition. Whereunto is added the Reasonableness of Christian Religion. London: 1691. V. 45

A View of the New Directory and a Vindication of the Ancient Liturgy of the Church of England. Oxford: 1646. V. 41

HAMMOND, ISAAC B.

Reminiscences of Frontier Life. Portland: 1904. V. 37; 42; 45; 46

HAMMOND, J. D.

Letter to the Hon. John C. Calhoun on the Annexation of Texas. Copperstown: 1844. V. 37; 39

HAMMOND, J. H.

The Farmer's and Mechanic's Practical Architect: and Guide in Rural Economy. Boston: 1858. V. 41

HAMMOND, JAMES

Love Elegies. Written in the Year 1732. London: 1743, 1742. V. 40

Love Elegies. Written in the Year 1732. London: 1762. V. 40

HAMMOND, JAMES HENRY

Gov. Hammond's Letters on Southern Slavery: Addressed to Thomas Clarkson, the English Abolitionist. Charleston: 1845. V. 44

The Railroad Mania; and Review of the Bank of the State of South Carolina, a Series of Essays. Charleston: 1848. V. 44

HAMMOND, JOHN

The Practical Surveyor, Containing the Most Approved Methods for Surveying of Lands and Waters . . . London: 1750. V. 45

HAMMOND, LUNA M.

Trials and Triumphs of an Orphan Girl. Cortland: 1859. V. 37

HAMMOND, NATHANIEL

The Elements of Algebra . . . to Which is Prefixed an Introduction . . . London: 1764. V. 40

HAMMOND, OTIS G.

Letters and Papers of Major-General John Sullivan, Continental Army. Concord: 1930-31-39. V. 39

The Utah Expedition 1857-1858. Concord: 1928. V. 46

HAMMOND, P. M.

The Book of the Piscatorial Society 1836-1936. London: 1936. V. 46

HAMMOND, ROBERT

The Electric Light in Our Homes. London: 1884. V. 44

Letters Between Col. Robert Hammond, Governor of the Isle of Wight, and the Committee of Lords and Commons . . . Relating to King Charles I . . . London: 1764. V. 39

HAMMOND, S. H.

Country Margins and Rambles of a Journalist. New York: 1855. V. 40

HAMMOND, THOMAS

These Four Views of the White Horse Hill . . . N.P.,: 1823. V. 46

HAMMOND TYPEWRITER COMPANY

Art in Typewriting. London: 1900. V. 41

HAMMOND, WILLIAM

Lectures on Veneral Diseases. Philadelphia: 1864. V. 42

HAMMOND, WILLIAM ALEXANDER 1828-1900

Insanity In Its Medico-Legal Relations. New York: 1866. V. 42

On Certain Conditions of Nervous Derangment . . . New York: 1881. V. 40

Physics and Physiology of Spiritualism. New York: 1871. V. 45; 46

Sexual Impotence in the Male. New York: 1883. V. 45

Sexual Impotence in the Male and Female. Detroit: 1887. V. 42

Sleep and Its Derangements. Philadelphia: 1869. V. 40; 45

Spinal Irritation. (Read Before the New York County Medical Society, Jan. 17, 1870). New York: 1870. V. 38

A Spiritualism and Allied Causes and Conditions of Nervous Derangement. London: 1876. V. 40; 41; 44

Spiritualism and Allied Cases and Conditions of Nervous Derangement. New York: 1876. V. 43

A Treatise on Hygiene with Special Reference to the Military Service. Philadelphia: 1863. V. 40

A Treatise on Insanity in Its Medical Relations. New York: 1883. V. 38; 42; 45

A Treatise on the Diseases of the Nervous System. New York: 1871. V. 42

HAMMOND'S Pictorial Atlas of the World. New York: 1907. V. 45

HAMMOND'S Standard Atlas of the World. New York: 1916. V. 45

HAMNER, LAURA V.

The No-Gun Man of Texas, 1938-1929. Amarillo: 1935. V. 37

HAMONIERE, G.

Vocabulaire Francais et Russe. Paris: 1815. V. 38

HAMOR, RALPH

A True Discourse on the Present State of Virginia . . . Richmond: 1860. V. 40; 45

HAMPSON, G. F.

Catalogue of the Lepidoptera Phaalaenae in the British Museum. London: 1898-1920. V. 37; 38

HAMPSTEAD ANTIQUARIAN & HISTORICAL SOCIETY

Transactions of the..for the Year 1899. Hampstead: 1900. V. 38

HAMPTON, RANDOLPH GORE

The Major in Washington City: A Series of Timely Letters From a Strict Southern Standpoint. New York: 1893. V. 37

HAMPTON, WADE

Reply of . . . Governor of South Carolina, and Others to the Chamberlain Memorial. Columbia: 1877. V. 44

HAMRICK, ALMA WARD

The Call of the San Saba, a History of San Saba County. San Antonio: 1941. V. 45

HAMSUN, KNUT 1859-1952

Hunger. London: 1899. V. 38

HAN, H.

Haploids of Higher Plants in Vitro. Beijing: 1986. V. 38

HANAFORD, PHEBE A.

The Life and Writings of Charles Dickens: a Woman's Memorial Volume. Augusta: 1871. V. 40; 43

HANAGHAN, JONATHAN

Eve's Moods Unveiled . . . Dublin;: 1957. V. 40; 42

HANBOROUGH PARROT PRESS

Hanborough Parrot Pieces, 1-4. Oxford: 1988. V. 42

HANBURY, DANIEL

Science Papers, Chiefly Pharmacological and Botanical. London: 1876. V. 38; 40; 41; 43

HANBURY, DAVID T.

Sport and Travel in the Northland of Canada. London: 1904. V. 37; 44; 45

HANBURY, THOMAS

The Garden at Mortola. V. 39; 40; 44

HANBURY, WILLIAM

A Complete Body of Planting and Gardening . . . London: 1770-71. V. 39

HANBURY-WILLIAMS, CHARLES

The Foundling Hospital for Wit. London: 1749-64. V. 38

HANCARVILLE, PIERRE FRANCOIS HUGHES, CALLED D'

Antiquities, Etrusques et Romaines. Paris: 1787. V. 37

HANCE, JOHN

Personal Impressions of the Grand Canyon of the Colorado River Near Flagstaff, Arizona as Seen through Nearly Two Thousand Eyes . . . San Francisco: 1899. V. 39

HANCHANT, W. L.

Mirth and Mocking on Sinner-Stocking! London: 1932. V. 40

HANCOCK, C. F.

Illustrated and Descriptive Catalogue of the Celebrated Devonshire Gems from the Collection of the Duke of Devonshire, K.G. Arranged and Mounted for His Grace, as a parure of Jewels. Westminster: 1857. V. 42

HANCOCK, JAMES

The Herons of the World. London: 1978. V. 40

HANCOCK, JOHN

Observations on the Climate, Soil and Productions of British Guiana, and on the Advantages of Emigration to and Colonising the Interior of That Country. London: 1840. V. 43

An Oration; Delivered March 5, 1774, at the Request of the Inhabitants of the Town of Boston; to Commemorate the Bloody Tragedy of the Fifth of March 1770. Boston: 1774. V. 37

HANCOCK, RICHARD RAMSEY

Hancock's Diary; or a History of the Second Tennessee Confederate Cavalry, with Sketches of First and Seventh Battalions . . . Nashville: 1887. V. 44

HANCOCK, SAMUEL

The Narrative of . . . 1845-1860. New York: 1927. V. 39; 45

HANCOCK, THOMAS

Exercitatio Medica Quaedam de Morbis Epidemicis . . . Edinburgh: 1806. V. 38

Personal Narrative of the Origin and Progress of . . . India-Rubber Manufacture in England. London: 1857. V. 42

Researches into the Laws and Phenomena of Pestilence; Including a Medical Sketch and Review of the Plague of London, in 1665; and Remarks on Quarantine. London: 1821. V. 42

HANCOCK, W. NEILSON

The Causes of Distress at Skull and Skibbereen During the Famine in Ireland. Dublin: 1850. V. 38

On the Prospects of the Beet-Sugar Manufacture in Ireland. Dublin: 1851. V. 38

HANCOCK, W. S.

Correspondence Between General W. T. Sherman, U. S. Army and Major General W. S. Hancock . . . Saint Paul: 1871. V. 38; 40; 45

Reports of Major General W. S. Hancock Upon Indian Affairs with Accompanying Exhibits. Washington: 1868. V. 45

HANCOCK, WILLIAM NEILSON

An Introductory Lecture on Political Economy. Dublin: 1849. V. 38; 39; 42

HANCOCK, WINFIELD S.

The Civil Record of Major-General Winfield S. Hancock During His Administration in Louisiana and Texas. N.P.: 1871. V. 41; 44

HANCOCK, WINFIELD S., MRS.

Reminiscences of . . . By His Wife. New York: 1987. V. 45

HANCOCKE, JOHN

Febrifugum Magnum; or, Common Water the Best Cure for Fevers and Probably for the Plague. London: 1723. V. 44

HAND, M. C.

From a Forest to a City: Personal Reminiscences of Syracuse. Syracuse: 1889. V. 41

THE HAND Phrenologically Considered: Being a Glimpse at the Relation of the Mind with the Organisation of the Body. London: 1848. V. 42

HAND, RICHARD A.

A Bookman's Guide to Hunting, Shooting, Angling and Related Subjects . . . Metuchen: 1991. V. 46

HAND, WILLIAM M.

The House Surgeon and Physician . . . Hartford: 1818. V. 42; 45

The House Surgeon and Physician. New Haven: 1820. V. 37; 38; 39; 40; 42

HANDASYDE, EMILY BUCHANAN

The Four Gardens. London: 1912. V. 38

THE HAND-BOOK of Pencil Drawing; Intended as a Key to All Drawing-Books Which Have No Written Instructions. London: 1843. V. 38

HAND-BOOK of the Oneida Community; with a Sketch of Its Founder, and an Outline of Its Constitution and Doctrines. Wallingford: 1867. V. 39

HAND-BOOK of Minneapolis, Prepared for the Thirty-Second Annual Meeting of the American Association for the Advancement of Science . . . 1883. Minneapolis: 1883. V. 39

HAND-BOOK Southern Kansas. Chicago: 1886. V. 42

HANDBOOK of Paleoichthyology. Volume 10: Otolithi Piscium. Stuttgart: 1985. V. 37

HANDBOOK of the Birds of Europe, The Middle East & North Africa. Volume 1. Ostrich to Ducks. London: 1977. V. 45

HANDBOOK of the Birds of Europe, The Middle East and North Africa. Volume 2. Hawks to Bustards. London: 1980. V. 45

HANDBOOK of the Birds of Europe, The Middle East and North Africa. Volume 2. Hawks to Bustards. London: 1982. V. 45

HANDBOOK of the Birds of Europe, The Middle East and North Africa. Volume 3. Waders to Gulls. London: 1983. V. 45

HANDBOOK of the Birds of Europe, The Middle East and North Africa. Volume 4. Terns to Woodpeckers. London: 1985. V. 45

HANDBOOK of the Birds of Europe, The Middle East and North Africa. Volume 5. Tyrant Flycatchers to Thrushes. London: 1985. V. 45

THE HANDBOOK of Turning. London: 1842. V. 40

THE HANDBOOK of Turning: Containing Instructions in Concentric, Elliptic, and Eccentric Turning: also Various Plates of Chucks, Tools and Instruments . . . London: 1852. V. 37

HANDBOOK to the Collection of British Pottery and Porcelain in the Museum of Practical Geology, Jermyn Street, London. London: 1893. V. 37

HANDBOOKS to the Cathedrals of England and Wales. London: 1869-87. V. 44

HANDBY, VIOLET E.

The Modern Kerry Blue Terrier. Manchester: 1933. V. 40

HANDEL, GEORGE FREDERICK

Hymen. A Serenata. Dublin: 1742. V. 38

Judas Macchabaeus. London: 1755. V. 38

Six Concertos, for the Harpsichord or Organ . . . 1760. V. 46

HANDEL, GEORGE FRIEDRICK

Judas Maccabaeus. London: 1850. V. 40

HANDFIELD-JONES, R. M.

Surgery of the Hand. Edinburgh: 1940. V. 42

HANDICRAFTS and Reconstruction. London: 1919. V. 44; 46

HANDLER, HANS

The Spanish Riding School. New York: 1972. V. 39

HANDLEY, JAMES

Colloquia Chirurgica. London: 1733. V. 38

HANDLEY, JAMES continued

Colloquia Chiurgica: or, the Whole Art of Surgery Epitomiz'd and Made Easie, According to Modern Practice. London: 1705. V. 37

HANDLEY-READ, C.

The Art of Wyndham Lewis. London: 1951. V. 42

HANDLIN, W. W.

American Poltics . . . New Orleans: 1864. V. 37; 39; 42

HANDMADE Papers of Japan. Tokyo: 1957. V. 38

HANDMADE Papers of Japan, Including an Abridged Reproduction of One of the Oldest Classics of Japanese Literature About Paper Making by Hand, Kamiskuki Japanese Literature About Paper Making . . . Tokyo: 1963. V. 46

THE HANDMAID To Arts, Sciences, Agriculture, &c. London: 1790. V. 41

HANDS, ELIZABETH

The Death of Amon. Coventry: 1789. V. 37

HANDSAKER, SAM

Pioneer Life. Eugene: 1908. V. 37; 42; 46

HANDSWORTH ECONOMICAL UNION

A Code of Laws for the Government of a Society of People Under the Appellation of the Handsworth Economical Union. Birmingham: 1830. V. 43

HANDY, ISAAC WILLIAM KER

Our National Sins. A Sermon, Delivered in the First Presbyterian Church, Portsmouth, Va. on the Day of Fasting, Humiliation and Prayer, Jan. 4, 1861. Portsmouth: 1861. V. 45

Salvation for the Sinner! N.P.: 1861. V. 38

HANDYSIDE, HENRY

A Treatise on an Improved Method for Overcoming Steep Gradients on Railways, Read Before the British Association in 1875, at Bristol. Bristol: 1878, V. 46

HANDYSIDE, PETER DAVID

A Probationary Essay on Osteo-Aneurism, or Aneurism of the Arterial Capillaries of Bone. Edinburgh: 1833. V. 42

HANEY, JOHN LOUIS

A Bibliography of Samuel Taylor Coleridge. Philadelphia: 1903. V. 43

HANGAY, G.

Biological Museum Methods. London: 1985. V. 38

HANGER, GEORGE

The Life, Adventures and Opinions of Col. George Hanger. London: 1801. V. 37; 38; 42; 43; 44; 45; 46

Military Reflections on the Attack and Defence of London . . . London: 1795. V. 37; 42

To All Sportsmen, and Particularly to Farmers and Gamekeepers. London: 1814. V. 45

HANHART, M.

Confederate Camp During the Late American War from the Original Painting by C. W. Chapman . . . 59th Virginia Regiment . . . London: 1871. V. 42

HANKEY, THOMSON

The Principles of Banking, Its Utility and Economy, with Remarks on the Working and Management of the Bank of England. London: 1887. V. 38; 39; 41

The Principles of Banking, its Utility and Economy; with remarks on the Working and Managment of the Bank of England. London;: 1873. V. 37

HANKINS, C.

Dakota Land: or, the Beauty of St. Paul. New York: 1868. V. 37; 42

HANKSHAW, JOHN

Letters Written from Colombia, During a Journey from Caracas to Bogota and Thence to Santa Martha in 1823. London: 1824. V. 39

HANLEY, JAMES

At Bay. London: 1935. V. 41; 42; 43; 44

Boy. Paris: 1936. V. 42

Broken Water - An Autobiographical Excursion. London: 1937. V. 38

Captain Bottell. Boriswood: 1933. V. 39

Captain Bottell. London: 1933. V. 38

Drift. London: 1930. V. 39; 41; 42

Ebb & Flood. London: 1932. V. 38; 39; 40; 41

The Furys. 1935. V. 37

The Furys. London: 1935. V. 38; 40

The German Prisoner. London: 1930. V. 43; 44; 45; 46

Grey Children. A Study in Humbug and Misery in South Wales. London: 1937. V. 42

Half an Eye; Sea Stories. London: 1937. V. 40

Hollow Sea. London: 1928. V. 37

The House in the Valley. London: 1951. V. 42

The Last Voyage. London: 1931. V. 39; 40; 42; 43

Levine. London: 1956. V. 38; 46

Lost - a Short Story. Vancouver: 1979. V. 41

Men in Darkness. London: 1931. V. 41

Men in Darkness. New York: 1932. V. 44

Quartermaster Clausen. London: 1934. V. 37

Resurrexit Dominus. London: 1934. V. 43; 46

Resurrexit Dominus. N.P.: 1934. V. 37

Stoker Haslett. London: 1932. V. 37; 38; 39; 42; 43

Stoker Haslett. London: 1932. V. 43

The Welsh Sonata. London: 1954. V. 44

HANMER, THOMAS

The Correspondence. London: 1838. V. 38

Philological Inquiries in three Parts. London: 1781. V. 38

HANNA, CHARLES A.

The Scotch-Irish; or, the Scot in North America, North Britain, and North Ireland. New York: 1902. V. 37; 39; 43; 46

The Wilderness Trail or the Ventures and Adventures of the Pennsylvania Traders of the Allegheney Path . . . New York: 1911. V. 37; 39; 41

The Wilderness Trail, or the Ventures and Adventures of the Pennsylvania Traders on the Allegheny Path . . . With some New Annals of the Old West, and the Records of some Strong Men and some Bad Ones. New York/London: 1911. V. 37

HANNA, JOHN SMITH

A History of the Life and Services of Captain Samuel Dewees, a Native of Pennsylvania, and a Soldier of the Revolution and the Last Wars. Baltimore: 1844. V. 39; 41

HANNA, PAUL R.

Frank Lloyd Wright's Hanna House; the Clients' Report. New York: 1981. V. 46

HANNA, WILLIAM

Memoirs of the Life and Writings of Thomas Chalmers. Edinburgh & London: 1849-52. V. 42

Memoirs of the Life and Writings of Thomas Chalmers, D.D., LL.D. Edinburgh: 1851-52. V. 43

HANNAFORD, SAMUEL

Jottings in Australia. Melbourne: 1856. V. 41

The Wild Flowers of Tasmania, or Chatty Rambles Afloat and Ashore, Amidst the Seawees and Flowering Plants . . . Melbourne: 1866. V. 46

HANNAH, BARRY

Airships. New York: 1978. V. 41; 46

Black Butterfly. 1982. V. 42

Geronimo Rex. New York: 1972. V. 37; 38; 39; 40; 42; 43; 44; 46

Neighborhood: an Early Fragment from Ray. University of Alabama: 1981. V. 38; 41

Nightswatchmen. New York: 1973. V. 39; 42; 45

Power and Light. N.P.: 1963. V. 42

Power and Light. Winston Salem: 1983. V. 41; 46

HANNAY, DAVID

A Short History of the Royal Navy, 1217 to 1688. London: 1898. V. 42

HANNAY, JAMES

The History of Acadia, From Its First Discovery to Its Surrender to Engand by the Treaty of Paris. St. John: 1879. V. 42; 43

History of the War of 1812, Between Great Britain and the United States of America. Canada: 1901. V. 41

History of New Brunswick. St. John: 1909. V. 42

HANNAY, JAMES OWEN 1865-1950

Irishmen All . . . London: 1913. V. 43

HANNEMAN, AUDRE

Ernest Hemingway, A Comprehensive Bibliography with Supplement to Ernest Hemingway, a Comprehensive Bibliography. Princeton: 1969. V. 41

HANNETT, JOHN

Bibliopegia; or, the Art of Bookbinding in All Its Branches. London: 1835. V. 44

Bibliopegia; or, the Art of Bookbinding In All Its Branches . . . London: 1836. V. 41

Bibliopegia; or, Bookbinding . . . London: 1865. V. 41

An Inquiry into the Nature and Form of Books of the Ancients; with a History of the Art of Bookbinding. London: 1837. V. 38; 41

HAOLE,

Sandwich Island Notes, an Account of Affairs in 1853, Past and Present Conditions and Origins, Treaties, Missionary Enterprises, Crime . . . New York & London: 1854. V. 41

HAPGOOD, HUTCHINS

Four Poets of the Ghetto. 1963. V. 46

HAPPOLD, D. C. D.

The Mammals of Nigeria. Oxford: 1987. V. 38; 39

HAPPY Birthday, George. 1979. V. 42

HAPPY Changes, or Story of John, Paul and David. London: 1850. V. 46

THE HAPPY Courtezan; or, The Prude Demolish'd. London: 1735. V. 45

THE HAPPY Man. The True Gentleman. N.P.: 1800-10. V. 45

THE HAPPY Negro, Being a True Account of an Extraordinary Negro in North America . . . York: 1825. V. 44

THE HAPPY Rock - A Book About Henry Miller. Berkeley: 1945. V. 46

HAPRER, WILLIAM

The Advice of a Friend to the Army and People of Scotland. N.P.: 1745. V. 39

HARA, H.

An Enumeration of the Flowering Plants of Nepal. London: 1978-82. V. 37; 38

HARADA, JIRO

The Gardens of Japan. London: 1928. V. 44

HARADA, YOSHITO

Mu-Yang-Ch'eng, Han and Pre-han Sites at the Foot of Mount Lao-Tieh in South Manchuria, Archaeologia Orientalis. Tokyo & Kyoto: 1931. V. 42

HARAPER, ROBERT GOODLOE

A Short Account of the Principal Proceedings of Congress . . . and a Sketch of the State of Affairs Between the United States and France in July 1798. Philadelphia: 1798. V. 38

HARASZTHY, A.

Grape Culture, Wines and Wine Making. New York: 1862. V. 37

HARASZTI, ZOLTAN

The Enigma of the Bay Psalm Book. Chicago and London: 1965. V. 40

HARBAUGH, H.

The Life of Rev. Michael Schlatter. Philadelphia: 1857. V. 43

HARBAUGH, HENRY

The Fathers of the German Reformed Church in Europe and America. Lancaster: 1857-81. V. 39

The Life of Rev. Michael Schlatter. Philadelphia: 1857. V. 39; 41; 43

HARBESON, GEORGIANA BROWN

American Needlework. New York: 1938. V. 42

HARBESON, JOHN F.

The Study of Architectural Design: With Special Reference to the Program of the Beaux Arts Institute of Design. New York: 1926. V. 42

The Study of Architectural Design. New York: 1927. V. 41

HARBEY, GIDEON

The City Remembrancer; being Historical Narratives of the Great Plague at London 1665; Great Fire 1666; Great Storm 1703 . . . The whole compiled from the curious and authentic Papers of the late very learned Dr. Harvey, his Majesty's Physician to the Tower . . . London: 1769. V. 37

HARBIN, GEORGE

The Hereditary Right of the Crowns of England Asserted . . . London: 1713. V. 38; 41; 42

THE HARBINGER - a May Gift. Boston: 1833. V. 38

HARBISON, MASSY

A Narrative of the Sufferings of Massy Harbison, from Indian Barbarity . . . Pittsburgh: 1828. V. 46

A Narrative of the Sufferings of Massy Harbison, from Indian Barbarity . . . Pittsburgh: 1829. V. 45

HARBORNE, J. B.

Plant Chemosystematics. London: 1984. V. 37

HARBOUR, JENNIE

My Book of Favourite Fairy Tales. London. V. 45

THE HARBRINGER - a May Gift. Boston: 1833. V. 39

HARCOUET DE LONGEVILLE

Long Livers: a Curious History of Such Persons of Both Sexes Who Have Liv'd Several Ages, and Grown Young Again . . . London: 1722. V. 37; 46

HARCOURT, G. J.

The Regimental Records of the First Battalion The Royal Dublin Fusiliers, Formerly the Madras Europeans, The Madras European Regiment, the First Madras Fusiliers, the 102nd Royal Madras fusiliers, 1644-1842. London: 1910. V. 41

HARCOURT, G. M.

Banking and Commercial Guide. Houston: 1891. V. 44

HARCOURT, ROBERT

A Relation of a Voyage to Guiana. London: 1613. V. 45

The Relation of a Voyage to Guiana. London: 1626. V. 41

HARCOURT-SMITH, SIMON

The Last of Uptake or the Estranged Sisters. London: 1942. V. 37; 40; 41

HARCUS, WILLIAM

Handbook for Emigrants Proceeding to Adelaid, South Australia . . . London: 1873. V. 43

South Australia: Its History, Resources and Productions. London: 1876. V. 38; 46

THE HARD Case of Mary Squires, the Gipsey, and Susanna Wells. London: 1753. V. 46

HARD, M. K.

Woman's Medical Guide: Being a Complete Review of the Peculiarities of the Female Constitution and the Derangements to Which It Is Subject. Mt. Vernon: 1848. V. 45

HARDCASTLE, EPHRAIM

Wine and Walnuts; or, After Dinner Chit-Chat. By Ephraim Hardcastle, Citizen and Dry-Salter. London: 1823. V. 37

HARDEE, WILLIAM J.

Memorial. Army of Tennessee . . . Richmond: 1863. V. 42; 44; 45

HARDEE, WILLIAM JOSEPH

Rifle and Light Infantry Tactis for the Exercise and Manoeuvres of Troops When Acting as Light Infantry or Riflemen. Philadelphia: 1855. V. 42

Rifle and Light Infantry Tactics: for the Exercise. Memphis: 1861. V. 38; 45

Rifle and Infantry Tactics, Revised and Improved. Mobile: 1861. V. 44

HARDEN, DONALD B.

Roman Glass from Karanis Found by the University of Michigan Archaeological Expedition in Egypt, 1924-29. Ann Arbor: 1936. V. 42

HARDEN, JACOB S.

Life Confession and Letters of Courtship of Jacob S. Harden, of the M.E. Church, Mount Lebanon, Hunterdon Co., N.J. Executed for the Murder of His Wife, on the 6th of July 1860, at Belvidere, Warren Co., N. J. Hackettstown: 1860. V. 41

HARDEN, SAMUEL

The Pioneer. Greenfield: 1895. V. 39

HARDENBURG, W. E.

The Putumayo, the Devil's Paradise, Travels in the Peruvian Amazon Region and an Account of the Atrocities Committed Upon the Indians Therein. London: 1913. V. 39

HARDESTY, H. H.

Hardesty's Historical and Geographical Encyclopedia . . . New York:/ Richmond:/: 1884. V. 45

HARDHAM, JOHN

The Fortune-Tellers; or the World Unmask'd. London: 1750? V. 40

HARDIE, JAMES

An Account of the Yellow Fever, Which Occured in the City of New York, in the Year, 1822. New York: 1822. V. 39

HARDIE, MARTIN

English Coloured Books. London: 1906. V. 37; 38; 40; 41; 45

English Colored Books. London: 1906. V. 38

English Coloured Books. (1906). V. 37

The Etched and Engraved Work of Sir Frant Short. 1918-20. V. 39

The Etched Work of W. Lee-Hankey, R.E. from 1904 to 1920. London: 1920. V. 42; 44

The Etched Work of W. Lee Hankey, R.E. from 1904 to 1920. London: 1921. V. 41

Etchings and Drypoints from 1902 to 1924 by James McBey. London: 1925. V. 38; 39; 41

Frederick Goulding, Master Printer of Copper Plates. 1910. V. 44

Frederick Goulding, Master Printer of Copper Plates. Stirling: 1910. V. 39; 41; 42; 44

HARDY, PHILIP DIXON

The Northern Tourist, or Stranger's Guide to the North and North West of Ireland, etc. Dublin: 1830. V. 37; 38

HARDY, RENE

Bitter Victory. Garden City: 1956. V. 41; 42

The Sword of God. Garden City: 1954. V. 44

HARDY, ROBERT WILLIAM HALE

Travels in the Interior of Mexico in 1825, 1826, 1827 and 1828. London: 1829. V. 38; 39; 42; 45

HARDY, THOMAS 1840-1928

A Changed Man, the Waiting Supper, and Other Tales, Concluding with the Romantic Adventures of a Milkmaid. London: 1913. V. 37; 38; 39; 40; 41; 44; 45

Compassion - an Ode - In Celebration of the Centenary of the Royal Society for the Prevention of Cruelty to Animals. London: 1924. V. 41; 44

The Duke's Reappearance: a Tradition. New York: 1927. V. 37; 39; 40

The Dynasts. London: 1903-06-08. V. 40

The Dynasts. London: 1904-06-08. V. 40; 41

The Dynasts. London: 1904-08. V. 42

The Dynasts. London: 1904-09-08. V. 38; 40

The Dynasts. London: 1927. V. 37; 38; 40; 41; 42; 43; 44; 45; 46

The Famous Tragedy of the Queen of Cornwall at Tintagel in Lyonnesse. 1923. V. 45

The Famous Tragedy of the Queen of Cornwall at Tintagel in Lyonnesse. London: 1923. V. 41

The Famous Tragedy of the Queen of Cornweall at Tintagel in Lyonesse . . . New York: 1923. V. 46

Far from the Madding Crowd. With twelve illustrations by Helen Allingham. London: 1874. V. 37

Far from the Madding Crowd. Cambridge: 1958. V. 38; 40; 41

Far From the Madding Crowd. London: 1958. V. 43

Far From the Madding Crowd. New York: 1958. V. 39; 41; 43

Fellow-Townsmen. New York: 1880. V. 41

A Group of Noble Dames.. London: 1891. V. 37; 38; 39; 42; 43

The Hand of Ethelberta. London: 1876. V. 37; 46

How I Built Myself a House. 1865. V. 41

Human Shows Far Phantasies. London: 1925. V. 41; 42; 45

Human Shows Far Phantasies. New York: 1925. V. 39; 41

An Indiscretion in the Life of an Heiress. London: 1934. V. 37

Jude the Obscure. London: 1896. V. 37; 38; 40; 41; 44; 46

Jude the Obscure. New York: 1896. V. 39; 40; 46

Jude the Obscure. London: 1896, 1895. V. 38; 46

Jude the Obscure. New York: 1896, 1895. V. 38

Jude the Obscure. A Letter and a Foreword. Lakewood: 1917. V. 46

Jude the Obscure. New York: 1969. V. 38; 41

A Laodicean; or, the Castle of the de Staneys. London: 1881. V. 43; 45

A Laodicean. New York: 1881. V. 46

Late Lyrics and Earlier. London: 1922. V. 40; 41; 45; 46

Late Lyrics and Earlier. London: 1922. V. 46

Life's Little Ironies. 1894. V. 46

Life's Little Ironies. London: 1894. V. 37; 38; 39; 40; 41; 43

The Mayor of Casterbridge: the Life and Death of a Man of Character. London: 1886. V. 44; 46

The Mayor of Casterbridge. London: 1887. V. 38

The Mayor of Casterbridge. New York: 1964. V. 38; 40; 42

Moments of Vision and Miscellaneous Verses. London: 1917. V. 39

Notes on 'The Dynasts' in Four Letters to Edward Clodd. Edinburgh: 1929. V. 37

Novels and Stories of . . . The Library Edition. London: 1951-61. V. 37

Old Mrs. Chundle: a Short Story. Los Angeles: 1978. V. 41

Our Exploits at West Poley. 1952. V. 45

The Oxen. Hove: 1915. V. 37; 40; 42; 44; 46

The Oxen. Hove: 1915. V. 44

The Oxen. N.P.: 1915. V. 43; 45

The Patriot. Addressed to the People, of the Present State of Affairs in Britain and in France. Edinburgh: 1793. V. 41

The Play of St. George. New York: 1928. V. 43

The Return of the Native. V. 46

The Return of the Native. London: 1878. V. 45

The Return of the Native. London: 1878. V. 37; 38; 41; 43; 45

The Return of the Native. New York: 1895. V. 39

Return of the Native. London: 1913. V. 38; 40; 43

The Return of the Native. London: 1929. V. 38; 40; 41; 42; 43; 44; 46

The Return of the Native. New York: 1929-. V. 46

The Return of the Native. New York: 1942. V. 42

Satires of Circumstance Lyrics and Reveries. London: 1914. V. 38; 46

Selected Poems of Thomas Hardy. Liverpool: 1916. V. 41

Selected Poems. London: 1916. V. 46

Selected Poems. 1921. V. 45

Selected Poems of Thomas Hardy. London: 1921. V. 37; 38; 39

Selected Poems of Thomas Hardy. London: 1926. V. 43

Selected Poems. 1980. V. 45

Selected Poems . . . Sussex: 1980. V. 38

Short Stories. London: 1928. V. 38; 40

Song of the Soldiers. Hove: 1915. V. 41

Song of the Soldiers. London: 1914. V. 37

Tess of the D'Urbervilles. London: 1891. V. 37; 38; 40; 41; 42; 43; 44; 45

Tess of the D'Urbervilles. London: 1892. V. 37; 38; 39; 42

Tess of the D'Urbervilles. London and New York: 1899. V. 39

Tess of the D'Urbervilles. London: 1903. V. 37

Tess of the D'Urbervilles. London: 1926. V. 37; 38; 41

Tess of the D'Urbervilles. New York: 1956. V. 38; 44; 46

The Three Wayfarers. New York: 1930. V. 44; 46

The Three Wayfarers. Dorchester, Dorset: 1935. V. 40

The Three Wayfarers. Dorset: 1935. V. 40

A Trampwoman's Tragedy. London: 1917. V. 37

The Trumpet-Major. London: 1880. V. 38

The Trumpet-Major. New York: 1880. V. 46

Two on a Tower, a Romance. London: 1883. V. 37

Under the Greenwood Tree - a Rural Painting of the Dutch School. London: 1913. V. 40

Under the Greenwood Tree or The Mellstock Quire. London: 1940. V. 42; 45

The Well-Beloved. 1897. V. 45

The Well-Beloved. London: 1897. V. 37; 39; 41; 46

Wessex Poems and Other Verses. London: 1898. V. 37; 40

Wessex Poems and Other Verses. London & New York: 1898. V. 39; 41; 42

Wessex Poems and Other Verses. New York: 1898. V. 46

Wessex Poems and Other Verses. New York: & London: 1899. V. 46

Wessex Tales Strange, Lively and Commonplace. London: 1888. V. 41; 45

Wessex Tales, Strange, Lively and Commonplace. New York: 1888. V. 37

Winter Words in Various Moods and Metres. London: 1928. V. 37; 43

Winter Words, in Various Moods and Metres. New York: 1928. V. 41

The Woodlanders. London: 1887. V. 38; 39; 42; 45

The Woodlanders. London: 1897. V. 38

The Woodlanders. London: 1903. V. 45

The Works of Thomas Hardy. London: 1907-14. V. 38

Works. New York: 1910. V. 46

The Works in Prose and Verse. London: 1917. V. 42

Works. London: 1919. V. 38; 42; 44; 45; 46

The Works. London: 1919-20. V. 37; 38; 43; 46

The Writings of Thomas Hardy. New York: London: V. 41

The Writings of Thomas Hardy in Prose and Verse. New York: 1915. V. 46

The Writings in Prose and Verse. New York: 1920. V. 42; 44

The Writings of Thomas Hardy in Prose and Verse. New York: & London: 1920. V. 43; 46

Yuletide in a Younger World. New York: 1927. V. 44

HARDY, THOMAS DUFUS 1804-1878

Rotuli Litterarum Clausarum in Turri Londinensi Asservati, 1204-1227. London: 1833/44. V. 40

HARDY, W. J.

Book-Plates. London: 1893. V. 41

Bookplates. New York & London: 1897. V. 40

The Handwriting of the Kings and Queens of England. London: 1893. V. 40

HARDY, WILLIAM

The Miner's Guide; or, Complete Miner. Sheffield: 1748. V. 40

The Miner's Guide; or Compleat Miner. Birmingham: 1762. V. 39

HARDY, WILLIAM BATE

Collected Scientific Papers . . . Cambridge: 1936. V. 40

HARDYNG, JOHN

The Chronicle From the First Begynnyng of Englande, Unto the Reigne of King Edward the Fourth Where He Made an End of His Chronicle . . . London: 1543. V. 41

HARDYNGE, HAL

Cheltenham Lyrics, Lays of a Modern Troubadour, and Other Poems. Cheltenham;: 1830. V. 42

HARE, AUGUSTUS J. C.

Memorials of a Quiet Life. London: 1874-76. V. 37; 40

HARE, AUGUSTUS J. C. continued

The Story of Two Noble Lives. London: 1893. V. 45

The Story of My Life. London: 1896-1900. V. 39

The Story of My Life. New York: 1896-1901. V. 41

The Story of Two Noble Lives. London: 1898. V. 38; 42

Walks in Rome. London: 1883. V. 39

HARE, BISHOP

Eleventh Annual Report of the Missionary Bishop of Niobrara. N.P.: 1883. V. 42

HARE, FRANCIS AUGUSTUS

The Last of the Bushrangers. London: 1892. V. 40

HARE, HOBART AMORY

A System of Practical Therapeutics. Philadelphia: 1891-97. V. 38

HARE, KENNETH

London's Latin Quarter. London: 1926. V. 37; 38

Three Poems. London: 1916. V. 46

HARE, ROBERT

On Electricity. Philadelphia: 1826. V. 43

HARE, W. LOFTUS

The Court of the Printer's Guild. London: 1914. V. 44

The Court of the Printer's Guild. New York: 1949. V. 45

The Court of the Printer's Guild. San Francisco: 1975. V. 45

HARFORD, FREDERICK K.

Epigrammatica, Serious, Semi-Serious and Divertive. London: 1890. V. 38

HARFORD, JOHN SCANDRETT

Considerations Upon the Pernicious Influence of the Bristol Gaol, Both in Relation to the Health and Morals of the Prisoners Confined Therein . . . Bristol: 1815. V. 43

HARGIS, O. P.

Thrilling Experiences of a First Georgia Cavalryman in the Civil War. Special Scout Under General Wheeler. Rose. V. 42

HARGRAVE, CATHERINE PERRY

A History of Playing Cards and a Bibliogrpahy of Cards and Gaming. Boston: 1930. V. 43

A History of Playing Cards and a Bibliography of Cards and Gaming. Boston and New York: 1930. V. 37; 39

A History of Playing Cards and a Bibliography of Cards and Gaming. New York: 1930. V. 41

HARGRAVE, FRANCIS

An Argument in Defence of Literary Property. London: 1774. V. 39; 42

Collectanea Juridica, Consisting of Tracts Relative to the Law and Constitution of England. London: 1792. V. 40

A Collection of Tracts Relative to the Law of England. London: 1787. V. 43

Juridical Arguments and Collection. London: 1797. V. 40

HARGRAVE, JAMES

The Hargrave Correspondence 1821-1843. Toronto: 1859. V. 38

The Hargrave Correspondence 1821-1843. Toronto: 1938. V. 38; 42

HARGRAVE, JOSEPH JAMES

Red River. Montreal: 1871. V. 37; 38; 39; 40; 41; 42; 43; 45

HARGRAVE, LETITIA

The Letters of Letitia Hargrave. Toronto: 1947. V. 38; 45

HARGROVE, ELY

Anecdotes of Archery, from the Earliest Ages to the Year 1791. York: 1792. V. 39; 46

Anecdotes of Archery, from the Earliest Ages to the Year 1791. York: 1845. V. 46

The History of the Castle, Town and Forest of Knaresborough, With Harrogate, and Its Medicinal Waters. York: 1789. V. 41

HARGROVE, WILLIAM

History and Description of the Ancient City of York . . . London: 1818. V. 44

HARICH-SCHNEIDER, ETA

A History of Japanese Music. London: 1973. V. 46

HARIKARANA, MULTANI

The Forms of Herkern Corrected from a Variety of manuscripts, Supplied with the Distinguishing Marks of Construction and Translated into English . . . Calcutta: 1781. V. 40

HARINGTON, EDWARD

A Schizzo on the Genius of Man. Bath: 1793. V. 41; 42

HARINGTON, JOHN

The Metamorphosis of Ajax. London: 1927. V. 42

HARIOT, THOMAS 1560-1621

Admiranda Narratio Fida Tamen, de Commodis et Incoloarum Ritibus Virginae. Frankfurt: 1590. V. 40; 41

Admiranda Narratio Fida Tamen, De Comodis et Incolarum Ritibus Virginiae . . . Francoforti ad Moenum: 1590. V. 38

Artis Analyticae Praxis ad Aequationes Algebraicas Nova, Expedita & Generali Methodo . . . London: 1631. V. 38; 41

HARISON, ROBERT

The Surgical Anatomy of the Arteries of the Human Body: Designed for the Use of Students in the Dissecting Room. Dublin: 1824-25. V. 37

HARKER, A.

The Tertiary Ingenous Rocks of Skye. London: 1904. V. 46

HARKER, W.

A Practical Grammar of Music . . . London: 1830. V. 42

HARKEY, DEE

Mean as Hell. 1948. V. 37

HARKIN, WILLIAM

Scenery and Antiquities of North West Donegal. Londonderry: 1893. V. 43

HARKINS, HENRY

The Treatment of Burns. London: 1942. V. 42

HARKNESS, JOHN GRAHAM

Stormont, Dundas and Glengarry: a History. 1784-1945. Oshawa: 1946. V. 38; 41; 42

HARLAN, JACOB WRIGHT

California, '46 to '88. Oakland: 1888. V. 40

California '46 to '88. San Francisco: 1888. V. 40; 41; 45

HARLAN, RICHARD 1796-1843

Fauna Americana . . . Philaelphia: 1825. V. 39; 40; 42; 43

Medical and Physical Researches. Philadelphia: 1835. V. 39

Refutation of Certain Misrepresentations Issued Against the Author of the 'Fauna Americana' in the Philadelphia Franklin Journal No. 1 1826 and in the North American Review No. 50. Philadelphia: 1826. V. 41; 45; 46

HARLAN, ROBERT D.

Bibliography of the Grabhorn Press 1957-1966 & Grabhorn-Hoyem 1966-1973. (With Check-List 1916-1956 and a Complete Specimen of Types). San Francisco: 1972. V. 37

HARLAND, HENRY

As It Was Written. New York: 1885. V. 42

As It Was Written: a Jewish Musician's Story. New York: 1885. V. 40

Comedies and Errors. London: 1898. V. 40

Grey Roses. London: 1896. V. 40

Mademoiselle Miss and Other Stories. London: 1893. V. 40

My Friend Prospero. New York: 1904. V. 38

HARLAND, J.

Historical Account of the Cistercian Abbey of Salley in Craven, Yorkshire Founded A.D. 1147 . . . London: 1853. V. 38; 41

HARLAND, JOHN WHITFIELD

The Printing Arts, an Epitome of the Theory, Practice, Processes and Mutual Relations of Engraving, Lithography & Printing, In Black and in Colours. London: 1892. V. 44

HARLE, JONATHAN

An Historical Essay on the State of Physick in the Old and New Testament, and the Apocryphal Interval. London: 1729. V. 41

HARLEIAN Miscellany. A Collection of Scarce, Curious and Entertaining Pamphlets and Tracts, As Well as In Manuscript as in Print. London: 1808-13. V. 38; 43

HARLEIAN Miscellany, or, a Collection of Scarce, Curious and Entertaining Pamphlets and Tracts, as Well in Manuscript as in Print, Found in the Latae Earl of Oxford's Library. London: 1744. V. 37

THE HARLEIAN Miscellany; or, a Collection of Scarce, Curious and Entertaining Pamphlets and Tracts . . . Found in the Late Earl of Oxford's Library. London: 1808-11. V. 46

HARLEQUIN Premier: a Farce, as It Is Daily Acted. London: 1769. V. 38

THE HARLEQUINS. London: 1753. V. 38

HARPER, IDA HUSTED

The Life and Work of Susan B. Anthony . . . Indianapolis: 1899/1908. V. 42

HARPER, J. R.

Paul Kane's Frontier. Austin: 1971. V. 39

HARPER, J. RUSSELL

Historical Directory of New Brunswick Newspapers and Periodicals. Fredericton: 1961. V. 37

Painting in Canada: A History. Toronto: 1966. V. 37

Portrait of a Period. A Collection of Notman Photographs 1856 to 1915. With an introduction by Edgar Andrew Collard. Montreal: 1967. V. 37; 39

HARPER, JOSEPH M.

Mr. Harper's Report to the Legislature of New Hampshire on the Culture of Silk. N.P.: 1830. V. 39

HARPER, L.

Preliminary Report of the Geology and Agriculture of the State of Mississippi. Jackson: 1857. V. 42; 43

HARPER, LATHROP C.

A Selection of Incunabula. New York: 1930. V. 40; 42

HARPER, MALCOLM M. I.

Rambles in Galloway. London: 1896. V. 41

HARPER, ROBERT FRANCIS

The Code of Hammurabi King of Babylon About 2250 B.C. Chicago: 1904. V. 40

HARPER, ROBERT GOODLOE

The Case of Georgia Sales on the Mississippi Considered . . . Philadelphia: 1799. V. 42

Correspondence Respecting Russia, Between Robert Goodloe Harper, Esq. and Robert Walsh, Jun. Philadelphia: 1813. V. 45

A Letter from Robert Goodloe Harper of South Carolina to His Constituents. Cambridge: 1801. V. 44

Observations on the Dispute Between the United States and France. London. V. 39

Observations on the Dispute Between the United States and France, Addressed by Robert Harper, Esq. Dublin: 1798. V. 42

Observations on the Dispute Between the United States and France, Addressed by Rober +Harper, Esq. Philadelphia printed: 1798. V. 46

A Short Account of the Principal Proceedings in Congress, in the Late Session and a Sketch of the State of Affairs Between the United States and France in July 1798; in a letter from Robt. Goodloe Harper, Esq. of South Carolina . . . London: 1798. V. 39

Speech on the Foreign Intercourse Bill: Delivered in the House of Representatives of the United States, on Friday, Marcy 2, 1798. London: 1798. V. 38; 39

HARPER, THOMAS

The Accomptant's Companion; or Young Arithmetician's Guide . . . London: 1765. V. 39

HARPER, WILLIAM

A Letter to the Archbishop of York: Humbly Offering to His Graces's Solution, Some Doubts and Scruples Suggested by His Late Speech to the Grand Meeting of the County of York, Called to Subscribe an Association for Supporting the German Government . . . N.P.: 1945. V. 39

Memoir on Slavery, Read Before the Society for the Advancement of Learning, of South Carolina, At Its Annual Meeting at Columbia, 1837. Charleston: 1838. V. 44

HARPER'S Encyclopaedia of U.S. History to 1905. New York: 1905. V. 44

HARPER'S History of the War in the Philippines. New York: & London: 1900. V. 46

HARPSFIELD, NICHOLAS

The Life and Death of Sr Thomas More, Knight, Sometimes Lord High Chancellor of England . . . Oxford: 1932. V. 46

THE HARPSICHORD Illustrated and Improved . . . London: 1731. V. 45

HARPUR, YVONNE

Decoration in Egyptian Tombs of the Old Kingdom. London: and New York: 1987. V. 44

HARRADEN, R.

Cantabrigia Depicta; A Series of Engravings Representing the Most Picturesque and Interesting Edifices in the University of Cambridge; With an Historical and Descriptive Account of each. Cambridge: 1809. V. 37

HARRAP, GEORGE G.

Love Lyrics from Five Centuries. London: 1932. V. 41; 46

HARRELL, JOHN M.

The Brooks and Baxter War: A History of the Reconstruction Period in Arkansas. St. Louis: 1893. V. 37; 39; 44

HARRER, WILLIAM

With Drum and Gun in '61. A Narrative of the Adventures of William Harrer of the Fourteenth New York State Volunteers. Greenville: 1908. V. 42

HARRIET & Mary. Being the Relations Between Percy Bysshe Shelley, Harriet Shelley, Mary Shelley, and Thos. Jefferson Hogg. (London): 1944. V. 37

HARRILL, LAWSON

Reminiscences 1861-1865. Statesville: 1910. V. 37; 42

HARRIMAN Alaska Expedition. New York: 1901. V. 37

HARRIMAN ALASKA EXPEDITION, 1899.

Alaska. London: 1901. V. 38

HARRIMAN-BROWNE, ALICE

Chaperoning Adrienne: a Tale of the Yellowstone National Park. Seattle: 1907. V. 39

HARRIMAN, EDWARD H.

Harriman Alaska Expedition. New York: 1901. V. 45

HARRINGTON, ALAN

Life in the Crystal Palace. New York: 1959. V. 46

The Revelations of Dr. Modesto. New York: 1955. V. 39

The Secret Swinger. New York: 1966. V. 39

HARRINGTON, CHARLES

Summering in Colorado. Denver: 1874. V. 37; 38

HARRINGTON, H. N.

The Engraved Work of Sir Francis Seymour Haden, P.R.E. an Illustrated and Descriptive Catalogue. Liverpool: 1910. V. 46

HARRINGTON, JAMES 1611-1677

The Censure of the Rota Upon Mr. Milton's Book, Entitled, the Ready and Easie Way to Establish a Free Common-Wealth. London: 1660. V. 45; 46

The Commonwealth of Oceana. London: 1656. V. 45

The Oceana . . . and His Other Works. London: 1700. V. 37; 41; 42; 45; 46

The Oceana . . . and His Other Works. Dublin: 1737. V. 37; 38; 39

The Oceana and Other Works. London: 1737. V. 38

The Perogative of Popular Government. London: 1657. V. 37

HARRINGTON, JOHN W.

The Jumping Kangaroo and the Apple Butter Cat. New York: 1900. V. 37

HARRINGTON, ROBERT

A Philosophical and Experimental Enquiry into the first and general Principles of animal and vegetable Life: likewise into Atmosperical Air . . . with a Refutation of Dr. Priestley's Doctrine of Air . . . London: 1781. V. 37

HARRINGTON, T.

The Maamtrasna Massacre. Dublin: 1884. V. 43

HARRINGTON, THOMAS FRANCIS

Harvard Medical School: a History, Narrative and Documentary. New York: 1905. V. 37; 38; 41; 42; 43

HARRIOT, THOMAS

Artis Analyticae Praxis . . . London: 1631. V. 38; 45; 46

HARRIOTT, JOHN

Struggles through Life, Exemplified in the Various Travels and Adventures in Europe, Asia, Africa and America. London: 1808. V. 39; 40

HARRIS, A. C.

Alaska and the Klondike Gold Fields Containing a Full Account of the Discovery of Gold; Enormous Deposits of the Precious Metal; Routes Traversed by Miners; How to fine Gold; Camp Life at Klondike . . . Including Mrs. Eli Gage's . . . Chicago: (1897?). V. 37

HARRIS, ALBERT W.

The Blood of the Arab. Chicago: 1941. V. 39

The Cruise of a Schooner. Chicago: 1911. V. 38; 40; 41; 42; 45

Cruise of a Schooner. Chicago: 1958. V. 38

HARRIS, ALEX

A World Unsuspected: Portraits of Southern Childhood. Chapel Hill: 1987. V. 46

HARRIS, ALEXANDER

A Review of the Political Conflict in America, from the Commencement of the Anti-Slavery Agitation to the Close of Southern Reconstruction. New York: 1876. V. 42

Settlers and Convicts; or Recollections of Sixteen Years' Labour in the Australian Backwoods. London: 1852. V. 46

HARRIS, BARTHOLOMEW

The True Copy of a Letter From Mr. Harris and Mr. Annesley, Two of the East-India-Companies Council, Left at Surrat by Their General Sir John Child Barronet . . . London: 1688. V. 42

HARRIS, BESS

Lawren Harris. Toronto: 1969. V. 44

HARRIS, BRANSON L.

Some Recollections of My Boyhood. Indianapolis: 1908. V. 38

HARRIS, BRET

V. 46

HARRIS, BURTON

John Colter: His Years in the Rockies. New York: 1952. V. 37

HARRIS, C. R. S.

The Heart and Vascular System in Ancient Greek Medicine from Alcmaeon to Galen. Oxford: 1973. V. 44

HARRIS, CLEMENT B.

Brief Memoir of the Late Lt. Col. Sir Thomas Noel Harris, K. H., Knight of the Royal Order of Military Merit of Prussia, and of the Imperial Orders of St. Anne and Vladimir of Russia. London: 1893. V. 41

HARRIS, DEAN

By Path and Trail. Chicago: 1908. V. 39; 43

HARRIS, E. C.

New Zealand Berries - New Zealand Flowers - New Zealand Ferns. Nelson: 1894. V. 40

HARRIS, EILEEN

British Architectural Books and Writers 1556-1785. Cambridge: 1990. V. 45

HARRIS, ELIZABETH M.

The Art of Medal Engraving. Newtown: 1991. V. 46

HARRIS, EMILY MARION

Benedictus. London: 1887. V. 41

HARRIS, FLETCHER

Sermons on Important Subjects . . . to Which is Prefixed a memoir of the Author's Life. Granville: 1821. V. 39

HARRIS, FRANK 1856-1931

Elder Conklin and Other Stories. New York: 1894. V. 43
Elder Conklin and Other Stories. London: 1895. V. 38
Joan La Romee. London. V. 43
Joan La Romee: a Drama. London: 1927. V. 46
Montes the Matador and Other Stories. London: 1900. V. 41
My Life and Loves. Paris and Nice: 1922-27. V. 44
My Life and Loves. Paris: 1922-7. V. 43
My Life and Loves. Paris: 1945. V. 41
New Preface to 'The Life and Confessions of Oscar Wilde'. London: 1925. V. 46
Oscar Wilde: His Life and Confessions. New York: 1916. V. 38; 46
The Women of Shakespeare. New York: 1912. V. 38

HARRIS, G. F.

The Yorkshire Jurassic Flora. London: 1961-79. V. 37

HARRIS, GEORGE 1809-1890

Civilization Considered as a Science, in Relation to Its Essence, Its Elements and Its End. London: 1861. V. 43
Observations Upon the English Language, in a Letter to a Friend. London: 1752. V. 39

HARRIS, GEORGE W.

George W. Harris. London: 1930. V. 39

HARRIS, GEORGE WASHINGTON

Sut Lovingood. Yarns Spun by a 'Nat'ral Born Durn'd Fool. Warped and Wove for Public Wear. New York: 1867. V. 38; 42

HARRIS, HELENA J.

Southern Sketches. Cecil Gray; or, the Soldier's Revenge (and Rosa Sherwood; or, the Avenger. New Orleans: 1866. V. 44

HARRIS, HENRY

California's Medical Story. San Francisco: 1932. V. 41; 45
California's Medical Story. Springfield: 1932. V. 42

HARRIS, ISAAC

Harris's General Business Directory, of the Cities of Pittsburgh & Allegheny; and Also of the Most Important Towns and Cities of Pennsylvania, Ohio, Western New York, Virginia, etc . . . Pittsburgh: 1841. V. 41; 42

HARRIS, J. RENDEL

Letters from the Scenes of the Recent Massacres in ARmenia. London: 1897. V. 46

HARRIS, JAMES

Hermes or a Philosophical Inquiry Concerning Universal Grammar . . . London: 1765. V. 44
Hermes or a Philosophical Enquiry Concerning Universal Grammar. London: 1771. V. 38; 41
Hermes or a Philosophical Inquiry Concerning Universal Grammar. London: 1794. V. 37; 43
Philological Inquiries . . . London: 1781. V. 37; 38; 41; 45; 46
Philological Inquiries. London: 1802. V. 40
Philosophical Arrangements. London: 1775. V. 38; 41; 44; 46
Three Treatises. The First Concerning Art. The Second Concerning Music, Painting, and Poetry. The Third Concerning Happiness. London: 1744. V. 38; 42; 44; 45
Three Treatises. The First Concerning Art. The Second Concerning Music Painting and Poetry. The Third Concerning Happiness. London: 1765. V. 41
Three Treatises, the First Concerning Art, the Second Concerning Music, Painting and Poetry, the Third Concerning Happiness. London: 1774. V. 40; 44
Three Treatises. The First Concerning Art. The Second Concerning Music, Painting and Poetry. The Third Concerning Happiness. London: 1792. V. 39; 40
Three Treatises: the First Concerning Art, the Second Concerning Music, Painting and Poetry; the Third Concerning Happiness. London: 1792. V. 39
the Works . . . London: 1801. V. 39; 41; 45

HARRIS, JAMES COFFEE

The Personal and Family History of Charles Hooks and Margaret Monk Harris. Rome: 1911. V. 43; 44

HARRIS, JOEL CHANDLER 1848-1908

Aaron in the Wildwoods. Boston & New York: 1897. V. 46
Balaam and His Master and Other Sketches and Stories. Boston & New York: 1891. V. 46
The Chronicles of Aunt Minervy Ann. New York: 1899. V. 37; 43; 46
Daddy Jake. The Runaway, and Short Stories Told After Dark. New York: 1889. V. 37; 39; 40; 41
Free Joe and Other Georgian Sketches. New York: 1887. V. 38; 39; 40; 41; 42; 46
Gabriel Tolliver: a Story of Reconstruction. New York: 1902. V. 45; 46
The Library of Souther Literature. Atlanta: (1909). V. 37
A Little Union Scout. New York: 1904. V. 41; 43; 44
Mingo and Other Sketches in Black and White. Boston: 1884. V. 37; 39; 41; 44; 46
Nights with Uncle Remus. Boston: 1883. V. 37; 41; 42
Nights with Uncle Remus. London: 1884. V. 39
Nights with Uncle Remus. London: 1913. V. 39; 42
On the Plantation. New York: 1892. V. 37; 41
The Shadow Between His Shoulder Blades. Boston: 1909. V. 38; 39; 40; 42
Tales of the Home Folks in Peace and War. Boston: 1898. V. 39
Tales of the Home Folks In Peace and War. Boston & New York: 1898. V. 37; 46
The Tar Baby and Other Rhymes of Uncle Remus. New York: 1904. V. 39; 40
Told by Uncle Remus: New Stories of the Old Plantation. New York: 1905. V. 39
Uncle Remus and His Legends of the Old Plantation. London: 1811. V. 40
Uncle Remus, His Songs and His Sayings. New York: 1881. V. 37; 39; 40; 42; 43; 44; 45; 46
Uncle Remus and Brer Rabbit. New York: 1907. V. 46
Uncle Remus, His Songs and His Sayings. London: 1920. V. 39
Uncle Remus, His Songs and His Sayings. New York: 1920. V. 44
Uncle Remus, or, Mr. Fox, Mr. Rabbit, and Mr. Terrapin. London: 1901. V. 39
Wally Wanderoon and His Story-Telling Machine. New York: 1903. V. 46

HARRIS, JOHN

Astronomical Dialogues Between a Gentleman and a Lady. London: 1725. V. 43; 44; 45
Astronomical Dialogues Between a Gentleman and a Lady. London: 1766. V. 39
A Catalogue of British Drawings for Architecture, Decoration, Sculpture, and Landscape Gardening 1550-1900 in American Collections. New York: 1971. V. 41
A Catalogue of British Drawings For Architecture, Decoration, Sculpture and Landscape Gardening, 1500-1900 in American Collections. Upper Saddle River: 1971. V. 38; 42
The Description and Uses of the Celestial and Terrestrial Globes; and of Collins's Pocket Quadrant. London: 1703. V. 37; 38; 44
Gardens of Delight, the Rococo English Landscape of Thomas Robins the Elder. London: 1978. V. 38; 40

HARRIS, JOHN continued

Historical Pastime or a New Game of the History of England from the Conquest to the Acession of George the Third. London: 1803/10. V. 46

Lexicon Technicum. London: 1704-10. V. 38; 46

Lexicon Technicum. London: 1736. V. 38

Navigation Atque Itinerantium Bibliotheca or a Complete Collection of Voyages and Travels . . . London: 1764. V. 46

HARRIS, JOSEPH

The Description and Use of the Globes and the Orrery to Which Is Prefixed the Way of Introduction a Brief Account of the Solar System. London: 1734. V. 41

The Description an Use of the Globes and the Orrery. London: 1740. V. 46

The Mistakes, Or, The False Report. London: 1691. V. 37

HARRIS, JULIA COLLIER

The Life and Letters of Joel Chandler Harris. Boston & New York: 1918. V. 44

HARRIS, LAWREN

Contrasts. A Book of Verse. Toronto: 1922. V. 38

The Story of the Group of Seven. Toronto: 1964. V. 43; 45

HARRIS, MARIA WELCH

United States Girls Across the Atlantic. Homer: 1876. V. 39

HARRIS, MARK

Bang the Drum Slowly. New York: 1956. V. 39; 45; 46

The Southpaw. Indianapolis: 1953. V. 44

HARRIS, MARTHA DOUGLAS

History and Folklore of the Cowichan Indians. Victoria: 1901. V. 37; 39; 43; 46

HARRIS, MATTIE

Pathway of Mattie Howard (to and From Prison). N.P.: 1937. V. 46

HARRIS, MOSES

The Aurelian; or, Natural History of English Insects. London: 1758-66. V. 39

The Aurelian: Or, Natural History of English Insects . . . London: 1778. V. 39; 45

The Aurelian; or, Natural History of English Insects . . . London: 1794. V. 40

The Aurelian, a Natural History of English Moths and Butterflies. London: 1840. V. 42

The English Lepidoptera; or, the Aurelian's Pocket Companion. London: 1775. V. 43

An Exposition of English Insects, with Curious Observations and Remarks, Wherein Each Insect is Particularly Described . . . London: 1776. V. 45

Exposition of English Insects, Including the Several Classes of Neuroptera, Hymenoptera & Diptera, or Bees, Flies & Libellulae . . . London: 1782. V. 39; 45

An Exposition of English Insects, Including Several Classes of Neuroptera, Hymenoptera and Diptera, or Bees, Flies and Libellulae. London: 1786. V. 37

HARRIS' Pittsburgh Business Directory, for..1837 . . . Names of Merchants, Manufacturers, Mecahnics . . . etc. Pittsburgh: 1837. V. 39

HARRIS, R.

Scriptural Researches on the Licitness of the Slave-Trade . . . Liverpool: 1788. V. 39

HARRIS, RICHARD

Mayfair to Millbank. London: 1870. V. 41

HARRIS, SAMUEL

Pernicious Fiction. New York: 1853. V. 37

HARRIS, SARAH HOLLISTER

An Unwritten Chapter of Salt Lake 1851-1901. New York: 1901. V. 39; 40; 42; 45

HARRIS, STANLEY

The Coaching Age. London: 1885. V. 39

Old Coaching Days. London: 1882. V. 39; 43

HARRIS, T.

A Short Way to Know the World. London: 1712. V. 39; 45; 46

HARRIS, THADDEUS M.

Biographical Memorials of James Oglethorpe, Founder of the Colony of Georgia. Boston: 1841. V. 41; 46

HARRIS, THADDEUS MASON

Constitutions of the Ancient and Honorable Fraternity of Free and Accepted Masons. Worcester: 1798. V. 38

Discourses, Delivered on Public Occasions, Illustrating the Principles, Displaying the Tendency, and Vindicating the Design, of Freemasonry. Charlestown: 1801. V. 40

The Journal of a Tour Into the Territory Northwest of the Alleghany Mountains . . . Boston: 1805. V. 37; 38; 39; 42; 43; 45; 46

The Journal of a Tour into the Territory Northwest of the Alleghany Mountains . . . Boston: 1805. V. 42

The Minor Encyclopedia. Boston: 1803. V. 40

HARRIS, THADDEUS WILLIAM

A Treatise on Some of the Insects Injurious to Vegetation. Boston: 1862. V. 38

HARRIS, THOMAS

Goya Engravings and Lithographs. San Francisco: 1983. V. 46

The Life and Services of Commodore William Bainbridge. Philadelphia: 1837. V. 46

A Narrative of the Rise and Progress of the Disputes Subsisting Between the Patentees of Covent-Garden Theatre. London: 1768. V. 39; 42

HARRIS, THOMAS LAKE

An Epic of the Starry Heaven. New York: 1855. V. 42

God's Breath in Man and in Humane Society. Santa Rosa: 1891. V. 37; 38; 42

A Lyric of the Morning Land. New York: 1854. V. 38; 41; 43; 44

A Lyric of the Golden Age. New York: 1856. V. 37; 42

A Lyric of the Morning Land. New York: 1856. V. 42

The New Republic: Prospects, Dangers, Duties and Safeties of the Times. Santa Rosa: 1891. V. 37; 42

Star Flowers: a Poem of the Woman's Mystery . . . Fountaingrove: 1886. V. 42

Star-Flowers: A Poem of the Woman's Mystery . . . Canto the Seventh. Fountaingrove, Ca.: 1887. V. 37

The Wisdom of Adepts, Esoteric Science in Human History. Fountain Grove: 1884. V. 41

HARRIS, W.

Sculptures Metopes Discovered Amongst the Ruins of The Temple of the Ancient City of Selinus in Sicily. London: 1826. V. 37

HARRIS, W. B.

The Elephant's Ball and Grand Fete Champetre Intended as a Companion to Those Much Admired Pieces . . . London: 1807. V. 42

HARRIS, WALTER

The Antient and Present State of the County of Down, Containing a Chorographical Description, with the Natural and Civil History of the Same . . . Dublin: 1744. V. 43

The Defence of the Scots Settlement at Darien, Answer'd Paragraph by Paragraph. London: 1699. V. 40

Hibernica; or, Some Antient Pieces Relating to Ireland. Dublin: 1757. V. 38; 42

Hibernica, or Some Antient Pieces Relating to Ireland. Dublin: 1770. V. 38

Hibernica, or Some Antient Pieces Relating to Ireland . . . a Project of King James for the Plantation of the Escheated Counties. The Report of the Commission to the Establishment of the Plantation and Nicholoas Pynner's Survey of said . . . Dublin: 1747. V. 37

The History and Antiquities of the City of Dublin, from the Earliest Accounts . . . London: 1766. V. 41

The Land of the African Sultan Travels in Morocco 1887, 1888 and 1889. London: 1889. V. 43

Pharmacologia Anti-Emperica: or a Rational Discourse of Remedies both Chymical and Galencial . . . Together with some Remarks on the Causes and Cure of the Gout, the Universal Use of the Cortex, of Jesuit's Power, and the most . . . London: 1683. V. 37

HARRIS, WALTER B.

A Journey through the Yemen and Some General Remarks Upon that Country. Edinburgh: 1893. V. 39

A Journey through the Yemen and Some General Remarks Upon that Country. London: 1893. V. 45

Tafilet: the Narrative fo a Journey of Explortion in the Atlas Mountains and the Oases of the North-West Sahara. Edinburgh & London: 1895. V. 41

HARRIS, WILLIAM

A Catalogue of the Library of the Royal Institution of Great Britian, Methodically Arranged, with an Alphabetical List of Authors. London: 1809. V. 39

An Historical And Critical Account of the Life and Writings of James the First, King of Great Britain. London: 1753. V. 38

An Historical and Critical Account of the Life of Oliver Cromwell . . . after the Manner of Mr. Bayle. London: 1762. V. 39; 46

An Historical and Critical Account of the Life and Writings of Charles I, King of Great Britain. London: 1772. V. 42; 43; 45

An Historical and Critical Account of the Lives and Writings of James I and Charles I and of the Lives of Oliver Cromwell and Charles II. London: 1814. V. 41

An Historical and Critical Account of the Life and Writings of Charles I, King of Great Britain. London: 1758. V. 39

HARRIS, WILLIAM continued

Outlines of Geography, Natural, Civil and Political . . . the Terraqueous Globe . . . Carlisle: 1808. V. 41

HARRIS, WILLIAM CORNWALLIS

The Angler's Guide Book and Tourist's Gazetter of the Fishing Waters of the United States and Canada. New York: 1885. V. 39

The Highlands of Ethiopia. London: 1844. V. 38; 41; 45

Portraits of the Game and Wild Animals of Southern Africa, Deliniated in the Native Haunts, During a Hunting Expedition from Cape Colony as Far as the Tropic of Capricorn in 1836 and 1837, with Sketches of Field Sports. London: 1840. V. 39; 42; 43; 44

Portraits of Game and Wild Animals of Southern Africa. London: 1969. V. 38

The Wild Sports of Southern Africa. London: 1839. V. 38; 40; 41; 42; 43; 44

The Wild Sports of Southern Africa. London: 1839. V. 41

The Wild Sports of Southern Africa . . . London: 1844. V. 42; 43; 46

The Wild Sports of South Africa . . . London: 1852. V. 38; 41; 42; 43

HARRIS, WILLIAM RICHARD

By Path and Trail. Chicago: 1908. V. 43

The Catholic Church in Utah . . . Salt Lake City: 1901. V. 38; 41

The Catholic Church in Utah 1776-1909. Salt Lake City: 1909. V. 37; 40; 42; 43; 46

HARRISON-AINSWORTH, E. D.

The History and War Records of the Surrey Yeomanary. London: 1928. V. 43; 44

HARRISON, ALFRED H.

In Search of a Polar Continent. London: 1908. V. 37; 39

HARRISON & SONS

Printing Types. London: 1889. V. 38; 42

HARRISON, BENJAMIN S.

Fortune Favors the Brave. Los Angeles: 1953. V. 43

HARRISON, CANON F.

English manuscripts of the 14th century (c. 1250 to 1400). 1937. V. 37

HARRISON, CHARLES

Theatricals and TAbleaux Vivants for Amateurs. London: 1885. V. 44

Theatricals and Tableaux Vivants for Amateurs. London: 1890. V. 46

A Treatise on the Culture and Management of Fruit Trees . . . Sheffield: 1823. V. 46

HARRISON, CHARLES YALE

Generals Die in Bed. New York: 1930. V. 43

HARRISON, CONSTANCE CARY 1843-1920

Bric-A-Brac Stories. New York: 1885. V. 43

Woman's Handiwork in Modern Homes. New York: 1881. V. 45

HARRISON, D. L.

The Mammals of Arabia. London: 1964-72. V. 40

HARRISON, E. J.

The Fighting Spirit of Japan and Other Studies. London: 1913. V. 45

HARRISON, EVELYN B.

Archaic and Archaistic Sculpture. Princeton: 1965. V. 42

HARRISON, FAIRFAX

The Belair Stud, 1747-1761. Richmond: 1929. V. 42

The Equine F. F. Vs. A Study of the Evidence for the English Horses Imported into Virginia Before the Revolution. Richmond: 1928. V. 42

The Harrison's of Skimino. New York: 1910. V. 39

The John's Island Stud (South Carolina) 1750-1788. Richmond: 1931. V. 40; 42

The Roanoke Stud 1795-1833. Richmond: 1930. V. 42

HARRISON, FLORENCE

Elfin-Song. New York: (1912). V. 37

In the Fairy Ring. London: 1906. V. 40

In the Fairy Ring. London: 1908. V. 46

The Pixy Book. London: 1918. V. 46

The Rhyme of a Run. London: V. 42; 45

HARRISON, FRANK MOTT

A Bibliography of the Works of John Bunyan. 1932 for 1930. V. 44

HARRISON, FREDERIC

Annals of an Old Manor House, Sutton Place, Guildford. London: 1893. V. 37; 39; 40; 41

HARRISON, G. B.

Elizabethan and Jacobean Quartos. Edinburgh: 1966. V. 41

HARRISON, G. J.

Clinical, Avian Medicine and Surgery. Philadelphia: 1986. V. 37

HARRISON, GABRIEL

The Life and Writing of John Howard Payne. Albany: 1875. V. 42

HARRISON, GEORGE

Songs by George Harrison. London: 1987. V. 42

HARRISON, GEORGE L.

Chapters on Social Science as Connected with the Administration of State Charities. Philadelphia: 1877. V. 39; 42

HARRISON, HELEN A.

Larry Rivers. New York: 1984. V. 43

HARRISON, HELEN MAYER

The Book of the Seven Lagoons: a Suite of 45 Images. La Jolla: 1987. V. 41

HARRISON, J. B.

The Geology of the Goldfields of British Guiana. London: 1908. V. 43

The Latest Studies on Indian Reservations. Philadelphia: 1887. V. 37; 42

HARRISON, J. C.

Game Birds of the British Isles. London: 1988. V. 40

HARRISON, J. E.

Greek Vase Paintings. London: 1894. V. 37; 40; 42; 44

HARRISON, J. M.

The Birds of Kent. London: 1953. V. 42

HARRISON, JACK C.

The Birds of Prey of the British Islands. London: 1980. V. 37; 40

HARRISON, JAMES

The Life of the Right Honourable Horatio Lord Nelson. London: 1806. V. 39

HARRISON, JIM

Farmer. New York: 1976. V. 43

5 Blind Men. Fremont: 1969. V. 42

A Good Day to Die. New York: 1973. V. 45

Just Before Dark: Collected Non-Fiction. Livingston: 1991. V. 45; 46

Just Before Dark. Montana: 1991. V. 46

Legends of the Fall. New York. V. 43; 44

Legends of the Fall. New York: 1979. V. 45

Letters to Yesenin. Fremont: 1973. V. 44; 46

Locations. New York: 1968. V. 42; 43; 44

The Natural World: a Bestiary. Barrytwon: 1981. V. 45

Outlyer. New York: 1971. V. 39; 40; 46

Plain Song. New York: 1965. V. 41; 45

Plain Song. New York: (1966). V. 37

Returning to Earth. N.P.: 1977. V. 44

Selected and New Poems. New York: 1982. V. 37; 40; 43; 45

Sundog. New York: 1984. V. 43

The Theory and Practice of Rivers. Seattle: 1986. V. 41; 42; 43; 44

Warlock. 1981. V. 43

Warlock. New York: 1981. V. 37; 38; 40; 41; 43; 44; 45; 46

Wolf. New York: 1971. V. 37; 43

The Woman Lit by Fireflies. Boston: 1900. V. 44

The Woman Lit by Fireflies. Boston: 1988. V. 44

HARRISON, JOHN

The Principles of Mr. Harrison's Time-Keeper, with Plates of the Same Published by Order . . . (French title) Principles de la Montre de Mr. Harrison . . . Impres a Londres 1767 par: 1767. V. 43

The Principles of Mr. Harrison's Time-Keeper, with Plates of the Same. London: 1767. V. 37

Survey of the Manor of Sheffield. London: 1908. V. 45; 46

Survey of the Manor of Sheffield. London: 1908. V. 45

HARRISON, JOSEPH

A Short View of Menckenism in Menckenese. Seattle: 1927. V. 46

HARRISON, MARY ST. LEGER KINGSLEY 1852-

Oddities and Outlines. London: 1806. V. 43

The Wages of Sin. London: 1891. V. 41; 45

HARRISON, MICHAEL

In the Footsteps of Sherlock Holmes. London: 1958. V. 46

HARRISON OF PARIS

A Typographical Commonplace Book. Paris: 1932. V. 44

A Typographical Commonplace-book. New York: 1932. V. 45

HARRISON, RICHARD 1837-1931

Recollections of a Life in the British ARmy During the Latter Half of the 19th century. London: 1908. V. 46

HARRISON, ROBERT

The Dublin Dissector. Washington: 1835. V. 41; 44

The Dublin Dissector. Washington: 1835. V. 41

Strange Relation of the Suddain and Violent Tempest, Which Happened at Oxford may 31, Anno Domini 1682. Together with An Enquiry into the Probable Cause and Usual Consequences of Such Like Tempests and Storms. Oxford: 1682. V. 43

HARRISON, SARAH

The House-Keeper's Pocket Book and Compleat Family Cook Containing Above Twelve Hundred Curious and Uncommon Receipts . . . London: 1764. V. 38

HARRISON, SHARON R.

The Etchings of Odilon Redon. New York: 1986. V. 44

HARRISON, T.

The Bookbinding Craft and Industry, an Outline of its History, Development and Technique. London: 1926. V. 41

The Bookbinding Craft and Industry, an Outline of Its History, Development and Technique . . . London: 1930. V. 41

HARRISON, THOMAS

Barrister at Law: The Law and Practice Relating to Ejectments in Ireland. Dublin: 1903. V. 39

HARRISON, THOMAS ERAT

VI Greek Myths. London: 1879. V. 40

HARRISON, TONY

Anno Forty Two - Seven New Poems. London: 1987. V. 40; 42

Continuous - 50 Sonnets from the School of Eloquence. London: 1981. V. 40; 41

Continuous: Poems. London: 1981. V. 42

Earthworks. Leeds: 1964. V. 41

The Fire-Gap; a Poem with Two Tails. London: 1985. V. 37; 40

The Loiners. London: 1970. V. 41

Losing Touch - In Memoriam George Cukor, Died 24.1.83. London: 1990. V. 44; 46

The Mother of the Muses. London: 1989. V. 42

Newcastle is Peru. Newcastle-upon-Tyne: 1969. V. 41

The Passion - Selected from the 15th Century Cycle of York Mystery Plays - in a Version by the Company with Tony Harrison. London: 1977. V. 46

Selected Poems. London: 1984. V. 40

Ten Sonnets from the School of Eloquence. London: 1987. V. 40

HARRISON, W.

Bibliotheca Nonensis, A Bibliographical Account of Works Relating to the Isle of Man. Douglas: 1876. V. 45

Bibliotheca Monesis, a bibliographical account of works relating to the Isle of Man. 1876. V. 37

Ripon Millenary (1886). Ripon: 1892. V. 46

HARRISON, W. P.

The Gospel Among the Slaves: A Short Account of Missionary Operations Among the African Slaves of the Southern States . . . Nashville: 1893. V. 43

HARRISON, W. RANDLE

Suggestions for Illuminating. London: 1863. V. 38

HARRISON, WALTER

Pickett's Men: a Fragment of War History. New York: 1870. V. 37; 39; 42

HARRISON, WILLIAM HENRY

A Discourse on the Aborigines of the Valley of the Ohio. Cincinnati: 1838. V. 37; 41; 44

The Humourist, a Companion for the Christmas Fireside. London. V. 42

HARRISON, WILMOT

Memorable London Houses, a Handy Guide. London: 1889. V. 37

HARRISSE, HENRY

Bibliotheca Americana Vetustissima. New York: 1866. V. 40

Bibliotheca Americana Vetustissima: a Description of Works relating to America Published between 1492-1551. Paris: 1877. V. 37

Decouverte et Evolution Cartographique de Terre-Neuve et des Pays Circonvoisins 1497-1501-1769. Paris: 1900. V. 39

HARRO-HARRING, PAUL

Dolores: a Novel of South-America . . . Montevideo: 1846. V. 43

HARROP, DOROTHY A.

A History of the Gregynog Press. London: 1980. V. 44

A History of the Gregynog Press. Middlesex: 1980. V. 44

A History of the Gregynog Press. Pinner: 1980. V. 40; 44

HARRSEN, META

Central European Manuscripts in the Pierpont Morgan Library. New York: 1958. V. 46

The Nekcseilipocz Bible: A Fourteenth Century Manuscript from Hungary in the Library of Congress. Ms. Pre-Acession 1. A Study. Washington: 1949. V. 44; 46

HARRY ANGELO CO., NEW YORK & PARIS.

Illustrations of the Model Gowns Displayed at Our Spring Opening, March, 1918. V. 43

HARRY'S Little Lessons. Philadelphia: 1850. V. 40

HARSHBERGER, JOHN

The Botanists of Philadelphia and Their Work. Philadelphia: 1899. V. 42

HARSHBERGER, JOHN W.

The Vegetation of the New Jersey Pine-Barrens. Philadelpia: 1916. V. 38; 39; 41; 45

HART, A.

Funeral Sermon on the Death of Maj. Jos. W. Anderson . . . with an Obituary. Richmond: 1863. V. 44

HART, A. B.

The American Nation. New York: 1904. V. 42

HART, ADOLPHUS M.

History of the Valley of the Mississippi. Cincinnati: 1853. V. 42

HART, ALBERT B.

Commonwealth History of Massachusetts Colony, Province and State. New York: 1927. V. 37; 40; 42; 44

HART, CHARLES

The History of the 1st Volunteer Battalion the Royal Warwickshire Regiment and Its Predecessors . . . Birmingham: 1906. V. 38

HART, CHARLES HENRY

Memoirs of the Life and Works of Jean Antoine Houdon, the Sculptor of Voltaire . . . Philadelphia: 1911. V. 43

HART, CYRUS WADSWORTH

Colloquy Between Two Deists, on the Immortality of the Soul. Poughkeepsie: 1816. V. 40

HART, DAVID BERRY

Atlas of Female Pelvic Anatomy. New York: 1884. V. 42

HART, FRANCES NOYES

The Bellamy Trial. 1927. V. 39

HART, FRANCIS R.

The Siege of Havanna, 1762. Boston: 1931. V. 42

HART, FRANCIS RUSSELL

Personal Reminiscences of the Caribbean Sea and the Spanish Main. Boston: 1914. V. 44

HART, FRED H.

The Sazerac Lying Club. San Francisco: 1878. V. 37; 38; 41

The Sazerac Lying Club. San Francisco & New York: 1878. V. 38

HART, GEORGE OVERBURY

George O. 'Pop' Hart: Twenty-Four Selections From His Work. New York: 1928. V. 38; 41

HART, GERALD E.

The Fall of New France, 1755-1760. Montreal: 1888. V. 42

HART, H. G.

The New Annual Army List, Militia List, Yeomanry Cavalry List, for 1890. London: 1890. V. 41

The New Annual Army List . . . 1891. London: 1891. V. 41

The New Annual Army List . . . 1892. London: 1892. V. 41

The New Annual Army List . . . 1893. London: 1893. V. 41

The New Annual Army List . . . 1894. London: 1894. V. 41

The New Annual Army List . . . 1895. London: 1895. V. 41

The New Annual Army List . . . 1896. London: 1896. V. 41

The New Annual Army List . . . 1897. London: 1897. V. 41

HART, H. G. continued

The New Annual Army List . . . 1898. London: 1898. V. 41

HART, HENRY CHICHESTER

Some Account of the Fauna and Flora of Sinai, Petra and Wady 'Arabah. London: 1891. V. 45

HART, HILDA

Fairytale Gems. London: 1920. V. 37; 46

HART, HORACE

A Bibliography of the History of Printing in the Library of Congress. Springwater: 1987. V. 38

Bibliotheca Typographica, a List of Books About Books. Rochester: 1933. V. 41

Notes on a Century of Typography at the University Press, Oxford, 1693-1794. 1900. V. 40

Notes on a Century of Typography at the University Press, Oxford, 1693-1794. Oxford: 1900. V. 46

Notes on a Century of Typography at the University Press, Oxford, 1693-1794. Oxford: 1970. V. 41

HART, JAMES

Argonaut Stories. Selected by James Hart. San Francisco: 1906. V. 37

A Practical Treatise on the Construction of Oblique Arches. London: 1848. V. 40

HART, JAMES D.

John Steinbeck, His Language. Aptos: 1970. V. 38

My First Publication; Eleven California Authors Describe their Earlies Appearances in Print. San Francisco: 1961. V. 37; 38; 41

An Original Leaf from the First Edition of Alexander Barclay's English Translation of Sebastian Brant's 'Ship of Fools.' San Francisco: 1938. V. 41; 42

HART, JOHN

The Trial of John Hart, Esq. Alderman of London: for Adultery and Cruelty . . . London: 1780. V. 38; 40

HART, JOHN A.

History of Pioneer Days in Texas and Oklahoma. Guthrie: 1909. V. 41

HART, JOHN S.

A Brief Exposition of the Constitution of the United States, for the Use of Common Schools. Philadelphia: 1848. V. 45

The Iris, an Illuminated Souvenir for 1852. Philadelphia: 1852. V. 42

HART, JOSEPH

Hymns, &c. Composed on Various Subjects. London: 1784. V. 37; 42

Hymns &c. Composed on Various Subjects . . . with the Author's Experience, the Supplement and Appendix . . . The Tenth Edition. Elizabeth Town: (1787?). V. 37

Miriam Coffin, or, the Whale Fisherman: a Romance. New York: 1842. V. 46

HART, JOSEPH C.

Miriam Coffin; or, The Whale Fisherman. New York: 1834. V. 37; 39; 43

Miriam Coffin, or the Whale Fishermen; a Tale. San Francisco: 1872. V. 41

The Romance of Yachting: Voyage the First. New York: 1848. V. 41

HART, JOSEPHINE

Damage. New York: 1991. V. 46

HART, LIDDELL

'T. E. Lawrence' - in Arabia and After. London: 1934. V. 38

HART, LOCKYER WILLIS

Character & Costumes of Afghuanistan . . . London: 1843. V. 46

HART, MARY

Pinto Ben: and Other Stories. New York: 1919. V. 42

HART, MOSS

Act One. New York: 1959. V. 41

I'd Rather Be Right. New York: 1937. V. 40

Lady in the Dark. New York: 1941. V. 45

Merrily We Roll Along. New York: 1934. V. 41

HART, SAMUEL

In Memoriam, Samuel Colt and Caldwell Hart Colt. Springfield: 1898. V. 37; 40

HART, WILLIAM

Fugitive Pieces, in Prose and Verse . . . London: 1801. V. 41

HART, WILLIAM S.

Hoofbeats. New York: 1933. V. 45

My Life East and West. Boston: 1929. V. 43

The Order of Chanta Sutas, a Ritual. Hollywood: 1925. V. 39; 45

Pinto Ben: and Other Stories. New York: 1919. V. 39; 45

HARTCLIFFE, JOHN

A Compleat Treatise of Moral and Intellectual Virtues . . . London: 1721. V. 40

A Treatise of Moral and Intellectual Vitures . . . London: 1691. V. 40; 44

HARTE, BRET 1836-1902

The Adventure of Padre Vicentio . . . Berkeley: 1939. V. 44

The Bell-Ringer of Angel's and Other Stories. Boston: 1894. V. 44

Bret Harte in California: A Character Study. San Francisco: 1951. V. 37

Clarence. London: 1895. V. 37; 44

Condensed Novels and Other Papers. New York: 1867. V. 37; 39; 40; 44

Cressy. Boston: 1889. V. 37; 38

Dickens in Camp. San Francisco: 1922. V. 37; 39; 42; 44

Dickens in Camp. San Francisco: 1923. V. 41

Drift from Two Shores. Boston: 1878. V. 39

Facsimile of the Original Manuscript of the Heathen Chinee, as Written for the Overland Monthly . . . Together with the Corrected Letter Press as Published in the Issue of September 1870. San Francisco: 1871. V. 40; 44; 45

A First Family of Tasajara. London: 1891. V. 39

Gabriel Conroy. Hartford: 1876. V. 44; 46

Gabriel Conroy. London: 1876. V. 41; 44

The Hathen Chinee. Chicago: 1870. V. 37

The Heath Chinee. Chicago: 1870. V. 37; 43; 45

The Heathen Chinee. Boston: 1871. V. 39

The Heaten Chinee: Plain Language from Truthful James. San Francisco: 1924. V. 41

The Heathen Chinee. San Francisco: 1936. V. 42

The Heritage of Dedlow Marsh, and Other Tales. London: 1889. V. 43

How Santa Claus Came to Simpson's Bar. Los Angeles: 1941. V. 46

In a Hollow of the Hills. London: 1895. V. 37; 44

In a Hollow of the Hills. Boston/New York: 1895. V. 37

The Lectures. Brooklyn: 1909. V. 44

The Lost Galleon and Other Tales. San Francisco: 1867. V. 37; 39; 41; 45; 46

Lothan by Mr. Benjamin. London: (1871). V. 37

The Luck of the Roaring Camp and Other Sketches. Boston: 1870. V. 38; 39; 40; 44; 45

Luck of Roaring Camp. Toronto: 1871. V. 41; 42

The Luck of the Roaring Camp and Other Sketches. London: 1872. V. 39

The Luck of the Roaring Camp and Other Sketches. Boston: 1875. V. 45

The Luck of the Roaring Camp. San Francisco: 1948. V. 38; 39; 41; 46

The Luck of the Roaring Camp. San Francisco: 1958. V. 46

A Millionaire of Rough and Ready. Boston: 1887. V. 41; 42

A Millionaire of Rough & Ready. Kentfield: 1955. V. 37; 38; 43; 45; 46

Mrs. Skagg's Husbands and Other Sketches. Boston: 1873. V. 45

Mliss, a Story . . . is From 'The Luck of Roaring Camp and Other Sketches.' San Francisco: 1948. V. 38

Mliss: a Story. San Francisco: 1958. V. 39; 46

Outcroppings. San Francisco: 1866. V. 37; 40; 44

Overland Sketches . . . New York: 1870. V. 42

The Pliocene Skull. Washington: 1871. V. 38; 40; 44

Poems. Boston: 1871. V. 37; 39; 42; 43; 44; 45

A Protege of Jack Hamlin's. London: 1894. V. 45

A Protegee of Jack Hamilin's. Boston: 1894. V. 41; 42

The Queen of the Pirate Isle. London: 1886. V. 37; 40; 41; 42; 43; 44

The Queen of the Pirate Isle. Boston & New York: 1887. V. 42

San Francisco in 1866. San Francisco: 1951. V. 37; 38; 44; 45

Snow-Bound at Eagle's. London: 1886. V. 40; 42; 44

Stories in Light and Shadow. London: 1898. V. 45

Sue: a Play in Three Acts. London: 1902. V. 44

Tales of the Argonauts and Other Sketches. Boston: 1875. V. 44; 46

Tales of the Gold Rush. New York: 1944. V. 43

Tennessee's Partner. San Francisco & New York: 1907. V. 46

Thankful Blossom. Toronto: 1877. V. 39

Two Men of Sandy Bar. Boston: 1876. V. 41; 42

Under the Redwoods. Boston & New York: 1901. V. 44

A Waif of the Plains. London: 1890. V. 37; 44; 46

A Ward of the Golden Gate. London: 1890. V. 40; 42; 44

The Wild West. Paris: 1930. V. 37; 39; 40; 42; 44; 45

The Wild West. 1936. V. 42

The Wild West. 1936. V. 40

The Wild West. 1936. V. 37

Complete Works. New York: 1885. V. 42

HARTE, BRET 1836-1902 continued

The Complete Works Collected and Revised by Author. London: 1890/96. V. 39

Works. New York: 1906. V. 46

The Works of Bret Harte. New York: 1912. V. 38

Works. Boston and New York: 1929. V. 42

The Writings. Boston: 1896. V. 42

The Writings of . . . Boston & New York: 1896. V. 44

The Writings. Boston: 1906. V. 42

The Writings of . . . Boston: 1914. V. 46

HARTE, BRETT 1836-1902

The Heathen Chinee and Other Poems Mostly Humorous. London: 1871. V. 42

HARTE, WALTER

An Essay on Reason. London: 1735. V. 37; 38; 40; 45; 46

Essays on Husbandry. London: 1764. V. 39; 40; 45

The History of the Life of Gustavus Adolphus, King of Sweden, sirnamed the Great. London: 1759. V. 38

Poems on Several Occasions. London: 1727. V. 38; 40; 45

HARTFORD COPPER & GOLD MINING CO.

Copper and Gold Alaska and Idaho the Hartford Copper and Gold Mining Co. Boston: 1901. V. 39

HARTFORD, FRANCES SEYMOUR, COUNTESS OF

Correspondence Between Frances, Countess of Hartford (afterwards Duchess of Somerset) and Henrietta Louisa, Countess of Pomfret, 1738-1741. London: 1806. V. 38

HARTFORD, PROVIDENCE AND FISHKILL RAILROAD COMPANY

Charter of the Hartford, Providence and Fishkill Railroad Company: Orginally the Manchester Railroad Company. Hartford: 1849. V. 37

HARTFORD UNION MINING & TRADING COMPANY

Around the Horn in '49. Journal of the Hartford Union Mining and Trading Company. Wetherfield: 1898. V. 45

HARTGERS, JOST

Tragicum Theatrum actorum & Casuum Tragicorum Londini Publice Celebratorum. Amsterdam: 1649. V. 40

HARTING, J. E.

British Animals Extinct Within Historic Times . . . London: 1880. V. 40

Glimpses of Bird Life, Pourtrayed with Pen and Pencil. London: 1880. V. 40

A Handbook of British Birds Showing the Distribution of the Resident and Migratory Species in the British Islands. London: 1901. V. 40

Hints on the Management of Hawks. London: 1898. V. 39; 40; 45

HARTING, JAMES EDMUND

Bibliotheca Accipitraria: a Catalogue of Books Ancient and Modern Relating to Falconry. London: 1891. V. 46

The Birds of Middlesex. London: 1866. V. 42

HARTLEY, DAVID 1732-1813

An Account of the Method of Securing Buildings (and Ships) Against Fire. London: 1774. V. 43

An Address to the Committee of the County of York, on the State of Public Affairs. York: 1781. V. 37

The Budget. London: 1764. V. 44

Considerations on the Proposed Renewal of the Bank Charter. London: 1781. V. 37

Letters on the American War. Bath: 1778. V. 40; 43

Letters on the American War. London: 1778. V. 38; 39; 40

Letters on the American War. Addressed to the Right Worshipful the Mayor and Corporation (etc.) . . . of the Town of Kingston-Upon-Hull. London: 1779. V. 46

Observations on Man, His Frame, His Duty and His Expectations. London: 1749. V. 42; 46

Observations on Man, His Frame, His Duty and His Expectations. London: 1791. V. 40

Observations on Man, His Frame, His Duty and His Expectations. London: 1801. V. 42; 43; 45

Observations on Man, His Fame, His Duty and His Expectations. London: 1810. V. 38

Observations on Man, in Two Parts. London: 1834. V. 38; 41

Pantheon, January 14, 1792. London: 1792. V. 43

Speech and Motions Made in the House of Commons on Monday, the 27th of March, 1775. Together with a Draught of a Letter of Requisition to the Colonies. London: 1775. V. 37; 46

The State of the Nation, with a Preliminary Defence of the Budget. London: 1765. V. 42; 44

A View of the Present Evidence for and Against Mrs. Stephens's Medicines, as a Solvent for the Stone. London: 1739. V. 37; 44

HARTLEY, DOROTHY

A Mediaeval Anthology Edited & Illuminated by Dorothy Hartley. London: 1930. V. 39

Thomas Tusser. London: 1931. V. 45

HARTLEY, HAROLD

Nineteen Drawings by Aubrey Beardsley from the Collection of Mr. Harold Hartley. London: 1919. V. 43

HARTLEY House, Calcutta. London: 1789. V. 43

HARTLEY, J.

History of the Westminster Election. London: 1784. V. 42

History of the Westminster Election, Containing Every Material Occurrence, From Its Commencement on the First Day of April, to the Final Close of the Poll, on the 17th of May . . . London: 1785. V. 38

HARTLEY, JOHN

Researches in Greece and the Levant. London: 1833. V. 37; 39

HARTLEY, L. P.

Eustace & Hilda. London: 1947. V. 43

My Fellow Devils. London: 1951. V. 37

Night Fears and Other Stories. London: 1924. V. 40

The Shrimp and the Anemone. London: 1944. V. 38; 42

The Shrimp and the Anemone. The Sixth Heaven. Eustace and Hilda. London: 1944/46/47. V. 37

Simonetta Perkins. London: 1925. V. 38; 39

Simonetta Perkins. New York: 1926. V. 40

The Travelling Grave and Other Stories. Sauk City: 1948. V. 44; 45

HARTLEY, LEONARD LAWRIE

A Catalogue of the Library of the Late Leonard Lawrie Hartley . . . London: 1885. V. 45

HARTLEY, LODWICK

Katherine Anne Porter: a Critical Symposium. Athens: 1969. V. 39

HARTLEY, MARSDEN

Adventures in the Arts: Informal Chapters on Painters, Vaudeville and Poets. New York: 1921. V. 40

Twenty Five Poems. Paris: 1923. V. 37; 41; 42; 44

HARTLEY, THOMAS

A Discourse on Mistakes Concerning Relation, Enthusiasm, Experiences, &c. Germantown: 1759. V. 41; 42; 43; 45

HARTLEY, WINCHCOMBE SAVILLE

An Account of the Invention and Use of Fire-Plates, for the Security of Buildings and Ships Against Fire by the Late David Hartley. London: 1834. V. 43

HARTLEY, WINCHOMBE HENRY

An Address to the Public, on the Subject of the Late Loan. London: 1781. V. 41

HARTLIB, SAMUEL

The Reformed Commonwealth of Bees, Presented in Severall Letters . . . London: 1655. V. 42

The Reformed Virginian Silk-Worm, or, A Rare and New Discovery . . . London: 1655. V. 40

Samuel Hartlib His Legacy of Husbandry. London: 1655. V. 37; 38; 40; 43; 44; 45; 46

HARTMAN, C. V.

Archaeological Researches in Costa Rica. Stockholm: 1901. V. 44

HARTMANN, A. T.

Die Hebraerin am Putztische und als Braut. Amsterdam: 1809-10. V. 45

HARTMANN, DANIEL

Burgerliche Wohnungs Baukunst. Basle: 1688. V. 46

HARTMANN, FRANZ

Diseases of Children and Their Homoeopathic Treatment. New York: 1853. V. 42

The Life of Philippus Theophrastus, Bombast of Hohenheim Known by the Name of Paracelsus . . . London: 1887. V. 46

The Life of Philippus Theophrastus Bombast of Hohenheim Known by the Name of Paracelsus . . . London: 1896. V. 46

HARTMANN, GEORGE

Wooed by a Sphinx of Aztlan . . . and Incidents of Interest from the Life of a Western Frontier. Prescott: 1907. V. 41

HARTMANN, L.

The Story of Champ D'Asile, as Told by Two of the Colonists. Dallas: 1937. V. 37; 38; 40

HARTMANN, L. continued

Le Texas, Ou Notice Historique Sur Le Champ d'Asile, Comprenant Tout Ce Qui S'est Passe Depuis La Formation Jusqu'a La Dissolution De Cette Colonie, Les Causes Oui L'ont Amenee, Et La Liste De Tous Le Colons Francais . . . Paris: 1819. V. 45

HARTMANN, ROBERT

Reise in Nordost Africa. Berlin: 1863. V. 40

HARTMANN, SADAKICHI

Buddha. New York: 1897. V. 40

The Last Thirty Days of Christ. New York: 1920. V. 42

HARTMANNO, JOHANNE

Officina Sanitatis Sive Praxis Chymiatrica . . . Noribergae: 1677. V. 46

HARTNOLL, PHYLLIS

The Grecian Enchanted. 1952. V. 39

The Grecian Enchanted. Great Britain (sic): 1952. V. 37; 39

The Grecian Enchanted. London: 1952. V. 39; 40; 41

HARTPENCE, WILLIAM ROSS

History of the Fifty-First Indiana Vetern Volunteer Infantry. Harrison & Cincinnati: 1894. V. 38

HARTSHORNE, ALBERT

Old English Glasses, an Account of Glass Drinking Vessels in England, From Early Times to the End of the Eighteenth Century, With Introductory Notices, Original Documents, etc. London: 1897. V. 38; 39; 40

HARTSHORNE, ANNA C.

Japan and Her People. Philadelphia: 1902. V. 43; 45

HARTSHORNE, C. H.

Salopia Antiqua, or, an Enquiry from Personal Survey into the 'Druidical' Military, and Other Early Remains in Shropshire and the North Welsh Broders . . . London: 1841. V. 41

HARTSHORNE, CHARLES

Reality as a Social Process. Glencoe: 1953. V. 45

HARTSHORNE, CHARLES HENRY

Ancient Metrical Tales. London: 1829. V. 38; 46

The Book Rarities in the University of Cambridge . . . London: 1829. V. 38; 41

The Book Rarities in the University of Cambridge. London: 1892. V. 37

The Homes of the Working Man. An Address . . . Northampton?: 1856. V. 38; 40

HARTSOEKER, NICHOLAS

Essay de Dioptrique. Paris: 1694. V. 42

HARTSON, HALL

Youth. A Poem. London: 1773. V. 42; 45

HARTWELL, JESSE

The Wars of Michael and the Dragon. Painesville: 1845. V. 40

HARTWIG, G.

The Sea and Its Living Wonders. London: 1860. V. 41

The Tropical World: a Popular Scientific Account of the Natural History of the Animal and Vegetable Kingdoms in the Equatorial Regions. London: 1863. V. 45

HARTWIG, GEORG

The Polar World: a Popular Description of Man and Nature in the Arctic and Antarctic Regions of the Globe. London: 1869. V. 39

The Polar World: a Popular Description of Man and Nature in the Arctic and Antarctic Regions of the Globe. New York: 1869. V. 42

HARTZELL, CHARLES

A Short and Truthful History of Colorado During the Turbulent Reign of 'Davis the First'. Denver: 1894. V. 37; 42

HARTZENBUSCH, JUAN EUGENIO

The Lovers of Teruel. London: 1938. V. 40; 43

The Lovers of Teruel. Newtown: 1938. V. 42; 43; 44; 45; 46

THE HARVARD Classics. V. 37

HARVARD COLLEGE

The Laws of Harvard College. Boston: 1790. V. 37

HARVARD COLLEGE. LIBRARY

The Kilgour Collection of Russian Literature 1750-1920. Cambridge: 1959. V. 46

HARVARD COLLEGE. LIBRARY. DEPT. OF PRINTING & GRAPHIC ARTS

Catalogue of Books and Manuscripts. Part I: French 16th Century Books. Cambridge: 1964. V. 40; 41; 44; 46

Catalogue of Books and Manuscripts. Part II. Italian 16th Century Books. Cambridge: 1974. V. 41; 42; 44

Catalogue of Books and Manuscripts. Part I: French 16th Century Books. Cambridge: 1964. V. 46

Catalogue of Books and Manuscripts. Part II. Italian 16th Century Books. Cambridge: 1974. V. 46

HARVARD UNIVERSITY

The Laws of Harvard College. Boston: 1790. V. 38

HARVARD UNIVERSITY. LIBRARY

Houghton Library, 1942-1967. A Selection of Books and Manuscripts in Harvard Collections. Cambridge: 1967. V. 38; 39; 42

The Kilgour Collection of Russian Literature, 1750-1920. Cambridge: 1959. V. 38; 40

HARVARD UNIVERSITY. LIBRARY. DEPARTMENT OF GRAPHIC ARTS

Harvard College Library Department of Printing and Graphic Arts: Catalogue of Books and Manuscripts. Part 2: Italian 16th Century Books. Cambridge: 1974. V. 39

Harvard College Library Department of Printing and Graphic Arts: Catalogue of Books and Manuscripts. Part I: French 16th Century Books. Cambridge: 1964. V. 39

HARVARD University. Library. DEPARTMENT OF PRINTING AND GRAPHIC ARTS Catalogue of Books and Manuscripts. Part 1. French 16th Century Books. 1964. V. 42

HARVARD UNIVERSITY. LIBRARY. HOUGHTON LIBRARY

A Selection of Books and Manuscripts in Haravard Collections. Cambridge: 1967. V. 44

HARVEIAN ORATIONS

A Collection of 31 Harveian orations from 1950 to 1983. V. 37

HARVERY, J. MARTIN

Character and the Actor: A Lecture Delivered Before the Ethological Society, by J. Martin Harvey. Florence: 1908. V. 37

HARVEST, GEORGE

A Sermon Preached Before the Honourable Trustees for Establishing the Colony of Georgia In America, and the Associates of the Late Reverend Dr. Bray . . . London: 1749. V. 39; 43

HARVEY & CO., LONDON

Short Account of Sir Astley Cooper's Vital Restorative, the only Acknowledged Successful Remedy for the Removal of General, Local and Nervous Debility . . . London: 1864. V. 39

HARVEY, CHARLES

The History of the 4th Battalion Norfolk Regiment (late East Norfolk Militi). London: 1899. V. 38

HARVEY, CHARLES T.

Special Report on Data Relating to the Maritime Canal of Nicaragua and the Regions of Tributary Thereto. New York: 1890. V. 42

HARVEY, CHRISTOPHER

The School of the Heart; or, the Heart . . . London: 1778. V. 44

The School of the Heart, or the Heart, (of itself gone away from God) Brought Back Again to Him and Instructed by Him. Bristol: 1808. V. 43

HARVEY CUSHING SOCIETY

A Bibliography of the Writings of Harvey Cushing Prepared on the Occasion of His Seventieth Birthday. Springfield: 1939. V. 41; 44; 45

A Bibliography of the Writings of Harvey Cushing Prepared on the Occasion of His Seventieth Birthday April 8, 1939 by the Harvey Cushing Society. Springfield: 1940. V. 44; 45

HARVEY Cushing's Seventieth Birthday Party, April 8, 1939. Springfield: 1939. V. 41; 44; 45; 46

HARVEY, EDWARD

The Manual Exercise, as Ordered by His Majesty, in the Year 1764. Together with PLans and Explanations of the Method Generally Practised at Reviews and Field Days. Philadelphia: 1776. V. 40

HARVEY, ELLWOOD

Valedictory Address to the Graduating Class of the Female Medical College of Pennsylvania . . . Philadelphia: 1854. V. 43; 45

HARVEY, G. H.

The Harvey Families of Inishowen, Co. Donegal and Maen, Cornwall. 1927. V. 43

HARVEY, GABRIEL

The Works. London: 1884. V. 45

HARVEY, GEORGE

On Old and New Inventions for Keeping Pictorial Works of Art. London: 1861. V. 38

HARVEY, GIDEON

Ars Curandi Morbos Expectatione: Item de Vanitatibus, Dolis & Mendaciis Medicorum . . . Amsterdam: 1695. V. 41

The Conclave of Physicians . . . London: 1686-85. V. 38

The Family Physician, and the House of Apothecary . . . London: 1676. V. 44

The Family Physician and the House Apothecary. London: 1678. V. 38; 40; 42

The Third Edition of the Vanities of Philosophy and Physick: enlarged . . . offering moreover at different hyoptheses in Metaphysicks . . . Physick . . . and other Diseases. London: 1702. V. 37; 40

HARVEY, HENRY

History of the Shawnee Indians, from the Year 1681 to 1854, Inclusive. Cincinnati: 1855. V. 37; 42

HARVEY, J. R.

Records of the Norfolk Yeomanry Cavalry, to Which is Added the Fencilbe and Provisonal Cavalry of the Same Country From 1780 to 1908 . . . London: 1908. V. 38

HARVEY, JAMES

A Collection of English Precedents Relating to the Office of a Justice of the Peace . . . London: in the Savoy: 1751. V. 46

Praesagium Medicum, or, the Prognostick Signs of Acute Diseases; London: 1706. V. 40; 41; 42; 44; 45; 46

HARVEY, JAMES M.

The State of Kansas. Thanksgiving Proclamation. Topeka: 1869. V. 40

HARVEY, JANE

The Castle of Tynemouth. Newcastle-upon-Tyne: 1830. V. 39

HARVEY, JOHN

English Medieval Architects. London: 1954. V. 45; 46

The Life of Robert Bruce King of Scots. Edinburgh: 1729. V. 41; 46

THE HARVEY Lectures. 1960-76. V. 42

HARVEY, MOSES

Lectures, Literary and Biographical. Edinburgh: 1864. V. 46

Newfoundland As It Is in 1894: a Handbook and Tourists' Guide. St. John's: 1894. V. 44

Newfoundland in 1897 Being Queen Victoria's Diamond Jubilee Year and the Four Hundredth Anniversary of the Discovery of the Island by John Cabot. London: 1897. V. 44

Newfoundland in 1900. New York: 1900. V. 43; 44

HARVEY, OSCAR J.

A History of Wilkes-Barre, Luzerne Co., Pennsylvania from the First Beginnings . . . Wilkes-Barre: 1909-30. V. 39; 41; 42

HARVEY, RICHARD

An Astrological Discourse Upon the Great and Notable Conjunction of the Two Superiour Planets Saturne and Jupiter Which Shall Happen the 28th Day of April 1583 with a Briefe Declaration of the Effects Which the Late Eclipse of the Sunne 1582 . . . London: 1583. V. 40; 45

HARVEY, W.

The Church of the Nativity at Bethlehem. London: 1910. V. 42

A Tale of Two Nations. 1894. V. 45

HARVEY, W. C.

Sensibility, the Stranger and Other Poems. London: 1818. V. 42

HARVEY, W. F.

Midnight House and Other Tales. London: 1910. V. 44

Strange Conquest. 1934. V. 44

HARVEY, W. W.

Sketches of Hayti: from the Expulsion of the French, to the Death of Christophe. London: 1827. V. 42

HARVEY, WILLIAM 1578-1657

The Anatomical Exercises of Dr. William Harvey. London. V. 45

Anatomical Exercitations, Concerning Generation of Living Creatures. London: 1653. V. 40; 41; 42

The Anatomical Exercises. London: 1673. V. 39; 41; 42

The Anatomical Exercises. London: 1928. V. 37; 38; 39; 40; 41; 42; 43; 44; 45; 46

De Motu Locali Animalium, 1627. Cambridge: 1959. V. 38; 45

Exercitat Anatomicae de Motu Cordis et Sanguinis Circulo. Rotterdam: 1671. V. 37

Exercitatio Anatomica De Motu Cordis et Sanguinis in Animalibus. Florence: 1928. V. 40; 41; 42; 43; 45

Exercitationes de Generatione Animalium. Amsterdam: 1651. V. 40; 41; 45

Exercitationes de Generatione Animalium. London: 1651. V. 37; 38; 39; 40; 43

Exercitationes Anatomicae. De Motu Cordis & Sanguinis Circulatione . . . London: 1660. V. 45

Exercitationes De Generatione Animalium. Patavii: 1666. V. 37; 38; 41

De Motu Cordis & Sanguinis in Animalibus, Anatomica Exercitatio. Leiden: 1639. V. 39; 43

De Motu Locali Animalium, 1627. Cambridge: 1959. V. 41; 42

On Excision of the Enlarged Tonsil, and Its Consequences in Cases of Deafness. London: 1850. V. 41

Opera Omnia. London: 1766. V. 40

Portraits of Dr. William Harvey. Oxford: 1913. V. 39; 44; 46

Prelections Anatomiae Universalis. London: 1886. V. 45

Scottish Chapbook Literature. Paisley: 1903. V. 41

The Works of William Harvey, M.D. London: 1846. V. 40

Works. London: 1847. V. 41

HARVEY, WILLIAM HENRY

Flora Capensis Being a Systematic Description of the Plants of Cape Colony, Caffraria & Port Natal (and Neighboring Territories); 173. V. 39

Flora Capensis, Being a Systematic Description of the Plants of the Cape Colony, Caffraira and Port Natal. London: 1859-1927, 1973. V. 38

Flora Capensis, Being a Systematic Description of the Plants of the Cape Colony, Caffraria and Port Natal. London: 1858-1927, 1973. V. 37

A Manual of the British Marine Algae. London: 1849. V. 37; 38

Nereis Boreali-Americana: or, Contributions to a History of the Marine Algae of North America. Part I. - Melanospermeae. Washington: 1852. V. 40

Phycologia Britannica; or a History of British Sea-Weeds . . . London: 1846-51. V. 43

Phycologia Britannica. London: 1871. V. 39; 40; 43

HARVEY, WILLIAN HENRY

Nereis Boreali-Americana . . . Washington: 1851-53-58. V. 44

HARVIE-BROWN, J. A.

A Fauna of the North-West Highlands and Skye. Edinburgh: 1904. V. 37; 38

The History of the Squirrel in Great Britain. Edinburgh: 1881. V. 44

A Vertebrate Fana of Argyll and the Inner Hebrides. Edinburgh: 1892. V. 40

HARVIE-BROWN, JOHN A.

A Fauna of the Tay Basin and Strathmore. London: 1906. V. 37; 38

A Vertebrate Fauna of Sutherland, caitheness and Est Cromarty. Edinburgh: 1887. V. 44

Vertibrate Fauna of Sutherland, etc. London: 1887. V. 37

HARWOOD, EDWARD

Biographica Classica; the Lives and Characters of the Greek and Roman Classics. London: 1778. V. 42; 44

Certaine Choise and Remarkable Observations Selected Out of a Discourse Written Long Since by the Late and Famous Earle of Essex, Very Useful for These Times. London: 1642. V. 37

A View of the Various Editions of the Greek and Roman Classics, with Remarks. London: 1775. V. 42

A View of the Various Editions of the Greek and Roman Classics. London: 1790. V. 45

HARWOOD, THOMAS

The History and Antiquities of the Church and City of Lichfield . . . Gloucester: 1806. V. 44

HARWOOD, WILLIAM

On the Curative Influence of the Southern Coast of England, Especially that of Hastings. London: 1828. V. 39; 46

HASCALL, F. K.

Harry Wearne. New York: 1933. V. 41

HASCLOCK, JOHN

A Letter from Lysbone, Directed to Captain Thomas Harrison. London: 1650. V. 43

HASELDEN, THOMAS

The Seaman's Daily Assistant. London: 1777. V. 40

The Seaman's Daily Assistant: Being a Short, Easy, and Plain Method of Keeping a Journal at Sea . . . London: 1778. V. 42

The Seaman's Daily Assistant, Being a Short, Easy and Plain Method of Keeping a Journal at Sea . . . London: 1779. V. 42

The Seaman's Daily Assistant, Being a Short, Easy and Plain Method of Keeping a Journal at Sea. V. 40

HASELER, H.

Scenery of the Southern Coast of Devonshire . . . Sidmouth: 1819. V. 41

A Series of Views of Sidmouth and Its Neighbourhood Drawn from Nature and Painting. Clifton Cottage, Sidmouth,: 1825. V. 40

HASELER, H. continued

A Series of Views of Sidmouth and Its Neighbourhood, Drawn from Nature and on Stone. London: 1825. V. 38

A Series of Sidmouth and Its Neighbourhood, Drawn from Nature and On Stone. Sidmouth: 1825. V. 40

HASELL, JOHN

Memorials and Other Papers, Relative to the Claims of Captain John Hasell on the Court of Portugal on Account of the Illegal Seizure of the Ship Argyle by the Governor of the Brasils. London: 1778. V. 39

HASKELL, ARNOLD

Balletomania. London: 1934. V. 45

HASKELL, ARNOLD L.

Some Studies in Ballet. South Kensington: 1928. V. 38

HASKELL, DANIEL

A Tenative Check-List of Early European Railway Literature 1831-1848. Boston: 1955. V. 46

HASKELL, DANIEL C.

The United States Exploring Expedition 1838-1842 and its Publication 1844-1874, a Bibliography. New York: 1942. V. 37

HASKELL, FRANKLIN ARETAS

The Battle of Gettysburg. Boston: 1908. V. 42

HASKELL, WILLIAM B.

Two Years in the Klondike and Alaskan Gold-Fields. Hartford: 1898. V. 37; 38; 40; 44; 45

HASKETT SMITH, W. P.

Climbing in the British Isles 1. - England. London: 1894. V. 40

HASKETT, WILLIAM J.

Shakerism Unmasked, or the History of the Shakers . . . Pittsfield: 1828. V. 39

HASKETT, WILLIAM JAY

An Abstract of the Laws of the State and Ordinances of the Corporation of the City of New York, in Relation to Vessels, Wharves, Piers, Slips, Basins, Wrecks and Salvage. New York: 1848. V. 41

HASKINS, C. W.

The Argonauts of California . . . New York: 1890. V. 44

The Argonauts of California: Being the Reminiscences of Scenes and Incidents that Occurred in California in Early Mining Days, by a Pioneer. N: 1890, c.1889. V. 40

HASKINS, DAVID GREENE

Ralph Waldo Emerson, His Materanl Ancestors. Boston: 1886. V. 43

HASKINS, R. W.

New England and the West. Buffalo: 1843. V. 40; 45

HASLAM, MALCOLM

Marks and Monograms of the Modern Movement, 1875-1930. New York: 1977. V. 43

HASLAM, S. M.

River Plants of Western Europe. London: 1987. V. 37

HASLEM, JOHN

The Old Derby China Factory . . . London: 1876. V. 40; 41; 42; 46

HASLEWOOD, FRANCIS

Memorials of Smarden, Kent. Ipswich: 1886. V. 39; 42

The Parish of Chislet, Kent. Ipswich: 1887. V. 40

HASLEWOOD, JOSEPH

The Dialogue of Creatures Moralised. London: 1816. V. 38

Hereafter Ensue the Trewe Encountre or Batayle Lately Don Betwene Englande and Scotlande. London: 1809. V. 45

(Introduction to The Mirror for Magistrates.) London: 1815. V. 37

Mirror of Magistrates, in Five Parts . . . Collated with Various Editions, and Historical Notes etc. London: 1815. V. 37

The Secret History of the Green Room. London: 1792. V. 39; 40; 45

Some Account of the Life and Publications of the Late Joseph Ritson, Esq. London: 1824. V. 39

HASLUCK, PAUL

The Book of Photography, Practical, Thoretic and Applied. London: 1905. V. 40

HASLUCK, PAUL N.

The Automobile. London: 1902. V. 41

HASLUND, HENNIN

Tents in Mongolia (Yabonah). Adventures and Experiences Among the Nomads of Central Asia. London: 1934. V. 39

HASPELS, C. H. EMILIE

The Highlands of Phrygia. Princeton: 1971. V. 40; 42; 44

HASSALL, ARTHUR HILL

History of British Freshwater Algae, Including Descriptions of the Desmideae and Diatomaceae. London: 1845. V. 38; 43; 45

The Microscopic Anatomy of the Human Body, in Health and Disease. London: 1849. V. 38

HASSALL, CHRISTOPHER

Christ's Comet. London: 1937. V. 38

Penthesperson. London: 1938. V. 41

HASSALL, JOAN

The ARtist. V. 45

Cranford. London: 1940. V. 46

Joan Hassall, Engravings and Drawings. Pinner: 1985. V. 37

To William Maxwell - Upon the Success of His Endeavours to Obtain a Grant . . . to Buy Equipment for the Book-Production Class in the College of Art, Edinburgh, 1943. Edinburgh: 1944. V. 40

The Wood Engravings of Joan Hassall. London: 1960. V. 40; 41; 43

HASSALL, JOHN

The Good Old Nursey Rhymes. London: 1920. V. 41

Tour of the Grand Junction Canal, Illustrating in a Series of Engravings, with an Historical and Topographical Description of Those Parts of the Counties of Middlesex, Hertfordshire, Buckinghamshire, Bedfordshire and Northamptonshire . . . London: 1819. V. 41

HASSALL, W. O.

The Holkham Bible Picture Book. London: 1954. V. 38; 45

The Holkham Library. Oxford: 1970. V. 38; 45

HASSAM, CHILDE

The Etchings and Drypoints of Childe Hassam. New York: 1925. V. 44

HASSAN, SELIM

Excavations at Giza 1929-1930. 1932. V. 46

Excavations at Giza, 1929-1930. Oxford: 1932. V. 42; 44

Excavations at Giza, 1935-1936. Volume VII: The Mastabas of the Seventh Season and Their Description. Cairo: 1953. V. 44

Excavations at Giza, 1936-37-38. Volume IX: The Mastabas of the Eighth Season and their Description. Cairo: 1960. V. 44

Excavations at Giza, 1938-39. Volume X: The Great Pyramid of Khufu and Its Mortuary Chapel. Cairo: 1960. V. 44

Excavations at Saqqara, 1937-1938. Cairo: 1975. V. 42

The Mastabas of the Seventh Season and Their Description. Cairo: 1953. V. 42

HASSARD, ANNIE

Floral Decorations for the Dwelling House. London & New York: 1876. V. 42

HASSAUREK, FRIEDRICH

Four Years Among Spanish Americans. New York: 1866. V. 40

Four Years Among Spanish Americans. New York: 1867. V. 40

HASSE, CHARLES E.

An Anatomical Description of the Diseases of Circulation and Respiration. London: 1846. V. 41; 42; 43

HASSELL, JOHN

Aqua Picture. No. 2. J. Hassell. Sherwood: 1812. V. 42

The Camera; or, Art of Drawing in Water Colours . . . London: 1823. V. 44; 45

Graphic Delineation. A Practical Treatise on the Art of Etching, or Manner of Copying Pictures and Drawings . . . London: 1826. V. 41

Memoirs of the Life of the Late George Morland with Critical and Descriptive Observations on the Whole of His Work Hitherto Before the Public. London: 1806. V. 39; 40; 44

Picturesque Rides and Walks, with Excursions by Water, Thirty Miles Round the British Metropolis. London: 1817. V. 37; 41; 44

Picturesque Rides and Walks, with Excursions by Water, Thirty Miles Round the British Metropolis. London: 1817-18. V. 38; 39; 40; 44

Tour of the Isle of Wight. London: 1790. V. 37; 41; 43; 45

Tour of the Grand Junction (Canal). Islington: 1819. V. 44

Tour of the Grand Junction. London: 1819. V. 37; 39; 40; 42; 44; 45

HASSELQUIST, FREDERICK

Voyages and Travels in the Levant in 1749-1752. London: 1766. V. 37; 39; 42; 44; 46

HASSENFRATZ, J. H.

La Siderotechnie, ou l'Art de Traiter les Minerais de Fer Pour en Obtenir de la Fonte, du Fer, ou de l'Acier. Paris: 1812. V. 40; 42

HASSLER, EDGAR W.

Old Westmoreland: a History of Western Pennsylvania During the Revolution. Pittsburgh: 1900. V. 42

HASSLER, F. R.

Documents Relating to the Construction of Uniform Standards of Weights and Measures for the United States from 1832 to 1835. New York: 1836. V. 45

HASSLER, FERDINAND R.

Elements of the Geometry of Planes and Solids. Richmond: 1828. V. 42

HASSLER, JON

An Interview with Jon Hassler. Minneapolis: 1990. V. 46

HASSRICK, PETER H.

Frederic Remington Paintings, Drawings and Sculpture in the Amon Carter Museum and the Sid W. Richardson Foundation Collections by Peter H. Hassrick. New York: 1973. V. 44

HASTAIN, E.

Hastain's Township Plats of the Creek nation. Muskogee: 1910. V. 46

HASTED, EDWARD

The History and Topographical Survey of the County of Kent. Canterbury: 1778-99. V. 39; 40; 41; 45

HASTELL, JOHN 1743-1820

Precedents of Proceedings in the House of Commons with Observations. London: 1785-1796. V. 40

HASTIE, T.

The Only Method to Make Reading Easy, or, Child's Best Instructor . . . Newcastle: 1839. V. 46

HASTINGS and Its Vicinity. London: 1817. V. 39

HASTINGS, FRANCIS RAWDON, 1ST MARQUIS OF

Summary of the Administration of the Indian Government from October 1813 to January 1823. Edinburgh: 1825. V. 40

HASTINGS, FRANK STEWART

A Ranchman's Recollections. Chicago: 1921. V. 37; 38; 42; 43; 46

HASTINGS, HUGH

Ecclesiastical Records, State of New York. Albany: 1901. V. 39; 40; 42; 44

HASTINGS, JAMES

Encyclopaedia of Religion and Ethics. Edinburgh: 1908. V. 46
Encyclopaedia of Religion and Ethics. Edinburgh: 1908-21. V. 40

HASTINGS, JOHN

The Practice of Surgey: Embracing Minor Surgery and the Application of Dressings. Philadelphia: 1850. V. 42

HASTINGS, LANSFORD W.

A New Description of Oregon and California . . . Cincinnati (sic): 1857. V. 43

HASTINGS, SALLY

Poems on Different Subjects. Lancaster: 1808. V. 41; 42; 44; 46

HASTINGS, SUSANNAH WILLARD JOHNSON

A Narrative of the Captivity of Mrs. Johnson. Windsor: 1814. V. 37; 38
A Narrative of the Captivity of Mrs. Johnson. Windsor: 1807. V. 37

HASTINGS, THOMAS

The Book of the Wars of Westminster . . . London: 1784. V. 43
Dissertation on Musical Taste; or, General Principles of Taste Applied to the Art of Music. Albany: 1822. V. 43
Etchings from the Works of Ric. Wilson. London: 1825. V. 38
The Regal Rambler; or, Eccentrical Adventures of the Deveil in London; with the Manoeuvres of His Ministers, Towards the Close of the Eighteenth Century. London: 1793. V. 46

HASTINGS, VISCOUNT

The Golden Octopus: Legends of the South Seas. London: 1928. V. 37

HASTINGS, WARREN 1732-1818

Debates of the House of Lords, on the Evidence Delivered in the Trial of Warren Hastings, Esquire. London: 1797. V. 40; 41; 46
The Defence of Warren Hastings, Esq. London: 1786. V. 41
The History of the Trial of Warren Hastings, Esq., Late Governor General of Bengal, Before the High Court of Parliament, on an Impeachment for High Crimes and Misdemeanours. London: 1796. V. 38; 46

A Letter from . . . Governor-General of Bengal, to the Honourable the Court of Directors of the East-India Company. London: 1784. V. 38
Memoirs Relative to the State of India. London: 1786. V. 37; 39

HASTLEY, THOMAS

A Discourse on Mistakes concerning Religion, Enthusiasm, Experiences &c. London: 1759. V. 37

HASTNOLL, PHYLLIS

The Grecian Enchanted. Great Britain: 1952. V. 41

HASWELL, ANTHONY

Memoirs and Adventures of Captain Matthew Phelps; Formerly of Harwington in Connecticut Now Resident in Newhaven in Vermont . . . Bennington: 1802. V. 39; 43; 45; 46

HATCH, BENTON L.

A Check-List of the Publications of Thomas Bird Mosher . . . 1966. V. 39; 45
A Check-List of the Publications of Thomas Bird Mosher. Amherst: 1966. V. 42
A Check List of the Publications of Thomas Bird Mosher of Portland, Maine, 1891-1923. London: 1966. V. 41
A Check List of the Publications of Thomas Bird Mosher of Portland, Maine, 1891-1923. Northampton: 1966. V. 38; 43; 45

HATCH, FREDERICK H.

The Gold Mines of the Rand Being a Description of the Mining Industry of Witwatersrand South African Republic. London: 1895. V. 42; 44; 45; 46

HATCH, Z. PATEN

The Christian Diadem. New York: 1851. V. 40

HATCHER, J. B.

Ceratopsia. (Horned Dinosaurs). Washington: 1907. V. 39

HATCHER, J. S.

Machine Guns. Mechanism: the Practical Handling of Machine Gun Fire: Machine Gun Tactics. London: 1917. V. 43
Machine Guns. mechanism: The Practical Handling of Machine Gun Fire: Machine Gun Tactics. Wisconsin: 1917. V. 44; 45; 46

HATCHER, MATTIE AUSTIN

Letters of an Early American Traveller: Mary Austin Holley, Her Life and Her Works, 1784-1846. Dallas: 1933. V. 42; 43
The Opening of Texas to Foreign Settlement, 1801-1821. Austin: 1927. V. 37; 38

HATCHER, ROBERT

The Pharmacopoeia and the Physician . . . Chicago: 1908. V. 42; 45

HATFIELD, EDWIN F.

St. Helena and the Cape of Good Hope. New York: 1852. V. 38; 45

HATFIELD, RICHARD

Geyserland Empiricisms in Social Reform Being Data and Observations Recorded by the Late Mark Stubble . . . Washington: 1908. V. 42

HATFIELD, S.

Letters on the Importance of the Female Sex . . . London: 1803. V. 42

HATFIELD, THOMAS DE

Hatfield's Survey: a Record of the Possessions of the See of Durham . . . Durham: 1857. V. 40

HATHAWAY, ANN

Muskoka Memories. Toronto: 1904. V. 44

HATHAWAY, CHARLES S.

Our Firemen: a Record of the Faithful and Heroic Men Who Guard the Property and Lives in the City of Detroit. Detroit: 1894. V. 44

HATHAWAY, ELLA C.

Battle of the Big Hole in August, 1877. N.P.: 1919. V. 42; 44; 46

HATHAWAY, J. W.

The Good Man Father Winslow; or, a Sketch of the Life of the Rev. Howard Winslow. Farmington: 1861. V. 43

HATSELL, JOHN

Precedents of the Proceedings in the House of Commons Under Separate Titles with Observations. London: 1781. V. 38

HATTON, EDWARD

Comes Commercii, or, the Trader's Companion. (with) A Supplement to Comes Commercii . . . London: 1754. V. 41; 46
A Mathematical Manual; or, Delightful Associate. London: 1728. V. 38; 46
A New View of London; or, an Ample Account of that City. London: 1708. V. 39
A New View of London . . . London: 1808. V. 44

HATTON, J.

Newfoundland: The Oldest British Colony. London: 1883. V. 39

HATTON, JOSEPH

Club-Land. London and Provincial. London: 1890. V. 44

Henry Irving's Impressions of America . . . London: 1884. V. 46

'The New Ceylon'. Being a Sketch of British North Borneo, or Sabah. London: 1881. V. 41

Newfoundland. Its History, Its Present Condition, and Its Prospects in the Future. Boston: 1883. V. 37; 40; 43

Provincial Papers, Being a Collection of Tales and Sketches. London: 1861. V. 46

HATTON, RICHARD G.

The Craftman's Plant-Book. London: 1909. V. 44

HATTON, THOMAS

A Bibliography of the Periodical Works of Charles Dickens. London: 1933. V. 37; 40; 41; 43

A Bibliography of the Periodical Works of Charles Dickens, Bibliographical, Analytical and Statistical. London: 1935. V. 39

A Bibliography of the Periodical Works of Charles Dickens. Bibliographical, Analytical and Statistical. 1933. V. 37

Catalogue of the Important Collections Mainly of the Writings of Charles Dickens and of Other XIX Century Authors Forming Part of the Library of Thomas Hatton . . . . .Which Will be Sold by Auction . . . 30th of Nov. 1931, . . . Sotheby & Co. London: 1931. V. 40

An Introduction to the Mechanical Part of Clock and Watch Work. London: 1773. V. 43; 45

HATZIMICHALI, ANGELIKI

Greek Folk Costume. Athens: 1984. V. 37; 39

HAUDICQUER DE BLANCOURT, FRANCOIS

The Art of Glass. London: 1699. V. 39; 40; 42; 43; 44

HAUDICQUER DE BLANCOURT, JEAN

De l'Art de la Verrerie . . . Ouvrage Rempli de Plusiers Secrets & Curiositez . . . Paris: 1697. V. 40; 44

L'Art de la Verrerie. Paris: 1718. V. 38

HAUF, F. J.

Margaritologie Vermischt mit Conchyliologischen Beytragen zur Naturkunde von Baiern. Munich: 1795. V. 43

HAUGHTON, GRAVES

Prodromus, or, an Inquiry into the First Principles of Reasoning . . . London: 1839. V. 46

HAUGHTON, S.

Sport and Travels. Dublin: 1916. V. 45

HAUGHTON, WILLIAM

Sylvicola; or, Songs from the Backwoods. Viroqua: 1878. V. 40

HAUGUM, J.

A Monograph of the Birdwing Butterflies, the Systematics of Ornithoptera, Troides and Related Genera. Klampenborg: 1978-85. V. 37

HAUKSBEE, FRANCIS

Physico-Mechanical Experiments on Various Subjects. London: 1719. V. 42; 44

HAULTAIN, THEODORE

Hints for Lovers. Boston: 1909. V. 46

HAUPT, A.

Renaissance Palaces of Northern Italy & Tuscany. London: 1931. V. 42

HAUPT-GRUND der Gebauden und des Gartens des Herrn Geheimden Raths, Baron von Vernezober in Berlin. Augsburg: 1740. V. 38

HAUPT, HERMAN

Reminiscences of General Herman Haupt. Milwaukee: 1901. V. 39; 46

HAURY, EMIL W.

The Stratigraphy and Archaeology of Vetana Cave, Arizona. Tucson: 1950. V. 42

HAUSLEUTNER, W. G.

Gallerie der Nationen . . . Amerikaner . . . Stuttgart: 1793. V. 38

HAUSTED, PETER

Ad Populum; or, a Lecture to the People. N.P.: n.d.: 1644. V. 40

Senile Odium. Comoedia. Cantabrigiae: 1633. V. 37

HAUTECOEUR, LOUIS

Les Mosques du Caiare. Paris: 1932. V. 38

HAUTEFEUILLE, JEAN DE 1647-1724

Moyen de Faire des Experiences Sensibles, qui Prouvent le Mouvement de la Terre Autour du Soleil, et la Verite du Sisteme de Copernic. Second Moyen de Faire des Experiences Sensibles. Orleans: 1721. V. 38

La Perfection des Instrumens der Mer. Paris?: 1715. V. 38

HAUY, M.

Essai sur l'Education des Aveugles. Paris: 1786. V. 46

HAUY, R. J.

An Elementary Treatise on Natural Philosophy. London: 1807. V. 40

HAUY, RENE JUST

Traite de Mineralogie . . . Paris: 1801. V. 38; 45

HAUY, VALENTIN

Essai sur l'Education des Aveugles, ou Expose de Differens Moyens . . . Paris: 1786. V. 45

HAVELL, E. B.

Indian Architecture; Its Psychology, Structure and History from the First Muhammadan Invasion to the Present Day. London: 1913. V. 39

HAVELL, R.

Sporting Miseries. London: 1817. V. 39

The Tour or Select Views on the Southern Coast. London: 1827. V. 39

HAVEN, ALICE BRADLEY

'All's Not Gold That Glitters;' Or the Young Californian. New York: 1853. V. 40; 41

HAVEN, CHARLES C.

Washington and His Army During Their March through and Return to New Jersey, in December 1776 and January 1777. Trenton: 1856. V. 42

HAVEN, JOSEPH

A Discourse at the Funeral of Rev. Ralph Emerson, D.D., Late Professor of Ecclesiastical History and Pastoral Theology in Andover Theological Seminary . . . Chicago: 1863. V. 39

HAVENS, MUNSON ALDRICH

Horace Walpole and the Strawberry Hill Press 1757-1789. Canton: 1901. V. 44

HAVERCAMP BEGEMANN, E.

Willem Buytewech. Amsterdam: 1959. V. 43

HAVERCOMP, SIGEBERT

Dissertationes de Alexandri Magni Numismate . . . Lugduni Batavorum: 1722. V. 46

HAVERFIELD, T. TUNSTALL

Feriae Sacrae; or, Short Notes on the Great Festivals of the Church . . . London: 1847. V. 42

HAVERGAL, FRANCES RIDLEY

Life Mosaic. The Ministry of Song and Under the Surface. London: 1879. V. 38

HAVERKAMP-BEGEMANN, EGBERT

Drawings from the Clark Art Instiute. New Haven: 1964. V. 42; 44

Drawings from the Clark Art Institute. A Catalogue Raisonne of the Robert Sterling Clark Collection of European and American Drawings. Sixteenth - Nineteenth Centuries. New Haven and London: 1964. V. 46

HAVERRGAL, FRANCES RIDLEY

Swiss Letters and Alpine Poems. London: 1882. V. 45

HAVERSCHMIDT, F.

Birds of Surinam. London: 1971. V. 42

HAVERSCHMIDT, FRANCOIS

Birds of Surinam. London: 1968. V. 38; 39; 40

HAVILAND, JOHN

Britannia's Pastorals. London: 1625. V. 44

HAVILAND, MAUD D.

A Summer on the Yenesel. 1915. V. 46

HAWAGUCHI, EKAI

Three Years in Tibet. Madras: 1909. V. 40

HAWAII

Compiled Laws of the Hawaiian Kingdom. Honolulu: 1884. V. 37

Hawaiian Islands: Report of the Committee on Foreign Relations. Washington: 1894. V. 37

Index of all Grants and Patents Land Seas. Honolulu: 1916. V. 37

HAWAII. CONSTITUTION

Constitution of the Republic of Hawaii Promulgated July 4th A.D. 1894. Honolulu: 1894. V. 37; 45

HAWAII. CONSTITUTION - 1841

Ke Kumu Kanawai, a Me Na Kanawai O Ko Hawaii Pae Aina. Ua Kauia I Ke Kauia Kamehameha III. Honolulu: 1841. V. 39

HAWAII. CONSTITUTION - 1894

Constitution of the Republic of Hawaii. N.P.: 1894. V. 40

HAWAIIAN Album No. 1, The Royal Family. Honolulu: 1880. V. 44

THE HAWAIIAN Almanac and Annual for 1898 . . . Honolulu: 1898. V. 39; 41

HAWAIIAN Cook Book Compiled by the Ladies' Society of Central Union Church. Honolulu: 1896. V. 41

HAWAIIAN HISTORICAL SOCIETY

Annual Reports. Honolulu: 1896-1925. V. 38

HAWAIIAN ISLANDS. LAWS, STATUTES, ETC.

Penal Code of the Hawaiian Islands, Passed by the House of Nobles and Representatives on the 21st of June, 1850; to Which are Appended the Other Acts Passed by the House of Nobles and Representatives During their General Session for 1850. Honolulu: 1850. V. 40

THE HAWAIIAN Islands. Their Resources . . . Coffee, The Coming Staple Product. Honolulu: 1896. V. 39; 43

HAWAIIAN MISSION CHILDREN'S SOCIETY

Second Annual Report of the Hawaiian Mission Children's Society. Honolulu: 1854. V. 37; 39

HAWARD, LAZARUS

The Charges Issuing Forth of the Crown Revenue of England, and Dominion of Wales. London: 1647. V. 38

HAWARDEN, EDWARD

Charity and Truth; or Catholics Not Uncharitable in Saying That None Are Saved Out of the Catholic Church. Dublin: 1809. V. 46

HAWEIS, H. R.

American Humorists. London: 1883. V. 40; 42

HAWEIS, H. R., MRS.

The Art of Beauty. London: 1883. V. 37; 41

The Art of Decoration. London: 1881. V. 38

HAWES, CHARLES BOARDMAN

The Dark Frigate. Boston: 1923. V. 42

HAWES, CHARLES H.

The Uttermost East Being an Account of Investigations Among the Natives and Russian Convicts of the Island of Sakhalin. London: 1904. V. 43

HAWES, G. H.

The Nature of Spiritual Existence and Spiritual Gifts, Given through the Mediumship of Mrs. Cora L. V. Richmond. San Francisco: 1884. V. 43

HAWES, GEORGE W.

. . . Ohio State Gazetteer and Business Directory for 1859 and 1860 . . . Cincinnati: 1860. V. 39; 40

Ohio State Gazetteer and Business Directory, for 1859 and 1860. Number One. Cincinnati, Ohio: 1859. V. 37

HAWES, HARRIET BOYD

Vasiliki nd Other Prehistoric Sites on the Isthmus of Hierapetra, Crete. Excavations of the Wekl-Houston-Cramp Expeditions 1901, 1903, and 1904. Philadelphia: 1908. V. 37; 44

HAWES, WILLIAM POST 1803-1841?

Sporting Scenes and Sundry Sketches . . . New York: 1842. V. 42; 44

HAWKE, CASSANDRA

Julia de Grammont. London: 1788. V. 42; 43

HAWKE, MICHAEL

The Grounds of the Lawes of England. London: 1657. V. 40

HAWKER, ESSEX

The Wedding: A Tragi-Comi-Pastoral-Farcical Opera. London: 1729. V. 38

HAWKER, PETER

The Diary of Colonel Peter Hawker, 1802-1853. London: 1893. V. 39; 42; 46

Instructions to Young Sportsmen in all that Relates to Guns and Shooting. London. V. 38

Instructions to Young Sportsmen on the Choice, Care and Management of Guns: Hints for the Preservation of Game, Directions for Shooting Wildfowl, &c, &c. London: 1816. V. 46

Instructions to Young Sportsmen in All That Relates to Guns and Shooting. London: 1824. V. 42

Instructions to Young Sportsmen in all that Relates to Guns and Shooting. London: 1826. V. 43; 46

Instructions to Young Sportsmen in All That Relates to Guns and Shooting. London: 1830. V. 39; 40

Instructions to Young Sportsmen in all that Relates to Guns and Shooting. London: 1833. V. 39

Instructions to Young Sportsmen in all That Relates to Guns and Shooting. London: 1838. V. 42

Instructions to Young Sportsmen in all that Relates to Guns and Shooting. Philadelphia: 1853. V. 39

Instructions to Young Sportsmen in All That Relates to Guns and Shooting. London: 1854. V. 45

Instructions to Young Sportsmen in All That Relates to Guns and Shooting. London: 1859. V. 39; 40

Instructions to Young Sportsmen on the Choice, Care and Management of Guns. London: printed for R.: 1816. V. 37

The Sportsman's Pocket Companion. No. 1. Croydon: 1801. V. 46

HAWKER, ROBERT STEPHEN 1809-1875

The Cornish Ballads and other Poems, The Quest of the Sangraal. Oxford & London: 1869. V. 39; 44

Ecclesia: A Volume of Poems. Oxford: 1840. V. 39; 45

Echoes from Old Cornwall. London: 1846. V. 39; 44

The Poetical Works . . . London: 1879. V. 38

The Quest of the Sangraal. Exeter: 1864. V. 37; 39

HAWKES, FRANCIS L.

Narrative of the Expedition of an American Squadron to the China Seas and Japan Performed in the Years 1852, 1853 and 1854. New York: 1856. V. 46

HAWKES, J.

Manufacturers of Every Description of Looking Glasses and Furniture by Steam Power. Birmingham: 1870. V. 37

HAWKES, JOHN

Adventures in the Alaskan Skin Trade. New York: 1985. V. 42

The Bettle Leg. New York: 1951. V. 44; 45; 46

The Blood Oranges. 1971. V. 42

The Cannibal. 1949. V. 44; 46

The Cannibal. Norfolk: 1949. V. 44

The Cannibal. London: 1962. V. 39

Death, Sleep and the Traveler. 1974. V. 42

The Goose on the Grave. New York: 1954. V. 41

Innocence in Extremis. 1985. V. 40; 45

Innocence in Extremis. New York: 1985. V. 46

The Innocent Party. 1966. V. 42

The Lime Twig. 1961. V. 42

The Lime Twig. New York: 1961. V. 45

The Lime Twig. New York: 1963. V. 39; 40; 41

Lunar Landscape. New York: 1969. V. 39; 40; 41; 44; 45; 46

The Passion Artist. New York: 1979. V. 42; 44

Second Skin. New York: 1964. V. 39; 40; 41

Travesty. 1976. V. 42

The Universal Fears. Northridge: 1978. V. 39

HAWKES, NATHAN MORTIMER

Hearths and Homes of Old Lynn, with Studies in Local History. Lynn: 1907. V. 46

HAWKESWORTH, JOHN 1715?-1773

An Account of the Voyages Undertaken by Order of His Present Majesty for Making Discoveries in the Southern Hemisphere, and Successively Performed by Commodore Byron, Capt. Wallis, Capt. Carteret, and Capt. Cook, in the Dolphin, the Swallow . . . London: 1773. V. 38; 41; 42; 43

An Account of the Voyages Undertaken by the Order of His Present Majesty, For Making Discoveries in the Southern Hemisphere . . . Dublin: 1775. V. 41; 45

An Account of the Voyages Undertaken by the Order of His Present Majesty for Making Discoveries in the Southern Hemisphere. London: 1785. V. 38; 41; 44

The Adventurer. London: 1753-1754. V. 37

Almoran and Hamet. Dublin: 1761. V. 43

Almoran and Hamet. London: 1761. V. 39; 40; 43

A New Voyage, Round the World, in the Years 1768, 1769, 1770 and 1771, Undertaken by Order of His Present Majesty, Performed by Capt. James Cook . . . New York: 1774. V. 42

Relation des Voyages Entrepris par Ordre de s Majeste Britannique . . . Paris: 1774. V. 45

HAWKESWORTH, MISS

Relics of Antiquity: or, Remains of Ancient Structures, with Other Vestiges of Early Times in Great Britain. London: 1811. V. 38

HAWNEY, WILLIAM

The Complete Measurer; or, the Whole Art of Measuring. London: 1789.
V. 42

HAWORTH, EUPHRASIA FANNY

Saint Sylvester's Day and Other Poems. London: 1847. V. 39

HAWORTH, M. E.

Road Scrapings; Coaches and Coaching. London: 1882. V. 39

HAWTHORN Presbyterian Church: Jubilee History 1864-1914. Melbourne:
1914. V. 41

HAWTHORN, R.

*Shipbuilding and Engineering - an Historical and Hundredth Anniversary
Photographic Brochure on the Engines Built, the Ships and Speedboats for
WWI.* London: 1917. V. 41

HAWTHORNE, JULIAN

Bressant. New York: 1873. V. 41; 44

Hawthorne and His Wife. Cambridge: 1884. V. 40

Hawthorne Reading: an Essay. Celveland: 1902. V. 44

Sebastian Strome. London: 1879. V. 42

*The Secret of Solomon. (with) Solomon Columbus Rhodes and Company.
(with) Julian Hawthorne and Company.* N.P.: 1909. V. 46

HAWTHORNE, NATHANIEL 1804-1869

The Blithedale Romance. Boston: 1852. V. 38; 39; 40; 41; 43; 44; 45; 46

The Blithedale Romance. London: 1852. V. 39

The Celestial Rail-Road. Boston: 1843. V. 40

Complete Writings. Boston: 1900. V. 45

Doctor Grimshawe's Secret. Boston: 1883. V. 37; 40; 42; 44; 45

Dr. Grimshawe's Secret. London: 1883. V. 44; 45

Famous Old People: Being the Second Epoch of Grandfather's Chair.
Boston: 1841. V. 38; 42; 44

Famous Old People: Being the Second Epoch of Grandfather's Chair.
Boston: 1842. V. 44

Fanshawe, a Tale. Boston: 1828. V. 41

The Gentle Boy; a Thrice Told Tale. Boston: 1839. V. 38; 43; 44; 46

The Golden Touch. San Francisco: 1927. V. 37; 38; 39; 40; 41; 43; 45; 46

Grandfather's Chair: a History for Youth. Boston: 1841. V. 41; 44

Grandfather's Chair: a History for Youth. Boston: 1842. V. 43; 44

Grandfather's Chair: A History for Youth. Boston/New York: 1841. V. 37

The House of the Seven Gables. Boston: 1851. V. 37; 38; 39; 40; 41; 42;
43; 44; 45; 46

The House of The Seven Gables. London: 1851. V. 40

The House of the Seven Gables. New York: 1935. V. 37; 38; 40; 41

Liberty Tree: With the Last Words of Grandfather's Chair. Boston: 1841.
V. 44

Liberty Tree: with the Last Words of Grandfather's Chair. Boston: 1842.
V. 44

Liberty Tree: With Last Words of Grandfather's Chair. Boston: 1851. V. 44

Life of Franklin Pierce. Boston: 1852. V. 37; 38; 40; 41; 43; 44; 45

The Marble Faun. Boston. V. 46

The Marble Faun. Boston: 1850. V. 42

The Marble Faun. Boston: 1860. V. 37; 38; 39; 40; 41; 42; 43; 44; 45; 46

The Marble Faun. Leipzig: 1860. V. 39

The Marble Faun: or, The Romance of Monte Beni. Boston: 1869. V. 37

The Marble Faun or the Romance of Monte Beni. Boston: 1889. V. 41

The Marble Faun or the Romance of Monte Beni. Cambridge: 1889. V. 40

The Marble Faun or the Romance of Monte Beni. New York: 1931. V. 44

The Marble Faun or the Romance of Monte Beni. Zurich: 1931.
V. 40; 42; 43

Mosses from an Old Manse. New York: 1846. V. 42; 44; 45

Mosses from an Old Manse. New York: 1852. V. 44

Mosses from an Old Manse. Boston: 1854. V. 44; 45

Our Old Home. Boston: 1863. V. 37; 38; 39; 40; 41; 42; 43; 44; 45; 46

Our Old Home. London: 1863. V. 38; 39; 41; 44

Pansie: a Fragment. London: 1864. V. 45

Passages from American Notebooks. Boston: 1868. V. 39; 44; 46

Passages from the American Note-Books. London: 1868. V. 40; 45; 46

Passages from the English Note-Books. Boston: 1870. V. 38; 39; 40;
44; 46

Passages from the English Note-books of Nathaniel Hawthorne. London:
1870. V. 40

Passages from French and Italian Notebooks. London: 1871. V. 40; 43

Passages from the French and Italian Notebooks. Boston: 1872. V. 44

Peter Parley's Universal History on the Basis of Geography. Boston: 1837.
V. 39; 44

The Scarlet Letter. 1850. V. 45

The Scarlet Letter. Boston: 1850. V. 37; 39; 40; 41; 42; 43; 44; 45; 46

The Scarlet Letter. Boston: 1851. V. 44

The Scarlet Letter. Toronto: 1879. V. 42

The Scarlet Letter. Cambridge: 1892. V. 40

The Scarlet Letter. New York: 1908. V. 42

The Scarlet Letter. London: 1920. V. 38; 41; 42

The Scarlet Letter. New York: 1928. V. 45; 46

The Scarlet Letter. San Francisco: 1928. V. 37

The Scarlet Letter. London: 1935. V. 38

The Scarlet Letter. New York: 1935. V. 37

The Scarlet Letter. New York: 1951. V. 40

Septimius Felton. Berlin: 1872. V. 46

Septimius Felton. Boston: 1872. V. 37; 38; 41; 43; 44; 45; 46

Sights from a Steeple. 1988. V. 45

The Snow Image and Other Tales. London: 1851. V. 39

The Snow Image and Other Twice Told Tales. Boston: 1852. V. 37; 40; 42;
43; 44; 45

The Snow Image. New York: 1864. V. 37

Tanglewood Tales. London. V. 39; 40

Tanglewood Tales. London: New York: Toronto. V. 41

Tanglewood Tales. Boston: 1853. V. 39; 40; 44

Tanglewood Tales. Chicago: 1913. V. 42

Tanglewood Tales. London: 1918. V. 37; 40; 41; 45

Tanglewood Tales. Philadelphia: 1921. V. 43

Tanglewood Tales. London: 1938. V. 38; 40

Transformation. London: (1850). V. 37

Transformation; or, the Romance of Monte Beni. Leipzig: 1860. V. 37; 38;
40; 41; 43; 46

Transformation: or, The Romance of Monte Beni. London: 1860. V. 37; 38;
40; 46

True Stories from History and Biography. Boston: 1851. V. 42; 43; 44; 46

Twice Told Tales. Boston: 1837. V. 42; 44

Twice Told Tales. Boston: 1851. V. 43; 44

A Virtuoso's Collection and Other Tales. Boston: 1877. V. 44

A Wonder Book. London. V. 44; 46

A Wonder Book for Girls and Boys. Boston: 1852. V. 38; 41; 43; 44

A Wonder Book for Girls and Boys. Boston: 1892. V. 41

Wonder Book for Girls and Boys. Boston: 1893. V. 41

A Wonder Book for Girls and Boys. London: 1893. V. 41

Wonder Book for Boys and Girls. London: 1898. V. 40

A Wonder Book and Tanglewood Tales. New York: 1910. V. 38; 45

A Wonder Book. London: 1922. V. 38; 39; 40; 41; 44; 46

A Wonder Book. London, New York & Toronto: 1922. V. 40

A Wonder Book and Tanglewood Tales. London: 1925. V. 42

A Wonder Book. New York: (1922). V. 37

Works. Edinburgh & London: 1850-52. V. 37

Works. Boston: 1865. V. 39

The Works of Nathaniel Hawthorne. 1880. V. 37

The Complete Works. Boston: 1882. V. 38

Works. Boston & New York: 1882. V. 40; 42

Works. Boston: 1883. V. 42; 44

The Complete Works. Cambridge: 1883. V. 38

The Complete Works. Cambridge: 1883-84. V. 40

The Complete Works. Boston: 1886. V. 42

The Complete Works. Boston & New York: 1886. V. 38

The Complete Works. Boston: 1891. V. 42

The Complete Works. Boston & New York: 1909. V. 44

Complete Writings. Boston: 1900. V. 38; 40; 41; 42

The Writings. Boston & New York: 1900. V. 45

The Writings Of . . . New York: 1900. V. 40; 41; 46

The Writings of . . . Boston: 1903. V. 46

HAWTHORNE, SOPHIA AMELIA PEABODY 1811-1871

Notes in England and Italy. New York: 1875. V. 43

HAWTREY, CHARLES

*Evidence that the Relation of Josephus Concerning Herod's Having New
Built the Temple at Jerusalem is Either False or Misinterpreted.* Oxford:
1786. V. 39

Various Opinion of the Philosophical Reformers Considered . . . London:
1792. V. 38; 39

HAWTREY, GEORGE P.

Chester Historical Pageant, July 18th to 23rd, 1910: Book of Words.
Chester: 1910. V. 46

HAWTREY, R. G.

Currency and Credit. London: 1919. V. 43

HAXTHAUSEN, AUGUST VON

Transaucasia. Sketches of the Nations and Races Between the Black Sea and the Caspian. London: 1854. V. 42

Transcaucasia. London: 1854. V. 45

HAY, A.

The History of Chichester. Chichester: 1804. V. 42

HAY, DAVID R.

The Geometric Beauty of the Human Figure Defined. Edinburgh: 1851. V. 43

The Laws of Harmonious Colouring Adapted to Interior Decorations, Manufactures and Other Useful Purposes. London: 1838. V. 39; 44

The Laws of Harmonious Colouring Adapted to Interior Decorations &c. London: 1844. V. 44

The Laws of Harmonious Colouring Adapted to Interior Decorations, with Observations on the Practice of House Painting. Edinburgh: 1847. V. 43; 44

The Laws of Harmonious Coloring, Adapted to Interior Decoration, &c. To which is now added, an attempt to Define Aesthetical Taste. London/Edinburgh: 1844. V. 37

A Nomenclature of Colours Applicable to the Arts and Natural Sciences, to Manufactures and Other Purposes of General Utility. Edinburgh & London: 1846. V. 39

HAY, EDWARD

History of the Insurrection of the County of Wexford, AD 1798. Dublin: 1803. V. 39; 40; 46

History of the Insurrection of the County of Wexford, A.D. 1798; including an Account of Transactions preceding that event, with an appendix.... London: 1803. V. 39

History of the Irish Insurrection of 1798. New York: 1846. V. 46

History of the Irish Insurrection of 1798... Boston: 1850. V. 38

History of the Insurrection of the County of Wexford A.D. 1798. Dublin: 1803. V. 37

HAY, GEORGE

An Essay on the Liberty of the Press. (with) An Essay on the Liberty of the Press, Shewing that the Requisition of Security for Good Behaviour from Libellers, is Perfectly Compatible with the Constitution and Laws of Virginia. Richmond: 1803. V. 42

Letters on Usury and Interest; Shewing the Advantage of Loams in the Support of Trade and Commerce. London: 1774. V. 38

Speech Delivered in the Legislature of Virginia. Richmond: 1817. V. 41; 44

A Treatise on Expatriation. Washington: 1814. V. 42; 45

HAY, JAMES

Johnson - His Charateristics and Aporisms. London: 1884. V. 45; 46

HAY, JOHN

Hay's Views of Aberdeen. London: 1840. V. 44

Jim Bludso of the Prairie Belle, and Little Breaches. Boston: 1871. V. 38; 40; 42; 43; 44; 46

The Life and Letters of John Hay. Boston: 1915. V. 38

The Pike Country Ballads. Boston: 1912. V. 41

HAY, JOHN C. DALRYMPLE 1821-192

Lines from My Log Books. Edinburgh: 1898. V. 46

HAY, O. P.

The Fossil Turtles of North America. Washington: 1908. V. 38

HAY, R.

The Dictionary of Garden Plants in Colour, with House and Greenhouse Plants. London: 1970. V. 39; 40; 42; 46

HAY, RICHARD

An Essay on the Origine of the Royal Family of the Stewarts, in Answer to Dr. Kennedy's Chronological, Genealogical and Historical Dissertation of the Royal Family of the Stewarts. Edinburgh: 1722. V. 37; 39

HAY, ROBERT

Illustrations of Cairo. London: 1840. V. 42

HAY, THOMAS

History of a Case of a Recurring Sarcomatous Tumor of the Orbit in a Child... Philadelphia. V. 42

HAY, THOMAS ROBSON

Hood's Tennessee Campaign. New York: 1929. V. 41; 42

HAY, WILLIAM

Mount Caburn. London: 1730. V. 37; 45

Religio Philosophicii. London: 1735. V. 38

Religio Philosophici. London: 1753. V. 37

HAYASHI, Y.

Illustrated Trees in Colour. Tokyo: 1985. V. 37

HAYCOX, ERNEST

By Rope and Lead. Boston: 1951. V. 41; 42

HAYDEN, ARTHUR

Royal Copenhagen Porcelain. Its History and Development From the Eighteenth Century to the Present Day. London: 1911. V. 41

Spode and His Successors. London: 1925. V. 40

HAYDEN, EVERETT

The Great Storm Off the Atlantic Coast of the United States - March 11-14, 1888. Washington: 1888. V. 42

HAYDEN, FERDINAND VANDIVEER 1829-1887

Geological and Geographical Atlas of Colorado and Portions of Adjacent Territories. Washington: 1877. V. 46

Geological and Geographical Atlas of Colorado and Portions of Adjacent Territory. New York: 1881. V. 39

Geological Report of the Exploration of the Yellowstone and Missouri Rivers. Washington: 1869. V. 37; 41

Preliminary Report of the United States Geological Survey of Wyoming and Portions of Contiguous Territories. Washington: 1872. V. 37; 38

Sun Pictures of Rocky Mountain Scenery, with a Description of the Geographical nd Geological Features, and Some Account of the Resources of the Great West. New York: 1870. V. 37; 38; 40; 44

Twelfth Annual Report of the United States Geological and Geographical Survey of the Territories: a Report of Progress of the Exploration in Wyoming and Idaho for the Year 1878. Part I: Geology, Paleontology, and Zoology. Washington: 1883. V. 38

HAYDEN, HORACE E.

Genealogical and Family History of the Wyoming and Lackawanna Valleys, Pennsylvania. New York: 1906. V. 39; 42

HAYDEN, HORACE EDWIN

A Refutation of the Charges Made Against the Confederate States of America of Having Authorized the Use of Explosive and Poisoned Musket and Rifle balls During the Late Civil War of 1861-65. Richmond: 1879. V. 44

HAYDEN, HORACE H.

Geological Essays; or an Enquiry into Some of the Geological Phenomena to be Found in Various Parts of America, and Elsewhere. Baltimore: 1820. V. 44; 45

HAYDN, JOSEPH

Dictionary of Dates and Universal Reference Relating to Ages and Nations. London: 1841. V. 38

HAYDOCK, ROGER 1643-1696

A Collection of the Christian Writings, Labours, Travels and Sufferings of... (with) An Account of His Death and Burial. London;: 1700. V. 39

HAYDON, A. L.

Stories of King Arthur. London: 1910. V. 37

HAYDON, BENJAMIN ROBERT 1786-1846

Correspondence and Table-Talk. London: 1876. V. 39; 42

Description of Haydon's Picture of the Great Meeting of Delegates Held... June 1840, for the Abolition of Slavery and the Slave Trade Throughout the World... London: 1841. V. 42

Descriptions of Eucles, and Punch, with Other Pictures, Drawings and Sketches... London: 1830. V. 38

Lectures on Painting and Design... London: 1844. V. 45

Life of Benjamin Robert Haydon, Historical Painter, from His Autobiography and Journals. London: 1853. V. 39; 42

New Churches; Considered with Respect to the Opportunities they Offer for the Encouragement of Painting. London: 1818. V. 41; 43

Painting, and the Fine Arts: Being the Articles Under Those Heads Contributed to the Seventh Edition of the Encyclopaedia Britannica. Edinburgh: 1838. V. 39; 44

HAYDON, F. STANSBURY

Aeronautics in the Union and Confederate Armies. With a Survey of Military Aeronatuics Prior to 1861. Baltimore: 1941. V. 39; 46

HAYDON, G. H.

Five Years' Experience in Australia Felix, Comprising a Short Account of Its Early Settlement and Present Position... London: 1846. V. 39; 46

HAYEK, FRIEDRICH A.

Geldtheorie und Konjunktur-Theorie... Vienna: 1929. V. 45

HAYES, A. A.

New Colorado and the Santa Fe Trail. New York: 1880. V. 46

HAYES, A. B.

History of the City of Lincoln, Nebraska... Lincoln: 1889. V. 43

HAYES, BENJAMIN

Pioneer Notes. Los Angeles: 1929. V. 40

HAYES, BENJAMIN continued

Pioneer Notes from the Diaries of Judge Benjamin Hayes 1849-1875. Los Angeles: 1929. V. 39; 40; 42; 43

HAYES, CHARLES

A Treatise of Fluxions: or an Introduction to Mathematical Philosophy. London: 1704. V. 38

HAYES, CHARLES W.

Galveston: History of the Island and the City. Austin: 1974. V. 37; 39; 41; 42; 43

HAYES, DANIEL

A Long Journey. The Story of Daniel Hayes. Portland: 1876. V. 40

A Long Journey, the Story of Daniel Hayes. Portland: 1876. V. 44; 45

HAYES, EDWARD

The Ballads of Ireland. Dublin. V. 38

The Ballads of Ireland. London: 1856. V. 38

HAYES, HARRIET

The Home Nurse and Nursery. New York: 1888. V. 42

HAYES, HELEN

On Reflection: an Autobiography. New York: 1968. V. 42; 45

Twice Over Lightly: New York Then and Now. New York: 1972. V. 42; 44; 45

HAYES, ISAAC I.

The Land of Desolation: Being a Personal Narrative of Observation and Adventure in Greenland, 1869. New York: 1872. V. 41

HAYES, ISAAC ISRAEL

The Open Polar Sea: a Narrative of a Voyage of Discovery Towards the North Pole, in the Schooner 'United States'. London: 1867. V. 38; 40; 42; 43; 46

HAYES, ISSAC I.

Pictures of Arctic Travel - Greenland. New York: 1881. V. 37

HAYES, J.

Gainsborough as Printmaker. London: 1971. V. 39

The Landscape Paintings of Thomas Gainsborough. London: 1982. V. 39

HAYES, J. GORDON

Antarctica: a Treatise on the Southern Continent. London: 1928. V. 39; 42

The Conquest of the South Pole. London: 1932. V. 43

HAYES, JOHN

Thomas Gainsborough, the Drawings. London: 1970. V. 39; 40; 46

HAYES, JOHN RUSSELL

Old Quaker Meeting-Houses. Philadelphia: 1911. V. 37

HAYES, JOHN WARNER

Ancient Lamps in the Royal Ontario Museum I: Greek and Roman Clay Lamps, a Catalogue. Toronto: 1980. V. 40; 42; 44

Roman and Pre-Roman Glass in the Royal Ontario Museum. A Catalogue. Toronto: 1975. V. 40; 42; 44

Roman Pottery in the Royal Ontario Museum: a Catalogue. Toronto: 1976. V. 42; 44

HAYES, M. HORACE

Among Men and Horses. London: 1894. V. 43

The Points of the Horse: a Familiar Treatise on Equine Conformation. London: 1893. V. 39

Points of the Horse. London: 1896. V. 39

Points of the Horse, a Familiar Treatise on Equine Conformation. London: 1897. V. 39

HAYES, MICHAEL ANGELO 1820-1877

Costumes of the British Army. London: 1845. V. 43

HAYES, RICHARD

Biographical Dictionary of Irishmen in France. Dublin: 1949. V. 38

An Estimate of Places for Life: Shewing How Many Years Purchase a Place for Life is Worth. London: 1728. V. 37; 38

Interest at One View Calculated to a Farthing. London: 1747. V. 37; 38

Ireland and Irishmen in the French Revolution. Dublin: 1932. V. 38; 40

Ireland and Irishmen in the French Revolution. London: 1932. V. 38; 39

The Negociator's Magazine of Monies and Exchanges. London: 1730. V. 38; 43

The Negociator's Magazine. London: 1740. V. 44

The Negociator's Magazine . . . London: 1777. V. 45; 46

A New Method for Valuing of Annuities upon Lives. London;: 1746. V. 37

Old Irish Links with France. Dublin: 1940. V. 38

The Register of Derry Cathedral . . . Parish of Templemore. Londonderry: 1642-1703. V. 37

HAYES, RUTHERFORD B.

Diary and Letters of Rutherford B. Hayes (Volumes 3-5). Columbus: 1924. V. 41

Diary and Letters of Rutherford B. Hayes. New York: 1971. V. 39; 40; 42; 44

Diary and Letters of . . . Nineteenth President of the United States. New York: 1071. V. 37

Message From . . . An Act Authorizing the President of the United States to Make Certain Negotiations with the Ute Indians in the State of Colorado. Washington: 1879. V. 37

HAYES, SAMUEL

Duelling: a Poems. Cambridge: 1775. V. 39; 40; 42

A Practical Treatise on Planting and the Management of Woods and Coppices. Dublin: 1794. V. 37; 40; 42; 45; 46

Prayer: a (Seatonian-prize) Poem. Cambridge: 1777. V. 39

HAYES, THOMAS

A Serious Address on the Dangerous Consequences of Neglecting Common Coughs and Colds, etc. Boston: 1796. V. 37

HAYES, WILLIAM

A Natural History of British Birds, etc. London: 1771?-75. V. 37; 42

Portraits of Rare and Curious Birds, and Their Descriptions, From the Menagery of Osterly Park, in the County of Middlesex. London: 1794. V. 40

Portraits of Rare and Curious Birds with Their Descriptions, from the Menagery of Osterly Park, in the County of Middlesex. London: 1794-99. V. 42

Portraits of the Curious Exotic Birds, Which Formerly Composed the Osterly Menagerie. London: 1846. V. 39

HAYES, WILLIAM C.

The Scepter of Egypt: a Background for the Study of the Egyptian Antiquities in the Metropolitan Museum of Art. New York: 1953/1960/1959. V. 42

The Scepter of Egypt: a back ground for the study of the Egyptian antiquities in the Metropolitan Museum of Art. New York: 1953-1968. V. 37

HAYGARTH, HENRY WILLIAM

Recollections of Bush Life in Australia, During a Residence of Eight Years in the Interior. London. V. 39

HAYGARTH, J.

A Sketch of a Plan to Exterminate the Casual Small-Pox from Great Britain and to Introduce General Inoculation . . . London: 1793. V. 43

HAYLEY, WILLIAM

Ballads . . . Founded on Anecdotes Relating to Animals, with Prints, Designed and Engraved by William Blake. Chichester: 1805. V. 45

A Catalogue of the Very Extensive Library of the Late William Hayley, Esq. Removed from His Seat at Felpham . . . Which will be sold by Auction, by Mr. Evans, at His House, No. 93, Pall Mall, on Tuesday, Feb. 13th, and twelve following days . . . London: 1821. V. 41

An Elegy on the Greek Model. Addressed to the Right Reverend Robert Lowth, Lord Bishop of London. Cambridge: 1779. V. 37

An Essay on History: in Three Epistles to Edward Gibbon, Esq. with Notes. London: 1780. V. 41; 45; 46

An Essay on Epic Poetry: in five Epistles to the Rev. Mr. Mason. London: 1782. V. 37

The Life and Posthumous Writings of William Cowper, Esq. Chichester: 1803. V. 45

The Life and Posthumous Writings of William Cowper. Chichester: 1803-04. V. 37; 41; 42; 43

The Life and Posthumous Writings of William Cowper. Chichester: 1803-06. V. 38

The Life and Posthumous Writings of William Cowper. Chichester: 1806. V. 38

the Life of George Romney. Chichester: 1809. V. 39; 42

The Life of Milton, in Three Parts. London: 1796. V. 39

Little Tom, the Sailor. London: 1917. V. 42

Occasional Stanzas, Written at the Request of the Revolution Society, and Recited on their Anniversary, November 4, 1788. London: 1788. V. 42

Ode, Inscribed to John Howard, Esq. F.R.S. London: 1780. V. 37; 42

A Philosophical, Historical and Moral Essay on Old Maids. London: 1785. V. 37; 38; 41; 42; 46

A Philosophical, Historical and Moral Essay on Old Maids. London: 1793. V. 43

Plays of Three Acts (in verse) Written for a Private Theatre. Dublin: 1784. V. 40; 44

Plays of Three Acts. London: 1784. V. 38; 40; 41; 42; 43; 45

Poems and Plays. London: 1785. V. 37; 39; 42; 45

The Poetical Works . . . Dublin: 1785. V. 45

The Triumphs of Temper. London: 1781. V. 38; 43

The Triumphs of Temper. Newburyport: 1794. V. 40

HAYLEY, WILLIAM continued

The Triumphs of Temper. Chichester: 1803. V. 37; 38; 39; 42; 44; 45

The Triumphs of Temper. Chichester: 1809. V. 44

The Triumphs of Temper, A Poem: in Six Cantos. Chichester: 1817. V. 46

The Triumphs of Temper. Chichester & London: 1803. V. 37

Two Dialogues; Containing a Comparative View of the Lives, Characters and Writings of Philip the Late Earl of Chesterfield and Dr. Samuel Johnson. London: 1787. V. 45; 46

HAYMO, BP. OF HALBERSTADT d. 853

In Omnes Psalmos Pia Breuis Ac Dilucida Explanatio. Coloniae: 1561. V. 40; 42

HAYMOND, CREED

The Central Pacific Railroad, its Relations with the Government. Washington: 1881. V. 39

The Central Pacific Railroad Co. Its Relation to the Government. San Francisco: 1888. V. 40; 44; 46

The Political Code of the State of California. Sacramento: 1872. V. 43

HAYNE, M. H. E.

The Pioneers of the Klondyke being an account of Two Years Police service on the Yukon by H. West Taylor. London: 1897. V. 37

HAYNE, PAUL H.

Poems. Boston: 1855. V. 41

HAYNE, ROBERT Y.

Speech of Mr. Hayne, of South Carolina, in the Senate of the United States, Jan. 218, 1830, on Mr. Foot's Resolution. Washington?: 1830. V. 42

HAYNES, ALFRED E.

Man-Hunting in the Desert, Being a Narrative of the Palmer Search Expedition (1882, 1883). London: 1894. V. 40; 46

HAYNES, C. M.

Elementary Principles of Electro Therapeutics. Cicago: 1896. V. 40

HAYNES, F. JAY

Catalogue Northern Pacific Views. Fargo: 1883. V. 43

Yellowstone Park Scenery/Northern Pacific Scenery. St. Paul. V. 39

Yellowstone National Park. Photo-Gravures from Nature. Fargo: 1887. V. 41

Yellowstone National Park in Photo Gravure. Saint Paul: 1891. V. 41

HAYNES, GIDEON

Pictures form Prison Life . . . Boston: 1869. V. 46

HAYNES, J. C.

Yellowstone National Park. Photogravures from Nature. New York: 1887. V. 37; 39

HAYNES, JAMES

Travels in Several Parts of Turkey, Egypt and the Holy Land. London: 1774. V. 45

HAYNES, LEMUEL

Universal Salvation, a Very Ancient Doctrine . . . concord: 1814. V. 45

HAYNES, R. E.

Man Hunting in the Desert, Being a Narrative of the Palmer Search Expedition. London: 1894. V. 45

HAYNES, THOMAS

A Treatise on the Improved Culture of the Strawberry, Raspberry and Gooseberry. London: 1812. V. 37; 45

A Treatise on the Improved Culture of the Strawberry, Raspberry and Gooseberry, Designed to prove the Present Common Mode of Cultivation Erroneous. London: 1814. V. 39

HAYNES, WILLIAM BARBER

Ducks and Duck Shooting. Chicago: 1924. V. 39; 43

HAYNIE, HENRY

Paris Past and Present. New York: 1902. V. 39

HAYS, GILBERT A.

Under the Red Patch. Pittsburgh: 1908. V. 42

HAYS, LOUISE FREDERICK

History of Macon County, Georgia. Atlanta: 1933. V. 42

The Rumph and Frederick Familes, Genealogical and Biographical. Atlanta: 1942. V. 42

HAYS, MARY

Female Biography. London: 1803. V. 37

HAYTER, CHARLES

An Introduction to Perspective, Drawing and Painting. London: 1825. V. 39; 41; 44

An Introduction to Perspective, Practical Geometry, Drawing and Painting. London: 1832. V. 39; 44

An Introduction to Perspective, Practical Geometry, Drawing and Painting . . . London: 1845. V. 44; 45

An Introduction to Perspective, Drawing and Painting, In a series of Pleasing and Familiar Dialogues between the Author's children . . . and a compendium of genuine instruction . . . carefully adapted for the use of females . . . London: 1820. V. 37

An Introduction to Perspective, Practical Geometry. London. V. 37

HAYTER, JOHN

A Report Upon the Herculaneum Manuscripts in a Second Letter . . . to H.R.H. the Prince Regent. London: 1811. V. 39

A Report Upon the Herculaneum Manuscripts . . . (with) Herculaneum Rolls. Correspondence Relative to a Proposition Made by Dr. Sickler of Hildbrughausen. London: 1811, 1817. V. 38

HAYTER, THOMAS

An Essay on the Liberty of the Press, Chiefly as It Respects Personal Salnder. London: 1755. V. 39; 41; 42

HAYWARD, ABRAHAM

Biographical and Critical Essays. London: 1858. V. 37

Verses of Other Days. London: 1847. V. 40; 42; 43

HAYWARD, GEORGE

Surgical Reports and Miscellaneous Papers on Medical Subjects. Boston: 1855. V. 41; 42; 45

HAYWARD, J. F.

The Art of the Gunmaker. London: 1963-65. V. 46

Virtuoso Goldsmiths and the Triumph of Mannerism. 1540-1620. London: 1976. V. 37

HAYWARD, JOHN

The Columbian Traveller and Statistical Register. Boston. V. 42

English Poetry - an Illustrated Catalogue of First and Early Editions Exhibited in 1947 at 7 Albemarle Street, London. London: 1950. V. 45

English Poetry. An Illustrated catalogue of first and early editions exhibited in 1947 at 7 Albemarle St., London. 1950. V. 37

English Poetry. An Illustrated Catalogue of First and Early Editions Exhibited in 1947 at 7 Albemarle Street, London. Cambridge: 1950. V. 37; 42

The First Part of the King Henrie the III. Extending to the End of the First Yeare of His Raigne. London: 1620-30. V. 38

The First Part of the Life and Raigne of King Henrie the IIII. London: 1638? V. 38; 40

The Life and Raigne of King Edward the Sixth. London: 1630. V. 37; 41

The Life and Raigne of King Edward the Sixt. London: 1636. V. 39

The Lives of the III Normans, Kings of England. London: 1613. V. 40; 46

Plays of Three Acts: Written for a Private Theatre. London: 1784. V. 41

A Reporte of a Discourse Concerning Supreme Power in Affaires of Religion. London: 1606. V. 43

HAYWARD, JOSEPH

The Science of Horticulture, Including a Practical System for the Management of Fruit Trees, Arranged on Demonstrative Physiological Principles. London: 1818. V. 39

The Science of Horticulture . . . London: 1824. V. 42

HAYWARD, THOMAS

The British Muse, of a Collection of Thoughts Moral, Natural and Sublime, of Our English Poets. London: 1738. V. 39; 42; 45

HAYWOOD, A.

The History of the Royal West African Frontier Force. Aldershot: 1964. V. 42

HAYWOOD, A. H. W.

Through Timbuctu and Across the Great Sahara - an Account of an Adventurous Journey of Exploration from Sierra Leone to the Source of the Niger . . . London: 1912. V. 45

HAYWOOD, ELIZA

The Invisible Spy. London: 1773. V. 40

Memoirs of a Certain Island Adjacent to the Kingdom of Utopia. London: 1725-26. V. 45

Memoirs of a Certain Island Adjacent to the Kingdom of Utopia. London: 1727. V. 40

The Secret History of the Present Intrigues of the Court of Carimania. London: 1727. V. 42

HAYWOOD, ELIZA FOWLER 1693-1756

The Female Spectator. London: 1748. V. 39

The Female Spectator. London: 1750. V. 43

The Female Spectator. London: 1755. V. 45

HAYWOOD, ELIZA FOWLER 1693-1756 continued

The Fortunate Foundlings; Being the Genuine History of Colonel M-rs. and His Sister, Madam du P-y, the Issue of the Hon. Ch-es M-rs. Son of the Late Duke of R-l-d. London: 1761. V. 43

Mary Stuart, Queen of Scots: Being the Secret History of Her Life and the Real Causes of all Her Misfortunes. London: 1725. V. 39

A Present for a Servant-Maid; or, the Sure Means of Gaining Love and Esteem. London: 1743. V. 40; 46

A Present for a Servant-Maid. Dublin: 1744. V. 40

The Wife. Also, the Husband, In Answer to the Wife. Dublin: 1756. V. 41

The Wife. London: 1756. V. 39

HAYWOOD, FRANCIS 1796-1858

An Analysis of Kant's Critick of Pure Reason by the Translator of the Work. London: 1844. V. 37; 45

HAYWOOD, JOHN

The Duty and Office of Justices of Peace, and of Sheriffs, Coroners, Constables &c. Halifax: 1800. V. 38; 40; 42

The Duty and Authority of Justices of the Peace, in the State of Tennessee. Nashville: 1810. V. 38

The Statute Laws of the State of Tennessee, of a Public and General Nature, Revised and Digested . . . by Order of the General Assembly. Knoxville: 1831. V. 37

HAYWOOD, WILLIAM

Report to the Special Committee Upon Improvements of the Honourable the Commissioners of Sewers of the City of London, on the Traffic and Improvements in the Public Ways of the City of London, 23rd March 1866. London: 1866. V. 38; 40

HAZARD, CAROLINE

The Illuminators: a Poem Read at the Installation of the Eta Chapter of the Phi Beat Kappa Society . . . Gloucesterhire: 1905. V. 46

Mission Verses. Santa Barbara: 1889. V. 41

HAZARD, EBENEZER

Historical Collections: Consisting of State Papers and Other Authentic Documents, Intended as Materials for an History of the United States of America. Philadelphia: 1792/94. V. 42; 46

HAZARD, JOSEPH

Poems on Various Subjects. Brooklyn: 1814. V. 40; 44

HAZARD, NATHAN

Observations on the Peculiar Case of the Whig Merchants, Indebted to Great Britain at the Commencement of the Late War . . . New York: 1785. V. 45

HAZARD, ROWLAND G.

Language: Its Connection with the Present Condition and Future Prospects of Man. Providence: 1836. V. 40

Two Letters on Causation and Freedom in Willing, Addressed to John Stuart Mill. Boston: 1869. V. 45; 46

HAZARD, SAMUEL

Cuba With Pen and Pencil. Hartford: 1871. V. 41

Hazard's United States Commercial and Statistical Register . . . Philadelphia: 1840-42. V. 46

Santo Domingo, Past and Present; with a Glance at Hayti. New York: 1873. V. 37; 40

HAZARD, THOMAS R.

Report on the Poor and Insane in Rhode-Island . . . Providence: 1851. V. 42; 45; 46

HAZELTON, WILLIAM

Wildfowling Tales from the Great Ducking Resorts of the Continent. Chicago: 1921. V. 45

HAZELTON, WILLIAM C.

Tales of Duck and Goose Shooting. Springfield: 1922. V. 39

HAZEN, A. T.

A Bibliography of the Strawberry Hill Press. New Haven: 1942. V. 39; 46

HAZEN, ALLEN T.

A Catalogue of Horace Walpole's Library. New Haven & London: 1969. V. 45

HAZEN, EDWARD

The Panorama of Professions and Trades; or Every Man's Book . . . Philadelphia: 1836. V. 40

The Panorama of Professions and Trades; or, Every Man's Book. Philadelphia: 1841. V. 38

Popular Technology; or, Professions and Trades. New York: 1841. V. 43

Popular Technology; or, Professions and Trades. New York: 1843. V. 39; 46

HAZEN, JACOB A.

Five Years Before the Mast, or Live in the Forecastle, Aboard a Whaler and Man of War. Philadelphia: 1856. V. 41

Five Years Before the Mast, or Life in the Forecastle Aboard of a Whaler and man-Of-War. Philadelphia: 1865. V. 41

HAZEN, REUBEN W.

History of the Pawnee Indians. Fremont: 1893. V. 40

HAZEN, WILLIAM B.

Our Barren Lands. Cincinnati: 1875. V. 38; 40; 43

HAZLEWOOD, D.

A Compendious Grammar of the Feejeean Language with Examples of Native Idioms. Vewa, Feejee: 1850. V. 40

HAZLITT, WILLIAM 1778-1830

An Abridgment of the Light of Nature Pursued by Abraham Tucker, Esq. London: 1807. V. 38; 43

Amoris; or, The New Pygmalion. London: 1823. V. 37

Characteristics: in the Manner of Rochefoucault's Maxims. London: 1823. V. 37

Characters of Shakespeare Plays. London: 1817. V. 37; 42; 45

Character's Of Shakespeare's Plays. London: 1818. V. 37

The Collected Works of William Hazlitt. London: 1902. V. 37; 40

The Collected Works . . . London: 1902-04. V. 46

Conversations of James Northcote, Esq. London: 1830. V. 39; 40; 42; 46

Criticisms on Art: and Sketches of the Picture Galleries of England. London: 1843-44. V. 39

Criticisms on Art; and Sketches of the Picture Galleries of England. London: 1853-54. V. 42

The Eloquence of the British Senate. London: 1807. V. 39; 42

The Eloquence of the British Senate. London: 1808. V. 40

Essays on the Principles of Human Action . . . London: 1836. V. 43

Lectures on the English Poets. London: 1818. V. 40; 44; 45

Lectures on English Comic Writers. London: 1819. V. 37; 38; 39; 40

Lectures on the English Poets. London: 1819. V. 37; 39; 42

Lectures Chiefly on the Dramatic Literature of the Age of Elizabeth. Delivered at the Surrey Institution. London: 1820. V. 39

A Letter to William Gifford, Esq. from William Hazlittt. London: 1820. V. 37

Letters on the English Poets. London: 1818. V. 42

Liber Amoris. London: 1823. V. 37; 38; 39; 40

Liber Amoris. London: 1893. V. 41; 43; 44

Liber Amoris. London: 1894. V. 39

Liber Amoris and Dramatic Criticisms. London: 1948. V. 46

The Life of Napoleon Buonaparte. London: 1830/1828-1830. V. 39

Life of Napoleon Buonaparte. London: 1852. V. 38

Literary Remains. With a notice of his life, by his son, and thoughts on his Genius and writings by E.L. Bulwer, Esq., M.P. In Two Volumes. London: 1836. V. 37; 39; 42; 43

The Miscellaneous Works. London: 1887. V. 42

Notes of a Journey through France and Italy. London: 1826. V. 40

Painting and the Fine Arts . . . Edinburgh: 1838. V. 42

The Plain Speaker. London: 1826. V. 37; 39; 42; 45

Political Essays with Sketches of Public Characters. London: 1819. V. 38; 39; 42

A Reply to the Essay on Population, by the Rev. T.R. Malthus. In a series of letters. To which are added, extracts from the esssay; with notes. London: 1807. V. 37

The Round Table: a Collection of Essays on Literature, Men and Manners. Edinburgh: 1817. V. 40; 43

The Round Table: a Collection of Essays and Literature, Men and Manners. London: 1817. V. 42

Selected Essays. London: 1930. V. 44

Shakespeare Jest-Book. London: 1881. V. 38

Sketches fo the Principal Picture-Galleries in England. London: 1824. V. 40; 44; 45

The Spirit of the Age; or Contemporary Portraits. London: 1825. V. 39; 40; 41; 42; 44; 46

Table-Talk or Original Essays. London: 1821. V. 38; 43

Table-Talk; or, Original Essays on Men and Manners. London: 1824. V. 39

Table Talk: Essays on Men and Manners. London: 1870. V. 41

A View of the English Stage. London: 1818. V. 37; 38; 39; 40; 42; 46

The Miscellaneous Works. Philadelphia: 1848. V. 37

The Collected Works. London: 1902. V. 37; 38

The Complete Works. London: 1930. V. 42

The Complete Works. London: 1930-34. V. 37; 39

HAZLITT, WILLIAM CAREW 1834-1913

The Coinage of the European Continent with an Introduction and Catalogues of Mints Denominations and Rulers. London: 1893. V. 38

HAZLITT, WILLIAM CAREW 1834-1913 continued

Four Generations of a Literary Family: the Hazlitts in England, Ireland and America, Their Friends and Fortunes 1725-1896. London: 1896. V. 46

Four Generations of a Literary Family. London: 1897. V. 44

Gleanings in Old Garden Literature. London: 1887. V. 40

History of the Venetian Republic; Her Rise, Her Greatness and Her Civilization. London: 1860. V. 39

Memoirs of William Hazlitt. London: 1867. V. 39

Old Cookery Books And Ancient Cuisine. New York: 1886. V. 39; 44

Popular Antiquities of Great Britain. London: 1870. V. 40

Remains of the Early Popular Poetry of England . . . London: 1864. V. 45

Remains of the Early Popular Poetry of England. London: 1864-66. V. 46

A Select Collection of English Plays. London: 1874-76. V. 38; 39

The Venetian Republic, Its Rise, Its Growth and Its Fall. London: 1915. V. 45

HAZZI, JOSEPH, RITTER VON 1768-1845

Letter from James Mease, Transmitting a Treatise on the Rearing of Silkworms; by Mr. De Hazzi, of Munich, April 21, 1828. Washington: 1828. V. 39; 45

HDRLICKA, ALFRED

Drei Zyklen: Winckelmann; Haarmann; Roll Over Mondrian. Vienna-Munich: 1968. V. 46

HEAD, F. B.

The Life of Bruce, the African Traveller . . . London: 1838. V. 40

HEAD, FRANCIS

Stokers and Pokers; or, the London and North-Western Railway, the Electric Telegraph and the Railway Clearing House. London: 1849. V. 41; 45

HEAD, FRANCIS BOND

Bubbles from the Brunnens of Nassau. London: 1834. V. 46

Bubbles from the Brunnens of Nassau. New York: 1836. V. 46

The Emigrant. London: 1846. V. 37; 38; 42; 43

A Fortnight in Ireland. London: 1852. V. 37; 38; 39; 41; 42

The Horse and His Rider. London: 1860. V. 43

Message from His Excellency Sir Francis Bond Head, Lieutenant Governor of Upper Canada: in Answer tot he Address of the House of Assembly of the 5th February, 1836, with Sundry Documents. (Tor.): 1836. V. 37

Message, from His Excellency the Lieutenant Governor, of the 30th January, 1836; Transmitting a Despatch from His Majesty's Government. (Tor.): 1936. V. 37

A Narrative. London: 1839. V. 37; 38; 41; 42; 44

Rough Notes Taken During Some Rapid Journeys Across the Tampas and Among the Andes. London: 1826. V. 39; 40; 42

HEAD, GEORGE

Forest Scenes and Incidents, in the Wilds of North America . . . London: 1838. V. 43

Forests Scenes and Incidents in the Wilds of North America. London: 1829. V. 39; 41; 44

A Home Tour through the Manufacturing Districts of England in the Summer of 1835. London: 1836. V. 38; 39

A Home Tour Through Various Parts of the United Kingdom . . . *Also, Memoirs of an Assistant Commissary-General.* London: 1837. V. 42; 43; 44

A Home Tour through the Manufacturing Districts of England in the SUmmer of 1835. London: 1836. V. 37

HEAD, HENRY

Studies in Neurology. London: 1920. V. 38; 41; 42

Studies in Neurology. Oxford: 1920. V. 37; 39; 40; 41

HEAD, JOHN

On the Rise and Progress of Steam Locomotion on Common Roads, with an Abstract of the Discussion Upon the Papers . . . London: 1873. V. 42

HEAD, RICHARD

The English Rouge Described, In the Life of Merion Latroon: a Witty Extravagant . . . London: 1672. V. 45

The English Rogue Described in the Life of Meriton Latroon, a Witty Extravagant . . . *(with) The English Rogue Continued* . . . London;: 1672, 1671. V. 39

The English Rogue (:) Described in the Life of Meriton Latroon, a Witty Extravagant (:) Comprehending the Most Eminent Cheats of Both Sexes. (With: The English Rogue Continued . . . *&c).* London: 1680. V. 37

The English Rogue; or Witty Extravagant: Described in the Life of meriton latroon . . . *The Four Parts. To which is added a Fifth Part, compleating the whole History of His Life.* London: 1688. V. 37; 38

Proteus Redivivus. London: 1675. V. 38; 40; 42; 44; 45

Proteus Redivivus. London: 1684. V. 42; 45

HEAD, THOMAS ANTHONY

Campaigns and Battles of the Sixteenth Regiment Tennessee Volunteers in the War Between the States . . . Nashville: 1885. V. 43

HEADLAM, CUTHBERT

History of the Guards Division in the Great War. 1914-1918. London: 1924. V. 37; 46

HEADLAM, JOHN

A Second Letter to the Right Honourable Robert Peel . . . *On Prison Labour, Containing a Vindication of the Principles and Practice of the Magistrates of the North Riding of the County of York with Respect to Their Treatment of Prisoners Before Trial.* London: 1824. V. 42

HEADLAND, FREDERICK WILLIAM

The Action of Medicines in the System. Philadelphia: 1963. V. 44

HEADLEY, HENRY

Poems and Other Pieces. London: 1786. V. 45

Select Beauties of Ancient English Poetry. London: 1787. V. 38; 39; 45

Select Beauties of Ancient English Poetry. London: 1797. V. 40

HEADLEY, J. T.

The Illustrated Life of Washington . . . . *Together with an Interesting Account of Mt. Vernon As It Is* . . . New York: 1860. V. 41

The Life and Travels of General Grant. Philadelphia: 1879. V. 39; 42

HEADLEY, JOHN W.

Confederate Operations in Canada and New York. New York: 1906. V. 37

HEAGERTY, JOHN J.

Four Centuries of Medical History in Canada and a Sketch of the Medical History of Newfoundland. Toronto: 1928. V. 46

HEAL, AMBROSE

The English Writing Masters, 1550-1800. Hildesheim: 1962. V. 40

The English Penmen; Their Portraits and Biographies. N.P.: 1945. V. 38

The English Writing-Masters and Their Copy-Books, 1570-1800. 1931. V. 38

English Writing-Masters and Their Copy-Books 1570-1800; a Biographical Dictionary and Bibliography. Hildensheim: 1962. V. 38; 39

The English Writing-Masters and their copy books 1570-1800/ A biographical dictionary & a bibliography. With an introduction on the development of hand writing by S. Morison. Cambridge: 1931. V. 37; 40

London Tradesman's Cards of the Eighteenth century. London: 1925. V. 37; 38; 41; 44; 45; 46

The London Furniture Makers from the Restoration to the Victorian Era 1660-1840. London: 1953. V. 37; 38; 39

London Tradesmen's Cards of the 16th Century. London: 1925. V. 37

The Signboards of Old London Shops. London: 1947. V. 41

HEALD, F. B.

A Selection of Suggestive Designs. Nottingham. V. 37

HEALDE, THOMAS

The New Pharmacopoeia of the Royal College of Physicians of London. London: 1788. V. 42

HEALEY, EDWARD

A Series of Picturesque Views of Castles and Country Houses in Yorkshire. Bradford: 1885. V. 39

HEALEY, GEORGE HARRIS

The Meditations of Daniel Defoe. Now First Printed. Edited by George Harris Healey. (Cummington): 1946. V. 37

THE HEALING Art; or, Chapters Upon Medicine, Diseases, Remedies, and Physicians, Historical and Biographical and Descriptive. London: 1887. V. 45

A HEALTH to the Northamptonshire Sneakers. London: 1705. V. 41

HEALY, JOHN

History of the Diocese of Meath . . . Dublin: 1908. V. 37; 43; 44

Maynooth College. Its Centenary History 1795-1895. Dublin: 1895. V. 38

HEALY, MICHAEL A.

Report of the Cruise of the Revenue Marine Steamer 'Corwin' in the Arctic Ocean in the Year 1885. Washington: 1887. V. 38; 42

A Report on the Cruise of the Revenue Marine Steamer Corwin in the Arctic Ocean in the Year 1884. Washington: 1889. V. 40; 41; 43

Report of the Cruise of the Revenue Marine Steamer Corwin in the Arctic Ocean in the Year 1885. Washington: 1885. V. 37

HEANEY, HOWELL J.

Thirty Years of Bird & Bull Press: A Bibliography, 1958-1988. Newtown: 1988. V. 40; 41; 42

HEANEY, SEAMUS 1939-

After Summer. Old Deerfield: 1978. V. 46

After Summer. Old Deerfield & Dublin: 1978. V. 43

After Summer, Illustrations by Timothy Engelland. Dublin: 1978. V. 37

Bog Poems. London: 1975. V. 39; 40; 43; 45

HEANEY, SEAMUS 1939- continued

A Boy Driving His Father to Confession. Frensham: 1965. V. 38

A Boy Driving His Father to Confession. Frensham: 1970. V. 39

Chaplet. Dublin: 1971. V. 40

Clearances. Amsterdam: 1986. V. 38

The Cure at Troy . . . Derry: 1990. V. 44; 46

Death of a Naturalist. 1966. V. 45

Death of a Naturalist. London: 1966. V. 41; 42

Death of a Naturalist. New York: 1966. V. 37; 39; 42

Door Into the Dark. 1969. V. 37; 45

Door into the Dark. London: 1969. V. 37; 38; 39; 41; 42; 43; 45

Eleven Poems. Belfast: 1965. V. 37; 40; 41; 42

Field Work. London: 1979. V. 38

Field Work. New York: 1979. V. 39; 41; 42; 43; 46

Glanmore Sonnets von Seamus Heaney. Hamburg: 1977. V. 46

The Government of the Tongue - the 1986 T. S. Eliot Memorial Lectures and Other Critical Writings. London: 1988. V. 40; 45

Gravities - a Collection of Poems and Drawings. Newcastle-upon-Tyne: 1979. V. 45

Hailstones. Dublin: 1984. V. 39; 41; 45; 46

The Haw Lantern. London: 1987. V. 41

The Haw Lantern. New York: 1987. V. 41; 42

Hedge School. 1979. V. 46

Hedge School. Salem: 1979. V. 37; 39; 42

A Lough Neagh Sequence. Manchester: 1959. V. 38

A Lough Neagh Sequence. Didsbury: 1969. V. 41

New Selected Poems 1966-1987. London: 1990. V. 44

North North. London: 1975. V. 37; 40; 43; 44; 45

North. New York: 1976. V. 45

The Place of Writing - the Inauguration of the Richmond Ellman Lectures in Modern Literature. Atlanta: 1989. V. 44; 46

Poemcards 3. London: 1973. V. 46

Poems 1965-1975. New York: 1980. V. 39; 44

Poems and a Memoir. 1982. V. 38; 39; 40; 41; 44

Poems and a Memoir. New York: 1982. V. 38; 39; 40; 41; 42; 44; 45

Poetry Ireland Presents a Reading to Mark the Sixtieth Birthday of John Montague and the Fiftieth Birthday of Seamus Heaney. Dublin: 1989. V. 45

Preoccupations. London: 1980. V. 39; 43

Preoccupations. New York: 1980. V. 42; 44

Robert Lowell - a Memorial Address and an Elegy. London: 1978. V. 39; 43; 46

Robert Lowell: a Memorial Address and an elegy. London and Boston: 1978. V. 40

Seeing Things. London: 1991. V. 45; 46

Selected Poems 1965-1975. London: 1980. V. 38; 39; 42

Selected Poems. New York: 1982. V. 39

The Sounds of Rain; a Poem. 1988. V. 44; 46

Special Agenda Issue. London: 1989. V. 41

Station Island. London: 1984. V. 43

Station Island. New York: 1984. V. 41

Stations. Belfast: 1975. V. 37

Sweeney Astray. Derry: 1983. V. 40; 46

Sweeney Astray. New York: 1984. V. 41; 45

The Tree Clock. Belfast: 1990. V. 44; 46

Ugolino. Dublin: 1979. V. 38

Verses for a Fordham Commencement. London: 1984. V. 42

Verses for a Fordham Commencement. New York: 1984. V. 39; 41; 45

Wintering Out. London: 1972. V. 38; 42

Wintering Out. New York: 1973. V. 39

HEAP, GWIN HARRIS

Central Route to the Pacific, from the Valley of the Mississippi to California. Philadelphia: 1854. V. 37; 38; 39; 40; 41; 42; 46

HEAR Him and His Neighbors. Letters and Documents of Distinguished Citizens of Tennessee, on the Buying and Selling of Human Beings. New York: 1828. V. 44

HEARD, FRANKLIN FISKE

Leavitt Alley Indicted for the Murder of Abijah Ellis, in the Supreme Judicial Court of Massachusetts. Boston: 1875. V. 38

HEARD, ISAAC V. D.

History of the Sioux War and Massacres of 1862 and 1863 . . . New York: 1863. V. 37; 39; 42; 43

History of the Sioux War and Massacres of 1862 and 1863. New York: 1864. V. 46

History of the Sioux War and Massacres of 1862 and 1863. New York: 1865. V. 41

HEARD, JAMES

A Practical Grammar of the Russian Language. St. Petersburg: 1827. V. 40

HEARN, CHARLES W.

The Practical Printer: a Complete Manual of Photographic Printing . . . Philadelphia: 1878. V. 39; 42

HEARN, GEORGE A.

A Collection of Carved Ivories. New York: 1908. V. 41; 42

HEARN, LAFCADIO 1850-1904

An American Miscellany. New York: 1924. V. 42

Appreciations of Poetry. New York: 1916. V. 39

Books and Habits: From the Lecutures of Lafcadio Hearn. New York: 1921. V. 37

The Boy Who Drew Cats. Tokyo. V. 45

Chita: a Memory of Last Ireland. New York: 1889. V. 39; 41; 43; 44; 46

La Cuisine Creole. New Orleans. V. 39

La Cuisine Creole. New York: 1885. V. 38; 43

La Cuisine Creole. New Orleans: 1922. V. 40; 41

A Drop of Dew. Tokyo: 1950. V. 46

Editorials. Boston: 1926. V. 38; 42; 44

Essays in European and Oriental Literature. New York: 1923. V. 37

Exotics and Retrospectives. Boston: 1898. V. 44

Gibbeted: Execution of a Youthful Murderer . . . Los Angeles: 1933. V. 44

Glimpses of Unfamiliar Japan. Boston: 1894. V. 42; 46

Glimpses of Unfamiliar Japan. Boston & New York: 1894. V. 39; 41

'Gombo Zhebes.' New York: 1885. V. 39; 41; 43; 45

Historical Sketch Book and Guide to New Orleans and Environs. New York: 1885. V. 37; 43

Historical Sketch Book and Guide to New Orleans and Environs. With Map . . . Edited and Compiled by Several Leading Writers of the New Orleans Press. New York: 1884. V. 37

Insects and Greek Poetry. New York: 1926. V. 44

Japan, an Attempt at Interpretation. New York: 1904. V. 38; 40; 42

Japanese Fairy Tales. Tokyo. V. 44

A Japanese Miscellany. Boston: 1901. V. 38; 39; 45; 46

Japanese Fairy Tales. New York: 1924. V. 44

Japanese Fairy Tales. 1931? V. 41

Japanese Fairy Tales. Philadelphia: 1931? V. 43

Japanese Fairy Tales. Tokyo: 1925. V. 39

Karma. New York: 1918. V. 42

Kokoro. Hints and Echoes of Japanese Inner Life. Boston: 1896. V. 43

Kokoro, Hints and Echoes of Japanese Inner Life. Boston & New York: 1896. V. 39

Kotto Being Japanese Curios, with Sundry Cobwebs. New York: 1902. V. 38; 40; 43

Kwaidan: Stories and Studies of Strange Things. Boston: 1904. V. 43

Kwaidan: Stories and Studies of Strange Things. London: 1904. V. 42

Kwaidan, Stories and Studies of Strange Things. New York: 1932. V. 41

Kwaidan Stories and Studies of Strange Things. Tokyo: 1932. V. 45; 46

Leaves From the Diary of an Impressionist. Boston: 1911. V. 39

Leaves from the Diary of an Impressionist: Early Writings of . . . Boston & New York: 1911. V. 44

Lectures on Shakspeare. Tokyo: 1928. V. 44

Letters from the Raven, Being Correspondence of Lafcadio Hearn. New York: 1907. V. 43; 44; 46

Letters from Shimane and Kyushu. Kyoto: 1934. V. 39

Miscellanies. Articles and Stories Now First Collected by Albert Mordell. London: 1924. V. 39; 44

La Nouvelle Atala ou la Fille de l'Espirit Legende Indienne par Chahta-Ima. Nouvelle Orleans: 1879. V. 43

'Out of the East' Reveries and Studies in New Japan. Boston: 1895. V. 43

Pre-Raphaelite and Other Poets: Lectures. New York: 1922. V. 45

The Romance of the Milky Way and Other Studies and Stories. Boston & New York: 1905. V. 39; 46

Shadowings. Boston: 1900. V. 37; 39; 40; 42; 46

Some New Letters and Writings. Tokyo: 1925. V. 39; 45

Stray Leaves from Strange Literature. Boston: 1884. V. 38; 39; 41; 43; 46

Talks to Writers. New York: 1920. V. 37; 41; 43; 44

Two Years in the French West Indies. New York: 1890. V. 38; 39; 41; 43; 44

The Writings. Boston & New York: 1923. V. 38

Youma, the Story of a West Indian Slave. New York: 1890. V. 39; 43

HEARN, THOMAS

A Short View of the Rise and Progress of Freedom in Modern Europe, as Connected with the Causes Which Led to the French Revolution . . . London: 1793. V. 45

HEATHCOTE, E. D.

Flowers of the Engadine. Winchester: 1891. V. 37

HEATHCOTE, GEORGE

A Letter to the Right Honourable the Lord Mayor, the Worshipful Aldermen, and Common Council ... London: 1762. V. 42; 45

HEATHCOTE, NORMAN

St. Kilda. London: 1900. V. 43

HEATHCOTE, RALPH

Sylva; or, the Wood; Being a Collection of Anecdotes, Dissertations, Characters, Apophihegms, Original Letters, Bons Mots, and Other little Things. London: 1786. V. 42

Sylva; or, the Wood. Dublin: 1789. V. 42; 46

Sylva; or, the wood. London: 1876. V. 46

HEATHER, WILLIAM

The New West India Pilot ... London: 1810. V. 43

HEATHERINGTON, ALEXANDER

A Practical Guide for Tourists, Miners and Investors and All Persons Interested in the Development of the Gold Fields of Nova Scotia. Montreal,: 1868. V. 38; 41; 45

HEATHERLEY, F.

The Peregrine Falcon at the Eyrie. 1913. V. 46

The Peregrine Falcon at the Eyrie. London: 1913. V. 45

HEATHFIELD,

A Catalogue of the Valuable Library of the Late Right Hon. Lord Heathfield. London: 1813. V. 44

HEATH'S Gallery of British Engravings. London: 1836-37. V. 44
HEATH'S Gallery of British Engravings. London: 1836-38. V. 46

HEATON, ERNEST

Problems of Colonization and the Science of Publicity in Empire Building. Toronto: 1912. V. 43

HEATON, JOHN HENNIKER 1848-1914

Australian Dictionary of Dates and Men of the Time. (with) History of Australia, 1542 to Date. London: Sydney, etc.: 1879. V. 39

HEAVENHILL, WILLIAM S.

Siege of the Alamo. San Antonio: 1888. V. 44

HEAVISIDE, JOHN T. C.

American Antiquities; or, the New World the Old and the Old World the New. London: 1868. V. 43

HEAVISIDE, OLIVER 1850-1925

Electromagnetic Theory. London: 1893-1912. V. 40

Electrical Papers. London & New York: 1892. V. 38

HEAVISIDES, EDWARD MARSH

The Poetical and Prose Remains. London: 1850. V. 40

HEAVISIDES, M.

The History of the First Public Railway (Stockton & Darlington), the Opening Day and What Followed. Stockton-on-Tees: 1912. V. 42

HEAVYSEGE, CHARLES

Saul: a Drama in Three Parts. Montreal: 1859. V. 43

Saul. Boston: 1869. V. 43

HEAWOOD, EDWARD

Watermarks, Mainly of the 17th and 18th Centuries. Hilversum: 1950. V. 41

Watermarks, Mainly of the 17th and 18th Centuries. Hilversum: 1957. V. 40

Watermarks, Mainly of the 17th and 18th Centuries. Hilversum: 1986. V. 38

HEBARD, GRACE RAYMOND

Ashakie: an Account of Indian Resistance of the Covered Wagon and Union Pacific Railroad Invasions of Their Territory. Cleveland: 1930. V. 45

The Bozeman Trail: Historical Accounts of the Blazing of the Overland Routes into the Northwest, and the Fights with Red Cloud's Warriors. Cleveland: 1922. V. 39; 43; 44; 46

The Bozeman Trail, Historical Accounts of the Blazing of the Overland Routes into the Northwest and the Fights with Red Cloud's Warriors. Glendale: 1922. V. 45

the Pathbreakers from River to Ocean. Glendale: 1932. V. 45

Sacaiawea. Glendale: 1957. V. 46

Sacajawea A Guide and Interpreter of the Lewis and Clark Expedition with an Account of the Travels of Toussaint Charbonneau and of Jean Baptiste, the Expedition Papoose. Glendale: 1933. V. 37; 40; 41; 42; 45

Washakie an Account of Indian Resistance of the Coveed Wagon and Union Pacific Railroad Invasions of Their Territory. Cleveland: 1930. V. 39; 41; 42; 43; 45; 46

HEBB, GEORGE

The Declaration of Rights and the Constitution of Maryland. Baltimore: 1824. V. 37

HEBENSTREIT, JOHANN ERNST

Museum Richterianum Continens Fossilia Animalia Vegetabilia Mar. Leipzig: 1743. V. 39

HEBER, AMELIA

The Life of Reginald Heber. London: 1830. V. 39; 43

HEBER-PERCY, ALGERNON

Moab, Ammon and Gilead. Market Drayton: 1896. V. 41

HEBER, REGINALD

A Ballad by the Revd Reginald Heber Late of Calcutta. Chester: 1830. V. 37; 40; 41; 42

Hymns Written and Adapted too the Weekly Church Serivce of the Year. London: 1827. V. 38

Hymns, Written or Selected for the Weekly Church Service of the Year. London: 1828. V. 41; 45

The Life of Jeremy Taylor ... with a Critical Examination of His Writings. London: 1824. V. 39; 45

The Life of Reginald Heber, D.D. Lord Bishop of Calcutta. London: 1830. V. 42

Narrative of a Journey through the Upper Provinces of India from Calcutta to Bomaby, 1824-1825, with Notes Upon Ceylon ... London: 1828. V. 39; 40; 41; 45

Narrative of a Journey through the Upper Provinces of India, from Calcutta to Bombay, 1824-25. Philadelphia: 1828. V. 43

Narrative of a Journey through the Upper Provinces of India ... Philadelphia: 1829. V. 43

HEBERDEN, WILLIAM 1710-1801

Commentaries on the History and Cure of Diseases. London: 1802. V. 37; 39

Commentaries on the History and Cure of Diseases. London: 1803. V. 44; 45

Commentaries on the History and Cure of Diseases. Philadelphia: 1845. V. 41

Commentaries on the History and Cure of Diseases. Boston: 1818. V. 37

An Introduction to the Study Physic .... New York: 1929. V. 40; 41

On Education. London: 1818. V. 43; 46

Oratio Harveiana in Honorem Medicinae. London: 1810. V. 38; 39

HEBERT, RICHARD A.

Modern Maine, Its Historic Background, People and Resources. New York: 1951. V. 38

HEBRA, FERDINAND

On Diseases of the Skin, Including the Exanthemata. London: 1866-80. V. 45

HEBREW EDUCATION SOCIETY OF PHILADELPHIA

Constitution and By-Laws ... Adopted at a Town Meeting of Israelites on June 4, 1848. Philadelphia: 1848. V. 43

HECHT, ANTHONY

Aesopic-Couplets to Accompany the Thomas Bewick Wood Engravings ... Northampton: 1967. V. 42

Aesopic: Twenty Four Couplets ... to Accompany the Thomas Bewick Engravings for 'Select Fables.' Northampton: 1967. V. 41; 44; 45

The Seven Deadly Sins; Poems. Northampton: 1958. V. 37

A Summoning of Stones. New York: 1954. V. 38; 41

The Venetian Vespers. Boston: 1979. V. 37; 41; 44

Voltaire - Poem Upon the Lisbon Earthquake. Lincoln: 1977. V. 46

HECHT, BEN

The Bewitched Tailor. New York: 1941. V. 37; 43

The Champion Far Away. New York: 1931. V. 44; 45

The Collected Stories of ... New York: (1945). V. 37

The Hero of Santa Maria. New York: 1920. V. 43

A Jew in Love. New York: 1931. V. 37; 43

The Kingdom of Evil. Chicago: 1924. V. 38; 39; 40; 42; 46

1001 Afternoons in Chicago. Chicago: 1922. V. 43

1001 Afternoons in New York. New York: 1941. V. 39

HECK, J. G.

Iconographic Encyclopaedia of Science, Literature and Art. New York: 1851. V. 39; 46

HECKER, CARL FRIEDRICH 1812-1878

Die Elpehantiasis Oder Lepra Arabica. Lahr: 1858. V. 42

HECKER, JOHANN JULIUS

Flora Berolinensis: das ist Abdruck der Krauter und Blumen nach der Besten Abzeichnung der Natur. Berlin: 1757-58. V. 37

HECKER, JUSTUS FRIEDRICH CARL 1795-1850

Der Schwarze Tod im Vierzehnten Jahrhundert. Berlin: 1832. V. 42

Epidemics of the Middle Ages. London: 1844. V. 39; 41; 43

The Epidemics of the Middle Ages. London: 1846. V. 37; 38; 41; 42

HECKETHORN, C. W.

The Printers of Basle in the XV & XVI Centuries their biographies, printed books and devices. 1897. V. 37

HECKETHORN, CHARLES WILLIAM

The Secret Societies of All Ages and Countries. London: 1897. V. 38

HECKEWELDER, JOHN 1743-1823

An Account of the History, Manners and Customs of the Indian Nations, Who Once Inhabited Pennsylvania and Neighbouring States. V. 39

An Account of the History, Manners and Customs of the Indian Nations Who Once Inhavited Pennsylvania and the Neighboring States. Philadelphia: 1819. V. 45

History, Manner and Customs of the Indian Nations Who Once Inhabited Pennsylvania and the Neighbouring States. Philadelphia: 1881. V. 39

History, Manners and Customs of the Indian Nations who Once inhabited Pennsylvania and the Neighbouring States. Philadelphia: 1876. V. 37

A Letter to a Friend; in Which Some Account is Given of the Brethren's Society for the Furtherance of the Gospel Among the Heathen. London: 1769. V. 42

A Narrative of the Mission of the United Brethren Among the Delaware & Mohegan Indians . . . 1740-1808. Philadelphia: 1820. V. 37; 39; 42; 43; 45; 46

A Narrative of the Mission of the United Brethren Among the Delaware and Mohegan Indians . . . Cleveland: 1907. V. 42

A Narrative of the Mission of the United Brethren Among the Delaware and Mohegan Indians 1740-1808. Philadelphia: 1920. V. 41

HECKMAN, A.

Modern Decorative Art in Confectionery 'Modeko' New Series. Nordhausen: 1925. V. 42

HECKMANN, A.

Zuckerarbeiten und Eismeisselei. Leipzig: 1925. V. 46

HECKSCHER, AUGUST

Memorial Day Address. Cambridge: 1957. V. 46

HECKSCHER, ELI F.

Mercantilism. London: 1934. V. 39

HECKSTALL-SMITH, B.

Yachts and Yachting in Contemporary Art. London: 1925. V. 41; 42

HECTOR, ANNIE FRENCH 1825-1902

A Choice of Evils. London: 1894. V. 41

HEDEGAARD, J.

Morphological Studies in the Genus Thododendron, Dealing with Fruits, Seeds, and Seedlings, and Their Associated Hairs. Copenhagen: 1980. V. 37

HEDELIN, FRANCOIS

The Whole Art of the Stage. London: 1684. V. 38

HEDENDAAGSCHE Historie, of Tegenwoordige Staat Van Amerika. Amsterdam: 1766. V. 45

HEDERICI Graecum Lexicon Manuale. London: 1803. V. 37

HEDGE, LEVI 1766-1844

Elements of Logick; or a Summary of the General Principles and Different Modes of Reasoning. Cambridge: 1816. V. 39; 46

Elements of Logick; or a Summary of the General Principles and Different Modes of Reasoning. Boston: 1836. V. 43

HEDGECOE, JOHN

Henry Moore. New York: 1968. V. 39; 43; 46

Henry Moore. N.P.: 1968. V. 41

HEDGELAND, ISABELLA KELLY

A Collection of Poems and Fables. London: 1794. V. 37

HEDGELAND, J. P.

A Description of the Splendid Decorations Recently Made to the Church of St. Neot, Cornwall. London: 1830. V. 45

HEDGES, ISAAC A.

Sorgo or the Northern Sugar Plant by the Pioneer Investigator in the Northern Cane Enterprise. Cincinnati: 1863. V. 37; 41; 43

HEDGES, PHINEAS

Stricutres on the Elementa Medicinae of Doctor Brown. Goshen: 1795. V. 38; 40

HEDIN, SVEN

Across the Gobi Desert. London: 1931. V. 38

Big Horse's Flight. London: 1936. V. 41

Central Asia and Tibet. London: 1903. V. 41; 46

Eine Routenaufnahme Durch Ostpersien. Stockholm: 1918/27. V. 46

Jehol. City of Emperors. London: 1932. V. 37; 46

Overland to India. London: 1910. V. 38; 41

Riddles of the Gobi Desert. New York: 1933. V. 43

The Silk Road. London: 1938. V. 41

Through Asia. London: 1898. V. 43

Through Asia. London & New York: 1899. V. 38

Through Asia. New York: 1899. V. 38; 41

Trans-Himalaya. London: 1909. V. 40; 42; 44

Trans-Himalaya. Discoveries and Adventures in Tibet. London: 1910-13. V. 46

HEDIN, THOMAS

The Sculpture of Gaspard and Balthazard Marsy. Art and Patronage in the Early Reign of Louis XIV. With a Catalogue Raisonne. Columbia: 1983. V. 42

HEDLEY, JOHN

A Practical Treatise on the Working and Ventilation of Coal Mining. London: 1851. V. 37; 38

HEDLEY, OSWALD DODD

Who Invented the Locomotive Engine? London: 1858. V. 46

HEDLEY, W. S.

Therapeutic Electricity and Practical Muscle Testing. London: 1899. V. 42

HEDLINGUER, JEAN CHARLES

Collection Complette de Toutes les Medailles du Chevalier Jean Charles Hedlinguer. Augsburg: 1782. V. 39; 41

HEDREN, PAUL L.

First Scalp for Custer, the Skrimish at War Bonnet Creek, Nebraska, July 17, 1876 with a Short History of the War Bonnet Battlefield. Glendale: 1980. V. 45

HEDRICK, ULYSESS PRENTISS

Pears of New York. Albany: 1921. V. 44

The Plums of New York. Albany: 1944. V. 45

HEDRICK, ULYSSES PRENTISS

The Cherries of New York. Albany: 1915. V. 45

The Grapes of New York. Albany: 1908. V. 40; 42; 45; 46

The Plums of New York. Albany: 1911. V. 40; 41

HEDRICK, ULYSSES PRESTISS

Peaches of New York. Albany: 1916. V. 44

HEER, J. C.

The Primaeval World of Switzerland. London: 1876. V. 42

HEER, OSWALD

The Primaeval world of Switzerland. London: 1876. V. 41

HEEREBOORD, ADRIAN

Collegium Ethicum sev Philosophia Moralis. London: 1658. V. 40

HEEREN, ARNOLD H. L.

Historical Researches into the Politics, Intercourse and Tradae of the Carthaginians, Ethiopians and Egyptians. London: 1850. V. 38

A Manual of the History of the Political System of Europe and Its Colonies . . . to . . . the Fall of Napoleon. Oxford: 1834. V. 38

Reflections of the Politics of Ancient Greece. Boston: 1824. V. 37; 42

Reflections on the Politics, Intercourse, and Trade of the Ancient Nations of Africa. Oxford: 1832. V. 46

HEERMANS, FORBES

Thirteen Stories of the Far West. Syracuse,: 1897. V. 37

HEFFRON, ROBERT

Pneumonia, with Special Reference to Pneumococcus Lobar Pneumonia. New York: 1939. V. 43

HEGAN, ALICE CALDWELL

Mrs. Wiggs of the Cabbage Patch. New York: 1901. V. 42

HEGARTY, REGINALD B.

Returns of Whaling Vessels Sailing from American Ports. New Bedford: 1959. V. 41

HEGARTY, SALLY

Twelve Mammal Skulls. 1989. V. 45

HEGEL, GEORG WILHELM FRIEDRICH 1770-1831

Encyclopadie der Philosophischen Wissenschaften im Grundrisse Zum Gebrauch Seiner Vorlesungen. Heidelberg: 1817. V. 40; 45

Grundlinien der Philosophie des Rechts. Berlin: 1821. V. 38; 41; 45

Lectures on the Philosophy of Religion. London: 1895. V. 43

The Logic of Hegel. Translated from the Encyclopaedia of the Philosophical Sciences with Prolegomena by William Wallace (1844-1897). Oxford: 1874. V. 37

System der Wissenschaft. Erster Theil (all published). Bamberg und Wurzburg: 1807. V. 39; 41

Wissenschaft der Logik. Nuremberg: 1812-13-16. V. 42

Wissenschaft der Logik. Nurnberg: 1812-16. V. 39; 43; 45

HEGEMANN, WERNER

The American Vitruvius: an Architects' Handbook of Civic Art. New York: 1922. V. 42

HEGENDORF, CHRISTOPH

Disserendi Demonstrandiue Ars Ita Iuri Ciuili ad Commodata. Basle: 1535. V. 40

Oratio De Artibvs, Fvtvro Ivrisconsvlto & Necessarijs & Frugiferis, Comparandis. Hagenau: 1529. V. 40

HEGENDORFF, CHRISTOPH 1500-1540

Encomium Ebrietatis. (with) Encomium Sobrietatis. France?: 1520. V. 43

HEGESIPPUS

De Bello Iudaico . . . Cum Eiusdem Anacephaleosi. Paris: 1511-12. V. 45

De Rebus a Judaeorum Principibus . . . Excidio Hierosolymorum. Cologne: 1525. V. 40; 45

HEGUERTY, PIERRE ANDRE

Remarques sur Plusieurs Branches de Commerce et de Navigation . . . N.P.: 1757. V. 45

HEIBLOCQ, JACOBUS

Farrago Latino-Belgica of Megelmoes Van Latijnsche en Duitsche Gedichten. Amsterdam: 1662/3. V. 37

HEIDE, ANTONIUS DE

Experimenta Circa Sanguinis Missionem, Fibras Motrices Urtica Marinam &c . . . Amsterdam: 1686. V. 46

HEIDEGGER, MARTIN

Die Kategorien- und Bedeutungslehre des Duns Scotus. Tubingen: 1916. V. 39

hebel der Hausfreund. Ufullingen: 1957. V. 45

Sein und Zeit. ERste Halfte. Niemeyer: 1927. V. 45

Sein und Zeit. ERste Halfte. Niemeyer, Halle: 1927. V. 41

HEIDEN, THOMAS

The Sculpture of Gaspard and Balthazard Marsy. Columbia: 1983. V. 44

HEIDMANN, CHRISTOPHER

Europa Siue Manuductio ad Geographiam Veterem . . . Wolffenbuttel: 1658. V. 45

HEILMANN, G.

The Origin of Birds. London: 1926. V. 39

HEILMANN, GERHARD

Danmarks Fugeliv. Copenhagen: 1939. V. 38

HEILNER, VAN CAMPEN

A Book of Duck Shooting. Philadelphia: 1939. V. 39

Our American Game Birds. Garden City: 1941. V. 39; 46

Salt Water Fishing. Philadelphia: 1937. V. 37; 39; 44

HEILPRIN, ANGELO

Alaska and the Klondike a Journey to the New Eldorado with Hints to the Traveller and Observations on the Physical History and Geology of the Gold Regions . . . New York: 1889. V. 39; 42; 43

HEIMBURGER, JOST

Der Volkommene Zimmermann Oder Vollstandige Anweisung zur Bau-Kunst . . . Frankfurt: 1761. V. 45

HEIN, O. L.

Memories of Long Ago. New York: 1925. V. 46

HEINE, HEINRICH

Atta Troll and Other Poems. London: 1876. V. 42

Atta Troll. New York: 1914. V. 43

Florentine Nights. London: 1927. V. 41; 42

Gods in Exile. Los Angeles: 1931. V. 42

Poems. Vienna: 1854. V. 37

The Prose and Poetical Works. New York: 1920. V. 42

Der Rabbi von Bacherach. Berlin: 1921. V. 41

Sammtliche Werke. Philadelphia: 1856-55. V. 42; 43

The Works. London: 1893. V. 42

The Works of Heinrich Heine. New York: 1920. V. 46

HEINECCIUS, JOHANN GOTTLIEB

A Methodical System of Universal Law . . . London: 1763. V. 46

HEINECKEN, K. H.

Idee Generale d'Une Collection Complete d'Estampes. Avec une Dissertation sur l'Origine de la Gravure & sur les Premiers Livres d'Images. Leipzig/Vienna: 1771. V. 40

HEINEMAN, JAMES H.

P. G. Wodehouse: a Centenary Celebration 1881-1981. New York: 1981. V. 46

P. G. Wodehouse: A Centenary Celebration 1881-1981. New York & London: 1981. V. 38

HEINEMANN, KATHERINE

Brandings. West Branch: 1968. V. 41

HEINEMANN, LARRY

Close Quarters. New York: 1977. V. 42; 45; 46

HEINIGER, ERNST A.

The Great Book of Jewels. Boston: 1974. V. 40

HEINLEIN, ROBERT A.

Job: a Comedy of Justice. New York: 1984. V. 41; 43; 45

HEINLEIN, ROBERT ANAON 1907-1988

Between Planets. New York: 1951. V. 37

The Menace from Earth. 1959. V. 43

HEINLEIN, ROBERT ANSON 1907-1988

Assignment in Eternity. 1953. V. 39; 43; 45

Assignment in Eternity. Pennsylvania: 1953. V. 39

Assignment in Eternity. Reading: 1953. V. 39; 41; 42

Beyond this Horizon. 1948. V. 43; 44; 45

The Cat Who Walks through Walls. 1985. V. 45

The Cat Who Walked through Walls. New York: 1985. V. 42

The Discovery of the Future. 1941. V. 43

The Discovery of the Future. Los Angeles: 1941. V. 43

The Door Into Summer. 1957. V. 37; 39

Double Star. 1956. V. 37; 39; 43; 45

Double Star. London: 1958. V. 44

Farmer in the Sky. New York: 1950. V. 42

Farnhams Freehold. New York: 1964. V. 43

Friday. 1982. V. 43

Friday. New York: 1982. V. 41; 42

The Green Hills of Earth. 1951. V. 44

The Green Hills of Earth. Chicago: 1951. V. 45; 46

Have Space Suit-Will Travel. New York: 1958. V. 39

I Will Fear No Evil. 1971. V. 37; 39

Job: a Comedy of Justice. 1984. V. 43; 45

The Man Who Sold the Moon. 1950. V. 39; 43; 44

The Man Who Sold the Moon. Chicago: 1950. V. 42

The Man Who Sold the Moon. The Green Hills of Earth. Revolt in 2100 and Methuselah's Children. 1950/51/53. V. 43

The Man Who Sold the Moon. The Green Hills of Earth. & Revolt in 2100. 1950-53. V. 45

The Man Who Sold the Moon; The Green Hills of Earth; Revolt in 2100 and Methuselah's Children. 1958.51/53. V. 44

The Man who sold the Moon, the Green Hills of Earth. Revolt in 2100 and methuselah's Children. 1958. V. 37

Methuselah's Children. New York: 1958. V. 42; 43

Methuselah's Children. 1959. V. 37; 44

Methuselah's Children. Hicksville: 1958. V. 37

The Moon is a Harsh Mistress. 1967. V. 44

Orphans of the Sky. London: 1963. V. 43

Orphans of the Sky. New York: 1964. V. 43; 44

Orphans of the Sky. 1964. V. 37

The Past Through Tomorrow. New York: 1967. V. 39; 43; 45

The Pupper Masters. New York: 1951. V. 44

The Puppet Masters. 1953. V. 39

Red Planet. 1949. V. 39

Revolt in 2100. 1953. V. 37; 39; 43

Revolt in 2100. Chicago: 1953. V. 41; 42

Rocket Ship Galileo. 1947. V. 39

Rocket Ship Galileo. New York: 1947. V. 42; 44; 45

HEINLEIN, ROBERT ANSON 1907-1988 continued

The Rolling Stones. New York: 1953. V. 43

The Sixth Column. 1949. V. 43

A Sixth Column. New York: 1949. V. 43

Space Cadet. New York: 1948. V. 44

The Star Beast. New York: 1954. V. 43; 44

Starman Jones. New York: 1953. V. 44; 45

Starship Troopers. 1959. V. 37; 43

Starship Troopers. New York: 1959. V. 39; 45

Stranger in a Strange Land. 1961. V. 43

Stranger in a Strange Land. New York: 1961. V. 46

Stranger in a Strange Land. New York: 1991. V. 44; 45

Three by Heinlein. 1956. V. 43

Tomorrow, the Stars. Garden City: 1952. V. 41; 42

Tunnel in the Sky. New York: 1955. V. 39; 44

The Unpleasant Profession of Jonathan Hoag. Hicksville: (1959). V. 37

Waldo and Magic, Inc. New York: 1950. V. 44

HEINROTH, JOHANN C. A. 1773-1843

Ueber die Wahrheit . . . Leipzig: 1824. V. 46

HEINS, HENRY HARDY

A Golden Anniversary Bibliography of Edgar Rice Burroughs. West Kingston;: 1964. V. 41

HEINSE, JOHANN JACOB WILHELM

Anastasia und das Schachspiel. Frankfurt: 1831. V. 38

HEINSIUS, D.

Rerum ad Sylvam-Ducis Atque Alibi in Belgio aut a Belgis anno MDCXXIX Gestarum Historia. 1631. V. 37

HEINSIUS, NICOLAUS

Bibliotheca Heinsiana Sive Catalogus Librorum, Quos, Magno Studio & Sumtu dum Viveret Collegit Nicolaus Heinsius, Dan. Fil. Leiden: 1682. V. 40

HEINTZELMAN, ARTHUR WILLIAM

H. de Toulouse-Lautrec, One Hundred and Ten Unpublished Drawings. Boston: 1955. V. 42

HEINZELMANN, F.

Reisebilder und Skizzen us der Pyrenaischen Halbinsel Nebst Blicken uf die Lander des Mejicanischen Golfes und Californien . . . Leipzig: 1851. V. 38

HEINZEN, KARL

The Rights of Women and Sexual Relations. Boston: 1891. V. 39

HEIRS of Hippocrates. Iowa City: 1991. V. 45

HEIRS of Hippocrates . . . Iowa City: 1990. V. 46

HEISTER, LORENZ

A General System of Surgery . . . to which is prefixed an introduction concerning th nature, origin, progress and imporvements of Surgery. London;: 1745. V. 37

Institvtiones Chirvrgicae, in Qvibvs Qvidqvid ad rem Chirvrgicam Pertinet, Optima et Novissima Ratione Pertractavr . . . Amstelaedami: 1750. V. 39

Medical, Chirurgical and Anatomical Cases and Observations. London: 1755. V. 39; 40

HEITLAND, WILLIAM EMERTON

The Roman Republic . . . Cambridge: 1909. V. 37

HEITMAN, F. B.

Historical Register of Officers of the Continental Army During the War of the Revolution. April 1775 to December 1783. Washington: 1893. V. 39

HEITMAN, FRANCIS B.

Historical Register of Officers of the Continental Army During the War of the Revolution, April, 1775 to December 1783. Washington: 1914. V. 44

HEITON, JOHN

The Castes of Edinburgh. Edinburgh: 1859. V. 42

HEITZMANN, CARL

Anatomy Descriptive and Topographical in 625 Illustrations. New York: 1887. V. 38

HEIZER, R. F.

The California Indians. Berkeley: 1951. V. 44

HEJDUK, J.

Judith Turner Photographs Five Architects. New York: 1980. V. 46

HEKLER, ANTON

Greek and Roman Portraits. London: 1912. V. 40; 42; 44

HELD, JULIUS S.

Peter Paul Rubens. The Oil Sketches. A Critical Catalogue. Princeton: 1980. V. 44

Rembrandt and the Book of Tobit. Northampton: 1964. V. 39; 41

Rubens: Selected Drawings . . . with a Critical Catalogue. London: 1959. V. 37; 40

HELFFERICH, KARL

Germany's Economic Progress and National Welath 1888-1913. Berlin: 1913. V. 43

HELIANUS, LODOVICUS

De Bello Suscipiendo Aduersus Venetianos & Turcas Oratio. Augsburg: 1510. V. 37

HELIODORUS

The Adventures of Theagenes and Chariclia, a Romance. London: 1717. V. 38; 40

Historia Aethopiacae Libri Decem. Numquam Antea in Lucem Editi. Basle: 1534. V. 45

HELL for Leather. New York: 1928. V. 45

HELLER, DAVID

A History of Cape Silver, 1700-1870. Cape Town: 1949. V. 38

HELLER, ELINOR RAAS

Bibliography of the Grabhorn Press, 1915-1940. San Francisco: 1940. V. 37; 43; 46

A Bibliography of the Grabhorn Press, 1915-1973. San Francisco: 1940/57/77. V. 45

Bibliography of the Grabhorn Press 1915-1956. San Francisco: 1975. V. 41; 43

HELLER, JOHN H.

Heller's Galveston Directory. 1878 and Portion of 1879. Glaveston: 1879. V. 45

HELLER, JOSEPH 1923-

Catch 22. 1961. V. 43

Catch-22. London: 1961. V. 39

Catch 22. New York: 1961. V. 37; 39; 40; 42; 43; 44; 45; 46

Catch 22. New York: 1973. V. 45

God Knows. New York: 1984. V. 41; 42; 45

Good as Gold. New York: 1979. V. 39; 40; 41; 43; 46

Something Happened. New York: 1974. V. 37; 39; 40; 41; 42; 43; 44; 46

We Bombed in New Haven - a Play. New York: 1968. V. 45; 46

HELLER, MICHAEL

Figures of Speaking. Mt. Horeb: 1977. V. 44

HELLFRIED, CARL F. VON

Outlines of a Political Survey of the English Attack on Denmark in 1807. London: 1809. V. 39

HELLINGA, WYTZE 1908-

Copy and Print in the Netherlands, an Atlas of Historical Bibliography. Amsterdam: 1962. V. 44; 46

The Fifteenth Century Printing Types of the Low Countires. Amsterdam: 1966. V. 39; 43; 44; 45

HELLMAN, ALFRED

A Collection of Early Obstetrical Books: An Historical Essay with Bibliographical Description of 37 Items. New Haven: 1952. V. 42

HELLMAN, LILLIAN 1905-

Days to Come. New York: 1936. V. 37; 46

The Little Foxes. New York: (1939). V. 37; 42

Pentimento. Boston: 1973. V. 43

Scoundrel Time. Boston: 1969. V. 44

Scoundrel Time. Boston: 1976. V. 44; 46

Scoundrel Time. New York: 1976. V. 41

Three (Unfinished Woman, Pentimento, Scoundrel Time). Boston: 1979. V. 39

Three. New York: 1979. V. 41

Watch on the Rhine. New York: 1942. V. 45

HELLMAN, SAM

Stanley and Livingstone. Bevely Hills: 1937. V. 45

HELLMUTH Weissenborn Engraver. Andoversford: 1983. V. 46

HELLOT, JEAN

L'Art de la Teinture des Laines, et des Etoffes de Laine, en Grand et Petit Teint avec une Insturction sur les Debouillis. Paris: 1730. V. 42

The Art of Dying Wool, Silk and Cotton. London: 1789. V. 44

HELLPRIN, ANGELO

Contributions to the Tertiary Geology and Paleontology of the United States. Philadelphia: 1884. V. 46

HELLSTROM, PONTUS

The Rock Drawings. Denmark: 1970. V. 40; 42; 44

HELLWIG, JOHANN OTTO VON

Arcana Maiora, Oder Curiose und Nutzliche Beschreibung Vieler Wahrhaften Physicalischen . . . Frankfurt & Leipzig: 1712. V. 46

HELLWIG, LUDWIG CHRISTOPH VON

Nosce te Ipsum, Velanatomicum Vivum, Moder . . . Erffurt: 1716. V. 45

HELM, H. T.

American Roadsters and Trotting Horses. Chicago: 1878. V. 46

HELM, MARY S.

Scraps of Early Texas History. Austin: 1884. V. 37; 38; 39; 42

HELM, W. H.

Vigee-Lebrun, 1755-1842: Her Life, Works and Friendships. Boston: 1915. V. 44; 45

HELME, ELISABETH

Rambles in London, and the Adjacent Villages. London: 1798. V. 40

HELMHOLTZ, HERMAN VON

Popular Lectures on Scientific Subjects. First Series and Second Series. London: 1881-91. V. 44

HELMHOLTZ, HERMANN LUDWIG FERDINAND VON 1821-1894

Beschreibung Eines Augen-Spiegels zur Untersuchung der Netzhaut im Lebenden Auge. Berlin: 1851. V. 42

Handbuch der Physiolgischen Optik. Leipzig: 1867. V. 37; 38; 42

The Sensations of Tone as a Physiological Basis for Music. London: 1875. V. 38

Treatise on Physiological Optics. Racine: 1924-25. V. 46

HELMONT, BAPTISTA VAN JOHANNES 1579-1652

Ortus Medicinae. Amsterdam: 1652. V. 46

HELMONT, JEAN BAPTISTE VAN

Ortus Medicinae . . . Venetiis: 1561. V. 37

HELMONT, JOHANNES BAPTISTA VAN 1579-1644

Ortus Medicinae. (with) Opuscula Medica Inaudita. Amsterdam: 1648. V. 38

HELMS, ANTHONY Z.

Travels in Buenos Ayres, by Potosi to Lima. London: 1807. V. 38; 40; 41

HELPER, HINTON R.

The Land of Gold. Baltimore: 1855. V. 43

HELPER, HINTON ROWAN

The Impending Crisis of the South: How to Meet It. New York: 1860. V. 43; 46

The Impending Crisis of the South: How to Meet It. New York: 1857. V. 37

The Three Americas Railway. St. Louis: 1881. V. 44

HELPRIN, MARK

A Dove of the East. New York: 1975. V. 43; 44; 46

Ellis Island and Other Stories. New York: 1981. V. 44

Refiners Fire. New York: 1977. V. 44

A Soldier of the the Great War. San Diego: 1991. V. 45

Winter's Tale. New York: 1983. V. 43

HELPS, ARTHUR

Casimir Maremma. London: 1870. V. 37; 38; 42

The Claims of Labour. London: V. 38; 42; 46

The Claims of Labour. London: 1844. V. 42

The Claims of Labour. London: 1845. V. 42

The Conquerors of the New Orld and Their Bondsmen. London: 1848-52. V. 41

The Life of Las Casas. London: 1868. V. 38

The Life of Hernando Cortes. London: 1871. V. 43

Life and Labours of Mr. Brassey 1805-1870. London: 1872. V. 46

Oulita the Serf. London: 1858. V. 46

Realmah. London: 1868. V. 38; 40; 44

The Spanish Conquest in America and Its Relation to the History of Slavery and to the Government of Colonies. London: 1855-61. V. 37; 40

Thoughts in the Cloister and the Crowd. London: 1835. V. 40

Thoughts Upon Government. London: 1872. V. 39; 42

HELPS to the Study of Presbyterianism; or, an Unsophisticated Exposition of Calvinism. With Hopkinsian Modifications and Policy with a View to a More Easy Interpretation of the Same. Knoville: 1834. V. 39

HELSHAM, RICHARD 1680-1733

A Course of Lectures in Natural Philosophy . . . London: 1739. V. 45

A Course of Lectures in Natural Philosophy. London: 1743. V. 42; 46

A Course of Lectures in Natural Philosophy. Philadelphia: 1802. V. 44

HELSMAH, RICHARD 1680-1733

A Course of Lectures in Natural Philosphy. London: 1777. V. 37

HELTEY, C., MRS.

The Native Flowers of New Zealand Illustrated in Colours . . . London: 1887-88. V. 41

HELUIS, JEAN

Le Mirover Dv Prince Chretien . . . Dedie a . . . Charles Monsieur d'Aumalle. Paris: 1566. V. 42

HELVETIORUM Respublica. Diversorum Autorum Quorum Nonnulli Nunc Primum in Lucem Prodiunt. Lugdunum Batavorum: 1627. V. 39

HELVETIUS, CLAUDE ADRIEN 1715-1771

De l'Esprit. Paris: 1758. V. 38; 39; 41; 45

De L'Esprit. Amsterdam & Leipsick: 1759. V. 46

De L'Esprit . . . London: 1759. V. 37; 38; 40; 41; 44; 45

A Treatise on Man; His Intellectual Faculties and Education. London: 1810. V. 37; 40

Oeuvres Complettes. Londres: 1776. V. 39

HELVETIUS, JEAN ADRIEN

Recueil des Methodes . . . pour la Guerison des Plus Dangereuses Maladies qui Attaqunet le Corps Humain . . . Trevoux: 1720-21. V. 37

HELWIG, SIMON

The Capture and Prison Life in Rebeldom for Fourteen Months of Simon Helwig, Late Private Co. F. 51st O.V.I. Canal Dover: 1900. V. 44

HELY-HUTCHINSON, JOHN

The Commercial Restraints of Ireland, Considered in a Series of Letters . . . Dublin: 1779. V. 45

HELYOT, PIERRE

Histoire des Ordres Monastiques, Religieux et Militaires, et des Congregations Seculieres de l'un et de l'Autre Sexe, Qui Ont Ete Establies Jusqu'a Present . . . Paris: 1721. V. 46

HEMANS, F.

The Poetical Works. Philadelphia: 1839. V. 41

HEMANS, FELICIA DOROTHEA BROWNE

The Forest Sanctuary and Other Poems. London: 1825. V. 45; 46

The Forest Sanctuary, With Other Poems. London: 1829. V. 40

Hymns on the Works of Nature . . . Boston: 1827. V. 42

The League of the Alps, the Siege of Valencia, the Vespers of Palermo and Other Poems. Boston: 1826. V. 44

Memorials of . . . New York: 1836. V. 39

Poems. Liverpool: 1808. V. 39

Poems. Edinburgh: 1854. V. 37; 39; 42

The Siege of Valencia. London: 1823. V. 43

Works. Edinburgh: 1839. V. 37; 40

The Works of Mrs. Hemans, with A Memoir by her Sister. Philadelphia: 1842. V. 42; 43

HEMENWAY, ABBY MARIA

Poets and Poetry of Vermont. Rutland: 1858. V. 41

HEMENWAY, CHARLES

Memoirs of My Day in and Out of Mormondom by . . . Salt Lake City: 1887. V. 42

HEMERE, CLAUDE

De Academia Parisiensi. Qvalis Primo Fvit In Insvla et Episcoporvm Scholis Liber. Paris: 1637. V. 42

HEMING, WILLIAM

The Eunuch. London: 1687. V. 41

HEMINGWAY, ERNEST MILLAR 1899-1961

Across the River and Into the Trees. London: 1950. V. 37; 42; 43; 45

Across the River and Into the Trees. New York: 1950. V. 37; 38; 39; 42; 43; 44; 45

The Dangerous Summer. New York: 1985. V. 39

Death in the Afternoon. London: 1932. V. 38

Death in the Afternoon. New York: 1932. V. 42; 43; 44; 45; 46

Death in the Afternoon. New York, London: 1932. V. 37; 38; 39

HENDERSON, GEORGE continued

Lahore to Yarkand. Incidents of the Route and Natural History of the Countries Traversed by the Expedition of 1870, under T.D. Forsyth, Esq. C.B. London: 1873. V. 39; 43; 46

Studies in Bible Illustration. London: 1987. V. 39

HENDERSON, GEORGE F. R.

Stonewall Jackson and the American Civil War. London: 1898. V. 43

HENDERSON, GEORGE F.R.

Stonewall Jackson and the American Civil War. London: 1906. V. 42; 44

Stonewall Jackson and the American Civil War. London/New York: 1898. V. 37

HENDERSON, HALTON

Artistry in Single Action. Dallas: 1989. V. 42

HENDERSON, HAMISH

Elegies for the Dead in Cyrenaica. London: 1948. V. 42

Elegies for the Dead in Cyrenaica. Edinburgh: 1971. V. 40

HENDERSON, HAROLD G.

The Surviving Works of Sharaku. New York: 1939. V. 38; 41; 44

HENDERSON, JAMES

A History of Brazil . . . London: 1821. V. 38; 45

Notes by the Way. During a Ramble Through Chihli, in March 1874. Tientsin: 1874. V. 41

HENDERSON, JAMES D.

Lilliputian Newspapers. Worcester: 1936. V. 42

HENDERSON, JENNIE CROCKER

California: the Library of Jennie Crocker Henderson. San Francisco: 1979-80. V. 46

HENDERSON, JOHN

Letters and Poems by the Late Mr. John Henderson. London: 1786. V. 38; 39; 40; 42; 45

Observations on the Colonies of New South Wales and Van Dieman's Land. Calcutta: 1832. V. 39

HENDERSON, JOHN B.

The Cruise of the Tomas Barrera. New York: & London: 1916. V. 45

The West Indies. London: 1905. V. 44; 45

HENDERSON, L. R. S., MRS.

The Magic Aeroplane: a Fairy Tale. Chicago: 1911. V. 45

HENDERSON, MARC ANTHONY

The Song of Milkanwatha. Cincinnati: 1856. V. 39

HENDERSON, MARC ANTONY

The Song of Milgenwater. Cincinnati: 1856. V. 43

HENDERSON, PAUL C.

Landmarks on the Oregon Trail. New York: 1953. V. 38; 39; 44

HENDERSON, ROBERT W.

Early American Sport. New York: 1937. V. 37; 39; 42; 46

HENDERSON, T. F.

James I and VI. London: 1904. V. 38

HENDERSON, THOMAS

An Epitome of the Physiology, General Anatomy and Pathology of Bichat. Philadelphia: 1829. V. 44

Hints on the Medical Examination of Recruits for the Army . . . Philadelphia: 1856. V. 42

Observations on the Comet of Encke, Made in June 1832. London: 1833. V. 37

HENDERSON, WILLIAM

Notes and Reminiscences of My Life as an Angler . . . London: 1876. V. 43

HENDERSON, WILLIAM AUGUSTUS

Common Sense in the Kitchen . . . New York: 1870. V. 45

The Housekeeper's Instructor. London. V. 38

The Housekeeper's Instructor. London: 1790. V. 37; 42

The Housekeeper's Instructor. London: 1805. V. 38

The Housekeeper's Instructor. Stratford: 1805. V. 39

Modern Domestic Cookery, and Useful Receipt Book, Adapted for Families. Boston: 1845. V. 37; 45

HENDERSON, Z.

The Anything Box. 1965. V. 43

The People: No Different Flesh. New York: 1967. V. 43

Pilgrimmage: the Book of the People. 1961. V. 43

HENDERSON'S New Belfast Directory and Northern Repository for 1843-44. Belfast: 1843. V. 43

HENDLEY, THOMAS HOLBEIN

Damascening on Steel or Iron, as Practiced in India. London: 1892. V. 42

The Rulers of India and the Chiefs of Rajputana, 1550 to 1897. London: 1897. V. 39

HENDRICKS, GORDON

The Life and Work of Winslow Homer. New York: 1979. V. 39

HENDY, JAMES

A Treatise on the Glandular Disease of Barbados, Providing It to Be Seated in the Lymphatic System. London: 1784. V. 42; 46

HENELY, WILLIAM

Universal Dictionary of Violin and Bow Makers. London: 1973. V. 38

HENERSON, HAROLD G.

The Surviving Works of Sharaku. New York: 1939. V. 46

HENEY, HOWELL J.

Thirty Years of Bird and Bull: a Bibliography 1958-1988. 1988. V. 45

HENING, WILLIAM WALLER

The New Virginia Justice . . . Richmond: 1810. V. 40

The Statutes at Large: Being a Collection of All the Laws of Virginia from the First Session of the Legislature in the Year 1619. Charlottesville: 1969. V. 44

HENING, WILLIAM WALTER

The Statutes at Large; being a Collection of all the Laws of Virginia, from the First Session of the Legislature, in the Year 1619. New York, Richmond: 1819-1823. V. 37

HENITZELMAN, ARTHUR WILLIAM

H. De Toulouse-Lautrec. Boston: 1955. V. 44

HENKEL, DAVID

Answer to Mr. Joseph Moore, the Methodist; with a Few Fragments of the Doctrine of Justification. New Market: 1825. V. 38

HENKEL, PAUL

The Christian Catechism. New Market: 1816. V. 41

HENKELS, STAN V.

Andrew Jackson and the Bank of the United States. Philadelphia: 1928. V. 39; 42

HENLE, FRITZ

The American Virgin Islands. New York: 1971. V. 42

HENLEY, DAVID

The Proceedings of the General Court-Martial Held at Cambridge, on Tuesday the Twentieth of January . . . Upon the Trial of Colonel David Henley. Boston: 1778. V. 46

HENLEY, JOHN

Law and Arguments in Vindication of the University of Oxford: In Two Seasonable Discourses . . . London: 1749? V. 41

HENLEY, LOIS B.

Winter Reason - One Woman's Words. Laguana: 1977. V. 37

HENLEY, SAMUEL

A Discourse Delivered in the Chapel of William and Mary College, Virginia; on the Anniversary of the College Foundation. Cambridge: 1776. V. 45

HENLEY, W. E.

The Tudor Translations. London: 1892-1905. V. 39

HENLEY, WILLIAM ERNEST 1849-1903

A Book of Verses. London: 1888. V. 37; 44; 46

Hawthorn and Lavender. Songs and Madrigals. London: 1901. V. 44; 46

Hawthorn and Lavender. New York: 1901. V. 44

Hawthorn and Lavender. London: 1910. V. 45

A London Garland, Selected from Five Centures of English Verse . . . London & New York: 1895. V. 39

London Types. London: 1898. V. 40; 42; 43

London Types. New York: 1898. V. 41; 43

London Voluntaries. Portland: 1910. V. 43

A London Garland: Selected from Five Centuries of English Verse. London: 1895. V. 37; 38

London Voluntaries, The Song of the Sword, and Other Verses. London: 1893. V. 38

Poems. London: 1905. V. 44

HENLEY, WILLIAM ERNEST 1849-1903 continued

Poems. London: 1913. V. 45

The Song of the Sword and Other Verses. London: 1892. V. 41; 46

Views and Reviews: Essays in Appreciation. London: 1890. V. 37; 46

The Works. London: 1908. V. 37; 42; 46

HENNE, JOHN

Principles of Military Surgery; comprising, observations on the arrangement, police and practice of hospitals, and on the history, treatment, and anomalies of Variola and Syphilis . . . Philadelphia: 1830. V. 37

HENNEBERG, FREIHERR ALFRED VON

The Art and Craft of Old Lace. New York: 1931. V. 45

HENNEBIQUE, FRANCOIS

Le Breton Arme. Organe des Agents et Concessionnaires du Systeme Hennebique. (and) Releve des Travaux Executes en Systeme Hennebique. Paris: 1903-13. V. 44

HENNELL, REGINALD

A Famous Indian Regiment, the Kali Panchwin 2/5th (Formerly the 105th) Mahratta Light Infantry 1768-1923. London: 1927. V. 42; 46

The History of the King's Body Guard of the Yeoman of the Guard. The Oldest Permanent Body Guard of the Sovereigns of England, 1485 to 1904. Westminster: 1904. V. 37

HENNELL, THOMAS

Six Poems. London: 1947. V. 40

HENNEN, JOHN

Observations on Some Important Poems in the Practice of Military Surgery and in the Arrangment and Police of Hospitals. Edinburgh: 1818. V. 44

Principles of Military Surgery, Comprising Observations on the Arrangement, Police and Practice of Hospitals, and on the History, Treatment and Anomalies of Variola and Syphillis. London: 1820. V. 38

Principles of Military Surgery Comprising Observations on the Arrangement, Police and Practice of Hospitals, and on the History, Treatment and Anomalies of Variola and Syphilis. Philadelphia: 1830. V. 38

HENNEPIN, LOUIS

Description de la Louisiane. Paris: 1688. V. 38

Description de la Louisane, Nouvellement Decouverte au Sud'Quest de la Nouvelle France, par Ordre du Roy . . . Paris: 1783. V. 39

A Description of Louisiana, By Father Louis Hennepin, Recollect Missionary. Translated from the Edition of 1683, and Compared with the Nouvelle Decouverte, The La Salle Documents . . . New York: 1880. V. 39

A New Discovery of a Vast Country in America, Extending About Four Thousand Miles, Between New France and New Mexico . . . London: 1698. V. 37; 38; 40; 42

A New Discovery of a Vast Country in America. Chicago: 1903. V. 42

Nouvelle Decouverte d'un Tres Grand Pays Situe dans l'Amerique. Utrecht: 1697. V. 38; 39; 40; 42; 43; 46

HENNEQUIN, JEAN

Le Gvidon General des Finaces. Contenant l'Instruction du Maniement de Toutes les Finances de France. Paris: 1596. V. 45

HENNESSEY, ESME F.

The Slipper Orchids. V. 45; 46

HENNESSY, GEORGE

Novum Repertorium Ecclesiasticum Parochiale Londiniense or London Diocesan Clergy Succession from the Earliest Time to the Year 1898. London: 1898. V. 41

HENNESSY, J. G.

Central Asian Carpets of Peshawar. Peshawar: 1916. V. 40

HENNESSY, JOHN BASIL

Ancient Near Eastern Pottery. New York: 1979. V. 44

HENNESSY, JOHN POPE

Sir Walter Raleigh in Ireland. London: 1883. V. 39

HENNESSY, W. M.

The Book of Fenagh in Irish and English, compiled by St. Caillin, Founder of Fenagh etc. Dublin: 1875. V. 37

HENNEZEL, HENRI D'

Decorations and Designs of Silken Masterpieces: Ancient and Modern. New York: 1925. V. 43

HENNICK, LOUIS C.

Louisiana: Its Street and Interurban Railways. Shreveport: 1962-65. V. 42

HENNIKER, FREDERICK

Notes During a Visit to Egypt, Nubia, the oasis Boeris, Mount Sinai and Jerusalem. London: 1824. V. 39; 41; 44; 45

HENNING, FRED

Fights for the Championship. London: 1900. V. 43

HENNING, WILLIAM WALLER

The Statutes at Large, being a Collection of all the Laws of Virginia . . . V. 40

The Virginia Justice . . . Richmond: 1825. V. 43

HENNINGS, JUSTIS CHRISTIAN 1731-1815

Von den Ahndungen und Visionen. Leipzig: 1777-83. V. 46

HENNINGSEN, CHARLES FRANCIS

The Last of the Sophis. London: 1831. V. 45

HENOCH, EDWARD

Lectures on Children's Diseases. London: 1889. V. 42

HENOT, GEORGES

The Countess Sarah from the French..by Lady . . . London: 1884. V. 43

HENREY, BLANCHE

Botanical and Horticultural Literature Before 1800. Oxford: 1975. V. 40; 41; 46

British Botanical and Horitcultural Literature Before 1800 . . . London: 1975. V. 37; 38; 39; 40; 44; 45; 46

HENRICUS, MARTIN

Epicedion in Obitvm Reverendi . . . Viri . . . D. Philippi Melanthonis. Wittenberg: 1560. V. 42

HENRION, DENIS

L'Usage du Compas de Proportion. Rouen: 1614? V. 41

HENRIQUES DE SOUSA, JOAO

Discurso Politico Sobre o Juro do Dinheiro. Lisbon: 1786. V. 45

HENRIQUES, J. O.

The War History of 1st Battalion Queen's Westmisnter Rifles. 1914-1918. London: 1923. V. 45

HENRISONE, ROBERT

The Trail of the Paddok & the Mous From the Morall Bagilillis of Esope. By Robert Henrisone. With watercolor illustrations by Nicholas Parry. Shropshire: 1986. V. 37

HENRY, A.

Biblia Pauperum. London: 1986. V. 39

HENRY, ALEXANDER

Henry's Journal, Covering Adventures and Experiences in the Fur Trade on the Red River, 1799-1801. Winnipeg: 1888. V. 37

The Manuscript Journals of Alexander Henry, Fur Trader of the Northwest Company, and of David Thompson, Official Geographer and Explorer of the Same Company. New York: 1897. V. 43; 46

New Light on the Early History of the Greater Northwest. New York: 1897. V. 37; 38; 39; 40; 42; 43; 44; 45; 46

Travels & Adventures in Canada and the Indian Territories Between the Years 1760 and 1776. Boston: 1901. V. 43

Travels and Adventures in Canada and the Indian Territories, Between the Years 1760 and 1766. New York: 1809. V. 38; 39; 40; 41; 42; 43; 46

Travels and Adventures in Canada and the Indian Territories Between the Years 1760 and 1776. Toronto: 1901. V. 44

HENRY, B. C.

Ling-Nam or Interior Views of Southern China Including Explorations in the Hithertoo Untraversed Island of Hainan. London: 1886. V. 43

HENRY, CHARLES

Elements d'une Theorie Generale de la Dynamogenie Autrement dit du Contraste, du Rythme et de la Mesure Avec Applications Speciales aux Sensations Visuelle et Auditive. Paris: 1889. V. 42

HENRY, DAVID 1710-1792

The Complete English Farmer. London: 1771. V. 42

An Historical Account of all the Voyages Round the World, Performed by English Navigators . . . London: 1773. V. 45

An Historical account of All the Voyages Around the World, Performed by English Navigators. London: 1774. V. 41; 45

An Historical Account of the Curiosities of London and Westminster . . . London: 1777. V. 43

An Historical Description of the Tower of London, and Its Curiousities. London: 1788. V. 38

HENRY, E. R.

Classification and Uses of Finger Prints. London: 1900. V. 45

HENRY, FREDERICK

Standard History of the Medical Profession of Philadelphia. Chicago: 1897. V. 38

HENRY, G. M.

Coloured Plates of the Birds of Ceylon. Ceylon: 1927-35. V. 46

Coloured Plates of the Birds of Ceylon. Colombo: 1927-35. V. 42

HENRY, GUSTAVUS A.

Speech of Hon. Gustavus A. Henry, of Tennessee, in the Senate of the Confederate States, November 29, 1864. Richmond: 1864. V. 38

HENRY, H. S.

De-Luxe Illustrated Catalogue of Paintings by 'The Men of 1830' Forming the Private Collection of . . . New York: 1907. V. 44

HENRY, J. T.

The Early and Later History of Petroleum . . . Its Development in Western Pennsylvania . . . Philadelphia: 1873. V. 38; 43; 45

HENRY, JAMES

An Account of the Proceedings of the Government Metropolitan Police in the City of Canton. Dublin: 1840. V. 40; 43; 45

Poems Chiefly Philosophical in Continuation of My Book and a Half Year's Poems. Dresden: 1856. V. 40

HENRY, JAMES P.

Resources of the State of Arkansas with Description of Counties, Railroads, Mines and the City of Little Rock. Little Rock: 1873. V. 45; 46

HENRY, JOHN JOSEPH

Account of Arnold's Campaign Against Quebec, and of the Hardships and Sufferings of that Band of Heroes and Travelers . . . Albany: 1877. V. 44

An Accurate and Interesting Account of the Hardships and Sufferings of that Band of Heroes, Who Traversed the Wilderness in the Campaign Against Quebec in 1775. Lancaster: 1812. V. 37; 39; 41; 43

HENRY, JOSEPH

The Papers of Joseph Henry. Washington: 1972-81. V. 42; 44

Report of the Trial of Joseph Henry, Esq. in the Sherrif's Court, on . . . Jan. 20, 1809 for Criminal Conversation with Lady Emily Best. London: 1809. V. 38

Scientific Writings of . . . Washington: 1887, 1886. V. 40

HENRY, LEIGH

A Musical Causerie. London: 1922. V. 41

HENRY, MATTHEW 1662-1714

The Communicant's Companion. Boston: 1716. V. 39

An Exposition of the Old and New Testament. London: 1800. V. 39

A Short Account of the Life of Lieutenant Illidge, Who Was in the Militia of the County of Chester Near Fifty Years. London: 1710. V. 41

HENRY, MATTHEW BARKER

Greenwich Hospital, a Series of Naval Sketches Descriptive of othe Life of a Man-of-War's Man. London: 1826. V. 39; 41; 43

HENRY; or the Juvenile Traveller. London: 1836. V. 45

HENRY, ROBERT

The History of Great Britain from the First Invasion of it by the Romans Under Julius Caesara. London: 1771-85. V. 37

HENRY, ROBERT SELPH

the Story of Reconstruction. Indianapolis: 1938. V. 41; 46

HENRY, SAMUEL

A New and Complete American Family Herbal. New York: 1814. V. 45

HENRY, STUART

Hours with Famous Parisians. Chicago: 1897. V. 38

HENRY, THOMAS CHARLTON

Letters to an Anxious Inquirer, Designed to Relieve the Difficulties of a Friend, Under Serious Impressions. Charleston: 1827. V. 44

HENRY, WILLIAM

An Appeal to the people of Ireland. Occasioned by the insinuations and misrepresentations of the author of a weekly paper, entitled, The Censor. Proving that the principles laid down in that paper, and the author's . . . Dublin: 1749. V. 37

The Elements of Experimental Chemistry . . . Philadelphia: 1817. V. 43

An Epitome of Chemistry, in Three Parts. Philadelphia: 1802. V. 42

HENRY, WILLIAM CHARLES

Memoirs of the Life and Scientific Researches of John Dalton. London: 1854. V. 42

HENRY, WILLIAM S.

Campaign Sketches of the War with Mexico. New York: 1847. V. 38; 40; 46

HENSHALL, JAMES A.

Bass, Pike, Perch and Others. New York: 1903. V. 37

Camping and Cruising in Florida. Cincinnati: 1888. V. 39

HENSHALL, SAMUEL

Strictures on the Late Motions of the Duke of Leinster, in the House of Peers. London: 1798. V. 39

HENSHAW, J. W.

Mountain Wild Flowers of America. Boston: 1906. V. 45

Wild Flowers of the North American Mountains. New York: 1915. V. 46

HENSLOW, J. S.

Syllabus of a Course of Botanical Lectures. Cambridge: 1828. V. 40

HENSLOW, T. GEOFFREY W.

Ye Sundial booke. London: 1935. V. 46

HENSLOWE, PHILIP

Henslowe's Diary. (with) Henslowe's Papers. London: 1904-08. V. 45

HENSMAN, HOWARD

The Afghan War of 1879-80. London: 1882. V. 42

HENSMAN, MARY

Dante Map. London: 1892. V. 38

HENSON, JOSIAH

Truth Stranger than Fiction. Father Henson's Story of His Own Life. Boston: 1858. V. 43; 46

HENTY, G. A.

St. Bartholomew's Eve. 1894. V. 41

HENTY, GEORGE ALFRED 1832-1902

At the Point of the Bayonet. London: 1902. V. 38

Brains and Bravery. London: 1903. V. 37; 46

By Sheer Luck. London: 1884/83. V. 46

By Conduct and Couragae. London: 1905. V. 37

A Roving Commission. Or Through the Black Insurrection of Hayti. London: 1900. V. 38

St. George for England. London: 1910. V. 46

A Search for a Secret. London: 1867. V. 43

Through Three Campaigns. The Story of Chitral, Tirah, and Ashantee. London: 1904. V. 38

The Treasure of the Incas. New York: 1902. V. 44

With Roberts to Pretoria. A Tale of the South African War. London. V. 39; 40

With Cochrane the Dauntless. London: 1897. V. 46

With Moore at Corunna. London: 1898. V. 46

With Roberts to Pretoria. London: 1902. V. 38

With the Allies to Pekin. London: 1904. V. 38

Won by the Sword. London: 1900. V. 38

HENTZE, C.

Chinese Tomb Figures. A Study in the Beliefs and Folklore of Ancient China. London: 1928. V. 39; 46

HENTZNER, PAUL

Travels in England, During the Reign of Queen Elizabeth . . . London: 1797. V. 37; 38

HENTZY, RODOLPHE

Promenade Pittoresque dans l'Eveche due Bale. The Hague: 1808-9. V. 46

HENWOOD, GEORGE

Four Lectures on Geology and Mining, Read at the Mechanics' Instituions, Leeds, Hull, Bradford, Harrogate &c. London: 1855. V. 40

HEPBURN, GEORGE BUCHAN

Observations on the Bill for the Sale of Corn by Weight, and for Preventing Frauds in the Sale of Corn by Allowance, or Addition, or by Adulteration . . . Edinburgh: 1796. V. 39

HEPBURN, H. P.

Reports of Cases Argued and Determined in the Supreme Court of the State of California, in the Year 1852. Philadelphia: 1854. V. 37

HEPBURN, J. D.

Twenty Years in Khama's Country, and Pioneering Among the Batauana of Lake Ngami, Told in the Letters. London: 1895. V. 39

HEPBURN, ROBERT

A Discourse Concerning the Character of a man of Genius. Edinburgh: 1715. V. 45

HEPPELWHITE, A.

The Cabinet Maker an Upholster's Guide; or, Repository of Designs for Every Article of Household Furniture . . . With a Scale to each, and an Explanation in Letterpress. Also the Plan of a Room, shewing the Proper Distribution of the Furniture . . . London: 1789. V. 37

HEPPENSTALL, RAYNER

Middleton Murry - a Study in Excellent Normality. London: 1934. V. 40

HEPWORTH, BARBARA

Carvings and Drawings. London: 1952. V. 46

HERACLIDES PONTICUS d. 307 BC

Allegoriae in Homeri Fabulas de Diis, Nunc Primum e Graeco Sermone in Latinum Translatae: Conrado Gesnero Medico Tigurino Interprete. Basle: 1544. V. 40

HERAD, ISAAC V. D.

History of the Sioux War and Massacres of 1862 and 1864. New York: 1863. V. 40

HERALD, CHANDOS

The Black Prince, an Historical Poem. London: 1842. V. 40

THE HERALDRY of Nature; or, Instructions for the King at Arms . . . London: 1785. V. 39; 45

HERALDRY of New Helvetia, With Thirty-Two Cattle Brands and Ear Marks Reproduced from the Original Certificates Issued at Sutter's Fort 1845 to 1848. San Francisco;: 1945. V. 37; 38

HERALD'S Commemorative Exhibition 1484-1934, Held at The College of Arms, Engraved and Illustrated Catalogue. London: 1936. V. 41; 42

HERALDUS, DESIDERIUS

Adversariorvm Libri Dvo. Paris: 1599. V. 44

HERAUD, JOHN A.

Voyages Up the Mediterranean and in the Indian Seas; with Memoirs . . . London: 1837. V. 42

HERBARIUS. Herbolario Volgare, Nelquale se Dimostra a Conoscer le Herbe & le Sue Virtu, & il Modo di Operale, con Molti Altri Simplici, di Novo Venute in Luce & di Latino in Volgare Tradutte . . . Venice: 1536. V. 46

HERBART, JOHANN FRIEDRICH

Allgemeine Padagogik aus dem Zweck der Erziehung Abgeleitet. Gottingen: 1806. V. 41; 45

A Text Book in Psychology: an Attempt to Fund the Science of Psychology on Experience, Metaphysics and Mathematics. New York: 1891. V. 42

HERBELOT, BARTH D'

Bibliotheque Orientale . . . Paris: 1697. V. 45

HERBERT, A. P.

Double Demon (In) Four One-Act Plays. Oxford: 1923. V. 44

Topsy, M.P. London: 1929. V. 44

HERBERT, ALAN PATRICK

No Boats on the River. London;: 1932. V. 37

Poor Poems and Rotten Rhymes. Winchester: 1910. V. 37; 41; 44

HERBERT, ANTHONY

Conquest to Nowhere. Herminie: 1955. V. 44

HERBERT, CHARLES

A Relic of Revolution . . . American Prisoners Captured on the High Seas and Carried into Plymouth England . . . 1776. Boston: 1847. V. 41; 42

Translations, Imitations and Other Poems. London: 1808. V. 45

HERBERT, D.

Fish and Fisheries. London: 1894. V. 40

HERBERT, EDWARD 1648?-1698

A Short Account of the Authorities in Law, Upon Whch Judgement was given in Sir Edw. Hales His Case, Written by Sir Edw. Herbert . . . London: 1688. V. 38; 40

Works. London: 1730. V. 38

HERBERT, EDWARD HERBERT, BARON 1583-1648

The Autobiography of Edward Lord Herbert of Cherbury. 1928. V. 38

The Autobiography of Edward Lord Herbert of Cherbury. Newtown: 1928. V. 38; 39; 40; 43; 44; 45

Dialogue Between a Tutor and His Pupil. London: 1768. V. 38

The Life and Raigne of King Henry the Eighth. London: 1649. V. 42

The Life and Reign of King Henry the Eighth. London: 1682. V. 41

Life of Edward, Lord Herbert of Cherbury, by Himself. Strawberry Hill: 1764. V. 39

The Life of Edward Herbert of Cherbury. Written by Himself. London: 1770. V. 38

The Life Written by Himself. Dublin: 1771. V. 44

The Life of Edward Lord Herbert of Cherbury. London: 1778. V. 38; 40; 41

HERBERT, FRANK

Chapter House Dune. 1985. V. 37; 39

Chapter House Dune. London: 1985. V. 45

The Dragon in the Sea. 1956. V. 43; 45

Dune. New York: 1963-65. V. 42

Dune. New York: 1965. V. 42

Dune. Philadelphia & New York: 1965. V. 39

Dune. London: 1966. V. 44; 45

Dune. London: 1966. V. 45

Dune Messiah. 1969. V. 43

Dune Messiah. New York: 1969. V. 37; 39; 42

God Emperor of Dune. New York: 1981. V. 46

Eye. Berkley: 1985. V. 44

40 Years Prospecting and Mining in the Black Hills of South Dakota. Rapid City: 1921. V. 39; 43; 45

God Emperor of Dune. New York: 1981. V. 39; 43; 44

Heretics of Dune. New York: 1981. V. 43

Heretics of Dune. London: 1984. V. 43

The Jesus Incident. 1969. V. 39

Whipping the Star. New York: 1970. V. 44

HERBERT, GEORGE 1593-1633

English Works. Boston: 1905. V. 40; 46

The English Works of George Herbert. Boston & New York: 1905. V. 41; 43; 46

The English Works. Boston and New York: 1915. V. 46

Herbert's Remains. London: 1652. V. 38; 39; 41; 44; 45

Poems. Newtown: 1923. V. 37; 40; 42

Poems. Newtown: 1928. V. 41

The Poetical Works of . . . New York: 1871. V. 45

A Priest to the Temple. London: 1675. V. 38; 43; 45

The Temple. Sacred Poems and Private Ejaculations. Cambridge: 1633. V. 42; 45

The Temple, Sacred Poems & Private Ejaculations. London: 1850. V. 37; 38; 40

The Temple. Sacred Poems and Private Ejaculations. Prefatory Note by Francis Meynell. London: 1927. V. 37; 39; 40; 41; 43; 44; 45

The Works and Bishop Hall's Satires and Psalms. London: 1861. V. 37; 39

The Works of George Herbert. London: 1861. V. 38; 41

The Works in Prose and Verse. London: 1865. V. 40

Works In Prose and Verse. London: 1853. V. 37

HERBERT, HENRY, & CO.

London (Illustrated). A Complete Guide to the Places of Amusement, Objects of Interest, Parks, Clubs, Markets . . . London: 1876. V. 40

HERBERT, HENRY WILLIAM 1807-1858

American Game in Its Seasons. New York: 1853. V. 44

The Brothers. New York: 1835. V. 43; 45

The Chevaliers of France from the Crusaders to the Marechals of Louis XIV. New York: 1853. V. 44

The Complete Manual for Young Sportsmen. New York: 1856. V. 40

Cromwell. New York: 1838. V. 39; 46

Field Sports in the United States, and the British Provinces of America. London: 1848. V. 39

Field Sports in the United States and the British Provinces of America. New York: 1849. V. 42; 44

Frank Forester and His Friends; or, Woodland Adventures in the Middle States of North America . . . London: 1849. V. 39

Frank Forester's Fish and Fishing of the United States and British Provinces of North America. London: 1849. V. 44

Frank Forester's Fish and Fishing of the United States and British Provinces of North America. (with) Supplement . . . New York: 1849/1850. V. 44

Frank Forester's Horse and Horsemanship of the United States and British Provinces of North America. New York: 1857. V. 40; 44

Frank Forester's Fugitive Sporting Sketches . . . Westfield: 1879. V. 44

Frank Forester's Sporting Scenes and Characters. Philadelphia: 1881. V. 39

Frank Forester's Field Sports of the United States . . . North America. New York: 1858. V. 37

Frank Forester's Sporting Scenes and Characters. Philadelphia: 1857. V. 44

The Miller of Martigne. New York: 1847. V. 43

My Shooting Box by Frank Forester . . . Philadelphia. V. 43

The Silent Rifleman. New York: 1875. V. 44

Sporting Scenes and Sundry Sketches. New York: 1842. V. 40; 41; 44

Sporting Scenes and Sundry Sketches; Being the Miscellaneous Writings of J. Cypress, Jr. New York: 1942. V. 44

HERBERT, HENRY WILLIAM 1807-1858 continued

The Tricks and Traps of Horse Dealers. New York: 1858. V. 42

Trouting Along the Catasauqua. New York: 1927. V. 43; 44

The Warwick Woodlands. New York: 1934. V. 44

HERBERT, J. A.

Illuminated Manuscripts. London. V. 40

Illuminated Manuscripts. London: 1911. V. 41; 42

Illuminated manuscripts. (1911). V. 37

Titus and Vespasian or the Destruction of Jerusalem in Rhymed Couplets. London: 1905. V. 44

HERBERT, JAMES

The Fog. London: 1975. V. 41

The Rats. London: 1974. V. 40

HERBERT, LUKE

The Engineer's and Mechanic's Encyclopaedia, Comprehending Practical Illustrations of the Machinery and Processes Employed in Every Description of Manufacture of the British Empire. London: 1847-35. V. 42

The Engineers and Mechanics Encyclopaedia. London: 1848. V. 42

HERBERT, MARY ELIZABETH

Abyssinia and Its Apostle. London: 1867. V. 37

HERBERT, MARY ELIZABETH A'COURT HERBERT, BARONESS 1822-1911

Impressions of Spain in 1866. London: 1867. V. 43

HERBERT, R. L.

Barbizon Revisited: Essays and Catalogue. San Francisco: 1963. V. 46

HERBERT, RICHARD A.

Modern Maine, Its Historic Background, People and Resources. New York: 1951. V. 38

HERBERT, THOMAS

A Relation of Some Yeares Travaile, Begunne anno 1626 Into Afrique and . . . Asia . . . London: 1634. V. 42; 44

Some Years Travels into Divers Parts of Asia and Afrique. London: 1638. V. 40

Some Years Travels into Divers Parts of Africa and Asia the Great. London: 1677. V. 42; 43; 45

HERBERT, WILLIAM 1771-1851

Antiquities of the Inns of Court and Chancery. London: 1804. V. 38; 40

The History of the Twelve Great Livery Companies of London . . . London: 1836-37. V. 37; 39; 41

Miscellaneous Poetry. London: 1804-06. V. 38; 39

Musae Etonenses. London: 1755. V. 38

Translations from the German, Danish, &c. To Which is Added Miscellaneous Poetry, Part Second, Translations from the Italian, Spanish, Portuguese, German &c. with Select Icelandic Poetry . . . London: 1804-06. V. 42; 43

Works. London: 1838-42. V. 43; 45

HERBERT, WILLIAM HARRIS

Field Sports in the United States, and the British Provinces of America. London: 1848. V. 42

HERBERT, WILLIAM V.

The Defence of Plevna 1877. London: 1895. V. 45

HERBERT, ZBIGNIEW

Selected Poems. Harmondsworth: 1968. V. 38

HERBERTS, K.

Oriental Lacquer: Art and Technique. New York. V. 38

Oriental Lacquer: Art and Technique. New York. V. 41

Oriental Lacquer; Art and Technique. New York: 1963. V. 40

HERBINIO, JOHANNE

Dissertationes de Admirandis Mundi Cataractis Supra & Subterraneis, Earumque Principio, Elementorum Circulatione . . . Amsterdam: 1678. V. 42

HERBINUS, JAN

Dissertationes de Admirandis Mundi Cataractis Supra & Subetrraneis, Earumque Principio, Elementorum Circulaione . . . Amsterdam: 1678. V. 43

HERBST, JOSEPHINE

Rope of Gold. New York: 1939. V. 46

HERD, DAVID

Ancient and Modern Spanish Songs, Heroic Ballads, etc. Glasgow: 1869. V. 43

HERDER, JOHANN GOTTFRIED

Abhandlung uber den Ursprung der Sprache. Berlin: 1772. V. 38

Ideen zur Philosophie der Geschichte der Menschheit. Riga und Leipzig: 1784-1891. V. 38; 41; 45

Outlines of a Philosophy of the History of Man. London: 1800. V. 39

Sammtliche Werke. Stuttgart und Tubingen: 1827-30. V. 43; 45

HERDER, JOHN N.

General Orders, No. 9. Head Quarters Post Pilot Knob. Pilot Knob: 1864. V. 39

HERDMAN, CHARLOTTE

The Return of the Fairies. Dublin: 1824. V. 39

HERDMAN, WILLIAM G.

Pictorial Relics of Ancient Liverpool. London: 1856. V. 37; 39

Pictorial Relics of Ancient Liverpool. Liverpool: 1857. V. 39

Pictorial Relics of Ancient Liverpool. Liverpool: 1878. V. 37; 39; 40; 46

Relics of Ancient Liverpool. London: 1878. V. 37

Views in Modern Liverpool. Liverpool: 1864. V. 44

HERDSON, HENRY

Ars Memoriae, the Art of Memory Made Plain. (with) Ars Mnemonica, sive Hersonus Bruxiatus. London: 1654. V. 46

HERE and There, a Book of Transformation Pictures. London: 1890. V. 38

HERE Begynneth a Lityll Treatise . . . of the Arte & Crafte to Knowe Well to Dye . . . N.P.. V. 38

HEREFORD, CHARLES

The History of France, from the First Establishment of that Monarchy to the Present Revolution. Dublin: 1791. V. 40

HERFORD, OLIVER

An Alphabet of Celebrities. Boston: 1889. V. 46

An Alphabet of Celebrities. Boston: 1899. V. 37; 40; 42

An Alphabet of Celebrities. Boston: 1900. V. 44

Artful Anticks. New York: 1894. V. 41

The Kitten's Garden of Verses. New York: 1911. V. 37

The Laughing Willow. New York: 1918. V. 46

HERGESHEIMER, JOSEPH

Berlin. New York: 1932. V. 44

The Limestome Tree. New York: 1931. V. 44

San Cristobal de la Habana. New York: 1920. V. 44

Sheridan: A Military Narrative. Boston: 1931. V. 44

Sheridan: a Military Narrative. Boston & New York: 1931. V. 45

Tampico: A Novel. New York: 1926. V. 37; 44

The Three Black Pennys. New York: 1930. V. 39

HERICOURT, LOUIS JULIEN

De Academia Suessionensi, Cum Epistolis Ad Familiares. Montalban: 1688. V. 45

HERIGONE, PIERRE

Cursus Mathematicus Nova, Brevi et Clara Methodo Demonstratus . . . Paris: 1634-37-42. V. 42

HERING, GEORGE

Sketches on the Danube in Hungary and Transylania. London: 1838. V. 43

HERING, GEORGE E.

The Mountains and Lakes of Switzerland, the Tyrol and Italy. London: 1847. V. 39; 41

HERING, OSWALD C.

Concrete and Stucco Houses. New York: 1912. V. 44

HERING, RUDOLPH

Survey of Water-Way From Lake Michigan to the Illinois River. Washington: 1890. V. 37

HERIOT, GEORGE

Analyses of New Voyages and Travels, Lately Published in London. London: 1807. V. 42

Geroge Heriot. Montreal: 1973. V. 43

Travels through the Canadas, Containing a Description of the Picturesque Scenery on Some of the Rivers and Lakes . . . London: 1807. V. 37; 38; 40; 42; 44; 45

Travels through the Canadas, Containing a Description of the Picturesque Scenery on Some of the Rivers and Lakes . . . . Philadelphia: 1813. V. 41

Travels through the Canadas . . . Edmonton: 1971. V. 42

HERIOT, JOHANNES

Liber Discipuli de Eruditione Christifdelum. Basel: 1485. V. 45

HERLE, CHARLES

Ahab's Fall by His Prophets Flatteries . . . London: 1644. V. 42

HERMAN MILLER FURNITURE CO.

THE Herman Miller Collection: Furniture Designed by George Nelson and Charles Eames with Occasional Pieces by Isamu Noguchi, Peter Hvidt and O.M. Nielsen. Zeeland: 1952. V. 46

HERMAN, WILLIAM

The Dance of Death. San Francisco: 1877. V. 38

HERMAN, WOLFFGANG

Mariae Ehren Kraentz-Lein. Augsburg: 1652. V. 38; 41

HERMANNIDES, RUTGER

Britannia Magna Sive Angliae, Scotiae, Hiberniae . . . Amstelodami: 1661. V. 43

HERMANT, ABEL

Entretiens sur la Grammaire Francaise. Paris: 1923. V. 37

HERMES, GERTRUDE

Wood Engravings by Gertrude Hermes Being Illustrations to Selborne . . . 1988. V. 44

Wood Engravings by Gertrude Hermes. Newtown: 1988. V. 42; 45

HERMES TRISMEGISTUS

Pymander Merevrii Trismegisti Cum Commento Fratris Hannibalis Rosseli . . . Liber III. Cracow: 1586. V. 45

HERMES TRISMEGISTUS, MERCURIUS

The Divine Pymander . . . London: 1650. V. 38

HERMES, WILLIAM

Studies of Trees. Berlin: 1860? V. 42

HERMETIC Waste. 1986. V. 40

THE HERMETICAL Triumph. London: 1723? V. 37

THE HERMIT of the Chesapeake; or, Lessons of a Lifetime. Philadelphia: 1869. V. 44

HERMITE, JAQUES L'

Journael van der Naussauche Vioot, ofte Beschrijvingh van der Voyagie om den Grantschen Aert-Kloot, Gerdaen met elf Schepen . . . Amsterdam: 1648. V. 41

HERNANDEZ DE CORDOBA, FRANCISCO

The Discovery of Yucatan . . . Berkeley: 1942. V. 42

HERNANDEZ, DON JOSE DE LA LUZ

Memoir on the Salubrity of the Isle of Pines. Habana: 1857. V. 41

HERNANDEZ, FRANCISCO

Nova Plantarum, Animalium, et Mineralium Mexicanorum Historia. Rome: 1651. V. 39; 45; 46

Quatro Libros. De la Naturaleza, y Virtudes de las Plantas, y Animales que Estan Recevidos en el Uso de Medicina en la Nueva Espana . . . Mexico: 1615. V. 41

HERNANDEZ, JAMES

A Philosophical and Practical Essay on the Gold and Silver Mines of Mexico and Peru. London: 1755. V. 43

HERNANDEZ, JOSE

The Gaucho Martin Fierro. Oxford: 1935. V. 41

HERNDERSON, J. T.

Manual of Cattle: for the Use of the Farmers of Georgia. Atlanta: 1880. V. 38

HERNDON, DALLAS T.

Centennial History of Arkansas. Chicago: 1922. V. 38; 39

HERNDON, SARAH RAYMOND

Days on the Road Crossing the Plains in 1865. New York: 1902. V. 37; 38; 39; 40; 43; 45

HERNDON, WILLIAM

Exploration of the Valley of the Amazon: Made Under Direction of the Navy Department. Washington: 1853. V. 44

Lincoln and Ann Rutledge: and the Pioneers of New Salem. Herrin: 1945. V. 44

HERNDON, WILLIAM H.

Abraham Lincoln: The True Story of a Great Life. New York: 1892. V. 40; 41; 43

Herndon's Lincoln. The True Story of a Great Life . . . The History & Personal Recollections of Abraham Lincoln. Chicago: 1889. V. 37; 39

Herndon's Lincoln: The True Story of a Great Life. Chicago and New York: and: 1889. V. 45

Herndon's Lincoln, the True Story of a Great Life. The History and Personal Recollections of Abraham Lincoln. Chicago, New York & San: 1889. V. 39

Herndon's Lincoln. The True Story of a Great Life. Chicago: 1890. V. 40

HERNDON, WILLIAM LEWIS

Exploration of the Valley of the Amazon. Washington: 1853. V. 39; 44

Exploration of the Valley of the Amazon, Made Under Direction of the Navy Department. Washington: 1853, 1854. V. 37; 39

Exploration of the Valley of the Amazon, Made Under the Direction of the Navy Department. Washington: 1854. V. 37; 39; 40; 43

HERNE, PEREGRINE

Perils and Pleasures of a Hunter's Life; or The Romance of Hunting. Philadelphia: 1859. V. 46

Perils and Pleasures of a Hunter's Life; or, the Romance of Hunting. Boston: 1854. V. 37

HERNE, SAMUEL

A Journey from Prince of Wales Fort in Hudson's Bay, to the Northern Ocean. London: 1795. V. 38

HERNMARCK, CARL

The Art of the European Silversmith 1430-1830. London: and New York: 1977. V. 44

HERO OF ALEXANDRIA

De Gli Automati, Overo Machine se Moventi, Libri Due, Tradotte dal greco da Bernardino Baldi Abbato di Guastalla. Venice: 1589. V. 41

Liber de Machinis Bellicis Necnon de Geodaesia. Venice: 1572. V. 39

(Pneumatics). Gli Artifitiosi et Curiosi Moti Spiritale di Herrone. Ferrara: 1589. V. 45

Spiritalium Liber. Urbino: 1575. V. 38; 41; 45

HERO OF ALEXNADRIA

Gli Artificiosi, e Cvriosi Moti Spiritali di Herone. Bologna: 1647. V. 39

HEROCIAL Epistle from Death to Benjamin Moseley, M.D. London: 1810. V. 39

HERODIAN

Historiarium Libri VIII. Basle: 1535? V. 40; 45

Historiarum Libri VIII. Genovae: 1581. V. 37; 38; 40

(Greek Title). Historiarum, Libri VIII. Lugduni: 1611. V. 40; 42; 44

Historie of Twenty Roman Caesars, and Emperors . . . London: 1635. V. 43

A Marci Principatu Historiarum Libri Octo. Louvain: 1525. V. 37; 42

HERODIANIUS

Der Fuertrefflich Griechisch Geschichtsschreiber Herodianus/ den der Hochgelert Angelus Politianus inn das Latein . . . Augsburg: 1531. V. 41

HERODIANUS

H. Herodiani Histor. Lib. VIII. cum Angeli Politiani Interpretatione . . . Geneva: 1581. V. 46

Historia de Imperio Post Marcum. Bologna: 1493. V. 46

Historiae de Imperio Post Marcum: vel, de Suis Temporibus. Lugduni: 1559. V. 46

HERODOTUS

Egypt. 1989. V. 44

Egypt. Greenbae: 1989. V. 44

(Greek title: then) Libri Novem, Quibus Musarum Indita Sunt Nomina . . . ad Haec Georgii Gemisti, qui et Pletho Dicitur, de iis Quae Post Pugnam ad Mantineam Gesta Sunt, Libri II. Basle: 1541. V. 43

(Greek Title) Followed by Latin title Herodoti Libri Novem Quibus Musarum Indita Sunt Nomina. Venice: 1502. V. 40

Herodotus, Translated from the Greek, with Notes. London: 1812. V. 45

Historia. Oxford: 1809. V. 43

Historiae Lib. IX. Frankfurt: 1594. V. 40; 45

Historiarum Libri IX. Leyden: 1715. V. 39

The Histories. Haarlem: 1958. V. 45

The History of Herodotus. London: 1737. V. 44

The History of Herodotus. Oxford: 1824. V. 43

History. London: 1875. V. 40

The History of Herodotus of Halicarnassus. Bloomsbury: 1935. V. 38; 39; 41; 45

The History. London: 1935. V. 38; 42; 44; 45

The Life and Travels of Herodotus. London: 1855. V. 44

THE HEROIC Epistle Answered: by the R---- H----- Lord C------. London: 1776. V. 40

HEROIC Epistle to Joseph Priestley. London: 1791. V. 40
HEROIC Epistle to Joseph Priestley. London: 1791. V. 39

AN HEROIC Epistle to Mr. Winsor, the Patentee of the Hydro-Carbonic Gas Lights, and Founder of the National Light and Heat Company. London: 1808. V. 40

HEROICAL Epistle from Death to Benjamin Moseley M.D. London: 1810. V. 42

HEROLT, JOHANNES

Liber Discipuli de Eruditione Christifidelium. Strassburg: 1490. V. 45

Sermones Discipuli (de Tempore per Circulum Anni. Sermones de Sanctis. Promptuarium Exemplorum De Miraculis BVM). Lyon: 1490. V. 38

HERON-ALLEN, EDWARD

Selsey Bill; Historic and Prehistoric. London: 1911. V. 38; 44; 45

Violin-Making, As It Was and Is . . . London: 1885. V. 42; 44; 45

HERON, DENIS CAULFIELD

The Constitutional History of the University of Dublin with Some Account of Its Present Condition and Suggestions for Improvement. Dublin: 1847. V. 42

HERON PRESS

Poems Between the Body & the Soul. Deefield: 1975. V. 37

HERON, ROBERT

The Comforts of Human Life; or Smiles and Laughter of Charles Chearful and Martin Merryfellow. London: 1807. V. 37; 42; 45

Notes; Printed but Not Published. Grantham: 1850. V. 39

Observations Made in a Journey Through the Western Counties of Scotland in the Autumn of MDCCXCII . . . Perth: 1793. V. 44; 46

HERONDAS

The Mimiambs of Herondas. London. V. 40; 43

The Mimiambs. London: 1926. V. 46

HERPORT, ALBRECHT

Eine Kurtze Ost-Indianischen Insulen und Landt-Schafften Gelegenheit de Einwohneren Sitten und gottes-Dienst Allerley Fruchten und Wilden Thieren Beschaffenheit Sampt Etlichen Nachdencklichen . . . Berne: 1669. V. 41

HERR, GEORGE

Episodes of the Civil War . . . San Francisco: 1890. V. 42

HERR, MICHAEL

Dispatches. New York: 1977. V. 39; 43; 45

Dispatches. New York: 1978. V. 44

HERRE, H.

The Genera of the Mesembryanthemaceae. Cape Town: 1971. V. 46

HERRENSCHWAND

De l'Economie Politique et Morale de l'Espece Humaine. London: 1796. V. 45

De l'Economie Politique et Morale de l'Espece Humaine. (with) Du Vrai Principe Actif de l'Economie Politique. London: 1796/97. V. 41

HERRERA, ANTONIO DE

Descripcion de las Indias Occidentales . . . (with) Historia General . . . Madrid: 1726-30. V. 38

The General History of the Vast Continent and Islands of America, Commonly Called the West Indies, etc. London: 1725. V. 37; 43

Prima (Secundo, Tercera) Parte de la Historia General del Mundo. Valladolid: 1606, 1612. V. 40

Prima (Secunda, Tercera) Parte de la Historia General dei Mundo. Valladolid: 1612. V. 45

HERRERA, GABRIEL ALONSO DE

Libro de Agricultura, que Tracta de la Labranca y Crianca, y de Muchas Otras Particularidades y Provechos del Campo. Medina del Campo: 1584. V. 37; 40

HERRERA Y TORDESILLAS, ANTONIO DE

Histoire General des Voyages et Conquestes des Castillans, dans les Isles & Terreferme des Indes Occidentales. Paris: 1660. V. 39

HERRICK, FRANCIS HOBART

The American Eagle. New York: 1934. V. 39; 40

Audubon the Naturalist. A History of His Life and Times. New York: 1917. V. 39

HERRICK, H. W.

Water Color Painting: Description of Materials with Direction for Their Use in Elementary Practice (and) Sketching from Nature in Water Color. New York: 1882. V. 46

HERRICK, JAMES

A Short History of Cardiology. Springfield: 1942. V. 42; 45

HERRICK, ROBERT 1591-1674

Chrysomela. A Selection from the Lyrical Poems of Robert Herrick. London: 1884. V. 37; 40

Chrysomela - a Selection from the Lyrical Poems of Robert Herrick. London: 1892. V. 44

Delighted Earth. London: 1927. V. 46

Delightful Earth: an Extensive Selection from the Hesperides. 1927. V. 40

Herrick's Content-His Grange and His Book of Littles. London and Belfast: 1884. V. 41

Hesperides. London: 1648. V. 39; 40; 43; 44; 45; 46

The Kelmscot Press edition of Poems Chosen Out of the Works of Robert Herrick. (1895). V. 37

Love's Dilemmas. Chicago: 1898. V. 37; 42

One Hundred and Eleven Poems. 1955. V. 38

One Hundred and Eleven Poems. London: 1955. V. 39; 41

One Hundred and Eleven Poems. Waltham St. Lawrence: 1955. V. 46

One Hundred and Eleven Poems. (London): 1934. V. 37

Complete Poems. London: 1876. V. 38; 39

Poems Chosen Out of the Works of Robert Herrick. Hammersmith: 1895. V. 37; 38; 39; 41; 42; 43

Poems Chosen Out of the Works of Robert Herrick. London: 1895. V. 45

Poems Chosen Out of the Work of Robert Herrick. London: 1896. V. 37; 41

The Poetical Works. London: 1928. V. 37; 39; 40; 41; 43; 45; 46

Select poems from the Hseperides, or works both human and divine, with occasional remarks by J.N. (John Nott). Bristol: (1810). V. 37

A Selection from the Lyrical Poems of Robert Herrick. London: 1911. V. 45

Selections from the Poetry. New York: 1882. V. 38; 42

Thanksgiving to God, for His House. Bronxville: 1960. V. 38

HERRICO, SCIPIONE

La Bablionia Distrutta: Poema Heroica; Aggiontovi Dire Idily del Medesimo. Venice: 1624. V. 39

HERRIES, CHARLES

Abstract of Colonel Herries's Instructions for Volunteer Corps of Cavalry, Adapted to the Use of the Volunteer and Militia Cavalry of the United States. Philadelphia: 1811. V. 37

HERRIES, JOHN CHARLES

A Reply to Some Financial Mistatements In and Out of Parliament. London: 1803. V. 39

HERRIES, ROBERT

Sketch of Financial and Commercial Affairs in the Autumn of 1797. London: 1797. V. 45

HERRIES, WILLIAM H.

The Successful Running and Sire Lines of the Modern Thoroughbred Horse . . . London: 1921. V. 42

HERRING, J. H.

Thames Bridges from London to Hampton Court. London. V. 43

HERRING, J. L.

Saturday Night Sketches: Stories of Old Wiregrass Georgia. Boston: 1918. V. 46

HERRING, RICHARD

Paper and Paper Making, Ancient and Modern. London: 1855. V. 46

Paper and Paper Making, Ancient and Modern. London: 1856. V. 38

A Practical Guide to the Varieties and Relative Values of Paper, Illustrated with Samples of Nearly Every Description, and Specially Adapted to the Use of Merchants, shippers, and the Trade . . . London: 1860. V. 38

HERRING, ROBERT

Adam and Evelyn at Kew. London: 1930. V. 38; 40; 42; 44; 45

Cactus Coast. Paris: 1934. V. 37

The Impecunious Captain or Love as Liv'd - a Play on the Lives of George Farquhar and Anne Oldfield. London: 1944. V. 43

HERRING, T. S.

Dover, a Poem Composed on the Top of Shakespear's Cliff. London: 1841. V. 37; 40

HERRLINGER, ROBERT

History of Medical Illustration from Antiquity to A.D. 1600. London: 1970. V. 39; 45

History of Medical Illustration from Antiquity to 1600. New York: 1970. V. 38; 40; 41; 42; 45

HERROD-HEMPSALL, W.

Bee-Keeping New and Old Described with Pen and Camera. London: 1930. V. 37; 38

HERRON-ALLEN, E.

Selsey Bill, Historic and Prehistoric. London: 1911. V. 42

HERRON, DON

Reign of Fear: Fiction and Film of Stephen King. Los Angeles: 1988. V. 40; 44

Reign of Fear: Fiction and Film of Stephen King. Los Angeles/Columbia: 1988. V. 41

HERRON, JOSEPH E.

Explorations in Alaska, 1899, for an All American Overland Route From Cook Inlet, Pacific Ocean, To the Yukon. Washington: 1901. V. 37

HERSCHEL, CAROLINE LUCRETIA

Catalogue of Stars, Taken from Mr. Flamsteed's Observations. London: 1798. V. 38; 41

HERSCHEL, JOHN FREDERICK WILLIAM

Account of a Series of Observations, Made in the Summer of the Year 1825, for the Purpose of Determining the Difference of the Meridians of the Royal Observatories of Greenwich and Paris. V. 40

The Bakerian Lecture on Certain Motions Produced in Fluid Conductors. London: 1824. V. 40

Essays from the Edinburgh and Quarterly Reviews, with Addresses and Other Pieces. London: 1857. V. 39; 45; 46

Light Encyclopaedia Metropolitana. London: 1827. V. 38

A Manual of Scientific Inqiury, Prepared for the Use of Her Majesty's Navy . . . London: 1849. V. 42

A Manual of Scientific Enquiry . . . London: 1851. V. 43

Memoirs of Francis Baily, Esq. London: 1845. V. 40

Observations of the Apparent Distances and Positions of 380 Double and Triple Stars Made in the Years 1821, 1822 and 1823 and Compared with Those of Other Astronomers . . . London: 1825. V. 38; 44

Outlines of Astronomy. London: 1849. V. 37; 38

Preliminary Discourse to the Study of Natural Philosophy. London: 1830. V. 40

Results of Astronomical Observations. London: 1847. V. 38; 40; 45; 46

Third Series of Observations with a Twenty-Feet Reflector . . . (with) Fourth Series of Observations With a Twenty-Feet Reflector . . . London: 1830. V. 41

A Treatise on Astronomy. London: 1833. V. 42; 44; 45

HERSEY, JOHN

Hiroshima. 1983. V. 39; 40; 41

Hiroshima. New York: 1983. V. 37; 38; 39; 40; 41; 42

HERSEY, S.

Business Directory and Gazetteer of Bucks County, Pennsylvania . . . Wilmington: 1871. V. 39; 41

HERSEY, THOMAS

The Midwife's Practical Directory; or, Woman's Confidential Friend. Philadelphia: 1861. V. 43

HERSHKOVITZ, P.

Living New World Monkeys (Platyrrhini). Chicago: 1977. V. 37

HERTELL, THOMAS

The People's Rights Re-Claimed . . . New York: 1826. V. 45

HERTER, CHRISTIAN ARCHIBALD

On Finfantilism from Chronic Intestinal Infection. New York: 1908. V. 46

HERTFELDER, BERHARD

Basilica S. S. Udalrici et Afrae . . . Historice Descripta . . . Augsburg: 1653. V. 44

HERTFORD, FRANCIS INGRAM SEYMOUR CONWAY, 2ND MARQUIS OF 1743-1822

A Letter to the Belfast Fist Company of Volunteers, in the Province of Ulster. Belfast: 1782. V. 46

HERTFORDSHIRE NATURAL HISTORY SOCIETY AND FIELD CLUB

Transactions. London: 1892-1908. V. 44

HERTODT, JOHANN FERDINAND

Crocologia Seu Curiosa Croci Regis Vegetabilium Enucleatio Continens Illius Etymologiam . . . Jena: 1671. V. 46

HERTSLET, EDWARD

The Map of Africa by Treaty. London: 1894. V. 42

HERTSLET, EVELYN M.

Ranch Life in California. London: 1886. V. 38

HERTSLET, LEWIS 1787-1870

A Complete Collection of the Treaties and Conventions at Present Subsisting Between Great Britain and Foreign Powers . . . London: 1820-27. V. 43

A Complete Collection of the Treatises and Conventions at Present Subsisting Between Great Britain and Foreign Powers . . . London: 1827. V. 46

A Complete Collection of the Treaties and Conventions and Reciprocal Regulations at Present Subsisting Between Great Britain and Foreign Powers, and of the Laws, Decrees and Orders in Council . . . London: 1827, 1835-45. V. 41

HERTZ, HEINRICH RUDOLPH

Gesammelte Werke . . . Band I Schriften vermischten Inhlts (II. Untersuchungen ueber Elektrischen Kraft . . . Leipzig: 1895/1894/1894. V. 38

Untersuchungen Ueber die Ausbreitung der Elektrischen Kraft. Leipzig: 1892. V. 38; 41; 42; 45

HERTZ, HENRIK

King Rene's Daughter. London: 1845. V. 43

HERTZ, J. H.

Sermons Addresses and Studies by The Chief Rabbi. London: 1938. V. 38

HERTZ, J. P.

A Familiar Dissertation on the Causes and Treatment of the Diseases of the Teeth . . . London: 1815. V. 38

HERTZKA, THEODORE

Freeland. A Social Anticipation. London: 1891. V. 40

A Trip to Freeland. Bow: 1905. V. 42

HERTZLER, ARTHUR

A Treatise on Tumors. Philadelphia: 1912. V. 42

HERVEUS NATALIS, BRITO

Quatuor Quodlibeta. Venice: 1486. V. 45

HERVEY, AUGUSTUS

Augustus Hervey's Journal. London: 1953. V. 45

HERVEY, ELIZABETH

Amabel; or, Memoirs of a Woman of Fashion. London: 1814. V. 42

The Mourtray Family. London: 1800. V. 40

HERVEY, JAMES

Dialogues Between Theron and Aspasio . . . Pontefract: 1805. V. 41

Meditations and Contemplations. London. V. 42

Meditations and Contemplations . . . to Which is Prefixed the Life of the Author . . . London: 1796. V. 41

HERVEY, JOHN

Ancient and Modern Liberty Stated and Compar'd. London: 1734. V. 42

An Answer to the Country Parson's Plea Against the Quakers-Tythe-Bill. In a Letter to the R. R. Author. London. V. 38

The Conduct of the Opposition and the Tendency of Modern Patriotism (More Particularly in a Late Scheme to Establish a Military Government in this Country) . . . London: 1734. V. 39

An Epistle from a Nobleman to a Doctor of Divinity . . . London: 1733. V. 42

Lady Suffolk: the Old Grey Mare of Long Island. New York: 1936. V. 39

Memoirs of the Reign of King George II. London: 1931. V. 41; 44

Messenger. The Great Progenitor. New York: 1935. V. 38; 39; 40; 46

Miscellaneous Thoughts on the Present Posture Both of Our Foreign and Domestic Affairs. London: 1742. V. 41

Observations on the Writings of the Craftsman. London: 1730. V. 41

Observations Upon a Pamphlet, Entitled, Miscellaneous Thoughts &c. in a Letter to the Noble Author. London: 1742. V. 41

Racing in America 1665-1959. New York: 1922-60. V. 43

Sequel to a Pamphlet Intitled Observations on the Writings of the Craftsman. London: 1730. V. 41

HERVEY, T. K., MRS.

Juvenile Calendar and Zodiac of Flowers. London: 1855. V. 39

HERVEY, THOMAS

A Letter from the Hon. Thomas Hervey, to Sir Thomas Hanmer. London: 1741. V. 39; 41

HERVEY, THOMAS K.

Australia; with other Poems. London: 1824. V. 43

HERVEY, THOMAS KIBBLE

The Poetical Sketch-Book, Including a Third Edition of Australia. London: 1829. V. 42

HERVIEUX DE CHANTELOUP, J. C. 1683-1747

A New Treatise of Canary Birds. London: 1718. V. 39

HERWARTH VON HOHENBURG, JOHN GEORGE 1553-1622

Theasurus Hieroglyphicorum e Museo Ioannis Georgij Herrart ab Hohenburg . . . Munich?: 1610. V. 44

HERZFELD, E.

Monumenta Asiae Minoris Antiqua. Manchester: 1930. V. 42

HERZFELD, ERNEST E.

Iran in the the Ancient East. London: 1941. V. 44

HERZOG, ISAAC

The Main Institutions of Jewish Law. 1936-1939. V. 40

HESELTINE, J. P.

Some Original Drawings by Anicent and Modern Artists Remaining in the Collection of J. P. H. London: 1917. V. 44

HESELTINE, PHILIP 1894-1930

Merry-Go-Down. A Gallery of Gorgeous Drunkards Through The Ages. Collected for the use, interest, illumination and delectation of serious topers. London. V. 39

Merry-Go-Down. A Gallery of Gorgeous Drunkards through the Ages . . . London: 1929. V. 38

HESIOD

Hesiodi Ascraei Opuscula Inscripta Erga Kai Hemerai. Paris: 1543. V. 45

Opera et Dies. Theogonia. Scutum Herculis. Omnia Vero Cum Multis Optimisque Expositionibus. Venice: 1537. V. 43

Opera. Basle: 1542? V. 44

Opera et Dies. Lyons: 1550. V. 45

HESLOP, R. O.

A Bibliographical List of Works Illustrative of the Dialect of Northumberland. London: 1896. V. 38; 40

HESS, ALFRED

Collected Writings. Springfield: 1936. V. 38; 40

Rickets Including Osteomalacia and Tetany. Philadelphia: 1929. V. 40

HESS, HANS

Lyonel Feininger. Stuttgart: 1959. V. 42

Lyonel Feininger. New York: 1961. V. 42; 43; 45; 46

HESS, WILLIAM

The Epistle of Paul the Apostle to the Philippians, the Epistle of Paul The Apostle to the Colossians, the Epistle of Paul the Apostle to. New York: 1836. V. 38

HESSE, HEINRICH

Neue Garten-Lust: das ist, Grundliche Vorstellung, wie ein Lust-Kuchen- und Baum-Garten under Unserem Teutschen Climate Fuglich Anzurichten . . . Leipzig: 1690. V. 46

HESSE, HERMANN

Die Morgenlandfahrt. Berlin: 1932. V. 45

Magister Ludi. New York: 1949. V. 42

Siddhartha. Berlin: 1922. V. 44

Sinclairs Notizbuch. Zurich: 1923. V. 45

Steppenwolf. 1929. V. 37

Steppenwolf. London: 1929. V. 42

Steppenwolf. 1977. V. 38

Unterwegs. 1911. V. 44

Unterwegs. Munchen: 1911. V. 45

HESSELGRAVE, RUTH AVELINE

The Batheaston Parnassus Fairs. San Francisco: 1963. V. 42

Lady Miller and the Batheaston Literary Circle. New Haven: 1927. V. 39

HESSELIUS, ANDREAS

Kort Berettelse om then Swenska Kyrkios. Norkioping: 1725. V. 39; 41; 43

HESSEMER, F. M.

Arabische und Alt-Italienische Bau-Verzierungen. Berlin: 1836-42. V. 41

HESSUS, HELIUS EOBANUS

De Tuenda Bona Valetudine, Libellus. Frankfurt: 1556. V. 37

Heroidum Libri Tres. Paris: 1546. V. 38

HESTER, JOHN

The Secrets of Physick and Philosophy, Divided into Two Books. London: 1633. V. 38; 40

HESTON, ALFRED M.

Absegami: Annals of Eyren Haven (Egg Harbor) & Atlantic City, 1609 to 1904. Camden: 1904. V. 39

Absegami: Annals of Eyren Haven and Atlantic City 1609 to 1904. N.P.: 1904. V. 41

South Jersey. A History, 1664-1924. New York: 1924. V. 42

HESTON, JACOB FRANKLIN

Moral and Political Truth; or Reflections Suggested by Reading History and Biography. Philadelphia: 1811. V. 37

HET Groote Tafereel der Dwaasheid, Vertoonende de Opkomst, Voortgang en Ondergang van de Actie, Bubbel en Windnegotie, in Vrankrijk, Engeland . . . N.P.,: 1722. V. 43

HETHERINGTON, A. L.

The Early Ceramic Wares of China. London: 1922. V. 38; 41; 42

The Early Ceramic Wares of China. London: 1924. V. 38

HETHERINGTON, JOHN

Yichud. Albion: 1991. V. 45

HETLEY, G. B.

The Native Flowers of New Zealand Illustrated in Colours . . . from Drawings Coloured to Nature. London: 1887-88. V. 42

HETLEY, THOMAS

Reports and Cases Taken in the Third, Fourth, Fifth, Sixth and Seventh Years of the Late King Charles I. London: 1657. V. 44; 45

HETON, THOMAS

Some Account of Mines and the Advantages of Them to This Kingdom. London: 1707. V. 40

HETTNER, HERMANN

Athens and the Peloponnese with Sketches of Northern Greece. Edinburgh: 1854. V. 39

HEURES Nouvelles Tirees de la Sainte Ecriture . . . Paris: 1670. V. 40

HEURNE, JOHAN VAN

Opera Omnia . . . luxta Otthonis Heurnii, Auctoris Filii . . . Lyon: 1658. V. 38

HEUSINGER, EDWARD W.

Early Explorations and Mission Establishments in Texas. San Antonio: 1936. V. 44

HEUSSER, ALBERT H.

The History of the Silk Dyeing Industry in the United States. Paterson: 1927. V. 42

HEVELIUS, JOHANNES

Selenographia: sive, Lunae Descriptio, Atque Accurata, Tam Macularum Eius, Quam Motuum Diversorum, Aliarumque Omnium Vicissitudinum, Phasiumque . . . Danzig: 1647. V. 44

HEVERLY, C. F.

History of Sheshequin 1777-1902. Towanda: 1902. V. 42

HEVIA BOLANOS, JUAN

Curia Filipica, Donde Breve y Compendioso se Trata de los Iuizios, Mayormente Forenses, Eclesiasticos, y Seculares, con lo Sobre Ellos Hasta Aora Dispuesto por Derecho . . . Madrid: 1635. V. 41

HEVIA BOLANOS, JUAN DE

Laberintho de Comercio Terrestre Y Naval. Lima: 1617. V. 38; 40

HEWARDINE, MR.

Collection of Odes, Songs and Epigrams, Against the Whigs, Alias the Blue and Buff. London: 1790. V. 45

HEWATT, ALEXANDER

An Historical Account of the Rise and Progress of the Colonies of South Carolina and Georgia. London: 1779. V. 39; 41; 42; 44; 45; 46

HEWES, ROBERT

An Elucidation of Regulations for the Formations and Movements of Cavalry. Salem: 1804. V. 37; 39

Rules and Regulations for the Sword Exercise of the Cavalry. To which is Added, The Review Exercise. Boston: 1802. V. 37

HEWETSON, W. B.

History of Napoleon Bonaparte, and Wars of Europe. London: 1815. V. 46

HEWETT, DANIEL

The Commercial Chart, and Universal Traveller . . . with Brief Description of New York, Boston, Philadelphia, Baltimore, Washington, Charleston and New Oreleans . . . New York: 1825. V. 41

HEWETT, SARAH

The Peasant Speech of Devon with Other Matters Connected Therewith. London: 1892. V. 41

HEWINS, W. A. S.

The Royal Saints of Britain from the Latter Days of the Roman Empire. London: 1929. V. 45

HEYLYN, PETER 1600-1662 continued

Cyprianus Anglicus: Or, the History of the Life and Death of . . . William, Lord Archbishop of Canterbury. Dublin: 1719. V. 39

Ecclesia Vindicata; or, the Church of England Justified . . . London: 1657. V. 46

Examen Historicum; or a Discovery and Examination of the Mistakes, Alsities and Defects in Some Modern Histories . . . London: 1659. V. 46

A Help to English History . . . Continued to 1680. London. V. 46

A Help to English History . . . London: 1670. V. 46

A Help to English History. London: 1680. V. 40; 44

A Help to English History. London: 1773. V. 40

The Historie of that Famous Saint and Souldier . . . St. George of Cappadocia . . . Colophon: 1631. V. 45

The History of . . . St. George of Cappadocia . . . London: 1631. V. 38; 39

The History of the Sabbath. London: 1636. V. 39

Microcosmos: a Little Description of the Great World. Oxford: 1636. V. 46

Mikrokosmos. A Little Description of the Great World. Oxford: 1639. V. 38

The Rebells Catechisme. London: 1643. V. 39; 43

HEYMAN, MAX L.

Prudent Soldier . . . E.R.S. Canby, 1817-1873 . . . Indian Campaigns, in the Mexican War, in California, New Mexico, Utah, and Oregon . . . Civil War. Glendale: 1859. V. 39

Prudent Soldier . . . E.R.S. Canby, 1817-1873 . . . Indian Campaigns, in the Mexican War, in California. Glendale: 195. V. 42

Prudent Soldier . . . E. R. S. Canby, 1817-1873 . . . Indian Campaigns in the Mexican War in California, New Mexico, Utah, and Oregon . . . Glendale: 1959. V. 39; 41; 42

HEYMANN, C. DAVID

Ezra Pound: the Last Rower. New York: 1976. V. 40

HEYMN, JEAN 1769-1821

Nouveau Dictionnaire Russe-Francois et Allemand. Moscow: 1799-01-02. V. 40

HEYNEMAN, JULIE HELEN

Arthur Putnam, Sculptor. San Francisco: 1932. V. 37; 40; 42

HEYNES, SAMUEL

A Treatise of Trigonometry, Plane and Spherical, Theoretical and Practical. London: 1701. V. 40; 41

HEYRICK, ELIZABETH

Immediate, Not Gradual Abolition; or, an Inquiry into the Shortest, Safest and Most Effectual Means of Getting Rid of West Indian Slavery. London: 1825. V. 42

HEYWARD, DOROTHY

Porgy. New York: 1927. V. 46

HEYWARD, DUBOSE

Brass Ankle. New York: 1931. V. 37; 39; 41; 43; 44; 46

Carolina Chansons Legends of the Low Country. New York: 1922. V. 37; 39; 43; 46

The Half Pint Flask. New York: 1929. V. 39; 43; 46

Jasbo Brown and Selected Poems. New York: 1911. V. 44

Jasbo Brown and Selected Poems. New York: 1931. V. 43

Mamba's Daughters. New York: 1939. V. 41; 42; 43; 44

Porgy. New York: 1925. V. 39

HEYWOOD, B. A.

A Vacation Tour at the Antipodes, Through Victoria, Tasmania, New South Wales, Queensland and New Zealand, in 1861-62. 1863. V. 46

HEYWOOD, CHESTER DODD

Negro Combat Troops in the World War the Story of the 371st Infantry. Worcester: 1928. V. 42; 46

HEYWOOD, E. W.

Uncivil Liberty: an Essay to Show the Injustice and Impolicy of Ruling Woman Without Her Consent. Princeton: 1870. V. 44; 45

HEYWOOD, ELLIS

Il Moro d'heliseo Heivodo Inglese. Florence: 1556. V. 37

HEYWOOD, JAMES

Illustrations of the Principal English Universities. N.P.: 1863. V. 38

Letters and Poems on Several Subjects. London: 1726. V. 41

HEYWOOD, JOHN

The Spider and the Flie. London: 1556. V. 37; 39

HEYWOOD, ROBERT

A Journey to America in 1834. Cambridge: 1919. V. 43

HEYWOOD, SAMUEL 1753-1828

A Dissertation Upon the Distinctions in Society, and Rank of the Pepole, Under the Anglo Saxon Governments. London: 1818. V. 41

HEYWOOD, THOMAS

The Actors Vindication, Containing, Three Brief Treatises . . . London: 1658. V. 40

A Challenge for Beavtie. London: 1636. V. 38

The General History of Women . . . London: 1657. V. 42

The Hierarchie of the Blessed Angells . . . London: 1635. V. 42; 43; 44

The Life of Merlin, Sirnamed Ambrosius. London: 1641. V. 45

The Life of Merlin, surnmaed Ambrosius. Carmarthen: 1812. V. 40

Pleasant Dialogues and Dramma's . . . London: 1637. V. 40; 45

Troia Britanica; or, Great Britaines Troy. London: 1609. V. 38; 44

HEYWOOD, V. H.

The Biology and Chemistry of the Compositae. London: 1977. V. 37

HEYWOOD-WAKEFIELD, GARDNER, MASSACHUSETTS.

Catalog no. 11: Reed and Rattan Furniture. 1910s. V. 45

HIATT, CHARLES

Picture Posters. London: 1895. V. 37; 38; 40; 46

Picture Posters. London: 1896. V. 44

HIBBARD, J. R.

Sermon on the Causes and Uses of the Present Civil War Delivered . . . in the New Jerusalem Temple. Chicago: 1862. V. 46

HIBBEN, PAXTON

Henry Ward Beecher: An American Portrait. New York: 1927. V. 38

HIBBEN, T. N.

Dictionary of the Chinook Jargon, or Indian Trade Language of the North Pacific Coast. Victoria: 1899. V. 41

HIBBEN, T. N., & CO.

Dictionary of the Chinook Jargon; or, Indian Trade Language of the North Pacific Coast. Victoria: 1878? V. 42; 45

HIBBERD, SHIRLEY

The Amateur's Greenhouse and Conservatory; a Handy Guide. London: 1883. V. 41

The Book of the Aquarium and Water Cabinet. Groombridge. V. 43

The Book of the Aquarium and Water Cabinet. London: 1850's. V. 38

Familiar Garden Flowers. London: 1880. V. 38

The Ivy, a Monograph, Comprising the History, Uses, Characteristics and Affinities of the Plant, and a Descriptive List of all the Garden Ivies in Cultivation. London: 1872. V. 37; 43

New and Rare Beautiful Leaved Plants. Boston: 1870. V. 39

New and Rare Beautiful Leaved Plants. London: 1870. V. 37; 38; 39; 40; 42

Rustic Adornments for Homes of Taste. London: 1857. V. 38; 43

Rustic Adornments for Homes of Taste. London: 1870. V. 39; 42; 43

Rustic Adornments for Homes of Taste. London: 1895. V. 44

HIBBERT, EDWARD

Narrative of a Journey from Santiago de Childe to Buenos Ayres in July and August 1821. London: 1824. V. 40; 43

HIBBERT, GEORGE

A Catalogue of the Library of George Hibbert. London: 1829. V. 39

HIBBERT, S.

History of the Foundations in Manchester of Christ's College. Chetham's Hospital (and) The Ancient Parish Church. London: 1834/48. V. 37

HIBBERT, SAMUEL 1782-1848

Sketches of the History of Apparitions; or, an Attempt to Trace Such Illusions to Their Physical Causes. Edinburgh: 1824. V. 45

Sketches of the Philosophy of Apparitions. Edinburgh: 1824. V. 38; 40

Sketches of the Philosophy of Apparitions; or, an Attempt to Trace Such Illusions to Their Physical Causes. Edinburgh: 1825. V. 43

HICHBORN, PHILIP

Standard Designs for Boats of the United States Navy. Washington: 1900. V. 42

HICHENS, R.

Flames. London: 1897. V. 44

HICHENS, ROBERT

The Call of the Blood. London: 1906. V. 45

The Green Carnation. London: 1894. V. 42; 46

HICKENLOOPER, FRANK

An Illustrated History of Monroe County, Iowa. Albia: 1896. V. 38; 44; 45

HICKERINGILL, EDMOND 1630-1708

The Horrid Sin of Man-Catching: Explain'd in a Sermon . . . London: 1681. V. 39

HICKERINGILL, EDMUND 1630-1708

The Black Non-Conformist, Discover'd in More Naked Truth. London: 1682. V. 40

HICKES, GEORGE 1642-1715

Grammatica Anglo-Saxonica ex Ling. Oxford: 1711. V. 38

Institutiones Grammaticae Anglo-Saxonicae. Oxoniae: 1689. V. 38

Linguarum Vett. Septentrionalium Thesaurus. Oxford: 1703-05. V. 38; 41

Linguarum Vett., Septentrionalium Thesaurus Grammatico-Criticus et Archaeologicus. Oxford: 1705. V. 39

Ravilla Redivius, Being a Narrative of the Late Tryal of Mr. James Mitchel a Conventicle-Preacher . . . London: 1678. V. 46

HICKEY, EMILY H.

Verse-Tales, Lyrics and Translations. London: 1889. V. 38

HICKEY, WILLIAM

Memoirs. London. V. 42

Memoirs. 1749-1809. London: 1913-25. V. 38

The Works of Martin Doyle. Dublin: 1834. V. 42

HICKLIN, JOHN

The History of Nottingham Castle. London and Nottingham: 1836. V. 37

The 'Ladies of Llangollen,' as Sketched by Many Hands . . . Chester: 1847. V. 38

HICKMAN, WILLIAM A.

Brigham's Destroying Angel. New York: 1872. V. 41; 42; 46

HICKOK, LAURENS P.

A System of Moral Science. Schenectady: 1853. V. 43

HICKS, ELIAS

Observations on the Slavery of the Africans and Their Descendants. New York: 1811. V. 44

Observations on the Slavery of the Africans and Their Descendants and on the Use of the Produce of Their Labor . . . New York: 1814. V. 44

HICKS, FRANCIS

Reminiscences of His Public Life. Montreal: 1884. V. 43

HICKS, GRANVILLE

One of Us. The Story of John Reed. New York: 1935. V. 39

HICKS, J. G.

The Percy Artillery. London: 1899. V. 42

HICKS, J. R.

A Contribution to the Theory of the Trade Cycle. Oxford: 1950. V. 46

The Theory of Wages. London: 1932. V. 43

HICKS, RATCLIFFE

Southern California, or the Land of . . . Springfield: 1898. V. 38

HICKS, URBAN EAST

Personal Recollections of Capt. U. E. Hicks. Scenes, Incidents, Dangers and Hardships Endured During the Yakima and Clickitat Indian War. Portland: 1886. V. 39

HICKSON, MARY

ireland in the Seventeenth Century, or The Irish Massacres of 1641-42 . . . illustrated by extracts from unpublished State Papers, Unpublished MSS . . . relating to the Plantations of 1610 and 1639, unpublished Depositions etc. etc. London: 1884. V. 37

HICKSON, SYDNEY J.

A Naturalist in North Celebes. A narrative of travel in Minahassa, the Sangir and Talaut Islands, with notices of the fauna, flora and ethnology of the districts visited. London: 1889. V. 37

HIEBNER, ISRAEL

Mysterium Sigillorum, Herabarum & Lapidarum Oder: Volkommene Cur und Heilung Aller Kranckheiten Schaden und Leibes Auch Gemuths-Beschwerungen . . . Erfurt: 1696. V. 43

HIENACH ist Begriffen alle Geschicht so Sich in Levant Oder gen auff Gang der Sunen in Orient Zwischen dem Gros en Thurcken un dem Soldan zu Allchayro unnd dem Soffi . . . N.P.: 1518. V. 45

HIEOVER, HARRY

Sporting Facts and Sporting Fancies. London: 1853. V. 42; 43

The Sportsman's Friend in a Frost. London: 1857. V. 42; 43

HIER Beghint een Schoone Boeck en is Geheten Die Vertroostinghe der Gelantenre Menschen en Van der Verclaringhe der Consciencie. Antwerp: 1517. V. 43

HIERLING Artifice Detected; or, the Profit and Loss of Great-Britain, in the Present War with Spain, Set In Its True Light; by Laying Before the Publick, As Full, Compleat, and Regular a List as Can be Had, of the British Ships Taken Since . . . London: 1742. V. 41

HIERO-MASTIX, a Satire, (in verse) Occasioned by Publications Which Have Recently Appeared in Connection with the Apocrypha Controversy. Edinburgh: 1828. V. 46

HIEROCLES

Commentarius in Aurea Pythagoreorum Carmina. Paris: 1583. V. 41

In Aureos Versus Pythagorae Opusculum . . . Padua: 1474. V. 40

In Aurea Pythagoreorum Carmina and De Providentia et Fata. London: 1673. V. 37

HIERON, SAMUEL

A Helpe vnto Deuotion . . . London: 1608. V. 44

HIERONYMUS, SAINT

Epistolae. Venice: 1476. V. 41

Epistolae Hieronymi. Parma: 1480. V. 39

Epistolae. Venice: 1496. V. 37

Epistolae. Venice: 1500? V. 45; 46

Epistole Sancti Hieronymi . . . Impressum Lugduni Per. V. 42

Eple & Tractatus. Lyon: 1513. V. 40

Vita de Sancto Hieronymo (The Life of St. Jerome). Cambridge: 1928. V. 40

Omnes Quae Extant . . . Basiliae: 1563. V. 42

La Reigle de Deuotion des Epistres de Moseigneur Sainct Ierosme a Ses Seurs Fraternelles en Religion; en Latin et en Francoys. Paris: 1500. V. 43

Saint Paul, the First Hermite: His Life by St. Jerome in the Translation of 1630. Lewisburg: 1988. V. 40; 41

Vita et Transitus. Treviso: 1478. V. 46

HIFFERN, PAUL

Remarks on an Ode on the Death of His Royal Highness Frederick, Prince of Wales. Dublin: 1752. V. 38

HIGBEE, ELIAS

'Latter Day Saints,' Alias Mormons. Washington: 1840. V. 39; 41; 43

HIGDEN, HENRY

A Modern Essay on the Tenth Satyr of Juvenal. London: 1687. V. 45

The Wary Widdow; or, Sir Noisy Parrat. London: 1693. V. 38

HIGDEN, RANULPH d.1364

Polychronicon. London: 1482. V. 44

Polychronicon. Westminster: 1482. V. 43; 45; 46

Polychronicon. Southwerke: 1527. V. 37; 39; 45

Polychronicon. colophon: MCCCCC . . . V. 43

Policronicon. Colophon: 1495. V. 43

HIGGIN, L.

Handbook of Embroidery. London: 1880. V. 41

HIGGINS, AILEEN CLEVELAND

Dream Blocks. New York: 1908. V. 46

HIGGINS, BELDEN & CO.

Illustrated Historical Atlas of Elkhart Co., Indiana. Chicago: 1874. V. 41

Illustrated Historical Atlas of St. Joseph Co., Indiana. Chicago: 1875. V. 42

HIGGINS, BRYAN

Experiments and Observations Made with a View of Improving the Art of Composing and Applying Calcareous Cements and of Preparing Quick Lime . . . London: 1780. V. 38; 41; 43; 44; 45

Minutes of the Society for Philosophical Experiments and Conversations. London: 1795. V. 40

HIGGINS, C. G.

The Oxfordshire and Buckinghamshire Light Infantry Chronicle. An Annual Record of the First and Second Battalions, fromerly the 43rd and 52nd. Light Infantry and the Territorial Battalions of the Regiment. London: 1947-1954. V. 37

HIGGINS, F. R.

Arable Holdings; Poems. Dublin: 1933. V. 40

HIGGINS, GODFREY

The Celtic Druids. London: 1829. V. 38; 39

The Celtic Druids. 1827. V. 37

HIGGINS, HENRY H.
Notes by a Field-Naturalist in the Western Tropics. Liverpool: 1877. V. 39

HIGGINS, JOSEPH T.
The Whale Ship Book. New York: 1927. V. 38; 42

HIGGINS, N.
The Bernards of Abington and Nether Winchendon. London: 1903. V. 43

HIGGINS, R. A.
Catalogue of the Terracottas in the Department of Greek and Roman Antiquities. London: 1969-70. V. 42; 44

HIGGINS, SOPHIA E.
The Bernards of Abington and Nether Winchendon; a Family History. London: 1903-04. V. 37

HIGGINS, WILLIAM
Experiments and Observations on the Atomic Theory and Electrical Phenomena. London: 1814. V. 45; 46
Experiments and Observations on the Atomic Theory, and Electrical Phenomena. V. 45

HIGGINS, WILLIAM MULLINGAR
Aristomenes: a Grecian Tale. London: 1838. V. 42

HIGGINS, WILLIAM MULLINGER
The Philosophy of Sound, and History of Music. London: 1838. V. 43

HIGGINSON, A. HENRY
British and American Sporting Authors. Berryville: 1949. V. 39
British and American Sporting Authors. London: 1951. V. 37; 39; 40; 44
The Hunts of the United States and Canada. Their Masters, Hounds and Histories. Boston: 1908. V. 39; 43
Letters from an Old Sportsman to a Young One. Garden City: 1929. V. 39; 42
Letters from an Old Sportsman to a Young One . . . New York: 1929. V. 43
Try Back. A Huntsman's Reminiscences. New York: 1931. V. 39; 46

HIGGINSON, FRANCIS
Nevv-Englands Plantation, or, a Short and Trve Description of the Commodities and Discommodites of that Countrey. London: 1630. V. 42; 44

HIGGINSON, FRED A.
Robert Graves: a Bibliography. 1987. V. 40; 42

HIGGINSON, T. W.
A Ride through Kanzas. New York: 1856-58. V. 42

HIGGINSON, THOMAS WENTWORTH 1823-1911
Army Life in a Black Regiment. Boston: 1870. V. 38; 39; 43
Army Life in a Black Regiment. Boston: 1890. V. 43
Atlantic Essays. Boston: 1871. V. 40
Old Cambridge. New York: 1899. V. 43; 44
Thalatta; a Book for the Sea-Side. Boston: 1853. V. 43

HIGGONS, BEVILL
The Generous Conqueror. London: 1702. V. 37; 38; 45
A Short View of the English History . . . Hague: 1727. V. 42

HIGHAM, C. S. S.
The Development of the Leeward Islands Under the Restoration 1660-1688. Cambridge: 1923. V. 40; 42

HIGHAM, R.
Report of the Engineer, to the Directors of the Ohio Rail Road Company, March 20, 1837. Painesville: 1837. V. 37

HIGHFILL, PHILIP H.
A Biographical Dictionary of Actors, Actresses, Musicians, Dancers, Managers and Other Stage Personnel in London, 1660-1800. Carbondale: 1973-76. V. 37

THE HIGHLAND Laddie, Dedicated to Their Graces the Duke & Duchess of Hamilton by Their Humble Ser.t. T. January. London: 1752. V. 45

HIGHMORE, ANTHONY
The History of the Honourable Artillery Company of the City of London. London: 1804. V. 41

HIGHMORE, NATHANEL
Case of a Foetus Found in the Abdomen of a Young Man (Thomas Lane), at Sherborne, in Dorsetshire. London: 1815. V. 42

HIGHMORE, NATHANIEL
Corporis Humani Disquisitatio Anatomica. The Hague: 1651. V. 38; 41

HIGHSMITH, PATRICIA
The Blunderer. New York: 1954. V. 44
The Blunderer. London: 1956. V. 43
Deep Water. London: 1957. V. 45
Miranda the Panda is on the Veranda. New York: 1958. V. 39
Plotting and Writing Suspense Fiction. Boston: 1966. V. 41
The Price of Salt. New York: 1952. V. 39
Strangers on a Train. London: 1950. V. 38; 41; 42; 46
Strangers on a Train. New York: 1950. V. 38; 43; 44
The Talented Mr. Ripley. 1955. V. 37; 39
The Talented Mr. Ripley. New York: 1955. V. 37; 41
The Talented Mr. Ripley. London: 1957. V. 38; 41; 42; 45; 46
This Sweet Sickness. London: 1961. V. 42

HIGHT, JOHN J.
History of the Fifty-Eighth Regiment of Indiana Volunteer Infantry . . . Princeton: 1895. V. 38

HIGHTOWER, JAMES
Happy Hunting Grounds. Colorado Springs: 1910. V. 42

HIGHTOWER, JOHN
Pheasant Hunting. New York: 1946. V. 39

HIGHWATER, JAMAKE
Kiowa Indian Art: Watercolor Paintings in Color by the Indians of Oklahoma. Sante Fe: 1979. V. 39

HIGSON, DANIEL
Seafowl Shooting Sketches. Preston, Lancs.: 1909. V. 39

HIGUELOS, OSCAR
Our House in the Last World. New York: 1982. V. 43

HILARIUS, BISHOP OF POITIERS
Lucubrationes Quotquot Extant, olim per Des. Basel: 1535. V. 38

HILARIUS, EPISCOPUS PICTAVIENSIS
De Trinitate Contra Arianos. Venice: 1489. V. 45

HILARY, SAINT
Opera Complura Sancti Hylarii Episcopi hac Serie Coimpressa . . . Colphon: 1510. V. 42

HILARY, ST., BP. OF POITIERS
Lucubrationes Quotquot Extant Olim per Des. Dersmum Rot. Haud Mediocribus Sudoribus Emandate . . . Basle: 1535. V. 43

HILBERRY, CONRAD
The Lagoon: Images from Oxbow. 1989. V. 42

HILDBURGH, W. L.
Medieval Spanish Enamels and Their Relation to the Origin and the Development of Copper Champleve Enamels of the 12th and 13th Centuries. London: 1936. V. 37

HILDEBRANDT, A.
Airships Past and Present Together with Chapters on the Use of Balloons in Connection with Meteorology, Photography and the Carrier Pigeon . . . London: 1908. V. 40

HILDEBRANDT, A. M.
Heraldic Bookplates. London: 1892-94. V. 42; 46

HILDEBRANDT, WOLFGANG
Magia Naturalis . . . Darmstadt: 1610. V. 46

HILDEBURN, CHARLES R.
A Century of Printing. The Issues of the Press in Pennsylvania. Philadelphia: 1885-1886. V. 42; 43; 44
The Charlemagne Tower Collection of American Colonial Laws. Philadelphia: 1890. V. 38
Issues of the Press in Pennsylvania, 1685-1784. Philadelphia: 1885-86. V. 41; 42
Sketches of Printers and Printing. New York: 1895. V. 46

HILDEN, WILHELM
Quaestionum et Commentariorum in Organon Aristotelis. Berlin: 1585. V. 37; 45

HILDENBRAND, JOHANN VALENTIN VON
Institutiones Practico Medicale Rudimenta Nosologiae et Therapiae Specilis Complectentes . . . Vienna: 1821-25. V. 45

HILDER, J. J.
The Art of J. J. Hilder. Sydney: 1918. V. 41
J. J. Hilder, Water-Colourist. Sydney: 1916. V. 41

HILDRETH, JAMES

The Dragoon Campaigns to the Rocky Mountains; Being a History of the Enlistment, Organization, and First Campaigns of the Regiment of the United States Dragoons . . . New York: 1836. V. 37; 38; 39; 40; 41; 42; 43; 45; 46

HILDRETH, RICHARD 1807-1865

Despotism in America . . . Boston: 1840. V. 46

The History of Banks. Boston: 1837. V. 38; 39; 41

The History of the United States of America. New York: 1849-1852. V. 44

The Slave; or Memoirs of Archy Moore. Boston: 1836. V. 42; 45

The Slave; or Memoirs of Archy Moore. Boston: 1840. V. 45

The Slave; or Memoirs of Archy Moore. Boston: 1846. V. 42

HILDRETH, SAMUEL P.

Original Contributions to the American Pioneer. Cincinnati: 1844. V. 37; 38; 39

Pioneer History: Being an Account of the First Examinations of the Ohio Valley . . . Cincinnati: 1848. V. 37

HILDROP, JOHN

Free Thoughts Upon the Brute-Creation or an Examination of Father Bougeant's Philosophical Amusements &c. London: 1742. V. 39

A Letter to a member of Parliament, Containing a Proposal for Bringing in a Bill to Revise, Amend or Repeal Certain Obsolete Statutes, Commonly Called the Ten Commandments. London: 1738. V. 41; 42; 45

A Modest Aplogy for the Ancient and Honourable Family of the Wrongheads. London: 1744. V. 38; 45

HILGARD, E. W.

Report on the Geology and Agriculture of the State of Mississippi . . . . Jackson: 1860. V. 43

HILL, A. P., MRS.

The Life and Services of Rev. John E. Dawson . . . Atlanta: 1872. V. 41

HILL, A. V.

Muscular Movement in Man: The Factors Governing Speed and Recovery from Fatigue. New York: 1927. V. 37

HILL, A. W.

Poisonous Plants - Deadly, Dangerous and Suspect. London: 1927. V. 44

HILL, AARON

The Art of Acting. London: 1746. V. 39

Essays, for the Month of December, 1716. London: 1716. V. 40

Free Thoughts Upon Faith; or, the Religion of Reason. London: 1746. V. 43

A Full and Just Account of the Present State of the Ottoman Empire in All Its Branches. London: 1709. V. 39

A Full and Just Account of the present State of the Ottoman Empire in all its Branches: with the Government, and policy, religion, customs, and way of life of the Turks in General. London: 1710. V. 37

The Northern-Star. London: 1725. V. 40; 45

HILL, ABRAHAM

Familiar Letters Which Passed Between Abraham Hill, Esq. Fellow and Treasurer of the Royal Society, One of the Lords of Trade, and Comptroller to His Grace the Archbishop of Canterbury. London: 1767. V. 41; 43; 44

HILL, ALEX STAVELEY

From Home to Home: Autumn Wanderings in the North-West, in the Years 1881, 1882, 1883, 1884. New York: 1885. V. 44

HILL, ALEXANDER STAVELEY

From Home to Home: Autumn Wandering in the North-West in the Years 1881, 1882, 1883, 1884. London: 1885. V. 39

HILL, ALFRED J.

History of Company E of the Sixth Minnesota Regiment of Volunteer Infantry. St. Paul: 1899. V. 38; 39; 40; 42; 43; 44

HILL, ALICE POLK

Tales of the Colorado Pioneers. Denver: 1884. V. 37; 39; 45

HILL & SONS

The Violin Makers of the Guarneri Family (1626-1762). London: 1931. V. 38

HILL, ARTHUR

Anicent Irish Architecture. Cork: 1874. V. 43; 44

Antonio Stradivari: His Life and Work. London: 1902. V. 37

Ariba: Ancient Irish Architecture. A Monograph of Cormac's Chapel Cashel, Co. Tipperary. Cork: 1874. V. 37

Gio: Paolo Maggini. His Life and Work. London: 1892. V. 37

The Violin Makers of the Guarneri Family (1626-1762). London: 1931. V. 37

HILL, BENJAMIN

Lectures on the American Eclectic System of Surgery. Cincinnati: 1850. V. 39

HILL, BENJAMIN H.

Public Meeting! (and) Address to the Citizens of Troup County. La Grange: 1855. V. 42

Speech of the Means of Success, The Sources of Danger, and the Consequences of Failure in the Confederate Struggle for Independence! Atlanta: 1874. V. 42

HILL, BENSON EARLE 1795-1845

A Pinch of Snuff. London: 1840. V. 38; 39; 40; 41

HILL, BERT HODGE

Corinth. Volume I, Part VI: The Springs, Peirene, Sacred Spring, Glauke. 1964. V. 40; 42

HILL, BRIAN

Henry and Acasto. London: 1798. V. 41; 42; 45

Observations and Remarks in a Journey through Sicily and Calabria, in the Year 1791: With a Postscript, Containing Some Account of the Ceremonies of the Last Holy Week at Rome, and of a Short Excrusion to Tivoli. London: 1792. V. 39

HILL, CHARLES 1745?-1825.

The Effects of Civilzation on the People in European States. London: 1805. V. 37

HILL, CONSTANCE

Jane Austen: Her Home and Her Friends. London: 1902. V. 39; 41; 43; 45

HILL, D. H.

North Carolina. Confederate Military History. Atlanta: 1899. V. 43

HILL, DANIEL HARVEY

Bethel to Sharpsburg. Raleigh: 1926. V. 39

HILL, DEREK

Islamic Architecture and Its Decoration, A.D. 800-1500. Chicago: 1964. V. 38

HILL, EDWIN DARLEY

The Northern Banking Co. Ltd. Belfast: 1925. V. 37

HILL, EMMA

A Dangerous crossing and What Happened on the Other Side. Denver: 1914. V. 44; 45

HILL Field: Poems and Memoirs for John Montague on His Sixtieth Birthday. Minneapolis: 1989. V. 42

HILL, FRANCIS

The Outlaws of Horseshoe Hole. New York: 1901. V. 45

HILL, FREDERIC S.

Twenty-Six Historic Ships, the Story of Vessels of War and Their Successors in the Navies of the U.S . . . 1775-1902. New York: 1903. V. 42

HILL, FREDERICK

Crime: Its Amount, Causes and Remedies. London: 1853. V. 46

HILL, G. BIRKBECK

The Boswell Centenary - May Nineteen MDCCCXCV. London: 1895. V. 44

HILL, GEOFFREY

Collected Poems. London: 1986. V. 38; 40; 42; 43; 45

For the Unfallen - Poems 1952-1958. London: 1959. V. 38; 42

King Log. London: 1968. V. 37; 38; 44

The Mystery of the Charity of Charles Peguy. London: 1983. V. 45

Oxford Poetry. Swinford: 1953. V. 44

Preghiere. Leeds: 1964. V. 44

Somewhere Is Such a Kingdom - Poems 1952-1971. Boston: 1975. V. 40; 41

Tenebrae. London: 1978. V. 44

HILL, GEORGE

An Historical Account of the MacDonnells of Antrim, Including Notices of Some Other Septs, Irish and Scottish. Belfast: 1873. V. 37; 43

An Historical Account of the Plantation in Ulster at the Commencement of the Seventeenth Century, 1608-1620. Belfast: 1877. V. 37; 43

The Montgomery Manuscripts, 1608-1706. Belfast: 1869. V. 37; 43

The Ruins of Athens, with Other Poems. Washington: 1831. V. 41

HILL, GEORGE BIRKBECK NORMAN 1835-1903

Dr. Johnson, His Friends and Critics. London: 1878. V. 40; 41

Footsteps of Dr. Johnson. London: 1890. V. 39; 40; 45; 46

HILL, GEORGE BIRKBECK NORMAN 1835-1903 continued

Johnsonian Miscellanies. New York: 1897. V. 39

Johnsonian Miscellanies. Oxford: 1897. V. 39; 45

HILL, GEORGE F.

A Corpus of Italian Medals of the Renaissance Before Cellini. London: 1930. V. 37

Select Greek Coins: a series of enlargements illustrated and described. Paris/Brussels: 1927. V. 37

HILL, GEORGE FRANCIS

Catalogue of the Greek Coins of Palestine (Galilee, Samaria, and Judaea). London: 1914. V. 45

HILL, GEORGE W.

History of Ashland County, Ohio . . . N.P.: 1880. V. 39; 46

HILL, GEORGE WILLIAM

New Theory of Jupiter and Saturn. Washington: 1890. V. 38

HILL, GEORGIANA

A History of English Dress from the Saxon Period to the Present Day. London: 1893. V. 40; 42

HILL, GRAY

With the Bedouins. London: 1891. V. 43; 45

HILL, IRA

Antiquities of America Explained. Hagerstown: 1831. V. 42; 45

HILL, ISABEL LOUISE

Fredericton, New Brunswick, British North America. Fredericton: 1968. V. 43

HILL, J. B.

The Geology of Falmouth and the Truro of the Mining District of Camborne and Redruth. London: 1906. V. 44; 46

HILL, J. L.

End of the Cattle Trail. (and) The Passing of the Indian and Buffalo. Long Beach: 1923. V. 42

HILL, JEROME

Trip to Greece. New York: 1936. V. 37

HILL, JOHN 1716?-1775

The Actor; A Treatise on the Art of Playing. London: 1750. V. 37; 40; 41; 42; 43

The Actor; or, a Treatise on the Art of Playing. London: 1755. V. 38; 40; 41

The British Herbal. London: 1756. V. 37; 38; 39; 41; 42; 45; 46

Circumstances Which Preceded the Letters to the Earl of -----; and May Tend to a Discovery of the author. London: 1775. V. 42

The Conduct of a Married-Life. London: 1753. V. 41; 45

The Construction of Timber, From Its Early Growth. London: 1770. V. 39

A Decade of Curious Insects . . . London: 1773. V. 42

Essays in Natural History and Philosophy. London: 1752. V. 42

The Family Herbal or an Account of all Those English Plants, Bungay: 1810? V. 37

The Family Herbal. Bungay: 1812. V. 37; 38; 40

The Family Herbal. Bungay: 1820. V. 41

The Family Herbal, or an Account of All Those English Plants Which are Remarkable for Their Virtues and of the Drugs Which are Produced by Vegetables of Other Countries. London: 1835. V. 46

The Family Herbal, or an Account of All Those English Plants. London: 1840. V. 43

Fossils Arranged According to Their Obvious Characters, with Their History and Description . . . London: 1771. V. 37

A General Natural History . . . London: 1751. V. 46

A History of Plants . . . London: 1751. V. 38

The History of a Woman of Quality: or, the Adventures of Lady Frail. By an Impartial hand. London: 1751. V. 37

The Inspector. London: 1753. V. 46

A Letter to Dr. Abraham Johnson, On the Subject of His New Scheme for the Propagation of the Human Species . . . London: 1750. V. 38; 43

Lucina Sine Concubitu. London: 1750. V. 38; 39; 40; 42; 43

Lucina Sine concubitu. London: 1761. V. 44

Lucina Sine Concubitu. 1930. V. 42

Lucina Sine Concubitu. London: 1930. V. 40

Lucina Sine Concubitu. Waltham St. Lawrence: 1930. V. 40; 41; 46

Observations on the Greek and Roman Classics. London: 1753. V. 37

A Review of the Works of the Royal Society of London . . . London: 1751. V. 37; 39; 42

A Review of the Works of the Royal Society of London. London: 1780. V. 38; 39

A Series of Progressive Lessons, Intended to Elucidate the Art of Flower Painting in Water Colours. Philadelphia: 1818. V. 44

The Sleep of Plants, and Causes of Motion in the Sensitive Plant . . . London: 1757. V. 38; 43

The Story of Elizabeth Canning Considered. London: 1753. V. 42; 46

The Useful Family Herbal. London: 1754. V. 42

The Vegetable System . . . London: 1762-61. V. 43

Virtues of British Herbs. London: 1771-2. V. 38

HILL, JOHN, gent.

The Young Secretary's Guide. London: 1764. V. 39

HILL, JONATHAN

Hill Collection of Pacific Voyages. San Diego: 1974. V. 40

The Hill Collection of Pacific Voyages. San Diego: 1974-82-84. V. 40

HILL, JOSEPH

The Book Makers of Old Birmingham. Birmingham: 1907. V. 44

The Interest of These United Provinces. Amsterdam: 1673. V. 43

HILL, JOSEPH J.

History of Warners Ranch and Its Environs. Los Angeles: 1927. V. 38; 39; 44

HILL, K. ETHEL

Evylena Nunn Miller's Travel Tree. Santa Ana: 1933. V. 39; 42; 44

HILL, LEONARD

The Physiology and Pathology of the Cerebral Ciruclation: and Experimental Research. London: 1896. V. 42

HILL, MATTHEW DAVENPORT

Suggestions for the Repression of Crime, Contained in Charges Delivered to Grand Juries of Birmingham, Supported by Additional Facts and Arguments. London: 1857. V. 39; 42

HILL, NORMAN NEWELL

History of Knox County, Ohio. Mt. Vernon: 1881. V. 46

HILL, OCTAVIA

Letter(s) to my Fellow Workers, 1873-1910. London: 1873-1910. V. 39; 41

HILL, OLIVER

The Fifth Essay of D.M. a Friend of Truth and Physick Against the Circulation of the Blood. London: 1700-01. V. 38

The Fifth Essay of Nine, Upon Several Subjects: This Being Against the Circulation of the Blood; in Two Parts; the First Being a Full Refutation of that Blind Hypothesis. The Second Shewing the Cause of the Pulse, or the Beating of the Hear and Arteries. London: 1702. V. 40

The Garden of Adonis. London: 1973. V. 37

A Rod for the Back of Fools in Answer to a Book of Mr. John Toland Called Christinaity not Mysterious . . . London: 1702. V. 38

HILL, PASOCE GRENFELL

Fifty Days on Board a Slave Vessel in the Mozambique Channel, in April and May, 1843. New York: 1844. V. 46

HILL, RICHARD

An Apology for Brotherly Love, and for the Doctrines of the Church of England, In a Series of Letters to the Revd. Charles Daubeny . . . London: 1798. V. 38; 45

The Blessings of Polygamy Displayed, in an Affectioante Address to the Rev. Mr. Madan, Occasioned by His Late Work, Entitled Thelphythora, or, a Treatise on Female Ruin. London: 1781. V. 44; 45

Pietas Oxoniensis; or, a Full and Impartial Account of the Expulsion of Six Students from St. Edmund Hall, Oxford . . . Cambridge: 1768. V. 44

The Sky-Rocket; or Thoughts During the Easter Recess of Parliament, on Several Very Important Subjects, and On Several Recent Events. London: 1782. V. 41

HILL, ROBERT G.

Geography and Geology of the Black and Grand Prairies, Texas. Washington: 1901. V. 44

HILL, ROBERT GARDINER

A Lecture on the management of Lunatic Asylums and the Treatment of the insane. Delivered at the Mechanics Institution Lincoln 1838. With Statistical tables Illustrative of the Complete Practicability of the System advocated in . . . London: 1839. V. 37

HILL, ROWLAND 1795-1879

The Life of Sir Rowland Hill and the History of His Penny Postage. London: 1880. V. 39; 41

The State and Prospects of Penny Postage, As Developed in the Evidence Taken Before the Postage Committee of 1843 . . . London: 1844. V. 42

HILL, S. B.

Souvenir of Austin, Texas. New York: 1888. V. 41

HILL, S. S.

The Dominions of the Pope and of the Sultan . . . Madden & Madden: 1845. V. 45

HILL, SAMUEL S.

Travels in the Sandwich and Society Islands. London: 1856. V. 38; 41

Travels in Peru and Mexico. London: 1860. V. 46

Travels in Egypt and Syria. London: 1866. V. 39

HILL, THOMAS

The Profitable Arte of Gardening, Now the Thirde Time set Forth ... London: 1574. V. 43

HILL, THOMAS E.

Manual of Social & Business Forms: A Guide to Correct Writing. Chicago: 1882. V. 37

HILL-TOUT, CHARLES

British North America. I. The Far West, Home of Salish and Dene. Toronto: 1907. V. 37

Ethnological Studies of the Mainland Halkomelem, a Division of the Salish of British Columbia. London: 1902. V. 43

The Native Races of the British Empire: British North America ... Toronto: 1907. V. 43

HILL, VERNON

Ballads Weird and Wonderful. London: 1912. V. 38; 40; 42; 43; 46

HILL, W. E.

A Short Account of a Violin by Stradivari, dated 1690. London: 1890. V. 46

HILL, WALTER B.

In the District Court of the United States for the Western Division of the Southern District of Georgia. John A. Kelly et al, vs. The State of Georgia ... Telfair County, Georgia ... Synopsis of the Testimony & Report of the Decision of Judge Emory Speer. Macon: 1895. V. 45

HILL, WILLIAM

Col. William Hill's Memoirs of the Revolution. Columbia: 1921. V. 44

Organization of the Territory of Oklahoma. Washington: 1684. V. 45

HILLAR, H. R.

The Dreamland Express. 1927. V. 42

HILLARD, E. B.

The Last Men of the Revolution. Hartford: 1864. V. 37

HILLARY, MAX

The Turn of the Tide. London: 1896. V. 42

HILLARY, WILLIAM

Observations on the Changes of Air and Concomitant Epidemical Diseases, in the Island of Barbadoes. London: 1766. V. 42; 44; 46

Observations on the Changes of the Air and Concomitant Epidemical Diseases in the Island of Barbadoes. Philadlephia: 1811. V. 37; 39; 40; 41; 42; 43; 44; 45; 46

HILLEBRAND, KARL

Six Lectures on the History of German Thought. London: 1880. V. 41

HILLER, J.

The Art of Hokusai in Book Illustration. (1980). V. 37

HILLER, JOHANN WOLFGANG

Tractatvs Theorico-Practicvs de Expensis Stvdirovm. Augsburg: 1619. V. 42

HILLERMAN, TONY

The Blessing Way. New York: 1970. V. 39; 45

Blessing Way. New York: 1990. V. 45

Coyote Waits. New York: 1990. V. 43; 44; 45; 46

Dance Hall of the Dead. New York: 1973. V. 42; 43

Dance Hall of the Dead. London: 1985. V. 42; 44

Dance Hall of the Dead. New York: 1990. V. 45

Dark Wind. New York: 1982. V. 45

The Fly on the Wall. New York: 1971. V. 43; 44

Fly on the Wall. New York: 1990. V. 45

The Great Taos Bank Robbery. Albuquerque: 1973. V. 43

Listening Woman. New York: 1978. V. 42; 43

New Mexico. Portland: 1974. V. 44; 45

People of My Darkness. New York: 1980. V. 43

Rio Grande. Portland: 1975. V. 45

Talking God. New York: 1989. V. 43; 44; 45

A Thief of Time. New York: 1988. V. 42; 43; 45

Words, Weather and Wolfmen. Gallup: 1989. V. 43; 44

HILLES, FREDERICK W.

New Light on Dr. Johnson. New Haven: 1959. V. 44; 46

HILLHOUSE, JAMES

Percy's Masque, a Drama. New York: 1820. V. 39

Propositions for Amending the Constitution of the United States, Submitted to the Senate, 12 April 1808, with Explanatory Remarks. New Haven: 1808. V. 38

HILLHOUSE, JAMES A.

Dramas, Discourses and Other Pieces. Boston: 1839. V. 38; 40

HILLHOUSE, MARY

German Songs in English Rhyme. Hartford: 1871. V. 46

THE HILLIAD; or, 'Hard Measure' versified, etc. London: 1796. V. 45

HILLIARD D'AUBERTEUIL, MICHEL RENE

Histoire de l'Administration de Lord North, Ministre des Finances en Angleterre, Depuis 1770 Jusqu'en 1782, 35 de la Guerre de l'Amerique Septentrionale ... Londres, et se trouve Paris: 1784. V. 41

HILLIARD, JOHN NORTHERN

Greater Magic, a Practical Treatise on Modern Magic. Minneapolis: 1945. V. 38

HILLICK, M. C.

Practical Carriage and Wagon Painting, a Treatise on the Painting of Carriages, Wagons and Sleighs, Embracing Full and Explicit Directions for Executing all Kinds of Work ... Chicago: 1906. V. 41

HILLIER, J.

The Art of Hokusai in Book Illustration (1980). London: 1980. V. 45

HILLIER, JACK

The Art of the Japanese Book. London: 1987. V. 39

Suzuki Harunobu. An Exhibition of the Colour-Prints and Illustrated Books on the Occasion of the Bicentenary of His Death in 1770. Philadelphia: 1970. V. 46

Japanese Prints and Drawings from the Vever Collection. London: 1976. V. 39

Japanese Prints and Drawings from the Vever Collection. London: 1977. V. 42

Landscape Prints of Old Japan. San Francisco: 1960. V. 37; 41

Twelve Woodblock Prints of Kitagawa Utamaro Illustrating the Process of Silk Culture. With an Introductory Essay by Jack Hillier. San Francisco: 1965. V. 37

The Uninhibited Brush. London: 1974. V. 42

HILLMAN, BRENDA

Coffee, 3 a.m. Lisbon: 1981. V. 39

HILLMAN, CARLOS H.

Old Timers: British and American in Chile. Santiago: 1900. V. 40

HILLMAN, H.

Cellular Structure of the Mammalian Nervous System. London: 1987. V. 38

HILLS, A. C.

Matrimonial Brokerage in the Metropolis. New York: 1st edition; V. 43

HILLS, CHESTER

The Builder's Guide. Hartford: 1846. V. 41

HILLS, JOHN

Points of a Racehorse. Edinburgh: 1903. V. 43

HILLS, JOHN WALLER

A History OF Fly Fishing for Trout. 1921. V. 40

A Summer on the Test. London: 1924. V. 40

HILLS, MARGARET T.

The English Bible in America. A Bibliography of Editions of the Bible and the New Testament Published in America 1777-1957. New York: 1961. V. 39

HILLS, MRS.

Fair Faces and True Hearts, a Novel. London: 1882. V. 43

HILLS, OSBORN C.

Saint Mary Stratford Bow. London: 1900. V. 44; 46

HILLYARD-SWINSTEAD, GEORGE

The Story of My Old World Garden and How I Made It In a London Suburb. London: 1910. V. 38

HILLYER, GEORGE

Battle of Gettysburg. N.P.: 1904. V. 44

HILLYER, GILES M.

Address Delivered at the Third Anniversary Celebration of the Alpha Delta Phi Society of Miami University, on the Triumphs of Mind. Cincinnati: 1839. V. 39

HILLYER, S. STEVENS

The Plumber and Sanitary Houses. A Practical Treatise on the Principles of Internal Plumbing Works or the Best Means for Effectually Excluding Noxious Gases from Our Houses. London: 1877. V. 38

HILPRECHT, HERMAN V.

The Babylonian Expedition of the University of Pennsylvania, Series D. Philadelphia: 1904. V. 37; 40

Business Documents of Murashu, Sons of Nippur, Dated in the Reign of Artaxerxes I (464-424 B.C.). Philadelphia: 1898. V. 40

Explorations in Bible Lands During the 19th Century. Philadelphia: 1903. V. 37; 40; 42

In the Temple of Bel at Nippur. Philadelphia: 1904. V. 37

Mathematical, Meterological and Chronological Tablets from the Temple Library of Nippur. Philadelphia: 1906. V. 40; 42; 44

HILPRECHT, HERMANN V.

The Excavations in Assyria and Babylonia. Philadelphia: 1904. V. 42

HILSOP, HERBERT R.

An Englishman's Arizona. Tucson: 1965. V. 42

HILTL, GEORGE

Preussens Heer . . . Seine Heutige Uniformirung und Bewaffnung Gezeichnet von C. F. Schindler, Pracht-Ausgabe. Berlin: 1875-76. V. 39

HILTON, ARTHUR CLEMENT

The Light Green. Cambridge: 1872. V. 40

HILTON, CONRAD

Inspirations of an Innkeeper. Los Angeles: 1963. V. 46

HILTON, HAROLD H.

The Royal and Ancient Game of Gold. London: 1912. V. 41

HILTON, JAMES 1900-1954

Catherine Herself. London: 1920. V. 37; 40; 44

Contango. London: 1932. V. 40

The Dawn of Reckoning. London: 1925. V. 44; 45

Good-Bye Mr. Chips. Boston: 1934. V. 46

Good-bye Mr. Chips. London: 1934. V. 39

Knight Without Armour. London: 1933. V. 40

Lost Horizon. London: 1933. V. 39; 42

Murder at School. London: 1931. V. 42

Nothing so Strange. Boston: 1947. V. 37

Rage in Heaven. 1932. V. 45

The Story of Dr. Wassell. Boston: 1943. V. 46

Terry. London: 1927. V. 37; 45

To You Mr. Chips. London: 1938. V. 39; 45

A Tribute to Charles Aubrey Smith. Los Angeles: 1948/49. V. 45

HILTON, JOHN

Change: the Beginning of a Chapter in Twelve Volumes. London: 1919. V. 38

HILTON, ROBERT

The British Art Printer and Lithographer. London: 1895-96. V. 41

HILTON-SIMPSON, M. W.

Land and Peoples of the Kasai. London: 1911. V. 39

HILTON, WILLIAM

Caps Well Fit: or, Select Epigrams, serious and comic. By Titus, in Sandgate, and Titus, Everywhere. Necastle: 1785. V. 37

Wee Whose Names Are Here Underwritten Who Were Employed and Sent in the Ship Adventure . . . Charlestown or Boston: 1662. V. 44

HILTY, STEVEN L.

A Guide to the Birds of Columbia. Princeton: 1986. V. 37; 38; 39

A Guide to the Birds of Colombia. 1986. V. 39

HILTZHEIMER, JACOB

Extracts from the Diary of Jacob Hiltzheimer of Philadelphia, 1765-1798. Philadelphia: 1893. V. 42

HILZINGER, JOHN GEORGE

Treasure Land. Tucson: 1897. V. 38; 39; 44

HIMES, CHARLES FRANCIS

Sketch of Dickinson College, Carlisle, Penn'a, Including the List of Trustees and Faculty from the Foundation and More Particular Account of the Scientific Department. Harrisburg: 1879. V. 37; 38

HIMES, CHESTER

Blind Man with a Pistol. 1969. V. 44

A Case of Rape. New York: 1980. V. 43

Cast the First Stone. 1952. V. 42

For Love of Imabelle. 1958. V. 39

If He Hollers, Let Him Go. 1945. V. 44

Lonely Crusade. New York: 1947. V. 42; 45

Pinktoes. Paris: 1961. V. 38; 41; 42

The Quality of Hurt. New York: 1972. V. 43

HIMES, JOSHUA V.

Millennial Harp. Designed for Meetings on the Second coming of Christ. Boston: 1843. V. 45

DER HIMMELWAGEN. Nuremberg: 1519. V. 40

HIMMELWRIGHT, ABRAHAM L. A.

In the Heart of the Bitteroot Mountains. The Story of the Carlin Hunting Party September-December, 1893. New York: 1895. V. 37; 38; 41; 45

HINCHLIFF, THOMAS W.

South American Sketches; or A Visit to Rio Janeiro, the Organ Mountains, La Plata and the Parana. London: 1863. V. 38; 45

HINCHMAN, WALTER

Sketches & Poems: 1845-1920. N.P.: 1920. V. 37; 38; 40; 42; 43

HINCKS, C. MALCOLM

A Commutation of Sentence and Other Incidents in the Life of Samuel Snubbins, Sneak Theif. London: 1906. V. 42

HINCKS, EDWARD

Buonaparte: a Poem. Cork: 1816. V. 42; 44

HINCKS, T.

A History of the British Marine Polyzoa. London: 1880. V. 37

HINCLIFF, THOMAS W.

South American Sketches; or a Visit to Rio Janeiro, the Organ Mountains, La Plata and the Parana. London: 1863. V. 41

HIND, ARTHUR MAYGER

A Catalogue of Rembrandt's Etchings . . . London: 1923. V. 44; 46

Catalogue of early Italian engravings preserved in the Dept. of Prints and Drawings in the British Museum. Edited by S. Covin. 1901-10. V. 37

Engraving in England in the Sixteenth Centuries and Seventeenth Centuries. Cambridge: 1952-64. V. 44

Engraving in England in the Sixteenth and Seventeenth Centuries. Cambridge: 1955. V. 41; 46

The Etchings of D. Y. Cameron. London: 1924. V. 39; 43; 44; 45; 46

Giovanni Battista Piranesi, a Critical Study with a List of His Published Works and Detailed Catalogues of the Prisons and Views of Rome. London: 1922. V. 38; 40

A History of Engraving and Etching from the 15th Century to the Year 1914 . . . Boston: 1923. V. 42; 44

A History of Engraving & Etching from the 15th Century to the Year 1914. Being the third and fully revised edition of A short history of engraving and etching. London: 1923. V. 37; 43

An Introduction to a History of Woodcut with Detailed Survey of Work Done in the 15th Century. 1935. V. 45

An Introduction to a History of Woodcut . . . Boston: 1935. V. 42

An Introduction to a History of Woodcut, with a Detailed Survey of Work Done in the Fifteenth Century. London: 1935. V. 37; 39; 40; 45

Rembrandt's Etchings, an Essay and a Catalogue. London: 1912. V. 39; 44

A Short History of Engraving and Etching for the Use of Collectors and Students. London: 1911. V. 41

A Short History of Engraving and Etching, for the Use of Collectors and Students. London: 1908. V. 38

Wenceslaus Hollar and His Views of London and Windsor in the Seventeenth Century. London: 1922. V. 38; 39; 40; 42; 43; 44; 45; 46

HIND, CHARLES LEWIS

Turner's Golden Visions. London: 1925. V. 42

HIND, E. CORA

The Story of the Big Ditch. (N.P.): 1912. V. 37

HIND, G. W.

A Series of Twenty Five Plates Illustrating the Causes of Displacement in the Various Fractures of the Bones of the Extremities. V. 37; 39; 40; 41; 44; 46

A Series of Twenty Plates Illustrating the Causes of Displacement in the Various Fractures of the Bones of the Extremities. London. V. 38

A Series of Twenty Plates Illustrating . . . Fractures of the Bones of the Extremities . . . London: 1836. V. 43

HIND, HENRY YOULE

British North Americaa. Reports of Progress, Together with a Preliminary and General Report, on the Assinniboine and Saskatchewan Exploring Expedition . . . London: 1860. V. 37

Essay on the Insects and Diseases Injurious to the Wheat Crops. Toronto: 1857. V. 43

HIND, HENRY YOULE continued

Explorations in the Interior of the Labrador Peninsula, the Country of the Montagnais and Nasquapee Indians. London: 1863. V. 44

Narrative of the Canadian Red River Exploring Expedition of 1857 and of the Assiniboine and Saskatchewan Exploring Expedition of 1858. London: 1860. V. 37; 38; 39; 41; 43; 44; 45

North-West Territory. Reports of Progress, Together with a Preliminary and General Report of the Assinboine and Saskatchewan Exploring Expedition, Made Under Instructions From the Provincial Secretary, Canada. Toronto: 1859. V. 37; 38; 39; 41; 43; 44

Report on a Topographical & Geological Exploration of the Canoe Route Between Fort William, Lake Superior and Fort Garry, Red River. Toronto: 1858. V. 40

Territoire du Nord-Ouest. Toronto: 1859. V. 46

HINDE, CAPTAIN

The Discipline of the Light Horse. London: 1778. V. 42

HINDE, G. J.

A Monograph of the British Fossil Sponges. London: 1887-1912. V. 37; 38

HINDE, M.

A New Royal and Universal Dictionary of Arts and Sciences. London: 1770-71. V. 38

HINDE, SIDNEY LANGFORD

The Fall of the Congo Arabs. London: 1897. V. 41; 45

The Last of the Masai. London: 1901. V. 40; 41

HINDERWELL, THOMAS

The History and Antiquities of Scarborough and the Vicinity. York: 1811. V. 40

The History and Antiquities of Scarborough and Vicinity. York: 1798. V. 38

HINDLEY & Wilkinson Ltd. London: 1890-1900. V. 46

HINDLEY, C.

The History of the Catnach Press, at Berwick-Upon-Tweed, Alnwick and New Castle-Upon-Tyne, in Nrothumberland, & Seven Dials. London: 1886. V. 37; 38; 39; 41; 42; 43; 44; 45

HINDLEY, CHARLES

A History of the Cries of London, Ancient and Modern. London: 1881. V. 41; 43

The Life and Times of James Catnach. London: 1878. V. 43; 44

The Old Book Collector's Miscellaney . . . or a Collection . . . of Literary Rarities . . . During the Sixteenth and Seventeenth Centuries. London: 1871-72. V. 40

The Old Book Collector's Miscellany. London: 1871-73. V. 39; 42

The Roxburghe Ballads. London: 1873. V. 43

The Roxburghe Ballads. London: 1874. V. 46

The True History of Tom and Jerry or Life in London. London: 1888. V. 39; 41; 42

HINDLEY, JOHN HADDON

Persian Lyrics, or Scattered Poems, from the Diwan-I-Hafiz. London: 1800. V. 40

HINDLIP, CHARLES ALLSOPP, 3RD BARON 1877-

Sport and Travel. Abyssinia and British East Africa. London: 1906. V. 43

HINDLIP, LORD

Sport and Travel Abyssinia and British East Africa. London: 1906. V. 40

HINDMARSH, ROBERT

Letters to Dr. Priestley . . . London: 1792. V. 40; 41; 42; 45; 46

Letters to Dr. Priestley . . . London: 1822. V. 40

HINDS, JOHN

Conversations on Conditioning. The Grooms' Oracle, and Pocket Stable-Directory; in which the managment of horses generally, as to health, dieting, and exercise, are considered, in a series of familiar dialogues, between . . . London: 1829. V. 37

The Veterinary Surgeon . . . London: 1827. V. 42

HINDS, WILLIAM ALFRED 1833-1910

American Communities . . . Oneida: 1878. V. 37; 39; 41; 42

HINE, DARYL

Five Poems, 1954. Toronto: 1954. V. 43

HINE, REGINALD L.

The History of Hitchin. London: 1927-29. V. 39; 42

HINES, DAVID

The Life, Adventures and Opinions of David Theo. Hines of South Carolina . . . New York: 1840. V. 46

HINES, E. CURTISS

The Haunted Barque and Other Poems. Auburn: 1848. V. 44

HINES, GUSTAVUS

A Voyage Round the World . . . Buffalo: 1850. V. 42; 45

HINES, JOSEPH WILKINSON

Touching Incidents in the Life and Labors of a Pioneer on the Pacific Coast Since 1853. San Jose: 1911. V. 37

HINGSTON, JAMES

Guide for Excursionists from Melbourne . . . Dedicated to all in Search of health, Recreation and Pleasure. Melbourne: 1868. V. 41

HINGTON, RICHARD J.

Rebel Invasion of Missouri and Kansas, and the Campaign of the Army of the Border, Against General Sterling Price, in October and November, 1864. Chicago: 1865. V. 42

HINKLE, GEORGE

Sierra-Nevada Lakes. Indianapolis: 1949. V. 44

HINKS, R. P.

Catalogue of the Greek, Etruscan and Roman Paintings and Mosaics in the British Museum. London: 1933. V. 42

HINKSON, KATHARINE TYNAN 1861-1931

Cuckoo Songs. Boston: 1894. V. 40

The Flower of Peace - a Collection of the Devotional Poetry of . . . London: 1914. V. 43

A Little Book of XXIV Carols. Portland: 1907. V. 41

Rose of the Garden. London: 1912. V. 39; 40

Twenty One Poems. 1907. V. 40

The Wild Harp. London: 1913. V. 39; 41

HINMAN, CHARLTON

The Printing and Proof Reading of the First Folio of Shakespeare. Oxford: 1963. V. 37; 39; 46

HINMAN, ROYAL R.

A Historical Collection, from Official Records, Files, Etc. Hartford: 1842. V. 46

Letters from the English Kings and Queens Charles Ii, James II, William and Mary, Anne, George II and c. to the Governors of the Colony of Connecticut . . . Hartford: 1836. V. 44

HINMAN, S. D.

Journal . . . Missionary to the Santee Sioux Indians. Philadelphia: 1869. V. 43

HINSDALE, GUY

Acromegaly Syringomyelia Crossed Knee-Jerk Anterior Poliomyelitis. Philadelphia: 1900. V. 38; 39; 40; 41

HINSDALE, WILBERT B.

Archaeological Atlas of Michigan. Ann Arbor: 1931. V. 37; 39; 45; 46

HINSHAW, GLENNIS

A Bibliography of Writings and Illustrations by Tom Lea. El Paso: 1971. V. 44

HINSHELWOOD, N. M.

Amidst the Laurentians, Being a Guide to Shawinigan Falls and Points on the Great Northern Railway of Canada. Montreal: 1902. V. 43

HINTON, H. E.

Biology of Insect Eggs. Oxford: 1981. V. 38

Biology of Insect Eggs. London: 1980. V. 37

HINTON, J. W.

Organ Construction. London: 1902. V. 40

HINTON, JOHN HOWARD

The History and Topography of the United States. London: 1830-32. V. 41

The History and Topography of the United States of North America . . . Boston: 1834. V. 37; 39; 40; 43

History & Topography of No. America. Boston: 1850. V. 39

HINTON, PERCIVAL

Eden Phillpotts: a Bibliography of First Editions. Birmingham: 1931. V. 42

HINTON, RICHARD

Rebel Invasion of Missouri and Kansas and the Campaign of the Army of the Border. Leavenworth: 1865. V. 43

HINTON, RICHARD J.

The Hand-Book to Arizona . . . San Francisco: 1878. V. 37; 42; 43; 44

Irrigation in the United States. A Report Prepared by . . . Under the Direction of the Commissioner of Agriculture. Washington: 1887. V. 39

HINTON, RICHARD J. continued

A Report on Irrigation and the Cultivation on the Soil Thereby. Washington: 1892. V. 37; 44

HINTON, S. E.

The Outsiders. New York: 1967. V. 42; 45

HINTS and Sketches, by an American Mother. New York: 1839. V. 43

HINTS for the Formation of a Fresh-Water Aquariam. London: 1857. V. 38

HINTS on the Impressment of Seamen. London: 1827. V. 40

HINTS Respecting the Improvement of the Literary and Scientific Education of Candidates for the Degree of Doctor of Medicine in the University of Edinburgh, Humbly Submitted to the Consideration of the Patrons and Professors of that Institution. Edinburgh: 1824. V. 39

HINTS to Farmers on the Nature, Purchase, and Application of Peruvian, Bolivian and African Guano; with a Series of Authenticated Experiments . . . London: 1844. V. 39

HINTS to the Bearers of Walking Sticks. London: 1809. V. 41; 44

HIORT, JOHN WILLIAM

A Practical Treatise on the Construction of Chimneys with Supplement. London: 1826. V. 45; 46

HIPKINS, ALFRED JAMES 1826-1903

Musical Instruments, Historic, Rare and Unique. Edinburgh: 1888. V. 46

Musical Instruments, Historic, Rare and Unique. London: 1921. V. 39; 40; 42; 46

Musical Instruments Historic, Rare and Unique. London: 1945. V. 38

Musical Instruments, Historic, Rare and Unique, the Selection, Introduction and Descriptive Notes . . . Reprint. 1921. V. 37

HIPKINS, JAMES

The Grecian Wanderer, and Other Poems. London: 1833. V. 42

HIPKINS, W. E.

The Wire Rope and Its Applications. Birmingham: 1896. V. 38; 41; 44

HIPPESLEY, R.

Bath and It's Environs, a Descriptive Poem, in Three Cantos. Bath: 1775. V. 40; 43

HIPPISLEY, GUSTAVUS

A Narrative of the Expedition to the Rivers Orinoco and Apure, in South America. London: 1819. V. 38; 41; 43

HIPPISLEY, J. H.

Chapters on Early English Literature. London: 1837. V. 43

HIPPISLEY, JOHN

A Dissertation on Comedy; in Which the Rise and Progress of that Species of the Drama is Particularly Consider'd and Deduc'd from the Earliest to the Present Age. London: 1750. V. 46

HIPPISLEY, JOHN COX 1748-1825

Prison Labour, etc., Correspondence and Communication Concerning the Introduction of Tread-Mills into Prisons . . . London: 1823. V. 39; 40; 41; 43

HIPPOCRATES

The Aphorismes of Hippocrates Prince of Physicians. London: 1655. V. 39

De Flatibus Liber, ab Adriano Alemano . . . Commentariis Illustratus. Paris: 1557. V. 46

The Genuine Works of Hippocrates. New York. V. 42; 44

The Genuine Works of Hippocrates. Translated from the Greek with a preliminary discourse and annotations by Francis Adams. London: 1840. V. 37

The Genuine Works of Hippocrates. London: 1849. V. 37; 38; 39; 40; 41; 44

The Genuine Works of Hippocrates. New York: 1886. V. 41; 42; 44; 45

Hippocrates cot Medicorum Omnivm Facile Principis Opera . . . Venetiis: 1575. V. 46

Hippocrates de Circuitu Sanguinis, Exercitatio III. Leiden: 1659. V. 45

Hippocrates Coi Medicorvm Omnivm Facile Principis Opera, Qvibvs Addidimvs . . . Venetiis: 1679. V. 44; 45

Hippocratis Coi, Medicorum Principis . . . Studio Ioannis Opsopoei Brettani. Frankfurt: 1587. V. 40

Octoginta Volumina . . . Nunc Tandem per M. Fabium Calvum Rhavennatem. Rome: 1525. V. 46

On Intercourse and Pregnancy. New York: 1952. V. 45

Opera Omnia Quae Extant in VIII Sectiones ex Erotiani Mente Distributa. Francofurti: 1595. V. 39

Opera Omnia, Gaece & Latine . . . Lugduni Batavorum: 1665. V. 39

Paul Offredi Medicinae Doctoris, in Librum Aphorismorum Hippocratis Commentaria Aphoristica, ad Methodum Analyticam Redacta. Aureliae Allobrogum,: 1606. V. 44; 46

Quarum Artium ac Linguarum Cognitione Medico opus sit . . . Aphorismi Hippocratis Graece. Hagenau: 1530. V. 37

Super Aphorismos Iacobi Foroliviensis in Hippocratis Aphorismos, et Galeni Super Eisdem Commentarios . . . Venice: 1546. V. 37

Upon Air, Water, and Situation, and Upon Prognosticks, in Acute Cases Especially. London: 1734. V. 42

Works. London: 1923-31. V. 46

HIRNHAIM, HIERONYMUS

De Typho Generis Humani, Sive Scientiarum Humanarum, Inani ac Ventoso Tumore . . . Prague: 1676. V. 44

HIROE, M.

Orchid Flowers. Kyoto: 1971. V. 37

Umbelliferae of the World. Kyoto: 1979. V. 37

HIRSCH, AUGUST

Biographisches Lexikon der Hervorragenden Aerzie aller Zeiten und Volker. Wien und Leipzig: 1884-88. V. 41

Handbook of Geographical and Historical Pathology. London: 1883-1886. V. 41; 42

HIRSCH, ROBERT

The Robert Hirsch Collection. Old Master Drawings, Paintings and Mediaeval Miniatures: Works of Art: Furniture & Porcelain, Impressionist & Modern Art . . . sold at auction by Sotheby . . . 20th June- 27th June 1978. London: 1978. V. 37

HIRSCH, SIDNEY M.

The Fire Regained. New York: 1913. V. 37; 39; 40; 42

HIRSCH, WEINTRAUB & CO., PHILADELPHIA.

Uniforms for Every Purpose. 1925. V. 46

HIRSCHBERG, JULIUS

The Treatment of Shortsight. New York: 1912. V. 44

HIRSCHFELD, ALBERT

The American Theatre As Senn by Hirschfeld. New York: 1916. V. 46

Harlem. New York: 1941. V. 39

HIRSCHFELD, SIADOR

The Toothbrush: Its Use and Abuse. New York: 1939. V. 40

HIRSCHMAN, JACK

Black Alephs - Poems 1960-1968. London: 1969. V. 39

A Correspondence of Americans. Bloomington: 1960. V. 43

Kline Sky. Los Angeles: 1965. V. 46

Two: Poems. Los Angeles: 1964. V. 46

Two: Ten Lithographs by Arnold, Poems by Jack Hirschman. Los Angeles: 1964. V. 42

HIRST, BARTON

A System of Obstetrics, by American Authors. Philadelphia: 1888. V. 42

HIRST, HENRY

The Coming of the Mammoth, The Funeral of Time. Boston: 1845. V. 45

HIRST, HENRY B.

Endymion: A Tale of Greece. Boston: 1848. V. 44

HIRST, J. CROWTHER

Hiram Greg. London: 1881. V. 40

HIRT, A. L.

Die Weihe des Eros Uranios. Berlin: 1818. V. 46

HIRTH, F.

Hsin-Kuan Wen-Chien-Lu. Text Book of Documentary Chinese . . . Shanghai: 1888. V. 43

HIRTZLER VICTOR

Hotel St. Francis. Book of Recipes and Model Menus. San Francisco;: 1910. V. 43

The Hotel St. Francis Cook Book. Chicago: 1919. V. 38; 40

HIRZEL, HANS K.

The Rural Socrates; or an Account of a Celebrated Philosophical Farmer . . . Hallowell: 1800. V. 45

HIS Catholic Majesty's Most Christian Manifesto, and Reasons for Not Paying the Ninety-Five Thousand Pounds . . . London: 1739. V. 42

HIS Catholick Majesty's Conduct Compared with that of His Britannick Majesty, As Well with Regard, to What Happened Before the Convention of the 14th January of This Year 1739, as to What Has Been Done Since . . . London: 1739. V. 40

HIS Imperial Highness the Grand Duke Alexis in the United States of America During the Winter of 1871-1872 . . . for Private Distribution. Cambridge: 1872. V. 38

HIS Maiesties Speach in This Last Session of Parliament. London: 1605. V. 41

HISCOX, GARDNER D.

Mechanical Movements, Powers and Devices. New York: 1927. V. 40

HISLOP, HERBERT R.

An Englishman's Arizona: The Ranching Letters of Herbert R. Hislop 1876-1878. Tucson: 1965. V. 39; 44

HISPERICA FAMINA

Hisperica Famina: The Garden of God. The Prologue and a Part of the Book of Days Translated by Winthrop Palmer Boswell. San Francisco: 1974. V. 40

HISS, ALGER

In the Court of Public Opinion. New York: 1957. V. 39

HISSEY, JAMES JOHN

Across England in a Dog-Cart from London to St. Davids and Back. London: 1891. V. 43

HISTOIRE D'OUTRE MER

The History of Over Sea. New York: 1902. V. 38

HISTOIRE du Chevalier Paris et de La Belle Vienne. Paris: 1835. V. 41; 45

HISTORIA Dorum Fatidicorum . . . Cum Eorum Iconibus. Frankfurt: 1680. V. 39

HISTORIA Quatuor Regum Angliae Heroico Carmine Conclusa. London: 1868. V. 40

A HISTORICAL Account of His Majesty's Visit to Scotland. Edinburgh: 1822. V. 37; 40; 46

AN HISTORICAL Account of Mandrakes, Both Male and Female. London: 1741. V. 39
AN HISTORICAL Account of Mandrakes, Both Male and Female. London: 1742. V. 39

AN HISTORICAL Account of the Circumnavigation of the Globe and of the Progress of Discovery in the Pacific Ocean from the Voyage of Magellan to the Death of Cook. Edinburgh: 1837. V. 45

AN HISTORICAL Account of the Curiosities of London and Westminster, in three parts: Tower of London, Westminster Abbey, Old and New Cathedral of St. Paul. London: 1782-84. V. 37

AN HISTORICAL Account of the Discovery of the Island of Madeira, Abridged from the Portuguese Original. London: 1750. V. 41; 42

AN HISTORICAL Account of the Heroick Life and Magnanimous Actions of the Most Illustrious and Magnanimous Actions of the Most Illustrious Protestant Prince, James, Duke of Monmouth. London: 1683. V. 38; 45

AN HISTORICAL Account of the Late Election of Knights of the Shire for the County of Down, Together with a Petition to Parliament Complaining of an Undue Election and Return for the Said County, and the Proceedings Thereof . . . printed in the year: 1784. V. 43

AN HISTORICAL Account of the Late Election of Knights of the Shire for the County of Down. Together with the Petition to Parliament, Complaining of an Undue Election and Return for the Said County . . . Dublin: 1784. V. 41

AN HISTORICAL Account of the Origin, Progress and Present State of the Benthlem Hospital, Founded by the Eighth, for the Cure of Lunatics and Enlarged by Subsequent Benefactors . . . London: 1783. V. 42

AN HISTORICAL Account of the Settlement and Possession of Bombay, by the English East India Company, and of the Rise and Progress of the War with the Mahratta Nation. London: 1781. V. 44

AN HISTORICAL Account of the Triumphant Spirit of the Whigs. Edinburgh: 1746. V. 39

HISTORICAL and Biographical Atlas of the New Jersey Coast. Philadelphia: 1878. V. 38; 44

HISTORICAL and Biographical Record of the Territory of Arizona. Chicago: 1896. V. 42

AN HISTORICAL and Descriptive Account of Iceland, Greenland, and the Faroe Islands. New York: 1841. V. 42

HISTORICAL and Descriptive of Fremont & Custer Counties with their Principal Towns. Canon City and Other Towns, Fremont County, ROsita, Silver Cliff, Ula . . . Canon City;: 1879. V. 37

THE HISTORICAL and Local New Bath Guide. Bath. V. 46

HISTORICAL and Scientific Sketches of Michigan: Comprising a Series of Discourses delivered before the Historical Society of Michigan, and other Interesting papers Relative to the Territory. Detroit: 1834. V. 37

HISTORICAL Atlas Map of Sonoma Conty, California. Oakland: 1877. V. 40

HISTORICAL Catalogue of Portraits, Representing Distinguished Persons in the History and Literature of the United Kingdom. London: 1820. V. 41; 46

HISTORICAL Collections of Louisiana, Embracing Many Rare and Valuable Documents Relating to the Natural, Civil and Political History of that State . . . N: 1846-53. V. 40

HISTORICAL Collections of Louisiana, Embracing Many Rare and Valuable Documents Relating to the Natural, Civil and Political History of that State Compiled with Historical and Biographical Notes . . . New York: 1846-53. V. 40

HISTORICAL Collections of the Mahoning Valley. Youngstown: 1876. V. 40; 43

AN HISTORICAL Compendium, from the Creation, to the Year of Our Lord 1726. Westmisnter: 1726. V. 41

AN HISTORICAL Description of the Tower of London and Its Curiosities. Giving an Account of Its Foundation . . . Government . . . Spoils of the Spanish Armada, . . . Armory . . . Jewel Office . . . London: 1759. V. 38; 41

AN HISTORICAL Description of Westminster-Abbey, Its Monuments and Curiosities. London: 1754. V. 39

A HISTORICAL Descriptive and Commercial Directory of Owyhee County, Idaho. Silver City, Idaho: 1898. V. 37

AN HISTORICAL Detail of the Most Remarkaable Pubick Occurrences, and the Newest Political Intelligence. London: 1765. V. 38; 45

AN HISTORICAL Dictionary of England and Wales. London: 1692. V. 39

AN HISTORICAL Digest of the Reports of Commissioners Appointed to Inquire into Abuses in the Public Departments of Government, Between the Years 1776 and 1812 . . . London: 1824. V. 39

AN HISTORICAL, Genealogical and Poetical Dictionary: Containing the Lives and Actions of all the Great Men Among the Grecians, Romans, Jews, etc . . . London: 1703. V. 41

HISTORICAL Memoranda Relative to the Discovery of Etherization and To the Connection With It of the Late Dr. William T. G. Morton. Boston: 1871. V. 45

THE HISTORICAL Mirror, or Biographical Miscellany, for the Instruction and Entertainment of Youth. London: 1775. V. 40

AN HISTORICAL Miscellany of the Curiosities and Rarities in Nature and Art. London: 1792-97? V. 46

AN HISTORICAL Narrative of the Great Plague at London, 1665 . . . and Some Account of Other Remarkable Plagues, Ancient and Modern . . . London: 1769. V. 38

HISTORICAL Narrative of the Turko-Russian War. London: 1880. V. 38

HISTORICAL Portraiture of Leading Events in the Life of Ali Pacha, Vizier of Epirus, Surnamed the Lion. London: 1823. V. 41

HISTORICAL Record of the First, or Royal Regiment of Foot: Containing an Account of the Origin of the Regiment in the Reign of King James VI of Scotland and of its subsequent Services to 1838. London: 1838. V. 37

AN HISTORICAL Record of the Light Horse Volunteers of London and Westminster. London: 1843. V. 38

HISTORICAL Records of the 2nd Battalion, 24th Regiment, for the Campaign in South Africa, 1877-78-79. India: 1882. V. 41

HISTORICAL Records of the Town of Cornwall. Litchfield County, Connecticut. Hartford: 1877. V. 46

HISTORICAL Remarks and Anecdotes on the Castle of the Bastille. London: 1780. V. 46

HISTORICAL Remarks on the Castle of the Bastille: with Curious and Entertaining Anecdotes of that Fortress &c. &c. From the French. London: 1789. V. 39

AN HISTORICAL Review of Pennsylvania, From Its Origin, Embracing, Among Other Subjects, the Various Points of Controversy, Which Have Arisen . . . Philadelphia: 1812. V. 42

A HISTORICAL Review of the Constitution and Government of Pennsylvania, From Its Origin . . . London: 1759. V. 42

HISTORICAL Sketch of Barton Lodge No. 6. G.R.C., A.F. and A.M. Hamilton: 1895. V. 42

AN HISTORICAL Sketch of Los Angeles County. Los Angeles: 1876. V. 37

HISTORICAL Sketches Illustrative of the Life of M. De Lafayette and the Leading Events of the American Revolution. New York: 1824. V. 45

HISTORICAL Sketches of the Missions Under the Care of the Board of Foreign Missions of the Presbyterian Church. Philadelphia: 1886. V. 44

HISTORICAL SOCIETY OF MONTANA

Contributions to the . . . Volume III. Helena: 1900. V. 38
Contributions to the Historical Society of Montana. Helena: 1876. V. 39; 40
Contributions to the . . . Volume II. Helena: 1896. V. 37; 38

HISTORICAL SOCIETY OF PENNSYLVANIA

Memoirs of the . . . . Philadelphia: 1826. V. 38

HISTORICAL SOCIETY OF SOUTHERN CALIFORNIA

Annula Publications. 1884-1934. V. 41

HISTORICAL Souvenir of San Francisco, California. Views of Prominent Buildings, the Bay, Islands, etc. San Francisco: 1887. V. 46

AN HISTORICAL View of the Principles, Chracterss, Persons &c. of the Political Writers in Great Britain . . . London: i.e.: 1740. V. 46

HISTORISCHE-GENEALOGISCHER Calendar, Oder Jahrbuch der Merkwuerdigsten Neun Welt-Bergenheiten fur 1784. Leipsig: 1793. V. 40

THE HISTORY and Adventures of Frank Hammond. London: 1754. V. 38

THE HISTORY and Antiquites of Rochester and Its Environs. Rochester: 1772. V. 40

A HISTORY and Biographical Cyclopaedia of Butler County, Ohio. Cincinnati: 1882. V. 46

HISTORY and Business Directory of Madison County, Iowa. Des Moines: 1869. V. 42

THE HISTORY and Defence of the Last Parliament. London: 1713. V. 42

HISTORY and Defense of Magna Charta. Dublin: 1769. V. 40

THE HISTORY and Description of Fossil Fuel, the Collieries and Coal Trade of Great Britain. London: 1835. V. 39

HISTORY and Description of the Public Charities in the Town of Frome. Frome: 1833. V. 37

HISTORY and Evidence of the Passage of Abraham Lincoln from Harrisburg, Pa. to Washington, D. C. on the 22d and 23d of February, 1861. 1892. V. 38

THE HISTORY and Legends of Old Castles and Abbeys. London: 1875. V. 39

HISTORY India. London: 1906. V. 46

THE HISTORY of a Little Silver-Fish. Hartford: 1819. V. 45

THE HISTORY of a Voyage to the Moon. With an Account of the Adventurer's Subsequent Dicoveries. An exhumed Narrative, Supposed to have been ejected from a Lunar Volcano. London: 1864. V. 37

HISTORY of Allegheny County, Pennsylvania. Chicago: 1889. V. 41; 42

HISTORY of Amador County, California, with Illustrations and Biographical Sketches of its Prominent Men and Pioneers. Oakland: 1881. V. 37; 38

HISTORY of American Field Service in France: 'Friends of France' 1914-1917. Boston: 1920. V. 39

HISTORY of Arizona Territory Showing Its Resources and Advantages . . . San Francisco: 1884. V. 42; 45

HISTORY of Ashtabula County, Ohio . . . 1798-1878. Philadelphia: 1878. V. 39; 46

HISTORY of Beaver Co., Pennsylvania; Including Its Early Settlement . . . Chicago: 1888. V. 41; 42

HISTORY of Bedford, Somerset and Fulton Counties, Pennsyvlania. Chicago: 1884. V. 42

HISTORY of Benton County, Iowa, Containing a History of the County, Its Cities, Towns, &c., A Biographical Directory of Its Citizens, War Record of Its Volunteers in the Late Rebellion. Chicago: 1878. V. 38

HISTORY of Benton, Washington, Carroll, Madison, Crawford, Franklin and Sebastian Counties, Arkansas. Chicago: 1889. V. 45

THE HISTORY of Bookbinding. 525-1950. Baltimore: 1957. V. 40

HISTORY of Boston, from 1630 to 1856. Boston: 1856. V. 43

HISTORY of Bradford County, Pennsylvania, 1770-1878. Philadelphia: 1878. V. 42

HISTORY of Butler and Bremer Counties, Iowa, Together with Sketches of Their Towns, Villages and Townships, Educational, Civil, Military and Political History. Springfield: 1883. V. 38

HISTORY of Butler County, Pennsylvania. N.P.: 1895. V. 41

HISTORY of Butler County, Pennsylvania, 1796-1883. Chicago: 1883. V. 41

THE HISTORY of Caledonia; or, the Scots Colony in Darien in the West Indies. London: 1699. V. 40

HISTORY of Chemung, Tompkins and Schuyler Counties, New York. Philadelphia: 1879. V. 44

HISTORY Of Cincinnati and Hamilton County, Ohio; Their Past and Present. Cincinnati: 1894. V. 46

THE HISTORY of Clark County, Ohio. Chicago: 1881. V. 38

HISTORY of Clear Creek and Boulder Valleys, Colorado. Chicago: 1880. V. 37; 43

THE HISTORY of Columbia County, Wisconsin. Chicago: 1880. V. 46

HISTORY of Coos County. Somersworth: 1972. V. 39

HISTORY of Crawford County, Pennsylvania. Chicago: 1885. V. 41; 42

HISTORY of Cumberland and Adams Counties, Pennsylvania. Chicago: 1886. V. 41

HISTORY of Dane County, Wisconsin. Chicago: 1880. V. 46

HISTORY of Davidson County, Tennessee, with Illustrations and Biographical Sketches of its Prominent Men and Pioneers. Philadelphia: 1880. V. 39

HISTORY Of Dearborn and Ohio Counties, Indiana. Chicago: 1885. V. 46

HISTORY of Dearborn, Ohio and Switzerland Counties, Indiana, from Their Earliest Settlement . . . Chicago: 1895. V. 46

HISTORY of Delaware County, New York (1797-1880). New York: 1880. V. 46

THE HISTORY of Don Juan, or the Libertine Destroyed. London: 1815. V. 44

THE HISTORY of Eliza Warwick. London: 1791. V. 45

THE HISTORY of England: Being a Compendium, Adapted to the Capacities and Memories of Youth at School. London: 1768. V. 42

HISTORY of Erie County, Pennsylvania. Chicago: 1884. V. 41; 42

THE HISTORY of Fanny Seymour. London: 1753. V. 40

HISTORY of First City Troop Philadelphia City Cavalry, 1774-1874. Philadelphia: 1875. V. 41

HISTORY of Franklin County, Pennsylvania . . . Chicago: 1887. V. 41; 42

HISTORY of Franklin, Jefferson, Washington, Crawford & Gasconade Counties, Missouri . . . Chicago: 1888. V. 38

THE HISTORY of George Barnwell the London Apprentice, Who Robbed His Master, and Murdered His Uncle, to Satisfy the Extravagance of His Mistress, Millwood . . . London: 1810. V. 44

HISTORY of Greene and Sullivan Counties, State of Indiana . . . Chicago: 1884. V. 46

HISTORY of Helyas. Knight of the Swan. New York: 1901. V. 46

HISTORY of Indiana County, Penn'a. 1745-1880. Newark: 1880. V. 39; 41; 42

THE HISTORY of Ink. New York: 1860. V. 38

THE HISTORY of Ireland, From the Earliest Authentic Accounts. Dublin: 1784. V. 46

THE HISTORY of Jack and the Bean Stalk. Glasgow: 1810. V. 39

THE HISTORY of Jane Grey, Queen of England. London: 1792. V. 39; 44

THE HISTORY of Jane Shore. Concubine to Edward IVth. Boston: 1801. V. 40

THE HISTORY of Johnny Quae Genus. London: 1822. V. 40

HISTORY of Jones County, Iowa, Containing a History of the County, Its Citites, Towns &c., Biographical Sketches of Citizens, War Record of Its Volunteers in the Late Rebellion. Chicago: 1879. V. 46

THE HISTORY of Julia and Cecilia de Valmont. Cork: 1797. V. 41

HISTORY of Kalamazoo County, Michigan. Philadelphia: 1880. V. 39

THE HISTORY of King-Killers; or, the 30th of January Commemorated: in the Lives of Thirty-One Fanatick Saints, Famous for Treason, Rebellion &c . . . London: 1719. V. 39

HISTORY of LaPorte County, Indiana . . . Chicago: 1880. V. 46

THE HISTORY of Little Billy & His Grand-Pa, A Tale for Young and Old. Batnstable: 1925. V. 37

THE HISTORY of Little Goody Two-Shoes. London: 1960. V. 46

THE HISTORY of Little Tom Thumb. London. V. 44

THE HISTORY of Lord North's Administration to the Dissolution of the Thirteenth Parliament of Great Britain. London: 1781. V. 37

HISTORY of Luzerne, Lackawanna and Wyoming Counties. New York: 1880. V. 41; 42; 44

HISTORY of Madison County, Illinois. Edwardsville: 1882. V. 46

THE HISTORY of Marion County, Ohio, Containing a History of the County; its Townships, Towns, Churches, Schools, etc., General and Local Statistics; Military Record; Portraits of Early settlers and Prominent Men; History . . . Chicago: 1883. V. 37; 38

HISTORY Of McDonough County, Illinois. Springfield: 1885. V. 46

HISTORY of McLean County, Illinois. Chicago: 1879. V. 46

HISTORY of Medicine and Surgery and Physicians and Surgeons of Chicago. Chicago: 1922. V. 42; 45

HISTORY of Medina County and Ohio. Chicago: 1881. V. 46

THE HISTORY of Miss Maria Barlowe. Dublin: 1778. V. 38

THE HISTORY of Mr. Byron and Miss Greville. London: 1767. V. 37

HISTORY of Monterey County . . . . Fresno: 1979. V. 44

HISTORY of Montgomery and Fulton Counties, New York, with Illustrations Descriptive of Scenery, Private Residences, Public Buildings, Fine Blocks, and Important Manufactories, from Original Sketches by Artists of the Highest Ability . . . New York: 1878. V. 38

THE HISTORY Of More Persons than One, or Entertaining and Instructive Anecdotes for Youth. London: 1823. V. 46

HISTORY of Morris County, New Jersey, with Illustrations, and Biographical Sketches of Prominent Citizens and Pioneers. New York: 1882. V. 38; 41; 42

HISTORY of Morrow County and Ohio. Chicago: 1880. V. 44

HISTORY of Muscatine County, Iowa. Chicago: 1879. V. 46

THE HISTORY of North Allerton, in the County of York. Northallerton: 1791. V. 45

THE HISTORY of Oliver and Arthur. Boston: 1903. V. 46
THE HISTORY of Oliver and Arthur. Boston and New York: 1903. V. 44
THE HISTORY of Oliver and Arthur. Cambridge: 1903. V. 45

HISTORY of Oswego County, New York. Philadelphia: 1877. V. 39

HISTORY of Pennsylvania Hall. Philadelphia: 1838. V. 43

THE HISTORY of Pews. Cambridge: 1841. V. 39

THE HISTORY of Philip de Commines, Knight, Lord of Argenton. London: 1674. V. 39

HISTORY Of Pike and Dubois Counties, Indiana. Chicago: 1885. V. 46

THE HISTORY of Poetry. With Such Alterations of Phrase as May be More Suitable to the Taste of This Age. London: 1735-36. V. 39

HISTORY of Portage County, Ohio, Containing a History of the County, Its Townships, Towns, Villages, Schools, Churches, Industries, etc., Portraits of Early Settlers and Prominent Men . . . Chicago: 1885. V. 39

THE HISTORY of Preston, in Lancashire; Together with the Guild Merchant and some Account of the Duchy and County Palatine of Lancaster. London: 1822. V. 46
THE HISTORY of Preston, in Lancashire; Together with the Guild Merchant, and Some Account of the Duchy and County Palatine of Lancaster. London: 1922. V. 42

THE HISTORY of Prince Lee Boo, a Native of the Pelew Islands Brought to England by Captain Wilson. Philadelphia: 1802. V. 37; 41; 42; 43

A HISTORY Of Prince Lee, Boo, Native of the Pelew Islands, Brought to England by Captain Wilson. London: 1808. V. 41; 42

THE HISTORY of Prince Mirabel's Infancy, Rise and Disgrace. London: 1712. V. 42; 45

THE HISTORY of Racine and Kenosha Counties, Wisconsin. Chicago: 1879. V. 46

THE HISTORY of Ripon, Comprehending a Civil and Ecclesiastical Account of that Ancient Borough. York: 1801. V. 44

THE HISTORY Of Robespierre, Political and Personal, Containing, His Principles and Actions and Design in the Jacobin Club, Commune of Paris, Constituent Assembly and the Convention. London: 1794. V. 41

THE HISTORY of Rock County, Wisconsin . . . Early Settlement, Growth, Development . . . Chicago: 1879. V. 46

HISTORY of Santa Ana City and Valley: Its Past, Flourishing Present and Bright Future. Santa Ana: 1887. V. 41

HISTORY of Santa Barbara County, California, with Illustrations and Biographical Sketches . . . Oakland: 1883. V. 38; 40

HISTORY of Santa Clara County, California. San Francisco: 1881. V. 45; 46

THE HISTORY of Sauk County, Wisconsin. Chicago: 1880. V. 44

HISTORY of Seneca County, Ohio. Chicago: 1886. V. 39

HISTORY of Shiawassee and Clinton Counties, Michigan, With Illustrations and Biographical Sketches of Their Prominent Men and Pioneers. Philadelphia: 1880. V. 42

THE HISTORY of Susanna. San Francisco. V. 46

HISTORY of Texas, Together with a Biographical History of the Cities of Houston and Galveston. Chicago: 1895. V. 38
HISTORY of Texas, Together With a Biographical History of the Cities of Houston and Galveston. Chicago: 1895. V. 38

HISTORY of Texas World War Heroes. Dallas: 1919. V. 42; 44

HISTORY of the 20th (Duke of Cambridge's Own) Infantry, Brownlow's Punjabis. Devonport: 1909. V. 38

HISTORY Of the 5th Royal Gurkha Rifles (Frontier Force). Volume II: 1929-1947. Aldershot: 1956. V. 41

THE HISTORY of the Abbey Church of St. Peter's Westminster, Its Antiquities and Monuments. London: 1812. V. 46

HISTORY of the American Field Service in France 'Friends of France' 1914-1917. Boston: 1920. V. 43

HISTORY of the Arkansas Valley, Colorado. Chicago: 1881. V. 37; 38; 40; 45

HISTORY of the Baldwin Locomotive Works from 1831 to 1897. Philadelphia: 1897. V. 41

HISTORY of the Bible. Boston: 1819. V. 41
HISTORY of the Bible. Lansingburgh: 1824. V. 45
HISTORY of the Bible. Bridgeport: 1831. V. 41
HISTORY of the Bible. Cooperstown: 1846. V. 41; 44

THE HISTORY of the Campaign of 1796, in Germany and Italy. London: 1797. V. 42
THE HISTORY of the Campaign of 1796 in Germany and Italy. London: 1800. V. 43

HISTORY of the Captivity and Sufferings of Mrs. Maria Martin, Who Was Six years a Slave in Algiers: Two of Which she was Confined in a Dark and Dismal Dungeon, Loaded with Irons. Boston: 1806? V. 37; 40

HISTORY of the Celebration of the Fiftieth Anniversary of the Taking Possession of California and Raising the American Flag at Monterey, Cal. Oakland: 1896. V. 41

HISTORY Of the City of Denver, Arapahoe County and Colorado. Chicago: 1880. V. 38; 39; 40; 42; 45

A HISTORY of the City of Newark, New Jersey, Embracing Practically Two and a Half Centuries, 1666-1913. New York: 1913. V. 41

HISTORY of the Counties of McKean, Elk, Cameron and Potter, Pennsylvania With Biographical Selections. Chicago: 1890. V. 41; 42

HISTORY of the County of Middlesex, Canada. Toronto: 1889. V. 41; 46

THE HISTORY of the County of Welland, Ontario, Its Past and Present . . . Welland: 1887. V. 44

THE HISTORY of the Discovery and Conquest of the Canary Islands. Dublin: 1767. V. 37

HISTORY of the Family of Daubeney from the Collections and Records of the Heralds College etc. N.P.. V. 39

THE HISTORY of the Famous Town of Hallifax . . . With a True Account of Their Antient Odd Customary Gibbet-Law. London: 1712. V. 44

THE **HISTORY** of the Feuds and Conflicts Among the Clans in the Northern Parts of Scotland and in the Western Isles, from the Year 1031 to the Year 1619. London: 1780. V. 42

HISTORY of the Fifty-Seventh Regiment, Pennsylvania Veteran Volunteer Infantry, First Brigade, First Division, Second Corps, Army of the Potomac. Meadville: 1904. V. 37

HISTORY of the First Baptist Church, Chicago: With the Articles of Faith, and Covenant and a Catalogue of Its Members, January 15th, 1866. Chicago. V. 46

HISTORY of the First Troop Philadelphia City Cavalry 1914-1948. Philadelphia: 1948. V. 42

THE **HISTORY** of the Fisherman and the Genius, Taken from the Real Manuscript of the Arabian Tales Recently Discovered in Bagdad. London: 1859. V. 41

HISTORY of the Great Western Sanitary Fair. Cincinnati: 1864. V. 41

HISTORY of the Guibord Case: Ultramontanism Versus Law and Human Rights. Montreal: 1875. V. 44

A **HISTORY** of the Japanese Arts. Tokyo: 1913. V. 46

A **HISTORY** of the Juniata Valley. Harrisburg: 1936. V. 39; 41; 42

THE **HISTORY** of the Late Revolution in England, with the Causes and Means by Which it Was Accomplished. London: 1689. V. 42

A **HISTORY** of the Life and Public Services of Major General Andrew Jackson, Impartially Compiled from the Most Authentic Sources. Philadelphia?: 1828. V. 42; 45

THE **HISTORY** of the Life of Tamerlane the Great. London: 1782. V. 44

THE **HISTORY** of the Little Old Woman Who Lived in a Shoe. London: 1860. V. 45
THE **HISTORY** of the Little Old Woman Who Lived in a Shoe. New York: 1860. V. 40

THE **HISTORY** Of the London Rifle Brigade 1859-1919. London: 1921. V. 42; 45; 46

THE **HISTORY** of the Man After God's Own Heart. London: 1761. V. 39

THE **HISTORY** of the Mitre and Purse, in Which the First and Second Parts of the Secret History of the White Staf are Fully Considered, and the Hypocrisy and Villanies of the Staff Himself are Laid Open and Detected. London: 1714. V. 38

THE **HISTORY** of the Most Remarkable Tryals in Great Britain and Ireland, in Capital Cases . . . London: 1715. V. 38

HISTORY of the One Hundred and Twenty-fifth Regiment Pennsylvania Volunteers, 1862-1863. Philadelphia: 1906. V. 42

HISTORY of the Organization of the Methodist Epsicopal Church, South . . . Nashville: 1845. V. 37; 43; 46

HISTORY of the Part of the Susquehanna and Juniata Valleys, Embraced in the Counties of Mifflin, Juniata, Perry, Union and Snyder, in the Commonwealth of Pennsylvania. Philadelphia: 1886. V. 41; 42

HISTORY of the Pirates Containing the Lives of Those Noted Pirate Captains Mission, Bowen, Kidd, Tew, Halsey, White, Condent, Bellamy, Fly, Howard, Lewis, Cornelius, Williams, Burgess, North, and their Several Crews . . . Haverhill: 1825. V. 37

THE **HISTORY** of the Popish-Sham-Plots from the Reign of Queen Elizabeth to this Present Time. Particularly of the Present Popish Plot. Being an Account of the several Methods the Papists have used to stifle it . . . London: 1682. V. 37

THE **HISTORY** Of the Rebellion in the Years 1745 and 1746. Oxford: 1944. V. 40

THE **HISTORY** of the Reign of George the Third, King of Great Britain, etc. to the Conclusion of the Session of Parliament . . . London: 1770. V. 46

THE **HISTORY** of the Rise, Progress and Extinction of the Late Rebellion in Scotland. Edinburgh: 1759. V. 46

A **HISTORY** of the Royal Toxophilite Society, from Its Institution to the Present Time (i.e. 1870). 1870. V. 46

A **HISTORY** of the Schuylkill Fishing Company of the State in Schuylkill 1732-1888. Philadelphia: 1889. V. 41

A **HISTORY** of the Schuylkill Fishing Company of the State in Schuylkill 1732-1888. (with) A History . . . 1888-1932. Philadelphia: 1889-1932. V. 41

HISTORY of the Sisters of Charity of Leavenworth, Kansas. Kansas City: 1898. V. 38

THE **HISTORY** of the Stage. In Which Is Included, the Theatrical Characters of the Most Celebrated Actors Who Have Adorn'd the Theatre. London: 1742. V. 46

HISTORY of the State of Nebraska; a Full Account of Its Growth . . . Chicago: 1882. V. 43

HISTORY of the Third Pennsylvania Cavalry, Sixteenth Regiment Pennsylvania Volunteers, in the American Civil War. Philadelphia: 1905. V. 42

THE **HISTORY** of the Times. London: 1935-1984. V. 41
THE **HISTORY** of the Times. London: 1950-52. V. 46

HISTORY of the Town of Hingham, Massachusetts. N.P.: 1863. V. 46

A **HISTORY** Of the University of Oxford, Its Colleges, Halls and Public Buildings. London: 1814. V. 46

THE **HISTORY** of the Venetian Conquests, from the Year 1684 to This Present Year 1688. London: 1689. V. 40

THE **HISTORY** of the Voyages of Christopher Columbus, in Order to Discover America and the West-Indies. London: 1777. V. 43; 46

THE **HISTORY** of the Witch of Endor. London: 1754. V. 39

HISTORY of the Works of the Learned. London: 1701, 1705. V. 38

THE **HISTORY** of the Works of the Learned; or, an Impartial Account of Books Lately printed in all Parts of Europe. London: 1699-1712. V. 38; 40; 42

HISTORY of Tioga County, Pennsylvania . . . Harrisburg: 1897. V. 41; 42

THE **HISTORY** of Tom Jones the Foundling, in His Married State. London: 1750. V. 39; 42; 46

A **HISTORY** of Trenton, 1679-1929: Two Hundred and Fifty Years of a Notable Town with Links in Four Centuries. Princeton: 1929. V. 38; 46

HISTORY of Trumbull and Mahoning Counties, with Illustrations and Biographical Sketches. Clevelnd: 1882. V. 38

HISTORY of Trumbull & Mahoning Counties, with Illustrations and Biographical Sketchs. Cleveland: 1882. V. 37; 46

HISTORY of Urology. Baltimore: 1933. V. 45

A **HISTORY** of Useful Arts & Manufactures. Dublin: 1822. V. 44; 45

THE **HISTORY** of Vanillo Gonzales, Surnamed the Merry Batchelor. London: 1797. V. 42

THE **HISTORY** of Vanillo Gonzales; Surnamed the Merry Batdhelor. London: 1797. V. 45

HISTORY of Venango County, Pennsylvania. Chicago: 1890. V. 41; 42

HISTORY of Western Maryland. Philadelphia: 1882. V. 40

HISTORY of York County Pennsylvania. Chicago: 1886. V. 41

HISTORY of Yuba County California with Illustrations Descriptive of Its Scenery, Residences, Public Buildings, Fine Blocks and Manufactories . . . Oakland: 1879. V. 42

THE **HISTORY** of Zoa, the Beautiful Indian, Daughter of Henrietta de Belgrave; and of Rodomond, Whom Zoa Releases from Confinement and with Him Makes Her Escape from Her Father, Who Was the Occasion of Rodomond's Imprisonment and Dreadful Sufferings. London: 1806. V. 38

HITCHCOCK, EDWARD

Final Report on the Geology of Massachusetts: In Four Parts . . . Amherst: 1841. V. 42

Final Report on the Geology of Massachusetts. Amherst and Northampton: 1841. V. 40

Ichnology of New England. A Report on the Sandstone of the Connecticut Valley, Especially its Fossil Footmarks . . . Boston: 1858, 1865. V. 38

Outline of the Geology of the Globe and of the United States in Particular . . . Boston: 1853. V. 42

The Religion of Geology and Its Connected Sciences. London: 1851. V. 40

Report on the Geology, Mineralogy, Botany and Zoology of Massachusetts. Amherst: 1833. V. 40; 43

Sketch of the Scenery of Massachsetts. Northampton: 1842. V. 39; 40

Supplement to the Ichnology of New England. Boston: 1865. V. 45; 46

HITCHCOCK, ENOS

Memoirs of the Bloomsgrove Family. Boston: 1790. V. 37; 41; 43; 44; 45; 46

HITCHCOCK, ETHAN ALLEN

Fifty Years in Camp and Field. New York: 1909. V. 37; 39; 40; 46

Remarks Upon Alchemy and the Alchemists . . . A True Method of Discovering the True Nature of Hermetic Philosophy . . . New York: 1865. V. 46

HITCHCOCK, ETHAN ALLEN continued

A Traveler in Indian Territory. Cedar Rapids: 1930. V. 39; 40; 43; 45

A Traveler in Indian Territory. Cedar Rapids: 1930. V. 42

HITCHCOCK, F. L.

History of Scranton and Its People. New York: 1914. V. 39; 41

HITCHCOCK, FRANK

A True Account of the Capture of Frank Rande, 'The Noted Outlaw' by the late Frank Hitchcock - Sheriff of Peoria County, Ill . . . Peoria: 1897. V. 37

HITCHCOCK, H. R.

An English-Hawaiian Dictionary . . . San Francisco: 1887. V. 38; 40; 42

HITCHCOCK, HENRY

The Alabama Justice of the Peace . . . Cahawba: 1822. V. 43

HITCHCOCK, HENRY RUSSELL

Early Victorian Architecture in Britain. London: 1954. V. 45

Early Victorian Architecture in Britain. New Haven: 1954. V. 41; 44

Modern Architecture, Romanticism and Reintegration. New York: 1929. V. 46

Modern Architecture in England. New York: 1937. V. 41

Philip Johnson: Architecture 1949-1965. New York: 1967. V. 43; 46

Rococo ARchitecture in Southern Germany. London: 1968. V. 42

Temples of Democracy, the State Capitols of the USA. New York: 1976. V. 41

HITCHCOCK, J. R. W.

Etching in America. New York: 1886. V. 40; 41; 44; 46

HITCHCOCK, PETER

Speech of . . . In the Senate of Ohio. February 2 and 3, 1835, On the Resolutions From the House of Represenatives, to Rescind Certain Resolutions of the Last General Assembly, Giving Instructions to Our Senators and Representatives in Congress. Columbus: 1835. V. 42

HITCHENER, ELIZABETH

Enigmas, Historical and Geographical, by a Clergyman's Daughter. London: 1834. V. 46

Letters of Elixabeth Hitchener to Percy Bysshe Shelley. New York: 1926. V. 37; 39

HITLER, ADOLF

Mein Kampf. New York: 1939. V. 38

Mein Kampf. Munich: 1925-27. V. 37

HITOPADESA

The Heetopades of Veeshnoo-Sarma, in a Series of Connected Fables . . . Bath: 1787. V. 42

Hitopadesa. London: 1847. V. 43; 44

Indian Fables from the Sanscrit of the Hitopadesa . . . London: 1862. V. 42

HITT, THOMAS

A Treatise on Fruit Trees. London: 1755. V. 38

A Treatise of Fruit-Trees. London: 1757. V. 45

A Treatise on Fruit Trees. Dublin: 1758. V. 37; 41; 43

A Treatise on Fruit-Trees. London: 1768. V. 37; 41; 43; 44

HITTEL, JOHN S.

The Resources of California. San Francisco: 1867. V. 41

HITTELL, J. S.

The Prospects of Vallejo: Or, Evidences that Vallejo will become a Great City. Vallejo: 1871. V. 37

HITTELL, JOHN S.

Commerce and Industries of the Pacific Coast of North America: Comprising the Rise, Progress, Products, Present Condition and Prospects . . . On the Western Side of Our Continent, and Some Account of Its Resources . . . San Francisco: 1882. V. 45

A History of the City of San Francisco and Incidentally of the State of California. San Francisco: 1878. V. 42; 44; 45

Hittell's Hand-Book of Pacific Coast Travel.. San Francisco: 1887. V. 40; 42

The Resources of California, Comprising the Society, Climate, Salubrity, Scenery, Commerce and Industry of the State. San Francisco: 1874. V. 40

HITTELL, THEODORE H.

The Adventures of James Capen Adams, Mountaineer and Grizzly Bear Hunter of California. V. 46

The Adventures of James Capen Adams, Mountaineer and Grizzly Bear Hunter, of California. Boston: 1860. V. 38; 39

The Adventures of James Capen Adams, Mountaineer & Grizzly Bear Hunter, of California. San Francisco: 1860. V. 39; 40; 46

The Adventures of James Capen Adams, Mountaineer and Grizzly Bear Hunter. Boston: 1861. V. 38; 39; 40; 41; 42; 43

History of California. San Francisco: 1885. V. 40; 41

HITTLE, JOHN S.

Hittle on Gold Mines and Mining. Quebec;: 1864. V. 38

HIXON, ADRIETTA APPLEGATE

On to Oregon! Weiser: 1947. V. 40; 43

HJORTSBERG, WILLIAM

Tales and Fables. Los Angeles: 1985. V. 40; 46

HJORTSBERG, WILLLIAM

Falling Angel. New York: 1978. V. 45

H.M.S. 'Parliament,' or, The Lady Who Loved a Government Clerk. Ottawa: 1880. V. 42

HOADLY, BENJAMIN

A Defence of the Enquiry Into the Reasons of the Conduct of Great Britain. London: 1729. V. 44

The Original and Institution of Civil Government. London: 1710. V. 38

Tracts Formerly Published: Now Collected in One Volume . . . London: 1715. V. 45

The Suspicious Husband, a Comedy. London: 1747. V. 40

The Thoughts of an Honest Tory, Upon the Present Proceedings of that Party. London: 1710. V. 43

HOADLY, JOHN

Jephtha, an Oratorio. London: 1737. V. 38; 39

HOAR, ALLEN

The Submarine Torpedo Boat, It's Characteristics and Modern Development. New York: 1916. V. 41

HOARD, H. ELIOT

The British Warblers, a History with Problems of Their Lives. London: 1907-15. V. 42

HOARE, CLEMENT

A Practical Treatise on the Cultivation of the grape Vine on Open Walls. London: 1837. V. 40

HOARE, L.

Hints for the Improvement of Early Education and Nursery Discipline. London: 1827. V. 39; 40

HOARE, LOUISA

Hints for the Improvement of Early Education and Nursery Discipline. London: 1819. V. 38; 42

Hints for the Improvement of Early Education and Nursery Discipline. London: 1820. V. 45

HOARE, MICHAEL M.

The 'Resolution' Journal of Johann Reinhold Forster, 1772-75. London: 1982. V. 46

HOARE, P. R.

An Examination of Sir John Sinclair's Observations on the Report of the Bullion Committee, and on the General Nature of Coin or Money, and the Avntges of Paper Circulation. London: 1811. V. 38

HOARE, PRINCE

Memoirs of Granville Sharp, Esq. Composed from His Own Manuscripts and Other Authentic Documents in the Possession of His Family and of the African Institution. London: 1820. V. 37

HOARE, RICHARD COLT

A Classical Tour through Italy and Sicily. London: 1819. V. 39; 42; 43

A Collection of Forty-Eight Views of Noblemen's and Gentlemen's Seats . . . and Romantic Places in North and South Wales. London: 1806. V. 37; 39

Hints to Travellers in Italy. London: 1815. V. 46

Journal of a Tour in Ireland. A.D. 1806. London: 1807. V. 46

Recollections Abroad, During the Year 1790. Bath: 1817. V. 40

HOBAN, JAMES

Gems of Irish Eloquence. Baltimore: 1841. V. 46

HOBAN, RUSSELL

Kleinzeit. London: 1974. V. 45

The Mouse and His Child. London: 1969. V. 41

Ridley Walker. London: 1980. V. 43

Turtle Diary. London: 1975. V. 41; 43

HOBART, CHAUNCEY

Recollections of My Life. Red Wing: 1885. V. 39; 42

HOBART-HAMPDEN, AUGUSTUS C.

Never Caught: Personal Adventures Connected with Twelve Successful Trips in Blockade Running During the American Civil War, 1863-64. New York: 1908. V. 42; 43

HOBART-HAMPDEN, AUGUSTUS CHARLES

Never Caught Personal Adventures Connected with Twelve Successful Trips in Blockade Running During the American Civil War 1863-64. London: 1867. V. 46

HOBART, HENRY d. 1625

The Reports of . . . London: 1650. V. 40

The Reports of That Reverend and Learned Judge, The Right Honourable Sir Henry Hobart . . . London: 1658. V. 42

The Reports of that Reverend and Learned Judge, the Right of Honourable Sir Henry Hobart . . . . Lord Chief Justice of His Majesties Court of Common Pleas; and Chancellor to both Their Highnesses Henry and Charles, Prince of Wales . . . London: 1678. V. 39

The Reports of that Reverend and Learned Judge, the Right Honourable Sir Henry Hobart . . . In the Savoy: 1724. V. 45

The Reports of that Reverend and Learned Judge, the Right Honourable Sir Henry Hobart . . . London: 1768. V. 40

HOBART, JOHN HENRY

The Correspondence of . . . 1757 - 1797. New York: 1911-12. V. 40; 42; 44; 45

HOBART, NASH

Ministers of the Gospel Considered as Fellow-Labourers. Boston: 1747. V. 42

HOBART, NOAH

An Attempt to Illustrate and Confirm the Ecclesiastical Constitution of the Consociated Churches in the Colony of Connecticut. Occasioned by a Late 'Explanation of the Saybrook Platform'. New Haven: 1765. V. 41; 45

HOBART Town Almanack and Van Dieman's Land Annual for 1838 . . . Hobart-Town: 1838. V. 38; 43

HOBBES, THOMAS 1588-1679

The Art of Rhetoric, with a Discourse of the Laws of England. London: 1681. V. 41

Considerations Upon the Reputation, Loyalty, Manners, and Religion, of Thomas Hobbes of Malmesbury. London: 1680. V. 40; 42; 45; 46

Elementa Philosophica de Cive. Amsterdam: 1742. V. 38

Elementa Philosophica de Cive. Lausanne: 1782. V. 46

Elementa Philosophica De Cive. Amsterdam: 1647. V. 37

Elementa Philosophica De Cive. Amstelodami: 1669. V. 37

An Historical Narration Concerning Heresie and the Punishment Thereof. London: 1680. V. 45

The History of the Grecian War. London: 1676. V. 38; 40; 42

Hobb's Tripos, in Three Discourses. London: 1684. V. 37; 40; 41; 42; 43; 45; 46

A Letter About Liberty and Necessity. London: 1677. V. 42; 43

Leviathan. London: 1651. V. 37; 41; 42; 43; 45; 46

De Mirabilibus Pecci: Being the Wonders of the Peak in Darby-Shire, Commonly Called the Devil's Arse of Peak. London: 1678. V. 40

De Mirabilibus Pecci. London: 1683. V. 40

The Moral and Political Works of Thomas Hobbes of Malmesbury. London: 1750. V. 39

Philosophicall Rudiments Concerning Government and Society. London: 1651. V. 37; 39

Tracts of Mr. Thomas Hobbes of Malmesbury. London: 1682. V. 41; 43; 45; 46

The Treatise on Human Nature and that on Liberty and Necessity with a Supplement. London: 1812. V. 37

A True Ecclesiastical History, From Moses to the Time of Martin Luther, In Verse Made English from the Latin Original. London: 1722. V. 40

English Works. London: 1839. V. 40

The English Works of Thomas Hobbes of Malmesbury. (with) Opera Latina. London: 1962, 1961. V. 39

HOBBS, JAMES

Wild Life in the Far West. Hartford: 1872. V. 37; 39; 40; 42; 46

Wild Life in the Far West: Personal Adventures of a Border Mountain Man. Hartford: 1873. V. 38; 40; 43

HOBBS, WILLIAM HERBERT

The Discoveries of Antarctica Within the American Sector, as Revealed by Maps and Documents. Philadelphia: 1939. V. 46

HOBBY Horse. London: 1888. V. 41

HOBBY, WILLIAM

An Inquiry Into the Itinerancy, and the Conduct of the Rev. Mr. George Whitefield, an Itinerant Preacher. Boston: 1745. V. 40

HOBBY, WILLIAM J.

Remarks Upon Slavery: Occasioned by Attempts Made to Circulate Improper Publications in the Southern States. Augusta: 1835. V. 43

HOBHOUSE, EMILY

The Brunt of the War and Where It Fell. London: 1902. V. 42

HOBHOUSE, J.

The Substance of Some Letters Written from Paris During the Last Reign of the Emperor Napoleon and Addressed Principally to the Right Hon. Lord. Byron. London: 1817. V. 40

HOBHOUSE, J. C.

A Journey through Albania, and other provinces of Turkey in Europe and Asia, to Constantinople during 1809 and 1810. London: 1813. V. 37

HOBHOUSE, JOHN

Historical Illustrations of the Fourth Canto of Childe Harold. London: 1818. V. 39; 42; 44

HOBHOUSE, JOHN CAM

Contemporary Account of the Separation of Lord and Lady Bryon; Also of the Destruction of Byron's Memoirs. London: 1870. V. 44

Imitations and Translations from the Ancient and Modern Classics, Together with Original Poems Never Before Published. London: 1809. V. 41; 44

The Wonders of a Week at Bath; in a Doggerel Address to the Hon. T. S . . . London: 1811. V. 42

HOBHOUSE, ROSA

The Man with the Leather Patch and Five Other Tales. Ditchling: 1928. V. 41

HOBKIRK, CHARLES P.

Huddersfield: Its History and Natural History. Huddersfield: 1868. V. 45

HOBO'S Code Book. Los Angeles: n.d. V. 37

HOBSON, A.

Great Libraries. 1970. V. 45; 46

Humanists and Bookbinders. Cambridge: 1989. V. 45

HOBSON, ANTHONY

Apollo and Pegasus. Amsterdam: 1975. V. 40; 41; 42; 44; 46

Great Libraries. New York: 1970. V. 44

Great Libraries. London: 197?. V. 40

Humanists and Bookbinders, the Origins and Diffusion of the Humanistic Bookbinding 1459-1559 with a Census of Historiated Plaquette and Medallion Bindings of the Renaissance. New York: 1989. V. 43

HOBSON, E. W.

Proceedings of the Fifth International Congress of Mathematicians. (Cambridge, 22-28 August, 1912); Cambridge: 1913. V. 37

HOBSON, G. D.

Les Reliures a la Fanfare . . . London: 1935. V. 40

HOBSON, GEOFFREY DUDLEY

Bindings in Cambridge Libraries. Cambridge: 1929. V. 37; 39; 41; 45

English Binding Before 1500. The Sandars Lectures 1927. 1929. V. 45

English Binding Before 1500. Cambridge: 1929. V. 37; 39; 41; 43; 45; 46

English Bindings 1490-1940 in the Library of J. R. Abbey. London: 1940. V. 43

Maioli, Canevari and Others. Boston: 1926. V. 37; 38; 40

Maioli, Canevari and Others. London: 1926. V. 41

Studies in the History of Bookbinding. London: 1988. V. 40

Thirty Bindings. Described by G. D. Hobson, Selected from the First Edition Club's Seventh Exhibition, Held at 25 Park Lane, by Permission of Sir Philip Sassoon. 1926. V. 39

Thirty Bindings Selected from the First Edition Club's Seventh Exhibition. London: 1926. V. 39; 40; 41; 43; 44; 45; 46

Thirty Bindings. London: 1926. V. 38

HOBSON, JOHN A.

The Social Problem: Life and Work. London: 1902. V. 46

HOBSON, R. L.

The Later Ceramic Wares of China. London: 1925. V. 46

HOBSON, ROBERT LOCKHART

The Art of the Chinese Potter from the Han Dynasty to the End of the Ming . . . New York: 1923. V. 41; 43

The Art of the Chinese Potter from the Han Dynasty to the End of the Ming. London: 1923. V. 37

A Catalogue of Chinese Pottery and Porcelain in the Collection of Sir Percival David. London: 1934. V. 37

Catalogue of Porcleain Furniture and Other Works of Art in the Collection of Lady Wantage. Enfield: 1912. V. 37

Chinese, Corean and Japanese Potteries. New York: 1914. V. 39; 42; 44

Chinese Pottery and Porcelain: an Account of the Potter's Art in China from Primitive Times to the Present Day. New York: 1915. V. 41

Chinese Ceramics in Private Collections. London: 1931. V. 42; 44

Chinese Ceramics in Private Collections. London: 1932. V. 42

Chinese Art. New York: 1927. V. 39; 44

Chinese Pottery and Porcelain. London: 1915. V. 39; 42; 44

HOBSON, ROBERT LOCKHART continued

The George Eumorfopoulos Collection: Catalogue of the Chinese, Corean and Persian Pottery and Porcelain. London: 1925. V. 42

The Later Ceramic Wares of China. London: 1925. V. 41; 42

The Later Ceramic Wares of China. New York: 1925. V. 38

The Wares of the Ming Dynasty. London. V. 38

The Wares of the Ming Dynasty. London: 1923. V. 39; 41; 42; 46

Worcester Porcelain. London: 1910. V. 45

Worcester Porcelain, a Description of the Ware from the Wall Period to the Present Day. London: 1910. V. 40; 42; 46

HOBSON, WILLIAM

The Miners Dictionary. Wrexham: 1747. V. 40

HOBSON'S Fox Hunting Atlas. London: 1875. V. 39

HOBY, EDWARD

A Counter-snarle for Ishamel Rabshacheh. London: 1613. V. 44

HOCCLEVE, THOMAS

Poems by Thomas Hoccleve, Never Before Printed . . . London: 1796. V. 45

HOCH, HANNAH

Miniaturen. 16 Linolschnitte. Berlin: 1964. V. 42

HOCHBERG, LEW

Thoracic Surgery Before the 20th Century. New York: 1960. V. 41; 45

HOCHMAN, SANDRA

The Vaudeville Marriage. Poems. New York: (1966). V. 37

HOCHSTETTER, F. VON

The Geology of New Zealand. (with) Geological and Topographical Atlas of New Zealand by . . . Auckland: 1864. V. 40; 44

HOCHSTETTER, FERDINAND VON

New Zealand and Its Physical Geography, Geology and Natural History . . . Stuttgart: 1867. V. 40

HOCKEN, EDWARD

A Treatise on Amaurosis. Philadelphia: 1842. V. 42

HOCKEN LIBRARY, DUNEDIN.

Catalogue of the Hocken Library, Dunedin. Dunedin: 1912. V. 46

HOCKEN, THOMAS MORLAND

Contributions to the Early History of New Zealand. London: 1898. V. 43

HOCKER, JOHANN LUDWIG

Hailsbronnischer Antiquitaten-Schatz. Ansbach and Nuremberg: 1731. V. 45

HOCKIN, THOMAS

A Discourse on the Nature of God's Decrees: Being an Answer to a Letter from a Person of Quality Concerning Them. London: 1684. V. 41; 43

HOCKNEY, DAVID

China Diary. London: 1982. V. 40

David Hockney: Paintings, Prints and Drawings, 1960-1970. Boston: 1970. V. 41

Martha's Vineyard and Other Places. My Sketchbook. London: 1985. V. 41

Martha's Vineyard and Other Places. New York: 1985. V. 42

HODDER, GEORGE

Memories of My Time, Including Personal Reminiscences of Eminent Men. London: 1870. V. 39

HODDER, JAMES

Hodder's Arithmetick. London: 1678. V. 45; 46

HODEGUS Confuted, In a Plain Demonstration, That the Pillar of a Cloud and Fire, Which Led the Israelites Thro' the Wildnerness; Was Not, As Mr. Toland Vainly Imagines . . . London: 1721. V. 39; 43

HODGE, A. TREVOR

The Woodwork of Greek Roofs. Cambridge: 1960. V. 40

HODGE, CHARLES

The State of the Country. New York: 1861. V. 42

HODGE, DAVID

Angling Days on Scotch Lochs. Edinburgh: 1884. V. 39

The Quest of the Gilt Edged Girl. London: 1897. V. 43

HODGE, FREDERICK

The Benavides Memorial of 1643. Albuquerque: 1954. V. 46

HODGE, FREDERICK WEBB

Handbook of American Indians North of Mexico. Washington: 1907. V. 38

Handbook of North American Indians, North of Mexico. Washinton: 1907, 1910. V. 38

Handbook of American Indians North of Mexico. Washington: 1911. V. 42

Handbook of American Indians North of Mexico. Washington: 1912. V. 37; 39; 45

Handbook of American Indians, North of Mexico. Washington: 1907-1910. V. 37

History of Hawikuh, New Mexico. Los Angeles: 1937. V. 40; 43

Spanish Explorers in the Southern United States, 1528-1543. New York: 1907. V. 37; 39

HODGE, GENE MEANY

The Kachinas are Coming. Flagstaff: 1967. V. 44

HODGE, HIRAM C.

Arizona As It Is; or The Coming Country. New York: 1877. V. 37; 38; 39; 40; 41; 42; 43; 44; 46

HODGE, HUGH

On Diseases Peculiar to Women Including Displacements of the Uterus. Philadelphia: 1860. V. 42

The Principles and Practice of Obstetrics. Philadelphia: 1866. V. 42

HODGE, ORLANDO JOHN

Reminiscences. Cleveland: 1902-10. V. 39; 42

HODGES, CHARLES CLEMENT

The Abbey of St. Andrew, Hexham. Hexham: 1888. V. 38

The Abbey of St. Andrew, Hexham. London: 1888. V. 38

Ecclesia Hagustaldensis. London: 1888. V. 45

HODGES, J.

The Abbey of St. Andrew, Hexham. London: 1888. V. 40; 46

HODGES, JAMES

A Defence of the Scots Abdicating Darien: Including an Answer to the Defence of the Scot's Settlement There. Edinburgh: 1700. V. 46

A Defence of the Scots Abdicating Darien: Including an Answer to the Defence of the Scots Settlement There. Edinburgh?: 1700. V. 39

A Defence of the Scots Abdicating Darien. N.P.: Edinburgh?: 1700. V. 40

Essay Upon the Union. London: 1706. V. 43

The Present State of England, as to Coin and Publick Charges. (with) A Supplement to the Present State of England as to Coin and Publick Charges. London: 1697. V. 46

HODGES, L. K.

Mining in the Pacific Northwest. Seattle: 1897. V. 45

HODGES, NATHANIEL

Loimologia (in Greek) sive Pestis Nuperae Apud Populum Londinensem Grassantis Narratio Historica. London: 1672. V. 38; 41

HODGES, RICHARD MANNING

A Narrative of Events Connected with the Introduction of Sulphuric Ether into Surgical Use. Boston: 1891. V. 46

HODGES, SYDNEY

A New Godiva. London: 1876. V. 40

When Leaves Were Green. London: 1896. V. 40

HODGES, THOMAS LAW

The Use and Advantages of Pearson's Draining Plough; Detailed in Paper Communicated to the Society for the Encouragement of Arts . . . London: 1839. V. 39

HODGES, W.

An Historical Account of Ludlow Castle. Ludlow: 1794. V. 37; 40

HODGES, WILLIAM

Travels in India, During the Years 1780, 1781, 1782 and 1783. London: 1793. V. 37; 38; 45; 46

Travels in India, During the Years 1780, 1781, 1782 and 1783. London: 1794. V. 42

HODGES, WILLIAM, 1ST BARONET 1645?-1714

Great Britain's Groans; or, an Account of the Oppression, Ruin, and Pay, Health and Lives, and Dreadful Ruin of Their Families. London: 1695. V. 38; 41

HODGKIN, FRANK E.

Pen Pictures of Representative Men of Oregon. Portland: 1882. V. 44

HODGKIN, J. E.

Rariora. London: 1900-02. V. 42; 45

HODGKIN, JOHANNES

Calligraphia Graeca et Poecilographia Graeca. London: 1807. V. 39; 40

HODGKIN, JOHN ELIOT

Rariora. London. V. 42

Rariora, Being Notes of Some of the Printed Books, Manuscripts, Historical Documents, Medals, Engravings, Pottery, etc. Collected (1858-1900). London: 1903. V. 39

HODGKIN, R. H.

A History of the Anglo-Saxons, from the Invasions of 360 A.D. to 897 A.D. Oxford: 1935. V. 39

HODGKIN, THOMAS

Italy and Her Invaders. Oxford: 1880-99. V. 39

Italy and Her Invaders. Oxford: 1885-1899. V. 43; 44

Italy and Her Invaders. 1892-99. V. 39

Italy and Her Invaders. Oxford: 1892-99. V. 37; 42

Lectures on the Morbid Anatomy of the Serous and Mucous Membranes. Volume 1. Philadelphia: 1838. V. 40

Narrative of a Journey to Morocco in 1863 and 1864. London: 1866. V. 46

On the Anatomical Characters of Some Adventitious Structures, Being an Attempt to Point Out the Relation Between the Microscopic Characters and Those Which are Discernible by the Naked Eye. 1843. V. 42

HODGKINS, E. M.

Catalogue of a Collection of Mounted Porcelain Belonging to E. M. Hodgkins. Paris: 1911. V. 43

HODGKINS, WILLIAM HENRY

The Battle of Fort Stedman (Petersburg, Va.) March 25, 1865. Boston: 1889. V. 46

HODGKINSON, CLEMENT

Australia, from Port Macquarie to Moreton Bay; with Descriptions of the Natives, Their Manners and Customs . . . London: 1845. V. 43

HODGKINSON, EATON

Experimental Researches on the Strength of Pillars of Cast Iron . . . London: 1846. V. 44

HODGSON, ADAM

A Letter to M. Jean-Baptiste Say, on the Comparative Expense of Free and Slave Labour. Liverpool: 1823. V. 37

Letters from North America. London: 1824. V. 40; 46

Letters from North America, Written During a Tour in the United States and Canada. London: 1824. V. 37; 38; 39; 43

Remarks During a Journey through North America in the Years 1819, 1820 and 1821. New York: 1823. V. 37; 38; 39

Remarks During a Journey through North America in the Years 1819, 1829 and 1821 in a Series of Letters . . . London: 1824. V. 45

HODGSON, CHARLES

Trial of Mr. Charles Hodgson for Adultery with Mrs. Fowler, Wife of Mr. Fowler of Blackfriars-road, Solicitor . . . Also William Reader, Esquire for Criminal Conversation with Mrs. Walker (etc.). London: 1808? V. 45

HODGSON, FRANCIS

Lady Jane Grey, a Tale, In Two Books, with Miscellaneous Poems, In English and Latin. London: 1809. V. 42

HODGSON, FRED

Commonsense Stair Building and Hand Railing. (with) Perspective Views and Floor Plans. Riverside: 1903. V. 46

HODGSON, J.

Beauties of England and Wales. Volume 12, Part I: Northumberland and Nottingham. London: 1813. V. 38

Northumberland, Nottinghamshire. London: 1813. V. 40

A Topographical and Historical Description of the County of Westmoreland. London: 1813. V. 38

Westmorland. London: 1813. V. 40

HODGSON, J. E.

Doctor Johnson on Ballooning and Flight. London: 1925. V. 39

The History of Aeronautics in Great Britain from the Earliest Times to the Latter Half of the 19th Century. London: 1924. V. 44; 45

THe History of aeronautics in Great Britain from the earliest times to the latter half of the 19th century. 1924. V. 37

HODGSON, JAMES

The Doctrine of Fluxions, Founded on Sir Isaac Newton's Method. London: 1758. V. 44

An Introduction to Chronology. London: 1747. V. 40

HODGSON, JOSEPH

The Cradle of the Confederacy . . . Mobile: 1876. V. 46

Engravings Intended to Illustrate Some of the Diseases of Arteries. London: 1815. V. 37; 39; 41

HODGSON, MR.

Westmoreland; or Original Delineations, Topographical, Historical and Descriptive, of that County. London: 1818. V. 42

HODGSON, RALPH

The Bull. London: 1913. V. 38; 44

Eve and Other Poems. London: 1913. V. 38

Eve and Other Poems. Westminster: 1913. V. 44

Hymn to Moloch. London: 1921. V. 37

The Last Blackbird and Other Lines. London: 1907. V. 37; 38; 40; 42; 44

The Mystery and Other Poems. London: 1913. V. 44

The Mystery. Bethesda: 1956. V. 44

Silver Wedding and Other Poems. Minerva: 1941. V. 46

The Skylark. London: 1958. V. 40; 42

Songs to Our Surnames. Cerne Abbas: 1960. V. 44

HODGSON, SHADWORTH H. 1832-1912

The Philosophy of Reflection. London: 1878. V. 42; 44

HODGSON, THOMAS

The London Catalogue of Books . . . London: 1846. V. 42

HODGSON, W. B.

On the Importance of the Study of Economic Science as a Branch of Education for All Classes. London: 1860. V. 42

Two Lectures on the Conditions of Health and Wealth Educationally Considered. Edinburgh: 1860. V. 42

HODGSON, WILLIAM B.

Notes on Northern Africa. New York: 1844. V. 43

HODGSON, WILLIAM BROWN

Memoir on the Megatherium, and Other Extinct Gigantic Quadrupeds of the Coast of Georgia, with Observations On Its Geologic Features. New York: 1846. V. 44

HODGSON, WILLIAM HOPE

Carnacki the Ghost Finder. London: 1913. V. 42

Carnacki, the Ghost Finder. 1947. V. 45

Carnacki: The Ghostfinder. Sauk City: 1947. V. 45

The Ghost Pirates. London: 1909. V. 40

The House on the Borderland. London: 1908. V. 42

The House of the Borderland and Other Novels. Sauk City: 1946. V. 39; 40; 41; 42; 43; 44; 45; 46

The House on the Borderland. S.C.: 1946. V. 37

HODGSON, WILLOUGHBY, MRS.

The Quest of the Antique. London: 1924. V. 41

HODIERNA, GIOVANNI BATTISTA

Archimede Redivivo con la Stadera del Momento . . . Palermo: 1644. V. 44

HODIN, J. P.

Barbara Hepworth. London: 1961. V. 45; 46

HODJASH, SVETLANA

The Egyptian Reliefs and Stelae in the Pushkin Museum of Fine Arts, Moscow. Leningrad: 1982. V. 44

HODNETT, E.

Five Centuries of English Book Illustration. London: 1988. V. 45

HODNETT, EDWARD

English Woodcuts, 1480-1535. London: 1935. V. 37; 38; 40

HODSON, ARNOLD W.

Trekking The Great Thirst. London: 1912. V. 39; 40; 45

Trekking the Great Thirst, Travel and Sport in the Kalahari Desert. New York: 1912. V. 46

HODSON, JAMES

Dame Parlet's Farm . . . London: 1834. V. 41

HODSON, JAMES LANSDALE

Red Night. A War Play in a Prologue and Four Acts. London: 1930. V. 46

HOE, R.

Anderson Auction Company Catalogue of the Library of Robert Hoe. New York: 1911-12. V. 44

HOE, ROBERT 1089-1909

A Catalogue of Books Printed in Foreign Languaes Before . . . 1600 Volumes I-II (with) A Catalogue of Books Printed in Foreign Languages After . . . 1600 Volumes I-IV (with) A Catalogue of Manuscripts (and) Catalogue of Books of Emblems. New York: 1907-09. V. 39

Catalogue of the Library of Robert Hoe. New York: 1911-12. V. 41

HOE, ROBERT 1089-1909 continued

Catalogue of (his) Library. Sold by the Anderson Auction Co., April 1911 - Nov. 1912. New York: 1912. V. 38

A Lecture on Bookbinding as a Fine Art. New York: 1886. V. 39; 41

The Library of Robert Hoe, A Contribution to the History of Bibliophilism in America. New York: 1895. V. 41

The Library of Robert Hoe of New York. New York: 1911. V. 46

One Hundred and Seventy-Six Historic and Artistic Book-Bindings, Dating from the Fifteenth Century to the Present Time . . . New York: 1895. V. 37; 45

One Hundred and Seventy-Six Historic Book-Bindings from the Fifteenth Century to the Present Time, Pictured by Etchings, Artotypes and Lithographs after the Originals Selected from the . . . New York: 1895. V. 44

HOEHNE, F. C.

Flora Brasilica. Sao Paulo: 1940-68. V. 37

HOESCHEL, DAVID

Nomenclator, Sive Index Vocvm Trilingvis. Augsburg: 1593. V. 40

HOEY, ABRAHAM VAN

Letters and Negociations of M. Van Hoey, Ambassador from the States-General to His Most Christian Majesty. London: 1743. V. 41

HOEY, P.

A Plain and Concise Method of Learning the Gregorian Note: Also a Collection of Church Music, Selected from the Roman Antiphonary and Gradual. Dublin: 1800. V. 46

HOFER, PHILIP

Baroque Book Illustration. Cambridge: 1951. V. 41

Baroque Book Illustration. A Short Survey from the Collection in the Department of Graphic Arts, Harvard College Library. Cambridge: 1970. V. 39

HOFF, EBBE C.

Bibliography of Aviation Medicine. Springfield: 1942, 1944. V. 40

Bibliography of Aviation Medicine. Springfield/Washington: 1942/1944. V. 41

HOFFENSTEIN, SAMUEL

Poems in Praise of Practically Nothing. 1928. V. 44

HOFFER, RAIMUND

A Practical Treatise on Caoutchouc and Gutta Percha. Philadelphia: 1883. V. 46

HOFFMAN, ABBIE

Soon to Be a Major Motion Picture. New York: 1980. V. 42

HOFFMAN, ALICE SPENCER

The Children's Shakespeare. London: 1911. V. 46

HOFFMAN, C. F.

The New York Book of Poetry. New York: 1837. V. 38

HOFFMAN, CHARLES FENNO

Greyslaer; a Romance of the Mohawk. New York: 1840. V. 42; 43; 44

Wild Scenes in the Forest and Prairie. London: 1840. V. 37

A Winter in the Far West. London: 1835. V. 38; 39

Winter in the West. New York: 1835. V. 37; 38

HOFFMAN, DAVID

Miscellaneous Thoughts on Men, Manners and Things by Anthony Grumbler. Baltimore: 1837. V. 44

HOFFMAN, ERNST THEODOR AMADEUS

Prinzessin Brambilla. Breslau: 1821. V. 39

HOFFMAN, EUGENE A.

Genealogy of the Hoffman Family, Descendants of Martin Hoffman. New York: 1899. V. 46

HOFFMAN, HERMAN

Californien, Nevada Und Mexico. 1871. V. 39

HOFFMAN, MALVINA

Heads and Tales. New York: 1936. V. 40

HOFFMAN, OGDEN

Opinion of His Honor . . . The United States vs. Andrew Castillero - 'New Almaden.' San Francisco: 1816. V. 42

Reports of Land Cases Determined in the United States District Court. San Francisco: 1862. V. 46

HOFFMAN, RICHARD

Florilegium Typographia, A Culling of Matrix Fonts for Line-Casting Machine Setting. Van Nuys: 1985. V. 37; 39; 45

HOFFMANN, CARL

A Practical Treatise on the Manufacture of Paper in All Its Branches. Philadelphia: 1873. V. 41

HOFFMANN, CARL AUGUST SIEGFRIED

Handbuch der Mineralogie. Freiberg: 1811-15. V. 43

HOFFMANN-DONNER, HEINRICH 1809-1894

The English Struwwelpeter. Leipsic: 1847. V. 42

The English Struwwelpeter. Leipsic: 1850. V. 40

The English Struwwelpeter. London: 1859. V. 44

The English Struwwelpeter. London: 1860. V. 40

The English Struwwelpeter. 1880. V. 41

The English Struwwelpeter. London: 1885. V. 41

Slovenly Peter. New York: 1935. V. 42

Slovenly Peter . . . New York & London: 1935. V. 40

HOFFMANN, E. T. A.

The Devil's Elixir. Edinburgh: 1824. V. 40; 42

Tales of Hoffman. London: 1932. V. 42; 43

Weird Tales. London: 1885. V. 38; 43

HOFFMANN, ERNST THEODOR AMADEUS 1776-1822

Tales of Hoffman. London: 1932. V. 44

HOFFMANN, FRIEDRICH

Observationum Physicochymicarum Selectionum Libri III. Halle: 1722. V. 45

HOFFMANN, H.

Modern Interiors in Europe and America. London: 1930. V. 37

HOFFMEISTER, W.

Travels in Ceylon and Continental India . . . Edinburgh: 1848. V. 40

HOFFY, A.

The Orchardist's Companion. Philadelphia: 1841. V. 39

HOFLAND, BARBARA

Little Manuel, the Captive Boy: a True Story. Dallas: 1979. V. 46

HOFLAND, BARBARA WREAKS HOOLE 1770-1844

Africa Described, In Its Ancient and Present State. London: 1828. V. 40

Daniel Dennison, and the Cumberland Statesman. London: 1848. V. 44

A Descriptive Account of the Mansion and Gardens of White-Knights, A Seat of His Grace the Duke of Marlborough . . . London: 1819. V. 38; 42

Patience and Perserverance; or, the Modern Griselda. London: 1813. V. 44; 45

Poems. Sheffield: 1805. V. 42; 45

Richmond, and Its Surrounding Scenery. London: 1832. V. 42

The Stolen Boy. New York: 1830. V. 37; 43

The Young Pilgrim, or Alfred Campbell's Return to the East. New York: 1828. V. 42

The Young Pilgrim, or Alfred Campbell's Return to the East and his Travels in Egypt, Nubia, Asia Minor, Arabia Petraea &c. New York: 1828. V. 45

HOFLAND, MRS.

The History of a Merchant's Widow and Her Young Family. London: 1818. V. 46

HOFLAND, T. C.

The British Angler's Manual. London: 1839. V. 39; 41; 43; 44; 46

The British Angler's Manual. London: 1841. V. 39

The British Angler's Manual, or, the Art of Angling in England, Scotland, Wales and Ireland. London: 1848. V. 46

Catalogue of Mr. Hofland's Pictures, Now Exhibiting at 106, New Bond Street. London: 1821. V. 45

HOFMAN, H. O.

Gold Milling in the Black Hills. New York: 1889. V. 39

HOFMANN, CARL

Praktisches handbuch der Papier - Fabrikation. Berlin: 1891-97. V. 38

HOFMANN, CASPAR

De Thorace Ejusque Partibus Commentarius Tripartitus. Frankfurt: 1627. V. 37

HOFMANN, I.

Genius Morborum Epidemicus Anno MDCCCXXXII Vindobonae Observatus. Vindobonae: 1833. V. 38

HOFMANN, JOHANN JACOB

lexicon Universale, Historiam Sacram et Profanam . . . Leyden: 1698. V. 46

HOFMANN, WERNER

Art in the Nineteenth Century. London: 1961. V. 42; 44

HOFMANN, WERNER continued

The Sculpture of Henri Laurens. New York: 1970. V. 43; 46

HOFMEISTER, WILHELM 1824–1877

On the Germination, Development and Fructification of the Higher Cryptogamia, and on the Fructification of the Coniferae. London: 1862. V. 37; 42

HOFSTATTER, HANS H.

Erotic Drawings. New York: 1980. V. 42

HOG, JAMES

Otia Christiana; or, Christian Recreations. Edinburgh: 1708. V. 44

HOGABOAM, JAMES J.

Bean Creek Valley, Incidents of Its Early Settlement. Hudson: 1876. V. 42

HOGAN, EDMUND

The Description of Ireland and the State Thereof, as It Is at Present in Anno 1598 . . . Dublin: 1878. V. 38

Onomasticon Goedelicum . . . an Index, with Indentifications to the Gaelic Names of Places and Tribes. Dublin: 1910. V. 37; 43

The Pennsylvania State Trials: Containing the Impeachment, Trial and Acquittal of Francis Hopkinson, and John Nicholson . . . the former Being Judge of the Court of Admiralty and the latter, the Comptroller-General of the Commonwealth of Pennsylvania. Philadelphia: 1794. V. 39

HOGAN, EILEEN

Ogham. London: 1979. V. 42

Ogham. N.P.: 1979. V. 39

Variations: Fragments of Sappho and Haiku. 1974. V. 40

Variations. London: 1974. V. 43; 45

HOGAN, FRANK

The Romantics, 1801–1820, An Exhibit of Books and Autograph Letters from the Collection of Frank J. Hogan. Los Angeles: 1938. V. 41; 45

HOGAN, JAMES FRANCIS

The Gladstone Colony. Sydney: 1898. V. 40

The Irish in Australia. London: 1888. V. 39

HOGAN, JOHN

Thoughts About the City of St. Louis Her Commerce and Manufactures, Railroads, &c. St. Louis: 1854. V. 37

HOGAN, P. EDMUNDO

Ibernia Ignatiana. Dublin: 1880. V. 46

HOGAN, ROBERT

Modern Irish Drama. Dublin: 1975-84. V. 43

HOGARTH, DAVID GEORGE

Carchemish. Report on the Excavations at Ejerabis on Behalf of the British Museum. London: 1914-52. V. 40

Carchemish: Report on the Excavations at Djerabis on Behalf of the British Museum. London: 1914-52. V. 37; 44

Devia Cypria. Notes of an Archaelogical Journey in Cyprus in 1888. London: 1889. V. 39

Excavations at Ephesus: the Archaic Artemisis. London: 1908. V. 40; 44

The Life of Charles M. Doughty. London: 1928. V. 44

The Life of Charles M. Doughty. Oxford: 1928. V. 38

The Nearer East. London: 1950. V. 45

The Penetration of Arabia . . . London: 1905. V. 45

The Penetration of Arabia. London: 1904. V. 46

HOGARTH, GEORGE

Memoirs of the Musical Drama. London: 1838. V. 43

HOGARTH PRESS

The Hogarth Essays. Garden City: 1928. V. 37

HOGARTH, T. W.

The Bull Terrier. Manchester: 1936. V. 40; 43; 45

HOGARTH, WILLIAM 1697–1764

The Analysis of Beauty. London: 1753. V. 38; 40; 44

The Analysis of Beauty. London: 1772. V. 40

Biographical Anecdotes of William Hogarth. London: 1782. V. 41; 44; 46

The Complete Engravings. New York. V. 44

The Complete Engravings. London: 1968. V. 40

The Genuine Works of William Hogarth. London: 1808. V. 46

Hogarth Illustrates From His Own Manuscript. London: 1812. V. 38

Hogarth Moralized: a Complete Edition of all the Most Capital and Admired Works of William Hogarth. London: 1831. V. 41

The Life and Works of William Hogarth. Philadelphia: 1900. V. 42

The Complete Works of . . . London. V. 44

The Works. London. V. 38; 40

The Works. London: 1795-1802. V. 40

The Genuine Works of William Hogarth. London: 1808-10. V. 46

The Works of William Hogarth. London: 1821. V. 37; 38; 40

The Works of William Hogarth . . . London: 1822. V. 38

The Works. London: 1823. V. 46

The Works of William Hogarth, Containing One Hundred and Fifty-Eight Engravings by Mr. Cooke and Mr. Davenport. London: 1827. V. 41

The Works. London: 1833. V. 37; 40; 45; 46

The Works of, In a Series of Engravings . . . London: 1835. V. 40

The Complete Works . . . London: and New York: 1860. V. 44

The Complete Works of William Hogarth . . . London: 1865. V. 45

The Complete Works. London: 1880. V. 37; 38

The Works. Philadelphia: 1900. V. 43; 46

HOGBEN, CAROL

From Manet to Hockney. London: 1985. V. 46

HOGDKIN, FRANK E.

Pen Pictures of Representative Men of Oregon. Portland: 1882. V. 38

HOGE, WILLIAM J.

Sketch of Dabney Carr Harrison, Minister of the Gospel and Captain in the Army of the Confederate States of America. Richmond: 1863. V. 44

HOGG, ALEX

A General Catalogue of Valuable New Books, Printed for and sold by Alex Hogg, at No. 16 Pater-Noster Row . . . London: 1780. V. 41

HOGG, J.

The Microscope: Its History, Construction and Applications. London: 1854. V. 45

HOGG, JAMES

Altrive Tales. London: 1832. V. 39; 46

The Brownie of Bodsbeck; and Other Tales. Edinburgh: 1818. V. 39; 42; 46

The Domestic Manners and Private Life of Sir Walter Scott. Glasgow: 1834. V. 39; 42

Dramatic Tales. Edinburgh: 1817. V. 45

The Jacobite of Scotland; Being the Songs, Airs and Legends of the Adherents to the House of Stuart. Edinburgh: 1819-21. V. 39; 40; 42; 46

The Jacobite Relics of Scotland; being the Songs, Airs, and Legends of the Adherents to the house of Stuart. Edinburgh: 1819. V. 37

The Jacobite Relics of Scotland, Being the Songs, Airs & Legends of the Adherents to the House of Stuart. Edinburgh: 1819, 1821. V. 38

The Mountain Bard; Consisting of Ballads and Songs Founded on Facts and Legendary Tales. Edinburgh: 1807. V. 39; 42

The Mountain Bard; consisting of legendary ballads and tales. Edinburgh: 1821. V. 37

The Pilgrims of the Sun; a Poem. Edinburgh: 1815. V. 40; 42; 46

The Poetic Mirror, or the Living Bards of Britain. London: 1816. V. 39; 42; 43

The Poetic Mirror, or Living Bards of Britain. London: 1929. V. 43

The Poetical Works. Edinburgh: 1822. V. 39; 41; 42; 46

The Poetical Works of the Ettrick Shepherd. Edinburgh & London: 1864. V. 39

The Poetical Works of the Ettrick Shepherd. With an autobiography . . . Glasgow/Edinburgh/London: (ca. 1864). V. 37

The Private Memoirs and Confessions of a Justified Sinner . . . London: 1824. V. 37; 39; 43

Queen Hynde. London: 1825. V. 40

The Queen's Wake. Edinburgh: 1813. V. 43

The Shepherd's Calendar. Edinburgh: 1829. V. 38

Songs. Edinburgh: 1831. V. 38

Tales and Sketches and Peotical Works. Glasgow: Edinburgh: &: 1836. V. 46

Tales and Sketches, Including Several Pieces Not Before Printed. London: 1878. V. 40

The Three Perils of Man; or, War, Women and Witchcraft. London: 1822. V. 39

Winter Evening Tales, Collected Among the Cottagers in the South of Scotland. Edinburgh: 1820. V. 39

Winter Evening Tales, Collected Among the Cottagers in the South of Scotland. Edinburgh & London: 1820. V. 40

The Works of the Ettrick Shepherd. London,: 1866. V. 42; 46

The Works of the Ettrick Shepherd. London, Glasgow & Edinburgh: 1866. V. 39

HOGG, LEWIS M.

A Letter to His Grace the Duke of Newcastle, Secretary of State for the Colonies, &c. &c. on Behalf of the Melanesian Mission of the Bishop of New Zealand. London: 1853. V. 40

HOGG, ROBERT

The Florist and Pomologist. London: 1863-69. V. 39

HOGG, ROBERT continued

A Selection of the Eatable Funguses of Great Britain. London. V. 40

The Wild Flowers of Great Britain. London: 1863-1880. V. 44

HOGG, THOMAS

A Concise and Practical Treatise on the Growth and Culture of the Carantion, Pink, Auricula, Polyanthus, Ranunculus, Tulip, and Other Flowers . . . London: 1820. V. 46

A Concise and Practical Treatise on the Growth and Culture of the Carnation, Pink, Auricula, Polyanathus, Ranunculus, Tulip, Hyacinth, Rose and Other Flowers. London: 1832. V. 37; 40

HOGG, THOMAS JEFFERSON 1792-1862

The Athenians. London: 1943. V. 40

The Athenians. Waltham St. Lawrence: 1943. V. 40; 46

The Life of Percy Bysshe Shelley. London: 1858. V. 37; 38; 40

The Life of Percy Bysshe Shelley . . . London: 1906. V. 42

HOGREWE, J. L.

Beschreibung der in England seit 1759 Angelegten . . . Schiffbarren Kanale. Hannover: 1780. V. 37; 38

HOHBURG, CHRISTIAN

Kurtzer und Erbaulicher Auszug-Oder; Denckwurdige Sprueche as Christian Hoburgs, Postilla Mystica Ueber die Evangelium . . . Germantown: 1748. V. 40; 41; 42

HOHENHAUSEN UND HOCHHAUS, S. J., FREIHERR VON

Die Alterthumer Daciens in dem Heutigen Siebenburgen. Vienna: 1775. V. 44

HOHL, REINHOLD

Alberto Giacometti. New York: 1971. V. 39; 43; 46

HOHMAN, ELMO P.

The American Whaleman: a Study of Life and Labor in the Whaling Industry. New York: 1928. V. 46

HOHNEL, LUDWIG VON

Discovery of Lakes Rudolf and Stefanie. London: 1894. V. 42; 43; 44; 45

Discovery by Count Teleki of Lakes Rudolph and Stephanie. London: 1894. V. 43

HOIER, H. M.

The Franco-Prussian War, Its Causes, Incidents and Consequences. London: 1870-72. V. 41

HOITT, IRA G.

Pacific Coast Guide and Programme of the Knights Templar Triennial Conclave . . . San Francisco: 1883. V. 38; 41

HOKE, HELEN

The Thrillers Chillers and Killers. London: 1979. V. 42

HOK'SAI

Two Drawings. Gloucestershire: 1910. V. 46

HOKUSAI: Master of the Japanese Ukiyo-Ye School of Painting. London. V. 45

HOLBACH, PAUL HENRI, BARON D'

Systeme de la Nature. London: 1770. V. 38; 41; 45

HOLBACH, PAUL HENRI THIRY

System of Nature; or, the Laws of the Moral and Physical World. Philadelphia: 1808. V. 39

HOLBACH, PAUL HENRI THIRY, BARON D'

The System of Nature; or, the Laws of the Moral and Physical World. London: 1817. V. 40; 41

HOLBACH, PAUL HENRY THIRY, BARON D'

Ethocratle ou le Gouvernement Fonde sur la Morale. Amsterdam: 1776. V. 42

HOLBEIN, HANS 1498-1554

The Celebrated Alphabet of Death. Paris: 1856. V. 38; 39; 41

Simolachri, Historie, e Figure de la Morte . . . Aiuntovi di Nuovo Molte Figure Mai Piu Stampate. Lyon: 1549. V. 40

The Dance of Death (Icones Mortis). Basilae: 1554. V. 38

The Dance of Death. Lyons: 1554. V. 40

The Dance of Death. London: 1804. V. 38; 39

The Dance of Death. London: 1816. V. 45

The Dance of Death through the Various Stages of Human Life. London: 1803. V. 37; 38; 45

Historiarum Veteris Testamenti Icones ad Viuum Expressae. Lyon: 1543. V. 43

Icones Historiarum Veteris Testamenti . . . Lyon: 1547. V. 39

Icones Veteris Testamenti: Illustrations of the Old Testament. London: 1830. V. 39

The Paintings. London: 1956. V. 44

Portraits of Illustrious Personages of the Court of Henry VIII. London: 1812. V. 39

Portraits of Illustrious Personages of the Court of Henry VIII. London: 1828. V. 41

HOLBERG, LUDVIG

Beschreibung der Beruhmten Haupt und Handelstadt Bergen in Norwegen. Copenhagen und Leipzig: 1753. V. 38

A Journey to the World Under-Ground. London: 1742. V. 37; 38; 39; 43; 46

HOLBERG, LUDVIG, BARON

Nicolai Klimi Iter Subterraneum Novam Telluris Theoriam ac Historiam Quintae Monarchiae Adhue Nobis Incognitae Exhibens e Bibiliotheca B. Abelini. Hafniae & Lipsiae: 1741. V. 40

HOLBERG, LUDWIG, BARON 1684-1754

An Introduction to Universal History. London: 1787. V. 39

HOLBERT, LUDVIG

Den Berommelige Norske Handel-Stad Bergens Beskrivelse. Copenhagen: 1757. V. 38

HOLBROOK, J. E.

Ichthyology of South Carolina. Charleston: 1860. V. 37; 38; 45

HOLBROOK, JOHN EDWARDS

North American Herpetology; or, a Description of the Reptiles Inhabiting the United States. Philadelphia: 1836-38. V. 43

North American Herpetology . . . Philadelphia: 1842. V. 41

HOLBROOK, SAMUEL

Threescore Years: an Autobiography, Containing Incidents of Voyages and Travels, Including Six Years in a man of War. Boston: 1857. V. 38; 39; 41

HOLBROOK, SILAS P.

Sketches by a Traveller. Boston: 1830. V. 38; 39; 43

HOLCOMBE, E. J.

Physical Decline of Leisure Class American Women. New York: 1893. V. 43

HOLCOMBE, HENRY

A Sermon, Occasioned by the Death of Lt. General George Washington, Late President of the United States . . . . Savannah: 1800. V. 43

HOLCOMBE, RETURN A.

An Account of the Battle of Wilson's Creek, or Oak Hills, Fought Between the Union Troops, Commanded by Gen. N. Lyon and the Southern or Confederate Troops Under Command of Gens. McCulloch and price. Springfield: 1883. V. 39

HOLCROFT, THOMAS

The Adventures of Hugh Trevor. London: 1794. V. 42

An Amourous Tale of the Chaste Loves of Peter the Long, and of His Most Honoured Dame Blanche Bazu, . . . London: 1786. V. 38

Herman and Dorothea. London: 1801. V. 41

A Letter to the Right Honourable William Windham on the Intemperance and Dangerous Tendency of His Public Conduct. London: 1795. V. 41

The Life of Baron Frederic Trenck. Dublin: 1790. V. 38

Memoirs of the Late Thomas Holcroft, Written by Himself, and Continued to the Time of His Death . . . London: 1816. V. 37

A Plain and Succinct Narrative of the Late Riots and Disturbances in the Cities of London and Westminster, and Borough of Southwark. London: 1780. V. 39

Tales of the Castle: or, Stories of Instruction & Delight. Being 'Les Veillees du Chateau' written in French by Madame La Comtesse de Genlis. In Five Volumes. London: 1806. V. 37

Travels from Hamburg through Westphalia, Holland and the Netherlands to Paris. London: 1804. V. 41

HOLDEN, EDITH B.

the Country Diary of an Edwardian Lady. London: 1984. V. 46

HOLDEN, EDWARD G.

Art Work of the Story of Detroit. Chicago: 1894. V. 44

HOLDEN, EDWARD S.

Catalogue of Earthquakes on the Pacific Coast 1769 to 1897. 1898. V. 45

Publications of the Lick Observatory of the University of California. Sacramento;: 1887. V. 40

HOLDEN, FRANCES MAYHUGH

Lambshead Before Interwoven. College Station: 1982. V. 46

HOLDEN, GEORGE H.

Canaries and Cage Birds. New York: 1895. V. 40; 46

HOLDEN, HAROLD

Noses. Cleveland: 1950. V. 42

HOLDEN, HORACE

A Narrative of Shipwreck, Captivity and Sufferings of Horace Holden and Benj. H. Nute . . . Boston: 1836. V. 41; 42; 46

HOLDEN, M.

A Small Celestial Atlas, or Maps of the Visible Heavens. Preston: 1818. V. 39

HOLDEN, OLIVER

Plain Psalmody, or Supplementary Music. Boston: 1800. V. 44

HOLDEN, RAYMOND

It Is Earlier Than You Think. N.P.: 1959. V. 39; 41; 43; 44

HOLDEN, WILLIAM C.

The Past and Future of the Kaffir Races. London: 1866. V. 42

HOLDEN, WILLIAM CURRY

Alkalai Trails or Social and Economic Movements of the Texas Frontier 1846-1900. Dallas: 1930. V. 37; 43; 44; 46

Hill of the Rooster. New York: 1956. V. 38

Rollie Burns. Dallas: 1932. V. 38; 42; 43

The Spur Ranch: A Study of the Inclosed Ranch Phase of the Cattle Industry of Texas. Boston: 1930. V. 38

The Spur Ranch. Boston: 1934. V. 37; 42; 43; 44; 46

HOLDER, CHARLES F.

The Big Game Fishes of the United States. New York: 1903. V. 37; 41

HOLDER, CHARLES FREDERICK

The Channel Islands of California: A Book for the Angler, Sportsman and Tourist. Chicago: 1910. V. 37; 46

Life in the Open. New York: 1906. V. 37; 42; 46

Recreations of a Sportsman on the Pacific Coast. New York: 1910. V. 37

HOLDER, WILLIAM

A Discourse Conceining Time, with Application of the Natural Day and Lunar Month, and Solar Year, as Natural . . . London: 1701. V. 42; 45

Introductio ad Chronologiam: sive ars Chronolgica in Expitomen Redacta. Oxoniae: 1691. V. 45

HOLDERLIN, JOHANN CHRISTIAN FRIEDRICH

Gedichte/Entwurfe zu Gedichten und Bruchstucke. Aurora & Lexington: 1946-49. V. 44

HOLDERMANN, J. B. D.

Grammaire Turque, ou Methode Courte & Facile pour Apprendre la Langue Turque. Constantinople: 1730. V. 39; 45

HOLDERNESS, MARY

New Russia. London: 1823. V. 44

HOLDING, T. H.

Coats: How to Cut and Try Them on. London: 1885. V. 37

Trousers, Vests, Breeches & Faiters. London: 1886. V. 37

Uniforms of British Army, Navy and Court. London: 1894. V. 38

HOLDSWORTH, EDMUND

Deep Sea Fishing and Fishing Boats, an Account of the Practical Working of the Various Fisheries Around the British Islands. London: 1874. V. 41

HOLDSWORTH, EDWARD 1684-1746

Muscipula; or, the Mouse Trap: a Poem in Latin and English. London: 1720. V. 39

HOLDSWORTH, JOHN T.

Financing an Empire. History of Banking in Pennsylvania. Chicago: 1928. V. 41

HOLDSWORTH, WINCH

A Defence of the Doctrine of the Resurrection of the Same Body. London: 1727. V. 45

HOLE in the Wall; or a Peep at the Creed-worshippers. N.P.: 1828. V. 46

HOLE, JAMES

The Homes of the Working Classes with Suggestions for Their Improvement. London: 1866. V. 38

HOLE, RICHARD

Remarks on the Arabian Nights' Entertainments . . . London: 1797. V. 37; 42

HOLE, S. R.

Our Gardens. London: 1899. V. 45

HOLE, S. REYNOLDS

A Little Tour in America. London: and New York: 1895. V. 44; 46

HOLE, SAMUEL REYNOLDS

A Little Tour in Ireland. London: 1859. V. 37; 38

A Little Tour in Ireland, by an Oxonian, illustrations by John Leech. London: 1892. V. 37

HOLEHOUSE, SAMUEL

Catalogue of Furniture . . . Telescopes . . . Medallions . . . Coins . . . Harp, Guitar and Fine Violins. London. V. 44

HOLFORD, G.

Observations ont he Necessity of Introducing a Sufficient Number of Respectable Clergyman into Our Colonies in the West Indies . . . London: 1807. V. 42

Observations on the Necessity of Introducing a Sufficient Number of Respectable Clergymen into Our Colonies in the West Indies and the Expediency of Establishing for that Purpose, by Subscription a College, in this Country . . . London: 1808. V. 43

HOLFORD, GEORGE

The Destruction of Jerusalem an Absolute and Irreistible Proof of the Divine Origin of Christianity. Burlington: 1807. V. 37; 40

The Holford Library. London: 1927-8. V. 39; 45

The Holford Library Catalogue . . . forming part of the Collections at Dorchester House, Park Lane, the property of Lt.Col. Sir George Holford . . . which will be sold by Auction by Messrs Sotheby and Co., 1927-28-29. V. 37

HOLFORD, GEORGE PETER

The Destruction of Jerusalem, an Absolute and Irresistable Proof of the Divine Origin of Christianity: Including a Narrative of the Calamities which Befell the Jews . . . With a Brief Description of the City and Temple. (Burlington/New York: 1807. V. 37

Substance of the Speech of George Holford, Esq. on the Motion Made by Him in the House of Commons, on Tuesday, the 14th of June, 1814, for Leave to Bring in a Bill for the Better Management of the Prisons Belonging to the City of London. London: 1814. V. 40

HOLFORD, MARGARET

Margaret of Anjou. London: 1816. V. 42

Wallace; or, the Fight of Falkirk; a Metrical Romance. London: 1809. V. 38; 39; 40

HOLIDAY, BILLIE

Lady Sings the Blues. Garden City: 1956. V. 42

HOLIDAY, HENRY

Stained Glass as an Art. London: 1896. V. 42

Stained Glass as an Art, by Henry Holiday. London: 1986. V. 37

HOLIDAY Hours. London: 1890. V. 45

HOLINSHED, RAPHAEL

The Fist and Second (Third) Volumes of Chronicles, Comprising 1 The Description and Historie of England 2 The Description and Historie of Ireland, 3 The Description and Historie of Scotland . . . London: 1587. V. 39

The First (Laste) Volume of the Chronicles of England, Scotlande, and Irelande. London: 1577. V. 38

Holinshed's Chronicles of England, Scotland and Ireland. London: 1807-08. V. 37; 44; 46

HOLITSCHER, ARTHUR

Amerika. Berlin: 1922. V. 45

THE HOLKHAM Bible Picture Book. London: 1954. V. 40; 41; 43; 45

HOLLADAY, BEN

Table of Distances of the Overland Daily Stage Line, from Atchison, Kansas to Great Salt Lake City, the Route Passing through Denver City, Thence by the Cherokee Trail Along Cache la Poudre River, through Laramie Plains . . . Denver: 1862. V. 41; 45

HOLLADAY, BENJAMIN

Table of Distances of the Overland Daily Stage Line from Athcinson, Kansas to Great Salt Lake City . . . New York: 1863. V. 42

HOLLAND

Articulen Van Vrede Ende Verbondt Tusfchen Den Doorluchtighsten Groomtmachtighsten Prins Ende Heere Karel . . . The Hague: 1667. V. 44

HOLLAND, ANNIE JEFFERSON

The Refugees: a Sequel to 'Uncle Tom's Cabin.' Austin: 1892. V. 40

HOLLAND, ELIZABETH VASSALL, LADY 1770-1845

A Memoir of Rev. Sydney Smith. London: 1855. V. 38

HOLLAND, F. W.

Sinai and Jerusalem. London. V. 40

HOLLAND, F. W. continued

Sinai and Jerusalem.. London: 1870. V. 46

Sinai and Jerusalem, or Scenes from Bible Lands. London: 1872. V. 39; 45

Sinai and Jerusalem. London: 1880. V. 38

HOLLAND, G. A.

History of Parker County and the Double Log Cabin. 1937. V. 42

History of Parker County and the Double Log Cabin. Weatherford: 1937. V. 40

HOLLAND, G. CALVERT

The Philosophy of Animated Nature. London: 1848. V. 37; 38; 39; 40; 41; 45

HOLLAND, HENRY

Chapters on Mental Physiology. London: 1852. V. 43

Chapters on Mental Physiology. London: 1853. V. 45

General View of the Agriculture of Cheshire . . . London: 1808. V. 44

General View of the Agriculture of Cheshire . . . London: 1813. V. 43; 46

Herwologia Anglica . . . V. 46

Herwologia Anglica hoc est Clarissimorum et Doctissimorum Aliquot Anglorum qui Floruerunt ab Anno Cristi M.D . . . . Impensis Crispini Passaei: 1620. V. 38

Herwologia Anglica . . . London?: 1620. V. 40

The Iceland Journal of Henry Holland 1810. London: 1987. V. 43

Medical Notes and Reflections. Philadelphia: 1839. V. 42; 45

Travels in the Ionian Isles, Albania, Thessaly, Macedonia, &c. London: 1815. V. 39

HOLLAND, HENRY RICHARD

Foreign Reminiscences. London: 1850. V. 43; 44

HOLLAND, HENRY RICHARD FOX

Some Account of the Lives and Writings of Lope Felix de Vega Carpio and Guillen de Castro. London: 1817. V. 42

Some Account of the Life and Writings of Lope Felix de Vega Carpio. London: 1806. V. 37

HOLLAND, HENRY RICHARD VASSALL FOX, 3RD BARON 1773-1840

Eve's Legend. London: 1928. V. 42

HOLLAND, J. G.

The Marble Prophecy and Other Poems. New York: 1872. V. 45

HOLLAND, JOHN

The Cottage of Pella, a Tale of Palestine. Sheffield: 1821. V. 42

The History and Description of the Town and Parish of Worksop, in the County of Nottingham. Sheffield: 1826. V. 42

The History, Antiquities and Description of the Town and Parish of Worksop, in the County of Nottingham. Sheffield: 1826. V. 42; 44

The History and Description of Fossil Fuel, The Collieries, and the Coal Trade of Great Britain. London: 1835. V. 37; 38; 42

The History and Description of Fossil Fuel, the Collieries, and Coal Trade of Great Britain. London: 1841. V. 37

The Hopes of Matrimony: a Poem. London: 1822. V. 38

The Negro's Friend, or, the Sheffield Anti-Slavery Album. Sheffield: 1826. V. 45; 46

Sheffield Park. A Descriptive Poem. Sheffield: 1820. V. 37

The Tour of the Don. London: 1837. V. 44

A Treatise on the Progressive Improvement and Present State of the Manufactures in Metal. London: 1831-33-34. V. 39

HOLLAND, JOSIAH GILBERT

History of Western Massachusetts. The Counties of Hmpden Hampshire, Franklin and Berkshire. Springfield: 1855. V. 38

History of Western Massachusetts. Springfield: 1865. V. 46

HOLLAND, MARY

Our Army Nurses: Interesting Sketches and Photographs of Over 100 of the Nobel Women Who Served in Hospitals and On Battle Fields During Our Late Civil War, 1861-1865. Boston: 1897. V. 42

HOLLAND, P.

Select Views of the Lakes in Cumberland, Westmorland and Lancashire From Drawings Made by P. Holland . . . Liverpool: 1792. V. 44

Select Views of the Lakes in Cumberland, Westmoreland and Lancashire. Liverpool: 1792. V. 39; 41

HOLLAND, RAY P.

Shotgunning in the Lowlands. West Hartford: 1945. V. 38; 43

HOLLAND, TREVENEN J.

Record of the Expedition to Abyssinia. London: 1870. V. 41

HOLLAND, VYVYAN

Hand Colored Fashion Plates 1770 to 1899. London: 1955. V. 41; 44

HOLLANDER, BERNARD 1864-1934

In Search of the Soul and the Mechanism of Thought, Emotion and Conduct. London: 1920. V. 43; 46

HOLLANDER, JOHN

A Crackling of Thorns. New Haven: 1958. V. 39; 41

Looking Ahead: Poems. 1982. V. 42

Looking Ahead; Poems. New York: 1982. V. 41

HOLLANDERS In Iowa. Brieven Uit Pella, van een Gelderschman. Met Twee Platen. Arnhem: 1858. V. 39

HOLLAND'S City Directory of Belvidere, From . . . 1894 to 1898. Chicago: 1895. V. 39; 43

HOLLAND'S Fond Du Lac City Directory, for the Years 1880-1884. Chicago: 1880. V. 43

HOLLANDUS, ISAAC

Curieuse und Rare Chymische Operationes, Worinnen Nicht Allein Einige Bifshero Unbekannte Geheimnisse die Rechte Universal-Tinctur . . . Leipzig and Gandeleben: 1714. V. 46

HOLLAR, WENZEL

Muscarum Scarabeorum Vermiumque Variae Figurae et Formae . . . Ex Collectione Arundeliana . . . Antwerp: 1646. V. 39

HOLLENBACK, FRANK

Pikes Peal by Rail. Denver: 1962. V. 46

HOLLES, DENZIL

Memoirs from the Year 1641, to 1648. London: 1699. V. 38

The Petition of the Members of the House of Commons, who are Accused by the Army. London: 1647. V. 38

HOLLES, DENZIL HOLLES, BARON

The Case Stated of the Jurisdiction of the House of Lords int he Point of Impositions . . . London: 1676. V. 42

Lord Hollis His Remains: Being a Second Letter to a Friend Concerning the Judicature of the Bishops in Parliament. London: 1682. V. 41

HOLLES, DENZIL, LORD

A True Relation of the Unjust Accusation of Certain French Gentlemen (Charged with Robbery, of Which They Were Most Innocent). London: 1671. V. 38; 40

HOLLEY, ALEXANDER L.

American and European Railway Practice in the Economical Generation of Steam . . . New York: 1861. V. 42

HOLLEY, FRANCES CHAMBERLAIN

Once Their Home; or, Our Legacy from the Dakotahs, Historical, Biographical and Incidental. Chicago: 1891. V. 37; 42; 46

HOLLEY, FRANCIS CHAMBERLAIN

Once Their Home or Our Legacy from the Dakotah. Chicago: 1890. V. 37; 44

HOLLEY, MARY AUSTIN 1784-1846

Texas. Observations, Historical, Geographical and Descriptive. Baltimore: 1833. V. 37; 38; 41; 42; 43; 45

Texas. Lexington: 1836. V. 37; 39; 42; 45

Texas. Austin: 1935. V. 37

Texas: Observations, Geographical and Descriptive, in a Series of Letters Written During a Visit to Austin's Colony. Austin: 1981. V. 37; 38; 39; 42; 44; 45; 46

HOLLEY, O. L.

A Description of the City of New York: With a Brief Account of the Citites, Towns, Villages, and Places of Resort Within Thirty Miles . . . New York: 1847. V. 41

HOLLEY, ORVILLE L.

The Picturesque Tourist . . . New York: 1844. V. 42; 43

HOLLICK, FREDERICK

The Matron's Manual of Midwifery, and the Diseases of Women During Pregnancy and in Childbed. New York: 1848. V. 46

Outlines of Anatomy and Physiology. Philadelphia: 1846. V. 40

HOLLIDAY, FRANCIS

An Introduction to Fluxions, Designed for the Use and Adapted to the Capacities of Beginners. London: 1777. V. 42

HOLLINGSHEAD, JOHN

Ragged London in 1861. London: 1861. V. 40

HOLLINGSOWRTH, JOHN MC HENRY

The Journal of . . . of the First New York Volunteers (Stevenson's Regiment), Sept. 1846 - August 1849 . . . San Francisco: 1923. V. 38

HOLLINGSWORTH, A. G. H.

The History of Stowmarket, the Ancient County Town of Suffolk, with Some Notices of the Hundred of Stow. Ipswich & London: 1844. V. 39

Rebecca; or, the Times of Primitive Christianity. A Poem, in Four Cantos. London: 1832. V. 37

HOLLINGSWORTH, JOHN MC HENRY

The Journal of . . . of the First New York Volunteers (Stevenson's Regiment) September 1846-August 1849. San Francisco: 1923. V. 45

The Journal of Lieut. John McHenry Hollingsworth of the First New York Volunteers (Stevenson's Regiment). San Francisco: 1924. V. 41; 45

HOLLINGSWORTH, JOHN MCHENRY

The Journal of Lieutenant John McHenry Hollingsworth of the First New York Volunteers (Stevenson's Regiment) September 1846-August 1849. San Francisco: 1923. V. 39; 40; 41

HOLLINGSWORTH, S.

A Dissertation on the Manners, Government and Spirit of Africa. Edinburgh: 1788. V. 40; 41

HOLLINGSWORTH, RICHARD 1639?-1701

Vindiciae Carolinae; or, a Defence of Eikon Basilike . . . London: 1692. V. 41

HOLLINS, WILLIAM

Rail Roads in the United States of America . . . Baltimore: 1827. V. 39; 41

HOLLINSHEAD, JOHN

Hints to Country Gentlemen and Farmers on the Importance of Using Salt as a General Manure. Blackburn: 1800. V. 43

HOLLIS, MARGERY

Through Thick and Thin. London: 1893. V. 44

Up In Arms. London: 1896. V. 41

HOLLISTER, G. H.

The History of Connecticut, from the First Settlement of the Colony. Hartford: 1857. V. 37

HOLLISTER, OVANDO J.

The Mines of Colorado. Springfield: 1867. V. 42

The Mines of Colorado. Springfield, Mass.: 1867. V. 37

The Resources and Attractions of Utah. Salt Lake City: 1882. V. 42; 43

HOLLISTER, URIAH S.

The Navajo and His Blanket. Denver: 1903. V. 37; 38

HOLLMAN, ALBERT M.

Pioneering in the Northwest Niobrara-Virginia City Wagon Road . . . Pioneers Short Sketches of Charles Floyd War EAgle Theophile Bruguier and Others . . . Sioux City: 1924. V. 39

HOLLOWAY, JAMES

The Free and Voluntary Confession and Narrative of . . . (Addressed to His Majesty) . . . Colophon: 1684. V. 42

HOLLOWAY, JOHN

The Very Remarkable Trial of John Holloway and Owen Haggerty, Who Were Found Guilty, at the Old-Bailey on Friday, February 20, 1807, of the Wilful Murder of Mr. J. C. Steele . . . London: 1807. V. 38; 42

HOLLOWAY, LAURA C.

Adelaide Neilson: a Souvenir. New York: and London: 1885. V. 46

The Ladies of the White House; or, in the Home of the Presidents. New York: 1886. V. 44

HOLLOWAY, ROBERT

The Phoenix of Sodom, or the Vere Street Coterie. London: 1813. V. 43

HOLLOWAY, W. R.

Indianapolis. A Historical and Statistical Sketch of the Railroad City . . . Indianapolis: 1870. V. 37; 42

HOLLOWAY, WILLIAM

The Baron of Laderbrooke. London: 1800. V. 40

The Peasants Fate; a Rural Poem. London: 1802. V. 42

HOLLOWELL, J. M.

War-Time Reminiscences and Other Selections. Goldsboro: 1939. V. 42

HOLLSTEIN, F. W. H.

German Engravings, Etchings and Woodcuts ca. 1400-1700. Volume VII: Albrecht and Hans Durer. Amsterdam: 1962? V. 41

HOLLY, HENRY HUDSON

Holly's Country Seats . . . New York: 1863. V. 38; 39; 44

Modern Dwellings in Town and Country, Adpated to American Wants and Climate with a Treatise on Furniture and Decoration. New York: 1878. V. 46

HOLLYBAND, CLAUDIUS

The Elizabethan Home; Dicovered in 2 Dialogues. London: 1925. V. 44

HOLMAN, ALBERT M.

Pioneering in the Northwest Niobrara-Virginia City Wagon Road. Sioux City: 1924. V. 38; 40; 41

HOLMAN, DAVID

Buckskin and Homespun. Austin: 1979. V. 37; 38; 39; 40; 41; 42; 43; 44; 45; 46

Letters of Hard Times in Texas 1840-1880. Austin: 1974. V. 37; 38; 40; 42; 45; 46

HOLMAN, FREDERICK V.

Dr. John McLoughlin, the Father of Oregon. Cleveland: 1907. V. 38

HOLMAN, JAMES

Travels through Russia, Siberia, Poland, Cracow, Austria, Bohemia, Saxony, Prussia, Hanover, etc. London: 1834. V. 41; 44

Travels in Madras, Ceylon, Mauritius, Cormoro Islands, Zanzibar, Calcutta, etc. London: 1840. V. 41

Travels in China, New Zealand, New South Wales, Van Diemen's Land, Cape Horn, etc. London: 1840. V. 42

Travels through Russia, Siberia, Poland, Austria, Saxony, Prussia, Hanover, &c. London: 1825. V. 42

A Voyage Round the World, Including Travels in Africa, Asia, Australasia, America. London: 1834. V. 40

HOLMAN, JOHN P.

Sheep and Bear Trails. New York: 1933. V. 43

HOLMAN, LOUIS A.

The Graphic Processes: Intaglio, Relief, Planographic. A Series of Actual Prints, Selected and Arranged with Notes. Boston: 1926. V. 38

The Graphic Processes. Intaglio, Relief and Planographic: With a set of Actual Prints Illustrative of the Text. Boston: 1929. V. 37

HOLMAN, WILLIAM R.

Library Publications. San Francisco: 1965. V. 37; 38; 39; 40; 41; 44; 45

Library Publications. San Francisco: (1965). V. 37

HOLMBERG, MAJ SANDMAN

The God Path. Lund: 1946. V. 40; 44

HOLMDAHL, GUSTAV

Gunnar Asplund, Architect, 1885-1940. Stockholm: 1950. V. 41

HOLME, BENJAMIN

A Collection of the Epistles and Works of Benjamin Holme. London: 1753. V. 40

HOLME, C.

Peasant Art in Sweden, Lapland and Iceland. London: 1910. V. 46

HOLME, C. G.

Lettering of Today. London: 1937. V. 41

HOLME, C. GEOFFREY

Modern Photography 1934-35. London. V. 46

HOLME, CHARLES 1848-1923

The Art of the Book. London: 1914. V. 38; 40; 41; 44

The Art of the Book. London: Paris: New York: 1914. V. 44

Colour Photography and Other Recent Developments of the Art of the Camera. London: 1908. V. 44

English Water Colour With Reproductions of Drawings by Eminent Painters. London: 1902. V. 43; 44

English Water-Colour with Reproductions of Drawings by Eminent Painters. New York: 1902. V. 42

Modern British Domestic Architecture and Decoration. London: 1901. V. 43

Modern Pen Drawings: European and American. London: 1901. V. 44

Modern Design in Jewellery and Fans. London: 1902. V. 40

The War. London: 1918. V. 45; 46

HOLME, GARNETT

Nanda: A Grove Play. San Francisco: 1928. V. 37

HOLME, GEOFFREY

Etchings of To-Day. New York: 1929. V. 39

Figure Painting in Water-Colours, by Contemporary British Artists. London: 1923. V. 39

Modern Woodcuts and Lithographs by British and French Artists. London: 1919. V. 40; 41

HOLME, TIMOTHY

A System of Surgery, Theoretical and Practical, In Treatises by Various Authors. Philadelphia: 1882. V. 42

HOLMELUND, ELSE

Little Bear. New York: 1957. V. 46

HOLMES, A. C.

Practical Shipbuilding, a Treatise on the Structural Design and Building of Modern Steel Vessels from the Making of the Raw Material to the Equipped Vessel. London: 1908-17-18. V. 42

HOLMES, A. S.

Belinda or the Rivals. Vancouver: 1970. V. 44

HOLMES, ABIEL

American Annals; or a Chronological History of America From Its Discovery in MCCCCXCII to MDCCCIV. Cambridge: 1805. V. 41; 43; 46

Annals of America, from the Discovery by Columbus in the Year 1492 to the Year 1826. Cambridge: 1829. V. 37; 42

A Family Tablet: Containing a Selection of Original Poetry. Boston: 1796. V. 41; 42

HOLMES, BAYARD

The Surgery of the Head. New York: 1903. V. 42

HOLMES, BETTIE FLEISCHMANN

The Log of the 'Laura' in Polar Seas. Cambridge: 1907. V. 43

HOLMES BOOK CO.

Descriptive and Priced Catalogue of Books, Pamphlets, and Maps Relating Directly or Indirectly to the History, Literature and Printing of California and the Far West Formerly the Collection of Thomas Wayne Norris, Livermore, Calif. Oakland: 1948. V. 38

HOLMES, C. J.

Constable and His Influence on Landscape Painting. New York: 1902. V. 41

Notes on the Post Impressionist Painters: Grafton Galleries 1910-11, by C.J. Holmes. London: 1910. V. 37

HOLMES, CHARLOTTE R.

The Burckmyer Letters, March 1863 to June 1865. Columbia: 1926. V. 44

HOLMES, ELEANOR

The Price of a Pearl. London: 1894. V. 41

HOLMES, ERNEST

The Science of Mind. New York: 1943. V. 46

HOLMES, FRANCIS S.

The Southern Farmer and Market Gardener . . . Charleston: 1842. V. 37

HOLMES, FRED L.

Wisconsin: Stability, Progress, Beauty. Chicago: 1946. V. 37; 38

HOLMES, ISAAC

An Account of the United States of America, Derived from Actual Observation, During a Residence of Four Years in that Republic . . . London: 1823. V. 39; 42

HOLMES, J. H. H.

A Treatise on Coal Mines of Durham and Northumberland. London: 1816. V. 38; 40; 41; 43; 46

HOLMES, JOHN

The Art of Rhetoric Made Easy. London: 1766. V. 46

A Descriptive Catalogue of Books, in the Library of John Holmes, F.S.A. Norwich: 1828-40. V. 39; 44

Historical Sketches of the Missions of the United Brethren for Propagating the Gospel Among the Heathen from Their Commencement to the Present Time. Dublin: 1818. V. 37; 38; 40

A System of Rhetoric, in a Method Entirely New. Dublin: 1786. V. 42

HOLMES, JOHN CLELLON

Get Home Free. New York: 1964. V. 37

Go. New York: 1952. V. 37; 39; 41; 42; 46

Gone in October. ailey: 1985. V. 39; 41

The Horn. New York: 1958. V. 37; 39; 41; 46

Nothing More to Declare. London: 1968. V. 46

HOLMES, JOHN M.

Colour in Interior Design. London: 1932. V. 38

HOLMES, KENNETH L.

Covered Wagon Women. Diaries, and Letters from the Western Trails 1840-1890. Glendale: 1983. V. 44

Covered Wagon Women: Diaries and Letters from the Western Trails, 1840-1890. Glendale: 1983-86. V. 37

HOLMES, LEWIS

Arctic Whaleman, or Winter in the Arctic Ocean, the narrative of wreck of whaleship 'Citizen' in Arcti Ocean, sufferings of crew during nine months among the natives, a brief history of whaling. Boston: 1857. V. 37

HOLMES, LOUIS A.

Fort McPherson, Nebraska, Fort Cottonwood, N.T.: Gaurdian of the Tracks and Trails. Lincoln: 1963. V. 43

HOLMES, MAURICE

Captain James Cook, R.N., F.R.S. A Bibliographical Excursion. London: 1952. V. 41; 46

HOLMES, OLIVER WENDELL 1809-1894

An Address Delivered at the Annual Meeting of the Boston Microscopical Society. Cambridge: 1877. V. 39; 44

Astraea. Boston: 1850. V. 38; 39; 41; 43; 44; 46

At Dartmouth. The Phi Beta Kappa Poem Read by Dr. Oliver Wendell Holmes at the Dartmouth Commencement Excercises July 24, 1839 Prior to His Appointment to the Chair of Anatomy and Physiology at Dartmouth Medical School. New York: 1940. V. 41

The Autocrat of the Breakfast Table. V. 39

The Autocrat of the Breakfast Table. Boston: 1858. V. 37; 38; 39; 40; 41; 42; 43; 44; 45; 46

The Autocrat of the Breakfast TAble. London: 1893. V. 41; 42

Autocrat of the Breakfast Table/Professor at the Breakfast Table/Poet at the Breakfast Table. London/Boston: 1902-13. V. 41

The Autocrat of the Breakfast Table; The Professor at the Breakfast Table; The Poet at the Breakfast Table. London: 1902-20. V. 39

The Autocrat of the Breakfast TAble. Cambridge: 1894. V. 37; 40

Before the Curfew and Other Poems, Chiefly Occasional. Boston: 1888. V. 43

Before the Curfew and Other Poems. Boston and New: 1888. V. 45

Before the Curfew and Other Poems, Chiefly Occasional. Boston & New York: 1888. V. 46

Before the Curfew and Other Poems. Boston/New York: 1888. V. 37

Border Lines of Knowledge in Some Provinces of Medical Science. Boston: 1862. V. 37; 42; 43; 44; 45; 46

Boylston Prize Dissertations for the Years 1836 and 1837. Boston: 1838. V. 40; 45; 46

The Brave Old South. Boston: 1879. V. 41

The Common Law. Boston: 1881. V. 37; 38; 39; 44; 46

The Common Law. Boston: 1881, 1909. V. 38; 40

The Contagiousness of Puerperal Fever. V. 39

The Correspondence of Mr. Justice Holmes and Sir Frederick Pollock 1874-1932. Cambridge: 1941. V. 40

Currents and Counter-Currents in Medical Science. Boston: 1861. V. 37; 40; 42; 44; 45; 46

Dedication of the New Building and Hall of the Boston Medical Library Association. Boston: 1881. V. 46

Dedication of the New Building and Hall of the Boston Medical Library Association . . . 1878 . . . Address of the President, Dr. Oliver Wendell Holmes. Cambridge: 1881. V. 40

Dorothy Q. Boston: 1893. V. 44; 46

Dorothy Q, Together with A Ballad of the Boston Tea Party and Grandmother's Story of Bunker Hill Battle. Cambridge: 1893. V. 40

Elsie Veneer: a Romance of Destiny. Boston: 1861. V. 37; 39; 40; 42; 43; 44; 45; 46

Essays 1842-1882. Boston: 1887. V. 40

The Guardian Angel. Boston: 1867. V. 38

The Harbinger - a May Gift. Boston: 1833. V. 37

Homoeopath, and Its Kindred Delusions. Boston: 1842. V. 38; 41; 42; 46

Humorous Poems. Boston: 1865. V. 40; 43; 45

The Iron Gate and Other Poems. Boston: 1880. V. 37; 39; 41

The Iron Gate. Boston & New York: 1881. V. 39

John Lothrop Motley. Boston: 1879. V. 37; 38; 41

Justice Oliver Wendell Holmes. New York: 1936. V. 43

The Last Leaf. Cambridge: 1895. V. 41; 45; 46

Library of Practical Medicine. Boston: 1836. V. 46

Mechanism in Thought and Morals. Boston: 1871. V. 38; 39; 41; 45

Medical Essays: 1842-1882. Birmingham: 1987. V. 41

A Moral Antipathy. Boston & New York: 1884. V. 40

A Moral Antipathy. Boston: 1888. V. 43

A Mortal Antipathy: First Opening of the New Portfolio. Boston: 1885. V. 37; 45

The New Century and the Building of the Harvard Medical School 1783-1883. Cambridge: 1884. V. 45

Old Ironsides. New York: 1922. V. 39

One Hundred Days in Europe. Boston: 1887. V. 41

One Hundredth Anniversary of the Foundation of the Medical School of Harvard University. Cambridge: 1884. V. 37

Over the Tea Cups. Boston: 1891. V. 41

Poems. Boston: 1836. V. 38; 39; 40; 41; 44; 46

Poems. Boston & New York: 1836. V. 39

Poems. London: 1846. V. 39; 40; 41; 45; 46

Poems. Boston: 1849. V. 43

Poems. Boston: 1881. V. 40; 41

HOLMES, OLIVER WENDELL 1809-1894 continued

Poems . . . Boston: 1891. V. 39; 40

The Poet at the Breakfast Table. Boston: 1872. V. 37; 40; 42; 44; 45; 46

The Professor at the Breakfast Table. With The Story of Iris. Boston: 1860. V. 38; 39; 41; 42; 43; 44; 45; 46

Puerperal Fever, as a Private Pestilence. Boston: 1855. V. 42; 46

The School Boy. Boston: 1878. V. 38

The School Boy. Boston: 1879. V. 46

Songs in Many Keys. Boston: 1862. V. 45; 46

Songs of Many Seasons 1862-1874. Boston: 1875. V. 40; 42

Songs and Poems of the Class of Eighteen Hundred and Twenty-Nine. Boston: 1868. V. 45

Soundings from the Atlantic. Boston: 1864. V. 43; 44; 46

Speeches. Boston: 1900. V. 38

Teaching from the Chair and at the Bedside- An Introductory Lecture delivered before the Medical Class of Harvard University 11/6/1867. Boston: 1867. V. 39

Urania; a Rhymed Lesson. Boston: 1846. V. 40; 46

The Vision of Sir Launfal. Cambridge: 1848. V. 39; 41

The Vision of Sir Launfal. Cambridge: 1948. V. 46

Visions: a Study of False Sight. Boston: 1878. V. 46

Welcome to All Nations. Philadelphia: 1876. V. 41

Works. Boston: 1892. V. 42

The Works. Boston & New York: 1892. V. 39; 40; 41

Works. Boston: (1892-1896). V. 37

The Works of Oliver Wendell Holmes. Boston: 1892-1896. V. 37

Writings. Boston: 1891. V. 46

The Writings of Oliver Wendell Holmes. Cambridge: 1891-92. V. 37; 38; 40

The Complete Writings of Oliver Wendell Holmes. Boston: 1892. V. 38; 40

The Writings of . . . With the Life and Letters by John T. Morse. Boston: 1896. V. 46

The Writings of Oliver Wendell Holmes. Cambridge: 1891-92. V. 37

HOLMES, R. S.

The History of Yorkshire County Cricket 1833-1903. Westminster: 1904. V. 46

HOLMES, RICHARD

Shelley: the Pursuit. London: 1974. V. 40

HOLMES, RICHARD RIVINGTON

Queen Victoria. London & Paris: 1897. V. 39

Specimens of Royal Fine & Historical Bookbinding, Selected from the Royal Library, Windsor Castle. London: 1893. V. 39; 45; 46

HOLMES, ROBERT

Ode for the Encaenia Held at Oxford, July, 1793, for the Reception of His Grace William Henry Cavendish, Duke of Portland. Oxford: 1793. V. 42

HOLMES, ROBERTA EVELYN

The Southern Mines of California: Early Development of the Sonora Mining Region. San Francisco: 1930. V. 39

HOLMES, SAMUEL

The Journal of Samuel Holmes, Sergeant-major of the XIth Light Dragoons During His Attendance as One of the Guard on Lord Macartney's Embassy to China and Tartary 1792-93. London: 1798. V. 39

HOLMES, SAMUEL J.

A Bibliography of Eugenics. Berkeley: 1924. V. 41

HOLMES, SHERLOCK

The Whole Art of Detection. Chicago: 1968. V. 38

HOLMES, THOMAS J.

Cotton Mather a Bibliography of His Works. Cambridge: 1940. V. 37; 38; 40; 43; 44

Increase Mather, His Works: Being a Short-Title Catalogue of the Published Writings That Can Be Ascribed to Him. Cleveland: 1930. V. 42

Increase Mather a Bibliography of His Works. Cleveland: 1931. V. 38; 43; 44

The Minor Mathers. A List of Their Works. Cambridge: 1940. V. 44

HOLMES, THOMAS JAMES

Cotton Mather. A Bibliography of His Works. Newton: 1974. V. 45; 46

The Minor Mathers: a List of Their Works. Cambridge: 1940. V. 43

HOLMES. W. H.

Aboriginal Pottery of the Eastern United States. (Washington: 1903). V. 37

HOLMES, WILLIAM

Religious Emblems. Boston: 1853. V. 40

Religious Emblems; being a Series of Emblematic Engravings . . . Designed to Illustrate Divine Truth. Cincinnati: 1851. V. 37

HOLMES, WILLIAM H.

Archaelogical Studies Among the Ancient Cities of Mexico. Chicago: 1895-97. V. 39; 42

HOLOGNE, GREGOIRE

Catharine Virginis, Doctoris & Martyris Certamine. Ad Generosvm Pvervm Lancelotum de Berlaymont. Antwerp: 1556. V. 42

Lambertias. Tragoedia de Oppresione B. Lamberti . . . quae nunc Leodium Translata est, Episcopi & Martyris Gloriossimi. Antwerp: 1556. V. 42

Lavrentias. Tragoedia de Martyrio Constantissimi Leuitae D. Laurentii, Romae sub Decio passi. Ad Generosum Adolescentem Ludouicum de Berlaymont. Antwerp: 1556. V. 42

HOLROYD, ABRAHAM

Spice Islands Passed in the Sea of Reading, a Series of Selections From Our Local Poetry. Bradford: 1859. V. 43

HOLROYD, JOHN BAKER

Observations on the Commerce of the American States with Europe and the West Indies . . . London: 1783. V. 38

HOLROYD, MICHAEL

Lytton Strachey. A Critical Biography. London: 1967/8. V. 40

HOLSINGER, H. R.

Holsinger's History of the Tunkers and the Brethren Church. Lathrop: 1901. V. 38

HOLST, HERMANN VON

The Constitutional and Political History of the United States. Chicago: 1889-1892. V. 37

HOLSTEIN, ANNA

Three Years in Field Hospitals of the Army of the Potomac. Philadelphia: 1867. V. 37; 42

HOLSTEIN, P.

Contribution a l'Etude des Armes Orientales: Inde et Archipel Malais. Paris: 1931. V. 39

HOLT, ARDERN

Fancy Dresses Described, or, What to Wear at Fancy Balls. London. V. 40; 46

Fancy Dress Described; or, What to Wear at Fancy Balls. London: 1887. V. 44

Fancy Dresses Described; or, What to Wear at Fancy Balls. London: 1882. V. 37

Fancy Dresses Described; or, What to Wear at Fancy Balls. London: (1887). V. 37

HOLT, E. EMMETT

The Diseases of Infancy and Childhood. New York: 1897. V. 41; 44; 45; 46

HOLT, J.

Characters of the Kings and Queens of England, Selected from Different Histories . . . Dublin: 1789. V. 38; 42

Report of the Judge Advocate General On 'The Order of American Knights,' Alias 'The Sons of Liberty', a Western Conspiracy in Aid of the Southern Rebellion. Washington: 1864. V. 42

HOLT, JOHN

Characters of the Kings and Queens of England, Selected from the Different Historians, with Observations and Reflections Chiefly Adapted in Common Life . . . London: 1786/87/88. V. 42

General View of the Agriculture of the County of Lancaster. London: 1794. V. 41

General View of the Agriculture of the County of Lancaster. London: 1795. V. 39; 41; 44

HOLT, JOSEPH

Reply of J. Holt to Certain Calumnies of Jacob Thompson. Washington: 1883. V. 40

HOLT, L. EMMETT

Diseases of Infancy and Childhood. New York: 1897. V. 37; 38; 39; 40; 42

HOLT, ROSA BELLE

Rugs, Oriental and Occidental Antique and Modern . . . Chicago: 1901. V. 44

Rugs Oriental and Occidental Antique and Modern. Chicago: 1927. V. 40

HOLT-WHITE, RASHLEIGH

The Life and Letters of Gilbert White of Selborne. London: 1901. V. 38

HOLTBY, WINIFRED

South Riding - an English Landscape. London: 1936. V. 41

Virginia Woolf. London: 1932. V. 39

HOLTEDAHL, O.

Report of the Scientific Results of the Norwegian Expedition to Novaya Zemlya, 1921. Oslo: 1924-30. V. 43

HOLTHAUS, P. D.

Wanderings of a Journeyman Tailor through Europe and the East, During the Years 1824 to 1840. London: 1844. V. 42; 45

HOLTHOER, ROSTISLAU

New Kingdom Pharaonic Sites: the Pottery. Denmark: 1977. V. 42; 44

HOLTON, DAVID P.

Winslow Memorial. Family Records of Winslows and Their Descendants in America, with the English Ancestry as Far As Is Known. New York: 1877-88. V. 39

HOLTON, E. D.

Our Claims to the Pacific Coast. Milwaukee: 1889. V. 39

Travels with Jottings. Milwaukee: 1880. V. 39; 45

HOLTON, ISAAC F.

New Granada: Twenty Months in the Andes. New York: 1857. V. 38; 42; 45; 46

HOLTZCLAW, WILLIAM H.

The Black Man's Burden. New York: 1915. V. 39

HOLUB, EMIL

Seven Years in South Africa: Travels, Researches and Hunting Adventures, Between the Diamond-Fields and the Zambesi (1872-79). Boston: 1881. V. 41

HOLWELL, J. Z.

A Genuine Narrative of the Deplorable Deaths of the English Gentleman, and Others Who Were Suffocated in the Black-Hole in Fort-William, at Calcutta, in the Kingdom of Bengal . . . London: 1758. V. 41

HOLWELL, JOHN

A Sure Guide to the Practical Surveyor. London: 1678. V. 37; 40

HOLWELL, JOHN ZEPHANIAH

India Tracts. 1. An Address to the Proprietors of the East-India Stock . . . II. A Refutation of a Letter from Certain Gentlemen of the Council at Bengal . . . III. Important Facts Regarding the East-India Company's Affaris in Bengal . . . IV A Narrative of . . . London: 1774. V. 44

THE HOLY Experiment. Philadelphia: 1950. V. 43

THE HOLY Fast of Lent. Defended Against All of Its Profaners; or, a Discourse, Shewing that Lent-Fast was First Taught the World by the Apostles, as Dr. Gunning, Now Bishop of Ely Learnedly Proved in a Sermon Printed by Him in the Yeare 1662 . . . London: 1677. V. 38

HOLY Songs and Sonnets Part I. Holy Songs and Sonnets Part II. Groningen: 1985. V. 45

HOLYOAKE, GEORGE JACOB

Among the Americans and a Stranger in America. Chicago: 1881. V. 40

The History of the Last Trial by Jury for Atheism in England . . . London: 1850. V. 42

The History of Co-Operation in England. Philadelphia: 1875. V. 39

The History of Co-operation in England; Its Literature and Its Advocates. London: 1875-79. V. 37; 39

Life and Last Days of Robert Owen. London: 1859. V. 38

Travels in Search of a Settler's Guide Book of America and Canada. London: 1884. V. 37; 38

HOLYOAKE, MANFRED

The Conservation of Pictures. London: 1870. V. 46

HOLYOKE, EDWARD

The Holyoke Diaries, 1709-1856. Salem: 1911. V. 46

HOLYOKE, SAMUEL

The Columbia Repository of Sacred Harmony. Exeter: 1802. V. 37

HOLZAPFEL, RUDOLF MELANDER

Shakespeare's Secret. Dublin: 1961. V. 46

HOMAGE To Baudelaire on the Centennial of Les Fleurs du Mal from Poets at the State University of Iowa. Iowa City: 1957. V. 46

HOMAGE to the Book. New York: 1968. V. 37; 45
HOMAGE to the Book. Westvaco: 1968. V. 44

THE HOME and Grave of Byron. London: 1852. V. 44

HOME Book of the Picturesque. New York: 1852. V. 45

HOME Cook Book. Tried, Tested, Proved. Compiled by Ladies of Toronto and Other Cities and Towns in Canada. Toronto: 1878. V. 37

HOME, EVERARD

A Dissertation on the Properties of Pus . . . London: 1788. V. 43

Lectures on Comparative Anatomy In Which are Explained the Preparations in the Hunterian Collection. London: 1814-28. V. 42; 43

Practical Observations on the Treatment of Stricutres in the Urethra, and the Esophagus. London: 1805-1821. V. 42

Practical Observations on the Treatment of Ulcers of the Legs, Considered As a Branch of Military Surgery. Philadelphia: 1811. V. 40

HOME, FRANCIS

Clinical Experiments, Histories and Dissections. Edinburgh: 1780. V. 44

Medical Facts and Experiments. London: 1759. V. 37; 38; 39

The Practice in the Clinical Wards of the Royal Infirmary from Feb. 8, 1778 to April 30 1778. Edinburgh: 1778. V. 42

Principia Medicinae. Edinburgh: 1770. V. 44

The Principles of Agriculture and Vegetation. London: 1759. V. 37; 38

HOME, HENRY LORD KAMES

The Gentleman Farmer. Being an attempt to improve agriculture, by subjecting it to the test of rational principles. Dublin: 1779. V. 37

HOME, JOHN 1722-1808

An Account of the Life and Writings of Henry Mackenzie (1745-1831). Edinburgh: 1822. V. 38

Alonzo, a Tragedy. London: 1773. V. 38

Douglas, a Tragedy. Edinburgh: 1798. V. 39

Dramatic Works. London: 1760. V. 38

The Siege of Aquileia. London: 1760. V. 41; 44

HOME Kindness. London: 1900. V. 45

HOME, or a Short Account of Charles Grafton. Boston: 1816. V. 43

HOME, ROBERT

Select Views in Mysore, the country of Tippoo Sultan . . . London: 1794. V. 45

HOME, WILLIAM

With the Border Volunteers to Pretoria. Hawick: 1901. V. 38

HOMEM, MANUEL

Memoria da Disposicam das Armas Castlehanas, que Injustamente, Invadirao o Reyno de Portugal, no anno de 1580 . . . Lisbon: 1655. V. 45

Resorreicam de Portugal, e Morte Fatal de Castella . . . Composta por Fernao Homem de Figueiredo. Nantes: 1641-45. V. 45

HOMER, HENRY

An Enquiry into the Means of Preserving and Improving the Publick Roads of this Kingdom. Oxford: 1767. V. 37

HOMERUS

The Battle of the Frogs and Mice. Wiltshire: 1988. V. 42

The Death of Hector: A Version After Iliad XXII. Wellingborough: 1973. V. 37

The Homeric Hymn to Aphrodite. London: 1948. V. 37; 38; 39; 40; 41; 43

The Homeric Hymn to Aphrodite. Printed in Great Britain: 1948. V. 37

The Homeric Hymn to Aphrodite. Waltham St. Lawrence: 1948. V. 46

Homer's Hymns to Aphrodite. London: 1928. V. 46

Hymns to Aphrodite. N.P.. V. 43

Six Hymns of Homer. Maastricht: 1929. V. 40; 41

Homeri Poetae Clarissimi Ilias. Coloniae: 1522. V. 40

The Iliad 'Homeri Poetate Clarissimi Ilias'. Coloniae: 1522. V. 44

The Iliad. Coloniae: 1522. V. 42

Ilias, Hoc Est, De Rebvs Ad Troiam Gestis Descriptio, iam Recens Latino Carmine Reddita, Helio Eobano Hesso Interprete. Basle: 1540. V. 39

Homeri Ilias, id es, De Rebus and Troiam Gestis. Paris: 1554. V. 38

(Greek title). Iliad. Worms: 1563. V. 43

Homeri Ilias, id est, de Rebus ad Troiam Gestis. London: 1591. V. 42

Homer, Prince of Poets: Translated According to the Greek in Twelve Books of His Iliads. London: 1610? V. 40

The Iliads of Homer. London: 1611? V. 37; 38

Homer His Iliads. London: 1660. V. 38

Homer. His Iliads. (with) Homer. His Odysses. London: 1660/1669. V. 43

The Iliad of Homer. London: 1715-20. V. 45

The Iliad. London: 1720. V. 39; 40

The Iliad of Homer. London: 1750. V. 43

Ilias. Londini: 1760. V. 43

Homeri Ilias Graece et Latine . . . London: 1760. V. 43

The Iliad of Homer. London: 1760. V. 43

The Iliad. Glasgow: 1771. V. 38

The Iliad . . . Glasgow: 1771. V. 41

The Iliad. Chiswick: 1825. V. 38

The Iliad of Homer. Chiswick: 1825. V. 43

HOMERUS continued

The Iliads of Homer . . . London: 1843. V. 38

The Iliad of Homer. London: 1871. V. 39

The Iliad . . . Boston & New York: 1905. V. 44

The Iliad. 1911. V. 40

Iliad. Munich: 1923. V. 40

The Iliad of Homer. London: 1928. V. 40

The Iliad . . . Haarlem: 1931. V. 41

The Iliad. London: 1931. V. 44

The Iliad. New York: 1931. V. 38

The Iliad of Homer. New York: 1931. V. 41

The Iliad. Chicago: 1962. V. 43

Pax: from Book XIX of the Iliad. London: 1967. V. 40

The Iliad. Philadelphia: 1974. V. 42

Ilias. Nova Recognitione Castigata. (vol. 2 Odyssea. Barrachomyomachia. Hymni xxxii). Colophon: 1551. V. 40

Ilias, Odysseia. London: 1831. V. 40

The Iliad & The Odyssey. Translated by Alexander Pope. V. 37

Ilias, Divo Justinopolitano Interprete. (with) Odyssea, Divo Justinopolitano Interprete. Batrachomyomachia, Aldo Manutio Interprete . . . Venice: 1537. V. 45

Opus Utrumque Homeri Iliados et Odyssae, Diligenti Opera Iacobi Micylli & Ioachimi Camerarii. Basle: 1541. V. 40

Ilias Seu Potius Omnia Eius Quae Extant Opera. Odyssea Eiusdem Batrachomyomachia, Hymni . . . Strassburg: 1572/c.1580. V. 45

Ilias et Odyssea. Cambridge: 1711. V. 40

The Iliad of Homer; The Odyssey of Homer. Translated by Mr. Pope. London: 1715-1726. V. 37

The Iliad & Odyssey of Homer. London: 1791. V. 41; 42

Iliad & Odyssey. Oxford: 1801. V. 45

The Iliad (& the Odyssey). London: 1802. V. 38

The Iliad of Homer. (with) the Odyssey of Homer. London: 1802. V. 45

The Iliad of Homer Engraved from the Compositions of John Flaxman, R. A. Sculptor London (with) The Odyssey . . . London: 1805. V. 41

The Iliad (&) The Odyssey of . . . London: 1825. V. 44

The Iliad & The Odyssey. London: 1831. V. 38; 46

The Iliad & Odyssey. London: 1890. V. 39

Iliad & Odyssey. Munich: 1923-24. V. 43

Iliad & Odyssey. N.P.: 1923-24. V. 45

The Iliad. (and) The Odyssey. 1931. V. 37

The Iliad. The Odyssey. London: 1931. V. 42; 45; 46

Iliad & Odyssey. London: 1931. V. 40; 43; 46

The Iliad & The Odyssey. N.P.: 1931. V. 40

The Iliad. 1928. V. 38

Navsikaa. Paris: 1899. V. 41

Homer's Odyssey. London: 1725. V. 43

The Odyssey of Homer. London: 1725-26. V. 38; 44; 45

The Odyssey. London: 1760. V. 43

The Odyssey of Homer. Boston: 1871-72. V. 38

The Odyssey. London: 1887. V. 42; 43; 45; 46

The Odyssey of Homer. London: 1901. V. 41

The Odyssey . . . New York: 1905. V. 44

The Odyssey: a Line for Line Translation in the Metre of the Original by H. B. Cotterill. London: 1911. V. 44

The Odyssey. London: 1924. V. 37; 39; 40; 41; 42; 44

The Odyssey. London and Boston: 1924. V. 43

The Odyssey of Homer. London/Boston: 1924. V. 37

the Odyssey of Homer. Boston: 1929. V. 39

The Odyssey of Homer. Cambridge: 1929. V. 46

The Odyssey of Homer. London: 1930. V. 39

L'Odyssee. Paris: 1930. V. 38

The Odyssey. Haarlem: 1931. V. 41

The Odyssey. London: 1931. V. 41

The Odyssey. New York: 1931. V. 38; 45

The Odyssey. England: 1932. V. 46

The Odyssey. London: 1932. V. 37; 39; 40; 43

The Odyssey of Homer. New York: 1933. V. 41

The Odyssey. London: 1935. V. 41; 46

The Odyssey of Homer. London: 1936. V. 39

The Odyssey. New York: 1981. V. 38

Quae Exstant Omnia . . . Basle: 1606. V. 38

Ton Toy Omeroy Sesomenon Apanton Tomoi Tessapes - General title transliterated from the Greek. Glaguae: 1756-58. V. 41; 42

The Works of. London. V. 38

Opera. Venice: 1524. V. 38

Opera Graecolatina Omnia. Basileae: 1567. V. 44

The Whole Works of Homer. London: 1616. V. 37; 44; 46

The Whole Works of Homer; Prince of Poetts, in His Iliads and Odysses. (with) The Crowne of All Homers Worckes Batrachomyomachia or the Battaile of Frogs and Mise. His Hymns' and Epigrams. London: 1616 & ?1624. V. 41

Works in Greek. Glasgow: 1756-58. V. 43; 45

The Works of Homer . . . London: 1780. V. 43

The Works. London: 1794. V. 41

The Whole Works of Homer . . . London: 1857. V. 43

The Whole Works of Homer. Oxford: 1930. V. 37; 43; 44; 45

The Whole Works. Oxford: 1930-31. V. 38; 39; 41; 42; 46

HOMES, GEOFFREY

Finders Keepers. New York: 1940. V. 44

HOMES in Arkansas! Buy Railway Lands Where the Title Comes from the United States . . . St. Louis: 1875. V. 43; 45

HOMES in Texas for Everybody: Valuable Information. St. Louis: 1887. V. 38

HOMES Of American Authors. New York: 1853. V. 38
HOMES of American Authors. New York: 1853. V. 37; 39; 40; 41; 43; 45; 46

HOMES of American Statesmen. New York: 1854. V. 39; 41; 43

HOMES of the Passing Show. London: 1900. V. 44

HOMESPUN, PRISCILLA

Universal Receipt Book. Being a Compendious Repository of Practical Information in Cookery, Preserving, Pickling, Distilling, and all the Branches of Domestic Economy. Philadelphia: 1818. V. 37

HOMILIARIUS Doctorum. Basel: 1493. V. 40; 43

HOMMAIRE DE HELL, XAVIER

Les Steppes de la Mer Caspienne, Le Caucase, La Crimee et la Russie Meridionale. Voyage Pittoresque, Historique et Scientifique. Paris: 1843/44/45. V. 39

Travels in the Steppes of the Caspian Sea, the Crimea, the Caucasus, &c. London: 1831. V. 46

Travels in the Steppes of the Caspian Sea, the Crimea, Caucasus &c. London: 1847. V. 41

THE HOMOLOGY of Economic Justice. An Essay by an East India Merchant, Showing that Political Economy is Sophistry, and Landlordism Usurpation and Illegality. London: 1884. V. 38

HONCE, CHARLES

Books and Ghosts. Mount Vernon: 1948. V. 42

Mark Twain's Associated Press Speech and Other News Stories on Murder, Modes, Mysteries, Music and Makers of Books. New York: 1940. V. 42; 44

The Public Papers of a Bibliomaniac. 1942. V. 39

Tales from a Beekman Hill Library. 1952. V. 39

HONDIUS, HENDRIK

Grondige Onderrichtinge in de Optica, of te Perspective Konste. Amsterdam: 1640. V. 45

HONDIUS, HENRICUS

Instrvction en la Science de Perspective. 's-Gravenhage: 1625. V. 43

THE HONDURAS Almanack, for 1828. Belize: 1828. V. 39

HONE, WILLIAM

Ancient Mysteries Described, Especially the Engish Miracle Plays. London: 1823. V. 38; 40; 41; 42; 44; 45

The Table Book. London: 1827-28. V. 37

The Everday Book: Or, Everlasting Calender on Popular Amusements . . . London: 1926-27. V. 37

Catalogue of the Valuable and Interesting Collection of Books, Tracts, Ballads, Prints &c. of Mr. William Hone. London: 1843. V. 44

The Every-Day Book; or, the Guide to the Year Relating to the Popular Amusements, Sports Ceremonies, Manners, Customs and Events. London: 1825-26. V. 45

The Every-Day Book and Table Book; or Everlasting Calendar of Popular Amusements, Sports, Pastimes, Ceremonies, Manners, Customs and Events.. London: 1838-47. V. 39

The Every-Day Book and Table Book; or, Everlsting Calendar of Popular Amusements, Sports, Pastimes, Ceremonies, Manners, Customs and Events. London: 1839. V. 46

The Every-Day Book and Table Book. (with) The Year Book of Daily Recreation and Informataion. London: 1832-35. V. 37

Every-Day Book: or the Guide to the year . . . London. V. 46

Facetiae and Miscellanies. London: 1827. V. 39

The Green Bag: a Dainty Dish to Set Before a King. London: 1820. V. 40

THE HONEST GRIEF of a Tory, Expressed in a Genuine Letter from a Burgess of-----, in Wiltshire, to the Author of the Monitor, Feb. 17, 1759. London: 1759. V. 42

HONEY, W. B.

European Ceramic Art; from the End of the Middle Ages to About 1815.
London: 1949/52. V. 46

HONEY, WILLIAM BOWYER

The Ceramic Art of China and Other Countries of the Far East. London:
1945. V. 38; 41

European Ceramic Art. New York. V. 42

European Ceramic Art, from the End of the Middle AGes to About 1815.
London: 1949/52. V. 42

HONEYMAN,

Honeyman Collection of Scientific Books and Manuscripts. London: 1978-80.
V. 42

The Honeyman Colletion of Scientific Books and Manuscripts. London:
1978-81. V. 39

HONEYMAN, A.

The Honeyman Collection of Scientific Books and Manuscripts. London:
1978-May 1981. V. 44

HONEYMAN, A. VAN DOREN

*The Honeyman Family (Honeyman, Honyman, Hunneman, etc.) in Scotland
and America, 1548-1908.* Plainfield: 1909. V. 46

*Joannes Nevius: Schepen and Third Secretary of New Amsterdam under the
Dutch . . . and His Descendants, A.D. 1627-1900.* Plainfield: 1900. V. 38

*The Van Doorn Family (Van Doorn, Van Dorn, Van Doren, etc.) in Holland
and America, 1088-1908.* Plainfield: 1909. V. 38

THE HONEYMAN Collection of Scientific Books and Manuscripts.
London: 1978/1981. V. 37

HONEYMAN, ROBERT

The Honeyman Collection of Scientific Books and Manuscripts. London:
1978-81. V. 43

HONIG, LOUIS O.

The Pathfinder of the West James Bridger. Kansas City: 1951. V. 45

Westport. Gateway to the Early West. Kansas City: 1950. V. 45

HONIG'S Owl Tower. Cambridge: 1829. V. 40

THE HONKONG Almanack and Directory for 1846, with an Appendix.
Hong Kong: 1846. V. 42

HONORE, MINIATURIST FL. 1288

*An Illuminated Manuscript of La Somme Le Roy Attributed to the Parisian
Miniaturist Honore.* 1953. V. 39

HONORIUS, AUGUSTODUNENSIS

Expositio in Librum Salomonis qui Dicitur Canticum Canticorum. Cologne:
1485. V. 46

HOOD, B. H., MRS.

Records and Reminiscences of Confederate Soldiers in Terrell County.
Dawson: 1914. V. 44

HOOD, D. D.

The Ecology and Management of Wetlands. London: 1987. V. 38

HOOD, JOHN B.

*Advance and Retreat. Personal Experiences in the United States and
Confederate States Armies.* New Orleans: 1880. V. 38; 39; 42

HOOD, R. B.

Occasional Addresses and Travel Tales. Fort Worth: 1927. V. 37; 39; 42

HOOD, SINCLAIR

Excavations in Chios 1938-1955: Prehistoric Emprio and Ayio Gala. London:
1981-82. V. 44

HOOD, THEODORE EDWARD

Sayings and Doings: a Series of Sketches from Life. London: 1824. V. 41

*Tentamen; or, an Essay Towards the History of Whittington, some Time
Lord Mayor of London.* London: 1820. V. 46

HOOD, THOMAS 1799-1845

The Epping Hunt. London: 1829. V. 37; 40

The Epping Hunt. New York: 1930. V. 39

Humorous Poems. London: 1893. V. 40

Odes and Addresses to Great People. London: 1825. V. 37; 42; 43; 44

The Plea of the Midsummer Fairies. London: 1827. V. 42

Poems . . . London: 1846-47. V. 38; 40

Poems. London: 1871. V. 39; 46

Poems. London: 1872. V. 39; 40

Poems. London: 1881. V. 46

Poems. First and Second Series. London: 1889. V. 40

The Serious Poems of Thomas Hood. London: 1876. V. 46

The Serious Poems of Thomas Hood. London: 1901. V. 38

Thomas Hood. London: 1870. V. 37

Whims and Oddities: Poems: Wit and Humour. London: 1860, 1863. V. 38

Whims and Oddities, in Prose and Verse; With Forty Original Designs.
London: 1826. V. 37

Works. New York: 1861. V. 38; 42

The Works. London: 1862. V. 38; 42

The Works, Comic and Serious, in Prose and Verse. (with) The Memorials.
London: 1862-69. V. 46

The Works of . . . New York: 1864. V. 40

The Works. London: 1869. V. 38; 40; 44

The Works . . . London: 1869-73. V. 46

The Works. London: 1882. V. 42

The Works, Comic and Serious, in Prose and Verse. London: 1882-84.
V. 38; 39

The Works, Comic and Serious, in Prose and Verse. London: 1869-72.
V. 37

HOOD, THOMAS H.

Notes of a Cruise H.M.S. 'Fawn' in the Western Pacific in the Year 1862.
V. 41

*Notes of a Cruise in H.M.S. 'Fawn' In the Western Pacific in the Year
1862.* Edinburgh: 1863. V. 42; 45; 46

HOOD, TOM

Griset's Grotesques. London: 1867. V. 46

Miss Kilmansegg and Her Precious Leg. Campden: 1904. V. 43

Miss Kilmansegg and Her Precious Leg: a Golden Legend. London: 1904.
V. 46

*Miss Kilmansegg and her Precious Leg. A golden legend; printed with three
drawings by Reginald Savage under the care of C.R. Ashbee at the Essex
House Press.* Gloucestershire: 1904. V. 37

HOOD, WHARTON P.

*On Bone-Setting and its relation to the treatment of joints crippled by injury,
rheumatism, inflammation, &c &c.* London: 1871. V. 37

HOOD'S Comic Annual: for the Years 1869 to 1892. London. V. 45

HOOFNAH, JOHN

*New Practical Improvements and Observations on Some of the Experiments
and Considerations Touching Colours of the Honourable and Judicious
Robert Boyle, Esq . . .* London: 1738. V. 40; 42; 46

HOOFS, Claws and Antlers of the Rocky Mountains. Denver: 1894.
V. 42

HOOGHE, ROMEYN DE

*Spiegel om Welte Sterven, Aanwyzende met Pretverbeeldingen van het
Lyden Onzes Saligmakers Jesu Christi . . .* Amsterdam: 1694. V. 39

HOOK, DIANA H.

The Haskell F. Norman Library of Science and Medicine. San Francisco.
V. 46

HOOK, JAMES

Guida di Musica. London: 1785. V. 39; 40; 43

Pen Owen. Edinburgh: 1822. V. 38

Pen Owen. London: 1822. V. 42

HOOK, THEODORE

Gilbert Gurney. London: 1836. V. 45

Gilbert Gurney. London: 1841. V. 40

Gurney Married; a Sequel to Gilbert Gurney. Philadelphia: 1839. V. 40

*The Life of General, the Right Honourable Sir David Baird, Bart, G.C.B.,
K.C. &c. &c.* London: 1832. V. 41

*Reminiscences of Michael Kelly, of the King's Theatre and Theatre Royal,
Drury Lane . . .* London: 1826. V. 46

HOOK, THEODORE EDWARD 1788-1841

The Invisible Girl. A Piece in One Act. Baltimore: 1807. V. 37

Jack Brag. London: 1837. V. 38

Sayings and Doings. London: 1824. V. 41; 44; 46

Sayings and Doings, or Sketches from Life. Second Series. London: 1825.
V. 44

Sayings and Doings; or, Sketches from Life. Third Series. London: 1828.
V. 44

Sayings and Doings: First, Second and Third Series Complete. London:
1834. V. 39

Sayings and Doings. London: 1824-5-8. V. 45

The Soldier's Return; Or, What Can Beauty Do? London: 1805. V. 37; 44

The Trial by Jury: a Comic Piece, in Two Acts. New York: 1811.
V. 37; 40; 46

HOOK, WALTER FARQUHAR

Lives of the Archbishops of Canterbury. London: 1861-76. V. 39

HOOK, WALTER FARQUHAR continued

Lives of the Archbishops of Canterbury. London: 1875-65-79. V. 39; 42

On the Means of Rendering More Efficient the Education of the People. London: 1846. V. 45

HOOKE, ANDREW

An Essay on the National Debt, and National Capital. London: 1750. V. 37; 38; 41; 42

An Essay on the National Debt and National Capital... London: 1751. V. 41; 45

HOOKE, NATHANIEL

An Account of the Conduct of the Dowager Duchess of Marlborough. London: 1742. V. 46

HOOKE, ROBERT 1635-1703

Micrographia; or Some Physiological Descriptions of Minute Bodies Made by magnifying Glasses... N.P.. V. 42

Micrographia. Weiler im Allgau, W.G.. V. 39

Micrographia; or Some Physiological Descriptions of Minute Bodies Made by the Magnifying Glasses... London: 1667. V. 42; 43

Micrographia: or Some Physiological Descriptions of Minute Bodies Made by Magnifying Glasses. London: 1665. V. 37; 42

Microscopic Observations of Dr. Hooke's Wonderful Discoveries by the Microscope. London: 1780. V. 42; 43

Miscroscopic Observations. London: 1781. V. 37; 38

Philosophical Collections. London: 1679-81. V. 40

Philosophical Experiments and Observations of the Late Eminent Dr. Robert Hooke. London: 1726. V. 37; 38; 41

The Posthumous Works... London: 1705. V. 37; 42

HOOKE, WILLIAM

The Every-day Book and Table Book. (with) The Year Book of Daily Recreation and Information... London: 1837-35-38-32. V. 38

HOOKER, JOHN

Some Reminiscences of a Long Life, with a Few Articles on Moral and Social Subjects of Present Interest. Hartford: 1899. V. 45

HOOKER, JOSEPH DALTON

The Botany of the Antarctic Voyage of H.M. Discovery Ships 'Erebus' and 'Terror'. London: 1963. V. 38

The Botany. The Antarctic Voyage of H. M. Discovery Ships :ERebus' and 'Terror' in the Years 1839-1843 Under the Command of Captain Sir James Clark Ross, Kt., R.N., F.R.S. &c. Weinheim: 1963. V. 46

The Botany of the Antaractic Voyage of H. M. Discovery Ships 'Erebus' and 'Terror.' London: 1844-60. V. 37

Flora Tasmaniae. London: 1963. V. 38

Flora of British India. 1978. V. 37; 39

Flora of British India. London: 1875-97. V. 37

Handbook of the New Zealand Flora. London: 1864-67. V. 37

Himalayan Journals... London: 1854. V. 46

Himalayan Journals. London: 1855. V. 43

Illustrations of Himalyan Plants Chiefly Selected from Drawings Made by the late J. F. Cathcart Esq. of the Bengal Secret Service. London: 1855. V. 42; 45

HOOKER, RICHARD

Of the Lawes of Ecclesiastical Politie. London. V. 39

Of the Lawes of Ecclesiastical Politie. London: 1593. V. 38

Of the Lawes of Ecclesiastical Politie. London: 1593-97. V. 41

Of the Lawes of Ecclesiasticall Politie. Eyght Bookes. (with) Of the Laws of Ecclesiasticall Politite. The Fift Booke. London: 1597. V. 40

Of the Lawes of Ecclesiastical Politie. London: 1632-31. V. 40

Of the Laws of Ecclesiastical Politie. London: 1632-31. V. 46

Of the Lawes of Ecclesiastical Politie. London: 1639. V. 45

Of the Lawes of Ecclesiastical Politie. London: 1676. V. 37; 45; 46

Of the Lawes of Ecclesiasticall Politie. London: 31/31/31/31. V. 43

Of the Lawes of Ecclesiasticall Politie. London: 1594-97. V. 37

Works. London: 1666. V. 38; 42

The Works... London: 1676. V. 42

The Works of That Learned and Judicious Divine... London: 1682. V. 37; 40

The Works of that Learned and Judicious Divine, Mr. Richard Hooker, in Eight Books... London: 1723. V. 40; 43

The Works. Oxford: 1841. V. 39

The Works of that Learned and Judicious Divine... 1845. V. 38

The Works. London: 1845. V. 39

The Works of that Learned and Judicious Divine, Mr. Richard Hooker... Oxford: 1845. V. 40; 46

The Works with an Account of His Life and Death by Isaac Walton. Oxford: 1850. V. 41

The Works of That Learned and Judicious Divine, Mr. Richard Hooker, Containing Eight Books of The Laws of Ecclesiastical Polity and Several Other Treatises, edited by Isaac Walton. Oxford: 1820. V. 37

HOOKER, THOMAS

The Christians Two Chiefe Lessons, viz. Self-Deniall and Self-Tryall. London: 1640. V. 40

A Survey of the Summe of Church-Discipline. London: 1648. V. 39

HOOKER, WILLIAM

Companion to the Botanical Magazine. London: 1835-36. V. 40; 41

The Paradisus Londinensis. London: 1806-07. V. 42

Pomona Londiensis... London: 1818. V. 42

HOOKER, WILLIAM DAWSON

Notes on Norway; or, a Brief Journal of a Tour Made to the Northern Parts of Norway in the Summer of 1836. Unpublished: 1837. V. 43

HOOKER, WILLIAM FRANCIS

The Prairie Schooner. Chicago: 1918. V. 39; 40

HOOKER, WILLIAM JACKSON

Botanical Miscellany. London: 1830-33. V. 37

The Botany of Captain Beechey's Voyage. London: 1825-28. V. 38

British Jungermanniae. London: 1816. V. 37; 43

A Century of Ferns. London: 1854. V. 38; 43

A Century of Ferns. London: 1854. V. 37

Companion to the Botanical Magazine; Being a Journal Containing Such Interesting Botanical Information... London: 1835. V. 42

Companion to the Botanical Magazine... London: 1835-36. V. 42

Copy of a Letter Addressed to Dawson Turner, Esq.... on the Occasion of the Death of the Duke of Bedford... Glasgow: 1840. V. 43

Exotic Flora. Edinburgh: 1823-27. V. 38

Figures and Descriptions of Ferns... Unnoticed by Botanists. London: 1831. V. 37

Flora Boreali-Americana or the Botany of the Northern Parts of British America. 1960. V. 39

Flora Boreali-Americana; or the Botany of the Northern Parts of British America. 1980. V. 46

Garden ferns... the drawings by Walter Fitch. London: 1862. V. 37

Icones Filicum, Figures and Descriptions of Ferns, Principally of Such as Have Been Altogether Unnoticed by Botanists, or Have Not Been Correctly Figured. London: 1829-31. V. 37

Journal of a Tour in Iceland in the Summer of 1809. Yarmouth: 1811. V. 38; 40; 42

Journal of a Tour in Iceland in the Summer of 1809. London: 1813. V. 38; 40; 42; 43

The Journal of Botany, Being a Second Series of the Botanical Miscellany. Dehra Dun: 1984. V. 38

Muscologia Britannica. London: 1827. V. 37

Pomona Londinensis. London: 1813-1818. V. 37

Species Filicum. London: 1846-64. V. 37; 38

Species Filicum. London: 1846-64, 1970. V. 38

Species Filicum. London: 1970. V. 37

Synopsis Filicum, or, a Synopsis of all Known Ferns... London: 1865-68. V. 42

Synopsis Filicum. London: 1868. V. 37; 38

Synopsis Filicum. London: 1874. V. 37

HOOKHAM, MARY ANN

The Life and Times of Margaret of Anjou, Queen of England and France. London: 1872. V. 38; 42

HOOLE, BARBARA

Poems. Sheffield. V. 37

A Season at Harrogate; in a Series of Poetical Epistles from Benjamin Blunderhead, Esquire, to His Mother in Derbyshire... Knaresborough: 1812. V. 38

HOOLE, CHARLES

The Common Accidence Examined and Explained by Short Questions and Answers... London: 1734. V. 41

An Easie Entrance to the Latine Tongue... London: 1649. V. 45

HOOLE, ELIJAH

Madras, Mysore and the South of India. London: 1844. V. 39; 45

HOOLE, JOHN

Cyrus; a Tragedy. London: 1768. V. 37; 38; 41; 42

Jerusalem Delivered... London: 1764. V. 44

Timanthes: a Tragedy. London: 1770. V. 37

HOOLE, SAMUEL

Aurelia; or, the Contest: an Heroi-Comic Poem: in Four Cantos. London: 1783. V. 39

Modern Manners. London: 1782. V. 38

HOOPER, CALVIN LEIGHTON

Cruise of the Revenue-Steamer Corwin in Alaska and the N.W. Arctic Ocean in 1881. Washington: 1883. V. 38

HOOPER, E. J.

Hooper's Western Fruit Book . . . Cincinnati: 1857. V. 45

HOOPER, GEORGE

A Discourse Concerning Lent, in Two Parts. London: 1696. V. 37; 43

De Valentinianorum Haeresi Conjecturae, Quibus Illius Origo ex Aegyptiaca Theologia Deducitur. 1711. V. 45

Waterloo: the Downfall of the First Napoleon: a History of the Campaign of 1815. London: 1862. V. 43

HOOPER, JACOB

An Impartial History of the Rebelion and Civil Wars in England, During the Reign of King Charles the First. London: 1738. V. 43

HOOPER, JAMES

Art and Artifacts of the Pacific, Africa and the Americas: the James Hooper Collection. London: 1976. V. 39

HOOPER, JOHN

A Declaration of the X Holie Commandements. London: 1588? V. 44

HOOPER, JOHNSON JONES

Some Adventures of Captain Simon Suggs . . . V. 43

HOOPER, ROBERT 1773-1835

The Anatomist's Vade-Mecum . . . Boston: 1801. V. 44

The Antatomist's Vade Mecum. Windsor: 1809. V. 44

Examinations in Anatomy, Physiology, Practice of Physic, Surgery, Materia Medica, Chemistry and Pharmacy for the Use of Students Who Are About to Pass the College of Surgeons, or the Medical or Transport Board. New York: 1815. V. 40; 42

The London Dissector; or, System of Dissection . . . Philadelphia: 1818. V. 43

The Morbid Anatomy of the Human Brain. London: 1828. V. 39; 45

The Physician's Vade-Mecum. Albany: 1809. V. 40

Quincy's Lexicon-Medicum. London: 1802. V. 38

HOOPER, W. H.

Ten Months Among the Tents of the Tuski, with Incidents of an Arctic Boat Expedition in Search of Sir John Franklin . . . London: 1853. V. 42; 45

HOOPER, WILLIAM

Fifty Years Since: an Address, Delivered Before the Alumni of the University of North Carolina . . . Chapel Hill: 1861. V. 41; 42

Rational Recreations, In Which the Principles of Numbers and Natural Philosophy are Clearly and Copiously Elucidated by a Series of Essay, Entertaining, Interesting Experiments. London: 1783. V. 38

Rational Recretations, in Which the Principles of Numbers and Natural Philosophy are . . . Elucidated by a Series of Easy Entertaining and Interesting Experiments. London: 1783-2. V. 42; 45

Rational Recreations . . . London: 1783-82. V. 38; 40; 42; 44

HOOPES, P. R.

Connecticut Clockmakers of the 19th Century. Hartford: 1930. V. 37

HOORNBEEK, JOHANNES

De Conversione Indorum & Gentilium. Amsterdam: 1669. V. 45

HOOTON, CHALRES

Colin Clink. London: 1841. V. 38; 45

HOOTON, CHARLES

St. Louis' Isle, or Texiana; with Additional Observations Made in the United States and Canada. London: 1847. V. 42; 43

HOOTON, EARNEST A.

The Indians of Pecos Pueblo: A Study of their Skeletal Remains. New Haven: 1930. V. 37

HOOVER, H. A.

Early Days in the Mogollons (Muggy-Yones). El Paso: 1958. V. 42

HOOVER, HERBERT

Addresses Upon the American Road 1955-1960. Caxton: 1961. V. 42

The Challenge to Liberty. New York: 1934. V. 40

On Growing Up. 1962. V. 42

The Ordeal of Woodrow Wilson. New York: 1958. V. 41

The Protection of Freedom. Iowa: 1954. V. 40

A Remedy for Disappearing Game Fishes. New York: 1930. V. 40

HOOVER, HERBERT CLARK 1874-1964

Addresses Upon the American Road 1933-1938. New York: 1938. V. 39

Addresses Upon the American Road . . . 1933-38. Philadelphia: 1948. V. 46

America's First Crusade. New York: 1942. V. 45

The Basis of Lasting Peace. New York: 1945. V. 38; 39

Bibliotheca De Re Metallica. The Herbert Clark Hoover Collection of Mining and Metallurgy. Claremont: 1980. V. 37; 38; 42; 45

The Challange to Liberty. New York: 1934. V. 38; 39; 44

The Challenge to Liberty. New York, London: 1935. V. 39

The Crisis in American Life, Address at the Republican National Convention, Philadelphia, Tuesday June 22, 1948. V. 46

The Crisis in American Life and The Meaning of America. N.P.: 1948. V. 39

This Crisis in American Life. Philadelphia: 1948. V. 43

The Herbert Clark Hoover Collection of Mining and Metallurgy. Bibliotheca de re Metallica. Claremont: 1980. V. 39

The Memoirs of Herbert Hoover. New York: 1951-52. V. 42; 44; 46

The Memoirs of . . . The Cabinet and the Presidency 1920-1933. New York: 1952. V. 43

The Memoirs of Herbert Hoover, The Cabinet and Presidency, 1920-1933. New York: 1952. V. 37

Principles of Mining. New York: 1909. V. 43

Remedy for Disappearing Game Fishes. New York: 1930. V. 38; 42

This Crisis in American Life. Philadelphia: 1948. V. 39

HOOVER, J. EDGAR

Masters of Deceit. New York: 1958. V. 41; 45

Persons in Hiding. Boston: 1938. V. 38

HOPE, ANNE FULTON 1809-1887

Memoir of the Late James Hope, M.D. Physician to St. George's Hospital. London: 1842. V. 40

HOPE, ARTHUR

A Manual of Sorrento and Inlaid Work for Amateurs. New York: 1877. V. 41

HOPE, JAMES

A Treatise on the Diseases of the Heart and Great Vessels . . . Philadelphia: 1846. V. 42

HOPE, JOHN

Occasional Attempts at Sentimental Poetry, by a Man in Business. London: 1769. V. 42; 45

HOPE, LORD FRANCIS 1866-

Catalogue of a Collection of Early Newspapers and Essayists . . . Presented to the Bodleian Library. Oxford: 1865. V. 40; 44

HOPE, MRS.

Memoir of the Late James Hope, M.D. London: 1848. V. 46

HOPE, STANLEY

A New Godiva. London: 1876. V. 41

HOPE, THEODORE C.

Memoirs of the Fultons of Lisburn. London: 1902. V. 38

HOPE, THOMAS 1770?-1831

Anastasius; or, Memoirs of a Greek. London: 1819. V. 40

Anastasius, or, Memoirs of a Greek; written at the close of the Eighteenth Century. London: 1820. V. 37; 42

Athanasius, or, Memoirs of a Greek. London: 1836. V. 40; 41

Costume of the Ancients. London: 1809. V. 39; 40; 43

Costume of the Ancients. London: 1841. V. 42

Costume of the Ancients. London: 1812. V. 38

An Essay on the Origin and Prospects of Man. London: 1831. V. 43

An Historical Essay on Architecture. London: 1835. V. 38

An Historical Essay on Architecture. (with) An Analytical Index to . . . London: 1835/36. V. 42

An Historical Essay on Architecture. London: 1840. V. 38

Household Furniture and Decoration. London: 1807. V. 37; 38

Minor Practicks, or, a Treatise of the Scottish Law (with) A Discourse on the Rise and Progress of the Law of Scotland and an Alphabetical Abridgment of the Acts of Sederunt, From the Restoration to the Present Year. Edinburgh: 1726. V. 40

HOPE, W. H. ST. JOHN

The Abbey of St. Mary in Furness, Lancashire. Kendal: 1902. V. 38; 40

The Architectural History of the Cathedral Church and Monastery of St. Andrew at Rochester. London: 1900. V. 44

Architectural Description of Kirkstall Abbey. Leeds: 1907. V. 45

Windsor Castle - an Architectural History. London: 1913. V. 39; 41; 43; 44

HOPE, WILLIAM H. ST. JOHN

Cowdray and Easebourne Priory in the County of Sussex. London: 1919. V. 37; 42; 46

HOPEGOOD, PETER

Peter Lecky by Himself. New York: 1936. V. 44

HOPEWELL-SMITH, ARTHUR

An Introduction to Dental Anatomy and Physiology Descriptive and Applied. London: 1913. V. 45

HOPGOOD, GEORGE

On the Management of the Hair and Scalp. Ryde, Isle of Wight: 1856. V. 42

HOPKINS, ALBERT A.

A Dickens Atlas Including Twelve Walks in London with Charles Dickens. New York: 1923. V. 38

Magic Stage Illusions and Scientific Diversions Including Trick Photography. New York: 1898. V. 43

Magic: Stage Illusions and Scientific Diversions Including Trick Photography. New York: 1901. V. 45

Magic Stage Illusions and Scientific Diversions Including Trick Photography. New York: 1911. V. 43

HOPKINS, ALFRED

The Fundamentals of Good Bank Building. New York: 1929. V. 45

HOPKINS, C. T.

Extracts from Report of the Committee Appointed Nov. 11, 1873, by the Chamber of Commerce of San Francisco . . . San Francisco: 1874. V. 39

HOPKINS, CHARLES

The Art of Love. London: 1704. V. 43

Boadicea Queen of Britain. London: 1696. V. 39; 44

Boadicea, Queen of Britain. London: 1697. V. 45

Friendship Improv'd. London: 1700. V. 37; 40; 41; 44

Friendship Improved. London: 1770. V. 38

Neglected Virtue. London: 1696. V. 38

Pyrrhus King of Epirus. London: 1695. V. 38; 39; 40; 41; 45; 46

HOPKINS, EDWARD J.

The Organ, Its History and Construction . . . London: 1877. V. 46

HOPKINS, EMMA CURTIS

First Lesson in Christian Science (and Third, Fourth, Sixth-Eleventh Lesson). Chicago: 1888-87-91. V. 43

HOPKINS, EZEKIEL

An Exposition on the Lord's Prayer, with a Catechistical Explication Thereof . . . London: 1692. V. 41

HOPKINS, G. H. E.

An Illustrated Catalogue of the Rothschild Collection of Fleas (Siphonaptera) in the British Museum (Natural History). London: 1953-66. V. 37; 38

An Illustrated Catalogue of the Rothschild Collection of Fleas (Siphonaptera) in the British Museum . . . Volume I. Tungidae and Pulicidae. London: 1953. V. 38

HOPKINS, G. M.

City Atlas of Auburn, New York. Philadelphia: 1882. V. 38

City Atlas of Philadelphia. Volume 2. 21st and 28th Wards. Philadelphia: 1875. V. 39

City Atlas of Philadelphia. Volume 3. 23rd Ward. Philadelphia: 1876. V. 39

City Atlas of Philadelphia. Volume 4. 25th Ward. Philadelphia: 1875. V. 39

Combined Atlas of the State of New Jersey and the City of Newark from Actual Survey Official Records and Private Plans. Philadelphia: 1873. V. 38

HOPKINS, G. M., & COMPANY

City Atlas of Philadelphia. Volume I. 22nd Ward. Philadelphia: 1876. V. 39

HOPKINS, GARLAND EVANS

The First Battle of Modern Naval History. Richmond: 1943. V. 45; 46

HOPKINS, GERARD MANLEY 1844-1889

A Book of Christmas Verse. London: 1895. V. 40

The Mind & Poetry of Gerard Manley Hopkins, S. J., by Bernard Kelly. Ditchling: 1935. V. 37

Poems of Gerard Manley Hopkins. London: 1930. V. 39; 41; 43

Poems of Gerard Manley Hopkins. Oxford: 1930. V. 38; 44

Poems of . . . Now First Published. London: 1918. V. 37

Selected Poems. London: 1954. V. 38; 44; 46

A Vision of the Mermaids. London: 1929. V. 41; 44; 46

A Vision of the Mermaids. A Prize Poem Dated Christmas, 1862 . . . now for the first time printed in full. Oxford: 1929. V. 37

HOPKINS, I. A.

New Form Book, or, Every Man's Legal Assistant. Milwaukee: 1848. V. 40

HOPKINS, JOHN HENRY

Essay on Gothic Architecture, with Various Plans and Drawings for Churches: Burlington: 1836. V. 45

HOPKINS, JOHN LIVINGSTON

Messalina's Questions; or, a Vindication of Slavery. Liverpool: 1821. V. 43

HOPKINS, JON H.

Orozco: A Catalogue of His Graphic Work. Flagstaff: 1967. V. 41

HOPKINS, JOSEPH R.

Report of the Case of Trespass & Assault and Battery, Wherein John Evans was Plantiff . . . Tried at a Court of Nisi Prius for the City and County of Philadelphia, Before the Hon. H. H. Brackenridge . . . Philadelphia: 1810. V. 43

HOPKINS, LEMUEL

The Democratized, a Poem. Philadelphia: 1795. V. 44

HOPKINS, LUTHER WESLEY

From Bull Run to Appomatox. a Boy's View. Baltimore: 1908. V. 42

HOPKINS, MANLEY

A Handbook of Average, for the Use of Merchants, Agents, Ship-Owners, Masters and Others . . . (with) Appendices . . . London: 1859. V. 38

Hawaii: the Past, Present and Future of Its Island Kingdom. London: 1866. V. 38; 41

Hawaii: The Past, Present, and Future of its Island-Kingdom. An Historical Account of the Sandwich Islands. (Polynesia). With a Preface by the Bishop of Oxford. London: 1862. V. 37; 44

HOPKINS, SAMUEL

A Discourse Upon the Slave-Trade, and the Slavery of the Africans. Providence: 1793. V. 43

Historical Memoirs, Relating to the Housatunnuk Indians . . . Boston: 1753. V. 38; 42; 46

Historical Memoirs, Relating to the Housatunnur Indians; or, An Account of the Methods Used, and Pains Taken for the Propagation of the Gospel Among the Heathenish Tribe. Boston: 1755. V. 44

Historical Memoirs, Relating to the Housatunnuk Indians; or, An Account of the Methods Used, and Pains Taken, for the Propagation of the Gospel Among the Heathenish Tribe. Boston;: 1753. V. 37

An Inquiry Concerning the Future State of Those Who Die In Their Sins . . . Newport: 1783. V. 43

An Inquiry Concerning the Future State of Those Who Die in Their Sins . . . And Wheter Endless Punishment be Consistent with Divine Justice . . . Newport: 1783. V. 45

The Life and Character of the Late Reverend Mr. Jonathan Edwards, President of the College of New Jersey. Boston. V. 44

The Life and Character of the Late Reverend Mr. Jonathan Edwards, President of the College of New Jersey. Boston: 1765. V. 43

The Puritans and Queen Elizabeth: or The Church, Court and Parliament of England . . . New York: 1875. V. 46

Sketches of the Life of the Late Rev. Samuel Hopkins, D.D . . . . Written by Himself . . . Hartford: 1805. V. 39

HOPKINS, SARAH WINNEMUCCA

Life Among the Piutes: Their Wrongs and Claims. Boston: 1883. V. 37; 39; 40; 44; 45

HOPKINS, THOMAS

Great Britain, for the Last Forty Years. London: 1834. V. 37; 42; 43; 46

HOPKINS, THOMAS SMITH

Colonial Furniture of West New Jersey. Haddonfield: 1936. V. 42; 46

HOPKINSON, CECIL

A Bibliography of the Musical and Literary Works of Hector Berlioz, 1803-1869. Edinburgh: 1951. V. 45

Collecting Golf Books 1743-1938. Droitwich: 1980. V. 38

HOPKINSON, FRANCIS

The Miscellaneous Essays and Occasional Writings. Philadelphia: 1792. V. 37

HOPKINSON, JOSEPH

What Is Our Situation? And What Our Prospects? Philadelphia: 1798. V. 46

What Is Our Situation? and What Our Prospects? or a Demonstration of the Insidious Views of Republican France. London: 1799. V. 39

HOPKINSON, TOM

Mist in the Tagus. London: 1946. V. 41

HOPLEY, CATHARINE C.

Stonewall Jackson, Late General of the Confederate States Army. A Biographical Sketch, and an Outline of His Virginian Campaign. London: 1863. V. 37

HOPLEY, CATHERINE C.

Life in the South; from the Commencement of the War. London: 1863. V. 37; 39; 40

HOPPE, DAVID HEINRICH

Ectypa Plantarum Ratisbonensium, Oder Abdrucke Derjenigen Pflanzen, Welche um Regensburg wild Wachsen. Regensburg: 1787-93. V. 37

HOPPE, E. O.

The Book of Fair Women. New York: 1922. V. 38

The Book of Fair Women. New York: 1922. V. 37; 45

HOPPER, CLARENCE 1817-1868

Catalogue of the Books, Manuscripts, Works of Art . . . Which are Preserved in the Shakespeare Library and Museum . . . London: 1868. V. 40

HOPPER, NORA

Ballads in Prose. London: 1894. V. 38; 41; 43

HOPPER, THOMAS

A Letter to Lord Viscount Melbourne on the Rebuilding of the Royal Exchange. London: 1839. V. 38

HOPPIN, AUGUSTUS

On the Nile. Boston: 1874. V. 37

HOPPIN, JOSEPH CLARK

Euthymides and His Fellows. Cambridge: 1917. V. 40; 42

A Handbook of Attic Red-Figured Vases Signed by or Attributed to the Various Masters of the Sixth and Fifth Centuries B.C. Cambridge: 1919. V. 44

A Handbook of Greek Black-Figured Vases With a Chapter on the Red Figured Southern Italian Vases. Paris: 1924. V. 42; 44

HOPPNER, JOHN

Oriental Tales, Translated into English Verse. London: 1805. V. 39

HOPPUS, EDWARD

Practical Measuring Made Easy to the Meanest Capacity, by a New Set of Tables. London: 1738. V. 40

Practical Measuring Made Easy to the Meanest Capacity, by a new Set of Tables. York: 1800. V. 46

HOPPUS, F

The Gentleman's and Builder's Repository. London: 1760. V. 38

HOPPUS, MARY

A Great Treason. London: 1883. V. 44; 46

HOPSON, WINTHROP H.

Memoirs of Dr. Winthrop Hartly Hopson. Cincinnati: 1887. V. 46

HOPWOOD, AUBREY

The Gunkum Book. London: 1900. V. 45

HORACE Wells, Dentist, Father of Surgical Anesthesia. Hartford: 1948. V. 42; 45

HORAE Sarisburienses. Salisbury: 1829. V. 44

HORAN, JAMES

Authentic Wild West: The Gunfighters. New York: 1976. V. 42

The Gunfighters: The Authentic Wild West. New York: 1976. V. 45

HORAN, JAMES D.

The Life and Art of Charles Schreyvogel, Painter-Historian of the Indian-Fighting Army of the American West. New York: 1969. V. 39; 41

The McKenney-Hall Portrait Gallery of American Indians. New York: 1971. V. 40

The McKenney-Hall Portrait Gallery of American Indians. New York: 1972. V. 37; 39; 41; 42

HORAPOLLO

De Sacris Notis & Sculpturis Libri duo . . . Paris: 1551. V. 37

(Greek title, then) De Sacris Notis & Sculpturis Libri duo . . . Paris: 1551. V. 38; 39

De Hieroglyphicis Notis. Lyon: 1542. V. 43

(Greek title) Ori Apollinis Niliaci, De Sacris Notis & Sculpturis Libri Duo, vbi ad Fidem Vetusti Codicis Manu Scripti Restituta Sunt Loca Permulta . . . Parisiis: 1551. V. 43

HORATIUS FLACCUS, QUINTIUS 65-8 BC

Opera. Paris: 1733. V. 46

HORATIUS FLACCUS, QUINTUS 65-8 BC

His Art of Poetry (etc.). London: 1640. V. 45

His Art of Poetry (etc.). London: O640. V. 40

L'Arte Poetica d'Horatio in Ottava Rima . . . Naples: 1610. V. 38

Bernardini Parthenii Spilimbergii in Horatii Flacci Carmina atq. Epodos Commentarii. Quibus Poetae Artificium & Via ad Imitationem, atq; ad Poetoce Scribendum Aperitur. Ad Stephanum Bathori Poteniss . . . 1584. V. 39

The Carmen Seculare of Horace. London: 1779. V. 39; 42

Carmina Alcaica - Carmina Sapphica. 1903. V. 37; 39; 44

Quinti Horati Flacci Carmina Alcaica. 1903. V. 45

Carmina Alcaica. Chelsea: 1903. V. 38; 44; 46

Quinti Horati Flacci Carmina Alcaica. Chelsea: 1903. V. 39; 44

Carmina Alcaica. London: 1903. V. 38

Carmina Sapphica. Boston: 1983. V. 38; 39

Carminum Libri Quatuor. V. 44

Horatii Carminum Libri IV. London: 1926. 43; 45

Cum Commentariis Selectiffimis Variorum: & Scholis Integris Johannis Bond . . . Lugd. Batav. & Roterod: 1670. V. 41

Cura H. H. Milman. London: 1853. V. 46

Q. Horatii Flacci Eclogae. London: 1701. V. 45

Epistolar(um) Liber. Leipzig: 1498. V. 38

Est Modus in Rebus: the First Satire. 1980. V. 40

Horatii F. Poemata . . . Florentiae: 1514. V. 44

Liber de Arte Poetica. Florentiae: 1550. V. 37

Liber de Arte Poetica Jacobi Grifoli Luciniane(n)sis Interpretatione Explicatus. Florence: 1550. V. 37

Lierzangen en Dichtkunst. Amsterdam: 1654. V. 38

The Lyrics of Horace. Chester: 1822. V. 38

The Odes, Satyrs and Epistles of Horace. London: 1684. V. 40

The Odes, Epodes and cArmen Seculare . . . London: 1741. V. 45

The Odes and Epodes . . . Boston: 1901. V. 42

Odes, Epodes, and Carmen Saeculare. London: 1850. V. 37

Works. Florence: 1482. V. 46

Q. Horacio Flacco Poeta Lyrico Latino. Granada: 1599. V. 37

The Poems of Horace . . . London: 1666. V. 39; 44

The Poems of Horace, Consisting of Satyres, and Epistles, Rendered in English and Paraphrased by Several Persons. London: 1671. V. 39; 40; 43; 44

The Poems of Horace, Consisting of Odes, Satyrs and Epistles. London: 1680. V. 39; 40; 44; 46

Poetae Venusini. Venetiis: 1549. V. 40

A Poetical Translation of the Works of Horace . . . London: 1765. V. 45

Poemata. Venice: 1509. V. 46

Poemata. Hagae Comitum: 1721. V. 37; 38

Poemata. Orleans: 1767. V. 37; 38

Quintus Horatius Flaccus. Birmingham: 1777. V. 39; 41

A Medicinable Morall, that is, the two bookes of Horace, His Satyres, Englyshed.. London: 1566. V. 38

Quintus Horatius Flaccus Accedunt nunc Danielis Heinsii de Satyra Horatiana Libri duo in Quibus Totum Poetae Institutum & Genius Expeditur. Lugdunum Batavorum: 1629. V. 39

Horace's First Satire Modernised and Addressed to Jacob Henriques. London: 1762. V. 40

(Opera) Horatius cum Quattuor Commentariis. Venice: 1495-96. V. 46

Opera. Venice: 1509. V. 46

Opera Omnia. Venice: 1519. V. 37

Opera, Dionysii Lambini . . . Emendatus. Venice: 1566. V. 45

Opera. Bernardini Parthenii . . . In Q. Horatii Flacci Carmina atq. Epodos Commentarii Quibus Poetae Artificum & Via ad Imitationem, atq. ad Poetice Scribendum Apcritur (and) Sermonum . . . Satyrarvm, Epistolarum. Venice: 1584. V. 37

L'Opere D'Oratio Poeta Lirico, Commentatae da Giouanni Fabrini de Fighine in Lingua Volgare Toscana . . . Venice: 1587. V. 38

Opera. Paris: 1642. V. 45

Q. Horatius Flaccus Cum Commentariis Selectissimis Variorum & Scholiis Integris Johannis Bond. Leyden & Rotterdam: 1670. V. 42

Quinti Horatii Flacci Opera ad Optimorum Exemplarum Fidem Recensita. Cambridge: 1699. V. 38

Opera ex Recensione & cum Notis Atque Emendationibus. Cambridge,: 1711. V. 45

Opera ex Recensione & Cum Notis Atque Emendationibus. Amsterdam: 1728. V. 45

Quinti Horatii Flacci Opera. Londini: 1733. V. 46

Opera. London: 1733. V. 45

Opera. Paris: 1733. V. 45

Quinti Horatii Flacci Opera. London: 1733-37. V. 38; 45; 46

Opera. London: 1733-37. V. 38; 39; 40; 42; 43

Opera. London: 1734-37. V. 42

The Works. London: 1741/43. V. 41

Opera. Glasgow: 1744. V. 38; 46

The Works of Horace. London: 1756. V. 38

Quintus Horatius Flaccus: ad Lectiones Probatiores Diligenter Emendatus, et Interpunctione Nova Saepius Illustratus. Glasguae: 1760. V. 43

The Works of Horace. Dublin: 1761. V. 42

Works. Birminghamiae: 1762. V. 44

The Works of Horace . . . London: 1767. V. 40

Opera. Birminghamiae: 1770. V. 38; 43

Opera. Birmingham: 1777. V. 40

HORATIUS FLACCUS, QUINTUS 65-8 BC continued

The Works of Horace, Translated Literally into English prose . . . Edinburgh: 1777. V. 38

Opera. Parma: 1791. V. 44

Opera. Glasgow: 1796. V. 37; 38; 39; 40; 41; 45; 46

Opera. Parisiis: 1799. V. 39; 45

Opera. London: 1826. V. 46

Opera Omnia Recensuit Filon. Paris: 1828. V. 39

The Works of . . . London: 1849. V. 37; 38; 44

Opera. London: 1853. V. 41

Quinti Horati Flacci Opera Omnia. London: 1910. V. 39; 40

HORBLIT, HARRISON

One Hundred Books Famous in Science, Based on an Exhibition Held at the Grolier Club. New York: 1964. V. 39; 41; 42; 43; 45

One Hundred Books Famous in Science basee on an exhibition held at the Grolier Library. 1964. V. 37

HORDEN, JOHN

Bibliography of Francis Quarles to the Year 1800. Oxford: 1953. V. 41

A Grammar of the Cree Language as Spoken by the Cree Indians of North America. London: 1881. V. 46

HORDER, T. J.

A History of Embryology. London: 1986. V. 37; 38

HORE, ANNIE

To Lake Tanganyika in a Bath Chair. London: 1889. V. 45

HORE, EDWARD

Tanganyika, Eleven Years in Central Africa. London: 1892. V. 39; 41; 43; 44; 45

HORE, J. P.

The History of Newmarket and the Annals of the Turf. London: 1886. V. 42; 43; 46

HOREAU, HECTOR 1801-1872

Panorama d'Egypte et de Nubie avec un portrait de Mehemet-Ali et un Texte orne de Vignettes. Paris: 1841. V. 44

HORETZKY, CHARLES

Canada on the Pacific. Montreal: 1874. V. 37; 44; 46

Some Startling Facts Relating to the Canadian Pacific Railway and the North West Lands . . . Ottawa: 1880. V. 37; 42

HORGAN, PAUL

Encounters with Stravinsky, a Personal Record. London: 1972. V. 46

The Great River. New York: 1954. V. 38; 39; 42

The Habit of Empire. Santa Fe: 1939. V. 38; 40; 42

The Habit of Empire. Santa Fe: (1939). V. 37

Lamy of Santa Fe. His Life and Times. New York: 1975. V. 38; 39; 41; 43

Publisher's Tea. Adam and Blaine Entertain. N.P.: 1935. V. 46

Under the Sangre De Cristo. Santa Fe: 1985. V. 43

HORIZON: a Review of Literature and Art. London: 1940-50. V. 37; 40

HORLER, SYDNEY

False-Face. London: 1926. V. 45

The Mystery of No. 1. London: 1925. V. 45

HORLOCK, K. W.

The Squire of Beechwood: A True Tale. London: 1857. V. 41

HORMAN, WILLIAM

Vulgaria. Oxford: 1926. V. 44

HORN, CALVIN

Confederate Victories in the Southwest and Union Army Operations in the Southwest. Albuquerque: 1961. V. 37

HORN, GEORG 1620-1670

Orbis Politicus Imperiorum, Regnorum, Principatiuum, Rerumpublicarum. Frankfurt: 1675. V. 38

HORN, GEORGE 1620-1670

Rerum Britannicarum Libri Septem, Quibus Res in Anglia, Scotia, Hibernia, an Anno MDCXLV Bello Gestae, Exponuntur. Leiden: 1648. V. 41

HORN, HOSEA B.

Horn's Overland Guide, from the U.S. Indian Sub Agency, Council Bluffs on the Missouri River, to the City of Sacramento, in California . . . New York: 1852. V. 38; 41; 43

Horn's Overland Guide, from the U.S. Indian Sub-Agency, Council Bluffs, on the Missouri River, to the City of Sacramento. New York: 1853. V. 41; 43

HORN, MADELINE DARROUGH

Farm on the Hill, by Madeline Darrough Horn. New York;: 1936. V. 37

HORN, THOMAS HARTWELL

An Introduction to the Study of Bibliography. London: 1814. V. 41

HORN, TOM

Life of Tom Horn, Government Scout and Interpreter. Denver: 1904. V. 43; 46

HORN, W. F.

The Horn Papers; Early Western Movement on the Monongahela and Upper Ohio, 1765-1795. Complete Set. Scottdale: 1945. V. 37

HORN, WALTER

The Plan of St. Gall: a Study of the Architecture and Economy of . . . 1979. V. 38

The Plan of Saint Gall. Berkeley: 1979. V. 41; 42

HORNADAY, WILLIAM T.

Camp-Fires in the Canadian Rockies. New York: 1906. V. 44

Camp-Fires in the Canadian Rockies. New York: 1907. V. 42; 43; 44

The Extermination of the American Bison. Washington: 1889. V. 40

HORNBECK, ROBERT

Robidoux's Ranch. Riverside: 1913. V. 39; 41; 44

HORNBEIN, THOMAS

Everest: The West Ridge. San Francisco: 1965. V. 37; 41

HORNBEIN, THOMAS F.

Everest: The West Ridge. London: 1966. V. 40

HORNBLOW, ARTHUR

A History of the Theatre in America . . . Philadelphia: 1919. V. 43

HORNBY, BEATRIX

The Children's Garden - A Memory of the Old Porch House. 1913. V. 37

The Children's Garden, a Memory of the Old Porch House. Chelsea: 1913. V. 38; 40

HORNBY, C. H. ST. J.

A Descriptive Bibliography of the New Books Printed at the Ashendene Press, MDCCCXV-MCMXXXV. Chelsea: 1935. V. 37; 43; 44; 45; 46

HORNBY, C. H. ST. JOHN

The Ashendene Press: C.H.St. J. Hornby's Foreword to His Descriptive Bibligoraphy. Meriden: 1939. V. 46

A Descriptive Bibliography of the Books Printed at the Ashendene Press MDCCXCV-MCMXXXV. San Francisco: 1976. V. 39; 40; 43

HORNBY, EMELIA BITHYNIA MACERONI, LADY d. 1866

Constantinople During the Crimean War. London: 1863. V. 40

HORNBY, HUGH FREDERICK

Catalogue of the Art Library Bequeated . . . to the Free Public Library of the City of Liverpool. Liverpool: 1906. V. 38

HORNBY, JAMES

Catalogue of the Library of Mr. James Hornby, Wigan. N.P.: 1888. V. 38; 40

HORNBY, LOUISA

Cottage Contrasts; or, After Pleasure Comes Pain. Warrington: 1820. V. 42

HORNE, BERNARD S.

The Compleat Angler 1653-1967. A New Bibliography. Pittsburgh: 1970. V. 39; 40; 44; 46

HORNE, CHARLES

Great Men and Famous Women: A Series of Pen and Pencil Sketches of the Lives of More than Two Hundred of the Most Prominent Personages in History. Edited by Charles Horne. 1894. V. 37

HORNE, G.

Savage Life in Central Australia. London: 1924. V. 40

HORNE, GEORGE

A Fair and Impartial State of the Case Between Sir Isaac Newton and Mr. Hutchinson. Oxford: 1753. V. 38; 42; 43

Observations on the Case of the Protestant Dissenters, with Reference to the Corporation and Test Acts. Oxford: 1790. V. 41

HORNE, HENRY

Essays Concerning Iron and Steel. London: 1773. V. 42; 44; 46

HORNE, HERBERT P.

The Binding of Books: And Essay in the History of Gold-Tooled Bindings. London: 1894. V. 37

HORNE, JOHN

Many Days in Morocco. London: 1925. V. 38; 46

HORNE, MELVILL

Letters on Misions. Schenectady: 1797. V. 39

HORNE, RICHARD HENGIST

Australian Facts and Prospects; to Which is Prefixed the Author's Australian Autobiography. London: 1859. V. 41

Ballad Romances. London: 1846. V. 45

Exposition of the False Medium and Barriers Excluding Men of Genius from the Public. London: 1833. V. 43; 45; 46

The Hamlet Controversy. Melbourne: 1867. V. 40

Orion: an Epic Poem in Three Books. London: 1843. V. 37; 40; 41; 42; 46

HORNE, RICHARD HENRY

A New Spirit of the Age. New York: 1844. V. 43

HORNE, RICHARD HENRY HENGIST

Memoirs of a London Doll. London: 1846. V. 38

HORNE, THOMAS HARTWELL

The Campaign of Waterloo. London: 1816. V. 46

A Catalogue of the Library of the College of St. Margaret and St. Bernard, Commonly Called Queen's College in the University of Cambridge . . . London: 1827. V. 46

The Complete Grazier; or Farmer's and Cattle Breeder's and Dealer's Assistant . . . London: 1833. V. 44

An Introduction to the Study of Bibliography. London: 1814. V. 38; 40; 42; 44

An Introduction to the Critical Study and Knowledge of the Holy Scriptures. London: 1828. V. 43

An Introduction to the Critical Study and Knowledge of the Holy Scriptures. London: 1839. V. 43

Landscape Illustrations of the Bible. London: 1835-36. V. 42

A Manual of Biblical Bibliography . . . London: 1839. V. 40

HORNE TOOKE, JOHN

A Letter to John Dunning, Esq. (on the conjunction 'That'). London: 1778. V. 38

A Letter to a Friend on the Reported Marriage of His Royal Highness the Prince of Wales. London: 1787. V. 39; 41

HORNE, WILLIAM ANDREW

A Geniune Account of the life and Trial of William Andrew Horne, Esq; of Butterly-Hall, in the County of Derby . . . London: 1760. V. 37

HORNECK, PHILLIP

The High German Doctor With Many Additions and Alterations to which is added a large explanatory index. London: 1720. V. 38

HORNEIUS, CONRAD

De Processv Dispvtandi Liber. Frankfurt a.M.: 1624. V. 39

HORNELL, JAMES

British Coracles and Irish Curraghs, with a Note on the Quffah of Iraq. London: 1938. V. 40

HORNEMAN, FREDERICK CONRAD

The Journal of Frederick Horneman's Travels, from Cairo to Mourzouk, the Capital of the Kingdom of Fezzan, in Africa, in the Years 1797-8. London: 1802. V. 38

HORNEMANN, BODIL

Types of Ancient Egyptian Statuary. Copenhagen: 1951-69. V. 44

HORNER, FRANCIS

Memoirs and Correspondence. London: 1843. V. 37

HORNER, GUSTAVUS RICHARD BROWN

Medical and Topographical Observations Upon the Mediterranean and Upon Portugal, Spain and Other Countries. Philadelphia: 1839. V. 42

HORNER, JOHN

Buildings in the Town and Parish of Halifax. Halifax: 1835. V. 38

HORNER, JOSHUA

Letters from an Artist Sojourning on the Continent . . . Halifax: 1841. V. 44

HORNER, WILLIAM E.

Lessons in Practical Anatomy, for the Use of Dissectors. Philadelphia: 1827. V. 42

Lessons in Practical Anatomy, for the Use of Dissectors. Philadelphia: 1823. V. 37

HORNER, WILLIAM EDMONDS 1793-1853

A Treatise on Pathological Anatomy. Philadelphia: 1829. V. 44

HORNIUS, GEORGIUS

De Originibus, Americanis. The Hague: 1652. V. 40

HORNOR, T.

Description of an Improved Method of Delineating Estates, with a Sketch of the Progress of Landscape Gardening in England . . . London: 1813. V. 46

HORNOR, THOMAS

View of London, and the Surrounding Country Taken with Mathematical Accuracy From an Observatory Purposely Erected Over the Cross of St. Pauls Cathedral . . . London: 1823. V. 41

HORNOR, WILLIAM MAC PHERSON

Blue Book Philadelphia Furniture. Philadelphia: 1935. V. 42

HORNOR, WILLIAM S.

This Old Monmouth of Ours. Freehold: 1932. V. 39; 41

HORNUNG, CLARENCE P.

Treasury of American Design. New York: 1972. V. 41

Treasury of American Design and Antiques. New York: 1972? V. 41

HORNUNG, E. W.

The Black Mask. London: 1901. V. 41

Mr. Justice Raffles. London: 1909. V. 38; 44

HORNUNG, JOHANNES

Cista Medica, qua in Epistolae Clarissimorum Germaniae Medicorum, Familiares & in Re Medica, Tam Quoad Hermetica & Chymica . . . Noribergae: 1652? V. 43

HORODISCH, ABRAHAM

Miniatur Exlibris. Amsterdam: 1966. V. 46

HOROVITZ, FRANCES

Poems. Aylesford: 1967. V. 42

Snow Light, Water Light. Newcastle upon Tyne: 1983. V. 44

HOROVITZ, MICHAEL

The Wolverhampton Wanderer - an Epic of Britannia - in Twelve Books with a Resurrection and a Life. London: 1971. V. 41

HOROWITZ, LOUIS J.

The Towers of New York: the Memoirs of a Master Builder. New York: 1937. V. 46

HORRALL, S. F.

History of the Forty-Second Indiana, Volunteer Infantry. 1892. V. 38

HORRAX, GILBERT

Neurosurgery: an Historical Sketch. Springfield: 1952. V. 41

HORREBOW, NIELS

The Natural History of Iceland. London: 1758. V. 40

HORROCKS, JEREMIAH

Opuscula Astronomica; viz. Astronomia Kepleriana, Defensa & Promota. London: 1672-73. V. 44

HORRY, P.

The Life of Gen. Francis Marion, A Celebrated Officer . . . in South Carolina and Georgia. Baltimore: 1814. V. 44

HORSBRUGH, B.

The Game-Birds and Water-Fowl of South Africa. London: 1912. V. 38

The Game-Birds and Water-Fowl of South Africa. London: 1912. V. 37

HORSBURGH, JAMES

Atmospherical Register or Weather Book. London: 1816. V. 40

Directions for Sailing to and From the East Indies, China and New Holland, Cape of Good Hope, and the Interjacent Ports . . . London: 1809. V. 39

The India Directory, or, Directions For Sailing to and From the East Indies, China, Australia, and the Interjacent Ports of Africa and South America. London: 1852. V. 38

The India Directory, or, Directions for Sailing to and from the East Indies, China, Australia and the Interjacent Ports of Africa and South America. London: 1855. V. 40

India Directory, or Directions for Sailing to an From the East Indies, China, Austrilia, Cape of Good Hope, Brazil . . . compiled chiefly from Original Journals of the Company's Ships . . . London: 1836. V. 37

HORSE-RACING: Its History and Early Records of the Principal and Other Race Meetings. London: 1863. V. 37

THE HORSE; with a Treatise on Draught; and a Copious Index. London: 1831. V. 43

HORSELY, J. W.

Jottings From Jail. London: 1887. V. 42

HORSEMANDEN, DANIEL

A Journal of the Proceedings in the Detection of the Conspiracy Formed by Some White People, In Conjunction with Negro and Other Slaves, For Burning the City of New York in America, and Murdering the Inhabitants . . . New York: 1744. V. 42

HORSFALL, J. G.

Plant Disease, an Advanced Treatise. London: 1977-78. V. 38

HORSFALL, THOMAS

Notes on the Manor of Well and Snape in the North Riding of the County of York. Leeds: 1912. V. 46

HORSFIELD, T.

Map of the Island of Java, to Illustrate the Researches of Thomas Horsfield . . . London: 1852. V. 38

HORSFIELD, THOMAS

A Catalogue of the Birds in the Museum of the Hon. East-India Company. London: 1854-58. V. 46

HORSFIELD, THOMAS WALKER

The History, Antiquities and Topography of the County of Sussex. Lewes: 1835. V. 39

The History, Antiquities and Topography of the County of Sussex. Lewes: 1835. V. 39; 45

The History, Antiquities and Topography of the County of Sussex. Lewes 1835 reprinted, with an Introduction by F. W. Steer. Dorking: 1974. V. 37

HORSFORD, EBEN NORTON

The Defences of Norumbega. Boston and New York: 1891. V. 38; 40; 43

Discovery of America by Northmen. Boston & New York: 1888. V. 38; 40; 42; 43

The Discovery of the Ancient City of Norumbega. Cambridge: 1889? V. 38; 40; 43

The Landfall of Leif Erikson A.D. 1000, and the Site of His Houses in Vinland. Boston: 1892. V. 38

Leif's House in Vinland (and) Graves of the Northmen. Boston: 1893. V. 38; 40; 43

The Problem of the Northmen. Boston & New York: 1890. V. 38; 40; 43

HORSLEY, HENEAGE

Tracts in Controversy with Dr. Priestley Upon the Historical Question of the Belief of the First Ages in Our Lord's Divinity. Dundee: 1812. V. 41; 45

HORSLEY, J. SHELTON

Surgery of the Blood Vessels. St. Louis: 1915. V. 42

HORSLEY, J. W.

Jottings From Jail. Notes and Papers on Prison Matters. London: 1887. V. 39

HORSLEY, JOHN

Britannia Romana; or the Roman Antiquities of Britian. London: 1732. V. 41

Britannia Romana or the Roman Antiquites of Britain. London: 1974. V. 38; 44

A Short and General Account of the Most Necessary and Fundamental Principles of natural Philosophy . . . Glasgow: 1743. V. 46

HORSLEY, JOHN JAMES

A Rough Diary of a Cruise Along the Coast of Norway, from Stavanger to the North Cape, August 1886. Alnwick: 1886? V. 43; 44

HORSLEY, SAMUEL

A Catalogue of the Entire and Very Valuable Library, of the Late Right Rev. Samuel Horsley, Lord Bishop of St. Asaph. London: 1807. V. 44

Elementary Treatises on the Fundamental Principles of Practical Mathematics for the Use of Students by Samuel Lord Bishop of Rochester. Oxford: 1801. V. 37; 40

The Speeches in Parliament. Dundee: 1813. V. 40

Statements Submitted to the Right Honourable Sir Joseph Banks, President of the Royal Society of London. Louth: 1803. V. 44

HORSLEY, VICTOR

The Cerebellum: Its Relation to Spatial Orientation and to Locomotion. Being the Boyle Lecture for 1905. London: 1905. V. 37

The Linacre Lecture. The Function of the So-Called Motor Area of the Brain. London: 1909. V. 39; 40

The Structure and Functions of the Brain and Spinal Cord. Philadelphia: 1892. V. 38

The Structure and Functions of the Cerebellum Examined by a New Method. 1908. V. 41

HORSLEY, WILLIAM

Serious Considerations on the High Duties Examin'd. Addressed to Sir Matthew Decker. London: 1744. V. 40; 41

A Treatise on Maritime Affairs; or a Comparison Between the Commerce and Naval Power of England and France. London: 1744. V. 40; 41; 45

HORSMAN, GILBERT

Precedents in Conveyancing . . . In the Savoy: 1744. V. 45

HORST, TIELEMAN VAN DER

Theatrum Machinarum Universale . . . Amsterdam: 1736-37. V. 43

Theatrum Machinarum Universale of Nieuwe Algemeene Bouwkunde. Amsterdam: 1739. V. 46

Theatrum Machinarum Universale, of Keurige Verzameling van Verscheide Grote en Zeer Fraaie Waterwerken . . . Amsterdam: 1794?-1774. V. 38

HORST, TIELEMANS VAN DER

Neue Bau-Kunst, worinn . . . Wie Man Vielerley Arten der Treppen . . . Nuremberg: 1763. V. 45

HORSTER, MARITA

Andrea del Castagno. London: 1980. V. 46

HORT, JOHN JOSIAH

The Horse Guards. London: 1850. V. 40

HORT, RICHARD 1803 or 4-1857

The Embroidered Banner, and Other Marvels. London: 1850. V. 40

The Guards and the Line. London: 1851. V. 44

The Horse Guards, by the Two Mounted Sentries. Dublin: 1850. V. 44

Penelope Wedgebone: The Supposed Heiress. London: (n.d. 1850). V. 37

HORTICULTURAL SOCIETY OF LONDON

Catalogue of the Fruits Cultivated in the Garden. London: 1831. V. 40

Transactions of the Horticultural Society of London. London: 1812-30. V. 39

Transactions of the Horticultural Society of London. London: 1812-48. V. 37

Transactions of . . . London: 1812-48. V. 39

Transactions. London: 184-. V. 37

HORTON, LYDIARD H.

Dream Problem and the Mechanism of Thought Viewed from the Biological Standpoint. Philadelphia: 1926. V. 45

HORTON, THOMAS F.

History of Jack County, Being Accounts of Pioneer Times, Excerpts from County Court Records, Indian Stories . . . Jacksboro: 1932. V. 46

HORTON, WILLIAM THOMAS

A Book of Iamges. 1898. V. 42

A Book of Images. London: 1898. V. 42

William Horton Thomas - a Selection of His Work. London. V. 42; 45

HORTULUS Animae. Lustgarten der Seelen; mit Schoenen Lieblichen Figuren. (with) Das Symbolum der Heiligen Aposteln . . . Wittenberg: 1550. V. 38

HORTULUS Anime Cum Aliis Q(uam) Orationibus. Lyons: 1513. V. 45

HORTUS Indicus Malabaricus, Continens Regni Malabarici Apud Indos Celeberrimis Generis Plantae Rarioi, Latinis, Malabricis, Arabicis et Bramanum Characteribus Expressas . . . 1979-1983. V. 39

HORTUS SANITATIS

Ortus Sanitatis. de Herbis et Plantis De Animalibus et Reptilibus. De Avibus et Voltilibus. De Piscibus et Natailibus De Lapidibus et in Terre Venis Nascenti(-bus). De Urinis et Earum Speciebus. Tabula Medicinalis cum Directorio Generali . . . Strasbourg: 1497. V. 39

HORWOOD, A. J.

Catalogue of the Ancient Mss. at Gray's Inn. London: 1869. V. 46

HOSACK, ALEXANDER

A Memoir Upon Staphyloraphy; with Cases and a Description of the Instruments Requisite for the Operation. New York: 1833. V. 42

HOSACK, DAVD

An Inaugural Discourse Delivered at the Opening of Rutgers Medical College . . . New York: 1826. V. 38

HOSACK, DAVID

Catalogue of the Entire Medical Library of the Late Doctor David Hosack . . . New York: 1867. V. 40; 41; 44

A Funeral Address . . . at the Interment of Doctor James Tillary, Late President of the City of New York. New York: 181. V. 43

A Funeral Address . . . at the Interment of Doctor James Tillary . . . New York: 1818. V. 45

An Inaugural Discourse Delivered at the Opening of Rutgers Medical College . . . New York: 1826. V. 37; 40; 41; 44; 45; 46

Lectures on the Theory and Practice of Physic, Delivered in the College of Physicians and Surgeons of the University of the State of New York . . . Philadelphia: 1838. V. 37; 43

Lectures on the Theory and Practice of Physic. Philadelphia: 1838. V. 40; 42

Observations on Vision. Read Before the Royal Society of London, May 1, 1794 . . . New York: 1813. V. 44

HOSACK, DAVID continued

Observations of the Medical Character. Addressed to the Graduates of the College of Physicians and Surgeons. New York: 1826. V. 37; 38

HOSE, CHARLES

The Field-Book of a Jungle-Wallah. London: 1929. V. 39

HOSHOUR, SAMUEL K.

Letters to Esq. Pedant, in the East, by Lorenzo Altisonant, an Emigrant to the West. Cambridge City: 1844. V. 42

Letters to Squire Pedant, in the East . . . Indianapolis: 1870. V. 42; 45

HOSKINS, CYRIL HENRY

The Third Eye - the Autobiography of a Tibetan Lama. London: 1956. V. 40

HOSKINS, G. A.

Travels in Ethiopia, Above the Second Cataract of the Nile . . . London: 1835. V. 42

HOSKINS, KATHERINE

A Penetential Primer: Poems, by Katherine Hoskins. Cummington, MA: 1945. V. 37

HOSKINS, NATHAN

A History of the State of Vermont From Its Discovery and Settlement to the Close of the year 1830. Vergennes: 1831. V. 37; 39

HOSMER, HEZEKIAH L.

Charge of Chief Justice Hosmer, to the Grand Jurdy of the First Judicial District, . . . Virginia City: 1864. V. 40; 42

HOSMER, SUSAN H. C.

Nantucket Receipts. Boston: 1880. V. 37

HOSMER, WILLIAM

Autobiography of Rev. Alvin Torry, First Missionary to the Six Nations and the Northwestern Tribes of British North America. Auburn: 1862. V. 43

THE HOSPITAL of the Protestant Episcopal Church in Philadelphia. Philadelphia: 1869. V. 41

THE HOT Springs of Arkansas. St. Louis: 1877. V. 43

HOT Sulphur Baths Combining Natural Heat Mineral Qualities Unrivaled Climate San Antonio Texas. San Antonio: 1901. V. 41

HOTCHISS, CHARLES F.

On the Ebb: a Few Log-Lines from an Old Salt. New Haven: 1878. V. 45

HOTCHKIN, JAMES H.

A History of the Purchase and Settlement of Western New York, and of the Rise, Progress and Present State of the Presbyterian Church in that Section. New York: 1848. V. 46

HOTCHKIN, S. F.

Ancient and Modern Germantown, Mount Airy and Chestnut Hill. Philadelphia: 1889. V. 39; 42; 44

Rural Pennsylvania in the Vicinity of Philadelphia. Philadelphia: 1897. V. 39; 41

HOTCHKISS, CHARLES F.

On the Ebb: a Few Log-Lines from an Old Salt. New Haven: 1878. V. 40; 46

HOTCHKISS, FELIX

The Art of Bowls. London: 1932. V. 42

HOTCHKISS, JEDEDIAH

Confederate Military History: Virginia. Atlanta: 1899. V. 46

HOTCHKISS, JEDIDIAH

The Virginias . . . Volume VI, 1885. Staunton: 1885. V. 42

HOTHAM, MISS

A Catalogue of the Very Extensive and Valuable Library . . . Richmond. V. 40

Catalogue of . . . Porcelain and . . . Articles of Rarity. Richmond, Surrey: 1817. V. 40

HOTMAN, FRANCOIS

Brutum Fulmen. N.P.: 1585. V. 41

Francogallia. Geneva: 1573. V. 42

HOTMAN, JEAN, SIEUR DE VILLIERS

L'Ambassadeur. N.P.: 1603. V. 40

HOTOMAN, FRANCIS

Franco-Gallia: or an Account of the Ancient Free State of France, and Most Other Parts of Europe Before the Loss of Their Liberties. London: 1711. V. 46

HOTSON, J. LESLIE

The Death of Christopher Marlowe. London: 1925. V. 40

HOTTEN, JOHN CAMDEN

Charles Dickens. The Story of His Life. London: 1870. V. 38

A Dictionary of Modern Slang, Cant, and Vulgar Words . . . London: 1859. V. 41

A Dictionary of Modern Slang, Cant and Vulgar Words . . . London: 1860. V. 41

The History of Signboards. London: 1866. V. 39

The Original Lists of Persons of Quality . . . London: 1874. V. 42

The Original Lists of Persons of Quality . . . New York: 1874. V. 46

Thackeray the Humourist and Man of Letters. London: 1864. V. 40

HOTTINGER, HENRY

The Henry Hottinger Collection. New York: 1967. V. 37

HOUCK, LOUIS

A History of Missouri from the Earliest Explorations and Settlements. Chicago: 1908. V. 38; 45

HOUCKGEEST, ANDRE EVERARD VAN BRAM

Voyage de l'Mbassade de la Compagnie des Indes Orientales Hollandaises, vers l'Empereur de la Chine, dans les Annees 1794 & 1795. Philadelphie: 1797-98. V. 41

HOUDIN, ROBERT

Memoirs of . . . Written by Himself. Philadelphia: 1859. V. 46

HOUDINI, HARRY

Houdini's Book of Magic and Party Pastimes: Fasincating Puzzles, Tricks and Mysterious stunts. New York: 1927. V. 46

Miracle Mongers and Their methods. New York: 1920. V. 46

The Unmasking of Robert-Houdin. London: 1910. V. 46

The Unmasking of Robert-Houdin. New York: 1908. V. 37

HOUGH, EMERSON 1857-1923

The Covered Wagon. New York: 1922. V. 37; 38; 39; 40

The Covered Wagon. New York: & London: 1922. V. 46

The Firefly's Light. New York: 1916. V. 42

The King of Gee Whiz. Indianapolis: 1906. V. 42

The Way to the West, and Live sof Three Early Americans: Boone, Crockett & Carson. Indianapolis: 1903. V. 39

HOUGH, FRANKLIN B.

Diary of the Siege of Detroit in the War with Pontiac. Albany: 1860. V. 37

A History of Jefferson County in the State of New York. Albany: 1854. V. 40

A History of St. Lawrence and Franklin Counties, New York. Albany: 1853. V. 40

Proceedings of the Commissioners of Indian Affiairs, Appointed by Law for the Extinguishment of Indian Titles in the State of New York. Albany: 1861. V. 37

The Siege of Savanah. Albany: 1866. V. 38; 39; 45

HOUGH, HENRY BEETLE

Melville in the South Pacific. Boston: 1960. V. 40

HOUGH, HORATIO GATES

Diving, or an Attempt to Describe Upon Hydraulic and Hydrostataic Principles . . . Hartford: 1813. V. 38; 46

Diving, or An Attempt to Describe Upon Hydraulic and Hydrostatic Principles, A Method of Supplying the Diver with Air Underwater. Hartford: 1871. V. 43

HOUGH, W.

A Narrative of the March and Operations of the Army of the Indus, in the Expedition into Afffganistan in the Years 1838-1839. Calcutta: 1840. V. 41

HOUGH, WILLIAM

Political and Military Events in British India, from the Years 1756-1849. London: 1853. V. 38

HOUGHTON, ARTHUR BOYD

Arthur Boyd Houghton a Selection from His Work in Black and White, Printed for the Most Part from the Original Wood-Blocks. London: 1896. V. 39

HOUGHTON, BENJAMIN

Considerations Humbly Addressed to the Magistrates of the City and County of Dublin . . . Dublin: 1764. V. 42

HOUGHTON, CLAUDE

Three Fantastic Tales. London: 1934. V. 37

HOUGHTON, JOHN

Husbandry and Trade Improv'd . . . London: 1727-28. V. 39; 42

HOUGHTON, RICHARD MONCKTON MILNES, 1ST BARON 1809-1885

The Events of 1848, Especially in Their Relation to Great Britain. London: 1849. V. 41

Good Night and Good Morning. London: 1860. V. 39

Life, Letters and Literary Remains of John Keats . . . London: 1848. V. 43

Life, Letters and Literary Remains. New York: 1848. V. 46

Some Writings and Speeches in the Last Year of His Life . . . London: 1888. V. 43; 46

HOUGHTON, T. S.

The Printers' Practical Every-Day-Book, Calculated to Assist the Young Printer to Work with Ease and Expedition. London: 1842. V. 43

HOUGHTON, THOMAS

Royal Institutions: Being Proposals for Articles to Establish and Confirm Laws, Liberties and Customs of Silver & Gold Mines, to All the King's Subjects, in Such Parts of Africa and America . . . London: 1694. V. 37; 38

HOUGHTON, W.

British Fresh Water Fishes. London: 1880. V. 40

British Fresh-Water Fishes. 1885. V. 46

British Fresh-Water Fishes. London: 1879. V. 37; 39; 42; 44

British-Fresh-Water Fishes. London: n.d.(1879). V. 37

HOUGHTON, WALTER R.

American Etiquette and Rules of Politeness. Indianapolis: 1882. V. 42

Conspectus of the History of Political Parties and the Federal Government. Indianapolis: 1880. V. 46

HOUGHTON, WILLIAM

Sketches of British Insects. London: 1875. V. 38

HOULDBROOKE

A Short Address tot he People of Scotland, on the Subject of the Slave Trade. Edinburgh: 1792. V. 42

HOULDER, J. A.

North-East Madagascar. Antananarivo: 1877. V. 40

HOUNSELL BROTHERS, LONDON.

Flags and Signals of All Nations by Hounsell Brothers. London: 1870. V. 41

HOURS PRESS

The Hours Press Booklet - Being a List of Books Published by Nancy Cunard at the Hours Press During 1929 and 1930 . . . Paris: 1930. V. 40

HOUSE, E.

A Narrative of the Captivity of Mrs. Horn and Her Two Children, with Mrs. Harris, by the Camanche Indians . . . St. Louis: 1839. V. 45

HOUSE, EDWARD J.

A Hunter's Camp-Fires. New York: 1909. V. 46

HOUSE, EDWARD M. 1858-1938

The Intimate Papers of Colonel House . . . Boston: 1926. V. 44

HOUSE, EDWARD MANDELL

The Intimate Papers of Colonel House. Boston: 1926-28. V. 38

HOUSE, H. D.

Wild Flowers of New York. Albany: 1923. V. 45

Wild Flowers of New York. Albany: 1918, 1923. V. 37; 38

HOUSE, HOMER D.

Wildflowers of New York. 1923. V. 40; 46

THE HOUSE-KEEPERS Cook Book, Containing a Great Variety of Unknown and Valuable Receipts . . . Philadelphia: 1838. V. 45

HOUSE, M. R.

The Ammonoidea, Evolution, Classification, Mode of Life and Geological Usefulness. London: 1981. V. 37

THE HOUSE of Windsor. A Book of Portraits. London: 1937. V. 44

A HOUSE Party. An Account of the Stories Told at at Gathering of Famous American Authors, The Story Tellers Being Introduced by Paul Leicester Ford. Boston: 1901. V. 40

THE HOUSE that Jack Built. London: 1830. V. 46
THE HOUSE That Jack Built. London: 1840. V. 45
THE HOUSE that Jack Built. London: 1850. V. 41
THE HOUSE that Jack Built. London: 1853. V. 38
THE HOUSE that Jack Built. London: 1875. V. 42

THE HOUSE We Live In. London. V. 46

A HOUSEHOLD Atlas of the World . . . Philadelphia/New York: 1898. V. 45

HOUSEHOLD Conveniences. Being the Experience of Many Practical Writers. New York: 1884. V. 42

HOUSEHOLD, GEOFFREY

Arabesque. London: 1948. V. 45

Rogue Male. London: 1939. V. 37; 45

The Spanish Cave. Boston: 1936. V. 38

The Third Hour. London: 1937. V. 41; 45

HOUSEHOLD Pictures for Home and School. London: 1868. V. 38

THE HOUSEKEEPER and Butler's Guide; or, a System of Cookery, and Making of Wines. Glasgow. V. 38

HOUSEKEEPER'S Assistant, Composed Upon Temperance Principles, with Instructions in the Art of Making Plain and Fancy Cakes, Puddings, Pastry, Confectionery, Ice Cream, Jellies, Blanc Mange, Also for the Cooking of All the Various Kinds of Meats . . . Boston: 1845. V. 37

THE HOUSEKEEPER'S Receipt Book, or, the Repository of Domestic Knowledge . . . London: 1813. V. 42; 43

HOUSER, LIONEL

Lake of Fire. (New York): (1933). V. 37

HOUSMAN, ALFRED EDWARD 1859-1936

Introductory Lecture: Delivered Before the Faculties of Arts and Laws of Science in University College London, October 3, 1892. Cambridge: 1933. V. 37

Last Poems. London: 1922. V. 39; 40; 41; 46

More Poems. London: 1936. V. 39; 44

Notes on Persius. London: 1913. V. 44

Odes from the Greek Dramatists. London: 1890. V. 41

A Shropshire Lad. London: 1896. V. 39; 41; 43; 44

A Shropshire Lad. New York: 1897. V. 39; 40; 44

A Shropshire Lad. London: 1914. V. 42; 46

A Shropshire Lad. London: 1921. V. 39

A Shropshire Lad and Last Poems. Chipping Campden: 1929. V. 41; 46

A Shropshire Lad. (and) Last Poems. London: 1929. V. 46

A Shropshire Lad. New York: 1935. V. 37; 39; 41; 44; 46

A Shrophsire Lad. New York: & London: 1935. V. 46

A Shropshire Lad. Market Drayton: 1990. V. 45

Sincerus & Lucretius III 717. London: 1909. V. 44

Some Poems, Some Letters, and a Personal Memoir by His Brother, Laurence Housman. London: 1937. V. 38

HOUSMAN, CLEMENCE

The Unknown Sea. London: 1898. V. 42

The Were-Wolf. Chicago: 1896. V. 43

The Were-Wolf. London: 1896. V. 37; 40; 41; 42; 45; 46

The Were-Wolf. London & Chicago: 1896. V. 39

HOUSMAN, JOHN

A Descriptive Tour and Guide to the Lakes, Caves, Mountains and Other Natural Curiosities, in Cumberland, Westmorland, Lancashire and Part of the West Riding of Yorkshire. Carlisle: 1817. V. 39; 42

A Topographical Description of Cumberland, Westmoreland, Lancashire, and a Part of the West Riding of Yorkshire. London: 1800. V. 38

HOUSMAN, LAURENCE 1865-1959

All Fellows: Seven Legends of Lower Redemption With Insets in Verse. London: 1896. V. 39; 41

Arthur Boyd Houghton. London: 1896. V. 38; 39

Bethlehem. London: 1902. V. 41; 43; 46

Blind Love. Boston: 1901. V. 41

The Blue Moon. London: 1904. V. 42

A Farm in Fairyland. London: 1894. V. 40; 42; 44; 46

The Field of Clover. London: 1898. V. 37; 38; 40; 41; 44

The Field of Clover. New York: 1902. V. 46

Green Arras. Chicago: 1896. V. 38

Green Arras. London: 1896. V. 37; 43

Hop-O-Me-Heart: A Grown-Up Fairy Tale. Flansham: 1938. V. 38

The House of Joy. London: 1895. V. 43

The Little Land. London: 1899. V. 38; 41

Mendicant Rhymes. Chipping Campden: 1906. V. 45; 46

Mendicant Rhymes. London: 1906. V. 37; 46

Princess Badoura. London. V. 45

Princess Badoura. London: 1913. V. 43; 45; 46

Prunella, or Love in a Dutch Garden. London: 1906. V. 38; 41; 46

Rue. London: 1899. V. 46

Stories from the Arabian Nights retold by Laurence Housman. London. V. 45

HOUSMAN, LAURENCE 1865-1959 continued

Stories from the Arabian Nights. London: 1907. V. 41; 45; 46

Stories from the Arabian Nights. Nottingham: 1910. V. 37; 38

The Story of the Seven Young Goslings. London. V. 43

The Story of Seven Young Goslings. London: 1899. V. 44

The Story of Seven Young Goslings. London: 1900. V. 43

A Tale from the Arabian Nights Retold by Laurence Housman. London: 1913. V. 41

Victoria Regina, a Dramatic Biography. New York. V. 46

HOUSSER, F. B.

A Canadian Art Movement. The Story of the Group Seven. Toronto: 1926. V. 45; 46

HOUSTON AND TEXAS CENTRAL RAILROAD

Lands Originally Granted to the Houston & Texas Central Galveston, Harrisburg & San Antonio Texas & New Orleans and Gulf, Western Texas & Pacific Railway Co.'s in Texas. Chicago: 1892. V. 39

HOUSTON, MATILDA

Texas and the Gulf of Mexico; or, Yachting in the New World. London: 1844. V. 44

HOUSTON, MATILDA CHARLOTTE

A Woman's Memories of World Known Men. London: 1883. V. 46

HOUSTON, PERCY HAZEN

Doctor Johnson, a Study in 18th Century Humanism. Cambridge: 1923. V. 39

THE HOUSTON Post Texas Almanac, for 1896. Houston: 1896. V. 38

HOUSTON, SAM

Case of Judge John C. Watrous: Charges Against the Judge of the District Court of the U.S. for the District of Texas. Washington: 1858. V. 37; 46

Ever Thin Truly. Love Letters from Sam Houston to Anna Raguet. Austin: 1975. V. 40

Life of General Houston. Washington: (1855). V. 37

Message from the President of the Republic . . . Houston: 1838. V. 37

Nebraska Bill-Indian Tribes. Speech of Hon. Sam Houston, of Texas, Delivered in the Senate of the United States, February 14 and 15, 1854, in Favor of Maintaining the Public Faith with the Indian Tribes. Washington: 1854. V. 42

The Writings of Sam Houston, 1813-1943. Austin: 1938-1943. V. 43

The Writings of Sam Houston 1813-1863. Austin: 1938-43. V. 42

The Writings of Sam Houston, American Giant. Washington: 1962. V. 41

Writings of Sam Houston. Austin: 1970. V. 37; 39; 41; 42; 44

HOUSTOUN, JAMES

Some New and Accurate Observations Geographical, Natural and Historical . . . London: 1725. V. 43

HOUSTOUN, MATILDA

Texas . . . Yachting in the New World. London: 1844. V. 37; 38

Texas and the Gulf of Mexico; or, Yachting in the New World. (and) The Englishwoman in Egypt. Philadelphia: 1845. V. 38; 39; 42

HOUSTOUN, MATILDA C.

Hesperos: or, Travels in the West. London: 1850. V. 37; 38; 46

Zoe's Brand. London: 1864. V. 42

HOUSTOUN, MATILDA CHARLOTTE

A Cruel Wrong. London: 1890. V. 39

His Besetting Sin. London: 1888. V. 39

Texas and the Gulf of Mexico. London: 1844. V. 39

HOUTEN, HENDRIK VAN

Verhandelinge van de Grontregelen der Door-zigtkunde of Tekenkonst (Perspectief). Amsterdam: 1705. V. 45

HOVER, JOHN C.

Memoirs of the Miami Valley. Chicago: 1919-20. V. 39; 46

HOVEY, ALVIN

General Orders No. 61. Helena: 1862. V. 41

General Orders No. 2. Helena: 1862. V. 41

HOVEY, ALVIN P.

To His Excellency the Governor of Wisconsin. Camp at Helena: 1862. V. 39

HOVEY, C. M.

The Fruits of America. Boston and New York: 1852-56. V. 39

HOVEY, RICHARD

Poems. Washington: 1880. V. 46

HOVEY, SYLVESTER

Letters from the West Indies . . . New York: 1838. V. 46

HOVGAARD, WILLIAM

General Design of Warships, Fifty Phrases Described in Detail . . . London: 1920. V. 39

HOVHANESS, ALAN

The Burning House: Opus 185. New York: 1960. V. 45

magnificat for Soli, Chorus and Orchestra. New York: 1961/58. V. 45

HOW, CHARLES

Devout Meditations . . . Edinburgh: 1752. V. 46

HOW, DAVID

Diary of David How, a Private in Col. Paul Dudley Sargent's Regiment of the Massachusetts Line in the Army of the American Revolution. Morrisania: 1865. V. 42; 43

HOW, G.

English and Scottish Silver Spoons, Medieval to Late Stuart and Pre-Elizabethan Hall-Marks on English Plate. London: 1952-57. V. 37

HOW, G. E. P.

English and Scottish Silver Sppons Mediaeval to Late Stuart and Pre-Elizabethan Hall-marks on English Plate. London: 1952. V. 44

HOW, LOUIS

The Penitentes of San Rafael. Indianapolis: 1900. V. 37

HOW, NEHEMIAH

A Narrative of the Captivity of Nehemiah How in 1745-1747. Cleveland: 1904. V. 37; 46

HOW Tis Done. Chicago.: 1879. V. 38

HOW 'Tis Done. A Thorough Ventilation of the Numerous Schemes Conducted by Wandering Canvassers, Together with the Various Advertising Dodges for the Swindling of the Public. Syracuse: 1890. V. 40

HOW to Buy and Sell Money. Plaistow & London: 1928-29. V. 38; 44
HOW to Buy and Sell Money. (London: 1929). V. 37

HOW to Go West, A Guide to Southern Iowa, Nebraska, Kansas, California and the Whole Great West . . . Chicago: 1873. V. 39

HOW to Keep a Husband, or Culinary Tactics. San Francisco: 1872. V. 40

HOW to Make Doll's Furniture and Furnish a Doll's House. London: 1871. V. 44

HOW to Make Japanese Color Prints. Yokohama: 1948. V. 38

HOWALAND, E. A., MRS.

New England Economical Housekeeper. Worcester: 1847. V. 45

HOWARD, ALICE WOODBURY

Ching-Li and the Dragons. New York: 1931. V. 42

HOWARD, BEN

Father of Waters, Poems 1965-1976. Omaha: 1979. V. 39

Father of Waters, Poems 1965-1976. University of Nebraska ata: 1979. V. 37

HOWARD, BENJAMIN C.

A Report of the Decision of the Supreme Court of the United States, and the Opinions of the Judges Thereof, in the Case of Dred Scott. New York: 1857. V. 42; 44

Report of the Decision of the Supreme Court of the United States, and the Opinions of the Judges Thereof, in the Case of Dred Scott Versus John F. A. Sandford, December Term 1856. Washington: 1857. V. 37; 43

HOWARD, BRIAN

First Poems. Paris: 1930. V. 40

God Save the King. Paris: 1931. V. 41

God Save the King. Paris: 1930. V. 37

HOWARD-BURY, C. K.

Mount Everest, the Reconnaissance, 1921. New York: 1922. V. 46

HOWARD, CHARLES

Historical Anecdotes of Some of the Howard Family. London: 1769. V. 38

HOWARD, DAVID SANCTUARY

China for the West. London: 1978. V. 44

Chinese Armorial Porcelain. London: 1974. V. 42; 45

HOWARD, DAVID SANTUARY

China for the West. Chinese Porcelain and other Decorative Arts for Export Illustrated from the Mottahedeh Collection. London and New York: 1978. V. 37

HOWARD, EBENEZER

To-morrow: a Peaceful Path to Real Reform. London: 1898. V. 38

HOWARD, EDWARD

Copernicans of all Sorts Convicted. London: 1705. V. 39

Jack Ashore. London: 1840. V. 42

The Old Commodore. London: 1837. V. 39; 40

Sir Henry Morgan, the Buccaneer. Paris: 1842. V. 43

The Usurper. London: 1668. V. 38

The Woman's Conquest. London: 1671. V. 42

HOWARD, EDWARD GLANVILLE

Outward Bound, or a Merchant's Adventures. London: 1838. V. 43

HOWARD, EDWARD GRANVILLE

Sir Henry Morgan the Buccaneer. London: 1842. V. 45; 46

HOWARD, EDWIN L.

Chinese Garden ARchitecture. New York: 1931. V. 39

HOWARD, F. E.

English Church Woodwork. New York: 1927. V. 41

HOWARD, FRANCES THOMAS

In and Out of the Lines. New York: & Washington: 1905. V. 44

HOWARD, FRANK 1805?-1866

Colour as a Means of Art . . . London: 1835. V. 42

Colour, as a Means of Art. London: 1838. V. 42; 44

Colour as a Means of Art. London: 1849. V. 42; 44

Colour as a Means of Art . . . London: 1880. V. 38; 41; 44

Lessons on Colour, Being an Exemplification of the Principles Described in Colour as a Means of Art . . . London: 1841. V. 46

HOWARD, G. S.

Report of the Trial of the Libel Suit of Dr. G. S. Howard, of Carleton Place, Ont. Against the 'Montreal Star'. Montreal: 1898. V. 40

HOWARD, GEOFFREY

Early English Drug Jars. London: 1931. V. 39

HOWARD, GEORGE

Lady Jane Grey, and Her Times. London: 1822. V. 41; 45

HOWARD, GEORGE ELLIOTT

A History of Matrimonial Institutions, Chiefly in England and the United States . . . London: 1904. V. 43

HOWARD, GEORGE SELBY

The New Royal Cyclopaedia and Encyclopaedia. London: 1788. V. 41; 46

HOWARD, GEORGE W.

The Monumental City, Its Past History and Present Resources. Baltimore: 1873. V. 46

HOWARD, GORGES EDMOND

A Treatise of the Exchequer and Revenue of Ireland. Dublin: 1776. V. 42

HOWARD, H. ELIOT

The British Warblers, a History with Problems of Their Lives. London: 1907-15. V. 38; 39; 40; 42; 43; 44; 45

The British Warblers; A History, with Problems of their Lives. London: 1907-1914. V. 37

An Introduction to the Study of Bird Behaviour. 1929. V. 46

An Introduction to the Study of Bird Behaviour. London: 1929. V. 45

HOWARD, H. R.

The History of Virgil A. Stewart, and His Adventure in Capturing & Exposing the Great 'Western Land Pirate' and His Gang, in Connexion with the Evidence . . . New York: 1836. V. 43; 45

The History of Virgil A. Stewart, and His Adventure in Capturing and Exposing the Great 'Western Land Pirate' and His Gang. New York: 1842. V. 39; 46

The Life and Adventures of Joseph T. Hare. New York: 1847. V. 46

The Life and Adventures of Joseph T. Hare. New York: 1847 or 1849. V. 45

HOWARD, HENRY

A Defensative Against the Poyson of Supposed Prophecies . . . London: 1620. V. 42

HOWARD, HILDA GLYNN

The Writing on the Wall. Vancouver: 1921. V. 45

HOWARD, JAMES H. W.

Bond and Freer; a True Tale of Slave Times. Harrisburg: 1886. V. 39

HOWARD, JEAN G.

Of Mice and Mice. Cranberry Isles: 1978. V. 42

Too Close Apart: Two Stories. Cranberry Isles: 1977. V. 42

HOWARD, JOHN 1726-1790

An Account of the Principal Lazarettos in Europe . . . Warrington: 1789. V. 38; 39; 40; 41; 43; 46

An Account of the Principal Lazarettos In Europe. London: 1791. V. 40; 44; 46

Historical Remarks and Anecdotes on the Castle of the Bastille. London: 1780. V. 42

The Life of the Late John Howard, Esq. London: 1790. V. 40; 42

The State of the Prisons in England and Wales, with Preliminary Observations, and an Account of Some Foreign Prisons and Hospitals. London: 1784. V. 40

The State of Prisons in England and Wales, With Preliminary Observations and an Account of Some Foreign Prisons and Hospitals . . . Warrington: 1784. V. 38; 39; 41; 43; 46

The State of the Prisons in England and Wales, With Preliminary Observations, and an Account of Some Foreign Prisons and Hospitals. London: 1792. V. 40; 46

The State of the Prisons in England and Wales . . . (with) An Account of the Principal Lazarettos in Europe . . . London: 1792, 1791. V. 38

The State of the Prisons in England and Wales. Warrington: 1780. V. 37; 38; 43

The State of the prisons in England and Wales, with preliminary observations and an account of some foreign prisons. Warrington: 1777. V. 37

The State of the Prisons in England and Wales, with Preliminary Observations and an Account of Some Foreign Prisons and Hospitals. Warrington/London: 1784. V. 37

A View of the Character and Public Services of the Late John Howard. London: 1792. V. 40

The Works of John Howard, Esq. London: 1791-92. V. 42; 44; 45

HOWARD, JOHN GALEN

Brunelleschi. a Poem. San Francisco: 1913. V. 42; 45

HOWARD, JOSEPH JACKSON

Baronets, the Wardour Press Series of Armorial Bookplates. London: 1895. V. 46

Genealogical Collections Illustrating the History of Roman Catholic Families of England, Based on the Lawson Manuscript. London: 1887-92. V. 39

HOWARD, LELAND O.

The Mosquitoes of North and Central America and the West Indies. 1912-17. V. 37; 38

HOWARD, LEONARD

Miscellaneous Pieces in Prose and Verse. London: 1765. V. 41

HOWARD, MC HENRY

Recollections of a Maryland Confederate Soldier and Staff Officer Under Johnston, Jackson & Lee. Baltimore;: 1914. V. 39

HOWARD, OLIVER O.

Headquarters, Department and Army of the Tennessee . . . Field Circular: the Following Rules and Regulations. East Point: 1864. V. 43

My Life and Experiences Among Our Hostile Indians . . . Hartford: 1907. V. 43

HOWARD, OLIVER OTIS

Autobiography of Oliver Otis Howard, Major General United States Army. New York: 1908. V. 39

Famous Indian Chiefs I Have Known. New York: 1908. V. 39; 45

General Taylor. New York: 1892. V. 45

My Life and Experiences Among Our Hostile Indians. Hartford: 1907. V. 45

Nez Perce Joseph, an Account of His Ancestors, His Lands, His Confederates, His Enemies, His Murders, His Wars, His Pursuit and Capture. Boston: 1881. V. 39; 43; 45

Statement of Br. Maj. Gen. O. O. Howard Before the Committee on Education and Labor in Defense Against the Charges Presented by Hon. Fernando Wood, and Argument of Edgar Ketchum, Esq. New York: 1870. V. 39

HOWARD, PYLE

The Line of Love. By James Branch Cabell. New York: 1905. V. 37

HOWARD, R. A. N.

Life's Real Romance. N.P.: 1883. V. 46

HOWARD, R. E.

Always Comes Evening. Sauk City: 1957. V. 44

HOWARD, RICHARD BARON

An Inquiry into the Morbid Effects of Deficiency of Food, Chiefly with Reference to their Occurrence Amongst the Destitute Poor. London: 1839. V. 38

HOWARD, ROBERT

The Duell of the Stags: a Poem. In the Savoy: 1668. V. 44

Four New Plays, Viz: The Suprisal, The Committee, Comedies, The Indian Queen, The Vestal Virgin, Tragedies . . . London: 1665. V. 42

A Free Discourse Wherein the Doctrines of Tyranny are Display'd. London: 1697. V. 45

The Great Varourite, or, the Duke of Lerma. In the Savoy: 1668. V. 44

Historical Observations upon the Reigns of Edward I, II, III and Richard II. With Remarks Upon Their Faithful Counsellors and False Favourites. London: Printed for J.: 1689. V. 37

The History of the Reigns of Edward & Richard II; With Reflections and Characters of Their Chief Ministers and Favourites. London: 1690. V. 41

The Life and Reign of King Richard the Second. London: 1681. V. 43; 45

Poems. London: 1660. V. 37; 40; 41; 44; 45; 46

HOWARD, ROBERT E.

The Coming of Conan. New York: 1953. V. 43; 46

The Coming of Conan. New York: (1953). V. 37

Conan the Conqueror: the Hyborean Age. New York: 1950. V. 46

Conan the Barbarian. New York: 1950-55. V. 42

Conan the Barbarian. New York: 1954. V. 43; 46

Conan the Barbarian. New York: (1954). V. 37

The Dark Man and Others. Sauk City: 1963. V. 39; 40; 42; 43; 45

The Dark Man and Others. SC: 1963. V. 39

The Darkman and Others. 1963. V. 45

Singers in the Shadows. West Kingston: 1970. V. 45

Skull Face and Others. 1946. V. 39; 45

Skull Face & Others. Sauk City: 1946. V. 37; 39; 40; 42; 45

Skull Face and others. Sauk City: 1946. V. 37; 39

The Sword of Conan. New York: 1952. V. 42; 43; 46

HOWARD, ROBERT MILTON

Reminiscences. Columbus: 1912. V. 42

HOWARD, SYLVANUS

Every Tradesman His Own Lawyer; or a Digest of the Law Concerning Trade, Commerce and Manufactures. London: 1794. V. 46

HOWARD, THOMAS

On the Loss of Teeth; and on the Best Means of Restoring Them . . . London: 1856. V. 45

On the Loss of Teeth and Loose Teeth; and on the Best Means of Restoring Them. London: 1860. V. 40

On the Loss of Teeth; and on the Best Means of Restoring Them . . . London: 1853. V. 37

HOWARD, WALDO

The Mistake of a Life-time; or, The Robert of the Rhine Valley. Boston: 1850. V. 43

HOWARD, WILLIAM TRAVIS

Public Health Administration and the Natural History of Disease in Baltimore, Maryland 1797-1920. Washington: 1924. V. 45

HOWARTH, HENRY H.

History of the Mongols from the 9th to the 19th Century. London: 1876/80/88. V. 39

HOWARTH, T.

Charles Rennie Mackintosh and the Modern Movement. London: 1977. V. 46

HOWARTH, THOMAS

Charles Rennie MacKintosh and the Modern Movement. London: 1952. V. 45

HOWAY, F.

British Columbia, from the Earliest Times to the Present. Vancouver: 1914. V. 43; 45

HOWAY, F. W.

The. V. 44

The Dixon-Meares Controversy Containing, Remarks on the Voyages of John Meares by George Dixon . . . Bath: 1842. V. 46

HOWAY, FREDERIC W.

British Columbia and the United States: the North Pacific Slope from Fur Trade to Aviation. Toronto: 1942. V. 44

Voyages of the 'Columbia' to the Northwest Coast, 1787-1790 and 1790-1793. (Boston): 1941. V. 37

HOWAY, FREDERIC WILLIAM

The Dixon-Mears Controversy. Toronto: 1929. V. 38; 44

Voyages of the 'Columbia' to the Northwest Coast 1787-1790 and 1790-1793. Boston: 1941. V. 37; 38; 42

HOWBERT, IRVING

Indians of the Pike's Peak Region. New York: 1914. V. 42

HOWE & STEVENS

Treatise Upon Dyeing and Scouring, as Adapted to Their Family Dye Colours with Many Other Valuable Receipts. Boston: 1863. V. 40

HOWE, ANDREW JACKSON

The Art and Science of Surgery. Cincinnati: 1879. V. 44

HOWE, CHARLES 1661-1742

Devout Meditations; or, a Collection of Thoughts Upon Religious and Philosophical Subjects. Edinburgh: 1752. V. 41

HOWE, EDGAR F.

The Story of the First Decade in Imperial Valley, California. Imperial: 1910. V. 43

HOWE, EDGAR WATSON

The Story of a Country Town. Atchison: 1883. V. 38; 40; 41; 43

HOWE, ELLIC

The London Compositor. London: 1947. V. 38; 42

The London Bookbinders 1780-1806. London: 1950. V. 45

The London Bookbinders, 1780-1806. London: 1950. V. 46

HOWE, FLORENCE

Story of the Battle Hymn of the Republic. New York: 1916. V. 45

HOWE, FRANCES R.

Story of a French Homestead in the Old Northwest. Columbus: 1907. V. 39; 41

HOWE, HENRY

Historical Collections of Virginia . . . Charleston: 1845. V. 43

Historical Collections of the Great West . . . New York: 1857. V. 39

Historical Collections of Ohio in Two Volumes. Ohio: 1896. V. 46

Historical Collections of Ohio: an Encyclopedia of the State. Cincinnati: 1900. V. 44

Memoirs of the Most Eminent American Mechanics; also Lives of Distinguished European Mechanics. New York: 1858. V. 42; 45

HOWE, HENRY MARION

The Metallurgy of Steel. New York: 1892. V. 44

HOWE, JOHN

The Blessednesse of the Righteous Discoursed from Psal. 17, 15 . . . London: 1668. V. 42

The Christian's Pocket Companion. Enfield: 1826. V. 45

HOWE, JOHN BADLAM

Mono-Metalism and Bi-Metalism; or, the Science of Monetary Values. Boston: 1879. V. 44

HOWE, JULIA WARD

At Sunset. Boston: 1910. V. 41

The Julia Ward Birthday Book. Boston: 1889. V. 41

Later Lyrics. Boston: 1866. V. 41

Memoir of Dr. Samuel Gridley Howe. Boston: 1876. V. 41; 43

Passion Flowers. Boston: 1854. V. 37; 43

The Story of Evangelina Cisneros. New York: 1898. V. 46

A Trip to Cuba. Boston: 1860. V. 38

The World's Own. Boston: 1857. V. 41

HOWE, M. A. DE WOLFE

The Humane Society of the Commonwealth of Massachusetts, an Historical Review 1785-1916. Boston: 1918. V. 41

HOWE-NURSE, WILFIRD

Berkshire Vale. London: 1927. V. 41

HOWE, OCTAVIUS T.

American Clipper Ships 1833-1858. Salem: 1926-27. V. 38

American Clipper Ships: 1833-1858. New York: 1967. V. 37

HOWE, PARKMAN DEXTER

The Parkman Dexter Howe Library. (Parts I through IV). Gainesville: 1983-86. V. 38

The Parkman Dexter Howe Library . . . Gainesville: 1983-87. V. 40

HOWE, S. FERDINAND

The Commerce of Kansas City in 1886, with a General Review of its Business Progress. Kansas City: 1886. V. 37

HOWE, S. G.

The Blind Child's First Book. Boston: 1838. V. 41

On the Causes of Idiocy. Edinburgh: 1858. V. 38

HOWE, SAMUEL GRIDLEY 1801-1876

Appeal to the People of the United States to Relieve from Starvation the Women and Children of the Greeks of the Island of Crete. Boston: 1867. V. 40; 41

The Cretan Refugees and Their American Helpers. Boston: 1868. V. 37

An Historical Sketch of the Greek Revolution. New York: 1828. V. 37; 39; 41

the Journals and Letters of Samuel Gridley Howe. Boston: 1909. V. 41; 44; 46

The Letters and Journals of . . . The Greek Revolution and the Servant of Humanity. Boston: 1909. V. 43

HOWE, SOLOMON

Worshipper's Assistant. Containing the Rules of Music, and a Variety of Easy and Plain Psalm Tunes. Northampton: 1799. V. 37

HOWE, W. E.

A History of the Metropolitan Museum of Art . . . New York. V. 46

HOWE, WILLIAM

The Narrative of Lieut. Gen. Sir William Howe, in a Committee of the House of Commons, on the 29th of April. London: 1780. V. 41; 46

HOWEL, JAMES 1594-1666

Londinopolis; an Historicall discourse or Perlustration of the City of London, the Imperial Chamber, and chief Emporium of Great Britain; whereun to is added another of the city of Westminster, with the Courts of Justice . . . London: 1657. V. 37

HOWEL, LAURENTIO

Synopsis Canonum Eccclesiae Latinae. London: 1710. V. 38

HOWELL & STEWART

A Catalogue of Books . . . of Oriental Literature . . . (and) Oriental Manuscripts. London: 1826. V. 38

HOWELL, ARTHUR H.

Revision of the North American Ground Squirrels, With a Classification of the North American Sciuridae. Washington: 1938. V. 39

HOWELL, CLARK

Pioneers of Wiregrass Georgia . . . Adel: 1959. V. 42

HOWELL, FRANCIS

The Characters of Theophrastus; translated from the Greek and illustrated by Physiognomical sketches . . . London: 1824. V. 37

HOWELL, JAMES 1594?-1666

Dendrologia (in Greek). Dodona's Grove. London: 1640. V. 46

(Greek Title, then) A Discourse Concerning the Precedency of Kings. London: 1664. V. 38

(Greek: Proedria Basilike), a Discourse Concerning the Precedency of Kings . . . London: 1668? V. 45

Dodona's Grove or the Vocall Forest. London: 1640. V. 41

Dodona's Grove, or, the Vocall Forrest. London: 1640. V. 37; 42; 43

Dodona's Grove, or the Vocall Forrest. Cambridge: 1645. V. 38; 43

Epistolae Ho-Elianae. Familiar Letters Domestic and Forren . . . . London: 1645. V. 42; 43

Epistolae Ho-Elianae. Familiar Letters Domestic and Forren. London: 1655. V. 40

Epistolae Ho-Elianae. Familiar Letters, Domestic and Forren. London: 1678. V. 40

Epistolae Ho-Elianae: Familiar Letters Domestick and Foreign . . . London: 1726. V. 43

Epistolae Ho-Elianae or the Familiar Letters. Boston: 1907. V. 41

Londinopolis: an Historical Discourse or Perlustration of the City of London. London: 1657. V. 45

Instructions for Forreine Travell. London: 1642. V. 42; 44

Lustra Ludovici, or the Life of . . . Lewis the XIII. V. 45

Lustra Ludovici, on the Life of the Late Victorious King of France, Lewis the XIII. London: 1646. V. 43; 46

A Survay of the Signorie of Venice, Of Her Admired Policy and Method of Government. London: 1651. V. 44; 45; 46

HOWELL, JOHN

California. Catalogue 50. Parts I-V (complete). San Francisco: 1979-1980. V. 37; 40

Londinopolis; an Historicall Discourse of Perlustration of the City of London. London: 1657. V. 38

HOWELL, LAURENCE 1664?-1720

The Orthodox Communicant, by Way of Meditation on the Order for the Administration of the Lord's Supper . . . London: 1721. V. 40

Synopsis Canonum Ecclesiae Latinae. London: 1710. V. 40

HOWELL, PETER

The Life and Travels of Peter Howell Written by Himself. Newbern: 1849. V. 39

HOWELL, WILLIAM

An Institution of General History, From the Beginning of the World to the Monarchy of Constantine the Great. London: 1661. V. 40

An Institution of General History, from the Beginning of the World to the Monarchy of Constantine the Great . . . London: 1662/1661. V. 43

HOWELLS, JOHN MEAD

The Architectural Heritage of the Piscataqua. New York: 1937. V. 42

The Architectural Heritage of the Merrimack: Early Houses and Gardens. New York: 1941. V. 41

Lost Examples of Colonial Architecture. New York: 1931. V. 38; 41; 42

HOWELLS, WILLIAM COOPER

Recollections of Life in Ohio, from 1813 to 1840. Cincinnati: 1895. V. 43

HOWELLS, WILLIAM DEAN 1837-1920

A Boy's Town . . . New York: 1890. V. 37; 41; 44; 46

A Chance Acquaintance. Boston: 1874. V. 42

A Counterfeit Presentment. Boston: 1877. V. 46

Criticism and Fiction. New York: 1891. V. 46

The Elevator. Boston: 1885. V. 39

Familiar Spanish Travels. New York: 1913. V. 43

The Flight of Pony Baker. New York: & London: 1902. V. 44

Imaginary Interviews. New York: 1910. V. 37; 41; 43; 44

An Imperative Duty. New York: 1892. V. 39

An Imperative Duty. New York: 1893. V. 41

Italian Journeys. New York: 1867. V. 44

The Leatherwood God. New York: 1916. V. 44

The Life and Public Services of Hon. Abraham Lincoln . . . and Hon. Hannibal Hamlin. Boston: 1860. V. 43

Literary Friends and Acquaintance. New York: 1902. V. 43

A Little Girl Among the Old Masters. Boston: 1884. V. 42; 46

The Minister's Charge, or the Apprenticeship of Lemuel Barker. Edinburgh: 1886. V. 44

Mrs. Farrell. New York: 1921. V. 46

My Mark Twain. New York: 1910. V. 41

The Niagara Book. V. 43

Poems of Two Friends. Columbus: 1860. V. 39; 44

Poems. Boston: 1886. V. 43

The Register. Boston: 1884. V. 39

The Rise of Silas Lapham. Boston: 1885. V. 37; 38; 40; 43; 45

Room Forty-Five, a Farce. Boston: 1900. V. 41

The Seen and the Unseen At Stratford-On-Avon. New York: 1904. V. 40

The Seen and the Unseen at Stratford-on-Avon. New York & London: 1914. V. 41

The Seen and Unseen at Stratford-On-Avon: A Fantasy. New York: 1914. V. 37

Stops of Various Quills. New York: 1895. V. 44

The Story of a Play. New York: 1898. V. 43

Suburban Sketches. New York: 1871. V. 41

Tuscan Cities. Boston: 1886. V. 46

The Undiscovered Country. Boston: 1880. V. 37

Venetian Life. New York: 1866. V. 46

Venetian Life. Boston: 1892. V. 44

Venetian Life. New York: 1892. V. 40

Years of My Youth. New York: & London: 1916. V. 46

HOWES, B. G.

Howes' Model Copy-Book, or System of Penmanship. Boston: 1867. V. 41

HOWES, WRIGHT

U.S. IANA (1700-1950). A Descriptive Check-List of 11,450 Printed Sources Relating to Those Parts of Continental North America . . . New York: 1954. V. 38; 39

U.S. IANA (1650-1950). New York: 1963. V. 42

U.S. IANA (1650-1950): a Selective Bibliography In Which are Described 11, 620 Uncommon and Significant Books Relating to the Continental Portion of the United States. New York: 1988. V. 44

U.S. IANA (1650-1950). New York: 1962. V. 38; 46

HOWGILL, FRANCIS

Mystery Babylon, the Mother of Harlots Discovered, Her Rise, and When with Many of His Sorceries, With HEr Merchants of Divers Orders and Ranks and Merchandize of Divers Sorts These Many Hundred Years. London: 1660. V. 40

HOWISON, JOHN

European Colonies in Various Parts of the World, Viewed in Their Social, Moral and Physical Condition. London: 1834. V. 37; 41

Sketches of Upper Canada. Edinburgh: 1821. V. 37; 38; 39; 41; 42; 43; 46

Sketches of Upper Canada, Domestic, Local and Characteristic . . . Edinburgh: 1825. V. 44

HOWISON, NEIL M.

Oregon: Report of Lieut. Neil M. Howison . . . Being the Result of an Examination in the Year 1846 of the Coast, Harbors, Rivers, Soil, Productions, Climate . . . Washington: 1st edition; V. 45

Report of Lieut. Neil M. Howison, United States Navy, to the Commander of the Pacific Squadron: Being the Result of an Examination in the Year 1846 of the Coast, Harbors, Rivers, Soil, Productions, Climate, and Population of the Territory of Oregon. Washington: 1848. V. 40

HOWITT, ANNA MARY

An Art Student in Munich. London: 1853. V. 45; 46

HOWITT, E.

Selections from Letters Written During a Tour through the United States, in the Summer and Autumn of 1819 . . . Nottingham: 1820. V. 37; 40; 46

HOWITT, MARGARET

Twelve Months with Fredrika Bremer in Sweden. London: 1866. V. 37; 45

HOWITT, MARY

The Cost of Caergwyn. London: 1864. V. 44

Mary Howitt: an Autobiography. London: 1891. V. 44

The Queens of England . . . London: 1860. V. 42

HOWITT, SAMUEL

The British Sportsman. London: 1812. V. 39

Howitt's Miscellaneous Etchings Old and New. London: 1812. V. 39

A New Work of Animals . . . London: 1811. V. 37; 43

Orme's Collection of British Field Sports. Guildford: 1955. V. 40

HOWITT, WILLIAM

The Book of the Seasons; or the Calendar of Nature. London: 1831. V. 41

The Boy's Country-Book. London: 1839. V. 38; 40

Homes and Haunts of the Most Eminent British Poets. London: 1847. V. 39

Land, Labor and Gold; or, Two Years in Victoria; with Visits to Sydney and Van Dieman's Land. Boston: 1855. V. 40; 45

Land, Labour and Gold or, Two Years in Victoria, with Visits to Sydney and Van Dieman's Land. London: 1855. V. 44; 45; 46

Land, Labour and Gold; or, Two Years in Victoria. London: 1885. V. 39

Land, Labor and Gold; or, Two Years in Victoria: with Visits to Sydney and Van Dieman's Land. Boston: 1895. V. 40

Life in Germany; or, Scenes, Impressions and Every-Day Life of the Germans, Including the Popular Songs, Sports and Habits of the Students of the Universities. London: 1849. V. 44; 46

The Northern Heights of London or Historical Associations of Hampstead, Highgate, Muswell Hill, Hornsey and Islington. London: 1869. V. 40

Ruined Abbeys and Castles of Great Britain. London: 1862. V. 37; 38; 43

Ruined Abbeys and Castles of Great Britain and Ireland. Second Series. London: 1864. V. 38; 39

The Rural Life of England. London: 1838. V. 38; 39; 44

The Rural and Domestic Life of Germany. London: 1842. V. 39; 40; 43

The Student Life of Germany. London: 1841. V. 45

Tallangetta, the Squatter's Home. London: 1857. V. 40; 46

Visits to Remarkable Places: Old Halls, Battle Fields, and Scences Illustrative of Striking Passages in English History and Poetry. London: 1840. V. 45

Visits to Remarkable Places. London: 1840-42. V. 37; 38; 39; 46

HOWLAND, ARTHUR

Materials Toward a History of Witchcraft Collected by Henry Charles Lea. Philadelphia: 1839. V. 45

HOWLAND, E.

Grant as Soldier and Statesman: Being a Succinct History of His Military and Civl Career. London: 1868. V. 38

HOWLAND, E. A., MRS.

The New England Economical Housekeeper and Family Receipt Book. Worcester: 1847. V. 44

HOWLAND, E. P.

A Tale of Home and War. Portland: 1888. V. 38; 39

HOWLAND, RICHARD HUBBARD

Greek Lamps and Their Survivals. Princeton: 1958. V. 44

HOWLAND, S. A.

Steamboat Disasters and Railroad Accidents in the United States . . . Worcester: 1840. V. 38; 46

HOWLET, ROBERT

The School of Recreation: or, Sure Guide to the Most Ingenious Exercises of Hunting, Riding, Racing, Fireworks, Military Discipline, the Science of Defence . . . London: 1710. V. 37

HOWLETT, RICHARD

The School of Recreation; or a Guide to the Most Ingenious Exercises of Hunting, Riding, Racing, Fireworks, Military Discipline, Science of Defence, Hawking, Tennis, Bowling . . . London: 1701. V. 43

HOWLETT, ROBERT

The Angler's Sure Guide; or, Angling Improved and Methodically Digested . . . London: 1706. V. 45

HOWLETT, W. J.

Life of the Right Reverend Joseph P. Machebeauf D.D . . . Pioneer Priest of New Mexico, Pioneer Priest of Colorado . . . Pueblo: 1908. V. 42; 44

HOWLEY, J. P.

The Beothucks or Red Indians: The Aboriginal Inhabitants of Newfoundland. 1915. V. 37

HOWLEY, JAMES P.

The Beothucks or Red Indians. Cambridge: 1915. V. 40; 44

HOWSE, ERNEST MARSHALL

Saints in Politics . . . London: 1952. V. 43

HOWSHIP, JOHN 1728-1793

Hunterian Oration Delivered . . . Royal College of Surgeons . . . London: 1833. V. 39; 40

Practical Observations on the Symptoms, Discrimination, and Treatment of Some of the Most Important Diseases of the Lower Intestines and Anus. London: 1821. V. 40; 42

HOWSON, E. W.

Harrow School. London: 1898. V. 37

HOWSON, J.

Foreign Scenes and Travelling Recreations. Edinburgh: 1825. V. 39

HOY, PATRICK C.

A Brief History of Bradford's Battery, Confederate Guards Artillery. Pontotoe: 1932. V. 44

HOY, WILLIAM

The Chinese Six Companies. San Francisco: 1942. V. 39

HOYEM, ANDREW

What If. Poems: 1967-1987. San Francisco: 1987. V. 39; 42

HOYER, LINDA GRACE

The Papier-Mache Santa Claus. 1983. V. 42

HOYER, M. A.

A Round Robin. London: 1890. V. 44

HOYER, MARIA A.

Good Dame Fortune. London: 1894. V. 41

HOYLAND, FRANCIS

Poems and Translations. London: 1763. V. 40; 42; 45

HOYLAND, JOHN 1750-1831

A Historical Survey of the Customs, Habits and Present State of the Gypsies Designed to Develope the Origin of This Singular People and to Promote the Amelioration of Their Condition. London: 1816. V. 42

A Historical Survey of the Customs, Habits and Present State of The Gypsies. York: 1816. V. 37; 38; 39; 41; 42; 43; 46

History as Direction. London: 1930. V. 38; 41; 45

HOYLE, EDMOND 1672-1759

Hoyle's Games Improved. London: 1775. V. 38

Hoyle's Games Improved. London: 1779. V. 38; 39; 40; 43; 45

Hoyle's Games Improved. Boston: 1814. V. 45

Hoyle's Games Improved. New York: 1821. V. 41

Hoyle's Games Improved being practical treatises on whist, quadrille, piquet, chess, back-gammon, draughts, cricket, tennis, quinze, hazard, lansquenet, billiards, faro, rough & noir, cribbage, matrimony, cassino, goff or golf . . . London: 1796. V. 37; 41

Mr. Hoyle's Games of Whist, Quadrille, Piquet, Chess and Back-Gammon . . . London. V. 44

HOYLE, EDMOND 1672-1759 continued

Mr. Hoyle's Games of Whist, Quadrille, Piquet, Chess and Back-Gammon . . . London: 1763. V. 43

Mr. Hoyle's Games of Whist, Quadrille, Piquet, Chess and Back-Gammon. London: 1765. V. 44

Mr. Hoyle's Games of Whist, Quadrille, Piquet, Chess and Back-Gammon . . . London: 1770. V. 42

Mr. Hoyle's Game of Whist, Quadrille, Piquet, Chess and Backgammon . . . London: 1785? V. 38

Mr. Hoyle's Games of Whist, Quadrille, Picquet, Chess and Backgammon. London: 1769. V. 38; 39

The New Pocket Hoyle, Containing the Games of Whist. London: 1802. V. 38

The New Pocket Hoyle, Containing the Games of Whist, Quadrille, Piquet, Vingt-un (etc.). Philadelphia: 1805. V. 41

The Polite Gamester. Dublin: 1752. V. 41

A Short Treatise on the Game of Whist. Bath printed and: 1743. V. 39

A Short Treatise on the Game of Whist . . . London: 1743. V. 38; 41

A Short Treatise on the Game of Whist . . . London: 1746. V. 38

HOYLE, JOHN

Dictionarium Musica, Being a Complete Dictionary . . . London: 1770. V. 41

HOYLE, RAFAEL LARCO

Checan- Essay on Erotic Elements in Peruvian Art. Geneva: 1965. V. 39

HOYLE, W. E.

Report on the Cephalopoda (of the Challenger Voyage). London: 1886. V. 43

HOYLE, WILLIAM

Crime in England and Wales in the Nineteenth Century. London: 1876. V. 43

HOYM, CHARLES HENRY

Catalogus Librorum Bibliothecae Illustrissimi Viri . . . Comitis de Hoym . . . Descriptius a Gabriele Martin. Paris: 1738. V. 38

HOYT, E.

Rules and Regulations for Drill, Sabre Exercise, Equitation, Formation and Field Movements of Cavalry . . . Greenfield: 1816. V. 42

A Treatise on the Military Art. Brattleborough: 1798. V. 38; 42

HOYT, ELIHU

A Brief Sketch of the First Settlement of Deerfield, Mass. Greenfield: 1833. V. 39; 45

HOYT, EPAPHRAS

Antiquarian Researches: Comprising a History of the Indian Wars in the Country Bordering the Connecticut River and Parts Adjacent . . . Greenfield: 1824. V. 39

Rules and Regulations for Drill, Sabre Exercise, Equitation, Formation and Field Movements of Cavalry. Greenfield: 1813. V. 37

A Treatise on the Military Art in Four Parts. Greenfield: 1798. V. 37

HOYT, GEORGE H.

Kansas and the Osage Swindle. A Letter to Hon. Sidney Clarke. Washington: 1868. V. 39; 43

HOYT, HENRY F.

A Frontier Doctor. Boston: 1929. V. 39

HOYT, JOHN W.

An Agricultural Survey of Wyoming. Washington: 1893. V. 39

HOYT, SHELLEY

The Circus of Most Inventions. Oakland: 1985. V. 39

Typographic Prints 1980 to 1984. Berkeley & Hitchin: 1987. V. 39

HOYTEMA, THEODOOR VAN

The Happy Owls. London: 1896. V. 37

HOZIER, H. M.

The Franco-Prussian War: Its Causes, Incidents and Consequences. London: 1870-72. V. 37; 38

The Russo-Turkish War: Including an Account of the Rise and Decline of the Ottoman Power, and History of the Eastern Question . . . London. V. 44; 46

The Russo-Turkish War . . . London: 1877-79. V. 42

HRDLICKA, ALES

Anthropological Survey in Alaska. By Ales Hrdlicka. Washington: 1930. V. 37

Anthropology of Kodiak Island. Philadelphia: 1944. V. 41

HROTSVIT OF GANDERSHEIM b. ca. 935

Abraham. London: 1922. V. 45

HUARD, CHARLES 1875-1965

Twelve Etchings Made on the Front by Ch. Ch. Huard. N.P.: 1916. V. 37; 40; 45; 46

HUARTE, JUAN

Essame de Gl'Ingegni de Gli Huomini, per Apprender le Scienze . . . Venice: 1582. V. 38

Examen de Ingenios. The Examination of Mens Wits. London: 1616. V. 39

Examen de Ingeinos; or, The Tryal of Wits, Discovering the Great Difference of Wits Among Men, and What Sort of Learning Suits Them . . . London: 1698. V. 39

HUBACH, R. R.

Early Midwestern Travel Negatives. Detroit: 1961. V. 39

HUBBACK, THEODORE R.

To Far Western Alaska for Big Game. London: 1929. V. 38

HUBBARD, ALICE

Garnett and the Brindled Cow, Also Other Mothers, by Alice Hubbard. East Aurora: 1913. V. 37

Life Lessons. East Aurora: 1909. V. 40

Woman's Work, Being an Inquiry and an Assumption by Alice Hubbard. East Aurora: 1908. V. 38; 46

Woman's Work: Being an Inquiry and an Assumption, by Alice Hubbard. East Aurora, NY: 1908. V. 37

HUBBARD, ELBERT 1856-1915

The City of Tagaste. 1900. V. 39; 40; 43

The Complete Writings of Elbert Hubbard. East Aurora: 1908-15. V. 46

Contemplations. 1902. V. 43

The Doctors. East Aurora: 1909. V. 37; 41

Justinian and Theodora. East Aurora: 1906. V. 38; 41; 45

Little Journeys to the Homes of Famous Women. East Aurora: 1898. V. 41

Little Journeys to the Homes of English Authors - S. T. Coleridge. East Aurora: 1900. V. 37; 38; 46

Little Journeys to the Homes of English Authors. Volume Six, New Series (Book 1) with Volume Seven, New Series (Book 2). East Aurora: 1900. V. 41

Little Journeys to the Homes of Great Musicians. New York: 1901. V. 41

Little Journeys to the Homes of the Great . . . New York & Chicago: 1916. V. 38

The Man of Sorrows. East Aurora: 1904. V. 40

A Message to Garcia. East Aurora. V. 46

A Message to Garcia and Thirteen Other Things. East Aurora: 1901. V. 44

This Then is A William Morris Book . . . East Aurora: 1907. V. 37

Old John Burroughs. East Aurora: 1901. V. 40

Pig-Pen Peter; or Some Chums of Mine . . . East Aurora: 1914. V. 40

Thomas Jefferson: a Little Journey . . . and an Address. East Aurora: 1906. V. 44

The Complete Writings of Elbert Hubbard. East Aurora: 1908-15. V. 38

The Complete Writings. East Aurora: 1914. V. 42

HUBBARD, GARDINER GREEN

Catalog of the Gardiner Green Hubbard Collection of Engravings. Presented to the Library of Congress by Mrs. Gardiner Green Hubbard. Washington: 1905. V. 41

HUBBARD, GURDON S.

Incidents and Events . . . Collected from Personal Narrations and Other Sources. Chicago: 1888. V. 42

HUBBARD, J. H.

Jane Austen's Sailor Brothers Biography of Two British Adrmirals, Naval Action from 1775 to 1848 . . . London: 1906. V. 42

HUBBARD, J. NILES

An Account of Sa-go-Ye-Wat-Ha, or Red Jacket and His People 1750-1830. Albany: 1886. V. 43; 45

HUBBARD, JEREMIAH

Forty Years Among the Indians. Miami: 1913. V. 39; 40; 42; 43

HUBBARD, JOHN

Sketches of Border Adventures in the Life and Times of Major Moses Van Campen, a Surviving Soldier of the Revolution. Bath: 1842. V. 37; 38; 46

HUBBARD, JOHN GELLIBRAND 1805-1889

The Currency and the Country. London: 1843. V. 41

HUBBARD, L. RON

Battlefield Earth. New York: 1982. V. 46

Buckskin Brigades. 1937. V. 45

HUBBARD, L. RON continued

Death's Deputy. 1948. V. 43; 44; 45

Dianetics. 1950. V. 43

Dianetics, the Modern Science of Mental Health. New York: 1950. V. 38; 39; 46

Dianetics. 1951. V. 43

Final Blackout. 1947. V. 39

Final Blackout. 1948. V. 43

From Death to the Stars. 1953. V. 44

The Kingslayer. 1949. V. 43

The Kingslayer. Los Angeles: 1949. V. 37

Slaves of Sleep. 1948. V. 44

Slaves of Sleep. Chicago: 1948. V. 37; 44

A Test of Whole Track Recall. 1968. V. 46

Triton & Battle of Wizards. 1949. V. 43

Typewriter in the Sky and Fear. New York: 1951. V. 42; 46

HUBBARD, LEONIDAS

A Woman's Way through Unknown Labrador. London: 1908. V. 44

HUBBARD, LUCIUS

Contributions Towards a Bibliography of Gulliver's Travels . . . Chicago: 1922. V. 42; 44

HUBBARD, R. B.

Oration of Gov. R. B. Hubbard of Texas, Delivered at Philadelphia at the United States Centennial Exposition. St. Louis: 1876. V. 41; 43

The United States in the Far East; or, Modern Japan and the Orient. Richmond: 1899. V. 39

HUBBARD, R. H.

Catalogue of Printing and Sculpture. Volume III: Canadian School. Ottawa: 1960. V. 43

HUBBARD, ROBERT

Historical Sketches of Roswell Franklin and Family. Dansville: 1839. V. 44; 45

Historical Sketches of Roswell Franklin and Family. New York: 1839. V. 45

HUBBARD, WILLIAM

The History of the Indian Wars in New England from the First Settlement to the Terminataion of the War with King Philip, in 1677. Roxbury: 1865. V. 37; 38; 43; 45

A Narrative of the Indian Wars in New England, from the First Planting Thereof in the Years 1607, to the Year 1677 . . . Worcester: 1801. V. 39

A Narrative of the Indian Wars in New England, from the First Planting Thereof in the Year 1607, to the Year 1677. Norwich: 1802. V. 42

A Narrative of the Indian Wars in New England, from the First Planting Thereo in the Year 1607, to the Year 1677. Brattleborough: 1814. V. 37

A Narrative of the Indian Wars in New-England, From the First Planting Thereof in the Year 1607, to the Year 1677. Boston: 1775. V. 37; 38

The Present State of New England . . . London: 1677. V. 43

HUBBELL, ALVIN A.

The Development of Ophthalmology in America, 1800 to 1870. Chicago: 1908. V. 39

HUBER, FRANCOIS

Nouvelles Observations sur les Abeilles, Adresses a M. Charles Bonnet. Geneve: 1792. V. 43

HUBER, JEAN PIERRE

The Natural History of Ants . . . London: 1820. V. 41

HUBER, VICTOR AIME

The English Universities. London: 1843. V. 38

HUBERT, GEORGE

South Sea Bubbles. By the Earl and the Doctor. London: 1872. V. 40

HUBLEY, BERNARD

The History of the American Revolution, Including the Most Importat Events and Resolutions of the Honourable Continental Congress During that Period and . . . Northumberland: 1805. V. 39; 43; 44; 45

HUBLY, RUSSELL C.

'G' Company, or Every-Day Life of the R. C.R. Montreal: 1902. V. 40

HUBNER, JOHANN

Curieuses Natur-Kunst-Gewerckund Handlungslexicon. Leipzig: 1712. V. 45

HUBNER, LE BARON DE

A Ramble Round the World. London: 1874. V. 39

HUC, E. R.

The Chinese Empire. London: 1855. V. 45

HUC, EVARISTE-REGIS

Travels in Tartary, Thibet and China. London: 1851-52. V. 38

HUC, M.

A Journey through the Chinese Empire. New York: 1856. V. 42

Travels in Tartary, Thibet and China During the Years 1844-5-6. 1850. V. 42

Travels in Tartary, Thibet, and China, during the years 1844-5-6. Translated from the French by W. hazlitt. (In Two Volumes). Illustrated with fifty engravings on wood. London: (1852). V. 37

HUCBALDUS

Egloga de Caluis. in Qua ab Una Littera. c. Singulae Dictiones Incipiunt. Erfurt: 1501. V. 40

HUCKE, AGNES

A Tale of Ten Little Toys. New York: 1920's. V. 46

HUCKELL, JOHN

Avon. Birmingham: 1758. V. 37; 38; 39; 45

HUCKS, J.

Poems by J. Hucks, A.M. Fellow of Catharine Hall, Cambridge. Cambridge: 1798. V. 43

HUDDART, JOSEPH

Memoirs of the Late Captain Joseph Huddart, F.R.S. London: 1821. V. 38

The Oriental Navigator. London: 1801. V. 40

The Oriental Navigator, or Directions for Sailing to and From the East Indies . . . Philadelphia: 1801. V. 42

HUDDESFORD, GEORGE

Bubble and Squeak, a Galli-Maufry of British Beef with Chopp'd Cabbage of Allic Philosophy and a Radical Reform. (with) Crambe Repetita, a Second Course of Bubble and Squake . . . London: 1799. V. 39

The Poems of . . . London: 1801. V. 37; 45

The Scum Uppermost When the Middlesex Porridge-Pot Boils Over!! London: 1802. V. 42

Topsy Turvy: With Anecdotes and Observations Illustrative of Leading Characters in the Present Government of France. London: 1793. V. 42

The Wiccamical Chaplet, a Selection of Original Poetry . . . London: 1804. V. 43

HUDLESTON, F. J.

Catalogue of the War Office Library. London: 1906-41. V. 44

HUDSON AND CLARK

A Catalogue of all the Genuine Stock of Cutlery, Hardware, Japaned Goods, &c. of Messrs. Hudson and Clark (leaving of business), Removed from Their Late House in Welclose Square, Which Will be Sold by Auction by Mr. Paullin . . . May 21, 1805 . . . London: 1805. V. 39

HUDSON, ANNE

English Wycliffite Sermons. 1983/88. V. 44

HUDSON, C. T.

The Rotifera; or Wheel-animalcules . . . London: 1868. V. 45

The Rotifera or Wheel Animacules. London: 1886-89. V. 42; 43; 46

HUDSON, CHARLES

Where There's a Will There's a Way; an Ascent of Mont Blanc by a New Route and Without Guides. London: 1856. V. 43

HUDSON, DAVID

History of Jemima Wilkinson, a Preacheress of the Eighteenth Century. Geneva: 1821. V. 40; 44

History of Jemima Wilkinson, a Preacheress of the Eighteenth Century. Geneva: 1822. V. 40

Memoir of Jemima Wilkinson, Preacheress of the Eighteenth Century . . . Bath: 1844. V. 46

HUDSON, DEREK

Arthur Rackham: His Life and Work. London: 1960. V. 38; 40

Arthur Rackham: His Life and Work. New York: 1960. V. 41; 45

Sir Joshua Reynolds. London: 1958. V. 40

HUDSON, HOBART

Dr. J. H. Barnard's Journal. Dec. 1835-June 1836. 1950. V. 44

HUDSON, J. K.

Letters to Governor Lewelling . . . Topeka: 1893. V. 44

HUDSON, JOHN

The Case and Appeal of John Hudson, one of the officers of His Majesty's Revenue of Excise; who was tried at the Old Bailey, in December 1779, upon a charge of commiting a robbery in the shop of Robert Davis, grocer. To which is added the whole . . . London: 1781. V. 37

The Florist's Companion. Newcastle-upon-Tyne: 1794. V. 46

HUDSON, JOSEPH

Remarks Upon the History of the Landed and Commercial Policy of England, from the Invasion of the Romans to the Accession of James the First. London: 1785. V. 37; 39

HUDSON, JOSHUA HILARY

Sketches and Reminiscences. Columbia: 1903. V. 41; 42; 45

HUDSON, MARIANNE SPENCER

Almack's: a Novel. London: 1826. V. 44

HUDSON, PETER

A New Introduction to Trade and Business, Very Useful for Youth of Both Sexes. London: 1809. V. 39

HUDSON, T. S.

A Scamper Through America. London: 1882. V. 38

HUDSON, THOMAS

Poems on Several Occasions. Newcastle-upon-Tyne: 1752. V. 41; 42

HUDSON, TRAVIS

The Material Culture of the Chumash Interaction Sphere. Los Altos: 1982. V. 46

The Material Culture of the Chumash Interaction Sphere. Los Altos & Santa Barbara: 1982. V. 46

HUDSON, WILLIAM

Flora Anglicana: . . . Londini: 1778. V. 44

Flora Anglica. London: 1778. V. 39; 42

HUDSON, WILLIAM HENRY 1841-1922

Adventures Among Birds. London: 1913. V. 37

Afoot in England. London: 1909. V. 44

Birds of La Plata. London: 1920. V. 37; 39; 42; 44; 46

Birds and Man. London: 1901. V. 42; 44

Birds and Man. London: 1915. V. 37

Birds from My Homeland. New York: 1958. V. 44

Birds in a Village. London: 1893. V. 37; 46

Birds in London. London: 1898. V. 37; 41; 44; 46

Birds in Town and Village. London: 1919. V. 37

Birds of La Plata. London & Toronto: 1920. V. 37

Birds of La Plata. London: & Toronto: J. M.: 1920. V. 44

The Collected Works of . . . London: 1922-23. V. 40; 42

The Collected Works of William Henry Hudson. London: 1923-24. V. 45

A Crystal Age. London: 1887. V. 41; 44; 46

Dead Man's Plack and An Old Thorn. London: 1920. V. 37; 41; 45

Fan. The Story of a Young Girl's Life. London: 1892. V. 37; 39; 40; 43

Fan. New York: 1926. V. 44

Far Away and Long Ago. London: 1918. V. 37; 38; 41; 42

Far Away and Long Ago. New York: 1918. V. 39

Far Away and Long Ago. Buenos Aires: 1943. V. 39; 43; 45

Far Away and Long Ago. London: 1931. V. 37

Gauchos of the Pampas and the Horses. Hanover: 1963. V. 40

Gauchos of the Pampas and Their Horses. Hanover, N.H.: 1963. V. 37

Green Mansions. London: 1904. V. 37; 39; 40; 43; 44; 46

Green Mansions. London: 1926. V. 39; 44

Green Mansions. Philadelphia: 1935. V. 45

Hampshire Days. London: 1903. V. 40; 44

Idle Days in Patagonia. London: 1893. V. 37; 39; 40; 42; 44

Idle Days in Patagonia. London: 1921. V. 37

The Land's End. London: 1908. V. 41; 44

The Land's End: a Naturalist's Impressions in West Cornwall. New York: 1908. V. 44

A Little Boy Lost. London: 1905. V. 37; 40; 41; 42; 43; 44

A Little Boy Lost. New York: 1920. V. 40; 41; 43

A Little Boy Lost. New York: 1929/c. 1920. V. 46

Men, Books and Birds. London: 1925. V. 44

The Naturalist in La Plata. London: 1892. V. 41; 43; 44

The Naturalist in La Plata. London: 1895. V. 39

The Naturalist in La Plata. London & New York: 1895. V. 40

The Naturalist in La Plata. London: 1903. V. 41

Nature in Downland. London: 1900. V. 37; 41; 42; 43; 44

El Ombu. London: 1902. V. 39; 42

153 Letters from . . . London: 1923. V. 38

The Purple Land That England Lost. London: 1885. V. 39; 40; 41; 44

The Purple Land. London: 1904. V. 37; 41

The Purple Land. London: 1929. V. 41

A Quiet Corner in a Library. Chicago: 1915. V. 40

Ralph Herne. New York: 1923. V. 44

Rare Vanishing and Lost British Birds. London: & Toronto: 1923. V. 44

Seagulls in London. N.P.: 1922. V. 46

A Shepherd's Life. 1977. V. 42

A Shepherd's Life. London: 1977. V. 42

A Shepherd's Life. Tisbury: 1977. V. 38

Tales of the Pampas. New York: 1916. V. 37

A Traveller in Little Things. London: 1921. V. 37; 41; 42; 43; 44

W. H. Hudson's Letters to R. B. Cunninghame Graham - with a Few to Cunninghame Graham's Mother Mrs. Bontine. London: 1941. V. 41

Complete Works. London: 1922-23. V. 37; 42; 44

Complete Works. London: 1922-23. V. 46

The Collected Works. London: 1922-23. V. 38; 42

Works of . . . London: 1922-29. V. 39

Collected Works. London: 1923. V. 39

HUDSON'S BAY COMPANY

Black's Rocky Mountain Journal 1824. London: 1955. V. 40

Copy-Book of Letters Outward &c. Begins 29th May, 1860; Ends 5 July, 1867. 1948. V. 40

Cumberland House Journals and Inland Journal 1775-82. First Series 1775-79. London: 1951. V. 40

Cumberland House Journals and Inland Journals 1775-82. Second Series 1779-82. London: 1952. V. 40

The History of the Hudson's Bay Company, 1670-1870. Volume One 1670-1763; Volume Two: 1763-1870. London: 1958-59. V. 40

Minutes of the Hudson's Bay Company 1679-1684. First Part 1679-82. London: 1945. V. 43

Minutes of Council, Northern Department of Rupert Land, 1821-1831. 1940. V. 40

Minutes of the Hudson's Bay Company, 1679-84. First Part, 1679-182. 1945. V. 40

Minutes of the Hudson's Bay Company, 1679-84. Second Part 1682-84. 1946. V. 40

Moose Fort Journals 1783-1785. London: 1954. V. 39; 42; 46

Ogden's Snake Country Journals, 1824-26. London: 1950. V. 40

Rae's Arctic Correspondence 1844-45. London: 1953. V. 40

A HUE and Cry After Beauty and Virtue. London: 1680. V. 38

HUES, ROBERT

Traicte des Globes, et de levr vsage. Paris: 1618. V. 44

HUESTIS, G. O.

Memorials of Wesleyan Missionaries and Ministers, Who Have Died Withing the Bounds of the Conference of Eastern British America, Since the Introduction of Methodism Into These Colonies. Halifax: 1872. V. 46

HUET, PIERRE DANIEL

Comercio de Holanda, o el Gran Thesoro Historial, y Politico del Florecinte Comercio que los Holandeses Tienen en Todos los Estados . . . Madrid: 1746. V. 45

The History of Romances. London: 1715. V. 42

The History of the Commerce and Navigation of the Ancients. London: 1717. V. 39; 42; 46

Traitte de la Situation du Paradis Terrestre. Paris: 1691. V. 38

HUFELAND, CHRISTOPH WILHELM 1762-1836

Die Kunst Das Menschliche Leben Zu Verlaengern. Jena: 1797. V. 38

HUGER, ELIZABETH PINCKNEY

Statement of the Attempted Rescue of General Lafayette from 'Olmutz'. Charleston: 1881? V. 46

HUGH, ALFRED H.

Catalogue of the Fifty Manuscripts and Printed Books Bequeathed to the British Museum by Alfred H. Huth. London: 1912. V. 42

HUGH Mac Diarmid, Selected Lyrics. Frenich, Foss: 1967. V. 41

HUGH MacDiarmid, Selected Lyrics. 1967. V. 46

HUGHES, CHARLES

The Compleat Horseman; or, the Art of Riding Made Easy. London: 1772. V. 38

HUGHES, DOROTHY B.

The So Blue Marble. New York: 1940. V. 46

HUGHES, EDITH W.

Motoring in White from Dakota to Cape Cod. New York: 1917. V. 38

HUGHES, ELIZABETH

The California of the Padres; or, Footprints of Ancient Communism. San Francisco: 1875. V. 38; 39; 45

HUGHES, GEORGE W.

Memoir Descriptive of the March of a Division of the United States Army, Under the Command of Brigadier General John E. Wool. Washington: 1846. V. 43; 46

Operations of the Army in Texas and Adjacent Mexican States. Washington: 1850. V. 37; 38; 39; 42; 43; 46

HUGHES, GRAHAM

Modern Jewelry. An International Survey 1890-1963. New York: 1963. V. 41

HUGHES, GRIFFITH fl. 1750

The Natural History of Barbados. London: 1750. V. 37; 39; 40; 42; 43; 45

HUGHES, H. D.

A History of Durham Cathedral Library. Durham: 1925. V. 44

HUGHES, HERBERT 1882-1937

The Joyce Book. London. V. 40

HUGHES, JOHN

The Boscobel Tracts. Edinburgh: 1830. V. 44

A Discussion of the Question, is the Roman Catholic Religion . . . Philadelphia: 1836. V. 43

The Ecstasy. London: 1720. V. 37; 45

An Ode to the Creator of the World. London: 1713. V. 38

Poems on Several Occasions. London: 1735. V. 38; 42; 45

HUGHES, JOHN CEIRIOG

Caneuon Ceiriog: Detholiad. Newtown: 1925. V. 41; 43; 45

HUGHES, JOHN TAYLOR

Doniphan's Expedition . . . Cincinnati. V. 39

Doniphan's Expedition: Containing an Account of the Conquest of New Mexico . . . Cincinnati: 1847. V. 43

Doniphan's Expedition. Cincinnati: 1848. V. 37; 38; 39; 40; 41; 42; 43; 44

Doniphan's Expedition. Cincinnati: 1851. V. 39

Doniphan's Expedition. Washington: 1914. V. 38

HUGHES, JOHN W.

The Trial of Dr. John W. Hughes, for the Murder of Miss Tamzen Parsons, with a Sketch of His Life, as Related by Himself. Cleveland: 1866. V. 40

HUGHES, JOSIAH

Australia Revisited in 1890, and Excursions to Egypt, Tasmania and New Zealand . . . Bangor: 1891. V. 46

HUGHES, LANGSTON

Ask Your Mama. New York: 1961. V. 42; 46

The Big Sea. New York: 1940. V. 43; 45

Black Magic. Englewood Cliffs: 1967. V. 42; 43

The Dream Keeper and Other Poems. New York: 1932. V. 43

Emperor of Haiti: an Historical Drama . . . N.P.: 1949. V. 43

Fields of Wonder. New York: 1947. V. 42

Fight for Freedom. New York: 1962. V. 39

Fine Clothes to the Jew. New York: 1927. V. 41

The First Book of Jazz . . . New York: 1955. V. 42

Four Negro Poets. New York: 1927. V. 42

Freedom's Plow. New York: 1943. V. 38; 39; 40; 42; 44; 46

I Wonder as I Wander. New York: 1956. V. 40; 42

Jim Crow's Last Stand. New York: 1943. V. 43

A New Song. New York: 1938. V. 38; 39; 40; 42; 44

New Negro Poets. Bloomington: 1964. V. 44

Not Without Laughter. New York: 1933. V. 45

Not Without Laughter. London/New York: 1930. V. 37

The Poetry of the Negro 1746-1949. Garden City: 1949. V. 41

Shakespeare in Harlem. New York: 1942. V. 41; 42

Shakespeare in Harlem. New York: 1947. V. 43

Simple Speaks His Mind. New York: 1950. V. 43; 46

Simple Takes a Wife. New York: 1953. V. 45

Simple Stakes a Claim. New York: 1957. V. 43; 46

Simple Takes a Wife. 1953. V. 43

Simple's Uncle Sam. New York: 1965. V. 43

The Sweet Flypaper of Life. New York: 1955. V. 39; 46

Tambourines to Glory. New York: 1958. V. 41; 46

The Ways of White Folks. London: 1934. V. 42

The Weary Blues. New York: 1926. V. 45; 46

HUGHES, R. E.

That Kentucky Campaign; or, the Law, the Ballot, and the People in the Goebel-Taylor Contest. Cincinnati: 1900. V. 46

HUGHES, RICHARD

Confessio Juvenis; Collected Poems. London: 1926. V. 37; 41

Ecstatic Ode on Vision. London: 1925. V. 46

The Fox in the Attic. London: 1961. V. 41

Gipsy-Night. Berkshire: 1922. V. 37; 43

Gipsy-Night and Other Poems. Chicago: 1922. V. 37

A High Wind in Jamaica. V. 37; 40; 42

A High Wind in Jamaica. 1929. V. 45

A High Wind in Jamaica. London: 1929. V. 37; 39; 42; 43; 46

The Innocent Voyage. 1944. V. 45

The Innocent Voyage. New York: 1944. V. 46

The Relation of Nationalism to Literature. London: 1932. V. 40

The Scouring of the White Horse. Cambridge: 1859. V. 41; 43; 44

The Sisters' Tragedy. Oxford: 1922. V. 37; 40

The Spider's Palace and Other Stories. London: 1931. V. 42

HUGHES, RICHARD B.

Pioneer Years in the Black Hills. Glendale: 1957. V. 37; 43

HUGHES, ROBERT

A Catalogue of the Genuine and Most Curious Collection of Sardonyx's . . . and Other Oriental Stones, Antique Cameo's and Intaglia's in Rings, Pictures and Miniatures, Curious Mathemataical and Optical Instruments. London: 1770. V. 38; 40

Coberley Hall. Cheltenham: 1824. V. 46

HUGHES, ROBERT E.

Two Summer Cruises with the Baltic Fleet, in 1854-5 . . . London: 1855. V. 38; 46

HUGHES, ROBERT M.

General Johnston. New York: 1893. V. 41; 42

HUGHES, ROSA PHILLIPS

Rebel on a Ranch. Dallas: 1915? V. 38

HUGHES-STANTON, BLAIR

*Pastoral or Virtue Requited, by H.H.M. (Higham): (1935). V. 37

HUGHES, SUKEY

Washi, the World of Japanese Paper. Tokyo: 1978. V. 38; 40; 41

Washi, the world of Japanese paper. Tokyo: (1978). V. 37

HUGHES, T. P.

Notes on Muhammadanism . . . London: 1875. V. 44

HUGHES, T. S.

The History of England, from the Accession of George III, 1760 to the Accession of Queen Victoria 1837. London: 1846. V. 46

HUGHES, TED 1930-

Adam and the Sacred Nine. London: 1978. V. 37; 41; 43

Adam and the Sacred Nine: Poems. 1979. V. 40

Adam and the Sacred Nine. (1929). V. 37

Animal Poems. 1967. V. 38

Animal Poems. London: 1967. V. 38

The Burning of the Brothel: a Poem. London: 1966. V. 41

Capriccio. Leeds: 1990. V. 45

The Cave Birds. 1975. V. 38

Cave Birds. London: 1975, 1979. V. 42

Cave Birds: an Alchemical Cave Drama. London: 1978. V. 41

Chiasmadon. 1977. V. 41

Chiasmadon. Maryland: 1977. V. 40

Couples Under Cover. London: 1979. V. 40

Crow: Poems. London: 1970. V. 41; 43

Crow Wakes. Woodford Green: 1971. V. 38; 40

Crow. London: 1973. V. 38; 39; 41; 42

The Earth-Owl and Other Moon-People. London: 1963. V. 38; 43

Earth-Moon. London: 1976. V. 38

Eat Crow. London: 1971. V. 40; 43; 44

February 17th. London: 1979. V. 40; 41

A Few Crows. Exeter: 1970. V. 38

Five Autumn Songs for Children's Voices. London: 1969. V. 40

Fly Inspects. London: 1983. V. 41

Four Tales Told by an Idiot. 1979. V. 41; 42; 43; 44; 46

From the Life and Songs of the Crow. London: 1973. V. 44

Gaudete. London: 1977. V. 38

The Hawk in the Rain. London: 1957. V. 39; 40; 43; 44; 46

The Hawk in the Rain. New York: 1957. V. 37; 38; 40; 42; 43; 44

Henry Williamson: A Tribute by Ted Hughes. London: 1977. V. 38

HUGHES, TED 1930- continued

Henry Williamson. London: 1979. V. 38; 41

How the Whale Became and Other Stories. London: 1963. V. 46

How the Whale Became. New York: 1966. V. 38

In the Little Girl's Angel Gaze. London: 1972. V. 44

Inspects. 1983. V. 42

The Iron Man. London: 1985. V. 46

Lupercal: Poems. London: 1959. V. 43

Lupercal. 1960. V. 38

Lupercal. London: 1960. V. 42; 44; 46

The Martyrdom of Bishop Farrar. N.P.: 1970. V. 38

Mice are Funny Little Creatures. 1983. V. 42

Mice are Funny Little Creatures. London: 1983. V. 41

Moortown Elegies: Thirty Four Poems. 1978. V. 40

Moortown. London: 1979. V. 38

Moortown Elegies. (N.P.): (1978). V. 37

Nessie the Mannerless Monster. London: 1964. V. 46

Orts. 1978. V. 37

Orts. London: 1978. V. 39

Poetry Is. New York: 1970. V. 46

Poetry From Cambridge, 1952-4. Edited by Karl Miller. Oxford: 1955. V. 37

A Primer of Birds. 1981. V. 39

A Primer of Birds. Devon: 1981. V. 38; 41; 42

A Primer of Birds. Lurley, Devon: 1981. V. 37; 39; 44

Prometheus on His Crag: 21 Poems. London: 1973. V. 46

Ravens. London: 1979. V. 40

Remains of Elmet: Sixty-Two New Poems. 1979. V. 37; 40

Remains of Elmet. London: 1979. V. 39; 40; 41; 42; 43; 44

River. London: 1983. V. 38

Roosting Hawk. N.P.: 1950's. V. 41; 42; 44

Season Songs. London: 1976. V. 37; 38

Shakespeare's Poems. London: 1971. V. 45

Spring Summer Autumn Winter. London: 1973. V. 39

T. S. Eliot: a Tribute. London: 1987. V. 44

Teaching a Dumb Calf. London: 1979. V. 41

The Threshold. London: 1979. V. 39

Weasels at Work. London: 1983. V. 41

Wessels at Work. 1983. V. 42

What is the Truth? London: 1984. V. 41

Wodwo: Poems, Stories and a Play. London: 1967. V. 41

HUGHES, THOMAS

Fifty Years Ago. London & New York: 1891. V. 38

G.T.T. Gone to Texas, Letters from Our Boys. London: 1884. V. 38; 40; 42; 43; 44; 45

G. T. T. Gone to Texas: Letters From Our Boys. New York: 1884. V. 37; 38; 39; 42

History of the Society of Jesus in North America, Colonial and Federal. London: 1908-10. V. 40; 44

A Manual for Co-operators. Prepared at the Request of the Co-operative Congress . . . April, 1879. London: 1881. V. 38

The Old Church; What Shall We Do With It? London: 1878. V. 38

Rugby Tennessee Being Some Account of the Settlement Founded on the Cumberland Plateau by the Board of Aid to Land Ownership, Limited, a Company Incorporated in England . . . London: 1881. V. 37; 38; 42; 43; 45

The Scouring of the White Horse. Cambridge: 1859. V. 37; 40; 42; 44; 46

The Scouring of the White Horse. Cambridge & London: 1859. V. 43

The Scouring of the White Horse . . . London: 1859. V. 41

Tom Brown's School Days. Cambridge: 1857. V. 39; 42

Tom Brown at Oxford. Cambridge: 1861. V. 37; 40; 41; 46

Tom Brown's School Days. London: 1869. V. 42

Tom Brown's School Days. Philadelphia: 1880. V. 44

Tom Brown's School Days. Cambridge: 1957. V. 40

Tracts for Priests and People. No. I. Religio Laici. Cambridge: 1861. V. 38

HUGHES, THOMAS ALOYSIUS 1849-1939

History of the Society of Jesus in North America, Colonial and Federal. London: 1908-10. V. 43; 45

HUGHES, THOMAS S.

Travels in Greece and Albania. London: 1830. V. 37; 39

Travels in Sicily, Greece and Albani. London: 1820. V. 37; 38; 39

HUGHES, TOM

The Remains of Elmet. London: 1979. V. 42

HUGHES, W. J.

Rebellious Ranger; Rip Ford and the Old Southwest. Norman: 1964. V. 42

HUGHES, W. R.

A Week's Tramp in Dickens-Land. London: 1891. V. 43

HUGHES, WENDELL

Reconstructive Surgery of the Eyelids. London: 1851. V. 39

Reconstructive Srugery of the Eyelids. St. Louis: 1943. V. 42

HUGHES, WILLIAM, of Gray's Inn

An Abridgement of the Statutes in Force and Use, Made in the 16th, 17th and 18th Years of the Reign of K. Charles the First, and in the 12th, 13th and 14th Years of the Reign of K. Charles II . . . London: 1663. V. 39

An Atlas of Classical Geography. Philadelphia: 1859. V. 41; 43

The Grand Abridgment of the Law, or a Collection of the Principal Cases and Points of the Common-Law of England . . . London: 1662/3. V. 40

The Practical Angler. London: 1842. V. 39

HUGHES, WILLIAM CARTER

The Ameri. V. 41

The American Miller, and Mill-Wright's Assistant. Detroit: 1850. V. 39; 41

HUGHES, WILLIAM EDGAR 1840-

The Journal of a Grandfather. St. Louis: 1912. V. 41; 42; 43; 44; 45

HUGHES, WILLIAM R.

A Week's Tramp in Dickens-Land. London: 1893. V. 40

HUGHS, FANNIE MAY BARBEE

Legends of Texas Rivers and Sagas of the Lone Star State. 1937. V. 42

HUGHS, MARY ROBSON

The Orphan Girl. Phildelphia: 1827. V. 38

HUGHSON, D.

the New Family Receipt Book . . . London: 1817. V. 46

HUGHSON, DAVID

London, Being an Accurate History and Description of the British Metropolis and Its Neighborhood, to Thirty Miles Extent . . . London: 1806-09. V. 39

HUGNET, GEORGES

Petite Anthologie Poetique du Surrealisme. Paris: 1934. V. 37

La Sphere de Sable. Illustrations de Jean Arp. Paris: 1943. V. 42

HUGO, ABEL

Histoire de la Campagne d'espagne en 1823. Paris: 1824-25. V. 38

HUGO, H.

De Militia Antiqua et Nova ad Regem Philippum IV. Antwerp: 1630. V. 37

Pia Desideriia, or Divine Addresses in Three Books. London: 1712. V. 46

HUGO, HERMAN

De Militia Eqvestri Antiqva et Nova Libri Qvinqve. Antwerpen: 1630. V. 43

Obsidio Bredana Armis Philippi IIII. Antwerpen: 1626. V. 43

HUGO, HERMANN

Pia Desideria. Antwerp: 1668. V. 38

Pia Desideria. Parisiis: 1670. V. 37

HUGO, HERMANNUS

De Prima Scribendi Origine et Universa rei Literariae Antiquitate, ad Reuserendeum Patrem Carolum . . . Antverpiae: 1617. V. 45

Pieux Desirs Imites des Latins du R. P. Herman Hugo de la Compe de Iesus. Paris: 1627. V. 40

HUGO, RICHARD

The Innocent Voyage. New York: 1944. V. 45

Road Ends a Tahola. Pittsburg: 1978. V. 46

A Run of Jacks. Minneapolis: 1961. V. 45

HUGO, T.

The Descriptive Catalogue of (and supplement to) The Works of Thomas and John Bewick. London: 1856-58. V. 44

HUGO, THOMAS 1820-1876

The Bewick Collector. London: 1866-68. V. 42; 45

HUGO, VICTOR 1802-1865

The Battle of Waterloo. East Aurora: 1907. V. 39

The Battle of Waterloo, from Les Miserables. Connecticut: 1977. V. 43

The Complete Works. London: 1910. V. 46

Hans of Iceland. London: 1825. V. 37; 38; 39; 40; 43

Hernani; or the Honour of a Castilian. London: 1830. V. 38

The Hunchback of Notre Dame. London: 1833. V. 46

The Last Days of a Condemned. London: 1840. V. 42

Le Livre D'Or de Victor Hugo. Paris: 1883. V. 46

HUGO, VICTOR 1802-1865 continued

The Man Who Laughs. New York: 1869. V. 39

Les Miserables. London: 1862. V. 38

Les Miserables. Richmond: 1863-1864. V. 40

Les Miserables. Boston: 1890. V. 39

Les Miserables. New York: 1938. V. 41; 44; 45; 46

Les Miserables. Harmondsworth: 1985. V. 40

Ninety Three. London: 1874. V. 37; 39; 41

Notre Dame de Paris . . . Paris: 1844. V. 46

Notre-Dame de Paris. New York: 1930. V. 38

Nortre-Dame De Paris. Paris: 1930. V. 42; 43; 45

The Novels, Complete and Unabridged. Philadelphia: 1894. V. 42

Novels. Philadelphia: 1895. V. 42; 44; 45

Ruy Blas. Paris: 1838. V. 46

So This Then is the Battle of Waterloo. East Aurora: 1907. V. 46

Toilers of the Sea. London: 1866. V. 38; 40; 42

The Toilers of the Sea. 1960. V. 40

The Toilers of the Sea. New York: 1960. V. 44; 46

The Toilers of the Sea. Verona: 1960. V. 42

The Toilers of the Sea. In the translation by Isabel F. Hapgood and with an introduction by Matthew Josephson. Illustrated with wood engravings by Tranquillo Marangoni. Verona: 1961. V. 37

Oeuvres Completes de Victor Hugo. Paris. V. 44

Works. New York: 1899. V. 37; 39

Works. Boston: 1900. V. 42

The Works. N.P.: 1907. V. 42

THE HUGO Winners. Garden City: 162. V. 45

HUGUENOT SOCIETY OF LONDON

Proceedings, 1887-1952. London. V. 39

Proceedings of the the Huguenot Society of London. London: 1887-1952. V. 42

HUI-MING, WANG

Wang Hui-Ming. (Woodcuts). Northampton: 1968. V. 37

HUIE, JAMES

An Abridgment of All the Statutes Now in Force, Relative to the Revenue of Excise, Methodically Arranged and Alphabetically Digested. Edinburgh: 1797. V. 45

HUIE, RICHARD

A Probationary Essay on Scirrhus and Cancer in General but Particularly as They are Met with in the Female Breasts. Edinburgh: 1822. V. 41

HUIE, WILLIAM BRADFORD

The Revolt of Mamie Stover. New York: 1951. V. 41; 42

HUISH, MARCUS

British Water-Colour Art, in the First Year of the Reign of King Edward the Seventh and During the Century Covered by the Life of the Royal Society of Painters in Water Colours . . . London: 1904. V. 39; 44

HUISH, MARCUS B.

The American Pilgrim's Way in England to Homes and Memorials of the Founder's of Virginia. London: 1907. V. 41

Samplers and Tapestry Embroideries. London: 1913. V. 43

HUISH, ROBERT

An Authentic History of the Coronation of His Majesty, King George the Fourth . . . London: 1821. V. 42

The Improved British Angler. Derby: 1830. V. 42

The Life of William Cobbett. London: 1835. V. 39

The Life of James Greenacre, Who was Executed at the Old Bailey for the brutal Murder of Mrs. Hannah Brown. London: 1837. V. 45

The Religious Ceremonies and Customs of Every Nation of the World. London: 1828. V. 44

HUISMAN, P.

Lautrec by Lautrec. New York: 1964. V. 45

HUISMAN, PHILIPPE

Lautrec by Lautrec. New York: 1976. V. 41

HULBERT, ARCHER B.

Marcus Whitman, Crusader. Denver: 1936/38/41. V. 40

HULBERT, ARCHER BUTLER

Historic Highways of America. Cleveland: 1902-05. V. 38; 39; 41; 46

The Ohio River, a Course of Empire . . . New York: 1906. V. 39

Where Rolls the Oregon: Prophet and Pessimist Look Northwest. Denver: 1933. V. 39

HULBERT, CHARLES

African fragments . . . Shrewsbury: 1826. V. 46

Museum Americanum . . . London: 1823. V. 43

Volcanic Wonders, or, Scenes of Astonishment . . . Shrewsbury: 1827. V. 46

HULET, JOHN

Murder and Suicide. Westmoreland: 1806. V. 41

HULL, A. GERALD

Jahr's New Manual of Homoeopathic Practice. Repertory. New York: 1850. V. 42

Jahr's New Manual of Homoeopathic Practice. Symptomatology. New York: 1851. V. 42

HULL, AUGUSTUS LONGSTREET

The Campaigns of the Confederate Army. Atlanta: 1901. V. 42

HULL, CORDELL

The Memoirs of . . . New York: 1948. V. 38

HULL, EDMUND

Adsonville; or Marrying Out. Albany: 1824. V. 43

HULL, EDWARD

The Coal-Fields of Great Britain. London: 1905. V. 38

Mount Seir, Sinai and Western Palestine Being a Narrative of a Scientific Expedition. London: 1889. V. 43

A Treatise on the Building and Ornamental Stones of Great Britain and Foreign Countries . . . London: 1872. V. 37; 39; 40; 43; 46

HULL, J.

The British Flora. Manchester: 1799. V. 38

HULL, LINDLEY M.

History of Central Washington Including the Famous Wenatchee, Entiat, Chelan and Columbia Valleys. Spokane: 1929. V. 42

HULL, ROBERT

Cursory Notes on the Morbid Eye. London: 1840. V. 40

HULL, THOMAS

Genuine Letters from a Gentleman to a Young Lady His Pupil . . . London: 1772. V. 40

Moral Tales in Verse, Founded on Real Events. London: 1797. V. 37

Richard Plantagenet a Legendary Tale. London: 1774. V. 42

The Royal Merchant: an Opera. London: 1768. V. 38

HULL, WILLIAM

Memoirs of the Campaign of the North Western Army of the United States, A.D. 1812. Boston: 1824. V. 45

Report of the Trial of Brig. General William Hull; Commanding the North-Western ARmy of the United States by a Court Martial Held at Albany on Monday 3d January 1814 and Succeeding Days. New York: 1814. V. 39

HULLAH, JOHN

The History of Modern Music. London: 1862. V. 43

HULLMANDEL, CHARLES

The Art of Drawing on Stone. London: 1824. V. 40; 42

The Art of Drawing on Stone. London: 1835. V. 40

The Art of Drawing on Stone. London: 1894. V. 38

The Art of Drawing on Stone. London: 1833. V. 38; 42

HULLS, JONATHAN

A Description and Draught of a New-Invented Machine . . . London: 1737. V. 38

HULME, E.

Leather for Libraries. London: 1905. V. 41; 44

HULME, F. EDWARD

Familiar Wild Flowers. London. V. 38; 39; 41; 43; 44

Familiar Garden Flowers. Series 1-5. London: 1882-86. V. 46

Familiar Wild Flowers. First, Second, Third, Fourth & Fifth Series. London: 1859-1870. V. 38

Familiar Wild Flowers. London: 1877-85. V. 38

The Flags of the World: Their History, Blazonry and Associations. London: 1899. V. 46

Plants. Their Natural Growth and Ornamental Treatment. London: 1874. V. 42

Principles of Ornamental Art. London: 1875. V. 38

A Series of Sketches from Nature of Plant Form. London: 1868. V. 38

Suggestions in Floral Design. London, Paris & New York: 1870-80. V. 39; 41

Suggestions in Floral Design. Paris & New York: 1870-80. V. 41

HULME, F. EDWARD continued

Suggestions in Floral Design. London: 1878. V. 43

Suggestions in Floral Design. London: 1880. V. 39

HULME, KERI

The Bone People. Auckland & London: 1985. V. 42

The Bone People. Baton Rouge: 1985. V. 42

Te Kaihau: the Windeater. New York: 1987. V. 45

HULME, T. E.

Speculations. London: 1924. V. 41

HULSE, ELIZABETH

A Dictionary of Toronto Printers, Publishers, Booksellers and the Allied Trades 1798-1900. Toronto: c. 1982. V. 37

HULSIUS, LEVINUS

XII Primorum Caesarum et LXIIII Ipsorum Uxorum et Parentum ex Antiquis Numismatibus, in Aere Incisae, Effigies . . . Frankfurt a.M.: 1597. V. 45

Vierte Schiffart. Wahrhafftige Historien. Einer Wunderbaren Schiffart, Welche Ulrich Schmidel von Straubing von Anno 1534 . . . 1554 in American Oder Neuwewelt, bey Brasilia und Rio della Plata Gethan. Nuremberg: 1602. V. 37

HULSKER, JAN

The Complete Van Gogh: Paintings - Drawings - Sketches. New York: 1984. V. 41

HULST, ROGER A. DE

Jordaens Drawings. London: 1974. V. 43; 45

HULTEN, E.

The Circumpolar Plants. Stockholm: 1962/1964-71. V. 37

Flora of Alaska and Yukon. Lund & Leipzig: 1941-50. V. 42

Flora of Alaska and Neighboring Territories . . . Stanford: 1968. V. 45

Flora of Kamtchatka and the Adjacent Islands. Stockholm: 1927-30. V. 37

HULTEN, K. G. PONTUS

Jean Tinguely. 'Meta'. Boston: 1972/75. V. 45

The Machine. As Seen at the End of the Mechanical Age. New York: 1968. V. 39

HULTEN, PONTUS

Brancusi and the Concept of Sculpture. London: 1988. V. 44

HULTON, PAUL

The American Drawings of John White 1577-1590. Chapel Hill: 1964. V. 42

The Work of Jacques Le Moyne de Morgues, a Huguenot Artist in France, Florida and England. London: 1977. V. 38; 40; 44

Work of Jacques Le Moyne De Morgues: A Huguenot Artist In France, Florida & Englnad. Foreword, catalogue & introduction studies by Paul Hulton. (1977). V. 37

HULTON, PAUL HOPE

American Drawings of John White, 1577-15790. London & Chapel Hill: 1946. V. 39

The American Drawings of John White 1577-1590. London: 1964. V. 39; 45

THE HUMANE Review. Volume 1. April, 1900 to January 1901. London: 1901. V. 41

HUMASON, WILLIAM LAWRENCE

From the Atlantic Surf to the Golden Gate, First Trip on the Great Pacific Railroad. Two Days and Nights Among the Mormons. Hartford: 1869. V. 38; 40; 42; 43; 46

HUMBER, W. W.

Orissa. London: 1872. V. 38

HUMBER, WILLIAM

A Comprenhensive Treatise on the Water Supply of Cities and Towns with Numerous Specifications of Exisiting Waterworks. London: 1876. V. 40; 41; 43

A Comprehensive Treatise on the Water Supply of Cities and Towns . . . . Chicago: 1879. V. 38; 41; 43; 46

A Record of the Progress of Modern Engineering. London: 1865. V. 37; 39; 42; 43

HUMBERTUS DE ROMANIS

Expositio Super Regulam Beati Augustini Episcopi. Expositio Hugonis de S. Victore Super Eandem Regulam Beati Augustini. Hagenau: 1505-06. V. 37

HUMBLE Address of the Archbishop, President of the Convocation of the Province of Canterbury; and of the Bishops and Clergy of the Same Province, in Convocation Assembled; Presented to His Majesty at St. James's on Sat. 23rd of Feb. 1716. London: 1716. V. 41

THE HUMBLE Address of the Lord Mayor, Aldermen and Commons of the City of London in Common Council Assembled . . . to the King's Most Excellent Majesty. London: 1682. V. 42

THE HUMBLE Address of the Publicans of New England, to Which You Please. London: 1691. V. 38; 40; 42; 44

A HUMBLE Petition Offered to the Right Reverend, Honoruable and Worshipfull Estates of This Present Parliament Assembled at Westminster Pallace . . . London: 1606. V. 44

THE HUMBLE Petitions (In Verse) of His Majesties Truly Loyal Protestant Subjects, By Some Called Presbyterians, for a Blessed Reformation. N.P.: 1680. V. 40

THE HUMBLE Remonstrance of the Five-Foot-Highians, Against the Antichristian Practice of Using a Standard in Enlisting of Soldiers. Dublin: 1733. V. 38; 45

THE HUMBLE Representation and Petition of the Justices of Peace, the Grand Juries and Other Well Affected Persons to This Commonwealth, at the General Sessions . . . . for the County Palatine of Chester . . . London: 1651. V. 43

THE HUMBLE Representations, or Addresses, of the . . . Lords Spiritual and Temporal . . . Presented to Her Majesty on Friday the Thirty First of March 1704. And Her Majesty's . . . Answer. London: 1704. V. 37

HUMBOLDT, FRIEDRICH HEINRICH ALEXANDER, BARON VON 1769-1859

Atlas Geographique et Physique du Royaume de la Nouvelle Espagne. Paris: 1811. V. 42; 43

Atlas Geographique et Physique des Regions Equinoxiales du Nouveau Continent. Paris: 1834. V. 42; 43

Cosmos: a Sketch of a Physical Description of the Universe. London: 1870. V. 39; 42

Essai Politique sur la Royaume de la Nouvelle Espagne . . . Paris: 1811. V. 38; 42; 43; 46

Experiences sur le Galvanisme, et en General sur Ilrritation des Fibres Musculaires et Nerveuses. Paris: 1799. V. 37

a Geognostical Essay on the Superposition of Rocks in Both Hemispheres. London: 1823. V. 45

The Island of Cuba, by Alexander Humboldt. New York: 1856. V. 39

The Island of Cuba. New York: 1856. V. 37; 38; 42; 45

Personal Narrative of Travels to the Equinoctial regions of the New Continent, During the Years 1799-1804. London: 1814-20. V. 40

Personal Narrative of Travels to the Equinoctial Regions of the New Continent, During the Years 1799-1804 . . . London: 1814-20. V. 37; 38; 40

Personal Narrative of Travels to the Equinoctial Regions of the New Continent, During the Years 1799-1804. Philadelphia: 1815. V. 37; 38

Personal Narrative of Travels to the Equinoctial Regions of the New Continent, During the Years 1799-1804 . . . London: 1822/25/21/26. V. 45

Personal Narrative of Travels to the Equinoctial Regions of the New Continent, During the Years 7199-1804 . . . London: 1822-29. V. 46

Personal Narrative of Travels to the Equinoctial Regions of America During the Years 1799-1804. London: 1852-53. V. 37

Political Essay on the Kingdom of New Spain. New York: 1811. V. 39; 41

Political Essay of the Kingdom of New Spain. London: 1822. V. 42

Researches, Concerning the Institutions & Monuments of the Ancient Inhabitants of America. London: 1814. V. 37; 38; 40; 41; 45

Selections from the Works of the Baron de Humboldt, Relating to the Climate, Inhabitants, Productions and Mines of Mexico. London: 1824. V. 38; 40; 43

Travels in the South of Europe and in Brazil. London: 1849. V. 41; 45

Versuche uber die Gereizte Muskel - und Nervenfaser Nebst Vermuthungen Uber den Chemischen Process des Lebens in der Their . . . Posen, Dekcer and: 1797. V. 42

Vues des Cordilleres et Monumens des Peuples Indigenes de l'Amerique. Paris;: 1810. V. 42

Views of Nature; or Contemplations on the Sublime Phenomena of Creation; with Scientific Illustrations. London: 1850. V. 40

Voyages aux Regions Equinoxales du Nouveau Continent. Amsterdam: 1971-73. V. 44

Vues des Cordillieres et Monuments des Peuples Indigenes de l'Amerique. Paris: 1816. V. 41

HUME, ALLAN OCTAVIAN

The Game Birds of India, Burmah and Ceylon. Calcutta: 1879-81. V. 43

Nests and Eggs of Indian Birds. London: 1889-90. V. 38

HUME, CYRIL

Cruel Fellowship. New York: 1925. V. 46

Wife of the Centaur. New York: 1923. V. 38

HUME, DAVID 1757-1838

Commentaries on the Law Respecting the Description and Punishment of Crimes. Edinburgh: 1797. V. 39; 40

Commentaries on the Law of Scotland, Respecting Trial for Crimes . . . Edinburgh: 1800. V. 38; 40

Dialogues Concerning Natural Religion. London: 1779. V. 37; 41; 42; 45

Discours Politiques de Monsieur Hume. Dresden: 1755. V. 45

An Enqiury Concerning the Principles of Morals. London: 1751. V. 37; 39; 45

HUME, DAVID 1757-1838 continued

Essays, Moral and Political. Edinburgh: 1742. V. 39

Essays and Treatises on Several Subjects. London: 1758. V. 39; 45; 46

Essays and Treatises on Several Subjects. London: 1764. V. 40; 41; 42; 43; 45

Essays and Treatises on Several Subjects. In two volumes ... Volume I: Containing Essays, Moral, Political and Literary (Volume II. Containing an Enquiry Concerning Human Understanding. An Enquiry Concerning the Principles of Morals and Natural History ... London: 1767. V. 37

Essays and Treatises on Several Subjects. London: 1768. V. 42; 43; 45

Essays and Treatises on Several Subjects in Two Volumes. Volume I Containing Essays, Moral, Political and Literary. Volume II Containing an Enquiry Concerning Human Understanding. London & Edinburgh: 1768. V. 41

Essays and Treatises on Several Subjects. London: 1770. V. 42; 43; 45

Essays and Treatises on Several Subjects. London: 1777. V. 39

Essays and Treatises on Several Subjects. Dublin: 1779. V. 41; 42; 46

Essays and Treatises on Several Subjects. London: 1788. V. 39; 42; 43; 46

Essays and Treatises on Several Subjects. Edinburgh: 1800. V. 45

Essays and Treatises on Several Subjects. Edinburgh: 1804. V. 37; 39; 40; 43; 45

Essays & Treatises on Several Subjects. In Two Volumes. A New Edition. Edinburgh/London: 1804. V. 37

Essays and Treatises on Several Subjects. Edinburgh: 1809. V. 41

Essays on Suicide and the Immortality of the Soul. London: 1783. V. 37; 39

Four Dissertations. 1. The Natural History of Religion. II. Of the Passions. III Of Tragedy. IV. Of the Standard of Taste. London: 1757. V. 37; 38; 41; 45

Histoire de la Maison de Tudor, sur le Trone d'Angelterre ... Amsterdam: 1763. V. 40; 41; 45

The History of England to the Reign of George the Third ... London. V. 45

The History of Great Britain. London: 1757. V. 42; 43; 45

The History of England Under the House of Tudor. London: 1759. V. 44

The History of England. London: 1762. V. 40

The History of England, from the Invasion of Julius Caesar to the Revolution in 1688. London: 1763. V. 42; 45

The History of England. London: 1773. V. 37; 38; 39; 40

The History of England, from the invasion of Julius Caesar to the Revolution in 1688. In eight volumes. A new edition, corrected. To which is added, a complete index. Dublin: 1780. V. 37

The History of England, from the Invasion of Julius Caesar to the Revolution in 1688. London: 1792/93. V. 43; 45

The History of England, from the Invasion of Julius Caesar to the Revolution in 1688. Edinburgh: 1805. V. 41; 45

The History of England from the Invasion of Julius Caesar to the Revolution of 1688. London: 1806. V. 37

The History of England, from the Invasion of Julius Caesar to the Revolution in 1688. London: 1809. V. 43

The History of England. New York: 1810. V. 40

The History of England ... to the Revolution in 1688. London: 1812. V. 40

The History of England, from the Invasion of Julius Caesar, to the Revolution in 1688. London: 1813. V. 39

The History of England from the Invasion of Julius Caesar to the Revolution of 1688. London: 1822. V. 37; 40; 46

The History of England. London: 1823. V. 38

The History of England from the Invasion of Julius Caesar to the Death of George the Second. London: 1825. V. 42

The History of England. Oxford: 1826. V. 42

The History of England. London: 1848. V. 37

History of England. London: 1864-56. V. 39

The History of England from the Invasion of Julius Caesar ... to the Death of George III ... and from the Accession of George III to the Thirty-Sixth Year of the Reign of Queen Victoria ... London: 1872. V. 39

The History of England, from the Invasion of Julias Caesar ... to the Death of George the Second. London: 1790. V. 46

The History of England, from the Invasion of Julius Caesar to the Revolution in 1688. London: 1767. V. 46

Huber die Menschliche Natur aus dem Englischen Nebst Kritischen Versuchen zur Beurtheilung Dieses Werks von Ludwig Heinrich Jakob. Halle: 1790-92. V. 40

A Letter from a Gentleman to His Friend in Edinburgh (1745). Edinburgh: 1967. V. 39

The Letters of David Hume. Oxford: 1969. V. 38

The Life of David Hume, Esq. Written by Himself. London: 1777. V. 37

Pensees Philosohiques, Morales, Critiques, Litteraires et Politiques de M. Hume. A Londres: 1767. V. 45

Pensees Philosophiques, Morales, Critiques, Litteraires et Politiques de M. Hume. Londres: 1767. V. 41

Pensees Philosophiques, Morales, Critiques, Litteraires et Politiques de M. Hume. Londres: Paris?: 1767. V. 41

Philosophical Essays Concerning Human Understanding ... London: 1748. V. 45

Philosophical Essays Concerning Human Understanding. London: 1751. V. 39

The Philosophical Works. Edinburgh: 1826. V. 38

Philosophical Essays Concerning Human Understanding. London: 1748. V. 37

Political Discourses. Edinburgh: 1752. V. 40; 41; 42; 45

Saggi Politici Sopra il Commercio ... Venezia: 1767. V. 39; 41

A Treatise of Human Nature. London: 1739, 1740. V. 39

A Treatise of Human Nature. London: 1817. V. 38; 42; 43; 45

A Treatise of Human Nature: Being an Attempt to Introduce the Experimental Method of Reasoning into Moral Subjects ... London: prtd. for John Noon: 1739, 1740. V. 37

A True Account of the Behaviour and Conduct of Archibald Stewart, Esq ... London: 1748. V. 42

La Vie de David Hume. Londres: 1777. V. 38

Oeuvres Philosophiques de M.D. Hume. London: 1764. V. 40

HUME, F.

For the Defense. 1898. V. 45

HUME, FERGUS W.

The Man With a Secret. London: 1890. V. 44

The Mystery of the Hansom Cab. 1887. V. 39

The Mystery of a Hansom Cab. London: 1887? V. 42; 43

The Mystery of a Hansom Cab. London: 1888. V. 44

HUME, GEORGE H.

Canada As It Is: Comprising Details Relating to the Domestic Policy, Commerce, and Agriculture, of the Upper and Lower Provinces ... New York: 1832. V. 38; 39

HUME, H. HAROLD

Camellias in America. Harrisburg: 1946. V. 46

HUME, JAMES DEACON 1774-1842

The Laws of the Customs. London: 1833. V. 40

HUME, JOSEPH 1777-1855

The Substance of the Speech ... at an Adjourned General Court of the Proprietors of Est India Stock ... in the India House, 19th January 1813 ... London: 1813. V. 38

HUME, MARTIN

The Courtships of Queen Elizabeth. London. V. 42

HUME, PATRICK

Annotations on Milton's Paradise Lost. London: 1695. V. 42

HUME, SOPHIA

An Exhortation to the Inhabitants of the Province of South Carolina, to Bring Their Deeds to the Light of Christ ... Philadelphia: 1748? V. 43

An Exhortation to the Inhabitants of the Province of South Carolina. London: 1752. V. 38; 40; 41; 44

An Exhortation to the Inhabitants of the Province of South Carolina, to Bring Their Deeds to the Light of Christ, in Their Own Consciences ... Dublin: 1754. V. 45

An Exhortation to the Inhabitants of the Province of South-Carolina ... Leedes: 1752. V. 37

An Exhortation to the Inhabitants of the Province of South Carolina to Bring Their Deeds to the Light of Christ, in Their Own Consciences. (with) An Epistle to the Inhabitants of South Carolina; Containing Sundry Observations Proper to be Considered ... London: 1752, 1754. V. 37

HUME, W. F.

The Topography and Geology of the Peninsula of Sinai (South Eastern-Portion). Cairo: 1906. V. 43

HUMELBERGIUS SECUNDUS, DICK, PSEUD.

Apician Morsels. New York: 1829. V. 39; 44

HUMES, THOMAS W.

Second Report to the East Tennessee Relief Assocation at Knoxville ... and the Report of the General Agent ... Knoxville: 1866. V. 46

HUMES, THOMAS WILLIAM

The Loyal Mountaineers of Tennessee. Knoxville: 1888. V. 43; 45

HUMFREVILLE, J. LE

Twenty Years Among the Savage Indians. Hartford: 1897. V. 45

HUMMEL, H. E.

Techniques in Pheromone Research. Berlin: 1984. V. 37

THE HUMOURIST. London: 1763. V. 38

THE HUMOURS of Plymouth. Plymouth: 1780. V. 41

HUMPHREY, A. W. H.

Narrative of a Voyage to Port Phillip and Van Dieman's Land. Melbourne: 1948. V. 41

HUMPHREY, JOHN H.

Roman Circuses: Arenas for Chariot Racing. London: 1986. V. 44

HUMPHREY, MAUD

A Treasury of Stories, Jingles and Rhymes. New York: (c. 1894). V. 37

HUMPHREY, OMAR

Wreck of the Rainier: a Sailor's Narrative. Portland: 1887. V. 41; 42

HUMPHREY, WILLIAM

The Last Husband. New York: 1953. V. 41; 42

HUMPHREYS, A. A.

Preliminary Report Concerning Explorations and Surveys Principally in Nevada and Arizona. Washington: 1871. V. 40

Report Upon the Physics and Hydraulics of the Mississippi River . . . Washington: 1876. V. 38; 42

HUMPHREYS, A. L.

A Handbook to County Bibliography, Being a Bibliography of Bibliographies Relating to the Counties and Towns of Great Britain and Ireland. London: 1917. V. 45

Old Decorative Maps and Charts. London: 1926. V. 45

HUMPHREYS, ANDREW ATKINSON

Report Upon the Physics and Hydraulics of the Mississippi River; Upon the Protection of the Alluvial Region Against Overflow; and Upon the Deepening of the Mouths . . . Philadelphia: 1861. V. 37; 38; 39; 42; 43

Report Upon the Physics and Hydraulics of the Mississippi River . . . Washington: 1867. V. 43

Preliminary Report Concerning Explorations and Surveys Principally in Nevada and Arizona. Washington: 1872. V. 37

HUMPHREYS, ARTHUR L.

Buckleberry. A Berkshire Parish the Home of Bolingbroke 1701-1715. Reading: 1932. V. 43

Bucklebury. A Berkshire Parish the Home of Bolingbroke 1701-1715. London: 1932. V. 37

A Handbook to County Bibliography, being a Bibliography of Bibliographies relating to the Counties and Towns of Great Britain and Ireland. 1917. V. 37

HUMPHREYS, ARTHUR LEE

Old Decorative Maps and Charts. London & New York: 1926. V. 39; 41; 43

HUMPHREYS, DAVID

Discours en vers, Adresse aux Officiers et aux Soldats des Differentes Armees Americaines. Paris: 1786. V. 40

An Essay on the Life and Late Honorable Major General Israel Putnam. Catskill: 1796. V. 40

An Essay on the Life of the Honorable Major-General Israel Putnam: Addressed to the State Society of the Cincinnati in Connecticut. Hartfod: 1788. V. 37

An Historical Account of the Incorporated Society for the Propagation of the Gospel in Foreign Parts. London: 1730. V. 37; 38; 39; 42; 43; 44; 46

The Miscellaneous Works. New York: 1790. V. 38; 39

The Miscellaneous Works of David Humphreys, Late Minister Plenipotentiary from the United States of America to the Court of Madrid. New York: 1804. V. 37; 42

A Poem on the Happiness of America; Addressed to the Citizens of the United States. London: 1790. V. 46

A Poem on Industry. Addressed to the Citizens of the United States of America. Philadelphia: 1794. V. 40

Poems by Col. David Humphreys, Late Aide-de-Camp to His Excellency General Washington. Philadelphia: 1789. V. 40

HUMPHREYS, EMYR

The Kingdom of Bran. 1979. V. 40; 45

Pwyll a Riannon. 1980. V. 40; 45

HUMPHREYS, FRANK L.

Life and Times of David Humphreys . . . New York: 1917. V. 46

HUMPHREYS, HENRY NOEL 1810-1879

Ancient Coins and Medals. London: 1850. V. 39

The Art of Illumination and Missal Painting. London: 1849. V. 39; 42; 43

British Butterflies and Their Transformations. London: 1841. V. 37; 43

British Butterflies and Their Transformations. (with) British Moths and Their Transformations. London: 1841-45. V. 38

British Moths and Their Transformations. London: 1845. V. 46

British Butterflies and Their Transformations. London: 1848. V. 46

British Butterflies and their Transformations. London: 1857. V. 41

The Butterfly Vivarium. London: 1858. V. 38

The Coinage of the British Empire. London: 1861. V. 39

The Coinage of the British Empire. London: 1863. V. 41

The Coinage of the British Empire. London: 1868. V. 39

The Coins of England . . . London: 1848. V. 43

The Genera of British Moths. London: 1860. V. 37; 39; 41; 46

The Genera of British Moths. London: (1860). V. 37

Hans Holbein's Celebrated Dance of Death . . . London: 1868. V. 41

A History of the Art of Printing From Its Invention to Its Wide-Spread Development in the Middle of the Sixteenth Century. London: 1867. V. 44

A History of the Art of Printing. London: 1868. V. 37; 38; 39; 40; 43; 45

A History of the art of printing from its invention to its widespread development in the middle of the 16the century. Preseded by a short account of the origin of the alphabet, and of the successive methods of recording events . . . 1868. V. 37

Illuminated Illustrations of Froissart. London: 1845. V. 42; 44

The Illuminated Books of the Middle Ages. London: 1849. V. 41; 43

Masterpieces of the Early Printers and Engravers. London: 1870. V. 37; 41; 44; 45

Masterpieces of the early printers & engravers. A series of facsimiles from rare and curious books, remarkable for illustrative devices, beautiful borders, decorative initials, printers' marks, elaborate title pages &c. 1870. V. 37

Maxims and Precepts of the Saviour. London: 1848. V. 37; 41; 45

The Miracles of Our Lord. London: 1848. V. 38; 43; 44

Ocean Gardens. London: 1857. V. 37; 42

The Origin and Progress of the Art of Writing. London: 1853. V. 38

The Origin and Progress of the Art of Writing. London: 1855. V. 38; 40; 44; 46

Our Life, Illustrated by Pen and Pencil. London: 1865. V. 43

Parables of Our Lord. London: 1848. V. 37

Picturesque Scenery in North Wales. Carnarvon,. V. 38

Picturesque Scenery in North Wales. Carnarvon: 1860. V. 40

The Record of the Black Prince. London: 1849. V. 37; 38; 39; 43; 45

A Record of the Black Prince. London: 1849/48. V. 46

Rembrandt's Etchings. London: 1871. V. 44

Rome, and Its Surrounding Scenery . . . London: 1840. V. 45

Sentiments and Similes of William Shakespeare. London: 1851. V. 38; 41

Stories by an Archaeologist and His Friends. London: 1856. V. 43

Ten Centuries of Art, Its Progress in Europe from IXth to the XIXth Century. London: 1852. V. 38

HUMPHREYS, MILTON WYLIE

Military Operations 1861-1864 Fayetteville, West Virginia and the Lynchburg Campaign. Fayetteville: 1926. V. 43

HUMPHREYS, PHEBE WESTCOTT

The Practical Book of Garden Architecture. Philadlephia: 1914. V. 46

HUMPHREYS, SAMUEL

Tales and Novels in Verse. London: 1735. V. 45; 46

HUMPHREYS, W. P.

Atlas of the City and County of San Francisco from Actual Surveys and Offical Records. Philadelphia: 1876. V. 38; 40

HUMPHRIES, SYDNEY

Oriental Carpets. London: 1910. V. 37; 39; 40; 41; 42; 44

HUMPHRY, GEORGE MURRAY

Old Age. The Results of Information Received Respecting Nearly Nine Hundred Persons Who Had Attained the Age of Eighty Years, Including Seventy-Four Centenarians. Cambridge: 1889. V. 41

HUN, HENRY

An Atlas of the Differential Diagnosis of the Diseases of the Nervous System: an Analytical and Semeiological Neurological Charts. Troy: 1913. V. 42

HUNDDESFORD, GEORGE

The Scum Uppermost when the Middlesex Porridge Pot Boils OVer!! An Heroic Election Ballad with explanatory notes. Accompanied with an admonitory not to a Blind Horse. London: 1802. V. 37

HUNDERTPFUND, LIBERTAT

The Art of Painting Restored to Its Simplest and Surest Principles. London: 1849. V. 38

HUNDLEY, D. R.

Social Relations in Our Southern States. New York: 1860. V. 46

HUNER, ROBERT

A Brief Account of a Tour Through some parts of Scotland. 1839. V. 37

HUNGERFORD, EDWARD

The Story of the Baltimore & Ohio Railroad 1827-1927. New York: 1928. V. 46

HUNGERFORD, MARGARET

Green Pleasure and Grey Grief. London: 1886. V. 37

HUNGERFORD, MARGARET WOLFE ARGLES

Portia. London: 1883. V. 38

HUNGERFORD, MARGARET WOLFE HAMILTON 1855?-1897

Molly Bawn. London: 1878. V. 44

HUNGERFORD, TOWNSEND

Report of Occurrences at Mhow During and Subsequent to the Mutiny of Native Troops at that Station in July 1857. Mhow?: 1858. V. 45

HUNNEWELL, JAMES F.

Bibliography of the Hawaiian Islands. Boston: 1869. V. 46

HUNNICUT, JAMES W.

The Conspiracy Unveiled. Philadelphia: 1863. V. 43

HUNSICKER, CLIFTON S.

Montgomery County, Pennsylvania, a History. New York: 1923. V. 41; 42

HUNT, AURORA

The Army of the Pacific 1860-1866. Glendale: 1951. V. 38; 39; 43; 45; 46

An Historical Narrative and Topographical Description of Louisiana, and West Florida, Comprehending the River Mississippi with Its Principal Branches and Settlements . . . Philadelphia: 1784. V. 39

HUNT BOTANICAL LIBRARY

Catalogue of Botanical Books in the Collection of Rachel McMasters Miller Hunt . . . Pittsburgh: 1958-61/91. V. 46

HUNT, CHARLES

A History of the Introduction of Gas Lighting. London: 1907. V. 37

HUNT, CHARLES HAVENS

Life of Edward Livingston . . . New York: 1864. V. 42; 46

HUNT, CORNELIUS E.

The Shenandoah; or, the Last Confederate Cruiser. New York: 1867. V. 46

The Shenandoah; or the last Confederate Cruiser. New York/London: 1867. V. 37

HUNT, F. KNIGHT

The Fourth Estate. London: 1850. V. 37; 42

HUNT, FREEMAN

Hunt's Merchants' Magazine. New York: 1849. V. 40

HUNT, G. H.

Outram and Havelock's Persian Campaign . . . London: 1858. V. 46

HUNT, GEORGE D.

History of Salem and the Immediate Vicinity, Columbia County, Ohio. Salem: 1898. V. 44

HUNT, GEORGE W.

A History of the Hunt Family. Boston: 1890. V. 39

HUNT, GILBERT J.

The Late War Between the United States and Great Britain, from June 1812 to February 1815. New York: 1816. V. 46

HUNT, H. LYONS

Plastic Surgery of the Head, Face and Neck. Philadelphia: 1926. V. 42

HUNT, HARRIOT K.

Glances and Glimpses; or Fifty Years Social, Including Twenty Years Professional Life. Boston: 1856. V. 43

HUNT, HENRY

Investigation at Ilchester Gaol, in the County of Somerset, Into the Conduct of William Bridle, the Gaoler, Before the Commissioners Appointed by the Crown. London: 1821. V. 41; 42

Memoirs of Henry Hunt, Esq., written by himself in His Majesty's Jail at Ilchester. London: 1820. V. 37

Visit to the Red Sulphur Spring of Virginia, During the Summer of 1837 . . . Boston: 1839. V. 46

HUNT, HERBERT

Tacoma. Its History and Its Builders. Chicago: 1916. V. 45

HUNT, HOLMAN

Notes on the Pictures of Mr. Holman Hunt. Exhibited at the Rooms of the Fine Arts Society, 1886. With Criticisms by John Ruskin and other comments. London: 1886. V. 37

HUNT, ISAAC

The Irish People and the Irish Land: a Letter to Lord Lifford with Comments on the Publications of Lord Duffern and Lord Reese. Dublin: 1867. V. 46

HUNT, J. H.

Indian 'Fakirs'. London: 1934. V. 40; 41; 43

HUNT, JAMES H.

Mormonism: Embracing the Origin, Rise and Progress of the Sec, with an Examination of the Book of Mormon. St. Louis: 1844. V. 40; 45

HUNT, JOHN

The Ascent of Everest. London: 1953. V. 40; 43

HUNT, JOHN WARREN

Wisconsin Gazetteer. Madison: 1853. V. 41

HUNT, L. A. BREWER

My Leigh Hunt Library. Cedar Rapids: 1932. V. 37; 45

HUNT, LEIGH 1784-1859

An Attempt to Shew the Folly and Dangers of Methodism. London: 1809. V. 43

The Autobiography of Leigh Hunt . . . London: 1850. V. 43; 44

The Autobiography of Leigh Hunt, with Reminiscences of Friends and Contemporaries. New York: 1850. V. 44; 45

The Autobiography . . . Westmisnter: 1903. V. 39

Bacchus in Tuscany. London: 1825. V. 39

A Book for a Corner; or Selections in Prose and Verse from Authors the Best Suited to That Mode of Enjoyment. London: 1849. V. 39; 41; 43; 44; 46

The Book of the Sonnet. Boston: 1867. V. 43

The Book of the Sonnet. London: 1867. V. 43

The Book of the Sonnet. Boston: 1885. V. 46

Captain Sword and Captain Pen. London: 1835. V. 38; 39; 43

Christianism; or Belief and Unbelief Reconciled; Being Exercises and Meditations. London: 1832. V. 39; 42; 43; 45

Classic Tales, Serious and Lively; With Critical Essays on the Merits and Reputations of the Authors. London: 1806-07. V. 43

The Companion. London: 1828. V. 44; 46

The Correspondence . . . London: 1862. V. 43; 44

Critical Essays on Performers of the London Theatres . . . London: 1807. V. 37; 43; 46

A Day by the Fire; and Other Papers, Hitherto Uncollected. London: 1870. V. 43

The Descent of Liberty. London: 1815. V. 40; 42

The Descent of Liberty, a Mask. To which is prefixed, an Essay on the Origin and Nature of Masks; and a Memoir of the Author. Philadelphia: (1816). V. 37

The Dramatic Works of Wycherley, Congreve, Vanbrugh and Farquhar, with Biographical and Critical Notices. London: 1840. V. 38

Essays. The Indicator. The Seer. London: 1842. V. 44

The Feast of the Poets, with Notes, and Other Pieces in Verse . . . London: 1814. V. 42

The Feast of the Poets, with Notes and Other Pieces in Verse. London: 1815. V. 43

Foliage; or Poems Original and Translated. London: 1818. V. 43

Hero and Leander, and Bacchus and Ariadne. London: 1819. V. 43

Imagination and Fancy; or, Selections from the English Poets, Illustrative of Those First Requisites of Their Art . . . London: 1844. V. 43

The Indicator, and the Companion . . . London: 1834. V. 39; 42; 43; 46

A Jar of Honey from Mount Hybla. London: 1847. V. 45

A Jar of Honey from Mount Hybla. London: 1848. V. 37; 38; 39; 40; 42; 43; 44; 45; 46

Juvenilia; or a Collection of Poems: Written Between the Ages of Twelve and Sixteen . . . London: 1801. V. 37; 39; 43; 44; 46

The King v. John and Leigh Hunt. A Report of the Trial 'The King v. John and Leigh Hunt', for a Libel on the Prince Regent . . . London: 1812. V. 38

Leigh Hunt's London Journal . . . London: 1834-35. V. 42

Leigh Hunt's London Journal. To Assist the Inquiring Animate the Struggling, and Sympatheize with All. London: 1834-35. V. 38

Lord Byron and Some of His Contemporaries. London: 1828. V. 39; 42; 46

Lord Byron and Some of His Contemporaries; with Recollections of the Author's Life and of His Visit to Italy. Philadelphia: 1828. V. 45

Lord Byron and Some of His Contemporaries. Paris: 1828. V. 37

Men, Women and Books. London: 1847. V. 39; 40; 42; 43; 44; 45; 46

Men, Women and Books. New York: 1847. V. 40

The Months, Descriptive of the Successive Beauties of the Year. London: 1821. V. 41

The Old Court Suburb. London: 1855. V. 39; 40

Old Court Suburb. London: 1902. V. 43; 45

One Hundred Romances of Real Life . . . London: 1843. V. 43; 44

HUNT, LEIGH 1784-1859 continued

One Hundred Romances Selected and Annotated . . . London: 1846. V. 39

The Palfrey; a Love Story of Old Times. London: 1842. V. 37; 42; 43

The Poetical Works. London: 1812. V. 42

The Poetical Works. London: 1832. V. 39; 42; 44; 45

Readings for Railways; or, Anecdotes and Other Short Stories, Reflections, Maxims, Characteristics, Passages of Wit, Humour and Poetry. London: 1849. V. 43

The Rebellion of the Beasts; or, the Ass is Dead. London: 1825. V. 42; 45

The Religion of the Heart. London: 1853. V. 39

A Saunter through the West End. London: 1861. V. 39; 43; 46

The Seer; or Common-Places Refreshed. Boston: 1864. V. 41

Sir Ralph Esher; or, Memoirs of a Gentleman of the Court of Charles II. London: 1830. V. 43

Stories from the Italian Poets. London: 1846. V. 40; 42; 45

The Story of Rimini. London: 1816. V. 42

Table Talk. London: 1851. V. 43

The Town; Its Memorable Characters and Events. London: 1848. V. 39; 41; 43; 44; 45

Ultra-Crepidarius; a Satire on William Gifford. London: 1823. V. 43

Wit and Humor, Selected from the English Poets. London: 1846. V. 38

Wit and Humor, Selected from the English Poets. New York: 1847. V. 39; 41; 43

HUNT, LENOIR

Bluebonnets and Blood: the Romance of Texas. Houston: 1938. V. 42

HUNT, LYNN BROGUE

An Artists Game Bag. New York: 1936. V. 39

HUNT, M. S.

Nova Scotia's Part in the Great War. Halifax: 1920. V. 45

HUNT, MARGARET RAINE

Our Grandmothers' Gowns. London: 1884. V. 42

Our Grandmother's Gown. London: 1895. V. 38

HUNT, MEMUCAN

Boundary: United States and Texas. Washington: 1837. V. 37

The Public Debt and Lands of Texas. New Orleans: 1849. V. 41

HUNT, P. F.

Orchidaceae. London: 1973. V. 37; 38

HUNT, RACHEL MC MASTERS MILLER

Catalogue of Botanical Books in the Collection of Rachel McMasters Miller Hunt. Pittsburgh: 1958-61. V. 39; 43; 46

Catalogue of Botanical Books in the Collection of Rachel McMasters Miller Hunt. New York: 1991. V. 46

HUNT, RACHEL MCMASTERS MILLER

Two Manuals of Gardening from English Manuscript Notebooks of the Seventeenth Century in the Library of Rachel McMasters Miller Hunt. Pittsburgh: 1952. V. 39

William Penn, Horticulturist. Pittsburgh: 1953. V. 39

HUNT, RICHARD

Then and Now Recollections and a Diatribe. Hayward's Heath, Sussex: 1928. V. 38

HUNT, RICHARD CARLEY

Salmon in Low Water. New York: 1950. V. 45

HUNT, RICHARD S.

Guide to the Republic of Texas . . . New York: 1839. V. 37; 38; 42; 46

A New Guide to Texas: Consisting of a Brief Outline of the History of Its Settlement . . . New York: 1845. V. 39

HUNT, ROBERT

The Island of Assada, Near Madagascar Impartially Defined. London: 1650. V. 40

A Manual of Photography. London: 1853. V. 37; 40; 42

Panthea, the Spirit of Nature. London: 1849. V. 43

A Popular Treatise on the Art of Photography. Glasgow: 1841. V. 46

Researches on Light In Its Chemical Relations . . . London: 1854. V. 37; 39; 41; 42; 44; 45

Researches on Light: An Examination of all the Phenomena Connected with the Chemical and Molecular Changes Produced by the Influence of the Solar Rays. London: 1844. V. 37; 42

A Treatise on the Progressive Improvement and Present State of the Manufactures in Metal. London: 1853. V. 37; 39

HUNT, ROBERT L.

A History of Farmer Movements in the Southwest, 1873-1925. College Station: 1926. V. 39

A History of Farmer Movements in the Southwest, 1873-1925. (College Station, Texas): (1926). V. 37

HUNT, ROCKWELL D.

California and Californians. Chicago: 1932. V. 41

HUNT, T. DWIGHT

Address Delivered Before the New England Society of San Francisco at the American Theatre. San Francisco: 1853. V. 43

The Past and Present of the Sandwich Islands . . . San Francisco: 1853. V. 41; 42

HUNT, T. F.

Architecttura Campestre . . . London: 1827. V. 40

Half a Dozen Hints on Picturesque Domestic Architecture, in a Series of Designs for Gate Lodges. London: 1826. V. 38

Half a Dozen Hints on Picturesque Domestic Architecture, in a Series of designs for Gate Lodges, Gamekeppers' Cottages, and other Rural Residences. London: 1833. V. 38

Half a Dozen Hints on Picturesque Domestic Architecture . . . London: 1841. V. 38

HUNT, T. STERRY

Petroleum Its Geological Relations. Quebec: 1865. V. 38; 42; 45

HUNT, THOMAS

De Antiquitate, Elegantia, Utilitate Linguae Arabicae Oratio. Oxford: 1739. V. 37

A Defence of the Charter and Municipal Rights of the City of London. London: 1683. V. 40; 44

The Rights of the Bishops to Judge in Capital Cases in Parliament Cleared. London: 1680. V. 40

HUNT, THOMAS FREDERICK 1791-1831

Architettura Campestre: Displayed in Lodges, Gardeners' Houses, and Other Buildings, Composed of Simple and Economical Forms in the Modern or Italian Style. London: 1827. V. 38; 39; 41; 44

Designs for Parsonage Houses, Alms Houses, etc. London: 1827. V. 38; 42; 44

Designs for Parsonage Houses, Alms Houses, etc., etc., with Examples of Gables, and Other Crurious Remains of Old English Architecture. London: 1841. V. 38; 44

Exemplars of Tudor Architecture, Adapted to Modern Habitations with Illustrative Details . . . London: 1830. V. 38; 40; 41

Exemplars of Tudor Architecture, Adapted to Modern Habitations . . . London: 1836. V. 39; 42

Expemplars of Tudor Architecture Adapted to Modern Habitations . . . and Observations on the Furniture of the Tudor Period. London: 1850. V. 38

Half a Dozen Hints on Picturesque Domestic Architecture, in a Series of designs for Gate Lodges, Gamekeepers' Cottages and Other Rural Residences. London: 1826. V. 38; 39; 42; 44

Half a Dozen Hints on Picturesque Domestic Architecture, in a Series of Designs for Gate Lodges, Gamekeepers' Cottages and Other Rural Residences. London: 1833. V. 38

Half a Dozen Hints on Picturesque Domestic Architecture, in a Series of Designs for Gate Lodges, Gamekeepers' Cottages and Other Rural Residences. London: 1841. V. 38; 39; 44

HUNT, THORNTON LEIGH

The Foster-Brother; a Tale of the War of Chiozza. London: 1845. V. 41

HUNT, VIOLET

The Tiger Skin. London: 1924. V. 44

HUNT, WILLIAM fl. 1673-1713

A Mathematical Companion, or the Description and Use of a New Sliding-Rule, by Which Many Useful and Necessary Questions in Arithmetick, Military Orders, Interest, Trigonometry, Planometry . . . London: 1697. V. 39

The Political History of England, From the Earliest Times to the Reign of Queen Victoria. London: 1906-10. V. 39

HUNT, WILLIAM GIBBES

An Address, Delivered at Nashville, Tenn., April 6, 1831 . . . Nashville: 1831. V. 39; 42

HUNT, WILLIAM HOLMAN

The Debating Hall, Oxford Union Society. Oxford: 1906. V. 42

Oxford Union Society: The Story of the Painting of the Pictures on the Walls and the Decorations on the Ceiling of the Old Debating Hall (now the Library) in the Years 1857-8-9, by W. Holman Hunt. Oxford: 1906. V. 37; 42

Pre-Raphaelitism and the Pre-Raphaelite Brotherhood. London: 1905. V. 37; 39; 42; 45

Pre-Raphaelitism and the Pre-Raphaelite Brotherhood. New York: 1905. V. 37; 41

HUNT, WILLIAM S.

Frank Forester . . . a Tragedy in Exile. Newark: 1933. V. 38; 40

HUNT, WILLIAM SHAPTER

Brown's Sporting Tour in India. London: 1865. V. 39

HUNTER, A.

Culina Famulatrix Medicinae; or, Receipts in Modern Cookery. York: 1810. V. 44

HUNTER, ALEXANDER

Culina Famulatrix Medicinae. York: 1804. V. 38; 39; 40; 41; 44; 45; 46
Georgical Essays. London: 1773. V. 39
Georgical Essays. York: 1777. V. 37
Georgical Essays. York: 1778. V. 38
Georgical Essays. York: 1803-04. V. 37
Johnny Reb and Billy Yank. New York: 1905. V. 42
Outlines of Agriculture, Addressed to Sir John Sinclair, Bart, President of the Board of Agriculture. York: 1797. V. 43

HUNTER, DANIEL J.

A Sketch of Chili, Expressly Prepared for Emigrants from the United States and Europe. New York: 1866. V. 41; 44; 46

HUNTER, DARD 1883-1966

Before Life Began 1883-1923. Cleveland: 1941. V. 37; 38; 46
Chinese Ceremonial Paper. Chillicothe: 1937. V. 37
Chinese Ceremonial Paper. A Monograph relating the fabrication of paper and the foil and the use of paper in Chinese rites and religious ceremonies. Chillicothe, Ohio: 1937. V. 37
Hand-Made Paper and Its Watermarks. Marlborough-Upon-Hudson: 1917. V. 41; 43
The Life Work of Dard Hunter. Chillicothe: 1981. V. 38
The Life Work of Dard Hunter . . . Chillicothe: 1981-83. V. 40; 42
The Life Work of Dard Hunter. Chillicothe: 1981-83, 1986. V. 39
The Life Work of Dard Hunter . . . Chillicothe: 1981-85. V. 44
The Life Work of Dard Hunter. Chillicothe: 1981-83 (86). V. 37
The Literature of Papermaking 1390-1800. Chillicothe: 1925. V. 38; 40
The Making of Books: The Lost Art of Making Books, Ancient Paper Making, Seventeenth Century Type-Making. Chillicothe: 1987. V. 38
My Life with Paper. New York: 1958. V. 37; 38; 39; 40; 41; 43; 44; 45
Old Papermaking. Chillicothe: 1923. V. 40; 45
Old Papermaking in China and Japan. Chillicothe: 1932. V. 45
On Papyrus, Excerpted from The Story of Early Printing. New Britain: 1971. V. 41
Paper-Making in the Classroom. Peoria: 1931. V. 38
A Papermaking Pilgrimage to Japan, Korea, and China. New York: 1936. V. 37
Papermaking by Hand in America. Chillicothe: 1950. V. 38; 39; 40; 46
Papermaking by Hand in India. New York: 1939. V. 37; 38; 39; 41; 43; 45; 46
Papermaking in Indo-China. 1932. V. 44
Papermaking in Indo-China. Chillicothe: 1947. V. 37; 38; 44
Papermaking in Pioneer America. Philadelphia: 1952. V. 38; 40; 42
Papermaking in Southern Siam. Chillicothe: 1938. V. 45
A Papermaking Pilgrimage to Japan, Korea and China. New York: 1936. V. 44; 45; 46
Papermaking: the History and Technique of an Ancient Craft. V. 39
Papermaking, the History and Technique of an Ancient Craft. New York: 1943. V. 37; 38; 40; 41; 42; 43
Papermaking through Eighteen Centuries. New York: 1930. V. 37; 38; 39; 41; 42; 43; 45; 46
Primitive Papermaking, an Account of a Mexican Sojourn and of a Voyage to the Pacific Islands . . . Chillicothe: 1927. V. 38
Romance of Watermarks. Cincinnati: 1940. V. 42
A Specimen of Type. Cambridge: 1940. V. 38; 41; 43; 45

HUNTER, E. R.

Thoreau MacDonald. Toronto: 1942. V. 43

HUNTER, EVAN

Blackboard Jungle. V. 42

HUNTER, FRANCIS

Dissertatio Chemica Inauguralis de Aetheribus. Edinburgh: 1808. V. 41

HUNTER, GEORGE

Reminiscences of an Old Timer . . . A Pioneer, Hunter, Miner and Scout of the Pacific Northwest . . . San Francisco: 1887. V. 37; 38; 42
Reminiscences of an Old Time. Battle Creek: 1888. V. 42; 46
Reminiscences of an Old Timer . . . Battle Creek: 1889. V. 45

HUNTER, GEORGE LELAND

Decorative Textiles. Philadelphia: 1918. V. 41; 42
Decorative Textiles. Philadlephia & London: 1918. V. 41
The Practical Book of Tapestries. Philadelphia & London: 1925. V. 38

Tapestries; Their Origin, History and Renaissance. New York: 1912. V. 42

HUNTER, H. L.

Leaves of Gold. London: 1951. V. 38

HUNTER, HENRY

Sacred Biography; or the History of the Patiarchs. London: 1820. V. 39

HUNTER, J.

A Complete Dictionary of Farriery & Horsemanship, Containing the Art of Farriery In All Its Branches . . . Dublin: 1796. V. 40

HUNTER, J. M.

The Trail Drivers of Texas. Nashville: 1925. V. 45

HUNTER, JAMES

A Lecture on the Grammatical Construction of the Cree Language, Delivered by the Ven. Archdeacon Hunter Before the Institute of Rupert's Land at the Court House, Fort Garry, Red River Settlement; on the 2nd April, 1862 . . . London: 1875. V. 40

HUNTER, JOHN 1728-1793

Essays and Observations on Natural History, Anatomy, Physiology, Psychology and Geology. London: 1861. V. 37; 42; 45; 46
An Historical Account of the Transactions at Port Jackson and Norfolk Island, with the Discoveries Which Have Been Made in New South Wales and in the Southern Ocean, Since the Publiction of Phillip's Voyage. London: 1793. V. 40; 42; 44; 45; 46
Lectures on Comparative Anatomy in Which are Explained the Preparations in the Hunterian Collection. London: 1814-28. V. 41
The Natural History of the Human Teeth; Explaining Their Structure, Use, Formation and Diseases. London: 1771. V. 42
Observations on Certain Parts of the Animal Oeconomy. London: 1786. V. 37; 39; 42
Observations on Certain Parts of the Animal Oeconomy . . . Philadelphia: 1841. V. 42
Observations on the Diseases of the Army in Jamaica; and On the Best Menas of Preserving the Health of Europeans, in That Climate. London: 1788. V. 42
Resa Til Nya Sodra Wallis, Aren 1787, Foljande; Jamte Nyaste Underrattelser om Engelska Nybygget i Port Jackson, Nya Holland och Norfoks . . . Stockholm: 1797. V. 46
Treatise on the Venereal Diseases. N.P.: 1786. V. 44
A Treatise on the Veneral Disease. London: 1788. V. 39
A Treatise on the Veneral Disease. Philadelphia: 1791. V. 40
A Treatise on the Blood, Inflammation and Gunshot Wounds to Which is Prefixed a Short Account of the Author's Life. London: 1794. V. 37; 45; 46
A Treatise on the Blood, Inflamation and Gun-Shot Wounds. Philadelphia: 1817. V. 41; 42
A Treatise on the Veneral Disease. London: 1818. V. 40; 41; 43; 44
A Treatise on the Venereal Disease with an Introduction and Commentary by Joseph Adams. Philadelphia: 1818. V. 46
A Treatise on the Blood, Inflammation, and Gun-Shot Wounds. Philadelphia: 1823. V. 42; 44
Treatise on the Natural History and Diseases of the Human Teeth: Explaining Their Structure, Use, Formation, Growth and Diseases. Philadelphia: 1841. V. 42
A Treatise on the Veneral Disease. Philadelphia: 1853. V. 39
A Treatise on the Venereal Disease. Philadelphia: 1859. V. 42
A Treatise on the Veneral Disease. London: 1786. V. 37
The Works of John Hunter, F.R.S. London: 1835-37. V. 45
The Works of John Hunter. London: 1837. V. 46
Works of John Hunter. Philadelhia: 1839. V. 45
Hunter's Works. Philadelphia: 1839-40. V. 39; 40; 41

HUNTER, JOHN DUNN

Manners and Customs of Several Indian Tribes Located West of the Mississippi . . . London: 1823. V. 39
Manners and Customs of Several Indian Tribes Located West of the Mississippi . . . Philadelphia: 1823. V. 37; 39; 40; 41; 43; 44
Memoirs of a Captivity Among the Indians of North America. London: 1823. V. 37; 39; 43
Memoirs of a Captivity Among the Indians of North America, from Childhood to the Age of Nineteen. London: 1824. V. 37; 38

HUNTER, JOHN MARVIN

The Album of Gunfighters. Bandera: 1951. V. 39; 40; 42; 46
The Boy Captives. N.P.: 1927. V. 44
Horrors of Indian Captivity: True Stories of the Texas Frontier, Based on Facts Given by Some of the Captives Themselves. Bandera: 1937. V. 38
Jack Hays - The Intrepid Texas Ranger. Bandera: 1927. V. 44
Pioneer History of Bandera County Seventy-Five Years of Intrepid History. Bandera: 1922. V. 39
The Trail Drivers of Texas. San Antonio: 1920. V. 39
The Trail Drivers of Texas. San Antonio: (1920), 1923. V. 39
The Trail Drivers of Texas. San Antonio: 1920/23/24. V. 42

HUNTER, JOHN MARVIN continued

The Trail Drivers of Texas. San Antonio: 1920-24. V. 37; 38; 46

The Trail Drivers of Texas. N.P.: 1920 & 1923. V. 43

The Trail Drivers of Texas. San Antonio: 1924. V. 39

The Trail Drivers of Texas. Nashville: 1925. V. 37; 39; 42; 46

Trail Drivers of Texas. New York: 1963. V. 37; 38

HUNTER, JOSEPH 1783-1861

Antiquarian Notices of Lupset, the Heath, Sharlston and Ackton in the County of York. London: 1851. V. 41

Collections Concerning the Church or Congregation of Protestant Separatists Formed at Scrooby in North Nottinghamshire, in the Time of King James I . . . London: 1854. V. 39

The Hallamshire Glossary . . . London: 1829. V. 42

Hallamshire. The History and Topography of Sheffield. Sheffield: 1869. V. 40

Hallamshire. The History and Topography of the Parish of Sheffield in the County of York. London: 1869. V. 37

New Illustrations of the Life, Studies and Writings of Shakespeare. London: 1845. V. 43

South Yorkshire. The History and Topography of the Deanery of Doncaster, in the County of York. London: 1828-31. V. 37

HUNTER, MARTHA TALIAFERRO

A Memoir of Robert M. T. Hunter. Washington: 1903. V. 46

HUNTER, NORMAN

The Incredible Adventures of Professor Branestawn. London: 1933. V. 45

Larky Legends. London: 1938. V. 45

HUNTER, RACHEL

Letters of Mrs. Palmerstone to Her Daughter . . . London: 1810. V. 43

HUNTER, RICHARD

Three Hundred Years of Psychiatry, 1535-1860. London: 1963. V. 42; 45

Three Hundred Years of Psychiatry 1535-1860. London: 1964. V. 46

Three Hundred Years of Psychiatry 1535-1860. Harsdale: 1982. V. 38; 46

HUNTER, ROBERT HANCOCK

Narrative of Robert Hancock Hunter, from His Arrival in Texas, 1822 through the Battle of San Jacinto, 1836. Austin: 1936. V. 37; 42

HUNTER, ROBERT MERCER TALLAFERRO

A Memoir of Robert M. T. Hunter . . . with an Address on His Life.. Washington: 1903. V. 45

HUNTER, SAM

Larry Rivers. New York. V. 43

Larry Rivers. New York: 1970. V. 46

HUNTER, SAMUEL J.

The Hunters' and Trappers' Illustrated Historical Guide, Treating Only of the Wild Animate Nature of North America. St. Louis: 1869. V. 37; 40

HUNTER, THOMAS

Reflections Critical and Moral on the Lettes of the Late Earl of Chesterfield. London: 1776. V. 38

HUNTER, W. A.

Fisherman's Pie: an Angling Symposium. London: 1926. V. 39

HUNTER, W. M. S.

Chisholm's Panoramic Guide for Niagara Fals to Quebec. Montreal: 1869. V. 38

HUNTER, W. S.

Hunter's Eastern Townships Scenery, Canada East. Montreal: 1860. V. 41

HUNTER, W. W.

The Imperial Gazetteer of India. London: 1885-87. V. 37

A Life of the Earl of Mayo. London: 1875. V. 43

Orissa. London: 1872. V. 43

A Statistical Account of Assam. London: 1879. V. 37

HUNTER, WILLIAM

Anatomia Uteri Humani Gravidi Tabulis Illustrata. London: 1851. V. 43

The Anatomy of the Human Gravid Uterus Exhibited Figures. London: 1851. V. 41; 44

Biggar and the House of Fleming. An Account of the Biggar District . . . Edinburgh: 1867. V. 38

Historical Account of Charing Cross Hospital and Medical School . . . London: 1914. V. 40

Hunter's Ottawa Scenery, in the Vicinity of Ottawa City, Canada. Ottawa: by the author,: 1855. V. 45

Medical Commentaries. London: 1762. V. 44; 45; 46

A Short View of the Political Situation of the Northern Powers. London: 1801. V. 38

Travels Through France, Turkey, and Hungary, to Vienna, in 1792. London: 1803. V. 40

Travels in the Year 1792 through France, Turkey and Hungary, to Vienna . . . In A Series of Letters, to a Lady in England. London: 1796. V. 37

Two Introductory Lectures, Delivered by William Hunter, to His Last Course of Anaomical Lectures, at His Theatre in Windmill Street. London: 1784. V. 41

HUNTER, WILLIAM S.

Chisholm's Panoramic Guide from Niagara Falls to Quebec. Montreal: 1869. V. 39; 42

Hunter & Pickup's Panoramic Guide from Niagara Falls to Quebec. Montreal: 1863. V. 42

Hunter & Pickup's Panoramic Guide from Niagara Falls to Quebec. Montreal: 1866. V. 37; 39

Hunter's Ottawa Scenery, in the Vicinity of Ottawa City, Canada. Ottawa City: 1855. V. 40; 43

Hunter's Panoramic Guide from Niagara Falls to Quebec. Boston: 1857. V. 37; 38; 40; 42; 46

Hunter's Panoramic Guide from Niagara Falls to Quebec. Montreal: 1857. V. 42

Hunter's Eastern Township Scenery, Canada East. Montreal: 1860. V. 43

Hunter's Panoramic Guide from Niagara Falls to Quebec. Boston & Cleveland: 1857. V. 38

HUNTER, WILLIAM WILSON

The Indian Empire: Its People, History & Products. London: 1893. V. 45

HUNTING Trails on Three Continents. New York: 1933. V. 46

HUNTINGDON, WILLIAM

Spiritual Birth. London: 1789. V. 40

HUNTINGTON, CHARLES B.

Charles B. Huntington for Forgery. Principal Defense: Insanity. New York: 1857. V. 38

HUNTINGTON, DAVID C.

The Landscapes of Frederic Edwin Church: Vision of an American Era. New York: 1966. V. 42

HUNTINGTON, ELLSWORTH

The Climatic Factor as Illustrated in Arid America. Washington: 1914. V. 42; 44

The Pulse of Asia. A Journey in Central Asia. London: 1907. V. 40

HUNTINGTON, GEORGE

Robber and Hero. Northfield: 1895. V. 39

HUNTINGTON, JOHN G.

Reminiscences of John G. Huntington a Pioneer of Kansas and the Two Mexico's. Willimasport: 1897. V. 45

HUNTINGTON, JONATHAN

Classical Sacred Musick. Boston: 1812. V. 43

HUNTINGTON, RANDOLPH

History in Brief of 'Leopard' and 'Linden'. Philadelphia: 1885. V. 37; 42

History in Brief of 'Leopard' and 'Linden', General Grant's Arabian Stallions, Presented to Him by the Sultan of Turkey in 1879. 1885. V. 38

HUNTINGTON, WILLIAM

A Divine Poem on the Shunamite. Addressed to a Friend. Lewes: 1787. V. 45

A Divine Poem on the Shunamite. London: 1787. V. 37

A Valuable and Rare Book Entitled William Huntington Upon Universal Charity . . . Macon: 1841. V. 45

HUNTLEY, HENRY VANE

Peregrine Scramble. London: 1849. V. 41

HUNTLEY, HENRY VERE

California: Its Gold and its Inhabitants. London: 1856. V. 37

HUNTLY, KATE HOPE

Wedlock, and Its Skeleton Key. London: 1891. V. 39

HUNTON, EPPA

Autobiography of Eppa Hunton. Richmond: 1933. V. 45

HUNTON, W. GORDON

English Decorative Textiles. London: 1930. V. 42

HURCOMB, W. E.

The Wetherfield Collection of 222 Clocks Sold on 1st May, 1928 . . . London: 1929. V. 44

HURD, ARCHIBALD

A Merchant Fleet at War. London: 1920. V. 39

HURD, D. HAMILTON

History of Bristol County, Massachusetts. Philadelphia: 1883. V. 46

History of Merrimack & Belknap Counties. Philadelphia: 1885. V. 39

History of Cheshire and Sullivan Counties, New Hampshire. Philadelphia: 1886. V. 46

HURD-MEAD, KATE CAMPBELL

A History of Women in Medicine from the Earliest Times to the Beginning of the Nineteenth Century. 1938. V. 41

A History of Women in Medicine from the Earliest Times to the Beginning of the Nineteenth Century. Haddam: 1938. V. 39; 42

Medical Women of America. New York: 1933. V. 39

HURD, PETER

The Lithographs. 1968. V. 42

The Lithographs. Lubbock: 1968. V. 46

Peter Hurd Sketch Book. Chicago: 1971. V. 38

Peter Hurd Sketch Book. Chicago: (1971). V. 37

HURD, RICHARD

Dialogues on the Uses of Foreign Travel; Considered as a Part of an English Gentleman's Education. London: 1764. V. 38; 39; 45

An Introduction to the Study of the Prophecies Concerning the Christian Church . . . London: 1772. V. 41

A Letter to Mr. Mason; on the Marks of Imitation. Cambridge: 1757. V. 41

Moral and Political Dialogues; Being the Substance of Several Conversations Between Divers Eminent Persons of the Past and Present Age. London: 1759. V. 41

Moral and Political Dialogues . . . London: 1765. V. 38; 40

HURD, RICHARD M.

Principles of City Land Values, the Record and Guide. New York: 1905. V. 38; 41

HURDIS, JAMES

Lectures showing the Several Sources of that Pleasure which the Human mind receives from Poetry. London: 1797. V. 37

Poems. London: 1790. V. 37

Reflections Upon the Commencement of a New Year. London: 1793. V. 41

Select Critical Remarks upon the English Version of the first ten chapters of Genesis. London: 1793. V. 37

Tears of Affection, a Poem, Occasioned by the Death of a Sister Tenderly Beloved. London: 1794. V. 43

The Village Curate, a Poem. London: 1788. V. 38

The Village Curate. Newburyport: 1793. V. 40

The Village Curate and Other Poems; Including Some Pieces Now First Published. London: 1810. V. 42; 44

HURHAM, J. D.

Memoir of Rev. John L. Prichard, Late Pastor of the First Baptist Church, Wilmington, N.C. Raleigh: 1867. V. 37; 44

HURIS, JAMES

Cursory Remarks upon the Arrnagement of the Plays of Shakespeare; occasioned by reading Mr. Malone's Essay on the chronological order of those celebrated pieces. London: 1792. V. 37

HURLBERT, J. BEAUFORT

Britain and Her Colonies. London: 1865. V. 37

HURLBERT, W. H.

Ireland Under Coercion. Edinburgh: 1888. V. 38

HURLBUTT, F.

Chelsea China. Liverpool University: 1937. V. 37

HURLBUTT, FRANK

Bow Porcelain. London: 1926. V. 40; 42; 44

Bristol Porcelain. London: 1928. V. 44; 46

Old Derby Porcelain and Its Artist-Workmen. London: 1925. V. 41

HURLEY, FRANK

Argonauts of the South. New York: 1925. V. 43

Pearls and Savages. New York: 1924. V. 38

HURLY, PATRICK

The Tryal and Conviction of Patrick Hurley . . . Dublin: 1701. V. 40

HURN, D.

Rural Rhymes; or, a Collection of Epistolary, Humorous and Descriptive Pieces. Spalding: 1813. V. 38

HURRAH We're Moving. 1950. V. 45

HURRY, JAMIESON B.

Imhotep, the Vizier and Physician of King Zoser and Afterwards the Egyptian God of Medicine. Oxford: 1926. V. 44

HURST, CHARLES CHAMBERLAIN

Experimetns in Genetics. Cambridge: 1925. V. 40

HURST, FANNIE

Lummox. New York: 1923. V. 44

HURST, H. R.

Excavations at Carthage: the British Mission. Sheffield: 1984. V. 40

HURST, SAMUEL H.

Journal-History of the Seventy-Third Ohio Volunteer Infantry. Chillicothe: 1866. V. 42; 46

HURSTHOUSE, CHARLES

An Account of the Settlement of New Plymouth in New Zealand, from Personal Observation, During a Residence There of Five Years. London: 1849. V. 38

New Zealand, or Zealandia, the Britain of the South. London: 1857. V. 39

HURSTON, ZORA NEALE

L'Arbalete. Paris: 1944. V. 46

Dust Tracks on Road. Philadelphia: 1942. V. 45

Moses Man of the Mountain. Philadelphia: 1939. V. 46

Mules and Men. Philadelphia: 1935. V. 44; 45

HURSTONE, J. P.

Royal Intrigues; or, Secret Memoirs of Four Princesses . . . London: 1808. V. 39

HURT, WALTER

The Scarlet Shadow. Girard: 1907. V. 46

HURTLEY, THOMAS

A Concise Account of Some Natural Curiosities in the Environs of Malham in Craven, Yorkshire. London: 1786. V. 44; 45; 46

HURTON, WILLIAM

A Voyage from Leith to Lapland; or Pictures of Scandinavia in 1850. London: 1852. V. 43; 44

HURWITZ, HYMAN

A Grammar of the Hebrew Language. London: 1835. V. 40

An Introductory Lecture Delivered in the University of London, on Tuesday, November 11, 1828. London: 1829. V. 42

HUSBANDS, JOHN

A Miscellany of Poems by Several Hands. Oxford: 1731. V. 40; 43

HUSE, CHARLES E.

Sketch of the History and Resources of Santa Barbara City and County, California. Santa Barbara: 1876. V. 43

HUSK, WILLIAM HENRY

An Account of the Musical Celbrations on St. Cecilia's Day in the Sixteenth, Seventeenth and Eighteenth Centuries. London: 1857. V. 43

HUSKE, JOHN

The Present State of North America. Boston: 1755. V. 38

The Present State of North America, &c. Part 1. London: 1755. V. 37; 44; 46

HUSKISSON, WILLIAM

Memoir of the Late Right Honourable William Huskisson, with Particulars of His Lamented Death. Liverpool: 1830. V. 46

The Question Concerning the Depreciation of Our Currency Stated and Examined . . . London: 1810. V. 37

The Speeches of the Right Honourable William Huskisson, with a Biographical Memoir, Supplied to the Editor from Authentic Sources. London: 1831. V. 40; 43

The Speeches, with a Biographical Memoir . . . London: 1831. V. 45

HUSMANN, GEORGE

American Grape Growing and Wine Making. New York: 1881. V. 46

HUSON, HOBART

Captain Phillip Dimitt's Commandancy of Goliad, 1835-1836. Austin: 1974. V. 37; 39; 42

District Judges of Refugio County. Refugio: 1941. V. 37; 38; 40

HUSON, THOMAS

Round About Helvellyn. London: 1895. V. 46

HUSS, IOANNES

De Anatomia Antichristi. De Mysteriis Iniquitatis. De Revelatione Christi & Antichristi. De Abolendis Sectis & Tradtionibus Hominum. De Unitate Ecclesiae & Schismate Vitando. De Evangelica Perfectione. De Pernicie Traditionum Humanarum. De Regno . . . Strasbourg: 1524. V. 38

HUSS, JOHANN

Epistolae Quaedam Piissimae & Eruditissimae Iohannis Hus . . . Wittenberg: 1537. V. 40

HUSSERL, EDMUND

Logische Untersuchungen. Halle: 1900-01. V. 45

HUSSEY, C.

The Picturesque Studies in a Point of View. London & New York: 1927. V. 37

The Work of Sir Robert Lorimer. London: 1931. V. 37

HUSSEY, CHRISTOPHER

English Country Houses, Mid and Late Georgian. London: 1935/58. V. 43

English Country Houses. Early Georgian 1715-1760. London: 1955. V. 37; 38; 43

English Country Houses, Early, Mid and Late Georgian; Caroline, Baroque. London: 1955/6/8/66/70. V. 46

English Country Houses. Early, Mid and Late Georgian, Caroline, Baroque. London: 1955-70. V. 45

English Country Houses, Early, Mid and Late Georgian. 1984. V. 45

English Country Houses: Early Georgian 1715-1760: Mid Georgian 1760-1800; Late Georgian 1800-1840. Suffolk: 1984. V. 39

English Country Houses: Mid Georgian 1760-1800. London: 1956. V. 38

English Gardens and Landscapes 1700-1750. London: 1967. V. 38; 44

The Life of Sir Edward Lutyens. London: 1950. V. 42; 45

The Life of Sir Edward Lutyens. London: 1953. V. 38; 40

The Picturesque Studies in a Point of View. London: 1927. V. 44; 45

Tait Mackenzie - a Sculptor of Youth. Philadelphia: 1930. V. 39

The Work of Sir Robert Lorimer. London: 1931. V. 40

HUSSEY, E. C.

Home Building, a Reliable Book of Facts, Relative to Building, Living, Materials, Cost, From New York to San Francisco. New York: 1876. V. 46

HUSSEY, GEORGE A.

History of the Ninth Regiment. New York: 1889. V. 45

HUSSEY, J. A.

Preliminary Survey of the History and Physical Structure of Fort Vancouver. N.P.: 1949. V. 39

HUSSEY, JOHN A.

A History of Fort Vancouver and Its Physical Structure. Portland: 1957. V. 39; 45

The Voyage of the Raccoon. San Francisco: 1958. V. 38; 44

HUSSON, A. M.

The Mammals of Suriname. Leiden: 1978. V. 37

HUSSON, JULES F.F.

Le Violon de Faience. Paris: 1885. V. 45

HUSTON, GARTH

Sir Kenelm Digby. Checklist. Los Angeles: 1969. V. 40; 41

HUSTON, JOHN

Frankie and Johnny. New York: 1930. V. 46

Humphrey Bogart. Los Angeles: 1957. V. 45

HUSUNG, MAX JOSEPH

Bucheinbande aus der Preussischen Staatsbibliothek zu Berlin. Leipzig: 1925. V. 38

HUTCHESON, ARCHIBALD

An Estimate of the Present National Debt: to which is added a Copy of Remarks Which Were Subjoined to Some Calculations Made in April 1717 Relating to the Publick Debts. London: 1718. V. 37

HUTCHESON, DAVID

Poems. Oban, Bonnytown, Port: 1858-67. V. 40

HUTCHESON, FRANCIS

Abhandlungen uber die Natur und Beherrschun der Leidenschaften und Neigungen und Uber das Moralische Gefuhl Insonderheit. Leipzig: 1760. V. 38

An Essay on the nature and Conduct of the Passions and Affections. London: 1728. V. 41; 43; 45

An Essay on the Nature and Conduct of the Passions and Affections. London: 1742. V. 42; 43; 45

An Essay on the Nature and Conduct of the Passions and Affections, with Illustrations on the Moral Sense. London: 1756. V. 42; 43; 45

An Essay on the Nature and Conduct of the Passions and Affections. Glasgow: 1769. V. 41; 45

An Inquiry in to the Original of Our Ideas of Beauty and Virtue . . . London: 1726. V. 39; 42

An Inquiry into the Original of Our Ideas of Beauty and Virtue. London: 1729. V. 38; 39; 40; 44

An Inquiry into the Original of our Ideas of Beauty and Virtue. In Two Treatises. I. Concerning Beauty, Order, Harmony, Design. II. Concerning Moral Good and Evil. The Fifth Edition, Corrected. London: 1753. V. 37

Letters Between the Late Mr. Gilbert Burnet, and Mr. Huchinson, Concerning the True Foundation of Virtue or Moral Goodness. London: 1735. V. 42; 43

Letters Concerning the True Foundation of Virtue or Moral Goodness, Wrote in a Correspondence Between Mr. Gilbert Burnet and Mr. Francis Hutcheson. (Thoughts on Laughter). (Observations on the Fable of the Bees.) Glasgow: 1772. V. 42; 43

A Short Introduction to Moral Philosophy . . . Glasgow: 1747. V. 39; 42

A Short Introduction to Moral Philosophy, in Three Books . . . Glagow: 1764. V. 46

A Short Introduction to Moral Philosophy, in Three Books . . . Glasgow: 1772. V. 42

A System of Moral Philosophy. Glasgow: printed and sold: 1775. V. 37

A System of Moral Philosophy, in Three Books. Glasgow: printed & sold by: 1755. V. 37

The Works. London: 1969-71. V. 39

HUTCHESON, GILBERT

A Treatise on the Offices of Justice of Peace . . . etc. in Scotland. Edinburgh: 1806. V. 38

Treatise on the Offices of Justice of Peace. Edinburgh: 1809. V. 40

HUTCHINGS, JAMES MASON

Hutching's California Scenes. San Francisco: 1854. V. 46

Hutchings' Tourist's Guide to the Yosemite Valley and the Big Tree Groves for the Sprint and Summer of 1877. San Francisco: 1877. V. 37

In the Heart of the Sierras: The Yosemite Valley, Both Historical and Descriptive; and Scenes by the Way. Old Cabin: 1886. V. 41

In the Heart of the Sierras; The Yo Semite Valley . . . Yo Semite Valley & Oakland: 1886. V. 43

In the Heart of the Sierras. The Yosemite Valley, Both Historical and Descritpive. Yosemite & Oakland: 1886. V. 39

In the Heart of the Sierras. Yosemite Valley and Oakland: 1886. V. 44

Scenes of Wonder and Curiosity in California. San Francisco: 1860. V. 39; 44

Scenes of Wonder and Curiosity in California. San Francisco: 1861. V. 44

Scenes of Wonder and Curiosity in California. London: 1865. V. 43

Scenes of Wonder and Curiosity in California. New York & San Francisco: 1870. V. 37; 38; 40

Scenes of Wonder and Curiosity in California. New York: 1871. V. 44

Scenes of Wonder and Curiosity in California. San Francisco: 1872. V. 44

HUTCHINS, D. E.

Report on the Forests of British East Africa. London: 1909. V. 41

HUTCHINS, HENRY CLINTON

Robinson Crusoe and Its Printing, 1719-1731. New York: 1925. V. 38; 43

HUTCHINS, JOHN

The History an Antiquities of the County of Dorset. London: 1774. V. 38

The History and Antiquities of the County of Dorset. London: 1861/63/68/70. V. 39

HUTCHINS, MAUDE PHELPS

Diagrammatics. New York: 1932. V. 38; 39; 40

HUTCHINS, PATRICIA

Ezra Pound's Kensington. London: 1964. V. 37; 38; 40

James Joyce's Dublin. Dublin: 1950. V. 41

HUTCHINS, THOMAS

An Historical Narrative and Topographical Description of Louisiana and West Florida, Comprehending the River Mississippi . . . Philadelphia: 1784. V. 38; 43

A Topographical Description of Virginia, Pennsylvania, Maryland and North Carolina. London: 1778. V. 46

HUTCHINSON, BENJAMIN

Kimbolton Park: a Poem. London: 1765. V. 41

HUTCHINSON, C. C.

Resources of Kansas, Fifteen Years Experience. Topeka: 1871. V. 37; 39

HUTCHINSON, EDWARD

The Victoria Nyanza, a Field for Missionary Enterprise. London: 1876. V. 43

HUTCHINSON, FRANCIS 1660-1739

A Defence of the Compassionate Address to Papists. London: 1718. V. 37

HUTCHINSON, FRANCIS 1660-1739 continued

An Historical Essay Concerning Witchcraft. London: 1718. V. 38; 43; 44

Historical Essay Concerning Witchcraft. London: 1720. V. 46

HUTCHINSON, FRANK

New South Wales. Sydney: 1896. V. 39

HUTCHINSON, GRAHAM SETON

The Thirty-Third Division in France and Flanders 1915-1919. London: 1921. V. 37

HUTCHINSON, H. D.

The Campaign in Tirah 1897-1898. London: 1898. V. 46

HUTCHINSON, H. G.

Golf. London: 1890. V. 40

HUTCHINSON, H. R.

The Lindley Library. Catalogue of Books, Pamphlets, Manuscripts and Drawings. London: 1927. V. 39; 44

HUTCHINSON, HAROLD F.

London Transport Posters. London: 1963. V. 41

HUTCHINSON, HORACE

Big Game Shooting. London: 1905. V. 37; 41

British Golf Links: a Short Account of the Leading Golf Links of the United Kingdom. London: 1897. V. 41

HUTCHINSON, I. R.

Reminiscences . . . Forty-Five Years in Mississippi, Louisiana and Texas. Houston: 1874. V. 38

HUTCHINSON, J.

A Botanist in Southern Africa. Los Angeles: 1946-53. V. 38

Flora of West Tropical Africa. London: 1954-72. V. 37

Genera of Flowering Plants (Angiospermae). 1980. V. 38

HUTCHINSON, J. H.

A Catalogue of Books Belonging to J. H. Hutchinson. London: 1882. V. 38; 40

HUTCHINSON, JOHN

A Botanist in Southern Africa. London: 1946. V. 39

Memoirs of the the Life of Colonel Hutchinson . . . London: 1806. V. 39

HUTCHINSON, JONATHAN

An Atlas of Portraits of Diseases of the Skin. London: 1860-75. V. 41

Atlas of Clinical Medicine, Surgery and Pathology . . . London: 1901-03. V. 43

Atlas of Clinical Medicine, Surgery and Pathology. Volume II. London: 1904-07. V. 43

A Clinical Memoir on Certain Diseases of the Eye and Ear, Consequent on Inherited Syphilis. London: 1863. V. 37; 38

Discussion on the Pathology of Syphilis. London: 1875-76. V. 39

A Smaller Atlas of Illustration of Clinical Surgery. London: 1895. V. 45

HUTCHINSON, K. M.

Memoir of Abijah Hutchinson, a Soldier of the Revolution. Rochester: 1843. V. 40

HUTCHINSON, LUCY

Memoirs of the Life of Colonel Hutchinson, Governor of Nottingham Castle and Town. London: 1808. V. 42

HUTCHINSON, MRS.

Fly-Fishing in Fresh and Salt Water. London: 1851. V. 39

HUTCHINSON, PETER ORLANDO

The Geology of Sidmouth. Sidmouth: 1843. V. 38

HUTCHINSON, THOMAS

Buenos Ayres and Argentine Gleanings . . . London: 1865. V. 45

A Collection of Original Papers Relative to the History of the Colony of Massachusetts-Bay. Albany: 1865. V. 38

Copy of Letters Sent to Great Britain by His Excellency Thomas Hutchinson, the Hon. Andrew Simon, and Several Other Persons. Boston: 1773. V. 45

The Diary and Letters of His Excellency . . . London: 1883. V. 39

The History of the Colony of Massachusetts Bay, from the First Settlement Thereof in 1628, Until Its Incorporation with the Colony of Plymouth, Province of Main. London: 1765. V. 38; 46

The History of the Province of Massachusetts-Bay, From the Charter of King William and Queen Mary, in 1691, Until the Year 1750. Boston: 1767. V. 39

The History of Massacnusetts, from the First Settlement Thereof in 1628, Until the Year 1750. Boston: 1795. V. 46

The History of Massachusetts from the First Settlement Thereof in 1628, Until the year 1750 . . . Salem/Boston: 1795. V. 41

The History of the Province of Massachusetts Bay, from 1749 to 11774 . . . London: 1828. V. 43; 46

HUTCHINSON, THOMAS J.

Impressions of West Africa. London: 1858. V. 39; 42

Parana; With Incidents of the Paraguayan War, and South American Recollections, From 1861 to 1868. London: 1868. V. 39

Ten Years' Wanderings Among the Ethiopians. London: 1861. V. 43

HUTCHINSON, THOMAS JOSEPH

Buenos Ayres and Argentine Gleanings . . . London: 1865. V. 38; 42

Narrative of the Niger, Tshadda and Binue Explroation: Including a Report on the Position and Prospects of Trade Up Those Rivers, With Remarks on the Malaria and Fevers of Western Africa. London: 1855. V. 46

Ten Years' Wanderings Among the Ethiopians. London: 1861. V. 38

HUTCHINSON, W. H.

A Note Book of the Old West. (with) One Man's West. Chico: 1947/48. V. 44

HUTCHINSON, W. N.

Dog Breaking. The Most Expeditious, Certain and Easy Method. London: 1848. V. 46

HUTCHINSON, WALTER

Hutchinson's Dog Encyclopaedia. London: n.d. V. 43

Hutchinson's Britian Beautiful, A Popular and Illustrated Account of the . . . Historical, Architectural . . . London: 1930. V. 39

Hutchinson's Dog Encyclopaedia. London. V. 39

HUTCHINSON, WILLIAM 1732-1801

An Excursion to the Lakes in Westmoreland and Cumberland . . . London: 1776. V. 44

The History and Antiquities of the County Baplatine of Durham. Newcastle: 1785-87-94. V. 46

The History and Antiquites of the County Palatine of Durham. Durham: 1821, 1823. V. 40

The History of the County of Cumberland. Carlisle: 1794. V. 40; 42

The Spirit of Masonry in Moral and Elucidatory Lectures. London: 1775. V. 42

HUTCHISON, G. S.

Footslogger - an Autobiography. Hutchinson: 1931. V. 44

HUTCHISON, I. R.

Reminiscences, Sketches and Addresses Selected from My Papers During a Ministry of Forty-Five Years in Mississippi, Louisiana and Texas. Houston: 1874. V. 39

HUTCHISON, J. R.

Reminiscences . . . Forty-Five Years in Mississippi, Louisiana and Texas. Houston: 1874. V. 39; 42

HUTCHISON, LT. COL.

History and Memoir of the 33rd Battalion Machine Gun Corps and of the 19th, 98th, 100th and 248th M.G. Companies. London: 1919. V. 45; 46

HUTCHISON, WILLIAM

The Spirit of Masonry. In Moral and Elucidatory Lectures. Carlisle: 1795. V. 45

HUTCHISSON,

Sixteen Sketches Illustrative of the Siege and Capture of Bhurtpore. Calcutta: 1826. V. 41; 44; 46

HUTCINSON, W. N.

Dog Breaking. London: 1848. V. 39

HUTH, A. H.

A Catalogue of Woodcuts and Engravings in the Huth Library. 1910. V. 37; 39

Catalogue of the 50 manuscripts & printed books bequethed to the British Museum by A.H. Huth. 1912. V. 37

HUTH, ALFRED H.

Catalogue of the Fifty Manuscripts & Printed Books Bequeathed to the British Museum by Alfred H. Huth. London: 1912. V. 38; 44

HUTH, ALFRED HENRY

A Catalogue of the Woodcuts and Engravings in the Huth Library. London: 1910. V. 41; 45; 46

Catalogue of the Famous Library of Printed Books (and) Illuminated Manuscripts . . . Collected by Henry Huth. London: 1911-18. V. 46

HUTH, F. H.

Works on Horses and Equitation. London: 1887. V. 42

HUTH, HANS

Roentgen Furniture. Abraham and David Roentgen. London: 1974. V. 42

HUTH, HENRY

Ancient Ballads and Broadsides . . . London: 1867. V. 45

Catalogue of the Famous Library of Printed Books, Illuminated Manuscripts, Autograph Letters and Engravings. London: 1911-20. V. 39; 44; 45

Catalogue of the Famous Library . . . Collected by Henry Huth. London: 1911-22. V. 39

The Huth Library. London: 1880. V. 39; 41

HUTNIK, JOSEPH

We Ripened Fast: the Unofficial History of the 75th Infantry Division. Frankfurt & Main. V. 45

HUTT, HENRY

The Henry Hutt Picture Book. New York: 1908. V. 44

HUTTEN, ULRICH VON 1488-1523

Ad Carolum Imperatorem, Adversus Intentatam Sibi a Romanistis vim & Iniuriam, Conquestio. Ad principes Ac Viros Germaniae de Eadem Reconquestio. Ad Albertum Brandepurgensem & Friderichum Saxonum Ducen, Principes Electores . . . Strasbourg: 1520. V. 38

Arminius Dilogus Huttenicus, Continens res Arminii in Germania Gestas. Wittenberg: 1538. V. 38

De Guaiaci Medicina et Morbo Gallico Liber Unus. Mainz: 1524. V. 37

Duo Volumina Epistolarum Obscurorum Virorum Ad D.M. Ortui. Rome: 1570. V. 40

De Guaiaci Medicina et Morbo Gallico Liber Unus. Mainz: 1524. V. 42

Oytie. Nemo. Augsburg: 1518. V. 37

HUTTICH, JOHANN

Collectanea Antiquitatum in Urbe, Atque Agro Moguntino Repertarum. Mainz. V. 39

Imperatorum et Caesarum Vitae, cum Imaginibus ad Vivam Effigiem Expressis. Strassburg: 1534-37. V. 38; 39; 44

Imperatorum & Caesarvm Vitae, Cvm Imaginibus ad Viuam Effigiem Expressis. Lyon: 1550. V. 39

HUTTON, ALFRED

The Sword and the Centuries. London: 1901. V. 41

The Swordsman. London: 1891. V. 40; 42

HUTTON, CATHERINE

The Tour of Africa. London: 1819. V. 46

HUTTON, CHARLES 1737-1823

A Course of Mathematics . . . London: 1799-98. V. 42; 45

A Course of Mathematics. London: 1800-01, 1811. V. 38

the Diarian Miscellany. London: 1775. V. 39

Elements of Conic Sections; with Select Exercises in Various Branches of Mathematics and Philosophy. London: 1787. V. 44

A Mathematical and Philosophical Dictionary. London: 1796. V. 46

A Mathematical and Philosophical Dictionary . . . London: 1796-5. V. 40; 43

A Mathematical and Philosophical Dictionary. London: 1796, 1795. V. 38

A Mathematical and Philosophical Dictionary: with an historical account of the rise, progress and present state of these Sciences; also memoirs of the lives and writings of the most eminent authors. London: 1795. V. 37

Mathematical Tables: containing Common, Hyperbolic and Logistic Logarithms. (with) A Large and Original History of the Discoveries and Writings relating to those Subjects. London: 1785. V. 37

Miscellanea Mathematica. London: 1775. V. 38; 43

A Treatise on Mensuration, Both in Theory and Practice. Newcastle Upon Tyne: 1770. V. 38; 40

HUTTON, CLARKE

Eleven Chinese Proverbs. Esher: 1975. V. 45

HUTTON, J.

Theory of the Earth. London: 1972. V. 37

HUTTON, JAMES

Abstract of a Dissertation Read in the Royal Society of Edinburgh Upon the Seventh of March, the Fourth of April MDCCLXXXV, Concerning the System of the Earth . . . Edinburgh: 1785. V. 41

Missionary Life in the Southern Seas. London: 1874. V. 43

Theory of the Earth, with Proofs and Illustrations. London: 1899. V. 45; 46

HUTTON, JOHN

A Tour to the Caves, in the Environs of Ingleborough and Settle in the West Riding of Yorkshire. London: 1781. V. 45

HUTTON, LAWRENCE

Literary Landmaraks of London. London: 1885. V. 38; 40

HUTTON, R. N.

Five Years in the East. London: 1847. V. 45

HUTTON, RICHARD 1561-1639

The Young Clerk's Guide. London: 1652. V. 38; 40

HUTTON, S. K.

Among the Eskimos of Labrador. Toronto: 1912. V. 44

HUTTON, W.

The Battle of Bosworth Field, Between Richard the Third and Henry Earl of Richmond, August 22, 1485. London: 1813. V. 41

HUTTON, WILLIAM

The Battle of Bosworth-Field, Between Richard the Third, and Henry Earl of Richmond, August 22, 1485 . . . Birmingham: 1788. V. 43

Courts of Requests. Birmingham: 1787. V. 40

A Dissertation on Juries. Birmingham: 1789. V. 40

A Journey from Birmingham to London. Birmingham: 1785. V. 40; 43; 46

The Life of William Hutton, F. A. S. S. London: 1817. V. 43

HUTTON, WILLIAM HOLDEN

By Thames and Cotswold. Westminster: 1903. V. 43

HUTTON, WILLIAM RICH

California 1847-1852. San Marino: 1942. V. 38; 44; 45

HUXFORD, FOLKS

Pioneers of Wiregrass Georgia. Homerville: 1951-60. V. 42

Pioneers of Wiregrass Georgia. Homerville: 1951-75. V. 42

HUXFORD, H. J.

History of the 8th Gurkha Rifles 1824-1949. Aldershot: 1952. V. 42

HUXHAM, JOANNE

Observationum de Aere et Morbis Epidemicis . . . London: 1752. V. 42

HUXHAM, JOHN

A Dissertation on the Malignant, Ulcerous Sore Throat. London: 1757. V. 38

An Essay on Fevers to Which is Now Added a Dissertation on the Malignant, Ulcerous Sore Throat. London: 1757. V. 38

An Essay on Fevers, To Which is Now Added, A Dissertation on the Malignant, Ulcerous Sore-Throat. London: 1764. V. 44

Medical and Chemical Observations Upon Antimony. London: 1756. V. 38

HUXLEY, ALDOUS LEONARD 1894-1963

After Many a Summer Dies the Swan. New York & London: 1939. V. 43

After Many a Summer. London: 1939. V. 37

Along the Road. Notes and Essays of a Tourist. New York: 1925. V. 37

Antic Hay. London: 1923. V. 39; 40; 41; 46

Antic Hay. London: 1926. V. 46

Ape and Essence. London: 1949. V. 39

Apennine. Gaylordsville: 1930. V. 39; 40; 42; 43

Arabia Infelix. New York: 1929. V. 39; 41; 42; 43; 44; 46

Beyond the Mexique Bay. London: 1934. V. 37; 38; 40; 41; 42; 43; 44

Brave New World. 1932. V. 37; 39; 43

Brave New World. Garden City: 1932. V. 41

Brave New World. London: 1932. V. 37; 38; 39; 40; 41; 42; 43; 44; 45; 46

Brave New World. New York: 1932. V. 44; 45

Brave New World Revisited. New York: 1958. V. 44

Brave New World. 1974. V. 39

Brave New World. Avon: 1974. V. 44; 46

Brief Candles. New York: 1930. V. 39; 43; 44; 46

The Burning Wheel. Oxford: 1916. V. 37; 38; 39; 40; 41; 42; 44

The Burning Wheel. Oxford: 1916. V. 37

The Cicadas and Other Poems. Garden City: 1931. V. 38; 39

The Cicadas and Other Poems. London: 1931. V. 38; 39; 43; 44; 46

The Defeat of Youth. Oxford: 1918. V. 37; 39; 40; 42; 44; 46

The Discovery. 1924. V. 45

Do What You Will. London: 1929. V. 37; 44; 46

An Encyclopedia of Pacifism. London: 1937. V. 38; 43

Ends and Means. London: 1937. V. 43

Ends and Means. An Enquiry into the Nature of Ideals and Into the Methods Employed for their Realization. London: 1937. V. 39; 41

Ends and Means. New York: 1937. V. 43

Essays New and Old. London: 1926. V. 39; 40; 41; 43; 44; 46

Essays New and Old. London: 1936. V. 42

Essays New and Old. London: 1926. V. 37; 38

Eyeless in Gaza. London: 1936. V. 37; 38; 41; 42; 46

The French of Paris. New York: 1954. V. 39

Holy Face and Other Essays. London: 1929. V. 37; 38; 39; 40; 41; 42; 44

Jesting Pilate. London: 1926. V. 43

Leda. London: 1920. V. 38; 41

HUXLEY, ALDOUS LEONARD 1894-1963 continued

Leda. Garden City: 1929. V. 39

Leda. New York: 1929. V. 37; 39; 40; 45

Little Mexican: & Other Stories. London: 1924. V. 46

Mortal Coils. London: 1922. V. 42; 44

The Most Agreeable Vice. Los Angeles: 1938. V. 39; 41; 42; 43

Music at Night. New York: 1931. V. 39; 42; 45; 46

New World. London: 1932. V. 43

The Olive Tree. London: 1936. V. 37; 41; 43; 46

On the Margin. London: 1923. V. 43

Point Count Point. London: 1928. V. 37; 38; 40; 41; 42; 43; 44

Point Counter Point. New York: 1928. V. 43

Prisons. London: 1949. V. 39

Prisons. Los Angeles: 1949. V. 37; 38; 40

Proper Studies. London: 1927. V. 44

Proper Studies. Garden City: 1928. V. 43

Rotunda. London: 1932. V. 40

Science Liberty and Peace. New York: 1946. V. 41; 42

Selected Poems. Oxford: 1925. V. 38; 39

Selected Poems. New York: 1925. V. 37

Selected Poems. Oxford: 1926. V. 38

T. H. Huxley as a Man of Letters. London: 1912. V. 41

Texts and Pretexts: an Anthology. London: 1932. V. 37; 40

Texts and Pretexts. London: 1935. V. 44

Texts and Pretexts. London: 1949. V. 39

They Still Draw Pictures! New York: 1938. V. 37

Those Barren Leaves. London: 1925. V. 39; 44; 46

Those Barren Leaves. New York: (1925). V. 37

Time Must Have a Stop. New York: 1944. V. 41; 42; 46

Tomorrow and Tomorrow and Tomorrow. New York: 1956. V. 41

Two or Three Graces and Other Stories. London: 1926. V. 41

Vulgarity in Language. London: 1930. V. 37; 43; 45; 46

What Are You Going to Do About It? London: 1936. V. 42; 43

Words and Their Meanings. Los Angeles: 1940. V. 39; 40

Words and Their Meanings. Los Angeles: (1940). V. 37

The World of Light. London: 1931. V. 42; 46

HUXLEY, ELSPETH

Red Strangers. London: 1939. V. 42

White Man's Country. London: 1935. V. 42

HUXLEY, JULIAN

The Uniqueness of Man. London: 1941. V. 45

HUXLEY, LEONARD

Life and Letters of Thomas Henry Huxley. London: 1900. V. 45

HUXLEY, THOMAS

The Monkey: an Essay. N.P.: 1959. V. 40

HUXLEY, THOMAS HENRY 1825-1895

Collected Essays. London: 1970. V. 39

Collected Essays. London: 1898. V. 37

The Crayfish. London: 1880. V. 39

Diary of the Voyage of H.M.S. Rattlesnake. London: 1935. V. 39; 46

An Elementary Atlas of Comparative Osteology, in Twelve Plates, the Objects Selected and Arranged by Professor Huxley and Drawn on Stone by B. Waterhouse Hawkins. London: 1864. V. 40

Essays of . . . London: 1901-04. V. 39

Evidence as to Man's Place in Nature. London: 1863. V. 38; 39; 43; 45; 46

Hume, Sa Vie -sa Philosophie . . . Paris: 1880. V. 43

An Introduction to the Classification of Animals. London: 1869. V. 41

A Manual of the Anatomy of Invertebrated Animals. London: 1871. V. 40

The Monkey: an Essay. N.P.: 1959. V. 42

The Oceanic Hydrozoa. London: 1858. V. 43; 45

The Oceanic Hydrozoa: a Description of the Calycophoridae and Physophoridae Observed During the Voyage of H. M. S. 'Rattlesnake' in the Years 1846-1850. London: 1859. V. 37; 43; 45

On the Morphology of the Cephalous Mollusca, as Illustrated by the Anatomy of Certain Heterpoda and Pteropoda Collected During the Voyage of H.M.S. 'Rattlesnake' in 1846-50. London: 1852. V. 43

On Our Knowledge of the Causes of the Phenomena of Organic Nature. London: 1863. V. 38

On the Origin of Species; or, the Cause of the Phenomena of Organic Nature. New York: 1863. V. 38; 45

On Our Knowledge of the Causes of the Phenomena of Organic Nature. London: 1863. V. 38

Science and Culture and Other Essays. London: 1881. V. 41

The Scientific Memoirs of Thomas Henry Huxley. London: 1898-1902. V. 38; 41; 42; 45

Selected Works. New York & London. V. 37

Touchstone for Ethics (1893-1943). New York: & London: 1943. V. 41

Works of . . . London: 1904-08. V. 46

HUYCKE, HAROLD D.

To Santa Rosalia, Further and Back. Newport News: 1970. V. 40

HUYGENS, CHRISTIAN

De Circuli Magnitudine Inventa. Leiden: 1654. V. 45

Cosmotheros; or Conjectures Concerning the Planetary Worlds and Their Inhabitants. Glasgow: 1757. V. 40

Horologium Oscillatorium. Sive de Motu Pendulorum ad Horologia Aptato Demonstrationes Geometricaae. Paris: 1673. V. 37

Kosmotheoros, Sive de Terris Coelestibus, Earumque Ornatu, Conjecturae. The Hague: 1698. V. 37; 44

Opera Varia. Leyden: 1724. V. 38

Opera Reliqua. Amsterdam: 1728. V. 46

Systema Saturnium, sive de Causis Mirandorum Saturni Phaenomenon, et Comite Ejus Planeta Novo. The Hague: 1659. V. 37

HUYGHE, RENE

L'Arte e l'Uomo. Turin: 1959-62. V. 38

Delacroix. London: 1963. V. 44

Delacroix. New York: 1963. V. 37; 40

HUYSCHE, G. L.

The Red River Expedition. London: 1871. V. 37; 42; 46

HUYSHE, G. L.

The Red River Expedition. London: & New York: 1871. V. 39; 44

The Red River Expedition. New York: 1871. V. 37

HUYSHE, JOHN

A Treatise on Logic, on the Basis of Aldrich, with Illustrative Notes. (with) Questions on Aldrich's Logic, with Reference to the Most Popular Treatises. Oxford: 1842/45. V. 43; 45

HUYSMANS, J. K.

Against the Grain. 1922. V. 44; 45

Down There. 1924. V. 43; 45

De Tout. Paris: 1902. V. 46

HUYSMANS, JORIS KARL

Croquis Parisiens, Eaux-Fortes de Forain & Raffaelli. Paris: 1880. V. 38

En Route. Paris: 1921. V. 38

HYAMS, EDWARD

The English Garden. London: 1964. V. 37

HYATT, H. S.

Manufacturing, Agricultural and Industrial Resources of Iowa with reliable Information to Capitalists Seeking the Best Fields for Investments, Also, Valuable Information for Emigrants Seeking the New and Desirable Homes . . . Des Moines,: 1872. V. 37; 38; 42

HYATT, THADDEUS

An Account of Some Experiments with Portland Cement Concrete Combined with Iron, as a Building Material, With Reference to Economy of Metal in Construction . . . London: 1877. V. 44

The Prayer of Thaddeus Hyatt to James Buchanan . . . In Behalf of Kansas, Asking for a Postponement of All the Land Sales in that Territory . . . Washington: 1860. V. 45

HYBINUS, GAIUS

The Poeticon Astronomicon. 1985. V. 44

THE HYBIRDS, an Epi-Comic Satire. Milwaukee: 1871. V. 38

HYDE, ALEXANDER

The Frozen Zone - and Its Explorers . . . Hartford: 1875. V. 39

HYDE, DOUGLAS

Catalogue of the Books and Manuscripts Comprising the Library of the Late Sir John Gilbert. Dublin: 1918. V. 43

Danta De, Hymns to God - Ancient and Modern. Dublin: 1928. V. 38

The Lad of the Ferule, Giolla an Fhiugha, or the Adventures of the Children of Norway. London: 1899. V. 43

The Religious Songs of Connacht. London: 1906. V. 43

HYDE, EDWARD

The History of the Rebellion and Civil Wars in Ireland. London: 1720. V. 37

The History of the Revellion and Civil Wars in Ireland. London: 1721. V. 37

HYDE, GEORGE E.

Rangers and Regulars. Denver: 1933. V. 42

HYDE, GEORGE E. continued

Red Cloud's Folk. Norman: 1937. V. 37

HYDE, HENRY

The Correspondence of Henry Hyde, Earl of Clarendon, and of His Brother, Laurence Hyde, Earl of Rochester . . . London: 1828. V. 39

HYDE, HENRY HYDE, BARON 1710-1753

The Mistakes; or the Happy Resentment. London: 1758. V. 43

HYDE, J. A. LLOYD

Oriental Lowestoft. New York: 1936. V. 39

Oriental Lowestoft: Chinese Export Porcelain, Porcelaine de la Cie. des Indes. Newport: 1964. V. 37; 38

Oriental Lowestaft Chinese Export Porcelain Porcelaine de la Cie des Indes. Newport: Monmouthshire: 1964. V. 40

HYDE, JAMES WILSON

The Royal Mail: Its Curiosities and Romance. Edinburgh: 1885. V. 42; 43

HYDE, JOHN

Mormonism: Its Leaders and Designs. New York: 1857. V. 43; 45

HYDE, LAURENCE

Southern Cross: a Novel of the South Seas . . . Los Angeles: 1951. V. 42

HYDE, MATILDA STRANGE HYDE

Little Captives of 1704. 1919. V. 41

HYDE Nugent. London: 1827. V. 42

HYDE, ORSON

A Sketch of the Travels and Ministry of . . . Salt Lake City: 1869. V. 42; 43

HYDE, RALPH

The Regent's Park Colosseum . . . London: 1982. V. 41

HYDE, T. K.

The Negro Sunday Scholar; or the Life of Catherine Chambers, Who Died, Oct. 31, 1823, in the Island of Montserrat, West Indies. New York: 1828. V. 44

HYDE, WALTER WOODBURN

Olympic Victor Monuments and Greek Athletic Art. Washington: 1921. V. 42

HYDE, WILLIAM L.

History of the One Hundred and Twelfth rEgiment N. Y. Volunteers. Fredonia: 1866. V. 39; 40; 43

HYES, RICHARD

The Last Invasion of Ireland. Dublin: 1939. V. 38

HYETT, FRANCIS ADAMS

The Bibliographer's Manual of Gloucestershire Lieterature . . . Gloucester: 1895-97. V. 39; 40; 42; 43; 44; 45

HYGINUS, mythographer

The Poeticon Astronomicon. 1985. V. 40

HYGINUS, C. JULIUS

Mythographi Latini. Amsterdam: 1681. V. 41

HYGINUS, GAIUS JULIUS

The Poeticon Astronomicon. Greenbae: 1985. V. 44

HYMAN, L.

The Invertebrates. New York: 1940-59. V. 37

The Inverterbrates. London: 1940-67. V. 37

HYMERS, JOHN

A Treatise on Differential Equations, and on the Calculus of Finite Differences. Cambridge: 1839. V. 37

HYMN on the Death of President Lincoln. London: 1900. V. 38

A HYMN to the Victory in Scotland. London: 1719. V. 41

HYMNI per Totum Annum: item Orationes Dominicales, Feriales, ac de Sanctis, cum Suis Antiphonis & Versiculis. Antwerp: 1601. V. 37

HYMNS and Prayers for Use at the Marriage of Michael Hornby and Nicolette Ward at St. Margaret's Church, Westminster, Nov. 15, 1928. Chelsea: 1928. V. 43; 46

HYMNS and Prayers for Use at the Marriage of Michael Hornby and Nicolette Ward at St. Margaret's Church. Chelsea: 1928. V. 37

HYMNS and Prayers for Use at the Marriage of Michael Hornby and Nicolette Ward at St. Margaret's Church Westminster, November XV, MCMXXVIII. V. 39

HYMNS and Prayers to Be Sung and Said at the Marriage of St. John Hornby and Cicely Barclay in the Parish Church, Bayford, on January XIX MDCCCXCVIII. Chelsea: 1898. V. 46

HYMNS for Divine Worship, Compiled for Use of the Methodist New Connexion. London: 1875. V. 40

HYMNS for Public and Social Worship. Maulmain: 1839. V. 40

HYMNS for the Camp. Raleigh: 1864. V. 39

HYMNS for the Liberator Soiree, Friday Evening, January 24th, 1851. ?Boston: 1851. V. 44

HYMNS for the Use of the Society of United Christian Friends Professing the Faith of Universal Salvation. New York: 1817. V. 43

HYMNS to Aphrodite. San Francisco: 1927. V. 42

HYNE, CUTCLIFFE

The Lost Continent. London: 1900. V. 42

HYNE, DOUGLAS

A Literary History of Ireland from the Earliest Times to the Present Day. London: 1910. V. 38

HYNES, FRANK W.

Nature's Romance 'Over the Loop' Clear Creek Canon and Adjacent Scenery. Denver: 1898. V. 39

HYSON, TIMOTHY

A Letter to Mr. Richard Twining, Tea Dealer, and One of the Candidates for the Present Vacancy in the East India Direction. London: 1827. V. 42

HYVOENEN, HEIKKI

Russian Porcelain. Collection Vera Saarela. The National Museum of Finland. Helsinki: (1982). V. 37

I

IAMBLICHUS

Chalcidensis ex Coele-Syria de Mysteriis Liber. Oxford: 1678. V. 39; 44

Life of Pythagoras, or Pythaagoric Life. London: 1816. V. 37

IAMBLICHUS, OF CHALCIS

De Mysteriis Aegyptiorum, Chaldaeorum, Assyriorum (and other Plantoic and Neo-Platonic Writings). Venice: 1497. V. 46

IBAR, FRANCISCO

Muerte Politica de la Republica Mexicana (with) Regeneracion Politica . . . Mexico: 1829-30. V. 39

IBBETSON, JULIUS CAESAR

An Accidence, or Gamut of Painting in Oil and Watercolors. London: 1803. V. 44

A Picturesque Guide to Bath, Bristol, Hot-Wells, the River Avon and Adjacent Country . . . London: 1793. V. 39; 43; 44

IBBETT, VERA

Flowers in Heraldry. Vancouver: 1977. V. 39

IBBETT, W. J.

Ten Lyrics. (Flanshom: 1924). V. 37

IBBETT, WILLIAM JOSEPH

Three Letters from W. J. Ibbett to His Friend H. Buxton Forman in Praise of Venus. London: 1894. V. 42

IBBOT, BENJAMIN

A Course of Sermons Preach'd for the Lecture Founded by Honourable Robert Boyle Esq . . . London: 1727. V. 46

IBN' ARABSHAH, AHMAD MUHAMMED 1392-1450

(Arabic title) Vitae & Rerum Gestarum Timuri, Qui Vulgo Tamerlanes Dicitur, Historia. Leiden: 1636. V. 39

IBN-BATUTA

Viagens Extensas e Dilatadas do Celebre Arabe Abu-Abdalah, Mais Conhecido Pelo Nome de Ben-Batuta. Lisbon: 1840-55. V. 45

IBN MASAWAYH, YUHANNA d. 857 or 8

I Libri di Gio. Mesue de i Semplici Purgativi, et Delle Medicine Composte, di Molte Annotationi e Dichiarationi Ornati & Illustrati. Venetiis: 1589. V. 39

Opera Medicinalia. Venice: 1495. V. 39

Opera de Medicamentorum Purgantium Delectu, Castigatione & Usu, Libri Duo . . . Venice: 1581. V. 41

IBN SHADDAD, BAHA AL-DIN YUSUF UBU RAFI

(Arabic & Latin) Vita et res Gestae Sultani,Almalichi Alnasiri, Saladini, Abi Modafiri Josephi F. Jobi . . . Leiden. V. 44

IBN TAGHRIBIRDI, ABU AL-MAHASIN YUSUF 1411-1470

History of Egypt. 1382-1469 A.D. Berkeley: 1954-63. V. 39

IBRAHIM-HILMY

The Literature of Egypt and Soudan from the Earliest Times to the Year 1885 Inclusive. London: 1886-88. V. 40

IBSEN, HENRIK 1828-1906

Bygmester Solness. Copenhagen: 1892. V. 38

En Folkefiende. Skuespil i Fem Akter. Kobenhavn: 1882. V. 39

Hedda Gabler. Kobenhavn: 1890. V. 38; 42; 45; 46

Hedda Gabler. London: 1891. V. 38; 46

Hedda Gabler . . . (with) The Master Builder. London: 1891/95. V. 44

The Oxford Ibsen. Oxford;: 1960-77. V. 38; 40

Peer Gynt. London: 1936. V. 37; 38; 40; 41; 42; 44; 45; 46

Peer Gunt. London: (1936). V. 37

The Pillars of Society and Other Plays. London: 1888. V. 44

Poems. New York: 1987. V. 45

The Vikings at Helgeland. Christiania: 1858. V. 46

Collected Works. London: 1908. V. 46

The Works. New York: 1911. V. 42; 44

The Collected Works. New York: 1912-16. V. 40

The Works. New York: 1917. V. 44; 45

The Works. The Viking Edition. With Introductions by William Archer and C.H. Herford. New York: 1911-12. V. 37

ICARD, S.

Dictionary of Greek Coin Inscriptions. Chicago: 1968. V. 40; 42; 44

Dictionary of Greek Coin Inscriptions. Chicago: (1968). V. 37

ICE-CREAM and Cakes. A New Collection of Standard Fresh and Original Receipts for Household and Commercial Use by an American. New York: 1883. V. 44

ICELAND, Greenland and the Faroe Islands. Edinburgh. V. 37

ICELANDIC Sagas, and Other Historical Documents Relating to the Settlements and Descents of the Northmen on the British Isles. London: 1887-94. V. 42

ICHTHYOLOGY for Youth; or, a History of Nearly All the Known Fishes of the Ocean. New York: 1810. V. 44

IDAHO. CONSTITUTION - 1890

The Constitution of the Proposed State of Idaho. Washington: 1890. V. 37; 38; 39

IDAHO. TERRITORY. LAWS, STATUTES, ETC.

Laws of the Territory of Idaho, First Session, Convened on the 7th Day of December 1863 and Adjourned on the 4th Day of February 1864, at Lewiston . . . Lewiston: 1864. V. 46

IDAHO. (TERRITORY). LAWS, STATUTES, ETC. - 1866

Laws of the Territory of Idaho Thir Session . . . At Boise City Containing Also the Territorial Organic Act . . . Boise City: 1866. V. 42

IDAHO. (TERRITORY). LAWS, STATUTES, ETC. - 1889

General Laws of the Territory of Idaho Passed at the Fifteenth Session of the Territorial Legislature . . . 1889 . . . at Boise City . . . Idaho: 1889. V. 42

IDAHO. (TERRITORY). LEGISLATIVE ASSEMBLY - 1881

Journal of the Council of the Eleventh Legislative Assembly of the Territory of Idaho . . . Boise City: 1881. V. 42

IDE, A. W.

Index to A. W. Ide's Map. Showing Towns, Counties, Lakes, Creeks, Mountains, Buttes, Rivers, Etc. Helena: 1890. V. 39

IDE, SIMEON

A Bibliographical Sketch of the Life of William B. Ide: with a Minute and Interesting Account of One of the Largest Emigrating Companies. Claremont: 1880. V. 38; 39; 40; 41; 42; 43

IDE, WILLIAM B.

Who Conquered California? Claremont: 1880. V. 43

IDEAS for Rustic Furniture Proper fro Garden Seats, Summer Houses, Hermitages, Cottages &c. London: 1780. V. 46

IDEM, SEMPER

The 'Blue Book'. A Bibliographical Attempt to Describe the Guide Books to the Houses of Ill Fame in New Orleans as They Were Published There. N.P.: 1936. V. 37; 40

IDES, EVERT YSBRANTS

Three Years Travels from Moscow Overland to China: Thro' Great Ustiga, Siriania, Permia, Sibiria, Daour, Great Tartary, &c. to Peking . . . London: 1706. V. 38; 40; 41

IDLE, CHRISTOPHER, PSEUD.

Hints on Shooting and Fishing, &c. London: 1855. V. 42

THE IDLER. London: 1761. V. 37; 38
THE IDLER. London: 1767. V. 38

IGNATIUS

Epistolae Genuinae S Ignatii Martyris; Quae Nunc Primum in Lucem Vident ex Bibliotheca Florentina. Amstelodami: 1646. V. 39

IGNATIUS, SAINT OF ANTIOCH

Epistolae Undecim. Basle: 1520. V. 42

IHNE, WILHELM

The History of Rome. London: 1871-82. V. 37

IHRE, JOHANN

Glossarium Suiogothicum, in Quo Hodierno Usu Frequentata Vocabula, Quam in Legum Patriarum Tabulis Aliisque Aevi Medii Scriptis Obvia Explicantur . . . Upsaliae: 1769. V. 38

IKTOMI, NIKOLA

America Needs Indians! Denver: 1937. V. 39

ILCHESTER, EARL OF

Letter to Henry Fox Lord Holland. 1915. V. 45

ILES, FRANCIS

Malice Aforethought. London: 1931. V. 44

ILEY, MATTHEW

The Life, Writings, Opinions, and Times of the Right Hon. George Gordon Noel Byron, Lord Byron . . . In the Course of the Biography is Also Separately Given Copious Recollections of the Lately Destroyed MSS, originally intended for posthumous publication . . . London: 1825. V. 37

ILF, ILYA

The Little Golden Calf. New York: 1932. V. 37

ILIFF, EDWARD H., MRS.

Poems Upon Several Subjects. London: 1808. V. 43; 45

ILIFF, JOHN W.

Iliff's Imperial Atlas of the World . . . Chicago: 1891. V. 45
Iliff's Imperial Atlas of the World. Chicago: 1897. V. 45

ILIVE, JACOB

The Book of Jasher . . . Bristol: 1829. V. 42

THE ILLEGAL Marriage; or, the Adventures of a Young Lady of Fortune, Who Was Seduced from Her Parents by a Military Officer . . .
Portsea: 1810. V. 44

ILLINGWORTH, A. HOLDEN

More Reminiscences. Bradford: 1936. V. 39
Reminiscences. Bradford: 1932. V. 37

ILLINGWORTH, CAYLEY

A Topographical Account of the Parish of Scampton . . . and of the Roman Antiquities Lately Discovered There. London: 1810. V. 41

ILLINOIS. BOARD OF COMMISSIONERS FOR PUBLIC WORKS

Report from the Commissioners of Public Works, In Reply to Resolutions of the Senate and House of Representatives of the State of Illinois, Transmitting Abstracts of Disbursements in Each Circuit. Vandalia: 1839. V. 43

ILLINOIS CENTRAL RAIL-ROAD COMPANY

Illinois Central Rail-Road Company Offers for Sale Over 2,000,000 Acres Selected Farming and Wood Lands . . . New York: 1856. V. 44

ILLINOIS CENTRAL RAILROAD CO.

The Illinois Central Rail-Road Company Offer for Sale Over 2,400,00 Acres Selected Prairie, Farm and Wood Lands, in Tracts of Any Size . . . New York: 1855. V. 37; 42
The Illinois Central Railroad Company Offers for Sale over 1,500,000 Acres Selected Farming and Wood Lands. Chicago: 1858. V. 42

ILLINOIS CENTRAL RAILROAD COMPANY

A Guide to the Illinois Central Railroad Lands. The Illinois Central Railroad Company Offer for Sale over 1,400,000 Acres of Selected Prairie and Wood Lands. Chicago: 1859. V. 37; 39
The Illinois Central Railroad Company offers for sale over 1,500,00 Acres selected Farming and Woodlands . . . Situated on each side of their Railroad . . . Boston: 1857. V. 37

ILLINOIS. CONSTITUTION - 1818

Constitution of the State of Illinois. Washington: 1818. V. 37

ILLINOIS. CONSTITUTION - 1870

Constitution of the State of Illinois, as Adopted in Convention, May 13, 1870, and Submitted to the People for Adoption or Rejection at an Election to Be Held July 2 . . . and the Address of the Convention . . . Springfield: 1870. V. 42

ILLINOIS. CONSTTUTIONAL CONVENTION - 1847

Journal of the Convention for Altering, Amending, or Revising the Constitution of the State of Illinois. Springfield: 1847. V. 37

ILLINOIS. LAWS, STATUTES, ETC.

Laws of the State of Illinois Relative to Justices of the Peace. Vandalia: 1839. V. 45

ILLINOIS. LAWS, STATUTES, ETC. - 1824

Laws of the State of Illinois Relating to Railroad Debits of Counties, Townships, Cities and Towns, and Supereme Court Decisions Relating Thereto. Chicago: 1868. V. 41

ILLINOIS. LAWS, STATUTES, ETC. - 1829

The Revised Code of Laws of Illinois. Cincinnati: 1829. V. 39

ILLINOIS. LAWS, STATUTES, ETC. - 1851

Laws of the State of Illinois. Springfield: 1851. V. 42

ILLINOIS MISSOURI & TEXAS RAILROAD COMPANY

The Illinois, Missouri & Texas Railway Company. Prospectus, Reports and Other Documents. St. Louis: 1873. V. 37

ILLINOIS ST. ANDREWS SOCIETY OF THE CITY OF CHICAGO

Constitution of the Illinois St. Andrews Society of the City of Chicago. Adopted 26th Jan. 1846. Chicago: 1846. V. 40

ILLINOIS. STATE BOARD OF AGRICULTURE

Catalogue of the American Fat Stock Show, American Horse Show, Held in the Expostion Building, Chicago, November 13-24, 1888. Chicago: 1888. V. 39

ILLINOIS TYPE-FOUNDING CO.

First Specimen of the Illinois Type-Founing Co. Chicago: 1873. V. 42

THE ILLUMINATED Calendar and Home Diary. London: 1844. V. 38
THE ILLUMINATED Calendar and Home Diary. London: 1845. V. 38; 39; 42

THE ILLUMINATED Calendar and Home Diary for 1845. London. V. 44

THE ILLUMINATED Calender and Home Diary. London: 1845/44. V. 44

ILLUMINATED Manuscripts, Incunabula, and Americana from Famous Libraries of the Marquess of Lothian . . . New York: 1932. V. 41

THE ILLUSTRATED Annual of Microscopy. London: 1898-1900. V. 45

ILLUSTRATED Atlas of Oakland County Michigan. Racine: 1896. V. 39

ILLUSTRATED Atlas of the Dominion of Canada . . . Toronto: 1880. V. 44
ILLUSTRATED Atlas of the Dominion of Canada . . . Toronto: 1881. V. 44

THE ILLUSTRATED Book of Natural History, Part III. Philadelphia: 1859. V. 46

ILLUSTRATED Catalogue of Spectacles and Eyeglasses in 8-K, 10-K and 14-K Gold, Platinum, Silver, Alumnico, Roman Alloy, German Silver, Filled Gold, Steel . . . Southbridge: 1894. V. 43

THE ILLUSTRATED Guide to the London and Dover Railway. London: 1844. V. 38

AN ILLUSTRATED Guide to the Most Favored Section of California. 1893. V. 41

ILLUSTRATED Historical Album of the Battalion, the Queen's Own Rifles of Canada, 1856-1894. Toronto: 1894. V. 45

ILLUSTRATED Historical Atlas of Berks County, Pennsylvania. Reading: 1876. V. 41

ILLUSTRATED History of New Mexico. Chicago: 1895. V. 37; 43

AN ILLUSTRATED History of North Idaho, Embracing Nez Perces, Idaho, Latah, Kootenai and Shoshone Counties, State of Idaho. 1903. V. 41

AN ILLUSTRATED History of Skagit and Snohomish Counties. Chicago: 1906. V. 45

AN ILLUSTRATED History of Sonoma County, California. Chicago: 1889. V. 41; 45

THE ILLUSTRATED London Almanack. London: 1858-75. V. 38

ILLUSTRATED London and Its Representatives of Commerce. London: 1893. V. 40

THE ILLUSTRATED London News. Her Majesty's Glorious Jubilee 1897; The Record Number of a Record Reign. London: 1897. V. 40

THE ILLUSTRATED London Spelling Book. London: 1849. V. 40

ILLUSTRATED Minneapolis 1891. Minneapolis: 1891. V. 37

AN ILLUSTRATED Record of Important Events in the Annals of Europe During the Years 1812, 1813, 1814 and 1815. London: 1815. V. 43

ILLUSTRATIONS of Armorial China. London: 1887. V. 41

ILLUSTRATIONS of Baptismal Fonts. London: 1844. V. 42

ILLUSTRATIONS of Lancashire. London: 1830. V. 37

ILLUSTRATIONS of Natural History . . . London: 1829-30. V. 44

ILLUSTRATIONS Of Eating; displaying the Omnivorous Character of Man; and exhibiting the Natives of Various Countries at Feeding Time. By A Beef-Eater. London: 1847. V. 39

ILLUSTRATIONS of Missionary Scenes, an Offering to Youth. Mainz. V. 39; 40

ILLUSTRATIONS of the Principal Regions of the Human Body, in Relation to Surgical Anatomy. New York: 1830. V. 41

ILLUSTRATIONS of Southern Chivalry as Shown by Photographic Portraits of Their Prisoners of War. London: 1865. V. 45

ILLUSTRATIONS of the Isle of Wight, From Original Drawings by Leitch, Clint, Cooke, Barry, etc . . . . Ryde: 1858. V. 39

ILLUSTRATORS of Children's Books 1744-1945. Compiled by Bertha E. Mahony, Louise Payson Latimer, Beulah Folmsbee. Boston: 1947. V. 37

IM THURN, EVERARD F.

Among the Indians of Guiana Being Sketches Chiefly Anthropologic from the Interior of British Guiana. London: 1883. V. 40; 43

IMAGE DU MONDE

The Mirrour of the World. Kentfield: 1964. V. 38; 39; 40; 42; 43; 44; 46

Mirroure of the Worlde. Oxford: 1980. V. 44

IMAGE, SELWYN

Art, Morals, and the War - a Lecture Delivered in the Ashmolean Museum. Oxford: 1914. V. 40

IMAGES of the Southern Writer. Athens: 1985. V. 41

IMAGIST Anthology - 1930. New York: 1930. V. 38; 40

DES IMAGISTES. An Anthology. New York: 1914. V. 41

IMBERDIS, J.

Papyrus, or the Craft of Paper. Hilversum: 1952. V. 38; 46

IMBERT, BARTHELEMY 1747-1790

Le judgement de Paris: Amsterdam: i.e. Paris: 1772. V. 45

IMBROGLIO. Leicester: 1968. V. 39

IMES, BIRNEY

Juke Joint. Jackson: 1990. V. 44; 45

IMES, BURNEY

Juke Joint Photographs. V. 43

IMFIELD, X.

Relief Model of Zermat. Maps and Photographs. Zurich: 1887. V. 41

IMISON, JOHN

The School of Arts. London: 1790. V. 38; 41; 42; 46

A Treatise of the Mechanical Powers. London: 1787. V. 42

IMITATIO CHRISTI

The Christian Pattern Paraphras'd; or, the Book of the Imitation of Christ . . . London: 1697. V. 46

An Extract from the Christian-Pattern; or, a Treatise on the Imitation of Christ. London: 1785. V. 39

Of the Imitation of Jesus Christ. V. 44

Contemptus Mundi Nuevamente Romanado. Colophon: Sevilla. V. 39

Contemptus Mundi Nuevamente Romancadeo. Seville: 1538. V. 40

Of the Imitation of Christ. London: 1602. V. 42

L'Imitation de Jesus-Christ . . . Paris: 1643. V. 38; 44

L'Imitation de Iesus Christ. Rouen: 1651. V. 45

Doctrinae Venerabilis Thomae a Kempis e libello de Imitatione Christi, pro singulis anni diebus selectae. Munich: 1699. V. 38

De l'Imitation de Jesus Christ. Paris: 1720. V. 40

De Imitatione Christi. Avignon: 1752. V. 44

L'Imitation de Jesus Christ. Paris: 1820. V. 38

De Imitatione Christi. Paris: 1824. V. 39

Of the Imitation of Christ. London: 1825. V. 45

Of the Imitation of Jesus Christ. London: 1828. V. 40

Of the Imitation of Jesus Christ. London: 1851. V. 40

L'Imitation de Jesus Christ. Paris: 1855. V. 39

L'Imitation de Jesus Christ. (with) Appendice a L'Imitation de Jesus Christ. Paris: 1856. V. 46

De L'Imitation de Jesus Christ. Paris: 1856-58. V. 37

Imitation de Jesus Christ. Paris: 1860. V. 38

The Imitation of Christ . . . London: 1896. V. 45

Of the Imitation of Christ. London: 1898. V. 46

Of the Imititation of Christ. Boston: 1899. V. 45

Of the Imitation of Christ. London: 1903. V. 41

The Imitation of Christ. Campden: 1904. V. 43

Of the Imitation of Christ. Chipping Campden: 1904. V. 44

The Imitation of Christ. Bijou Edition. With a preface by W.J. Knox-Little. London: 1906. V. 37

Of the Imitation of Christ. London: 1911? V. 37

Imitation of Christ. London: 1923. V. 41

Of the Imitation of Christ. London: 1935. V. 44

L'Imitation du Christ. Paris: 1957. V. 41

IMITATIONS of the Characters of Theophrastus. London: 1774. V. 41; 42; 46

IMLAH, JOHN

May Flowers. Poems and Songs. Some in the Scottish Dialect. London: 1827. V. 43

IMLAY, GEORGE

A Topographical Description of the Western Territory of North America. London: 1793. V. 37; 38; 40; 41; 43; 45; 46

A Topographical Description of the Wetern Territory of North America . . . New York: 1793. V. 46

A Topographical Description of the Western Territory of North Americaa . . . London: 1792. V. 37; 38; 39; 45

IMLAY, GILBERT

A Description of the Western Territory of North America. Dublin: 1793. V. 42

A Topographical Description of the Western Territory of North America. London: 1797. V. 38; 39; 41; 42

IMLAY, RICHARD

Richard Imlay's Patent for Improvement in the Mode of Supporting the Bodies of Railroad Cars and Carriages. Philadelphia: 1852. V. 39

IMMERWAHR, HENRY R.

Attic Script: a Survey. Oxford: 1990. V. 44

THE IMMIGRANT'S Guide to Minnesota in 1856. St. Anthony: 1856. V. 39; 40; 42

THE IMMORALITY of Stage-Plays in General and of the Tragedy Called Douglas, in Particular. Edinburgh: 1757. V. 43

IMMORTALIA. An Anthology of American Ballads, Sailors' Songs, Cowboy Songs, College Songs, Parodies, Limericks, and Other Humorous Verses and Doggerel Now for the First Time Brought Together in Book Form by a Gentleman about Town. New York: 1927. V. 37

THE IMPARTIAL Accomptant. To All Lovers of Great-Britain, First to the King, Lords and Commons, Then to the Whole Nation, is Demonstratively Made Known How to Pay the National Debts, if 48 Millions in Seven Years . . . London: 1739. V. 38

AN IMPARTIAL Account of the Doctrines of the Church of Rome . . . Shewing what Rome was in its pristine purity, and how it has degenerated. London: 1679. V. 37

AN IMPARTIAL Account of the Life and Writings of the Late Reverend William Dodd, LL.D. London: 1777. V. 38

AN IMPARTIAL and True History of the Life and Services of Major General Andrew Jackson. N.P.: 1828. V. 39; 42

AN IMPARTIAL Enquiry in the Management of the War in Spain . . . London: 1712. V. 42

AN IMPARTIAL History of the French Revolution From Its Commencement. Perth: 1795. V. 41

AN IMPARTIAL Review of the Conduct of the Admirals M----ws and L----k, in the Late Engagement in the Mediterranean . . . by an Officer on Board at the Time of Action. London: 1745. V. 41

IMPARTIAL Review of Two Pamphlets Lately Published, One Entituled, An Apology for the Late Resignation (by Chesterfield and Marchmont); the Other, The Resignation Discussed, &c. London: 1748. V. 41

AN IMPARTIAL Sketch of the Life of Thomas Paine . . . London: 1792. V. 38

IMPARTIAL Strictures on the Poem called 'The Pursuits of Literature:' and Particularly a Vindication of the Romance of 'The Monk.' London: 1798. V. 40

AN IMPARTIAL View of English Agriculture, for Permitting the Exploration of Corn, in the Year 1663, to the Present Time. London: 1766. V. 43

IMPEACHMENT of Mr. La Fayette: Containing His Accusation . . . Supported by Mr. Brissot of Warville; and His Defence by Mr. Vaublanc; with a Supplement. Philadelphia: 1793. V. 37

IMPERIAL BRAZILIAN MINING ASSSOCIATION

Reports of the Directors Addressed to the Share-Holders, Reports 'I' (Encompassing reports 1-4), 2, 3, 6-14, 17, 18 and 45. London: 1826-48. V. 43

IMPEY, JOHN

The Office of Sheriff Shewing Its History and Antiquity . . . Dublin: 1788. V. 42

THE IMPORTANCE of Literature to Men of Business: a Series of Addresses Delivered at Various Popular Institutions. London: 1852. V. 42

THE IMPORTANCE of the Liberty of the Press. London: 1748. V. 40

IMPORTANT Considerations on the true Nature of Government. Wherein Various Notions Relating to the British Constitution (are) . . . Fairly Stated. By a Love of Truth. London: 1741. V. 41

IMPORTANT New Etchings. New York: 1888. V. 46

IMPORTANT Old Masters of the Italian, Flemish, Dutch, French, and English Schools. New York: 1931. V. 40

IMPOSITION de Quatre Millions sur la Colonie de St. Domingo, en Execution du Memoire du Roi du 15 Aout 1763. Cap Francois: 1764. V. 40

THE IMPOSTURE Detected; or, the Mystery and Iniquity of Elizabeth Canning's Story Displayed . . . London: 1753. V. 46

IMPRESSIONS de Voyages. Paris. V. 41; 45

IMPREY, ELIJAH BARWELL
Poems. London: 1811. V. 45

THE IMPRINT. 1913. V. 45
THE IMPRINT. London: 1913. V. 40; 44

IMPROVEMENTS in the Microscope. London: 1832-33. V. 45

IMRAY, JAMES
Sailing Directions for the Gulf of Mexico and Islands of Porto Rico, Jamaica, Haiti, Cuba, the Bahamas, &c. London: 1863. V. 40

IMRAY, JAMES FREDERICK
Sailing Directions for the West Coast of North America. London: 1853. V. 38

IM THURN, EVERARD F.
Among the Indians of Guiana. London: 1883. V. 44

IN Convention of the Representatives of the State of New York, Kingston, April 1, 1777. Fishkill: 1777. V. 45

IN Council. In Philadelphia, September 4, 1777. Resolved. Philadelphia: 1777. V. 40

IN Memoriam. Albert Pike. N.P.: 1895. V. 39
IN Memoriam. Albert Pike. N.P.: 1897. V. 39
IN Memoriam. Albert Pike. N.P.: 1900. V. 39

IN Memoriam: Edward Thomas - Being No. Two of the Green Pastures Series. London: 1919. V. 44

IN Memoriam. Edwin Grabhorn, 1889-1968. San Francisco: 1969. V. 40

IN Memoriam. Edwin R. Purple. New York: 1881. V. 38

IN Memoriam: Isaac Todhunter. Cambridge: 1884. V. 39

IN Memoriam of John Rylands, Born February 7, 1801. Died December 11, 1888. Manchester: 1889. V. 40

IN Memoriam Vladimir Nabokov 1899-1977. New York: 1977. V. 38

IN Memoriam, William Loring Andrews. New York: 1921. V. 46
IN Memoriam: William Loring Andrews. New York: 1921. V. 40

IN Memory of Brother Albert Pike. N.P.: 1894. V. 39

IN Principio. Hammersmith: 1911. V. 41; 45

IN School and Out of School. By One Who Knows Both. London: 1825. V. 40

IN the American and Mexican Joint Commission William E. Barron and William Barron vs. the United States. San Francisco?: 1870's. V. 40

IN the Clutch of Circumstance, My Own Story. New York: 1922. V. 43

INAYAT ALLAH
Bahar-Danush; or, Garden of Knowledge. Shrewsbury: 1799. V. 43

INCE, JOSEPH MURRAY
Seven Views Illustrating the County of Radnor, from Drawings Taken on the Spot. London: 1832. V. 43

INCHBALD, ELIZABETH
The British Theatre, or, a Collection of Plays. London: 1970. V. 39
The British Theatre. London: 1806-09. V. 37
The Marked Man, a Comedy . . . London: 1780. V. 42
The Married Man. London: 1780. V. 40
The Married Man, a Comedy. Philadelphia: 1796. V. 39; 40
Memoirs of Mrs. Inchbald, Including Her Familiar Correspondence With the Most Distinguihsed Persons of Her Time. London: 1833. V. 39; 41; 43; 45
The Modern Theatre. London: 1811. V. 37; 43
The Modern Theatre: a Collection of Successful Modern Plays. London: 1973. V. 39
Simple Histoire. Paris: 1790's. V. 39; 41; 45
A Simple Story. Dublin: 1791. V. 37; 39; 41; 43; 45
A Simple Story. London: 1791. V. 39; 40; 43; 45; 46

INCHBOLD, A. C.
Under the Syrian Sun. London: 1906. V. 41; 44; 46

INCHBOLD, T.
Harrogate and Its Environs. Leeds: 1828. V. 40

INCHOFER, MELCHIOR
Tractatus Syllepticus, in Quo, Quid de Terrae, Solisque Motu, vel Statione, Secundum S. Scripturam & Sanctos Patres Sentiendum Quave Certitudine Alterutra Sententia Tenenda sit, Breviter Ostenditur. Rome: 1633. V. 38

INCIPIT Liber Beati Hieronimi de Essencia Diuinitatis. (with) Incipit Summa Edita a Tratre Thomas de Aquino de Articulis Fidei et Ecclesie Sacramentis. Augsburg: 1474. V. 38

INDAGINE, JOANNES
Introductiones Apotelesmatice Elegantes, in Chyromantiam, Physionomiam, Astrologiam Naturalem, Complexiones Hominum, Naturas Planetarum. Lyons: 1556. V. 38

INDAGINE, JOHANNES
Chiromantia. Strasbourg: 1534. V. 40

THE INDEPENDENT Briton. London: 1742. V. 40

THE INDEPENDENT Gold Hunter on His Way to California. New York: 1849. V. 39

THE INDEPENDENT Republic of Liberia . . . Philadelphia: 1848. V. 39; 45

THE INDEPENDENT Whig. London: 1721. V. 40

INDER, W. S.
On active Service with the S. J. A. B. South African War 1899-. Kendal: 1903. V. 42

INDERWICK, F. P. 1836-1904
A Calendar of Inner Temple Records (1505-1714). London: 1896-1901. V. 40

THE INDESTRUCTIBLE Reading Book. Boston: 1851. V. 38

INDEX Expurgatorius Librorum qui Hoe Sacculo Prodierunt, vel Doctrinae non Sanae Erroribus Inspersis, vel Inutilis & Offensivae Maledictentiae . . . Strassburg: 1599. V. 45

INDEX Kewensis, an Enumeration of the Genera and Species of Flowerin Plants from the Time of Linnaeus to 1885. Oxford: 1977-83. V. 37; 38

INDEX Kewensis. Supplement 17. London: 1987. V. 38

INDEX Kewensis. Supplement 18. For the Period January 1981 to December 1985. London: 1987. V. 38

INDEX Librorum Prohibitorum. Paris: 1599. V. 41

INDEX Librorum Prohibitorum, cum Regulis Confectis Per Patres a Tridentina Synodo Delectos, Auctoritate Sanctiss. Venice: 1564. V. 40

INDEX Londinensis to Illustrations of Flowering Plants, Ferns and Fern Allies. London: 1929-80. V. 37

INDEX to the General Naval Instructions, for the Edition of 1808. N.P.(London?): (1809?). V. 37

INDEX to the Original and Inserted Illustrations Contained in 'The Complete Angler.' New York: 1866. V. 37; 39

INDIA HOUSE, INC., NEW YORK.
A Descriptive Catalogue of the Marine Collection to be Found at India House. New York: 1935. V. 41

INDIA OFFICE
A Catalogue of Manuscript and Printed Reports, Field Books, Memoirs, Maps, etc. of the Indian Surveys Deposited in the Map Room of the India Office. London: 1878. V. 44

INDIA. PERSIAN BOUNDARY COMMISSION
Eastern Persia an Account of the Journeys of the Persian Boundary Commission 1870-71-72. London: 1876. V. 40

INDIAE, FRANCISCI
Hygiphilus Tertius vel de Symptomatur Febri Malignae Supervenientium natura, et Curatione. Veronae: 1596. V. 39

INDIAN Anecdotes and Barbarities. Barre: 1837. V. 37; 46

INDIAN Basket Weaving by the Navajo School of Indian Basketry. Los Angeles: 1903. V. 37

THE INDIAN Fighter!! And Ghost of Morgan!! Mucklebrowst: 1832. V. 40

INDIAN Outfits and Establishments: a Practical Guide for Persons About to Reside in India; Detailing the Articles Which Should be Taken Out; and the Requirements of Home Life and Management. London: 1882. V. 39

INDIAN SOCIETY OF ORIENTAL ART

Journal of the Indian Society of Oriental Art. 1967/68-84/85. V. 41

INDIAN Treaties Printed by Benjamin Franklin, 1736-1762. Philadelphia: 1938. V. 37; 38; 39; 42

INDIANA. CONSTITUTION

Constitution of the State of Indiana: Adopted in Convention . . . Washington: 1816. V. 46

INDIANA. CONSTITUTION - 1851

Constitution of the State of Indiana, and the Address of the Consituttional Convention. New Albany: 1851. V. 37

INDIANA. CONSTITUTIONAL CONVENTION - 1851

Journal of the Convention of the People of the State of Indiana to Amend the Constitution, Assembled October, 1850. Indianapolis: 1851. V. 37

INDIANA. LAWS, STATUTES, ETC. - 1825

Laws of the State of Indiana Passed and Published at the Ninth Session of the General Assembly. Indianapolis: 1825. V. 41

INDIANA. LAWS, STATUTES, ETC. - 1831

The Revised Laws of Indiana. Indianapolis: 1831. V. 39; 44

INDIANA Magazine of History . . . Bloomington: 1905-88. V. 40

INDICE de Las Ordenes Y Decretos Espedidos Por El Honorable Congreso De Este Estado, Desde el Ano de 1824, Hasta Fine de El de 1828. Leona Vicario: 1829. V. 40

THE INDIVIDUAL. Cambridge: 1837. V. 40

INDUSTRIAL WORKERS OF THE WORLD

Proceedings of the First Convention of the Industrial Workers of the World, Founded at Chicago June 27- July 8, 1905. New York: 1905. V. 42

INDUSTRIES of New Jersey, Part II. Cumbeland, Salem, Gloucester, Atlantic, Camden and Cape May Counties. New York: 1882. V. 44

THE INDUSTRY of all Nations 1851: the Art Journal Illustrated Catalogue. London: 1851. V. 42

INETT, JOHN

Origines Anglicanae; or, a History of the English Church. London: 1704. V. 44

AN INFALLIBLE Remedy for the High Prices of Provisions. Together with a Scheme for Laying Open the Trade to the East-Indies. London: 1768. V. 38

INFANTINE Complaints; or, Rather, Complaints of Infants, and Hints to Mothers. London: 1842. V. 38

THE INFANTRY Exercise of the United States Army, Abridged for the Use of the Militia of the United States. Philadelphia: 1819. V. 41

THE INFANT'S Battledore. London: 1830. V. 46

INFIDELITY and Abolitionism. An Open Letter to the Friends of Religion, Morality and the American Union. Washington: 1856. V. 39

INFORMATION for the People on Cholera: Including a Sketch of Its History, Symptoms, Preventives and Treatment. Philadelphia: 1832. V. 37

INFORMATION Relative to an Alleged Unlawful Traffic with Rebels in the State of Texas During the Late War . . . Washington: 1871. V. 41

INFORME de la Comision Pesquisidora de la Frontera del Norte . . . Sobre Depredacions de los Indios (and) Appendice . . . Mexico: 1874. V. 38

INGALIS, E. FLETCHER

Diseases of the Chest, Throat and Nasal Cavities. New York: 1900. V. 40

INGALLS, FAY

About Dogs - and Me. Hot Springs: 1939. V. 39

INGALLS, RACHEL

Mrs. Caliban. London: 1982. V. 46

Theft and the Man Who Was Left Behind. 1970. V. 45

Theft. London: 1970. V. 43; 45

INGE, WILLIAM

4 Plays. New York: 1958. V. 46

My Son is a Splendid Driver. Boston: 1971. V. 39

Summer Brave and Eleven Short Plays. New York: 1962. V. 46

INGELBY, C. M.

A Complete View of the Shakespeare Controversy, Concerning Manuscript Matter . . . published by Mr. J. Payne Collier as the Fruits of is Researches. London: 1861. V. 38

INGELBY, THOMAS

Ingelby's Whole Art of Legerdemain . . . London: 1815. V. 42

INGELO, NATHANIEL

Bentivolio and Urania. London: 1660-64. V. 41

Bentivolio and Urania, in Four Books . . . (with) Bentivolio and Urania, The Second Part in Two Books. London: 1660/64. V. 42

INGELOW, JEAN

Fated to Be Free. London: 1875. V. 45

Poems. Boston: 1867. V. 37

Poems. London: 1867. V. 38; 39; 44

Poems. New York: 1921. V. 41

Poems. London: 1968. V. 46

INGEN HOUSZ, JAN

Experiments Upon Vegetables, Discovering Their Great Power of Purifying the Common Air in the Sun-Shine, and of Injuring It in the Shade and at Night . . . London: 1779. V. 38; 43

INGEN, WILHELMINA VAN

Figures from Seleucia on the Tigris Discovered by the Expeditions Conducted by the University of Michigan with the Cooperation of the Toledo Museum of Art and Cleveland Museum of Art 1927-1932. Ann Arbor: 1939. V. 40

INGERSOLL, CHARLES

A Letter to a Friend in a Slave State. Philadelphia: 1862. V. 46

INGERSOLL, CHARLES JARED

A Discourse Concerning the Influence of America on the Mind; Being the Annual Oration Delivered Before the American Philosophical Society, at the University of Philadelphia, on the 18th Oct. 1823. Philadelphia: 1823. V. 37; 45

INGERSOLL, ERNEST

The Crest of the Continent. A Record of a Summer's Ramble in the Rocky Mountains and Beyond. Illustrations after photographs by W.H. Jackson. Chicago: 1885. V. 37

INGERSOLL, I. A.

Ingersoll's Century Annals of San Bernardino County, 1769 to 1904 . . . Los Angeles: 1904. V. 40

INGERSOLL, ROBERT G.

The Works. New York: 1929. V. 42

INGERSOLL, ROBERT H. 1833-1899

The Works. New York: 1902. V. 46

INGHAM CLARK, R.

A Few Notes on Varnishes and Fossil Resins. London: 1890. V. 44

INGHAM, G. THOMAS

Digging Gold Among the Rockies, or Exciting Adventures of Wild Camp Life in Leadville, Black Hills and the Gunnison Country. Philadelphia: 1880. V. 37; 40; 46

INGHAM, HARVEY

The Northern Border Brigade. Des Moines: 1926. V. 38; 41; 42; 43; 46

The Northern Border Brigade: A Story of Military Beginnings. (Des Moines: 1926). V. 37

Ten Years on the Iowa Frontier . . . Des Moines: 1915. V. 38

INGHIRAMI, FRANCESCO

Pitture de Vasi Fittili . . . 1833-37. V. 40

INGHOLT, HARALD

Gandharan Art in Pakistan. New York: 1957. V. 38

INGLEBY, C. M.

An Introduction to Metaphysic. London: 1869. V. 40; 41

Reflections Historical and Critical on the Revival of Philosophy at Cambridge. Cambridge: 1870. V. 45

INGLEFIELD, JOHN NICHOLSON

Capt. Inglefield's Narrative, Concerning the Loss of His Majesty's Ship the Centaur . . . and the Miraculous Preservation of the Pinnace . . . in a Traverse of Near 300 Leauges on the Great Western Ocean. London: 1783. V. 46

INGLEFIELD, JOHN RICHARDSON

Capt. Inglefield's Narrative, concerning the Loss of His Majesty's Ship The Centaur . . . London: 1783. V. 45

INGLIS, HENRY D.

Ireland in 1834. London: 1835. V. 39

The New Gil Blas . . . London: 1832. V. 42

INGLIS, HENRY DAVID 1795-1835

The Channel Islands. London: 1835. V. 44

Rambles in the Footsteps of Don Quixote. London: 1837. V. 37; 38; 39; 41; 43

INGLIS, JAMES

Tent Life in Tigerland, With Which is Incoporated Sport and Work on the Nepal Frontier . . . London: 1892. V. 40

INGLIS, JOHN

A Dictionary of Aneityumese Language. London: 1882. V. 43

INGLIS, RICHMOND GARDINER

Anna and Edgar; or Love and Ambition. Edinburgh: 1781. V. 40

INGLIS, RICHMOND, MRS.

Anna and Edgar; or, Love and Ambition. Edinburgh: 1781. V. 42

INGOLD, ERNEST

The House in Mallorca. San Francisco: 1950. V. 40

INGPEN, ABEL

Instructions for Collecting, Rearing and Preserving British and Foreign Insects . . . London: 1839. V. 43

INGPEN, ARTHUR ROBERT

Master Worsley's Book on the History and Continuation of the Honourable Society of the Middle Temple. London: 1910. V. 41

The Middle Temple Bench Book, Being a Register of Benchers of the Middle Temple . . . London: 1912. V. 41

INGPEN, R.

Shelley in England. New Facts and Letters from the Shelley-Whitton Papers. London: 1917/ V. 37

INGRAHAM, EDWARD DUNCAN

A Sketch of the Events Which Preceded the Capture of Washington, by the British, on the Twenty-Fourth of August, 1814. Philadelphia: 1849. V. 44; 46

INGRAHAM, GRANVILLE S.

History Gillette Murder Trial and Grace Brown's Love Letters. New York: 1907. V. 38

INGRAHAM, HENRY ANDREWS

American Trout Streams. New York: 1926. V. 39

INGRAHAM, J. H.

The Rose of the Rio Grande. Glasgow & London: 1870. V. 41

INGRAHAM, JOSEPH

Joseph Ingraham's Journal of the Brigantine Hope on a Voyage to the Northwest Coast of North America, 1790-92. Barre: 1917. V. 37

INGRAHAM, JOSEPH HOLT 1809-1860

Alice May and Bruising Bill. Boston: 1845. V. 45

The American Lounger; or Tales, Sketches and Legends Gathered in Sundry Journeyings. Philadelphia: 1839. V. 43

Burton; or, the Sieges. New York: 1838. V. 40

The Dancing Feather, or the Amateur Freebotters. Boston: 1842. V. 38; 40

Edward Austin; or, The Hunting Flask. Boston: 1845. V. 39

Edward Manning; or, the Bride and the Maiden. Boston: 1847. V. 40

Frank Rivers; or, The Dangers of the Town. New York: 1880. V. 43

The Knights of Seven Lands. Boston: 1845. V. 43; 44

The Lady of the Gulf. Boston: 1846. V. 45

Lafitte: the Pirate of the Gulf. New York: 1836. V. 43

Morris Graeme; or, the Cruise of the Sea Slipper. Boston: 1843. V. 38; 40; 43

The Quadroone; or, St. Michael's Day. New York: 1841. V. 38; 40; 43; 46

The South West. New York: 1835. V. 37; 38; 39; 42; 43; 44; 45; 46

The Spanish Galleon, or the pirate of the Mediterranean. Boston: 1845. V. 38

The Sunny South; or, the Southerner at Home, Embracing Five Years' Experience of a Northern Governess in the Land of the Sugar and the Cotton. Philadelphia: 1860. V. 42

INGRAM, HENRY

Matilda, a Tale of the Crusades, a Poem in Six Books. London: 1830. V. 43

INGRAM, J. FORSYTH

The Story of a Gold Concession, and Other African Tales and Legends. Pietermartizburg, natal: 1893. V. 40

INGRAM, JAMES

Memorials of Oxford. Oxford: 1837. V. 41; 44

Memorials of the Parish of Codford St. Mary, in the County of Wilts. Oxford: 1844. V. 37

INGRAM, JOHN HENRY

Edgar Allan Poe, His Life, Letters and Opinions. London: 1880. V. 37

Oliver Madox Brown. London: 1883. V. 40

The Raven by Edgar Allan Poe. London: 1885. V. 42

INGRAM, REX

Mars in the House of Death. New York: 1939. V. 44; 45

INGRAM, ROBERT ACKLOM 1763-1809

The Cause of the Increase of Methodism and Dissension and Popularity of What is Called Evangelical Preaching. London: 1807. V. 41

INGRAM, WILLIAM

Poems, in the English and Scottish Dialects. Aberdeen: 1812. V. 39

INGRATITUDE. A Poem. London: 1764. V. 40

INGRSOLL, LUTHER A.

Ingersoll's Century Annals of San BErnardino County 1769-1904 . . . Los Angeles: 1904. V. 43

THE INJURIOUS Effects of Slave Labour: an Impartial Appeal to the Reason, Justice, and Patriotism of the People of Illinois on the Injurious Effects of Slave Labour. Philadelphia, London: 1824. V. 37

INLAND TYPE FOUNDERY

Specimen Book and Catalog. Saint Louis: 1907. V. 43

INLAND TYPE FOUNDRY

Specimen Book and Catalog. Saint Louis: 1897. V. 38; 43

INMAN, HENRY 1837-1899

Buffalo Jones' Forty Years of Adventure. London: 1899. V. 38

Buffalo Jones' Forty Years of Adventure. Topeka: 1899. V. 37; 38; 39; 43; 45

The Great Salt Lake Trail. New York: 1898. V. 42; 43; 46

The Great Salt Lake Trail . . . New York: 1989. V. 42

The Old Santa Fe Trail. New York: 1897. V. 37; 38; 39; 40; 42; 45; 46

The Old Santa Fe Trail: The Story of a Great Highway. Topeka: 1899. V. 43

Stories of the Old Santa Fe Trail. Kansas City: 1881. V. 45

Tales of the Trail. Topeka: 1898. V. 37

INN, H.

Chinese Houses and Gardens. New York: 1950. V. 45

INNER TEMPLE. LONDON. LIBRARY

Catalogue of manuscripts in the Library . . . of Inner Temple. 1972. V. 40

Catalogue of the Printed Books in the Library of the Inner Temple. London: 1843. V. 40

INNES, HAMMOND

Wreckers Must Breathe. London: 1940. V. 44

INNES, HARRY

Mr. Rowan's Motion for an Inquiry into the Conduct of Harry Innis (sic) District Judge of the U.S. for the District of Kentucky. Washington: 1808. V. 37; 38

INNES, JOHN 1739-1777

A Short Description of the Human Muscles, Chiefly as They Appear on Dissection. Edinburgh: 1778. V. 39; 41; 45

A Short Description of the Human Muscles, Arranged as They Appear on Dissection. New York: 1818. V. 41

INNES, MICHAEL

Appleby's End. London: 1945. V. 38

The Daffodil Affair. New York: 1942. V. 39

Death at the President's Lodging. London: 1936. V. 37

From London Far. London: 1946. V. 38

A Night of Errors. London: 1948. V. 38

The Weight of the Evidence. London: 1944. V. 38

What Happened at Hazlewood. London: 1946. V. 38

INNES, P. R.

The History of the Bengal European Regiment, Now the Royal Munster Fusiliers, and How It Helped to Win India. London: 1885. V. 40; 42

INNES, THOMAS

A Critical Essay on the Ancient Inhabitants of the Northern Parts of Britain and Scotland. London: 1799. V. 37; 41

INNES, WILLIAM

Liberia; or the Early History and Signal Preservation of the American Colony of Free Negroes on the Coast of Africa. Edinburgh: 1831. V. 37

INNIS, HAROLD A.

The Fur Trade in Canada. New Haven: 1930. V. 43

Peter Pond: Fur Trader and Adventurer. Toronto: 1930. V. 42; 45

Select Documents in Canadian Economic History. Toronto: 1929/33. V. 45

Select Documents in Canadian Economic History, 1783-1885. Toronto: 1933. V. 42

INNOCENT III, POPE 1160-1216.

De officio Missae & sacramento altaris. Paris: 1518. V. 37

Fundamentum Eterne Felicitatis. Colophon: 1509. V. 40

Opera. Venice: 1578. V. 37

INNOCENT VIII, POPE 1432-1492.

Bulla canonizationis Sancti Leopoldi Marchionis. (Vienna: 1484). V. 37

INOUYE, JUKICHI

Home Life in Tokyo. Tokyo: 1911. V. 38

INQUIRES by the Agricultral Society. Boston: 1800. V. 37; 46

AN INQUIRY into the Causes of Our Naval Miscarriages . . . London: 1707. V. 43

AN INQUIRY into the Causes of Our Naval Miscarriages; With Some Thoughts on the Interest of this Nation as to a Naval War . . . Dublin: 1707. V. 42

AN INQUIRY into the Causes of the Insurrection of the Negroes in the Island of St. Domingo to Which are Added, Observations of M. Garran-Coulon on the Same Subject . . . 29th Feb. 1792. London: 1792. V. 40

INQUIRY into the Fitness of Attending Parliament: In a Letter from a Member to His Friend, Who Has Absented. London: 1739. V. 41

AN INQUIRY into the Medical Curriculum by the Edinburgh Pathalogical Club. Edinburgh: 1919. V. 39

AN INQUIRY into the Rights of Free Subjects: in Which the Cases of the British Sailors and Common Soldiers are Distinctly Consider'd and Compar'd. London: 1749. V. 41

THE INS and Outs; or, the True Inwardness of Political Reform, by the Author. Omaha: 1877. V. 42

THE INSCRIPTIONS at Tor House and Hawk Tower. Los Angeles: 1989. V. 41

INSIDE Sebastopol, and Experiences in Camp. London: 1856. V. 42

INSIGNIUM Aliquot Virorum Icones. Lyon: 1559. V. 41; 45

THE INSTANT It Happened. N.P.: 1972. V. 41

INSTITORIS, HENRICUS d. ca. 1500

Malleus Maleficarum. Speyer: 1487. V. 39

Malleus Maleficorum Maleficas et Earum Heresin ut Phramea Potentissima Conterens. Paris: 1510-15. V. 40

INSTITUICAO da Companhia Geral do Grao Para, Emaranhao. Lisbon: 1755. V. 40

INSTITUTION OF CIVIL ENGINEERS

The Civil Engineer in War. London: 1948. V. 43

THE INSTITUTION of the Society of the Cincinnati. Formed by the Officers of the Army of the United States. Boston: 1801. V. 38

INSTRUCTION for Field Artillery. Philadelphia: 1863. V. 38

INSTRUCTION for Heavy Artillery. Charleston: 1861. V. 37; 41

INSTRUCTIONS and Regulations for the Formations and Movements of the Cavalry. 1807. V. 37

INSTRUCTIONS for a Young Lady. Edinburgh: 1770. V. 39

INSTRUCTIONS for Cutting Out Apparel for the Poor . . . London: 1789. V. 37

INSTRUCTIONS for the Guidance of Her Majesty's Naval Officers Employed in the Suppression of the Slave Trade. London: 1844. V. 39

INSTRUCTIONS in Household Matters. Or, the Young Girl's Guide to Domestic Service. London: 1847. V. 39

INSTRUCTIONS to Medical Officers of the United States Navy. Washington: 1867. V. 42

THE INTELLECTUAL Observer, Review of Natural History, Microscopic Reseaarch, etc. London: 1862-65. V. 38

THE INTELLECTUAL Observer: Review of Natural History, Microscopic Research and Recreative Science. London: 1862-68. V. 44; 46

THE INTER-OCEANIC Canal and the Monroe Doctrine. New York: 1800. V. 41

THE INTER-OCEANIC Canal of Nicaragua: Its History, Physical Condition, Plans and Prospects. New York: 1891. V. 38

AN INTERESTING Account of the Voyages and Travels of Captain Lewis and Clark, in the Years 1804, 1805 and 1806 . . . Baltimore: 1812. V. 38; 41

THE INTERESTING and Affecting History of Prince Lee Boo. London: 1789. V. 38

AN INTERESTING Appendix to Sir William Blackstone's Commentaries on the Laws of England. Philadelphia: 1773. V. 41

INTERESTING Particulars of the Loss of the Admiral Gardner & Britannia, Outward-Bound Indiamen, and of the Appollo, a Large Brig, Which with other Vessels, Were Wrecked on the Goodwins, Jan. 24, 1809 . . . London: 1809. V. 41

INTERESTING Tracts, Relating to the Island of Jamaica, Consisting of Curious State-Papers, Councils of War, Letters, Petitions, Narratives &c. St. Jago de la Vega: 1800. V. 44

THE INTERESTS of the British Empire in North America. Ottawa: 1868. V. 43

THE INTERESTS of the Empress Queen, the King of France and Spain, and Their Principal Allies, with Respect to Their Glory, the Essential Advantage of Their Crowns, and Their Conscience, Betrayed in the Preliminary Articles, signed at Aix-la-Chapelle . . . N.P.: 1748. V. 41

THE INTERESTS of the Protestant Dissenters Considered. London: 1732. V. 40

INTERIANO, PAOLO

Ristretto delle Historie Genovesi. Lucca: 1551. V. 37

INTERNAL Mining and Exchange Company. Chicago: 1871. V. 42

INTERNATIONAL & GREAT NORTHERN RAILROAD

Homes in Texas on the Line of the International & Great Northern R.R. 1880-81. New York: 1880. V. 44

INTERNATIONAL ASSOCIATION OF BIBLIOPHILES

A Bibliophile's Los Angeles, Essays . . . on the Occasion of Its 14th Congress, 30 September to 11 October 1985. Los Angeles: 1985. V. 41

INTERNATIONAL COMPANY OF MEXICO

Tierra Perfecta Or 'Perfect Land' of the Mission Fathers Lower California, The Peninsula, Now Open to Colonists. New York. V. 45

THE INTERNATIONAL Competition for a New Administration Building for the Designs Submitted in Response to the Chicago Tribune's $100,000 Offer . . . Chicago: 1923. V. 38; 45

INTERNATIONAL CONFERENCE ON AERIAL NAVIGATION, CHICAGO, 1893

Proceedings of . . . New York: 1894. V. 40

INTERNATIONAL CONGRESS OF PHILOSOPHY

Philosophie Generale et Metaphysique; Morale Generale; Logique et Histories des Sciences; Histoire de la Philosophie. Paris: 1900-02. V. 41

INTERNATIONAL COTTON EXPOSITION, ATLANTA, 1881.

The Products, Machinery and Manufactures. Atlanta: 1881. V. 41

INTERNATIONAL EXPOSITION, ST. LOUIS, 1904.

Official Catalogue of the Exhibition of the German Empire. Berlin: 1904. V. 39

INTERNATIONAL Journal of Surgery and Antiseptics 1888-1892. V. 37

INTERNATIONAL METEOROLOGICAL CONGRESS

International Cloud-Atlas Published by Order of the Committee. Paris: 1896. V. 41

INTERNATIONAL PRIMATOLOGICAL SOCIETY CONGRESS, 10TH

Selected Proceedings. London: 1986. V. 38

THE INTERNATIONAL Railway & Steam Navigation Guide No. 262, May 1886. Montreal: 1886. V. 45

INTERNATIONAL RUBBER & ALLIED TRADES EXHIBITION, 3RD, N.Y.

The Official Handbook on India Rubber and Catalogue. London: 1911. V. 39

THE INTERNATIONAL Unbound Anthology Consul's Series. New York: 1930. V. 38

INTERNATIONAL UNIVERSAL EXPOSITION, PARIS, 1900.

Report of the Commissioner-General for the United States to the International Universal Exposition, Paris, 1900. Washington: 1901. V. 38

INTERPRETACION de Los Motivos; Que en Los Papeles Impresos Que an Parecido Sobre La Conspiracion de la Luisiana. N.P.: 1769. V. 44

INTRODUCTION 2: Stories by New Writers. London: 1964. V. 39

THE INTRODUCTION of Parliamentary Government in New South Wales. Dinner of the Surviving Members of the First Legislative Assembly at Parliament House, May 23, 1887. Sydney: 1887. V. 39

AN INTRODUCTION of the Ancient Greek and Latin Measures Into British Poetry. London: 1737. V. 41

INTRODUCTION To American Indian Art. New York: 1931. V. 41

AN INTRODUCTION to English Grammar. Brentford: 1817. V. 41

AN INTRODUCTION to the History of the Kingdoms and State of Asia, Africa and America, both Ancient and Modern According to the Method of Samuel Puffendorf, Counsellor of State to the Late King of Sweden. London: 1705. V. 39

AN INTRODUCTION to the Knowledge of Fungusses. London: 1820. V. 39

INVASION; or the Duty of Every Briton to be Prepared; With the Most Effectual Means of Resisting the Threat of Our Inveterate Enemy. London: 1805. V. 38

AN INVENTORY of the Historical Monuments in Westmorland. London: 1936. V. 40

INVERARITY, ROBERT BRUCE

Movable Masks and Figures of the North Pacific Coasts Indians. Cranbrook: 1941. V. 44

INVESTIGATION by the City Council of Salt Lake City of Rumors Affecting the Peace, Reputation and Welfare of the City and Its Inhabitants. Salt Lake City: 1885. V. 45

INVESTIGATION of the Assassination of President John F. Kennedy. Hearings before the President's Commission . . . Washington: (1964). V. 37

THE INVITATION To Sir Rupert to Dine. London: 1908/09/10. V. 45

INWOOD, HENRY WILLIAM

The Erechtheion at Athens. London: 1827. V. 39

The Erectheion at Athens, Fragments of Athenian Architecture, and a Few Remains in Attica, Megara and Epirus . . . London: 1831. V. 38; 40; 44

IONESCO, EUGENE

Journeys Among the Dead. 1987. V. 42; 45

Journeys Among the Dead. New York: 1987. V. 39; 40

Present Past Past Present. New York: 1971. V. 45

Rhinoceros. London: 1964. V. 40

A Stroll in the Air and a Frenzy for Two or More. New York: 1965. V. 45

IONNESCU-GION, G. I.

Istoria Bucurescilor. Bucharest: 1899. V. 37

IOWA. BOARD OF EDUCATION

Journal of the Board of Education of the State of Iowa, At Its First Session . . . at the City of Des Moines. Des Moines: 1858. V. 37; 39

IOWA. BOARD OF RAILROAD COMMISSIONERS

First Annual Report of the Board of Railroad Commissioners, State of Iowa. Des Moines: 1878. V. 39

IOWA. CENSUS BOARD - 1857

The Census Returns of the Different Counties of the State of Iowa, for 1856. Iowa City: 1857. V. 38

IOWA CENTRAL RAILROAD

The Central Railroad of Iowa . . . From St. Louis to St. Paul . . . New York: 1870. V. 37

IOWA. CONSTITUTION - 1846

Constitution of the State of Iowa, Adopted in Convention, May 18, 1846. Washington: 1846. V. 43

IOWA. CONSTITUTION - 1857

The Debates of the Constitutional Convention of the State of Iowa, Assembled at Iowa City, 1857. Davenport: 1857. V. 37; 38; 39

IOWA. GENERAL ASSEMBLY - 1851

The Code of Iowa Passed at the Session of the General Assembly. Iowa City: 1851. V. 43

IOWA. GENERAL ASSEMBLY - 1860

Journal of the Senate of the Eighth General Assembly of the State of Iowa. Des Moines: 1860. V. 37; 39

IOWA. GEOLOGICAL SURVEY

First and Second Annual Report of Progress by the State Geologist and the Assistant and Chemist of the Geological Survey of the State of Iowa. Des Moines: 1868. V. 39

IOWA Journal of History and Politics. Iowa City: 1903-1960. V. 37

IOWA. LAWS, STATUTES, ETC.

Special Acts and Resolutions . . . of the Eighth General Assembly of the State of Iowa. Des Moines: 1860. V. 44

IOWA. LAWS, STATUTES, ETC. - 1839

The Statute Laws of the Territory of Iowa, Enacted at the First Session of the Legislative Assembly of Said Territory, Held at Burlington, A.D. 1838-'39. Du Buque: 1839. V. 37

IOWA. LAWS, STATUTES, ETC. - 1841

Laws of the Territory of Iowa, Enacted at the Session of the Legislature Which Commenced on the First Monday of December, A.D., 1841. Iowa City: 1841. V. 37

IOWA. LAWS, STATUTES, ETC. - 1843

Revised Statutes of the Territory of Iowa. Iowa City: 1843. V. 37

IOWA. LAWS, STATUTES, ETC. - 1848

Acts, Resolutions and Memorials Passed at the Extra Session of the First General Assembly of the State of Iowa. Iowa City: 1848. V. 40

IOWA. LAWS, STATUTES, ETC. - 1851

The Code of Iowa Passed at the Session of the General Assembly. Iowa City: 1851. V. 37; 38; 39

IOWA. LAWS, STATUTES, ETC. - 1853

Acts, Resolutions and Memorials Passed at the Regular Session of the Fourth General Assembly of the State of Iowa . . . Iowa City: 1853. V. 43

Laws of the State of Iowa in Relation to Corporations for Rail Road Purposes, and Articles of Incorporation of the Mississippi and Missouri Railroad Company. Davenport: 1853. V. 42

IOWA. LEGISLATURE

H. R. Journal Of . . . of the 11th General Assembly of the State of Iowa. Des Moines: 1866. V. 45

IOWA. (TERRITORY). LAWS, STATUTES, ETC.

The Statute Laws of the Territory of Iowa. Eancted at the First Session of the Legislative Assembly . . . Held at Burlington, A.D. 1838-39. Dubuque: 1839. V. 39; 40; 43; 46

IOWA. (TERRITORY). LAWS, STATUTES, ETC. - 1841

Laws of the Territory of Iowa, Enacted at the Session of the Legislature Which Commenced on the First Monday of Decemer, A.D. 1841. Iowa City: 1841. V. 39

IOWA. (TERRITORY). LAWS, STATUTES, ETC. - 1843

Revised Statutes of the Territory of Iowa. Iowa City: 1843. V. 39; 43

IOWA: The Home for Immigrants. Being a treatise on the resources of Iowa, & giving useful information with regard to the state, for the benefit of immigrants & others. Des Moines: 1870. V. 37; 39

IOWA WESTERN RAILROAD

Report of the Engineer of the Iowa Western Railroad. Muscatine: 1851. V. 42

IRAN BASTAN MUSEUM, TEHERAN.

Oriental Ceramics. Tokyo: 1981. V. 42

IRBY, CHARLES LEONARD

Travels in Egypt and Nubia, Syria and Asia Minor; During the Years 1817 and 1818. London: 1884. V. 40

Travels in Egypt and Nubia, Syria and Asia Minor; During the Years 1817 and 1818. London: 1823. V. 39; 40

IRBY, L. HOWARD L.

The Ornithology of the Straits of Gibraltar. London: 1875. V. 45

The Ornithology of the Straits of Gibraltar. London: 1895. V. 38; 45

IRBY, RICHARD

Historical Sketch of the Nottoway Grays, Afterwards Company G, Eigtheenth Virginia Regiment, Army of Northern Virginia . . . Richmond: 1878. V. 44

IRCASTRENSIS, PSEUD.

Love and Horror; an Imitation of the Present, and a Model for all Future Romances. London: 1815. V. 38

IREDALE, TOM

Birds of New Guinea. Melbourne: 1956. V. 37; 42; 43; 46

Birds of Paradise and Bower Birds. Melbourne: 1950. V. 37; 42

IRELAND, ALEXANDER

The Book-Lover's Enchiridion. London: 1888. V. 37; 44; 45

List of the Writings of William Hazlitt and Leigh Hunt, Chronologically Arranged.. London: 1868. V. 43

IRELAND and America; a Letter to the O'Donoghue, M.P. by an American Citizen. New York: 1862. V. 37

IRELAND, E. H.

The Napoleon Anecdotes. London: 1822-25. V. 38

IRELAND, GEOFFREY

Epstein: a Camera Study of the Sculptor at Work. London: 1957. V. 41

IRELAND, JOHN d. 1808

Hogarth Illustrated. London: 1793-1804. V. 39; 40

Hogarth Illustrated. (with) A Supplement . . . London: 1806/1798. V. 40

Hogarth Illustrated. London: pub. by W. Bulmer: 1806/1804. V. 45

Hogarth Illustrated from His Own Manuscripts . . . London: 1812. V. 46

IRELAND. LAWS, STATUTES, ETC. - 1723

A Collection of all the Statutes Now In Use; with Notes in the Margin. Dublin: 1723. V. 40

IRELAND. LAWS, STATUTES, ETC. - 1800

The Irish Statutes of the Parliament Held in Ireland from 1300 to 1800 (Act of Union). Dublin: 1800. V. 43

IRELAND. LAWS, STATUTES, ETC. - 1865

Ancient Laws of Ireland. Senchus Mor. Dublin: 1865-1901. V. 38

IRELAND, M. W.

The Medical Department of the U. S. Army in the World War. Washington: 1921-29. V. 42

IRELAND. PARLIAMENT - 1784

The Parliamentary Register, or History of the Proceedings and Debates of the House of Commons of Ireland. Dublin: 1784-88. V. 40

IRELAND. REPORT OF THE SELECT COMMITTEE ON FISHERIES.

Report of the Select Committee on Fisheries, Ireland, with the Minutes of Evidence. London: 1849. V. 37

IRELAND, SAMUEL d. 1800

Graphic Illustrations of Hogarth, from Pictures . . . London: 1794. V. 40; 46

Graphic Illustrations of Hogarth. London: 1794-99. V. 45

A Picturesque Tour Through Holland, Brabane and Part of France, Made in the Autumn of 1789. London: 1790. V. 40; 41; 44

Picturesque Views on the River Thames . . . London: 1792. V. 37; 39; 44

Picturesque Views on the River Medway, from the Nore to the Vicinity of Its Source in Sussex. London: 1793. V. 45

A Picturesque Tour through Holland, Brabant, and Part of France; Made in the Autumn of 1789. London: 1796. V. 37; 39; 41; 43

Picturesque Views on the River Wye, from Its Source at Plinlimmon Hill, to its Junction with Severn Below Chepstow. London: 1797. V. 38

Picturesque Views, with an Historical Account of the Inns of Court in London and Westmisnter. London: 1800. V. 39; 40

Picturesque Views on the River Thames, from Its Source in Gloucestershire to the Nore . . . London: 1801-02. V. 39

Picturesque Views, with an Historical Account of the Inns of Court, in London and Westminster. London: 1880. V. 38

Picturesque Views on the Upper or Warwickshire Avon, from its Source at Naseby to is Junction with the Severn at Twekesbury . . . London: 1795. V. 37; 38; 46

IRELAND, WILLIAM

Historical Sketch of the Zulu Mission, in South Africa, as Also of the Gaboon Mission in Western Africa. Boston: 1864. V. 39

IRELAND, WILLIAM HENRY 1777-1835

An Authentic Account of the Shakesperian Manuscripts. London: 1796. V. 40; 45

The Confessions Containing the Particulars of His Fabrication of the Shakespeare Manuscripts; together with Anecdotes and Opinions . . . London: 1805. V. 37; 39; 44

The Confessions of William Henry Ireland. New York: 1874. V. 41

Effusions of Love from Chatelar to Mary Queen of Scotland. London: 1805. V. 40; 42

England's Topographer, or a New and Complete History of the County of Kent; from the Earliest Records to the Present Time . . . London: 1828-30. V. 41

The Fisher Boy. A Poem comprising his several avocations, during the four seasons of the year. By H.C. Esq. London: (1808). V. 37

Memoirs of a Young Greek Lady, Madame Pauline Adelaide Alexander panam, against his Serene Highness the Reigning Prince of Saxe-Coburg. London: 1823. V. 37

Miscellaneous Papers and Legal Instruments Under the Hand and Seal of William Shakespeare . . . London: 1796. V. 37; 41; 42

Passages Selected by Distinguished Personages on the Great Literary Trial of Vortigern and Rowena! London: 1795-96. V. 42

Scribbleomania; or, the Printer's Devil's Polichronicon. London: 1815. V. 40; 41; 42

Stultifera Navis; the Modern Ship of Fools. London: 1807. V. 38; 41; 45

Vortigern; an Historical Play . . . London: 1832. V. 38; 42; 44

IRELAND, WILLIAM WOTHERSPOON 1832-1909

The Mental Affections of Children: Idiocy, Imbecility and Insanity. London: 1898. V. 43; 45

Randolph Methyl: a Story of Anglo Indian Life. London: 1863. V. 40; 42

IRENAEUS, SAINT

Opus Eruditissimum . . . Basle: 1526. V. 38

IRENAEUS, SAINT, BP. OF LYONS c. 130-200

Contra Omnes Haereses Libri Quinque. Oxford: 1702. V. 39

IRENE. N.P.: 1952. V. 46

IRENICUS, FRANCISCUS

Germaine Exegeseos Volumina Duodecima . . . Hagenau: 1518. V. 40

IRIARTE, FRANCISCO

Manifesto Que a Los Pueblos du Su Estado Dirije el Congreso de Occidente, Sobre La Conducta Politia Del Ciudadano Francisco Iriarte . . . Estado de Occidente: 1829. V. 46

IRIARTE, TOMAS

Fabulas Literarias. Barcelona: 1782. V. 40; 41; 44

THE IRIS: an Illuminated Souvenir for 1853. Philadelphia: 1853 (1852). V. 44

THE IRISH Abroad and At Home at the Court and In the Camp With Souvenir of 'The Brigade'. New York: 1857. V. 46

IRISH ARCHAEOLOGICAL SOCIETY

The Miscellany of the Irish Archaeological Society. Dublin: 1846. V. 44

Tracts Relating to Ireland for the Irish Archaeological Society. Dublin: 1841. V. 46

IRISH, C. W.

An Account of the Detonating Meteor, or February 12, 1875. Iowa City: 1875. V. 37

THE IRISH Canadian Calendar for 1878. V. 44

THE IRISH Compendium, or Rudiments of Honor, Containing the Descent, Marriage, Issue Titles, Posts and Seats of all the Nobility of Ireland, with Their Arms, Crestes . . . London: 1756. V. 38

IRISH, JOSEPH

The Abolitionists' Mirror. Union: 1860. V. 42

IRONS, NEVILLE JOHN

Fans of Imperial China. Fans of Imperial Japan. Hong Kong: 1981. V. 44

IRONSIDE, GILBERT

A Dissertation of Horses. London: 1800. V. 38

IRUINE, WILLIAM FERGUSON

A Short History of the Township of Rivington in the County of Lancaster . . . Edinburgh: 1904. V. 39

IRVIN, S. M.

Sophie Rubeti. Philadelphia: 1865. V. 38

The Waw-ru-haw-a. The Decline and Fall of Indian Superstitions . . . Philadelphia: 1871. V. 45

IRVIN, TERESA W.

Let the Tail Go with the Hide: the Story of Ben F. Williams. El Paso: 1984. V. 42

IRVINE, ALEXANDER

The Souls of Poor Folk. London: 1927. V. 43

IRVINE, ANDREW

Reflections on the Education of the Poor, submitted particularly to the consideration of the Landholders and Principal Manufactures. London: 1815. V. 37

IRVINE, JOHN

'Mormon' Protest Against Injustice. Salt Lake City: 1885. V. 42

IRVINE, LYN L.

Ten Letter-Writers. London: 1932. V. 42

Ten Letter-Writers. London: (1932). V. 37

IRVINE, WILLIAM 1776-1811

Letters on Sicily. London: 1813. V. 39

IRVING, ALEXANDER

The Man From World's End . . . London: 1920. V. 37

IRVING, B. A.

The Theory and Practice of Caste . . . London: 1853. V. 42

IRVING, WASHINGTON 1783-1859 continued

Salmagundi; or, the Whim-Whams and Opinions of Launcelot Langstaff . . . New York: 1807-08. V. 40

Salmagundi; or, the Whim-Whams and Opinions of Launcelot Langstaff, Esq. and Others. New York: 1820. V. 43

Salmagundi. London: 1824. V. 37; 41

Salmagundi; or, the Whim-Whams and Opinions of Launcelot Langstaff . . . New York: 1814. V. 45

The Sketch Book of Geoffrey Crayon . . . No. III. New York: 1819. V. 38; 40; 43

The Sketchbook of Geoffrey Crayon. New York: 1819/19-20. V. 41

The Sketch Book. London: 1820. V. 42; 44

Sketch Book of Geoffrey Crayon. New York: 1865. V. 39; 45; 46

The Sketch Book of Geoffrey Crayon. New York: 1894. V. 40

The Sketch-Book of Geoffrey Crayon, Gent. New York: 1895. V. 37; 38; 39

The Sketch Book of Geoffrey Crayon, Gent. New York: & London: 1895. V. 43

The Sketchbook of Geoffrey Crayon, Gent. New York: 1899. V. 40

Tales of a Traveller. London: 1824. V. 37; 39; 40; 42; 43

Tales of a Traveller, part I (-IV). Philadelphia: 1824. V. 45

Tales of a Traveller. London: 1848. V. 41

Tales of a Traveller. New York: 1895. V. 37; 39; 40

Three Choice Sketches by Geoffrey Crayon. San Mateo: 1941. V. 37; 38; 39; 40; 43; 44

A Tour of the Prairies. London: 1835. V. 37; 40; 42; 43; 45; 46

Tour of the Prairies. Philadelphia: 1835. V. 37; 38; 39; 40; 41; 42; 45; 46

Voyages and Discoveries of the Companions of Columbus. Paris: 1831. V. 40

Voyages and Discoveries of the Companions of Columbus. Philadelphia: 1831. V. 46

Wolfert's Roost and Other Papers Now First Collected. New York: 1855. V. 38; 39; 40; 43

Wolfert's Roost: and Other Papers, Now Collected. New York: 1855/54. V. 44

The Works of Washington Irving. London: 1850. V. 46

The Works. New York: 1860. V. 38

Works. London: 1868-1877. V. 37

Works . . . New York: 1869. V. 40

Complete Works. New York: 1897. V. 37

Works. New York: 1901. V. 42

The Works. New York & London: 1901. V. 39

Writings. New York: 1896-97. V. 40

IRWIN, DAVID

English Neoclassical Art. Studies in Inspiration and Taste. London: 1966. V. 42; 44

Scottish Painters at Home and Abroad 1700-1900. London: 1975. V. 42; 44

IRWIN, EYLES

Bedukah, or the Self Devoted. London: 1776. V. 40; 42

Eastern Eclogues; Written During a Tour through Arabia, Egypt and Other Parts of Asia and Africa in the Year MDCCLXXVII. London: 1780. V. 40; 42

An Epistle to the Right Honourable George Lord Pigot, on the Anniversary of Raising the Siege of Madras, Written During His Lordship's Confinement at St. Thomas's Mount. London: 1778. V. 40

Occasional Epistles, Written During a Journey from London to Busrah, in the Gulf of Persia, in the Years 1780 and 1781. London: 1783. V. 40

Saint Thomas's Mount. a Poem. London: 1774. V. 37; 40; 42

A Series of Adventures in the Course of a Voyage Up the Red Sea, on the Coasts of Arabia and Egypt . . . London: 1787. V. 38; 41

IRWIN, FRED CHIDLEY

The State and Position of Western Australia, Commonly Called the Swan-River Settlement. London: 1835. V. 39; 41; 43

IRWIN, JOHN

Origins of Chintz. London: 1970. V. 37; 41

IRWIN, RICHARD B.

History of the Nineteenth Army Corps. New York: 1893. V. 39

ISAAC, FRANK

English and Scottish Printing Types, 1501-1535 and 1508-1541. N.P.: 1930. V. 37; 43

English and Scottish Printing Types 1501-35 & 1508-41; . . . 1535-58 & 1552-8. London: 1930-32. V. 45

English and Scottish Printing Types 1535-1558 & 1552-1558. N.P.: 1932. V. 37; 41; 43

English Printers' Types of the Sixteenth Century. 1936. V. 43

English Printers' Types of the Sixteenth Century. London: 1936. V. 42

English Printers' Types of the Sixteenth Century. Oxford: 1936. V. 42

ISAAC, PAUL E.

Prohibition and Politics in Tennessee 1885-1920. V. 39

ISAACS, NATHANIEL

Travel and Adventures in Eastern Africa. London: 1836. V. 38; 41; 43

Travel and Adventures in Eastern Africa, Descriptive of the Zoolus, Their Manners, Customs, etc., etc . . . . Cape Town: 1970. V. 44; 45

ISAACS, NICHOLAS PETER

Twenty Years Before the Mast, or Life in the Forecastle. New York: 1845. V. 38

ISABELLA. London: 1823. V. 41; 43; 44; 45

ISABEY, JEAN BAPTISTE

Divers Essais Lithographiques. Paris. V. 45

ISAVERDENTZ, HAGOPOS 1834-

Armenia and the Armenians. Venice: 1878. V. 39

The Island of San Lazzaro, or the Armenian Monastery Near Venice. Venice: 1879. V. 39

ISBELL, F. A.

Mining and Hunting in the Far West, 1852-1870. Burlingame: 1948. V. 44

ISELIN, MARC

Surgery of the Hand: Wounds, Infections and Closed Traumata. London: 1940. V. 42

ISHAM, ASA B.

Prisoners of War and Military Prisons. Cincinnati: 1890. V. 38

ISHAM, JAMES

Observations on Hudson's Bay 1743, and Notes and Observations on a Book Entitled 'Voyage to Hudson's Bay in the Dobbs Galley, 1749'. London: 1949. V. 43; 44

James Isham's Observations on Hudsons Bay, 1743 and Notes and Observations on a Book Entitled A Voyage to Hudsons Bay in the Dobbs Gallery, 1749. Toronto: 1949. V. 42

ISHAM, NORMAN

Early Connecticut Houses . . . Providence: 1900. V. 46

ISHERWOOD, B. F.

The Official Reports of the inefficiency of the U. S. S. Wampanoag, and Mr. Isherwood's Defence. New York: 1868. V. 43

ISHERWOOD, CHRISTOPHER 1904-

All the Conspirataors. London: 1928. V. 37

The Berlin Stories. New York: 1945. V. 37; 39; 43

Christopher and His Kind: 1929-1939. Los Angeles: 1976. V. 39; 44

Christopher and His Kind 1929-1939. New York: 1976. V. 40; 41; 43

Christopher and His Kind 1929-1939. New York: (1976). V. 37

The Condor and the Cows. New York: 1949. V. 37; 38

Down There on a Visit. New York: 1962. V. 40

Goodbye to Berlin. London: 1939. V. 39; 40; 41

How to Know God. New York: 1953. V. 42

Journey to a War. New York: 1939. V. 39

Kathleen and Frank. London: (1971). V. 37

The Last of Mr. Norris. New York: 1935. V. 42

Lions and Shadows. London: 1938. V. 38; 40; 46

Lions and Shadows - and Education in the Twenties. Norfolk: 1947. V. 42; 44

A Meeting by the River. New York: 1967. V. 43

A Melodrama in Three Acts. On the Frontier. London: 1938. V. 39

The Memorial. London: 1932. V. 38; 41; 45

Mr. Norris Changes Trains. London: 1935. V. 38

My Guru and His Disciple. London: 1980. V. 40

Prater Violet. New York: 1945. V. 42

Sally Bowles. London: 1937. V. 38; 41; 43; 46

A Single Man. London: 1964. V. 45

A Single Man. New York: 1964. V. 40

A Single Man. 1980. V. 40; 45

Vedanta for Modern Man. New York: 1951. V. 39; 42; 46

ISHIGURO, KAZUO

The Remains of the Day. London: 1989. V. 41; 45; 46

ISHIGURO, KRAUZO

Three Stories. V. 45

ISHILL, JOSEPH

Elisee and Elie Reclus: in Memoriam. 1927. V. 46

An Evolutionary Psychologist. Theodore Schroeder's Thumbnail Essays Culled by Joseph Ishill. 1965. V. 46

ISHILL, JOSEPH continued

Free Vistas; (Volume II) a Libertarian Outlook on Life and Letters. 1937. V. 46

Theodore Schroeder. An Evolutionary Psychologist. 1964. V. 46

ISIDORE OF SEVILLE, SAINT

De Summo Bono et Soliloquiorum Eius. Basel: 1505. V. 37

ISIGURO, KAZUO

The Remains of the Day. London: 1989. V. 43

ISLA, JOSE FANCISCO DE

The History of the famous Preacher Friar Gerund de Campazas: otherwise Gerund Zotes. Translated from the Spanish. London: 1772. V. 37

ISLER, M.

The Tanagers. Washington: 1986. V. 38

ISLES, K. S.

An Economic Survey of Northern Ireland. Belfast: 1957. V. 38

ISLES, L. S.

An Economic Survey of Northern Ireland. Belfast: 1957. V. 43

ISOCARTES

Opera. Basle: 1594. V. 40; 45

ISOCRATES

Orationes et Epistolae. Geneva: 1593. V. 37; 38

The Orations and Epistles of Isocrates. London: 1752. V. 42

Scripta, Quae Quidem Nunc Extant, Omni Graecolatina, Postremo Recognita . . . Basiliae: 1571. V. 45

Trois Liures d'Isocartes. Le Premier Contient Enseignemens Pour Induire les Ieunes Gens a Uiure Honnestement & Aimer la Uertu . . . Paris: 1551. V. 41

Tvite le Orationi. Venice: 1555. V. 37; 40

ISOCRATIS

Orationes Duae. 1. Ad Demonicum. 2. Ad Nicoclem. Oxon: 1677. V. 39

ISOLA, AGOSTINO

Pieces Selected From the Italian Poets . . . Cambridge: 1778. V. 42

ISOLANUS, ISIDORUA DE

Ex Humana Divinaque Sapientia Tractatus Du Futura Noua Mundi Mutatione. Bologna: 1523. V. 38; 40

ISON, WALTER

The Georgian Buildings of Bath, 1700-1830. New York. V. 40

ISSACHAR Ryback. Zein Leven und Shafen. Paris: 1937. V. 45

ISSAVERDENS, JAMES

Armenia and the Armenians. Venice: 1878. V. 37

ISUMBRAS

The Romance of Syr Ysambrace. 1897. V. 39; 40

Syr Isambrace. Hammersmith: 1897. V. 38; 41

Syr Ysambrace. London: 1897. V. 41; 42

ITALIAN Furniture, Interiors and decoration. New York. V. 46

ITALIAN Renaissance: Measured Drawings with Details from the 13th to the 16th Century. New York: 1890. V. 39

ITALIAN Tales. London: 1824. V. 40; 41; 42

L'ITALIE. La Sicile, Les Iles Eoliennes, L'Ile d'Elbe, La Sardagne, Malte L'Ile de Calypso, etc. d'Apres les Inspirations, les Recherches et les Travaux de MM. le Viconte de Chateaubriand, de Lamartine, (etc.). Paris: 1834036. V. 46

ITCHWYRTH, AGATHA

The Cheese Girl in New Bench. Paris: 1927. V. 42; 43

ITHACUS, PSEUD.

A Letter to the Author of the National Journal. Tuesday, June 10, 1746. Edinburgh?: 1746. V. 39

THE ITINERARY of John Leland the Antiquary. Oxford: 1745-44. V. 40

ITOH, TEIJI

The Essential Japanese House: Craftsmanship, Function, Style in Town and Country. Tokyo/New York: 1967. V. 41

Imperial Gardens of Japan. New York: and Tokyo: 1970. V. 45

ITTEN, JOHANNES

The Art of Color. 1973. V. 43

Tagebuch. Berlin: 1930. V. 38

IUMO, TAKEDA

Chushingura, or the Treasury of Loyal Retainers. Tokyo: 1910. V. 44

IUSTA Oxoniensium . . . London: 1612. V. 38

IVERNOIS, FRANCIS D'

An Historical and Political View of the Constitution and Revolutions of Geneva, in the Eighteenth Century. London: 1784. V. 44

IVERSEN, ERIK

The Myth of Egypt and Its Hieroglyphs in European Tradition. Copenhagen: 1961. V. 42

Obelisks in Exile. Copenhagen: 1968/72. V. 44

IVERY, JOHN

The Hertfordshire Melody. London: 1773. V. 40

IVES, BRAYTON

Deluxe Catalogue of the Art and Literary Treasures Collected by the Late General Brayton Ives of New York. New York: 1915. V. 40

IVES, CHARLES

The Isles of Summer; or Nassau and the Bahamas. New Haven: 1880. V. 38; 40

IVES, EDWARD

A Voyage from England to India, in the Year MDCCLIV and an Historical Narrative of the Operations of the Squadron and Army in India, Under the Command of Vice-Admiral Watson and Colonel Clive . . . London: 1773. V. 45

IVES, JOHN

Remarks Upon the Garianonum of the Romans. London: 1774. V. 38

IVES, JOSEPH CHRISTMAS 1828-1868

Report Upon the Colorado River of the West. Washington: 1861. V. 37; 38; 39; 40; 41; 42; 43; 44; 45; 46

Report Upon the Colorado River of the West Explored in 1857 and 1858. New York: 1969. V. 41

IVEY, F. S.

Contemporaries from Tennessee: an Anthology of University of Tennessee Verse. Knoxville: 1930. V. 41

IVINS, VIRGINIA WILCOX

Pen Pictures of Early Western Days. Keokuk: 1905. V. 40

Pen Pictures of Early Western Days. N.P.: 1908. V. 39

IVORY, THOMAS 1709-1779

(Sale) Catalogue of . . . Pictures, Drawing Pictures . . . at St. Helen's Place . . . Norwich: 1803. V. 40; 44

IWAMIYA, TAKEJI

Forms, Textures, Images: Traditional Japanese Craftsmanship in Everyday Life. New York: 1982. V. 45

IWASAKI, KANEN

Honzo Zufu. Illustrated Manual of Plants. 1828-30. V. 44

IZACKE, RICHARD 1624-1700

Antiquities of the City of Exeter. London: 1677. V. 39; 44

Remarkable Antiquities of the City of Exeter. London: 1681. V. 42; 44

Remarkable Antiquities of the City of Exeter . . . London: 1723. V. 38; 40; 46

Remarkable Antiquities of the City of Exeter . . . L: 1724. V. 41

Remarkable Antiquities of the City of Exeter . . . Laws and Customs . . . London: 1724. V. 37; 39; 45

IZARD, MARK W.

Annual Message of Mark W. Izard, Governor of the Territory of Nebraska. Addressed to the Legislative Assembly. 1855. V. 45

Annual Message of . . . Governor of the Territory of Nebraska. Addressed to the Legislative Assembly. December 18, 1855. Omaha: 1855. V. 45

IZIKOWITZ, KARL GUSTAV

Musical and Other Sound Instruments of the South American Indians. Goteborg: 1935. V. 42

IZLAR, WILLIAM V.

A Sketch of the War Record of the Edisto Rifles, 1861-1865. Columbia: 1914. V. 40; 42

IZUMI, SEIICHI

Excavations at Kotosh, Peru: a Report of the Third and Fourth Expeditions. Tokyo: 1972. V. 42

IZZO, JOHANN BAPTIST

Elemens de l'ARchitecture Civile a l'Usage des Cavaliers du College Roial Theresien. Vienna: 1772. V. 45

J

J., A.

An Apology for Camp-Meetings, Illustrative of Their Good Effects and Answering the Principal Objections Urged Against Them. New York: 1810. V. 45

J., P.

The Constable's Guide and Pocket Companion; or, plain and easy instructions for high and petty constables, headboroughs, bursholders, tithingmen, &c. for passing through their several offices: with some useful observations. To which . . . London: 1771. V. 37

J., S.

Poetical Beauties of Modern Writers. London: 1798. V. 43

J., W.

Wonderful Relations; Being a Serious Inquiry Concerning the Nature, Subsistence & Operations of the Soul, or Spirit of Man, Immediately after the Death of the Body: . . . Fully confirmed . . . by Twelve wonderful, yet well-attested . . . . London: 1784. V. 37

JABET, G.

Notes on Noses . . . London: 1852. V. 46

JABIR IBN HAIYAN, AL TARASUSI, 8th century

Alchimiaegebri Arabis . . . Berne: 1545. V. 46

JACK Gannon. Jack of All Trades and Master of One. San Francisco: 1986. V. 40

JACK-A-NORY. Rhymes Illustrated by Richard Pope. (Bristol): 1987. V. 37

JACK, ALEXANDER

Six Views of Kot Kangra. London: 1847. V. 39

JACK, FLORENCE B.

The Woman's Book. London: 1911. V. 43

JACK, RICHARD

Elements of Conic Sections in Three Books; in which are demonstrated the principal Properties of the Parabola, Ellipse, and Hyperbola. Edinburgh: 1742. V. 37

JACK Tench; or, The Midshipman Turned Idler. London: 1841. V. 40

JACK Tench: or The Midshipman Turned Idler - The humors of the midshipman's berth in the Royal Navy. London: 1841/1842. V. 37

JACK, THOMAS

Onomasticon Poeticvm Siue, Propriorvm Qvibvs In Svis Monvmentis Vsi Svnt Veteres Poetae, Brevis Descriptio Poetica. Edinbvrgi: 1592. V. 37

JACK Wright and His Prairie Engine or Among the Bushmen of Australia. New York: 1918. V. 40

JACKMAN, W. J.

Flying Machines: Construction and Operation. Chicago: 1910. V. 37; 40; 42

JACKO'S Merry Method of Learning. London: 1843. V. 45

JACKO'S Merry Method of Learning the Pence Table. London: 1840. V. 39

JACKSON, A. P.

Oklahoma Politically and Topographically Described. Kansas City: 1885. V. 45

JACKSON, A. T.

Picture Writing of Texas Indians. Austin: 1938. V. 40

JACKSON, A. V. WILLIAMS

From Constantinople to the Home of Omar Khayyam. New York: 1911. V. 44

History Of India. London: 1906. V. 40

History of India. London: 1906-07. V. 38; 41; 43; 46

Persia Past and Present: A Book of Travel and Research. New York: & London: 1906. V. 44

JACKSON, A. Y.

A. Y.' Canada. Toronto: 1968. V. 44

Banting as an Artist. Toronto: 1943. V. 43; 44

A Painter's Country. Vancouver & Toronto: 1958. V. 42

JACKSON and a Standing Army. Philadelphia: 1828. V. 40

JACKSON, ANDREW

An Address to the People of Maryland, From Their Delegates in the Late National Republican Convention; Made in Obedience to a Resolution of that Body. Baltimore: 1832. V. 46

Annual Messages, Protest &c. Baltimore: 1835. V. 41

Correspondence Between General Jackson and Mr. Monroe, as Published at the National Intelligencer. Washington: 1824. V. 44

Correspondence Between . . . on the Subject of the Course of the Latter, In Deliberations of the Cabinet of Mr. Monroe, on the Occurences in the Seminole War. Washington: 1831. V. 38

Messages of Gen. Andrew Jackson, with a Short Sketch of His Life. Concord: 1837. V. 37; 39; 42

The Presidential Election, Written for the People of the United States, But Particularly for Those of the State of Kentucky. Fourth Series. Frankfort: 1824. V. 44

The Proclamation of Andrew Jackson, President to the People of the United States of America . . . New York: 1832. V. 42

Robert O'Hara Burke and the Australian Exploring Expedition of 1860. London: 1862. V. 40

JACKSON, ARTHUR 1593?-1666

Annotations Upon the Whole Book of Isaiah. London: 1682. V. 39

JACKSON, BENJAMIN DAYDON

Guide to the Literature of Botany. London: 1881. V. 37

Vegetable Technology. London: 1882. V. 39

JACKSON, C. C.

The Works. London: 1900. V. 38; 42

JACKSON, C. F. W.

Bull Dog Pedigrees. Bath: 1892-98. V. 43; 45

JACKSON, CATHERINE

The Works of . . . London: 1899. V. 38

JACKSON, CHARLES

The Fall of Valour. London. V. 40

A Treatise on the Pleadings and Practice in Real Actions. Boston: 1828. V. 40

JACKSON, CHARLES JAMES

English Goldsmiths and Their Marks: a History of the Goldsmiths, and Plateworkers of England, Scotland and Ireland. London: 1905. V. 40

English Goldsmiths and Their Marks. London: 1921. V. 42

An Illustrated History of English Plate, Ecclesiastical and Secular . . . London: 1911. V. 42

JACKSON, CHARLES REGINALD 1903-1968

The Lost Week-End. London: 1945. V. 40

JACKSON, CHARLES T.

Final Report on the Geology and Mineralogy of the State of New Hampshire . . . Concord: 1844. V. 38

A Manual of Etherization . . . Boston: 1861. V. 37; 39; 46

Report on the Gegological and Agricultural Survey of Rhode Island. Providence: 1840. V. 38

Report to the House of Representatives of the United States of America, Vindicating the Rights of Charles T. Jackson to the Discovery of the Anaesthetic Effects of Ether Vapor . . . Washington: 1850. V. 46

A Statement of the Claims of Charles T. Jackson, MD to the Discovery of the Applicability of Sulphuric Ether to the Discovery of Pain in Surgical Operations. Boston: 1847. V. 39

JACKSON, CHEVALIER

Bronchoscopy, Esophagoscopy and Gastroscopy. Philadelphia: 1934. V. 44

Peroral Endoscopy and Laryngael Surgery. St. Louis: 1915. V. 37

Traheo-Bronchoscopy, Esopagoscopy and Gastroscopy. St. Louis: 1907. V. 37

JACKSON, CLARENCE

Picture Maker of the Old West, William H. Jackson. New York: 1947. V. 37; 44; 46

JACKSON, DONALD

Johann Amerbach. Iowa City: 1956. V. 38; 40

JACKSON, EDGAR ALLEN

Letters of Edgar Allen Jackson, September 7, 1860-April 15, 1863. Franklin: 1939. V. 44

JACKSON, EDITH

Annals of Ealing. London: 1898. V. 44

JACKSON, EMILY

A History of Hand-Made Lace. London: 1900. V. 39; 43

Silhouette. London: 1938. V. 38; 40; 41; 45

Silhouette. New York: 1938. V. 42

JACKSON, FREDERICK

The Victim of Chancery. New York: 1841. V. 40

A Week in Wall Street. New York: 1841. V. 38; 43

JACKSON, FREDERICK GEORGE

The Great Frozen Land . . . London: 1895. V. 37; 44; 46

A Thousand Days in the Arctic. New York: 1899. V. 42; 43

A Thousand Days in the Arctic. New York: London: 1899. V. 37; 43

JACKSON, FREDERICK JOHN

The Birds of Kenya Colony and the Uganda Protectorate. London: 1938. V. 37; 43

Notes on the Game-Birds of Kenya and Uganda. London: 1926. V. 37

JACKSON, GEORGE

Sixty Years in Texas. Dallas: 1908. V. 39; 41; 45

Sixty Years in Texas. N.P.: 1908? V. 44

Sixty Years in Texas. Dallas: (1908). V. 37

JACKSON, GEORGE A.

Jackson's diary of '59' . . . Idaho Springs: 1929. V. 38

Jackson's Diary of '59. N.P.: 1929. V. 37; 40; 42

JACKSON, H. W. R.

Confederate Monitor and Patriot's Friend . . . Important and Thrilling Events of the Present Revolution . . . Atlanta: 1862. V. 40

JACKSON, HALLIDAY

Civlization of the Indian Natives: or, a Brief View of the Friendly Conduct of William Penn Towards Them in the Early Settlement of Pennsylvania . . . Philadelphia: 1830. V. 37; 44

JACKSON-HAY, GEORGE

The Records of the Third Battalion Prince of Wales' Own West Yorkshire Regiment, Late Second West York Light Infantry Militia, or 'York Regiment'. N.P.: 1897. V. 38

JACKSON, HELEN HUNT 1830-1885

A Century of Dishonor; a Sketch of the United States Government Dealings with Some of the Indian Tribes. New York: 1881. V. 40; 43; 45

Hetty's Strange History. Boston: 1877. V. 37; 39; 42

Ramona. Boston: 1884. V. 42

Ramona. Boston: 1900. V. 40; 45

Ramona. Boston: 1913. V. 37; 44

Ramona. Los Angeles: 1959. V. 38; 39; 46

The Training of Children. New York: 1882. V. 43

Verses. Boston: 1870. V. 42

JACKSON, HENRY

An Essay on Bread; Wherein the Bakers and Millers are Vindicated from the Aspersions Contained in Two Pamphlets; one Intitled Poison Detected; and the Other, The Nature of Bread Honestly and Dishonestly Made. London: 1758. V. 39

JACKSON, HENRY R.

Tallulah and Other Poems. Savannah: 1850. V. 41

JACKSON, HOLBROOK

The Anatomy of Bibliomania. 1930. V. 39; 41; 46

The Anatomy of Bibliomania. London: 1930. V. 37; 40; 42; 43

The Anatomy of Bibliomania. London: 1930-31. V. 37; 38; 40; 41; 43

The Anatomy of Bibliomania. New York: 1931. V. 37; 42; 44

The Eighteen Nineties. London: 1913. V. 46

The Eighteen Nineties Prelude to the Nineteen-Hundreds the Recapture of Something of a Remkarable Era. 1964. V. 46

Platitudes in the Making - Precepts and Advices for Gentlefolk. London: 1911. V. 43

The Printing of Books. 1938. V. 37

XX Unpublished Letters of Holbrook Jackson to Joseph Ishill with an Appreciation by John Brophy. 1960. V. 46

William Morris and the Arts and Crafts. 1934. V. 46

JACKSON, ISAAC R.

A Sketch of the Life and Public Services of William Henry Harrison. New York: 1836. V. 45

A Sketch of the Life and Public Services of William Henry Harrison . . . Columbus: 1840. V. 42

JACKSON, J.

European Hand Firearms of the 16th, 17th and 18th Centuries with a Treatise of Scottish Hand Firearms by Charles E. Whitelaw. London: 1923. V. 37

JACKSON, J. B. S.

A Descriptive Catalogue of the Anatomical Museum of the Boston Society for Medical Improvement. Boston: 1847. V. 37; 42

JACKSON, J. L.

The Art of Riding; or, Horsemanship made Easy. London: 1765. V. 37; 40

JACKSON, J. Q.

Valuable Receipts; or, Secrets Revealed! Boston: 1846. V. 44

JACKSON, J. R.

Minerals and Their Uses in a Series of Letters to a Lady. London: 1849. V. 42

Observations on Lakes. London: 1833. V. 40

JACKSON, JAMES 1777-1867

Letters to a Young Physician Just Entering Upon Practice. Boston: 1855. V. 41; 42; 44

A Memoir of James Jackson, Jr., M.D. Boston: 1835. V. 45

Memoir of . . . Boston: 1836. V. 38

A Report on Spasmodic Cholera. Boston: 1832. V. 45

A Syllabus of the Lectures Delivered at the Massachusetts Medical College to the Medical Students of Harvard University. Boston: 1816. V. 42

JACKSON, JAMES GREY

An Account of the Empire of Morocco and the District of Suse . . . London: 1809. V. 46

An Account of the Empire of Morocco and the District of Suse . . . Philadelphia: 1810. V. 43

An Account of Timbuctoo and Housa, Territories in the Interior of Africa. London: 1820. V. 46

JACKSON, JOHN

Chronological Antiquities; or the Antiquities and Chronology of the Most Ancient Kingdoms, from the Creation of the World. London: 1752. V. 44

The History of the Scottish Stage, from Its First Establishment to the Present Time; with Distinct Narrative of Some Recent Theatrical Transactions . . . Edinburgh: 1793. V. 39; 40; 43; 45

Reflections on the Commerce of the Mediterranean, Deduced from Actual Experience During a Residence on Both Shores of the Mediterranean Sea. New York: 1806. V. 39; 45

Strictures Upon the Merits of Young Roscius. London: 1804. V. 40

A Treatise on Wood Engraving, Historical and Practical. London: 1839. V. 41; 44; 46

A Treatise on Wood Engraving. London: 1861. V. 38; 40; 43

JACKSON, JOHN BAPTIST

An Essay on the Invention of Engraving and Printing in Chiaro Oscuro, as Practised by Albert Durer . . . London: 1754. V. 42

Printing in Chiaro Oscuro. London: 1754. V. 46

JACKSON, JOHN HUGHLINGS

Neurological Fragments. Oxford: 1925. V. 40

Selected Writings of John Hughlings Jackson. London: 1931. V. 42

Selected Writings of John Hughlings Jackson. London: 1932. V. 39; 41; 44

Selected Writings of John Hughlings Jackson. New York: 1958. V. 41

JACKSON, JOHN, OF TANFIELD MILL

The Practical Fly-Fisher. London: 1862. V. 38

The Practical Fly-Fisher. London: 1889. V. 38

The Practical Fly-Fisher, More Particularly for Grayling or Umber. London: 1899. V. 39; 40; 45

JACKSON, JOSEPH

Encyclopedia of Philadelphia. Harrisburg: 1931. V. 39; 41; 42

JACKSON, LEROY F.

The Peter Patter Book. Chicago & New York: 1919. V. 42

JACKSON, LUCRETIA E.

The Health Reformer's Cook Book; or How to Prepare Food from Grains, Fruits and Vegetables. Dansville: 1874. V. 45

JACKSON, MARGARET HASTINGS

Catalogue of the Frances Taylor Pearsons Plimpton Collection of Italian Books and Manuscripts in the Library of Wellesley College. Cambridge: 1929. V. 46

JACKSON, MARIA ELIZABETH

Botanical Dialogues Between Hortensia and Her Four Children, Designed for the Use of Schools. London: 1797. V. 37; 41; 42

The Florist's Manual; or, Hints for the Construction of a Gay Flower Garden. London: 1816. V. 38

JACKSON, MARIA ELIZABETH continued

The Florist's Manual. London: 1822. V. 37; 46

The Florist's Manual, or, Hints for the Construction of a Gay Flower-Garden. London: 1827. V. 37

JACKSON, MARY E.

The Life of Nellie C. Bailey; or, a Romance of the West. Topeka: 1885. V. 38

JACKSON, MASON

The Pictorial Press: Its Origin and Progress. London: 1885. V. 41; 44

JACKSON, MURRAY COSBY

A Soldier's Diary. South Africa 1899-1901. London: 1913. V. 41

JACKSON, P.

The Timurid and Sefavid Periods. Editors P. Jackson and L. Lockhart. 1986. V. 37

JACKSON, RANDLE 1757-1837

The Speech of Randle Jackson, Esq. Addressed to the Honorable the Committee of the House of Commons, Appointed to Consider of the State of the Woollen Manufacture of England . . . London: 1806. V. 43; 46

JACKSON, RICHARD

An Historical Review of the Constitution and Government of Pensylvania, From Its Origin . . . London: 1759. V. 45

The Interest of Great Britain Considered, with Regard to Her Colonies and the Acquisitions of Canada and Gaudaloupe . . . London: 1760. V. 41; 42

JACKSON, ROBERT

Remarks on the Epidemic of Yellow Fever, Which Has Appeared at Intervals on the South Coasts of Spain Since the Year 1800. London: 1821. V. 44

A Sketch, (Analytical) of the History and Cure of Contagious Fever. London: 1819. V. 44

A Systematic View of the Formation, Discipline and Economy of Armies. London: 1804. V. 37; 38; 39; 40; 41; 42; 44; 45; 46

A Treatise on the Fevers of Jamaica, with Some Observations on the Intermitting Fever of American and an Appendix . . . Philadelphia: 1795. V. 37; 38; 40; 41; 43; 44

A View of the Formation, Discipline and Economy of Armies . . . Stockton: 1824. V. 43

JACKSON, SHELDON

Alaska, and Missions on the North Pacific Coast . . . New York: 1880. V. 39

Alaska, and Missions on the North Pacific Coast . . . Fully Illustrated. New York: (1880). V. 37

Fifteenth Annual Report on Introduction of Domestic Reindeer into Alaska. Washington: 1906. V. 38

JACKSON, SHIRLEY

The Bird's Nest. New York: 1954. V. 44

The Haunting of Hill House. New York: 1959. V. 39; 46

Life Among the Savages. New York: 1953. V. 44

The Lottery. New York: 1949. V. 37; 42; 44

The Road through the Wall. 1948. V. 45

The Road Through the Wall. New York: 1948. V. 37; 38

The Sundial. New York: 1958. V. 37

JACKSON, T. G.

Dalmatia the Quarnero and Istria with Cettigne in Montenegro and the Island of Grado. Oxford: 1887. V. 39

JACKSON, T. STURGES

Logs of the Great Sea Fights 1794-1805. London: 1899. V. 41

JACKSON, THOMAS

An Affectionate Address to Sailors, Occasioned by the Wreck of the Trent and the Oak, to Which is Prefixed Some Particulars of the Wreck Itself. Yarmouth: 1836. V. 46

Industry Illustrated; a Memoir of Thomas Jackson, of Eltham Park, Kent . . . London: 1884. V. 43

JACKSON, THOMAS GRAHAM

Byzantine and Romanesque Architecture. Cambridge: 1920. V. 41; 42; 44

The Church of St. Mary the Virgin. Oxford: 1897. V. 38; 44; 46

Gothic Architecture in France, England and Italy. Cambridge: 1915. V. 42

The Renaissance of Roman Architecture. Cambridge: 1921-23. V. 38; 42

JACKSON, W.

An Abstract of the Several Deeds and Muniments That Relate to, or Concern the, Charitable Donations Belonging to the Parish of Hampton, in the County of Middlesex. London: 1816. V. 40

JACKSON, W. C.

Memoir of the Public Conduct and Services of Williams Collins Jackson, Senior Merchant on the Company's Madras Establishment. London: 1809. V. 38

JACKSON, W. H.

The Texas Stock Directory; or, Book of Marks and Brands. San Antonio: 1865. V. 42; 46

The Texas Stock Directory, or Book of Marks and Brands. New Braunfels: 1950's. V. 41

JACKSON, WILLIAM

A Full Report of All the Proceedings on the Trial of the Rev. William Jackson at the Bar of His Majesty's Court of King's Bench, Ireland, on an Indictment for High Treason. Dublin: 1795. V. 46

Memoirs of Dr. Richard Gilpin, of Scaleby Castle in Cumberland . . . London: 1879. V. 44

The New and Complete Newgate Calendar; or, Villany Displayed In All Its Branches. London: 1795. V. 40

The New and Complete Newgate Calendar; or, Malefactor's Universal Register. London: 1807. V. 39

Observations in Answer to Mr. Thomas Paine's 'Age of Reason'. Dublin: 1795. V. 43

JACKSON, WILLIAM A.

An Annotated List of the Publications of the Reverend Thomas Frognall Dibdin, D.D. Cambridge: 1965. V. 37; 39; 40; 42; 43

An Annotated List of the Publications of the Reverend Thomas Frognall Dibdin, D.D. . . . London: 1965. V. 40; 42

Appendix to Jackson's Map of Mining Districts of California . . . New York: 1851. V. 37

JACKSON, WILLIAM ALEXANDER

Records of a Bibliographer. Cambridge: 1967. V. 45

JACKSON, WILLIAM H.

Life and Confession of Sophia Hamilton, Who Was Tried, Convicted and Sentenced to Be Hung, at Frederickton, on the 8th Day of April, 1845, for the Prepetration of the Most Shocking Murders and Daring Robberies Perhaps Recorded in the Annals of Crime. Frederickton: 1845. V. 45

Picture Maker of the Old West. New York: 1947. V. 38

JACKSON, WILLIAM HENRY

The Canons of Colorado. Denver: 1890-1900. V. 45

Descriptive Catalogue of the Photographs of the United States Geological Survey of the Territories for the Years 1869 to 1873. Washington: 1874. V. 39

Descriptive Catalogue of Photographs of North American Indians. Washington: 1877. V. 37; 39

Time Exposure. The Autobiography of William Henry Jackson. New York: 1940. V. 37

William Henry Jackson's Rocky Mountain Railroad Album: Steam and Steel Across the Great Divide. Silverton: 1976. V. 39; 46

JACOB, GILES 1686-1744

The Compleat Court-Keeper; or Land Steward's Assistant. London: 1715. V. 42; 43

The Compleat Sportsman. London: 1718. V. 39

The Compleat Court-Keeper; or, Land Steward's Assistant. London: 1724. V. 40

The Compleat Parish-Officer . . . In the Savoy: 1731. V. 43

The Compleat Parish-Officer; . . . The Second Edition with Additions. In the Savoy: 1720. V. 37

The Complete Court-Keeper; or, Land-Steward's Assistant. London: 1764. V. 44

Every Man His Own Lawyer; or, a Summary of the Laws of England . . . New York: 1768. V. 43

Every Man his own Lawyer: or A summary of the laws of England . . . The Fourth edition, with additions. In the Savoy: 1750. V. 37

A Law Grammar; or Rudiments of the Law. London: 1749. V. 40

The Law Dictionary. London: 1809. V. 39; 40

The Law Dictionary Explaining the Rise, Progress and Present State of the English Law. Philadelphia and New York: 1811. V. 45

A Law Grammar; or, Rudiments of Law. Dublin: 1772. V. 39

Lex Constitutions: or, the Gentleman's Law. Being a compleat treatise of all the laws and statutes relating to the King . . . In the Savoy: 1719. V. 37

Memoirs of the Life of the Right Honourable Joseph Addison. London: 1719. V. 41; 45

The Modern Justice . . . In the Savoy: 1720. V. 42

A New Law-Dictionary . . . London: 1736. V. 45

The New Law-Dictionary. 1743. V. 39

A New Law-Dictionary. In the Savoy: 1744. V. 41

A New Law Dictionary. London: 1772. V. 39; 46

A New Law-Dictionary. In the Savoy: 1774. V. 43

A New Law-Dictionary . . . London: 1782. V. 45

A New Law-Dictionary. London: 1739. V. 37

The Poetical Register. London: 1723. V. 38; 41; 42; 44

The Rape of the Smock. London: 1717. V. 45

JACOB, HEINRICH EDUARD

The Sage of Coffee, the Biography of an Economic Portrait. London: 1935. V. 46

JACOB, HILDEBRAND

Bedlam. London: 1723. V. 38; 45

Callistia; or the Prize of Beauty. A Poem. London: 1738. V. 38

Chiron to Achilles: a Poem. London: 1732. V. 41

The Fatal Constancy. London: 1723. V. 41

Hymn to the Goddess of Silence. London: 1734. V. 38

JACOB, J.

Observations on the Structure and draught of Wheel Carriages. London: 1773. V. 38; 39; 40; 44

JACOB, JOHN

(Hebrew Title) The Jew Turned Christian; or, The Corner-Stone. London: 1678-9. V. 40

JACOB, JOHN G.

The Life and Times of Patrick Gass, Now Sole Survivor of the Overland Expedition to the Pacific . . . Wellsburg: 1859. V. 37; 46

JACOB, JOHN JEREMIAH

Biographical Sketch of the Life of the Late Capt. Michael Cresap. Cumberland: 1826. V. 39; 45

A Biographical Sketch of the Life of the Late Captain Michael Cresap. Cincinnati: 1866. V. 37; 41

A Biographical Sketch of the Life of the Late Capt. Michael Cresap. Cumberland: 1881. V. 45

Biographical Sketch of the Life of the late Captain Michael Cresap. Cincinnati: 1826. V. 37

JACOB, MIRA

Paul Delvaux: Graphic Work. New York: 1976. V. 39; 43

JACOB, N. H.

Storia Naturale delle Scimie e dei Maki. Turin and Genoa: 1816. V. 42

JACOB, S. S.

Jeypore Portfolio of Architectural Details. London: 1890. V. 38

JACOB, WILLIAM

an Historical Inquiry Into the Production and Consumption of the Precious Metals. London: 1831. V. 39; 43; 46

Observations on the Benefits Arising from the Cultivation of Poor Soils, by the application of pauper Labour: as exemplified in the Colonies for the Indigent and for Orphans in Holland: printed for the Society for Improving the condition . . . London: 1828. V. 37

Tracts Relating to the Corn Trade and Corn Laws . . . London: 1828. V. 43

Travels in the South of Spain, in Letters Written A.D. 1809 and 1810. London: 1811. V. 40; 41

JACOBAEUS, OLIGERUS

Museum Regium Seu Catalogus Rerum Tam Naturalium, Quam Artifialum, Quae in Basilica Bibliothecae . . . Copenhagen: 1696-99. V. 40

JACOBI, A.

Therapeutics of Infancy and Childhood. Philadelphia: 1896. V. 44

JACOBI, ABRAHAM

The Intestinal Diseases of Infancy and Childhood. Detroit: 1887. V. 37

JACOBI, CARL GUSTAV JACOB

Disquistiones Analyticae de Fractionibus Simplicibus. Berlin: 1725. V. 38

JACOBI, CHARLES THOMAS

Ten Variations of the Same Title-Pages Each in Black Ink and Also Rubricated. V. 44

JACOBI, EDUARD

Portfolio of Dermachromes . . . London: 1903-06. V. 43

Portfolio of Dermochromes. New York: 1905. V. 42

Portfolio of Dermochromes . . . New York: and London: 1905-06. V. 45

JACOBI, JOHANNES

A Litil Booke the Whiche Traytied and Reherced Many Gode Things Necessaries for the . . . Pestilence . . . Made by the . . . Bisshop of Arusiens . . . Manchester: 1910. V. 41

JACOBI, MARY PUTNAM

Essays on Hysteria, Brain-Tumor and Some Other Cases of Nervous Disease. New York: 1888. V. 39; 46

A Pathfinder in Medicine with Selections from Her Writings and a Complete Bibliography. New York: 1925. V. 44

JACOBI, MAXIMILIAN

On the Construction and Management of Hospitals for the Insane. London: 1841. V. 39

JACOBKI, FRIEDRICH HEINRICH

David Hume Uber den Glauben Oder Idealismus und Realismus. Ein Gesprach. Breslau: 1787. V. 45

JACOBS, HARRIET B.

Incidents in the Life of a Slave Girl. Boston: 1861. V. 39

JACOBS, JEAN BERNARD 1734-1790

Ecole Pratique des Accouchemens . . . Paris: 1785. V. 42

JACOBS, JOSEPH

The Book of Wonder Voyages. London: 1896. V. 43

Celtic Fairy Tales. London: 1892. V. 43

English Fairy Tales. London: 1890. V. 39

Indian Fairy Tales. London: 1892. V. 37; 41

More English Fairy Tales. London: 1894. V. 38; 43

JACOBS, LEONEBEL

Portraits of 30 Authors. New York: 1937. V. 41

JACOBS, ORANGE

The Memoirs of Orange Jacobs. Seattle: 1908. V. 40; 45

JACOBS, PETER

Journal of the Reverend Peter Jacobs, Indian Wesleyan Missionary, from Rice Lake to the Hudson's Bay Territory, and Returning. New York: 1857. V. 40

JACOBS, THOMAS JEFFERSON

Scenes, Incidents, and Adventures in the Pacific Ocean, or the Islands of the Australasian Seas, During the Cruise of the Clipper Margaret Oakley Under Capt. Benjamin Morrell . . . New York: 1844. V. 38; 45; 46

JACOBS, WILLIAM WYMARK 1863-1943

Many Cargoes. London: 1896. V. 37; 39; 41; 46

A Master of Craft. London: 1900. V. 38; 39; 41; 46

JACOBSEN, HERMANN

A Handbook of Succulent Plants. London: 1954, 1960. V. 39

A Handbook of Succulent Plants. London: 1986. V. 38

JACOBSEN, THORKILD

Sennacherib's Aqueduct at Jerwan. Chicago: 1935. V. 40; 42

Sennacherib's Aqueduct at Jerwan. Chicago: (1935). V. 37

JACOBSON & COMPANY

The General Catalogue . . . Architectural and Decorative Ornaments. New York: 1913 & 1929. V. 38; 40; 44

JACOBSON, EGBERT

The Color Harmony Manual. Chicago: 1942. V. 38

JACOBSTHAL, PAUL

Greek Pins and Their Connexions with Europe and Asia. Oxford: 1956. V. 40; 44

JACOBUS A SANCTO MICHAELE

Sacrovm Novi Testamenti Librorvm Omnivm Analysis Catholica, Et Oeconomia Generalais. Lyon: 1670. V. 37

JACOBUS DE GRUYTRODE

Lavacrum Conscientiae. Omnibus Sacerdotibus Summe Utile ac Necessarium. Paris: 1500. V. 37

JACOBUS DE THERAMO 1349-1417

Der Teutsch Belial. Augsburg: 1500. V. 40

JACOBUS DE VARAGINE 1230-1298

Lombardica Hystoria (Legenda Aurea Sanctorum); Ulm: 1488. V. 38

The Golden Lgend. London: 1527. V. 43

The Golden Legend. London: 1572. V. 41

The Golden Legend. 1892. V. 38

The Golden Legend. Hammersmith: 1892. V. 37; 38

The Golden Legend. London: 1892. V. 41

In the State of Innocensye. Beckenham: 1988. V. 41; 42

Legenda Aurea. Strassburg: 1476. V. 42

La Legende Doree en Francoys Nouvellement Imprimee. Lyon: 1518. V. 40; 45

The Life of St. George. From Caxton's Translation of the Golden Legend. London: 1919. V. 46

The Life of St. George. From Caxton's Translation of the Golden Legend. London: 1912. V. 46

Mariale: sive Sermones de Beata Maria Virginia. Venice: 1597. V. 45; 46

JACOBUS X

Untrodden Fields of Anthropology . . . 1930. V. 45

JACOBUS X continued

Untrodden Fields of Anthropology, Observations on the Esoteric Manners and Customs of Semi Civilized peoples . . . 1930. V. 39

JACOBY, HELMUT

New Architectural Drawings. 1969. V. 46

JACOMBE, SAMUEL

Moses, His Death: Opened and Applyed, in a Sermon at Christ-Church in London, Decemb. 23 MDCLVI (1656). At the Funeral of Mr. Edward Bright, M.A. Fellow of Emmanuel College in Cambridge and Minister of the Gospel There . . . London: 1657. V. 38; 41

JACOMBE, THOMAS

Several Sermons Preach'd on the Whole Eighth Chapter of the Epistle to the Romans . . . London: 1672. V. 45

JACQUARD, P.

Genetic Differentiaition and Dispersal in Plants. Berlin: 1985. V. 37

JACQUEMONT, VICTOR

Letters from India; Describing a Journey in the British Dominions of India, Tibet, Lahore and Cashmere, During the Years 1828, 1829, 1830, 1831. London: 1834. V. 38; 41

JACQUES, D. H.

The Rural Carolinian: an Illustrated Magazine of Agriculture, Horticulture and the Arts. Volume I. Charleston: 1870. V. 40

JACQUES DE GUYSE

Les Illustrations de la Gaule Belgique . . . Paris: 1531-1532. V. 37; 38; 40

JACQUES, HENRY

Moulin Rouge. Paris: 1925. V. 41

JACQUET, EUGENE

Histoire et Technique de la Montre Suisse de ses Origines a Nos Jours. 1945. V. 41

Technique and History of the Swiss Watch from Its Beginnings to the Present Day. Olten: 1953. V. 41

JACQUIN, JOSEPH FRANZ VON

Beytrage zur Geschichte der Vogel. Vienna: 1784. V. 46

JACQUIN, NICOLAUS JOSEPH VON 1727-1817

Oxalis. Monographia, Iconibus Illustrata. Vienna: 1794. V. 43; 46

Selectarum Stirpium Americanarum Historia. Vienna: 1763. V. 38; 40; 42; 43; 46

Selectarum Stirpium Americnarum Historia in Qua ad Linneanum Systema Determinatae Descriptaeque Sistunter Plantae . . . Vindobonae,: 1763. V. 42; 45

Stapeliarum in Hortis Vindobonensibus Cultarum. Sandton: 1982. V. 46

JACQUINOT, DOMINIQUE

L'Usage de l'Astrolabe, avec un petit Traicte de la Sphere . . . Paris: 1573. V. 38

JACSON, M.

The Record of a Regiment of the Line Being a Regimental History of the 1st Battalion Devonshire Regiment During the Boer War 1899-1902. London: 1908. V. 41

JAEGER, B.

The Life of North American Insects. Providence: 1854. V. 37; 39; 43; 45

JAEGER, DORIS U.

The Faculty of the College of Physicians and Surgeons Columbia University in the City of New York: Twenty-Four Portraits. New York: 1919. V. 37; 41; 42; 45

JAEGER, EDUARD VON

Ophthalmoskopischer Hand-Atlas. Wien: 1869. V. 42

JAEGER, WERNER

Paideia: the Ideals of Greek Culture. Oxford: 1944-46. V. 45

JAFFE, MICHAEL

Van Dyck's Antwerp Sketchbook. London: 1966. V. 37; 44; 46

JAGGARD, WILLIAM

Shakespeare Bibliography. Stratford-on-Avon,: 1911. V. 37; 39; 42; 45; 46

JAGO, F. W. P.

An English-Cornish Dictionary. London: & Plymouth: 1887. V. 45

JAGO, RICHARD

Edge-Hill, or, the Rural Prospect Delineated and Moralized. London: 1767. V. 38; 40; 43

Poems Moral and Descriptive. London: 1784. V. 46

JAGO, WILLIAM

A Text-Book of the Science and Art of Bread Making . . . London: 1895. V. 45

JAHR, G. H. G.

The New Homoeopathic Pharmacopoeia and Posology, or the Preparation of Homoeopathic Medicines and the Administrations of Doses. Philadelphia: 1842. V. 42

JAHR, GOTTLIEB HEINRICH GEORG

General and Special Therapeutics of Mental Diseases and Psychical Disorder. Manchester: 1857. V. 40

JAKOB, CHRISTFIELD

Atlas of the Nervous System. New York: 1896. V. 42

JAKOBSON, ROMAN

Selected Writings. (Volume I): Phonological Studies. The Hague: 1962. V. 46

JALOVEC, KAREL

German and Austrian Violin Makers. London: 1967. V. 37

German and Austrian Violin-Makers. Translated by George Theiner. London: (1967). V. 37

Italian Violin Makers. London: 1958. V. 38

Italian Violin Makers. New York: n.d. V. 37

Italian Violin Makers. London: 1965. V. 37

The Violin Makers of Bohemia. London: 1959. V. 37

THE JAMAICA Alamanck for the Year 1823. Kingston: 1822. V. 37

JAMAICA. ASSEMBLY

Proceedings of the Honourable House of Assembly Relative to the Maroons; Including Correspondence Between the Right Honourable Earl of Balcarres and the Honourable Major-General Walpole, During the Maroon Rebellion . . . St. Jago de la Vega: 1796. V. 39

Votes of the Honourable House of Assembly of Jamaica, in a Session Begun October 20, and Ended December 12, 1801 . . . Begun October 29 and Ended Dec. 11, 1811 . . . Begun Oct. 27 and Ended Dec. 11, 1812 . . . Begun Oct. 26 and Ended Dec. 4, 1813. Jamaica: 1802-12-13-14. V. 40

JAMAICA: Enslaved and Free. London: 1846. V. 41

JAMAICA. GENERAL ASSEMBLY - 1796

The Proceedings of the Governor and Assembly of Jamaica, in Regard to the Maroon Negroes . . . London: 1796. V. 38

JAMAICA. LAWS, STATUTES & ETC. - 1684

The Laws of Jamaica, Passed by the Assembly, and Confirmed by His Majesty in Council, April 17, 1684. To Which is Added, the State of Jmaica, as It is Now Under the Government of Sir Thomas Lynch. London: 1684. V. 38; 40; 41

JAMAICA. LAWS, STATUTES, ETC. - 1716

The Laws of Jamaica, Pass'd by the Governours, Council and Assembly in that Island, and Confirm'd by the Crown. London: 1716. V. 39

JAMAICA. LAWS, STATUTES, ETC. - 1789

The New Act of Assembly of the Island of Jamaica . . . Commonly Called the New Consolidated Act . . . Being the Present Code Noir of that Island . . . London: 1789. V. 37; 40

JAMAICA. LAWS, STATUTES, ETC. - 1793

An Abridgment of the Laws of Jamaica; Being an Alphabetical Digest of all the Public Acts of Assembly Now in Force . . . St. Jago de la Vega: 1793. V. 40

JAMAICA. LAWS, STATUTES, ETC. - 1841

The Laws of Jamaica Passed in the Fourth Year of the Reign of Queen Victoria. Jamaica: 1841. V. 39

JAMBLICHUS, OF CHALCIS d. 339

De Mysteriis Aegyptiorum. Chaldaeorum Assyriorum (and other works). Venice: 1497. V. 45

(Greek title, then) De Vita Pythagorae & Protrepticae Orationes ad Philosophiam Lib. II. Nunquam Hactenus Visi: Nunc Vero Graece & Latine Primum Editi cum Necessariis Castigationibus & Notis . . . Colophon: Excudebat: 1598. V. 45

(Greek title, then): De Vita Pythagorae & Protrepticae Orationes ad Philosophiam Lib. II. Nunquam Hactenus Visi. Heidelberg: 1598. V. 40

JAMES, Prince of No-Land: or, An Answer to Dr. Woodward's false Friend, in Vindication of the Reverand Mr. Sharp, the Curate of Stepney. Part 1. London: 1709. V. 39

JAMES, ARTHUR E.

Chester County Clocks and Their Makers. 1947. V. 39; 41; 42

The Potters and Potteries of Chester County, Pennsylvania. West Chester: 1945. V. 39; 41; 42

JAMES, BENJAMIN

A Treatise on the Management of Teeth. Boston: 1814. V. 37

JAMES BURNET

Of the Origin and Progress of Language . . . Edinburgh: 1774-89. V. 37

JAMES, BUSHROD W.

Alaskana, or Alaska in Descriptive and Legendary Poems. Philadelphia: 1892. V. 46

JAMES, C. H.

Small Houses for the Community. London: 1924. V. 38

JAMES, C. L. R.

Minty Alley. London: 1936. V. 44; 46

Party Politics in the West Indies. San Juan: 1962. V. 46

Trinidad - Short Stories, Articles and Poems. Port of Spain: 1929. V. 38

JAMES, CARY

The Imperial Hotel: FLW and the Architecture of Unity. Rutland: 1968. V. 46

JAMES, CHARLES

A New and Enlarged Military Dictionary, . . . London: 1802. V. 46

Poems by the author of Hints to Lord Rawdon on Some Military Abuses (etc.). London: 1792. V. 42

A Poetical Epistle from Petrarch to Laura. London: 1780. V. 43

Prince of No-Land: or, An Answer to Dr. Woodward's false Friend, in Vindication of the Reverend Mr. Sharp, the Curate of Stepney. London: 1709. V. 43

JAMES Clyman Frontiersman. Portland: 1960. V. 39

JAMES, EDWARD

The Adventures of Propaganda, the Propagrandissimo Dog, A Sequel to the Conquest of Abyssinia. The MAtter is Variously compiled by Mr. E.W. Selsey. c. 1952). V. 37

La Belle Au Bois Dormant and Other Poems. London: 1933. V. 38

The Bones of My Hand. London: 1938. V. 38; 42; 43; 44

Carmina Amico; Opus Quintum. 1932. V. 40; 44; 45

Carmina Amico, Opus Quintum. Verona: 1932. V. 38; 39; 40; 42

For the Lonely. London: 1960? V. 39

The Gardener Who Saw God. London: 1937. V. 40; 42

The Gardener Who Saw God. New York: 1937. V. 45

The Next Volume. London: 1933. V. 41

The Next Volume. London: 1939. V. 40

The Perfectly Ended Chapter - a Poem to the Memory of George V - an Irreproachable and Saintly King - on the Occasion of His Late Majsety's Jubilee . . . Oxford: 1936. V. 44

Reading Into the Picture. London: 1934. V. 42; 43; 45

JAMES, EDWIN 1797-1861

Account of an Expedition from Pittsburgh to the Rocky Mountains, in . . . 1819, 1820. London: 1823. V. 37; 38; 39; 40; 41; 43; 45

Account of an Expedition from Pittsburgh to the Rocky Mountains, Performed in the Years 1819 and 20. Philadelphia: 1823. V. 38; 39; 41; 42; 43; 44; 45

Account of an Expedition from Pittsburgh to the Rocky Mountains, Performed in the Years 1819, 1820. London: 1828. V. 45

Account of an Expedition from Pittsburgh to the Rocky Mountains, Performed in the Years 1819, 1820. Cleveland: 1905. V. 37

Memoires de John Tanner. Paris: 1835. V. 40; 41; 45

A Narrative of the Captivity and Adventures of John Tanner (U. S. Interpreter at the Saut de Ste. Marie) During Thirty Years Residence Among the Indians in the Interior of North America. New York: 1830. V. 37; 38; 39; 41; 43; 45

JAMES, ELLSWORTH DE KAY

Zoology of New York. Albany: 1844. V. 44

JAMES, F. L.

The Unknown Horn of Africa: an Exploration from Berbera to the Leopard River. London: 1890. V. 46

The Wild Tribes of the Soudan. London: 1883. V. 43; 45

JAMES F. WHITE & CO., INC., NEW YORK.

Trade Catalogue of Brassiere and Corset Fabrics. New York: 1920's. V. 43

JAMES Forbes; a Tale, Founded on Facts. London: 1824. V. 39

JAMES, G. P. R.

The Ancient Regime. New York: 1841. V. 45

The Desultory Man. New York: 1836. V. 45

Heidelberg. New York: 1846. V. 45

The Jacquerie. New York: 1842. V. 45

Memoirs of Celebrated Women. London: 1837. V. 43

On the Educational Institutions of Germany. London: 1835. V. 41

JAMES, GEORGE PAYNE RAINSFORD 1799-1860

Adrian; or the Clouds of the Mind. New York: 1852. V. 42

Agincourt. London: 1844. V. 46

Arrah Neil; or, Times of Old. London: 1845. V. 39; 46

Attila. London: 1837. V. 39; 46

Attila, a Romance. New York: 1837. V. 45

A Book of the Passions. London: 1839. V. 46

The Cavalier. Philadelphia: 1859. V. 44

The Commissioner; or, De Lunatico Inquirendo. Dublin: 1843. V. 40; 46

De l'Orme. London: 1830. V. 40; 42

Henry Masterton; or the Adventures of a Young Cavalier. London: 1832. V. 39; 46

The Huguenot: a Tale of the French Protestants. London: 1839. V. 46

The Huguenot. New York: 1839. V. 45

The King's Highway. London: 1840. V. 46

The Last of the Fairies. London: 1848. V. 44

Letters Illustrative of the Reign of William III, from 1696 to 1708. London: 1841. V. 46

The Life and Times of Louis the Fourteenth. London: 1838. V. 46

Mary of Burgundy, or the Revolt of Ghent. London: 1833. V. 40; 41; 43; 44

Morley Ernstein or the Tenants of the Heart. London: 1842. V. 40; 46

One in a Thousand; or, the Days of Henry Quatre . . . London: 1835. V. 38; 46

Philip Augustus; or, the Brothers in Arms. London: 1831. V. 40

Richelieu, a Tale of France. London: 1829. V. 38

The Robber. London: 1838. V. 39; 46

A Romance of Old Times. London: 1843. V. 39

Russell: A Tale of the Reign of Charles II. London: 1847. V. 41; 44

The Smuggler. London: 1845. V. 39; 46

Speech . . . at the Conservative Dinner at Sandwich, on Friday, the 4th of June, 1841, on Prosposing the Health of Sir Robert Peel, and the Conservative Members of the House of Commons. Dover: 1841. V. 40

The Works. London: 1844-49. V. 38; 46

JAMES, GEORGE WHARTON

The H.M.M.B.A. In California. Pasadena: 1896. V. 37; 40

In and Around the Grand Canyon. Boston: 1900. V. 37; 38; 39; 43; 44

In and Out of the Old Missions of California. Boston: 1905. V. 43

Indian Basketry. Los Angeles: 1901. V. 38

Indian Baskerty. Phoenix: 1902. V. 46

Indian Blankets and Their Makers. New York: 1937. V. 37; 39

The Indians of the Painted Desert Region. Boston: 1903. V. 46

The 1910 Trip of the H.M.M.B.A. to California and the Pacific Coast. San Francisco: 1911. V. 37

The Wonders of the Colorado Desert. Boston: 1906. V. 37; 40; 45; 46

JAMES, GILBERT

Fourteen Drawings Illustrating Rubaiyat of Omar Khayyam. London: 1898. V. 45

JAMES, GRACE

Green Willow and Other Japanese Fairy Tales. London: 1910. V. 37; 38; 39; 41; 42; 44; 45; 46

Green Willow and Other Japanese Fairy Tales. London: 1912. V. 42

JAMES, H. E.

Pedigrees of the Family of James of Culgarth, West Auckland and Barrock, and their Kinsfolk. Exter: 1913. V. 37

JAMES, H. E. M.

The Long White Mountain or a Journey in Manchuria. London: 1888. V. 40

JAMES, HENRY 1843-1916

The Ambassadors. London: 1903. V. 37

The Ambassadors. New York: 1903. V. 37; 38; 39; 40; 42; 44; 46

The Ambassadors. New York: & London: 1903. V. 46

The American. London: 1866. V. 39

The American. Boston: 1877. V. 43

The American. Leipzig: 1878. V. 46

The American. London: 1879. V. 37; 44

The American Scene. London: 1907. V. 37; 39; 45

The American Scene. New York: 1907. V. 38; 40; 45

The American Scene. New York: & London: 1907. V. 44

The American Volunteer Motor-Ambulance Corps in France. London: 1914. V. 44

The Aspern Papers. London: 1888. V. 41; 42; 45

The Apsern Papers. New York: 1888. V. 46

The Aspern Papers, Louisa Pallant, The Modern Warning. London: & New York: 1888. V. 37

The Author of Beltraffio, Pandora, Georgina's Reasons, the Path fo Duty, Four Meetings. Boston: 1885. V. 45; 46

The Awkward Age. New York: 1899. V. 37; 39; 42; 43; 44; 45; 46

JAMES, HENRY 1843-1916 continued

The Awkward Age. New York: & London: 1899. V. 42; 44

The Beast in the Jungle. Kentfield: 1963. V. 37; 38; 40; 42

The Better Sort. London: 1903. V. 42

The Better Sort. New York: 1903. V. 38; 40; 41; 44

The Bostonians. London: 1886. V. 37; 45

The Bostonians. London: & New York: 1886. V. 44

The Bostonians. New York: 1886. V. 38

A Bundle of Letters. Boston: 1880. V. 45; 46

Charles W. Eliot. Boston: 1930. V. 38

Confidence. Boston: 1880. V. 37; 38; 39; 40; 41; 43; 44; 45; 46

Confidence. New York: 1880. V. 37

Confidence. London: 1880, 1879. V. 42

Daisy Miller. New York: 1877/78. V. 46

Daisy Miller. Leipzig: 1879. V. 41

Daisy Miller: a Study. London: 1879. V. 42; 46

Daisy Miller. New York: 1879. V. 41; 45

Daisy Miller. Boston: 1883. V. 42; 44; 46

Daisy Miller and an International Episode. New York: 1892. V. 37; 44

Daisy Miller. Cambridge: 1969. V. 46

Daisy Miller. New York: 1969. V. 38

The Diary of a Man of Fifty and a Bundle of Letters. New York: 1880. V. 37; 41; 44; 45

Embarrassments. New York: 1896. V. 37; 45; 46

English Hours. Boston: 1905. V. 44

English Hours. Boston & New York: 1905. V. 37; 41

English Hours. Cambridge: 1905. V. 39

English Hours. London: 1905. V. 37

Essays in London. New York: 1893. V. 43; 44

Essays on Money, Exchanges, and Political Economy, Showing the Cause of the Fluctuations in Prices and of the Depreciation in the Value of Property of Late Years. London: 1820. V. 37

The Europeans. London: 1878. V. 42

The Europeans. Boston: 1879. V. 37; 43; 44; 45; 46

Facsimiles of National Manuscripts from William the Conqueror to Queen Anne . . . Southampton: 1865. V. 46

The Finer Grain. London: 1910. V. 41; 43

The Finer Grain. New York: 1910. V. 39

The Finer Grain. London: (1910). V. 37

French Poets and Novelists. London: 1878. V. 39; 45

Gabrielle de Bergerac. New York: 1918. V. 37; 41; 42; 46

The Golden Bowl. New York: 1904. V. 41; 45

The Golden Bowl. London: 1905. V. 43; 45; 46

The Great Streets of the World. New York: 1892. V. 41; 42

Hawthorne. London: 1879. V. 44

Hawthorne. New York: 1880. V. 43; 44

The Henry James Year Book. Boston: 1911. V. 45

In the Cage. Chicago: 1898. V. 38; 40; 41; 44; 45

In the Cage. Chicago: New York: 1898. V. 37; 39; 41; 42

In the Cage. London: 1898. V. 37

Instructions for Taking Meteorological Observations with Tables for Their Correction and Notes on Meteorological Phenomena. (with) Appendix. London: 1860. V. 45

An International Episode. New York: 1878. V. 43

An International Episode. New York: 1879. V. 41

Italian Hours. Boston: 1909. V. 45

Italian Hours. Boston & New York: 1909. V. 38; 40; 41; 43

Italian Hours. London: 1909. V. 43

The Ivory Towery. London: 1917. V. 46

The Ivory Tower. New York: 1917. V. 37; 45

Julia Bride. New York: 1909. V. 37; 45

A Landscape Painter. New York: 1919. V. 37; 41; 45

The Lesson of the Master. London: 1892. V. 38; 43; 45

The Lesson of the Master. New York: 1892. V. 37; 38; 39; 40; 45

The Letters. London: 1920. V. 40; 42; 46

Letters . . . to Walter Berry. Paris: 1928. V. 37

A Little Tour in France. Boston: 1885. V. 45; 46

A Little Tour in France. London: 1885. V. 42

A Little Tour in France. London: 1900. V. 37; 40

A London Life. London: 1889. V. 45

A London Life. New York: 1957. V. 44

The Madonna of the Future and Other Tales. London: 1879. V. 37; 41

Master Eustace. New York: 1920. V. 39; 43; 45

The Middle Years. London: 1917. V. 44; 45; 46

A Most Unholy Trade. Being Letters on Drama. Cambridge: 1923. V. 39; 46

A Most Unholy Trade Being Letters on the Drama. (Cambridge): 1923. V. 37

Note on the Block of Tin Dredged Up in Falmouth Harbour. London: 1872. V. 40

Notes on the Great Pyramid of Egypt, and the Cubits Used In Its Design. Southampton: 1869. V. 44

Notes of a Son and Brother. London: 1914. V. 42; 43; 45; 46

Notes on Novelists. London: 1914. V. 37; 40

Notes and Reviews. Cambridge: 1921. V. 46

The Novels and Tales. New York. V. 38

The Novels and the Tales. New York: 1907. V. 42

The Novels and Tales. New York: 1907-09. V. 42

The Novels and Tales. New York: 1907-09/17. V. 46

The Novels and Tales of . . . New York: 1907-18. V. 41

The Novels and Tales. New York: 1907-20. V. 42

The Novels and Tales. New York: 1922. V. 38; 44

Novels and Tales. New York: 1907-1917. V. 37

The Other House. London: 1896. V. 39; 43

The Other House. New York: 1896. V. 37; 45

The Other House. London: 1897. V. 41; 44; 45

The Outcry. London: 1911. V. 37; 44

The Outcry. New York: 1911. V. 42; 45

Partial Portraits. London: 1888. V. 37; 45

Partial Portraits. London: & New York: 1888. V. 37; 44

A Passionate Pilgrim. Boston: 1875. V. 37; 39; 41; 43; 44; 45

Picture and Text. New York: 1893. V. 41; 45

The Portrait of a Lady. Boston: 1882. V. 39; 40; 44; 45

The Portrait of a Lady. Boston: 1882, 1881. V. 41

The Portrait of a Lady. London: 1883. V. 39; 42

The Portrait of a Lady. Baltimore: 1967. V. 43

The Portrait of a Lady. New York: 1967. V. 38; 44; 46

Portraits of Places. London: 1883. V. 41; 43; 46

Portraits of Places. Boston: 1884. V. 37; 39

The Princess Casamassima. 1886. V. 46

The Princess Casamassima. London: 1886. V. 44

The Princess Casamassima. London: & New York: 1886. V. 46

The Princess Cassamassima; a Novel. London: 1887. V. 42

The Private Life. Lord Beaupre. The Visits. New York: 1893. V. 38; 44; 45; 46

The Question of Our Speech; the Lesson of Balzac; Two Lectures. Boston: 1905. V. 38

The Question of Our Speech/The Lesson of Balzac. Boston & New York: 1905. V. 46

The Real Thing. London: 1893. V. 41; 45

The Real Thing. New York: 1893. V. 45; 46

Refugees in Chelsea. Chelsea: 1920. V. 38

The Restless Analyst, Twelve Essays. Toronto: 1979 (1981). V. 37

The Reverberator. London: 1888. V. 38; 42; 43

The Reverberator. London: and New York: 1888. V. 37; 41; 44; 45

Roderick Hudson. Boston: 1876. V. 43; 44; 46

Roderick Hudson. Boston: 1879. V. 41

Roderick Hudson. London: 1883. V. 39

The Sacred Fount. London: 1901. V. 43; 45

The Sacred Fount. New York: 1901. V. 45

A Sense of the Past. London: 1917. V. 45; 46

The Sense of the Past. New York: 1917. V. 37; 40; 41; 42

The Siege of London. Boston: 1883. V. 41; 45

A Small Boy and Others. London: 1913. V. 42; 43; 46

A Small Boy and Others. New York: 1913. V. 45; 46

The Social Significance of Our Institutions: an Oration. Boston: 1861. V. 46

The Soft Side. London: 1900. V. 37; 41; 43

The Soft Side. New York: 1900. V. 44; 45

The Spoils of Poynton. Boston: 1897. V. 37; 40; 41; 45

The Spoils of Poynton. Boston & New York: 1897. V. 38; 40; 46

The Spoils of Poynton. London: 1897. V. 37; 38; 40; 41; 43; 45

Tales of Three Cities. Boston: 1884. V. 41; 45

Tales of Three Cities. London: 1884. V. 39; 44; 45

Tales of Three Cities. London: 1888. V. 46

Terminations. London: 1895. V. 37; 38

Terminations. New York: 1895. V. 37; 44; 45; 46

Theatricals. Two Comedies. Tenants. Disengaged. New York: 1894. V. 45

Theatricals Second Series. The Album. The Reprobate. London: 1895. V. 45

Theatricals. Two Comedies Tenants Disengaged. London: 1894. V. 38

The Tragic Muse. Boston: 1890. V. 38; 45

The Tragic Muse. London: 1890. V. 39; 41

Transatlantic Sketches. Boston: 1875. V. 39; 40; 41; 43; 44; 46

JAMES, HENRY 1843-1916 continued

Travelling Companions. New York: 1919. V. 44; 45

The Turn of the Screw. London: 1925. V. 46

The Turn of the Screw. Los Angeles: 1949. V. 42

The Turn of the Screw. New York: 1949. V. 38

The Two Magics, the Turn of the Screw, Covering End. London: 1898. V. 37; 41; 43; 46

Views and Reviews. Boston: 1908. V. 37; 44; 45

Washington Square. V. 41

Washington Square. London: 1881. V. 43; 44; 45; 46

Washington Square. New York: 1881. V. 37; 39; 40; 41; 43; 44

Washington Square. New York: 1971. V. 38

Watch and Ward. Boston: 1878. V. 44; 45; 46

What Maisie Knew. Chicago: 1897. V. 37; 44; 45

What Maisie Knew. Chicago & New York: 1897. V. 39; 46

What Maisie Knew. London: 1898. V. 37

The Wheel of Time. New York: 1893. V. 38; 42; 44; 45

The Whole Family. New York: 1908. V. 44

William Wetmore Story and His Friends. Boston: 1903. V. 41; 45

William Wetmore Story and His Friends. New York: 1903. V. 41

The Wings of the Dove. New York: 1902. V. 37; 40; 44

The Wings of the Dove. Westminster: 1902. V. 40; 41

Within the Rim. London: 1919. V. 39

JAMES, HENRY, OF BIRMINGHAM of Birmingham

State of the Nation. London: 1835. V. 40; 43; 46

JAMES I, KING OF GREAT BRITAIN 1566-1625

Apologia pro Iuramento Fidelitatis, Primum Quidem . . . Londini: 1609. V. 40; 43; 44; 46

Basilikon Doron (Graece). London: 1603. V. 38; 41; 45

By the King. Whereas We Did Lately Prorogue Our Parliament. London: 1608. V. 41

Daemonologie, in Forme of a Dialogue, Divided Into Three Books. London: 1603. V. 38

His Maiesties Speach in the Starre-Chamber, the XX of Ivne Anno 1616. London. V. 40

His Maiesties Speach In the Last Session of Parliament, as Neere His Very Words As Could be Gathered at the Instant. London: 1605. V. 38

King James His Judgment by Way of Counsell and Advice . . . Extracted Out of His Own Speeches by Doctor Willet. London: 1642. V. 43

The Kings Majesties Declaration to His Subjects, Concerning Lawfull Sports to Be Used. London: 1618. V. 45

The Quair Maid Be King James of Scotland the First Callit the Kingis Quair and Maid Quhen His Majestie Wes in Ingland. London: 1903. V. 44; 46

The True Lawe of Free Monarchies. Or The Reciprock and Mutuall Dutie Betwix a Free King and His Naturall Subjects. London: 1603. V. 45

Whereas We Did Lately Prorogue Our Parliament. London: 1608. V. 45

The Workes of . . . London: 1616. V. 41; 42

Opera . . . Londini: 1619. V. 42; 43

JAMES I, KING OF GREAT BRITIAN 1566-1625

The Kings Majesties Speech to the Lords and Commons . . . at Whitehall, on Wednesday the XXI of March. Anno Dom. 1609. London: 1609. V. 46

Royal Proclamation Proclaiming Friendship with all the Princes of Christendom, Forbidding Armed Vessels from England Attacking Spanish Merchant Ships, and Revoking Letters of Marque Held by the Elizabethan Privateer. London: 1603. V. 40

JAMES I, KING OF SCOTLAND

The Kingis Quair. London: 1903. V. 44; 46

JAMES II, KING OF GREAT BRITAIN 1633-1701

Papers of Devotion of James II. Oxford: 1925. V. 38; 40

The Royal Charter of Confirmation Granted . . . to the Trinity-House of Deptford-Strond. London: 1685. V. 40; 44

JAMES, ISAAC

Providence Displayed. Bristol: 1800. V. 38; 42

JAMES IV, KING OF SCOTLAND

Epistolae Jacobi Quarti. Edinburgi: 1722-24. V. 40

JAMES, J. H.

A Winter in Bath. London: 1808. V. 39

JAMES, JASON W.

Memorable Events in the Life of Capt. Jason W. James. Roswell: 1911? V. 45

Memories and Viewpoints. Roswell: 1928. V. 39; 44; 46

JAMES, JESSE

Jesse James, My Father. Westbrook,: 1906. V. 41

JAMES, JOHN S.

Stroud's Judicial Dictionary of Words and Phrases. London: 1971-82. V. 40

JAMES, JOHN THOMAS

The Flemish, Dutch and German Schools of Painting. (with) The Italian Schools of Painting. London: 1820. V. 40

The Flemish, Dutch and German Schools of Painting. London: 1822. V. 44

The Flemish, Dutch and German Schools of Painting. (with) The Italian Schools of Painting. London: 1822, 1820. V. 38

Journal of a Tour in Germany, Sweden, Russia, Poland, During the Years 1813 and 1814. London: 1816. V. 38; 39; 40

Journal of a Tour in Germany, Sweden, Russia, Poland, During the Years 1813 and 1814. London: 1817. V. 46

Journal of a Tour in Germany, Sweden, Russia, Poland in 1813-14. London: 1819. V. 38; 39; 40; 41; 42; 43

JAMES, LIONEL

The History of King Edward's Horse. 1921. V. 46

The History of King Edward's Horse. Sifton: 1921. V. 45

The Indian Frontier War, Being an Account of the Mohmund and Tirah Expeditions 1897. London: 1898. V. 42

JAMES, M. E.

The Heir of Aylmer's Court. London: 1884. V. 40; 44

JAMES, M. R.

Address at the Unveiling of the Roll of Honour of the Cambridge Tipperary Club on July 12, 1916. Cambridge: 1916. V. 41

The Five Jars. London: 1922. V. 38; 44

Ghost Stories of an Antiquary. 1904. V. 43

Ghost Stories of an Antiquary. London: 1904. V. 38

More Ghost Stories of an Antiquary. London: 1911. V. 44

A Petersborough Psalter and Bestiary of the 14th Century. Oxford: 1921. V. 45

A Thin Ghost and Others. London: 1919. V. 41; 45

Wailing Well. 1928. V. 45

The Wailing Well. Stanford Dingley: 1928. V. 41; 46

JAMES, MARQUIS

The Raven: a Biography of Sam Houston. Indianapolis: 1929. V. 37; 39; 42; 46

JAMES, MONTAGUE RHODES

The Western Manuscripts in the Library of Trinity College, Cambridge, a Descriptive Catalogue. Cambridge: 1900. V. 39

JAMES, M.R. 1862-1936

Collected Ghost Stories. London: 1931. V. 46

The Collected Ghost Stories of . . . London: 1934. V. 46

The Five Jars. 1922. V. 46

JAMES, NORAH C.

Sleeveless Errand. London: 1929. V. 41

JAMES, P. D.

The Blood Tie. London: 1980. V. 46

Cover Her Face. New York: 1962. V. 46

Cover Her Face. 1966. V. 39

Death of an Expert Witness. New York: 1977. V. 45; 46

The Skull Beneath the Skin. New York: 1982. V. 46

An Unsuitable Job for a Woman. London: 1972. V. 45

JAMES, PHILIP

A Butler's Recipe Book 1719. London: 1935. V. 41

Early Keyboard Instruments, From Their Beginnings to the Year 1820. London: 1930. V. 40

JAMES, PHILLIP

Henry Moore on Sculpture. London: 1966. V. 44

JAMES, Prince of No-Land; or, An Answer to Dr. Woodward's False Friend, in Vindication of the Reverend Mr. Sharp, the Curate of Stepney. London: 1709. V. 40

JAMES, R. RUTSON

Studies in the History of Ophthalmology in England Prior to the Year 1800. Cambridge: 1933. V. 42

JAMES, ROBERT

A Dissertation on Fevers and Inflammatory Disorders. London: 1748. V. 38

A Dissertation on Fevers and Inflammatory Distempers. London: 1764. V. 38

A Dissertation on Fevers, and Inflammatory Distempers. London: 1778. V. 42

Pharmacopoeia Universalis. London: 1747. V. 40

A Treatise on Canine Madness. London: 1760. V. 37; 38

JAMES, ROSS

A Coming of Winter. Markham, Ontario: 1981. V. 39

JAMES, SILAS

A Narrative of a Voyage to Arabia, India, &c. London: 1797. V. 38; 42

JAMES Sprunt Studies in History and Political Science. Chapel Hill: 1900-70. V. 38; 40

JAMES, STANLEY

Cannibals and Convicts. London: 1886. V. 38

The Vagabond Papers, Sketches of Melbourne Life in Light and Shade. Melbourne: 1877/78. V. 46

JAMES Stern - Some Letters for His Seventieth Birthday, 1974. London: 1974. V. 41

JAMES, T. G. H.

The Hekanakhte Papers and Other Early Middle Kingdom Documents. New York: 1962. V. 42

JAMES, THOMAS

Captain James Thomas's Strange and Dangerous Voyage in His Intended Discovery of the North-West Passage into the South Sea in the Years 1631 and 1632. London. V. 43

The Dangerous Voyage of Capt. Thomas James, In His Intended Discovery of a North West Passage into the South Sea. London: 1740. V. 39

The Strange and Dangerous Voyage of Captaine Thomas James, In His Intended Discovery of the Northwest Passage into the South Sea. London: 1633. V. 41

The Jesuits Downfall, Threatened Against Them by the Secvlar Priests for Their Wicked Lives . . . Oxford: 1612. V. 43

Three Years Among the Indians and Mexicans. St. Louis: 1916. V. 42; 46

A Treatise of the Corruption of Scripture, Councils and Fathers, by the Prelats, Pastors and Pillars of the Church of Rome, for Maintenance of Popery. London: 1688. V. 40

JAMES, THOMAS ANDREW

Count Cagliostro. London: 1838. V. 38; 42

JAMES V, KING OF SCOTLAND

Two Ancient Scottish Poems the Gaberlunzie-Man, and Christ's Kirk on the Green. Edinburgh: 1782. V. 38

JAMES, VINTON LEE

Frontier and Pioneer Recollections of Early Days in San Antonio and West Texas. 1938. V. 42

JAMES, W. N.

A Word or Two on the Flute. Edinburgh: 1826. V. 46

A Word or Two on the Flute. London: 1826. V. 44

JAMES, WILL 1892-1942

Cow-Boy Life in Texas; or, 27 Years a MAvrick . . . Chicago: 1893. V. 43; 46

Cow-Boy Life in Texas . . . or . . . 27 Years a Maverick. Donohue: 1893. V. 44

Cow-Boy Life in Texas; or, 27 years a Mavrick: A Realistic and True Recital of Wild Life on the Boundless Plains of Texas . . . As a Geniune Cow-Boy Among the Roughs and Toughs of Texas. Chicago: (1893). V. 37

Cowboy in the Making. New York: 1937. V. 39

Cowboys North and South. New York: 1924. V. 43

The Drifting Cowboy. New York: 1925. V. 43

Lone Cowboy. New York: 1930. V. 38; 40; 46

Lone Cowboy. New York: London: 1930. V. 43

Lone Cowboy. My Life Story. Illustrated by the Author. New York/London: 1932. V. 37

Look-See with Uncle Bill. New York: 1938. V. 46

Sand. New York: 1929. V. 37

Scorpion: a Good Bad Horse. New York: 1936. V. 44; 46

Smoky. New York: 1926. V. 41

Smoky. The Cow Horse. New York: 1929. V. 43

Uncle Bill: A Tale of Two Kids and a Cowboy. Illustrated by the author. New York/London: 1932. V. 37

JAMES, WILLIAM

The Experience of Activity. New York: 1905. V. 41

A Full and Correct Account of the Chief Naval Occurrences of the Late War Between Great Britain and the United States. London: 1817. V. 42

A Full and Correct Account of the Military Occurrences of the Late War Between Great Britain and the United States of America . . . London: 1818. V. 40; 43; 46

The Meaning of Truth. London: 1909. V. 37

The Naval History of Great Britain, from the Declaration of War by France in 1793 . . . London: 1837. V. 37; 43

The Naval History of Great Britain, from the Declaration of War by France in 1793 to the Accession of George IV. London: 1886. V. 45

The Naval History of Great Britain from the Declaration of War by France in 1793 to the Accession of George IV. London: 1902. V. 37

A Pluralistic Universe. New York: 1909. V. 45

A Pluralistic Universe. 1909. V. 37

The Principles of Psychology. New York: 1890. V. 37; 39; 42; 43; 44; 45

JAMES, WILLIAM D.

A Sketch of the Life of Brig. Gen. Francis Marion, and a History of His Brigade, From Its Rise in June 1780 Until Disbanded in December 1782. Charleston: 1821. V. 41; 44; 45; 46

JAMES, WILLIAM F.

History of San Jose California. San Jose: 1933. V. 37; 38

JAMESON, ANNA BROWNELL MURPHY 1794-1860

The Beauties of the Court of King Charles the Second. London: 1833. V. 38; 39; 42; 44

Characteristics of Women, Moral, Poetical and Historical. Philadelphia: 1833. V. 44; 45

Companion to the Most Celebrated Private Galleries of Art in London. London: 1844. V. 39

Handbook to the Public Gatherings of Art in and Near London. London: 1842. V. 38; 40

The History of Our Lord as Exemplified in Works of Art . . . (with) Legends of the madonna as Represented in the Fine Arts. London: 1865, 1872. V. 37

Legends of the Monastic Orders, as Represented in the Fine Arts. London: 1850. V. 46

Legends of the Monastic Orders. London: 1891. V. 46

Memoirs of the Beauties of the Court of Charles the Second With Their Portraits . . . London: 1838. V. 45

Memoirs of Celebrated Female Sovereigns. London: 1840. V. 44; 45

Memoirs of the Beauties of the Court of Charles II. London: 1851. V. 46

Visits and Sketches at Home and Abroad with Tales and Miscellanies Now First Collected and a New Edition of the Diary of an Ennuyee. London: 1834. V. 43

Visits and Sketches at Home and Abroad. London: 1835. V. 46

Winter Studies and Summer Rambles in Canada. London: 1838. V. 44

JAMESON, E. W.

The Hawking of Japan. 1962. V. 39

JAMESON, HORATIO

The American Domestick Medicine; or, Medical Admonisher. Baltimore: 1817. V. 42; 43

JAMESON, J. FRANKLIN

American Historian's Raw Materials, an Address . . . with the Presentation and Other Exercises at the Dedication of the William L. Clements Library of Americana, June 15, 1923. Ann Arbor: 1923. V. 45

JAMESON, JAMES S.

Story of the Rear Column of the Emin Pasha Relief Expedition. London: 1890. V. 39; 40; 41; 42; 45

JAMESON, ROBERT 1774-1854

Mineralogical Travels through the Hebrides, Orkney and Shetland Islands and Mainland of Scotland . . . Edinburgh: 1800-13. V. 38

A Mineralogical Description of the County of Dumfries. Edinburgh: 1805. V. 41; 43

Mineralogy of the Scottish Isles. Edinburgh: 1800. V. 37

System of Mineralogy, Comprehending Oryctognosie, Geognosie, Mineralogical Chemistry, Mineralogical Geography, and Oeconomical Mineralogy. Edinburgh: 1808. V. 38

JAMESON, THOMAS

Essays on the Changes of the Human Body, At Its Different Ages . . . London: 1811. V. 44; 45; 46

JAMI 1414-1492

Salaman and Absal. London: 1856. V. 39; 42

Salaman & Absal. Ipswich: 1871. V. 39

JAMIESON, ALEXANDER

A Treatise on the Construction of Maps; in Which the Principles of the Projections of the Sphere are Demonstrated. London: 1814. V. 39; 42; 43

JAMIESON, JOHN

An Etymological Dictionary of the Scottish Language . . . to Which is Prefixed a Dissertation on the Origin of the Scottish Language. Paisley: 1789/1882. V. 40

An Etymological Dictionary of the Scottish Language. Paisley: 1789/82. V. 45

An Etymological Dictionary of the Scottish Language. Edinburgh: 1808. V. 37; 38; 39

An Etymological Dictionary of the Scottish Language. Edinburgh: 1818. V. 40; 41

An Etymological Dictionary of the Scottish Language . . . Edinburgh: 1840-41 & 1825. V. 43

JAMIESON, JOHN continued

An Etymological Dictionary of the Scottish Language . . . 1878/82. V. 46

An Etymological Dictionary of the Scottish Language . . . Paisley: 1878-82. V. 44

An Etymological Dictionary of the Scottish Language . . . Paisley: 1879/1882. V. 39

An Etymological Dictionary of the Scottish Language . . . 1879-87. V. 38; 46

JAMIESON, MRS.

Popular Voyages and Travels throughout the Continent and Islands of Europe. London: 1820. V. 41; 44

JAMIESON, ROBERT

Accidental Death from Chloroform (From the London Medical Gazette). London: 1848. V. 39

Popular Ballads and Song from Tradition, Manuscripts and Scarce Editions . . . Edinburgh: 1806. V. 37; 43

JAMIN, LEON

L'Enseignement Professionel du Menuisier. Paris: 1896-1899. V. 40; 41

JAMISON, D. F.

The Life and Times of Bertrand Du Guesclin: a History of the Fourteenth Century. Charleston: 1864. V. 42; 45

JAMISON, JAMES CARSON

With Walker in Nicaragua or Reminiscences of an Officer of the American Phalanx. Columbia: 1909. V. 39; 41; 42; 46

JAMISON, MATTHEW H.

Recollections of Pioneer and Army Life. Kansas City: 1911. V. 39; 40

JAMISON, R.

A Trip to London; or, the Humours of a Berwick Smack. Edinburgh: 1815. V. 45

JAMOT, FREDERIC

Varia Poemata Graeca et Latine. Antwerp: 1593. V. 40; 45

JANE, FRED T.

All the World's Fighting Ships. London: 1898. V. 41

Blake of the 'Rattlesnake' or the Man Who Saved England. London: 1895. V. 44

The World's Warships. 1915. London: 1915. V. 43; 44

JANE'S All the World's Aircraft, 1940. Compiled and Edited by D.G. Grey and Leonard Bridgman. 1941. V. 37

JANE'S All the World's Aircraft 1941. New York: 1942. V. 45

JANE'S Fighting Ships. 1941. London: 1941. V. 38
JANE'S Fighting Ships, 1941. London: 1942. V. 40

JANES, THOMAS P.

Hand-Book of the State of Georgia Accompanied by a Geological Map of the State. Atlanta: 1876. V. 41; 44

A Manual of Georgia for the Use of Immigrants and Capitalists. Atlanta: 1878. V. 44

JANET, PIERRE

The Major Symptoms of Hysteria. New York: 1907. V. 42

Psychological Healing: a Historical and Clinical Study. London: 1925. V. 43

JANEWAY, HENRY H.

Radium Therapy in Cancer at the Memorial Hospital, New York (First Report: 1915-1916). New York: 1917. V. 40

JANIS, EUGENIA PARRY

Degas Monotypes: Essay, Catalogue and Checklist. Cambridge: 1968. V. 41

JANIS, HARRIET

Pablo Picasso. The Recent Years 1939-1946. New York: 1946. V. 39

Picasso, the Recent Years, 1939-1946. Garden City: 1947. V. 38; 40

JANIVER, FRANCIS DE HAES

The Sleeping Centinel. Philadelphia: 1863. V. 40

JANIVER, THOMAS

Dutch Founding of New York . . . New York: 1903. V. 39

JANIVER, THOMAS A.

In Old New York. New York: 1894. V. 44

JANNEAU, GIULLAUME

Modern Glass. London: 1931. V. 40

JANNEAU, GUILLAUME

Le Luminaire et les Moyens a Eclairages Nouveaux. Paris: 1926/29. V. 43

JANNEY, SAMUEL M.

Memoirs of Samuel M. Janney, Late of Lincoln, Loudon County, Va. Philadelphia: 1881. V. 42; 44

JANSON: A Definitive Collection. San Francisco: 1954. V. 40

JANSON, CHARLES WILLIAM

The Stranger in America: Containing Observations made during a long Residence in that Country, on the Genius, Manners and Customs of the People of the United States . . . and the Slave Trade. London: 1807. V. 37; 39; 41; 43; 45

JANSSEN, J. J.

Two Ancient Egyptian Ship's Logs: Papyrus Leiden I 350 verso and Papyrus Turin 2008. Leiden: 1961. V. 40

JANSSEN, STEPHEN THEODORE

The Wealth of Great Britian in the Ocean, Exemplified from Materials Laid Before the Committee of the House of Commons Appointed Last Session of Parliament to Examined Into the State of the British Fisheries. London: 1749. V. 40; 41; 45

JANSSEN, THEODORE

A Discourse Concerning Banks. London: 1742. V. 43

JANSSON, JACOB

In Psalterium, et Cantica Quibus per Horas Canonicas Romana Utitur Ecclesia. Louvain: 1597. V. 46

JANUARY, MARJORIE

Ninety Years the Story of William Parmer Fuller. San Francisco: 1939. V. 41

JANUS PRESS

Bread and Puppet: White Horse Butcher. (Newark, VT): 1977. V. 37

The Janus Press 1955-1980: Silver Anniversary Miscellany. 1982. V. 40

The Janus Press 1955-1980: Silver Anniversary Issue. Newark: 1982. V. 39

JANVIER, LUDOVIC

Pour Samuel Beckett. Paris: 1966. V. 46

JANVIER, T. A.

The Aztec Treasure House, a Romance of Contemporaneous Antiquity. New York: 1890. V. 40

JANVIER, THOMAS A.

In Old New York. New York: 1894. V. 41; 43

JANVIER, THOMAS ALLIBONE

Color Studies. New York: 1885. V. 37

JAPAN: Her Strength and Her Beauty. New York: 1904. V. 39; 40; 42; 45

JAPAN SOCIETY OF NEW YORK

Chinese, Corean and Japanese Potteries. Descriptive Catalogue of Loan Exhibition of Selected Examples. 1914. V. 41

Chinese, Corean, and Japanese Potteries. Descriptive Catalogue of Lon Exhibition of Selected Examples. 1914. V. 38

JAPAN TEXTILE COLOR DESIGN CENTER, OSAKA.

Textile Designs of Japan. Volume III. Okinawan, Ainu & Foreign Designs. Tokyo: 1980. V. 44

JAPAN TEXTILE COLOUR DESIGN CENTRE

Textile Designs of Japan. Designs composed mainly in Free Style . . . Osaka: 1959-61. V. 37

JAPANESE Children. Tokyo: 1940. V. 46

JAPANESE in Southern California. 'A History of 70 Years'. (Los Angeles): 1960. V. 37

JAQUES, FLORENCE PAGE

Francis Lee Jaques Artist of the Wilderness World. 1973. V. 38

Francis Lee Jaques: Artist of the Wilderness World. Garden City: 1973. V. 43

JAQUES, JOHN

Catechism for Children, Exhibiting the Prominent Doctrines of the Church of Jesus Christ of Latter-Day Saints . . . Liverpool: 1887. V. 42

JAQUES, MARY J.

Texan Ranch Life, with Three Months through Mexico in a Prairie Schooner. London: 1894. V. 38; 44; 46

JAQUET, EUGENE

Technique and History of the Swiss Watch . . . Boston: 1953. V. 42

Technique and History of the Swiss Watch. Olten: 1953. V. 37; 38; 44

JARDI, ENRIC

Torres Garcia. Barcelona: 1974. V. 46

JARDINE, DAVID

A Reading on the Use of Torture in the Criminal Law of England Previously to the Commonwealth. London: 1837. V. 37

JARDINE, GEORGE

Outlines of Philosophical Education, Illustrated by the Method of Teaching the Logic or the First Class of Philosophy, in the University of Glasgow. Glasgow: 1818. V. 43

Outlines of Philosophical Education, Illustrated by the Method of Teaching the Logic Class in the University of Glasgow. Glasgow: 1825. V. 41

JARDINE, WILLIAM

Birds of Great Britain and Ireland. Edinburgh: 1840. V. 40; 42

Birds of Great Britain and Ireland. Edinburgh: 1838-4-. V. 37

British Salmonidae. Edinburgh: 1839-41. V. 39

British Salmonidae. 1979. V. 46

British Salmonidae. London: 1979. V. 39; 45

A Catalogue of the Birds Contained in the Collection. London: 1874. V. 43

Humming-Birds. Edinburgh: 1833. V. 37; 38

Humming Birds. 1834. V. 46

Humming Birds. London: 1834. V. 45

Illustrations of Ornithology. Edinburgh: 1826-35. V. 42

The Natural History of Humming Birds. Edinburgh. V. 37

The Natural History of Humming-Birds. Edinburgh: 1833-34. V. 45

The Natural History of Game-Birds. Edinburgh: 1834. V. 46

The Natural History of Humming Birds. Edinburgh: 1834. V. 39; 44

The Natural History of Gallinaceous Birds. Edinburgh: 1834. V. 37

The Natural History of the Birds of Great Britain and Ireland. Edinburgh: 1838. V. 46

The Natural History of the Birds of Great Britain and Ireland. Edinburgh: 1838-43. V. 42

The Natural History of Humming-Birds. Edinburgh: 1840. V. 38

The Naturalist's Library. Edinburgh: 1834-43. V. 46

The Naturalist's Library: Ichthyology. Edinburgh: 1835. V. 39

Nautical Surveying. New York: 1878. V. 42

Sun-birds. Edinburgh: 1843. V. 37

JARDINE'S Naturalist's Library. Ichthyology. Edinburgh. V. 37

JARMAN, RICHARD

Omnipotence! A Poem. London: 1831. V. 43

JARMAN, WILLIAM

U.S.A. Uncle Sam's Abcess, or Hell Upon Earth for U.S. Uncle Same. Exeter: 1884. V. 37; 42

JARRATT, DEVEREUX

A Sermon Preached Before the Convention of the Protestant Episcopal Church in Virginia. At Richmond May 3, 1792. New London: 1792. V. 46

JARRATT, RIE

Gutierrez de Lara, Mexican-Texan. Austin: 1949. V. 37; 38; 44; 45

JARRATT, W. O.

Reminiscences of a Tour in Scotland. London: 1854. V. 42

JARRELL, RANDALL

Blood for a Stranger. New York: 1942. V. 38; 39; 40; 42; 44; 45

Blood for a Stranger. 1942. V. 46

Little Friend, Little Friend. New York: 1945. V. 37; 42; 45; 46

Losses. New York: 1948. V. 37; 40; 41; 42; 45

The Lost World. New York: 1965. V. 46

The Lost Children. 1980. V. 42

Pictures from an Insitution. New York: 1954. V. 39; 40; 41; 42; 44; 46

Randall Jarrell 1914-1965. New York. V. 44

Selected Poems. New York: 1955. V. 46

Seven League Crutches. New York: 1951. V. 37; 40; 42; 43; 45; 46

The Woman at the Washington Zoo: Poems and Translations. New York: 1960. V. 37

JARRETT, T.

A New Lexicon of the Hebrew Language . . . London: 1848. V. 38

JARRIGE, PIERRE

A Further Discovery of the Mystery of Jesuitisme, in a Collection of Severall Pieces. London: 1658. V. 40

JARRY, MADELEINE

The Carpets of the Manufacture de la Savonnerie. Leigh-on-Sea: 1966. V. 40

JARVES, JAMES JACKSON 1818-1888

History of the Hawaiian or Sandwich Islands, Embracing Their Antiquities, Mythology, Legends, Discovery by Europeans, in the Sixteenth Century . . . Boston: 1843. V. 37; 38; 44; 46

History of the Hawaiian or Sandwich Islands. Boston: 1844. V. 38

History of the Hawaiian Islands. Honolulu: 1847. V. 38; 40; 46

History of the Hawaiian Islands. Honolulu: 1872. V. 38; 46

JARVIS, EDWARD 1803-1884

Criminal Insane: Insane Transgressors and Insane Convicts. Utica: 1857. V. 43

Report on Insanity and Idiocy in Massachusetts. Boston: 1855. V. 39; 43; 45

JARVIS, J. W.

On the Origin of Sam Weller and the Real Cause of the Success of the Posthumous Papers of the Pickwick Club. London: 1883. V. 45; 46

JARVIS, JOHN B.

Report of John B. Jarvis, Relative to the Survey of the Proposed Caughnawaga Canal, and Documents Relative to the Survey and Improvements of the Rapids of the River St. Lawrence, by Messrs. Maillefert and Raasloff, Civil Engineers. Quebec: 1855. V. 38

JARVIS, RUSSEL

A Biographical Notice of Commander Jesse D. Elliott . . . & a History of the Figurehead of the U.S. Frigate 'Constitution'. Philadelphia: 1835. V. 42

JARVIS, T. M.

Accredited Ghost Stores. London: 1823. V. 37; 39; 43

JASEN, DAVID A.

P. G. Wodehouse: a Portrait of a Master. New York: 1974. V. 42

THE JASPER National Park. N.P.: 1927. V. 39

JAUNIN, CLAUDE

Les Complimens de la Langue Francoise. Rouen: 1628. V. 46

JAVACHEFF, CHRISTO

Christo: Valley Curtain, Rifle, Colorado 1970-72. New York: 1973. V. 41

JAVITCH, GREGORY

A Selective Bibliography of Ceremonies, Dances, Music and Songs of the American Indian, from Books in the Library of Gregory Javitch . . . Montreal: 1974. V. 37; 40; 41; 42; 44

JAY, HARRIET

The Dark Colleen. London: 1876. V. 38

JAY, JAMES

A Letter to the Governors of the College of New York; Respecting the Collection that was Made in This Kingdom in 1762 and 1763, . . . London: 1771. V. 37; 38; 46

JAY, JOHN

Caste and Slavery in the American Church. New York & London: 1843. V. 42

The Correspondence and Public Papers of . . . First Chief Justice of the U.S. &c. 1763-1826. New York: 1890. V. 39

JAY, JOHN C.

A Catalogue of Shells, Arranged According to the Lamarckian System; Together with Descriptions of New or Rare Species, Contained in the Collection of John C. Jay, M.D. New York: 1839. V. 38; 40; 42; 45

A Catalogue of the Shells, Arranged According to the Lamarckian System. New York: & London: 1839. V. 46

JAY, WILLIAM

Letter to Hon. William Nelson, M.C. on Mr. Clay's Compromise. New York: 1850. V. 39; 42

A Review of the Causes and Consequences of the Mexican War. Boston: 1849. V. 37; 38; 42; 44

A View of the Action of the Federal Government in Behalf of Slavery. New York: 1839. V. 37; 39; 42

War and Peace: the Evils of the First, and a Plan for Preserving the Last. New York: 1842. V. 37

JAYNE, CAROLINE FURNESS

String Figures. New York: 1906. V. 39

JAZZ Forum 1-4. Fordingbridge, Hampshire: 1946-47. V. 41

JEAFFERSON, CHRISTOPHER

A Young Squire of the Seventeenth Century. London: 1878. V. 39

JEAFFRESON, JOHN CORDY

A Book About Doctors. London: 1860. V. 42

A Book About Doctors. New York: 1861. V. 43

A Book About Lawyers. London: 1867. V. 38; 40

JEAFFRESON, JOHN CORDY continued

Book About the Table. London: 1875. V. 44

The Life of Robert Stephenson, F.R.S. etc., etc . . . . London: 1864.
V. 45; 46

The Real Lord Byron. Real. London: 1883. V. 46

JEAMSON, THOMAS d. 1674

Artificiall Embellishments. Oxford: 1665. V. 40

JEAN-AUBRY, G.

Eugene Boudin. Greenwich: 1968. V. 37; 40; 43; 44

Joseph Conrad in the Congo. Boston: 1926. V. 43; 44

Joseph Conrad in the Congo. London: 1926. V. 40; 46

Joseph Conrad. Life and Letters. London: 1927. V. 38

Joseph Conrad, Life and Letters. New York: 1927. V. 39; 43; 46

Twenty Letters to Joseph Conrad. 1926. V. 40; 45

JEAN DE CHANTAL KENNEDY, SISTER

Biography of a Colonial Town with Maps and Drawings by the Author.
Hamilton: 1961. V. 40

JEAN DE MEUN

*Le Plaisant Iev Dv Dodechedron de Fortune, non Moins Recreatif, Que
Subtil & Ingenieux.* Paris: 1577. V. 40

JEAN, MARCEL

The History of Surrealist Painting. New York: 1960. V. 39

Sites. Paris: 1953. V. 37

JEAN, THE HERMIT fl. 1180-1182

La Vie de Monseigneur Sainct Bernard . . . Paris: 1510-15. V. 45

JEANCON, J. A.

Pathological Anatomy, Pathology and Physical Diagnosis. Cincinnati: 1883.
V. 37; 38; 39; 40; 41; 44; 45; 46

Pathological Anatomy, Pathology and Physical Diagnosis. Cincinnati: 1885.
V. 42

JEANES, HENRY 1611-1662

A Mixture of Scholastical Divinity with Practicall, in Several Tractates . . .
Oxford: 1656. V. 38

JEANES, WILLIAM

The Modern Confectioner. London;: 1864. V. 37

JEANNERET-GRIS, CHARLES EDOUARD 1887-1965

Des Canons, des Munitions? Merci: Des logis . . . s.v.p. Boulogne: 1938.
V. 39; 43

Creation is a Patient Search. New York: 1960. V. 46

*Des Canons, des Munitions! Merci! Des Logis . . . s.v.p. Monographie du
Pavillon des Temps Nouveaux a l'Expostion Internationale Art et Technique
de Paris 1937.* Boulogne (Seine): 1938. V. 41

The Modulor: a Harmonious Measure to the Human Scale. London:
1954/58. V. 44

My Work. London: 1960. V. 41

Poeme de l'Angle Droit. Teriade: 1955. V. 38

JEANS, J. S.

Steel: Its History, Manufacture and Uses. London: 1880. V. 38; 40; 41;
43; 44

JEANS, JAMES HOPWOOD 1877-1946

The Dynamical Theory of Gases. Cambridge: 1925. V. 40

Problems of Cosmogony and Stellar Dynamics. Cambridge: 1919. V. 42

JEANS, JAMES STEPHEN

*Jubliee Memoiral of the Railway System. A History of the Stockton and
Darlingotn Railway and a record of its results.* London: 1875. V. 37

JEBB, BERTHA

A Strange Career. Edinburgh and London: 1894. V. 43

*A Strange Career, Life and Adventures of John Gladwyn Jebb, by His
Widow.* London: 1894. V. 37; 40

JEBB, FRED

*Considerations on the Expediency of a National Circulation Bank at this
time in Ireland.* Dublin: 1780. V. 37

*The Letters of Guatimozin on the Affairs of Ireland . . . to which are added
Letters of Causidicus, i.e. (Robert Johnson) that accompanied the Essays
of Guatimozin.* Dublin: 1779. V. 37

JEBB, JOSHUA 1793-1863

*Report on the Discipline and Construction of Portland Prison, and Its
Connection with the System of Convict Discipline Now in Operation.*
London: 1850. V. 40

*Report on the Discipline and Construction of Portland Prison, and Its
Connection with the System of Convict Discipline Now In Operation.*
Clowes: 1850. V. 38

JEBB, SAMUEL

Bibliotheca Literaria. London: 1722-24. V. 43

JEBOULT, EDWARD

*A General Account of West Somerset, Description of the Valey of the Tone
and History of Taunton . . .* Taunton, Somerset & Bristol: 1873. V. 38

JEFFERIES, DAVID

A Plain Narrative of a Journey from London to Rome, etc. Liverpool: 1750.
V. 46

Traite des Diamants et des Perles . . . Ouvrage Traduit de l'Anglois . . .
Paris: 1753. V. 38

JEFFERIES, RICHARD 1848-1887

Amaryllis at the Fair. London: 1887. V. 37; 43; 46

The Amateur Poacher. London: 1879. V. 40; 43; 46

Bevis. The Story of a Boy. London: 1882. V. 37; 41; 43; 46

*The Birth of a Naturalist: an Unpublished Chapter from Round About a
Great Estate by Richard Jefferies.* Market Drayton: 1985. V. 45

By The Brook. (London): 1981. V. 37

By The Brook. Edited and with an introduction by George Miller. London:
1981. V. 37

The Dewy Morn. London: 1884. V. 41; 43; 46

The Early Fiction . . . London: 1896. V. 40

Field and Hedgegrow. London: 1889. V. 40

The Gamekeeper at Home: Sketches of Natural History and Rural Life.
London: 1878. V. 37

Greene Ferne Farm. London: 1880. V. 40

Hodge and His Masters. London: 1880. V. 37; 38; 40; 41; 42; 43; 44; 46

Jack Brass, Emperor of England. London: 1873. V. 40; 43

The Life of the Fields. London: 1884. V. 40; 43

Nature Near London. London: 1883. V. 40; 43; 44; 46

The Nature Diaries and Notebooks of Richard Jefferies. 1941. V. 37

The Open Air. London: 1885. V. 37; 40; 41; 43; 44; 46

Red Deer. London: 1884. V. 40; 43; 45; 46

Restless Human Hearts. London: 1875. V. 37

Round about a Great Estate. London: 1880. V. 37; 40; 42; 43; 46

The Scarlet Shawl. London: 1874. V. 38; 40

The Story of a Boy. London: 1882. V. 42

The Story of My Heart. Boston: 1883. V. 39

The Story of My Heart. London: 1883. V. 37; 41; 45

The Toilers of the Field. London: 1892. V. 37; 39; 40; 43; 46

Wild Life in a Southern County. London: 1879. V. 37; 38; 42; 43; 44;
45; 46

Wood Magic: a Fable. 1881. V. 37; 40; 41

Wood Magic. London: 1881. V. 37; 38; 39; 40; 41; 42; 43; 44; 45

Wood Magic, a Fable. London (etc.): 1881. V. 37; 38

Works. London: 1905. V. 40; 46

JEFFERS, ROBINSON 1887-1962

The Alpine Christ and Other Poems. 1973. V. 39

The Alpine Christ and Other Poems. Aptos: 1973. V. 42

Apology for Bad Dreams. San Francisco: 1966. V. 37

Be Angry at the Sun. New York: 1941. V. 43; 45; 46

Una and Robinson. A Book of Gaelic Airs for Una's Melodeon. San
Francisco: 1989. V. 44

Brides of the South Wind - Poems 1917-1922. 1974. V. 39

Brides of the South Wind. Poems 1917-1922. Aptos: 1974. V. 42

Brides of the South Wind, Poems 1917-1922. Santa Barbara: 1974. V. 42

Californians. New York: 1916. V. 37; 39; 40; 42; 43; 45; 46

Cawdor and Other Poems. New York: 1928. V. 37; 38; 39; 40; 41; 42;
43; 46

Cawdor. Covelo: 1983. V. 37; 44; 46

Dear Judas. New York: 1929. V. 37; 39; 43; 44; 46

Descent to the Dead. New York: 1931. V. 37; 39; 40; 42; 43; 45

Descent to the Dead. New York: (1931). V. 37

The Desert. Los Angeles: 1976. V. 42

The Double Axe and Other Poems. New York: 1948. V. 45; 46

Flagons and Apples. Los Angeles: 1912. V. 41; 44; 46

Give Your Heart to the Hawks. New York: 1933. V. 37; 39; 46

Granite and Cypress. Rubbings from the Rock. Santa Cruz: 1976. V. 40

The Inscriptions at Tor House and Hawk Tower. Los Angeles: 1989. V. 42

The Loving Shepherdess. New York: 1956. V. 37; 40; 43; 46

Medea. New York: 1946. V. 41; 45

Not Man Apart. San Francisco: 1965. V. 41; 44

Poems. San Francisco: 1928. V. 41; 43; 44

Point Lobos. Oakland: 1987. V. 41; 42; 44

*A Portrait Written by Louis Adamic. With Foreword by Garth Sherwood
Jeffers.* Covelo: (1983). V. 37

JEFFERS, ROBINSON 1887-1962 continued

Return. An Unpublished Poem. San Francisco: 1934. V. 38

The Roan Stallion. New York: 1925. V. 41

Roan Stallion, Tamar and Other Poems. New York: 1935. V. 46

The Selected Poetry of Robinson Jeffers. New York: 1938. V. 39; 46

Shine, Perishing Republic. San Francisco: 1987. V. 39

Solstice. New York: 1935. V. 39; 41; 42; 43; 46

Songs and Heroes. Los Angeles: 1988. V. 43; 45; 46

Stars. Pasadena: 1930. V. 37

Such Counsels You Gave to Me & Other Poems. New York: 1937. V. 38; 39; 43; 46

Tamar and Other Poems. New York: 1924. V. 38

Themes in My Poems. San Francisco: 1956. V. 38; 39; 44; 46

Thurso's Landing. New York: 1932. V. 38; 39; 40; 41; 46

Tragedy Has Obligations. Santa Cruz: 1973. V. 37; 38; 40; 42; 43; 46

Two Consolations. San Mateo: 1940. V. 37; 39; 40; 41; 42

Two Consolations. San Mateo: 1940. V. 39

Where Shall I Take You To; the Love Letters of Una and Robinson Jeffers. Covelo: 1987. V. 40

The Women at Point Sur. New York: 1927. V. 37; 40; 42; 44

JEFFERS, UNA

Visits to Ireland: Travels and Diaries of . . . Los Angeles: 1954. V. 42; 44

JEFFERS, WILLIAM N.

Nautical Surveying. New York: 1878. V. 41

JEFFERSON Celebration. Washington Hall. Washington: 1834. V. 41

JEFFERSON, GEOFFREY

Selected Papers (of Sir Geoffrey Jefferson). London: 1960. V. 40

JEFFERSON, JOSEPH

The Autobiography of Joseph Jefferson. New York: 1890. V. 46

JEFFERSON, SAMUEL

The History and Antiquities of Allerdale Ward, Above Derwent in the County of Cumberland. Carlisle: 1842. V. 37; 40

The History and Antiquities of Allerdale Ward, Above Derwent, in the County of Cumberland. London: 1842. V. 38

JEFFERSON, T. H.

Map of the Emigrant Road from Independence, Mo. to St. Francisco, California. San Francisco: 1945. V. 40; 41; 44

JEFFERSON, THOMAS

The Address of Thomas Jefferson . . . Delivered . . . ON HIS Taking the Oath of Office as President. Baltimore: 1801. V. 40

The Age. V. 40

Catalogue of the Library of Thomas Jefferson. Charlottesville: 1983. V. 46

An Essay Towards Facilitation Instruction in the Anglo-Saxon and Modern Dialects of the English Language for the Use of the University of Virginia. New York: 1851. V. 39

A Manual for the Use of the Senate of the United States. Washington: 1801. V. 40

A Manual of Parliamentary Practice: for the Use of the Senate of the United States. Washington: 1812. V. 40

A Manual of Parliamentary Practice for the Use of the Senate of the United States. Lancaster;: 1813. V. 40

A Manual of Parliamentary Practice. Washington City: 1801. V. 37

Memoir, Correspondence and Miscellanies from the Papers of Thomas Jefferson. Charlottesville: 1829. V. 39

Memoir, Correspondence and Miscellanies, from the Papers of Thomas Jefferson. Boston: 1830. V. 40; 46

Message from . . . President of the United States to Both Houses of Congress at the Commencement of the Second Session of the Tenth Congress. Washington: 1808. V. 37

Message from . . . to both Houses of Congress at the Commencement of the Session. (Washington): 1803. V. 37

Notes on the Establishment of a Money Unit, and of an Coinage for the United States. Paris: 1785. V. 45

Notes on the State of Virginia. London: 1787. V. 38; 40; 42; 44

Notes on the State of Virginia. Philadelphia: 1794. V. 46

Notes on the State of Virginia. New York: 1801. V. 39

Notes on the State of Virginia. Newark: 1801. V. 40; 41

Notes on the State of Virginia. Boston: 1802. V. 43; 45

Notes on the State of Virginia. Trenton: 1803. V. 37

Observations sur la Virginie. Paris: 1786. V. 37; 38; 44

The Papers of Thomas Jefferson 1760-1791. Princeton: 1950-82. V. 46

Plan for Establishing Uniformity in the Currency, Coins, Weights and Measures of the United States. Philadelphia: 1790. V. 45

The Proceedings of the Government of the United States in Maintaining the Public Right to the Beach of the Mississippi, Adjacent to New Orleans Against the Intrusion of Edward Livingston. Baltimore: 1814. V. 40

A Summary View of the Rights of British America. Williamsburg: 1774. V. 45; 46

The Works of . . . New York: 1904. V. 39

The Writings of . . . New York: 1853. V. 39

The Writings of Thomas Jefferson. New York: 1892-99. V. 38

The Writings. Lunenburg: 1967. V. 46

JEFFERY, ALFRED

Notes on the Marine Glue. London: 1843. V. 38; 40

JEFFERY, L. H.

The Local Scripts of Archaic Greece. Oxford: 1963. V. 40

The Local Scripts of Archaic Greece . . . Oxford: 1990. V. 44

JEFFERY, L.H.

The Local Scripts of Archaic Greece; a study of the Origin of the Greek Alphabet and Its Development from the Eighth to the Fifth Centuries BC. 1989. V. 45

JEFFERY, ROBERT

A Narrative of the Life and Sufferings, and Deliverance of Robert Jeffery, the Seaman . . . London: 1811. V. 41

JEFFERYS, CHARLES W.

Canada's Past in Pictures. Toronto: 1934. V. 44

JEFFERYS, THOMAS

The American Atlas; or, a Geographical Description of the Whole Continent of America . . . London: 1776. V. 44; 45; 46

The American Atlas: or, A Geographical Description of the Whole Continent of America . . . London: 1976. V. 39

The County of York, Survey'd in MDCLXX. London: 1771-72. V. 39

A Description of the Maritime Ports of France. London: 1761. V. 37

A Description of the Maritime Parts of France . . . London: 1774. V. 43

A Description of the Spanish Islands and Settlements on the Coast of the West Indies. London: 1774. V. 43

An Exact Chart of the River St. Laurence, from Fort Frontenac to the Island of Anticosti Shewing the Soundings, Rocks, Shoals &c. with Views of the Lands. London: 1771. V. 42; 43

The Memorials of the English and French Commissaries Concerning the Limits of Nova Scotia or Acadia. London: 1755. V. 37

The Natural and Civil History of the French Dominions in North America and South America . . . London: 1760. V. 37; 38; 39; 42; 43; 44

Voyages from Asia to America . . . London: 1761. V. 46

Voyages from Asia to America, for Completing the Discoveries of the North West Coast of America. London: 1764. V. 37; 38

Voyages from Asia to America, for Completing the Discoveries of the North West Coast of America. Amsterdam & New York: 1967. V. 43

JEFFREY, FRANCIS 1773-1850

Combinations of Workmen. Edinburgh: 1825. V. 46

Contributions to the Edinburgh Review. London: 1844. V. 43

Contributions to the Edinburgh Review. London: 1846. V. 46

JEFFREY, J. K.

The Territory of Wyoming: Its Hisotry, Soil, Climate, Resources. Laramie City: 1874. V. 37

JEFFREY, OF MONMOUTH

The British History . . . London: 1718. V. 44

JEFFREYS, ELIZABETH

The Whole Tryal of John Swann and Elizabeth Jeffreys, at Walthamstow, in Essex, on the Third Day of July 1751 . . . London: 1752. V. 43; 46

JEFFREYS, GEORGE WASHINGTON

A Series of Essays on Agriculture & Rural Affairs. Raleigh: 1819. V. 38; 39; 40

JEFFREYS, J. B.

British Conchology. London: 1862-69. V. 37

JEFFREYS, KETURAH

The Widowed Missionary's Journal Containing Some Account of Madagascar. Southampton: 1827. V. 39; 44

JEFFRIES, B. JOY

Color-Blindness: Its Dangers and Its Detection. Boston: 1879. V. 42

JEFFRIES, C.

Wabash Captives; or the Awful Sentence . . . Lafayette: 1846. V. 45

JEFFRIES, DAVID

A Treatise on Diamonds and Pearls. London: 1771. V. 46

JEFFRIES, JOHN

A Narrative of the Two Aerial Voyages of Doctor Jeffries with Mons. Blanchard; with Meteorological Observations and Remarks. N.P.. V. 40; 45

JEFFRIES, JOHN continued

A Narrative of the Two Aerial Voyages of Doctor Jeffries with Mons, Blanchard . . . London: 1786. V. 40

JEFFRYES, ELIZABETH

Authentick Memoirs of the Wicked Life and Transactions of Elizabeth Jeffryes, Spinster. London: 1752. V. 43

JEHL, FRANCIS

Menlo Park Reminiscences. Dearborn: 1937-41. V. 40

JEKYLL: a Political Eclogue. London: 1788. V. 40

JEKYLL, GERTRUDE

Colour in the Flower Garden. London: 1908. V. 41

Gardens for Small Country Houses. London: 1920. V. 42

Garden Ornament. London: 1927. V. 38; 39; 40; 45; 46

Lilies for English Gardens. London: 1910. V. 42

Old West Surrey, Some Notes and Memories. London: 1904. V. 39

Roses for English Gardens. London: 1902. V. 38

Some English Gardens. London: 1904. V. 44; 46

Some English Gardens. London: 1905. V. 39; 41

Wall and Water Gardens. London: 1901. V. 38

Wood and Garden. London: 1899. V. 38

Wood and Garden, Notes and Thoughts, Prctical and Critical. London: 1900. V. 44

JELENSKI, CONSTANTIN

Leonor Fini. New York: 1968. V. 41; 43; 46

JELITTO, L.

Hardy Herbaceous Perennials. Portland: 1990. V. 45

JELLICOE, G. A.

Baroque Gardens of Austria. London: 1932. V. 45; 46

The Shakespeare Memorial Theatre, Stratford-upon-Avon. London: 1933. V. 37; 43

JELLIFFE, ROBERT A.

Faulkner at Nagano. Tokyo: 1956. V. 37

JELLISON, WILLIAM W.

Campaign of the 96 Ill. Volunteer Infantry. Cleveland: 1864. V. 43

JEMMAT, CATHERINE

Miscellanies in Prose and Verse. London: 1766. V. 38; 39; 41

Miscellanies in Prose and Verse. London: 1771. V. 40

JENCKS, E. N.

A Plea of Polygamy. Paris: 1898. V. 37

JENINGS, EDMUND

Considerations on the Mode and Terms of a Treaty of Peace. Hartford: 1779. V. 41; 45

A Full Manifestation of What Mr. Henry Laurens Falsely Denominates Candor in Himself, and Tricks in Mr. Edmund Jenings. London: 1783. V. 45

JENKINS, A. O.

Olive's Last Roundup. N.P.: 1930. V. 43

JENKINS, C. FRANCIS

The Boyhood of an Inventor. Washington: 1931. V. 38

Radiomovies, Radiovision, Television. Washington: 1929. V. 40; 46

Vision by Radio Photographs, Radio Photograms. Washington: 1925. V. 40; 46

Vision by Radio, Radio Photographs, Radio Photgrams. Washington: 1925. V. 40; 42; 44; 45; 46

JENKINS COMPANY

A Full Howes: A Catalogue of Books and Pamphlets Listed in Howes' U.S. Iana. Austin: 1981. V. 37

JENKINS, DAVID

Eight Centuries of Reports; or, Eight Hundred Cases Solemnly Adjudged in the Exchequer Chamber. In the Savoy: 1734. V. 45

The Works of That Grave and learned Lawyer Judge Jenkins, Prisoner in Newgate, Upon Divers Statues, Concerning, the Liberty and Freedome of the Subject. London: 1648. V. 38; 40; 44

The Works of . . . London: 1681. V. 40

JENKINS, GEORGE H.

Victoria: A Short History and Description of the Parliament House, Melbourne, Prepared at the Request of the Royal Commission on the Parliament Buildings. Melbourne: 1886. V. 41

JENKINS, HOWARD M.

Historical Collections Relating to Gwynedd, a Township of Montgomery County . . . Philadelphia: 1897. V. 42

Pennsylvania Colonial and Federal . . . Philadelphia: 1903. V. 41; 42

Pennsylvania, Colonial and Federal: a History, 1608-1906. Philadelphia: 1906. V. 43

JENKINS, J. T.

A History of the Whale Fisheries. London: 1921. V. 38

JENKINS, JAMES fl.1817

The Martial Achievements of Great Britain and Her Allies; from 1799 to 1815. London: 1814. V. 39

Martial Achievements of Great Britain and Her Allied from 1799-1815. London: 1814-15. V. 37; 38; 42; 45; 46

The Martial Achievements of Great Britain and Her Allies From 1799 to 1815. (with) the Naval Achievements of Great Britain from the Year 1793 to 1817. London: 1814/1817. V. 43

The Martial Achievements of Great Britain and Her Allies from 1799 to 1815. London: 1815-16. V. 45

The Martial Achievements of Great Britain and Her Allies; from 1799 to 1815. London: 1814-15 (1829). V. 38

The Naval Achievements of Great Britain, from the Year 1793 to 1817. London: 1817. V. 42; 43

The Naval Achievements of Great Britain, from the Year 1793 to 1817. London: 1816-17. V. 38

JENKINS, JAMES TRAVIS

Whales and Modern Whaling. London: 1932. V. 37

JENKINS, JEFF

The Northern Tier, or Life Among the Homestead Settlers. Topeka: 1880. V. 44

JENKINS, JOHN

The Art of Writing. Cambridge: 1813. V. 37; 39; 40; 43

JENKINS, JOHN CARMICHAEL

Three Letters, by 'Conestoga', to a Friend in Lancaster County, Pennsylvania, Upon Slavery and the Fugitive Law. Lancaster: 1851. V. 39

JENKINS, JOHN EDWARD

Lord Bantam. London: 1872. V. 37; 41; 46

JENKINS, JOHN H.

Along the Early Trails of the Southwest. Austin: 1969. V. 37; 39

Basic Texas Books. Austin: 1983. V. 37; 38; 40; 42; 43

Bluebonnets and Cactus: An Album of Southwestern Paintings by Porfirio Salinas. Austin: 1967. V. 37

Cracker Barrel Chronicles. A Bibliography fo Texas Town and County Histories. Austin: 1965. V. 40

The Most Remarkable Texas Book: an Essay on Heartsill's 1491 Days in the Confederatae Army, With a Leaf from the Original Printing. Austin: 1980. V. 37; 38; 39; 40

The Papers of the Texas Revolution, 1835-1836. Austin: 1973. V. 37; 38; 39; 40; 41; 42; 44; 45

Recollections of Early Texas . . . Austin: 1958. V. 43

JENKINS, JOHN S.

The Life of John Caldwell Calhoun. Auburn: 1850. V. 46

Recent Exploring Expeditions to the Pacific, and the South Seas, Under the American, English and French Governments. London: 1853. V. 38; 42; 43

Voyage of the U. S. Exploring Squadron Commanded by Captain Charles Wilkes in 1838, 1839 and 1840, 1841 and 1842 . . . Auburn: 1850. V. 39; 43

JENKINS, JOSEPH

A Sermon Occasioned by a Dreadful-Explosion of Gun-Powder, in Chester. Wrexham: 1772. V. 42

JENKINS, LADY MINNA

Sport and Travel in Both Tibets. London: 1909. V. 37; 39

JENKINS, PAUL B.

The Battle of Westport. Kansas City: 1906. V. 46

JENKINS, RHYS

Collected Papers, Links in the History of Technology from Tudor Times. Cambridge: 1936. V. 37

JENKINS, RICHARD

The Ode, Songs, Chorusses, &c. for the Concert in Commemoration of Chatterton, the Celebrated Bristol Poet. Bristol: 1784. V. 38

JENKINS, ROBERT

Spanish Insolence Corrected by English Bravery. London: 1739. V. 39; 41

JENKINS, THOMAS

Libel. Sir John Carr Against Hood and Sharpe. London: 1808. V. 43; 46

JENKINS, THOMAS continued

The Life Voyages and Travels of Thomas Jenkins and David Lowellin Through the Unknown Tracts of Africa. London: 1792. V. 40

JENKINS, THOMAS J.

Six Seasons on Our Prairies and Six Weeks in Our Rockies. Louisville: 1884. V. 38

JENKINSON, HILARY

The Later Court Hands in Englaand from the 15th to the 17th Century. 1927. V. 38

The Later Court Hands in England from the 15th to the 17th Century. Cambridge: 1927. V. 40; 44; 45

JENKS, SILVESTER

An Essay Upon the Art of Love. Oxon (London)?: 1702. V. 38

JENKS, STEPHEN

The Delights of Harmony . . . Dedham: 1805. V. 43

JENKS, WILLIAM

The Explanatory Bible Atlas and Scripture Gazetteer . . . Boston: 184. V. 45

JENNER, CHARLES

Letters from Lothario to Penelope. London: 1769. V. 44

Louisa; a Tale to Which is Added an Elegy to the Memory of Lord Lyttleton. London: 1774. V. 40; 43

The Placid Man; or Memoirs of Sir Charles Belville. London: 1770. V. 40

Poems. Cambridge: 1766. V. 41

Town Eclogues. London: 1773. V. 45

JENNER, EDWARD

An Enquiry into the Causes and effects of the Variolae Vaccinae . . . 1923. V. 44

An Inquiry into the Causes and Effects of the Variolae Vaccinae. Birmingham: 1978. V. 40

Some Observations on the Migration of Birds. V. 45

JENNER, JOHN

The Life of Edward Jenner, M.D. . . . with Illustrations of His Doctrines and Selections from His Correspondence. London: 1838. V. 41

JENNER, THOMAS

Londons Blame, If Not Its Shame . . . London: 1651. V. 42

JENNER, WALKER

Fragments of Letters and other Papers, Written in different Parts of Europe, at Sea and on the Asiatic and African Coasts or Shores of the Mediterranean, at the close of the Eighteenth . . . London: 1802. V. 37

JENNER, WILLIAM

Lectures and Essays on Fevers and Diptheria, 1849 to 1879. New York: 1893. V. 38

JENNESS, DIAMOND

Indians of Canada. Ottawa: 1932. V. 44

JENNESSEY, J. B.

Stephania: a Middle and Late Bronze-Age Cemetery in Cyprus. London: 1963. V. 42

JENNEWEIN, J. LEONARD

Black Hills Booktrails. Mitchell: 1962. V. 42

JENNEY, WALTER P.

Letter from the Secretary of the Interior, Transmitting . . . the Report of Prof. Walter P. Jenney Upon the Agriculture, Climate and Resources of the Black Hills. Washington: 1876. V. 37; 43

The Mineral Wealth, Climate and Rain-Fall, and Natural Resources of the Black Hills of Dakota. Washington: 1876. V. 37; 39

Report on the Mineral Wealth, Climate and Rain Fall and Natural Resources of the Black Hills of Dakota. 1876. V. 37

JENNING, EDMUND, MRS.

Thyra Gascoigne. London: 1863. V. 41

JENNINGS, ALPHONSO J.

Through the Shadows with O. Henry. New York: 1921. V. 39

Through the Shadows with O. Henry. New York: (1921). V. 37

JENNINGS, ARTHUR SEYMOUR

Wallpapers and Wall Coverings. A Practical Handbook for Decorators, Paper-hangers, Architects . . . showing the latest designs. New York: 1903. V. 37

JENNINGS, BRENDAN

Michael O Cleirigh, Chief of the Four Masters, and His Associates. Dublin: 1936. V. 38

JENNINGS, DAVID

An Introduction to the Use of the Globes and the Orrery. London: 1739. V. 40

An Introduction to the Use of Globes, and the Orrery. London: 1752. V. 38

An Introduction to the Knowledge of Metals. Birmingham: 1775. V. 38

Jewish Antiquities, or a Course of Lectures on the First Three Books of Godwin's Moses and Aaron. Edinburgh: 1808. V. 37; 43

JENNINGS, EDMUND

The Candor of Henry Laurens, Esa. London: 1783. V. 38

A Full Manifestation of What Mr. Henry Laurens Falsely Denominates Candor in Himself, and Tricks in Mr. Edmund Jennings. London: 1787. V. 38

JENNINGS, EDWARD

Practical Hints Addressed to Seamen, for Preventing Accidents on Board Ship and Especially for Guarding Against Hurricanes, Collision, Fire. London: 1844. V. 41

JENNINGS, ELIZABETH

A Dream of Spring. Stratford-upon-Avon: 1920. V. 37

In Shakespeare's Company. Shipston-on-Stour: 1985. V. 42

In Shakespeare's Company. (Shipson-on-Stour): (1985). V. 37

Italian Light and Other Poems. Hove: 1980. V. 42

Italian Light & Other Poems. (Hove): (1980). V. 37

Poems. Swinford, Eynsham: 1953. V. 41

JENNINGS, GEORGE HENRY

An Anecdotal History of the British Parliament, from the Earliest Periods to the Present Time. London: 1880. V. 44

JENNINGS, HENRY CONSTANTINE

A Catalogue of the Celebrated Collection of Beautiful Subjects of Natural History, a Chiefly in Conchology and Mineralogy, of Henry Constantine Jennings, Esq . . . Which Will be sold by Auction, by Mr. H. Phillips at His Great Rooms, no. 73. Bond Street . . . 1816. V. 37

An Endeavour to Prove that Reason is Alone Sufficient to the Firm Establishment of Religion, Which Must on Principles of Faith be Ever Precarious. Chelmsford: 1785. V. 45

A Physical Enquiry Into the Powers and Properties of Spirit, and How Far by Analogical Inference Resulting from Experimental and Natural Phenomena . . . Chelmsford: 1787. V. 45

Summary and Free Reflections, in Which the Great Outline Only, and Principal Fieatures, of the Following Subjects are Impartially traced, and Candidly Examined. Chelmsford: 1783. V. 45

Summary and Free Reflections, in Which the Great Outline Only, and Principal Features, of Several Interesting Subjects . . . . London: 1798. V. 42; 43

JENNINGS, HERBERT S.

Contributions to the Study of the Behavior of Lower Organisms. Washington: 1904. V. 38

JENNINGS, JAMES

The Family Cyclopaedia. London: 1821. V. 39

The Family Cyclopaedia, or manual of Useful and Necessary Information, Alphabetically Arranged . . . London: 1822. V. 46

Observations on Some of the Dialects in the West of England, Particularly Somersetshire . . . London: 1825. V. 41; 45

A Practical Treatise on the History, Medical Properties and Cultivation of Tobacco. London: 1830. V. 43; 45

JENNINGS, JOHN

Two Discourses; the First, Of Preaching Christ; the second, Of Particular and Experimental Preaching. Boston: 1740. V. 40; 44

JENNINGS, LOUIS J.

The Millionaire. Edinburgh/London: 1883. V. 37

JENNINGS, LOUIS JOHN

The Philadelphian. London: 1891. V. 41; 46

JENNINGS, N. A.

A Texas Ranger. New York: 1899. V. 37; 38; 42; 46

JENNINGS, OBIDIAH

Debate of Cambellism: Held at Nashville, Tennessee. Pittsburgh: 1832. V. 40

JENNINGS, OSCAR

Early Woodcut Initials. London: 1908. V. 38; 39; 40; 45; 46

On the Cure of the Morphia Habit. London: 1890. V. 43

JENNINGS, PRESTON J.

A Book of Trout Flies. New York: 1935. V. 43; 44

JENNINGS, S.

Orchids and How to Grow Them in India and Other Tropical Climates. London: 1875. V. 41

JENNINGS, W.

The Foundling of Belgrade. New York: 1808. V. 37

JENNISON, JOHN C.

Eurydice. Guide to Beauty. Self Preservation. Book of Receipts. New York: 1850s. V. 43

JENNISON, WILLIAM

Outline of Political Economy. Philadelphia: 1828. V. 39; 41; 44

JENNY, ADELLE

Early American Trade Cards. New York: 1927. V. 46

JENSEN, JENS MARINUS

Early History of Provo, Utah. Provo: 1924. V. 41

JENSEN, LAURA

Tapwater. Port Townsend: 1979. V. 41

JENSON, ANDRE

Day by Day with the Utah Pioneers, 1847. Salt Lake City: 1934. V. 41

JENSON, ANDREW

Day by Day with the Utah Pioneers 1847. A Chronological Record of the Trek Across the Plains. Salt Lake City: 1934. V. 42

JENTY, CHARLES NICHOLAS

A Course of Anatomico-Physiological Lectures on the Human Structure and Animal Oeconomy. London: 1757. V. 42; 45; 46

Uteri Praegnantis & Ad Partum Maturi Demonstrationes. London: 1757. V. 43

JENYNS, SOAME

Chinese Art: The Minor Arts. London: 1963-65. V. 42

Chinese Art, the Minor Arts II: Textiles, Glass and Painting on Glass, Carvings in Ivory and Rhinoceros Horn, Carving in Hardstones, Snuff-Bottles, Ink Cakes and Inkstoves. New York: 1965. V. 41

Chinese Art: The Minor Arts. London: 1965. V. 42

Disquisitions on Several Subjects. London: 1782. V. 42; 45

Every Man His Own Law-Maker. London: 1785. V. 38; 43

A Free Inquiry into the Nature and Origin of Evil. London: 1757. V. 42; 45

A Free Inquiry Into the Nature and Origin of Evil. London: 1761. V. 42; 45

Miscellaneous Pieces . . . London: 1716. V. 45

Miscellaneous Pieces. London: 1761. V. 40; 41; 44; 45

An Ode. London: 1780. V. 40

Poems. London: 1732. V. 45

Poems. London: 1752. V. 41; 42

A Scheme for the Coalition of Parties Humbly Submitted to the Publick. London: 1772. V. 39; 42

A View of the Internal Evidence of the Christian Religion. London: 1776. V. 40; 41; 42; 45; 46

A View of the Internal Evidence of the Christian Religion. Boston: 1793. V. 44

The Works of Soame Jenyns, Esq. London: 1790. V. 37; 41; 42; 43; 44; 45

Works of . . . London: 1792. V. 38

JEPHSON, J. M.

Shakespeare: His Birthplace, Home and Grave. London: 1864. V. 40; 44; 46

JEPHSON, MAURICE DENHAM

An Anglo-Irish Miscellany. Dublin: 1964. V. 38

JEPHSON, ROBERT 1736-1803

The Count of Narbonne, a Tragedy. London: 1781. V. 37; 38; 40; 42

An Epistle (in verse) to G(orges) E(dmund H(owa)rd, Esq. to Alderman George Faulkner. Barataria (i.e. Dublin): 1772. V. 40

Roman Portraits, a Poem in Heroick Verse. London: 1794. V. 37; 38; 41

JEPPE, C. B.

Gold Mining on the Witwatersrand. 1946. V. 37

JEPPESEN, KRISTIAN

Swedish Excavations and Researches. Lund: 1955-63. V. 40

JEPSON, EDWARD

Memories of an Edwardian and Neo-Georgian. London: 1937. V. 40

JEPSON, W. L.

A Flora of California. Berkeley: 1909-39. V. 45

JEPSON, WILLIS LINN

The Silva of California. Berkeley: 1910. V. 44

JERDAN, WILLIAM

The Autobiography. London: 1852. V. 44

Illustrations of the Plan of a National Association for the Encouragement and Protection of Authors, and Men of talent and Genius. London: 1839. V. 38

A Voyage to the Isle of Elba. London: 1814. V. 40

JERDON, T. C.

The Birds of India. Calcutta: 1862-64. V. 43

The Mammals of India. London: 1874. V. 41

JEREMIE, NICHOLAS 1669?-1732

Twenty Years of York Factory, 1694-1714. Ottawa: 1926. V. 44

JERMAN, MICHAEL

Parphrastical Meditations, by Way of Commentarie Upon the Whole Book of Proverbs of Solomon. London: 1638. V. 38

JERNINGHAM, EDWARD

The Deserter. London: 1770. V. 40

The Fall of Mexico. London: 1775. V. 40; 42; 45

The Nun: an Elegy. London: 1764. V. 37; 40

The Old Bard's Farewell; a Poem. London: 1811. V. 42; 46

Poems. London: 1774. V. 40; 42; 45; 46

Poems. Dublin: 1790. V. 40; 41

Poems and Plays. London: 1806. V. 40

JEROME, CHAUNCEY

History of the American Clock Business. New Haven: 1860. V. 38; 39; 40; 44

JEROME, IRENE

I Have Called you Friends. Boston: 1893. V. 38

JEROME, JEROME K.

The Diary of a Pilgrimage (and Six Essays). Bristol: 1891. V. 39

My First Book. London: 1894. V. 40

Three Men in a Boat. Bristol: 1889. V. 40

Three Men in a Boat, to Say Nothing of the Dog. London: 1889. V. 41

Three Men on Wheels. New York: 1900. V. 41

Three Men in a Boat to Say Nothing of the Dog! Ipswich: 1975. V. 38; 43

Three Men in a Boat. New York: 1975. V. 38

Told After Supper. London: 1891. V. 42

JEROME, JUDSON

Seranade. Berkeley: 1967. V. 46

JERRARD

The Night Flyers. London: 1852. V. 44

JERRARD, PAUL

The Floral Offering. London: 1852. V. 43

The Floral Offering. London: 1855. V. 41

JERROLD, ALICE

A Cruise in the Acorn . . . London: 1875. V. 45

JERROLD, BLANCHARD 1826-1884

The Book of Menus. London: 1876. V. 46

Cent per Cent. London: 1871. V. 46

How to See the British Museum. London: 1852. V. 40

The Life and Remains of Douglas Jerrold. London: 1859. V. 43; 46

The Life of George Cruikshank. London: 1882. V. 37; 39; 40; 46

The Life of George Cruikshank. Picadilly: 1882. V. 38

The Life of George Cruikshank . London: 1883. V. 39; 42

Life of Gustave Dore. London: 1891. V. 40

London, a Pilgrimage. London: 1872. V. 40; 46

London: a Pilgrimage. New York: 1890. V. 38; 40; 43

On the Boulevards; or Memorable Men and Things Drawn on the Spot, 1853-1866. Philadelphia: 1867. V. 46

JERROLD, DOUGLAS

The Big Book of Fairy Tales. London. V. 44

Cakes and Ale. London: 1842. V. 38; 45

Mrs. Caudle's Curtain Lectures. London: 1866. V. 39

A Man Made of Money. London: 1848-49. V. 42

A Man Made of Money. London: 1849. V. 38; 41

A Man Made of Money. London: (1848)-49. V. 37

Men of Character. London: 1838. V. 37

The Story of a Feather. London: 1867. V. 38; 39; 40; 46

Works. London: 1863. V. 40

The Works. London: 1863-64. V. 39

Works. London: 1865. V. 46

JERROLD, WALTER

The Big Book of Fairy Tales. London: 1911. V. 45

The Big Book of Fables. London: 1912. V. 38; 40

Bon Mots of Charles Lamb and Douglas Jerrold. London: 1893. V. 43

Bon-Mots of Sydney Smith and R. Brinsley Sheridan; Bon-Mots of Charles Lamb and Douglas Jerrold; Bon-Mots of Samuel Foote and Theodore Hook. London: 1893-94. V. 37

The Silvery Thames. Leeds & London: 1906. V. 39

JERRY Diddle and His Fiddle. London: 1830. V. 39

JERSEY, GEORGE VILLIERS, 3RD EARL OF

A Letter to Miss F--d. London: 1761. V. 43; 46

THE JERSEYMAN. Flemington: 1891-1905. V. 38

JERVES, JOHN JERVIS WHITE

A Refutation of M. M. de Montgaillard's Calumnies Against British Policy . . . London: 1812. V. 44

JERVEY, CLARE

Inscriptions on the Tablets and Gravestones in St. Michael's Church and Churchyard, Charleston, S.C. Columbia: 1906. V. 40

JERVIS, H.

Narrative of a Journey to the Falls of the Cavery, with an Historical and Descriptive Account of the Neilgherry Hills. London: 1834. V. 40

JERVIS, HENRY JERVIS WHITE

History of the Island of Corfu, and of the Republic of the Ionian Islands. London: 1852. V. 37; 39; 40; 41

JERVIS, THOMAS BEST

Records of Ancient Science, Exemplified and Authenticated in the Primitive Universal Standard of Weights and Measures. Calcutta: 1835. V. 43; 46

JERVISE, ANDREW

The History and Traditions of the Land of the Lindsays in Angus and Mearns with Notices of Alyth and Meigle. Edinburgh: 1882. V. 40

JESS, ZACHARIAH

A Compendious System of Practical Surveying and Dividing of Land . . . Wilmington: 1799. V. 42; 46

JESSE, CAPTAIN

The Life of George Brummell, Esq. London: 1886. V. 44

JESSE, EDWARD

Anecdotes of Dogs. London: 1858. V. 46

Anecdotes of Dogs. London: 1891. V. 40

Favorite Haunts and Rural Studies. London: 1847. V. 42; 43; 44

Gleanings in Natural History; with Local Recollections. Philadelphia: 1833. V. 44

Gleanings in Natural History. London: 1834-35. V. 39; 45

Gleanings in Natural History. London: 1843. V. 42

JESSE, F. TENNYSON

The City Curious. London: 1920. V. 44; 46

The Solange Stories. 1931. V. 46

JESSE, GEORGE R.

Researches into the History of the British Dog, &c &c. London: 1866. V. 37; 39; 45

JESSE, J. HENEAGE

London: Its Celebrated Characters and Remarkable Places. London: 1870. V. 38

London: Its Celebrated Characters and Remarkable Places. London: 1871. V. 37; 41

JESSE James: The Life and Daring Adventures of This Bold Highwayman and Bank Robber and His No Less Celebrated Brother, Frank James. Together with The Thrilling Exploits of the Younger Boys. Philadelphia: 1883. V. 40; 42

JESSE James: The Life and Daring Adventures of This Bold Highwayman and Bank Robber and His No Less Celebrated Brother, Frank James. Together with the Thrilling Exploits of the Younger Boys. Written By (One Who Dare Not Now Disclose His Identity). Philadelphia: 1882. V. 39; 45

JESSE, JOHN HENEAGE

George Selwyn, and His Contemporaries. London: 1882. V. 41; 44

Memoirs of the Life and Reign of King George the Third. London: 1867. V. 44

The Works of . . . London: 1901. V. 40; 46

JESSE, WILLIAM 1809-1871

Notes of a Half-Pay in Search of Health; or Russia, Circassia, and the Crimea in 1839-40. London: 1841. V. 42

JESSEL, FREDERIC

A Bibliography of Works in English on Playing Cards and Gaming. London: 1905. V. 39

JESSEN, BURCHARD H.

W. N. MacMillan's Expeditions and Big Game Hunting in Sudan, Abyssinia & British East Africa. London: 1906. V. 43

JESSOP, EDMOND

A Discovery of the errors of the English Anabaptists. As also an admonition to all such as are led by the like spirit of error. Wherein is set down all their severall and main points of error, which they hold. With a full answer . . . London: 1623. V. 37; 43; 44; 45

JESSOP, J. P.

Flora of South Australia. Netley: 1986. V. 38

JESSOP, THOMAS

The Jesuites Ghostly Wayes to Draw Other Persons Over to Their Damnable Principle of the Meritoriousness of Destroying Princes . . . London: 1679. V. 42

JESSOP, WILLIAM R. H.

Flindersland and Sturtland; or the Inside and Outside of Australia. London: 1862. V. 43

JESSOPP, AUGUSTUS

William Cecil, Lord Burghley. London: 1904. V. 40

JESSUP, EDWARD

The Lives of Picus and Pascal, Faithfully Collected from the Most Authentick Accounts of Them . . . London: 1723. V. 38

JESSUP, HENRY H.

Fifty-Three Years in Syria. New York: 1910. V. 39

JESSUP, THOMAS

Annual Report of the Quartermaster General, of the Operations of the Quartermaster's Department, For the Fiscal Year Ending On the 30th June, 1850. Washington: 1851. V. 45

JESTY, SIMON

River Niger. London: 1935. V. 38

THE JESUITS Justification (in Verse) Proving they Died as Innocent as the Child Unborn. N.P.: 1679. V. 40

JESUS MARIA, MANUEL

Copia Autentica De Carta del Illustrissimo Y Reverendissimo Senor Doct. Fr. Manuel de Jesus Maria, Dignissimo Obispo de Nankim y Governador Apostolico del Obispado de Pekim, Metropoli del Imperio de la China. N.P.: 1733. V. 43

JESUS MARIA Y HUALDE, MIGUEL DE

Destierro Merecido de Opiniones Equivocadas . . . Madrid: 1758 and 1765. V. 45

JETTE, JULIUS

Yoyit Rokanga Nulator Roka Do-Daletloye. Winnipeg: 1904. V. 42

JEVONS, FRANK BYRON

A History of Greek Literature. London: 1908. V. 38

JEVONS, HENRY STANLEY

The Future of Exchange and the Indian Currency. Allahabad: 1922. V. 45

JEVONS, WILLIAM

Systematic Morality, or, a Treatise on the Theory and Practice of Human Duty on the Grounds of Natural Religion. London: 1827. V. 39; 41

JEVONS, WILLIAM STANLEY 1835-1882

The Coal Question; and Inquiry Concerning the Progress of the Nation and the Probable Exhaustion of Our Coal Mines . . . London: 1866. V. 46

The Coal Question an Inquiry Concerning the Progress of the nation, and the Probable Exhaustion of Our Coal Miners . . . London: 1906. V. 37

Essays and Addresses, by Professors and Lecturers of the Owens College, Manchester. London: 1874. V. 40

Investigations in Currency and Finance. London: 1884. V. 39; 41; 42

Letters and Journal of W. Stanley Jevons. London: 1886. V. 39; 43

Methods of Social Reform and Other Papers. London: 1883. V. 42

Money and Mechanism of Exchange. London: 1875. V. 41

Money and Mechanism of Exchange. New York: 1875. V. 41; 45

Money and the Mechanism of Exchange. New York: 1878. V. 41

Papers and Correspondence. 1972-3. V. 41

The Principles of Science: a Treatise on Logic and Scientific Method. London: 1874. V. 37; 41

Principles of Science. London: 1877. V. 45

The Principles of Science. London: 1879. V. 40; 45

JEVONS, WILLIAM STANLEY 1835-1882 continued

The Principles of Economics. A Fragment of a Treatise on the Industrial Mechanism of Society and Other Papers. London: 1905. V. 38; 41; 42; 43

Pure Logic or the Logic of Quality Apart from Quantity: With Remarks on Boole's System and on the Relation of Logic and Mathematics. London: 1864. V. 37

Science Lectures for the People. Science Lectures Delivered in Manchester, 1866-67 and 1870-71. First and Second Series. Manchester: 1871. V. 46

The State in Relation to Labour. London: 1882. V. 37; 41; 42; 45; 46

Studies in Deductive Logic. London: 1880. V. 37; 38

The Theory of Political Economy. London & New York: 1871. V. 38

The Theory of Political Economy . . . London: 1911. V. 43

THE JEW, at Home and Abroad. Philadelphia: 1845. V. 45

JEWEL, JOHN 1522-1571

Aplogie Ecclesiae Anglicanae. London: 1599. V. 37; 42

Apologia Ecclesiae Anglicanae. Londini: 1581. V. 45

Certaine Sermons Preached Before the Queenes Majestie, and at Paules Crosse . . . London: 1583. V. 41

An Exposition Vpon the Two Epistles of the Apostle S. Paul to the Thessalonians. London: 1584. V. 45

The Works. London: 1609. V. 38; 41

The Works of the Very Learned and Reuerend Father in God Iohn Ievvell, not Long Since Bishop of Sarisbvrie. London: 1609. V. 40

JEWERS, ARTHUR J.

Wells Cathedral: Its Monumental Inscriptions and Heraldry. London: 1892. V. 46

JEWETT, ALBERT HENRY CLAY

A Boy Goes to War . . . Memories of 1860 to 1864. Bloomington: 1944. V. 43

JEWETT, D.

A Treatise on Early Marriage. Hartford: 1813. V. 39

JEWETT, HELEN

The Truly Remarkable Life of the Beautiful Helen Jewett, Who Was So Mysteriously Murdered. Philadelphia: 1880. V. 41

JEWETT, HENRY J.

The Archive of Texas. New Orleans: 1859. V. 42

The Archive War of Texas. New Orleans: 1859. V. 39

JEWETT, PAUL

New England Farrier; or, a Compendium of Earriery (sic), in Four Parts. Newburyport: 1795. V. 39; 44

The New England Farrier; Being a Compendium of farriery. Salem: 1807. V. 45

The New England Farrier . . . Exeter: 1822. V. 43

JEWETT, SARAH ORNE 1849-1909

Country By-Ways. Boston: 1881. V. 39

A Country Doctor. Boston: 1884. V. 40

The Country of the Pointed Firs. Boston: 1896. V. 40; 46

The Country of the Pointed Firs. Boston & New York: 1896. V. 46

The Country of the Pointed Firs. Boston: 1897. V. 46

The Country of the Pointed Firs. Boston & New York: 1897. V. 46

Deephaven. 1877. V. 46

Deephaven. Boston: 1877. V. 38; 40; 42; 45; 46

The King of Folly Island. Boston: 1888. V. 40; 44

Letters. Boston: 1911. V. 43

The Life of Nancy. Boston: 1895. V. 40

The Life of Nancy. Boston & New York: 1895. V. 39

A Marsh Island. Boston: 1885. V. 40; 43; 46

A Marsh Island. Boston and New York: 1885. V. 39; 41

A Native of Winby and Other Tales. Boston & New York: 1893. V. 39

A Native of Winby and Other Tales. Boston & New York: 1894. V. 46

Old Friends and New. Boston: 1879. V. 39

The Queen's Twin and Other Stories. Boston: 1899. V. 38; 39

The Queen's Twin and Other Stories. Boston and New York: 1899. V. 39; 41

Tales of new England. Boston: 1895. V. 40

The Tory Lover. Boston: 1901. V. 40

The Tory Lover. Boston and New York: 1901. V. 39; 40; 41

Verses. Boston: 1916. V. 46

A White Heron and Other Stories. Boston & New York: 1886. V. 39

JEWITT, EDWIN

Manual of Illuminated and Missal Painting. London: 1860. V. 44

Manual of Illuminated and Missal Painting. London: 1870's. V. 46

JEWITT, JOHN R. 1783-1821

A Narrative of the Adventures and Sufferings of John R. Jewitt; Only Survivor of the Crew of the Ship Boston, During a Captivity of Nearly Three Years Among the Savages of Nootka Sound. Middletown: 1815. V. 37; 46

Narrative of the Adventures and Sufferings of John R. Jewitt . . . New York: 1815. V. 38; 45

Narrative of the Adventures and Sufferings of John R. Jewitt . . . New York: 1849. V. 42

Narrative of the Adventures and Sufferigns (sic) of John R. Jewitt, Only Survivor of the Crew of the Ship Boston, During a Captivity of Nearly 3 Years Among the Savages of Nootka Sound. Ithaca: 1851. V. 37

JEWITT, LLEWELLYNN

The Ceramic Art of Great Britain. London: 1878. V. 38; 42

Handbook of English Coins. London: 1879. V. 41

The Life and Works of Jacob Thompson. London: 1882. V. 38; 40

The Wedgewoods. London: 1865. V. 38

JEWRY, MARY

Warne's Model Cookery and Housekeeping Book, Containing Complete Instructions in Household Management. London: 1868. V. 40

Warne's Every Day Cookery: Containing One Thousand Nine Hundred Receipts and Other Valuable Instructions. London: 1889. V. 42

JEWS. LITRUGY & RITUAL. HAGADAH

Haggadah for Passover. Paris: 1966. V. 40; 41; 45

JEWS. LITURGY & RITUAL. HAGADAH

The Haggadah. London: 1939. V. 46

Haggadah for Passover. Boston: 1965. V. 42

Haggadah for Passover. London: 1965. V. 39; 40; 41

Offenbacher Haggadah. Offenbach am Main: 1927. V. 45

A Passover Haggadah. New York: 1974. V. 41

JEWS. LITURGY & RITUAL. HAGGADAH

The Haggadah. Jerusalem: 1956. V. 39

The Haggadah. Executed by Arthur Szyk. Jerusalem & Tel Aviv: 1957. V. 39

JEWS. LITURY & RITUAL. HAGADAH

Haggadah for Passover Copied and Illustrated by Ben Shahn. Paris & London: 1966. V. 43

JEWSBURY, MARY JANE

Phatasmagoria; or, Sketches of Life and Literature. London: 1825. V. 37

JEX-BLAKE, SOPHIA

Medical Women: Two Essays. 1. Medicine as a Profession of Women. II. Medical Education of Women. Edinburgh: 1872. V. 42

The Practice of Medicine by Women, an Essay . . . Edinburgh: 1876. V. 42

JEYES, S. H.

Life and Times of the Marquis of Salisbury: History of the Conservative Party During the Last Forty Years. London: 1895. V. 39

JHABVALA, RUTH PRAWER

Amrita. New York: 1955. V. 41

A Backward Glance. London: 1965. V. 38

The Householder - a Screenplay. Delhi. V. 40

The Householder. London: 1960. V. 38

The Nature of Passion. London: 1956. V. 38; 45

The Nature of Passion. London: 1956. V. 43

To Whom She Will: A Novel. London: 1955. V. 42

JIM Crow's Vagaries, or Black Flights of Fancy . . . London: 1845? V. 42

JINGLE, BOB, PSEUD.

The Association &c. or the Delegates of the Colonies, at the Grand Congress, Held at Philadlephia Sept. 1, 1774 . . . New York: 1774. V. 37; 46

JITTA, A. N.

Roman Bronze Statuettes from the Netherlands. Groningen: 1967-69. V. 40

JOAD, C. E. M.

The Adventures of the Young Soldier in Search of the Better World. London: 1943. V. 45

JOAN, NATALIE

The Joyous Book. London: 1924. V. 38

Little Mothers. Milford. V. 44

The Pleasant Book. London. V. 38

JOAN, the Maid of Orleans . . . San Francisco;: 1938. V. 46

JOANNES DE GARLANDIA ca. 1195 - ca. 1272

Johannis De Garlandia. De Triumphis Ecclesiae Libri Octo. London: 1856. V. 40

JOANNES DE JANDUNO

Qudestiones Super Libros Arisotelia de Anima. Venice: 1480. V. 46

JOANNES PHILOPONUS

In Primos Qvatvor Aristotelis de Natvrali Avscvltatione Libros Commentaria. Comentatis in Libros de Anima Aristotelis. Contra Proclvm de Mvndi Aeternitate. Venice: 1535. V. 41; 43

John the Grammarian on the First Four Books of Aristole 'On Natural Ausculation'. Venice: 1535. V. 44

JOANNIDES, PAUL

The Drawings of Raphael with a Complete Catalogue. Oxford: 1983. V. 46

JOAO IV, KING OF PORTUGAL

Regimento da Forma Porque se ha de Fazer o Lancamento, e Cobranca das Decimas que os Tres Estados do Reyno Offerecerdo em Estas Vltimas Cortes, para a Desperza da Guerra. Lisbon: 1654. V. 41

JOAQUIN Murieta. The Brigand Chief of California. San Francisco: 1932. V. 38; 46

JOBE, JOSEPH

Extended Travels in Romantic America. Lausanne: 1966. V. 38

Extedned Travels in Romantic America. Switzerland: 1966. V. 44

Great Tapestries: The Web of History from the 12th to the 20th Century, by Verlet, Florisoone, Hoffmeister and Tabard. Lusanne: 1965. V. 40

JOBERT, LOUIS 1637-1719

The Knowledge of Medals. London: 1697. V. 39; 42

The Knowledge of Medals. London: 1715. V. 38; 45

La Science des Medailles, Nouvelles Edition Avec des Remarques Historiques et Critiques. Paris: 1739. V. 40

JOBERT, PAUL

Croquis de Guerre. 1916-1916. Paris: 1916. V. 43

JOBLOT, L.

Observations d'Histoire naturelle Faites avec le Microscope. Paris: 1754-55. V. 41

JOBSON, F. J.

Chapel and School Architecture, as Appropriate to the Buildings of Nonconformists . . . London: 1850. V. 38; 45

JOCELIN, SIMEON

The Chorister's Companion. New Haven: 1788. V. 45

JOCELYN, A.

Awards of Honour The Orders, Decorations, Medals and Awards of Great Britain and the Commonwealth from Edward III to Elizabeth II. London: 1956. V. 37

JOCELYN, ALICE

Mistrees Alice Jocelyn Her Letters. Chicago: 1903. V. 40; 41; 43

JOCELYN, ROBERT

Six Months with the Chinese Expedition; or, Leaves from a Soldier's Note-Book. London: 1841. V. 46

JOCELYN, STEPHEN PERRY

Mostly Alkali. Caldwell: 1953. V. 46

JOCK and Jerry. London: 1890. V. 39

JOCKNICK, SIDNEY

Early Days on the Western Slope of Colorado and Campfire Chats with Otto Mears the Pathfinder from 1870 to 1883. Denver: 1913. V. 37; 40; 43

JOCOSERIUS, WAHRMUND

Wol-Geschliffener Narren-Spiegel. Freystadt Berlin?: 1710? V. 40

JOE Beeler: in the Cradle of the Cattle Kingdom. N.P.: 1985. V. 42

JOE Miller's Jests; or, the Wits Vade-Mecum. London: 1754? V. 43
JOE Miller's Jests: or, the Wits Vade-Mecum. London: 1770. V. 37

JOEL, L.

Catalogue of a Major Collection of Rare Australiana, Pacific Voyages and Other Books. Sold by Auction on 29th, 30th & 31st August, 1988. Collingwood: 1988. V. 45

JOERG, JOHANN CHRISTIAN GOTTFRIED

Ueber Das Gebaerorgan des Menschen und der Saeugthiere im Schwangern und nicht-schwangern Zustande. Leipzig: 1808. V. 45

JOESTING, EDWARD

The Islands of Hawaii. N.P.: 1954. V. 41

The Islands of Hawaii. Honolulu: 1958. V. 44

The Islands of Hawaii. N.P.: 1958. V. 46

The Islands of Hawaii. Photography by Ansel Adams. (Honolulu): 1958. V. 37

JOHANNES DE CAPISTRANO, SAINT

Tractatus de Cupiditate. Cologne: 1842. V. 45

JOHANNES DE LAPIDE

Resolutorium Dubiorum Circa Celebrationem Missarum Occurrentium. Cologne: 1495. V. 43

JOHANNES DE SANCTO GEMINIANO

Opusculum de Quibusdam Materijs Predicabilibus de Operibus Sex Dieuorum Predicatum. Paris: 1512. V. 38; 44

JOHANNES DE TAMBACO 1288-1372

Consolatio Theologiae. Strassburg: 1479. V. 38

JOHANNES JACOBI

A Litil Boke of the Whiche Traytied and Reherced Many Gode Thinges Necessaries for the . . . Pestilence . . . Made by the . . . Bisshop of Arusiens . . . Manchester: 1910. V. 43

JOHANNSEN, ALBERT

The House of Beadle and Adams and Its Dime and Nickel Novels. Norman: 1950. V. 38; 39; 40; 44; 45; 46

The House of Beadle and Adams and Its Dime and Nickel Novels. London: 1950. V. 46

The House of Beadle and Adams and Its Dime Novels, the Story of a Vanished Literature. Norman: 1950/1962. V. 43

House of Beadle and Adams and Its Dime and Nickle Novels. Norman: 1950-62. V. 38

The House of Beadle and James and Its Dime and Nickel Novels. Norman: 1962. V. 39

Phiz: Illustrations from the Novels of Charles Dickens. Chciago: 1956. V. 41

JOHANNSON, C.

French Music Publishers' Catalogues of the Second Half of the Eighteenth Century. Stockholm: 1955. V. 39

JOHANSEN, HJALMAR

With Nansen in the North. Toronto: 1899. V. 44

JOHAS, MAURICE

Notes of an Art Collector. London: 1908. V. 37

JOHN Barnard and His Associates. Cambridge: 1927. V. 46

JOHN, BISHOP OF DURHAM

Historia Transubstantiantionis Papalis. London: 1675. V. 40

JOHN Brown and 'The Union Right or Wrong' Songster: Containing all the Celebrataed John Brown and Union Songs Which Have Become So Immensely Popular Throughout the Union. San Francisco: 1863. V. 38

THE JOHN Bull Magazine and Literary Recorder. London: 1824. V. 42

JOHN Cheap the Chapman's Library: the Scottish Chap Literature of Last Century, Classified. Glasgow: 1877. V. 42

JOHN CHECKLEY; or the Evolution of Religious Tolerance in Massachusetts Bay . . . 1719-1774. Boston: 1897. V. 43

JOHN, DENNYS

The Secrets of Angling 1613. London: 1883. V. 40

JOHN Elliott, the Reformed. An Old Sailor's Legacy. Boston: 1841. V. 43

JOHN Hayward 1904-1965: Some Memories. London: 1965. V. 40

JOHN MURRAY EXPEDITION, 1933-34.

Scientific Reports. London: 1935-67. V. 37; 38

JOHN, OF SALISBURY, BP. OF CHARTRES d.1180

Policraticus Contenta. De Nugis Curialiu(m). Paris: 1513. V. 37; 38; 45

Policraticus: sive De Nugis Curalium & Vestigiis Philosophorum Libri Octo. Lugduni Batavorum: 1595. V. 39

JOHN Paul Jones - Commemoration at Annapolis - April 24, 1906. Washington: 1907. V. 39

JOHN RYLANDS LIBRARY, MANCHESTER

Catalogue of a Selection of Mediaeval Manuscripts and Jewelled Book Covers Exhibited in the Main Library. Manchester: 1939. V. 40; 44

JOHN Stuart Mill, His Life and Works. Twelve Sketkches by Herbert Spencer, Henry Fawcett, Frederic Harrison, and other Distinguished Authors. New York: 1873. V. 37

JOHN Updike: In Memoriam. New York: 1977. V. 39

JOHN, W. D.

The Nantgarw Porcelain Album. Newport: 1975. V. 37; 39

Pontypool and Usk Japanned Wares. Newport: 1953. V. 42

Swansea Porcelain. Newport: 1958. V. 42

Swansea Porcelain. Newport: 1978. V. 37

William Billingsley, His Outstanding Achievements as an Artist and Porcelain Maker. Newport: 1968. V. 37; 38; 40

JOHNES, ARTHUR JAMES

Philological Proofs of the Original Unity and Recent Origin of the Human Race. London: 1843. V. 40

JOHNES, THOMAS

North of England and Scotland in MDCCIV. Edinburgh: 1818. V. 46

JOHNS, AYRESOME

Pattern of Terror. 1987. V. 42

JOHNS, C. H. W.

Assyrian Deeds and Documents Recording the Transfer of Property Including the So Called Private Contracts, Legal Decisions and Proclamations Preserved in the Kouyunjik Collections of the British Museum . . . Cambridge: 1898-1901. V. 40

Babylonian and Assyrian Laws, Contracts and Letters. New York: 1904. V. 44

JOHNS, CHARLES ALEXANDER

Monthly Gleanings from the Field and Garden. London: 1859. V. 42

JOHNS, E. B.

Camp Tavis and Its Part in the World War. New York: 1919. V. 44

JOHNS, GEORGE S.

Philip Henson, the Southern Union Spy. St. Louis: 1887. V. 44

JOHNS, HENRY T.

Life with the Forty-Ninth Massachusetts Volunteers. Pittsfield: 1864. V. 42

JOHNS, JASPER

Technics and Creativity II: Gemini G.E.L. New York: 1971. V. 38; 39

JOHNS, MAJOR

The naval and Military Heroes of Great Britain or Calendar of Victory Being a Record of British Valour and Conquest by Sea and Land on Every Day in the year from the Reign of William the Conqueror to the Battle of Inkermann. London: 1860. V. 38

JOHNS, ORRICK

Asphalt and Other Poems. New York: 1917. V. 37; 41; 42; 43; 44

JOHNS, RICHARD

Ascension, a Poem. London: 1836. V. 42

JOHNSON, A. E.

Brush Pen and Pencil. The Book of W. Heath Robinson. London: 1930. V. 43

The Russian Ballet. Boston & New York: 1913. V. 39

the Russian Ballet. Boston: 1913. V. 40

JOHNSON, A. H.

The History of the Worship Company of the Drapers of London . . . Oxford: 1914-22. V. 42

JOHNSON, ADAM R.

The Partisan Rangers of the Confederate States Army. Louisville: 1904. V. 37; 39; 42

JOHNSON, ALEXANDER

Relief from Accidental Death; or, Summary Directions, in Verse. London: 1789. V. 39

JOHNSON, ALEXANDER BRYAN

A Treatise on Language; of the Relation Words Bear to Things . . . New York: 1836. V. 45

JOHNSON, ALFRED

A Collection of Pictures Including Many American Vessels Painted by Antoine Roux and His Sons. Salem: 1925. V. 46

JOHNSON, ALFRED FORBES

A Catalogue of Engraved and Etched English Titlepages Down to the Death of William Faithorne, 1691. 1933. V. 45

A Catalogue of Engraved and Etched English Title-Pages Down to the Death of William Faithorne, 1691. London: 1933. V. 39

A Catalogue of Engraved and Etched English Title-pages Down to the Death of Wailliam Faithorne, 1691. London: 1934. V. 39; 40; 42; 46

A Catalogue of Engraved and Etched English Title-Pages Down to the Death of William Faithorne, 1691. Oxford: 1934. V. 42; 44

A Catalogue of Engraved and Etched English Titlepages Down to the Death of William Faithorne, 1691. 1934/for 1933. V. 43; 44

Decorative Initial Letters. London: 1931. V. 38; 40; 46

German Renaissance Title Borders. N.P.. V. 43

German Renaissance Title Borders. Oxford: 1929. V. 40

A History of the Old English Letter Foundries with Notes Historical and Bibliographical on the Rise and Progress of English Typography. London: 1952. V. 38

One Hundred Title-Pages 1500-1800. V. 46

One Hundred Title Pages 1500-1800. London: 1928. V. 39

One Hundred Title-Pages, 1500-1800. New York: 1928. V. 37; 38

Selected Essays on Books and Printing. Amsterdam: 1970. V. 37; 39; 41; 46

Selected Essays on Books and Printing. London: 1970. V. 39

Selected Essays on Books and Printing. Amsterdam: 1971. V. 39

Selected Essays on Books and Printing edited by P.H. Muir. Amsterdam: 1970 (1971). V. 37

JOHNSON, ALLEN

The Chronicles of America Series. New Haven: 1921. V. 37

Dictionary of American Biography. New York: 1953. V. 40; 41

JOHNSON, ALVIN

Johnson's New Natural History. New York: (1894). V. 37

Johnson's New Natural History. New York: (1994). V. 37

JOHNSON, ALVIN JEWETT

Johnson's New Illustrated (Steel Plate) Family Atlas . . . New York: 1860. V. 45

Johnson's New Illustrated (Steel Plate) Family Atlas, with Descriptions, Geographical, Statistical and Historical. New York: 1861. V. 45

Johnson's New Illustrated Family Atlas of the World. New York: 1862. V. 45

Johnson's New Illustrated (Steel Plate) Family Atlas, with Physical Geography . . . New York: 1863. V. 45

Johnson's New Illustrated (Steel Plate) Family Atlas, with Physical Geography . . . New York: 1864. V. 45

Johnson's New Illustrated Family Atlas of the World . . . New York: 1866. V. 45

Johnson's New Illustrated Family Atlas, with Physical Geography . . . New York: 1867. V. 45

Johnson's New Illustrated Family Atlas of the World . . . New York: 1868. V. 45

Johnson's New Illustrated Family Atlas of the World . . . New York: 1870. V. 45

JOHNSON, AMANDUS

The Swedish Settlements on the Delaware. 1911. V. 39; 41

The Swedish Settlements on the Delaware 1638-1664. Philadelphia: 1911. V. 38; 41; 44; 45

Swedish Contributions to American Freedom, 1776-1783. Philadelphia: 1953-57. V. 42

Swedish Contributions to American Freedom 1776-1783 . . . Philadelphia: 1953-57. V. 39; 40; 44

JOHNSON, ANDREW 1808-1875

Message of the President . . . Transmitting . . . From the State of Colorado and other Information Relating to the Admission of that State into the Union. Washington: 1866. V. 37

Trial of Andrew Johnson, President of the United States, Before the Senate of the United States, on Impeachment by the House of Representatives for High Crimes and Misdemeanors. Washington: 1868. V. 37; 38; 39; 43

JOHNSON, ANDREW, defendant 1808-1875

Supplement to the Congressional Globe: Containing the Proceedings of the Senate Sitting for the Trial of Andrew Johnson. Washington City: 1868. V. 40

JOHNSON, ANNA C.

The Iroquois; or, The Bright Side of Indian Character. New York: 1855. V. 37

JOHNSON, ANNA CUMMING

The Cottages of the Alps; or, Life and Manners in Switzerland. London: 1860. V. 46

JOHNSON, B. S.

Everyone Knows Somebody Who's Dead. London: 1973. V. 45

House Mother Normal. London: 1971. V. 45

Poems. London: 1964. V. 41

Poems Two. London: 1972. V. 41; 43

Statement Against Corpses - Stories. London: 1964. V. 45

Travelling People. Letchworth: 1963. V. 37; 40; 42

Travelling People. London: 1963. V. 38; 41; 45

Trawl. London: 1966. V. 45

JOHNSON, B. S. continued

The Unfortunates. London: 1969. V. 41; 43

JOHNSON, BARBARA

The Barbara Johnson Whaling Collection. New York: 1981-83. V. 38; 42

JOHNSON, BARRY

Flipper's Dismissal. London: 1980. V. 45

JOHNSON, BENJAMIN 1572-1637

The Works. London: prtd. by Richard: 1640. V. 37

The Works. With a Memoir of his Life and Writings by Barry Cornwall. A New Edition. London: 1838. V. 37

JOHNSON, Boswell and their Circle. Essays Presented to Lawrence Fitzroy Powell in Honour of His 84th Birthday. Oxford: 1965. V. 46

JOHNSON, BRADLEY T.

A Memoir of the Life and Public Serive of Joseph E. Johnston, Once the Quartermaster General of the Army of the United States, and a General in the Army of the Confederate States of America. Baltimore: 1891. V. 37; 38

JOHNSON, BURGES

More Necessary Nonsense. New York: 1931. V. 39

JOHNSON, C. P.

Hints to Collectors of Original Editions of the Works of William Makepeace Thackeray. London: 1885. V. 38

JOHNSON, C. PIERPOINT

British Wild Flowrs. London. V. 46

JOHNSON, CECIL

Notes from Below the Arctic Circle in the Letters of Cecil Johnson. 1944. V. 38

Notes From Below the Arctic Circle in the Letters of Cecil Johnson. San Francisco: 1944. V. 46

JOHNSON, CHARLES

Black Humor. Chicago: 1970. V. 46

British Poisonous Plants. London: 1856. V. 42

British Poisonous Plants. London: 1861. V. 42

Caelia; or, the Perjur'd Lover. London: 1733. V. 46

The Cobler of Preston. As It is acted at the Theatre-Royal in Dury-Lane, by His Majesty's Servants. London: 1716. V. 38

English Court Hand A.D. 1066 to 1500. Oxford: 1915. V. 37; 38; 40; 43; 44; 45

English Court Hand A.D. 1066-1500 Illustrated Chiefly from the Public Records. Oxford: 1915. V. 38

The Ferns of Great Britain. London: 1855-56. V. 38

The Force of Friendship. London: 1710. V. 38

A General History of the Pyrates. London: 1726. V. 38

A General History of the Pirates. Kensington: 1925-27. V. 45

A General History of the Pirates. Kensington: 1925/27. V. 42

A General History of the Lives and Adventures of the Most Famous Highwaymen, Murderers, Street-Robbers &c. from the Famous Sir John Falstaff in the Reign of K. Henry IV, 1399 to 1733. to which is added, A Genuine Account of the Voyages & Plunders... London: 1736. V. 38

A General History of the Lives and Adventures of the Most Famous Highwaymen, Murderers, Street-Robbers, &c... To which is added a Genuine Account of the Voyages and Plunders of the most Notorious Pyrates... London;: 1726. V. 37

The History of the Pirates, Containing the Lives of Those Noted Pirate Captains... and Their Several Crews. Norwich: 1814. V. 39

A History of the Lives and Actions of the most Famous Highwaymen, Stree-Robbers... to which is added a genuine account of the voyages and plunders of the most noted pirates. Edinburgh: 1814. V. 37

Middle Passage. New York: 1990. V. 46

The Sorcerer's Apprentice. Tales and Conjurations. New York: 1986. V. 46

The Tragedy of Medea... London: 1731. V. 38; 39; 43

The Victim. London: 1714. V. 38

The Village Opera, As It Is Acted at the Theatre-Royal... London: 1729. V. 45

JOHNSON, CHARLES BRITTEN 1788?-1835

Letters from the British Settlement in Pennsylvania. London: 1819. V. 39; 41; 42

Letters from the British Settlement in Pennsylvania. Philadelphia: 1819. V. 39; 41

JOHNSON, CHARLES F.

Angling in the Lakes of Northern Illinois. Chicago: 1896. V. 40

The Long Roll Being a Journal of the Civil War, As Set Down During the Years 1861-1863. East Aurora: 1911. V. 43

JOHNSON, CHARLES P.

Hints to Collectors of Original Editions of the Works of Charles Dickens. London: 1885. V. 39

Hints to Collectors of Original Editions of the Works of William Makepeace Thackeray. London: 1885. V. 39

JOHNSON, CHRISTOPHER TURNER

A Practical Essay on Cancer. Philadelphia: 1811. V. 45

JOHNSON, CLIFTON

The Parson's Devil. Springfield: 1927. V. 40

An Unredeemed Captive... Being the Story of Eunice Williams, Who at the Age of Seven Years Was Carried Away from Deerfield by the Indians in the Year 1704, and Who Lived Among the Indians in Canada as One of Them for the Rest of Her Life. Holyoke: 1897. V. 39

JOHNSON, CLIVE W.

With Memsaab on Safari. Los Angeles: 1956. V. 43

JOHNSON, CRISFIELD

Centennial History of Erie County, New York. Buffalo: 1876. V. 38

JOHNSON, CUTHBERT WILLIAM

The Farmer's Encyclopaedia and Dictionary of Rural Affairs... London: 1842. V. 46

On Fertilizers. London: 1839. V. 46

On Guano as a Fertilizer. London: 1843. V. 39

On Rendering Manures More Portable and Applicable by the Drill. London: 1841. V. 39

JOHNSON, DANIEL

Sketches of Indian Field Sports... London: 1827. V. 37; 45

JOHNSON, DAVID E.

A History of Middle new River Settlements and Continguous Territory. Huntington: 1906. V. 38

JOHNSON, E. PAULINE

The White Wampum. London: 1895. V. 43

JOHNSON, EDMUND C.

Tangible Typography: or, How the Blind Read. London: 1853. V. 38

JOHNSON, EDWARD

The Domestic Practice of Hydropathy. New York: 1849. V. 39

A History of New-England. London: 1654. V. 42; 44

Wonder-Working Providence of Sions Saviour in New England. Andover: 1867. V. 39

JOHNSON, EDWARD JOHN

Description of the Coast of Northumberland, from Sunderland Point to Warnham Flats... London: 1781. V. 42

Description of the Coast of Horthumberland, From Sunderland Point to Warnham Flats. London: 1819. V. 39; 42; 44

JOHNSON, EDWIN

The Navigation of the Lakes and Navigable Communications Therefrom to the Seaboard, and to the Mississippi River, and Relation of the Former to the Lines of Railway Leading to the Pacific. Hartford: 1866. V. 37

JOHNSON, EDWIN F.

Railroad to the Pacific. Northern Route. New York: 1854. V. 40; 41; 43

JOHNSON, F. C.

The Historical Record. A Quarterly Devoted Principally to the Early History of the Wyoming valley and Contiguous Territory with Notes and Queries Biographical, Antiquarian, Genealogical. Wilkes-Barre: 1896-1908. V. 39; 41

The Historical Record. A Quarterly Publication Devoted Principally to the Early History of the Wyoming Valley and Contiguous Territory with Notes and Queries Biographical, Antiquarian, Genealogical. Wilkes-Barre: 1896-1908. V. 39

JOHNSON, F. H.

Every Man His Own Guide at Niagaara Falls... Rochester: 1852. V. 38

Guide to Niagara Falls and Its Scenery, Including All the Points of Ineterest Both on the American and Canadian Side. Philadelphia: 1863. V. 43

Guide to Niagara Falls and Its Scenery, Including All the Poings of Interest Both of the American and Canadian Side... New York: 1868. V. 41; 46

JOHNSON, FOSTER MACY

A Backward Glance. 1975. V. 37

JOHNSON, FRANCIS

A Dictionary, Persian, Arabic and English. London: 1852. V. 46

JOHNSON, FRANCIS W.

A History of Texas and Texans, by... a Leader in the Texas Revolution. Chicago: 1914. V. 37

JOHNSON, FRANK M.

Forest, Lake and River: the Fishes of New England and Eastern Canada. Boston: 1902. V. 39

JOHNSON, FRIDOLF

Nasty Nancy and Her Cat. New York: 1962. V. 37; 38; 41

JOHNSON, G. W.

A History of English Gardening. London: 1829. V. 43

JOHNSON, GEORGE

Johnson's Graphic Statistics. Ottawa: 1887. V. 43

JOHNSON, GEORGIA DOUGLAS

An Autumn Love Cycle. New York: 1928. V. 46

JOHNSON, GUY B.

John Henry. Tracking Down a Negro Legend. Chapel Hill: 1929. V. 38; 39; 40

JOHNSON, H. H.

British Central Africa, Territories Under British Influence North of the Zambez. London: 1897. V. 37

JOHNSON, H. U.

From Dixie to Canada. Orwell: 1896. V. 41

JOHNSON, HANNIBAL AUGUSTUS

The Sword of Honor. A Story of the Civil War. Hallowell: 1906. V. 42

JOHNSON, HARRISON

Johnson's History of Nebraska. Omaha: 1880. V. 38

JOHNSON, HARRY

Liberia. London: 1906. V. 38

JOHNSON, HENRY LEWIS

Gutenberg and the Book of Books with Bibliographical Notes, Reproductions of Specimen Pages and a List of Known Copies . . . New York: 1932. V. 37; 44

JOHNSON, HERBERT CLARK

Poems from Flat Creek. Francistown: 1943. V. 46

JOHNSON, HONOR

Herbal: Poems. Woodside: 1980. V. 37; 45

JOHNSON, HOWARD F.

The Treatment of Incurable Diseases. London: 1851. V. 45

JOHNSON, J. fl. 1832

An Historical and Descriptive Account of the Island of Antigua. London: 1832. V. 43

Instruction in the Mosaic Religion. Philadelphia: 1830. V. 41

JOHNSON, J. NEELY

Annual Message of the Governor of the State of California. Sacramento: 1857. V. 37; 39

JOHNSON, JACK

Jack Johnson - In the Ring - and Out. 1927. V. 45

Jack Johnson - in the Ring - and Out. Chicago: 1927. V. 39; 45

JOHNSON, JAMES 1777-1845

Change of Air, or the Pursuit of Health . . . London: 1831. V. 39; 40; 41; 44; 45; 46

Change of Air, or, the Pursuit of Health . . . (with) The Recess or Autumnal Relaxation in the Highlands and Lowlands. London: 1831, 1834. V. 39

The Influence of Tropical Climates on European Constitutions . . . New York: 1826. V. 45; 46

Nuts to Crack. Droll Stories of Droll Folks. London: 1860. V. 43

The Oriental Voyager; or Descriptive Sketches and Cursory Remarks on a Voyage to India and China in His Majesty's Ship Caroline, Performed in the Years 1803-04-05-06. London: 1807. V. 38; 41

The Patentee's Manual: Being a Treatise on the Law and Practice of letters Patent, Especially Intended for the Use of Patentees and Inventors. London: 1853. V. 43; 46

Pilgrimages to the Spas in Pursuit of Health and Recreation, with an Inquiry into the Comparative Merits of Different Mineral Waters. London: 1841. V. 41

The Recess, or Autumnal Relaxation in the Highlands and Lowlands. London: 1834. V. 40

A Tour in Ireland with Meditations and Reflections. London: 1844. V. 39

JOHNSON, JAMES GIBSON

Southern Fiction Prior to 1860. Charlottesville: 1909. V. 37

JOHNSON, JAMES SYDNEY

The Persian Garden. San Francisco: 1929. V. 42

The Press of the Renaissance in Italy. 1927. V. 38

JOHNSON, JAMES WELDON

Along This Way: the Autobiography of . . . New York: 1933. V. 42

The Autobiography of an Ex-coloured Man. New York: 1927. V. 44

The Book of American Negro Poetry . . . New York: 1922. V. 43

The Book of American Negro Spirituals. New York: 1925. V. 43

Fifty Years and Other Poems. Boston: 1917. V. 37

God's Trombones. New York: 1927. V. 37; 38; 44; 46

Saint Peter Relates an Incident of the Resurrection Day. New York: 1930. V. 37; 39; 43; 44

Saint Peter Relates an Incident. New York: 1935. V. 44

JOHNSON, JOHN 1777-1848

An Abridgment of Johnson's Typographia, or the Printers' Instructor. Boston: 1828. V. 39

The Defense of Charleston Harbor, Including Fort Sumter and Adjacent Islands 1863-1865. Charleston: 1890. V. 42

Print and Privilege at Oxford to the Year 1700. Oxford: 1946. V. 41

Reliques of Ancient English Architecture. London. V. 40; 41

Typographia. London: 1824. V. 39; 42

Typographia, or the Printers' Instructor. London: 1824. V. 37; 38; 39; 40; 41; 44; 45; 46

JOHNSON, JOHN, BART 1742-1830

Orderly Book of . . . During the Oriskany Campaign, 1776-1777, Annotated by William L. Stone . . . Albany: 1882. V. 39; 42

JOHNSON, JOHN JAY

Directions for Using the Patent Excelsior Tanning Process. West Springfield: 1866. V. 42

JOHNSON, JOHN LIPSCOMB

Autobiographical Notes . . . (Aug. 12 1835 - March 2 1915). Boulder: 1958. V. 42; 43

JOHNSON, JOHN, Lt. Col.

A Journey from India to England, through Persia, Georgia, Russia, Poland and Prussia in the Year 1817. London: 1818. V. 41; 42; 45

JOHNSON, JOSEPH

Traditions and Reminiscences Chiefly of the American Revolution in the South. Charleston: 1851. V. 41; 45; 46

JOHNSON, JOYCE

Minor Characters. Boston: 1983. V. 45

JOHNSON, KENNETH M.

Famous California Trials. Los Angeles: 1961-75. V. 46

Jose Yves Limantour v. the United States. Los Angeles: 1961. V. 38; 42

San Francisco As It Is: Gleanings from the Picayune. Georgetown: 1964. V. 42

The Sting of the Wasp. San Francisco: 1967. V. 37; 46

JOHNSON, L.

The Book of Specimens of Plain and Fancy Printing Types, Borders, Cuts, Rules &c. manufactured at L. Johnson & Company's Foundry. Philadelphia: 1865. V. 46

An Elementary Arithmetic, Designed for Beginners. Raleigh, NC: 1864. V. 37

JOHNSON, LAURA W.

Eight Hundred Miles in an Ambulance. Philadelphia: 1889. V. 38

JOHNSON, LAURENCE

A Manual of the Medical Botany of North America. New York: 1884. V. 41; 42

JOHNSON, LESLIE L.

Notes on US Cavalry 1865-1890. Little Rock: 1960. V. 45

JOHNSON, LIONEL 1867-1902

The Art of Thomas Hardy. London: 1894. V. 40; 46

Ireland, With Other Poems. London: 1897. V. 37; 38; 40; 41

Poems by Lionel Johnson. Boston: 1895. V. 37; 38

Poems. London: 1895. V. 37; 41; 43

Poetry and Ireland. Dundrum: 1908. V. 41

Post Liminium: Essays and Critical Papers by Lionel Johnson. London: 1911. V. 38; 41

The Religious Poems of Lionel Johnson. London: 1916. V. 37; 38; 41; 46

Selected Letters. Edinburgh: 1988. V. 46

Sir Walter Raleigh in the Tower. Winchester: 1885. V. 41

Twenty One Poems by Lionel Johnson. 1904. V. 42

Twenty One Poems Written by Lionel Johnson: Selected By William Butler Yeats. Dundrum: 1904. V. 41

JOHNSON, LYNDON BAINES

No Retreat from Tomorrow: President Johnson's 1967 Messages to the Congress. Washington: 1967. V. 39

The Vantage Point. New York: 1971. V. 39; 44

JOHNSON, M. E.

Seashore Animals of the Pacific Coast. New York: 1927. V. 45

JOHNSON, MARY

Madam Johnson's Present; or, Every Young Woman's Companion . . . London: 1769. V. 42

JOHNSON, MATTHEW

America Pictorially Described. London: 1882. V. 43

JOHNSON, MELVIN

The Little Bombardier and Pocket Gunner. London: 1801. V. 38

JOHNSON, MERLE

American First Editions. New York: 1929. V. 45

American First Editions. New York: 1932. V. 45

American First Editions. New York: 1936. V. 38; 41; 43; 46

American First Editions Revised and Enlarged by Jacob Blanck. New York: 1949. V. 41

American First Editions, Revised and Englarged by Jacob Blanck. Waltham: 1965. V. 41

American First Editions. Waltham: 1969. V. 37; 43

A Bibliography of the Work of Mark Twain. New York: 1910. V. 38; 43; 46

A Bibliography of the Works of Mark Twain. New York: 1935. V. 40; 43; 44; 46

The Devil in Search of a Wife. New York: 1908. V. 43

High Spots of American Literature. New York: 1929. V. 38; 39; 40; 41; 42; 44; 45; 46

You Know These Lines . . . A Bibliography of the Most Quoted American Poems. New York: 1935. V. 46

JOHNSON, NORA

The World of Henry Orient. New York: 1963. V. 40; 46

JOHNSON, OVERTON

Route Across the Rocky Mountains, With a Description of Oregon and California. Lafayette: 1846. V. 37; 40; 41; 42

JOHNSON, PETER

The Nasmyth Family of Painters. Leigh-on Sea: 1977. V. 39

JOHNSON, R. BYRON

Very Far West Indeed, a Few Rough Experiences on the North-West Pacific Coast. London: 1872. V. 37; 38; 42

JOHNSON, RAY

The Paper Snake. New York: 1965. V. 41

JOHNSON, REBEKAH BAINES

The Johnsons. N.P.,: 1956. V. 38

JOHNSON, RICHARD

An Address to the Inhabitants of the Colonies Established in New South Wales and Norfolk Island. London: 1794. V. 45

Aristarchus anti-Bentleianus. Nottingham: 1717. V. 38; 41

Choice Scraps, Historical and Geographica, Consisting of Pleasing Stories and Diverting Anecdotes. London: 1790. V. 45

Grammatical Commentaries . . . London: 1718. V. 45

Grammatical Commentaries. London: 1706. V. 38

The Hermit of the Forest, and the Wandering Infants. Hudson: 1804. V. 40

The History of North America. Lansingburgh: 1795. V. 40

The Picture Exhibition . . . Worcester: 1788. V. 43

JOHNSON, RICHARD W.

Manual of Arms for Sharps' Carbine and Colt's Navy Revolver. San Antonio: 1860. V. 40

JOHNSON, RISSITER

Campfire and Battle-Field. History of the Conflicts and Campaigns of the Great Civil War in the U.S. New York: 1897. V. 41

JOHNSON, ROBBINS, & CO.

Descriptive Catalogue of the American Seed Garden. Wethersfield: 1855. V. 38

JOHNSON, ROBERT

Adventures of Captain Robert Johnson, In the Northern Circars of India . . . London: 1808. V. 43

Nova Britannia. London: 1609. V. 38; 40; 44

The Paintings of Robert Johnson. Sydney: 1947. V. 41

JOHNSON, ROBERT G.

An Historical Account of the First Settlement of Salem, in West Jersey. Philadelphia: 1839. V. 37; 38; 41

JOHNSON, ROBERT J.

Specimens of Early French Architecture, Selected Chiefly from the Churches of the Ile de France. Newcastle: 1864. V. 40; 44

JOHNSON, ROBERT UNDERWOOD

Battles and Leaders of the Civil War. New York: 1956. V. 44

JOHNSON, ROBERT WALLACE

Friendly Cautions to the Heads of Families and Others . . . Philadelphia: 1804. V. 40; 41; 44; 45

JOHNSON, RONALD

The Aficionado's Southwestern Cooking. N.P.: 1968. V. 46

Assorted Jungles: Rousseau. San Francisco: 1966. V. 37; 42

A Line of Poetry, a Row of Trees. Highlands: 1964. V. 37

Reading 1, Reading 2. Urbana: 1968. V. 45

Three Conceret Poems. Urbana: 1968. V. 42

JOHNSON, ROSSITER

Little Classics. Childhood. Boston: 1875. V. 44

JOHNSON, RUTH

The Adventures of Boo and Sam. and The Return of Boo and Sam. Meriden: 1968/69. V. 44

Bookman's Holiday. Meriden: 1971. V. 37; 44

JOHNSON, SAMUEL 1709-1784

An Account of the Life of Mr. Richard Savage, Son of the Earl Rivers. London: 1744. V. 43

An Account of the Life of Dr. Samuel Johnson, From His Birth to His Eleventh Yeara, Written by Himself. London: 1804. V. 37

An Account of the Life of Dr. Samuel Johnson from His Birth to His Eleventh Year, Written by Himself. London: 1984. V. 40; 45

Additional Volume to the Works of Samuel Johnson, LL.D. London: 1792. V. 41; 42; 46

Anecdotes of the Late Samuel Johnson, During the Last Twenty Years of His Life. By Hester Lynch Piozzi. London: 1786. V. 37

The Beauties of Johnson. London: 1781, 1782. V. 40

The Beauties of Johnson. Dublin: 1782. V. 45

The Beauties of Samuel Johnson. London: 1787. V. 39; 40

The Beauties of Johnson. London: 1792. V. 38; 39; 40; 41; 43; 45; 46

The Beauties of Samuel Johnson. London: 1804. V. 46

The Beauties of Samuel Johnson, LL.D. London: 1828. V. 40

The Beauties of Johnson: Consisting of Maxims and Observations, Moral, Critical and Miscellaneous. London: 1781. V. 37

The Celebrated Letter from Samuel Johnson, LL.D. to Philip Dormer Stanhope, Earl of Chesterfield . . . Buffalo: 1927. V. 45; 46

Christian Morals . . . The Second Edition. With a life of the Author, by Samuel Johnson; and explanatory notes. London: 1756. V. 37

The Collected Works. London: 1818. V. 39; 40; 45

The Collected Works. London: 1824. V. 45

The Collected Works. Glasgow: 1825. V. 45

Debates in Parliament. London: 1811. V. 40; 41; 43; 44

A Diary of a Journey into North Wales. London: 1816. V. 37; 38; 39; 40; 42; 43; 45; 46

A Dictionary of the English Langauge. London. V. 46

A Dictionary of the English Langauge. London: 1755. V. 37; 40; 41; 42; 43; 45; 46

A Dictionary of the English Language. London: 1755-56. V. 38

A Dictionary of the English Language. London: 1755-84. V. 37

A Dictionary of the English Language . . . London: 1756. V. 46

A Dictionary of the English Language . . . London: 1760. V. 37; 38

A Dictionary of the English Language. London: 1765. V. 39; 40; 41

A Dictionary of the English Language. London: 1766. V. 38; 40; 41; 42; 43

A Dictionary of the English Language. Dublin: 1768. V. 39; 41

A Dictionary of the English Language. London: 1770. V. 37; 41; 43; 44; 46

A Dictionary of the English Language. London: 1773. V. 37; 38; 44; 45; 46

A Dictionary of the English Language. London: 1774. V. 39

Dictionary. Dublin: 1775. V. 37; 40; 41; 43; 46

A Dictionary of the English Language. London: 1778. V. 41; 42; 43

A Dictionary of the English Language. London: 1783. V. 37

A Dictionary of the English Language. London: 1784. V. 37; 38; 40; 44

A Dictionary of the English Language. London: 1785. V. 37; 38; 40; 41; 42; 45; 46

A Dictionary of the English Language. London: 1786. V. 37; 41; 43; 45; 46

A Dictionary of the English Language. London: 1792. V. 41; 43

A Dictionary of the English Language. Edinburgh: 1797. V. 45

A Dictionary of the English Language. Dublin: 1798. V. 37; 38; 41

JOHNSON, SAMUEL 1709-1784 continued

A Dictionary of the English Language. London: 1799. V. 39; 40; 41; 43; 45; 46

A Dictionary of the English Language. London: 1800. V. 41

A Dictionary of the English Language, in Miniature. London: 1805. V. 41

A Dictionary of the English Language. Philadelphia: 1805. V. 41; 44

A Dictionary of the English Language. London: 1806. V. 38; 41; 42; 46

A Dictionary of the English Language. Baltimore: 1810. V. 41

A Dictionary of the English Language. London: 1810. V. 45; 46

A Dictionary of the English Language . . . London: 1813. V. 41

A Dictionary of the English Language. London: 1815. V. 39

A Dictionary of the English Language. London: 1818. V. 42

A Dictionary of the English Language. Philadelphia: 1818. V. 45

A Dictionary of the English Language. Philadelphia: 1818-19. V. 40

A Dictionary of the English Language in Miniature. London: 1819. V. 40

A Dictionary of the English Language. Philadelphia: 1819. V. 38

A Dictionary of the English Language. London: 1820. V. 39; 40; 46

A Dictionary of the English Language. London: 1822. V. 40

A Dictionary of the English Language. London: 1824. V. 40

A Dictionary of the English Language. London: 1827. V. 38; 39; 40; 41

Johnson's English Dictionary, as Improved by Todd and Abridged by Chalmers, with Walker's Pronouncing Dictionary . . . Boston: 1828. V. 39

A Dictionary of the English Language. London: 1828. V. 46

Johnson's Pocket Dictionary of the English Language . . . London: 1856? V. 42

A Dictionary of the English Language. London: 1872. V. 45; 46

A Dictionary of the English Language. 1979. V. 37

A Dictionary of the English Language. London: 1979. V. 39

A Dictionary of the English Language. London: 1990. V. 46

Dinarbas: a Tale. London: 1792. V. 46

Dr. Johnson's Table Talk. London: 1798. V. 37; 39; 41; 43; 45; 46

Dr. Johnson's Table-Talk. London: 1807. V. 37; 38; 41

Table Talk. Boston: 1809. V. 46

The Table Talk . . . London: 1818. V. 40

Dr. Johnson & Mrs. Thrale: including Mrs. Thrale's Unpublised Journal of the Welsh Tour Made in 1774 and Much Hitherto Unpublished Journal of the Welsh Tour Made in 1774 and Much Hitherto Unpublished Correspondence of the Streatham . . . London: 1910. V. 37

An English and Hebrew Grammar, Being the First Short Rudiments of Those Two Languages, Taught Together. To which is added, A Synposis of all the Parts of Learning. London: 1771. V. 37

The False Alarm. London: 1770. V. 39; 41; 42; 46

Forty Four Letters. Chelsea: 1931. V. 44

The Fountains. London: 1927. V. 38; 40; 45

The Fountains: a Fairy Tale. 1984. V. 40; 45

The Fountains, a Fairy Tale. Brisbane: 1984. V. 37; 39; 40; 46

The Harleian Miscellany. London: 1744-46. V. 37

The History of Rasselas, Prince of Abyssinia. London: 1817. V. 42

The History of Rasselas, Prince of Abissinia. Philadelphia: 1850. V. 40

The History of Rasselas, Prince of Abissinia. Oxford: 1927. V. 40

Hurlothrumbo. London: 1729. V. 38; 39; 40; 42; 46

The Idler. London: 1761. V. 37; 38; 39; 40; 41; 45

The Idler. London: 1767. V. 38; 39; 40; 45; 46

The Idler. London: 1783. V. 43; 46

The Idler. Newburyport: 1803. V. 46

The Idler, the first collected edition. Dublin: 1762. V. 37

Irene. Dublin: 1749. V. 37; 38; 41

Irene. London: 1749. V. 38; 40; 43; 46

Irene: a Tragedy. London: 1794. V. 40

Johnson and Queeney. London: 1932. V. 40

Johnsoniana. London: 1820. V. 45

Johnsoniana; or, Supplement to Boswell . . . London: 1836. V. 40; 46

Johnsoniana: a Collection of Miscellaneous Anecdotes and Sayings . . . London: 1845. V. 41

Johnson's English Dictionary: To Which is annexed The Pronunciation . . . Glasgow: 1809. V. 43

A Journey to the Western Islands of Scotland. Dublin: 1775. V. 37; 38; 39; 40; 41; 43; 44; 45; 46

A Journey to the Western Island Of Scotland. London: 1775. V. 39

A Journey to the Western Island of Scotland. London: 1775. V. 37; 38; 39; 40; 41; 42; 43; 44; 45; 46

A Journey to the Western Islands of Scotland. London: 1785. V. 40

A Journey to the Western Islands of Scotland. London: 1791. V. 39; 40; 44; 46

A Journey to the Western Islands of Scotland. Edinburgh: 1792. V. 39

A Journey to the Western Islands of Scotland. Edinburgh: 1798. V. 37

A Journey to the Western Islands of Scotland. A New Edition. Edinburgh/Glasgow: 1798. V. 37

A Journey to the Western Islands of Scotland. Baltimore: 1810. V. 38; 39; 40; 44

A Journey to the Western Islands of Scotland . . . Glasgow: 1817. V. 43

A Journey to the Western Islands of Scotland . . . Alnwick: 1819. V. 44

Julian's Arts to Undermine and Extirpate Christianity. London: 1689. V. 44

The Letters of Samuel Johnson. New York: 1892. V. 37; 39; 40; 44; 45

Letters to and From the Late Samuel Johnson, LL.D. Dublin: 1788. V. 38; 40; 41; 46

Letters from the Late Samuel Johnson, LL.D. To Which are Added Some Poems Never Before Printed. London: 1788. V. 41

Letters to and From the Late Samuel Johnson. London: 1788. V. 37; 38; 39; 40; 41; 43; 45; 46

The Letters of Samuel Johnson . . . Oxford: 1892. V. 39

The Letters of Samuel Johnson with Mrs. Thrale's Genuine Letters to Him. 1952. V. 40

The Letters of Samuel Johnson with Mrs. Thrale's Genuine Letters to Him. London: 1952. V. 44

The Letters of Samuel Johnson with Mrs. Thrale's Genuine Letters to Him. Oxford: 1952. V. 42; 43; 44

Letters. Collected and Edited by George Birkbeck Hill. London: 1982. V. 38

The Letters of Samuel Johnson with Mrs. Thrale's Genuine Letters to Him. Oxford: 1984. V. 38; 39

The Life of Mr. Richard Savage Son of the Earl Rivers. London: 1777. V. 42; 46

The Life of Mr. Richard Savage, Son of the Earl Rivers . . . To which are added, the Lives of Sir Francis Drake and Admiral Blake. London: 1769. V. 38

The Life of Samuel Johnson, LL.D. with critical observations on his works. London/Edinburgh: 1795. V. 37

The Lives of the English Poets. Dublin: 1779. V. 37; 38

Lives of the English Poets. (1779-1781). V. 37

Lives of The Most Eminent English Poets, with Prefaces, Biographical & Critical to the Works of the English Poets, etc. London: 1779-1781. V. 37

The Lives of the English Poets. Dublin: 1779-81. V. 37; 38; 39; 41; 42

The Lives of the Most Eiminent English Poets. London: 1781. V. 37; 38; 39; 40; 41; 42; 43; 44; 45; 46

The Lives of the Most Eminent English Poets . . . London: 1781. V. 43

The Lives of the Most Eminent English Poets. London: 1783. V. 37; 38; 39; 40

The Lives of the Most Eminent English Poets, with Critical Observations On Their Works . . . London: 1790. V. 42

The Lives of the Most Eiminent English Poets . . . London: 1790-91. V. 38; 41; 42; 43; 45; 46

The Lives of the English Poets. London: 1794. V. 39

The Lives of the Most Eminent English Poets. London: 1794. V. 38; 41; 43

Johnson's Lives of the English Poets, Abridged . . . London: 1797. V. 42

The Lives of the Most Eminent English Poets. Philadelphia: 1803. V. 41

The Lives of the Most Eminent English Poets . . . London: 1806. V. 41

The Lives of the Most Eminent English Poets. Charlestown: 1810. V. 39

The Lives of the Most Eminent English Poets. London: 1820. V. 39; 40

The Lives of the Most Eminent English Poets. London: 1821. V. 40; 43

The Lives of the Most Eminent English Poets with Critical Observations on Their Work. Halifax: 1836. V. 45

Lives of the Most Eminent English Poets. London: 1854. V. 37

Lives of the Most Eminent English Poets. London: 1854. V. 40

London: a Poem. London: 1738. V. 38

London: a Poem and the Vanity of Human Wishes. London: 1930. V. 39; 41; 42; 44; 46

Memoirs of Charles Frederick, King of Prussia. London: 1786. V. 38

Miscellaneous and Fugitive Pieces. Dublin: 1774. V. 38; 45

Miscellaneous and Fugitive Pieces. London: 1774. V. 37; 38; 40; 43

Johnsonian Miscellanies. London: 1897. V. 38

A Miscellany of Poems by Several Hands. Oxford: 1731. V. 41

Morceaux Choisis du Rambler, ou du Rodeur . . . Paris: 1785. V. 46

New Mode of Printing. Banbury: 1804. V. 43

The New London Letter Writer. London: 1948. V. 37; 42

The New London Letter Writer . . . Waltham: 1948. V. 44

Parliamentary Logick to which are subjoined Two Speeches and Other Pieces by William Gerard Hamilton. With an Appendix containing Considerations on the Corn Laws by Samuel Johnson never before printed. London: 1806. V. 37

A Pastoral Ballad in Four Parts. London: 1774. V. 40

The Plan of a Dictionary of the English Language. London: 1747. V. 41; 44; 45

The Plan of a Dictionary of the English Language. London: 1747-55. V. 45

The Poetical Works. Dublin: 1785. V. 37; 38; 39; 40; 45; 46

The Poetical Works. London: 1785. V. 37; 39; 40; 42; 43; 45; 46

The Poetical Works. London: 1789. V. 38; 41; 42; 46

Political Tracts. London: 1776. V. 37; 41; 42; 43

Political Tracts. Containing, The False Alarm. Falkland's Islands. The Patriot; and Taxation No Tyranny. Dublin: 1777. V. 45

Prayers and Meditations. Dublin: 1785. V. 39; 41; 42; 46

JOHNSON, SAMUEL 1709-1784 continued

Prayers and Meditations. London: 1785. V. 37; 38; 40; 41; 43

Prayers and Meditations. London: 1796. V. 41

Prayers and Meditations. London: 1807. V. 45

Prayers and Meditations. London: 1807. V. 40; 45

Prayers and Meditations. Oxford: 1973. V. 43

The Prefaces, Biographical and Critical, to the Works of the English Poets. London: 1779-81. V. 37; 38; 41; 45

Prefaces Biographical and Critical to the Works of the English Poets. London: 1779/81. V. 39; 40

The Prince of Abissinia. Dublin: 1759. V. 37; 38; 41; 45

The Prince of Abissinia. London: 1759. V. 37; 38; 39; 40; 42; 43; 44; 45; 46

The Prince of Abissinia. London: 1760. V. 41

The Prince of Abissinia. London: 1766. V. 37; 38; 39

The Prince of Abissinia. London: 1786. V. 37; 39; 46

The Prince of Abissinia, a Tale. London: 1796. V. 40

The Prince of Abissinia, a Tale. London: 1799. V. 40

The Prince of Abissinia. Oxford: 1816. V. 39

The Prince of Abissinia. Chiswick: 1817. V. 39

Proposals for the Publisher, 1774. Oxford: 1930. V. 44

The Rambler. London: 1752. V. 37; 38

The Rambler. London: 1753. V. 43

The Rambler. London: 1756. V. 41

The Rambler. London: 1763. V. 38; 41

The Rambler. London: 1771. V. 39; 45

The Rambler. (Edinburgh?): 1772. V. 37; 41

The Rambler. London: 1772. V. 45

The Rambler. London: 1784. V. 37; 40; 45

The Rambler. London: 1789. V. 41

The Rambler. London: 1791/92. V. 46

The Rambler. London: 1791-93. V. 43; 46

The Rambler. London: 1794. V. 38; 45

The Rambler. London: 1798. V. 46

The Rambler and The Idler. London: 1824. V. 40

Rasselas. London: 1786. V. 38; 40

Rasselas, Printed with Patent Types in a Manner Never Before Attempted. Banbury: 1804. V. 46

Rasselas. London: 1805. V. 38

Rasselas a Tale and Dinarbas a Tale. London: 1817. V. 46

Rasselas. London: 1818. V. 45

Rasselas. London: 1819. V. 41; 42; 45

Rasselas. With Engravings by A. Raimbach from Pictures by R. Smirke. London/Edinburgh: 1819. V. 37; 38

Rasselas: a Tale. (and) Dinarbas: a Tale. London: 1823. V. 44

Rasselas, Prince of Abissinia. (Birmingham: 1898). V. 37

Rasselas, Prince of Abissinia. Birmingham: 1898. V. 37; 41; 43

Sale Catalogue of Dr. Johnson's Library. Philadelphia: 1925. V. 39

Samuel Johnson's Prologue Spoken at the Opening of the Theatre in Drury-Lane in 1747 with Garrick's Epilogue. New York: 1902. V. 44

Select Essays. London: 1889. V. 40

A Selection from the Harleian Miscellany of Tracts, which principally regard English History; of which many are Referred to by Hume. London: 1793. V. 37

Sermons, on Different Subjects, Left for Publication by John Taylor, LL.D. London: 1800. V. 46

Sermons . . . Left for Publication by John Taylor, LL.D. Prebendary of Westminster. Ripon: 1835. V. 42

Taxation no Tyranny. London: 1775. V. 44; 45; 46

Thoughts on the Late Transactions Respecting Falkland's Islands. London: 1771. V. 38

The Vanity of Human Wishes. London: 1749. V. 38; 40; 44

Vanity of Human Wishes and Parnell's Hermit with Copious Notes and a Glossary . . . Serampore: 1858. V. 45

The Vanity of Human Wishes. 1984. V. 38

The Vanity of Human Wishes . . . Cambridge: 1984. V. 37; 46

The Vanity of Human Wishes. London: 1984. V. 39; 40

A Voyage to Abyssiania, by Father Jerome Lobo, a Portuguese Missionary. Containing the history, natural, civial & ecclesiastical, of that remote and unfrequented coutnry. To which . . . London: 1789. V. 37

A Voyage to Abyssinia. 1735. V. 37

A Voyage to Abyssinia, by Father Jerome Lobo, a Portuguese Missionary. Containing the history, natural, civil & Ecclesiastical, of that remote & unfrequented country. To which are added various other tracts by the same author . . . Stockdale: 1789. V. 37

The Witticisms, Anecdotes, Jests and Sayings of Dr. Samuel Johnson . . . London: 1793. V. 46

The Works of the English Poets. London: 1779-81. V. 38

The Works of the English Poets. London: 1790. V. 38

The Works. Boston: 109/11/12. V. 44

The Works of the English Poets. London: 1779. V. 46

The Works of the English Poets. London: 1779-81. V. 41; 45

The Works. London: 1787. V. 41; 43; 44

The Works of the English Poets. London: 1790. V. 40; 42

The Works. London: 1792. V. 38; 41

The Works of Samuel Johnson LL.D. A New Edition, in Six Volumes. With an Essay on His Life & Genius, by Arthur Murphy, Esq. Dublin: 1793. V. 37

The Works. London: 1796. V. 38

The Works. London: 1796-1811. V. 42

The Works, a new edition with an Essay on His Life and Genius by Arthur Murphy. London: 1806. V. 37

The Works.. Boston, New York: 1809/11/12. V. 40

The Works of . . . London: 1810. V. 37; 40

The Works. London: 1816. V. 37; 38

The Works. Dublin: 1816-17. V. 40

Works. London: 1823. V. 38

The Works. London: 1824. V. 40; 41; 42

The Works . . . with an Essay on His Life and Genius by Arthur Murphy. Glasgow: 1825. V. 46

The Works. With Murphy's Essay. London: 1825. V. 37; 38; 39

The Works. Oxford: 1825. V. 37; 38; 40; 41

The Works. Oxford & London: 1825. V. 38; 39; 41

The Works. New York: 1835. V. 41; 42; 43

Works. Troy: 1903. V. 39; 42

The Yale Editions of the Works. Volume One. Oxford: 1958. V. 45

The Yale Editions of the Works of Samuel Johnson: Volume One, Diaries, Prayers and Annals. New Haven: 1960. V. 39

Yale Edition of the Works of Samuel Johnson. Volume Two. 1963. V. 45

The Yale Editions of the Works of Samuel Johnson: Volume Two, The Idler and the Adventurer. New Haven: 1963. V. 39; 46

Yale Edition of the Works of Samuel Johnson. The Rambler. 1964. V. 45

The Works. New Haven: 1967-78. V. 46

Yale Edition of the Works of Samuel Johnson. Volumes 7 & 8. Johnson on Shakespeare. 1968. V. 45

The Yale Edition of the Works of Samuel Johnson: Volumes 7 and 8 Johnson on Shakspeare. New Haven: 1968. V. 39; 46

Yale Edition of the Works of Samuel Johnson. Volumes 3, 4 & 5. 1969. V. 45

The Yale Edition of the Works of Samuel Johnson. Volume 10, The Political Writings. New Haven: 1977. V. 39

The Yale Editions of the Works of Samuel Johnson. Volume One. 1986. V. 45

The Yale Edition of the Works of Samuel Johnson. Volume I: Diaries, Prayers and Annals. New Haven: 1958. V. 46

The Yale Edition of the Works of Samuel Johnson. Volume I, Diaries, Prayers and Annals. New Haven: 1986. V. 46

Yale Edition of the Works of Samuel Johnson. Volumes, III, IV and V. New Haven: 1969. V. 46

JOHNSON, SIDNEY SMITH

Texans Who Wore the Gray. Tyler: 1907. V. 37; 38; 44

JOHNSON, SOPHIA

The Friendless Orphan, an Affecting Narrative of the Trials and Afflictions of Sophia Johnson . . . New York: 1841. V. 45

The Friendless Orphan. New York: 1842. V. 39

The Friendless Orphan, an Affecting Narrative of the Trials and Afflictions of Sophia Johnson. Pittsburgh: 1842. V. 41

JOHNSON, STEPHEN

The Everlasting Punishment of the Ungodly . . . New London: 1786. V. 39

JOHNSON, SUSANNAH

A Narrative of the Captivity of Mrs. Johnson. Windsor: 1807. V. 40; 41

A Narrative of the Captivity of Mrs. Johnson, Containing an Account of Her Sufferings, During Four Years, with the Indians and French. New York: 1841. V. 39; 40; 44; 45

JOHNSON, T. BROADWOOD

Tramps Round the Mountains of the Moon, and Through the Back Gate of the Congo State. London: 1908. V. 45

JOHNSON, THEODORE T.

California and Oregon . . . Philadelphia: 1851. V. 42

Sights in the Gold Region. New York: 1849. V. 37; 38; 39; 40; 45; 46

Sights in the Gold Region, and Scenes by the Way. Dublin: 1850. V. 39

JOHNSON, THOMAS

Chippendale's Ornaments, and Interior Decorations, in the Old French Style. London: 1834. V. 45

JOHNSON, THOMAS B. d. 1840

The Complete Sportsman. London: 1817. V. 40

JOHNSON, THOMAS B. d. 1840 continued

The Game Keeper's Directory. London: 1851. V. 39

The Gamekeeper's Directory, and Complete Vermin Destroyer. London: 1838. V. 40

Hunting Directory. London: 1826. V. 42

The Shooter's Guide; or, Sportman's Companion . . . London: 1811. V. 41

The Shooter's Companion. London: 1823. V. 43

The Shooter's Guide; or, Complete Sportman's Companion: . . . London: 1824. V. 43

The Sportsman's Cycopedia. London: 1831. V. 40; 43; 44; 45

JOHNSON, THOMAS L.

A True Likeness. The Black South of Richard Samuel Roberts 1920-1936. Columbia & Chapel Hill: 1986. V. 41

JOHNSON, UNA F.

Ambroise Vollard, Editeur, 1867-1939: an Appreciation. New York: 1944. V. 46

JOHNSON, W. B.

History of the Progress and Present State of Animal Chemistry. London: 1803. V. 37

JOHNSON, W. M.

The Imperial Encyclopaedia; or Dictionary of the Sciences and Arts . . . London: 1811. V. 46

JOHNSON, W. R.

The History of England in Easy Verse. London: 1806. V. 45

Lilac Wind. Newark: 1983. V. 39; 42; 44; 46

Narcissus. Newark: 1990. V. 44; 46

JOHNSON, WALTER R.

A Report to the Navy Department of the United States, on American Coals Applicable to Steam Navigation and to Other Purposes. Washington: 1844. V. 45

JOHNSON, WARREN B.

From the Pacific to the Atlantic, Being an Account of a Journey from Eureka, Humboldt Co., California, to Webster, Worcester Co., Mass., with a Horse, Carriage, Cow and Dog. Webster: 1887. V. 42; 44; 45

JOHNSON, WILLIAM

The Imperial Cyclopaedia of Machinery Being a Series of Plans, sections and Elevations of Stationary, Marine and Locomotive Engines, Spinning Machinery, Grinding Mills, Tools &c. Glasgow: 1856. V. 38; 42

Lexicon Chymicum Obscuriorum Verborum et Rerum Hermeticarum, Tum Phrasium Paracelsicarum, in Scriptis Ejus . . . London: 1652-53. V. 46

Lexicon Chymicum cum Obscuriorum Verborum, et Rerum Hermeticarum . . . Frankfurt & Leipzig: 1678. V. 46

Lexicon Chymicum cum Obscuriorum Verborum, et Rerum Hermeticarum, Tum Phrasium Paracelsiorum . . . London: 1660. V. 38

The Papers of Sir William Johnson. Albany: 1921-1965. V. 39; 43

Poema Latinum Numismate Annuo Dignatum et in Curia Cantabrigiensi Recitatum Comitiis Maximis. Cambridge: 1844. V. 45

Relacao de Huma Batalha, Succedida No Campo de Lake Giorge Na America Septentrional, Entre as Tropas Inglezas Commandada Pelo Coronel Guilelmo . . . Lisbon: 1757. V. 38; 40

Remarks, Critical and Historical, on an Article in the Forty-Seventh number of the North American Review, Relating to Count Pulaski. Charaleston: 1825. V. 37

Sketches of the Life and Correspondence of Nathaniel Greene, Major General of the Armies of the United States in the War of the Revolution. Charleston: 1822. V. 44

JOHNSON, WILLIAM ERNEST 1858-1931

Logic. By W.E. Johnson, M.A . . . . Cambridge: 1921. V. 37

JOHNSON, WILLIAM SAMUEL

Glamourie. New York: and London: 1911. V. 43

JOHNSON, WILLIAM SAVAGE

An Account of a Summer's Pilgrimage. Meriden: 1972. V. 39; 46

JOHNSON, WILLIAM WICKLIFFE

Sketches of the Late Depression. Montreal: 1882. V. 40

JOHNSON, WILLIS F.

The History of Cuba. New York: 1920. V. 45

JOHNSONIANA: Being Anecdotes and Sayings . . . London: 1836. V. 37

JOHNSON'S England: an Account of the Life and Manners of His Age. Oxford: 1933. V. 37; 42

JOHNSTON, ABRAHAM ROBINSON

Marching with the Army of the West, 1846-1848. Glendale: 1936. V. 45

JOHNSTON, ALBERT SIDNEY

Lines on the Death of the Confederate Gen. Albert Sidney Johnston of Ky. N.P.. V. 39

Orders: No. 41. Head Quarters. Department of Texas. San Antonio: 1856. V. 45

JOHNSTON, ALEXANDER KEITH

Handy Royal Atlas of Modern Geography Exhibiting the Present Condition of Geographical Discovery and Research . . . London: 1885. V. 45

The Physical Atlas of Natural Phenomena. Edinburgh: 1850. V. 39

The Physical Atlas of Natural Phenomena. Edinburgh & London: 1850. V. 37; 38

The Physical Atlas of Natural Phenomena. London: 1856. V. 41

Royal Atlas of Modern Geography. Edinburgh: 1886. V. 41

Royal Atlas of Modern Geography. Edinburgh: 1895. V. 41

A School Atlas of Astronomy. Edinburgh & London: 1856. V. 43

JOHNSTON, C. GRANVILLE

Every Horse Owners' Training Manual and Horseman's Guide . . . San Francisco: 1871. V. 39

JOHNSTON, CHARLES b. 1768

Narrative of the Incidents Attending Capture, Detention and Ransom. New York: 1827. V. 37; 38; 39; 40; 41; 42; 45; 46

Sonnets, Original and Translated. London: 1823. V. 43

JOHNSTON, D. C.

The Aurora Borealis. Boston: 1831. V. 38

Scraps Nos. 1, 1849 New Series. Boston: 1849. V. 41

JOHNSTON, DAVID

The Uncomfortable Situation of the Blind, with the Means of Relief, Represented in a Sermon, Preached in the Tron Church, Edinburgh on Tuesday, May 15, 1793, at the Request of the Society for the Relief of the Indigent Blind. Edinburgh: 1793. V. 40

JOHNSTON, DAVID CLAYPOOL

Jeff Davis After the Fall of Fort Sumter 1861. Boston: 1863. V. 43

JOHNSTON, DAVID E.

A History of the Middle New River Settlements and Contiguous Territory. Huntington: 1906. V. 39; 46

JOHNSTON, DAVID EMMONS

The Story of a Confederate Boy in the Civil War . . . Portland: 1914. V. 44

JOHNSTON, EDWARD

A Carol and Other Rhymes. London: 1915. V. 43

Formal Penmanship Defined by the Thing. Berkeley: 1980. V. 44

Writing and Illuminating, and Lettering. London: 1906. V. 38; 41; 42

JOHNSTON, ELIZA GRIFFIN

Texas Wild Flowers. Austin: 1972. V. 44

Texas Wild Flowers. Austin: 1976. V. 38; 39; 41

JOHNSTON, ELIZABETH BRYANT

Original Portraits of Washington Including Statues, Monuments and Medals. Boston: 1882. V. 39

JOHNSTON, ELIZABETH L.

Recollections of a Georgia Loyalist. New York: 1901. V. 44; 45

JOHNSTON, ELLEN

Autobiography, Poems and Songs of Ellen Johnston. Glasgow: 1867. V. 46

JOHNSTON, FRANCES BENJAMIN

The Early Architecture of North Carolina. Chapel Hill: 1941. V. 39

The Early Architecture of North Carolina, a Pictorial Survey. Chapel Hill: 1947. V. 44

JOHNSTON, FREDERICK

Terracina Cloud. Verona: 1936. V. 42

JOHNSTON, G. HARVEY

Notes on the Ruddimans. London: 1887. V. 38

JOHNSTON, GEORGE

A Flora of Berwick-upon-Tweed. Edinburgh: 1829-31. V. 37

A History of British Sponges and Lithophytes. Edinburgh: 1842. V. 45

History of Cecil County, Md. and the Early Settlements Around the Head of the Chesapeake Bay and on the Delaware River, with Sketches of Some of the Old Families of Cecil County. Elkton: 1881. V. 39

A History of British Zoophytes. Edinburgh: 1838. V. 37

JOHNSTON, GEORGE, LT. COL.

Proceedings of a General Court Martial, Held at Chelsea Hospital . . . for the Trial of Lieut.-Col. Geo. Johnston Major 102nd REgiment, Late the New South Wales Corps on a Charge of Mutiny . . . London: 1811. V. 40

JOHNSTON, H. H.

The Kilima-Njaro Expedition. London: 1886. V. 40; 42

The River Congo from Its Mouth to Bolobo with a General Description of the Natural History and Anthropology of Its Western Basin. London: 1895. V. 46

JOHNSTON, H. P.

Memoir of Colonel Benjamin Tallmadge (Continental Light Dragoons 1776-1783). New York: 1904. V. 42

JOHNSTON, H. W.

Legends of Normandy . . . Paris: 1854. V. 42

JOHNSTON, HARRY

George Grenfell and the Congo. London: 1908. V. 38; 40; 45

Liberia. London: 1906. V. 38

The Nile Quest. A Record of the Exploration of the Nile and Its Basin. London: 1903. V. 43

JOHNSTON, HARRY H.

British Central Africa an Attempt to Give Some Account of a Portion of the Territories Under British Influence North of the Zambezi. London: 1897. V. 39; 43; 44; 46

British Central Africa. An Attempt to Give Some Account of a Portion of the Territories Under British Influence North of the Zambesi. New York: 1897. V. 41

George Grenfell and the Congo. London: 1908. V. 39; 41

The Nile Quest. London: 1903. V. 41

The Opening Up of Africa. London. V. 41

The Uganada Protectorate. London: 1902. V. 38; 40; 41; 46

The Uganda Protectorate. New York: 1904. V. 38; 41

JOHNSTON, HENRY P.

The Storming of Stony Point on the Hudson: Midnight July 15, 1779. New York: 1900/ V. 37

JOHNSTON, HENRY PHELPS

Memoir of Colonel Benjamin Tallmadge. New York: 1904. V. 46

JOHNSTON, ISAAC N.

Four Months in Libby, and the Campaign Against Atlanta. Cincinnati: 1893. V. 42

Four Months in Libby, and the Campaign Against Atlanta. Cincinnati: 1864. V. 37

JOHNSTON, ISABEL M.

The Jeweled Toad. Indianapolis: 1907. V. 45

JOHNSTON, J. P.

Twenty Years of Hus'Ling. Chicago: 1900. V. 42

JOHNSTON, JAMES

Reality Versus Romance in South Central Africa. London: 1893. V. 40; 42; 43; 44; 45

JOHNSTON, JAMES F. W.

The Chemistry of Common Life. Edinburgh & London: 1855. V. 42

Notes on North America. Edinburgh: 1851. V. 39; 45

Notes on North America: Agricultural, Economical and Social. Edinburgh & London: 1851. V. 39; 42

Notes on North America Agricultural, Economical, and Social. Boston/Edinburgh: 1851. V. 37

JOHNSTON, JENNIFER

The Captains and the Kings. London: 1972. V. 40

JOHNSTON, JOHN 1603-1675

Dendrographias, Sive Historiae Naturalis de Arboribus Et Fruticibus tam Nostri Quam Peregriniorbis. Francofurt ad Moenum: 1662. V. 38

Inscriptiones Historicae Regum Scotorum (in verse) . . . Amsteldami: 1602. V. 37; 42; 44

JOHNSTON, JOHN MOORE

Heterogenea, or Medley. Downpatrick: 1803. V. 38

JOHNSTON, JOSEPH E.

Narrative of Military Operations. New York: 1874. V. 37; 44

Reconnaissances of Routes from San Antonio to El Paso . . . also The Report of Captain R. B. Marcy's Route from Fort Smith to Santa Fe; and the Report of Lieut. J. H. Simpson of an Expedition into the Navajo Country. Washington: 1850. V. 41

Reports of the Secretary of War with Reconnaissances of Routes. Washington: 1850. V. 37; 38

Southern Boundary Line of Kansas; Report of Col. Johnston's Survey with the Accompanying Paper and Map. Washington: 1858. V. 40; 41

JOHNSTON, L. H.

The Duke of Lancaster's Own Yeomanry Cavalry, 23rd Co., I.Y. Bolton: 1902. V. 38

JOHNSTON-LAVIS, HENRY JAMES

Bibliography of the Geology and Eruptive Phenomena of the More Important Volcanoes of Southern Italy. London: 1918. V. 37; 42

The Eruption of Vesuvius in April, 1906. Dublin: 1909. V. 40

Monograph of the Earthquakes of Ischia. London & Naples: 1885. V. 38

JOHNSTON, LEWIS F. C.

Institutes of the Civil Law of Spain . . . London: 1825. V. 40

JOHNSTON, LEXANDER KEITH

The Physical Atlas . . . Edinburgh: 1849. V. 38

JOHNSTON, MARY

To Have and To Hold. Boston: 1900. V. 42

JOHNSTON, N. R.

Looking back from the Sunset Land; or, People Worth Knowing. Oakland: 1898. V. 46

JOHNSTON, NATHANIEL

The Excellency of Monarchical Government, Especially of the English Monarchy . . . London: 1686. V. 39; 46

JOHNSTON, PRISCILLA

The Mill Book. Ditchling: 1916. V. 37

JOHNSTON, PRISICLLA

The Mill Book. Ditchling: 1926. V. 43

JOHNSTON, RICHARD

Biomedical Results from Skylab. Washington: 1977. V. 45

Follow Me, 2nd Marine Division in WWII. New York: 1948. V. 39

JOHNSTON, RICHARD M.

Autobiography of Col. Richard Malcolm Johnston. Washington: 1901. V. 43; 46

JOHNSTON, RICHARD MALCOLM

Autobiography of Col. Richard Malcolm Johnston. Washington: 1900. V. 41

Pearce Amerson's Will. Chicago: 1898. V. 37

JOHNSTON, ROBERT

Travels through Part of the Russian Empire and the Country of Poland. London: 1815. V. 40

JOHNSTON, S. H. F.

The History of the Cameronians (Scottish Rifles), 1689-1946. Aldershot and London: 1949/57/61. V. 41

JOHNSTON, THEODORE

Sights in the Gold region and Scenes by the Way. New York: 1849. V. 45

JOHNSTON, WILLIAM

The Bibliography and Extant Portraits of Arthur Johnston, M.D. Aberdeen: 1895. V. 39

JOHNSTON, WILLIAM G.

Experiences of a Forty Niner. Pittsburgh: 1892. V. 37; 38; 40; 42; 43; 45

Life and Reminiscences from Birth to manhood of Wm. G. Johnston. Pittsburgh: 1901. V. 37

JOHNSTON, WILLIAM PRESTON

The Life of Gen. Albert Sidney Johnston. New York: 1878. V. 37; 38; 39; 42; 44

The Life of Gen. Albert Sidney Johnston. New York: 1880. V. 40

Seekers After God: Sonnets. Louisville: 1898. V. 44

JOHNSTONE, C. L.

Winter and Summer Excursions in Canada. London: 1893? V. 42

JOHNSTONE, CHARLES 1719?-1800?

Chrysal. London: 1760. V. 38; 40

Chrysal, or the Adventures of Cuinea . . . London: 1767. V. 38

Chrysal, or the Adventures of a Guinea . . . London: 1767-71. V. 43

Chrysal; or, the Adventures of a Guinea. London: 1771. V. 40

Chrysal, or the Adventures of a Guinea . . . London: 1771/68/67/67. V. 41

Chrysal. London: 1794. V. 37; 39

Chrysal. London: 1821. V. 38; 39; 43

Chrysal. London: 1822. V. 37; 38; 42

Chrystal . . . London: 1764. V. 42

The History of Arsaces, Prince of Betlis. London: 1774. V. 38; 41; 45

JOHNSTONE, CHARLES 1719?-1800? continued

The Reverie; or, a Flight to a Paradise of Fools. London: 1763. V. 37; 39; 40; 41; 42; 43; 45

JOHNSTONE, CHRISTIAN ISOBEL

The Edinburgh Tales. Edinburgh: 1845-46. V. 41

JOHNSTONE, DAVID LAWSON

The Brotherhood of the Coast. London: 1895. V. 46

JOHNSTONE, DR.

The Conspiracy. London: 1834. V. 45

JOHNSTONE, G. H.

Asiatic Magnolias in Culitvation. London: 1955. V. 37; 42; 44; 45; 46

JOHNSTONE, JAMES d.1798

Antiquitates Celto-Normannicae . . . the Chronicle of Man and the Isles, now first published complete from the original MSS. (and) Antiquitates Celto-Scandicae. Copenhagen: 1786. V. 37; 40; 46

Lodbrokar-Quida; or the Death-Song of Lodbrog. N.P.: Copenhagen: 1782. V. 38

The Norwegian Account of Haco's Expedition Against Scotland. Copenhagen: 1782. V. 37

JOHNSTONE, JAMES, CHEVALIER DE 1719-1800

Memoirs of the Rebellion in 1745 and 1746. London: 1820. V. 39

JOHNSTONE, JAMES JOHNSTONE, CHEVALIER DE

Memoirs of the Chevalier de Johnstone in three Volumes Translated from the Original French M.S. of the Chevalier. Aberdeen: 1870, 1871. V. 38

JOHNSTONE, JOHN 1797-1834

An Account of the Most Approved Mode of Draining Land. Edinburgh: 1797. V. 39; 42; 46

An Account of the Mode of Draining Land According to the System Practised by Mr. Joseph Elkington. London: 1801. V. 43

An Account of the Mode of Draining Land, According to the System Practised by Mr. Joseph Elkington. London: 1808. V. 42

A Systematic Treatise on the Theory and Practice of Draining Land. Edinburgh: 1834. V. 39

JOHNSTONE, WALTER

A Series of Letters, Descriptive of Prince Edward Island. Dumfries: 1822. V. 40

Travels in Prince Edward Island . . . Edinburgh: 1823. V. 40

JOHNSTONE, WILLIAM GROSART

The Nature-Printed British Seaweeds. 1859. V. 38; 39

The Nature Printed British Sea-Weeds: A History Accompanied by Figures and Dissections of the Algae of the British Isles. London: 1859. V. 43

The Nature-Printed Seaweeds. 1859/60. V. 43

The Nature Printed British Sea Weeds. London: 1859-60. V. 39; 41; 43; 46

JOHNSTON, WILLIAM PRESTON

The Life of General Albert Sidney Johnston. New York: 1879. V. 44

JOHONNOT, JACKSON

The Remarkable Adventures of . . . of Massachusetts, Who Served as a Soldier in the Western Army, in the Expedition Under Gen. Harmar, and St. Clair Containing an Account of His Captivity, Sufferings and Escape from the Kickapoo Indians. Greenfield: 1816. V. 37; 40; 46

JOINT Maps of the Northern Boundary of the United States, from the Lake of the Woods to the Summit of the Rocky Mountains. Washington: 1878. V. 40

JOINVILLE, JEAN DE

Histoire de Saint Louis, credo et lettre a Louis X. Paris: 1874. V. 37

The History of Saint Louis. 1937. V. 38

The History of Saint Louis by Jon, Lord of Joinville, Seneschal of Champagne. Montgomeryshire: 1937. V. 45

The History of Saint Louis. Newtown: 1937. V. 37; 38; 42; 43; 44; 45; 46

Memoirs . . . Written by Himself. London: 1807. V. 38; 40

JOKAI, MARUS

Timar's Two Worlds. Edinburgh & London: 1888. V. 37; 38

JOKELSON, PAUL

One Hundred of the Most Important Paper-Weights. (London: ca. 1966). V. 37

JOKER, WILHELM

Farbige Raume und Bauten. Stuttgart: 1929. V. 40

JOLAS, EUGENE

I Have Seen Monsters and Angels. Paris: 1983. V. 41

Transition Stories; Twenty-Three Stories from 'Transition'. New York: 1929. V. 39; 41

Vertical. A Yearbook for Romantic-Mystic Ascensions. New York. V. 41

Vertical: A Yearbook for Romantic Ascensions. New York: (1941). V. 37

Vertical: A Yearbook for Romantic-Mystic Acensions. New York: (1947). V. 37

JOLAS, MARIA

A James Joyce Yearbook. Paris: 1949. V. 46

JOLINE, ADRIAN H.

The Diversions of a Book-Lover. New York/London: 1903. V. 37

Meditations of an Autograph Collector. New York/London: 1902. V. 37

JOLLEY, JOHN

The Head Constable's-Assistant . . . London: 1726. V. 43

JOLLIFFE, JOHN

Belle Scott; or, Liberty Overthrown! Columbus: 1856. V. 43

JOLLIFFE, ROBERT A.

Faulkner at Nagano. Tokyo: 1956. V. 42

JOLLIVET, ADOLPHE

Documents Americains. Paris: 1845. V. 42

JOLLY, EMILY

Caste. London: 1857. V. 45

JOLY DE ST. VALIER

An Exposure, or, Examination of the Operations of the British Ministers, From the Commencement of the War Against the Americans, Till the Present Time. London: 1781. V. 40

JOLY DE ST. VALTER, LE SIEUR

Lettre Du . . . A Mr. Le Chevalier Yorke, Cedevant Ambassadeur d'Angleterre a La Haie, Suivie d'Observations et de Details Interressants Sur Les Evenements Que Cette Lettre a Produit. Londres: 1784. V. 44

JOLY, GUY 1607-1700

Memoires. (with) Memoires de Madame la Duchesse de Nemours. Geneva: i.e. Paris: 1751. V. 42

JOMBERT, CHARLES ANTOINE

Architecture Moderne, ou l'Art Bien Batir Pour Toutes Sortes de Personnes. Paris: 1764. V. 38; 42; 46

JONAH Judith Ruth. Greenbrae: 1984. V. 41

JONAS, EDWARD ASHER

Matthew Harris Jouett, Kentucky Portrait Painter (1787-1827). Louisville: 1938. V. 39; 42

JONCQUET, DIONYSIUS

Hortus Regius. Paris: 1665. V. 40

JONES, A.

The Art of Playing at Skittles; or, the Laws of Nine-Pins Displayed. London: 1773. V. 43; 46

JONES, A. H. M.

The Cities of the Eastern Roman Provinces. Oxford: 1937. V. 37

The Greek City from Alexander to Justinian. Oxford: 1940. V. 37; 40; 42; 44

JONES, ABNER D.

Illinois and the West. Boston: 1838. V. 37

JONES, ALEXANDER

Historical Sketch of the Electric Telegraph: Including Its Rise and Progress in the United States. New York: 1852. V. 38

JONES, AMANDA T.

A Prairie Idyl and Other Poems. Chicago: 1882. V. 45

JONES & CO.

Garden, Lawn, Cemetery and Park Adornments. Illustrated Catalog. Boston: 1893. V. 37

Jones' Views of the Seats, Mansions, Castles, etc. of Noblemen and Gentlemen in England, Wales, Scotland and Ireland. London: 1829-31. V. 37; 38; 39

Jones' Views of the Seats, Mansions, Castles &c. of Noblemen and Gentlemen in England, Wales, Scotland and Ireland, and Other Picturesque Scenery. London: 1829. V. 39

JONES & LAUGHLINS

Standard Steel Construction. Pittsburgh: 1898. V. 44

JONES, ANSON

Memoranda and Official Correspondence Relating to the Republic of Texas, Its History and Annexation. New York: 1859. V. 37; 38; 39; 41; 42

JONES, ANSON continued

Memoranda and Official Correspondence Relating to the Republic of Texas, Its History and Annexation. Chicago: 1966. V. 44

JONES, BARBARA

The Isle of Wight. London: 1950. V. 40

JONES, BENCE

The Life and Letters of Faraday. London: 1870. V. 40

JONES, BUEHRING H.

The Sunny Land; or, Prison Proe and Poetry. Baltimore: 1868. V. 38

JONES, C. BRYNER

Live Stock of the Farm. London: 1915-16. V. 39
Live Stock of the Farm. 1919. V. 45

JONES, C. HANDFIELD

Clinical Observations on Functional Nervous Disorders. Philadelphia: 1867. V. 38; 39

JONES, CHARLES A.

The Outlaw, and Other Poems. Cincinnati: 1835. V. 40

JONES, CHARLES C.

Antiquities of the Southern Indians, Particularly of the Georgia Tribes. New York: 1873. V. 37; 39; 44; 45
Biographical Sketches of the Delegates from Georgia to the Continental Congress. Boston: 1891. V. 43
Biographical Sketches of the Delegates from Georgia to the Continental Congress. Boston and New York: 1891. V. 41
The Dead Towns of Georgia. Savannah: 1878. V. 39; 46
Historical Sketch of Tomo-Chi-Chi, Mico of the Yamacraws. Albany: 1868. V. 37; 46
The Life and Services of Commodore Josiah Tattnall. Savannah: 1878. V. 37; 42; 43
Monumental Remains of Georgia. Savannah: 1861. V. 38; 40; 41; 43; 45
The Religious Instruction of the Negroes in the United States. Savannah: 1842. V. 42
Religious Instruction of the Negroes. An Address delivered before the General Assembly of the Presbyterian Church, at Augusta, Ga. December 10, 1861. Richmond: (1862). V. 37
Sergeant William Jasper. An Address Delivered Before the George Historical Society of Savannah, Georgia . . . Albany: 1876. V. 41; 42; 43; 44
The Siege of Savannah, in 1779, as Described in Two Contemporaneous Journals of French Officers in the Fleet of Count D'Estaing. Albany: 1874. V. 42
The Siege of Savannah in December, 1864, and the Confederate Operations in Georgia and . . . South Carolina During General Sherman's March from Atlanta to the Sea. New York: 1874. V. 43

JONES, CHARLES COLCOCK

Suggestions on the Religious Instruction of the Negroes in the Southern States. Philadelphia: 1847. V. 45

JONES, CHARLES E.

The Life and Confessions . . . Convicted of the Murder of Isaac Jackson, a Jew Peddler, at Springfield Masss. December 7, 1857, Together with an Appendix, Embracing His Trial and the Speeches of Counsel. Montpelier: 1860. V. 41

JONES, CHARLES EDGEWORTH

Georgia in the War 1861-1865. Atlanta: 1909. V. 42; 44

JONES, CHARLES H.

Appleton's Hand-Book of American Travel. New York: 1874. V. 38

JONES, CHRISTOPHER

The Monuments and Inscriptions of Tikal: The Carved Monuments. Philadelphia: 1982. V. 45

JONES, D. G.

The Lines of the Poet. Toronto: 1981. V. 39

JONES, DAN BURNE

The Prints of Rockwell Kent - a Catalogue Raisonne. Chicago: 1975. V. 39; 45

JONES, DANIEL W.

Forty Years Among the Indians. Salt Lake City: 1890. V. 37; 39; 40; 42; 46

JONES, DAVID 1895-1974

Anathemata. 1952. V. 43
The Anathemata. London: 1952. V. 37; 38; 40; 42; 43; 46
Aspidistras and Parlers. Ditching: 1927. V. 41
The Book of Jonah. 1979. V. 42
The Book of Jonah. London: 1979. V. 39; 41

A Compleat History of Europe; or, a View of the Affairs Thereof, Civil and Military . . . London: 1699. V. 39; 44
David Jones - 1895-1974. London: 1975. V. 41
Diary with Dominican Calendar and XII Wood-Engravings. Ditchling: 1928. V. 46
The Engravings of David Jones. London: 1981. V. 39; 40
Epoch and Artist. London: 1959. V. 37; 40; 42
The Fatigue. London: 1965. V. 41; 42; 43
In Parenthesis. London: 1937. V. 37; 41; 46
In Parenthesis. London: 1938. V. 45; 46
In Parenthesis. London: 1961. V. 42; 46
An Introduction to the Rime of the Ancient Mariner. 1972. V. 40; 45
An Introduction to the Rime of the Ancient Mariner. London: 1972. V. 42
Journal of Two Visits Made to Some Nations of Indians on the West Side of the River Ohio, in the Years 1772 and 1773 . . . New York: 1865. V. 38; 40; 45
Libellus Lapidum. Ditchling: 1924. V. 42
Libellus Lapidum. London: 1924. V. 40
The Life of James II, Late King of England. London: 1703. V. 45
Llfer Y Pregeteth-wr. Newtown: 1927. V. 44
On the Value of Annuities and Reversionary Payments with Numerous Tables. London: 1843. V. 38
The Secret History of White-Hall, from the Restoration of Charles II, Down to the Abdication of the Late K. James. London: 1697. V. 37; 39; 40; 42; 44; 46
A Simple Rosary Book. Ditchling, Sussex: 1927. V. 46
The Sleeping Lord. London: 1974. V. 37; 39; 43; 46
Thirteen Wood Engravings for the Book of Jonah. London: 1979. V. 37; 39
The Tribune's Visitation. London: 1967. V. 40
The Tribune's Visitation. London: 1969. V. 42; 43; 46
The Tribune's Visitation. Suffolk: 1969. V. 41
A True History of Laying on of Hands Upon Baptized Believers as Such . . . Burlington: 1805. V. 37

JONES, E.

A New Pocket Dictionary of the Welsh and English Languages . . . Caernarfon: 1840. V. 38

JONES, E. ALFRED

The Gold and Silver of Windsor Castle. London: 1911. V. 40

JONES, EBENEZER

Studies of Sensation and Event; Poems . . . London: 1843. V. 42
Studies of Sensation and Event: Poems . . . London: 1879. V. 41

JONES, EDWARD

The Bardic Museum of Primitive British Literature; and Other Admirable Rarities . . . London: 1802. V. 41
Index to Records Called the Originalia and The Memoranda on the Lord Treasurer's Remembrancer's Side of the Exchequer. London: 1793-95. V. 39; 40
Musical and Poetical Relicks of the Welsh Bards . . . London: 1794. V. 41

JONES, EDWARD T.

Jones's English System of Book-Keeping, by Single or Double Entry, In Which It is Impossible for an Error of the Most Trifling Amount to be Passed Unnoticed . . . New York: 1797. V. 39

JONES, ELECTA F.

Stockbridge, Past & Present, or Records of an Old Mission Station. Springfield: 1854. V. 39; 45

JONES, ERNEST

Life and Work of Sigmund Freud. New York: 1953-57. V. 44

JONES, EVAN R.

The Emigrant's Friend . . . London: 1881. V. 39; 42

JONES, FREDERIC CONINGESBY

The Attorney's New Pocket Book, and Conveyancer's Assistant. London: 1798. V. 40

JONES, FREDERIC WOOD

The Principles of Anatomy as Seen in the Hand. Baltimore: 1942. V. 42

JONES, G. D.

Life and Adventures in the South Pacific. New York: 1861. V. 37

JONES, GEORGE

Excursions to Cairo, Jerusalem, Damascus, and Balbec, from the United States Ship Delaware, During Her Recent Cruise. New York: 1836. V. 38; 39; 45
Sketches of Naval Life, with Notices of Men, Manners and Scenery, on the Shores of the Mediterranean. New Haven: 1829. V. 37

JONES, JOHN BEAUCHAMP 1810-1866

A Rebel War Clerk's Diary at the Confederate States Capital. Philadelphia: 1866. V. 37; 38; 39

JONES, JOHN G.

Mississippi Writers Talking. Jackson: 1982. V. 46

JONES, JOHN P.

Borger, The Little Oklahoma. Read It and Weep. N.P.. V. 45

JONES, JOHN PAUL

The Interesting Life, Travels, Voyages and Daring Engagements of the Celebrated Paul Jones . . . New York: 1823. V. 39

Life and Correspondence of John Paul Jones, Including His Narrative of the Campaign of the Liman, from Original Letters and Manuscripts . . . New York: 1830. V. 38; 42

Memoires de Paul Jones, Ou il Expose ses Principaux Services . . . Paris: 1798. V. 39

JONES, JOHN W.

Christ in the Camp, or Religion in Lee's Army. Richmond: 1887. V. 42

JONES, JOSEPH

Agricultural Resources of Georgia. Augusta: 1861. V. 44

Explorations of the Aboriginal Remains of Tennessee. Washington: 1876. V. 37

JONES, JOSEPH SEAWELL

A Defence of the Revolutionary History of the State of North Carolina from the Aspersions of Mr. Jefferson. Boston: 1834. V. 45

JONES, JUSTIN

The Nun of St. Ursula, or the Burning of the Convent. Boston: 1845. V. 40; 44; 45

JONES, KENNETH

Stone Soup. Portland: 1985. V. 41

JONES, L. T.

An Historical Journal of the British Campaign on the Continent, in the Year 1794. Birmingham: 1797. V. 38

JONES, LESLIE WEBBER

The Miniatures of the Manuscripts of Terence Prior to the 13th Century. Princeton: 1931. V. 43; 45; 46

The Script of Cologne from Hildebald to Hermann. Cambridge: 1932. V. 38; 40; 41

JONES, LIVINGSTON F.

Indian Vengeance. Boston: 1920. V. 44

JONES, MARGARET BELLE

Bastrop. Bastrop: 1936. V. 44; 45

JONES, MARY

Miscellanies in Prose and Verse. London: 1750. V. 42; 44

Miscellanies in Prose and Verse. Oxford: 1750. V. 37; 42

JONES, MICHAEL

Lieut. General Jones's Letter to the Councel of State, of a Great Victory Which Hath Pleased God to Give the Forces in the City of Dublin . . . London: 1649. V. 43

JONES, MRS.

The Housewife's Complete Guide, or an economical system of modern cookery, containing rudiments of cookery, directions how to roast and boil; how to make gravies, sauces, fricasees . . . Liverpool: (c. 1850). V. 37

JONES, MOTHER

Autobiography of Mother Jones. Chicago: 1925. V. 44

JONES, OWEN

The Book of Common Prayer. London: 1850. V. 37; 38; 41; 45; 46

Examples of Chinese Ornament Selected from Objects in the South Kensington Museum and Other Collections. London: 1867. V. 40; 44; 45; 46

The Fine Arts Courts in the Crystal Palace. London: 1854. V. 38

Flowers and Their Kindred Thoughts. London: 1848. V. 38; 44; 46

Fruits from the Garden and Field. London: 1850. V. 44; 46

The Grammar of Ornament. London: 1856. V. 38; 41; 42; 45; 46

The Grammar of Ornament. London: 1865. V. 39; 44

The Grammar of Ornament. London: 1868. V. 37; 38; 43; 45; 46

The Grammar of Ornament. London: 1910. V. 37; 41; 42; 43; 46

The Grammar of Ornament. London: 1874-76. V. 37

The History of Joseph and His Brethren. London: 1870. V. 42

Holy Matrimony. London: 1849. V. 42

Joseph and His Brethren. London: 1865. V. 41

One Thousand and One Initial Letters. London: 1864. V. 42; 45

Paradise and the Peri. London: 1860. V. 38

Plans, Elevations, sections and Details of the Alhambra; from Drawings Taken on the Spot in 1834 . . . and 1837. London: 1842. V. 40

Plans, Elevations, Sections and Details of the Alhambra: from Drawings Taken on the Spot. London: 1842-45. V. 39; 44

The Preacher. London: 1849. V. 41

Winged Thoughts. London: 1851. V. 42; 44; 46

JONES, OWEN GLYNN

Rock-Climbing in the English Lake District. London: 1897. V. 43

JONES, OWEN GLYNNE

Rock Climbing in the English Lake District. Keswick: 1900. V. 41; 44

JONES, PAUL

An Alphabet of Aviation. Philadlephia: 1928. V. 42

Flora Superba. London: 1971. V. 45; 46

Flora Magnifica. London: 1976. V. 43; 44; 46

JONES, PETER

A Collection of Chippeway and English Hymns. Toronto: 1840. V. 39

A Collection of Chippeway and English Hymns, for the Use of the Native Indians. New York: 1890. V. 39; 42

History of the Ojebway Indians. London: 1861. V. 42; 45

History of the Ojebway Indians, with Especial Reference to Their Conversion to Christianity . . . London: 1862? V. 38

Life and Journals of Kah-Ke-Wa-Quo-Na-By . . . Toronto: 1860. V. 42

Ojebway Hymns. Translated by Peter Jones. Toronto: 1877. V. 37

JONES, POMROY

Annals and Recollections of Oneida County. Rome: 1851. V. 40

JONES, R. E.

Greek and Cypriot Pottery . . . Athens: 1986. V. 40; 42; 44

JONES, R. HERVEY

To San Francisco and Back. London: 1878. V. 44

To San Francisco and Back. By a London Parson . . . London: (1878). V. 37

JONES, RHYS

Gorchestion Beirdd Cymru; Neu Flodau Godidowgrwydd Awen . . . Amwythig: 1773. V. 43

JONES, RICHARD d. 1855

Literary Remains, Consisting of Lectures and Tracts on Political Economy . . . London: 1859. V. 39; 42; 43

JONES, ROBERT

Artificial Fire-Works, Improved to the Modern Practice . . . London: 1766. V. 38

Artifical Fireworks, Improved to the Modern Practice, from the Minutest to the Highest Branches . . . London: 1776. V. 39

Orthopaedic Surgery of Injuries by Various Authors. London: 1921. V. 42

Orthopedic Surgery. New York: 1924. V. 42

JONES, ROWLAND

The Circles of Gomer, or, an Essay Towards an Investigation and Introduction of the English, as an Universal Language. London: 1771. V. 41; 43

JONES, RUPERT T.

Manual of the Natural History, Geology and Physics of Greenland, and the Neighbouring Regions . . . London: 1875. V. 40

JONES, S.

Fishes of the Laccadive Archipelago. Trivandrum: 1980. V. 37

JONES, S. I.

The Melange. London: 1831. V. 43

JONES, SAMUEL

The Siege of Charleston. New York: 1911. V. 39; 40; 42

JONES, SHIRLEY

Backgrounds. South Croydon: 1979. V. 39

Backgrounds. N.P.: 1980. V. 42

A Dark Side of the Sun. Croydon: 1985. V. 37; 39; 40

A Dark Side of the Sun. London: 1985. V. 38; 40; 44

Ello-Gast. London: 1986. V. 38

Ellor-Gast. Croydon: 1986. V. 39; 40

Ellor-Gast. 1986. V. 45

Five Flowers for My Father. 1990. V. 45

Five Flowers for My Father. London: 1990. V. 44

JONES, SHIRLEY continued

For Gladstone. N.P.: 1988. V. 41

For Gladstone. South Croydon: 1988. V. 46

Greek Dance. 1980. V. 45

Impressions. 1984. V. 45

Impressions. Croydon: 1984. V. 39

Impressions. N.P.: 1984. V. 38; 40

Nocturn for Wales. N.P.: 1981. V. 38

Nocturne for Wales: Five Stories with Three Early Poems. 1987. V. 40

Rhymes for Our Times. South Croydon: 1976. V. 39

The Same Sun. N.P.: 1978. V. 38; 44

Scop Hwilum Sang: Sometimes a Poet Sang. 1983. V. 40

Scop Hwilum Sang. London: 1983. V. 39; 40; 41

Scop Hwilum Sang. N.P.: 1983. V. 39; 40; 41; 44

Soft Ground, Hard Ground. 1989. V. 45

Soft Ground, Hard Ground. Croydon: 1989. V. 43; 45

Soft Ground, Hard Ground & A Little Light Relief with Shirley Jones. London: 1989. V. 41

Two Moons. London: 1991. V. 46

Windows: Five Poems and Five Etchings. 1977. V. 40

JONES, STEPHEN

A General Pronouncing and Explanatory Dictionary of the English Language, for the Use of Schools, Foreigners etc. on the Plan of Mr. Sheridan. London: 1813. V. 46

Rudiments of Reason; or, the Young Experimental Philosopher. London: 1805. V. 41

Sheridan Improved. London: 1798. V. 38

Sheridan Improved. London: 1800. V. 41

JONES, SYDNEY R.

Posters and Their Designers. London: 1924. V. 46

JONES, THEOPHILUS 1758-1812

A History of the County of Brecknock, in Two Volumes. Brecknock: 1805-09. V. 37; 41; 46

A History of the Couny of Brecknock. Brecknock: 1909-30. V. 42

JONES, THOMAS

A Diary of the Quorndon Hunt, From the Year 1791 to 1800, Inclusive. Derby: 1816. V. 39

The Gregynog Press: A Paper Read to the Double Crown Club on 7 April 1954. 1954. V. 37; 38

The Gregynog Press: a Paper Read to the Double Crown Club on 7 April 1954. London: 1954. V. 46

History of New York During the Revolutionary War and of the Leading Events in the Other Colonies. New York: 1879. V. 44

A Theme with Variations. Newtown: 1933. V. 37; 45

JONES, THOMAS AP CATESBY

The Proceedings of a Court-Martial on Commodore Thomas Ap Catesby Jones. Washington: 1851. V. 37; 39; 42

Taking Possession of Monterey . . . Washington: 1843. V. 39

JONES, THOMAS GOODE

Last Days of the Army of Northern Virginia. Richmond?: 1893. V. 44

JONES, THOMAS GWYNN

Detholiad o Ganiadau. Newtown: 1926. V. 37

JONES, THOMAS H.

Experience and Personal Narrative of Uncle Tom Jones; Who Was for Forty Years a Slave. New York: 1854. V. 40

The Experience of Thomas H. Jones, Who Was a Slave for Forty-Three Years. Boston: 1862. V. 42; 45

The Experience of Thomas H. Jones Who Was a Slave for Forty-Three Years. New Bedford: 1868. V. 46

JONES, THOMAS RYMER

A History of British Birds. London: 1843. V. 44

A History of British Fishes. London: 1859. V. 44

JONES, THOMAS WALLACE

The Last of the Buffalo. Cincinnati: 1909. V. 45

JONES, THOMAS WHARTON

The Principles and Practice of Opthalmic Medicine and Surgery. Philadelphia: 1863. V. 42

A Treatise on the Principles and Practice of Ophthalmic Medicine and Surgery. London: 1865. V. 44

JONES, TOM

The Last of the Buffalo, Comprising a History of the Buffalo Herd of the Flathead Reservation and an Account of the Great Round Up. With Illustrations. Cincinnati: 1909. V. 37

JONES, U. J.

History of the Early Settlement of the Juniata Valley. Philadelphia: 1856. V. 42

JONES' Views of Seats, Mansions, Castles &c. of Nobelmen adn Gentlmen of England, Scotland, Wales and Ireland and Other Picturesque Scenery with Historical Descriptions of the Mansions. London: 1829. V. 44; 45; 46

JONES, W. H. S.

Malaria and Greek History. Manchester: 1909. V. 37; 38; 41

JONES, W. HENRY

United States, Dept. of Interior, Before Hon. Sec. of the Interior, W. Henry Jonmes and Joseph S. Cutter VS. City of Petaluma. San Francisco: 1867. V. 37

JONES, WILFRED

How the Derrick Works. New York: 1930. V. 39

JONES, WILLIAM

Dissertations and Miscellaneous Pieces Relating to the History and Antiquities, the Arts, Sciences and Literature of Asia. London: 1792-96. V. 44

An Essay on the Church . . . Glocester: 1787. V. 45

An Essay on the Character of the Welsh as a Nation, in the Present Age. London: 1841. V. 42

A Grammar of the Persian Language. London: 1771. V. 43; 44; 45

A Grammar of the Persian Language. London: 1775. V. 37; 45

The History of the Life of Nader Shah, King of Persia . . . London: 1773. V. 40

Manava-Dherma-Sastra; or the Institutes of Menu . . . London: 1825. V. 44

Memoirs of the Life, Writings and Correspondence of Sir William Jones. V. 40

Memoirs of the Life, Studies, and Writings of the Right Revd. George Horne, D.D. Late Lord Bishop of Norwich. London: 1799. V. 41; 45

Observations in a Journey to Paris By Way of Flanders, In the Month of August 1776. London: 1777. V. 45

An Ode in Imitation of Alcaeus. Colophon: N.P.: London: ptd.: 1782. V. 41

Physiological disquisitions; or, Discourses on the Natural Philosophy of the Elements. London: 1781. V. 40

Poems, Consisting Chiefly of Translations from the Asiatick Languages. London: 1777. V. 40; 43

Poikilographia, or Various Specimens of Ornamental Penmanship, Comprising Twenty Two Different Alphabets. London: 1827. V. 39

Poikilographia. London: 1830. V. 46

Poikilographia. Or, Various Specimens of Ornamental Penmanship . . . London: 1846. V. 40

Poikilographia; or, The Various Specimens of Ornamental Penmanship . . . London: 1880. V. 38; 42; 44

A Popular Sketch of the Various Proposed Systems of Atmospheric Railway, Demonstrating the Applicability of the Mechanical Properties of the ATmosphere . . . London: 1845. V. 46

Remarks on the Proposed Breakwater at Cape Henlopen . . . To Which are Added the Report of the Board of Engineers, and Captain Bainbridge of the Navy . . . Philadelphia: 1826. V. 41; 44

Remarks on the Proposed Breakwater at Cape Henlopen . . . to Which are Added, the Report of Engineers and Captain Bainbridge of the Navy . . . Philadelphia: 1828. V. 41

Report . . . Reconnaissance of Northwestern Wyoming . . . Yellowstone Park Summer 1873. Washington: 1875. V. 37

A Treatise on the Art of Music. Colchester: 1784. V. 40

The Works. London: 1799. V. 38

The Works . . . London: 1807. V. 40

JONES, WILLIAM A.

Report Upon the Reconnaissance of Northwestern Wyoming Made in the Summer of 1873. Washington: 1874. V. 45

Report Upon the Reconnaissance of Northestern Wyoming Including Yellowstone National Park, Made in the Summer of 1873. Washington: 1875. V. 37; 40

JONES, WILLIAM D.

Army of Northern Virginia Memorial Volume. Richmond: 1880. V. 39

JONES, WILLIAM, of Nayland

An Essay on the First Principles of Natural Philosohy. Oxford: 1761. V. 46

An Essay on the First Principles of Natural Philosophy. Oxford: 1762. V. 40; 43

A Small Whole-Length of Dr. Priestley, from His Printed Works; or a Free Account (In Consequence of a Free Inquiry) of His Style, His Politics, His Feelings, His Logic, His Religion, His Philosophy. London: 1792. V. 39

JONSIUS, JOH 1624-1659.

De scriptoribus historiae philosophicae. Frankfurt: 1659. V. 37

JONSON, BEN 1573?-1637

The Alchemist. A Comedie. Acted in the year 1610. By The King's Maiesties Servants. London: 1616. V. 37

JONSON, BEN 1573?-1637 continued

Ben Jonson. Oxford: 1965-70. V. 44

A Croppe of Kisses, Selected Lyrics of Ben Jonson. Waltham St. Lawrence: 1937. V. 44; 46

A Croppe of Kisses. 1937. V. 38

The Dramatic Works of Ben Jonson and Beaumont & Fletcher. London: 1811. V. 39; 41; 45

Epicoene, or the Silent Woman. London: 1640. V. 46

Every Man In His Humour. London: 1755. V. 45

The Masque of Queens. London: 1930. V. 37; 38; 39; 40

Part of the King's Entertainment in Passing to His Coronation. London: 1616. V. 42

Songs by Ben Jonson. Hammersmith: 1906. V. 37; 39; 40; 43

Songs by Ben Jonson. London: 1906. V. 40; 41

His Volpone; or the Foxe. London: 1898. V. 37; 38; 39; 40; 44; 45; 46

Volpone. New York: 1898. V. 40; 41; 43

Volpone. Berlin: 1910. V. 37; 43

Volpone, or the Fox. Oxford: 1952. V. 46

The Workes . . . London: 1616-40, ie. 41. V. 46

The Workes. London: 1640. V. 38

The Workes. London: 1641. V. 45

The Works of Ben Jonson. London: 1692. V. 42; 43; 44; 45

The Works of . . . London: 1716. V. 38

The Works. London: 1756. V. 38; 43; 45

The Works. London: 1816. V. 38; 39; 41; 43; 44; 45

The Works. London: 1875. V. 42; 43; 45; 46

The Works of Ben Jonson. London: 1925-50. V. 46

JONSSON, ARNGRIMUR

Specimen Islandia Historicum . . . Amstelodami: 1643. V. 38

JONSTON, JOHANNES

Theatrum Univerale Omnium Animalium Piscium, Avium, Quadrupedium, Exanguium, Aquaticorum, Inscetorum, et Angium . . . Amsterdam: 1718. V. 43

JONSTONUS, J.

Historia Ciuilis & Ecclesiastica . . . Amsterdam: 1644. V. 46

JONSTONUS, JOANNES

Historiae Naturali de Quadrupedibus . . . Amsterdam: 1657. V. 42

JONVEAUX, EMILE

Two Years in East Africa. London: 1875. V. 46

JOPE, E. M.

An Archaeological Survey of Co. Down. Belfast: 1966. V. 38; 43

Studies in Building History. London: 1961. V. 38

JOPLIN, THOMAS 1790-1847

Views on the Subject of Corn and Currency. London: 1826. V. 41

JOPPIEN, RUDIGER

The Art of Captain Cook's Voyages. Melbourne: 1985. V. 41

The Art of Captain Cook's Voyages . . . New Haven & London: 1985. V. 40

The Art of Captain Cook's Voyages. New Haven: 1985-88. V. 40

The Art of Captain Cook's Voyages. New Haven & London: 1985-88. V. 45

The Art of Captain Cook's Voyages, by R. Joppien and B. Smith. New Haven: 1985. V. 37

JORAY, MARCEL

Vasarely. Neuchatel: 1965. V. 43; 46

Vasarely II. Neuchatel: 1971. V. 43; 46

Vasarely IV. Neuchatel: 1979. V. 43; 46

JORDAN, DAVID

The Fishes of Samoa. 1905. V. 41

JORDAN, DAVID STARR

American Food and Game Fishes. New York: 1903. V. 42

The Days of a Man. Yonkers on Hudson: 1922. V. 40

The Days of a Man: Being Memories of a Naturalist, Teacher and Minor Prophet of Democracy. Yonkers-on-Hudson: 1922. V. 39

Fishes of North and Middle America: A Descriptive Catalogue. V. 38; 39

The Fishes of North and Middle America. Washington: 1896-1900. V. 40

The Voice of the Scholar with Other Addresses on the Problems of Higher Education. San Francisco: 1903. V. 39

JORDAN, JIM M.

The Paintings of Arshile Gorky: a Critical Catalogue. New York: 1982. V. 43; 45; 46

The Paintings of Arshile Gorky: a Critical Catalogue. New York: 1982. V. 46

JORDAN, JOHN

Serious ACtual Dangers of Foreigners and Foreign Commerce in the Mexican States . . . Philadelphia: 1826. V. 39; 45

Welcombe Hills, Near Stratford Upon Avon. London: 1777. V. 40; 45

JORDAN, JOHN W.

Colonial and Revolutionary Families of Pennsylvania. New York: 1911. V. 39; 41; 42

Genealogical and Person History of Fayettee County, Pennsylvania. New York: 1912. V. 39; 41

Genealogical and Personal History of Beaver County, Pennsylvania. New York: 1914. V. 39; 41; 42

Historic Homes and Institutions and Genealogical and Personal Memos of the Lehigh Valley, Pennsylvania. New York: 1905. V. 42

A History of Delaware County, Pennsylvania and Its People. New York: 1914. V. 41; 42

A History of the Juniata Valley, and Its People. New York: 1913. V. 42

JORDAN, NEIL

The Past. London: 1980. V. 42; 46

JORDAN, SAMUEL

The Ensign of Liberty and the Wicked One Revealed . . . Fraiserville: 1849. V. 44

JORDAN, TED

Norma Jean. My Secret Life with Marilyn Monroe. New York: 1989. V. 45

JORDAN, THOMAS

The Campaigns of Lieut.-Gen. N.B. Forrest and of Forrest's Cavalry. America: 1868. V. 41

The Campaigns of Lieut. Gen. N. B. Forrest and Forrest's Cavalry . . . Cincinnati & St. Louis: 1868. V. 45

The Campaigns of Lt. Gen. N.B. Forrest. Memphis & New York: 1868. V. 39

JORDAN, WILFRED

Colonial Revolutionary Families of Pennsylvania. New York: 1936. V. 42

Colonial and Revolutionary Families of Pennsylvania. New Series. New York: 1939. V. 42

JORDAN, WILLIAM

The Creation of the World, with Noah's Flood. London: 1827. V. 40

JORDANES, BISHOP OF RAVENNA

Jornades de Rebus Gothorum. Paulus Diaconus Forojuliensis de gestis Langobardorum. 1515. V. 37

JORDANES, BP. OF RAVENNA

Jornandes de Rebus Gothorum. Colophon: 1515. V. 38; 40; 42; 43

JORDANUS, FRIAR

Mirabilia Descripta. The Wonders of the East . . . London: 1683. V. 41

JORDIN, JOHN F.

Memories . . . Being a Story of Early Times in Daviess County, Missouri . . . Gallatin: 1905. V. 38

JORGENSEN, JORGEN

A Treatise of Formal Logic. Copenhagen: 1931. V. 41; 43

JORIO, ANDREA DE

Real Museo Borbonico. Officina de Papiri Descritta. Naples: 1825. V. 38

JORTIN, JOHN

the Life of Erasmus. London: 1758. V. 45

Sermons on Different Subjects. London: 1787. V. 39

Tracts, Philological, Critical and Miscellaneous. London: 1790. V. 45

JOSE, ARTHUR

The Art of George Lambert. Sydney: 1924. V. 40

JOSE, ARTHUR W.

The Illustrated Australian Encyclopedia. Waterloo: 1925. V. 43

JOSEPH Delteil: Essays in Tribute. 1962. V. 39

JOSEPH, EDWARD L.

Warner Arundell: the Adventures of a Creole. London: 1845. V. 46

JOSEPH, H. S.

Memoirs of Convicted Prisoners . . . London: 1853. V. 42

JOSEPHSON, MATTHEW

Galimathias. New York: 1923. V. 38

JOSEPHUS, BEN GORION

The Wonderful and Most Deplorable History of the Latter Times of the Jews with the Destruction of the City of Jerusalem . . . Leonmister: 1803. V. 43

JOSEPHUS, FLAVIUS

De Antiquitatibus ac be Bello Judaico. Colophon: Venice: 1499. V. 43

De Antiquitatibus Ac De Bello Judaico. Venice: 1499. V. 40

Antiquitatum Judaicarum Libri XX. Paris: 1535. V. 37

De Bello Judaico. De Antiquitate Judaeorum Contra Apionem. Verona: 1480. V. 44

The Famous and Memorable Workes . . . London: 1620. V. 46

The Genuine Works of Flavius Josephus. Edinburgh: 1777. V. 43; 44

Opera. Basel: 1544. V. 42

Opera Quae Extant. Geneva: 1611. V. 40

Opera Quae Exstant, Nempe Antiquitatum Iudiacarum . . . Genevae: 1634. V. 40; 43

Que hoc Volumine Contineantur Josephi Historiographi . . . (Works). Paris: 1511. V. 39

The Works . . . London: 1702. V. 41

The Works. (with) Two Discourses, and Several Remarks and Observations Upon Josephus. London: 1725. V. 38

The Whole Works. Dundee: 1765. V. 39

The Whole Genuine and Complete Works of . . . London: 1800. V. 46

The Whole Genuine and Complete Works of . . . London: 1800/1785-86. V. 44

The Works of Flavius Josephus. London: 1811. V. 43

The Works of . . . Glasgow: 1814. V. 46

The Works of Flavius Josephus. Philadelphia: 1773-74. V. 37

JOSI, CHRISTIAN

A Catalogue of the Collection of Engravings, Etchings, and Original Drawings, and Books of Prints of Christian Josi Esq. Deceased . . . London: 1829. V. 38

JOSLIN, SESYLE

Brave Baby Elephant. New York: 1959. V. 40; 42

JOSSELYN, IRENE M.

Journal of the American Academy of Childe Psychiatry. New York: 1962-1981. V. 39

JOSSELYN, JOHN

An Account of Two Voyages to New England. London: 1674. V. 38; 39; 40; 42; 44

An Account of Two Voyages to New Englnad Made During the Years 1638, 1663, together with Chronological Observations of America, 1673. A Facsimile reprint of 75 copies. Valuable observations of the country and many curious and valuable particulars . . . Boston: 1865. V. 37

New-Englands Rarities Discovered: in Birds, Beasts, Fishes, Serpents, and Plants of That Country . . . London: 1672. V. 37; 42; 44

JOUBERT, LOUIS

Knowledge of Metals. London: 1715. V. 38

Oratio de Praesidiis Futuri Excellentis Medici..Adjecta Chr Schillingii Epigrammata Graeca & Latina. Geneva: 1580. V. 38; 39

JOUENNEAUX, GUY d. 1507

In Latine Lingue Elegantias/ Tam a Laurentio Valle q a Gellio Memorie Probitas Interpretatio Dilucida Thematis Creberrime Adhibitis. Paris: 1515. V. 40

Reformationis Monastice Vindicieseu Defensio. Paris: 1503. V. 38; 40

JOULE, JAMES PRESCOTT

The Scientific Papers. London: 1844-87. V. 37

JOURDAIN, A. M.

La Perse, ou Tableau de l'Histoire, du Governement, de la Religion, de la Litterature, etc, de cet Empire . . . Paris: 1814. V. 42

JOURDAIN, H. F. N.

The Connaught Rangers. London: 1924. V. 42

JOURDAIN, MARGARET

English Decoration and Furniture of the Early Renaissance (1500-1650). (with) English Decoration and Furniture of the Later XVIIIth Century (1760-1820). London: 1922-24. V. 40

English Decorative Plasterwork of the Reinaissance. London: 1926. V. 38; 46

English Decorative Plasterwork of the Renaissance. New York: 1926. V. 41

English Interior Decoration 1500 to 1800. A Study in Development and Design. London: 1950. V. 37; 39

English Furniture: The Georgian Period 1750-1830. London: 1953. V. 37; 42

The Morant Collection of Old Velvets, Damasks, Brocades, etc. at 91 New Bond St. London W. With a Description of English Upholstery During the 17th and 18th Centuries. London: 1910s. V. 41

The Morant Collection of Old Velvets, Damasks, Brocades, Etc. At 91 New Bond Street, London . . . With a Description of English Upholstery During the 17th and 18th Centuries. London: (ca. 1910). V. 37

Regency Furniture 1795-1820. London: 1934. V. 39

THE JOURNAL of the Household Brigade for the Year 1862 to 1890. London: 1862-1890. V. 46

NORTH Pacific Coast. A Journal Devoted to Home Life, Schools, Agriculture, Horticulture, Commerce, Mines, Manufactures and Other Resources of Washington Territory. New Tacoma: 1881.; V. 45

A JOURNAL of Romano-British and Kindred Studies. London: 1970-83. V. 45

JOURNAL des Dames et des Modes. Paris: 1801-22. V. 41

JOURNAL des Demoiselles. Paris: 1856-74. V. 39

JOURNAL of a Hunting Excursion to Louis Lake 1851. New York: 1961. V. 46

JOURNAL of a Soldier of the 71st, or Glasgow Regiment, Highland Light Infantry, from 1806-1815. Edinburgh: 1819. V. 40

JOURNAL of a Tour and Residence in Great Britain, During the Years 1810 and 1811, by a French Traveller. Edinburgh: 1815. V. 43

JOURNAL Of Animal Ecology. London: 1948-82. V. 38

A JOURNAL of Book-Lore. Volumes I-Vi. (All published). London: 1882-1884. V. 37

THE JOURNAL of Decorative Art. London: 1881-83. V. 40

THE JOURNAL of Egyptian Archaeology. London: 1914-1972. V. 40

JOURNAL Of Eight Days Journey from Portsmouth to Kingston upon Thames . . . . By A Gentleman of the Partie. London: 1756. V. 39

JOURNAL of Fish Biology. London: 1969-86. V. 37; 38

THE JOURNAL of General Psychology. Experimental, Theoretical, Clinical and Historical Psychology. Worcester: 1928-30. V. 46

JOURNAL of Health, Conducted by an Association of Physicians. Philadelphia: 1830-31. V. 42

JOURNAL of Medical Research. 1901-17. V. 42; 45

JOURNAL of Medical Research 1910-1917. V. 37

JOURNAL Of the Convention of the People of North Carolina Held on the 20th Day of May, A.D., 1861. Raleigh: 1862. V. 38

JOURNAL of the Expedition to La Guira and Porto Cavallos in the West-Indies, under the Command of Commodore Knowles. In a Letter from an Officer on board the Burford to his Friend at London. London: 1744. V. 37

JOURNAL of the History of Medicine and Allied Sciences. London: 1946-60. V. 42

JOURNAL of the History of Medicine and Allied Sciences. London: 1956-72. V. 37

THE GREAT Illegitimates!! Public and Private Life of that Celebrated Actress Miss Blank, otherwise Miss Ford, or Mrs. Jordan. London: 1831. V. 37

THE JOURNEY of Francisco Vazquez de Coronado, 1540-1542. San Francisco: 1933. V. 46

JOURNEYS Into the Moon, Several Planets and the Sun. Philadelphia: 1837. V. 37; 41

JOUSEE, MATHURIN

Le Theatre de l'Art de Charpentier, Enrichi de Diverses Figures, avec l'Interpretation d'Icelles. La Fleche: 1650. V. 44

JOUSSE, MATHURIN

L'Art de Charpenterie. Paris: 1751. V. 38; 44

JOUTEL, HENRI

Decouvertes et Etablissements des Francais Dans l'Uest et Dans le Sud de l'Amerique . . . 1614-1754: Memoires et Documents Originaux. Paris: 1876. V. 39

Diario Historico del Ultimo Viaje que Hizo M. de la Sale Para Descubrir el Desembocdero y Curso del Missicipi . . . New York: 1831. V. 38

Journal Historique de Dernier Voyage Que Feu M. De La Sale. Paris: 1713. V. 37; 38; 39; 40; 42; 43; 45; 46

A Journal of the Last Voyage Perform'd by Monsr de la Sale, to the Gulph of Mexico, To Find Out the Mouth of the Missipi (sic) River. London: 1714. V. 42

Journal of La Salle's Last Voyage . . . Chicago: 1896. V. 38; 42

Joutel's Journal of La Salle's Last Voyage 1684-7. Albany: 1906. V. 42; 46

JOVELLANOS, GASPAR MELCOR DE

Informe de la Sociedad Economica de Esta Corte al Real y Supremo Consejo de Castilla an el Expediente de ley Agraria. Madrid: 1795. V. 38

THE JOVIAL Songster, or, Sailor's Delight. London: 1795. V. 37

THE JOVIAL Songster, or, Sailor's Delight: a choice collection of cheerful and humourous songs, that are sung by the brave tars of old England, and other merry companions ... London: (c. 1800). V. 37

JOVII, PAULI

Pavli Jovii Novocomensis Episcopi Nucerini Elogia Virorum Bellica Virtute Illustruim. Basil: 1575-77. V. 41

JOWERS, W. G. W.

General Order No. 2. Palestine: 1861. V. 39; 40

JOWETT, W.

Christian Researches in the Mediterranean, from 1815 to 1820, in Furtherance of the objects of the Church Missionary Society. London: 1824. V. 39

JOY, HENRY

Historical Collections Relative to the Town of Belfast, from the Earliest Period to the Union with Great Britain. Belfast: 1817. V. 38; 43

JOY, NORMAN H.

A Practical Handbook of British Beetles. London: 1932. V. 41

JOYCE, JAMES 1882-1941

Anna Livia Plurabelle. New York: 1928. V. 37; 38; 39; 41; 42; 44; 45; 46

Anna Livia Plurabelle. London: 1930. V. 39; 42; 43

Anna Livia Plurabelle: a Fragment from Finnegan's Wake. 1985. V. 40

The Cat and the Devil. New York: 1964. V. 39

Chamber Music. London: 1907. V. 37; 39; 41

Chamber Music. Boston: 1918. V. 38; 39; 40; 42; 43; 45; 46

Chamber Music. London: 1918. V. 37; 42

Chamber Music. New York: 1918. V. 39; 42; 45

Chamber Music. London: 1923. V. 37; 38; 39; 42

Chamber Music. London: 1927. V. 40; 46

Collected Poems. New York: 1936. V. 42

Collected Poems. New York: 1937. V. 39

Corrections of Misprints in Finnegans Wake by James Joyce - as Prepared by the author After Publication of the First Edition. London: 1945. V. 46

The Dead. 1928. V. 37

The Dead. 1967. V. 42

The Dead. 1982. V. 45

The Dead. Verona: 1982. V. 40

Dubliners. London: 1914. V. 39; 41; 44; 45

Dubliners. New York: 1926. V. 42

Gens de Dublin. Paris: 1926. V. 42; 46

Dubliners. New York: 1986. V. 38; 39; 43; 44; 46

Dubliners - Illustrated by Louis Le Brocquy. Dublin: 1986. V. 37

Epiphanies. Buffalo: 1956. V. 46

The Epiphanies. New York: 1988. V. 44; 45

Exiles. 1918. V. 46

Exiles. London: 1918. V. 38

Exiles - a Play in Three Acts. New York: 1918. V. 37; 40; 41

Exiles. London: 1921. V. 40; 45

Exiles. New York: 1924. V. 38; 40

Exiles. New York: 1951. V. 38; 42; 45

Finnegan's Wake. London: 1939. V. 38; 39; 41; 42; 43; 44; 45; 46

Finnegans Wake. London & New York: 1939. V. 37; 39

Finnegan's Wake. New York: 1939. V. 37; 39; 40; 42; 43; 44; 45; 46

Finnegan's Wake. New York: 1947. V. 38

Finnegan's Wake. London: (1939). V. 37

Giacomo Joyce. New York: 1989. V. 46

Haveth Childers Everywhere. New York: 1930. V. 43

Haveth Childers Everywhere. Paris: 1930. V. 37; 40; 42

Haveth Childers Everywhere. London: 1931. V. 39; 46

I Hear an Army. London: 1929. V. 44

The Joyce Book. London: 1933. V. 43

A Key to the Ulysses of James Joyce. Chicago: 1927. V. 40

Letters of ... London: 1957/1966. V. 43

Letters. London: 1957-66. V. 42

Letters of James Joyce. New York: 1957-66. V. 46

Letters of James Joyce, Volumes Two and Three. London: 1966. V. 43

Letters. New York: 1966. V. 40; 46

The Mime of Mick, Nick and the Maggies. The Hague: 1933. V. 41

The Mime of Mick Nick and the Maggies. London and the Hague: 1934. V. 40

The Mime of Mick Nick and the Maggies. The Hague: 1934. V. 37; 39; 42

The Mime of Mick, Nick and the Magpies ... The Hague & Paris: 1934. V. 45

The Mime of Mick, Nick and the Maggies. The Hague/ New York: 1934. V. 43

The Mime of Mick Nick and the Maggies. London: 1934. V. 38

The Mookse and the Gripes. Portage: 1977. V. 42

Pastimes of James Joyce. New York: 1941. V. 45; 46

Pomes Pennyeach. Paris: 1927. V. 37; 38; 42; 45; 46

Pomes Pennyeach. London: 1933. V. 39

Pomes Pennyeach. London: (1933). V. 37

A Portrait of the Artist as a Young Man. 1916. V. 43

A Portrait of the Artist as a Young Man. New York: 1916. V. 37; 39; 42; 44

A Portrait of the Artist as a Young Man. London: 1916, 1917. V. 41

A Portrait of the Artist as a Young Man. London: 1917. V. 42; 44

Portrait of the Artist as a Young Man. London: 1918. V. 38

Dedalus, Portrait de l'Artise Jeune Par Lui-Meme. Paris: 1924. V. 40; 46

Jugendbildnis. Basel, etc.: 1926. V. 39

A Portrait of the Artist as a Young Man. London: 1926. V. 40

A Portrait of the Artist as a Young Man. Leipzig: 1930. V. 38

A Portrait of the Artist as a Young Man. London: 1965. V. 37; 39

A Portrait of the Artist as a Young Man. 1968. V. 39

Portrait of the Artist as a Young Man. New York: 1968. V. 39; 45

A Shorter Finnegans Wake. New York: 1967. V. 37

Stephen Hero. London: 1944. V. 37; 38; 40

Stephen Hero. New York: 1944. V. 37; 38; 40; 42; 44; 46

Storiella as She is Syung. 1937. V. 38

Storiella as She is Syung. London: 1937. V. 37; 38; 40; 41; 42; 43

Storiella as She is Syung. V. 37

Storiella as She Is Syung. (London: 1937). V. 37

Tales of Shem and Shaun. Paris: 1929. V. 39; 40; 42; 44

Two Tales of Shem and Shaun. London: 1932. V. 42; 45; 46

Topf! London: 1976. V. 45

Two Songs. In the Venture. London: 1903 & 1904. V. 41

Ulysses. V. 44

Ulysses. London: 1922. V. 38; 39; 42; 43

Ulysses. London & Paris: 1922. V. 37; 38; 40

Ulysses. Paris: 1922. V. 37; 38; 39; 40; 41; 42; 43; 44; 45; 46

Ulysses. Paris: 1924. V. 42; 43

Ulysses. Paris: 1925. V. 42; 43; 45

Ulysses. Paris: 1926. V. 39; 40; 43; 45

Ulysses. Paris: 1927. V. 39; 43

Ulysses. Paris: 1928. V. 43

Ulysse. 1929. V. 40

Ulysse. Paris: 1929. V. 37; 40

Ulysses. Paris: 1930. V. 43; 44

Ulysses. Zurich: 1930. V. 46

Ulysses. Hamburg: 1932. V. 37; 38; 40; 42; 46

Ulysses. Hamburg etc.: 1932. V. 39

Ulysses. Hamburg/Paris: 1932. V. 39; 43

Ulysses. London: 1932. V. 37

Ulysses. New York: 1934. V. 39; 41; 42; 44

Ulysses. Hamburg: 1935. V. 39; 43

Ulysses. New York: 1935. V. 37; 38; 39; 42; 43; 45; 46

Ulysses. London: 1936. V. 37; 39; 40; 41; 42; 43; 46

Ulysses. London: 1937. V. 37; 41; 43; 46

Ulysses. Hamburg: 1939. V. 38

(Title in Greek). Ulysses. Athens: 1969. V. 46

Ulysses: a Critical and Synoptic Edition. New York: 1984. V. 37; 42

Ulysses. New York: 1986. V. 44

Ulysses. San Francisco: 1988. V. 40

The Venture, 1905. London: 1905/1904. V. 42

Verbannte. Zurich: 1919. V. 45

JOYCE, JOHN

Confession of John Joyce, Alias Davis, Who Was Executed on Monday, the 14th of March, 1808, for the Murder of Mrs. Sarah Cross ... Philaelphia: 1808. V. 42

JOYCE, JOHN A.

A Checkered Life. Chicago: 1883. V. 37; 41; 44; 46

JOYCE, P. W.

Atlas and Cyclopedia of Ireland. New York: 1914. V. 38; 39

Atlas and History of Ireland. A Comprehensive Description of Each County, with A.M. Sullivan, The Story of Ireland. New York: 1899. V. 37

Old Irish Folk Music and Songs. London: 1909. V. 38

The Origin and History of Irish Names and Places. 1870. V. 46

The Origin and History of Irish Names of Places. London: 1898/1913. V. 43

A Social History of Ancient Ireland. Dublin: 1903. V. 46

A Social History of Ancient Ireland. London: 1903. V. 39

JOYCE, P. W. continued

A Social History of Ancient Ireland Treating of the Government, Military System, Law, Religion, Learning and Art, Trades, Industries and Commerce, Manners, Customs and Life of the Ancient Irish People. Dublin: 1913. V. 43

A Social History of Ancient Ireland, Treating of the Government, Law, Religion, Art, Trade and Commerce, Manners and Customs, etc. Dublin: 1920. V. 38

JOYCE, STANISLAUS

The Early Joyce: the Book of Reviews. 1902-1903. Colorado Springs: 1955. V. 40; 42

Le Journal de Dublin. Paris: 1967. V. 42

JOYCE, T. ATHOL

Women of All Nations. London: 1908. V. 44; 45

JOYCELYN, N.

Bible Atlas: Consisting of Nine Maps, with Explanations . . . New Haven: 1819. V. 45

JOYCELYN, SIMEON S.

College for Colored Youth. An Account of the New Haven City Meeting and Resolutions, with Recommendations of the College and Strictures Upon the Doings of New Haven. New York: 1831. V. 45

JOYNER, GEORGE

Display Work: The Principles and Practice; Commercial and Artistic Display, Type Selection Hints. London: 1909. V. 41

JOYNER, WILLIAM

The Roman Empress. London: 1671. V. 37; 45

THE JOYS of the Table, a Favourite Collection of Hunting, Drinking, Humorous, Comic, Queer and Funny Songs, Toasts, Sentiments, and Hobnobs. Dublin: 1808. V. 37

JUAN DE SANTA MARIA

Republica y Policia Christiana, Para Reyes y Principes y Para Los Que en el Govierno Tienen sus Vezes. Lisbon: 1621. V. 38

JUAN, JORGE

Noticias Secretas de America, Sobre El Estado Naval Militar, y Politico de los Reynos del Peru y Provincias de Quinto . . . London: 1826. V. 41; 43

Voyage to South America, Describing Spanish Cities, Towns, Customs, Manners . . . 1760. V. 45

A Voyage to South America. London: 1760. V. 46

A Voyage to South America . . . London: 1806. V. 42

A Voyage to South America . . . London: 1807. V. 46

JUAN Y SANTACILIA, JORGE

Dissertacion Historica y Geographica Sobre el Meridiano de Demaracion Entre los Dominios de Espana y Portugal y los Parages por Donde Passa en la America Meridional . . . Madrid: 1749. V. 41

Relacion Historica del Viage a la America Meridional. Madrid: 1748. V. 38

JUARROS, DOMINGO

Compendio de la Historia de la Ciudad de Guatemala. Guatemala: 1809, 1818. V. 43

A Statistical and Commercial History of the Kingdom of Guatemala, in Spanish America. London: 1823. V. 39; 43

LE JUBILE de l'An MDCC, Publie Par la Bulle d'Innocent XII, du 28 Mars 1649 . . . Amsterdam: 1701. V. 38; 40

JUDAH, SAMUEL BENJAMIN H.

Gotham and the Gothamites. New York: 1823. V. 40; 43

A Tale of Lexington. New York: 1823. V. 44

JUDAH, THEODORE D.

Report of the Chief Engineer Upon Recent Surveys. Progress of Construction and an Approximate Estimate of Cost of First Division of Fifty Miles of the Central Pacific Railroad of California, July 1st, 1863. Sacramento: 1863. V. 46

Report of the Chief Engineer on the Preliminary Survey, Cost of Construction and Estimated Revenue, of the Central Pacific Railroad of California, Across the Sierra Nevada Mountains, from Sacramento to the Eastern Boundary of California. Sacramento: 1862. V. 40; 46

JUDD, DAVID W.

Life and Writings of Frank Forester. New York: 1882. V. 38; 44

The Story of the Thirty-Third N.Y.S. Vols., or Two Years Campaigning in Virginia and Maryland. Rochester: 1864. V. 39

JUDD, DONALD

Complete Writings, 1959-1975: Gallery Reviews, Book Reviews, Articles, Letters to the Editor, Reports, Statements, Complaints. Halifax/New York: 1975. V. 46

JUDD, JOHN W.

The Geology of Rutland and the Parts of Lincoln, Leicester, Northampton, Huntingdon and Cambridge . . . London: 1875. V. 44; 46

JUDD, LAURA FISH

Honolulu Sketches of the Life Social, Political and Religious, in the Hawaiian Islands from 1828 to 1861 . . . With a Supplementary Sketch of Events to the Present Time. Honolulu: 1928. V. 39

JUDD, NEIL M.

The Architecture of Pueblo Bonito. Washington: 1964. V. 39

JUDD, SILAS

A Sketch of the Life and Voyages of Captain Alvah Dewey. Chittenango: 1838. V. 38; 46

A Sketch of the Life and Voyages of Captain Alvah Dewey. New York: 1838. V. 41

JUDD, SYLVESTER

History of Hadley Including the Early History of Hatfield, South Haldey, Amherst and Granby, Massachusetts. Springfield: 1905. V. 46

Philo: an Evangeliad. Boston: 1850. V. 43

THE JUDGEMENT OR Resolution of all Lords, the Judges and Other Lords Assembled in Starchamber . . . N.P.: 1679. V. 42

JUDICUM & Decretum Universitatis Oxoniensis Latum in Convocatione Habita Jul. 21. An 1683. Oxford: 1683. V. 45

JUDSON, A.

A Dictionary of the Burman Language, with Explanations in English. Calcutta: 1826. V. 40

JUDSON, ADONIRAM BROWN

The Influence of Growth on Congenital and Acquired Deformities. New York: 1905. V. 42

JUDSON, E. Z. C.

The Mysteries and Miseries of New York . . . New York: 1848. V. 44

JUDSON, EDWARD ZANE CARROLL

The Mysteries and Miseries of New York: a Story of Real Life. New York: 1848. V. 43

JUDSON, EMILY CHUBBOCK

Lillian Fane, and Other Tales. Boston: 1846. V. 40

JUDSON, EMILY CHUBBUCK

Alderbrook: a Collection of Fanny Forester's Village Sketches, Poems, etc. Boston: 1847. V. 43

JUDSON, J. RICHARD

The Drawings of Jacob de Gheyn II. Northampton: 1972. V. 37; 44; 45; 46

THE JUDYCYALL of Uryns: Consyderynege That It Is Expedyent For Every Man to Know the Operation and Qualities of His Body, and To Know In What State and Condicyion His Body Standeth In . . . London: 1527? V. 40

JUETTNER, OTTO

Daniel Drake and His Followers: Historical and Biographical Sketches. Cincinnati: 1909. V. 42

JUGAKU, BUNSHO

Hand-made Paper of Japan. 1938. V. 41

Paper-Making by Hand in Japan. Tokyo: 1959. V. 38; 41; 46

Paper-making by Hand in Japan. Tokyo: 1969. V. 43

JUGLAR, CLEMENT 1819-1905

A Brief History of Panics and Their Periodical Occurence in the United States. New York: 1893. V. 39

Des Crises Commerciales et de Leur Retour Periodique en France, en Angleterre et aux Etats-Unis. Paris: 1889. V. 41; 45

De Crises Commerciales et de Leur Retour Periodique en France, en Angleterre et aux Etats-Unis . . . Paris: 1862. V. 38

JUKES-BROWN, A. J.

The Creataceous Rocks of Britain. London: 1900-04. V. 43

JUKES, JOSEPH BEETE 1811-1869

Excursions in and About Newfoundland During the Years 1839 and 1840. London: 1840. V. 45

Excursions in and about Newfoundland during the Years 1839 and 1840. London: 1842. V. 37; 42; 46

Lectures on Gold for the Instruction of Emigrants About to Proceed to Australia. London: 1852. V. 46

Narrative of the Surveying Voyage of H. M. S. Fly, Commanded by Captain F. P. Blackwood, R. N., in Torres Strait, New Guinea, and Other Islands of the Eastern Archipelago, During the Years 1842-6. London: 1846. V. 42

JUKES, JOSEPH BEETE 1811-1869 continued

Narrative of the Surveying Voyage of HMS Fly, Commanded by Captain F. P. Blackwood, R.N. in Torres Strait, New Guinea, and Other Islands of the Eastern Archipelago, During the Years 1842-1846 . . . London: 1847. V. 39; 44; 46

On the Mode of Formation of Some of the River-Valleys in the South of IReland. London. V. 46

On the Mode of Formation of Some of the River Valleys in the South of Irelan. London: 1862. V. 41

JULER, HENRY E.

A Handbook of Opthalmic Science and Practice. London: 1893. V. 44

JULIAN, ANTONIO

La Perla de la America, Provincia de Santa Marta, Reconcida Observada, y Expuesta en Disursos Historicaos . . . Madrid: 1789. V. 43

JULIEN, ANDRE

The Topography of all the Known Vineyards. London: 1824. V. 40

JULIETTA. London: 1802. V. 39

JUNG, CARL GUSTAV 1875-1961

Analytical Psychology. New York: 1926. V. 41

Collected Works. New York: 1953-57. V. 42

Collected Works of C. G. Jung. Princeton: 1970-83. V. 45

Psychologische Typen. Zurich: 1921. V. 38

Pshychology of the Unconscious: a Study of the Transformations and Symbolisms of the Libido. London: 1916. V. 45

Psychology of the Unconscious. New York: 1916. V. 41

Studies in Word-Association. New York: 1919. V. 41

JUNG, JOACHIM 1587-1657

Opuscula Botanico-Physica ex Recensione et Distinctione Martini Folegii et Ioh. Vagetti cum Eorundem Annotationibus. Coburg: 1747. V. 46

JUNG-STILLING, JOHANN HEINRICH 1740-1817

Theory of Pneumatology, In Reply to the Question, What Ought to be Believed or Disbelieved Concerning Presentiments, Visions, Apparitions, According to Nature, Reason, and Scripture. London: 1834. V. 39

JUNGE, CARL S.

Ex Libris. New York: 1935. V. 43; 44

JUNIPER, B. E.

The Carnivorous Plants. London: 1989. V. 46

JUNIUS

Junius. London: 1772. V. 37

The Letters. London: 1772. V. 38; 40

Letters. Complete in One Volume, with a Copious Index. Philadelphia: 1791. V. 46

Letters. London: 1799. V. 38

The Letters. (with) His Confidential Correspondence with Mr. Wilkes, and His Private Letters Addressed to H. S. Woodfall. London: 1812. V. 38; 39

Letters. London: 1895. V. 44

JUNIUS, FRANCISCUS 1545-1602

Etymologicum Anglicanum. Oxford: 1743. V. 38; 44; 45

JUNIUS, HADRIANUS

Emblemata, ad Arnoldum Cobelium, Ejusdem Aenigmatum Libellus, ad D. Arnold Rosenbergum. Antwerp: 1565. V. 40

Emblemata. Leyden: 1585. V. 40

JUNIUS, MELCHOIR 1545-1604.

Animorum conciliandorum et movendorum ration. (Montbeliard: 1596. V. 37

JUNIUS, PSEUD.

Stat Nominis Umbra. London: 1797. V. 37; 38; 39

Stat Nominis Umbra. (The Letters of Junius). London: 1810. V. 37

The Letters of the Celebrated Junius. London: 1783. V. 40

Stat Nominis Umbra. London: 1772. V. 40; 41; 43

Stat Nominis Umbra. London: 1801. V. 38

JUNKER, WILHELM

Travels in Africa During the Years 1875-1878; (1879-1883); (1884-1886). London: 1890-92. V. 41

Travels in Africa, 1879-1883. London: 1891. V. 42

JURGENSEN, JORGEN

Travels through France and Germany, in the Years 1815, 1816 and 1817. London: 1817. V. 38

JURKOVIC, DUSAN

Prace Lidu Naseho. Lidove Stavby, Zarizeni A Vyzdoba Obydli, Drobne Prace. Wien: 1905. V. 46

JUS Imperii & Servitutis; or, the Law concerning Masters, Apprentices, Bayliffs, Receivers, Stewards, Attorneys, Factors, . . . London: 1707. V. 37

JUSSERAND, J. J.

The English Novel in the Time of Shakespeare. London: 1840. V. 39

The English Novel in the Time of Shakespeare. London: 1890. V. 39; 42

JUSSIEU, ANTOINE LAURENT DE

Genera Plantarum Secundum Ordines Naturales Disposita Juxta Methodum in Horto Regio Parisiensi Exaratam . . . Paris: 1789. V. 38; 39; 40; 42; 46

JUSSIM, ESTELLE

Slave to Beauty: The Eccentric Life and Controversial Career of F. Holland Day. Boston: 1981. V. 38; 39; 41; 42

JUST and Legal Exeptions Against the Late Act for Preventing Multiplicity of Buildings, Erected Within the Suburbs of the City of London, and Ten Miles Thereof, Since March 1620. London: 1657? V. 41

A JUST Reply to a Certain Apology Address'd to a Noble Lord in the Opposition, Particularly with Regard to France. London: 1748. V. 41

JUSTA Funebria Serenissimo Principi Ioanni Friderico, Brunsvicensium et Luneburge Duci a Revermo, et Sermo, Fratre Ernesto Augusto Episcopo Osnabrugensi Duci Brunsv et Luneb. Persoluta. Rinteln: 1685. V. 38

JUSTI, JOHANN HEINRICH GOTTLOB VON

Die Grundfeste zu der Macht und Gluckseeligkeit der Staaten . . . Konigsberg und Leipzig: 1760, 1761. V. 38

JUSTICE, ALEXANDER

A General Treatise on the Dominion of the Sea and a Compleat Body of Sea-Laws . . . In Ancient and Modern Authors . . . London: 1709-10. V. 37; 38; 40

JUSTICE, DONALD

A Local Storm. Iowa City: 1963. V. 39

The Summer Anniversaires. Middletown, Conn.: 1960. V. 37

JUSTICE, JAMES

The Scots Gardiners Director, containing Instructions to those Gardiners, who make a Kitchen Garden and the Culture of Flowers their Business: . . . and the Culture of all Herbs . . . . Edinburgh: 1754. V. 39

JUSTICE, JEAN

Dictionary of Marks and Monograms of Delft Pottery. London: 1930. V. 41; 42

THE JUSTICE of Parliaments On Corrupt Ministers, in Impeachments and Bills of Attainder, Consider'd. London: 1725. V. 39

THE JUSTICE of the Peace His Calling A Moral Essay. London: 1684. V. 38; 40

JUSTIN MARTYR

Opera. Paris: 1551. V. 44

JUSTINIAN

(Novellae Constitutiones). (Greek Title). Paris: 1542. V. 45

JUSTINIAN I, EMPEROR 483-565

Codex Justinanus. (with the Glossa Ordinaria of Accursius). Nuremburgh: 1475. V. 45

Codex and Corpus Iuris Civillis. Geneva: 1624. V. 41

Digestorum seu Pandectarum Libri Quinquaginta ex Florentinis Pandectis Repraesentati. Florence: 1553. V. 44

Institutiones. Rome: 1475. V. 38

Institutionum Libri Quatuor. London: 1761. V. 38; 43

Institutionum Libri IIII. Paris: 1534. V. 40; 45

Institutionum Juris Civilis Libri Quatuor. Paris: 1560. V. 40

JUSTINIANO, LAURENZO

Dottrina Della Vita Monastica. Venice: 1494. V. 39

JUSTINIANUS, LAURENTIUS 1381-1455

Opera and Vita. Paris: 1524. V. 40

JUSTINUS, MARCUS JUNIANUS

Epitomae in Trogi Pompeii Historias. Venice: 1470. V. 38; 39; 40; 41

Epitomae in Trogi Pompeii Historias. Venice: 1497. V. 46

Epitomae in Trogi Pompeii Historias. Venice: 1740. V. 43

Ex Trogo Pompeio Historia. Hagenau: 1526. V. 37

In Trogi Pompaei Historiarum. Florence: 1510. V. 39; 43

Justini Ex Trogo Pompeio Historia . . . Cologne: 1533. V. 45

Trogi Pompeii Historiarum Philippicarum Epitoma . . . Paris: 1581. V. 46

Trogi Pompei Externae Historiae in Compendium ab Justino Redactae . . . Venice: 1522. V. 37

THE JUTLAND Battle by Two Who Took Part In It. London: 1916. V. 38

JUVENAL DE CARLENAS, FELIX DE

The History of the Belles Lettres, and of the Arts and Sciences from Their Origin, Down to Present Time. London: 1740. V. 41

JUVENAL DE CARLENCAS, FELIX DE

The History of the Belles Lettres, and of Arts and Sciences, From Their Origin, Down to the Present Times. London: 1741. V. 45

JUVENALIS, DECIMUS JUNIUS 55-140

Decimus Junius Juveanlis, and Aulus Persius Flaccus . . . . Oxford: 1673. V. 43

Iuvenalis. Persius (Satyrae). Venice: 1501. V. 40; 41

Ivvenal Tradotto Di Latino in Volgar Lingva Per Georgio Summaripa Veronese, Novamente Impresso. Toscolano: 1525. V. 38

Juveanlis, Persii, Sulpitiae, Satirae. Cameraci: 1822. V. 45

Opus Quidem Divinu Antea . . . Colophon: 1514. V. 42

Satirae. Paris: 1684. V. 46

D. Ivnii Ivvenalis Satyrae. Paris: 1664. V. 41; 45

The Satires of Decimus Junius Juvenalis. London: 1693. V. 38; 39; 45

Satyrae. Birmingham: 1761. V. 39; 40; 41; 43

The Satires of Juvenal Paraphrastically Imitated. London: 1763. V. 42

The Satires of Juvenal . . . London: 1785. V. 42

A New Translation, with Notes, of the Third Satire of Juvenal. New York: 1806. V. 39

Satyra Quinta. Iowa City: 1979. V. 37

Satyrae . . . Acesserunt Variae Lectiones Notabiliores. Dublini: 1728. V. 42

Satyrae. Dublin: 1746. V. 38

Juvenal's Sixteen Saytrs, or, a Survey of the Manners and Actions of Mankind . . . London: 1647. V. 39; 40; 44; 46

JUVENALIS, Persius. Venetiis: 1501. V. 38

A JUVENILE Guide, or Manual of Good Manners. Canterbury: 1844. V. 39
A JUVENILE Guide, or Manual of Good Manners. New Lebanon: 1844. V. 42

JUVENILE Speaker; or, Selections for Reading or Recitation; with Introductory remarks on Elocution, and Plates, Exhibiting Attitudes of Gesture, and Examples of Inflection. London: 1829. V. 41

JUVENIS, JOHANNES

De Antiquitate et Varia Tarentinorum Fortuna, Libri Octo. Neapoli: 1589. V. 38

K

K., G.

The History and Adventures of Amedlia Meanwell . . . London: 1780. V. 45

K., H.

Chaplains in Khaki. Methodist Soldiers in Camp, on the Field and on the March. London: 1900. V. 41

K., W.

An English Answer to the Scotch Speech. London: 1668. V. 39

KA *Mooleloo O Heneri Opukahaia, Ua Hanauia Ma Hawaii M. H. 1787, A Ua Make Ma Amerika, Feberuari 17, 1818. Oia Ka Hua Mua O Hawaii Nei.* New York: 1867. V. 41

KABERRY, C. J.

Our Little Neighbors. London: 1921. V. 45

KABERRY, CHARLES

The Book of Baby Dogs. London. V. 46

KAEGEBEN, CHARLES F.

Souvenir Album of Paintings. Hoboken: 1907. V. 40

KAEMPFER, ENGELBERT

Amoenitatum Exoticarum Politico-Physico-Medicarum Fasciculi V, Quibus Continentur Variae Relationes, Observationes & Descriptiones Rerum Persicarum & Ulterioris Asiae . . . Lemgoviae: Typis &: 1712. V. 45

The History of Japan. Glasgow: 1906. V. 43

KAESER, H. J.

Mimff. London: 1939. V. 42

KAFKA, FRANZ

Amerika. 1927. V. 44

Amerika. Munich: 1927. V. 42; 46

Amerika. Norfolk: (1940). V. 37

Beim Bau der Chinesischen Mauer. Berlin: 1931. V. 42

Beim Bau der Chineslschen Mauer. Kiepenheuer: 1931. V. 44

Der Kubelreiten/ The Bucket Rider. West Burke: 1973. V. 39; 42; 43; 44

The Castle. New York: 1930. V. 42

Conversation with the Supplicant. West Burke: 1971. V. 39

Conversation with the Supplicant. West Burke: 1973. V. 39; 42; 44

The Country Doctor. Oxford: 1945. V. 42

Das Schloss. 1926. V. 44

The Diaries of Franz Kafa. London: 1948-49. V. 44

Ein Landarzt. 1919. V. 44

Ein Landarzt. Kleine Erzahlungen. Leipzig: 1919. V. 42

Ein Hungerkunstler. 1924. V. 44

Ein Hungerkunstler. Berlin: 1924. V. 46

Gesammelte Schriften. 1935-37. V. 44

Der Heizer. 1913. V. 44

In der Strafkolonie. 1919. V. 44

In the Penal Colony. 1987. V. 45

In the Penal Colony. New York: 1987. V. 39; 40

The Metamorphosis. London: 1937. V. 39; 40

Metamorphosis. New York: 1984. V. 43; 45; 46

Parables. New York: 1947. V. 44

Parables and Pieces. New York: 1990. V. 45

Das Schloss. Munich: 1926. V. 42

Der Prozess. Roman. Berlin: 1925. V. 41

The Trial. Avon: 1975. V. 38; 46

KAFTAL, GEORGE

Iconography of the Saints in Tuscan Painting. Florence: 1952. V. 43; 46

Iconography of the Saints in the Painting of North East Italy. Florence: 1978. V. 46

Saints in Italian Art. Florence: 1978. V. 42

KAGAN, SOLOMON

Jewish Contributions to Medicine in America (1656-1934) With Medical Chronology, Bibliography and 69 Illustrations. Boston: 1934. V. 45

Jewish Contributions to Medicine in America From Colonial Times to the Present. Boston: 1939. V. 37; 45

Life and Letters of Fielding H. Garrison. Boston: 1938. V. 41

KAHANE, JACK

Daffodil. New York: 1934. V. 38

Memoirs of a Booklegger. London: 1939. V. 38

KAHLER, WILLIAM R.

My Holidays in China. Shanghai: 1895. V. 43

KAHN, ALBERT E.

Days with Ulanova. New York: 1962. V. 40; 46

KAHN, LOUIS I.

Louis I. Kahn, Complete Works, 1935-74. Boulder: 1977. V. 41

The Notebooks and Drawings of . . . New York: 1973. V. 41

KAHNWEILER, DANIEL HENRY

Juan Gris. His Life and Work. London: 1947. V. 42

Juan Gris: His Life and Work. New York: 1969. V. 43

KAHOE, WALTER

The Golden Door, a Magazine Anthology for Bookish Folk. Yellow Springs: 1939. V. 40

KAHRL, WILLIAM L.

The California Water Atlas. Sacramento: 1979. V. 38; 46

KAIN, CONRAD

Where the Clouds Can Go. Boston: 1954. V. 44

KAINES, J.

Seven Lectures on the Doctrine of Positivism, Delivered at the Postitivist School in 1879 by J. Kaines. London: 1880. V. 41

KAISER, HENRY J.

Twenty-Six Addresses Delivered During the War Years. San Francisco: 1945. V. 39; 40; 46

KAISER, T. E.

Historic Sketches of Oshawa. Oshawa: 1921. V. 44

KALADLIT *Assilialiait, or Woodcuts, Drawn and Engraved by Greenlanders.* Godthaab in South Greenland: 1860. V. 42

KALAKAUA, DAVID

The Legends and Myths of Hawaii. New York: 1888. V. 38

KALAW-LEDESMA, PURITA

The Biggest Little Room: Philippine Art Gallery. N.P.: 1987. V. 41

KALDEWEY, GUNNAR

California Time. Poestenkill: 1987. V. 42

Clouds. Dusseldorf: 1981-82. V. 42

Clouds. Dusseldorf & New York: 1982. V. 38

KALER, JAMES OTIS

Toby Tyler or Ten Weeks with a Circus. New York: 1881. V. 44

KALISH, MAX

Labor Sculpture. New York: 1938. V. 44

KALLIR, O.

Grandma Moses. New York: 1973. V. 46

KALLIR, OTTO

Egon Schiele: Oeuvre Catalogue of the Paintings. New York: 1966. V. 41

Egon Schiele: the Graphic Work. New York: 1970. V. 41

KALLMAN, FRANZ J. 1897-1965

The Genetics of Schizophrenia: a Study of Heredity and Reproduction in the Familes of 1,087 Schizophrenics. New York: 1938. V. 43; 45

KALM, PETER

Kalm's Account of His Visit to England on His Way to America in 1748. London: 1892. V. 43

Peter Kalm's Travels in North America (From) the English Version of 1770. New York: 1937. V. 39; 42; 44; 45

Travels into North America. Warrington: 1770-71. V. 39; 41

Travels into North America . . . Warrington/London: 1770-71. V. 41; 42

Travels into North America. London: 1772. V. 38; 39; 41; 43; 45

KALONYMOS, ISAAC NATHAN BEN fl. 1438-1455. .

(Hebrew) Concordantiarum Hebraicarum Capita. Basel: 1556. V. 43

KANSAS. (TERRITORY).

Journal of the Council of the Territory of Kansas, at Their First Session. Shawnee: 1855. V. 45

KANT, IMMANUEL

Anthropologie in Pragmatischer Hinsicht Abgefasst. Konigsberg: 1798. V. 38; 42; 45

Critik der Practischen Vernunft. Riga: 1788. V. 38; 39; 40; 41; 43; 45

Critik der Practischen Vernunft. Zweyte Auflage. Riga: 1792. V. 41

Critique de la Raison Pure . . . Paris: 1835-36. V. 43; 45

Critick of Pure Reason. London: 1838. V. 37; 38; 45

Critick of Pure Reason. London: 1848. V. 41; 43

Critik der Reinen Vernunft. Riga: 1781. V. 42

Critik der Reinen Vernunft. Riga: 1787. V. 38; 39

Critik der Reinen Vernunft. Frankfurt & Leigzig: 1791. V. 41

Critik der Urtheilskraft. Berlin und Libau: 1790. V. 41; 45

Critik der Urtheilskraft. Zweite Auflage. Berlin: 1793. V. 41

Die Personlichkeit als Einfuhrung in das Werk. Munchen: 1905. V. 41

Elements of the Critical Philosophy. London: 1798. V. 38

An Enquiry, Critical and Metaphysical, into the Grounds of Proof for the Existence of God, and Into the Theodicy, a Sequel to the Logic and Prolegomena . . . London: 1836. V. 43; 45

Immanuel Kant's Vermischte Schriften. Aechte und Vollstandige Ausgabe. Halle: 1799. V. 45

Immanuel Kant's Vermischte Schriften. Halle/Konigsberg: 1799/1807. V. 41

Kant's Cosmogony, as In His Essay on the Retardation of the Rotation of the Earth and His Natural History and Theory of the Heavens. Glasgow: 1900. V. 41

Kritik of Judgment. London: 1892. V. 42; 45

Logic, from the German of . . . London: 1819. V. 43; 45

Logik. Ein Handbuch zu den Vorlesungen. Konigsberg: 1800. V. 45

The Metaphysic of Ethics. Edinburgh: 1836. V. 41; 42; 45

Metaphysical Works. London: 1836. V. 46

Metaphysiche Anfangsgrunde der Naturwissenschaft. Riga: 1786. V. 40; 41

A Philosophical Treatise on Perpetual Peace. London: 1884. V. 45

Prolegomena zu Einer Jeden Kunfligen Metaphysik die als Wissenschaft Wird Auftreten Konnen. Riga: 1783. V. 45

Prolegomena to Every Future Metaphysic, Which Can Appear as a Science. London: 1819. V. 45

Religion within the Boundary of Pure Reason. Edinbrugh: 1838. V. 40; 41

La Religion Dans Les Limites de la Raison. Paris: 1841. V. 39

Sammtliche Kleine Schriften. Konigsberg und Leipzig: 1797. V. 40; 41

Sammtliche Werke. Leipzig: 1838-1842. V. 41; 45

Versuch den Begriff der Negativen Grossen in die Weltweisheit Einzufuhren. Konigsberg: 1763. V. 45

Werke Sorgfaitig Reviderte Gesammtausgabe in Zehn Banden. Leipzig: 1838-39. V. 40; 43; 45

Zwei Schriften Uber die Grundlegenden Begriffe der Naturwissenschaften. Berlin: 1920. V. 38; 42

KANTOR, MACKINLAY

Andersonville. Cleveland/New York: 1935. V. 42

Andersonville. Cleveland/New York: 1955. V. 41

Diversey. New York: 1928. V. 46

Here Lies Holly Springs. New York: 1938. V. 38; 40; 42; 46

KAPLAN, EMANUEL

Functional and Surgical Anatomy of the Hand. Philadelphia: 1953. V. 42

KAPLAN, HAROLD I.

Comprehensive Textbook of Psychiatry/III. Baltimore/London: 1980. V. 45

KAPP, FRIEDRICH

Immigration, and the Commissioners of Emigration, of the State of New York. New York: 1870. V. 46

KAPPEL, A. W.

British and European Butterflies and Moths. London: 1895. V. 37; 38; 40; 42; 45; 46

KAPPLER, CHARLES J.

Indian Treaties 1778-1883. New York: 1973. V. 45

KAPROW, ALLAN

Assemblage, Environments & Happenings. New York: 1966. V. 46

KAPSNER, O. L.

A Benedictine Bibliography, an Author-Subject Union List. Minnesota: 1962. V. 38

KARABACEK, J.

Papyrus Erzherzog Rainer. Vienna: 1894. V. 37

KARAGEORGHIS, VASSOS

Excavations in the Necropolis of Salamis II. Nicosia: 1970. V. 40

Excavations in the Necropolis of Salamis III. Nicosia: 1973-74. V. 40

Excavations at Kition. Nicosia: 1974. V. 44

Excavations in the Necropolis of Salamis IV. Nicosia: 1978. V. 40; 44

Sculptures from Salamis I-II. Nicosia: 1964-66. V. 44

KARAKA, DOSABHAI FRAMJI

History of the Parsis Including Their Manners, Customs, Religion and Present Position. London: 1884. V. 37

KARALUS, KARL E.

The Owls of North America. Garden City: 1974. V. 38; 41; 44; 45

KARAMSIN, NICOLAI

Travels from Moscow, Through Prussia, Germany, Switzerland, France and England. London: 1803. V. 45

KARAMZIN, NIKOLAI MIKHAILOVICH

Istoria Gosoodarstva Rossiskavo. (The History of the Russian State). Saint Petersburg: 1818-29. V. 41

Tales, from the Russian. London: 1804. V. 40

KARL THEODOR, ABP. AND ELECTOR OF MAINZ 1744-1817

The Connection Between Moral and Political Philosophy, Considered . . . London: 1787. V. 43

KAROLIK, M.

M. & M. Karolik Collection of American Watercolors and Drawings, 1800-1875. Boston: 1962. V. 42

KARPFEN, FRITZ

Das Egon Schiele Buch. Vienna: 1921. V. 45

KARPINSKI, LOUIS CHARLES

Bibliography of the Printed Maps of Michigan 1804-1880, With a Series of Over 100 Reproductions of Maps. Lansing: 1931. V. 38; 42; 46

KARSH, JOUSUF

Portraits of Greatness. Toronto: 1960. V. 44

KARSH, YOUSUF

Faces of Destiny. Portraits by Karsh. Chicago: 1946. V. 37

Portraits of Greatness. London: 1960. V. 40

Portraits of Greatness. 1960. V. 37

KARSHAN, DONALD

Malevich: the Graphic Work, 1913-1930. Jerusalem: 1975. V. 46

KARSLAKE, FRANK

Guild of Women-Binders. London: 1898. V. 46

Notes from Sotheby's, Being a Compilation of 2032 Notes from Catalogues of Book-Sales Which Have Taken Place in the Rooms . . . Between the Years 1885-1909. London: 1909. V. 38; 40

KARSTEN, DIETRICH LUDWIG GUSTAV

Tablas Mineralogicas Dispuestas Segun Los Descrubrimientos mas Recientes e Illustradas con Notas. Mexico: 1804. V. 40

KARSTEN, P. A.

Mycologia Fennica. Heisingfors: 1871-79. V. 37

KASCHNITZ-WEINBERG, GUIDO

Sculture del Magazzino del Museo Vaticano. Citta del Vaticano: 1937. V. 40; 42; 44

KASPAR Kroak's Kaleidoscope. New York: 1890. V. 45

KASSABIAN, MIHRAN KRIKOR

Roentgen Rays and Electro-Therapeutics . . . Philadelphia: 1907. V. 38

KASSNER, THEO

Gold Seeking in South Africa. London: 1902. V. 38

KASSNER, THEODORE

My Journey from Rhodesia to Egypt Including an Ascent of Ruwenzori and a Short Account of the Route from Cape Town to Broken Hill and Lado to Alexandria. London: 1911. V. 45

KASSON, GRACIA

Tin Tan Tales: a Book for Children. London & New York: 1900. V. 40

Tin Tan Tales. London: 1912. V. 41

KATENSTEIN, H. JACOB

The History of Tyre from the Beginning of the Second Millenium B.C.E. until the Fall of the Neo-Babylonian Empire in 538 B.C.E. Jerusalem: 1973. V. 40

KATHE Kallwitz -Einundzivanzig Zeichnungen der Spaten Jahre. Berlin: 1948. V. 46

KATO, GENICHI

The Theory of Decrementless Conduction in Narcotised Region of Nerve. (with) The Further Studies of Decrementless Conduction. Tokyo: 1924/26. V. 39; 41; 44; 45; 46

KATZ, D. MARK

Custer in Photographs. Gettysburg: 1985. V. 45

KATZENSTEIN, H. JACOB

The History of Tyre, from the Beginning of the Second Millenium B.C.E. Until the Fall of the Neo-Babylonian Empire in 538 B.C.E. Jerusalem: 1973. V. 42; 44

KAUFFER, E. MC KNIGHT

The Art of the Poster: Its Origin, Evolution & Purpose. London: 1924. V. 37

The Art of the Poster: Its Origin, Evolution and Purpose. New York: 1925. V. 46

The World in 2030 A.D., by the Right Honourable the Earl of Birkenhead (i.e., Frederick Edwin Smith). London: (dated 1930). V. 37

KAUFFMAN, ANGELICA

Angelica's Ladies Library. London: 1794. V. 39; 41; 43

KAUFFMAN, C. H.

The Dictionary of Merchandize, and nomenclature in all languages for the use of Counting Houses . . . in all European languages. London: 1805. V. 37

The Dictionary of Merchandise and Nomenclature in all European Languages, for the Use of Counting-Houses, etc. London: 1815. V. 38; 39; 41

KAUFFMANN, JOHN

The Art of John Kauffmann. Melbourne: 1919. V. 41

KAUFMAN, GEORGE S.

The American Way. New York: 1939. V. 37; 38; 41; 42; 43; 45

Beggar on Horseback. New York: 1924. V. 38; 39; 40

Dinner at Eight. Garden City: 1932. V. 45

The Man Who Came to Dinner. New York: 1939. V. 45

KAUFMAN, M.

Dictionary of American Medical Biography. Westport: 1984. V. 45; 46

KAUFMAN, MARGARET

Aunt Sallie's Lament. West Burke: 1988. V. 40; 42

Sarah's Sacrifice: Poems. 1988. V. 45

Sarah's Sacrifice. London: 1988. V. 41

KAUFMANN, EDGAR

Taliesin Drawings: Recent Architecture of Frank Lloyd Wright Selected from His Drawings. New York: 1952. V. 46

KAUKOL, MARIA JOSEPH CLEMENT

Christlicher Seelen-Schatz Ausserlesener Gebetter. Bonn: 1729. V. 41

KAUNTZE, GEORGE E. F.

Historical Record of the Third, or King's Own Regiment of Light Dragoons; Containing an Account of the Formation of the Regiment in 1685 and its Subsequent Services to 1857. London: 1857. V. 41

KAUS, GINA

Luxury Liner. New York: 1932. V. 42; 44

KAVANAGH, ARTHUR

The Cruise of the R. Y. S. Eva. Dublin: 1865. V. 43

KAVANAGH, JAMES W.

Mixed Education, The Catholic Case Stated. Dublin: 1895. V. 42

KAVANAGH, JULIA

Daisy Burns, a Tale. London: 1853. V. 39

Woman in France During the Eighteenth Century. London: 1850. V. 40

KAVANAGH, MORGAN

Origin of Language and Myths. London: 1871. V. 43; 46

KAVANAGH, PATRICK

Collected Poems. London: 1964. V. 40; 45

Come Dance with Kitty Stobling and Other Poems. London: 1960. V. 38

The Great Hunger. Dublin: 1942. V. 38

The Great Hunger. London: 1966. V. 38

Ploughman and Other Poems. London: 1936. V. 40

A Soul for Sale - Poems. London: 1947. V. 38; 40; 46

KAVANAGH, PATRICK F.

A Popular History of the Insurrection of 1798. Cork: 1898. V. 38

KAVANAGH, THOMAS HENRY

Guilty or Not Guilty, or Conduct Unbecoming an Officer and a Gentleman. Lucknow: 1876. V. 38

KAVANAGH, W. J.

Mixed Education. Dublin: 1859. V. 38

KAWAGUCHI, EKAI

Three years in Tibet. 1909. V. 37

KAY, GERTRUDE ALICE

Helping the Weatherman. 1920. V. 46

KAY, JOHN

A Series of Original Portraits and Caricature Etchings by the Late John Kay, Miniature Painter, Edinburgh . . . Edinburgh: 1838. V. 40

KAY, JOSEPH

The Education of the Poor in England and Europe. London: 1846. V. 38

KAY, R.

The New Preceptor, or Young Lady's and Gentleman's True Instructor in the Rudiments of the English Tongue . . . Newcastle: 1801. V. 42

KAY-SHUTTLEWORTH, JAMES PHILLIPS

Ribblesdale or Lancashire Sixty Years Ago. London: 1874. V. 42

Scarsdale; or Life in the Lancashire and Yorkshire Border Thirty Years Ago. London: 1860. V. 42; 46

Thoughts and Suggestions on Certain Social Problems Contained Chiefly in Addresses to Meetings of Workmen in Lancashire. London: 1873. V. 42

KAY, STEPHEN

Travels and Researches in Caffraria. New York: 1834. V. 37; 39; 43

KAY, THOMAS

The Life of Sir John Fowler, Engineer. London: 1900. V. 46

KAY, ULYSSES

Symphony. N.P.: 1967. V. 45

KAY, WILLIAM

Accuracy in Blood Urea Estimation and Its Application to the Study of the Elimintion of Urea by the Normal Rabbit Kidney. V. 39

KAYE, J. W.

Lives of Indian Officers. London: 1895. V. 45

KAYE, JOHN WILLIAM

History of the War in Afghanistan. London: 1878. V. 45

Jerningham; or, The Inconsistent Man. London: 1836. V. 39

Peregrine Pultuney; or, Life in India. London: 1844. V. 45

KAYE, M. M.

The Far Pavilions. London: 1978. V. 41

KAYE-SMITH, SHELIA

Green Apple Harvest. London: 1920. V. 37; 38

The Tramping Methodist. London: 1908. V. 37; 40; 46

KAYLL, ROBERT

The Trades Increase. London: 1615. V. 41

KAYSERLING, M.

Christopher Columbus and The Participation of the Jews in the Spanish and Portuguese Discoveries. New York: 1894. V. 42

KAZANTZAKIS, NIKOS

Christopher Columbus. 1972. V. 44

Christopher Columbus. Kentfield: 1972. V. 39

The Odyssey. A Modern Sequel. New York: 1958. V. 46

Zorba the Greek. New York: 1953. V. 42

Zorba the Greek. 1952. V. 37

Zorba The Greek. London: 1952. V. 37; 39

KAZIN, ALFRED

On Native Grounds. New York: 1942. V. 37

KEACH, BENJAMIN

Antichrist Stormed; or, Mystery Babylon the Great Whore, and Great City, Proved to be the Present Church of Rome. London: 1689. V. 40

KEALTIE, J. S.

History of the Scottish Highlands, Highland Clans and Highland Regiments. With an Account of the Gaelic Language, Literature, and Music . . . and an Essay on the Highland Scenery . . . A New Edition, with the Regimental Portion brought . . . London: (c. 1890). V. 37

KEAN, B. H.

Tropical Medicine and Parasitology; Classic Investigations. 1978. V. 37; 42

KEARNEY, ELEANOR

Pattie: or, Leaves from a Life, and Other Articles. Lamoni: 1892. V. 39

KEARNEY, P. J.

The Private Case. An Annotated Bibliography of the Private Case Erotica Collection in the British Museum Library. London: 1981. V. 38; 42; 46

KEARNEY, RICHARD

A Plan for the Payment of the National Debt. Parsonstown: 1816. V. 38

KEARNY, S. W.

Proclamation to the People of California. Proclama al Pueblo de California. San Francisco: 1847. V. 38

KEARTON, CHERRY

Wild Life Across the World. London. V. 40

Wild Life Across the World . . . London. V. 39; 42; 43; 44; 45

Wild Life Across the World. London: (ca. 1915). V. 37

KEARY, ANNIE

Oldbury. London: 1869. V. 44

KEARY, E.

The Magic Valley of Patient Antoine. London: 1877. V. 44

KEASEBY, LINDLEY MILL

The Nicaragua Canal and the Monroe Doctrine. New York: 1896. V. 41

KEAST, JOHN

The Naturalist in Vancouver Island and the British Columbia. London: 1866. V. 45

KEATE, GEORGE

An Account of the Pelew Islands, Situated in the Western Part of the Pacific Ocean . . . 1788. V. 42

An Account of the Pelew Islands. London: 1788. V. 37; 38; 40; 41; 42; 46

An Account of the Pelew Islands, Situated in the Western Part of the Pacific Ocean . . . 1789. V. 42

An Account of the Pelew Islands . . . Basil: 1789. V. 42; 45

Account of the Pelew Islands . . . Capt. H. Wilson in 1783 in the Antelope. London: 1789. V. 39

An Account of the Pelew Islands, Situated in the Western Part of the Pacific Ocean. Philadelphia: 1789. V. 40

An Account of the Pelew Islands, Situated in the Western Part of the Pacific Ocean. Dublin: 1793. V. 39; 43

An Account of the Pelew Islands . . . Stanford: 1802. V. 41; 42

An Account of the Pelew Islands . . . London: 1803. V. 42

Affecting the Interesting Narrative of the Loss of the Antelope Packet, Capt. Wilson, Off the Pelew Islands, August 10th, 1782. London: 1800. V. 42

Ancient and Modern Rome, a Poem. London: 1760. V. 40; 41

An Epistle From Lady Jane Grey to Lord Guildford Dudley Supposed to Have Been Written in the Tower, a Few Days Before They Suffered. London: 1762. V. 37; 40; 43

An Epistle to Angelica Kauffman. London: 1781. V. 40; 43

Ferney: an Epistle to Monsr. de Voltaire. London: 1768. V. 37

The Monument in Arcadia. London: 1773. V. 38; 40; 43

Narrative of the Shipwreck of the Antelope East India Pacquet, on the Pelew Islands, Situated on the Western Part of the Pacific ocean, in August 1785. Perth: 1788. V. 41; 42

Netley Abbey, an Elegy. London: 1796. V. 37

A Short Account of the Ancient History, Present Government and Laws of the Republic of Geneva. London: 1761. V. 37; 39; 41

Sketches from Nature; Taken and Coloured, in a Journey to Margate. London: 1779. V. 42; 44; 45

Sketches from Nature, Taken and Coloured in a Journey to Margate. London: 1802. V. 38; 40

KEATE, THOMAS

Observations on the Fifth Report of the Commissioners of General. London: 1808. V. 42

KEATIN, C. A.

Keating and Forbes Familes and Reminisceces of C. A. Keating . . . Dallas: 1920. V. 44

KEATING, G. P.

The Keating Family. Dublin: 1938. V. 38

KEATING, GEOFFREY

The History of Ireland from the Earliest Periods to the English Invasion. New York: 1837. V. 39

KEATING, GEORGE T.

A Conrad Memorial Library. New York: 1929. V. 46

A Conrad Memorial Library. The Collection of George T. Keating. Garden City: 1929. V. 37; 39

KEATING, H. R. F.

Murder Must Appetize. London: 1975. V. 38

KEATING, HENRY SHEEHY

Remarks on the Defence of Ireland: Including Observations on Some Other Subjects Connected Therewith . . . Belfast: 1796. V. 45

KEATING, JEOFFREY

The General History of Ireland Collected by the Learned Jeoffrey Keating. Dublin: 1841. V. 46

Tri Bior-ghaoithe and Bhais. Dublin: 1890. V. 46

KEATING, JOHN

Cyclopedia of the Diseases of Children Medical and Surgical. Philadelphia: 1889. V. 42

Cyclopedia of the Diseases of Children. Philadelphia: 1890. V. 40; 41

KEATING, WILLIAM H.

Narrative of an Expedition to the Source of St. Peter's River, etc., in the Year 1823, Under the Command of Stephen H. Long. Philadelphia: 1824. V. 37; 38; 39; 42; 43; 44; 45; 46

Narrative of an Expedition to the Source of St. Peter's River, Lake Winnepeek, Lake of the Woods &c. Performed in the Year 1823. London: 1825. V. 37; 38; 39; 41; 43; 45; 46

KEATS, JOHN 1795-1821

La Belle Dame Sans Merci. Hammersmith: 1906. V. 39; 40; 43

The Collected Sonnets of John Keats. Maastricht: 1930. V. 38; 40

Endymion. London: 1818. V. 37; 39; 42; 44; 45

Endymion. Boston: 1888. V. 38; 40

Endymion. New Rochelle: 1902. V. 46

Endymion. New York: 1902. V. 40

Endymion. London: 1947. V. 37; 38; 40; 41; 42; 46

Endymion, a Poetic Romance. London: 1947. V. 38; 46

The Eve of Saint Agnes. London: 1880. V. 43

The Eve of Saint Agnes. New York: 1880. V. 41; 43

The Eve of St. Agnes. Chicago: 1896. V. 38

The Eve of St. Agnes. London: 1900. V. 37; 40; 41; 45

Hyperion. London: 1945. V. 46

Isabella or the Pot of Basil. London: 1898. V. 37; 39; 42

Isabella or the Pot of Basil. London: 1907. V. 42

John Keats Unpublished Poem to His Sister Fanny, April, 1818. Boston: 1909. V. 38; 44

The Keats Letters, Papers and other Relics Forming the Dilke Bequest in the Hampstead Public Library. London: 1914. V. 37

Lamia, Isabella, the Eve of St. Agnes and Other Poems. London: 1820. V. 40; 43; 44; 46

Lamia, and Other Poems. Berkshire: 1928. V. 44; 46

Lamia, Isabella, the Eve of Saint Agnes and Other Poems. London: 1928. V. 41

Lamia, Isabella, the Eve of Saint Agnes & Other Poems. Waltham St. Lawrence: 1928. V. 37; 38; 39; 41; 42; 44; 46

The Letters and Poems of John Keats. New York: 1883. V. 45

Letters of John Keats to Fanny Brawne. London: 1878. V. 37; 40; 41; 43; 45; 46

Letters of John Keats to Fanny Brawne. New York: 1878. V. 43; 45

The Letters . . . London: 1895. V. 39

The Letters of John Keats. 1931. V. 37; 40

The Letters. London: 1931. V. 43

Letters of John Keats to Fanny Brawne, with Three Poems and Three Additional Letters. Maastricht: 1931. V. 38

The Letters. 1958. V. 46

Life, Letters and Literary Remains. London: 1848. V. 37; 39; 42; 45

Life, Letters and Literary Remains of John Keats. New York: 1848. V. 43; 45; 46

Ode to a Grecian urn. Bronxville: 1952. V. 37; 44; 45

Odes, Sonnets & Lyrics. Oxford: 1895. V. 42; 43; 46

Odes. Maastricht: 1927. V. 39

Poems. London: 1817. V. 40; 44; 46

The Poems. 1894. V. 38

The Poems of John Keats. Hammersmith: 1894. V. 37; 41; 46

The Poems of John Keats. London: 1894. V. 41

Poems by John Keats. London: 1897. V. 46

Poems. London: 1898. V. 39; 40; 41; 46

KEATS, JOHN 1795-1821 continued

The Poems. 1904. V. 45

The Poems. London: 1905. V. 42

Poems of John Keats. Florence: 1906. V. 38; 41

Poems. Hammersmith: 1914/15. V. 45

The Poems of John Keats. London: 1920. V. 44

Poems of Keats: an Anthology in Commemoration of the Poet's Death February 23, 1821. Thavies Inn: 1921. V. 46

The Poems. London: 1928. V. 41

The Poems and Verses. London: 1930. V. 38

The Poems of John Keats. Cambridge: 1966. V. 44; 46

The Poems. New York: 1966. V. 38; 41

Poems Selected and Arranged by T. J. Cobden-Sanderson. 1914. V. 37

The Poetical Works of . . . London: 1841. V. 41

The Poetical Works. London: 1849. V. 39

Poetical Works. London: 1854. V. 39; 42

The Poetical Works. London: 1858. V. 42

The Poetical Works. London: 1865. V. 42

The Poetical Works. London: 1866. V. 40

The Poetical Works and Other Writings of John Keats . . . (with) Poetry and Prose by John Keats. London: 1883-90. V. 39

The Poetical Works and Other Writings of John Keats. London: 1889. V. 37; 46

The Poetical Works and Other Writings. London: 1889-90. V. 38; 40

The Poetical Works and Other Writings. London: 1890. V. 46

The Poetical Works. Philadelphia: 1895. V. 40

The Poetical Works. London: 1925. V. 39

Poetical Works. Oxford: 1925. V. 41

Poetical Works and Other Writings. New York: 1938. V. 38; 41; 42; 46

The Poetical Works. New York: 1938-39. V. 44

The Poetical Works. London: 1922. V. 37

The Poetical Works of John Keats. London: 1851. V. 37

Selections from the Poems of John Keats: Isabella or the Pot of Basil. Florence: 1906. V. 40

Two Odes: On Melancholy, On Autumn. Providence: 1989. V. 41

Unpublished Poem to His Sister Fanny. Boston: 1909. V. 38; 41; 46

The Complete Works. London: 1904. V. 42

The Complete Works and Life of John Keats. London & Boston: 1904. V. 41

KEAY, ISAAC

The Practical Measurer His Pocket Companion. London: 1724. V. 46

KEBLE, JOHN

The Christian Year. Oxford: 1827. V. 37; 38

National Apostasy Considered in a Sermon Preached in St. Mary's Oxford Before His Majesty's Judges of Assize, on Sunday, July 14, 1833. Oxford: 1833. V. 38

Lyra Innocentium: Thoughts in Verse on Christian Children, Their Ways and Their Privileges. Oxford: 1846. V. 37; 41

KEBLE, JOSEPH

An Assitance to Justices of the Peace, for the Easier Performance of their Duty. London: 1683. V. 38; 40

KEBLE MARTIN, W.

The Concise British Flora in Colour. London: 1969. V. 41

KEBLE'S Morning Hymn. London: 1861. V. 44

KECKERMANN, B.

Systema Physicum . . . Anno Christi MDCVII Publice Propositum in Gymnasio Dantiscano . . . Hanover: 1612. V. 41

KEEFE, CHARLES S.

The American House Being a Collection of Illustrations and Plans of the Best Country and Suburban Houses Built in the United States During the Last Few Years. New York: 194. V. 41

KEELE, K. D.

Leonardo Da Vinci on Movement of the Heart and Blood. London: 1952. V. 42

KEELER, BRONSON C.

Where to Go to Become Rich. Farmers', Miners' and Toursits' Guide. Chicago: 1880. V. 40

KEELER, N. E.

A Trip to Alaska and the Klondike in the Summer of 1905. Cincinnati: 1906. V. 41; 42

KEELER, S.

The Mechanics (and Kinematics) of Web - Work Plot Construction with Diagrams. 1955. V. 43; 46

KEELEY, EDMUND

Cavafy's Alexandria. Study of a Myth in Progress. London: 1977. V. 40

KEELEY, R. N.

In Arctic Seas, the Voyage of the 'Kite' with the Peary Expedition, Together with a Transcript of the Log. London: 1893. V. 41

KEELIVINE, CHRISTOPHER

Tales and Sketches of the West of Scotland. Glasgow: 1824. V. 46

KEELY, ROBERT N.

In Arctic Seas - The Voyage of the 'Kite.' Philadelphia: 1892. V. 37

KEEN, RALPH HOLBROOK

The Little Ape and Other Stories. London: 1921. V. 44

KEEN, WILLIAM WILLIAMS

An American Text-Book of Surgery. Philaelphia: 1892. V. 42

Surgery: Its Principles and Practice by Various Authors. Philadelphia: 1907-13. V. 42

Surgery. Its Principles and Practice. Philadelphia: 1910-26. V. 37; 38; 39; 40; 41; 44

Surgery. Its Principles and Practice. Philadelphia: 1912-21. V. 45

Surgery: Its Principles and Practice by Various Authors. Philadelphia: 1914. V. 42

The Surgical Operations on President Cleveland in 1893. Philadelphia: 1917. V. 41

The Treatment of War Wounds. Philadelphia: 1917. V. 42

KEENE, CHARLES

Mrs. Caudle's Curtain Lectures. By Douglas Jerrold. Illustrated by Charles Keene. London: 1866. V. 37

KEENE, DEREK

A Survey of Medieval Winchester. Oxford: 1985. V. 37

KEENE, HENRY GEORGE

Ex Eremo. Poems Chiefly Written in India. Edinburgh & London: 1855. V. 37

KEENE, J. M.

Fishing Tackle, Its Materials and Manufactures. London: 1886. V. 39

KEENE, JOHN HARRINGTON

Fly-Fhsing and Fly-Making for Trout. New York: 1887. V. 40; 43

KEENE, RICHARD RAYNAL

A Letter of Vindication to His Excellency Colonel Monroe . . . Philadelphia: 1824. V. 37

KEEP, JOHN

An Address Delivered December 22, 1837 in the Village of Lockport, N.Y. Commemorative of the Martyrdom of Rev. E. P. Lovejoy, Who Was Killed by the Mob in the City of Alton III on the Night of Nov. 7, 1837. Lockport: 1838. V. 40

KEEPE, HENRY

Monumenta Westmonasteriensio. London: 1682. V. 39; 41

Monuments Westmonasteriensia. London: 1683. V. 38

THE KEEPSAKE. London: 1827-36. V. 45

THE KEEPSAKE 1852. London: 1852. V. 40

THE KEEPSAKE: a Gift for the Holidays. New York: 1854. V. 40

THE KEEPSAKE For 1829. London: 1828. V. 43; 45

THE KEEPSAKE for MDCCCXXX. London: 1829. V. 39; 43
THE KEEPSAKE for MDCCCXXX. London: 1830. V. 39

THE KEEPSAKE for MDCCCXXXI. London: 1831. V. 39

THE KEEPSAKE for MDCCCXXXII. London. V. 38

THE KEEPSAKE for 1853. London: 1853. V. 39

KEES, WELDON

The Fall of the Magicians. New York: 1947. V. 46

Fall Quarter. Brownsville: 1990. V. 44

The Last Man. San Francisco: 1943. V. 39

Poems 1947-1954. San Francisco: 1954. V. 37; 39; 44

Two Prose Sketches. West Chester: 1984. V. 38; 40; 42; 46

KEESE, JOHN

The Floral Keepsake, with Thirty Engravings Elegantly colored from Nature. New York: 1854. V. 37

The Poets of America: Illustrated by One of Her Painters. New York: 1840/42. V. 41

KEFFER, FRANK M.

History of San Fernando Valley. Glendale: 1934. V. 42

KEGLEY, F. B.

Kegley's Virginia Frontier: The Beginning of the Southwest. Roanoke: 1938. V. 39; 45

KEHR, HANS

Introduction to the Differential Diagnosis of the Separate Forms of Gallstone Disease Based Upon His Own Experience Gained in 433 Laparotomies for Gallstones. Philadelphia: 1901. V. 42

KEIGHTLEY, THOMAS

An Account of the Life, Opinions and Writings of John Milton. London: 1855. V. 44

The Fairy Mythology. 1828. V. 43

Fairy Mythology. London: 1828. V. 39

History of the War of Independence in Greece. Edinburgh: 1830. V. 39

KEILL, JOANNE

Introductio Ad Veram Astroniam, Seu Lectiones Astronomicae Habitae in Schola Astronomica Academiae Oxoniensis. Oxoniae: 1718. V. 40

KEILL, JOHN

Introductio ad Veram Physicam: Seu Lectiones Physicae Habitae in Schola Naturalis Philosophiae Academiae Oxoniensis. Oxford: 1705. V. 45

An Introduction to the True Astronomy. London: 1769. V. 38; 39; 40

Introducto ad Veram Physicam; seu Lectiones Physicae Habitae in Schola Naturalis Philosophiae Academiae Oxoniensis An. Dom. 1700 . . . London: 1719. V. 41; 42

Lectures (on Optics and Hydrostatics). (Oxford: c. 1707). V. 37

KEIM, DE BENNEVILLE RANDOLPH

Sheridan's Troopers on the Borders. Philadelphia: 1870. V. 37; 38; 39

KEIMER, SAMUEL

Caribbeana. Containing Letters and Dissertations, Together with Poetical Essays, on Various Subjects and Occasions; Chiefly Wrote by Several Hands in the West Indies . . . London: 1741. V. 39

KEIR, JAMES

An Account of the Life and Writings of Thomas Day, Es. London: 1791. V. 37; 43

KEIR, SUSANNA HARVEY

Interesting Memoirs. Edinburgh: 1785. V. 41

KEISER, CLARENCE E.

Cuneiform Bullae of the Third Millenium B.C. New Haven;: 1920. V. 40

KEITH, ALEXANDER

Observations on the Act of Preventing Clandestine Marriages. London: 1753. V. 46

KEITH, ARTHUR

Menders of the Maimed. London: 1919. V. 38

KEITH, ARTHUR B.

Responsible Government in the Dominions. Oxford: 1912. V. 40

Responsible Government in the Dominions. Oxford: 1928. V. 41

KEITH, CHARLES

The Har'st Rig, and the Farmer's Ha': Two Poems in the Scottish Dialect. Edinburgh: 1801. V. 40

KEITH, CHARLES P.

The Provincial Councilors of Pennsylvania Who Held Office Between 1733 and 1776 and Those Earlier Councilors Who Were Some Time Chief Magistrates of the Province and Their Descendants. Philadelphia: 1883. V. 39; 41; 42; 46

KEITH, E. C.

A Countryman's creed. London: 1938. V. 44; 46

Gun for Company. London: 1937. V. 39

KEITH, ELMER

Big Game Rifles and Cartridges. Plantersville: 1936. V. 40

Sixguns. Harrisburg: 1955. V. 46

KEITH, GEORGE

A Journal of Travels from New Hampshire to Caratuck, on the Continent of North America. London: 1706. V. 41; 44; 46

The Presbyterian and Independent Visible Churches in New England and Else-Where, Brought to the Test, and Examined . . . With a Call and a Warning to the People of Boston and New England . . . London: 1691. V. 38; 40

A Serious Call to the Quakers Inviting Them to Return to Christianity. London: 1700. V. 41

KEITH, GEORGE MOUAT, BART.

A Voyage to South America and the Cape of Good Hope, in His Majesty's Brig Protector. London: 1819. V. 45

KEITH, GEORGE SKENE

Tracts on Weights, Measures and Coins. London: 1791. V. 37

KEITH, NOEL L.

The Brites of Capote. Fort Worth: 1950. V. 45; 46

KEITH, ROBERT

An Historical Catalogue of the Scottish Bishops Down to the Year 1688. Edinburgh: 1824. V. 38

A Large New Catalogue of the Bishops of the Several Sees, Within the Kingdom of Scotland, Down to the Year 1688. Edinburgh: 1755. V. 39

KEITH, ROBERT MURRAY 1730-1795

Memoirs and Correspondence of Sir Robert Murray Keith. London: 1849. V. 39

KEITH, THOMAS

An Introduction to the Theory and Practice of Plane and Spherical Trigonometry and the Orthographic and Stereographic Projections of the Sphere . . . London: 1801. V. 44

A New Treatise on the Use of the Globes, or a Philosophical View of the Earth and Heavens. New York: 1826. V. 39; 40

Struggles of Capt. Thomas Keith in America Including the Manner In Which He, His Wife and Child Were Decoyed by the Indians; Their Temporary Captivity, and Happy Deliverance . . . London: 1808? V. 37; 39; 46

A Treatise on the Use of the Globes, or a Philosophical View of the Earth and Heavens . . . London: 1821. V. 41

KEITH, WILLIAM

A Collection of Papers and Other Tracts, Written Occasionally on Various Subjects . . . London: 1740. V. 45

Keith, Old Master of California. New York & Berkeley: 1942. V. 46

Keith, Old Master of California. Fresno: 1956. V. 46

KELD, CHRISTOPHER

An Essay on the Polity of England; with a View to Discover the True Principles of the Government, What Remedies Might Be Likely to Cure the Grievances. London: 1785. V. 42

KELDANI, E. H.

A Bibliography of Geology and Related Sciences Concerning Egypt Up to the End of 1939. Cairo: 1971. V. 43

KELEHER, WILLIAM A.

The Fabulous Frontier: Twelve New Mexico Items. Santa Fe: 1945. V. 39; 43; 44; 46

The Fabulous Frontier: Twelve New Mexico Items. Albuquerque: 1962. V. 39

Maxwell Land Grant. 1942. V. 42

Maxwell Land Grant. A New Mexico Item. Santa Fe: 1942. V. 39; 42; 45; 46

A New Mexico Item. Santa Fe: 1942. V. 37

Turmoil in New Mexico 1846-1868. Santa Fe: 1952. V. 39; 42; 43

Violence in Lincoln County 1869-1881. Albuquerque: 1957. V. 39; 40; 41

KELELRMAN, W. A.

Ohio Fungi Exsiccati. Columbus: 1901-05. V. 46

KELEMEN, P.

Medieval American Art. London: 1943. V. 46

Medieval American Art: a Survey in Two Volumes. New York: 1943. V. 41; 42; 44

Medieval American Art. New York: 1944. V. 45

KELHAM, ROBERT

A Dictionary of the Norman or Old French Language . . . London: 1779. V. 42; 43

Domesday Book Illustrated. London: 1788. V. 42

KELIHER, J. J.

The Keliher Recipe Book. London: 1940's. V. 38

KELKER, LUTHER R.

History of Dauphin County, Pennsylvania . . . New York: 1907. V. 41; 42; 46

KELL, JOHN MC INTOSH

Recollections of a Naval Life, Including the Cruises of the Confederate States Steamers 'Sumter' and 'Alabama'. Washington: 1900. V. 42; 43

KELLAR, HUGH

Presbyterian Pioneer Missionaries in Manitoba, Saskatchewan, Alberta and British Columbia. Toronto: 1924. V. 43

KELLER, D.

The Eternal Conflict. 1949. V. 43

KELLER, DAVID H.

The Sign of the Burning Hart, a Tale of Arcadia. N.P.: 1938. V. 40

The Sign of the Burning Hart, a Tale of Arcadia. N.P.: 1948. V. 41

KELLER, DIETHELM

Kunstliche und Aigendtliche Bildtnussen der Rhomischen Keyseren, Ihrer Weybern und Kindern, Auch Anderer Verrumpten Personen, Wie die Auf Alten Pfenningen Erfunden sind, Sampt Ainer Kurtzen Beschreybung Ihrens Harkommens, Labens und Abschaids. Zurich: 1558. V. 45

KELLER-DORIAN, LYON

Trade Catalogue of Gold and Silver-Foil Textured and Embossed Paper Samples. 1920's. V. 43

KELLER, FERDINAND

The Lake Dwellings of Switzerland and Other Parts of Europe. London: 1878. V. 38; 41; 44

KELLER, FRANZ

The Amazon and Madeira Rivers; Sketches and Descriptions from the Notebook of an Explorer. London: 1874. V. 38; 40; 42

KELLER, HELEN

Double Blossoms: Helen Keller Anthology. New York: 1931. V. 42; 46

Helen Keller's Journal 1936-1937. Garden City: 1938. V. 39; 43

Let Us Have Faith. New York: 1940. V. 45

Our Duties to the Blind. Boston. V. 43

Our Duties to the Blind. Boston: 1904. V. 43; 44

Peace at Eventide. London: 1932. V. 39

The Song of the Stone Wall. New York: 1910. V. 42

Teacher. Anne Sullivan Macy. A Tribute by the Foster-Child of Her Mind. Garden City: 1955. V. 39

KELLER, HELEN ADAMS 1880-1968

Optimism, My Key of Life. New York: 1903. V. 38

The Story of My Life. With Her Letters (1887-1901), and a Supplementary Account of Her Education, etc. New York: 1927. V. 37

KELLETT, JOSEPHINE

That Friend of Mine. A Memoir of Magueritee McArthur. London: 1920. V. 46

KELLEY, ALLYN L.

The Pottery of Ancient Egypt: Dynasty I to Roman Times. Toronto: 1976. V. 40

KELLEY, ANTHONY M.

In Vinculis; or, the Prisoner of War . . . Petersburg: 1866. V. 42

KELLEY, CHARLES FABENS

Chinese Bronzes from the Buckingham Collection. Chicago: 1946. V. 44

KELLEY, DANIEL G.

What I Saw and Suffered in Rebel Prions. Buffalo: 1868. V. 44

KELLEY, E. G.

A Popular Treatise on the Human Teeth and Dental Surgery, Being a Practical Guide for the Early Management of the Health and Teeth of Children. Boston: 1843. V. 39

KELLEY, EMMA DUNHAM

Megda. Boston: 1892. V. 44

KELLEY, HALL J.

A General Circular to All Persons of Good Character, Who Wish to Emigrate to the Oregon Territory, Embracing Some Account of the Character and Advantages of the Country . . . Charlestown: 1831. V. 37; 38; 40; 41; 42; 46

A Geographical Sketch of that Part of North America Called Oregon . . . Tarrytown: 1919. V. 41; 44

A Geographical Sketch of that Part of North America, Called Oregon: Containing an Account of the Indian Title; the Nature of a Right of Sovereignty; the First Discoveries . . . Boston: 1830. V. 37; 38

A Narrative of Events and Difficulties in the Colonization of Oregon, and the Settlement of California. Boston: 1852. V. 39; 40; 43

Settlement on the Oregon River. Washington: 1828. V. 39

KELLEY, J. D.

Our Navy. Hartford: 1892. V. 45

KELLEY, JOSEPH

Thirteen Years in the Oregon Penitentiary. Portland: 1908. V. 41

KELLEY, ROBERT F.

Racing in America, 1937-1959. New York: 1960. V. 41

KELLEY, TOM, MRS.

From the Fleet in the Fifties - a History of the Crimean War, with Stothert Letters 1854-6 . . . London: 1902. V. 39

KELLEY, WILLIAM D.

The New Northwest; an Address on the Northrn Pacific Railway. Philadelphia: 1871. V. 41

The Old South and the New: a Series of Letters. New York: 1888. V. 39; 41

Why Colored People in Philadelphia are Excluded from the Street Cars. Philadelphia: 1866. V. 42

KELLISON, MATTHEW

A Survey of the New Religion. Douai: 1603. V. 38; 40

KELLOG, ROBERT B.

Life and Death in Rebel Prisons: Giving a Complete History of the Inhuman and Barbarous Treatment of Our Brave Soldiers by Rebel Authorities . . . Hartford: 1866. V. 38

KELLOGG, EDWARD

Labor and Other Capital: The Rights of Each Secured and the Wrongs of Both Eradicated . . . New York: 1849. V. 45

KELLOGG, GEORGE J.

Narative (sic) of Geo. J. Kellogg from 1849 to 1915. Janesville: 1915. V. 40; 43

KELLOGG, J. H.

Dr. Kellogg's Temperance Charts . . . Battle Creek: 1882. V. 44

Household Manual of Hygiene, Food and Diet, Common Diseases, Accidents and Emergencies, and Useful Hints and Recipes. Battle Creek: 1877. V. 46

Household Manual of Domestic Hygiene, Food and Diet, Treatment of Common Diseases, Accidents and Emergencies, and Healthful Cookery . . . (with) The Hygienic Cook Book. Battle Creek: 1882, 1875. V. 37

Ladies' Guide in Health and Disease, Girlhood, Maidenhood, Wifehood, Motherhood. Battle Creek: 1891. V. 42

Plain Facts for Old and Young. Burlington: 1882. V. 42

Sunbeams of Health and Temperance. Battle Creek: 1888. V. 39

KELLOGG, JAY C.

The Broncho Busted and Other Messages. Tacoma: 1932. V. 37

KELLOGG, LOUISE P.

Frontier Advance on the Upper Ohio, 1778-1779. Madison: 1916. V. 42; 46

Frontier Advance on the Upper Ohio. 1779-1781. Madison: 1917. V. 42

KELLY, CHARLES

Holy Murder, The Story of Porter Rockwell. New York: 1934. V. 46

Journals of John D. Lee 1846-47 and 1859. Salt Lake City: 1938. V. 42

Miles Goodyear First Citizen of Utah, Trapper, Trader and California Pioneer. Salt Lake City: 1937. V. 39; 42; 44; 45

Old Greenwood. Salt Lake City: 1936. V. 40; 42; 43; 45

Old Greenwood: the Story of Caleb Greenwood: Trapper, Pathfinder and Early Pioneer. Georgetown: 1965. V. 42

Outlaw Trail. Salt Lake City: 1838. V. 39; 45; 46

Outlaw-Trail a History of Butch Cassidy and His Wild Bunch Hole-in-the-Wall Brown's Hole Robber's Roost. Salt Lake City: 1938. V. 46

Salt Desert Trails. Salt Lake City: 1930. V. 38; 40; 41; 42; 44; 45; 46

KELLY, CHARLES ARTHUR

Delhi and Other Poems. London: 1864. V. 38; 40

KELLY, CHRISTOPHER

A Full and Circumstantial Account of the Memorable Battle of Waterloo. London: 1817. V. 40

A Full and Circumstantial Account of the Memorable Battle of Waterloo . . . and the Deportation of Napoleon Bonaparte to the Island of St. Helena . . . London: 1818. V. 40

History of the French Revolution, and the Wars Produced by that Memorable Event . . . London: 1817. V. 46

History of the French Revolution and of the Wars Produced by that Memorable Event, from the Commencement of Hostilities in 1792 . . . London: 1818. V. 46

KELLY, EDMOND 1851-1909

The Elimination of the Tramp. New York: 19808. V. 41

KELLY, FANNY

Narrative of My Captivity Among the Sioux Indians. Toronto: 1872. V. 39; 42

KELLY, H.

American Medical Biographies. New York: 1920. V. 45

KELLY, H. A.

Dictionary of American Medical Biography. New York: 1928. V. 41

KELLY, HOWARD

A Cyclopedia of American Medical Biography Comprising the Lives of Eminent Deceased Physicians and Surgeons from 1610 to 1910. Philadelphia: 1912. V. 39; 42

Electrosurgery. Philadelphia & London: 1932. V. 43

Gynecology and Abdominal Surgery. Philadelphia: 1908. V. 42

Medical Gynecology. New York: 1908. V. 44

Myomata of the Uterus. Philadelphia: 1909. V. 42

Operative Gynecology. New York: 1898. V. 42

Report in Gynecology I. Baltimore: 1890. V. 42

Some American Medical Botanists. Troy: 1914. V. 40; 43

KELLY, HUGH

The Babler. London: 1767. V. 38

False Delicacy, a Comedy. Boston: 1809. V. 44

Thespis; or, a Critical Examination inot the Merits of All the Principle Performers Belonging to Drury Lane Theatre. (with) . . . . Book the Second. London: 1764/67. V. 43

Thespis; or, a Critical Examination (in verse) Into the Merits of All the Principal Performers Belonging to Drury Lane Theatre. London: 1766. V. 40; 45

Thespis: or, a Critical Examination into the Merits of all the Principal Performers Belonging to Drury Lane Theatre. Dublin: 1767. V. 38

A Word to the Wise, a Comedy, As It is Performed at the Theatre Royal . . . London: 1770. V. 42

KELLY, ISABEL

The Archaeology of the Autlan-Tuxcacuesco Area of Jalisco I-II. Berkeley: 1945-49. V. 42; 44

KELLY, J. FREDERICK

The Early Domestic Architecture of Connecticut. New Haven: 1924. V. 44

Early Connecticut Meetinghouses Being an Account of the Church Edifices Built Before 1830 Based Chiefly Upon Town and Parish Records. New York: 1948. V. 39

KELLY, JAMES

A Complete Collection of Scottish Proverbs. London: 1721. V. 37; 38; 40; 41; 42; 46

KELLY, JOHN

Etchings and Drawings of Hawaiians. Honolulu: 1943. V. 37

Notes Upon the Errors of Geology Illustrated by Reference to Facts Observed in Ireland. London: and Dublin: 1864. V. 45

KELLY, JOSEPH

Thirteen Years in the Oregon Penitentiary. Portland: 1908. V. 43

KELLY, L. V.

The Range Men. The Story of the Ranchers and Indians of Alberta. Toronto: 1913. V. 37; 38; 39; 40; 41; 42; 43; 45; 46

KELLY, LUTHER S.

Yellowstone Kelly. New Haven: 1926. V. 41; 42; 43; 45

KELLY, MATTHEW

Cambrensis Eversus . . . in Rebus Hibernicis, edited with translation and notes by Rev. M. Kelly. Dublin: 1848. V. 37

KELLY, MICHAEL

Reminiscences. London: 1825. V. 43

Reminiscences of Michael Kelly, of the King's Theatre, and Theatre Royal Drury Lane . . . London: 1826. V. 38; 39; 40; 45

KELLY, MRS.

The Fatalists; or, Records of 1814 and 1815. London: 1821. V. 41

KELLY PATRICK 1756-1842

The Universal Cambist, and Commercial Instructor. London: 1811. V. 38; 39

The Universal Cambist and Commercial Instructor . . . London: 1835. V. 39

The Universal Cambist and Commerical Instructor . . . on the Exchanges, Monies, Weights . . . of all Trading Nations and their Colonies . . . banks, public funds and paper currencies. London: 1821. V. 37

KELLY, R. TALBOT

Burma. London: 1905. V. 45

Egypt. London: 1902. V. 46

KELLY, ROB ROY

American Wood Type 1828-1900. New York: 1969. V. 46

KELLY, ROBERT

Axon Dendron Tree. Cleveland: 1967. V. 43

Finding the Measure. 1968. V. 42; 43; 44

Ralegh. Los Angeles: 1972. V. 37

Sonnets. 1968. V. 42; 43; 44

Statement. 1968. V. 42; 43; 44

The Tears of Edmund Burke. (New York): 1973. V. 37

KELLY, THOMAS

Kelly's Practical Builder's Price Book or Safe Guide to the Valuation of All Kinds of Articifer's Work with the Modern Practice of Measuring . . . London: 1861. V. 42

Kelly's Practical Builder's Price Book. London: 1867. V. 38; 40

Practical Carpentry, Joinery and Cabinet-Making . . . London: 1840. V. 44

KELLY, THOMAS ALEXANDER ERSKINE, 6TH EARL OF 1732-1781

Minuets and Songs, Composed by the Right Honorable Thomas Earl of Kelly, Now for the First Time Published . . . Edinburgh: 1839. V. 40

KELLY, TOM, MRS.

From the Fleet in the Fifties. A History of the Crimean War. London: 1902. V. 41

KELLY, WALTER K.

Syria and the Holy Land. London: 1844. V. 45

KELLY, WILLIAM

Across the Rocky Mountains, from New York to California . . . London: 1852. V. 37; 42; 45

An Excursion to California Over the Prairie, Rocky Mountains and Great Sierra Nevada. London: 1851. V. 38; 39; 40; 41; 42; 45; 46

A Stroll through the Diggings of California. London: 1852. V. 39; 41; 43

KELLY'S Directory of Chemists and Druggists . . . and Other Trades Connected Therewith. London: 1896. V. 45

KELLY'S Directory of Nottinghamshire. London: 1904. V. 39

KELMAN, JOHN

The Holy land. London: 1902. V. 46

The Holy Land. London: 1912. V. 44

KELMO, F.

Watch-Repairer's Hand-Book . . . Boston: 1869. V. 42

KELMSCOTT, Doves and Ashendene: the Private Press Credos. San Francisco: 1952. V. 46

KELMSCOTT PRESS

Kelmscott Paper Specimen. Cambridge: 1974. V. 41

Syr Isambrace. (Edited by F.S. Ellis). (Hammersmith, England: 1897). V. 37

KELSALL, CHARLES

Horae Viaticae; the Author Mela Britannicus. Clifton & Bristol: 1839. V. 43

KELSEY, ALBERT W.

Autobiographical Notes and Memoranda . . . 1840-1910. Baltimore: 1911. V. 38; 42; 44

KELSEY, HENRY

The Kelsey Papers. Ottawa: 1929. V. 41; 43; 44; 45

KELSEY, S. T.

The Blue Ridge Highlands of Western North Carolina. Atlanta: 1878. V. 39; 42

KELSO, ISAAC

The Stars and Bars; or, the Reign of Terror in Missouri. Boston: 1863. V. 40

KELSO, JOHN J.

The Plantation of Ireland. A Review of Her Earlier Colonial Settlements. Belfast: 1865. V. 37

KELSON, GEORGE M.

The Salmon Fly: How to Dress It and How to Use It. London: 1895. V. 37; 39; 40; 46

Tips. London: 1901. V. 39

KELTIE, J. SCOTT

History of the Scottish Highlands, Highland Clans and Highland Regiments. London: 1890. V. 39

The Partition of Africa. London: 1893. V. 46

The Story of Emin's Rescue as Told in Stanley's Letters. New York: 1890. V. 39

KELTIE, JOHN S.

A History of the Scottish Highlands, Highland Clans and Highland Regiments . . . London. V. 44

A History of the Scottish Highlands, Highland Clans and Highland Regiments . . . Edinburgh & London: 1875. V. 44

History of their Scottish Higlanders, Highland Clans, and higland Regiments. With an Account of the Gaelic Language, Literature, and Music by the Rev. Thomas MacLauchlan, LL.D., F.S.A. (Scot.) and an Essay on Highland . . . Glasgow: (c. 1885). V. 37

KELTY, MARY ANN

The Favourite of Nature. London: 1822. V. 38

The Favourite of Nature. London: 1821. V. 37

Osmond, a Tale. London: 1822. V. 37; 38; 43

Trials; a Tale. London: 1824. V. 38

KELVIE, C. L.

The Grouse, Studies in Words and Piectures. V. 45; 46

KELVIN, LORD

Treatise on Natural Philosophy. Cambridge: 1912. V. 45

KELVIN, WILLIAM THOMPSON

Mathematical and Physical Papers. Cambridge: 1882/1884/1890. V. 38

KELVIN, WILLIAM THOMSON

Popular Lectures and Addresses. London: 1889-91. V. 45

KELYNG, JOHN d. 1671

A Report of Divers Cases in Pleas of the Crown . . . in the Reign of King Charles II (1662-169) With Three Modern Cases. London: 1708. V. 38; 40

KELYNGE, WILLIAM

A Report of Cases in Chancery, The King's Bench &c. In the Fourth, Fifth, Sixth, Seventh and Eighth Years of His late Majesty King George the Second . . . London: 1764. V. 45

KEMBLE, EDWARD C.

A History of California Newspapers, 1846-1858. Los Gatos: 1962. V. 41

KEMBLE, EDWARD W.

The Blackberries and Their Adventures. New York: 1897. V. 45

Kemble's Coons: a Collection of Southern Sketches. New York: 1896. V. 45

KEMBLE, FRANCES ANNE 1809-1893

Francis the First, an Historical Drama. London: 1832. V. 45

Journal of Frances Anne Butler. London: 1835. V. 43

Journal. Philadelphia: 1835. V. 41; 43; 44; 45

Journal . . . Philadelphia: 1835. V. 41

Journal of a Residence on a Georgia Plantation in 1838-1839. London: 1863. V. 38; 42; 46

Journal of a Residence on a Georgian Plantation in 1838-1839. New York: 1863. V. 40; 42; 43; 44; 45; 46

Poems. London: 1844. V. 45; 46

Record of a Girlhood. London: 1878. V. 40

Records of Later Life . . . London: 1882. V. 41; 43; 45

Records of a Later Life. New York: 1882. V. 42; 45

The Star of Seville. London: 1837. V. 42; 45; 46

The Views of Judge Woodward and Bishop Hopkins on Negro Slavery at the South. Philadelphia: 1863. V. 45

The Views of Judge Woodward and Bishop Hopkins on Negro Slavery at the South, Illustrated from the Journal of a Residence on a Georgian Plantation. Philadelphia: 1864. V. 44

KEMBLE, JOHN H.

Gold Rush Steamers. California: 1958. V. 42

KEMBLE, JOHN HASKELL

The Panama Route, 1849-1869. Berkeley & Los Angeles: 1943. V. 40; 45

KEMBLE, JOHN PHILIP

An Authentic Narrative of Mr. Kemble's Retirement from the Stage, Including Farewell Address . . . London: 1817. V. 43

Fugitive Pieces . . . York: 1800. V. 38; 41

KEMLO, F.

Kemlo's Watch Repairer's Hand Book. Boston: 1869. V. 40

KEMP, A. C.

The Biography of Claude Gibney Finch-Davies 1875-1920, Observer, Student and Highly Skilled Illustrator of South African Birds. Pretoria: 1976. V. 37; 38

KEMP, DIXON

A Manual of Yacht and Boat Sailing. London: 1888. V. 38; 40

A Manual of Yacht and Boat Sailing. London: 1895. V. 42

Yacht Architecture. London: 1885. V. 38

KEMP, EMILY GEORGIANA

The Face of Manchuria, Korea and Russian Turkestan. New York: 1911. V. 46

KEMP, LOUIS W.

The Signers of the Texas Declaration of Independence. Houston: 1944. V. 38

The Signers of the Texas Declaration of Independence. Salado: 1959. V. 40

KEMP, M. A., MRS.

Little Maids. Rhymes with Illustrations. London: 1876. V. 39

KEMP, ROBERT 1820-1897

Father Kemp's Old Folks Concert Tunes. Boston: 1860. V. 40

KEMPE, A. J.

The Loseley Manuscripts, and Other Rare Documents, Illustrative of Some of the Most Minute Particulars of English History, Biography and Manners, from the Reign of Henry VIII to That of James I Preserved in the Muniment Room of James More Molyneux, Esq, at.. London: 1836. V. 46

KEMPNER, STANLEY

Television Encyclopedia. New York: 1948. V. 40

THE KEMSLEY Manual of Journalism. London: 1950. V. 39

KEN, THOMAS

A Manual of Prayers For the Use of the Scholars of Winchester College. London: 1705. V. 37

KENADAY, ALEXANDER M.

Prospectus of a History of the Mexican War. Washington: 1875. V. 40

KENAN, THOMAS S.

Sketch of the Duplin Rifles. Raleigh?: 1895. V. 44

Sketch of the Forty-Third Regiment North Carolina Troops. (Raleigh: 1895). V. 37

KENDAL, OTIS

Atlas of the Heavens; Showing the Places of the Principal Stars, Clusters and Nebulae . . . Philadelphia: 1845. V. 39

KENDAL, SAMUEL

A Sermon, Delivered at Weston, January 12, 1813, on the Terimination of a Century Since the Incorporation of the Town. Cambridge: 1813. V. 39

KENDALL, A.

Tales of the Abbey; Founded on Historical Facts. London: 1800. V. 45; 46

KENDALL, AMOS

Kendall's Expositor for 1841 (through 1843). Washington: 1841-43. V. 43

Letters to John Quincy Adams, Relative to the Fisheries and the Mississippi, First Published in the Argus of Western America. Lexington: 1823. V. 40

Morse's Patent. Full Exposure of Dr. Chas. T. Jackson's Pretensions to the Invention of the American Electro-Magnetic Telegraph. Washington: 1852. V. 39

Secession. Letters of Amos Kendall: also, His Letters to Col. Orr and President Buchanan. Washington: 1861. V. 43

KENDALL, EDWARD AUGUSTUS

Parental Education; or, Domestic Lessons; a Miscellany, Intended for Youth. London: 1803. V. 40

The Swallow; a Fiction. London: 1800. V. 41

Travels Through the Northern Parts of the United States, in the Years 1807 & 1808. New York: 1809. V. 37; 38; 40; 42; 46

KENDALL, GEORGE W.

Narrative of the Texan Santa Fe Expedtion . . . V. 43

Narrative of the Texan Santa Fe Expedtion. London: 1844. V. 45

Narrative of the Texan Santa Fe Expedition. New York: 1844. V. 37; 38; 39; 40; 41; 42; 43; 44; 45; 46

Narrative of the Texan Santa Fe Expedition. New York: 1844-47. V. 40

Narrative of an Expedition Across the Great Southwestern Prairies, From Texas to Santa Fe . . . London: 1845. V. 37; 38; 39; 40; 41; 42; 44; 45

Narrative of the Texan Santa Fe Expedition, Comprising a Tour through Texas . . . London: 1847. V. 39; 42

Narrative of the Texan Santa Fe Expedition. New York: 1856. V. 37; 39; 40; 41; 42; 43; 46

KENDALL, GEORGE WILKINS

The War Between the United States and Mexico, Illustrated, Embracing Pictorial Drawings of all the Principal Conflicts.. New York & Philadelphia: 1851. V. 37; 39; 40; 41; 43; 44; 45; 46

KENDALL, H. B.

The Origin and History of the Primitive Methodist Church. London: 1906-07. V. 38

KENDALL, HENRY

Songs from the Mountains. Sydney: 1880. V. 37

KENDALL, HENRY EDWARD

Designs for Schools and School Houses, Parochial and National. London: 1847. V. 38

KENDALL, JOHN

An Elucidation of the Principles of English Architecture, Usually Denominated Gothic. London: 1831. V. 40; 44

KENDALL, JOSEPH

A Landsman's Voyage to California Being the Account . . . San Francisco: 1935. V. 45

KENDALL, KATHARINE

The Interior Castle: a Poem. 1968. V. 38; 46

The Interior Castle. Worcester: 1968. V. 41; 42; 43

KENDALL, OLIVER

Memorial of Josiah Kendall, One of the First Settlers of Sterling, Mass. and of Some of His Ancestors and of His Descendants. Providence: 1884. V. 46

KENDALL, PERCY F.

Geology of Yorkshire. 1924. V. 42

Geology of Yorkshire. London: 1924. V. 38; 40; 42; 43; 44

KENDALL, PERCY FRY

Geology of Yorkshire. N.P.: 1924. V. 38

KENDALL, WILLIAM

Poems. Exeter: 1793. V. 38

KENDERDINE, THADDEUS S.

A California Tramp and Later Footprints. Newtown: 1888. V. 39; 40; 42

KENDRICK, A. C.

The Life and Letters of Mrs. Emily C. Judson. New York: 1861. V. 40

KENDRICK, A. F.

A Book of Old Embroidery. Edited by Geoffrey Holme. London: 1921. V. 37

Catalogue of Textiles from Burying-Grounds in Egypt. London: 1920-22. V. 40; 41; 42; 44

Fine Carpets in the Victoria and Albert Museum. London: 1924. V. 41

Hand Woven Carpets, Oriental & European. London: 1922. V. 38; 39; 42

KENDRICK, T. D.

The County Archaeologies. London: 1930-37. V. 39

KENDRICKEN, PAUL H.

Memoirs of Paul Henry Kendricken. Boston: 1910. V. 46

KENEALLY, THOMAS

Bring Larks and Heroes. Melbourne: 1967. V. 40

The Place at Whitton. London: 1964. V. 37

KENEALY, EDWARD V. H.

Brallaghan, of the Deipnosophists (verse and Prose). London: 1845. V. 46

KENERDINE, THADDEUS S.

A California Tramp and Later Footprints. Newtown: 1888. V. 38

KENILWORTH Illustrated: or the History of the Castle, Priory and Church of Kenilworth. Chiswick: 1821. V. 39

KENLY, JOHN R.

Memoirs of a Maryland Volunteer. War with Mexico in the Years 1864-7-8. Philadelphia: 1873. V. 39; 41

KENNA, V. E. G.

Cretan Seals, with a Catalogue of the Minoan Gems in the Ashmolean Museum. Oxford: 1960. V. 37; 42

KENNAN, GEORGE

Russia and the West Under Lenin and Stalin. London: 1961. V. 39

Siberia and the Exile System. New York: 1891. V. 43; 46

Tent Life in Siberia. New York: 1881. V. 40

KENNAN, GEORGE F.

Memoirs 1925-1950. Boston: 1967. V. 44

KENNARD, EDWARD

Norwegian Sketches. London: 1899. V. 38

KENNARD, EDWARD A.

Hopi Kachinas. New York: 1938. V. 37; 40

KENNARD, JOSEPH SPENCER

The Italian Theatre From Its Beginnings to the Close of the Seventeenth Century. V. 46

KENNARD, MARY E.

The Sorrows of a Golfer's Wife. London: 1896. V. 44

KENNAWAY, JOHN H.

On Sherman's Track; or, the South After the War. London: 1867. V. 39

KENNE, CHARLES

Our People . . . London: 1888. V. 42

KENNE, JOHN HARRINGTON

Fly-Fishing and Fly-Making for Trout . . . New York: 1887. V. 39

KENNEBEC TRADING & MINING CO.

Constitution & By-Laws, of the Kennebec Trading and Mining Company. Organized January 19, 1849. New Bedford: 1849. V. 46

KENNEDY, A. W. M. C.

The Birds of Berkshire and Buckinghamshire. Eton & London: 1868. V. 37

KENNEDY, ADMIRAL

Sporting Sketches in South America. London: 1892. V. 40

KENNEDY, ALEXANDER B. W.

Petra: Its History and Monuments. London: 1925. V. 43; 45

KENNEDY, ALEXANDER, W. M. CLARK

The Birds of Berkshire and Buckinghamshire. Eton: 1868. V. 41

KENNEDY, DAVID

Incidents of Pioneer Days at Guelph and the County of Bruce. Toronto: 1903. V. 43

KENNEDY, EDWARD GUTHRIE 1849-1932

The Etched Work of Whistler. San Francisco: 1978. V. 39

KENNEDY, EVENDER C.

Osseo, the Spectre Chieftain. a Poem. Leavenworth: 1867. V. 37; 38

KENNEDY, EVORY

Observations on Obstetric Ausculation, with an Analysis of the Evidences of Pregnancy. New York: 1843. V. 42

KENNEDY, G. W.

The Pioneer Campfire in Four Parts. Portland: 1914. V. 40

KENNEDY, GRACE

Anna Ross, a Story for Children. Edinburgh: 1824. V. 45

Anna Ross; a Story of Children. New York: 1827. V. 41

Dunallan; or, Know What You Judge. Edinburgh: 1825. V. 38; 44; 46

Dunallan; or, Know What You Judge. New York: 1828. V. 46

KENNEDY, HUGH A. STUDDERT

The Visitor. San Francisco: 1930. V. 39

KENNEDY, JAMES

Conversations on Religion, with Lord Byron and Others, Held in Cephalonia . . . London: 1830. V. 37; 44

A Description of the Antiquities and Curiosities in Wilton House . . . Salisbury: 1769. V. 38; 42

Dictionary of Anonymous and Pseudonymous English Literature (Samuel Halkett and John Laing). New York: 1971. V. 44

The History of the Contagious Cholera. London: 1831. V. 40; 42

KENNEDY, JOHN

The First and Second Advents of Our Lord . . . Maidstone: 1785. V. 41

The History of Steam Navigation. Liverpool: 1903. V. 38

A Treatise Upon Planting, Gardening and the Management of the Hot House. Dublin. V. 39; 42

A Treatise on Planting, Pruning and on the Management of Fruit Trees. London: 1777. V. 46

A Treatise Upon Planting, Gardening and the Management of the Hot-House. Dublin: 1784. V. 37; 42; 46

A Treatise upon Planting, Gardening, and the management of the Hot-House. The Second Edition, Corrected and Greatly Enlarged. London: 1777. V. 37

KENNEDY, JOHN FITZGERALD 1917-1963

As We Remember Joe. Cambridge: 1945. V. 38

Profiles in Courage. New York: 1936. V. 40

Profiles in Courage. New York: 1955. V. 43

Profiles in Courage. New York: 1956. V. 39; 41; 43; 46

Some Elements of the American Character. 1976. V. 37; 40

The Strategy of Peace. New York: 1960. V. 37; 39; 42; 43; 45

Why England Slept. London: 1940. V. 42

Why England Slept. New York: 1940. V. 37; 39; 40; 43

Why England Slept. 1941. V. 43

Why England Slept. London: 1940? V. 37

Why England Slept. London: 1941. V. 37

KENNEDY, JOHN P.

Autograph Leaves of Our Country's Authors. Baltimore: 1864. V. 37

KENNEDY, JOHN PENDLETON

The Blackwater Chronicle. New York: 1853. V. 45

Letters of a Man of the Times to the Citizens of Baltimore. Baltimore: 1836. V. 45

Memoirs of the Life of William Wirt, Attorney Genl. of the U.S. Philadelphia: 1850. V. 40

Quodlibet: Containing Some Annals Thereof, with an Authentic Account of the Origin and Growth of the Borough and the Sayings and Doings of Sundry of the Townspeople . . . Philadelphia: 1840. V. 43; 44

Rob of the Bowl. Philadelphia: 1838. V. 40; 43; 46

Swallow Barn. Philadelphia: 1832. V. 41; 43; 45

The Collected Works. New York: 1969. V. 39

KENNEDY, JOSEPH P.

The Story of Films: as Told by Leaders of the Industy. Chicago/New York: 1927. V. 45

KENNEDY, LEO

The Shrouding. Toronto: 1933. V. 43

KENNEDY, MARGARET

The Constant Nymph. London: 1924. V. 46

Dewdrops. London: 1928. V. 42; 44

KENNEDY, MICHAEL S.

The Red Men's West. New York: 1965. V. 44; 45

The Red Man's West: True Stories of the Frontier Indians. N.P.: 1965. V. 42

KENNEDY, MILWARD

Death to the Rescue. London: 1931. V. 44

KENNEDY, PHILIP P.

The Blackwater Chronicle. New York: 1853. V. 41; 42; 44; 46

KENNEDY, QUINTIN, ABBOT OF CROSSRAGUELL 1520-1564

Ane Oratioune set Furth by Master Quintine Kennedy, Commendatour of Corsraguell, ye Zeir of Gode, 1561. Edinburgh: 1812. V. 37; 46

KENNEDY, R.

Squibs and Other Papers in Prose and Rhyme. Madras: 1862-63. V. 37

KENNEDY, ROBERT F.

The Enemy Within. New York: 1960. V. 46

An Honorable Profession. V. 39

Just Friends and Brave Enemies. New York: 1962. V. 46

KENNEDY, RUTH WEDGEWOOD

The Renaissance Painter's Garden. New York & Washington: 1948. V. 37

KENNEDY, RUTH WEDGWOOD

The Renaissance Painter's Garden. New York: 1948. V. 39

KENNEDY, THEO

Farnorth. London: 1866. V. 46

KENNEDY, THOMAS

A History of the Irish Protest Against Over Taxation from 1853-1892. Dublin: 1897. V. 46

Poems. Washington City: 1816. V. 41

KENNEDY, VANS

Researches into the Origin and Affinity of the Principal Languages of Asia and Europe. London: 1828. V. 40

Researches into the Nature and Affinity of Ancient and Hindu Mythology. London: 1831. V. 37; 38

KENNEDY, WILLIAM 1928-

Billy Phelan's Greatest Game. New York: 1978. V. 39; 42; 44; 45

The Cotton Club. San Francisco. V. 43

The Cotton Club. Astoria: 1983. V. 43

The Ink Truck. New York: 1969. V. 37; 38; 39; 42; 44; 45; 46

The Ink Truck. London: 1970. V. 37; 40; 41; 42; 44; 45; 46

Ironweed. N.P.: 1985. V. 42; 44

Ironweed. New York: 1983. V. 37; 41; 42; 43; 45; 46

Legs. 1975. V. 43

Legs. New York: 1975. V. 41; 42; 43; 44; 45

O Albany! New York: 1983. V. 44

Quinn's Book. Los Angeles: 1987. V. 44

Texas: the Rise, Progress and Prospects of the Republic of Texas. London: 1841. V. 37; 40; 42

Texas: Its Geography, Natural History and Topography. New York: 1844. V. 37; 42

KENNEDY, WILLIAM S.

Plan of Union; or, a History of the Presbyterian and Congregational Churches of the Western Reserve . . . Hudson: 1856. V. 43

KENNER, HUGH

Paradox in Chesterton. London: 1948. V. 38; 40; 43

KENNETH, GRAHAME

The Wind in the Willows. New York: 1940. V. 43

KENNETT, BASIL

The Antiquities of Rome. London: 1699. V. 40

An Essay Towards a Paraphrase of the Psalms, In English verse. London: 1706. V. 45

The Lives and Characters of the Ancient Grecian Poets. London: 1697. V. 37; 38; 45; 46

Romae Antiquae Notitia; or the Antiquities of Rome . . . London: 1696. V. 40

Romae Antiquae Notitia: or the Antiquities of Rome. London: 1699. V. 39; 41

Romae Antiquae Notitia. London: 1708. V. 39

Romae Antiquae Notitia, or, the Antiquities of Rome. London: 1737. V. 42

Rome Antiquae Notitia. Dublin: 1767. V. 39

KENNETT, WHITE

Bibliothecae Americanae Primordia. London: 1917. V. 38; 41

The Excellent Daughter. London: 1771. V. 40; 42; 44

Parochial Antiquities Attempted in the History of Ambrosden, Burcester, and Other Adjacent Parts in the Counties of Oxford and Bucks. Oxford: 1695. V. 37; 40

KENNEY, ARTHUR H.

Facts and Documents Illustrative of the Period Immediately Preceding the Accession of William III. London: 1827. V. 40

KENNEY, CHARLES LAMB

A Memoir of Michael William Balfe. London: 1875. V. 44

KENNEY, JAMES F.

The Sources for the Early History of Ireland. New York: 1929. V. 38

KENNEY, JOHN HENRY

The Burniad; an Epistle to a Lady, in the Manner of Burns. London: 1808. V. 43

KENNEY, JOHN P.

The Border States: Their Power and Duty in the Present Disordered Condition of the Country. Philadelphia: 1861. V. 45

KENNEY, LOUIS A.

Catalogue of the Rare Astronomical Books in the San Diego State University Library. San Diego: 1988. V. 42; 45

KENNION, EDWARD

An Essay on Trees in Landscape. London: 1815. V. 45

KENNION, R. L.

By Mountain Lake and Plain, Being Sketches of Sport in Eastern Persia. London: 1911. V. 46

Sport and Life in the Further Himalaya. Edinburgh: 1910. V. 44

Sport and Life in the Further Himalaya. Edinburgh & London: 1910. V. 40

KENRICK, JOHN

Horrors of Slavery. Cambridge: 1817. V. 42

Phoenicia. London: 1855. V. 45

KENRICK, MR.

Elements of the History of England: From the Invasion of the Romans to the Reign of George II. London: 1771. V. 46

KENRICK, WILLIAM

The American Silk Grower's Guide. Boston: 1839. V. 39; 40; 44

An Epistle to G. Colman, from W. Kenrick. London: 1768. V. 38

Epistles Philosophical and Moral. London: 1759. V. 37; 39

Free Thoughts on Seduction, Adultery and Divorce. London: 1771. V. 41

The Kapelion, or Poetical Ordinary. N.P.,: 1750. V. 37; 40

A Letter to Dr. Abraham Johnson, on the Subject of His New Scheme for the Propagation of the Human Species . . . London: 1750. V. 46

KENSHAW, RICHARD

Voyage to the Cape of Good Hope, Indian Ocean and Up the Red Sea . . . Manchester: 1813. V. 46

KENT, C. H.

Texas. The Future Home of the Emigrant. Davenport: 1878. V. 45

KENT, CHARLES

By Celtic Waters. Holiday Jaunts. With Rod, Camera & Paint Brush. London: 1894. V. 39

The Charles Dickens Dinner. London: 1867. V. 43

Charles Dickens as a Reader. London: 1872. V. 39

KENT, H. W.

Bibliographical Notes on 100 books famous in English Literature. New York: 1903. V. 37

KENT, HENRY B.

Graphic Sketches of the West. Chicago: 1890. V. 39; 41; 42

KENT, HENRY W.

Bibliographical Notes on One Hundred Books Famous in English Literature. New York: 1903. V. 41

One Hundred Books Famous in English Literature with Facsimiles of the Titlepages. With Bibliographical Notes on One Hundred Books Famous in English Literature. New York: 1902, 1903. V. 41

KENT, J. P. C.

Roman Coins. New York: 1978. V. 40; 42; 44

KENT, JACK

Racking Life of Lord George Cavendish Bentinck, M.P. and Other Reminiscences. Edinburgh: 1892. V. 43

KENT, JAMES

An Anniversary Discourse, Delivered Before the New York Historical Society, December 6, 1828. New York: 1829. V. 44

Commentaries on American Law. New York: 1826-28. V. 38

A Course of Reading, Drawn Up by the Hon. James Kent . . . New York: 1840. V. 45

Dissertations: Being the Preliminary Parat of a Course of Law Lecture s. New York: 1795. V. 37; 42

An Introductory Lecture to a Course of Law Lectures, Delivered November 17, 1794. New York: 1794. V. 45

KENT, L. A.

Leadville. The City. Denver: 1880. V. 37; 38

KENT, NATHANIEL

General View of the Agriculture of the County of Norfolk . . . 1794. V. 45

General View of the Agriculture of the County of Norfolk. London: 1796. V. 44

General View of the Agriculture of the County of Norfolk . . . Norwich: 1796. V. 42

Hints to Gentlemen of Landed Property. London: 1775. V. 42; 43

Hints to Gentlemen of Landed Property. London: 1776. V. 38; 41; 44

KENT, ROCKWELL

After Long Years: Being a Story of Which the Author, for a Change, is Not the Hero. Ausable Forks: 1968. V. 37

Alaska Drawings. New York: 1919. V. 38

Architec-Tonics: The Tales of Thom Thumbtrack Architect. New York: 1924. V. 37

A Basket of Poses. New York: 1924. V. 42

Beowulf. New York: 1932. V. 37

A Birthday Book. New York: 1931. V. 40; 42

The Bookplates and Marks of Rockwell Kent. 1929. V. 37; 39; 41

The Bookplates and Marks of Rockwell Kent. New York: 1929. V. 39; 42; 44; 46

The Decorative Work of T. M. Cleland. A Record and Review. With a Bibliographical and Critical Introduction by Alfred E. Hamill. New York: 1929. V. 37

Deep Water. V. 45

The Evolution of a Bookplate. Ausable Forks & New York: 1937-38. V. 45

Forty Drawings Done by Rockwell Kent to Illustrated the Works of William Shakespeare. Garden City: 1936. V. 41

Gabriel A Poem in One Son. By Alexander Pushkin. New York: 1929. V. 37

Greenland Journal. New York: 1962. V. 37; 38; 40; 43

How I Make a Wood Cut. Pasadena: 1934. V. 42

The Jewel - A Romance of Fairyland. Portland: 1990. V. 44; 45

Later Bookplates and Marks of . . . New York: 1937. V. 37; 42; 44; 45; 46

N by E. New York: 1930. V. 37; 39; 40; 41; 43; 44

N by E. Mocba: 1962. V. 40

Of Men and Mountains . . . An Account of the European Travels of the Author and His Wife. New York: 1959. V. 37

The Prints of Rockwell Kent. Chicago: 1975. V. 41

Rockwell Kent's Greenland Journal. New York. V. 37

Rockwellkentiana. New York: 1933. V. 37; 39; 41; 43; 44; 46

Salamina. New York: 1935. V. 37; 38; 44; 45

This Is My Own. New York: 1940. V. 37; 41; 43; 44

To Thee! Manitowoc: 1946. V. 40

Voyaging, Southward from the Straits of Magellan . . . New York: 1924. V. 39; 41

Voyaging Southward from the Strait of Magellan. New York & London: 1924. V. 39; 40

Voyaging Southward from the Strait of Magellan. New York & London: 1924/24. V. 42

Wilderness. New York: 1920. V. 37; 42

Wilderness: a Journal of Quiet Adventure in Alaska. New York & London: 1920. V. 42

Wilderness. Los Angeles: 1970. V. 41; 42; 43; 44

Wilderness: A Journal of Quiet Adventure in Alaska. 1974. V. 38

Wilderness. Including extensive hitherto unpublished passages from the original journal. Los Angeles: (c. 1970). V. 37

World Famous Paintings. New York: 1939. V. 37; 39

KENT, S. H.

Within the Artic Circle. London: 1877. V. 37

KENT, SAMUEL

The Banner Difplay'd; or, an Abridgement of Guillim: Being a Compleat System of heraldry in All Its Parts. London: 1726. V. 45

The Grammar of Heraldry. London: 1716? V. 37

KENT, W. S.

A Manual of the Infusoria, Including a Description of All Known Flagelalte, Ciliate and Tentaculiferous Protozoa . . . London: 1880-82. V. 42; 44; 46

KENT, WILLIAM

The Designs of Inigo Jones, Consisting of Plans and Elevations for Public and Private Buildings, with Some Additional Designs. London: 1727. V. 38

The Plans, Elevations and Sections; Chimney-Pieces, and Ceilings of Houghton in Norfolk . . . London: 1735. V. 38; 41; 45

Reminiscences of Outdoor Life. San Francisco: 1929. V. 38; 44

KENT, WILLIAM SAVILLE d. 1908

The Great Barrier Reef of Australia. London: 1893. V. 43

A Manual of Infusoria. London: 1880-82. V. 43

The Naturalist in Australia. London: 1897. V. 43

THE KENTISH Petition. The Humble Petition of the Gentlemen, Justices of the Peace, Grand Jury and Other Freeholders, at the General Quarter Sessions of the Peace Holden at Maidstone, the 29th of April in the Thirteenth Year of the Reign of Our Sovereign . . . N.P.: 1701. V. 42

KENTMANN, JOHANNES

Calculorum Qui in Corpore Ac Membris Hominum Innascuntur Genera XII. Zurich: 1565. V. 37

KENTUCKY

Preamble and Resolution Adopted by the General Assembly of Kentucky, Vindicating the Constitutionality of Replevin Laws, and the Right of the Legislature to Remove Judges for Error of Opinion; in Reply to the Response of the Judges of the . . . Frankfort: 1823. V. 44

Preamble and Resolutions of the Legislature of Kentucky, in Relation to the Late Decision of the Court of Appeals of the Replevin and Endorsement Laws, and of the Supreme Court of the United States on the Occupying Claimant Laws of Said State. Frankfort: 1824. V. 44

KENTUCKY ANTI-SLAVERY SOCIETY

Proceedings of the Kentucky Anti-Slavery Society, Auxillary to the American Anti-Slavery Society, At Its First Meeting in Danville, Ky. March 19th, 1835. Danville: 1835. V. 40

KENTUCKY. CONSTITUTIONAL CONVENTION - 1849

Report of the Debates and Proceedings of the Convention for the Revision of the Constitution of the State of Kentucky. Frankfort: 1849. V. 37; 39; 45

KENTUCKY. GENERAL ASSEMBLY - 1839

Journal of the House of Representatives of the Commonwealth of Kentucky . . . Frankfort: 1839. V. 37

KENTUCKY. GEOLOGICAL SURVEY, 1854-1860.

(First-Fourth) Report of the Geological Survey in Kentucky, Made in the Years 1854-1859. Frankfort: 1856-61. V. 38

KENTUCKY. HOUSE OF REPRESENTATIVES

Journal of the Called Session of the House of Representatives of the Commonwealth of Kentucky. Frankfort: 1861. V. 46

KENYATTA, JOMO

Facing Mount Kenya. The Tribal Life of the Gikuyu. London: 1938. V. 39

KENYON, F. G.

Ancient Books and Modern Discoveries. Chicago: 1927. V. 37; 38; 39; 41; 42; 43; 45; 46

KENYON, FREDERIC G.

Facsimiles of Biblical Manuscripts in the British Museum. London: 1900. V. 39

KENYON, FREDERIC G. continued

John Locke, Directions Concerning Education, Being the First Draft of His Thoughts. London: 1933. V. 39

KENYON, JOHN LOCKE

Directions Concerning Education Being the First Draft of His Thoughts Concerning Education Now Printed from Additional MS. 38771 in the British Museum . . . Oxford: 1933. V. 46

KENYON, KATHLEEN M.

Excavations at Jericho. Jerusalem: 1960. V. 40

Excavations at Jericho. Jerusalem & London: 1960-1965. V. 37; 40; 42

Excavations at Jericho. London: 1982. V. 40

Excavations at Jericho. London: 1983. V. 40; 44

KENYON-KINGDON, MAUD

From Out the Dark Shadows. San Diego: 1925. V. 42

KENYON, R. L.

The Gold Coins of England Arranged and Described . . . . London:: 1885. V. 40

KEOGH, J.

Zoologia Medicinalis Hebernica; or a Treatise of Birds, Beasts, Fishes, Reptiles or Insects . . . Dublin: 1737. V. 43

KEOHAN, EDMOND

Illustrated History of Dungarvan, Co. Waterford. Waterford: 1924. V. 37; 38

KEOWN, ERIC

The Tale of an Old Tweed Jacket. London. V. 40

KEPLER, JOHANNES

Astronomia Nova, Seu Physica Coelestis Tradita Commentariis de Motibus Stellae Martis, ex Observationibus G. V. Tychonis Brahe . . . Prague or Heidelberg: 1609. V. 38

Epistolae ad Joannem Kepplerum Mathematicum Caesareum Scriptae; Insertis ad Easdem Responsionibus Kepplerianis . . . Opus Novum, Quo Recondita Kepplerianae Doctrinae Capita Dilucide Explicantur . . . Ex Manscripta Editum. Frankfurt & Leipzig: 1718. V. 42

Tabulae Rudolphinae, Quibus Astronomicae Scientiae, Temporum Longinquitate, Collapsae Restauratio Continetur . . . Ulm: 1627. V. 42

KEPPEL, ARNOLD

Grizzlies at Bear Lake, Caribous, B.C. N.P.: 1900. V. 46

KEPPEL, AUGUSTUS

An Authentic and Impartial Copy of the Trial of the Hon . . . . Admiral of the Blue, Held at Portsmouth on the 7th of January 1779 and Continued by Several Adjournments to the 11th Day of Feb. 1779 . . . Portsmouth: 1779. V. 40

KEPPEL, FREDERICK

The Golden Age of Engraving: a Specialist's Story About Fine Prints. New York: 1910. V. 37; 46

KEPPEL, GEORGE

Narrative of a Journey Across the Balcan, by the Two Passes of Selimno & Pravadi . . . London: 1831. V. 42; 45

Personal Narrative of a Journey from India to England, by Bussorah, Bagdad, the Ruins of Babylon, Curdistan, the Court of Persia, the Western Shore of the Caspian Sea, Astrakhan . . . in the Year 1824. London: 1827. V. 37; 39

Personal Narrative of Travels in Babylonia, Assyria, Media and Scythia, in the Year 1824. London: 1827. V. 37; 39

KEPPEL, HENRY

The Expedition to Borneo of H.M.S. Dido for the Suppression of Piracy. London: 1846. V. 40; 45

Expedition to Borneo of the H.M.S. Dido for the Suppression of Piracy . . . New York: 1846. V. 43

The Expedition to Borneo of the H.M.S. Dido for the Suppression of Piracy . . . London: 1847. V. 37

A Visit to the Indian Archipelago, in H.M. Ship Maeander, with Portions of the Private Journal of Sir James Brooke, K.C.B. London: 1853. V. 37; 40

KEPPLER, VICTOR

The Eighth Art: A Life of Color Photography. New York: 1938. V. 39

KER, ANITA M.

Mexican Government Publications: a Guide to the More Important Publications of the National Government of Mexico 1821-1936. Washington: 1940. V. 40; 42

KER, DAVID

On the Road to Khiva. London: 1874. V. 41

KER, HENRY

Travels through the Western Interior of the United States, from the Year 1808 up to the Year 1816. Elizabethtown: 1816. V. 37; 38; 39; 40; 41; 45

KER, JOHN

The Memoirs of John Ker, of Kersland in North Britain Esq. London: 1726. V. 40; 44; 45

Slectarum de Lingua Latina . . . London: 1709. V. 40; 45

KER, N.

Fragments of Medieval Manuscripts Used as Pastedowns in Oxford Bindings with a Survey of Oxford Binding c. 1515-1620. Oxford: 1954. V. 41

KER, WILLIAM

Un Receuil Tire des Autheurs Francois, Tant en Prose qu'en vers, Pour l'Utilite de la Jeunesse qui desire de s'avancer dans la Langue Francoise. Edinburgh: 1727. V. 40

KERCHEVAL, SAMUEL

A History of the Valley of Virginia. Winchester: 1833. V. 45

A History of the Valley of Virginia. Woodstock: 1850. V. 45

A History of the Valley of Virginia. Woodstock: 1864. V. 39

A History of the Valley of Virginia. Woodstock: 1902. V. 37; 40; 42

KERENYI, CHARLES

Asklepios: Archetypal Image of the Physician's Existence. London: 1960. V. 45

KERFOOT, J. B.

American Pewter. Boston: 1924. V. 39

KERGUELEN-TREMAREC, YVES JOSEPH DE

Relation d'un Voyage dans la Mer du Nord, aux Cotes d'Islande, du Groenland, de Ferro, de Schettland, des Orcades & de Norwege; Fait en 1767 & 1768. Paris: 1771. V. 39

KERKUT, G. A.

Comprehensive Insect Physiology, Biochemistry and Pharmcology. London: 1985. V. 37; 38

KERN, JEROME

The Library. New York: 1929. V. 46

KERNER, ARNOLD

Tetras Chymiatrica, Proponens Praestantiam et in Medicina Efficaciam, Auri, Mercurii, Antiomonii . . . Erfurth: 1618. V. 43

KERNER, JOHANN SIMON VON

Hortus Sempervirens Exhibens Icones Plantarum Selectiorum Quotquot ad Vivorum Exemplorum Normam Reddere Licuit. (Band 45-48, 53-55 and 64). Stuttgart & Mannehime: 1810-20. V. 39

KERNER VON MAILAUN, A.

The natural History of Plants, Their Forms, Growth, Reproduction and Distribution. London: 1894-95. V. 46

KERNER VON MARILAUN, ANTON

The Natural History of Plants, Their Forms, Growth, Reproduction and Distribution . . . London: 1896. V. 39

KERNODLE, GEORGE R.

From Art to Theatre. Form and Convention in the Renaissance. Chicago: 1944. V. 37

KEROUAC, JACK 1922-1969

Big Sur. New York: 1962. V. 41; 42; 43; 44; 45; 46

Book of Dreams. San Francisco: 1960. V. 45

Desolation Angels. New York: 1963. V. 38

Desolation Angels. New York: 1965. V. 37; 42; 45

Desolation Angels. London: 1966. V. 41

The Dharma Bums. New York: 1958. V. 38; 39; 40; 42; 43; 44; 45; 46

Doctor Sax. New York: 1959. V. 37; 39; 42; 43; 44

Visions of Cody. Excerpts. New York. V. 45

Excerpts from Visions of Cody. New York: 1959. V. 44

Excerpts from Visions of Cody. Norfolk: 1959. V. 41; 45; 46

Excerpts from Visions of Cody. New York: 1960. V. 42

Visions of Cody. New York: 1972. V. 45; 46

Excerpts from Visions of Cody. New York: 1959. V. 39; 41; 44

Lonesome Traveller. New York: 1960. V. 38; 42; 44

Mexico City Blues. New York: 1959. V. 43

Not Long Ago Joy Abounded at Christmas. New York: 1972. V. 45

On the Road. New York: 1957. V. 38; 39; 41; 42; 43; 45; 46

On the Road. London: 1958. V. 41; 43; 45

A Portents Semina, Portents #6. N.P.: 1967. V. 45

Pull My Daisy. New York: 1961. V. 45

A Pun for Al Gelpi . . . Cambridge: 1966. V. 45

Rimbaud. San Francisco: 1960. V. 45

Satori in Paris. New York: 1966. V. 37; 41; 42; 45

Someday You'll be Lying. Pleasant Valley: 1967. V. 43; 46

KEROUAC, JACK 1922-1969 continued

The Subterraneans. New York: 1958. V. 44

The Subterraneans. London: 1960. V. 45

Take Care of My Ghost, Ghost. N.P.: 1977. V. 39

The Town and the City. New York: 1950. V. 37; 38; 39; 40; 42; 43; 44; 45; 46

The Town and the City. London: 1973. V. 37; 39

Two Early Stories. New York: 1973. V. 39

Vanity of Duluoz. New York: 1968. V. 37; 41; 44; 46

Visions of Gerard. New York: 1963. V. 38; 39; 44; 45

KERR, HENRY

Travels through the Western Interior of the United States, from the year 1808, up to the year 1816. With a Particular Description of a Great Part of Mexico, or New-Spain . . . Elizabethtown: 1816. V. 37

KERR, HUGH

A Poetical Description of Texas, and Narrative of Many Interesting Events in that Country . . . New York: 1838. V. 42

KERR, J. B.

Biographical Dictionary of Well-Known British Columbians with a Historical Sketch. Vancouver: 1890. V. 44

KERR, J. H.

Glimpses of Life in Victoria. Edinburgh: 1872. V. 46

KERR, JOHN

The Golf Book of East Lothian. Stevenage: 1987. V. 38

KERR, ROBERT

The English Gentleman's House. London: 1864. V. 40

A General History and Collection of Voyages and Travels, Arranged in Systematic Order . . . London: 1824. V. 41; 42; 46

The Gentleman's House. London: 1864. V. 37; 40; 41; 44

The Gentleman's House; or, How to Plan English Residences from the Parsonage to the Palace. London: 1871. V. 41

The Gentleman's House; or, How to Plan English residences, from the parsonage to the palace; with tables of accommodation and cost and a series of selected plans. Second edition, revised with a supplement on works of alterations . . . London: 1865. V. 37

KERR, W. H.

The Kidnappers. N.P.: 1867. V. 46

KERR, WILLIAM J.

The Genealogical Tree of the Family of Jarrett of Orange Valley, Jamaica, and Camerton Court, Somerset. Southampton: 1896. V. 37

KERR, WILLIAM MONTAGU

The Far Interior: a Narrative of Travel and Adventure From the Cape of Good Hope Across the Zambesi to the Lake Regions of Central Africa. London: 1886. V. 39

KERRIDGE, PHILIP MARKHAM

An Address on Angling Literature. Fullerton: 1970. V. 37; 43

KERRISON, ROBERT MASTERS

A Letter to the Rt. Hon. Robert Peel on the Supply of Water for the Metropolis, and a Refutation of the Mis-statements of an Anonymous Writer, Under the Designations of 'An Old Housekeeper.' (with) A Letter on the Supply of Water. London: 1828. V. 37

Observations and Reflections on the Bill Now in Progress . . . London: 1815. V. 42

KERRY, CHARLES

A History of Waverley Abbey, in the County of Surrey. Guildford: 1872. V. 41

KERRY-NICHOLLS, J. H.

The King Country; or, Explorations in New Zealand . . . London: 1884. V. 45

KERSEY, JOHN

Dictionarium Anglo-Britannicum; or, a General English Dictionary . . . London: 1708. V. 41

The Elements of that Mathematical Art Commonly Called Algebra, Expounded in Four Books. London: 1673. V. 45

The Elements of the Mathematical Art Commonly Called Algebra, Expounded in Four Books . . . London: 1673-4. V. 38; 42; 44

The Elements of that Mathematical Art Commonly Called Algebra . . . London: 1717. V. 41; 45

A New English Dictionary: Or, A Compleat Collection of the most Proper & Significant Workds, & Terms of Art . . . The Sixth Edition, carefully revised: With many important Additions & Improvements. London: 1752. V. 37

KERSH, GERALD

Faces in a Dusty Picture. London: 1944. V. 42

KERSHAW, S. W.

Art Treasures of the Lambeth Library. London: 1873. V. 41

KERSLAKE, JOHN

Early Georgian Portraits. London: 1977. V. 44

KERTESZ, ANDRE

Andre Kertesz. Sixty Years of Photography. New York: 1978. V. 41

Distortions. New York: 1976. V. 41

Hungarian Memories. Boston: 1982. V. 41

J'aime Paris. New York: 1974. V. 41

Of New York . . . New York: 1976. V. 41

KESCHINGER, PETRUS DE fl. late 15th century

Clavis Theolgiae Sive Reptorium . . . in Summam Doctoris Irrefragabilis Alexander de Hales. Basle: 1502. V. 45

KESEY, KEN 1935-

The Day After Superman Died. Northridge: 1980. V. 37; 39

The Further Inquiry. New York: 1990. V. 44

Kesey. 1977. V. 46

Kesey's Garage Sale. New York: 1973. V. 39; 43; 44; 46

One Flew Over the Cuckoo's Nest. London: 1962. V. 37; 39; 40; 42; 45

One Flew Over the Cuckoo's Nest. New York: 1962. V. 37; 38; 39; 40; 41; 42; 43; 44; 45; 46

Sometimes a Great Notion. V. 40

Sometimes a Great Notion. New York: 1964. V. 37; 38; 43; 44

KESLAR, FRANCOIS

Espargne-Bois C'Est a Dire, Nouvelle et Parci-Devant Non Commune, Ni Mise en Lumiere, Invention de Certains et Divers Fournneaux Artificiels . . . Oppenheim: 1619. V. 42

KESSEL, JOSEPH

Kisling. New York: 1971. V. 43

KESSLER, L.

Valuation Plan of the Witwatersrand Goldfields. London: 1902. V. 41

KESTER, JESSE Y.

The American Shooter's Manual. Philadelphia: 1827. V. 38; 43; 45

KETCHUM, RICHARD

The World of George Washington by Richard Ketchum. 1974. V. 37

KETCHUM, WILLIAM

An Authentic and Comprehensive History of Buffalo, with Some Account of Its Early Inhabitants Both Savage and Civilized . . . Buffalo: 1864. V. 39

Authentic and Comprehensive History of Buffalo. Buffalo: 1864-65. V. 46

KETCHUM, WILLIAM M.

History of the Corn Exchange, New York City, from the Time of Its Organisation in 1852 to March 1923. New York: 1923. V. 41

KETEL, RICHARD

De Elegantiori Latinitate Comparanda Scriptores Selecti. Amstelaedami: 1713. V. 44

KETHAM, JOHANNES DE

Fasciculus Medicinae. Venice: 1500. V. 45

Fasciculus Medicinae. 1970. V. 44

KETT, HENRY

Elements of General Knowledge Introductory to Useful Books in the Principal Branches of Literature and Science . . . London: 1815. V. 41

Emily, a Moral Tale, Including Letters from a Father to His Daughter, Upon the Most Important Subjects. London: 1809. V. 39

KETTEL, DANIEL WALTER

Pens, Ink and Paper. A Discourse Upon the Calligraphic Art with Curiosa, and an Appendix . . . London: 1885. V. 40

KETTEL, SAMUEL

Specimens of American Poetry. Boston: 1829. V. 41

KETTELL, R. H.

Early American Rooms. Portland: 1936. V. 37

Pine Furniture of Early New England. New York: 1929. V. 37; 46

KETTELL, ROBERT

The Animal Alphabet. Oxford: 1988. V. 42

KETTELL, RUSSELL HAWES

Pine Furniture of Early New England. Garden City: 1929. V. 38; 39

KEYSSLER, JOHANN GEORG 1693-1743

Travels Through Germany, Bohemia, Hungary, Switzerland, Italy and Lorrain. London: 1756-57. V. 42; 43; 45; 46

KEYSTONE TYPE FOUNDRY

Catalogue and Specimen Book. Chicago: 1915. V. 42

Keystone Type Foundry. Philadelphia: 1901. V. 38

Some Keystone Type Faces. with Borders. with Brass Good. with Cuts, Ornaments, Initials. with Miscellaneous Material and Machinery for Printers, Bookbinders' Supplies. Philadelphia. V. 38

KHAIN, V. E.

Geology of the U.S.S.R., Volume 1: Old Crters and Paleozoic Fold Belts. Stuttgart: 1985. V. 37; 38

KHANDALAVALA, KARL

New Documents of Indian Painting - a Reappraisal. Bombay: 1969. V. 43

Pahari Miniature Painting. Bombay: 1958. V. 39

KHAYYAT, ABU ALI YAHYA IBN GHALIB

De Judiciis Nativitatum Liber Unus, Antehac non Editus. Nuremberg: 1546. V. 38

KHELL VON KHELLBURG, JOSEPH

Physica ex Recentiorum Observationibus Accommodata Usibus Academicis . . . Vienna: 1754-55. V. 43

KHERDIAN, DAVID

Homage to Adana. Mount Horeb: 1970. V. 42

KHLIEBNIKOV, K. T.

Materialy Dlia Istorii Russkikh Zaselenii po Beregam Vostochnogo Okeana . . . St. Petersburg: 1861. V. 38

KHUEN, J. C.

Magnus in Ortu. Munich: 1727. V. 46

KHULMAN, A., & CO.

Catalogue of Surgical Instruments, Hospital Equipment and Supplies. Detroit: 1931. V. 42

KICK, CHARLES PAUL DE

The Works. Boston: (1902). V. 37

KICKHAM, CHARLES J.

Sally Cavanagh; or, the Untenanted Graves. Dublin: 1869. V. 41

KIDD, DUDLEY

Echoes from the Battlefields of South Africa. London: 1900. V. 45

KIDD, JAMES H.

Personal Recollections of a Cavalryman with Custer's Michigan Cavalry Brigade in the Civil War. Ionia: 1908. V. 40

KIDD, JOHN

On the Adaptation of External nature to the Physical Condition of Man. London: 1833. V. 38

The Parting of Sir William Wallace and His Bride and Other Poems. Alloa: 1843. V. 44

KIDD, SAMUEL

Catalogue of the Chinese Library of the Royal Asiatic Society. London: 1838. V. 42; 45

China, or Illustrations of the Symbols, Philosophy, Antiquities, Customs, Superstitions, Laws, Government, Education and Literature of the Chinese. London: 1841. V. 42; 46

KIDD, WALTER

The Direction of Hair in Animals and Man. London: 1903. V. 42

KIDDER, ALFRED VINCENT

The Artifacts of Uaxactun Guatemala. Washington: 1947. V. 42

Excavations at Kaminaljuyu. Washington: 1946. V. 42

An Introduction to the Study of Southwestern Archaeology with a Preliminary Account of the Excavations at Pecos. New Haven: 1924. V. 39; 42

The Pottery of Pecos. New Haven: 1931. V. 39

The Pottery of Pecos. New Haven: 1931 & 1936. V. 38

The Pottery of Pecos. New Haven: 1936. V. 42

KIDDER, D. P.

Brazil and Brazilians, Portrayed in Historical and Descriptive Sketches. Philadelphia: 1857. V. 38; 41

Brazil and the Brazilians, Portrayed in Historical and Descriptive Sketches. Philadelphia & Boston: 1857. V. 38

KIDDER, DANIEL P.

Brazil and the Brazilians, Historical and Descriptive Sketches. 1857. V. 42

Sketches of Residence and Travels in Brazil. Philadelphia: 1845. V. 39; 40; 41; 45

Sketches of Residences and Travels in Brazil. Philadelphia & London: 1845. V. 39

KIDDER, FREDERIC

Abenaki Indians: Their Treaties of 1713 and 1717. Portland: 1859. V. 42

History of the First New Hampshire Regiment in the War of the Revolution. Albany: 1868. V. 39

KIDDER, J. EDWARD

Japanese Temples, Sculpture, Paintings, Gardens and Architecture. Tokyo. V. 38; 41

Japanese Temples Sculpture Paintings, Gardens and Architecture. London: 1964. V. 43

Japanese Temples: Sculpture, Paintings, Gardens, Architecture. Tokyo/Amsterdam: 1964. V. 41

Masterpieces of Japanese Sculpture. Tokyo/Rutland: 1961. V. 41

Prehistoric Japanese Arts: Jomon Pottery. Tokyo: 1968. V. 38; 41

KIDDER, TRACY

The Road to Yuba City: a Journey Into the Juan Corona Murders. Garden City: 1974. V. 45

KIDGELL, JOHN

The Card. London: 1755. V. 38; 44; 45

A Genuine and Succinct Narrative of a Scandalous, Obscene and Exceedingly Profane Libel, Entitled an Essay on Woman . . . London. V. 42

A Genuine and Succint Narrative of a Scandalous, Obscene, and Exceedingly Profane Libel, Entitled, an Essay on Woman, as Also, of Other Poetical Pieces, containing the Most Atrocious Blasphemies. London: 1763. V. 37; 45

KIDNER, MICHAEL

The Elastic Membrane. Guildford: 1979. V. 41; 43

KIDO, HIRAKU

Handmade Papers of the World. Tokyo: 1979. V. 38; 43

KIDSON, JOSEPH R.

Historical Notices of the Leeds Old Pottery with a Description of Its Wares. Leeds: 1892. V. 40; 41; 46

KIDSTON, GEORGE J.

Despatch of His Majesty's Minister at Peking, Inclosing a Report . . . on a Journey in Mongolia . . . (with) Map to Accompany Despatch. London: 1904. V. 40

KIEFER, W. R.

History of the 153rd Regiment, Pennsylvania Volunteer Infantry. Easton: 1909. V. 42

KIERAN, JOHN

The American Sporting Scene. New York: 1941. V. 39; 46

KIERKEGAARD, SOREN

Af en Endnu Levendes Papirer. Kjobenhavn: 1833. V. 43; 45

Afsluttende Uvidenskabelif Efterskrift . . . Copenhagen: 1846. V. 40

KIERNAN, R. H.

The Unveiling of Arabia The Story of Arabian Travel and Discovery. London: 1937. V. 46

KIERNANDER, JONAS

Utkast til Medicinal-Lagfarenheten, Domare til Uplysning, Stockholm: 1776. V. 43

KIESTER, J. A.

History of Faribault County Minnesota From Its First Settlement to the Close of the Year 1879. Minneapolis: 1896. V. 43

KIEWIET, C. W. DE

Dufferin-Carnarvon Correspondence, 1874-1878. Toronto: 1955. V. 37

KIJIMA, T.

The Original Orchids, a Tribute to Nature's Spectacle of Orchids in Brilliant Sunshine. Tokyo: 197. V. 38

KIKI'S Memoirs. Paris: 1930. V. 38

KIKUCHI, SADAO

A Treasury of Japanese Wood Block Prints: Ukiyo-e. New York: 1969. V. 37; 38

KILBOURNE, D. W.

Strictures of Dr. I. Galland's Pamphlet Entitled 'Villainy Exposed'. With Some Account of His Transactions in Lands of the Sac and Fox Reservation, etc. Fort Madison: 1850. V. 43; 46

KILBURN, RICHARD

Choice Presidents Upon all Acts of Parliament, Relating to the Office and Duty of a Justice of Peace, Including Those Made and Passed in the First Year of the Reign of Queen Anne. London: 1703. V. 37; 43; 46

Choice Precedents Upon all Acts of Parliament, Relating to the Office and Duty of a Justice of Peace . . . London: 1715. V. 37

KILBURNE, RICHARD

A Topographie or Survey of the County of Kent. London: 1659. V. 39

KILBY, HENRY

Trips to Algeria, Holland, the North Cape, etc. London: 1895. V. 40

KILGORE, D. E.

A Ranger Legacy - 150 Years of Service to Texas. Austin: 1973. V. 42

THE KILGOUR Collection of Russian Literature, 1750-1920. Cambridge: 1959. V. 38

KILLBOURN, JOHN

The Ohio Gazetteer, or Topographical Dictionary. Chillicothe: 1819. V. 41

KILLEBREW, J. B.

Mineral and Agricultural Resources of the Portion of the Tennessee Along the Cincinnati Southern and Knoxville & Ohio Railroads . . . Nashville: 1876. V. 42

Oil Region of Tennessee with Some Account of Its Other Resources and Capabilities. Nashville: 1877. V. 42

KILLENS, JOHN O.

Youngblood. New York: 1954. V. 41; 42; 43

Youngblood. London: 1956. V. 40; 42; 44

KILLIGREW, HENRY

The Conspiracy. London: 1638. V. 37; 44

KILLIGREW, THOMAS

Comedies and Tragedies. London: 1664. V. 38; 43; 44

Miscellanea Aurea: or the Golden Medley. London: 1720. V. 38

The Prisoners. London: 1641. V. 37

KILLIKELLY, SARAH H.

Curious Questions in History, Literature, Art and Social Life. Philadelphia: 1886/89. V. 45

KILLINGTON, F. J.

A Monograph of the British neuroptera. London: 1937-37. V. 38

KILLION, TOM

Fortress Marin; an Aesthetic and Historical Description of the Coastal Fortifications of Southern Marin County. Santa Cruz: 1977. V. 37; 39; 42; 44

KILLITS, JOHN M.

Toledo and Lucas County, Ohio, 1623-1923. Chicago: 1923. V. 39; 42; 44

KILLMISTER, A. K.

The Shooter's Handbook Being the Treatise on Shooting . . . Edinburgh: 1842. V. 45

KILLON, TOM

Walls: a Journey Across Three Continents. Santa Cruz: 1990. V. 45

KILMER, JOYCE

The Circus and Other Essays. New York: 1916. V. 41; 42

Literature in the Making. New York: London: 1917. V. 43

Poems, Essays and Letters. New York: 1918. V. 43

Summer of Love. New York: 1911. V. 37; 39; 40; 41; 45; 46

Trees and Other Poems. New York: 1914. V. 37; 39; 41; 42; 43

Trees and Other Poems. New York: 1914. V. 44

KILNER, DOROTHY

Father's Advice to His Son. London: 1790? V. 45

KILOHANA ART LEAGUE

Six Prize Hawaiian Stories of the . . . Honolulu: 1899. V. 41

KILPATRICK, J. H. T.

The Reviewer, Re-Viewed; or a Rejoinder to the Rev. J. J. Triggs' 'Review' of the Controversy on Baptism. Augusta: 1844. V. 37; 38; 39

KILPATRICK, JACK FREDERICK

Sequoyah of Earth and Intellect. Austin: 1965. V. 38; 39; 40

KILPECK

The Sculptures of Kilpeck. Hereford: 1987. V. 40

KILTY, WILLIAM

Laws of, to Which are Prefixed the Original Charter, . . . with an Index. Rev. & Coll. by William Kilty. Annapolis: 1799-1800. V. 37

KILVERT, FRANCIS

The Curate of Clyro: . . . 1983. V. 44

KIMBALL, CHARLES P.

The San Francisco City Directory. September 1, 1850. San Francisco: 1890. V. 44

KIMBALL, F.

Thomas Jefferson Architect. Boston: 1916. V. 37

KIMBALL, FISKE

Domestic Architecture of the American Colonies and of the Early Republic. New York: 1922. V. 42

Mr. Samuel McIntire, Carver. The Architect of Salem. Portland: 1940. V. 38; 41; 44

KIMBALL, HEBER C.

President Heber C. Kimball's Journal. Salt Lake City: 1882. V. 42; 43

KIMBALL, J. P.

Laws and Decrees of the State of Coahuila and Texas, in Spanish and in English, to Which is Added the Constitution of Said State, Also the Colonization Law . . . and the Naturralization law . . . 1839. V. 37

Laws and Decrees of the State of Coahuila and Texas, in Spanish and in English, to Which is Added the Constitution of Said State, Also the Colonization Law . . . and the Naturalization Law. Houston: 1839. V. 38

KIMBALL, JACOB

The Rural Harmony, Being an Original Composition, in Three and Four Parts. Boston: 1793. V. 39

KIMBALL, MARIA BRACE

My Eight Years. N.P.. V. 41

KIMBALL, RICHARD B.

Virginia Randall; or, To-Day in New York. London: 1870. V. 40

KIMBALL, RICHARD BURLEIGH

Saint Leger; or, the Threads of Life. London: 1850. V. 37

KIMBALL, SARAH

Mormon Women's Protest. Salt Lake City: 1886. V. 42

KIMBALL, THEODORA

Manual of Information on City Planning and Zoning. (with) Planning Information Up to Date, a Supplement, 1923-1928 to Kimball's Manual . . . Cambridge: 1928. V. 41

KIMBALL, THOMAS

The Railroad Problem. Memorial to the Legislature of the State of Kansas. Topeka: 1883. V. 37

KIMBER, EDWARD

The History of the Life and Adventures of Mr. Anderson. Berwick: 1782. V. 40

Itinerant Observations in America . . . Savannah: 1878. V. 46

The Life and Adventures of Joe Thompson. London: 1751. V. 42

The Life, Extraordinary Adventures, Voyages and Surprising Escapes of Capt. Neville Frowde of Cork. Berwick: 1792. V. 46

KIMBER, HUGH

San Fairy Ann. London: 1927. V. 43; 44

KIMBER, ISAAC

The Life of Oliver Cromwell, Lord Protector of the Common-Wealth of England, Scotland and Ireland. London: 1724. V. 41; 43; 44

The Life of Oliver Cromwell, Lord-Protector of the Commonwealth of England, Scotland and Ireland. London: 1743. V. 39

KIMBER, W. C.

Etching and Plate Printing Materials, Copper Plate Presses, etc. London: 1924-28. V. 46

KIMBULL, EDMUND

Reflelctions Upon the Law of Libel, in a Letter Addressed to 'A Member of the Suffok Bar.' Boston: 1823. V. 37

KIMCHI, DAVID ca 1160-1235

Commentarri . . . in Haggaeum, Zachariam & Malachiam prophetas. Paris: 1557. V. 37

KIMCHI, DAVID BEN JOSEPH 1160-1245

Sefer Schoraschim. Venice: 1546. V. 40

KIMES, WILLIAM

John Muir. A Reading Bibliography. Palo Alto: 1977. V. 37; 43; 44; 45

KIMMEL, STANLEY

Mr. Davis's Richmond. New York: 1958. V. 38

KIMURA, SHOTARO

Sword and Blossom Poems from the Japanese. Tokyo: 1900. V. 41

KINAHAN, G. A.

Economic Geology of Ireland. London: 1889. V. 43; 44

KINAHAN, G. HENRY

Manual of the Geology of Ireland. London;: 1878. V. 37

KINCAID, J.

Adventures in the Rifle Brigade, in the Peninsula, France and the Netherlands from 1809 to 1815. London: 1830. V. 44

KINCAID, JAMAICA

At the Bottom of the River. New York: 1983. V. 46

KINCAID, JOHN

Random Shots from a Rifleman. London: 1835. V. 37; 39; 41

KINCAID, ZOE

Kabuki. The Popular Stage of Japan. London: 1925. V. 37

KINDERLEY, NATHANIEL

The Ancient and Present State of the Navigation of the Towns of Lyn, Wisbeach, Spalding and Boston . . . Lyn: 1751. V. 42

KINDERSLEY, DAVID

Graphic Sayings. London: 1972. V. 39

Twelve Alphabetick Images in Colour. Linton: 1983. V. 41; 45

KINDERSLEY, JEMIMA

Letters from the Island of Teneriffe, Brazil, the Cape of Good Hope and the East Indies. London: 1777. V. 37; 46

KINDIG, R. H.

Pictorial Supplement to Denver, South Park and Pacific. Denver: 1959. V. 43; 45

KING, A. S.

Form and Function in Birds. London: 1979-85. V. 40

Form and Function in Birds, Volume 3. London: 1985. V. 37; 38

KING, ALEXANDER WILLIAM

An Aubrey Beardsley Lecture. London: 1924. V. 38; 40; 41; 42; 43; 44

KING, C. W.

Antique Gems: Their Origin, Uses and Value. London: 1860. V. 44

The Handbook of Engraved Gems. London: 1886. V. 39

KING, CHARLES

The British Merchant. London: 1721. V. 44; 45

Campaigning with Crook and Stories of Army Life. New York: 1890. V. 37; 46

Circular Letter From Capt. Charles King Dated Milwaukee, Feb. 28, 1891. Milwaukee: 1891. V. 41

The Fifth Cavalry in the Sioux War of 1876. Milwaukee: 1800. V. 40

The Fifth Cavalry in the Sioux War of 1876. Milwaukee: 1880. V. 39; 40; 42; 43

KING, CHARLES WILLIAM

The Natural History of Precious Stones and of the Precious Metals. London: 1867. V. 46

KING, CLARENCE

Memoirs. New York: 1904. V. 45

Mountaineering in the Sierra Nevada. Boston: 1872. V. 39; 40; 41; 44

Mountaineering in the Sierra Nevada. London: 1872. V. 43

Mountaineering in the Sierra Nevada. London: 1874. V. 44

Mountaineering in the Sierra Nevada. London: 1947. V. 44

Report of the Geological Exploration of the Fortieth Parallel. Washington: 1870-80. V. 39; 42

U. S. Exploration of the Fortieth Parallel. Washington;: 1870-1880. V. 38

United States Geological Exploration of the Fortieth Parallel. Washington: 1878-80. V. 38

KING, DANIEL

The Vale-Royall of England. London: 1656. V. 39; 45

KING, DOROTHY N.

Find the Animals. N.P.: 1941. V. 39

KING, E. S. J.

Surgery of the Heart. Baltimore: 1941. V. 42

KING, EDWARD

An Essay on the English Constituion and Government. London: 1767. V. 38

An Essay on the Creation and Advantages of a Cultural and Commercial Triform Stock, as a Counter-Fund to the National Debt . . . London: 1825. V. 42

The Great South: a Record of Journeys in Louisiana, Texas, the Indian Territory, Missouri, Arkansas, Mississippi, Alabama, Georgia, Florida, South Carolina, North Carolina, Kentucky, Tennessee, Virginia, West Virginia and Maryland. Hartford: 1875. V. 38; 39; 40; 45

Morsels of Criticism Tending to Illustrate Some few Passages in the Holy Scriptures Upon Philosophical Principles and an Enlarged View of Things. London: 1788. V. 38

Vestiges of Oxford Castle. London: 1796. V. 40; 42

KING, FRANK M.

Longhorn Trail Drivers. Burbank: 1940. V. 38; 45

Longhorn Trail Drivers, Being a True Story of Cattle Drives of Long Ago. N.P.: 1940. V. 43

Mavericks, the Salty Comments of an Old-Time Cowpuncher. Pasadena: 1947. V. 42

Pioneer Western Empire Builders. Pasadena: 1946. V. 42

Wranglin' the Past. Los Angeles: 1935. V. 37; 38; 39; 45

KING, G.

The Orchids of the Sikkim-Himalaya. Lehre: 1967. V. 46

The Species of Ficus of the Indo-Malayan and Chinese Countries. Calcutta and London: 1887. V. 45; 46

KING George and the Turkish Knight. Ditchling: 1921. V. 40; 41

KING, GRACE

New Orleans: the Place and the People. New York: 1904. V. 44; 46

KING Grisly Beard's Picture Book. London. V. 43

KING, HENRY, BP. OF CHICHESTER

The Pslames of David, From the New Translation of the Bible Turned Into Meter; to be Sung After the Old Tunes Used in the Churches. London: 1651. V. 41

KING, J. ANTHONY

Twenty-Four Years in the Argentine Republic. New York: 1846. V. 40; 45; 46

KING, J. C. H.

Artificial Curiosities From the Northwest Coast of America. London: 1981. V. 46

KING, J. G.

Nummi Familiarum et Imperatorum. London: 1787. V. 46

KING, J. L.

History of the San Francisco Stock and Exchange Baord. San Francisco: 1910. V. 46

KING, JEFF

Where the Two Came to Their Father. New York: 1943. V. 45

KING, JESSIE M.

Books and Bookplates. Edinburgh: 1905. V. 43

Budding Life - A Book of Drawings. London: & Glasgow: 1907. V. 43

The Grey City of the North - a Book of Drawings. Edinburgh & London: 1910. V. 44

The Grey City of the North. London: 1910. V. 42

How Cinderella Was Able to Go to the Ball. A Brochue on Batik Written and Illustrated in Colour by . . . London. V. 39

Kirkcudbright: a Royal Burgh. Glasgow: 1934. V. 38

Kirkcudbright - a Royal Burgh - A Book of Drawings. London: 1934. V. 40

KING, JOHN

The American Family Physician; or, Domestic Guide to Health. Indianapolis: 1864. V. 42

Lectvres Vpon Ionas, Delivered at Yorke. Oxford: 1597. V. 37

Vitis Palatina. A Sermon Appointed to be Preached at Whitehall Upon the Tuesday After the Marriage of the Ladie Elizabeth her Grace. London: 1614. V. 39; 41; 44

KING, JOHN ANTHONY

Twenty Four Years in the Argentine Republic . . . New York: 1845. V. 42

KING, JOHN GLEN 1732-1787

The Rites and Ceremonies of the Greek Church, in Russia. London: 1772. V. 37; 39

KING, JOHN H.

Three Hundred Days in a Yankee Prison, Reminiscences of War Life, Captivity, Imprisonment at Camp Chase, Ohio. Atlanta: 1904. V. 39

KING, JOHN LYLE

Trouting on the Brule River, or, Lawyers' Summer-Wayfaring in the Northern Wildnerness. Chicago: 1879. V. 39

KING, LAVINIA

Poem on a Tour to North Cape. Dublin: 1885. V. 43; 44

KING, LEONARD W.

Bronze Reliefs from the gates of Shalmaneser, King of Assyria B. C. 860-825. London: 1915. V. 40; 42; 43

First Steps in Assyrian: A Book for Beginners. London: 1898. V. 37; 40

A History of Babylon. London: 1915. V. 42

The Sculpture and Inscription of Darius the Great on the Rock of Behistun in Persia. London: 1907. V. 42; 43; 44

Studies in Eastern History. London: 1904-07. V. 44

KING, LORD

The Life of John Locke . . . London: 1829. V. 45

KING *Luckieboy's Picture Book.* London: 1875. V. 38

KING, MARGARET RIVES

Memoirs of the Life of Mrs. Sarah Peter. Cincinnati: 1889. V. 46

KING, MARTIN LUTHER

The Measure of a man. Philadelphia: 1959. V. 45

Strength to Love. New York: 1963. V. 41

Stride Toward Freedom. New York: 1958. V. 39; 44; 45

Where Do We Go From Here. 1967. V. 45

KING, MOSES

King's Views of New York 1909. New York. V. 44

King's Views of New York 1908-9. New York: 1909. V. 39

Philadelphia and Notable Philadelphians. Philadelphia: 1902. V. 39; 41; 42

The Poets' Tributes to Garfield. Cambridge: 1882. V. 41

KING *Orfeo.* Kingston: 1989. V. 45

KING, PAULINE

American Mural Painting. Boston: 1901. V. 45

KING, PETER, 7TH BARON 1775-1833

The Life of John Locke . . . London: 1829. V. 37; 41

The Life of John Locke . . . London: 1830. V. 41

A Selection from the Speeches and Writings of the Late Lord King,. London: 1844. V. 38; 42

KING, PHILIP PARKER

Narrative of a Survey of the Intertropical and Western Colonies of Australia. London: 1827. V. 42; 45

KING, RICHARD ASHE

Love the Debt. London: 1882. V. 37; 38

Love's Legacy. London: 1890. V. 38

KING, RICHARD JOHN

Handbook to the Cathedrals of England. 1861-1874. V. 37

Handbook to the Cathedrals of England. London: 1869-87. V. 39

Handbook to the Cathedrals of England, Southern Division, Part I, Winchester, Salisbury, Exeter and Wells. London: 1876. V. 45

KING, ROBERT

A Memoir Introductory to the early History of the Primacy of Armagh. Armagh: 1854. V. 38; 43

KING, RONALD

Canga: Ten Hand Colored Etchings. 1976. V. 40

The White Alphabet. Guildford: 1984. V. 37; 39

The White Alphabet. Surrey: 1984. V. 37; 42

KING, ROY

The World of Currier and Ives. New York: 1968. V. 40

KING, S. W.

The Italian Valleys of the Pennine Alps: A Tour through all the Romantic and Less-Frequented 'Vals' of Northern Piedmont, from the Tarentaise to the Gries. London: 1858. V. 41

KING-SALTER, PETER

Whitepatch. London: 1887. V. 38

KING, STEPHEN 1947-

The Bachman Books. 1985. V. 44; 46

The Bachman Books: Four Early Novels . . . Rage. The Long Walk, Roadwork, The Running Man. New York: 1985. V. 46

Bare Bones. Columbia: 1988. V. 43

Bare Bones. Los Angeles: 1988. V. 39; 41

Bare Bones. Los Angeles/Columbia: 1988. V. 40

The Breathing Method. 1984. V. 43; 46

Brooklyn August. V. 45

Carrie. 1974. V. 37; 39

Carrie. Garden City: 1974. V. 42; 45

Carrie. London: 1974. V. 41

Carrie. New York: 1974. V. 37; 39; 45

Christine. 1983. V. 37; 39

Christine. West Kingston: 1983. V. 41; 42; 43

Cujo. New York: 1981. V. 39; 42

Cycle of the Werewolf. 1983. V. 37; 39; 46

Cycle of the Werewolf. Westland: 1983. V. 37; 38; 42

Danse Macabre. 1981. V. 43

Danse Macabre. New York: 1981. V. 45

The Dark Half. New York: 1989. V. 41; 42; 43; 46

The Dark Tower II. Rhode Island: 1987. V. 37

The Dark Tower II: The Drawing of the Three. 1987. V. 37; 39

The Dark Tower II: The Drawing of the Three. W. Kingston: 1987. V. 40; 41; 42; 45

The Dark Tower: The Gunslinger. 1982. V. 39; 43; 44; 46

The Dark Tower: The Gunslinger. W. Kingston: 1982. V. 41

The Dead Zone. 1979. V. 37; 39; 43

The Dead Zone. London: 1979. V. 41

Different Seasons. New York: 1982. V. 37; 45

Dolan's Cadillac. Northridge: 1988. V. 41; 42

Dolan's Cadillac. 1989. V. 43

Dolan's Cadillac. Northridge: 1989. V. 41; 42

The Drawing of the Three. 1989. V. 46

Es. 1986. V. 37; 43

Eyes of the Dragon. 1984. V. 43

The Eyes of the Dragon. Bangor: 1984. V. 45; 46

The Eyes of the Dragon. New York: 1987. V. 37; 42

Firestarter. Huntington: 1980. V. 41; 42; 43

Firestarter. Huntington Woods: 1980. V. 42; 46

Firestarter. London: 1980. V. 37; 40

Firestarter. New York: 1980. V. 37; 42

Four Past Midnight. New York: 1990. V. 44; 45

The Hardcase Speaks. 1971. V. 45

It. London: 1986. V. 37

It. New York: 1986. V. 37

It. Paris: 1988. V. 45

It Grows on You. 1973. V. 45

Letters from Hell. Northridge: 1988. V. 39

The Long Walk. New York: 1979. V. 45

Misery. 1987. V. 37; 43

Misery. New York: 1987. V. 37

My Pretty Pony. New York: 1988. V. 41

My Pretty Pony. 1989. V. 44; 46

My Pretty Pony. New York: 1989. V. 45; 46

Night Shift. 1978. V. 39

Night Shift. Garden City: 1978. V. 43; 45

The Night Flier in Prime Evil. West Kingston: 1988. V. 45

Night Shift. New York: 1978. V. 37

Pet Sematary. Garden City: 1983. V. 44; 45

The Plant. Bangor: 1982-83-85. V. 45

The Plant. (Part II). 1983. V. 39; 46

The Plant. (Part III). 1985. V. 37

Prime Evil. New York: 1988. V. 42

Rage. New York: 1977. V. 46

Roadwork. New York: 1981. V. 45

The Running Man. New York: 1982. V. 45

Salem's Lot. Garden City: 1975. V. 43

Salem's Lot. London: 1976. V. 38

Salem's Lot. New York: 1976. V. 44; 46

Salem's Lot. New York: 1975. V. 37

The Shining. 1977. V. 37; 39

The Shining. Garden City: 1977. V. 37; 38; 40; 43; 45

The Shining. London: 1977. V. 41

The Shining. New York: 1977. V. 37; 39; 43

Sister Carrie. Garden City: 1974. V. 44

Skeleton Crew. 1984. V. 39

Skeleton Crew. New York: 1984. V. 46

Skeleton Crew. 1985. V. 43

KING, STEPHEN 1947- continued

Skeleton Crew. Santa Cruz: 1985. V. 42

The Stand. Garden City: 1978. V. 41; 43; 46

The Stand. New York: 1978. V. 37; 39; 44; 45; 46

The Stand. London: 1979. V. 44

The Stand. New York: 1990. V. 43; 44; 46

Stephen King's Danse Macabre. New York: 1981. V. 44; 46

The Talisman. 1984. V. 39

The Talisman. New York: 1984. V. 43; 46

The Talisman. West Kingston: 1984. V. 40; 41; 42

Thinner. New York: 1984. V. 37; 42

The Tommy-Knockers. London: 1988. V. 38

Whispers, 17-18. Binghamton: 1982. V. 37; 39

KING, T. BUTLER

Correspondence on the Subject of Appraisements &c. Between T. Butler King, Collector and J. Vincent Browne, Appraiser, Custom House, San Francisco, Ca. Washington: 1852. V. 42

Joint Resolutions, Proposing the Establishment of Lines of Government War Steamers from the Port of Monterey or San Francisco. Washington: 1848. V. 39

Letter from the Hon. T. Butler King to the Hon. William C. Dawson. New York: 1855. V. 44

Report . . . on California. Washington: 1850. V. 39; 40

T. Butler King's Report on California. Washington: 1850. V. 38

KING, THOMAS

Love at First Sight: a Ballad Farce, of Two Acts. London: 1763. V. 41

KING, THOMAS BUTLER

California: The Wonder of the Age. A Book for every one going to or having an Interest in that Golden Region . . . New York: 1850. V. 37; 45

KING, THOMAS H.

The Study Book of Mediaeval Architecture and Art. London: 1858, 1859. V. 38

KING, THOMAS STARR

A Vacation Among the Sierras. San Francisco: 1962. V. 38

KING, THOROLD

Haschisch A Novel. New York: 1888. V. 37

KING, W. F.

Report Upon The Title of Canada to the Islands North of the Mainland of Canada. Confidential. Ottawa: 1905. V. 42

KING, W. L. MAC KENZIE

The Message of the Carillon and Other Addresses. Toronto: 1927. V. 46

KING, W. N.

Story of the War of 1898 - On-the-scene reporting, the naval and military hundred day engagement against Spain. New York: 1898. V. 37

KING, W. R.

Counterpoise Gun-Carriages and Platforms . . . for the Use of Officers of the Corps of Engineers. Washington: 1869. V. 42

KING, W. ROSE

The Sportsman and Naturalist in Canada. London: 1856. V. 38

The Sportsman and Naturalist in Canada. London: 1866. V. 37; 38

KING, WILLIAM

The Art of Cookery. London: 1708. V. 37; 38; 40; 42; 43; 45

The Art of Love. London: 1708. V. 38; 40; 41; 42; 45

The Art of Cookery; a Poem. London: & Westminster: 1708. V. 44

The Art of Cookery, in Imitation of Horace's Art of Poetry. London: 1708 or 1709. V. 39; 40

The Art of Cookery, in Imitation of Horace's Art of Poetry. London: 1712. V. 46

Chelesea Porcelain. London: 1922. V. 39; 42; 46

A Discourse Concerning the Inventions of men in the Worship of God. London: 1704. V. 44

Doctor King's Apology; or, Vindication of Himself from the Several Matters Charged on Him by the Society of Informers. Oxford: 1755. V. 42

Epistola Objurgatoria ad Gulielmum King, LL.D. (with) Epistola Canonici . . . ad Archdiaconum. London: 1744. V. 39

A Friendly Letter from Honest Tom Boggy, to the Reverend Mr. G(oddar)d, Canon of Windsor. (with) A Second Letter from Tom Boggy. London: 1710. V. 40

Miltonis Epistola ad Polionem. Londini: 1738. V. 42; 44

Miscellanies in Prose and Verse. London: 1705. V. 38; 41; 45

Miscellanies in Prose and Verse. London: 1707. V. 37; 41; 45

Miscellanies in Prose and Verse. London: 1709. V. 38; 43; 46

Rufinus; or An Historical Essay on the Favourite Ministry Under Theodosius the Great and His Son Arcadius. London: 1712, 1711. V. 38

Some Remarks on the Tale of Tub. London: 1704. V. 39

KING, WILLIAM, ABP. OF DUBLIN 1650-1729

An Admonition to the Dissenting Inhabitants of the Diocese of Derry Concerning A Book Lately PUblished by Mr. J. Boyse entitled Remarks on a Late Discourse of William, Ld. Bp. of Derry etc. Dublin: 1694. V. 43

An Essay on the Origin of Evil. Cambridge: 1739. V. 39

The State of the Protestants of Ireland Under the Late King James's Government . . . London: 1691. V. 42; 44; 46

The State of the Protestants of Ireland Under the Late King James's Government . . . London: 1692. V. 37; 38; 43

The State of the Protestants of Ireland Under the Late King James's Governement . . . Dublin: 1730. V. 44

KING, WILLIAM HARVEY

History of Homoeopathy and its Institutions in America. New York: 1905. V. 37

KING, WILLIAM L.

Newspaper Press of Charleston, S. C., a Chronological and Biographical History, Embracing a Period of One Hundred and Forty Years. Charleston: 1872. V. 42

KING, WILLIAM ROSS 1822-1890

The Sportsman and Naturalist in Canada. London: 1866. V. 39; 42; 43

KINGALE, ALEXANDER WILLIAM 1809-1891

The Invasions of the Crimea. London: 1877-88. V. 46

KINGDOM, WILLIAM

America and the British Colonies. London: 1820. V. 45

KINGDON, J.

African Mammal Drawings. Islip: 1987. V. 38

East African Mammals, a Atlas of Evolution in Africa. London: 1971-84. V. 37; 38; 42

KINGDON, J. A.

Richard Grafton, Citizen and Grocer of London and One Time Master of His Company . . . London: 1901. V. 41

KINGDON, JONATHAN

East African Mammals. An Atlas of Evolution in Africa. Volume I, Volumes III. London: 1977-82. V. 46

KINGDON-WARD, FRANCIS 1885-1958

Burma's Icy Mountains. London: 1949. V. 46

Plant Hunter in Manipur. London: 1952. V. 46

Plant Hunter's Paradise. London: 1937. V. 40

KINGHAM, W. R.

London Gunners. The Story of the H.A.C. Siege Battery in Action. London: 1919. V. 44; 45; 46

KINGLAKE, ALEXANDER WILLIAM 1809-1891

Eothen: or Traces of Travel Brought Home from the East. Philadelphia. V. 45

Eothen, or Traces of Travel Brought Home From the East. London: 1844. V. 39; 45

Eothen, or Traces of Travel Brought Home from the East. London: 1845. V. 38; 40; 41; 43

Eothen. Paris: 1846. V. 42

Eothen, or Traces of Travel Brought Home from the East. New York: 1848. V. 45

Eothen. London: 1913. V. 37; 38; 45

The Invasion of the Crimea . . . London: 1863. V. 45

The Invasion of the Crimea: its Origin, and an Account of Its Progress Down to the Death of Lord Raglan. Edinburgh: 1868-87. V. 38

The Invasion of the Crimea: Its Origina and an Account of Its Progress to the Death of Lord Raglan. London: 1874-87. V. 39

The Invasion of the Crimea, Its Origin, and an Account of Its Progress Down to the Death of Lord Raglan. New York: 1888. V. 45

The Invasion of the Crimea . . . Edinburgh and London: 1888-91. V. 40

The Invasion of the Crimea. Edinburgh and London: 1890-96. V. 37

A Portrait of Lady Hester. Marlborough: 1987. V. 40; 44

KINGMAN BROTHERS, CHICAGO.

Combination Atlas Map of Miami County, Indiana. 1877. V. 42

KINGMAN, LEROY WILSON

Owego Early Owego. Owego: 1987. V. 39

THE KINGS Cabinet Opened; or, Certain Packets of Secret Letters & Papers, Written with the Kings Own Hand, and Taken in his Cabinet at Nasby-Field, June 14, 1645. London: 1645. V. 38

KING'S Cliffe. A Short Account of the Two Charitable Foundations at King's Cliffe in the County of Northampton, The One Founded in the Year 1745, by Mrs. Elizabeth Hutcheson of King's Cliffe . . . The Other Founded in the Year 1727, by William Law . . . Stamford: 1755. V. 40

THE KING'S Royal Rifle Corps Chronicle, 1901-65. London: 1904-06. V. 42

KINGSBOROUGH, EDWARD KING

Antiquities of Mexico; comprising Facsimiles of Ancient Mexican Painting and Hieroglyphics. London: 1831-48. V. 42

KINGSBURY, ALICE

Ho! For Elf-Land! San Francisco: 1878. V. 42

Ho! For Elf-Land! San Francisco: 1877. V. 37

KINGSBURY, BENJAMIN

A Treatise on Razors . . . London: 1806. V. 46

KINGSBURY, GAINES P.

Colonel Doge's Journal . . . a Report of the Expedition of the Dragoons Under the Command of Colonel Dodge, to the Rocky Mountains. Washington: 1836. V. 40; 42

Journal of the March of a Detachment of Dragoons Under the Command of Colonel Dodge, During the Summer of 1835. Washington: 1836. V. 41

Report of the Expedition of the Dragoons, Under the Command of Colonel Henry Dodge to the Rocky Mountains, During the Summer of 1835 &c. Washington: 1836. V. 38

KINGSBURY, GEORGE W.

History of Dakota Territory. Chicago: 1915. V. 45

KINGSBURY, J. E.

The Telephone and Telephone Exchanges, Their Invention and Development. London: 1915. V. 37; 40; 42

KINGSBURY, JEROME

Dermochromes. New York: 1914. V. 41

The Portfolio of Dermochromes. New York: 1913. V. 38

KINGSBURY, SUSAN MYRA

The Records of the Virginia Company of London. Washington: 1906. V. 40

The Records of the Virginia Company of London, the Court Book, From the Manuscript in the Library of Congress. Washington: 1906-35. V. 42

KINGSFORD, WILLIAM

The Canadian Camels: Their History and Cost . . . Toronto: 1865. V. 41; 44

KINGSFORD, WILLIAM M.

Impressions of the West and South During a Six Weeks' Holiday. Toronto: 1858. V. 44

KINGSLEY, CHARLES 1819-1875

Alton Locke, Tailor and Poet. London: 1850. V. 38; 41; 44; 46

Andromeda and Other Poems. London: 1858. V. 46

At Last: A Christmas in the West Indies. London: 1871. V. 38

At Last: a Christmas in the West Indies. London: & New York: 1871. V. 39; 42

At Last: A Christmas in the West Indies. New York: 1871. V. 40; 42

Glaucus; or, the Wonders of the Shore. Cambridge: 1855. V. 40

Glaucus. Cambridge & London: 1859. V. 37

Glaucus, or the Wonders of the Shore. London: 1903. V. 37

Herewrd the Wake, 'last of the English'. London: 1866. V. 40

Hereweard the Wake, 'Last of the English'. London: & Cambridge: 1866. V. 46

The Hermits. London: 1868. V. 46

The Heroes. Cambridge: 1856. V. 38

The Heroes. 1912. V. 45

The Heroes or Greek Fairy Tales for My Children. London: 1912. V. 37; 41; 43

The Heroes or Greek Fairy Tales. London: 1914. V. 44

The Heroes or Greek Fairy Tales. London: (ca. 1920). V. 37

Hints to Stammerers, by a Minute Philosopher. London: 1864. V. 46

Hypatia; or, New Foes With an Old Face. London: 1853. V. 40; 41; 42; 46

The Life and Works. London: 1901. V. 37; 38; 42; 46

The Life and Works of . . . London: 1901-03. V. 46

Miscellanies. London: 1859. V. 40; 43; 46

The Novels. London: 1881. V. 38

The Novels and Poems. New York: 1897-1900. V. 42; 44

The Novels and Poems. Boston: 1899. V. 38

Poems. London: 1897. V. 44

Politics for the People. London: 1848. V. 46

The Roman and the Teuton. London: 1881. V. 42

The Saint's Tragedy. London: 1848. V. 37; 38; 39; 40; 41; 45; 46

South by West or Winter in the Rocky Mountains and Spring in Mexico. London: 1874. V. 37; 38; 41; 42

Two years Ago. Cambridge: 1857. V. 46

The Water Babies. London. V. 45

The Water Babies. New York. V. 44

The Water Babies. London: 1863. V. 37; 38; 39; 41; 43; 46

The Water Babies. London & Cambridge: 1863. V. 39; 41; 42; 45

The Water Babies: A Fairy Tale for a Land-Baby. London/Cambridge: 1863. V. 37

The Water Babies. London: 1885. V. 41

The Water Babies. New York: 1895. V. 44

The Water Babies. New York: 1900. V. 39

The Water Babies. London: 1909. V. 37; 43; 44; 45

The Water Babies. Boston: 1915. V. 42; 46

The Water Babies. London: 1915. V. 41

The Water Babies. New York: 1916. V. 46

The Water Babies. London: 1924. V. 46

The Water Babies. London: (n.d.). V. 37

Westward Ho. Boston: 1855. V. 37; 46

Westward Ho! Cambridge: 1855. V. 37; 38; 39; 40; 42; 43

Westward Ho! New York: 1947. V. 44

The Works. (with) Charles Kingsley, His Letters and Memories of His Life. London: 1879-1902. V. 37

The Works. London: 1968-69. V. 39

KINGSLEY, GEORGE HENRY

Notes on Sport and Travel. London: 1900. V. 41

KINGSLEY, HENRY

The Grange Garden, a Romance. London: 1876. V. 38

Ravenshoe. Cambridge & London: 1862. V. 46

KINGSLEY, J. STERLING

Nature's Wonderland. New York: 1894. V. 37

KINGSLEY, MARY HENRIETTA

Travels in West Africa. London: 1897. V. 41; 45; 46

KINGSLEY, SIDNEY

The Patriots. New York: 1943. V. 45

KINGSLEY, VINE W.

Reconstruction in America. New York: 1865. V. 38; 39; 44

KINGSLEY, ZAPHANIAH

A Treatise on the Patriarchal or Co-Operative System of Society, As It Exists in Some Governments and Colonies in America, and in the United States Under the Name of Slavery, With Its Necessity and Advantages . . . Tallahassee: 1829. V. 37; 38; 39; 44; 45

KINGSMILL, JOSEPH

Chapters on Prisons and Prisoners, and the Prevention of Crime.. London: 1854. V. 39; 42

THE KINGSPORT Book of Type Faces. Kingsport: 1950's. V. 46

THE KINGSPORT Book of Type Faces. Kingsport: 1960's. V. 46

KINGSTON, ELIZABETH CHUDLEIGH, DUCHESS OF

An Authentic Detail of Particulars Relative to the Late Duchess of Kingston. London: 1788. V. 38

KINGSTON, MAXINE HONG

Hawaii One Summer. San Francisco: 1987. V. 39; 40; 42; 43

The Woman Warrior. New York: 1976. V. 44; 45

KINGSTON, R.

A True History of the Several Designs and Conspiracies Against His Majesties Sacred Person and Government . . . London: 1698. V. 44

KINGSTON, WILLIAM

Infant Amusements; or, How to Make a Nursery Happy. London: 1867. V. 38

KINGSTON, WILLIAM H. G.

The Cruise of the 'Frolic'; or, Yachting Experiences of Barnaby Brine, Esq., R.N. London: 1860. V. 42

Lusitianian Sketches of the Pen and Pencil. London: 1845. V. 45

Manco, The Peruvian Chief. London: 1853. V. 40

Old Jack, a Man-of-War's Man and South-Sea Whaler. London: 1859. V. 41

Voyages and Travels of Count Funnibos and Baron Stilkin. London: 1890? V. 43

KINIETZ, W. VERNON

John Mix Stanley and His Indian Paintings. Ann Arbor: 1942. V. 40; 42

KINKEAD, A. S.

Landscapes of Corsic and Ireland. London: 1921. V. 38

KINKLE, ROGER D.

The Complete Encyclopedia of Popular Music and Jazz, 1900-1950. New Rochelle: 1974. V. 44

KINLOCH, ALEXANDER A. A.

Large Game Shooting in Thibet and the North West. London: 1869/76. V. 46

KINLOCH, ARCHIBALD GORDON

The Trial of Sir Archibald Gordon Kinloch, of Gilmerton, Bart. For the Murder of Sir Francis Kinloch, Bart, His Brother-German . . . Edinburgh: 1795. V. 37

KINLOCH, CHARLES WALTER

De Zeike Reiziger, or Rambles in Java and the STraits in 1852. London: 1853. V. 40

KINNAIRD, LAWRENCE

The Frontiers of New Spain: Nicolas de Lafora's Description, 1766-1768. Berkeley: 1958. V. 37

KINNEAR, JOHN G.

The Crisis and the Currency; with Comparison Between the English and Scotch Systems of Banking. London: 1847. V. 45

KINNELL, GALWAY

Avenue Bearing Initial of Christ Into New World. Boston: 1974. V. 39

Body Rags: Poems. Boston: 1968. V. 46

Body Rags. London: 1969. V. 39

The Book of Nightmares. Boston: 1971. V. 46

Brother of My Heart. A Poem. Toronto: 1977. V. 39

Fergus Falling. 1979. V. 39

Fergus Falling. Newark: 1979. V. 38; 39

First Poems 1946-1954. Mt. Horeb: 1970. V. 46

Fisherman. Toronto: 1980. V. 39

Flower Herding on Mount Monadnock. Boston: 1964. V. 44

The Hen Flower. 1969. V. 39

The Last Hiding Places of Snow. New York: 1980. V. 39; 42; 44

Poems of Night. London: 1967. V. 39; 45

Three Poems. New York: 1976. V. 37; 39; 40; 42

Two Poems. Newark: 1979. V. 41; 46

Two Poems. New York: 1981. V. 37; 39

What a Kingdom It Was. Boston: 1960. V. 37; 41; 42

KINNEY, ABBOT

Eucalyptus. Los Angeles: 1895. V. 43

KINNEY, ARTHUR F.

The Birds and Beasts of Shakespeare. Easthampton: 1990. V. 45; 46

KINNEY, COATES

Keeuka and Other Poems. Columbus: 1855. V. 40

KINNEY, HANNAH

A Review of the Principal Events of the Last Ten Years in the Life of . . . Boston: 1841. V. 44; 45

KINNEY, JAMES R.

How to Raise a Dog: In the City . . . in the Suburbs. New York: 1938. V. 39; 43

KINNEY, TORY

The Etchings of Troy Kinney. Garden City: 1929. V. 40; 46

KINNEY, WILLIAM A.

Hawaii's Capacity for Self-Government all but destroyed. Salt Lake City: 1927. V. 38

KINNIER, JOHN MAC DONALD

A Geographical Memoir of the Persian Empire . . . London: 1813. V. 39

KINO, EUSEBIO

Kino's Historical Memoir of Pimeria Alta a Contemporary Account of the Beginnings of California, Sonora and Arizona. Cleveland: 1919. V. 37; 39; 43; 46

KINO, EUSEBIO FRANCISCO

Lettres Edifiantes et Curieuses, Ecrites des Missions Etrangeres par Quelques Missionnaires de la Compagnie de Jesus. Paris: 1705. V. 40

KINROSS, JOHN

Details from Italian Buildings, Chiefly Renaissance . . . Edinburgh: 1882. V. 40; 44

KINSAKU, MATSUO

Traveler, my Name: Haiku of Basho. 1984. V. 39

KINSALE, IRELAND. CORPORATION

The Council Book of Kinsale (Co. Cork), from 1652 to 1800. Guildford: 1879. V. 45

KINSBERGEN, JAN HENDRICK VAN

Grondbeginselen der Zee Tacticq. Amsterdam: 1782. V. 41

KINSELLA, THOMAS 1928-

Another September. Dublin: 1958. V. 38

Ely Place. Dublin: 1972. V. 41

The Messenger. Dublin: 1978. V. 40; 41; 42; 44

Moralities. Dublin: 1960. V. 40

Nightwalker and Other Poems. Dublin. V. 42

Nightwalker. Dublin: 1967. V. 40; 41

Nightwalker and Other Poems. Dublin: 1968. V. 40

Notes from the Land of the Dead. Dublin: 1972. V. 39

Poems. Dublin: 1956. V. 40

The Starlit Eye. Dublin: 1952. V. 38; 40

Tear. Cambridge: 1969. V. 43

Wormwood. Dublin: 1966. V. 40; 41

KINSELLA, W. P.

Five Stories. Vancouver: 1986. V. 41; 42

Scars. N.P.: 1978. V. 43; 44

Scars. Toronto: 1978. V. 42; 43

Shoeless Joe Jackson Comes to Iowa. N.P.: 1980. V. 43; 44

Shoeless Joe. Boston: 1982. V. 42; 43; 44; 45; 46

Shoeless Joe Jackson Comes to Iowa. 1980. V. 43

KINSEY, ALFRED C.

Sexual Behaviour in the Human Male (and) Female. Philadelphia & London: 1948-53. V. 46

KINSEY, DARIUS

Kinsey, Photographer. A Half Century of Negatives by Darius and Tabitha May Kinsey. San Francisco: 1975. V. 41

KINSEY, W. M.

Portugal Illustrated: in a Series of Letters. London: 1828. V. 37; 38; 40; 43

KINSMAN, H. J.

Tactical Notes. Dublin & London: 1916. V. 41

KINZIE, JULIETTE A.

Narrative of the Massacre at Chicago, August 15, 1812, and of Some Preceding Events. Chicago: 1844. V. 37; 39; 40

Wau-Bun, the 'Early Day' in the North-West. New York: 1856. V. 37; 38; 40; 42; 46

Wau-Bun, the 'Early Day' of the North-West. Chicago: 1901. V. 37; 38

KINZINE, JOHN H., MRS.

Wan-Bun, the 'Early Day' in the North West. Chicago: 1856. V. 45

KIP, J.

Britannia Illustrata or Views of Several of the Queens Palaces as Also of the Principal Seats of the Nobility and Gentry of Great Britain. London: 1714-17. V. 42

KIP, JOHN

Nouveau Theatre de la Grande Bretagne, ou Description Exacte des Palais du Roy et des Maisons les Plus Considerables des Seigneurs et des Gentilshommes du Dit Royaume . . . London: 1715-28. V. 46

Nouveau Theatre de la Grande Bretagne. London: 1728. V. 39

KIP, L.

Hannibal's Man and Other Tales. 1878. V. 44

KIP, LAWRENCE

Army Life on the Pacific; a Journal of the Expedition Against the Northern Indians, The Tribes of the Coeur d'Alenes, Spokans, and Pelouzes, in the Summer of 1858. New York: 1859. V. 37; 38; 39; 41; 42; 43; 45; 46

The Indian Council At Walla Walla. May and June, 1855. Eugene: 1897. V. 45

KIP, LEONARD

California Sketches, with Recollections of the Gold Mines. Albany: 1850. V. 37; 39

KIP, WILLIAM I.

The Early Jesuit Missions in North America. New York: 1846. V. 42; 46

Early Jesuit Missions in North America . . . London: 1847. V. 41; 45

KIPLING, ARTHUR WELLESLEY

The Shadow of Glory Being a History of the Great War of 1910-11. London: 1910. V. 42

KIPLING, JOHN LOCKWOOD

Beast and Man in India. London: 1891. V. 42

KIPLING, RUDYARD 1865-1936

Abaft the Funnel. New York: 1909. V. 37; 40; 42; 44; 45

The Absent-Minded Beggar. London: 1899. V. 40; 43; 46

Actions and Reactions. London: 1909. V. 39

Actions and Reactions. New York: 1909. V. 37; 44

An Almanac of Twelve Sports. London: 1898. V. 37

American Notes. New York: 1891. V. 40

Barrack Room Ballads. London: 1892. V. 37; 39; 40; 44; 46

The Brushwood Boy. New York: 1899. V. 37; 38

Captains Dourageous. London: 1897. V. 38; 39; 40; 41; 42; 43; 45; 46

Captains Courageous. New York: 1897. V. 37; 44; 45; 46

La Chasse de Kaa. Paris: 1930. V. 38

A Choice of Songs. Garden City: 1925. V. 39

The City of Dreadful Night and Other Places. 1891. V. 39

The City of Dreadful Night and Other Places. Allaghabad & London: 1891. V. 43

The City of the Dreadful Night and Other Places. Allahabad: 1891. V. 39; 41; 42; 44

The City of the Dreadful Night and Other Places. London: 1891. V. 40; 45

Collected Verse of Rudyard Kipling. New York: 1910. V. 44; 46

Collected Verse. Toronto: 1910. V. 43

Collected Verse. London: 1912. V. 40

Collected Dog Stories. Garden City: 1934. V. 38

Collected Dog Stories . . . New York: 1934. V. 45

The Courting of Dinah Shadd and Other Stories. New York: 1890. V. 40

The Day of the Dead. Garden City: 1930. V. 39; 45

The Days Work. London: 1898. V. 39

The Dead King. London: 1910. V. 39

Debits and Credits. Garden City: 1926. V. 43

Debits and Credits. London: 1926. V. 37; 43; 44

Departmental Ditties and Other Verses. Calcutta: 1886. V. 40

Departmental Ditties and Other Verses. Lahore: 1886. V. 42

Departmental Ditties and Other Verses. Calcutta: 1888. V. 40

Departmental Ditties and Other Verses. Calcutta: 1890. V. 40

Departmental Ditties and Other Verses. Calcutta: 1892. V. 40

Departmental Ditties and Other Verses. London: 1897. V. 38

Departmental Ditties nd other Verses. New York: 1898. V. 38

Departmental Ditties and Other Verses. To all Heads of Depa . . . and all Anglo-Indians. Rudyard Kipling Assistant. Department of public Journalism, Lohore District. (1886). V. 37

Departmental Ditties, Barrack-Room Ballads and Other Verses. New York: 1890. V. 37; 38; 39; 40

Destroyers at Jutland. Garden City: 1916. V. 39

The Dipsy Chanty and Other Selected Poems. New York: 1898. V. 39

Doctors: an Address Delivered to the Students of the Medical School of the Middlesex Hospital, 1st October, 1908. London: 1908. V. 39; 41

Echoes by Two Writers. Lahore: 1884. V. 40

The Eyes of Asia. New York: 1918. V. 44

The Eyes of Asia. Garden City, New York: 1918. V. 37

The Feet of the Young Men. New York: 1920. V. 39

The Feet of the Young Men. Garden City: 1920. V. 37; 39; 44

The Five Nations. London: 1903. V. 45; 46

A Fleet In Being. London: 1898. V. 44

The Fringes of the Fleet. Garden City: 1915. V. 39

From Sea to Sea. Letters of Travel. New York: 1899. V. 41

From Sea to Sea and Other Sketches - Letters of Travel. London: 1900. V. 41

The Greek National Anthem. Garden City: 1918. V. 39

Ham and the Porcupine. Garden City: 1935. V. 45

The Haulahka, a Story of East and West. London: 1892. V. 40

Healing by the Stars. Garden City: 1928. V. 45

The Holy War. Garden City: 1917. V. 39

In Black and White. Allahabad: 1888. V. 39; 43; 45

Independence. Garden City: 1923. V. 45

Indian Tales. New York: 1890. V. 39

The Irish Guards in the Great War. V. 45

The Irish Guards. Garden City: 1918. V. 39

The Irish Guards. New York: 1918. V. 42

The Irish Guards in the Great War. London: 1923. V. 37; 39

Le Livre de La Jungle. Paris. V. 39; 41

The Jungle Book. London: 1894. V. 46

The Jungle Book. New York: 1894. V. 43

The Jungle Book and the Second Jungle Book. London: 1894-1895. V. 37; 39; 40; 41; 42; 43; 44; 45

The Jungle Book. London: 1895. V. 40; 46

Le Livre de la Jungle. Paris: 1910? V. 46

The Jungle Book: The Second Jungle Book. London: 1929. V. 45

The Jungle Book. New York: 1894/1985. V. 37

Just So Stories for Little Children. London: 1955. V. 44

Just So Stories for Little Children. London: 1902. V. 37; 38; 39; 41; 43; 45; 46

Justice. Garden City: 1918. V. 39

Kim. London: 1901. V. 37; 39; 41; 43

Kim. New York: 1901. V. 40; 41; 42; 46

Kim. New York: 1962. V. 44; 46

The King's Pilgrimage. Garden City: 1922. V. 45

Land and Sea Tales for Boys and Girls. Garden City: 1923. V. 37

Land and Sea Tales for Boys and Girls. New York: 1923. V. 44

Land and Sea Tales for Scouts and Guides. London: 1923. V. 38; 45

Letters of Marque. Allahabad: 1891. V. 38; 40; 44

Life's Handicap. London: 1891. V. 41; 44; 46

Life's Handicap. London: 1892. V. 40

The Light that Failed. London: 1891. V. 41

Limits and Renewals. New York: 1932. V. 37; 39; 42; 44; 46

Mesopotamia. Garden City: 1917. V. 39

The Naulahka: a Story of West and East. London: 1892. V. 40

The Naulahka. London: 1925. V. 37

Neighbours. Garden City: 1932. V. 45

The Nerve That Conquers. Garden City: 1928. V. 39

On Dry Cow Fishing as a Fine Art. Cleveland: 1926. V. 37; 40; 41; 43; 45

Our Lady of the Sack-Cloth. Garden City: 1935. V. 45

The Phantom Rickshaw and Other Tales. Allabadhad: 1885. V. 41

The Phantom Rickshaw and Other Eerie Tales. London: 1888. V. 40

The Phantom Rickshaw and Other Eerie Tales. London & Allahabad: 1888. V. 38

The Phantom 'Rickshaw and Other Eerie Tales. Allahabad, n.d.: 1890. V. 39; 40

The Phantom Rickysham and Other Tales. London: (1890). V. 37

Plain Tales from the Hills. London: 1888. V. 40

Plain Tales from the Hills. London: 1923. V. 46

Plain Tales from the Hills. Calcutta: 1888. V. 37; 38; 39; 40; 41; 44

Poems. Chicago: 1899. V. 40

Poems 1886-1929. Garden City: 1930. V. 39; 43; 45

Poems, 1886-1929. New York: 1930. V. 39

Poems 1886-1929. London: 1929. V. 37; 41

Puck of Pook's Hill. London: 1906. V. 43; 46

Puck of Pook's Hill. New York: 1906. V. 39; 40; 41; 42; 45

Puck of Pook's Hill. London: 1927. V. 46

Rewards and Fairies. London: 1910. V. 39; 43; 45

Rudyard Kipling's Verse - Inclusive Edition - 1885-1918. London: 1919. V. 40; 41

Rudyard Kipling's Verse. Garden City: 1945, (1940). V. 39

The Scholars. 1919. V. 41

The Science of Rebellion: a Tract for the Times. London: 1901. V. 44

The Sea and Sussex: from Rudyard Kipling's Verse. Garden City: 1926. V. 39; 45

Sea and Sussex from Rudyard Kipling's Verse. London: 1927. V. 41

Sea and Sussex from Rudyarad Kipling's Verse. London: 1926. V. 37; 41; 46

Sea and Sussex, from Rudyard Kipling's Verse. New York: 1926. V. 37; 41

The Second Jungle Book. London: 1895. V. 38; 40; 42; 44; 46

The Second Jungle Book. New York: 1895. V. 39

A Series of Thirty Etchings . . . London: 1901. V. 46

The Servant a Dog Told by Boots. London: 1930. V. 46

The Seven Seas. London: 1896. V. 41; 46

The Shipping Industry. Garden City: 1925. V. 39

The Sin of Witchcraft. London: 1901. V. 38

Soldier Tales. London: 1896. V. 41

Soldier Stories. New York & London: 1896. V. 40

Soldiers Three. Allahabad: 1888. V. 38; 39

Some Notes on a Bill. Little Rock: 1920. V. 37; 45

A Song of the English. London. V. 37

A Song of the English. London: 1909. V. 37; 38; 40; 41; 45

A Song of the English. New York: 1909. V. 43

A Song of the English. London: 1910. V. 42

A Song of the English. London: 1913. V. 42; 46

KIPLING, RUDYARD 1865-1936 continued

A Song of the English. London: 1916. V. 38

The Song of the Lathes. Garden City: 1918. V. 39

Stalky & Co. London: 1899. V. 40; 43

The Story of the Gadsbys. Allahabad: 1888. V. 43; 46

The Story of the Gadsbys, A Tale Without a Plot. Allahabad;: 1890. V. 39

The Story of the Gadsbys. Allahabad: 1898. V. 45

Tales of 'The Trade.' Garden City: 1916. V. 39

Tales of the East and West. Avon: 1973. V. 46

They. London: 1905. V. 40

They. New York: 1906. V. 40; 41

Thy Servant a Dog by Boots. London: 1930. V. 37

Traffics and Discoveries. London: 1904. V. 37; 38; 40; 41; 42; 44; 46

Twenty Poems From Rudyard Kipling. London: 1918. V. 40

The Two Jungle Books. London: 1924. V. 37; 45

Under the Deodars. Allahabad: 1888. V. 38

Under the Deodars . . . Allahabad: 1890. V. 39

Verse. New York: 1922. V. 42

Wee Willie Winkie and Other Child Stories. Allahbabad: 1888. V. 41

Wee Willie Winkie and Other Stories. Allahabad: 1890. V. 38

White Horses. London: 1897. V. 45

With the Night Mail: a Story of 2000 A.D. New York: 1909. V. 37; 39; 42; 46

Works. London: 1896-1918. V. 37; 39

The Works. London: 1913. V. 38

The Works of . . . Bombay Edition. London: 1913-1919. V. 37

Works. London: 1913-20. V. 46

The Bombay Edition of the Works of Rudyard Kipling. London: 1913-20. V. 46

The Works of . . . London: 1913-27. V. 41; 44; 46

Works in Prose and Verse. London: 1913-38. V. 37

The Works of Rudyard Kipling. Garden City: 1914-1915. V. 46

Works. London: 1915-37. V. 41

The Complete Works in Prose and Verse. London: 1937-39. V. 41; 44

Works. New York: 1941. V. 38; 42; 45

The Collected Works. New York: 1941. V. 37; 43; 46

The Writings in Prose and Verse . . . London: 1897-1907. V. 46

The Writings in Prose and Verse. (with) Departmental Ditties. London: 1898. V. 45

The Writings in Prose and Verse. New York: 1907. V. 42

Writings in Prose and Verse. New York: 1913. V. 38

The Writings in Prose and Verse of . . . New York: 1913-19. V. 44

The Writings in prose and verse. London: 1897-1938. V. 37

The Years Between. London: (1919). V. 37; 39; 41; 44; 46

KIPNESS, ROBERT

A Suite of Ten Lithographs Drawn by Robert Kipness for the Selected Poems of Rainer Maria Rilke. New York: 1979. V. 37

KIPPIS, ANDREW 1725-1795

An Account of the Voyages Round the World Performed by Captain James Cook, with an Account of His Life During the Previous and Intervening Periods. New York: 1825. V. 40; 42

Biographia Britannica. London: 1778-1783. V. 38; 46

Considerations on the Provisional Treaty with America, and the Preliminary Articles of Peace with France and Spain. London: 1783. V. 46

The Life of Captain James Cook. Dublin: 1788. V. 38; 41; 42; 45; 46

The Life of Captain James Cook. London: 1788. V. 37; 44

A Narrative of the Voyages Round the World Performed by Captain James Cook . . . London: 1814. V. 45

A Narrative of the Voyages Round the World, Performed by Captain James Cook. Chiswick: 1820. V. 41

A Narrative of the Voyages Round the World Performed by Captain James Cook . . . London: 1878. V. 39

A Narrative of the Voyages Round the World Performed by Captain James Cook, with an Account of His Life, During the Previous and Intervening Periods . . . London: 1893. V. 38; 39

Vie du Capitaine Cooke. Paris: 1789. V. 42

KIRBY, CHARLES F.

The Adventures of Arcot Rupee. London: 1867. V. 38

KIRBY, EPHRAIM

Reports of Cases Adjudged in the Superior Court of the State of Connecticut . . . Litchfield: 1789. V. 38; 42; 45

KIRBY, FREDERICK VAUGHAN

In Haunts of Wild Game. Edinburgh: 1896. V. 39

KIRBY, FREDERICK VAUGHN

In Haunts of Wild Game A Hunter-Nationalists Wanderings from Kahlamba to Libombo. 1896. V. 37

KIRBY, JOHN 1690-1753

The Capacity and Extent of the Human Understanding Exemplified in the Extraordinary Case of Automathes . . . Dublin: 1747. V. 42

The Suffolk Traveller. Ipswich: 1735. V. 38; 42; 44

The Suffolk Traveller. London: 1764. V. 45

The Suffolk Traveller . . . an actual Survey of the Whole County in the Years 1732, 1733 and 1734 to Which is Added an Appendix. Woodbridge: 1800? V. 41

KIRBY, JOHN JOSHUA 1716-1774

Dr. Brook Taylor's Method of Perspective Made Easy, Both in Theory and Practice. Ipswich: 1755. V. 38; 40; 41

An Historical Account of the Twelve Prints of Monasteries, Castles, Antient Churches, and Monuments, in the County of Suffolk, Which were Drawn by Joshua Kirby, Painter in Ipswich . . . Ipswich: 1748. V. 38; 40; 44

The Perspective of Architecture. London: 1761. V. 41; 44

KIRBY, M.

Beautiful Birds in Far-Off Lands; Their Haunts and Homes. London: 1873. V. 38

KIRBY, MARY

Rose-Coloured Spectacles. London: 1859. V. 38

KIRBY, PERCIVAL R.

The Musical Instruments of the Native Races of South Africa. Johannesburg: 1953. V. 42; 44

KIRBY, RICHARD

The Marrow of Astrology. London: 1687. V. 42

KIRBY, THOMAS

An Essay on Criticism. London: 1757. V. 37

KIRBY, WILLIAM

Mormonism Exposed and Refuted or True and False Religion Contrasted Forty Years' Experience and Observation Among the Mormons. Nashville: 1893. V. 41

On the Power Wisdom and Goodness of God as Manifested in the Creation of Animals and in Their History Habits and Instincts. London: 1835. V. 38

KIRBY, WILLIAM F.

The Butterflies and Moths of Europe. London: 1903. V. 37; 38; 39; 44

Elementary Text-book of Entomology. London: 1892. V. 45

European Butterflies and Moths. London: 1882. V. 37; 43; 45; 46

European Butterfiles and Moths . . . London: 1889. V. 38; 43; 46

A Hand-Book to the Order Lepidoptera. London: 1896-97. V. 40

An Introduction to Entomology. London: 1815. V. 44

An Introduction to Entomology or Elments of the Natural History of Insects. London: 1816-26. V. 39

An Introduction to Entomology; or Elements of the Natural History of Insects. London: 1822-23-26. V. 38

An Introduction to Entomology. London: 1822-26. V. 42

An Introduction to Entomology: or Elements of the Natural History of Insects. Fifth Edition. London: 1828. V. 37; 41; 43; 45

KIRCHEISEN, F.

Bibliography of Napoleon: a Systematic Collection Critically Selected. London: 1902. V. 46

KIRCHEN Gesaeng. Aus den Wittengergischen und Allen Andern den Besten Gesangbuechern Colligirt und Gesamelet . . . Frankfurt: 1569. V. 38

KIRCHENORDNUNG Wie es inn Des Durchleuchtigen . . . Herren Wolffgangs, Pfaltzgraven Bey Rhein, Gravens zu Veldentz unnd Sponhaim &c . . . Nurnberg: 1570. V. 37

KIRCHER, ANATHASIUS 1602-1680

China Monumentis Qua Sacris Qua Profanis, Nec non Variis Naturae & Artis Spectacularis, Aliarumque Rerum Memorabilium Argumentis Illustrata . . . Amsterdam: 1667. V. 39

KIRCHER, ATHANASIUS 1602-1680

Arithmologia Sive De Abditis Numerorum Mysteriis. Rome: 1665. V. 40

Diatribe De Prodigiosis Crucibus, Quae tam Supra Vestes Hominum, Quam res Alias, non Pridem Post Ultimum Incendium Vesuvij Montis Neapoli Comparverunt. Romae: 1661. V. 38

Latium. Id est, Nova & Parallela Latii tum Veteris tum Novi Descriptio . . . Amsterdam: 1671. V. 46

Magnes sive de Arte Magnetica. Rome: 1654. V. 38

Mundus Subterraneus. Amstelodami: 1665. V. 40

Mundus Subetrraneus. Amsterdam: 1678. V. 39

Musurgia Universalis sive Ars Magna Consoni et Dissoni in X. Libros Digesta. Rome: 1650. V. 41

KIRCHER, ATHANASIUS 1602-1680 continued

Obelisci Aegyptiaci Nuper Inter Isaei Romani Rudera Effossi Interpretatio Hieroglyphica. Rome: 1666. V. 45

Phonurgia Nova Sive Conjugium Mechanico-Physicum Artis & Naturae Paranympha Phonosophia Concinnatum . . . Kempten: 1673. V. 45

Primitiae Gnomonicae Catoptricae hoc est Horologiographiae Novae Specularis. Avignon: 1635. V. 38; 41

Prodromus Coptus Sive Aegyptiacus . . . Rome: 1636. V. 46

Scrutinium Physico-Medicum Contagiosae Luis, Quae Dicitur Pestis Quo Origo, Caussae, Signa, Prognostica Pestis Nec Non Insolentes . . . Leipzig: 1659. V. 45

KIRCHWEGER, ANTON d. 1746

Microscopium Basilii Valentini . . . Berlin: 1790. V. 46

KIREEFF, O.

Skobeleff and the Slavonic Cause. London: 1883. V. 39

KIRK, CHARLES D.

The Story of Canetuckey; Wooing and Warring in the Wilderness. Derby: 1860. V. 46

KIRK, CHARLES H.

History of the Fifteenth Pennsylvania Volunteer Cavalry, Which was Recruited and Known as the Anderson Cavalry in . . . 1861-65. Philadelphia: 1906. V. 39; 42; 44

KIRK, MALCOLM

Man As Art. New Guinea Body Decoration. London: 1981. V. 40

KIRK, ROBERT

An Essay of the nature and Actions of the Subetrranean (and for the Most Part), Invisible People, Here to Foir Going Under the Name of Elves, Faimes and fairies . . . Edinburgh: 1815. V. 38

KIRK, ROBERT C.

Twelve Months in Klondike. London: 1899. V. 37; 44

KIRK, RUSSELL

The Surly Sullen Bell. 1962. V. 42; 43

The Surly Sullen Bell. London: 1962. V. 45

KIRK, T.

The Forest Flora of New Zealand. London: 1889. V. 44; 46

KIRKALDY, DAVID

Results of an Experimental Enquiry into the Comparative Tensile Strength and Other Properties of Various Kinds of Wrought-Iron and Steel. Glasgow: 1862. V. 44

KIRKALDY, WILLIAM G.

Illustrations of David Kirkaldy's System of Mechanical Testing as Originated and Carried on by Him During a Quarter of a Century. London: 1891. V. 44

KIRKBRIDE, JOHN

The Northern Angler; or, Fly-Fisher's Companion. 1837. V. 40

The Northern Angler; or, Fly-Fisher's Companion. Carlisle: 1837. V. 43

The Northen Angler or Fly-Fisher's Companion. London: 1837. V. 45

KIRKBRIDE, THOMAS 1809-1883

On the Construction, Organization and General Arrangements of Hospitals for the Insane. Philadelphia: 1854. V. 43; 45

On the Construction, Organization and General Arrangements of Hospitals for the Insane. Philadelphia/London: 1880. V. 43

KIRKE, JOHN

The Seven Champions of Chritendome. London: 1638. V. 37

KIRKE, THOMAS

A Modern Account of Scotland. London: 1714. V. 42

KIRKE-WHITE, HENRY

Poetical Works. London: 1850. V. 37

KIRKEN, A.

A Brief Grammar of the English Language. Venice: 1853. V. 38

KIRKLAND, CAROLINE MATILDA STANSBURY 1801-1864

Forest Life. New York: 1842. V. 46

Montacute; or, a New Home . . . London: 1840. V. 43

A New Home-Who'll Follow? or, Glimpses of Western Life by Mrs. Mary Clavers. New York: 1839. V. 37; 43

Western Clearings. London: 1846. V. 45

KIRKLAND, FRAZAR

The Pictorial Book of Anecdotes and Incidents of the War of the Rebellion . . . Hartford: 1867. V. 38

KIRKLAND, FREDERICK R.

Letters on the American Revolution in the Library at 'Karolfred' Wyneewood, Pa. Philadelphia: New York: 1941, 1952. V. 40

KIRKLAND, JOHN

The Modern Baker, Confectioner and Caterer. London: 1924. V. 39

KIRKLAND, JOSEPH

Zury: the Meanest Man in Spring County, a Novel of Western Life. Boston & New York: 1887. V. 38

KIRKLAND, THOMAS J.

Historic Camden (SC): Part One: Colonial and Revolutionary. Part Two: Nineteenth Century. Columbia: 1905, 1928. V. 40

Historic Camden. Columbia: 1905/26. V. 46

KIRKMAN, F. B.

The British Bird Book. London: 1911-13. V. 37; 44; 45

KIRKMAN, JAMES THOMAS

Memoirs of the Life of Charles Macklin, Esq. London: 1799. V. 38; 41

KIRKMAN, MARSHALL M.

Classical Portfolio of Primitive Carriers . . . (with) 1500 Engravings Portraying the Primitive People of the World and Their Method of Carriage in Every Age and Quarter of the Globe. Chicago: 1895. V. 37; 41; 46

KIRKPATRICK, CYNTHIA

Poems for the Times. Parkersburg: 1865. V. 45

KIRKPATRICK, J. M.

The Heroes of Battle Rock, or the Miners' Reward . . . N.P.: 1904. V. 38; 39

KIRKPATRICK, JAMES

The Sea-Piece a Narative, Philosophical and Descirptive Poem. London: 1750. V. 46

KIRKPATRICK, T. PERCY

The Book of the Rotunda Hospital. London: 1913. V. 38

KIRKUP, THOMAS

A History of Socialism. London & Edinburgh: 1892. V. 41

KIRKWOOD, CHARLOTTE

The Nez Perce Indian War Under War Chiefs Joseph and Whitebird. N.P.: 1952. V. 46

KIRKWOOD, JAMES P.

Report on the Filtration of River Waters, for the Supply of Cities, as Practised in Europe, Made to the Board of Water Commissioners of the City of St. Louis. New York: 1869. V. 45

KIRKWOOD, KENNETH P.

Unfamiliar Lafcadio Hearn. Tokyo: 1936. V. 42

KIRKWOOD, S. J.

Letter . . . in Response to Senate Resolution of January 6, 1882, the Report of the Commissioner of the General Land Office Upon the Survey of the United States and Texas Boundary commission. Washington: 1882. V. 43

KIRKWOOD, SAMUEL J.

Special Message of Governor Samuel J. Kirkwood, in Reply to a Resolution of Inquiry Passed by the House of Representatives, March 2d, 1860, in Relation to the Requisition of the Gov. of Virginia, for One Barclay Coppic. Des Moines: 1860. V. 37

KIRMSE, MARGUERITE

Dogs. New York: 1930. V. 40; 43; 46

KIRMSE, MARGUERTIE

Dogs in the Field. New York: 1935. V. 39; 46

KIRSTEIN, LINCOLN

Paul Cadmus. New York: 1984. V. 43; 45

Rhymes of a PFC. New York & Tokyo: 1964. V. 41

KIRTIKAR, K. R.

Indian Medicinal Plants. 1984. V. 39

Indian Medicinal Plants. Dehra Dun,: 1976, 1981. V. 37; 38

KIRWAN, RICHARD

Elements of Mineralogy. London: 1794-96. V. 38

An Essay on the Analysis of Mineral Waters. London: 1799. V. 37; 38; 40

An Estimate of the Temperature of Different Latitudes. 1787. V. 40

An Estimate of the Temperature of Different Latitudes. London: 1787. V. 38; 46

KISBY, T. A.

The Young Curate, a Tale of the Times. Cambridge: 1854. V. 46

KISER, CAROLYN

Poems. Portland: 1959. V. 37

KISSAM, BENJAMIN

Dissertatio Medica Inauguralis . . . De utero Gravido . . . Edinburgh: 1783. V. 39; 40

KISSINGER, HENRY

White House Years. Boston: 1979. V. 39; 41; 42

Years of Upheaval. Boston: 1982. V. 39; 41; 42

THE KIT Book for Soldiers, Sailors and Marines. Chicago: 1942. V. 38; 42; 45

KITAGAWA, M.

Neo-Lineamenta Florae Manshuricae or; Enumeration of the Spontaneous Vascular Plants Hitherto Known from Manchuria (North Eastern China). 1979. V. 39

KITAJ. R. B.

Struggle in the West, The Bombing of London. London: 1967-69. V. 37

THE KITBOOK for Soldiers, Sailors and Marines. Chicago: 1943. V. 46

KITCHEN, B. F.

The Wormwood Star. Houston: 1981. V. 39

THE KITCHEN Directory, and American Housewife: Containing the Most Valuable and Original Receipts, in all the Various Branches of Cookery . . . New York: 1841. V. 37; 44

KITCHEN, KENNETH A.

Catalogue of the Egyptian Collection in the National Museum, Rio de Janeiro. Warminster: 1990. V. 44

KITCHEN, PADDY

English as She is Spoke. London: 1960. V. 38

KITCHIN, C. H. B.

The Sensitive One. London: 1931. V. 41

Streamers Waving. London: 1925. V. 40

Winged Victory. Oxford: 1921. V. 38

KITCHIN, G. W.

A History of France. Oxford: 1896-1903. V. 38; 39

KITCHIN, JOHN

Jurisdictions: or, the Lawful Authority of Courts Leets, Courts Baron . . . (with) Brevia Selecta of Choice Writs . . . London: 1663; V. 38

KITCHIN, THOMAS

The Traveller's Guide through England and Wales . . . Routs from Stage to Stage . . . London: 1783. V. 44; 46

KITCHINER, WILLIAM 1775-1827

The Art of Invigorating and Prolonging Life by Food, Clothing, Air, Exercise, Wine, Sleep and Pepetic Percepts . . . London: 1821. V. 40

The Cook's Oracle: Containing Receipts for Plain Cookery on the Most Economical Plan for Private Families. Boston: 1822. V. 40; 44

The Cook's Oracle . . . Edinburgh: 1822. V. 46

The Cook's Oracle. London: 1823. V. 46

The Cook's Oracle. New York: 1825. V. 39

The Cook's Oracle. London: 1829. V. 38; 41

The Cook's Oracle; and Housekeeper's Manual. New York: 1830. V. 38; 39; 40

Cook's Oracle: and Housekeeper's Manual, Containing Receipts for Cookery, and Directions for Carving. New York: 1832. V. 37; 45

The Economy of the Eyes. London: 1826-25. V. 38

The Housekeeper's Oracle; or, Art of Domestic Management . . . London: 1829. V. 46

Sure Methods of Improving Health and Prolonging Life . . . London: 1828. V. 43

The Traveller's Oracle. London: 1827. V. 39

KITE'S Philadelphia Directory for 1814. Philadelphia: 1814. V. 46

KITSON, SYDNEY D.

The Life of John Sell Cotman. London: 1937. V. 37; 39; 43; 46

KITTEL, F.

A Kannada-English Dictionary . . . Mangalore: 1894. V. 38

KITTENBERGER, KALMAN

Big Game Hunting and Collecting in East Africa 1903-1926. New York: 1929. V. 43

KITTLITZ, F. H. VON

Twenty Four Views of the Vegetation of the Coasts and Islands of the Pacific with Explanatory Descriptions Taken During the Exploring Voyage of the Russian Corvette 'Senjawin' Under the Command of Capt. Lutke, in the Years 1827, 1828 & 1829 . . . London: 1861. V. 41

KITTO, JOHN

A Cyclopedia of Biblical Literature. Philadelphia: 1866. V. 39

KITTON, FRED

Dickensiana, a Bibliography of the Literature Relating to Charles Dickens and His Writings. London: 1886. V. 39

KITTON, FREDERIC GEORGE

Dickens and His Illustrators: Cruikshank, Seymour, Buss, 'Phiz'.. London: 1899. V. 37; 41; 43; 44; 46

Dickens Illustrations . . . London: 1900. V. 40; 43; 46

KITTON, FREDERICK GEORGE

Charles Dickens by Pen and Pencil. London: 1890-91. V. 37

KITTON, JOHN G.

John Leech, Artist and Humorist. London: 1883. V. 37; 38; 39; 41; 43; 46

KITTREDGE, WILLIAM

We Are Not In this Together. Port Townsend: 1984. V. 42

KIZER, CAROLYN

Midnight Was My Cry: New and Selected Poems. Garden City: 1971. V. 44

The Ungrateful Garden. 1961. V. 38

The Ungrateful Garden: Poems. Bloomington: 1961. V. 37; 45

KJAERBOLLING, N.

Ornithologia Danica. Danmarks Fugle I 304 Afbildninger af de Gamle Hanner Med Saerskilt. (with) Ornithologia Danica. Danmarks Fugle I 252 Afbildninger af de Dragtskiftende . . . Kjobenhavn: 1851/54-56. V. 41

KLAH, HASTEEN

Navajo Creation Myth: The Story of the Emergence. Santa Fe: 1942. V. 39

KLAPP, H. MINOR

Krider's Sporting Anecdotes, Illustrative of the Habits of Certain Varieties of American Game. Philadelphia: 1853. V. 44

KLAPROTH, HEINRICH JULIUS VON

Abhandlung uber die Sprache und Schrift der uigiren . . . Paris: 1820. V. 38

KLAPROTH, HEIRNICH JULIUS VON

Travels in the Caucasus and Georgia, Performed in the Years 1807, and 1808 by Command of the Russian Government . . . London: 1814. V. 41; 44

KLAUBER, LAURENCE M.

Rattlesnakes, Their Habits, Life Histories and Influence on Mankind. Berkeley: and Los Angeles: 1956. V. 43

Rattlesnakes. Their Habits, Life Histories, and Influence on Mankind. 1972. V. 38

KLAUDER, CHARLES Z.

College Architecture in America. New York & London: 1929. V. 40

KLEE, FELIX

The Diaries of Paul Klee, 1898-1918. London: 1965. V. 44

KLEE, FREDERICK

Amerika Isoer I Den Nyeste Tid, en Histoisk-Statistisk Haaendbog, Ved. Kjobenhavn: 1837-39. V. 39

KLEE, PAUL

The Inward Vision: Watercolors, Drawings, Writings. New York: 1959. V. 46

Notebooks. Volume I: The Thinking Eye. London: 1969. V. 46

Paul Klee: Paintings, Watercolors, 1913 to 1939. New York: 1941. V. 41

Peadagogical Sketch Book. New York: 1944. V. 41; 45

KLEEBERG, LEVI

Eulogy in Commemoration of the Deceased Poetess Minna Kleeberg . . . New Haven: 1879. V. 45

KLEEN, TYRA DE

Mudras, the Ritual Hand-Poses of the Buddha Priests and the Shiva Priests of Bali. London: 1924. V. 42

KLEFEKER, JOHANN

Bibliotheca Eruditorum Praecocium. Hamburg: 1717. V. 38

KLEIN, A. M.

The Second Scroll. New York: 1951. V. 44

KLEIN, ADRIAN BERNARD

Colour Music. The Art of Light. London: 1926. V. 40

KLEIN, AUGUSTA

Among the Gods. Edinburgh & London: 1895. V. 45

KLEIN, F. A.

The Religion of Islam. London: 1906. V. 44

KLEIN, H. M. J.

Lancaster County, Pennsylvania: a History. New York: 1924. V. 41; 42; 46

KLEIN-NICOLAI, GEORG

The Everlasting Gospel, Commanded to Be Preached by Jesus Christ, Judge of the Living and Dead, Unto All Creatures, Mark XVI 15. V. 41

The Everlasting Gospel, Commanded to be Preached by Jesus Christ, Judge of the Living and Dead, Unto All Creatures, Mark XVI, 15. Germantown: 1753. V. 40

KLEIN, WILLIAM

Moscow. New York: 1964. V. 45

Rome: The City and Its People. New York: 1959. V. 41; 46

KLEINER, SALOMON

Das Prachtige Rath Hauss der Stadt Augspurg . . . L'Hotel Superbe dela Ville d'Augusbourg . . . Augsburg: 1732. V. 40

Representation Naturelle et Exacte de la favorite de Son Altesse Electorale de Mayence, en Quatorze Differentes Vues et Autant de Plans. Augsburg: 1726. V. 39

Representation au naturel des Chateaux de Weissenstein au Dessus de Pommersfeld et . . . Geubach . . . Augsburg: 1728. V. 44; 45

KLEINHOLZ, FRANK

Frank Kleinholz: A Self Portrait. New York: 1964. V. 39

Kleinholz Graphics: Catalogue Raisonne 1940-75. Miami: 1975. V. 46

KLEMP, EGON

Africa on Maps Dating from the Twelfth to the Eighteenth Century. Leipzig: 1968. V. 43

America in Maps Dating from 1500 to 1856. Leipzig: 1976. V. 43

KLIMIUS, NICHOLAS

A Journey to the World Under-Ground. London: 1742. V. 45

KLIMT, GUSTAV

Erotic Drawings. New York: 1980. V. 40

Gustav Klimt, Erotic Drawings. London: 1980. V. 43

KLINE, ARTHUR A.

El Paso and Ciudad Juarez. El Paso: 1905. V. 39

KLINEFELTER, WALTER

A Bibliographical Check-List of Christmas Books. Portland: 1936. V. 42

Christmas Books. with A Bibliographical Check-List of Christmas Books. With More Christmas Books. Portland: 1936. V. 40

Christmas Books. With a Bibliographical Check-List of Christmas Books. With More Christmas Books. Portland: 1936-38. V. 41

Ex-Libris A. Conan Doyle. Chicago: 1938. V. 46

The Fortsas Bibliohoax. Evanston,: 1986. V. 40

More Christmas Books. Portland: 1938. V. 42

A Packet of Sherlockian Bookplates. Nappanee: 1964. V. 40; 42

KLING, HERR

The Chess Euclid . . . London: 1849. V. 37; 39

KLINGEN, MELCHIOR

Das Ganze Sechsisch Landrecht. Leipzig: 1572. V. 41; 42

KLIPPART, J. H.

The Wheat Plant; Its Origin, Culture, Growth, Development, Composition, Varities, Diseases, etc . . . . Cincinnati: 1860. V. 45; 46

KLONDIKE AND BOSTON GOLD MINING AND MANUFACTURING COMPANY

Prospectus fo the Klondike and Boston Gold Mining and Manufacturing Co. Boston: 1898. V. 39

KLOPSTOCK, FRIEDERICH GOTTLIEB

The Messiah. London: 1825. V. 43

KLOPSTOCK, FRIEDRICH GOTTLIEB 1724-1803

Klopstock and His Friends. A Series of Familiar Letters Written During the Years 1750 and 1803. London: 1814. V. 45; 46

The Messiah, Attempted from the German of mr. Klopstock by Joseph Collyer. In Fifteen Books. Elizabeth Town: 1788. V. 37

KLOSS, C. B.

In the Andamans and Nicobars, the Narrative of a Cruise in the Schooner 'Terrapin' . . . New York: 1903. V. 43

KLOSS, GEORGE FRANZ BURKHARD 1787-1854

Catalogue of the Library of Dr. Kloss . . . London: 1835. V. 38; 45

KLUCHEVSKY, V. O.

A History of Russia. 1911-31. V. 45

KLUCKING, E. P.

Leaf Venation Patterns, Volume 2, Lauraceae. Berlin: 1987. V. 38

Leaf Venation Patterns. Volume I: Annonaceae. Berlin: 1986. V. 37; 38

KLUVER, HEINRICH

Mescal: The 'Divine' Plant and Its Psychological Effects. London: 1928. V. 38

KNAAP, JAN

De Mirandis Antiqvorvm Operibus, Opibus et Veteris Aevi Rebus, Pace, Belloque Magnifice Gestis. Lubeck: 1600. V. 39

KNAPP, ADELINE

This Then is Upland Pastures, Being Some Out Door Essays Dealing with the Beautiful Things That the Spring and Summer Bring. East Aurora: 1897. V. 41

KNAPP, ANDREW

Criminal Chronology; or, the Newgate Calendar. Liverpool: 1809-10? V. 40

The New Newgate Calendar . . . London: 1826? V. 46

KNAPP, ARTHUR MAY

Feudal and Modern Japan. Boston: 1900. V. 39

KNAPP, GEORG FRIEDRICH

The State Theory of Money. London: 1924. V. 43

KNAPP, H. S.

History Of the Maumee Valley Commencing With Its Occupation by the French in 1680. Toledo: 1872. V. 40

KNAPP, HERMANN

Cocaine and Its Use in Opthalmic and General Surgery . . . New York: 1885. V. 41

KNAPP, JOHN LEONARD 1767-1845

The Journal of a Naturalist. London: 1829. V. 37; 41

KNAPP, LYMAN

Territory of Alaska, Executive Office, Thanksgiving Proclamation 1891. Sitka: 1891. V. 39

KNAPP, MOSES L.

Researches on Primary Pathology and the Origin and Laws of Epidemics. Philadelphia: 1860. V. 42

KNAPP, SAMUEL LORENZO

The Bachelors and Other Tales, Founded on American Incidents and Character. New York: 1836. V. 45

Biographical Sketches of Eminent Lawyers, Statesmen and Men of Letters. Boston: 1821. V. 42

Extracts from the Journal of Marshal Soult, Addressed to a Friend. Newburyport: 1817. V. 38; 43

Lectures on American Literature, with Remarks on Some Passages of American History. New York: 1829. V. 39

The Life of Thomas Eddy. New York: 1834. V. 39

Sketches of Public Characters. New York: 1830. V. 39

KNAPPE, KARL ADOLF

Durer: The Complete Engravings. New York. V. 43

Durer: The Complete Engravings, Etchings, and Woodcuts. New York. V. 40

Durer: The Complete Engravings, Etchings and Woodcuts. London: 1965. V. 44

Durer: the Complete Engravings, Etchings and Woodcuts. New York: 1965. V. 46

Durer: The Complete Engravings, Etchings and Woodcuts. New York: (n.d.). V. 37

KNAPPENBERGER, PHILIP

An Inquiry into the Rights of Holding Negroes as Slaves, Substantially Proven and Made to Appear from Natural Facts and Copious Extracts from the Bible. Strasburg: 1862. V. 42

KNAPSACK, a Daily Journal of the Seventh Regiment New Armory Fair. New York: 1879. V. 38

KNATCHBULL, NORTON 1602-1683

Annotations Upon Some Difficult Texts in all the Books of the New Testament. Cambridge: 1693. V. 39

KNAUSS, WILLIAM H.

The Story of Camp Chase. Nashville: 1906. V. 39

KNECHT, EDMUND

The Principles and Practice of Textile Printing. London: 1952. V. 40

The Principles and Practice of Textile Printing. London: 1912. V. 37; 41

KNEEDLER, HIRAM S.

The Coast Country of Texas. Cincinnati: 1896. V. 39

Through Storylnd to Sunset Seas. Chicago: 1895. V. 38; 41; 44

KNEELAND, ABNER

A Funeral Sermon on the Death of Captain Abijah Harding, Who Was Killed by the Fall of a Tree, in Barre, Masss. New York: 1826. V. 44

KNEELAND, SAMUEL

The Wonders of the Yosemite Valley and of California . . . Boston: 1871. V. 37; 44

Wonders of the Yosemite Valley, and of California. Boston: 1872. V. 37; 38; 41; 44

The Wonders of the Yosemite Valley . . . Boston & New York: 1872. V. 37; 39

KNELLER, GODFREY

The Kit-Kat Club Done from the Original Paintings of Sr. Godfrey Kneller by Mr. Faber. London: 1735. V. 39; 46

KNIBBS, HENRY HERBERT

Temescal. Boston: 1925. V. 37

THE KNICKERBOCKER Gallery: a Testimonial to the Editor of the Knickerbocker Magazine from Its Contributors. New York: 1855. V. 46

THE KNIFE-GRINDER'S Budget of Pictures and Poetry, for Boys and Girls. London: 1829. V. 39

KNIGGE, ADOLPH FRANCIS FREDERICK, BARON VON

Practical Philosophy of Social Life. London: 1799. V. 40

KNIGHT, ALFRED E.

Amentet: an Account of the Gods, Amulets and Scarabs of the Ancient Egyptians. London: 1915. V. 40

KNIGHT AND PERRY

A Synopsis of the Coniferious Plants Grown in Great Britain. London: 1850. V. 40

KNIGHT, C. MORLEY

Hints on Driving. London: 1911. V. 43

KNIGHT, CHARLES 1791-1873

Capital and Labour; Including the Results of Machinery. London: 1853. V. 46

The English Cyclopaedia. London: 1854-61. V. 38

Half-Hours with the Best Authors. London. V. 45

Knight's Excrusion Companion. London: 1851. V. 40

Knowledge is Power; a View of the Productive Forces of Modern Society, and the Results of Labour, Capital and Skill. London: 1855. V. 45

The Land We Live In. London: 1854-56. V. 44

Mind Amongst the Spindles. London: 1844. V. 45

Old England: a Pictorial Musuem of Regal, Ecclesiastical, Municipal, Baro¬ial and Popular Antiquities. London: 1844. V. 40; 41; 44

Old England: a Pictorial Museum of Regal, Ecclesiastical, Baronial, Municipal and Popular Antiquities. London: 1845. V. 46

Old England, a Pictorial Museum of Regal, Ecclesiastical, Baronial, Municipal and Popular Antiquities From the Earliest Period to the Present Time. London: 1860. V. 44; 46

Old England: A Pictorial Museum, Regal, Ecclesiastical, Municipal, Baronial and Popular Antiquities. (with) Old England's Worthies. London: 1865. V. 38

Old England; a Pictorial Museum of Regal, Ecclesiastical, Municipal, Baronial and Popular Antiquities. Boston: 1870. V. 44

Old England: a Pictorial Museum o Regal, Ecclesiastaical, Municipal, Baronial and Popular Antiquities. London: 1860? V. 37; 40

The Old Printer and the Modern Press. London: 1854. V. 40; 43; 46

Passages of a Working Life, During Half a Century . . . London: 1864. V. 40; 42; 46

The Penny Cyclopaedia of the Society for the Diffusion of Useful Knowledge. London: 1833-46. V. 38

The Pictorial History of England (to 1760). (with) The Pictorial History of the Reign of George III. London: 1838-44. V. 39

The Popular History of England . . . London: 1856-1860. V. 44

The Popular History of England: an Illustrated history of Society and Government from the earliest period to the present times. Volume I (to 8). London: 1856-62. V. 37; 39; 42; 45

Shadows of the Old Booksellers. London: 1865. V. 40; 46

Trade's Unions and Strikes. London: 1834. V. 38

The Working Man's Companion. London: 1831. V. 40

The Working Man's Companion, The Results of Machinery, Namely Cheap Production and Increased Employment, Exhibited . . . (with) The Working Man's Companion. Philadelphia & Boston: 1832. V. 41

KNIGHT, CHARLES WILLIAM ROBERT

The Book of the Golden Eagle. London: 1927. V. 46

KNIGHT, E. H.

The Practical Dictionary of Mechanics: Being a Description of Tools, Instruments, Machines, Processes and Engineering; History of Inventions . . . (with) Supplement. London: 1877-84. V. 37; 42

KNIGHT, EDWARD FREDERICK

Where Three Empires Meet: a Narrative of Recent Travel in Kashmire, Western Tibet, Gilgit and the Adjoining Countries. London: 1893. V. 41

KNIGHT, ELLIS CORNELIA 1757-1837

The Autobiography of Miss Corenlia Knight with Extracts from Her Journals and Anecdote Books. London: 1861. V. 39

Description of Latium; or La Campagna di Roma. London: 1805. V. 41; 46

Dinarbas: a Tale: Being a Continuation of Rasselas. London: 1779. V. 42; 45

Dinarbas. London: 1790. V. 37; 38; 39; 40; 42; 43; 44; 45; 46

Dinarbas, a Tale. London: 1792. V. 42

Marcus Flaminius; or, a View of the Military, Political and Social Life of the Romans. London: 1792. V. 37; 40

KNIGHT, F.

Knight's scroll ornaments, designed for the use of silversmiths, chasers, die-sinkers, modellers, &c &c. The writing by J.H. Whiteman. London: (1883?). V. 37

Knight's vases and ornaments. Designed for the use of architects, silversmiths, jewellers, modellers, chasers, die sinkers, founders, carvers, and all ornamental manufacturers. London: 1833. V. 37

Ornamental Alphabets, Engraved by the First Artists of the Day . . . London: 1820. V. 45

KNIGHT, FLEMING ANN CUTHBERT

THe Prompter, Containing the Principles of the English Language and Suggestions to Teachers. With a Appendix in which are stated the opinions of different Grammarians by Mrs. Fleming (Ann Cuthbert Knight). Montreal: 1844. V. 37

KNIGHT, GARETH

A Practical Guide to Qabalistic Sympolism. London: 1972. V. 43

KNIGHT, H. G.

The Northern Territory of South Australia. Adelaide: 1880. V. 39

KNIGHT, H. GALLY

Ilderim: a Syrian Tale. London: 1816. V. 45

KNIGHT, HENRY COGSWELL

The Cypriad in Two Cantos; with Other Poems and Translations. Boston: 1809. V. 41; 42

Letters from the South and West. Boston: 1824. V. 38; 46

KNIGHT, HENRY G.

Saracenic and Norman Remains to Illustrate the Normans in Sicily. London: 1840. V. 38

KNIGHT, HENRY UNTON

Correspondence of Sir Henry Unton Knight Ambassador from Queen Elizabeth to Henry IV King of France. London: 1847. V. 40

KNIGHT, J.

Cultivation of the Plants Belonging to the Natural Order Proteeae. Cape Town: 1987. V. 38

English and Tamil Dictionary. Jaffna: 1852. V. 40

KNIGHT, J. H.

Notes on Motor Carriages with Hints for Purchasers and Users. London: 1896. V. 38

KNIGHT, JAMES

Some Observations on the Assiento Trade, as it Hath Been Exercised by the South-Sea Company . . . London: 1728. V. 38

The State of the Island of Jamaica. Chiefly in Relation to Its Commerce and the Conduct of the Spaniards in the West Indies. London: 1726. V. 39

KNIGHT, JOHN

Indian Artrocities. Narrative of the Perils and Sufferings of Dr. Knight and John Slover . . . Cincinnati: 1867. V. 38; 42

KNIGHT, JOHN ALDEN

Ruffed Grouse. New York: 1947. V. 39; 43

Woodcock. New York: 1944. V. 39

KNIGHT, LAURA

A Book of Drawings. London: 1923. V. 42

A Book of Drawings. London: 1932. V. 45

The Magic of a Line - the Autobiography of . . . London: 1965. V. 44

A Proper Circus Home. London: 1962. V. 44

KNIGHT, LUCIAN L.

Georgia's Roster of the Revolution . . . Officers and Men; Soldiers and Sailors; Partisans and Regulars . . . Atlanta: 1920. V. 42; 44

History of Fulton County, Georgia. Narrative and Biographical. Atlanta: 1930. V. 42

KNIGHT, O. W.

The Birds of Maine. Bangor: 1908. V. 39

KNIGHT, RICHARD PAYNE 1750-1824

An Account of the Remains of the Worship of Priapus, Lately Existing at Isernia, in the Kingdom of Naples . . . London: 1786. V. 42

An Analytical Essay on the Greek Alphabet . . . London: 1791. V. 40

An Anayltical Inquiry Into the Principles of Taste . . . London: 1805. V. 40; 42; 44; 45

An Analytical Inquiry into the Principles of Taste. London: 1806. V. 40

An Analytical Inquiry into the Principles of Taste. London: 1808. V. 46

A Discourse on the Worship of Priapus and Its Connection with the Mystic Theology of the Ancients . . . London: 1865. V. 44

A Discourse on the Worship of Pirapus, and Its Connection with the Mystic Theology of the Ancients . . . London: 1894. V. 39

The Landscape a Didactic Poem. London: 1794. V. 37; 39; 40; 41; 44; 45

The Landscape, a Didactic Poem. London: 1795. V. 44

A Monody on the Death of the Right Honourable Charles James Fox. London: 1806-7. V. 39; 42

KNIGHT, SAMUEL

The Life of Erasmus . . . an Account of His Learned Friends, and the State of Religion and Learning at the Time in Both Our Universities. Cambridge: 1726. V. 37

KNIGHT, SARAH

The Private Journal of a Journey from Boston to New York in the Year 1704, Kept by Madam Knight. Albany: 1865. V. 40

KNIGHT, T.

An Elegy On the Death of the Late Revd. Mr. George Whitefield, A.M. London: 1771. V. 45

KNIGHT, T. A.

Pomona Herefordiensis. London: 1811. V. 37

KNIGHT, THOMAS ANDREW

A Treatise on the Culture of the Apple and Pear, and on the Manufacture of Cider and Perry. Ludlow: 1797. V. 38

A Treatise on the Culture of the Apple and Pear, and on the Manufacture of Cider and Perry. Ludlow: 1809. V. 45

A Treatise on the Culture of the Apple and Pear, and on the Manufacture of Cider and Perry. London: 1802. V. 37

KNIGHT, WILLIAM

The Life of William Wordsworth. Edinburgh: 1889. V. 38

KNIGHT, WILLIAM H.

Hand-Book Almanac for the Pacific States: an Official Register and Yearbook of Facts, for the Year 1862. San Francisco: 1862. V. 40; 42; 44

KNIGHT, WILLIAM HENRY

Diary of a Pedestrian in Cashmere and Thibet. London: 1863. V. 40; 46

KNIGHTON, HENRY

Chronicon Henrici Knighton, vel Cnitthon, Monachi Leycestrensis. London: 1889-95. V. 44

KNIGHTON, WILLIAM

Elihu Jan's Story, of the Private Life of an Eastern Queen. London: 1865. V. 43

KNIGHTS OF LABOR

Constitution of the General Assembly, District Assemblies and Local Assemblies of the Order of the Knights of Labor of North America. N.P.: 1883. V. 39

KNIGHTS OF MALTA

Statuta Hospitalis Hierusalem. Rome: 1588. V. 40; 43

KNIP, ANTOINE PAULINE JACQUELINE

Les Pigeons. Paris: (Vol. I) Mme. Knip &: 1809-11/1838-43. V. 37

KNIPE, HENRY R.

Nebula to Man. London: 1905. V. 39

KNIPE, WILLIAM

Criminal Chronology of York Castle with a Register of the Criminals Capitally Convicted . . . York: 1867. V. 46

KNIPPING, JOHN B.

Iconography of the Counter Reformation in the Netherlands. Nieuwkoop: 1974. V. 44

KNISTER, RAYMOND

Collected Poems. Toronto: 1949. V. 44

My Star Predominant. London: 1934. V. 43

KNOBLOCK, BYRON W.

Banner Stones of the North American Indian. 1939. V. 38

Banner-Stones of the North American Indian. La Grange: 1939. V. 37

KNOEDLER, M. & CO., NEW YORK.

Dali 1943. April 14 to May 5, 1943. V. 39

KNOEPFEL, W. H.

An Account of Knoepfel's Schoharie Cave, Schoharie County, New York: With the history of its Discovery, Subterranean Lake, Minerals, and Natural Curiosities. New York: 1853. V. 37; 39; 42

KNOEWKA, PAUL

Illustrations to Goethe's Faust. Boston: 1871. V. 41

KNOLLES, RICHARD

The Generall Historie of the Turkes . . . London: 1621. V. 39

The Turkish History, Comprehending the Origin of that Nation . . . London: 1704. V. 38

The Turkish History, from the Original of the Nation to the Growth of the Ottoman Empire. London: 1687. V. 37

KNOLLYS, HENRY

The Life of General Sir Hope Grant, with Selections from His Correspondence. London: 1894. V. 38

KNOPF, ALFRED A.

Sixty Photographs by Alfred A. Knopf. New York: 1975. V. 42; 45

Some Random Recollections: an Informal Talk Made at the grolier Club, New York 21, Oct., 1948. New York: 1949. V. 44

KNOPKEN, ANDREAS 1468-1539

In Epistolam ad Romanos Interpretatio. Wittenberg: 1524. V. 38

KNORR VON ROSENROTH, BARON CHRISTIAN

Kabbala Denudata seu Doctrina Hebraeorum Transcendentailis et Metaphysica atque Theologica. Sulzbach and Frankfurt: 1677-84. V. 41

KNOTT, J. FORTUNE

Wild Animals, Photographed and Described. London: 1886. V. 44; 45

KNOUS, CAROLINE BOARDMAN S.

Ancestry Sketches Compiled for the Children. Hartford: 1900. V. 46

KNOWER, DANIEL

The Adventures of a Forty-Niner. Albany: 1894. V. 37; 43

THE KNOWLEDGE and Practice of Christianity Made Easy to the Meanest Capacities; or, an Essay Towards and Instruction for the Indians. London: 1770. V. 37

KNOWLES, CHARLES

An Account of the Expedition to Carthagena, with Explanatory Notes and Observations. London: 1743. V. 41; 45

KNOWLES, DAVID

The Religious Orders in England. 1961-62. V. 39

The Religious Orders in England. Cambridge: 1957-62. V. 37

KNOWLES, EDWARD

A Prospect from Forborough-Hill Near Reading in Berks . . . Reading: 1755. V. 42

KNOWLES, FRANCIS C.

The Monetary Crisis Considered Being Incidentally a Reply to Mr Horsley Palmer's Pamphlet 'on the Action of the Bank of Englnd, etc.' and a Defence of the Joint-Stock Banks Against His Accusations. London: 1837. V. 38

KNOWLES, HORACE J.

Countryside Treasures. London: 1946. V. 44

Peeps Into Fairyland. London: 1924. V. 46

KNOWLES, JAMES SHERIDAN

The Dramatic Works of . . . London: 1841. V. 46

Dramatic Works. London: 1841-43. V. 38; 40; 41; 43; 44

Fortescue. London: 1846. V. 42

KNOWLES, JAMES SHERIDAN continued

George Lovell. London: 1847. V. 42

KNOWLES, JOHN

An Inquiry into the Means Which Have Taken to Preserve the British Navy . . . London: 1821. V. 43

The Life and Writings of Henry Fuseli. London: 1831. V. 39

A Separate Peace. London: 1959. V. 42; 45

A Separate Peace. 1960. V. 44

A Separate Peace. New York: 1960. V. 38; 42

KNOWLSON, JAMES

Samuel Beckett: an Exhibition Held at Reading University Library, May to July, 1971. London: 1971. V. 43

KNOWLTON, CHARLES 1800-1850

Elements of Modern Materialism; Inculcating the Idea of a Future State, In Which All Will Be More Happy. Adam: 1829. V. 37; 41

Elements of Modern Materialism. London: 1829. V. 39

KNOWLTON, I. C.

Annals of Calais, Maine and St. Stephen, New Brunswick, Including the Village of Milltown, Me. and the Present Town of Milltown, N.B. Calais: 1875. V. 41

KNOWN Fables. New York: 1964. V. 40

KNOX, A. E.

Autumn on the Spey. London: 1862. V. 38

KNOX, ALEXANDER

The Climate of the Continent of Africa. Cambridge: 1911. V. 45

A History of the County of Down . . . its Early Colonization . . . Geography, Antiquities, Topography and Natural History. Dublin: 1875. V. 37; 38

The Irish Watering Places, Their Climate, Scenery and Accomodations . . . Dublin: 1845. V. 42

KNOX, CHARLES H.

Hardness, or the Uncle. London: 1841. V. 40

KNOX, DR.

Fish and Fishing in the Lone Glens of Scotland, with a History of the Progapation, Growth and Metamorphoses of the Salmon. London: 1854. V. 46

KNOX, DUDLEY W.

Naval Sketches of the War in California. New York: 1939. V. 37; 39; 41; 43; 44; 45

KNOX, GEORGE

A Study and Catalogue Raisonne of the Chalk Drawings of Giambattista and Domenico Tiepolo. Oxford: 1980. V. 40; 44

KNOX, HENRY

A Plan for the General Arrangement of the Militia of the United States. Philadlephia: 1791. V. 42

KNOX, JAMES

The Topography of the Basin of the Tay. Edinburgh: 1831. V. 40

KNOX, JOHN

An Answer to a Great Number of Blasphemous Cauillations by an Anabaptist, and Aduersarie to God and Predestination. Geneva: 1560. V. 37

Heir Followeth the Coppie of the Ressoning Which was Betuix the Abbote of Crossaguell and John Knox. Edinburgh: 1812. V. 37; 40

Historical Journal of the Campaigns in North America, for the Years 1757, 1758, 1759, and 1760: Containing the Most Remarkable Occurrences of that Period: Particularly the Two Sieges of Quebec, &c. &c. London: 1769. V. 39; 40

Historical Journal of the Campaigns in North America 1757-1760. Toronto: 1914-16. V. 37; 38; 42; 44; 45

The Historie of the Reformatioun of Religioun Within the Realm of Scotland. Edinburgh: 1732. V. 38

A New Collection of Voyages, Discoveries and Travels . . . in Europe, Asia, Africa, and America. London: 1767. V. 39

A Tour through the Highlands of Scotland, and the Hebride Isles in 1786. London: 1787. V. 42; 43; 44; 46

A View of the British Empire, More Especially Scotland. London: 1785. V. 39

KNOX, JOHN P.

A Historical Account of St. Thomas, W.I., with Its Rise and Progress in Commerce; Missions and Churches . . . New York: 1852. V. 37; 39; 40

KNOX, KATHLEEN

Fairy Gifts; or a Wallet of Wonders. London. V. 43

KNOX, ROBERT

Engravings of the Cardiac Nerves, the Nerves of the Ninth Pair, the Gloss-Pharyngeal, and the Pharyngeal Branch of the Pneumo-Gastric; copied from the Tabulae Neurologicae of Antonio Scarpa. By Edward Mitchell, Engraver . . . Edinburgh: 1832. V. 37; 41; 43; 45

Great Artists and Anatomists; a Biographical and Philosophical Study. London: 1852. V. 38

An Historical Relation of the Island of Ceylon in the East-Indies: Together With an Account of the Detaining in Captivity (of) the Author and Divers Other Englishmen Now Living There, and of the Author's Miraculous Escape. London: 1681. V. 37; 40

Man: His Structures and Physiology. London: 1858. V. 38

Observations Upon a 'Report by the Select Committee on Salmon Fisheries, Scotland: Together with the Minutes of Evidence, Appendix and Index, 30th June 1836. Edinburgh: 1837. V. 39

KNOX, RONALD

Essays in Satire. London: 1928. V. 46

Hilario Belloc MDCCCLXX-MCMXXX. 1930. V. 40

On English Translation. The Romanes Lecture Delivered in the Sheldonian Theatre 11 June 1957. Oxford: 1957. V. 44

An Open-air Pulpit. London: 1926. V. 44

Sanctions: a Frivolity. London: 1924. V. 40

KNOX, RONALD ARBUTHNOTT 1888-1957

A Selection from the Occasional Sermons of . . . Ronald Arbuthnott Knox. London: 1949. V. 38; 41; 44

Signa Severa. 1906. V. 38

KNOX, SAMUEL

An Essay on the Best System of Liberal Education, Adapted to the Genius of the Government of the United States. Baltimore: 1799. V. 43

KNOX, SEYMOUR H.

Aurora in England 1934. N.P.. V. 43

Polo Tales and Other Tales 1921-1971. N.P.. V. 43

To B.A. and Back 1932. Buffalo: 1969. V. 43

KNOX, THOMAS W.

The Boy Travellers on the Congo. New York: 1887. V. 39

Camp-Fire and Cotton-Field: Southern Adventure in Time of War. New York: 1865. V. 42

Overland through Asia. Hartford: 1870. V. 42

The Travels of Marco Polo for Boys and Girls. New York: 1885. V. 46

Underground, or Life Below the Surface. Hartford: 1874. V. 40

KNOX, VICESIMUS 1752-1821

Elegant Extracts . . . from the Most Eminent Prose Writers . . . London: 1810. V. 42

Elegant Extracts . . . from the Most Eminent Prose Writers . . . London: 1810-20. V. 44; 46

Essays Moral and Literary. London: 1782. V. 38

Essays Moral and Literary. London: 1795. V. 40

Essays Moral and Literary. Basil: 1800. V. 41

Liberal Education; or, a Practical Treatise on the Methods of Acquiring Useful and Polite Learning. London: 1781. V. 38; 41; 43

Liberal Education: or, a Practical Treatise on the Methods of Acquiring Useful and Polite Learning. London: 1795. V. 41

The Poetical Epitome; or, Elegant Extracts Abridged from the Larger Volume . . . London: 1792. V. 37; 41

Remarks on the Tendency of Certain Clauses in a Bill Now Pending in Parliament to Degrade Grammar Schools, with Cursory Strictures on the National Importance of Preserving Inviolate the Classical Discipline Prescribed by their Founders. London: 1821. V. 38

KNOX, WILLIAM 1732-1810

Extra Official State Papers. Addressed to the Rt. Hon. Lord Rawdon, and the Other Members of the Two Houses of Parliament, Associated for the Preservation of the Constitution and Promoting the Prosperity of the British Empire . . . Dublin: 1789. V. 38; 39

Extra Official State Papers. Addressed to the Right Honorable Lord Rawdon. London: 1789. V. 42

The Interest of the Merchants and Manufacturers of Great Britain, in the Present Contest with the Colonies, Stated and Considered. London: 1774. V. 37

The Present State of the Nation. London: 1768. V. 37; 38

KNUTTEL, GERARD

The Letter as a Work of Art. Amsterdam: 1951. V. 39; 42

The Letter as a Work of Art. Netherlands: 1951. V. 46

KOBAL, JOHN

Art of the Great Hollywood Portrait Photographers 1924-1940. New York: 1980. V. 45

KOBAYASHI, K.

The Eggs of Japanese Birds. Kobe: 1932-40. V. 37

KOBER, GEORGE MARTIN

Reminiscences of George Martin Kober, M.D., LL.D. Washington: 1930. V. 37; 38; 41; 43; 44

KOBYLANSKA, KRYSTYNA

Chopin in His Own Land. Crackow: 1955. V. 39

KOCH, C. L.

Ubersicht des Arachnidensystems. Nuremberg: 1837-50. V. 39

KOCH, CHARLES R. E.

History of Dental Surgery. Ft. Wayne: 1910. V. 38

KOCH, FREDERICK H.

Carolina Folk-Plays. Second Series. New York: 1924. V. 39

KOCH, KENNETH

From the Air: Poems. London: 1979. V. 45

Poems. New York: 1953. V. 41; 46

Poems from 1952-1953. 1968. V. 41; 42; 43; 44

When the Sun Tries to Go On. 1969. V. 37; 42; 44

When the Sun Tries to Go On. Los Angeles: 1969. V. 45

KOCH, ROBERT

Investigations Into the Etiology of Traumatic Infective Diseases. London: 1880. V. 38; 42; 43

Untesuchungen Uber die Aetiologie der Wundinfectionskrankheiten . . . Leipzig: 1878. V. 37; 46

KOCH, RUDOLF

The Book of Signs, Which Contains all Manner of Symbols Used from the Earliest Times to the Middle AGes . . . London: 1930. V. 43

Das Blumenbuch. Darmstadt: 1929-30. V. 45

KOCH, RUDOLPH

Buchstabenfreude, the Delight of Letters: a Collection of Quotations fro m the Works of Rudolph Koch. Kalamazoo & Toronto: 1976. V. 39

KOCH, T. W.

Catalogue of the Dante Collection Presented by Willard Fiske. Ithaca: 1898-1900. V. 44

KOCH, THEODORE WESLEY

On University Libraries. Paris: 1924. V. 46

KOCHAN, BERNICE

The Little Book of Hawaiian Flowers. Cleveland: 1964. V. 44

KOCHER, FRANZ

Die Babylonisch-Assyrische Medizin in Texten und Untersuchungen. Berlin: 1963-80. V. 44

KOCHER, THEODOR

Text-Book of Operative Surgery. New York: 1911. V. 44; 45; 46

KOCHS, THEO A., COMPANY, CHICAGO.

Modern Mirror Cases by Kochs. Catalog No. 45. 1931. V. 46

KOCIEJOWSKI, MARIUS

The Testament of Charlotte B. 1988. V. 44

The Testament of Charlotte B. Marlborough: 1988. V. 41

The Testament of Charlotte B. Wiltshire: 1988. V. 41; 42

KOCK, CHARLES PAUL DE 1794-1871

Edmond and His Cousin. New York: 1904. V. 46

The Flower Girl. New York: 1905. V. 41

Frederique. New York: 1907. V. 39

Jean. Boston: 1903. V. 40; 41

Madame Pantalon. Boston: 1904. V. 41

The Masterpieces of Charles Paul de Kock. Philadelphia: 1903. V. 38

Memoirs of Paul de Kock. London: 1899. V. 43; 45

Monsieur Dupont. Boston: 1902. V. 43

Sister Anne. London: 1902. V. 43

The Works. Boston: 1904. V. 43

KOCOUREK, ALBERT

Sources of Ancient and Primitve Law. Boston: 1915. V. 43

KODO Kawaraski. Kashishu. (Collection of Flowers and Poems). Kyoto: 1934. V. 39

KOEBEL, W. H.

Argentina Past and Present. London: 1914. V. 44

KOECHLIN, R.

Oriental Art: Ceramics, Fabrics, Carpets. New York. V. 38; 41

Oriental Art. New York: 1930. V. 45

KOECKER, LEONARD

Principles of Dental Surgery. Baltimore: 1842. V. 42

KOEHL, HERMANN

The Three Musketeers of the Air: Their Conquest of the Atlantic from East to West. New York: 1928. V. 38; 45

KOEHLER, S. R.

Etching. An Outline of Its Technical Processes and Its History, with Some remarks on Collections and Collecting. London: 1885. V. 40

KOEHN, ALFRED

japanese Tray Landscapes. Peking: 1937. V. 40; 46

KOEHOORN, MINNO, BARON OF

The New Method of Fortification. London: 1705. V. 37; 43

KOELLIKER, RUDOLPH ALBERT VON 1817-1905

Handbuch der Gewebelehre des Menschen fur Aerzte und Studirende. Leipzig: 1852. V. 38; 41; 45

Manual of Human Histology. London: 1853/54. V. 37; 45

Mikroskopische Anatomie oder Gewebelehre des enschen; Specielle Gewebelehre. Leipzig: 1805/52/54. V. 42

KOELS, A. E.

Report to the Batopilas Mining Company, on the Mineral District of Batopilas, State of Chihuahua, Mexico. San Francisco: 1866. V. 41

KOENIG, ARTHUR

Authentic History of the Indian Campaign Which Culminated in 'Custer's Last Battle,' June 25, 1876. N.P.. V. 37

KOENING, ARTHUR

Authentic History of the Indian Campaign Which Culminated in Custer's Last Battle June 25, 1876. St. Louis. V. 45

KOERNER, CARL THEODOR

The Life . . . London: 1827. V. 40

KOERNER, GUSTAVE

Memoirs of . . . 1809-1896: Life Sketches Written at the Suggestion of His Children. Edited by Thomas J. McCormack. Cedar Rapids, Iowa: 1909. V. 37

KOESTER, F.

Under the Desert Stars. Washington Square Pub.,: 1923. V. 44

KOESTLER, ARTHUR

Darkness at Noon. London: 1940. V. 40

The Practice of Sex. The Crisis of Civilisation and the Sexual Mass Misery of Our Time. London: 1936. V. 40

Theives in the Night. New York: 1947. V. 37

KOHL, JOHANN G.

Austria, Vienna, Prague, Hungary, Bohemia and the Danube; Galicia, Styria, Moravia, Bukovina and the Military Frontier. London: 1843. V. 39

Ireland, Dublin, the Shannon, Limerick, Cork and the Kilkenny Races . . . London: 1843. V. 42

Ireland, Scotland and England. London: 1844. V. 42

Russia. London: 1844. V. 43

KOHL, JOHANN GEORG

Travels in Canada, and Through the States of New York and Pennsylvania. London: 1861. V. 40; 42

KOHL, JOHANN GEORGE

Kitchi-Gami. Wanderings Round Lake Superior. London: 1860. V. 38; 41; 43; 46

KOHLHANS, TOBIAS LUDWID

Dilucidationes Quaedam Valde Necessariae in Gerardi Croesi Historiam Quakerianam Editae a Philaletha. Amsterdam: 1696. V. 44

KOHN, D.

The Darwinian Heritage. London: 1986. V. 37

KOHN, DAVID

Internal Improveiment in South Carolina 1817-1828. Washington: 1938. V. 39; 46

KOHN, FERDINAND

Iron and Steel Manufacture. London: 1869. V. 44

KOIZUMI, G.

Lacquerwork: a Prctical Exposition of the Art of Lacquering Together with Valuable Notes for the Collector. London: 1925. V. 38; 41; 44

KOIZUMI, SETSUKO

Reminiscences of Lafcadio Hearn. Boston: 1918. V. 43

KOHHLER, S. R.

American Art. London: 1886. V. 44

KOKOSCHKA, OSKAR

Die Traeumenden Knaben. Wien/Leipzig: 1908/17. V. 42
Kokoschka: Drawings. London: 1962. V. 38; 41
Saul and David. London: 1973. V. 38

KOLBEN, PTER

The Present State of the Cape of Good Hope. London: 1731.
V. 41; 43; 44

KOLDEWEY, KARL

*The German Arctic Expedition of 1869-70 and Narrative of the Wreck of
the Hansa in the Ice.* London: 1874. V. 38; 40; 42; 44; 46

KOLDEWEY, ROBERT

The Excavations at Babylon. London: 1914. V. 40

KOLFF, D. H.

*Voyages of the Dutch Brig of War :Dourga'; through the . . . Moluccan
Archipelago . . . Southern Coast of New Guinea . . . the Arafura Sea. Lt.
Kolff was the first to accurately chart the numerous islands lying between
the Moluccas and the Northern . . .* London: 1840. V. 37; 46

KOLHANS, JOHANN

*Tractatus Opticus, Qui Res Quam Plurimas, Utiles, Jucundas, ludicras &
Admirandas, Naturaliter Sistere Docet . . .* Leipzig: 1663. V. 44

KOLLE, FREDERICK STRANGE

Plastic and Cosmetic Surgery. New York: 1911. V. 42

KOLLMANN, AUGUSTUS FREDERIC CHRISTOPHER 1756-1829

*An Essay of Musical Harmony, According to the Nature of That Science,
and the Principles of the Greatest Musical Authors.* Utica: 1817. V. 40

KOLLMANN, PAUL

*The Victoria Nyanza. The Land, the Races and Their Customs, with
Specimens of Some of the Dialects.* London: 1899. V. 39; 41

KOLLOCK, HENRY

Sermons on Various Subjects . . . with a Memoir of the Life of the Author.
Savannah, (GA): 1822. V. 37

KOLLWITZ, KAETHE

Kaethe Kollwitz. New York: 1946. V. 44

KOLODIN, IRVING

The Continuity of Music: a History of Influence. New York: 1969. V. 45
The Metropolitan Opera 1883-1935. New York: 1936. V. 45

KOLODNY, ANATOLE

*Bone Sarcoma: the Primary malignant Tumors of Bone and the Giant Cell
Tumor.* Chicago: 1927. V. 42

KOLOKOTRONES, J. THEODORE

Writings and Letters on the Greek Revolution, 1821-1827. Athens: 1884.
V. 37

KOMARKOVA, V.

Alpine Vegetation of the Indian Peaks Area. 1979. V. 39

KOMAROV, V. L.

Flora SSSR. Leningrad & Wiesbaden: 1934-73. V. 38

KOMENSKY, JOHN AMOS

*The Labyrinth of the World, and the Paradise of the heart. By John Amos
Komensky. Translated by Count Lutzow. Illustration by Dorothea Braby.*
London: 1950. V. 37; 39; 41; 43; 44; 46

KOMISARJEVSKY, THEODORE

The Costume of the Theatre. London: 1931. V. 39; 45

KOMROFF, MANUEL

The Voice of Fire. Paris: 1927. V. 37

KONDAKOV, N. P.

The Russian Icon. I. Album of LXV Coloured Plates. Prague: 1928.
V. 37; 43

KONDOLEON, HARRY

*Points Along the Cote D'Azur Triangle. A Play by Harry Kondoleon. With
etchings and lithographs by Mark Beard.* New York: 1985. V. 37; 39;
40; 44

KONEIGSBERGER, LEO

Hermann Von Helmholts. Braunschweig: 1902. V. 46

KONEWKA, PAUL

Illustrations to Goethe's Faust. Boston: 1871. V. 41; 44

KONIG, CARL HINDRICH fl. 1743-1752

Inledning Til Mecaniken och Bygnigs-Konstan . . . Stockholm: 1752. V. 46

THE KONIGSMARK Drawings. London: 1952. V. 40

KONODY, P. G.

The Art of Walter Crane. London: 1902. V. 39; 46
Sir William Orpen. Artist and Man. London: 1932. V. 43

KONRAD, P.

Icones Selectae Fungorum. London: 1985. V. 38

KONSTAM, GERTRUDE A. M.

The May Pole. London: 1882. V. 46

KONSTANTINOS O SINAITIS, PATRIARCHIS K.

Constantiniade ou Description de Constantinople Ancienne et Moderne.
Constantinople: 1846. V. 45

KONUNGS SKUGGSJA

*Kongs-Skugg-Sio Utlogd a Daunsku og Latinu. Det Kongelige Speil med
Dansk og Latinsk Oversaettelse . . .* Sorae: 1768. V. 38; 40

KONWISER, HARRY M.

Texas Republic Postal System . . . New York: 1933. V. 37

KOONTZ, DEAN R.

After the Last Race. New York: 1974. V. 39; 44
The Bad Place. New York: 1990. V. 43
Blood Risk. Indianapolis: 1973. V. 42
Chase. New York: 1972. V. 44
Chase. London: 1974. V. 46
Cold Fire. New York: 1991. V. 44; 45; 46
Dragonfly. New York: 1975. V. 39
Hanging On. New York: 1973. V. 45
Lightning. New York: 1988. V. 44
Night Chills. New York: 1976. V. 44
Nightmare Journey. New York: 1975. V. 44
Phantoms. New York: 1983. V. 43
Prison of Ice. Philadelphia: 1976. V. 42
Prison of Ice. Philadelphia: 1976. V. 44
Shattered. New York: 1973. V. 43
The Wall of Masks. 1975. V. 44
The Wall of Masks. Indianapolis: 1975. V. 42
Writing Popular Fiction. 1973. V. 44

KOOP, ALBERT J.

Early Chinese Bronzes. London: 1924. V. 42; 46

KOOPMAN, HARRY LYMAN

Miniature Books. Los Angeles: 1968. V. 37; 41; 42

KOOPS, MATTHIAS

*A Development of the Views and Designs of the French Nation, and the
Advantages Which They Will Derive to Them, If They Should Be Able, by
a Peace, or Otherwise, to Secure Themselves the Free Navigation of the
Rivers Rhine, Maese, and Scheldt . . .* Dublin: 1796. V. 38; 39
*Historical Account of the Substances Which Have Been Used to Describe
Events, and to Convey Ideas, from the Earliest Date to the Invention of
Paper.* London: 1800. V. 44
*Historical Account of the Substances Which Have Been Used to Describe
Events and to Convey Ideas . . .* London: 1801. V. 38; 41; 45

KORAN

The Alcoran of Mahomet. London: 1649. V. 37; 39; 41; 42; 43; 46
The Koran, Commonly called the Alcoran of Mohammed. London: 1734.
V. 37; 39; 40
*The Koran, Commonly Called the Alcoran of Mohammed, Translated into
English . . .* London: 1764. V. 41
THE Koran . . . London: 1801. V. 43
The Koran, Commonly Called the Alcoran of Mahomet. Springfield: 1806.
V. 43
The Koran. New York: 1958. V. 40; 45

KORAN - 1543

*Machvmetis Saracenorvm Principis, Eivsqve Svccessorvm Vitae, ac Doctrina,
Ipeseque Alcoran . . .* Basel: 1543. V. 38

KORAN - 1766

The Morality of the East; Extracted from the Koran of Mahammed. London:
1766. V. 38

KORESH

The Cellular Cosmogony or-Earth A Concave Sphere . . . 1905. V. 44

KORETSKY, ELAINE

Color fro the Hand Papermaker. Brookline: 1983. V. 38

KORMONDY, E. J.

Handbook of Contemporary Developments in World Ecology. London: 1982. V. 37

KORN, CHRISTOPHER

Geschichte der Kriege in Und Ausser Europa Von Anfange Des Ausstandes der Brittischen Kolonien in Nordamerika. Nuremburg: 1776-77. V. 40; 42

KORNBLUTH, C.

Takeoff. New York: 1952. V. 43

KORNER, GUSTAVE P.

Memoirs of Gustave Koerner 1809-1896. Cedar Rapids: 1909. V. 39

KORNFELD, E. W.

Catalogue Raisonne de l'Oeuvre Grave et Lithographie de Paul Signac. Berne: 1974. V. 40

KORNFELD, EBERHARD W.

Verzeichnis des Graphischen Werkes von Paul Klee. Bern: 1963. V. 41

KORNWOLF, JAMES D.

M. H. Baillie Scott and the Arts and Crafts Movement. Baltimore: 1972. V. 42; 46

KORT Berattelse Om Wast Indien Eller America, som Elliest Kallas Nya Werlden. N.P.: 1675. V. 38; 40
KORT Berattelse Om Wast Indien Eller America, Som Elliest Kallas Nya Werlden. Wysingsborg: 1675. V. 40; 44

KORTRIGHT, F. H.

The Ducks, Geese and Swans of North America. Washington: 1942. V. 39

KORTRIGHT, FANNY AIKIN

On Latmos. London: 1881. V. 44

KOSINSKI, JERZY 1933-1991

The Art of the Self, Essays A Propos Steps. New York: 1968. V. 37; 45
Being There. 1970. V. 37; 43
Being There. New York: 1970. V. 39; 41; 43
Blind Date. Boston: 1977. V. 41; 46
Cockpit. Boston: 1977. V. 39
The Future is Ours, Comrade. Garden City: 1960. V. 45
The Future is Ours, Comrade. New York: 1960. V. 39; 40; 41; 46
No Third Path. Garden City: 1962. V. 42
The Painted Bird. 1965. V. 43; 46
The Painted Bird. Boston: 1965. V. 38; 39; 41; 42; 43; 46
The Painted Bird. New York: 1965. V. 38
Passion Play. New York: 1979. V. 46
Steps. New York: 1968. V. 41
To Hold a Pen. N.P.: 1973. V. 37

KOSSUTH, LOUIS

Kossuth in New England . . . Boston & Cleveland: 1862. V. 42

KOSTER, EDWARD

Travels in Brazil. London: 1817. V. 39

KOSTER, HENRY

Travels in Brazil. London: 1816. V. 41
Travels in Brazil. London: 1817. V. 41

KOTSILIBAS-DAVIS, JAMES

The Barrymores: The Royal Family in Hollywood. New York: 1981. V. 45

KOTZEBUE, A.

Rolla; or, The Peruvian Hero: A Tragedy in Five Acts. Translated from the German of Kotzebue. By M.G. Lewis, Esq. M.P. Author of the Monk, Castle Spectre, Love of Gain, etc. London: 1799. V. 37

KOTZEBUE, AUGUSTUS VON 1761-1819

Travels through Italy in the Years 1804 and 1805. London: 1806. V. 41; 44

KOTZEBUE, MORITZ VON

Narrative of a Journey into Persia, in the Suite of the Imperial Russian Embassy, in the Year 1817. Philadelphia: 1817. V. 46
Narrative of a Journey Into Persia in the Suite of the Imperial Russian Embassy, in the Year 1817. London: 1819. V. 37; 46

KOTZEBUE, OTTO VON

Entdeckungs-Reise in Die Sud-See Und Nach der Berings-Strasse Zur Erforschung Einer Nordostlichen Durchfahrt. Unternommen in den Jahren 1815, 1816, 1817 und 1818. Weimar: 1821. V. 39; 40
Neue Reise Um Die Welt, in den Jahren 1823, 24, 25 und 26. Weimar: 1830. V. 40; 41; 42
Neue Reise um die Welt, in den Jahren 1823-1826. Weimar & St. Petersburg: 1830. V. 38
A New Voyage Round the World, in the Years 1823, 24 and 26. London: 1830. V. 38; 39; 40
Reise um die Welt, in den Jahren 1823, 24, 25 und 26. Weimar: 1830. V. 38; 41
A Voyage of Discovery, into the South Sea and Beering's Straits, for the Purpose of Exploring a North-East Passage, Undertaken in the Years 1815-1818 . . . London: 1821. V. 38; 39; 41; 43

KOWALCZYK, GEORG

Decorative Sculpture. New York: 1930. V. 39

KOYAMA, FUJIO

The Heritage of Japanese Ceramics. New York: 1973. V. 38
Two Thousand years of Oriental Ceramics. New York. V. 38; 41
Two Thousand Years of Oriental Ceramics. New York: 1960. V. 46

KOZAKIEWICZ, STEFAN

Bernardo Bellotto. London: 1972. V. 40; 43; 44

KOZLOWSKI, T. T.

Seed Biology. New York: 1972. V. 46

KRAAY, COLIN M.

Archaic and Classical Greek Coins. Berkeley: 1976. V. 44

KRAELING, CARL H.

The Synagogue. With contributions by C.C. Torrey, C.B. Welles and B. Geiger. New Haven: 1956. V. 37; 40

KRAEPELIN, EMIL 1856-1926

General Paresis. Nervous and Mental Disease Monograph Series No. 14. New York: 1913. V. 45

KRAFFT-EBING, RICHARD FREIHERR VON 1840-1902

An Experimental Study in the Domain of Hypnotism. New York: 1889. V. 40; 43; 45; 46
An Experimental Study in the Domain of Hypnotism. New York: 1896. V. 42
Psychopathia Sexualis. Philadelphia: 1893. V. 40
Text-Book of Insanity Based on Clinical Observations. Philadelphia: 1904. V. 42

KRAFFT, J. C.

Plans, Coupes et Elevations de Diverses Productions de l'Art de la Charpente Executees tant en France que dans le Pays Etrangers. Paris. V. 44
Portes Cocheres, Portes d'entree, Balcons, Entablemens et Details de Menuiserie et de Serrurerie des Edifices les Plus Remarquables de Paris. Paris: 1810. V. 39
Traite des Echafaudages ou Choix des Meilleurs Modeles de Charpentes Executees tant en France qu'a l'Etranger Contenant la Description des Ouvrages en sous-oeuvre, des Etayements, des Differentes Especes de Cintres, des Applications de la Charpente aux.. Paris: 1856. V. 44

KRAG, MARTHA ANN

Martha-Jane: Nursery Nonsense. Indianapolis: 1897. V. 45

KRAKEL, DEAN

James Boren a Study in Discipline. Flagstaff: 1968. V. 38; 39
Tom Ryan. A Painter in Four Sixes Country. Flagstaff, Arizona: (1971). V. 37

KRAKEL, DEAN F.

The Saga of Tom Horn. Laramie: 1940. V. 43
The Saga of Tom Horn: The Story of a Cattlemen's War. Laramie: 1954. V. 38; 40; 42; 43; 46
South Platte Country, a History of Old Weld County, Colorado 1739-1900. Laramie: 1954. V. 43; 46

KRAMER, HILTON

Richard Lindner. Boston: 1975. V. 39; 42; 43; 45; 46
Richard Lindner. London: 1975. V. 44; 46

KRAMER, SIDNEY

A History of Stone and Kimball and Herbert S. Stone & Co. with a Bibliography of Their Publications, 1893-1905. Chicago: 1940. V. 39; 43

KRAMER, WILLIAM M.

Hans G. Burkhardt. Artist and Patron of the Arts. Northridge: 1982. V. 43; 44

KRAMERS, H. A.

The Atom and the Bohr Theory of Its Structure, an Elementary Presentation. London, Cophenhagen and: 1923. V. 38

KRAPF, J. L.

Outline of the Elements of the Kisuaheli Language, with Special Reference to the Kinika Dialect. Tubingen: 1850. V. 45

KRAPF, J. LEWIS

Travels, Researches, and Missionary Labours, during an Eighteen Years' Residence in Eastern Africa. Boston: 1860. V. 38

Travels, Researches and Missionary Labours, During an Eighteen Year's Residence in Eastern Africa. Together with Journey's to Jagga, Usambara, Ukambani, Shoa Abessinia and Kharatoum . . . London: 1860. V. 39; 40

KRASA or, The Merchant of Prague: a Bohemian Tale of the Fifteenth Century. Dublin: 1840? V. 40

KRASCHENINNIKOV, STEPHAN PETROVICH

The History of Kamtschatka, and the Kurilski Islands, with the Countries Adjacent. London: 1764. V. 41

KRASHENINNIKOV, STEPHAN PETROVICH

The History of Kamschatka, and the Kurilski Islands . . . Gloucester: 1764. V. 38; 39; 40; 41; 45; 46

KRASINSKI, HENRYK

The Poles in the Seventeenth Century. London: 1843. V. 37

KRASNA, NORMAN

Dear Ruth: A Comedy. New York: 1945. V. 45

KRASNOFF, PETER NIKOLAYEVICH

The Black Mass. New York: 1931. V. 44

KRAUS, HANS P.

The Cradle of Printing. New York: 1954-71. V. 45

the Ninetieth Catalogue. New York. V. 46

Sir Francis Drake: a Pictorial Biography. Amsterdam: 1970. V. 39; 41; 43

Thirty-Five Manuscripts Including the St. Blasien Psalter . . . Catalogue 100. New York: 1962. V. 46

KRAUS, JOHANN ULRICH

Labyrinte de Versailles. Augsburg: 1690. V. 42

Tapisseries Du Roy, ou Sont Represenentez les Quatre Elemens et les Quatre Saisons. Augsburg: 1690. V. 41

KRAUS, THEODOR

Pompeii and Herculaneum: the Living Cities of the Dead. New York: 1975. V. 40

KRAUSE, ALLEN K.

Studies on Tuberculous Infection . . . Baltimore: 1928. V. 43

KRAUSE, FEDOR

Surgery of the Brain and Spinal Cord Based on Personal Experiences. New York: 1909-12. V. 42; 46

Surgery of the Brain and Spinal Cord Based on Personal Experiences. New York: 1911. V. 44; 45; 46

KRAUSS, JOHANN ULRICH

Tapisseries du Roy. Augsburg: 1690. V. 45

KRAUSS, RUTH

A Hole is to Dig. New York: 1952. V. 42

Somebody Else's Nut Tree and Other Tales from Children. Lenox: 1971. V. 45

A Very Special House. New York: 1953. V. 41

KRAUSZ, SIGMUND

Street Types of Great American Cities with Literary Sketches by Well Known Authors. Chicago: 1896. V. 38; 45

KRAUTHEIMER, RICHARD

Lorenzo Ghiberti. Princeton: 1956. V. 45

KRAVCHINSKY, SERGYEI MIKHAILOVICH

King Stork and King Log. London: 1895. V. 43

KREBS, BENJAMIN 1785-1858

Handbuch der Buchdruckerkunst. Frankfurt: 1827. V. 46

KREBS, F. L.

Vollstandige Beschreib7ng und Abbildung der Sammtlichen Holzarten Welche Im Mittleren und Nordichen Deutschland Wild Wachsen. Erster Theil. Brunswick: 1826-35. V. 39

KREDEL, FRITZ

Dolls and Puppets of the Eighteenth Century. Lexington: 1958. V. 39

KREHBIEL, HENRY EDWARD

Afro-American Folksongs. A Study in Racial and National Music. New York: 1914. V. 45

KREIDOLF, ERNST

Ein Wintermarchen. Zurich: 1924. V. 37

THE KRESS Library of Business and Economics: Catalogue (Volume 1). Fairfield: 1977. V. 40

KRESS, SAMUEL

The Gospels of Saint Matthew, Saint Mark, Saint Luke and Saint John. Together with Acts of the Apostles. According to the Authorized King James Version with Reproductions of Religious Paintings in the Samuel H. Kress Collection. New York: 1959. V. 41

KREYMBORG, ALFRED 1883-

Others: an Anthology of the New Verse. New York: 1916. V. 42

Others. An Anthology of New Verse (1917). New York: 1917. V. 38; 46

Plays for Merry Andrews. New York: 1920. V. 38

KRIDER, JOHN

Krider's Sporting Anecdotes. Philadelphia: 1853. V. 44

KRIEBEL, REUBEN

Genealogical Record of the Descendants of the Schwenkfelders, Who Arrived in Pennsylvania in 1733, 1734, 1736, 1737 . . . Manayunk: 1879. V. 45

KRIEG, WENDELL J. S.

Architectonics of the Human Cerebrl Fiber Systems. Evanston: 1973. V. 38

Interpretive Atlas of the Monkey's Brain. Evanston: 1975. V. 38

Interpretive Atlas of the Monkey's Brain. Illinois,: 1975. V. 38

KRISHNAMURTI, G.

Women Writers of the 1890's. London: 1991. V. 46

KRISS Kringle's Raree Show, for Good Boys and Girls. New York: 1847. V. 38

KRISSMANN, G.

Manual of Cultivated Broad-Leaved Trees and Shrubs. London: 1985-86. V. 37

KRISTELLER, PAUL

Andrea Mantegna. London: 1901. V. 46

Early Florentine Woodcuts. London: 1897. V. 39; 44

KROEBER, ALFRED L.

Archaeological Explorations in Peru. Chicago: 1926-30. V. 42; 44

Handbook of the Indians of California. Washington: 1925. V. 37; 42

KROEBER, THEODORA

The Inland Whale. Covelo: 1987. V. 44; 46

KROGH, AUGUST

Anatomy and Physiology of the Capillaries. 1936. V. 44

KROLL, H. D.

Kelly Field in the Great War. San Antonio: 1919. V. 37; 39

KROMBHOLZ, JULIUS VINZENZ VON

Naturgetreue Abbildungen und Beschreibungen der Essbaren, Schadlichen und Verdachtigen Schwamme. Prague: 1831. V. 39

KROMER, TOM

Wainting for Nothing. New York: 1935. V. 42

KRON, KARL

Ten Thousand Miles on a Bicycle. New York: 1887. V. 38

KRONHAUSEN, PHYLLIS

A Survey of Erotic Fact and Fancy in the Fine Arts. New York: 1968/70. V. 41

KROODSMA, D. E.

Acoustic Communication in Birds. London: 1983. V. 37

KROPOTKIN, PETR ALEKSEEVICH

Kropotkin. Selections from His Writings. London: 1942. V. 39

KROUPA, B.

An Artist's Tour: Gleanings and Impressions of Travels in North and Central America and the Sandwich Islands. London: 1890. V. 38

KRUEGER, MAX

Pioneer Life in Texas. San Antonio: 1930. V. 37

KRUG, WILHELM TRAUGOTT

Allgemeines Handworterbuch der Philosophischen Wissenschaften, Nebst Ihrer Literatur und Geschichte. Leipzig: 1827-29. V. 41

Handbuch der Philosophie und der Philosophischen Literatur. Leipzig: 1820-21. V. 38

KRULL, GERMAINE

100 X Paris. Berlin-Westend: 1929. V. 37

KRUSENSTERN, ADAM JOHANN VON

Atlas de l'Ocean Pacifique. St. Petersburg: 1824. V. 39

Resa Omkring Jorden, Forrattad Uren 1803, 1804, 1805 och 1806. Orebro: 1811-12. V. 40

Voyage Round the World in the Years 1803, 1804, 1805 & 1806 . . . London: 1813. V. 45

KRUSINSKI, JUDAS THADEUS

The Chronicles of a Traveller. London: 1840. V. 40

KRUSINSKI, S. J.

The History of the Revolution of Persia; Taken from the Memoirs of Father Krusinski, Procurator of the Jesuits of Isphahan . . . London: 1728. V. 43

KRUSSMANN, G.

Manual of Cultivated Broad-Leaved Trees and Shrubs. Portland: 1984-85-86. V. 45

Manual of Cultivated Broad-Leaved Trees and Shrubs. London: 1985-86. V. 37; 38

Manual of Cultivated Broad-Leaved Trees & Shrubs. V. 39

KRUTCH, JOSEPH WOOD

Herbal. New York: 1965. V. 37

Was Europe a Success? New York: 1934. V. 46

KU KLUX KLAN

Constitution of the Women of the Ku Klux Klan. Little Rock: 1923. V. 37

KU KLUX KLAN. CONSTITUTION

Constitution and Laws fo the Knights of the Ku Klax Klan. Atlanta: 1921. V. 45

KUCHLER, BALTHASAR

Repraesentatio der Fubrstlichen Auffzug und Ritterspil . . . Ehrnfest den 6 Novemb. A(nn)o 1609. 1609/11. V. 44

KUDRNA, O.

Butterflies of Europe: Volume 8: Aspects of the Conservation of Butterflies in Europe. Wiesbaden: 1986. V. 37

Butterflies of Europe. Volume I: Concise Bibliography of European Butterflies. Wiesbaden: 1985. V. 37

KUESTER, LUDOLF

Bibliotheca Librorum Novorum. Utrecht: 1697. V. 37

KUGLER, FRANCIS

History of Frederick the Great with Five Hundred Original Designs by Adolph Menzel. London. V. 41

KUGLER, FRANZ THEODOR 1808-1858

Handbook of Painting. German, Flemish and Dutch Schools. Remodeled by Prof. Dr. Waagen and thoroughly revised and in part rewritten by Sir Joseph A. Crowse. London: 1898. V. 40

Handbook of Painting: Italian Schools, Thoroughly Revised and in Part Rewritten by Austen Henry Layard. London: 1900. V. 40

KUHLMAN, CHARLES

Custer and the Gall Saga. Billings: 1940. V. 45

KUHN, CHARLES L.

Romanesque Mural painting of Catalonia. Massachusetts: 1930. V. 43

KUHNEL, ERNST

The Textile Museum: Catalogue of Dated Tiraz Fabrics . . . Washington: 1952. V. 41

KULETRMANN, UDO

Trova. New York: 1978. V. 46

KULL, IRVING S.

New Jersey. a History. New York: 1930. V. 42; 44

New Jersey, a History. New York: 1930-32. V. 39; 46

KULP, GEORGE F.

Families of the Wyoming Valley Biographical, Genealogical and Historical. Sketches of the Bench and Bar of Luzerne County, Pennsylvania. Wilkes Barre: 1885-89-90. V. 39; 41; 42; 46

KULTERMANN, U.

Kenzo Tange, Architecture and urban Design 1946-69. 1970. V. 46

KUMAR, SATISH

Learning by Heart: an Anthology of Poetry. Devon: 1986. V. 40

KUME, YASUO

Tesuki Washi Shuno. Tokyo: 1980. V. 38; 39; 40; 41; 44; 45; 46

KUMM, H. KARL W.

From Hausaland to Egypt, through the Sudan. London: 1910. V. 39; 40; 42; 43; 44; 45

The Sudan. London: 1907. V. 42

KUNCKEL VON LOEWENSTERN, JOHANN

Collegium Physico-Chymicum Experimentale, Oder Laboratorium Chymicum. Hambrug & Leipzig: 1716. V. 40; 42; 44; 45

KUNDERA, MILAN

Immortality. New York: 1990. V. 46

Immortality. New York: 1991. V. 45; 46

The Joke. London: 1969. V. 44; 45; 46

KUNDMANN, JOHANN CHRISTIAN

Rariora Naturae & Artis item in red Medica, Oder Seltenheiten der natur und Kunst des Kundmannischen Naturalien-Kabinets, wie auch in der Artzeney-Wissenschafft . . . Breslau and Leipzig: 1737. V. 38

KUNHARDT, C. P.

Small Yachts. Their Deisgn and Construction Exemplified by the Ruling Types of Modern Practice. (with) Supplement to 'Small Yachts.' New York: 1891. V. 39

Steam Yachts and Launches, Their Machinery, Design and Construction . . . New York: 1891. V. 42

KUNHERT, WILHELM

In Den Wildnissen Afrikas und Asiens. Berlin: 1908. V. 40

KUNISADA: Two Japanese Ukiyoe Books Illustrated by the Artist Utagawa Kunisada (1786-1864). 1844. V. 45

KUNISAKI, JIHEI

Kamisuki Chohoki: a Handy Guide to Papermaking. Berkeley: 1948. V. 38; 39; 41

KUNITZ, STANLEY

The Coat Without a Seam. Northampton: 1974. V. 39; 40

KUNIYOSHI, YASUO

Catalogue of His Posthumous Exhibition Held at the National Museum of Modern Art, Tokyo. Tokyo: 1954. V. 39

KUNNEN, N. P.

Voyage Agricole en Russie Pendant l'Annee 1885. Luxembourg: 1886. V. 45

KUNO, TAKESHI

A Guide to Japanese Sculpture. Tokyo: 1963. V. 42

KUNOS, I.

Fourty-Four Turkish Fairy Tales. London. V. 42

KUNSTLERGABE Zum XII. Zionisten-Kongress Karlsbad 1921. Berlin: 1921. V. 45

KUNTZ, ALBERT

The Autonomic Nervous System. Philadelphia: 1934. V. 38

KUNZ, GEORGE FREDERICK

Birth Stones: Natal Stones, Sentiments and Supersititions Associated with Precious Stones. New York: 1931. V. 39

The Curious Lore of Precious Stones. Philadelphia: 1913. V. 39; 43; 44

The Curious Lore of Precious Stones. Philadelphia & London: 1913. V. 44

Gems and Precious Stones of North America. New York: 1890. V. 45

Ivory and the Elephant in Art, in Archaeology, and in Science. Garden City: 1916. V. 43

Ivory and the Elephant in Art, in Archaeology, and In Science. New York: 1916. V. 42

The Magic of Jewels and Charms. 1915. V. 42

Rings for the Finger. Philadelphia: 1917. V. 43

Shakespeare and Precious Stones. Philadelphia: 1916. V. 46

KUNZEL, HEINRICH

Upper California. Translated from the German by Anthony & Max Knight. San Francisco: 1967. V. 37; 46

KUROSAWA, REIKICHI

Imperial Chinese Art. A Catalogue of Writings and Paintings by the Chinese Emperors, Empresses and Princes Dating from the T'ang Dynasty to the end of the Ch'ang Dynasty, A.D. 618-1912. Shanghai: 1919. V. 40

KURTH, JULIUS

Sharaku. Munich: 1922. V. 38; 41

KURTZ, BENJAMIN P.

An Original Leaf from the Polychronicon Printed by William Caxton at Westminster for the year 1482 . . . San Francisco: 1938. V. 45

KURTZ, DONNA CAROL

Athenian White Lekythoi. Oxford: 1975. V. 40

The Berlin Painter. Oxford: 1983. V. 40; 42; 44

KURTZER Einhalt und Bedeutung des Ballets . . . Marburg: 1639. V. 46

KURTZES Hand-Buechlein, und Experiment, Vieler Artzneyen. Strassburg: 1659. V. 37

KURU, SACHIKO

Sachiko Kuru Photographs Sennen: First a Road. Tokyo: 1982. V. 39

KURZ, LOUIS

Battles of the Civil War, 1861-1865, The Complete Kurz and Allison Prints. Birmingham: 1976. V. 38

Buffaloes at Rest. Chicago. V. 44

KURZ, RUDOLPH FRIEDRICH

Journal of Rudolph Friedrich Kurz. Washington: 1937. V. 37; 38; 39; 41; 46

KURZE Geographie von Asia, Afrika, Amerika, und den Sudlandern. Versuch einer Fortsetzung von Raffs Geographie fur Kinder. Mit einer Neuen Illuminirten Weltkarte. Nurnberg: 1790. V. 38

KUSSMAUL, ADOLF

Disturbances of Speech. An Attempt in the Pathology of Speech. New York: 1877. V. 42

KUTTNER, CHARLES GOTTLOB

Travels through Denmark, Sweden, Austria and part of Italy in 1798 and 1799. London: 1805. V. 40; 42

KUTTNER, H.

Ahead of Time. 1953. V. 39

KUTZ, M. JENNIE

Wah-Ah-See, a Legend of the Sleeping Dew. Chicago: 1868. V. 40; 44

KUYKENDALL, IVAN L.

Ghost Riders of the Mogollon. San Antonio: 1954. V. 37; 38; 39; 42

KUYKENDALL, WILLIAM L.

Frontier Days. Denver: 1917. V. 40

Frontier Days. N.P.: 1917. V. 38; 39; 43; 46

KUZMA, GREG

A Day in the World. Omaha: 1976. V. 42

KWOK, LO KWAI

Useful Manual for the Use of Traders in China. Hong Kong: 1899. V. 40

KYAN, JOHN HOWARD

On the Elements of Light and Their Identity With Those of Matter, Radiant and Fixed. London: 1838. V. 37

KYNE, PETER B.

The Book I Never Wrote. San Francisco: 1942. V. 37

Outlaws of Eden. New York: 1930. V. 37

THE KYNOCH Press Book of Type Specimens. Birmingham: 1927. V. 40

KYOTO. Japan: 1931. V. 45

KYSS, ALEXANDER

Elementare Universale Totius Generis Humani Alphabetum . . . Budapest: 1813. V. 38

KYTCHIN, JOHN

Le Court Leete, et Court Baron. London: 1580. V. 46

L

L, D. C.

The Education Craze and Its Results. School Boards, Their Extravagances and Inefficiency. London: 1878. V. 37

L., R.

A Copye of a Letter Contayning Certain Newes, & the Articles or Requestes of the Devonshyre & Cornyshe Rebelles. London: 1549. V. 41

L., R. S.

The Unknown: a Tale of Truth and Fiction. Brighton: 1857. V. 40

L., T.

England's Almanack Shewing How the East-India Trade is Predudicial to this Kingdom. London. V. 45

LAAMB, LARNED

The Militia's Guide. Montpelier: 1807. V. 37

LABACCO, ANTONIO

Libro Appartenente a l'Architettura . . . Rome: 1559. V. 37; 40

Libro d'Antonio Labacco Appartenente a l'Architettura nel qual di Figurano alcune Notabili Antiquita di Roma. V. 37

LABAGH, ISAAC P.

The Mediatorial Reign of Christ on the Earth, Revealed in a Series of Essays . . . New York: 1844. V. 45

LABARRE, E. J.

A Dictionary of Paper and Paper Making Terms with Equivalents in French, German, Dutch and Italian. Amsterdam: 1937. V. 38

Dictionary and Encyclopaedia of Paper and Papermaking. London: 1952. V. 41

LABAT, GASTON LOUIS 1877-1934

Regional Anesthesia. Philadelphia: 1922. V. 42

Regional Anesthesia. Its Technic and Clinical Application. Philadlephia & London: 1923. V. 45

LABATT, HENRY J.

The Practice Act of California, Entitlted 'An Act to Regulate Proceedings in Civil Cases in the Courts of Justice in This State.' San Francisco: 1856. V. 43

Reports of Cases Determined in the District Courts of the State of California. San Francisco: 1857. V. 37; 39

LABAUME, EUGENE

A Circumstantial Narrative of the Campaign in Russia, Embellished with Plans of the Battles of Moscow and Malo-Jaroslavitz. London: 1815. V. 39; 43; 46

LA BEAUME, MICHAEL

Cases of Indigestion, From Disorders of the Stomach, Liver and Bowels and Other Complaints . . . London: 1827. V. 42

LA BEAUMELLE, LAURENT ANGLIVIEL DE

Memoirs for the History of Madame de Maintenon and the Last Age. London: 1757. V. 41; 46

LABELYE, CHARLES

A Description of Westminster Bridge. London: 1731. V. 42

The Present State of Westminster Bridge. London: 1743. V. 38; 40; 41

A Short Account of the Methods Made Use of In Laying the Foundation of the Piers of Westminster Bridge . . . London: 1739. V. 41

LABERINTO. Twenty Broadsides 1981-1982. Minneapolis: 1982. V. 44

LABILLARDIERE, JACQUES JULIEN HOUTEN DE

An Account of a Voyage in Search of La Perouse, Undertaken by Order of the Constituent Assembly of France and Performed in the Years 1791, 1792 and 1793, in the Recherche and Esperance, Ships of War Under the Command of Rear Admiral Bruni D'Entrecasteaux. London: 1800. V. 38; 41; 44

LABILLARDIERE, JACQUES JULIEN HOUTON DE

Relation du Voyage a la Recherche de la Perouse, Fait par Ordre de l'Assemblee Constituante, Pendant les Annees 1791, 1792 et Pendant la Lere et la 2e Annee de la Republique. Paris: 1800. V. 45

LABILLARDIERE, JAQUES JULIEN HOUTON DE

Novai Hollandiae Plantarum Specimen. Paris: 1804-1806. V. 42

Relation du oyage a la Recherche de La Perouse . . . Paris: 1799-1800. V. 42

LABILLIERE, FRANCIS PETER

Early History of the Colony of Victoria from Its Discovery to Its Establishment as a Self Government Province of the British Empire. London: 1879. V. 46

LA BIZARDIERE, MICHEL DAVID DE

An Historical Account of the Divisions in Poland: from the Death of k. Sobieski, to the Settlement of the Present King on the Throne. London: 1700. V. 39

LA BLANCHERE, HENRI DE

Monographie du Stereoscope et des Epreuves Stereoscopiques. Paris: 1861. V. 40

LABORDE, ALEXANDRE DE

Description des Nouveaux Jardins de la France et de ses Anciens Chateaux. Paris: 1808-15. V. 38; 42; 46

LABORDE, BENJAMIN

Choix de Chansons Mises en Musique. Paris: 1773. V. 40

LABORDE, CHARLES

Le Cotillion. Paris. V. 38

LABORDE, LEON DE

Journey through Arabia Petraea, to Mount Sinai, and the Excavated City of Petra, the Edom of the Prophecies. London: 1836. V. 39; 42

Journey through Arabia Petraea, to Mount Sinai and the Excavated City of Petra, the Edom of the Prophecies. London: 1838. V. 39; 45

LABOUCHERE, NORNA

Ladies Book Plates. London & New York: 1895. V. 40

LABOULAYE, EDOUARD

Fairy Tales. London: 1908. V. 40; 43

THE LABOURERS' Friend: A Selection from the Publictions of the . . . . Society . . . London: 1835. V. 38

LABREE, BEN

The Confederate Soldier in the Civil War. Louisville: 1895. V. 39; 44; 46

LA BROCQUIERE, BERTRANDON DE

The Travels of . . . Hafod: 1807. V. 44

LA BROSSE, JEAN BAPTISTE DE

Nehiro-Iriniui Aiamihe Massinahigan, Shatshegutsch, Mitinekapitsh, Askuamiskutsch, Netsherkatsch, Misht . . . Uabistigulatsh: 1767. V. 39; 42; 44

LA BRUYERE, JEAN DE

The Works of Monsieur de la Bruyere. London: 1713. V. 41

The Works . . . London: 1776. V. 42; 44

LABRUZZI, CARLO

Figure Fatti da Cinque Punti Obbligati. Rome?: 1790. V. 39

Raccolta di Venti Gruppi di Figure Disegnati dal Vero. Rome: 1790. V. 39

LABUTTE, R.

A French Grammar to Which is Prefixed an Analysis Relating to that Subject. Cambridge: 1784. V. 39

LABYRINTE de Versailles, Suivant la Copie. Paris. V. 40

LA CAILLE, M.

Journal Historique du Voyage Fait au Cap de Bonne Esperance. Paris: 1763. V. 45

LACAITA, J. P.

Catalogue of the Library at Chatsworth. London: 1879. V. 46

LA CALPRENEDE, GAULTIER DE COSTE, SEIGNEUR DE

Cassandra; the Fam'd Romance. London: 1661. V. 42

Cassandra: the Fam'd Romance. London: 1664. V. 45

Cassandra: the Fam'd Romance. London: 1652. V. 38

The Famous History of Cassandra . . . London: 1703. V. 46

Hymen's Praeludia; or, Loves Master-piece. London: 1659. V. 46

LACEPEDE, B. D. E. DE

Oeuvres Comprenant l'Histoire Naturelle des Quadrupedes, Ovipares, des Serpents, des Poissons et des Cetaces. Paris: 1826-33. V. 39

LACEPEDE, BERNARD GERMAIN ETIENNE, COMTE DE

Discours d'Ouverture et de Cloture du Cours d'Histoire Naturelle des Animaux Vertebres et a Sang Rouge, Donne dans le Museum National d'Histoire Naturelle. Paris: 1798-1802. V. 46

LACEY, ADIN BENEDICT

American Competitions. Philadelphia: 1907. V. 39

LACH, DONALD F.

Asia in the Making of Europe. Chicago: 1965-77. V. 42

LACH-SZYRMA, W. S.

Aleriel or a Voyage to Other Worlds. London: 1883. V. 45

LACHAISE, GASTON

Gaston Lachaise. Sixteen Reproductions in Collotype of the Sculptor's Work. New York: 1924. V. 38

LA CHALOTAIS, RENE LOUIS DE CARADEUC DE 1701-1785

Essai d'Education Nationale, ou Plan d'Etudes pour la Jeunesse. N.P.: 1763. V. 41; 43

LACHAMBRE, HENRI

Andree and His Balloon. Westmisnter: 1898. V. 46

Andree's Balloon Expedition in Search of the North Pole. New York: 1898. V. 42

LA CHAMBRE, MARIN

Discours sur les Causes du Desbordement du Nii. Paris: 1665. V. 46

dISCOURS. V. 46

LA CHAMBRE, MARIN CUREAU DE

The Art How to Know Men. London: 1665. V. 39; 43

LA CHESNEE MONSTEREUL, CHARLES DE

Traite des Tulipes avec la Maniere de les Bien Cultiver, Leurs Noms, Leurs Couleurs & Leur Beate. Paris: 1678. V. 46

LACHLAN, ELIZABETH

Leonora; or, the Presentation at Court. London: 1829. V. 46

LACINIUS, JANUS

Pretiosa Margarita Novella de Thesauro, Ac Pretiosissimo Philosphorum Lapide. Venice: 1546. V. 46

LACKINGTON, ALLEN & CO.

General Catalogue of Books for the Year 1808 . . . London: 1808. V. 38; 42; 44

LACKINGTON, JAMES 1746-1815

The Confessions of J. Lackington, Late Bookseller, at the Temple of the Muses, in a Series of Letters to a Friend . . . London: 1804. V. 39; 41; 42; 43; 45

The Confessions of J. Lackington, Late Bookseller at the Temple of the Muses. New York: 1808. V. 38; 42; 44

Memoirs of the First Forty-Five Years of the Life of James Lackington, the Present Bookseller in Chiswell Street, Moorfields, London . . . London: 1791. V. 37; 39; 41; 42; 43; 45

Memoirs of the Forty-Five First Years of the Life of James Lackington, the Present Bookseller in Chiswell Street, Finsbury Square, London. London: 1794. V. 39

Memoirs of the Forty-Five First Years of the Life of . . . London: 1795. V. 38; 40

Memoirs of the Forty-Five First Years of the Life of James Lackington. London: 1800. V. 38; 40; 42; 44

Memoirs of the Forty-Five First Years of . . . London: 1803. V. 38

LACLOS, PIERRE AMBROISE FRANCOIS CHODERLOS DE 1741-1803

Dangerous Connections. London: 1812. V. 41

Les Liaisons Dangereuses. Paris. V. 41

Les Liaisons Dangereuses. Amsterdam: 1784. V. 38

Les Liaisons Dangereuses. 1922. V. 40

Les Liasions Danguereuses. 1929. V. 45

Les Liaisons Dangereuses. Paris: 1929. V. 43; 44; 46

Les Liaisons Dangereuses. Paris: 1929-30. V. 38; 44

Les Liaisons Dangereuses. Amsterdam: 1782. V. 42

LACLOS, PIERRE AMBROISE FRANCOIS, CHOLDERLOS DE 1741-1803

Dangerous Connections; or, Letters Collected in a Society . . . London: 1784. V. 43

LACOMBE, J. M.

The History of Christina, Queen of Sweden. London: 1766. V. 39

LACOMBE, JEAN DE, SIEUR

A Compendium of the East Being an Account of Voyages to the Grand Indies. London: 1937. V. 44

LA CONDAMINE, CHARLES MARIE DE 1701-1774

Journal du Voyage Fait par Ordre du Roi, a l'Equateur, Servant d'Introduction Historique a la Mesure des Trois Premiers Degres du Meridien. Paris: 1751. V. 39

Journal of a Tour to Italy. Dublin: 1763. V. 40

Journal of a Tour to Italy. London: 1763. V. 40; 46

A Succinct Abridgment of a Voyage Made Within the Inland Parts of South America . . . London: 1747. V. 39; 43

LACONICS; or, New Maxims of State and Conversation. London: 1701. V. 42

LACONICS; or, New Maxims of State and Conversation. London: 1702. V. 41

LA COURT, PIETER DE

The True Interest and Political Maxims, of the Republic of Holland . . . London: 1746. V. 40

LA COURT VAN DER VOORT, PIETER DE

Les Agremens de la Campagne, ou Remarques Particulieres sur la Construction des Maisons de Campagne plus ou Moins Magnifiques, des Jardins de Plaisance . . . Leiden: 1750. V. 43

LA CREQUINIERE, M. DE

The Agreement of the Customs of the East Indians, With Those of the Jews and Other Ancient People . . . London: 1705. V. 45

LA CROIX, A. PHEROTEE DE ca. 1640-1715

L'Art de la Poesie Francoise et Latine, avec une Idee de la Musique sous Une Nouvelle Methode. Lyon: 1694. V. 41; 46

LA CROIX DU MAINE, FRANCOIS GRUDE, SIEUR DE

Premier Volvme De la Bibliotheqve . . . Qui est vn Catalogue General de Toutes Sortes d'Autheurs, qui ont Escrit en Francois depuis Cinq Cents ans & plus, lusques a ce lourd'huy. Paris: 1584. V. 38

LACROIX, IRENEE AMELOT DE

Rules and Regulations for the Field Exercise and Manoeuvres of the French Infantry, Issued August 1, 1791. Abridged. And all the Manoeuvres Added, Which Have Been Since Adopted by the Emperor Napoleon. Boston: 1809. V. 37

Rules and Regulations for the Field Exercise, and Manoeuvres of the French Infantry, Issued August 1, 1791. And the Manoeuvres Added, Which Have Been Adopted by the Emperor Napoleon. Boston: 1810. V. 37

LACROIX, PAUL 1806-1884

The Arts in the Middle Ages, and the Period of the Renaissance. London: 1870. V. 42

The Arts in the Middle Ages, and at the Period of the Renaissance. London: 1880's. V. 45

The Arts in the Middle Ages and the Renaissance. London: 1886. V. 41

Contes du Bibliophile Jacob a ses Petits-enfants. Paris: 1831. V. 46

Manners, Customs and Dress During the Middle Ages and During the Renaissance. London: 1874. V. 37; 44

Manners, Customs and Dress During the Middle Ages . . . London: 1880's. V. 45

Military and Religious Life in the Middle Ages and At the Period of the Renaissance. London: 1880's. V. 45

Science and Literature in the Middle Ages, and at the Period of the Renaissance. London: 1878. V. 45

LACROIX, SYLVESTRE FRANCOIS

An Elementary Treatise on the Different and Integral Calculus. Cambridge: 1816. V. 43

LA CROSE, J. DE

Memoirs for the Ingenious. London: 1693. V. 45

LACRYMAE Cantabrigienses in Obitum Serenissimae Reginae Mariae. Cantabrigiae: 1694-95. V. 44; 46

LACTANTIUS, LUCIUS COELIUD FIRMIANUS fl.300-320

A Relation of the Death of the Primitive Persecutors. Amsterdam: 1687. V. 44

LACTANTIUS, LUCIUS COELIUS FIRMIANUS

V. 45

Divinarum Institutionum Libri VII. De Ira Dei. De Opificio Dei. Epitome . . . Phoenix. Carmen de Dominica Resurrectione. Venice: 1515. V. 38

Divinarum Institutionum Libri Septem, Iam Novissime ad Vetusta Exemplaria Manuscripta Sedulo Collari . . . Coloniae: 1544. V. 43; 46

Divinarum Institutionum Libri VII, etc. Lugduni: 1615. V. 43

Opera . . . Accurate Castigata . . . Venice: 1502. V. 40

Opera Quae Extant, ad Fidem MSS. Recognita et Commentariis Illustrata a Tho. Spark. Oxford: 1684. V. 41

Opera, Quae Extant Omnia . . . Cantabrigiae: 1685. V. 41

Opera Quae Extant Omnia; Ad Fidem Codicum tam Impressorum, Quam Manu Scriptorum Recensita. Cambridge: 685. V. 45

LACY, BENJAMIN

The Vanity of the World; or, the Folly of Those Who Lead Wicked and Profane Lives and Yet Wish and Desire to Die the Death of the Righteous. London: 1720. V. 42

LACY, CHARLES DE LACY

The History of the Spur. London: 1904. V. 43

LACY, CHARLES DE LACY continued

The History of the Spur. London: 1910. V. 46

LACY, GEORGE L.

The Angler's Handbook for India. Calcutta: 1905. V. 39

LACY, JOHN

The Dramatic Works. Edinburgh & London: 1875. V. 46

The Prophetical Warnings of. London: 1707. V. 39

LACY, N. J.

The Legacy of Chretien de Troyes. London: 1986/87. V. 39

LACY, THOMAS

England and Ireland; or Home Sketches on Both Sides of the Channel. London: 1852. V. 43; 45

LADA-MOCARSKI, VALERIAN

Bibliography of Books on Alaska Published Before 1868. New Haven & London: 1935. V. 37

Bibliography of Books on Alaska published before 1868. New Haven: 1969. V. 37; 39; 43; 44; 45

Bibliography of Books on Alaska Published Before 1868. New Haven & London: 1969. V. 38; 41; 43

LADBROKE, MISS

Catalogue of the . . . Books and Other Effects. London: 1818. V. 40; 44

LADBROOKE, H.

The Presentation of the Address of the Mayor, Coporation and Burgesses of King's Lynn on His (Cresswell's) return from the Arctic Regions . . . V. 45

LADD, B. F.

History of Vineland. Vineland: 1881. V. 41

LADD, SAMUEL G.

State of Maine Head-Quarters, Portland, July 6, 1830. Portland: 1830. V. 42

LADD, WILLIAM

An Address . . . Portland, Feb. 6, 1824, Before the Peace Society of Maine. Portland: 1824. V. 37

An Essay on a Congres of Nations, for the Adjustment of International Disputes Without Resort to Arms. London: 1840. V. 37

Prize Essays on a Congress of Nations, for the Adjustment of International Disputes and for the Promotion of Universal Peace. Boston: 1840. V. 39

LADE, ROBERT

Voyages du Capitaine Robert Lade en Differentes Parties de l'Afrique, de l'Asie et de l'Amerique . . . Paris: 1744. V. 46

THE LADIES Amusement, or Whole Art of Japanning Made Easy. Newport: 1966. V. 40

THE LADIES Delight. Containing, I. An Address to Well Provided Hibernians. II. The Arbor Vitae; or, Tree of Life . . . . III. The Natural History of the Arbor Vitae . . . IV. Ridotto al' Fresco. London: 1732. V. 43; 45

THE LADIES Diary or Woman's Almanac, for the Year of Our Lord 1765 (to 1768). London: 1765-68. V. 39

LADIES' Indespensable Assistant. Being a Companion for Sister, Mother, and Wife . . . New York: 1853. V. 39

LADIES' Indispensable Assistant, Being a Companion for the Sister, Mother and Wife. New York: 1851. V. 37; 45

THE LADIES' Indispensable Companion and Housekeeper's Guide . . . New York: 1859. V. 39

THE LADIES Library, Written by a Lady. London: 1722. V. 38

THE LADIES Of Cabinet of Fasion, Music and Romances. London: 1837. V. 46

THE LADIES' Own Memorandum-Book: or, Daily Pocket Journal for the Year 1800. London: 1799. V. 46

THE LADIES Tales; Exemplified in the Vertues and Vices of the Quality with Reflections. London: 1714. V. 37; 42

LADISLAS OF MACEDONIA

Oratio ad Carolvm V . . . pro Hungaris & Slauis. Augsburg: 1530. V. 37

LADRON DE GUEVARA, ANTONIO

Noticias de los Poblados y Tratos de que se Componen el Nuevo Reyno de Leon, Provincia de Coaguila, Nueva Estremdura, y Provincia de las Texas . . . Mexico: 1739. V. 38

LADVOCAT, MONSIEUR

An Historical and Biographical Dictionary . . . Four Volumes. Cambridge: 1799. V. 37

LADY Jane Grey, an Historical Tale. London: 1791. V. 40

A LADY'S Diary of the Siege of Lucknow. London: 1858. V. 42

LADY'S Diary; or, the Women's Almanack. London: 1708. V. 37

THE LADY'S Drawing Room. London: 1744. V. 38

THE LADY'S Economical Assistant . . . London: 1819. V. 44

THE LADY'S Monthly Museum, or Polite Reposititory of Amusement and Instruction . . . London: 1798. V. 46

THE LADY'S Rhetorick . . . London: 1707. V. 46

THE LADY's Work-Box Companion. New York: 1844. V. 41

LAENNEC, RENE THEOPHILE HYACINTHE

De L'Auscultation mediate, Du Traite Du Diagnostic Des Maladies Des Poumons et Du Coeur. Paris: 1819. V. 43; 46

Traite de l'Auscultation et des Maladies des Poumons et Du Coeur. Paris: 1826. V. 37; 42

A Treatise on the Diseases of the Chest and on Mediate Ausculation . . . Philadelphia: 1823. V. 37; 41; 45

A Treatise on the Disease of the Chest and on Mediate Auscultation. New York: 1830. V. 38; 42; 45

A Treatise on the Diseases of the Chest and on Mediate Auscultation. London: 1834. V. 43

A Treatise on the Diseases of the Chest and on Mediate Auscultation . . . New York: 1835. V. 45

A Treatise on the Diseases of the Chest and on Mediate Auscultation. Philadelphia: 1835. V. 38; 42

A Treatise on Diseases of the Chest, and on Mediate Ausculation. New York: 1838. V. 37; 38; 43; 44; 45; 46

A Treatise on the Diseases of the Chest and on Mediate Auscultation. Translated from the latest French edition, with Notes and a Sketch of the author's Life, by John Forbes, M.D. Third edition, revised with additional Notes . . . London: 1829. V. 37

LAENNEC, RENE THEOPHILE HYANCINTHE

A Treatise on Mediate Auscultation, and On Diseases of the Lungs and Heart . . . London: 1846. V. 44

LAET, JOANNES DE

L'Histoire du Nouveau Monde ou Description des Indes Occidentales, Contenant Di-Huit Liures. Leyden: 1640. V. 43

Nieuwe Wereldt Ofte Beschrivjinghe Van West-Indien Wt Veelerhande Schriften Ende . . . Leyden: 1625. V. 43

Novus Orbis Seu Descriptionis Indiae Occidentalis Libri XVIII. Leyden: 1633. V. 37; 43; 44

LA FAGE, RAIMOND

Receuil des Meilleurs Dessins . . . Grave par Cinq des Plus Habiles Graveurs. Amsterdam: 1689. V. 39; 40

LA FARGE, JOHN

The Higher Life in Art. New York: 1908. V. 40

LA FARGE, OLIVER

Laughing Boy. Cambridge: 1929. V. 41

Tribes and Temples: A Record of the Expedition to Middle America. New Orleans: 1926. V. 43

LA FAYETT, MADAME DE

The Death of Madame. Paris: (1931). V. 37

LAFAYETTE, GILBERT DE MOTIER

Memoirs, Correspondence and Manuscripts of . . . Published by His Family. New York: 1838. V. 38

LA FAYETTE, MARIE JOSEPH PAUL YVES ROCH GILBERT DU MOTIER 1757-1834

Epistle from the Marquis De La Fayette to General Washington. Edinburgh: 1800. V. 39

Lafayette in the Age of the American Revolution: Selected Letters and Papers, 1776-1790. Ithaca: 1977-80. V. 43

LA FAYETTE, MARIE MADELEINE, COMTESSE DE

Fatal Gallantry. London: 1722. V. 39; 40

LA FAYETTE, MARIE MADELEINE PLOCHE DE LA VERGNE, COMTESSE DE

The Death of madame. Paris: 1931. V. 42; 44

Death of Madame. New York: 1931. V. 38

The Princess of Cleves. London: 1777. V. 43

La Princesse de Montpensier. Paris: 1662. V. 41

Zayde, Histoire Espagnole. Paris: 1780. V. 41

LAFEVER, MINARD

The Beauties of Modern Architecture. New York: 1835. V. 40

LAFEVER, MINARD continued

The Modern Builder's Guide. New York: 1833. V. 39

LAFFONT, ROBERT

The Ancient Art of Warfare. Volume I - 1300 B.C./1650 A.D. Volume II - 1700 to Our Times. Greenwich: 1966. V. 38

LAFITAU, JOSEPH FRANCOIS

Customs of the American Indians Compared with the Customs of Primitive Times. Toronto: 1974/77. V. 43

Customs of the American Indians Compared with the Customs of Primitive Times . . . Toronto: 1974-77. V. 45

De Zeden der Wilden van Amerika. In's Gravenhage: 1731. V. 39

Moeurs des Sauvages Ameriquains, Comparees aux Moeurs des Premiers Temps. Paris: 1724. V. 38; 39; 40; 41; 42; 43; 44; 45; 46

LAFITTE, JEAN BAPTISTE PIERRE

Adventures of an Actor. London: 1842. V. 39

LA FONTAINE, JEAN DE 1621-1695

Contes et Nouvelles en Vers. Paris: 1777. V. 42

The Fables of La Fontaine. London. V. 45

Fables Choisies Pour les Enfants. Paris. V. 46

Fables and Tales from La Fontaine. London: 1734. V. 43

Fables Choisies. Paris: 1755-59. V. 39; 40; 42; 44

Fables Choises, Mises en vers . . . Paris: 1765-1775. V. 41; 44; 45

Fables de la Fontaine . . . Paris: 1811. V. 44

Fables of La Fontaine. Paris: 1838. V. 41

Fables of Fontaine. Boston: 1841. V. 39; 41

Fables. Paris: 1864. V. 46

The Fables of . . . London: 1867. V. 45

The Fables. London: 1867-70. V. 37

Fables. Paris: 1868. V. 37

The Fables . . . London: 1870's? V. 42

The Fables of La Fontaine. Boston: 1884. V. 44

Fontaine's Fables. London: 1905. V. 46

Forty-Two Fables of La Fontaine. London: 1924. V. 40; 41; 42; 43

Fables. Paris: 1929. V. 38

The Fables . . . 1930. V. 42

The Fables. New York: 1930. V. 38; 39; 40; 41; 44

The Fables. London: 1931. V. 37; 41; 42; 46

The Fables. London & New York: 1931. V. 38; 39; 40

Vingt Fables. Lausanne: 1950. V. 37; 38; 39

The Fables of La Fontaine. New York: 1954. V. 38; 39; 40; 41; 42; 43; 44; 46

Fables. Lausanne: 1955. V. 41

Fables Choisies. Antwerp: 1688-94. V. 37

The Fables of Jean De La Fontaine. Translated into English verse by Walter Thornbury. 1885. V. 37

La Fontaine's Tales. London: 1814. V. 46

The Loves of Cupid and Psyche. London: 1744. V. 37; 38

Les Amours de Psyche et de Cupidon. Paris: 1791. V. 41

Les Oeuvres Postumes. Paris: 1696. V. 37

Poeme du Quinquina, et Autres Ouvrages en Vers. Paris: 1682. V. 40

The Raven and the Fox and Other Fables. 1986. V. 38

Selected Fables of La Fontaine. London: 1955. V. 41; 46

Tales and Novels in Verse. London: 1735. V. 42

Tales. London: 1814. V. 42; 46

Tales and Novels in Verse of J. De La Fontaine. Paris & New York: 1883. V. 43

Tales and Novels. Hollan,: 1929. V. 45

Tales and Novels. Nijmegan: 1929. V. 42

LAFORGUE, JULES

Moralites Legendaires. London: 1897-98. V. 44; 46

Moralities Legendaires. London: 1897. V. 37

Some Poems of Jules Lafourgue With Illustrations by Patrick Cauldfield. 1973. V. 40

Some Poems of Jules Laforgue. London: 1972. V. 37

LAFOSSE, PHILIPPE-ETIENNE

Cours d'Hippiatrique, ou Traite Complet de la Medicine des Chevaux. Paris: 1772. V. 42

LAFOY, J. B.

The Complete Coiffeur; or an Essay on the Art of Adorning Natural, and Creating Artificial Beauty. New York: 1817. V. 43

LAFRENTZ, FERDINAND W.

Cowboy Stuff: Poems. New York: 1927. V. 37; 38; 40

LAFRERY, ANTOINE

Illustrium Virorum ut Exstant in Urbe Expressi Vultus. Rome: 1569. V. 37

LAFUENTE FERRARI, ENRIQUE

Goya: His Complete Etchings, Aquatints and Lithographs. New York. V. 40

LA GAL, EUGENE

The School of the Guides, for the Use of the Army of the Confederate States with Questions. Griffin: 1861. V. 44

LAGALLA, GUILIO CAESARE 1577-1652

De Phoenomenis in Orbe Lunae Novi Telescopii Usu a D. Gallileo Gallileo nunc Iterum Suscitatis Physica Disputatio . . . Venice: 1612. V. 38; 46

LA GARDE CHAMBONAS, AUGUSTE, COMTE DE

Journal of a Nobleman; Comprising an Account of His Travels and a Narrative of His Residence at Vienna, During the Congress. London: 1831. V. 46

LA GARDE, LOUIS A.

Gunshot Injuries: How They Are Inflicted, Their Complications and Treatment. New York: 1914. V. 41

LAGARDELLE, FIRMIN

Soldier's Heart and the Effort Syndrome. London: 1918. V. 43

LAGERKVIST, PAR

The Dwarf. London: 1953. V. 40

The Marriage Feast and Other Stories. London: 1955. V. 40

LAGNY, GERMAIN DE

The Knout and the Russians; or the Muscovite Empire, the Czar and His People. London: 1854. V. 42

LA GOURNERIE, J. DE

Traite de Perspective Lineaire. Paris: 1859. V. 45

LA GRANGE DE CHESSLEUX, GILBERT ARNAUD FRANCOIS SIMON DE

La Conduite des Francois Justifee, ou Observations Sur un Escrit Anglois, Intitule: Conduite des Francois a L'egard de la Nouvelle-Ecosse.. Paris: 1756. V. 44

LA GRANGE, HELEN

Clipper Ships of America and Great Britain, 1833-69. A panorama of shipping from colonial days to the close of the clipper-ship era. New York: 1936. V. 37

LAGRANGE, JOSEPH LOUIS

Mechanique Analitique. Paris: 1788. V. 43

LAGUMA, ALEX

A Walk in the Night. Ibadan: 1962. V. 45

LAGUNA, D. M.

Flora Forestal Espanola . . . Madrid: 1883-90. V. 37

LAHACHE, THEO VON

Confederates' Polka March. New Orleans: 1862. V. 41

LA HIRE, PHILIPPE DE 1640-1718

Gnomonicks, or the Art of Shadows Improved. London: 1709. V. 46

Tabulae Astronomicae Ludovici Magni Jussu et Munificentia Exaratae et in Lucem Editae. Paris: 1727. V. 44; 46

Traite de Mecanique . . . Paris: 1695. V. 42

LA HIRE, PHILLIPE DE 1640-1718

Memories de Mathematique et de Physique, Contenant un Traite des Epicycloides, & Leurs Usages dans les Mechaniques. Paris: 1694. V. 38

LAHONTAN, LOUIS ARMAND DE LOM D'ARCE, BARON DE 1666-1715?

New Voyages to North America. London: 1703. V. 37; 39; 40; 42; 43; 46

Voyage Dans l'Amerique Septentrionale, Qui Contiennent une Relation des Differens Peuples qui y Habitent . . . A la haye: 1706. V. 43

Voyages du Baron de Lahonton dans l'Amerique Septentrionale, Qui Continent une Relation des Differens Peuples qui y Habitent, le Nature de Leur Gouvernement . . . Amsterdam: 1728. V. 43

LAHONTAN, LOUIS ARMOND DE LOM D'ARCE, BARON DE 1666-1715?

Nouveaux Voyages . . . Dans l'Amerique Septentrionale. (with) Memoires de l'Amerique Septentrionale, ou la Suite des Voyages. The Hague: 1709-03. V. 38; 39

New Voyages to North America. London: 1735. V. 37; 40

New Voyages to North America. Chicago: 1905. V. 38; 39

New Voyages to North-America. Containing An Account of the several Nations of that vast Continent; their Customs, Commerce, and Way of Navigation upon the Lakes and Rivers, the several Attempts of the English and French . . . Hague: 1703. V. 37

LAINEZ, MANUEL MUJICA

Cantata de Bomarzo. 1981. V. 38

Cantata di Bomarzo. Verona: 1981. V. 44

LAING, ALEXANDER

The Haunted Omnibus. London: 1937. V. 44

LAING, ALEXANDER GORDON

Travels in Western Africa in the Timannee, Kooranko and Soolina Countries. London: 1823. V. 46

LAING, ALLAN M.

Prayers and Graces. London: 1944. V. 37

LAING, BLAIR

Memoirs of an Art Dealer. Toronto: 1979-82. V. 43

Memoirs of an Art Dealer. Toronto: 1979/82. V. 42

LAING, D.

Hints for Dwellings . . . London: 1804. V. 44

LAING, DAVID

Early Metrical Tales; Including the History of Sir Egeir, Sir Gryme and Sir Gray-Steill. Edinburgh: 1826. V. 42

Plans, Elevations and Sections of Buildings Public and Private, Executed in Various Parts of England, & Including the New Custom-House. London: 1818. V. 37; 38; 39

Select Remains of the Ancient Popular Poetry of Scotland. Edinburgh: 1884. V. 46

LAING, G. BLAIR

Memoirs of an Art Dealer. Toronto: 1979-82. V. 37

LAING, JOHN

An Account of a Voyage to Spitzbergen. London: 1815. V. 37; 42

A Voyage to Spitzbergen. Edinburgh: 1818. V. 38; 40; 42; 43; 46

Voyage to Spitzbergen. London: 1818. V. 38

A Voyage to Spitzbergen. Edinburgh: 1822. V. 38; 41

LAING, S.

Prehistoric Remains of Caithness, with Notes on the Human Remains by T. H. Huxley. London: 1866. V. 38; 40

LAING, SAMUEL

The Heimskringla. London: 1889. V. 37

Journal of a Residence in Norway During the Years 1834, 1835 and 1836. London: 1837. V. 39; 41; 42; 44

Observations on the Social and Political State of Denmark, and the Duchies of Sleswick and Holstein in 1851. London: 1852. V. 43

A Tour in Sweden in 1838 . . . London: 1839. V. 41; 43; 44; 45

LAING, SETON

The Great City Frauds of Cole, Davidson and Gordon, Fully Exposed. London: 1856. V. 39

LAING, WILLIAM

A Catalogue of Books for the Year 1815, Now on Sale for Ready Money. Edinburgh: 1815. V. 38; 40

LAIRD, MAC GREGOR

Narrative of an Expedition Into the Interior of Africa, by the River Niger in the Steam Vessels Qourra and Alburkah, in 1832, 1833 and 1834. London: 1837. V. 40; 42; 43; 44; 45

LAIRD, MARY

The Eggplant Skin Plants and Poems. Mt. Horeb: 1973. V. 44

LAIRESSE, GERARD DE

The Art of Painting In all Its Branches. London: 1778. V. 38; 40

Les Principes du Dessin, ou Methode Courte et Facile pour Appendre cet art en Peu de Tems. Amsterdam: 1719. V. 39

LA JEUNESSE, ERNEST

In Memoriam Oscar Wilde, by Ernest la Jeunesse, Andre Gide and Granz Blei. Translation and Introduction by Percival Pollard. V. 37

LAKE, A.

Prose and Poetry. N.P.: 1905. V. 41

LAKE, ARTHUR

The Christians Wary Walking and Improving of Time. London: 1663. V. 41

LAKE, CHARLES S.

The World's Locomotives. London: 1900. V. 46

LAKE, JAMES WINTER

A Catalogue of a Genuine and Extensive Collection of Engraved Prints, Portraits, Illustrated Books, Books of Prints, Atlases and British Topography . . . London: 1808. V. 46

THE LAKE Ports (Saginaw and East Saginaw - from cover.) Historical and Descriptive Review of the Lakes, Rivers, Islands, Cities, Towns, Watering Places, Fisheries, Vessels, Steamers, Captains, Disasters, Early Navigators, Mineral Wealth, Trade . . . Detroit: 1877. V. 39

LAKE SHORE AND MICHIGAN SOUTHERN RAILROAD

1861 Summer Arrangement, 1861 Condensed Time Table of . . . Between Buffalo and Cleveland, Toledo, Chicago, Milwaukee, Cincinnati, St. Louis and the West and Southwest. Buffalo: 1861. V. 39

LAKEMAN, STEPHEN

What I Saw in Kaffir-Land. Edinburgh: 1880. V. 39

LAKES, ARTHUR

Prospecting for Gold and Silver. Scranton: 1895. V. 43

THE LAKESIDE Classics. Chicago: 1904-1986. V. 37

LAKIN, THOMAS

Potting, Enamelling and Glass Staining. Leeds: 1824. V. 39

LAKING, GUY FRANCIS

The Armory of Windsor Castle: European section. London: 1904. V. 40; 42; 44; 46

Sevres Porcelain of Buckingham Palace and Windsor Castle. London: 1907. V. 40

LAKING, GUY THOMAS

The Furniture of Windsor Castle. London: 1905. V. 37; 42

LAKNISKY, V. E.

Construction of the Panama Canal: A Personal Study of American Operations on the Isthmus of Panama. St. Petersburg: 1913. V. 37

LA LANDE, JOSEPH

Art de Faire le Papier. N.P.: 1761. V. 38

The Art of Papermaking. Kilmurray: 1976. V. 38

LALANDE, JOSEPH JEROME LEFRANCAIS DE

Des Canaux de Devigation et Specialment du Canal du Midi. Paris: 1778. V. 38

LA LANDE, M. DE

Art de Faire le Papier. Paris: 1761. V. 41

LALLEMAND, HENRI DOMINIQUE

A Treatise on Artillery; to Which is Added, a Summary of Military Reconnoitering, of Fortification, of the Attack and Defence of Places, and of Castrmentation. New York: 1820. V. 40

LALLY TOLLENDAL, THOMAS ARTHUR, COMTE

Memoirs of Count Lally, From His Embarking for the East Indies, as Commander of the French Forces in That Country . . . London: 1766. V. 39; 40; 45

LALLY TOLLENDAL, TROPHIME GERARD DE, MARQUIS 1751-1830

A Defence of the French Emigrants. Addressed to the People of France. London: 1797. V. 41

LALOR, JOHN 1814-1856

Money and Morale; A Book for the Times. London: 1852. V. 40; 43

LA LOUBERE, SIMON DE

A New Historical Relation of the Kingdom of Siam . . . London: 1693. V. 45

LA LOUPE, VINCENT DE

Annotationes in Aelium Spartianum, Iulium Capitolinum, Aelium Lampridium, Vulctium Gallicanum, Trebellium Pollionem, Flauium Vopiscum. Paris: 1560. V. 37; 38

LAMA, GIUSEPPE DE 1756-1833

Vita del Cavaliere Giambattista Bodoni, Tipografo Italiano. Parma: 1816. V. 40; 41; 44

LAMA, PIETRO DE

Tavola Alimentaria Velejate detta Trajana Restituita alla Sua Vera Lezione . . . Parma: 1819. V. 38

THE LAMA-SABACHTANI, or, Cry of the Son of God. London: 1691. V. 39

LA MAIRE DE BELGES, JEAN

La Traicte Intitule de la Difference des Scismes et des Concilles de l'Eglise. Paris: 1512. V. 38

LA MAMYE CLAIRAC, LOUIS A. DE

The Field Engineer of M. le Chevalier de Clairac. London: 1773.
V. 38; 41; 43

LAMANTIA, PHILIP

Erotic Poems. Berkeley: 1946. V. 37

LAMAR, JOHN BASIL

Address of the Executive Committee to the Constitutional Union Party of Georgia (and) Address of a Portion of the Executive Committee . . . Atlanta?: 1852. V. 45

Head-Quarters, Georgia . . . Orders. The Review and Inspection of the Militia, for the Year, 1834, Will Commence Soon. Milledgeville: 1834. V. 45

LAMAR, MIRABEAU B.

Address of Gen. Lamar to the Army of Texas. Baltimore: 1836. V. 37

Gen. Mirabeau B. Lamar's Letter to the People of Georgia. N.P.: (1850). V. 37

Gen. Mirabeau B. Lamar's Letter to the People of Georgia. N.P.: 1850. V. 39

LAMAR, MIRABEAU BUONAPARTE 1798-1859

The Papers of Mirabeau Buonaparte Lamar. Austin: 1968. V. 38

Verse Memorials. New York: 1857. V. 38; 40

LAMARCK, JEAN BAPTISTE

Flore Francaise. Paris: 1811. V. 38

Histoire Naturelle des Animaux sans Animaux leur Distribution, Leurs Classes, Leurs Familles, Leurs Genres . . . Paris: 1835-45. V. 42

Hydrogeologie ou Recherches sur l'Influence qu'ont les Eaux sur la Surace du Globe Terrestre . . . Paris: 1802. V. 40

Philosophie Zoologique ou Exposition des Considerations Reltives a l'Histoire des Animaux . . . Paris: 1809. V. 38

LAMARCK'S Genera of Shells, with a Catalogue of Species. Boston: 1833. V. 46

LAMARTINE, ALPHONSE DE

Bibliotheca Curiosa. The Life and Times of Christopher Columbus. Edinburgh: 1887. V. 40

A Biographical Sketch, the Poetical Meditations and Poetical and Religious Harmones of . . . London: 1849. V. 37; 43

Oeuvres. Paris: 1826; V. 41

Travels in the East, Including a Journey in the Holy Land. Edinburgh: 1850. V. 42

LAMARTINE, ANTOINE DE

Memoirs of My Youth. London: 1849. V. 46

LA MARTINIERE, PIERRE MARTIN DE

A New Voyage into the Northern Countries, Describing the Manners, Customs and Superstition, Buildings and Habits . . . London: 1674. V. 43; 44

Voyage des Pais Septentrionaux. Paris: 1671. V. 44; 46

LA MASTER, S.

The Phantom in the Rainbow. 1929. V. 44

LAMB, ARTHUR H.

Tragedies of the Osage Hills. Pawhuska. V. 43

LAMB, CAROLINE 1785-1828

Ada Reis, a Tale. London: 1823. V. 40

Glenarvon. London: 1816. V. 37; 38; 39; 40; 42; 44; 45

Graham Hamilton. London: 1822. V. 37

A New Canto. London: 1819. V. 42

LAMB, CHARLES 1775-1834

The Adventures of Ulysses. London: 1808. V. 37; 38; 42; 43; 46

Album Verses, With a Few Others. London: 1830. V. 38; 39; 40; 41; 42; 45

Beauty and the Beast. London. V. 42

Beauty and the Beast, or a Rough Outside with a Gentle Heart, a Poem. London: 1886. V. 46

Bon Mots. London: 1893. V. 43

The Child Angel: a Dream. London: 1910. V. 46

The Correspondence: with an Essay on His Life and Genius by Thomas Purnell, Aided by the Recollections of the Author's Adopted Daughter. London: 1870. V. 39

A Dissertation Upon Roast Pig. London: 1895. V. 38

A Dissertation Upon Roast Pig. Concord: 1904. V. 37; 38; 40; 41; 43; 44

A Dissertation Upon Roast Pig. Park Ridge: 1904. V. 44

Dissertation Upon Roast Pig. New York: 1932. V. 43

Elia. Essays Which Have Appeared Under that Signature in the London Magazine. London: 1823. V. 37; 39; 41

Elia. Essay Which Have Appeared Under that Signature in the London Magazine. (with) Last Essays of Elia. London: 1823/33. V. 37; 41; 42

Elia, Essays Which Have Appeared Under That Name in the London Magazine. Philadelphia: 1828. V. 40; 42

Elia. Essays Which Have Appeared Under the Signature in the London Magazine. (with) The Last Essays of Elia. London: 1833. V. 37; 38; 46

Elia. First (and Second) Series. London: 1835. V. 39

The Essays of Elia. Philadelphia & London: 1902. V. 39

The Essays of Elia. Last Essays of Elia. London: 1915-19. V. 39

Elia, and the Last Essays of Elia. Newtown: 1929-30. V. 37; 39; 44; 45; 46

Elia and Last Essays of Elia. 1930. V. 39

Elia and the Last Essays of Elia. Newtown: 1931. V. 45

Eliana: Being the Hitherto Uncollected Writings. London: 1864. V. 39

Eliana: Being the Hitherto Uncollected Writings of . . . New York: 1864. V. 39

Essays of Elia & Last Essays of Elia. Edinburgh: 1885. V. 43

Everybody's Lamb. London: 1950. V. 44

Final Memorials of Charles Lamb. London: 1848. V. 38; 39; 42

Final Memorials of Charles Lamb. London: 1850. V. 39

John Woodvil, a Tragedy. London: 1802. V. 39; 40; 43; 44

The Last Essays of Elia; Being a Sequel to Essays Published Under That Name. London: 1833. V. 43

The Letters of Charles Lamb, with a Sketch of His Life. London: 1837. V. 46

Letters. Boston: 1905. V. 40; 41; 42

The Letters. Ithaca: 1975. V. 40

The Life, Letters and Writings of Charles Lamb. London: 1876. V. 39; 41

The Life, Letters and Writings of Charles Lamb. London: 1895. V. 39; 42

The Life and Works. London: 1899. V. 39; 42

The Life and Works. London: 1899-1900. V. 42

The Life and Works. New York: 1900. V. 42

A Masque of Days from the Last Essays of Elia. London: 1901. V. 39; 41; 45

Mrs. Leicester's School. London. V. 44

Mrs. Leicester's School. London: 1808. V. 41; 42

Mrs. Leicester's School. London: 1809. V. 37; 39; 45

Mrs. Leicester's School . . . London: 1814. V. 42

Mrs. Leicester's School. London: 1895. V. 41

The New Year's Feast on His Coming of Age. London: 1824. V. 38

Poems, Letters and Remains. London: 1874. V. 39; 42; 45

Prince Dorus. London: 1889. V. 38; 41

The Prose Work. London: 1835. V. 37; 42

Satan in Search of a Wife. London: 1831. V. 37; 39; 40

Specimens of English Dramatic Poets, who Lived About the Time of Shakespeare. London: 1808. V. 38; 40

Specimens of English Dramatic Poets, Who Lived About the Time of Shakespeare . . . London: 1813. V. 42

A Tale of Rosamund Gray and Old Blind Margaret. London: 1798. V. 37; 39; 41; 42; 43; 45

A Tale of Rosamund Gray and Old Blind Margaret. London: 1928. V. 37; 38; 42; 43

Tales from Shakespeare. London. V. 42

Tales from Shakespeare. London: 1807. V. 37; 44

Tales from Shakespeare, Designed for the Use of Young Persons. London: 1816. V. 39; 41; 42

Tales from Shakespeare, Including Those by Charles and Mary Lamb, with a Contunation by Harrison S. Morris. Philadelphia: 1893. V. 40

Tales from Shakespeare. London: 1909. V. 37; 39; 40; 41; 42; 44; 45

Tales from Shakespeare. Philadelphia: 1922. V. 44

Tales from Shakespeare. London: 1923. V. 40

Tales from Shakespeare. Illustrated by Arthur Rackham. London/New York: 1909. V. 37

Witches and Other Night-Fears. Los Angeles: 1968. V. 41

The Works. London: 1818. V. 37; 38; 39; 40; 42; 43; 44; 45

The Works. London: 1838. V. 39; 42

The Works. London: 1850. V. 42

The Works. Boston: 1865. V. 40

Works. London: 1901-08. V. 37

Works. London: 1903. V. 39; 41; 42

The Works. London: 1903-05. V. 42; 46

LAMB, DANA

The Fishing's Only Part of It. New Jersey: 1982. V. 39

LAMB, DANA S.

Bright Salmon and Brown Trout. Barre: 1964. V. 39; 43

On Trout Streams and Salmon Rivers. Barre: 1963. V. 43

Wood-Smoke and Water Cress. Barre: 1965. V. 39; 43

LAMB, EDWARD BUCKTON

Studies of Ancient Domestic Architecture, Principally Selected from the Original Drawings in the Collection of the Late Sir William Burrell. London: 1846. V. 38

LAMB, ELKIN

Except It Die. Toronto: 1945. V. 45

Things New and Old. Toronto: 1945. V. 45

LAMB, M. C.

Leather Dressing Including Dyeing, Staining and Finishing. London: 1925. V. 37; 39; 40; 41

LAMB, MARTHA J.

History of the City of New York: Its Origin, Rise and Progress. New York: & Chicago: 1877-1880. V. 46

History of the City of New York: Its Origin, Rise, and Progress. New York: 1877. V. 37

The Story of the Washington Centennial. N.P.: 1889. V. 42; 45

LAMB, MARY

Poems, Letters, and Remains, Now First Collected with Reminiscences and Notes . . . London: 1874. V. 41

LAMB, PATRICK

Royal Cookery. London: 1710. V. 40; 42

LAMB, R.

An Original and Authentic Journal of Occurences During the Late American War, from Its Commencement to the Year 1783. Dublin: 1809. V. 37

LAMB, ROBERT

Memoir of My Own Life. Dublin: 1811. V. 39; 41

LAMB, SERJEANT ROGER

An Original And Authentic Journal of Occurrences During the Late American War. Dublin: 1809. V. 37; 39; 40; 41; 42; 44; 45; 46

LAMB, WINIFRED

Excavations at Thermi in Lesbos. Cambridge: 1936. V. 40; 44

LAMBARD, WILLIAM

Archeion; or, a Discourse Upon the High Courts of Justice in England . . . London: 1635. V. 43

The Duties of Constables, Borsholders, Tythingmen and Such Other Love Ministers of the Peace . . . London: 1594. V. 45

Eirenarcha, or Of the Office of the Justices of Peace . . . (with) The Duties of Contables, Borsholders, Tythingmen. 1607, 1606. V. 38

Eirenarcha, or of the Office of the Iustices of Peace, in Foure Bookes . . . London: 1619. V. 37; 42; 45

Eirenarcha, or of the Office of the Justices of Peace, in Foure Books etc. (with) The Duties of Constables, Borsholders, Tythingmen and Such Other Lowe and Lay Ministers of the Peace. London: 1614. V. 44; 45

The Orders, Proceedings, Punishments, and Privildges of the Commons House of Parliament in England. London?: 1641. V. 46

A Perambulation of Kent. Conteining the Description, Hystorie & Customes of that Shyre. London: 1576. V. 38

LAMBART, RICHARD

A New System of Military Discipline, Founded Upon Principle. Philadelphia: 1776. V. 39; 45

LAMBE, R.

The History of Chess, Together with Short and Plain Instructions . . . London: 1765. V. 42

LAMBE, ROBERT

An Exact and Circumstantial History of the Battle of Floddon. Berwick upon Tweed: 1774. V. 43

LAMBER, JOHN

Travels through Canada and the United States of North America, in the Years 1806, 1807 & 1808. Two which are added, Biographical Notices and Anecdotes of some of the Leading Characters in the United States . . . Second Edition, Corrected and Improved. London;: 1813. V. 37

LAMBERT, A.

The Hand-Book of Needlework. London: 1842. V. 40

LAMBERT, A. B.

A Description of the Genus Pinus. London: 1832. V. 38; 42; 43; 44

An Illustration of the Gems Cinchona . . . London: 1821. V. 43

LAMBERT, ANNE THERESE, MARCHIONESS DE

Essays on Friendship and Old-Age. London: 1780. V. 37; 41; 43; 45

The Works of the Marchioness de Lambert. London: 1749. V. 38; 40

LAMBERT, AUGUSTE

Systeme Financier et Colonial . . . Paris: 1832. V. 38

LAMBERT, AYLMER BOURKE

A Description of the Genus Cinchona, Comprehending the Various Species of Vegetables from Which the Peruvian and Other Barks of a Similar Quality are Taken. London: 1797. V. 37; 41

A Description of the Genus Prinus, with Directions Relative to the Cultivation and Remarks on the Uses of the Various Species . . . London: 1832. V. 44

LAMBERT, CHARLES J.

The Voyage of the Wanderer. London: 1883. V. 38

LAMBERT, CONSTANT

Summer's Last Will and Testament - a Masque for Orchestra, Chorus and Baritone Solon, to Words Taken from the Pleasant Comedy of that Name Written in 1593 by Thomas Nashe. London: 1946. V. 46

LAMBERT DE SAUMERY, PIERRE

The Devil Turn'd Hermit; or, the Adventures of Ashtaroth banish'd from Hell. London: 1741. V. 45

LAMBERT, ELIZABETH

The Right Honorable Elizabeth Lambert . . . Against Richard Tattersall . . . for a Libel, in Which her Ladyship is Charged with Unchastity, in Eloping with Her Footman. London: 1792. V. 38

LAMBERT, FRANCOIS

In Divi Lucae Evangelium Commentarii. Nuremburg: 1524. V. 42; 44

LAMBERT, GAVIN

GWTW: The Making of Gone with the Wind. Boston: 1973. V. 45

LAMBERT, GEORGE C.

Gems of Reminiscence. Salt Lake City: 1915. V. 42; 43

LAMBERT, JOHANN HEINRICH

Cosmologische Briefe uber die Einrichtung des Weltbaues. Augspurg: 1761. V. 42

LAMBERT, JOHN

Travels through Canada and the United States of North America. London: 1813. V. 38; 39; 42; 43; 45; 46

Travels through Canada, and the United States of North America, in 1806, 1807, & 1808. London: 1814. V. 40; 44

Travels Through Canada, and the United States . . . 1806, 1807 & 1808. London: 1816. V. 40

LAMBERT, JOHN JAMES

Records of the Skinners of London. London: 1933. V. 44

LAMBERT, JOSEPH

Observations on the rural affairs of Ireland; or a practical treatise on farming, planting and gardening, adapted to the circumstances, resources, soil and climate of the country; including some remarks on the . . . Dublin: 1829. V. 37

LAMBERT, JOSEPH I.

One Hundred Years with Second Cavalry. Fort Riley: 1939. V. 44

One Hundred Years with the Second Cavalry. Topeka: 1939. V. 41

LAMBERT, MISS

The Hand-Book of Needlework with Numerous Illustrations Engraved by J. J. Butler. New York: 1842. V. 38; 41; 42; 43

LAMBERT, SAMUEL

Information Useful for Navigators. Salem: 1821. V. 38; 41

LAMBERT, T. S.

Practical Anatomy, Physiology and Pathology. Portland: 1852. V. 45

LAMBERT, T. W.

Fishing in British Columbia. London: 1907. V. 42

LAMBERT VON HERSFELD

Germanorvm Res Praeclare Olim Gestae. Tubingen: 1533. V. 38

LAMBERT, W. G.

Babylonian Wisdom Literature. Oxford: (1975). V. 37

LAMBERT, WILL

Report of the Ceremonies of the Laying of the Corner Stone of the Capitol of Texas. Austin: 1885. V. 39; 42

LAMBERT, WILLIAM

Abstracts of Calculations to Ascertain the Longitude of the Capitol in the City of Washington, from Greenwich Observatory, in England. Washington City: 1817. V. 46

Abstracts of Calculations to Ascertain the Longitude of the Capitol in the City of Washington, From Greenwich Observatory, in England. (with) To the Critical Reviewers of Boston, in the State of Massachusetts. Washington City: 1810. V. 37

LAMBETH, JOSEPH A.

Lambeth Method of Cake Decoration & Practical Pastries. London: 1937. V. 44

LAMBETH, WILLIAM ALEXANDER

Thomas Jefferson as an Architect and a Designer of Landscapes. Boston and New York: 1913. V. 42

LAMBINET, PIERRE

Recherches Historiques, Litteraires et Critiques sur l'Origine de l'Imprimerie. Brussels: 1799. V. 38

LAMBOURNE, ALFRED

Scenic Utah Pen and Pencil. New York: 1891. V. 37; 42

LAMBTON, A. H.

From Prison to Power. London: 1893. V. 42

LAMENTATIONES Germanicae nationis. Schlettstadt: 1526. V. 37

LAMI, EUGENE

Voyage en Angleterre. Paris: 1829-30. V. 46

LAMM, CARL JOHAN

Cotton in Mediaeval Textiles of the Near East. Paris: 1937. V. 37; 43

LAMON, ROBERT S.

Megiddo I: Seasons of 1924-34, Strata I-V. Chicago: 1939. V. 40

LAMOND, HENRY

The Sea Trout. London: 1916. V. 41

The Sea-Trout: a Study in Natural History. London & Manchester: 1916. V. 41

LA MONNOYE, BERNARD DE 1641-1728

Noei Bourguignon . . . Dijon: 1720. V. 46

Traduction des Noels Bourguignons. Paris: 1802. V. 39

LAMONT, DANIEL S.

In the Senate of the United States . . . Transmitting Report of Board of Engineers Regarding Obstructions in the Columbia River. Washington: 1893. V. 42

LAMONT, JAMES

Seasons with the Sea-Horses. London: 1861. V. 38; 40; 43; 45

Seasons with the Sea-Horses; or, Sporting Adventures in the Northern Seas. New York: 1861. V. 37; 43

LA MOTE FOUQUE, friedrich, baron de 1874-

uNDINE & aSLAUGA'S kNIGHT. London. V. 46

LA MOTRAYE, AUBRY DE

Travels through Europe, Asia and into Part of Africa. London: 1723/1732. V. 38; 43

LAMOTTE, A.

Voyage dans le Nord de l'Europe . . . Londres: 1813. V. 43

LA MOTTE, ANTOINE HOUDART DE

Fables Nouvelles, Dediees au Roy . . . Paris: 1719. V. 39

LA MOTTE FOUQUE, FRIEDRICH HEINRICH KARL, FREIHERR DE 1777-1843

The Magic Ring . . . Edinburgh: 1825. V. 46

Undine. London: 1888. V. 37

Undine. London: 1897. V. 40; 41

Undine & Aslauga'a Knight. London: 1901. V. 46

Undine. 1909. V. 45

Undine. London: 1909. V. 40; 41; 45

Ondine. Paris: 1912. V. 46

Undine. London: 1919. V. 40; 44; 46

Undine. 1930. V. 43; 45

Undine. New York: 1930. V. 40; 44; 46

L'AMOUR, LOUIS

Heller with a Gun: A Gold Medal Original. Greenwich: (1958-1955). V. 37

Hopalong Cassidy and the Trail to Seven Pines. Garden City: 1951. V. 44

Smoke from this Altar. Oklahoma City: 1939. V. 46

LAMPE, JOHN FREDERICK

A Plain and Compendious Method of Teaching Thorough Bass After the Most Rational Manner with Proper Rules for Practice. London: 1737. V. 38; 40

LAMPEDUSA, GIUSEPPE DE

The Leopard. New York: 1989. V. 44

LAMPEDUSA, GIUSEPPE DI

The Leopard. 1988. V. 42

LAMPERT, W.

Food Limitation and the structure of Planton Communities. Stuttgart: 1986. V. 38

LAMPMAN, ARCHIBALD

At the Long Sault and Other New Poems. Toronto: 1943. V. 44

LAMPMAN, BEN HUR

Centralia Tragedy and Trial. Tacoma: 1920. V. 43

LAMSON, DAVID R.

Two Years' Experience Among the Shakers. West Boylston: 1848. V. 40

LAMSON, J.

Round Cape Horn. Bangor: 1878. V. 39; 40; 42

LAMSON, MARY SWIFT

Life and Education of Laura Dwey Bridgman, The Deaf, Dumb and Blind Girl. Boston: 1879. V. 37

LAMY, BERNARD 1640-1715

Apparatus Biblicus. Lyons: 1723. V. 42

The Art of Speaking. London: 1676. V. 38; 42; 44; 46

Traite de Perspective, ou Sont Contenus les Fondements de la peinture. Paris: 1701. V. 44

LANA TERZI, FRANCESCO 1631-1687

Magisterium naturae, et Artis, Opus Physico-Mathematicorum . . . Brescia: 1684-86, 1692. V. 38

Magisterium Naturae, et Artis. Parma: 1692. V. 45

Prodromo Overo Saggio di Alcune Inventioni Nuove Premesso all'Arte Maestra . . . Brescia: 1670. V. 37; 40; 43

LANCASHIRE & YORKSHIRE RAILWAY

By-Laws, Rules and Regulataions of the Lancashire and Yorkshire Railway Co., 1861. Manchester: 1861. V. 38

THE LANCASHIRE Garland; or Sir William Stanley's Travels. N.P.. V. 42

LANCASTER, I.

The Soaring Brids. ?Chicago: 1900. V. 43

LANCASTER, JOSEPH

The British System of Education. Washington: 1812. V. 39

Epitome of Some of the Chief Events and Transactions in the Life of Joseph Lancaster . . . New Haven: 1833. V. 39; 42

Improvements in Education As It Respects the Industrious Classes of the Community. London: 1805. V. 45

Improvements in Education. London: 1806. V. 37; 41

Improvements in Education, As It Respects the Industrious Classes of the Community. New York: 1807. V. 39

The Lancasterian System of Education, with Improvements. Baltmire: 1821. V. 44

Manual of the Lancasterian System, of Teaching, Reading, Writing, Arithmetic and Needle-Work. New York: 1820. V. 39

LANCASTER, NATHANIEL

The Plan of an Essay upon Delicacy. With a Specimen of the Work. In Two Dialogues. London: 1748. V. 39

The Pretty Gentleman; or Softness of Manners Vindicated from the False Ridicule Exhibited Under the Character of William Fribble, Esq. London: 1747. V. 43

LANCASTER, OSBERT

All Done from Memory. London: 1953. V. 45; 46

Classical Landscape with Figures. London: 1947. V. 45

Here of All Places. London: 1959. V. 38

Progress at Pelvis Bay. London: 1936. V. 38

With an Eye to the Future. London: 1967. V. 43; 44

LANCASTER, ROBERT A.

Historic Virginia Homes & Churches. Philadelphia: 1915. V. 37; 42; 46

LANCASTER, WILLIAM T.

Chartulary of the Cistercian Abbey of Fountains in the West Riding of the County of York. Leeds: 1915. V. 45

LANCELLOTTI, SECONDO

Farfalloni De gli Antichi Historici. Venetia: 1636. V. 37

LANCELOT, CLAUDE 1615?-1695

A New Method of Learning . . . the Greek Tongue . . . London: 1808. V. 39

A New Method of Learning the Italian Tongue. To which is added, an Italian Vocabulary, Choice Italian Phrases, Familiar Dialogues, Entertaining Stories . . . London: 1750. V. 37

LANCELOTTI, GIOVANNI PAULI 1510-1591

Corpus Juris Canonici, Emendatum et Notis Illustratum. Lyons: 1591. V. 40

LANCHESTER, ELSA

Charles Laughton and I. New York: 1938. V. 42; 45

LANCISI, GIOVANNI MARIA 1654-1720

De Motu Coprdis et Aneurysmatibus. Rome: 1728. V. 38; 40

LAND, ANDREW

Tales of a Fairy Court. London: (ca. 1907). V. 37

THE LAND of Sunshine, Fruit and Flowers. Columbus: 1898. V. 44

LANDACRE, PAUL

California Hills and Other Wood Engravings. Los Angeles: 1931. V. 37; 38; 39; 45; 46

LANDAIS, PETER

Memorial, to Justify Peter Landai's (sic) Conduct During the Late War. Boston: 1784. V. 38; 40; 43; 46

LANDAUER, BELLA CLARA

Bookplates from the Aeronautica Collection of . . . New York: 1930. V. 42

Early American Trade Cards from the Collection of . . . New York: 1927. V. 37; 42; 44

Some Aeronautical Music from the Collection of . . . Paris: 1933. V. 42

LANDE, LAWRENCE

The Development of the Voyageur Contract (1686-1821). 1989. V. 42

The Development of the Voyageur Contract, (1686-1821). Montreal: 1989. V. 43; 44

The Lawrence Lande Collection of Canadiana in . . . McGill University, with Rare and Unusual Candiana; First Supplement to the Lande Bibliography. Montreal: 1965/71. V. 42

The Lawrence Lande Collection of Canadiana in the Redpath Library of McGill University A Bibliography. Montreal: 1965. V. 37

The Lawrence Lande Collection of Canadiana in the Redpath Library of McGill University. A Bibliography. (with) . . . the first supplement. Montreal: 1971. V. 37

Rare and Unusual Canadiana, First Supplement to the Land Bibliography. Montreal: 1971. V. 40

LANDE, LAWRENCE M.

A Checklist of Printed and Manuscript Material Relating to the Canadian Indian . . . Montreal: 1974. V. 41

John Law: Banque Royale and Compagnie des Indes: a Bibliographical Monograph. Montreal: 1980. V. 46

Old Lamps Aglow. Montreal: 1957. V. 44

LANDELLS, E.

The Boy's Own Toy-Maker. New York: 1860. V. 40; 45

The Girl's Own Toy-Maker and Book of Recreation. London: 1860. V. 38

LANDEN, JOHN

A Dicourse Concerning the Residual Analysis . . . London: 1758. V. 43

Mathematical Memoirs Respecting a Variety of Subjects . . . London: 1780/89. V. 43

LANDER, FREDERICK WEST

Additional Estimate for For Kearney, South Pass, and Honey Lake Wagon Road. Letter from . . . Transmitting a Communication from Colonel Lander. Washington: 1861. V. 39; 41

Practicability of Railroads through the South Pass. Letter from the Secretary of the Interior, Transmitting a Report from . . . Washington: 1858. V. 37

LANDER, GEORGE

Bleak House; or Poor 'Jo'. A Drama in Three Acts. London: 1883? V. 40

LANDER, RICHARD

Journal of an Expedition to Explore the Course and Termination of the Niger; with a Narrative of a Voyage Down that River to Its Termination. London: 1832. V. 39; 40; 43

Journal of an Expedition to Explore the Course and Termination of the Niger with a Narrative of a Voyage Down the River to Its Termination. London: 1845. V. 41

Records of Captain Clapperton's Last Expedition to Africa . . . London: 1830. V. 42; 43

LANDER, S.

Our Own School Arithmetic. Greensborog: 1863. V. 38

LANDI, GUILIO, CONTE

La Vita Di Esopo Tradotta et Adornata dal Signor Conte Givlio Landi. Venice: 1550. V. 44

LANDI, ORTENSIO

Incerti Authoris Brevis Elucubrtio Super Inventa, de His Morbis a Quibus Humana Corpora Infestari . . . Venetiis: 1553. V. 40

LANDIS, CHARLES K.

Carabajal, the Jew. Vineland: 1894. V. 44

LANDMANN, GEORGE

A Universal Gazetteer; or, Geographical Dictionary of the World . . . London: 1835. V. 45

LANDMANN, GEORGE THOMAS 1780-1854

Adventures and Recollections of Colonel Landmann. London: 1852. V. 41

LANDMARKS Club Cook Book. Los Angeles: 1903. V. 45

LANDOLPHE, JEAN FRANCOIS

Memoires . . . Contenant L'Histoire de Ses Voyages Pendant Trente-Six ans, Aux Cotes D'Afrique et Aux Deux Ameriques. Paris: 1823. V. 37

LANDOLPHO DI SASSONIA

Vita di Giesu Christo Nostro Redentore Fatta Volgare da M. Francesco Sansovino. Venice: 1576. V. 37

LANDON, JOSPEH

Angle of Attack. Garden City: 1952. V. 37

LANDON, LETITIA ELIZABETH

Ethel Chruchill: or, The Two Brides. London. V. 39

The Golden Violet, With Its Tales of Romance & Chivalry; and Other Poems. London: 1827. V. 42; 44; 45

The Improvistrice; and Other Poems. London: 1824. V. 40

The Poetical Works of . . . London: 1827. V. 38

Poetical Works. London: 1853. V. 43

Romance and Reality. London: 1831. V. 43

LANDOR, ARNOLD HENRY SAVAGE 1865-1924

Across Widest Africa. London: 1907. V. 39; 40

Across Unknown South America. Boston: 1913. V. 41; 42

Across Unknown South America. London: 1913. V. 42; 46

China and the Allies. London: 1901. V. 38

The Gems of the East. London: 1904. V. 42

In the Forbidden Land. London: 1898. V. 42

In the Forbidden Land. London: 1899. V. 45

In the Forbidden land. New York: 1899. V. 38; 41

LANDOR, EDWARD WILSON

Adventures in the North of Europe. London: 1836. V. 43; 44

LANDOR, ROBERT EYRES

Selections from His Poetry and Prose. London: 1927. V. 37

LANDOR, WALTER SAVAGE 1775-1864

Andrea of Hungary, and Giovanna of Naples. London: 1839. V. 38; 39

Dry Sticks Fagoted. Edinburgh: 1858. V. 39

Epicurus, Leontion and Ternissa. London: 1896. V. 38; 41; 43; 44

Friendship and Love from the Philosophers. London: 1909. V. 41

Gebir; a Poem. Oxford: 1803. V. 39; 40; 42

Gebir, Count Julian, and Other Poems. London: 1831. V. 46

The Hellenics. London: 1847. V. 39

The Hellenics. Edinburgh: 1859. V. 39

Heroic Idyls, with Additional Poems. London: 1863. V. 39; 42

Idyllia Heroica decem Librum Phaleuciorum Unum Partim Jam Primo Partim Iterum Atq Tertio Edit Savagius Landor . . . 1820. V. 40

Imaginary Conversations of Literary Men and Statesmen. London: 1824. V. 45; 46

Imaginary Conversations of Literary Men and Statesmen. London: 1826-28. V. 38; 40; 46

Imaginary Conversations of Literary men and Statesman. London: 1826-29. V. 39

Imaginary Conversations of Literary Men and Statesmen. London: printed for Taylor: 1829. V. 37

Imaginary Conversations of Greeks and Romans. London: 1853. V. 39

Imaginary Conversations. London: 1891. V. 39

Imaginary Conversations. 1936. V. 39

Imaginary Conversations. New York: 1936. V. 44

Imaginary Conversations. Verona: 1936. V. 38; 39; 42

Imaginary Conversation of King Carlo-Alberto and the Duchess Belgioioso, on the Affairs and Prospects of Italy. London: 1848. V. 37

The Last Fruit Off an Old Tree. London: 1853. V. 39; 40

Letters of an American. London: 1854. V. 40; 42; 46

Literary Hours. Liverpool: 1837. V. 41

The Pentameron and Pentalogia. London: 1837. V. 39; 42

Pericles and Aspasia. London: 1836. V. 38; 39; 40; 42; 43; 44

Pericles and Aspasia. London: 1903. V. 46

Pericles and Aspasia. New York: 1903. V. 43

LANDOR, WALTER SAVAGE 1775-1864 continued

Poemata et Inscriptiones. London: 1847. V. 39

Popery: British and Foreign. London: 1851. V. 42

The Sculptured Garland. London: 1948. V. 37

The Works of Walter Savage Landor. London: 1846. V. 40; 42

The Works and Life. London: 1874-76. V. 39; 42

The Works. London: 1876. V. 38

Works. London: 1891-93. V. 46

Complete Works. London: 1927. V. 38; 40; 42

The Complete Works. London: 1927-36. V. 37; 38; 39; 40; 41; 44; 46

Complete Works. London: 1969. V. 37

The Complete Works . . . New York: 1969. V. 38

Complete Works. New York & London: 1969. V. 39; 40

The Works and life. London: 1876. V. 37

LANDRE, CHRISTOPHE

Hauss Artzney. Augusburg: 1578. V. 38; 42; 44

LANDRIANI, PAOLO

Osservazioni sui Difetti Prodotti Nei Teatri Dalla Cattiva Construzione del Palco Scenico e su Alcune Inavvertenze nel Dipingere le Decorazioni . . . Milan: 1815-24. V. 40; 44

Osservazioni sui Difetti Prodotti Nei Teatri Dalla Cattiva Construzione del Palco Scenico e su Alcune Inavvertenze nel Dipingere le Decorazioni con un'Aggiunta ed un'Appendice . . . Milan: 1825. V. 37; 42

LANDRIN, M. H. C.

A Treatise on Steel. Philadelphia: 1868. V. 44

LANDSBOROUGH, D.

A Popular History of British Seaweeds, Comprising Their Structure, Fructification, Specific Characters, Arrangement, and General Distribution, with Notices of Some of the Fresh Water Algae. London: 1857. V. 45

LANDSDORFF, ALEXANDER

Tall-i-Bakun A, season of 1932. Chicago: (1942). V. 37

LANDSEER, EDWIN

The Sportsman's Annual. First Series: Dogs. London: 1836. V. 39

The Works. London: 1879-80. V. 37

The Works of Sir Edwin Landseer. Illustrated by Forty-Four Steel Engravings and about two hundred woodcuts . . . with a history of his art-life by W. Cosmo Monkhouse. 1880. V. 37

LANDSEER, JOHN

Lectures on the Art of Engraving. London: 1807. V. 38; 42; 43

Sabaean Researches . . . London: 1823. V. 42

LANDSEER, THOMAS

Characteristic Sketches of Animals, Principally from the Zoological Gardens . . . London: 1832. V. 37; 41; 43; 44; 46

Life and Letters of William Beewick. London: 1871. V. 44

Monkey-ana or Men in Miniature, Designed and Etched . . . London: 1827. V. 39

LANDSELL, HENRY

Through Siberia. London: 1882. V. 40

LANDSTROM, BJORN

Ships of the Pharaohs. 4000 Years of Egyptian Shipbuilding. Garden City: 1970. V. 40; 44

LANDWEHR, JOHN

Emblem Books in the Low Countries, 1554-1949. Utrecht: 1970. V. 40; 43

Emblem and Fable Books printed in the Low Countries 1542-1813. Utrecht: 1988. V. 44

Romeyn De Hooghe (1645-1708) as Book Illustrator. Amsterdam: 1970. V. 40

V. O. C. A Bibliography of Publications Relating to the Dutch East Indian Company 1602-1800. Utrecht: 1990. V. 44

LANDY, JAMES

Cincinnati Past and Present. Cincinnti: 1872. V. 38

LANE, ALLEN STANLEY

Emperor Norton, the Mad Monarch of America. Caldwell: 1939. V. 46

LANE, J. C.

Hawaiian Directory and Hand Book of the Kingdom of Hawaii. San Francisco: 1888. V. 38

LANE, JOHN

Aubrey Beardsley and the Yellow Book. London: 1903. V. 40; 43

LANE, JOSEPH

Biography of Joseph Lane, 'Not Inappropriately Styled by His Brother Officers and Soldiers, The Marion of the War . . . ' Washington: 1852. V. 37; 41

LANE, LEVI COOPER

The Surgery of the Head and Neck. Philadelphia: 1898. V. 37; 41; 42

LANE, LUNSFORD

The Narrative of Lunsford Lane, Formerly of Raleigh N.C. Boston: 1842. V. 42

LANE, MOSES

The Protestant School. London: 1698. V. 39

LANE-POOLE, STANLEY

Coins and Medals: Their Place in History and ARt. London: 1885. V. 41

LANE, RICHARD

Images from the Floating World: the Japanese Print. New York: 1978. V. 39; 41

LANE, RICHARD JAMES

Reproductions in Photography of the First Proofs of Early Lithographic Drawings. London: 1868. V. 40

LANE, SAMUEL

Fifty Years and Over of Akron and Summitt County . . . Akron: 1892. V. 37; 40; 43; 44

LANE, W. ARBUTHNOT

Cleft Palate: Treatment of Simple Fractures, by Operation; Diseases of Joints; Antrechtomy; Hernia, Etc. London: 1897. V. 42

LANE, WALTER P.

The Adventures and Recollections of Gen. Walter P. Lane, with Sketches of the Texian, Mexican and Late Wars and Indian Fights. Marshall: 1928. V. 39

LANES, SELMA G.

The Art of Maurice Sendak. New York: 1980. V. 39

The Art Of Maurice Sendak. London: 1981. V. 41

LANFRANC OF MILAN

Lanfrank's 'Science of Cirurgie.' London: 1894. V. 42

LANFREY, PIERRE 1828-1877

The History of Napoleon the First. London: 1871. V. 39

LANG, ANDREW

Angling Sketches. London: 1891. V. 39; 41; 42

The Animal Story Book. London: 1896. V. 40; 41

Ballades in Blue China. Portland: 1907. V. 43

Ballads and Lyrics of Old France; with Other Poems. London: 1872. V. 42

Ban and Arriere Ban - a Rally of Fugitive rhymes. 1894. V. 46

A Batch of Golfing Papers. London: 1892. V. 40

The Blue Fairy Book. London: 1889. V. 42

The Blue Poetry Book. London: 1891. V. 37; 41; 42; 44; 46

The Book of Dreams and Ghosts. London: 1897. V. 39

The Book of Romance. London: 1902. V. 40

The Book of Saints and Heroes. London: 1912. V. 43

The Brown Fairy Book. London: 1904. V. 43; 46

The Brown Fairy Book. London: 1911. V. 40

The Brown Fairy Book. Edited by Andrew Lang. New York: 1904. V. 37

Cock Lane and Common Sense. London: 1894. V. 39

Complete Set of the Lang Fairy Books. The Blue, The Red, The Green, the Yellow, the Pink, the Grey, the Violet, the Crimson, the Brown, the Orange, the Olive, the Lilac. London: 1889-1910. V. 46

The Crimson Fairy Book. London: 1903. V. 39; 42; 46

The Crimson Fairy Book. Edited by Andrew Lang. New York: 1903. V. 37

The Fairy Books. London: 1889-1910. V. 44

The Green Fairy Book. London: 1892. V. 37; 42

The Grey Fairy Book. London: 1900. V. 40; 42; 45

A History of Scotland from the Roman Occupation. Edinburgh: 1900-07. V. 38

A History of Scotland from the Roman Occupation. London: 1900-07. V. 42

The Idylls of Theocritus, Bion & Moschus. London: 1922. V. 37

Letters to Dead Authors. London: 1886. V. 41

Letters on Literature. London: 1889. V. 39

The Library. London: 1892. V. 38; 40

The Life and Letters of John Gibson Lockhart. London: 1897. V. 43

The Life and Letters of John Gibson Lockhart. New York: 1897. V. 44

Lost Leaders. London: 1889. V. 44

Myth, Ritual and Religion. London: 1887. V. 42

LANG, ANDREW continued

The Nursery Rhyme Book. London: 1897. V. 46

Ode on a Distant Memory of 'Jane Eyre.' N.P.. V. 38

The Olive Fairy Book. London: 1907. V. 41; 44

Oxford Brief Historical and Descriptive Notes. London: 1880. V. 38

The Pink Fairy Book. London: 1897. V. 41

The Pink Fairy Book. London: New York: & Bombay: 1897. V. 45

Poetical Works. London: 1923. V. 38

Prince Prigio. Bristol: 1889. V. 42; 44

Prince Ricardo of Pantouflia. London: 1893. V. 45; 46

Prince Charles Edward. London: 1900. V. 40

Prince Charles Edward. London, Paris & New York: 1900. V. 40

Prince Charles Edward. Paris: 1900. V. 44; 46

Princes and Princesses. London: 1908. V. 45

The Princess Nobody - a Tale of Fairyland. London. V. 44

The Princess Nobody. London: 1884. V. 42; 43; 45

The Red Fairy Book. London: 1890. V. 43

The Red True Story Book. London: 1895. V. 41

The Red Book of Animal Stories. London: 1899. V. 44

The Red Romance Book. London: 1905. V. 40

The Red Book of Heroes. London: 1909. V. 40; 42

St. Andrews. London: 1893. V. 44

Tales of a Fairy Court. London: 1907. V. 40

Tales of Troy and Greece. London: 1907. V. 45

XXXII Ballads in Blue China. London: 1899. V. 40

The True Story Book. London: 1893. V. 42; 43

XXII Ballades in Blue China. London: 1880. V. 43; 45

The Violet Fairy Book. London: 1901. V. 42; 44; 45; 46

The Yellow Fairy Book. London: 1894. V. 39; 42; 44

LANG, E. M.

The Etchings of Anders Zorn. London: 1923. V. 40

LANG, H. C.

Rhopaloccera Europae Descripta et Delineata. London: 1884. V. 42; 43

LANG, HENRY C.

The Butterflies of Europe Described and Figured. London: 1884. V. 38; 40

LANG, HERBERT H.

Nineteenth Century Historians of the Gulf States. Austin: 1954. V. 39

LANG, JOHN D.

Report of a Visit to Some of the Tribes of Indians, Located West of the Mississippi River. New York: 1843. V. 37; 40; 41; 44; 45; 46

Report of a Visit to Some of the Tribes of Indians Located West of the Mississippi River. Providence: 1843. V. 37; 41; 46

LANG, JOHN DUNMORE

The Australian Emigrant's Manual. London: 1852. V. 41

Cooksland in North-Eastern Australia ... London: 1847. V. 38

New Zealand in 1839 ... London: 1839. V. 46

Queensland Australia. London: 1861. V. 38

LANG, LEONORA BLANCHE

The All Sorts of Stories Book. London: 1911. V. 41

The Book of Princes and Princesses. London: 1908. V. 38; 39

LANG, PAUL HENRY

Music in Western Civilization. New York: 1941. V. 45

LANG, THEODORE F.

Loyal West Virginia from 1861 to 1865 with an Introductory Chapter on the Status of Virginia for Thirty Years Prior to the War. Baltimore: 1895. V. 40; 42

LANG, WILLIAM

History of Seneca County, from the Close of the Revolutionary War to July, 1880. Springfield: 1880. V. 46

LANG, WILLIAM BAILEY

Views, with Ground Plans, of the Highland Cottages at Roxbury, Near Boston. Boston: 1845. V. 40

LANG, WILLIAM W.

A Paper on the Resources and Capabilities of Texas ... to which is Added a Brief Summary of the Advantages of the State as a Field for Immigration. New York: 1881. V. 37

Texas And Her Capabilities by Wm. W. Lang of Marlin, Texas. (New York): 1881. V. 37

LANGAARD, JOHAN H.

Edvard Munch: Masterpieces from the Artist's Collection in the Munch Museum in Oslo. New York: 1972. V. 46

LANGALLERIE, MARQUESS DE

The Memoirs of the Marquess de Langallerie ... London: 1708. V. 38

LANGBAINE, GERALD 1656-1692

An Account of the English Dramatick Poets, or Some Observations and Remarks on the Lives and Writings ... Oxford: 1691. V. 37; 39; 40; 41; 42; 43; 44; 45; 46

LANGBAINE, GERARD 1656-1692

An Account of the English Dramatick Poets ... (with) The Lives and Characters of the English Dramatick Poets. Oxford: 1699. V. 46

The Lives and Characters of the English Dramatic Poets. London: 1698. V. 38; 43

The Lives and Characters of the English Dramatick Poets. London: 1699. V. 40; 45

LANGDON, EMMA F.

The Cripple Creek Strike 1903-1904. Victor: 1904. V. 42

LANGDON, JOHN EMERSON

Canadian Silversmiths & Their Marks 1667 = 1867. Lunenburg: 1960. V. 43

Canadian Silversmiths, 1700-1900. Toronto: 1966. V. 43; 44

LANGDON, STEPHEN

Babylonian Liturgies: Sumerian Texts from the Early Period and from the Library of Ashurbanipal ... Paris: 1913. V. 44

Excavations at Kish. Paris: 1924. V. 40; 42; 44

Sumerian and Babylonian Psalms. Paris: 1909. V. 44

Tablets from the Archives of Drehem ... Paris: 1911. V. 44

The Venus Tablets of Ammizaduga. London: 1928. V. 40; 42

LANGDON, WILLIAM B.

Ten Thousand Chinese Things. A Descriptive Catalogue of the Chinese Collection, Now Exhibiting at the St. George's Place, Hyde Park Corner, London, with Condensed Accounts of the Genius, Government, History ... London: 1842. V. 40

Ten Thousand Things Relating to China and the Chinese ... Together with a Synopsis of the Chinese Collection. London: 1842. V. 41

LANGE, ANDREW

The Tercentenary of Izaak Walton. London: 1893. V. 37

LANGE, DOROTHEA

An American Exodus. New York: 1939. V. 37; 41

LANGE, FRED W.

History of Baseball in California and Pacific Coast Leagues, 1847-1938. Oakland: 1938. V. 37; 40

LANGE, FREDERICK ALBERT

History of Materialism and Criticism of Its Present Importance. London: 1892. V. 39

LANGE, GERALD

Starless & Bible Black. Poynette: 1975. V. 39; 42; 44

Starless & Bible Black. Poynette: (1975). V. 37

LANGE, HENRY

Atlas von Nord-Amerika. Nach den Neuesten Materialien ... Braunschweig: 1854. V. 38

LANGE, K.

Egypt: Architecture-Sculpture-Painting in Three Thousand Years. London: 1968. V. 40; 44

LANGER, SUSAN K.

Philosophy in a New Key. Cambridge: 1942. V. 45

LANGER VON BOLKENHAYN, JOHANNES 1484-1548

Ursach ... Von Ceremonien Christlichen ... Wittenberg: 1529. V. 46

LANGEVIN, HECTOR L.

Cinq Mois Chez. V. 44

LANGEWIS, LAURENS

Decorative Art in Indonesian Textiles. Amsterdam: 1964. V. 37

LANGFORD, J. A.

Staffordshire and Warwickshire, Past and Present. London. V. 38; 41

LANGFORD, NATHANIEL PITT

Diary of the Washburn Expedition to the Yellowstone and Firehole Rivers in the Year 1870. N.P.: 1905. V. 45; 46

Diary of the Washburn Expedition to the Yellowstone and Firehold Rivers in the Year 1870. St. Paul: 1905. V. 38; 44; 45

LANGFORD, NATHANIEL PITT continued

Diary of the Washburn Expedition to the Yellowstone and Firehole Rivers in the Year 1870. N.P.: (1905). V. 37

Diary of the Washburn Expedition to the Yellowstone and Fireholes Rivers in the year 1870. (St. Paul, Minn.): 1905. V. 37

Vigilante days and Ways: the Pioneers of the Rockies. Boston: 1890. V. 39; 45; 46

Vigilante Days and Ways: the Pioneers of the Rockies: The Makers and Making of Montana, Idaho, Oregon, Washington and Wyoming. New York: 1893. V. 44

Vigilante Days and Ways, the Pioneers of the Rockies the Makers and Making of Montana, Idaho, Oregon, Washington and Wyoming. New York: & St. Paul: 1893. V. 42

LANGFORD, T.

Plain and Full Instructions to Raise all Sorts of Fruit-Trees that Prosper in England . . . London: 1681. V. 39

Plain and Full Instructions to Raise All Sorts of Fruit Trees that Prosper in England, in that Method and Order . . . London: 1696. V. 37; 45

LANGHAM, WILLIAM

The garden of Health. London: 1597. V. 39

LANGHORNE, JOHN

The Correspondence of Theodosius and Constantia, from Their First Acquaintance to the Departure of Theodosius. London: 1766. V. 40

The Country Justice. London: 1774. V. 41

The Fables of Flora. London: 1804. V. 39

The Letters that Passed Between Theodosius and Constantia. London: 1764. V. 40; 46

Owen of Carron: a Poem. London: 1778. V. 37

The Poetical Works of . . . London: 1766. V. 38; 39; 40; 42; 43; 45

Solyman and Almena. London: 1762. V. 40; 42; 44

The Viceroy; a Poem. London: 1762. V. 42

LANGIUS, J. P.

Democritus Ridens, Sive Campus Recreationum Honestarum. Amsterdam: 1649. V. 37

LANGLAND, JOSEPH

A Dream of Love, by Joseph Langland. (Bradenton, Fl): 1986. V. 37

LANGLAND, ROBERT

Visio Willi' de Petro Plouhman. London: 1813. V. 42

LANGLAND, WILLIAM

The Vision of Pierce Plowman, Now Fyrste Imprynted by Roberte Crowley, Dwellyng in Ely rentes in Holburne. London: 1550. V. 38

The Vision of Pierce Plowman . . . London: 1561. V. 41

The Vision and Creed of Piers Ploughman. London: 1836. V. 42; 45

The Vision of William Concerning Piers the Plowman in Three Parallel Texts Together with Richard the Redeless. Oxford: 1886. V. 45

The Vision of William Concerning Piers the Plowman. New Rochelle: 1901. V. 38

LANGLES, LOUIS MATHIEU

Catalogue des Livres, Imprimes et Manuscrits. Paris: 1825. V. 38

LANGLEY, BATTY 1696-1751

Ancient Architecture, Restored and Improved, By a Great Variety of Grand and Usefull Designs, Entirely New in the Gothick Mode for the Ornamenting of Buildings and Gardens Exceeding Every Thing Thats Extant. N.P.: 1742. V. 42

The Builder's Compleat Assistant or a Library of Arts and Sciences Absolutely Necessary to be Understood by Builders and Workmen in General. London: 1738. V. 44; 45

The Builder's Director, or Bench Mate. London: 1751. V. 38

The Builder's Jewel; or, the Youth's Instructor . . . London: 1757. V. 40; 44; 46

The Builder's Director, or Bench-Mate. London: 1763. V. 38; 45

The Builder's Jewel; or the Youth's Instructor . . . Dublin: 1766. V. 44

The Builder's Complete Assistant. London: 1766. V. 41

The Builder's Jewel . . . London: 1768. V. 42

The Builder's Jewel; or the Youth's Instructor and Remembrancer. London: 1787. V. 41

The Builder's Jewel . . . London: 1794. V. 45; 46

The Builder's Jewel; or the Youth's Instructor and Workman's Remembrancer. London: 1797. V. 43

The Builder's Jewel. Haddington: 1805. V. 38

The Builder's Jewel; or, the Youth's Instructor and Workman's Remembrancer . . . Haddington: 1805. V. 41

The City and Country Builder's and Workman's Treasury of Designs. London: 1740. V. 41

The City and Country Builder's and Workman's Treasury of Designs. London: 1741. V. 38

The City and Country Builder's and Workman's Treasury of Designs. London: 1741? V. 39

The City and Country Builder's and Workman's Treatment of Designs . . . London: 1750. V. 43

The City and Country Builder's and Workman's Treasury. London: 1756. V. 38

The City and Country Builder's and Workman's Treasury of Designs; or, the Art of Drawing and Working the Ornamental Parts of Architecture. London: 1770. V. 41

The City and Country builder's and workman's treasure of designs: or the art of drawing and working the ornamental parts of architecture . . . with an appendix . . . By B.L. London: (1741). V. 37

Gothic Architecture, Improved by Rules and Proportions. London: 1747. V. 38; 42

Gothic architecture, improved by rules and proportions. In many grand desigs of columns, doors, windows, chinmey pieces, arcades, colonades, porticos, umbrellos, temples, and pavilions &c. With plans, elevations and profiles . . . London: (c. 1790). V. 37

The London Prices of Bricklayers Materials and Works . . . London: 1749. V. 38

New Principles of Gardenings. London: 1728. V. 38

Practical Geometry Applied to the Useful Arts of Building, Surveying, Gardening and Mensuration . . . London: 1726. V. 45

A Sure Method of Improving Estates. London: 1728. V. 38; 40; 42; 43

The Young Builder's Rudiments. London: 1730. V. 38

LANGLEY, CLARA A.

South Carolina Deed Abstracts, 1719-1772. Easley: 1983-1984. V. 40; 42

LANGLEY, E. A.

Narrative of a Residence at the Court of Meer Ali Moorad; with Wild Sports in the Valley of the Indus. London: 1860. V. 40

LANGLEY, HENRY G.

A Directory of the City of Oakland and the Town of Alameda. Oakland: 1875. V. 46

A Directory of the City of Oakland and Its Enivrons Including Alameda, Berkeley and Temescal for the Year Ending April 1, 1879. Oakland: 1878. V. 46

Pacific Coast Business Directory for 1867 . . . San Francisco: 1867. V. 42

The San Francisco Directory for the Year Commencing March, 1877. San Francisco: 1877. V. 46

LANGLEY, NOEL

Somebody's Rocking My Dreamboat. London: 1949. V. 45

LANGLEY, SAMUEL PIERPONT 1834-1906

Address of S. P. Langley, President of the American Association for the Advancement of Science, Delivered at the Cleveland Meeting. 1888. V. 41

Experiments in Aerodynamics. Washington: 1891. V. 38; 39; 44

Experiments in Aerodynamics. Washington: 1902. V. 38; 40; 42; 45

Langley Memoir of Mechanical Flight. Washington: 1911. V. 38; 40; 41; 42; 44; 46

Langley Memoir on Mechanical Flight. Washington City: 1911. V. 40; 45

The 1900 Solar Eclipse Expedition of the Astrophysical Observatory of the Smithsonian Institution. Washington: 1904. V. 40

LANGLEY, THOMAS

A New Almanacke and Prognosticaion for the Yeere . . . 1636. Lodnon: 1635. V. 39

LANGLEY, WILLIAM

The Persecuted Minister in Defence of the Ministrie. London: 1656. V. 38

LANGLOIS, DE FANCAN, FRANCOIS

The Favorites Chronicle. London: 1621. V. 46

The Favourites Chronicle. N.P.: 1621. V. 43; 45

The Favourites Chronicle. N.P.: London: 1621. V. 40

LANGLOTZ, ERNST

The Art of Magna Graecia: Greek Art in Southern Italy. London: 1965. V. 40; 42; 44; 45

LANGMAN, I. K.

A Selected Guide to the Literature on the Flowering Plants of Mexico. Philadelphia: 1964. V. 46

LANGMUIR, IRVING

The Collected Works . . . London: 1960-62. V. 40

LANGRISH, BROWNE

Physical Experiments upon Brutes: in Order to discover a Safe and Easy Method of dissolving the Stone in the Bladder by Injections. To which is added, a Course of Experiments with the Lauro-Cerasus . . . London: 1746. V. 37

Physical Experiments upon Brutes: in Order to discover a Safe and Easy Method of dissolving the Stone in the Bladder by Injections. To which is added, a Course of Experiments with the Lauro-Cerasus . . . Likewise an Account . . . London: 1745. V. 37

LANGSDORFF, GEORG HEINRICH VON

Bemerkungen auf Einer Reise um Die Welt in den Jahren 1803 bis 1807. Frankfurt: 1812. V. 38; 39; 40; 41

Bermerkungen auf Einer Reise um die Welt in den Jahren 1803 bis 1807. Frankfurt am Main: 1812. V. 37

Voyages and Travels in Various Parats of the World, During the Years 1803-07. London: 1813. V. 38; 41; 46

Voyages and Travels in Various Parts of the World During the Years 1803, 1804, 1805, 1806 and 1807. Carlisle: 1817. V. 39; 45

LANGSTON, CAROLYN LAVINIA

History of Eastland County, Texas. Dallas: 1904. V. 37

LANGSTON, JOHN

Early Days in Upper Canada: Letters of John Langton. Toronto: 1926. V. 44

LANGSTON, ROBERT

The Childhood and Youth of Charles Dickens. London: 1891. V. 37; 42

LANGTOFT, PETER

Chronicle from the Death of Cadwalader to the end of K. Edward the First's Reign. Oxford: 1725. V. 39

LANGTON, HUGH HORNBY

James Douglas, a Memoir. Toronto: 1940. V. 37; 40; 42; 45

LANGTON, RICHARD

Narrative of a Captivity in France, from 1809 to 1814. London: 1836. V. 40; 41

LANGTON, ROBERT

The Childhood and Youth of Charles Dickens. London: 1891. V. 41

The Pilgrimage of Robert Langton. Cambridge: 1924. V. 39

LANGUET, HUBERT

De La Pvissance Legitime dv Prince svr Le Pevple, et du Peuple sur le Prince. N.P.: 1581. V. 37; 42

Vindiciae Contra Tyrannos; sive, de Principis in Populum, Populique in Principem, Legitima Potestate, Stephano Iunio Bruto (pseud.). Hanau: 1595. V. 37

Vindiciae Contra Tyrannos. Strassburg?: 1580. V. 38

Vindiciae Contra Tyrannos: A Defence of Liberty Against Tyrants. London: 1689. V. 37

LANGWORTHY, A.

The Constitution of the Republic of Mexico, and the State of Coahuila & Texas... New York: 1832. V. 45

LANGWORTHY, EDWARD

Anecdotes of the Late Charles Lee, Esq. Lt. Colonel of the Forty-Fourth Regiment... London: 1797. V. 40

The Life and Memoirs of the Late Major General (Charles) Lee, Second in Command to General Washington, During the American Revolution... New York: 1813. V. 42; 45; 46

LANGWORTHY, FRANKLIN

Scenery of the Plains, Mountains, and Mines. Ogdensburgh: 1855. V. 37; 38; 40; 41; 42; 44; 45; 46

LANGWORTHY, LUCIUS

Dubuque: Its History, Mines, Indian Legends, etc. Dubuque: 1855. V. 39

LANHAM, EDWIN

The Wind Blew West. New York & Toronto: 1935. V. 37; 38; 40; 42

LANIER, HENRY WYSHAM

A. B. Frost: The American Sportsman's Artist. New York: 1933. V. 39; 43; 44; 45

Greenwich Village Today & Yesterday. New York: 1949. V. 39

LANIER, JAMES FRANKLIN DOUGHTY

Sketch of the Life of J. F. D. Lanier. N.P.: 1877. V. 41

Sketch of the life of... New York: 1870. V. 37

LANIER, SIDNEY 1842-1881

The Boy's Froissart... New York: 1879. V. 44

The Boy's King Arthur. New York: 1880. V. 44

The Boy's Own King Arthur. New York: 1880. V. 43

The Boy's Mabinogion. New York: 1881. V. 44

The Boy's King Arthur. New York: 1926. V. 37

The Centennial Meditation of Columbia. New York: 1876. V. 46

Florida: Its Scenery, Climate and History. Philadelphia: 1875. V. 41

Florida; Its Scenery, Climate and History. Philadelphia: 1876. V. 42

Letters; Sidney Lanier to Col. John G. James. Austin: 1942. V. 38; 39; 43; 44

Poems of Sidney Lanier. New York: 1884. V. 46

The Science of English Verse. New York: 1880. V. 46

Select Poems of Sidney Lanier. New York: 1895. V. 39

LANIGAN, JOHN

An Ecclesiastical History of Ireland. Dublin: 1829. V. 38; 43

LANIGAN, STEPHEN M.

Science and Scepticism: a Study of Some Principles Which Influence Modern Thought. Dublin: 1880. V. 42

LANKESTER, E. RAY

Extinct Animals. London: 1905. V. 39

Monograph of the Okapi. 1910. V. 46

LANKESTER, EDWIN

A Description and History of Vegetable Substances, Used in the Arts and in Domestic Economy. London: 1829. V. 43

LANMAN, CHARLES

Adventures of an Angler in Canada, Nova Scotia and the United States. London: 1848. V. 39; 44

Adventures in the Wilds of North America. London: 1854. V. 44

Adventures in the Wilds of the United States and British American Provinces. Philadelphia: 1856. V. 38; 40; 45

Farthest North. New York: 1885. V. 44; 45

The Japanese in America. New York: 1872. V. 38; 39; 43

Letters from the Alleghany Mountains. New York: 1849. V. 44

Summer in the Wilderness; Embracing a Canoe Voyage Up the Mississippi and Around Lake Superior. New York: 1847. V. 45

A Summer in the Wilderness; Embracing a Canon Voyage Up the Mississippi and Around Lake Superior. New York: & Philadelphia: 1847. V. 44

A Tour to the River Saguenay, in Lower Canada. Philadelphia: 1848. V. 44

LANNEL, JEAN DE

Le Romant Saytriqve. Paris: 1624. V. 42

LANNER, JOSEPH

The Boz Waltzes, as Performed by Dodsworth's Band, at the Grand Festival Park Theatre. New York: 1841. V. 40

LANNING, JOHN TATE

The Spanish Missions of Georgia. Chapel Hill: 1935. V. 44

LA NOUE, FRANCOIS DE 1531-1591

Discours Politiques et Militaires... Geneva: 1587. V. 40; 46

LANQUET, THOMAS

Coopers Chronicle Contenynge the vvhole Discourse of the Histories as Well of Thys Realme as All Other Countries... London: 1565. V. 45

Coopers Chronicle, Conteininge the Whole Discourse of the Histories as Well of This Realme, as All Other Countries. London: 1560. V. 37

LANSBURGH, MARK

An Illustrated Check List of Manuscript Leaves in the Collection of Mark Lansburgh. Santa Barbara: 1962. V. 39

LANSDELL, HENRY

Russian Central Asia including Kulkja, Bokhara, Khiva and Merv. London: 1885. V. 37

Through Siberia. London: 1882. V. 40

LANSDOWN, HENRY

Recollections of the Late William Beckford, of Fonthill, Wilts; and Lansdown, Bath. London: 1893. V. 39

LANSDOWNE, GEORGE GRANVILLE, BARON 1667-1735

The British Enchanters; or, No Magic-like Love. London: 1706. V. 41; 45

The Dramatic Works. Glasgow: 1752. V. 41

Heroick Love: a Tragedy. London: 1698. V. 38; 40

The Jew of Venice. London: 1701. V. 41

A Letter from a Noble Man Abroad, to His Friend in England. London: 1722. V. 41

Poems on Several Occasions. London: 1712. V. 38; 39; 41

The She-Gallants: a Comedy. London: 1696. V. 45

Three Plays, viz. The She-Gallants, a comedy. Heroick-Love, a Tragedy. And the Jew of Venice, a Comedy. London: 1713. V. 42; 45

The Genuine Works in Verse and Prose. London: 1732. V. 38

LANSDOWNE, J. FENWICK

Birds of the Eastern Forest. Toronto: 1968. V. 46

Birds of the Eastern Forest. Toronto and Montreal: 1968. V. 44

Birds of the Eastern Forest: Paintings... Toronto: 1968-70. V. 45

Birds of the West Coast. Toronto: 1976. V. 39

Birds of the West Coast. Toronto: 1976/80. V. 42

Birds of the West Coast: Paintings, Drawings... Toronto: 1976-80. V. 45

LANSDOWNE, J. FENWICK continued

Birds of the Eastern Forest. London: 1968-70. V. 37

Birds of the West Coast: Paintings, Drawings and Text. Toronto: 1980. V. 37

LANSIUS, THOMAS

Orationes Aliquot. Tubingen: 1616. V. 39

LANSTON MONOTYPE CORPORATION

Pastonchi a specimen of a new letter for use on the 'Monotype'. (1928). V. 37

LANTE, LOUIS MARIE

Costumes des Femmes de Hambourg, du Tyrol, de la Hollande, de la Suisse, de la Franconie, de l'Espagne, du Royaume de Naples, etc. Paris: 1827. V. 42

LANTHENAS, FRANCOIS

Convention Nationale. Rapport et Projet de Decret sur l'Organisation des Ecoles Primaires, Presentes a La Convention Nationale, au Nom de Son Comite d'Instruction Publique. Paris: 1790. V. 38

LANTHORN CLUB

The Lanthorn Book. New York: 1898. V. 41

LANTIER, ETIENNE FRANCOIS DE

The Travels of Antenor in Greece and Asia. London: 1799. V. 39

LANY, JOHN D.

Report of a Visit to Some of the Trives of Indians, located West of the Mississippi River. New York: 1843. V. 37

LANZ, PHILIPPE LOUIS

Essay on the Construction of Machines. London: 1825. V. 40

LANZI, LUIGI

The History of Painting in Italy . . . London: 1828. V. 42

LAON, JEAN DE

Relation du Voyage des Francois Fait Au Cap de Nord en Amerique. Paris: 1654. V. 40; 43

LAPELLETRIE, E.

Report of the Rev. E. Lapelletrie, to the Synod of the Presbysterian Church in Canada, in Connection with the Church of Scotland. Montreal: 1850. V. 41

LA PEROUSE, JEAN FRANCOIS DE GALAUP

Voyage de La Perouse Autour du Monde. Paris: 1797. V. 42

A Voyage Round the World, which was Performed in the Years 1785-1788 . . . Edinburgh: 1798. V. 46

The Voyage of La Perouse Round the World in the Years 1785, 1786, 1787 and 1788. London: 1798. V. 38; 39; 42

Voyage de La Perouse Autour du Monde, Public Conformement au du 22 Avril 1791 . . . Paris: 1798. V. 41

A Voyage Round the World 1785-1788 . . . London: 1799, 1798. V. 38

A Voyage Round the World. Performed in the Years 1785, 1786, 1787, 1788 . . . To Which are Added, A Voyage from Manilla to California, by Don antonio Maurelle: and an Abstract of the Voyage and Discoveries of the Late Capt. G. Vancouver. Boston: 1801. V. 39

LA PEYRERE, ISAAC DE

An Account of Greenland. London. V. 40

An Account of Greenland. (London: 1704). V. 37

Prae-Adamitae Sive Exercitatio Super Versibus XII-XIV Epistolae D. Pauli ad Romanos, Quibus Inducuntur Primi Homines Ante Adamum Conditi. Systema Theologicum Ex Prae-Adamitarum Hypothesi. Amsterdam: 1655. V. 38

Relation du Groenland. Paris: 1647. V. 37; 38

Relation du Groenland. (with) *Relation de L'Islande.* Paris: 1663. V. 38

LAPHAM, ISAAC A. 1793-1859

The Antiquities of Wisconsin, as Surveyd and Described. 1855. V. 43

The Antiquities of Wisconsin, as Surveyed and Described. Washington: 1855. V. 39; 42

The Antiquities of Wisconsin, as surveyed and described. London: (1855). V. 37

Report of the Diastrous Effects of the Destruction of Forest Trees, Now Going on so Rapidly in . . . Wisconsin. Madison: 1867. V. 45

LAPHAM, WILLIAM B.

History of Rumford, Oxford Co., Maine from Its First Settlement in 1779 to the Present Time. Augusta: 1890. V. 39

History of Rumford, Oxford County, Maine, from Its First Settlement in 1779 to the Present Time. Augusta: 1890. V. 46

My Recollections of the War of the Rebellion. Augusta: 1892. V. 45

LAPIDE, CORNELIUS

Commentaria in Ecclesiasticum. Antwerp: 1634. V. 37

Commentaria in Pentateuchum Mosis. Antwerp: 1623. V. 37

LAPIDE, JOHANNES DE

Resolutorum Dubiorum Circa Celebrationem Missarum Occurentium. Basle: 1492. V. 45

LAPLACE, CYRILLE PIERRE THEODORE

Voyage Autour du Monde par les Mers de L'Inde et de Chine Execute sur la Corvette de l'Etat La Favorite Pendant Les Annees 1830, 1831, et 1832. Paris: 1833. V. 42

LA PLACE, PIERRE DE

Politique Discourses, Treating of the Differences and inequalities of Vocations, as well Publique as Priuate. London: 1578. V. 37

LAPLACE, PIERRE SIMON

Essai Philosophique sur les Probabilites. Paris: 1814. V. 38

Exposition du Systeme du Monde. Paris: 1796. V. 38; 40; 41; 42; 45

Traite de Mecanique Celeste. Paris: 1798-1827. V. 42

Mecanique Celeste . . . Boston: 1829-39. V. 42; 45; 46

The System of the World. London: 1809. V. 38

The System of the World. Dublin: 1830.I. V. 38

LA PLACETE, J.

The Christian Casuist; or, a Treatise of Conscience. London: 1705. V. 39

LAPLAND Sketches, or, Delineations of the Costume, Habits, and Peculiarities of Jens Holm and His Wife Karina Christian, with Accurate Representations of the Deer, Sledges, Huts, &c. as Exhibited at Bullock's Museum. London: 1824? V. 37

LA POIX DE FREMINVILLE, EDME DE 1680-1778

Dictionnaire ou Traite de la Police Generale . . . Paris: 1758. V. 46

LA POPELINIERE, LANCELOT VOISON, SIEUR DE

L'Histoire de France Enrichie des Plus Notables Occurances Suruenues ez Prouinces de l'Europe & Pays Voisins, Soit en Paix Soit en Guerre. La Rochelle: 1581. V. 40

LAPORTE, JOHN

Of the Characters of Trees, Drawn and Engraved. London: 1795-98. V. 38; 40

The Progress of a Water-Coloured Drawing. London: 1802. V. 44

LAPRAIK, JOHN

Poems, On Several Occasions. Kilmarnock: 1788. V. 40

LA QUINTINIE, JEAN DE 1626-1688

The Compleat Gardner. London: 1699. V. 37; 39

The Complete Gardner. London: 1701. V. 39

Instruction Pour les Jardins Fruitiers et Potagers. Paris: 1690. V. 39; 41; 46

Instruction Pour les Jardins Fruitiers et Potagers, avec un Traite des Orangers, Suivy de Quelques Reflexions sur l'Agriculture. Amsterdam: 1692. V. 46

LA QUINTINYE, JEAN DE 1626-1688

The Compleat Gard'ner . . . London: 1693. V. 41; 42

LARAMIE, Hahns Peak and Pacific Railway System. The Direct Gateway to Southern Wyoming, Northern Colorado and Eastern Utah. Boston: 1910. V. 38; 40

LARAMIE, Hans Peak and Pacific Railway System. The Direct Gateway to Southern Wyoming, Northern Colorado and Eastern Utah. Boston: (1910). V. 37

LARBAUD, VALERY

Rues et Visages de Paris. Paris: 1926. V. 40

LARCOM, LUCY

Roadside Poems for Summer Travellers. Boston: 1876. V. 40

LARD, MOSES E.

A Review of Rev. J. B. Jeter's Book Enttitled 'Campbellism Examined.' Philadelphia: 1857. V. 42

LARDNER, DIONYSIUS 1793-1859

The Cabinet Cyclopaedia. London: 1830-31. V. 38

Common Things Explained. London: 1856. V. 38; 39

Lardner's Cyclopaedia. A Treatise on the Progressive Improvement and Present State of the Manufacture in Metal. London: 1853. V. 41

Lectures on the Steam-Engine, In Which Its Construction and Operation are Familiarly Explained . . . London: 1832. V. 37; 42

Museum of Science and Art. London: 1854-56. V. 38; 42; 43

The Museum of Science and Art. London: 1860. V. 38; 41

Railway Economy: a Treatise on the New Art of Transport, Its Management, Prospects and Relations . . . London: 1580. V. 46

Railway Economy; a Treatise on the New Art of Transport . . . London: 1850. V. 42

LARDNER, DIONYSIUS 1793-1859 continued

A Series of Lectures Upon Locke's Essay. Dublin: 1831. V. 41

The Steam Engine Familiarly Explained and Illustrated. London: 1836. V. 37; 42

A Treatise on the Origin, Progressive Improvement, and Present State of the Silk Manufacture. London: 1831. V. 38

A Treatise on the Progressive Improvement and Present State of the Manufactures in Metal. London: 1831/33/34. V. 44

LARDNER, NATHANIEL

The Historie of the Heretics of the First Two Centuries After Christ . . . Published from the manuscript of Nathaniel Lardnera, with larage additions by John Hogg. London: 1780. V. 37

A Large Collection of Ancient Jewish and Heathen Testimonies to the Truth of the Christian Religion, with Notes and Observations. London: 1764-65-66-67. V. 38

The Works. London: 1827-28. V. 39

LARDNER, RING, JR.

The Lardners (My Family Remembered). New York: 1976. V. 44

LARDNER, RING W. 1885-1933

Bib Ballads. Chicago: 1915. V. 37; 39; 41; 42; 43; 44; 45; 46

Bib Ballads. New York: 1915. V. 43; 45

Gullible's Travels, Etc. Indianapolis: 1917. V. 38; 39

How to Write Short Stories. New York: 1924. V. 46

How to Write Short Stories. New York/London: 1924. V. 41

June Moon. New York: 1930. V. 39; 41; 44

'Little Puff of Smoke' 'Good Night' A Southern Coon. V. 46

Lose with a Smile. New York: 1933. V. 38

Round Up. New York: 1929. V. 37; 39; 40; 41; 44; 45

Say It With Evil. Say It With Bricks. New York: 1923. V. 42

Say It With Oil: Few Remarks About Wives. New York: 1923. V. 39

Say it With Oil. New York: (1923). V. 37

Treat 'Em Rough: Letters from Jack the Kaiser Killer. Indianapolis: 1918. V. 39; 40; 41; 42

Treat'Em Rough. 1918. V. 37

The Young Immigrunts. Indianapolis: 1920. V. 42; 43; 46

LAREN, A. J. VAN

Cactus. Los Angeles: 1935. V. 39; 46

Succulents Other than Cacti. Los Angeles: 1935. V. 39

LA REYNIE DE LA BRUYERE, J. B. M. L.

The Livre Rouge, or Red Book. London: 1790. V. 39; 42; 44

LARGE, R. G.

Soogwilis a Collection of Kwakiutl Indian Designs and Legends. Toronto: 1951. V. 43

LARID, MAC GREGOR

Narrative of an Expedition Into the Interior of Africa, by the River Niger, in the Steam Vessels Quorra and Alburkah in 1832, 1833 and 1834. London: 1837. V. 46

LARIMER, SARAH L.

The Capture and Escape; or, Life Among the Sioux. Philadelphia: 1870. V. 38; 44; 45

LARIMER, WILLIAM H. H.

Reminiscences of General William Larimer and His Son William H. H. Larimer Two of the Founders of Denver City. V. 39; 40

LARISON, CORNELIUS W.

The Tenting School: a Description of the Tours Taken and of the Field Work Done . . . Ringos: 1883. V. 44

THE LARK. San Francisco: 1895-97. V. 41
THE LARK. San Francisco: 1895-April 1897. V. 46
THE LARK. San Francisco: 1895, etc. V. 37
THE LARK. San Francisco: 1896. V. 46

LARKIN,

Sketch of a Tour in the Highlands of Scotland, through Perthshire, Argylshire and Inveness-Shire, in September and October 1818 . . . London: 1819. V. 41

LARKIN, DAVID

The Unknown Painting of Kay Nielsen. London: 1977. V. 46

LARKIN, EDWARD

Speculum Patrum: a Looking-Glasse of the Fathers . . . London: 1659. V. 37; 45

LARKIN, PHILIP 1922-

All What Jazz. London: 1970. V. 40

Aubade. 1980. V. 39; 41; 43

Aubade. London: 1980. V. 39

Aubade. Salem: 1980. V. 40; 42; 45

Collected Poems. London: 1988. V. 41

The Explosion. London: 1970. V. 45

The Fantasy Poets Number Twenty One. Swinford: 1954. V. 38

A Girl in Winter. London: 1947. V. 37

Jill. Leicester: 1946. V. 41

Jill. London: 1946. V. 37; 38; 42; 45; 46

Jill. London: 1964. V. 42; 46

The Less Deceived. Hessle: 1955. V. 37; 41; 44

The Less Deceived: Poems. London: 1955. V. 37

New Poems 1958. London: 1958. V. 38

The North Ship. London: 1945. V. 43; 44; 45

The North Ship. London: 1965. V. 44

The North Ship. London: 1966. V. 41; 45

XX Poems. Belfast: 1951. V. 40

XX Poems. N.P.: 1951. V. 44

XX Poems. London: 1951. V. 37

The Whitsun Weddings. London: 1964. V. 38; 39; 40; 41; 42; 43; 44; 45

LARKIN, THOMAS

California in 1846 Described in Letters from . . . San Francisco: 1934. V. 42

LARKIN, THOMAS OLIVER

The Larkin Papers . . . Berkeley: 1951-64. V. 41; 45

The Larkin Papers: Personal, Business and Official Correspondence . . . Berkeley: Los Angeles: 1951-64. V. 40

The Larkin Papers: Business and Official Corresopondence of Thomas Oliver Larkin. Berkeley: 1951-64, 68. V. 45

The Larkin Papers: Business and Official Correspondence of Thomas Oliver Larkin . . . Edited by George P. Hammond. Berkeley: 1959. V. 37

LARKSPUR a Lyric Garland. Sussex: 1922. V. 42

LARMOR, JOSEPH

Aether and Matter. Cambridge: 1900. V. 40

Mathematical and Physical Ppaers. Cambridge: 1929. V. 45

LARNER, EDGAR T.

Practical Television. London: 1928. V. 40; 42; 43; 45

LAROCHE-GUILHEM, ANNA DE

The History of Female Favoruites, of mary de Padilla, Under Peter the Cruel . . . Livia Under the Emperor Augustus; Julia Farnesa, Under Pope Alexander . . . London: 1772. V. 42

Zingis; a Tartarian History. London: 1692. V. 37; 42

LA ROCHEFOUCAULD, FRANCOIS DUC DE 1613-1680

Maximes et Reflections Morales. Parma: 1811. V. 40; 41

Epictetus Junior, or Maximes of Modern Morality. London: 1670. V. 40

Maxims. London: 1902. V. 46

Maxims. London: 1913. V. 41; 42

Maxims. London: 1931. V. 39

Moral Maxims: by the Duke de la Roche Foucault. London: 1649. V. 45

Moral Maxims and Reflections. London: 1694. V. 38; 41

Moral Maxims and Reflections. London: 1706. V. 39

Moral Maxims. London: 1749. V. 39; 40

LA ROCHEFOUCAULD, FRANCOIS, DUCE DE 1613-1680

The Management of the Tongue . . . London: 1707. V. 43; 46

LA ROCHEFOUCAULD-LIANCOURT, FRANCOIS ALEXANDRE FREDERIC

Finances, Credit National, Interet Politique et de Commerce; Forces Militaires de la France. N.P.: 1789. V. 41

Travels through the United States of North America. London: 1799. V. 38

Voyage dans Les Etats-Unis d'Amerique, Fait en 1795, 1796 et 1797. Paris: 1799. V. 40

LA ROQUE, JEAN DE

A Voyage to Arabia the Happy, by way of the Eastern Ocean and the Streights of the Red-Sea: with a Journey from Moka to the King of Yemen . . . ; also, an Account of the Coffee-Tree with an historical treatise of Coffee. London: 1726. V. 37

LAROUSSE, PIERRE

Grand Dictionnaire Universel du XIXe Siecle. Paris: 1866-78 & n.d. V. 46

LARPENTEUR, CHARLES

Forty Years a Fur Trader on the Upper Missouri the Personal Narrative of Charles Larpenteur 1833-1872 . . . New York: 1898. V. 37; 41

LARRAINZER, MANUEL

Estudios Sobre la Historia de America sus Ruinas y Antiguedades. Mexico: 1875-78. V. 41

LARREMORE, THOMAS A.

The Marion Press: A Survey and Checklist. Jamaica: 1943. V. 41

The Marion Press: a Survey and Checklist. New York: 1943. V. 37; 43

LARREY, DOMINIQUE JEAN

Memoires de Chirurgie Militaire, et Campaignes. Paris: 1812-17. V. 42

Observations on Wounds, and their Complications by Erysipelas, Gangrene and Tetanus, and on the Principal Diseases and Injuries of the Head, Ear and Eye . . . Philadelphia: 1832. V. 38

Surgical Memoirs of the Campaigns of Russia, Germany and France. Philadelphia: 1832. V. 42

LARSEN, ELLOUISE B.

American Historical Views on Staffordshire China. New York: 1939. V. 39

LARSEN, HELGE

Ipiutak and the Arctic Whale Hunting Culture. New York: 1948. V. 42

LARSEN, SOFUS

Danish Eighteenth Century Bindings 1730-1780. Copenhagen: 1930. V. 41; 42; 44; 46

Danish Eighteenth Century Bindings 1730-1780. Copenhagen & London: 1930. V. 39

Danish Eighteenth Century Bindings, 1730-1780. Copenhagen: Levin U: 1930. V. 46

LARSON, BRUCE L.

Lindbergh of Minnesota: a Political Biography. New York: 1973. V. 43

LARSON, J. A.

Single Fingerprint System. New York: 1924. V. 46

LARSON, JAMES

Sergeant Larson, 4th Cav. San Antonio: 1935. V. 39; 44

LARSSON, CARL

Ett Hem. Stockholm: 1910. V. 38

Spadarfvet. Stockholm: 1906. V. 38

LARTET, E.

Reliquiae Aquitanicae. London: 1875. V. 38

LARTIGUE, JACQUES HENRI

Boyhood Photos of J. H. Lartigue. Lausanne: 1966. V. 41; 46

Boyhood Photos of J. H. Lartigue; The Family Album of a Guilded Age. N.P.: 1966. V. 37; 40

Diary of a Century. New York: 1970. V. 39

LAS Vegas Hot Springs. Springfield: 1883. V. 39

LA SALLE, ANTOINE DE

One Hundred Merrie and Delightsome Stories. Caarbonnek,: 1924. V. 38

LA SALLE, NICHOLAS DE

Relation of the Discovery of the Mississippi River Written from the Narrative of . . . Chicago: 1898. V. 42

LA SALLE, NICOLAS DE

Relation of the Discoveries and Voyages of Cavelier de La Salle from 1679 to 1681. The Official Narrative. Chicago: 1901. V. 38

LA SALLE, ROBERT CAVELIER DE

Relation of the Discoveries and Voyages of Cavelier de La Salle from 1679 to 1681. Chicago: 1901. V. 37; 40

LASCARIS, CONSTANTINUS

De Octo Partibus Orationis Lib. I (and other grammatical works). Venice: 1512. V. 40

LASCARIS, EVADNE

The Golden Band. London: 1935. V. 42

The Golden Bed of Kydno. London: 1935. V. 37; 40; 44

LAS CASES, EMMANUEL E. M. J., COMTE DE 1766-1842

A Complete Genealogical, Historical, Chronological and Geographical Atlas.. Philadelphia: 1821. V. 41; 43

LAS CASES, EMMANUEL E.M.J. COMTE DE 1766-1842

Journal of the Private Life and Conversations of the Emperor Napoleon at St. Helena. London: 1823. V. 41; 43

Journal of the Private Life and Conversations of the Emperor Napoleon at Saint Helena. London: 1824. V. 39

LA SERNA SANTANDER, CHARLES ANTOINE DE

An Historical Essay on the Origin of Printing. Newcastle: 1819. V. 40

LASERON, E.

A Dictionary of the Malayalim and English and the English and Malayalim Languages . . . Cottayam: 1856. V. 40

LASINIO, CARLO

Ornati Presi da Graffiti e Pitture Antiche Esistenti in Firenze. Florence: 1789. V. 44

LASLEY, M. E. A.

Across America in the Only House on Wheels; or, Lasley's Traveling Palace. N.P.: 1901. V. 37; 38

LA SOLLE, HENRI FRANCOIS DE

Bok et Zulba. Histoire Allegorique Traduite du Portugais de Dom Anrel Eniner. N.P.: 1740? V. 38

Memoirs of a Man of Pleasure, or the Adventures of Versorand. London: 1751. V. 38; 43

LA SPINA, GEORGE

Invaders from the Dark. Sauk City: 1960. V. 42; 45

LASSAIGNE, JACQUES

The Ceiling of the Paris Opera. New York: 1966. V. 39; 42

Chagall. Paris: 1957. V. 41

Marc Chagall, The Ceiling of the Paris Opera. New York: 1966. V. 39; 43; 45; 46

Marc Chagall, Drawings and Watercolors for the Ballet. New York: 1969. V. 41; 46

Spanish Painting from Catalan Frescos to El Greco; from Velazquez to Picasso. Geneva: 1952. V. 38; 42

LASSALLE, FERDINAND 1825-1864

Science and the Workingmen. New York: 1900. V. 39

LASSELS, RICHARD

A Most Excellent Way of Hearing Masse, With Profit and Devotion. London: 1686. V. 42; 44

The Voyage of Italy; or, A Complet Journey Through Italy. London: 1686. V. 38

LASSENIUS, JOHANNES

Versuessete Bitterkeit/im Leben, Lieben und Leiden/ zu Allgemeinem Trost in Allerhand Geistlichen und Leiblichen Anfechtungen . . . Copenhagen: 1685. V. 38

LASSEPAS, ULISES URBANO

De La Colonizacion de La Baja California Y Decreto de 10 Marzo de 1857. Mexico City: 1859. V. 38

LASSITER, GERALD

The Novels and Short Stories of . . . London: 1937. V. 46

LASSWELL, MARY

John Henry Kirby Prince of the Pines. Austin: 1967. V. 37; 38; 40; 43; 46

THE LAST of the Medici. Florence: 1930. V. 43

THE LAST Words of Polly Goold . . . Boston: 1817? V. 41

LASTEYRIE DU SALLANT, CHARLES PHILBERT, COMTE DE

Typographie Economique, ou l'Art de l'Imprimerie . . . Paris: 1837. V. 42; 44

LASZLO, FULOP 1869-

Selections from the Work of P. A. De Laszlo. London: 1921. V. 39

THE LATE Insurrection in Demerara, and Riot in Barbados. Colophon: 1823. V. 40

THE LATE Minister Unmask'd; or, an Answer to a Late Pamphlet, Entitled the Conduct of the Late Administration, with Regard to Foreign Affairs, from 1722 to 1742. London: 1742. V. 41

LATER Struggles in the Journey of Life . . . of a Country Bookseller. Edinburgh: 1833. V. 38

LATHAM, CHARLES

The Gardens of Italy. London: 1905. V. 37; 39

In English Homes. London: 1907. V. 44

In English Homes. London: 1907-09. V. 37; 38

In English Homes, the Internal Character, Furniture and Adornments. London: 1908. V. 40

LATHAM, HENRY

Black and White A Journal of a Three Months' Tour in the United States. London: 1867. V. 40

LATHAM, JOHN

An Essay on the Tracheae or Windpipes of Various Kinds of Birds. London: 1798. V. 43

A General Synopsis of Birds - Supplements 1 and 2 - Index Ornithologicus. London: 1781-1802. V. 38

A General Snyopsis of Birds. (with) Supplment to the General Synopsis of Birds. London: 1781-5/87-1802. V. 43

General Synopsis of Birds. London: 1781-87. V. 39

LATHAM, JOHN continued

A General History of Birds. Winchester: 1821-28. V. 42

A General History of Birds. Winchester: 1821-24. V. 37

A General Synopsis of Birds. London: 1781-1801. V. 37

LATHAM, JOHN HERBERT

The Construction of Wrought Iron Bridges ... Cambridge: 1858. V. 44

LATHAM, PETER M.

The Collected Works of Dr. P. M. Latham, with Memoir by Sir Thomas Watson. London: 1876-78. V. 41; 42; 45

Lectures on Subjects Connected with Clinical Medicine. Philadelphia: 1837. V. 46

Lectures on Subjects Connected with Clinical Medicine: Comprising Diseases of the Heart. Philadelphia: 1847. V. 42; 44

LATHAM, ROBERT GORDON

A Dictionary of the English Language. London: 1882. V. 43

The Ethnology of the British Colonies and Dependencies. London: 1851. V. 43

Norway and Norwegians. London: 1840. V. 37; 40

Opuscula: Essays Chiefly Philogocial and Ehtnographical. London: 1860. V. 38; 39

LATHAM, SIMON

Falconry or the Faulcons Lure and Cure in Two Books. London: 1633. V. 44

LATHAM, WILFRID

The States of the River Plate: Their Industries and Commerce, Sheep Farming, Sheep-Breeding, Cattle-Feeding and Meat Preserving: Employment of Capital: Land and Stock, and Their Values ... London: 1866. V. 39

The States of the River Plate. London: 1868. V. 41

LATHEN, EMMA

Murder, Sunny Side Up. New York: 1968. V. 45

LATHROP, DAVID

The History of the Fifty Ninth Regiment Illinois Volunteers ... Indianapolis: 1865. V. 42; 46

LATHROP, DOROTHY P.

Animals of the Bible. New York: 1937. V. 45

The Fairy Circus. New York: 1931. V. 43; 45

LATHROP, ELISE

Historic Houses of Early America. New York: 1927. V. 37

LATHROP, G. P.

A Masque of Poets. Boston: 1878. V. 41

LATHROP, GEORGE

Some Pioneer Recollections. Philadelphia: 1927. V. 40; 46

LATHROP, GEORGE PARSONS

A Study of Hawthorne. Boston: 1876. V. 44

LATHROP, JOHN

A Compendious History fo the Late War ... Boston: 1815. V. 43

A Discourse Before the Society for 'Propogating the Gosepl Among the Indians, and Others, in North America.' Boston: 1804. V. 39; 42

LATHROP, JOSEPH

Waiting on God for Rain. Springfield: 1805. V. 45

LATHROP, LEONARD E.

The Farmer's Library, or Essays Designed to Encourage the Pursuits and Promote the Science of Agriculture. Rutland: 1825. V. 41

The Farmers' Library; or Essays Designed to Encourage the Pursuits, and Promote the Science of Agriculture. Rochester: 1828. V. 41; 44

LATHY, T. P.

The Angler; a Poem, in Ten Cantos. London: 1820. V. 39

LATHY, THOMAS P.

The Angler; a Poem, in Ten Cantos ... London: 1819. V. 43

LATILLA, EUGENIO

Cartoons in Outline Illustrative of the Gospels with Illuminated Text. Florence: 1848. V. 44

LATIMER, ELIZABETH WORMELEY

Salvage. Boston: 1880. V. 42

LATIMER, HUGH 1485?-1555

Fruitfull Sermons ... London: 1635. V. 38

Sermon of the Plow. (Birmingham: n.d.). V. 37

LATIMER, JONATHAN

The Mink Lined Coffin. London: 1960. V. 42

LATIMORE, SARA BRIGGS

Arthur Rackham: a Bibliography. Los Angeles: 1936. V. 37; 38; 39; 40; 41; 42; 43; 44

LATIN Hymns Sung at the Church of Saint Hugh Letchworth. London: 1913. V. 38

LATIN Hymns Sung at the Church of Saint Letchworth. Letchworth: 1913. V. 40

LATINI, BRUNETTO 1230-1294

L'Ethica d'Aritistotile Ridotta in Compendio. Lyons: 1568. V. 40

LATINI, LATINO

Biblioteca Sacra et Profana Sive Observationes, Correctiones, Coniecturae & Variae Lectiones in Sacros, et Profanos Scriptores e Marginalibus Notis Codicum Eiusdem a Dominico Marco ... Rome: 1677. V. 37

LATOMUS, BARTHOLOMAEUS

Ad Christianissimum Galliarvm Regem Franciscvm ... Bombarda. Paris: 1536. V. 43

LA TOUCHE, J. D. D.

A Handbook of the Birds of Eastern China. London: 1925-34. V. 37; 45

LATOUCHE, JOHN

Travels in Portugal. London: 1875. V. 46

LATOUR, ARSENE LACARRIERE

Historical Memoir of the War in West Florida and Louisian in 1814-1815. Philadelphia: 1816. V. 42; 43; 46

LA TOUR DU PIN, PATRICE

Bestiaire Fabuleux. Paris: 1951. V. 38; 39

LA TOUR LANDRY, GEOFFREY DE

The Book of the Knight of La Tour Landry. 1930. V. 40

The Book of the Knight of La Tour Landry. London: 1930. V. 43

LATOUR, T.

The Favorite Airs from the Ballet of La Dansomanie, Performed at the King's Theatre Haymarket, Arranged for the Piano Forte with Additional Movements Composed ... London: 1806. V. 40

LATROBE, BENJAMIN HENRY

An Answer to the Joint Committee of the Select and Common Councils of Philadelphia, on the Subject of a Plan for Supplying the City with Wter. Philadelphia: 1799. V. 37; 46

Characteristic Anecdotes, and Miscellaneous Authentic Papers, Tending to Illustrated the Character of Frederic II, Late King of Prussia. London: 1788. V. 46

Description of a New Form of Edge Rail to be Called the Zrail with Its Supports, Fastenings, &c ... Baltimore: 1840. V. 46

LATROBE, C. I.

Journal of a Visit to South Africa in 1815 and 1816. London: 1818. V. 42; 44; 45

LATROBE, CHARLES JOSEPH

The Pedestrian: A Summer's Ramble in the Tyrol and Some of the Adjacent Provinces, 1830. London: 1832. V. 39

The Rambler in North America. London: 1835. V. 39; 41; 44

The Rambler in North America MDCCCXXXII-MDCCCXXXIII. New York: 1835. V. 41; 44

The Rambler in Mexico. London: 1836. V. 38; 42; 43; 45

LATROBE, CHRISTIAN IGNATIUS

Journal of a Visit to South Africa in 1815 and 1816. London: 1818. V. 41; 46

Journal of a Visit to South Africa, With Some Account of the Missionary Settlements of the United Brethren, Near the Cape of Good Hope. London: 1821. V. 38; 41

LA TROBE, J. A.

Scripture Illustrations. London: 1838. V. 38; 40; 46

LATROBE, JOHN H. B.

Memoir of Benjamin Banneker, Read Before the Maryland Historical Society, at the Monthly Meeting, May 1, 1845. Baltimore: 1845. V. 40

LATTA, F. F.

California Indian Folklore. Shafter: 1936. V. 38

California Indian Lore (as Told To). Shafter: 1976. V. 46

LATTA, ROBERT RAY

Reminiscences of Pioneer Life. Kansas City: 1912. V. 38

LATTIMORE, S. C., MRS.

Incidents in the History of Dublin, Texas. Dublin: 1914. V. 38; 43

LATTRE, JEAN

Atlas of Maps Showing the Briare, Orleans and Loing Canals. 1730? V. 39

LATYMER, HUGH

Fruitfull Sermons Preached by the Right Reverend Father, and Constant Martyr of Iesus Christ M. Hugh Latymer, Newly Imprinted with Others, Not Heretofore Set Forth in Print . . . London: 1584. V. 37; 41

LAUD, WILLIAM

the History of the Troubles and Tryal of the Most Reverend Father in God, and Blessed Martyr, William Laud. London: 1695. V. 45

A Relation of the Conference Betweene William Laud, the Lord Bishop of St. Davids . . . London: 1639. V. 38; 44; 45

A Relation of the Conference Between William Laud, Archbishop of Canterbury and Mr. (John) Fisher the Jesuite . . . London: 1673. V. 44

The Second Volume of the Remains . . . London: 1700. V. 42; 44

A Speech Delivered in the Starr Chamber . . . at the Censure of John Bastwick . . . & William Prinn . . . London: 1637. V. 46

A Summarie of Devotions . . . Oxford: 1667. V. 46

The Works. Oxford: 1976. V. 39

LAUDE Spirituale. Nella Quale si Contengono le Parti Principali della Dottrina Christiana. Turin: 1673. V. 37

LAUDER, T. D.

The Miscellany of Natural History. Volume I: Parrots. Edinburgh: 1833. V. 37

LAUDER, THOMAS DICK

An Account of the Great Floods of August 1829, in the Province of Moray and Adjoining Districts. Edinburgh: 1830. V. 41

Lochandhu. Edinburgh: 1825. V. 37; 38; 44

Memorial of the Royal Progress in Scotland. Edinburgh: 1843. V. 38

The Miscellany of Natural History. Volume I: Parrots. Edinburgh: 1833. V. 38; 43

Parrots. Edinburgh: 1833. V. 37

The Wolfe of Badenoch; a Historical Romance of the Fourteenth Century. Edinburgh: 1827. V. 38

LAUDER, WILLIAM

An Essay on Milton's Use and Imitation of the Moderns, in His Paradise Lost. London: 1750. V. 45

LAUDERDALE, JAMES MAITLAND, 8TH EARL OF 1759-1839

The Depreciation of the Paper Currency of Great Britain Proved. London: 1812. V. 37; 38

An Inquiry into the Nature and Origin of Public Wealth. London: 1804. V. 38

An Inquiry Into the Practical Merits of the System for the Government of India, Under the Superintendence of the Board of Contro ul. Edinburgh: 1809. V. 42

An Inquiry into the Nature and Origin of Public Wealth, and Into the Means and Causes of Its Increase. Edinburgh: 1804. V. 37

A Letter on the Present Measures of Finance, In Which the Bill Now Depending in Parliament is Particularly Considered. London: 1798. V. 39; 41; 45

A Letter on the Corn Laws. London: 1814. V. 38; 41

Letters to the Peers of Scotland. London: 1794. V. 40; 43

Lettre a Mylord Lauderdale. London: 1795. V. 40

LAUDERDALE, R. J.

Life on the Range and On the Trail. 1936. V. 42; 45

LAUDES Beatae Mariae Virginis. Hammersmith: 1896. V. 39; 41; 42; 43; 45

LAUDIVIO VEZZANENSE

Epistolae Thurci per Laudivium Hierosolimitanum Equitem Aggregate. Lugduni: 1520. V. 45

LAUER, JEAN PHILIPPE

Saqqara, the Royal Cemetary of Memphis: Excavations and Discoveries Since 1850. New York: 1976. V. 44

LAUFER, BERTHOLD

Archaic Chinese Jades . . . New York. V. 42

Archaic Chinese Jades Collected in China by A. W. Bahr Now in Field Museum of Natural History, Chicago. New York: 1927. V. 42

Chinese Pottery of the Han Dynasty. Leiden: 1909. V. 42

Notes on Turquois in the East. Chicago: 1913. V. 44

Paper and Printing in Ancient China. Chicago: 1931. V. 38

LAUGH and Be Fat, or the Merry Jester, Containing the Newest, Drollest, Queerest, Compleatest, Most Comical, Most Facetious and Best Collection, Ever Offered to the Inhabitants of the United Kingdoms. Manchester: 1793? V. 37

THE LAUGHING Philosopher. Dublin: 1777. V. 38; 39; 42; 46

LAUGHLIN, CLARENCE JOHN

Ghosts Along the Mississippi. New York: 1948. V. 41

New Orelans and Its Living Past. Boston: 1941. V. 45

LAUGHLIN, J. LAURENCE 1850-1933

The History of Bimetallism in the United States. New York: 1892. V. 38

LAUGHLIN, JAMES

Gists & Piths. Iowa City: 1982. V. 37; 38; 40; 42; 44

The House of Light: Poems. 1986. V. 40; 45

Stolen & Contaminated Poems. Isla Vista: 1985. V. 44

LAUGHLIN, LEDLIE IRWIN

Pewter in America; Its Makers and Their Marks. Boston: 1940. V. 39

LAUGHTON, BRUCE

The Euston Road School. London: 1986. V. 44

Philip Wilson Steer 1860-1942. Oxford: 1971. V. 44

LAUGHTON, JOHN KNOX

The Nelson Memorial. London: 1896. V. 38

LAUGHTON, L. G. CARR

Old Ship Figure-Heads & Sterns. London: 1925. V. 39; 40; 46

LAUGIER, MARC ANTOINE

Essai sur l'architecture. Paris: 1753. V. 37

LAUNAY, MARIA DE

L'Architecture Ottomane. Constantinople: 1873. V. 44

LAUNCHBERRY, JAMES

A Bouquet of Pheasants. Brighton: 1981. V. 37

LAUNCHBURY, JANE

A Bouquet of Pheasants. Brighton: 1981. V. 42

LAURA, AUNT, PSEUD.

Orphan Willie. Buffalo: 1862. V. 39

A Talk with the Little Folks, by Aunt Laura. Buffalo: 1863. V. 39

LAURANA, FRANCESCO

Four Portrait Busts by Francesco Laurana. Northampton: 1962. V. 37; 41

LAURANT DE LARA, DAVID

Elementary Instruction in the Art of Illuminating and Missal Painting on Vellum, a Guide to Modern Illuminators . . . London: 1857. V. 44

LAUREDNEAU, ANDRE

Witness for Quebec. Toronto: 1973. V. 39

LAUREL Leaves. Boston: 1876. V. 42

LAURENCE, EDWARD

A Dissertation on Estates Upon Lives and Years Whether in Lay on Church Hands. London: 1730. V. 42

The Duty of a Steward to His Lord. London: 1727. V. 39

The Duty and Office of a Land Steward. (with) an Appendix, Shewing the Way to Plenty; Proposed to the Farmers. London: 1743. V. 37; 38

LAURENCE, H.

London in Olden Time. London: 1825-27. V. 38

LAURENCE, JOHN

The Clergy-Man's Recreation. London: 1714. V. 39; 42; 43

The Fruit Garden Kalendar; or, a Summary of the ARt of Managing the Fruit Garden. London: 1718. V. 46

A New System of Agriculture. London: 1726. V. 42; 46

LAURENCE, MARGARET

This Side Jordan. London: 1960. V. 46

LAURENCIN, MARIE

Petit Bestiare, Poemes Inedites par . . . Paris: 1926. V. 43

LAURENCIO DE S. NICOLAS

Segunda Ympresion del Primera Parte del Arte Y Uso de Architectura. Madrid: 1667. V. 39

LAURENS, HENRY

The Papers of Henry Laurens. Columbia: 1968-81. V. 38; 44

The Papers of Henry Laurens, 1747-1777. Columbia: 1968-88. V. 40

The Physiological Effects of Radiant Energy. New York: 1933. V. 42

LAURENS, JOHN

The Army Correspondence of Colonel John Laurens in the Years 1777-8 Now First Printed from Original Letters Addressed to His Father Henry Laurens, President of Congress. New York: 1867. V. 42

LAURENT, AUGUSTE

Chemical Method, Notation, Classification and Nomenclature. London: 1855. V. 38; 46

LAURENT DE LARA, DAVID

Elementary Instruction in the Art of Illuminating and Missal Painting on Vellum. London: 1857. V. 38; 46

LAURENT, JOSEPH

New Familiar Abenakis and English Dialogues . . . Quebec: 1884. V. 37; 38; 43

LAURENT, PETER EDMUND

Recollections of a Classical Tour through Various Parts of Greece, Turkey and Italy, made in the Years 1818 and 1819. London: 1822. V. 37

LAURENTIUS, OF SCHNUFFIS 1633-1702

Mirantisches Floetlein, Oder Geistliche Schaefferey, In Welcher Christus Under dem Namen Daphnis, Die in Dem Suenden-Schlaff Vertiefte Seel Clorinda zu Einem Besseren Leben Auferweckt . . . Bischoefl: 1682. V. 40

LAURIE, R.

New Travellers Companion. London: 1807. V. 42; 43

LAURIE, R. H.

Catalogue of Perspective Views, Coloured for the Shew Glass or Diagonal Mirror. London: 1824. V. 40

LAURIE, RICHARD H.

The Virgin Islands Trigonmetrically Surveyed and Adjested by Accurate Astronomic Observations. London: 1821. V. 42

LAURIE, SIMON SOMERVILLE 1843-1916

On the Philosophy of Ethics, an Analytical Essay. Edinburgh: 1866. V. 42

LAURIE'S New Traveller's Companion, and Guide through the Roads of England and Wales . . . London: 1830. V. 40

LAURVIK, J. NILSEN

Is It Art? New York: 1913. V. 38; 39; 41

LAUT, AGNES C.

The Blazed Trail of the Old Frontier . . . New York: 1926. V. 42

LAUTERS, PAUL

Souvenir du Sacre-Coeur. Brussels: 1850. V. 38

LAUTS, JAN

Carpaccio: Paintings and Drawings. London: 1962. V. 37; 40; 42; 44

LAVAL, M. LOTTIN DE

Voyage dans la Peninsule Arabique du Siani et l'Egypte Moyenne Histoire, Geographie, Epigraphie. Paris: 1855-59. V. 43

LAVAL, PERE ANTOINE JEAN DE

Voyage de la Louisiane, Fait Par Ordre du Roy En l'Annee Mil Sept Cent Vingt . . . Paris: 1728. V. 40; 43

LAVALETTE, S.

Fables. Paris: 1847. V. 39

LAVALLEE, JOSEPH

Galerie du Musee Napoleon. Paris: 1808-1815. V. 40

Voyage Pittoresque et Historique de l'Istrie et de la dalmatie, Redige d'Apres l'Itineraire de L. F. Cassas. Paris: 1802. V. 38

LAVALLEYE, JACQUES

Pieter Bruegel the Elder and Lucas Van Leyden: The Complete Engravings. London: 1967. V. 37; 40; 43; 44

LA VALLIERE, CHEVALIER DE

The Art of War. Philadelphia: 1776. V. 44

LAVARDIN, JACQUES DE d. after 1587

Histoire de Georges Castriot, Surnomme Scanderbeg, Roy d'Albanie. Paris: 1621. V. 37; 40

The Historie of George Castriot, Surnamed Scanderbeg, King of Albanie. London: 1596. V. 41; 44

LAVATER, JOHANN CASPAR 1741-1801

Aphorisms on Man. London: 1788. V. 42; 44; 46

Aphorisms on Man. London: 1794. V. 37; 43

Essays on Physiognomy; for the Promotion of the Knowledge and the Love of Mankind. London: 1789. V. 37; 38; 41; 44

Essays on Physiognomy. London: 1789-92-98. V. 38; 40; 42

Essays on Physiognomy, Designed to Promote the Knowledge and Love of Mankind. London: 1789-98. V. 37; 41; 42; 43; 45; 46

Essays on Physiognomy. London: 1792. V. 41; 46

Essays on Phsysiognomy . . . Written in the German Language . . . Boston: 1794. V. 41; 43; 44

Essays on Physiognomy: For the Promotion of the Knowledge and the Love of Mankind: Abridged from Mr. Holcroft's trans. Boston: (1794). V. 37

Essays on Physiognomy . . . London: 1794. V. 38; 40

Essays on Physiognomy . . . London: 1797. V. 37; 38; 40; 41; 42; 45

Essays on Physiognomy . . . London: 1800. V. 38; 44

Essays on Physiognomy; for the Promotion of the Knowledge and Love of Mankind . . . To which are Added, One hundred Physiognomical Rules; A Posthumous Works by mr. Lavater, and Memoirs of the Life of the Author. London: 1804. V. 37

Essays on Physiognomy . . . London: 1810. V. 45

Essays on Physiognomy: . . . London: 1867. V. 46

Letter to the French Directory. London: 1799. V. 42

Secret Journal of a Self Observer; or, Confessions and Familiar Letters. London: 1795. V. 42; 46

The Whole Works of Lavater on Physiognomy. London: 1800. V. 38; 46

LAVATER, LUDWIG 1527-1586

De Spectris, Lemuribus et Magnis Atque Insolitis Fragoribus, Variisque Praesagitionibus, Quae Plerunque Obitum Hominum, Magnas Clades, Mutationesque Imperiorum Praecedunt, Liber Unus. Geneva: 1580. V. 45

LAVAYASSE, J. J. D.

A Statistical, Commercial and Political Description of Venezuela, Trinidad, Margarita and Tobago . . . London: 1820. V. 43

LAVEDANI, ANTONIO 1596-1670

De Anno Sancto sive Jubileo Christianorum. Toulouse: 1650. V. 38

LAVELLEE, JOSEPH

Galerie du Musee Napoleon. Paris: 1808-15. V. 44

LAVER, JAMES

Cervantes. Oxford: 1921. V. 40

A Complete Catalogue of the Etchings and Dry Points of Arthur Briscoe. London: 1930. V. 41

A History of British and American Etching. London: 1929. V. 42; 46

Ladies' Mistakes. Cupid's Changeling. A Stitch in Time. Love's Progress. Bloomsbury: 1933. V. 45

LAVERACK, EDWARD

The Setter . . . London: 1872. V. 45

LAVERAN, A.

Paludism. London: 1893. V. 38; 39; 40; 41; 42

LAVERAN, CHARLES L. A.

Trypanosomes and Trypanosomiases. London: 1907. V. 43

LA VERENDRYE, PIERRE GAUTIER DE VARENNES, SIEUR DE 1685-1749

Journals and Letters of Pierre Gautier de Varennes de La Verendrye and His Sons . . . Toronto: 1927. V. 38; 39; 44; 46

LAVIN, IRVING

Bernini and the Unity of the Visual Arts. Oxford: 1980. V. 39

Renaissance Painting in Honour of Millard Meiss. 1977. V. 44

Studies in Late Medieval And Renaissance Painting in Honor of Millard Meiss. New York: 1977. V. 42; 44

LAVIN, MARY

The Patriot Sun. London: 1956. V. 44

LAVIN, S. R.

Cambodian Spring. Deerfield: 1973. V. 37; 40; 42

The Stonecutters at War with the Cliff Dwellers. Nine Poems by . . . Williamsburgh: 1971. V. 38; 39; 46

LAVINGTON, GEORGE

The Enthusiasm of Methdists and Papists Compared. London: 1749/51. V. 44

LAVOISIER, ANTOINE LAURENT 1743-1794

Elements of Chemistry, in a New Systematic Order . . . Edinburgh: 1790. V. 41

Elements of Chemistry. Edinburgh: 1793. V. 38; 41; 46

Elements of Chemistry. Edinburgh: 1799. V. 40

Memoires de Chimie. Paris: 1805. V. 40

Methode de Nomenclature Chimique, Proposee par MM. de Morveau, Lavoisier, Berthelet & de Fourcroy. Paris: 1787. V. 38

Opuscules Physiques et Chimiques. Paris: 1801. V. 39

Traite Elementaire de Chimie, Presente dans un Ordre Nouveau et d'Apres les Decouvertes Modernes. Paris: 1789. V. 38

LAVOISIER, ANTOINE LAURENT 1743-1794 continued

Traite Elementaire de Chimie. Paris: 1798. V. 38

LAVOISNE, C. V.

A New Genealogical, Historical and Chronological Atlas . . . London: 1807. V. 45

LAVOISNE, M.

A Complete Genealogical, Historical, Chronological and Geographical Atlas. Philadelphia: 1820. V. 44

LAW, ALICE

Emily Jane Bronte and the Authorship of Wuthering Heights. Accrington: 1928. V. 41

LAW, EDMUND 1703-1787

An Enquiry Into the Ideas of Space, Time, Immensity and Eternity . . . Cambridge: 1734. V. 42; 43

LAW, ERNEST

The History of Hampton Court Palace. London: 1885-1891. V. 39

The History of Hampton Court Palace. London: 1891-1903. V. 42

The Royal Gallery of Hampton Court Illustrated. London: 1898. V. 43; 44

THE LAW-FRENCH Dictionary Alphabetically Digested; . . . In the Savoy: 1718. V. 41; 43

LAW, H. B.

The Second Army Air Service Book. Toul, France,: 1919. V. 38

LAW, J. S.

An Essay on the Religious Oral Instruction of the Colored Race . . . Penfield: 1846. V. 43

LAW, JOHN

Address Delivered Before the Vincennes Historical and Antiquarian Society, Feb. 22, 1839. Louisville: 1839. V. 37; 42; 43; 46

Colonial History of Vincennes. Vincennes: 1858. V. 37; 38; 39; 44

A Full and Impartial Account of the Company of Mississippi, Otherwise Call'd the French East-India Company, Projected and Settled by Mr. Law. London: 1720. V. 45

Het Groote Tafereel der Dwaasheid. Amsterdam: 1720. V. 38

Money and Trade Considered, with a Proposal for Supplying the Nation with Money. Edinburgh: 1705. V. 38

Money and Trade Considered: With a Proposal for Supplying the Nation with Money. Glasgow: 1750. V. 41

LAW, JOY

The Lion and Unicorn Press. A Short History . . . London: 1953-78. V. 46

THE LAW of Covenants. London: 1712. V. 42

THE LAW of Ejectments. In the Savoy: 1713. V. 38

THE LAW of Testaments and Wills. In the Savoy: 1744. V. 38

LAW, WILLIAM 1686-1761

A Demonstration of the Gross and Fundamental Errors of a Late Book, Called 'A Plain Account of the Nature and End of the Sacrament of the Lord's Supper.' London: 1737. V. 37; 43; 44

The Oxford Methodists. London: 1733. V. 39

A Practical Treatise Upon Christian Perfection. London: 1726. V. 44

A Serious Call to a Devout and Holy Life. London: 1729. V. 38; 39; 40; 42; 45

A Sermon, Preach'd at Hazelingfield, in the County of Cambridge, on Tuesday July 7, 1713. London: 1713. V. 38; 40; 41

The Spirit of Love, Being an Appendix to the Spirit of Prayer. London: 1752-65. V. 39; 40; 43

LAWALL, CHARLES H.

Four Thousand Years of Pharmacy: an Outline of the History of Pharmacy and the Allied Sciences. Philadelphia: 1927. V. 38; 42

LAWALREE, ANDRE

Pierre Joseph Redoute. Pittsburgh: 1972. V. 40

LAWLER, C. F.

The Elegant Sharper. London: 1804. V. 40

The Mixicologist or How to Mix All Kinds of Fancy Drinks. Cincinnati: 1899. V. 46

LAWLER, JOHN

Book Auctions in England in the Seventeenth Century (1676-1700). London: 1898. V. 42

LAWLESS, EMILY

Grania, the Story of an Island. London: 1892. V. 39; 46

Major Lawrence F. L. S. London: 1887. V. 44

LAWLESS, JOHN 1773-1837

A Compendium of the History of Ireland from the Earliest Period to the Reign of George I. Edinburgh: 1823. V. 43

LAWLOR, H. C.

A History of the Family of Cairnes or Cairns and Its Connections. London: 1906. V. 43

LAWRENCE, A. B.

A History of Texas, or the Emigrant's Guide to the New Republic . . . New York: 1844. V. 44; 45

History of Texas, or the Emigrant's Guide to the New Republic. New York: 1845. V. 39; 40; 46

Texas in 1840, or the Emigrant's Guide to the New Republic. New York: 1840. V. 37; 39; 40; 45

LAWRENCE, A. W.

Letters to T. E. Lawrence. London: 1962. V. 38

T. E. Lawrence by His Friends. London: 1954. V. 38

LAWRENCE, ADA

The Early Life of D. H. Lawrence. Florence: 1931. V. 38

Young Lorenzo. Florence: 1931. V. 37; 40; 42

LAWRENCE, AMOS

Extracts from the Diary and Correspondence . . . Boston: 1855. V. 40

LAWRENCE-ARCHER, J. H.

The British Army: Its Regimental Records, Badges, Devices, etc. London: 1888. V. 38

Monumental Inscriptions of the British West Indies, from the Earliest Date, with Genealogical and Historical Annotations . . . London: 1875. V. 40; 41

LAWRENCE, BOYLE

Celebrities of the Stage. London: 1890. V. 38; 45

LAWRENCE, CHARLES

History of the Philadelphia Almshouses and Hospitals from the Beginning of the Eighteenth to the Ending of the Nineteenth Centuries . . . Philadelphia: 1905. V. 45

Liverpool and Manchester Railway. Liverpool: 1832. V. 46

LAWRENCE, DAVID HERBERT 1885-1930

A Propos of Lady Chatterley's Lover. London: 1930. V. 42

Aaron's Rod. London: 1922. V. 39; 44

Aaron's Rod. New York: 1922. V. 39

Amores. London: 1916. V. 37; 38; 39; 43

Amores. New York: 1916. V. 40; 43

Apocalypse. Florence: 1931. V. 37; 38; 40; 41; 45

Apocalypse. London: 1932. V. 38; 44

Assorted Articles. London: 1930. V. 41; 42; 43; 44

Assorted Articles. New York: 1930. V. 43

Bay. London: 1929. V. 40

A Bibliography of the Writings of D.H. Lawrence. Philadelphia: 1925. V. 37

Birds, Beasts and Flowers. London: 1930. V. 39; 44

Birds, Beasts and Flowers. New York: 1923. V. 38

The Boy in the Bush. London: 1924. V. 41

The Boy in the Bush. New York: 1924. V. 39

Collected Poems. London: 1928. V. 38

The Collected Poems. London: 1929. V. 38

The Complete Poems of D. H. Lawrence. London: 1964. V. 43

Consciousness. Los Angeles: 1974. V. 42

Consciousness. N.P.: 1974. V. 39

Consciousness. Santa Barbara: 1974. V. 39

David: a Play. London: 1926. V. 37; 40; 44

David: a Play. New York: 1926. V. 39

England My England and Other Stories. New York: 1922. V. 39; 46

England, My England. London: 1924. V. 42; 46

The Escaped Cock. Paris: 1929. V. 37; 38; 39; 41; 43; 46

The Escaped Cock. Paris: 1929. V. 39

The Escaped Cock. 1973. V. 37; 42; 44

Etruscan Places. London: 1932. V. 41

Etruscan Places. New York: 1932. V. 40

Fantasia of the Unconscious. New York: 1922. V. 39

Fantasia of the Unconscious. London: 1923. V. 38; 41

Les Filles du Pasteur. Paris: 1933. V. 40

Fire and Other Poems. San Francisco: 1940. V. 38; 41

Fire and Other Poems. (San Francisco): 1940. V. 37

Fire and other Poems with a Foreword by Robinson Jeffers. San Francisco: 1930. V. 37

Glad Ghosts. London: 1926. V. 37; 38; 39; 41; 42; 45

LAWRENCE, RAWSTORNE

Gamonia, Art of Perserving Game Improved Method of Plantations and Covers. London: 1929. V. 37

LAWRENCE, RICHARD

The Complete Farrier and British Sportsman. London: 1816. V. 38

Elgin Marbles, from the Parthenon at Athens . . . London: 1818. V. 45

An Inquiry into the Structure and Animal Oeconomy of the Horse . . . Birmingham: 1801. V. 37; 42

An Inquiry into the Structure and Animal Economy of the Horse . . . with Proper Directions for Shoeing. London: 1803. V. 37

The Interest of Ireland in Its Trade and Wealth Stated. Dublin: 1682. V. 38

LAWRENCE, RICHARD HOE

Catalogue of the Engravings Issued by the Society of Iconophiles of the City of New York 1894-1908. New York: 1908. V. 39; 46

History of the Society of Iconophiles of the City of New York: MDCCCXCV; MCMXXX and Catalogue of its Publications . . . New York: 1930. V. 42; 43

LAWRENCE, SIMON

Forty Five Wood Engravers. 1982. V. 44

S. T. E. Lawrence: Boxwood Blockmaker. 1980. V. 44

S. T. E. Lawrence Boxwood Blockmaker. London: 1980. V. 41

LAWRENCE, THOMAS

Engravings from the Choicest Works. London: 1845. V. 40

Franci Nichollsii, M.D . . . Vita: cum Conjecturis Ejusdem de Natura et Usu Partium Humani Corporis Similarium. London: 1780. V. 39; 41; 45

Hydrops; Disputatio Medica. London: 1756. V. 42

Mercurius Centralis. London: 1664. V. 38

LAWRENCE, THOMAS DAWSON

The Miscellaneous Works. Dublin: 1789. V. 41; 42

LAWRENCE, THOMAS EDWARD 1888-1935

A Brief Account of the Advance of the Egyptian Expeditionary Force. Cairo: 1919. V. 38

Crusader Castles. Berkshire: 1936. V. 46

Crusader Castles. London: 1936. V. 37; 38; 40; 41; 43; 44; 46

Crusader Castles. Waltham St. Lawrence: 1936. V. 44; 45

The Diary. 1937. V. 44

The Diary of T. E. Lawrence. London: 1937. V. 44; 46

Eight Letters from T.E.L. to H. Granville-Barker. London: 1939. V. 38

An Essay on Flecker. Garden City: 1937. V. 41

From a Letter of T. E. Lawrence. Verona: 1959. V. 40

The Home Letters of T. E. Lawrence and His Brothers. Oxford: 1954. V. 38; 41

The Letters of T. E. Lawrence. London: 1938. V. 38; 41; 46

The Letters . . . London: 1938. V. 46

Letters to T. E. Lawrence. London: 1962. V. 41

T. E. Lawrence: Letters to E. T. Leeds. Glouchestershire: 1987. V. 39

Letters to E. T. Leeds. 1988. V. 39; 40; 45

Letters from T. E. Shaw to Bruce Rogers. New York: 1933. V. 45

Men in Print. 1940. V. 38; 39; 43

Men in Print. Waltham St. Lawrence: 1940. V. 44

Men in Print. London: 1940. V. 37

Men in Print. Essays in Literary Criticism. (1940). V. 37

Minorities. London: 1971. V. 41

The Mint. 1955. V. 41

The Mint. Garden City: 1955. V. 37; 40; 42; 46

The Mint. London: 1955. V. 37; 38; 39; 40; 44; 45; 46

The Mint. New York: 1955. V. 38

Oriental Assembly. London: 1939. V. 37; 40; 41; 42; 44; 46

Oriental Assembly. New York: 1940. V. 37; 39; 44

Oriental Assembly. London: (1939). V. 37

Revolt in the Desert. London: 1927. V. 38; 39; 46

Revolt in the Desert. New York: 1927. V. 39; 46

Al-Thawra Fi Al-Sahra. (Revolt in the Desert). Cairo: 1949. V. 41

Secret Despatches from Arabia. London: 1939. V. 41

Secret Despatches from Arabia. Waltham St. Lawrence: 1939. V. 44; 46

Secret Despatches from Arabia. 1939. V. 38

Seven Pillars of Wisdom. Oxford: 1922. V. 43

Seven Pillars of Wisdom, a Triumph. London: 1926. V. 46

The Seven Pillars of Wisdom. New York: 1926. V. 40

Seven Pillars of Wisdom. Garden City: 1935. V. 38; 40; 41; 42

Seven Pillars of Wisdom. London: 1935. V. 37; 38; 39; 40; 41; 42; 43; 44; 45; 46

Seven Pillars of Wisdom. New York: 1935. V. 37; 38; 40; 42

Seven Pillars of Wisdom: a Triumph. Garden City: 1938/26. V. 44

Seven Pillars of Wisdom. Garden City: (1935). V. 37

Shaw-Ede; T. E. Lawrence's Letters to H. S. Ede 1927-1935. London: 1942. V. 37; 40

Shaw-Ede. T. E. Lawrence's Letters to H. S. Ede 1927-1935. Waltham St. Lawrence: 1942. V. 44

A Short Note on the Design and Issue of Postage Stamps. Cairo: 1919. V. 40

The Suppressed Opening Chapter. London: 1977. V. 41

T. E. Lawrence to His Biographer Robert Graves. (with) T. E. Lawrence to His Biographer Liddell Hart. London: 1938. V. 37; 38

T. E. Lawrence to His Biographer. New York: 1938. V. 38; 39; 43; 45; 46

T. E. Lawrence: Letters to E. T. Leeds. 1988. V. 44

T. E. Lawrence: Letters to E. T. Leeds. Gloucestershire: 1988. V. 39; 40; 45

The Wilderness of Zin. London: 1915. V. 38

LAWRENCE, W. J.

The Life of Gustavus Vaughan Brooke, Tragedian. Belfast: 1892. V. 38

LAWRENCE, WILLIAM

The Autobiography of Sergeant William Lawrence, A Hero of the Peninsular and Waterloo Campaigns. London: 1886. V. 38

An Introduction to Comparative Anatomy and Physiology. London: 1816. V. 38

Lectures on Physiology, Zoology and the Natural History of Man, Delivered at the Royal College of Surgeons. London: 1819. V. 41; 42

Lectures on Physiology, Zoology and Natural History of Man, Delivered at the Royal College of Surgeons. London: 1822. V. 40; 42; 43; 46

Lectures on Physiology, Zoology and the Natural History of Man, Delivered at the Royal College of Surgeons. Salem: 1828. V. 37; 39

Lectures on Surgery Medical and Operative, as Delivered in the Theatre of St. Bartholomew's Hospital. London: 1832. V. 39

A Treatise on the Diseases of the Eye. Washington: 1834. V. 38; 40

A Treatise on the Diseases of the Eye. London: 1844. V. 44

A Treatise on the Diseases of the Eye. Philadelphia: 1847. V. 42

A Treatise on Hernia, being the Essay which gained the Prize offered by the Royal College of Physicians. London: 1806-1807. V. 37

Two Great Questions Determined by the Principles of Reason and Divinity. London: 1681. V. 43

LAWRENCE, WILLIAM BEACH

Address, Delivered Before the American Academy of Fine Arts. New York: 1825. V. 45

The Origin and Nature of the Representative and Federative Insitutions of the United States . . . New York: 1932. V. 45

Two Lectures on Political Economy, Delivered at Clinton Hall, Before the Mercantile Library Association of the City of New York. New York: 1832. V. 45; 46

LAWRENCEBURGH & UPPER MISSISSIPPI RAILROAD CO.

Acts Incorporating the . . . Indianapolis: 1852. V. 43

THE LAWS and Customs, Rights, Liberties and Privileges of the City of London. London: 1765. V. 40

THE LAWS Respecting Women, as They Regard Their Natural Rights, or Their Connections and Conduct. London: 1777. V. 39

THE LAWS of Cricket. London: 1907. V. 44

LAWS and Documents Showing the Organization, Powers, and Rights of the Western Pacific Railroad Co. of California. San Francisco: 1865. V. 42

LAWS Concerning the Poor Wherein is Treated of Overseers and Their Office, of Rates . . . of Settlements, of Families, Vagrants, Children, Servants etc. What shall Make or Amount to a Settlement by the Former and Later Statutes . . . London: printed by the: 1708. V. 37

THE LAWS Concerning Travelling &c. London: 1718. V. 39; 40

THE LAWS concerning Travelling, &c. Viz. I. Robbery. 2. Of such accidents . . . In the Savoy: 1718. V. 37

THE LAWS of Jamaica, Passed by the Assembly, and Confirmed by His Majesty in Council, April 17, 1684. To Which is Added, The State of Jamaica, As It Is Now Under the Government of Sir Thomas Lynch. London: 1684. V. 44

LAWS, R. M.

Antarctic Ecology. London: 1984. V. 37; 38

THE LAWS Respecting the Ordinary Practice of Impositions in Money-Lending and Buyring and Selling of Public Offices. London: 1787. V. 39; 42

LAWSON, ALEXANDER

The Compositor as Artist, Craftsman and Tradesman. Athens: 1990. V. 45

LAWSON, ANDREW C.

The California Earthquake of April 18, 1906. Washington: 1969-70. V. 41

LAWSON, CECIL C. P.

History of the Uniforms of the British Army 1961-1967. V. 37

LAWSON, CHARLES ALLEN

British and Native Cochin. London: 1861. V. 44

LAWSON, GEORGE

Injuries of the Eye, Orbit and Eyelids: Their Immediate and Remote Effects. Philadelphia: 1867. V. 42

Politica Sacra 7 Civilis; or, a Model of Civil and Ecclesiastical Government. London: 1689. V. 40

The Royal Water-Lily of South America, and the Water Lilies of Our Own Land . . . Edinburgh: 1851. V. 37; 44

LAWSON, J. MURRAY

Record of the Shipping of Yarmouoth, N.S. Yarmouth: 1876. V. 37

Record of the Shipping of Yarmouth, N.S. V. 37

LAWSON, JOHN

The History of Carolina . . . London: 1714. V. 45

The History of Carolina, Containing an Exact Description and Natural History of that Country . . . Raleigh: 1860. V. 39; 41

Lectures Concerning Oratory. Dublin: 1758. V. 41; 43

Lectures Concerning Oratory. Dublin: 1759. V. 46

Lectures Concerning Oratory. London: 1759. V. 42

A New Voyage to Carolina . . . London: 1714. V. 40

LAWSON, JOHN PARKER

Scotland Delineated. London: 1854. V. 39; 44

Scotland Delineated. London: 1854. V. 44

LAWSON, L. M.

A Practical Treatise on Phthisis Pulmonalis: Embracing Its Pathology, Causes, Symptoms and Treatment. Cincinnati: 1861. V. 42

LAWSON, PETER, & SON

The Agriculturist's Manual. Edinburgh: 1836. V. 39; 41

LAWSON, ROBERT

I Discover Columbus. Boston: 1941. V. 45

LAWSON, THOMAS

Meteorological Register for the Years 1826, 1827, 1828, 1829 and 1830. Philadelphia & New Orleans: 1840. V. 37; 38

LAWSON, WILL

Pacific Steamers. Glasgow: 1927. V. 45

LAWSON, WILLIAM

A New Orchard and Garden . . . London: 1631. V. 45

Ten Years of Gentleman Farming at Blennerhasset, with Co-Operative Objects. London: 1874. V. 43; 46

LAWTON, GEORGE

The Religious Houses of Yorkshire. London: 1853. V. 38

LAWTON, LANCELOT

Empires of the Far East. London: 1912. V. 40

LAX, ERIC

Woody Allen. New York: 1991. V. 46

THE LAY of Corneelis: The Three Cantos. Calcutta: 1812. V. 45

THE LAY of John Haroldson. Philadelphia: 1866. V. 42

LAY, WILLIAM

A Narrative of the Mutiny, on Board the Ship Globe, of Nantucket, in the Pacific Ocean. Jan 1824. New London: 1828. V. 40; 41; 43; 44; 46

LAYARD, AUSTEN HENRY 1817-1894

Discoveries in the Ruins of Nineveh and Babylon. London: 1853. V. 43

Early Adventures in Persia, Susiana and Babylonia. London: 1887. V. 39; 40

Early Adventures in Persia, Susiana and Bablonia Including a Residence Among the Bakhtiyari and Other Wild Tribes Before the Discovery of Nineveh. New York: 1887. V. 44

Early Adventures in Persia, Susiana and Babylonia Including a Residence Among the Bakhtiyari and Other Wild Tribes BEfore the Discovery of Nineveh. London: 1894. V. 40

The Monuments of Nineveh. (with) A Second Series of the Monuments of Nineveh. 1849, 1853. V. 40

The Monuments of Nineveh. (with) A Second Series of the Monuments of Nineveh . . . London: 1849, 1853. V. 42

The Monuments of Nineveh. London: 1849-53. V. 40

Ninevah and Its Remains. London: 1849. V. 37; 38; 39; 40; 42; 44; 46

Nineveh and its Remains. New York: 1849. V. 39

Nineveh and Its Remains . . . London: 1850. V. 38; 46

A Popular Account of Discoveries at Nineveh. London: 1851. V. 40

LAYARD, EDGAR LEOPOLD

The Birds of South Africa. London: 1875-1884. V. 37; 38; 39; 42

LAYARD, EDWARD LEOPOLD

The Birds of South Africa. Cape Town: 1867. V. 43

LAYARD, GEORGE SOMES

Catalogue Raisonne of Engraved British Portraits from Altered Plates. London: 1927. V. 42; 46

The Life and Letters of Charles Samuel Keene. London: 1892. V. 38; 39; 41; 44; 45

Suppressed Plates Wood Engravings, Etc. Together With Other Curiosities Germane Thereto. London: 1907. V. 37; 40; 41

Tennyson and His Pre-Raphaelite Illustrators. London: 1894. V. 37; 39; 40; 41; 44; 46

LAYARD, HENRY

Early Adventures in Persia, Susiana and Babylonia. London: 1887. V. 42

LAYCOCK, BENJAMIN

A Portion of the Life, Sufferings, Persecution and Punishment Inflicted Upon Benjamin Laycock an Englishman, of Myrtle Place, Bingley . . . Bingley: 1856. V. 46

LAYER, CHRISTOPHER

Report from the Committee . . . House Commons to Examine Christopher Layer and others . . . Relating to the Conspiracy . . . 1st of March 1722. London: 1722. V. 38

LAYNE, J. GREGG

Annals of Los Angeles from the Arrival of the First White Men to the Civil War 1769-1861. San Francisco: 1935. V. 40; 42; 44

Western Wayfaring: Routes of Exploration and Trade in the American Southwest. Los Angeles: 1954. V. 40

LAYNG, HENRY

The Rod, a Poem. Oxford: 1754. V. 37; 42; 46

LAYS of Ancient Babyland. London: 1849. V. 37

LAYS of the Belvoir Hunt. Grantham: 1866. V. 39

LAYS Of the Minnesingers or German Troubadours of the Twelfth and Thirteenth Centuries . . . With Historical and Critical Notices. London: 1825. V. 40

LAYS of the Western World. New York. V. 44

LAYTON, IRVING

The Cold Green Element. N.P.: 1955. V. 37

Dudek. Toronto: 1953. V. 43

Here and Now. Montreal: 1945. V. 43

The Improved Binoculars. Highlands: 1956. V. 44

In the Midst of My Fever. Palma de Mallorca: 1954. V. 43

The Love Poems of Irving Layton. Toronto: 1978. V. 37; 39; 44

Seventy-Five Greek Poems 1951-1974. Athens: 1974. V. 37

There Were No Signs: with Fifteen Etchings by Aligi Sassu. Toronto: 1979. V. 42; 44

LAYTON, T. B.

Catalogue of the Onodi Collection in the Museum of the Royal College of Surgeons of England. London: 1934. V. 39

LAZAMON, OF ERNLEY

Lazamon's Brut, or Chronicle of Britain. London: 1847. V. 38

LAZARUS, E. S.

The Form of Daily Prayers, According to the Custom of the Spanish and Portuguese Jews. New York: 1826. V. 43

LAZARUS, EMMA

The Dance to Death. New York: 1882. V. 43

LAZELL, FREDERICK JOHN

Some Winter Days in Iowa. (with) Some Spring Days in Iowa. (&) Some Summer Days in Iowa. (&) Some Autumn Days in Iowa. Cedar Rapids: 1907-11. V. 37; 38

LAZHECHNIKOV, IVAN IVANOVICH

The Heretic. Edinburgh & London: 1844. V. 38

LAZIUS, WOLFGANG

Fragmenta Qvaedam Caroli Magni Imp. Rom. Aliorumq; Incerti Nominis de Veteris Ecclesiae Ritibus ac Ceremonijs, a VVolgango Lazio eruta a Tineis. Antwerp: 1560. V. 39

LAZZARI, ANTONIO

Nuova Raccolta delle Principali Vedute Della R. Citta de Venezia. Venice: 1831. V. 38; 41; 44

LEA, HENRY C.

Supperstition and Force. Essays on the Wager of Law - The Wager of Battle - The Ordeal - Torture. Philadelphia: 1866. V. 37

LEA, HENRY CHARLES

A History of the Inquisition of the Middle Ages. New York: 1888. V. 40

A History of the Inquisition of Spain. New York: 1922. V. 46

Materials Toward a History of Witchcraft. New York: London: 1957. V. 43

LEA, J. HENRY

The Ancestry of Abraham Lincoln. Boston: 1909. V. 42

LEA, JAMES H.

The Ancestry and Posterity of John Lea of Christian Malford, Wilshire, England and of Pennsylvania in America. Philadelphia: 1906. V. 39

LEA, KENNETT

Poemata Melica. London: 1863. V. 37

LEA, TOM 1907-

The Brave Bulls. Boston: 1949. V. 46

87 Paintings and Drawings by Tom Lea. El Paso: 1971. V. 44

A Grizzly From the Coral Sea. El Paso: 1944. V. 38; 45

The Hands of Cantu. Boston: 1964. V. 44

In the Crucible of the Sun. Kingsville: 1974. V. 40; 43

The King Ranch. Boston: 1957. V. 37; 38; 39; 40; 42; 43; 44; 45; 46

The King Ranch. Kingsville: 1957. V. 38; 39; 44; 45; 46

The King Ranch. Kingsville: 1967. V. 42

The King Ranch. Boston: (1957). V. 37

The King Ranch. Boston and Toronto: 1957. V. 37

Peleliu Landing. El Paso: 1945. V. 37; 38; 39; 40; 42; 43; 44

A Picture Gallery, Paintings & Drawings by Tom Lea, with Text by the Artist. Boston: (1968). V. 37

A Picture Gallery. Boston: 1968. V. 37; 38; 39; 42; 43; 44

A Portfolio of Six Paintings. Austin: 1953. V. 41

Randado. El Paso: 1941. V. 42

Tcm Lea, A Selection of Paintings and Drawings from the Nineteen Sixties. San Antonio: 1969? V. 39

A Selection of Paintings and Drawings from the Ninetten-Sixties. San Antonio: (1969). V. 37

Western Beef Cattle: a Series of Eleven Paintings by Tom Lea Depicting the Origin and Development of the Western Range Animal. Austin: 1967. V. 38; 44

Western Beef Cattle: a Series of Eleven Printings Depicting the Origin and Development of the Western Range Animal. El Paso: 1967. V. 38; 46

LEACH, A. J.

Early Day Stories. The Overland. Norfolk: 1916. V. 40; 42; 43; 45; 46

LEACH, BERNARD

A Potter's Portfolio. London: 1951. V. 38; 42

LEACH, D. G.

Rhododendrons of the World. London: 1962. V. 43

LEACH, JAMES

A New Sett (-a Second Sett) of Hymns and Psalm Tunes Adapted for the Use of Churches, Chapels and Sunday Schools, with Accompaniments . . . London: 1789-94. V. 41

LEACH, JOHN 1760-1834

The Speech in the Committee of the Whole House, Upon the State of the nation, on Monday, December 31, 1810 Upon the Question of Limitations to the Royal Authority in the Hands of the Rent. London: 1811. V. 38; 40

LEACH, JOSIAH GRANVILLE

Genealogical and Biographical Memorials of the Reading, Howell, Yerkes, Watts, Latham and Elkins Families. Philadelphia: 1898. V. 39; 46

History of the Grinhurst Family with Notes on the Clarkson, DePeyster and Boude Families. Philadelphia: 1901. V. 46

Some Account of Capt. John Frazier and His Descendants. Philadelphia: 1910. V. 46

LEACH, MACEDWARD

The Book of Ballads. Mt. Vernon: 1967. V. 45

LEACH, W. E.

Malacostraca Podophtalmata Britanniae. London: 1815-75. V. 38

LEACH, WILLIAM

The Zoological Miscellany . . . London: 1814-17. V. 43

LEACOCK, STEPHEN

Canada. The Foundation of Its Future. Montreal: 1941. V. 38

The Greatest Pages of American Humour . . . New York: 1936. V. 43

The Hohenzollerns in America and Other Impossibilities. London: 1919. V. 44

Literary Lapses. Montreal: 1910. V. 40; 41; 42; 43; 44

The Marionettes' Calendar 1916. London: 1916. V. 41

My Discovery of England. London: 1922. V. 38

Over the Footlights. New York: 1923. V. 46

Over the Footlights. Toronto: 1923. V. 37; 40; 42

The Unsolved Riddle of Social Justice. London: 1920. V. 37; 40; 42

Winnowed Wisdom. New York: 1926. V. 43

LEADAM, I. S.

The Domesday of Inclosures 1517-1518. London: 1897. V. 44

LEADBEATER, MARY

The Leadbeater Papers. London: 1862. V. 43

Poems by Mary Leadbeater, Late Shackleton to Which is Prefixed Her Translation of the Thirteenth Book of the Aeneid, etc. Dublin: 1808. V. 43

LEADBETTER, CHARLES

Astronomy; or, the True System of Planets Demonstrated. London: 1727. V. 38; 41; 45

The Royal Gauger; or, Guaging made Perfectly Easy, As it is actually practised by the Officers of His Majesty's Revenue of Excise. Part I . . . also the established rules for finding the Contents of All Sorts of Cisterns, Coppers . . . London: 1755. V. 37

LEADER, JOHN DANIEL

Mary Queen of Scots in Captivity . . . Sheffield: 1880. V. 42

The Records of the Burgery of Sheffield, Commonly Called the Town Trust. London: 1897. V. 39

THE LEADING Industries of the West . . . Chicago: 1883. V. 38

LEAF and Flower Pictures, and How to Make Them. New York: 1857. V. 38

A LEAF from the Letters of St. Jerome. Los Angeles: 1981. V. 46

LEAF, MUNRO

The Story of Ferninand. New York: 1936. V. 38

The Story of Ferdinand. London: 1937. V. 39; 41; 45

Wee Gillis. New York: 1938. V. 37

LEAF, WALTER

Strabo on the Troad: Book XIII, Cap. I. Cambridge: 1923. V. 42

LEAFLETS OF MEMORY: An Illuminated Annual for 1852. Philadelphia: 1852, 1851. V. 38

LEAK, ANN E.

The Autobiography of Miss Ann E. Leak, Born Without Arms; Containing an Interesting Account of Her Early Life and Subsequent Travels in These United States. Boston: 1871. V. 41

LEAKE, CHAUNCEY

Letheon: the Cadenced Story of Anesthesia. Austin: 1947. V. 45

LEAKE, ISAAC Q.

Memoir of the Life and Times of General John Lamb. Albany: 1850. V. 39

Memoir of the Life and Times of General John Lamb, an Officer of the Revolution . . . Albany: 1857. V. 42; 45

LEAKE, JOHN

The Scholar's Manual. Oxford: 1733. V. 40

LEAKE, STEPHEN MARTIN

Heraldo Memoriale, or Memoirs of the College of Arms from 1727 to 1744. 1981. V. 44

An Historical Account of English Money from the Conquest to the Present Time. London: 1745. V. 37; 38; 40; 41; 43

An Historical Account of English Money from the Conquest to the Present Time . . . London: 1793. V. 41; 42

Nummi Britannici Historia. London: 1726. V. 37; 39; 40; 42

LEAKE, WILLIAM MARTIN 1777-1860

An Historical Outline of the Greek Revolution, with a Few Remarks on the Present State of Affairs in that Country. London: 1826. V. 39

Journal of a Tour in Asia Minor, with Comparative Remarks on the Ancient and Modern Geography of that Country. London: 1824. V. 37; 39; 45

Peloponnesiaca: a Supplement to Travels in the Morea. London: 1846. V. 37

Researches in Greece. London: 1814. V. 45

The Topography of Athens, with Some Remarks on Its Antiquities. London: 1821. V. 37; 39; 46

Travels in Northern Greece. London: 1835. V. 39

LEAKE, WILLIAM MARTIN 1777-1860 continued

Travels in the Morea. Amsterdam: 1968. V. 37

LEAKEY, M. D.

Laetoli: A :liocene Site in Northern Tanzania. London: 1986. V. 37

Laetoli: A Pliocene Site in Northern Tanzania. London: 1986. V. 37

LEAMING, JAMES ROSEBRUGH 1820-1892

Contributions to the Study of the Heart and Lungs. New York: 1890. V. 45

LEAMING, JEREMIAH

A Defence of the Episcopal Government of the Church . . . New York: 1766. V. 45

LEAN, COLONEL

Compendium of Kaffir Laws and Customs, Including Genealogical Tables of Kaffir Chiefs and Various Tribal Census Returns. Mount Coke: 1858. V. 39

LEAN, FLORENCE MARRYAT CHURCH 1837-1899

Life and Letters of Captain Marrayt. London: 1872. V. 43

LEAN, GORDON LINDSAY

Ducks of Sub-Saharan Africa. Randburg: 1986. V. 39

LEAN, VICNENT STUCKEY

Lean's Collectiana. Bristol: 1902. V. 37; 42

LEAO, MANUEL DE

Triumpho lusitano. Brussels: 1688. V. 38

LEAR, EDWARD 1812-1888

The Book of Nonsense. London. V. 38; 40

A Book of Nonsense. 1862. V. 45

A Book of Nonsense. London: 1862. V. 41

Edward Lear's Nonsense Songs and Laughable Lyrics. Larchmont: 1935. V. 40

Edward Lear's Nonsense Songs and Laughable Lyrics. New York: 1935. V. 38

Illustrations of the Family of Psittacidae, or Parrots . . . London: 1830-32. V. 40; 43

Illustrations of the Family of Psittacidae, or Parrots. New York: 1978. V. 38

Journal of a Landscape Painter in Albania. London: 1851. V. 39; 42

Journal of a Landscape Painter in Albania &c. London: 1853. V. 42

Journal of a Landscape Painter in Corsica. London: 1870. V. 37; 38; 39; 40; 42; 43

Journals of a Landscape Painter in Southern Calabria. London: 1852. V. 45; 46

The Jumblies. London: 1900. V. 46

Laughable Lyrics. London: 1877. V. 38; 41; 42; 43; 44

Laughable Lyrics, a Fourth Book of Nonsense Poems, Songs, Botany, Music &c. London: 1877/76. V. 43

Laughable Lyrics, French Book of Nonsense Poems, Songs, Botany and Music. V. 37

Letters to Chichester Fortescue Lord Carlingford and Frances Countess Waldegrave. (with) Later Letters. London: 1907-11. V. 37

More Nonsense Pictures, Rhymes, Botany, etc. London: 1872. V. 37

Nonsense Songs, Stories, Botany and Alphabets. Boston: 1871. V. 43

Nonsense Songs, Stories, Botany and Alphabets. London: 1871. V. 39; 44

The Pobble Who Has No Toes. Brisbane: 1979. V. 37

The Story of the Four Little Children Who Went Round the World (and) The History of the Seven Families of the Lake Pipple-Popple . . . 1920. V. 45

Views in Rome and Its Environs Drawn from Nature and on Stone. London: 1841. V. 39

Views in the Seven Ionian Islands. London: 1863. V. 42

Views in the Seven Ionian Islands. London: 1980. V. 39

Views in the Seven Ionian Islands. 1980. V. 37

LEAR, HENRIETTA L. FARRER

Life of Robert Gray. London: 1876. V. 39

LEARED, ARTHUR 1822-1879

Marocco and the Moors . . . London: 1891. V. 38; 45; 46

LEARMONT, JOHN

Poems Pastoral, Satirical, Tragic and Comic. Edinburgh: 1791. V. 41; 42

LEARMONTH, NOEL F.

The Portland Bay Settlement. Portland: 1934. V. 41

LEARNED, EDWARD

Tehuantepec Inter-Ocean Railroad. New York: 1882. V. 43

LEARNED, MARION DEXTER

Guide to the Manuscript Materials Relating to American History in the German State Archives. Washington: 1912. V. 42

The Life of Francis Daniel Pastorius, the Founder of Germantown. Philadelphia: 1908. V. 42

LEARNING by Heart. Devon: 1986. V. 43; 45

LEARNING by Heart: Poems. London: 1986. V. 40

LEARY, FREDERICK

The Earl of Chester's Regiment of Yeomanry Cavalry - Its Formation and Services 1797 to 1897. Edinburgh: 1898. V. 38

LEARY, PETER J.

Newark, New Jersey, Illustrated. New York: 1893. V. 39; 41

LEARY, TIMOTHY

Flashbacks, An Autobiography. Boston: 1983. V. 37

Interpersonal Diagnosis of Personality. New York: 1957. V. 39

LEASK, J. C.

The Regimental Records of the Royal Scots (The First or The Royal Regiment of Foot). Dublin: 1915. V. 37

LEATHABY, W. R.

The Church of Sancta Sophia Constantinople. London: 1894. V. 46

LEATHAM, ISAAC

General View of the Agriculture of the East Riding of Yorkshire, and the Ainsty of the City of York. London: 1794. V. 41

LEATHAM, WILLIAM HENRY

Poems. London: 1843. V. 42

LEATHER; a Discourse, Tendered to the High Court of Parliament. Of the General Use of Leather. London: 1629. V. 41

THE LEATHER Bottle. Concord: 1903. V. 40; 41; 44

LEATHER, ROBINSON K.

The Student and the Body-Snatcher. London: 1890. V. 41

LEATHES, HILL MUSSENDEN

Reminiscences of Waterloo. N.P.,: 1895. V. 41

LEAVES from the Medicine Tree, A History of the Area Influenced by the Tree and Biographies of Old Timers and Pioneers Who Came Under Its Spell Prior to 1910. Lethbridge: 1960. V. 46

LEAVIS, F. R.

Gerard Manley Hopkins: Reflections After Fifty Years. London: 1971. V. 40

LEAVITT, DUDLEY

The Teacher's Assistant and Scholar's Mathematical Directory. Concord: 1830. V. 42

LEAVITT, JONATHAN

A Summary of the Laws of Massachusetts, Relative to the Settlement, Support, Employment and Removal of Paupers. Greenfield: 1810. V. 45

LEAVITT, JOSHUA

Cheap Postage. Remarks and Statistics on the Subject of Cheap Postage and Postal Reform in Great Britain . . . Boston: 1848. V. 42

An Essay on the Best Way of Developing Improved Political and Commercial Relations Between Great Britain and America. London: 1869. V. 45

LEAVITT, M. B.

Fifty Years in Theatrical Management 1859-1909. New York: 1912. V. 46

LEAVITT, NANCY

Familiar Fruits and Vegetables. Amherst: 1986. V. 45

LEAVITT, RICHARD F.

The World of Tennessee Williams. New York: 1978. V. 37; 43; 44; 45; 46

LEAVITT, WILLIAM

A Short and Easy Method of Obtaining the True Lunar Distance. Salem: 1856. V. 41

LEAY, WILLIAM

Granada, Equatorial South America. London: 1869. V. 39

LEAZMIS, JOSE DE

Vida del Apostol Santiago el Mayor. Mexico City: 1699. V. 38

LE BAS, C. W.

Review of the Life and Character of Lord Byron. London: 1833. V. 44

LE BAS, CHARLES W.

The Life of Thomas Fanshaw Middleton. London: 1831. V. 39

LE BEAU, CLAUDE

Avantures du Sr. C. Le Beau, Avocat en Parlement, ou Voyage Curieux et Nouveau, Parmi les Sauvages de l'Amerique Septentrionale. Amsterdam: 1738. V. 39

LEBEAUD, M.

The Principles of the Art of Modern Horsemanship, for Ladies and Gentleman . . . Philadelphia: 1833. V. 43; 45

LE BEGUE, FRANCOIS

Traicte et Avis sur les Desordres des Monnoyes et Diversite d'y Remedier. Paris: 1600. V. 40

LEBEL, ROBERT

Marcel Duchamp. New York: 1959. V. 39

DAS LEBEN und Die Verwegenen Ubenado. (The Life and Tragic Death of Jesse James). Philadelphia: 1883. V. 39

LEBER, FERDINAND

Praelectiones Anatomicae . . . Edinburgi: 1790. V. 46

LE BLANC & ARMENGAUD

The Engineer and Machinist's Drawing Book, A Complete Course of Instruction for the Practical Engineer on the Basis of the Works of M. Le Blanc and M. M. Armengaud. Glasgow: 1855. V. 41

LE BLANC, H.

The Art of Tying the Cravat. London: 1828. V. 40

LEBLANC, MAURICE

The Exploits of Arsene Lupin. 1907. V. 39

The Hollow Needle. London: 1911. V. 39

LE BLOND, ELIZABETH ALICE FRANCES HAWKINS-WHITSHED

Adventures on the Roof of the World. London: 1904. V. 43

Mountaineering in the Land of the Midnight Sun. London: 1908. V. 43

True Tales of Mountain Adventure. London: 1903. V. 43

LE BLOND, JEAN

Deux Exemples des Cinq Ordres de l'Architecture Antique, et des Quatre plus Excelens Autheurs qui en ont Traitte, Scavoir, Palladio, Scamozzi, Serlio, et Vignole. Paris: 1683. V. 38

LEBOE, FRANS DE SYLVIUS

Opera Medica. Geneva: 1698. V. 38

LE BOUCHER, MICHEL

Catalogue Extrait Des Livres d'Assortimens, Qui se Vendent Chez Le Boucher, Libraire. Paris: 1778. V. 38

LEBOUCHER, ODET JULIEN

Histoire de la Derniere Guerre, Entre La Grande-Bretagne, et Les Etats-Unis de l'Amerique, La France, L'Espagne et La Hollande . . . Paris: 1787. V. 44; 46

LE BOURSIER DU COUDRAY, ANGELIQUE MARGUERITE

Abrege de l'Art des Accouchements, dans Lequel on Donne les Preceptes Necessaires Pour le Mettre Heureusement en Practique . . . Paris: 1777. V. 39

LE BOVIER DE FONTENELLE, BERNARD

Conversations on the Plurality of Worlds. Translated from the last Paris edition. By William Gardiner. London: 1715. V. 37

LE BRIGANT, JACQUES

Observations Fondamentales sur les Langues Anciennes et Modernes . . . Paris: 1787. V. 46

LE BROCQUY, LOUIS

Eight Irish Writers. Dublin: 1981. V. 40

LE BRUN

A New and more Correct Translation . . . of Mr. Cornelius Le Brun's Travels into Muscovy, Persia, and divers Parts of the East-Indies; containing an Accurate Description of all such Articles as are most remarkable in each of those . . . London: 1759. V. 37

LEBRUN, CHARLES

The Conference of Monsieur Le Brun, Chief Painter to the French King . . . Upon Expression, General and Particular. London: 1701. V. 44

Divers Desseins de Decorations de Pavillons. Paris: 1680's? V. 39

Handwoerterbuch der Seelen Mahlerey m Gebrauch Besonders Fuer Zeichner, Mahler und Liebhaber . . . Vienna/Prague: 1804. V. 40

Les Peintures de Charles Le Brun et D'Eustache le Sueur. Paris: 1740. V. 46

LE BRUN, CORNEILLE DE

Voyages par la Moscovie, en Perse, et Aux illustrationsndes Orientales. Avsterdam: 1718. V. 38

LEBRUN, FEDERICO

Drawings for Dante's Inferno. New York: 1963. V. 41

LE BRUN, LAURENT

Institvtio Ivventvtis Christianae. Paris: 1653. V. 42

LEBRUN, RICO

Drawings for Dante's Inferno. N.P.: 1963. V. 46

LE CARON, LOUIS 1534-1613

Pandectes ou Digestes du droit Francois. Paris: 1587. V. 37; 40

LE CARPENTIER, MATTHIEU

Receuil des Plans, Coupes et Elevations du Nouvel Hotel de Ville de Rouen . . . Paris: 1758. V. 38; 40; 44

LE CARRE, JOHN 1931-

Call for the dead. New York: 1962. V. 39; 45

The Clandestine Muse. 1986. V. 41; 46

The Clandestine Muse. Newark;: 1986. V. 40; 42; 43

The Honourable Schoolboy. London: 1977. V. 37; 44

The Little Drummer Girl. New York: 1923. V. 40

The Little Drummer Girl. New York: 1983. V. 37; 39; 42; 45; 46

The Little Drummer Girl. London: 1984. V. 40; 44

The Looking Glass War. London: 1965. V. 38; 40; 41; 42; 43

The Looking-Glass War. London: (1965). V. 37

A Murder of Quality. 1963. V. 39

The Naive and Sentimental Lover. London: 1971. V. 41

The Naive and Sentimental Lover. New York: 1971. V. 45

A Perfect Spy. London: 1936. V. 43

A Perfect Spy. V. 41

A Perfect Spy. London: 1986. V. 38; 39; 40; 41

The Russia House. London: 1989. V. 41; 42; 43; 44; 45

The Russia House. New York: 1989. V. 41; 42; 43

A Small Town in Germany. 1968. V. 46

A Small Town in Germany. London: 1968. V. 37; 38; 43

A Small Town in Germany. New York: 1968. V. 43

Smiley's People. 1979. V. 46

Smiley's People. London: 1980. V. 38; 41

Smiley's People. New York: 1980. V. 42

The Spy Who Came in From the Cold. London: 1963. V. 38; 39; 40; 41; 42; 43; 45; 46

The Spy Who Came In From the Cold. New York: 1964. V. 37; 39

Tinker Tailor Soldier Spy. 1974. V. 37

LE CAT, CLAUDE NICHOLAS

Traite de la Couleur de la Peau Humaine en General de celle des Negres en Particulier . . . Amsterdam: 1765. V. 41; 45

LE CAT, CLAUDE NICOLAS

Traite des Sens . . . Amsterdam: 1744. V. 38

LECHEVALIER, JEAN BAPTISTE

Descritpion of the Plain of Troy. Edinburgh: 1791. V. 41

LECHFORD, THOMAS

Plain Dealing: or, Newes from New-England . . . London: 1642. V. 44

Plain Dealing or News from New England. Boston: 1867. V. 40

LECHMERE, EDMUND

A Dispuration of the Church, Wherein the old Religion is Maintained . . . Doway: 1632. V. 43

A Disputation of the Church Wherein the Old Religion is Maintained. Douai: 1640. V. 41; 44

LECHMERE, NICHOLAS

The Messenger Defeated; or, the Lawyer's Escape. Colophon: 1705. V. 41

LECIESTER, ROBERT DUDLEY, EARL OF

Leycesters Common-Wealth: Conceived, Spoken, and Published with Protestation of all Dutifull Good Will and Affection Towards This Realme . . . London: 1641. V. 46

LECKENBY, CHARLES HARMON

The Tread of Pioneers. Steamboat Springs: 1944. V. 37; 39; 43; 46

The Tread of Pioneers . . . Some Highlights in the Dramatic and Colorful History of the Northwestern Colorado. Steamboat Springs: 1945. V. 46

LECKIE, GOULD FRANCIS

An Historical Research into the Nature and Balance of Power in Europe . . . (with) Essay on the Practice of the British Government . . . London: 1817/1812. V. 41

LEDERER, WILLIAM J.

The Ugly American. New York: 1958. V. 44

LEDIARD, THOMAS

The Life of John, Duke of Marlborough, Prince of the Roman Empire . . . London: 1743. V. 46

LEDOUX, C. N.

L'Architecture Consideree Sous le Rapport de l'Art, des Moeurs et de la Legislation. Paris: 1804. V. 38

L'Architecture Consideree Sous le Rapport de l'Art, des Moeurs et de la Legislation. Paris: 1961. V. 38

LEDOUX, LOUIS V.

An Essay on Japanese Prints. New York: 1938. V. 38; 41

LE DRAN, HENRI FRANCOIS

Consultation on Most of the Disorders that Require the Assistance of Surgery. London: 1766. V. 38

Observations in Surgery: Containing One Hundred and Fifteen Cases. London: 1740. V. 37; 39

The Operations in Surgery of Mons. Le Dran . . . London: 1768. V. 45

Parallele des Differentes Manieres de Tirer la Pierre hors de la Vessie. (with) Suite du Parallele des Differentes Manieres de faire l'Extraction de la Pierre qui est dans la Vessie Urinarie. (with) Recit d'une Guerison Singuliere. Paris: 1756. V. 38

LE DRAN, HENRY FRANCOIS

Parallele Des Differentes Maniers de Tirer la Pierre Hors de La Vessie. (with) Suite du Parallele des Differentes Manieres de Faire l'Extraction de la Pierre qui est dans la Vessie Urinaire. (with) Recit d'une Guerison Singuliere. Paris: C Osmont, 1730;. V. 41

LEDRU, NICHOLAS PHILIPPE

V. 45

LE DUC, W. G.

Minnesota Year Book for 1852. St. Paul: 1852. V. 45

LEDWICH, EDWARD

Antiquitates Sarisburienses, containing a Dissertation on the Ancient Coins . . . the Salisbury Ballad . . . Historical Memoirs Relative to the City . . . Salisbury: 1771. V. 38; 40

Antiquities of Ireland. Dublin: 1790. V. 39; 42

LEDYARD, ISAAC

An Essay on Matter. Philadelphia: 1784. V. 45

LEDYARD, JOHN

A Journal of Captain Cook's Last Voyage to the Pacific Ocean, and in Quest of a North-West Passage, Between Asia and America . . . Hartford: 1783. V. 39; 42; 43; 46

LEE, AGNES

The Round Rabbit. Boston: 1898. V. 43; 44

LEE, ALBERT

Tommy Toddles. New York: 1896. V. 37; 41

LEE, AMY FREEMAN

Hobby Horses. New York: 1940. V. 43

LEE, ANNA MARIA

Memoirs of Eminent Female Writers, Of All Ages and Countries. Philadelphia: 1827. V. 42

LEE, ARTHUR

A Second Appeal to the Justice and Interests of the People, on the Measures Respecting America. London: 1775. V. 41

A Speech, Intended to Have Been Delivered in the House of Commons In Support of the Petition from the General Congress at Philadelphia. London: 1775. V. 37; 41

LEE, BRIAN NORTH

Bookplates and Labels by Leo Wyatt. 1988. V. 45

Bookplates and Labels by Leo Wyatt. Wakefield: 1988. V. 40; 41; 42

Bookplates by Simon Brett. London: 1989. V. 44

Bookplates by Simon Brett. Wakefield: 1989. V. 43

LEE, CHARLES

Proceedings of a General Court Martial, Held at Brunswick in the State of New Jersey, by Order of His Excellency General Washington . . . for the Trial of Major General Lee July 4th 1778. Cooperstown: 1823. V. 46

Strictures on a Pamphlet, Entitled 'A Friendly Address to All Reasonable Americans, On the Subject of Political Confusion.' Newport: 1775. V. 40

LEE, CHAUNCEY

The American Accomptant. Lansingburgh: 1797. V. 38; 40; 41; 44; 46

The Trial of Virtue, a Sacred Poem. Hartford: 1806. V. 40

LEE, CUTHBERT

Contemporary American Portrait Painters. New York: 1929. V. 38; 44

LEE, DANIEL

Ten Years in Oregon. New York: 1844. V. 38; 40; 43; 46

LEE, E. C.

E. C. Lee, Saddlery, Manufacturer of Lee Saddles. Catalogue No. 20. Pierre: 1926. V. 44

LEE, EDMUND JENNINGS

Lee of Virginia, 1642-1892. Biographical & Genealogical Sketches of the Descendants of Colonel Richard Lee, with Brief Notices of Related Families . . . Philadelphia: 1895. V. 37

LEE, FITZHUGH

Chancellorsville. Richmond: 1879. V. 44

General Lee of the Confederate Army. London: 1895. V. 41

LEE, FLORENCE S.

Handbook for Hospital Sisters. London: 1874. V. 40

LEE, FRANCIS BAZLEY

Genealogical and Memorial History of the State of New Jersey. New York: 1910. V. 41; 42; 44

History of Trenton, New Jersey. Trenton: 1895. V. 46

History of Trenton, New Jersey. Trenton: 1895/98. V. 41

History of Trenton, New Jersey. The Record of Its Early Settlement and Corporate Progress . . . 1895. V. 41

LEE, GEORGE J.

The Voice; Its Artistic Production, Development and Preservation. London: 1870. V. 42; 43

LEE GRAD, BONNIE

Milton Avery. Michigan: 1981. V. 44

LEE, GUY CARETON

The History of North America. Philadelphia: 1903. V. 40

LEE, GUY CARLETON

The History of North America. Philadelphia: 1903-07. V. 44; 45; 46

LEE, GYPSY ROSE 1914-1979

The G-String Murders. New York: 1941. V. 42

LEE-HANKEY, HARDIE

The Etched Work of W. Lee-Hankey, R.E. from 1904-1920. London. V. 39

LEE, HANNAH FARNHAM

Memoir of Pierre Toussaint, Born a Slave in St. Domingo. Boston: 1854. V. 39; 42; 45

LEE, HANNAH FARNHAM SAWYER

The Backslider. Boston: 1835. V. 43

Elinor Fulton. Boston: 1837. V. 43

Historical Sketches of the Old Painters. Boston: 1838. V. 43

LEE, HARPER

To Kill a Mockingbird. London: 1960. V. 37; 39; 42; 45

To Kill a Mockingbird. New York: 1960. V. 42

To Kill a Mockingbird. Philadelphia: 1960. V. 44; 45

To Kill a Mockingbird. Philadelphia & New York: 1960. V. 38

To Kill A Mockingbird. Philadelphia/New York: (1960). V. 37

LEE, HARRIET

The Three Strangers. London: 1826. V. 38

LEE, HENRY

The Address of the Minority in the Virginia Legislature to the People of that State . . . Richmond: 1799. V. 42

The Life of the Emperor Napoleon . . . London: 1834. V. 44

Memoirs of the War in the Southern Department of the United States. Philadelphia: 1812. V. 41

Memoirs of the War in the Southern Department of the United States. Washington: 1827. V. 46

Memoirs of the War in the Southern Department of the United States . . . London: 1869. V. 41

Memoirs of the War in the Southern Department of the United States. New York: 1869. V. 37

Observations on the Writings of Thomas Jefferson. New York: 1832. V. 40

Observations on the Writings of Thomas Jefferson. Philadelphia: 1839. V. 41; 46

LEE, HOLME

Gilbert Massinger. London: 1855. V. 37

Hawksview: A Family history of our own times. London: 1859. V. 37

LEE, HOLME continued

Kathie Brande; A Fireside History of a Wuiet Life. In Two Volumes. London: 1856. V. 37

Maude Talbot. In Three Volumes. London: 1854. V. 37

Thorney Hall: A Story of an old family. London: 1854. V. 37

LEE, J. R.

A History of Market Drayton, with Some Account of Ashley, Betton, Norton, Cheswardine, and Other Villages. London: 1861. V. 42

LEE, JAMES

An Introduction to Botany. London: 1776. V. 39

LEE, JAMES ARTHUR

Three in Norway, by Two of Them. London: 1883. V. 44

LEE, JESSE

A Short Account of the Life and Death of the Rev. John Lee, A Methodist Minster in the United States of America. Baltimore: 1805. V. 37

A Short History of the Methodists in the United States of America . . . Baltimore: 1810. V. 37

LEE, JOHN

Catalogue of the Egyptian Antiquities in the Museum of Hartwell House. London: 1858. V. 40; 42; 44

Hand-Book for Coroners . . . Philadelphia: 1881. V. 42; 45

LEE, JOHN D.

Journals of John D. Lee, 1846-47 and 1859. Salt Lake City: 1938. V. 40

A Mormon Chronicle. San Marino: 1955. V. 38; 40; 43; 46

The Mormon Menace: Being the Confession of John D. Lee, an Official Assasin of the Mormon Church Under the Late Brigham young. New York: 1905. V. 37

Mormonism Unveiled; or the Life and Confessions of the Late Mormon Bishop . . . St. Louis: 1877. V. 45

Mormonism Unveiled; or the Life and Confessions of the Late Mormon Bishop, John D. Lee . . . St. Louis: 1878. V. 42; 46

LEE, L. P.

History of the Spirit Lake Massacre! New Britain: 1857. V. 37; 38; 40; 45; 46

LEE, LAURIE 1914-

As I Walked Out One Midsummer Morning. London: 1967. V. 38

Cider with Rosie. London: 1959. V. 37; 45

The Voyage of Magellan - a Dramatic Chronicle for Radio. London: 1948. V. 38

LEE, LAWRENCE

A Hawk from Cuckoo Tavern. Gaylordsville: 1930. V. 43

LEE, LUTHER

Woman's Right to Preach the Gospel. A Sermon Preached at the Oration of the Rev. Miss Antoinette L. Brown, at South Butler, Wayne County, N.Y. Sept. 15, 1853. Syracuse: 1853. V. 37

LEE, MARTHA A.

Mother Lee's Experience in Fifteen Years' Rescue Work with Thrilling Incidents of Her Life . . . Omaha: 1906. V. 38

LEE, N. K. M., MRS.

The Cook's Own Book . . . Boston: 1832. V. 45

The Cook's Own Book . . . Boston: 1838. V. 45

The Cook's Own Book, and Housekeeper's Reigster. Boston: 1842. V. 45

LEE, NATHANIEL 1653?-1692

Caesar Borgia, Son of Pope Alexander the Sixth. London: 1660. V. 42; 44

Caesar Borgia. London: 1680. V. 37; 38; 40; 42; 45

Constantine the Great. London: 1684. V. 39; 40

Gloriana, or the Court of Augustus Caesar. London: 1676. V. 38; 39; 44; 45; 46

Lucius Junius Brutus, Father of His Country. London: 1681. V. 37; 39; 44; 45; 46

The Massacre of Paris: a Tragedy. London: 1690. V. 45

The Princess of Cleve. London: 1689. V. 42

Sophonisba, or Hannibal's Overthrow. London: 1676. V. 45

The Tragedy of Nero, Emperour of Rome. London: 1675. V. 39; 44; 46

Two Tragedies of Mr. Lee, Namely Theodosius and Oedipus . . . N.P.: 1786. V. 43

The Works of Mr. Nathaniel Lee. London: 1713. V. 37; 40

LEE, NELSON

Three Years Among the Camanches, the Narrative of Nelson Lee, the Texas Ranger . . . Albany: 1859. V. 41; 42; 43; 44; 45

LEE, NORMAN

The Journal of Norman Lee, 1898, Which is the Account of a Cattle-Drive from the Chilcotin Country to Teslin Lake by the Telegraph Trail. Vancouver: 1959. V. 40

LEE, RACHEL FRANCES ANTONIA

A Vindication of Mrs. Lee's Conduct Towards the Gordons. London: 1807. V. 39; 42

LEE, RAWDON B.

A History and Description, with Reminiscences, of the Fox Terrier. London: 1889. V. 39; 43

A History and Description with Reminiscences of the Fox Terrier. London: 1890. V. 46

Modern Dogs. (Sporting Division). London: c. 1910. V. 37

LEE, RICHARD

Flowers from Sharon; or Original Poems on Divine Subjects. London: 1794. V. 41

A Treatise of Captures in War. London: 1759. V. 42

LEE, RICHARD HENRY

An Address from the Delegates of the Twelve United Colonies to the People of England. Newport: 1775. V. 39; 44; 45

Life of Arthur Lee, L.L.D. Boston: 1829. V. 37; 38; 39; 42; 43; 46

LEE, ROBERT

The Anatomy of the Nerves of the Uterus. London: 1841. V. 42

Clinical Reports of Ovarian and Uterine Diseases. Edinburgh: 1853. V. 42

LEE, ROBERT E.

Circular. Head Quarters of the Confederate States. Richmond: 1865. V. 39

General Orders No. 76. N.P.: 1863. V. 40

Reports of the Operations of the Army of Northern Virginia, from June 1862 to and Including the Battle at Fredericksburg Dec. 13, 1862. Richmond: 1864. V. 40

LEE, ROBERT M.

China Safari. 1986. V. 38

LEE, SAMUEL PHILLIPS

Report and Charts of the Cruise of the U.S. Brig Dolphin. Washington: 1854. V. 37; 38; 44

LEE, SAMUELS

A Hemingway Check List. New York: 1951. V. 37

LEE, SARAH BOWDICH

Adventures in Australia; or the Wanderings of Captain Spencer in the Bush and the Wilds . . . London: 1851. V. 37

LEE, SARAH R.

Memoirs of Baron Cuvier. London: 1833. V. 37

LEE, SARAH WALLIS BOWDICH 1791-1856

Trees, Plants and Flowers; Their Beauties, Uses and Influences. London: 1854. V. 37; 42

LEE, SIDNEY

A Life of William Shakespeare. London: 1908. V. 41

Shakespeare's England. Oxford: 1926, 1917. V. 38

LEE, SOPHIA 1750-1824

A Hermit's Tale: Recorded by His Own Hand, and Found in His Cell. London: 1787. V. 38

The Life of a Lover. London: 1804. V. 44

The Recess; or, a Tale of Other Times. London: 1785. V. 42; 45

The Recess; or, a Tale of Other Times. London: 1786. V. 38

The Recess; or a Tale of Other Times. London: 1787. V. 40

The Recess; or, a Tale of the Time. London: 1792. V. 41; 42; 45

The Recess; or a Tale of Other Times. London: 1804. V. 38

LEE, TANITH

The Secret Books of Paradys I & II: The Book of the Damned and The Book of the Beast. London: 1988. V. 42

LEE, W.

Ancient and Modern History of Lewes and Brightelmston in Which are Compressed the Most Interesting Events of the County at Large, Under the Regnian, Roman Saxon, and Norman Settlements. Lewes: 1795. V. 39

LEE, WEYMAN

An Essay to Ascertain the Value of Leases and Annuities for Years and Lives, and to Estimate the Chances of the Duration of Lives . . . London: 1738. V. 37; 38

LEE, WILLIAM

A Chronological Catalogue of the Works of Daniel Defoe. London: 1869. V. 37; 39; 40

The Currency of the Confederate States of America. Washington: 1875. V. 38

Daniel Defoe: His Life, and recently discovered writings: extending from 1716 to 1729. London: 1869. V. 37

The True and Interesting Travels of William Lee. London: 1808. V. 40; 46

LEECH, ARTHUR B.

Irish Riflemen in America. London: 1875. V. 39

LEECH, JOHN 1817-1864

Follies of the Year: A Series of Coloured Etchings from Punch's Pocket Books 1844-64. London: 1865. V. 39

Follies of the Year. London: 1866. V. 38; 42; 46

John Leech's Etchings . . . London: 1843. V. 44

A Little Tour in Ireland. Being a Visit to Dublin, Galway, Connamara, Atholone, Limerick, Killarney, Glengarriff, Cork, Etc. By an Oxonian. London: 1859. V. 37

Pictures of Life and Character from the Collection of Mr. Punch. Series 1-5. London: 1855-69. V. 38

Pictures of Life and Character. London: 1857-69. V. 43

Pictures of Life and Character, from the Collection of 'Mr. Punch'. London: 1886. V. 46

John Leech's Pictures of Life and Character. London: 1886-87. V. 46

Pictures of Life and Character, from the Collection of 'Mr. Punch.' 1st, 2nd & 3rd Series. London: 1887. V. 41

Pictures of Life & Character: From the Collection of Mr. Punch. London: 1855. V. 37

Pictures of Life and Character. From the collection of Mr. Punch. London: n.d. 1869. V. 37

The Porcelain Tower; or, Nine Stories of China. Compiled from original sources by 'T.T.T.' (i.e. Thomas Henry Sealy). London;: 1841. V. 37

Punch's Pocket Book. London: 1845-50, 1862. V. 38

Punch's Snapdragons for Christmas. London: 1845. V. 37

LEECH, JOHN HENRY

Butterflies from China, Japan and Corea. London: 1892-94. V. 37

LEECH, SAMUEL

Thirty Years from Home, or A Voice from the Main Deck. Boston: 1843. V. 41

LEEDHAM-GREEN, E. S.

Books in Cambridge Inventories. Cambridge: 1986. V. 46

THE LEEDS Guide; Including a Sketch of the Environs and Kirkstall Abbey. Leeds: 1806. V. 44

LEEDS, HERBERT COREY

Log of the Columbia. Cambridge: 1900. V. 42

LEEDS, LEWIS W.

Treatise on Ventilation: Comprising Seven Lectures Delivered Before the Franklin Institute. Philadelphia: 1866-68. V. 41

A Treatise on Ventilation: Comprising Seven Lectures Delivered Before the Franklin Institute, Philadlephia 1866-68. New York: 1871. V. 42; 45

LEEKE, WILLIAM

The History of Lord Seaton's Regiment (The 52nd Light Infantry), at the Battle of Waterloo . . . London: 1866. V. 42

LEEKEY, WILLIAM

A Discourse on the Use of the Pen. London. V. 39

LEEPER, DAVID ROHER

The Argonauts of 'Forty-Nine. South Bend: 1894. V. 39; 40; 41; 42; 45; 46

LEES, FREDERIC RICHARD

An Argument Legal and Historical for the Legislative Prohibition of the Liquor Traffic. Manchester: 1856. V. 46

LEES, G. R.

The Life and Adventures Beyond Jordan. London: 1906. V. 44

LEES, J. A.

B. C. 1887: a Ramble in British Columbia. London: 1888. V. 37; 39

LEES, JAMES ARTHUR

Three in Norway, by Two of Them. London: 1883. V. 43

Three In Norway. Philadelphia: 1883. V. 43; 44

LEES, JOHN

Journal of J. L. Of Quebec, Merchant. Detroit: 1911. V. 46

LEES-MILNE, J.

English Country Houses. Baroque 1685-1715. London: 1970. V. 37

LEES-MILNE, JAMES

English Country Houses. Baroque 1685-1715. London: 1970. V. 46

Harold Nicolson - a Biography. London: 1980-81. V. 44

LEES, THOMAS J.

The Musings of Carol. Wheeling: 1831. V. 39; 41

LEESE, ELIZABETH

Costume Design in the Movies. New York: 1977. V. 40

LEESER, ISAAC

The Book of Daily Prayer for Every Day in the Year According to the Custom of the German and Polish Jews. Philadelphia: 1848. V. 40

LEETE, JOSEPH

The Family of Leete. Written in conjunction with J.C. Anderson. London: 1906. V. 37

LEEUWENHOEK, ANTON VAN 1631-1723

Epistolae Physiologicae Super Compluribus Naturae Arcanis . . . Delft: 1719. V. 42

Opera Omnia, Seu Arcana Naturae, ope Exctissimorum Microscopiorum Detecta, Experimentis Variis Comprobata, Epistolis ad Varios Illustres Viros ut et ad Integram . . . Leyden: 1719. V. 38

Opera Omnia, seu Arcana Naturae, ope Exactissimorum Microscopiorum Detecta, Experimentis Variis Comprobata, Epistolas ad VArios Illustres Viros . . . Leiden & Delft: 1719-30. V. 46

The Select Works . . . London: 1798-1807. V. 40

The Selected Works . . . London: 1800-07. V. 39

LEEUWENHOEK, DOBELL

Antony van Leeuwenhoek and His 'Little Animals' . . . New York: 1932. V. 41; 44

LE FALLIENNE, RICHARD

Limited Editions Confessio Amantis. London: 1893. V. 37

LE FANU, ALICIA

Memoirs of the Life and Writings of Mrs. Frances Sheridan . . . London: 1824. V. 44

LE FANU, JOSEPH SHERIDAN 1814-1873

All in the Dark. London: 1866. V. 38

The Cock and the Anchor, Being a Chronicle of Old Dublin City. Dublin: 1845. V. 41

The Evil Guest. London: 1895. V. 37; 41

The Fortunes of Colonel Torlogh O'Brien; a Tale of the Wars of King Jmes. Dublin: 1847. V. 38

Green Tea and Other Stories. Sauk City: 1945. V. 42; 43; 45

Guy Deverell. London: 1865. V. 42

The House by the Church-Yard. London: 1897. V. 46

In a Glass Darkly. London: 1929. V. 45

A Lost Name. London: 1868. V. 42

The Purcell Papers. London: 1880. V. 42

The Rose and The Key. London: 1871. V. 42

The Tenants of Malory. London: 1867. V. 38; 42; 43; 45

The Tenants of Malory. New York: 1867. V. 39

Uncle Silas. London: 1886. V. 38

Wylder's Hand. London: 1870? V. 38; 46

LE FANU, W. R.

A Bio-Bibliography of Edward Jenner 1749-1823. London: 1951. V. 38; 42

LE FAUCHEUR, MICHEL

An Essay Upon the Action of an Orator . . . London: 1680? V. 42

LE FEBVRE, NICAISE

Traite de la Chymie. Paris: 1660. V. 42

LE FERON, JEAN

Catalogue des Tres Illustres Ducz et Connestables de France. Paris: 1555. V. 39; 42; 43

Catalogue des Noms . . . Paris: 1598. V. 38; 40

LE FEVRE D'ETAPLES, JACQUES

In Hoc Libro Continetur. Paris: 1517. V. 46

LEFEVRE, EDMOND

Le Commerce et l'Industrie de la Plume Pour Parure. Paris: 1914. V. 41

LEFEVRE, GEORGE WILLIAM

The Life of a Travelling Physician . . . London: 1833. V. 42

LE FEVRE, JEAN

Dictionnaire Des Rymes Francoises Redvict en Bon Ordre, et Augmente d'vn Grand Nombre de Vocables & Monosyllables Francois. Paris: 1572. V. 42

LEFEVRE, L. A.

The Lions Gate and the Beaver to the Empress. Vancouver: 1903. V. 39

LEFEVRE, RAOUL

The Recuyell of the Historyes of Troye. London: 1892. V. 41; 45
The Recuyell of the Historyes of Troye. Hammersmith: 1892. V. 37

LEFFEL, JAMES & CO.

The Construction of Mill Dams: Comprising also the Building of Race and Reservoir Embankments and Head Gates, the masurement of Streams, Gauging of Water Supply, &c. Springfield: 1874. V. 38

LEFFERTS, CHARLES M.

Uniforms of the American, British, French and German Armies in the War of the American Revolution, 1775-1783. New York: 1926. V. 38

LEFFINGWELL, WILLIAM BRUCE

Shooting on Upland, Marsh and Stream. Chicago: 1890. V. 45
Shooting on Upland, Marsh and Stream. London: 1890. V. 39; 40
Wild Fowl Shooting. Chicago: 1889. V. 39

LEFFMAN, HENRY

Under the Yellow Flag . . . N.P.: 1896. V. 42; 46

LEFLER, HEINRICH

Mozart. Bienna: (before 1919). V. 37

LEFLON, J.

Eugene de Mazenod. Bishop of Marseilles. New York: 1961-70. V. 43

LE FLORES, JOE

Wyoming Peace Office. An Autobiography. Laramie: 1953. V. 44

LEFROY, J. H.

Memorials of the Discovery and Early Settlement of the Bermudas or Somers Islands 1515-1685. 1932. V. 38

LEFROY, W. CHAMBERS

The Ruined Abbeys of Yorkshire. London: 1883. V. 40; 45

LEFT to Their Own Devices. New York: 1937. V. 37
LEFT to Their Own Devices. New York: 1938. V. 40

LE GALLIENNE, RICHARD 1866-1947

Beds. Leeds and Nottingham: 1929. V. 41
The Book-Bills of Narcissus An Account Rendered By . . . Derby: 1891. V. 37; 38; 39
The Book-Bills of Narcissus. London: 1894. V. 40
The Book-Bills of Narcissus. London: 1895. V. 43
Confessio Amantis. London: 1893. V. 41
English Poems. London: 1892. V. 38; 43; 46
English Poems. London: & New York: 1892. V. 46
George Meredith, Some Characteristics, with A Bibliography by John Lane. London: 1890. V. 41; 43
Limited Editions Confessio Amantis. London: 1893. V. 38
New Poems. London: 1910. V. 38; 41
An Old Country House. 1902. V. 43
An Old Country House. New York: 1902. V. 41; 43
A Prose Fancy; Together with Confessio Amantis, A Sonnet. London: 1893. V. 41
Prose Fancies. London: 1894. V. 38; 41; 42
The Quest of the Golden Girl. London: 1900. V. 42
The Religion of a Literary Man. London: 1893. V. 38; 43; 46
The Religion of a Literary Man. London: 1894. V. 41
The Religion of a Literary Man. London: 1895. V. 38
Robert Louis Stevenson An Elegy and Other Poems Mainly Personal. Boston: 1895. V. 41; 42
The Romance of Perfume. New York: 1928. V. 44; 46
The Romance of Perfume. New York/Paris: 1928. V. 37; 41
The Romance of Zion Chapel. London: 1898. V. 41
The Romantic 90s. London: 1926. V. 41
Two Essays by Richard Le Gallienne. Chicago and Skokie: 1961. V. 41
Volumes in Folio. London: 1889. V. 37; 38; 40; 41; 43; 46
Young Lives. New York: 1899. V. 41

LEGARE, HUGH SWINTON

Writings of Hugh Swinton Legare. Charleston: 1846. V. 40

LEGATIA David Aethiopiae Regis. Bologna: 1533. V. 39

LE GEAY, G. L.

Collection de Divers Sujets de Vases, Tombeaux, Ruines et Fontaines. Paris: 1770. V. 38

THE LEGEND of Liberty! and Force of Truth, Containing the Thoughts, Words and Deeds of Some Prominent Apostles, Champions and Martyrs. (with) The Legion of Liberty! and Force of Truth . . . New York: 1842. V. 42

THE LEGEND of Saint Ursula . . . London: 1869. V. 38; 40; 44

LEGENDARY Ballads. London: 1908. V. 42

THE LEGENDARY History of the Cross in a Series of Sixty-Four Woodcuts from a Dutch Book Published in 1483. New Britain: 1965. V. 44

LEGENDRE, ADRIEN MARIE

Essai sur la Theorie des Nombres. Paris: 1798. V. 46
Nouvelles Methodes Pour la Determination des Orbites des Cometes. Paris: 1805. V. 46

LE GENDRE, FRANCOIS

L'Arithmetique en sa Perfection Mise en Pratique Selon l'Usage des Financiers . . . Paris: 1673. V. 41; 45

LE GENDRE, L., ABBE

Les Moeurs et Coutumes des Francois dans les Premiers Tems de la Monarchie. Paris: 1753. V. 45

LE GENDRE, LOUIS

The History of the Reign of Lewis the Great, Till the General Peace Concluded at Reswick, in the Year 1697. London: 1699. V. 45

LEGER, ALEXIS SAINT-LEGER 1889-

Anabasis. London: 1930. V. 39; 40; 43; 45; 46
Anabasis. New York: 1938. V. 43
Anabasis. London: 1959. V. 39; 40
Birds. New York: 1966. V. 42
Exil. Buenos Aires: 1942. V. 46
Exil: suivi de Poemes a L'Etrangere Pluie-Neiges. Paris: 1946. V. 39
Winds. New York: 1953. V. 39; 41; 45

LEGER, JEAN 1615-1670

Histoire Generale des Eglises Evangeliques des Vallees de Piemont, ou Vaugoises. Leyden: 1669. V. 38

LEGEZA, IRENEUS LASZLO

Malcolm MacDonald Collection of Chinese Ceramics. London: 1972. V. 42; 46

LEGG, J, WICKHAM

The Coronation Order of King James I. London: 1902. V. 37

LEGGAT BROTHERS

Catalogue of Superior Old and New Books, in Theology, Biography, Antiquities . . . Now on Sale at the Very Low Prices Affixed, by Leggat Brothers . . . New York: 1855. V. 45

LEGGATT, ASHLEY

Stalking Reminiscences 1914-1920. London: 1921. V. 43

LEGGATT, WILLIAM

The Theory and Practice of the Art of Weaving Linen and Jute Manufactures by Power Loom . . . Dundee: 1907. V. 45

LEGGE, ALFRED O.

Sunny Manitoba Its Peoples and Its Industries. London: 1893. V. 43

LEGGE, JAMES

The Notions of the Chinese Concerning God and Spirits. Hongkong: 1852. V. 43

LEGGE, W. V.

A History of the Birds of Ceylon. London: 1878-80. V. 42
A History of the Birds of Ceylon. London: 1880. V. 43

LEGGE, WILLOW

An African Folktale. Guildford, Surrey: 1979. V. 39

LEGGETT, WILLIAM

Naval Stories. New York: 1835. V. 39
Tales and Sketches. New York: 1829. V. 42

LEGH, GERARD

The Accedence of Armorie. Colophon: 1597. V. 40
The Accedence of Armorie. London: 1597. V. 42
The Accedens of Armory. London: 1568. V. 38; 40
The Accedens of Armory. London: 1586. V. 37

LEGH, THOMAS

Narrative of a Journey in Egypt and the Country Beyond the Cataracts. London: 1816. V. 40

Narrative of a Journey in Egypt and the Country Beyond the Cataracts. London: 1817. V. 40

Narrative of a Journey in Eygpt and the Country Beyond the Cataracts. Philadelphia: 1817. V. 43

THE LEGION of Liberty! and Force of Truth . . . New York: 1843. V. 42

LEGMAN, GERSHON

The Limerick. Paris: 1953. V. 38

LE GOBIEN, CHARLES

Histoire des Isles Marianes, Nouvellement Converties a la Religion Chrestienne: & de la Mort Glorieuse des Premiers Missionaries qui y ont Preche la Foy. Paris: 1700. V. 41; 46

LE GORCE, JOHN OLIVER

The Book of Fishes. Washington: 1939. V. 46

LEGRAIN, LEON

Archaic Seal-Impressions. Oxford: 1936. V. 37; 40; 42

Business Documents of the Third Dynasty of Ur. London and Philadelphia: 1947-37. V. 42

Seal Cylinders. London: 1951. V. 37; 44

LE GRAND, ANTHONY

An Entire Body of Philosophy, According to the Principles of the Famous Renate des Cartes, in Three Books . . . London: 1694. V. 44

LE GRAND, ANTOINE

Dissertatio de Carentia Sensus & Cognitionis in Brutis. London: 1675. V. 43

Historia Naturae, Variis Experimentis et Ratiociniis Elucidata. Secumdum Principia Stabilita in Institutione Philosophiae edita ab eodem authore. 1680. V. 37

LE GRAND D'AUSSY, PIERRE JEAN BAPTISTE 1737-1800

Fabilaux or Tales Abridged from French Manuscripts of the XIIth and XIIIth Centuries. London: 1796. V. 41

Fabilaux or Tales . . . London: 1815. V. 44; 45

Fabilaux or Tales . . . London: 1796, 1800. V. 41

Fabliaux or Tales. London: 1796-1800. V. 40

Norman Tales from the French. London: 1789. V. 46

LE GRAND, JULIA

The Journal of . . . New Orleans 1862-1863. Richmond: 1911. V. 39; 44

LEGRAND, MARC ANTOINE 1637-1728

Theatre . . . Paris: 1742. V. 41; 45

LEGROS, LUCIEN ALPHONSE

Typographical Printing-Surfaces, the Technology and Mechanism of Their Production. London: 1916. V. 45

LE GUIN, URSULA

Always Coming Home. London: 1986. V. 45

The Compass Rose. Portland: 1982. V. 46

The Dispossessed. New York: 1974. V. 39

Dreams Must Explain Themselves. 1975. V. 44

The Farthest Shore. 1972. V. 39

The Farthest Shore. New York: 1972. V. 37

The Lathe of heaven. New York: 1971. V. 39

The Left Hand of Darkness. London: 1969. V. 37; 46

The Tombs of Atuan. New York: 1971. V. 37

LEHIGH COAL & NAVIGATION COMPANY

Facts Illustrative of the Character of the Anthracite or Lehigh Coal, Found in the Great Pines at Mauch Chunk, in Possession of the Lehigh Coal and Navigation Co . . . . Boston: 1825. V. 43

LEHMAN, ANTHONY L.

Paul Landacre: a Life and a Legacy. Los Angeles: 1983. V. 39; 42

LEHMANN, C. G.

Physiological Chemistry in a New Systematic Order . . . London: 1851-54. V. 38

LEHMANN-FELSKOWSKI, G.

The Shipbuilding Industry of Germany, Development from the 15th Century . . . London: 1904. V. 41

LEHMANN-HAUPT, H.

Bookbinding in America. 1941. V. 39

LEHMANN-HAUPT, HELLMUT

Two Essays on the Decretum of Gratian. Los Angeles: 1971. V. 37; 46

Two Essays on the Decretum of Gratian Together with an Original Leaf Printed on Vellum by Peter Schoeffer at Mainz in 1472. Los Angeles & San Francisco: 1971. V. 42; 45

LEHMANN, HERMAN

The Last Captive: The Lives of Herman Lehmann. Austin: 1972. V. 40; 41

Nine Years Among the Indians, 1870-1879. 1927. V. 42

Nine Years Among the Indians, 1870-1879 . . . The Life of a Texan Among the Indians. Austin: 1927. V. 46

LEHMANN, JOHN

New Writing and Daylight. London: 1942. V. 38

Poets of Tomorrow. Third Selection . . . London: 1942. V. 38

The Reader at Night, and Other Poems. Toronto: 1974. V. 39

LEHMANN, MILTON

This High Man: the Life of Robert H. Goddard. New York: 1963. V. 39; 45

LEHMANN, PHYLLIS WILLIAMS

The Hieron, Samothrace. London: 1969. V. 45

Roman Wall Paintings from Boscoreale in the Metropolitan Museum of Art. Cambridge: 1953. V. 42; 44

LEHMANN, ROSAMOND

Dusty Answer. London: 1927. V. 45

The Echoing Grove. London: 1953. V. 42

Invitation to the Waltz. London: 1982. V. 46

LEHMANN, ROSAMUND

Invitation to the Waltz. V. 41

LEHMANN, V. W.

Forgotten Legions, Sheep in the Rio Grande Plain of Texas. El Paso: 1969. V. 37; 44; 45

LEHNER, JOSEPH

Neue Schriften und Firmenschilder im Modernen Style. Vienna: 1899. V. 41; 43; 45

LEHRER, WARREN

Versations. Mattapoinset: 1980. V. 38; 39; 41

LEHRMAN, DANIEL S.

Advances in the Study of Behavior. 1965-78. V. 38

LEIB, CHARLES

Nine Months in the Quartermaster's Department of the Chances for Making a Million. Cincinnati: 1862. V. 44

LEIBER, FRITZ

Night's Black Agents. 1947. V. 45

Night's Black Agent. Sauk City: 1947. V. 37; 42; 43; 45

The Saga of Fafhrd and the Gray Mouser. New York: 1977. V. 39

The Secret Songs. 1968. V. 39

The Wanderer. 1967. V. 39

LEIBIG, JUSTUS VON FREIHERR

Researches on the Chemistry of Food and the Motion of the Juices in the Animal Body. Lowell: 1848. V. 42

LEIBNIZ, GOTTFRIED WILHELM

A Collection of Papers, Which Passed Between . . . Mr. Leibnitz, and Dr. Clarke in the Years 1715 and 1716, Related to othe Principles of Natural Philosophy and Religion . . . London: 1717. V. 37; 38

Commercium Philosohicum et Mathematicum . . . Lausanne & Geneva: 1745. V. 41; 43; 45; 46

Otium Hanoveranum Sive Miscellnia. Leizpzig: 1718. V. 38

LEICESTER, EARLS OF. LIBRARY. (HOLKHAM HALL)

The Holkham Library. 1970. V. 40

The Holkham Library, Illuminations and Illustrations in the Manuscript Library of the Earl of Leicester. Oxford: 1970. V. 39; 41; 45

THE LEICESTERSHIRE Poll, As the Same Was Taken at the County-Court, Holden at the Castle of Leicester, on Thursday the Seventeenth day of December, 1719 . . . London: 1720. V. 45

LEICHARDT, LUDWIG

Journal of an Overland Expedition in Australia, from Moreton Bay to Port Essington . . . During the Years 1844-45. London: 1847. V. 39

LEICHHARDT, F. W. LUDWIG

The Letters. Cambridge: 1968. V. 46

LEIDEN. KERN INSTITUTE

Annual Bibliography of Indian Archaeology. Leiden: 1930-172. V. 41

LEIDY, JOSEPH

An Elementary Treatise on Human Anatomy. Philadelphia: 1861. V. 38; 43

LEIGH, ALFRED

Maud Atherton. London: 1879. V. 38

LEIGH, AUSTEN

Recollections of the Early Days of the Vine Hunt and of Its Founder, William John Chute, Esq. M.P . . . London: 1865. V. 39; 44

LEIGH, BENJAMIN WATKINS 1781-1849

Letters of Algernon Sydney, In Defence of Civil Liberty and ATaingst Encroachments of Military Despotism. Richmond: 1830. V. 39

LEIGH-BENNETT, E. P.

Match Making, Being Some Glances at the British Match Making Industry in the Factories of Bryant and May Ltd. London: 1931. V. 43

LEIGH, CHANDOS

The View, and Other Poems. London: 1820. V. 42

LEIGH, CHARLES

The Natural History of Lancashire, Cheshire and the Peak, in Derbyshire. Oxford: 1700. V. 37; 38; 39; 44; 46

LEIGH, DELL

East Coasting. London: 1931. V. 42

LEIGH, EDWARD

Critica Sacra in Two Parts . . . *(with) A Supplement to the Critica Sacra* . . . London: 1650/62. V. 44

Critica Sacra in two Parts: The First containing Observations on all the Radices, or Primitive Hebrew Words of the Old Testament . . . *The Second Philolgicall and Theologicall Observations upon all the Greek Words of the* . . . London: 1650. V. 37; 42

A Philologicall Commentary; or, an Illustration of the Most Obvious and Useful Words in the Law . . . London: 1658. V. 46

Select and Choice Observations, containing all the Romane Emperours. The first eighteen by Edward Leigh . . . *the others added by his son Henry Leigh. Certain choice French proverbs, alphabetically disposed and Englished added also by the same* . . . London: 1657. V. 37

LEIGH, EGERTON

Ballads & Legends of Cheshire. (Collected by Egerton Leigh). London: 1867. V. 37

Considerations on Certain Political Transactions of the Province of South Carolina. London: 1774. V. 40

LEIGH FERMOR, PATRICK

The Violins of Saint Jacques. London: 1953. V. 41

LEIGH, GEORGE

The Leigh Peerage; a Full and Complete History of the Claim of George Leigh to the Dormant title of Baron Leigh of Stoneley. London: 1834. V. 39

The Leigh Peerage; a full and complete history of the claim of George Leigh to the dormant title of Baron Leigh of Stonely. London: (1834). V. 37

Mary Grainger. London: 1874. V. 41

LEIGH, GERARD

The Accedence of Amory. London: 1568. V. 45

The Accedence of Armorie. London: 1591. V. 45

The Accedence of Armorie. London: 1597. V. 45

LEIGH, JAMES HENRY 1765-1823

Poems on Several Occasions. London: 1790. V. 46

LEIGH, OLIVER

Edgar Allan Poe: The Man: The Master: The Martyr. Chicago: 1906. V. 39

THE LEIGH Peerage: Being a Full and Complete History of the Claim of George Leigh, Esq. to the Dormant Title of Baron Leigh, of Stoneley, in the County of Warwick . . . London: 1834. V. 37

LEIGH, PERCIVAL

The Comic English Grammar. London: 1840. V. 39

Manners and Customs of ye Englyshe . . . London: 1849. V. 43

LEIGH, SAMUEL

Leigh's New Picture of England and Wales. London: 1820. V. 44

Leigh's New Pocket Road-Book of England and Wales . . . London: 1831. V. 42

LEIGH, SAMUEL EGERTON

Munster Abbey, a Romance. Edinburgh: 1797. V. 40; 41

LEIGH, WILLIAM R.

The Western Pony. New York: 1933. V. 39; 42; 46

LEIGHLY, JOHN

California as an Island. San Francisco. V. 44

California as an Island. San Francisco: 1972. V. 37; 40; 43; 44; 46

LEIGHTON, CAROLINE C.

Life at Puget Sound with Sketches of Travel in Washington Territory, British Columbia, Oregon and California 1865-1881. Boston: 1883. V. 41

Life at Puget Sound, with Sketches of Travel in Washington territory, British Columbia, Oregon and California. Boston: 1884. V. 45

LEIGHTON, CLARE

The Farmer's Year. London: 1933. V. 37; 38; 40; 44; 45

The Farmer's Year. New York: 1933. V. 39

Four Hedges - a Gardener's Chronicle. London: 1935. V. 41; 42; 44

Four Hedges: a Gardener's Chronicle. New York: 1935. V. 44; 46

The Musical Box . . . London: 1936. V. 45

Wood Engraving and Woodcuts. London: 1932. V. 42; 43

Woodcuts - Examples of the Work of Clare Leighton. London: 1930. V. 39; 40

LEIGHTON, DOROTHY

Disillusion. London: 1894. V. 38

LEIGHTON, ELLIS

Answer of the Company of Royal Adventurers of England Trading into Africa . . . London: 1667. V. 43

The Several Declarations of the Company of Royal Adventurers of England Trading to Africa . . . London: 1667. V. 43

LEIGHTON FIRM, BOOKSELLERS, LONDON.

Early Printed Books Arranged by Presses. Offered for Sale by J. and J. Leighton, 40 Brewer St. Regent St., London W. Parts I-III. London: 1910. V. 42

LEIGHTON, FRANCIS

The Muse's Blossoms' or, Juvenile Poems. London: 1769. V. 37; 45

LEIGHTON, JOHN

The Diverting History of John Gilpin. London: 1845. V. 37

The Life of Man Symbolised by the Months of the Year. London: 1866. V. 42

London Cries and Public Edifices from Sketches on the Spot. London: 1847. V. 40

London Out Of Town, or the Adventures of the Browns at the Sea Side. London: 1850. V. 40

Madre Natura Versus the Moloch of Fashion. London: 1874. V. 42; 44

Paris Under the Commune: or, The Seventy-Three Days of the Second Siege. London: 1871. V. 40

Suggestions in Design. London: 1853. V. 39; 41; 45

Suggestions in Design, Being a Comprehensive Series of Original Sketches in Various Styles or Ornament Arranged for Application in the Decorative and Constructive Arts. London: 1880. V. 37; 39; 43; 46

Suggestions in Design . . . for Application in the Decorative and Constructive Arts. London: 1881. V. 40

Suggestions in Design. London: (1880-1881). V. 37

Swan's Views of the Lakes in Scotland. Glasgow: 1836. V. 40

LEIGHTON, JOHN M.

The Lakes of Scotland, a Series of Views, from Paintings Taken Expressly for the Work by John Fleming . . . Glasgow: 1834. V. 43

Select Views on the River Clyde . . . London: 1830. V. 44

LEIGHTON, MARIE CONNOR

Husband and Wife. London: 1888. V. 41

LEIGHTON, ROBERT

The New Book of the Dog. London: 1907. V. 40

A Practical Commentary Upon the First Epistle General of Saint Peter. London. V. 42

A Practical Commentary Upon the First Epistle General of Saint Peter. London: 1848. V. 42

A Practical Commentary Upon the First Epistle General of Saint Peter. London: 1870. V. 45

LEIGHTON, STANLEY

Shropshire Houses Past and Present. London: 1901. V. 38; 40

LEIGHTON, W. A.

A Flora of Shropshire. London: 1841. V. 39; 40

LEIGHTON, WILLIAM

History of Oliver and Arthur. Done into English by William Leighton and Eliza Barrett. Boston: 1903. V. 37

LEINSTER, M.

Operation: Outer Space. 1954. V. 44

LEINSTER, MURRAY

The Last Space Ship. New York: 1949. V. 39

LEIPNIK, F. L.

A History of French Etching. London: 1924. V. 40; 44

LEIRIS, MICHEL

Francis Bacon Full Face and in Profile. London: 1983. V. 41

Joan Miro Lithographs. New York: 1972. V. 44; 46

Joan Miro Lithographs. Volume 2. New York: 1975. V. 46

Wilfredo Lam. New York: 1970. V. 39; 43

LEISY, ERNEST E.

The Letters of Quintus Curtius Snodgrass. Dallas: 1946. V. 44

LEITCH, R. P.

A Course of Painting in Neutral Tint. London: 1880. V. 41

A Course of Water-Colour Painting. London: 1875. V. 44

A Course of Sepia Painting. London: 1880. V. 41

LEITH, GEORGE

A Short Account of the Settlement, Produce and Commerce of Prince of Wales Island in the Straits of Malacca. London: 1805. V. 45

LEITNER, QUIRIN

Die Waffensammlung des Oesterreichischen Kaiserhauses im k.k. Artillerie-Arsenal Museum in Wien. Vienna: 1866-70. V. 44

LEIVA Y AGUILAR, FRANCISCO DE

Decission de la Duda, en Que se Pregunta, si Puede por la Urina ser Concoida en las Mugeres la Prenez. Cordova: 1633. V. 42

Desengano Contra el Mal Uso del Tabaco. Cordoba: 1634. V. 38

LEJEUNE, C. A.

Cinema. London: 1931. V. 40

LE JEUNE DE BOULENCOURT

Description Generale de l'Hostel Royale des Invalides . . . avec les Plans, profiles & Elevations de ses Faces, Coupes & Apparatements. Paris: 1683. V. 38

LE JEUNE, J. P.

English Manual or Prayers and Catechism in English Typography; Chinook Manual . . . ; Latin Manual . . . in Use by Indians of British Columbia. Kamloops: 1896. V. 43

LE JEUNE, PAUL

Relation de Ce Qvi S'est Passe de Plvs Remarqvable Avx Missions des Peres de la Compagnie de Iesvs, en la Nouvvelle France, es Annees 1660 & 1661 . . . Paris: 1662. V. 41; 42; 44

LEJUNE, J. M.

Skawmish Manual, or Prayers, Hymns and Catechism in Skwamish. V. 44

LEKTECHSYRIO CORPORATION

Species of Wild Flowers of the U.S.S.R. Descriptive Catalogue of Bulbs and Roots. Moscow: 1935. V. 37

LELAND, CHARLES G.

The English Gipsies and Their Language. London: 1873. V. 41; 45

Gypsey Sorcery and Fortune Telling. Illustrated by Numerous Incantations, Specimens of Medical Magic, Anecdotes and Tales. Copiously illustrated by the Author. London;: 1901. V. 37

The Hundred Riddles of the Fairy Bellaria. London: 1892. V. 40; 42

LELAND, CHARLES GODFREY

The Union Pacific Railway, Eastern Division or Three Thousand Miles in a Railway Car. Philadelphia: 1867. V. 37; 40; 46

LELAND, CHARLES P.

Capt. Leland's Report of the Horrible Sacrifices of Human Victims Among the Various Tribes of India. New York: 1851. V. 45

LELAND, CHARLES PALMER

English - Gipsy Songs in Romany with Metrical English Translations. London: 1875. V. 42

The English Gipsies and Their Language. London: 1893. V. 42

Gypsy Sorcery and Fortune Telling. London: 1891. V. 42

LELAND, F. W.

With the M.T. In Mesopotamia. London: 1920. V. 46

LELAND, JOHN 1691-1766

The Advantage and Necessity of the Christian Revelation, Shewn from the State of Religion in the Antient Heathen World. London: 1764. V. 38

Genethliacon Illustrissimi Eaduerdi Principis Cambriae. L: 1543. V. 40

Genethliacon Illustrissimi Eaduerdi Principis Cambriae, Ducis Coriniae . . . London: 1543. V. 38; 41; 43; 45

The Itinerary of John Leyland the Antiquary. Oxford: 1744-45. V. 44

The Itinerary of John Leland the Antiquary. Oxford: 1768-69. V. 41; 46

The Itinerary published by Mr. Thomas Hearne. The Third Edition, printed from Mr. Hearne's corrected copy in the Bodleian Library. Oxford: 1770. V. 37

A View of the Principal Deistical Writers That Have Appeared in England in the Last and Present Century with Observations Upon Them and Some Account of the Answers that Have Been Published Against Them. London: 1754. V. 38; 41

A View of the Principal Deistical Writers of the Last and Present Century. London: 1755. V. 39

A View of the Principal Deistical Writers That Have Appeared in England in the Last and Present Century. London: 1757. V. 41; 43; 45

A View of the Principal Deistical Writers That Have Appeared in England in the Last and Present Century. London: 1807. V. 42

A View of the Deistical Writers that Have Appeared in England in the Late and Present Century. London: 1764. V. 39

LELAND, JOHN A.

A Voice from South Carolina. Charleston: 1879. V. 38; 40

LELAND, JOSEPH

The Farmer's Diary; or the United States Alamanack, for . . . 1792. Danbury: 1791. V. 40

LELAND, SAMUEL PHELPS

Peculiar People. Cleveland: 1891. V. 37

LELAND, THOMAS

The History of Ireland from the Invasion of Henry II. Dublin: 1773. V. 38; 40; 41; 45

The History of Ireland from the Invasion of Henry II. London: 1773. V. 39; 44

The History of Ireland from the Invasion of Henry II. Philadelphia & New York: 1774. V. 39

The History of Ireland From the Invasion of Henry II with a Prelimary Discourse on the Ancient State of that Kingdom. Dublin: 1814. V. 43; 46

Longsword, Earl of Salisbury. London: 1762. V. 40; 41; 42; 45

The Orations of Demosthenes. Dublin: 1777. V. 40

A View of the Principal Deistical Writers that Have Appeared in England in the Last and Present Century . . . London: 1754-56. V. 45

LELARGE DE LOUROUEIX

Les Folies du Siecle. Parisi: 1817. V. 37

LE LIEUR, JACQUES

Les Principaux Edifices de la Ville de Rouen en 1525 . . . Rouen: 1845. V. 38

LE LOUTEREL, FRANCOIS PHILLIPPE

Manual of Military Reconnaissances, Temporary Fortification and Partisan Warfare, for Officers of Infantry and Cavalry . . . Atlanta: 1862. V. 43

LE LOYER, PIERRE 1550-1634

Des Spectres ou Apparations et Visions d'Esprits, Anges et Demons, se Monstrans Sensiblement aux Hommes . . . 1586. V. 39

LE MAIR, H. WILLEBEEK

Granny's Little Rhyme Book. London. V. 46

Little Songs of Long Ago. London: 1912. V. 46

Nursie's Little Rhyme Book. London. V. 46

Our Old Nursery Rhymes. London & Philadelphia: 1911. V. 38

LE MAIRE DE BELGES, JEAN 1473-1525

L'Epistre du Roy a Hector de Troye. Paris: 1513. V. 41

Le Traictie Intiule de la Difference des Scismes et des Concilles de Leglise. Lyon: 1511. V. 38

LE MAIRE DES BELGES, JEAN 1473-1525

Les Illustrations de Gaule et Singularitez de Troye . . . avec La Couronne Margaritique . . . Lyon: 1549. V. 39

La Legende des Venitiens. A Plaincte du Desir. Les Regretz de la Dame Infortunee. Paris: 1512 and 1516. V. 39

Lepistre du Roy a Hector de Troye. Et Aucunes Aultres Oeuures Assez Dignes de Veoir. Paris: 1513. V. 39

LE MAIRE, HENRI

The French Gil Blas; or Adventures of Henry Lanson. London: 1793. V. 45

LEMAIRE, JOSEPH JEAN FRANCOIS 1782-1834

Le Deniste des Dames. Paris: 1818. V. 45

LEMAISTRE, JOHN GUSTAVUS

Frederic Latimer: or, the History of a Young Man of Fashion. London: 1799. V. 38; 40

LEMAN, TANFIELD

An Historical Deduction of Government; in a Letter to a Friend in the Country. London: 1748. V. 41

LE MARCHANT, JOHN GASPARD

Rules and Regulations of the Sword Exercise of Cavalry. London: 1796.
V. 38

LE MARIE, JEHAN

Turchiche Spurcitie et Perfidiae Suggillatio et Confutatio. Paris: 1514. V. 45

LE MASCRIER, JEAN B.

*Memoires Historiques sur La Louisiane, Contenant ce Qui Y Est Arrive de
Plus Memorable Depuis L'Annee 1687 . . .* Paris: 1753. V. 46

LE MAY, REGINALD

A Concise History of Buddhist Art in Siam. Cambridge: 1938. V. 38

LEMBEYE, J.

Aves de la Isla de Cuba. Havana: 1850. V. 40

LEMERCIER, LOUIS JEAN NEPOMUCENE

*Essais Poetiques sur la Theorie Newtonienne, Tirees de l'Atlantiade, Poeme
Inedit.* Paris: 1808. V. 43

LEMERY, NICHOLAS 1645-1715

A Course of Chymistry. London: 1686. V. 42

A Course of Chymistry . . . London: 1720. V. 42

A Course of Chymistry . . . London: 1677. V. 37

A Course of Chymistry . . . London: 1698. V. 37

LEMERY, NICOLAS

Dictionaire ou Traite Universel des Drogues Simples. Rotterdam: 1727.
V. 44

Modern Curiosities of Art and Nature. London: 1685. V. 43

*New Curiosities in Art and Nature: or, A Collection of the most Valuable
Secrets in All Arts and Sciences . . . Being very Useful for all Persons who
are desirous to consult their Health, pleasure or Beauty; enrich'd with an
Infinite . . .* London;: 1711. V. 37

LE MESURIER, THOMAS

Translations Chiefly from the Italian of Petrarch and Metastasio. Oxford:
1795. V. 41

LEMKE, THEODOR

Geschichte Deutschthums von New York Von 1848 bis auf die Gegenwart.
New York: 1891. V. 39

LEMKE, W. J.

The Battle of Prairie Grove, Arkansas, December 7, 1862. Fayetteville:
1967. V. 39

LEMLEY, JOHN

*Autobiography and Personal Recollections of John Lemley, Editor of the
Zion's Watchman . . .* Albany: 1885-6. V. 38

LEMMON, NANNIE

The Battle of the Stove Pipes. N.P.: 1862. V. 45

LEMNIUS, LEVINUS 1505-1568

*Levini Lemnii . . . Occulta Naturae Miracula, ac Varia Rerum Documenta,
Probabili Ratione Atque Artifici Coniectura Explicata.* Antverpiae: 1567..
V. 40

De Miraculis Occultis Naturae, Libri IIII. Antverpiae: 1574. V. 46

De Miraculis Occultis Naturae, Libri III. Antwerp: 1581. V. 39; 40

De Miraculis Occultis Naturae. Leiden: 1666. V. 38

Occulta Naturae Miracula . . . Antwerp: 1559. V. 40

Occulta Naturae Miracula . . . De Habitu et Constitutione Corporis.
Antwerpiae: 1561. V. 37

LEMOINE, H.

Typographical Antiquities. London: 1813. V. 42

LEMOINE, HENRY

Typographical Antiquities, History, Origin and Progress of Printing . . .
London: 1797. V. 37; 38; 39; 40; 45; 46

LE MOINE, J. M.

The Chronicles of the St. Lawrence. Montreal: 1878. V. 42

The Sword or Brigadier-General Richard Montgomery: a Memoir. Quebec:
1870. V. 41

LEMOISNE, P. A.

Degas et Son Oeuvre. Paris: 1949. V. 42; 44

Gothic Painting in France Fourteenth and Fifteenth Centuries. Florence:
1931. V. 43; 46

LEMON, GEORGE WILLIAM

English Etymology; or, a Derivative Dictionary of the English Language.
London: 1783. V. 41

LEMON, MARK

The Chimes . . . A Drama in Four Quarters . . . London: 1845. V. 40

The Chimes. London: 1887. V. 40

Fairy Tales. London: 1868. V. 45; 46

The Heir of Applebite and Our Lodgers. London: 1856. V. 43

The Jest Book, The Choicest Anecdotes and Sayings. London: &
Cambridge: 1864. V. 43; 44

LEMON, ROBERT

*Catalogue of a Collection of Printed Broadsides in the Possession of the
Society of Antiquaries of London . . .* London: 1866. V. 42

LE MONNIER, G. P. d. 1766

*Dissertation sur les Maladies des Dents, avec Les Moyens d'y Remedier &
de les Guerir.* Paris: 1753. V. 42

LE MONNIER, PIERRE CHARLES

Memoires Concernant Diverses Questions d'Astronomie et de Physique.
Paris: 1781-88. V. 41; 45

LEMOS DE AFFONSECA, RAPHAEL DE

*Commento Portugues dos Quatro Livros da Instituta do Emperador
Iustiniano ou Breve Resumo do Direito Civil.* Lisbon: 1656. V. 37

LE MOYNE, LOUIS V.

Country Residences in Europe and America. New York: 1921. V. 39

Country Residences in Europe and America. New York: 1908. V. 37

LE MOYNE, PIERRE

La Gallerie des Femmes Fortes. Leyden: 1660. V. 38

LEMOYNE, SIMON SYLVESTRE CLEMENT 1727-1806

*Idees Preliminaires, Et Prospectus d'un Ouvrage sur les Peches Maritimes
de France.* Paris: 1777. V. 39

L'EMPEREUR CONSTANT

The Tale of the Emperor Coustans and Over the Sea. 1894. V. 44

The Tale of the Emperor Coustans and of Over Sea. Hammersmith: 1894.
V. 38; 39; 40; 42; 45; 46

The Tale of the Emperor Coustans and of Over Sea. London: 1894. V. 41

LEMPERLY, PAUL

Books and I. Cleveland: 1938. V. 39

LEMPRIERE, C.

Notes in Mexico in 1861 and 1862; Politically and Socially Considered.
London: 1862. V. 38

LEMPRIERE, J.

Universal Biography . . . London: 1808. V. 38

*Universal Biography: Containing A copious Account Critical and Historical, of
the Life and Character, Labors and Actions of Eminent persons, In all
Ages and countries, Conditions and Professions. In Two Volumes.* New
York: 1810. V. 37; 40

LEMPRIERE, JOHN c. 1765-1824

Bibliotheca Classica; or, a Classical Dictionary . . . London: 1792. V. 45

Bibliotheca Classica . . . . London: 1797. V. 41; 43

LEMPRIERE, WILLIAM

*Report on the Medicinal Effects of an Aluminous Chalybeate Water, Lately
Discovered at Sandrocks in the Parish of Chale . . .* Neport, Isle of Wight:
1811. V. 41

*A Tour from Gribraltar to Tangier . . . and Thence over Mount Atlas to
Morocco.* London: 1791. V. 46

*A Tour from Gibraltar to Tangier, Sallee, Mogodore, Santa Cruz, and
Tarudant . . .* Philadelphia: 1794. V. 40

A Tour thorugh the Dominions of the Emperor of Morocco. Newport: 1813.
V. 44

LE NAIN DE TILLEMONT, LOUIS SEBASTIAN 1637-1698

An Account of the Life of Apollonius Tyaneus . . . London: 1702. V. 46

LENCCIUS, JOANNES BAPTISTA

*Observationes Politicae, ex Varijs Historiarum a Civillis Doctrinae
Scriptoribus . . .* Strasbourg: 1606. V. 42

L'ENCLOS, NINON DE 1615-1705

Letters to the Marquiss De Sevigne. London: 1751. V. 38; 39

The Memoirs . . . London: 1776. V. 38

*The Memoirs . . . with her letters to Monsr de St. Evremond and to the
Marquis de Sevigne. Collected and Translated from the French, By A
Lady. In Two Volumes.* London: 1761. V. 37

LENDERMAN

Adventures Among the Spiritualists and Free-Lovers . . . Cincinnati: 1860.
V. 46

LENDRUM, J.

A Concise and Impartial History of the American Revolution. Boston: 1795.
V. 41

LE NEVE, JOHN 1679-1741

Fasti Ecclesiae Anglicanae; or, an Essay Towards Deducing a Regular Succession, of all the Principal Dignitaries in Each Cathedral, Collegiate Church or Chapel. London: 1716. V. 38; 39

Monumenta Anglicana; Being Inscriptions on the Monuments of Several Eminent Persons Deceased in Or Since the Year 1700, to the End of the Year 1715. (with) Monumenta Anglicana . . . in or Since the Year 1650 to the End of the Year 1718 . . . London: 1717, 1719. V. 41

LENG, JOHN

America in 1876. Dundee: 1877. V. 38; 41; 42

LENGENFELDER H.

World Guide to Libraries. London: 1987. V. 38

L'ENGLE, MADELAINE

Camilla Dickinson. New York: 1951. V. 43
Ilsa. New York: 1946. V. 42
The Small Rain. New York: 1945. V. 43; 46
The Young Unicorns. New York: 1968. V. 43

LENGLEN, SUZANNE

Lawn Tennis. The Game of Nations. New York: 1925. V. 43

LENGLET-DUFRESNOIS, NICOLAS

De l'Usage des Romans, avec une Bibliotheque des Romans . . . Amsterdam: 1734. V. 38

LENGLET-DUFRESNOY, ABBE NICOLAS

Histoire de la Philosophie Hermetique . . . La Haye: 1742. V. 46

LENIN, VLADIMIR ILYICH 1870-1924

Marx, Engels, Marxism. Moscow: 1973. V. 40
Proletarskaia Revoliutsiia i Renegt Kautskii Izdanie Tsentrispolkoma. N.P.: 1920. V. 38
Ciito Delat? Nabolevshie Voprosy Nashego Dvizheniia. (What Is to Be Done? Burning Questions of Our Movement). Stuttgart: 1902. V. 38; 40

LENK, TORSTEN

The Flintlock: Its Origin and Development. London: 1965. V. 42

LENNARD, EMMA BARRETT

Constance Rivers. London: 1867. V. 38

LENNON, JOHN

Power to the People. London: 1972. V. 38

LENNOX, CHARLOTTE RAMSEY 1720-1804

The Female Quixote; or, the Adventures of Arabella. London: 1752. V. 38; 40; 42
The Female Quixote, or The Adventures of Arabella. London: 1810. V. 38; 41; 42
Henrietta. London: 1758. V. 40
Shakespear Illustrated. London: 1753. V. 43
Shakespeare Illustrated; or the Novels and Histories on Which the Plays of Shakespeare are Founded, Collected and Translated from the Original Authors . . . (with) The Third and Last Volume. London: 1753, 1754. V. 41; 46
The Sister. London: 1769. V. 43

LENNOX, WILLIAM

Epilepsy and Related Disorders. Boston: 1950. V. 42
Recreations of a Sportsmen. London: 1862. V. 41

LENNOX, WILLIAM PITT

Coaching, with Anecdotes of the Road. London: 1876. V. 37; 43

LE NOBLE, EUSTACHE

Moliere Le Critique, et Mercure, Aux Prises Avec Les Philosohes. Holland: 1709. V. 38

LENOBLE, EUSTACHE, BARON DE SAINT GEORGES ET DE TENNELIERE

Contes et Fables. Lyon: 1697. V. 37
Zulima: or, Pure Love. London: 1719. V. 37

LENOIR, ALEXANDER

Museum of French Monuments; or, an Historical and Chronological Description of the Monuments in Marble, Bronze and Bas-Relief Collected in the Museum at Paris . . . Paris: 1803. V. 44

LENOIR, ALEXANDRE

Antiquities Mexicaines. Relation des Trois Expeditions du Capitaine Dupaix, Ordonnes en 1805, 1806 and 1807 . . . Paris: 1834. V. 42

LENOIR, M. ALBERT

Architecture Monastique. Paris: 1852. V. 38

LE NORMAND, MARIE ANN ADELAIDE

The Oracle of Human Destiny; or, the Unerring Foreteller of Future Events, and Accurate Interpreter of Mystical Signs and Influences through the Medium of Common Cards. London: 1826. V. 39; 42

LENORMANT, FRANCOIS

Chaldean Magic; Its Origin and Development. London: 1878. V. 44

LENOTRE, G.

Works. London: 1906-1924. V. 40

LENOX, EDWARD H.

Overland to Oregon in the Tracks of Lewis and Clark. Oakland: 1904. V. 40; 45

LENS, BERNARD

A New and Compleat Drawing Book . . . London: 1751. V. 40; 44

LENTORE, G.

Romances of the French Revolution. London: 1908. V. 37

LENTZ, HAROLD B.

The 'Pop-Up' Cinderella and Other Tales by . . . New York: 1933. V. 42

LENYGON, FRANCIS

The Decoration and Furniture of English Mansions, During the Seventeenth and Eighteenth Centuries. London: 1909. V. 39
Decoration in England from 1660 to 1770. (together with) Furniture in England from 1660 to 1760. London: 1924/1914. V. 40; 46
Decoration in England from 1640-1760. London: 1927. V. 39
Furniture in England from 1660 to 1760. London: 1920. V. 39

LEO AFRICANUS, JOANNES

De Totius Africae Descriptione, Libri IX . . . Recens in Latinam Linguam Conversi Joan. Floriano Interprete . . . Antverpiae: 1556. V. 45

LEO HEBRAEUS

De Amore Dialogi Tres. Venice: 1564. V. 38

LEO Holub, Photographer. Stanford: 1982. V. 46

LEO I, POPE

Epistolae Catholicae et Sanctae. Paris: 1511. V. 38; 41

LEO I, THE GREAT, SAINT, POPE d. 461

On the Birthday of Our Lord Jesus Christ. Worcester: 1958. V. 46
Sermones. Cologne. V. 39
Sermones et Opusculae. Rome: 1470-71. V. 40
Sermones. 1482. V. 42
Sermones Quam Diligentissime Nuper Rime Castigati & Quantum Anniti ars Potuit Fide Liter Impressi. Venice: 1505. V. 45

LEOB, ISADOR

Debates of the Missouri Constitutional Convention of 1875 . . . Columbia, Mo.: 1930-44. V. 37

LEON & BROTHER

Catalogue of First Editions of American Author . . . New York: 1885. V. 38; 42; 43; 44; 45; 46

LEON DE LABORDE, M.

Journey through Arabia Petraea, to Mount Sinai and the Excavated City of Petra, the Edom of the Prophecies. London: 1838. V. 40

LEON, H.

Flora de Cuba. 1979. V. 39

LEON, L.

Diary of a Tar Heel Confederate Soldier. Charlotte: 1913. V. 37

LEON, NICOLAS

La Obstetricia en Mexico. Mexico: 1910. V. 42

LEON Y GAMA, ANTONIO DE

Descripcion Historica y Cronologica de las dos Piedras Que con Ocasion del Nuevo Empedrado Que se Esta Formando en la Plaza Principal de Mexico . . . Mexico: 1792. V. 45

LEONARD, ARTHUR GLYN

The Lower Niger and Its Tribes. London: 1906. V. 39

LEONARD, ELMORE

The Big Bounce. 1989. V. 43
The Big Bounce. New York: 1989. V. 42; 44
The Bounty Hunters. 1953. V. 39
The Bounty Hunters. Boston: 1954. V. 43
Dutch Treat. New York: 1977. V. 43
Fifty-Two Pick Up. London: 1974. V. 38

LEONARD, ELMORE continued

Fifty-Two Pickup. New York: 1974. V. 42; 44

Glitz. New York: 1985. V. 43

Hombre. 1989. V. 46

The Moonshine War. Garden City: 1969. V. 43; 44; 45

Swag. New York: 1976. V. 41; 42; 43; 44; 45

LEONARD, HUGH F.

A Hand-Book of Wrestling. New York: 1897. V. 40

LEONARD, IRVING A.

Spanish Approach to Pensacola, 1689-1693. Albuquerque: 1939. V. 39; 42

LEONARD, JOHN W.

The Gold Fields of the Klondike Fortune Seekers' Guide to the Yukon Region of Alaska and British America. London: and Chicago: 1897. V. 45

LEONARD, PETER

The Western Coast of Africa. Philadelphia: 1833. V. 46

LEONARD, WILLIAM

Reports and Cases of Law . . . (1540-1615). London: 1658-75. V. 40

Reports and Cases of Law: (In Four Parts) Argued and Adjudged in the Courts of Law at Westminster. London: 1675. V. 45

Reports and Cases of Law . . . (1540-1615). London: 1687. V. 40; 45

LEONARD, WILLIAM E.

Two Lives a Poem. New York: 1925. V. 38

LEONARD, WILLIAM ELLERY

Gilgamesh. Avon: 1974. V. 44

LEONARD, ZENAS

Adventures of Zenas Leonard: Fur Trader and Trapper, 1831-1836. Cleveland: 1904. V. 37; 39; 41

LEONARDI, DOMENICO FELICE

Le Delizie della Villa di Castellazzo. Milan: 1743. V. 38; 39; 42; 44

LEONARDO DA VINCI 1452-1519

Leonardo da Vinci on the Human Body. New York: 1952. V. 38; 44

Leonardo Da Vinci. New York: 1956. V. 41

The Literary Works of Leonardo da Vinci. 1939. V. 46

The Madrid Codices. Lucerne: 1974. V. 46

The Madrid Codices. New York: 1974. V. 39

The Madrid Codices. New York: 1976. V. 38; 46

The Notebooks of Leonardo Da Vinci. London: 1938. V. 44

The Notebooks. New York: 1938. V. 43

The Notebooks of Leonardo Da Vinci. London: 1945. V. 38; 39; 40

On the Human Body. New York: 1952. V. 39

Thoughts on Art and Life . . . Boston: 1906. V. 40

Traite de la Peinture de Leonardo da Vinci Donne au Public et Traduit de l'Italien en Francois . . . Paris: 1651. V. 41

Traite de la Peinture de Leonardo da Vinci Donne au Public et Traduit de l'Italien en Francois par R. F. S. D. CX. Paris: 1651. V. 37

Trattato della Pittura di Leonardo da Vinci Nuovamente dato in Luce, Colla Vita Dell'istesso Autore, Scritta da Rafaelle du Fresne. Naples: 1733. V. 42

Trattato Della Puttura di Lionardo da Vinci Ridotto Alla Sus Vara Lezione Sopra Una Copia a Penna Di Mano Di Stefano Della Bella . . . Firenze: 1792. V. 41

Trattato della Pittura di Leonardo da Vinci Nuovamente dato in Luce, Colla Vita dell'Istesso Autore, Scritta da Rafaelle du Fresne. Naples: 1733. V. 37

A Treatise of Painting. London: 1721. V. 41; 42; 46

A Treatise of Painting. Translated from the Original Italian and adorned with a great number of cuts. London: 1721. V. 37

LEONARDO, RICHARD

History of Surgery. New York: 1943. V. 37; 41; 42; 45

History of Gynecology. New York: 1944. V. 46

LEONARDUS DE UTINO d. 1470

Sermones Aurei de Sanctis. Nuremberg: 1478. V. 43

Sermones Aurei de Sanctis. Venice: 1743. V. 40

Sermones Aurei de Sanctis. Venice: 1475. V. 37

LEONICENI, NICOLAI

Opuscula. Basel: 1532. V. 37

LEONICENUS, OMNIBONUS d. 1493

De Octo Partibus Orationis et de Arte Metrica. Padua: 1474. V. 38

LEONICUS THOMAEUS, NICOLAUS 1456-1531

Dialogi Nunc Primum in Lucem Editi. Venice: 1524. V. 40

LEOPOLD, ALDO

A Sand Country Almanac. New York: 1949. V. 42; 43

A Sand Country Almanac. Oxford: 1949. V. 44

LEOPOLD CASSELLA & CO., FRANKFURT/NEW YORK.

The Printing of Cotton Fabrics, with Dyestuffs of Leopold Cassella & Co. 1905. V. 46

LEOPOLD, RUDOLF

Egon Schiele: Paintings, Watercolours, Drawings. London: 1973. V. 41; 43

LEOTARDO, ONORATO d. 1650

Liber Singularis de Usuris et Contractibus Usuraiis Coercendis. Venice: 1655. V. 40

LEOVY, HENRY J.

The Laws and General Ordinances of the City of New Orleans . . . Revised and Digested . . . New Orleans: 1866. V. 37

LEOWITZ, CYPRIANUS VON

Eclipsium Omnium ab anno domini 1554. Usque in Annum Domini 1606, Accurata Descriptio & Pictura, ad Meridianum Augustanum Ita Supputata, ut Quibusius Alijs Facilime Accomodari Possit . . . colophon: 1556. V. 44

LE PAGE DU PRATZ d. 1775

Histoire de la Louisiane. Paris: 1758. V. 39; 42; 43; 46

The History of Louisiana, or the Western Parts of Virginia and Carolina. London: 1763. V. 40; 46

The History of Louisiana, or the Western Parts of Virginia and Carolina. London: 1774. V. 38; 39

LE PAN, DOUGLAS

The Wounded Prince and Other Poems. London: 1948. V. 44

LE PAUTRE, ANTOINE

Les Oeuvres d'Architecture. Paris: 169-1737. V. 44

Le Oeuvres d'Architecture. Paris: 1691-1737. V. 38; 40

Les Oeuvres d'Architecture d'Anthoine Le Pautre. Paris: 1692. V. 39

Les Oeuvres d'Architecture d'Anthoine Le Pature Architecte Ordinaire du Roy. Paris: 1710. V. 38

LE PAUTRE, JEAN

Oeuvres d'Architecture. Paris: 1751. V. 41; 46

L'EPEE, CHARLES MICHEL DE

La Veritable Maniere d'Instruire les Sourds et Muets . . . Paris: 1784. V. 38

LE PEROUSE, JEAN FRANCOIS

Voyage de la Perouse Autour du Monde . . . Paris: 1796-97. V. 46

LE PETIT, FRANCOIS

La Grande Chronique . . . de Hollande, Zelande, Westfirse, Utrecht, Frise, Overyssel & Groeningen. Dordrecht: 1601. V. 44

LE PEYROUSE, M. DE LA

A Voyage Around the World + a Voyage from Manila to California by Don Maurelle + Abstract of the Voyages and Discoveries of the late Capt. G. Vancouver. Boston: 1801. V. 39

LEPICIE, FRANCOIS BERNARD

Catalogue Raisonne des Tableaux Du Roy. Paris: 1752. V. 38

LEPINE, ERNEST

The Days of Chivalry, or, The Legends of Croquemitaine. London. V. 37

The Legend of Cronquemitaine, and the Chivalric Times of Charlemagne. London: 1870. V. 41

LEPLONGEON, AUGUSTUS

Queen Moo and the Egyptian Sphinx. London: 1896. V. 39

Queen Moo and the Egyptian Sphinx. New York: 1900. V. 37

LE POIVRE, MS.

Travels of a Philosopher. Dublin: 1770. V. 44

LEPORINUS, GABRIEL

Dialogus De Immortalitate Intellectivae Animae . . . Vienna: 1566. V. 43

LEPPER, J. H.

History of the Grand Lodge of Free and Accepted Masons of Ireland. Dublin: 1925/57. V. 43

LE PRESTRE DE VAUBAN, SEBASTIAN DE

The New Method of Fortification, As Practised by Monsieur de Vauban, Engineer General of France. London: 1693. V. 43

LEPSIUS, RICHARD

Discoveries in Egypt, Ethiopia and the Peninsula of Sinai, in the Years 1842-1845, During the Mission Sent Out by His Majesty Frederick William IV of Prussia. London: 1852. V. 40

LEPSIUS, RICHARD continued

Letters from Egypt, Ethiopia, and the Peninsula of Sinai. London: 1853. V. 40

LE QUANG, BA

The Story of a Vietnamese Freedom Fighter. N.P.. V. 45

LEQUEL, LOUIS

Identity; or, No Thoroughfare. New York: 1870? V. 40; 43

LE QUEUX, W.

Devil's Dice. 1897. V. 46

LE QUEX, WILLIAM

The Unborn Tomorrow - How the World Will Be Divided After the Ar. London: c. 1917. V. 46

LERIS, MICHEL

Wilfredo Lam. New York: 1970. V. 42

LERMAN, LOUIS

Winter Soliders. The Story of a Conspiracy Against the Schools. New York: 1941. V. 41

LERMONTOV, MIKHAIL YUREVICH 1814-1841

The Demon: a Poem. London: 1875. V. 38

A Song About Tsar Ivan Vasilyevitch His Young Bodyguards and the Valiant Merchant Kalashnikov. London: 1929. V. 38; 40

LERMONTOV, MIKHAIL YUREVITCH 1814-1841

A Song About Tsar Ivan Vasilyevitch His Young Bodyguard and the Valiant Merchant Kalashnikov. 1929. V. 42

LERNER, ALAN JAY

Camelot. New York: 1961. V. 42

LEROQUAIS, V.

Le Breviaire de Philippe le Bon. 1929. V. 46

LE ROUGE, GEORGE LOUIS

Atlas nouveau Portatif . . . Pour Usage des Militaires Colleges et du Voyageur. Paris: 1767-73. V. 38

LE ROUGE, SIEUR

Description de Chambord . . . Paris: 1750. V. 44

LEROUX, GASTON

Phantom of the Opera. New York. V. 39

The Phantom of the Opera. 1911. V. 42; 43

The Phantom of the Opera. London: 1911. V. 46

The Phantom of the Opera. New York: 1911. V. 42; 45

LEROUX, HUGUES

Acrobats and Mountebanks. London: 1890. V. 43

LE ROUX, PHILIBERT JOSEPH

Dictionnaire Comique, Satyrique, Critique, Burlesque, Libre et Proverbial . . . Amsterdam: 1718. V. 38

Dictionnaire Comique, Satyrique, Critique . . . Libre et Proverbial. Lyon: 1752. V. 37

LE ROY, DAVID

Les Ruines des Plus Beaux Monuments de la Grece, Considerees du Cote de l'Architecture . . . Paris: 1770. V. 39; 42

LE ROY, FRANCOIS fl. 1499-1512

Le Liure de la Femme Forte et Vertueuse . . . Paris: 1517. V. 45

LEROY, L. ARCHIER

Wagner's Music Drama of the Ring. London: 1925. V. 42; 45

Wagner's Music Drama of the Ring, by L. Archier Leroy. London: (preface 1925). V. 37

LE ROY, LOUIS 1510-1577

Of the Interchangeable Covrse, Or Variety of Things in the Whole World. London: 1594. V. 38

La Vicissitudine o Mutabile Varieta delle Cose Nell'Universo . . . Venice: 1585. V. 40; 43

LE ROY, M. SIEUR DE GOMBERVILLE

Moral Virtue Delineated. London: 1726. V. 42

LE ROY, PIERRE

Statuts et Privileges du Corps des Marchands Orfevres-Joyailliers de la Ville de Paris . . . Paris: 1759. V. 40

LERY, JEAN

Historia Navigationis in Brasiliam Quae et America Dicitur. Geneva: 1594. V. 37; 39; 40

LERY, JEAN DE

Historia Navigationis In Brasiliam Quae Et America Dicitur. Geneva: 1586. V. 40

LE SAGE, ALAIN RENE 1668-1747

The History and Adventures of Gil Blas of Santillane. London: 1725. V. 40

Histoire de Gil Blas. London: 1769. V. 37; 39

The Adventures of Gil Blas of Santillana. Dublin: 1777. V. 38

The Adventures of Gil Blas of Santillana. London: 1792. V. 41

The Adventures of Gil Blas of Santillana. London: 1798. V. 38

The Adventures of Gil Glas, of Santillane. London: 1802. V. 37

The Adventures of Gil Blas of Santillana. London: 1807. V. 37; 46

The Adventures of Gil Blas. London: 1809. V. 37; 38; 42

Histoire de Gil Blas de Santillane. Londres: 1809. V. 40; 43

The Adventures of Gil Blas. London: 1819. V. 37; 38; 40; 41; 43; 44; 45

The Adventures of Gil Blas of Santillana. London: 1823. V. 39

Histoire de Gil Blas de Santillane. Paris: 1835. V. 45

The Adventures of Gil Blas of Santillane. London: 1836. V. 43

The Adventures of Gil Blas of Santillane. (with) Asmodeus, or the Devil on Two Sticks. London: 1836-41. V. 38

The Adventures of Gil Blas of Santillane. Exeter: 1839. V. 40

The Adventures of Gil Blas of Santillana. London: 1881. V. 37; 40

The Adventures of Gil Blas of Santillane. London: 1937. V. 40

The Adventures of Gil Blas of Santillane. Oxford: 1937. V. 40; 41

Les Aventures de M. Robert Chevalier, dit de Beauchene, Capitaine de Flibustiers dans la Nouvelle France. Amsterdam: 1783. V. 39

Asmodeus: or the Devil on Two Sticks. London: 1841. V. 41; 46

Asmodeus, or the Devil Upon Two Sticks. London: 1881. V. 41

Le Bachelier de Salamanque, ou Les Memoires de D. Cherubin de la Ronda. Paris & A. L. Haye,: 1736 & 1738. V. 37

The Bachelor of Slamanaca; or, Memoirs of Don Cherubim. London: 1767. V. 37; 38; 40

The Devil Upon Two Sticks. London: 1785. V. 40

Le Diable Boiteux; or, The Devil Upon Two Sticks. London: 1708. V. 38; 45

Works. London: 1881. V. 37

LESCARBOT, MARC

Histoire de la Novvelle-France. Paris: 1618. V. 41; 42; 44

The History of new France. Toronto: 1907/11/14. V. 45

Les Muses de la Novvelle France. Paris: 1612. V. 41; 42; 44

The Theatre of Neptune in New France. Boston: 1927. V. 44

LESCARBOURA, AUSTIN C.

Behind the Motion Picture Screen. London: 1920. V. 41

LESCENE-DES-MAISONS, JACQUES

Contrat Conjugal, ou Lois du Mariage, de la Repudiation et du Divorce. n.p. Paris?: 1781. V. 45

LESLEY, J. P.

A Geological Hand Atlas of the Sixty-Seven Counties of Pennsylvania, Embodying The Results of the Field Work of the Survey, 1874-1884. Harrisburg: 1885. V. 37

The Iron Manufacturer's Guide to the Furnaces, Forges and Rolling Mills of the United States, with Discussions of Iron as a Chemical Element.. New York: 1859. V. 38; 42

Petroleum: Geological Report on Lands of Paint Lick Fork of Sand River, In Eastern Kentucky. Philadelphia: 1865. V. 38

LESLEY, LEWIS B.

Uncle Sam's Camels: the Journal of May Humphreys Stacey, Supplemented by the Report of E. F. Beale, 1857-1858. Cambridge: 1929. V. 37; 39

LESLEY, PARKER

Renaissance Jewels and Jewelled Objects. The Melvin Gutman Collection. Baltimore: 1968. V. 46

LESLIE, ALEXANDER

The Arctic Voyages of Adolf Erik Nordenskiold, 1858-1879. London: 1879. V. 39; 41; 44

LESLIE, C. R.

Memoirs of the Life of John Constable. London: 1937. V. 42; 44

LESLIE, CHARLES

The Constitution, Laws and Government of England Vindicated. London: 1709. V. 42

An Essay Concerning the Divine Right of Tythes. London: 1700. V. 43

The Finishing Stroke. London: 1711. V. 39

Gallienus Redivivus, or Murther Will Out. Edinburgh: 1695. V. 37

Masonry: a Poem. Edinburgh: 1739. V. 45

The Massacre of Glenco. London: 1703. V. 43

A New History of Jamaica from the Earliest Accounts to the Taking of Porto Bello by Vice-Admiral Vernon. London: 1740. V. 37; 38; 39; 41; 45

LESLIE, CHARLES continued

A New and Exact Account of Jamaica. Edinburgh: 1839. V. 41

Reflections Upon a Late Scandalous and Malicious Pmphlet Entitiul'd 'The Shortest Way with the Dissenters; or Proposals for the Establishment of the Church.' London: 1703. V. 38

A Reply to a Book entitul'd Anguis Flagellatus, or, a Switch for the Snake . . . London: 1702. V. 38

A Short and Easie Method with the Desits. London: 1723. V. 43; 45

The Snake in the Grass, or, Satan Transformed into an Angel of Light, Discovering the Deep and Unsuspected Subtility Which is Couched Under the Pretended Simplicity of Many of the Principal Leaders of Those People Called Quakers. London: 1698. V. 38

The Socinian Controversy Discuss'd; Wherein the Chief of the Socinian Tracts. are Consider'd. London: 1708. V. 40

A View of the Times, Their Principles and Practices, in the First Volume of the Rehearsals. 1708. V. 44

LESLIE, CHARLES ROBERT

Autobiographical Recollections. London: 1860. V. 37; 39; 43; 45; 46

LESLIE, DAVID

Among the Zulus and Amatongas; With Sketches of the Natives. Edinburgh: 1875. V. 40

LESLIE, ELIZA

The American Girl's Book; or, Occupation for Play Hours. New York: 1864. V. 46

Domestic French Cookery . . . Philadelphia: 1832. V. 43

Mr. and Mrs. Woodbridge, with Other Tales. Providence: 1841. V. 41; 43

LESLIE, FRANK

Frank Leslie's Illustrated Famous Leaders and Battle Scenes of the Civil War . . . New York: 1896. V. 46

Historical Register of the United States Centennial Exposition, 1876. New York: 1877. V. 45

LESLIE, JAMES B.

Armagh Clergy and Parishes . . . Dundalk: 1911. V. 43

Clogher Clergy and Parishes . . . from the Earliest Period . . . Enniskillen: 1929. V. 43

Ossory Clergy and Parishes . . . Enniskillen: 1933. V. 43

Raphoe Clergy and Parishes . . . Enniskillen: 1940. V. 43

LESLIE, JOHN 1766-1832

An Experimental Inquiry into the Nature, and Propagation of Heat. London: 1804. V. 40; 42

Killarney: a Poem. London: 1772. V. 43

Killarney. A Poem. London: 1773. V. 40

Narrative of Discovery and Adventure in the Polar Seas and Regions . . . Edinburgh: 1830. V. 46

Narrative of Discovery and Adventure in the Polar Seas and Regions . . . New York: 1833. V. 43

De Origine, Moribus et Rebus Gestis Scotorum. Rome: 1578. V. 41

De Origine Moribus & Rebus Gestis Scotorum. Romae: 1675. V. 38; 44

The Philosophy of Arithmetic. Edinburgh: 1817. V. 38; 45

LESLIE, JOHN H.

A List of the Officers Who Have Served in the Madras Artillery, from Its Foundation in 1748 down to 1861. N.P.,: 1900. V. 38

LESLIE, MISS

Miss Leslie's New Receipts for Cooking. Philadelphia: 1854. V. 37; 46

Miss Leslie's New Cookery Book. Philadelphia: 1857. V. 37; 45

LESLIE, SHANE

An Anthology of Catholic Poets. London: 1925. V. 37; 40

The Greek Anthology Selected and Translated with a Prolegomenon. London: 1929. V. 41

The Poems. London: 1928. V. 41

The Skull of Swift. London: 1928. V. 46

LESLIE, THOMAS EDWARD CLIFFE

Essays in Political and Moral Philosophy. Dublin: 1879. V. 37; 40

Essays in Political Economy. Dublin: 1888. V. 42

Essays in Political Economy . . . London: 1888. V. 43

L'ESPINE, JEAN DE c. 1506-1597

Dialogue de la Cene de Nostre Seigneur Jesus Christ. N.P.: 1566. V. 40

LESQUEREUX, LEO

Contributions to the Fossil Flora of the Western Territories. Part 3: The Creaceous and Tertiary Floras. Washington: 1883. V. 44

LESSAIGNE, JACQUES

The Ceiling of the Paris Opera. New York: 1966. V. 43

LESSEPS, FERDINAND DE

Percement de l'Isthme de Suez. Atlas des Cartes, Plans, Sondages, Profils et Forages a l'Appui du Projet de la Commission Internationale. Paris: 1856. V. 41

Recollections of Forty Years. London: 1887. V. 37

LESSEPS, JEAN BAPTISTE B. DE

Journal Historique du Voyage de M. De Lesseps, Consul de France, Employe Dans L'Expedition de M. Le Comte de La Perouse, en Qualite d'Interprete du Roi . . . Paris: 1790. V. 38; 41; 42; 43; 46

Travels in Kamtschatka, During the Years 1787 and 1788. London: 1790. V. 42; 43; 45; 46

LESSER, FRIEDRICH CHRISTIAN

Testaceo-Theologia, Oder Grundlicher Beweis des Daseyns und der Vollkommnesten Eigenschaften Eines Gottlichen Wesens, aus Naturlicher und Geistlicher Betrachtung der Schnecken und Muschelen, . . . Leipzig: 1744. V. 43

LESSING, DORIS 1919-

Canopus in Argos: Archives. New York: 1979-83. V. 40; 42

Fourteen Poems. London: 1959. V. 46

Fourteen Poems. Middlesex: 1959. V. 38

Fourteen Poems. Northwood: 1959. V. 38; 42

The Golden Notebook. London: 1962. V. 42

The Golden Notebook. New York: 1962. V. 42

The Good Terrorist. London: 1985. V. 46

The Grass is Singing. London: 1950. V. 37; 38

The Grass is Singing. New York: 1950. V. 39; 42

The Habit of Loving. London: 1957. V. 40

In Pursuit of the English - a Documentary. London: 1960. V. 43

Martha Quest. London: 1952. V. 39; 42

The Story of a Non-Marrying Man and Other Stories. London: 1972. V. 39

The Summer Before the Dark. London: 1973. V. 45

This Was the Old Chief's Country. London: 1951. V. 43; 44

This Was the Old Chief's Country. New York: 1951. V. 46

This Was the Old Chief's Country. New York: 1952. V. 39

LESSING, GOTTHOLD EPHRAIM

Laokoon, Oder ueber die Grenzen der Mahlerey und Poesie. Berlin: 1766. V. 40; 41

Nathan der Weise. Berlin: 1779. V. 41

Three Comedies. Colchester: 1838. V. 40

LESSIUS, LEONARD

De Justitia et Jure Caeterisque Virtutibus Cardinalibus Libri Quatuor. Paris: 1613. V. 37

Hygiasticon; or, the Right Course of Preserving Life and Health Unto Extream Old Age. London: 1634. V. 45

De Justitia et Jure . . . Antwerp: 1632. V. 45

The Temperate Man, or the Way of Preserving Life & Health, together with Soundness of the Senses, Judgment and memory unto Extream Old Age . . . London: 1678. V. 38

A LESSON In Seeing. London: 1897. V. 42

LESSON, RENE PRIMEVERE

Histoire Naturelle des Oiseaux-Mouches. Paris: 1829. V. 40

Histoire Naturelle des Oiseaux-Mouches . . . Paris: 1829-30. V. 39

Histoire des Oiseaux-Mouches. (with) Histoire Naturelle de Colibris, Suivie d'un supplement . . . (with) Les Trochilidees ou les Colibris et les Oiseaux-Mouches . . . (with) Histoire Naturelle des Oiseaux de Paradis et des Epimaques . . . Paris: 1829-35. V. 41; 42

Histoire Naturelle des Oiseaux de Paridis et des Epimaques. Paris: 1834-35. V. 45

Les Trochilidees; ou les Colibris et les Oiseaux-Mouches, Suivis d'un Index General . . . Paris: 1832-33. V. 39

A LESSON to Youth. London: 1720? V. 41

LESSONS On Thrift. London: 1820. V. 40

LESTER, CHARLES EDWARDS

The Artist, the Merchant, and the Statesman, of the Age of the Medici and of Our Own Times In Two Volumes. New York: 1845. V. 40

The Artists of America . . . New York: 1846. V. 42; 46

The Life of Sam Houston. New York: 1855. V. 37; 39; 42

The Life of Sam Houston . . . New York: etc.,: 1855. V. 39

Life and Public Services of Charles Sumner. New York: 1874. V. 42

Sam Houston and His Republic. New York: 1846. V. 37

LESTER, HORACE FRANCIS

Hartas Maturin. London: 1888. V. 40; 46

LESTER, J. C.

Ku Klux Klan. Its Origin, Growth and Disbandment. Nashville: 1884. V. 46

LESTER, J. C. continued

Ku Klux Klan: Its Origin, Its Growth and Disbandment. New York: 1905. V. 43

Ku Klux Klan: Its Origin, Growth and Disbandment. New York & Washington: 1905. V. 38

LESTER, JOHN E.

The Atlantic to the Pacific. What to See and How to See It. London: 1873. V. 40

The Yo-semite: Its History, Its Scenery, its Development. Profidence: 1873. V. 38

LESTER, KATHERINE MORRIS

Accessories of Dress. Peoria: 1940. V. 44

LESTER, W. W.

A Digest of the Military and Naval Laws of the Confederate States . . . Columbia: 1864. V. 37; 44

L'ESTRANGE, A. G.

The Life of Mary Russell Mitford. London: 1870. V. 40; 41

LE STRANGE, G.

Description of Syria, Including Palestine. London: 1886. V. 44

L'ESTRANGE, HAMON

The Alliance of Divine Offices Exhibiting All the Liturgies of the Church of England Since the Reformation, as Also the Late Scotch Service-Book . . . London: 1659. V. 43; 44

The Alliance of Divine Offices, Exhibiting all the Liturgies of the Church of England Since the Reformation . . . London: 1690. V. 46

The Reign of King Charles: an History Faithfully and Impartially Delivered and Disposed into Annals. London: 1655. V. 43

L'ESTRANGE, M.

Heligoland; or, Reminiscences of Childhood. London: 1850. V. 44; 46

L'ESTRANGE, ROGER

A Discourse of the Fishery. London: 1674. V. 41; 45

Fables and Storyes Moralized . . . London: 1699. V. 40

The Free-Born Subject; or, the Englishmans Birthright . . . London: 1679. V. 42

A History of the Life of Aesop, according to Sir Roger l'Estrange. to which is added a Choice Collection of Fables, with Instructive Morals. Portsmouth: 1808. V. 38

Interest Mistaken, or the Holy Cheat; Proving from Undeniable Practises and Positions of the Presbyterians, that the Design of that Party is to Enslave Both King and People Under the Masque of Religion . . . London: 1661. V. 40

Narrative of the Plot. Set Forth for the Edification of His Majesties Liege-People. London: 1680. V. 41

The Observator. London: 1684-87. V. 44

Seneca's Morals, by Way of Abstract. London: 1806. V. 43

L'ESTRANGE, W. D.

Under Fourteen Flags; Being the Life and Adventures of Brigadier-General MacIver, a Soldier of Fortune. London: 1884. V. 41

LESUEUR, CHARLES A.

Dessins de Ch. A Lesueur Executes Aux Etats-Unis de 1816 a 1837. Paris: 1927? V. 38; 39

LETAROUILLY, PAUL

Edifices de Rome Moderne ou Recueil des Palais, Maisons, Eglises, Couvents et Autres Monuments Publics et Particuliers les Plus Remarqables de la Ville Rome. Rome: 1857. V. 38

Edifices De Rome Moderne. Paris: 1868-74. V. 44

Edifices de Rome Moderne our Recueil des Palais, Maisons, Eglises, Couvents et Autres Monuments Publics et Particuliers les Plus Remarquables de la Ville de Rome. Paris: 1857. V. 37

Le Vatican et la Basilique de Saint-Pierre de Rome. Paris: 1882. V. 37

LETCHER, OWEN

Big Game Hunting in North-Eastern Rhodesia. London: 1911. V. 39

LETCHER, ROBERT PERKINS

Message of Governor Letcher, to the Legislature of Kentucky, at December Session, 1841. Frankfort: 1841. V. 44

LETCHWORTH, WILLIAM PRYOR 1823-1910

Care and Treatment of Epileptics. New York: 1900. V. 38; 39

The Insane in Foreign Countries. New York: 1889. V. 40

The Insane in Foreign Countries. New York: London: 1889. V. 43

LETHABY, W. R.

The Church of Sancta Sophia Constantinople. London: 1894. V. 43

Ernest Gimson: His Life and Work. 1924. V. 40

Ernest Gimson: His Life and Work. Stratford-upon-Avon: 1924. V. 40; 42

Greek Buildings Represented by Fragments in the British Museum. London: 1908. V. 40; 42

Philip Webb and His Works. London: 1935. V. 37; 40

Scrips and Scraps. Cirencester: 1953. V. 41

LETHEM, JONATHAN

Historical and Dscriptive Review of Kansas. Topeka: 1890-91. V. 39

LETI, GREGORIO 1630-1701

Il Putanismo di Roma, or the History of the Whores and Whoredom of the Popes, Cardinals and Clergy of Rome. London: 1670. V. 43; 46

The Life of Donna Olimpa Maldachini, Who Governed the Church During the Time of Innocent the X. London: 1667. V. 43

The Life of Pope Sixtus the Fifth . . . Dublin: 1779. V. 42

LETROSNE, GUILLAUME FRANCOIS

De l'Ordre Social, Ouvrage Suivi d'un Traite Elemntaire sur la Valeur, l'Argent la Circulation, l'Industrie & le Commerce (sic) Interieur & Exterieur. Paris: 1777. V. 41

LETT, KATHERINE LUCY

Records of the Lett Family in Ireland. Dublin: 1925. V. 38

LETTER, Addressed to the Legislators of the Several States, Composing the Federal Union; Recommending an Uniform Continental Currency. New York: 1797? V. 45

LETTER Addressed to Two Great Men, on the Prospect of Peace; and on the Terms to Be Insisted On . . . London: 1760. V. 38

A LETTER Concerning the Consequences of an Incorporating Uniou(sic), In Relation to Trade. Edinburgh: 1706. V. 42

A LETTER Concerning the Disabling Clauses Lately Offered to the House of Commons for Regulating Corporations. London: 1690. V. 41

A LETTER Concerning the Disabling Clauses Lately Offered to the House of Commons for Regulating Corporations. London: 1960. V. 39

A LETTER from a Clergyman to Miss Mary Blandy, Now a Prisoner in Oxford Castle; with Her Answer Thereto. As Also Miss Blandy's Own Narrative of the Crime for Which She is Condemn'd to Die. London: 1752. V. 45

A LETTER from a Gentleman in London to His Friend in the Country, Concerning the Treaty of Aix-La-Chapelle, Concluded on the 8th of October, 1748. London: 1748. V. 46

A LETTER from a Gentleman in the West of England to His Friend In London. London: 1754. V. 43

A LETTER from a Gentleman in Town to a Friend in the Country, Concerning the Present State of the Fishing-Copartnery in North-Briton. Edinburgh: 1723. V. 42

LETTER from a Gentleman in Town to His friend in the Country, Relating to the Royal Infirmary of Edinburgh. Edinburgh: 1739. V. 39

A LETTER from a Member of the States General in Holland to a Member of Parliament in England; by Which the Saddle is Put Upon the Right Horse, and the True Origin of the Present Confusion in Europe Plainly Demonstrated. London: 1743. V. 41

A LETTER from a Merchant in the City of London, to the R--t. H--ble W-- P-- Esq; upon the Affairs and Commerce of North America, and the West Indies; Our African Trade; the Destination of Our Squadrons and Convoys . . . London: 1757. V. 37; 41

A LETTER from a Person of Distinction to the Rt. Hon. J(ohn) E(arl) of Eg(mon)t. Occasioned by the Publication of three Late Pamphlets, entitled. An Examination of Principles . . . An Occasional Letter . . . A Second Series of Facts. London: 1749. V. 41

A LETTER from a Soldier, Being Some Remarks Upon a Late Scandalous Pamphlet; entitled, An Address of Some Irish-Folks to the House of Commons. Dublin?: 1702. V. 42

A LETTER from a Spaniard in London to His Friend in Madrid. Setting Forth the Happy Consequences That Must Accrue to Spain, from the Late Conduct of Her Great Friend at the Court of England. London: 1739. V. 41

A LETTER from a West-India Merchant to a Gentleman at Tunbridg, Concerning that Part of the French Proposals, Which Relates to North America . . . London: 1712. V. 42

A LETTER from a West India Merchant to A Gentleman at Tunbridge, Concerning that Part of the French Proposals . . . London: 1712. V. 41

A LETTER from an English Traveller at Rome to His Father, of the 6th of May 1721. London?: 1721. V. 41

A LETTER from an Officer Retired to His Son in Parliament. Edinburgh: 1776. V. 37

A LETTER from Flanders, Giving an Account of the Present State of the War in the Netherlands, the Weakness of the Allies and Strength of the French . . . London: 1744. V. 41

A **LETTER** from Hanover, Shewing the True Cause of the Present Broils of Germany and Confusions of Europe . . . Done into English from the Original High Dutch. London: 1744. V. 41

A **LETTER** from One of the Society of Friends, Relative to the Conscientious Scrupulousness of Its Members to Bear Arms. Philadelphia?: 1795. V. 39

A **LETTER** from the Mayor of the Antient Borough of Guzzle-Down, to Sir Francis Wronghead, Their R------ve in P--------t. London: 1733. V. 42

A **LETTER** of Advice to a Young Gentleman of an Honourable Family, Now in His Travels Beyond the Seas . . . London: 1688. V. 38

A **LETTER** of Private Direction by the Author of 'The Cloud of Knowing.' London: 1963. V. 42

LETTER of the Delegate of the Territory of Utah in Congress, Enclosing the Memorial of Delegates of the Convention. Washington: 1858. V. 39

THE **LETTER** of the Right Hon. C.J. Fox to the Electors of Westmisnter, Anatomized . . . London: 1793. V. 44

LETTER, S. L.

The Encyclopaedia of the New York Stage, 1920-1930. London: 1985. V. 39

A **LETTER** (Second Letter) to the Author of an Examination of the Principles (by John Perceval); and an Enquiry in to the Conduct of the Two B-----rs. London: 1749. V. 41

A **LETTER** To a Friend in the Country, in Relation to the New Law Concerning Spiritous Liquors. London: 1743. V. 43

A **LETTER** to a Gentleman Relating to the Office of Ruling Elders in the Churches. Boston: 1731. V. 37; 40

LETTER to a Great Man in France (?Bolingbroke); in Which are Briefly Considered, the Following Popular Points: viz The Conduct of Mr. P(ultene)y. The Right of Instructing Members . . . Of Limiting the Number of Placemen. London: 1743. V. 41

A **LETTER** to a Member of Parliament Concerning the Four Regiments Commonly Called Mariners. London: 1699. V. 40; 44

A **LETTER** to a Member of Parliament, Concerning the Repeal of the Corporation and Test Acts. London: 1739. V. 41

A **LETTER** to a Member of Parliament, Relating to the Bill for the Opening of a Trade, to and From Persia through Russia. London: 1741. V. 46

A **LETTER** to a Member of Parliament, Shewing, that a Restraint on the Press is Inconsistent with the Protestant Religion, and Dangerous to the Liberties of the Nation. London: 1698. V. 37

A **LETTER** To a Member of Parliament, Wherein the Power of the British Legislature, and the Case of the Colonists, are Briefly and Impartially Considered. London: 1765. V. 40

A **LETTER** To a Noble Lord, Concerning the British Navy, &c. in Our Present Critical Situation. London: 1776. V. 42

A **LETTER** to a Noble Lord; Containing Some Remarks On the Nature and Tendencey of Two Acts Past Last Session of the Last Parliament, Namely, An Act for Vesting In His Majestie the Estates of Certain Traytors, &c. & an Act for Taking Away & Abolishing . . . London: 1748. V. 41

A **LETTER** to a Noble Negotiator Abroad (i.e. John Montagu, Earl of Sandwich). On the Present Prospect of a Speady Peace. In Which the True Senses of the Several Articles of the Preliminaries Is Inquired and the French Views in Granting Them Exposed. London: 1748. V. 41

LETTER to a Proprietor of the East-India Company. London: 1750. V. 41; 45

A **LETTER** to a Right Honourable Member of Parliament, Demonstrating the Absolute Necessity of Great Britain's Assisting the House of Austria . . . London: 1742. V. 41; 45

A **LETTER** to a Young Gentleman Upon His Admission into the University. London: 1753. V. 39

A **LETTER** To Dr. Sangrado, in Answer to Thomsonus Redivivus. London: 1746. V. 42

A **LETTER** to George Cheyne, M.D.F.R.S., Shewing, The Danger of Laying Down General Rules to Those Who are not Acquainted with the Animal Oeconomy, &c. for Preserving and Restoring Health, Occasion'd by His Essay on Health and Long Life. London: 1724. V. 38

A **LETTER** to His Grace the Duke of N********, on the Present Crisis in the Affairs of Great Britain. Containing, Reflections on a Late Great Resignation. London: 1761. V. 37

A **LETTER** to Jasper Vaux, Esq. Chairman of the Meeting at Lloyds, on Monday, the 29th January Last, in Which the Nature and Principles and the Past and Present Extent of Marine Assurance are Examined . . . London: 1810. V. 43

A **LETTER** to John Trot-Plaid, Esq., Author of the Jacobite Journal, Concerning Mr. Carte's General History of England . . . London: 1748. V. 46

A **LETTER** to Lord -----. With an Address to the Town. London: 1768. V. 45

A **LETTER** To Richard Brinsley Sheridan, Esq. on the Proposed Renewal of the Charter of the East India Company. London: 1793. V. 41

A **LETTER** to Sir George Saville, Bart, Upon the Allegiance of a British Subject; Occasioned by His Late Bill in Parliament in Favour of the Roman Catholics of This Kingdom. London: 1778. V. 41

A **LETTER** to Sir John Phillips, Bart. Occasion'd by a Bill Brought Into Parliament to Naturalized Foreign Protestants. London: 1747. V. 41; 43; 46

A **LETTER** to Sir R----d C--x, on Occasion of a Pamphlet Ascribed to His Intituled, Ireland Disgraced, etc. London: 1758. V. 41

A **LETTER** to the Author of a Pamphlet Entitled, Some Thoughts on the Nature of Paper Credit. Dublin: 1760. V. 40

A **LETTER** to the Author of Considerations on Several Proposals for the Better Maintenance of the Poor. London: 1752. V. 40

A **LETTER** to the Author of the History and Mystery of Good-Friday. Cambridge: 1782. V. 45

A **LETTER** to the Bishop of London, On His Public Conduct. London: 1772. V. 45

A **LETTER** to the Earl of Sherburne on the Peace. London: 1783. V. 39

A **LETTER** to the Gentlemen of the Army. London: 1757. V. 41

A **LETTER** to the Landholders of Great Britain on the Present Important Crisis: Containing Some Interesting Observations to Stockholders. London: 1798. V. 39

A **LETTER** to the Merchants of the Portugal Committee, from a Lisbon Trader. London: 1754. V. 46

A **LETTER** to the Most Noble Thomas, Duke of Newcastle, On Certain Points of the Last Importance to These Nations . . . London: 1746. V. 43

A **LETTER** to the Negroes Lately Converted to Christ in America . . . London: 1743. V. 43

LETTER to the President of the United States, Touching the Prosecutions, Under His Patronage, Before the Circuit Court in the District of Columbia . . . New Haven: 1808. V. 45

A **LETTER** to the Reverend The Moderator and Members of the Presbytery of Haddington. Edinburgh: 1757. V. 43

A **LETTER** to the Right Hon. George Grenville. London: 1763. V. 38

LETTER to the Right Hon. Lord Kenyon, Lord Chief Justice of the King's Bench, On the Present High Prices of Corn and Other Provisions. London: 1880. V. 42

A **LETTER** to the Right Hon. Lord Tenterden, Justices Bayley, Littledale and Parke, On Martial, Military and Civil Law; and on the word 'Crime.' London: 1829. V. 39

A **LETTER** TO the Right Honourable Charles Townshend . . . London: 1764. V. 45

A **LETTER** to the Right Honourable J- P-, Speaker of the House of Commons in Ireland. London: 1767. V. 39

A **LETTER** to the Right Honourable the E--l of T-q-r. London: 1748? V. 38; 41

A **LETTER** to the Right Honourable the Earl of B***, on A Late Important Resignation, and Its Probabale Consequences. London: 1761. V. 37

LETTER to the Right Honourable the Earl of Haddington, Lord Lieutenant of the County of Haddington . . . London: 1810. V. 39

A **LETTER** to the Right Honourable the Earls of Egremont and Halifax, His Majesty's Principal Secretaries of State on the Seizure of Papers. London: 1763. V. 37

A **LETTER** to the Right Honourable the Lord B---y. London: 1757. V. 44

A **LETTER** to the Right Honourable The Lord Provost of Edinburgh, on the Subject of the Proposed New Streets and Approaches to the City; in Answer to a Letter on that Subject, By 'A Builder'. Edinburgh: 1825. V. 41

A LETTER to the Right Honourable William Pulteney Esq. Occasion'd by a Bill Depending in the House of Commons for Raising One Hundred Thousand Pounds Upon the Roman Catholicks. London: 1723. V. 39

A LETTER To the Rt. Hon. the Lord Mayor, Aldermen, Sheriffs and Clergy of the City of Dublin. Dublin: 1763. V. 40

A LETTER to the Secret Committee. Containing Certain Extraordinary Practices of the Late M----r, Intended to Have Been Laid Before Them in a Private Manner and Now Submitted to Their Publick Consideration. London: 1742. V. 41

A LETTER to the Town, Concerning the Man and the Bottle. London: 1749. V. 41; 44

A LETTER to the Whigs. London: 1729. V. 37
A LETTER to the Whigs. London: 1779. V. 38; 43

A LETTER TO Viscount Milton, M.P. By One of His Constituents . . . London: 1827. V. 44; 46

A LETTER Upon the Distillery to the Framers of the Prth-Shire Resolutions. Perth?: 1784? V. 42

A LETTER Without Any Superscription, Intercepted in the Way to London. N.P.: 1643. V. 40; 43

LETTERA Annua del Giappone dell'anno 1596. Padua: 1599. V. 44

LETTRE Volgari di Diversi Eccellentissimi Huomini, in Diverse Materie. Venice: 1545. V. 40

LETTERS, in the Original, with Translations and Messages, That Passed Between the King and Queen, Prince and Princess of Wales. London: 1737. V. 39

LETTERS Addressed to Martin Van Buren, Esq., Secretary of State; Correcting Many Important Errors in a Late Biography of that Gentleman. By Corrector. New York: 1830. V. 43

LETTERS Addressed to Two Young Married Ladies, on the Most Interesting Subjects . . . London: 1782. V. 42

LETTERS and Papers on Agriculture and Planting & Selected from the Correspondence-Book of the Society Instituted at Bath, for the Encouragement of Agriculture, Arts, Manufactures and Commerce, within the Counties of Somerset . . . Bath: 1783. V. 39; 42; 44

LETTERS and Papers on Agriculture, Planting &c. Selected from the Correspondence of the Bath and West of England Society. Bath: 1802. V. 39

LETTERS Concerning the Present State of England. London: 1772. V. 41; 42

LETTERS From a Portuguese Nun. Gloucestershire: 1986. V. 39

LETTERS from Captain Barclay, Mr. Frquharson, General Burnett and Mr. Stuart: With a Statement of Facts, Addressed to the Impartial; by the Injured Party. Leith: 1814. V. 38

LETTERS From Golden Latitudes . . . St. Paul: 1885. V. 42

LETTERS from Settlers & Labouring Emigrants in the New Zealand Company's Settlements of Wellington, Nelson and New Plymouth . . . London: 1843. V. 45

LETTERS of Abbe Salemankis (Pseud.) to a Friend in Ireland. Philadelphia: 1810. V. 41

LETTERS OF Captain Don Pedro Fages and the Reverend President Fr. Junipero Serra . . . San Francisco: 1936. V. 46

LETTERS Of Religion and Vertue, to Several Gentlemen and Ladies. London: 1695. V. 40; 43

LETTERS of the Ghost of Alfred, Addressed to the Hon. Thomas Erskine, and the Hon. Charles James Fox, on the Occasions of the State Trials at the Close of the Ear 1794, and the Beginning of the Year 1795. London: 1798. V. 39

THE LETTERS of Wyoming, to the People of the United States, on the Presidential Election and in Favour of Andrew Jackson. Philadelphia: 1824. V. 42

LETTERS on Malvern . . . an Account of the Various Seats in the Neighbourhood. Worcester: 1815. V. 37; 40

LETTERS On the Manners of the French, and on the Follies and Extravagances of the Times. Dublin. V. 46

LETTERS Patent, Establishing a Supreme Court of Judicature, at Fort-William, in Bengal. London: 1774. V. 37; 38

LETTERS Poems and Drawings for Vernon Scannell. London: 1967. V. 38

LETTERS Redrawn from the Trajan Inscription in Rome. Davenport: 1961. V. 40

LETTERS to a Friend in England, on the Actual State of Ireland. London: 1828. V. 38; 42

LETTERS to Benjamin Franklin from his Family and Friends 1751-1790. New York: 1859. V. 37

LETTERS to Conrad. London: 1926. V. 41

LETTERS to the King, from an Old Patriotic Quaker, Lately Deceased. London: 1778. V. 37

LETTERS Written During the Late Voyage of Discovery in the Western ARctic Sea. London: 1821. V. 42

LETTICE, JOHN
Letters on a Tour through Various Parts of Scotland, in the Year 1792. London: 1794. V. 41; 43

LETTOW-VORBECK, PAUL EMIL VON 1870-
My Reminiscences of East Africa. London: 1922. V. 41

LETTRE, EMIL
Kleinodien. Potsdam: 1922. V. 38

LETTRES Edifiantes et Curieuses, Ecrites des Missions Etrageres par Quelques Missionnaires de la Compagnie de Jesus. V. Recueil. Paris: 1705. V. 39

LETTRES Edifiantes et Curieuses, Escrites des Missions Estrangeres. Lyon: 1819. V. 46

LETTRES Infernales et les Tisons. 1740. V. 38

LETTRES Patentes en Forme d'Edit, Portant Establissement d'une Compagnie de Commerce, Sous le Nom de Compagnie d'Occident . . . Donne a Paris au Mois d'Aout 1717. Paris: 1717. V. 38; 44

LETTS, JOHN M.
California Illustrated: Including a Description of the Panama and Nicaragua Routes by a Returned Californian. New York: 1852. V. 39
California Illustrated . . . . New York: 1853. V. 42
A Pictorial View of California . . . New York: 1853. V. 37; 39; 40; 46

LETTSOM, JOHN COAKLEY
Grove-Hill: an Horticultural Sketch. London: 1794. V. 38
Hints Designed to Promote Beneficence and Temperance & Medical Science. London: 1801. V. 38; 40; 42
History of the Origin of Medicine: An Oration, Delivered at the Anniversary Meeting of the Medical Society of London . . . London: 1778. V. 41
Medical Memoirs of the General Dispensatory of London, for Part of the Years 1773 and 1774. London: 1774. V. 46
Museum Lettsomianum. A Catalogue of the Entire Museum. London: 1816. V. 40
The Naturalist's and Traveller's Companion. London: 1799. V. 41; 43
The Naturalist's and Traveller's Companion . . . London: 1774. V. 37; 41
Some Account of the Late John Fothergill, M.D. London: 1783. V. 45

LETTSOM, JOHN CROAKLEY
Reflections on the General Treatment and Cure of Fevers. London: 1772. V. 39

LETTY, C.
Wild Flowers of the Transvaal. Pretoria: 1962. V. 45

LE TURC, M.
Echelles Pour les Bibliotheques, Plus Commodes et Plus Solides que Celles Dont on Fait Actuelement Usage. London: 1781. V. 40

LEUCHARS, ROBERT B.
A Practical Treatise on the Construction, Heating and Ventilation of Hot-Houses . . . Boston: 1851. V. 44

LEUCHT, CHRISTIAN LEONHARD
Neuer Muntz-Tractat von Approbirten and Devalvirten Guldinern, und Andern Muntz-Sorten, was Dieselbe Sowol vor Geprag, als Auch an Schrott und Korn Halaten . . . Nurnberg & Leipzig: 1692. V. 37

LEUNCLAVIUS, JOHN
Historiae Musulmanae Turcorum, de Monumentis Issorum Exscriptae Libri XVIII . . . Frankfurt: 1591. V. 37

LEUPOLD, JACOB
Theatrum Machinarum Generale. 1724-39. V. 39
Theatrum Machinarum Generale. Leipzig and Dresden: 1724-39. V. 40

LEURECHON, JEAN
Mathematical Recreations. Or, a Collection of many Problems, extracted out of the Ancient and Modern Philosophers, as Secrets and Experiments in Arithmetick, Geometry, Cosmographie, Horologiographie . . . London: 1653. V. 37

LEVAILLANT, FRANCOIS

Histoire Naturelle des Oiseaux d'Afrique. Paris: 1796-1805-08-12. V. 37; 42

Histoire Naturelle des Oiseaux d'Afrique. Paris: 1805-08. V. 41

Traveller in South Africa and His Collection of 165 Watercolour Paintings 1781-1784. Cape Town: 1973. V. 44

Travels from the Cape of Good Hope, Into the Interior Parts of Africa. London: 1790. V. 43

Voyage de M. Le Vaillant dans l'Interieur de l'Afrique . . . Paris: 1790. V. 38

LEVARIE, NORMA

The Art and History of Books. New York: 1968. V. 38

LEVASSEUR, PIERRE EMILE 1828-1911

The American Workman. Baltimore: 1900. V. 41

LE VAYER DE BOUTIGNY, ROLLAND

A Dissertation Shewing the Invalidity of All Proof by Similitude of Hands, in Criminal Cases . . . London: 1744. V. 41; 42

The Famous Romance of Tarsis and Zelie Digested into Ten Books. London: 1685. V. 39; 40; 42; 44; 46

LEVELING, HEINRICH PALMAZ

Anatomische Erklarung der Original-Figuren von Andreas Vesal, Samt Einer Anwendung der Winslowischen Zergliederungslehre in Sieben Buchern. Ingolstadt: 1783. V. 42; 43

LEVENS, HENRY C.

A History of Cooper County, from the First Visit My White Men, in February 1804 to the Fifth Day of July 1876. St. Louis: 1876. V. 38; 39; 42; 43; 46

LEVENS, PETER

A Right Profitable Booke for all Diseases Called, The Path-Way to Health, Wherein are to Bee Found Most Excellent and Approved Medicines of Great Vertue . . . London: 1632. V. 37

LEVER, C.

Naturalized Birds of the World. Harlow: 1987. V. 38

LEVER, CHARLES JAMES 1806-1872

Arthur O'Leary. His Wanderings and Ponderings in Many Lands. London: 1844. V. 38; 40; 42; 43

Arthur O'Lery: His Wanderings and Ponderings in Many Lands. London: 1845. V. 44

Charles O'Malley, the Irish Dragoon. Dublin: 1841. V. 38; 39; 40; 41

Charles O'Malley, the Irish Dragoon. London: 1857. V. 43; 46

Charles O'Malley. London: 1897. V. 40

Confessions of Con. Cregan: the Irish Gil Blas. London: 1849. V. 37; 42; 46

The Confessions of Harry Lorrequer. Dublin: 1839. V. 37; 41

The Daltons or Three Roads in Life. London: 1852. V. 38; 40; 41; 43

Davenport Dunn, a Man of Our Day. London: 1859. V. 39

Davenport Dunn, a Man of Our Day. London: 1862. V. 43; 46

The Dodd Family Abroad. London: 1852-54. V. 40

The Dodd Family Abroad. London: 1854. V. 44

The Fortunes of Glencore. London: 1857. V. 38; 41

The Knight of Gwynne. London: 1846-47. V. 39

The Knight of Gwynne. London: 1847. V. 40

The Knight of Gwynne; a Tale of the Time of the Union. London: 1848. V. 40; 46

The Knight of Gwynne. London: 1851. V. 43; 46

Luttrell of Arran. London: 1865. V. 39

The Martins of Cro'Martin. London: 1854-56. V. 46

The Martins of Cro-Martin. London: 1856. V. 38; 39; 41

Novels. London: 184-165. V. 43

Novels. London: 1841-65. V. 46

The Novels of . . . London: 1897. V. 41; 46

The Novels. London: 1897-1899. V. 37; 40

The O'Donoghue; a Tale of Ireland Fifty Years Ago. Dublin: 1845. V. 40

The O'Donoghue: A Tale of Ireland. New York: 1902. V. 38

Our Mess . . . Dublin: 1843-4. V. 41

Paul Goslett's Confessions in Love, Law and the Civil Service. London: 1868. V. 39

Roland Cashel. London: 1850. V. 37; 40; 42

St. Patrick's Eve. London: 1845. V. 44

Sir Brook Fossbrooke. Edinburgh: 1866. V. 37

LEVER, DARCY

The Young Sea Officer's Sheet Anchor; or A Key to the Leading of Rigging and to Practical Seamanship. London: 1808. V. 38; 42; 43

The Young Sea Officer's Sheet anchor. London: 1835. V. 41

The Young Officer's Sheet Anchor. New York: 1843. V. 40

The Young Sea Officer's Sheet Anchor; or, a Key to the Leading of Rigging and to Practical Steamanship. Boston: 1930. V. 41

The Young Sea Officer's Sheet. Anchor or a Key to the leading of Rigging and Practical Seamanship. (1819). V. 37

LEVER, JOHN C. W. 1811-1858

A Practical Treatise on Organic Diseases of the Uterus. Newburgh: 1845. V. 44

LEVERHULME, WILLIAM HESKETH LEVER, 1ST VISCOUNT 1851-1925

The Art Collections. New York: 1926. V. 38; 40

LEVERING, JOSEPH M.

A History of Bethlehem, Pennsylvania, 1741-1802. Bethelehem: 1903. V. 42; 46

LE VERT, OCTAVIA WALTON

Souvenirs of Travel. Mobile: 1857. V. 46

LEVERTOV, DENISE 1923-

The Double Image. London: 1946. V. 37; 38; 39; 40; 42; 44; 45; 46

Embroideries. Los Angeles: 1969. V. 46

Life in the Forest. 1978. V. 42

Mass for the Day of St. Thomas Didymus. 1981. V. 39

A New Year's Garland for My Students. MIT 1969-1970. Mt. Horeb: 1970. V. 37

Pig Dreams. Woodstock: 1981. V. 42

Summer Poems/ 1969. Berkeley: 1970. V. 46

Three Poems. Mt. Horeb: 1968. V. 43

A Tree Telling of Orpheus. Los Angeles: 1968. V. 38

Wanderer's Daysong. Copper Canyon: 1981. V. 38; 40; 42; 43

Wanderer's Daysong. 1981. V. 37

With Eyes at the Back of Our Heads. Norfolk: 1960. V. 42; 43

LEVESON GOWER, GRANVILLE

Genealogical Memoranda Relating to the Family of Gresham. London: 1884. V. 38

LEVESON, HENRY A.

Sport in Many Lands. London: 1877. V. 43

Sport in Many Lands. Africa and America. London: 1880. V. 46

LEVESQUE DE POUILLY, LOUIS JEAN

The Theory of Agreeable Sensations. London: 1749. V. 39

The Theory of Agreeable Sensations: In Which the Laws Observed by nature in the Distribution of Pleasure are Investigated . . . London: 1774. V. 46

LEVETT, HANSON

An Acurate Historical Account of all the Orders of Knighthood . . . London: 1802? V. 45

LEVI, A. J.

Conversion of Mr. and Mrs. Levi. New York: 1852. V. 44

LEVI, DAVID 1740-1799

A Defence of the Old Testament, in a Series of Letters Addressed to Thomas Paine. Philadelphia: 1798. V. 37; 43

LEVI, DORO

Early Hellenic Pottery of Crete. Amsterdam: 1969. V. 40

Festos e la Civilta Minoca. Roma: 1976-81. V. 40

LEVI, PETER

The Light Garden of the Angel King - Journeys in Afghanistan. London: 1972. V. 44; 45; 46

LEVICK, G.

Antarctic Penguins. London: 1914. V. 41

LEVIN, IRA

The Boys from Brazil. New York: 1976. V. 42

Rosemary's Baby. New York: 1967. V. 42; 45

The Stepford Wives. New York: 1972. V. 42

LEVINE, DAVID

Pens & Needles. Boston: 1969. V. 39; 44

A Summer Sketchbook. New York: 1963. V. 38

LEVINE, PHILIP

On the Edge. Iowa City: 1963. V. 46

LEVINE, SAMUEL

Coronary Thrombosis: its Various Clinical FEatures. Baltimore: 1931. V. 42

LEVINE, SAMUEL ALBERT

Clinical Heart Disease. Philadelphia: 1936. V. 45

LEVINGE, RICHARD

Jottings for Early History of the Levinge Family. Dublin: 1873. V. 38

LEVINS, PETER

Manipulus Vocabulorum: a Rhyming Dictionary of the English Language. London: 1867. V. 38; 44

LEVINSOHN, ISAAC BEER

Efes Dammin. London: 1841. V. 37

LEVINSON, ABRAHAM

Pioneers of Pediatrics. New York: 1943. V. 45

LEVINSON, ANDRE

La Argentina: a Study in Spanish Dancing. Paris: 1928. V. 45

Histoire de Leon Bakst. Paris: 1924. V. 38; 46

Marie Taglioni (1804-1884). London: 1930. V. 43

L'Oeuvre de Leon Bakst Pour 'La Belle au Bois Dormant'. Paris: 1922. V. 46

The Story of Leon' Bakst's Life. New York: 1922. V. 42

LEVINSTEIN, EDWARD

Morbid Craving for Morphia. London: 1878. V. 40

LEVINZ, CRESWELL 1627-1700

Reports of . . . Cases . . . in the Court of King's Bench (and Common Pleas) During the Time that Sir Robert Foster, Sir Robert Hyde and Sir John Kelyng Were Chief Justices . . . London: 1722. V. 40

LEVIS, H. C.

Baziliologia A Booke of Kings. New York: 1913. V. 46

LEVIS, HOWARD C.

A Bibliography of American Books Relating to Prints and the Art and History of Engraving. London: 1910. V. 43

Catalogue of Engraved Portraits, Views, etc. Connected with the Name of Levis. London: 1914. V. 40

A Descriptive Bibliography of the Most Important Books in the English Language Relating to the Art and History of Engraving and the Collecting to Prints. London: 1912. V. 41

A Descriptive Bibliography of the Most Important Books in the English Language Relating to the Art and History of Engraving and Collecting Prints. London: 1912-13. V. 40; 42; 44; 46

LEVISON, J. B.

Memories for My Family. San Francisco: 1933. V. 39; 42; 45

LEVITT, HELEN

A Way of Seeing. New York: 1965. V. 37; 41

A Way of Seeing. New York: 1981. V. 41

LEVY, JEAN BAPTISTE MICHEL DE

Journal Historique Ou Fastes du Regne de Louis XV Surnomme Le Bien-Aime. Paris?: 1757. V. 39

LEVY, JULIEN

Surrealism. New York: 1936. V. 39

LEVY, SAMUEL YATES

The Italian Bride. Savannah: 1856. V. 37

LEWELLIN, J. L.

A Prince Edward Island: a Brief but Faithful Account of This Fine Colony: Shewing Some Of Its Advantages as a Place of Settlement . . . London: 1834. V. 40

LEWER, H. W.

The Church Chests of Essex. London: 1913. V. 41

LEWES, CHARLES LEE

Comic Sketches . . . London: 1804. V. 42

Memoirs, Containing Anecdotes Historical and Biographical, of the English and Scottish Stages, During a Period of Forty Years. London: 1805. V. 42

LEWES, GEORGE HENRY

The Biographical History of Philosophy, From Its Origin in Greece Down to the Present Day. London: 1857. V. 37

Comte's Philosophy of the Sciences . . . London: 1853. V. 40; 42

The History of Philosophy from Thales to Comte. London: 1867. V. 38

The Life of Maximillien Robespierre; with Extracts from His Unpublished Correspondence. London: 1849. V. 46

The Life of Goethe. London: 1864. V. 39

On Actors and the Art of Acting. London: 1875. V. 43

The Physical Basis of Mind. London: 1877. V. 45

Problems of Life and Mind, Second Series: The Physical Basis of Mind and Third Series: Problem the First, The Study of Psychology. Problem the Second, Mind as a Function of the Organism. Problem the Third, The Sphere of Sense & Logic of Feeling . . . London: 1877/1879. V. 39

The Spanish Drama. London: 1846. V. 43

LEWES, JOHN LEE

Memoirs of Charles Lee Lewes . . . London: 1805. V. 38

LEWIN, E.

Subject Catalogue of the Library of the Royal Empire Society, Formerly Royal Colonial Institute. London: 1930-37. V. 39

LEWIN, LOUIS 1850-1929

Phantastica: Narcotic and Stimulating Drugs. New York: 1931. V. 43

LEWIN, WILLIAM

The Birds of Great Britian, with their Eggs Accurately Figured. London: 1789-94. V. 39

The Birds of Great Britain. London: 1795-1801. V. 42

The Birds of Great Britain . . . London: 1795-97. V. 39

Les Oiseaux De La Grande Bretagne, Ranges Dans Un Ordre Systematique, Graves Avec Sain et Peints d'Apres Nature . . . 1800. V. 40

LEWINE, J.

Bibliography of Eighteenth Century Art and Illustrated Books . . . London: 1898. V. 42

LEWIS, A. G.

Sport, Travel and Adventure. New York: 1916. V. 42

LEWIS, A. H.

Chemainus and Crofton Districts, Vancouver Island, British Columbia, Headquarters for Lumbering and Mining Industries. Chemainus: 1910. V. 43

LEWIS, ALBERT ADDISON

Boxwood Gardens. Richmond: 1924. V. 38

LEWIS, ALETHEA BRERETON

Isabella. London: 1823. V. 38; 39; 42; 43; 46

Rhoda. London: 1816. V. 38

Things by Their Right Name. London: 1812. V. 38

Things by Their Right Names. London: 1814. V. 39

LEWIS, ALFRED HENRY

Sandburrs. New York: 1900. V. 40

Wolfville. New York: 1897. V. 38; 43

Wolfville Days. New York: 1902. V. 39; 40

Wolfville Nights. New York: 1902. V. 39

LEWIS, ALONZO

Poems. Portsmouth: 1823. V. 46

Poems. Boston: 1831. V. 40

LEWIS, ALUN

Ha! Ha! Among the Trumpets . . . London: 1945. V. 42

In the Green Tree. London: 1948. V. 42

The Last Inspection and Other Stories. London: 1942. V. 42

Letters from India. London: 1946. V. 40

Raider's Dawn and Other Poems. London: 1942. V. 39

LEWIS, ANDREW

the Orderly Book of that Portion of the American Army Stationed at or Near Williamsburg, Va. Under the Command of General Andrew Lewis, from Marh 18th, 1776 to August 28th 1776. Richmond: 1776. V. 46

The Orderly Book of that Portion of the American Army Stationed at or Near Williamsburg, Va. Under the Command of General Andrew Lewis from March 18th, 1776 to August 28th 1776. Richmond: 1860. V. 39; 45

LEWIS, ANGELO JOHN 1839-1919

Drawing Room Conjuring. London and New York: 1887. V. 42

Tricks with Cards: a Complete manual of Card Conjuring. London: & New York: 1889. V. 46

LEWIS, AUSTIN

Montmartre (March 18, 1871). San Francisco: 1896? V. 42

LEWIS, B. ROLAND

Shakespeare Documents, Facsimiles, Transliterations, Translations and Commentary. Stanford: 1943. V. 41

LEWIS, C. DAY

Posthumous Poems. By C. Day Lewis. With an introduction by Jill Balcon. Gloucestershire: 1979. V. 37

LEWIS, CECIL

The Trumpet is Mine. London: 1938. V. 38; 40

LEWIS, CHARLES BERTRAND

Brother Gardner's Lime-Kiln Club. Chicago: 1882. V. 40

LEWIS, CHARLES THOMAS COURTNEY

George Baxter the Picture Printer. London: 1894. V. 44

George Baxter (Colour Printer) His Life and Work. London: 1908. V. 38; 40; 42; 43; 44

George Baxter, the Picture Printer. London: 1924. V. 45; 46

The Le Blond Book. 1920. Being a History & detached Catalogue of the Work of Le Blond & Co. by the Baxter PRocess, with a Glance at the other Licensees. 1920. V. 37

The Picture Printer of the Nineteenth Century: George Baxter 1804-1867. L: 1911. V. 40

The Picture Printer of the 19th Century. George Baxter 1804-1867. London: 1911. V. 37; 41; 42; 43; 44; 46

The Picture Printer of the 19th century. 1804-67. V. 37

The Story of Picture Printing in England During the Nineteenth Century or Forty Years of Wood and Stone. London. V. 40; 46

The Story of Picture Printing in England During the 19th Century or 40 Years of Wood and Stone. London: 1928. V. 38; 39; 40; 46

The Story of Picture Printing in England During the Nineteenth Century, or Forty Years of Wood and Stone. London: 1930. V. 45

The Story of Picture Printing in England during the 19th Century or 40 years of wood and stone. 1928. V. 37

The Story of Picture Printing in England during the Nineteenth Century; or, Forty years of wood and stone. London: (1928). V. 37

LEWIS, CLARENCE I.

An Analysis of Knowledge and Valuation. La Salle: 1946. V. 45

LEWIS, CLIVE STAPLES 1898-1963

Mark vs. Tristram - Correspondence Between C. S. Lewis and Owen Barfield. Cambridge: 1967. V. 40

Dimer. London: 1926. V. 41

The Great Divorce. London. V. 41

The Great Divorce. London: 1945. V. 37; 38; 40; 42; 44

A Grief Observed. London: 1961. V. 45

The Horse and His Boy. London: 1954. V. 40

The Horse and His Boy. New York: 1954. V. 43

The Last Battle. London: 1956. V. 38

The Lion, The Witch and the Wardorbe. London: 1950. V. 38; 43; 44

The Magician's Nephew. London: 1955. V. 38; 45

A Note on Comus. London: 1932. V. 46

Out of the Silent Planet. London: 1938. V. 42

Perelandra. New York: 1944. V. 44

The Personal Heresy - Controversy. London: 1939. V. 40

The Pilgrim's Regress. London: 1933. V. 44

Prince Caspian. New York: 1951. V. 43

Rehabilitations and Other Essays. London: 1939. V. 41

The Screwtape Letters. London: 1942. V. 43; 44; 45; 46

A Story of Children. London: 1956. V. 45

The Trouble with X. London. V. 40

The Voyage of the Dawn Treader. London: 1952. V. 40; 46

The Voyage of the Dawn Treader. New York: 1952. V. 43

LEWIS, DAVID

Miscellaneous Poems by Several Hands. London: 1726. V. 46

Miscellaneous Poems, by Several Hands. London: 1726-30. V. 39; 42

Miscellaneous Poems, by Several Hands. (with) Miscellaneous Poems, by Several Hands. London: 1726/30. V. 43

LEWIS, E. GOODWYN

Shakesperean Creations. London: 1865. V. 44

LEWIS, E. J.

Hints to Sportsmen, Containing Notes on Shooting . . . Philadelphia: 1851. V. 40; 43

LEWIS, EDWARD W.

Lectures on the Geology of Leighton Buzzard and Its Neighbourhood Delivered Before the Working Mens Club and Insitute of that Town. Leighton Buzzard: 1879. V. 41

LEWIS, EDWIN

Duty, Not Decay. A Poem. London: 1902. V. 38

LEWIS, ELDAD

An Eulogy, on the Life and Character of His Excellency George Washington, Esqr . . . Pittsfield: 1800. V. 40

LEWIS, ELISHA J.

the American Sportsman . . . Philadelphia: 1855. V. 45

The American Sportsman. Philadelphia: 1857. V. 39

The American Sportsman. Philadelphia: 1863. V. 39

LEWIS, F.

The Pontremoli Collection of Carpets and Textiles. Leigh-on-Sea: 1942. V. 37

LEWIS, FLORENCE

China Painting. London: 1883. V. 38

LEWIS, FRANK

Myles Birket Foster 1825-1899. Leigh-on-Sea: 1973. V. 39

LEWIS, FRANKLIN

The Cleveland Indians. New York: 1949. V. 39

LEWIS, FREDERICK CHRISTIAN

Scenery of the River Dart. London: 1821. V. 38; 45; 46

The Scenery of the River Exe. London: 1827. V. 38

LEWIS, G. GRIFFIN

The Practical Book of Oriental Rugs. Philadelphia and London: 1920. V. 40

The Practical Book of Oriental Rugs. Philadelphia: 1921. V. 44

LEWIS, G. R.

Illustrations of Kilpeck Church, Herefordshire. London: 1842. V. 37; 38; 40

LEWIS, G. W.

The Campaigns of the 124th Regiment Ohio Volunteers Infantry with Roster and Roll of Honor. Akron: 1894. V. 46

The Campaigns of the 124th Regiment, Ohio Volunteer Infantry with Roster and Roll of Honor. Akron: 1899. V. 45

LEWIS, GEORGE CORNEWALL 1806-1863

An Essay on the Influence of Authority in Matters of Opinion. London: 1849. V. 37

An Examination of Some Passages in Dr. Whately's Elements of Logic. Oxford: 1829. V. 43; 45

On Local Disturbances in Ireland and on the Irish Church Question. London: 1836. V. 38; 42; 43

A Treatise on the Methods of Observation and Reasoning in Politics. London: 1852. V. 43

LEWIS, GEORGE CORNEWALL, 2ND BARONET 1806-1863

Remarks on the Use and Abuse of Some Political Terms. London: 1832. V. 41

LEWIS, GRACE HEGGER

Half a Loaf. New York: 1931. V. 37; 40; 42

LEWIS, H. C.

A Descriptive bibliography of the most important books in the English language relating to the art & histroy of engraving and the collecting of prints; . . . supplement and index. 1913-13. V. 37

LEWIS, HARRY

Pulsars: Three States of a Single Poem. N.P.: 1974. V. 39

LEWIS, HENRY

Das Illustrirte Mississippithal . . . vom Wasserfalle su St. Anthony an bis zum Golf von Mexico . . . Dusseldorf: 1854. V. 38; 39

The Valley of the Mississippi Illustrated. St. Paul: 1867. V. 42

The Valley of the Mississippi Illustrated. St. Paul: 1967. V. 43; 46

LEWIS, HENRY CLAY

Odd Leaves from the Life of a Louisiana 'Swamp Doctor.' Philadelphia. V. 43

The Swamp Doctor's Adventures in the Southwest. Philadelphia: 1858. V. 39

LEWIS, JAMES HENRY

The Best Method of Pen-Making . . . London: 1826. V. 44

LEWIS, JAMES OTTO

Aboriginal Portfolio. Philadelphia: 1835-36. V. 39

The American Indian Portfolio. Kent: 1980. V. 38; 39; 41

LEWIS, JANE

Narrative of the Captivity and Providential Escape of Mrs. Jane Lewis . . . Who, with a Son and Daughter . . . and an Infant Babe, Were Made Prionsers Within a Few Miles of Indian Creek, by a Party of Indians of the Tribes of Sacs and Foxes . . . New York: 1824. V. 39

Narrative of the Captivity and Providential Escape of Mrs. Jane Lewis. New York: 1834. V. 42; 45

LEWIS, JANET

The Earth Bound 1924-1944. Aurora: 1946. V. 38; 46

The Wheel in Midsummer. Lynn, Mass.: 1927. V. 37

LEWIS, JENNY

Catalogue of an Exhibition of Poetry Manuscripts in the British Museum. London: 1967. V. 46

LEWIS, JOHN

Analytical Outlines of the English Language, or a Cursory Examination of Its Materials and Structure. Richmond: 1825. V. 37

Christianity and the Social Revolution. 1937. London: 1935. V. 45

A Complete History of the Several Translations of the Holy Bible, and New Testament in English. London: 1739. V. 39; 45; 46

A Complete History of the Several Translations of the Holy Bibl and New Testament into English, Both in MS and in Print . . . London: 1939. V. 39

Graphic Design with Special Reference to Lettering, Typography and Illustration. London: 1954. V. 45

John Nash, the Painter as Illustrator. N.P.: 1978. V. 43

John Nash: The Painter as Illustrator. Surrey: 1978. V. 37; 40; 41

The Life of Mayster Wyllyam Caxton, of the Weald of Kent; the first printer in England. London: 1737. V. 40

The Painter as an Illustrator. Surrey: 1978. V. 44

Printed Ephemera. Ipswich: 1926. V. 41

Printed Ephemera. Ipswich: 1962. V. 40

LEWIS, JOHN FREDERICK

Sketches and Drawings of Alhambra. London: 1835. V. 45

LEWIS, JOHN L.

The Miner's Fight for American Standards. Indianapolis. V. 46

LEWIS, JOHN W.

The Life, Labors and Travels of Elder Charles Bowles, of the Free Will Baptist Denomination, Together with an Essay on the Character and Condition of the African Race . . . Watertown: 1852. V. 41; 42

LEWIS, LAWRENCE

The Advertisements of the Spectator. Boston & New York: 1909. V. 38

A History of the First Bank Chartered in the United States. Philadelphia: 1882. V. 38

LEWIS, M. J. T.

Temples in Roman Britain. Cambridge: 1966. V. 42; 44

LEWIS, MADAN

The Lewis Carroll Centenary in London. London: 1932. V. 45

LEWIS, MATTHEW GREGORY 1775-1818

Abaellino, the Bravo of Venice. Ballston Spa: 1811. V. 39

Ambrosio, or the Monk: a romance. London: 1798. V. 37

The Bravo of Venice. London: 1805. V. 42

The Castle of Lindenberg; or, the History of Raymond and Agnes with the story of the Bleeding Nun: and the method by which the Wandering Jew quieted the Nun's Troubled spirit. London: 1798. V. 37

Journal of a West India Proprietor, Kept During a Residence in the Island Of Jamaica. London: 1834. V. 38; 40; 42

Le Moine. Paris: 1840. V. 40

The Monk. London: 1796. V. 37

The Monk: a Romance. London: 1797. V. 39; 45; 46

The Monk, a Romance. Waterford: 1818. V. 39

The Monk. London: 1825. V. 41

The Monk, a Romance. London: 1830? V. 39; 42

The Monk. Paris: 1832. V. 40

The Monk. N.P.: 1845. V. 39; 42

The Monk. London: 1880. V. 43

The Monk. London: 1884? V. 39

Poems. London: 1812. V. 37; 38; 39; 42; 45

Tales of Wonder . . . Dublin: 1801. V. 37; 42

Tales of Wonder. London: 1801. V. 39; 42; 43; 45; 46

LEWIS, MERIWETHER 1774-1809

History of the Expedition Under the Command of Captain's Lewis and Clark. Philadelphia: 1814. V. 37; 38; 39; 40; 41; 43; 44; 46

History of the Expedition Under the Command of Captains Lewis and Clarke (sic). New York: 1842. V. 40

History of the Expedition of Captains Lewis and Clark 1804-5-6. Chicago: 1902. V. 37; 39; 44

History of the Expedition of Captain's Lewis and Clark, 1804-5-6. Chicago: 1903. V. 38; 44

History of the Expedition of Captains Lewis and Clark 1804-05-06. Chicago: 1905. V. 37

History of the Expedition Under the Command of Captains Lewis and Clarke to the Sources of the Missouri . . . New York: 1922. V. 46

In Memoriam: Sergeant Charles Floyd. Report of the Floyd Memorial Association prepared on behalf of the Committee on Publication by Elliott Coues. Sioux City: 1897. V. 37

The Journals of Lewis and Clark, to the Mouth of the Columbia River Beyond the Rocky Mountains in the Years 1804-05 & 6. Dayton: 1840. V. 38; 40

Journals of Captain Meriwether Lewis & Sergeant John Ordway Kept on the Expedition of Western Exploration 1803-1806. Madison: 1916. V. 38

The Journals of the Expedition Under the Command of Captains Lewis and Clark. New York: 1962. V. 37; 42; 43

Journals of the Expedition Under the Command of Captains Lewis and Clark. New York: 1967. V. 46

Original Journals Of the Lewis and Clark Expedition 1804 - 1806 Printed from the Original Manuscripts . . . New York: 1904-05. V. 38; 39; 40; 41

Original Journals of the Lewis and Clark Expedition, 1804-1806. New York: 1959. V. 41

Original Journals of the Lewis and Clark Expedition, 1804-1806. New York: 1969. V. 37; 43; 44; 45

Travaels in the Interior Parts of America. London: 1807. V. 37

Travels to the Source of the Missouri River and Across the American Continent to the Pacific Ocean. London: 1814. V. 37; 38; 39; 40; 46

Travels to the Source of the Missouri River, and Across the American Continent to the Pacific Ocean . . . 1804, 1805 and 1806. London: 1815. V. 39

Travels to the Source of the Missouri River, and Across the American Continent to the Pacific Ocean. London: 1817. V. 42

LEWIS, OSCAR 1893-

California in 1846 Described in Letters from Thomas O. Larkin . . . San Francisco: 1934. V. 39; 40; 45

Hearn and His Biographers: the Record of a Literary Controversy . . . San Francisco: 1930. V. 38; 39

The Origin of the Celebrated Jumping Frog. San Francisco: 1931. V. 37; 38; 43

The Wonderful City of Carrie Van Wie. San Francisco: 1963. V. 38; 39; 43; 46

LEWIS, ROBERT BENJAMIN

Light and Truth. Boston: 1844. V. 38; 42; 44

LEWIS, SAMUEL

Atlas to the Topographical Dictionary of Ireland. London: 1849. V. 41

Supplementary (Atlas) Volume To 'A Topographical Dictionary of Scotland . . .' London: 1846. V. 38

A Topographical Dictionary of England, Comprising the Several Counties. London: 1831. V. 44

A Topographical Dictionary of England, Comprising the Several Counties, Cities, Boroughs, Corporate and Market Towns . . . London: 1833. V. 42

Topographical Dictionary of Ireland. London: 1839. V. 38

A Topographical Dictionary of Scotland . . . London: 1856. V. 38

A Topographical Dictionary of Ireland, comprising the several counties, cities, market and post towns and villages, with historical and statistical descriptions etc. etc. of Ireland. London;: 1837. V. 37

LEWIS, SARAH

Woman's Mission. Boston: 1840. V. 44; 45

LEWIS, SINCLAIR 1885-1951

Ann Vickers. Garden City: 1933. V. 45

Arrowsmith. New York: 1925. V. 39; 43; 44; 45; 46

Babbitt. New York: 1922. V. 41; 44; 46

Bethel Merriday. New York: 1940. V. 37

Cas Timberlane. London: 91946). V. 37

Cheap and Contented Labor. New York: 1929. V. 43

Cheap & Contented Labor: The Picture of a Southern Mill Town in 1929. New York: (1929). V. 37

Dodsworth. 1929. V. 46

Dodsworth. New York: 1929. V. 39; 41

Dodsworth. 1932. V. 40; 41; 42; 43; 44

Elmer Gantry. London: 1927. V. 43

Elmer Gantry. New York: 1927. V. 39; 43; 46

Elmer Gantry. 1927. V. 37

The Innocents. New York: 1917. V. 41; 44

Jayhawker: a Play. Garden City: 1935. V. 39

Keep Out of the Kitchen. New York: 1929. V. 37; 38; 40; 42; 43; 46

Kingsblood Royal. New York: 1947. V. 38; 39; 40; 41; 42; 43; 46

Main Street. New York: 1920. V. 38; 46

Main Street. Chicago: 1937. V. 37; 38; 39; 45; 46

Main Street. New York: 1937. V. 40; 41; 42; 43; 46

The Man Who Knew Coolidge. 1928. V. 43

The Man Who Knew Coolidge. New York: 1928. V. 37

The Man who Knew Coolidge: Being the Soul of Lowell Schmaltz. London: (1928). V. 37

Sinclair Lewis on the Valley of the Moon. N.P.: 1932. V. 37

The Trail of the Hawk. London: 1923. V. 39

The Trail of the Hawk. A Comedy of the Seriousness of Life. New York: (1915). V. 37

Work of Art. Garden City: 1934. V. 39; 40; 41

LEWIS, THOMAS 1881-1945

The Blood Vessels of the Human Skin and Their Respondes. London: 1927. V. 42

LEWIS, THOMAS 1881-1945 continued

Clinical Disorders of the Heartbeat. London: 1912. V. 42

Clinical Electrocardiography. London: 1913. V. 42; 45

Clinical Disorders of the Heartbeat. London: 1924. V. 45

Diseases of the Heart Described for Practitioners and Students. New York: 1933. V. 45

Electrocardiography and Clinical Disorders of the Heart Beat. London: 1949. V. 45

Lectures on the Heart. New York: 1915. V. 42

The Mechanism and Graphic Registration of the Heart Beat. London: 1920. V. 43

The Mechanism and Graphic Registration of the Heart Beat. London: 1925. V. 42; 43

Origines Hebraeae: the Antiquities of the Hebrew Republick. London: 1724-1725. V. 42

The Soldier's Heart and the Effort Syndrome. London: 1918. V. 41

The Soldier's Heart and the Effort Syndrome. New York: 1920. V. 43; 44

LEWIS, TIMOTHY RICHARDS

A Report of Microscopical and Physiological Researches into the Nature of the Agent of Agents Producing Cholera. Calcutta: 1533. V. 41

A Report on the Microscopic Objects Found in Cholera Evacuations &c. Calcutta: 1870. V. 41

A Report of Microscopical and Physiological Researches into the Nature of the Agent or Agents Producing Cholera. Calcutta: 1872. V. 41

LEWIS, WILLIAM 1714-1781

Commercium Philophico-Technicum; or, the Philosphical Commerce of Arts, Designed as an Attempt to Improve Arts, Trades and Manufactures. London: 1763. V. 45

Commercium Philosophical Commerce of Arts: Designed as an Attempt to Improve Arts, Trades and Manufactures. London: 1765. V. 42

A Course of Practical Chemistry. London: 1746. V. 37

The Edinburgh New Dispensatory . . . Edinburgh: 1801. V. 39; 43

Elements of the Game of Chess, or a New Method of Instruction in that Celebrated Game . . . New York: 1827. V. 40; 43

An Experimental History of the Materia Medica, or the Natural and Artificial Substances Made Use of In Medicine. London: 1761. V. 40; 41

An Experimental History of the Materia Medica, or of the Natural and Afritifical Substances Made Use of in Medicine. London: 1791. V. 40

An Experimental History of the Materia Medica, or of the Natural and Artificial Substances Made use of in Medicine. London: 1768. V. 38

The New Dispensatory . . . London: 1753. V. 37; 45

The New Dispensatory. London: 1785. V. 38; 40

Oriental Chess, or Specimens of Hindoostanee Excellence in that Celebrated Game . . . London: 1817. V. 40

Report of the Chief Engineer of the Pacific and Atlantic Railroad Company January, 1855. San Francisco: 1855. V. 37

LEWIS, WILLIAM BEVAN

Text-book of Mental Diseases with Special Reference to the Pathological Aspects of Insanity. Paris: 1890. V. 45

LEWIS, WILLIAM DRAPER

The Life of Theodore Roosevelt. N.P.: 1919. V. 40

LEWIS, WILLIAM J.

Report of the Engineers on the Survey of the Marysville and Benicia National Rail Road. Marysville: 1853. V. 42; 45

LEWIS, WILLIAM S.

The Journal of John Work. Cleveland: 1923. V. 37; 39; 45; 46

Ranald MacDonald. The Narrative of His Early Life on the Columbia Under the Hudson's Bay Company's Regime . . . Pacific Whale Fishery . . . Adventures to Japan . . . 1824-1894. Spokane: 1923. V. 37; 38; 39; 44

Reminiscences of Joseph H. Boyd. Seattle: 1924. V. 38; 39; 44

LEWIS, WILLIE NEWBURY

Between Sun and Sod. Clarendon: 1938. V. 37; 43

LEWIS, WILMARTH S.

Collector's Progress. New York: 1951. V. 40

Collector's Progress. London: 1952. V. 41

LEWIS, WYNDHAM 1882-1957

America and Cosmic Man. London: 1948. V. 38; 41; 42

Anglosaxony: a League that Works. Toronto: 1941. V. 41

The Apes of God. London: 1930. V. 38; 39; 40; 41; 42; 45

The Apes of God. London: 1955. V. 39; 40

The Apes of the Gods. New York: 1932. V. 37

The Art of Being Ruled. London: 1926. V. 37

Blast - Numbers 1 and 2 (all published). London: 1914-15. V. 42; 45

Blast I. Blast II. 1981. V. 42; 44

Blast I, II and III. Santa Barbara: 1981/84. V. 42

Blasting & Bombardiering. London: 1937. V. 37; 40; 41; 42; 43; 44; 45; 46

The Caliph's Design. London: 1919. V. 37

The Childermass - Section 1. London: 1928. V. 40; 42; 45

The Childermass - Section 1. 1928. V. 37

A Christmas Book: An Anthology for Moderns. London: 1928. V. 38

Count Your Dead: They Are All Alive! London: 1927. V. 39

Count Your Dead - They Are Alive! London: 1937. V. 40; 41; 42; 45

The Diabolical Principle and the Dithyrambic Spectator. London: 1931. V. 37; 41

Doom of Youth. London: 1932. V. 37; 42; 45

The Doom of Youth. New York: 1932. V. 42

The Enemy No. 3. - a Review of Art and Literature. London: 1929. V. 40

Enemy of the Stars. Harmsworth: 1932. V. 40

Enemy of the Stars. London: 1932. V. 37; 40; 41; 42

Filibusters in Barbary. 1932. V. 42

Filibusters in Barbary. New York: 1932. V. 40; 44

The Ideal Giant: The Code of Herdsman; Cantleman's Spring-Mate. London: 1917. V. 39

The Jews Are Human? London: 1939. V. 40; 42

Left Wings over Europe. London: 1936. V. 39; 40; 42; 46

The Lion and the Fox. London: 1927. V. 37; 38; 40; 41

Men Without Art. London: 1934. V. 37

Morrow, Bradford and Lafourcade, Bernard. A Bibliography of the Writings of Wyndham Lewis. Santa Barbara: 1978. V. 37

The Mysterious Mr. Bull. London: 1938. V. 45

The Old Gang and the New Gang. London: 1933. V. 41; 42

One Way Song: Poems. London: 1933. V. 40; 42; 45; 46

Paleface. The Philosophy of the 'Melting-Pot.' London: 1929. V. 37; 41

Roaring Queen. London: 1973. V. 37; 45

Rude Assignment; a Narrative of My Career Up-to-Date. London: 1950. V. 40

Rude Assignment: an Intellectual Autobiography. 1984. V. 42; 43; 44

Satire and Fiction. London: 1930. V. 40; 41

The Sea-Mists of the Winter. 1981. V. 42; 43; 44

Self Condemned. London: 1954. V. 43

Self Condemned. Chicago: 1955. V. 43

Snooty Baronet. London: 1932. V. 37

Tarr. London: 1918. V. 37; 39; 40; 41

Tarr. New York: 1918. V. 37; 38

Tarr. London: 1919. V. 42

Tarr. London: 1928. V. 42

Thirty Personalities and a Self Portrait. London: 1932. V. 39; 40; 41; 42; 43

Time and Western Man. London: 1927. V. 42

Timon of Athens. London: 1913. V. 39

The Tyro. London: 1921 & 1922. V. 40

The Wild Body. London: 1927. V. 37; 38; 40; 41; 43; 46

Wings Over Europe. London: 1936. V. 43

Wyndham Lewis the Artist. London: 1939. V. 37; 42; 43; 45

LEWISHON, FLORENCE

St. Croix Under Seven Flags. Hollywood: 1970. V. 42

LEWISOHN, LUDWIG

The Case of Mr. Crump. Paris: 1926. V. 38; 39; 40; 46

The Romantic. Paris: 1931. V. 44

LE WRIGHT, J.

Two Proposals Becoming England at this Juncture to Undertake. One, for Securing a Collony (sic) in the West Indies, as Her Majesty's Propriety Now to be Enter'd Upon, or for Ever Lost. And the Other for Advancing Merchandise and the Crown-Revenue to . . . London: 1706. V. 46

LEX Londinensis; or, the City Law. London: 1680. V. 46

THE LEX Scripta of the Isle of Man; Comprehending the Ancient Ordinances and Statute Laws. From the Earliest to the Present Times. Douglas (Isle of Man): 1819. V. 40

LEY, J. W. T.

The Dickens Circle. London: 1918. V. 40

LEY, JOHN

A Discourse Concerning Puritans. London: 1641. V. 40

LEYBOURN, WILLIAM 1626-1700

The Compleat Surveyor: Containing the Whole Art of Surveying of Land . . . London: 1653. V. 43; 45

Compleat Surveyor; or, the Whole Art of Surveying of Land. London: 1722. V. 38; 39; 41

Cursus Mathematicus. Mathematical Sciences in Nine Books. London: 1690. V. 45

LEYBOURN, WILLIAM 1626-1700 continued

Dialing: Plain, Concave, Convex, Projective, Reflective, Refractive, Shewing How to Make all Such Dials, and to Adorn Them with all Useful Furniture . . . London: 1682. V. 37; 38

An Introduction to Astronomy and Geography. London: 1675. V. 45

Panarithmologia. London: 1776. V. 41

LEYBURN, GEORGE

Holy Characters. Douay: 1662. V. 41

LEYCESTER, PETER

Historical Antiquities, in Two Books. The First Treating in General of Great-Brettain and Ireland. The Second Containing Particular Remarks concerning Cheshire. Faithfully Collected out uthentick Histories, Old Deeds, Records . . . London: 1673. V. 37

LEYCESTERS Common-Wealth Conceived, Spoken and Published with the Most Earnest Protestation of all Dutifull Good Will and Affection Towards This Realme; For Whose Good Onely it is Made Common to Many. London: 1641. V. 38

LEYDA, JAY

The Years and Hours of Emily Dickinson. New Haven: 1960. V. 45

LEYDEN, JOHN

Historical and Philosophical Sketch of the Discoveries and Settlements of the Europeans in Northern and Western Africa at the Close of the Eighteenth Century. Edinburgh: 1799. V. 40

Historical Account of Discoveries and Travels in Africa . . . Edinburgh & London: 1817. V. 37

Malay Annals: Translated from the Malay Language by . . . London: 1821. V. 37

Scottish Descriptive Poems . . . Edinburgh: 1803. V. 42

Scottish Descriptive Poems; with some illustrations of Scottish Literary Antiquities. Edinburgh/London: 1803. V. 37

LEYDEN. RIJKSUNIVERSITEIT.

Illustrium Hollandiae Vvestfrisleae Ordinvm Alma Academia Leidensis. Lvgdvni Batavorvm: 1614. V. 39

LEYES Conciernientes a la Indemnidad y Relevacion de Los Pueblos. Seville: 1491. V. 40

LEYES DE TORO GLOSADAS

Utilis et Aurea Glosa Domini Didaci Castelli . . . Super Leges Tauri . . . Burgos: 1527. V. 41

LEYLAND, FRANCIS

The Bronte Family. London: 1886. V. 41; 43

LEYMARIE, JEAN

Art Since Mid-Century: The New Internationalism. Volume I: Abstract Art. Volume II: Figurative Art. Greenwich: 1971. V. 39

Balthus. New York: 1979. V. 39

French Painting. The Nineteenth Century. Geneva: 1962. V. 39

The Graphic Works of the Impressionists: Monet, Pissarro, Renoir, Cezanne, Sisley. New York: 1972. V. 42

The Jerusalem Windows. Monte Carlo: 1962. V. 44

The Jerusalem Windows. New York: 1962. V. 45; 46

Marc Chagall: The Jerusalem Windows. New York: 1962. V. 41

Marc Chagall Monotypes 1966-1975. Geneve: 1966. V. 41; 42; 44

LEYS, LEONARD

Hygiasticon seu Vera Ratio Valitudinis Bonae et Vitae una Cum Sensuum, Iudicii & Memoriae Integritate ad Extremam Senectutem Conservandae. Antverpiae: 1614. V. 37

LEYS, NORMAN

Kenya. 1924. V. 39

L'HERITIER DE BRUTELLE, CHARLES LOUIS

Sertum Anglicum Seu Plantae Rariores Quae in Hortis Juxta Londinum, Imprimis in Horto Regio Kewensi Excoluntur, ab anno 1786 ad annum 1787 observatae. Paris: 1788. V. 43

L'HERITIER DE VILLANDON, MARIE JEANNE 1664-1734

Oeuvres Meslees . . . Paris: 1696. V. 46

LHOMOND, CHARLES FRANCOIS

Elements of French Grammar. Hallowell: 1837. V. 38; 40

LHOMOND, M.

Elements of French Grammar. Boston: 1831. V. 45

L'HOPITAL, MICHEL DE

Epistolarum Libri Sex. Paris: 1585. V. 44; 45

LI, H. L.

Flora of Taiwan. Taipei: 1976-79. V. 37

LI PO 705?-762

Fifty Poems. Lexington: 1984. V. 40; 45

LIARDET, JOHN

An Appeal to the Public on the Right of Using Oil Cement, or Composition for Stucco &c Containing the Provisos in Letters Patent Granted for Inventions, and the Provisos in the Act of Parliament for Extending the Term of the Patent Granted . . . London: 1778. V. 44

LIBANIUS

Pro Templis Gentilium Non Exscendendis Theodosium M. Imp. Oratio . . . N.P.: 1634. V. 44

LIBAVIUS, ANDREAS

Alchemia . . . Opera Dispersis Passim optimorum Autorum, Veterum & Recentium Exemplis Potissimum . . . Francofurti: 1597. V. 38

Analysis Dialectica Colloquii Ratisbonensis 1601. Frankfurt: 1601. V. 43

LIBBIE, C. F. & CO.

Catalogue of the Valuable Private Library of the Late Frederick W. French. Boston: 1901. V. 42

LIBBY, O. G.

The Arikara Narrative of the Campaign Against the Hostile Dakotas June 1876. Bismarck: 1920. V. 45

LIBBY, WILLARD F.

Radiocarbon Dating. Chicago: 1952. V. 38

THE LIBELLE of Englyshe Polycye A Poem on the Use of Sea Power, 1436. Oxford: 1926. V. 39; 41

LIBELLI Sev Decreta A Clodoveo, Et Childeberto & Clothario Prius Aedita, ac Postremem a Caraolo Lucide Emendata, Auctaque Plurimum. ?Paris: ?1550. V. 37

LIBER Ardmachanus. The Book of Armagh. Dublin: 1913. V. 45

LIBER Hysagoge Joannici . . . and Other Works. Venetiis: 1502. V. 38; 40

LIBER Mirabilis . . . qui Prophetias Revelationesque Necnon res Mirandas . . . Sensuit la Secunde Partie de ce Livre. Paris: 1522. V. 40

LIBER Precvm Pvlicarvm, Sev Ministerij Ecclesiastice Administrationis Sacramentorum. London: 1574. V. 38

LIBER Processionum Secundum Ordinem Fratrum Predicatorum Impressum per Meynardum Ungut Alemanum & Stanislaum Polonum Socios. Seville: 1494. V. 40

LIBER Scriptorum. The First Book of the Author's Club. New York: 1893. V. 38

LIBER Uagatorum der Betler Orden. Strassbourg?: 1510. V. 44

THE LIBERAL. London: 1822-23. V. 46

LIBERATI, FRANCESCO

La Perfettione Del Cavallo Libri Tre Di . . . Romano. Roma: 1669. V. 37; 38

LIBERMAN, ALEXANDER

The Art and Technique of Color Photography. New York: 1951. V. 41

The Artist in His Studio. New York: 1960. V. 37; 38; 40; 42; 43; 46

LIBERTY & COMPANY, LONDON.

Modern Silver Designed and Made by Liberty & Company. London: 1924-25. V. 43

THE LIBERTY Bell. Boston: 1847. V. 40

LIBERTY Evolution in Costume: Illustrated by Past Fashion Plates and Present Adaptations of the Empire and Early Victorian Period. London: & Paris,: 1893. V. 44

LIBMAN, EMANUEL

Subacute Bacterial Endocarditis. New York: 1941. V. 42

LIBRAIRIE DE LA CONSTURCTION MODERNE

Garages et Salles d'Esposition. Paris: 1928. V. 42

THE LIBRARY. London: 1900. V. 41

THE LIBRARY Atlas of Modern Geography . . . New York: 1892. V. 45

THE LIBRARY of Agricultural and Horticultural Knowledge . . . London: 1832. V. 40

THE LIBRARY of Agriculture and Horticultural Knowledge with an Appendix Containing an Abridgement of the Principal Laws Relating to Farming and Rural Affairs.. Lewes: 1832. V. 37

THE LIBRARY of Fiction, or Family Story-Teller. London: 1836-37. V. 40

THE LIBRARY of Southern Literature. Atlanta: 1909. V. 39

LIBRI, GUGLIELMO

Catalogue of the Choicer Portion of the Magnificent Library . . . Unknown Block-Books . . . 1859. V. 46

Catalogue of the Choicer Portion of the Magnificent Library Formed by M. Guglielmo Libri. London: 1859. V. 37; 39; 41

Catalogue of the Extraordinary Collection of Splendid Manuscripts, Chiefly Upon Vellum in Various Languages of Europe and the East. London: 1859. V. 45

LIBRO de Marchi de Cavalli . . . Venetia: 1588. V. 43

LIBRO Di Novelle, et di Bel Parlar Gentile. Florence: 1572. V. 40

LIBURNIO, NICOLO

Elegantissime Sentenze et Avrei Detti de Diversi Eccellentissimi Antiqui Savi . . . Aggiuntovi Molti Ornati et Arguti Motti de Piu Boni Authori, in Vulgar . . . Venice: 1543. V. 43

LICEAGA, J. M. DE

Adiciones y Rectificaciones a la Historia de Mexxico que Escribio D. Lucas Alaman . . . Guanajuato: 1868. V. 42

LICETI, FORTUNIO

De Lucernis Antiquorum Reconditis Lib. Sex.. Udine: 1652. V. 40

LICETUS, FORTUNIUS

De Monstris. Ex Recensione Geraldi Blasii, M.D. & P.P. Qui Monstra Quaedam Nova & Rariora Ex Recentiorum Scriptis Addidit. Amsterdam: 1665. V. 37

LICHTENBERGER, J. F.

Histoire de l'Invention de l'Imprimerie. Strasbourg & Paris: 1825. V. 38

LICHTENSTEIN, H.

Beitrag zur Ornithologischen Fauna von Californien, nebst Bemerkungen uber die Artkennzeichen der Pelicane und Uber . . . Berlin: 1938. V. 44

LICHTENSTEIN, HENRY

Travels in Southern Africa, in the Years 1803, 1804, 1805, and 1806. London: 1812-15. V. 43

LIDDELL, DONALD M.

Chessmen. London: 1938. V. 42

LIDDELL, E. G. T.

Discovery of Reflexes. Oxford: 1960. V. 41

LIDDELL HART, BASIL HENRY, 1895-

Lawrence of Arabia. London: 1936. V. 44; 46

LIDDELL, R. S.

The Memoirs of the Tenth Royal Hussars rince of Wales' Own) Historical and Social. London: 1891. V. 37

LIDELL, JOHN A.

A Treatise on Apoplexy, Cerebral hemorrhage, Cerebral Embolism, Cerebral Gout, Cerebral Rheumatism and Epidemic Cerebro-Spinal Meningitis. New York: 1873. V. 44; 46

LIDGATE, JOHN

The Life and Death of Hector. London: 1614. V. 39

LIDSAY, ALEXANDER WILLIAM CRAWFORD

LEtter on Egypt, Edom and the Holy Land. London: 1839. V. 37

LIEBAULT, AMBROISE AUGUSTE 1823-1904

Du Sommeil et des Etats Analogues Consideres Surtout au Point de Vue de l'Action du Moral sur le Physique. Paris: 1866. V. 45; 46

LIEBER, FRANCIS

Legal and Political Hermeneutics, or Principles of Interpretation and Construction in Law and Politics, with Remarks on Precedents and Authorities. Boston: 1839. V. 38

Letters to a Gentleman in Germany, Written After a Trip from Philadelphia to Niagara. Philadelphia: 1834. V. 38; 40

A Popular Essay on Subjects of Penal Law, and on Uninterrupted Solitary Confinement at Labor . . . Philadelphia: 1838. V. 41; 43; 45

The Stranger in America . . . London: 1835. V. 42; 46

LIEBERKUHN, SAMUEL

The History of Our Lord and Saviour Jesus Christ. New York: 1821. V. 37; 40

LIEBIG GOLD MINING AND MILL COMPANY

Prospectus of the Liebig Gold Mining & Mill Co. of Colorado . . . New York: 1864. V. 37

LIEBIG, JUSTUS

Animal Chemistry. London: 1842. V. 37; 38; 42; 44; 46

Chemistry in Its Applications to Agriculture and Physiology. London: 1842. V. 39; 43

Chemistry In Its Applications to Agriculture and Physiology. London: 1843. V. 39

Chemistry and Physics in Relation to Physiology and Pathology. London: 1846. V. 40

Die Organische Chemie in Ihrer Anwendung auf Physiologie und Pathologie. Braunschweig: 1842. V. 46

Familiar Letters on Chemistry, and Its Relation to Commerce, Physiology and Agriculture. (with) Familiar Letters on Chemistry. Second Series. London: 1843-44. V. 46

Instructions for the Chemical Analysis of Organic Bodies. Glasgow: 1839. V. 40

The Natural Laws of Husbandry. London: 1863. V. 37; 45

Organic Chemistry in Its Applications to Agriculture and Physiology. London: 1840. V. 42; 43

Researches on the Chemistry of Food. London: 1847. V. 40

Researches on the Motion of the Juices in the Animal Body . . . London: 1848. V. 42; 44; 45

LIEBIG, JUSTUS VON

Animal Chemistry, or Organic Chemistry in Its Applications to Physiology and Pathology . . . New York: 1842. V. 45

LIEBLING, A. J.

Back Where I Came From. New York: 1938. V. 45

LIECHTENSTEIN, MARIE, PRINCESS OF

Holland House. London: 1874. V. 37

LIEHGTON, JOHN M.

The Lakes of Scotland: a Series of Views . . . Glasgow: 1834. V. 42

LIETZE, ERNST

Modern Heliographic Processes. New York: 1888. V. 37; 41

LIEUTAUD, JOSEPH

Essais Anatomiques . . . Paris: 1742. V. 45

Synopsis of the Universal Practice of Medicine. Philadelphia: 1816. V. 39; 40; 42

LIEVEN, DAR'IA KHRISTOFOROVNA BENCKENDORFF 1785-1857

Letters of Princess Lieven to Lady Holland 1847-57. Oxford: 1856. V. 38

Letters of Princess Lieven to Lady Holland 1847-1857. Oxford: 1956. V. 40; 44

LIEVRE, EDOUARD

Works of Art in the Collection of England. London: 1880. V. 39

THE LIFE, Accouchement, and Death of the Princess Charlotte; with a Portrait Taken from Her Death-Bed. London: 1817. V. 44

THE LIFE and Actions of that Notorious Old Bawd Susannah Wells and Mary Squires, (an Old Travelling Gipsey), Who Were Both Convicted at Justice-Hall in the Old Baily, on Thursday the 22d of February, 1753, for a Felony and Robbery on Elizabeth Canning . . . London: 1753. V. 46

LIFE and Adventure in the South Pacific. New York: 1861. V. 41

THE LIFE and Adventures of Bampsylde-Moore Carew, Commonly Called King of the Beggars. London: 1788. V. 39

THE LIFE and Adventures of Henry Lanson. London: 1805. V. 42

THE LIFE and Adventures of John Nicol, Mariner. Edinburgh: 1822. V. 39

THE LIFE and Adventures of Mrs. Christian Davies, Commonly Call'd Mother Ross; Who, in Several Campaigns Under King William and the Late Duke of Marlborough, in the Quality of a Foot-Soldier and Dragoon . . . London: 1740. V. 41; 44

THE LIFE and Adventures of Obadiah Benjamin Franklin Bloomfield, M.D. Philadelphia: 1818. V. 40

THE LIFE and Adventures of that Most Eccentric Character James Hirst of Rawcliffe, Yorkshire. Knottingly (Yorkshire): 1860. V. 37

THE LIFE and Adventures of the Celebrated Walking Stewart. London: 1822. V. 39

THE LIFE and Amours of Owen Tideric, Price of Wales, Otherwise Owen Tudor . . . . London: 1751. V. 42

THE LIFE and Aventures of the Golden Farmer, Including Likewise the Histories of His Companion, Old Mobb and Servant, Long Robin. London: 1802. V. 46

THE LIFE and Death of John Carpenter, Alias Hell Fire Jack, the Noted Horse Stealer, Who was Executed April 4, 1805; Also the Particulars of Eliz. Barber, alias Mrs. Daley, Hanged for Murder . . . London: 1805. V. 45

THE LIFE and Dreadful Sufferings, of Captain James Wilson, In Various Parts of the Globe, Including a Faithful Narrative of Every Circumstance During the Voyage . . . Portsea: 1810. V. 40

LIFE And Dying Confession of John Van Alstine, Executed March 19, 1819, for the Murder of William Huddleston, Esq., Deputy Sheriff of the County of Scoharie. Schoarie: 1819. V. 40

THE LIFE and Glorious Actions of His Grace James Duke of Ormond; with His Conduct in the Campaign of 1712. London: 1715. V. 41

THE LIFE and Martyrdom of Saint Katherine of Alexandria, Virgina and Martyr. London: 1884. V. 40

THE LIFE and Memoirs of Mr. Ephraim Tristram Bates, Commonly Called Corporal Bates, A Broken Hearted Soldier. London: 1756. V. 40

THE LIFE, and Military Achievement of Toussant Loverture (sic), late General in Chief of the Armies of Santo Domingo, from the Year 1792 . . . N.P.: 1804. V. 46

THE LIFE and Reign of Her Late Excellent Majesty Queen Anne. London: 1738. V. 45

THE LIFE and Singular Adventures of jack Shepherd. London: 1787. V. 46

THE LIFE and Times of Louis the Fourteenth. London: 1838. V. 41

THE LIFE and Times of Sam. Claremont: 1855. V. 43

LIFE, History and Handcuff Secrets of Houdini. New York: 1907. V. 43

LIFE in Bombay, and the Neighbouring Out-Stations. London: 1852. V. 43

LIFE in Philadelphia. A Black Ball. La Pastorelle. London: 1820? V. 39

LIFE Military and Civil of the Duke of Wellington . . . London: 1852. V. 42

THE LIFE, Misfortunes and Adventures of Indiana, the virtuous orphan. Written by himself. Illustrated with several Copper Plates. The Third Edition. London: 1755. V. 37

THE LIFE of Alexander Pope, Esq. with a True copy of his last Will and Testament. London: 1744. V. 38

THE LIFE of Christ as Told In Selections from the New Testament. New York: 1951. V. 41

THE LIFE of Dick En-l--d, Alias Captain En-l--d; of Turf Memory. London: 1792. V. 41

THE LIFE of Dr. Oliver Goldsmith: Written from Personal Knowledge, Authentic Papers, and other Indubitable Authorities. London: 1774. V. 39

THE LIFE of General Tom Thumb. Troy. V. 39

LIFE of George Frederick Handel. London: 1784. V. 45

THE LIFE of Jack Rann, Otherwise Sixteen-String Jack, the Noted Highwayman, Who was Executed at Tyburn, Nov. 30, 1744. Durham: 1838. V. 45

THE LIFE of James Fitz-James, Duke of Berwick . . . Containing an Account of His Birth, Education and Military Exploits in Ireland, Flanders, Spain , the Sevegnnes, Dauphiny and on the Rhine . . . London: 1738. V. 46

LIFE of John C. Calhoun Presenting a Condensed History of Political Events from 1811 to 1843. New York: 1843. V. 46

THE LIFE of John Metcalfe, Commonly Called Blind Jack of Knaresborough. York: 1795. V. 45

THE LIFE of Lamenther: a True History. London: 1771. V. 46

THE LIFE of Mahomet; or, the History of that Imposture Which was Begun Carried On, and Finally Established by Him in Arabia . . . New York: 1813. V. 40

THE LIFE of Mahomet; or, the History of the Imposture Which Was Begun, Carried on and Finally Established by Him in Arabia . . . Worcester: 1802. V. 43

THE LIFE of Man. London: 1866. V. 44

THE LIFE of Miss Marion Smith. Boston: 1844. V. 37; 40

THE LIFE of Mrs. Abington (Formerly Miss Barton) Celebrated Comic Actress . . . London: 1888. V. 45

THE LIFE of Mr. James Quin, a Comedian. London: 1766. V. 38

THE LIFE of Napoleon. London: 1817. V. 43

THE LIFE of Saint David. Newtown: 1927. V. 42

THE LIFE of St. George. Printed from the Golden Legend of William Caxton. New Fairfield: 1957. V. 38

THE LIFE of the Celebrated Mail Robber and Daring Highwayman Joseph Thompson Hare who Committed Depredations in the Cities of New York and Philadelphia to the Amount of Nearly Ninety Thousand Dollars. Also of the Cruel and Ferocious Pirate, Alexander Tardy. Philadelphia: 1844. V. 37

THE LIFE of the Late Earl of Chesterfield: or, the Man of the World. London: 1774. V. 38

THE LIFE of Tom Thumb. Troy: 1863. V. 41

LIFE Songs. London: 1884. V. 38; 39; 40; 42

THE LIFE, Travels and Adventures of Christopher Wafstaff, Gentleman, Grandfather of Tristram Shandy. London: 1762. V. 40

THE LIFE, Travels and Opinions of Benjamin Lundy, Including His Journeys to Texas and Mexico . . . Philadelphia: 1847. V. 46

THE LIFE, Travels, Voyages and Daring Engagements of Paul Jones . . . Albany: 1809. V. 43; 46

THE LIFE, Trial, Condemnation, and Dying Address of the Three Thayers! Who Were Executed for the Murder of John Love, at Buffao, New York, June 17th, 1825. Buffao: 1825. V. 42

LIFE'S Comedy: Second Series. New York: 1897. V. 46

LIGER, LOUIS
Le Jardinier Fleuriste, ou la Culture Universelle des Fleurs, Arbres, Arbustes, Arbrisseaux Servant a l'Embellissement des Jardins . . . Paris: 1763. V. 39
La Nouvelle Maison Rustique, ou economie Generale de Tous les Biens de Campagne; La Maniere de les Entretenir & del les Multiplier . . . Paris: 1740. V. 39
La Nouvelle Maison Rustique, ou Economie Generale de Tous les Biens de Campagne. Paris: 1768. V. 39

THE LIGHT and Truth of Slavery. Aaron's History. Worcester: 1847? V. 44

LIGHT, EDWARD
Introduction to the Art of Playing on the Harp-Lute & Apollo-Lyre. London: 1798? V. 45

THE LIGHT-Horse Drill: Describing the Several Evolutions, in a Progressive Series. London: 1801. V. 38

THE LIGHT-HORSE Drill: Describing the Several Evolutions, In a Progressive Series, From the First Rudiments, to the Manoeuvres of the Squadron. London: 1800. V. 38

LIGHTBODY, JAMES
Every Man His Own Gauger . . . London: 1695. V. 43

LIGHTBOWN, RONALD
Sandro Botticelli: Life and Work. Berkeley: 1978. V. 37; 43

LIGHTBROWN, RONALD
Mantegna: With a Complete Catalogue of the Paintings, Drawings and Prints. Oxford: 1986. V. 46

LIGHTFOOT, J.
Flora Scotia. London: 1777. V. 37; 38

LIGHTFOOT, JOHN 1602-1675
Opera Omnia. Rotterdam: 1686. V. 40

LIGHTHILL, E. BUNFORD
A Popular Treatise on Deafness: Its Causes and Prevention. New York: 1862. V. 43

LIGHTOLER, TIMOTHY
The Gentleman and Farmer's Architect . . . London: 1762. V. 38

LIGHTON, WILLIAM B.
Memoirs of the Life of . . . Minister of the Gospel. Wells River: 1835. V. 42
Narrative of the Life and Sufferings of . . . Troy: 1846. V. 37; 41; 42

LIGHTS and Shadows of American Life. London: 1892. V. 46

LIGNE, CHARLES DE
Coup d'Oeil sur Beloeil. Beloeil: 1781. V. 38

LIGNE, CHARLES, PRINCE DE
Mon Refuge; ou Satyre sur les Abus des Jardins Modernes . . . London: 1801. V. 44

LIGON, RICHARD
A True and Exact History of the Island of Barbados. London: 1657. V. 41
A True and Exact History of the Island of Barbadoes. London: 1673. V. 40; 46

LIGUORI, ALPHONSO MARIA DE', SAINT 1696-1787

The Way of Salvation. London: 1836. V. 45

LILFORD, THOMAS LITTLETON POWYS, 4TH BARON 1833-1896

Coloured Figures of the Birds of the British Islands. London: 1885-97. V. 37; 38; 42

Coloured Figures of the Birds of the British Islands. London: 1891-97. V. 43

Notes on the Birds of Northamptonshire and Neighbourhood. London: 1895. V. 40

LILIENTHAL, DAVID E.

The Journals of David E. Lilienthal. New York: 1964-66. V. 44

LILIENTHAL, LILLIE BERNHEIMER

In Memoriam: Jesse Warren Lilienthal. San Francisco: 1921. V. 39; 42

LILIENTHAL, OTTO

Birdflight as the Basis of Aviation. London: 1911. V. 42; 45

LILIKALANI, E. K.

Move! Excel the Highest! The Celebrated Lilikalani Manifesto of the Election Campaign of February, 1882. Honolulu: 1882. V. 41; 44

LILIUOKALANI, QUEEN OF HAWAIIAN ISLANDS 1838-1917

An Account of the Creation of the World According to Hawaiian Tradition. Boston: 1897. V. 38

LILJEVALCH, C. F.

Chinas Handel, Industri Och Statsforfattning, Jemte Underrattelser om Chinesernes . . . Stockholm: 1848. V. 46

LILLINGSTON, LUKE

Reflections on Mr. Burchet's Memoirs. 1704. V. 45

Reflections on Mr. Burchet's Memoirs. London: 1704. V. 38; 40; 44

LILLO, GEORGE

Fatal Curiosity. London: 1737. V. 38; 46

Fatal Curiosity: a True Tragedy. London: 1762. V. 46

George Barnwell. Boston: 1828. V. 42

The London Merchant, or the History of George Barnwell. London: 1731. V. 38

LILLY, ELI

Prehistoric Antiquities of Indiana. Indianapolis: 1937. V. 37

LILLY, JOHN

A Collection of Modern Entries . . . (with) the Method of Suing to and Reversing Outlawries by Writ of Error (with) A Collection of Writs . . . Dublin: 1792. V. 40

The Dramatic Works . . . London: 1858. V. 42

Modern Entries . . . a Collection of Select Pleadings in the Courts of King's Bench, Common Pleas and Exchequer . . . London: 1741. V. 40

The Practical Conveyancer. London: 1719. V. 40

The Practical Conveyancer . . . In the Savoy: 1742. V. 45

LILLY LIBRARY

Notable Medical Books from the Lilly Library. Indianapolis: 1976. V. 38

LILLY, WILLIAM

Anima Astrologiae . . . London: 1676. V. 46

History of His Life and Times from the Year 1602 to 1681 . . . London: 1822. V. 38; 42

Merlini Anglici Ephemeris; or, Astrologicall Predictions for the Year 1651. London: 1651. V. 43

A Short Introduction of Grammar. Oxford: 1714. V. 41

The Starry Messenger. London: 1645. V. 38

William Lilly's History of his Life and Times, from the year 1602 to 1681. Written by Himself, in the sixty-sixth year of his age, to his worthy friend, Elias Ashmole, Esq. Published from the original MS. London: 1715. V. 37

LILLYWHITE, FRED

The English Cricketers' Trip to Canada and the United States. London: 1860. V. 42; 43

LILY, GEORGE

Chronicon Sive Brevis Enumeratio Regum et Principium. Frankfurt: 1565. V. 38; 41; 45

LILY, WILLIAM

A Short Introduction to Grammar. London: 1725. V. 42

A Short Introduction to Grammar. London: 1760. V. 40; 41

LIMA, ELADIO DA CRUZ

Mammals of Amazonia. Rio de Janeiro: 1943. V. 38

Mammals of Amazonia. Volume I. General Introduction and Primates. Rio de Janeiro: 1945. V. 37; 38

LIMA, MATIAS

A Encadernacao em Portugal. Gaia: 1933. V. 38

LIMBORCH, PHILIP

The History of the Inquisition . . . London: 1731. V. 46

LIMBORGH, PHILIP A.

The History of the Inquisition. London: 1731. V. 38; 44

LIMBOUR, GEORGES

Andre Beaudin. London: 1961. V. 39; 43; 46

LIMBOURG, JEAN PHILIPPE DE

New Amusements of the German Spa. London: 1764. V. 37; 45

LIMBURG, K. E.

The Hudson River Ecosystem. Berlin: 1986. V. 38

LIMEBEER, ENA

To a Proud Phantom. Richmond: 1923. V. 37; 44

LIMITED EDITIONS CLUB

Bibliography, 1929-1985. New York: 1985. V. 38; 39; 40; 41

Bibliography of the Fine Books Published by the Limited Editions Club 1929-1985. V. 38

Quarto Millenary, the first 250 publications and the first 25 years 1929-1954 of the Limited Editions Club. New York: 1959. V. 37; 38; 39; 41; 46

LIMOJON DE ST. DIDIER, ALEXANDRE T.

The City and Republic of Venice. London: 1699. V. 43

LIN, TSAN-PIAO

Native Orchids of Taiwan. Taiwan: 1975-87. V. 38

LINACRE, THOMAS

De Mendata Strvctvra Latini Sermonis, Libri VI. Coloniae: 1555. V. 46

LINATI, C.

Costumes Civiles, Militaires et Religieux de Mexique . . . Bruxelles: 1828. V. 42

LINCK, JOANNES BERNARD

Annales Austrio-Clara-Vallenses. Vienna: 1723. V. 46

LINCK, JOHANN HEINRICH

De Stellis Marinis Liber Singularis. (with) Stellarum Marinarum Tabulae. Leipzig: 1733. V. 42

LINCKLAEN, JOHN

Travels in the Years 1791 and 1792 in Pennsylvania, New York and Vermont. New York: 1897. V. 40; 41; 42

LINCOLN, ABRAHAM 1809-1865

Abraham Lincoln, Selections from His Writings. Worcester: 1950. V. 39; 45

The Address of the Hon. Abraham Lincoln, in Indication of the Policy of the Framers of the Constitution and the Principles of the Republican Party, Delivered at Cooper Institute, Feb. 27th, 1860, Issued by the Young Men's Republican Union . . . New York: 1860. V. 41

Addresses of Abraham Lincoln. Kingsport: 1929. V. 46

Collected Works. Rutgers: 1953. V. 42

The Collected Works. 1953. V. 37

The Collected Works of Abraham Lincoln. New Brunswick: 1953. V. 37

Discoveries and Inventions: a Lecture by Abraham Lincoln Delivered in 1860. San Francisco: 1915. V. 39

General Orders. No. 139. War Department. Adjutant General's Office. Washington, Sept. 24, 1862 . . . A Proclamation. Washington: 1862. V. 46

The Gettysburg Speech . . . Delivered on Nov. 19, 1863 . . . Delivered on Nov. 19, 1863. New York: 1924. V. 44; 45

The Gettysburg Address. Los Angeles: 1961. V. 41

The Gettysburg Address. Lafayette: 1973. V. 44

The Gettysburg Address (November 19, 1863). New York: 1988. V. 39

Life and Public Service of General Zachary Taylor. An Address. Boston & New York: 1922. V. 38

Political Debates Between Hon. Abraham Lincoln and Hon. Stephen A. Douglas, in the Celebrated Campaign of 1858, in Illinois . . . Columbus: 1860. V. 42; 46

Proclamation of Emancipation. Davenport: 1865. V. 40

Proclamation of Emancipation. N.P.: 1865? V. 40

Speech of Hon. Abraham Lincoln, Delivered in Springfield, Saturday Evening July 17, 1858. Springfield: 1858. V. 42

Complete Works of Abraham Lincoln. Cumberland Gap: 1903. V. 42

Complete Works. New York: 1905. V. 46

Complete Works. N.P.: 1920's. V. 42

Complete Works of Abraham Lincoln. New York: 1939. V. 42

The Writings . . . New York: 1905. V. 42

LINCOLN Campaign Songster. Philadelphia: 1864. V. 40

THE LINCOLN Centennial Medal. New York: 1908. V. 38; 40

LINCOLN, E. H.

Wild Flowers of New England. Pittsfield: 1911-14. V. 40; 42

LINCOLN GOLD MINING COMPANY

Prospectus and By-laws of the Lincoln Gold Mining Company of Colorado . . . Philadelphia: 1866. V. 37

LINCOLN, JOSEPH C.

Cape Cod Ballads. Trenton: 1902. V. 37; 39; 40; 42; 43

LINCOLN, MARY JOHNSON BAILEY 1844-1921

Mrs. Lincoln's Boston Cook Book. Boston: 1884. V. 38; 45

Mrs. Lincoln's Boston Cook Book: What to Do and What Not to Do In Cooking. Boston: 1899. V. 46

LINCOLN, R. J.

British Marine Amphipoda: Gammaridea. London: 1979. V. 37; 38

LINCOLN, ROBERT T.

Letter from . . . Transmitting . . . . a Progress Report of the Mississippi River Commission. Washington: 1881. V. 39

LINCOLN, WILLIAM

The Journals of Each Provincial Congress of Massachusetts in 1774 and 1775 and of the Committee of Safety. Boston: 1838. V. 40

LINCOLN, WILLIAM S.

Alton Trials . . . New York: 1838. V. 38; 40; 44; 46

Life with the Thirty-Fourth Mass. Infantry in the War of the Rebellion. Worcester: 1879. V. 38; 39; 42

LINCOLN'S INN, LONDON.

The Records of the Honorable Society. Lincoln's Inn: 1897-1902. V. 40

LINCON, ROBERT T.

Letter from the Secretary of War . . . Official Report of Schwatka of His Military Reconnaissance of 1883 in Alaska . . . Washington: 1884. V. 37

LIND-GOLDSCHMIDT, JENNY

Memoir of . . . Her Early Art-Life and Dramatic Career 1820-1851. London: 1891. V. 40

LIND, J.

An Essay on Diseases Incidental to Europeans in Hot Climates . . . London. V. 43

LIND, JAMES

An Essay on Diseases Incidental to Europeans In Hot Climates, with the Method of Preventing Their Fatal Consequences. Philadelphia: 1811. V. 40

An Essay on Diseases Incidental to Europeans in Hot Climates. London: 1777. V. 37

Traite du Scorbut . . . Paris: 1756. V. 37

LIND, JOHN

An Answer to the Declaration of the American Congress. London: 1776. V. 37; 38; 42

Defence of Lord Pigot. Damnatus Absens. London: 1777. V. 43

LINDBERG, PEHR

Architectura Mechanica, of Moolen-Boek Vaneenige Opstallen Van Moolens, Nevens Hunne Gronden. Amsterdam. V. 41

LINDBERGH, ANNE MORROW

Dearly Beloved. New York: 1962. V. 38

North to the Orient. New York: 1935. V. 39

LINDBERGH, CHARLES A.

Boyhood on the Upper Mississippi . . . St. Paul: 1972. V. 39; 45; 46

The Spirit of St. Louis. New York: 1953. V. 39; 40; 42; 43; 45

'We'. New York: 1927. V. 46

We. The Famous Flier's own story of His Life and His Transatlantic Flight . . . London: 1928. V. 37

LINDE, A. VAN DER

The Haarlem Legend or the Invention of Printing by Lourens Janszoon Coster, from the Dutch by J. H. Hessels . . . London: 1871. V. 44

LINDEBERG, H. T.

Domestic Architecture of H. T. Lindeberg. New York: 1940. V. 43

LINDEBOOM, G. A.

Dutch Medical Biography: a Biographical Dictionary of Dutch Physicians and Surgeons 1475-1975. Amsterdam: 1984. V. 41; 42; 45

LINDEGREN, ERIK

ABC of Lettering and Printing Types. New York: 1965. V. 44

LINDELBACH, MICHAEL

Praecepta Latinitatis. Heidelberg: 1486. V. 38; 39; 40

LINDEMAN, M. H.

The Quarter Horse Breeder. Wichita Falls: 1959. V. 45

LINDEN, DIEDERICK WESSEL

Three Letters on Mining and Smelting; in Which a Method is Laid Down, Whereby These Useful Sciences May be Greatly Improved. London: 1750. V. 45

LINDEN, JAMES

Printers to the Club. San Francisco: 1986. V. 39; 41

LINDEN, JOHANNES VAN DER 1756-1835

Institutes of the Laws of Holland. London: 1828. V. 40

LINDERMAN, FRANK B.

Blackfeet Indians. St. Paul: 1935. V. 38; 39; 44

Indian Why Stories. Sparks From War Eagles Lodge-Fires. New York: 1915/25. V. 44

Indian Why Stories. Sparks from War Eagle's Lodge-Fire. New York: 1915. V. 37

Out of the North. St. Paul: 1940. V. 44; 45

LINDESAY, PATRICK

The Interest of Scotland Considered, With Regard to Its Police in Imploying of the Poor, Its Agriculture, Its Trade, Its Manufactures and Fisheries. Edinburgh: 1733. V. 45

LINDESTOLPE, JOHAN 1678-1724

Liber de Venenis. Francofvrti et Lipsiae: 1739. V. 38

THE LINDFIELD Reporter, or Philanthropic Magazine. Lindfield: 1836=42. V. 37

LINDGREN, WALDEMAR

The Gold and Silver veins of Silver City, De Lamar and Other Mining Districts of Idaho. Washington: 1897. V. 37

LINDHOUT, HENRI VAN ca. 1550-ca.1620

Introductio in Physicam Iudiciariam. Hamburg: 1597. V. 43

LINDLEY, AUGUSTUS

After Ophir: a Search for the African Gold Fields. London: 1870. V. 43

LINDLEY, AUGUSTUS F.

Adamantia. The Truth About the South African Diamond Fields; or, Vindication of the Orange Free State to that Territory and an Analysis of British Diplomacy and Aggression Which Has Resulted in Its Illegal Seizure by the Governor of the Cape of Good Hope. London: 1873. V. 41

LINDLEY, GEORGE

A Guide to the Orchard and Kitchen Garden. London: 1831. V. 37; 38; 39; 40; 46

LINDLEY, JOHN 1799-1865

Folia Orchidacea. London: 1852-59. V. 43

The Fossil Flora of Great Britain. London: 1831-37. V. 37; 39

An Introduction to Botany. London: 1848. V. 44

Ladies Botany. London: 1834-37. V. 41; 46

Ladies Botany; or, a Familiar Introduction to the Study of the Natural System of Botany. London: 1835. V. 40

Ladies' Botany; or a Familiar Introduction to the Study of the Natural System of Botany. London: 1837. V. 43

Ladies Botany; or a Familiar Introduction to the Study of the Natural System of Botany. London: 1837-40. V. 46

Ladies Botany. London: 1841. V. 42; 43

Ladies' Botany. London: 1865. V. 37

An Outline of the First Principles of Horticulture. London: 1832. V. 39; 41

Paxton's Flower Garden. London: 1850-53. V. 41

Paxton's Flower Garden. London: 1853. V. 38

Rosarum Monogrpahia; or, a Botanical History of Roses. London: 1820. V. 43

Rosarum Monographia; or, a Botanical History of Roses. London: 1830. V. 37

The Treasury of Botany: a Popular Dictionary of the Vegetable Kingdom. New York: 1872. V. 38; 41

The Vegetable Kingdom. London: 1853. V. 41; 46

LINDLEY, KENNETH

A Hereford Window. (Hereford): 1979. V. 37

LINDLEY, NATHANIEL 1828-1921

An Introduction to the Study of Jurisprudence. Philadelphia: 1855. V. 40

LINDLEY, THOMAS

Narrative of a Voyage to Brasil. London: 1805. V. 40; 46

LINDLEY, WALTER

California of the South . . . New York: 1888. V. 42

LINDSAY, ALEXANDER WILLIAM CRAWFORD

Letters on Egypt, Edom and the Holy Land. London: 1839. V. 40

LINDSAY, CAROLINE BLANCHE ELIZABETH

Bertha's Earl. London: 1891. V. 40; 44

LINDSAY, D.

A Blade for Sale. 1927. V. 44

LINDSAY, DAVID

Adventures of Monsieur de Mailly. London: 1925. V. 43

Facsimile of an Ancient Heraldic Manuscript Emblazoned by Sir David Lindsay of the Mount, Lyon King of Arms. 1542. Edinburgh: 1822. V. 39

A Voyage to Arcturus. London: 1920. V. 43

The Works of the Famous and Worthy Knight, Sir David Lindsay of the Mount . . . Edinburgh: 1720. V. 43

LINDSAY, DAVID MOORE

A Voyage to the Arctic in the Whaler Aurora. Boston: 1911. V. 39; 41; 43

LINDSAY, HOWARD

State of the Union. New York: 1946. V. 39

LINDSAY, JACK

The Collected Poems. Lake Forest: 1981. V. 39

Death of a Spartan King and Two Other Stories of the Ancient World. London: 1974. V. 43

Dionysos, Nietzsche Contra Nietzsche: an Essay in Lyrical Philosophy. 1928. V. 40

Fauns and Ladies. Sydney: 1923. V. 41

Helen Comes of Age. London: 1927. V. 39; 43; 46

Loving Mad Tom: Bedlamite Verses of the LXVI and XVII Centuries. London: 1927. V. 42; 43; 45

The Passionate Neatherd. London. V. 40

Storm at Sea. London: 1935. V. 37; 38; 41; 42; 44

LINDSAY, JOHN

A View of the Coinage of Ireland, from the Invasion of the Danes to the Reign of George IV. Cork: 1839. V. 42; 43

A View of the Coinage of Scotland, with Copious Tables, Lists, Descriptions and Extracts from Acts of Parliament . . . Cork: 1845. V. 42; 43

LINDSAY, LIONEL

A Book of Woodcuts Drawn on Wood and Engraved by Lionel Lindsay. Sydney: 1922. V. 41

Conrad Martens: the Man and His Art. Sydney: 1920. V. 41

LINDSAY, LORD

Letters on Egypt, Edom and the Holy Land . . . London: 1838. V. 44

LINDSAY, NICHOLAS VACHEL 1879-1931

The Chinese Nightingale and Other Poems. New York: 1917. V. 38; 39

The Chinese Nightingale. New York: 1920. V. 37

Collected Poems. New York: 1923. V. 41

Collected Poems. New York: 1925. V. 39; 46

The Congo and Other Poems. New York: 1919. V. 38

Every Soul is a Circus. New York: 1929. V. 43

General William Booth Enters into Heaven and other Poems. New York: 1913. V. 39

The Golden Book of Springfield. New York: 1920. V. 39; 43

The Golden Whales of California. New York: 1920. V. 37

A Handy Guide for Beggars . . . Being Sundry Explorations Made While Afoot and Penniless in Florida, Georgia, North Carolina . . . (New York): 1916. V. 37

A Memorial of Lincoln, Called the Heros of Time. Springfield: 1910. V. 39

The Moon-Worms. Springfield: 1910. V. 39; 42

Proclamation of the Gospel of Beauty. Springfield: 1912. V. 38; 39; 40; 42

Rhymes to be Traded for Bread. Springfield: 1912. V. 37; 39; 42

Rhymes to be Traded for Bread. Springfield: 1912. V. 37

The Soul of the City Receives the Gift of the Holy Spirit. Springfield: 1913. V. 37

The Tramps' Excuse and Other Poems. Springfield: 1909. V. 44

The Tree of Laughing Bells. N.P.: 1905. V. 39

War Bulletin Number Five. Springfield: 1909. V. 42

War Bulletin Number Three. Springfield: 1909. V. 42

We Who are Playing Tonight. Springfield: 1905. V. 39

The Wedding of the Rose and the Lotus. Springfield: 1912. V. 39

LINDSAY, NORMAN

The Cautious Amorist. 1932. V. 37

The Magic Pudding. New York: 1936. V. 40

Micomicana. Carlton: 1979. V. 41

Paintings in Oil. Sydney: 1945. V. 42

Pen Drawings. Sydney: 1931. V. 42

Water Colour Book - Eighteen Reproductions. Sydney: 1939. V. 41

LINDSAY, OWEN

Verbatim Report of the Trial of Owen Lindsay, for the Murder of Francis A. Colvin, Containing the Testimony in Full: Opening and Closing Speeches of Counsel; Charge to the Jury, Etc . . . Syracuse: 1875. V. 39

LINDSAY, PATRICK

The Interest of Scotland Considered, With Regard to Its Police in Imploying of the Poor, Its Agriculture, Its Trade, Its Manufactures, and Fisheries. Edinburgh: 1733. V. 37; 38

The Interest of Scotland Considered, with Regard to Its Police in Employing the Poor, Its Agriculture, Its Trade, Its Manufacture and Fisheries. London: 1736. V. 39

LINDSAY, PHILIP

An Account Biographical and Informative of the Later Days of Sir Henry Morgan Admiral of Buccaneers . . . London: 1930. V. 40; 46

LINDSAY, ROBERT

The History of Scotland: from 1436 to 1565. Glasgow: 1749. V. 41

LINDSAY, ROBERT STRATHERN

A History of the Mason Lodge of Holyrood House (St. Luke's) No. 44 Holding of the Grand Lodge of Scotland with Roll of Members 1734-1934. London: 1935. V. 38

LINDSAY, W. C.

A Letter to His Grace the Lord Primate of Ireland: In Which is Vindicated the Principles and Conduct of Orange-Men. Dublin: 1798. V. 42

LINDSAY, W. S.

History of Merchant Shipping and Ancient Commerce. London: 1874/76. V. 40

History of Merchant Shipping and Ancient Commerce. London: 1874-76. V. 38

LINDSEY, CHARLES

Clergy Reserves: Their History and Present Position Showing the Systematic Attempts that Have Been MAde to Establish in Connection with the State. Toronto: 1851. V. 42; 46

The Life and Times of Wm. Lyon Mackenzie. Toronto: 1862. V. 42

LINDSEY, WILLIAM

Apples of Istakhar. Boston: 1895. V. 37; 38; 41

Cinder-Path Tales. Boston: 1896. V. 39

LINDSLEY, A. L.

Sketches of an Excursion to Southern Alaska. Portland: 1881. V. 46

LINDSLEY, PHILIP

An Address, Delivered in Nashville, January 12, 1825, at the Inauguration of the President of Cumberland College. Nashville: 1825. V. 37; 40

Baccalaureate Address, Pronounced on the Sixth Anniversary Commencement of the University of Nashville, Octover 5, 1831. Nashville: 1831. V. 39

Baccalareate Address, Pronounced on the Seventh Anniversary Commencement of the University of Nashville, Oct. 3, 1832. Nashville: 1832. V. 44

A History of Greater Dallas and Vicinity. Chicago: 1909. V. 38

LINDT, JOHANN

The Paper Mills of Berne and Their Watermarks, 1465-1859. Hilversum: 1964. V. 38; 41

LINE, JOHN, & SONS

Newest Designs in Wallpapers for Stock Buyers Only. London and Reading,: 1895. V. 37

LINEBARGER, P.

The Political Doctrines of Sun Yatsen. 1937. V. 43

LINEHAN, JOHN

The Drainage Engineer and General Land Improver . . . all Connected with the Improvement or Management of Landed Property, Waterworks, etc . . . Dublin: 1849. V. 38

LINES, Composed on the Dreadful and Untimely Death of Daniel Brown and John Harvey, both of Nottingham, N. H . . . Who Had Been Burning a Coal Pit in a Solitary Wood . . . N.P.: 1816. V. 39

LINES, KATHLEEN

Once in Royal David's City. Oxford: 1956. V. 43

LINTON, WILLIAM JAMES

The English Republic. God and the People. London: 1851. V. 38

LION-GOLDSCHMIDT, DAISY

Bronze, Jade, Sculpture, Ceramics. New York: 1960. V. 46

Chinese Art: Bronze, Jade, Sculpture, Ceramics. New York: 1962. V. 41

Chinese Art: Bronze, Jade, Sculpture, Ceramics. New York: 1966. V. 38; 41

Chinese Art. Oxford: 1980-81. V. 42

Ming Porcelain. London: 1978. V. 42; 46

LION-GOLDSCMIDT, DAISY

Chinese Art: Bronze, Jade, Sculpture, Ceramics. London: 1960. V. 39

LIONI, OTTAVIO

Ritratti di Alcuni Celebri Pittori del Secolo XVII . . . con le Vite de' Medesimi Tratte da Vari Autori . . . Rome: 1731. V. 38; 40

LIONNE, ARTUS DE

Chinese Manual. London: 1854. V. 41

THE LION'S Masquerade; The Elephant's Ball. London: 1883. V. 38

LIOT, W. B.

Panama, Nicaragua and Tehuantepec . . . London: 1849. V. 45

LIPEN, MARTIN

Bibliotheca Recalis Medica, Omnium Materiarum, Rerum et Titulorum in Universa Medicina Occurentium . . . Francofurti: 1679. V. 42

LIPMAN, JEAN

American Primitive Painting. London: 1942. V. 41

Calder's Universe. New York: 1976. V. 43; 46

LIPMAN, M.

The Chatterlings. 1928. V. 43; 46

LIPPARD, GEORGE

Legends of Mexico. Philadelphia: 1847. V. 43

Original Revolutionary Chronicle. Philadelphia: 1843. V. 37

Washington and His Generals; or Legends of the Revolution. Philadelphia: 1847. V. 41

LIPPARD, LUCY

The Graphic Work of Philip Evergood. New York: 1966. V. 43; 46

LIPPARD, LUCY R.

Ad Reinhardt. New York: 1981. V. 39

LIPPINCOTT, Grambo & Co.'s Gazeteer. Philadelphia: 1854. V. 45

LIPPINCOTT, H. C.

A Report of the Trial of Sir H. C. Lippincott, Bart. on a Charge of Rape, Committed on the Person of Mary Milford, Spinster, aged 17 Years . . . London: 1810. V. 37

LIPPINCOTT, SARA JANE

Greenwood Leaves: a Collection of Sketches and Letters. Boston: 1850. V. 44

LIPPINCOTT, SARA JANE CLARKE 1823-1904

New Life in New Lands: Notes of Travel . . . New York: 1873. V. 39; 41

LIPPMAN, FRIEDRICH

Drawings by Sandro Botticeli for Dante's Divina Comedia. London: 1896. V. 45

LIPPMANN, F.

The Art of Wood Engravings in Italy in the 15th Century. Englis edition with extensive corrections and additions by the author, which have not appeared in the German original. 1888. V. 37

LIPPMANN, WALTER 1899-1974

United States in World Affairs: An Account of American Foreign Relations, 1931-40 and 1945-67. By Walter Lippmann in collaboration with William O. Scroogs. New York: 1932-68. V. 37; 42

LIPPS, OSCAR H.

A Little History of the Navajos. Cedar Rapids: 1909. V. 46

LIPSCOMB, GEORGE

The History and Antiquities of the County of Buckingham. London: 1847. V. 38; 39; 44

LIPSCOMB, H. C.

History of Staindrop Church. London: 1852. V. 37; 40

LIPSCOMB, WILLIAM

Verses on the Beneficial Effects of Inoculation, Which Obtained One of the Chancellor's Prizes at the University of Oxford in the Year 1772. London: 1793. V. 42

LIPSCOMBE, WILLIAM

Poems. Oxford: 1784. V. 40; 43

LIPSIUS, JUSTUS

De Amphitheatro Liber. In Quo Forma Ipsa Loci Expressa & Ratio Spectandi. Cum Aeneis Figuris. Omnia Auctiora vel Meliora. Antwerp: 1598. V. 45

De Bibliothecis Syntagma. Antwerp: 1619. V. 38

De Cruce Libri Tres, Ad Sacram Profanamque Historiam Utiles. Antverpiae: 1594. V. 43

De Amphitheatro Liber. Antwerp: 1585. V. 37

Epistolarum Selectarum Centuria Prima Miscellanea. Antwerp: 1611-14. V. 44

I. Lipsi Saturnalium Libri Duo, De Gladiatoribus. Antwerp: 1585. V. 45

Los sys Libros de las Politicas o Doctrina Civil de Iusto Lipsio, que Siruen Para el Goueirno del Reyno, o Principado. Madrid: 1604. V. 41

Opera Omnia . . . Antwerp: 1637. V. 40

Poliorceticon Sive de Machinis Tormentis Telis. Antverpiae: 1599. V. 39

LIPSKI, LOUIS L.

Dated English Delftware. Tin-glazed Earthenware 1600-1800. London: 1984. V. 39; 42; 46

Dated English Delftware. Tin-glazed Earthenware 1600-1800. London: 1894. V. 37

LISCH, G. C. F.

Geschichte der Buchdruckerkunst in Mecklenburg. Schwerin: 1839. V. 38

LISFRANC, JACQUES

Diseases of the Uterus, a Series of Clinical Lectures, Delivered at the Hospital La Pitie. Boston: 1839. V. 46

LISIANSKY, UREY

A Voyage Round the World, in the Year 1803, 4, 5, & 6; Peformed by Order of His Imperial Majesty Alexander the First, Emperor of Russia, in the Ship Neva. London: 1814. V. 38; 40; 42; 43; 46

L'ISLA, JOSE FRANCISCO DE

The History of the Famous Preacher Friar Gerund de Campanzas, Otherwise Gerund Zotes. London: 1772. V. 45

LISLE, EDWARD

Observations in Husbandry. London: 1757. V. 37; 40; 42; 46

LISLE, JOE

Play Upon Words. London: 1828. V. 46

LISNEY, A. A.

A Bibliography of British Lepidoptera 1608-1799. London: 1960. V. 39; 44; 46

A Bibliography of British lepidoptera 1608-1799. 1960. V. 37

LISOLA, LE BARON FRANCOIS PAUL 1613-1675

The Buckler of State and Justice Against the design Manifestly Discovered of the Universal Monarchy, Under the Vain Pretext of the Queen of France her Pretensions. London: 1667. V. 38; 41

The Buckler of State and Justice Against the Design Manifestly Discovered of the Universal Monarchy, Under the Vain Pretext of the Queen of France Her Pretensions. London: 1667. V. 41

LISSAGARAY, PROSPER O.

History of the Commune of 1871. New York: 1898. V. 39; 41

LISSIM, SIMON

The Art of Raymond Lister. Cambridge: 1958. V. 40

An Artist's Interpretation of Nature. New York: 1958. V. 40

Simon Lissim Interviewed by Raymond Lister. Cambridge: 1962. V. 40

LISSITZKY, E.

Die Kunstismen. Les Ismes de l'Art. The Isms of Art. Erlenbach-Zurich/: 1925. V. 42

LISSITZKY, ELIEZER

Die Kunstismen. Les Ismes de l'Art. Erlenbach: 1925. V. 41

LIST, FRIEDRICH

Gesammelte Schriften. Stuttgart und Tubingen: 1850-51. V. 38; 39

National System of Political Economy . . . Philadelphia: 1856. V. 42

Outlines of American Political Economy, in a Series of Letters Addressed by . . . Philadelphia: 1827. V. 37

LIST, N. A.

The Wisdom of Solomon: a Key to the Bible, and the Ancient Americans. Omaha: 1889. V. 46

A **LIST** of all the Officers of the Army and Royal Marines on Full and Half Pay, with an Index; and a Succession of Colonels. London: 1807. V. 46

A **LIST** of Copies of Charters, From the Commissioners for Trade and Plantations Presented to the Honourable the House of Commons . . . 25th of April 1740 . . . London: 1741. V. 41

LIST of Etonians Who Fought in the Great War, 1914-1919. London: 1921. V. 45; 46

LIST of Fugitives from Justice for 1900, Compiled from the Revised Reports of Sherriffs. Austin: 1900. V. 38

LIST of Officers of the Royal Regiment of Artillery, They Stood in the Year 1763, with a Continuation to the Present Time . . . Greenwich: 1815. V. 41; 46

A **LIST** of Officers Who Died, Were Killed, or Broke on the Expedition of the West Indies, Commencing Oct. 26th 1740 and ending February the 20th 1741-2. V. 44

A **LIST** of Several Ships Belonging to English Merchants, Taken by French Privateers, Since December One Thousand Six Hundred and Seventy Three . . . Amsterdam: 1677. V. 37

A **LIST** of the Names of Persons to Whom Military Patents Have Issued Out of the Secretary's Office and To Whom Delivered. New York: 1793. V. 41

A **LIST** of the Officers of the Milita of the United Kingdom and of the Yeomanry Cavalry of Great Britain. London: 1817. V. 37

LISTA de Los Ciudadanos Que Deberan Companer Los Jurados . . . Santa Fe: 1834. V. 41

LISTER, G.
A Monograph of the Mycetozoa, a Descriptive Catalogue of the Spcies in the Herbarium of the British Museum. London: 1925. V. 46

LISTER, JOSEPH 1827-1912
The Collected Papers of Joseph, Baron Lister. London: 1909. V. 37; 38
The Collected Papers. Oxford: 1909. V. 38; 39; 40
The Collected Papers of Joseph, Baron Lister. Birmingham: 1979. V. 38; 41; 45
A Further Contribution to the Natural History of Bacteria and the Germ Theory of Fermentative Changes. London: 1873. V. 37
Joseph Baron Lister: Centenary Volume, 1827-1927. Edinburgh &c.: 1927. V. 38
On the Coagulation of the Blood. London: 1863. V. 38

LISTER, MARTIN
Historiae Animalium Angliae tres Tracatus. London: 1678. V. 37; 42; 46
Historiae Sive Synopsis Methodicae Conchyliorum. London: 1685-97. V. 45
Historiae Sive Synopsis Methodicae Conchyliorum et Tabularum Anatomicarum Editio Altera. Oxford: 1770. V. 43
A Journey to Paris in the Year 1698. London: 1699. V. 39; 41
Martini Lister Sex Exceritationes Medicinales De Quibusdam Morbis Chronicus . . . London: 1694. V. 38; 42
Octo Exercitationes Medicinales . . . London: 1697. V. 42

LISTER, RAYMOND
Bergomask. (Cambridge): (ca. 1960). V. 37
Decorated Porcelains of Simon Lissim, by Raymond Lister. Cambridge, England: 1955. V. 37
The Emblems of Theodosius or, the Unity of Endymion and Prometheus, by Raymond Lister. N.P. (Cambridge, England): 1969. V. 37
Gabha. Cambridge: 1964. V. 43
Hammer and Hand. Cambridge: 1969. V. 37; 41; 45
Song of Theodosius. Cambridge: 1963. V. 43
The Song of Theodosius. Cambridge: 1953. V. 37
There Was a Star Danced. Cambridge: 1933. V. 45
There was a Star Danced. Cambridge: 1983. V. 37
A Title to Phoebe. Cambridge: 1972. V. 46

LISTER, REGINALD
Jean Goujon, His Life and Work. London: 1903. V. 38; 40

LISTER, THOMAS
A Correct Alphabetical List of All the Ships and Vessels Belonging to the Several Ports of Whitehaven, Workington, Maryport and Harrington . . . Whitehaven: 1810. V. 40

LISTER, THOMAS HENRY
Arlington. London: 1832. V. 42; 46
Granby. London: 1826. V. 38; 40

LISTON, ROBERT
Elements of Surgery. Philadelphia: 1837. V. 42; 44
Elements of Surgery. London: 1840. V. 43; 46

Lectures on the Operations of Surgery and on Diseases and Accidents Requiring Operations . . . Philadelphia: 1846. V. 42
Practical Surgery: With 120 Engravings on Wood . . . with Notes and Additional Illustrations by George W. Norris, M.D. Philadelphia: 1838. V. 42

LISTS of the Chiefs, Officers, Court of Assistants &c. &c of the Honourable Artillery Company. London: 1804-20. V. 41

LITANIAE In Alm Domo Luretana, Omnibus Diebus Sabbati, Vigilarum & Festorum Beatissimae Virginis Musice Decantari Solitae. Paris: 1578. V. 38

THE LITANY. N.P.: 1843. V. 42

THE LITANY of the D. of B. London: 1679? V. 41; 45

LITCH, JOSIAH
Dialogue on the Nature of Man, His State in Death, and the Final Doom of the Wicked. Philadelphia: 1850? V. 45

LITCH, WILBUR F.
The American System of Dentistry, in Treatises by Various Authors. Philadelphia: 1886. V. 39; 42

LITCHFIELD, FREDERICK
Illustrated History of Furniture from the Earliest to the Present Time. London: 1899. V. 39
Pottery and Porcelain: a Guide to Collectors. London: 1925. V. 41

LITCHFIELD, PAUL W.
Autumn Leaves: Reflections of an Industrial Lieutenant. Cleveland: 1945. V. 46

LITCHFIELD, R. B.
Tom Wedgwood, the First Photographer, an Account of His Life . . . London: 1903. V. 39

THE LITERARY and Philosophical Repertory: Physical Scienes; the Liberal and Fine Arts. Middlebury: 1812-17. V. 39

LITERARY Gazette; or, Journal of Criticism, Science and the Arts. Philadelphia: 1821. V. 46

THE LITERARY Miscellany . . . Cambridge: 1805-06. V. 40

THE LITERARY Miscellany, Including Dissertations and Essays on Subjects of Literature, Science and Morals . . . Cambridge: 1805. V. 44

THE LITERARY Miscellany; or, Elegant Selections of the Most Admired Fugitive Pieces and Extracts. Manchester: 1794. V. 46

THE LITERATURE of Letterpress Printing 1849-1900. 1986. V. 45

LITHGOVY, WILLIAM
The Totall Discourse, of the Rare Adventures, and Painefull Peregrinations of Long Nineteene Yeares Trauayles, from Scotland to the Most Famous Kingdomes in Europe, Asia and Africa . . . London: 1622. V. 43

LITHGOW, WILLIAM
A True and Experimentall Discourse, Upon the Beginning, Proceeding and Victorious Event of This Last Siege of Breda. London: 1637. V. 40; 42

LITHOPINION, The Graphic Arts and Public Affairs Journal of Local One, Amalgamated Lithographers of America. New York: 1965-75. V. 46

LITT, WILLIAM
Wrestliana; or, an Historical Account of Ancient and Modern Wrestling. Whitehaven: 1823. V. 40

LITTA, CONTE POMPEO
Celebri Famiglie Italiane. Milan: 1839. V. 41; 44

LITTAUER, VLADIMIR S.
Jumping the Horse. New York: 1931. V. 43

LITTEL, JOHN
Family Records: or Genealogies of the First Settlers of Passaic Valley, (and Vicinity) Above Chatham-with Their Ancestors and Descendants, as Far as Can Now be Ascertained. Feltville: 1851, ie 1852. V. 37

LITTELL, JOHN
Family Records; or, Genealogies of the First Settlers of Passaic Valley. Feltville: 1851. V. 39; 41

LITTELL, WILLIAM
Festoons of Fancy, Consisting of Compositions Amatory. Louisville: 1814. V. 42; 46

A **LITTLE** Anthology of Hitherto Uncollected Poems by Modern Writers. Flansham: 1922. V. 38

LITTLE Child's Home ABC Book. New York: 1870. V. 46

LITTLE, DAVID F.
The Wanderer, and Other Poems. Los Angeles: 1880. V. 39

LITTLE, DAVID MASON

Pineapples of Finest Flavour. Cambridge: 1930. V. 44

LITTLE Dot and Her Friends. London: 1880. V. 39

THE LITTLE Flowers of St. Francis of Assisi. Translaed by T.W. Arnold. Illustrations taken from a Manuscript at the Laurentian Library, Florence. London: 1909. V. 37

LITTLE Folks Fair. London: 1890. V. 39

LITTLE, G.

The Angler's Complete Guide and Companion. London: 1882. V. 40

LITTLE, GEORGE

Life On the Ocean, or Twenty Years at Sea . . . Aberdeen & Ipswich: 1847. V. 45

LITTLE, GEORGE THOMAS

Genealogical and Family History of the State of Maine. New York: 1909. V. 46

THE LITTLE Gleaner. Fredericksburg: 1868-69. V. 39

THE LITTLE Graves. New York: 1830. V. 44

LITTLE, HENRY W.

H. M. Stanley: His Life, Travels and Explorations. London: 1890. V. 44

LITTLE, J. J.

The J. J. Little Book of Types, Specimen Pages, and Book Papers . . . New York: 1923. V. 38

LITTLE, JAMES A.

From Kirtland to Salt Lake City. Salt Lake City;: 1890. V. 37; 39; 40; 42; 43; 45; 46

Jacob Hamblin, a Narrative of His Personal Experience, as a Frontiersman, Missionary to the Indians and Explorer. Salt Lake City: 1881. V. 42; 46

What I Saw on the Old Santa Fe Trail. Plainfield: 1904. V. 41

LITTLE, JANET

The Poetical Works of Janet Little, the Scotch Milkmaid. Air: 1792. V. 42; 45

LITTLE, JOHN

Dr. Johnson and Noah Webster, Two Men and Their Dictionaries. San Francisco: 1971. V. 45

THE LITTLE Learner's Toy Book. London. V. 40

LITTLE, MALCOLM 1925-1965

The Autobiography of Malcolm X. New York: 1965. V. 39

LITTLE Marian. Philadelphia: 1878. V. 46

LITTLE Nancy, or the Punishment of Greediness. Philadelphia: 1824. V. 38

LITTLE, NINA FLETCHER

Little by Little. New York: 1984. V. 45

LITTLE, O. H.

The Geography and Geology of Makalla (South Arabia). Cairo: 1925. V. 43

LITTLE, OTIS

The State of Trade in the Northern Colonies Considered . . . London: 1748. V. 41; 43

LITTLE Red Riding Hood. London: 1866. V. 45
LITTLE Red Riding Hood. London: 1880. V. 39
LITTLE Red Riding Hood. London: 1890. V. 39
LITTLE Red Riding Hood. London: 1900. V. 43

LITTLE, SHELBY

George Washington. New York: 1929. V. 39

LITTLE Songs of Long Ago. London: 1912. V. 45

LITTLE Stories About Mark Twain. New York: 1911. V. 43

LITTLE Stories of One or Two Syllables for Little Children. London: 1849. V. 45

LITTLE Tales, with Lots of Pretty Pictures, for Little Folks. London: 1850. V. 39

LITTLE Tots' Holiday Book. London: 1900. V. 45

LITTLE Tot's Pleasure Book. London. V. 40

A LITTLE Treasury of Modern Verse. New York: 1946. V. 46

LITTLE, W. J.

Medical and Surgical Aspects of In-Knee (Genu-Valgum): Its Relation to Ricketts, Its Prevention and Treatment with and Without Surgical Operation. New York: 1882. V. 39

On Spinal Weakness and Spinal Curvatures: Their early recognition and treatment. London: 1868. V. 37

LITTLE, W. L.

Staffordshire Blue, Underglaze Blue Transfer-Printed Earthenware. London: 1969. V. 39

THE LITTLE Warbler: Volume I: Scottish Songs. Edinburgh: 1820. V. 39

LITTLE, WILLIAM

The Easy Instructor, or, A New Method of Teaching Sacred Harmony. Albany: 1828. V. 40

The Easy Instructor; or a New Method of Teaching Sacred Harmony. Albany, New York: (1810). V. 37

History of Warren; a Mountain Hamlet, Locted Among the White Hills of New Hampshire. Manchester: 1870. V. 38

LITTLEDALE, WILLOUGHBY

The Registers of St. Bene't and St. Peter, Paul's Wharft, London, Christenings, Marriages and Burials 1607-1837. London: 1909-12. V. 41

LITTLEFIELD, GEORGE EMERY

The Early Massachusetts Press 1638-1711. Boston: 1907. V. 37

LITTLEJOHN, DAVID

Dr. Johnson and Noah Webster. San Francisco: 1971. V. 38; 45

LITTLER, F. M.

A Handbook of the Birds of Tasmania and Its Dependencies. Launceston: 1910. V. 37; 38

LITTLETON, ADAM 1627-1694

Latin Dictionary, in Four Parts. London: 1735. V. 45

Linguae Latinae Dictionaris Quadripartitus. London: 1678. V. 38; 40; 41; 43; 46

Linguae Latinae Liber Dictionarius Quadripartitus. London: 1684. V. 45

LITTLETON, EDWARD

The Groans of the Plantations. London: 1689. V. 41; 44

LITTLETON, THOMAS

An Abridgment of the First Part of Ld. Coke's Institutes; with Great Additions . . . London: 1751. V. 40

Littletons Tenures. London: 1557. V. 37; 40

Tenures in Englishe. London: 1574. V. 46

Les Tenures de Monsieur Littleton. London: 1604. V. 40

Les Tenures de Monsieur Littleton. London: 1612. V. 40

Littleton's Tenvres in English . . . London: 1616. V. 43

Littleton's Tenures in English, Lately Perused and Amended. London: 1627. V. 38

Littleton's Tenures in French and English. London: 1671. V. 40

Littleton's Tenures, in English. London: 1825. V. 40

LITURGIA Britannica. London: 1845. V. 40

LA LITURGIA Ynglesa, o El Libro de la Orocion Comun . . . Segun el Uso de la Yglesia Anglicana . . . Londres: 1715. V. 43

LA LITURGIE de l'Eglise Anglicane . . . Roy George . . . Prince de Galles. Londres: 1715. V. 43

LIU, T. S.

Quarternary Geology and Environment of China. Beijing: 1985. V. 37; 38

LE LIURE du Faulcon des Dames. Paris: ?1520's. V. 39

LIVELY, EDWARD

A True Chronologie of the Times of the Persian Monarchie, and After to the Destruction of Jerusalem by the Romanes. London: 1597. V. 37

LIVELY, PENELOPE

Moon Tiger. London: 1987. V. 45

LIVERANI, G.

Five Centuries of Italian Majolica. 1960. V. 42

LIVERANI, GIUSEPPE

Five Centuries of Italian Majolica. New York: 1960. V. 38; 42

Five Centuries of Italian Majolica. New York, Toronto & London: 1960. V. 39

LIVERMORE, ABIEL ABBOT

The War with Mexico Reviewed. Boston: 1850. V. 37

LIVERMORE, D. P.

Comfort in Sorrow: a Token for the Bereaved. Chicago: 1866. V. 44

LIVERMORE, GEORGE

An Historical Research . . . Opinions of the Founders of the Republic of Negroes as Slaves, as Citizens and as Soldiers. Boston: 1862. V. 38; 40

LIVERMORE, MARY

My Story of the War: a Woman's Narrrative of Four Years Personal Experience as a Nurse in the Union Army . . . Hartford: 1889. V. 42

My Story of the War: a Woman's Narrative of Four Years Personal Experience as a Nurse in the Union Army . . . Hartford: 1890. V. 41; 45

LIVERMORE, SAMUEL T.

A History of Block Island from Its Discovery in 1514, to the Present Time, 1876. Hartford: 1877. V. 40

LIVERMORE, THOMAS LEONARD

History of the Eighteenth New Hampshire Volunteers 1864-65. Boston: 1904. V. 42

THE LIVERPOOL And Manchester Photographic Journal. 1858. V. 37

LIVERPOOL, CECIL GEORGE SAVILE, 4TH EARL

Catalogue of Portraits, Miniatures, etc. in the Possession . . . Hull: 1905. V. 38

LIVERPOOL, CHARLES JENKINSON, 1ST EARL OF 1727-1808

A Treatise on the Coins of the Realm in a Letter to the King. Oxford: 1805. V. 37; 38; 39; 40; 41; 45

A Treatise of the Coins of the Realm: in a Letter to the King. London: 1880. V. 42

LIVERPOOL, ROBERT BANKS JENKINSON, 2ND EARL OF

The Speech of the Right Hon. The Earl of Liverpool, in the House of Lords, on Friday the 26th of May, 1820, on a Motion of the Marquis of Lansdown, 'That a Select Committee Be Appointed to Inquire into the Means of Extending and Securing the Foreign . . . London: 1820. V. 40; 43

LIVERSEEGE, HENRY

Engravings from the Works of Henry Liverseege. London: 1835. V. 40; 46

A LIVERYMAN'S Reply to Sir Crisp Gascoigne's Address. London: 1754. V. 46

LIVES and Confessons of John Williams, Francis Frederick, John P. Rog, and Peter Peterson, Who Were Tried at the United States Circuit Court in Boston, for Murder and Piracy, Sentenced to be Executed Jan. 21, 1819 and afterwards reprieved . . . Boston: 1819. V. 42

THE LIVES and Last Wills and Testaments of the Following Eminent Persons. I. Dr. Gilbert Burnet . . . II. Dr. Thomas Burnet . . . III. Dr. George Hickes . . . IV. Dr. Daniel Williams . . . V. Joseph Addison . . . VI. Mr. Mahomet . . . with several other valuable tracts . . . London: 1728. V. 39

THE LIVES of all the Lords Chancellors, Lords Keepers and Lord Commissioners, of the Great Seal of England . . . London: 1708. V. 40

THE LIVES of the Ancient Philosophers, Containing An Account of their Several Sects, Doctrines, Actions and Remarkable Sayings . . . With an Appendix containing the Lives of Several Later Philosophers not confined to particular Sects . . . NewboroughL: 1702. V. 37

LIVES, Trials, Behaviour, Execution and the Last Dying Words of ARthur Thistlewood, William Davidson, James Ings, John Thoms Brunt and Richard Tidd, for High Treason. Stood: 1820. V. 40

LIVESAY, DOROTHY

Day and Night. Poems. Toronto: 1944. V. 43

Green Pitcher. Toronto: 1928. V. 43

Poems for People. Toronto: 1947. V. 43

Signpost. Toronto: 1932. V. 43

LIVING English Poets. London: 1883. V. 43

LIVINGS, F.

Twelve White Flowers. London: 1888. V. 44

LIVINGSTON, EDWARD

An Answer to Mr. Jefferson's Justification of His Conduct in the Case of the New Orleans Batture. Philadelphia: 1813. V. 40

A Faithful Picture of the Political Situation of New Orleans. Boston: 1808. V. 37

Introductory Report to the Code of Prison Discipline; Explanatory of the Principles on Which the Code is Founded. London: 1827. V. 41; 45

Introductory Report to the Code of Prison Discipline . . . Being Part of the System of Penal law Prepared for the State of Louisiana. Philadelphia: 1827. V. 37

A Personal History of the San Francisco Earthquake and Fire of 1906. 1941. V. 38

Remarks on the Expediency of Abolishing the Punishment of Death. Philadelphia: 1831. V. 43

Report Made to the General Assembly of the State of Louisiana, on the Plan of a Penal Code fro the Said State. New Orleans: 1822. V. 38

LIVINGSTON, EDWIN B.

The Livingstons of Callendar and their Principal Cadets. (Edinburgh): 1887-92. V. 37

LIVINGSTON, FLORA

Bibliography of the Works of Rudyard Kipling. New York: 1927. V. 43

LIVINGSTON, JOHN

Catalogue of Law Books, Comprising a Catalogue of a Select Law Library. New York: 1856. V. 45

LIVINGSTON, JOHN A.

Birds of the Northern Forest. Toronto: 1977. V. 42

Birds of the Eastern Forest. Two Volumes. Paintings by J. Fenwick Lansdowne. Text by John A. Livingston. Toronto and Montreal: c. 1968-70. V. 37

LIVINGSTON, JOHN HENRY

The Constitution of the Reformed Dutch Church, in the United States of America. New York: 1793. V. 41

Two Sermons, Delivered Before the New York Missionary Society . . . New York: 1799. V. 42

LIVINGSTON, LUTHER

A Bibliography of the First Editions In Book Form of the Writings of Charles and Mary Lamb. New York: 1903. V. 40

Franklin and His Press at Passy. New York: 1914. V. 38; 40; 45

LIVINGSTON, PHILIP

the Other Side of the Question; or, a Defence of the Liberties of North America. New York: 1774. V. 45

LIVINGSTON, ROBERT R.

Essay on Sheep: Their Varities - Account of the Merinoes of Spain, France, etc. New York: 1809. V. 40

Essay on Sheep: Their Varieties--Account of the Merinoes . . . Reflections on the Best Method of Treating Them and Raising a Flock in the United States . . . Concord: 1813. V. 44

LIVINGSTON, WILLIAM

A Funeral Elogium on the Reverend Mr. Aaron Burr, Late President of the College of New Jersey. New York: 1758. V. 45

The Papers of William Livingston. Trenton: 1979-87. V. 44

A Review of the Military Operations in North America . . . New York: 1770. V. 44; 46

LIVINGSTONE, DAVID 1813-1873

Dr. Livingstone's Cambridge Lectures. Cambridge: 1858. V. 38; 46

The Last Journals of David Livingstone, in Central Africa, from 1865 to His Death. London: 1874. V. 38; 41; 42; 46

The Last Journals of David Livingstone in Central Africa, from 1865 to His Death Continued by a Narrative of His Last Moments . . . New York: 1875. V. 45; 46

The Last Journals of David Livingstone in Central Africa, from 1865 to His Death. London: 1880. V. 45

Life and Explorations, Carefully Compiled from Reliable Sources . . . London: 1875. V. 44

Livingstone's Travels and Researches in South Africa. Philadelphia: 1858. V. 40; 45

Missionary Travels and Researches in South Africa. London: 1857. V. 38; 39; 40; 41; 42; 43; 44; 45; 46

Missionary Travels and Researches in South Africa. New York: 1858. V. 37; 38; 41; 43; 45; 46

A Narrative of Dr. Livingston's (sic) Discoveries in South-Central Africa, from 1849 to 1856. London: 1857. V. 39

Narrative of an Expedition to the Zambesi and Its Tributaries; and of the Discovery of the Lakes Shirwa and Nyassa. London: 1865. V. 40; 42; 43

Narrative of an Expedition to the Zambesi and Its Tributaries. New York: 1866. V. 37; 39; 41; 42; 46

The Zambesi Expedition of David Livingstone 1858 to 1863. London: 1956. V. 45

LIVINGSTONE, PAEDAR

The Monaghan Story. Enniskillen: 1980. V. 43

LIVINGSTONE, PHILIP

The Other Side of the Question; or, a Defence of the Liberties of North America. New York: 1774. V. 42; 44

LIVINGSTONE, WILLIAM

A Funeral Elogium on the Reverend Mr. Aaron Burr, Late President of the College of New Jersey. New York/Boston: 1758. V. 37

LIVIUS, TITUS

Ab Urbe Condita Libri Qui Extant XXXXV. Venice: 1592. V. 40

LIVIUS, TITUS continued

Decas Tertia. Venice: 1519. V. 37

The First Five Books of the Roman History. Edinburgh: 1722. V. 39

The First Five Books of the Roman History. Edinburgh: 1822. V. 37; 40

Historae Romanae Decades. Milan: 1495. V. 39

Latinae Historiae Principis Decades tres cum Dimidia . . . Basiliae: 1539. V. 39

Romanae Historiae Decades Tres, cvm Dimidia, Partim Caelii Secvndi Cvrionis Industria, Partim Collatione Meliorum Codicum Iterum Diligenter Emendatae. Basileae: 1555. V. 39

Historiaraum ab Urbe Condita, Libri qui Exstant XXXV, cum Universae Historiae Eptimois Caroli Sigonii Scholia . . . Multis in Partibus Aucta. Venice: 1572. V. 37

Historiarum ab Urbe Condita. Cum Universae Historiae Epitomis a Carolo Sigonio Emendati. Venice: 1555. V. 45

Historiarum Quod Extant, cum Perpetuis Caroli Signonii et J. Fr. Gronovii Notis . . . Amsterdam: 1679. V. 46

Historiarum ab Urbe Condita Libri Qui Supersunt, cum Omnium Epitomis . . . Edinburgh: 1751. V. 45

Historiarum ab Urbe condita . . . Boston: 1788. V. 45

Historiarum Libri . . . Oxonii Impensis: 1840/41. V. 46

The Romane Historie Written By . . . London: 1600. V. 37; 38; 39; 46

Historiarum Libri. Leyden: 1634. V. 38; 42

The History of Rome. London: 1952-67. V. 45

The History of Early Rome. New York: 1970. V. 38

The History of Early Rome. Verona: 1970. V. 46

Latinae Historiae Principis Decades Tres, cum . . . Emendatiores . . . Caelii Secundi Curionis.. Basileae: 1549. V. 37

T. Liuii Patauini, Historiarum ab Urbe Condita, Libri, qui Extant, XXXV. Venetiis: 1555. V. 37

T. Livius Patavinus Historicus. Duobus Libris Auctus Cum L. Flori Epitome. Mainz: 1518. V. 37

LE LIVRE de la Verite de Parole. Paris: 1929. V. 39

LE LIVRE de Quatre Couleurs. Paris: 1760. V. 43

LIVRE d'Images Parlantes Pour Amuser les Chers Bebes. Paris: 1885. V. 46

LE LIVRE et Ses Amis. Paris: 1945-47. V. 40

LE LIVRE Rouge . . . Paris: 1790. V. 46

LES LIVRES de l'Enfance Du XVe Au XIXe Siecle. London: 1978. V. 40

LIVRES de Prieres, tisse d'Apres les Enluminures des Manuscrits du XIVe au XVIe siecle. Lyon: 1886-87. V. 46

LIVY

The History of Early Rome. Verona: 1970. V. 43

LIZARS, JOHN 1783-1860

A System of Anatomical Plates of the Human Body . . . Edinburgh: 1822-26. V. 41

A System of Anatomical Plates of the Human Body. Edinburgh: ca. 1825. V. 37

LIZARS, ROBINA

In the Days of the Canada Company. Toronto: 1896. V. 38; 42

LIZARS, WILLIAM HOME

Eight Engravings of the Ruins Occasioned by the Great Fires in Edinburgh on the 15th, 16th and 17th Novr. 1824. Edinburgh: 1825. V. 39

Eight Engravings of the Ruins Occasioned by the Great Fires in Edinburgh on the 15th, 16th and 17th Novr. 1824. Edinburgh: 1825? V. 42

LLANOS Y GUTIERREZ, VALENTIN MARIA

Don Esteban; or Memoirs of a Spaniard. London: 1825. V. 40

Don Esteban; or, Memoirs of a Spaniard. London: 1826. V. 42

LLEWELLYN, MARTIN

Men-Miracles. London: 1679. V. 39

LLEWELLYN, RICHARD

How Green Was My Valley. London: 1939. V. 37; 39; 41; 42; 46

None but the Lonely Heart. London: 1943. V. 37

LLEWELYN, THOMAS

Historical and Critical Remarks on the British Tongue and Its Connection with Other Languages Founded On Its State in the Welsh Bible. London: 1769. V. 42

LLORENTE, JUAN ANTONIO

The History of the Inquisition of Spain, from the Time of Its Establishment to the Reign of Ferdinand VII . . . London: 1826. V. 42

LLOYD, A. ALAN

Some Outstanding Clocks over Seven Hundred Years, 1250-1950. London: 1958. V. 37

LLOYD, A. B.

In Dwarf Land and Cannibal Country, a Record of Travel and Discovery in Central Africa. London: 1899. V. 46

LLOYD, BENJAMIN E.

Lights and Shades in San Franciso. San Francisco: 1876. V. 40

LLOYD, CHARLES

The Anatomy of a Late Negotiation. London: 1763. V. 37; 38

The Conduct of the Late Administration Examined. London: 1767. V. 40; 41

Desultory Thoughts in London, Titus and Gisippus, with Other Poems. London: 1821. V. 41

Nugae Canorae. Poems. London: 1819. V. 39

Poems on Various Subjects. Carlisle: 1795. V. 46

The Tragedies of Vittorio Alfieri. London: 1815. V. 43

LLOYD, DAVID

Desgrifiad O Diriogaeth Wisconsin, a Rhai o'R Taleithian A'r Tiriogaethau Agosap Idoi Yn Mharthau Gorllewinol Unol Daleithiau America. Bangor: 1845. V. 39

Economy of Agriculture. Germantown: 1832. V. 41

Fair Warnings to a Careless World; In the Pious Letters Written by the Right Honourable James Earl of Marleburgh, A Little Before His Death . . . London: 1665. V. 43

Memoires of the Lives, Actions, Sufferings and Deaths of those . . . Personages that Suffered by Death, Sequestration, decimation, or Otherwise for the Protestant Religion . . . from the Year 1637 to . . . 1660 . . . continued to 1666. London: 1668. V. 38; 46

State-Worthies; or, the Statesmen and Favourites of England from the Reformation to the Revolution. London: 1766. V. 39

State-Worthies, or the Statesman and Favourites of England since the Reformation . . . during the Reigns of King Henry VIII, Edward VI, Queen Mary, Queen Elizabeth, King James and King Charles I. London: 1670. V. 37; 38; 41

The States-Men and Favourites of England Since the Reformation. London: 1665. V. 38; 41

LLOYD, E. W.

Artillery: Its Progress and Present Position. Portsmouth: 1893. V. 42

LLOYD, EVAN

The Powers of the Pen, a Poem Addressed to Jon Curre, Esqr. London: 1766. V. 39

LLOYD, FREDERICK

Life of Viscount Nelson, Also of Sir R. Abercrombie and Marquis Cornwallis. Omskirk: 1806. V. 44

LLOYD-GEORGE, DAVID LLOYD GEORGE, 1ST EARL OF 1863-1945

War Memoirs. London: 1933. V. 40

LLOYD, HENRY

The History of the Late War in Germany Between the King of Prussia, and the Empress of Germany and Her Allies . . . London: 1766. V. 38

The History of the Late War in Germany, Between the King of Prussia, and the Empress of Germany and Her Allies. London: 1781. V. 40

LLOYD, HENRY DEMAREST

Wealth Against Commonwealth. New York: 1894. V. 39

LLOYD, HUMPHREY

Elementary Treatise on the Wave-Theory of Light. London: 1857. V. 40

A Treatise on Light and Vision. London: 1831. V. 44; 45

LLOYD, J. U.

The Chemistry of Medicine . . . Cincinnati: 1881. V. 42

LLOYD, JAMES T.

Lloyd's Steamboat Directory, and Disasters on the Western Waters, Containing the History of the First Application of Steam . . . Cincinnati: 1856. V. 38; 42

LLOYD, JOHN

The Early History of the Old South Wales Iron Works 1760 to 1840. London: 1906. V. 44

Historical Memoranda of Breconshire; a Collection of Papers . . . 1903. V. 42

Thesaurus Ecclesiasticus . . . London: 1796. V. 44

LLOYD, JOHN URI

Etidorphia or the End of the Earth. Cincinnatti: 1896. V. 42

Etidorpha or the End of the Earth. New York: 1901. V. 42

The Right Side of the Car. Boston: 1897. V. 41

LLOYD, JONES

Caneuon Ceiriog Detholiad. Newtown: 1925. V. 45

LLOYD-JONES, W.

Havash! Frontier Adventures in Kenya. London: 1925. V. 39

LLOYD, LLEWELLYN

Field Spots of the North of Europe: Comprised in a Personal Narrative of a Residence in Sweden and Norway in the Years 1827-28. London: 1830. V. 39; 43

Field Sports of the North of Europe. London: 1831. V. 39

The Field Sports of the North of Europe . . . London: 1885. V. 43; 44

The Game Birds and Wild Fowl of Sweden and Norway; Together with an Account of the Seals and Salt Water Fishes of those Countries. London: 1867. V. 37; 40; 42; 43; 45

Scandinavian Adventures During a Residence of Upwards of Twenty Years. London: 1854. V. 39; 40; 43

LLOYD, LODOWICK

The Marrow of History, or the Pilgrimage of Kings and Princes, Truly Representing the Variety of Dangers Inherent to Their Crowns . . . London: 1653. V. 41

The Stratagems of Ierusalem: with the Martiall Lawes and Militarie Discipline, as Well of the Iewes, as of the Gentiles. London: 1602. V. 39

LLOYD, MARY

Meditations on divine Subjects . . . . New London: 1802. V. 40

LLOYD, MILDRED

Type and the Alphabet. Lafayette: 1973. V. 42

LLOYD, NATHANIEL

Garden Craftsmanship in Yew and Box. London: 1925. V. 42

A History of English Brickwork. London: 1925. V. 42; 45

A History of the English House. 1931. V. 45; 46

A History of the English House from Primitive Times to the Victorian Period. London: 1949. V. 39

History of the English House from Primitive Times to the Victorian Period. London: 1951. V. 40; 43

LLOYD, ROBERT

The Actor. A Poetical Epistle to Bonnell Thornton. London: 1760. V. 37; 38

The Actor. A Poem By . . . London: 1926. V. 42; 44

Poems. London: 1762. V. 37; 38; 39; 40; 41; 42; 43; 45

The Poetical Works.. London: 1774. V. 41; 42; 45; 46

Shakespeare: an Epistle (in verse) to Mr. Garrick; with an Ode to Genius. London: 1760. V. 39; 40; 42; 45

LLOYD, SETON

Beycesultan. London: 1962. V. 40

LLOYD, THOMAS

The Trials of William S. Smith and Samuel G. Ogden, for Misdeameanours . . . New York: 1807. V. 42; 43; 44

LLOYD THOMAS, M. G.

Traveller's Verse. London: 1946. V. 38

Travellers' Verse. London: 1946. V. 42

Travellers' Verse. London: 1947. V. 46

LLOYD, THOMAS W.

History of Lycoming County, Pennsylvania. Topeka: 1929. V. 46

LLOYD, W. W.

P. & O. Pencillings. London: 1895. V. 40

LLOYD, WILLIAM

Narrative of a Journey from Caunpoor to the Boorendo Pass in the Himalaya Mountains, via Gwalior, Agra, delhi and Sirhind . . . London: 1840. V. 43

Narrative of a Journey from Caunpoor to the Boordeno Pass in the Himalaya Mountains, Via Gwalior, Agra, Delhi and Sirhind . . . London: 1846. V. 45

The Pretences of the French Invasion Examined. London: 1692. V. 44

LLOYD, WILLIAM P.

History of the First Regiment Pennyslvania Reserve Cavalry. Philadelphia: 1864. V. 46

LLOYD, WILLIAM WATKISS

Elijah Fenton: His Poetry and Friends. 1894. V. 46

Elijah Fenton: His Poetry and Friends. Hanley: 1894. V. 43

LLOYD, WILLIAM WHITELOCK

Union Jottings. London: 1896. V. 46

LLOYD, WILLIAM WHITLOCK

On Active Service. London: 1890. V. 44

LLOYDS, F.

Practical Guide to Scene Painting and Painting in Distemper. London: 1875. V. 44

Practical Guide to Scene Painting and Painting in Distemper. London: 1870's? V. 37

Practical Guide to Scene Painting and Painting on Distemper. London: 1860. V. 38

LLOYD'S Nataural History. London: 1896-97. V. 37

LLUELYN, MARTIN

Men-Miracles. With Other Poems. N.P.: Oxford: 1646. V. 39

LLWYD, RICHARD

Beaumaris Bay, a Poem. Chester: 1800. V. 37

The Poetical Works . . . London: 1837. V. 45

LLYFR y Pregeth-Wr. Newtown: 1927. V. 41

LOBB, THEOPHILUS.

Medicinal Letters. London: 1763. V. 38

LOBDELL, LUCY

Narrative of Lucy Ann Dobdell, the Female Hunter of Delaware and Sullivan Counties. New York: 1855. V. 39

LOBEL, MATHIAS DE

Plantarum Seu Stripium Historia . . . (with) Nova Stirpium Adversaria, Perfacilis Vestigatio, Luculenta qua Accessio ad Priscorum . . . Antwerp: 1576. V. 39

LOBEL MATTHIAS DE

Seu Stirpium Historia . . . Cui Annexum est Adversariorum Volumen . . . Antwerp: 1676. V. 39

LOBENSTINE, BELLE W.

Extracts from the Diary of William C. Lobenstine. December 31, 1851-1858. N.P.: 1920. V. 46

LOBENSTINE, WILLIAM C.

Extracts from the Diary of William C. Lobenstine Dec. 31, 1851-1858. N.P.: 1920. V. 40; 42

Extracts from the Diary of William C. Lobenstine Dec. 31, 1851-1858. 1920. V. 39; 42

LOBO, JERONYMO 1596?-1678

A Voyage to Abyssinia. London: 1735. V. 37; 38; 40; 41; 42; 44; 45

A Voyage to Abyssinia. London: 1789. V. 44; 45

A Voyage to Abyssinia. London: 1789. V. 37

LOBSCHEID, WILLIAM

English and Chinese Dictionary, with the Punti and Mandarin Prnunciation. Hong Kong: 1886-9. V. 43

LOBSTEIN, JOHANN FRIEDRICH DANIEL

A Treatise on the Structure, Function and Diseases of the Human Sympathetic Nerve. Philadelphia: 1831. V. 38; 45; 46

Treatise Upon the Semeiology of the Eye, for the Use of Physicians . . . New York: 1830. V. 45

LOBWASSER, AMBROSIUS

Die Psalmen Davids . . . In Teutsche Reimen Gebracht, Samt andern Haus-Gesaengen. St. Gallen: 1709-15. V. 38

LOCATION Register of Twentieth-Century English Literary Manuscripts and Letters. A Union List of Papers of Modern English, Irish, Scottish and Welsh Authors in the British Isles. London: 1988. V. 42

LOCCENIUS, JOHANNES

Rervm Svecicaraum Historia A Rege Berone Tertio Usque ad Ericum Decimum Quartum Deducta . . . Stockholm: 1654. V. 37

LOCH, JAMES

An Account of the Improvements on the Estates of the Marquess of Stafford in the Counties of Stafford and Salop, and on the Estate of Sutherland. London: 1820. V. 37

Memoir of George Granville, Late Duke of Sutherland. London: 1834. V. 41

LOCHEE, LEWIS

Elements of Fortification. London: 1780. V. 38

A System of Military Mathematics. London: 1776. V. 37

LOCHER, J. L.

Escher: With a Complete Catalogue of the Graphic Works . . . London: 1981. V. 42

LOCKE, JOHN 1632-1704 continued

The Works of John Locke Esq. London: 1727. V. 41

The Works. London: 1751. V. 39

The Works of John Locke, Esq. London: 1759. V. 37; 41; 43; 45

The Works of . . . London: 1777. V. 46

The Works. London: 1801. V. 37; 39; 40; 42; 44; 46

The Works. London: 1823. V. 39

The Clarendon Edition of the Works. London: 1970-1988. V. 41

LOCKE, L. L.

The Ancient Quipu or, Peruvian Knot Record, by L.L. Locke. New York: 1923. V. 37

LOCKE, RICHARD

The Circle Squared. London: 1730. V. 39; 40

LOCKE, SAMUEL

Die Verbindung und Uebereinanderstellung de Saulen, oder Anweisung wie bey der Baukunst die funf Saulenordnungen auf Eine Sehr Leichte und Bequeme Art . . . Dresden: 1783. V. 44

LOCKE, WILLIAM J.

Flower of the Rose - a Romantic Play. London: 1909. V. 41

LOCKE WYNNE, JOHN

An Abridgement of Mr. Locke's Essay concerning Humane Understainding. The Second Edition, Corrected and Enlarged. London: 1700. V. 37

LOCKER, EDWARD HAWKE

Memoirs of Celebrated Naval Commanders, from Howard to Nelson . . . London: 1831-32. V. 39

Memoirs of Celebrated Naval Commanders . . . London: 1832. V. 38

Views in Spain. London: 1824. V. 45

LOCKER-LAMPSON, FREDERICK 1821-1895

An Appendix to the Rowfant Library. London: 1900. V. 41

A Catalogue of the Printed Books, Manuscripts, Autograph Letters, Drawings and Pictures Collected by Frederick Locker-Lampson. (with) Appendix to the Rowfant Library; a Catalogue. London: 1886/1900. V. 39

London Lyrics. London: 1881. V. 39; 41; 42; 43

London Rhymes. London: 1882. V. 42

London Lyrics. London: 1885. V. 42

Memories of Men, Places and Things. London: 1895. V. 41

Poems by . . . London: 1868. V. 37; 41

A Selection from the Works of . . . London: 1864. V. 46

A Selection from the Works of . . . London: 1865. V. 38; 39; 43

LOCKER-LAMPSON, GODFREY

An Appendix to the Rowfant Library. A Catalogue of the Printed Books, Manuscripts, Autograph Letters, etc, Collected Since the Printing of the First Catalouge . . . London: 1900. V. 43

LOCKER-LAMPSON, HANNAH JANE LAMPSON

What the Blackbird Said. London: 1881. V. 38

LOCKHART, GEORGE

The Case of Mr. Greenshields, Fully Stated and Discuss'd in a Letter from a Commoner of North Britain, to an English Peer. Edinburgh?: 1711. V. 45

The Lockhart Papers . . . Published from Original Manuscripts in the Possession of Anthony Aufrere, of Hoveton, Norfolk. London: 1817. V. 39

Memoirs Concerning the Affairs of Scotland, from Queen Anne's Accession to the Throne, to the Commencement of the Union of the Two Kingdoms of Scotland and England, in May 1707 . . . London: 1714. V. 38; 42; 43; 46

LOCKHART, JOHN GIBSON 1784-1854

Ancient Spanish Ballads: Historical & Romantic. Edinburgh: 1823. V. 39

Ancient Spanish Ballads: Historical and Romantic. London: 1841. V. 38; 42; 43; 44; 46

Ancient Spanish Ballads: Historical and Romantic. London: 1842. V. 39; 44; 45

The History of Matthew Wald. Edinburgh: 1824. V. 40; 43

Janus; or, the Edinburgh Literary Alamanck. Edinburgh: 1826. V. 42

Life of Sir Walter Scott, Bart. Edinburgh: 1853. V. 39

Life of Robert Burns. Edinburgh: 1828. V. 37

The Life of Robert Burns. Liverpool: 1914. V. 37

The Life of Sir Walter Scott. Edinburgh: 1902-03. V. 37

Lockhart's Spanish Ballads. London: 1856. V. 39

Memoirs of the Life of Sir Walter Scott. Edinburgh: 1837. V. 41

Memoirs of the Life of Sir Scott, Bart. Edinburgh: 1837-38. V. 37; 39; 42; 44

Memoirs of the Life of Sir Walter Scott. London: 1837-38. V. 46

Memoirs of the Life of Sir Walter Scott. Paris: 1838. V. 38

Memoirs of the Life of Sir Walter Scott. Philadelphia: 1838. V. 39

Memoirs of the Life of Sir Walter Scott, Bart. Edinburgh: 1839. V. 37; 39; 40; 42

Memoirs of Sir William Scott. London: 1914. V. 42

Peter's Letters to His Kinfolk. Edinburgh: 1819. V. 39; 46

Peter's Letters to His Kinsfolk. Edinburgh, London & Glasgow: 1819. V. 38

Reginald Dalton. Edinburgh: 1823. V. 37; 39; 46

Reginald Dalton. Edinburgh & London: 1823. V. 38

Valerius: a Roman Story. Edinburgh: 1821. V. 39; 41; 43; 44; 46

LOCKHART, ROBERT BRUCE

My Rod My Comfort. London: 1949. V. 37; 45

LOCKHART, STEVE

The Lockhart Papers. London: 1817. V. 42

LOCKHART, WILLIAM

The Medical Missionary in China: a Narrative of Twenty Years Experience. London: 1861. V. 43

LOCKMAN, JOHN

The Entertaining Instructor; in French and English. London: 1765. V. 38; 46

A New Roman History, by Question and Answer in a Method Much More Comprehensive Than Any of the Kind Extant Extracted from Ancient Authors and the Most Celebrated Among the Modern. London: 1754. V. 38

Pastoral Stanzas. London: 1743. V. 37

Travels of the Jesuits, Into Various Parts of the World . . . London: 1743. V. 45

Travels of the Jesuits, into Various Parts of the World. London: 1743-62; V. 40

Travels of the Jesuits, into Various Parts of the World . . . London: 1743/62. V. 41

Travels of the Jesuits, Into Various Parts of the World. London: 1762. V. 41

LOCKRIDGE, RICHARD

Mr. and Mrs. North. New York: 1936. V. 46

LOCKRIDGE, ROSS

Raintree County. Boston: 1948. V. 45

LOCKWOOD, ALICE G. B.

Gardens of Colony and State. New York: 1931. V. 37; 39; 42

LOCKWOOD, C. B.

My Trip to California in 1850. Daytona, Fla.: 1910. V. 37

LOCKWOOD, FRANK C.

The Apache Indians. New York: 1938. V. 39

Arizona Characters. Los Angeles: 1928. V. 39

The Life of Edward E. Ayer. Chicago: 1929. V. 39

Pioneer Days in Arizona. New York: 1932. V. 37; 39; 40; 44; 45; 46

Story of the Spanish Missions of the Middle Southwest. Santa Ana: 1934. V. 42; 43; 44

LOCKWOOD, HENRY FRANCIS

The History and Antiquities of the Fortifications to the City of York. London: 1834. V. 42

LOCKWOOD, JAMES D.

Life and Adventures of a Drummer Boy or Seven Years a Soldier. Albany: 1893. V. 44

LOCKWOOD, JOHN H.

Westfield and Its Historic Influences 1669-1919. 1922. V. 37

LOCKWOOD, JOSEPH

Guide to St. Helena, Descriptive and Historical with a Visit to Longwood and Napoleon's Tomb. St. Helena: 1851. V. 40

LOCKWOOD, LUKE VINCENT

Colonial Furniture in America. New York: 1901. V. 39

Colonial Furniture in America. London: 1902. V. 39

Colonial Furniture in America. New York: 1926. V. 38; 39; 41

LOCKWOOD, M. S.

Art Embroidery. A Treatise on the Revived Practice of Decorative Needlework. London: 1878. V. 41; 43

A Treatise on the Revived Practice of Decorative Needlework. London: 1878. V. 42

LOCKWOOD, RUFUS A.

The Vigilance Committee of San Francisco. Metcalf vs. Argenti et al. Speech of R. A. Lockwood. San Francisco: 1852. V. 40

LOCKYER, CHARLES

An Account of the Trade in India . . . London: 1711. V. 40; 43

LOCOMOBILE COMPANY OF AMERICA

The Locomobile Book. A Description of the Latest Models. Bridgeport: 1915. V. 37

LOCUS Solus I–V. Mallorca: 1961–62. V. 37

LODDIGE, CONRAD & SONS

The Botanical Cabinet. London: 1818/21/23. V. 41

LODER, ROBERT

The Statutes, and Ordinances, for the Government of the Alms-Houses, in Woodbridge, in the County of Suffolk. Woodbridge: 1792. V. 42; 46

LODEWIJCKSZ, WILLEM

Premier Livre de l'Histoire de la Navigation aux Indes Orientales par les Hollandois . . . Amsterdam: 1598. V. 39

LODGE, DAVID

The British Museum is Falling Down. London: 1965. V. 38

Ginger You're Barmy. London: 1962. V. 38

Rolfe's Bestiary. Aylesford: 1961. V. 40

Rolfe's Bestiary. N.P.: 1963. V. 44

LODGE, EDMUND

Life of Sir Julius Caesar, Knt. Judge of the High Court of Admiralty, Master of the Rolls, Chancellor of the Exechequer, and a Privy Councellor to King James, and Charles, the First . . . London: 1810. V. 39

The Peerage, Baronetage, Knightage and Companionage of the British Empire. London: 1905. V. 44

Portraits of Illustrious Personages of Great Britain . . . London: 1821. V. 44

Portraits of Illustrious Personages of Great Britain. London: 1835. V. 37; 39

Portraits of Illustrious Personages of Great Britain. London: 1844–50. V. 46

Portraits of Illustrious Personages of Great Britain. London: 1849. V. 37; 41

Portraits of Illustrious Personages of Great Britain . . . London: 1860. V. 39

Portraits of Illustrious Personages of Great Britain. Boston: 1902. V. 42

Portraits of Illustrious Personages of Great Britain, engraved from authentic pictures in the galleries of the nobility, and the public collections of the country, with biographical and historical memoirs, etc. London: (c. 1860). V. 37

LODGE, G.

Memoirs of an Artist Naturalist. London: 1946. V. 37; 39; 40; 43

LODGE, HENRY CABOT

Hero Tales. New York: 1897. V. 46

Life and Letters of George Cabot. Boston: 1877. V. 46

LODGE, JOHN

Introductory Sketches, Towards a Topographical History, of the County of Hereford. Kington: 1793. V. 37; 40; 43

LODGE, OLIVER

The Work of Hertz and Some of His Successors, Being the Substance of a Lecture Delivered at the Royal Inst. on June 1, 1894. London: 1894. V. 39

LODGE, OLIVER J.

Signalling Across the Space Without Wires. New York: 1906? V. 41

LODGE, THOMAS

Glaucus and Silla with Other Lyrical and Pastoral Poems. 1819. V. 43

Rosalynde. New Rochelle: 1902. V. 42

LODOISKA; or, the Tartar Robber. London: 1810. V. 44

LOEB, HAROLD

Technocracy. The Plan of Plenty. Los Angeles: 1933. V. 46

LOEB, ISADOR

Debates of the Missouri Constitutional Convention of 1875 . . . Columbia: 1803/1944. V. 44

Debates of the Missouri Constitutional Convention of 1875 . . . Columbia: 1830, 1944. V. 40; 42

LOEB, JACQUES 1859–1924

Comparative Physiology of the Brain and Comparative Psychology. New York: 1900. V. 45

LOEBER, E. G.

Paper Mould and Mouldmaker. Amsterdam: 1982. V. 43

Paper Mould and Mouldmaker. Amsterdam: 1983. V. 38

LOEHR, CHARLES THEODORE

War History of the Old First Virginia Infantry Regiment, Army of Northern Virginia. Richmond: 1884. V. 38; 44

LOEHR, MAX

Chinese Bronze Age Weapons: The Werner Jannings Collection in the Chinese National Palace Museum. Ann Arbor: 1956. V. 41

LOENING, GROVER C.

Military Aeroplanes . . . London: 1916. V. 40

LOESCHER, VALENTIN ERNST 1673–1749

Vollstandige Reformations - Acta und Documenta, Oder Umstandliche Vorstellung des Evangelischen Reformations-Wercks . . . Leipzig: 1720/23/29. V. 38

LOEWE, EDWARD JOSEPH

Ferns British and Exotic. London: 1872. V. 44

LOEWE, LOUIS

A Dictionary of the Circassian Language. London: 1854. V. 41

LOEWY, RAYMOND

Industrail Design. Woodstock: 1979. V. 46

The Locomotive. London: 1937. V. 44

Locomotive, the New Vision. Norwich;: 1937. V. 42

LOFFT, CAPELL

Laura: or an Anthology of Sonnets . . . London: 1814-1813-1814. V. 39; 40; 46

LOFTHOUSE, J.

A Thousand Miles from a Post Office. London: 1922. V. 42

LOFTIE, W. J.

Lessons in the Art of Illuminating, With Practical Instructions and a Sketch of the History of the Art, by W.J. Loftie. London: (late 1970s). V. 37

Orient Line Guide - Chapters for Travellers by Sea. London: 1890. V. 39

LOFTING, HUGH

Doctor Dolittle's Caravan. New York: 1926. V. 44

Doctor Doolittle in the Moon. New York: 1928. V. 45

Gub Gub's Book. London: 1932. V. 42

LOFTUS, CHARLES

My Youth by Sea and Land From 1809 to 1816. London: 1876. V. 44

LOFTUS, WILLIAM

The Brewer: a Familiar Treatise on the Art of Brewing. London: 1857. V. 37; 41; 43; 46

LOFTUS, WILLIAM KENNETT

Travels and Researches in Chaldaea and Susiana . . . London: 1857. V. 46

LOGAN, ELIZA

St. Johnstoun; or, John Earl of Gowrie. Edinburgh: 1823. V. 37; 38; 42; 46

LOGAN JACK, ROBERT

Northmost Australia Three Centuries of Exploration, Discovery and Adventure in and Around the Cape York Peninsula, Queensland . . . London: 1921. V. 41

LOGAN, JAMES

The Clans of the Scottish Highlands, Illustrated by Appropriate Figures . . . London: 1845-47. V. 39; 42

The Clans of the Scottish Highlands, Illustrated by Appropriate Figures, Displaying their Dress, Arms, Tartans, Armorial Insignia and Social Occupations . . . London: 1847. V. 37

The Scottish Gael, or Celtic Manners as preserved among the Highlanders . . . London: 1831. V. 37

LOGAN, JOHN

The House That Jack Built . . . Omaha: 1974. V. 42

Poems. London: 1781. V. 40

Poems. Londonderry?: 1872. V. 37

LOGAN, JOHN H.

A History of the Upper Country of South Carolina, from the Earliest Periods to the Close of the War of Independence. Charleston: 1859. V. 45

LOGAN, MARY SIMMERSON CUNNINGHAM 1838–1923

Reminiscences of a Soldier's Wife: an Autobiography. New York: 1913. V. 44

LOGAN, OLIVE

Apropos of Women and Theatres. New York: 1869. V. 39; 44; 45

Before the Footlight and Behind the Scenes. Philadelphia: 1870. V. 40; 43

LOGAN, SAMUEL C.

A City's Danger and Defense, or Issues and Results of the Strikes of 1877. Scranton: 1877. V. 42; 46

LOGAN, WALTER S.

Irrigation for Profit. N.P.: 1890. V. 45

LOGGAN, DAVID

Cantabrigia Illustrata, Sive Omnium Celeberrimae Istius Universitatis, Aularum, Bibliothecae Academicae, Scholarum Publicarum, Sacelli Coll. Regalis, nec Non Totius Oppidi Ichnographia. Cambridge: 1690. V. 45

Cantabrigia Illustrata . . . a Series of Views of the University and Colleges and of Eton College. Cambridge: 1905. V. 39; 40

LOGGIN, ROBERT

The Present Management of the Customs Being a Detection of Grand Frauds in That Branch of His Majesty's Royal Revenue to the Value of Five Hundred Thousand Pounds Per Annum . . . London: 1720, 1719. V. 42

LOGICAL Nonsense. The Works of Lewis Carroll . . . with an Introduction, Biography, Notes and a Bibliography. New York: 1934. V. 37

LOGIER, J. B.

A System of the Science of Music and Practical Compsotion.. London: 1827. V. 39

LOGOS. Tubingen: 1910-33. V. 39

LOGUE, CHRISTOPHER

Devil, Maggot, and Son. Tunbridge Wells: 1956. V. 37

The Girls. London: 1969. V. 37

Red Bird. Guildford: 1979. V. 37

Wand and Quadrant. Paris: 1953. V. 37

LOHENSTEIN, DANIEL CASPER VON 1635-1683

Werke. Breslau: 1685-89. V. 39; 41

LOHNIS, F.

Studies Upon the Life Cycles of the Bacteria. Part I. Review of the Literature 1838-1918. Washington: 1921. V. 45

LOLLIUS, ANTONIUS

Oratio Circumcisionis Dominicae Coram Innocentis VIII Habita. Rome: 1485. V. 44

LOLME, J. L. DE 1745-1807

The Constitution of England; or, An Account of the English Government. London: 1821. V. 41

The Constitution of England; In Which It Is Compared Both with the Republican Form of Government, and the Other Monarchies in Europe. London: 1826. V. 45

The History of the Flagellants. London: 1783. V. 40

LOMAN, AL

Remembering Carl Herzog: a Texas Printer and His Books. Dallas: 1985. V. 37

LOMAX, DAVID ALEXANDER NAPIER 1868-

A History of the Services of the 41st (the Welch) Regiment, (Now 1st Battalion the Welch Regiment) from Its Formation in 1719 to 1895. Davenport: 1899. V. 40

LOMAX, EDWARD

Encyclopedia of Architecture. London: 1852. V. 39

LOMAX, JAMES

Diary of Otter Hunting. From A.D. 1829 to 1871. 1910. V. 37

Otter Hunting Diary 1829 to 1871 of the Late James Lomax, Esq. of Clayton Hall. Blackburn: 1910. V. 37; 46

Otter Hunting Diary. London: 1910. V. 39

LOMAX, JOHN A.

American Ballads and Folk Songs. New York: 1934. V. 38; 39; 40; 41; 42; 46

Cowboy Songs and Other Frontier Ballads. New York: 1910. V. 38

Songs of the Cattle Trail and Cow Camp. New York: 1919. V. 38

LOMAX, THOMAS J.

Recollections of a Busy Life. Cresco: 1923. V. 43

LOMAZZO, GIOVANNI PAOLO 1538-1600

Trattato dell'Arte Della Pittura, Scoltura, et Architecttura . . . Milano: 1585. V. 38

A Tracte Containing the Artes of Curious Paintinge Caruinge & Buildinge. Oxford: 1598. V. 37; 38

LOMBARD, DANIEL

A Succinct History of Ancient and Modern Persecutions. London: 1747. V. 45

LOMBARDELI, ORAZIO

Gli Aforismi Scolastici. Siena: 1603. V. 42

LOMENIE DE BRIENNE, LOUIS HENRI

Actis, et Epistolis, Itinerarium. Parisiis: 1662. V. 38

LOMERIRUS, JOHANNES 1636-1699

De Veterum Gentilium Lustrationibus Syntagma. Utrecht: 1681. V. 40

LOMMIUS, JODOCUS

A Treatise of Continual Fevers . . . To Which are Added Medicinal Observations. London: 1732. V. 37

LONCIER, ADAM

Volstaendiges Kraeuterbuch. Augsburg: 1783. V. 44

LONDESBOROUGH, ALBERT DENISON, 1st BARON 1805-1860

Miscellanea Graphica: Represetations of Ancient, Mediaeval and Reanissance Remains in the Possession of Lord Londesborough. London: 1856. V. 46

Miscellanea Graphica: Representations of Ancient, Mediaeval and Renaissance Remains in the Possession of Lord Londesborough. London: 1857-54-57. V. 42

LONDON

Report Improvements and Town Planning Committee . . . London: 1944. V. 45

LONDON Almanack for the Year 1794. London. V. 39

LONDON Almanack for the Year 1795. London: 1795. V. 46

LONDON Almanack for the Year 1838. London: 1837. V. 46

LONDON Almanack for the Year of Christ 1779. London: 1779. V. 43

LONDON Almanack for the Year of Christ 1784. London: 1783. V. 38

LONDON Almanack for the Year of Christ 1787. V. 45

THE LONDON Almanack for the Year of Christ 1795. London: 1794. V. 38

LONDON Almanack for the Year of Christ 1810. London. V. 43

LONDON Almanack for the year of Christ 1812. (London): (1811). V. 37

LONDON & BLACKWALL RAILWAY

Statements Illustrative of the Necessity for Additional Means of Communication Between London and Blackwall. London: 1836. V. 46

THE LONDON and Country Brewer: a Treatise on Milling Science and Practice. (with) Recent Progress in Flour Manufacture, Supplement. London: 1888. V. 45

THE LONDON and Country Brewer, Containing the Whole Art of Brewing All Sorts of Malt-Liquors . . . London: 1758-59. V. 45

LONDON and Its Environs Described. London: 1761. V. 39

LONDON & Its Environs Described, Containing an Account of Whatever is Most Remarkable . . . London: 1761. V. 44

LONDON & NORTH EASTERN RAILWAY

On Either Side. London: 1930's. V. 46

LONDON & SOUTH WESTERN RAILWAY COMPANY

Rules and Regulations for the Guidance of the Officers and Servants of the London & South Wester Railway Company. London: 1856. V. 37

THE LONDON Angler's Book, or Waltonian Chronicle. London: 1834. V. 40

THE LONDON Aphrodite. 1928-9. V. 43

LONDON Aphrodite. A Miscellany of Poems, Stories and Essays by Various Hands Eminent or Rebellious . . . . London: 1929. V. 42

LONDON, ARCHIBALD

The Wonderful Magazine and Extraordinary Museum: Being a Complete Repository of the Wonders, Curiosities, and Rarities of Nature and Art. Carlisle: 1808. V. 38

LONDON ARTISTS' ASSOCIATION

Recent Paintings by Vanessa Bell with a Foreword by . . . Feb. 4th to March 8th 1930. London: 1930. V. 39

LONDON Catalogue of Books, With Their Sizes, Prices and Publishers, Containing the Books Published in London, and Those Altered in Size Or Price Since the Year 1800 to October 1822. London: 1822. V. 40

LONDON, CHARMIAN K.

The Book of Jack London. New York: 1921. V. 38

The Log of the Snark. New York: 1915. V. 46

The Log of the Snark. London: New York: 1925. V. 43

The New Hawaii. V. 39

The New Hawaii. London: 1923. V. 41

Our Hawaii. New York: 1917. V. 39

LONDON. CHARTERS

The Royal Charter of Confirmation Granted by King Charles II to the City of London. London: 1680. V. 46

LONDON City Directory, 1874-5. Detroit: 1874. V. 40

THE LONDON Companion: or, an Account of the Fares of Hackney Coachmen, Chairmen, and Watermen. London: 1773. V. 38

THE LONDON Company of Virginia. New York: 1908. V. 40

LONDON, G.

The Retir'd Gardener. London: 1706. V. 39

LONDON. GREAT EXHIBITION OF THE WORKS OF INDUSTRY ... 1851.

The Industry of Nations 1851. The Art Journal Illustrated Catalogue. London: 1851. V. 39; 41; 42; 44; 46

LONDON, H. A.

Memorial Address on the Life Services of Gen. Bryan Grimes, a Major General . . . Army of the Confederate States . . . Raleigh: 1886. V. 43

LONDON, HANNAH R.

Portraits of Jews by Gilber and Other Early American Artists. New York: 1927. V. 46

LONDON, HENRY ARMAND

An Address on the Revolutionary History of Chatham County, N.C. Delivered . . . . 1876. Sanford: 1894. V. 42

LONDON in 1838. New York: 1839. V. 37

LONDON Institution: Catalogue of the Library, Systematically Classed. London: 1835-52. V. 38

LONDON Interiors: A Grand National Exhibition of the Religious, Regal and Civic Solemniies, Public Amusements, Scientific Meetings and Commercial Scenes of the British Capital . . . London: 1850. V. 39; 44

LONDON Interiors with Their Costumes and Ceremonies. London: 1841. V. 38; 43

LONDON INTERNATION EXHIBITION, 1871.

Official Reports on the Various Sections of the Exhibition. Volume II. Woollen Fabrics and Machinery. Education. Scientific Inventions. London: 1871. V. 41

LONDON, JACK 1876-1916

The Abysmal Brute. New York: 1913. V. 39; 41; 42; 43; 44; 45; 46

The Abysmal Brute. Toronto: 1913. V. 38; 46

The Acorn Planter. New York: 1916. V. 42; 45; 46

Adventure. London: 1911. V. 39

Adventure. New York: 1911. V. 37; 40; 43; 46

The Apostate. Chicago: 1912. V. 39

Before Adam. New York: 1907. V. 37; 38; 39; 40; 43; 45; 46

Before Adam. Toronto: 1907. V. 39

Before Adam. New York: 1913. V. 45

Brown Wolf and Other Jack London Stories. New York: 1920. V. 43

Burning Daylight. New York: 1910. V. 37; 40; 41; 42; 46

Burning Daylight. London: 1911. V. 40

The Call of the Wild. 1903. V. 44

The Call of the Wild. London: 1903. V. 39; 40; 43

The Call of the Wild. New York: 1903. V. 37; 39; 40; 42; 43; 44; 46

The Call of the Wild. Toronto: 1903. V. 39

The Call of the Wild. New York: 1914. V. 40; 41

The Call of the Wild. New York: 1926. V. 38

The Call of the Wild. 1960. V. 39

The Call of the Wild. Los Angeles: 1960. V. 37; 39; 42; 44

The Call of the Wild. New York: 1960. V. 37; 43

The Cruise of the Dazzler. New York: 1902. V. 37; 40; 42

The Cruise of the Snark. New York: 1911. V. 37; 39; 40; 43; 45; 46

A Daughter of the Snows. Philadelphia: 1902. V. 38; 39; 42; 43; 46

The Dream of Debs. Chicago: V. 41

The Dream of Debs. Chicago: 1909. V. 42

The Dream of Debs. Chicago: 1909 or later. V. 42

The Dream of Debs. Chicago: 1912. V. 42; 43

The Dream of Debs. Chicago: 1929. V. 38

Dutch Courage and Other Stories. New York: 1922. V. 39; 41; 43; 45; 46

The Faith of Men and Other Stories. London: 1904. V. 39

The Faith of Men and Other Stories. New York: 1904. V. 38; 40

The Game. London: 1905. V. 42; 46

The Game. New York: 1905. V. 37; 41; 42; 43; 44; 45; 46

The Game. Toronto: 1905. V. 40

The God of His Fathers. New York: 1901. V. 37; 40; 41; 42; 43; 45

The God of His Fathers. 1902. V. 46

Hearts of Three. London: 1920. V. 43

Hearts of Three. New York: 1920. V. 39; 40; 43; 45

The House of Pride and Other Tales of Hawaii. London: 1912. V. 46

The Human Drift. London: 1917. V. 39

The Human Drift. New York: 1917. V. 43; 45

The Iron Heel. New York: 1908. V. 38; 39; 40

The Iron Heel. London: 1966. V. 43

Jerry of the Islands. New York: 1917. V. 38; 39; 40; 42; 43; 46

John Barleycorn. New York: 1913. V. 37; 39; 40; 44; 46

John Barleycorn or Alcoholic Memoirs. London: 1914. V. 40; 42

John Barleycorn; Or, Alcoholic Memoirs. London: (1914). V. 37

A Klondike Trilogy: Three Uncollected Stories. Santa Barbara: 1983. V. 37; 46

The Little Lady of the Big House. New York: 1916. V. 39; 40; 42; 43

The Little Lady of the Big House. New York: 1918. V. 46

The Little Lady of the Big House by Jack London. 1916. V. 37

Lost Face. New York: 1910. V. 40; 46

Love of Life and Other Stories. New York: 1907. V. 39; 43; 45

Love of Life. London: 1946. V. 37; 40; 42

Martin Eden. New York: 1909. V. 38; 39; 40; 42; 43; 46

Martin Eden. London: 1910. V. 40

Michael, Brother Jerry. New York: 1917. V. 38; 39; 40; 42; 43

Moon Face and Other Stories. London: 1906. V. 43

Moon Face and Other Stories. New York: 1906. V. 40; 41; 42; 43; 44; 45

The Mutiny of the Elisnore. New York: 1914. V. 39; 40; 43; 46

The Mutiny of the Elsinore. London: 1915. V. 38; 39; 40

The Night Born. New York: 1913. V. 39; 40; 42; 43; 44; 46

On the Makaloa Mat. New York: 1919. V. 37; 40; 43

The People of the Abyss. New York: 1903. V. 40; 43; 45

The Red One. New York: 1918. V. 43

The Red One. London: 1919. V. 38; 39; 40

The Red One. V. 37

Revolution. Chicago: 1909. V. 39; 43

Revolution and Other Essays. New York: 1910. V. 43; 45; 46

The Road. London: V. 41

The Road. New York: 1907. V. 40; 41; 42; 43

The Scarlet Plague. New York: 1915. V. 37; 39; 40; 41; 43; 45; 46

The Sea-Wolf. London: 1904. V. 40

The Sea Wolf. New York: 1904. V. 39; 40; 42; 43; 45

The Sea Sprite and the Shooting Star. N.P.: 1932. V. 39

Smoke Bellew. New York: 1912. V. 38; 39; 40; 41; 42; 43; 45

The Son of the Wolf, Tales of the Far North. Boston: 1900. V. 37; 38; 40; 43; 44; 45

The Son of the Wolf. Boston & New York: 1900. V. 39; 40; 41; 46

Son of the Sun. Garden City: 1912. V. 40

A Son of the Sun. New York: 1912. V. 43

The Star Rover. 1915. V. 43

The Star Rover. New York: 1915. V. 39; 46

The Strength of the Strong. New York: 1914. V. 43; 45; 46

Tales of the Fish Patrol. New York: 1905. V. 43; 45

Tales of the Fish Patrol. London: 1906. V. 37; 39

Theft. New York: 1910. V. 43

The Turtles of Tasman. New York: 1916. V. 37; 40; 43

The Valley of the Moon. New York: 1913. V. 38; 39; 43

War of the Classes. London: 1905. V. 46

War of the Classes. New York: 1905. V. 43; 45

The War of the Classes. New York: 1912. V. 42

What Life Means to Me. Princeton: V. 43; 45

When God Laughs and Other Stories. New York: 1911. V. 43; 45

When Jack Laughs and Other Stories. New York: 1911. V. 41

White Fang. London: 1906. V. 46

White Fang. New York: 1906. V. 37; 39; 40; 41; 42; 43

White Fang. New York: & London: 1906. V. 46

White Fang. New York: 1914. V. 39

White Fang. New York: (1914). V. 37

LONDON, JOHN

An Answer to the Pretended Remarks on Mr. Webber's Scheme and the Draper's pamphlet . . . London: 1741. V. 43

THE LONDON Kalendar; or Court and City register, for England, Scotland, Ireland and America for . . . 1803. London: 1803. V. 40

LONDON Kalendar; or, Court and City Register, for England, Scotland, Ireland and the Colonies, for the Year 1809 . . . London: 1808. V. 46

THE LONDON Medley: Containing The Exercises Spoken by Several Young Noblemen and Gentlemen, at the Annual Meeting of the Westminster Scholars, on the 28th of Jan. 1730-1, at Westminster School . . . London: 1731. V. 43

THE LONDON Mercury. London: 1919-23. V. 41

LONDON MISSIONARY SOCIETY

Circular Letters Giving the First News of the Abandonment of the Tahitian Mission. London: 1799. V. 41

The London Missionary Society's Report of the Proceedings Against the Late Rev. J. Smith of Demerara, Minister of the Gosepl Who Was Tried Under Martial Law . . . London: 1824. V. 42

A Missionary Voyage to the Southern Pacific Ocean, Performed in the years 1796, 1797, 1798 in the Ship Duff, Commanded by Captain James Wilson. London: 1799. V. 41; 45; 46

A Small Collection of 4 Reports by the Directors of the Annual General Meeting of the Missionary Society (Known as the London Missionary Society). London: 1926/28/29. V. 39

THE LONDON Modern Atlas. London: 1860. V. 45

LONDON Oddities; or, the Theatrical Cabinet; Being Neat Tit Bits for the Lovers of Humour and Eccentricity and a Glorious Collection of Nerve Working . . . London: 1823. V. 46

LONDON, PERCEVAL

The Opening of Tibet. New York: 1905. V. 43

LONDON. ROYAL ACADEMY

Burlington House. A Commemorative Catalogue of the Exhibition of Italian Art . . . London: 1931. V. 41

A Commemorative Catalogue of the Exhibition of Italian Art Held in the Galleries of the Royal Academy, Burlington House. London: 1930. V. 42

LONDON. ROYAL ACADEMY OF ARTS

Commemorative Catalogue of the Exhibition of British Art. London: 1934. V. 42

LONDON. ROYAL COLLEGE OF PHYSICIANS

Pharmacopoeia Collegii Regalis Medicorum Londinensis. London: 1746. V. 45

LONDON SAND BLAST DECORATIVE WORKS LTD.

Glass. London: 1935. V. 37

THE LONDON Singer's Magazine. London. V. 38

LONDON. STATIONERS' COMPANY

Records of the Court of the Stationers' Company, 1576 to 1602, from Register B . . . . (with) Records of the Court of the Stationers' Company, 1602 to 1640. London: 1930, 1957. V. 39

THE LONDON Theatre. London: 1815. V. 45

THE LONDON Universal Letter Writer; or, Whole Art of Polite Correspondence . . . London: 1800. V. 41

LONDON. UNIVERSITY. LIBRARY.

The Sterling Library. A Catalogue of the Printed Books, and Literary Manuscripts: Collected by Sir Louis Sterling and Presented by Him to the University of London. Cambridge: 1954. V. 39

LONDON Unmask'd: or the New Town Spy. London: 1784? V. 37

LONDON vs. New York. By an English Workman. London: 1859. V. 45

LONDONDERRY, CHARLES WILLIAM STEWART VANE, 3RD MARQUESS OF

Narrative of the War in Germany and France, in 1813 and 1814. London: 1830. V. 41; 43

Recollections of a Tour in the North of Europe in 1836-1837. London: 1838. V. 38; 39; 44

LONDONDERRY, CHARLES WILLIAM STEWART VANE, 3rd OF

Recollections of a Tour in the North of Europe in 1836-1837. London: 1828. V. 38

LONDONDERRY, FRANCES ANNE VANE, MACHIONESS OF

A Journal of a Three Months' Tour in Portugal, Spain, Africa &c. London: 1843. V. 38

LONDON'S Dreadful Visitations. London: 1665. V. 41

LONDONS Flames Discovered by Informations Taken Before the Committee, Appointed to Enquire After the Burning of the City of London. London: 1667. V. 43

LONDON'S Flames Reviv'd: or, An Account of the Several Informations Exhibited to a Committee Appointed by Parliament, September the 25th 1666 to Enquire into the Burning of London. London: 1689. V. 39

LONDON'S Liberties; or a Learned Argument of Law and Reason, Upon Saturday, Dec. 14, 1650, Before the Lord Major, Court of Aldermen and Common-Councell at Guild Hall . . . London: 1651. V. 43

LONDONS Loyalty to Their King and Country, and the Protestant Religion. London: 1679? V. 42

LONELICH, HENRY

The Holy Grail. 1861-63. V. 45

LONG, B. S.

British Miniaturists. London: 1968. V. 39

LONG, BASIL S.

British Miniaturists. London: 1929. V. 39; 46

LONG, C. CHAILLE

Central Africa: Naked Truths of Naked People. New York: 1877. V. 45

LONG, C. E.

Royal Descents, a Genealogical List of the Several Persons Entitled to Quarter the Arms of the Royal Houses of England. London: 1845. V. 41

LONG, CHARLES

A Temperate Discussion of the Causes Which Have Led to the Present High Price of Bread. London: 1800. V. 42

LONG, EDWARD

The History of Jamaica. London: 1774. V. 39

LONG, ESMOND

A History of Pathology. Baltimore: 1928. V. 45

LONG, F. B.

The Goblin Tower. 1935. V. 39

LONG, FRANK BELKNAP

The Horror from the Hills. Sauk City: 1963. V. 42; 43; 45

The Hounds of Tindalos. Sauk City: 1946. V. 39; 42; 43; 45

LONG, GEORGE

Marcus Aurelius Antoninus, the Emperor. London: 1898. V. 46

The Penny Cyclopaedia of the Society for the Diffusion of Useful Knowledge. London: 1833-43. V. 46

LONG, GEORGE WASHINGTON

The Voyage of the Jeannette . . . Boston: 1883. V. 43

Voyage of the Jeannette. New York: 1883. V. 37

LONG, HANIEL

Interlinear to Cabeza de Vaca. His Relation of the Journey from Florida to the Pacific 1825 - 1536. Santa Fe: 1936. V. 37

Malinche (Dona Marina). Santa Fe: 1939. V. 42

Pittsburgh Memoranda. Santa Fe: 1935. V. 41; 42; 46

Poems. New York: 1920. V. 42; 46

LONG, HENY LAWES

Hannibal's Passage of the Alps. London: 1830. V. 46

LONG, HUEY P.

Every Man a King. New Orleans: 1933. V. 39

LONG, JAMES

The Book of the Pig. London: 1886. V. 37

Strike, but Hear! Evidence Explanatory of the Indigo System in Lower Bengal. Calcutta: 1861. V. 45

LONG, JOHN

Voyages and Travels of an Indian Interpreter and Trader. London: 1791. V. 37; 38; 40; 41; 42; 43; 44; 45; 46

Voyages and Travels of an Indian Interpreter and Trader, Describing the Manners and Customs of the North American Indians.. Paris: 1793. V. 38

LONG, LESSEL

Twelve Months in Andersonville. Huntington;: 1886. V. 42

LONG, ROGER

The Music Speech, Spoken at the Public Commencement in Cambridge July the 6th, 1714. London: 1714. V. 41; 45

LONG, STEPHEN H.

Descriptions of Col. S. H. Long's Bridges, Together with a Series of Directions to Bridge Builders. Philadelphia: 1841. V. 43

Narrative of the Proceedings of the Board of Engineers, of the Baltimore and Ohio Rail Road Company, from Its Organization to Its Dissolution . . . Baltimore: 1830. V. 43

Rail Road Manual, or a Brief Exposition of Principles and Deductions Applicable in Tracing the Route of a Rail Road. Baltimore: 1829, 1836. V. 42

Voyage in a Six-Oared Skiff to The Falls of Saint Anthony in 1817. Philadelphia: 1860. V. 38; 39; 42; 43

LONG, THOMAS

A Compendious History of All the Popish and Fanatical Plots and Conspiracies Against the Established Government in Church and State, in England, Scotland and Ireland, from the First Year of Qu. Eliz. Reign to this Present Year 1684. London: 1684. V. 44

The History of the Donatists. London: 1677. V. 39

Vox Cleri: or, the Sense of the Clergy, Concerning the Makings of Alterations in the Established Liturgy . . . Vox Regis & Regni: or a Protest Against Vox Cleri. London: 1690. V. 39

LONG, W. H.

Medals of the British Navy and How They Were Won. London: 1895. V. 42

LONGACRE, J. J.

Craniofacial Anomalies: Pathogenesis and Repair. Philadelphia: 1968. V. 42

LONGCHAMPS, PIERRE CHARPENTIER DE 1740-1812

Histoire Impartiale des Evenemens Militaires et Politiques de la Derniere Guerre. Amsterdam & Paris: 1785. V. 42

LONGCHAMPS, PIERRE DE 1740-1812

Histoire Impartiale des Evenemens Miltaires et Politiques de La Derniere Guerre . . . Paris: 1785. V. 44

LONGFELLOW, HENRY WADSWORTH 1807-1882

The Belfry of Bruges and Other Poems . . . Cambridge: 1845. V. 39

The Belfry of Bruges and Other Poems. Cambridge: 1846. V. 44; 45; 46

The Belfry of Bruges and Other Poems. Cambridge: 1846, 1845. V. 41

The Birds of Killingworth. New York: 1974. V. 39

The Courtship of Miles Standish. Boston: 1858. V. 37; 38; 39; 40; 41; 42; 43; 44; 45

Courtship of Miles Standish and Other Poems. London: 1858. V. 46

The Courtship of Miles Standish. Boston: 1858, 1859. V. 40

The Courtship of Miles Standish, and Other Poems. Boston: 1858-59. V. 39

The Courtship of Miles Standish. Boston: 1920. V. 45

The Courtship of Miles Standish. London: 1920. V. 46

The Courtship of Miles Standish. By Henry Wadsworth Longfellow. Indianapolis: (c. 1903). V. 37

The Early Poems of Henry Wadsworth. London: 1878. V. 45

The Estray. Boston: 1847. V. 40; 46

Evangeline. Boston: 1847. V. 42

Evangeline: a Tale of Acadie. Boston: 1850. V. 39

Evangeline. London: 1856. V. 38

Evangeline. Boston: 1886. V. 41

Evangeline, a Tale of Arcadie. Boston: 1897. V. 42

Evangeline. Indianapolis: (c. 1905). V. 37

The Golden Legend. London. V. 44

The Golden Legend. Boston: 1851. V. 37; 39; 40; 41; 43; 45

The Golden Legend. London: 1851. V. 40; 45

The Golden Legend. Boston: 1852. V. 45; 46

The Golden Legend. London: 1910. V. 42; 43; 45

The Golden Legend. London;: (n.d.). V. 37

The Hanging of the Crane. Boston: 1875. V. 44

The Hanging of the Crane . . . Boston & New York: 1907. V. 39

Hyperion. New York: 1839. V. 39; 41; 42; 43; 45

Hyperion, a Romance. Boston: 1848. V. 46

Hyperion. London: 1865. V. 37; 41

Kavanagh, a Tale. Boston: 1849. V. 45

Manuel De Proverbes Dramatiques. Portland: 1830. V. 45

Manuel De Proverbes Dramatiques. Boston: 1832. V. 45

Manuel de Proverbes Dramatiques. Boston: 1840. V. 39

The Masque of Pandora and Other Poems. Boston: 1875. V. 44

The New England Tragedies. Boston: 1868. V. 44; 46

The New England Tragedies. London: 1868. V. 46

Outre Mer; a Pilgrimage Beyond the Sea. New York: 1835. V. 38; 43; 46

Poems on Slavery. Cambridge: 1842. V. 39; 41

Poems on Slavery. Boston: 1843. V. 39

Poems. Boston: 1857. V. 43

Poems. Boston: 1866. V. 37

Poems of Places. Volume I France. Volume II France and Savoy. Boston: 1877. V. 38

The Poetical Works of . . . London. V. 40

The Poetical Works of . . . London: 1865. V. 39

Poetical Works of . . . London: 1871. V. 39

The Poetical Works of Henry Wadsworth Longfellow. Boston: 1881/82. V. 46

The Poetical Works of . . . Longfellow and The Complete Prose Works of Longfellow With His Later Poems. Boston: 1886. V. 42

The Poetical Works of . . . Boston & New York: 1888. V. 46

The Complete Poetical Works of . . . Boston & New York: 1914. V. 38; 40

Poetical Works. London: 1904. V. 37

The Poetical Works of . . . London: 1867. V. 38

The Poets and Poetry of Europe . . . Philadelphia: 1845. V. 44

Saggi de Novellieri Italiani. Boston: 1832. V. 41; 43; 44; 45; 46

The Seaside and Fireside. Boston: 1850. V. 37; 38; 43; 44

The Seaside and the Fireside. Liverpool: 1850. V. 41

The Song of Hiawatha. London. V. 40

The Song of Hiawatha. Boston: 1844. V. 39

Song of Hiawatha. Boston: 1855. V. 37; 38; 39; 40; 41; 42; 43; 44; 45; 46

The Song of Hiawatha. London: 1855. V. 37; 38; 39; 40; 41; 42; 44

The Song of Hiawatha. Boston: 1856. V. 41

The Song of Hiawatha. Boston: 1891. V. 41; 46

The Song of Hiawatha. Boston & New York: 1891. V. 39

The Song of Hiawatha. Boston: 1911. V. 46

Tales of a Wayside Inn. Boston: 1863. V. 37; 38; 39; 41; 42; 43; 44; 45; 46

The Village Blacksmith in Yankee Farmer. Boston: 1941. V. 37

Voices of the Night. Cambridge: 1839. V. 39; 45; 46

Voices of the Night. Cambridge: 1840. V. 39; 41

The Waif: a Collection of Poems. Cambridge: 1845. V. 38; 39

Complete Works . . . Poetry (and) Prose. Boston: 1866. V. 40

The Complete Work..the Prose Works. (with) The Complete (Poetry) Works. Boston: 1866/1871. V. 39

The Works. Boston: 1886. V. 38; 42

The Works. Boston and New York: 1886-91. V. 45

The Wreck of the Hesperus. Boston: 1845? V. 44

The Writings, with Bibliographical and Critical Notes. 1886. V. 46

The Writings. Cambridge: 1886. V. 42; 45; 46

The Writings. Cambridge: 1886-87. V. 40

The Complete Writings. Boston: 1904. V. 41; 42

LONGFELLOW, SAMUEL

A Book of Hymns for Public and Private Devotion. Boston: 1866. V. 44

LONGHURST, M. H.

English Ivories. 1926. V. 42

LONGHURST, P.

hibiscus. Melbourne: 1978-79. V. 42

LONGINUS, DIONYSIUS

De Grandi Loquentia. Oxford: 1636. V. 41

On the Sublime . . . London: 1739. V. 44

On the Sublime. London: 1743. V. 42

On the Sublime. London: 1770. V. 43

On the Sublime: Translated from the Greek. With Notes and Observations and some account of the Life, Writings and Character of the Author. By William Smith. London: 1819. V. 37

Quae Supersunt. Oxonii: 1778. V. 43; 46

The Works of Dionysius Longinus, on the Sublime . . . London: 1712. V. 44

LONGINUS,DIONYSIUS

De Sublimitate Commentarius. Dublin: 1797. V. 45

LONGLEY, ALCANDER

What is Communism? St. Louis: 1890. V. 40

LONGLEY, ELIAS

American Manual of Phonography. Cincinnati: 1854. V. 43

Pronouncing Vocabulary of Geographical and Personal Names. Cincinnati: 1857. V. 45

LONGLEY, MICHAEL

Ten Poems. Belfast: 1965. V. 38; 41

LONGMAN, C. J.

Archery. London: 1894. V. 40; 46

LONGMAN, E. D.

Pins and Pincushions. London: 1911. V. 42; 44

LONGMAN, HURST, REES & ORME

A General Catalogue of Valuable and Rare Old Books. London: 1814. V. 39

LONGMAN, W.

Tokens of the Eighteenth Century Connected with Booksellers and Bookmakers. Bombay: 1916. V. 44

Tokens of the Eighteenth Century Connected with Booksellers and Bookmakers. London: 1916. V. 40

LONGMAN, WILLIAM

A Lecture on Switzerland. London: 1857. V. 43; 46

LONGMANS' New Atlas, Political and Physical for the Use of Schools and Private Persons. London: 1889. V. 45

LONGMORE, T.

The Sanitary Contrasts of the British and French Armies During the Crimean War. London: 1883. V. 39

A Treatise on Gunshot Wounds. Philadelphia: 1862. V. 38; 42

LONGRIDGE, MICHAEL

Specification of John Birkinshaw's Patent, for an Improvement in the Construction of Malleable Iron Rails, to be Used in Rail Roads . . . Newcastle: 1824. V. 44

LONGSHORE, JOSEPH SKELTON

An Introductory Lecture, Delivered Before the Class, at the Opening of the Female Medical College of Pennsylvnaia . . . Philadelphia: 1850. V. 43

LONGSTAFF, F. V.

The Book of the Machine Gun. London: 1917. V. 43; 44; 45; 46

LONGSTAFF, GEORGE B.

The Langstaffs of Teesdale and Weardale; materials for a history of a yeoman family. London: 1906. V. 37; 38

LONGSTAFFE, W.

The History and Antiquities of the Parish of Darlington. Darlington: 1854. V. 37

LONGSTREET, AUGUSTUS BALDWIN 1790-1870

Georgia Scenes, Characters, Incidents &c. In the First Half Century of the Republic. Augusta: 1835. V. 38; 43

Georgia Scenes. Characters, Incidents &c. in the First Half entury of the Republic. New York: 1850. V. 46

Georgia Scenes, Characters, Incidents, etc. in the First Half Century of the Republic . . . New York: 1851. V. 43

Georgia Scenes. Characters, Incidents, &c. New York: 1858. V. 46

Letters on the Epistle of Paul to Philemon, or the Connection of Apostolical Christianity with Slavery. Charleston: 1845. V. 44

A Voice from the South: Comprising Letters from Georgia to Massachusetts, and to the Southern States. Baltimore: 1847. V. 43; 44

LONGSTREET, JAMES

From Manassas to Appomatox. Philadelphia: 1896. V. 38; 39; 40; 41; 44

LONGUEIL, CHRISTOPHE DE

Epistolarvm Libri IIII. item Bartolomaei Ricci de Imitatione Libri Tres. Lyon: 1563. V. 39

LONGUEVILLE, PETER

The Hermit; or, The Unparalleled Sufferings and Surprising Adventures of Mr. Philip Quarll, an Englishman. Wesminster: 1727. V. 45

The Hermit. London: 1759. V. 40

The Hermit; or, The Unparallel'd Sufferings and Surprising Adventures of Mr. Philip Quarli . . . London: 1780. V. 37; 42

The Hermit. London: 1786. V. 37; 40

LONGUS

Les Les Amours Pastorales de Daphnis et Chloe. Lille: 1792. V. 46

Les Amours Pastorales de Daphnis et Chloe. Chelsea: 1933. V. 40; 41; 43; 44; 46

Les Amours Pastorales de Daphnis et Chloe. London: 1933. V. 39; 40; 42; 45

Daphnis and Chloe. London: 1893. V. 37

Daphnis and Chloe. Waltham St. Lawrence: 1923. V. 46

Daphnis and Chloe. London: 1937. V. 41

Daphnis and Chloe. New York: 1977. V. 46

Daphnis and Chloe. By Longus. Translated by George Moore. New York: (1977). V. 37

Daphnis and Chloe. London: 1982. V. 37; 44; 46

Daphnis & Chloe. A Most Sweet, and Pleasant Pastoral Romance for Young Ladies, translated out of the Greek of Longus by Geo. Thornley. (Waltham Saint Lawrence): 1923. V. 37

Daphnis & Chloe. London: 1925. V. 39; 44; 45; 46

the Pastoral Loves of Daphnes and Chloe. London: 1924. V. 44

The Pastoral Lvoes of Daphnis & Chloe. 1984. V. 40

Les Pastorales de Longus, ou Daphnis et Chloe. Paris: 1902. V. 42

Les Pastorales de Longus ou Daphnis & Chloe. Paris: 1937. V. 39

LONGWORTH, DAVID

Longworth's American Almanac, New York Register and City Directory . . . New York: 1798. V. 45

LONGWORTH, J. A.

A Year Among the Circassians. London: 1840. V. 40

LONGWORTH, MARIA THERESA

Zanita a Tale of the Yosemite. New York: 1872. V. 42

LONGWORTH, THOMAS

Longworth's American Almanac, New York Register and City Directory for 1835-36. New York: 1835. V. 40

LONGWORTH'S American Alamanc, New York Register and City Directory . . . 1840-41. New York: 1840. V. 39

LONICER, JOHANN ADAM

Stand und Orden der Heil Romischen Catholischen Kirchen Darinn Aller Geistlichen Personen, H. Rittern und dero Verwandten Herkommen . . . Frankfurt: 1585. V. 42

LONICER, PHILIP

Chronicorum Turcicorum . . . Frankfurt: 1584. V. 37; 39

LONN, ELLA

Reconstruction in Louisiana After 1868. New York: 1918. V. 43

LONNEUX, MARTIN

The Graded Catechism in Innuit. Chaneliak: 1951. V. 42

LONSDALE, HENRY

The Life and Works of Musgrave Lewthwaite Watson, Sculptor. London: 1866. V. 39

The Worthies of Cumberland. London: 1867-75. V. 41

LOOK Before You Leap; or, a Few Hints to Such Aritzans, Mechanics, Labourers, Farmers and Husbandmen, as are Sesirous of Emigrating to America . . . London: 1796. V. 39; 42

LOOK, HENRY M.

Cui Bono? A Serious Satire. Pontiac: 1871. V. 40

LOOMIS, AUGUSTUS W.

Scenes in the Indian Country. Philadelphia: 1859. V. 37; 42; 46

LOOMIS, CHESTER A.

Journey on Horseback through the Great West in 1825. Bath: 1927. V. 41; 46

LOOMIS, ELIAS

A Treatise on Meterology. New York: 1868. V. 38

LOOMIS, JOHN L.

Leadville Colorado. The Most Wonderful Mining Camp in the World. Colorado Springs: 1879. V. 40

LOOMIS, LEANDER VANESS

A Journal of the Birmingham Emigranting Company. Salt Lake City: 1928. V. 39; 43; 45

Journal of the Birmingham Emigrating Company. 1928. V. 38

LOOMIS, WILLIAM ISAACS

Discovery of the Origin of Gravitation, and the Majestic Motive Force Which Generated the Diurnal and Yearly Revolutions of the Heavenly Bodies. Martindale Depot,: 1866. V. 39

LOOS, ANITA

Gentlemen Prefer Blondes. 1925. V. 46

Gentlemen Prefer Blondes - the Illuminating Diary of a Professional Lady. 1926. V. 37

A Mouse is Born . . . New York: 1951. V. 39

LOOSCAN, ADELE LUBBOCK BRISCOE

A Brief Sketch of the Life and Characteristics of Mrs. Mary Jane Briscoe . . . Houston: 1904. V. 40

LOPATE, PHILLIP

In Coyoacan. New York: 1971. V. 45

LOPE DE VEGA

The Star of Seville. Newtown: 1935. V. 40; 43

LOPES DE CASTANHEDA, FERNAO

Historia del Descubrimiento y Conquista dela India por Los Portugueses . . . Antwerp: 1554. V. 41

LOPEZ, BARRY

Coyote Love. Portland: 1989. V. 46

Coyote Love: Native American Folk Tales. Maine: 1991. V. 46

Desert Notes. Kansas City: 1976. V. 43; 44; 45

Giving Birth to Thunder Sleeping with His Daughter. 1977. V. 42

Giving Birth to Thunder, Sleeping With His Daughter, Coyote Builds North America. Kansas City: 1977. V. 42; 44; 45

Of Wolves and Men. New York: 1978. V. 44

Winter Count. New York: 1981. V. 44

LOPEZ DE CASTANEDA, FERNANDEZ

The First Booke of the Historie of the Discoverie and Conquest of the East Indies, Enterprised by the Portingales, in Their Daungerous Navigations, in the Time of King Don John, the Second of that Name. London: 1582. V. 40

LOPEZ DE CASTRO, BALTASAR

Relacion de la Execucion del Arbitrio, Para el Remedio de Los Rescates, en el Isla Espanola, y Comprouacion Della. Madrid: 1605. V. 40

LOPEZ DE PALACIOS RUBIOS, JUAN d. 1524

Libellus de Beneficiis in Curia Vacantibus. Salamanca: 1517. V. 44; 46

LOPEZ DE STUNIGA, DIEGO

Annotationes Contra Erasmvm Roterodamvm in Defensionem Tralationis Novi Testamenti. Alcala de Henares: 1520. V. 38

LOPEZ DE UBEDA, FRANCISCO

Libro de Entretenimiento, de la Picara Justina, en el Qual Debaxo de Graciosos Discursos, se Encierran Provechosos Avisos . . . Medina del Campo: 1605. V. 39; 41

LOPEZ DE VARGAS MACHUCA, TOMAS

Atlas Geografico del Reyno de Espana e Islas Adyacentes. Madrid: 1755. V. 45

LOPEZ DE VILLALABOS, FRANCISCO

The Medical Works . . . now first translated with commentary and Biography. By George Gaskoin. London: 1870. V. 37

LOPEZ DE ZARATE, FRANCISCO

Poema Heroico de la Invencion de la Cruz, por el Emperador Constantino Magno. Madrid: 1648. V. 38

LOPEZ GOMARA, FRANCISCO

La Terza Parte Delle Historie Dell' Indie Nella Quale Particolarmente Si Tratta dello Scoprimento Della Provinca De Iucatan Detta Nuova Spagana & Delle Cose Degne Di Memoria . . . Venetia: 1566. V. 37

LOPEZ, JOSE HILARIO

Memorias del General . . . , Antiguo Presidente de la Nueva Granada, Escritas por el Mismo. Paris: 1857. V. 38

LOPEZ, JUAN

De Libertate Ecclesiastica Tractatus. Eiusdem Tractatus Dialogicus de Confederatione Principum & Potentatum. Strassburg: 1511. V. 38

LOPEZ-REY, JOSE

Velazquez: a Catalogue Raisonne of His Oeuvre. London: 1963. V. 40; 44

LORAIN, JOHN

Nature and Reason Harmonized in the Practice of Husbandry. Philadelphia: 1825. V. 37; 43

L'ORANGE, H. P.

Apotheosis in Ancient Portraiture. Oslo: 1947. V. 37

LORCA, FEDERICO GARCIA

Ballad of the Little Square. London: 1984. V. 39

Bodas de Sangre. Madrid: 1936. V. 38

Cina Jardins Cinq Sens. Paris: 1982. V. 46

Eleven Poems by Federico Garcia Lorca Illustrated with Eleven Original Colour Etchings by Terry Frost. London: 1989. V. 41

Lament for Ignacio Sanchez Meijias. V. 46

Lament for the Death of a Bullfighter and Other Poems. New York: 1937. V. 44

Poems. London: 1939. V. 41

LORD Berners. London: 1922. V. 40

LORD Byron's Farewell to England, with Three Other Poems, Viz. Ode to St. Helena, To My Daughter, on the Morning of Her Birth, and To the Lily of France. London: 1816. V. 45; 46

LORD Ch----n's Prophecy, an Ode; Addressed to Lieutenant General G-ge. London: 1776. V. 39

LORD, ELIOT

Comstock Mining & Miners. Washington: 1883. V. 38; 45

LORD, ELIZABETH

Reminiscences of Eastern Oregon. Portland: 1903. V. 37

LORD, G. A.

A Short Narrative of the Life and Conversion of Rev. G.A. Lord, Fomerly a french Canadian Roman Catholic and Now Engaged as the People's Independent Colporteur . . . N.P.: 1855. V. 41

LORD, JAMES

Alberto Giacometti Drawings. Greenwich: 1971. V. 39; 46

LORD, JOHN

Beacon Lights of History. New York: 1885-88. V. 38

Beacon Lights of History. New York: 1886-1902. V. 45

The Christian Philosopher, and Metaphysician . . . Portland: 1852. V. 42

Memoir of John Kay of Bury, County of Lanceaster, Inventor of the Fly Shuttle, Metal Reeds . . . Rochdale: 1903. V. 42

LORD, JOHN C.

The Popular Objections of Infidelity, Stated and Answered in a Series of Lectures Addressed to the Young Men of Buffalo. Buffalo: 1838. V. 41

LORD, JOHN KEAST

The Naturalist in Vancouver Island and British Columbia. London: 1866. V. 38; 39

LORD, JOSEPH

The Militiaman's Pocket Companion . . . Hudson: 1822. V. 38; 43

LORD, JOSEPH L

A Defence of Dr. Charles T. Jackson's Claims to the Discovery of Etherization. Boston: 1848. V. 40; 41; 45

LORD, NATHAN

A True Picture of Abolition. Boston: 1863. V. 42

LORD, PERCEVAL BARTON

Algiers, With Notices of the Neighbouring States of Barbary. London: 1835. V. 45

LORD, THOMAS

Entire New System of Ornithology or Oecumenical History of British Birds. London: 1791-96. V. 37

Entire New System of Ornithology or Oecumenacal History of British Birds. London: 1796-96. V. 42

LORD, W. B.

Shifts and Expedients of Camp Life, Travel and Exploration. London: 1871. V. 37

LORD, WALTER

A Time to Stand. New York: 1961. V. 37; 40

LORD, WILLIAM

A Sermon Preached Before . . . the Society for the Propagation of the Gospel in Foreign Parts . . . February 21, 1794. London: 1794. V. 45

LORD, WILLIAM BARRY

The Corset and the Crinoline. A Book of Modes and Costumes from Remote Periods to the Present Time. By W.B.L. London: (1868). V. 37

LORD, WILLIAM R.

Reminiscences of a Sailor, from Cabin Boy to Shipmaster . . . London: 1894. V. 39

LORD, WILLIS

Nature of a Call to, and Preparations for the Work of the Gospel Ministry. Chicago: 18965. V. 39

LORDELOT, BENIGNE 1639-1720

I Doveri Della Vita Domestica di Un Padre di Famiglia. Parma: 1794. V. 42

LORD'S PRAYER. DAKOTA

The Lord's Prayer in Dahcota. N.P.. V. 39

THE LORDS Protest. Die Veneris 2 do Maii, 1746. N.P.: 1746. V. 39

LOREDANO, GIOVAN FRANCISCO

Il Cimeterio. Epitafij Giocosi. Venice: 1645. V. 37

LORENTZ, HENDRIK ANTOON 1853-1928

Lectures on Theoretical Physics Delivered at the University of Leiden. London: 1927. V. 38

The Theory of Electrons and Its Applications to the Phenomena of Light and Radiant Heat, a Course of Lectures Delivered in Columbia University. 1906. V. 40

The Theory of Electrons and Its Applications to the Phenomena of Light and Radiant Heat. Leipzig: 1909. V. 42

LORENZ, FRIEDRICH AUGUST

Chemisch Physicalische Untersuchung des Feuers. Kopenhagen und Leipzig: 1789. V. 42

LORENZ, LINCOLN

John Paul Jones Fighter for Freedom and Glory. Annapolis: 1943. V. 41

LORENZANA Y BUITRON, FRANCISCO ANTONIO DE

Cartas Pastorales, y Edictos del Illmo. Senor D. Francisco Antonio Lorenznana, y Buitron, Arzobispo de Mexico. Mexico: 1770. V. 45

Historia de Nueva-Espana . . . Mexico: 1770. V. 41; 42; 43; 45

LORENZINI, CARLO 1829-1890

The Adventures of Pinocchio. New York: 1929. V. 45

Le Adventure di Pinocchio. Milano: 1944. V. 43

LORENZO GIUSTINIANO, SAINT 1381-1455

Trattato della Disciplina et della Perfettion Monastica. Venice: 1569. V. 38

LORI, DANIEL

Hassliebe. San Francisco: 1988. V. 39

LORICHIUS, JODOCUS

Cura Corporis Humani Pia & Salubris. Ingolstadt: 1587. V. 38

LORICHIUS, JOHANNES

Aenignmatum Libellus, Rerum Cognitione VAria, Simul ac Festivo Sale Refertus, Ex Optimis Authoribus, Cum Sacris, Tum Ethnicis, Non Vulga Istudio (sic) Collectus. Marpurg: 1540. V. 43

LORIMER, H. L.

Homer and the Monuments. London: 1950. V. 40; 42; 44

LORIMER, J. G.

The Gazeteer of the Persian Gulf, Oman and Central Arabia. United Kingdom: 1986. V. 37

LORIMER, NORMA

By the Waters of Egypt, Voyage of the S. S. 'Cairo' Bound for Alexandria in 1907. London: 1909. V. 41

LORIMER, ROBERT

The Work of Sir Robert Lorimer. London: 1931. V. 43

LORING, EDWARD G.

Text-book of Ophthalmoscopy. New York: 1893-91. V. 44

LORING, ROSAMOND B.

Decorated Book Papers, Being an Account of Their Designs and Fashions. Cambridge: 1942. V. 38; 41; 42; 45

Decorated Book Papers Being an Account of Their Designs and Fashions. Harvard: 1942. V. 45

Marbled Papers, by Rosamond B. Loring. Boston: 1933. V. 37

L'ORME, PHILIBERT DE

Nouvelles Inventions Pour Bien Bastir et a Petits Fraiz . . . Paris: 1561. V. 38; 40

Le Premier Tome de l'Architecture. Paris: 1568. V. 38; 40

LORNA, ANTON MARIA

Fabbrica ed Usi Principali della Squaccra di Proporzione. Verona: 1767. V. 38

LORNE, MARQUIS

Candadian Pictures Drawn with Pen and Pencil. London: 1884. V. 38

LORREQUER, HARRY

The Irish Dragoon. Dublin: 1841. V. 37

LORRY, ANN CHARLES

De Melancholia et Morbis melancholicis. Paris: 1765. V. 42; 46

LORRY, ANNE CHARLES

De Melancholia et Morbis Melancholicis. Lutetiae Parisiorum: 1765. V. 40

Tractatus de Morbis Cutaneis. Paris: 1777. V. 38

LORTET, LOUIS

La Faune Momifiee de l'Ancienne Egypte. Serie 1-5. Lyon: 1905-09. V. 44

LORY, GABRIEL

Picturesque Tour through the Oberland in the Canton of Berne, in Switzerland. London: 1823. V. 45

LORYOT, FRANCOIS 1571-1640

Les Secretz Moraux, Concernants les Passions du Coeur Humaine . . . Paris: 1614. V. 43

LOS Angeles, from the Mountains to the Sea. Chicago: 1922. V. 38

THE LOS Angeles Saturday Post Unrivaled Atlas of the World. Chicago/New York: 1901. V. 45

LOS ANGELES COUNTY, CALIFORNIA. MUSEUM. LOS ANGELES.

The Los Angeles County Museum Presents a Retrospective Exhibition of the Walt Disney Medium. N.P.: 1940. V. 39

LOSCHAK, DAVID

The Art of Thomas Girtin. London: 1954. V. 46

LOSKIEL, GEORGE HENRY

History of the Mission of the United Brethern Among the Indians of North America . . . London: 1794. V. 37; 38; 39; 40; 43; 45; 46

LOS RIOS, JEAN FRANCOIS DE

Bibliographie Instructive, ou Notice de Quelques Livres Rares, Singuliers & Difficiles a Trouver. Avignon & Lyons: 1777. V. 38

LOSSAEUS, NICHOLAS

De Ivre Vniversitatvm Tractatvs Omnibus Legum Studiosis, & in Foro & in Scholis Versantibus maxime Vtilis, ac Necessarius. Turin: 1601. V. 42

LOS SANTOS, FRANCISCO DE

A Description of the Royal Palace, and Monastery of St. Laurence, Called the Escurial and of the Chapel Royal of the Pantheon. London: 1760. V. 38

LOSSING, BENSON JOHN

The American Centennial, a History of the Progress of the Republic of the United States. Philadelphia: 1876. V. 40

The American Historical Record. Two Volumes. Philadelphia: 1872-1873. V. 37

A History of the Civil War. New York: 1912. V. 39; 42

History of New York City, Embracing an Outline Sketch of Events from 1609 to 1830 and a Full Account of Its Development from 1830 to 1884. New York: 1884. V. 39

Memoir of Lieut. Col. John T. Greble of the United States Army. Philadelphia: 1870. V. 39

A Memorial of Alexander Anderson, M.D., the First Engraver of Wood in America. Read Before the New York Historical Society, Oct. 5, 1870. New York: 1872. V. 41

Our Country: a Household History for All Readers, From Discovery of America to the Present Time. New York: 1877. V. 42

Our Country. New York: 1877-78. V. 39; 42

The Pictorial Field Book of the Revolution. New York: 1850. V. 40

The Pictorial Field-Book of the Revolution. New York: 1851. V. 44; 46

The Pictorial Field-Book of the Revolution . . . New York: 1851-52. V. 46

The Pictorial Field Book of the Revolution. New York: 1852. V. 42; 43

The Pictorial Field Book of the Revolution. New York: 1855. V. 44

Pictorial Field Book of the American Revolution. New York: 1859. V. 40

The Pictorial Field-Book of the Revolution, or Illustrations by Pen and Pencil of the History, Biography, Scenery, Relics and Traditions of the War of Independence. New York: 1860. V. 46

Pictorial Field Book of the War of 1812. New York: 1869. V. 39; 44; 46

The Pictorial Field Book of the Civil War in the United States of America. New Haven: 1878. V. 40

Pictorial History of the Civil War in the United States of America. Philadelphia: 1868. V. 39

Washington and the American Republic. New York: 1870. V. 39

Washington & The American Republic. New York: (1870). V. 37

LOSSIUS, KASPAR FRIEDRICH

Gamal and Lina; or, the African Children. London: 1817. V. 37; 45

Moralische Bilderbibel mit Kupfern nach Schubertschen Zeichnungen und mit Erklarungen. Gotha: 1805-12. V. 42

LOSSIUS, LUCAS

Annotationes Scholaasticae in Evangelia Dominicalia . . . Frankfurt: 1578. V. 37

LOSTELNAU, SIEUR DE

Le Mareschal de Bataille. Contenant Le Mainement des Armes. Les Evolutions. Plusieurs Bataillons. Paris: 1647. V. 37

LOTH, JOHANN THOMAS

The Ancient and Accepted Scottish Rite. London: 1876. V. 38

LOTHIAN, WILLIAM

The History of the United Provinces of the Netherlands, from the death of Philip II, King of Spain, to the Truce Made with Albert and Isabella . . . London: 1780. V. 41

The History of the United Provinces of the Netherlands, from the Death of Phillip II, King of Spain, to the Truce Made with Albert and Isabella. London: 1780. V. 41; 42

LOTHIAN, WILLIAM S. R. KERR, MARQUESS OF 1832-1870

Fragment of a Parallel Between the History, Literature and Art of Italy in Middle Ages. Edinburgh: 1863. V. 42

LOTHROP, J. S.

J.S. Lothrop's Champaign County Directory, 1870-71, with a History of the Same and of Each Township Therein. Chicago: 1871. V. 41

LOTHROP, S. K.

Archaeology of Southern Veraquas, Panama. Cambridge: 1950. V. 42

Cocle: an Archaeological Study of Central Panama. Cambridge: 1937-1942. V. 42

Pre-Columbian Art. Robert Woods Bliss Collection. New York: 1957. V. 37

LOTHROP, S. K. continued

Pre-Columbian Art. Robert Woods Bliss Collection. New York: 1959. V. 44; 46

Robert Woods Bliss Collection: Pre-Columbian Art. London: 1959. V. 42; 44

Treasures of Ancient America. Geneva: 1964. V. 39

Treasures of Ancient America. Geneva: 1972. V. 42; 44

Zacualpa: A Study of Ancient Quiche Artifacts. Washington: 1936. V. 38

LOTI, PIERRE

Impressions. Westminster: 1898. V. 44

The Romance of a Child. Chicago & New York: 1891. V. 46

Un Pelerin D'Angkor. Paris: 1930. V. 46

LOTT, EMMELINE

Harem Life in Egypt and Constantinople. London: 1866. V. 42

LOTT, LEWIS

Collection of Beautiful Miniatures, Reproduced in Facsimile from Original Paintings . . . London. V. 45

Collection of Beautiful Miniatures . . . Vienna: 1880. V. 45

LOTTINI, GIOVANNI FRANCESCO 1512-1572

Avvedimenti Civilii. Florence: 1574. V. 46

LOTTO, FRANK

Fayette County; her History and Her People. Schulenberg: 1902. V. 37; 38; 41; 42

LOTZE, HERMANN 1817-1881

Mikrokosmus. Ideen zur Naturgeschichte und Geschichte der Menschheit. Leipzig: 1856-64. V. 41; 45

LOUANDRE, CHARLES

Les Arts Somptuaires. Paris: 1857-58. V. 38; 41; 42

LOUBAT, JOSEPH F.

The Medallic History of the United States of America 1776-1876. New York: 1878. V. 46

Narrative of the Mission to Russia, in 1866 of the Hon. Gustavus Vasa Fox, Assistant Secretary to the Navy. New York: 1873. V. 43; 46

LOUD, GORDON

Khorsabad, Parts I & II. Chicago: 1936. V. 40

The Megiddo Ivories. Chicago: 1939. V. 40

LOUDON, and Loudon County, Tennessee. Herein You Will Find a faithful and Accurate Description of Loudon and Loudon County, the Fairest Portion of Tennessee . . . Loudon: 1890. V. 44

LOUDON, ARCHIBALD

A Selection of Some of the Most Interesting Narratives of Outrages Committed by the Indians in Their Wars with the White People. Carlisle: 1808. V. 45

The Wonderful Magazine, and Extraordinary Museum. Carlisle: 1808. V. 40

LOUDON, J. H.

James Scott and William Scott, Bookbinders. London: 1980. V. 40

James Scott and William Scott, Bookbinders. (London): (1980). V. 37

LOUDON, JANE 1807-1858

The Amateur Gardener's Calendar . . . London: 1847. V. 45

British Wild Flowers. London: 1849. V. 43

Gardening for Ladies; and Companion to the Flower Garden. New York: 1860. V. 37

The Ladies' Flower-Garden of Ornamental Annuals. London: 1840. V. 44

The Ladies Magazine of Gardening. London: 1842. V. 43

The Ladies Country Companion . . . London: 1846. V. 46

The Ladies Flower-Garden of Ornamental Greenhouse Plants. London: 1850. V. 39

Loudon's Encyclopaedia of Plants. London: 1866. V. 38

My Own Garden; or, the Young Gardener's Year Book. London: 1855. V. 42

LOUDON, JOHN CLAUDIUS 1783-1843

Arboretum et Fruitecetum Britannicum . . . London: 1838. V. 37; 38; 41; 42; 43; 46

Arboretum et Fruiticetum Britannicum . . . London: 1844. V. 37; 42; 44

The Architectural Magazine and Journal. London: 1834. V. 44

The Architectural Magazine and Journal. London: 1838. V. 46

The Architectural Magazine and Journal of Improvements in Architecture. London: 1972-1973. V. 46

The Derby at Arboretum, Containing a Catalogue of the Trees and Shrubs Included in It . . . London: 1840. V. 44

An Encyclopaedia of Agriculture . . . London: 1826. V. 45; 46

An Encyclopaedia of Agriculture. London: 1831. V. 40

An Encyclopaedia of Agriculture . . . London: 1835. V. 39

An Encyclopaedia of Agriculture. London: 1844. V. 45

An Encyclopaedia of Cottage, Farm and Villa Architecture and Furniture. London: 1833. V. 38

An Encyclopaedia of Cottage, Farm & Villa Architecture & Furniture. London: 1839. V. 38

An Encyclopaedia of Cottage, Farm and Villa Architecture and Furniture . . . London: 1842. V. 46

An Encyclopaedia of Gardening . . . London: 1824. V. 37; 41

An Encyclopaedia of Gardening. London: 1825. V. 39

An Encyclopaedia of Gardening; Comprising the Theory and Practice of Horticulture, Floriculture, Arboriculture, and Landscape-Gardening . . . London: (1830). V. 37

An Encyclopaedia of Gardening. London: 1835. V. 38; 39

An Encyclopaedia of Gardening. London: 1860. V. 40; 41

An Encyclopaedia of Gardening . . . . Horticulture, Floriculture, Arboriculture and Landscape Gardening . . . London: 1878. V. 43

Loudon's Encyclopaedia of Plants. London: 1855. V. 44

An Encyclopaedia of Plants. London: 1829. V. 37; 38; 39; 40

An Encyclopaedia of Plants. London: 1836. V. 44; 45

An Encyclopaedia of Trees and Shrubs. London: 1869. V. 44

The Gardener's Magazine, and Register of Rural and Domestic Improvement. London: 1826-34. V. 46

Hints on the Formation of Gardens and Pleasure Grounds . . . London: 1812. V. 38

Loudon's Hortus Britannicus. London: 1830. V. 39

The Magazine of Natural History and Journal of Zoology, Botany, Mineralogy, Geology and Meteorology. London: 1829-1833. V. 40

A Manual of Cottage Gardening. London: 1830. V. 37; 40

Observations on Laying Out Farms in the Scoth Style, Adapted to England . . . London: 1812. V. 45; 46

Observations . . . on the Theory and Practice of Landscape Gardening and on Gaining Land from Rivers or the Sea. Edinburgh: 1804. V. 45

The Suburban Gardener and Villa Companion. London: 1838. V. 38; 39

The Suburban Gardener and Villa Companion. London: 1938. V. 37

The Suburban Horticulturlist . . . London: 1842. V. 41; 45

A Treatise on Forming, Improving and Managing Country Residences. London: 1806. V. 38; 39; 41; 44; 46

Trees and Shrubs: an Abridgment of the Arboretum at Fruticetum Britannicum . . . London: 1883. V. 46

The Villa Gardener. London: 1850. V. 41

LOUDON, MARGRACIA

Philanthropic Economy; or the Philosophy of Happiness, Practically Applied tot he Social, Political and Commercial relations of Great Britain. London: 1835. V. 42

LOUGH, THOMAS

England's Wealth, Ireland's Poverty. London: 1896. V. 38

LOUGHBOROUGH, J. N.

Rise and Progress of the Seventh-Day Adventists with Tokens of God's Hand in the Movement and a Brief Sketch of the Advent Cause from 1831 to 1844. Battle Creek: 1892. V. 44

LOUGHBOROUGH, JOHN

The Pacific Telegraph and Railway. St. Louis: 1849. V. 37; 38; 39; 40; 41; 42; 43; 46

LOUGHBRIDGE, ROBERT MC GILL

English and Muskokee Dictionary. St. Louis: 1890. V. 46

LOUGHLIN, G. F.

Mineral Resources of the U.S., 1918, by G.F. Loughlin. Washington: 1921. V. 37

LOUIS, ANTOINE

Dissertation sur la Question . . . . Comment se Fait le Transmission des Maladies Hereditaires? (with) Observation et Remarques sur les Effects du Virux Cancereux. Paris: 1749. V. 43

LOUIS, MORRIS

Morris Louis. New York: 1979. V. 41

LOUIS, PIERRE

Anatomical, Pathological and Therapeutic Researches on the Yellow Fever of Gibraltar of 1828. Boston: 1839. V. 42

LOUIS, PIERRE CHARLES ALEXANDRE

Anatomical, Pathological and Therapeutic Researches Upon the Disease Known Under the Name of Gastro-Enterite, Putrid, Ataxic, or Typhoid Fever, etc. Boston: 1836. V. 38

Pathological Reasearches on Phthisis. London: 1835. V. 38

Pathological Researches on Phthisis. Boston: 1836. V. 38

Recherches Anatomicao Pathologiques sur la Phthisie . . . Paris: 1825. V. 38

LOUIS, PIERRE CHARLES ALEXANDRE continued

Recherches Anatomiques, Pathologiques et Therapeutiques sur la Maladie Connue Sous les Noms de Gastro-Enterite . . . Paris & London: 1829. V. 38

LOUIS, VICTOR

Salle de Spectacle de Bordeaux. Paris: 1782. V. 37; 38; 42; 44

LOUIS XIV, KING OF FRANCE

Edit Du Roy, Portant Revocation de la Compagnie des Indes Occidentales, et Union au Domaine de la Couronne des Terres, Isles, Pais & Doits de Ladite Compagnie . . . Donne a Saint Germain . . . Decembre 1674. Paris: 1675. V. 40

LOUIS XIV The Great Bastard, Protector of the Little One. London: 1702. V. 46

LOUIS XV, KING OF FRANCE

Declaration du Roy, Concernant L'imprimerie. N.P.,: 1729. V. 38

LOUISA; a Narrative of Facts . . . New York: 1801. V. 45; 46

LOUISIANA

Third Grand State Fair of Mechanic's and Agricultural Fair Association of Louisiana. To Commence on Tuesday, April 6yh, 1869 . . . In the City of New Orleans . . . New Orleans: 1869. V. 37

LOUISIANA BIBLE SOCIETY

Second Report of the Board of Managers of the Louisiana Bible Society. New Orleans: 1816. V. 45

LOUISIANA. CONSTITUTION - 1815

The Constitutions of the United States of America, with Their latest Amendments. Boston: 1815. V. 37

LOUISIANA. CONSTITUTION - 1879

Constitution of the State of Louisiana, Adopted in the Convention at the City of New Orleans, 1879. New Orleans: 1879. V. 37; 39

LOUISIANA. CONSTITUTIONAL CONVENTION, 1864

Journal Officiel des Travaux de la Convention Reunie Pour Reviser et Amender la Constitution de l'Etat de la Louisiane. New Orleans: 1864. V. 39

LOUISIANA. CONVENTION, 1861.

Ordinances Passed by the Convention of Louisiana, at Its First Session, Together with the Constitution of the State, as Amended. New Orleans: 1861. V. 39

LOUISIANA. LAWS, STATUTES, ETC. - 1813

Acte Pour Reglet L'Organisation et la Descipline des Milices de L'Etat et de la Louisiane. New Orleans: 1813. V. 40

LOUISIANA. LAWS, STATUTES, ETC. - 1834

An Act for the Organization and Discipline of the Militia of the State of Louisiana, Approved 8th March 1834. New Orleans: 1834. V. 37

LOUISIANA. LAWS, STATUTES, ETC. - 1864

Acts Passed by the Twenty Seventh Legislature of the State of Louisiana, in Extra Session at Opelousas, December 1862 and January, 1863. Natchitoches: 1864. V. 42

LOUISIANA. LEGISLATURE - 1850

Rules and Orders of the House of Representatives: To which is Annexed the Constitution of the States of Louisiana. New Orleans: 1850. V. 37

LOUISIANA NATIVE AMERICAN ASSOCIATION

Address of the Louisiana Nataive American Associataion, to the Citizens of Louisiana and the Inhabitants of the United States. New Orleans: 1839. V. 37

LOUISVILLE, CINCINNATI & CHARLESTON RAIL ROAD CO.

Charter of the Louisville, Cincinnati & Charleston Rail Road Co. Columbia: 1836. V. 44

LOUKOMSKI, G. K.

Jules Romain. Paris: 1930. V. 37

THE LOUNGER. a Periodical paper. Edinburgh: 1785/1786. V. 37

LOUNSBERRY, ALICE

A Guide to the Trees. New York: 1900. V. 37

LOUNSBERRY, CLEMENT A.

Early History of North Dakota. Washington: 1919. V. 42; 44; 45
North Dakota. A History and People. Chicago: 1916. V. 45

LOUNSBURY, RALPH GREENLEE

The British Fishery at Newfoundland, 1634-1763. New Haven: 1934. V. 37

LOUNSBURY, THOMAS R.

James Fenimore Cooper. London: 1884. V. 46

LOURVIK, J. NILSEN

Is It Art? Post-Impressionism. Futurism. Cubism. New York: 1913. V. 44

LOUSTAUNAU Huit Vues Representatn les Plus Beaux Sites des Differents Villages de Pargolova aux Environs de St. Petersbourg . . . St. Petersbourg: 1833. V. 39

LOUTHERBOURG, P. J. DE 1740-1812

The Romantic and Picturesque Scenery of England and Wales. London: 1979. V. 39; 44

LOUTHERBOURG, P.J. DE 1740-1812

The Romantic and Picturesque Scenery of England and Wales, from Drawings, Made Expressly for This Undertaking . . . London: 1805. V. 41
The Romantic and Picturesque Scenery of England and Wales . . . 1979. V. 40

LOUVET DE COUVRAY, JEAN B.

Interesting History of the Baron de Lovzinski. New York: 1807. V. 39
Narrative of the Dangers To Which I Have Been Exposed, Since the 31st of May, 1793. Dublin: 1795. V. 42

LOUYMER, JEAN FRANCOIS NICHOLAS

Costumes Usos e Trajos de Todos os Povos do Mundo em Face de Documentos Authenticos e das Mais Recentes Viagens. Lisboa: 1872-74/76/78. V. 40

LOUYS, PIERRE

Aphrodite. Paris: 1909. V. 39
Aphrodite. Paris: 1896. V. 46
Aphrodite. London: 1926. V. 42
Leda Ou La Louange des Biehneureuses Tenebres. Paris: 1898. V. 46
Psyche. New York: 1928. V. 41
Satyrs and Women translated by Pierre Loving, Drawings by majeska. New York: 1930. V. 37
The Song of Bilitis. 1928. V. 38
The Songs of Bilitis. New York: 1926. V. 38; 46
The Songs of Bilitis. London: 1928. V. 41
The Songs of Bilitis. New York: (1926). V. 37
The Twilight of the Nymphs. London: 1928. V. 39; 44; 45; 46
Woman and Puppet. 1927. V. 43

LOVAT FRASER, CLAUD

The Two Wizards and Other Songs. London: 1913. V. 38

LOVAT, SIMON FRASER, 12TH BARON 1667-1747

A Candid and Impartial Account of the Behaviour of Simon Lord Lovat. London: 1747. V. 38
Memoirs of Simon Lord Lovat . . . Now First Translated, from the Original Manuscript. London: 1797. V. 40
The Whole Proceedings in the House of Peers, Upon the Impeachment for High Treason . . . March 9th-19 1746-7 . . . London: 1747. V. 38

LOVAT, SIMON JOSEPH FRASER, BARON 1871-1933

Genuine Memoirs of the Life of Simon Lord Fraser of Lovat. London: 1746. V. 39
Memoirs of the Life of Simon Lord Lovat. London: 1797. V. 40; 44; 45

LOVE, Marriage and Divorce, and the Sovereignty of the Individual. Boston: 1889. V. 41

LOVE and Revenge; or, the Vintner Outwitted: an Opera as Acted at the New Theatre in the Hay-Market. London: 1729. V. 46

LOVE, ANNIE C.

History of Navarro County. Dallas: 1933. V. 44

LOVE, AUGUSTUS EDWARD HOUGH 1863-1940

A Treatise on the Mathematical Theory of Elasticity. Cambridge: 1892-93. V. 40

LOVE, CHRISTOPHER

Prophecies of the Reverend Christopher Love; and His Last Words on the Scaffold; Who Was Beheaded at Tower-Hill, London: on the Twenty-Second Day of August, 1651. Boston: 1793. V. 40
The Whole Triall of Mr. Love, Before the High Court of Justice in Westminster Hall . . . London: 1652. V. 45

LOVE, EMANUEL KING

History of the First African Baptist Church, From Its Organization, January 20th, 1788 to July 1st, 1888. Savannah: 1888. V. 40

LOVE, H. D.

Description List of Pictures in the Government House. Madras: 1903. V. 38; 40

LOVE in Extasie. Ilkley: 1981. V. 44

LOVE, JOHN

Geodaesia; or, the Art of Surveying and Measuring Land Made Easy. London: 1745. V. 43

Geodaesia; or, the Art of Surveying and Measuring Land Made Easy. London: 1768. V. 39; 42; 44

Geodaesia; or, the Art of Surveying and Measuring Land Made Easy. London: 1786. V. 44; 45

Geodaesia; or, the Art of Surveying and Measuring Land Made Easy. New York: 1796. V. 42

The New Waymouth Guide; or, Useful Pocket Companion. Waymouth: 1788. V. 41

THE LOVE, Joy and Distress of the Beautiful and Virtuous Miss Fanny Adams, that Was Trapan'd in a False Marriage, to Lord Whatley, His Base and Ungenerous Treatment of Her in Marrying Another Lady . . . London: 1725. V. 37; 40
THE LOVE, Joy and Distress of the Beautiful and Virtuous Miss Fanny Adams, That Was Trapan'd in a False Marriage to Lord Whatley, His Base and Ungenerous Treatment of Her in Marrying Another Lady . . . London: 1760. V. 46

LOVE, NATH

The Life and Adventures of Nat Love, Better Known as Deadwood Dick. Los Angeles: 1907. V. 39

LOVE, ROBERTUS

The Rise and Fall of Jesse James. New York: 1926. V. 40; 45

LOVE, THOMAS

The Art of Dyeing, Cleaning, Scouring and Finishing on the Most Approved English and French Methods. Philadelphia: 1869. V. 40

LOVE, WILLIAM DE LOSS

The Colonial History of Hartford. Hartford: 1935. V. 44

LOVE Without Artifice; or, the Disappointed Peer. London: 1733. V. 39; 45

LOVECRAFT, H. P.

At the Mountains of Madness and Other Novels. Sauk City: 1964. V. 45

Beyond the Wall of Sleep. 1943. V. 46

Beyond the Wall of Sleep. Sauk City: 1943. V. 44

A History of the Necronomicon. 1938. V. 43

Lovecraft at Last. Arlington: 1975. V. 46

The Shadow Over Innsmouth. Everett: 1936. V. 46

The Survivor and Others. Sauk City: 1957. V. 45; 46

3 Tales of Horror. Sauk City: 1967. V. 43

LOVECRAFT, HOWARD PHILLIPS

Collected Poems. Sauk City: 1963. V. 37; 42

The Dark Brotherhood and Other Pieces. 1966. V. 45

The Dark Brotherhood and Other Stories. Sauk City: 1966. V. 37

The Dream Quest of Unknown Kadath. Buffalo: 1955. V. 40; 42

Dreams and Fancies. 1962. V. 45

Dreams and Fancies. Sauk City: 1962. V. 37; 39

The Dunwich Horror and Others. Sauk City: 1963. V. 37

The Lurker at the Threshold. 1945. V. 46

The Lurker at the Threshold. Sauk City: 1945. V. 37; 39; 42; 43; 45; 46

The Lurker at the Threshold. Sauk City: 1947. V. 45

Marginalia. 1944. V. 37

Marginalia. Sauk City: 1944. V. 39; 42; 43; 44; 45

Selected Letters. Sauk City: 1965-76. V. 37; 42; 45

The Shunned House. Athol: 1928. V. 42

The Shuttered Room and Other Pieces. 1959. V. 45

The Shuttered Room and Other Pieces. Sauk City: 1959. V. 37; 42; 45

Something About Cats. Sauk City: 1949. V. 37; 39; 42; 43; 44; 45; 46

Supernatural Horror in Literature. New York: 1945. V. 42

LOVEJOY, J. C.

Narratives of the Sufferings of Lewis and Milton Clarke, Songs of a Soldier of the Revolution . . . Boston: 1846. V. 42

LOVEJOY, JOSEPH C.

Memoir of the Rev. Elijah P. Lovejoy, Who Was Murdered in Defence of the Liberty of the Press, at Alton, Illinois No. 7, 1873. New York: 1836. V. 46

Memoir of the Rev. Elijah P. Lovejoy; Who Was Murdered in Defence of the Liberty of the Press, at Alton, Illinois, Nov. 7, 1837. New York: 1838. V. 37; 42

LOVELACE, RALPH MILBANKE, EARL OF

Astarte. London: 1921. V. 46

LOVELACE, RICHARD

Lucasta. London: 1649. V. 38; 40; 41; 45

Lucasta . . . to Which is Added Aramantha. (&) Posthume Poems . . . Chiswick: 1827/8. V. 44

Lucasta, The Poems of Richard Lovelace. Now first edited by W. Carew Hazlitt. London: 1864. V. 37

The Poems. Oxford: 1925. V. 43; 46

LOVELESS, PETER

The Law's Disposal of a Person's Estate Who Dies Without Will or Testament . . . London: 1792. V. 45

LOVELING, BENJAMIN

Latin and English Poems. London: 1741. V. 39; 40; 43; 45

LOVELL, ARCHIBALD

A Summary of Material Heads Which may Be Enlarged and Improved Into a Compleat Answer to Dr. Burnet's Theory of the Earth. London: 1696. V. 42

LOVELL, GEORGE W.

The Wife's Secret. London: 1869. V. 45

LOVELL, GEORGE WILLIAM

The Provost of Bruges: a Tragedy. London: 1836. V. 39

LOVELL, JAMES

An Oration Delivered April 2d, 1771. At the Request of the Inhabitants of the Town of Boston; to Commemorate the Bloody Tragedy of the Fifth of March, 1770. Boston: 1771. V. 41

LOVELL, JOHN

The Canada Directory for 1857-58. Montreal: 1857. V. 37

LOVELL, MANSFIELD

Correspondence Between the War Department and General Lovell Relating to the Defences of New Orleans. Submitted in Response to a Resolution of the House of Representatives Passed Third Feb. 1863. Richmond: 1863. V. 45

LOVELL, ROBERT

Panzooructologia (graece) Sive Panzoologicomieralogia. Oxford: 1661. V. 38; 40; 41; 45

Poems, Containing The Retrospect, Odes, Elegies, Sonnets &c. Bath: 1795. V. 45

LOVELL, THOMAS

The Auctioneer's Pocket Companion and Complete Ready Reckoner . . . London: 1818. V. 39

The Builder's Assistant, and Complete Ready Reckoner; . . . Also, a variety of newly constructed tables, ... London: 1813. V. 39

LOVEMAN, ROBERT

the Gates of Silence with Interludes of Song. New York: 1903. V. 46

LOVER, SAMUEL 1797-1868

The Collected Writings of . . . New York. V. 46

The Collected Writings of Samuel Lover. New York: 1901. V. 40; 42; 44

Handy Andy; A Tale of Irish Life. London: 1842. V. 43

Legends and Stories of Ireland. London: 1848. V. 39

Rory O'Mare. London: 1837. V. 39; 40

Songs and Ballads. London: 1839. V. 46

Treasure Trove. London: 1844. V. 40; 43

LOVERING, T. S.

Geology and Ore Depostis of the Breckenridge Mining District, Colorado. Washington: 1934. V. 41

THE LOVER'S Secretary; or, the Adventures of Lindamira, a Lady of Quality. London: 1734. V. 42

LOVETT, A. C.

The Armies of India. Painted by . . . Described by Major G.F. McMunn, D.S.O. with a Foreword by Field-Marshal Earl Roberts. London: 1911. V. 37

LOVETT, H. A.

Canada and the Grand Trunk 1829-1924. (Montreal): (1924). V. 37

LOVETT, HENRY WILLIAM

Thoughts on the Cause of Evil, Physical and Moral. London: 1810. V. 42

LOVETT, R.

The Electrical Philosopher Containing a New System of Physics Founded Upon the Principle of an Universal Plenum of Elementary Fire . . . Worcester: 1774. V. 38

LOVETT, RICHARD

The Electrical Philosopher. Worcester: 1774. V. 37

The English Bible in the - 1525 to 1640. 1899. V. 38

The History of the London Missionary Society 1795-1895, London: 1899. V. 44

LOVETT, RICHARD continued

The History of the London Missionary Society 1795-1895. London: 1899. V. 37; 38; 41; 44

London Pictures Drawn with Pen and Pencil By . . . 1890. V. 37; 40

Norwegian Pictures . . . London: 1890. V. 43; 44

United States Pictures. London: 1891. V. 42

LOVETT, ROBERT W.

Lateral Curavture of the Spine and Round Shoulders. Philadelphia: 1907. V. 42; 45

LOVETT, WILLIAM 1800-1877

Elementary Anatomy and Physiology for Schools and Private Instruction, with Lessons on Diet, Intoxicating Drinks, Tobacco and Disease. London: 1853. V. 41

Manifesto of the General Convention of the Industrious Classes. London: 1839. V. 42

LOVIBOND, EDWARD

Poems on Several Occasions. London: 1785. V. 42; 45

LOVING, J. C.

The Loving Brand Book. Austin: 1965. V. 37; 38; 43; 44; 46

LOVING Man Tom. 1938. V. 39

LOW, A. P.

Report on the Dominion Government Expedition to Hudson Bay and the Arctic Islands on Board the D. G. S. Neptune 1903-1904. Ottawa: 1906. V. 37; 42; 44

LOW, CHARLES RATHBONE

Her Majesty's Navy, Including Its Deeds and Battles. London and New York: 1890-1893. V. 41

Soldiers of the Victorian Age. London: 1880. V. 41

LOW, DAVID 1786-1875

The Breeds of the Domestic Animals of the British Islands . . . London: 1842. V. 38

Dear David, Dear Graham. Oxford: 1989. V. 46

Elements of Practical Agriculture. London: 1847. V. 37

On Landed Property and the Economy of Estates. London: 1844. V. 38; 42

On the Domesticated Animals of the British Islands. London. V. 37

LOW, FRANCES H.

The Little Men in Scarlet and Other New Fairy Tales. London: 1896. V. 43

Queen Victoria's Dolls. London: 1894. V. 42; 44; 45

LOW, GEORGE

Fauna Occadensis; or, The Natural History of the Quadrupeds. Edinburgh: 1813. V. 43; 45

LOW, HUGH

Sarawak: Its Inhabitants and Productions: Being Notes During a Residence in that Country with His Excellency Mr. Brooke. London: 1848. V. 45

LOW, JOSEPH

Heads. Newton: 1960. V. 37

LOW-LIFE; or One Half of the World, Knows Not How the Other Half Live, Being a Critical Account of What is Transacted . . . In The Twenty-Four Hours, Between Saturday-Night and Monday-Morning. London: 1764. V. 40

LOW, NATHANAEL

An Astronomical Diary; or Almanack for . . . 1767. Boston: 1767. V. 40; 44

An Astronomical Diary, or Almanack, for the Year of Christian Aera, 1776. Massachusetts-Bay: 1775. V. 38

LOW, NATHANIEL

An Astronomical Diary; or, Almanack for 1777. Boston: 1776. V. 42

LOW, ROSEMARY

Amazon Parrots. London: 1983. V. 37; 38; 39; 43

The Parrots of South America. London: 1972. V. 38

LOW, SAMPSON

The English Catalogue of Books, Comprising the Contents of the 'London' and the 'British Catalogues, and The Principal Works Published in the United States of America and Continental Europe with Dates of Publication . . . London: 1873-1937. V. 39; 43

LOW, WILL H.

Ex Libris. Cleveland: 1896. V. 41

LOWBURY, EDWARD

Goldrush: Poems. (Shipston-on-Stour): (1983). V. 37

A Letter from Masada. Richmond: 1982. V. 38

Poetry and Paradox - an Essay with Nineteen Relevant Poems. Richmond: 1976. V. 38

LOWDERMILK, WILL H.

History of Cumberland from the Time of the Indian Town, Caluclucuc in 1728 Up to the Present Day, Embracing an Account of Washington's First Campaign, and Battle of Fort Necessity, Together with a History of Braddock's Expedition. Washington: 1878. V. 46

LOWE, ARTHUR CHARLES

The Diary of an Officer of the 16th (Queen's) Lancers, June 16, 1822 to June 16, 1840. Calcutta: 1894. V. 38

LOWE BROTHERS CO.

Counter Price List and Color Book of the Manufactures of the Lowe Bros. Co. Dayton: 1900? V. 37

LOWE, C. BRUCE

Breeding Racehorses by the Figure System. London: 1913. V. 37

LOWE, CONSTANCE M.

Merry Surprises: a Novel Picture Book for Children. London: 1900. V. 45

Pictures Everywhere. Printed in Bavaria: 1900. V. 40

What a Surprise. A Mechanical Book for Children. London: 1900. V. 38

LOWE, E. A.

Palaeographical Papers, 1907-1965. Oxford: 1972. V. 46

LOWE, EDWARD JOSEPH

Beautiful Leaved Plants. London: 1861. V. 37; 38; 39; 40

Beautiful Leaved Plants. London: 1864. V. 39; 42; 43; 45

Ferns: British and Exotic. London: 1856. V. 37; 38; 39

Ferns: British and Exotic. (with) A Natural History of New and Rare Ferns. London: 1871-72. V. 42

Ferns: British and Exotic. London: 1872. V. 38; 39; 40; 41; 42; 43; 44; 46

Ferns: British and Exotic. London: 1866-67. V. 37

A Natural History of British Grasses. London: 1858. V. 42; 43; 44

A Natural History of New and Rare Ferns . . . London: 1862. V. 39

A Natural History of New and Rare Ferns. London: 1864. V. 39

A Natural History of British Grasses. London: 1868. V. 43

A Natural History of British Grasses. London: 1891. V. 44

Our Native Ferns. London: 1865. V. 38

Our Native Ferns; or a History of the British Species and Their Varities. London: 1874-76. V. 37; 39; 42; 46

LOWE, HELEN

Unprotected Females in Norway; or, the Pleasantest Way of Travelling there, passing through Denmark and Sweden. With Scandinavian Sketches from Nature. London: 1857. V. 37

LOWE, JOHN

A Treatise on the Solar Creation and Universal Deluge of the Earth . . . London: 1795. V. 42

LOWE, JOSEPH

The Present State of England in Regard to Agriculture, Trade and Finance; With a Comparison of the Prospects of England and France . . . London: 1823. V. 39; 41

LOWE, PERCIVAL G.

Five Years a Dragoon. Kansas City: 1906. V. 38; 40; 41; 42; 44; 45; 46

LOWE, R. T.

A History of the Fishes of Madeira. London: 1843-60. V. 42

Protest Against the Ministrations in Madeira of the Reverend T. K. Brown in Opposition to Episcopal Authority and in Violation of the Laws and Constitution of the Church of England. Funchal: 1848. V. 42; 44

LOWE, ROBERT

General View of the Agriculture of the County of Nottingham, with Some Observations on the Means of Its Improvement. London: 1794. V. 41

General View of the Agriculture of the County of Nottingham. London: 1798. V. 46

LOWE, ROBERT W.

Bibliographical Account of English Theatrical Literature, from the Earliest Times to the Present Day. New York: 1888. V. 38

LOWE, T. S. C.

The Air-Ship City of New ; a Full Description of the Air Ship and the Apparatus to Be Employed in the Aerial Voyage to Europe. New York: 1859. V. 39; 40

LOWELL, AMY 1874-1925

Can Grande's Castle. New York: 1918. V. 40; 46

John Keats. Boston: 1925. V. 37; 42; 43; 45

John Keats. Boston and New York: 1925. V. 43

Legends. Boston/New York: 1921. V. 43

LOWELL, AMY 1874-1925 continued

The Madonna of Carthagena. 1927. V. 39

Pictures of the Floating World. New York: 1919. V. 43; 46

Some Imagist Poets an Anthology. (with) Some Imagist Poets, 1916: An Annual Anthology. (with) Some Imagist Poets, 1917: An Annual Anthology. Boston: 1915-17. V. 37

Sword Blades and Poppy Seed. New York: 1914. V. 37; 39; 41; 43

What's O'Clock. Boston: 1925. V. 46

LOWELL, G.

American Gardens. Boston: 1902. V. 45

More Small Italian Villas and Farm Houses. New York: 1920. V. 46

Smaller Italian Villas and Farmhouses. New York: 1916. V. 46

Smaller Italian Villas & Farmhouses. New York: 1922. V. 39

Smaller Italian Villas and Farmhouses. (with) More Small Italian Villas and Farmhouses. New York: 1916, 1920. V. 37

LOWELL, JAMES RUSSELL 1819-1891

The Anti-Slavery Papers of James Russell Lowell. Boston: 1902. V. 39; 41; 42

The Anti-Slavery Paper. Boston & New York: 1902. V. 39; 40

The Biglow Papers. Cambridge: 1848. V. 42; 44; 45

The Biglow Papers. Cambridge and London: 1848. V. 43

The Biglow Papers. (and) The Biglow Papers. Second Series. Cambridge: 1848, 1888. V. 40

The Biglow Papers. London: 1859. V. 45

The Biglow Papers. London: 1865. V. 43

The Cathedral. Boston: 1870. V. 44

Class Poem. Cambridge: 1838. V. 45

Collected Writings. London: 1892. V. 46

The Complete Writings. Boston: 1904. V. 42

Complete Writings. Cambridge: 1904. V. 38

Conversations of Some of the Old Poets. Cambridge: 1845. V. 37; 41; 43; 46

The Courtin'. Boston: 1874. V. 39; 41; 42; 46

Death of President Garfield. London: 1881. V. 39; 46

Democracy and Other Addresses. Boston & New York: 1887. V. 41

A Fable for Critics. New York: 1848. V. 39; 41

A Fable for Critics. Boston: 1859. V. 40

A Fable for Critics. Boston: 1891. V. 40; 41; 43; 44

Fireside Travels. Boston: 1864. V. 43

Heartsease and Rue. Boston: 1888. V. 44

Heartsease and Rue. London: 1888. V. 40

Heartsease and Rue. Boston and New York: 1888. V. 37

Impression of Spain. Boston: 1899. V. 43

In Memoriam James Abram Garfield. London: 1881. V. 38; 40; 42

Lectures on English Poets. Cleveland: 1897. V. 46

Lowell Calendar. Boston: 1886. V. 39

Meliboeus-Hipponax: the Bigelow Papers. Cambridge & London: 1848. V. 38; 40

Ode Recited at the Commemoration of the Living and Dead Soldiers of Harvard University, July 21, 1865. Cambridge: 1865. V. 42

On the Capture of Certain Fugitive Slaves Near Washington. N.P.: 1845? V. 42; 43

On Democracy: An Address Delivered in the Town Hall, Birmingham, on the 6th of October 1884. Birmingham: 1884. V. 37; 40

Il Pesceballo. Cambridge: 1862. V. 39; 41

Poems. Boston: 1848. V. 43

Poems. Second Series. Cambridge and Boston: 1848. V. 43

Poems. Boston: 1849. V. 40; 42; 45

The Poetical Works. London: 1896. V. 38

The Poetical Works. London and New York: 1903. V. 42

The Present Crisis. Portland: 1918. V. 37

The President's Policy. N.P., n.d. Philadelphia: 1864. V. 37

Under the Willows. Boston: 1869. V. 40; 42

The Vision of Sir Launfal. Cambridge: 1848. V. 38; 44; 45

The Vision of Sir Launfal. 1928. V. 44

Works. Boston: 1892. V. 42

Works. Boston & New York: 1899-1901. V. 40

The Writings. Cambridge: 1890-92. V. 37; 40; 43

Complete Writings. Cambridge: 1904. V. 40

A Year's Life. Boston: 1841. V. 37; 40; 42; 44

LOWELL, JOHN

The New-England Patriot . . . Boston: 1810. V. 46

Peace Without Dishonour - War Without Hope. Boston: 1807. V. 46

LOWELL, MARIA

The Poems of Maria Lowell. Cambridge: 1907. V. 43

The Poems of Maria Lowell. Cambridge: 1855. V. 37

THE LOWELL Offering, Written, Edited and Published by Female Operatives Employed in the Mills. Lowell: 1844-45. V. 37

LOWELL, PERCIVAL

Annals of the Lowell Observatory. Boston, New York: and: 1898-1905. V. 45

Mars and its Canals. New York: 1906. V. 37

LOWELL, ROBERT 1917-1977

Buckshee. 1966. V. 39

For the Union Dead. New York: 1964. V. 37; 38; 40; 42; 45

4 by . . . Cambridge: 1969. V. 38; 39; 42

4. Massachusetts: 1969. V. 41; 44

History. New York: 1973. V. 40

Imitations. New York: 1961. V. 39

Land of Unlikeness. 1944. V. 39; 40; 45

Life Studies. London: 1959. V. 40; 42; 43

Life Studies. New York: 1959. V. 37; 38; 40; 42; 45

Lord Weary's Castle. New York: 1946. V. 37; 38; 40; 42; 45; 46

The Mills of the Kavanaughs. New York: 1951. V. 37; 38; 39; 40; 42; 45

Near the Ocean. London: 1967. V. 45

Near the Ocean. New York: 1967. V. 40

The Old Glory. New York: 1965. V. 38; 40; 41; 42; 44

Poems 1938-1949. London: 1950. V. 37; 38; 42; 43

Promethus Bound. London: 1970. V. 45

The Voyage and Other Versions of Poems by Baudelaire. London: 1968. V. 40; 45; 46

LOWER, M. A.

A Compendious History of Sussex, Topographical, Archaeological and Anecdotal . . . Lewes, London & Brighton: 1870. V. 39

LOWER, MARK ANTHONY 1813-1876

Sussex Martyrs . . . Lewes: 1851. V. 40

LOWER, WILLIAM

The Phaenix in Her Flames. London: 1639. V. 37; 38

LOWERY, WOODBURY

The Lowery Collection. A Descriptive List of Maps of the Spanish Possessions Within Present Limits of the United States, 1502-1820. Washington: 1912. V. 39; 40; 43

The Spanish Settlements Within the Present Limits of the United States 1513-1561. New York: 1901. V. 38; 42

LOWES, JOHN LIVINGSTON

The Road to Xanadu: a Study in the Ways of the Imagination. Boston: 1927. V. 44

The Road to Xanadu. Boston & New York: 1927. V. 39

LOWMAN, ALBERT TERRY 1935-

Printer at the Pass: The Work of Carl Hertzog. San Antonio: 1972. V. 40

Printing Arts in Texas. Austin: 1975. V. 38; 39; 40; 41; 42; 43; 45; 46

Printing Arts in Texas. Austin: 1981. V. 37

Remembering Carl Hertzog. Dallas: 1985. V. 37; 38; 42; 43; 45

This Bitterly Beautiful Land. Austin: 1972. V. 38; 40; 41; 42; 43; 44

This Bitterly Beautiful Land. Austin: 1974. V. 40

LOWMAN, MOSES

A Dissertation on the Civil Government of the Hebrews . . . London: 1745. V. 38

A Rational of the Ritual of the Hebrew Worship. London: 1816. V. 40

Three Tracts. I. Remarks Upon . . . Whether the Appearances Under the Old Testament Were Appearances of the True God Himself . . . II. An Essay on the Schechinah . . . III. Texts of Scriptures Relating to the Logos Considered. London: 1756. V. 40

LOWNDES, HANNAH MARIA JONES

The Gipsey Chief; or, The Haunted Oak. London: 1840. V. 38

Trials of Love; or Woman's Reward . . . London: 1849. V. 42

LOWNDES, THOMAS

A Method to Prevent, Without a Register, the Running of Wool from Ireland to France, and to Other Foreign Parts. London: 1745. V. 40; 43

A State of the Coal-Trade to Foreign Parts, by Way of Memorial to a Supposed Very Great Assembly. London: 1744-45. V. 40

LOWNDES, WILLIAM

A Catalogue of Books, Pamphlets, Prints, Oratorios and Plays. London: 1790. V. 38

A Report Containing an Essay for the Amendement of the Silver Coins. London: 1695. V. 37; 38; 39; 40; 43

LOWNDES, WILLIAM THOMAS 1798?-1843

The Bibliographer's Manual of English Literature. London: 1834. V. 38; 40; 45

The Bibliographers Manual of English Literature . . . London: 1857. V. 39

Bibliographer's Manual of English Literture. London: 1857-64. V. 38

The Bibliographer's Manual of English Literature. London: 1857-65. V. 44

The Bibliographer's Manual of English Literature. London: 1869. V. 42

The Bibliographer's Manual of English Literature Containing an Account of Rare, Curious and Useful Books, Published in or Relating to Great Britain and Ireland . . . London: 1871. V. 46

The Bibliographer's Manual of English Literature. London: 1864. V. 37

The Bibliographer's Manual of English Literature . . . New edition, revised, corrected and enlarged. 1857-64. V. 37

LOWREY, MALCOLM

Ultramarine. Philadelphia: 1962. V. 37

LOWRIE, JOHN C.

A Manual of Missions; or, Sketches of the Foreign Missions of the Presbyterian Church . . . New York: 1854. V. 45

LOWRY, L. S.

Drawings. London: 1963. V. 37

Drawings of L. S. Lowry. 1963. V. 38

LOWRY, MALCOLM 1909-1957

Dark as The Grave Wherein My Friend is Laid. New York: 1968. V. 40; 41; 42; 44

Hear Us O Lord from thy Dwelling Place. 1961. V. 43

Hear Us O Lord from Heaven Thy Dwelling Place. Philadelphia and New York: 1961. V. 38

Hutton Street. Cincinnati: 1940. V. 40

Lunar Caustic. Paris: 1963. V. 46

October Ferry to Gabriola. New York: 1970. V. 39; 44

October Ferry to Gabriola. London: 1971. V. 45

Ultramarine. London: 1933. V. 37; 42; 43

Ultramarine. Philadelphia: 1962. V. 39; 45

Ultramarine. London: 1963. V. 45

Under the Volcano. London: 1947. V. 38; 40; 43; 44; 45

Under the Volcano. New York: 1947. V. 38; 39; 40; 42; 43; 44; 45; 46

Under Vulkanen. Kobenhavn: 1949. V. 39; 44

Unter Dem Vulkan. Stuttgart: 1950. V. 39; 44

LOWRY, MARTIN

Venetian Printing: Nicolas Jenson and the Rise of Roman Letterform. Herning: 1989. V. 45

LOWRY, ROBERT

The Blaze Beyond the Town: The Toy Balloon; Phisterus. Bari: 1945. V. 40

Hutton Street. Cincinnati: 1940. V. 37

The Journey Out. 3 Stories. Bari: 1945. V. 42

LOWRY, T. K.

The Hamilton Manuscripts, Containing an Account of the Settlement of the Territories of Upper Clandeboyse, Great Andes, and Dufferin in County Down . . . Belfast: 1867. V. 37; 38

LOWRY, WALKER

Tumult at Dusk. San Francisco: 1963. V. 38; 40; 46

LOWSLEY, BRAZILLAI

A Glossary of Berkshire Words and Phrases. London: 1888. V. 41

LOWTH, ROBERT

Billesdon Coplow, a Poem. February 24, A.D. 1804. Montreal: 1809. V. 43

Billesdon Coplow, a Poem on Foxhunting . . . London: 1833. V. 44; 46

Isaiah. A New Translation; with a Preliminary Dissertation and Notes Critical, Philological, and Explanatory. London: 1778. V. 38

The Life of William of Wykeham, Bishop of Winchester. London: 1759. V. 39

De Sacra Poesi Hebraeorum. Oxford: 1753. V. 38

De Sacra Poesi Hebraeorum . . . Oxonii: 1763. V. 38

A Sermon Preached Before the Governors of the Radcliffe Infirmary at St. Mary's Church in Oxford, on Wednesday, July 3, 1771. Oxford: 1771. V. 38

A Short Introduction to English Grammar. London: 1763. V. 41

A Short Introduction to English Grammar. London: 1769. V. 41

A Short Introduction to English Grammar. London: 1772. V. 41; 42; 46

A Short Introduction to English Grammar. London: 1783. V. 43; 46

A Short Introduction to English Grammar; with Critical Notes. London: 1789. V. 41; 42; 46

A Short Introduction to English Grammar. London: 1791. V. 41

LOWTHER, ALICE

When It Was June. London: 1923. V. 41

LOWTHER, GEORGE FRANCIS 1913-

The Adventures of Superman. New York: 1942. V. 42

LOWTHER, GEORGES

Gerald; a Tale of Conscience. London: 1840. V. 42

LOWY, A.

The History of Chivalry and Ancient Armour, with Descriptions of the Feudal System, the Usages of Knighthood, the Tournament and Trials by Single Combat . . . London: 1857. V. 40

THE LOYAL Address of the Eminent Town of Lynn-Regis in the County of Norfolk. London: 1681. V. 42

LOYAL Attachment; a Poem. London: 1795. V. 42

THE LOYAL Convenanter, or, Peace and Truth Revived. London: 1648. V. 43

THE LOYALIST; or, Anti-Radical; Consisting of Three Departments. London: 1820. V. 38

LOYALTY and Nonconformity; or, a Loyal Nonconformist Decently Interr'd. London: 1669. V. 40

LOZANO, CHRISTOBAL

Los Reyes Nuevos de Toledo. Descrivense las Cosas mas Augustas, y Notables de Esta Ciudad Imperial . . . Madrid: 1667. V. 45

LOZANO, PEDRO

A True and Particular Relation of the Dreadful Earthquake Which Happen'd at Lima, the Capital of Peru, and the Neighboring Port of Callao, On the 28th of October 1746 . . . London: 1748. V. 40; 41; 42

LTICHFIELD, SAMUEL

The Dresden Gallery. Marks and Monograms on Old China. Litchfields: 1884. V. 44

LUACH for the Year 5541 (i.e. 1781-82). London: 1781. V. 39

LUARD, JOHN

A History of the Dress of the British Solldier, from the Earliest Period to the present Time. London: 1852. V. 37

LUARREA, JUAN

Guernica. New York: 1947. V. 40

LUBBOCK, BASIL

Adventures by Sea from Art of Old Time. London: 1925. V. 38; 39; 42

Barlow's Journal of His Life at Sea in King's Ships, East and West Indiamen and Other Merchantmen from 1659 to 1703. London: 1934. V. 41

Bully Hayes, South Sea Pirate, Unbelievable Saga of Adventures in the Days of Iron Men and Wooden Ships . . . Boston: 1931. V. 41

The Last of the Windjammers. London: 1927 & 1929. V. 41

Sail, the Romance of the Clipper ships. London: 1927. V. 38; 44

LUBBOCK, FRANCIS R.

In the Name of the State of Texas, To All To Whom These Presents Shall Come. Austin. V. 39

Six Decades in Texas; or, Memoirs of Francis R Lubbock, Governor of Texas in Wartime. Austin: 1900. V. 37; 38; 39; 42; 45

LUBBOCK, J. G.

Art and the Spiritual Life. Leicester: 1967. V. 37; 40

Aspects of Art and Science. Leicester: 1969. V. 37; 40; 45; 46

From Garden to Galaxy. London. V. 41

From Garden to Galaxy. London: 1980. V. 39; 40; 41; 45; 46

From the Snows to the Seas. Cambridge: 1986. V. 38; 40

From the Snows to the Seas. London: 1986. V. 43; 46

Love for the Earth. 1990. V. 45

pERECEPTIONS OF THE eARTH. London. V. 46

Perceptions of the Earth. 1977. V. 40

Perceptions of the Earth. London: 1977. V. 38; 39; 40; 41; 43; 44; 45; 46

Reflections from the Sea. 1971. V. 42

Reflections from the Sea. Leicester: 1971. V. 37; 39; 40; 41; 46

The Sphere of Rocks and Water. 1983. V. 38

The Sphere of Rocks and Water. London: 1983. V. 38; 43; 44; 46

LUBBOCK, JOHN

Monograph of the Collembola and Thysanura. London: 1873. V. 38; 43

LUBBOCK, JOHN WILLIAM 1803-1865

Remarks on the Classification of the Different Branches of Human Knowledge. London: 1838. V. 45

LUBERSAC, ABBE DE 1730-1804

Discours sur les Monumens Publics. Paris: 1775. V. 38; 39; 40; 41

LUBIENICKI, STANISLAW

Theatrum Cometicum . . . Amsterdam: 1668-66-68. V. 42

LUBKE, WILHELM

History of Sculpture, from the Earliest Ages to the Present Time. London: 1872. V. 40; 44

LUBY, CATHERINE

The Spirit of the Lakes (:Killarney); or, Mucruss Abbey. London: 1822. V. 43; 46

LUC, JEAN ANDRE DE

Geological Travels in some parts of France, Switzerland and Germany. Translated from the French Manuscript. London: 1813. V. 37

LUCA, MARK

Back to the Cave. San Francisco: 1956. V. 44

LUCAN, LORD

English Cavalry in the Army of the East. 1854 & 1855. London: 1856. V. 41

LUCAN, MARCUS ANNAEUS 39-68

Lucan's Pharsalia, or the Civil Warres of Rome, Between Pompey the Great, and Julius Caesar . . . London: 1627. V. 45

LUCANUS, MARCUS ANNAEUS 39-68

De Bello Civili Libri Decem. Paris: 1545. V. 40

De Bello Civili, Libri Decem. Frankfurt: 1551. V. 40

De Bello Civili Velpharsaliae Libri X. Antverpiae: 1592. V. 40

De Bello Civili, cum Hug. Grotii, Farnabii, Notis Integris, et Variorum Selectissimis. London: 1818. V. 42

De Bello Civili Lbiri Decem. Lutetiae: MDXLV. V. 45

Delle guerre Civili . . . con Aggiunta sino Alla Morte di Cesare. Ravenna: 1587. V. 38

Lucano Traduzido de Verso Latino en Prosa Cstellana. Burgos: 1578. V. 38

Lvcano Tradvzido De Verso Latino En Prosa Castellana, Por Martin Laso De oropesa . . . Burgos: 1588. V. 38

Pharsalia. Venice: 1502. V. 41

Pharsalia. Venice: 1515. V. 37

Pharsalia. London: 1614. V. 40; 45

Lucan's Pharsalia. London: 1718. V. 38; 43; 44; 46

Pharsalia Sive Belli Civilis Libri Decem. Lugduni Batavorum (Leyden): 1728. V. 46

Pharsaliae, cum Commentario Petri Burmanni. Leyden: 1740. V. 46

Pharsalia, cum Notis Hugonis Grotii et Richrdi Bentleii . . . 1760. V. 43

Pharsalia, cum Notis Hugonis Grotii et Richardi Bentleii. London: 1760. V. 40

Pharsalia. Strawberry Hill: 1760. V. 38; 40; 41; 43

Pharsalia, Sive de Bello Civili, Libri X. Glasguae: 1785. V. 44

LUCAS, ARTHUR

John Lucas, Portrait Painter, 1828-1874: A Memoir of His Life Mainly Deduced From Correspondence of His Sisters. London: 1910. V. 44

LUCAS, CHARLES

An Appeal to the Commons and Citizens of London. London: 1756. V. 40

The Complaints of Dublin . . . In Behalf of Himself. Dublin: 1748. V. 40; 41; 46

Cursory Remarks on the Method of Investigating the Principles and Properties of Bath and Bristol Waters. Bath: 1764. V. 38

An Essay on Waters. London: 1756. V. 42

The Old Serpentine Temple of the Druids, at Avebury, in North Wiltshire, a Poem. Marlborough: 1795. V. 46

LUCAS, CORYDON L.

The Milton Lott Tragedy and A Sketch of the Life of Col. Nathan Boone. Madrid: 1905. V. 38

The Milton Lott Tragedy. Madrid: 1906. V. 43

LUCAS, E. V.

All the World Over. London: 1899. V. 45

At 'The Pines.' A Visit to A. C. Swinburne. London: 1916. V. 38

Edwin Austin Abbey, R.A. The Record of His Life and Work. London: 1921. V. 39

Edwin Austin Abbey, Royal Academician: The Record of His Life and Work. New York: 1921. V. 42; 43

Edwin Austin Abbey. New York & London: 1921. V. 42

Four and Twenty Toilers. London. V. 46

John Constable the Painter. London: 1924. V. 39; 41

Playtime and Company. London: 1925. V. 40; 41; 42; 45; 46

Whenever I See a Grey Horse. London. V. 46

LUCAS, ELIZA

Journal and Letters of Eliza Lucas (1741-1744). Wormsloe: 1850. V. 42

LUCAS, E.V.

Playtime & Company. A Book for Children. Verses by E.V. Lucas. Pictures by E.H. Shepard. London: (1925). V. 37

LUCAS, F. L.

Gilgamish, King of Erech. London: 1948. V. 37; 44; 46

The Golden Cockerel Anthology. Waltham St. Lawrence: 1937. V. 45

LUCAS, FRED W.

The Annals of The Voyages of the Brothers Nicolo and Antonio Zeno. London: 1898. V. 40; 42; 43; 45

Appendiculae Historicae. London: 1891. V. 40

LUCAS, GEORGE

Star Wars. N.P.. V. 42

LUCAS, HERMAN W.

The Raven's Leaf. Poems. Los Angeles: 1907. V. 45

LUCAS, JOHN

Miscellanies in Verse and Prose . . . Salisbury: 1776. V. 41

LUCAS, JOSEPH

The Yetholm History of the Gypsies. London: 1882. V. 42

LUCAS-LUCAS, H. F.

The Fox Hunting Alphabet. London: 1910. V. 42

LUCAS, PAUL

Voyage du Sieur Paul Lucas, fait en 1714 . . . Rouen: 1719. V. 44

Voyage Du Sieur Lucas, fait en MDCCXIV &c. Amsterdam: 1720. V. 43

LUCAS, RICHARD 1648-1715

An Enquiry After Happiness, in Several Parts. London: 1704-1700-1696. V. 42; 45

Humane Life; or, a Second Part of the Enquiry After Happiness. London: 1690. V. 42

An Inquiry After Happiness. Edinburgh: 1754. V. 44

Religious Perfection: or, a Third Part of the Enquiry After Happiness. London: 1696. V. 39

LUCAS, S. E.

The Catalogue of Sassoon Chinese Ivories. London: 1950. V. 37; 42

LUCAS, ST. JOHN

The Oxford Book of French Verse: XIIIth to XXth Century. Oxford: 1910. V. 44

LUCAS, THEOPHILUS

Memoirs of the Lives, Intrigues and Comical Adventures of the Most Famous Gamesters and Celebrated Sharpers in the Reigns of Charles II, James II, William III and Queen Anne. London: 1714. V. 41

LUCAS, THOMAS J.

Camp Life and Sport in South Africa. London: 1878. V. 37; 39; 40; 41; 42; 43; 45

Pen and Pencil Reminiscences of a Campaign in South Africa. London: 1861. V. 44

The Zulus and the British Frontiers. London: 1879. V. 41

LUCAS, W. J.

British Dragonfiles. (Odonata). London: 1900. V. 38; 39; 41; 43

LUCAS, WILLIAM

The Duellists; or, Men of Honour . . . London: 1805. V. 45

LUCATT, EDWARD

Rovings in the Pacific from 1837 to 1849; with a Glance at California . . . London: 1851. V. 42; 44

LUCCA. LAWS, STATUTES, ETC.

Lucensis Civitatis Statuta . . . Lucca: 1539. V. 40

LUCCHESE, MATTEO

Riflessioni Sulla Pretesa Scoperta del Sopranornato Toscano . . . Venice: 1730. V. 38

LUCCHINI, ANTONIO-MARIA

La Nouvelle Magnificence Royale sur les Ondes, on Soit, le Bucintor . . . Venice: 1776. V. 38

LUCCOCK, JOHN

The Nature and Properties of Wool. Leeds: 1805. V. 37

LUCE, CLARE BOOTH

Kiss the Boys Good-bye. New York: 1939. V. 45

LUCE, EDWARD S.

Keogh, Comanche and Custer. N.P.: 1939. V. 37; 38

Keogh, Comanche and Custer. Ashland: 1974. V. 45

LUCE, G. H.

Poems. London: 1924. V. 40

Poems . . . Richmond: 1923. V. 38

LUCE, S. B.

Seamanship . . . New York: 1898. V. 39

LUCE, STEPHEN B.

Steamship: Compiled from Various Authorities . . . For the Use of the United States Naval Academy . . . New York: 1866. V. 40

LUCETT, EDWARD

Rovings in the Pacific, from 1837 to 1849. London: 1851. V. 38

LUCIAN SAMOSATENSIS

Dialogi Selectiores Coelestes, Marini & Inferni, Graece & latine edite in Usum Puerorum. Basle: 1560. V. 40

LUCIANUS SAMOSATENSIS

Dialogi & Alia Emuncta. Paris: 1514. V. 40

I Dialogi Piacevoli, le Vere Narrationi, le Facete Epistole . . . di Greco in Volgare Tradotte per M. Nicolo da Lonigo. Venice: 1541. V. 45

Dialogues of Lucian from the Greek. London: 1773. V. 46

Dialogues. Paris: 1951. V. 42; 43; 45

Dorum Dialogi Numero 70. Strassburg: 1515. V. 44

Lucian of Samosata. From the Greek. London: 1820. V. 46

Lucian's True History. London: 1894. V. 37; 40; 42

Opera, Quae Graece Extant . . . Omnia Multo Quam Ante, Tum Ex Diversorum Codicum Collatione. Basle: 1555. V. 40; 43

The Select Dialogues of . . . To Which is Added. A New Literal Translation in Latin, with Notes in English . . . London: 1744. V. 41

The True Historie of Lucian the Samosatenian. Berkshire: 1927. V. 41

The True Historie of Lucian, the Samosantenian. Waltham St. Lawrence: 1927. V. 37; 39; 44; 45

De Veris Narrationibus Commentarii Duo Festivissimi. Basle: 1524. V. 40

The Works of Lucian. London: 1780. V. 43; 46

LUCIE-SMITH, EDWARD

Seven Colours . . . Cambridge: 1974. V. 40; 42

LUCILIUS, GAIUS

Satyrarvm Quae Supersunt Reliqviae. Lvgdvni Batavorvm: 1597. V. 46

LUCIUS, HORATIUS

Tractatvs de Privilegiis Stvdentivm . . . Caroli Girardi . . . Epistola, de Ivris Volvminibvs . . . Ex Bibliotheca Casparis Barthi. Frankfurt: 1625. V. 42

Tractatvs, De Priuilegiis Scholarium. Padua: 1564. V. 38

LUCIUS, JOHANNES

Placitorvm Summae apud Gallos Curiae Libri XII. Multis a Secunda Editione, Placitis Insignibus Adaucti . . . Paris: 1559. V. 45

LUCKENBACH, A.

Forty-Six Scripture Narratives from the Old Testament. New York: 1838. V. 38

LUCKENBACH, ABRAHAM

A Collection of Hymns for the Use of the Delaware Christian Indians, of the Missions of the United Brethren in North America. Bethlehem: 1847. V. 45

LUCKENBILL, DANIEL DAVID

Ancient Records of Assyria and Babylonia. Chicago: 1926-27. V. 37; 44

The Annals of Sennacherib. Chicago: 1924. V. 40; 42; 44

The Annals of Sennacherib. Chicago: (1924). V. 37

LUCKOMBE, PHILIP

A Concise History of the Origin and Progress of Printing with Practical Intructions to the Trade in General Compiled from Those Who Have Wrote on this Curious Act. London: 1770. V. 37

The History and Art of Printing. London: 1770-71. V. 39

The History and Art of Printing. London: 1771. V. 37; 42; 44

A Tour Through Ireland. London: 1783. V. 38

A Tour Through Ireland . . . prefixed a description of that Kingdom. London: 1780. V. 37

LUCRETIUS CARUS, TITUS 99-55 BC

Della Natura delle Cose. Amsterdamo: i.e. Paris: 1754. V. 40; 44

Della Natura Delle Cose. In Amsterdamo: 1754. V. 41; 42

The Nature of Things . . . London: 1813. V. 40; 41; 42; 45

Of the nature of Things. London: 1743. V. 38; 43; 46

De Rerum Natura. Venice: 1515. V. 38; 40

De Rerum Natura Libri Sex. Paris & Lyon: 1563. V. 45

De Rerum Natura Libri Sex. Antwerp: 1566. V. 37

De Rerum Natura, Libri VI . . . Lutetiae: 1570. V. 44

De Rerum Natura Libri Sex. Paris: 1570. V. 37; 40

De Rerum Natura Libri VI. Frankfrut: 1583. V. 40; 44

De Rerum Natura Libri Sex . . . Lugduni Batuorum: 1595. V. 41

De Rerum Natura Libri Sex. Saumur: 1662. V. 38

De Rerum Natura. Cantabrigiae: 1675. V. 40; 42

De Rerum Natura Libri Sex . . . Oxford: 1695. V. 43

De Rerum Natura Sex, ad Optimorum Exemplarium Fidem Recensiti. London: 1712. V. 41; 45

De Rerum Natura Libros Sex, Interpretatione et Notis Illustravit Thomas Creech . . . London: 1717. V. 41

De Rerum Natura Libri Sex, Cum Notis Integris Dionysii Lambini, Oberti Gifanii, Tanaquilli Fabri . . . Leiden: 1725. V. 43

De Rerum Natura Libri Sex, Cum Notis Integris Dionysii Lambini, Oberti Gifanii, Tanaquilli Fabri . . . Lugduni Batavorum: 1725. V. 45

De Rerum Natura Libri Sex. Lutetiae Parisiorum: 1744. V. 45

De Rerum natura Libri Sex, Accedunt Selectae Lectiones Dilucidando Poemati Apposita. Paris: 1744. V. 45

De Rerum Natura. Glasgow: 1749. V. 45

De Rerum Natura Libri Sex. Glasgow: 1759. V. 41; 45

Titi Lucretii Cari de rerum Natura libri sex. Ex Editione Thomae Creech. Glasguae: 1759. V. 39

De Rerum Natura. Birmingham: 1772. V. 38; 40; 42; 43; 45

De Rerum natura Libri Sex. Birmingham: 1773. V. 41; 44

De Rerum Natura Libros Sex . . . London: 1796. V. 40; 43

De Rerum Natura Libri Sex. London: 1823. V. 40

De Rerum Natura, Libri Sex. Londini: 1824. V. 40; 45

De Rerum Natura Libri Sex. Chelsea: 1913. V. 45

De Rerum Natura: Of the Nature of Things. Los Angeles: 1957. V. 43; 46

Titus Lucretius Carus, His Six Books of Epicurean Philosophy, Done Into English Verse, with Notes. London: 1683. V. 41; 46

LUCY. a Tale. Belfast: 1822. V. 38

LUCY, H. W.

Peeps at Parliament: Taken from Behind the Speaker's Chair. London: 1903. V. 39

LUDECUS, MATTHIAS d. 1601

Historia Von der Erfindung Wunderwereken und Zersdorung des Vermeinten Beiligen Bluts zur Wilsnagk . . . Wittenberg: 1586. V. 45

LUDENDORFF, GENERAL

The General Staff and Its Problems. New York: 1920. V. 46

LUDLAM, WILLIAM

Essays on Scripture Metaphors, Divine Justice, Divine Mercy, and the Doctrine of Satisfaction. London: 1785. V. 44

LUDLOW, EDMUND 1617-1692

Memoirs of Edmund Ludlow, Esq; Lt. General of the Horse Commander in Chief of the Forces in Ireland, One of the Council of State, and a Member of the Parliament Which Began on November 3, 1640. Switzerland: 1698-99. V. 42; 44

Memoirs. London: 1751. V. 39; 45

Memoirs . . . with a Collection of Original Papers, and the Case of King Charles the First. London: 1771. V. 37; 41; 42

LUDLOW, EDWARD

Memoirs. Switzerland. (with) *Memoirs . . . the Third and Last Part.* London: 1698, 1720. V. 40

LUDLOW, FITZ HUGH

The Hasheesh Eater: Being Passages from the Life of a Pythagorean. New York: 1857. V. 42; 46

The Heart of the Continent . . . New York: 1870. V. 39; 42

The Opium habit. New York: 1868. V. 37; 38; 40

LUDLOW, NOAH M.

Dramatic Life as I Found It. St. Louis: 1880. V. 38; 39; 40; 41; 42

LUDLOW, WILLIAM

Appendix PP. Report of a Reconnaissance of the Black Hills of Dakota. Made in the Summer of 1874. Washington: 1875. V. 46

Report of a Reconnaissance of the Black Hills of Dakota. Washington: 1875. V. 39; 41; 43; 44; 45; 46

Report of a Reconnaissance from Carroll, Montana Territory, on the Upper Missouri, to the Yellowstone National Park & Return, Made in the Summer of 1875. Washington: 1876. V. 37; 38; 39; 41; 45

LUDLUM, ROBERT

The Scarlatti Inheritance. 1971. V. 39

LUDLUM, ROBERT continued

The Scarlatti Inheritance. New York: 1971. V. 39

The Scarlatti Inheritance. New York & Cleveland: 1971. V. 40

Trevayne. 1973. V. 46

Trevayne. New York: 1973. V. 41; 42; 43

LUDOLF, HIOB 1625-1704

Lexicon Aethiopico-Latinum. Grammtica Aethiopica. Confessio Fidei Claudii Regis. London: 1661. V. 37; 38; 40

LUDOLPH, HIOB 1625-1704

A New History of Ethiopia. London: 1682. V. 43; 46

LUDOLPHUS DE SAXONIA

Vita Christi, ex Evangeliis et Scriptoribus Orthodoxis per Ludolphum Saxonium, Sacri Ordinis Carthusiensium Excerpta. Paris: 1534. V. 41; 45

LUDOVICO DEGLI ARRIGHI, VINCENTINO fl. 1522

The Calligraphic Models of Ludovico Degli Arrighi surnamed Vicentino. Paris: 1926. V. 39; 40

Regola da Imparare Scrivere Varii Caratteri de Littere con Li Svoi Compassi et Misvre et il Modo de Temperare le Penne Secondo la Sorte de Littere Che orrai Scrivere, Ordinato per Ludovico Vicentino con Una Recetta da Far Inchiostro Fino . . . Venice: 1533. V. 40

LUFF, JOHN N.

The Postage Stamps of the United States. New York: 1907. V. 46

LUFF, JOSEPH

Autobiography of Elder . . . One of the Twelve Apostles of the Reorganized Church of Jesus Christ of Latter Day Saints. Lamoni: 1894. V. 37; 38

LUFFMAN, JOHN

The Charters of London Complete; also Magna Charta and the Bill of Rights. London: 1793. V. 46

LUGAR, ROBERT

Architectural Sketches for Cottages, Rural Dwellings, and Villas, in the Grecian, Gothic and Fancy Styles, with Plans. London: 1805. V. 38; 42

The Country Gentleman's Architect. London: 1805. V. 38

The Country Gentleman's Architect. London: 1807. V. 38; 40; 42; 45; 46

The Country Gentleman's Architect. London: 1823. V. 38; 46

The Country Gentleman's Architect. London: 1838. V. 38

Plans and Views of Ornamental Domestic Buildings Executed in the Castellated and Other Styles. London: 1836. V. 42

Villa Architecture . . . London: 1828. V. 42

LUGARD, FREDERICK D.

The Rise of Our East African Empire. Edinburgh: 1893. V. 38; 41

The Rise of Our East African Empire, Early Efforts in Nyasaland and Uganda. London: 1893. V. 46

LUGARD, JOHN

The Antiquities of the Anglo-Saxon Church. Philadelphia: 1841. V. 46

LUGO, BERNARDO DE

Gramatica en La Lengua General Del Nuevo Reyno Llamada Mosca. Madrid: 1619. V. 37; 40

LUHAN, MABEL DODGE

Edge of Taos Desert. New York: 1937. V. 41; 46

Lorenzo in Taos. New York: 1932. V. 41

Movers and Shakers. New York: 1936. V. 41

Taos and Its Artists. New York: 1947. V. 41; 42; 43; 44; 46

Winter in Taos. New York: 1935. V. 41; 42

LUIGI AMEDEO OF SAVOY, DUKE OF THE ABRUZZI

On the 'Polar Star' in the Arctic Sea. London: 1903. V. 37; 40

LUINO, FRANCESCO

Delle Progressioni E Serie. Milan: 1767. V. 45

LUIS DE GRANADA 1504-1588

Memorial de la Vida Christiana: en el Qual se Ensefia Todo lo Que un Christiano Deue Hazer Dende (sic) el Principio de Su Conuersion, Hasta el Fin dela Perfection . . . Salamanca: 1578-79. V. 45

Primera (-Quinto) Parte de la Introduction del Symbolo de la Fe. Gerona: 1620. V. 40; 45

Rosario Figurato della Sacratissima Vergine Madre di Dio Nostra Avocata dall' Opere del Rev. P. F. Luigi di Granata . . . Venice: 1578. V. 43

Rosario della sacr(issi)ma Vergine Maria . . . e Sette Devotissimi Orationi . . . Rome?: 1573. V. 37

Specchio della Vita Humana, nel Quale si Contiene il Libro Della Contemplatione . . . (bound with) Trattato della Confessione et Communione. (bound with) Essercitio et Ammaestramento del Buon Christiano. Venice: 1568. V. 43

LUISINI, FRANCESCO 1523-1568

In Librum Q. Horatii Flacci de Arte Poetica Commentarius. Venice: 1554. V. 43

LUISINO, ALOYSIO

Aphrodisiacus, Sive de Lue Venerea . . . Leyden: 1728. V. 38; 45

LUKE, B.

John Bon and Mast Person. London: 1807. V. 37; 42

LUKE Darrell, the Chicago Newsboy. Chicago: 1865. V. 40; 42

LUKE, L. D.

A Journey from the Atlantic to the Pacific Coast, By Way of Salt Lake City Returning by Way of the Southern Rome. New York: 1884. V. 44

A Journey from the Atlantic to the Pacific Coast. Utica: 1884. V. 37; 40; 43; 44

LUKIN, JAMES

The Lathe and Its Uses; or, Instruction in the Art of Turning Wood and Metal. London: 1874. V. 45

LUKIN, ROBERT

A Treatise on Tennis. London: 1822. V. 39

LUKIS, W. C.

An Account of Church Bells. London: 1857. V. 38; 40

LULL, RAMON

Libro de la Concepcion Virginal . . . Brussels: 1664. V. 37

Raymundi Lulli . . . Mercuriorum Liberiam Tandem Subsidio Manuscripti Exemplaris . . . Coloniae: 1567. V. 41

Opera ad Inventam. Strasbourg: 1598. V. 37

The Order of Chivalry. Translated by William Caxton and L'Ordene de Chevalerie. Translated by William Morris. London: 1893. V. 41

Raymundi Lulli . . . De Secretis Naturae, seu de Quinta Essentia Liber Unus, in Tres Distinctiones Diuisus . . . Coloniae: 1567. V. 41

LULLIES, REINHARD

Greek Sculpture. London: 1960. V. 40; 42

LULLIN DE CHATEAUVIEUX, FREDERIC 1772-1841

Manuscript Transmitted from St. Helena, by an Unknown Channel. London: 1817. V. 39

LULLIUS, RAIMUNDUS

Arbor Scientiae Venerabilis ac Celitus Illuminati Partis Raymundi Iulii Majoricensis . . . Lyon: 1515. V. 46

Codicillus Seu Vade Mecum, in Quo Fontes Alchimicae Artis ac Philosophiae Reconditioris Uberrime Traduntur. Rouen: 1651. V. 46

Libelli Aliquot Chemici . . . Basle: 1572. V. 46

Opera ea Quae ad Adinventam ad Ipso Artem Universalem, Scientarum Artiumque Omnium Breui Compendio . . . Strasbourg: 1609. V. 46

Practica Compendiosa Artis Raymundi Lul. Lyon: 1523. V. 46

De Secretis Naturae Siue Quinta Essentia Libri Duo. Venice;: 1542. V. 46

De Secretis Naturae, Seu de Quinta Essentia Liber Unus, in Tres Distinctiones Divisus . . . Cologne: 1567. V. 46

Testamentum . . . Duobus Libris Universam Artem Chymicam Compleetens. Cologne: 1753. V. 46

LULLY, JEAN BAPTISTE 1632-1687

Armide. Paris: 1686. V. 40; 43

Roland, Tragedie Mise en Musique. Paris: 1685. V. 40

Thesee, Tragedie Mise en Musique. Paris: 1688. V. 40

LUMBY, EDWIN

Edwin Lumby's Illustrated Catalogue of Wrought Welded Boilers, Cisterns, etc. Halifax: 1880. V. 37

LUMHOLTZ, CARL

Among Cannibals. London: 1889. V. 39; 45; 46

Among Cannibals. New York: 1889. V. 38; 42

El Mexico Desconocido . . . New York: 1904. V. 41

New Trails in Mexico. New York: 1912. V. 39; 40; 41; 42; 46

Through Central Borneo. London: 1921. V. 42; 46

Unknown Mexico. New York: 1902. V. 38; 39; 40; 45

Unknown Mexico. London: 1903. V. 40

THE LUMIERE; Containing a Variety of Topographical Views in Europe and America. New York: 1831. V. 41

LUMISDEN, ANDREW 1720-1801

Remarks on the Antiquities of Rome and Its Environs . . . London: 1797. V. 37; 39; 44; 45

LUMLEY, L. R.

History of the Eleventh Hussars (Prince Albert's Own) 1908-1934. London: 1936. V. 41

LUMLEY, WILLIAM GOLDEN

The Art of Further Amendment of the Laws Relating to the Poor in England, with Other Statutes Affecting the Poor Law . . . of 1844. London: 1844. V. 39

LUMMIS, CHARLES F.

The Awakening of a Nation: Mexico of To-Day. New York: (1898). V. 37

Flowers of Our Lost Romance. Boston & New York: 1929. V. 45

The Gold Fish of Gran Chimu. Boston & New York: 1896. V. 37; 38; 41

The King of the Broncos and Other Stories of New Mexico. New York: 1898. V. 39

A Tramp Across the Continent. New York: 1892. V. 39; 40; 45

LUMMIS, W.

The Roll of the Victoria Cross. India: 1926. V. 42

LUMPKIN, C. P.

History of the Waco Baptist Association of Texas. Waco: 1897. V. 45

LUMPKIN, WILSON

The Removal of the Cherokee Indians from Georgia. New York: 1907. V. 38

The Removal of the Cherokee Indians from Georgia. Savannah: 1907. V. 42; 45

LUMSDEN & SON, (JAMES)

Lumsden & Son's Steam-boat Companion . . . Glasgow: 1831. V. 43

LUMSDEN, E. S.

The Art of Etching. London: 1925. V. 38

LUMSDEN, H.

History of the Hammermen of Glasglow. Paisley: 1912. V. 44

LUMSDEN, JAMES

American memoranda. Glasgow: 1844. V. 38; 42; 46

LUMSDEN, THOMAS

A Journey from Meerut in India, to London, Through Arabia, Persia, Armenia, Georgia, Russia, Austria, Switzerland and France During the Years 1819 and 1820. Edinburgh: 1822. V. 43

LUNARDI, VINCENZO

An Account of Five Aerial Voyages in Scotland, In a Series of Letters to His Guardian . . . London: 1786. V. 42

LUNCH, WILLIAM F.

Naval Life; or, Observations Afloat and on Shore. The Midshipman. New York: 1851. V. 37

LUND, FREDRIK MACODY

Ad Quadratum. A Study of the Geometrical Bases of Classic and Medieval Religious Architecture. London: 1921. V. 42

LUND, JOHANNES

Die Alten Juedischen Heiligthuemer. Hamburg: 1738. V. 44

LUNDQUIST, ROBERT

Before the Rain. Santa Cruz: 1985. V. 39

LUNDY, BENJAMIN

The Genuis of Universal Emancipation. Baltimore: 1830-33. V. 42

Life, Travels and Opinions of Benjamin Lundy, Including His Journeys to Texas and Mexico. Philadelphia: 1847. V. 43; 44; 45

The Origin and True Causes of the Texas Insurrection, Commenced in the Year 1835. Philadelphia: 1836. V. 38; 46

The War in Texas; a Review of Facts and Circumstances, Showing That This Contest is the Result of a Long Premeditated Crusade Against the Government . . . Philadelphia: 1836. V. 37; 42; 46

The War in Texas. Philadelphia: 1837. V. 41; 42; 44; 45

LUPI REBELLO, JACOBUS

Fructus Sacramenti Penitentiae. Paris: 1494. V. 42

LUPICINI, ANTONIO

Breve Discorso Sopra la Reduzione dell'anno, & Emendazione del Calendario. Florence: 1580. V. 38

Discorso Sopra la Fabrica, e Uso Delle Nuove Verghe Astronomiche. Firenze: 1582. V. 38

LUPOFF, RICHARD A.

Edgar Rice Burroughs: Master of Adventure. New York: 1965. V. 46

LUPTON, DONALD

The Glory of Their Times, or, the Lives of Ye Primitive Fathers . . . London: 1640. V. 44

LUPTON, THOMAS

A Thousand Notable Things of Sundry Sorts, Enlarged. London: 1686. V. 43

LUPTON, WILLIAM

A Discourse of Murther, Preach'd in the Chapel at Lincoln's Inn, and Publish'd at the Request of the Worshipful the Masters of the Bench. London: 1725. V. 37

LUQMAN

Sapientis Fabulae et . . . Arabum Adagia. Leiden: 1625. V. 40

LURCAT, ANDRE

Architecture. Paris: 1929. V. 42

LURIE, ALISON

V. R. Lang: a Memoir. Munich: 1959. V. 37; 46

V. R. Lang. A Memoir. Munich: 1939. V. 37

LUSCOMBE, MICHAEL H. T.

The Pleasures of Society, a Poem. London: 1824. V. 40; 43

LUSHINGTON, FRANKLIN

Background. London: 1931. V. 37

The Gambardier Giving Some account of the Heavy and Siege Artillery in France, 1914-1918. London: 1930. V. 43; 44; 45; 46

Memoir of Henry Fitmaurice Hallam. London: 1850. V. 46

LUSHINGTON, HENRY

A Great Country's Little Wars; or England, Affghanistan and Sinde . . . London: 1844. V. 38; 41; 44

LUSHINGTON, S. G.

The Statutes Relating to Lunacy, Comprising the Law With Respect To Pauper Lunatics, Hospitals and Licensed Hosued . . . London: 1890. V. 42

LUSHINGTON, S. R.

The Life and Services of General Lord Harris, During His Campaigns in America, the West Indies and India. London: 1840. V. 38

LUSIGNAN, SAUVEUR

A Genuine Voyage to Smyrna and Constantinople, and a Journey from Thence Overland to England . . . London: 1801. V. 45

Letters Addressed to Sir William Fordyce, Containing a Voyage and Journey from England to Smyrna, from thence to Constantinople and from that Place Over Land to England . . . London: 1788. V. 37

LUSSAN, MARGUERITE DE

The Life of the Countess de Gondez. London: 1729. V. 41; 42; 45

LUST, HERBERT C.

Giacometti: The Complete Graphics and 15 Drawings. New York: 1970. V. 39; 46

LUSTER, MARY R.

Autobiography of Mary R. Luster, Springfield, Missouri. Springfield: 1935. V. 38; 40; 42

The Autobiography of . . . Springfield, Missouri. Written in her eighty-first and eighty-second years . . . Springfield, Mo.: (1935). V. 37

LUSUS Westmonasterienses, Sive Epigrammatum et Poematum Minorum Delectus. Westmonasterii: 1730. V. 39

THE LUTE of Love. London: 1920. V. 38; 44

LUTHER, MARTIN 1483-1546

Ain Christlyche und Vast Wolgegruente Beweysung von dem Juengsten Tag/Und von Seinen Zaichen . . . Witemberg: 1522. V. 38

An Die Pfarrhern Wider den Wucher zu Predigen. Wittemberg: 1540. V. 38

Antwortt Deutsch Mart. Luthers Auff Koenig Henrichs Von Engelland Buch. Wittemberg: 1522. V. 38; 40; 42

Auf Das Ubir Christlich Ubirgeystlich, und Ubirkunstlich Buch Bocks Emszers u Leypptzick Antwortt D.M.L. Wittenberg: 1521. V. 40

Colloquia Oder Tischreden Doctor Martini Lutheri, so er in Vilen Jaren, die Zeyt Seines Lebens, Gegen Gelehrten Leuthen Auch Frombden Gesten und Seinen Tischgesellen Gefuret . . . Getruckt zu Franckfurt am: 1568. V. 40

A Commentarie Upon the Epistle of S. Paul to the Galathians. London: 1644. V. 41

A Commentary Upon the Fifteen Psalmes, Called Psalmi Graduum, that is Psalmes of Dgrees . . . London: 1615. V. 46

Der Sechs und Dreissiste Psalm David, Eynen Christlichen Menschen tzu Leren und Troesten . . . Wittenberg: 1521. V. 38

Der Kleiner Catechismus. Germanton: 1785. V. 44; 45

Deutsch Auszlegung des 67. Wittenberg: 1521. V. 38; 41

Die Syben Beuszpsalmen. Strasbourg: 1519. V. 42

LUTHER, MARTIN 1483-1546 continued

Die Zwo Epsiteln Sant Peters. Augsburg: 1522. V. 38

Die Lugend von S. Johanne Chrysostomo and die Heiligen Veter in dem Vermeinten Concilio zu Mantua, Durch D. Marti. Luther Gesand. Wittemberg: 1537. V. 38

Das Diese wort Christi (Das ist Mein Leib. Etce) Noch Fest Stehen Widder die Schwermgeister. Wittemberg: 1527. V. 38

Dris Martini Lutheri Colloquia Mensalia . . . London: 1651. V. 45

Dris Martini Lutheri Colloquia mensala; or, Dr. Martin Luther's Divine Discourses at His Table. London: 1652. V. 46

Ein Sermon von dem Wucher, Doctor Martini Luther Augustiner zu Wittemberg. Nuremberg: 1520. V. 42

Ein Brieff Von Seinem Buch der Winckel Messen, an Einen Guten Freund. Wittemberg: 1534. V. 42

Ein Sermon Vber das Evangelion Johannis an XXV. Von Maria Magdalena. Wittemberg: 1531. V. 37

Epistolarum Reverendi Patris Domini D. Martini Lutheri, Tomus Primus, Continens Scripta viri Dei, ab Secundum. Ihenae (Jena): 1556. V. 38

Epistolarum Reverendi Partis . . . Tomus Primus . . . (with) Secundus Tomus. Jena & Eisleben: 1556-65. V. 40

Evangelium von den Tzehen Auszsetzigen. Wittemberg: 1521. V. 38

Eyn Sermon D. Martini Luthers. Wittemberg: 1522. V. 45

Katechesis Marteinou tou Loutherou, he Mikra Kaloumene, Hellenikolatine. Catechesis Martini Lutheri Parva, Graecolatina, Postremum Recognita. Basel: 1567. V. 38

Loci Communes . . . Excriptis Ipsius Latinis Forma Gnomologica & Aphoristica Collecti & in Quinque Classes Distributi . . . Magdeburg: 1594. V. 46

Das Magnificat Vorteutschet Unnd Auszgelegt. Wittemberg: 1521. V. 38

Samtliche Schriften . . . Halle: 1740-53. V. 38

Schrifften und Wercke . . . Leipzig: 1729-33. V. 38

Sermo Elegantissimus, Super Sacramento Corporis & Sanguinis Christi. Hagenau: 1527. V. 43

Several Choice Prophecyes of the Incomparable and Famous Dr. Martin Luther, . . . London: 1666. V. 43

Das Siebed Capitel S. Paul zu den Chorinthern Ausgelegt Durch Maartinum Luther. Wittemberg: 1523. V. 38

Sylvula Sententiarum, Exemplorum, Historiarum, Allegoriarum, Similitudinum, Facetirum, Partim ex Reverendi Viri, D. Martini Luther . . . Francofurti: 1566. V. 38

Vermanung zum Sacrament des Leybs und Bluts Unsers Herren. Wittemberg: 1530. V. 38

Von der Beicht ob Die der Bapst Macht Habe zu Gepitenn. Doctor Martinus Luther. Witttenberg: 1521. V. 38

Von der Beycht; ob die der Bapst Macht Habe zu Gebieten. Wittenberg: 1522. V. 38

Von Welltlicher Uberkeytt wie Weytt man yhr Gehorsam Schuldig sey Mart. Luther. Vuittemberg: 1523. V. 38

Von Kuffshandlung und Wucher. Vuittemberg: 1524. V. 38

Von Den Falschen Betler Buberey, Mit Einer Vorrede Martini Luther. Und Hinden an Ein Rotwelsch Vocabularius. Wittemberg: 1528. V. 44

Von den Letzten Worten Davids. Wittemberg: 1543. V. 38

Warnunge D Martini Luther; an Seine Lieben Deudschen, Vor Etlichen Jren Geschrieben, auff Diesen Fall, so Die Feinde Christlicher Warheit diese Kirchen und Land . . . Wittemberg: 1547. V. 38

LUTHER, SETH

An Address to the Working Men of New England, on the State of Education and on the Condition of the Producing Classes in Europe and America. New York: 1833. V. 45

LUTTIG, JOHN C.

Journal of a Fur Trading Expedition on the Upper Missouri, 1812-13. St. Louis: 1920. V. 38; 42; 43

LUTTON, ANNE

Poems on Moral and Religious Subjects. Dublin: 1829. V. 37; 42

LUTTRELL, HENRY

Advice to Julia. A Letter to Rhyme. London: 1820. V. 41

Advice to Julia. A Letter in Rhyme. London: 1829. V. 42

Crockford House, A Rhapsody (and) A Rhymer in Rome. London: 1827. V. 37; 44

LUTTRELL, NARCISSUS 1657-1752

A Brief Historical Relation of State Affairs from September 1678 to April 1714. Oxford: 1857. V. 37; 40; 45

LUTYENS, EDWIN

The Architecture of Sir Edwin Lutyens. V. 46

The Architecture of Sir Edwin Lutyens . . . London: 1950. V. 45

LUTYENS, ROBERT

The Old Burgundians. Portraits of Eleven of the Members. London: 1962. V. 45

LUTZ, HENRY FREDERICK

Early Babylonian Letters from Larsa. New Haven: 1917. V. 44

LUXBOROUGH, LADY

Letters Written by the Late Right Honourable Lady Luxborough to William Shenstone, Esq. London: 1775. V. 41

LUYKEN, JAN

Afbeelding der Menschelyke Bezigheden, Bestaande in Hondert Onderscheiden Printverbeeldingen, Vertonende Allerhande Stantspersonen, zo van Regeeringe, Konsten . . . Amsterdam: 1698. V. 46

LUYS, JULES BERNARD

Recherches sur le Systeme Nerveux Cerebro-Spinal sa Structure, ses Fonctions et ses Maladies . . . Paris: 1865. V. 37

LVRES de Prieres, Tisse d'Apres les Enluminures. Lyon: 1886-87. V. 46

LYALL, ALFRED COMYN

Verses Written in India. London: 1889. V. 45

LYALL, ROBERT

The Character of the Russians, and a Detailed History of Moscow. London: 1823. V. 38; 41; 43; 44; 45

Travels in Russia, the Krimea, the Caucasus and Georgia. London: 1825. V. 40; 46

LYCETT, J.

Views in Australia. Melbourne &c.: 1973. V. 41

LYCOPHRON

Cassandra. Cambridge: 1806. V. 43

Lycophronis Chalcidensis Alexandra, cum Graecis Isaacii Tzetzis Commentariis. Oxford: 1697. V. 45

LYCOSTHENES, CONRAD

Prodigionum ac Ostento Chronicon. Basle: 1557. V. 44

Die Wunder Gottes in der Natur, bey Erscheinung der Cometen, oder Besondere Anmerckung der Vornehmsten Cometen . . . Frankfurt & Leipzig: 1744. V. 38

LYDDEL, RICHARD

An Account of the Tryal of Richard Lyddel, Esq; at His Majesty's Court of Common-Pleas, Before the Right Honourable Lord - Chief - Justice Eyre, for Carrying on a Criminal Converstation with the Late Lady Abergavenny; on Monday the 16th of Feb. 1729/30. London: 1730. V. 42

LYDEKKER, R.

Library of Natural History. New York & Chicago: 1901. V. 37

LYDEKKER, RICHARD

Animal Portraiture. V. 46

Animal Portraiture. London. V. 45

Animal Portraiture. 1912. V. 46

Animal Portraiture. London: 1912. V. 39; 40

Animal Portraiture. London: n.d. V. 37

Animal Portraiture with Fifty Studies in Full Colour, reporduced from original painting. London: (1912). V. 37

Catalogue of the Fossil Birds in the British Museum. London: 1891. V. 44

Catalogue of the Ungulate Mammals in the British Museum (Natural History). London: 1913-15. V. 45

Catalogue of the Ungulate Mammals in the British Museum. London: 1913-16. V. 37; 38; 39

Catalogue of the Heads and Horns of Indian Big Game Bequeathed by A. O. Hume, C.B. to the British Museum (Natural History) London. London: 1913. V. 38

The Game Animals of Africa. London: 1908. V. 39; 40; 46

The Game Animals of Africa. London: 1926. V. 38; 45

The Royal Natural History. V. 46

The Royal Natural History. London. V. 45

The Royal Natural History. London: 1893-1896. V. 39; 42; 43; 44; 46

The Royal Natural History. London: 1893-94. V. 44

The Sheep and Its Cousins. London: 1912. V. 39

Wild Life of the World. London: 1915. V. 44

LYDGATE, JOHN

The Chorale and the Bird. Chelsea: 1929. V. 37

Table Manners for Children . . . 1989. V. 45

LYDIAT, THOMAS

De Variis Annorum Formis (etc.). London: 1605. V. 40; 45

LYDON, A. F.

English Lake Scenery. London: 1880. V. 38; 43; 46

Fairy Mary's Dream. London: 1870. V. 45

Gems from the Poets Illustrated from Original Designs by . . . London: 1855. V. 45

Scottish Loch Scenery. London: 1882. V. 43; 44; 46

LYDSTON, G. FRANK

Panama and Sierras. Chicago: 1900. V. 43

LYE, EDWARD 1694-1767

Dictionarium Saxonico et Gothico-Latinum . . . London: 1772. V. 38

LYE, LEN

No Trouble. Deya, Majorca: 1930. V. 37; 38
No Trouble. Mallorca: 1930. V. 40; 41; 42; 46
No Trouble. Deya: Majorca,: 1830. V. 37

LYEGE, JEAN, 16th century

De Humani Corporis Harmonia Libri IIII. Lutetiae: 1555. V. 40

LYELL, CHARLES 1797-1875

Elements of Geology. London: 1838. V. 46
Elements of Geology. Philadelphia: 1839. V. 40
Elements of Geology. Boston: 1841. V. 40; 43
The Geological Evidence of Antiquity of Man With Remarks on Theories of the Origin of Species by Variation. London: 1863. V. 38; 39; 40; 41; 43; 44; 45; 46
The Geological Evidences of the Antiquity of Man, with Remarks on Theories of the Origin of Species by Variation. Philadelphia: 1863. V. 42
The Geological Evidences of the Antiquity of Man, with an Outline of Glacial and Postertiary Geology and Remarks on the Origin of Species. London: 1873. V. 37; 38
Life, Letters and Journals of Sir Charles Lyell, Bart. London: 1881. V. 39
Principles of Geology, Being an Attempt to Explain the Former Changes of the Earth's Surface, by Reference to Causes Now in Operation. London: 1830/32/33. V. 37; 42
Principles of Geology . . . London: 1830-33. V. 37; 41; 42
Principles of Geology. London: 1832-33. V. 44; 46
Principles of Geology . . . Philadelphia: 1837. V. 45
Principles of Geology. London: 1840. V. 40; 45
Principles of Geology. London: 1847. V. 43; 44; 46
Principles of Geology. London: 1867-68. V. 43; 44; 46
Principles of Geology. London: 1872. V. 43; 45
Principles of Geology. New York: 1877. V. 40
Principles of Geology. London: 1970. V. 37; 38
Principles of Geology. London: 1853. V. 37
Reisen in Nord Amerika. Halle: 1846. V. 39
A Second Visit to the United States of North America. New York: 1849. V. 37; 46
A Second Visit to the United States of North America. New York: & London: 1850. V. 46
Travels in North America; with Geological Observations on the United States, Canada, and Nova Scotia. London: 1845. V. 41; 42; 43; 46
Travels in North America, in the Years 1841-2. New York: 1845. V. 38; 40
Zweite Reife Nach den Vereinigten Staaten Von Nordamerita. Braunschweig: 1851. V. 39

LYELL, DENIS

The Hunting and Sppor of Central African Game. London: 1928. V. 37

LYELL, DENIS D.

The African Elephant and Its Hunters. London. V. 39; 40
The African Elephant and Its Hunters. London: 1924. V. 38; 44; 45
Hunting Trips in Northern Rhodesia. London: 1910. V. 39
The Hunting and Spoor of Central African Game. London: 1929. V. 38
Memories of an African Hunter. London: 1923. V. 39
Nyasaland for the Hunter and Settler. London: 1912. V. 37; 38
Wild Life in Central Africa. London: 1913. V. 39

LYELL, J. C.

Fancy Pigeons. London: 1887. V. 38

LYELL, JAMES P. R.

Early Book Illustration in Spain. With an introduction by Dr. Konrad Haebler. 1926. V. 37

LYELL, JAMES PATRICK RONALDSON

Early Book Illustration in Spain. London: 1926. V. 37; 38; 44; 46

LYER, MICHAEL

Cultur Anatomicus. Hoc Est: Methodus Brevis Facilis ac Perspicuna Arteficiose & Compendiose Human Incidendi Cadavaera. Hafniae: 1665. V. 38

LYFORD & BOYCE

The Art of Lettering and Sign painter's Manual. Boston: 1870. V. 40

LYFORD, WILLIAM G.

The Westen Address Directory . . . Baltimore: 1837. V. 38; 39; 43; 46

LYLE, JOHN N.

The Revised Statutes of Texas. Galveston;: 1879. V. 38

LYLE, R. C.

The Aga Khan's Horses. London: 1938. V. 43
Brown Jack. London: 1934. V. 37; 42
Royal Newmarket. London: 1945. V. 40; 42

LYLTE, ANDREW

A Name for Evil. (1947). V. 37

LYLY, JOHN

The Complete Works. Oxford: 1902. V. 37; 39
Euphues. (with) Euphues and His England. London: 1623. V. 39
Euphues: the Anatomie of Wit. London: 1636. V. 39
Sixe Covrt Comedies. London: 1632. V. 46

LYMAN, ALBERT

Journal of a Voyage to California, and Life in the Gold Diggings. Hartford: 1852. V. 40; 42; 43

LYMAN, GEORGE D.

The Book and the Doctor. San Francisco: 1933. V. 38; 46
John Marsh, Pioneer. New York: 1930. V. 38; 42; 46

LYMAN, HENRY

Artifical Anaesthesia and Anaesthetics. New York: 1881. V. 42; 45

LYMAN, HENRY M.

The Practical Home Physician. Albany: 1888. V. 38

LYMAN, JOSEPH B.

The Philosophy of House-Keeping. Hartford: 1867. V. 39

LYMBURNER, ADAM

The Paper Read at the Bar of the House of Commons, by Mr. Lymburner; Agent for the Subscribers to the Petitions from the Province of Quebec. Quebec: 1791. V. 43

LYMINGTON, LORD

Spring Song of Iscariot. Paris: 1929. V. 37

LYN, SAMUEL

A Short Narrative of the Case of Samuel Lynn, Esq . . . London: 1720. V. 43

LYNCH, ANNE C.

The Rhode Island Book. Providence: 1841. V. 40

LYNCH, ANNE CHARLOTTE 1815-1891

Poems. New York: 1849. V. 37; 39; 41; 43

LYNCH, BERNARD

A Guide to Health through the Various Stages of Life. London: 1744. V. 43; 45

LYNCH, BOHUN

A History of Caricature. Boston: 1927. V. 41
Max Beerbohm in Perspective. London: 1921. V. 41
The Prize Ring. London: 1925. V. 40

LYNCH, E. M.

Killboylan Bank or Every Man His Own Banker. London: 1896. V. 39

LYNCH, H. F. B.

Armenia. Travels and Studies. Beirut: 1965. V. 39
Armenia. Travels and Studies. London: 1901. V. 37

LYNCH, JAMES

With Stevenson to California 1846. N.P.: 1896. V. 40; 45

LYNCH, JAMES D.

The Bench and Bar of Texas. St. Louis: 1885. V. 37; 38; 41

LYNCH, JAMES K.

With Stevenson to California 1846. N.P.: 1896? V. 40

LYNCH, P.

The Life of St. Patrick Apostle of Ireland. Dublin: 1828. V. 46

LYNCH, PATRICIA

The Turf-Cutter's Donkey. London: 1934. V. 41

LYNCH, THEODORA ELIZABETH

The Cotton-Tree; or, Emily, the Little West-Indian. London: 1847. V. 44

LYNCH, W. F.

Narrative of the U. S. Expedition to the River Jordan and the Dead Sea. Philadelphia: 1850. V. 42

Naval Life; or Observations Afloat and On Shore - the Midshipman. New York: 1851. V. 42

Naval Life; or, Observations Afloat and on Shore - the Midshipman. Washington: 1851. V. 39

LYND, JOHN

United States of America. City of New Orleans. State of Louisiana. Be it known that on this 18th Day of December 1815 . . . Joseph Donitien Boulet . . . deposed that he was an inhabitant of the province of Louisiana on the 30th day of April, 1803 . . . New Orleans: 1815. V. 37

LYNDE, HUMPHREY 1579-1636

Via Devia: The By-Way: Mis-leading the Weake and Unstable into Dangerous Paths of Error . . . London: 1630. V. 39

Via Tuta: the Safe Way . . . (with) Via Devia: the By-Way. London: 1630. V. 39

LYNDSAY, DAVID

Facsimile of an Ancient Heraldic Manuscript Emblazoned by Sir David Lyndsay of the Mount, Lyon King of Armes 1542. Edinburgh: 1822. V. 46

The Poetical Works. London & Edinburgh: 1806. V. 38

The Poetical Works. Edinburgh: 1871. V. 40

The Poetical Works . . . with Memoir, Notes, and Glossary by David Laing. Edinburgh: 1879. V. 37

LYNE, CHARLES

The Industries of New South Wales. Sydney: 1882. V. 39

LYNE, MICHAEL

Horse, Hounds, and Country. London: 1938. V. 39

The Michael Lyne Sketch Book. London: 1979. V. 39; 46

A Parsons Son. London: 1974. V. 39

LYNK, MILES V.

The Black Troopers or the Daring Heroism of the Negro Soldier in the Spanish American War. Jackson: 1899. V. 46

LYNN, ELWYN

Sidney Nolan: Myth and Imagery. London & Melbourne: 1967. V. 41

LYNN, NEVILLE

Lynn's Acting Edition. London: 1893-96. V. 42

LYNN, SAMUEL

A Short Narrative of the Case of Samuel Lynn, Esq. London: 1720. V. 40

LYNN, WALTER

An Essay Towards a More Easie and Safe Method of Cure in the Small Pox. London: 1714. V. 43

LYNTON Abbott's Children. London: 1879. V. 40

LYON, A. B.

Lyon Memorial. Massachusetts Familes Including Descendants of the Immigrants William Lyon, of Roxbury, Peter Lyon, of Dorchester, George Lyon, of Dorchester with Introduction Treating of the English Ancestry of the American Families. Detroit: 1905. V. 44

LYON & HEALY

Rare Old Violins, Violas, Violoncellos. Chicago: 1922. V. 37

Rare Old Violins, Volas and Violoncellos. Chicago: 1929. V. 37

LYON, B. B. VINCENT

Non-Surgical Drainage of the Gall Tract. Philadelphia: 1923. V. 45

LYON, C. J.

History of St. Andrews, Episcopal, Monastic, Academic and Civil . . . Edinburgh: 1843. V. 41

LYON, D. S.

Tariff, or Rates of Duties Payable from And After the 3d of March, 1833 on all Goods, Wares, and Merchandise, Imported into the United States of America. V. 40

LYON, DANNY

The Bikeriders. New York: 1968. V. 45; 46

LYON, EMMA

Miscellaneous Poems. Oxford: 1812. V. 42

LYON, GEORGE FRANCIS 1795-1832

A Brief Narrative of an Unsuccesful Attempt to Reach Repulse Bay, through Sir Thomas Rowe's 'Welcome' in His Majesty's Ship Griper . . . London: 1825. V. 37; 38; 39; 40; 41; 42; 43; 44; 46

Journal of a Residence and Tour in the Republic of Mexico in the Year 1826. With some Account of the Mines of that Country. London: 1828. V. 37

A Narrative of Travels in Northern Africa in the Years 1818, 19 and 20. London: 1821. V. 38; 40

The Private Journal of Captain G. F. Lyon, of HMS Hecla During the Recent Voyage of Discovery Under Captain Parry. London: 1824. V. 37; 42; 43; 45; 46

The Private Journal of . . . During the Recent Voyage of Discovery Under Captain Parry, 1821-1823. Barre: 1970. V. 45

Twenty-Six Original Proof Plates for Parry's Second Voyage Drawn by Captain G. F. Lyon and Engraved by Edward Finden. London: 1824. V. 40

LYON, IRVING WHITALL

Colonial Furniture of New England. A Study of the Domestic Furniture in Use in the Seventeenth & Eighteenth Centuries. Boston & New York: 1891. V. 39

The Colonial Furniture of New England. Boston: 1924. V. 39; 42

Colonial Furniture of New England. Boston & New York: 1925. V. 45

LYON, JAMES

Four Essays on the Right and Propriety of Secession by Southern States. Richmond: 1861. V. 46

Urania, a Choice Collection of Psalmtunes Anthems . . . Philadelphia?: 1773? V. 38

LYON, JOHN

Experiments and Observations Made with a View to point Out the Errors of the Present Received Theory of Electricity. London: 1780. V. 43; 45

The Harp of Zion. Liverpool: 1853. V. 37; 42

The History of the Town and Port of Dover, and of Dover Castle; with a Short Account of the Cinque Ports. Dover: 1813-14. V. 42; 43

LYON, LEMUEL

The Military Journals of Two Private Soliders, 1758-1775 . . . a Supplement Containing Official Papers on the Skirmished at Lexington and Concord. Poughkeepsie: 1855. V. 37

LYON, MAX

Catalogue of . . . Works of Art, Chiefly Italian of the Mediaeval and Renaissance Periods . . . London: 1914. V. 44

LYON, P.

Observations of the Barrenness of Fruit Trees, and of the Means of Preventions and Cure. Edinburgh: 1813. V. 43; 45

LYON, WILLIAM P.

Reminiscences of the Civil War. Compiled from the war correspondence of Colonel . . . & from his personal letters & diary by Mrs. Adelia C. Lyon. (San Jose, CA): 1907. V. 37

LYONS, ARTHUR

All God's Children. New York: 1975. V. 42; 45

LYONS, CICELY

Salmon, Our Heritage: the Story of a Province and an Industry. Vancouver: 1969. V. 43

LYONS, H. G.

A Report on the Temples of Philae. Cairo: 1908. V. 43

LYRA Germanica. London: 1861. V. 42; 44
LYRA Germanica. London: 1864. V. 41
LYRA Germanica. London: 1868. V. 39; 42; 45

THE LYRIC Year. One Hundred Poems. New York: 1912. V. 38

LYRICAL Ballads, with a Few Other Poems. London: 1798. V. 37

LYSACHT, A. M.

Joseph Banks in Newfoundland and Labrador, 1766. London: 1971. V. 38; 41

LYSAGHT, ELIZABETH J.

The Gold of Ophir. London: 1890. V. 44

LYSER, ALICE

Spain and Spanish America in the Libraries of the University of California: a Catalogue of Books. Berkeley: 1928-30. V. 45

LYSIAS

Eratosthenes, Hoc est, Brevis et Lvculenta Defensio Lysiae pro Caede Eratosthenis, Praelectionibus Illustrata Andreae Dvnaei. Cantabrigiae: 1593. V. 46

LYSONS, DANIEL

The County Palatine of Cheshire. London: 1810. V. 44

Derbyshire. London: 1817. V. 44

The Environs of London. London: 1792-96. V. 42

The Environs of London: Being an Historical Account of the Towns, Villages, and Hamlets Within Twelve Miles of that Capital. London: 1800/1795/1796. V. 39

An Historical Account of Those Parishes in the County of Middlesex . . . London: 1800. V. 42; 46

LYTTON, EDWARD GEORGE EARLE LYTTON BULWER-LYTTON, 1ST BARON 1803-1873 continued

Collected Works. London: 1852-74. V. 38

Works. London: 1877-1883. V. 42

Works. Boston: 1890. V. 42

Works. Boston: 1891. V. 42

LYTTON, EDWARD ROBERT

Tannhauser: or, the Battle of the Bards. Mobile: 1863. V. 46

LYTTON, EDWARD ROBERT BULWER-LYTTON, 1ST EARL OF 1831-1891

Confessions of a Water-Patient; in a Letter to W. Harrison Ainsworth, Esq. London: 1845. V. 41

The Earl's Return. London: 1887. V. 42

Lucile. London: 1860. V. 39

Lucretia, or, the Children of Night. London: 1846. V. 41

M

MAC ADAM, JOHN LOUDON 1756-1836

Directions for Repairing Roads. Pembroke: 1819? V. 38

Observations on the Management of Trusts for the Care of Turnpike Roads, as Regards the Repair of the Road, the Expenditure of the Revenue, and the Appointment and Quality of Executive Officers. London: 1825. V. 38

A Practical Essay on the Scientific Repair and Preservation of Public Roads. London: 1819. V. 37

Remarks on the Present System of Road Making . . . Bristol: 1816. V. 37; 39; 42

Remarks On the Present System of Road Making . . . London: 1820. V. 39; 42

Remarks on the Present System of Road Making . . . with a View to a Revision of the Existing Laws . . . Defending the Road Funds from Misapplication . . . London: 1821. V. 39

Remarks on the Present System of Road Making . . . London: 1822. V. 39; 42

Remarks on the Present System of Road Making . . . London: 1823. V. 38; 39

MAC ADAM, M. F. LAMING

The Temples of Kawa. Oxford: 1949-55. V. 37; 40

MC ADAMS, W E.

A Lecture on the Colony of New Zealand, Addressed to the Working Classes. London: 1873. V. 43

MC ADIE, ALEXANDER

The Clouds and Fogs of San Francisco. San Francisco: 1912. V. 45

MC AFEE, ROBERT B.

History of the Late War in the Western Country. Lexington: 1816. V. 38; 42; 44; 46

History of the Late War in the Wester Country, Comprising a Full Account of all Transactions in that Quarter, from the Commencement of Hostilitites at Tippecanoe, tot he Termination of the Contest at New Orleans. Lexington, Ky.: 1816. V. 37

MC ALEER, GEORGE

Gathered Waiflets. Worcester: 1913. V. 43

MC ALEXANDER, U. G.

History of the Thirteenth regiment United States Infantry. 1905. V. 46

MAC ALISTER, R. A.

The Excavation of Gezer 1902-1905 and 1907-1909. London: 1912. V. 37

MAC ALISTER, R. A. S.

The Book of MacCarthaigh Riabach, Otherwise Called the Book of Lismore. Dublin: 1950. V. 43

Ireland in Pre Celtic Times. Dublin: 1921. V. 38; 43

A Text Book of European Archaeology. Volume I: The Paleolithic Period. Cambridge: 1921. V. 38

MAC ALISTER, R. A. STEWART

The Excavation of Gezer 1902-1905 and 1907-1909. London: 1912. V. 42

The Secret Languages of Ireland, with Special Reference to the Origin and Nature of the Shelta Language . . . Cambridge: 1937. V. 42

MAC ALLESTER, OLIVER

A Series of Letters, Discovering the Scheme Porjected by France, in MDCCLIX. For an Intended Invasion upon England with Flat Bottom'd Boars . . . London: 1767. V. 37

MC ALLISTER, ISABEL

Alfred Gilbert. London: 1929. V. 39; 41

MC ALLISTER, JAMES GRAY

Sketch of Captain Thomas McAllister Co. A. 27th Virginia Regiment. Petersburg: 1896. V. 42

MC ALLISTER, JOSEPH THOMPSON

Virginia Militia in the Revolutionary War. Hot Springs: 1913. V. 45; 46

MC ALLISTER, WARD

Society As I Have Found It. New York: 1890. V. 42

MC ALMON, ROBERT

Being Geniuses Together. London: 1938. V. 37; 38; 40; 42; 45

A Companion Volume. Paris: 1923. V. 37; 44

Contact Collection of Contemporary Writers. Paris: 1925. V. 40; 41

Distinguished Air: Grim Fairy Tales. Paris: 1925. V. 43

Explorations. London: 1921. V. 37

A Hasty Bunch. Paris: 1923. V. 37; 38; 40; 42; 45; 46

A Hasty Bunch. Paris: 1923. V. 45

A Hasty Bunch. Paris: 1922. V. 37

Indefinite Huntress and Other Stories. Paris: 1932. V. 43

Not Alone Lost. Norfolk: 1937. V. 41

The Portrait of a Generation. 1926. V. 41

The Portrait of a Generation. Dijon: 1926. V. 39

The Portrait of a Generation. Paris: 1926. V. 42; 43; 45

Post Adolescence. Dijon. V. 38; 41

Post Adolescence. Paris: 1920. V. 42

Post-Adolescence. Dijon: 1923. V. 39; 40; 42; 44; 46

Post-Adolescence. Dijon: 1923. V. 46

Village: as It Happened through a Fifteen Year Period. Dijon: 1923. V. 46

Village. Paris: 1924. V. 41

M'ALPINE, D.

The Botanical Atlas, A Guide to the Practical Study of Plants. Edinburgh: 1883. V. 44

The Botanical Atlas, a Guide to the Practical Study of Plants. Edinburgh: 1883. V. 42; 43; 44; 46

MAC ALPINE, I.

Three Hundred Years of Psychiatry 1535-1860. Hartsdale: 1928. V. 40

Three Hundred Years of Psychiatry 1535-1860. Hartsdale: 1982. V. 39; 41

M'ALPINE, JOHN

Genuine Narratives and Concise Memoirs of Some of the Most Interesting Exploits and Singular Adventures of John M'Alpine, a Native Highlander, from the Time of His Emigraation from Scotland to America 1773 . . . till December 1779. 1985. V. 38; 40

Genuine Narratives and Concise Memoirs of Some of the Most Interesting Exploits and Singular Adventures of John M'Alpine. London: 1985. V. 39

M'ALPINE, NEIL

A Pronouncing Gaelic Dictionary . . . Edinburgh: 1832. V. 42

A Pronouncing Gaelic Dictionary. Edinburgh: 1833. V. 37; 40; 41; 42; 44

MAC ANDREW, ISAAC FORSYTH

Memoir of Isaac Forsyth, Bookseller in Elgin. London: 1889. V. 40; 44

MC ANDREW, JOHN

Venetian Architecture of the Early Renaissance. Cambridge: 1980. V. 46

MAC ARTHUR, BLANCHE

Lessons in Figure Painting in Water Colors. London: 1880. V. 46

Lessons in Figure Painting in Water Colours. London: 1885. V. 40

MAC ARTHUR, DOUGLAS

Reminiscences. New York: 1964. V. 41; 45

MAC ARTHUR, JAMES

New South Wales, It's Present State and Future Prospects.. London: 1837. V. 40; 44; 46

MC ARTHUR, JOHN

The Army and Navy Gentleman's Companion: or, a New and Complete Treatise . . . on Fencing. London: 1784. V. 44

Financial and Political Facts of the Eighteenth and Present Century . . . London: 1803. V. 38; 42; 46

MC ARTHUR, JOHN W.

New Developments: Including the Grange, Anti-Monopoly, Farmers' Alliance, Co-operative Fire Insurance and the Economic Barn, to Which is Added an Account of Artificial Butter. Oneonta: 1886. V. 44

MAC ARTHUR, MILDRED YORBA

California Spanish Proverbs. San Francisco: 1954. V. 42

MAC ARTNEY, EARL

An Authentic Account of an Embassy for the King of Great Britain and the Emperor of China. London: 1797. V. 37

MAC ARTNEY, M.

English Houses and Gardens in the 17th and 18th Centuries. London: 1908. V. 37

MAC ASKILL, WALLACE R.

Out of Halifax. New York: 1937. V. 39

MC AULEY, JEREMIAH

Transford, or the History of a River Thief, Briefly Told. New York?: 1876. V. 44

MC AULIFFE, E.

History of the Union Pacific Coal Mines 1868-1940. Omaha. V. 43

History of the Union Pacific Coal Mines, 1868 to 1940. Omaha: 1940. V. 39; 46

MC AVITY, J. M.

Lord Strathcona's Horse (Royal Candians). Toronto: 1947. V. 44

MAC AVOY, R. A.

Tea with a Black Dragon. 1987. V. 44

MAC BEAN, ALEXANDER

A Dictionary of the Bible; or, an Explanation of the Proper Names and Difficult Words in the Old and New Testament . . . London: 1766. V. 38

A Dictionary of Ancient Geography, Explaining the Local Apellations in Sacred, Grecian and Roman History . . . London: 1773. V. 41; 44

MC BEAN, S.

England, Palestine, Egypt & India, Connected by a Railway System. Popularly Explained, with a Map. London: 1876. V. 37

MC BEY, JAMES

Etchings and Dry Points from 1902 to 1924. London: 1925. V. 42

The Etchings of James McBey. London: 1929. V. 38

MAC BRIDE, DAVID

Experimental Essays on Medical and Philosophical Subjects. Dublin: 1767. V. 43

An Historical Account of a New Method of Treating the Scurvy at Sea. London: 1767. V. 37

MC BRIDE, JOHN R.

History of the Thirty-Third Indiana Veteran Volunteer Infantry . . . 1861-1865. Indianapolis: 1900. V. 42; 46

MAC BRIDGE, DAVID

Experimental Essays on Medical and Philosophical Subjects. London: 1767. V. 42

MAC BRIDGE, J. D.

The Mohammedan Religion Explained . . . London: 1857. V. 44

MC BRIDGE, JAMES

Symmes's Theory of Concentric Spheres. Cincinnati: 1826. V. 40

MC BURNEY, WILLIAM HARLIN

A Check List of English Prose Fiction 1700-1739. 1960. V. 42

MAC CABE, FREDERICK

Mac Cabe's Art of Ventriloquism and Vocal Illusions, with Full Directions to Learners . . . New York: 1875. V. 43

MC CABE, JAMES D.

The Aid-De-Camp; a Romance of the War. Richmond: 1863. V. 40

The Illustrated History of the Centennial Exhibition . . . Philadelphia: 1876. V. 40

Life and Campaigns of General Robert E. Lee. Atlanta: 1866. V. 37

M'CABE, JOHN COLLINS

Scraps. Richmond: 1835. V. 46

MC CAFFERY, STEVE

In England Now That Spring, Polaroid Poems, Found Texts, Visions & Collaborations Records of a Journey thru Scotland and England May 1878. Toronto: 1979. V. 39

MC CAFFREY, A.

Dragonflight. 1969. V. 39

The Year of the Lucy. 1986. V. 39; 43

MC CAFFREY, ANNE

The Ship Who Sang. London: 1971. V. 41

MAC CAIG, DONALD

A Reply to John Stuart Mill on the Subjection of Women. Philadelphia: 1870. V. 40

MAC CAIG, NORMAN

Far Cry. London: 1943. V. 45

MC CAIN, CHARLES

History of the SS. 'Beaver'. Vancouver: 1894. V. 39; 40; 41; 42; 43

MC CALEB, WALTER F.

The Aaron Burr Conspiracy, a History Largely from Original and Hitherto Unused Sources. New York: 1903. V. 42; 46

MC CALL, BERTRAM HARDY

The History and Antiquities of the Parish of Mid Calder with Some Account of the religious House of Torphichen Founded Upon Record. Edinburgh: 1894. V. 38

MC CALL, GEORGE A.

Letters from the Frontiers. V. 40; 45

Letters from the Frontiers Written During a Period of Thirty Years' Service in the Army of the United States. Philadelphia: 1868. V. 46

A Pennsylvania Reserves in the Peninsula. Philadelphia?: 1862. V. 44

Report of the Secretary of War Communicating . . . Colonel McCall's Reports in Relation to New Mexico. Washington: 1851. V. 37; 44; 46

MC CALL, HUGH

The History of Georgia, containing Brief Sketches of the Most Remarkable Events, Up to the Present Day. Savannah: 1811-16. V. 40; 43; 44; 46

The History of Georgia, Containing Brief Sketches of the Most Remarkable Events, up to the Present Day. Savannah: 1811, 1816. V. 37

MC CALLA, WILLIAM L.

Adventures in Texas, Chiefly in the Spring and Summer of 1840. Philadelphia: 1841. V. 39; 42

MAC CALLUM, ESTHER D.

The History of St. Clement's Church, El Paso, Texas, 1870-1925. El Paso: 1925. V. 37; 39

MC CALLUM, HUGH

An Original Collection of the Poems of Ossian, Orrann, Ulin and Other Bards Who Flourished in the Same Age. Montrose: 1816. V. 39

M'CALLUM, PIERRE F.

Travels in Trinidad During the Months of February, March and April, 1803, in a Series of Letters. Liverpool: 1805. V. 40

M'CALLUM, PIERRE FRANC

The Rival Queens, or Which is the Darling? London: 1810. V. 38

MAC CALLUM, WILLIAM

A Text-Book of Pathology. Philadelphia: 1916. V. 42

The William Stewart Halsted, Surgeon. Baltimore: 1931. V. 42

MC CALMONT, HUGH

The Memoirs of Major-General Sir Hugh McCalmont, K.C.B. London: 1924. V. 38

MC CANLISS, IRENE

Weight on the Thoroughbred Racehorse. N.P.: 1967. V. 39

MC CANN, CHARLES

A Shikari's Pocket-Book: with Hints on Preserving and Skinning Trophies in the Field. London: 1927. V. 37

MC CANN, IRVING GOFF

With the National Guard on the Border; Our National Military Problem. St. Louis: 1917. V. 37; 39; 42; 46

MAC CANN, WILLIAM

Two Thousand Miles' Ride Through the Argentine Provinces; Being an Account of the Natural Products of the Country, and the Habits of the People. London: 1853. V. 41

MC CARTHY, CARLTON

Contributions to a History of the Richmond Howitzer Battalion. Richmond: 1883-86. V. 44

Detailed Minutiae of Soldier Life in the Army of Northern Virginia 1861-1865. Richmond: 1882. V. 37; 42

Walks About Richmond. A Story for Boys and a Guide to Persons Visiting the City . . . Richmond: 1870. V. 39

MC CARTHY, CHARLES H.

Lincoln's Plan of Reconstruction. New York: 1901. V. 40; 46

MAC CARTHY, CORMAC

All the Pretty Horses. New York: 1992. V. 46

Blood Meridian. New York: 1985. V. 43; 44

The Orchard Keeper. New York: 1965. V. 38; 44; 45; 46

The Orchard Keeper. London: 1966. V. 43

Outer Dark. New York: 1968. V. 46

Suttree. New York: 1979. V. 44; 45; 46

MC CARTHY, DANIEL

The Siege of Florence: an Historical Romance. London: 1840. V. 46

MC CARTHY, EUGENE

Familiar Fish . . . A Practical Book on Fresh-Water Game Fish. New York: 1900. V. 37

MC CARTHY, EUGENE J.

And Time Began. N.P.: 1968. V. 45

MC CARTHY, F. D.

Australia's Aborigines, Their Life and Culture. Melbourne: 1957. V. 38

MC CARTHY, J.

A History of Our Own Times, from the Accession of Queen Victoria to the General Election of 1800. London: 1886-87. V. 38

MC CARTHY, J. T.

The Poetry and Oratory of Ireland. New York: 1880. V. 39

MC CARTHY, JUSTIN 1830-1912

A History of Our Own Times. London: 1901. V. 41

Irish Literature. New York: 1904. V. 37

MC CARTHY, LEE

Histopathology of Skin Diseases. St. Louis: 1931. V. 42

MC CARTHY, MARY

The Company She Keeps. New York: 1942. V. 37

Kaltenborn Edits the News. New York: 1937. V. 44

MAC CARTHY, THOMAS

Montalto; or the Heart Unveiled. London: 1819. V. 42

Montalto; or the heart unveiled. A Poem, in Two Cantos with Other Poems. London: 1809. V. 37

MC CARTNEY, W. A.

The Statutes of Oklahoma, 1893; Being a Compilation of all the Laws now in Force in the Territory of Oklahoma. Guthrie: 1893. V. 37

MC CARTY, J. HENRICKSON

Two Thousand Miles Through the Heart of Mexico. New York: 1886. V. 46

MC CARTY, WILLIAM

Geographical Memoir Upon Upper California by John Charles Fremont. Philadelphia: 1849. V. 45

MC CARVER, NORMAN

Hearne on the Brazos. 1958. V. 42

MC CAULEY, JAMES EMMIT

A Stove-Up Cowboy's Story . . . Austin: 1943. V. 39

MC CHESNEY, J. H.

Lake Como Gold and Silver Mines, San Juan County, Colorado. (New York: 1879). V. 37

MC CHESNEY, WILLIAM R.

A Discourse Delivered at Louisville, Ky., on the Second Sunday in May, 1843, before the First English Evan. Lutheran Church: Exhibiting a Concise view of the Doctrines, Pratices, and Government of the Evan. Lutheran Church in the United States. Louisville: 1843. V. 37

MC CLANAHAN, E.

The Natural man. New York: 1983. V. 46

MC CLELLAN, CARSWELL

Notes on the Personal Memoirs of P. H. Sheridan. St. Paul: 1889. V. 44

MC CLELLAN, ELISABETH

Historic Dress in America 1607-1800. Philadelphia: 1904-10. V. 39

Historic Dress in America 1607-1800. With an introductory chapter on dress in the Spanish and French settlements in Florida & Louisiana. Philadelphia: (1904-10). V. 37

MC CLELLAN, GEORGE

Anatomy in Relation to Art. Philadelphia: 1900. V. 41

Regional Anatomy In Its Relation to Medicine and Surgery. Philadelphia: 1891. V. 38

Regional Anatomy In Its Relation to Medicine and Surgery. Philadelphia: 1892. V. 42

Regional Anatomy in its relation to Medicine and Surgery. Philadelphia: 1891-92. V. 37

MC CLELLAN, GEORGE B.

General Orders, No. 163, Headquarters, Army of the Potomac. Camp Near Sharpsburg: 1862. V. 43; 46

MC CLELLAN, GEORGE BRINTON 1826-1885

Manual of Bayonet Exercise: Prepared for the Use of the Army of the U. S. Philadelphia: 1861. V. 39

MC CLELLAN, H. B.

The Life and Campaigns of Major General J. E. B. Stuart. Richmond: 1885. V. 39

MC CLELLAN, HENRY BRAINERD

The Life and Campaigns of Major General J. E. B. Stuart. Commander of the Cavalry of the Army of Northern Virginia. Boston: 1885. V. 42

The Life and Campaigns of Major-General J. E. B. Stuart, Commander of the Cavalry of the Army of Northern Virginia. Boston & New York: 1885. V. 37

MC CLELLAN, ISAAC

The Fall of the Indian, With Other Poems. Boston: 1830. V. 40

M'CLELLAND, JOHN

Report on the Physical Conditions of the Assam Tea Plant, with Reference to geolgoical Structure, Soil and Climate. Calcutta: 1837. V. 45

MC CLELLAND, NANCY

Duncan Phyfe and the English Regency, 1795-1830. New York: 1939. V. 40

Historic Wall-Papers, from their Inception to the Introduction of Machinery. Philadelphia & London: 1924. V. 39; 41

Historic Wallpapers, from Their Inception to the Introduction of Machinery. Philadelphia and London: 1924. V. 39

MC CLELLAND, R.

Report of . . . Communicating . . . a copy of the Correspondence Between the Department of the Interior and the Indian Agents and Commissioners in California. Washington: 1853. V. 39

MC CLERNAND, EDWARD J.

With the Indian and Buffalo in Montana, 1870-1878. Glendale: 1969. V. 38; 41; 44

MC CLINTOCK, FRANCIS L.

A Narrative of the Discovery of the Fate of Sir John Franklin and His Companions. London: 1859. V. 44; 45

A Narrative of the Discovery of the Fate of Sir John Franklin & His Companions. Boston: 1860. V. 43

The Voyage of the 'Fox' in the Arctic Seas. London: 1859. V. 43

M'CLINTOCK, FRANCIS LEOPOLD

A Narrative of the Discovery of the Fate of Sir John Franklin and His Companions. London: 1859. V. 38; 40; 42; 44

A Narrative of Discovery of the Fate of Sir John Franklin and His Companions. Boston: 1860. V. 39

The Voyage of the 'Fox' in the Arctic Seas. London: 1859. V. 41; 42

The Voyage of the Fox in the Arctic Seas. London: 1859. V. 37; 38; 40; 42; 45; 46

The Voyage of the 'Fox' in the Arctic Seas. Boston: 1860. V. 37; 41; 42

The Voyage of the 'Fox' in the Arctic Seas. London: 1860. V. 44; 45

The Voyage of the 'Fox' in the Arctic Seas in Search of Franklin and His Companions. London: 1881. V. 42

MC CLINTOCK, JAMES H.

Mormon Settlement in Arizona. Phoenix: 1921. V. 39; 43; 44

MC CLINTOCK, JOHN S.

Pioneer Days in the Black Hills. Deadwood: 1939. V. 38; 40; 45

M'CLINTOCK, LEOPOLD

A Narrative of the Discovery of the Fate of Sir John Franklin and His Companions. Boston: 1860. V. 37

MC CLINTOCK, WALTER

The Old North Trail or Life, Legends and Religion fo the Blackfeet Indians. London: 1910. V. 39; 43; 46

Old Indian Trails. Boston & New York: 1923. V. 45

Old Indian Trails. New York: 1923. V. 40

MC CLINTON, KATHARINE MORRISON

The Chromolithographs of Louis Prang. New York: 1973. V. 46

M'CLUNG, JOHN

Sketches of Western Adventure. Maysville: 1832. V. 37; 39; 46

M'CLUNG, JOHN A.

Sketches of Western Adventure . . . Philadelphia: 1832. V. 41; 44; 45; 46

Sketches of Western Adventure, Containing an Account of the Most Interesting Incidents Connected with the Settlement of the West from 1755 to 1794. Dayton: 1847. V. 39

MC CLUNG, NELLIE L.

Before They Call. N.P.: 1937. V. 42

When Christmas Crossed 'The Peace' Bringing the Joys of Christmas to the North Country. Toronto: 1923. V. 46

MC CLURE, ALEXANDER

Three Thousand Miles through the Rocky Mountains . . . Philadelphia: 1869. V. 37; 40

MC CLURE, DAVID

Diary of David McClure, Doctor of Divinity, 1748-1820 . . . New York: 1899. V. 40

Memoirs of the Rev. Eleazar Wheelock, Founder and President of Dartmouth College and Moor's Charity School . . . Newburyport: 1811. V. 42

MC CLURE, FLOYD ALONZO

Chinese Handmade Paper. 1986. V. 40

Chinese Handmade Paper. Newtown: 1986. V. 37; 38; 39; 40; 42; 44; 45

MC CLURE, LEWIS

The McClure Press, Plans for Reconstructing the 15th Century Printing Press of Johann Gutenberg. Salisbury: 1984. V. 40; 41

MC CLURE, MICHAEL

The Book of Benjamin. Berkeley: 1982. V. 40

Dark Brown. San Francisco: 1961. V. 39

The Grabbing of the Fairy. St. Paul: 1978. V. 38; 40

Little Odes and the Raptors. 1969. V. 41; 42; 43

Passage. Big Sur: 1956. V. 39

M'CLURE, ROBERT

The Arctic Dispatches Containing an Account of the Discovery of the North-West Passage . . . London: 1853. V. 41

The Discovery of the North-West Passage by H.M.S. 'Investigator', Capt. R. M'Clure, 1850-54. London: 1856. V. 38; 41; 43

The Discovery of the North-West Passage . . . London: 1857. V. 39

MC CLURE, SAMUEL SIDNEY 1857-1949

My Autobiography. New York: 1914. V. 38; 40; 43

M'CLYMONT, J. A.

Greece. London: 1906. V. 44

MAC COLL, D. S.

Nineteenth Century Art . . . Glasgow: 1902. V. 41; 42; 44

MAC COLL, HUGH

Symbolic Logic and Its Applications. London: 1906. V. 41; 43

MC COMB, ARTHUR

Agnolo Bronzino: His Life and Works. Cambridge: 1928. V. 43; 45

MC CONATHY, DALE

Hollywood Costume: Glamour! Glitter! Romance! New York: 1976. V. 39; 43; 46

MC CONKEY, HARRIET E.

Dakota War Whoop; or, Indian Massacres and the War in Minnesota of 1862-3. St. Paul: 1864. V. 40; 45

M'CONKEY, HARRIET E. BISHOP

Dakota War Whoop; or, Indian Massacres and War in Minnesota. Saint Paul: 1863. V. 39; 42

MC CONKEY, JOHN C.

From New York to Portland, Oregon via Straits of Magellan, with a History of the Voyage, Scenes, Places, Incidents and Notes of the Journey. Walla Walla: 1879. V. 43

MC CONNELL, H. H.

Five Years a Cavalryman; or, Sketches of Regular Army Life on the Texas Frontier Twenty Odd Years Ago. Jacksboro: 1889. V. 37; 38; 39; 42; 43; 44

Five Years a Cavalryman; or, Sketches of Regular Army Life on the Texas Frontier, Twenty Odd Years Ago. Jacksboro, TX: 1889. V. 37

MC CONNELL, MATTHEW

An Essay on the Domestic Debts of the United States of America. Philadelphia: 1787. V. 37; 42

MC CONNELL, W. J.

Early History of Idaho. Caldwell: 1913. V. 44

MC CONNELL, WILLIAM

Upside Down; or Turnover Traits from Original Sketches. London: 1868. V. 42

MC CONNOCHIE, A. I.

The Deer and Deer Forests of Scotland: Historical, Descriptive, Sporting. London: 1923. V. 46

MC COOK, H. C.

American Spiders and Their Spinningwork, a Natural History of the Orbweaving Spiders of the United States . . . Philadelphia: 1890. V. 42

The Natural History of the Agricultural Ant of Texas. Philadelphia: 1880. V. 42

MC COOK, HENRY C.

American Spiders and Their Spinningwork. Philadelphia: 1889-90-93. V. 40

American Spiders and their Spinningwork. Philadelphia: 1889-93. V. 39

The Natural History of the Agricultural Art in Texas. Philadelphia: 1879. V. 37

MC COOK, HENRY CHRISTOPHER

Old Farm Fairies. Philadelphia: 1895. V. 45

MC CORCKLE, JILL

The Cheerleader. Chapel Hill: 1984. V. 42; 44

July 7th. Chapel Hill: 1984. V. 42; 44

MC CORCKLE, SAMUEL

Incident on the Bark Columbia. Cummington: 1941. V. 41

MC CORKLE, JOHN

Three Years with Quantrell. Armstrong: 1914. V. 39; 42

MAC CORMAC, WILLIAM

An Address of Welcome Delivered on the Occasion of the Centenary Festival of the Royal College of Surgeons of England . . . London: 1900. V. 39

MAC CORMACK, SAMUEL

A View of the State of Parties in the United States of America . . . Edinburgh: 1812. V. 46

M'CORMICK, CHARLES

Memoirs of the Right Honourable Edmund Burke. London: 1797. V. 39; 42

Memoirs of the Right Honourable Edmund Burke; or, an Impartial Review of His Private Life, His Public Conduct, His Speeches in Parliament . . . London: 1798. V. 43

MC CORMICK, HARRIET HAMMOND

Landscape Art, Past and Present. New York: 1923. V. 37; 38; 41; 45

MC CORMICK, HENRY

Across the Continent in 1865. Harrisburg: 1937. V. 40

Across the Continent in 1865. Harrisburg: 1944. V. 45

M'CORMICK, R.

Voyages of Discovery in the Arctic and Antarctic Seas and Round the World . . . London: 1884. V. 43

MC CORMICK, RICHARD

Arizona: Its Resouces and Prospects. New York: 1865. V. 37; 39; 40; 41; 42; 43; 44; 45; 46

Arizona: It's Resources and Prospects. New York: 1865. V. 44

A Visit to the Camp Before Selastopol. New York: 1855. V. 37

MC CORMICK, S. J.

McCormick's Almanac for the Year 1869 . . . Portland: 1868. V. 42

MC CORMICK, WILLIAM THOMAS

A Ride Across Iceland in the Summer of 1891. Digby: 1892. V. 42

MC COSH, JAMES

The Laws of Discursive Thought . . . London: 1870. V. 40; 41; 43; 45

The Scottish Philosophy. London: 1875. V. 41; 42

The Supernatural in Relation to the Natural. Cambridge: 1862. V. 40

MC COWAN, DAN

A Naturalist in Canada. Toronto: 1941. V. 46

MC COWN, DONALD E.

Nippur I: Temple of Enlil, Scribal Quarter and Soundings. Chicago: 1967. V. 44

MC COY, ESTHER

Francisco, Artigas, (1950-1970). Mexico City: 1972. V. 42

MC COY, HORACE

I Should Have Stayed Home. New York: 1938. V. 44

No Pockets in a Shroud. London: 1938. V. 44

They Shoot Horses, Don't They? London: 1935. V. 44

They Shoot Horses Don't They? New York: 1935. V. 43

Walk Three Steps Down. Los Angeles: 1950. V. 46

MC COY, ISAAC

The Annual Register of Indian Affairs Within the Indian (or Western) Territory. No. 1. Shawanoe Mission: 1835. V. 42

The Annual Register of Indian Affairs Within the Indian (Or Western) Territory . . . No. 2. 1836. V. 38

The Annual Register of Indian Affairs Within the Indian (or Western) Territory. Shawane Baptist Mission,: 1836. V. 42

MAC DONALD, MURDOCH

Nile Control. A Statement of the Necessity for Further Control of the Nile to Complete the Development of Egypt and Develop a Certain Area in the Sudan . . . Cairo: 1920. V. 40

MAC DONALD, PHILIP

The Link. Garden City: 1930. V. 44

MC DONALD, R.

A Grammar of the Tukudh Language. London: 1911. V. 45

MC DONALD, R. H.

Illustrated History and Map of Chicago. New York: 1872. V. 44

MAC DONALD, R. J.

The History of the Dress of the Royal Regiment of Artillery, 1625-1897. London: 1899. V. 37; 41; 42

MAC DONALD, RANALD

Ranald MacDonald: the Narrative of His Early Life on the Columbia Under the Hudson's Bay Company's Regime . . . Spokane: 1923. V. 37; 41

MAC DONALD, ROGER

The British Martial Register, Comprising a Complete Chronological History of all the Most Celebrated Land Battles, by Which the English Standard has Been Distinguished in the Field of Wars . . . London: 1806. V. 37

MAC DONALD, ROSS

Black Money. New York: 1966. V. 37; 39; 42; 46

Blue City. New York: 1947. V. 43

The Chill. New York: 1964. V. 39; 42

A Collection of Reviews. Northridge: 1979. V. 37; 40

The Doomsters. London: 1958. V. 46

The Doomsters. New York: 1958. V. 44

The Drowning Pool. New York: 1950. V. 46

The Far Side of the Dollar. New York: 1965. V. 46

The Far Side of the Dollar. New York: 1976. V. 39

Find a Victim. New York: 1954. V. 44; 45

The Galton Case. New York: 1959. V. 43

The Goodbye Look. New York: 1969. V. 37; 42

The Instant Enemy. New York: 1968. V. 39; 42; 46

The Ivory Grin. New York: 1952. V. 44; 46

Lew Archer Private Investigator. New York: 1977. V. 37; 43; 46

Meet Me at the Morgue. New York: 1953. V. 44

The Name is Archer. New York: 1955. V. 39

Self Portrait: Ceaselessly into the Past. Santa Barbara: 1981. V. 41; 44; 46

Trouble Follows Me. 1946. V. 46

The Zebra - Striped Hearse. New York: 1962. V. 44; 45; 46

MAC DONALD, THOREAU

The Group of Seven. Toronto: 1944. V. 43

Woods and Fields. Toronto: 1951. V. 44

MC DONALD, WILLIAM

A History of the Laurel Brigade Originally the Ashby Cavalry of the Army of Northern Virginia. Baltimore: 1907. V. 37

Poems. Edinburgh: 1809. V. 41; 42; 46

MC DONALD, WILLIAM N.

A History of the Laurel Brigade, Originally the Ashby Cavalry of the Army of Northern Virgina and Chew's Battery. Baltimore: 1907. V. 37; 39; 45

A History of the Laurel Brigade. (Baltimore): 1907. V. 37

MAC DONALD, WILLIAM RUSSELL

The Dublin Mail; or, Intercepted Correspondence. London: 1821. V. 37; 41; 43

MAC DONELL, J. A.

Sketches Illustrating the Early Settlement and History of Glengarry in Canada . . . Montreal: 1893. V. 44

MAC DONGAH, DONAH

Veterans and Other Poems. Dublin: 1941. V. 39

MAC DONNEL, DAVID EVANS

A Dictionary of Quotations, in Most Frequent Use. London: 1798. V. 41

M'DONNELL, ALEXANDER

Considerations on Negro Slavery. London: 1824. V. 38

MAC DONNELL, ARTHUR A.

Camping Voyages on German Rivers . . . London: 1890. V. 41

MAC DONNELL, ENEAS

The Hermit of Glenconella. London: 1820. V. 37; 40

MC DONNELL, J.

Gold Tooled Bookbindings Commissioned by Trinity College Dublin in the Eighteenth Century. Dublin: 1987. V. 43

Gold-tooled Bookbindings Commissioned by Trinity College Dublin in the Eighteenth Century. London: 1987. V. 39

MAC DONNELL, R. G.

Laws and Ordinances of the British Settlements in the Gambia and Their Dependencies (1843-1852). London: 1852. V. 40

MAC DONNELL, RICHARD G.

Australia: What It Is, and What It May Be: a Lecture . . . Dublin: 1863. V. 45

MC DONNELLY, J.

Gilt Tooled Bookbindings, commissioned by Trinity College Dublin in the Eighteenth Century. Dublin: 1987. V. 37

M'DONOUGH, FELIX

The Hermit in London; or, Sketches of English Manners. London: 1821. V. 39

The Hermit in London; or, Sketches of English Manners. London: 1822. V. 42

The Hermit in Edinburgh; or, Sketches of Manners and Real Characters and Scenes in the Drama of Life. London: 1824. V. 41

MAC DOUALL, JOHN

Narrative of a Voyage to Patagonia and Terra Del Fuego, Through the Straits of Magellan, in H. M. S. Adventure and Beagle, in 1826 and 1827. London: 1833. V. 39; 43

MAC DOUGALL, ARTHUR R.

Dud Dean and His Country. New York: 1946. V. 43

MAC DOUGALL, ELIZABETH B.

Fons Sapentiae Renaissance Garden Fountains. Washington: 1978. V. 46

MAC DOUGALL, FRANCES HARRIET

Elleanor's Second Book. Providence: 1839. V. 37; 38

M'DOUGALL, GEORGE F.

The Eventful Voyage of H.M. Discovery Ship 'Resolute' to the Arctic Regions in search of Sir John Franklin and the Missing Crews of H.M. Discovery Ships 'Erebus' and 'Terror', 1852, 1853, 1854 . . . London: 1857. V. 37

MC DOWELL, ROBERT HARBOLD

Stamped and inscribed objects from Seleucia on the Tigris. Ann Arbor: 1935. V. 37

MC DOWELL, ROBERT HAROLD

Coins from Seleucia on the Tigris. Ann Arbor: 1935. V. 40

MC DOWELL, WILLIAM A.

A Demonstration of the Curability of Pulmonary Consumption, In All Its Stages. Louisville: 1843. V. 39

MC DUFFIE, GEORGE

Speech of . . . on the Proposed Amendment to the Constitution of the United States Respecting the Election of the President and Vice President in the House of Representatives Feb. 15, 16, 1826. Washington: 1826. V. 40

Speech of the Hon. George McDuffie, at a Public Dinner Given Him by the Citizens of Charleston, SC May 19, 1831. Georgetown: 1831. V. 46

MAC ECHERN, DUGALD

The Sword of the North: Highland Memories of the Great War. Inverness: 1923. V. 46

MC ELRATH, THOMSON P.

A Press Club Outing. New York: 1893. V. 37; 38; 42

Yellowstone Valley: What It Is, Where It Is, and How to Get To It. St. Paul: 1880. V. 42

MAC ELREE, WILMER W.

Along the Western Brandywine. West Chester: 1912. V. 41; 42; 46

Around the Boundaries of Chester County. West Chester: 1934. V. 46

Down the Eastern and Up the Black Brandywine. N.P.: 1906/ V. 46

MC ELROY, HARRY

Desert Hawing II. London: 1977. V. 39

MC ELROY, JOSEPH

Ancient History: a Parapharse. New York: 1971. V. 39

Hind's Kidnap. New York: 1969. V. 45

Plus. New York: 1977. V. 39

A Smuggler's Bible. New York: 1966. V. 39; 40; 41; 42; 43; 46

A Smuggler's Bible. New York: (1966). V. 37

Women and Men. 1987. V. 43

MC ELROY, JOSEPH continued

Women and Men. New York: 1987. V. 37; 39

MC ELROY, PENNY

Allegory. Word and Visual Images. Redlands: 1988. V. 44

MC ELWAINE, EUGENE

The Truth About Alaska, the Golden Land of the Midnight Sun. 1901. V. 46

The Truth About Alaska. The Golden Land of the Midnight Sun. Chicago: 1901. V. 45

MC ELWEE, THOMAS B.

A Concise History of the Eastern Penitentiary fo Pennsylvania, Together with a Detailed STatement of the Proceedings of the Committee . . . for the Purpose of Examining into the Economy and Management of that Institution . . . Philadelphia: 1835. V. 46

MC EVOY, BERNARD

From the Great Lakes to the Wild West: Impressions of a Tour Between Toronto and the Pacific. Toronto: 1902. V. 46

MC EWAN, CALVIN W.

Soundings at Tell Fakhariyah. Chicago: 1958. V. 44

MC EWAN, IAN

First Love, Last Rites. London: 1975. V. 40; 43

In Between the Sheets and Other Stories. London: 1978. V. 40; 41; 45

MC EWEN, JEAN

Les Iles Reunies. Montreal: 1975. V. 39

MAC EWEN, WILLIAM

The Growth of Bone. Observations on Osteogenesis. Glasgow: 1912. V. 40; 41

The Growth and Shedding of the Antler of the Deer. Glasgow: 1920. V. 43

Pyogenic Infective Diseases of the Brain and Spinal Cord. Glasgow: 1893. V. 40; 44

MAC FADDEN, HARRY A.

Rambles in the Far West. Hollidaysburg: 1906. V. 39; 41; 46

MAC FAIT, EBENEZER

Remarks on the Life and Writings of Plato. Edinburgh: 1710. V. 38

Remarks on the Life and Writings of Plato, with Answers to the Principal Objections Against Him . . . Edinburgh: 1760. V. 39

MC FALL, CRAWFORD

With the Zhob Field Force 1890. London: 1895. V. 46

MC FALL, FRANCES ELIZABETH

The Heavenly Twins. London: 1893. V. 37; 38; 41; 44

MC FALL, FRANCES ELIZABETH CLARK

The Heavenly Twins. New York: 1893. V. 39; 45

MAC FALL, HALDANE

The Art of Hesketh Hubbard. London: 1924. V. 39; 41

Aubrey Beardsley. 1927. V. 40

Aubrey Beardsley. New York: 1927. V. 37; 38; 41

Aubrey Beardsley - the Man and His Work. London: 1928. V. 40; 41; 42; 43; 45

Aubrey Beardsley, the Man and His Work. London: (1928). V. 37

The Book of Lovat Claud Fraser. London: 1922. V. 40; 42; 44

The Book of Claud Lovat Fraser. London: 1923. V. 38; 41; 42; 44; 46

The Clown, The Harlequin, The Pierrot of His Age. New York: 1927. V. 39

The French Pastellists of the Eighteenth Century. London: 1909. V. 42

A History of Painting. Boston: 1916. V. 41

The Splendid Wayfaring. London: 1913. V. 40; 41; 42; 43

Whistler: Butterfly, Wasp, Wit, Master of the Arts, Enigma. London: 1905. V. 41

The Wooings of Jezebel Pettyfer. London: 1898. V. 37; 39; 40; 41; 44

The Wooings of Jezebel Pettyfer, Being the Personal History of Jehu Sennacherib Dyle Commonly called Masheen Dyle. London: 1913. V. 41

MAC FARLAN, ALLAN

American Indian Legends. Los Angeles: 1968. V. 46

MC FARLAN, JOHN

Inquiries Concerning the Poor. Edinburgh: 1780. V. 43

MAC FARLAN, ROBERT

The History of the Reign of George the Third. London: 1770-96. V. 46

MC FARLAND, ASA

Five Months Abroad: or Letters from the Ocean and the Land. Concord: 1851. V. 43

MC FARLAND, J. HORACE

Getting Acquainted with Trees. New York: 1904. V. 41

MC FARLAND, W. L.

Salmon of the Atlantic. New York: 1925. V. 39; 41; 45

MAC FARLANE, CHARLES

The Book of Table Talk. London: 1836. V. 42

The Camp of Refuge. London: 1844. V. 40; 42

Constantinople in 1828. London: 1829. V. 40; 46

The Lives and Exploits of Banditti and Robbers in All Parts of the World . . . London: 1837. V. 45

The Lives of Banditti and Robbers In All Parts of the World. London: 1933. V. 45

MAC FARLANE, JAMES

The Coal-Regions of America: Their Topography, Geology and Development . . . New York: 1873. V. 43

MAC FARLANE, JOHN

Antoine Verard. London: 1900. V. 39

A Trip to Parnassus; or, Pieces in Verse. Edinburgh: 1820. V. 39; 42

MAC FARLANE, NIGEL

Handmade Papers of the Himalayas. London: 1986. V. 40

Handmade Papers of the Himalayas. Winchester: 1986. V. 38

Handmade Papers of India. Winchester: 1987. V. 38; 43; 45

MAC FARLANE, ROBERT

The History of the Reign of George the Third . . . to the Conclusion of the Session of Parliament, Ending in May, 1770. London: 1770. V. 46

MAC FARLANE, WALTER

Illustrated Catalogue of Castings. (with) Railings and Gtes Supplement. Glasgow: 1900-30. V. 37

MAC FARLANE, WALTER, & CO.

Illustrated Catalogue of Macfarlane's Castings. Glasgow: 1880's. V. 44

Illustrated Catalogue of Castings. Glasgow: 1900 & ca. 1930. V. 40

Illustrated Catalogue of Macfarlane's Castings. Glasgow: 1906. V. 44

Illustrated Examples of Macfarlane's Architectural Ironwork. Glasgow: 1920. V. 44

Illustrated Catalogue of Macfarlane's Castings. Glasgow: 1932. V. 44

MC FEE, WILLIAM

The Captain Macedonie Cocktail. 1930. V. 46

Casuals of the Sea. London: 1916. V. 37; 38; 39; 41

Command. London: 1922. V. 39

The Harbourmaster. New York: 1931. V. 43

Harbours of Memory. London: 1922. V. 38

Letters from an Ocean Tramp. London: 1908. V. 39

North of Suez. Garden City: 1930. V. 42; 43

The Reflections of Marsyas. Gaylordsville: 1933. V. 39; 41; 42; 43

Watch Below. New York: 1940. V. 43

MAC FIE, MATTHEW

Vancouver Island and British Columbia. London: 1865. V. 37; 38; 39; 42; 43; 46

MAC GAHAN, J. A.

Campaigning on the Oxus and the Fall of Khiva. London: 1874. V. 42; 45

Under Northern Lights. London: 1876. V. 41; 43

MC GAHERN, JOHN

The Dark. London: 1965. V. 42

MC GAULEY, J. W.

The Elements of Architecture. Dublin: 1846. V. 38

M'GAVIN, JAMES R.

The Loss of the Austalia: a Narrative of the Loss of the Big Australia, by Fire, on Her Voyage from Leith to Sydney . . . New York: 1849. V. 38

MC GAW, JAMES F.

Philip Seymour, or Pioneer Life in Richland County, Ohio. Mansfield: 1858. V. 38

MC GAW, LISA

Rex Brasher's Birds & Trees of North America Comprising 875 Full Color Paltes . . . New York: 1961. V. 46

MC GEE, THOMAS D.

A History of the Attempts to Establish the Protestant Reformation in Ireland and the Successful Resistance of that People. Boston: 1853. V. 46

MC GEHEAN, THOMAS

History of the Life and Trials of . . . Who Was Charged with the Shooting and Killing of Thomas S. Myers. In the City of Hamilton, Butler County, Ohio . . . Biographical Sketch of Hon. C. L. Vallandigham . . . the Notorious Whisky Ring of Southern Ohio. Cincinnati: 1874. V. 39

MAC GEORGE, A.

An Inquiry As to the Amorial Insignia of the City of Glasgow. Glasgow: 1866. V. 41; 44

MAC GEORGE, ANDREW

The Bairds of Gartsherrie; Some Notices of their Origin and history. Glasgow: 1875. V. 37

MAC GEORGE, NORMAN

The Arts in Australia. Melbourne & London: 1948. V. 41

MAC GHEE, ROBERT J. L.

How We Got to Pekin. London: 1862. V. 45

MAC GIBBON, DAVID

The Castellated and Domestic ARchitecture of Scotland from the 12th to the 18th Century. Edinburgh: 1887-1892. V. 39

The Castellated and Domestic Architecture of Scotland from the Twelffth to the Eighteenth Century. Edinburgh: 1977. V. 38

The Ecclesiasatical Architecture of Scotland. Edinburgh: 1896-97. V. 37; 39; 40; 44

The Ecclesiastical Architecture of Scotland from the Earliest Times to the Seventeenth Century. Edinburgh: 1896. V. 39

MC GIBBON, ELMA

Leaves of Knowledge. Spokane: 1904. V. 41; 44

MC GILL, JOHN

Faith, the Victory. Richmond: 1865. V. 40

MAC GILL, PATRICK

Soldiers and Songs. London: 1917. V. 43; 46

MC GILL, SAMUEL D.

Narrative of Reminiscences in Williamsburg County. Columbia: 1897. V. 42

MAC GILL, STEVEONS

Remarks on Prisons. Glasgow: 1810. V. 43

MAC GILL, THOMAS

Travels in Turkey, Italy and Russia, During the Years 1803, 1804, 1805 and 1806. London: 1808. V. 43

MC GILL UNIVERISTY. LIBRARY

The Lawrence Lande Collection of Canadiana in the Redpath Library of McGill University. Montreal: 1965. V. 42; 43; 44; 45

MC GILL UNIVERSITY. LIBRARY

The Lawrence Lande Collection of Canadiana in . . . McGill University. (with) Rare and Unusual Canadiana: First Supplement to the Lande Bibliography. Montreal: 1965/71. V. 44

The Lawrence Lande Collection of Canadiana in the Redpath Library of McGill University: a Bibliography (and) Rare Unusual Canadiana. Montreal: 1965-71. V. 39

M'GILLIVRAY, DUNCAN

The Journal of Duncan M'Gillivray, of the North West Company at Fort George on the Saskatchewan, 1794-95. Toronto: 1929. V. 40; 42; 45

MAC GILLIVRAY, W.

A History of British Birds. London: 1837-52. V. 37; 38; 42

The Natural History of Dee Side and Braemar. London: 1855. V. 37

MAC GILVRAY, JOHN

Poems. London: 1787. V. 41; 42

MC GLASHAN, C. F.

History of the Donner Party. Truckee: 1879. V. 37; 38; 43; 44

History of the Donner Party. Sacramento: 1907. V. 44

History of the Donner Party: a Tragedy of the Sierra. Sacramento: 1907, 1880. V. 38

MC GLASHAN, CHARLES F.

History of the Donner Party. Sacramento. V. 40; 43

History of the Donner Party. San Francisco: 1880. V. 39; 46

History of the Donner Party. San Francisco: 1922. V. 39

MC GONNIGLE, ROBERT D.

When I Went West. From the Bad Lands to California. Pittsburgh: 1901. V. 39; 40; 41; 43

MC GOUGH, ROGER

Crocodile Puddles. London: 1984. V. 40; 43; 45

MAC GOWAN, ALICE

The Last Word. Boston: 1903. V. 46

MC GOWAN, EDWARD

McGowan vs. California Vigilantes. Oakland: 1946. V. 40

Narrative of Edward McGowan, Including a Full Account of the Author's Adventures and Perils . . . San Francisco: 1857. V. 44; 46

Report of the Committee on Mines and Mining Interests, to Whom was Referred the Memorial of Citizens of San Francisco. Sacramento: 1856. V. 39

MAC GOWAN, JOHN

Infernal Conference; or Dialogues of Devils. Lexington: 1804. V. 40

MC GRANDLE, LEITH

Europe: The Quest of Unity. London: 1975. V. 37; 39

MC GRATH, EILEEN

The Work of Eileen McGrath. Sydney: 1931. V. 41

MAC GRATH, JOHN RICHARD

The Obituary Book of Queen's College, Oxford: An Ancient Sarum Kalender with the Obits of the Founders and Benefactors of the College. Oxford: 1910. V. 37

MC GRATH, RAYMOND

Glass in Architecture and Decoration. London: 1937. V. 37; 41; 43; 44

Glass in Architecture and Decoration. With a section on the nature and properties of glass by H.E. Beckett. London: 1937. V. 37

MC GRAW, ELOISE JARVIS

Merry Go Round in Oz. 1963. V. 46

Merry Go Round in Oz. Chicago: 1963. V. 46

MC GREE, THOMAS D.

Historical Sketches of O'Connell and His Friends Including the Right Reverend Doyle and Milner Moore, Lawless, Furling, Sheil, etc. Boston: 1845. V. 46

A Life of Right Rev. Edward Maginn, Coajutor Bishop of Derry with Selections of His Correspodence. New York: 1857. V. 46

MAC GREGOR, A. WALLACE

Fifty Years of Lawn Tennis in Scotland. Edinburgh: 1927. V. 43

MAC GREGOR, ALASDAIR ALPIN

Percyval Tudor-Hart 1873-1954. Portrait of an Artist. London: 1961. V. 41

MAC GREGOR, BARRINGTON

King Longbeard. London: 1898. V. 40; 42

MC GREGOR, CHARLES

History of the Fifteenth Regiment, New Hampshire Volunteers, 1862-1863. Concord: 1900. V. 38; 43

MAC GREGOR, CHARLES METCALFE

Wanderings in Balochistan. London: 1882. V. 40

MC GREGOR, DION

The Dream World of Dion McGregor. New York: 1964. V. 45

MC GREGOR, DUNCAN

A Narrative of the Loss of the 'Kent' East Indiaman, by Fire, in the Bay of Biscay, on the 1st of March, 1825. Edinburgh: 1825. V. 37; 46

MC GREGOR, E. R.

Jewish Chronicle-Extra. New York: 1852. V. 45

M'GREGOR, JAMES

Medical Sketches of the Expedition to Egypt from India. London: 1804. V. 43

M'GREGOR, JOHN

British America. Edinburgh: 1833. V. 45

British America. London: 1833. V. 38

Commercial Statistics. London: 1844-47. V. 43; 46

Commercial Tariffs and Regulations, Resources and Trade, the Several States of Europe and America . . . Parth the Sixteenth. States of Mexico. London: 1846. V. 39

Commercial. London: 1847. V. 40

My Note Book. London: 1835. V. 40

The Progress of America, from the Discovery by Columbus to the Year 1846. London: 1847. V. 39

M'GREGOR, JOHN JAMES

New Picture of Dublin, Comprehending a History of the City, an Account of Its Various Establishments and Institutions . . . Dublin: 1821. V. 43

MAC GREGOR, MIRIAM

Weeds in My Garden. Fullerton: & Andoversford,: 1986. V. 37

MC GREGOR, R. C.

A Manual of Philippine Birds. Manila: 1909. V. 37

MC GREGOR, ROBERT

The Byron Gallery of Highly Finished Engravings, Illustrating Lord Byron's Works. New York: 1849. V. 44

M'GREGOR, W. L.

The History of the Sikhs; Containing the Lives of the Gooroos; the History of the Independent Sirdars, or Missuls, and the Life of the Great Founder of the Sikh Monarchy, Maharajah Runjeet Sing. London: 1846. V. 39

MC GREGORE, DAVID

The Spirits of the Present Day Tried. Boston: 1742. V. 43; 44

MAC GREGORY, JOHN

Commercial Tariffs and Regulations, Resources and Trade, the Several States of Europe and America . . . Part the Sixteenth States of Mexico. London: 1846. V. 41

MC GREW, CHARLES B.

Italian Doorways. Cleveland: 1929. V. 38; 43

MC GROARTY, JOHN STEVEN

History of Los Angeles County. Chicago: 1923, V. 39; 46

History of Los Angeles County. Chicago/New York: 1923. V. 37

Los Angeles: from the Mountains to the Sea. Chicago: 1921. V. 44

MC GUANE, THOMAS

The Bushwhacked Piano. New York: 1971. V. 44

In the Crazies. Seattle: 1985. V. 43

Keep the Change. Boston: 1989. V. 43; 45

Ninety-Two in the Shade. New York: 1973. V. 44

Ninety-Two in the Shade. London: 1974. V. 46

Nobody's Angel. New York: 1981. V. 46

Panama. New York: 1978. V. 44; 45

The Sporting Club. New York: 1968. V. 37; 38; 40; 44; 45; 46

MAC GUIRE, CATHAL

Amabel. London: 1893. V. 46

MC GUIRE, HUNTER

The Memory of 'Stonewall' Jackson. New York: 1898. V. 42

MC GUIRE, J. A.

In the Alaska-Yukon Gamelands. Cincinnati: (1921). V. 37

MC GUIRE, JOHN A.

In the Alaska Yukon Gamelands. Cincinnati: 1921. V. 39

MC GUIRE, JUDITH W.

Diary of a Southern Refugee During the War, by a Lady of Virginia. New York: 1867. V. 38

MAC GUNN, JOHN

The Making of Character. Cambridge: 1905. V. 38

MC GURK, RUTH

Bad Changes. Oakland: 1986. V. 38

MC HALE, JOHN

An An. V. 46

M'HARRY, SAMUEL

The Practical Distiller or an Introduction to Making Whiskey, Gin, Brandy, Spirits &c &c. Harrisburgh: 1809. V. 44

MC HENRY, JAMES

Rules and Regulations Respecting the Recruiting Service. Philadelphia: 1799. V. 44

MC HENRY, LAWRENCE

Garrison's. Springfield: 1969. V. 40; 42

MC HUGH, GLEN

An Appraisal. A Letter by Glenn McHugh Addressed to Frank Hall, January 1946. Hillsborough: 1946. V. 46

MC HUGH, R. J.

Modern Mexico. New York: 1914. V. 42

MC IAN, ROBERT RONALD

The Clans of the Scottish Highlands, Illustrated by Appropriate Figures, Displaying Their Dress, Tartans, Arms, Armorial Insignia and Social Occupations. London: 1857. V. 44

MC ILHANEY, EDWARD WASHINGTON

Recollections of a '49er. Kansas City: 1908. V. 38; 40; 43; 44; 46

MC ILVAINE, CHARLES

One Thousand American Fungi. Indianapolis: 1900. V. 37; 45

M'ILVAINE, WILLIAM

Sketches of Scenery and Notes of Personal Adventure in California and Mexico. Philadelphia: 1850. V. 38; 39; 40; 42

Sketches of Scenery and Notes of a Personal Adventure in California and Mexico. San Francisco: 1951. V. 37; 38; 40; 41; 45; 46

MC ILVANNEY, WILLIAM

Landscapes and Figures. Guildford: 1973. V. 37

Remedy is None. London: 1966. V. 41

MC ILWAINE, H. R.

Journals of the Council of the State of Virginia: 1776-1791. Richmond: 1931-82. V. 37

Legislative Journals of the Council of Colonial Virginia. Richmond: 1918. V. 46

MC ILWRAITH, T. F.

The Bella Coola Indians. Toronto: 1948. V. 40

MC INDOE, G.

Poems and Songs, Chiefly in the Scottish Dialect. Edinburgh: 1805. V. 41; 42

MC INERNEY, JAY

Bright Lights, Big City. New York: 1984. V. 43

MAC INNES, C. M.

In the Shadow of the Rockies. London: 1930. V. 46

MAC INNES, COLIN

Absolute Beginners. London: 1959. V. 40

June in Spring. London: 1952. V. 38

To the Victors the Spoils. London: 1950. V. 40

MAC INNES, TOM

The Complete Poems of . . . Toronto: 1923. V. 45

MC INTOSH, A.

A Linguistic Atlas of Late Medieval English. 1986. V. 38

MC INTOSH, A. H.

Artistic Furniture. Kircaldy: 1900. V. 45

MC INTOSH, A. J.

Best Thoroughbreds Bloodlines in Australia. Volume Two. Kensington: 1982. V. 37

M'INTOSH, CHARLES

The Flower Garden. London: 1839. V. 44

The Flower Garden. London: 1838. V. 37; 38; 44

The Greenhouse, Hot House and Stove Including Selected Lists of the Most Beautiful Species of Exotic Flowring Plants . . . London: 1838. V. 40; 44

The Greenhouse, Hot House and Stove. London: 1840. V. 37; 45

The New and Improved Practical Gardener, and Horticulturalist . . . London: 1851. V. 41; 42; 46

The New and Improved Gardener, and Modern Horticulturalist . . . London: 1854. V. 39; 42; 46

The New and Improved Practical Gardener, and Modern Horticulturist. London: 1861. V. 40

The Practical Gardener and Modern Horticulturalist. London: 1828. V. 44

The Practical Gardener and Modern Horticulturist. London: 1828-30. V. 38

The Practical Gardener and Modern Horticulturist. London: 1828-9. V. 43

MAC INTOSH, CHARLES A.

Popular Outlines of the Press, Ancient and Modern. N.P.: 1858? V. 38

MAC INTOSH, DAVID

A Collection of Gaelic Proverbs, and Familiar Phrases. Edinburgh: 1785. V. 38

MC INTOSH, DAVID GREGG

The Campaign of Chancellorsville. Richmond: 1915. V. 44

MAC INTOSH, JAMES

Vindiciae Gallicae. Dublin: 1791. V. 39

MC INTOSH, JOHN

The Discovery of America, by Christopher Columbus; and the Origin of the North American Indians. Toronto: 1836. V. 40

The Origin of the North American Indians . . . New York: 1843. V. 41; 43; 44

MC INTOSH, JOHN continued

The Origin of the North American Indians. New York, etc.: 1843. V. 38

MC INTOSH, MARIA J.

Woman in America, Her Work and Her Reward. New York: 1850. V. 44; 45

MC INTOSH, W. C.

The Resources of the Sea. Cambridge: 1899. V. 42

The Resources of the Sea, as Shown in the Scientific Experiments to Test the Effects of Trawling and of the Closure of Certain Areas off the Scottish Shores. London: 1899. V. 45

MC INTYRE, ARCHIBALD

A Letter to His Excellency Daniel D. Tompkins, Late Governor of the State of New York. Albany: 1819. V. 41

MAC INTYRE, D.

Hindu-Koh Wanderings and Wild Sport on and Beyond the Himalyas. London: 1891. V. 42

MAC INTYRE, DONALD

Hindu-Koh; Wanderings and Wild Sport on and Beyond the Himalayas. Edinburgh: 1889. V. 39; 40

Hindu Koh. Wanderings and Wild Sport On and Beyond the Himalays. London: 1889. V. 41; 44

MC INTYRE, JAMES

Poems. Ingersoll: 1889/91. V. 44

MC INTYRE, ROBERT C.

Martin Johnson Heade, 1819-1904. New York: 1948. V. 46

MAC INTYRE, W. IRWIN

Colored Soldiers. Macon: 1923. V. 46

MAC ISSAC, F.

The Mental Marvel. 1930. V. 44

MC IVER, MARY A.

Poems. Ottawa: 1869. V. 43

MAC KALL, WILLIAM W.

A Son's Recollections of His Father. New York: 1930. V. 44

MAC KAY, AENEAS JAMES GEORGE 1839-1911

The Practice of the Court of Session. Edinburgh: 1877-79. V. 40

MAC KAY, ALEXANDER

The Western World; or, Travels in the United States in 1846-47. London: 1849. V. 42; 43; 46

The Western World. Philadelphia: 1849. V. 38; 44

Western India. London: 1853. V. 43; 46

MAC KAY, ANDREW

The Complete Navigator; or, An Easy and Familiar Guide to the Theory and Practice of Navigation . . . Philadelphia: 1807. V. 37; 40; 42

MC KAY, BARRY

Marbling Methods and Receipts from Four Centuries, with Other Instructions Useful to Bookbinders. Oxford: 1990. V. 45

Patterns and Pigments in English Marbled Papers. 1988. V. 40; 45

Patterns and Pigments in English Marbled Papers. iddlington: 1988. V. 44

Patterns and Pigments in English Marbled Papers. Kidlington: 1988. V. 40; 42

Patterns and Pigments in English Marbled Papers: An Account of the Origins, Sources, and Documentary Literature to 1881. Oxford: 1988. V. 39

MAC KAY, CHARLES

The Gaelic Etymology of the Languages of Western Europe and More Especially of the English and Lowland Scotch, and of Their Slang, Cant, and Colloquial Dialects. London: 1877. V. 39

The Home Affections, Pourtrayed by the Poets. V. 38; 41

The Home Affections Protrayed by the Poets. London: 1858. V. 42

Life and Liberty in America; or Sketches of a Tour in the United States and Canada in 1857-8. London: 1859. V. 39; 42; 45; 46

Life and Liberty in America . . . London: 1859. V. 46

Life and Liberty in America: Sketches of a Tour in the U.S. and Canada in 1857-8. New York: 1859. V. 46

Memoirs of Extraordinary Popular Delusions. London: 1841. V. 38

The Mormons; or Latter-Day Saints. London: 1841. V. 45

The Mormons, or Latter-Day Saints. London: 1851. V. 42

The Salamandrine. London: 1853. V. 43

The Whisky Demon; or, the Dream of the Reveller. Edinburgh: 1860. V. 46

MC KAY, CLAUD

Songs of Jamaica. Kingston: 1912. V. 46

MC KAY, CLAUDE

Banana Bottom. New York: 1933. V. 38; 39; 42; 45

Banjo. New York: 1929. V. 38; 41; 44; 45

Harlem Shadows. New York: 1922. V. 38

Home to Harlem. 1928. V. 45

Spring in New Hampshire and Other Poems. London: 1920. V. 38

MC KAY, DONALD

Daring Donald McKay or, the War Trail of the Modocs. Chicago: 1884. V. 40

MAC KAY, HELEN

Dream Boats and Other Stories. New York: 1918. V. 43

Stories for Pictures. New York: 1912. V. 43; 45

MAC KAY, HENRY

An Abridgement of the Excise-Laws, and of the Custom-Laws, Now in Force in Great Britain. Edinburgh: 1779. V. 40

MAC KAY, J. N.

History of 7th Duke of Edinburgh's Own Gurkha Rifles. Edinburgh: 1962. V. 42

MAC KAY, J. W. C.

The Port Elizabeth Directory and Guide to the Eastern Province of the Cape of Good Hope for 1872. London: 1871. V. 43

MAC KAY, JAMES T.

Flora Hibernica, Comprising Flowering Plants, Ferns . . . Dublin: 1836. V. 43

MAC KAY, JOHN HENRY

The Anarchists. A Picture of Civilization at the Close of the Nineteenth Century. Boston: 1891. V. 41

M'KAY, LAUCHLAN

The Practical Ship-Builder. New York: 1839. V. 41

MAC KAY, MALCOLM S.

Cow Range and Hunting Trail. New York: 1925. V. 39; 42

MC KAY, RICHARD C.

Some Famous Sailing Ships and Their Builder Donald McKay, A Study of the American Sailing Packet and Clipper Eras. New York: 1928. V. 44

Some Famous Sailing Ships and Their Builder Donald McKay. New York: 1931. V. 46

South Street A Maritime History of New York. New York: 1934. V. 44

MC KAY, ROBERT H.

Little Pills an Army Story. Pittsburg, KS: 1918. V. 37; 38; 40; 45

MAC KAY, ROBERT W. STUART

The Canada Directory. Montreal: 1851. V. 37

The Strangers' Guide to the Cities of Montreal and Quebec, together with sketches of the Cities of Toronto, Kingston, and Hamilton, and of the Towns of Bytown, London, &c., and a glance at the most remarkable cataracts and falls, mineral . . . Montreal: 1852. V. 37

MC KAY, SETH S.

Seven Decades of the Texas Constitution of 1876. Lubbock: 1942. V. 37

Texas Politics, 1906-1944. Lubbock: 1952. V. 38

MAC KAY, SHELIA

The Forth Bridge. A Picture History. Edinburgh. V. 43

MC KAY, W. J. S.

The History of Ancient Gynaecology. New York: 1901. V. 42

MC KAY, WILLIAM

John Hoppner, R. A. London: 1909. V. 39; 44

The Popular Idol. London: 1876. V. 40

MAC KAYE, PERCY

The Far Familiar; Fifty New Poems. London: (1938). V. 37

Johnny Crimson: a Legend of Hollis Hall. Boston: 1895. V. 37

The Mystery of Hamlet King of Denmark or What We Will. New York: 1950. V. 46

Poesia Religio. France: 1939. V. 42

The Roll Call: a Masque of the Red Cross. Washington: 1918. V. 46

Sanctuary. Bird Masque. New York: 1914. V. 38

MC KECHNIE, SUE

British Silhouette Artists and Their Work. 1760-1860. London: 1978. V. 39

MC KEE, JAMES C

Narrative of the Surrender of a command of U.S. Forces at Fort Fillmore, N.M. in July, A.D. 1861, at the Breaking Out of the Civil War . . . New York: 1881. V. 37

MC KEE, JAMES H.

Back in War Times . . . History of the 144th Regiment. New York: 1903. V. 46

MC KEE, R. E.

The McKee Collection of Paintings. El Paso: 1968. V. 41

MC KEE, THOMAS JEFFERSON

Catalogue of the Library of the Late Thomas Jefferson McKee. New York: 1900-06. V. 39

M'KEEVOR, THOMAS

A Voyage to Hudson's Bay, During the SUmmer of 1812. Containing a Particular Account of the Icebergs and other Phenomena which present themselves in those Regions; also, a Description of the Esquimeaux and North American Indians; . . . London: 1819. V. 37

MAC KELLAR, SMITHS AND JORDAN

1796-1896, One Hundred Years, MacKellar, Smiths and Jordan Foundry. Philadelphia: 1896. V. 37; 44

MAC KELLAR, THOMAS

The American Printer, a Manual of Typography. Philadelphia: 1879. V. 46
The American Printer; A Manual of Typography. Philadelphia: 1866. V. 38

MC KELLOP, A. P.

Constitution and Laws of the Muskogee Nation. Muskogee: 1893. V. 37; 38

MC KELVEY, S. D.

The Lilac, a Monograph. New York: 1928. V. 42; 43; 45; 46
The Lilac, a Monograph. London: 1928. V. 37

MC KELVEY, SUSAN

Botanical Exploration of the Transmississippi West. Jamaica Plain: 1955. V. 39; 40; 43

MC KELVEY, SUSAN DELANO

Botanical Exploration of the Trans-Mississippi West, 1790-1850. Cambridge: 1955. V. 46
Botanical Exploration of the Transmississippi West. Jamaica Plain: 1955. V. 39

MC KELVIE, C. L.

J. C. Harrison's Gamebirds of the British Isles. London: 1989. V. 42
The Snipe, Studies in Words and Pictures. V. 46
The Spine, Studies in Words and Pictures. London: 1989. V. 43
The Woodcock, a Study in Words and Pictures. 1988. V. 39

MC KELVIE, COLIN LAURIE

J. C. Harrison's Gamebirds of the British Isles. London: 1989. V. 41
The Woodcock, a Study in Words and Pictures. Norfolk: 1988. V. 41

MAC KENNA, F. SEVERNE

Chelsea Porcelain. Leigh-on-Sea: 1951. V. 42

M'KENNA, J. E.

Diocese of Clogher. Enniskillen: 1920. V. 43

MC KENNA, ROLLIE

Rollie McKenna: a Life in Photography. New York: 1991. V. 46

MAC KENNA, THEOBALD

Address to the Roman Catholics of Ireland, Relative to the Late Proceedings, and the Means and Practicability of a Tranquil Emancipation. Dublin: 1792. V. 41
An Essay on Parliamentary Reform and on the evils likely to ensue, from a Republican Constitution in Ireland. Dublin: 1793. V. 37
Political Essays relative to the affairs of Ireland, in 1791, 1792, and 1793; with remarks on the present state of that country. London: 1794. V. 37
Thoughts on the Civil Condition and Relations of the Roman Catholic Clergy, Religion and People in Ireland. London: 1805. V. 43

MAC KENNEA, F. SEVERNE

Chelsea Porcelain, the Triangle and Raised Anchor Wares. Leigh on Sea: 1948. V. 37

M'KENNEDY, THOMAS LORRAINE

Memoirs Officil and Personal; With Sketches of Travels Among the Northern and Southern Indians. New York: 1846. V. 38

MC KENNEY, COLONEL

Catalogue of One Hundred and Seventeen Indian Portraits, Representing Eighteen Different Tribes . . . N.P.: 1836. V. 43

MC KENNEY, L. M.

McKenney's Business Directory of the Principal Towns of California, Nevada, Utah, Wyoming, Colorado and Nebraska. Sacramento: 1882. V. 39; 42

MC KENNEY, THOMAS

The Indian Tribes of North America . . . Edinburgh: 1933-34. V. 40

MC KENNEY, THOMAS LORRAINE 1785-1859

Catalogue of One Hundred and Fifteen Indian Portraits, Representing Eighteen Different Tribes, Accompanied by a Few Brief Remarks on the Character &c. of Most of Them. Philadelphia: 1836. V. 41
History of the Indian Tribes of North America. Philadelphia: 1855. V. 37; 38
History of the Indian Tribes of North America . . . Philadelphia: 1870. V. 43
History of the Indian Tribes of North America. Philadelphia: 187? V. 44
History of the Indian Tribes of North America. Edinburgh: 1933. V. 45
History of the Indian Tribes of North America. Kent: 1978. V. 37; 39; 40; 41; 44
The Indian Tribes of North America, with Biographical Sketches and Anecdotes of the Principal Chiefs. Edinburgh: 1933. V. 38; 42; 45
The Indian Tribes of North America. Edinburgh: 1933-34. V. 39; 40; 41; 43
Memoirs Official and Personal. New York: 1846. V. 37; 39; 40; 42; 44; 45
Reply to Kosciursko Armstraong's Assault Upon Col. M'Kenney's Narrative of the Causes that Lead to General Armstrong's Resignation of the Office of Secretary of War in 1814. New York: 1847. V. 41
Sketches of a Tour to the Lakes, of the Character and Customs of the Chippeway Indians, and of the Incidents Connected with the Treaty of Fon Du Lac . . . also a Vocabulary of the Algic, or Chippeway Language. Baltimore: 1827. V. 40; 44
To the Public. N.P.: 1828. V. 45

MC KENNY, THOMAS LORRAINE

The Indian Tribes of North America. Edinburgh: 1933-34. V. 38

MAC KENZIE, A.

A Woollen Draper's Letter on the French Treaty, to His Friend's and Fellow Tradesmen all Over England. London: 1786. V. 38

MC KENZIE, ALEX

Regimental Orders: 35th Battalion, Head Quarters, Barrie, March 18th, 1882. V. 43

MAC KENZIE, ALEXANDER

History of the Frasers of Lovat with Genealogies of the Principal Families of the Name to Which is Added Those of Dunballoch and Phopachy. Iverness: 1896. V. 37; 40
The Life of Paul Jones. Boston: 1841. V. 40; 42
The Life of Paul Jones. New York: 1845. V. 46
Proceedings of the Naval Court Martial in the Case of Alexander Slidell Mackenzie, a Commander in the Navy of the United States . . . to Which is Annexed, an Elaborate Review by James Fenimore Cooper. New York: 1844. V. 40
Reisen von Montreal Durch Nordwestamerika Nach dem Eismeer und der Sud-See. Hamburg: 1902. V. 42
Speeches of the Hon. Alexander MacKenzie During His Recent Visit to Scotland. Toronto: 1876. V. 43
Voyages from Montreal on the River of St. Laurence through the Continent of North America, to the Frozen and Pacific Oceans; in the Years 1789 and 1793. London: 1801. V. 37; 38; 40; 41; 42; 45; 46
Voyages from Montreal on the River St. Lawrence through the Continent of North America, to the Frozen and Pacific Oceans in the Years 1789 and 1793. London: 1802. V. 41
Voyages from Montreal . . . Through the Continent of North America, to the Frozen and Pacific Oceans. New York: 1802. V. 37
Voyages d'Alex.dre Mackenzie Dans l'Interieur de l'Amerique Septentrionale. Paris: 1802. V. 41; 42; 43
Voyages from Montreal on the River St Lawrence through the Continent of North America to the Frozen and Pacific Oceans in the Years 1789 and 1793 . . . Toronto: 1927. V. 38; 40
A Year in Spain. Boston: 1829. V. 42
A Year in Spain by a Young American. London: 1831. V. 41

MAC KENZIE, ARTHUR F.

Chess: its Poetry and Its Prose. Kingston: 1887. V. 40

MAC KENZIE, CECIL W.

Donald Mackenzie. Los Angeles: 1937. V. 43

MAC KENZIE, CHARLES

Notes on Haiti, Made During a Residence in that Republic. London: 1830. V. 39; 42

MC KENZIE, CHARLES H.

The Religious Sentiments of Charles Dickens, Collected from His Writings. London: 1884. V. 40; 43

MAC KENZIE, COLIN

Five Thousand Receipts in all the Useful and Domestic Arts. Philadelphia: 1829. V. 39; 41
MacKenzie's Five Thousand Receipts in all the Useful and Domestic Arts . . . Philadelphia: 1831. V. 38

MAC KENZIE, COMPTON

Gallipoli Memories. London: 1929. V. 42; 43

MAC KENZIE, COMPTON continued

Greek Memories. London: 1932. V. 38; 39; 45

My Life and Times. London: 1963-71. V. 42

My Life and Times: Octave One - Octave 10. London: 1963/71. V. 45

Poems. London: 1907. V. 37; 46

Poems. Oxford: 1907. V. 39; 41; 42

Poems. Oxford & London: 1907. V. 37; 38; 40

Santa Claus in Summer. Oxford. V. 42

Sinister Street. London: 1913-14. V. 39; 40; 41

MC KENZIE, D. A.

Egyptian Myth and Legend. London. V. 40

MC KENZIE, D. F.

The Cambridge University Press 1696-1712. Cambridge: 1966. V. 44

MAC KENZIE, DUNCAN

Excavations at Ain Shems (Beth-Shemesh). London: 1913. V. 40; 42

MAC KENZIE, E.

A Descriptive and Historical Account of the Town and County of Newcastle Upon Tyne, Including the Borough of Gateshead. Newcastle-upon-Tyne: 1827. V. 39; 46

An Historical, Topographical, and Descriptive View of the United States of America, and of Upper and Lower Canada. Newcastle-upon-Tyne: 1819. V. 38; 39; 40

An Historical, Topographical and Descriptive View of the County of Northumberland . . . Newcastle-upon-Tyne: 1825. V. 37; 38; 40; 42

An Historical, Topographical and Descriptive View of the County Palatine of Durham. Newcastle upon Tyne: 1834. V. 42

MAC KENZIE, FRANCIS ALEXANDER

Hints for the Use of Highland Tennants. Inverness: 1838. V. 37

MAC KENZIE, FREDERICK

The Architectural Antiquities of the Collegiate Chapel of St. Stephens, Westminter; the Late House of Commons. High Holborn: 1774. V. 37

Diary of Frederick Mackenzie, 1775-1781. Cambridge: 1930. V. 38; 44; 45

MAC KENZIE, G. M.

Travels in the Slavonic Provinces of Turkey-in-Europe. London: 1867. V. 45

Travels in the Slavonic Provinces of Turkey-in-Europe. London: 1877. V. 45

MAC KENZIE, GEORGE 1636-1691

The Antiquity of the Royal Line of Scotland Farther Cleared and Defended Against the Exceptions Lately Offer'd by Dr. Stillingfleet . . . London: 1686. V. 41; 42

Essays Upon Several Moral Subjects. London: 1713. V. 40

Idea Eloquentiae Forensis Hodiernae; unda Cum Actione Forensi Ex Unaquaque Juris Parte. Edinburgh: 1681. V. 38; 40

An Idea of the Modern Eloquence of the Bar. Together with a Pleading Out of Every Part of Law. Edinburgh: 1711. V. 38

The Institutions of the Law of Scotland, by Sir George Mackenzie of Rosehaugh . . . Edinburgh: 1706. V. 45

The Institutions of the Law of Scotland. Edinburgh: 1688. V. 38

Jus Regium; or, the Just and Solid Foundations of Monarchy in General . . . London: 1684. V. 38; 42

A Moral Essay preferring Solitude to Publick Employment, and all it's Appanages; such as Fame, Command, Riches, Pleasures, Conversation, &c. Edinburgh: 1665. V. 39

Moral Gallantry. Edinburgh: 1667. V. 41; 45; 46

A Moral Paradox . . . Edinburgh: 1667. V. 45

Moral Gallantry. A Discourse, wherein the Author endeavours to prove, that Pointof Honour (abstracting from all other tyes) obliges Men to be Virtuous. And that there is nothing so mean (or unworthy of a Gentleman) as Vice. Edenburgh, London: 1669. V. 39

Moral Gallantry. London: 1669. V. 40; 41

A Moral Essay. London: 1685. V. 46

The Moral History of Frugality with its opposite Vices, Covetousness, Niggardliness,Prodigality, and Luxury. London;: 1691. V. 39

Observations on the Acts of Parliament Made by King James the First (etc.). Edinburgh: 1686. V. 38; 40

Observations Upon XVIII. Act Parliament XXIII K. James VI. Against Dispositions Made in Defraud of Creditors, etc. Edinburgh: 1699. V. 40

Pleadings, in Some . . . Cases, Before the . . . Courts of Scotland, Since . . . 1661. Edinburgh: 1704. V. 38

Reason. An Essay. London: 1695. V. 41; 44; 45

The Science of Herauldry, treated as a part of the Civil Law & Law of Nations. Bound with: Observations upon the Laws & Customs of Nations, as to Precedency. Edinburgh: 1680. V. 37

A Vindication of the Government in Scotland. London: 1691. V. 45

MAC KENZIE, GEORGE STEUART

Travels in the Island of Iceland, During the Summer of the Year MDCCCX. Edinburgh: 1811. V. 42; 44

MAC KENZIE, GEORGIANNA MUIR

Travels in the Slavonic Provinces of Turkey-in-Europe. London: 1867. V. 39

Travels in the Slavonic Pronvinces of Turkey in Europe. London: 1877. V. 37

Travels in the Slavonic Provinces of Turkey-in-Europe. London & New York:;: 1866. V. 37; 40

MAC KENZIE, GERALDINE

The First Australian's First (Second, Third, Fourth, Fifth, Sixth) Book . . . Melbourne: 1951. V. 41

MAC KENZIE, HENRY 1745-1831

An Account of the Life and Writings of John Home, Esq. Edinburgh: 1822. V. 41

Julia de Roubigne. London: 1777. V. 45

Julia de Roubigne, a Tale in a Series of Letters. London: 1781. V. 40

Julia de Roubigne, a Tale in a Series of Letters . . . London: 1782-81. V. 39

The Lounger. Dublin: 1787. V. 41

The Lounger. London: 1788. V. 39

The Man of Feeling. London: 1771. V. 39; 41

The Man of the World. London: 1773. V. 37; 38; 40; 43; 45

The Man of Feeling. Berwick: 1800. V. 40

The Man of Feeling. The Second Edition, Corrected. London: 1771. V. 37

The Man of the World. London: 1795. V. 40

The Mirror. Edinburgh: 1779-80. V. 41

The Mirror, a Periodical Paper, Published at Edinburgh in the Years 1779 and 1780. London: 1783. V. 38

The Miscellaneous Works. London: 1806/1805. V. 40

The Miscellaneous Works. Leith: 1815. V. 41

The Pursuit of Happiness (a poem). London: 1771. V. 40

The Pursuit of Happiness. London: 1781. V. 42

Report of the Committee of the Highland Society of Scotland, Appointed to Inquire Into the Nature and Authenticity of the Poems of Ossian. Edinburgh: 1805. V. 37; 42; 46

The Works . . . Edinburgh: 1824. V. 45; 46

MAC KENZIE, J.

Voyage from Montreal, on the River St. Laurence, through the Continent of North America, to the Frozen and Pacific Oceans; in the Years 1789 and 1793. New York: 1802. V. 45

A Woollen Draper's Letter on the French Treaty to His Friends and Fellow Tradesmen all Over England. London: 1786. V. 40; 42; 46

MAC KENZIE, J. B.

Thayendanegea: an Historico-Military Drama. Toronto: 1898. V. 38

MAC KENZIE, J. S. E.

British Orchids: How to Tell One from Another. London: 1918. V. 42

MAC KENZIE, JAMES

Angina Pectoris. London: 1923. V. 42

Diseases of the Heart. London: 1910. V. 38

Diseases of the Heart. New York: 1910. V. 42

Diseases of the Heart. London: 1918. V. 43

The Future of Medicine. London: 1919. V. 44

The Study of the Pulse: Arterial, Venous and Heaptic and of the Movements of the Heart. Edinburgh: 1902. V. 42

The Study of the Pulse Arterial, Venous and Hepatic and of the Movements of the Heart. Edinburgh & London: 1902. V. 37

MAC KENZIE, JOHN

Austral Africa Losing It or Ruling It. London: 1887. V. 42; 43; 46

Ocean, Stella and Other Poems. Edinburgh: 1815. V. 41; 42

Ten years North of the Orange River. Edinburgh: 1871. V. 38

MAC KENZIE, JOHN STUART

An Introduction to Social Philosophy. Glasgow: 1890. V. 42; 45

MAC KENZIE, JOHN WHITEFOORD

Catalogue of the First (-Second) Part of the . . . Library of Rare and Curious Books . . . Edinburgh: 1886. V. 45

MAC KENZIE, MARY JANE

Geraldine; or, Modes of Faith and Practice. London: 1820. V. 38; 40; 42

Private Life. London: 1829. V. 38

Private Life: or Varities of Character and Opinion. New York: 1829. V. 44

Private Life; or Varieties of Character and Opinion. New York: 1829. V. 41; 43

MAC KENZIE, MORELL

Diseases of the Throat and Nose. Philadelphia: 1880-1884. V. 42

The Fatal Illness of Frederick the Noble. London: 1888. V. 39; 43

A Manual of Diseases of the Throat and Nose. New York: 1880-84. V. 43

MAC KENZIE, MORRELL

Diseases of the Pharynx, Larynx and Trachea. (with) Diseases of the Oesophagus, Nose and Naso-Pharynx. New York: 1880. V. 42

The Use of the Laryngoscope in Diseases of the Throat. Philadelphia: 1865. V. 42

MAC KENZIE, MURDO

View of the Salmon Fishery of Scotland. Edinburgh & London: 1860. V. 37

MAC KENZIE, MURDOCH

A Treatise on Marine Surveying. London: 1819. V. 40

MAC KENZIE, RANALD S.

Ranald S. MacKenzie's Official Correspondence Relating to Texas, 1871-1873 (and) 1873-1879. Lubbock: 1968. V. 41; 42; 44

MAC KENZIE, RODERICK

Strictures on Lt. Col. Tarleton's History 'of the Campaigns of 1780 and 1781, In the 'Southern Provinces of North America' . . . London: 1787. V. 41; 44

MAC KENZIE, T. A.

Historical Records of the 79th Queen's Own Cameron Highlanders. London: 1887. V. 40

MAC KENZIE, W. B.

Married Life . . . London: (1867). V. 37

MAC KENZIE, W. R.

Ballads and Sea Songs from Nova Scotia. Cambridge: 1928. V. 43

MAC KENZIE, WILLIAM

A Practical Treatise on the Diseases of the Eye. London: 1840. V. 42

A Practical Treatise on the Diseases of the Eye . . . London: 1854. V. 44

A Practical Treatise on the Diseases of the Eye . . . Philadelphia: 1855. V. 42; 44

A Practical Treatise on the Diseases of the Eye. Boston: 1833. V. 38

MAC KENZIE, WILLIAM LYON

The Lives and Opinions of Benj'n Franklin Butler, U.S. District Attorney for Southern District of New york and Jesse Hoyt, Counsellor at Law . . . Boston: 1845. V. 42

MAC KENZIES Five Thousand Receipts . . .

Philadelphia: 1854. V. 45

M'KEOWN, WILLIAM A.

A Treatise on Unripe Cataract. London: 1898. V. 43

MC KERROW, R. B.

Title-page Borders Used in England and Scotland 1485-1640. London: 1932 for 1931. V. 44

Title-page Borders Used in England and Scotland, 1485-1640. London: 1932. V. 37; 38; 40; 44; 45

MC KERROW, R.B.

Dictionaries of the Printers and Booksellers who Were at Work in England, Scotland and Ireland 1557-1775. London: 1907-32. V. 39

Printer's & Publishers' Devices in England & Scotland 1485-1640. London: 1949. V. 37

MC KERROW, RONALD BAINES

Title-Page Borders Used in England and Scotland 1485-1640. London: 1931. V. 38; 39; 43

M'KEWAN, DAVID HALL

Lessons on Trees in Water Colours. London: 1850. V. 45

MAC KEY, AIDAN

Mr. Chesterton Comes to Tea, or; How the King of England Captures Redskin Island. Beford: 1978. V. 41

MAC KEY, MARGARET GILBERT

California Adventures. Los Angeles: 1937. V. 38

MAC KEY, SAMPSON ARNOLD

The Mythological Astronomy of the Ancients Demonstrated by Restoring to Their Fables and Symbols Their Original meanings. Norwich: 1822-23. V. 46

MAC KIE, CHARLES FRANCIS

The Heroines of '76' Their Trials, Tribulations and Triumphs. Written by a Soldier Man, a Sailor Man, and a Railroad Man and Edited by the Editor. Philadelphia: 1876. V. 37

M'KIE, JAMES

Title pages (and imrprints) of the Books in the Private Library of James M'Kie, Kilmarnock. Kilmarnock: 1867. V. 44

MC KILLIP, P.

The House on Parchment Street. 1973. V. 44

MC KILLIP, PATRICIA

The Forgotten Breasts of Eld. New York: 1974. V. 42

The Riddle-Master of Hed. 1976. V. 44

MC.KILLIP, PATRICIA A.

The Riddle of the Stars: The Riddle-Master of Hed; Heir of Sea and Dire; Harpist in the Wind. London: 1979. V. 39; 42

M'KIM, J. M.

A Sketch of the Slave Trade in the District of Columbia, Contained in Two Letters. Pittsburgh: 1838. V. 43

MC KIM MEAD & WHITE

A Monograph of the Work of McKim Mead and White, 1879-1915. Volume IV. New York: 1915. V. 45

MC KINLAY, D. A.

Facts about Minnesota: Reliable Information for Immigrants, with a Valuable Map, Presented by the St. paul Minneapolis & Manitoba Railway. St. Paul: 1879. V. 37; 39

MC KINLAY, JAMES

McKinlay's Journal of Exploration in the Interior of Australia. (Burke Relief Expedition). Melbourne: 1863. V. 43

MC KINLAY, JOHN

Journal of Exploration in the Interior of Australia. Melbourne: 1862. V. 45

M'KINLEY, ANDREW

The Trial of Andrew M'Kinley, Before the High Court of Justiciary, at Edinburgh on the 1st Day of July 1817, for Administering Unlawful Oaths. Edinburgh: 1818. V. 41

MC KINLEY, R.

Beauty. 1978. V. 44

MC KINLEY, WILLIAM

Speeches and Addresses . . . From March 1, 1897 to May 30, 1900. New York: 1900. V. 39

MAC KINNEY, LOREN

Medical Illustraions in Medieval Manuscripts. London: 1965. V. 41; 42; 45

MC KINNEY, WILSON

Fred Carrasco: the Heroin Merchant. Austin: 1975. V. 44

MAC KINNON, DANIEL 1791-1836

Origin and Services of the Coldstream Guards. London: 1833. V. 40

MAC KINNON, JAMES

South African Traits. Edinburgh: 1887. V. 39; 40; 44; 45

MAC KINNON, L. B.

Atlantic and Transatlantic Sketches, Afloat and Ashore. London: 1852. V. 40

MAC KINNON, LAUCHLAN BELLINGHAM

Steam Warfare in the Parana. London: 1848. V. 39

MAC KINNON, W. H.

The Origins and Services of The Coldstream Guards. London;: 1833. V. 37

MAC KINNON, WILLIAM ALEXANDER

On the Rise, Progress and Present State of Public Opinion, in Great Britain, and Other Parts of the World. London: 1828. V. 40; 42

MAC KINTOSH, ALEXANDER

The Driffield Angler. Lincs.: 1806. V. 40

The Driffield Angler: to Which are Added, Instructions for Shooting, Rules for Training and Managing Pointers, Spaniels and Greyhounds &c . . . Gainsborough: 1806. V. 39

The Modern Fisher; or, Driffeld Angler. Derby: 1821. V. 43; 45

MAC KINTOSH, ANGUS

Mad Doctors, Mad Houses and Laws. Edinburgh: 1864. V. 43

MAC KINTOSH, CHARLES RENNIE

Haus Eines Kunstfreundes. Darmstadt: 1902. V. 42

MAC KINTOSH, ELIZABETH 1896-1952

The Man in the Queue. New York: 1929. V. 37; 40

MAC KINTOSH, HAROLD

Early English Figure Pottery. London: 1938. V. 37; 46

MAC LEAN, JAMES

A Genuine Account of the Life and Actions of James Maclean, Highwayman, To the Time of His Trial and Receiving Sentence at the Old-Bailey. London: 1750. V. 45

Seventeen Years' History, of the Life and Sufferings of James M'Lean. Hartford: 1814. V. 46

MC LEAN, JAMES HENRY

Ukase. We Command All Nations to Keep the Peace. Peace-Makers. New York: 1880. V. 37

MAC LEAN, JOHN

Canadian Savage Folk: the Native Tribes of Canada. Toronto: 1896. V. 44

Notes of a Twenty Five Years' Service in the Hudson's Bay Territory. London: 1849. V. 38; 39; 41; 45

Notes of a Twenty-Five Years' Service in the Hudson's Bay Territories. Toronto: 1932. V. 39; 45

MAC LEAN, JOHN HUGH

Remarks on Fair Prices and Produce Rents. Edinburgh: 1825. V. 39; 42; 46

MAC LEAN, L.

An Inquiry into the Nature, Causes and Cure of Hydrothorax. Hartford: 1814. V. 37; 44

MC LEAN, MALCOLM D.

Papers Concerning Robertson's Colony in Texas. Ft. Worth and Arlington: 1974. V. 42

Papers Concerning Robertson's Colony in Texas. Ft. Worth & Arlington: 1974. V. 39

Papers Concerning Robertson's Colony in Texas. Ft. Worth/Arlington: 1974. V. 37

MAC LEAN, NORAMN

A River Runs Through It and Other Stories. Chicago: 1976. V. 44; 45; 46

MAC LEAN, NORMAN

A River Runs Through It. West Hatfield: 1989. V. 45

MC LEAN, RUARI

Benjamin Fawcett Engraver and Colour Printer, with a List of His Books and Plates. Hampshire: 1988. V. 40; 46

Motif: A Journal of Visual Arts. London: 1958-1965. V. 41

Motif: a Journal of Visual Arts. London: 1958-1964. V. 39

Victorian Book Design and Colour Printing. London: 1963. V. 37; 38; 40; 41; 42

Victorian Book Design and Colour Printing. Berkeley & Los Angeles: 1972. V. 42

Victorian Book Design and Colour Printing. London: 1972. V. 38; 39; 40; 45; 46

Victorian Book Design and Colour Printing. N.P.: 1972. V. 37; 38; 39; 44

Victorian Publisher's Book-Bindings in Cloth & Leather. London: 1974. V. 42; 43; 45

Victorian Publishers' Book-bindings in Cloth and Leather. London: 1974. V. 46

Victorian Publishers' Bookbindings in Cloth and Leather. Berkeley: 1973. V. 37

MC LEAN SILVER MINING CO.

The McLean Silver Mining Co. of Montana. Philadelphia: 1865. V. 37

MC LEAN, THOMAS

The Devils at Home. London: 1829. V. 44

The Looking Glass, or Caricature Annual 1830, & 1831. V. 40

MC LEAN, WILLIAM EDWARD

Forty-Third Regiment of Indiana Volunteers. Terre Haute: 1903. V. 43

MC LEES, ARCHIBALD

A Series of Alphabets Designed as a Text Book for Engravers and Painters of Letters by Archibald McLees, Bank Note Engraver. New York: 1871. V. 37

MAC LEISH, ARCHIBALD

Einstein: Paris: 1929. V. 46

An Evening's Journey to Conway Massachusetts: an Outdoor Play. Northampton. V. 46

An Evening's Journey to Conway Massachusetts. Northampton: 1967. V. 42

Happy Marriage and Other Poems. Boston: 1924. V. 37; 39

Land of the Free. New York: 1938. V. 37; 38; 39; 46

New Found Land. Boston: 1930. V. 37; 42

Nobodaddy - a Play. Cambridge: 1926. V. 37; 39; 40; 45

The Pot of Earth. Boston: 1925. V. 41

Public Speech. New York: 1936. V. 41; 42; 45

Songs for Eve. Boston: 1954. V. 39

Streets in the Moon. Boston: 1926. V. 41; 42

MC LELLAN, LEIGH

Artist's Proof. Brief History, Type Specimen and Checklist of the Meadow Press. San Francisco: 1990. V. 45

MAC LENNAN, HUGH

Barometer Rising. New York: 1941. V. 43

MC LENNAN, J. S.

Louisbourg from Its Foundation to Its Fall 1713-1758. London: 1918. V. 37; 39

M'LEOD, ALEXANDER

Negro Slavery Unjustifiable. A Discourse. New York: 1802. V. 42

Trial of Alexander M'Leod, for the Murder of Amos Durfee; and as an Accomplice in the Burning of the Steamer Caroline, in the Niagara River, During the Canadian Rebellion in 1837-38. New York: 1841. V. 45

MAC LEOD, ALLAN

The Bishop of Llandaff's 'Apology for the Bible' Examined. London: 1796. V. 46

MAC LEOD, CATHERINE MARTIN

The Silent Sea. London: 1892. V. 38

M'LEOD, DONALD

Brief Reivew of the Settlement of Upper Canada by the U. E. Loyalists & Scotch Highlnders, in 1783. Cleveland: 1841. V. 38; 42

History of Wiskonsan, From Its First Discovery to the Present Period. Buffalo: 1846. V. 42; 45; 46

MAC LEOD, E. H., MRS.

Geraldine Hamilton; or, Self-Guidance. London: 1832. V. 37

MAC LEOD, GEORGE

Notes on the Surgery of the War in the Crimea, With Remarks on the Treatment of Gunshot Wounds. Philadelphia: 1862. V. 39; 42

MAC LEOD, HENRY DUNNING

The Principles of Economical Philosophy. London: 1872. V. 42

MAC LEOD, HUGH

Casus Principis; or, an Essay Towards a History of the Principality of Scotland . . . London: 1791. V. 43

M'LEOD, JOHN 1777?-1820

Narrative of a Voyage, in His Majesty's Late Ship Alceste, to the Yellow Sea. London: 1817. V. 38; 39; 40; 42; 44; 45

Narrative of a Voyage in His Majesty's Late Ship 'Alceste' to the Yellow Sea, Along the Coast of Corea, and through its Numerous Hitherto Undiscovered Islands, to the Island of Lewchew . . . London: 1818. V. 38

Voyage of His Majesty's Ship Alceste Along the Coast of Corea, to the Island of Lewchew. London: 1818. V. 37; 38; 39; 40; 41

Voyage of His Majesty's Ship Alceste, to China, Corea, and the Island of Lewchew. London: 1819. V. 37; 38; 40; 41

Voyage of His Majesty's Ship Alceste, to China, Corea and the Island of Lewchew, with an Account of Her Shipwreck. London: 1820. V. 38; 41

A Voyage to Africa. London: 1820. V. 42

A Voyage to Africa with Some Account of the Manners and Customs of the Dahomian People. London: 1820. V. 43

MAC LEOD, JOHN MAC LEOD HENRY

Practical Handbook of the Pathology of the Skin. London: 1903. V. 38

MC LEOD, LYONS,

Travels in Eastern Africa. London: 1860. V. 40; 46

MC LEOD, MALCOLM

The Pacific Railway. Britannicus' Letters from the Ottawa Citizen. Ottawa: 1875. V. 45

MC LEOD, ROBERT R.

Markland or Nova Scotia. Its History, Natural Resources and Native Beauties. 1903. V. 40

MC LEOD, ROBERTS RANDALL

Markland or Nova Scotia. Its History, Natural Resources and Native Beauties. N.P.: 1903. V. 37

MAC LEOD, RODERICK

On Rheumatism in Its Various Forms and on the Affections of Internal Organs, More Especially the Heart and the Brain . . . London: 1842. V. 37; 42

MAC LEOD, XAVIER DONALD

History of the Devotion to the Blessed Virgin Mary in North America. New York: 1866. V. 44

MC LEVY, JAMES

Curiosities of Crime in Edinburgh During the Last Thirty Years. Edinburgh: 1861. V. 39; 45

MAC LISE, JOSEPH

Surgical Anatomy. London: 1851. V. 42

Surgical Anatomy. Philadelphia: 1851. V. 41; 42; 43

MC LISH, JOHN

The North American Tourist. New York: 1839. V. 44; 45

MC LOUGHLIN, JOHN

The Letters of John McLoughlin from Port Vancouver to the Governor and Committee First Series, 1825-38. London: 1941. V. 44

The Letters of John McLoughlin, from Fort Vancouver to the Governor and Committee, 1825-46. Toronto: 1941-44. V. 40; 43

The Letters of . . . From Fort Vancouver to the Governor and Committee. Third Series. London: 1944. V. 43

The Letters of . . . From Fort Vancouver to the Governor and Committee. First Series 1825-1838. Toronto: 1941. V. 37

MC LUHAN, HERBERT MARSHALL

The Mechanical Bride. New York: 1951. V. 40; 42; 43

MC LUHAN, MARSHALL

The Gutenberg Galaxy. Toronto: 1962. V. 40

The Gutenberg Galaxy. 1962. V. 37

Through the Vanishing Point. New York: 1968. V. 42

MAC LYSAGHT, EDWARD

Irish Familes: Their Names, Arms and Origins. Dublin: 1957. V. 41; 42

MAC MAGHAN, J. A.

Campaigning on the Oxus, and the Fall of Khiva. London: 1874. V. 46

MAC MAHON, A. RUXTON

Far Cathay and Farther India. London: 1893. V. 46

M'MAHON, BERNARD

The American Gardener's Calendar. Philadelphia: 1806. V. 38; 39

MC MAHON, JOHN V. L.

A Historical View of the Government of Maryland, from Its Colonization to the Present Day. Baltimore: 1831. V. 37

MAC MAHON, T. W.

Cause and Contrast: an Essay on the American Crisis. Richmond: 1862. V. 37; 38; 46

MC MASTER, ELIZABETH WARING

The Girls of the Sixties. Columbia: 1937. V. 40

MC MASTER, JOHN BACH

A History of the People of the United States, from the Revolution to the Civil War. New York: 1907-13. V. 38

MC MASTER, S. W.

60 Years on the Upper Mississippi. Rock Island: 1893. V. 42; 43; 46

60 Years on the Upper Mississippi. Rock Island: 1895. V. 46

MC MECHEN, EDGAR C.

Walter Scott Cheesman A Pioneer Builder of Colorado. Denver: 1914. V. 41

Walter Scott Heesman A Pioneer Builder of COlorado. (Denver: 1914). V. 37

MAC MICHAEL, MORTON

A Land Lubber's Log of a Voyage Round the Horn, Being a Journal . . . During the Voyage from Philadelphia to San Francisco via Cape Horn . . . Philadelphia: 1879. V. 39; 41

MAC MICHAEL, WILLIAM 1784-1839

The Gold Headed Cane. London: 1827. V. 37; 38; 39; 41; 42; 45

The Gold Headed Cane. London: 1828. V. 38; 39; 40; 41; 44; 45; 46

The Gold Headed Cane. New York: 1915. V. 41; 42

The Gold-Headed Cane. London: 1927. V. 37

The Gold-Headed Cane, edited by William Munk. London: 1884. V. 37

Journey from Moscow to Constaninople in the Years 1817, 1818. London: 1819. V. 39; 40; 41; 44; 45

MAC MILLAN & CO.

A Bibliographical Catalogue of Macmillan & Co.'s Publications from 1843 to 1889. London: 1891. V. 40; 42; 44; 45

MAC MILLAN, CYRUS

Canadian Fairy Tales. London: 1922. V. 44

Canadian Wonder Tales. London: 1920. V. 44

MAC MILLAN, DONALD B.

Four Years in the White North Voyage of the S. S. Diana by the Crocker Land Expedition, from the Brooklyn Navy Yard to upeernavik and Northern Areas. New York: 1918. V. 41

MAC MILLAN, JOHN C.

The Early History of the Catholic Church in Prince Edward Island. Quebec: 1905. V. 43

MAC MINN, EDWIN

On the Frontier with Colonel Antes; or, the Struggle for Supremacy of the Red and White Races in Pennsylvania. Camden: 1900. V. 41; 42; 44; 46

MC MORRIES, EDWARD YOUNG

History of the First Regiment, Alabam: Volunteer Infantry, C. S. A. Montgomery: 1904. V. 42; 43; 45

MC MULLEN, THOMAS

Hand-Book of Wines, Practical, Theoretical and Historical . . . New York: 1852. V. 45

MAC MUNN, G. F.

The Armies of India. London: 1911. V. 41; 42; 44; 46

MAC MUNN, GEORGE

Egypt and Palestine. London: 1928-30. V. 46

The History of the Sikh Pioneers (23rd, 32nd, 34th). London: 1930's. V. 42

MAC MURRAY, JOHN V. A.

Treatise and Agreements with and Concerning China 1894-1919. New York: 1921. V. 41

MC MURRAY, W. J.

History of the Twentieth Tennessee Regiment Volunteer Infantry, C.S.A. Nashville: 1904. V. 39; 44

MC MURRICH, J. PLAYFAIR

Leonardo da Vinci, the Anatomist. Baltimore: 1930. V. 39; 41; 42; 46

MC MURTRIE, DOUGLAS

The First Printing in South America. Profidence: 1926. V. 44

Plantin's Index Characterum of 1567. New York: 1924. V. 44; 46

MC MURTRIE, DOUGLAS C.

The Beginnings of Printing In Utah. Chicago: 1931. V. 42

A Bibliography of Mississippi Imprints 1798-1830. Beauvoir Community: 1945. V. 40

The Book: the Story of Printing & Bookmaking. New York: 1937. V. 40

Early Printing in New Orleans 1764-1810. New Orleans: 1929. V. 40

Early Printing in Wisconsin. Seattle: 1931. V. 44

Early Printing in Tennessee with a Bibliography of the Issues of the Tennessee Press 1793-1830. Chicago: 1933. V. 42

Early Printing in Colorado. Denver: 1935. V. 41; 45

Early Printing in Wyoming and the Black Hills. Hattiesburg: 1943. V. 40

Early Printing in Colorado. Denver: 1935. V. 37

Early Printing in Wyoming and the Black Hills. Hattiesburg, Miss.: 1943. V. 37

Eighteenth Century North Carolina Imprints 1749-1800. Chapel Hill: 1938. V. 41

The General Epistle of the Latter Day Saints Dated . . . Chicago: 1935. V. 42

A History of Printing in the United States. New York: 1936. V. 39; 40; 42; 44

Jotham Meeker, Pioneer Printer of Kansas. Chicago: 1930. V. 38; 42

New York Printing 1693, Facsimile in the Full Scale of the Originals of all Known New York Imprints of that Year. Chicago: 1928. V. 37; 42

M'MURTRIE, HENRY

The Gentleman's Medical Vade-Mecum and Traveling Companion . . . Philadelphia: 1824. V. 43

Sketches of Louisville and Its Environs. Louisville: 1819. V. 46

MC MURTRIE, M.

Wild Flowers of Scotland. 1982. V. 39

MC MURTRY, LARRY 1936-

All My Friends Are Going to Be Strangers. 1972. V. 43

All My Friends are Going to Be Strangers. New York: 1972. V. 41; 42; 44; 46

Anything for Billy. New York: 1988. V. 38; 43; 44

Buffalo Girls. New York: 1990. V. 43; 44; 45

Cadillac Jack. New York: 1982. V. 37; 38; 40; 41; 43; 44

The Desert Rose. New York: 1983. V. 37; 39; 40; 42; 43; 44; 46

Film Flam. New York: 1987. V. 38; 39; 43

Flim Flam. New York: (1987). V. 37

Horseman, Pass By. New York: 1961. V. 37; 38; 39; 41; 42; 44; 45

In a Narrow Grave. Austin: 1968. V. 38; 43; 44

It's Always We Rambled. New York: 1974. V. 38; 39; 43; 44; 45

The Last Picture Show. 1966. V. 46

The Last Picture Show. New York: 1966. V. 39; 42; 44; 46

MC MURTRY, LARRY 1936- continued

The Last Picture Show. New York: 1966. V. 46

Leaving Cheyenne. Stanford: 1962. V. 42

Leaving Cheyenne. New York: 1963. V. 37; 44

Lonesome Dove. 1985. V. 44; 46

Lonesome Dove. New York: 1985. V. 40; 41; 42; 43; 44; 45; 46

Lonesome Dove. New York: (1985). V. 37

Lonesome Dove. New York: (1986). V. 37

Montana. Los Angeles: 1988. V. 42

Moving On. New York: 1970. V. 37; 40; 41; 42; 44; 45; 46

Moving On. London: 1971. V. 45

In a Narrow Grave. Austin: 1968. V. 37

Pigs on the Porch. New York: 1985. V. 43

Some Can Whistle. New York: 1989. V. 42; 43; 44

Some Can Whistle. New York: 1990. V. 46

Somebody's Darling. New York: 1978. V. 45

Terms of Endearment. New York: 1975. V. 45

Terms of Endearment. New York: 1975. V. 37; 38; 39; 40; 41; 44; 45; 46

Terms of Endearment. London: 1977. V. 42

Texasville. V. 41

Texasville. New York: 1986. V. 37; 38; 39

Texasville. New York: 1987. V. 37; 38; 39; 40; 41; 42; 43; 44; 45

MC MURTRY, OSCAR

A Short History of the Capture by Indians of Mrs. Mary Kinnan, and Subsequent Rescue from Captivity by Her Brother 1791-1794. N.P.: 1903. V. 45

MAC NAB, D.

An Exact Description of the Island and Kingdom of Sicily, Its Provinces, Towns and Remarkable Places ... Falkirk: 1784. V. 42

M'NAB, W.

A Treatise on the Propagation, Cultivation, and General Treatment of Cape Heaths, in a Climate Where they Require Protection During the Winter Months. Edinburgh: 1832. V. 37

M'NAB, WILLIAM

Hints on the Planting and General Treatment of Hardy Evergreens in the Climate of Scotland. Edinburgh: 1831. V. 37; 40

MC NABB, F. VINCENT

God's Book and Other Poems. Ditchling: 1930. V. 46

MC NABB, VINCENT

Francis Thompson and Other Essays. Ditchling: 1935. V. 42

Geoffrey Chaucer. A Study in Genius and Ethics. Ditchling and London: 1934. V. 38

Geoffrey Chaucer: A Study in Genius & Ethics. Ditchling: 1934. V. 37

Geoffrey Chaucer: A Study in Genius and Ethics. Ditchling: 1934. V. 37

God's Book and Other Poems. Ditchling: 1930. V. 40; 42

MC NAGHTEN, MELVILLE LESLIE

Sketchy Memories of Eton. 1866-1872. Calcutta: 1885. V. 45

MC NAIR, J. F. A.

Prisoners Their Own Warders. A Record of the Convict Prison at Singapore in the Straits Settlements Established 1825, Discontinued 1873 ... London: 1899. V. 41

MAC NAIR, PETER

The Geology of the Grampians and the Valley of Strathmore. Glasgow: 1908. V. 41

MC NAIR, ROBERT FRENCH

The Colours of the British Army; Comprising the Standards, Guidons, and Flags of Every Regiment in Her Majesty's Serivce. The Grenadier Guards. London: 1869. V. 41

MAC NAMARA, JOHN

In Perils by Mine Own Countrymen Three Years on the Kansas Border. New York & Auburn: 1856. V. 40; 41; 46

MAC NAMARA, N. C.

The Story of an Irish Sept; their Character and Struggle to maintain Their lands in Clare. London;: 1896. V. 37

MAC NAMEE, JAMES J.

History of the Diocese of Ardagh. Dublin: 1954. V. 46

MC NASPY, S. J.

At Face Value. New Orleans: 1978. V. 42

MC NAUGHTON, J. H.

Onnalinda, a Romance. London: 1886. V. 42

MC NAUGHTON, MARGARET

Overland to Cariboo. Toronto: 1896. V. 37; 38; 39; 40; 42; 45

MC NEALUS, VIRGINIA QUITMAN

Code Duello, Letters Concerning the Prentis-Tucker Duel of 1842. Dallas: 1931. V. 39

MAC NEICE, LOUIS

Autumn Journal. London: 1939. V. 40; 41; 42; 45

Blind Fireworks. London: 1929. V. 41; 42; 45

Blind Fireworks. London: 1929. V. 45

Collected Poems 1925 -1948. London: 1949. V. 43; 44

Holes in the Sky. Poems 1944 - 1947. London: (1948). V. 37

I Crossed the Minch. London: 1938. V. 45

I Crossed the Minch. London/New York/Toronto: 1938. V. 40

I Crossed the Minch. London, New York & Toronto: 1938. V. 37

The Last Ditch. Dublin: 1940. V. 44; 46

The Last Ditch. Dublin: 1940. V. 41

Meet the U.S. Army. London: 1943. V. 37; 41; 46

Out of the Picture: a Play. London: 1937. V. 37; 40

Poems. London: 1935. V. 40; 41

Poems. 1937. V. 41

Round the Corner. London: (1963). V. 37

Round the Corner. London: 1963. V. 37

Selected Poems. London: (1940). V. 37

The Sixpence Rolled Away. London: 1956. V. 40; 41

Springboard: Poems 1941-1944. London: 1944. V. 41

Springboard. Poems 1941 - 1944. (London): (1944). V. 37

The Strings are False - an Unfinished Autobiography. London: 1965. V. 41

Ten Burnt Offerings: Poems. London: 1952. V. 43

MAC NEIL, HECTOR

Scotland's Skaith. Edinburgh: 1795. V. 39

The Waes o' War; or, The Upshot o' the History o' Will and Jean. Edinburgh: 1796. V. 39

MC NEIL, MORRIS

Hokum. Wellesley Hills: 1978. V. 40; 44

MC NEILE, H. C.

Bulldog Drummon Strikes Back. Garden City: 1933. V. 46

MC NEILL, A. J.

With Horse and Hound in Worcestershire. London: 1880. V. 37

MAC NEILL, ALYSON

Twenty-Three Wood Engravings for the Song of the Forest by Colin Mackay. Llandago: 1987. V. 39

MAC NEILL, HECTOR

Bygane Times, and Late Come Changes; or, a Bridge Street Dialogue. Edinburgh: 1811. V. 42

The Poetical Works. London: 1801. V. 40

The Poetical Works of ... Philadelphia: 1815. V. 39

The Poetical Works. New York: 1802. V. 37

Scotland's Skaith; or, the History O'Will and Jean. Edinburgh: 1795. V. 40; 42

Scotland's Skaith; or, The History o'Will and Jean ... (with) The Waes o' War ... Edinburgh: 1796. V. 42

Town Fashions, or Modern Manners Delineated, a Satirical Dialogue; with James and Mary ... Edinburgh: 1810. V. 42

MAC NEILL, JOHN

On the Means of Comparing the Respective Advantages of Different Lines of Railway; and on the Use of Locomotive Engines. London: 1836. V. 46

MAC NEILL, MAIRE

The Festival of Lughnasa. A Study of the Survival of the Celtic Fetival of the Beggining of Harvest. London: 1962. V. 38

M'NEMAR, RICHARD

The Kentucky Revival ... New York: 1846. V. 42

A Memorial, Remonstrating Against a Certain Act of the Legislature of Kentucky, entitled 'An Act to Regulate Civil Proceedings Against Certain Communities Having Property in Common' ... Harrodsburg: 1801. V. 39

MC NETT, E. A.

Cataloque of the McNett Nursery ... Lampasas: 1875-85. V. 45

MAC NICHOL, JOHN R.

A Review (of the) National Liberal-conservative Convention Held at Winnipeg, Manitoba, October 10th to 12th, 1927. Toronto: 1930. V. 45

MAC QUOID, PERCY continued

A History of English Furniture from the Middle Ages to the Late Georgian Period. London: 1924-27. V. 45

A History of English Furntiure: The Age of Oak: The Age of Walnut: The Age of Mahogany: the Age of Satinwood. History: 1925-28. V. 39

A History of English Furniture: The Age of Oak: The Age of Walnut: The Mage of Mahogany and the Age of Satinwood. 1987. V. 39

A History of English Furniture: the Age of Oak and Walnut and the Age of Mahogany and Satinwood. London: 1987. V. 39

A History of English Furniture. Vol. I-Parts 1 & 2. The Age of Oak. The Age of Walnut. London: 1904-5. V. 37

MAC RAE, ALEXANDER

A Handbook of Deer-Stalking . . . Edinburgh: 1880. V. 43

MAC RAE, DAVID

The Americans at Home: Pen and Ink Sketches of American Men, Manners and Institutions. Edinburgh: 1870. V. 38

MC RAE, JOHN FINDLAY

Two Centuries of Typefounding. London: 1920. V. 40; 42

MAC RAY, JOHN

The Golden Lyre. Specimens of the Poets of England, France, Germany and Italy. London: 1829. V. 43

MAC RAY, WILLIAM DUNN

Annals of the Bodleian Library, Oxford. Oxford: 1890. V. 46

A Manual of British Historians to A.D. 1600. London: 1845. V. 39; 40

MAC READY, WILLIAM CHARLES

Mac Ready's Reminiscences, and Selections From His Diaries and Letters. London: 1875. V. 39; 40

MC REYNOLDS, ROBERT

Thirty Years on the Frontier. Colorado Springs: 1906. V. 37; 38; 39; 40; 43; 45

MAC RITCHIE, DAVID

Scottish Gypsies Under the Stewarts. London: 1894. V. 42

MC ROBBIE, KENNETH

Eyes Without a Face. Toronto: 1960. V. 44

MC ROBIE, WILLIAM ORME

Fighting the Flames? Montreal: 1881. V. 38; 40

MC ROSKEY, RACINE

The Missions of California. San Francisco: 1914. V. 43

MC SHERRY, JAMES

History of Maryland: From Its First Settlement in 1634 to the Year 1848. Baltimore: 1849. V. 46

M'SHERRY, RICHARD

El Punchero; or, a Mixed Dish from Mexico, Embracing General Scott's Campaign, with Sketches of Military Life in Field and Camp . . . Philadelphia: 1850. V. 37; 39

Essays and Lectures on 1. The Early History of Maryland. 2. Mexico and Mexican Affairs. 3. A Mexican Campaign. 4. Homoeopathy. 5. Elements of Hygiene. 6. Health and Happiness. Baltimore: 1869. V. 46

MC SHINE, KYNASTON

Joseph Cornell. Essays: Dawn Ades, Ratcliff & Others. New York: 1981. V. 44; 45

M'SPARRAN, ARCHIBALD

The Irish legend or M'Donnell and the Norman De Borgos. Philadelphia: 1846. V. 37

MC SPARRAN, F.

Cambridge Unviersity Library MS. F.f.2.38. London. V. 39

Cambridge University Library MS. F.f.s.38. London: 1979. V. 39

MC TAGGART, ANN

Memoirs of a Gentlewoman of the Old School. London: 1830. V. 38; 39; 42

M'TAGGART, ANNE

Plays . . . London: 1832. V. 44; 45

MC TAGGART, JOHN MC TAGGART ELLIS

A Commentary on Hegel's Logic. Cambridge: 1910. V. 41

Studies in the Hegelian Dialectic. Cambridge: 1896. V. 41

Studies in Hegelian Cosmology. Cambridge: 1901. V. 41

MC TAGGART, JOHN MCTAGGART ELLIS

Some Dogmas of Religion. London: 1906. V. 40

MC TAGGART, M. F.

From Colonel to Subaltern Some Keys for Homeowners, Illustrated by the Wag of the Regiment (Charles Simpson). London: 1928. V. 37

MAC TAVISH, NEWTON

The Fine Arts in Canada. Toronto: 1925. V. 37; 44

MAC VICAR, JOHN G.

On the Beautiful, the Picturesque, the Sublime. London: 1837. V. 46

MAC VICAR, JOHN V.

An Enquiry into Human Nature. Edinburgh: 1853. V. 41

MAC VICAR, W. M.

A Short History of Annapolis Royal the Port Royal of the French, From Its Settlement in 1604 to the Withdrawal of the British Troops in 1854. Toronto: 1897. V. 44

MC VICKAR, H. W.

Our Amateur Circus or a New York Season. New York: 1892. V. 37

M'WATT, DAVID

Letter to the Officers, Non Commissioned Officers and Privates, of the Berwickshire Yeomanry Cavalry. Edinburgh: 1825. V. 38

MAC WATT, JOHN

The Primulas of Europe. London: 1923. V. 40

MAC WHORTER, ALEXANDER

A Series of Sermons, upon the most Important Principles of our Holy Religion . . . Newark: 1803. V. 37

MC WHORTER, G. C.

Incident in the War of the U.S. With Mexico, Illustrating the Services of Wm. Maxwell Wood, Surgeon U.S.N. Oswego: 1872. V. 39; 42

MC WHORTER, L. V.

Hear Me, My Chief! Nez Perce History and Legend. Caldwell: 1952. V. 46

MC WHORTER, L.V.

The Border Settlers of North-Western Virginia from 1768 to 1795. Hamilton;: 1905. V. 41

The Crime Against the Yakimas. Yakima: 1913. V. 42

MC WILLIAM, JAMES ORMISTON

Medical History of the Expedition to the Niger During the Years 1841-2 . . . London: 1843. V. 37; 41; 45

MC WILLIAM, ROBERT

An Essay on the Origin and Operation of the Dry Rot. London: 1818. V. 37; 38; 40; 41; 46

MC WILLIAMS, JOHN

Recollections of John McWilliams. Princeton. V. 40; 42

Recollections of John McWilliams. Princeton: 1919. V. 40; 44; 45

Recollections of John McWilliams: His Youth, Experiences in California, and the Civil War. Princeton: 1921. V. 42; 44

Recollections of John McWilliams. Princeton, N.J.: n.d. V. 37

M., A.

The Reformed Gentleman: or, the Old English Morals Rescued from the Immoralities of the Present Age. London: 1693. V. 39

M., E. A.

The Truth of the Raid of the Confederate General, John Morgan and Command through Portions of the States of Kentucky, Indiana and Ohio During the War of the Rebellion. N.P.: 1894. V. 44

M., H. H.

Pastoral or, Virtue Requited, by H.M.M. Colchester: 1935. V. 37

M., J.

A Few Local Sketches. Calcutta: 1844. V. 41

The Shadow of the Tree of Life: Or, a Discourse of the Divine Institution and most effectural Application of Medicinal Remedies. In order to the Preservation and Restauration of Health. London: 1673. V. 37

M., R.

A General Survey of that Part of the Island of St. Christophers, Which Formerly Belonged to France . . . London: 1722. V. 45

M., W.

The Compleat Cook. London: 1658. V. 41; 42

M., W. F.

The Principles of Gambling, Speculative Trade, and Usury and Considerations on the Hon. Mr. Westropp's Bill to Amend Act XII, of 1848, for Avoidance of Wages. Bombay: 1863. V. 40

M., W. H.

The Life and Adventures of the Celebrated Pie-Bald Man. Hanley?: 1867. V. 43

M*****, CAPTAIN

The Handbook of Horsemanship. London: 1842. V. 40

MA-KA-TAI-ME-SHE-KIA-KIAK; of, Black Hawk, and Scenes in the West. New York: 1848. V. 37

MAARPERGER, PAUL JACOB

Beschreibung der Banquen. Halle und Leipzig: 1717. V. 38

MAARTENS, MAARTEN

An Old Maid's Love. London: 1891. V. 41

MAASKAMP, EVERT

Costumes, Moeurs et Habillements dans les Pays-Bas-Unis, Dessines et Colores d'Apres Nature. Amsterdam: 1814. V. 43

Representations of Dresses, Morals and Customs in the Kingdom of Holland . . . Amsterdam: 1808. V. 45

MABERLY, CATHERINE CHARLOTTE

Emily; or, the Countess of Rosedale. London: 1840. V. 39

MABINOGION

The Golden Cockerel Mabinogion. 1948. V. 39

The Mabinogion. London: 1877. V. 38; 43

The White Book Mabinogion. Pwllheli: 1907. V. 40

The Mabinogion. London: 1948. V. 40; 41

The Golden Cockerel Mabinogion. London: 1948. V. 40; 41; 43

The Golden Cockerel Mabinogion. Waltham St. Lawrence: 1948. V. 40; 41

MABLY, GABRIEL BONNOT DE

Doutes Proposes Aux Philosophes Economistes, sur l'Ordre Naturel et Essentiel des Societes Politiques. The Hague and Paris: 1768. V. 41; 45

Entretiens de Phocion, sur le Rapport de la Morale avec la Politique. Amsterdam: 1763. V. 45

Lettres a Madame la Mrquise de P(ompadour) sur l'Opera. Paris: 1741. V. 38

Observations sur le Gouvernement et Les Loix des Etats-Unis d'Amerique. Amsterdam: 1784. V. 45

Phocion's Conversations; or, the Relation Between Morality and Politics. London: 1769. V. 41

MABLY, GABRIEL BONNOT L'ABBE DE

Doutes Proposes aux Philosophes Economistes, sur l'Ordre Naturel et Essentiel des Societes Politiques. Paris & Hague: 1768. V. 42

Des Droits et des Devoirs du Citoyen. Kell: 1789. V. 42

MAC NEICE, LOUIS

Blind Fireworks. London: 1929. V. 37

MAC NEVEN, WILLIAM JAMES

Exposition of the Atomic Theory of Chymistry; and the Doctrine of Definite Proportions. New York: 1819. V. 37

MAC PHERSON, JAMES

Fingal, an ancient epic poems . . . London: 1762. V. 37

MACALLESTER, OLIVER

A Series of Letters, Discovering the Scheme Projected by France, in 1759 for an Intended Invasion Upon England with Flat-Bottom'd Boats . . . London: 1767. V. 39; 42

MACARDLE, DOROTHY

The Irish Republic. Dublin: 1951. V. 43

MACARDY, JOSEPH

The Commercial Cyclopaedia . . . Manchester: 1833. V. 42

MACARIUS, AEGYPTIUS

(Greek title: then) Homiliae Quinquaginta. Ex Bibliotheca Regia. Paris: 1559. V. 43; 44

MACARTNEY, GEORGE MACARTNEY, 1ST EARL 1737-1806

Correspondence Betweeen Lord Macartney and Major-General Stuart, Since Lord Macartney's Arrival in England, from the 10th Jan. to 8th June 1786. London: 1786. V. 42

MACARTNEY, JAMES

A Treatise on Inflammation. London: 1838. V. 38; 42; 44

MACARTY, CAPTAIN

An Appeal to the Candour and Justice of the People of England, in Behalf of the West India Merchants and Planters, Founded on Plain Facts . . . London: 1792. V. 45

MACAULAY, AULAY

The History and Antiquities of Claybrook, in the County of Leicester. Leicester: 1791. V. 46

Polygraphy, or Shorthand Made Easy to the Meanest Capacity being an Universal Character fitted to all Languages. London: 1757. V. 37

MACAULAY, CATHARINE

The History of England from the Revolution to the Present Time, in a Series of Letters to the Reverend Doctor Wilson. Bath: 1768. V. 46

Loose Remaraks on Certain Positions to be Found in Mr. Hobbe's Philosophical Rudiments of Government and Society. London: 1767. V. 37

Observations on a Pamphlet, entitled, Thoughts on the Cause of the Present Discontents. London: 1770. V. 41

MACAULAY, G.

The History of England. London: 1869. V. 45

MACAULAY, J. J.

A Whip at the Mast. 1910. V. 46

MACAULAY, ROSE

Abbots Verney. London: 1906. V. 43

Orphan Island. 1924. V. 44

Orphan Island. London: 1924. V. 46

Pleasure of Ruins Interpreted in Photographs by Roloff Beny. London: 1974. V. 37

The Writings of E. M. Forster. London: 1938. V. 39; 44

MACAULAY, THOMAS BABINGTON MACAULAY, 1ST BARON 1800-1859

Biographies . . . Contributed to the Encyclopaedia Britannica. Edinburgh: 1860. V. 37

The Complete Writings. Boston and New York: 1901. V. 45

The Complete Works of . . . The Albany Edition. London: 1898. V. 37

Critical and Historical Essays. London: 1849. V. 46

Critical and Historical Essays Contributed to the Edinbrugh Review. London: 1858. V. 45

Critical and Historical Essays, Contributed to the Edinburgh Review. London: 1862. V. 46

Critical and Historical Essays. London: 1852. V. 37

Evening. A Poem . . . Cambridge: 1821. V. 40

The History of England from the Accession of James II. New York: 1849. V. 42

The History of England from the Accession of James the Second. London: 1849-55. V. 46

The History of England from the Accession of James the Second. (with) Critical and Historical Essays, Contributed to the Edinburgh Review. London: 1852-61. V. 39

The History of England From the Accession of James the Second. London: 1856. V. 43

The History of England from the Accession of James the Second. London: 1856-1861. V. 40

The History of England from the Accession of James the Second. London: 1858-61. V. 43

The History of England from the Accession of James the Second. London: 1860. V. 46

The History of England from the Accession of James the Second. London: 1863/55/61. V. 46

The History of England from the Accession of James the Second. London: 1881. V. 38

The History of England from the Accession of James II. London: 1849-61. V. 37

Lays of Ancient Rome. London: 1842. V. 40

Lays of Ancient Rome. London: 1867. V. 43; 45

The Life and Works. Edinburgh: 1896-97. V. 46

Macaulay's Essays. London: 1866. V. 43

Macaulay's Essays, Critical, Historical and Miscellaneous Essays. New York: 1866. V. 42

The Miscellaneous Writings. London: 1860. V. 42

The Miscellaneous Writings. London: 1860. V. 37

On the Durability of American Institutions: A Letter Written in 1857. San Francisco: 1941. V. 46

'On the Durability of American Institutions.' A Letter Written in 1857. San Francisco: 1941. V. 38

Pompeii. A Pome Which Obtained the Chancellor's Medal at the Cambridge Commencement, July 1819. Cambridge: 1819. V. 38

Pompeii. Cambridge: 1819. V. 39

Selected Letters. 1982. V. 40

The Works of Lord Macaulay. London: 1866. V. 39

The Works Complete. London: 1876. V. 38

The Complete Works. London: 1898. V. 43

Works. London: 1898-1903. V. 43

Works. London: 1913. V. 40

MACAULAY, ZACHARY

Negro Slavery; or a View of Some of that State of Society As It Exists in the United States of America and In the Colonies of the West Indies . . . London: 1823. V. 42

MACAULEY, JAMES

Observations on Gymnastics, and the Gymnasium. Dublin: 1828. V. 38

MACAULEY, THOMAS BABINGTON, MACAULEY, 1ST BARON 1800-1859

The History of England from the Accession of James the Second. London: 1853-61. V. 39

MACBETH, a Poem in Six Cantos. London: 1817. V. 42

MACCHETTA, BLANCHE ROOSEVELT TUCKER

The Copper Queen, a Romance of To-day and Yesterday. Covent Garden: 1886. V. 46

MACCHIAVELLI, LUCA

Oratio de Liberali Educatione Habita Bononiae in Alma Academia Divi Joannis in Monte. Bologna: 1561. V. 38

MACCIO, PAOLO

Emblemata . . . Bologna: 1628. V. 39

MACDERMOT, E. T.

Illustrations by Lionell Edwards, the Devon and Somerset Staghounds. London: 1936. V. 37

MACE, ARTHUR C.

The Tomb of Senebtisi et Lisht. New York: 1916. V. 40; 42; 44

The Tomb of Senebtisi et Lisht. New York: 1973. V. 40

MACE, FAYETTE

Familiar Dialogues on Shakerism, In Which the Principles of the United Society are Illustrated and Defended. Portland: 1837. V. 44

Familiar Dialogues on Shakerism: In Which the Principles of the United Society are Illustrated and Defended. Portland: 1838. V. 46

MACE, THOMAS

Musick's Monument, or a Remembrancer of the Best Practical Musick, Both Divine and Civil, That Has Ever Been Known to Have Been in the World. London: 1676. V. 40; 44

MACEDO, FRANCISCO 1596-1618

Elogia Poetica in Serenissimam Rempublicam Venetam, Ejusque Augustum Senatum Tribunalia Pontifices Duces . . . Padua: 1680. V. 46

MACEDO, JOSE AGOSTINHO DE

Newton Poema . . . Lisbon: 1815. V. 38

MACELLARD, JEAN fl. 1420

A Picutre Book of the Life of Saint Anthony the Abbot. 1937. V. 39

MACER FLORIDUS

De Viribus Herbarum . . . Paris: 1506. V. 37

MACERONE, FRANCIS

Defensive Instructions for the People: Containing the New and Improved Combination of Arms Called Foot Lancers . . . London: 1832. V. 45

MACH, ERNST

The Principles of Physical Optics. London: 1926. V. 42

MACHADO, ANTONIO

Times Alone: 12 Poems from 'Soledades' by Antonio Machado. Port Townsend: 1983. V. 42

MACHADO DE ASSIS, JOAQUIM MARIA

Chrysalidas. Poesias . . . Rio de Janeiro: 1864. V. 38

Resurreicaeo. Rio de Janeiro: 1872. V. 39

MACHAR, AGNES MAULE

The Story of Old Kingston. Toronto: 1908. V. 42; 44; 45

MACHELLUS, JACOBUS

Patrocinia Forensia. Venice: 1560. V. 38; 40

MACHEN, ARTHUR 1863-1947

The Anatomy of Tobacco; or Smoking Methodised, Divided and Considered After a New Fashion. London: 1884. V. 39; 43; 46

The Anatomy of Tobacco. New York: 1926. V. 40; 46

Bridles and Spurs. 1951. V. 44

Bridles and Spurs. Cleveland: 1951. V. 42

Casanova's Escape from the Leads. London: 1925. V. 46

The Children of the Pool and Other Stories. London: 1936. V. 40

The Chronicle of Clemendy. London: 1888. V. 46

The Chronicle of Clemendy. London: 1925. V. 46

The Cosy Room and Other Stories. London: 1936. V. 40

Dr. Stiggins: His Views and Principles. Westminster: 1906. V. 46

Dog and Duck. London: 1924. V. 43

Dog & Duck. New York: 1924. V. 39

Fantastic Tales of Beroalde de Cverville. Carbonek: 1923. V. 39; 41

Fantastic Tales or the Way to Attain. Carbonnek: 1923. V. 46

Far Off Things. London: 1922. V. 39; 43; 46

A Few Letters from Arthur Machen. Cleveland: 1932. V. 42; 43; 45; 46

The Glorious Mystery. Chicago: 1924. V. 46

The Great God Pan and the Inmost Light. London: 1894. V. 45

The Green Round. London: 1933. V. 40

The Heptameron - or - Tales & Novels of Marguerite, Queen of Navarre. 1905. V. 37

The Hill of Dreams. London. V. 43; 44

The Hill of Dreams. London: n.d. V. 37

The Hill of Dreams. London: (1922). V. 37

The Hill of Dreams. London: 1922. V. 37

The London Adventure or the Art of Wandering. London: 1924. V. 41; 46

Notes and Queries. London: 1926. V. 40; 46

One Hundred Merrie & Delightsome Stories. V. 39; 41

Ornaments in Jade. New York: 1924. V. 44; 45

Precious Balms. London: 1924. V. 39; 40

Precious Balms. London: 1924. V. 40

The Shining Pyramid. London: 1925. V. 38; 39; 40

Starrett vs. Machen. St. Louis: 1977. V. 40

Strange Roads-With the Gods of Spring. London: 1924. V. 39; 46

Things Near and Far. London: 1921. V. 39; 40; 41

Things Near and Far. London: 1923. V. 44; 46

The Three Imposters or the Transmutations. London: 1895. V. 38; 39; 44

Tom O'Bedlam and His Song. Westport: 1930. V. 46

The Caerleon Edition of the Works. London: 1923. V. 40

The Works. London: 1923. V. 38; 40; 42

MACHERCRIER, VALERANDUS

Methodus Artis Poeticae. Paris: 1529. V. 40

MACHIAVELLI, NICCOLO 1469-1527

A Translation of Part of the First book of Machiavell's Art of War. London: 1774. V. 40; 41

The Art of War. Albany: 1815. V. 39; 40; 41

Discorsi . . . Sopra la Prima Deca di Tito Livio. Nuovamente Corretti & con Diligenza Ristampati. Venice: 1540. V. 40

Les Discours de l'Estat de Paix et de Guerre . . . Paris: 1572. V. 40

Machiavels Discourses . . . London: 1636. V. 41; 45

Machiavel's Discourses Upon the First Decade of T. Livius. London: 1674. V. 41

Disputationum de Republica . . . Libri III. Montbeliard: 1588. V. 42

The Florentine Historie. London: 1595. V. 40; 46

The Florentine History in VIII Books. London: 1674. V. 41; 44

Historie Florentine. Florence: 1532. V. 41

I Discorsi di Nicolo Machiavelli, Sopra la Prima Deca di Tito Livio . . . Palermo: 1584. V. 38

Machiavel's Discourses Upon the First Decade of T. Livius . . . to which is added his Prince. With some marginal animadversion noting and taxing his errors . . . etc. London: 1674. V. 37

Opere. Cosmpoli (Venise),: 1769. V. 43

The Prince. New York: 1954. V. 37

Il Prencipe de Nicolo Machiavelli. Venice: 1540. V. 45

Il Principe. Milan: 1947. V. 41

A Translation of Part of the First Book of Machiavell's Art of War . . . London: 1744. V. 41; 46

Tutte le Opere di Nicolo Machiavelli Cittadino et Secretario Fiorentino . . . 1609-19. V. 38; 41

The Works of . . . London: 1675. V. 37; 39

The Works of the Famous . . . . London: 1720. V. 37; 42

The Works. London: 1775. V. 37; 38; 40

MACHIAVELLI, NICHOLAS 1469-1527

The Works of the Famous Nicholas Machiavel . . . London: 1680. V. 46

MACK, EBENEZER

The Cat-Fight; a Mock Heroic Poem. New York: 1824. V. 43

MACK, EFFIE MONA

Nevada, A History of the State From the Earliest Times through the Civil War. Glendale: 1936. V. 37

MACK, RICHARD

The Widening Stream. San Francisco?: 1965. V. 39

MACKAIL, JOHN WILLIAM

An Address Delivered the XIth November MDCCCC at Kelmscott House, Hammersmith, Before the Hammersmith Socialist Society. Hammersmith: 1901. V. 39

An Address Delivered the XIth November DCCCC at Kelmscott House Hammersmith Before the Hammersmith Socialist Society. Hammersmith: 1905. V. 43

Biblia Innocentum. 1892. V. 38

Biblia Innocentum: Being the Story of God's Chosen People Before the Coming of Our Lord Jesus Christ Upon Earth, Written Anew for Children. 1892. V. 37; 39

Biblia Innocentium: Being the Story of God's Chosen People Before the Coming of Our Lord Jesus Christ Upon Earth. Hammersmith: 1892. V. 44

Biblia Innocentium . . . London: 1892. V. 42

Cornelii Taciti de Vita et Moribus Iulii Agricolae Liber. London: 1900. V. 44

Homer. An Address Delivered on Behalf of the Independent Labour Party. Hammersmith: 1905. V. 38; 46

The Life of William Morris. London: 1899. V. 39; 41

The Parting of the Ways: an Address. Hammersmith: 1903. V. 40; 46

Pervigilium Veneris. Hammersmith: 1910. V. 37

Socialism and Politics: an Address and a Programme. Hammersmith: 1903. V. 37; 46

Socialism and Politics: an Address and a Programme. London: 1903. V. 45

William Morris: an Address Delivered . . . Before the Hammersmith Socialist Society. Hammersmith: 1901. V. 37; 39; 46

William Morris: an Address Delivered the XIth November MDCCCC at Kelmscott House, Hammersmith Before the Hammersmith Socialist Society. Hammersmith: 1902. V. 40; 41; 46

MACKAIL, LEONARD L.

Abel Buell the First Type Cutter and Caster in English America. Mount Vernon: 1930. V. 40; 42

MACKALL, WILLIAM W.

A Son's Recollections of His Father. New York: 1930. V. 42

MACKE, AUGUST

August Macke Tunisian Watercolours and Drawings. New York: 1959. V. 46

MACKELLAR, C. D.

Scented Isles and Coral Gardens Torres Straits, German New Guinea and the Dutch East Indies. London: 1912. V. 43

MACKELLAR, SMITHS AND JORDAN FOUNDRY

1796-1896. One Hundred Years. Philadelphia: 1896. V. 39

MACKELLAR, SMITHS & JORDAN, TYPE FOUNDERS

Fourteenth Specimen Book . . . Philadelphia: 1881. V. 42

MACKELLAR, THOMAS

The American Printer: a Manual of Typography. Philadelphia: 1974. V. 44

MACKERN, H. F.

Side-Lights on the March, the Experiences of an American Journalist in South Africa. London: 1901. V. 46

MACKEY, AIDAN

Mr. Chesterton Comes to Tea, or, How the King of England Captured Redskin Island. Bedford: 1978. V. 42; 44

MACKEY, FRANK J.

Forward March! The Photographic Record of America in the World War . . . Chicago: 1834. V. 42

MACKEY, JAMES

Compositions In Verse; With an Essay on Female Education. Dublin: 1819. V. 42; 46

MACKEY, T. J.

The Hazen Court Martial: The Responsibility for the Disaster to the Lady Franklin Bay Polar Expedition. New York: 1885. V. 38

MACKINTOSH, JAMES

Vindiciae Gallicae, Defence of the French Revolution and its English Admirers Against the Accusations of the Right Hon. Edmund Burke . . . London: 1791. V. 44

MACKLEY, GEORGE

Confessions of a Woodpecker. Old Working: 1981. V. 46

Engraved in the Wood. London: 1968. V. 37; 39; 40; 41

Monica Poole: Wood Engraver. 1984. V. 44; 45

Monica Poole: Wood Engraver. Kent: 1984. V. 40

Monica Poole, Wood Engraver. 1987. V. 38

Wood Engraving. London: 1948. V. 40

MACKLIN, CHARLES

The Case of Charles Macklin Comedian. London: 1743. V. 42; 43

The Man of the World. London: 1793. V. 38; 40; 45

Mr. Macklin's Reply to Mr. Garrick's Answer. To which are prefix'd all the papers, which have publickly aappeared in regard to this important dispute. London: 1743. V. 37

The True-Born Irishman. Dublin: 1783. V. 40

MACKLIN, W. R.

The Decorative Paintings in Christ's Hospital Chapel MCMXIII-MCMXXIII. Ditchling: 1925. V. 42

MACKMURDO, A. H.

Wren's City Churches. Orpington: 1883. V. 37; 38; 39; 41

MACKMURDO, ARTHUR H.

Wren's City Churches. London: 1883. V. 37

MACKWORTH, HUMPHREY

The Cast of Sir Humphrey Mackworth, and the Mine Adventures, With Respect to the Extraordinary Proceedings of the Agents, Servants and Dependents, of the Right Honourable Sir Thomas Mansell, Bar. London: 1707. V. 39

Sir H. Mackworth's Proposal in Miniature, As It Has Been Put in Practice in New York, in America. London: 1720. V. 44

MACKWORTH-PRAED

Birds of East and North East Africa. Birds of the Southern Third of Africa. London: 1957-60-62-63. V. 37

MACKWORTH-PRAED, CYRIL WINTHROP

Birds of the Southern Third of Africa. 1962. V. 46

Birds of the Southern Third of Africa. 1962-63. V. 38

MACKY, JOHN

A Journey through the Austrian Netherlands. London: 1725. V. 42; 46

A Journey through the Austrian Netherlands. London: 1732. V. 38

Memoirs of the Secret Service of . . . During the Reigns of King William, Queen Anne, and King George I. London: 1733. V. 37; 41

MACLAREN-ROSS, JULIAN

Of Love and Hunger. London: 1947. V. 38

MACLAY, EDGAR S.

History of American Privateers. New York: 1899. V. 44

MACLAY, EDWARD STANTON

A History of the U.S. Navy from 1775 to 1898. New York: 1898. V. 39

MACLAY, SAMUEL

Journal of Samuel Maclay, While Surveying the West Branch of the Susquehanna. Williamsport: 1887. V. 46

MACLAY, W. W.

Portland Cement for Engineering Works. New York: 1890. V. 44

MACLAY, WILLIAM

Sketches of Debates in the First Senate of the United States in 1789-91. Harrisburg: 1880. V. 37; 38

MACLEAY, W. S.

Illustrations of the Annulosa of South Africa . . . Chiefly Collected During an Expedition into the Interior of South Africa Under the Direction of Dr. Andrew Smith in the Years 1834, 1835 and 1836. London: 1838. V. 39

MACLISE, D.

A Gallery of Illustrious Literary Characters (1830-1838). London: 1873. V. 38

MACLISE, JOSEPH

Comparative Osteology . . . London: 1847. V. 45

Surgical Anatomy. Philadelphia: 1859. V. 38

MACLURE, ROBERT

The Arctic Dispatches Containing an Account of the Discovery of the North-West Passage. London: 1853. V. 45; 46

MACLURE, WILLIAM

Opinions on Various Subjects, Dedicated to the Industrious Producers. New Harmony: 1831. V. 41; 44; 45

Opinions on Various Subjects. New Harmony: 1831-1837. V. 39

MACMURDO, A. H.

Wren's City Churches. Orpington, Kent: 1883. V. 42

MACOMB, ALEXANDER

A Treatise on Martial Law, and Courts-Martial; as Practised in the United States of America. Charleston: 1809. V. 38

MACOMB, J. N.

Report of an Exploring Expedition from Santa Fe, New Mexico, to the Junction of the Grand and the Green Rivers of the Great Colorado of the West in 1859. Washington: 1876. V. 40; 41; 42; 43; 45

MACOMBER, H. P.

A Descriptive Catalogue of the Grace K. Babson Collection of the Works of Sir Isaac Newton and the Material relating to him in the Babson Institute Library, Babson park, Mass. With an introduction by Roger Babson Webber; A Supplement . . . New York/Babson Park;: 1950-5. V. 37

MACOMBER, JOB

A Poem, Delivered in Bowdoingham, to a Respectable Audience of the Fourth of July, 1806. Exeter: 1826. V. 40

MACON, T. J.

Reminiscences of the First Company of Richmond Howitzers. Richmond. V. 37; 39

MACON, THOMAS JOSEPH

Reminiscences of the First Company of Richmond Howitzers. Richmond: 190-. V. 46

MACON, THOMAS L.

Protest of the State of Louisiana to the Senate of the United States. N.P.: 1868. V. 39

MACOUN, JOHN

Catalogue of Canadian Birds. 1909. V. 42

Manitoba and the Great North-West. The Field for Investment. The Home of the Imigrant. V. 39

Manitoba and the Great North-West. Guelph: 1882. V. 43

Manitoba and the Great Northwest; the Field for Investment. The Home for the Emigrant. London: 1883. V. 37; 39; 42

Manitoba and the Great North-West. Guelph: 1882. V. 38

MACRAY, WILLIAM DUNN

A Manual of British Historians to A.D. 1600. London: 1845. V. 38

MACREADY, WILLIAM CHARLES

The Diaries . . . 1833-1851. London: 1912. V. 46

Macready's Reminiscences, and Selections from His Diaries and Letters. London: 1875. V. 46

MACRERY, JOSEPH

An Inaugaral Disseration on the Principle of Animation. Wilmington: 1802. V. 37

MACROBIUS

Macrobii Avrelii Theodosii Viri Consularis et Illustris, in Somnius Scipionis, Lib. II. II. Saturnaliorum Lib. VII. Venice: 1565. V. 37

MACROBIUS, A. A. T.

Opera. Lug. Batav: 1597. V. 45

MACROBIUS, AMBROSIUS

Somnium Scipionis Libri II. Saturnaliorum Libri VII. London:ugduni: 1538. V. 41

Somnium Scipionis Libri II. Saturnaliorum Libri VII. Lugduni: 1538. V. 39

MACROBIUS, AMBROSIUS AURELIUS THEODOSIUS

In Somnium Scipionis, Libri II. Eiusdem Saturnaliorum Libri VII. Coloniae: 1527. V. 38

MACROBIUS, AMBROSIUS THEODOSIUS

In Somnium Scipionis ex Ciceronis. Venice: 1528. V. 43; 45

In Somnium Scipionis Lib. II. Saturnaliorum. Lib. VII. Lyon: 1556. V. 42

MACROBIUS, AMBROSIUS THODOSIUS

Opera. Leyden: 1670. V. 40

MACY, OBED

The History of Nantucket . . . Boston: 1835. V. 37; 42; 45

The History of Nantucket, Being a Compendious Account of the First Settlement of the Islands by the English, Together with the Rise and Progress of the Whale Fishery . . . Mansfield: 1880. V. 41

MACY, WILLIAM F.

The Nantucket Scrap Basket. Nantucket: 1916. V. 42

MACY, WILLIAM HUSSEY

There She Blows! Or, the Log of the Arethusa. Boston & New York: 1877. V. 41

MACY'S Atlas of the World. New York: 1896. V. 45

MACY'S Garden and Where the Flowers Went. London: 1873. V. 45

MADAN, F. F.

The Daniel Press, Memorials of C.H.O. Daniel with a bibliography of the Press. 1845-1919. Oxford: 1921. V. 37

A New bibliography of the Eikon Basilike of King Charles I with a note on the authorship. Oxford: 1950. V. 37

MADAN, FALCONER

Books in Manuscript. London: 1893. V. 41

A Chart of Oxford Printing 1468-1900. Oxford: 1903. V. 40

A Chart of Oxford Printing '1468'-1900. London: 1940. V. 39

The Daniel Press. Memorials of C. H. O. Daniel with a Bibliography of the Press 1845-1919. V. 41

Lewis Carroll Centenary in London. London: 1932. V. 43

Oxford Books. A Bibliography of Printed Works Relating to the University and City of Oxford or Printed or Published There (1468-1680). Oxford: 1895-1931. V. 46

MADAN, FRANCIS F.

A New Bibliography of the Eikon Basilike of King Charles I . . . London: 1950. V. 38; 40

MADAN, MARTIN

Thelyphthora; or, a Treatise on Female Ruin . . . London: 1780. V. 46

Thelyphthoria. London: 1781. V. 37; 38

MADAN, RICHARD ROBERT

The Literary Life and Correspondence of the Countess of Blessington. London: 1855. V. 37

MADAN, SPENCER

A Letter to Doctor Priestley in Consequence of His 'Familiar Letters Addressed to the Inhabitants of the Town of Birmingham &c. Birmingham: 1790. V. 39

The Principal Claims of the Dissenters, Considered in a Sermon Preached at St. Philip's Church in Birmingham . . . the 14th of Feb. 1790. Birmingham: 1790. V. 41

MADARIAGA, SALVADOR DE

Don Quixote, an introductory Essay in Psychology. London: 1934. V. 38

Don Quixote: An Introductory Essay in Psychology. Newtown: 1934. V. 37; 38; 40; 44; 46

MADDEN, DANIEL OWEN

Revelations of Ireland in the Past Generation. Dublin: 1818. V. 44

MADDEN, FREDERICK

Privy Purse Expenses of the Princess Mary. London: 1831. V. 37; 38

MADDEN, HENRY MILLER

Xantus, Hungarian Naturalist in the Pioneer West. Palo Alto: 1949. V. 38; 41

MADDEN, JEROME

The Lands of the Southern Pacific Railroad Company of California. San Francisco: 1982. V. 39

Lands of the Southern Pacific Railroad Company of California; Their situation, Soil, Climiate, Vegetation, Presetn & Prospective Values, Price & The Terms Under Which They are Offered For Sale; with General Information on the Resources . . . San Francisco: 1877. V. 37

MADDEN, R. R.

Travels in Turkey, Egypt, Nubia and Palestine in 1824, 1825, 1826 and 1827. London: 1829. V. 41; 42

A Twelvemonth Residence in the West Indies, During the Transition from Slavery to Apprenticeship, with Indicental Notices of the State of Society . . . Philadelphia: 1835. V. 40; 41

MADDEN, RICHARD ROBERT 1798-1886

The Connexion Between the Kingdom of Irelnd and the Crown of England . . . Dublin: 1845. V. 38

Historical Notice of Penal Laws Against Roman Catholics. London: 1865. V. 39

The Literary Life and Correspondence of the Countess of Blessington. London: 1855. V. 38; 41; 43; 44; 45; 46

The Mussulman. London: 1830. V. 37

Phantasmata or Illusions and Fanatacisms of Protean Forms Productive of Great Evils. London: 1857. V. 37; 39; 43; 46

Travels in Turkey, Egypt, Nubia and Palestine in 1824, 1825, 1826 and 1827. London: 1829. V. 43

Travels in Turkey, Egypt, Nubia and Palestine in 1824, 1825, 1826 and 1827. London: 1833. V. 37

The Turkish Empire. London: 1862. V. 37

The United Irishmen, Their Lives and Times. Philadelphia: 1842. V. 43

The United Irishmen, Their Lives and Times . . . Dublin: 1857/60. V. 38

MADDEN, SAMUEL

A Proposal for the General Encouragment of Learning in Dublin-College. Dublin: 1732. V. 39; 46

A Proposal for the General Encouragement of Learning in Dublin-College. Dedicated to his Grace the Lord Primate; and humbly offer'd to the Consideration of all that wish well to Ireland. London: 1732. V. 39

Reflections and Resolutions Proper for the Gentlemen of Ireland. Dublin: 1738. V. 42

Reflections and Resolutions Proper for the Gentlemen of Ireland, As To Their Conduct for the Service of Their Country . . . Dublin: 1816. V. 42

MADDEN, SAMUEL continued

Themistocles, the Lover of His Country. London: 1729. V. 39

MADDOCK, ALFRED BEAUMONT

Practical Observations on Mental and Nervous Disorders. London: 1857. V. 45

MADDOCK, HENRY d. 1824

A Treatise on the Principles and Practice of the High Court of Chancery . . . Hartford: 1822. V. 40

MADDOCK, JAMES

The Florist's Directory . . . London: 1810. V. 37; 45

MADDOCK, JAMES C.

The Florist Directory. London: 1792. V. 38; 40

MADDOW, BEN

Edward Weston: Fifty Years. Millerton: 1973. V. 44

Edward Weston. His Life and Photographs. Millerton: 1979. V. 41

Faces: a Narrative History of the Portrait in Photography. Boston: 1977. V. 45

MADDOX, BRENDA

Nora: The Real Life of Molly Bloom. Boston: 1988. V. 41; 42; 44

MADDOX, WILLES

Views of Lansdown Tower, Bath. Bath: 1844. V. 39

MADEIRA, PERCY C.

Hunting in British East Africa. Philadelphia: 1909. V. 39

MADHLOOM, T. A.

The Chronology of Neo-Assyrian Art. London: 1970. V. 42

MADIGN, THOMAS F.

Word Shadows of the Great; the Lure of Autograph Collecting. New York: 1930. V. 38

MADISON, CHARLES

Book Publishing In American Culture. N.P.. V. 46

MADISON, JAMES

An Examination of the Conduct of Great Britain, Respecting Neutrals. Philadelphia: 1807. V. 41

Letters from . . . to Messrs. Monroe and Pinkney on Subjects Committed to Their Joint Negotiation: With Their Communications to the Secretary of State. Washington: 1808. V. 42

Letters and Other Writings. Philadelphia: 1865. V. 40

The Papers of James Madison, Purchased by Order of Congress . . . and His Reports of Debates in the Federal Convention . . . Washington: 1840. V. 41

The Papers of James Madison, Purchased by Order of Congress, Being His Correspondence and Reports of Debates During the Confederation and in the Federal Convention. Mobile: 1842. V. 39

Selections from the Private Correspondence of . . . from 1813-1836. Washington: 1853. V. 37; 43

Speech in the House of Representatives of the Congress of the United States, Delivered Jan. 14, 1794, by James Madison, of Virginia, in Support of His Propositions for the Promotion of the Commerce of the United States and in Reply . . . New York: 1794. V. 44

MADISON, LUCY FOSTER

Joan of Arc, the Warrior Maid, by Lucy Foster Madison. Philadelphia: 1929. V. 37

MADISON: The Capital of Wisconsin, Its Progress, Capabilities and Destiny. Madison: 1855. V. 39; 42

MADISON: The Capital of Wisconsin: Its Progress, Capabilities and Destiny. Madison: 1855. V. 42

MADOU, J.

Costumes Belgiques Anciens et Modernes, Militaires, Civils et Religieux. Brussells: 1830. V. 42

MADOX, THOMAS 1666-1727

Baronia Anglica. London: 1736. V. 39

Baronia Anglica. An History of Land-Honors and Baronies, and of Tenure in Capite, Verified by Records. London: 1741. V. 37; 38; 43

Firma Burgi, or an Historical Essay Concerning the Cities, Towns and Burroughs of England . . . London: 1726. V. 38; 40; 42

The History and Antiquities of the Exchequer of the Kings of England . . . London: 1711. V. 37; 39; 42

The History and Antiquities of the Exchequer of the Kings of England. London: 1769. V. 38; 40; 41

THE MADRAS Almanac . . . 1835, Calculated for the Meridian of Fort St. George. Madras: 1835. V. 40

MADRAS; An Account of the Origin, Progress and Consequences of the Late Discontents of the Army on the Madras Establishment. London: 1810. V. 41

MADSEN, STEPHAN TSHUDI

Sources of Art Nouveau. Oslo: 1956. V. 42

MAELEN, P. VAN DER

Atlas Universel de Geographie Physique, Politique, Statistique et Mineralogique . . . Brussels: 1827. V. 43

MAEMPEL, JOHAN CHRISTIAN

The Young Rifleman's Comrade. London: 1826. V. 37; 39; 40; 42

MAERZ, A.

A Dictionary of Color. New York: 1930. V. 38

MAESTLIN, MICHAEL

Disputatio de Eclipsibus Solis et Lunae . . . Tubingen: 1596. V. 38

MAETERLINCK, MAURICE

The Blue Bird. New York: 1911. V. 41; 46

The Blue Bird. New York: 1920. V. 38; 41

The Blue Bird. London: (c. 1911). V. 37

The Blue Bird. A Fairy Play in Six Acts. Translated by Alexander Teixera de Mattos. With Twenty-Five Illustrations in Colour by F. Cayley Robinson. London: (1911). V. 37

Douze Chansons. Bruxelles: 1929. V. 38

Douze Chansons. Paris: 1896. V. 37

Douze Chansons. Brussels: 1929. V. 37

Hours of Gladness. London: 1912. V. 41; 45; 46

The Intelligence of the Flowers. New York: 1907. V. 42

The Life of the Bee. London: 1911. V. 44; 46

The Life of the Bee. London: 1912. V. 42; 44

News of Spring and Other Nature Studies. New York: 1913. V. 41

The Treasure of the Humble. London: 1906. V. 46

XII Songs. Chicago: 1902. V. 38

Works. New York: 1901-16. V. 46

Works of . . . New York: 1907. V. 40; 46

THE MAFEKING Mail. Siege Numbers, Nov. 1st, 1899-March 31st, 1900. Mafeking: 1900. V. 38

MAFFEI, GIOVANNI PIETRO

L'Historie des Indes Orientals, et Occidentales . . . Paris: 1665. V. 45

Rerum a Societate Jesu in Oriente Gestarum Ad Annum Usque a Deipara Virgine MDLXVIII. Dillingen: 1571. V. 40

MAFFEI, IOANNES PETRUS 1535-1603

De Vita et Moribus Ignatii Loiolae. Rome: 1585. V. 38

MAFFEI, PAOLO ALESSANDRO

Raccolta di Statue Antichi e Moderne . . . Illustratae Colle Sposizioni a Ciascheduna Immagine. Rome: 1740. V. 37

MAFFEI, RAFFAELE

Commentariorum Urbanorum . . . octo & Triginta Libri cum Duplici Eoru(n)dem Indice Secundum Tomos Collecto. Paris: 1511. V. 37

Commentariorum Urbanorum Libri . . . Paris: 1526. V. 37

MAFFEI, RAFFAELLE

Commentariorum Urbanorum . . . Octo & Triginta Libri, Accuratius Quam Antehac Excusi, cum Duplici Eorundem Indice, Secundum Tomos Collecto. Basel: 1530. V. 37

MAFFEI, SCIPIONE

Museum Veronense hoc est Antiquarum Inscriptionum Atque Anaglyphorum . . . Veronae: 1749. V. 42; 46

MAFFITT, JOHN N.

Tears of Contrition: or Sketches of the Life of John N. Maffitt . . . to which are appended Several Poetic Effusions. New London: 1821. V. 38

MAFFITT, JOHN NEWLAND

Ireland: a Poem. Louisville: 1839. V. 40

MAGALOTTI, GREGORIO

Securitatis ac Salvi Conductus Tractatus Perutilis & Quotidianus. Rome: 1538. V. 37

MAGALOTTI, LORENZO

Travels of Cosmo the Third, Grand Duke of Tuscany, Through England, During the Reign of King Charles the Second (1669). London: 1821. V. 41

MAGAZINE of American History. New York & Chicago: 1877-1893. V. 40

THE MAGAZINE of Domestic Economy. London: 1836-44. V. 39; 42

MAGAZZARI, GIOVANNI

Trattato Della Composizione e Dell'Ornamento de'Giardini . . . Bologna: 1841. V. 41

MAGDELAINE, PIERRE DE SAINTE MARIE

Traitte d'Horlogiographie, Contenant Plvsievrs manieres de Constrive svr Tovtes Svrfaces . . . Paris: 1645. V. 42

MAGEE, DAVID

The Ballad of the Hollow Leg. Kentfield: 1955. V. 41

Catalogue of Some Five Hundred Examples of the Printing of Edwin and Robert Grabhorn 1917-1960. Two Gentlemen from Indiana Now Resident in California . . . Offered for Sale at the Book Shop of David Magee. San Francisco: 1960. V. 41; 44

A Course in Correct Cataloguing, or Notes to the Neophyte. San Francisco: 1958. V. 42; 44

Fine Printing and Bookbinding from San Frncisco and Its Environs . . . San Francisco: 1961. V. 38

The Hundredth Book. A Bibliography of the Publications of the Book Club of California and a History of the Club. San Francisco: 1958. V. 38; 40; 41; 45; 46

The Spider and the Flie. San Francisco: 1939. V. 42; 44

Victoria R.I.: A Collection of Books, Manuscripts, Autograph Lettes, Original Drawings, Etc., by the Lady Herself and Her Loyal Subjects, Produced During Her Long and Illustrious Reign. San Francisco: 1969-70. V. 37

MAGEE, DOROTHY

Bibliography of the Grabhorn Press. 1940.1956. San Francisco: 1957. V. 37; 38; 39; 46

MAGENDIE, FRANCOIS

An Elementary Compendium of Physiology. Philadelphia: 1824. V. 42

Formulary for the Preparation and Mode of Employing Several New Remedies. Philadelphia: 1824. V. 44

Formulary for the Preparation and Employment of Several New Remedies . . . London: 1830. V. 44

Physiological and Chemical Research on the Use of the Prussic or Hydro-Cyanic Acid in the Treatment of the Breast and Particularly in Phthisic Pulmonale. New Haven: 1820. V. 40; 41

Physiological and Chemical Research on the Use of the Prussic or Hydro-Cyanic Acid in the Treatment of the Brest and particularly in Phthisic Pulmonale. New Haven;: 1820. V. 37; 39

A Summary of Physiology . . . Baltimore: 1822. V. 45

MAGGI, GIROLAMO d.1572

Della fortificatione delle Citta . . . Venice: 1563. V. 37

MAGGS BROS.

The Art of Writing. 2800 B.C. to 1930 A.D. Illustrated in a Collection of Documents Written on Vellum, Papyrus, Silk, Linen, Bamboo or Inscribed on Clay, Marble Steatite, Jasper, Haematite, Matrix of Emerald and Chalcedony. London: 1931? V. 42

Manuscripts and Books on Medicine, Alchemy, Astrology and natural Sciences Arranged in Chronological Order & Portraits and Autographs of Eminent Physicians and Scientists. London: 1929. V. 42; 45

MAGGS BROTHERS

Bookbindings Historic and Artistic. London: 1914. V. 41

Book Bindings: Historical and Decorative. No. 489. London: 1927. V. 41

Biblioteca Brasiliensis . . . London: 1930. V. 40

A Collection of French XVIIIth Century Illustrated Books . . . Issued in Commemoration of the Seventieth Birthday of Maggs Bros. London: 1930. V. 40; 41

An Illustrated Catalogue Raisonne of One Hundred and Six Original Manuscripts, Autographs, Maps and Printed Books Illustrating the Discovery and History of America from 1492 to 1814. Washington: 1929. V. 41

A Selection of Books, Manuscripts, Engravings and Autograph Letters, Remarkable for Their Interest and Rarity, Being the Five Hundred Catalogue Issued by Maggs Bros. Booksellers. London: 1928. V. 40

MAGIC Books from Mexico. Harmondsworth: 1953. V. 42

THE MAGIC Horse. London: 1930. V. 43

MAGIE, DAVID

Roman Rule in Asia Minor. Princeton: 1950. V. 42

MAGILL, ROBERT MC CORKLE

Magill Family Record. Richmond: 1907. V. 43; 46

MAGINI, GIOVANNI ANTONIO

Novae Coelestium Orbium Theoricae Congruentes cum Observationibus N. Copernici. Venice: 1589. V. 38; 41; 44

MAGINN, JAMES DOWAL

Fitzgerald the Fenian. London: 1889. V. 40

MAGINN, WILLIAM

A Gallery of Illustrious Literary Characters (1830-1838), Drawn by Daniel Maclise . . . London: 1873. V. 45

Miscellaneies in Prose and Verse. London: 1885. V. 40

The Red Barn, a Tale. London: 1828. V. 43

The Red Barn, a tale, founded on fact. London: 1831. V. 37

Whitehall; or, the Days of George IV. London: 1827. V. 46

MAGINNIS, ARTHUR J.

The Atlantic Ferry, Its Hips, Men and Working. London: 1892. V. 37

MAGINOGION

The Maginogion from the Welsh of the Llyfr Coch o Hergest . . . London: 1877. V. 42

MAGIRUS, JOHANN

Physiologiae Peripateticae Libri Sex cum Commentariis. London: 1619. V. 41

A MAGISTRATE'S Guide; and Citizen's Counsellor, Being a Digested Abstract of Those Laws of the State of Maryland Most Necessary . . . Frederick-Town: 1805. V. 40

MAGISTRIS, JOHANNES DE

Quaestiones sup Totu Cursum Logice. Basle: 1490. V. 37

Quaestiones Veteris et Novae Logicae. Colophon: 1488. V. 37

MAGIUS, HIERONYMUS

Variarum Lectionum Seu Miscellaneorum Libri IIII. 1564. V. 42

Variarum Lectionum Seu Miscellaneorum Libri IIII. Venice: 1564. V. 38

MAGNA Charta cum Statutis, Tum Antiquis, Tum Recentibus, Maximopere, Animo Tenendix, Nunc Demum ad Unum, Tipis Aedita. London: 1587. V. 37

MAGNE, A.

Monographie de Nouveau Theatre du Vaudeville Erige par la ville de Paris. Paris: 1873. V. 37; 42

MAGNEL, GUSTAVE

Prestressed Concrete. London: 1948. V. 44

MAGNET: Devoted to the Investigation of Human Physiology, Embracing Vitality, Pathetism, Psychology, Phrenopathy, Phrenology, Nerology . . . New York: 1843. V. 46

MAGNI, PIETRO PAOLO b. 1525

Discorsi . . . Sopra il Modo di Sanguinare; Discorso . . . Sopra il Modo di Fare i Cauterii . . . Brescia: 1618/18. V. 42

Discorsi . . . Sopra il Modo di Sanguinare; Discorso . . . Sopra il Modo di Fare i Cauterii . . . Brescia: 1618, 1618. V. 37

MAGNIAC, HOLLINSWORTH

The Collection of Works of Art. Pictures . . . at Tredegar House, Monmouthshire. 1916. V. 38

THE MAGNOLIA For 1836. New York: (1835). V. 37

MAGNUS, CHARLES

In Commemoration of the Glorious Victories of the 3rd and 9th of April 1865. New York: 1865. V. 39

MAGNUS, OLAUS 1490-1558

A Compendious History of the Goths, Swedes & Vandals and Other Northern Nations. London: 1658. V. 40; 42; 46

Historia de Gentibus Septentrionalibus. Antwerp: 1562. V. 38

Historia Delle Genti et Della Natvra Delle Cose Settentrionali. In Vinegia: 1565. V. 38; 40

Historia de Gentibus Septentrionalibus. Antwerp: 1562. V. 37

Historia de Gentibus Septentrionalibus . . . sic in Epitomen Redacta, ut Non Minus Clare Quam Breviter . . . Antwerp: 1558. V. 38; 39

Storia d'Olao Magno . . . de Costumi de Popoli Settentrionali . . . Venice: 1561. V. 38; 40; 42

MAGOFFIN, SUSAN SHELBY

Down the Santa Fe Trail and into Mexico. New Haven: 1926. V. 38; 39; 42; 44

MAGOUN, F. ALEXANDER

The Frigate Constituion and Other Historic Ships. Salem: 1928. V. 39; 40; 46

MAGRA, JAMES MARIA

A Journal of a Voyage Round the World, in His Majesty's Ship Endeavour, in the Years 1768, 1769, 1770 and 1771. London: 1771. V. 42

MAGRATH, JOHN RICHARD

The Obituary Book of Queen's College, Oxford. Oxford: 1910. V. 38

The Queen's College. Oxford: 1921. V. 38

MAGRE, M.

La Montee Aux Enfers. Poesies. Paris: 1920. V. 38

Les Soirs d'Opium. Poemes. Paris: 1921. V. 38

MAGRE, MAURICE

Confessions sur les Femmes, l'Amour, l'Opium, l'Ideal. Paris: 1930. V. 43

MAGRUDER, J. BANKHEAD

General Orders No. 29. Houston: 1863. V. 41

Special Orders. No.---- Head Quarters, Bureau of State Troops, District of Texas, New Mexico and Arizona. Houston: 1863. V. 39

MAGUIRE, JOHN F.

The Industrial Movement in Ireland, as Illustrated by the National Exhibition of 1852. Cork: 1863. V. 42; 44

The Irish in America. London: 1868. V. 41; 43; 46

MAGUIRE, JOHN FRANCIS 1815-1872

The Industrial Movement in Ireland. Cork: 1853. V. 46

MAHABHARATA

The Mahabharata of Krishna-Dwalpayana Vyasa. Calcutta: 1955. V. 45

MAHABHARATA. BHAGAVADGITA

The Bhagvat-Geeta . . . London: 1785. V. 39; 42

The Song Celestial or Bhagavad-Gita. Philadelphia: 1934. V. 40

MAHAFFY, J. P.

The Particular Book of Trinity College, Dublind. London: 1904. V. 43

Rambles and Studies in Greece. Philadelphia: 1892? V. 44

MAHAM, D. H.

An Elementary Course of Civil Engineering. London: 1859. V. 43; 46

MAHAN, A. T.

The Life of Nelson. London: 1899. V. 45

The South African War. New York: 1900. V. 39

MAHAN, ALFRED THAYER

The Gulf and Indland Waters. New York: 1883. V. 46

The Influence of Sea Power Upon History 1660-1783. Boston: 1890. V. 42; 43

The Influence of Sea Power Upon History. London: 1890. V. 40

Influence of Sea Power upon History 1660-1783; and French Revolution & Empire 1793-1812 in two volumes. Boston: 1894. V. 37

The Life of Nelson. London: 1897. V. 41; 42; 43

Major Operations of the Royal Navy 1762-1783. Boston: 1898. V. 42

Sea Power In Its Relations to the War of 1812. London: 1905. V. 37; 38; 46

MAHAN, BRUCE E.

Old Fort Crawford and Frontier. Iowa City: 1926. V. 38

MAHAN, D. H.

A Complete Treatise on Field Fortification, with General Outlines of the Principles Regulating the Arrangement, the Attack and the Defence of Permanent Works. New York: 1836. V. 43; 44

An Elementary Course of Civil Engineering, for the Use of the Cadets of the U.S. Military Academy. New York: 1838. V. 37; 39

MAHAN, DENNIS HART

Industrial Drawing: Comprising the Description and Uses of Drawing Instruments . . . New York: 1852. V. 40

MAHFOUZ, NAGUIB

The Beginning and the End. New York: 1989. V. 46

Palace Walk. New York: 1990. V. 45

MAHFOUZ, NAGUIB PACHA

Atlas of Mahfouz's Obstetric, and Gynaecological Museum Altrincham, England, 1949. V. 43

MAHOMED, S. D.

Shampooing; or, Benefits Resulting from the Use of the Indian Medicated Vapour BAth . . . Brighton: 1826. V. 38; 44

MAHON, DEREK

Design for a Grecian Urn - Poems. Cambridge: 1966. V. 38

Ecclesiastes. Didsbury: 1970. V. 45

Twelve Poems. Belfast: 1965. V. 38

MAHON, LORD VISCOUNT

Considerations on the Means of Preventing Fraudulent Practices of the Gold Coin. London: 1775. V. 42; 46

MAHONEY, BERTHA E.

illustrators of Children's Books 1744-1945. Boston: 1947. V. 46

MAHONEY, FRANCIS SYLVESTER

Facts and Figures from Italy . . . Addressed During the Last Two Winters to Charles Dickens, Esq . . . London: 1847. V. 43

MAHONEY, JAMES W.

The Cherokee Physician, or Indian Guide to Health, as Given by Richard Foreman. Asheville: 1849. V. 45

MAHONY, BERTHA E.

Illustrators of Children's Books. Boston: 1947. V. 39; 42

Illustrators of Children's Books 1744-1945. Boston: 1970. V. 40

MAHONY, FRANCIS SYLVESTER

Facts and Figures from Italy. London: 1847. V. 40; 42; 43

The Reliques of Father Prout. London: 1836. V. 37; 45

MAHONY, JAMES

The Book of the Baltic, Being the North of Europe Steam Company's Route to Denmark, Sweden and Russia, Norway, Prussia and the Hanseatic Ports . . . London: 1857. V. 42

MAHOOD, RUTH I.

Photographer of the Southwest-Adam Clark Vroman, 1856-1916. Los Angeles: 1961. V. 41

MAHR, ADOLF

Christian Art in Ancient Ireland. Dublin: 1932. V. 43

MAIDEN, J. H.

The Flowering Plants and Ferns of New South Wales . . . Sydney: 1895-98. V. 42

MAIDLOW, JOHN M.

Essays on Commons Preservation . . . London: 1867. V. 45

MAIDMENT, JAMES 1795?-1879

Ane Declaration of the lust and Necessar Causis, Moving Us of the Nobilitie of Scotland . . . to Repair to His Ienes Presence, and to Remane with Him for Resisting of the Present Daingeris Appearing to Goddis Trew Religion. 1822. V. 41

A Book of Scotish Pasquils. 1568-1715. Edinburgh: 1868. V. 44

Catalogue of the Library. Edinburgh: 1880. V. 38

Cocke Lorelle's Bote. Edinburgh: 1841. V. 46

A New Book of Old Ballads. Edinburgh: 1844. V. 43

A New Book of Old Ballads. N.P.: 1844. V. 42

A North Countrie Garland. Edinburgh: 1824. V. 38

Templaria. N.P.: Edinburgh?: 1828. V. 43

THE MAIDSTONE Garland. N.P.. V. 42

MAIER, MICHAEL

De Circulo Physico . . . Oppenheimii: 1616. V. 46

Viatorium, Hoc Est, de Montibus Planetarum Septem Seu Metallorum . . . Rouen: 1651. V. 46

THE MAIL Souvenir of Toronto. Toronto: 1891? V. 43

MAILE, JOHN LEVI

Prison Life in Andersonville . . . Los Angeles: 1912. V. 42; 43

MAILER, NORMAN 1923-

Ancient Evenings. 1983. V. 46

Ancient Evenings. Boston: 1983. V. 41; 42; 43; 46

The Armies of the Night: History as a Novel, The Novel as History. New York: 1968. V. 46

Barbary Shore. New York: 1951. V. 37; 38; 40; 42; 45; 46

Barbary Shore. New York & Toronto: 1951. V. 39

Cannibals and Christians. New York: 1966. V. 42; 44

Deaths for the Ladies (and Other Disasters). New York: 1962. V. 37; 40; 42

The Executioner's Song. Boston: 1979. V. 43; 45

The Faith of Graffiti. New York: 1974. V. 37; 40; 42

Harlot's Ghost. New York: 1991. V. 46

Huckleberry Finn, Alive at 100. New Jersey: 1985. V. 43

the Last Night. New York: 1984. V. 41; 42; 46

Marilyn a Biography. 1973. V. 43

Marilyn. New York: 1973. V. 39; 45; 46

The Naked and the Dead. 1948. V. 43

The Naked and the Dead. New York: 1948. V. 38; 39; 40; 42; 44; 46

The Naked and the Dead. New York & Toronto: 1948. V. 39

The Naked and the Dead. New York: Toronto: 1948. V. 41; 42

The Naked and the Dead. London: 1949. V. 41; 42; 45

The Naked and the Dead. New York: (1948). V. 37

Of a Fire on the Moon. Boston: 1970. V. 46

Of a Small and Modest Malignancy, Wicked and Bristling with Dotes. Northridge: 1980. V. 37; 39; 40; 42; 43

Tough Guys Don't Dance. New York: 1974. V. 43

Tough Guys Dont' Dance. New York: 1984. V. 41; 42; 44; 45

MAILER, NORMAN 1923- continued

A Transit to Narcissus. New York: 1978. V. 37; 40; 42; 43

MAILER, TEOBERT

Researches in the Central Portion of the Usumatsintla Valley. Cambridge: 1901-1903. V. 37

MAILLARD, ANDRE

Apologie. s.l., s.n.: 1588. V. 38

MAILLARD, MARIE

A True Relation of the Wonderful Cure of Marie Maillard. (Lame almost ever since she was born). On Sunday, the 26 of November 1693 . . . London: 1787. V. 38

MAILLARD, N. D.

The History of the Republic of Texas from the Discovery of the Country to the Present Time, and the Cause of Her Separation from the Republic of Mexico. London: 1842. V. 40; 42; 45

MAILLET, BENOIT DE

Telliamed ou Entretiens d'un Philosphe Indien avec un Missionaire Francais sur la Diminution de la Mer, la Formation de la Terre, l'Origine de l'Homme. Amsterdam: 1748. V. 38

Telliamed. London: 1750. V. 38; 45

Telliamed; or, The World Explain'd. Baltimore: 1797. V. 37; 42

MAILS, THOMAS E.

The People Called Apache. Englewood Cliffs: 1974. V. 44

The People Called Apache. New York: 1974. V. 45

Sundancing at Rosebud and Pine Ridge. Lake Mills: 1978. V. 45

MAIMBOURG, LOUIS

Histoire De La Ligue. Paris: 1683. V. 37; 39

The History of the League. London: 1684. V. 37; 38; 39; 41; 44; 46

History of Arianism: Shewing Its Influence Upon Civil Affairs, and the Causes of the Dissolution of the Roman Empire. London: 1727. V. 44

MAIMON, SALOMON

Streiferen im Gebiete der Philosophie. Verlin: 1793. V. 40

Versuch Einer Neuen Logik oder Theorie des Denkens. Berlin: 1794. V. 45

MAIMONIDES 1135-1204

Doctor Perplexorum: ad Dubia & Obscuriora Scripturae Loca Rectius Intelligenda Veluti Clavem Continens . . . Basileae: 1629. V. 39

Tractatus Rabbi Moysi de Regimine Sanitatis ad Soldanum Regem. Augsburg: 1513. V. 38

MAIN, ALEXANDER

Life and Conversations of Dr. Samuel Johnson (Founded Chiefly Upon Boswell). London: 1874. V. 39

MAIN, DAVID M.

Three Hundred English Sonnets. Edinburgh: 1884. V. 43

MAIN, JAMES

Hints on Landscape Gardening. London: 1842. V. 44

MAINDRON, MAURICE

St-Cendre. Paris: 1930. V. 40

MAINE. CONSTITUTION - 1819

Petition of a Convention of the People of the District of Maine Praying to be Admitted Into the Union as a Separate and Independent State, Accompanied with a Constitution for Said State. Washington: 1819. V. 37

MAINE. CONSTITUTIONAL CONVENTION - 1820

The Debates, Resolutions, and Other Proceedings, of the Convention of Delegates, Assembled . . . for the Purpose of Forming a Constitution for the State of Maine. Portland: 1820. V. 38

MAINE, HENRY SUMNER

Ancient Law and Its Connection with the Early History of Society, and Its Relation to Modern Ideas. New York: 1888. V. 38

A Brief Memoir of His Life by the Rt. Hon. Sir M.E. Grant Duff with Some of His Indian Speeches and Minutes . . . V. 40

International Law, a Series of Lectures Delivered Before the University of Cambridge, 1887. London: 1888. V. 37

Popular Government: Four Essays. London: 1885. V. 42

MAINTENON, FRANCOIS D'AUBIGNE, MADAME DE

The Letters of Madame de Maintenon; and Other Eminent Persons in the Age of Lewis XIV. London: 1753. V. 45

MAINTENON, FRANCOISE D'AUBIGNE, MADAME DE

The Letters of Madame de Maintenon; and Other Eminent Persons in the Age of Lewis XIV. London: 1755. V. 43

MAINTENON, MADAME DE

Memoirs for the History of Madame de Maintenon and of the Last Age. London: 1757. V. 38

MAINWARING, JOHN

Memoirs of the Life of the Late Frederic Handel. London: 1760. V. 41; 45

MAINWARING, THOMAS

A Defence of Amicia, Daughter of Hugh Cyveliok, Earl of Chester. London: 1673. V. 44

A Reply to an Answer of the Defence of Amicia . . . London: 1673. V. 42; 44; 46

MAIOLO, SIMEONE, BP. OF VOLTURARA

Dies Caniculares. Mainz: 1607. V. 44

MAIOR, GEORG 1502-1574

Vitae Patrum . . . Wittenberg: 1544. V. 38

MAIORAGIUS, MARCUS ANTONIUS 1514-1555

De Senatu Romano Libellus. Milan: 1561. V. 43

MAIORICA, GIRONIMO

De Novis Christianae Religionis Progressibus, et Certaminibus in Iaponia, Anno 1622. 1627. V. 45

MAIR, CHARLES

Through the Mackenzie Basin. Toronto: 1908. V. 38; 42; 43; 44

MAIRET, ETHEL M.

a Book of Vegetable Dyes. Ditchling: 1917. V. 46

A Book of Vegetable Dyes, by Ethel M. Mairet. Hammersmith: 1916. V. 37

Vegetable Dyes. Ditchling: 1924. V. 41

MAIS, CHARLES

The Surprising Case of Rachel Baker, Who Prays and Preaches in Her Sleep . . . New York: 1814. V. 45

MAISON, MARGARET

John Oliver Hobbes: Her Life and Work. London: 1976. V. 41

MAISSIN, EUGENE

The French in Mexico and Texas (1838-1839). Salado: 1961. V. 37

MAISTER, GEORG

Panegyricus Francisco et Mariae Theresiae Augustis . . . Vienna: 1756. V. 42

MAISTRE, XAVIER DE

Voyage Autour de Ma Chambre. Boston: 1901. V. 44

MAITLAND CLUB

Miscellany Consisting of Original Papers and Other Documents Illustrative of the History and Literature of Scotland. Edinburgh: 1840. V. 40

MAITLAND, EDWARD

Clothed With the Sun . . . the Illuminations of Anna (Bonus) Kingsford. New York: 1889. V. 43

The Pilgrim and the Shrine . . . London: 1868. V. 37; 43

MAITLAND, FREDERIC W.

The Life and Letters of Leslie Stephen. London: 1906. V. 38; 45

MAITLAND, FREDERICK LEWIS

Narrative of the Surrender of Buonaparte, and of His Residence on Board H.M.S. Bellerophon. Boston: 1826. V. 40

MAITLAND, JOHN

Observations on the Impolicy of Permitting the Exportation of British Wool and of Preventing the Free Importation of Foreign Wool. London: 1818. V. 42

MAITTAIRE, MICHAEL

The English Grammar; or, an Essay on the Art of Grammar, Applied to and Exemplified in the English Tongue. London: 1712. V. 45

MAITTAIRE, MICHEL

Miscellanea Graecorom Aliquot Scriptorum Carmina, Cum Versione Latina Et Notis. Londini: 1722. V. 46

Senilia, Sive Poetica Aliquot in Argumentis Varii Generis Tentamina. Londini: 1742. V. 38

MAJDRAKOFF, IVAN

Heads. San Francisco: 1961. V. 45

MAJOR, ALBANY F.

Early Wars of Wessex Being Studies from England's School of Arms in the West by . . . Cambridge: 1913. V. 40

MAJOR, EMIL

Urs Graf. London: 1947. V. 41

MAJOR, FREDERICK WILLIAM

Manitoulin. The Isle of the Ottawas. Gore Bay: 1934. V. 37

MAJOR, HENRY

The Room in the McLean House, at Appomatox, C.H. In Which Gen. Lee Surrendered to Gen. Grant. New York: 1867. V. 45

MAJOR, HOWARD

The Domestic Architecture of the Early American Republic. The Greek Revival. Philadelphia: 1926. V. 44

Domestic Architecture of the Early American Republic: The Greek Revival. Philadelphia & London: 1926. V. 39

MAJOR, JOHANN DANIEL

Historia Anatomes Kilonis Primae. Kiloni: 1666. V. 38; 42

MAJOR, JOHANNES 1469-1550

Historia Majoris Britanniae, Tam Anglie Atque Scotie. Paris: 1521. V. 42

MAJOR, JOSHUA

A Treatise on the Insects Most Prevalent on Fruit Trees, and Garden Produce . . . Leeds: 1829. V. 43

MAJOR, RALPH

A History of Medicine. Springfield: 1954. V. 40; 41; 42; 45

MAJOR, RALPH H.

Classic Descriptions of Disease. Springfield: 1932. V. 38

A History of Medicine. Springfield: 1954. V. 38; 39

MAJOR, THOMAS

Les Ruines de Paestum ou de Poisdonie dans la Grande Greece. London: 1768. V. 42

MAJORIBANKS, J.

Slavery: an Essay in Verse. Edinburgh: 1792. V. 37

MAJORS, ALEXANDER

Seventy Years on the Frontier. Chicago and New York: 1893. V. 40; 42; 43; 45

Seventy Years on the Frontier. Denver: 1893. V. 40; 42

Seventy Years on the Frontier . . . Memoirs of a Life time on the Border. With a PReface by 'Buffalo Bill' (General W.F. Cody). Edited by Colonel PRentiss Ingraham. Chicago/New York: 1893. V. 37

MAKE Money a Great and Safe Enterprise. Cutting the Backbone of the American Continent, by the Atlantic-Pacific Tunnel, To Take Out Millions of Dollars . . . Denver: 1882. V. 37
MAKE Money a Great and Safe Enterprise. Cutting the Backbone of the American Continent, by the Atlantic-Pacific Tunnel, to Take out Millions of Dollars . . . Denver, Co.: 1882. V. 37

MAKOVSKI, L. W.

Land and Labout. The Opportunity of British Columbia. Vancouver: 1914. V. 46

MALACARNE, CLARO GIUSEPPE

Catalog di una Collezione di Minerali Disposta Secondo il sistema del Celebre Werner ed Acquistata per Uso de'Licei del Regno d'Italia a Freyberg . . . Milano: 1813. V. 46

MALACOLOGICAL SOCIETY OF LONDON

Proceedings. London: 1935-69. V. 37

MALAMUD, BERNARD 1914-1986

The Assistant. New York: 1957. V. 39; 45

God's Grace. New York: 1982. V. 41; 42

The Natural. New York: 1952. V. 38; 39; 41; 42

The Natural. London: 1963. V. 37; 41; 42; 44

Rembrandt's Hat. New York: 1973. V. 45

The Stories of Bernard Malamud. New York: 1983. V. 45

The Stories of Bernard Malamud. New York: 1983. V. 41; 45; 46

Two Fables. Pawlet: 1978. V. 42; 43

MALAN, A. H.

Famous Homes of Great Britain and Their Stories. (with) More Famous Homes. New York: 1902. V. 46

MALAPERT, CHARLES

Austriaca Sidera Heliocyclia Astronomicis Hypothesibus Illigata. Douai: 1633. V. 41

MALASPINA DI SANAZZARO, LUIGI 1754-1834

Delle Leggi del Bello Applicate alla Pittura ed Architettura. Pavia: 1791. V. 43

MALCOLM, A. G.

The History of the General Hospital, Belfast and Other Medical Institutions of the Town, etc. Belfast: 1851. V. 43

MALCOLM, ALEXANDER

A New System of Arithmetick, Theoretical and Practical. London: 1730. V. 38; 39

MALCOLM, HOWARD

Travels in South-Eastern Asia, Embracing Hindustan, Malaya, Siam and China . . . Boston: 1839. V. 41; 44

MALCOLM, J. P.

An Historical Sketch of the Art of Caricaturing. London: 1813. V. 38; 39; 41; 45

MALCOLM, JAMES PELLER

Londinium Redivivum; or, an Antient History and Modern Description of London. London: 1803-1807. V. 37

Topographical and Antiquarian Authors. London: 1808. V. 38

MALCOLM, JAMES PELLOR

Miscellaneous Anecdotes Illustrative of the Manners and History of Europe During the Reigns of Charles II, James II, William III and Q. Anne. London: 1811. V. 43; 46

MALCOLM, JOHN

The History of Persia, from the Most Early Period to the Present Time. London: 1815. V. 37; 41; 44

The Life of Robert, Lord Clive . . . London: 1836. V. 42

A Memoir of Central India, Including Malwa, and Adjoining Provinces. London: 1823. V. 39

Memoir of Central India, Including Malwa and Adjoining Provinces. London: 1824. V. 44

A Memoir of Central India, Including Malwa and Adjoining Provinces. London: 1832. V. 40

A Memoir of Central India, Including Malwa and Adjoining Provinces . . . Parbury,: 1932. V. 37

Miscellaneous Poems by . . . Bombay: 1829. V. 37; 43; 44

The Political History of India, from 1784 to 1823. London: 1826. V. 39; 42; 46

MALCOLM, ROBERT

The Life of Oliver Goldsmith. London: 1890. V. 41

MALCOLM, SARAH

A True Copy of the Paper Delivered the Night Before Her Execution . . . to the Rev. Mr. Piddington . . . London: 1732. V. 38

A True Copy of the Paper, Delivered the Night Before Her Execution by Sarah Malcolm, to the Rev. Mr. Piddington, Lecturer of St. Bartholomew the Great March 6th, 1732-3. London: 1732/33. V. 45; 46

MALCOLME, DAVID

Letters, Essays and Other Tracts Illustrating the Antiquities of Great Britain and Ireland, Together with Many Curious Discoveries of the Affinity Betwixt the Languages of the Americans and the Ancient Britons, etc. London: 1744. V. 43

MALDINEY, HENRI

Derriere Le Miroir. Paris: 1964. V. 44; 46

MALDONATUS, IOANNES

Commentarii in Quattuor Evangelistas. Pont a Mousson: 1596-97. V. 40

MALEBRANCHE, NICOLAS

Father Malebranche's Treatise Concerning the Search After Truth. Oxford: 1694. V. 43

His Treatise Concerning the Search After Truth. London: 1700. V. 39; 40

MALEBRANCHE, NICOLAS DE

Father Malebranche's Treatise Concerning the Search After Truth. Oxford & London: 1694. V. 38; 41; 45

Malebranche's Search after Truth. London: 1694. V. 41; 42; 45

MALEBRANCHE, P. B. MAXIMILIEN

Le Microscope Bibliographique. Amsterdam: 1771. V. 39

MALER, TEOBERT

Explorations in the Department of Peten Guatemala and Adjacent Region. Cambridge: 1908. V. 42; 44

Explorations of the Upper Usumatsintla and Adjacent Region. Cambridge: 1908. V. 42

Researches in the Central Portion of the Usumatsintla Valley. Cambridge: 1901-1903. V. 42

MALESHERBES, CHRETIEN GUILLAUME DE LAMOIGNON DE

Memoires Pour Servir a l'Histoire du Droit Public de la France en Matieres d'Impots, ou Receuil de ce Qui s'est Passe de Plus Interessant a la Cour des Aides . . . Bruxelles: 1779. V. 38

MALESPINI, RICORDANO d. 1281

Historia Antica . . . dall'edificazione di Fiorenza per Insino all'anno MCCLXXXI. Florence: 1568. V. 39; 40

MALET, CAPTAIN

Annals of the Road or Notes on Mail and Stage Coaching. London: 1876. V. 37; 42; 43

MALET, MARIANNE DORA

Violet; or, the Danseuse; a Portraiture of Human Passions and Character. London: 1836. V. 44

MALET, MARIANNE DORA, LADY

Violet Woodville; or, the Life of an Opera Dancer. Boston: 1843. V. 44

MALET, RAWDON

When the Red Gods Call. London: 1934. V. 43; 45

MALET, WILLIAM WYNDHAM

An Errand to the South in the Summer of 1862. London: 1863. V. 39

MALETO, PIETRO FRANCISCO

Historia del Beato Amadeo Terzo Duca di Savoia. Turin: 1613. V. 37

MALEVOLTI, ANGELO

The School of Fencing, with a General Explanation of the Principal Attitudes and Positions Peculiar to the Art. N.P.: 1968. V. 43

MALGAIGNE, J. F.

Surgery and Ambroise Pare. Norman: 1965. V. 42; 45

MALHAM, JOHN

The Naval Gazetteer. Boston: 1797. V. 38

MALHERBE, ALFRED

Monographie des Picidees ou Histoire Naturelle des Picides, Picumnines, Yuncines ou Torcols. Metz: 1859-62. V. 37; 42

MALHERBE, FRANCOIS DE 1555-1628

Les Oeuvres. Troyes: 1635. V. 38

Les Oeuvres. Paris: 1638-1648. V. 40

THE MALIBU. Rancho Topanga Malibu Sequit: An Historical Approach by W. W. Robinson. II. Personal Considerations: Essays by Lawrence Clark Powell. Los Angeles: 1958. V. 41; 42

MALICKY, H.

Atlas of European Trichoptera. The Hague: 1983. V. 37

MALIM, MARGARET F.

Old English Wood-Carving Patterns from Oak Furniture of the Jacobean Period. London: 1906. V. 46

MALINES, GERARD

An Essay on the Fishing Trade. Edinburgh: 1720. V. 43

MALING, PETER BROMLEY

Early Charts of New Zealand 1542-1851. Wellington: 1969. V. 39; 43

MALINGRE, CLAUDE

Traicte De La Loy Saliqve, Arms, Blasons, & Deuises des Francois. Paris: 1614. V. 37; 40

MALINIAC, JACQUES

Breast Deformities and Their Repair. V. 42

MALINOWSKI, BRONISLAW

Coral Gardens and Their Magic: a Study of the Methods of Tilling the Soil and of Agricultural Rites in the Trobriand Islands. New York: 1935. V. 46

Crime and Custom in Savage Society. London: 1926. V. 43

The Sexual Life of Savages in North-Western Melanesia. London: 1929. V. 37; 43

MALINS, GEOFFREY H.

How I Filmed the War. London: 1920. V. 43

MALKIN, BENJAMIN

Classical Disquisitions and Curiosities, Critical and Historical. London: 1825. V. 45

A Father's Memoirs of His Child . . . London: 1806. V. 45

MALKIN, BENJAMIN HEATH

Essays on Subjects Connected with Civilisation. London: 1795. V. 42

Essays on Subjects Connected with Civilization. London: 1795. V. 40; 42

A Father's Memoirs of His Child. London: 1806. V. 39; 46

The Scenery, Antiquities and Biography of South Wales, From Materials Collected During Two Excursions in the Year 1803. London: 1804. V. 41

MALL, THOMAS

A Cloud of Witnesses; or, the Sufferers Mirrour . . . London: 1665. V. 44

The History of the Martyrs Epitomised. Boston: 1747. V. 37; 38; 44; 46

MALLANDAINE, E.

The British Columbia Directory . . . Victoria: 1887. V. 43

MALLANDAINE, EDWARD

First Victoria Directory . . . San Francisco: 1860. V. 42

MALLARME, S.

Un Coup de Des Jamais n'Abolira le Hasard. Verona: 1987. V. 41

MALLARME, STEPHANE

L'Apres-Midi d'un Faune. London: 1956. V. 41; 42

Pages. Brussels: 1891. V. 38

Preface to Vatahek. Paris: 1876. V. 38

MALLARY, R. DE WITT

Lenox and the Berkshire Highlands. New York & London: 1902. V. 38

MALLE, LUIGI

Figurative Art in Piedmont. Volume 1 (of 2): From the Prehistoric Period to the Sixteenth Century. Turin: 1972. V. 46

MALLEMONT, A.

History of Ladies' Hairdressing from the Earliest Periods to the End of the XIXth Century. London: 1904. V. 39; 40

MALLERY, GARRICK

Pictographs of the North American Indians. (Washington: 1887). V. 37

MALLESON, GEORGE BRUCE

Herat: the Granary and Garden of Central Asia. London: 1880. V. 46

MALLET, CHARLES EDWARD

A History of the University of Oxford. London: 1924-27. V. 45

A History of the University of Oxford. London: 1924-7. V. 37

MALLET, DAVID

Alfred: a Masque. London: 1740. V. 37; 41

Alfred; a Masque. London: 1751. V. 38; 41; 44; 46

Amyntor and Theodora; or, the Hermit. A Poem. London: 1747. V. 40

Ballads and Songs. London: 1857. V. 42

A Congratulatory Letter to Selim (i.e. Lyttelton) on Three Letters to the Whigs (by Horace Walpole). London: 1748. V. 41; 42; 46

Edwin and Emma. Birmingham: 1760. V. 37; 39; 40; 41; 42; 43; 45; 46

The Life of Francis Bacon. London: 1740. V. 38; 39; 40; 42; 45

Poems on Several Occasions. London: 1762. V. 42; 45

The Works. London: 1759. V. 40

MALLET DU PAN, J.

The History of the Destruction of the Helvetic Union and Liberty. Boston: 1799. V. 37; 38; 39; 40; 41

MALLET DU PAN, JACQUES

The British Mercury, or, Historical and Critical Views of the Events of the Present Times. London: 1798-1800. V. 46

The Dangers Which Threaten Europe . . . To Which is Added, The Aeras of Events Subsequent to the Resolution of France. New York: 1795. V. 37

MALLET, FRANCIS

The Life of Francis Bacon, Baron of Verulam . . . London: 1760. V. 39

MALLET, H. E.

Annals of the Road or Notes on Mail and Stage Coaching in Great Britain . . . to which are added Essays on the Road by Nimrod. London: 1876. V. 37

MALLET, PAUL HENRI

Northern Antiquities; or, a Description of the Manners, Customs, Religions and Laws of the Ancient Danes . . . London: 1770. V. 38; 43

MALLET, ROBERT

On The Physical Conditions Involved in the Construction of Artillery: with an Investigation of the Relative and Absolute Values of the Materials Principally Empolyed and of Some Hiterto Unexplained Causes of the Destruction . . . London: 1856. V. 37; 44

MALLET-STEVENS, ROBERT 1886-1945

Grandes Constructions. Paris: 1928. V. 38

MALLETT, DAVID

Ballads and Songs. London: 1857. V. 43

MALLEUS Maleficarum. N.P.: 1928. V. 43

MALLEY, CHARLES D.

Leonardo da Vinci on the Human Body. New York: 1952. V. 39

MALLING, OVE

Great and Good Deeds of Danes, Norwegians and Holsteninians . . . London: 1807. V. 37; 39; 43

MALLISON, SAM T.

The Great Wildcater. Charleston: 1953. V. 44

MALLISON, WILLIAM HENRY

The Seaman's Friend. London. V. 38; 39; 44

MALLOCK, W. H.

Every Man His Own Poet. Chicago: 1903. V. 40

The Heart of Life. London: 1895. V. 40

A Romance of the Nineteenth Century. London: 1881. V. 41

MALLOCK, WILLIAM HURRELL

The New Republic; or, Culture, Faith and Philosophy in an English Country House. London: 1877. V. 37

Verses. London: 1893. V. 43

MALLORY, JOHN

Objections Humbly Offer'd Against Passing the Bill, Intitled, a Bill for the More Easy and Speedy Recovery of Small Debts, into Law. London: 1730. V. 46

MALLOWAN, M. E. L.

Nimrud and Its Remains. 1966. V. 42

Nimrud and Its Remains. New York: 1966. V. 42

Prehistoric Assyria: the Excavations at Tall Arpachiyah, 1933. London: 1935. V. 40

MALLOWNEY, M. G.

Gunnison City the Future Metropolis of the Western Slope. Gunnison: 1882. V. 37

MALLOY, WILLIAM M.

Treaties, Conventions, International Acts, Protocols and Agreements Between the United States of America and Other Powers 1776-1909. Washington: 1910. V. 40

MALMESBURY, JAMES EDWARD, EARL OF

Half a Century of Sport in Hampshire, Being Extracts from the Shooting Journals of James Edward, Second Earl of Malmesbury. London: 1905. V. 42

MALMESBURY, JAMES HARRIS, 1ST EARL OF 1746-1820

Diaries and Correspondence. London: 1844. V. 39

MALO, DAVID

Hawaiian Antiquities. Honolulu: 1908. V. 46

MALONE, ANTHONY

A Letter from a P--me S--j---t, to a H-gh P----t, Concerning the Present Posture of Affairs, With Advice From a Certain Great E----l, Who Lately Had a Private Conference with a Cr--n-d h--d. 1754. V. 41

MALONE, DUMAS

The Fry and Jefferson Map. Princeton: 1950. V. 45

Jefferson and His Time. Boston: 1948-81. V. 39

MALONE, EDMOND

A Biographical Memoir of the Late Right Honourable William Windham. London: 1810. V. 37; 39; 40; 45; 46

An Inquiry into the Authenticity of Certain Miscellaneous Papers and Legal Instruments, Published Dec. 24, 1795 and Attributed to Shakespeare, Queen Elizabeth, and Henry, Earl of Southhampton. London: 1796. V. 38; 39; 40; 41; 42; 45; 46

MALONE, JAMES H.

The Chickasaw Nation. Louisville: 1922. V. 40

MALONE, R. EDMOND

Three Years' Cruise in the Australian Colonies. London: 1854. V. 45

MALONE, THOMAS H.

Memoir of Thomas H. Malone: an Autobiography Written for His Children . . . Nashville: 1928. V. 39

MALONE, WILLIAM

A Reply to Mr. James Ussher his Answer. Douai,: 1627. V. 37

MALONEY, T. J.

U. S. Camera 1937. New York: 1937. V. 37

MALORY, THOMAS d. 1471

The Birth, Life, and Acts of King Arthor of His Noble Knights of the Round Table . . . London: 1893-94. V. 37; 40

The Birth and Life and Acts of King Arthur . . . London: 1893 & 1894. V. 43

The Birth, Life and Acts of King Arthur, of His Noble Knights of the Round Table . . . London: 1909. V. 45

The Birth, Life and Acts of King Arthur. London: 1927. V. 41; 45; 46

The Birth Life and Acts of King Arthur . . . Le Morte Darthur . . . (London): 1927. V. 37

Lancelot & Elaine . . . 1948. V. 43

Lancelot and Elaine. Buckinghamshire: 1948. V. 45

Lancelot and Elaine. N.P.: 1948. V. 46

Lancelot and Elaine - Being the Eighth to the Twentieth Chapters of the Eighteenth Book of Le Morte d'Arthur. Pigotts: 1948. V. 37; 42; 45

Le Morte D'Arthur. By Sir Thomas Malory. The text of William Caxton in modernized spelling, edited by Alfred Pollard. Illustrated by W. Russell Flint. London: 1910-1911. V. 37

Le Morte D'Arthur printed by William Caxton 1485. Reproduced in facsimile from the copy in the Pierpont Morgan Library, New York with an introduction by P. Needham. 1976. V. 37

Le Morte D'Arthur. London: 1889-91. V. 40

Le Morte D'arthur. London: 1893. V. 43; 46

Le Morte D'Arthur. London: 1893-94. V. 37; 40

Le Morte d'Arthur. London: 1893-94. V. 43

Le Morte d'Arthur. London: 1899. V. 40

Le Morte d'Arthur. London: 1909. V. 43

Le Morte d'Arthur. London: 1910-11. V. 38; 39; 40; 42; 44; 46

The Romance of King Arthur and His Knights of the Round Tables, Abridged from Malory's Morte D'Arthur. London: 1917. V. 37; 39; 41; 43; 44; 46

Le Morte D'Arthur. London: 1920. V. 45

Le Morte D'Arthur. London: 1920. V. 42

Le Morte D'Arthur. London: 1921. V. 38; 40

Le Morte d'Arthur. London: 1927. V. 42

Le Morte d'Arthur. London: 1927. V. 39; 40

Le Morte Darthur. New York: 1927. V. 42; 43

Le Morte d'Arthur. New York: 1927. V. 41

The Nobel & Joyous Boke Entytled Le Morte Darthur. Oxford: 1933. V. 39; 41; 42; 44; 46

The Noble and Joyous Boke Entytled le Morte d'Arthur. Stratford-upon-Avon: 1933. V. 41

Le Morte D'Arthur. London: 1936. V. 38; 41; 42; 45

Le Morte d'Arthur. London: 1936. V. 39

Le Morte d'Arthur. London: 1936. V. 43

Le Morte D'Arthur. New York: 1936. V. 46

Le Morte D'Arthur. New York: 1936. V. 38; 39; 43; 44

Le Morte d'Arthur, 1485. London: 1976. V. 39; 45

Le Morte D'arthur. New York: 1982. V. 43

The Most Ancient and Famous History of the Renowned Prince ARthur King of Britaine. London: 1634. V. 44

The Noble and Joyous Book Entyled Le Morte Darthur. Chelsea: 1914. V. 43; 44

The Noble & Joyous Boke Entytled le Morte Darthur. Oxford: 1923. V. 37; 45

The Romance of King Arthur and His Knights of the Round Table . . . New York: 1917. V. 44; 45

The Story of King Arthur and of His Noble Knights of the Round Table. New York: 1936. V. 40

Works. Oxford: 1947. V. 39

The Works. 1948. V. 46

MALOUF, DAVID

Bicycle and Other Poems. St. Lucia: 1970. V. 44

Child's Play. London: 1982. V. 45

MALOUIN, PAUL JACQUES

Description et Details des Arts du Meunier, du Vermiceller et du Boulenger . . . Paris: 1767. V. 42

MALPIGHI, MARCELLO 1628-1694

Anatome Plantarum. London: 1675-79. V. 46

Consultationum Medicarum Nonnullarumque Dissertationum Collectio, Ante hac Plurimum Desiderata, Nunc Denique in Lucem Edita . . . Venice: 1747. V. 41; 45

The Correspondence of Marcello Malpighi. Ithaca: 1975. V. 40; 41

Disertatio Epistolica de Formatione Pulli in Ovo. London: 1673. V. 37

Dissertatio Epistolica de Bombyce, Societati Regiae, Londini ad Scientiam Naturalem Promovendam Institutate, Dicata. Londini: 1669. V. 38

Epistolae Anatomicae. Amsterdam: 1669. V. 37; 39; 41; 42; 43

Opera Posthuma, Figuris Aeneis Illustrata. London: 1697. V. 41; 45

Opera Omnia. London: 1686. V. 37

De Structura Glandularum Conglobatarum Consimiliumque Partium Epistola. London: 1689. V. 41; 43

De Viscerum Structura Exercitatio Anatomica . . . Amsterdam: 1669. V. 44; 46

MALRAUX, ANDRE

Antimemoires. Paris: 1967. V. 46

The Metamorphosis of the Gods. New York: 1960. V. 41

The Psychology of Art: Museum Without Walls. New York: 1950. V. 40

The Psychology of Art: Museum Without Walls; the Creative Act; The Twilight of the Absolute. Translated by Stuart Gilbert. Bollingen Series XXIV. New York: (1950). V. 37

The Voices of Silence. Garden City: 1953. V. 37

MALTBY, CHARLES

The Life and Public Services of Abraham Lincoln. Stockton: 1884. V. 43

MALTBY, W. J.

Captain Jeff; Or, Frontier Life in Texas with the Texas Rangers. Colorado, Texas: 1906. V. 37; 41

MALTBY, WILLIAM J.

Captain Jeff or Frontier Life in Texas with the Texas Rangers . . . Colorado: 1906. V. 38; 46

MALTE-BRUN, M. CONRAD 1775-1826

Universal Geography, or, a Description of all the Parts of the World in a New Plan. Edinburgh: 1822-33. V. 39

MALTHUS, THOMAS ROBERT

Additions to the Fourth and Former Editions of an Essay on the Principle of Population . . . London: 1817. V. 37

Definitions in Political Economy, Preceded by an Inquiry into the Rules Which Ought to Guide Political Economists in the Definition and Use of Their Terms . . . London: 1827. V. 38; 39; 41; 45

Definitions in Political Economy, Preceded by an Inquiry Into the Rules Which Ought to Guide Political Economists in the Definition and Use of Their Terms . . . London: 1853. V. 39; 41

An Essay on the Principle of Population. London: 1803. V. 38; 39; 41; 42; 45

An Essay on the Principle of Population. London: 1806. V. 37; 38; 39; 42

An Essay on the Principle of Population. (and) Additions to the Fourth and Former Editions of An Essay on the Principle of Population. London: 1806, 1817. V. 40

An Essay on the Principle of Population. London: 1807. V. 37; 38; 39; 41; 42; 43; 45

An Essay on the Principle of Population. George Town: 1809. V. 38; 41; 43; 45

Essai sur le Principe de Population. Paris: 1809. V. 38

An Essay on the Principle of Population. Washington: 1809. V. 38

An Essay on the Principle of Population. Washington City: 1809. V. 38; 39; 40; 41; 42; 45; 46

An Essay on the Principle of Population . . . London: 1817. V. 37; 39; 43

An Essay on the Principle of Population. London: 1826. V. 39; 41; 42

First Essay on Population 1798. London: 1926. V. 41

The Grounds of an Opinion on the Policy of Restricting the Importation of Foreign Corn; Intended as an Appendix to 'Observations on the Corn Laws. London: 1815. V. 39; 41

An Inquiry Into the Nature and Progress of Rent, and the Principles by Which it Is Regulated . . . London: 1815. V. 39

An Inquiry into the Nature and Progress of Rent, and the Principles By Which It Is Regulated. London: 1934. V. 41

Observations on the Effects of the Corn Laws, and of the Rise or Fall in the Price of Corn on the Agriculture and General Wealth of the Country. London: 1814. V. 45

Principles of Political Economy Considered With a View to Their Application. London: 1820. V. 37; 38; 39; 40; 42; 43; 45; 46

Principles of Political Economy. Boston: 1821. V. 37; 38; 39; 41; 45

Principles of Political Economy Considered with a View to Their Practical Application. London: 1836. V. 38; 39; 41; 43; 45

Principes d'Economie Politique Consideres sous la Rapport de leur Application Pratique. Paris: 1846. V. 39; 42

Reply to the Chief Objections Which Have Been Urged Against the Essay on the Principle of Population. London: 1806. V. 37; 38

Statements Respecting the East India College, with an Appeal to Facts, in Refutation of the Charges Lately Brought Against It, in the Court of Proprietors. London: 1817. V. 45

A Summary View of the Principle of Population. London: 1830. V. 41

MALTON, JAMES

A Collection of Designs for Rural Retreats, as Villas Principally in the Gothic and Castle styles of Architecture. London: 1802. V. 45

Dublin Views, in Colour. Dublin: 1981. V. 43

An Essay on British Cottage Architecture. London: 1798. V. 38; 42; 45; 46

The Young Painter's Maulstick. London: 1800. V. 38; 41; 44; 46

The Young Painter's Maulstick . . . London: 1803. V. 41

MALTON, THOMAS

A Compleat Treatise on Perspective. London: 1776. V. 44

Oxford. London: 1802-04. V. 44

Views of Oxford. London: 1810. V. 39; 41; 44

THE MALTSTER'S Guide, containing the Substance of the several Excise Laws and Regulations to which Maltsters are subject; and also a variety of Information relating to the Excise in general. London: 1811. V. 39

MALTZ, ALBERT

The Journey of Simon McKeever. Boston: 1949. V. 46

MALTZ, MAXWELL

Evolution of Plastic Surgery. New York: 1946. V. 43

MALVASIA, CARLO CESARE 1616-1693

Felsina Pittrice vite de Pittori Bolognesi. Bologna: 1678. V. 37; 40

Le Pitture di Bologna . . . Rendono il Passeggiere Disingannato ed Instrutto dell'Ascoso Accademica Gelato . . . Bologna: 1686. V. 40

Le Pittvre Di Bologna Che Nella Pretesa, e Rimostrata sin Hora da Altri Maggiore Antichita & Impareggiabile Eccellenza Nella Pittura . . . Bologna: 1686. V. 43

MALVEZZI, VIRGILIO

Considerations Upon the Lives of Alcibiades and Coriolanus . . . London: 1650. V. 44

Discourses Upon Cornelius Tacitus. London: 1642. V. 38; 41; 44; 46

The Pourtract of the Politicke Christian-Favourite. London: 1647. V. 37; 38

MAMBELLI, GIULIANO

Gli Annali delle Edizzioni Dantesche. Bologna: 1931. V. 46

MAMERANUS, NICOLAS

Catalogus Familiae Totius Aulae and Catalogus Omnium Generalium and Catalogus Expeditionis. Cologne: 1550. V. 38

MAMEROT, SEBASTIEN

Les Passages de Oultre Mer. Du Noble Godefroy De Buillon Quit Fut Roy de Hierusalem. Paris: 1525. V. 44

MAMET, DAVID

The Frog Prince. New York: 1984. V. 46

MAMMA'S Tales: Farmer Fallowfield's Pretty Stories for Good Girls and Boys. Philadelphia: 1850. V. 46

MAMMATT, E.

A Collection of Facts and Practical Observations Intended to Elucidate the Formation of the Ashby Coal-Field in the Parish of Ashby-de-la-Zouch and the Neighbouring District. London: 1836. V. 46

MAMOULIAN, ROUBEN

Abigayil: the Story of the Cat at the Manger. Greenwich: 1964. V. 45

MAN-EATERS and Other Denizens of the Indian Jungle. Calcutta & Simla: 1928. V. 39

MAN, F. H.

150 Years of Artists' Lithographs 1803-1953. London: 1953. V. 40

MAN, FELIX H.

Eight European Artists. New York: 1954. V. 42; 45

THE MAN of Honour. London: i.e. Edinburgh: 1737. V. 45

THE MAN of Honour (in verse). London: 1737. V. 40; 41

THE MAN of Taste, Occasion'd by an Epistle of Mr. Pope's on that Subject. London: 1733. V. 46

THE MANAGEMENT of the Revenue; with Queries Relative Thereto. Dublin: 1758. V. 40

MANARDI, GIOVANNI 1462-1535

Epistolarum Medicinalium Libri Duodeviginti. Basle: 1535. V. 38

MANARIN, LOUIS H.

North Carolina Troops 1861-1865: A Roster. Raleigh, NC: 1966-1985. V. 37

MANASSES, CONSTANTINE

Annales, Nunc Primum in Lucem Prolati & de Graecis Latini Facti, per I. Leuvenclaium ex Io. Sambuci V.C. Biblotheca. Basel: 1573. V. 45

MANBY, G. W.

An Essay on the Preservation of Shipwrecked Persons. London: 1812. V. 42; 43

MANBY, GEORGE WILLIAM 1765-1864

An Historic and Picturesque Guide from Clifton, through the Counties of Monmouth, Glamorgan, and Brecknock with Representations of Ruins, Interesting Antiquities &c. Bristol: 1802. V. 39; 41

Journal of a Voyage to Greenland, in the Year 1821. London: 1823. V. 39; 43; 46

Journal of a Voyage to Greenland, in the Year 1821. London: 1822. V. 37

MANCHEE, THOMAS JOHN

The Bristol Charities, Being the Report of the Commissioners for Enquiring Concerning Charities in England and Wales . . . Bristol: 1831. V. 39; 44

MANCHESTER ANGLERS' ASSOCIATION

Angler Eveings. Papers by Members of the . . . 1st-3rd Series. Manchester: 1880/1882/1894. V. 39

MANCHESTER, DUKE OF

Court and Society From Elizabeth to Anne. London: 1864. V. 41

MANCHESTER, HENRY MONTAGU, 1ST EARL OF

Contemplatio Morti, et Immortalitatis. London: 1631. V. 45

MANCHESTER, HERBERT

Four Centuries of Sport in America, 1490-1890. New York: 1931. V. 39

MANCHESTER LIBRARY

Catalogue of Medical Books in Manchester University Library 1480-1700. Manchester: 1972. V. 38

THE MANCHESTER Songster: Being a Collection of the Most Favourite Songs, That Have Been Sung at the Public Places of Entertainment in London, and at the Theatre-Royal, Manchester. Manchester: 1792. V. 46

MANCHESTER UNIVERSITY. LIBRARY.

Catalogue of Medical Books in Manchester U. Library 1480-1700. Manchester: 1972. V. 39

MANCHESTER, WILLIAM DROGO MONTAGU, 7TH DUKE OF 1823-1890

Court and Society from Elizabeth to Anne. London: 1864. V. 42

MANCINELLI, ANTONIO

De Oratore Brachylogia. Rome: 1487. V. 42

Versilogus de Heroici, Saphici . . . Versuum Compositione & syllabarum Quantitate. Leipzig: 1513. V. 40

MANCINUS, DOMINICUS

Tractatus de Passione Domini. Leipzig: 1509. V. 38

MANCUR, JOHN H.

Everard Norton. New York: 1844. V. 40

MANDAT-GRANCEY, EDMOND

Cow-Boys and Colonels Narrative of a Journey Across the Prairie and Over the Black Hills of Dakota . . . New York: 1887. V. 46

MANDELBAUM, ALLEN

A Lied of Letterpress for Moser and McGrath. Northampton: 1980. V. 40

MANDELSLO, JOHAN ALBRECHT VON

Morgenlandische Reise Beschreivung. Schleswig: 1658. V. 38; 40

MANDELSLO, JOHANN ALBRECHT VON

Morgenlaendische Reisebeschreibung, Worinnen Zugleich der Zustand der Fuernembsten Ost-Indianischen Laender . . . Schleswig: 1658. V. 38

MANDELSLO, JOHANN ALBRECHT VON

The Voyages and Travels of the Ambassadors Sent by Frederick Duke of Holstein, to the Great Duke of Muscovy, and the King of Prussia. London: 1669. V. 41

MANDER, JAMES

The Derbyshire Miner's Glossary. Bakewell: 1824. V. 40

MANDER, RAYMOND

Theatrical Companion to Coward - a Pictorial Record of the First Performances of the Theatrical Works of Noel Coward. London: 1957. V. 41

MANDERSON, CHARLES F.

The Twin Seven-Shooters. New York: 1902. V. 41; 42

MANDEVILLE, BERNARD

The Fables of the Bees. London: 1725. V. 38

The Fable of the Bees. London: 1732-3. V. 40

The Fable of the Bees. London: 1732/3. V. 41

La Fable des Abeilles, ou Des Fripons Devenus Honnetes Gens . . . Londres: 1750. V. 46

The Fable of the Bees. Edinburgh: 1772. V. 41

The Fable of the Bees: or, Private Vices, Public Benefits . . . The Third Edition. To which is added A Vindication of the Book . . . (With) The Fable of the Bees. Part II. London: 1724-29. V. 37

The Fable of the Bees: or, Private Vices, Publick Benefits. With an Essay on Charity and Charity Schools. And A Search into the Nature of Society. The Fourth Editio. To which is added, a vindication of the book from the . . . London: 1725. V. 37

The Virgin Unmask'd . . . London: 1709. V. 41

MANDEVILLE, BERNARD DE

An Enquiry into the Origin of Honour, and the Usefulness of Christianity in War. London: 1732. V. 43

The Fable of the Bees . . . London: 1723. V. 38; 42

The Fable of the Bees. London: 1724. V. 38; 39; 43

The Fable of the Bees . . . (with) The Fable of the Bees, Part II. London: 1724/29. V. 41; 45

The Fable of the Bees. (with) The Fable of the Bees. Part II. London: 1725/29. V. 42

The Fable of the Bees; or, Private Vices, Publick Benefits. London: 1729. V. 42; 43

The Fable of the Bees: or, Private Vices, Publick Benefits. London: 1732/33. V. 45

The Fable of the Bees . . . Edinburgh: 1772. V. 39

A Treatise of the Hypochondriack and Hysterick Diseases. London: 1730. V. 45

MANDEVILLE, G. HENRY

Flushing, Past and Present: a Historical Sketch. Flushing: 1860. V. 38

MANDEVILLE, JOHN

Qual Tracta de le Piu Maravegliose Cose e Piu Notabile (che) se Trovino. Venice: 1521. V. 40

The Travels of Sir John Maneville. London: 1900. V. 37

The Voiage and Travaile of Sir John Maundeville, Kt. London: 1725. V. 45

The Voiage and Travaile of Sir John Maundeville, Kt . . . 1928. V. 37

The Voiage and Travaile of Sir John Maundeville, Kt. San Francisco: 1928. V. 37

The Voiage and Travaile of Sir John Maundevile, Kt. New York: 1928. V. 39

MANDEY, VENTERUS

Mellificium Mensionis; or, the Marrow of Measuring. London: 1717. V. 40

MANDIARGUES, ANDRE PIEYRE DE

Chagall. New York: 1974. V. 46

MANDIROLA, AGOSTINO

Manuale di Giardinieri Diviso in Tre Libri. Venice: 1661. V. 43

MANDOWSKY, ERNA

Pirro Ligorio's Roman Antiquities. London: 1963. V. 44

MANE-KATZ, R. S.

Aries Mane-Katz. 1894-1962. London: 1970. V. 46

MANEKEN, CAROLUS

Formule Epistolaru. Strassburg: 1493. V. 44

MANET, EDUARD

Letters with Aquarelles. New York: 1925. V. 41

Watercolors and Pastels. New York: 1959. V. 41

MANETTI, X.

Ornithologia Methodice Digesta Atque Iconibus Aeneis ad Vivum Illuminatis Ornata. Mouckianis: 1767-76. V. 42

MANFRED, FREDERICK FEIKEMA 1912-

Boy Almighty. St. Paul: 1945. V. 41

The Golden Bowl. St. Paul: 1944. V. 41

MANFREDI, GIROLAMO

Libro Intitulato il Perche, Tradotto di Latino in Italiano, dall'Eccel. Medico & Astrologo, M. Hieronimo Manfredi. Venetia: 1588. V. 39

MANGAM, WILLIAM D.

The Clarks. An American Phenomenon. New York: 1941. V. 37; 40; 42; 43; 45

MANGET, JEAN JACQUES

Bibliotheca Chemica Curiosa . . . Genevae: 1702. V. 37

MANGET, JOHANNES JACOB

Bibliotheca Pharmaceutico°Medico, Seu Rerum ad Pharmaciam Galenico-Chymicam Spectantium Thesaurus Refertissimus . . . Genevae: 1703. V. 46

MANGIN, E.

Piozziana or Recollections of the Late Mrs. Piozzi, with Remarks by a Friend. London: 1833. V. 46

MANGIN, EDWARD 1772-1852

George the Third. London: 1807. V. 46

A Letter to the 'Admirers of Chatterton.' 1838. V. 38

Oddities and Outlines. London: 1806. V. 38

MANGINN, WILLIAM

Military Sketch-Book. London: 1831. V. 45

MANGOURIT, M. O. B.

Travels in Hanover, During the Years 1803 and 1804. London: 1806. V. 40

MANHATTAN CO.

An Act of Incorporation of the Manhattan Company. New York: 1799. V. 45

MANHEIM, EMILY

Selections from the Hop McCormick Collection of Staffordshire Pottery. Chicago: 1980. V. 41

MANHEIM, FREDERIC

Affecting History of the Dreadful Distresses of Frederic Manheim's Family. Philadelphia: 1794. V. 40

Affecting History of the Dreadful Distresses of Frederic Manheim's Family... Philadelphia: 1800. V. 37; 42; 46

MANHOOD, H. A.

Crack of Whips. London: 1934. V. 39

MANIGAULT, GABRIEL

Saint Cecilia. London: 1872. V. 38

MANILIO, SEBASTIANO

Pistole del Moralissimo Seneca Nuovamente Fatte Volgare. Venice: 1944. V. 45

MANILIUS

M. Manilii Astronomicon Interpretatione et Notis ac Figuris Illustravit Michael Fayus. Paris: 1679. V. 41

MANILIUS, MARCUS

Astronomicon and Caesarem Augustum. Lyons: 1566. V. 40

Manilii Astronomicon Interpretatione t Notis Ac Figuris Illustravit Michael Fayvs Bacc. Theol. & P. Eccl. De Putangelis Jussu Christianissimi Regis, In Usum Serenissimi Delphini. Parisiis: 1679. V. 46

M. Manilii Astronomicon... London: 1739. V. 38; 44

Astronomicon Libri Quinque. Paris: 1579. V. 37

The Five Books.... Containing a System of the Ancient Astronomy and Astrology; Together with the Philosophy of the Stoicks. London: 1700. V. 43

MANING, FREDERICK EDWARD

Old New Zealand: A Tale of the Good Old Times. Auckland: 1863. V. 40

MANINGTON, GEORGE

A Soldier of the Legion. London: 1907. V. 41

MANJE, J. M.

Unknown Arizona and Sonora 1693-1721... Luz de Tierra Incognita... Tucson: 1954. V. 39

MANKOWITZ, WOLF

Wedgwood. New York: 1953. V. 44

MANLEY, MARY DE LA RIVIERE

Almyna; or, the Arabian Vow. London: 1707. V. 41

Court Intrigues, in a Collection of Original Letters from the Island of the New Atalantis &c. London: 1711. V. 39; 43

Letters Written to Mrs. Manley. To Which is Added a Letter from a Supposed Nun in Portugal, to a Gentleman in France, in Imitation of the Nun's Five Letters in Print, by Colonel Pack. London: 1696. V. 40

Memoirs of Europe Towards the Close of the Eighth Century. London: 1710-11. V. 42

Memoirs of Europe, Towards the Close of the Eighth Century. London: 1711. V. 45

Memoirs of the Life of Mrs. Manley. London: 1717. V. 40

Memoirs of Europe, Towards the Close of the Eighth Century. Written by Eginardus, Secretary and Favourite to Charlemagne; and done into English by the Translator of the New Atlantis. London: 1710. V. 37; 45

The Power of Love.. London: 1720. V. 45

The Power of Love: in Seven Novels. London: 1741. V. 43; 45

The Royal Mischief. London: 1696. V. 41; 44

Secret Memoirs and Manners of Several Persons of Quality, of Both Sexes. London: 1709. V. 38; 39; 40; 42; 43; 46

Secret Memoirs and Manners of Several Persons of Quality, of Both Sexes. (with) Memoirs of Europe. London: 1709-10. V. 41; 45

Secret Memoirs and Manners of Several Persons of Both Sexes. London: 1720. V. 39; 41

The Secret Memoirs and Manners of Several persons of Quality of Both Sexes from the New Atlantis, an Island in the Mediterranean. London: 1736. V. 40

The Secret History of Queen Zarah, and the Zarazians. Wherein the Amours, Intrigues, and Gallantries of the Court of Albigion are pleasantly expos'd... Suppos'd to be translated from the Italian... in the Vatican... London: 1743. V. 37

MANLEY, ROGER

The Russian Impostor... London: 1674. V. 42

MANLEY, THOMAS

The Interpreter, Containing the Genuine Signification of Such Obscure Words and Terms Used Either in the Common or Statute Lawes of this Realm. London: 1684. V. 43

MANLEY, W. B. L.

A Field Guide to the Butterflies and Burnets of Spain. London: 1970. V. 40

MANLEY, WILLIAM

A Collection of the Laws of the Customs Now in Force to Prevent Frauds and Abuses in the Revenue... London: 1742. V. 41

MANLY, JOHN

The Text of the Canterbury Tales. Studied on the Basis of All Known Manuscripts. Chicago: 1940. V. 38

MANLY, WILLIAM L.

Death Valley in '49. San Jose: 1894. V. 37; 38; 39; 40; 41; 45

MANN, ALBERT W.

History of the 45th Regiment, Massachusetts Volunteer Militia. Boston: 1908. V. 46

History of the Forty-Fifth Regiment, Massachusetts Volunteer Militia. Jamaica Plain: 1908. V. 38

MANN, CHARLES

Merv, the Queen of the World; and the Scourge of the Man Stealing Turcomans. London: 1881. V. 43

MANN, D. D.

the Present Picture of New South Wales... London: 1811. V. 45

Views of Old Sydney. Sydney: 1884. V. 45

MANN, EDWARD

A Manual of Psychological Medicine and Allied Nervous Diseases. Philadelphia: 1883. V. 42

MANN, EDWIN JOHN

The Deaf and Dumb; or, a Collection of Articles Relating to the Condition of Deaf Mutes... Boston: 1836. V. 41

MANN, ELIAS

The Northampton Collection of Sacred Harmony. Northampton: 1802. V. 46

MANN, ERNEST A.

Brooke House, Hackney. London: 1904. V. 40

MANN, HEINRICH

Berlin. London: 1929. V. 46

In the Land of Cockaigne. New York: 1929. V. 44

The Little Town. Boston: 1931. V. 45

MANN, HERMAN 1729-1796

The Female Review; or, Memoirs of an American Young Lady. Dedham: 1797. V. 37; 38; 39; 40

The Female Review. The Life of Deborah Sampson, the Female Soldier in the War of the Revolution. Boston: 1866. V. 38; 46

MANN, HORACE

An Oration, Delivered at Dedham (Mass.) July 4th, 1823. Dedham: 1823. V. 37

Slavery: Letters and Speeches. Boston: 1951. V. 46

MANN, HORACE, MRS.

Christianity in the Kitchen. Boston: 1857. V. 41

MANN, IDA

Developmental Abnormalities of the Eye. Cambridge: 1937. V. 41; 42; 44

MANN, JAMES

Medical Sketches of the Campaigns of 1812, 13, 14. Dedham: 1816. V. 42; 45

MANN, MARY E.

In Summer Shade. London: 1893. V. 40; 42

MANN, MATTHEW

A System of Gynecology. Philadelphia: 1887. V. 42

MANN, THOMAS

Bekenntnisse Des Hochstaplers Felix Krull. Wien, Leipzig & Muenchen: 1922. V. 41

The Beloved Returns. New York: 1940. V. 37; 39; 40; 41; 43; 44; 45; 46

Buddenbrooks. New York: 1924. V. 46

Death in Venice and Other Stories. New York: 1925. V. 45

Death in Venice. London: 1928. V. 42; 46

Death in Venice. New York: 1925. V. 38

Death in Venice. New York: 1935. V. 37

MANSFIELD, EDGAR continued

The Work of Edgar Mansfield. London: 1966. V. 41

MANSFIELD, EDWARD D.

Memoirs of the Life and Services of Daniel Drake, M.D. Cincinnati: 1855. V. 41; 46

MANSFIELD, EDWARD DEERING

The Mexican War: A History of Its Origin. New York: 1848. V. 38

MANSFIELD, JARED

Essays, Mathematical and Physical. New Haven: 1801. V. 46

MANSFIELD, JOSEPH K. F.

Colonel J. K. F. Mansfield's Report of the Inspection of the Department of Texas in 1856. Austin. V. 46

MANSFIELD, KATHERINE 1888-1923

The Aloe. London: 1930. V. 38; 41

The Aloe. New York: 1930. V. 46

Bliss: and Other Stories. London: 1920. V. 46

Bliss and Other Stories. Toronto: 1923. V. 39

The Collected Stories. London: 1945. V. 41

The Dove's Nest and Other Stories. London: 1921. V. 38

The Doves' Nest and Other Stories. London: 1923. V. 39; 42

The Garden Party and Other Stories. London: 1922. V. 43; 46

The Garden Party. 1939. V. 41

The Garden Party. London: 1939. V. 37; 40; 41; 44

In a German Pension. London: 1911. V. 37; 40; 46

Je ne Parle Pas Francais. Hampstead: 1919. V. 40

The Journal of Katherine Mansfield 1914-1922. London: 1727. V. 41

Journal 1914-1922. London: 1927. V. 42

The Journal of Katherine Mansfield. London: 1927. V. 38; 42; 43; 44

The Letters of Katherine Mansfield. London: 1828. V. 41

The Letters of Katherine Mansfield. London: 1928. V. 38; 42; 43; 44

The Little Girl and Other Stories. New York: 1924. V. 41

Poems. London: 1923. V. 45

Poems. New York: 1924. V. 43; 45

Prelude. London: 1918. V. 41

Prelude. Richmond: 1918. V. 38

Something Childish and Other Stories. London: 1924. V. 38; 41; 42; 43; 44

Something Childish and Other Stories. Toronto: 1924. V. 39

To Stanislaw Wyspianski. London: 1938. V. 38

MANSFIELD, LEWIS WILLIAM

The Morning Watch: a Narrative. New York: 1850. V. 45

MANSFIELD, S. M.

Proccedings of the Boundary Between the United States and Texas. N.P.: 1886. V. 45

MANSFIELD, W. W.

A Digest of the Statutes of Arkansas, Embracing All Laws of a General and Permanent Character. Little Rock: 1884. V. 45

MANSION, HORACE

Old French Nursery Songs. London: 1920. V. 46

MANSION, LEON LARUE

Letters Upon the Art of Miniature Painting. London: 1822. V. 42; 46

Letters Upon the Art of Miniature Painting. London: 1823. V. 39; 42; 44

MANSO, GIOVANNI BATTISTA

Vita di Torquato Tasso . . . Venice: 1621. V. 40

MANSO, PETER

Mailer, His Life and Times. New York: 1984. V. 38

Mailer, His Life and Times. Peter Manso. New York: (1984). V. 37

MANSON, JACQUES CHARLES DE 1724-1809

Traite du Fer et de l'Acier . . . Paris: 1804. V. 40

MANSON, PATRICK

Tropical Diseases. London: 1898. V. 44

MANSON, W. L.

The Highland Bagpipe, Its History, Literature and Music, with Some Account of the Traditions, Superstitions, etc. Paisley: 1901. V. 43

MANSTEIN, CHRISTOF HERMANN VON 1711-1757

Memoirs of Russia, Historical, Political and Military, for the Year 1727 to 1744. London: 1770. V. 37; 40

MANSTEIN, CHRISTOPH H. VON 1711-1757

Memoirs of Russia, Historical, Political and Military, from the Year MDCCXXVII, to MDCCLXLIV. Dublin: 1770. V. 39

MANT, ALICIA CATHERINE

Ellen; or, the Young Godmother. Philadelphia: 1816. V. 45

MANTELL, GIDEON ALGERNON

The Fossils of the South Downs. London: 1822. V. 37; 38; 39; 42; 43

Geological Excursions round the Isle of Wight, and along the adjacent Coast of Dorsetshire . . . Second edition with important additions. London;: 1851. V. 37

The Geology of the South-East of England. London: 1833. V. 37; 42

A Narrative of the Visit of Their Most Gracious Majesties William IV, and Queen Adelaide, to the Ancient Borough of Leaves, on the 22d of October 1830. London: 1831. V. 45

A Pictorial Atlas of Fossil Remains. London: 1850. V. 37; 38; 42; 43; 44; 46

Thoughts on Animalcules. London: 1846. V. 42; 43; 44; 46

The Wonders of Geology. London: 1838. V. 42; 43; 44

MANTICA, FRANCESCO MARIA

De Coniecturis Ultimarum Voluntatum Libri Duodecim. Frankfurt: 1580. V. 40

MANTLE, BURNS

The Best Plays of 1899 . . . -1960. New York: 1920-60. V. 46

MANTLE, MICKEY

The Mick. Garden City: 1985. V. 44

MANTUANUS, BAPTISTA

De Patientia Aurei Libri Tres. Basel: 1499. V. 40

MANTZ, RUTH ELVISH

The Critical Bibliography of Katherine Mansfield. London: 1931. V. 41

MANUAL Shewing the System of Survey of the Dominion Lands, with Instructions to Surveyors . . . Ottawa: 1883. V. 46

MANUAL Exercise and Evolutions of the Cavalry. As Practised in the Late American Army. Materially Corrected and Amended for Use of the Cavalry Throughout the United States. East Windsor: 1799. V. 37

THE MANUAL Exercise, with Explanations, as Ordered by His Majesty. London: 1770. V. 41

MANUAL of Artificial Limbs, Copiously Illustrated. New York: 1912. V. 42

THE MANUAL of Catholic Piety. New York: 1851. V. 44

A MANUAL of Catholic Prayers. Philadelphia: 1774. V. 41

A MANUAL of Devout Prayers, Fitted for all Persons and Occasions. Paris: 1671. V. 37

A MANUAL of Military Surgery. Prepared for the Use of the Confederate States ARmy. Richmond: 1863. V. 38

MANUAL of the Practical Naturalist; or Directions for Collecting, Preparing and Preserving Subjects of natural History. Boston: 1831. V. 43

MANUEL DE MELLO, FRANCISCO

Aula Politica, Curia Militar: Epistola Declamatoria ao Serenissimo Principe D. Theodozio: & Politica Militar . . . Lisbon: 1720. V. 38

MANUEL II, KING OF PORTUGAL 1889-

Early Portuguese Books 1489-1600 in the Library of His Majesty. London: 1929-35. V. 39

THE MANUFACTORY of Sheffield, Consists of Children's and Toy Knives, from 3d. Halfpenny. London? Sheffield?: 1790. V. 42

THE MANUSCRIPT of Diedrich Knickerbocker, Jun. New York: 1824. V. 40

MANUTIUS, PAULUS

Antiquitatum Romanorum Liber de Legibus. Venice: 1569. V. 44

De Antiquitatum Romanarum, Liber de Legibus. Venetiis: MDLVII. V. 42

Epistolarum Libri III. Venice: 1560. V. 40

MANUZIO, ALDO PIO 1449 or 50-1515

Aldi Manutii Romani Grammaticae Institutiones Graecae. colophon: 1515. V. 45

Aldi Manutii Romani Institutionum Grammaticarum Libri Tres. Cologne: 1517. V. 40

MANUZIO, PAOLO

Antiquitatum Romanarum Pauli Manutii Libri Duo, Unus de Legibus alter de Senatu. Geneva: 1595. V. 44

MANVILL, P. D., MRS.

Lucinda; or, the Mountain Mourner. Johnstown: 1807. V. 44

Lucinda; or the Mountain Mourner. Ballston Spa: 1817. V. 37; 40; 42; 44

MANWARING, CHRISTOPHER

Essays, Historical, Moral, Political and Agricultural. New London: 1829. V. 46

MANWOOD, JOHN d. 1610

An Abridgment of Manwood's Forrest Laws and Of all the Acts Parliament Made Since . . . London: 1696. V. 40

A Treatise and Discovrse of the Lawes of the Forrest . . . London: 1958. V. 39; 40; 45

A Treatise of the Lawes of the Forest . . . London: 1615. V. 37; 38; 40; 43; 45

A Treatise of the Laws of the Forest, Wherein is Declared Not Onely Those Laws, As They Are Now in Force . . . London: 1665. V. 40; 46

MANYPENNY, GEORGE W.

Letter from the Commissioner of Indian Affairs to Colonel Benton. Washington: 1855. V. 42

Our Indian Wards. Cincinnati: 1880. V. 40; 45; 46

Our Indian Wards. Cincinnati: 1880. V. 37

MANZANO, JUAN F.

Poems by a Slave in the Island of Cuba, Recently Liberated . . . London: 1840. V. 40; 46

MANZINI, CESARE

Instruction Pour Elever, Nourir, Dresser, Instruire & Penser Toutes Sortes de Petis Oyseaux de Voliere, Que l'on Tient en Cage Pour Entendre Chanter. Paris: 1674. V. 44

MANZINI, GIOVANNI BATTISTA

Les Harangves Academiqves. Paris: 1641. V. 37

MANZINI, LUIGI

Applausi Festivi Fatti in Roma per l'Elezione de Ferdinando III al Regno di Romani . . . Rome: 1637. V. 46

MANZONI, ALESSANDRO

I Promessi Sposi (The Brethrothed). New York: 1951. V. 43

I Promessi Sposi. Verona: 1951. V. 42; 46

MAO TSE-TUNG

Quotations form Chairman Mao Tse-Tung. Peking: 1966. V. 44

THE MAP Collector. Great Britain: 1977-86. V. 40

MAP Collectors' Series. London: 1963-75. V. 40

MAPEL, CAMILLO

Italy, Classical, Historical and Picturesque. London: 1847. V. 45

MAPLE, WILLIAM

A Method of Tanning Without Bark. Dublin: 1729. V. 37

MAPLESON, T. W. GWILT

Lays of the Western World. New York: 1848. V. 45

Pearls of American Poetry. New York: 1853. V. 43; 45

Pearls of American Poetry. New York: (c. 1853). V. 37

MAPPLETHORPE, ROBERT

Certain People: a Book of Portraits. Pasadena: 1985. V. 43

Lady Lisa Lyons. New York: 1983. V. 44; 46

Photographs. Norfolk. V. 45

Photographs. Norfolk: 1978. V. 45

MAPS of the Several Counties and Shires in England, with the Principality of Wales, &c. London: 1804. V. 38

MAPS, Reports, Estimates &c. Relative to Improvements of the Navigation of the River St. Lawrence and a Proposed Canal Connecting the River St. Lawrence and Lake Champlain. Toronto: 1856. V. 42

MARADERSTEIG, GIOVANNI

The Officina Bodoni. Verona: 1980. V. 37

On G. B. Bodoni's Type Faces. Verona: 1968. V. 37

MARALDI, JEAN DOMINIQUE

Connoissance des Temps Pour l'Annee Bissextile 1748. Au Meridier de Paris, Publiee par l'Ordre de l'Academie Royale des Sciences. Paris: 1747. V. 42

MARAN, RENE

Batouala. New York: 1932. V. 37; 39; 44

MARANA, GIOVANNI

Letters Writ by a Turkish Spy, who Lived Five and Forty Years Undiscovered at Paris. London: 1770. V. 38; 40; 41; 43; 44

MARANGOU, LILA

Benaki Museum, Athens. Bone Carvings from egypt I: Graeco-Roman Period. Rubengen: 1976. V. 40

MARANTA, BARTOLOMEO d. 1571

Libri Duo, de Theriaca et Mithridatio . . . Frankfurt: 1576. V. 37; 42; 44

Methodi Cognoscendorum Simplicium Libri Tres, Cum Indice Copioso. Venice: 1559. V. 37

MARAT, JEAN PAUL

Fire and the Terror Recherches Physiques sur le Feu. Paris: 1780. V. 38

MARATELLI, LODOVICO

Opere . . . Aggiunto vi il Quarto di Vergilio, Tradotto dal Medesimo. Florence: 1548. V. 37

MARBAKER, THOMAS D.

History of the 11th New Jersey Volunteers from Its Organization to Appomattox. Trenton: 1898. V. 46

MARBAULT, M. DE

Essai Sur le Commerce de Russie, avec l'Histoire de Ses Decouvertes. Amsterdam: 1777. V. 38; 40

MARBECKE, JOHN

The Lyves of Holy Sainctes, Prophetes, Patriarches and Others. London: 1754. V. 45

THE MARBLE-WORKERS' Manual. Philadelphia: 1865. V. 39; 41

MARBLING Methods and Receipts from Four Centuries, with Other Instructions Useful to Bookbinders. 1990. V. 45

MARBODIUS

De Lapidibus Preciosis Enchiridion. Paris: 1531. V. 37

MARBOT, JEAN BAPTISTE ANTOINE MARCELLIN, BARON

The Memoirs. London: 1892. V. 45

MARBURY, MARY ORVIS

Favorite Flies and Their Histories. Boston: 1892. V. 46

Favorite Flies and Their Histories with Many Replies from Practical Anglers to Inquiries Concerning How, When and Where to Use Them. Boston & New York: 1892. V. 39

MARCADE, JEAN

Roma Amor Essay on Erotic Elements in Etruscan and Roman Art. Geneva: 1961. V. 39

MARCASSUS, PIERRE DE 1584-1664

Les Dionysiaques ou Le Parfait Heros. Paris: 1631. V. 43

MARCEAU, MARCEL

The Story of Bip. New York: 1976. V. 38; 39; 40; 42

MARCEL, GUILLAUME 1647-1708

Tablettes Chronologiques, Contenant Avec Ordre, l'Etat de l'Eglise en Orient & en Occident . . . Amsterdam: 1687. V. 39

MARCEL, J. J.

Alphabet Irlandais Precede d'une Notice Historique, Litteraire et Typographique. Paris: 1804. V. 45

Oratio Dominica CL Linguis Versa, et Propriis Cujusque Linguae Characteribus Plerumque Expressa. Paris: 1805. V. 45

MARCEL, JEAN

The History of Surrealist Painting by Marcel Jean with the Collaboration of Arpad Mezei. London: 1960. V. 41

MARCELIN, PIERRE

Canape-Vert. New York: 1944. V. 45

The Pencil of God. Boston: 1951. V. 45

MARCELLINO, MARCO VALERIO

Il Diamerone . . . Ove con Vive Ragioni si Mostra, la Morte Non Esser Quel Male, Che'l Senso si Persuade. Venice: 1565. V. 45

MARCELLINUS, AMMIANUS

The Roman Historie, Containing Such Acts and Occurents as Passed Under Constantius, Iulianus, Iovianus, Valentinianus and Valens . . . London: 1609. V. 40; 43

MARCELLO, PIETRO

Vite de Prencipi di Vinegia . . . Venice: 1557. V. 37; 38; 41

Vite de' Prencipi di Vinegia . . . Venetia: 1557. V. 37

MARCELLUS and Julia: a Dialogue. London: 1788. V. 39

MARCELLUS EMPIRICUS

De Medicamentis Empiricis Physicis, ac Rationabilibus Liber, Ante Mille ac Ducentos Plus Minus Annos Scriptus . . . Basel: 1536. V. 42

MARCELLUS'; Published in the Virginia Gazette, November and December, 1794. Richmond: 1794? V. 46

MARCET, ALEXANDER 1770-1822

An Essay on the Chemical History and Medical Treatment of Caluculous Disorders. London: 1819. V. 40

MARCET, JANE

Conversations on Chemistry, in Which the Elements of that Science are Familiarly Explained and Illustrated by Experiments and Plates. New Haven: 1813. V. 40; 41; 42; 45

Conversations on Chemistry . . . New Haven: 1814. V. 43; 44; 45

Conversations on Political Economy . . . London: 1819. V. 39; 41

Conversations on Political Economy . . . London: 1821. V. 43; 46

Conversations on Political Economy . . . London: 1827. V. 41; 42

Conversations on Mineralogy. London: 1822. V. 38

Conversations on Political Economy. London: 1817. V. 37; 42

Conversations on Political Economy. In which the elements of that science are familiarly explained. London: 1816. V. 37

John Hopkins's Notions on Political Economy. London: 1833. V. 43

MARCET, WILLIAM

A Contribution to the History of the Respiration of Man . . . London: 1897. V. 38; 42

An Experimental Inquiry into the Action of Alcohol on the Nervous System. London: 1860. V. 37

MARCGRAVE, J.

Historia Natural do Brasil. Sao Paulo: 1942. V. 39

MARCH, HARRY A.

Pro Football. Its 'Ups' and 'Downs'. Albany: 1934. V. 43

MARCH, J.

The Jolly Angler; or, Waterside Companion. London: 1833. V. 39; 40; 44

The Jolly Angler, or Water Side Companion . . . London: 1842. V. 41

The Jolly Angler; or, Waterside Companion. London: 1850. V. 40

The Jolly Angler; or, Waterside Companion. London: 1883. V. 40

MARCH, JOHN 1612-1657

Reports: or, New Cases with Divers Resolutions and Judgements Given Upon Solemn Arguments, and with Great Deliberation. London: 1648. V. 38; 40

MARCH, JOSEPH M.

The Set Up. New York: 1928. V. 39; 43; 46

MARCH PHILLIPS, L. F.

Mill and Hamilton. The Battle of Two Philosophers. London: 1866. V. 38

MARCH, RANDOLPH BARNES 1812-1887

Explorations of the Red River of Louisiana, in the Years 1852 . . . Washington: 1853. V. 38

MARCH, T. C.

Flower and Fruit Decoration. London: 1862. V. 37; 38; 39

MARCH, WILLIAM

Company K. New York: 1933. V. 46

The Little Wife. New York: 1935. V. 38; 40; 42

MARCHAND, ETIENNE

Voyage Autour du Monde, Pendant les Annees 1790, 1791 et 1792, Precede d'une Introduction Historique . . . Paris: 1798. V. 38

MARCHAND, LESLIE A.

Byron: a Biography. New York: 1957. V. 38

MARCHANT,

Observations on Mr. Fielding's Plan for a Preservatory and Reformatory. London: 1758. V. 39

MARCHANT, JOHN

Lusus Juveniles: or, Youth's Recreation. London: 1753. V. 37; 39

A New Complete English Dictionary, Peculiarly Adapted to the Instruction and Improvement of Those Who Have Not Had the Benefit of a Learned or Liberal Education . . . London: 1760. V. 41

MARCHANT, MR.

Observations on Mr. Fielding's Plan for a Preservatory and Reformatory. London: 1758. V. 37

MARCHESINUS, JOHANNES

Mammotrectus Super Bibliam. Venice: 1479. V. 37

Mamotrectus Super Bibliam. Venice: 1506. V. 39

MARCHINI, G.

Italian Stained Glass Windows. London: 1957. V. 41

marchini, giuseppe

Italian Stained Glass Windows. New York: 1956. V. 42

MARCHIS, L.

L'Epopee Aerienne. Paris: 1910. V. 42

MARCHMONT

A Selection from the Papers of the Earls of Marchmont, in the Possession of the Right Honble. Sir George Henry Rose, Illustrative of Events from 1685 to 1750. London: 1831. V. 37

MARCHMONT, HUGH HUME, EARL OF

The Present Interest of the People of Great Britain, at Home and Abroad, Consider'd: In a Letter to a Member of Parliament. London: 1758? V. 41

A Serious Exhortation to the Electors of Great Britain; Wherein the Importance of the Approaching Elections is Particularly Proved from the Present Situation Both at Home and Abroad. London: 1740. V. 41

A State of the Rise and Progress of Our Disputes With Spain, and Of the Conduct of Our Ministers Relating Thereto. London: 1739. V. 41; 45

MARCI, JOANNES MARCUS THAUMANTIAS

Liber de Arcu Coelesti Deque Colorum Apparentium Narura, Ortu, et Causis. Pragae: 1648. V. 40

MARCON, F.

Wonderful Balloon Ascents; or, the Conquest of the Skies. London: 1870. V. 41

MARCOT, R.

Spencer Repeating Firearms. Irvine: 1983. V. 38

MARCOU, JULES

Report on Geology and Topography of California. (with) Agricultural Resources and Mineral Productions . . . (with) Le Terrain Carbonifere . . . Washington & Sacramento: 1850. V. 43

MARCOY, PAUL

A Journey Across South America, from the Pacific Ocean to the Atlantic Ocean. London: 1874. V. 43

Travels in South America from the Pacific Ocean to the Atlantic Ocean. New York: 1875. V. 38; 39; 46

MARCUELLO, FRANCISCO

Primera Parte de la Historia Natural y Moral de la Aves. Saragossa: 1617. V. 43

MARCUS, JACOB ERNST

Studie Beelden en Fragmenten . . . Amsterdam: 1807-14. V. 39

MARCUS, STANLEY

The Book Club of Texas. Dallas: 1989. V. 41; 46

MARCY, HENRY

The Anatomy and Surgical Treatment of hernia. New York: 1892. V. 42

MARCY, RANDOLPH BARNES 1812-1887

Border Reminiscences. New York: 1872. V. 39; 42

Exploration of the Red River of Louisiana, in the Year 1852. Washington: 1853. V. 37; 39; 41; 42; 43; 46

Exploration of the Red River of Louisiana, In the Year 1852. Washington: 1854. V. 38; 39; 40; 41; 42

Explorations of the Big Wichita and Headwaters of the Brazos Rivers. Washington: 1856. V. 41; 42

The Prairie Traveler. New York: 1859. V. 37; 38; 40; 41; 42; 43; 44; 45

The Prairie and Overland Traveller: a Companion for Emigrants, Traders, Travellers, Hunters and Soldiers Traversing the Great Plains. London: 1860. V. 38

The Prairie Traveler, A Hand-Book for Overland Expeditions. London: 1863. V. 41; 42; 45

Route from Fort Smith to Santa Fe. Washington: 1850. V. 40; 41

Thirty Years of Army Life on the Border. New York: 1866. V. 37; 38; 39; 40; 42; 43; 46

MARDEN, GEORGE N.

The Growth and Grip of Mormonism. Boston: 1885. V. 37; 39

MARDERSTEIG, GIOVANNI 1892-1977

The Alphabet of Francesco Torniello da Novara (1517). Verona: 1971. V. 39; 40; 42

The Alphabetum Romanum of Felice Feliciano da Verona. Verona: 1960. V. 39

Felice Feliciano Veronese, Alphabetum Romanum. Verona: 1960. V. 41

Giovanni Mardersteig on G. B. Bondoni's Type Faces. Verona: 1968. V. 40; 41

MARDERSTEIG, GIOVANNI 1892-1977 continued

The Making of a Book at the Officina Bodoni. Verona: 1973. V. 41; 42; 43; 45

The Officina Bodoni. Verona: 1980. V. 37; 38; 39; 41; 42; 43; 45; 46

The Officina Bodoni: an Account of the Work of a Hand Press . . . 1981. V. 45

The Officina Bodoni. An Account of the Work of a Hand Press 1923-77. Edited and translated by H. Schmoller. Verona: (1980). V. 37

On G. B. Bodoni's Type Faces. Verona: 1968. V. 41; 42; 45

MARDERSTEIG, HANS

Officina Bodoni. Verona: 1929. V. 45

MARDIE, MARTIN

Water-Colour Painting in Britain. London: 1869. V. 41

MARDIKIAN, GEORGE

Dinner at Omar Khayyam's. New York: 1944. V. 44

MARDON, EDWARD RUSSELL

Billiards: Game, 500 Up. Played at Brighton on the 18th of January, 1844. An Account of the Above Game. Brighton: 1844. V. 38

MARDRUS, J. C.

Le Livre de la Verite de Parole. Paris: 1929. V. 44

Ruth et Booz. Paris: 1930. V. 41

MARES, CARL

The History of the Typewriter. London: 1909. V. 42; 44

MAREY, E. J.

Animal Mechanism: a Treatise on Terrestrial and Aerial Locomotion. London: 1874. V. 37; 40

MARGAM Abbey, an Historical Romance of the Fourteenth Century. London: 1837. V. 42

MARGARET Mitchell and Her Novel 'Gone With the Wind.' New York: 1936. V. 39; 44; 45

MARGARITA DAVITICA

Margarita Davitica, seu Expositio Psalmorum. Augsburg: 1475-76. V. 45

MARGARY, AUGUSTUS RAYMOND

The Journey of Augustus Raymond Margary, from Shanghae to Bhamo . . . London: 1876. V. 43

MARGARY, IVAN D.

Roman Roads in Britain. London: 1955-57. V. 42

THE MARGATE Guide. London: 1770. V. 38

MARGESON, CHARLES

Experiences of Gold Hunters in Alaska. N.P.: 1899. V. 37; 38

MARGOLIOUTH, D. S.

Cairo, Jerusalem and Damascus. London: 1907. V. 44

A Commentary on the Book of Daniel . . . Oxford: 1889. V. 44

MARGOLIOUTH, G.

Catalogue of the Hebrew and Smaritan Manuscripts in the British Museum. London: 1905. V. 46

MARGOLIOUTH, J. P.

Supplement to the Thesaurus Syriacus of R. Payne Smith . . . Collected and Arranged by His Daughter. Oxford: 1927. V. 38

MARGRY, PIERRE

Decouvertes et Etablissements des Francais dans l'Ouest et Dans Sud l'Amerique Septentrionale. Paris: 1876-86. V. 38; 42; 43; 44; 46

Les Navigations Francaises et la Revolution Maritime du XIVe au XVIe Siecle. Paris: 1867. V. 39

MARGUERITE D'ANGOULEME, QUEEN OF NAVARRE 1492-1549

Contes et Nouvelles . . . Amsterdam: 1698. V. 40

The Fortunate Lovers. Twenty-Seven Novels of the Queen of Navarre. London: 1887. V. 38

Heptameron Francois. Les Nouvelles de Marguerite, Reine de Navarre. Berne: 1792. V. 40

The Heptameron. London: 1894. V. 43

The Heptameron . . . London: 1894. V. 43; 46

The Heptameron . . . London: 1904. V. 45

The Heptameron - or, Tales and Novels of Marguerite, Queen of Navarre. 1905. V. 39; 43

The Heptameron of the Tales of Margaret, Queen of Navarre. London: 1922. V. 43

MARGUERITE DE VALOIS 1553-1615

Les Memoires de la Roine Marguerite. Paris: 1628. V. 43

The Memorialls of Margaret de Valoys, First Wife to Henry the Fourth, King of France and Navarre. London: 1641. V. 37

MARIA, CONSORT OF FERDINAND I, KING OF RUMANIA

The Lily of Life. A Fairy Tale. London: 1915. V. 40

MARIA DE AGREDA 1602-1665

Mystica Ciudad de Dios, Milagros su Omnipotencia y Abismo de la Gracia. Lisboa: 1681. V. 38

MARIA THERESA, QUEEN OF HUNGARY

Memoirs of the Queen of Hungary. London: 1741. V. 41

The Queen of Hungary's Manifesto; Being a Full Answer to the French Declaration of War . . . London: 1744. V. 41

The Queen of Hungary's Reply to the Manifesto, Which Count Dohna, Minister from the King of Prussia, Read at the Court of Vienna. Vienna: 1744. V. 41

MARIA to Henric, and Henric to Maria; or, the Queen to the King in Holland, and His Majesty's Answer . . . London: 1691. V. 41; 45

MARIA, VICENZO

Il viaggio All'Indie Orientali . . . Con le Osservationi, e Successi nel Medesimo, i Costumi, Kiti di Varie Nationi . . . Venice: 1678. V. 45

MARIACHER, GIOVANNE

Italian Blown Glass from Ancient Rome to Venice. New York: 1961. V. 38; 42

MARIAN

An Old Manuscript: A Story by Marian. Written at the Request of the Little Ones. To whom it is Dedicated. (N.P.: c. 1870?). V. 37

MARIANA, JUAN DE

The General History of Spain, from the First Peopling of It by Tubal, Till the Death of King Ferdinand . . . London: 1699. V. 41

Historiae de Rebus Hispaniae Libri XXX. Moguntiae: i.e. Mainz,: 1605. V. 40

De Ponderibus et mensuris. Toledo: 1599. V. 45; 46

MARIANI, GIOVANNI c. 1535

Tariffa Perpetua con le Ragion fatte per Scontro di Qualunque Mercandante si Voglia. Venetia: 1559. V. 38

MARIANI, PAUL

Timing Devices: Poems. Easthampton: 1977. V. 40; 45

Timing Devices: Peoms. By Paul Mariani. With wood engravings by Barry Moser. Easthampton, Mass.: 1977. V. 37

MARIANI, VALERIO

Michelangelo the Painter. New York: 1973. V. 41

MARIANUS DE ORSCELAR, F.

Gloriosus Franciscus Redivivus Sive Chronica Observantiae Strictioris, Reparatae, Reductae, ac Reformatae . . . Ingolstadt: 1625. V. 39

MARIE, PIERRE

Lectures on Diseases of the Spinal Cord. London: 1895. V. 42

MARIE, QUEEN OF ROUMANIA

The Dreamer of Dreams. London: (1915). V. 37

The Lost Princess. London: 1924. V. 42

Peeping Pansy. London. V. 42

The Story of Naughty Kildeen. London. V. 45

The Story of Naughty Kildeen. Oxford: 1922. V. 41

MARIET, ETHEL M.

A Book of Vegetable Dyes. A.D. 1917. Ditchling: 1917. V. 44

MARIETTE, AUGUSTE

Voyage dans la Haute-Egypte d'Apres les Monuments Antiques Entre le Caire et la Premiere Cataracte. Paris & Leipzig: 1893. V. 40; 42

MARIETTE, PIERRE JEAN

Description des Travaux qui ont Precede et Accompagne et Suivi la fonte en Bronze d'un Seul jet de la Statue Equestre de Louis XV, le Bien Aime. Paris: 1768. V. 38; 42

Recueil des Plans, Elevations, Profiles et Decorations de l'Architecture Francaise a Paris. Parais: 1727 onwards. V. 38

Traite des Pierres Gravees . . . Paris: 1750. V. 41; 42; 46

MARIGNY, CHEVALIER TAITBOUT DE

Three Voyages in the Black Sea to the Coast of Circassia. London: 1837. V. 39; 45

MARILLIER, H. C.

The Early Work of Aubrey Beardsley. The Later Work of Aubrey Beardsley. London: 1912, 1920. V. 40

The Early Work of Aubrey Beardsley. The Later Work of Aubrey Beardsley. London: 1912/20. V. 43

MARILLIER, HENRY CURRIE

A Brief Sketch of the Morris Movement and of the Firm Founded by William Morris . . . London: 1911. V. 41

MARIN, JOHN

Drawings and Watercolors. New York: 1950. V. 37; 38

John Marin. Watercolors, Oil Paintings, Etchings. New York: 1936. V. 42

MARIN, SAMUEL

A Plan for Establishing and Disciplining a National Militia in Great Britain, Ireland and In All the British Dominions in America. London: 1745. V. 41

MARINARO, V. C.

A Modern Dry Fly Code. New York: 1976. V. 37

MARINATOS, SPYRIDON

Crete and Mycenae. New York. V. 38; 42

Crete and Mycenae. New York: 1960. V. 40; 41; 42

Crete and Myceane. New York: (1960). V. 37

Excavations at Thera. Athens: 1968-76. V. 40

MARINDIN, A. H.

The Salamanca Campaign. London: 1906. V. 42

MARINE BIOLOGICAL ASSOCIATION OF THE UNITED KINGDOM

Journal, First Series. New Series. London: 1887-1974. V. 38

MARINE SOCIETY, LONDON.

The Bye-Laws and Regulations of the Marine Society, Incorporated in MDCCLXXII. London: 1792. V. 42

The Bye-Laws and Regulations of the Marine Society . . . London: 1792. V. 39

The Bye-Laws and Regulations of the Marine Society . . . London: 1809. V. 41; 42; 46

The Bye-Laws and Regulations of the Marine Society . . . London: 1820. V. 42

MARINELLI, GIOVANNI

Le Medicine Partenenti Alle Infermita Delle Donne . . . Venice: 1574. V. 38

MARINEO SICULO, LUCIO

Opus de Rebus Hispaniae Memorabilibus. Alcala: 1533. V. 41; 42

MARINER, WILLIAM

An Account of the Natives of the Tonga Islands, in the South Pacific Ocean . . . London: 1818. V. 41

An Account of the Natives of the Tonga Islands, in the South Pacific Ocean. Boston: 1820. V. 41; 42

THE MARINER'S Chronicle. New Haven: 1836. V. 41; 42; 45

THE MARINER'S Chronicle: Containing Narratives of the Most Remarkable Disasters at Sea . . . New Haven: 1834. V. 45

MARINETTI, F. L.

Les Mots en Liberte Futuristes. Milan: 1919. V. 38

MARINI, MARINO

Idea a Spazio. Paris: 1963. V. 38

MARINIS, GIROLAMO

Genva, Sive Dominii, Gvbernationis, Potentiae, Dignitatis, Sereniss. Genoa: 1666. V. 40

MARINO, GIAMBATT

Dicierie Sacre . . . In quest'ultima Impressione Ricorette . . . Venetia: 1626. V. 37

MARINO, GIAMBATTISTA 1569-1625

La Sampogna . . . Divisa in Idilly, Favolosi, et Pastorali. Paris: 1620. V. 43

MARINOFF, ELAINE

Windows. Los Angeles: 1988. V. 42

MARINONI, GIOVANNI JACOPO DE

De Astronomica Specula Domestica et Organico Apparatu Astronomico Libri Duo Reginae Dicati . . . Vienna: 1745. V. 44

MARION

Mummy's Bedtime Story Book. London: 1929. V. 42

MARION-DUMERSAN, THEOPHILE

Guide des Curieux et des Etrangers dans les Bibliotheques Publiques de Paris . . . Paris: 1818. V. 38

MARION, F.

The Wonders of Optics. London: 1868. V. 38; 39

MARIOTTE, EDME

The Motion of Water, and Other Fluids. London: 1718. V. 37; 38

MARIS, M.

Souvenirs d'Amerique. Relations d'un Voyage au Texas et en Haiti. Brussels: 1863. V. 38

MARIS, ROGER

Slugger in Right. Larchmont: 1963. V. 46

MARITAIN, RAISSA

Patriarch Tree. Thirty Poems. 1965. V. 38

Patriarch Tree. Worcester: 1965. V. 37; 38; 39; 40; 41; 45; 46

THE MARITIME Campaign of 1778. A Collection of all the Papers Relative to the Operations of the English and French Fleets. London: 1778. V. 39

MARIUS, C. F. P.

Icones Selectae Plantarum Cryptogamicarum quas in Itinere per Brasiliam Annis 1817-20. Munich: 1828-34. V. 41

MARIUS, JOANNES BOLLENSIS J. F.

Castorologia Explicans Castoris Animalis Naturam & Usum Medico-Chemicum Antidhac a Joanne Mario Bollensi & Physico Ulmano Postea Celeberrimo Labori Insolito Subjects. Augsburg: 1685. V. 39

MARIUS, SIMON 1570-1624

Mundus Jovialis anno MDCIX Detectus ope Perspicilii Belgici. Nurnberg: 1614. V. 46

MARIZ CARNEIRO, ANTONIO DE

Roteiro da India Oriental. Com as Emmendas Que Nouamente se Fizerao a elle. Lisbon: 1666. V. 41

MARJORIBANKS, ALEXANDER

Travels in New Zealand. London: 1846. V. 41

Travels in New South Wales. London: 1847. V. 46

Travels in New South Wales. London & Edinburgh: 1847. V. 39

MARJORIBANKS, J.

Trifles in Verse. Kelson: 1784. V. 41

MARK, AMY

The Sea King's Daughter. Birmingham: 1895. V. 37; 42

MARK, DON

Seven Persian Fables. Columbus: 1983. V. 42

MARK, ENID

An Afternoon at Les Collettes. Wallingford: 1988. V. 43

MARK, JOHN

Genealogy of the Family of Mark or Marke, Cumberland; Pedigree and Arms of the Bowscale Branch of the Family. Manchester: 1898. V. 39

MARK THE ANCHORITE

Marci Eremitae, Nicolae, Hesychii Presbyteri Opera Quae Extant. Paris: 1563. V. 39

MARKEVITCH, MARIE ALEXANDRE

The Epicure in Imperial Russia. San Francisco: 1941. V. 42

MARKEY, JOSEPH I.

From Iowa to the Philippines A History of Company M. Fifty-First Iowa Infantry Volunteers. Red Oak: 1900. V. 43

MARKHAM, A. H.

A Polar Reconnaissance, Being the Voyage of the 'Isbjorn' to Novaya Zemlya. London: 1881. V. 43

MARKHAM, ALBERT HASTINGS

The Great Frozen Sea. London: 1878. V. 42; 46

A Whaling Cruise to Baffin's Bay and the Gulf of Boothia. London: 1875. V. 37; 41; 44

MARKHAM, C. A.

The History of the Northamptonshire and Rutland Militia . . . London: 1924. V. 38

MARKHAM, CLEMENTS ROBERT 1830-1916

A History of the Abyssinian Expedition. London: 1869. V. 38

The Lands of Silence. Cambridge: 1921. V. 44

A Memoir of the Lady Ana de Osorio, Countess of Chinchon and Vice-Queen of Peru . . . London: 1874. V. 44

Narratives of the Mission of George Bogle to Tibet and of the Journey of Thomas Manning to Lhasa. London: 1876. V. 39

The Threshold of the Unknown Region. London: 1873. V. 38; 45

The Threshold of the Unknown Region. London: 1876. V. 43

MARKHAM, CLEMENTS ROBERT 1830-1916 continued

Travels in Peru and India While Superintending the Collection of Chincona Plants and Seeds In South America. London: 1862. V. 38

The Voyages of William Baffin, 1612-1622. London: 1881. V. 45

MARKHAM, CLEMENTS ROBERTS 1830-1916

Cuzco: a Journal to the Ancient Capital of Peru . . . London: 1856. V. 42

Life of Sir Leopold McClintock. London: 1909. V. 38

MARKHAM, EDWIN

Lincoln and Other Poems. New York: 1908. V. 39; 43

The Man with the Hoe and Other Poems. New York: 1899. V. 38; 39; 40; 42

The Man with the Hoe. San Francisco: 1899. V. 39

The Man With the Hoe. San Francisco: 1899. V. 37; 38; 39; 40; 42; 43; 46

The Man with the Hoe and Other Poems. New York: 1900. V. 40; 42

The Man with the Hoe. New York: 1900. V. 42

The Man With the Hoe. San Francisco: 1916. V. 42

The Younger Choir. New York: 1910. V. 39

MARKHAM, FRANCIS

Five Decades of Epistles of Warre. London: 1622. V. 46

MARKHAM, FRED

Shooting in the Himalayas. London: 1854. V. 41; 44

MARKHAM, GERVASE

Cheape and Good Husbandry for the Well-Ordering of All Beastes and Fowles, and for the Generall Cure of Their Diseases. London: 1631. V. 45

Cheape and Good Husbandry, for the Well-Ordering of all Beasts and Fowles . . . Cattell, Horse, Oxe, Cos, Sheepe, Goats, Swine and Tame Conies. London: 1653. V. 37

The Citizen & Countryman's Experienced Farrier . . . Baltimore: 1803. V. 37

Countrey Contentments, or, The English Huswife . . . London: 1623. V. 37

Country Contentments; or, the Husbandmans Recreations. London: 1633. V. 43

Country Contentments; or the husbandmans Recreation. . . . . Hunting, Hawking, Coursing, Laws of the Lease, Shooting in the Long bow, Cross Bow. London: 1664. V. 37; 39

The English House-Wife. London: 1631. V. 40; 45

The English House-Wife . . . London: 1683. V. 39; 40

The English Husbandman. (with) The Second Booke of the English Husbandman. London: 1613-15. V. 37

The Inrichment of the Weald of Kent . . . London: 1636. V. 41; 44; 45

The Inrichment of the Weald of Kent . . . London: 1675. V. 39; 44

The Inrichment of the Weald of Kent. London: 1683. V. 41; 42

Markham's Maister-Peece, Containing all Knowledge Belonging to Smith, Farrier, or Horse-Leech Touching the Curing of all Diseases in Horses . . . London: 1631. V. 41

Markham's Farewell to Husbandry. London: 1638. V. 39; 44

Markhams Farewell to Husbandry. London: 1656. V. 39; 40

Markham's Farewel to Husbandry. London: 1668. V. 39; 41

Markham's Masterpiece . . . London: 1717. V. 43

Markham's Master-Piece, Containing All Knowledge Belonging to the Smith, Farrier, or Horse-Leach . . . London: 1734. V. 38

Markham's Farewell to Husbandry . . . London: 1631. V. 37

The Pleasures of Princes or Good Mens Recreations. London: 1927. V. 41; 46

A Way to Get Wealth . . . London: 1631. V. 43

A Way to Get Wealth. London: 1638. V. 37

MARKHAM, H. H.

Resources of California. Sacramento: 1893. V. 37; 46

MARKHAM, MRS.

New Children's Friend, Consisting of Tales and Conversations. London: 1832. V. 42

MARKHAM, WILLIAM

A General Introduction to Trade and Business. London: 1738. V. 41

An Introduction to Spelling and Reading English: Being the Most Plain and Easy Method of Teaching Young Children to Read.. Derby: 1824. V. 44

MARKLAND, ABRAHAM 1645-1728

Pteryplegia; or, The Art of Shotting-Flying. 1727. V. 43

Pteryplegia; or, the Art of Shooting-Flying. London: 1735. V. 40; 42; 43

Pteryplegia; or, the Art of Shotting-Flying. London: 1767. V. 40

MARKLAND, GEORGE

Pteryplegia; or, The Art of Shooting-Flying. London. V. 45

Pteryplegia; or, the Art of Shooting-Flying. London: 1727. V. 40; 45

Pteryplegia: The Art of Shooting-Flying. New York: 1931. V. 37

MARKLAND, J.

Typographia, an Ode on Printing. Roanoke: 1926. V. 41

MARKLOVE, H.

Views of Berkeley Castle. Taken on the Spot, and Drawn on Stone . . . London: 1840. V. 41

Views of Berkeley Castle. London: 1840. V. 41; 43

MARKOE, PETER

The Algerine Spy in Pennsylvania; or Letters Written by a Native of Algiers on the Affairs of the United States of America . . . Philadelphia: 1787. V. 43

MARKS, A. A.

A Treatise on Artifical Limbs with Rubber Hands and Feet. New York: 1903. V. 39

MARKS, DAVID

The Life of David Marks, to the 26th Year of His Age. Limerick: 1831. V. 43; 46

Memoirs of the Life of David Marks, Minister of the Gospel. Dover: 1846. V. 39; 42; 43; 46

Memoirs of the Life of David Marks, Minister of the Gospel. Dover: 1846. V. 43

Memoirs of the Life of David Marks, Minister of the Gospel . . . Dover: 1846. V. 42

MARKS, H. M.

Pastoral or Virtue Requited. London: 1935. V. 38

MARKS, HAWYARD

Proofs of Some Early Nineteenth-Century Woodblocks for Tea and Tobacco Papers . . . Kensington: 1948. V. 45

MARKS, HENRY STACY

Pen and Pencil Sketches. London: 1894. V. 39

MARKS, JOHN GEORGE

Life and Letters of Frederick Walker, A.R.A. London: 1896. V. 39

MARKS, LILLIAN

Saul Marks and the Plantin Press: the Life and Work of a Singular Man. Los Angeles: 1980. V. 37; 40; 42

MARKS, MARY A. M. HOPPUS

Dr. Willoughby Smith. London: 1892. V. 41

MARLBOROUGH, GEORGE SPENCER, 4TH DUKE OF 1739-1817

Gemmarum Antiquarum Delectus, ex Praestantioribus Desumptus, Quae in Dactyliothecis Ducis Marlburiensis Conservantur . . . London: 1845. V. 40

MARLBOROUGH, JOHN CHURCHILL, DUKE OF

The Case of His Grace the D--- of M----------. As design'd to be Represented by Him to the . . . House of Commons, in Vindication of Himself from the Charge of the Commissioners of Accounts. London: 1712. V. 38

MARLBOROUGH, SARAH CHURCHILL, DUCHESS OF

An Account of the Conduct of the Dowager Duchess of Marlborough, from Her First Coming to Court, to the Year 1710. London: 1742. V. 41

Private Correspondence. London: 1838. V. 41

MARLBOROUGH, SARAH JENNINGS CHURCHILL, DUCHESS OF 1660-1744

Private Correspondence, Illustrative of the Court and Times of Queen Anne, With Her Sketches and Opinions of Her Contemporaries . . . London: 1838. V. 41; 42

MARLEN, G.

Earl Browder - Communist or Tool of Wall Street or Stalin, Trotsky or Lenin. 1937. V. 46

MARLETTE, S. H.

Report of the Surveyor-General of Nevada for 1865. Carson City: 1865. V. 37

Report on the Surveyor-General of Nevada for 1866. Carson City: 1867. V. 37

MARLIANI, B.

Urbis Romae Topographia. Rome: 1544. V. 37

MARLIANI, GIOVANNI BARTOLOMEO

Topographia Antiqvae Romae. Lyons: 1534. V. 42

MARLIANUS, JOANNES BARTHOLOMAEUS

Urbis Romae Topographia Accurate, Tum ex Veterum . . . Venice: 1588. V. 41

MARLIN, T. J.

Sketches by a Color Sergeant. Tarkio: 1904? V. 44; 45

MARLOTH, R.

The Flora of South Africa. London: 1913-32. V. 38; 42

The Flora of South Africa. Volume 3. London: 1932. V. 38

MARLOW, JEREMIAH

A Book of Cyphers or Letters Reverst. London: 1683. V. 46

MARLOW, LOUIS

The Puppets' Dallying. London: 1905. V. 42

MARLOWE, CHRISTOPHER 1564-1593

Doctor Faustus. London: 1903. V. 40; 42; 43

Edward the Second. Kensington: 1929. V. 42; 46

Edward the Second. London: 1929. V. 38; 43

The Famous Tragedy of the Rich Jew of Malta. 1933. V. 46

The Famous Tragedy of the Rich Jew of Malta. London: 1933. V. 37; 42

Four Plays. (Tamburlaine the Great, Parts I & II. The Tragical History of Dr. Faustus. The Troublesome Reign of Edward the Second.) New York: 1966. V. 37; 38

Hero and Leander. Edinburgh: 1909. V. 46

The Life and Death of Tamburlaine the Great. London: 1930. V. 44

The Tragicall History of Doctor Faustus. London: 1932. V. 37; 41; 42; 46

The Works. London: 1826. V. 40; 44; 46

The Works of Christopher Marlowe. London: 1826. V. 45

The Works. London: 1850. V. 45

The Works. London: 1885. V. 40; 46

The Works and Life. London: 1930-33. V. 38; 40

The Works and Life of Christopher Marlowe. New York: London: 1930/33. V. 46

The Complete Works. Cambridge: 1973. V. 42

MARMADUKE, M. M.

Journal of M. M. Marmaduke of a Trip from Franklin, Missouri to Santa Fe, New Mexico in 1824. Columbia: 1911. V. 37

MARMADUKE'S Multiply's Merry Method of Making Minor Mathematicians. London: 1832. V. 39

MARMELSZADT, WILLARD

Musical Sons of Aesculapius. New York: 1946. V. 38; 40; 41; 42; 43; 45

MARMET, MELCHIOR DE

Entertainments of the Cours; or, Academical Conversations. London: 1658. V. 40; 42; 43

MARMIER, XAVIER

Voyage En Suisse. Paris: 1862. V. 38

MARMION, ANTHONY

The Ancient and Modern History of the Maritime Ports of Ireland. London: 1858. V. 43

MARMION, SHACKERLEY

The Dramatic Works. Edinburgh & London: 1875. V. 46

The Dramatic Works . . . London: 1875. V. 41

MARMION, SHAKERLEY

The Antiqury. London: 1641. V. 45

A Fine Companion. London: 1633. V. 37; 43

MARMONT, MARSHAL

The Present State of the Turkish Empire. London: 1839. V. 37

MARMONTEL, JEAN FRANCOIS 1723-1799

Belisaire. Paris: 1767. V. 38

Belisarius. London: 1767. V. 40

Belisarius. Brussels: 1792. V. 40

Belisarius. London: 1800? V. 40

Belisarius. To which are Added Fragments of Moral Philosophy. Harding: 1794. V. 37

Chefs-d'Oeuvre Dramatique, ou Recueil des Meilleures Pieces du Theatre Francois . . . Paris: 1773. V. 39

The Incas; or, the Destruction of the Empire of Peru. London: 1777. V. 39; 40; 45

The Incas; or the Destruction of the Empire of Peru. Alston, Cumberland: 1808. V. 40

Moral Tales. London: 1766. V. 43

Oeuvres Complettes De . . . A Liege: 1777. V. 43

MARMORA, ANDREA

Della Historia di Corfu. Venice: 1672. V. 37; 39

MARMORA Arundelliana; Sive Saxa Graece Incisa. London: 1629. V. 37

MARMORA RAILROAD

Chairman's Remarks and Engineer's Report. Belleville: 1858. V. 45

MAROLLES, LEWIS DE

An Essay on Providence. London: 1790. V. 44

MAROLOIS, SAMUEL

The Art of Fortification, or Architecture Militaire, as Well Offensive as Defensive . . . Amsterdam: 1638. V. 38

Opera Mathematica ou Oeuvres Mathematiques Traictans de Geometrie, Perspective, Architecture et Fortification. Amsteram: 1662. V. 40

MAROT, JEAN

L'Architecture Francaise, ou Recueil de Plans, Elevations, Coupes et Profiles des eglises, Palais, Hotels et Maisons de Campagne ou de Plaisance des Environs et de Plusieurs Autres Endroits de France. Paris. V. 38

Le Magnifique Chasteau de Richelieu, en General et en Particulier . . . Paris: 1660. V. 38

Recueil des plus Beaux Edifices et Frontispices des Eglizes de Paris . . . Paris: 1650. V. 44

Recueil des Plans, Profils et Elevations de Plusiers Palais, Chasteaux, Eglises, Sepultures, Grottes et Hostels Batis dans Paris et aux Environs . . . Paris: 1738. V. 38; 42

MAROTH, R.

The Flora of South Africa. London: 1913-32. V. 37

MAROZZO, ACHILLE

Arte dell'Armi di Achille Marozzo Bolognese Ricorretto, et Ornato di Nuoue Figure in Rame. Venetia: 1568. V. 40

MARPERGER, PAUL JACOB

Beschreibung der Banquen. Leipzig: 1717. V. 39

Das Neu-Eroffnete Manufacturen-Hauss. Hamburg: 1707. V. 38

Neu-Eroffnetes Handels-Bericht oder Wohlbestelltes Commercien-Collegium . . . Hamburg: 1709. V. 40; 41

MARPERGER, PAUL JAKOB

Curieuses und Reales Natur-, Kunst-, Berg-, Gewerckund Handlungs - Lexicon. Leipzig: 1731. V. 41

MARPURG, FRIEDRICH WILHELM

Anleitung zum Clavierspielen, der Schoenen Ausuebung der Heutigen Zeit Gemaess Entworfen. Berlin: 1755. V. 40

Handbuch Bey Dem Generalbasse Und Der Composition mit Zwey Drey Vier Fuenf Sechs Sieben Acht und Mehreren Stimmen. Berlin: 1755/77/58. V. 40

MARQUAND, ALLAN

Andrea Della Robbia and His Atelier. Princeton: 1922. V. 42

MARQUAND, ERNEST DAVID

Flora of Guernsey and the Lesser Channel Islands . . . London: 1901. V. 39

MARQUAND, JOHN

Sincerely, Willis Wayde. Boston: 1955. V. 41

MARQUAND, JOHN P.

Mr. Motto is So Sorry. New York: 1938. V. 45

No Hero. Boston: 1935. V. 43

Point of No Return. Boston: 1949. V. 40

Sincerely Willis Wayde. Boston: 1955. V. 39

MARQUAND, JOHN PHILLIPS

Do Tell Me, Doctor Johnson. Cleveland: 1928. V. 37; 44

MARQUARDT VON FIRSCH, VALENTIN

Des Westindischen Kleinen Albertus, Eines Pennsylvaniers Aus Philadelphia und der Schoenen Europaeischen Adolpha von Tanoy auf der Insel Martinque Merkwuerdige Reise Geschichte. Frankfurt/Leipzig: 1757. V. 40; 41

MARQUES PEREIRA, NUNO

Compendio Narrativo do Peregrino da America em que se Tratam Varios Discursos Espirituaes . . . Lisboa Occidental: 1731. V. 45

Compendio Narrativo do Peregrino da America, em Que se Tratam Various Discursos Espiritues, e Moraes, com Muitas Advertencias . . . Lisbon: 1760. V. 41

MARQUIS, DON

Archy's Life of Mehitabel. Garden City: 1933. V. 41; 42

Carter. New York: 1921. V. 39

Chapters for the Orthodox. Garden City: 1934. V. 37

Danny's Own Story. Garden City: 1912. V. 41; 42

Noah an' Jonah an' Cap'n John Smith. New York: 1921. V. 45

The Old Soak's History of the World. Garden City: 1924. V. 39

Poems and Portraits. Garden City: 1922. V. 39

Sonnets to a Red-Haired Lady. Garden City: 1922. V. 39

MARQUIS of Carabas; or New Puss in Boots. London: 1850. V. 39

MARQUIS, T. G.

Canada's Sons on Kopje and Veldt; a Historical Account of the Canadian Contingents. N.P.: 1900. V. 40

MARRA, JOHN

Journal of the Resolution's Voyage in 1772, 1773, 1774 and 1775. On Discovery to the Southern Hemisphere . . . London: 1775. V. 42

MARRANT, JOHN

A Narrative of the Life of . . . , of New York, in North America: Giving an Account of his Conversion when only Fourteen Years of Age . . . being . . . taken by an Indian Hunter among the Cherokees, where he was condemned to die. With an Account . . . Leeds: 1810. V. 37

MARRIAGE Asserted: in Answer to a Book Entituled Conjugium Conjurgium; or, Some Serious Considerations on Marriage . . . . London: 1674. V. 43

MARRIAGE Costumes of Various Nations. London: 1820's. V. 45

THE MARRIAGE of the Coquet and the Alwine. Newcastle-upon-Tyne: 1817. V. 37

MARRIOTT, ALICE

Maria: The Potter of San Ildefonso. Norman: 1948. V. 39

MARRIOTT, CHARLES

The Cooperative Principle Not Opposed to a True Political Economy, or Remarks on Some Recent Publications on Subjects Relative to the Intercommunion of Labour, Capital and Consumption. Oxford: 1855. V. 38; 45

Laura Knight - A Book of Drawings. London: 1923. V. 38

MARRIOTT, ERNEST

Jack B. Yeats Being a True Impartial View of His Pictorial and Dramatic Art . . . London: 1911. V. 39

MARRIOTT, JAMES

Memoire Justicatif de la Conduite de la Grande Bretagne, en Arretant les Navires Etrangers et les Munitions de Guerre destinees aux Insurgens de l'Amerique. Londres: 1779. V. 38

Poems Written Chiefly at the University of Cambridge; together With a Latin Oration Upon the History and Genius of the Roman and Canon Laws . . . London: 1760. V. 41

Poems Written Chiefly at the University of Cambridge; Together with a Latin Oration Upon the History and Genius of the Roman and Canon Laws. N.P.: 1760. V. 42

Poems Written Chiefly at the University of Cambridge . . . N.P.: London: 1760. V. 45

Poems written chiefly at the University of Cambridge; together with a Latin oration upon the history and genuis of the Roman and Canon laws . . . (London: 1706). V. 37

MARRIOTT, JOHN

A Short Account of John Marriott, Including Extracts from Some of His Letters. Doncaster: 1803. V. 40

MARRIOTT, THOMAS

Female Conduct. London: 1759. V. 40; 41; 43

MARRIOTT, W. F.

A Grammar of Political Economy. London: 1874. V. 42

MARRIOTT-WATSON, ROSAMUND

Vespertilia and Other Verses. London: 1895. V. 38

MARRIOTT, WILLIAM

The Country Gentleman's Lawyer; and the Farmer's Complete Law Library . . . London: 1797. V. 40

The Country Gentleman's Lawyer. London: 1802. V. 38

MARROT, H. V.

A Bibliography of the Works of John Galsworth. 1928. V. 37; 40

Bulmer and Bensley. London: 1930. V. 45

William Bulmer - Thomas Bensley, a Study in Transition. London: 1930. V. 37

MARRYAT, C. B.

A Diary in America with Remarks on Its Institutions. London: 1839. V. 37

MARRYAT, EMILIA

Henry Lyle, or Life and Existence. London: 1856. V. 39

MARRYAT, FLORENCE

Life and Letters of Captain Marryat. London: 1872. V. 42

MARRYAT, FRANK

Borneo and the Indian Archipelago. London: 1848. V. 39; 43

Mountains and Molehills or Reflections of a Burnt Journal. London: 1855. V. 37; 44; 46

Mountains and Molehills or Recollections of a Burnt Journal. New York: 1855. V. 38; 39; 46

MARRYAT, FREDERIC

The Phantom Ship. 1839. V. 44

MARRYAT, FREDERICK 1792-1848

The Children of the New Forest. London: 1847. V. 43

A Diary in America, with Remarks on Its Institutions. London: 1839. V. 38; 39; 42; 46

A Diary in America, with Remarks on Its Institutions. New York: 1839. V. 40

The Floral Telegraph. London: ?1850. V. 43

Jacob Faithful. London: 1834. V. 43

Japhet, in Search of a Father. London: 1836. V. 41; 43; 44

Joseph Rushbrook; or the Poacher. London: 1841. V. 37; 40; 41; 43; 44

The King's Own. London: 1830. V. 43

The Little Savage. London: 1848-49. V. 43

The Little Savage. London: 1849/49. V. 44

Masterman Ready or The Wreck of the Pacific. London: 1841/2. V. 39

Masterman Ready. London: 1841-42. V. 42

Masterman Ready, or the Wreck of the Pacific. London: 1841/42. V. 44

Midshipman Essay. London: 1836. V. 39

The Mission: or, Scenes in Africa. London: 1845. V. 43

Mr. Midshipman Easy; Poor Jack; Frank Mildmay; The King's Own; The Phantom Ship; Japhet; Jacob Faithful; The Pirate and the Three Cutters; Snarleyyow; Masterman Ready; Peter Simple; Newton Foster. London: 1895-1901. V. 44

Narratives of the Travels and Adventures of Monsieur Violet, in California, Sonora, and Western Texas. London: 1843. V. 42; 43

Newton Forster; or, The Merchant Serive. London: 1832. V. 41; 43

The Novels. London. V. 38; 42

The Novels. London: 1895. V. 42

The Novels. London: 1896-98. V. 38

Olla Podrida. London: 1840. V. 38; 43

The Pacha of Many Tales. London: 1835. V. 42; 43

Percival Keene. London: 1842. V. 38; 39; 43

Peter Simple. London: 1834. V. 38

Peter Simple. London: 1837. V. 43

The Pirate, and the Three Cutters. London: 1836. V. 37; 38; 39; 41; 42; 43

The Pirate, The Three Cutters and Moonshine, or tales of the Sea. New York: 1836. V. 46

Poor Jack. London: 1840. V. 38; 39; 41; 43; 45

Poor Jack. London: 1860. V. 44

The Privateer's Man One Hundred Years Ago. London: 1846. V. 42; 43

The Settlers in Canada. London: 1844. V. 43

Snarleyvow, or the Dog Fiend. London: 1837. V. 39; 43

Travels and Romantic Adventures of Monsieur Violet, Among the Snake Indians and Wild Tribes of the Great Western Prairies. London: 1843. V. 37; 38

The Travels and Adventures of Monsieur Violet in California, Sonora and Western Texas. London: 1884. V. 45

Valerie, an Autobiography. London: 1849. V. 43; 46

The Works. Boston: 1896. V. 39

MARRYAT, HORACE

One Year in Sweden; Including a Visit to the Isle of Gotland. London: 1862. V. 39

A Residence in Jutland, the Danish Isles and Copenhagen. London: 1860. V. 43

MARRYAT, JOSEPH

Collections Towards a History of Pottery and Porcelain in the 15th, 16th, 17th and 18th Centuries. London: 1850. V. 40

Joseph Rushbrook; or, the Poacher. London: 1842. V. 46

Observations on the Application of the West India Dock Company for a Renewal of Their Character. London: 1823. V. 37

Pottery & Porcelain, Collections Towards a History of in the 15th, 16th, 17th & 18th Centuries. London: 1850. V. 39; 43

The Substance of a Speech . . . In the House of Commons, on Thursday, July 25th, 1822, Upon Mr. Humes Motion for Appointing a Commission of Enquiry to Report on the Statae of the Island of Trinidad. London: 1823. V. 38

Thoughts on the Abolition of the Slave Trade, and Civilisation of Africa . . . London: 1816. V. 39

MARRYAT, R. N.

The Little Savage. London: 1848/49. V. 42

MARRYAT, SAMUEL FRANCIS

Mountains and Molehills, or, Recollections of a Burnt Journal. London: 1855. V. 39

MARRYOT, THOMAS

Sentimental Fables. Designed chiefly for the Use of the Ladies. London;: 1772. V. 37

MARS, AMAURY

Reminiscences of Santa Clara Valley and San Jose, with the Souvenir of the Carnival of Roses . . . San Francisco: 1901. V. 38

MARS, JAMES

Life of James Mars, a Slave Born and Sold in Connecticut. Hartford: 1866. V. 42; 44

MARSCHNER, H.

The Mineral Nutrition of Higher Plants. London: 1986. V. 37

MARSDEN, E. W.

Greek and Roman Artillery. Oxford: 1969-71. V. 37

MARSDEN, KATE

On Sledge and Horseback to Outcast Siberian Lepers. London: 1892. V. 46
On Sledge and Horseback to Outcast Siberian Lepers. London: 1893. V. 40

MARSDEN, PETER

An Account of the Island of Jamaica . . . Newcastle: 1788. V. 40; 46

MARSDEN, WILLIAM

The History of Sumatra. London: 1811. V. 39; 41; 44
The History of Sumatra, Containing an Account of the Government, Laws, Customs and Manners of the Native Inhabitants, with a Description of the Natural Productions, and a Relation of the Ancient Political State of the Island. London: 1784. V. 37

MARSH, ANDREW J.

Marsh's Manual of Reformed Phonetic Shorthand. San Francisco: 1868. V. 40

MARSH, ANNE

Emilia Wyndham. London: 1848. V. 40
Two Old Men's Tales. The Deformed and the Admiral's Daughter. London: 1834. V. 37; 44

MARSH, ANNE CALDWELL

Tales of the Woods and Fields. London: 1836. V. 44

MARSH, BARTON W.

The Uncompahgre Valley and the Gunnison Tunnel. Montrose: 1905. V. 43

MARSH, CHARLES

The Winter's tale, a Play. London: 1756. V. 45

MARSH, CHARLES F.

Reinforced Concrete. London: 1904. V. 44

MARSH, E. L.

Where the Buffalo Roamed. Toronto: 1908. V. 41; 42

MARSH, EDWARD

Edward Marsh's Little Book: Reproduced in Facsimile. Eton: 1990. V. 45
Forty-Two Fables of La Fontaine. London: 1924. V. 44
Georgian Poetry. 1911-1922. London: 1913-22. V. 38
Rupert Brooke: a Memoir. London: 1918. V. 41

MARSH, GEORGE P.

The Camel: His Organization, Habits, and Uses Considered with Reference to His Introduction into the United States. Boston: 1856. V. 37; 46
Lectures on the English Language. (with) The Origins and History of the English Language. (with) Man and Nature; or, Physical Geography as Modified by Human Action. New York: 1867. V. 40
The Origin and History of the English Language and of the Early Literature It Embodies. London: 1862. V. 39
Report on the Artificial Propagation of Fish. Burlington: 1857. V. 40

MARSH, HENRY

Palace Hotel Waltz. San Francisco: 1875. V. 40

MARSH, HERBERT

The History of the Politicks of Great Britain and France, from the Time of the Conference at Pillnitz, to the Declaration of War Against Great Britain . . . London: 1800. V. 43; 46

MARSH, HIPPISLEY CUNLIFFE

A Ride through Islam . . . London: 1877. V. 46

MARSH, HONORIA D.

Shades from Jane Austen. London: 1975. V. 39; 40; 42; 43; 44
Shades from Jane Austen. London: 1975. V. 40

MARSH, J. B. T.

The Story of the Jubilee Singers. Cleveland: 1892. V. 44

MARSH, JAMES B.

Four Years in the Rockies; or the Adventures of Isaac P. Rose. New Castle: 1884. V. 40; 42; 43; 46

MARSH, JOHN

The Story of Commander Allen Gardiner, R.N., with Sketches of Missionary Work in South America. London: 1867. V. 46

MARSH LAMBERT, H. G. C.

The Tot and Tim ABC. London: 1925. V. 46

MARSH, NGAIO

Clutch of Constables. London: 1968. V. 40

MARSH, O. C.

Dinocerata. Washington: 1884. V. 37; 39

MARSH, REGINALD

Sister Carrie. New York: 1939. V. 46

MARSH, RICHARD

The Joss: a Reversion. London: 1901. V. 41; 46

MARSH, S. N.

A Plain and Popular Explanation of the nature, Varieites, Treatment and Cure of Hernia. New York: 1870. V. 39

MARSH, THOMAS

Annals of the Hospital, of S. Wulstan, or Commandery in the City of Worcester . . . Worcester: 1890. V. 44

MARSH, W. LOCKWOOD

Aeronautical Prints and Drawings. London: 1924. V. 37; 40

MARSHALL,

Catalogue of Five Hundred Celebrated Authors of Great Britain, Now Living . . . London: 1788. V. 42

MARSHALL, AGNES B.

Fancy Ices. London: 1890. V. 42

MARSHALL, ALFRED

Elements of Economics of Industry. London & New York: 1892. V. 38
Fiscal Policy of International Trade . . . Ordered by the House of Commons, to Be Printed, 11 Nov. 1908. London: 1908. V. 43
Industry and Trade. A Study of Industrial Technique and Business Organization; and of Their Influences on the conditions of Various Classes and Nations. London: 1919. V. 37; 46
Money Credit & Commerce. London: 1923. V. 42; 43
Official Papers. London: 1926. V. 38; 39
Principles of Economics. London: 1890. V. 37
The Pure Theory of Foreign Trade. The Pure Theory of Domestic Values. London: 1935. V. 43

MARSHALL, ARTHUR

Explosives, Their Manufacture, Properties, Tests and History. London: 1915. V. 40

MARSHALL, ARTHUR MILNES

Lectures on the Darwinian Theory. London: 1894. V. 40

MARSHALL, C. F. DENDY

The British Post Office From Its Beginnings to the End of 1925. Oxford: 1926. V. 40
Early British Locomotives. Early. London: 1939. V. 46
A History of Railway Locomotives Down to the End of the Yeat 1831. London;: 1953. V. 37
Two Essays in Early Locomotive History. I. The First Hundred Railway Engines. II. British Locomotives in North America. London: 1928. V. 46

MARSHALL-CALDER, ARTHUR

A Crime Against Cania. London: 1934. V. 38

MARSHALL, CHARLES

Playing Trades. London: 1875? V. 42

MARSHALL, EDWARD

The Story of the Rough Riders, 1st U.S. Volunteer Cavalry: the Regiment in Camp and On the Battle Field. New York: 1899. V. 45

MARSHALL, F. H.

Catalogue of Jewellery, Greek, Etruscan and Roman, in the Departments of Antiquities, British Museum. London: 1911. V. 44
Catalogue of the Jewellery, Greek, Etruscan, and Roman, in the Departments of Antiquities, British Museum. London: (1969). V. 37

MARSHALL, FLORENCE ASHTON THOMAS 1843-1922

The Life and Letters of Mary Wollstonecraft Shelley. London: 1889. V. 42

MARSHALL, FREDERICK

Population and Trade in France in 1861-62. London: 1862. V. 40

MARSHALL, GEORGE

Epistles in Verse, Between Cynthio and Leonora. Newcastle: 1812. V. 37; 38; 40; 41

MARSHALL, H. G. HAYES

British Textile Designers Today . . . Leigh-on-Sea: 1939. V. 44

Interior Decoration To-Day. Leigh-On-Sea, Essex: 1938. V. 42

MARSHALL, H. RISSIK

Coloured Worcester Porcelain of the First Period (1751-1783). Newport: 1954. V. 41

MARSHALL, HENRY

Ceylon; a General Description of the Island and Its Inhabitants . . . London: 1846. V. 42; 45

MARSHALL, HERBERT

Cathedral Cities of France. London: 1907. V. 38

MARSHALL, HUMPHREY 1760-1841

History of Kentucky. Frankfort: 1824. V. 38

MARSHALL, HUMPHRY 1722-1801

Arbustrum Americanum: The American Grove; or, an Alphabetical Catalogue of Forest Trees and Shrubs, Natives of the American United States. Philadelphia: 1785. V. 38

MARSHALL, J. U.

The Times: or Chaos Has Come Again. Charleston: 1868. V. 44

MARSHALL, JOHN

Atlas to Marshall's Life of Washington. New York?: 1832. V. 42

Atlas to Marshall's Life of Washington. Philadelphia: 1832. V. 38

A History of the Colonies Planted by the English On the Continent of North America, from Their Settlement, the Commencement of that War Which Terminated in Their Independence. Philadelphia: 1824. V. 37; 40

The Life of George Washington, Commander in Chief of the American Forces During the War Which Established the Independence of His Country . . . London: 1804-07. V. 44

The Life of George Washington, Commander in Chief of the American Forces, During the War Which Established the Independence of His Country . . . Philadelphia: 1804-07. V. 38; 39; 41; 43

Vie de George Washington. Paris: 1807. V. 40

Mohenjo-Daro and the Indus Civilization. London: 1931. V. 37; 46

Opinion Delivered by Mr. Chief Justice Marshall, in the Case of Samuel A. Worcester. Verses the State of Georgia. Washington: 1832. V. 41; 43

Royal Naval Biography; or Memoirs of the Services of all the Flag-Officers . . . London: 1823. V. 38

The Writings of . . . Late Chief Justice of the United States, Upon the Federal Constitution. Boston: 1839. V. 39

MARSHALL, JOSEPH

Travels through Holland, Flanders, Germany, Denmark, Sweden, Lapland, Russia, the Ukraine and Poland. London: 1772. V. 41

MARSHALL, JULIAN, MRS.

The Life and Letters of Mary Wollstonecraft Shelley. London: 1889. V. 37

MARSHALL, MARK

The King of Fowls. Sydney: 1958. V. 43

MARSHALL, MRS. A. B.

Fancy Ices. With 86 Illustrations. London: (n.d.). V. 37

MARSHALL, NATHANIEL

A Defence of Our Constitution in Church and State; or, an Answer to the Late Charge of the Non-Jurors, Accusing Us of Heresy and Shism, Perjury and Treason . . . London: 1717. V. 45

MARSHALL, PARK

A Life of William B. Bate, Citizen, Soldier and Statesman. Nashville: 1908. V. 42

MARSHALL, PAULE

Praisesong for the Widow. New York: 1983. V. 43; 45

Soul Clap Hands and Sing. New York: 1961. V. 45; 46

MARSHALL, ROBERT

An Examination into the Repsective Merits of the Proposed Canal and Iron Railway, from London to Portsmouth. London: 1803. V. 46

MARSHALL, SAMUEL VANCE

The Importance of Letters in the Mississippi Valley. Natchez: 1838. V. 44

MARSHALL, T. W. M.

Christian Missions: Their Agents and Their Results. New York: 1870. V. 43

MARSHALL, THOMAS

The Catechism Set Forth in the Book of Common-Prayer, Briefly Explained by Short Notes . . . Oxford: 1679. V. 44

MARSHALL, THOMAS M.

A History of the Western Boundary of the Louisiana Purchase 1819-1841. Berkeley: 1914. V. 38

MARSHALL, W.

The Yorkshire Archaeological and Topographical Journal. London: 1870-1902. V. 37

MARSHALL, W. G.

Through America; or, Nine Months in the United States. London: 1881. V. 37; 38

MARSHALL, W. P.

Afloat on the Pacific Ocean or Notes of Three Years Life at Sea. Zanesville: 1876. V. 44

Descritpion of the Patent Locomotive Steam Engine of Messrs. Robert Stephenson and Co., Newcastle Upon Tyne. London: 1838. V. 40

MARSHALL, W. T.

Cactaceae, with Illustrated Keys of all Tribes, Sub-Tribes and Genera. Pasadena: 1941. V. 37; 38

MARSHALL, WILLAIM

Minutes, Experiments, Observations and General Remarks on Agriculture, In the Southern Counties . . . London: 1799. V. 42

MARSHALL, WILLIAM 1745-1818

Minutes of Agriculture, Made on a Farm of 300 Acres of Various Soils, Near Coyrdon, Surry. To Which is Added, a Digest . . . London: 1778. V. 40

Minutes of Agriculture, Made on a Farm of 300 Acres of Various Soils, Near Croydon, Surry. London: 1788. V. 41

Minutes of Agriculture, made on a farm of 300 acres of various soils, near Croydon. Surry: 1778. V. 37

On Planting and Rural Ornament. London: 1803. V. 38; 44

On the Landed Property of England, an Elementary and Practical Treatise. London: 1804. V. 40

Planting and Ornamental Gardening. London: 1785. V. 37; 38; 39; 40; 41; 44

Planting and Rural Ornament. London: 1796. V. 37; 38; 39; 40; 41; 44; 46

A Review of the Landscape, a Didactic Poem: Also an Essay on the Picturesque . . . London: 1795. V. 38

The Rural Economy of Norfolk. London: 1787. V. 39; 40

The Rural Economy of Gloucestershire . . . Glocester: 1789. V. 42

The Rural Economy of the Midland Counties. Dublin: 1793. V. 38

The Rural Economy of the Midland Counties . . . London: 1890. V. 46

The Rural Economy of Glocestershire. Glocester: 1789. V. 40

The Rural economy of the West of England. London: 1796. V. 37; 41

MARSHALL, WILLIAM I.

Acquisition of Oregon and Long Suppressed Evidence About Maracus Whitman. Seattle: 1911. V. 38; 39; 41

MARSHAM, JOHN 1602-1685

Canon Chronicus Aegyptiacus, Ebraicus, Graecus. Franequerae: 1696. V. 40

MARSHMAN, JOHN

Dissertation on . . . the Chinese Language. Serampore: 1809. V. 45

MARSILIIS, HIPPOLYTUS DE

Practica Causaru Criminaliumuna Cum Theorica & Repertorio . . . Lugduni (Lyon): 1529. V. 38

Practica Causarum Criminalium . . . Nuperrime Castigata . . . Curavimus Etiam Excudendum Materiarum Scitu Dignarum Repertorium Alphabeticum. Lugduni: apud Iacobum Giunta: 1546. V. 39

MARSOLLIER, JACQUES 1647-1724

The Life of St. Francis de Sales, Bishop and Prince of Geneva . . . London: 1737. V. 38

MARSTON, AFLRED

British Ferns, Nature Printed by . . . Ludlow: 1860. V. 40

MARSTON, ANNA LEE

Records of a California Family: Journal and Letters of Lewis C. Gunn and Elizabeth Le Breton Gunn. San Diego: 1928. V. 37; 38; 39

MARSTON, EDWARD

Frank's Ranche; or, My Holiday in the Rockies. Boston: 1886. V. 39; 43

Frank's Ranche or My Holiday in the Rockies, Being a Contribution to the Inquiry into What We Are To Do with Our Boys. London: 1886. V. 40; 43

MARSTON, GEORGE WHITE

A Family Chronicle. V. 43

MARSTON, JOHN

The Metamophosis of Pigmalions Image. Waltham St. Lawrence: 1926. V. 37; 40; 41; 45

The Metamorphosis of Pigmalions Image. 1926. V. 38; 42

The Works. London: 1887. V. 40; 44

MARSTON, PHILIP BOURKE

Song-Tide and Other Poems. London: 1871. V. 46

MARSTON, WESTLAND

Our Recent Actors. London: 1888. V. 44

MARSTON, WILLIAM MOULTON

The Lie Detector Test. New York: 1938. V. 46

MARSY, F. M. DE

Analyse Raisonnee de Bayle, ou Abrege Methodique de ses Ouvrages, Particuliereument de Son Dictionnaire Historique et Critique . . . V. 41

MARTEL, T.

Wounds of the Skull and Brain . . . London: 1918. V. 39

MARTEN, JOHN

A Treatise of All the Degrees and Symptoms of the Venereal Disease, in Both Sexes . . . London: 1706? V. 42

A Treatise of the Veneral Disease. The Seventh Edition, as also the Second Edition of his Appendix . . . London: 1711. V. 37

MARTENS, FRANZ HEINRICH

Ueber Eine Sehr Complicirte Hasenscharte Oder Einen Sogenannten Wolfsrachen, mit Einer an Demselben Subjeckte Befindlcihen Merkwurdigen Misstaltung der Hande und Fusse . . . Leipzig: 1804. V. 43

MARTENS, FRIEDRICH

Friderich Martens vom Hamburg Spitzbergische oder Groenlandische Reise Beschreibung Gethan im Jahr 1671. Aus Eigner Erfahrunge Beschreiben/ . . . . Hamburg: 1675. V. 45

MARTENS, M. DE

An Essay on Privateers, Captures, and Particularly on Recaptures, According to the Laws, Treaties, and Usages of the Maritime Powers of Europe . . . London: 1801. V. 37

THE MARTIAL Achievements of Great Britain and Her Allies from 1799 to 1815. London: 1814-15. V. 43; 44

MARTIAL D'AUVERGNE

Aresta Amorvum LII. Paris: 1555. V. 38

MARTIAL, MARCUS VALERIUS

Epigrammaton Libri XII. Ingelstadij: 1599. V. 37

Select Epigrams of Martial English (by Henry Killigrew). London: 1689. V. 44

MARTIALIS, MARCUS VALERIUS

Epigramaton Libri Duodecim . . . Basle: 1559. V. 43

Epigrammata. Parma: 1480. V. 46

Epigrammata. Venice: 1495. V. 46

Epigrammata. Leyden: 1670. V. 40

The Epigrams of M. Val. Martial. London: 1782. V. 38

The Epigrams, in 12 Books. London: 1783. V. 43

Martialis Cum duobus Commentis (Epigrams). Venice: 1495. V. 42

Martialis (Opera). Venice: 1501. V. 43

Select Epigrams of Martial . . . London: 1689. V. 42

MARTIALUS, MARCUS VALERIUS

Epigrammata. Venice: 1501. V. 41; 46

MARTIN, A. C.

The Durban Light Infantry. Volume I - 1854 to 1934. Durban: 1969. V. 41

MARTIN, ANNIE

Home Life on an Ostrich Farm. London: 1890. V. 40

MARTIN, ARCHER

Hudson Bay Company's Land Tenures and the Occupation of Assiniboia by Lord Selkirk's Settlers. London: 1898. V. 43

MARTIN, BARTHELEMY

Traite sur l'usage du lait. Paris: 1684. V. 37

MARTIN, BENJAMIN

Biographica Philosophica: Being an Account of the Lives, Writings and Inventions of the Most Eminent Philosophers and Mathematicians Who Have Flourished from the Earliest Ages of the World to the Present Time. London: 1764. V. 42; 46

The Description and Use of Both the Globes, the Armillary, Sphere and Orrery. London: 1758. V. 40

The Description and Use of a Case of Mathematical Instruments . . . London: 1771. V. 43

The Description and Use of Both Globes, the Armillary Sphere, and Orrery . . . London: 1773. V. 46

A New and Comprehensive System of Philology. London: 1759. V. 40

A New Compleat and Universal System or Body of Decimal Arithmetick, containing, I. The whole doctrine of decimal numbers . . . II. The application and use of decimal arthmetick in all the parts or branches of arithmetical science . . . London: 1763. V. 37

A Panegyrick on the Newtonian Philosophy. London: 1749. V. 41

Philosohia Britannica. London: 1759. V. 38

The Philosophical Grammar. London: 1735. V. 39

The Philosophical Grammar . . . London: 1755. V. 42

The Philosophical Grammar. London: 1778. V. 38

The Universal Gazetteer . . . Dublin: 1759. V. 45

The Young Gentleman and Lady's Philosophy, in a Continued Survey of the Works of Nature and Art. London: 1759-63. V. 42

The Young Gentleman and Lady's Philosophy in a Continued Survey of Nature and Art. London: 1781-1782. V. 38

MARTIN, CAROLINE

Lap Games and Other Songs for Children. Gloucestershire: 1989. V. 42

MARTIN, CHESTER

Empire and Commonwealth. Oxford: 1929. V. 41

MARTIN, COLONEL

A Plan for Establishing and Disciplining a National Militia in Great Britain, and in All the British Dominions of America. London: 1745. V. 37; 40; 43

MARTIN, DAVID

Histoire du Vieux et du Nouveau Testament. Amsterdam: 1700. V. 45

MARTIN, DOUGLAS

A Song in Favour of Bundling. Leicester: 1961. V. 39

MARTIN, E. G.

Principles of the Gold Water Treatment of Diseases and Its Application. London: 1843. V. 44

MARTIN, EDUARD

Atlas of Gynaecology and Obstetrics . . . Cincinnati: 1881. V. 38; 46

MARTIN, EDWARD

The Twenty-Eighth Division Pennsylvania's Guard in the World War Forwards by Commanding Generals . . . Pittsburgh: 1923-24. V. 45

The Twenty-Eighth Pennsylvania's Guard in the World War Forwards by Commanding Generals. Pittsburgh: 1923-4. V. 46

MARTIN, FRANCIS XAVIER

A Treatise on the Powers and Duties of Executors and Administrators According tot he Law of North Carolina. Newbern: 1803. V. 42

MARTIN, FRANCOIS XAVIER

The History of Louisiana from the Earliest Period. New Orleans: 1827-29. V. 41

The History of North Carolina, from the Earliest Period. New Orleans: 1829. V. 45

The History of Louisiana, from the Earliest Period. New Orleans: 1827. V. 37

MARTIN, FRED

A Travel Book. San Francisco: 1976. V. 39; 44

MARTIN, FREDERICK

The History of Lloyd's - and of Marine Insurance of Great Britain. London: 1896. V. 39

The Life of John Clare. London: 1865. V. 39; 42

MARTIN, FREDRIK ROBERT

The Miniature Painting and Painters of Persia, India and Turkey from the 8th to the 18th Century. London: 1912. V. 41

MARTIN, G. R.

Wild Cards - A Mosiac Novel. 1987-90. V. 43

MARTIN, GEOFFREY THORNDIKE

Corpus of Reliefs of the New Kingdom from the Memphite Necropolis and Lower Egypt. London: 1987. V. 42; 44

MARTIN, GEORGE

The Heredity Right of the Crown of England Asserted; the History of the Succession Since the Conquest Clear'd . . . London: 1713. V. 43

MARTIN, GEORGE M.

British Masonic Miscellany. Dundee: 1935. V. 38

MARTIN, GREGORY

A Discoverie of the Manifold Corruptions of the Holy Scriptures by the Heretikes of Our Daies, Specially the English Sectaries, and of Their Foule Dealing Herein . . . Printed at Rhemes: 1582. V. 41

A Discoverie of the Manifold Corruptions of the Holy Scriptures by the heretikes of our daies, specially the Englishectaries, and of their foule dealing herein, by partial & false translation to the advantage of their heresies, in . . . London: 1582. V. 37

A Discovery of the Manifold Corruptions of the Holy Scriptures. Reims: 1582. V. 38

MARTIN, HENRY

Arman. New York. V. 39; 46

MARTIN, HORACE T.

Castorologia or the History and Traditions of the Canadian Beaver. London: 1892. V. 37; 38; 42

Castorologia or History and Traditions of the Canadian Beaver. Montreal: 1892. V. 40; 41; 42

MARTIN, J.

Bibliographical Catalogue of Privately Printed Books. London: 1854. V. 38

MARTIN, J. C.

Maps of Texas and the Southwest, 1513-1900. Albuquerque: 1984. V. 45

MARTIN, JACK

Border Boss: Captain John R. Hughes Texas Ranger. San Antonio: 1942. V. 42

Border Boss: Captain John R. Hughes Texas Ranger. San Antonio: 1942. V. 42

MARTIN, JAMES A.

Minutes of the Fortieth Annual Session of the Brier Creek Association Convened at the Cool Spring Meeting House, Wilkes County, N.C. Saturday Before the 4th Lord's-Day in September, 1861. Salem: 1861. V. 44

MARTIN, JOHN

An Account of the Natives of the Tonga Islands in the South Pacific. London: 1817. V. 42; 46

An Account of the Natives of the Tonga Islands, in the South Pacific. Boston: 1820. V. 37

Bibliographical Catalogue of Privately printed Books. London: 1854. V. 41; 42

Cherokee Indians. Memorial of a Delegation of the Cherokee Tribe of Indians. Washington: 1832. V. 39

The Dance: the Story of the Dance Told in Pictures and Text. New York: 1946. V. 45

The History and Antiquities of Naseby in the County of Northampton. Cambridge: 1792. V. 38

MARTIN, JOHN A.

Address . . . Delivered in Kansas. Topeka: 1888. V. 39; 43

MARTIN, JOHN BIDDULPH

The Grasshopper in Lombard Street. London: 1982. V. 41

MARTIN, JOHN C.

Lest We Forget: a Chronicle of Important Events of the Civil War. Madison: 1920. V. 46

MARTIN, JOHN H.

Columbus, Geo . . . History - Incident - Personality. Part II - 1846 to 1865. Columbus: 1875. V. 43

A Manual of Microscopic Mounting: With Notes on the Collection and Examination of Objects. London: 1872. V. 40

MARTIN, JOHN HILL

Martin's Bench and Bar of Philadelphia, Together with Other Lists of Persons Appointed to Administer the Laws in the City and County of Philadelphia and the Province and Commonwealth of Pennsylvania. Philadelphia: 1883. V. 38

MARTIN, JOHN RUPERT

The Illustration of the Heavenly Ladder of John Climacus. Princeton: 1954. V. 38; 43

MARTIN, JONATHAN

The Life of Jonathan Martin, of Darlington, Tanner. Lincoln: 1828. V. 46

MARTIN, JOSEPH G.

Seventy-Three Years' History of the Boston Stock Market, from January 1, 1798 to January 1, 1871 . . . Boston: 1871. V. 45

MARTIN, MARCUS J.

Wireless Transmission of Photographs. London: 1916. V. 45

MARTIN, MARIA

An Historical Account of the Kingdom of Algiers . . . Rutland: 1815. V. 46

MARTIN, MARTIN

A Description of the Western Islands of Scotland. London: 1703. V. 41; 45

A Description of the Western Isles of Scotland. London: 1716. V. 46

MARTIN, MARY E.

From the Silent Path. London: 1886. V. 42

MARTIN, MATTHEW

Letter to the Right Hon. Lord Pelham, on the State of Mendicity in the Metropolis. London: 1803. V. 40

Substance of a Letter, Dated Poet's Corner, Westminster, 3rd March, 1803, to the Right Hon. Lord Pelham on the State of mendicity in the Metropolis. London: 1811. V. 45

MARTIN, P. I.

A Geological Memoir on a Part of Western Sussex. London: 1828. V. 37; 39; 43

MARTIN, P. S.

Quaternary Extinctions, a Prehistoric Revolution. London: 1984. V. 37; 38

MARTIN, PERCY F.

Mexico's Treasure House (Guanajuato) . . . New York: 1906. V. 44

MARTIN, PHILIP

Earnest Pennies. London: & Oxford: 1973. V. 46

Earnest Pennies, an Anthology of Prayers and Meditations on the Holy Eucharist. London: and Oxford: 1973. V. 41

MARTIN, R. M.

The Hudson's Bay Territories and Vancouver's Island. London: 1849. V. 37

Ireland Before and After the Union with Great Britain. London: 1848. V. 41

MARTIN, ROBERT MONTGOMERY 1803?-1868

The British Colonies: Their History, Extent, Condition and Resources. London & New York: 1851-57? V. 42

China: Political, Commercial and Social . . . London: 1847. V. 39

History of the British Colonies . . . London: 1834-35. V. 40

History of the British Colonies. Volume IV Possessions in Africa and Austral-Asia. London: 1835. V. 46

History of the British Possessions in the Indian and Atlantic Oceans . . . London: 1837. V. 39

History of Nova Scotia, Cape Breton, the Sable Islands, N.B., P.E.I., the Bermudas, Newfoundland, &c. London: 1837. V. 43; 44

History of Nova Scotia, Cape Breton, the Sable Islands, New Brunswick, Prince Edward Island, the Bermudas, Newfoundland &c. Whittaker,: 1837. V. 42

History, Statistics and Geography of Upper and Lower Canada in the British Colonial Library. London: 1838. V. 42

The History of the Indian Empire. London: 1860. V. 42

The Hudson's Bay Territories and Vancouver's Island. London: 1849. V. 43

The Hudson's Bay Territories, and Vancouver's Island . . . London: 1849. V. 42

The Indian Empire: History, Topography, Geology, Climate, Population, Chief Cities and Provinces . . . London. V. 45

Ireland Before and After the Union with Great Britain. London: 1848. V. 39

Statistics of the Colonies of the British Empire in the West Indies, South America, North America, Asia, Austal-Asia, Africa and Europe . . . London: 1839. V. 40; 45

MARTIN, ROSCOE

The People's Party in Texas: A Study in Third Party Politics. Austin: 1933. V. 37; 46

MARTIN, S.

A Sister's Stories. London: 1833. V. 39

MARTIN, SAMUEL

Extra Work of a London Pastor. London: 1863. V. 43

MARTIN, SAMUEL MC DONALD

New Zealand: In a Series of Letters . . . London: 1845. V. 45

MARTIN, SARAH CATHERINE

The Comic Adventures of Old Mother Hubbard, and Her Dog. London: 1805. V. 40

A Continuation of the Comic Adventures of Old Mother Hubbard, and Her Dog. London: 1807. V. 40

MARTIN, T.

The Life of His Royal Highness the Prince Consort. London: 1878-80. V. 44

Mary Magdalen's Tears Wip't Off . . . London: 1676. V. 42

MARTIN, THEODORE

The Book of Ballads. Edinburgh and London: 1877. V. 46

The Book of Ballads. London: 1845. V. 37

MARTIN, THEODORE continued

The Life of His Royal Highness the Prince Consort. London: 1875-80.
V. 38; 45

MARTIN, THOMAS

The Carpenters' and Joiners' Instructor in Geoemtrical Lines . . . London:
1826. V. 44

The Circle of the Mechanical Arts. London: 1813. V. 46

MARTIN, THOMAS H.

*Atlanta and Its Builders. A Comprehensive History of the Gate City of the
South.* N.P.: 1902. V. 39

MARTIN, VICTORIA CLAFLIN WOODHULL 1838-1921

Memorial to the House Judiciary Committee, January 1871. V. 43

The Origin, Tendencies and Principles of Government . . . New York: 1871.
V. 43

MARTIN, W.

The Alps. London: 1904. V. 44

MARTIN, W. C.

Flora of New Mexico. 1980-81. V. 39

MARTIN, WILLIAM

*The Christian Philosopher's Explanation of the General Deluge, and the
Proper Cause of all the Different Strata.* Newcastle: 1834. V. 40; 42

A New System of Natural Philosophy, on the Principle of Perpetual Motion.
Newcastle: 1821. V. 38

The Taranaki Question. London: 1861. V. 40

MARTIN, WILLIAM T.

History of Franklin County. Columbus: 1858. V. 43

MARTIN, WILLIAM YOUNG

*The East: Being a Narrative of Personal Impressions of a Tour in Egypt,
Palestine and Syria.* London: 1876. V. 46

MARTINDALE, ADAM

The Country-Survey-Book; or Land-Meters Vade-Mecum. London: 1692.
V. 41

MARTINDALE, ANDREW

Simone Martini. Oxford: 1988. V. 46

MARTINDALE, F. W.

Alice in Holidayland. London: 1920. V. 42

MARTINDALE, FRANCES

Words of Hope and Comfort for the Sorrowful. London: 1850. V. 39

Words of Hope and Comfort for the Sorrowful. London: 1860. V. 41

Words of Hope and Comfort for the Sorrowful. London: 1867. V. 38; 41

Words of Hope and Comfort for the Sorrowful. N.P.: 1867. V. 38

Words of Hope & Comport for the Sorrowful. London: (c. 1860). V. 37

MARTINDALE, JAMES WHITE

Sporting Scenes and Country Characters. London: 1840. V. 46

MARTINE, GEORGE

Essays Medical and Philosophical. London: 1740. V. 46

*Reliquae Divi Andreae, of the State of the Venerable and Primital See of
St. Andrews . . .* St. Andrews: 1797. V. 38; 42; 43

MARTINEAU & SMITH

Patent Globe Cock. Birmingham: 1860. V. 44

Patent Globe Cock. Birmingham, n.d., ca.: 1860. V. 40

MARTINEAU, HARRIET 1802-1876

Autobiography. Boston: 1877. V. 38

Autobiography. London: 1877. V. 38; 41; 42

British Rule in India; an Historical Sketch. London. V. 46

British Rule in India; an Historical Sketch. London: 1857. V. 38; 41; 43; 46

A Complete Guide to the English Lakes. London: 1855. V. 43; 44

Corporate Tradition and National Rights. London: 1857. V. 39

Dawn Island. Manchester: 1845. V. 38; 44

Dawn Island. Manchester: J.: 1845. V. 45

Dawn Island. Manchester: 1845. V. 37

Deerbrook. London: 1839. V. 37; 38; 39; 41

Deerbrook: a Novel. New York: 1839. V. 42

Eastern Life, Present and Past. London: 1848. V. 37

England and Her Soldiers. London: 1859. V. 42

The English Lakes. Windermere: 1858. V. 40

Eyre's Acquittal. London: 1884. V. 44

The Factory Controversy. Manchester: 1855. V. 38; 43

Feats On The Fiord. London: 1914. V. 41

The History of England During the Thirty Years' Peace: 1816-1846. London:
1849-50. V. 42

A History of the American Compromises. London: 1856. V. 45

A History of the Thirty Years Peace, A.D. 1816-1846. London: 1877. V. 41

A History of the Thirty Years Peace, A.D. 1816-1846. Shannon: 1971.
V. 41

The Hour and the Man. New York: 1841. V. 42

Household Education. London: 1849. V. 41; 42; 45

How to Observe. Morals and Manners. London: 1838. V. 37; 42

Illustrations of Political Economy . . . Brooke and Brooke Farm, a Tale.
Boston: 1832. V. 44

Illustrations of Political Economy. London: 1832-34. V. 39; 42

Illustrations of Political Economy . . . London: 1832-34. V. 46

*Illustrations of Political Economy . . . (with) Illustrations of Taxation. (with)
Poor Laws and Paupers Illustrated. (with) Forest and Game-Law Tales.*
London: 1832-45. V. 38

Illustrations of Political Economy. Boston: 1833. V. 41; 42

*Illustrations of Political Economy . . . (with) Poor Laws and Paupers
Illustrated . . .* London: 1833-34. V. 39

*Introduction to the History of the Peace. From 1800 to 1815. (and) The
History of England During the Thirty Years' Peace 1816-1846.* London:
1851/1849-50. V. 39

Letters on the Laws of Man's Nature and Development. London: 1851.
V. 42

The Martyr Age of the United States of America . . . Newcastle-upon-Tyne:
1840. V. 43

Miscellanies. Boston: 1836. V. 37; 38; 39; 41

Retrospect of Western Travel. London: 1838. V. 42

Retrospect of Western Travel. New York: 1838. V. 40

Society in America. London: 1837. V. 38; 41; 42; 46

Suggestions Towards the Future Government of India. London: 1858. V. 40

Traditions of Palestine. London: 1830. V. 44

Views of Slavery and Emancipation; from 'Society in America.' New York:
1837. V. 40

MARTINEAU, JAMES 1805-1900

Discourses Theological and Philosophical (spines so lettered). Liverpool &
London. V. 40

Endeavours after the Christian Life: Discourses. London: 1867. V. 37; 40

Essays, Reviews, and Addresses. London: 1890/91. V. 39

MARTINELL, C.

Gaudi, His Life, His Theories, His Work. 1967. V. 46

MARTINELLI, D. AGOSTINO

*Descrittione di Diversi Ponti Esistenti Sopra li Fiumi Nera, e Tevere con un
Discorso Paraticolare della Navigatione da Perugia a Roma.* Rome: 1676.
V. 37

*Stato del Ponte Felice Rappresentato alli . . . Signori Cardinali della S. C.
dell'acque.* Rome: 1682. V. 37

MARTINENT, LOUIS

*Manual of Pathology . . . . Applicable to Affections of the Head, Chest and
Abdomen.* London: 1826. V. 43

MARTINET, FRANCOIS NICOLAS

*Histoire des Oiseaux, Peints dans Tous Leurs Aspects, Ornee de Planches
Coloriees.* Paris: 1787-90. V. 39

MARTINEZ CARO, RAMON

*Verdadera Idea de la Primera Campagna de Tejas y Sucesos Ocurridos
Depues de la Accion de San Jacinto.* Mexico: 1837. V. 38; 39; 41; 42; 45

MARTINEZ DE LA PUENTE, D. JOSEPH

*Comprendio De Las Historias De Los Descubrimientos, Conquistas, y
Guerras De La Indian Oriental, y sus Islas, Desde Los Tiempos del Infante
Don Enrique de Portugal su Inventor, Hermano del Rey D. Duarte . . .*
Madrid: 1681. V. 38; 40

MARTINEZ, MARTIN

*Libri Decem Hypotyposeon Theologicarum, Sive Regularum Intelligendum
Scripturas Divinas, in Duas Partes Distributi.* Salamanca: 1582. V. 38

MARTINEZ, MARTINUS

*Libri decem Hypotyposeon Theologicarum, sive Regularaum ad Intelligendum
Scripturas Divinas . . .* Salmantaicae: 1582. V. 37

MARTINEZ, PABLO L.

*Guia Familiar de Baja California, 1700-1900: Vital Statistics of Lower
California.* Mexico City: 1965. V. 40

MARTINGALE, JAMES WHITE

Sporting Scenes and Country Characters. London: 1840. V. 46

MARTINIER, P.

*Injuries of the Face and Jaw and the Repair and Treatment of Fractured
Jaws.* New York: 1917. V. 42

MARTINIUS, PETRUS

The Key of the Holy Tongue. Leyden: 1593. V. 40

MARTINO, E.

Oratorio Pro Crepitu Ventris Habita ad patres Crepitantes. Cosmopoli: 1768. V. 39

MARTINS PEREIRA, ANTONIO

Relacao da Infeliz, a Deploravel Viagem, que Fez . . . D. Fr. Joao de Faro para Sua Se da Cidade da Ribeira Grande . . . Lisbon: 1741. V. 38

MARTIN'S Sportsman's Almanack, Kalendar and Traveller's Guide for 1819. London: 1819. V. 40

MARTION, JOHN

An Account of the Natives of the Tonga Islands, in the South Pacific Ocean . . . Edinburgh: 1827. V. 44

MARTIUS, C. F. P.

Icones Selectae Plantarum Cryptogamicarum Quas in Itinere Per Brasiliam Annis 1817-20. Munich: 1828-34. V. 39; 40

MARTIUS, GALEOTTUS

De Homini Libri Duo. Georgii Merulae in Galeotum Annotationes. Basileae: 1517. V. 38

MARTORELLI, GIACOMO

De Regia Theca Calamaria. Naples: 1756. V. 38

MARTYN, BENJAMIN

An Impartial Enquiry into the State and Utility of the Province of Georgia. London: 1741. V. 38; 40; 42; 44; 46

Reasons for Establishing the Colony of Georgia. London: 1733. V. 40; 43

Timoleon. London: 1730. V. 41; 45

MARTYN, HENRY 1781-1812

Journals and Letters. 1837. V. 39

MARTYN, JOHN

The Georgics of Virgil, with an English Translation and notes by John Martyn. London: 1741. V. 37

MARTYN, T.

Flora Rustica . . . London: 1792-94. V. 41; 43

MARTYN, THOMAS

Aranei, or a Natural History of Spiders, Including the Principal Parts of the Well Known Work on English Spiders . . . London: 1793. V. 37; 39

A Chronological Series of Engravers from the Invention of the Art. Cambridge: 1770. V. 40; 41; 42; 44

The English Entomologist Exhibiting all the Coleopterous Insects Found in England. London: 1792. V. 37; 38

Entomologist Anglois Ouvrage ou l'on a Rafsemble tous les Insectes Coleopteres Qui se Trouvent en Angleterre et qui Forment plus de 500 Especes different d'Insectes . . . London: 1792. V. 42; 45

Letters on the Elements of Botany, Addressed to a Lady by the Celebrated J. J. Rousseau. London: 1787. V. 37

Thirty Eight Plates, with Explanations, Intended to Illustrate Linnaeus's System of Vegetables. London: 1788. V. 44

Thirty Eight Plates with Explanations Intended to Illustrate Linnaeus's System of Vegetables and Particularly Adapted to the Letters on the Elements of Botany. London: 1799. V. 38; 40

A Tour Through Italy. London: 1791. V. 37; 39; 40; 41

The Universal Conchologist . . . London: 1785. V. 41

The Universal Conchologist . . . London: 1789. V. 37; 42

The Universal Conchologist, Exhibiting the Figure of Every Known Shell . . . (with) Figures of Non Descript Shells . . . London: 1789/64. V. 45

MARTYN, WILLIAM

The Historie & Lives, of the Kings of England, from William the Conqueror Unto . . . Henry the Eighth. London: 1628. V. 46

MARTYR, PETER 1455-1526

. . . De Rebus Oceanicis & Orbe Novo Decades Tres: Quibus Quicquid de Inventis Nuper Terris Traditum, Novarum Rerum Cupidum Lectorem Retinere Possit, Copiose, Fideliter, Eruditeque Docetur. Basle: 1533. V. 37

The Common Places of the Most Famous and Renowned Diuine Doctor Peter Martyr . . . London: 1583. V. 43

De Rebus Oceanicis et Novo Orbe . . . et Item de Rebus Aethiopicis . . . Cologne: 1574. V. 43

THE MARTYROLOGY Of Donegal. A Calendar of the Saints of IReland. Dublin: 1864. V. 44

MARULLO TARCANIOTA, MICHELE d. 1500

Poetae tres Elegantissimi Emendati & Aucti: Michael Marullus. Hieronymus Angerianus. Ioannes Secundus. Paris: 1582. V. 39

MARULLUS, MICHAEL

Epigrammata & Hymni. Paris: 1561. V. 38

Hymni et Epigrammata Marulli. Florence: 1497. V. 45

MARULUS, MARACUS

Evangelistarium. Venice: 1516. V. 37

A MARVEL Among Citites: Spokane Falls. A Western Wonder . . . Untold Mineral and Agricultural Wealth . . . Description of the Marvelous Water Power. ST. Paul: 1888. V. 39

MARVELL, ANDREW 1621-1678

An Account of the Growth of Popery, and Arbitrary Government in England . . . Amsterdam: 1677. V. 38

The Garden. Boston: 1970. V. 37

The Garden. Boston: 1970. V. 37

A Letter from a Gentleman in Ireland to His Brother in England, Relating to the Concerns of Ireland in the Matter of Trade. London: 1677. V. 38; 45

Miscellaneous Poems. London: 1681. V. 37; 40; 43; 44; 45; 46

Miscellaneous Poems. London: 1923. V. 44; 45

The Poems and Letters of . . . Oxford: 1927. V. 43

The Rehearsal Transpos'd . . . . with The Rehearsal Transpos'd, the Second Part. London: 1672, 1673. V. 38

The Rehearsal Transpos'd; or Animadversions Upon a Late Book, Entitled, A Preface, Shewing What Grounds There are For Rears and Jealousies of Popery. (with) The Rehearsal Transpos'd: the Second Part . . . London: 1672/73. V. 44

A Short Historical Essay touching General Councils, Creeds, and Impositions in Matters of Religion, Very Seasonable for Allaying the Heats of the Church. London: 1680. V. 37

The Works. London: 1726. V. 38

The Works of Andrew Marvell, Esq., Political, Controversial and Political. London: 1776. V. 38; 42; 43; 44

MARVIN, C. F.

Kite Experiments at the Weather Bureau. Washington: 1896. V. 40

MARVIN, CHARLES

The Eye-Witnesses' Account of the Diastrous Russian Campaign Against Akhal Tekke Turcomans. London: 1880. V. 43

The Russians at Merv and Herat, and Their Power of Invading India. London: 1883. V. 41

MARVIN, CHARLES THOMAS

Reconnoitring Central Asia. Pioneering Adventures in the region lying between Russia and India. London: 1885. V. 37

MARVIN, EDWIN E.

The Fifth Regiment Connecticut Volunteers A History. Hartford: 1889. V. 42

MARVIN, FRANCIS M.

The Van Horn Family History. East Stroudsbourg,: 1929. V. 42

MARX, ENID

An ABC of Birds and Beasts. London: 1985. V. 37; 39

MARX, GROUCHO

Beds. New York: 1930. V. 41

The Groucho Letters. New York: 1967. V. 41; 42

The Marx Bros. Scrapbook. New York: 1973. V. 45

MARX, KARL 1818-1883

Le Capital . . . Paris: 1872-75. V. 41

Le Capital. Paris: 1878. V. 45

Capital; a Critical Analysis of Capitalist Production. London: 1887. V. 41; 42

Capital: a Critical Analysis of Capitalist Production . . . London: 1887. V. 41

Capital. A Critical Analysis of Capitalist Production. London: 1889. V. 39

Capital. A Critique of Political Economy. Chicago: 1921/19/09. V. 38

Capital: A Critical Analysis of Capitalist Production. New York: 1889. V. 37

A Contribution to the Critique of Political Economy. Chicago: 1913. V. 39

Der Achtzehnte Brumaire . . . dritte Auflage. Hamburg: 1885. V. 38

The Eastern Question: A Reprint of Letters Written 1853-1856 Dealing with the Events of the Crimean War by Karl Marx. London: 1897. V. 37

Manifesto of the Communist Party. Moscow: 1977. V. 40

The Poverty of Philosophy being a translation of the 'Misere de la Philosophie.' London: 1900. V. 39

MARY Queen of Scots. The Authentic Portraits. London: 1903. V. 41

MARYAN, WILLIAM

A Treatise Explaining the Impossibility of the Disease Termed Hydrophabia. London: 1809. V. 43; 46

MARYE, GEORGE T.

From '49 to '83 in California and Nevada. San Francisco: 1923. V. 37; 38; 43; 45

MARYLAND.

The Report of and Testimony Taken Before the Joint Committee of the Senate and house of Delegates of Maryland. Annapolis: 1836. V. 45

MARYLAND. (COLONY). LAWS, STATUTES, ETC.

Act of Assembly Passed in December, 1754 . . . an Act for Taking and Detaining Able-Bodied Men for His Majesty's Service. Annapolis: 1755. V. 44

Acts of the Province of Maryland, Made and Passed at a Session of Assembly, on Saturday the Twenty-Second Day of February . . . Annapolis: 1755. V. 44

Acts of the Province of Maryland, Made and Passed at a Session of the Assembly, Begun and Held at Baltimore Town, on Friday the Eighth Day of April . . . Annapolis: 1757. V. 44

Votes and Proceedings of the Lower House of Assembly of the Province of Maryland . . . Annapolis: 1755. V. 44

MARYLAND. LAWS, STATUTES, ETC. - 1765

The Laws of Maryland at Large, with Proper Indexes. Annapolis: 1765. V. 40; 43

MARYLAND. LAWS, STATUTES, ETC. - 1787

Laws of Maryland, Made Since 1763, Consisting of Acts of Assembly Under the Proprietary Government . . . and, Acts of Assembly Since the Revolution. Annapolis: 1797. V. 42

MARYLAND. LEGISLATURE - 1810

Votes and Proceedings of the Senate of the State of Maryland. Annapolis: (1810). V. 37

MARYLAND. SENATE - 1810

Votes and Proceedings of the Seante of the State of Maryland. Annapolis: 1810. V. 39

MARYLEBONE CRICKET CLUB

The Memorial Biography of Dr. W. G. Grace. London: 1919. V. 40

MARZIALS, THEO

Pan Pipes. A Book of Old Songs. London. V. 43

Pan Pipes. A Book of Old Songs. London: 1883. V. 38; 43

MARZIN, CARDINAL

Letters to Lewis XIV. The Present King of France, on His Love to the Cardinal's Niece. Together with his secret negotiation with Don Lewis D'Haro. London: 1691. V. 37

MARZIO, GALEOTTO

De Homine Libri Duo. Basel: 1517. V. 37

MAS, ALPHONSE

Le Verger, ou Histoire, Culture et Description des Varietes de Fruits, Le Plus Generalement Connues. Paris: 1873. V. 42

MASARYK, THOMAS GARRIGUE

The Spirit of Russia. London & New York: 1919. V. 37

MASCAGNI, PAOLO 1752-1815

Prodrome d'un Ouvrage sur le Systeme des Vaisseaux Lymphatiques. Siena: 1784. V. 43

Vasorum Lymphaticorum Corporis Humani Historia et Ichnographia. Senis (Siena): 1787. V. 38

Vasosum Lymphaticorum Corporis Humani Historia et Ichnographia . . . Senis: 1787. V. 37; 39; 43; 45

MASCAGNI, PAULO 1755-1815

Vasorum Lymphaticorum Corporis Humani Historia et Ichnographia. Siena: 1787. V. 42

MASCOV, JOHN JACOB

The History of the Ancient Germans. London: and Westminster: 1737-38. V. 44

The History of the Ancient Germans. Westminster: 1737-38. V. 42

MASEFIELD, JOHN 1878-1967

At. Katherine of Ledbury and Other Ledbury Papers. London: (1951). V. 37

Ballads. London: 1903. V. 38; 40

The Bird of Dawning. London: 1933. V. 37

The Box of Delights Or When the Wolves Were Running. London: 1935. V. 41

Chaucer. Cambridge: 1931. V. 43

The Country Scene. London: 1937. V. 41; 44; 46

End and Beginning. London: 1933. V. 39

The Ledbury Scene as I Have Used it in My Verse. (Hereford: 1951). V. 37

Melloney Holtspur. London: 1922. V. 38

Odtaa. London: 1926. V. 41

Reynard the Fox, or the Ghost Heath Run. London. V. 41

Right Royal. London: 1922. V. 37; 39; 41

Salt Water Ballads. London: 1902. V. 37; 38; 39; 40; 41; 42; 46

So Long to Learn. Chapter of an Autobiography. London: (1952). V. 37

Some Memories of W. B. Yeats. Dublin: 1940. V. 37; 39

The Taking of Helen. London: 1923. V. 46

A Tarpaulin Muster. London: 1907. V. 38

Tribute to Ballet. London: 1938. V. 45

MASEREEL, FRANS

The Making of a Book at the Officina Bodoni: Twelve Woodcuts. Verona: 1973. V. 45

My Book of Hours. 1922. V. 45

My Book of Hours: 167 Designs Engraved on Wood. N.P.: 1922. V. 37; 39

My Book of Hours. Paris: 1922. V. 44

MASERES, FRANCIS

The Canadian Freeholder: a Dialogue Shewing, the Sentiments of the Bulk of the Freeholders of Canada Concerning the Late Quebeck-act . . . (with) The Canadian Freeholder: in Three Dialogues Between an Englishman and a Frenchman, Settled in Canada. London: 1776, 1779. V. 37

Considerations on the Expediency of Admitting Representatives from the American Colonies Into the House of Commons. London: 1770. V. 46

Considerations on the Bill Now Depending in the House of Commons, for Enabling Parishes to Grant Life-Annuities to Poor Persons. London: 1773. V. 45

An Enquiry into the Extent of the Power of Juries, on Trials of Inditments or Informations for Publishing Seditious, or Other Criminal Writings, or Libels Extracted from a Miscellaneous Collection of the Papers that Were Published in 1776 . . . London: 1785. V. 38

An Enquiry into the Extent of the Power of Juries, on Trails of Indictments or Informations, for Publishing Seditious, or Other Criminal Writings . . . Dublin: 1792. V. 38; 45; 46

The Principles of the Doctrine of Life-Annuities . . . London: 1783. V. 38; 45

A Review of the Government and Grievances of the Province of Quebec, Since the Conquest of It by the British Arms. London: 1788. V. 41; 42

Select Tracts Relating to the Civil Wars in England, in the Reign of King Charles the First. London: 1815. V. 43

Tracts on the Resolution of Affected Algebrick Equations. London: 1800. V. 38; 41

THE MASK. The Journal of the Art of the Theatre. Florence: 1929. V. 37

MASKELL, ALFRED

Ivories. London: 1905. V. 41

Ivories. New York: 1905. V. 41

Wood Sculpture. New York: 1911. V. 41

MASKELL, WILLIAM

A History of the Martin Marprelate Controversy. London: 1845. V. 46

MASKELYNE, NEVIL

Tables Requisite to be used with the Nautical Ephemeris, for finding the Latitude and Longitude at Sea. Published by Order of the Commissioners of Longitude. London: 1802. V. 37

MASON, ALFRED EDWARD WOODLEY

At the Villa Rose. London: 1910. V. 39

The Broken Road. London: 1907. V. 39

Clementina. London: 1901. V. 39

The Courtship of Morrice Buckler. New York: 1896. V. 39

Ensign Knightley: and Other Stories. Westminster: 1901. V. 39

The Four Feathers. London: 1902. V. 39; 45

Konigsmark. London: 1938. V. 41; 45

Lawrence Clavering. London: 1897. V. 39

Miranda of the Balcony. London and New York: 1899. V. 39

Parson Kelly. London: 1900. V. 39

The Philanderers. London & New York: 1897. V. 39

A Romance of Wastdale. London: 1895. V. 39; 44

Running Water. London: 1907. V. 39

The Truants. London: 1904. V. 39

The Turnstile. London: 1912. V. 39

The Watchers. Bristol: 1899. V. 39

The Witness for the Defence. London: 1913. V. 38

MASON, AMELIA GERE

The Women of the French Salons. New York: 1891. V. 41; 43; 45

MASON, BENJMAIN F.

Through War to Peace. N.P.: 1891. V. 41

MASON, BOBBIE ANN

Nabakov's Garden: a Guide to Ada. Ann Arbor: 1974. V. 39; 42

Shiloh. New York: 1982. V. 42; 43; 44; 45; 46

MASON, CHARLES H.

Our Prize Dogs. New York: 1888. V. 45

MASON, CHARLOTTE

The Lady's Assistant . . . A Complete System of Cookery . . . London: 1805. V. 45

MASON, EDWARD G.

Chapters from Illinois History. Chciago: 1901. V. 40

Early Chicago and Illinois. Chicago: 1890. V. 43

MASON, EUGENE

Old World Love Stories. London: 1913. V. 42

MASON, G. H.

The Punishments of China. London: 1801. V. 46

The Punishments of China. London: 1808. V. 41

The Punishments of China. London: 1822. V. 46

MASON, GEORGE

An Essay on Design in Gardening. London: 1768. V. 42; 44

An Essay on Design in Gardening. London: 1795. V. 40

Ode On the Loss of the Steamship 'Pacific', November 4th, 1875. Nanaimo: 1875. V. 45

A Supplement to Johnson's English Dictionary. New York: 1803. V. 37

A Supplement to Johnson's English Dictionary of which the palpable errors are attempted to be rectified and its material omissions supplied. Together with a 16 page Appendix bound in at the end, and which was published shortly . . . London: 1801. V. 37; 39

MASON, GEORGE C.

The Application of Art to Manufactures. New York: 1858. V. 37; 38; 42

MASON, GEORGE CHAMPLIN

Newport Illustrated. New York: 1854. V. 39

MASON, GEORGE HENRY

The Costume of China. London: 1800. V. 44

MASON, HENRY

The New Art of Lying, Covered by Iesuites Under the Vaile of Equivocation (etc). London: 1624. V. 44

MASON, HENRY J. MONCK

Primitive Christianity in Ireland. Dublin: 1836. V. 40

MASON, J. M.

In the Senate of the United States . . . Report. The Select Committee of the Senate Appointed to Inquire into the late Invasion and Seizure of the Public Property at Harper's Ferry, Beg leaf to Submit their report. Washington: 1860. V. 37

MASON, JEREMIAH

Memoir and Correspondence. Cambridge: 1873. V. 37

MASON, JESSE D.

History of Santa Barbara County, California, with Illustrations and Biographical Sketches of Its Prominent Men and Pioneers. Oakland: 1883. V. 40

History of Santa Barbara & Ventura Counties, California . . . Berkeley: 1961. V. 40

MASON, JOHN

A Brief History of the Pequot War. New York: 1869. V. 40

An Essay on Elocution or, Pronunciation. London: 1751. V. 39; 41; 42; 43

An Essay on Elocution or, Pronouniciation. London: 1757. V. 44

An Excellent Tragedy of Mulleasses the Tvrke, and Borgias Governour of Florence. London: 1632. V. 37

More Papers Hand Made. Leicester: 1960. V. 41

More Papers Hand Made by John Mason. Leicester: 1966. V. 43

More Papers Hand Made. New York: 1966. V. 43; 46

More Papers Hand Made by John Mason. Leicester: 1967. V. 38; 41; 43; 46

More Papers Handmade by John Mason. London: 1966. V. 37; 39

Paper Making as an Artistic Craft. Leicester. V. 46

Paper Making as an Artistic Craft. Leicester: 1963. V. 39

The Paper makers crafts, verse by -; illustrations by R. Graham. Leicester: 1965. V. 37

Paper Making as an Artistic Craft. Leicester: 1963. V. 37; 38; 39; 40; 42; 43; 46

Self Knowledge: a Treatise. London: 1769. V. 46

Some Papers Hand Made by John Mason. London: 1959. V. 37; 38; 46

Spiritual Songs; or, Songs of Praise, with Penitential Cries to Almighty God . . . Bocking: 1795. V. 46

Twelve Papers by John Mason. London: 1959. V. 37; 38

MASON, JOHN MONCK

Comments on the Several Editions of Shakespeare's Plays, Extended to those of Malone and Steevens . . . Dublin: 1807. V. 45

Remarks Upon Poyning's Law, and the Manner of Passing Bills in the P-------t of I-----d. Dublin: 1758. V. 40

MASON, KENNETH

Abode of Snow. A History of Himalayan Exploration and Mountaineering. London: 1955. V. 44

MASON, LAURIS

The Lithographs of George Bellows: a Catalogue Raisonne. Millwood: 1977. V. 43

MASON, M.

The Pictorial Press Its Origin and Progress . . . London: 1885. V. 45

MASON, MICHAEL H.

The Arctic Forests. London: 1924. V. 39; 42

MASON, MISS

Kate Gearey; or, Irish Life in London. London: 1853. V. 46

MASON, MONCK

Account of the Late Aeronautical Expedition from London to Weilburg . . . London: 1836. V. 45

Account of the Late Aeronautical Expedition from London to Weilburg . . . New York: 1837. V. 42

MASON, OTIS TIFTON

Indian Basketry. New York: 1904. V. 40

MASON, R.

Robes of Thespis, Costume Designs by Modern Artists. London: 1928. V. 44

MASON, RICHARD

The Gentleman's New Pocket Farrier. Richmond: 1825. V. 45

The Gentleman's New Pocket Farrier, Comprising a General Description of the Noble and Useful Animal the Horse . . . Richmond: 1828. V. 41

The Gentleman's New Pocket Farrier, Comprising a General Description of the Noble and Useful Animal the Horse . . . Richmond: 1830. V. 42; 45

The Gentleman's New Pocket Farrier, Comprising a General Description of the Noble and Useful Animal the Horse . . . Richmond: 1835. V. 39; 40; 42

MASON, RICHARD ANGELUS

A Liturgical Discourse of the Mass. London: 1670-69. V. 37

MASON, RICHARD LEE

Narrative of . . . in the Pioneer West. 1819. New York: 1915. V. 39; 42

MASON, RUPERT

Robes of Thespis; Costume Designs by Modern Artists. London: 1928. V. 39

MASON, SIMON

A Narrative of the Life and Distresses of Simon Mason, Apothecary. Birmingham: 1754? V. 41

Practical observations in Physick, Wherein is Exhibited the Aetiology, or the Rise and Nature of the Most Prevelant Distempers. Birmingham: 1757. V. 37

MASON, STUART

Bibliography of Oscar Wilde. London: 1914. V. 39; 40; 41; 45

MASON, THOMAS

Chips from Dickens. New York. V. 43

Chips From Dickens. New York: 1884. V. 40

Public and Private Libraries of Glasgow. Glasgow: 1885. V. 44

MASON, W.

Crumbs from the Master's Table; or, Select Sentences, Doctrinal, Practical and Experimental. New York: 1831. V. 39

MASON, WALT

Uncle Walt. Chicago: 1910/11. V. 41

Uncle Walt. The Poet Philosopher. Chicago: 1911. V. 46

Uncle Walt. Chicago: 1910, 1911. V. 37

MASON, WILLIAM 1725-1797

An Archaeological Epistle to the Reverend and Worshipful Jeremiah Miles, D.D., Dean of Exeter . . . London: 1782. V. 38

Caracticus, a Dramatic Poem: written on the Model of the Ancient Greek Tragedy. London: 1759. V. 37

Crumbs from the Master's Table; or Select Sentences, Doctrinal, Practical, Experimental. New York: 1831. V. 41

The English Garden: a Poem. London: 1772. V. 37; 39; 42

MASON, WILLIAM 1725-1797 continued

The English Garden: a Poem. London: & York: 1772/77/79/81. V. 45

The English Garden: a Poem. London & York: 1777-81. V. 41

The English Garden. Cork: 1783. V. 42

The English Garden. York: 1783. V. 38

The English Garden; a Poem. York: 1783. V. 40; 41

The English Garden: a Poem. York: 1783. V. 46

The English Garden. London: 1825. V. 39

The English Garden: A Poem. In Four Books . . . With a Sketch of His Life. London: 1803. V. 37

An Epistle to Dr. Shebbeare: to which is Added an ode to Sir Fletcher Norton, in Imitation of Horace, Ode VIII, Book IV. London: 1777. V. 38

Isis. London: 1749. V. 40; 41; 45

Musaeus: A Monody to the Memory of Mr. Pope, in Imitation of Milton's Lycidas. London: 1747. V. 37

Ode to Mr. Pinchbeck, Upon His Newly Invented Patent Candle Snuffers. London: 1776. V. 38; 40; 44; 46

Odes. Cambridge: 1756. V. 38; 44

Poems. Dublin: 1764. V. 39

Poems. London: 1764. V. 38; 41; 45

The Poetical Works of the Author of the Heroic Epistle to Sir William Chambers. London: 1805. V. 38

Saffo Dramma Lirico in Tre Atti Sul Modello Toscano dall' Inglese . . . London: 1809. V. 40

MASON, WILLIAM L.

The History of Antiquities of Birkenhead Priory . . . Oxford and London: 1854. V. 44

MASONRY Further Dissected; or More Secrets of that Mysterious Society Reveal'd. London: 1738. V. 42

MASPERO, G.

The History of Egypt, Chaldea, Syria, Babylonia, and Assyria. London: 1903-06. V. 37; 42

MASPERO, GASTON

History of Egypt, Chaldea, Syria, Babylonia and Assyria. London: 1903. V. 37; 40

History of Egypt, Chaldea, Syria, Babylonia and Assyria. London: 1904. V. 42

THE MASQUE: A Theatre Notebook. London: 1946-49. V. 45
THE MASQUE. a Theatre Notebook. London: 1946-9. V. 37

A MASQUE of Poets. Boston: 1878. V. 43

THE MASQUE of the Edwards of England: Being a Coronation Pageant to Celebrate the Crowning of the King. London: 1902. V. 46

MASQUERIER, LEWIS

Sociology; or, the Reconstruction of Society, Government and Property. New York: 1877. V. 37

MASSA, NICCOLO 1489-1569

Lo(g)ica . . . Venice: 1549. V. 43

MASSA, NICOLO

Loica Distinta in Sette Libri . . . Venice. V. 45

MASSACHSETTS. BOARD OF INTERNAL IMPROVEMENTS

Report of the Board of Directors of Internal Improvements of the State of Massachusetts on The Practicability and Expediency of a Rail-Road from Boston to the Hudson River, and from Boston to Providence, Submitted to the General Court, Jan. 16, 1829. Boston: 1829. V. 37

MASSACHUSETTS

A Defence of the Legislature of Massachusetts, or the Rights of New England Vindicated. Boston: 1804. V. 37

Journal of Debates and Proceedings in the Convention of Delegates Chosen to Revised the Constitution of Massachusetts, Begun and Holden at Boston, Nov. 15, 1820 and Continued by Adjournment to Jan. 9, 1821. Boston: 1853. V. 43

Report of the Evidence and Points of Law Arising in the Trail of John Francis Knapp for the Murder of Joseph White. Salem: 1830. V. 37

MASSACHUSETTS. BOARD OF INTERNAL IMPROVMENTS - 1829

Report of the Board of Internal Improvements of the Practicability and Expediency of a Railroad from Boston to the Hudson River. Boston: 1829. V. 37

MASSACHUSETTS CHARITABLE FIRE SOCIETY

The Constitution of the Massachusetts Charitable Fire Society. Boston: 1794. V. 46

MASSACHUSETTS. (COLONY).

The Charter Granted by Their Majesties King William and Queen Mary, to the Inhabitants of the Province of the Massachusetts-Bay . . . (with) Acts and Laws of His Majesty's Province of the Massachusetts-Bay in New England. Boston: 1726. V. 39

MASSACHUSETTS. (COLONY). LAWS, STATUTES, ETC. - 1775

In the Fifteenth Year of the Reign of George the Third . . . Acts and Laws, Passed by the Great and General Court of Assembly of the Colony of the Massachusetts Bay in New England. Watertown: 1775. V. 41

MASSACHUSETTS. (COMMONWEALTH). CONSTITUTION - 1781

The Constitution or Frame of Government for the Commonwealth of Massachusetts. Boston: 1781. V. 40

MASSACHUSETTS. CONSTITUTION

The Constitution of the State of Massachusetts, and that of the United States. Brookfield: 1807. V. 42; 46

MASSACHUSETTS. CONSTITUTION - 1787

The Constitution or Frame of Government for the Commonwealth of Massachusetts. Worcester: 1797. V. 37

MASSACHUSETTS. CONSTITUTIONAL CONVENTION

A Constitution or Frame of Government, Agreed Upon by the Delegates of the People of the State of Massachusetts Bay, in Convention Begun and Held at Cambridge on the First of September 1779 and Continued by Adjournments to the Second of March, 1780 . . . Boston: 1780. V. 44

The Constitution or Frame of Government for the Commonwealth of Massachusetts. Boston: 1781. V. 44

Debates, Resolutions and Other Proceedings of the Convention of the Commonwealth of Massachusetts, Convened at Boston, on the 9th of January, 1788 . . . for the Purpose of Assenting to and Ratifying the Constitution . . . Boston: 1788. V. 40; 41

MASSACHUSETTS. CONSTITUTIONAL CONVENTION - 1821

Journal of Debates and Proceedings in the Convention of Delegates, Chosen to Revise the Constitution of Massachusetts. Boston: 1821. V. 37

MASSACHUSETTS. CONSTITUTIONAL CONVENTION - 1832

Journal of the Convention for Framing a Constitution of Government for the State of Massachusetts, 1779-1780. Boston: 1832. V. 37

MASSACHUSETTS. GENERAL COURT. HOUSE OF REPRESENTATIVES

State of Massachusetts Bay in the House of Representatives, February 5, 1777. Resolved, that When Any Wagon-Master . . . Boston: 1777. V. 40

MASSACHUSETTS. GENERAL COURT. JOINT COMM. ON THE LIBRARY

State Papers on Nullification: Including the Public Acts of the Convention of the People of South Carolina. Boston: 1834. V. 40

MASSACHUSETTS GENERAL HOSPITAL

Address of the Board of Trustees of the Massachusetts General Hospital to the Public. Boston: 1814. V. 43

Massachusetts General Hospital Neurological Clinic Reports: Cases Presented At Staff Meetings in the Neurological Service Massachusetts General Hospital 1833-1944. V. 42

MASSACHUSETTS HORTICULTURAL SOCIETY

Catalogue of the Library of the Massachusetts Horticultural Society. Cambridge: 1918/20. V. 45

MASSACHUSETTS. HOUSE OF REPRESENTATIVES

Journals of the House of Representatives of Massachusetts 1715-1777. Boston: 1919-87. V. 40

Journals of the House of Representatives of Massachusetts, 1715-1779. Boston: 1919-90. V. 45

MASSACHUSETTS. LAWS, STATUTES, ETC. - 1789

The Perpetual Laws of the Commonwealth of Massachusetts, from the Commencement of the Constitution in October 1780 to the Last Wednesday, in May, 1789 . . . . Boston: 1789. V. 42

MASSACHUSETTS. LAWS, STATUTES, ETC. - 1799

An Act to Incorporate the Boston Marine Insurance Company. Boston: 1799. V. 41

MASSACHUSETTS. LAWS, STATUTES, ETC. - 1814

The Charters and General Laws of the Colony and Province of Massachusetts by Carefully Collected from the Publick Records and Ancient Printed Books (etc.). Boston: 1814. V. 37; 38

MASSACHUSETTS. LEGISLATURE. HOUSE OF REPRESENTATIVES

Journals of the House of Representatives of Massachusetts, 1715-1777. Boston: 1919-87. V. 42

MASSACHUSETTS MEDICAL SOCIETY

Acts of Incorporation and Acts Regulating the Practice of Physic and Surgery, with the By-Laws and Orders of the Massachusetts Medical Society. Boston: 1826. V. 41; 46

Acts of Incoporation and Acts Regulating the Practice of Physic and Surgery, with the By-Laws and Orders. Boston: 1832. V. 40; 41; 45; 46

The Pharmacopeia of the Massachusetts Medical Society. Boston: 1808. V. 40

A Report on Spasmodic Cholera, Prepared by a Committee Under the Direction of the Counsellors of the . . . Boston: 1832. V. 45

MASSACHUSETTS PEACE SOCIETY

Constitution of the Massachusetts Peace Society. Boston: 1815. V. 45

MASSACHUSETTS SOCIETY FOR PROMOTING AGRICULTURE

Laws and Regulations of the Massachusetts Society for Promoting Agriculture. Boston: 1793. V. 42

MASSACHUSETTS Soldiers, Sailors and Marines in the Civil War. Norwood & Boston: 1931-1937. V. 38

MASSACHUSETTS STATE TEXAS COMMITTEE

How to Settle the Texas Question. Boston: 1845. V. 41; 45

MASSACRE of Cheyenne Indians. Washington: 1865. V. 37; 41

THE MASSACRE of Glenco. London: 1703. V. 37; 42

MASSACRE OF Lieutenant Grattan and His Command by Indians. Glendle: 1983. V. 38

MASSARI, FRANCESCO

In Nonum Plini De Naturali Historia Librum Castigationes et Annotations. Basel: 1537. V. 42; 44

MASSCHUSETTS. LAWS, STATUTES, ETC. 1775

. . . Acts and Laws, Passed by the Great General Court of Assembly of the Colony of the Massachusetts-Bay in New England; Begun and Held at Watertown . . . the Nineteenth Day of July, Anno Domini, 1775. Watertown: 1775. V. 38

MASSE, GERTRUDE C. E.

A Bibliography of First Editions of Books Illustrated by Walter Crane. London. V. 39; 43

MASSE, J. N.

A Pocket Atlas of the Descriptive Anatomy of the Human Body. N: 1846. V. 42

MASSEREENE & FERRARD, JOHN SKEFFINGTON FOSTER SKEFFINGTON, 10TH VISCOUNT 1812-1863 Church Melodies. London: 1847. V. 43

MASSETT, STEPHEN C.

'Drifting About', or What 'Jeems Pipes of Pipesville' and Saw-and-Did. New York: 1863. V. 37; 38; 39; 42

MASSEY, EDMUND

A Letter to Mr. Maitland, in Vindication of the Sermon Against Inoculation. London: 1722. V. 42

MASSEY, FRANK E.

Portrait Sketches of Cheshire Hunting Men from 1850 to 1890. Manchester: 1903. V. 42

MASSEY, G. BETTON

Conservative Gynecology and Electro-Therapeutics. Philadelphia: 1905. V. 42

Electricity in the Diseases of Women, with Special Reference to the Application of Strong Currents. Philadelphia: 1890. V. 42

MASSEY, JOHN E.

Autobiography of . . . New York: 1909. V. 42

MASSEY, VINCENT

The Sword of Lionheart and Other Wartime Speeches. Toronto: 1942. V. 45

MASSEY, W.

The Origin and Progress of Letters. An Essay in Two Parts. London: 1763. V. 38; 41; 45

MASSIALOT, FRANCOIS

Le Confiteur Royal, ou Nouvelle Instructions Pour les Confitures, les Liqueurs et les Fruits. Paris: 1776. V. 41

Le Cuisinier Roial et Bourgeois; qui Apprend a Ordonner Toute Sorte de Repas en Gras & Maigre, & la Meilleure Maniere des Ragouts les Plus Delicats & Plus a la Mode. Paris: 1710. V. 39

Nouvelle Instruction Pour les Confitures, les Liqueurs et les Fruits, avec la Maniere de Bien Ordonner un Dessert & Tout le Reste qui est du devoir des Maitres d'Hotels, Sommeliers, Confiseurs, & Autres Officiers de Bouche. Paris: 1710. V. 39

MASSIE, J. W.

Continental India, Travelling Sketches and Historical Recollections, Illustrating the Antiquity, Religion and Manners of the Hindoos . . . London. V. 46

Continental India, Travelling Sketches and Historical Recollections . . . London: 1840. V. 42

MASSIE, JAMES W.

America: The Origin of Her Present Conflict; Her Prospect for the Slavery and Her Claim fro Anti-Slavery Sympathy. London: 1864. V. 40; 41; 43

MASSIE, JOSEPH

An Essay on the Causes of the Natural Rate of Interest. London: 1750. V. 41

A Representation Concerning the Knowledge of Commerce As a National Concern . . . London: 1760. V. 42

MASSIE, W.

Sydenham; or, Memoirs of a Man of the World. London: 1830. V. 40; 42; 46

MASSILLON, J. B. 1663-1742

Sermons. London;: 1797-98. V. 39

MASSILLON, JEAN BAPTISTE

Sermons 'On the Duties of the Great'. London: 1769. V. 38

MASSINELLO; Or A Satyr Against the Association, and the Guildhall Riot. London: 1683. V. 37; 38; 45

MASSINGER, PHILIP

The Dramatic Works. London: 1839. V. 38

The Dramatic Works. London: 1840. V. 39

The Duke of Millaine. London: 1638. V. 39; 44

The Dvke of Millaine. London: 1638. V. 37; 42

The Fatall Dovvry: a Tragedy. London: 1632. V. 37

The Great Dvke of Florence. London: 1636. V. 37

The Maid of honovr. London: 1632. V. 37

The Pictvre. London: 1630. V. 37

The Plays. London: 1805. V. 39; 40; 43

Plays. London: 1813. V. 42; 45

Plays, with Notes Critical and Explanatory by W. Gifford. London: 1813. V. 37

The Renegado, a Tragaecomedie. London: 1630. V. 37

The Roman Actor. London: 1629. V. 37

The Unnatural Combat. London: 1639. V. 39; 44

The Virgin Martyr; a Tragedie. London: 1631. V. 37

MASSINGHAM, H. J.

The Great Victorians. London: 1932. V. 44

MASSINGHAM, P.

The Dramatic Works. With an Introduction by Hartley Coleridge. London: 1839. V. 37

MASSMANN, ROBERT E.

Alpha and Omega, the Christian Symbol that Was Haddon Klingberg. New Britain: 1971. V. 44

A Dard Hunter Keepsake. New Britain: 1971. V. 41

MASSON, ANDRE

Mythology of Being. New York: 1942. V. 44

Nocturnal Notebook. New York: 1944. V. 42

MASSON, ARTHUR

An English Spelling Book, for the Use of Schools, in Three Parts . . . London: 1765. V. 41

MASSON, C. F. P.

Secret Memoirs of the Court of Petersburg Particularly Towards the End of the Reign of Catherine II and the Commencement of that of Paul I. London: 1800. V. 37; 40

MASSON, CHARLES

Narrative of Various Journeys in Balochistan, Afghanistan, and the Punjab . . . London: 1842. V. 45

Narrative of Various Journeys in Balochistan, Afghanistan, the Panjab & Kalat, and a Memoir on Eastern Balochistan. London: 1844. V. 39; 42

Secret Memoirs of the Court of Petersburg . . . London: 1800-1802. V. 42

MASSON, DAVID

The Life of John Milton: Narrated in Connexion with the Political, Ecclesiastical and Literary History of His Time. Cambridge: 1859-80. V. 45

MASSON, F.

Stapeliae Novae. London: 1796-97. V. 38

MASSON, FREDERIC

Livre du Sacre de l'Empereur Napoleon. Paris: 1908. V. 41

MASSON, FREDERICK

Cavaliers de Napoleon. Paris: 1895. V. 38

MASSON, G.

Italian Gardens. New York: 1961. V. 41; 45

Italian Gardens. New York: 1965. V. 37

MASSON, GEORGINA

Italian Villas and Palaces. New York: 1959. V. 44

Italian Gardens. London: 1961. V. 39

MASSON, IRVINE

The Mainz Psalters and Canon Missae 1457-1459. London: 1954. V. 38; 40; 46

MASSORILLI, LORENZO d. 1560

Aureum Sacrorum Hymnorum Opus. Foligno: 1547. V. 43

MASSOUF, or the Philosophy of the Day. London: 1802. V. 40

MASSOUL, CONSTANT DE

A Treatise on the Art of Painting, and the Composition of Colours, Containing Instructions for All the Various Processes of Painting. London: 1797. V. 41; 44

MASSY, RICHARD TUTHILL

Analytical Ethnology; the Mixed Tribes in Great Britain and Ireland Examined, and the Political, Physical and Metaphysical Blunderings on the Celt and the Saxon Exposed. London: H. Bailliere; Bath: 1855. V. 44

MAST, C. .

Annals of the Conestoga Valley in Lancaster, Berks, and Chester Counties, Pennsylvania. Scottdale: 1942. V. 41

MAST, ISAAC

The Gun, Rod and Saddle. Philadelphia: 1875. V. 38

MASTER, GEORGE STREYNSHAM

Some Notices of the Family of Master of East Langdon and Yotes in Kent, New Hall and Croston in Lancashire and Barrow Green in Surrey. London: 1874. V. 42; 46

MASTER Peter Patalan. A Fifteenth Century French Farce. Iowa City: 1975. V. 39

MASTERMAN, GEORGE FREDERICK

Seven Eventful Years in Paraguay. London: 1869. V. 46

THE MASTERPIECES of the Centennial International Exhibition. Philadelphia: 1876-78. V. 40

THE MASTERPIECES of the Centennial International Exposition Illustrated. Philadelphia: 1876. V. 42

MASTERS, EDGAR LEE 1868-1950

A Book of Verses. Chicago: 1898. V. 41

Lee, a Dramatic Poem. New York: 1926. V. 38; 41

Maximilian. Boston: 1902. V. 41

The New Star Chamber and Other Essays. Chicago: 1904. V. 41

The New Spoon River. New York: 1924. V. 39; 41

The Serpent in the Wilderness. New York: 1932. V. 46

The Serpent in the Wilderness. New York: 1933. V. 39

Skeeters Kirby. New York: 1923. V. 41

Spoon River Anthology. New York: 1905. V. 39

Spoon River Anthology. New York: 1915. V. 39; 40; 42; 43

Spoon River Anthology. New York: 1942. V. 45

MASTERS, J. E.

Old English Cordials - Rules and Receipts for Making All Sorts of English Wines and All of the Choicest Cordials for the Closet -1737. Bristol: 1938. V. 44

MASTERS, JOHN

Bhowani Junction. London: 1954. V. 45

MASTERS, JOSEPH

Little Stories of One and Two Syllables for Little Children. London: 1849. V. 39

MASTERS, JOSEPH G.

Shadows Across the Little Big Horn. Laramie: 1951. V. 45

MASTERS, MARY

Familiar Letters and Poems on Several Occasions. London: 1755. V. 43

MASTERS, MAXWELL T.

Vegetable Teratology . . . London: 1869. V. 43

MASTERS of Medicine. London: 1897-1900. V. 39

MASTERSON, WILLIAM BARCLAY

The 75th Anniversary Edition of Famous Gun Fighters of the Western Frontier. Monroe: 1982. V. 41

MASTIN, JOHN

The History and Antiquities of Naseby, in the County of Northampton. Cambridge. V. 45

The History and Antiquities of Naseby in the County of Northampton. Cambridge: 1792. V. 39; 46

MASUDA, H.

The Fishes of the Japanese Archipelago. Tokyo: 1984. V. 37; 38

MASUI, MITSUZO

Bibliography of Finance. 1935. V. 39

MASURY, JOHN W.

A Popular Treatise on the Art of House Painting - Plain and Decorative. New York: 1872. V. 40

Superfine Coach Colors for Coach, Carriage and Car Painting. New York & Chicago: 1895. V. 42

MASZEWSKI, W. M.

Index to the Trail Drivers of Texas. Houston: 1983. V. 45

THE MATABELE Gold Reefs and Estates Company Limited. London: 1898. V. 45

MATARATIUS, FRANCISCUS

De Componendis Versibus Hexametro et Pentametro. Venice: 1482. V. 38

MATCHETT, RICHARD J.

Baltimore Directory for 1853-54. Baltimore: 1853. V. 46

THE MATCHLESS Rogue: or, an Account of the Contrivances, Cheats, Stratagems and Amours of Tom Merryman, Commonly Called Newgate Tom. London: 1725. V. 46

THE MATCHLESS Rogue: or, n Account of the Contrivances, Cheats, Stratagems and Amours of Tom Merryman, Commonly Called Newgate Tom . . . London: 1725. V. 38; 46

MATELEIF, CORNELIS

Journael, Ende Historische Verhael, van de Treffeelijcke Reyse, Gedaen Naer Oost-Indien, ende China met elf Schepen. Amsterdam: 1648. V. 45

MATEMAN, CHARLES S. L.

The First Ascent of the Kasai. New York: 1889. V. 40

MATHE, CHARLES

History of Kidney Surgery. Baltimore: 1933. V. 38

THE MATHEMATICAL Monthly. Cambridge: 1858-1861. V. 40

MATHER, AMASA STONE

Extracts from the Letters, Diary and Note Books of . . . June 1907 to December 1908. Cleveland: 1910. V. 40

MATHER, COTTON 1662-1727

Baptistes. Boston: 1724. V. 39; 45

The Christian Phililosopher . . . London: 1721. V. 41; 46

Diary of . . . 1681-1708. Boston: 1911-12. V. 42

Eleutheria: or, an Idea of the Reformation in England: and a History of Non-Conformity in and Since that Reformation, with Predictions of a More Glorious Reformation and Revolution at Hand . . . London: 1698. V. 38; 40

India Christiana. Boston: 1721. V. 40

The Life and Death of the Renown'd Dr. John Eliot, Who Was the First Preacher of the Gospel to the Indians in America . . . London: 1691. V. 38

The Life and Death of the Reverend Mr. John Eliot Who was the First Preacher of the Gospel to the Indians in America. London: 1694. V. 42; 44

Magnalia Christi Americana. London: 1702. V. 38; 40; 41; 44; 45; 46

Magnalia Christi Americana; or, the Ecclesiastical History of New England. Hartford: 1820. V. 39; 41

Magnalia Christi Americana . . . Hartford: 1853-55. V. 43

Pietas in Patriam: the Life of His Excellency Sir William Phips, Knt. Late Captain General, and Governour in Chief of the Province of the Massachuset-Bay, New England. London: 1697. V. 42; 44; 46

Psalterium Americanum. Boston: 1718. V. 41; 45

Ratio Disciplinae Fratrum Nov Anglorum: a Faithful Account of the Discipline Professed and Practiced: in the Churches of New England. Boston: 1726. V. 38; 44

The Wonders of the Invisible World: Being an Account of the Tryals of Several Witches . . . London: 1693. V. 43

MATHER, FREDERIC GREGORY

The Refugees of 1776 from Long Island to Connecticut. Albany: 1913. V. 44

MATHER, GEORGE R.

Two Great Scotsmen, the Brothers William and John Hunter. Glasgow: 1893. V. 42

MATHER, INCREASE 1639-1723

A Discourse Proving that the Christian Religion, is the Only True Religion. Boston: 1702. V. 43

A Discourse Concerning Faith and Fervency in Prayer, and the Glorious Kingdom of the Lord Jesus Christ, on Earth, Now Approaching. Boston: 1710. V. 40; 43

MATHER, INCREASE 1639-1723 continued

A Disquisition Concerning Ecclesiastical Councils. Boston: 1716. V. 40; 42; 45

Early History of New England. Albany: 1864. V. 40

The First Principles of New England, Concerning the Subject of Baptisme & Communion of Churches . . . Cambridge: 1675. V. 38

The Mystery of Israel's Salvation, Explained and Applyed: or, A Discourse Concerning the General Conversion of the Israelitish Nation. London: 1669. V. 37

The Order of the Churches in New England Vindicated. Boston: 1700. V. 44

The Order of the Gospel, Professed and Practiced by the Churches of Christ in New England, Justified. Boston: 1700. V. 42; 44; 45

A Sermon . . . Preached at Roxbury, Oct. 29, 1718 When Mr. Thomas Walter Was Ordained a pastor in the Church, by His Grandfather . . . Boston: 1718. V. 39

MATHER, JAMES

The Herring, Its Natural History and National Importance; Edinburgh: 1864. V. 38

MATHER, RICHARD

V. 44

Church-Government and Church-Covenant Discussed, in an Answer to the Elders of the Several Churches in New England . . . London: 1643. V. 39

A Defence of the Answer and Arguments of the Synod Met at Boston in the Year 1662. Cambridge: 1664. V. 45

A Platform of Church Discipline, Gathered Out of the World of God, and Agreed Upon by the Elders and Messengers of the Churches Assembled in the Synod at Cambridge in New England . . . London: 1653. V. 42

A Platform of Church Discipline, Gathered Out of the World of God, and Agreed Upon by the Elders and Messengers of the Churches Assembled in the Synod at Cambridge in New England . . . Printed in New England: 1653. V. 44

MATHER, SAMUEL 1706-1785

An Abridgement of the Life of the Late Reverend and Learned Dr. Cotton Mather, of Boston in New England. London: 1744. V. 42

All Men Will Not Be Saved Forever; or, an Attempt to Prove. Boston: 1782. V. 43

An Attempt to Shew That America Must Be Known to the Ancients. Boston: 1773. V. 38; 40

The Fall of the Mighty Lamented: A Funeral Discourse Upon the Death of Wilhelmina Dorothea Carolina, Queen-Consort to His Majesty. Boston: 1738. V. 38; 40

The Life of the Very Reverend and Learned Cotton Mather. Boston: 1729. V. 37; 38; 39; 40; 42; 45

Memoirs of the Life of the Late Reverend Increase Mather, D.D. Who Died August 23, 1723. London: 1725. V. 41; 44

The Right of the Government of Connecticut to Claim and Hold the lands Within the Limits of Their Charter . . . Hartford: 1773. V. 44

MATHERS, C. W.

The Far North. Edmonton: 1902. V. 42

MATHERS, E. POWYS

A Circle of the Seasons. Waltham St. Lawrence: 1929. V. 38

A Circle of the Seasons. London: 1929. V. 38

Eastern Love. London: 1927-30. V. 42; 44; 45

Illustrations by Franz Felix. New York. V. 46

Love Night. London: 1936. V. 41

Love Night. A Laothian Gallantry. Waltham St. Lawrence: 1936. V. 42

Love Night: A Laotian Gallantry. (London): (1936). V. 37

Maxims and Considerations of Chamfort. Waltham St. Lawrence: 1926. V. 42

Procreant Hymn. Waltham St. Lawrence: 1926. V. 37; 39; 42; 43

Red Wise. Waltham St. Lawrence: 1925. V. 44

Red Wise. London: 1926. V. 38; 42

Red Wise. N.P.: 1926. V. 39

Red Wise. Waltham St. Lawrence: 1926. V. 37; 40; 42; 44; 45

Red Wise. Waltham Saint Lawrence: 1926. V. 38; 41

Red Wise. (Waltham St. Lawrence): 1926. V. 37

MATHERS, EDWARD P.

South Africa and How to Reach It by the Castle Line. London: 1889. V. 39; 40

MATHERS, JAMES

Dedication to Be Sung at the Dedication of the Howard Street Presbyterian Church, San Francisco, June 15, 1851. San Francisco: 1851. V. 43

MATHERS, JOHN, PSEUD.

The History of Mr. John Decastro and His Brother Bat, Commonly Called Old Crab. London: 1815. V. 40; 46

MATHES, J. HARVEY

The Old Guard in Gray. Memphis: 1897. V. 40; 42; 44

MATHES, W. MICHAEL

Mexico on Stone. San Francisco: 1984. V. 37; 38; 39; 40; 41; 42; 44; 45; 46

Spanish Approaches to the Island of California 1628-1632. San Francisco: 1975. V. 37; 39

MATHESIUS, JOHANNES 1504-1565

Historien, Von des Ehrwirdigen in Gott Seligen Thewren Manns Gottes, Doctoris Martini Luthers, anfang, lehr, leben und sterben, Alles Ordendich der Jarzal nach, Wie Sich alle Sachen zu Jeder Zeyt Haben Zugetragen . . . Nurnberg: 1566. V. 38

MATHESON, EWING

Works in Iron, Bridge and Roof Structures. London: 1873. V. 44

Works in Iron. Bridge and Roof Structures. London: 1877. V. 38

MATHESON, JOHN

England to Delhi: a Narrative of Indian Travel. London: 1870. V. 46

MATHESON, R.

Born of Man and Woman. 1954. V. 43

MATHESON, RICHARD

Bid Time Return. New York: (1949). V. 37

Born of Man and Woman. Philadelphia: 1954. V. 38; 40; 42

Hell House. New York: 1971. V. 39

A Stir of Echoes. 1958. V. 39

MATHESON, WILLIAM

Printer's Choice. A Selection of American Press Books 1968-1978. Austin: 1983. V. 44

MATHEWS, ALFRED

History of the Counties Lehigh and Carbon . . . Philadelphia: 1884. V. 46

MATHEWS, ALFRED E.

Gems of Rocky Mountain Scenery, Containing Views Along and Near the Union Pacific Railroad. New York: 1869. V. 39; 42; 43; 46

Pencil Sketches of Montana. New York: 1868. V. 45; 46

Pencil Sketches of Colorado, Its Cities, Principal Towns and Mountain Scenery. Denver: 1961. V. 41

MATHEWS, AMANDA

The Hieroglyphics of Love. Stories of Sonoratown and Old Mexico. Los Angeles: 1906. V. 39

MATHEWS, ANNE

Anecdotes of Actors. London: 1844. V. 43

MATHEWS, CHARLES

Catalogue Raisonee of Mr. Mathew's Gallery of Theatrical Portraits . . . London: 1833. V. 38; 40

The London Mathews: Containing an Account of this Celebrated Comedian's Trip to America. New York: 1824. V. 39

The London Mathews: Containing a Copious Narration of all the Celebrated Entertainments of the Inimitable Charles Mathews . . . London: 1824-26. V. 39

MATHEWS, CHARLES EDWARD

The Annals of Mont Blac. London: 1898. V. 41; 43; 44

MATHEWS, CORNELIUS

Big Abel and Little Manhattan. New York: 1845. V. 45

Chanticleer: a Thanksgiving Story. Boston & New York: 1850. V. 39

The Motley Book: a Series of Sketches of American Life. New York: 1840. V. 40

MATHEWS, EDWARD J.

Crossing the Plains. N.P.: 1930. V. 38; 40; 42

Crossing the Plains. Adventures of Edward James Mathews in '59. N.P.: (1930). V. 37

MATHEWS, G. M.

The Birds of Norfolk and Lord Howe Islands, and the Australasian South Polar Quadrant . . . London: 1928. V. 43

MATHEWS, HARRY

The Conversions. New York: 1962. V. 44

Out of Bounds: Poems. Providence: 1989. V. 46

Singular Pleasures. New York: 1988. V. 42

Tlooth. 1966. V. 44

The Way Home. 1988. V. 40; 45

The Way Home. New York: 1988. V. 42; 44

MATHEWS, JOANNA

Belle's Pink Boots. New York: 1881. V. 41; 43

MATHEWS, JOHN

A Voyage to the River Sierra-Leone, on the Coast of Africa. London: 1788. V. 43

MATHEWS, M. M., MRS.

Ten Years in Nevada or Life on the Pacific Coast. Buffalo: 1880. V. 37; 38; 40; 46

MATHEWS, R. G.

Men and Women Merely Players. Montreal: 1903. V. 37

MATHEWS, SALLIE

Interwoven, a Pioneer Chronicle. El Paso: 1958. V. 39

MATHEWS, THOMAS

The History of the mediterranean Fleet from 1741 to 1744, with the Original Letters, &c. that Passed Between Admirals Matthews (sic) and Lestock. London: 1745. V. 38

A Narrative of the Proceedings of His Majesty's Fleet in the Mediterranean, and the Combined Fleets of France and Spain, from the Year 1741 to March 1744. London: 1744. V. 43

A Narrative of the Proceedings of His Majesty's Fleet in the Mediterranean and the Combined Fleets of France and Spain, from the Year 1741 to March 1744. London: 1745. V. 41; 46

MATHIAS, THOMAS JAMES

Componimenti Lirici de' Piu Illustri Poeti d'Italia. Londra: 1802. V. 39

An Epistle in Verse to the Rev. Dr. Randolph, English Preceptor to H.R.H. the Princess of Wales, Occasioned by the Publication of the Correspodnence Between the Earl, and Countess of Jersey, and the Doctor, Upon the Subject of Some Letters . . . London: 1796. V. 40

An Essay on the Evidence, External and Internal, Relating to the Poems Attributed to Thomas Rowley. London: 1783. V. 41

Poesie Liriche Toscane . . . Naples: 1824. V. 44

The Pursuits of Literature . . . London: 1797. V. 45

The Pursuits of Literature. London: 1798. V. 39; 40; 42; 45

Pursuits of Literature. Philadelphia: 1800. V. 37

The Pursuits of Literature, a Satirical Poem in Four Dialogues. London: 1812. V. 37

The Shade of Alexander Pope on the Banks of the Thames. Dublin: 1799. V. 40

MATHIAS, WILLEM

Libellus de Bello Iusto & Licito. Antwerp: 1514. V. 43

MATHIASSEN, T.

Prehistory of the Angmagssalik Eskimos. Copenhagen: 1933. V. 39

MATHIASSEN, THERKEL

Archaeological Collections from the Western Eskimos. By Therkel Mathiassen. Copenhagen: 1930. V. 37

MATHIESEN, KENNETH

How We Saw the United States of Ameica. Edinburgh: 1883. V. 39; 42

MATHIESON, KENNETH

How We Saw the United States of America. Dunfermline: 1883. V. 39

MATHIESSEN, PETER

Partisans. London: 1956. V. 38

The Snow Leopard. New York. V. 42

MATHIEU DE DOMBASLE, CHRISTOPHE JOSEPH ALEXANDRE

Essai Sur l'Analyse Des Eaux Naturelles, Par les Reactifs. Nancy: 1810. V. 39

MATHIEU, PIERRE LOUIS

Gustave Moreau: With a Catalogue of the Finished Paintings, Watercolors and Drawings. Boston: 1976. V. 39; 40; 45

Gustave Moreau. London: 1977. V. 46

MATHISON, GILBERT FARQUHAR

Narrative of a Visit to Brazil, Chile and Peru, and the Sandwich Islands During the Years 1821 and 1822. London: 1825. V. 39; 40; 42; 43

MATILLA, ROBERT W.

A Chronological Bibliography of Works of Vilhjalmur Stefansson (1879-1962) . . . Hanover: 1978. V. 44

MATISSE, HENRI

Camera Work. New York: 1912. V. 39

Cinquante Dessins . . . (Paris): 1920. V. 37

Jazz. New York: 1983. V. 39

Portraits. Monte Carlo: 1955. V. 37

Portraits. Monte Carlo: 1955. V. 37

MATLOCK, J. EUGENE

Gone Beyond the Law. Dallas: 1940. V. 38

MATON, WILLIAM GEORGE

Observations Relative Chiefly to the Natural History, Picturesque Scienery and Antiquities of the Western Counties of England. Salisbury: 1797. V. 40

MATRAINI, CHIARA

Breve Discorso Sopra la Vita e Laude Della Beatiss(ima) Verg(ine) e Madre del Figliuol(o) di Dio. Lucca: 1590. V. 45

THE MATRIOMINIAL Preceptor. London: 1765. V. 42

MATRIX 1. 1985. V. 40
MATRIX 1. Andoversford: 1988. V. 42

MATRIX 10. 1990. V. 45
MATRIX 10. Andoversford: 1990. V. 44
MATRIX 10. Gloucestershire: 1990. V. 46

MATRIX 11. 1991. V. 46

MATRIX 3. Andoversford: 1983. V. 42

MATRIX 4. Andoversford: 1984. V. 42

MATRIX 5. Andoversford: 1985. V. 38
MATRIX 5. Gloucestershire: 1985. V. 40

MATRIX 6. 1986. V. 40
MATRIX 6. Andoversford: 1986. V. 38; 39; 41; 44; 45
MATRIX 6. Gloucestershire: 1986. V. 40; 41
MATRIX 6. London: 1986. V. 41

MATRIX 7. 1987. V. 40; 45
MATRIX 7. Andoversford: 1987. V. 40; 42; 44
MATRIX 7. Gloucestershire: 1987. V. 40; 41
MATRIX 7. Gloucestershrie: 1987. V. 46
MATRIX 7. London: 1987. V. 41; 44

MATRIX 8. Manor Farm: 1986. V. 40
MATRIX 8. Andoversford: 1988. V. 40; 42; 44
MATRIX 8. Gloucestershire: 1988. V. 41
MATRIX 8. London: 1988. V. 41; 44

MATRIX 9. N.P.: 1949. V. 44
MATRIX 9. N.P.: 198. V. 42
MATRIX 9. Manor Farm: 1986. V. 45
MATRIX 9. 1989. V. 42
MATRIX 9. Gloucestershire: 1989. V. 41
MATRIX 9. London: 1989. V. 44
MATRIX 9. N.P.: 1989. V. 42; 44

MATRIX; A Review for Printers and Bibliophiles. Glouchestershire: 1981-85. V. 39

MATRIX Seven. Manor Farm: 1986. V. 39
MATRIX Seven. Manor Farm: 1986. V. 38; 46
MATRIX Seven. Manor Farm: 1987. V. 39

MATSON, HENRY JAMES

Remarks on the Slave Trade and African Squadron. London: 1848. V. 42; 43

MATSON, NEHEMIAH

Memories of Shabena. Chicago: 1878. V. 38; 40; 45

Reminiscences of Bureau County . . . Princeton, Ill: 1872. V. 37

MATTES, MERRILL J.

Platte River Road Narratives. Urbana: 1988. V. 38; 40; 41

MATTESON, ANTONETTE

The Occult Family Physician; and Botanic Guide to Health . . . Buffalo: 1894. V. 45

MATTEUCCI, CARLO

Lectures on the Physical Phenomena of Living Beings. London: 1847. V. 40

MATTHAEUS, ANTONIUS 1601-1654

De Criminibus Ad Lib XLVIII et XLVIII. Dig. Commentarius . . . Vesasliae: 1679. V. 46

MATTHES, FRANCOIS

Geologic History of the Yosemite Valley. Washington: 1930. V. 44

MATTHESON, JOHANN

Kleine General-Bass-Schule, Worin Nicht nur Lernende, Sondern Vornehmlich Lehrende, Aus den Allerersten Anfangsgruenden des Clavier Spielens . . . Hamburg: 1735. V. 40

MATTHEW, OF WESTMINSTER

Flores Historiarum per Matthaeum Westmonasteriensem Collecti . . . Londini: 1570. V. 43; 45

Flores Historiarum. London: 1890. V. 44

Flores Historiarum. London: 1570. V. 37

MATTHEWS, A.

The Birds of Oxfordshire and the Neighbourhood. 1849-52-49-80. V. 46

MATTHEWS, A. continued

A Monograph of the Coleopterous families. London: 1899. V. 39; 40

Trichopterygia. Illustrata et Descripta. A Monograph of the Trichopterygia (and) Supplement. London: 1872, 1900. V. 39

Trichopterygia Illustrata et Descripta. A Monograph of the Trichopterygia (and) Supplement. London: 1872 & 1900. V. 40

MATTHEWS, BRANDER

Bookbindings, Old and New. London: 1896. V. 39; 44

Pen and Ink. Papers on Subjects of More or Less Importance. New York/London: 1888. V. 37

MATTHEWS, CORNELIUS

Poems on Man, In His Various Aspects Under the American Republic. New York: 1843. V. 45

The Various Writings of Cornelius Matthews. New York: 1843. V. 45

MATTHEWS, ELIZA KIRKHAM

What Has Been. Alexandria: 1803. V. 45; 46

MATTHEWS, FREDERICK C.

American Merchant Ships 1850-1900 (-Series Two). Salem: 1930-31. V. 39; 41; 46

MATTHEWS, HENRY

The Diary of an Invalid Being the Journal of a Tour in Pursuit of Health in Portugal, Italy, Switzerland and France in the Years 1817, 1818, 1819. London: 1820. V. 39; 40; 43; 45

The Diary of an Invalid . . . . London: 1835. V. 42

MATTHEWS, J. W.

Incwadi Yami, or Twenty Years' Personal Experience in South Africa. New York: 1887. V. 40

MATTHEWS, JAMES M.

The Statutes at Large of the Provisional Government of the Confederate States of America . . . Richmond: 1864. V. 40

MATTHEWS, JOHN

Eloisa in Deshabille: a Satirical Poem. London: 1819. V. 46

A Voyage to the River Sierra-Leone, On the Coast of Africa. London: 1791. V. 39

MATTHEWS, JOHN N.

The Statutes at Large of the Provisional Government of the Confederate States of America . . . February 8, 1816. to . . . February 18, 1862. Richmond: 1864. V. 42

MATTHEWS, LEONARD

A Long Life in Review. St. Louis?: 1927. V. 40; 43

A Long Life in Review. (St.Louis?: 1927). V. 37

MATTHEWS, MARY M.

Ten Years in Nevada; or, Life on the Pacific Coast. Buffalo: 1880. V. 37; 43

MATTHEWS, R. BORLASE

The Aviation Pocket Book for 1913. London: 1913. V. 40

The Aviation Pocket-Book for 1919-20. London: 1919. V. 40

MATTHEWS, SALLIE REYNOLDS

Interwoven, a Pioneer Chronicle. Houston: 1936. V. 37; 44; 45; 46

Interwoven. 1958. V. 45

Interwoven. A Pioneer Chronicle. El Paso: 1958. V. 37; 39; 42; 46

Interwoven: a Pioneer Chronicle (and) Lambshead Before Interwoven: a Texas Range Chronicle, 1848-1878. College Station: 1982. V. 46

MATTHEWS, T.

Advice to the Young Whist Player . . . Bath: 1814. V. 45

MATTHEWS, THOMAS

A Narrative of the Proceedings of His Majesty's Fleet in the Mediterranean, and the Combined Fleets of France and Spain, from the Year 1741, to March 1744. London: 1744. V. 45

MATTHEWS, W.

Charlotte Bronte. A Tribute to Her Genius & Works. London: 1897. V. 43

MATTHEWS, WASHINGTON

The Night Chant, a Navaho Ceremony. Washington: 1902. V. 37

MATTHEWS, WILLIAM

Bookbinding, a Manual for Those Interested in the Craft of Bookbinding. London: 1929. V. 44

A Collection of Affidavits and Certificates, Relative to the Wonderful Cure of Mrs. Ann Mattingly . . . City of Washington: 1824. V. 43

Modern Bookbinding Practically Considered: a Lecture Read Before the Grolier Club of New York, March 25, 1885. New York: 1889. V. 37; 39; 41

MATTHEY, C. G. R.

Catalogue of Works on Fencing and Duelling, Forming the Private Collection of . . . London: 1898. V. 45

MATTHIAE, AUGUSTUS

A Copious Greek Grammar. London: 1829. V. 38

MATTHIAS, BENJAMIN

The Politician's Register. Philadelphia: 1835. V. 42

MATTHIASON, J. H.

Bedford and Its Environs, or an Historical and Topographical Sketch of the Town of Bedford, and Places Adjacent . . . Bedford: 1831. V. 41

MATTHIESSEN, PETER

The Cloud Forest. New York: 1961. V. 39

In the Spirit of Crazy Horse. New York: 1983. V. 38; 40; 42; 43; 44; 45; 46

Indian Country. New York: 1984. V. 45

Killing Mr. Watson. New York: 1989. V. 45

Men's Lives. N.P.: 1983. V. 44

Men's Lives. New York: 1986. V. 45

Men's Lives. N.P.: 1986. V. 39; 43

Nine Headed Dragon River. Boston: 1986. V. 42

On the River Styx and Other Stories. New York: 1988. V. 45

On the River Styx and Other Stories. New York: 1989. V. 46

Partisans. London: 1955. V. 41

Partisans. New York: 1955. V. 42; 46

Paritsans. London: 1956. V. 37; 42; 46

Race Rock. London: 1954. V. 41

Race Rock. New York: 1954. V. 37; 38; 42; 45; 46

Raditzer. New York: 1961. V. 44; 45

Raditzer. London: 1963. V. 42

The Shorebirds of North America. 1967. V. 46

The Shorebirds of North America. London: 1967. V. 45

The Shorebirds of North America. New York: 1967. V. 39; 44

The Snow Leopard. New York. V. 39

The Snow Leopard. New York: 1978. V. 42

Under the Mountain Wall. New York: 1962. V. 42

Wildlife in America. V. 39

Wildlife in America. New York: 1959. V. 37; 39; 43; 46

MATTHIEU, PIERRE

La Conivration De Conchine. Paris: 1618. V. 37

The Heroyk Life and Deplorable Death of the most Christian King Henry the Fourth . . . Translated by Ed Grimestone, Esquire. London: 1612. V. 37

The Povverfull Favorite, or, the Life of Aelius Seianus. 1628. V. 41

MATTHIOLI, PIETRO ANDREA

Commentarii Secundo Aucti in Libros Sex Pedacii Dioscoridis Anarzabei de Medica Materia. Venetiis: 1558. V. 39

Epistolarum Medicinalium Libri Quinque. Prague: 1561. V. 38

Opera Omnia. Frankfurt: 1598. V. 38

Opusculum de Simplicium Medicamentorum Facultatibus Secundum Locos & Genera . . . Venetiis: 1569. V. 38; 39

Opusculum, de Simplicium Medicamentorum Facultatibus Secundum Locos & Genera. Venice: 1569. V. 39

MATTHISON, ARTHUR

Enoch Arden, a Drama, in Five Acts, Founded on Tennyson's Great Poem. New York: 1969. V. 43

MATTIEU, PIERRE

The Powerfull Favorite, or the Life of Aelius Seianus. London: 1628. V. 45

MATTILA, ROBERT W.

A Chronological Bibliography of Works of Vilhjalmur Stefansson (1879-1962). Hanover: 1978. V. 45

MATTIOLI, LODOVICO 1662-1747

Primi Elementi Della Pittura Raccolti da Varj Auttori per Uso de Principianti del Dissegno, et Intagliati ad Instanza di Lelio dalla Volpe in Bologna. Bologna: 1728. V. 39

MATTIOLI, PIER ANDREA

Commentarii in VI. Libros Pedacii Dioscoridis Anazarbei de Medica materia, ab Ipso Autore Recogniti . . . Venice: 1583. V. 43

MATTIOLI, PIETRO ANDREA 1501-1577

Apologia Adversus Amathum Lusitanum. Venice: 1558. V. 42

Commentarii, in Libros Sex . . . Dioscorides . . . De Medica Materia. Venetiis: 1554. V. 37; 42; 44

Commentarii, in Libros Sex . . . De Materia Medica . . . Venetijs: 1554. V. 37

MATTIOLI, PIETRO ANDREA 1501-1577 continued

Commentarii Secundo Aucti, in Libros Sex Pedacii Dioscoridis Anazarbe de Medica Maateria. (with) Apologia Adversus Amathum Lusitanum . . . Venice: 1558. V. 37

Compendium de Plantis Omnibus. Venetiis: 1571. V. 37; 42; 44

Opera Quae Extant Omnia: hoc Est, Commentarii in VI. Frankfurt: 1598. V. 37

MATTSON, MORRIS

Paul Ulric, or, the Adventures of an Enthusiast. New York: 1835. V. 45

MATURIN, C. R.

The Melmoth the Wanderer: a Tale. London: 1892. V. 43

MATURIN, CHARLES ROBERT

The Albigenses, a Romance. London: 1824. V. 39

Bertram; or, The Castle of St. Aldobran, an Italian Tale . . . London: 1816. V. 38; 45

Melmoth the Wanderer. Edinburgh: 1820. V. 39

Melmoth the Wanderer. Edinburgh: 1820-21. V. 38

Melmoth the Wanderer. London: 1892. V. 38; 40

The Wild Irish Boy. London: 1808. V. 38; 46

Woman; or, Pour et Contre. Edinburgh: 1818. V. 38; 39; 40

MATURIN, EDWARD

Montezuma: the Last of the Aztec. New York: 1845. V. 43

MATURIN, R. C.

Bertram, or The Castle of St. Aldobrand, Being the Romance of the Tragedy. London: 1816. V. 41

MATZ, B. W.

Character Sketches from Dickens. London: 1924. V. 38

MATZ, FRIEDRICH

Die Dionysischen Sarkophage. Berlin: 1968-75. V. 44

MAU, AUGUST

Pompei: Its Life and Art. New York: 1899. V. 41

MAUCH Chunk and Vicinity: With a Description of the Famous Switch-Back Railroad. Mauch Chunk: 1872. V. 46

MAUCLAIR CAMILLE, AMES BRETONNES

Trois Contes Illustres par J. Wely. Paris: 1907. V. 46

MAUDE, A. H.

The 47th (London) Division, 1914-1919. London: 1922. V. 45

MAUDE, AYLMER

A Peculiar People. The Dukhobors. London: 1905. V. 40

MAUDE, FRANCIS C.

Five Years in Madagascar with Notes on the Military Situation. London: 1895. V. 45

MAUDE, JOAN

Behind the Night-Light: The By-World of a Child of Three. London: 1912. V. 46

MAUDE, JOHN

Visit to the Falls of Niagara in 1800. London: 1826. V. 37; 46

MAUDE, THOMAS

Verbeia; or Wharfdale, a Poem, Descriptive and Didactic with Historical Remarks. York: 1782. V. 40; 42

Viator, a Poem. London: 1782. V. 42

Wensley-Dale; or Rural Contemplations; a Poem. London: 1772. V. 40; 43

Wensley-Dale; or Rural Contemplations, a Poem. London: 1780. V. 40; 42

MAUDSLAY, ALFRED PERCIVAL

Biologia Centrali-Americana; or, Contributions to the Knowledge of the Fauna and Flora of Mexico and Central America. New York: 1974. V. 42

MAUDSLAY, ANNE C.

A Glimpse at Guatemala and Some Notes on the Ancient Monuments of Central America. London: 1899. V. 37; 38; 42

MAUDSLAY, ATHOL

Highways and Horses. London: 1888. V. 37

MAUDSLEY, HENRY 1835-1918

Body and Will: Being an Essay Concerning Will In Its Metaphysical, Physiological and pathological Respects. London: 1883. V. 45

The Pathology of Mind. London: 1879. V. 43; 45

MAUDUIT, ISRAEL

The Case of the Dissenting Ministers Addressed to the Lords Spiritual and Temporal . . . London: 1772. V. 39

Considerations on the American War. Addressed to the People of England. London: 1776. V. 37

A Short View of the History of the Colony of Massachusetts Bay, with Respect to Their Charters and Constitutions. London: 1774. V. 39

MAUGHAM, R. C. F.

Wild Game in Zambezia. London: 1914. V. 39; 43

MAUGHAM, WILLIAM SOMERSET 1874-1965

Ah King. London: 1933. V. 40; 41; 42; 43; 44

Ah King. London: (1933). V. 37

Ashenden. London: 1928. V. 42; 44; 45

The Bishop's Apron. London: 1906. V. 38

The Book Bag. Florence: 1932. V. 37; 39; 43; 44; 45

Cakes and Ale . . . London. V. 43

Cakes and Ale. Garden City: 1930. V. 46

Cakes and Ale. London: 1930. V. 38; 39; 42; 46

Cakes and Ale. London: 1954. V. 37; 38; 39; 40; 44

The Casuarina Tree. London: 1926. V. 46

Christmas Holiday. London: 1939. V. 39; 43

The Circle. London: 1921. V. 41

The Collected Plays. (with) The Selected Novels. London: 1951-53. V. 39

Cosmopolitans. London: 1936. V. 41

Creatures of Circumstance. London: 1947. V. 40; 46

Don Fernando or Variations on Some Spanish Themes. Garden City: 1935. V. 46

Don Fernando. London: 1935. V. 40; 41; 42; 46

Don Fernando, or Variations on Some Spanish Themes. London & Toronto: 1935. V. 37; 38

Don Fernando, or Variations on Some Spanish Themes. London and Toronto: 1935. V. 39; 40

The Gentleman in the Parlour: a Record of a Journey from Rangoon to Haiphong. London: 1930. V. 38; 39; 44

Home and Beauty. London: 1923. V. 46

The Judgement Seat. London: 1934. V. 38; 39; 43; 44; 45

The Land of the Blessed Virgin. London: 1905. V. 45; 46

The Letter. New York: 1925. V. 46

A Letter from Pontus. New York: 1936. V. 41

Lisa of Lambeth. London: 1897. V. 37; 38; 42; 44; 45

Liza of Lambeth. London. V. 39

Liza of Lambeth. London: 1947. V. 37; 39; 43

The Magician. London: 1908. V. 39; 40; 41

The Making of a Saint. 1898. V. 46

Making of a Saint. London: 1898. V. 37; 38; 46

A Man of Honour. London: 1903. V. 38; 45

The Moon and Sixpence. London: 1919. V. 39; 43

My South Sea Island. Chicago and Skokie: 1964. V. 41

The Narrow Corner. London: 1932. V. 41

Of Human Bondage. Garden City: 1915. V. 46

Of Human Bondage. London: 1915. V. 39; 40; 41; 45

Of Human Bondage. New York: 1915. V. 40; 41; 42; 45

Of Human Bondage. Garden City: 1936. V. 37; 44; 46

Of Human Bondage. New York: 1936. V. 38

Of Human Bondage. 1938. V. 44

Of Human Bondage. New Haven: 1938. V. 40; 42; 45; 46

Of Human Bondage. New York: 1938. V. 44

Of Human Bondage. Washington: 1946. V. 37; 40; 42; 43

On a Chinese Screen. London: 1922. V. 44

On a Chinese Screen. London: 1932. V. 45

Orientations. London: 1899. V. 37; 38; 39; 40

Our Betters. London: 1923. V. 44

Points of View. London: 1959. V. 38

The Razor's Edge. Garden City: 1944. V. 37; 38; 39; 45

The Selected Novels. London: 1953. V. 38; 45

The Selected Novels. London: (1953). V. 37

Strictly Personal. 1941. V. 43

Strictly Personal. Garden City: 1941. V. 39; 42; 45; 46

Strictly Personal. New York: 1941. V. 41

The Summing Up. London: 1938. V. 44

The Summing Up. Garden City: 1954. V. 39; 46

The Summing Up. New York: 1954. V. 41; 45

Ten Novels and Their Authors. London: 1954. V. 38

Theatre. New York: 1937. V. 38

Theatre. N.P.: 1947. V. 41

MAUGHAM, WILLIAM SOMERSET 1874-1965 continued

Theatre. London: 1937. V. 39; 46

The Trembling of a Leaf. London: 1921. V. 40; 42

The Unconquered. New York: 1944. V. 38; 41

The Vagrant Mood. London: 1952. V. 38; 39; 45

A Writer's Notebook. Garden City: 1949. V. 40; 42; 43; 46

A Writer's Notebook. Garden City: 1949. V. 46

A Writer's Notebook. London: 1949. V. 39; 40; 41

A Writer's Notebook. New York: 1949. V. 41; 42

MAUGHAN, WILLIAM C.

The Alps of Arabia. London: 1873. V. 45

MAUGHAN, WILLIAM SOMERSET 1874-1965

Cakes and Ale. V. 37

MAULE, FRANCIS I.

The Tame Trout and Other Fairy Tales. N.P.. V. 43

MAULEON, AUGER DE, SEIGNEUR DE GRANIER d. ca. 1650

Recveil de Divers Memoires, Harangves, Remonstrances et Lettres Servans a l'Histoire de Nostre Temps. Paris: 1623. V. 43

MAULSBY, O. W.

Rolling Stone: The Autobiography of O. W. Maulsby. Los Angeles: 1931. V. 39; 43; 46

MAUN-GWU-DAUS

An Account of the North American Indians, Written For Maun-Gwu-Daus, a Chief of the Indians. Leicester: 1848. V. 44

MAUND, BENJAMIN

The Botanic Garden. London: 1835-36. V. 39

The Botanic Garden. London: 1825. V. 37

The Botanic Garden. London: 1825-1830. V. 38

The Botanic Garden. London: 1878. V. 37

The Botanist. London: 1837-46. V. 39

The Botanist . . . London: 1893. V. 44

The Fruitist, a Treatise on Orchard and Garden Fruits, Their Description, History and Management. London: 1850. V. 44

MAUNDER, E. WALTER

The Indian Eclipse 1898. London: 1899. V. 42

MAUNDER, SAMUEL

The Treasury of History . . . New York: 1851. V. 45

MAUNDEVILLE, JOHN

The Travels of Sir John Mandeville. London: 1900. V. 38

The Voiage and Travaile of Sir John Maundevile, Ktd. Which Treateth of the Way to Hierusalem. New York: 1928. V. 37; 38

MAUNDREL, HENRY

A Journey from Aleppo to Jerusalem. New Haven: 1814. V. 40

maundrell, ehrny

a Journey from Aleppo to Jerusalem at Easter, A.D., 1697. Oxford: 1707. V. 45

MAUNDRELL, HENRY

A Journey from Aleppo to Jerusalem at Easter, A.D. 1697. Oxford: 1732. V. 38; 45

A Journey from Aleppo to Jerusalem: at Easter, A.D. 1697. Oxford: 1749. V. 45

A Journey from Aleppo to Jerusalem at Easter A.D. 1697. Oxford: 1703. V. 37

MAUNSELL, R.

A Grammar of the New Zealand Language. Auckland: 1842. V. 45

MAUNZIO, PAOLO 1512-1574

Epistolarum . . . Libri Decem, Quinque Nuper Additis, Eiusdem Que Praefationes Appellantur. Lyon: 1574. V. 43

MAUNZIO, PAOLOS 1512-1574

Orthographiae Ratio. Venice: 1566. V. 46

MAUPAS, CHARLES

A French Grammar and Syntaxe, containing most exact and certaine rules, for the prounuciation, orthography, construction, and use of the French language. Translated into English, with many additions and explications, peculiarly usefull to . . . London: 1634. V. 37

MAUPASSANT, GUY DE

Claire de Lune. Leipzig: 1916. V. 45

La Main Gauche. Paris: 1889. V. 43

The Wretch. Cazenovia: 1966. V. 44

MAUPERTIUS, PIERRE LOUIS MOREAU DE

The Figure of the Earth, Determined from Observations . . . at the Polar Circle. London: 1738. V. 39; 40; 41; 42; 44

MAUPERTUIS, PIERRE LOUIS MOREAU DE

Astronomie Nautique; ou Elemens d'Astronomie, Tant Pour un Observatoire Fixe, Que Pour un Observatoire Mobile. Paris: 1743. V. 44

Dissertation Physique a l'occasion du Negre Blanc. Leyden: 1744. V. 38

La Figure de la Terre, Determinee par les Observations de Messieurs de Maupertuis, Clairault, Camus, Le Monnier . . . Paris: 1738. V. 38; 41; 44; 45

MAUQUEST DE LA MOTTE, GUILLAUME 1665-1737

A General Treatise of Midwifery. 1746. V. 39

A General Treatise on Midwifery; Illustrated with Upward of Four Hundred Curious Observations and Reflexions Concerning that Art. London: 1746. V. 41; 43

MAURAN, G.

Essai sur les Maladies qui Attaquent le Plus Communement les Gens de Mer. Marseilles: 1766. V. 42; 45

MAURER, CHRISTOPH

XL Embelmata Miscella Nova. Zurich: 1820. V. 39

MAURICE, F.

The History of the Scots Guards from the Creation of the Regiment to the Eve of the Great War. London: 1934. V. 41

MAURICE, FREDERICK DENISON

Modern Philosophy; or, a Treatise of Moral and Metaphysical Philosophy from the Fourteenth Century to the French Revolution, with a Glimpse into the Nineteenth Century. London: 1862. V. 38

MAURICE, H.

A Letter Out of the Country, to a Member of This Present Parliament . . . London: 1689. V. 42

MAURICE, J. F.

The Diary of Sir John Moore. London: 1904. V. 41

MAURICE, PRINCE OF ORANGE

The Triumphs of Nassau; or, a Description and Representation of all the Victories Both by Land and Sea . . . London: 1613. V. 38; 42

maurice, thomas

The Crisis of Britain: a Poem . . . London: 1803. V. 43

Grove-Hill, a Descriptive Poem, With an Ode to Mithra, by the Author of Indian Antiquities. London: 1799. V. 41

Grove Hill: A Descriptive Poem. To which is added, An Ode to Mithra. London: 1813. V. 37

Observations Connected with Astronomy and Ancient History, Sacred and Profane, On the Ruins of Babylon, as Recently Visited and Described . . . (with) Observations on the Remains of Ancient Egyptian Grandeur and Superstition . . . London: 1816/1818. V. 42

Observations Connected with Astronomy and Ancient History, Sacred and Profane, on the Ruins of Bablyon, as Recently Visited and Described by Claudius James Rich, Esq., Resident for the East India Company at Bagdad . . . London: 1816. V. 37

The Oxonian. Oxford: 1778. V. 44

The School-Boy. Oxford: 1775. V. 40; 42

Westminster Abbey with Occasional Poems and a Free Translation of the Oedipus Tyrannus of Sophocles. London: 1813. V. 40; 46

MAURICEAU, A. M.

The Married Woman's Private Medical Companion . . . Discovery to Prevent Pregnancy. New York: 1847. V. 41; 42

The Married Woman's Private Medical Companion . . . New York: 1854. V. 45

The Married Woman's Private Medical Companion, Embracing the Treatment of Menstruation . . . Pregnancy, and How it may be Determined . . . Discovery to Prevent Pregnancy . . . New York;: 1848. V. 37

MAURICEAU, FRANCISCO

De Mulierum Praegnantium, Parturientium, et Puerperarum Morbis Tractatus. Paris: 1681. V. 37

MAURICEAU, FRANCOIS

Observations sur la Grossesse et l'Accouchement des Femmes et Sur Leurs Maladies & Celles des Enfants Nouveau-Nez. Paris: 1694. V. 42

Traite des Maladies des Femmes Grosses, et de Celles qui Sont Nouvellement Acouchees . . . Paris: 1675. V. 38; 41

Traite des Maladies des Femmes Grosses. Paris: 1694. V. 40

MAURO, LUCIO

Le Antichita de la Citta di Roma. Venice: 1566. V. 42; 45

MAUROIS, ANDRE

Ariel. Paris: 1924. V. 40

Chelsea Way. London: 1930. V. 43

The Silence of Colonel Bramble. London: 1919. V. 37; 40; 42

MAUROLICO, FRANCESCO

Cosmographia . . . in Tres Dialogos Distincta. Venice: 1542. V. 37; 42

Cosmographia. Venice: 1543. V. 44

MAURY, ABRAM P.

Address of the Honorable Abram P. Maury, on the Life and Character of Hugh Lawson White, Delivered at Franklin, May 9, 1840. Franklin: 1840. V. 43

MAURY, DABNEY H.

Recollections of a Virginian in the Mexican, Indian and Civil Wars. New York: 1894. V. 38; 39; 45

MAURY, F.

Treatise on the Dental Art . . . Philadelphia: 1843. V. 37

MAURY, JEAN SIFFREIN

The Principles of Eloquence; Adapted to the Pulpit and the Bar. London: 1793. V. 41; 42

MAURY, MATTHEW FONTAINE

Explanations and Sailing Directions to Accompany the Wind and Current Charts . . . Philadelphia: 1854. V. 37; 44

Explanations and Sailing Directions to Accompany the Wind and Current Charts. Washington: 1858. V. 37

Maury's Investigations of the Winds and Currents of the Sea. Washington: 1851. V. 38

The Physical Geography of the Sea. New York: 1855. V. 37; 38; 41; 42; 43; 44; 45

The Physical Geography of the Sea. New York: 1859. V. 46

The Physical Geography of the Sea. London: 1855. V. 37; 38

The Physical Geography of the Sea. London: 1856. V. 37; 38

The Physical Geography of the Sean. New York/London: 1857. V. 37

Physical Survey of Virginia. Richmond: 1868. V. 40; 41

Resources of West Virginia . . . Wheeling: 1876. V. 45

MAURY, NANNIE BELLE

Whalers and Whaling. New Bedford: 1896. V. 41

MAURY, RICHARD L.

The Battle of Williamsburg and the Charge of the 24th Virginia, of Early's Brigade. Richmond: 1880. V. 37; 44

MAUS, L. MERVIN

An Army Officer on Leave in Japan. Chicago: 1911. V. 40

MAVERICK, GEORGE

Ye Maverick-Authentic Account of the Term 'Maverick' as Applied to Unbranded Cattle. San Antonio: 1889. V. 38

Ye Mavericks. San Antonio: 1905. V. 43

MAVERICK, MARY A.

Memoirs of Mary A. Maverick, San Antonio's First American Woman. San Antonio: 1921. V. 45

MAVERICK, MARY ANN

Memoirs . . . San Antonio: 1921. V. 37; 39; 43; 44; 45; 46

MAVERICK, SAMUEL A.

Notes on the Storming of Bexer in the Close of 1835. San Antonio: 1942. V. 37

MAVONIUS, RICHARD

Exercitationum Linguae Graecae. Paris: 1599. V. 40

Exercitationum linguae Graecae. Paris: 1559. V. 37

MAVOR, JAMES

Book of the Victorian Era Ball Given at Toronto on the Twenty Eighth of December MDCCCXCVII. Toronto: 1898. V. 44

MAVOR, WILLIAM

The British Tourists. London: 1798. V. 37; 38

The English Spelling Book. London: 1802. V. 44

The English Spelling Book, Accompanied by a Progressive Series of Easy and Familiar Lessons . . . London: 1809. V. 46

The English Spelling Book. London: 1885. V. 37; 38; 39; 40; 41; 43; 46

Historical Account of the Most Celebrated Voyages, Travels and Discoveries from the Time of Columbus to the Present Period. London: 1796-7. V. 45

Historical Account of the Most Celebrated Voyages, Travels and Discoveries from the Time of Columbus to the Present Period. London: 1796-97. V. 41

Universal History, Ancient and Modern. London: 1802. V. 38

MAVOR, WILLIAM F.

A Tour in Wales, and Through Several Counties of England Including Both the Universities, Performed in the Summer of 1805. London: 1806. V. 39; 41

MAVOR, WILLIAM FORDYCE

The Juvenile Olio . . . London: 1796. V. 42

Miscellanies in Two Parts: I. Prose. II. Verse. Oxford: 1829. V. 42

MAW, G.

A Monograph of the Genus Crocus. London: 1886. V. 37; 40; 42

MAW, HENRY LISTER

Narrativa da Passagem do Pacifico ao Atlantico, a Travez dos Andes Nas Provincias do Norte do Peru e Descendo Pelo Rio Amazonas ate ao Para. Liverpool: 1831. V. 45

MAWE, J.

Familiar Lessons on Mineralogy and Geology. London: 1822. V. 42

Familiar Lessons on Mineralogy and Geology, to Which is Added a Practical Description of the Use of the Lapidaryy's Apparatus. London: 1828. V. 37

MAWE, JOHN

A Descriptive Catalogue of Minerals, intended for the use of students; by which they may arrange the specimens they collect: also the catalogue accompanying portable collections. Soldy by J. Mawe. Second Edition. To which . . . London: 1816. V. 37

Familiar Lessons on Mineralogy and Geology . . . London: 1820. V. 45

Familiar Lessons on Mineralogy and Geology. London: 1821. V. 38

Familiar Lessons on Mineralogy and Geology. London: 1822. V. 39; 43

Familiar Lessons on Mineralogy and Geology. London: 1826. V. 38

Familiar Lessons on Mineralogy and Geology. London: 1829. V. 40

The Mineralogy of Derbyshire. London: 1802. V. 40; 41; 43

Travels in the Interior of Brazil. London: 1812. V. 46

Travels in the Interior of Brazil, Particularly in the Gold and Diamond Districts of That Country, by Authority of the Prince Regent of Portugal, Including a Voyage to the Rio de la Plata, and an Historical Sketch of the Revolution of Buenos Ayres. London: 1812. V. 37; 40

A Treatise on Diamonds, and Precious Stones: Including Their History - Natural and Commercial, to Which is Added, the Methods of Cutting and Polishing. London: 1823. V. 45

The Voyager's Companion, or Shell Collector's Pilot . . . London: 1825. V. 42

MAWE, T.

Every Man His Own Gardener. London: 1800. V. 45

MAWE, THOMAS

Every Man His Own Gardner. London: 1773. V. 38

Every Man His Own Gardner. London: 1784. V. 38

Every Man His Own Gardner. London: 1788. V. 42

Every Man His Own Gardner. London: 1803. V. 39

Every Man His Own Gardner. London: 1805. V. 38; 41

Every Man His Own Gardner. London: 1813. V. 38

Everyman His Own Gardener. London: 1829. V. 39

The Universal Gardener and Botanist. London: 1797. V. 37; 38; 42

MAWMAN, JOSEPH

Catalogue of Established and Approved Books . . . with the Opinions and Characters of the Reviewers of a Considerable Portion of the Publications. London: 1804. V. 38

An Excursion to the Highlands of Scotland and the English Lakes . . . London: 1805. V. 37; 45

A Picturesque Tour through France, Switzerland, on the Banks of the Rhine, and through Part of the Netherlands; in the Year MDCCCXVI. London: 1817. V. 40

MAWSON, DOUGAS

Home of the Blizzard. London: Philadelphia. V. 46

MAWSON, DOUGLAS

The Home of the Blizzard . . . London: 1915. V. 43

The Home of the Blizzard. Philadelphia: 1915. V. 37; 38; 42; 46

The Home of the Blizzard Being the Story of the Australasian Antarctic Expedition 1911-14. Philadelphia: (1915). V. 37

MAWSON, THOMAS A.

Calgary. London: 1914. V. 42

MAWSON, THOMAS H.

The Art and Craft of Garden Making. London: 1900. V. 44

The Art and Craft of Garden Making. London: 1901. V. 37; 38; 39; 40

The Art and Craft of Garden Design. London: 1926. V. 38

The Art & Craft of Garden Making. Fifth Edition. London: (1926). V. 37

MAWSON, THOMAS H., & SONS

Amounderness: Being the Report of the Regional Planning Committee for the Area of Fylde. London: 1937. V. 39

MAXCY, VIRGIL

Address to the Agricultural Society of Maryland, Delivered at Their Anniversary Meeting, held in the Chamber of the House of Delegates. Annapolis: 1820. V. 46

MAXEY, VIRGIL

The Maryland Resolutions, and the Objections to Them Considered. Baltimore: 1822. V. 44

MAXFIELD, A.

The True Story of One Regiment: 11th Maine Inf. Vols. in the War of the Rebellion. New York: 1896. V. 39

MAXFIELD, THOMAS

A Short and True Account of the Most Material Circumstances that Happened the Last Seven Days Before the Death of Thomas Sherwood, who was Executed on Friday, May 22, 1778. London: 1778. V. 39

MAXIM, HIRAM S.

Artificial and Natural Flight. London: 1909. V. 38

Artificial and Natural Flight. London & New York: 1908. V. 38

MAXIMILIAN, COUNT OF LODRON IN HAAG

Conspectus Assertionum Ex Universa Philosophia et Institutionibus Mathematicis. Munich: 1764. V. 39

MAXIMILIAN, PRINCE

Travels in Brazil, in 1815, 1816, and 1817. Translated from the German. Illustrated with Engravings. London: 1820. V. 37

MAXIMS and Precepts of the Saviour. London: 1848. V. 43

MAXIMUM TYRIUS

Sermones e Craeca in Latinam Linguam Versi. Rome: 1517. V. 40

MAXIMUS, TYRIUS

Sermones Sive Disputationes XLI. Geneva: 1557. V. 37

MAXWELL, ARCHIBALD M.

A Run through the United States During the Autumn of 1840. London: 1841. V. 39

MAXWELL, DONALD

Wembley in Color. London: 1924. V. 38

MAXWELL, GEORGE CLERK

Observations on the Method of Growing of Wool in Scotland, and Proposals for Improving the Quality of Our Wool. Edinburgh: 1756. V. 38

MAXWELL, HENRY

An Essay Towards an Union of Ireland with England. London: 1703. V. 43

MAXWELL, HERBERT

British Fresh Water Fishes. London: 1904. V. 41

Chronicles of the Houghton Fishing Club, 1822-1908. (with) Further Chronicles of the Houghton Fishing Club. London: 1908, 1932. V. 39

Fishing at Home and Abroad. London: 1913. V. 39

Fishing at Home and Abroad. Printed at the Arden Press,: 1913. V. 37

The Life of Wellington. London: 1900. V. 42

Life and Times of the Right Honourable William Henry Smith, M.P. Edinburgh & London: 1893. V. 37

The Lowland Scots Regiments. Their Origin, Character and Services Previous to the Great War of 1914. Glasgow: 1918. V. 37

Salmon & Sea Trout. London: 1898. V. 39

Scalacronica. Glasgow: 1907. V. 37

Scottish Gardens. London: 1908. V. 37

Sixty Years a Queen. London: 1897. V. 38; 41

MAXWELL, HU

History of Tucker County, West Virginia, from the Earliest Explorations and Settlements to the Present Time. Kingwood: 1884. V. 38; 39; 42

The History of Randolph County, West Virginia. Morgantown: 1898. V. 37

History of Tucker Coutny, West Virginia, from the Earliest Explorations and Settlements to the Present Time. Kingwood, W. Va.: 1884. V. 37

MAXWELL-HYSLOP, K. R.

Western Asiatic Jewellery c. 3000 - 612 BC. London: 1971. V. 40; 44

MAXWELL, J.

Sacro-Sancta Regum Majestas. 1644. V. 39

MAXWELL, J. G.

Sighs, Smiles and Sketches. London: 1860. V. 39

MAXWELL, JAMES CLERK

An Elementary Treatise on Electricity. Oxford: 1881. V. 37; 46

Matter and Motion. London: 1882. V. 41

On Stresses in Rarified Gases Arising from Inequalities of Temperature. London: 1879. V. 38; 41

On Stresses in Rarified Gases Arising from Inequalities of Temperature. London. V. 38

The Scientific Papers . . . Cambridge: 1890. V. 37

A Treatise on Electricity and Magnetism. Oxford: 1873. V. 42; 43

A Treatise on Electricity and Magnetism. Oxford: 1881. V. 39

A Treatise on Electricity and magnetism. London: 1904. V. 45

MAXWELL, JOHN I.

The Spirit of Marine Law, or Compendium of the Statutes Relating to the Admirality. London: 1800. V. 37

MAXWELL, JOSEPH

Metaphysical Phenomena, Methods and Observations. New York: 1905. V. 44

MAXWELL, MARIUS

Stalking Big Game with a Camera in Equatorial Africa. London: 1925. V. 37; 39; 41; 42; 44; 46

Stalking Big Game with a Camera in Equatorial Africa. New York: 1924. V. 37; 46

MAXWELL, MARY ELIZABETH BRADDON 1837-1915

All Along the River. London: 1893. V. 38; 44

Asphodel: a Novel. London: 1882. V. 44

Birds of Prey. London: 1867. V. 43; 44

Birds of Prey. London: 1868. V. 43

The Cloven Foot. London: 1879. V. 38

Eleanor's Victory. London: 1863. V. 38; 43

The Fatal Three. London: 1888. V. 38

Henry Dunbar. London: 1864. V. 38; 41

Henry Dunbar Histoire d'un Reprouve. Paris: 1865. V. 46

Hostages to Fortune. London: 1875. V. 43

Just As I Am. London: 1880. V. 45; 46

Lady Audley's Secret. London: 1862. V. 38; 41; 43; 44

Milly Darrell and Other Tales. London: 1873. V. 44

Mohawks. London: 1886. V. 38

Mount Royal. London: 1882. V. 38

Only a Clod. London: 1865. V. 44

The Story of Barbara: Her Splendid Misery, and Her Gilded Cage. London: 1880. V. 41

The Story of Barbara. London: 1895? V. 38

Vixen. London: 1879. V. 38

MAXWELL, MONTGOMERY

My Adventures. London: 1845. V. 39

MAXWELL, ROBERT

The Practical Husbandman . . . Edinburgh: 1757. V. 37; 42; 46

Selection Transactions of the Honourable The Society of Improvers in the Knowledge of Agriculture in Scotland. Edinburgh: 1743. V. 39

MAXWELL, SPENCER

Collecting Abbey. Santa Fe: 1991. V. 45

MAXWELL, THOMAS H.

Irish Land Purchase Cases 1904-11. London: 1912. V. 44; 45

MAXWELL, W. H.

The Field Book: or, Sports and Pastimes of the United Kingdom. London: 1833. V. 39; 43

The Fortunes of Hector O'Halloran and His Man, Mark Anthony O'Toole. London: 1842. V. 40

The History of the Irish Rebellion in 1798; with Memoirs of the Union and Emmet's Insurrection in 1803. London: 1852. V. 39

Life of His Grace the Duke of Wellington, K.G. &c. &c. London: 1839-41. V. 41

Rambling Recollections of a Soldier of Fortune. Dublin: 1842. V. 43

Wanderings in the Highlands and Islands, with Sketches Taken on the Scottish Border . . . London: 1844. V. 40

MAXWELL, WILLIAM

The Chateau. New York: 1961. V. 44

Five Tales . . . Printed to Celebrate His Eightieth Birthday. 1988. V. 45

Five Tales. Omaha: 1988. V. 42

From the Yalu to Port Arthur, a Personal Record. London: 1906. V. 46

The Heavenly Tenants. New York & London: 1946. V. 37

They Came Like Sparrows. New York: 1937. V. 39

MAXWELL, WILLIAM continued

Time Will Darken It. New York: 1948. V. 44

The Virginia Historical Register. Richmond: 1848. V. 40

The Writer as Illusionist. New York: 1955. V. 45

The Writer as Illusionist. N.P.: 1955. V. 45

MAXWELL, WILLIAM HAMILTON 1792-1850

The Dark Lady of Doona. London: 1834. V. 38

The Field Book; Sports and Pastimes of the British Islands . . . London. V. 42

The Fortunes of Hector O'Halloran and His Man Mark Anthony O'Toole. London: 1842/3. V. 38

Military Heroes That Have Distinguished Themselves During the Late Wars, Embellished with Equestrian Portraits. London: 1817-20. V. 38

The Soldier on Service; or, Adventures in the Camp and Field. London: 1849. V. 46

The Victories of the British Armies. London: 1839. V. 38

Wild Sports of the West. London: 1832. V. 42; 44

MAY, ALFRED

Exercises for Conversation in English and Swedish, Together with Examples on the Use of the Particles, Forms for Letters &c. Stockholm: 1844. V. 45

MAY, CHARLES A.

A Card. N.P.: 1848. V. 37

MAY, E. S.

Achievements of Field Artillery. Woolwich: 1893. V. 42

MAY, GEORGE

A Descriptive History of the Town of Evesham . . . Evesham: Ptd. & Pub. by: 1845. V. 41

A Descriptive History of the Town of Evesham . . . London: 1845. V. 45

MAY, HANS

Reconstructive and Reparative Surgery. Philadelphia: 1947. V. 42

MAY, HERBERT GORDON

Material Remains of the Megiddo Cult. Chicago: 1935. V. 42

MAY, J.

Brede's Tale. 1982. V. 44

MAY, J. LEWIS

John Lane and the Nineties. London: 1936. V. 40

MAY, PHIL

Gutter-Snipes. London: 1896. V. 38; 39

The Phil May Folio of Caricature Drawings and Sketches in Line Block, Half Tone and Photogravure with a Biography. London. V. 38

The Phil May Album. London: 1900. V. 46

Phil May in Australia. Sydney: 1904. V. 42; 46

MAY, ROBERT L.

Rudolph the Red-Nosed Reindeer. Evanston: 1963. V. 38

MAY, T.

Arbitrary Government Displayed to the Life, in the Tyrannic Usurpation of a Junto of Men Called the Rump Parliament. London: 1682. V. 39

MAY This New House be Built to Endure . . . San Francisco: 1931. V. 46

MAY, THOMAS

Arbitrary Government Display'd to the Life, in he Tyrannick Usurpation of a Junto of Men Called the Rump Parliament . . . London: 1683. V. 40; 43; 45

A Discourse Concerning the Successe of Former Parliaments. Imprinted at London: 1642. V. 44

A Discourse Concerning the Successe of Former Parliaments. London: 1642. V. 45

The Heire. London: 1633. V. 37

The History of the Parliament of England: Which Began November the Third, M.DC.XL, with Short and Necessary View of Some Precedent Yeares. London: 1647. V. 37; 46

The Pottery Found at Silchester. 1916. V. 42

Supplementum Lucani Libri VII. Leiden: 1640. V. 43

Two Tragedies. Viz. Cleopatra Queene of Aegypt. And Agrippina Empress of Rome. London: 1654. V. 42

The Victorious Reigne of King Edward the Third. London: 1635. V. 38; 45

MAY, W. E.

Swords for Sea Service. London: 1970. V. 42; 44

MAY, WALTER W.

Marine Painting. With Sixteen coloured plates. London: 1899. V. 37

MAYBANK, THOMAS

Mirth for Young & Old Alike. London: 1937. V. 46

MAYBECK, BERNARD R.

Palace of Fine Arts and Lagoon: Pan Pacific International Expo, 1915. San Francisco: 1915. V. 46

MAYBERRY, DAVID F.

Trial of David F. Mayberry, for the Murder of Andrew Alger . . . . Reported by Ira C. Jenks, Esq . . . Janesville: 1895. V. 40

MAYDON, H. C.

Big Game Shooting in Africa. London: 1932. V. 39; 42

Big Game Shooting in Africa. London: 1951. V. 42

MAYEN, JOHANN FRIEDRICH

die Kunst der Vernuftigen Kinderzucht in den Nothigsten Grundsatzen. Helmstadt: 1753. V. 44

MAYER, A. M.

Sport with Gun and Rod in American Woods and Waters. London: 1883. V. 38

MAYER, ALFRED M.

Sport with Gun and Rod in American Woods and Waters. New York: 1883. V. 39; 43; 44; 46

Sport with Gun and Rod in American Woods and Waters. Edinburgh: 1884. V. 39

MAYER, AUGUST L.

Velazquez: a Catalogue Raisonne of the Pictures and Drawings. London: 1936. V. 42; 44

MAYER, BRANTZ

Captain Canot or, Twenty Years of an African Slaver . . . From the Captain's Journals. New York: 1854. V. 38

Mexico As It Was and As It Is. New York: 1844. V. 42; 46

Mexico As It Was and as It Is. New York: & London: 1844. V. 44

Mexico, As It Was and As It Is. Philadelphia: 1847. V. 43

Mexico, Aztec, Spanish and Republican: a Historical, Geographical, Political, Statistical and Social Account of that Country from the Period of the Invasion by the Spaniards to the Present Time . . . Hartford: 1853. V. 41

Revelations of a Slave Trader; or Twenty Years' Adventures of Captain Canot. London: 1854. V. 39

MAYER, GRACE M.

Once Upon a City. New York 1890-1910. New York: 1958. V. 37

MAYER, HENRY

The Adventures of a Japanese Doll. London. V. 42

The Adventures of a Japanese Doll. London: 1901. V. 42

MAYER, HENRY A.

Hawaii: Its Stamps and Postal History. New York: 1948. V. 46

MAYER, JOHANN TOBIAS

Opera Inedita. Gottingen: 1775. V. 38

MAYER, JOHN

The Sportsman's Directory; or Park and Gamekeeper's Companion . . . Colchester: 1817. V. 37; 43

The Sportsman's Directory; or Park and Gamekeeper's Companion . . . London: 1817. V. 39

The Sportsman's Directory. London: 1819. V. 40

The Sportsman's Directory and Park and Gamekeeper's Companion . . . London: 1838. V. 45

MAYER, JOSEPH

Early Exhibitions of Art in Liverpool. Liverpool: 1876. V. 37

MAYER, L. A.

Eretz-Israel: Archaeological, Historical and Geographical Studies. Jerusalem: 1964. V. 40; 42

Islamic Astrolabists and Their Works. Geneva: 1956. V. 43

Islamic Woodcarvers and Their Works. Geneva: 1958. V. 37

MAYER, LUIGI 1776-1815

Interesting Views in Turkey, Selected from The Original Drawings . . . London: 1819/36. V. 46

Views in Egypt from the Original Drawings . . . London: 1804. V. 38

Views in the Ottoman Dominions, in Europe and Asia, and Some of the Mediterranean Islands, from the Original Drawings Taken for Sir Robert Ainslie, by . . . London: 1810. V. 37; 39

MAYER, TOM

The Weary Falcon. Boston: 1971. V. 42

MAYER, WOLFGANG

Chirist Fasciculus Heroyci Poematis Charactere Digestus. Landshut: 1515. V. 45

Christi Fasciculus Florido Heroyci Poematis Charactere Digestus. Landshut: ?1515. V. 40

MAYERNE, THEODORE TURQUET DE 1573-1665

Praxeos Mayernianae ... London: 1690. V. 38

MAYERS, WILLIAM F.

The Treaty Ports of China and Japan. London and Hong Kong: 1867. V. 39

MAYES, EDWARD

Lucius Q.C. Lamar: His Life, Times, and Speeches, 1825-1893. Nashville: 1896. V. 37

MAYES, FRANCES

The Arts of Fire. Woodside: 1982. V. 37; 39; 43; 45

The Arts of Fire. 1983. V. 38

MAYFIELD, JOHN

The Trial of the Mutineers, Late of His Majesty's Ship Temeraire, Held on Board the Gladiator, In Portsmouth Harbour, Jan. 6, 1802. (A Continuation of the Trial of the Mutineers .... Jan. 14 ... London: 1802. V. 38; 45

MAYFIELD, JOHN S.

Mark Twain vs. the Street Railway Company. N.P.: 1926. V. 45

Mark Twain vs. the Street Railway. N.P.: 1926. V. 42; 45

MAYFIELD, MILLIE

Progression; or, the South Defended. Cincinnati: 1860. V. 40

MAYGRIER, J. P.

Midwifery Illustrated ... New York: 1833. V. 45

MAYHALL, JOHN

The Annals of Yorkshire From the Earliest Pierod to the Present Time. Leeds: 1866. V. 39

MAYHEW, AUGUSTUS

Acting Charades. London: 1850. V. 37; 38; 40; 42

The Image of His Father, or, One Boy is More Trouble than Two Dozen Girls. London: 1848. V. 38

Paved With Gold. London: 1858. V. 39; 40; 44; 46

MAYHEW, AUGUSTUS SEPTIMUS

The Greatest Plague of Life. London: 1847. V. 41; 42

MAYHEW, EXPERIENCE 1673-1758

Grace Defended, in a Modest Plea for an Important Truth ... Boston: 1744. V. 44

Indian Converts: or, Some Account of the Lives and Dyring Speeches of a Considerable Number of the Christianized Indians of Martha's Vineyard, in New England. London: 1727. V. 45

MAYHEW, HENRY

The Criminal Prisons of London and Scenes of Prison Life. London: 1862. V. 37; 39; 42

1851, or, the Adventures of Mr. and Mrs. Sandboys and Family, Who Came to London to 'Enjoy Themseleves' and to See the Great Exhibition. London: 1851. V. 39; 46

The Image of His Father. London: 1851. V. 40

London Labour and the London Poor. London: 1851. V. 40

London Labour and the London Poor. London: 1861. V. 40

London Labour and the London Poor: the Condition and Earnings of Those That Will Work, Those That Cannot Work and Those That Will Not Work. London: 1861, 1862. V. 39

London Labour and the London Poor ... (with) Those That Will Not Work, Comprising Prostitutes, Swindlers, Thieves, Beggars ... London: 1861-62. V. 40

London Labour and the London Poor ... Those That Will Not Work. London: 1862. V. 40

London Labour and the London Poor. London: 1865. V. 39

London Labour and the London Poor. London: 1865? V. 40

London Labor and the London Poor: The Condition and Earnings of Those That Will Work, Cannot Work and Will Not Work. London: 1866. V. 40

London Characters. London: 1874. V. 40

London Labour and the London Poor ... London: 1967. V. 40; 41

The Lower Rhine and Its Picturesque Scenery. London: 1860. V. 45

The Rhine and Its Picturesque Scenery. London: 1856. V. 37; 41; 43

The Upper Rhine. London: 1858. V. 44; 46

MAYHEW, HORACE

The Comic Almanack for 1848. London: 1847. V. 41

MAYHEW, JONATHAN 1720-1766

Discourse on Rev. XV. 3d 4th Occasioned by the Earthquakes in November 1755. Delivered in the Wes-Meeting House, Boston, Thursday December 18, Following. Boston: 1755. V. 38; 43

The Expected Dissolution of All Things ... Two Sermons ... Boston: 1755. V. 38

God's Hand and Providence to be Religiously Acknowledged in Public Calamities. Boston: 1760. V. 38; 43

Practical Discourses Delivered on Occasion of the Earthquakes in November, 1755. Boston: 1760. V. 45

Sermons Upon the Following Subjects ... Boston: 1755. V. 44

The Snare Broken. A Thanksgiving Discourse, Preched at the Desire of the West Church in Boston, N.E. Friday May 23, 1766, Occasioned by the Repeal of the Stamp Act. Boston: 1766. V. 37; 38

Two Discourses Delivered October 25th 1759 ... A Day of Public Thanksgiving, for the Success of His Majesty's Arms, More Particularly in the Reduction of Quebec, the Capital of Canada. Boston: 1759. V. 37; 38

MAYHEW, THE BROTHERS

Acting Charades or Deeds not Words. London: 1850. V. 45; 46

The Greatest Plague of Life. London: 1847. V. 39

The Image of His Father. London: 1851. V. 43

The Magic of Kindness. London: 1849. V. 43

Whom to Marry and How to Get Married, or, the Adventures of a Lady. London: 1848. V. 39; 43

MAYLAND, H. J.

Grosse Aquarienpraxis. Hanover. V. 38

MAYNARD, C. J.

The Butterflies of New England, With Original Descriptions and Six Species. Newtonville: 1891. V. 37; 41; 43; 45

Handbook of the Sparrows, Finches, etc. of New England. Newtonville: 1897. V. 39

MAYNARD, CHARLES J.

A Manual of North American Butterflies. Boston: 1891. V. 43

MAYNARD, FREDERIC W.

Descriptive Notice of the Drawings and Publications of the Arundel Society. London: 1869. V. 38; 46

Descriptive Notice of the Drawings and Publications of the Arundel Society from 1869 to 1873 Inclusive ... London: 1873. V. 46

MAYNARD, G. S.

All Alaska Sweepstakes. Rome, April 1st, 1909. Nome: 1909. V. 43

MAYNARD, HENRY M.

Handbook to the Crumlin Viaduct, Monmouthshire; with Copious Details of the Design, Dimensions, and General proportions of the Structure, Description of the Locality, Etc. The Mechanical and Engineering Details being Deduced ... Crumlin/London: 1862. V. 37

MAYNE, ETHEL COLBURN

The Life and Letters of Anne Isabella, Lady Noel Byron from Unpublished Papers in the Possession of the Late Ralph, Earl of Lovelace. London: 1929. V. 42

MAYNE, F.

The Perilous Nature of the Penny Periodical Press. London: 1852. V. 38

MAYNE, JOHN D.

A Treatise on Hindu Law and Usage. Madras/London;: 1888. V. 40

MAYNE, JONATHAN

Barnett Freedman. London: 1948. V. 38

MAYNE, JOSEPH

The Amorovs Warre. London: 1648. V. 38

MAYNE, R. C.

Four Years in British Columbia and Vancouver Island. London. V. 42

Four Years in British Columbia and Vancouver Island. An Account of the Forests, Rivers, Coasts, Gold Fields and Resources for Colonization. London: 1862. V. 39; 43

Four Years in British Columbia and Vancouver Island. London: 1862. V. 43; 44; 45

MAYNE, REID 1818-1883

The Quadroon; or, a Lover's Adventures in Louisiana. London: 1856. V. 44

The Scalp Hunters ... Philadelphia: 1851. V. 44

MAYNWARING, EVERARD

Tutela Sanitatis ... The Protection of Long Life, and Detection of Its Brevity, from Diaetetic Causes and Common Customs. London: 1664. V. 37

MAYO, HERBERT 1796-1852

Letters on the Truths Contained in Popular Superstitions. Frankfurt am Main: 1849. V. 46

The Nervous System and Its Functions. London: 1842. V. 38

Observations on Injuries and Diseases of the Rectum. London: 1833. V. 42

The Philosophy of Living. London: 1837. V. 45

MAYO, JOHN HORSLEY

Medals and Decorations of the British Army and Navy. London: 1897. V. 37

MAYO, RICHARD SOUTHWELL BOURKE, 6TH EARL OF

St. Petersburg and Moscow: a Visit to the Court of the Czar. London: 1846. V. 37

MAYO, ROBERT

The Affadavit of Andrew Jackson, Taken by the Defendants in the Suit of Robert Mayo vs. Blair and Rives for a Libel, Analysed and Refuted. Washington: 1840. V. 44

Political Sketches of Eight Years in Washington, in Four Parts, with Annotations to Each. Baltimore: 1839. V. 45; 46

MAYO, THOMAS

Remarks on Insanity Founded on the practice of John Mayo, and tending to illustrate the Physical Symptoms and Treatment. London: 1817. V. 37

THE MAYOR and the Monks of Tynemouth. Newcastle: 1843. V. 38; 39

MAYOR, F. M.

The Room Opposite and Other Tales of Mystery and Imagination. London: 1935. V. 46

MAYOR, WILLIAM

A Brief Chronological Description of a Collection of Original Drawings by the Old Masters . . . London: 1875. V. 44

MAYRONIS, FRANCISCUS DE

Sermones ab Adventu cum Quadragesimali. Venice: 1491/2. V. 44

MAY'S Garden and Where the Flowers Went. London: 1873. V. 46

MAZAR, BENJAMIN

Views of the Biblical World. Chicago: 1959. V. 42

MAZARIN, HORTENSE DE LA PORTE, DUCHESSE DE

The Memoirs of the Dutchess Mazarine. London: 1676. V. 39; 40; 43; 44; 46

MAZARIN, JULES

Cardinal Mazarin's Letters to Lewis XIV, the Present King of France, on His Love to the Cardinal's Niece. Together with his secret Negotiation with Don Lewis d'Haro, Chief Minister to the King of Spain. London: 1691. V. 37

Epilogo De'Dogmi Politici Secondo i Dettami Rimastine dal Cardinal Mazzarino. Cologne: 1698. V. 37

Lettres . . . ou lon Voit Le Secret de la Negotiation de la Paix des Pirenees; & la Relation des Conferences qu'il a eues pour ce Sujet avec D. Louis de Haro, Ministre d'Espagne. Amsterdam: 1690. V. 37

MAZOCHIUS, ALEXIUS SYMMACHIUS

In Mutilum Campani Amphitheatri Titulum . . . Commentarius. Napoli: 1727. V. 38

MAZYCK, ARTHUR

Guide to Charleston Illustrated. Charleston: 1875. V. 44

MAZZEI, FILIPPO

Recherches Historiques et Politiques sur les Etats-Unis de l'Amerique Septentrionale, ou l'on Traite des Etablissemens des Treize Colonies . . . Colle: 1788. V. 44

Recherches Historiques et Politiques sur les Etats-Unis de l'Amerique Septentrionale . . . Colle & Paris: 1788. V. 38

Recherches Historiques et Politiques sur les Etats-Unis de l'Amerique Septentrionale . . . Paris: 1788. V. 43; 45

MAZZINI, JOSEPH

Life and Writings. London: 1890. V. 38; 42

MAZZOLINI, SILVESTRO

Errata et Argvmenta Martini Lvteris Recitata, Detecta, Repvlsa et Copiossime TRita. Rome: 1520. V. 44

MAZZONI, JACOPO

Della Difesa Della Comedia di dante . . . Nellaa Quale si Risponde alle Oppositioni Fatte al Discorso di M. Jacopo Mazzoni, e si Tratta . . . dell'artre Poetica . . . alla Philosophia & alle Belle Lettere. Cesena: 1587. V. 37

MAZZULLA, FRED

Brass Checks and Red Lights. Denver?: 1966? V. 42

MEACHAM, A. B.

Wi-Ne-Ma (The Woman-Chief) and Her People. Hartford: 1876. V. 38; 45

MEACHAM, A. G.

A Compendious History of the Rise and Progress of the Methodist Church, Both in Europe and America. Hallowell: 1832. V. 42

MEACHAM, ALFRED B.

Wigwam and War Path; or the Royal Chief in Chains. Boston: 1875. V. 42

MEACHAM, CHARLES M.

A History of Christian County Kentucky from Oxcart to Airplane . . . Nashville: 1930. V. 42

MEAD, C. J. H.

Cornwall's Royal Engineers. Plymouth: 1947. V. 42

MEAD, DANIEL W.

Report on the Dam and Water Power Development at Austin, Texas . . . Nov. 1917. Madison: 1. V. 44

MEAD, EDWARD C.

Genealogical History of the Lee Family of Virginia and Maryland from AD 1300 to AD 1866. New York: 1871. V. 45

Historic Homes of the South-West Mountains Virginia. Philadelphia: 1899. V. 40

MEAD, HENRY

The Sepoy Revolt; its Causes and Consequences. London: 1857. V. 43

MEAD, HOMER

The Eighth Iowa Cavalry in the Civil War. Carthage: 1927. V. 44

MEAD, KATE CAMPBELL HURD

A History of Women in Medicine from the Earliest Times to the Beginning of the Nineteenth Century. Haddam: 1938. V. 38

MEAD, MARGARET 1901-1978

Growing Up in New Guinea. New York: 1930. V. 38

Male and Female: a Study of the Sexes in a Changing World. New York: 1949. V. 38

MEAD, MATTHEW

The Almost Christian Discoveed; or, the False Professor Tried and Cast . . . to Which is Added, the Believer's Triumph in God's Promises . . . Lexington: 1824. V. 44

MEAD, PETER B.

An Elementary Treatise on American Grape Culture and Wine Making. New York: 1867. V. 40

MEAD, RCHARD

A Discoursse on the Small Pox and Measles . . . London: 1755. V. 44

MEAD, RICHARD

Bibliotheca Meadiana, sive Catalogue Librorum Richardi Mead, M.D. London: 1755. V. 38; 42

Catalogue of the Pictures. London: 1754. V. 45

A Certain Cure for the Bite of a Mad Dog. N.P.: 1750. V. 41; 42

A Discourse Concerning the Action of the Sun and Moon. London: 1708. V. 38; 41

A Discourse on the Small Pox and Measles . . . London: 1755. V. 42

A Mechanical Account of Poisons. London: 1702. V. 44

A Mechanical Account of Poisons in Several Essays. London: 1708. V. 37; 38; 41; 43

A Mechanical Account of Poisons in Several Essays. Dublin: 1736. V. 44

Medica Sacra; Sive de Morbis Insignioribus, Kvi in Bibliis Memorantur, Commentarius. London: 1749. V. 39; 41; 42

Medica Sacra; or, a Commentary on the most remarkable Diseases, mentioned in theHoly Scriptures. London: 1755. V. 39

Medica Sacra; sive. De Morbis Insigniioribus, qvi in Bibliis Memorantur Commentarius. London: 1759. V. 37; 39; 41; 44; 45; 46

The Medical Works of Richard Mead, M.D. Physician to His Late Majesty King George II . . . London: 1762. V. 38; 42; 44

The Medical Works of Richard Mead, M.D., Physician to His Late Majesty K. George II . . . Edinburgh: 1765. V. 41

Medical Works of . . . Dublin: 1767. V. 41

Monita et Praecepta medica. Londini: 1751. V. 43

Museum Meadianum, Sive, Catalogus Nummorum Quae vir Clarissimus Richardus Mead, M.D. Nuper Defunctus Comparaverat. London: 1755. V. 39; 44

A Short Discourse concerning Pestilential Contagion, and the Methods to be used to Prevent it. London;: 1720. V. 37

A Treatise on the Small Pox and Measles . . . London: 1747. V. 43

A Treatise Concerning the Influence of the Sun and Moon Upon Human Bodies and the Diseases Tehreby Produced. London: 1748. V. 37; 40; 41; 44; 45

MEAD, RICHARDO

Monita et Praecepta Medica. Londini: 1751. V. 40

MEAD, SPENCER P.

Ye Historie of ye Town of Greenwich. New York: 1911. V. 42

MEAD, WILLIAM

Family Prayers. Alexandria: 1834. V. 40

MEADE, E. R.

Argument in the Matter of the Union Pacific Railway Co., Eastern Division. Washington: 1865. V. 39

MEADE, GEORGE G.

Report of Major General Meade's Military Operations and Administration of Civil Affairs in the Third Military District and Department of the South, for the Year 1868 with Accompanying Documents. Atlanta: 1868. V. 39; 41; 42; 44

MEADE, GEORGE GORDON

General Order No. 68. Head Quarters Army of the Potomac. Gettysburg: 1863. V. 40

Head Quarters Army of the Potomac, July 4th, 1863. General Orders No. 68. N.P.: 1863. V. 40

MEADE, HERBERT

A Ride through the Disturbed Districts of New Zealand. London: 1871. V. 40; 41; 43

MEADE, R.

The Coal and Iron Industries of the United Kingdom . . . London: 1882. V. 42

MEADE, RICHARD

A History of Thoracic Surgery. Springfield: 1961. V. 41

MEADE, WILLIAM

An Enquiry into the Chymical Character and Properties of that Species of Coal, Lately Discovered at Rhode Islande . . . Boston: 1808. V. 46

Sermon Preached by Bishop Meade at the Opening of the Convention of the Protestant Episcopal Church of Virginia. Richmond: 1861. V. 44

Sketches of Old Virginia Family Servants. Philadelphia: 1847. V. 37

MEADES, ANNA

The History of Sir William Harrington. London: 1771. V. 38; 43

MEADMORE, C.

The Modern Chair: Classics in Production. New York: 1975. V. 46

MEADOWCRAFT, WILLIAM H.

The Boy's Life of Edison. New York: (1921). V. 37

MEADOWCROFT, WILLIAM H.

The Boy's Life of Edison. New York: 1921. V. 45

MEADOWS, ARTHUR

Hints to Farmers on the Cultivation of Mangel Wurzel, Beans, Carrots and Parsnips. Dublin: 1828. V. 37

MEADOWS, JOSEPH KENNEY

Home for the Holidays: a Pleasant Remembrance of My Early Days. Philadelphia & New York: 1849. V. 39

MEADOWS, KENNY

Heads of People: Portraits of the English. London: 1840. V. 43

MEADOWS, MARY JANE

The Life, Voyages and Surprising Adventures, of Mary Jane Meadows - Voyage of the 'Grosvenor: wreck on African Coast at Caffraria, and nine years' imprisonment. A shipwreck and castaway narrative. London: 1802. V. 37

MEADOWS, PHILIP

A Narrative of the Principal Actions Occurring in the Wars Between Sueden and Denmark. London: 1677. V. 40; 43; 44

MEADOWS, THOMAS TAYLOR

The Chinese and Their Rebellions . . . to Whcih is Added an Essay on Civilization and Its Present State in the East and West . . . London: 1856. V. 41

MEAGER, LEONARD

The English Gardener; or, a Sure Guide to Young Planters and Gardeners in Three Parts. London: 1670. V. 43

The English Gardener or a Sure Guide to Your Planters and Gardeners in Three Parts . . . London: Printed for P.: 1670. V. 37

The New Art of Gardening . . . London: 1699. V. 37

MEAGHER, ANDREW

The Popish Mass. Limerick: 1771. V. 46

MEAGHER, THOMAS FRANCIS

Memoirs . . . Including Personal Reminiscences by Michael Cavanagh . . . Worcester: 1892. V. 39

MEANS, JAMES

Epitome of the Aeronautical Annual. Boston: 1910. V. 40; 42

Five Patents Relating to Aviation. Boston: 1900. V. 40

Manflight. Boston: 1891. V. 40

MEANY, EDMOND S.

History of the State of Washington. New York: 1924. V. 45

Mount Rainier. New York: 1916. V. 38; 45

Vancouver's Discovery of Puget Sound. New York: 1907. V. 40

MEARA, BARRY E.

Napoleon in Exile: or, a Voice from St. Helena. London: 1831. V. 41

MEARES, JOHN

Viaggi Dalla China Alla Costa Nord-Ovest D'America Fatti Negli Anni 1788 e 1789 Dal Capitano G. Meares . . . Firenze: 1796. V. 46

Voyage Made in the Years 1788 and 1789, From China to the Northwest Coast of America . . . London: 1790. V. 37; 38; 39; 40; 41; 42; 43; 45

Voyages Made in the Years 1788 and 1789, from China to the Northwest Coast of America. London: 1791. V. 37; 38; 39; 41

Voyages de la Chine a l Cote Nord-Ouest d'Amerique . . . (with) Atlas. Paris: 1794. V. 38; 39; 40; 42

Voyages Made in the Years 1788 and 1789, from China to the North West Coast of America. Amsterdam & New York: 1967. V. 43

Voyages Made in the Years 1788 and 1789, from China to the North West Coast of America. Amsterdam: 1967. V. 37; 43

MEARS, ELIZABETH FARNSWORTH

Voyage of Pere Marquette, and Romance of Charles de Langlade: or, the Indian Queen. An Historical Poem of the 17th and 18th Centuries. FOnd ud Lac: 1860. V. 39

MEARS, W.

A Compleat Catalogue of All the Plays That Were Ever Yet Printed in the English Language. London: 1719. V. 38; 40

MEARS, WILLIAM

A Compleat Catalouge of All the Plays That Were Ever Yet Printed in the English Language. London. V. 41

MEASE, JAMES

Observations on the Arguments of Professor Rush, in Favour of the Inflammatory Nature of the Disease Produced by the Bite of a Mad Dog. Whitehall: 1801. V. 42

The Picture of Philadelphia, Giving an Account of its Origin, Increase and Improvements in Arts, Sciences, Manufactures, Commerce and Revenue with a Compendious View of its Societies, Literary, Benevolent, Patriotic and Religious . . . Philadelphia: 1811. V. 41; 43; 44; 45; 46

Picture of Philadelphia for 1824. Philadelphia: 1823. V. 42; 46

A Reply to the Criticisms by J. N. Barker, on the Historical Facts in the Picture of Philadelphia. Philadelphia: 1828. V. 46

MEASON, MALCOLM RONALD LAING

The Profits of Panics. London: 1866. V. 37

THE MEASURES of the Late Administration Examin'd. With an Enquiry into the Grounds of the Present Revolution. London: 1745. V. 41

MECHAM, C. H.

Sketches and Incidents of the Siege of Lucknow. London: 1858. V. 37; 39; 40

MECHEL, C. DE

Oeuvre de Jean Holbein, ou Receuil de Gravures d'Apres ses Plus Beaux Ouvrages. Basle: 1780-95. V. 39

MECHLING, W. T.

Regulations of the Army of the Confederate States, 1862 . . . Austin: 1862. V. 42

MECHNIKOV, IL IA IL'ICH 1845-1916

Immunity in Infective Diseases. Cambridge: 1905. V. 42; 45; 46

Lectures on the Comparative Pathology of Inflammation. London: 1893. V. 42

The Nature of Man, Studies in Optimistic Philosophy. London: 1903. V. 42; 45

MECKEL, JOHANN FRIEDRICH 1781-1833

De Duplicitate Monstrosa Commentarius. Halle & Berlin: 1815. V. 42

MECKLENBURG, ADOLF FRIEDRICH, DUKE OF

From the Congo to the Niger and the Nile . . . London: 1913. V. 42; 44

MECKLENBURG, ADOLPHUS FREDERIC, DUKE OF

In the Heart of Africa. London: 1910. V. 39

MEDAGLIA d'Onore Decretata dal Pubblico di Parma al Celebre Tipografo Gio: Battista Bodoni. Parma: 1806. V. 38

MEDALLIC History of Napoleon: a Collections of All the Medals, Coins, and Jettons Relating to His Actions and Reign, from the Year 1796 to 1815. London: 1819. V. 46

MEDE, JOSEPH

The Works. London: 1672. V. 38

MEDER, JOHANNES fl. 1495

Quadragesimale de Filio Prodigo. Colophon: Basle: 1495. V. 40

Quadragesimale Novum de Filio Prodigo et de Angeli Ipsius Admonitione. Basel: 1495. V. 44; 45

MEDFORD, MACALL

Oil Without Vinegar, and Dignity Without Pride. London: 1807. V. 40

MEDHURST, G.

Calculations and Remarks, Tending to Prove the Practicability, Effects and Advantages of a Plan for the Rapid Conveyance of Goods and Passengers Upon an Iron Road through a Tube of 30 Feet in Area . . . London: 1812. V. 46

MEDHURST, WALTER HENRY

Ancient China the Shoo King, or the Historical Classic . . . Shanghae: 1846. V. 46

China: its State and Prospects, with Especial Reference to the Spread of the Gospel . . . London: 1838. V. 45

Pamphlets Issued by the Chinese Insurgents at nan-king; to Which is Added a History of the Kwang-Se Rebellion, Gathered From PUblic Documents . . . Shanghai: 1853. V. 41; 44

A MEDIAEVAL Dream Book. London: 1963. V. 38; 42

MEDIAEVAL Latin Student Songs. San Francisco: 1928. V. 39; 46

MEDIAEVAL Latin Students Songs. Rendered into English Verse by John Addington Symonds. 1928. V. 38

MEDICAE Artis Principes, Post Hippocratem & Galenum . . . Geneva: 1567. V. 43

MEDICAL and Physical Journal. London: 1799-1804. V. 37; 42

THE MEDICAL and Surgical History of the War of the Rebellion. Washington: 1875-88. V. 45

THE MEDICAL and Surgical History of the War of the Rebellion (1861-1865) . . . Washington: 1870/77/83. V. 40

THE MEDICAL and Surgical Register: Consisting Chiefly of Cases in the New-York Hospital by John Watts, Jun., Valentine Mott and Alexauder H. Stevens. New York: 1818. V. 42

MEDICAL and Surgical Register of the United States. Detroit: 1896. V. 38

MEDICAL AND SURGICAL SOCIETY OF LONDON

A Catalogue of the Library of the Medical and Chirurgical Society of London with A Supplement. London: 1816. V. 40

MEDICAL Botany. London: 1821. V. 41; 42

MEDICAL Botany; or, History and Plants in the Materia Medica of the London, Edinburgh and Dublin Pharmacopoeias . . . London: 1821-22. V. 38

MEDICAL Classics. Baltimore: 1936. V. 41
MEDICAL Classics. Baltimore: 1936-40. V. 37; 38; 41

MEDICAL Essays: Compiled from Reports to the Bureau of Medicine and Surgery by Medical Officers of the U.S. Navy. Washington: 1872. V. 41

MEDICAL History. A Quarterly Journal Devoted to the History and Bibliography of Medicine and the Related Sciences. London: 1957-76. V. 37

MEDICAL Leaves 1939. Chicago: 1939. V. 45

MEDICAL Library and Historical Journal. New York: 1903-07. V. 44
MEDICAL Library and Historical Journal. New York: 1904-07. V. 44

THE MEDICAL Repository. Volume I. New York: 1804. V. 45

MEDICAL SOCIETY OF LONDON

Catalogue of Books Contained in the Library. London: 1803. V. 45

MEDICAL SOCIETY OF THE DISTRICT OF COLUMBIA

Constitution of the Medical Society of the District of Columbia; to Which is Prefixed the Act of Incorporation. Washington: 1820. V. 43

MEDICI Antiqui. Omnes, Qui Latinis Literis Diversorum Morborum Genera & Remedia Persecuti Sunt, Undique Conquisiti & Uno Volumine Comprehensi, ut Eorum, Qui se Medicinae Studio . . . Venice: 1547. V. 45

MEDICI, LORENZO DE 1449-1492

Ballatette . . . Florence: 1499. V. 46

MEDIEVAL Latin Student Songs. San Francisco: 1928. V. 46

MEDILL, JOSEPH

Educational. An Easy Method of Spelling the English Language. Chicago: 1867. V. 38

Educations. An Easy Method of Spelling the English Language. Chicago: 1867. V. 42

MEDINA, CIPRIANO DE

Sermon a La Fiesta Real del Santissimo Sacramento Del Altar, Y Segundo Corpus de Espana . . . Lima: 1641. V. 40

MEDINA DE LAS TORRES, GASPAR DE, DUQUE DE

Muerte de Pie de Paolo. Segunda Relacion, Y Muy Copiosa de Una Carta Que Embio el Senor Duque de Medina a la Contracion de Seville. Madrid: 1638. V. 40

Muerte de Pie de Palo. Segunda Relacion, Y Muy Copiosa de Una Carta Que Embio el Senor Duque de Medina A La Contractacion de Seville . . . Madrid: 1638. V. 43

MEDINA, JOSE T.

Biblioteca Hispano-Americana (1493-1810). Santiago: 1958-62. V. 40; 42

Biblioteca Hispano-Americana 1493-1810. Amsterdam: 1968. V. 40

La Imprenta en Mexico 1539-1821. Amsterdam: 1965. V. 40

MEDINA, PEDRO DE

Regimiento de Navegacion. Contiene las Cosas que los Pilotos han de Saber. colophon: 1563. V. 41

MEDINA, PEDRO DE MEDINA

Libro de Grandezas y Cosas Memorables de Espana. Alcala: 1566. V. 43

MEDINA, PIETRO DA

Arte del Navigare. Venice: 1609. V. 40; 45

THE MEDLEY, a New Song Book, Being a Choice Collection of 27 Celebrated New Songs. Newcastle: 1810. V. 38

MEDLEY, J. B.

Catalogue of the Library, Tynesfield. Bristol: 1894. V. 38; 40

MEDLEY, J. G.

Professional Papers on Indian Engineering. Roorkee: 1864-70. V. 40

A MEDLEY of the Cries of London> London: 1775. V. 39

MEDLICOTT, WILLIAM G.

Catalogue of a Collection of Books formed by William G. Medlicott, of Longmeadow, Mass. Boston: 1878. V. 41

MEDOWS, PHILIP

Observations Concerning the Dominion and Sovereignty of the Seas. London: 1689. V. 44

MEDWIN, THOMAS

The Angler in Wales, or, Days and Nights of Sportsmen. London: 1834. V. 39; 46

Conversations of Lord Byron . . . London: 1824. V. 39; 40; 41; 42; 43; 44; 45

Journal of the Conversations of Lord Byron; Noted During a Residence with His Lordship at Pisa, in the Years 1821 and 1822. London: 1824. V. 39; 40; 41; 42; 44; 45

Journal of the Conversations of Lord Byron . . . New York: 1824. V. 43; 46

Journal of the Conversations of Lord Byron; Noted During a Residence with His Lordship at Pisa, in the Years 1821 and 1822. Paris: 1824. V. 46

The Life of Percy Bysshe Shelley. London: 1847. V. 37; 39; 42

The Shelley Papers. London: 1833. V. 39; 42; 43

MEEHAN, C. P.

The Fate and Fortunes of Hugh O'Neill, Earl of Tyrone and Rory O'Donel, Earl of Tyrconnel. Dublin: 1870. V. 39

MEEHAN, THOMAS

The American Handbook of Ornamental Trees. Philadelphia: 1853. V. 43

The Gardener's Monthly and Horticultural Advertiser. Volume II. Philadelphia: 1860. V. 39

Native Flowers and Ferns of the United States. Boston & Philadelphia. V. 46

The Native Flowers and Ferns of the United States in Their Botanical, Horticultural and Popular Aspects. (with) The Native Flowers and Fersn of the United States in Their Botanical, Horticultural and Popular Aspects. Series II. Boston: 1800. V. 46

The Native-Flowers and Ferns of the United States in Their Botanical, Horticultural and Popular Aspects. Boston: 1878-79. V. 38; 43

Native Flowers and Ferns of the United States. Boston & Philadelphia: 1878-79-80. V. 39; 41; 44; 46

The Native Flowrs and Ferns of the United States. Boston: 1878-9. V. 46

MEEHAN, THOMAS continued

The Native Flowers and Ferns of the United States in Their Botanical, Horticultural and Popular Aspects. (with) The Native Flowers and Ferns of the United States . . . Boston: 1880. V. 42

The Native Flowers and Ferns of the United States in their Botanical, Horticultural, and Popular Aspects. Illustrated with Chromolithographs. Boston: 1879-1880. V. 37

MEEK, C. K.

A Sudanese Kingdom an Ethnographical Study of the Jukun-Speaking Peoples of Nigeria. London: 1931. V. 39

Tribal Studies in Northern Nigeria. London: 1931. V. 39

MEEK, CHARLES

The Will to Funtion: A Philosophical Study. Bisley: 1929. V. 37

MEEK, F. B.

A Report on the Invertebrate Cretaceous and Tertiary Fossils of the Upper Missouri Country. Washington: 1876. V. 41

MEEK, JOE

Oregon, Memorial of the Legislative Assembly of Oregon Territory Relative to Their Present Situation and Wants. Washington: 1848. V. 45

MEEKE, MARY

Les Mariages Nocturnes, ou Octave et la Famille Browning. Paris: 1820. V. 41

The Mysterious Wife. London: 1797. V. 37

MEEKER, EZRA

Pioneer Reminiscences of Puget Sound. Seattle: 1905. V. 45

Washington Territory West of the Cascade Mountains. Olympia: 1870. V. 42

Washington Territory West of the Cascade Mountains, Containing a Description of Puget Sound and Rivers Emptying into It . . . Olympia: 1870. V. 38; 41; 43; 45

MEEKER, N. C.

First Annual Report of the Union Colony of Colorado, Including a History of the Town of Greeley, from the Date of Settlement to the Present Time. New York: 1871. V. 37

Life in the West; or Stories of the Mississippi Valley. New York: 1868. V. 39

MEEKEREN, JOB JANSZOON VAN

Observationes Medico-Chirurgicae, ex Belgico in Latinum Translatae ab Abrahamo Blasio. Amstelodami: 1682. V. 38; 43; 46

MEEKS, CARROLL L. V.

Italian Architecture, 1750-1914. New York: 1966. V. 42

MEERMAN, GERARDO

Origines Typographicae. The Hague: 1765. V. 40

MEERMAN, WILLEM

Comoedia Vetus. Antwerp: 1612. V. 43

MEET the Detective. London: 1935. V. 46

MEFFRETH

Sermones Dormi Secure De Sanctis. Basle: 1489. V. 46

MEGGENDORFER, LOTHAR

Bestie Mobili e Parlanti. Milano. V. 45

Comic Actors. London: 1890. V. 45; 46

Die Grobe Wurst (The Giant Sausage). Munchen. V. 40

Lebende Bilder. Munich: 1895. V. 41

Neue Lebende Bilder: ein Ziehbilderbuch. Munchen: 1880. V. 46

Neue Thierbilder. Munchen: 1890. V. 40; 46

Tiny Tim, Prince of Liliput. London: 1898. V. 46

What's O'Clock. London: 1895. V. 42

MEGINESS, JOHN F.

History of the West Branch Valley of the Susquehanna . . . Williamsport: 1888-89. V. 41; 42

MEGINNESS, JOHN F.

Biography of Frances Slocum, the Lost Sister of Wyoming. Williamsport: 1891. V. 40; 45

MEGROZ, R. L.

Dante Gabriel Rossetti. New York: 1929. V. 44

MEHTA, NANALA CHAMANLAI

Studies in Indian Painting. Bombay: 1926. V. 44

MEHTA, VED

Three Stories of the Raj. Berkeley: & London: 1986. V. 46

MEIBOMIUS, MARCUS

Antiquae Musicae Scriptores Septem. Amsterdam: 1652. V. 40

MEIDINGER, CARL VON

Icones Piscium Austriae Indigenorum Quos Collegit Vivisque Coloribus Expressos Edidit . . . Vienna: 1785-94. V. 39

MEIER, GEORGE FREDERICK

The Merry Philosopher. London: 1764. V. 38

MEIER-GRAEFE, JULIUS

Degas. London: 1923. V. 44

Modern Art. London: 1908. V. 42

Vincent Van Gogh. London: 1926. V. 44

MEIGE, HENRY 1866-1940

Tics and Their Treatment. New York: 1907. V. 45

MEIGGS, RUSSELL

Roman Ostia. Oxford: 1960. V. 40

MEIGS, ARTHUR

An American Country House: the Property of Arthur E. Newbold, Jr., Esq. of Laverock, Pa. Mellor, Megis and Howe, Architects. New York: 1925. V. 44

The Origin of Disease, Especially of Disease Resulting from Intrinsic as Opposed to Extrinsic Causes. Philadelphia: 1897. V. 42

A Study of the Human Blood-Vessels in Health and Disease. Philadelphia: 1907. V. 42

MEIGS, CHARLES

Obstetrics: The Science and The Art. Philadelphia: 1849. V. 42

On the Nature, Signs and Treatment of Childbed Fevers. Philadelphia: 1854. V. 42

A Treatise on the Acute and Chronic Diseases of the Neck of the Uterus. Philadelphia: 1854. V. 42; 45; 46

MEIGS, CHARLES D.

A Memoir of Samuel George Morton, M.D., Late President of the Academy of Natural Sciences of Philadelphia . . . Philadelphia: 1851. V. 40

MEIGS, J. AITKEN

Catalogue of Human Crania, in the Collection of the Academy of Natural Sciences of Philadelphia. Philadelphia: 1857. V. 41

MEIGS, JOHN

The Cowboy in American Prints. Chicago: 1972. V. 44; 46

MEIGS, JOHN FORSYTH

The Story of the Seaman: and Account of the Ways and Appliances of Seafarers and of Ships from the Earliest Time until now. With an Introduction by Admiral William L. Rodgers. Philadelphia: 1924. V. 37

MEIGS, M. C.

Outline Description of U.S. Military Posts and Stations in the Year 1871. Washington: 1872. V. 41

War Department, Quartermaster General's Office . . . Outline Descriptions of U.S. Military Posts and Stations in the Year 1871. Washington: 1872. V. 37

MEIGS, MONTGOMERY C.

Papers on Practical Engineering: Prepared by Officers of the United State Corps of Engineers. Washington: 1849. V. 38

MEIGS, WILLIAM M.

The Life of John Caldwell Calhoun. New York: 1917. V. 45

MEIJER, LODEWIJK

Philosophia S. Scripturae Interpres; Exercitatio Paradoxa, In qua Veram Philosophiam Infallibilem S. Literas Interpretandi Normam Esse . . . Amsterdam: 1666. V. 40; 41; 45

MEIKELEHAM, ROBERT STUART

The History and Art of Warming and Ventilating Rooms and Buildings by Open Fires, Hypocausts, German, Dutch, Russian and Swedish Stoves . . . London: 1845. V. 43

MEIKLE, R. D.

Flora of Cyprus. London: 1977-85. V. 37; 38

MEIKLEHAM, ROBERT STUART

A Descriptive History of the Steam Engine. London: 1824. V. 40

MEIKLEJOHN, I. M. D.

The Golden Primer. London: 1910. V. 41

MEIKLEJOHN, J. M. D.

English Literature. A New History and Survey. London: 1904. V. 38

MEILAN, MARK ANTHONY

Holy Writ Familiarized to Juvenile Conceptions. London: 1791. V. 46

MEINADIER, A.

The World in Miniature. New Orleans: 1857. V. 42; 45

MEINE, FRANKLIN J.

Tall Tales of the Southwest: an Anthology of Southern and Southwestern Humor, 1830-1860. New York: 1930. V. 37; 38; 39; 40

MEINERS, CHRISTOPHER

History of the Female Sex Comprising a View of the Habits, Manners and Influence of Women, Among all Nations, From the Earliest Ages to the Present Time. London: 1808. V. 37; 44; 45

MEINERTZHAGAN, R.

Birds of Arabia. London: 1980. V. 44

MEINERTZHAGEN, DAN

Bird Life in an Arctic Spring: the Diaries of . . . London: 1899. V. 39; 40; 43

MEINERTZHAGEN, R.

Army Diary 1899-1926. Edinburgh: 1960. V. 40

Birds of Arabia. London: 1954. V. 37; 38; 39; 43

Diary of a Black Sheep. London: 1964. V. 43

Nicoll's Birds of Egypt. London: 1930. V. 40; 42; 46

MEINERTZHAGEN, RICHARD

Birds of Arabia. Edinburgh: 1954. V. 39

Birds of Arabia. Edinburgh & London: 1954. V. 39

Birds of Arabia. London: 1980. V. 37; 38; 39

Kenya Diary 1902-1906. London: 1957. V. 37; 41

Nicholl's Birds of Egypt. London: 1930. V. 37; 38; 39; 41; 44; 45

Pirates and Predators. London: 1959. V. 37; 38; 39; 40; 43; 44; 45

MEINESTRIER, CLAUDE FRANCOIS

Traite des Tournois, Joustes, Carrousels, et Autres Spectacles Publics. Lyon: 1669. V. 37

MEINHOLD, WILHELM

The Amber Witch. London: 1903. V. 39

Mary Schweidler, the Amber Witch. London: 1903. V. 39

Sidonia the Sorceress. Hammersmith: 1893. V. 37; 38; 39; 42; 44; 46

Sidonia the Sorceress. London: 1926. V. 42

Sidonia the Sorceress. Translated by Francesca Speranza Lady Wile. (Hammersmith: 1893). V. 37

The Sorceress. London: 1926. V. 39; 41

MEINHOLD, WILLIAM

Sidonia the Sorceress. London: 1893. V. 37; 38; 41

MEISS, MILLARD

The Belles Heures of Jean, Duke of Berry. New York: 1974. V. 46

Essays in Honor of Erwin Panofsky. New York: 1961. V. 44

French Painting in the Time of Jean De Berry. London: 1967. V. 38; 40

French Painting in the Time of Jean de Berry. London: 1968. V. 42; 46

French Painting in the Time of Jean de Berry. The Limbours and Their Contemporaries. London: 1974. V. 38; 46

The Visconti Hours. New York: 1972. V. 41

MEISSNER, AUGUST GOTTLEIB

Historisch-Malerische Darstellungen aus Bohmen. Prague: 1798. V. 39; 40; 44

MEISSONNIER, JUSTE AURELE

Oeuvre de Juste Aurele Meissonnier. Paris: 1750. V. 38

MEITNER, LISE

On the Products of the Fission of Uranium and Thorium Under Neutron Bombardment. Copenhagen: 1939. V. 46

MEJIA, FELIX

La Fayette en Monte Vernon, en 17 de Octubre 1824. Philadelphia: 1825. V. 45

MELA, POMONIUS

Julius Solinus. Itinerarium Antonini Aug. Vibius Sequester. Venice: 1518. V. 44

MELA, POMPONIUS

Cosmographia, sive De Situ Orbis. Venice: 1478. V. 38

De Orbis Situ. Paris: 1530. V. 41; 42

Pomponii Mele Scriptoris Luculentis Simi Maxima Cura Recogniti Cosmographia . . . Paris: 1513. V. 40; 43

Pomponii Melae de Orbis Situ Libri Tres, Accuratissime Emendati, Vna Cvm Commentariis Ioachimi Vadiani Helvetii Castigatiori . . . Paris: 1540. V. 41; 43

De Sito Orbis Libri Tres . . . Paris: 1539. V. 46

Venice, in Aedibus Aldi et Andreae Soceri, Oct. 1518. V. 45

MELANCHTHON, PHILIP

Enrratio Epistolae Pauli ad Colossenses Praelectae anno MDLVI. Wittemberg: 1559. V. 37

Erotemata Dialectices, Continentia Fere Integram Artem, Ita Scripta ut Iuventuti Utiliter Proponi Possint. Wittenberg: 1548. V. 37

Erotemata Dialectices Continentia Integram Artem, ita Scripta ut Iuventuti Utiliter Proponi Possint. Wittenberg: 1579. V. 37

Gemeine Anweissung Ynn die Heylige Schrifft durch Georg Spalatin Vordeutschet. Wittenberg: 1526. V. 37

MELANCHTHON, PHILIPP 1497-1560

Brevis et Utilis Commentius in Priorem Epistolam Pauli ad Corinthios & in Aliquot Capita Secundae (with) Enarratio Epistolae Prioris ad Timotheum, et Duorum Capitum Secundae, Scripta & Dictata in Praelectione Public Anno 1550 et 1551. Vitebergae: 1561. V. 38

Compendiaria Dialctices (sic) Ratio. Augsburg: 1523. V. 42

De Dialectia Libri Quatuor . . . Accesserunt Enim Caeteris Aeditionibus Praeter Regulas Consequentiarum. Strassburg: 1545. V. 42

Die Haubt Artickel und Furnemesten Punckt der Gantzen Hayligen Schrift . . . Augsburg: 1522. V. 38

Elementorum Rhetorices Libri Duo . . . Basle: 1564. V. 42

Erotemata Dialectices Continenta Fere Integram Artem Ita Scripta ut Iuventute Utiliter Proponi Possit. Wittenberg: 1547. V. 40

Erotemata Dialectices, Continentia fere Integram Artem, Ita Scripta, ut Juventuti Utiliter Proponi Poussint. Lipsiae: 1562. V. 38

Initia Doctrinae Physicae. Witebergae: 1559. V. 40

Instituiones Rhoetricae. Wittenberg: 1521. V. 37; 40

Liber de Anima. (with) Initia Doctrinae Physicae. Liepsig: 1561 & 1560. V. 40

Philippi Melanchthonis ad Doctorem Albertum Hardenbergium Epistolae. Bremae: 1589. V. 38

MELANCTHON, PHILIPP 1497-1560

Selectarum Declamationum . . . Argentorati: 1564. V. 42

MELBOURN, JULIUS

Life and Opinions of . . . . New York: 1847. V. 39

MELBOURNE PUBLIC LIBRARY

Catalogue of the Casts, Busts, Reliefs, and Illustrations of the School of Design and Ceramic Art in the Museum of Art at the Melbourne Public Library. Melbourne: 1865. V. 41

THE MELBOURNE Quarterly: a Family Journal of Original and Selected Literature, in Thirteen Parts. Melbourne: 1883. V. 41

MELDRUM, JOHN

The Copy of a Letter Sent to the King. London: 1642. V. 45

MELEAGER, OF GADRA

The Songs of Meleager. London: 1937. V. 38; 39; 41; 43

MELENDY, H. B.

The Governors of California: Peter H. Burnett to Edmund G. Brown. Georgetown: 1965. V. 44

MELETIUS

De Natura Structuraque Hominius Opus, Polemonis Atheniensis Insignis Philosophi Naturae Signorum Interpretationis . . . Venetia: 1552. V. 39

MELETOPOULOS, IOANNIS

Athinai 1650-1870. New York: 1986. V. 37

MELINE, JAMES

Two Thousand Miles on Horseback. New York: 1867. V. 39; 42

MELISH, JOHN

A Geographical Description of the United States, with the Contiguous British and Spanish Possession, Intended as an Accompaniment to Melish's Map of These Countries. Philadelphia: 1816. V. 41; 43; 45; 46

A Geographical Description of the United States, with the Contiguous Countries, Including Mexico and the West Indies; Intended as an Accompaniment to Melish's Map of theses Countries. A New Edition, Greatly Improved. Philadelphia: 1822. V. 37

Letter to James Monroe, Esq. Philadelphia: 1820. V. 46

The North American Tourist. New York: 1839. V. 38

The Traveller's Directory through the United States. Philadelphia: 1819. V. 41; 43

The Traveller's Directory through the United States . . . Philadelphia: 1822. V. 45

MELL, PATRICK HUGHES

A Calm Appeal to Southern Baptists, in Advocacy of Separation from the North . . . By a Southern Baptist. Athens: 1846. V. 44

MELLAART, JAMES

Excavations at Hacilar. Edinburgh: 1970. V. 42; 44
Excavations at Hacilar. Edinburgh: (1970). V. 37

MELLADEW, H.

Sport and Travel Papers. London: 1909. V. 39; 43

MELLAND, FRANK

Elephants in Africa. London: 1938. V. 39

MELLEN, GRENVILLE

The Martyr's Triumph. Boston: 1833. V. 43
Sad Tales and Glad Tales. Boston: 1828. V. 43; 44

MELLEN, PETER

Jean Clouet. London: 1971. V. 42

MELLICK, ANDREW D.

The Story of an Old Farm, or, Life in New Jersey in the Eighteenth Century. Somerville: 1889. V. 38

MELLIN, GEORGE SAMUEL ALBERT

Immanuel Kant's Biographie. Leipzig: 1804. V. 40; 41; 45

MELLISH, KATHERINE

Cookery and Domestic Management, Including Economic and Middle Class Practical Cookery. London & New York: 1902. V. 37

MELLISS, J. C.

St. Helena: a . . . Description of the Island, Including Its Geology, Fauna, Flora and Meterology. London: 1875. V. 43

MELLO AZEVEDO E BRITO, PAULO JOSE DE

Carta de Hum membro da Preterila Junta do Governo Provisional da Provincia da Bahia, Com Hum Appendice. Lisbon: 1822. V. 46

MELLO FRANCO, FRANCISCO DE

Reino da Estupidez, Poema. Paris: 1818. V. 41

MELLON, HARRIOT

A Tale of the Last Century. London: 1825. V. 45

MELLON, JAMES

African Hunter. New York: 1975. V. 44

MELLON, PAUL

Books on the Horse and Horsemanship, Riding, Hunting, Breeding and Racing 1400-1941 by John B. Podeschi; British Sporting and Animal Paintings 1655-1867 by Judy Egerton; British Sporting and Animal Prints 1658-1874 by Dudley Snelgrove. London: 1978-81. V. 41
Books on the Horse and Horsemanship. Riding, Hunting, Breeding & Racing. 1400 to 1941. A Catalogue of the Paul Mellon Collection . . . London: 1981. V. 39

MELLOR, MEIGS & HOWE

A Monograph of the Works of Mellor, Meigs & Howe. New York: 1923. V. 39; 40; 44

MELLOW, JAMES R.

Charmed Circle: Gertrude Stein and Co. New York: 1974. V. 41

MELMOTH, HENRY

Sorrows of Memory and Other Poems. London: 1807. V. 42

MELMOTH, WILLIAM

Of Active and Retired Life, and Epistle. London: 1735. V. 37

THE MELODIST: a New Song Book. Newcastle: 1810. V. 38

MELON, J. F.

Essai Politique sur le Commerce. Paris?: 1736. V. 42

MELON, JEAN FRANCOIS

Essai Politique sur le Commerce. Amsterdam: 1736. V. 45

MELONE, HARRY R.

History of Central New York Embracing Cayuga, Seneca, Wayne, Ontario, Tompkins, Cortland, Schuyler, Yates, Chemung, Steuben and Tioga Counties. Indianapolis: 1932. V. 39

MELOY, ARTHUR S.

Theatres and Motion Picture Houses. New York: 1916. V. 37

MELROSE, W.

An Address, Delivered at a Public Meeting Held in the City of Macon, for . . . Considering . . . Our Currency, and the Present System of Banking. Macon: 1840. V. 45

MELTON, A. B.

Seventy Years in the Saddle and then Some. Kansas City: 1950. V. 46

Seventy Years in the Saddle. Kansas City, Mo.: 1948. V. 37

MELTON, EDWARD

Eduward Meltons, Engelsch Edelmans, Zeldzaame en Gedenkwaardige Zee-en Land-Reizen; Door Egyptien, West-Indien, Perzien, Turkyen Oost-Indien . . . Amsterdam: 1702. V. 43; 44

MELTZER, MILTON

In Their Own Words: a History of the American Negro 1916-1966. New York: 1967. V. 45

MELVILL, DAVID

A Facsimile of the Letters Produced at the Trial of the Rev. Ephraim K. Avery, on an Indictment for the Murder of Sarah Maria Cornell, Taken with Great Care by Permission of the Hon. Supreme Judicial Court of Rhode Island . . . Newport: 1833. V. 41

MELVILLE, E. J. WHYTE

The Arab's Ride to Cairo A Legend of the Desert. Edinburgh: 1855. V. 43

MELVILLE, ELIZABETH HELEN

A Residence at Sierra Leone. London: 1849. V. 45
A Residence at Sierre Leone. London: 1861. V. 45

MELVILLE, GEORGE JOHN WHTYE

Market Harborough; or, How Mr. Sawyer Went to the Shires. London: 1861. V. 39

MELVILLE, GEORGE W.

In the Lena Delta: a Narrative of the Search for Lieut. Commander DeLong and His Companions Followed by an Account of the Greely Relief Expedition and a Proposed Method of Reaching the North Pole. Boston: 1885. V. 38; 43; 44

MELVILLE, HENRY

Australasia and Prison Discipline. London: 1851. V. 39; 44
The Trial of Henry Lord Viscount Melville, Before the Right Honorable the House of Peers . . . for High Crimes and Misdeameanours Upon an Impeachment . . . London: 1806. V. 45

MELVILLE, HENRY, 1ST VISCOUNT

A Letter From Lord Viscount Melville to the Right Hon. Spencer Perceval, on the Subject of Naval Timber. London: 1810. V. 42

MELVILLE, HERMAN 1819-1891

The Apple-Tree Table and Other Sketches. Princeton. V. 37
Battle Pieces and Aspects of the War. New York: 1866. V. 37; 39; 40; 42; 43; 45; 46
Benito Cereno. London: 1926. V. 37; 40; 41; 43; 44; 45; 46
Benito Cereno. Barre: 1972. V. 38; 41
Billy Budd and Other Prose Pieces. London: 1924. V. 37; 40
Billy Budd Foretopman. London: 1946. V. 40
Billy Budd Sailer. Mount Holly: 1987. V. 46
Cetology. A Systematized Exhibition of the Whale in His Broad Genera . . . New York: 1973. V. 41; 43
Cetology. New York: 19743. V. 46
Clarel. A Poem and Pilgrimage in the Holy Land. New York: 1876. V. 44
Clarel a Poem and Pilgrimage to the Holy Land. London: 1924. V. 40
Cock-a-doodle-doo! Or the Crowing of the Noble Cock Beneventano. Hamburg: 1986. V. 38
The Confidence Man. New York: 1857. V. 40; 44
The Encantadas: or, Enchanted Isles. Burlingame: 1940. V. 46
Israel Potter: His Fifty Years in Exile. London: 1855. V. 40
Israel Potter: His Fifty Years of Exile. New York: 1855. V. 39; 40; 42; 43; 45; 46
John Marr and Other Poems. Princeton: 1922. V. 41
Journal Up the Straits. October 11, 1856-May 5, 1857. New York: 1935. V. 37; 41
Life and Adventure in the South Pacific. New York: 1861. V. 40
The Lightning Rod Man. Minneapolis: 1982. V. 42
The Lightning-Rod Man. N.P.: 1982. V. 46
Mardi and a Voyage Thither. New York: 1849. V. 45
Mardi, and a Voyage Thither. New York: 1849. V. 37; 39; 40; 41; 42; 45
Moby Dick; or, The Whale. New York: 1851. V. 37; 38; 39; 40; 43; 44; 45
Moby-Dick: or, the Whale. New York: 1855. V. 44
Moby Dick. Chicago: 1930. V. 37; 38; 41; 42; 43; 45; 46
Moby Dick. New York: 1930. V. 37; 39; 40; 41; 42
Moby Dick, the White Whale. London: 1940's. V. 38
Moby Dick, or, The Whale. New York: 1943. V. 39; 41
Moby Dick. San Francisco;: 1979. V. 37; 38; 41; 43; 46
Moby Dick, or The Whale. New York: 1851. V. 37
Moby Dick; or, The Whale. New York: 1871. V. 37
Moby Dick. Mt. Vernon: 1975. V. 37
Moby Dick - a reprint of the 265 copy edition of the 1970 Arion Press. Berkley: 1981. V. 37

MELVILLE, HERMAN 1819-1891 continued

Narrative of a Four Month's Residence Among the Natives of a Valley of the Marquesas Islands. London: 1846. V. 38; 39; 40; 41; 43; 45

Omoo: a Narrative of Adventures in the South Seas. London: 1847. V. 38; 39; 41; 42

Omoo: Narrative of Adventures in the South Seas. London: 1847. V. 46

Omoo. New York: 1847. V. 37; 38; 39; 40; 41; 42; 43; 44; 46

Omoo. New York: 1847. V. 40

Omoo. New York: 1850. V. 39

Omoo. New York: 1852. V. 41

Omoo. New York: 1855. V. 41

Omoo. 1961. V. 45

Omoo. Oxford: 1961. V. 43; 44

Omoo: a Narrative of Adventures in the South Seas. London: 1849. V. 38

'Passages from Mr. Melville's 'Omo', contained in the Literary World. A Gazette for Authors, Readers and Publishers. Edited by C.F. Hoffman. Volume I. New York: 1847. V. 37

A Perfect Prodigy: Melville on the Birith of Malcolm. New York: 1986. V. 46

The Piazza Tales. London: 1856. V. 42

The Piazza Tales. New York: 1856. V. 37; 39; 40; 44

Pierre; or, the Ambiguities. New York: 1851. V. 39; 40; 44; 46

Pierre; or, the Ambiguities. New York: 1852. V. 41; 42; 43; 44; 45

Poems Containing Battle-Pieces, John Marr and Other Sailors, Timoleon and Miscellaneous Poems. London: 1924. V. 40

Redburn. London: 1849. V. 42

Redburn. New York: 1849. V. 40; 46

Redburn . . . Paris: 1850. V. 42

Redburn: His First Voyage. New York: 1863. V. 45

Redburn: His First Voyage. Being the Sailor-Boy Confessions and Reminiscences of the Son-of-a-Gentleman, in the merchant Service. V. 37

Rock Rodondo, Sketches Third and Fourth of 'The Encantadas.' New York: 1981. V. 39; 40; 45

Typee: a Peep at Polynesian Life. New York: 1846. V. 38; 39; 41; 42; 43; 44; 45; 46

Typee. London: 1847. V. 39; 41

Typee; a Peep at Polynesian Life. New York: 1847. V. 39; 40; 44; 45; 46

Typee: a Peep at Polynesian Life. New York: 1849. V. 40; 45

Typee. New York: 1935. V. 40; 41; 43

White Jacket; or, the World in a Man-Of-War. London: 1850. V. 41

White Jacket. New York: 1850. V. 37; 39; 40; 42; 43; 44; 45; 46

White-Jacket. New York & London: 1850. V. 39

Works. London: 1922. V. 42; 44; 46

The Works of Herman Melville. London: 1922-24. V. 40

The Works . . . London: 1922-28. V. 43

MELVILLE, JAMES

The Memoires of Sir James Melvil o Hal Hil. London: 1683. V. 46

MELVILLE, LEWIS

The Life of William Makepeace Thackeray. London: 1899. V. 46

The Life and Letters of William Cobbett in England and America. London: 1913. V. 45

The London Scene. London: 1926. V. 46

The Trial of the Duchess of Kingston. Edinburgh & London: 1927. V. 42

MELVILLE, ROBERT

Henry Moore: Sculpture and Drawings 1921-1969. New York. V. 46

Henry Moore: Sculpture and Drawings, 1921-1969. New York. V. 43

Henry Moore, Sculpture and Drawings. London: 1970. V. 46

MELZO, LODOVICO

Regole Militari Sopra il Governo a Servitio Particolare della Cavalleria. Antwerpen: 1611. V. 43

A MEMENTO of the Quarter-Centenary Year of William Shakespeare, 1564-1964, April 23. Worcester: 1964. V. 46

MEMENTOES, Historical and Classical, of a Tour through Part of France, Switzerland, and Italy, in the Years 1821 and 1822. London: 1824. V. 46

MEMMINGER, CHRISTOPHER GUSTAVUS

The Book of Nullification, by a Spectator of the Past. Charleston: 1830. V. 44

MEMMO, FRANCESCO

Vite e Macchine di Bartolommeo Ferracino Celebre Bassanese Ingegnere. Venice: 1754. V. 37

A MEMOIR of Field-Marshall the Duke of Wellington; With Interspersed Notices of His Principal Associates in Council and Companions and Opponents in Arms. London. V. 40

MEMOIRE sur les Enfans-Trouves, Presente a MM. les Procureurs du Pays de Provence par les Recteurs de l'Hopital General St. Jacques de la Ville d'Aix. Aix: 1780. V. 45

MEMOIRES de l'Institut National des Science et Arts . . . Literature et Beaux Arts . . . Paris: 1798-1804. V. 42

MEMOIRES Des Contraventions Faites par la france; au Traitte de Paix Conclu a Nimmegue Entre Sa Majeste & le Roy tres-Chrestien. N.P.: 1682. V. 37

MEMOIRES of the Love and State Intrigues of the Court of H(anover) . . . London: 1743. V. 44

MEMOIRS Concerning the Life and Manners of Captain Macheath. London: 1728. V. 39; 45

MEMOIRS Illustrative of the History and Antiquities of Wiltshire and the City of Salisbury, Communicated to the Annual Meeting of the Archaelogical Inst. of Great Britian and Ireland, Held at Salisbury July 1849. London: 1851. V. 41

MEMOIRS of a Coquet or the History of Miss Harriot Airy. London: 1765. V. 40

MEMOIRS of Allegheny County, Pennsylvania, Personal and Genalogical. Madison: 1904. V. 41; 42

MEMOIRS OF Charley Crofts, Containing Numerous Highly Entertaining Anecdotes. Cork: 1829. V. 40

MEMOIRS of George Anne Bellamy, Including All Her Intrigues, With Genuine Anecdotes of All Her Public and Private Connections. By a Gentleman of Covent-Garden Theatre. London: 1785. V. 42; 46

MEMOIRS of His Royal Highness the Prince of Wales. London: 1808. V. 38

MEMOIRS of M. de Brinboc: Containing Some Views of English and Foreign Society. London: 1805. V. 46

MEMOIRS of the Antiquities of Great Britain, Relating to the Reformation, etc . . . . London: 1723. V. 41

MEMOIRS of the Bashaw Count Bonneval, from His Birth to His Death . . . London: 1750. V. 41

MEMOIRS of the Celebrated Persons Composing the Kit-Kat Club. London: 1821. V. 38

MEMOIRS of the Chevalier de St. George (the Old Pretender). With Some Private Passages of the Life of the Late King James II, Never Before Publish'd. London: 1712. V. 39; 46

MEMOIRS of the Countess de Bressol. London: 1743. V. 40; 41

MEMOIRS of the Foreign Legion. London: 1924. V. 43

MEMOIRS of the Life and Gallant Exploits of the Old Highlander, Sergeant Donald Macleod, Who Having Returned, Sounded, with the Corpse of General Wolfe, from Quebec was Admitted an Out-Pensioner of Chelsea Hospital in 1759 . . . London: 1791. V. 38; 42; 46

MEMOIRS of the Life and Most Memorable Transactions of Capt. William Henry Cranstoun. London: 1752. V. 45

MEMOIRS of the Life and Writings (Prose and verse) of R-ch-d G-rd-n-r, Esq. Alias Dick Merry-Fellow, of Serious and Facetious Memory! London: 1782. V. 46

MEMOIRS of the Life of Andrew Hofer. London: 1820. V. 42

MEMOIRS of the Life of Lord Nelson Containing a Particular Account of All His Victories. Boston: 1806. V. 43

MEMOIRS of the Life of Mr. Booth, Containing a True Settlement of all the Circumstances Attending His Engagements at the Rival Theatres with a Few Remarks Upon His Conduct. London: 1817. V. 39

MEMOIRS of the Life of Sir Stephen Fox, Kt. From His First Entrance Upon the Stage of Action, Under the Lord Piercy, Till His Decease . . . London: 1717. V. 40

MEMOIRS of the Lives of King Edward IV and Jane Shore. London: 1714. V. 37

MEMOIRS of the Love and State-Intrigues of the Court of H-----; From the Marriage of the Princess of Z-----, to the Tragical Death of Count K-----k . . . London: 1743. V. 42

MEMOIRS of the Miami Valley. Chicago: 1919-20. V. 46

MEMOIRS of the Northern Impostor. London: 1786. V. 38

MEMOIRS of the Present Countess of Derby, (Late Miss Farren) . . . London: 1797? V. 39; 42

MEMOIRS of the Public and Private Life of Napoleon Bonaparte. London: 1844. V. 42

MEMOIRS Of the Secret Societies of the South of Italy, Particularly the Carbonari. London: 1821. V. 39

MEMOIRS of Westminster Hall, A Collection of Interesting Incidents, Anecdotes and Historical Sketches, Relating to Westminster Hall . . . St. Louis: 1874. V. 37

MEMORANDUM of the Picture Called the Chapeau de Paille, by P. P. Rubens; Exhibiting at Mr. Stanley's Room, No. 21, Old Bond Street. London: 1823. V. 45

MEMORANDUMS of a Residence in France, in the Winter of 1815-1816. London: 1816. V. 44

MEMORIAE V.CL.D. Ioannis Placotomi, Medici Illustris Carmina Amicorum. Rostock: 1578. V. 38

THE MEMORIAL. New York: 1851. V. 43; 44; 46

MEMORIAL and Biographical History of Northern California. Chicago: 1891. V. 43

A MEMORIAL and Biographical History of the Coast Counties of Central California . . . Chicago: 1893. V. 45

MEMORIAL and Genealogical Record of Southwest Texas. Chicago: 1894. V. 43; 46

MEMORIAL and Protest of the Cherokee Nation. Memorial of the Cherokee Representatives, Submitting the Protest of the Cherokee Nation Against Ratification . . . of the Treaty Negotiated at New Echota, in December, 1835. Washington: 1836. V. 37

MEMORIAL Ceremonies, Mark Twain, Samuel Langhorne Clements, 1835-1910. New York: 1910. V. 41

MEMORIAL for Archibald Douglas . . . and for Margaret Duchess of Douglas and Charles Duke of Queensberry and Dover, His Curators, Defenders Against George James, Duke of Hamilton, Lord Douglas Hamilton & Their Tutors and Sir Hew Dalrymple.. London: 1766. V. 39

MEMORIAL for George-James Duke of Hamilton . . . and Sir Hew Dalrymple . . . Pursuers, Against the Person Pretending to Be Archibald Stewart, Alias Douglas, . . . Defender. To Which are Annexed, Sequel of the Memorial . . . London: 1767. V. 41

MEMORIAL for George-James Duke of Hamilton, Marquis of Douglas . . . Lord Douglas Hamilton, and Their Tutors, and Sir Hew Dalrymple . . . Pursuers, Against the Person Pretending to be Archibald Stewart, Alias Douglas, Only Son Now on Life of the Marriage . . . Edinburgh: 1767. V. 40

A MEMORIAL for the City of Milwaukee, on the Subject of a Naval Depot, an Armory and an Arsenal. Milwaukee: 1861. V. 42

A MEMORIAL Keepsake for Paul A. Bennett 1897-1966. Gathered Together by Friends. New York: 1967-68. V. 42

A MEMORIAL Keepsake. Paul Bennett 1897-1966. New York: 1967. V. 43; 45

MEMORIAL of a Delegation from the Cherokee Indians. Washington: 1831. V. 37

MEMORIAL of Citizens of the U.S. Praying for the Establishment of a Distinct Territorial Government . . . Dec. 2, 1845. Washington: 1845. V. 42

MEMORIAL of Henry O'Reilly, Proposing a System of Inter-Communication, by Mail and Telegraph, Along a Military Road through Our Own Territories Between the Atlantic and the Pacific States . . . Washington: 1852. V. 39

A MEMORIAL of John Greenleaf Whittier from His Native City, Haverhill, Massachusetts. Haverhill: 1893. V. 39

MEMORIAL of John Ross and Others, Representatives of the Cherokee Nation of Indians, on the Subject of The Existing Difficulties in the Nation, and Their Relations with the United States. Washington: 1846. V. 37

MEMORIAL of Major General Andrew Jackson. Washington: 1820. V. 42; 46

MEMORIAL of Samuel Finley Breese Morse, Including Appropriate Ceremonies of Respect at the National Capitol, and Elsewhere. Washington: 1875. V. 38

MEMORIAL of the Convention of the People of the State of Alabama, Assembled to form a Constitution and State Government. Washington: 1821. V. 39

MEMORIAL Of the Illinois and Wabash Land Company. Philadelphia: 1797. V. 37

MEMORIAL of the San Francisco Land Association and Brief of Memorialists in Support Thereof. Philadelphia: 1872. V. 42

MEMORIAL of the Senators and Representatives, and the Constitution of the State of Kansas. Washington: 1856. V. 39; 46

MEMORIAL of the Six Chinese Companies. An Address to the Senate and House of Representatives of the United States. San Francisco: 1877. V. 42

MEMORIAL Record of Southwestern Minnesota. Chicago: 1897. V. 46

MEMORIAL Sketch of Dr. William Frederick Poole MDCCCXXI. Chicago: 1895. V. 41

THE MEMORIAL to the Church of England Humbly Offer'd to the Consideration of All True Lovers of Our Church and Constitution, Seriously Consider'd Paragraph by Paragraph. London: 1705. V. 45

MEMORIAL to the Government of the United States, From the Citizens of Chicago, Illinois, Setting Forth the Advantages of that City as a Site for a National Armory and Foundry. Chicago: 1861. V. 41; 44

MEMORIAL to the President and Congress for the Admission of Wyoming Territory to the Union. Cheyenne: 1889. V. 39

MEMORIAL to the Senators and Representatives of the Forty-First Congress. Memorial from the Commissioners Elected by the Reconstruction Convention of the State of Texas . . . Washington: 1869. V. 45

MEMORIALS Concerning Deceased Friends; Being a Selection from the Records of the Yearly Meeting for Pennsylvania &c. from the Year 1788 to 1819, Inclusive. Philadelphia: 1821. V. 37; 40

MEMORIALS of C. H. C. Daniel with a Bibliography of the Press 1845-1919. Oxford: 1921. V. 38; 44

MEMORIALS of Christie's: a Record of Art Sales from 1766 to 1796. London: 1896. V. 45

MEMORIALS of Old Boys and Masters of the Dragon School, Oxford Who Fell in the Great War. 1922. V. 45
MEMORIALS of Old Boys and Masters of the Dragon School, Oxford Who Fell in the Great War. London: 1922. V. 46

THE MEMORIALS of the English and French Commissaries Concerning the Limits of Nova Scotia or Acadia. London: 1755. V. 38; 42; 43; 44; 46

MEMORIALS of the Senators and Representatives, and the Constitution of the State of Kansas. Washington: 1856. V. 39

MEMORIALS on Both Sides, from the Year 1687, to the Death of K. James II. With Divers Original Papers Never Before Publish'd. London: 1711. V. 39

LES MEMORIE della Signora Dvchessa Mazarini. Cologne: 1678. V. 37

MEMORIES des Commissaires du Roi et de Ceux de sa Majeste Britannique, Sur Les Possessions & les Droits Respectifs Des Deux Couronnes en Amerique, avec les Actes Publics & Pieces Justificatives. Paris: 1755-57. V. 38; 40; 41; 42

MEN and Women of the Day. A Picture Gallery of Contemporary Portraiture. London: 1888/89. V. 44

MEN of Affairs and Representative Institutions of Oklahoma. Tulsa: 1916. V. 37

MEN of Mark. A Gallery of Contemporary Portraits of Men Distinguished in the Senate, the Church, in Science, Literature and Art, the Army, Navy, Law, Medicine, etc. London: 1876-83. V. 37
MEN Of Mark. A Gallery of Contemporary Portraits of Men Distinguished in the Senate, the Church, in Science, Literature and Art, the Army, Navy, Law, Medicine, Etc. London: 1880. V. 44

MEN of Note Affliated with Mining and Mining Interests in the Cripple Creek District. N.P.: 1905. V. 42

MEN of Texas. A Collection of Portraits of Men . . . of the State of Texas. Houston: 1903. V. 37; 43

MEN of the Period: England. London: 1890. V. 39

MEN of the Time In Australia: Victorian Series, 1878. Melbourne: 1878. V. 41

MENA, JUAN DE

Copilacion de Todas las Obras del Famossimo Poeta . . . Colophon: Valladolid: 1536. V. 45

MENABONI, ATHOS

Menaboni's Birds. New York: 1950. V. 38
Menaboni's Birds. New York: 1951. V. 39

MENANDER

The Bad-Tempered Man or the Misanthrope. London: 1960. V. 40
Takton Menandroi Sozomena. (with) Ex Comoediis Menandri Quae Supersunt. Parisiis: 1553. V. 38

MENCKEN, HENRY LOUIS 1880-1956

The American Language. New York: 1919. V. 45
Americana 1925. New York: 1925. V. 40

MENCKEN, HENRY LOUIS 1880-1956 continued

Americana 1925. New York: 1925. V. 40

Americana 1926. New York: 1926. V. 37; 40; 42; 45

The Artist. Boston: 1912. V. 41; 42; 45; 46

A Book of Burlesques. New York: 1916. V. 45

Damn! A Book of Calumny. New York: 1918. V. 44

The Diary of H. L. Mencken. New York: 1990. V. 43

Europe After 8:15. New York: 1914. V. 39; 43; 45

Friedrich Nietzsche. Boston: 1908. V. 37; 40; 41

George Bernard Shaw and His Plays. Boston: 1905. V. 40; 42; 44

George Bernard Shaw: His Plays. Boston & London: 1905. V. 46

The Gist of Nietsche. Boston: 1910. V. 39

The Gist of Nietzsche. Boston: 1910. V. 39; 41; 44

Happy Days 1880-1892. London: 1940. V. 45

Happy Days. New York: 1940. V. 40; 43; 44; 45

Happy Days. Heathen Days. Newspaper Days. New York: 1940-43. V. 45

Heathen Days, 1890-1936. New York: 1943. V. 44; 46

In Defense of Women. New York: 1918. V. 39

In Defence of Women. Leipzig: 1927. V. 40

In the Footsteps of Gutenberg. Princeton: 1954. V. 44

James Branch Cabell. New York: 1927. V. 39

A Little Book in C Major. New York: 1916. V. 37

Men vs. the Man. A Correspondence Between Robert Rives La Monte, Socialist and H. L. Mencken, Individualist. New York: 1910. V. 37; 45

Menckeniana. New York: 1928. V. 43; 44

A New Dictionary of Quotations on Historical Principles from Ancient and Modern Sources. New York: 1942. V. 39

Newspaper Days, 1899-1906. New York: 1941. V. 44

Notes on Democracy. New York: 1926. V. 40; 41; 43; 45; 46

Notes on Democracy. London: 1927. V. 45

Prejudices: Second Series. New York: 1920. V. 40

Prejudices: Fifth Series. London. V. 40

Prejudices: Fifth Series. New York: 1926. V. 40

The Philosophy of Friedrich Nietzsche. (with) The Gist of Nietzsche. Boston: 1908, 1910. V. 39

The Philosophy of Friedrich Nietzsche. Boston: 1908. V. 37

Pistols for Two. New York: 1917. V. 39

Prejudices. Second Series. New York: 1920. V. 42

Prejudices Third Series. New York: 1922. V. 38; 40; 45

Prejudices Sixth Series. London: 1927. V. 46

Prejudices: Sixth Series. New York: 1927. V. 46

Prejudices. Fifth Series. London. V. 42

Prejudices. Fifth Series. New York: 1926. V. 39; 42

Selected Prejudices. New York: 1927. V. 42

Selected Prejudices. New York: 1927. V. 40; 42

The Sunpapers of Baltimore. New York: 1937. V. 37; 45

Supplement I The American Langauge. New York: 1945. V. 43

Treatise on the Gods. New York: 1930. V. 39; 40; 45

Treatise on the Gods. New York & London: 1930. V. 39; 46

Treatise on Right and Wrong. New York: 1934. V. 41

Treatise on the Gods. New York: 1946. V. 39; 45

MENDALL, P.H., MRS.

The New Bedford Practical Receipt Book. New Bedford: 1862. V. 45

MENDEL, G. J.

Il Tesoro Dell'Ornato Collezione do Scelti Ornati di Tutte le Epoche dell'Arte. Roma: 1886-87. V. 45

MENDEL, MISS

Notes on Travel and Life. New York: 1854. V. 38; 39; 40

MENDELEEFF, DMITRY IVANOVICH

The Principles of Chemistry. London: 1891. V. 40

The Principles of Chemistry. London: 1905. V. 40

MENDELL, G. H.

Report of the Various Projects for the Water Supply of San Francisco, Cal. Made to the Mayor, the Auditor, and the District Attorney, Constituting the Board of Water Commissioners. San Francisco: 1877. V. 37; 40; 42; 44

MENDELSOHN, MOSES

Memoirs of Moses Mendelsohn, The Jewish Philosopher. London: 1825. V. 41

MENDELSOHN, OZENFANT A.

Eric Mendelsohn. V. 44

MENDELSSOHN-BARTHOLDY, FELIX

Elijah. An Oratorio. London. V. 40

MENDELSSOHN, MOSES

Phaedon; or, The Death of Socrates . . . London: 1789. V. 41

MENDELSSOHN, SIDNEY

South African Bibliography . . . London: 1910. V. 39

South African Bibliography . . . London: 1957. V. 45

South African Bibliography. London: 1968. V. 45

MENDES, ALFRED H.

Pitch Lake - a Story from Trinidad. London: 1934. V. 45

MENDES, CATULLE

Hesperus. Paris: 1904. V. 39; 41; 46

MENDES DA COSTA, EMANUEL

Elements of Conchology . . . London: 1776. V. 43

MENDES PINTO, FERDINANDO

The Voyages and Adventures of Ferdinand Mendez Pinto, a Portugal, During His Travels for the Space of One and Twenty Years in the Kingdoms of Ethiopia, China, Tartaria, Cauchinchina, Calaminham, Siam, Pegu, Japan and a Great Part of the East Indies. London: 1663. V. 40

MENDEZ SILVA, RODRIGO

Vida y Hechos Heroicos del Gran Condestable de Portugal D. Nuno Alvarez Pereyra Conde de Barcelos . . . Madrid: 1640. V. 45

MENDOZA, DANIEL

The Art of Boxing; with a Statement of the Transactions That Have Passed Between Mr. Humprheys and Myself Since Our Battle at Oldham. London: 1789. V. 42

MENDOZA Y RIOS, JOSEPH DE

A Complete Collection of TAbles for Navigation and Nautical Astronomy. London: 1809. V. 46

MENEFEE, C. A.

Historical and Descriptive Sketch Book of Napa, Sonoma, Lake and Mendocino, Comprising Sketches of Their Topography, Productions, History, Scenery and Peculiar Attractions. Napa City: 1873. V. 40; 46

MENESES, AFFONSO DE

Varios versos ao Felix Nacimento, do Serenissimo Infante Dom Pedro Manoel. Lisbon: 1648. V. 45

MENESES, FERNANDO DE, CONDE DA ERICEIRA

Historia de Tangere, que Comprehende as Noticias Desde a Sua Primeira Conquista ate a Sua Ruina. Lisbon: 1732. V. 38

MENEZES, LUIZ DE, CONDE DE ERICEIRA

Compendio Panegirico da Vida, e Accoens do Excellentissimo Senhor Luis Alverez de Tavora, Conde de S. Joao, Marquez de Tavora . . . Lisbon: 1674. V. 41

MENGER, ANTON

Das Recht Auf Den Vollen Arbeitsertrag in Geschichtlicher Darstellung. Stuttgart: 1886. V. 45

MENGIN, E.

Corpus Codicum Americanorum Medii Aevi . . . Copenahgen: 1942-52. V. 42

MENGS, ANTHONY RAPHAEL

Sketches on the Art of Painting. (with) Description of the Three Celebrated Pictures by Rubens, in the Museum at Antwerp: the Cruccifixion the Adoration of the Kings; and the Entomment. London: 1782, 1819. V. 37

The Works of . . . London: 1796. V. 42

MENHART 1896-1962. Bloomington: 1966. V. 40; 41

MENINSKI, FRANCOISE DE MESGNIER

Linguarum Orientalium Institutiones . . . seu Grammatica Turcica . . . Vienna: 1680. V. 45

MENKEN, ADAH I.

Infelicia. Philadelphia: 1869. V. 46

MENNELL, ARTHUR

Die Konigsphantasien, Eine Wanderung zu den Schlossern Konig Ludwigs II. von Bayern. Leipzig: 1892. V. 38

MENNELL, JAMES B.

The Treatment of Fractures by Mobilisationa and Massage. London: 1911. V. 45

MENNENIUS, FRANCISCUS

Deliciae Eqvestrivm Sive Militarivm Ordinum. Cologne: 1638. V. 37

MENNIE, DONALD

The Grandeur of the Gorges. Shanghai: 1926. V. 37; 45

The Grandeur of the Gorges. 1926. V. 38

MENNIE, DONALD continued

The Pageant of Peking. Shanghai: 1920. V. 42

The Pageant of Peking. Shanghai: 1922. V. 40

MENNIS, JOHN

Facetiae Musarum Deliciae: or, the Muse's Recreation. London: 1874. V. 38

MENNO SIMONS

Ein Fundament und Klare Anweisung von der Seligmachenden Lehre Unsers Heern Jesu Christi aus Gottes Wort Kurz Begriffen. Pennsylvanien: 1794. V. 38

MENNO SYMONS 1492-1559

Opera Omnia Theologica, of Alle de Godtgellerde Wercken . . . Amsterdam: 1681. V. 38

MENOCAL, A. G.

Report of the U. S. Nicaragua Surveying Party, 1885. Washington: 1886. V. 38; 41

MENPES, D.

Venice, the Character and Mood of the City of Canals During the Varied Seasons, Architecture and the Gondolas . . . London: 1904. V. 41; 42; 46

MENPES, DOROTHY

Brittany. London: 1905. V. 46

Paris by Mortimer Menpes. London: 1909. V. 46

World Pictures by . . . London: 1902. V. 44

World's Children. London: 1903. V. 44; 46

MENPES, M.

Japan a Record in Colour by . . . London: 1901. V. 44

MENPES, MORTIMER

Japan. A record in color by . . . London: 1903. V. 38; 40

Japan, a Record in Colour. London: 1905. V. 46

Japan. A Record in Colour. London: 1904. V. 46

War Impressions. London: 1901. V. 42; 43; 44

Whistler As I Knew Him. London: 1904. V. 39; 42; 46

MENSA Philosophica. Cologne: 1500. V. 38
MENSA Philosophica. Cologne: 1500). V. 37

MENSHIKOV, ALEKSNDR DANILOVICH

Steigen und Fall Eines Frossen Ministers in der Vollstandigne Lebensbeschreibung des Nunmehro Verungluckten Fursten von Menzikoff Gezeigt. N.P.: 1728. V. 38

MENSING, ANTON W. M. 1866-1936

Catalogue of the Very Valuable and Important Library Formed by the Late Ant. W. M. Mensing. London: 1936-37. V. 41

The Mensing Library. London: 1936-37. V. 39; 45

The Mensing Library. Catalogue of the Very Valuable and Important Library . . . London: 1936-7. V. 39

MENSSHENGEN, FRANTZ MARTIN

Ausfurliche und Grundrichtige Beschreibung des Ganzen Elb-Stroms . . . Nurnberg: 1687. V. 41

THE MENTAL Guide, Being a Compend of the First Principles of Metaphyscis . . . Boston: 1828. V. 42

MENTEITH, ROBERT fl. 1621-1660

The History of the Troubles of Great Britain (1633-1650). London: 1735. V. 39

MENTMORE

Catalogue of French and Continental Furniture, Tapestries and Clocks; Works of Art and Silver; Porcelain; Paintings, Prints and Drawings. London: 1977. V. 39; 46

MENZ, BALTHASAR

Stambuch, Darinnen Vermeldet wie das Konigreich zu Sachen ein Herzogthumb Worden, die Religion und Herrschafft Geendert . . . Wittenberg: 1601. V. 37

MENZEL, WOLFGANG

German Literature. Oxford: 1840. V. 37; 42

MENZIES, A.

Menzies' Journal of Vancouver's Voyage April to October 1792. Victoria: 1923. V. 37; 45

MENZIES, G. K.

The Story of the Royal Society of Arts. London: 1935. V. 38

MENZIES, WILLIAM

Catalogue of the Books, Manuscripts and Engravings Belonging to William Menzies of New York. New York: 1875. V. 44

MENZIES, WILLIAM G.

Collecting Antiques. London: 1928. V. 41

MEONI, DOMENICO

Relazione Distinta della Feste e Dimostrazioni di Giubilo fatte dalla Citta di Viterbo pel'Esaltazione Coronazione della Sntita di Nostro Signore Papa Innocenzo XIII . . . Viterbo: 1721. V. 46

MERA, H. P.

The Alfred I. Barton Collection of Southeastern Textiles. Santa Fe: 1949. V. 39

Pueblo Indian Embroidery. Santa Fe: 1943. V. 42

The 'Rain Bird' a Study in Pueblo Design. Sante Fe: 1937. V. 37; 39

Style Trends of Pueblo Pottery: In the Rio Grande and Little Colorado Cultural Areas from the Sixteenth to the Nineteenth Century. Sante Fe: 1939. V. 39

MERBECKE, JOHN

The Book of Common Prayer Noted . . . 1550. London: 1844. V. 44

MERCADO, TOMAS DE

De' Negotii et Contratti de Mercanti, et de Negotianti, Trattato Utilissimo non Solamente a chi Essercita la Mercatura, ma ncora a Confessori, Predicatori & Lettori. In Brescia: 1591. V. 38

THE MERCANTILE Agency Reference Book (and Key) for the Within States with a List of Banks and Bankers: Also State Collection and Assignment Laws. New York: 1899. V. 42; 45

MERCATI, MICHEL 1541-1593

Metallotheca. Opus Posthumum, Auctoritate, & Munificentia Clementis Undecemi Pontificis Maximi ex Tenebris in Lucem Eductum . . . Rome: (colphon 1717). V. 46

MERCATI, MICHELE

Metallotheca. Opus Posthumum . . . Romae: 1717-19. V. 40

MERCATOR GERARD

Virginae Item et Floridae Americae Profinciarum Nova Descriptio. Amsterdam: 1606. V. 45

MERCENARIUS, ARCHANGELUS

Iudicium Super Rationibus Aristotelis Primo de Partibus Animalium Capite Primo. Padua: 1570. V. 38

MERCER, A. S.

The Banditti of the Plains, or the Cattlemen's Invasion of Wyoming in 1892. San Francisco: 1935. V. 37; 38; 41; 42; 43; 44

MERCER & MONOD

The Monod Pattern. Improved Two Wheeled Velocipede. New York: 1868. V. 39

MERCER, ASA S.

The Banditti of the Plains; or, the Cattleman's Invasion of Wyoming in 1892. Cheyenne: 1894. V. 38; 39; 40; 44; 45

The Banditti of the Plains. Denver: 1894. V. 37; 40; 46

MERCER, ASA SHINN

The Banditti of the Plains; or, the Cattlemen's Invasion of Wyoming in 1892 (The Crowning Infamy of the Ages.) (Cheyenne: 1894). V. 37

MERCER, CAVALIE

Journal of the Waterloo Campaign Kept throughout the Campaign of 1815. London: 1870. V. 41

MERCER, DAVID

The Bankrupt and Other Plays. London: 1974. V. 43

The Monster of Karlovy Vary and Then and Now. London: 1979. V. 43

MERCER, HENRY C.

Ancient Carpenters' Tools Illustrated and Explained Together with the Implements of the Lumberman, Joiner and Cabinet Maker, in Use in the Eighteenth Century. Doylestown: 1929. V. 45

MERCER, SAMUEL A. B.

The Tell El-Amarna Tablets. Toronto: 1939. V. 42

MERCER, THOMAS

The Sentimental Sailor, or St. Preux to Eloisa. Edinburgh: 1772. V. 39; 40

The Sentimental Sailor or St. Preux to Eloisa. Edinburgh: 1782. V. 41

MERCER, WILLIAM T.

The Gynandriad: A Satire of the Day on Woman's Rights. London: 1873. V. 37

THE MERCHANT and Trader's Daily Companion. Dublin: 1776. V. 40

MERCHANT, PAUL

Salt Water Island. (Madley): 1983. V. 37

Stones. Exeter: 1973. V. 38; 45

MERCHANT Vessels of the United States. Washington: 1881-1957. V. 45

MERCHANT'S ASSOCIATION OF NEW YORK

The Natural Resources and Economic Conditions of the State of Texas . . . New York: 1901. V. 38

MERCIER, CHARLES

A New Logic. London: 1912. V. 43; 45

MERCIER, CHARLES ARTHUR 1852-1919

Criminal Responsibility. Oxford: 1905. V. 45

MERCIER DE COMPIEGNE

Eloge du Sein des Femmes Ouvrage Curieux dans Lequel on Examine s'il Doit Etre Decouvert . . . Paris: 1873. V. 41

MERCIER DE LA RIVIERE, PIERRE PAUL

L'Ordre Naturel et Essentiel des Societes Politique. Londres: 1767. V. 39; 41

MERCIER-DUPARTY, CHARLES

Sentimental Letters on Italy; Written in French . . . in 1785. London: 1789. V. 41; 42

MERCIER, LOUIS SEBASTIEN 1740-1814

L'An Deux Mille Quatre Cent Quarante. Londres: 1772. V. 38

Du Theatre, ou Nouvel Essai sur l'Art Dramatique. Amsterdam: 1773. V. 43

Memoirs of the Year Two Thousand Five Hundred. London: 1772. V. 37; 41; 43

Memoirs of the Year Two Thousand Five Hundred. Translated form the French by W. Hooper, M.D. London: 1772. V. 37

The Nightcap. Dublin: 1786. V. 39

MERCURIALE, GIROLAMO 1530-1606

De Arte Gymnastica Libri Sex - Secunda Editione Aucti & Multis Figuris Ornati. Giunta: 1573. V. 42

De Arte Gymnastica Libri Sex . . . Secunda . . . Paris: 1577. V. 43

De Arte Gymnastica, Libri Sex. Amsterdam: 1672. V. 43; 45

De Morbis Muliebribus Praelectiones. Venice: 1591. V. 45

Variarum Lectionum, in Medicinae Scriptoribus et Aliis, Libri Sex . . . Venice: 1598. V. 43

MERCURIALE, SCIPIONE d. 1615

La Commare Oriccoglitrice . . . Divisa in tre Libri. Ristampata Correcta et Accresciuta dall'Istesso Autore. Venice: 1621. V. 42

MERCURIALIS, GIROLAMO 1530-1606

De Arte Gymnastica Libri Sex. Venice: 1573. V. 45

MERCURIALIS, HIERONYMUS

De Arte Gymnastica, Libri Sex . . . Parisiis: 1577. V. 37; 39; 41

MERCURIES Message (in verse), or the Coppy of a Letter sent to William Laud Late Archbishop of Canterbury, Now Prisoner in the Tower. N.P.: London: 1641. V. 39

MERCURIO, SCIPIONE GIROLAMO

La Commare, o Riccoglitrice. Venice: 1621. V. 41

MERCURIUS, OXONIENSIS

The Letters of, by Mr. Osbert Lancaster. London: 1970. V. 40

MERCY the Truest Heroism: Display'd in the Conduct of Some of the Most Famous Conquerors and Heroes of Antiquity, viz; Cyrus, Alexander, Julius, Caesar, Augustus, Flavius, Vespasianus, Titus, M. Anoninus, Alphonsus, King of Arragon . . . London: 1746. V. 41

MERE, ANTOINE GOMBAUD, CHEVALIER DE

Les Oeuvres. Amsterdam: 1692. V. 37

MEREDITH, DE WITT

Voyages of the Velero IIII . . . Los Angeles: 1939. V. 42

MEREDITH, GEORGE 1828-1909

The Adventures of Harry Richmond. London: 1871. V. 40; 42

The Amazing Marriage. Westminsner: 1895. V. 38; 39; 40

Beauchamp's Career. London: 1876. V. 38; 41; 42

Diana of the Crossways. London: 1885. V. 40; 42; 43

The Egoist. London: 1879. V. 38; 39; 40; 41; 42; 44

Emilia in England. London: 1864. V. 40; 42; 45

Evan Harrington; or, He Would be a Gentleman. New York: 1860. V. 45; 46

Evan Harrington. London: 1861. V. 40; 42

Farina; a Legend of Cologne. London: 1857. V. 40

Jump to Glory Jane. London: 1892. V. 37; 44; 46

Letters . . . to Algernon Charles Swinburne and Theodore Watts-Dunton. Pretoria: 1922. V. 40

The Letters of George Meredith to Alice Meynell. London & San Francisco: 1923. V. 41

Letters from George Meredith to Various Correspondents. Pretoria: 1924. V. 46

Lord Ormont and His Aminta. London: 1894. V. 38; 39; 42; 43; 46

Modern Love. London: 1862. V. 38; 39; 40; 41; 45

Modern Love and Poems of the English Roadside, with Poems and Ballads. London: 1862. V. 43

Modern Love. Portland: 1891. V. 42

Modern Love. Portland: 1898. V. 43

One of Our Conquerors. London: 1891. V. 37; 38; 40; 41; 42; 43; 44; 46

The Ordeal of Richard Feverel. London: 1849. V. 40

The Ordeal of Richard Feverel. London: 1859. V. 40; 41; 42

Poems. London: 1851. V. 39

Poems: The Empty Purse, with Odes to the Comic Spirit, to Youth in Memory and Verses. London: 1892. V. 40; 42

Rhoda Fleming. London: 1865. V. 37; 40; 42

Selected Poems. London: 1897. V. 41

The Shaving of Shagpat. London: 1856. V. 37; 38; 40; 42; 43; 46

A Tour to the Rhine. With Antiquarian and Other Notices. London: 1825. V. 39

The Tragic Comedians. London: 1880. V. 41; 43

The Tragic Comedians. London: 1881. V. 38; 41

Vittoria. London: 1867. V. 42

The Works. London: 1896-1911. V. 42

Complete Works. London: 1896-1912. V. 38

Works. London: 1909. V. 42; 44

The Works of . . . London: 1909-11. V. 37

The Works of . . . (with) The Letters of . . . London: 1909-11 & 1912. V. 44

The Works. London: 1912. V. 40; 46

The Works. London: 1914-20. V. 38

MEREDITH, GRACE E.

Girl Captives of the Cheyennes. Los Angeles: 1927. V. 45

MEREDITH, HENRY

An Account of the Gold Coast of Africa. London: 1812. V. 41; 46

MEREDITH, LOUISA ANNE TWAMLEY 1812-1895

Bush Friends in Tasmania, Native Flowers, Fruits and Insects, Drawn From Nature . . . London: 1891. V. 43

My Home in Tasmania During a Residence of Nine Years. London: 1852. V. 41

Notes and Sketches of New South Wales, During a Residence in that Colony from 1839 to 1844. London: 1846. V. 39

Our Wild Flowers Familiarly Described and Illustrated. London: 1839. V. 38

Some of My Bush Friends in Tasmania. London: 1860. V. 39; 41; 44

MEREDITH, ROYSTON

Mr. Steele Detected. London: 1714. V. 41

MEREDITH, SAMUEL

Accounts of Payments and Receipts of Public Monies, from the 1st of January to the 30th of September, 1792. Philadelphia: 1792. V. 39

MEREDITH, WILLIAM

Letter to Dr. Blackstone, by the Author of the Question Stated. London: 1770. V. 38

Love Letter from an Impossible Land. New Haven: 1944. V. 46

Ships and Other Figures. 1948. V. 40; 41

Ships and Other Figures. Princeton: 1948. V. 42; 43; 44

The Wreck of the Thresher and Other Poems. New York: 1964. V. 38; 39; 46

The Wreck of the Thresher and Other Poems. New York: 1965. V. 41

MERGANTHALER LINOTYPE CO.

Linotype Faces. New York: 1905. V. 44

MERHAV, RIVKA

A Glimpse into the Pase: the Joseph Ternbach Collection. Jerusalem: 1981. V. 40; 42; 44

MERIAN, MARIA SIBYLLA

Metamorphosis Insectorum Surinamensium. Hamburg: 1964. V. 38

The Wondrous Transformation of Caterpillars. London: 1978. V. 42

MERIAN, MATTHAUS 1593-1650

Historiae Sacrae Veteris et Novi Testamenti Bybelsche Figuren Vertoonende de Voornamste Historien der Heylighe Schrifture. Amsterdam;: 1650. V. 41

MERIDA, CARLOS

Mexican Costume. Chicago: 1941. V. 39

MERIDIAN and East Mississippi. Meridian: 1900. V. 44

MERIGOT, J.

Promenade Ou Itineraire des Jardins d'Ermenonville. Paris: 1788. V. 46

Promenades ou Itineraire des Jardins de Chantilly. London: 1785. V. 44

Promenades ou Itineraire des Jardins de Chantilly . . . Paris: 1791. V. 39; 44; 45

Promenade ou Itineraire des Jardins d'Ermenoville. Paris: 1811. V. 39; 44

MERIGOT, JAMES

The New Drawing Magazine . . . London: 1814. V. 45

A Select Collection of Views and Ruins in Rome and Its Vicinity. London. V. 43; 45

MERIMEE, J. F. L.

The Art of Painting in Oil, and in Fresco; Being a History of the Various Processes and Materials Employed . . . London: 1839. V. 38; 40

MERIMEE, PROSPER

Carmen. London. V. 41

Carmen. Winchester: 1896. V. 44; 45

Carmen. London: 1916. V. 38; 40; 41; 45

Carmen and Letters from Spain. Paris: 1931. V. 43; 46

Carmen. Paris: 1935. V. 42

Carmen. New York: 1941. V. 40; 41

Carmen. New York: 1941. V. 38

Carmen. Sydney: 1984. V. 41

The Plays of Clara Gazul, a Spanish Comedian. London: 1825. V. 43

MERINO DE JESUCRISTO, ANDRES

Escuela Paleographica, o de Leer Letras Antiguas, Desde la Entrada de los Godos en Espana Hasta Nuestros Tiempos. Madrid: 1780. V. 37; 42; 45

MERITON, G.

The Touchstone of Wills, Testaments and Administrations. London: 1674. V. 38

MERITT, BENJAMIN DEAN

The Athenian Calendar in the Fifth Century Based on a Study of the Detailed Accounts of Money Borrowed by the Athenian State I.G. Cambridge: 1928. V. 44

Athenian Financial Documents of the Fifth Century. Ann Arbor: 1932. V. 44

The Athenian Tribute Lists. Cambridge: 1939-53. V. 44

MERIVALE, CHARLES

A History of Romans Under the Empire. London: 1850-62. V. 46

History of the Romans Under the Empire. London: 1852-62. V. 37

MERIVALE, JOHN HERMAN 1779-1844

A Letter to William Courtenay, Esq. on the Subject of the Chancery Commission. London: 1827. V. 40

MERIWETHER, LEE

The Tramp at Home. New York: 1889. V. 41; 45

MERK, F.

Fur Trade and Empire. George Simpson's Journal; Remarks Connected with the Fur Trade in the Course of a Voyage from York Factory 1824-1828. Cambridge: 1931. V. 37; 46

MERKELEY, CHRISTOPHER

Biography of Christopher Merkley, Written by Himself. Salt Lake City: 1887. V. 37; 45; 46

MERKEN, JOHANN

Liber Artificiosus Alphabeti Maioris, Oder Neu Inventirtes Kunst-Schreib-und Zeichenbuch . . . Erster (-Anderer) Theil. Elberfeld: 1785. V. 46

MERKLEY, C.

Biography. Salt Lake City: 1887. V. 43; 44

MERREM, B.

Avium Rariorum et Minus Cognitarum Icones et Descriptiones. Leipzig: 1786-87. V. 43

MERRETT, C.

Pinax Rerum Naturalium Britannicarum Continens Vegetabilia, Animalia, et Fossilia in Hac Insula Reperta Inchoatus. Londini: 1667. V. 39

MERRIAM, C. HART

The Dawn of the World. Cleveland: 1910. V. 37; 45

MERRIAM Webster International Dictionary Unabridged. 1961. V. 45

MERRICK, GEORGE B.

Old Times on the Upper Mississippi: The Recollections of a Steamboat Pilot from 1854 to 1863. The levees, the engine room, wooding up, the 'old man', art of steering, the wrecks, Civil War time, with appendix list of . . . Cleveland: 1909. V. 37; 45

MERRICK, GEORGE BYRON

Old Times on the Upper Mississippi the Recollections of a Steamboat Pilot From 1854 to 1863. Cleveland: 1909. V. 40; 46

MERRICK, JAMES

The Destruction of Troy, Being the Sequel of the Iliad. Oxford: 1742. V. 39

The Destruction of Troy, Being a Sequel of the Iliad. Oxford: 1742? V. 43

MERRICK, JOHN

Heliocrene. Reading: 1744. V. 45

MERRICK, LEONARD

Four Stories. London: 1925. V. 37

The Man Who Was Good. London: 1892. V. 41

The Works. New York: 1919-27. V. 46

MERRIDEW'S Leamington Guide: Excursions in the Neighbourhood of Leamington Spa . . . Leamington: 1843. V. 45

MERRIFIELD, MARY

Dress as a Fine Art. Boston: 1854. V. 41; 43; 44; 45

MERRIFIELD, MARY PHILADELPHIA

The Art of Fresco Painting, as Practised by the Old Italian and Spanish Masters . . . Brighton: 1846. V. 44

The Art of Fresco Painting. London: 1846. V. 39

MERRILL, ELMER

A Bibliography of Eastern Asiatic Botany (and) Supplement I. Jamaica Plain: 1938-60. V. 39; 40

MERRILL, ELMER D.

Enumeration of Philippine Flowering Plants. 1968. V. 39

MERRILL, JAMES

Angel. Stonington: 1959. V. 40

Bronze. London: 1984. V. 42

Bronze. New York: 1984. V. 39; 41; 46

The Country of a Thousand Years of Peace. New York: 1959. V. 39; 40; 45; 46

The (Diblos) Notebook. New York: 1965. V. 37

Divine Comedies. New York: 1976. V. 38; 39; 41

Feathers from the Hill. Iowa City: 1978. V. 46

First Poems. New York: 1951. V. 37; 39; 44

Japan: Prose of Departure. N.P.: 1987. V. 42

Marbled Paper. Salem: 1982. V. 45; 46

Overdue Pilgrimage to Nova Scotia. New York: 1990. V. 43; 46

Prose in Departure. New York: 1987. V. 41

Robert the Devil. Iowa City: 1981. V. 46

Samos. Los Angeles: 1980. V. 39; 45; 46

The Seraglio. London: 1958. V. 41

Souvenirs. London: 1984. V. 42

Souvenirs. New York: 1984. V. 41; 46

Two First Editions: Divine Comedies. (and) Scripts for the Pageant. New York: 1976/80. V. 45

Yannina. New York: 1973. V. 39; 43

The Yellow Pages. Cambridge: 1974. V. 38

MERRILL, SELAH

East of the Jordan: a Record of Travel and Observation in the Countries of Moab Gilead and Bashan During the Years 1875-1877. New York: 1881. V. 44

MERRILL, WILLIAM E.

Iron Truss Bridges for Railroad. New York: 1878. V. 43

MERRIMAN, HENRY SETON

The Money-Spinner. London: 1896. V. 37

Prisoners and Captives. London: 1891. V. 37

Young Mistley. London: 1888. V. 37; 44

MERRIMAN, SAMUEL

A Dissertation on Retroversion of the Womb, Including Some Observations on Extra-Uterine Gestation. Philadelphia: 1817. V. 42

MERRITT, A.

The Moon Pool. New York: 1919. V. 42

The Ship of Ishtar. New York: 1926. V. 42

MERRITT, EDWARD PERCIVAL

Horace Walpole, Printer. Boston: 1907. V. 45

MERRITT, FRANK C.

History of Alameda County, California. Chicago: 1928. V. 38

MERRITT, HENRY 1822-1877

Art Criticism and Romance with Recollections . . . London: 1879. V. 38

MERRITT, PERCIVAL

The True Story of the So-Called Love Letters of Mrs. Piozzi. Cambridge: 1927. V. 39; 45

THE MERRY and Facetious Companion, in French and English . . . London: 1746. V. 46

MERRY, ANDREW

The Last Dying Words of the Eighteenth Century. London: 1800. V. 37

THE MERRY Cobler and His Musical Alphabet. Glasgow: 1815. V. 43

THE MERRY Fellow's Companion; or American Jest Book. Harrisburgh: 1797. V. 44

THE MERRY Frolics of the Comical Cheats of Swalpo, a Notorious Pickpocket. London: 1800. V. 38

THE MERRY Frolics or the Comical Cheats of Swalpo, a Notorious Pickpcoket and the Merry Pranks of Roger the Clown. London: 1826. V. 46

MERRY, J.

The Witticisms, Anecdotes, Jests and Sayings of Dr. Samuel Johnson During the Whole of His Life. London: 1793. V. 45

MERRY, ROBERT

The Pains of Memory. London: 1796. V. 42

THE MERRY-THOUGHT: or, the Glass-Window and Boghouse Miscellany. London: 1731. V. 38

MERRY Times. London: 1895. V. 39

MERRYMAN, MR.

The Child's Book of Shadows, or, Amusement for Long Evenings. London: 1854-61. V. 46

MERRYMOUNT PRESS

Merrymount Press New Year's Greeting Cards. Boston: 1912-1942. V. 41

MERRYWEATHER & SONS, LTD.

Merryweather's Illustrated Catalogue. London: 1906. V. 38

MERRYWEATHER, F. SOMNER

Bibliomania in the Middle Ages . . . London: 1849. V. 38

MERRYWEATHER, JAMES COMPTON

Fire Protection of Mansions. London: 1886. V. 40

MERSHON, W. B.

The Passenger Pigeon. New York: 1907. V. 39

MERSIUS, JOHN

Creta, Cyprus, Rhodus. Sive De Nobilissimarum Harum Insularum Rebus & Antiquitatibus. Amsterdam: 1675. V. 37

MERTENS, HIERONYMUS ANDREAS

Kurzgefabte Vorschlage fur die Schuler des Augspurgischen Evangel. Augsburg: 1779-1782. V. 42

MERTINS, LOUIS

The Intervals of Robert Frost: a Critical Bibliography. Berkeley: 1947. V. 44

MERTON, THOMAS 1915-1968

The Alaskan Journal of Thomas Merton. Isla Vista: 1988. V. 40; 41; 42; 43; 45; 46

The Alaskan Journal of Thomas Merton, with Sixteen Letters. 1988. V. 40; 45

A Catalogue of Pictures and Drawings from the Collection of Sir Thomas Merton. London: 1950. V. 40

The Christmas Sermons of Blessed Guerric of Igny. Abbey of Gethsemeni: 1958. V. 39

The Christmas Sermons of Bl. Guerric of Igny. 1959. V. 41

The Christmas Sermons of Bl. Guerric of Igny. Kentucky: 1959. V. 45

The Christmas Sermons of Blessed Guerric of Igny. 1958. V. 38

Eighteen Poems. New York: 1985. V. 38; 41; 42; 43; 44; 45

Eighteen Poems. (New York): (1985). V. 37

Elected Silence. London: 1949. V. 43

Encounter. 1988. V. 41; 42

Encounter. Monterey: 1988. V. 41; 42; 43

Encounter. N.P.: 1988. V. 43

Father Louie. New York. V. 45

Figures for an Apocalypse. New York: 1947. V. 46

Gethesemani. A Life of Praise. Kentucky: 1966. V. 45

A Hidden Wholeness: Thomas Merton and John Howard Griffin. Boston: 1970. V. 44

Life and Holiness. New York: 1963. V. 46

A Man in the Divided Sea. 1946. V. 42

Monk's Pond, Old Hermit. Monterey: 1988. V. 45; 46

Nicholas of Cusa/Dialogue About the Hidden God. New York. V. 46

Notes on Sacred and Profane Art. New York: 1956? V. 43

On the Solitary Life. 1977. V. 39

On the Solitary Life, by Guigo. Pawlet: 1977. V. 41

Original Child Bomb, Points for Meditation to Be Scratched on the Walls of a Cave. New York: 1961. V. 44

The Ox Mountain Parable of Meng Tzu. Lexington: 1960. V. 42

The Pax. New York: 1957-58. V. 45

Seeds of Contemplation. Mt. Vernon: 1949. V. 43

The Tears of the Blind Lions. New York: 1949. V. 43

Thirty Poems. Norfolk: 1944. V. 38; 43; 46

The Tower of Babel. New York: 1955? V. 43

Waters of Silence. London: 1950. V. 42; 43

MERTON, WILFRED

A Descriptive Catalogue of the Greek Papyri in the Collection of Wilfred Merton, F.S.A. London: 11948, 1959. V. 41

A Descriptive Catalogue of the Greek Papyri in the Collection of Wilfred Merton, F.S.A. London & Dublin: 1948-59. V. 40

MERVAULT, PETER

The Last Famous Siege of the City of Rochel: Together with the Edict of nantes. London: 1680. V. 37

MERWIN, RAYMOND E.

The Ruins of Holmul, Guatemala. Cambridge: 1932. V. 42

MERWIN, W. S.

Apparitions. Northridge: 1981. V. 39

Feathers from the Hill. Iowa City: 1978. V. 41; 45

Green with Beasts. London: 1956. V. 37; 39

Koa. New York: 1988. V. 41

The Lice - Poems. New York: 1967. V. 41

Mary. Brooklyn: 1976. V. 38; 39

Mary. New York: 1982. V. 40

Mary. A Story. New York: (1982). V. 37

A Mask for Janus. New Haven: 1952. V. 39; 46

One Story. New York: 1989. V. 43

The Poem of the Cid. London: 1959. V. 41

Robert the Devil. Iowa City: 1981. V. 38; 45

Signs. Iowa City: 1971. V. 43

Three Poems. New York: 1968. V. 42

MERWIN, W.S.

The Dancing Bears. New Haven: 1954. V. 45

MERYMAN, RICHARD

Andrew Wyeth. Boston: 1968. V. 37; 38; 39; 40; 41; 42; 43; 44; 46

Andrew Wyeth. Boston: 1969. V. 38; 39

MERZ, JOHN THEODORE

A History of European Thought in the Nineteenth Century. Edinburgh: 1903-14. V. 38

MESMER, FRANZ ANTON

Essai sur les Probabilites du Somnambulisme Mgnetique, Pour Servir l'Histoire du Mgnetisme Animal. Amsterdam: 1785. V. 38

Memoire Sur la Decouverte du Magnetisme Animal. A Geneve: 1779. V. 45; 46

Memoire sur la Decouverte du Magnetisme Animal . . . Geneva and Paris: 1779. V. 40

Memoire Sur la Decouverte du Magnetisme Animal. Geneva & Paris: 1779. V. 46

Precis Historique des Faits Relatifs au Magnetisme-Animal Jusques en Avril 1781. London: 1781. V. 38; 45

MESOPOTAMIA EXPEDITIONARY FORCE, 1915-1919.

Survey of the Fauna of Iraq. Mammals, Birds, Reptiles, etc., made by Members of the Mesopotamia Expeditionary Force, D, 1915-1919. Bombay: 1923. V. 38

MESSALINA. London: 1821. V. 39

THE MESSENGER Defeated; or the Lawyer's Escape. London: 1705. V. 45

MESSINK, JAMES

Airs, Duets, Etc. in the New Pantomime, Called the Norwood Gypsies. London: 1777. V. 39

MESSISBUGO, CHRISTOFORO DI

Banchetti. Compositioni di Vivande, et Apparecchio Generale. Ferrara: 1549. V. 38; 40

Libro Nuovo Nel Qual S'Insegna Il Modo d'Ordinar Banchetti, Apparecchiar Tavole . . . Venetia: 1617. V. 38

MESSITER, CHARLES A.

Sport and Adventures Among the North American Indians. London: 1890. V. 37

MESSLER, ABRAHAM

Centennial History of Somerset County. Somerville: 1878. V. 44

First Things in Old Somerset. A Collection of Articles Relating to Somerset County, N.J . . . Somerville: 1899. V. 41

MESSNER, REINHOLD

The Big Walls. New York: 1978. V. 44

MESUE 928-1018

De Re Medica Tres, Iacobo Sylvio Medico Interprete Lyons, apud Gulielmum Rovillium. colophon: 1550. V. 40

METALIOUS, GRACE

Peyton Place. New York: 1956. V. 46

METASIO, PIETRO ANTONIO DOMENICO BUONAVENTURA 1698-1782

Opere Scelte: Publicate da A. Buttura. Paris: 1823. V. 39

METASTASIO, PIETRO ANTONIO DOMENICO BOUNAVENTURA 1698-1782

Demetrius. London: 1737. V. 39

METASTASIO, PIETRO ANTONIO DOMENICO BUONAVENTURA 1698-1782

Dramas and Other Poems. London: 1800. V. 37; 38; 40

Observations on the Poetics of Aristotle, by Metastasio, Rendered Into English. Sydney: 1842. V. 41

Opere di Pietro Metastasio. Mantova: 1817. V. 46

METCALF, J.

Eight Views of Fountains Abbey. Ripon. V. 45

Eight Views of Fountains Abbey, Intended to Illustrate the Architecture and Picturesque Scenery of that Celebrated Ruin. London: 1832. V. 41

METCALF, JOHN

The Life of John Metcalf, Commonly Called Blind Jack of Knaresborough. London: 1795. V. 40

METCALF, PAUL

Genoa: a Telling of Wonders. Highlands: 1965. V. 44; 46

Willie's Throw. New York: 1981. V. 38

METCALF, SAMUEL L.

A Collection of Some of the Most Interesting Narratives of Indian Warfare in the West . . . Lexington: 1821. V. 45

METCALFE, C. R.

Anatomy of the Monocotyledons. Volume 7: Helobiae (Alismatidae). Oxford: 1982. V. 39

Anatomy of the Monocotyledons. Oxford: 1960-82. V. 37; 38

METCALFE, CHARLES THEOPHILUS

Farewell Addresses of the Inhabitants of Jamaica to the Right Honorable . . . Kingston: 1842. V. 40

METCALFE, CHARLES THEOPHILUS METCALFE, BARON 1785-1846

Selections from the Papers of Lord Metcalfe. London: 1855. V. 42

METCALFE, FREDERICK 1815-1885

The Oxonian in Norway. London: 1856. V. 39

METCALFE, JOHN

The Feasting Dead. Sauk City: 1954. V. 42; 43; 45

METCALFE, SAMUEL LYTLER

A New Theory of Terrestrial Magnetism. New York: 1833. V. 40

METCHIM, DON BRIDGMAN

Wild West Poems. London: 1889. V. 37

METCHNIKOFF, ELIE

Immunity in Infective Diseases. Cambridge: 1905. V. 40

THE METEOR. London: 1901-08. V. 38

METEREN, EMANUEL VAN

Niederlandische Historien Oder Geschichten Aller Deren Handel . . . Arnhem: 1612. V. 43; 44

A Trve Discovrse Historicall of the Svcceeding Governors in the Netherlands . . . London: 1602. V. 41; 44

METEYARD, ELIZA

Choice Examples of Wedgwood Art. London: 1879. V. 37; 41; 42

Choice Examples of Wedgwood Art. London: 1879. V. 37

A Group of Englishmen (1795-1815), London: 1871. V. 44; 45

The Lady Herbert's Gentlewomen. London: 1862. V. 43

The Life of Josiah Wedgewood. London: 1865. V. 38; 39; 40

The Life of Josiah Wedgwood. London: 1980. V. 38

Memorials of Wedgwood. London: 1874. V. 37; 41

Wedgwood and His Works. London: 1873. V. 37; 41; 42

The Wedgwood Handbook. London: 1875. V. 37

Wedgwood's Catalogue of Cameos, Intaglios, Medals, Bas-Reliefs, Busts and Small Statues. London: 1873. V. 40; 44

METEYARD, ELIZABETH

Choice Examples of Wedgwood Art. London: 1879. V. 46

A METHOD is Here Humbly Propos'd That Will Enable the Government to Pay Off that Part of the Publick Debt, Which is Redeemable. N.P.: 1715. V. 40

A METHOD Most Humbly Proposed, to Prevent the Running of Wooll (sic) from Ireland to Foreign Parts. London: 1739. V. 40

A METHODICAL Treatise of Replevins, Distresses, Avowries . . . London: In Savoy,: 1739. V. 37

METHODIST EPISCOPAL CHURCH

The Doctrines and Discipline of the Methodist Episcopal Church in Canada. Hamilton, Ont.: 1872. V. 37

METHODIUS

De Revelatione Facta ab Angelo Beato Methodio in Carcere Detento. Basle: 1504. V. 38

METHODIUS, SAINT

Titulus in Libellus . . . Contines in se Reuelationes Diuinas a Sanctis Angelis Factas de Principio Mundi & Eradicatione Variou Regno Atq Ultimi Regis Romanorum Gestis U Futuro Triumpho in Turcos . . . Augsburg: 1496. V. 40

METHODUS Discendi Artem Medicam, in Duas Partes Divisa . . . Londini: 1734. V. 39; 40

METHVEN, ROBERT

The Log of a Merchant Officer. London: 1854. V. 42; 45

METHVIN, J. J.

Andele, or the Mexican-Kiowa Captive. Louisville: 1899. V. 37; 46

In the Limelight or History of Anadarko (Caddo County) and Vicinity From the Earliest Days. Oklahoma City. V. 39

METIUS, ADRIAN

De Genvino Usu Utriusque Globi Tractatus. Amstelodamens: 1624. V. 37

METLAKE, GEORGE

The Life and Writings of St. Columban, 542?-615. Philadelphia: 1914. V. 39

METROPOLITAN MUSEUM OF ART

19th Century America: Furniture and Other Decorative Arts. New York: 1970. V. 45

METROPOLITAN MUSEUM OF ART. NEW YORK.

The Architect and the Industrial Arts. An Exhibition of Contemporary American Design. 1929. V. 46

METROPOLITAN RAILWAY TERMINI

Report of the Commissioners Appointed to Investigate the Various Projects for Establishing Railway Termini within or in the Immediate Vicinity of the Metropolis. (with) Maps, Plans . . . London: 1846. V. 46

METSCHAL, JOHN

Rudolph J. Nunnenmacher Collection of Projectile Arms. Milwaukee: 1928. V. 37; 38

METTLER, CECILIA

History of Medicine. Philadelphia: 1947. V. 37; 38; 41

METZ, C. M.

Studies for Drawing the Human Figure. Philadelphia. V. 46

METZ, LEON CLAIRE

The Shooters. El Paso: 1976. V. 41

METZDORF, ROBERT F.

The Tinker Library. A Bibliographical Catalogue of the Books and Manuscripts Collected by Chauncey Brewster Tinker. New Haven: 1959. V. 38

METZEROTT, W. G.

Our National Buildings! Views of Washington. Washington: ?1845-50. V. 41

METZGAR, JUDSON D.

Adventures in Japanese Prints. Los Angeles: 1943. V. 46

METZGER, JOHANN

An Historical Description of the Castle of Heidelberg and Its Gardens . . . Heidelberg: 1830. V. 39

MEUNIER, C.

La Flore Ornamentale Appropriee aux Decors des Reliures. Paris: 1938. V. 40; 44

MEURSIUS, JOHN

Athenae Atticae. Leyden: 1624. V. 37

De Regno Laconico Libri II. Piraeeus. Sive, De Piraeo, Atheniensium Portu Celeberrimo & Ejusdem Antiquitatibus, Liber Singularis. Utrecht: 1687-86-86. V. 37

MEW, CHARLOTTE

The Rambling Sailor. London: 1929. V. 42; 43; 44

MEXIA, PEDRO

Les Diverses Lecons . . . avec Trois Dialogues, Mises en Francais par Claude Gruget . . . Lyon: 1577. V. 37; 40

The Imperiall Historie of the Lives of the Emperours. London: 1623. V. 40

THE MEXICAN Colonies. Valuable Information to Intending Settlers and Tourists. Salt Lake City: 1890. V. 39

THE MEXICAN Petroleum Co., Ltd. A Booklet of Photographs Illustrating a Trip Over Some of the Properties of the Company. In Two Parts. N.P., n.d.: 1913. V. 37

MEXICO (CITY). CONSULADO

Ordenanzas Del Consulado De La Universidad De Los Mercaderes De Esta Nueva Espana. Mexico City: 1772. V. 40

MEXICO. CONSTITUTION - 1824

Acta Constitutiva de la Federacion Mexicana. Mexico: 1824. V. 39

Constitucion Federal de Los Estados Unidos Mexicanos, Sancionada por el Congreso General Constituyente, el 4 de Octubre de 1824. Mexico: 1824. V. 39

MEXICO. (ECCLESIASTICAL PROVINCE) COUNCIL, 1585

Sanctum Provinciale Concilium Mexici Celebratum Anno Domini Millessimo Quingentessimo Octuaagessimo Quinto, Praesidente in eo Illmo. ac Rmo. D. D. Petro Moya de Conteras Archiepo. Mexicano . . . nunc vero ad instantiam et ex sumptibus . . . Mexico: 1622. V. 38

MEXICO. TREATIES ETC.

Tratado de Paz, Amistad, Limites y Arreglo Definitivo Entre la Republica Mexicana y los Estados-Unidos de Norte America . . . Mexico: 1848. V. 45

The Treaty of Guadalupe Hidalgo, February Second, 1848. Berkeley: 1949. V. 44

MEXICO. TREATIES, ETC. - 1848

Tratado de Paz Amistad y Limites Entre la Republica Mexicana y Los Estados-Unidos de Norte America . . . Queretaro: 1848. V. 40

Treaty of Gudalupe Hidalgo. Lara: 1848. V. 38

MEYEN, SERGEI V.

Fundamentals of Palaeobotany. London: 1987. V. 38

MEYENDORFF, GEORGES DE

Voyage d'Orenbourg a Boukhara, Fait en 1820, a Travers les Steppes. Paris: 1826. V. 40; 46

MEYER, A. B.

The Birds of Celebes and the Neighbouring Islands. Berlin: 1898. V. 40

MEYER, ADOLF 1866-1950

The Collected Papers of Adolf Meyer. Baltimore: 1952. V. 39; 43

MEYER, AGNES

Chinese as Reflected in the Thought and Art of Li Lung-Mien . . . New York: 1922. V. 46

MEYER, AGNES E.

Chinese Painting as Reflected in the Thought and Art of Li Lung-Mien, 1070-1106. New York: 1923. V. 38; 41

MEYER, CARL

Nach Dem Sacramento. Reisebilder Eines Heimgekerten. Aurau: 1855. V. 37

MEYER DE SCHAUENSEE, R.

A Guide to the Birds of South America. London: 1971. V. 37

A Guide to the Birds of Venezuela. Princeton: 1978. V. 37

MEYER, F. S.

A Handbook of Art Smithing for the Use of Practical Smiths, Designers of Ironwork, Technical and Art Schools, Architects, etc. London: 1896. V. 40

MEYER, FRANZ

Marc Chagall: Life and Work. New York. V. 39; 41; 43; 46

Marc Chagall. New York: 1963. V. 46

Mark Chagall: Life and Work. New York: 1964. V. 46

MEYER, G.

Lehrbuch der Schonen Gartenkunst. Berlin: 1873. V. 41

MEYER, G. F. W.

Flora des Konigreichs Hannover. Gottingen: 1842-54. V. 43

MEYER, GEORG

Bergwercks Geschopff, vnd Wunderbare Eigenschafft der Metalsfruchte. Leipzig: 1595. V. 40

MEYER, H. L.

Colored Illustrations of British Birds and Their Eggs. London: 1844-57. V. 40

Coloured Illustrations of British Birds and Their Eggs. London: 1842-50. V. 37; 42; 43

Coloured Illustrations of British Birds and Their Eggs. London: 1853-57. V. 40; 41; 44

Coloured Illustrations of British Birds and Their Eggs. London: 1857. V. 38; 40

Illustrations of British Birds. London: 1835-44. V. 44

Illustrations of British Birds. London: 1837. V. 39

MEYER, HANS

Across East African Glaciers. London: 1891. V. 37; 38; 43; 46

Der Kilimandjaro. Reisen und Studien. Berlin: 1900. V. 43

Ostafrikanische Gletscherfahrten Forschungsreisen im Kilimandscharo-Gebiet . . . Leipzig: 1890. V. 46

MEYER, HENRY CODINGTON

Civil War Experiences Under Bayard, Gregg, Kilpatrick, Custer, Raulston and Newberry 1862, 1863, 1864. New York: 1911. V. 42

MEYER, H.L.

Illustrations of British Birds. London: 1837-44. V. 37

MEYER, JOHANN GEORG, CALLED MEYER VON BREMEN

Meyer von Bremen Gallery: Selected Photographs of His Latest and Choicest Works. New York: 1876? V. 41

MEYER, JOHANN JAKOB

Mahlerische Reise auf der Neuen Kunst-Strasse aus dem Etschthal im Tyrol uber das Stilfser Joch durch das Veltlin Langs dem Somersee Nach Manland . . . Zurich: 1831. V. 39

MEYER, KLAUS

Prepositions: Fifteen Relief Prints in Colour. 1987. V. 40

MEYER, THOMAS

Blind Date. Guildford: 1979. V. 37

Sappho's Raft. V. 37; 40; 42

Sappho's Raft. Highlands: 1982. V. 44; 46

The Umbrella of Aesculapius. Highlands: 1975. V. 46

The Umbrella of Aesculapius. Highlands: 1975. V. 37; 40; 42

MEYERHOF, OTTO FRITZ

Chemical Dynamics of Life Phenomena. Philadelphia & London: 1924. V. 41

MEYERS, R. C. V.

Life and Adventures of Lewis Wetzel, the Renowned Virginia Ranger and Scout . . . Philadelphia: 1883. V. 46

MEYERS, WILLIAM H.

Jouranl of a Cruise to California and the Sandwich Islands in the United States SllopOof-War Cyane. San Francisco: 1935. V. 43

Journal of a Cruise to California and the Sandwich Islands 1841-1844. San Francisco: 1955. V. 37; 38; 40; 45; 46

Naval Sketches of the War in California. New York: 1939. V. 37; 45; 46

Naval Sketches of the War in California. San Francisco: 1939. V. 38

Sketches of California and Hawaii. 1970. V. 38; 44

Sketches of California and Hawaii. N.P.: 1970. V. 39

Sketches of California and Hawaii. San Francisco: 1970. V. 38; 40; 41; 45; 46

MEYERSTEIN, E. H. W.

Goemagog & Corineus. V. 45

The Pageant and Other Stories. London. V. 46

MEYGRET, AMADEUS

Questiones in Libros de Celo & Mundo Aristotelis. Paris: 1514. V. 44

MEYNELL, ALICE

A. M. A Keepsake for the A. I. G. A. London: 1930. V. 37

The Children. London: 1897. V. 41

Collected Poems. London: 1913. V. 42

The Colour of Life and Other Essays on Things Seen and Heard. Chicago: 1896. V. 38

Mary, the Mother of Jesus: an Essay. London: 1912. V. 44

Poems and The Rhythm of Life and Other Essays. London: 1893. V. 43

The Poems of . . . London: 1923. V. 42; 44

Preludes. London: 1875. V. 38; 39

MEYNELL, FRANCIS

A(lice) M(eynell). A Keepsake for the A.I.G.A. from Francis Meynell. London: 1930. V. 46

Fleuron Anthology. V. 46

My Lives. London: 1971. V. 39

The Nonesuch Century. London: 1936. V. 40; 42

Poems & Pieces 1911-1961. London: 1961. V. 40

Typography. London: 1923. V. 37; 40; 41; 42; 43; 45

The Typography of Newspaper Advertisements. London: 1929. V. 37; 40; 41

The Week-End Book. London: 1939. V. 44

MEYNELL, GERARD T.

Pages from Books. London. V. 46

Pages from Books. London: 1927. V. 41

MEYNELL, HUGO

The Meynellian Science; or Fox-Hunting Upon System. Kew Gardens: 1926. V. 41

MEYNELL, KATHERINE

Seas of the Moon. London: 1988. V. 41

MEYNELL, WILFRID

the Child Set in the Midst. London: 1892. V. 41

THE MEYNELLIAN Science of Foxhunting Upon System. New York: 1926. V. 39; 43

MEYNEN, EMIL

Bibliography on German Settlements in Colonial North America. Leipzig: 1937. V. 41; 42; 46

MEYRICK, SAMUEL RUSH

The Costume of the Original Inhabitants of the British Islands, and Adjacent Coasts of the Baltic . . . London: 1815. V. 37; 38; 45

The Costume of the Original Inhabitants of the British Islands, from the Earliest periods to the Sixth Century. London: 1821. V. 38; 41; 42; 43

A Critical Enquiry into Ancient Armour, as It Existed in Great Britain, from the Norman Conquest to the Reign of King Charles II. London: 1824. V. 46

A Critical Inquiry into Antient Armour as It Existed in Europe, but Particularly in England, from the Norman Conquest to the Reign of King Charles II. London: 1837. V. 41

A Critical Enquiry into Ancient Armour, As It Existed in Europe, But Particularly in England from the Norman Conquest to the Regin of King Charles the Second . . . London: 1842. V. 41; 43

Engraved Illustrations of Antient Armour. London: 1854. V. 41; 42; 44; 46

MEYRICK, WILLIAM

The New Family Herbal; or, Domestic Physician . . . Birmingham: 1802. V. 45

MEYRINK, G.

The Golem. 1928. V. 44

MEZERAY, FRANCOIS

A General Chronological History of France. London: 1683. V. 45

MEZERAY, FRANCOIS EUDES DE 1610-1683

Histoire de France Depuis Pharamond jusqu'a Mainetenant, Avec un Abrege de la Vie de Chaque Reine. Paris: 1643-51. V. 40

MEZEY, ROBERT

White Blossoms. West Branch: 1965. V. 40

MEZGER, G. C.

Augsburgs Alteste Druckdenkmale und Formschneiderarbeiten. Augsburg: 1840. V. 38

MICALORI, JACOMO

Crisis . . . de Eryci Puteani Circulo Urbaniano in Qua Disputatur, an sit Constituendum Dierum in Orbe Principium ab Ipso Puteano Excogitatum. Urbini: 1632. V. 44; 45

MICHAEL, ALBERT D.

British Oribatidae. London: 1884-88. V. 43

MICHAEL DE DALEN

Casus Breves Decretalium Sexti et Clementinarum. Strassburg: 1485. V. 41; 42

MICHAELIS, ADOLF

Ancient Marbles in Great Britain. Cambridge: 1882. V. 37; 40; 44

MICHAELIS, H. VON

Birds of Prey, a Kinship. Knysna: 1987. V. 42

MICHAELIS, M. GEORG

Vortheile Allerhand Arten von Sonnen-Uhren zu Verfertigen, Nebst Verschiedenen Angenehmen Erfindungen und Vielen Kupffern Vermehrter . . . Jena und Leipzig: 1735. V. 46

MICHAELIS, SEBASTIAN

The Admirable Historie of the Possession and Conversion of a Penitent Woman. London: 1613. V. 43

MICHAELIUS, JONAS

Manhattan in 1628 as Described in the Recently Discovered Autograph Letter of . . . Written from the Settlement on the 8th of August of That Year and Now First Published. New York: 1904. V. 37

MICHALOWSKI, KAZIMIERZ

Art of Ancient Egypt. New York. V. 38; 41

Art of Ancient Egypt. New York. V. 41

Art of Ancient Egypt. New York: 1968. V. 42; 44

Art of Ancient Egypt. New York: 1969? V. 41

Art of Ancient Egypt. 1968. V. 37

MICHAUD, LOUIS GABRIEL

Biographie Universelle, Ancienne et Moderne, ou Histoire, par Ordre Alphabetique, de la Vie Publique et Privee de Tous les Hommes Qui se Sont fait Remarquer par Leurs Ecrits . . . Paris: 1811-33. V. 40

MICHAUD, M.

Correspondence d'Orient (1830-1831). Brussels: 1841. V. 37

MICHAUX, FRANCOIS ANDRE 1770-1855

Flora Boreali-Americana, Sistens Caracteres Plantarum Quas in America Septentrionali Collegit et Detexit Andreas Michaux . . . Paris: 1803. V. 38; 43

Flora Boreali-Americana, Sistens Caracteres Plantarum Quas in America Septentrionali Collegit et Detexit. Paris & Strasbourgh: 1803. V. 39

Histoire des Arbres Forestiers de l'Amerique Septenrionale. Paris: 1810-13. V. 38; 40; 43

The North American Sylva. Paris: 1817-19. V. 38

The North American Sylva, or a Description of the Forest Trees, of the United States, Canada and Nova Soctia. Philadelphia: 1817-19. V. 40

The North American Sylva, or a Description of the Forest Trees of the United States, Canada and Nova Soctia. Paris: 1819. V. 37; 40

The North American Sylva, or a Description of the Forest Trees of the United States, Canada and Nova Scotia. Philadelphia: 1871. V. 45

The North American Sylva, or a Description of the Forest Trees . . . Philadelphia: 1871. V. 42; 43; 45

The North American Sylva . . . Philadelphia: 1871. V. 42

Travels to the Westward of the Allegany Mountains, in the States of Ohio, Kentucky, and Tennessee, and Return to Charlestown, through the Upper Carolinas . . . London: 1805. V. 37; 38; 40; 41; 42; 43; 45; 46

Travels to the Westward of the Allegany Mountains, in the States of the Ohio, Kentucky and Tennessee, in the Year 1802. London: 1805. V. 40

Travels to the Westward of the Allegany Mountains, in the States of the Ohio, Kentucky and Tennessee, in the Year 1802. London: 1805. V. 46

Voyage a l'Ouest des Monts Alleghanys, dans les Etats de l'Ohio, du Kentucky et du Tennessee, et Retour a Charleston par les Hautes-Carolines. Paris: 1804. V. 38

MICHAUX, HENRI

A Selection. 1979. V. 39

MICHEAUX, OSCAR

The Masquerade. New York: 1947. V. 37; 42

The Story of Dorothy Stanfield. 1946. V. 37

MICHEL, DAN, of Northgate fl. 1340

The Ayenbite of Inwyt Written in the Dialect of the County of Kent by Dan. Michel of Northgate in the Year 1340. London: 1855. V. 40

MICHEL, EMILE

Great Masters of Landscape Painting. London: 1910. V. 41

MICHEL, EMILE continued

Rembrandt, His Life, His Work and His Time. London: 1894. V. 39

Rubens: His Life, His Work and His Time. London: 1899. V. 40

MICHEL, FRANCISQUE

A Critical Inquiry into the Scottish language with the view of Illustrating the Rise and Progress of Civilisation in Scotland. London: 1882. V. 37

MICHEL, WALTER

Wyndham Lewis Paintings and Drawings. Berkeley: 1971. V. 39; 43; 44; 45; 46

Wyndham Lewis: Paintings and Drawings. Berkeley & Los Angeles: 1971. V. 41

MICHELANGELO BUONARROTI

Le Rime . . . Pittore Scultore e Architetto Cavate Dagli Autografi e Pubblicate da Cesare Guasti . . . Firenze: 1863. V. 39

MICHELENA, JUAN ANGEL DE

Parlamento Dirixido por el Capitan de Navio . . . a la Junta de Buenos-Ayres y Contestacion de Esta. Colophon: 1811. V. 40

Parlamento Dirixido por el Capitan de Navio . . . Montevideo: 1811. V. 46

MICHELET, JULES

The Bird. London: 1869. V. 41

The Insect. London: 1875. V. 41

MICHELI, MARIO DE

Siqueiros. New York: 1968. V. 38; 44; 46

MICHELI, PIER ANTONIO 1679-1737

Nova Plantarum Genera Iuxta Tournefortii Methodum Disposita. Florence: 1729. V. 38

MICHELI Y MARQUEZ, JOSEPH fl. 1642-1648

Tesoro Militar de Cavalleria Antiguo y Moderno. Madrid: 1642. V. 43

MICHELINI, FAMIANO 1604-1665

Trattato della Direzione de'Fiumi Nel Quale si Dimostrano da' Suoi Veri Principi i Modi Piu Sicuri . . . Firenze: 1664. V. 38

Trattato della Direzione de Fiumi.. Florence: 1664. V. 40

MICHELL, E. B.

The Art and Practice of Hawking. London: 1900. V. 39; 42

MICHELL, JOHN 1724-1793

Conjectures Concerning the Cause and Observations Upon the Phaenomena of Earthquakes . . . London: 1760. V. 43

A Treatise of Artifical Magnets. Cambridge: 1751. V. 41; 42; 46

MICHELL, THOMAS

Russian Pictures Drawn with Pen and Pencil. New York: 1889. V. 46

MICHELSON, ALBERT ABRAHAM

Light Waves and Their Uses. Chicago: 1903. V. 42; 44; 45; 46

MICHELTORENA, MANUEL

La Ecsma. Asamblea Departamental con Fecha 20 del Corriente me Ha Dirijido la Acta Siguiente . . . Monterey: 1844. V. 39; 40; 41; 46

MICHENER, JAMES ALBERT 1907-

Alaska. New York: 1988. V. 39

Alaska. New York: 1988. V. 39; 41; 45; 46

The Bridges at Toko-Ri. 1953. V. 46

The Bridges at Toko-Ri. (New York: 1953). V. 37

The Caribbean. New York. V. 43

The Caribbean. New York: 1989. V. 41; 42

The Caribbean. New York: 1989. V. 42

Chesapeake. New York: 1978. V. 39; 42; 43; 45

Collectors, Forgers - and a Writer: a Memoir. New York: 1983. V. 41; 42

Collectors, Forgers -- and a Writer. A Memoir. 1983. V. 39

The Covenant. New York: 1980. V. 39; 43

The Drifters. New York: (1971). V. 37

The Drifters. New York: 1971. V. 46

Facing East. New York: 1970. V. 42; 46

Facing East. New York: 1973. V. 39

The Fires of Spring. New York: 1949. V. 42

The Fires of Spring. New York: (1949). V. 37

Hawaii. Hollywood. V. 45

Iberia. New York: 1968. V. 43; 44

Japanese Prints from the Early Masters to the Modern. Rutland & Tokyo: 1959. V. 44; 45

Legacy. New York: 1987. V. 37; 38

The Modern Japanese Print. Rutland: 1962. V. 40

Poland. New York: 1983. V. 43; 45; 46

Return to Paradise. 1951. V. 43

Sayonara. New York: 1954. V. 44; 45

Space. New York: 1982. V. 37; 40; 42; 45

Sports in America. New York. V. 45

Tales of the South Pacific. New York: 1947. V. 46

Tales of the South Pacific. New York: 1950. V. 39

Tales of the South Pacific. London: 1951. V. 46

Texas. New York: 1985. V. 38; 39; 40; 45

Texas. Austin: 1986. V. 37; 38

The World is My Home. New York: 1992. V. 46

MICHIE, ALEXANDER

The Siberian Overland Route from Peking to Petersburg, through the Deserts and Steppes of Mongolia, Tartary. London: 1864. V. 46

MICHIE, ARCHIBALD

Readings in Melbourne. London: 1879. V. 39

MICHIE, THOMAS JOHNSON

The Virginia Scrivener . . . Staunton: 1833. V. 41; 45

MICHIGAN

Manual Containing the Rules of the Senate and House of Representatives of the State of Michigan and Joint Rules of the Two Houses and Other Matter. Michigan: 1848. V. 42; 45

MICHIGAN. CONSTITUTION

Constitution of the State of Michigan as Adopted in Convention, Begun and Held at . . . Detroit 11 May 1835. Detroit: 1835. V. 39; 42

MICHIGAN. CONSTITUTION - 1835

A Constitution and Form of Government by the Inhabitants of the Territory of Michigan. Washington: 1835. V. 37

MICHIGAN. LAWS, STATUTES, ETC.

Acts of the Legislature of the State, with an Appendix. Detroit. V. 44

MICHIGAN. LAWS, STATUTES, ETC. - 1840

An Act to Incorporate the Macomb & Sasginaw Railroad Company, and for Other Purposes. Together with the Subsequent Amendements &c. Mount Clemens: 1840. V. 37

MICHIGAN. (TERRITORY). LAWS, STATUTES, ETC. - 1821

Laws of the Territory of Michigan with Marginal Notes and an Index; to Which are Prefixed, the Ordinance and Several Acts of Congress Relating to this Territory. Detroit: 1821. V. 38

MICHLER, NATHANIEL

Routes from the Western Boundary of Arkansas to Santa Fe and the Valley of the Rio Grande. Washington: 1850. V. 40; 41

MICKLE, ISAAC

Reminiscences of Old Gloucester; or Incidents in the History of the Counties of Gloucester, Atlantic and Camden, New Jersey. Philadelphia: 1845. V. 41

MICKLE, WILLIAM JULIUS

The Lusiad or the Discovery of India, and Epic Poem Translated from the original Portuguese of Luis de Camoens. London: 1778. V. 37

Pollio, an Elegiac Ode. Oxford: 1766. V. 38; 40; 43

Pollio: an Elegiac Ode. Oxford: 1766. V. 38

The Prophecy of Queen Emma. London: 1782. V. 38

MICKWITZ, A.

The A. E. Nordenskiold Collection . . . Annotated Catalogue of Maps Made Up to 1800. Helsinki: 1979. V. 40

MICQUEAU, JEAN LOYS

Aureliae Urbis memorabilis ab Anglis Obsidio, anno 1428. Orleans: 1560. V. 38

THE MICROCOSM of London. London: 1808-10. V. 46

THE MICROCOSM of London. London: 1904. V. 44

MIDDIMAN, SAMUEL

Select Views of Great Britain Engraved by S. Middiman from Pictures and Drawings by the Most Eminent Artists with Descriptions. London: 1812. V. 37; 40

Select Views in Great Britian . . . London: 1813. V. 41

Select Views in Great Britain, Engraved from Pictures and Drawings by the Most Eiment Artists. London: 1913. V. 44

THE MIDDLE States: a Handbook for Travellers. Boston: 1879. V. 42

MIDDLEBROOK, LOUIS F.

The Frigate 'South Carolina'. Salem: 1929. V. 46

History of Maritime Connecticut, During the Revolution, 1775-83 . . . Salem: 1925. V. 41

MIDDLETON, A. H.

Records of the Stirlingshire, Dumbarton, Clackmannan, and Kinross Militia, Highland Borderers Lifght Infantry, Now 3rd Battalion Argyll and Sutherland Highlanders (Princess Louise's). Stirling: 1904. V. 38

MIDDLETON, ARTHUR E.

Sir Gilbert de Middleton and the Part He Took in the Rebellion in the North of England in 1317. Newcastle-upon-Tyne: 1918. V. 37

MIDDLETON, B.

The Whole Art of Bookbinding; The Whole Process of Marbling Paper. Austin: 1987. V. 41

MIDDLETON, CHARLES

The Architect and Builder's Miscellany, or Pocket Diary. London: 1799. V. 46

Picturesque and Architectural Views for Cottages, Farm Houses, and Country Villas. London: 1793. V. 39; 42

MIDDLETON, CHARLES S.

Shelley and His Writings. London: 1858. V. 37

MIDDLETON, CHARLES T.

A New and Complete System of Geography. London: 1777. V. 39

MIDDLETON, CHRISTOPHER

Nocture in Eden. London: 1945. V. 40

Poems. London: 1944. V. 40

A Reply to the Remarks of Arthur Dobbs, Esq., On Captain Middleton's Vindication of His Conduct on Board His Majesty's Ship the Furnance . . . London: 1744. V. 43

A Vindication of the Conduct of Captain Christopher Middleton, in a Late Voyage on Board His Majesty's Ship the Furnance . . . London: 1743. V. 43

MIDDLETON, COLIN

The Fool of Destiny. London: 1894. V. 41

MIDDLETON, CONYERS

A Dissertation Concerning the Origin of Printing in England. Cambridge: 1735. V. 42

Dissertationis de Servili Medicorum Conditione Appendix, seu Defension pars Secundus. London: 1761. V. 38

A Free Inquiry Into the Miraculous Powers, Which are Supposed to Have Subsisted in the Christian Church, from the Earliest Ages Through Several Sucessive Centuries. London: 1749. V. 39; 40

A Full and Impartial Account of all the Late Proceedings in the University of Cambridge Against Dr. Bentley . . . London: 1719. V. 39

The History of the Life of Marcus Tullius Cicero. London: 1750. V. 44

The History of the Life of M. Tullius Cicero. London: 1755. V. 43

The History of the Life of Marcus Tullius Cicero. London: 1741. V. 37

The Life of M. Tullius Cicero. London: 1824. V. 42; 44; 46

De Medicorum apud Veteres Romanos Degentium Conditione Dissertationem, Qua Servilem Atque Ignobilem eam Suisse Contendit . . . London: 1727. V. 44

The Miscellaneous Works of the Late Reverend and Learned . . . London: 1752. V. 38

Oratio De Novo Physiologiae Explicandae Munere Ex Celeberrimi Woodwardi Testamento Instituto . . . London: 1732. V. 40

MIDDLETON, J. HENRY

The Engraved Gems of Classical Times with a Catalogue of Gems in the Fitzwilliam Museum. Cambridge: 1891. V. 37; 40; 42; 44

Illuminated Manuscripts in Classical and Mediaeval Times, Their Art and Their Technique. Cambridge: 1892. V. 45

MIDDLETON, J. J.

Grecian Remains in Italy, a Description of Cyclopian Walls, and of Roman Antiquities. London: 1812. V. 41

MIDDLETON, JOHN

View of the Agriculture of Middlesex . . . London: 1798. V. 41

View of Agriculture of Middlesex. London: 1807. V. 46

MIDDLETON, R. HUNTER

Cherryburn Prints I and II. Chicago: 1973. V. 41

MIDDLETON, RICHARD

Epigrams and Satyres; Made by Richard Middleton of Yorke, Gentleman. Edinburgh: 1840. V. 44

The Ghost Ship. Eden: 1926. V. 39

Letters to Henry Savage. London: 1929. V. 40

MIDDLETON, THOMAS

Women Beware Women. London: 1657. V. 42

The Works. London: 1840. V. 38; 39; 46

The Works. London: 1885. V. 44

MIDDLETON, W. M.

Chirk Castle Accounts, A.D. 1666-1753. Manchester: 1931. V. 44

MIDGLEY, SAMUEL

Hallifax, and Its Gibbet-Law Placed in a True Light. London: 1708. V. 40; 45

MIDIVANI, BARBARA

The Enchanted: Poems. London: 1934. V. 39

THE MIDLAND Counties' Railway Companion, with Topographical Descriptions of the Country through which the Lines Passes, and Time, Fare and Distance Tables, Corrected to the 24th August. Also, Complete Guides to the London and Birmingham . . . London: 1840. V. 38

MIDNIGHT Scenes and Social Photographs; Being Sketches of Life in the Streets, Wynds and Dens of the City. Glasgow: 1858. V. 46

MIDON, FRANCIS

The History of the Rise and Fall of Masaniello, the Fisherman of Naples, Containing a . . . Relation of the Tumults and Popular Insurrections that Happened in that Kingdom . . . on Account of the Tax Upon Fruits. London: 1756. V. 38

MIDSUMMER Holidays at Briar's Hall; or, Summer Mornings Improved. London: 1828. V. 40

MIEGE, GUY

A Complete History of the Late Revolution, from the First Rise of It to this Present Time. London: 1691. V. 43

The Great French Dictionary. London: 1688. V. 45

Miscellanea; or, a Choice Collection of Wise and Ingenious Sayings . . . London: 1694. V. 43

A New French Grammar; or, a New Method for Learning of the French Tongue. To Which are Added . . . a Large Vocabulary . . . London: 1678. V. 42

The Present State of Denmark. London: 1683. V. 37; 43; 44

A Relation of Three Embassies from His Sacred Majestie Charles II to the Great Duike of Moscovie, the King of Sweden and King of Denmark. London: 1669. V. 40; 42; 43; 44

A Short Dictionary English and French, with Another French and English. London: 1685. V. 39

The Short French Dictionary, in Two Parts. Hague: 1699. V. 38

MIEL, F. M.

Histoire du Sacre de Charles X, dans ses Rapports avec les Beaux Arts . . . Paris: 1825. V. 46

MIELIKIAN-CHIRVANI, A. S.

Islamic metalwork from the Iranian world, 8th-18th centuries. 1982. V. 37

MIERIS, FRANS VAN

Beschryving der Stad Leyden. Leyden: 1762-84. V. 44

MIERS, EARL SCHENCK

Big Ben: a Novel. Philadelphia: 1942. V. 39

MIERS, JOHN

Travels in Chile and La Plata, ... and the Mining Operations in Chile. London: 1826. V. 38; 39; 45

MIERT, A. S. J. P. A. M. VAN

Comparative Veterinary Pharmacology, Toxicology and Therapy. London: 1986. V. 37

MIFFLIN, J. HOUSTON

Rhymes of an Artist. Philadelphia: 1835. V. 40; 41

MIGEON, GASTON

1900: L'Exposition Retrospective de l'Art Decoratif Francais. Paris: 1901. V. 40; 41

MIGHELS, HENRY R.

Sage Brush Leaves. San Francisco: 1879. V. 43

MIGNAN, ROBERT

Travels in Chaldea, Including a Journey from Bussorah to Baghdad, Hillah, and Babylon, Performed on Foot in 1827 . . . London: 1829. V. 38

MIGNAULT, CLAUDE

Discovrs svr la Chrestienne & Louable Enterprinse (sic) de Monseigneur Charles de Lorraine . . . Paris: 1572. V. 44

MIGNET, AUGUSTE FRANCOIS

History of the French Revolution, from 1789 to 1814. London: 1826. V. 40

MIJANGOS, JUAN DE

Espeio Divino en Lengua Mexicana . . . En Mexico: 1607. V. 37

Primera Parte Del Sermonario Dominical Y Sanctoral, en Lengua Mexicana. En Mexico: 1624. V. 37

MIKEL, W. C.

City of Belleville History. Picton: 1943. V. 44

MIKHAILOV, VASILII VASIL'EVICH

Adventures of (Vasily) Michailow, a Russian Captive; Among the Kalmucs, Kirghiz and Kiwenses. Written by Himself. London: 1822. V. 39

MIKI, TEIICHI

(wrapper title) Short Biographies of Eminent Japanese in Ancient and Modern Times . . . Tokyo: 1890. V. 43

MIKKELSEN, EJNAR

Lost in the Arctic. London: 1913. V. 39; 43; 44; 45

MIKOLOWSKI, KEN

Thank You, Call Again. Mt. Horeb: 1973. V. 44

MILBANK, JEREMIAH

The First Century of Flight in America. Princeton: 1943. V. 40

MILBANK, KITTY

The Flighty Prince. New York: 1963. V. 43

MILBERT, JACQUES GERARD

Itineraire Pittoresque du Fleuve Hudson et des Parties Laterales de l'Amerique du Nord, d'Apres les Dessins Originaux Pris sur Les Lieux. Paris: 1828-29. V. 42

MILBOURNE, LUKE

The Christian Pattern Paraphras'd; or, the Book of the Imitation of Christ, Commonly Ascribed to Thomas A Kempis. London: 1697. V. 44; 45

Tom of Bedlam's Answer to His Brother Ben Hoadly, St. Peter's Poor Parson, Near the Exchange of Principles. London: 1709. V. 39; 43; 45

MILBURN, WILLIAM HENRY

The Pioneers, Preachers and People of the Mississippi Valley. New York: 1860. V. 37; 38; 39; 40

MILBURNE, H.

A Narrative of Circumstances Attending the Retreat of the British Army Under the Command of the Late Lieut. Gen. Sir John Moore, K.B . . . London: 1809. V. 39

THE MILD-WHITE Torn A Book of Old Fairy Tales. London. V. 44

MILDMAY, WILLIAM

An Account of the Southern Maritime Provinces of France, Respecting the Distress to Which They Were Reduced at the Conclusion of the War in 1748 . . . London: 1764. V. 43; 46

The Police of France; or, an Account of the Laws and Regulations Established in that Kingdom for the Preservation of Peace and the Preventing of Robberies. London: 1763. V. 43; 46

MILDRED. Shaftesbury: 1926. V. 45

MILDRED Norman the Nazarene. London: 1858. V. 40

MILEHAM, GEOFFREY S.

Churches in Lower Nubia. Philadelphia: 1910. V. 40; 42

MILES, ALFRED H.

Heroes of History. London: 1924. V. 44

The Poets and the Poetry of the Century - Robert Bridges and Contemporary Poets. London. V. 44

The Poets and Poetry of the Century. London: 1890. V. 41

MILES, ALLIE LOWE

Old San Francisco. New York: 1927. V. 42

MILES CITY SADDLERY CO.

Illustrated Catalogue and Price List No. 12. St. Paul: 1912. V. 41

MILES, EDMUND

An Epitome, Historical and Statistical, Descriptive of Miles, R.D. London: 1841. V. 41

An Epitome, Historical and Statistical, Descriptive of the Royal Naval Service of England. London: 1844. V. 38

MILES, GEORGE

Collis P. Huntington. New York: 1890's. V. 37

MILES, HENRY A.

Lowell, As It Was, and As It Is. Lowell: 1845. V. 42; 43; 44

Lowell, As It Was and As it Is. Lowell: 1845. V. 43

MILES, HENRY DOWNES

The Book of Field Sports and Library of Vetinary Knowledge. London: 1861-63. V. 39

British Field Sports; a Valuable Work of Reference for the Gentleman, the Sportsman, the Farmer, the Members of the Volunteer Rifle Corps . . . London: 1870. V. 42

Pugilistica. The History of British Boxing. Edinburgh: 1906. V. 38; 40; 46

MILES, J.

Vindication of Admiral Nelson's Proceedings in the Bay of Naples. London: 1843. V. 39

MILES, J. S.

A Historical Sketch of Roxborough, Manayunk, Wissahickon 1690-1940. N.P.: 1940. V. 41; 42; 46

MILES, NELSON A.

Letter from the Secretary of War . . . Transmitting . . . Correspondence with General Miles relative to the Surrender of Geronimo. Washington: 1887. V. 37

Personal Recollections of General Nelson A. Miles. 1896. V. 39

Personal Recollections and Observations Embracing a Brief View of the Civil War . . . Chicago: 1896. V. 38; 39; 40; 42; 46

Personal Recollections and Observations of . . . Chicago and New York: 1896. V. 40; 45

Personal Recollection Of . . . New York: 1896. V. 45

Report of Brig-General N.A. Miles . . . Commanding the Department of the Columbia, 1884. Vancouver Barracks: 1884. V. 37

Serving the Republic. New York: 1911. V. 37

MILES, PLINY

The Advantages of Ocean Steam Navigation and Coastwise, to the Commerce of Boston . . . Boston: 1857. V. 44

The Social, Political and Commercial Advantages of Direct Steam Communication and Rapid Postal Intercourse Between Europe and America . . . London: 1859. V. 43

MILES, S. B.

The Countries and Tribes of the Persian Gulf. London: 1919. V. 45

The Countries and Tribes of the Persian Gulf. London: 1966. V. 45

MILES, W.

The Horse's Foot, and How to Keep It Sound. V. 38

MILES, W. J.

Modern Practical Farriery. London. V. 38; 40

Modern Practical Farriery. London: 1840. V. 39; 40; 41

Modern Practical Farriery . . . London: 1868/69. V. 45

Modern Practical Farriery, a Complete System of the Veterinary Art. London: 1880. V. 44

Modern Practical Farriery. A Complete guide to all that relates to the horse . . . forming a complete system of veterinary art . . . with numerous illustrations and series of anatomical plates . . . London: c. 1840. V. 37

MILES, WILLIAM

General Remarks on Stables and Examples of Stable Fittings. London: 1860. V. 37; 40

Journal of the Sufferings and Hardships of Capt. Parker H. French's Overland Expedition to California, Which Left New York City, May 13th, 1850 and Arrived at San francisco Dec. 14. New York: 1916. V. 45

A Letter to Henry Duncombe, Esq. London: 1796. V. 39; 43

MILES, WILLIAM P.

Republican Government Not Everywhere and Always the Best; and Liberty not the Birth-right of Mankind. Charleston: 1852. V. 42

MILET, PETER

Captivity of Father Peter Milet, S.J. Among the Oneida Indians. New York: 1888. V. 46

MILFORD HAVEN, LOUIS ALEXANDER, MARQUESS OF

British Naval Medals . . . London: 1919. V. 42

Naval Medals: Commemorative Medals, Naval Rewards, War Medals, Naval Tokens, &c. of France, the Netherlands, Spain and Portugal. London: 1921. V. 42

MILFORD, JOHN

Norway, and Her Laplanders, in 1841 . . . London: 1842. V. 44

Norway and Her Laplanders, in 1841. London: 1842. V. 40; 43; 44

MILFORT, JEAN ANTOINE LE CLERC

Memoire ou Coup-D'Oeil Rapide sur Mes Differens Voyages et Mon Sejour Dans la Nation Creck. Paris: 1802. V. 42; 44; 45

MILINA, JUAN IGLESIAS

The Geographical, Natural and Civil History of Chili. Middletown: 1808. V. 45

MILITARY and Other Poems Upon Several Occasions, and to Severl Persons. By an Officer of the Army. London: 1716. V. 38

THE MILITARY Costume of Europe. London: 1812-22. V. 40

THE MILITARY Costume of Turkey. London: 1818. V. 45

A **MILITARY** Dictionary. Explaining All Difficult Terms in Martial Discipline, Fortification and Gunnery. London: 1704. V. 46

MILITARY Expedition Against the Sioux Indians. Washington: 1876. V. 46

THE **MILITARY** History of Kentucky. Frankfort: 1939. V. 38

MILITARY Laws, Containing . . . Richmond, VA: 1820. V. 37

MILITARY Maps Illustrating the Operations of the Armies of Potomac & James May 4th, 1864 to April 9th 1865. Washington: 1869. V. 45

THE **MILITARY** Mentor: Being a Series of Letters Recently Written by a General Officer to His Son, on His Entering the Army. London: 1809. V. 42

MILITARY Mentor Being a Series of Letters Recently Written by a General Officer to His Son on His Entering the Army . . . Salem: 1808. V. 37; 38

MILITARY Orders and Instructions for the Wiltshire Battalion of Militia; Beginning XIV August, MDCCLVIII and ending XX October, MDCCLXX. Chelsea: 1772. V. 46

MILIZIA, FRANCESCO

Del Teatro. Venice: 1773. V. 37

The Lives of Celebrated Architects, Ancient and Modern. London: 1826. V. 45

The Lives of Celebrated Architects, Ancient and Modern. London: 1862. V. 45

MILL, HUGH ROBERT

The Siege of the South Pole. London: 1905. V. 41; 45

The Siege of the South Pole. New York: 1905. V. 41

MILL, JAMES 1773-1836

Analysis of the Phenomena of the Human Mind. London: 1829. V. 38; 40; 42

Analysis of the Phenomena of the Human Mind. London: 1869. V. 41

The Article Colony. London: 1820? V. 40

The Article of Education. London: 1824. V. 40

The Article Liberty of the Press. London: 1825? V. 38

The Article of the Press, Reprinted from the Supplement to the Encyclopedia Britannica. London: 1825? V. 37

Elements of Political Economy. London: 1821. V. 40; 41

Elements of Political Economy. London: 1824. V. 37; 39; 40; 42; 45; 46

Elements of Political Economy. London: 1826. V. 37; 38; 39; 41

Elements of Political Economy. London: 1826. V. 41

Elements of Political Economy . . . London: 1844. V. 39; 42; 43

Essays on Government, Jurisprudence, Liberty of the Press, and Law of Nations. London: 1823. V. 41

Essays on Government, Jurisprudence, Liberty of the Press and Law of Nations. London: 1823? V. 42

Essays on Government, Jurisprudence, Liberty of the Press, and Law of Nations. London: 1825. V. 37

Essays on Government, Jurisprudence, the Liberty of the Press, and Law of Nations. London: 1829. V. 46

A Fragment on Mackintosh. London: 1835. V. 38; 39

The History of British India. London: 1826. V. 42

MILL, JOB

The Present Practice of Conveyancing or Select Precedents of Coveyances, Chosen from Great Variety of Original Draughts . . . In the Savoy: 1746. V. 45

MILL, JOHN STUART 1806-1873

Auguste Comte and Positivism. London: 1865. V. 39; 45

Autobiography. London: 1873. V. 37; 38; 39; 40; 41; 42; 45; 46

Autobiography. London: 1873. V. 39

Autobiography. London: 1873. V. 39

Autobiography. London: 1873. V. 42

Autobiography. London: 1873. V. 42

Chapters and Speeches on the Irish Land Question. London: 1870. V. 39

Considerations on Representative Government. London: 1861. V. 37; 39; 40; 41; 42; 43

Considerations on Representative Government. London: 1865. V. 39; 41; 43; 44

Considerations on Representative Government. London: 1865. V. 43

Die Inductive Logik. Braunschweig: 1849. V. 41

Dissertations and Discussions. Boston: 1864. V. 40

Dissertations and Discussions. London: 1859. V. 38; 41; 42; 43; 45

Dissertations and Discussions: Political, Philosophical and Historical. Boston: 1864-67. V. 45

Dissertations and Discussions: Political, Philosophical and Historical. London: 1867. V. 41

Dissertations and Discussions, Political, Philosophical and Historical. London: 1867-1875. V. 39; 43; 45

Dissertations and Discussions - Political, Philosophical and Historical. London: 1875. V. 39

England and Ireland. London: 1868. V. 38

Essays on Some Unsettled Questions of Political Economy. London: 1844. V. 38; 39; 41; 45

Essays on Some Unsettled Questions. London: 1874. V. 41

An Examination of Sir William Hamilton's Philosophy and of the Principal Philosophical Questions Discussed in His Writings. London: 1865. V. 39; 41; 43; 45

An Examination of Sir William Hamilton's Philosophy and of the Principal Questions Discussed in His Writings. London: 1865. V. 45

An Examination of Sir William Hamilton's Philosophy and of the Principal Philosophical Questions Discussed in His Writings. London: 1867. V. 42

Inaugural Address, Delivered to the University of St. Andrews Feb. 1st 1867. London: 1867. V. 37; 40

The Letters. London: 1910. V. 40; 41; 43

Nature, the Utility of Religion and Theism. London: 1874. V. 37; 38; 39; 40; 42; 45

Nature, the Utility of Religion and Theism. London: 1874. V. 38

Nature the Utility of Religion and Theism. London: 1874. V. 37

On Liberty . . . London: 1849. V. 45

On Liberty. London: 1859. V. 38; 39; 43; 44; 45; 46

On Liberty. Boston: 1863. V. 42; 46

On Liberty. London: 1864. V. 37; 39; 45

On Liberty. London: 1869. V. 40

Personal Representation. Speech of John Stuart Mill, Esq. M.P. Delivered in the House of Commons, May 29, 1867. London: 1867. V. 37

Principles of Political Economy, with Some of Their Applications to Social Philosophy. London. V. 39

Principles of Political Economy. London: 1848. V. 37; 38; 39; 41; 43; 44; 45

Principles of Political Economy with Some of Their Applications to Social Philosophy. London: 1848/49. V. 38

Principles of Political Economy with Some of Their Applications to Social Philosophy. London: 1849. V. 38; 39; 43

Principles of Political Economy, with Some of Their Applications to Social Philosophy. London: 1852. V. 39; 43

Principles of Political Economy with Some of Their Applications to Social Philosophy. London: 1857. V. 37; 42; 43

Principles of Political Economy with Some of Their Applications to Social Philosophy. London: 1862. V. 40

Principles of Political Economy with Some of the Applications to Social Philosophy. London: 1865. V. 39

Principles of Political Economy. London: 1871. V. 39

Principles of Political Economy with Some of Their Applications to Social Philosophy. London: 1878. V. 39

Principles of Political Economy. London: 1886. V. 40; 42

The Subjection of Women. London: 1869. V. 37; 39; 40; 41; 42; 43; 45

The Subjection of Women. New York: 1869. V. 37; 38

The Subjection of Women. Philadelphia: 1869. V. 37

The Subjection of Women. London: 1870. V. 40

The Subjection of Women. London: 1883. V. 39

A System of Logic, Ratiocinative and Inductive. London: 1843. V. 38; 40

A System of Logic, Radtiocinative and Inductive, Being a Connected View of the Principles of Evidence and the Methods of Scientific Investigation. London: 1846. V. 38; 39

A System of Logic, Ratiocinative and Inductive . . . New York: 1846. V. 45

A System of Logic . . . New York: 1848. V. 37; 42

A System of Logic, Ratiocinative and Inductive, Being a Connected View of the Principles of Evidence, and the Methods of Scientific Investigation. London: 1851. V. 39; 43; 45

A System of Logic, Ratiocinative and Inductive . . . London: 1856. V. 43; 45

A System of Logic, Rationcinative and Inductive . . . London: 1875. V. 43; 45

A System of Logic . . . London: 1879. V. 40; 42; 46

A System of Logic. New York: 1848. V. 37

Thoughts on Parliamentary Reform. London: 1859. V. 37; 38

Three Essays on Religion, Nature, the Utility of Religion, and Theism. London: 1874. V. 39

Three Essays on Religion. Nature, the Utility of Religion and Theism. London: 1885. V. 40

Utilitarianism . . . London: 1864. V. 42

The Utility of Religion and Theism. London: 1874. V. 39

MILL, NICHOLAS

The History of Mexico, from the Spanish Conquest to the Present Era. London: 1824. V. 42

MILLAIS, JOHN EVERETT 1829-1896

Millais's Illustrations. A Collection of Drawings on Wood. London: 1865. V. 38

MILLAIS, JOHN EVERETT 1829-1896 continued

Millais' Illustrations. A Collection of Drawings on Wood. London: 1866, 1865. V. 38

Millais's Illustrations: a Collection of Drawings on Wood. London: 1866. V. 39; 42

MILLAIS, JOHN GUILLE 1865-1931

A Breath from the Veldt. London: 1895. V. 39; 43; 44; 45

A Breath from the Veldt. London: 1899. V. 37; 40; 42

British Deer and Their Horns. London: 1897. V. 39; 40

British Deer and Ground Game, Dogs, Guns and Rifles. London: 1913. V. 46

British Diving Ducks. London: 1913. V. 39; 42; 45; 46

British Deer and Their Horns. London: 1982. V. 43

Far Away Up the Nile. London: 1924. V. 40; 42; 44; 45

Far Away Up the Nile. London: 1924. V. 40

Game Birds and Shooting Sketches. London: 1892. V. 38; 39; 42; 44; 46

Game Birds and Shooting-Sketches. London: & Manchester: 1892. V. 42

Game Birds and Shooting-Sketches, Illustrating the Habits, Modes of Capture, Stages of Plumage . . . London: 1894. V. 46

The Gun at Home and Abroad. London: 1913. V. 45

The Life and Letters of Sir John Everett Millais. London: 1899. V. 38; 39; 44; 45

The Life and Letters of Sir John Everett Millais, President of the Royal Academy. London: 1899. V. 45

Life of Frederick Courtenay Selous, D.S.O. 25th Royal Fusiliers. London: 1918. V. 40; 42

The Mammals of Great Britain and Ireland. London: 1904. V. 40; 44; 46

The Mammals of Great Britain and Ireland. London: 1904-06. V. 37; 39; 45

The Natural History of British Suface Feeding Ducks. London: 1902. V. 37; 38; 39; 40; 43; 44; 45; 46

The Natural History of British Game Birds. London: 1909. V. 39; 42; 46

A Naturalist's Sketch Book. London: 1919. V. 46

New Foundland and Its Downtrodden Ways. New York: 1907. V. 45

Newfoundland and Its Untrodden Ways. London: 1907. V. 38; 40

Newfoundland, and Its Untrodden Ways. London: 1907. V. 38

Rhododendrons. London: 1917. V. 37

The Wildfowler in Scotland. London: 1901. V. 39; 43; 45; 46

MILLANT, ROGER

The Life and Work of J. B. Fuillaume. London: 1972. V. 37; 38

MILLAR, DONALD

Measured Drawings of Some Colonial and Georgian Houses. New York: 1915. V. 45; 46

MILLAR, ERIC GEORGE

English Illuminated Manuscripts from the Tenth to the Thirteenth Century. Paris: 1926. V. 42; 44

English Illuminated Manuscripts from the Xth to the XIIIth Century. Paris & Brussels: 1926-28. V. 39

The St. Trond Lectionary. 1949. V. 39

A Thirteenth Century York Psalter. 1952. V. 39

A Thirteenth Century Bestiary in the Library of Alnwick Castle. 1958. V. 39

MILLAR, G. H.

A New . . . Body or System of Natural History. London: 1785. V. 41

MILLAR, JOHN

An Historical View of the English Government, from the Settlement of the Saxons in Britain to the Accession of the House of Hanover. Dublin: 1789. V. 40

A History of the Witches of Renfrewshire . . . Paisley: 1809. V. 46

Observations Concerning the Distinction of ranks in Society. London: 1771. V. 40; 42

Observations Concerning the Distinctions of Ranks in Society. London: 1773. V. 46

The Origin of the Distinction of Ranks . . . Edinburgh: 1806. V. 42

MILLAR, MARGARET

Do Evil in Return. London: 1952. V. 44

MILLAR, OLIVER

Italian Drawings and Paintings in the Queen's Collection. London: 1965. V. 42

The Later Georgian Pictures in the Collection of Her Majesty the Queen. London: 1963. V. 42

The Later Georgian Pictures in the Collection of Her Majesty the Queen. London: 1969. V. 39

The Later Georgian Pictures in the Collection of Her Majesty the Queen by Oliver Millar. 1969. V. 37

The Tudor, Stuart and Early Georgian Pictures in the Collection of Her Majesty the Queen. London: 1963. V. 38; 39; 42

MILLAR, WILLIAM

The Fairy Minstrel, and Other Poems. Edinburgh: 1822. V. 40; 42

Plastering Plain and Decorative. London: 1927. V. 39

MILLARD, BAILEY

History of the San Francisco Bay Region. Chicago: 1924. V. 38

MILLARD, CHRISTOPHER

The Printed Work of Claud Lovat Fraser. London: 1923. V. 39; 41; 43

MILLARD, DAVID

A Journal of Travels in Egypt, Arabia Petrae, and the Holy Land During 1841-42. Rochester,: 1843. V. 40

MILLARD, E. E.

Random Casts; or Odds and Ends from an Angler's Note Book. New York: 1878. V. 42

MILLARD, EDWARD EAMES

Days on the Nepigon. New York: 1917. V. 43

MILLARD, JOHN

The Gentleman's Guide in His Tour Through France. London: 1788. V. 45

MILLARY, EDNA ST. VINCENT

Huntsman, What Quarry? New York: 1939. V. 37

MILLAY, EDNA ST. VINCENT 1892-1950

Aria Da capo - A Play In One Act. New York: 1920. V. 38; 40

Aria Da Capo (A Play in One Act). New York: 1920. V. 40

Aria Da Capo. New York: 1921. V. 39; 40; 42; 43; 46

Aria Da Capo. New York: 1921. V. 40

Aria Da Capo. New York: 1921. V. 39

The Ballad of the Harp Weaver. New York: 1922. V. 37; 42

The Ballad of the Harp-Weaver. New York: 1922. V. 37

The Buck in the Snow. New York: 1928. V. 43; 46

The Buck in the Snow and Other Poems. New York: 1928. V. 46

The Buck in the Snow and Other Poems. New York: and London: 1928. V. 43

Conversation at Midnight. New York: 1937. V. 40; 46

Conversation at Midnight. New York & London: 1937. V. 39

Conversation at Midnight. Los Angeles: 1964. V. 42; 44; 45

Fear. New York: 1927. V. 42

Fear. New York: 1929. V. 46

Huntsman, What Quarry? New York: 1939. V. 37; 40; 41; 42; 44; 46

The King's Henchman. New York: 1927. V. 42

The King's Henchman. New York & London: 1927. V. 39

The Lamp and the Bell. New York: 1921. V. 39; 40

A Landscape of Edna St. Vincent Millay Sonnets. Oakland: 1987. V. 41

Renascence and Other Poems. New York: 1917. V. 37; 39; 42; 43; 44; 46

Wild Swans. Leverett: 1979. V. 38

Wine From these Grapes. New York: 1934. V. 38; 42; 45

Works. New York: 1930. V. 42

MILLER, A. E. HASWELL

Military Designs and Paintings. London: 1969. V. 39

Military Drawings and Paintings in the Royal Collection. London: 1970. V. 44

MILLER, A. P.

Tom's Experiences in Dakota; Why He Went, What He Did There. Minneapolis: 1883. V. 39; 46

MILLER, ALEXANDER

Incidents of a Continental Tour in 1877. Liverpool: 1877. V. 43

MILLER & RICHARD

Specimens of Book Newspaper, Jobbing and Ornamental Types. Edinburgh: 1865. V. 38

MILLER, ANDREW

New States and Territories, or the Ohio, Indiana, Illinois, Michigan, North-Western, Missouri, Louisiana, Mississippi (sic) and Alabama, in Their Real Characters in 1818. Kenne: 1819. V. 46

MILLER, ANNA 1741-1781

Letters from Italy, Describing the Manners, Customs, Antiquities, etc. in 1770 and 1771. London: 1777. V. 39; 43

MILLER, ANNA RIGGS

Poetical Amusements at Villa Near Bath. Bath: 1775. V. 46

MILLER, ARTHUR 1915-

After the Fall. New York: 1964. V. 37; 38; 43; 46

MILLER, ARTHUR 1915- continued

After the Fall. New York: 1967. V. 41

All My Sons. New York: (1947). V. 37

The Crucible. New York: 1953. V. 46

Death of a Salesman - Certain Private Conversations in Two Acts and a Requiem. London: 1949. V. 43

Death of a Salesman. New York: 1949. V. 42; 43; 44; 46

Death of a Salesman. New York: 1981. V. 39; 43

Death of a Salesman. 1984. V. 38; 39; 41; 42; 45

Death of a Salesman. New York: 1984. V. 39; 41

Situation Normal. 1944. V. 46

Situation Normal. New York: 1944. V. 43

A View from the Bridge. Paris: 1981. V. 39

MILLER, BENJAMIN S.

Ranch Life in Southern Kansas and the Indian Territory. New York: 1896. V. 46

Ranching in the Southwest. New York: 1896. V. 39; 40; 46

MILLER, C. WILLIAM

Benjamin Franklin's Philadelphia Printing 1728-1766. Philadelphia: 1974. V. 46

MILLER, CHARLES

The Correction of Featural Imperfections. Chicago: 1907. V. 42

Cosmetic Surgery: The Correction of Featural Imperfections. Philadelphia: 1924. V. 42; 44

MILLER, DAVID

Arbroath and Its Abbey or the Early History of the Town and Abbey of Aberbrothock. Edinburgh: 1860. V. 40

MILLER, DIANE DISNEY

The Story of Walt Disney. New York: (1957). V. 37

MILLER, E. D.

Modern Polo. London: 1902. V. 43

MILLER, E. MORRIS

Australian Literature: A Bibliography to 1938, Extended to 1950. London: 1956. V. 39; 40

MILLER, E. T.

A Financial History of Texas. Austin: 1916. V. 37; 44

MILLER, EDMOND

An Account of the University of Cambridge, and the Colleges There. London: 1717. V. 39

MILLER, EDMUND THORNTON

A Financial History of Texas. Austin: 1916. V. 38

MILLER, EDWARD

The History and Antiquities of Doncaster and Its Vicinity, with Anecdotes of Eminent Men. Doncaster: 1804. V. 45

The Medical Works of Edward Miller. New York: 1814. V. 38; 41; 44; 46

The Medical Works of Edward Miller, M.D. Later Professor of the Practice of Physic in the University of New York . . . New York: 1814. V. 41

MILLER, EDWARD G.

Captain Edward Gee Miller of the 20th Wisconsin: His War 1861-1865. Fayetteville, Ark.: 1960. V. 37

MILLER, EMILY VAN DORN

A Soldier's Honor, with Reminiscences of Major General Early Van Dorn, by His Comrades. New York: 1902. V. 44

MILLER, ERIC

Camps, Tramps and Trenches. The Diary of New Zealand Sapper, 1917. New Zealand: 1939. V. 45

MILLER, FRANCIS TREVELYAN

Lindbergh: His Story in Pictures. New York: 1929. V. 45

The Photographic History of the Civil War. New York: 1911. V. 37; 42; 46

The Photographic History of the Civil War. New York: 1911-12. V. 42

The Photographic History of the Civil War. New York: 1957. V. 46

The World in the Air. New York: 1930. V. 37; 42

MILLER FURNITURE CO.

The Herman Miller Collection: Furniture Designed by George Nelson, Charles Eames, Isamu Noguchi, Paul Laszlo. Zeeland: 1949. V. 40

MILLER, GEORGE

A Description of the Cathedral Church of Ely. London: 1834. V. 40

Later Struggles in the Journey of Life; or, the Afternoon of My Days . . . the Real Life of a Country Bookseller. Edinburgh: 1833. V. 38; 39; 40; 41; 42; 44; 45

Missouri's Memorable Decade, 1860-1870: an Historical Sketch Personal-Political-Religious. Columbia: 1898. V. 46

MILLER, HENRY fl. 1856

Account of a Tour of the California Missions, 1856. San Francisco: 1952. V. 41; 46

The Air-Conditioned Nightmare. New York: 1945. V. 45

Aller Retour New York. Paris: 1935. V. 39

The Amazing and Invariable Beauford de Lancy. New York: 1945. V. 39

Black Spring. Paris: 1936. V. 39; 41; 42; 46

Black Spring. Paris: 1936. V. 39

Black Spring. Paris: 1938. V. 38; 46

The Books in My Life. New York: 1952. V. 42

The Colossus of Maroussi. Norfolk: 1961. V. 44

The Colossus of Maroussi. San Francisco: (1941). V. 37

The Cosmological Eye. 1939. V. 39

The Cosmological Eye. New Directions: 1939. V. 39

The Cosmological Eye. Norfolk: 1939. V. 37; 39; 40; 42; 45; 46

Echolalia: Reproductions of Water Colours by Henry Miller. Berkeley: 1945. V. 43

Echolalia - Reproductions of Water Colours. London: 1945. V. 38

Greece. New York: 1964. V. 46

Hamlet. Santurce: 1939. V. 44; 45

Hamlet. New York: 1939, 1941. V. 39

Hamlet: Volume 1. Santurce: 1953. V. 45

Hamlet. The Franenkel-Miller Correspondence. London: 1962. V. 42

Hamlet I & II. Santurce & New York: 1939, 1941. V. 39

Henry Miller Miscellanea. Berkeley: 1945. V. 41

Henry Miller Miscellanea. San Mateo: 1945. V. 44

Henry Miller, Watercolors, Drawings and His Essay the Angel Is My Watermark! New York: 1962. V. 45

Henry Miller's Book of Friends. Santa Barbara: 1976. V. 38

Henry Miller Letters to Anais Nin. New York: 1965. V. 37

Insomnia or the Devil at Large. Albuquerque: 1970. V. 39; 45

Into the Night. Berkeley: 1947. V. 45

Into the Night Life. (Berkeley: 1947). V. 37

Joey. Santa Barbara: 1979. V. 43

The Journals and Drawings of . . . San francisco: 1952. V. 38

Journey to an Antique Land. Big Sur: 1960. V. 39

Letters of Henry Miller and Wallace Fowlie (1943-1972). New York: 1975. V. 39

Love Between the Sexes. 1978. V. 39

Marizius Forever. San Francisco: 1946. V. 37; 39; 40; 44

Maurizius Forever. 1946. V. 39

Max and the White Phagocytes. Paris: 1938. V. 37; 39; 46

Max et les Phagocytes. Paris: 1947. V. 42

Max et les Phagocytes. Paris: 1947. V. 40; 42; 44

Michael Fraenkel. Hamlet. Puerto Rico: 1939. V. 46

Miscellanea. London: 1945. V. 45

Money and How It Gets That Way. Paris. V. 39

Money and How It Gets That Way. Paris: 1938. V. 39; 41; 42

Murder the Murderers. Big Sur: 1944. V. 39

My Life and Times. New York: 1975. V. 38; 39; 44; 46

My Bike and Other Friends. Santa Barbara: 1978. V. 39

My Life and Times. Playboy Press, n.d.. V. 44

The Nightmare Book. New York: 1975. V. 39; 43; 45

The Nightmare Notebook. New Directions. New York: (1975). V. 37

Notes on 'Aaron's Rod' and Other Notes on Lawrence. Santa Barbara: 1980. V. 43

Of, By and About Henry Miller. Yonkers: 1947. V. 44

An Open Letter to Stroker! New York: 1978. V. 39

Order and Chaos Chez Hans Reichel. New Orleans: 1966. V. 37; 38; 42; 44

Order and Chaos Chez Hans Reichel. Tucson: 1966. V. 37; 39; 43; 46

Order and Chaos Chez Hans Reichel. New Orleans: (1966). V. 37

The Paintings of Henry Miller. Santa Barbara: 1982. V. 39; 41; 43

Plexus: La Crucifixion en Rose. Paris: 1952. V. 44

Plexus. Paris: 1953. V. 39; 42; 43; 45

Plexus. Paris: 1953. V. 43

Reflections on the Death of Mishima. Santa Barbara: 1972. V. 39

The Rosy Crucifixion. Book One. Sexus. Paris: 1949. V. 41

the Rosy Crucifixion. Book Two: Plexus. Paris: 1953. V. 39; 45

Scenario (A Film With Sound). Paris: 1937. V. 43

Semblance of a Devoted Past. Berkeley: 1944. V. 39; 44

Sexus. Paris: 1949. V. 39; 46

The Smile at the Foot of the Ladder. San Francisco: 1955. V. 46

Stand Still Like the Hummingbird. New York: 1962. V. 45

MILLER, HENRY fl. 1856 continued

Sunday After the War. Norfolk: 1944. V. 44

Sunday After the War. London: 1945. V. 45

The Theatre and Other Pieces. New York: 1979. V. 43

The Time of the Assassins. New York: 1956. V. 45

Tropic of Cancer. Paris: 1934. V. 37; 42; 43; 46

Tropic of Cancer. Paris: 1935. V. 39; 40

Tropic of Cancer. New York: 1940. V. 37

Tropique du Cancer. Paris: 1945. V. 43

Tropique du Cancer. Paris: 1947. V. 39

Tropic of Capricorn. Paris: (1939). V. 37

Tropic of Capricorn. Paris: 1939. V. 37; 39; 41; 42

Un Etre Etoilique. N.P.: 1937. V. 41

What Are You Going to Do About Alf. London: 1971. V. 39

The Wisdom of the Heart. London: 1941. V. 45

The World of Sex. Chicago: 1940. V. 43

The World of Lawrence: a Passionate Appreciation. Santa Barbara: 1980. V. 45

MILLER, HENRY ERNEST

The Art and Planning of Landscape Gardening. London: 1890. V. 43

MILLER, HERMAN P.

Outline Maps of the Counties of Allegheny, Berks, Bucks, Cambria, Dauphin . . . Harrisburg: 1901. V. 45

MILLER, HUGH

A Collection of the Important Works of this Eminent Geologist . . . Edinburgh. V. 46

The Cruise of the Betsey. Edinburgh: 1858. V. 38

The Old Red Sandstone; or New Walks in an Old Field. Edinbrugh: 1841. V. 39; 42; 44

The Old Red Sandstone; or New Walks in an Old Field . . . Edinburgh: 1859. V. 40

Poems Written in the Leisure Hours of a Journeyman Mason. Inverness: 1829. V. 37; 42

Sketch Book of Popular Geology. Edinburgh: 1859. V. 39; 40; 42; 44

The Testimony of the Rocks; or Geology in Its Bearings on the Two Theologies, Natural and Revealed. Edinburgh: 1857. V. 44

MILLER, J. HILLIS

Thomas Hardy: Distance and Desire. 1970. V. 40

MILLER, J. I.

The Spice trade of the Roman Empire, 29 BC to AD 641. Oxford: 1969. V. 37

MILLER, J. MARTIN

The Monarch Standard Atlas of the Commercial, Geographical and Historical World . . . Chicago: 1904. V. 45

The Monarch Standard Atlas of the Commercial, Geographical and Historical World . . . Chicago: 1905. V. 45

The Twentieth Century Atlas of the Commercial, Geographical and Historical World . . . Chicago: 1902. V. 45

MILLER, J. R.

Insect Plant Interactions. Berlin: 1986. V. 37

MILLER, J. S.

A Natural History of the Crinoidea, or Lily-Shaped Animals; with Observations on the Genera Asteria, Euryale, Comatula and Marsupites. Bristol: 1821. V. 37

MILLER, JACOB W.

9'-51': or, the Jamestwon's Horizon. Gowen: 1882. V. 46

MILLER, JAMES 1706-1744

Art and Nature. London: 1738. V. 42

Harlequin-Horace; or the Art of Modern Poetry. London: 1731. V. 41; 45

The Humours of Oxford. London: 1730. V. 39; 42

Observations on Trial by Jury in Civil Causes in Scotland and Remedial Measures for Its Abuse. Edinburgh: 1848. V. 45

The Practice of Surgery. Philadelphia: 1846. V. 42

St. Baldred of the Bass, a Pictish Legend. Edinburgh: 1824. V. 42

Seasonable Reproof, a Satire, in the Manner of Horace . . . London: 1735. V. 46

MILLER, JEFFREY

Paul Bowles: a Descriptive Bibliography. Santa Barbara: 1986. V. 39; 46

MILLER, JOAQUIN 1841-1913

The Building of the City Beautiful. Cambridge & Chicago: 1893. V. 45

First Families of the Sierras. Chicago: 1876. V. 43

An Illustrated History of the State of Montana Containing A History of the State of Montana from the Earliest Period of its Discovery to the Present Time. Chicago: 1894. V. 45

The One Fair Woman. London: 1876. V. 46

The Ship in the Desert. Boston: 1875. V. 45

Songs of the Sierras. Boston: 1871. V. 46

True Bear Stories. Covelo: 1985. V. 37; 46

Unwritten History; Life Amongst the Modocs. Hartford: 1874. V. 38; 39; 40; 41

MILLER, JOHN

The Country Gentleman's Architect, in a Great Variety of Designs . . . London: 1797. V. 40; 44

The Country Gentleman's Architect, in a Great Variety of New Designs . . . London: 1797. V. 44

Memoirs of General Miller, in the Service of Peru. London: 1828. V. 43

New York Considered and Improved, 1695. Cleveland: 1903. V. 39; 40

A 20th Century History of Erie County, Pennsylvania. Chicago: 1909. V. 42

MILLER, JOHN G.

The Great Convention. Description of the Convention of the People of Ohio, Held at Columbus. Columbus: 1840. V. 45

MILLER, JOSEPH

The Family Jo: Miller; A drawing-room jest book. Jo: Miller,-A Biography. London: 1848. V. 37

MILLER, KARL

Poetry from Cambridge 1952-54. Swinford, Eynsham: 1955. V. 41

MILLER, KELLY

The Everlasting Stain. Washington: 1924. V. 43

Race Adjustment Essays on the Negro in America. New York: 1908. V. 45

MILLER, LADY

Letters from Italy, Describing the Manners, Customs, Antiquities, Painting, etc. of that Country, in the Years MDCCLXX and MDCCLXXI, to a Friend Residing in France, by an English Woman. London: 1776. V. 38

MILLER, LEWIS B.

A Crooked Trail, the Story of a Thousand-Mile Saddle Trip Up and Down the Texas Frontier in Pursuit of a Runaway Ox, with Adventures by the Way. Pittsburgh: 1908. V. 42

MILLER, LINUS W.

Notes of an Exile to Van Dieman's Land . . . Fredonia: 1846. V. 40; 43

Notes of an Exile to Van Dieman's Land . . . New York: 1846. V. 43; 46

MILLER, MARION M.

Great Debates in American History, from the Debates in the British Parliament on the Stampe Act 1764-5 to the Debates in Congress, 1913. New York: (1913). V. 37

MILLER, MERLE

The Judges and the Judged. Garden City: 1952. V. 39

MILLER, MURIEL

Homer Watson: The Man of Doon. Toronto: 1938. V. 42

MILLER, NATHAN L.

Public Papers of Nathan L. Miller, Forty-Sixth Governor of the State of New York: Albany: 1924. V. 43

MILLER, OLIVE BEAUPRE

Book House for Children - A Picturesque Tale of Progress. Chicago: 1929/35. V. 45

Engines and Brass Bands. 1933. V. 46

My Bookhouse. Chicago: 1920. V. 45

My Book of History. 1929. V. 46

Sunny Rhymes for Happy Children. 1917. V. 46

MILLER, PATRICK

Ana and the Runner. London: 1937. V. 41

Ana the Runner. Waltham St. Lawrence: 1937. V. 40; 45

The Green Ship. V. 41

The Green Ship. Waltham St. Lawrence: 1936. V. 45

Woman in Detail. London: 1947. V. 38; 40; 41

Woman in Detail. Waltham St. Lawrence: 1947. V. 46

MILLER, PHILIP

the Abridgement of the Gardener's Dictionary . . . London: 1711. V. 45

The Abridgement of the Gardener's Dictionary. London: 1763. V. 40

The Abridgement of the Gardener's Dictionary. London: 1771. V. 37; 39

Fiugres of the Most Beautiful, Useful and Uncommon Plants Described in the Gardeners Dictionary, Exhibited on Three Hundred Copper Plates. London: 1755-60. V. 44

The Gardener's Dictionary. London: 1731. V. 37; 39; 42; 46

MILLER, PHILIP continued

The Gardener's Dictionary. London: 1733. V. 39; 40

The Gardener's Dictionary. London: 1737. V. 41

The Gardeners Dictionary. London: 1743/40. V. 45

The Gardeners Kalendar. London: 1751. V. 38; 43; 44

The Gardeners Dictionary. London: 1752. V. 43

The Gardener's Dictionary. London: 1759. V. 39; 41

The Gardeners Kalendar. London: 1760. V. 43

The Gardeners Kalendar . . . London: 1769. V. 45; 46

The Gardener's Dictionary. Codicote: 1969. V. 45

The Gardener's and Botanist's Dictionary. London: 1807. V. 37

MILLER, S. G., MRS.

Sixty Years in the Nueces Valley, 1870 to 1930. San Antonio: 1930. V. 44

MILLER, SAMUEL

A Brief Retrospect of the Eighteenth Century . . . New York: 1830. V. 39

MILLER, STEPHEN F.

The Bench and Bar of Georgia. Philadelphia: 1858. V. 37; 38; 41; 45; 46

Memoir of Gen. David Blackshear . . . in the War of 1813-14 on the Frontier and Sea-Coast of Georgia . . . Philadlephia: 1858. V. 44; 45

MILLER, STEVE

Caroline's Poem. Madison: 1977. V. 42

Hurricane Lake. Madison: 1979. V. 44

Hurricane Lane. Madison: 1979. V. 42

Wild Night Irises. Madison: 1976. V. 41; 42

Wild Night Irises. A Book of Poems, by Steve Miller. (Madison): 1976. V. 37

MILLER, SUSAN G.

Sixty Years in the Nueces Valley. 1870 to 1930. San Antonio: 1930. V. 38; 39; 44; 46

Sixty Years in The Nueces Valley. 1870-1930. San Antonio: (1930). V. 37

MILLER, THEODORE W.

Theodore W. Miller, Rough Rider: His Diary as a Soldier Together with the Story of His Life. Akron: 1899. V. 44

MILLER, THOMAS

Common Wayside Flowers. London: 1860. V. 42; 45

Historical and Genealogical Record of the First Settlers of Colchester County. Halifax: 1873. V. 42; 43

The Romance of Nature; or, the Poetical Language of Flowers. New York: 1860. V. 38

Turner and Girtin's Picturesque Views. London: 1854. V. 37; 38; 39; 40

Turner and Girtin's Picturesque Views, Sixty Years Since. London: 1854. V. 37

MILLER, TOWNSEND

A Letter from Texas. Dallas: 1944. V. 39

A Letter From Texas. Dallas: 1939. V. 37

MILLER, W. W.

Forty Years at El Paso, 1858-1898. El Paso: 1962. V. 46

MILLER, WALTER

A Canticle for Leibowitz. 1960. V. 37; 39; 43

A Canticle for Leibowitz. London: 1960. V. 38

A Canticle for Leibowitz. Philadelphia: 1960. V. 44; 45

A Canticle for Leibowitz. Philadelphia: 1960. V. 44

Daedalus and Thespis. New York: 1929/31/32. V. 38

MILLER, WILLIAM 1769-1844

The Costume of the Russian Empire. London: 1803. V. 39

The Costume of the Russian Empire. London: 1822. V. 46

Essays on the Latin Orient. Cambridge: 1921. V. 45

Evidence from Scripture and History of the Second Coming of Christ, About the Year 1843. New York: 1836. V. 41

Evidence from Scripture and History of the Second Coming of Christ About the Year 1843; Exhibited in a Course of Lectures. Boston: 1840. V. 39; 45

Evidence from Scripture and History of the Second Coming of Christ, About the Year 1843. Boston;: 1842. V. 45

Reunion in Barcelona. 1959. V. 39

A Thrilling Narrative of the Life, Adventures and Terrible Crimes of James Bagwell . . . N.P.: 1851. V. 42; 45

Views of the Prophecies and Prophetic Chronology, Selected from the Manuscripts of William Miller; with a Memoir of His Life. Boston: 1841. V. 45

MILLER, WILLIAM H.

The History of Kansas City, Together with a Sketch of the Commerical Resources of the Country with Which It is Surrounded. Kansas City: 1881. V. 37; 39

Sixth Annual Report of the Trade and Commerce of Kansas City, Missouri. Kansas City: 1883. V. 37

MILLER, WILLIAM HALLOWES 1801-1880

The Elements of Hydrostatics and Hydrodynamics. Cambridge: 1831. V. 40

MILLER, WILLOUGHBY D.

The Micro-organisms of the Human Mouth. Philadelphia: 1890. V. 38

MILLERN, ALEXANDER VON

All About Petroleum, and the Great Oil Districts of Pennsylvania, West Virginia, Ohio, &c. The most Complete and most Reliable Description of this Remarkable Region ever Issued. New York: 1864. V. 37

MILLERS, GEORGE

A Description of the Cathedral Church of Ely. London: 1807. V. 38

MILLER'S Planters' and Merchants' Almanac, for the Year of Our Lord 1846 . . . Calculaed by David Young, for the States of Carolina and Georgia. Charleston: 1845. V. 44

MILLER'S Planters' and Merchants' Almanac, for the Year of Our Lord 1849 . . . Calculated by David Young, for the States of Carolina and Georgia. Charleston: 1848. V. 44

MILLES, T.

Nobilitas Politica vel Civilis. London: 1608. V. 37

MILLET, GABRIEL

Byzantine Painting at Trebizond. London: 1936. V. 45

MILLET, SAMUEL

A Whaling Voyage in the Bark 'Willis'. Boston: 1924. V. 37; 38; 41; 42; 46

MILLETOT, BENIGNE

L' Homme Dv Pape Et Dv Roy. Ov Reparties Veritables Sur les Imputations Calomnieuses d'un Libelle Diffamatoire, seme Contre sa Sainctete & sa Majeste Tres-Chrestienne. Brussels: 1636. V. 37

L' Homme Dv Pape et Dv Roy. Ov, Reparties Veritables Sur les Imputations Calomnieuses d'un Libelle Diffamatoire, Semme Contre sa Sainctete & sa Majeste Tres-Chrestienne. Brussels: 1635. V. 37

MILLETT, KATE

Elegy for Sita. New York: 1979. V. 46

MILLHOUSE, ROBERT

Blossoms, Being a Selection of Sonnets from His Various Manuscripts with Prefatory Remarks by the Rev. Luke Booker. London: 1823. V. 42

Sherwood Forest, and Other Poems. London: 1827. V. 42

The Song of the Patriot, Sonnets and Songs. London: 1826. V. 42

MILLICAN, JOHN

Rivers in the Desert. Esher: 1982. V. 37

MILLIER, A.

Millard Sheets. Los Angeles: 1935. V. 46

MILLIKAN, ROBERT ANDREWS

The Electron. Its Isolation and Measurement and the Determination of Some of Its Properties. Chicago: 1923. V. 38

MILLIN, A. L.

Peintures de Vases Antiques Vulgairement Appeles Etrusques Tirees de Differentes Collections. Paris: 1808, 1810. V. 39

Travels through the Southern Departments of France. Performed in the Years 1804 and 1805. London: 1808. V. 40

MILLINGEN, FREDERICK

Wild Life Among the Koords. London: 1870. V. 45

MILLINGEN, JOHN GIDEON 1782-1862

Curiosities of Medical Experience. Philadelphia. V. 43

Curiosities of Medical Experience. Philadelphia: 1838. V. 39; 42; 45

The History of Duelling. London: 1841. V. 40; 42

The Passions: or Mind and Matter. London: 1848. V. 45

MILLINGTON, S. M. T.

The Servant's Companion and Useful Guide. Liverpool: 1864. V. 40

MILLIS, CHRISTOPHER

Diary of the Delphic Oracle. Cortona: 1991. V. 46

MILLIS, JOHN

The Citizen and Countryman's Experienced Farrier. London: 1764. V. 45

MILNE, ALAN ALEXANDER 1882-1956 continued

Michael and Mary. London: 1930. V. 45; 46

Now We Are Six. London: 1927. V. 37; 38; 39; 40; 41; 42; 43; 44; 45; 46

Now We Are Six. London: 1927. V. 46

Now We Are Six. London: 1927. V. 46

Now We Are Six. London: 1927. V. 45

Now We Are Six. London: 1927. V. 40

Now We Are Six. New York: 1927. V. 42; 45; 46

Now We Are Six. London: (1927). V. 37

Once a Week. London: 1926. V. 41

The Pooh Calendar. New York: 1929. V. 45

The Pooh Books. London: 1982. V. 44

The Pooh Books. London: 1989. V. 43

The Secret. New York: 1929. V. 37; 41; 43; 46

Songs from Now We Are Six. London: 1927. V. 46

Teddy Bear and Other Songs from When Were Very Young. London: 1926. V. 46

Those Were the Days. London: 1929. V. 37; 39; 41; 43

Tigger Comes to the Forrest. London. V. 45

Toad of Toad Hall. London: 1929. V. 37; 42; 44; 46

Toad of Toad Hall. A Play from Kenneth Grahame's Book 'The Wind in the Willows.' London: (1929). V. 37

When We Were Very Young. London. V. 45

When We Were Very Young. London: 1924. V. 37; 42; 43; 46

When We Were Very Young. Winnie the Pooh. Now We Are Six. The House at Pooh Corner. London: 1924/26-28. V. 45

When We Were Very Young. New York: 1925. V. 46

When I Was Very Young. New York: 1930. V. 39; 43

When We Were Very Young. London: 1974. V. 42

When We Were Very Young; Winnie the Pooh; Now We ARe Six; House at Pooh Corner. London: 1989. V. 46

When We Were Very Young. N.P.: 1924. V. 37

Winnie-the Pooh and the Bees. London. V. 41

The Winnie-The Pooh Quartet. London: 1924-28. V. 44

Winne the Pooh. London: 1926. V. 37; 38; 39; 40; 41; 43; 44; 45; 46

Winnie The Pooh. Toronto: 1926. V. 39

Winnie the Pooh. London: 1928. V. 42

Winnie the Pooh. London: 1973. V. 42; 46

Winnie-the-Pooh. London: (1926). V. 37

MILNE, CHRISTIAN

Simple Poems on simple subjects. Aberdeen: 1805. V. 37

MILNE, DAVID

On the Mid-Lothian and East-Lothian Coalfields. London. V. 42

MILNE-HOLME, MARY PAMELA

Mamma's Black Nurse Stories; West Indian Folk Lore. Edinburgh & London: 1890. V. 40; 42

MILNE, JOHN S.

Surgical Instruments in Greek and Roman Times. Oxford: 1907. V. 39; 40

MILNE, JOSHUA 1776-1851

A Treatise on the Valuation of Annuities and Assurances on Lives and Survivorships. London: 1815. V. 39; 40

MILNE, LESLIE

Shans at Home. London: 1910. V. 41

MILNE, SAMUEL

The Standards and Colours of the Army, From the Restoration, 1661, to Introduction of the Territorial System, 1881. Leeds: 1893. V. 41

MILNER, HENRY ERNEST

The Art and Planning of Landscape Gardening. London: 1890. V. 37; 41

The Art and Practice of Landscape Gardening. London: 1890. V. 44

The Art and Planning of Landscape Gardening. London: 1890. V. 37

MILNER, HENRY M.

Frankenstein; or, The Man and the Monster!. London: 1830? V. 42

MILNER, J.

An Inquiry Into Certain Vulgar Opinions Concerning the Catholic Inhabitants and the Antiquities of Ireland. London: 1800. V. 46

MILNER, JOE E.

California Joe, Noted Scout and Indian Fighter . . . Caldwell: 1935. V. 40; 41; 44

California Joe, Noted Scout and Indian Fighter. 1935. V. 37

MILNER, JOHN

The Cruise of H.M.S. 'Galatea'. London: 1869. V. 37; 41; 44

The Ecclesiastical History, & Survey of the Antiquities of Winchester. Winchester: 1809. V. 46

A Treatise on the Ecclesiastical Architecture of England, during the Middle Ages. London: 1811. V. 37

MILNER, JOSEPH

Essay on Several Religious Subects, Chiefly Tending to Illustrate the Scripture-Doctrine of the Influence of the Holy Script. York: printed by Ward &: 1789. V. 44

Gibbon's Account of Christianity Considered . . . York: 1781. V. 42

The History of the Church of Christ. London: 1827. V. 39

MILNER, T. H.

On the Regulation of Floating Capital, and Freedom of Currency. London: 1848. V. 38; 39; 41

MILNER, THOMAS

Descriptive Atlas of Astronomy, and of Physical and Political Geography . . . London: 1853. V. 39

The Elevation of the People, moral, instructional and social. London: 1846. V. 37

The Gallery of Geography. Glasgow: 1872. V. 40

MILNES, CHARLOTTE

The Loves of Hally and Sophy. London: 1795-96. V. 46

MILNES, JACOB

Sectionum Conicarum Elementa Nova Methodo Demonstrata. Oxford: 1723. V. 40

MILNES, R. MONCKTON

The Real Union of England and Ireland. London: 1845. V. 38

MILNES, RICHARD MONCKTON 1809-1885

Life, Letters and Literary Remains of John Keats. London: 1848. V. 37

MILNOR, WILLIAM

An Authentic Historical Memoir of the Schuylkill Fishing Company of the State in Schuylkill. Philadelphia: 1830. V. 42; 43

An Authentic Historical Memoir of the Schuylkill Fishing Company of the State in Schuylkill. Philadelphia: 1862-1903. V. 42

Memoirs of the Gloucester Fox Hunting Club Near Philadelphia. New York: 1927. V. 41; 42

MILNS, WILLIAM

The Penman's Repository. London: 1787. V. 41; 46

The Penman's Repository, Containing Twenty Correct Alphabets . . . Manchester: 1860's. V. 41

The Well-Bred Scholar, or Practical Essays on the Best Methods of Improving the Taste, and Assisting the Extertions of Youth in Their Literary Pursuits. London: 1794. V. 46

MILOSZ, ARS MAGNA

Poemes. 1895-1927. Paris: 1929. V. 37

MILOSZ, CZESLAW

The Captive Mind. 1983. V. 39

The Captive Mind. New York: 1983. V. 38; 44; 46

MILOSZ, O. V. DE L.

Fourteen Poems by . . . San Francisco: 1952. V. 44

MILROY, JACK

Portraits of the Queen, the Stamp Collages of.. Dallas: 1979. V. 39

MILTON, FRANCIS

The Automobilist Abroad. With Many Illustrations from Photographs, Deocrations, Maps and Plans by Blanche McManus. London: 1907. V. 37

MILTON, JOHN 1608-1674

Accedence Commenc't Grammar, Supply'd with Sufficient Rules, for the Use of Such (Younger or Elder) as are Desirious . . . London: 1669. V. 42; 43

L'Allegro. London: 1849. V. 39

L'Allegro and Il Pensoroso. London: 1855. V. 44

L'Allegro and Il Penseroso. New Rochelle: 1903. V. 43

Allegro and Penseroso. Leipzig: 1921. V. 40

L'Allegro and Il Penseroso. New York: 1954. V. 38

L'Allegro and Il Penseroso. London: 1859. V. 37

Apple Orchard. Kent: 1940's. V. 46

Areopagitica. New York: 1890. V. 37; 41; 43

Areopagitica. Hammersmith: 1903. V. 39; 40; 46

Areopagitica. London: 1903. V. 44

Areopagitica. 1903-04. V. 42

Areopagitica. 1904. V. 40; 45

MILTON, JOHN 1608-1674 continued

Paradise Lost (and) Paradise Regain'd. Hammersmith: 1902/05. V. 37; 43; 44

Paradise Lost. Liverpool: 1906. V. 38; 45

Paradise Lost. London: 1931. V. 38; 39; 41; 44; 46

Paradise Lost (and) Paradise Regain'd. San Francisco: 1936. V. 40; 46

Paradise Lost. London: 1937. V. 37; 41; 42

Paradise Lost. Waltham St. Lawrence: 1937. V. 37; 40; 41; 44; 46

Paradise Regaind. V. 46

Paradise Regain'd. Samson Agonistes, A Dramatic Poem. Comus. A Mask: With Poems on Several Occasions. London. V. 38

Paradise Regain'd. A Poem. In IV Books. To Which is added Samson Agonistes. London: 1671. V. 41

Paradise Regain'd. A Poem . . . to which is added Samson Agonistes. London: 1680. V. 43; 46

Paradise Regain'd. (with) Samson Agonistes. London: 1688. V. 46

Paradise Regain'd. A Poem. In Four Books. To Which is added Samson Agonistes. And Poems Upon Several Occasions. London: 1713. V. 37; 42

Paradise Regain'd . . . London: 1727. V. 45

Paradise Regain'd . . . (with) Samson Agonistes; and Poems Upon Several Occasions . . . London: 1743. V. 42; 43

Paradise Regain'd. Birmingham: 1758. V. 38

Paradise Regain'd . . . From the text of Doctor Newton. To which are added Poems on Several Occasions. Philadelphia: 1791. V. 37

Paradise Regained, a Poem. London: 1795. V. 40; 41

Paradise Regained and Other Poems. London: 1825. V. 46

Paradise Regain'd: A Poem in IV Books. Hammersmith: 1905. V. 46

Paradise Regained. London: 1924. V. 38; 39

Poems on Affairs of State. V. 39

Poems in English. London. V. 44

Poems. London: 1645. V. 39; 40; 43; 44; 45; 46

Poems, &c. Upon Several Occasions. London: 1673. V. 38; 41; 42; 45

The Shorter Poems of John Milton. London: 1889. V. 37; 38; 40; 44

The Shorter Poems of John Milton. London: 1899. V. 37

Poems in English. London: 1926. V. 37; 40; 41; 44; 45; 46

Poems Upon Several Occasion, English, Italian and Latin with Translations. London: 1785. V. 38; 40; 46

Poetical Works of John Milton. London: 1760 & 1766. V. 39

The Poetical Works. Springfield: 1794. V. 40; 41; 43; 44

The Poetical Works . . . From the text of Doctor Newton. With the Life of the Author. in Two Parts. Springfield, Mass./Boston: 1794. V. 37

Poetical Works. London: 1794-95-97. V. 46

Poetical Works. London: 1794-97. V. 38; 39; 40; 43; 44; 45; 46

The Poetical Works. Boston: 1796. V. 37; 38; 40

The Poetical Works of John Milton. London: 1808. V. 38

Poetical Works. London: 1809. V. 38; 39; 40

The Poetical Works of John Milton. Oxford: 1824. V. 40; 44; 46

The Poetical Works. London: 1826. V. 38; 40

The Poetical Works. London: 1835. V. 40; 41; 43; 44

The Poetical Works. London: 1836. V. 38

The Poetical Works. London: 1839. V. 39

The Poetical Works . . . London: 1841. V. 40

The Poetical Works. L: 1852. V. 40

The Poetical Works of . . . London: 1852. V. 37; 44

The Poetical Works. London: 1853. V. 37; 39

Poetical Works. Philadelphia: 1864. V. 41

The Poetical Works. London: 1890. V. 42

The Poetical Works of John Milton. London: 1904. V. 38; 45

The Poetical Works. London: 1874. V. 37

Pro Popvlo Anglicano Defensio, Contra Clavdii Anonymi, Alias Salmasii . . . London: 1651. V. 39; 44; 45

Pro Populo Anglicano Defensio, Contra . . . Salmasii Defensionem Regiam. London: 1652. V. 37

The Prose Works . . . with a Life of the Author . . . London: 1806. V. 39

A Selection from the English Prose Works. Boston: 1826. V. 46

Complete Prose Works of John Milton. New Haven: 1953-80. V. 46

Complete Prose Works. New Haven & London: 1959-80. V. 46

Samson Agonistes. New Rochelle: 1904. V. 44; 46

Samson Agonistes: a Dramatic Poem. Florence: 1930-31. V. 45

Samson Agonistes, a Dramatic Poem. 1931. V. 45

Samson Agonistes. Harrow: 1931. V. 37

Samson Agonistes. Harrow Weald, Middlesex: 1931. V. 44

Samson Agonistes. Middlesex: 1931. V. 37; 42

Samson Agonistes. New Rochelle: 1940. V. 43

Samson Agonistes. Norwich: 1979. V. 37

Tetrachordon: Expositions Upon the Four Chief Places in Scripture, Which Treat of Marriage, or Nullities in Mariage. London: 1645. V. 45

Three Poems . . . 1896. V. 45

A Tractate of Education . . . To which are added, four paper on the same subject from the spectator. Glasgow: 1746. V. 37

The Works. London: 1697. V. 38; 41

The Works. London: 1850-51. V. 45

The Works in Prose and Verse. London: 1851. V. 40; 41; 46

Works in Verse and Prose, printed from the Original Editions with a Life of the Author by the Rev. John Mitford. London: 1863. V. 37; 40; 42

MILTON, LOUISE CHANDLER

In Garden of Dreams: Lyrics and Sonnets. Boston: 1890. V. 38

MILTON, THOMAS

The Chimney-Piece Maker's Daily Assistant. London: 1766. V. 40; 44

A Compleat Treatise on Perspective, in Theory and Practice . . . London: 1779. V. 44

MILTON, WILLIAM FITZWILLIAM, VISCOUNT 1839-1877

British Columbia. London: 1864. V. 38; 40; 41; 43

A History of the San Juan Water Boundary Question. London: 1869. V. 37; 41

The North-West Passage by Land. London: 1865. V. 45

The North-West Passage by Land. London: 1866. V. 40; 42

Voyage de l'Atlantique au Pacifique a Travers le Canada, Les Montagnes Rocheuses et La Colombie Anglaise. Paris: 1866. V. 41

MILTOUN, FRANCIS

The Automobilist Abroad. London: 1907. V. 44

MIMPRISS, ROBERT

A Chronological and Geographical Chart . . . London: 1835. V. 44

MIMS, WILBUR F.

War History of the Prattville Dragoons. Thurber. V. 39

MINADOI, GIOVANNI TOMMASO

Historia della Guerra fra Turchi et Persani . . . Con Una Descrittione di Tutte le Cose Pertinenti alla Religione, alle Forze al Governo & al Paese del regno de Persani . . . Venetia: 1588. V. 39; 41; 42

Historia Della Guerra fra Turchi et Persani . . . Venetia: 1558. V. 37

MINAMOTO, HOSHU

An Illustrated History of Japanese Art. Kyoto: 1935. V. 38; 41; 44

MINASIAN, KHATCHIK

Five Poems. Mt. Horeb: 1971. V. 44

The Simple Songs of . . . Fresno: 1950. V. 46

The Simple Songs of . . . San Francisco: 1950. V. 37; 39

MINCE Pies for Christmas and for All Merry Seasons. London: 1812. V. 37; 40

MINCHIN, H. COTTON

The Legion Book, by Captain H. Cotton Minchin. London: 1929. V. 37

MINCOFF, E.

Pillow Lace. London: 1907. V. 42

MINER, CHARLES

Essays from the Desk of Poor Robert the Scribe. Doylestown: 1815. V. 39; 41; 42

History of Wyoming, in a Series of Letters, from Charles Miner to His Son William Penn Miner, Esq. Philadelphia: 1845. V. 39

MINER, DOROTHY

Studies in Art and Literature for Belle da Costa Greene. Princeton: 1954. V. 42

MINER, H. S.

Orchids, the Royal Family of Plants. Boston: 1885. V. 45; 46

THE MINERAL and Agricultural Resources of East Tennessee: Her Inducements to Those Who Seek Wealth and Health. Knoxville: 1883. V. 44

THE MINER'S Own Book. San Francisco: 1858. V. 38

THE MINES of New Mexico. Inexhaustible Deposits of Gold and Silver . . . Santa Fe: 1896. V. 39

MINET, WILLIAM

Some Account of the Hughenot Family of Minet from Their Coming Out of France at the Revocation of the Edict of Nantes MDCLXXXVI Founded on Isaac Minet's Relation of Our Family. London: 1892. V. 41

MINGAUD, M.

The Noble Game of Billiards. London: 1831. V. 38; 39

MINGAY, CHARLES

A Series of Lectures on the Most Approved Principles and Practices of Modern Surgery. London: 1821. V. 42

MINGHETTI, MARCO

The Masters of Raffaello. London: 1882. V. 42; 45

MINIATURE History of England. London: 1850's. V. 46

A MINIATURE History of the Holy Bible. Hartford: 1821. V. 43

MINIATURES and Drawings by an English Artist of the 14th Century Reproduced from Royal Ms. 2 B. VII in the British Museum. London: 1912. V. 39

MINICK, A. RACHEL

A History of Printing in Maryland, 1791-1800. With A Bibliography of Works Printed in the State During the Period. Baltimore: 1949. V. 41

MINICK, ROGER

Delta West. Berkeley: 1969. V. 37

MINIFIE, MARGARET

The Histories of Lady Frances S----and Lady Caroline S----. London: 1763. V. 42

The Picture. Dublin: 1766. V. 39

MINIFIE, WILLIAM

A Text Book of Geometrical Drawing, for the Use of Mechanics and Schools . . . Baltimore: 1857. V. 39

MINISTERIAL Artifice Detected, or, a Full Answer to a Pamphlet Lately Published, Intitled, The Interests of the Empress Queen, the Kings of France and Spain &c. Betryaed in the Preliminar Articles at Aix-la-Chapelle. London: 1749. V. 41

MINISTERIAL Prejudices in Favour of the Convention. Examind' and Answer'd. London: 1739. V. 41

MINKOFF, GEORGE ROBERT

A Bibliography of the Black Sun Press. Great Neck: 1970. V. 41

A Bibliography of the Black Sun Press. New York: 1970. V. 39

MINNESOTA

Annals of the Minnesota Historical Society . . . Number IV. St. Paul: 1853. V. 37

Statement of the St. Paul & Chicago Railway Company Respecting Its land Grant Bonds. St. Paul: 1867. V. 37

MINNESOTA; a Brief Sketch of Its History, Resources, and Advantages. St. Paul: 1893. V. 42

MINNESOTA. CONSTITUTION - 1858

Report Communicating a Copy of the Constitution of Minnesota. Washington: 1858. V. 37

MINNESOTA. CONSTITUTIONAL CONVENTION - 1858

Debates and Proceedings of the Constitutional Convention for the Territory of Minnesota . . . Saint Paul: 1858. V. 37; 39

MINNESOTA. GOVERNOR - 1861

Annual Message of Governor Ramsey to the Senate and House of Representatives of the State of Minnesota. St. Paul: 1861. V. 39

THE MINNESOTA Guide: A Handbook of Information for Travellers, Pleasure Seekers and Immigrants. St. Paul: 1869. V. 37

MINNESOTA HISTORICAL SOCIETY

Annals of the Minnesota Historical Society. St. Paul: 1850. V. 38; 39; 42

Annals of the Minnesota Historical Society for 1853. No. IV. St. Paul: 1853. V. 37; 42

MINNESOTA History. St. Paul: 1915-1980. V. 37; 40

MINNESOTA in the Civil and Indian War. 1891. V. 45

MINNESOTA in the Civil and Indian Wars 1861-1865. St. Paul: 1890. V. 44

MINNESOTA in the Civil War and Indian Wars, 1861-1865. St. Paul: 1861-1865. V. 37

MINNESOTA In the Civil War and Indian Wars, 1861-65. St. Paul: 1891. V. 39

MINNESOTA: Its Progress and Capabilities. Being the Second Annual Report of the Commissioner of Statistics. Saint Paul: 1862. V. 37

MINNESOTA: Its Resources and Progress; Its Beauty, Healthfulness and Fertility; and Its Attractions and Advantages as a Home for Immigrants. St. Paul: 1870. V. 37

MINNESOTA. STATE BOARD OF IMMIGRATION

Minnesota, the Empire State of the North West: The Commercial, Manufacturing and Geographical Centre of the American Continent. St. Paul: 1878. V. 42

MINNESOTA. (TERRITORY). GOVERNOR

Fourth Annual Message of the Governor of the Territory of Minnesota; with the Accompanying Documents. St. Paul: 1853. V. 42

MINNESOTA. (TERRITORY). LAWS, STATUTES, ETC. - 1851

Revised Statutes of the Territory of Minnesota, Passed at the Second Session of the Legislative Assembly. St. Paul: 1851. V. 39

MINNESOTA. The Empire State of the New North-West, The Commercial, Manufacturing and Geographical Centre of the American Continent. St. Paul: 1865. V. 38
MINNESOTA, the Empire State of the New North-West, the Commercial, Manufacturing and Geographical Centre of the American Continent. St. Paul: 1878. V. 37

MINOR, D. K.

American Railroad Journal. New York: 1832. V. 43

MINOR, DOROTHY

Studies in Art and Literature for Belle de Costa Greene. Princeton: 1954. V. 38; 40

MINORSKY, V.

The Chester Beatty Library. A Catalogue of the Turkish manuscripts and minatures. With an introduction by J.V.S. Wilkinson. Dublin: 1958. V. 37

MINOT, GEORGE R.

The History of the Insurrections in Massachusetts in 1786 and the Rebellion Consequent Thereon. Worcester: 1788. V. 38

MINOT, GEORGE RICHARDS

Continuation of the History of the Province of Massachusetts Bay. Boston: 1798, 1803. V. 40; 41; 46

The History of the Insurrections in Massachusetts. Boston: 1810. V. 38

MINOT, LAURENCE

Poems on Interesting Events in the Reign of King Edward III, Written by Laurence Minot. London: 1795. V. 38; 39

MINOT, WILLIAM

Private Letter of William Minot Collected and Arranged by His Son. N.P.: 1895. V. 42; 43

MINOTATURE. Paris: 1933-May 1939. V. 46

MINOTAURE. Revue Artistique et Litteraire. Paris: 1933-39. V. 45

MINSHEU, JOHN

Ductor in Linguas, the Guide into Tongues. London: 1617. V. 43; 45

The Guide Into Tongues . . . London: 1627. V. 40

Minshaei Emendatio, vel a Mendis Expurgatio, Seu Augmentatio Sui Ductoris in Linguas, the Guide Into Tongues . . . London: 1627. V. 38; 40; 42; 45; 46

MINSHEV, JOHN

Minshaei Emendatio, Vel a Mendis Expurgatio . . . London: 1626. V. 44

MINSHULL, JOHN

A Comic Opera, Entitled Rural Felicity; with the Humour of Patrick, and Marriage of Shelty. New York: 1801. V. 45

MINTO, GILBERT ELLIOT MURRAY, 1ST EARL OF

The Speech of Lord Minto, in the Hose of Peers, April 11, 1799 . . . Respecting the Union Between Great Britain and Ireland. Dublin: 1799. V. 39

MINTO, WALTER

an Inaugural Oration, on the Progress and Importance of the Mathematical Sciences. Delivered at Princeton on the Evening Preceding the Annual Commencement 1788. Trenton: 1788. V. 45

MINTON, HOLLINS & CO.

Patent Tile Works. Manufacturers of Encaustic, Venetian and Plain Tiles for Mosiac Pavement . . . Stoke-upon-Trent: 1875. V. 37

MINTON, JOHN

Speculations on the Contemporary Painter - a Lecture Delivered at the City of Birmingham College of Arts and Crafts on 25 June 1952. 1952. V. 44

MINTON, W. L.

Alexander Begg's Red River Journal and Other Papers Relative to the Red River Resistance of 1869-1870. Toronto: 1956. V. 37

MINTORN, JOHN

The Hand-Book for Modelling Wax Flowers. London: 1844. V. 44

MINTURN, R. B.

From New York to Delhi, by Way of Rio De Janeiro, Australia, and China. New York: 1858. V. 38

MINTURNO, ANTONIO

Rime e Prose. Venice: 1559. V. 40

MINTURNUS, ANTONIUS

De Poeta. Venice: 1559. V. 39

A **MINUTE** and Circumstantial Narrative of the Loss of the Steam-Packet Pulaski, Which Burst Her Boiler and Sunk On the Coast of North Carolina, June 14, 1838. Providence: 1839. V. 45

MINUTES of the First Hebrew-Christian Conference of the United States. Held at Mountain Lake Park, Md. July 28-30, 1903. Pittsburgh?: 1903. V. 37

MINUTES to Go. San Francisco: 1968. V. 45

MIR HASSAN ALI, B., MRS.

Observations on the Mussulmauns of India . . . London: 1832. V. 45

MIRAB MUNIS, S. M.

Firdaws aliqbal. History of Khorezm. Edited by Y. Bregel. 1987/88. V. 37

MIRABAUD, JEAN BAPTISTE DE

Opinion des Anciens sur les Juifs. Paris: 1750. V. 43

MIRABEAU, HONORE GABRIEL RIQUETTI, COMTE DE 1749-1791

Considerations on the Order to Cincinnatus. To Which are Added Several Original Papers Relative to that Insitution. Philadelphia: 1786. V. 37

Errotika Biblion. Paris: 1792. V. 45

Gallery of Portraits of the National Assembly, Supposed to Be Written by Count de Mirabeau. London: 1790. V. 42

Mirabeau's Letters, During His Residence in England . . . London: 1832. V. 42; 45

Oeuvres Posthumes et Faceties de Mirabeau le Jeune. Paris: 1798. V. 39

MIRABEAU, OCTAVE

Aristide Maillol. Paris: 1921. V. 44

MIRABEAU, VICTOR RIQUETI, MARQUIS DE 1715-1789

L'Ami des Hommes, out Traite de la Population. A La Haye: 1758. V. 38

Theorie de l'Impot. Paris?: 1760. V. 38

MIRABEAU, VICTOR RIQUETTI, MARQUIS DE 1715-1789

L'Ami des Hommes, ou Traite de la Population. Avignon: 1756-1760. V. 38; 41; 45

MIRACLES of Madame Saint Katherine of Fierbois. Chicago: 1897. V. 37

THE **MIRACLES** of Our Lord. London: 1848. V. 42

MIRAEUS, AUBERTUS

Elogia Belgica sive Illustrium Belgi(i) Scriptorum, Qui Nostra Patrumque Memoria . . . London: 1609. V. 45

MI'RAJ NAMAH

The Miraculous Journey of Mahomet. London: 1977. V. 39

MIRANDA, GIOVANNI

Osservationi Della Lingua Castigliana . . . Divise in Quatro Libri . . . Venice: 1566. V. 40

MIRANDA, or the Discovery. Norwich: 1800. V. 43

MIRANDOLAM, OCTAVIANUM fl.1507

Flores Illustrium Poetarum. Geneva: 1653. V. 40

MIRANDULAM, OCTAVIANUM fl. 1507

Illustrium Poetarum Flores. Lugduni: 1553. V. 39; 41; 46

Illustrium Poetarum Flores! Lugduni: 1553. V. 46

Illustrium Poetarum Flores . . . De Poetica Virtute et Studio Humanitatis Impellente ad Bonum. Strassburg: 1544. V. 37

Viridarium Illustrium Poetarum. Haguenau: 1517. V. 37

MIREHOUSE, JOHN

A Practical Treatise on the Law of Tithes. London: 1818. V. 38; 40

MIRICK, B. L.

The History of Haverhill, Massachusetts. Haverhill: 1832. V. 46

MIRISON, ROBERT

Hortus Blesensis Auctus, cum Notulis Durationis & Charactismis Plantarum tam Additarum, Quam non Scriptarum . . . (with) Hallucinationes Caspari Bauhini in Pinace . . . London: 1669. V. 46

MIRKUS, A. MARY

Robert Gibbings: a Bibliography. London: 1962. V. 42

MIRO, JOAN

Joan Miro Lithographs. New York: and Paris: 1972/75/77/81. V. 46

Lithographs. Volumes I-III. (1972-7). V. 37

Miro: Recent Paintings. New York: 1953. V. 41

Miro, 1959-1960. New York: 1961. V. 41

Oiseau Solaire, Oiseau Lunaire, Etincelles. New York: 1967. V. 41

LE **MIROUER** Historial de France. Paris: 1516. V. 38

MIRRLEES, HOPE

Paris: a Poem. Richmond: 1919. V. 46

A **MIRROR** for the Intemperate. Boston: 1830. V. 41

THE **MIRROR** of the Graces. Boston: 1831. V. 45

MIRROR of the Graces; or the English Lady's Costume. London: 1811. V. 41

THE **MIRROR** of the Graces; or, The English Lady's Costume . . . Fashion in Dress . . . New York: 1815. V. 39

MISCELLANEA. London: 1727. V. 38

MISCELLANEA Parliamentaria. London: 1681. V. 40

MISCELLANEOUS Pieces of Antient English Poesie. London: 1660. V. 40

MISCELLANEOUS Pieces of Antient English Poesie. London: 1764. V. 39

MISCELLANEOUS Poems and Translations. London: 1762. V. 40

MISCELLANEOUS Poems by Several Hands. London: 1726-30. V. 38; 41; 45

MISCELLANEOUS Poems Selected from the United States Literary Gazette. Boston: 1826. V. 37; 43

MISCELLANEOUS Reflections Upon the Peace, and Its Consequences. London: 1749. V. 41

MISCELLANEOUS Remarks on the Police of Boston . . . Boston: 1814. V. 44; 45

MISCELLANEOUS State Papers: from 1501 to 1726. London: 1778. V. 39

MISCELLANIES. London: 1742. V. 40

A **MISCELLANY.** New York: 1958. V. 43

MISCELLANY, Being a Collection of Poems. London: 1685. V. 41

A **MISCELLANY** of American Poetry 1920. New York: 1920. V. 39

A **MISCELLANY** of American Poetry, 1925. New York: 1925. V. 39

A **MISCELLANY** of Poems by Several Hands. Oxford: 1731. V. 38

A **MISCELLANY** of Type. 1990. V. 45

A MISCELLANY of Type. Gloucestershire: 1990. V. 46

MISCELLANY Poems and Translations by Oxford Hands. London: 1685. V. 38; 41

MISCELLANY Poems and Translations by Oxford Hands. London: and Oxford: 1685. V. 45

MISHIMA, YUKIO

Confessions of a Mask. Norfolk: 1958. V. 46

Five Modern No Plays. New York: 1957. V. 43; 45

Naked Festival. New York: Tokyo: 1969. V. 42

The Sailor Who Fell From Grace with the Sea. New York: 1965. V. 46

The Sea of Fertility Cycle. New York: 1972-74. V. 37; 46

The Sound of Waves. New York: 1956. V. 43; 46

The Sound of Waves. New York: 1856. V. 45

Sun and Steel. Tokyo: 1970. V. 42

Twilight Funflower - a Play in Four Acts. Tokyo: 1958. V. 45

MISS Browne. The Story of a Superior Mouse. London: 1895. V. 46

MISS Canning and the Gypsey; or, a More Particular Inlet Into the Knowledge of that Paradoxical Affair, Than Any Attempts Hitherto Made to Bring It to Light. London: 1754. V. 46

MISS Milly Millefleur's Career. New York: 1869. V. 44

MISSION Furniture: How to Make It. Part I, II, III. Chicago: 1909-10-12. V. 38

MISSIONS in Ireland, Especially with Reference to the Proselytizing Movement . . . Dublin: 1855. V. 38

MISSISSIPPI

Resolution of the Legislative Council and House of Representatives of the Mississippi Territory, Relative to . . . British Ministers at Ghent. Washington: 1815. V. 44

MISSISSIPPI BAPTIST ASSOCIATION

Minutes of the Nineteenth Anniversary of the Mississippi Baptist Association, Held with the Salem Church, Livingston Parrish, La., September 21-23, 1861. New Orleans: 1861. V. 44

MISSISSIPPI. CONSITITUION - 1817

Letter from His Excellency Daivd Holmes, Governor of the State of Mississippi, Transmiting a Copy of the Constitution and Form of Government of the Said State. Washington: 1817. V. 37

MISSISSIPPI. CONSITUTIONAL CONVENTION - 1865

Journal of the Proceedings and Debates in the Constitutional Convention of the State of Mississippi August, 1865. Jackson: 1865. V. 37; 39; 43; 45

MISSISSIPPI. CONSTITUTION

Constitution and Form of Government for the State of Mississippi. Nathchez: 1817. V. 42

MISSISSIPPI. HIGH COURT OF ERRORS AND APPEALS.

The State of Mississippi V. Hezron A. Johnson, Involving the Liability of the State of Mississippi for the Payment of the Bonds Issued for and on Account of the Mississippi Union Bank . . . Jackson: 1853. V. 44

MISSISSIPPI. LAWS, STATUTES, ETC.

Laws of the State of Mississippi. Passed at a Called Session of the Mississippi Legislature Held in Columbus, Feb. and March 1865. Meridian: 1865. V. 43

MISSISSIPPI. LEGISLATURE

Journal of the State Convention and Ordinances and Resolutions Adopted in January, 1861, with an Appendix. Jackson. V. 45

MISSISSIPPI. STATE GEOLOGICAL SOCIETY

Report on the Agriculture and Geology of Mississippi. E. Barksdale: 1854. V. 46

MISSISSIPPI. STATE GEOLOGIST

Preliminary Report on the Geology and Agriculture of the State of Mississippi. Jackson: 1857. V. 46

Report on the Geology and Agriculture of the State of Mississippi. Jackson: 1860. V. 46

MISSISSIPPI. (TERRITORY). LAWS, STATUTES, ETC. - 1816

Statutes of the Mississippi Territory . . . the Ordinance for the Government of the Territory of the United States, North-West of the River Ohio . . . and Such Acts of Congress as Relate to the Mississippi Territory . . . Natchez: 1816. V. 40

MISSISSIPPI Writers: Reflections of Childhood and Youth. Jackson: 1985/86. V. 42

MISSISSIPPI Writers: Reflections of Youth and Childhood. Jackson: 1985. V. 45

MISSON, MAXIMILIAN

A new Voyage to Italy. Four Volumes. London: 1714. V. 37

MISSOURI

Messages and Proclamations of the Government of the State of Missouri (1820-1964). Columbia: 1922-64. V. 42

MISSOURI. CONSTITUTION

Constitution of the State of Missouri. Washington: 1820. V. 37; 39; 44

MISSOURI. CONSTITUTIONAL CONVENTION - 1861

Journal and Proceedings of the Missouri State Convention Held at Jefferson City and St. Louis, March, 1861. St. Louis: 1861. V. 37; 39

MISSOURI. CONSTITUTIONAL CONVENTION - 1930

Debates of the Missouri Constitutional Convention. Columbus, Mo.: 1930-1944. V. 37

MISSOURI HISTORICAL AND PHILOSOPHICAL SOCIETY

Annals of the Missouri Historical and Philosophical Society. Jefferson City: 1848. V. 37; 39

MISSOURI IRON COMPANY

Prospectus of the Missouri Iron Company and Missouri and Iron Mountain Cities, Together With a Map of the States of Missouri and Plan of the Cities. Boston: 1837. V. 37

Prospectus of the Missouri Iron Company and Iron Mountain Cities, Together with a Map of the State of Missouri and Plans of the Cities. Hartford: 1837. V. 37; 43

Prospectus of the Missouri Iron Company. With the Acts of Incorporation. N.P.: 1873. V. 46

MISSOURI. LAWS, STATUTES, ECT. - 1841

The Revised Statutes of the State of Missouri Revised and Digested by the Eighth General Assembly . . . With the Constitution of Missouri. St. Louis: 1941. V. 37

MISSOURI. LAWS, STATUTES, ETC. - 1841

The Revised Statutes of the State of Missouri Revised and Digested by the Eight General Assembly . . . St. Louis: 1841. V. 37

MISSOURI. LAWS, STATUTES, ETC. - 1843

Laws of the State of Missouri Passed at the First Session of the Twelfth General Assembly. Jefferson City: 1843. V. 37; 42

MISSOURI. LAWS, STATUTES, ETC. - 1849

Laws of the State of Missouri. City Of Jefferson: 1849. V. 37

MISSOURI. LAWS, STATUTES, ETC. - 1858

Laws of the State of Missouri, Passed at the First Session of the Eighteenth General Assembly . . . December A.D. 1854. Jefferson City: 1855. V. 37; 39

MISSOURI PACIFIC RAILRAOD

Statistics and Information Concerning Indian Territory, Oklahoma and The Cherokee Strip. St. Louis: 1893. V. 45

MISSOURI PACIFIC RAILROAD

Scenes Along the Houston North Shore Railway. 1927. V. 46

MISSOURI. STATE GEOLOGIST

The First and Second Annual Reports of the Geological Survey of Missouri. Jefferson City: 1855. V. 39; 42

Geological Report of the Country Along the Line of the South-Western Branch of the Pacific Railroad, State of Missouri. St. Louis: 1859. V. 39; 41; 42; 43

MRS. Greet's Story of the Golden Owl. London: 1892-1893. V. 38

THE MISTLETOE: a German Tale of Christmas. London: 1847. V. 42

MISTRAL, GABRIELA

Selected Poems of Gabriela Mistral. Bloomington: 1957. V. 44

MITCHEL, JOHN

The History of Ireland to 1884. New York: 1884. V. 39

Jail Journal; or, Five Years in British Prisons. New York: 1854. V. 43

MITCHEL, MARTIN

History of the County of Fond du Lac, Wisconsin, From Its Earliest Settlement to the Present Time. Fond du Lac: 1854. V. 42

MITCHEL, O. M.

The Planetary & Stellar Worlds: a Popular Exposition of the Great Discoveries & Theories of Modern Astronomy. New York: 1849. V. 45

MITCHEL, THOMAS LIVINGSTONE

Three Expeditions into the Interior of Eastern Australia . . . London: 1839. V. 39

MITCHELL, ADRIAN

For Beauty Douglas: Collected Poems 1953-79. London: (1982). V. 37

MITCHELL, ALBERT

Recollections of One of the Light Brigade. Canterbury: 1884. V. 42

MITCHELL, ARTHUR

The Insane in Private Dwelling. Edinburgh: 1864. V. 42

List of Travels and Tours in Scotland, 1296 to 1900. Edinburgh: 1902. V. 38

MITCHELL, B. W.

Trail Life in the Canadian Rockies. New York: 1924. V. 41; 44

MITCHELL, C. H.

The Illustrated Books of the Nanga, Maruyama, Shijo and Other Related Schools of Japan: a Bibliography. Los Angeles: 1972. V. 43

MITCHELL, CAROLINE A.

Records of the Royal Horse Artillery, From Its Formation to the Present Time. London: 1888. V. 42; 46

MITCHELL, CLARENCE BLAIR

The 'ABC' of Riding to Hounds. Princeton: 1916. V. 43

MITCHELL, D. W.

Ten Years in the United States: Being an Englishman's Views of Men and Things in the North and South. London: 1862. V. 40; 46

MITCHELL, DONALD GRANT 1822-1908

Bound Together: a Sheaf of Papers. New York: 1893. V. 43

Dream Life: a Fable of the Seasons. New York: 1851. V. 46

MITCHELL, DONALD GRANT 1822-1908 continued

Dream Life. New York: 1884. V. 43

First Gleanings; or, a New Sheaf from the Old Fields of Continental Europe. New York: 1851. V. 43; 46

The Lorgnetee, or Studies of the Town by an Opera Gower. New York: 1850. V. 42

Reveries of a Bachelor by Ik Marvel. New York: 1850. V. 42; 45; 46

The Works. New York: 1907. V. 42

MITCHELL, E. B.

In Western Canada Before the War: A Study of Communities. London: 1915. V. 44

MITCHELL, ELISHA

Arguments for Temperance: a Sermon Addressed to the Students of the University of North Carolina . . . Raleigh: 1831. V. 39

MITCHELL, F. S.

The Birds of Lancashire. London: 1885. V. 41

MITCHELL, FLORA

Vanishing Dublin. Dublin: 1966. V. 37; 38; 43

MITCHELL, FRANK

The 17 Horse Songs of Frank Mitchell. London: 1969. V. 39

MITCHELL, GEORGE

A Catalogue of the Library. London: 1869. V. 45

MITCHELL-HENRY, L.

Tunny Fishing at Home and Abroad. London: 1934. V. 39; 40; 43

MITCHELL, ISAAC

The Asylum; or Alonzo and Melissa. Poughkeepsie: 1811. V. 43

MITCHELL, J.

The Philosophy of Witchcraft. Glasgow: 1839. V. 43

MITCHELL, J. L.

Grand Trunk Railway Gazetteer, Commercial Advertiser and Business Directory, 1862-1863. Toronto: 1862. V. 37

MITCHELL, J. LESLIE

Three Go Back. Indianapolis: 1932. V. 39

MITCHELL, JAMES

Parochial History of Saint Neots, in Cornwall and an Historical Sketch of the Life and Miracles of Saint Neot. Bodim: 1833. V. 40

The Portable Encyclopaedia . . . London: 1828. V. 46

MITCHELL, JOHN

Jail Journal, or Five Years in British Prisons. New York: 1854. V. 46

A Night on the Banks of Doon, and Other Poems. Paisley: 1838. V. 38

The Present State of Great Britain and North America, With Regard to Agriculture, Population, Trade and Manufactures, Impartially Considered. London: 1767. V. 37; 41; 44

Treatise on the Falsifications of Food, and the Chemical Means Employed to Detect Them. London: 1848. V. 42

MITCHELL, JOHN AMES

The Last American. New York: 1902. V. 42

MITCHELL, JOHN KEARSLEY

Five Essays by John Kearsley Mitchell. Philadelphia: 1859. V. 41; 42; 45

Remote Consequences of Injuries of Nerves and Their Treatment. Philadelphia: 1895. V. 42

MITCHELL, JOHN M.

The Herring. Its Natural History and National Importance. Edinburgh: 1864. V. 46

MITCHELL, JONATHAN

Propositions Concerning the Subject of Baptism and Consociation of Churches, . . . Cambridge: 1662. V. 38

MITCHELL, JOSEPH

The Highland Fair; or, Union of the Clans. London: 1731. V. 37; 46

The Missionary Pioneer, or a Brief Memoir of the Life, Labours, and Death of John Stewart . . . New York: 1827. V. 38; 39

Poems on Several Occasions. London: 1729. V. 42

MITCHELL, LEON

Prisoners of War in the Trans-Mississippi. Austin: 1961. V. 39

MITCHELL, MARGARET 1900-1949

Gone With the Wind. London: 1936. V. 42

Gone with the Wind. New York: 1936. V. 37; 38; 39; 42; 44; 45; 46

Gone with the Wind. Toronto: 1936. V. 39

Gone with the Wind. London: 1937. V. 46

Gone with the Wind. London: 1939. V. 39; 42; 45

Gone With the Wind. New York: 1939. V. 38; 39; 42; 46

Gone with the Wind. New York: 1939 (1936). V. 45

Gone with the Wind. London: 1940/1939. V. 45

Gone with the Wind. New York: 1961. V. 42; 44; 45

Gone With the Wind. New York: 1968. V. 39; 41; 42; 43; 45

Gone With the Wind. (New York: ca. 1940). V. 37

Vom Winde Verweht (Gone with the Wind). Hamburg: 1937. V. 44

MITCHELL, MARTIN

Geographical and Statistical History of the County of Winnebago. Oshkosh: 1856. V. 39

MITCHELL MOTOR WORKS

Motor Roads to London. London: 1907. V. 42

MITCHELL, NAHUM

History of the Early Settlement of Bridgewater, In Plymouth County, Massachusetts . . . Boston: 1840. V. 46

MITCHELL, P.

The West and North-West. Montreal: 1880. V. 42; 45

MITCHELL, PETER

Jan Van Os 1744-1808. Leigh on Sea: 1968. V. 44

MITCHELL, PIER ANTONIO 1679-1737

Nova Plantarum Genera Iuxta Tournefortii Methodum Disposita. Florence: 1729. V. 40

MITCHELL, ROBERT

Plans, and Views in Perspective, with Descriptions, of Buildings Erected in England and Scotland, and also an Essay, to Elucidate the Grecian, Roman and Gothic Architecture . . . London: 1801. V. 38

MITCHELL, S. L.

Secret Springs of Dublin Song. Dublin: 1918. V. 43

MITCHELL, SAMUEL AUGUSTUS 1792-1868

An Accompaniment to Mitchell's Reference and Distance Map of the United States . . . . Philadelphia: 1834. V. 41; 43; 46

An Accompaniment to Mitchell's Map of the World . . . Philadelphia: 1843. V. 42; 44; 45

An Accompaniment to Mitchell's Reference and Distance Map of the United States . . . Philadelphia: 1845. V. 46

Accompaniment to Mitchell's New Map of Texas, Oregon, and California, with the Regions Adjoining. Philadelphia: 1846. V. 41; 42

Accompaniment to Mitchell's New Map of Texas, Oregon and California . . . Tacoma: 1925. V. 45

A General View of the World . . . Philadelphia?: 1845. V. 38

A General View of the World . . . Philadelphia: 1846. V. 45

Illinois in 1837. Philadelphia: 1837. V. 37; 38; 43; 46

Illinois in 1837; a Sketch Descriptive of the Situation, Boundaries, Face of the Country, Prominent Districts, Prairies, Rivers, Minerals, Animals, Agricultural Productions . . . of the State of Illinois. Philadelphia: 1838. V. 40; 41

Mitchell's Compendium of the Internal Improvements of the United States. Philadelphia: 1835. V. 42; 45

Mitchell's Traveller's Guide through the United States, Containing the Principal Cities, Towns, &c . . . Philadelphia: 1838. V. 38; 40

Mitchell's Traveller's Guide Through the United States . . . Philadelphia: 1838. V. 43; 46

Mitchell's School Atlas: Comprising the Maps, etc. Designed to Illustrate Mitchell's School and Family Geography. Philadelphia: 1852. V. 37; 39; 41

Mitchell's New General Atlas . . . Philadelphia: 1867. V. 45

Mitchell's New General Atlas, Containing Maps of the Various Countries of the World, Plans of Cities, etc. Philadelphia: 1868. V. 41

Mitchell's New General Atlas, Containing Maps of the Various Countries of the World . . . Philadelphia: 1872. V. 45

Mitchell's New General Atlas, Containing Maps of the Various Countries of the World . . . Philadelphia: 1885. V. 45

MITCHELL'S School Atlas: Comprising the Maps and Tables designed to Accompany Mitchell's School and Family Geography. Philadelphia: 1859. V. 40

A New Map of Texas Oregon and California with the Regions Adjoining. Philadelphia: 1846. V. 40; 42

A New Universal Atlas Containing Maps of the Various Empires, Kingdoms, States and Republics of the World . . . Philadelphia: 1847. V. 45

A New Universal Atlas Containing Maps of the Various Empires . . . Philadelphia: 1854. V. 45

A New Universal Atlas Containing Maps of the Various Empires . . . Philadelphia: 1855. V. 45

MITCHELL, SAMUEL L.

A Concise Description of Schooley's Mountain in New Jersey, with Some Experiments on the Water of Its Chalybeate Spring. New York: 1810. V. 45

MITCHELL, SAMUEL L. continued

Devotional Somnium; or, a Collection of Prayers and Exhortations, Uttered by Miss Rachel Baker, in the City of New York, in the Winter of 1815, During Her Abstracted and Unconscious State. New York: 1815. V. 37; 38

The Medical Repository, and Review of American Publications on Medicine, Surgery, and the Auxiliary Branches of Philosophy. New York: 1802-09. V. 40

The Medical Repository and Review of American Publications on Medicine, Surgery and the Auxiliary Branches of Science . . . Volume VI - Second Hexade Volume IV. New York: 1803-07. V. 41

The Medical Repository, Comprehending Original Essays and Intelligence Relative to Medicine, Chemistry, Natural History. New York: 1810-12. V. 38

Medical Repository. New York: 1804. V. 38

MITCHELL, SILAS WEIR 1829-1914

A Brief History of Two Families. Philadelphia: 1912. V. 43

The Comfort of the Hills and Other Poems. New York: 1910. V. 42

A Diplomatic Adventure. New York: 1906. V. 37

Fat and Blood: and How to Make Them. Phildelphia: 1877. V. 38

Fat and Blood and How to Make Them. First English from second American. London: 1878. V. 37

Fat and Blood: and How to make Them. Philadelphia: 1879. V. 42

Fat and Blood: and How to Make Them. Philadelphia/London: 1879. V. 43

Hugh Wynne - Free Quaker. 1897. V. 46

Hugh Wynne, Free Quaker. New York: 1897. V. 37; 46

Injuries of Nerves and Their Consequences. Philadelphia: 1872. V. 42

Lectures on Diseases of the Nervous System, Especially in Women. Philadelphia: 1881. V. 42

Lectures on the Diseases of the Nervous System, Especially in Women. Philadelphia: 1885. V. 42

Mary Reynolds: a Case of Double Consciousness. Philadelphia: 1889. V. 46

Reflex Paralysis. New Haven: 1941. V. 41

Researches Upon the Venom of the Rattlesnake. Washington: 1861. V. 40; 41; 44

Researches Upon the Venoms of Poisonous Serpents. Washington: 1886. V. 45

Some Recently Discovered Letters fo William Harvey with Other Miscellanea. Philadelphia: 1912. V. 42; 45; 46

Two Lectures on the Conduct of the Medical Life . . . Addressed to the Students of the University of Pennsylvania and the Jefferson Medical College. Philadelphia: 1893. V. 38

The Wager and Other Poems. New York: 1900. V. 42

MITCHELL, T., MRS.

Gleanings from Travels in England, IReland and Through Italy; or, Comparative Views of Society at Home and Abroad. Belfast: 1825. V. 42; 44

MITCHELL, THOMAS LIVINGSTON

Journal of an Expedition into the Interior of Tropical Australia. London: 1848. V. 41; 42; 46

MITCHELL, WESLEY CLAIR 1874-1948

A History of the Greenback. Chicago: 1903. V. 38; 39

MITCHELL, WILLIAM A.

On the Pleasure and Utility of Angling. Newcastle-Upon-Tyne: 1824. V. 40

MITCHELL, WILLIAM ANDREW

An Essay on Capacity and Genius . . . Edinburgh: 1820. V. 43

An Essay on Capacity and Genius; to Prove that There is No Original Mental Superiority Between the Most Illiterate and the Most Learned of Mankind, and that no Genius, Whether Individual or National, is Innate . . . London: 1820. V. 42; 46

An Essay on Capacity and Genius: To prove that there is no original mental superiority between the most literate and the most learned of mankind, and that no genius, whethe individual or national, is innate, but . . . London: (1820?). V. 37

An Essay on Capcity and Genius. London: 1820? V. 37

MITCHENER, C. H.

Historic Events in the Tuscarawas and Muskingum Valley, and in Other Portions of the State of Ohio. Dayton: 1876. V. 40

Ohio Annals. Dayton: 1876. V. 46

MITCHILL, SAMUEL L.

Catalogue of the Organic Remains, Which, With Other Geological and Some Mineral Articles Were Presented to the New York Lyceum of Natural History in August 1826. New York: 1826. V. 41

MITCHILL, SAMUEL LATHAM 1764-1831

The Picture of New-York . . . New York: 1807. V. 46

MITCHISON, NAOMI

The Alban Goes Out. London: 1939. V. 40

Beyond This Limit. London: 1935. V. 37; 45

MITE. Grimsby: 1893. V. 38

MITFORD, EARDLEY

The Law of Wills, Codicils and Revocations. London: 1800. V. 40

MITFORD, EDWARD LEDWICH

A Land March from England to Ceylon Forty Years Ago. London: 1884. V. 38

MITFORD, JOHN

Adventures of Johnny Newcomb in the Navy. London: 1819. V. 37; 38; 40; 41; 43

The Adventures of Johnny Newcome in the Navy. London: 1823. V. 37; 39

The Correspondence of Thomas Fray and William Mason to Which are Added Some Letters Addressed to by Gray to the Rev. James Brown, D.D. London: 1853. V. 42

A Description of the Crimes and Horrors in the Interior of Warburton's Private Made-House at Hoxton, Commonly Called Whitmore House. London: 1825. V. 41

The Military Adventures of Johnny Newcome . . . London: 1816. V. 42

My Cousin in the Army. London: 1822. V. 38; 40; 42; 43

My Cousin in the Army. London: 1825. V. 40

My Cousin in the Army; or, Johnny Newcome on the Peace Establishment. London: n.d. V. 37

Peninsular Sketches During a Recent Tour. London: 1816. V. 41

A Treatise on the Pleadings in Suits in the Court of Chancery by English Bill. London: 1787. V. 38; 45

MITFORD, MARY RUSSELL 1787-1855

Belford Regis. London: 1835. V. 43; 44; 45; 46

Christina, the Maid of the South Seas. London: 1811. V. 38

Dramatic Scenes, Sonnets and Other Poems. London: 1827. V. 42

Finden's Tableaux; The Iris of Prose, Poetry and Art for MDCCCXI. London: 1839. V. 41

Foscari and Julian. London: 1827. V. 42

Our Village. London: 1824-32. V. 37; 42; 44

Our Village. London: 1879. V. 43; 45

Our Village. London: 1893. V. 37; 38; 42

Our Village. London: 1910. V. 44

Our Village. London: 1947. V. 38

Our Village. London: 1949. V. 44

Our Village. London: 1824/28/30/32. V. 37

Poems. London: 1810. V. 37; 40; 41

Recollections of Literary Life. New York: 1852. V. 41

Watlington Hill: a Poem. London: 1812. V. 44

MITFORD, NANCY 1904-1973

Don't Tell Alfred. London: 1960. V. 44

Noblesse Oblige. London: 1956. V. 38; 39

The Sun King. London: 1969. V. 41

Voltaire in Love. London: 1957. V. 40; 44

Wigs on the Green. London: 1935. V. 38

MITFORD, WILLIAM

An Essay Upon the Harmony of Language, Intended Principally to Illustrate That of the English Language. London: 1774. V. 38; 41; 42; 46

The History of Greece. London: 1814-21. V. 38; 41; 43; 46

The History of Greece. London: 1822. V. 42

The History of Greece. London: 1829. V. 37; 40

The History of Greece. London: 1838. V. 41; 44

An Inquiry into the Principles of Harmony in Language, and of the Mechanism of Verse, Modern and Antient. London: 1804. V. 46

MITOUFLET, MARC THOMIN

Traite d'Optique Mechanique, Dans Lequel on Donne les Regles et les Proportions . . . Paris: 1749. V. 41; 45

MITRA, DEBALA

Ratnagiri (1958-61). New Delhi: 1981, 1983. V. 38

MITRA, S. M.

The Life and Letters of Sir John Hall . . . London: 1911. V. 46

MITSOU. Quarante Images par Baltusz. Zurich: 1921. V. 39

MITTELBERGER, GOTTLIEB

Gottlieb Mittelbergers Reise nach Pennsylvanien im Jahr 1750. Stuttgart: 1756. V. 40

Gottlieb Mittelberger's Journey to Pennsylvania in the Year 1750 and Return to Germany in the Year 1754. Philadelphia: 1898. V. 41; 42; 46

MITTEN, DAVID GORDON

Classical Bronzes. Providence: 1975. V. 44

MITTON, G. E.

Normandy by Nico Jungman. London: 1905. V. 46

MIURA, EINEN

The Art of Marbled Paper, Marbled Patterns and How to Make Them. London: 1898. V. 46

MIURA, KERSTIN TINI

My World of Bibliophile Binding. Berkeley: 1984. V. 37; 43

My World of Bibliophile Binding. Japan: 1980. V. 37; 46

MIVART, ST. G.

A Monograph of the Lories, or Brush-Tongued Parrots . . . London: 1896. V. 42

MIVART, ST. GEORGE

Dogs, Jackals, Wolves and Foxes. London: 1890. V. 41

On the Genesis of Species. New York: 1871. V. 41; 43

MIX, GEORGE

Report Given by Col. Geo. A. Mix, Dubuque of the Exploration of the Prosposed Route of the Dubuque & Pacific Railroad. Dubuque: 1855. V. 42

MIXSON, FRANK M.

Reminiscences of a Private. Columbia: 1910. V. 42

MIYABE, K.

Icones of the Essential Forest Trees of Hokkaido. Tokyo: 1983. V. 37

MIYOSHI, E.

The World Orchid Stamps. Tokyo: 1987. V. 38

MIZAULD, ANTOINE

Hortorum Secreta, Cultus et Auxilia, Amoenae Voluptatis, & Inenarrabilis Utilitatis Abunde Plena . . . Lutetiae: 1575. V. 39

Meteorologia, Sive Rerum Aeriarum Commentariolus. Paris: 1547. V. 39; 41

Le Mirouer du Temps, Autrement Dict Ephemerides Perpetuelles de l'Air. Paris: 1547. V. 39; 41

Secretorum, Agri enchiridion Primum, Hortorum Curam, Auxilia, Secreta & Medica Praesidia Inventu Prompta, ac Paratu Facilia Libris Tribus Pulcherrimis Complectens. Lutetia: 1560. V. 39

MIZNER, ADDISON

Florida Architecture of Addison Mizner. New York: 1928. V. 40; 44; 46

MO, TIMOTHY

The Monkey King. London: 1978. V. 38; 41; 44

Sour Sweet. London: 1982. V. 40; 45

MOAT, LOUIS S.

Frank Leslie's Illustrated Famous Leaders and Battle Scenes of the Civil War. New York: 1896. V. 39

MOAT, S. SHEPHEARD

Practical Proofs of the Soundness of the Hygeian System of Physiology . . . New York: 1834. V. 41

A MOB in the Pit; or, Lines Addressed to the D--ch-ss of A-----ll. London: 1773. V. 42

MOBERLY, GEORGE

Introduction to Logic. Oxford: 1830. V. 37

MOBERLY, WALTER

Early History of Canadian Pacific Railway. Vancouver: (1908). V. 37

The Rocks and Rivers of British Columbia. London: 1885. V. 39

MOBLEY, CHRISTOPHER DARLINGTON 1890-1957

Where the Blue Begins. Philadelphia: 1922. V. 39; 40; 41

MOCENIGO, ANDREA

Bellum Cameracense. Venice: 1525. V. 44

MOCHET, RICHARD

Tractatus de Politia Ecclesiae Anglicanae. Londini: 1705. V. 46

MOCHIZUKI, KOTARO

The Proposed Reduction of the Naval Armaments of the United States and Japan. N.P., N.d.: 1925. V. 40

MOCK, HARRY E.

Industrial Medicine and Surgery. Philadelphia & London: 1919. V. 43

MOCKLER-FERRYMAN, A. F.

British West Africa Its Rise and Progress. London: 1900. V. 46

MODDIE, JOHN WEDDERBURN

Ten Years in South Africa. London: 1835. V. 38

A MODEL of the Royal Marriage of Windsor . . . London: 1863. V. 38; 40

MODELLO, e Fabrica del Conclave per la Creatione del Nuouo Papa. Con gli Ordini, e Prouisioni che si Fanno del Cammerlengo . . . 1590. V. 42

MODELS of Letters, for the Use of Schools and Private Students. London: 1794. V. 39

MODENA, LEO DE

Kerk-Zeeden en de Gewoonten, Die Huiden in Gebruik zyn Onder de Jooden. Amsterdam: 1700. V. 45

MODERN Arabia Displayed, in Four Tales. London: 1811. V. 43

MODERN Art. Indianapolis: 1893-95. V. 44

THE MODERN Art of Boxing, as Practised by Mendoza, Humphreys, Ryan, Ward, Watson, Johnson and Other Eminent Pugilists. London: 1790. V. 37

MODERN Athenians. Edinburgh: 1882. V. 46

MODERN Ballads. Preston: c. 1780. V. 46

A MODERN Bill of Fare for Seven, As It Was Perform'd by Their Own Desire and Approbation in May, Anno Domini 1751 and Compared with a Bill of Fare Provided for King Henry the 8th and His Queen the Foreign Ministers, Lord-Mayor, Judges &c. London: 1751. V. 42

MODERN Book Production. London: 1928. V. 37; 40; 41

MODERN Bookbindings and their Designers. London: 1899-1900. V. 38

THE MODERN Boxer, or Scientific Art and Practice of Attack and Self Defence . . . London: 1847. V. 39

MODERN British Liveries. London: 1880. V. 41

MODERN Building Record. A Record of the Most Notable and Interesting Buildings in Recent Years. London: 1910-14. V. 45

MODERN Cases in Law and Equity. London: 1730. V. 38

MODERN Characters. Annapolis: 1819. V. 44

A MODERN Delineation of the Town and Port of Kingston Upon Hull Being an Accurate Guide to all the Various Objects of Public Interest . . . Hull: 1805. V. 39

MODERN Design in Jewellery and Fans. London: 1901-1902. V. 37

A MODERN Dissertation on a Certain Necessary Piece of Household Furniture. London: 1752. V. 40; 41; 44; 46

THE MODERN Family Physician, or the Art of Healing Made Easy. London: 1775. V. 43
THE MODERN Family Physician, or the Art of Healing Made Easy. Dublin: 1776. V. 38

MODERN Furniture Designs, Adapted from the English Periods. London: 1922. V. 44

THE MODERN Light Aeroplane. London: (c. 1930). V. 37

THE MODERN Minerva; or, the Bat's Seminary for Young Ladies. London: 1810. V. 43

THE MODERN Miniature. London: 1792. V. 38; 40

THE MODERN Monitor; or, Flyn's Speculations. Cork: 1771. V. 41

THE MODERN Motor Car. London: (c. 1930). V. 37

MODERN Pen Drawings: European and American. London: 1901. V. 46

THE MODERN Practice of the London Hospitals. London: 1785. V. 42; 46

THE MODERN Songster; or Universal Banquet of Vocal Music. Baltimore: 1805. V. 44

A MODEST Vindication of Oliver Cromwell from the Unjust Accusations of Lieutenant-General Ludlow in His Memoirs. London: 1698. V. 43

A MODEST Vindication of the Right Honourable Sir Gilbert Heathcote, Knight, Late Lord-Mayor of the City of London. Plainly Proving that the Act Past for Regulating the Election of Alderman, Was by a High-Church-Tack, forc'd on him, Contrary to . . . London: 1711. V. 41

MODUS Salium. A Collection of Such Pieces of Humour (not to be found in others of this kind) as Prevail'd in Oxford, in the Time of Mr. Anthony a Wood. Oxford: 1751. V. 46

MODY, N. H. N.

A Collected Nagasaki Colour Prints and Paintings Showing the Influence of Chinese and European Art on that of Japan. Rutland and Tokyo: 1969. V. 43

MOELLENBROCK, ANDREAS VALENTIN

Cochlearia Curiosa; or the Curiosities of Scurvygrass . . . London: 1676.
V. 42

MOERAN, J. W.

Mccullagh of Aiyansh. London: 1922. V. 37

MOESHSEN, JOHANN CARL WILHELM 1722-1795

Verzeichnis Einer Samlung von Bildnissen, Grostentheils Beruhmter
Aerzie . . . Berlin: 1771. V. 41

MOESTISSIMAE Ac Laetissimae Academiae Cantabrigiensis Affectus,
Decedente Carlo II. Cantabrigiae: 1684-5. V. 37; 38; 44; 45

MOESTISSIMAE ac Laetissimae Academiae Cantabrigiensis Carmina
Funebria & Triumphalia. Cantabrigiae: 1714. V. 44

MOEVS, MARIA TERESA MARABINI

The Roman Thin Walled Pottery from Cosa (1948-1954). Rome: 1973.
V. 42; 44

MOFFAT, A. S.

The Secrets of Angling. Edinburgh: 1865. V. 41

MOFFAT, ALFRED

Our Old Nursery Rhymes. 1911. V. 44
Our Old Nursery Rhymes. London: 1911. V. 37; 46

MOFFAT, ROBERT

Missionary Labour and Scenes in Southern Africa. London: 1842.
V. 38; 41; 45

MOFFAT, W. GRAHAM

What's the World Coming To? London: 1893. V. 42

MOFFATT, JAMES

The Moffatt New Testament Commentary. London: 1947-52. V. 43; 44

MOFFET, THOMAS 1553-1604

Health's Imrpvoement, or Rules Comprizing the Nature, Method and Manner
of Preparing All Sorts of Foods Used in this Nation. London: 1746. V. 39

MOFFETT, E. C.

With the Eighth Division: a Souvenir of the South African Campaign.
London: 1903. V. 38

MOFFETT, KENWORTH

Kenneth Noland. New York: 1977. V. 42; 43

MOFFETT, THOMAS

The Silkewormes, and Their Flies: Lively Described in Verse, by T. M. a
countrie f aramer, and an apprentice in physicke . . . London: 1599. V. 37

MOFFETT, WILLIAM

Hesperi-Neso-Graphia. Dublin: 1724. V. 40; 42

MOFFETTE, JOSEPH F.

The Territories of Kansas and Nebraska. New York: 1856. V. 37; 40; 41

MOGFORD, HENRY

Hand-Book for the Preservation of Pictures. London: 1845. V. 38; 40; 41;
44; 45
Handbook for the Preservation of Pictures. London: 1845. V. 44

MOGG, EDWARD

Mogg's Pocket Itinerary. London: 1826. V. 39; 44
Paterson's Roads. London: 1829. V. 39; 41
Paterson's Roads . . . London: 1831. V. 46
Paterson's Roads . . . (with) Appendix. London: 1832. V. 44

MOGGRIDGE, J. T.

Harvesting Ants and Trapdoor Spiders. London: 1873-74. V. 43

MOGRIDGE, GEORGE

The Celestial Empire: or, Points and Pickings of Information About China
and the Chinese. London: 1844. V. 46
Loiterings Among the Lakes of Cumberland and Westmoreland. London:
1849. V. 41
Points and Pickings of Information About the Chinese. London: 1844. V. 46
Sergeant Bell and His Raree-Show. London: 1839. V. 43

MOHANTY, BIJOY CHANDRA

Block Printing and Dyeing of Bagru, Rajsthan. Ahmedabad: 1983. V. 38

MOHN, ISABELLA

Geraldine Hamilton; or Self-Guidance. London: 1832. V. 40

MOHOLY-NAGY, L.

The New Vision, from Material to Architecture. New York: 1930. V. 45

Vision in Motion. Chicago: 1947. V. 37; 41; 46

MOHOLY-NAGY, S.

Carlos Raul Villanueva & the Architecture of Venezuela. New York: 1964.
V. 46

MOHOLY-NAGY, SIBYL

Pedagogical Sketchbook. London. V. 44

MOHR, EDWARD

To the Victoria Falls of Zambesi. London: 1876. V. 45

MOHRENHEIM, JOSEPH

Abhandlung uber die Entbindungskunst. St. Petersburg: 1791. V. 46

MOIR, D. M.

Outlines of the Ancient History of Medicine: Being a View of the Progress
of the Healing Art Among the Egyptians, Greeks, Romans and Arabians.
Edinburgh: 1831. V. 42

MOIR, DAVID MACBETH 1798-1851

Domestic Verses. Edinburgh: 1871. V. 40; 41; 46
Sketches of Poetical Literature of the Past Half Century. Edinburgh &
London: 1846. V. 42; 46
Sketches of the Poetical Literature of the Past Half Century in Six Lectures
Delivered at the Edinburgh Philosophical Association. London: 1852. V. 45

MOIR, GEORGE T.

Sinners and Saints. Victoria: 1948. V. 46

MOIR, JOHN

Preventive Policy; or the Worth of each, the Safety of All . . . London:
1796. V. 43

MOISE, LUCIUS CLIFTON

Biography of Isaac Harby with an Account of the Reformed Society of
Israelites of Charleston, S.C. 1824-1833. Columbia: 1931. V. 45

MOIVRE, ABRAHAM DE 1667-1754

Annuities Upon Lives. London: 1725. V. 37
Annuities Upon Lives; or, the Valuation of Annuities Upon Any Number of
Lives. Dublin: 1731. V. 43
Annuities on Lives. London: 1752. V. 39
The Doctrine of Chances; or, a Method of Calculating the Probability of
Events in Play. London: 1718. V. 37; 42; 46
The Doctrine of Chances. London: 1756. V. 39

MOKLER, ALFRED JAMES

Fort Casper (Platte Bridge Station). Casper, Wyoming: 1939. V. 37
History of Natrona County Wyoming 1888-1922. Chicago: 1923. V. 37
Transition of the West. Chicago: 1927. V. 37; 45

MOLENGRAAFF, G. A. F.

Borneo-Expedition: Geological Explorations in Central Borneo (1893-94).
Leyden & Amsterdam: 1902. V. 40

MOLESWORTH, MARY LOUISA STEWART 1842-1921

The Adventures of Herr Baby. London: 1881. V. 43
The Cuckoo Clock. London: 1931. V. 40
Four Winds Farm, A Christmas Child, an Old Fashioned Story. London:
1880/85/87. V. 41
Two Little Waifs. London: 1883. V. 46

MOLESWORTH, MRS.

The Magic Nuts. London: 1898. V. 40
The Talking Clock. London: 1890. V. 44

MOLESWORTH, ROBERT 1656-1725

An Account of Denmark, As It Was in the Year 1692. London: 1694.
V. 38; 41; 45
An Account of Denmark As It Was in the Year 1692. N.P.: 1694. V. 40
A Letter from a Member of the House of Commons to a Gentleman
without Doors, relating to the Bill of Peerage lately brought into the House
of Lords. Together with Two Speeches for and againts the Bill. London:
1719. V. 37

MOLESWORTH, WILLIAM NASSAU

Prize Essay, on the Great Importance of an Improved System of Education
for the Upper and Middle Classes. London: 1867. V. 45

MOLEVILLE, BERTRAND DE

A Chronological Abridgement of the History of Great Britain, from the First
Invasion of the Romans to the Year 1763 . . . London: 1812. V. 46

MOLEVILLE, M. BERTRAND DE

The Costume of the Hereditary States of the House of Austria. London:
1804. V. 37; 39; 42

MOLIEN, G.

Travels in Africa to the Sources of the Senegal and Gambia in 1818. London: 1820. V. 40; 42; 43; 44; 45

MOLIERE, JEAN BAPTISTE POQUELIN DE 1622-1673

Select Comedies of Mr. de Moliere. London: 1732. V. 39; 41; 46

Monsieur de Pourceaugnac, or, Squire Trelooby. London: 1704. V. 38

Tartuffe, or the Hypocrite. Leipzig: 1930. V. 40

Tartuffe or the Hypocrite. In a Verse Translation by Curtis Page. New York: 1930. V. 37

The Works of . . . Paris & Philadelphia. V. 46

Oeuvres. A Amsterdam: 1675. V. 39; 40; 42

Oeuvres. Paris: 1734. V. 40

The Works of Moliere. London: 1739. V. 46

The Works of Moliere. Glasgow: 1751. V. 38

The Works of . . . London: 1755. V. 37

Oeuvres. Paris: 1791. V. 41

The Dramatic Works. Edinburgh: 1875. V. 42

Oeuvres Completes de Moliere . . . Paris: 1880-85. V. 46

The Works of Moliere. Illustrations by Mm. Louis Leloir, Maurice Leloir, Jacques Leman, Edmond Hedouin. Paris/Philadelphia: (1891) V. 37

The Works of . . . Paris: 1900. V. 46

Works. Paris & Philadelphia: 1910. V. 41

MOLINA, ALONSO DE

Vocabulario en Lengua Castellana y Mexicana . . . Mexico: 1571. V. 39; 41

MOLINA, FELIPE

Bosquejo de la Republica de Costa Rica, Seguido de Apuntamientos Para su Historia. New York: 1851. V. 38; 41

MOLINA, JUAN DE

Descripcion del Reyno de Galizia y de las Cosas Notables. Mondonedo: 1551. V. 38

MOLINA, JUAN IGNACIO DE

The Geographical, Natural and Civil History of Chili. Middletown: 1808. V. 37; 38; 39; 40; 41; 46

The Geographical, Natural and Civil History of Chile. London: 1809. V. 39; 42; 43

MOLINA, JUAN IGNATIO DE

Compendio de la Historia Geografica, natural Y Civil del Reyno De Chile. Madrid: 1788. V. 38

MOLINA, LOUIS DE 1535-1601

Liberi Arbitrii cum Gratiae Donis, Divina Praescientia, Providentia, Praedestinatione, et Reprobatone . . . Antwerp: 1595. V. 41

MOLINAEUS

Tragicum Theatrum Actorum & Cauum Tragicorum Londini Publice Celebratorum Quibus. Amstelodami: 1649. V. 46

MOLINET, CLAUD DU

Le Cabinet de la Bibliotheque de Sainte Genevieve, Contenant les Antiquites de la Religion des Chretiens des Egyptiens & des Romains . . . Paris: 1692. V. 38; 44

MOLINEUX, THOMAS

A Concise Introduction to the Knowledge of the Globes . . . London: 1829. V. 38

An Introduction to Byrom's Universal English Short-Hand. Macclesfield: 1823. V. 44

An Introduction to Mr. Byrom's Universal English Shorthand. Stockport: 1804. V. 38

MOLINI, GUISEPPE

Catalogues. Florence: 1835-34. V. 40

MOLL, HERMAN

Thirty-Two Maps . . . Geography of the Ancients as Contained in . . . Greek and Latin Classicks . . . Dublin: 1735. V. 42

Thirty-Two Maps . . . Geography of the Ancients as Contained In . . . Greek and Latin Classicks . . . London: 1755. V. 42

The Traveller's Companion. London: 1780. V. 39

MOLL, HERMANN

Geographia Classica: The Geography of the Ancients, so Far Describ'd as It is Contain'd in the Greek and Latin Classicks . . . London: 1712. V. 45

MOLLER, ARVID

Kort Beskrifning Ofwer Est-och Lifland . . . Wasteras: 1756. V. 38

MOLLET, ANDRE

Le Jardin de Plaisir, Contenant Plusieurs Dessins de Jardinage Tant Parterres en Broderie, Compartiments de Gazon, Que Bosquets et Autres . . . Stockholm: 1651. V. 46

MOLLHAUSEN, BALDWIN

Diary of a Journey from the Mississippi to the Coasts of the Pacific with a United States Government Expedition. London: 1858. V. 37; 38; 40; 41; 42; 43; 45; 46

Reis Van den Mississippi Naar de Kusten van Den Grotten Oceaan, Door B. Mollhausen, Met Een Voor-Berigt Van Alexnader von Humboldt. Tezutphen: 1858-59. V. 41

Tagebuch Einer Reise vom Mississippi Nach dem Kusten der Sudsee . . . Leipzig: 1858. V. 38; 40; 42; 43; 45

Vandringer Gjennem Det Vestilige Nordamerikas Prairier . . . Kjobenhavn: 1862. V. 38

MOLLIEN, G.

Travels in the Republic of Columbia, in the Years 1822 and 1823. London: 1824. V. 39

MOLLIEN, GASPARD T.

Travels in Africa, to the Sources of the Senegal and Gambia in 1818. London: 1820. V. 41

MOLLISON, JOHN R.

The New Practical Window Gardener. London: 1879. V. 38

MOLLOY, CHARLES

Common Sense; or, the Englishman's Journal. London: 1738/39. V. 46

The Coquet; or, the English Chevalier. London: 1718. V. 41

De Jure Martimo et Navali: or, a Treatise of Affaires Maritime and of Commerce. London: 1677. V. 40

De Jure Maritimo et Navali: or, a Treatise of Affaires Maritime and of Commerce. London: 1682. V. 40

De Jure Maritimo et Navale or, a Treatise Affairs Maritime and of Commerce . . . London: 1682-1722. V. 42

De Jure Maritimo et Navali. London: 1701. V. 40

De Jure Maritimo et Navali: or a Treatise of Affairs Maritime and of Commerce. London: 1707. V. 39

Treatise of Affairs Maritime and Commerce. London: 1701. V. 39

MOLLOY, FITZGERALD

The Russian Court in the Eighteenth Century. London: 1905. V. 39

MOLLOY, J. FITZGERALD

Famous Plays, with a Discourse by Way of Prologue on the Playhouses of the Restoration. London: 1886. V. 40

Royalty Restored or London Under Charles II. London: 1885. V. 38

MOLMENTI, POMPEO

The Life and Works of Vittorio Carpaccio. London: 1907. V. 40; 43

MOLNAR, FERENC

The Play's The Thing. New York: 1927. V. 42

The Plays. New York: 1929. V. 39; 41

MOLNAR, J. E.

Author-title Index to Joseph Sabin's Dictionary of Books Relating to America. Metuchen: 1974. V. 39; 40

THE MOLOCH of Orthodoxy, or the Two Faces of That System Exhibited in Caricature; with a Burlesque on the Sophistry by Which the Two are Attempted to be Reconciled Together. Boston: 1820. V. 40

MOLYNEUX, THOMAS MORE

Conjunct Expeditions; or Expeditions that Have Been Caried on Jointly by the Fleet and Army, with a Commentary on a Littoral War. London: 1759. V. 37; 46

MOLYNEUX, WILLIAM

The Case of Ireland's being bound by Acts of Parliament made in England Stated. To which are added Letters to the Men of Ireland, b Owen Roe O'Nial. (Joseph Pollock). Dublin. V. 37

The Case of Ireland's Being Bound by Acts of Parliament in England Stated. Dublin: 1698. V. 37; 38

The Case of Ireland's Being Bound by Acts of Parliament in England Stated . . . Dublin?: 1706. V. 37; 38

MOMADAY, N. SCOTT

House Made of Dawn. New York: 1968. V. 38; 40; 43

The Names. New York: 1978. V. 45

The Way to Rainy Mountain. Albuquerque: 1969. V. 37; 42; 44

MOMBERT, J. I.

An Authentic History of Lancaster County, Pennsylvania. Lancaster: 1869. V. 41

MOMENTS of Truth. London: 1965. V. 38; 40

MOMMSEN, THEODOR

The History of Rome. London: 1867. V. 41; 46

The History of Rome. London: 1881. V. 45

MONACHUS, ROBERTUS

Bellvm Christianorvm Principvm, Praecipve Gallorvm, Contra Saracenos, Anno Salutis MLXXXVIII Pro Terra Sancta Gestum and Other Works. Basel: 1533. V. 41; 42

MONACO, DOMENICO

Specimens from the Naples Museum. London: 1884. V. 38

MONAGHAN, F.

French Travellers in the United States 1675-1932. New York: 1933. V. 40

MONAGHAN, FRANK

French Travellers in the United States, 1765-1932. New York: 1933. V. 42

MONAGHAN, JAY

Lincoln Bibliography 1839-1939. Springfield: 1934-45. V. 43
Lincoln Bibliography 1839-1939. Springfield: 1943. V. 40; 42; 44
Lincoln Bibliography 1839-1939. Springfield: 1943-45. V. 45
Swamp Fox of the Confederacy: the Life and Military Services of M. Jeff Thompson. Tuscaloosa: 1956. V. 45

MONAHAN, J.

Canon: Records Relating to the Dioceses of Ardagh and Clonmacnoise. Dublin: 1886. V. 43

MONAHAN, JOHN

Records Relating to the Diocese of Ardagh and Clonmacnoise. Dublin: 1886. V. 39

THE MONARCH Souvenir of Sunset City and Sunset Scenes, Being Views of Ca lifornia Midwinter Fair and Famous Scenes in the Golden State. San Francisco: 1894. V. 41

MONARDES, NICHOLAS 1512-1588

Delle Cose Che Vengono Portate Dall'Indie Occidentali Pertinenti All' Uso Della Medicina... Venice: 1575. V. 40; 43; 44; 46
Delle Cose che Vengono Portate dall'Indie Occidentali Pertinenti all'Uso Della Medicina... Parte Prima. Novamente Recata Dalla Spagnola Nella Nostra Lingua Italiana. Dove Ancho Tratta de Veneni & Della lor Cura... Parte Seconda... Venetia: 1582. V. 39
Joyfull Newes Out of the Newfound Worlde... London: 1580. V. 42
Joyfull Newes Out of the New-Founde Worlde. London: 1596. V. 37; 38; 39; 40; 43; 44
Joyfull News Out of the New Founde Worlde Written in Spanish by Nicholas Monardes, Physician of Seville and Englished by John Frampton, Merchant Anno 1577. London: 1925. V. 39; 41; 42; 45
De Secanda Vena in Pleuriti, Inter Graecos & Arabes Concordia. Antwerp: 1564. V. 38
Simplicium Medicamentorum Ex Nova Orbe... Antwerp: 1579. V. 38
Simplicum Medicamentorum ex Novo Orbe Delatorum, Quorum in Medicina Usus est, Historiae Liber Tertius... Antwerp: 1582. V. 39

MONASTICON Anglicanum. A History of the Abbies and Other Monasteries, Hospitals, Friaries and Cathedrals and Collegiate Churches, with their Dependencies, in England and Wales... London: 1846. V. 44

MONBODDO, JAMES BURNET, LORD

Of the Origin and Progress of Language. Edinburgh: 1774-86-87-89. V. 39

MONBODDO, JAMES BURNETT, LORD

Antient Metaphysics. Edinburgh: 1799-1784. V. 38
Of the Origin and Progress of Language. Edinburgh and London: 1774-1809. V. 44

MONCAEIUS, FRANCISCUS

Heden siue Paradisus. Rigiaci Atrebatium, Apud Aegidium Balduinum. (colophon: 1593. V. 37

MONCALM SAINT-SERVAN, LOUIS JOSEPH DE MONCALM GAZON, MARQUIS

Letters from the Marquis de Moncalm, Governor-General of Canada; to Messers de Berryer & de la Mole; in the Years 1757, 1758, and 1759. London: 1777. V. 39

MONCK, FRANCES E. O.

My Canadian Leaves. London: 1891. V. 41; 44

MONCK, JOHN BERKELEY

General Reflections on the System of the Poor Laws, with a Short View of Mr. Whitbread's Bill, and a Comment On It. London: 1807. V. 42

MONCK, MARY

Marinda. London: 1716. V. 38; 41

MONCORNET, BALTHAZAR

Le Magnifique Carousel Fait sur le fleuve de l'Arne a Florence Pour le Mariage du Grand Duc. Paris: 1631-2. V. 46

MONCREIFF, JAMES

Introductory Address on Jurisprudence and the Amendment of the Law, Delivered to the Association for the Promotion of Social Science at Glasgow, on Tuesday, September 25, 1860. Edinburgh: 1860. V. 46

MONCRIEFF, A. R. HOPE

Surrey. London: 1906. V. 40

MONCRIEFF, GUY

The Letters of Abelard and Heloise. London: 1925. V. 41

MONCRIEFF, JOHN

Galba. A Dialogue on the Navy. London: 1748. V. 41; 45
The Scale; or, Woman Weighed with Man. (with) The Scale... London: 1752, 1753. V. 41
The Twenty-Fourth of May. London: 1742. V. 41

MONCRIEFF, W. T.

The March of Intellect. London: 1830. V. 38

MONCRIEFF, WILLIAM

Camillus. A Dialogue on the Navy. London: 1748. V. 41; 45

MONCRIEFF, WILLIAM T.

The Pickwickians; or, The Peregrinations of Sam Weller. London: 1872? V. 40
The Pickwickians. London: 1875? V. 40

MONCRIF, FRANCOIS AUGUSTIN PARADIS DE

Moncrif's Cats. London: 1961. V. 37; 39; 46
Cats. Translated by Reginald Bretnor. With 10 Illustrations by Copyel reproduced by collotype from the original edition. London: 1962. V. 37
Moncrif's Cats. Waltham St. Lawrence: 1961. V. 45

MOND, ROBERT

The Bucheum. London: 1934. V. 40
Catalogue of the Collection of Drawings by the Old Masters. London. V. 40; 42; 44
Cemeteries of Armant I. London: 1937. V. 37; 40; 42

MONDINO DE LUZZI

Anatomia Mundini, ad Vetustissimorum, Erundemque Aliquot Manuscriptorum Codicum Fidem Collata Iustoq suo Ordini Restituta... Marburg: 1541. V. 37

MONDRIAN, PIET

Plastic Art and Pure Plastic Art. New York: 1945. V. 43

MONEGLIA, GIOVANNI ANDREA

Ercole in Tebe, Festa Teatrale Rappresentata in Firenze per le Reali Nozze de' Serenissimi Sposi Cosimo Terzo, Principe di Toscana, e Margherita Luisa, Principessa d'Orleans. Florence: 1661. V. 37

MONELL, S. H.

A System of Instruction in X-Ray Methods and Medical Uses of Light, Hot-Air, Vibration and High-Frequency Currents. New York: 1902. V. 42

MONELLS, S. H.

The Treatment of Disease by Electric Current. New York: 1900. V. 42

MONETTE, JOHN W.

History of the Discovery and Settlement of the Valley of the Mississippi. New York: 1846. V. 37; 38; 39; 40; 42
History of the Discovery and Settlement of the Valley of the Mississippi. New York: 1848. V. 38; 42

MONEY, A. W.

Guns, Ammunition & Tackle. New York: 1904. V. 37; 43

MONEY, ALBERT W.

Pigeon Shooting. New York: 1896. V. 39

MONEY-COUTTS, FRANCIS BURDETT

Peoms. London: 1896. V. 37

MONEY, EDWARD

The Cultivation and Manufacture of Tea. London: 1878. V. 44

MONEY, J. W. B.

Java; or How to Manage a Colony. London: 1861. V. 39

MONEY, MESSENGER

A Sketch of the Life and Character of the Late Dr. Money, Physician to the Royal Hospital at Chelsea... London: 1789. V. 46

MONFAUCON DE VILLARS, NICOLAS DE

The Count de Gabalis. London: 1714. V. 38

MONGAN, AGNES

Drawings in the Fogg Museum of Art. Cambridge: 1946. V. 38; 42; 46

MONGE, GASPARD 1746-1818

Description de l'Arrete du Comite de Salut Public. Paris: 1794. V. 41; 45

An Elementary Treatise on Descriptive Geometry, with A Theory of Shadows and of Perspective . . . London: 1851. V. 46

Geometrie Desriptive . . . Paris: 1798-99. V. 42

Geometrie Descriptive. Paris: 1799. V. 38; 41; 45

MONGINOT, FRANCOIS

De La Guerison des Fievres par le Quinquina. Paris: 1680. V. 41; 45

MONGREDIEN, AUGUSTUS

The Western Farmer of America. London: 1880. V. 44

MONGTOMERY, B.

Poems from the Desert. London: 1944. V. 37

MONICART, JEAN BAPTISTE DE

Versailles Immortalise par les Merveilles Parlant de Batimens, Jardins, Bosquets, Parcs, Statues . . . Paris: 1720. V. 38

MONIER, PIERRE

The History of Painting, Architecture, Sculpture, Graving. London: 1699. V. 37

MONIER-WILLIAMS, MONIER

Religious Thought and Life in India. London: 1883. V. 46

MONINO, ANTONIO

Historia de los Catalogos de Libreria Expanoles (1661-1840). Madrid: 1966. V. 38

MONIPENNIE, JOHN

The Abridgement or Summarie of the Scots Chronicles (etc). Edinburgh: 1633. V. 44

An Abridgement, or Summarie of the Scots Chronicles. Edinburgh: 1818. V. 42

MONIS DE CARVALLO, ANTONIO fl. 1641-1644

Francia Interessada con Portugal en la Separacion de Castilla. Paris: 1644. V. 43

THE MONK and His Sister or Ruins of the Castle del Rivino. London: 1811. V. 46

MONK, CHARLES JAMES

The Golden Horn; and Sketches in Asia Minor, Egypt, Syria and the Hauraan. London: 1851. V. 40

MONK, JAMES

State of the Present Form of Government of the Province of Quebec. London: 1789. V. 39; 45; 46

MONK, JAMES H.

The Life of Richard Bentley, Master of Trinity College, Cambridge. London & Cambridge: 1830. V. 39

MONK, JOHN

An Agricultural Dictionary, Consisting of Extracts from the Most Celebrated Authors and Papers. London: 1794. V. 42

MONK, MARIA

Awful Disclosures, by Maria Monk, of the Hotel Dieu Nummery of Montreal . . . New York: 1836. V. 41

MONK, MARY MOLESWORTH d. 1715

Marinda. London: 1716. V. 37; 38; 40; 42; 45

THE MONK of the Moutains; or, a Description of the Joys of Paradise . . .* Indianapolis: 1866. V. 37

MONK, SAMUEL H.

The Sublime, a Study of Critical Theories in Eighteenth Century England. New York: 1935. V. 40

MONKEHOUSE, ALLAN

The Rag: an Incident in Three Acts. London: 1928. V. 45

THE MONKEYS in Red Caps, an Old Story, Newly Inscribed to the Club of Jacobins . . .* London: 1792. V. 43

MONKHOUSE, COSMO

The Christ Upon the Hill. London: 1895. V. 41; 42

The Christ Upon the Hill: a Ballad. London: 1905. V. 38

A History and description of Chinese Porcelain. London. V. 40

A History and Description of Chinese Porcelain. London: 1901. V. 38; 41

The Life and Works of Sir John Tenniel. London: 1901. V. 43

MONKHOUSE, W.

The Churches of York. London: 1843. V. 41; 46

MONKHOUSE, WILLIAM COSMO

A Dream of Idleness and Other Poems. London: 1865. V. 37; 44

The Earlier English Water-Colour Painters. London: 1890. V. 39

The Works of John Henry Foley, R.A. Sculptor. London: 1875. V. 39

MONKLAND, ANNE CATHERINE

Life in India; or, the English at Calcutta. London: 1828. V. 41

MONMOUTH, ROBERT CAREY, EARL OF

Memoirs of the Life of Robert Carey, Baron of Leppington and Earl of Monmouth. London: 1759. V. 43; 45

MONNETT, HOWARD N.

Action Before Westport, 1964. V. 45

MONNETTE, ORRA EUGENE

First Settlers of ye Plantations of Piscataway and Woodbridge, Olde East New Jersey 1664-1714. Los Angeles: 1930-35. V. 40; 43

MONNIER, HENRY

Recontres Parisiennes Macedoine Pitoresque. Paris: 1820's. V. 44

MONNIER, M.

Martinique. Hydrographical Atlas. Paris: 1827-31. V. 45

MONNIER, PIERRE CHARLES

Description et Usage des Principaux Instruments d'Astronomie. Paris: 1774. V. 45

MONOD, E.

L'Exposition Universelle de 1889. Paris: 1890. V. 44

MONODY: Inscribed, with Respect and Affection, to Lady Byron. London: 1824. V. 38

MONODY, on the Death of Brigadier-General Zebulon Montgomery Pike; Who Fell at the Battle of York, Upper Canada, April 27, 1813. N.P.: 1816. V. 40

MONOTYPE CORPORATION, LTD., LONDON.

Leaves Out of Books, Brought Together as Examples of 20 Classic 'Monotype' Faces at Work Helping British Publishers and Printers to achieve Typographic Distinction in Trade Manufacture. London: 1938. V. 40

Monotype Flower Decorations. London: 1924. V. 40

Pastonchi. London: 1928. V. 44

Pastonchi. A Specimen of a New Letter for the Use on the 'Monotype'. Verona: 1928. V. 42

MONPLAISIR, H.

Foletta; or the Enchanted Bell. New York: 1849. V. 45

MONRAVA E ROCA, ANTONIO

Academicas Oracoens Phisico-anatomico-medico-cirurgicas, em que Practicam os Mais Eruditos Discipulos da Nova Academia das Quatro Sciencias, para a Comvercam do Errado Lastimoso Povo Apolino . . . Antwerp: 1732. V. 38

MONRO, ALEXANDER

An Account of the Inoculation of Small Pox in Scotland. Edinburgh: 1765. V. 43

Elements of the Anatomy of the Human Body of Its Sound State. Edinburgh: 1831. V. 41

History, Geography, and Statistics of British North America. Montreal: 1864. V. 43

New Brunswick: with a Brief Outline of Nova Scotia, and Prince Edward Island . . . Halifax: 1855. V. 37; 40; 43

Outlines of the Anatomy of the Human Body, in Its Sound and Diseased State. Edinburgh: 1813. V. 43

The Structure and Physiology of Fishes Explained and Compared With Those of Man and Other Animals. Edinburgh: 1785. V. 40

The Structure and Physiology of Fishes Explained and Compared with Those of Man and Other Animals. London: 1785. V. 46

Traite d'Osteologie Traduit de l'Anglois de M. Monro. Ou l'on a Ajoute des Planches en Taille Douce Qui Representent au naturel Tous les os de l'Adulte et du Foetus . . . Paris: 1759. V. 43

MONRO, DAVID

'Landlords' Rents' and 'Tenants' Profits;' or Corn-farming in Scotland. Edinburgh & London: 1849. V. 38

MONRO, DONALD

Praelectiones Medicae ex Cronii Instituto, Annis 1774 et 1775 . . . London: 1776. V. 45

MONRO, EDWARD

Basil, The Schoolboy; or, the Heir of Arundel. London: 1854. V. 45

MONRO, G.

Extracts . . . from the Writings . . . London: 1836. V. 41

MONRO, HAROLD

Before Dawn (Poems and Impressions). London: 1911. V. 43

Children of Love. London: 1914. V. 43

The Collected Poems of Harold Monro. London: 1933. V. 39; 43

The Earth for Sale. London: 1928. V. 44

On Day Awake. London: 1922. V. 43

Poems. London: 1906. V. 43

Strange Meetings. London: 1917. V. 41; 43; 44

Trees. London: 1916. V. 44; 46

MONRO, ROBERT

His Expedition With the Worthy Scots Regiment. London: 1637. V. 41

The Scotch Military Discipline Learnd from the Valiant Swede, and Collected for the Use of All Worthy Commanders Favouring the Laudable Proffession of Armes. London: 1644. V. 38; 42; 43; 44

MONRO, THOMAS 1764-1815

Essays on Various Subjects. London: 1790. V. 42; 46

The Olla Podrida, a Periodical Work. London: 1788. V. 44

MONRO, VERE

A Summer Ramble in Syria, with a Tatar Trip from Aleppo to Stamboul. London: 1835. V. 45

MONROE, ALEXANDER 1697-1767

The Anatomy of Human Bones, Nerves and Lacteal Sac and Duct. Edinburgh: 1782. V. 45

The Works of Alexander Monro, M.D . . . . Edinburgh: 1781. V. 41

MONROE, DONALD

A Treatise on Medical and Pharmaceutical Chemistry, and the Materia Medica. London: 1788. V. 38

MONROE, HARRIET

The Columbian Ode. Chicago: 1893. V. 37

Valeria and Other Poems. Chicago: 1891. V. 37

MONROE, JAMES

The Memoir of James Monroe. Charlottesville: 1828. V. 46

Message from . . . Relative to the Arrest and Imprisonment of Certain American Citizens at Santa Fe. Washington: 1818. V. 42

Message from . . . Transmitting a Report of the commissioners . . . to Establish a National Armory on the Western Waters. Washington: 1825. V. 37

A Narrative of a Tour of Observation, Made During the Summer of 1817, by . . . President of the United States . . . Philadelphia: 1818. V. 38; 40; 46

A View of the Conduct of the Executive, in the Foreign Affairs of the United States, Connected with the Mission to the French Republic, During the Years 1794, 5 & 6. Philadelphia: 1797. V. 40; 42

A View of the Conduct of the Executive in the Foreign Affairs of the United States, as Connected with the Mission to the French Republic in the Years 1795 . . . Philadelphia: 1798. V. 46

MONROE, THOMAS

Essays on Various Subjects. London: 1790. V. 43

MONSEY, R.

Ad Virum Ornatissimum Totiq; Clero Summe Observadum D. Jacobum Astley Eq. Barttum. Norwich: 1710? V. 39; 42

MONSIEUR Thing's Origin. London: 1722. V. 38

MONSON, WILLIAM JOHN

Extracts from a Journal (Tour in Istria and Dalmatia, 1817 - Sicily, Malta and Calabria, 1819). London: 1820. V. 42

THE MONSTER of Monsters; a True and Faithful Narrative of a Most Remarkable Phaenomenon Lately Seen in This Metropolis . . . N.P.: 1754. V. 43

MONSTRELET, ENGUERRAND DE

The Chronicles of Enguerrand de Monstrelet, a Gentleman Formerly Resident at Cambray in Cambresis . . . London: 1809. V. 37; 44

The Chronicles of Enguerrand de Monstrelet . . . N.P.: 1809. V. 38

The Chronicles . . . 1400-1516. London: 1810. V. 46

The Chronicles of . . . London: 1845. V. 46

MONTAGU, BARBARA

A Description of Millenium Hall, and the Country Adjacent . . . London: 1762. V. 42; 45

A Description of Millennium Hall and the County Adjacent. London: 1767. V. 40

MONTAGU, BASIL

The Opinions of Different Authors Upon the Punishment of Death, Selected by Basil Montagu, Esq. of Lincolns Inn. London: 1809. V. 42

Selections from the Works of Taylor, Hooker, Hall and Lord Bacon. With an Analysis of the Advancement of Learning. London: 1805. V. 37

MONTAGU, EDWARD WORTLEY 1713-1776

Reflections on the Rise and Fall of the Antient Republics. Adapted to the Present State of Great Britain. London: 1759. V. 39; 42

Reflections on the Rise and Fall of the Ancient Republicks, Adapted to the Present State of Great Britain. London: 1778. V. 38

MONTAGU, ELIZABETH ROBINSON 1720-1800

An Essay on the Writings and Genius of Shakespear, Compared with the Greek and French Dramatic Poems. London: 1769. V. 38; 40; 43; 44; 46

An Essay on the Writings and Genius of Shakespear, Compared with Some Remarks Upon Misrepresentation of Mons. de Voltaire. London: 1770. V. 38; 39; 43

An Essay on the Writings and Genius of Shakespeare, Compared with the Greek and French Dramatic Poets . . . London: 1772. V. 41; 42

An Essay on the Writings & Genius of Shakespear, compared with the Greek and French Dramatic Poets. London: 1777. V. 38; 41; 44; 46

A Lady of the Last Century: Illustrated in Her Unpublished Letters. London: 1873. V. 41

The Letters, With Some of the Letters of Her Corrspondents. London: 1809. V. 38

The Letters of . . . with Some of the letters of Her Correspondents . . . London: 1810/13. V. 37; 46

The Letters of . . . with Some of the Letters of Her Correspondents. Boston: 1825. V. 46

Mrs. Montagu, Queen of the Blues. Boston: 1923. V. 46

MONTAGU, GEORGE

Ornithological Dictionary, or, Alphabetical Synopsis of British Birds. London: 1802-13. V. 37; 38

Ornithological Dictionary. London: 1813. V. 43

Ornithological Dictionary of British Birds. London: 1831. V. 42; 44

Testacea Britannica; or, Natural History of British Shells . . . London: 1803-08. V. 46

MONTAGU, H. W.

The Campaigns of Wellington. London: 1833. V. 40

Monsieur Mallet. London: 1830. V. 38; 41

MONTAGU, HENRY

Al Mondo. Contemplatio Mortis, & Immortalitatais. London: 1636. V. 37

MONTAGU, MARY PIERREPONE WORTLEY, LADY 1689-1762

Complete Letters. 1965-67. V. 46

The Complete Letters . . . Oxford: 1967. V. 45

Letters of the Right Honourable Lady M--Y W---Y M----E. (with) An Additional Volume to the Letters. London: 1763. V. 40; 41; 44

Lettres . . . Rotterdam: 1763. V. 39; 40; 45

Letters of the Right Honourable Lady . . . Written During Her Travels in Europe, Asia and Africa . . . (with) An Additional Volume of Letters. London: 1763/67. V. 39; 45

Lettres de Milady Marie Wortley Montague . . . Rotterdam: 1764. V. 41

Letters . . . . London: 1769. V. 40

Letters of the Right Honourable Lady M--y W---y M---e: Written During her Travels in Europe, Asia, and Africa. London: 1784. V. 40; 43

The Letters and Works of Lady Mary Wortley Montagu. London: 1837. V. 37; 39; 41; 44; 45

The Letters and Works. Paris: 1837. V. 39; 42

Letters from the Levant During the Embassy to Constantinople 1716-18. London: 1838. V. 42

Letters . . . Written During Her Travels . . . London: MDCCLXIII. V. 42

Letters . . . Written During Her Travels in Europe, Asia and Africa . . . to Which are Added, Poems, by the Same Author. London: 1789. V. 37

The Poetical Works . . . London: 1767. V. 42; 45

The Poetical Works of the Right Honourable . . . . London: 1768. V. 40; 43

The Poetical Works of the Right Honourable Lady . . . London: 1784. V. 42

Verses Adddress'd to the Imitator of the First Satire of the Second Book of Horace. London: 1716. V. 45

Verses Address'd to the Imitator of the First Satire of the Second Book of Horace. London: 1733. V. 38; 40; 41; 42

The Works. Including Her Correspondence, Poems and Essays . . . London: 1803. V. 38; 39; 42; 43

The Works of the Right Honourable Lady Mary Wortley Montagu . . . London: 1805. V. 45

Works. London: 1817. V. 39; 40

The Works of the Right Honourable Lady Mary Wortley Montague. London: 1895. V. 40; 41

MONTAGU, PIERREPONE WORTLEY, LADY 1689-1762

Letters of the Right Honourable Lady M--y W---y M----e: Written, During Her Travels in Europe, Asia and Africa, etc. Dublin: 1763. V. 38

MONTAGU, RICHARD 1577-1641

The Acts and Monuments of the Church Before Christ Incarnate. London: 1642. V. 39

Analecta Ecclesiasticarum Exercitationum. London: 1622. V. 38

Appello Caesarem. I Iust Appeale from Two Uniust Informers. London: 1625. V. 43; 44

Diatriabe Upon the First Part of the Late History of Tithes (by John Selden). London: 1621. V. 40

MONTAGU, ROBERT

Naval Architecture. London: 1852. V. 38

MONTAGUE, BASIL

Some Thoughts Upon Liberty and the Rights of Englishmen. London: 1819. V. 38

MONTAGUE, CHARLES

The Hind and the Panther Transvers'd to the Story of the Country Mouse and the City-Mouse. London: 1687. V. 43

The Works and Life of the righ Honourable Charles Late Earl of Halifax. London: 1715. V. 39

MONTAGUE, CHARLES EDWARD

A Hind Let Loose. London: 1910. V. 42

Right Off the Map. London: 1927. V. 42

MONTAGUE, GEORGE

Ornithological Dictionary of British Birds. London: 1831. V. 46

Ornthological Dictionary; of, Alphabetical Synopsis of British Birds. London: 1802/1813. V. 46

MONTAGUE, JOHN

Forms of Exile. Dublin: 1958. V. 38; 43

Poisoned Lands. 1977. V. 42

Poisoned Lands. London: 1977. V. 42

The Rough Field. 1972. V. 42

The Rough Field. (Dublin): (1972). V. 37

A Slow Dance. 1975. V. 42

MONTAGUE OF BEAULIEU, LORD

Cars and Motor-Cycles. London: 1929. V. 38

MONTAGUE, S. S.

Report of the Chief Engineer Upon Recent Surveys, Progress of Construction and Estimated Revenue of the Central Pacific Railroad of California. Sacramento: 1864. V. 38

MONTAGUE, W.

The Youth's Encyclopedia of Health with Games and Playground Amusements. London: 1838. V. 39; 45

MONTAGUE, W. E.

Campaigning in South Africa. Edinburgh: 1880. V. 41

MONTAIGNE, MICHEL DE 1533-1592

The Essayes or Morall, Politike, and Militarie Discourses . . . London: 1632. V. 43

Les Essais. Paris: 1595. V. 38

The Essayes. London: 1603. V. 37; 38; 39; 40; 42; 43; 45

Les Essais. Paris: 1604. V. 45

Essays. London: 1613. V. 37; 38; 39; 40; 42; 44; 46

Essays. London: 1700. V. 37; 38; 45

Essais. Paris: 1725. V. 40; 41; 46

Essais de . . . London: 1739. V. 40

The Essays. London: 1759. V. 38

The Essays. London: 1776. V. 38

The Essays. London: 1811. V. 39

Essays. London: 1877. V. 41; 45

Essays. Boston: 1902-04. V. 37; 40; 42; 45

Essays. Boston & New York: 1903-04. V. 41

The Essayes of Michael Lord of Montaigne Done Into English by John Florio. London: 1908. V. 44

Essays of Montaigne. New York: 1910. V. 46

Essays. London: 1931. V. 39; 41; 44; 45; 46

The Essays. New York: 1946. V. 40

The Essays. 1947. V. 44

Essays of Michel de Montaigne. Garden City: 1947. V. 37; 43; 44

Essays of Michel de Montaigne. New York: 1947. V. 46

Essays of Montaigne. Hillsborough: 1948. V. 41; 42; 44; 46

The Works of. New York: 1910. V. 37; 41

MONTALE, EUGENIO

Botta e Risposta (Lettera da Asolo); a Poem. Verona: 1976. V. 45

Mottetti. The Motets of Eugenio Montale in Italian with Facing English Translations by Lawrence Kart. San Francisco: 1973. V. 46

Le Occasioni. Torino: 1939. V. 39

Il Poeta, Diario. Verona: 1972. V. 41

MONTALEMBERT, CHARLES, COMTE DE

The Monks of the West from St. Benedict to St. Bernard. London: 1896. V. 39

MONTALEMBERT, CHARLES FORBES RENE, COMTE DE'

The Political Future of England. London: 1856. V. 37

MONTALTUS, ANTONIUS LUDOVICUS

Tractatus Reprobationis Sententiae Pilati. Paris: 1493. V. 38

MONTANA

Proceedings Relating to the Northern Pacific Railroad Company's Claim to the Mineral Lands of Montana. Helena: 1890. V. 37

MONTANA, a State Guide Book. New York: 1939. V. 46

MONTANA. BOARD OF RAILROAD COMMISSIONERS

Annual Report . . . 1907-1908-1916. Helena: 1908-16. V. 41

MONTANA. CONSTITUTION

Constitution of the State of Montana. Helena: 1889. V. 37; 38; 39; 41; 43; 44; 45

MONTANA. CONSTITUTION - 1915

Constitution of the State of Montana. Helena: 1915. V. 41

MONTANA Exhibit at the World's Fair and a Description of the Various Resources of the State, Mining, Agriculture and Stock Growing. Butte: 1893. V. 42

MONTANA. GOVERNOR - 1888

Report of the Governor of Montana to the Secretary of the Interior. Washington: 1888. V. 39

MONTANA HISTORICAL SOCIETY

Montana Historical Society Contributions. Helena: 1876-1940. V. 42

MONTANA - History, Resources, Possibilities. Butte: 1893. V. 38

MONTANA STOCK GROWERS ASSOCIATION

Brand Book of the Montana Stock Growers Association for 1886. Chicago: 1886. V. 43

Brand Book of the Montana Stock Growers Association for 1910. Helena: 1910. V. 40

MONTANA. (TERRITORY). LAWS, STATUTES, ETC.

Laws, Memorials and Resolutions of the Territory of Montana. Helena: 1869. V. 44

Organic Act of Montana Territory. (Caption title reads: An Act to Provide a Temporary Government for the Territory of Montana). Virginia City: 1867. V. 42; 43

MONTANA. (TERRITORY). LAWS, STATUTES, ETC. - 1874

Laws, Memorials and Resolutions of the Territory of Montana, Passed at the Extraordinary Session of the Legislative Assembly . . . Helena: 1874. V. 42

MONTANA. (TERRITORY). LAWS, STATUTES, ETC. - 1876

Laws, Memorials and Resolutions of the Territory of Montana, Passed at the Ninth Regular Session of the Legislative Assembly. Helena: 1876. V. 42

MONTANO, GIOVANNI BATTISTA 1532-1621

Le Cinque Libri di Architettura. Rome: 1691. V. 37; 42

MONTANUS, ARNOLD

Ambassades Memorables de la Compagnie des Indes Orientales des Provinces Unies, Vers les Empereurs du Japon. Amsterdam: 1680. V. 40

MONTANUS, JOANNES BAPTISTA

Consultationes Medicae, olim Quidem Ioannis Cratonis Vratislaviensis Medici Caesarei Opera atque Studio Correctae Ampliataeque. N.P.: 1583. V. 37

MONTANUS, NICOLO

Oratio ad Lucenses. Rome: 1481-87. V. 43

MONTARA, ALESSANDRO

Catalogo dei Manoscritti Italiani che sotto la Denominazione di Codici Canoniciani Italici. Oxford: 1864. V. 46

MONTAUS, ARNOLDUS

De Nieuwe en Onbekende Weereld . . . Amsterdam: 1671. V. 44

MONTBARD, GEORGES

Among the Moors, Sketches of Oriental Life. London: 1894. V. 38

MONTCALM, MARQUIS DE

Letters from . . . Governor General of Canada . . . London: 1777. V. 42; 46

MONTE, GIOVANNI BATTISTA DA

In Libros Galeni de Arte Curandi ad Glauconem Explanationes . . . Venice: 1554. V. 45

MONTE, GUIDOBALDO, MARCHESE DEL

In Duos Archimedis Aequeponderantium Libros Paraphrasis Scholiis Illustrata. Pisa: 1587. V. 38; 43

In Duos Archimedis Aequeponderantium Libros Paraphrasis Scholiis Illustrata. Pesaro: 1588. V. 38

MONTE-SNYDER, JOHANN DE

Tractus de Medicina Universali. (with) Metamorphosis Planetarum. Franckfurt am Mayn: 1709. V. 38

MONTEATH, GEORGE C.

Sale-Catalogue of the Valuable Medical Library. Glasgow: 1828. V. 38

MONTEATH, R.

Guide and Profitable Planter . . . London: 1824. V. 44

MONTEFALCHIUS, PETRUS IACOBUS

De Cognomibus Deorum. Perugia: 1525. V. 45

MONTEFIORE, JOSHUA

Commercial and Notarial Precedents . . . Philadelphia: 1803. V. 40

MONTEFIORE, MOSES

Diaries of Sir Moses and Lady Montefiore . . . from 1812 to 1883. London: 1890. V. 45

MONTEIRO DE CARVALHO, JOSE

Diccionario Portuguez das Plantas, Arbustos, Matas, Arvores, Animaes Quadrupedes . . . Lisbon: 1756. V. 45

MONTEIRO, J. J.

Angola and the River Congo. London: 1875. V. 39; 41; 44

MONTEITH, JOHN B.

The Status of Young Joseph and His Band of Nez-Perce Indians Under the Treaties Between the United States and the Nez Perce Tribe of Indians, and the Indian Title to Land. Portland, Oregon: 1876. V. 37

MONTEITH, R.

The True and Genuine Art of Exact Pointing. Edinburgh: 1704. V. 38

MONTEITH, ROBERT

Description of the Islands of Orkney and Zetland. Edinburgh: 1845. V. 40; 43

An Theater of Mortality; or, the Illustrious Inscriptions Extant Upon the Several Monuments . . . Edinburgh: 1704. V. 46

An Theater of Mortality; or, a Further Collection of Funeral-Inscriptions Over Scotland. Edinburgh: 1713. V. 41; 43

MONTEMAYOR Y CORDOBA DE CUNENCA, JUAN FRANCISCO

Excubationes Semicentum ex Decisionibus Regiae Chancellariae Santi Dominici . . . Mexici: 1667. V. 40

MONTEMERLI, MARIE, COUNTESS

The Florentines. London: 1870. V. 46

MONTENARI, GIOVANNI

Del Teatro Olimpico di Andrea Palladio in Vicenza. Padua: 1733. V. 37

MONTENAY, GEORGETTE DE

Emblematum Christianorum Centuria, cum Eorumdem Interpretatione. Zurich: 1584. V. 40

MONTENEGRO, ROBERT

Vaslav Nijinsky. An Artistic Appreciation of his Works in Black, White and Gold. V. 37

MONTEREY LIBRARY ASSOCIATION

Constitution and Rules of the Monterey Library Association Together with a Catalogue of Books. San Francisco: 1854. V. 41; 43

MONTES DE OCA, J. M.

Vida de San Felipe de Jesus Protomartir de Japon y Patron de su Patria Mexico. Mexico: 1801. V. 39; 43

MONTESPAN, FRANCOISE

Memoirs of Madame la Marquise de Montespan. London: 1895. V. 42

MONTESSORI, MARIA

The Montessori Method. London: 1912. V. 45

MONTEUX, JEROME DE, 16th century

Compendiolum Curatricis Scientiae Longe Utilissimum . . . Lugduni: 1556. V. 40

MONTFAUCON, BERNARD DE 1655-1741

L'Antiquite Expliquee et Representee en Figures. Paris: 1722. V. 39

L'Antiquitie Expliquee et Representee en Figures. (with) Supplement au Livre de l'Antiquitie Expliquee et Representee en Figures. Paris: 1719-24. V. 39

The Antiquities of Italy. London: 1725. V. 39; 44

L'Antiquite Expliquee et Representee en Figures. (with) Supplement Au Livre de l'Antiquite. Paris: 1719/1757. V. 44

Antiquity Explained and Represented in Sculptures . . . Cambridge: 1721-25. V. 44

A Collection of Regal and Ecclesiastical Antiquities of France. London: 1750. V. 38

Diarium Italicum sive Monumentorum Veterum, Bibliothecarum, Musaeorum . . . Paris: 1702. V. 38

MONTFORD, GUILLAUME

Traite Elementaire de l'Art d'Ecrire. Paris: 1800. V. 45

MONTGOMERIE, T. G.

Routes in the Western-Himalays, Kashmir . . . Dehra Doon: 1875. V. 40

MONTGOMERY, ALEXANDER

The Poems of . . . Edinburgh: 1821. V. 38

MONTGOMERY, B. L.

Personal Messages to 21 Army Group - Normandy to the Baltic 6 June 1944 - 8 May 1945. London: 1945. V. 38

MONTGOMERY, CHARLES

American Furniture: The Federal Period. New York: 1966. V. 41

MONTGOMERY, ELIZABETH

Reminiscences of Wilmington. Philadelphia: 1851. V. 46

MONTGOMERY, FLORENCE

A Very Simple Story; Being a Chronicle of the Thoughts and Feelings of a Child . . . Sealford: 1867. V. 42

MONTGOMERY, FLORENCE M.

Printed Textiles. English and American Cottons and Linens 1700-1850. New York: 1970. V. 41

MONTGOMERY, G. W.

Narrative of a Journey to Guatemala in Central America, in 1838. New York: 1839. V. 39

MONTGOMERY, H.

The Life of Major General Zachary Taylor. Auburn: 1850. V. 37

MONTGOMERY, JAMES

The Abolition of the Slave Trade. London: 1814. V. 39; 42

Art in the Blood and What Is This Thing Called Music? N.P.: 1950. V. 43

A Case of Identity. Philadelphia: 1955. V. 43

Greenland and Other Poems. London: 1819. V. 37; 42; 43

Journal of Voyages and Travels by the Rev. Daniels Tyerman and George Bennett . . . London: 1831. V. 42

Journal of Voyages and Travels by the Rev. Daniels Tyerman and George Bennett . . . London: 1832. V. 42

Memorial for John Duncan. London: 1761. V. 42

Pelican Island and Other Poems. London: 1827. V. 43

Poems on the Abolition of the Slave Trade. London: 1809. V. 38; 40; 42; 45; 46

Poems by William Cowper . . . Glasgow: 1824. V. 42

Poems of . . . London: 1860. V. 45

Poems. London: 1865. V. 39; 45

The Poetical Works of James Montgomery. Boston: 1825. V. 46

The Poetical Works of James Montgomery Collected by Himself. London: 1856. V. 41

A Poet's Porfolio; or, Minor Poems. London: 1835. V. 40

A Practical Detail of the Cotton Manufacture of the United States of America. Glasgow: 1840. V. 39

Prison Amusements and Other Trifles; Principally Written During Nine Months Confinement in the Castle of York. London: 1797. V. 37; 46

Prose, by a Poet. London: 1824. V. 38

Shots from the Canon. N.P.: 1953. V. 43

Sidelights on Sherlock. N.P.. V. 43

A Study in Pictures. 1954. V. 39

A Study in Pictures . . . Philadelphia: 1954. V. 43; 44

Three Trifling Monographs. (1) Four Birds in a Gilded Cage. (2) Those Gorgeous Magazines. (3) Speculation in Diamonds. N.P.: 1952. V. 43

MONTGOMERY, L. M.

Ann of Green Gables. London: 1908. V. 43

Chronicles of Avonlea. London: 1912. V. 43

Kilmeny of the Orchard. Boston: 1910. V. 44

MONTGOMERY, MAJ. GENERAL

The Story of the Fourth Army in the Battles of the Hundred Days, August 8th to November 11th, 1918. London: 1919. V. 45; 46

MONTGOMERY-MASSINGBERD, HUGH

Burke's Presidential Families of the United States of America. London: 1975. V. 37

MONTGOMERY, MORTON L.

Historical and Biographical Annals of Berks County, Pennsylvania. Chicago: 1909. V. 41; 42

History of Berks County in the Revolution, from 1774 to 1783. Reading: 1894. V. 41; 42

MONTGOMERY OF ALAMEIN, BERNARD LAW MONTGOMERY, 1ST VISCOUNT 1887-

Eighth Army. Some Notes on High Command in War. Tripoli: 1943. V. 41

Eighth Army. Some Brief Notes for Senior Officers on the Conduct of Battle. Africa: 1942. V. 41

El Alamein to the River Sangro. London: 1946. V. 42

A History of Warfare. London: 1969. V. 46

Lecture on Military Leadership Given at the University of St. Andrews by Field-Marshal Sir Bernard Montbomery on 15 November 1945. Germany: 1945. V. 41

21 Army Group. The Armoured Division in Battle. Holland: 1944. V. 41

21st (British) Army Group in the Campaign in North-West Europe, 1944-45. 1945. V. 41

21 Army Group. High Command in War. Germany: 1945. V. 41

21 Army Group. Modern Administration in the field in European Warfare. Germany: 1945. V. 41

21 Army Group. Some Notes on the Use of Air Power in Support of Land Operations and Direct Air Support. Holland: 1944. V. 41

21 Army Group. Some Notes on the Conduct of War and the Infantry Division in Battle. Belgium: 1944. V. 41

MONTGOMERY; or *The West Indian Adventurer.* Kingston: 1812, 1813. V. 40; 42

MONTGOMERY, ROBERT

The Omnipresence of the Deity. London: 1828. V. 43

The Sacred Annual: Being the Messiah, a Poem. London: 1834. V. 38; 39; 45

MONTGOMERY, ROBERT BRUCE

The Long Divorce. New York: 1951. V. 38

MONTGOMERY, RUTHERFORD G.

High Country. New York: 1938. V. 44

MONTGOMERY, W. F.

An Exposition of the Signs and Symptoms of Pregnancy. Philadelphia: 1857. V. 40; 41

MONTGOMERY, ZACHARY

The Poison and Fountain, or, Anti-Parental Education, Essays and Discussions on the School Question. San Francisco: 1878. V. 38

MONTHAN, D.

R. C. Gorman: the Lithographs. Flagstaff: 1978. V. 46

MONTHAN, GUY

Art and Indian Individualists; the Art of Seventeen Contemporary Southwestern Artists and Craftsmen. Flagstaff: 1975. V. 45; 46

THE MONTHS Of the Year. New York: 1924. V. 39

A MONTH'S Vacation Being an Account of the Manner in Which a Juvenile Party Passed Their Time in Baker Street . . . London: 1825. V. 46

MONTI, PHILIPPO MARIO

Elogia . . . Illustrium Pontificatu Alexandri III ad Benedictum XIII. Eorum Imaginibus Quae in Pinacotheca Philippi Cardinalis de Montibus Spectantur. Rome: 1751. V. 38

MONTIGNY, FRANCOIS DE

Relation de la Mission du Missisip (sic) du Seminaire de Quebec, en 1700. Nouvelle York: 1861. V. 39

MONTJOSIEU, LOUIS DE 16th century

Gallus Romae Hospes, Ubi Multa Antiquorum Monimenta Explicantur . . . Rome: 1585. V. 40; 44

MONTLEZUN, BARON DE

Voyage Fait Dans les Annees 1816 et 1817, De New Yorck a La Nouvelle-Orleans, et de L'Orenoque au Mississippi . . . Paris: 1818. V. 38; 45; 46

MONTOLIEU, ISABELLE POLIER, BARONNE DE 1751-1832

Caroline of Lichtfield. London: 1786. V. 38; 41

MONTORGUEIL, GEORGE

Blanc et Rouge Rose et Noir, Bleu, Blanc Rose. Paris: 1930/31/32. V. 45

MONTORGUEIL, GEORGES

Les Chants Nationaux de Tous les Pays. Paris: 1901. V. 42

MONTOYA, JUAN DE

New Mexico in 1602 . . . Relataion of the Discovery of New Mexico. Albuquerque: 1938. V. 37; 38; 42

MONTREAL AMATEUR ATHLETIC ASSOCIATION

M.A.A.A. Souvenir - of New Club House 1905. Montreal: 1905. V. 45

MONTREAL & BOSTON AIR LINE AND PASSUMPSIC RAILROAD

Grand Excursion Tours - 1879. N.P.: 1879. V. 45

MONTREAL & NEW YORK RAILROAD CO.

Report of the Directors of the Montreal & New York Railroad Company to the Proprietors. Montreal: 1853. V. 45

MONTREAL. BOARD OF TRADE

Illustrated Edition of Montreal: The Splendour of Its Location, the Grandeur of Its Scenery, The Stability of Its Buildings, Its Great Harbour . . . Montreal: 1909. V. 45

MONTREAL GENERAL HOSPITAL

Montreal General Hospital Reports: Clinical and Pathological by the Medical Staff. Volume I. Montreal: 1880. V. 42

MONTREAL NATURAL HISTORY SOCIETY

Consitution and By-Laws of the . . . with the Amending Act, 20th Vict. Ch. 118. Montreal: 1859. V. 46

MONTREAL NORTHERN COLONIZATION RAILWAY CO.

The 'Times' and Its Corresponents on Canadian Railways. London: 1875. V. 45

MONTRESOR, CLAUDE BOURDEILLE, COMTE DE

Memoires. Leyden: 1665-67. V. 37

MONTUCCI, ANTONIO

The Amusing Instructor; or, a Key to the Italian Classics . . . London: 1793. V. 41

MONTUFAR Y CORONADO, MANUEL

Memorias Para la Historia de la Revolucion de Centro-America, por un Guatemalteco. Jalapa: 1832. V. 38

MONTULE, EDOUARD DE

A Voyage to North America and the West Indies in 1817. London: 1821. V. 38; 39; 40; 41; 44; 45; 46

A MONUMENT, Dedicated to Posterity in Commemoration of ye Incredible Folly Transacted in the Year 1720. London: 1764. V. 45

MONUMENTA Historica Britannica, or Materials for the History of Britain, from the Earliest Period to the End of the Reign of King Henry VII. London: 1848. V. 41

MONUMENTA Ordinis Minorum. Salamanca: 1511. V. 42

MONUMENTS of Washington's Patriotism. Washington: 1838. V. 40

MONYPENNY, WILLIAM FLAVELLE 1866-1912

The Life of Benjamin Disraeli Earl of Beaconsfield. London: 1910-20. V. 38

The Life of Benjamin Disraeli, Earl of Beaconsfield. New York: 1910-20. V. 38; 42

MONZA, ANTONIO MARIA

La Medicina Difesa. Ragionamento Accademico. Crema: 1655. V. 37

MONZA, LOUIS

Graphic Works of Louis Monza. 1973. V. 40

MOODEY, SAMUEL

Judas the Traitor Hung Up in Chains, to Give Warning to Professors. New Haven: 1761. V. 43

MOODIE, JOHN WEDDERBURN 1797-1869

Ten Years in South Africa: Including a Particular Description of the Wild Sports of that Country. London: 1835. V. 37

MOODIE, JOHN WEDDERBURN DUNBAR

Scenes and Adventures, as a Soldier and Settler, During Half a Century. Montreal: 1866. V. 39

MOODIE, SUSANNA

Roughing It in the Bush; or, Life in Canada. New York: 1852. V. 37; 42

Roughing It in the Bush; or, Life in Canada. London: 1852. V. 37

MOODIE, WILLIAM

Old English, Scotch and Irish Songs, with Music. Edited by William Moodie. New York: 1900. V. 37

MOODY, CHRISTOPHER LAKE

A Sketch of Modern France. London: 1798. V. 46

MOODY, DWIGHT L.

The North-Western Hymn Book. A Collection Adapted to Church, Sunday School and Revival Services. Chicago: 1868. V. 37

MOODY, LORING

Facts for the People, Showing the Relations of the U.S. Government to Slavery: Embracing a History of the Mexican War. Boston: 1847. V. 37; 39; 42

Facts for the People, or a History of the Mexican War, Showing the Relation of the U.S. Government to Slavery. Boston: 1848. V. 37; 38; 39

MOODY, T. W.

The Londonderry Plantation, 1609-1641. Belfast: 1939. V. 43

MOODY, WILLIAM VAUGHAN

The Masque of Judgment. Boston: 1900. V. 40; 43

MOON, A. M.

A Family Memorial. London: 1872. V. 42

MOON, ALEXANDER

A Catalogue of the Indegenous and Exotic Plants Growing in Ceylon . . . with a Sketch of the Divisions of Genera and Species in Use Amongst the Singhalese. Colombo: 1824. V. 43

MOON, GEORGE WASHINGTON

The Oldest Type-Printed Book in Existence . . . London: 1901. V. 42

MOON, R. C.

The Morris Family of Philadelphia, Descendants of Anthony Morris 1654-1721. 1908-09. V. 46

MOON, WILLIAM

Light for the Blind: a History of the Origin and Success of Moon's System of Reading . . . London: 1875. V. 42

MOON, WILLIAM LEAST HEAT

Blue Highways - a Journey Into America. 1982. V. 46

Blue Highways. Boston: 1983. V. 46

MOONSHINE, MAURITIUS, PSEUD.

The Battle of the Bards. London: 1800. V. 45

MOOR, EDWARD

Oriental Fragments. London: 1834. V. 43

MOOR, JOHN HENRY

Notices of the Indian Archipelago, and Adjacent Countries . . . Singapore: 1837. V. 43; 46

MOOR, RICHARD

Accurate and Compendious Tables of Interest . . . London: 1751. V. 38

MOORAT, JOSEPH

Thirty Old Time Nursery Songs. London. V. 42

MOORAT, S. A.

Catalogue of Western Manuscripts on Medicine and Science in the Wellcome Historical Medical Library. London: 1962. V. 42

MOORCOCK, MICHAEL

The Land Leviathon. London: 1974. V. 40

MOORE, A. W.

The Alps in 1864. A Private Journal . . . London: 1867. V. 40

The Alps in 1864. Edinburgh: 1902. V. 43

A History of the Isle of man. London: 1900. V. 37; 44

Manx Names. The Surnmes and Place Names of the Isle of man. London: 1903. V. 38

MOORE, ADA SMALL

A Study of Chinese Paintings in the Collection of Ada Small Moore. London: 1940. V. 42

MOORE, ALAN

Sailing Ships of War 1800-1860 Including Transition to Steam. London: 1926. V. 37; 42; 45

Sailing Ships of War, 1800-1860 . . . London: and New York: 1926. V. 46

MOORE, ALBERT B.

History of Alabama and Her People. Chicago: 1927. V. 42

MOORE, ANNE CARROLL

A Century of Kate Greenaway. New York & London: 1946. V. 43

MOORE, ARTHUR

The Knight Punctilious. London: 1903. V. 46

MOORE, BENJAMIN, & CO.

Practical Suggestions for Interior and Exterior Decoration. New York: 1930. V. 41

MOORE, BRIAN

The Executioners. Toronto: 1951. V. 43

The Feast of Lupercal. Boston & Toronto: 1957. V. 42

The Feast of Lupercal. London: 1958. V. 40

Intent to Kill. London: 1956. V. 44; 46

Judith Hearne. London: 1955. V. 44

Lies of Silence. London: 1990. V. 44

The Lonely Passion of Judith Hearne. Boston: 1955. V. 41

The Luck of Ginger Coffey. London: 1960. V. 44

The Mangan Inheritance. London: 1979. V. 41; 42; 45; 46

Murder in Majorca. London: 1958. V. 44

Sailor's Leave. New York: 1953. V. 43

Two Stories. 1978. V. 41; 42; 45

MOORE, C. L.

Shambleau. New York: 1953. V. 43; 46

MOORE, CAROLINE T.

Abstracts of the Wills of the State of South Carolina, 1670-1784. Columbia: 1960-69. V. 40; 42

MOORE, CHARLES 1743-1811

A Full Inqiury Into the Subject of Suicide. London: 1790. V. 40; 45

The Improvement of the Park System of the District of Columbia. Washington: 1902. V. 38

Plan of Chicago Prepared Under the Direction of the Commercial Club During the Years 1906-08 . . . Chicago: 1909. V. 44

MOORE, CLARA SOPHIA

Social Ethics and Society Duties, Thorough Education of Girls for Wives and Mothers for Professions. Boston: 1892. V. 37

MOORE, CLARENCE B.

Antiquities of the Ouachita Valley. Philadelphia: 1909. V. 42

Certain Aboriginal Mounds of the Coast of South Carolina. Philadelphia: 1898. V. 42

Certain Aboriginal Remains of the Northwest Florida Coast. Part I (and) Certain Aboriginal Remains of the Tombigbee River. Philadelphia: 1901. V. 42

Certain Aboriginal Remains of the Northwest Florida Coast. Philadlephia: 1901-02. V. 37; 42

Certain Mounds of Arkansas and of Mississippi. Philadelphia: 1908. V. 39; 42

The Northwestern Florida Coast Revisited. Philadelphia: 1918. V. 44

Some Aboriginal Sites in Louisiana and in Arkansas. Philadelphia: 1913. V. 42

MOORE, CLEMENT C.

Account of a Visit from St. Nicholas. Pasadena: 1962. V. 41

The Night Before Christmas. New York: 1928. V. 46

The Night Before Christmas. London: 1931. V. 40; 41

The Night Before Christmas. Philadelphia: 1931. V. 40

The Night Before Christmas. Philadelphia: 1942. V. 40; 42

The Night Before Christmas. London: (1931). V. 37

The Night Before Christmas. A Visit from St. Nicholas, by Clement C. Moore. Illustrated by Winfield Nash. Chicago: (1940). V. 37

Observations Upon Certain Passages in Mr. Jefferson's Notes on Virginia, Which Appear to Have a Tendency to Subvert Religion and Establish a False Philosophy. New York: 1804. V. 40; 44; 45

A Plain Statement, Addressed to the Proprietors of Real Estate, in the City and County of New York. New York: 1818. V. 45

Poems. New York: 1844. V. 37; 42; 44

A Sketch of Our Political Condition Addressed to the Citizens of the United States, Without Distinction of Party. New York: 1813. V. 45

A Visit from St. Nicholas. Windham: 1937. V. 46

MOORE, CORNELIUS

The Craftsman, and Freemason's Guide. Cincinnati: 1846. V. 43

MOORE, DAVID

Concise Notices of the Indigenous Grasses of Ireland. Glasnevin: 1843. V. 38

MOORE, DECIMA

We Two in West Africa. New York: 1909. V. 39

MOORE, E. HAMILTON

Fifteen Roes, Being Our Lady's Rosary in Verse. Oxford: 1926. V. 38

MOORE, EDWARD

Fables for the Female Sex. London: 1766. V. 43
Fables for the Female Sex. London: 1771. V. 37; 41; 42
The Foundling. London: 1748. V. 46
Poems, Fables and Plays. London: 1756. V. 37; 38
Studies in Dante. First to Fourth Series. Oxford: 1968-69. V. 44
The World for the Year 1753-1756. London: 1753-56. V. 45

MOORE, EDWARD A.

The Story of a Cannoneer Under Stonewall Jackson. Lynchburg: 1910. V. 42; 43; 44
The Story of a Connoneer Under Stonewall Jackson. New York/Washington: 1907. V. 37

MOORE, EDWARD CROZIER SIBBALD

Sanitary Engineering . . . London: 1898. V. 42

MOORE, EDWARD MARTIN

The Spoil of the North Wind. Chicago: 1900. V. 41

MOORE, EDWIN

Elementary Drawing Book. York: 1840. V. 43

MOORE, F.

The Lepidoptera of Ceylon. London: 1880-87. V. 43

MOORE, FRANCES

Historical Life of Joanna of Sicily Queen of Naples and Countess of Provence. London: 1824. V. 37

MOORE, FRANCIS

The History of Lady Julia Mandeville. London: 1763. V. 40
Map and Description of Texas, Containing Its History, Geology, Geography and Statistics. Philadelphia: 1840. V. 39; 42
Map and Description of Texas . . . Philadelphia & New York: 1840. V. 39
Travels into the Inland Parts of Africa . . . London: 1738. V. 45

MOORE, FRANK

Diary of the American Revolution. New York: 1859-1860. V. 39
Diary of the American Revolution. New York: 1865. V. 40
Rebel Rhymes and Rhapsodies Collected and Edited By . . . New York: 1864. V. 42
The Rebellion Record. New York: 1861-64. V. 38; 46
The Rebellion Record: a Diary of American Events . . . New York: 1861-68. V. 42
Rebellion Record: a Diary of American Events, with Documents, Narratives, Illustrative Incidents, Poetry, Etc. New York: 1862-71. V. 38

MOORE, FREDERICK H.

Mistress Haselwode, a Tale of the Reformation Oak. London: 1876. V. 46

MOORE, GEORGE 1852-1933

Abel Allnutt. London: 1837. V. 46
An Anthology of Pure Poetry. New York: 1924. V. 39
Aphrodite in Aulis. London: 1930. V. 41; 43; 46
Apostle. London: 1923. V. 46
Avowals. London: 1919. V. 46
The Brook Kerith. Edinburgh: 1916. V. 40
The Brook Kerith. London: 1929. V. 37; 39; 40; 42; 43; 44; 46
The Brook Kerith. New York: 1929. V. 38; 40; 46
The Collected Works. New York: 1922-24. V. 37; 38; 42; 44
The Coming of Gabrielle. London: 1920. V. 44; 45
Confessions of a Young Man. London: 1888. V. 41
Confessions of a Young Man. London: 1917. V. 38
Conversations in Ebury Street. London: 1924. V. 46
Esther Waters, a Novel. London: 1894. V. 38; 40; 46
Esther Waters. Chicago: 1899. V. 41
Evelyn Innes. London: 1898. V. 40; 42
Hail and Farewell! I. Ave. II. Salve. III. Vale. London: 1911/12/14. V. 41
Heloise and Abelard. 1920-21. V. 46
Heloise and Abelard. London: 1921. V. 40
Impressions and Opinions. London: 1891. V. 41; 42
In Single Strictness. London: 1922. V. 39
Literature at Nurse, or Circulating Morals. London: 1885. V. 38
Martin Luther: A Tragedy in Five Acts. London: 1879. V. 41
Memoirs of My Dead Life. London: 1906. V. 42; 44

Memoirs of My Dead Life. London: 1921. V. 46
A Modern Lover. London: 1883. V. 40
Pagan Poems. London: 1881. V. 41
The Passing of the Essenes. London: 1930. V. 43; 44; 46
Peronnik the Fool. London: 1933. V. 37; 39; 40; 41; 42; 43; 44; 45; 46
Peronnik the Fool, by George Moore. Eure, France: 1928. V. 37
Reminiscences of the Impressionist Painters. Dublin: 1906. V. 38
Sister Teresa. London: 1901. V. 42; 45; 46
Spring Days. London: 1888. V. 41; 46
Tales of the Passions; in Which is Attempted an Illustration of Their Effects on the Human Mind. London: 1808-11. V. 38
The Talking Pine. Paris: 1931. V. 37; 38; 39; 45
Ulick and Soracha. London: 1926. V. 37; 39; 46
The Untilled Field. Philadelphia: 1903. V. 46
The Use of the Body in Relation to the Mind. London: 1846. V. 38

MOORE, GEORGE AUGUSTUS

Memoirs of My Dead Life . . . London: 1906. V. 42
Memoirs of My Dead Life. London: 1908. V. 42

MOORE, GEORGE EDWARD

Principia Ethica. 1903. V. 43; 45
Principia Ethica. Cambridge: 1903. V. 37; 38; 39; 41; 44
Principia Ethica. Cambridge: 1922. V. 45

MOORE, GEORGE FLETCHER

Extracts from the Letters and Journals of . . . London: 1834. V. 46

MOORE, GEORGE H.

Historical Notes on the Employment of Negroes in the American Army of the Revolution. New York: 1862. V. 42
The Treason of Charles Lee, Major General, Second in Command in the American Army of the Revolution. New York: 1860. V. 42
Washington as an Angler. New York: 1887. V. 39; 44; 45; 46

MOORE, H. JUDGE

Scott's Campaign in Mexico . . . Charleston: 1849. V. 37; 39; 42; 46

MOORE, HARRY THORNTON

John Steinbeck and His Novels. London: 1939. V. 39

MOORE, HENRY 1732-1802

Poems Lyrical and Miscellaneous. London: 1803. V. 39; 40; 42

MOORE, HENRY, Drawing Master

Picturesque Excursions from Derby to Matlock Bath, and Its Vicinity . . . Derby: 1818. V. 39; 44
Picturesque Excursions in the High Peak of derbyshire. Derby: 1819. V. 39; 44

MOORE, HENRY SPENCER 1898-

As the Eye Moves . . . :a Sculpture by Henry Moore. New York: 1973. V. 41
Heads, Figures and Ideas. London: 1958. V. 41; 45
Henry Moore. New York: 1968. V. 37; 38; 44
Henry Moore's Sheep Sketchbook. London: 1980. V. 42
Henry Moore at the British Museum. New York: 1982. V. 43
Moore Lithographs. London: 1974. V. 37; 40
Sculpture and Drawings. London: 1944. V. 44
Shelter Sketch Book. London: V. 38
Shelter Sketch Book. London: 1940. V. 39; 41; 43
Shelter-Sketch-Book. Berlin: 1967. V. 37; 40

MOORE, HUGH 1808-1834

Memoir of Co. Ethan Allen; Containing the most Interesting Incidents Connected with his Private and Public Career. Plattsburgh, New York: 1834. V. 37
Memoir of Col. Ethan Allen . . . New York: 1834. V. 44
Memoir of Col. Ethan Allen . . . Plattsburgh: 1834. V. 40

MOORE, ISABELLA

The Useful and Entertaining Family Miscellany. London: 1766. V. 42

MOORE, J. A.

Physiology of the Amphibia. London: 1964-76. V. 37

MOORE, J. G.

Patent Office and Patent Laws; or, a Guide to Inventors and a Book of Reference fro Judges, Lawyers, Magistrates and Others . . . Philadelphia: 1855. V. 43

MOORE, J. H.

The Political Condition of the Indians and the Resources of the Indian Territory. St. Louis: 1874. V. 37; 42; 46

MOORE, J. HAMILTON

The Gentleman and Lady's Minitor and English Teacher's Assistant . . . London: 1791. V. 38

Young Gentleman and Lady's Monitor, and English Teacher's Assistant . . . New York: 1792. V. 46

MOORE, J. STAUNTON

Annals of Henrico Parish by Rt. Rev. L. W. Burton . . . History of St. John's P.E. Church, Together with . . . the Bishops of Virginia . . . A Complete Roster of Vestries from 1741 to 1904 . . . Richmond: 1904. V. 39; 42

MOORE, JAMES

The History and Practice of Vaccination. London: 1817. V. 44

Twenty-Five Views in the Southern Part of Scotland. London: 1794. V. 37; 39

MOORE, JOHN

A Checklist of the Writings of Daniel Defoe. Bloomington: 1960. V. 44

A Congratulatory Poem on the Wonderful Atchievments (sic) of Sir John Mandevil, &c. London: 1683. V. 37; 38; 41; 43; 44

England's Interest: or, The Gentleman and Farmer's Friend (with) The Angler's Guide. London: 1721. V. 39

The Fleet Air Arm - A Short Account of Its History and Achievements. London: 1943. V. 38

An Inaugural Dissertation on Digitalis Purpurea, or Fox-Glove; and Its Use in Some Diseases: Submitted to the Examination of the Rev. John Ewing, S.T.P. Provost. Philadelphia: 1800. V. 37

A Journal During a Residence in France, from the Beginning of August to the Middle of September 1792 . . . Dublin: 1793. V. 38; 40

A Journal During a Residence in France from the Beginning of August to the Middle of December, 1792. London: 1793. V. 37; 38; 39; 41; 43; 44

A Journal During a Residence in France, from the Beginning of August to the Middle of December, 1792 . . . Chambersburg; &: 1797, 1794. V. 40

Medical Sketches, in Two Parts. Providence: 1794. V. 38; 40; 43; 44

Mordaunt. Sketches of Life, Character and Manners . . . London: 1800. V. 39; 42; 45

Various Views of Human Nature, Taken from Life and Manners, Chiefly in England by the Author of Zeluco. London: 1796. V. 37; 38; 39; 40; 42; 46

Various Views of Human Nature, Taken from Life and Manners, Chiefly in England. London: 1796. V. 37; 38; 39; 42

Various Views of Human Nature, Taken from Life and Manners, Chiefly in England. New York: 1798. V. 40

A View of Society and Manners in France, Switzerland and Germany. London: 1779. V. 46

A View of Society and Manners in France, Switzerland, and Germany; with Anecdotes Relating to Some Eminent Characters. London: 1780. V. 40

A View of Society and Manners in France, Switzerland and Germany. Dublin: 1781. V. 45

A View of Society and Manners in Italy, with Anecdotes Relating to Some Eminent Characters. London: 1781. V. 37; 39; 42; 45; 46

A View of Society and Manners in France, Switzerland, and Germany. London: 1783. V. 43

A View of Society and Manners in France, Switzerland and Germany. London: 1786. V. 40; 41; 43

A View of Society and Manners in Italy . . . London: 1790. V. 45

View of Society and Manners in France, Switzerland and Germany . . . Boston: 1792. V. 38; 44

A View of Society and Manners in Italy. Boston: 1792. V. 46

A View of Society and Manners in Italy, with Anecdotes . . . Boston: (England): 1792. V. 43

A View of the Causes and Progress of the French Revolution. London: 1795. V. 43

A View of the Society and Manners in Italy. London: 1783. V. 39

A View of Society and Manners in France, Switzerland and Germany. London: 1789. V. 39

Zeluco. Dublin: 1789. V. 40

Zeluco. London: 1789. V. 37; 40

MOORE, JOHN BASSETT

Four Phases of American Development. Baltimore: 1912. V. 45; 46

History and Digest of the International Arbitrations to Which the United States Has Been a Party, Together With Appendices . . . Washington: 1898. V. 42

MOORE, JOHN CARRICK 1763-1834

The Life of Lieutenant-General Sir Joh Moore. London: 1833. V. 40

The Life of Lieutenant General Sir John Moore, by His Brother. London: 1834. V. 41; 45; 46

A Narrative of the Campaign of the British Army in Spain . . . London: 1809. V. 42

A Narrative of the Campaign of the British Army in Spain, Commanded by His Excellency Lieut. General John Moore K.B. & c. London: 1809. V. 42; 46

MOORE, JOHN HAMILTON

A New and Complete Collection of the Voyages and Travels, Including Those of Byron, Wallis, Furneaux, Cook, Parkinson, Forster, Bouganville . . . London: 1778. V. 39; 41

The New Practical Navigator. Newburyport: 1800. V. 41; 42

The New Practical Navigator; Being an Epitome of Navigation . . . Twelfth Edition. London: 1796. V. 39

The Seaman's Complete Daily Assistant, and New Mariner's Compass. London: 1792. V. 45

MOORE, JOHN M.

Instructions to the Surveyor General of Oregon . . . Washington: 1851. V. 41

MOORE, JOHN W.

Roster of North Carolina Troops in the War Between the States. Raleigh: 1882. V. 38

MOORE, JONAS 1617-1679

Modern Fortification. London: 1673. V. 38

MOORE, JOSEPH WEST

Picturesque Washington: Pen and Pencil Sketches of Its Scenery, History, Traditions, Public and Social Life. Providence: 1884. V. 40

MOORE, JULIA A.

The Sentimental Song Book. Grand Rapids: 1876. V. 40; 42; 45

MOORE, M. B.

The Dixie Speller to Follow the First Dixie Reader. Raleigh: 1864. V. 40

The First Dixie Reader Designed to follow the Dixie Primer. Raleigh: 1863. V. 40

MOORE, MARIANNE 1887-1972

The Absentee. New York: 1952. V. 39

The Absentee. New York: 1962. V. 38; 40; 42

Collected Poems. New York: 1951. V. 38; 39

Collected Poems. New York: 1953. V. 41

The Complete Poems of Marianne Moore. New York: 1967. V. 46

Eight Poems. New York: 1962. V. 43; 46

Eight Poems. New York: 1963. V. 39

Letters From and to the Ford Motor Company. New York: 1958. V. 38

Like a Bulwark. New York: 1956. V. 41; 44; 45

like a Bulwark. London: 1957. V. 39; 42

A Marianne Moore Reader. New York: 1961. V. 39; 42

Marriage. New York: 1923. V. 38; 42

Marriage. (New York: 1923). V. 37

Nevertheless. New York: (1944). V. 37

O To Be a Dragon. New York: 1959. V. 41; 42; 44; 46

Occasionem Cognesce. 1963. V. 39

Occasionem Cognosce. Cambridge: 1963. V. 40; 41; 42

Occasionem Cognosce. Lunenberg: 1963. V. 40

The Pangolin & Other Verses. London: 1936. V. 37; 41; 42; 44; 45; 46

Poems. London: 1921. V. 37; 38; 39; 40; 41; 42; 44; 45

Predilections. New York: 1955. V. 41; 42; 45; 46

Selected Poems. London: 1935. V. 37; 42

Selected Poems. New York: 1935. V. 39

Selected Poems . . . With an Introduction by T.S. Eliot. London: (1935). V. 37

Tell Me, Tell Me, Granite, Steel and Other Topics. New York: 1966. V. 41; 42

Tipoo's Tiger. New York: 1967. V. 46

What Are Years. New York: 1941. V. 37; 42; 46

William Keinbush. New York: 1963. V. 39

MOORE, MARINDA BRANSON

The Dixie Speller. Raleigh, NC: 1864. V. 37

The Geographical Reader for the Dixie Children. Raleigh: 1863. V. 37; 38; 40

Primary Geography, Arranged as a Reading Book, with Questions and Answers Attached. Raleigh: 1864. V. 38

MOORE, MARTIN

Memoirs of the Life and Character of Rev. John Eliot, Apostle to the N.A. Indians. Boston: 1822. V. 38

MOORE, MERRILL

Cross Currents - a Selection of Sonnets 1903-1957. Christchurch: 1961. V. 38

Illegitimate Sonnets. New York: 1950. V. 37; 39; 46

A Miscellany. First Series. I-X. Boston: 1939. V. 46

More Clinical Sonnets. New York: 1953. V. 39

Six Sides to a Man. New York: 1935. V. 41; 42; 43; 44; 46

MOOREHEAD, WARREN K. continued

The Stone Age in North American. Boston: 1910. V. 38

The Stone Age in North America. Boston & New York: 1910. V. 44

The Stone Age in North America. New York: 1910. V. 39

Stone Ornaments Used by Indians. Andover: 1917. V. 40; 42; 44; 45

The Stone Age in North America. Sullivan: 1987. V. 39

MOORES, I. R.

Statement of Facts Relative to the Incorporation and Organization of the Oregon Central Railroad Co. of Salem Oregon. Portland: 1868. V. 42

MOOREY, P. R. S.

Catalogue of the Ancient Persian Bronzes in the Ashmolean Museum. Oxford: 1971. V. 40; 42

Kish Excavations 1923-1933 . . . Oxford: 1978. V. 44

MOORHOUSE, EDWARD

The History and Romance of the Derby. London: 1911. V. 43

The Romance of Derby. London: 1908. V. 39; 42; 46

MOORHOUSE, MAJOR LEE

Souvenir Album of Noted Indians Photographed by . . . Pendleton: 1906. V. 37

MOORMAN, F. W.

The Place-Names of the West Riding of Yorkshire. Leeds: 1910. V. 45

MOORSOM, W. S.

Historical Record of the Fifty-Second Regiment (Oxfordshire Light Infantry) from the Year 1755 to the year 1858. London: 1860. V. 37; 44

MOOSO, JOSIAH

The Life and Travels of Josiah Mooso. Winfield: 1888. V. 37; 42

MOOTZ, HERMAN E.

'Pawnee Bill' a Romance of Oklahoma. Los Angeles: 1928. V. 46

MORABIN, JACQUES 1687-1762

The History of Cicero's Banishment. London: 1725. V. 38

MORAGNE, MARY ELIZABETH

The British Partizan: a Tale of the Olden Time. Macon: 1864. V. 44

MORAIS, HENRY S.

The Jews of Philadelphia. Philadelphia: 1894. V. 41; 42

MORAL and Instructive Tales for the Improvement of Young Ladies; calculated to amuse the mind, and form the heart to virtue. London: (1786). V. 37

MORAL and Instructive Tales for the Improvement of Young Ladies; Calculated to Amuse the Mind, and to Form the Heart of Virtue. London: 1786. V. 41; 45

MORAL Essays, Chiefly Collected from Different Authors. Liverpool: 1796. V. 42

THE MORAL Miscellany: or, a Collection of Select Pieces, in Prose and Verse, for the Instruction and Entertainment of Youth. London: 1765. V. 37

THE MORAL Statistics of Glasgow in 1863, Practically Applied. Glasgow: 1864. V. 42

MORAN, JAMES

The Double Crown Club. London: 1974. V. 41

Heraldic Influence on Early Printers' Devices. Leeds: 1978. V. 44

Printing Presses. History and Development from the Fifteenth Century to the Modern Times. Berkeley: 1973. V. 45

Printing Presses. History and Development from the Fifteenth Century to Modern Times. Berkeley & Los Angeles: 1973. V. 39

Printing Presses. London: 1973. V. 41; 43

MORAN, PATRICK

Spicilegium Ossoriense. Dublin: 1874. V. 46

MORAN, PATRICK FRANCIS

The Pastoral Letters and Other Writings of Cardinal Cullen, Archbisiohp of Dublin. Dublin: 1882. V. 39

MORAND, P.

Ferme la Nuit. Paris: 1925. V. 38

MORAND, PAUL

Open All Night. London: 1923. V. 42

Rues et Visages de New-York de Chas. Laborde. Paris: 1950. V. 41

MORANDI, MORANDO 1693-1756

Della Cura Preservativa della Rabbia Canina . . . Ancona: 1755. V. 42

MORANDO, BERNARDO

La Rosalinda. Libri Diece. Venice: 1680. V. 37

MORANT, PHILIP

The History and Antiquities of the County of Essex. London: 1768. V. 39; 44; 46

The History and Antiquities of the County of Essex. London: 1978. V. 42

MORANY, PHILIPPE

A Woorke Concerning the Trewness of the Christian Religion, Written in French Against Atheists, Epicures . . . London: 1587. V. 37

MORASSI, ANTONIO

A Complete Catalogue of the paintings of G.B. Tiepolo Including Pictures by His Pupils and Followers Wrongly Attraituted to Him. London: 1962. V. 37

Guardi: I Dipiniti. Venice: 1984. V. 45

MORAVIAN CHURCH. LITURGY & RITUAL

Liturgy and Hymns for the Use of the Protestant Church of the United Bretheran or Unitas Fratrum. Bethelehem: 1853. V. 39; 41

MORDECAI, ALFRED

Report of the Experiments on Gunpowder Made At Washington Arsenal in 1843 and 1844. Washington: 1845. V. 40

MORDECAI, SAMUEL

Richmond in By-Gone Days. Richmond: 1856. V. 41

MORDEN, ROBERT

Geography Rectified; or, a Description of the World. London: 1680. V. 39

MORE, ALEXANDER GOODMAN

Life and Letters of Alexander Goodman More. Dublin: 1898. V. 39; 42; 43

MORE, FRANK FRANKFORT

One Fair Daughter: Her Story. London: 1894. V. 46

MORE, HANNAH 1745-1833

Bible Rhymes, on the names of all the books of the Old and New Testament: With allusions to some of the principal incidents and characters. London: 1821. V. 37

Bishop Bonner's Ghost. Strawberry Hill: 1789. V. 41; 45

Christian Morals. London: 1813. V. 42

Coelebs in Search of a Wife. London: 1808. V. 38

Coelebs in Search of a Wife. London: 1809. V. 44

A Country Carpenter's Confession of Faith . . . London: 1794. V. 43

Essays on Various Subjects. London: 1777. V. 37; 39; 41; 43; 45

Essays On Various Subjects Principally Designed for Young Ladies. London: 1778. V. 42; 46

Essays on Various Subjects, Principally Designed for Young Ladies. Chambersburg: 1796. V. 45

Florio; a Tale, for Fine Gentlemen and Fine Ladies. London: 1786. V. 37; 40; 42

Florio: A Tale for Fine Gentlmen & Ladies: and The Bas Bleu; or Conversation. (bound with) Sir Eldred of the Bower & The Bleeding Rock. (bound with) Ode to Dragon.. London: 1787, 1777. V. 38

Hints Towards Forming the Character of a Young Princess. London: 1805. V. 39; 40; 43; 45; 46

Moral Sketches of Prevailing Opinions & Manners, Foreign and Domestic: With Reflections on Prayer. London: 1819. V. 38

Ode to Dragon, Mr. Garrick's House-Dog, at Hampton. London: 1777. V. 37

The Pilgrims. Philadelphia: 1807. V. 42

Poems. London: 1816. V. 38

The Riot: or Half a Loaf is Better than no Bread. 1794. V. 42

Sacred Dramas: Chiefly Intended for Young Persons. London: 1782. V. 40

Sacred Dramas. London: 1818. V. 46

Sacred Dramas: the Searh after Happiness and Other Poems. London: 1825. V. 39

The Search after Happiness: a Pastoral Drama. Brisol: 1774. V. 39

Sir Eldred of the Bower, and the Bleeding Rock. London: 1770. V. 39

Sir Eldred of the Bower, and the Bleeding Rock. London: 1776. V. 37; 39; 40; 41; 43; 45; 46

Slavery, a Poem. London: 1788. V. 40; 42

Slavery: a Poem. Philadelphia: 1788. V. 39

Strictures on the Modern System of Female Education. London: 1799. V. 38; 41; 42; 45; 46

Strictures on the Modern System of Female Education with a View of the Principles and Conduct Prevalent Among Women of Rank and Fortune. Charlestown: 1800. V. 42; 44; 45

Strictures on the Modern System of Female Education. Dublin: 1800. V. 42

Strictures on the Modern System of Female Education. Philadelphia: 1800. V. 44

Strictures on the Modern System of Female Education. London: 1826. V. 38; 39

MOREHEID, J. N.

Lives, Adventures, Anecdotes, Amusements and Domestic Habits of the Siamese Twins . . . Raleigh: 1848. V. 45

MOREL, EDMUND D.

The British Case in French Congo. The Story of a Great Injustice, Its Causes and Its Lessons. London: 1903. V. 39

Great Britain and the Congo. London: 1909. V. 42

MOREL-VINDE, VICOMTE DE

Essai sur les Constructions Rurales Economiques . . . Paris: 1824. V. 38

MORELAND, ELEANOR

The Life of . . . in a Letter to Her Niece. Cambridge: 1822. V. 45; 46

MORELAND Vale; or the Fair Fugitive. New York: 1801. V. 43

MORELIET, ABBE ANDRE 1727-1819

Theorie du Paradoxe. Amsterdam: 1775. V. 39

MORELL, CHARLES

The Tales of The Genii: Or, The Delightful Lessons of Horam the Son of Asmar. Translated from the Persian. London: 1805. V. 37

MORELL, J. D.

An Historical and Critical View of the Speculative Philosohy of Europe in the Nineteenth Century. London: 1847. V. 42; 43; 45

An Introduction to Mental Philosophy, on the Inductive Method. London: 1862. V. 42

MORELL, JOHN REYNELL

Algeria: the Topography and History, Political, Social and Natural of French Africa. London: 1854. V. 42; 43; 45

MORELL, THOMAS

Robert Ainsworth's Dictionary, English and Latin. London. V. 40

Robert Ainsworth's Dictionary, English and Latin. London: 1773. V. 40

Thesaurus Graecae Posseos, sive Lexicon Graeco-Prosodiacum. Eton: 1762. V. 45

MORELL, W. W.

The History and Antiquities of Selby, in the West Riding of the County of York. London: 1867. V. 41

The History and Antiquities of Selby, in the West Riding of the County of York. Selby: 1867. V. 39; 44

MORELLI, COSIMO 1731-1812

Pianta, e Spaccato del Nuovo Teatro d'Imola. Rome: 1780. V. 37; 42

MORELLY, ABBE

Code de La Nature, ou Les Veritable Esprit de ses Loix, De Tout Tema Neglige ou Meconnu . . . Amsterdam: 1755. V. 45

MORELY, HENRY

A Defence of Ignorance. London: 1851. V. 41

MORENO-GALAVAN, JOSE MARIA

The Latest Avant Garde. Greenwich. V. 39

MORERI, LOUIS

Le Grand Dictionnaire Historique ou le Melange Curieux de l'Histoire Fabuleuse des Dieux & des Heros de l'Antiquite Paienne . . . Paris: 1759. V. 39

The Great Historical, Geographical and Poetical Dictionary; being a Curious Miscellany of Sacred and Prophane history . . . Collected from the best Historians, Chronologers, and Lexicographers . . . But more especially out of Lewis Morery, D.D . . . London: 1694. V. 37

MORES, EDWARD ROWE

A Dissertation Upon English Typographical Founders and Founderies . . . New York: 1924. V. 44

A Dissertation Upon English Typographical Founders. 1963. V. 40

Nomina et Insignia Gentilicia Nobilium Equitumque Sub Edoardo Prime Rege Militantium. Oxford: 1749. V. 46

MORESBY, JOHN

Discoveries and Surveys in New Guinea and the D'Entrecasteaux Islands. London: 1876. V. 37; 40

New Guinea and Polynesia. London: 1876. V. 46

MORESTEL, PIERRE 1575-1658

Artis Kabbalisticae, Sive Sapientiae Divinae Academia; in Novem Classes Amicissima Cum Brevitate, Tum Claritate Digesta. Paris: 1621. V. 40

MORETON, C. O.

Old Carnations and Pinks . . . London: 1955. V. 38

MORETTI, THOMASO

A General Treatise of Artillery; or, Great Ordnance. London: 1683. V. 46

MORFI, JUAN AUGUSTIN

Excerpts from Memorias for the History of the Province of Texas . . . San Antonio: 1932. V. 42

History of Texas, 1673-1779. Albuquerque: 1935. V. 37; 38; 42

MORFIT, CAMPBELL

The Arts of Tanning, Currying, and Leather Dressing. Philadelphia: 1852. V. 39

MORFIT, HENRY M.

Condition of Texas: The Political, Military and Civil Condition of Texas. Washington: 1836. V. 37; 38; 39; 44; 46

Message From the President of the U.S., Relative to the 'Political, Military, & Civil Condition of Texas.' Washington: 1836. V. 37

MORFORD, HENRY

John Jasper's Secret. Philadelphia: 1871. V. 42

John Jasper's Secret. London: 1872. V. 40; 43

MORGA, ANTONIO DE

History of the Philippine Islands. From Their Discovery by Magellan in 1521 to the XVII Century . . . Cleveland: 1907. V. 41

MORGAGNI, GIOVANNI BATTISTA 1682-1771

Adversaria Anatomica Omnia. Venice: 1762. V. 38

Adversaria Anatomica Omnia . . . together with Opuscula Miscellanea Quorum. Venice: 1762 & 1763. V. 43

Epistolae Anatomicae Duae Novus Observationes & Animadversiones . . . Leyden: 1728. V. 38

The Seats and Causes of Diseases, Investigated by Anatomy. Boston: 1824. V. 46

The Seats and Causes of Diseases Investigated by Anatomy. New York: 1960. V. 38; 39; 40; 41

The Seats and Causes of Diseases. Birmingham: 1983. V. 39

The Seats and Causes of Diseases Investigated by Anatomy. London: 1769. V. 37

De Sedibus, et Causis Morobrum . . . Venice: 1761. V. 37

De Sedibus et Causis Moroborum per ntomen Indagatis. 1779. V. 38

MORGAN, A.

Drawings in the Fogg Museum of Art. Cambride: 1946. V. 46

MORGAN, AL

The Great Man. New York: 1955. V. 45

MORGAN, ALBERT T.

Yazoo; or, On the Picket Line of Freedom in the South. Washington: 1884. V. 39; 42; 44

MORGAN, AUGUSTUS DE

Arithmetical Books from the Invention of Printing to the Present Time. London: 1847. V. 38

The Differential and Integral Calculus. London: 1842. V. 38

MORGAN, BARBARA

Martha Graham. Sixteen Dances in Photographs. New York: 1941. V. 37; 38

MORGAN, CHARLES H.

Corinth. Volume XI: the Byzantine Pottery. Cambridge: 1942. V. 40

MORGAN, CHARLES LANGBRIDGE

The Flashing Stream. London: 1938. V. 46

The Gunroom. London: 1917. V. 41

The Gunroom. London: 1919. V. 39; 42

MORGAN, CONWY LLOYD

An Introduction to Comparative Psychology. London: 1894. V. 37

MORGAN, DALE L.

Jedediah Smith and the Opening of the West. Inianapolis & New York: 1943. V. 42

Jedediah Smith and the Opening of the West. New York: 1953. V. 40; 41; 45

Jedediah Smith and His Maps of the American West. San Francisco: 1954. V. 38; 39; 40; 45; 46

The Overland Diary of James A. Pritchard from Kentucky to California in 1849. Denver: 1959. V. 46

Overland in 1846. Georgetown: 1963. V. 38; 41; 43

The Rocky Mountain Journals of Wm. Marshall Anderson - The West in 1834. San Marino: 1967. V. 37

The West of William Ashley. Denver: 1963. V. 46

The West of William H. Ashley. Denver: 1964. V. 37; 38; 40; 41; 43

MORGAN, DAN J.

Historical Lights and Shadows of the Ohio Penintentiary. Columbus: 1895. V. 45

MORGAN, EMANUEL

A Book of Poetic Experiments. New York: 1916. V. 43

MORGAN, FREDERICK

Eleven Poems. London: 1983. V. 41

MORGAN, GWENDA

The Wood-Engravings of Gwenda Morgan. 1985. V. 44

The Wood-Engravings of Gwenda Morgan. Andoversford: 1985. V. 43

The Wood-engravings of Gwenda Morgan. Gloucestershire: 1985. V. 38

MORGAN, HECTOR DAVIES

The Doctrine and Law of Marriage, Adultery and Divorce. Oxford: 1826. V. 46

MORGAN, HENRY J.

Bibliotheca Canadensis: or a Manual of Canadian Literature. Ottawa: 1867. V. 43; 44

Sketches of Celebrated Canadians, and Persons Connected with Canada, from the Earliest Period to the History of the Province to the Present Time. Quebec: 1862. V. 40; 42; 43; 44

The Tour of H. R. H. The Prince of Wales through British American and the United States by a British Canadian. Montreal: 1860. V. 43

MORGAN, J.

Phoenix Britannicus: Being a Miscellaneous Collection of Scarce and Curious Tracts. London: 1732. V. 38; 42

MORGAN, J. R.

The History of Wichita Falls. Wichita Falls: 1931. V. 37

MORGAN, JAMES MORRIS

Recollections of a Rebel Reefer. Boston: 1917. V. 39; 40; 41; 42; 44

MORGAN, JOHN

A Discourse Upon the Institution of Medical Schools In America, Delivered at a Public Anniversary Commencement, Held in the College of Philadelphia, May 30 and 31, 1765. Philadelphia: 1765. V. 44

Essays Upon I: The Law of Evidence. II: New Trials. III: Special Verdicts. IV: Trials at Bar., and V: Repleaders. Dublin: 1789. V. 38

The Journal of Dr. John Morgan of Philadelphia from the City of Rome to the City of London 1764 . . . Philadelphia: 1907. V. 40; 42; 44; 46

Reminiscences of the Founding of a Christian Mission on the Gambia. London: 1864. V. 39; 45

MORGAN, JOHN HILL

The Life Portraits of Washington and Their Replicas. Philadelphia: 1931. V. 37

MORGAN, JOHN MINTER

The Critics Criticised: with Remarks on a Passage in Dr. Chalmer's Bridgewater Treatise. London: 1834. V. 40

MORGAN, JOHN PIERPONT 1837-1913

Catalogue of Twenty Renaissance Tapestries from the J. Pierpont Morgan Collection. Paris: 1913. V. 39

Pictures in the Collection of J. Pierpont Morgan at Prince's Gate and Dover HOuse, London. London: 1907. V. 40

MORGAN, LEWIS H.

The American Beaver and His Works. Philadelphia: 1868. V. 40

Houses and House Life of the American Aborigines. Washington: 1881. V. 40; 44

League of the Ho-De'-No-Sau-Nee, or Iroquois. Rochester: 1851. V. 45

League of the Ho-De-No Sau-Nee or Iroquois. New York: 1901. V. 45

League of the Ho-De-No-Sau-Nee or Iroquois. New York: 1904. V. 39

Systems of Consanguinity and Affinity of the Human Family. Washington: 1871. V. 38

Systems of Consanguinity and Affinity of the Human Family. 1870. V. 37

MORGAN, LOUISA

Baron Bruno; or, the Unbelieving Philosopher, and Other Fairy Stories. London: 1875. V. 44

MORGAN, MAC NAMARA

The Piscopade: a Panegyri-Satiri-Serio-Comical Poem. London: 1748. V. 46

The Sequel. London: 1745. V. 42

The Triumvirade; or, Broad Bottomry. London: 1743. V. 46

The Triumvirade; or Broad Bottomry. London: 1745. V. 42

MORGAN, MACNAMARA

The Causidicade. London: 1743. V. 40

A Letter to Miss Nossiter, Occasioned by Her First Appearance on the Stage. London: 1753. V. 39

MORGAN, MAURICE

An Essay on the Dramatic Character of Sir John Falstaff. London: 1777. V. 38; 39; 40; 42; 45

MORGAN, MISS

The Gaol of the City of Bristol Compared With What a Gaol Ought to Be. Bristol: 1815. V. 42; 43; 46

MORGAN, OCTAVIUS 1803-1888

Notice of Tessellated Pavement, Discovered in the Churchyard Caerleon (with) Essay on Mazes and Labyrinhts by Edward Trollope. Newport: 1846. V. 38

MORGAN, OLGA

As They Were and As They Should Have Been. London. V. 40

MORGAN, RICHARD P.

Report of the Survey of the Route of the Galena and Chicago Union Railroad . . . Chicago: 1847. V. 37; 42; 45

MORGAN, SYDNEY OWENSON, LADY 1783?-1859

Absenteeism. London: 1825. V. 37; 44

The Book of the Boudoir. London: 1829. V. 37; 41

Florence Macarthy: an Irish Tale. London: 1818. V. 38; 40; 44

Florence Macarthy; an Irish Tale. London: 1818-19. V. 42

Florence McCarthy; an Irish Tale. London: 1819. V. 42

France. London: 1817. V. 41

Irish Tales and Romances. London: 1833. V. 46

L'Italie. Paris: 1821. V. 44

Italy. London: 1821. V. 38

Italy. New York: 1821. V. 46

Lady Morgan's Memoirs. London: 1862. V. 41; 42; 46

Lady Morgan's Memoirs: Autobiography, Diaries and Correspondence. London: 1863. V. 40

The Life and Times of Salvator Rosa. London: 1824. V. 37; 39; 40; 42; 44

A National Tale. London: 1814. V. 41

The Novice of Saint Dominick. London: 1806. V. 40

O'Donnel. London: 1814. V. 38; 43; 45

O'Donnel. London: 1815. V. 38; 44

Patriotic Sketches of Ireland, Written in Connaught. London: 1807. V. 45; 46

The Princess; or the Beguine. Paris: 1833. V. 42

The Princess, or the Beguine. Paris: 1835. V. 39

The Wild Irish Girl. London: 1806. V. 37; 40

The Wild Irish Girl . . . London: 1807. V. 37; 44

Woman and Her Master. London: 1840. V. 37

Woman: or, Ida of Athens. By Miss Owenson. London: 1809. V. 37

MORGAN, SYLVANUS 1620?-1693

The Sphere of Gentry. London: 1661. V. 38; 39; 42

MORGAN, T.

The Mechanical Practice of Physick . . . London: 1735. V. 46

MORGAN, THOMAS

My Story of the Last Indian War in the Northwest. The Bannock, Puite, Yakima and Sheepeater Tribes. Forest Grove: 1954. V. 46

Philosophical Principles of Medicine, in Three Parts. London: 1725. V. 39

Physico-Theology. London: 1741. V. 40

Romano-British Mosaic Pavements. London: 1886. V. 38; 41; 46

MORGAN, THOMAS CHARLES

Sketches of the Philosophy of Life. London: 1819. V. 43

Sketches of the Philosophy of Morals. London: 1822. V. 39; 40; 41; 42; 43

MORGAN, THOMAS HUNT

Heredity and Dex. New York: 1913. V. 40

The Theory of the Gene. New Haven: 1926. V. 45

MORGAN, WILLIAM

The Doctrine of Annuities and Assurances on Lives and Survivorships. London: 1779. V. 41

Facts Addressed to the Serious Attention of the People of Great Britain Respecting the Expence of the War, and the State of the National Debt. London: 1796. V. 37; 39; 41

The Homoeopathic Treatment of Indigestion, Constipation and Haemorrhoids. Philadelphia: 1854. V. 42

Illustrations of Masonry, by One of the Fraternity. New York: 1827. V. 43

A Narrative of the Facts and Circumstances Relating to the Kidnapping and Presumed Murder of William Morgan, and of an Attempt to Carry Off David C. Miller and to Ruin or Destroy the Printing Office of the Latter . . . Batavia: 1827. V. 40; 41; 46

Ogilby's and Morgan's Pocket-Book of the Roads. London: 1732. V. 43

Psalmau Dafydd. Newtown: 1929. V. 46

MORGENSTERN, CHRISTIAN

Gallowsongs. Los Angeles: 1970. V. 38

MORGHEN, FILIPPO

Le Antichita di Pozzuoli, Baja e Cuma . . . Naples: 1769. V. 40

MORGULIS, SERGIUS

Fasting and Undernutrition: A Biological and Sociological Study of Inanitation. New York: 1923. V. 42

MORI, ARINORI

Life and Resources in America. Washington: 1871. V. 45

MORI, GIOVANNI MARIA

Opere . . . all'Illustrissimo Signor Gio. Battista Ravascheri Conte di Lavagna, Signor del Taro, e Baron Della Rocca di Piamonte. Venice: 1649. V. 41

MORIA. For Sale to Actual Settlers. N.P.: 1815. V. 40

MORICAND, CONRAD

Portraits Astrologiques. Paris: 1933. V. 43

MORICE, A. G.

The Carrier Language (Dene Family): a Grammar and Dictionary Combined. Vienna/Winnipeg: 1932. V. 45

The History of the Northern Interior of British Columbia. Toronto: 1904. V. 37; 43

MORICE, JOHN

Catalogue of the Valuable Library of the Late John Morice. London: 1844. V. 44

MORIER, DAVID R.

Photo the Suliote: A Tale of Modern Greece. London: 1857. V. 37

MORIER, JAMES JUSTINIAN 1780?-1849

Abel Allnutt. London: 1834. V. 44

Abel Allnutt. London: 1837. V. 38; 43

The Adventures of Hajji Baba, of Ispahan. London: 1824. V. 38

The Adventures of Haji Baba of Ispahan. London: 1828. V. 38; 39; 40; 41; 43

Ayesha, the Maid of Kars. London: 1834. V. 37; 45

Ayesha, the Maid of Kars. Philadelphia: 1834. V. 45

A Journey through Persia, Armenia and Asia Minor, to Constantinople in 1803-9. London: 1812. V. 41; 44

A Journey Through Persia, Armenia, and Asia Minor, to Constantinople, in the Years 1808 and 1809 . . . (and) A Second Journey . . . Between the Years 1810 and 1816 . . . London: 1812-18. V. 42

The Mirza. London: 1841. V. 39; 41

An Oriental Tale. Brighton: 1839. V. 40; 42; 46

Zohrab the Hostage. London: 1832. V. 43; 45

MORIGI, PAOLO 1525-1604

Histori dell'Origine di Tutte le Religioni. Venice: 1590. V. 41

MORIGIA, PAOLO

Historia dell' Antichita di Milano, Divisa in Quattro Libri. Venice: 1592. V. 38

MORIN, JEAN 1591-1659

Exercitationes Ecclesiasticae in Utrumque Samaritanorum Pentateuchum . . . Paris: 1631. V. 46

MORIN, JEAN BAPTISTE

Ad Australes et Boreales Astrologis; pro Astrologia Restituenda Epistolae. Paris: 1628. V. 40

MORIN, PIERRE

Instructions Facile pour Connoitre Toutes Sortes d'Orangers, et Citronniers. Paris: 1680. V. 45

Nouveau Traite des Oeillets, la Facon la Plus Utile et Facile de les Bien Cultiver . . . Paris: 1676. V. 38

MORING, THOMAS

50 Book Plates Engraved on Copper. London: 1901. V. 41

One Hundred Book Plates, Engraved on Wood. London: 1900. V. 38; 40; 42

MORISON, ALEXANDER

Outlines of Lectures on Mental Diseases. London: 1826. V. 46

MORISON, DOUGLAS

Views of Haddon Hall. London: 1842. V. 42

MORISON, GEORGE ERNEST

An Australian in China Being the Narrative of a Quiet Journey Across China to Burma. London: 1895. V. 46

MORISON, JOHN 1791-1859

Family Prayers for Every Morning and Evening Throughout the Year. London: 1837. V. 39

MORISON, SAMUEL

Talbot Baines Reed, Author, Bibliographer, Typefounder. Cambridge: 1960. V. 39

MORISON, SAMUEL ELIOT

Admiral of the Ocean Sea. A Life of Christopher Columbus. Boston: 1942. V. 39

Christopher Columbus Admiral of the Ocean Sea. Boston: 1942. V. 39

Journal and other Documents on the Life and Voyages of Christopher Columbus - Translated and Edited by S.E.M., illustrated by Limas de Freitas. New York: 1963. V. 37; 44; 46

Journals and Other Documents on the Life and Voyages of Christopher Columbus. New York: 1963. V. 46

The Life and Letters of Harrison Gray Otis, Federalist, 1765-1848. Boston: 1913. V. 39

The Maritime History of Massachusetts 1783-1860. Boston: 1921. V. 39

Massachusettensis de Conditoribus or the Builders of the Bay Colony . . . Boston: 1930. V. 39

MORISON, STANLEY 1889-1967

The Art of the Printer. London: 1925. V. 39; 40; 45

The Art of the Printer: 250 Title and Text Pages Selected from Books Composed in the Roman Letter Printed from 1500 to 1900. New York: 1925. V. 37; 38

The Calligraphic Models of Ludovico degli Arrighi Surnamed Vincentino. Montagnola: 1926. V. 42

Catalogue of an Exhibition of Books Illustrating British and Foreign Printing 1919-1929. London: 1929. V. 40

The Craft of Printing. London: 1921. V. 37; 38

The Craft of Printing: a Brief Review of the Progress and Present State of the Printing Arts. Manchester: 1922. V. 40

The English Writing-Masters and Their Copy-Books, 1750-1800. Cambridge: 1931. V. 40

The English Newspaper. Cambridge: 1932. V. 37; 38; 39; 42

Eustachio Celebrino da Udene. Paris: 1929. V. 42; 45

The Fleuron a Journal of Typography. Cambridge: 1926. V. 40

The Fleuron: a Journal of Typography. Cambridge: 1930. V. 42

Four Centuries of Fine Printing, Upwards of Six Hundred Examples of the Work of Presses Established During the Years 1500-1914. London: 1924. V. 37; 38; 44

Fra Luca de Pacioli of Borgo S. Sepolcro. New York: 1933. V. 37; 38; 39; 44; 45

German Incunabula in the British Museum. London: 1928. V. 45

German Incunabula in the British Museum Printed in the Fifteenth Century in Gothic Letter and Derived Founts. London: 1929. V. 44

German Incunabula in the British Museum: One Hundred and Fifty-Two Facsimile Plates . . . London: 1975. V. 45

German Incunabula in the British Museum. New York: 1975. V. 43

History of the Times. London: 1935-84. V. 44

The History of the Times. London: 1950-52. V. 39; 40; 46

Ichabod Dawks and His News-Letter, with an Account of the Dawks Family of Booksellers and Stationers, 1635-1731. Cambridge: 1931. V. 38

John Fell 1745-1831. London: 1930. V. 38; 40; 42; 45; 46

John Fell, 1745-1831, Bookseller, Printer, Publisher, Typefounder, Journalist &c . . . 1930. V. 38

John Fell, 1745-1831, Bookseller, Printer, Publisher, Typefounder, Journalist &c. Cambridge: 1930. V. 37; 39; 40

John Fell the University Press and the 'Fell' Types. Oxford: 1967. V. 37; 38; 39; 40; 42; 43; 44

Modern Fine Printing. London: 1925. V. 37; 45

On Type Faces. Examples of the Use of Type for the Printing of Books. London: 1923. V. 40; 44

Printing 'The Times' Since 1785. London: 1953. V. 37; 39

The Punches and Matrices Designed for Printing in the Greek, Latin, English, and Oriental Languages Bequeathed in 1686 to the University of Oxford by John Fell, D.D. Oxford: 1925. V. 46

Recollections of Daniel Berkeley Updike. Boston: 1943. V. 37; 41; 43

Selected Essays on the History of Letter Forms, I.E. Manuscript and Print. Cambridge: 1981. V. 45

Selected essays on the history of letter forms in manuscript and print. Edited by D. McKitterick. Cambridge: (1981). V. 37

Splendour of Ornament. 1968. V. 40

Splendour of Ornament. London: 1968. V. 37; 40; 41; 42

Stanley Morison and D. B. Updike, Selected Correspondence. New York: 1979. V. 39

Talbot Baines Reed: Author, Bibliographer, Typefounder. Cambridge: 1960. V. 38; 40; 41; 45

A Tally of Types Cut for Machine Composition and Introduced at the University Press, Cambridge. Cambridge: 1953. V. 39; 41; 45; 46

The Typographic Arts - Past, Present and Future. Edinburgh: 1944. V. 42

Typographic Design in Relation to Photographic Composition. San Francisco: 1959. V. 37; 41; 45; 46

The Typographic Book 1450-1935. Chicago: 1963. V. 37; 42; 43; 44

The Typographic Book 1450-1935. London: 1963. V. 42; 45; 46

MORISON, STANLEY 1889-1967 continued

The University Press and the 'Fell' Types, the Punches and Matrices Designed for Printing in the Greek, Latin, English and Oriental Languages Bequeathed in 1686 to the University of Oxford by John Fell. Oxford: 1967. V. 43

MORISON, TONI

Beloved. London: 1987. V. 41

MORISOT, BERTHE

The Correspondence of Berthe Morisot with Her Family and Her Friends Manet, Puvis de Chavannes, Degas, Monet, Renoir and Mallarme. London: 1957. V. 45

MORKILL, JOHN WILLIAM

The Parish of Kirkby Malhamdale in the West Riding of Yorkshire. Gloucester: 1933. V. 45

MORLAND, SAMUEL 1625-1695

Elevation des Eaux par Toute Sorte de Machines Reduite a la Mesure, au Poids a la Balance, par le Moyen d'un Nouveau Piston & Corps de Pompe . . . Paris: 1685. V. 42

MORLAND, THOMAS HORNBY

The Genealogy of the English Race Horse . . . London: 1810. V. 42; 43

MORLEY, C.

Ichneumonologia Britannca, The Ichneumons of Great Britain. Plymouth & London: 1903-14. V. 38

MORLEY, CHRISTOPHER DARLINGTON 1890-1957

The Haunted Bookshop. Garden City: 1919. V. 40

The Palette Knife. Chelsea: 1929. V. 45

The Palette Knife. New York: 1929. V. 39

Parnassaus on Wheels. New York: 1917. V. 39; 40

Parnassus on Wheels. Garden City: 1917. V. 41; 44; 46

Passivity Program. Chicago: 1939. V. 42

Paumanok. Garden City: 1926. V. 41; 42

Travels in Philadelphia. Philadelphia: 1920. V. 39

Where the Blue Begins. Garden City: 1922. V. 39; 41; 42

Where the Blue Begins. New York: 1922. V. 40; 41

Where the Blue Begins. New York: 1922, 1925. V. 40

Where the Blue Begins. New York: (1925). V. 37

Where the Blue Begins. New York: 1925. V. 38; 44

The Works. New York: 1927. V. 38; 42

MORLEY, FRANCES TALBOT PARKER, COUNTESS OF 1781-1857

Portraits of the Spruggins Family, Arranged by Richard Suclethumkin Spruggins, Esq. London: 1829. V. 39

MORLEY, HENRY

English Writers. London: 1887-95. V. 43

Palissy the Potter. The Life of Bernard Palissy, of saintes, His Labours and Discoveries in Art and Science . . . London: 1852. V. 37

MORLEY, JOHN

An Essay on the Nature and Cure of Scrophulous Disorders, Vulgarly Called the King's Evil . . . London: 1773. V. 38

MORLEY, JOHN, VISCOUNT 1838-1923

Diderot and the Encyclopaedists. London: 1878. V. 39; 41

The Works of Lord Morley. London: 1921. V. 38; 41; 42

MORLEY, STEPHEN

Memoirs of a Serjeant of the 5th Regt. of Foot . . . Ashford: 1842. V. 42

MORLEY, SYLVANUS G.

Guide Book to the Ruins of Quiviqua. Washington: 1935. V. 44

The Inscriptions of Peter, by S.G. Morley. Washington: 1937-38. V. 37

An Introduction to the Study of the Maya Hieroglyphs. Washington: 1915. V. 37; 45

MORLEY, THOMAS 1557-1603

A Plain and Easy Introduction to Practical Music, Set Down in Form of a Dialogue, Divided Into Three Parts. London: 1771. V. 40

MORNAND, PIERRE

Artistes du Livre. Paris: 1938-50. V. 42

MORNAY, BONINGTON 1824

A Practical Treatise on the Breeding, Rearing and Fattening of all Kinds of Domestic Poultry, Pheasants, Pigeons, and Rabbits. London: 1824. V. 37

MORNINGTON, GARRETT COLLEY WELLESLEY, 1ST EARL OF 1735-1781

A Catalogue of the Extensive and Valuable Library . . . Dengan Castle . . . Part the First: Containing the Books. Dublin: 1795. V. 38

A MORNYNGE Remembraunce. London: 1906. V. 46

MORO, ANTONIO LAZARRO

De' Crostacei e Degli Altri Marini Corpi che si Truovano su'montil Libri Due. Venice: 1740. V. 43

MORONI, LINO

Descrizione del Sacro Monte della VErnia. Florence: 1612. V. 45; 46

MORPHET, RICHARD

The Prints of Cecil Collins. London: 1981. V. 46

MORPHIS, J. M.

History of Texas, from Discovery and Settlement. New York: 1874. V. 39; 43

History of Texas, from the Discovery and Settlement. New York: 1875. V. 41

MORRELL, ABBY JANE

Narrative of a Voyage to the Ethiopic and South Atlantic Ocean, Indian Ocean, Chinese Sea, North and South Pacific Ocean in the Years 1829, 1830, 1831. New York: 1833. V. 41; 42; 43

MORRELL, BENJAMIN

A Narrative of Four Voyages, to the South Sea, North and South Pacific Ocean, Chinese Sea, Ethiopic and Southern Atlantic Ocean, Indian and Antarctic Ocean. New York: 1832. V. 37; 38; 41; 42

MORRELL, CHARLES

The tales of the Genii. London: 1820. V. 46

MORRELL, DAVID

First Blood. New York: 1972. V. 42

MORRELL, E.

The Twenty-Fifth Man. Montclair: 1924. V. 39; 40; 45

MORRELL, LUKE A.

The American Shepherd . . . New York: 1845. V. 43

MORRELL, OTTOLINE

Ottoline: the Early Memoirs - Ottoline at Garsington; the Memoirs. London: 1963-74. V. 43

MORRELL, W. WILBERFORCE

The History and Antiquities of Selby, in the West Riding of the County of York . . . Selby: 1867. V. 46

MORRELL, Z. N.

Flower and Fruits in the Wilderness; or, 46 Years in Texas. St. Louis: 1882. V. 38; 39; 42; 44

Flowers and Fruits in the Wilderness . . . St. Louis: 1882 (1872). V. 45

Flowers and Fruits in the Wilderness; or Forty Six Years in Texas and Two Winters in Honduras. Dallas: 1886. V. 45

MORRES, HERVEY REDMOND, VISCOUNT

The Prodigal: or, Marriage A-La Mode. London: 1794. V. 37

MORRICE, ALEXANDER

A Practical Treatise on Brewing the VArious Sorts of Malt Liquor. London: 1834. V. 46

A Treatise on Brewing. London: 1815. V. 40

A Treatise on Brewing. London: 1915. V. 37; 44

MORRICE, BEZALEEL

A Voyage from the East Indies. London: 1716. V. 37; 39

MORRILL, V. E.

Men of Today in the Eastern Townships. Sherbrooke: 1917. V. 46

MORRIS, ALEXANDER

Nova Britannia; or, British North America, Its Extent and Future. Montreal: 1858. V. 46

Prize Essay. Canada and Her Resources: an Essay. Montreal: 1855. V. 46

The Treaties of Canada with the Indians of Manitoba and the North-West Territories . . . Toronto: 1880. V. 37; 42

MORRIS, B. F.

The Life of Thomas Morris: Pioneer and Long a Legislator of Ohio and U.S. Senator from 1833 to 1839. Cincinnati: 1856. V. 46

MORRIS, BEVERLEY R.

British Game Birds and Wildfowl. London: 1864. V. 38

MORRIS, BEVERLEY ROBINSON

British Game Birds and Wildfowl. London. V. 45

British Game Birds and Wildfowl. London: 1855. V. 37; 38; 44

British Game Birds and Wildfowl. London: 1889. V. 39

MORRIS, BISHOP

The Horizon History of the Medieval World by Morris Bishop. 1968. V. 37

MORRIS, CHARLES

The Autobiography of Commodore Charles Morris, U.S. Navy . . . Boston and Annapolis: 1880. V. 46

MORRIS, CORBYN

An Essay Towards Fixing the True Standards of Wit, Humour, Raillery, Satire and Ridicule. London: 1744. V. 41; 44

An Essay Towards Deciding the Important Question, Whether It be a National Advantage to Britian to Insure the Ships of Her Enemies? London: 1747. V. 41; 45

An Essay towards illustrating the Science of Insurance. Wherein it is attempted to fix, by precise calculation, several important maxims . . . ; to solve various problems, and cases of contest . . . London: 1747. V. 37

A Letter to the Mayor of . . . . . Wherein the Discouragement of the Seamen Employed in His Majesty's Navy, and the Merits of the Bill Brought Into Parliament in the Last Session, for Their Relief, are Impartially Explained. London: 1758. V. 42

A Letter from a By-Stander to a Member of Parliamant (sic): Wherein is Examined What Necessity There is for the Maintenance of a Large Regular Land-Force in This Island; What Proportions the Revenues of the Crown Have Born to Those of the People . . . London: 1743. V. 41; 45

A Letter to the Reverend Mr. Thomas Carte, Author of the Full Answer to the Letter from a Bystander. London: 1743. V. 41; 45

MORRIS, D.

The Colony of British Honduras, Its Resources and Prospects . . . London: 1883. V. 45

MORRIS, EARL H.

Archaeological Studies in the Lat Plata District: Southwestern Colorado and Northwestern New Mexico. Washington: 1939. V. 42

The Temple of the Warriors at Chichen Itza, Yucatan. Washington: 1931. V. 42

MORRIS, EDMUND

Derrick and Drill. New York: 1865. V. 38; 39; 40; 42; 44

MORRIS, EDWARD JOY

Notes of a Tour through Turkey, Greece, Egypt, Arabia Petrae, to the Holy Land . . . Aberdeen: 1847. V. 45

MORRIS, EDWARD ROWE

A Dissertation Upon English Typographical Founders and Founderies, With Appendix by John Nichols. New York: 1924. V. 37

MORRIS, FRANCIS ORPEN 1810-1893

All the Articles of the Darwin Faith. London: 1875. V. 40

The Ancestral Homes of Britian. London: 1868. V. 38; 42

Bible Natural History. London: 1852. V. 38

Castles and Halls of England Forming a New Series of Ancestral Homes. London: 1870. V. 39

The County Seats of the Noblemen and Gentlemen of Great Britain and Ireland. London. V. 39

A History of British Birds. Leeds & London. V. 42

A History of British Birds. London: 1851-53. V. 39

History of British Birds. Grrombridge: 1851-57. V. 39

A History of British Birds. London: 1851-57. V. 37; 39; 42; 43; 44

A History of British Birds. London: 1860-66. V. 39

A History of British Birds. (and) Nest and Eggs. London: 1863-61. V. 37

A History of British Birds. London: 1863-67. V. 42; 43; 45

A History of British Birds. London: 1865. V. 38

A History of British Birds. London: 1870. V. 39; 40

A History of British Birds. London: 1888. V. 39; 45

A History of British Birds. London: 1891. V. 43

A History of British Birds. London: 1895. V. 42

A History of British Birds. London: 1897. V. 38

A History of British Birds. London: 1903. V. 37

A History of British Birds. London: 1970. V. 38

A History of British Butterflies. London: 1851-53. V. 37

A History of British Butterflies. London: 1852-1853. V. 37; 38

A History of British Butterflies. London: 1853. V. 38; 39; 40; 42

A History of British Butterflies. London: 1860. V. 37; 38

A History of British Butterflies. London: 1864. V. 43

A History of British Butterflies. London: 1865. V. 46

A History of British Butterflies. London: 1870. V. 38

A History of British Butterflies. London: 1872. V. 38

A History of British Butterflies. London: 1891. V. 37; 41; 42; 45

A History of British Butterflies. London: 1893. V. 37

A History of British Butterflies. London: 1904. V. 42; 43; 44

A History of British Butterflies. London: 1908. V. 38; 40

A History of British Moths. London: 1896. V. 42; 43

A History of British Moths. London: 1903. V. 37; 38

A Natural History of British Birds. London: 1870. V. 42

Natural History of British Moths. London: 1871. V. 38

A Natural History of British Moths. London: 1872. V. 37

A Natural History of British Moths. London: 1894. V. 37

A Natual History of the Nests and Eggs of British Birds. London: 1853/55/56. V. 45

A Natural History of the Nests and Eggs of British Birds. London: 1861. V. 43

A Natural History of the nests and eggs of British birds. (In three volumes). London: 1866/7. V. 37

A Natural History of the Nests and Eggs of British Birds. London: 1875. V. 37; 39; 40; 42; 43; 45

Natural History of the Nests and Eggs of British Birds. London: 1879. V. 37; 43; 44

A Natural History of the Nests and Eggs of British Birds. London: 1892. V. 38

A Natural History of the Nests and Eggs of British Birds. London: 1896. V. 37; 39; 40; 43

A Series of Picturesque Views of Seats of the Noblemen and Gentlemen of Great Britain and Ireland . . . London. V. 38; 40; 46

A Series of Picturesque Views of Seats of the Noblemen and Gentlemen of Great Britain . . . (with) Facsimiles of Autographs of Subscribers to the Picturesque Views of Seats of Noblemen and Gentlemen . . . Leeds: 1860-80. V. 41

A Series of Picturesque Views of the Seats of the Nobleman and Gentlemen of Great Britain and Ireland, with Descriptive and Historical Letterpress. London: 1860-80. V. 39

A Series of Picturesque Views of Seats of Noblemen and Gentlemen of Great Britian and Ireland. London: 1864-80. V. 38

A Series of Picturesque Views of Seats of the Noblemen and Gentlemen of Great Britain and Ireland. London: 1866-80. V. 44

A Series of Picturesque Views of the Seats of Noblemen and Gentlmen of Great Britain and Ireland. London: 1866-c.1885. V. 45

A Series of Picturesque Views of the Seats of the Nobleman and Gentleman of Great Britain and Ireland . . . Leeds: 1867. V. 41

A Series of Picturesque Views of Seats of the Noblemen and Gentlemen of Great Britain with Descriptive and Historical Letterpress. Leeds: 1880. V. 41

A Series of Picturesque Views of Seats of the Noblemen and Gentlemen of Great Britain and Ireland. London: 1880. V. 39; 44

A Series of Picturesque Views of Seats of the Noblemen and Gentlemen of Great Britain and Ireland. London, Edinburgh & Dublin: 1880. V. 38

A Series of Picturesque Views of Seats of the Noblemen and Gentlemen of Great Britain and Ireland, with descriptive and historical letterpress. London: 1870-1880. V. 37

MORRIS, FRANK

Impressions of Waterfowl of Australia. Australia: 1977. V. 45

MORRIS, FRANK T.

Birds of Prey of Australia. Melbourne: 1973. V. 38; 39; 41; 42; 46

Birds of the Australian Swamps. East Melbourne: 1978. V. 37

Finches of Australia. Melbourne: 1976. V. 39

Impression of Waterfowl of Australia. 1977. V. 46

Pigeons and Doves of Australia. Melbourne: 1976. V. 42

Robins and Wrens of Australia. Melbourne/New York: 1979. V. 37

MORRIS, GEORGE POPE

The Deserted Bride, and Other Poems. New York: 1838. V. 41; 43

The Little Frenchman and His Water Lots, with Other Sketches of the Times. Philadelphia: 1839. V. 43; 45

MORRIS, GOUVERNEUR

The Diary and Letters of Gouverneur Morris Minister of the United States to France . . . New York: 1888. V. 46

Notes on the United States of America. Philadelphia: 1806. V. 40

MORRIS, GOVERNIEUR

An Oration in Honor of the Memory of George Clinton, Late Vice-President of the United States. Delivered May 19, 1812. New York: 1812. V. 45

MORRIS, HENRY 1925-

The Bird and Bull Commonplace Book. North Hills: 1971. V. 44

Bird and Bull Number 13. North Hills: 1972. V. 45

Bird & Bull Pepper Pot. 1977. V. 37; 39; 40; 42

Bird & Bull Pepper Pot. North Hills: 1977. V. 38; 40; 43; 45; 46

Coast to Coast in Forty-Three Hours: the Flight of RB-1. North Hills: 1980. V. 42

The First Fine Silver Coinage of the Republic of San Serriffe: The Bird & Bull Commemorative 100 Coronas. Newtown: 1988. V. 39; 40; 42; 44; 45

Five on Paper. North Hills: 1963. V. 41; 43; 45

The Flight of the RB-1. Coast to Coast in Forty-Three Hours. North Hills: 1980. V. 39; 43

Guilford & Green. North Hills: 1970. V. 39; 40; 46

Japanese Paper Balloon Bombs: The First ICBM. North Hills: 1982. V. 41

MORRIS, HENRY 1925- continued

Japonica. The Study and Appreciation of the Art of Japanese Paper. North Hills: 1981. V. 37; 38; 40; 42; 46

No. V-109, The Biography of a Printing Press. N.P.: 1978. V. 39

Omnibus: Instructions for Amateur Papermakers with Notes and Observations on Private Presses, Book Printing . . . 1967. V. 40; 45

Omnibus, Instructions for Amateur Papermakers. Newtown: 1967. V. 39

Omnibus. North Hills: 1967. V. 37; 38; 46

The Origin and Progress of Renal Surgery. London: 1898. V. 45

A Pair on Paper: Two Essays on Paper History and Related Matters. North Hills: 1976. V. 46

The Paper Maker. A Survey of Lesser-Known Hand Paper Mills in Europe and North America. Compiled and Edited by Henry Morris. North Hills: 1974. V. 37

Pepperpot. North Hills: 1977. V. 37; 38; 40

The Private Press-Man's Tale. Newtown: 1990. V. 43; 44

Roller-Printed Paste Papers for Bookbinding. North Hills: 1975. V. 37; 38

Surgical Diseases of the Kidney and Ureter Including Injuries, Malformations and Misplacements. London: 1901. V. 42

Trade Tokens of British and American Booksellers and Bookmakers. Newtown: 1989. V. 41; 42; 44

Twenty-One Years of Bird & Bull: a Bibliography, 1958-1979. Austin: 1980. V. 46

V-109 The Biography of a Printing Press. North Hills: 1978. V. 43

A Visit to Hayle Mill, Written from Notes Made During a Visit to J. Barcham Green, Ltd. North Hills: 1970. V. 37; 44

MORRIS, HERVEY REDMOND

The Prodigal; or Marriage A-La-Mode. London: 1794. V. 42

MORRIS, IVAN

The Tale of Genji Scroll. Tokyo: 1971. V. 46

MORRIS, J.

Makers of Japan. London: 1906. V. 40

MORRIS, JOSEPH

The German Air Raids on Great Britain. 1914-1918. London: 1922. V. 45

The 'Spirit Pervails'. San Francisco: 1886. V. 42

MORRIS, LEOPOLD

Pictorial History of Victoria and Victoria County. 1953. V. 42

MORRIS, LEWIS

The Epic of Hades. London: 1883. V. 38

MORRIS, LUCILLE

Bald Knobbers. Caldwell: 1939. V. 43

MORRIS, M. C. F.

Francis Orpen Morris. A Memoir. London: 1897. V. 41

MORRIS, MARGARET H.

A Praise Meeting of the Birds. Philadelphia: 1878. V. 42

MORRIS, MAURICE O'CONNOR

Hibernia Venatica. London: 1878. V. 43

Rambles in the Rocky Mountains. London: 1864. V. 37; 38; 40; 41; 42; 43; 45; 46

Triviata or Crossroad Chronicles of Passages in Irish Hunting History During the Season of 1875-76. London: 1877. V. 38

MORRIS, MAY

William Morris; Artist, Writer, Socialist. Oxford: 1936. V. 37; 41

MORRIS, MOWBRAY

Poet's Walk, An Introduction to English Poetry. London: 1870? V. 44

MORRIS, R. H.

Chester in the Plantagenet and Tudor Reigns. Chester. V. 38

Chester in the Plantaganet and Tudor Reigns. London. V. 40

MORRIS, RALPH

The Life and Astonishing Adventures of John Daniel, a Smith at Royston in Hertfordshire . . . London: 1770. V. 42

MORRIS, RICHARD

Flora Conspicua; A Selection of the Most Ornamental Flowering Hardy, Exotic and Indigenous Trees, Shrubs, and Herbaceous Plants for Embellishing Flower Gardens and Pleasure Grounds. London: 1830. V. 41

Flora Conspicua; a Selection of the Most Ornamental Flowering, Exotic and Indigenous Trees, Shrubs and Herbaceous Plants for Embellishing Flower-Gardens and Pleasure Grounds. London: 1825-26. V. 37

The Life and Mysterious Transactions of Richard Morris, Esq. London: 1798. V. 45

MORRIS, ROBERT

An Essay in Defence of Ancient Architecture. London: 1728. V. 38; 39

Fatal Necessity. London: 1742. V. 38

Freemasonry in the Holy Land; or, Handmarks of Hiram's Builders. New York: 1872. V. 42

Lectures on Architecture: Consisting of Rules Founded Upon Harmonick and ARithmetical Proportions in Building. London: 1759. V. 39

A Letter to Sir Richard Aston, Knt. One of the Judges of His Majesty's Court of King's Bench, and Late Chief Justice of the Common Pleas in Ireland . . . London: 1770. V. 37; 42

Select Architecture: Being Regular Designs of Plans and Elevations Well Suited to Both Town and Country . . . London: 1757. V. 39

MORRIS, ROBERT C.

Collections of the Wyoming Historical Society. Cheyenne: 1897. V. 38; 45

MORRIS, THOMAS

A House for the Suburbs; Socially and Architecturally Sketched. London: 1860. V. 40

MORRIS, W. A.

A Review of Dr. Wooten's Review of the Causes that Led to the Death of the Late Adjt. Gen. John B. Jones. Austin: 1882. V. 39; 41

MORRIS, WILLIAM 1834-1896

An Address Delivered by William Morris at the Distribution of Prizes to Students of the Birmingham Municipal School of Art on Feb. 21, 1894. London: 1898. V. 39; 40; 41; 44; 45; 46

An Address Delivered XIth November, MDCCC, etc. London: 1901. V. 37; 38; 40; 43; 44

The Aims of Art. London: 1887. V. 37

Architecture and History, and Westminster Abbey. London: 1900. V. 45

Architecture, Industry and Wealth. London: 1902. V. 41; 43; 46

Art and the Beauty of the Earth. London: 1898. V. 37; 40; 41; 42; 44

Art and the Beauty of the Earth. London: 1899. V. 41; 44; 45

Art and its Producers, and the Arts and Crafts of Today. London: 1899. V. 41

Art and Its Producers, and the Arts and Crafts of Today; Two Addresses Delivered Before the National Association for the Advancement of Art. London: 1901. V. 39; 44

The Art and Craft of Printing. New Rochelle: 1902. V. 37

The Art and Craft of Printing. New York: 1902. V. 46

Arts and Crafts Essays by Members of the Arts and Crafts Exhibition Society. London: 1893. V. 46

A Book of Verse. London: 1980. V. 38; 39; 40; 41; 42; 44

Chants for Socialists. London: 1885. V. 38; 46

Child Christopher and Goldilind the Fair. 1895. V. 37; 38; 40

Child Christopher and Goldilind the Fair. Hammersmith: 1895. V. 37; 40; 45

Child Christopher and Goldilind the Fair. London: 1895. V. 41

Child Christopher and Goldilind the Fair. Portland: 1900. V. 37

The Decorative Arts. London: 1878. V. 38; 41; 43; 46

The Defence of Guenevere. London: 1858. V. 37; 39; 40; 41; 42; 46

The Defence of Guinevere and Other Poems. 1892. V. 44

The Defence of Guenevere, and Other Poems. London: 1892. V. 38; 41

The Defence of Guenevere and Other Poems. London: 1904. V. 37; 41; 44; 46

The Defence of Guenevere and Other Poems. London: & New York: 1904. V. 43

The Defence of Guenevere and Other Poems. Hammersmith: 1892. V. 37

Doom or King Acrisius. New York: 1902. V. 44

A Dream of John Bull and a King's Lesson. 1892. V. 45

A Dream of John Bull and a Kings Lesson. London: 1892. V. 38; 41

Early Poems. London: 1914. V. 41; 42; 44; 46

The Earthly Paradise. London: 1868-70. V. 41; 44; 46

The Earthly Paradise. London: 1870. V. 40; 42; 44

The Earthly Paradise. London: 1890. V. 38; 44

The Earthly Paradise. 1896. V. 38

The Earthly Paradise. London: 1896. V. 42

The Earthly Paradise. Hammersmith: 1896-1897. V. 44

The Earthly Paradise. London: 1896-97. V. 40; 41

Earthly Paradise. London: 1905. V. 37; 42; 44

Five Arthurian Poems. New Rochelle: 1902. V. 46

Five Arthurian Poems: The Defence of Guenevere; King Arthur's Tomb; Sir Galahad - a Christmas Mystery; The Chapel in Lyoness; A Good Night in Prison. New York: 1902. V. 41

The God of the Poor. London. V. 46

Gossip About an Old House on the Upper Thames. New York: 1901. V. 44

Gothic Architecture. 1893. V. 37; 38; 39; 42

Gothic Architecture. A Lecture for the Arts and Crafts Exhibition Society. Hammersmith: 1893. V. 37; 42; 44; 45

Gothic Architecture. London: 1893. V. 38

MORRIS, WILLIAM 1834-1896 continued

Gothic Architecture: A Lecture for the Arts and Crafts Exhibition Society, by William Morris. (London: 1893). V. 37

Guenevere. Two Poems by William Morris, The Defence of Guenevere and King Arthur's Tomb. London: 1930. V. 37; 38; 39

The History of Over Sea. New York: 1902. V. 41

The History of Sigurd the Volsung and the Fall of the Nibelungs. Hammersmith: 1897. V. 46

The History of Sigurd The Volsung and the Fall of the Niblungs. London: 1898. V. 39; 41

The Hollow Land and Other Contributions to the Oxford and Cambridge Magazine. London: 1903. V. 42

The Hollow Land. Hingham: 1905. V. 37

Hopes and Fears for Art. London: 1902. V. 45

The House of the Wolfings and all the Kindreds of the Mark. London: 1901. V. 45

How I Became a Socialist. London: 1896. V. 46

The Ideal Book. 1899. V. 46

The Ideal Book. New York: 1899. V. 41

The Ideal Book. London: 1907, but 1908. V. 44

A King's Lesson. Aberdeen: 1891. V. 46

A King's Lesson. Madison: 1934. V. 40; 41; 42

Kunst en Maatschappij. Lezingen - Vertaald Door M. Hugenholtz-Zeeven en van een Levens Schets Voorzien door Henri Polak. Amsterdam: 1903. V. 43

Lectures on Art Delivered in Support of the Society for the Protection of Ancient Buildings. London: 1882. V. 43; 46

The Life and Death of Jason. Boston: 1867. V. 42

The Life and Death of Jason. London: 1867. V. 37; 42

The Life and Death of Jason. London: 1895. V. 41

The Life and Death of Jason. London: 1925. V. 39

Love is Enough. London: 1873. V. 41; 46

Love is Enough, or the Freeing of Pharamond. 1897. V. 42

Love is Enough. Hammersmith: 1897. V. 42

Love is Enough, or the Freeing of Pharamond, a Morality. London: 1897. V. 41

Love is Enough, Or the Freeing of Pharamond: a Morality. Hammersmith: 1879. V. 37

Monoploy: or, How Labour is Robbed. London: 1890. V. 46

News from Nowhere. London: 1891. V. 42; 43; 46

News from Nowhere. Hammersmith: 1892. V. 45

News From Nowhere: or An Epoch of Rest Being Some Chapters from a Utopian Romance. London: 1891. V. 37

A Note by William Morris on His Aims in Founding the Kelmscott. Hammersmith: 1898. V. 39; 41; 45

A Note by William Morris on His Aims In Founding the Kelmscott Press. London: 1898. V. 38; 41

A Note by William Morris On His Aims in Founding the Kelmscott Press. London: 1934. V. 37; 39; 42

A Note by William Morris on His Aims in Founding the Kelmscott Press, Together with a Short Description of the Press by S. C. Cockerell . . . 1969. V. 42

A Note on His Aims in Founding the Kelmscott Press. Together with a Short Description of the Press by S. C. Cockerell, and an Annotated List of the Books Printed in Golden Thereat. 1898. V. 37

Of the Friendship of Amis and Amile. Hammersmith: 1894. V. 38

Of the Friendship of Amis and Amile. London: 1894. V. 41

Of the Freindship of Amis and Amile. (Hammersmith, England: 1894). V. 37

Old French Romances done into English. London: 1896. V. 41

The Pilgrims of Hope. Portland: 1901. V. 40

Poems by the Way. 1891. V. 37; 38

Poems by the Way. Hammersmith: 1891. V. 37; 39; 40; 46

Poems by the Way. London: 1891. V. 40; 41; 42; 43; 44; 46

Poems by the Way. (Hammersmith: 1891). V. 37

Poetical Works. London: 1896. V. 39

Pre-Raphaelite Ballads. New York: 1900. V. 37; 40; 41; 42; 45

Printing, an Essay. Park Ridge: 1903. V. 37

Pygmalion and the Image. New York: 1903. V. 42

The Reward of Labour: a Dailogue. N.P.: 1893? V. 46

The Roots of the Mountains. London: 1889. V. 41; 44

Roots of the Mountains. London: 1890. V. 46

The Roots of the Mountains. London: 1901. V. 41; 45

Sir Galahad. New Rochelle: 1902. V. 45

Sir Galahad. Chicago: 1904. V. 38; 41; 42

Sir Galahad, A Christmas Mystery. Decorations and two full page illustrations by H.M. O'Kane. (New Rochelle: 1902). V. 37

Socialism, Its Growth and Outcome. London: 1893. V. 42

The Socialist Ideal of Art. London: 1891. V. 46

The Society for the Protection of Ancient Buildings Concerning Westminster Abbey. London: 1893. V. 46

Some Hints on Pattern Designing. London. V. 46

Some Hints on Pattern-Designing. London: 1881. V. 40

Some Hints on Pattern Designing: A Lecture Delivered by William Morris at the Working mens College, London on December 10, 1881. London: 1889. V. 41

Some Hints on Pattern-Designing. Colophon: 1899. V. 45

Some Hints on Pattern Designing. London: 1899. V. 41; 42

Some Thoughts on Ornamented MSS. of the Middle Ages. New York: 1934. V. 38

Some Notes on Early Woodcut Books; With a Chapter on Illuminated Manuscripts. New Rochelle: 1902. V. 37

The Stories of the Kings of Norway. London: 1893. V. 46

The Story of Cupid and Psyche. 1974. V. 40; 45

The Story of Cupid and Psyche. By William Morris. With wood engravings designed by Edward Burne-Jones and engraved by William Morris. London: 1974. V. 37

The Story of Cupid and Psyche. London & Cambridge: 1974. V. 37; 42

The Story of Sigurd the Volsung and the fall of the Niblungs. London: 1877. V. 38; 40; 45

The Story of Sigurd the Volsung and the Fall of the Niblungs. Hammersmith: 1898. V. 37; 39; 46

The Story of Sigurd the Volsung and the Fall of the Niblungs. London: 1898. V. 42

The Story of the Glittering Plain. 1891. V. 45

The Story of the Glittering Plain. London: 1891. V. 40

The Story of the Glittering Plain, or The Land of Living Men. By William Morris. Hammersmith: (1894). V. 37

The Story of the Volsungs and Niblungs with Certain Songs from the Elder Eda. London: 1870. V. 37

The Sundering Flood. London: 1897. V. 41

The Sundering Flood. Hammersmith: 1897/98. V. 45

The Tables Turned; or, Numpkins Awakened, a Socialist Interlude . . . London: 1887. V. 38; 39; 41; 43; 46

A Tale of the House of the Wolfings and All the Kindreds of the Mark . . . London: 1889. V. 42

A Tale of the House of the Wolfings and all the Kindreds of the Mark . . . London: 1901. V. 38

The Tale of King Florus and the Fair Jehane. Translated by William Morris of the French 13the century. (Hammersmight: 1893). V. 37

Textile Fabrics. A Lecture Delivered in the Lecture Room of the Exhibition, July 11th 1884. London: 1884. V. 37

This Earthly Paradise. 1896. V. 37

True and False Society. London: 1888. V. 46

The Tryal Between Sir W---m M--rr--s . . . and Lord A---gst---s F---tz-R--y for Criminal Conversation with the Plaintiff's Wife. London: 1742. V. 41

The Two Sides of the River. Hapless Love and the First Foray of Aristomenes. London: 1890. V. 38; 44

Two Poems: the Defence of Guenevere, and, King Arthur's Tomb. London: 1930. V. 46

Under an Elm-Tree; or, Thoughts in the Countryside. Aberdeen: 1891. V. 41

Useful Work Verses Useless Toil. London: 1893. V. 38

The Water of the Wonderous Isles. Hammersmith: 1897. V. 38; 42; 45; 46

The Water of the Wondrous Isle. London: 1897. V. 40; 41; 42; 46

The Well at the World's End. 1896. V. 45

The Well at the World's End. Hammersmith: 1896. V. 37; 42; 45

The Well at the World's End. London: 1896. V. 41; 43; 46

Why I Am a Communist. London: 1984. V. 46

William Morris to Whistler. Papers and Addresses on Art and Craft and the Commonweal. London: 1911. V. 38; 41

The Wood Beyond the World. 1894. V. 42; 44; 45

The Wood Beyond the World. Hammersmith: 1894. V. 37

The Wood Beyond the World. London: 1894. V. 41

The Wood Beyond the World. Boston: 1895. V. 41; 43

The Wood Beyond the World. London: 1895. V. 40; 43; 46

The Wood Beyond the World. (Hammersmith: 1894). V. 37

Works. London: 1901-02. V. 37; 38

The Collected Works of William Morris with Introductions by his Daugher May Morris. London: 1910. V. 37

The Collected Works. London: 1910-15. V. 38

MORRIS, WILLIAM G.

An Essay on the Manufacturing Interests of California, the Causes that Impede and Those that Would Aid their Development. San Francisco: 1872. V. 37; 38

MORRIS, WILLIAM MEREDITH

British Violin-Makers, Classical and Modern. London: 1904. V. 40

MORRIS, WILLIE

North Toward Home. London: 1968. V. 39

MORRIS, WRIGHT 1910-

About Fiction. New York: 1975. V. 45

The Cat's Meow. 1975. V. 39

MORRIS, WRIGHT 1910- continued

The Cat's Meow. Los Angeles: 1975. V. 39; 44; 46

A Cloak of Light. New York: 1985. V. 40; 42; 44

The Deep Sleep. New York: 1953. V. 44; 45; 46

Fire Sermon. New York. V. 45

God's Country and My People. 1968. V. 46

God's Country and My People. New York: 1968. V. 44

Green Grass, Blue Sky, White House. 1970. V. 39

Here is Einbaum. Los Angeles: 1973. V. 39

The Home Place. New York: 1948. V. 38

The Inhabitants. New York: 1946. V. 37; 39; 40; 42; 45; 46

Love Among the Cannibals. New York: 1957. V. 43

The Man Who Was There. New York: 1945. V. 38; 46

Man and Boy. New York: 1951. V. 40; 46

My Uncle Dudley. New York: 1942. V. 39; 40; 42; 44; 46

The Origins of Sadness. Alabama: 1984. V. 46

Plains Song for Female Voices. New York: 1980. V. 42; 46

War Games. 1972. V. 46

MORRISON, ALFRED

The Blessington Papers. London: 1895. V. 44

MORRISON & FOURMY

General Directory of the City of Denison 1887-88. Galveston: 1887. V. 44

Morrison & Fourmy's General Directory of the City of San Antonio for 1879-80. Marshall: 1879. V. 37

MORRISON, ARTHUR

Chronicles of Martin Hewitt Being the Second Series of the Adventures of Martin Hewitt . . . London: 1895. V. 45

The Hole in the Wall. London: 1902. V. 39

The Painters of Japan. London: 1911. V. 37; 38; 40; 44

Tales of Mean Streets. London: 1894. V. 41; 42

MORRISON, C.

An Essay on the Relations Between Labour and Capital. London: 1854. V. 42

MORRISON, HETTY A.

My Summer in the Kitchen. Indianapolis: 1878. V. 37; 44; 45

MORRISON, J. S.

Greek Oared Ships 900-322 B.C. Cambridge: 1968. V. 42

MORRISON, JIM

The Lords and New Creatures. New York: 1970. V. 44; 45

MORRISON, JOHN E.

History of the New York Shipyards, 1613-1869 . . . New York: 1909. V. 42

MORRISON, JOHN H.

History of American Steam Navigation. New York: 1903. V. 37; 42; 46

MORRISON, LEONARD A.

The History of Windham, in New Hampshire (Rockingham County), 1718-1883 . . . Boston: 1883. V. 42

History of the Alison or Allison Family in Europe and America, AD 1135 to 1893. Boston: 1893. V. 46

MORRISON, MOLLIE N.

The Silversmiths and Goldsmiths of the Cape of Good Hope 1652-1850. Johannesburg: 1936. V. 40

MORRISON, PEGGY

Cosy Chair Stories. London: 1924. V. 45

MORRISON, ROBERT

A Grammar of the Chinese Language. Serampore: 1815. V. 40

Plantarum Umbelliferarum Distributio Nova, per Tabulas Cognationis et Affinitatis ex Libro Naturae Observata & Detecta. (with) Plantarum Historiae Universalis Oxoniensis pars Secunda seu Herbarum Distributio Nova. Oxford: 1672-80. V. 42; 45

A View of China, for Philological Purposes. Macao: 1817. V. 40

MORRISON, TONI

Beloved. New York: 1987. V. 39; 42; 43; 44

The Bluest Eye. New York: 1970. V. 45

The Bluest Eye. London: 1979. V. 39; 42; 43; 46

The Bluest Eye. 1970. V. 44

Jazz. New York: 1992. V. 46

Song of Solomon. New York: 1977. V. 46

Sula. London: 1974. V. 44

Sula. New York: 1974. V. 42; 45

Tar Baby. New York: 1981. V. 42; 43; 44; 45; 46

MORRISON, W. H.

Morrison's Stranger's Guide for Washington City. Washington: 1872. V. 43

MORRISON, WILLIAM B.

Military Posts and Camps in Oklahoma. Oklahoma City: 1936. V. 37; 38; 45

MORROW, BRADFORD

A Bibliography of the Writings of Wyndham Lewis. Los Angeles: 1978. V. 39

A Bibliography of the Writings of Wyndham Lewis. Santa Barbara: 1978. V. 37; 38; 39; 40; 42; 43; 46

A Bibliography of the Black Sparrow Press: 1966-1978. 1981. V. 42; 44

A Bibliography of the Black Sparrow Press: 1966-1978. Santa Barbara: 1981. V. 37; 40; 45

Passing from the Provinces: Three Fragments. Santa Barbara: 1981. V. 41

MORROW, PRINCE A.

Atlas of Skin and Veneral Diseases. New York: 1889. V. 38; 40; 41; 45; 46

MORROW, R. A. H.

Story of the Spring Hill Disaster . . . St. John: 1891. V. 43

MORROW, W. C.

The Ape, The Idiot and Other People. 1897. V. 43

The California Literary Pamphlets, Nos. 1-6. V.P.: 1936. V. 43

MORSCH, E.

Concrete-Steel Construction (Der Eisenbetonbau). London: 1909. V. 44

MORSE, A. REYNOLDS

Dali, a Study of His Life and Work. Greenwich: 1958. V. 40

MORSE, ALEXANDER PORTER

A Treatise on Citizenship, by Birth and By Naturalization . . . Boston: 1881. V. 40

MORSE, CHARLES F.

Letters Written During the Civil War. Boston: 1898. V. 46

MORSE, CHARLES W.

The Diamond Atlas. New York: 1858. V. 45

MORSE, EDWARD S.

Glimpses of China and Chinese Homes. Boston: 1902. V. 42

Japanese Homes and Their Surroundings. Boston: 1886. V. 39; 43

Japanese Homes and Their Surroundings. London: 1886. V. 46

Japanese Homes and Their Surroundings. New York: 1895. V. 44

Japanese Homes and Their Surroundings. New York: 1904. V. 38

MORSE, JEDIDIAH 1761-1826

An Abridgement of the American Gazetteer Exhibiting . . . Boston: 1798. V. 39

The American Geography; or a View of the Present Situation of the United States of America. London: 1792. V. 39; 40; 41; 43; 44

The American Geography. London: 1794. V. 44

The American Gazetteer, Exhibiting, in Alphabetical Order, a Much More full and Accurate Account, Than Has Been Given, of the States, Provinces, Counties, Cities . . . . Boston: 1797. V. 40

The American Gazetteer . . . Charlestown: 1802. V. 40; 43

The American Gazetteer, Exhibiting a Full Account of the Civil Divisions, Rivers, Harbours, Indian Tribes &c. Charlestown: 1804. V. 38; 41

The American Gazetteer, Exhibiting a Full Account of the Civil Divisions, Rivers, Harbours, Indian Tribes, &c of the American Continent, also the West Indian and other Appendant Islands; with a Particular Description of Louisiana. Charlestown/Boston: 1804. V. 37

The American Gazetteer, Exhibiting A Full Account of the Civil Divisions, Rivers, Harbours, Indian Tribes &c . . . (with) A New Gazetteer of the Eastern Continent . . . Charlestown: 1804/02. V. 46

American Geography or, a View of the present Situation of the United States of America. Elizabeth Town: 1789. V. 37

The American Universal Geography . . . Charlestown: 1819. V. 40

Annals of the American Revolution. Hartford: 1824. V. 40

A Compendious History of New England, Designed for Schools and Private Families. Charlestown: 1804. V. 39

A Comendious History of New England, Exhibiting an Interesting View of the First Settlers of that Country, Their Character, Their Sufferings and Their Ultimate Prosperity. London: 1808. V. 42; 44

Geography Made Easy: Being an Abridgement of the American Universal Geography. Boston: 1796. V. 42

New and Correct Edition of the American Geography . . . Edinburgh: 1795. V. 38; 45

A New Gazetteer of the Eastern Continent; or, a Geographical Dictionary . . . Charlestown: 1802. V. 38

MORSE, JEDIDIAH 1761-1826 continued

A New Universal Gazetteer, or Geographical Dictionary . . . With an Appendix, Containing an Account of the Monies, Weights and Measures of Various Countries, with Tables Illustrating the Population, Commerce, and . . . New Haven: 1823. V. 37

A Report to the Secretary of War of the United States, on Indian Affairs, Comprising a Narrative of a Tour Performed in the Summer of 1820. New Haven: 1822. V. 37; 38; 39; 41; 42; 43; 45; 46

A Sermon, Exhibiting the Present Dangers, and Consequent Duties of the Citizens of the United States of America . . . Charlestown: 1799. V. 41

The Traveller's Guide; or Pocket Gazetteer of the United States Extracted from the Latest Edition of Morse's Universal Gazetteer. New Haven: 1823. V. 37; 45

The Traveller's Guide. New Haven: 1826. V. 42

MORSE, JOHN

Life and Letters of Oliver Wendell Holmes. Boston: 1896. V. 40

MORSE, JOHN F.

Illustrated Historical Sketches of California, with a Minute History of Sacramento Valley. Together with an Appendix of General News. Sacramento: 1854. V. 39

MORSE, JOHN T.

American Statesmen. Boston: 1898. V. 46

Life and Letters of Oliver Wendell Holmes. Cambridge: 1896. V. 38; 44; 45

Life and Letters of Oliver Wendell Holmes. Boston: 1897. V. 46

MORSE, O. A.

A Vindication of the Claim of Alexander M. W. Ball, of Elizabeth, N.J. to the Authorship of the Poem, 'Rock Me to Sleep, Mother . . . ' New York: 1867. V. 40

MORSE, PETER

Jean Charlot's Prints: a Catalogue Raisonne. Honolulu: 1976. V. 41

John Sloan's Prints: A Catalogue Raisonne of the Etchings, Lithographs and Posters. New Haven: 1969. V. 43; 45

John Sloan's Prints: A Catalogue Rasionne of the Etchings, Lithographs and Posters. New York: 1969. V. 46

Popular Art: The Example of Jean Charlot. Santa Barbara: 1978. V. 41

MORSE, SAMUEL FRENCH

Five Cummington Poems. 1939(. V. 37

Time of Year. 1943. V. 43

Time of Year a First Book of Poems Introduced by Wallace Stevens. Cummington: 1943. V. 37

Wallace Stevens: a Preliminary Checklist of His Published Writings 1898-1954. New Haven: 1954. V. 46

MORSE, SIDNEY E.

A Geographical View of Greece and an Historical Sketch of the Recent Revolution in that Country. New Haven: 1824. V. 39

Morse's North American Atlas Containing the Following Beautifully Colored Maps . . . New York: 1842. V. 45

Morse's Cerographic Maps . . . New York: 1845. V. 45

Morse's North American Atlas. New York: 1845? V. 39

MORSE, WILLARD S.

Howard Pyle. A Record of His Illustrations and Writings. Wilmington: 1921. V. 43; 46

MORSE, WILLIAM INGLIS

Nordic Trails. Boston: 1930. V. 43

MORSELS for Merry and Melancholy Mortals. Ipswich: 1815. V. 43

MORTIMER, ALFRED

S. Mark's Church Philadelphia and Its Lady Chapel: With an Account of Its History and Treasures. New York: 1909. V. 41; 42; 44

MORTIMER, CHAPMAN

Reflections in a Golden Eye. (Screenplay). New York: 1966. V. 44

MORTIMER, GEORGE

Observations and Remarks Made During a Voyage to the Islands of Teneriffe, Amsterdam, MAria's Islands near Van Dieman's Land . . . London: 1791. V. 46

MORTIMER, J. R.

Forty Years' Researches in British and Anglo Saxon Burial Mounds of East Yorkshire. London: 1905. V. 37; 39; 40; 44; 45

MORTIMER, JOHN

Three Plays: The Dock Brief, I Spy and What Shall We Tell Caroline? London: 1958. V. 42

The Whole Art of Husbandry; or, The Way of Managing and Improving Land. London: 1712. V. 42

The Whole Art of Husbandry . . . London: 1721. V. 45

The Whole Art of Husbandry . . . London: 1761. V. 42

MORTIMER, JOHN HAMILTON

Original Etchings . . . Illustrations of the Principal Characters in Shakspeare (sic). S.N., s.l.. V. 38

MORTIMER, RUTH

The Bewildering Thread. Wallingford: 1986. V. 44

Catalogue of Books and Manuscripts. Part I. French 16th Century Books. Cambridge: 1964. V. 43

Catalogue of Books and Manuscripts. Part II. Italian 16th Century Books. Cambridge: 1974. V. 43; 45

Harvard College Library Department of Printing and Graphic Arts, Catalogue of Books and Manuscripts. Part I: French 16th Century Books. Cambridge: 1964. V. 38

Harvard College Library . . . Italian 16th Century Books. Cambridge: 1974. V. 38

MORTIMER, THOMAS

The Elements of Commerce, Politics and Finances, in Three Treatises on Those Important Subjects. London: 1772. V. 38

Every Man His Own Broker; or, a Guide to Exchange-Alley. London: 1765. V. 41

Every Man His Own Broker; or, a Guide to Exchange Alley. (with) A New Book of Interest. London: 1765/66. V. 41

A Grammar Illustrating the Principles and Practice of Trade and Commerce; for the Use of Young Persons Intended for Business. London: 1810. V. 38

MORTIMER, W. GOLDEN

Peru - History of Coca, the Divine Plant of the Incas. New York: 1901. V. 37; 38; 39; 40; 41; 42; 44; 46

MORTLOCK, C. B.

Famous London Churches. London: 1934. V. 38

MORTON, A. S.

Beyond the Palaeocrystic Sea or the Legend of Halfjord. Chicago: 1895. V. 44

MORTON & CO.

An Illustrated and Descriptive Guide to the Great Railways of England and Their Connections with the Continent. London: 1886-7. V. 46

MORTON, ANDRE

The Sword is Drawn. Boston: 1944. V. 44

MORTON, ARTHUR S.

A History of the Canadian West to 1870-1871. London: 1939. V. 41; 44; 45

A History of the Canadian West to 1870-71. London, Edinburgh, Paris: 1939. V. 40

A History of the Candian West to 1870-1871. New York: 1939. V. 44

The Journal of Duncan M'Gillivray of the North West Company at Fort George on the Saskatchewan, 1794-95. Toronto: 1939. V. 44

Sir George Simpson. Toronto and Vancouver: 1944. V. 42; 44

MORTON, DESMOND

Telegrams of the North-West Campaign. Toronto: 1972. V. 37; 43; 44

MORTON, EDWARD

Travels in Russia, and a Residence at St. Petersburg and Odessa, in the Years 1827-29. London: 1830. V. 37; 40

MORTON, FRANCIS

A Manual of Optics. London: 1855. V. 44

MORTON, G. H.

The Geology of the Country Around Liverpool . . . London: 1891. V. 38

MORTON, H. V.

In the Steps of St. Paul. London: 1920. V. 38

MORTON, HAMILTON

The Americas Cup, a Nautical Poem. New York: 1874. V. 39

MORTON, HENRY

Report of the Committee Appointed by the Philomathean Society of the University of Pennsylvania to Translate the Inscription on the Rosetta Stone. Philadelphia: 1859. V. 37

MORTON, J. F.

Atlas of Medicinal Plants of Middle America. Springfield: 1981. V. 45

MORTON, JOHN

The Natural History of Northampton-shire. London: 1712. V. 37; 38; 39; 41; 44

MORTON, JOHN BRUCE

Memories of Merton. Madras: 1865. V. 42

MORTON, JOHN CHALMERS 1821-1888

A Cyclopedia of Agriculture, Practical and Scientific. Glasgow: 1855. V. 41

A Cyclopedia of Agriculture, Practical and Scientific . . . . Glasgow, Edinburgh &: 1855. V. 42

MORTON, JOHN LOCKHART

The Resources of Estates. London: 1858. V. 38

MORTON, JOHN WATSON

The Artillery of nathan Bedford Forrest's Cavalry. Nashville: 1909. V. 37; 44

MORTON, L.

A Medical Bibliography. London: 1970. V. 44

MORTON, LESLIE T.

Garrison and Morton's Medical Bibliography. London: 1954. V. 42

A Medical Bibliography (Garrison & Morton). An Annotated Check List of Texts Illustrating the History of Medicine. London: 1970. V. 46

A Medical Bibliography. (Garrison & Morton). An Annotated Check-List of Texts Illustrating the History of Medicine. London: 1976. V. 45

A Medical Bibliography (Garrison & Morton): an Annotated Check-List of Texts Illustrating the History of Medicine. Hampshire: 1983. V. 42; 45

A Medical Bibliography (Garrison and Morton). An Annotated Check-List of Texts Illustrating the History of Medicine. London: 1983. V. 39

MORTON, NATHANIEL

New England's Memorial. Newport: 1772. V. 38; 40; 42; 44; 46

New England's Memorial. Boston: 1826. V. 38

The New England's Memorial. Plymouth: 1826. V. 38; 39; 40

MORTON, OHLAND

Teran and Texas. Austin: 1948. V. 37; 38; 44

MORTON, RICHARD

Opera Medica. Amsterdam: 1699. V. 40; 44

Phthisiologia Seu Exercitationes de Phthisi. Tribus Libris Comprehensae. Totumque Opus Varlis Historiis Illustaratum. London: 1689. V. 43

Phthisiologia; or, a Treatise of Consumptions. London: 1694. V. 41

Phthisiologia seu Exercitationes de Phthisi. Frankfurt & Leipzig: 1691. V. 37

Pyretologia (Graece). Pars Altera . . . London: 1694. V. 38

MORTON, SAMUEL GEORGE 1799-1851

Crania Americana; or, a Comparative View of the Skulls of Various Nations of North and South America . . . Philadelphia: 1839. V. 38

Crania Americana. London: 1839. V. 38

Illustrations of Pulmonary Consumption, Its Anatomical Characters, Causes, Symptoms and Treatment. Philadelphia: 1834. V. 37; 39; 43

Illustrations of Pulmonary Consumption . . . Philadelphia: 1837. V. 39; 42; 43

illustrations of Pulmonary Consumption, Its Anatomical Characters, Causes, Symptoms and Their Treatment. Philadelphia: 1937. V. 37

MORTON, SARAH W.

Beacon Hill: A Local Poem, Historic and Descriptive. Book I. Boston: 1797. V. 37

MORTON, SARAH W. A.

Ouabi: Or the Virtues of nature. An Indian Tale. In Four Cantos. Boston: 1790. V. 38

MORTON, THOMAS

Apologia Catholica ex Meris Jesuitarum Contradictionibus Conflata (etc.). London: 1605. V. 41; 44

Columbus; or, a World Discovered. London: 1792. V. 38

Engravings Illustrating the Surgical Anatomy of the Head and Neck, Axilla, Bend of the Elbow and Wrist, with Descriptions. London: 1845. V. 37; 40; 42

New English Canaan or New Canaan. Amsterdam: 1637. V. 37; 38; 40; 44

MORTON, THOMAS, BP. OF DURHAM 1564-1659

A Defence of the Innocencie of the Three Ceremonies of the Church of England. London: 1619. V. 40

A Discharge of Five Imputations of Mis-Allegations, Falsely Charged Upon the Bishop of Durseme by an English Baron. 1633. V. 41

A Discharge of Five Imputations of Mis-Allegations, Fallsly Charged upon the (Now) Bishop of Duresme, by an English Baron. London: 1633. V. 42

An Exact Discoverie of Romish Doctrine In the Case of Conspiracie and Rebellion . . . London: 1605. V. 43

A Full Satisfaction Concerning a Double Romish Iniquitie. London: 1606. V. 40

The Grand Imposture of the (Now) Church of Rome . . . London: 1628. V. 42

MORTON, THOMAS G.

The History of the Pennsylvania Hospital, 1751-1895. Philadelphia: 1895. V. 42; 45; 46

MORTON, W. L.

Alexander Begg's Red River Journal and Other Documents Relating to the Red River Reistance of 1869-70. Toronto: 1956. V. 45

MORTON, WILLIAM

U.S. 32nd Congress, 1st Session, House (Report of) The Select Committe to Whom was Referred the Memorial of Dr. William T. G. Morton, Asking Renumeration from Congress for the Discovery of the Anesthetic or Pain-Subduing Properties of Sulphuric Ether. Washington: 1852. V. 45

MORTON, WILLIAM J.

The X Ray or Photography of the Invisible and Its Value in Surgery. London: 1896. V. 43

The X Ray or Photography of the Invisible and Its Value in Surgery. New York: 1896. V. 37; 41; 42

MORTON, WILLIAM T. G.

Minority Report . . . Concerning the Discovery of the Anaesthetic Property of Sulphuric Ether. (Washington: 1849). V. 37

On the Physiological Effects of Sulphuric Ether and Its Superiority to Chloroform. Boston: 1850. V. 41

Trails of a Public Benefactor, as illustrated in the Discovery of Etherization by Nathan P. Rice. New York: 1859. V. 37

MORTON'S Medical Bibliography. 1991. V. 46

THE MORTONS of Bardon. London: 1863. V. 42; 46

MORUS, THOMAS

La Description de L'Isle de l'Utopie ou est Compris le Miroer des Republiques du Monde & l'Exemplaire de vie Heureuse. Paris: 1550. V. 38

MORVAN DE BELLEGARDE, JEAN BAPTISTE

Reflexions upon Ridicule; or What It Is That Makes a Man Ridiculous and the Means to Avoid It. London: 1727. V. 41

Reflexions Upon Ridicule; or, What It Is That Makes a Man Ridiculous . . . London: 1739. V. 44

Reflexions upon Ridicule; or What it is that makes a man ridiculous; and the means to avoid it. Wherein are represented the different manners and characters of persons of the present age . . . London: 1707. V. 37

MORYSEN, FYNES 1566-1630

A History of Ireland from the Year 1599 to 1603 with a Short Narration of the State of the Kingdom from the Year 1169. To Which is Added a Description of Ireland. Dublin: 1735. V. 46

MORYSON, FYNES 1566-1630

Itinerary. London: 1617. V. 37; 41; 43; 45

Itinerary Containing His Ten Yeeres Travel through the Twelve Dominions of Germany, Bohmerland, Sweitzerland, Netherland, Denmarke, Poland, Italy, Turky, France, England, Scotland & Ireland. Glasgow: 1907-08. V. 37; 38; 39; 42; 46

An Itinerary, Containing His Ten Yeers Travel through the Twelve Dominios of Germany, Bohmerland, Sweitzerland, Scotland and Ireland. Glasgow: 1908. V. 46

MOSBY, JOHN SINGLETON

Stuart's Cavalry in the Gettysburg Campaign. New York: 1908. V. 45

MOSCARDO, LODOVICO

Note Overo Memorie del Museo di Lodovico Moscardo Nobile Veronese, Accademico Filarmonico, dal Medisimo Descritte, et in Tre Libri Distinte . . . con l'Aggiunta in Questa Seconda Parte Dello Stesso Autore Acccresciuta di Cose Sepattati . . . Verona: 1672. V. 37

MOSCATI, SABATINO

The Phoenicians. Milan: 1988. V. 40

The World of the Phoenicians. New York: 1968. V. 42

MOSCHINI, VITTORIO

Canaletto. Milan: 1954. V. 43

MOSCHOPOULOS, MANUEL

De Ratione Examinandae Orationis Libellus. Paris: 1545. V. 38; 45

MOSELEY, BENJAMIN

On Hydrophobia, Its Prevention and Cure: with a Dissertation on Canine Madness . . . London: 1813. V. 38

A Treatise on Sugar. London: 1800. V. 45

A Treatise Concerning the Properties and Effects of Coffee. Philadelphia: 1796. V. 37

MOSELEY, HENRY GWYN JEFFREYS

The High Frequency Spectra of the Elements. 1913. V. 37

MOSELEY, HENRY N.

Notes by a Naturalist. London: 1892. V. 38; 41

Oregon: Its Resources, Climate, People, and Productions. London: 1878. V. 37; 45

MOSELEY, HUMPHREY

Courteous Reader, These Books Following are Printed for Humphrey Moseley at the Princes Armes in St. Paul's Churchyard. London: 1656. V. 44

MOSELEY, MARTIN E.

The Dry-Fly Fisherman's Entomology. London: 1921. V. 38

The Fly-Fishing Fisherman's Entomology. London: 1921. V. 40

MOSELEY, MARY

The Bahamas Handbook. Nassau: 1926. V. 38

MOSELEY, WALTER MICHAEL

An Essay on Archery; Describing the Practice of that Art, in all Ages and Nations. London: 1792. V. 38; 39; 46

An Essay on Archery; Describing the Practice of that Art in All Ages and Nations. Worcester: 1792. V. 42; 43

MOSELEY, WILLIAM WILLIS

Eleven Chapters on Nervous or Mental Complaints, and on Two Great Discoveries . . . London: 1841. V. 43

MOSELY, EPHRAIM

Teeth, Their Natural History. London: 1862. V. 40; 45

MOSELY, MARTIN E.

The Dry-Fly Fisherman's Entomology. London: 1921. V. 43

MOSELY, WILLIAM

Baptist Discipline Together with the Necessary Forms in Constituting Churches, Ordaining Deacons and Ministers, with the Order of Buisness, Abstract of Principles, Decorum and the Powers of an Association. Griffin: 1854. V. 44

MOSEMAN, C. M.

Moseman's Illustrated Guide for Purchasers of Horse Furnishing Goods, Novelties and Stable Appointments, Imported and Domestic. New York: 1900. V. 37

MOSENTHAL, JULIUS DE

Ostriches and Ostrich Farming. London: 1877. V. 39; 40

MOSER, BARRY

A Family Letter. 1979. V. 39

Fifty Wood Engravings. Northampton: 1978. V. 38; 39; 43

Fifty Wood Engravings. Easthampton: 1978. V. 37

Gold Rush. Los Angeles: 1985. V. 39; 42

Twelve Woodengravings of Cirsia & Various. Northampton: 1978. V. 46

Wood Engraving, Notes on the Craft. Northampton: 1979. V. 42

MOSER, GEORGE

A Family Letter Written in Nineteen Thirty-Two by George Moser to His Nephew Arthur Moser and Published by His Great Nephew Barry Moser. Easthampton: 1979. V. 37

MOSER, JEFFERSON F.

The Salmon and Salmon Fisheries of Alaska. Washington: 1899. V. 38

MOSER, JOSEPH

The Adventures of Timothy Twig, Esq. London: 1794. V. 39; 40; 42; 45; 46

MOSES, ADOLF

Luser the Watchmaker. Cincinnati: 1880. V. 37

MOSES, ANNA MARY ROBERTSON 1860-

Grandma Moses, American Primitive. New York: 1947. V. 39

Grandma Moses. My Life's History. New York: 1952. V. 45

MOSES BEN MAIMON 1135-1204

Doctor Perplexorum: ad Dubia & Obscuriora Scripturae Loca Rectius Intelligenda Veluti Clavem Continens . . . Basle: 1629. V. 40

Shemonah Peraquim sive Canones Ethici . . . Amstelodami;: 1640. V. 42

Tractatus Rabbi Moysi de Regimine Sanitatis ad Soldanum Regem. Augsburg: 1513. V. 40

MOSES, HENRY

Ancient Vases from the Collection of Sir Henry Englefield, Drawn and Engraved by Henry Moses. London: 1848. V. 37; 44

Vases from the Collection of Sir Henry Englefield, Bart. London: 1819. V. 44

Visit of William the Fourth When Duke of Clarence, as Lord High Admiral, to Portsmouth, in the Year 1827, With Views of the Russian Squadron. London: 1830. V. 39; 41

Visit of William the Fourth When Duke of Clarence, as Lord High Admiral to Portsmouth, in the Year 1827 with Views of the Russian Squadron. London: 1840. V. 40

MOSES, JOHN

Illinois, Historical and Statistical Comprising the Essential Facts of Its Planting and Growth as a Province, County, Territory and State. Chicago: 1889. V. 38

MOSES, MYER

Full Annals of the Revolution in France, 1830. New York: 1830. V. 37

Oration, Delivered at Tammany-Hall on the Twelfth May, 1831 . . . New York: 1831. V. 45

MOSES, ROBERT

Yale Verse: 1898-1908. New Haven: 1909. V. 44

MOSGROVE, GEORGE DALLAS

. . . Kentucky Cavaliers in Dixie or, the Reminiscences of a Confederate Cavalryman . . . Louisville: 1895. V. 43

MOSHEIM, JOHANN L. VON 1694-1755

An Ecclesiastical History, Antient and Modern, from the Birth of Christ, to the Beginning of the Present Century . . . London: 1765. V. 42; 43

An Ecclesiastical History, Ancient and Modern. London: 1811. V. 37; 39

De Rebus Christianorum Ante Constantinum Magnum Commentarii. Helmstadt: 1753. V. 39

MOSHEIM, JOHN L. VON 1694-1755

Institutes of Ecclesistical History Ancient and Modern. London: 1850. V. 38

MOSHER, RICHARD

A Short Narrative Containing the Birth, Education, Accidents, Awakening, Conversion, Call to the Ministry, Travels, Events and Reflections. Union Mills: 1846. V. 39; 44

MOSHER, THOMAS BIRD

Amphora. A Collection of Prose and Verse Chosen by the Editor of the Bibleot. Portland: 1912. V. 42

The Mosher Books. Portland: 1910. V. 44

MOSIN, VLADIMIR

Anchor Watermarks. Amsterdam: 1973. V. 38

MOSKOWITZ, IRA

Ira Moskowitz: Graphics - a Catalogue Raisonne 1929-1975. Baltimore: 1975. V. 39; 44

Satan in Goray. By Isaac Bashevis Singer. Etchings and drawings by Ira Moskowitz. New York: (c. 1981). V. 37

MOSLEY, OSWALD

Fascism: 100 Questions Asked and Answered. London: 1936. V. 43

MOSLEY, SETH LISTER

An Account of the Birds of the Huddersfield District. Huddersfield: 1915. V. 37

A History of British Birds, Their Nests and Eggs. Huddersfield: 1881-94. V. 37

MOSQUERA, T. C.

Memoir on the Physical and Political Geography of New Granada. New York: 1853. V. 46

MOSS, CELIA

Early Efforts: a Volumes of Poems by the Misses Moss, of the Hebrew Nation, Aged 18 and 16. London: 1839. V. 45

MOSS, CHARLES

The Evidence of the Resurrection Cleared from the Exceptions of a Late Phamphlet, Entitled the Resurrection of Jesus Considered by a Moral Philosopher, in Answer to the Tryal of the Witnesses, &c. London: 1744. V. 42

MOSS, EDWARD L.

Shores of the Polar Sea, a Narrative of the Arctic Expedition of 1875-76. London: 1878. V. 46

MOSS, FRANK

Persecution of Negroes by Roughs and Policemen, in the City of New York, August 1900. New York: 1900. V. 45

MOSS, FREDERICK J.

Through Atolls and Islands in the Great South Sea. London: 1889. V. 41

MOSS, GEOFFREY

Defeat. New York: 1924. V. 45

MOSS, HOWARD

Finding Them Lost and Other Poems. New York: 1965. V. 41

Instant Lives. New York: 1974. V. 41

The Toy Fair. New York: 1954. V. 41

A Winter Come. A Summer Gone. Poems 1946-1960. New York: 1956. V. 41

The Wound and the Weather. New York: 1946. V. 41; 46

MOSS, HUGH

By Imperial Command. An Introduction to Ch'ing Imperial Painted Enamels. Hong Kong: 1976. V. 38

MOSS, THOMAS

Poems on Several Occasions. Wolverhampton: 1769. V. 42

Poems Upon Several Occasions. London: 1827. V. 43

A Treatise of Gauging, Containing not only What is Common on the Subject, But Likewise a Great Variety of New and Interesting Improvements. London: 1765. V. 44

MOSS, W. G.

The History and Antiquities of the Town and Port of Hastings. London: 1824. V. 39; 44

MOSSE, A. H. E.

My Somali Book a Record of Two Shooting Trips. London: 1913. V. 41

MOSSE, HENRIETTA ROUVIERE

Craigh-Melrose Priory; or, Memoirs of the Mount Linton Family. London: 1816. V. 37

MOSSER, MARJORIE

Good Maine Food. New York: 1939. V. 38

Good Maine Food. New York: 1940. V. 41

MOSSMAN, SAMUEL

Narrative of the Shipwreck of the 'Admella' Inter-Colonial Steamer, on the Southern Coast of Australia. Melborune: 1859. V. 40

Our Australian Colonies. London: 1836. V. 38

THE MOST Effectual Way of Detecting Forged Notes. London: 1818. V. 39

A MOST Execrable and Barbarous Murder Done by an East-Indian Devil, or a Native of Java Major, in the Road of Bantam, Aboard and English Ship Called the Coster on the 22 of October last in 1641. London: 1642. V. 45

A MOST Valuable Collection of Exotica and Scarce Aquatic Plants, Orange Trees, and Camellias . . . Clapton: 1822. V. 38; 40

MOSTEL, ZERO

Zero by Mostel. New York: 1965. V. 39; 40

MOTHER GOOSE

Aunt Louisa's London Picture Book. London: 1868. V. 38

The Boyd Smith Mother Goose. New York: 1919. V. 42

The Jessie Willcox Smith Mother Goose . . . New York: 1914. V. 42; 46

Mother Goose's Melodies. Philadelphia: 1860. V. 44

Mother Goose's Melodies. Philadelphia: 1870. V. 41

Mother Goose. London: 1881. V. 38; 43; 45; 46

Mother Goose, or the Old Nursey Rhymes. London & New York: 1881. V. 39

Mother Goose, or the Old Nursey Rhymes. New York: 1881. V. 39

Mother Goose. New York: 1904. V. 46

Mother Goose in Silhouettes cut by Katharine G. Buffum. Boston and New York: 1907. V. 41

The Complete Mother Goose. New York: 1909. V. 38

Mother Goose: the Old Nursery Rhymes. London: 1913. V. 38; 41

Mother Goose. Chicago: 1915. V. 40

Mother Goose's Nursery Tales. London: 1923. V. 45

Mother Goose. Book 1. New York: 1923. V. 39

Mother Goose. New York: 1928. V. 45

Mother Goose. London: 1938. V. 46

Mother Goose. The Old Nursery Rhymes. London: 1958. V. 39

Mother Goose: Twenty Nursery Rhymes. San Fransisco: 1970. V. 38; 39

Mother Goose; The Old Nursery Rhymes. London: (1913). V. 37

Mother Goose or the Old Nursery Rhymes. Illustrated by Kate Greenaway. Engraved and Printed by Edmund Evans. New York: n.d. (1881). V. 37

Mother Goose or the Old Nursery Rhymes. London & New York: 1918. V. 38

My Book of Mother Goose Nursery Rhymes. London. V. 40

My Book of Mother Goose Nursery Rhyme. London: 1927. V. 46

The Old Fashioned Mother Goose Melodies. New York: 1879. V. 37; 43

The Real Mother Goose. Chicago: 1916. V. 46

The Real Mother Goose. London: 1925. V. 42

Ridiculous Rhymes. London: 1870. V. 38

VerBeck's Bears in Mother Goose-Land . . . London. V. 42

Willy Pogany's Mother Goose. New York: 1928. V. 41; 46

MOTHER Shipton Part I & II. London: 1771. V. 46

MOTHER'S Little Rhyme Book. V. 44
MOTHER'S Little Rhyme Book. London. V. 43

THE MOTHER'S Own Book, Containing Important and Useful Preparations, &c. Ipswich: 1834. V. 42; 46

MOTHERWELL, ROBERT

The Dada Painters and Poets. New York: 1951. V. 39; 41; 42

Dada Painters and Poets: an Anthology. Wittenborn: 1951. V. 45

Robert Motherwell. New York: 1983. V. 43

MOTHERWELL, WILLIAM

Minstrelsey: Ancient and Modern, with an Historical Introduction and Notes. Glasgow: 1827. V. 39; 46

Minstrelsy, Ancient and Modern. Boston: 1846. V. 39

MOTIF: a Journal of Visual Arts. London: 1958-65. V. 40

MOTION, ANDREW

Goodnestone - a Sequence. London: 1972. V. 38

MOTLEY, JOHN

The History of the Life of Peter I, Emperor of Russia. London: 1739. V. 40; 46

MOTLEY, JOHN L.

(Collected Historical) Works. London: 1903-04. V. 39

MOTLEY, JOHN LOTHROP 1766-1851

History of the United Netherlands. London: 1867. V. 40

History of the United Netherlands from the Death of William the Silent to the Twelve Years' Truce 1609. New York: 1869. V. 40

Merry-Mount; a Romance of the Massachusetts Colony. Boston & Cambridge: 1849. V. 43

Morton's Hope; or The Memoirs of a Provincial. New York: 1839. V. 43

The Rise of the Dutch Republic. New York: 1856. V. 41; 43

The Rise of the Dutch Republic. New York: 1869. V. 40

The Rise of the Dutch Republic, a History. London: 1892. V. 38

The Rise of the Dutch Republic. London: 1900. V. 38

THE MOTOGRAPH Moving Picture Book. London: 1898. V. 42

MOTOJIRO, K.

The Japanese Iris. Tokyo: 1971. V. 45

THE MOTORGRAPH Moving Picture Book. 1898. V. 44

MOTT, A.

Biographical Sketches and Interesting Anecdotes of Persons of Color. New York: 1837. V. 39

Biographical Sketches and Interesting Anecdotes of Persons of Color. New York: 1839. V. 39

MOTT, ABIGAIL 1766-1851

Biographical Sketches and Interesting Anecdotes of Persons of Color. New York: 1838. V. 38

MOTT, ABIGAIL FIELD

Observations on the Importance of Female Education, and Maternal Instruction, With Their Beneficial Influence on Society. New York: 1825. V. 41

Observations on the Importance of Female Education and Maternal Instruction with Their Beneficial Influence on Society. New York: 1827. V. 37

MOTT, EDWARD HAROLD

Between the Ocean and the Lakes The Story of Erie. New York: 1901. V. 40

MOTT, FRANK LUTHER

A History of American Magazines, 1741-1850, 1850-1865, 1865-1885, 1885-1905, 1905-1930. Cambridge: 1967-68. V. 37

MOTT, J. L.

J. L. Mott Iron Works. Illustrated Catalogue of Artistic Grates, Fenders, Andirons, Fire Irons and Other Goods for the Fitting and Decorating of the Fire Place. New York: 1882. V. 41

MOTT, LUCRETIA

Discourse on Woman. Philadelphia: 1850. V. 43

A Sermon to the Medical Students . . . at Cherry Street Meeting, Philadelphia on First-Day Evening, Second Month, 11th 1849. Philadelphia: 1849. V. 43

MOTT, SMITH B.

The Campaigns of the Fifty-Second Regiment, Pennsylvania Volunteer Infantry, Second Regiment, Pennsylvania Volunteer Infantry . . . Philadelphia: 1911. V. 42

MOTTE, ANDREW d. 1730

A Treatise of the Mechanical Powers, Wherein the Laws of Motion, and the Properties of Those Powers are Explained and Demonstrated. London: 1727. V. 37; 42

MOTTE, BENJAMIN

Oratio Dominica . . . Nimirum, Plus Centum Linguis, Versionibus, aut Characteribus Reddita & Expressa. London: 1700. V. 46

MOTTELAY, PAUL F.

Frank Leslie's Illustrations: the Soldier in Our Civil War. New York: 1893. V. 42

MOTTELAY, PAUL FLEURY

Bibliographical History of Electricity and Magnetism Chronologically Arranged . . . London: 1922. V. 39; 42; 45

MOTTEUX, PETER ANTHONY

Beauty in Distress. London: 1698. V. 42; 44

Love's a Jest. London: 1696. V. 38; 45

Love's Triumph: an Opera. London: 1708. V. 44

Maria. A Poem Occasioned by the Death of Her Majesty. London: 1695. V. 41; 45

MOTTLEY, JOHN

The History of the Life and Reign of the Empress Catherine: Containing, A Short History of the Russian Empire . . . London: 1744. V. 37

The History of the Life of Peter I, Emperor of Russia. London: 1739. V. 37

Joe Miller's Jests; or, the Wits Vade-Mecum. London: 1739. V. 45

Joe Miller's Jests . . . London: 175-? V. 42

Joe Miller's Jests; or, the Wits Vade-Mecum. London: 1751. V. 42; 44

MOTTRAM, RALPH HALE

The Crime at Vanderlynden's. London: 1926. V. 38

Sixty-Four, Ninety-Four! London: 1925. V. 38

The Spanish Farm. A Story of Flanders. London: 1924. V. 44

The Spanish Farm Trilogy, 1914-1918. London: 1927. V. 40

The Spanish Farm. Sixty-Four, Ninety-Four! The crime at Vanderlynden's. London: 1924-25-26. V. 37

Strawberry Time and the Banquet. London: 1934. V. 44

Ten Years Ago. London: 1928. V. 38; 44; 45; 46

Three Personal Records of the War. London: 1929. V. 44

MOUAT, FREDERIC J.

Adventures and Researches Among the Andaman Islanders. London: 1863. V. 38

Hospital Construction and Management. London: 1883. V. 39

MOUBRAY, BONINGTON

A Practical Treatise on the Breeding, Rearing and Fattening of all Kinds of Domestic Poultry. London: 1824. V. 37; 41; 43

MOUFFLE D'ANGERVILLE d. ca. 1794

The Private Life of Lewis XV. Dublin: 1781. V. 39

MOUHY, CHARLES DE FIEUX, CHEVALIER DE

The Fortunate Country Maid . . . London: 1789. V. 46

MOULE, THOMAS

Antiquities in Westminster Abbey. London: 1825. V. 37

An Essay on the Roman Villas of the Augustan Age, Their Architectural Disposition and Enrichments . . . London: 1833. V. 38; 40; 45

Great Britain Illustrated. London: 1830. V. 42; 46

Heraldry of Fish, Notices of the Principal Families Bearing Fish in their Arms. London: 1842. V. 39

The Landscape Album; or, Great Britain Illustrated: in A Series of Views by W. Westall. London: 1832. V. 42

MOULIN, R. P.

Cree Hymns: Recueil de Cantiques Cris. Edmonton: 1929. V. 45

MOULTON, JOSEPH W.

New York 170 Years Ago, with a View and Explanatory Notes. New York: 1843. V. 44

View of the City of New-Orange. New York: 1825. V. 41; 46

MOULTON, LOUISE CHANDLER

Arthur O'Shaughnessy His Life and Works. Cambridge & Chicago: 1894. V. 42

In Garden of Dreams: Lyrics and Sonnets. Boston: 1890. V. 41

My Third Book. A Collection of Tales. New York: 1859. V. 40; 41

MOULTRIE, WILLIAM

Memoirs of the American Revolution, So Far As It Is Related to the States of North and South Carolina, and Georgia. New York: 1802. V. 44; 45

MOUNSEY, A. H.

A Journey through the Caucasus and the Interior of Persia, 1872. London: 1872. V. 37; 39; 45

MOUNT-EDGCUMBE, RICHARD EDGCUMBE, 2ND EARL OF 1764-1839

Musical Reminiscences of an Old Amateur. London: 1824. V. 40

Musical Reminiscences, Containing an Account of the Italian Opera in England from 1773. London: 1834. V. 45

MOUNTAIN, ARMINE W.

A Memoir of George Jehoshaphat Mountain, D.D., D.C.L., Late Bishop of Quebec. London: 1866. V. 44

A Memoir of George Jehoshphat Mountain, D.D., D.C.L., Late Bishop of Quebec. Montreal: 1866. V. 38; 44

MOUNTAIN, JAMES

The History of Selby, Ancient and Modern. York: 1800. V. 39; 44; 45

MOUNTAIN, R. G.

Songs of the Wilderness. London: 1846. V. 43

THE MOUNTAINS of Wales: An Anthology in Verse and Prose. 1987. V. 40

MOUNTBATTEN, LOUIS, EARL OF

An Introduction to Polo. London: 1931. V. 39

MOUNTENEY, BARCLAY

Selections from the Various Authors Who Have Written Concerning Brazil. London: 1825. V. 39; 40; 43

MOUNTENEY-JEPHSON, A. J.

Emin Pasha and the Rebellion at the Equator. London: 1890. V. 39; 41; 42; 45

Emin Pasha and the Rebellion at the Equator. New York: 1890. V. 44; 45

MOUNTFAUCON DE VILLARS, NICOLAS DE

The Count de Gabalis: Being a Diverting History of the Rosicrucian Doctrine of Spirits. London: 1714. V. 39; 42

MOUNTFORD, C. P.

Records of the American Australian Scientific Expedition to Arnhem Land. Volume I Art, Myth and Symbolism. 1956. V. 38

MOUNTFORD, WILLIAM

Martyria: a Legend. Boston: 1846. V. 38; 40

MOUNTFORT, WILLIAM

Greenwich-Park: a Comedy. London: 1691. V. 45

Six Plays Written by Mr. Mountfort . . . London: 1720. V. 46

MOUNTMORRES, HERVEY REDMOND MORRES

Plan of an Universal Fishing Company in Ireland. Dublin: 1773. V. 42

MOURELLS, FRANCISCO ANTONIO

Voyage to the Sonora in the Second Bucareli Expedition. San Francisco: 1920. V. 37

MOURIKI, DOULA

The Mosaics of the nea Moni of Chios. Athens: 1985. V. 45

The Mosaics of the Nea Moni, Chios. New York: 1986. V. 37; 39

MOURLOT, FERNAND

Art in Posters: the Complete Original Posters of Braque, Chagall, Dufy, Leger, Matisse, Miro, Picasso. Monte Carlo: 1959. V. 46

Braque Lithographe. Monte Carlo: 1963. V. 42

The Lithographs of Chagall: 1957-1962. Monte Carlo: 1963. V. 41

Picasso Lithographe. Monte Carlo: 1949-64. V. 41

Picasso Lithographs. Boston: 1970. V. 41; 43; 46

Souvenirs et Portraits d'Artistes. Paris: 1972. V. 41

MOURRA, MAURICE

'Creations Maurice Mourra.' Paris: n.d. V. 37

MOURT, GEORGE

Mourt's Relation, or Journal of the Plantation at Plymouth. Boston;: 1865. V. 39

A Relation or Iournall of the Beginning and Proceedings of the English Plantation Setled at Plimoth in New England, by Certaine English Aduenturers Both Merchants and Others. London: 1622. V. 37; 38

MOURY, SYLVESTER

Arizona and Sonora: The Geography. New York: 1864. V. 39

MOUSSINAC, LEON

The New Movement in the Theatre. London: 1931. V. 38

Tapis. Paris: 1925. V. 37; 40

MOUTON, GABRIEL

Observationes Diametrorum Solis et Lunae Apparentium, Meridianarumque Aliquot Altitudinum Soli & Paucarum Fixarum. Lyon: 1670. V. 44

MOWAT, FARLEY

Never Cry Wolf. Toronto: 1963. V. 39

Wale of the Great Sealers. Toronto: 1973. V. 45

MOWER, ARTHUR

Zulneida; a Tale of Sicily. London: 1837. V. 43; 45

MOWRIS, J. A.

A History of the 117th Regiment. Hartford: 1866. V. 46

MOWRY, SYLVESTER

Arizona and Sonora. New York: 1864. V. 42; 43

Memoir of the Proposed Territory of Arizona. Washington: 1857. V. 39

MOXON, ELIZABETH

English Housewifery. Leeds: 1790. V. 38; 42

English Housewifry. Leedes: 1750. V. 37

MOXON, JOSEPH 1627-1700

Mechanick Exercise on the Whole Art of Printing 1683-84. London: 1962. V. 38; 40; 43

Mechanick Exercise on the Whole Art of Printing (1683-4). London: 1958. V. 38; 46

Practical Perspective. London: 1670. V. 46

A Tutor to Astronomy and Geography, or an Easie and Speedy Way to Know the Use of Both the Globes, Coelestial and Terrestrial. London: 1674. V. 38

A Tutor to Astronomy and Geography . . . London: 1686. V. 38; 42

A Tutor to Astronomy and Geography, or an Easie and Speedy Way to Know the Use of Both Globes . . . London: 1699. V. 40; 42

A Tutor to Astronomie and Geograpahie: or an Easie and Speedy Way to Know the Use of Both the Globes, Coelestial and Terrestrial . . . London: 1659. V. 38

MOYENS et Conditions A Redresser Le Pont Des Arches Establis Du Temps Des Nobles Seignevrs Les Bovrgvemaistres Fovollon Et Beeckman Avec la Suitte & le Compte Final, Rendu l'An 1663. Liege: 1663. V. 37

MOYER, H. P.

History of the Seventeenth Regiment Pennsylvania Volunteer Cavalry, or One Hundred and Sixty-Seconds in the Line of Pennsylvania Volunteer Regiments, War to Suppress the Rebellion, 1861-1865. Lebanon: 1911. V. 39; 42

MOYERS, WILLIAM H.

Sketches of California and Hawaii. San Francisco: 1970. V. 40

MOYLE, ROBERT

An Exact Book of Entries, of the Most Select and Judicial Writs Used in the Common Law. London: 1658. V. 38; 40

MOYLE, WALTER

The Works of Walter Moyle Esq; None of Which Were Ever Before Publish'd. London: 1726. V. 39; 42

The Whole Works that were Published by Himself. London: 1727. V. 39

MOYNIHAN, BERKELY

The Operative Treatment of Gastric Ulcers. London: 1903. V. 37

MOYSEY, ABEL

The Confederates; a Story. London: 1823. V. 40; 42; 46

MOZART, LEOPOLD

leopold Mozarts Hochfurstl. Augsburg: 1787. V. 45

MOZART, WOLFGANG AMADEUS 1756-1791

Letter of Mozart and His Family. London: 1938. V. 45

The Letters of Wolfgang Amaedus Mozart. New York: 1866. V. 41; 43

A Selection from the Vocal Compositions of Mozart, United to English Verse Never Before Published . . . piano-forte accompaniments arranged from the original scores by Muzio Clementi. The poetry, by David Thomson . . . London: 1816. V. 37

Songs, Duets, Recitative, Etc. Etc. in Don Juan. London: 1833. V. 39

MOZEEN, THOMAS

A Collection of Miscellaneous Essays. London: 1762. V. 37

The Lyrick Pacquet. London: 1764. V. 37

Young Scarron. London: 1752. V. 37; 42

MROUEH, A.

An Anthology of Arab Humour in 8 volumes: Poets and writers/Egyptians/Emigrants/Judges and Lawyers/Varieties. 1987. V. 37

MT. PRINCETON Hot Springs Townsite and Improvement Co. Quincy, Ill.: 1890. V. 37

MUCHA, ALPHONSE M.

Figures Decoratives. Paris: 1905. V. 41

MUCHA, JIRI

Alphonse Mucha: The Master of Art Nouveau. London: (1967). V. 37

MUCHALL-VIEBROOK, T. W.

Flemish Drawings of the Seventeenth Century. London: 1926. V. 42; 46

MUCKAWI, ABDUL KADIR MAHOMED

Anglo-Arabic Rudimentary Teacher. Bombay: 1884. V. 44

MUCKLE, HUGH

Tetecan: an Aztec Tragedy. San Francisco: 1950. V. 39

MUDD, HARVEY

The Plain of Smokes. Santa Barbara: 1981. V. 38; 40; 42; 45; 46

The Plain of Smokes. 1982. V. 42

The Plain of Smokes. 1982. V. 43; 44

MUDD, JOSEPH ALOYSIUS

With Porter in North Missouri, a Chapter in the History of the War Between the States. Washington: 1909. V. 43; 46

MUDD, NETTIE

Life of Doctor Samuel A. Mudd. N.P.: 1906. V. 42; 46

MUDFORD, WILLIAM

An Historical Account of the Campaign in the Netherlands in 1815 . . . London: 1817. V. 45

Nubilia in Search of a Husband. Philadelphia: 1809. V. 39

Stephen Dugard. London: 1840. V. 43

MUDGE, EDWARD

An Account of the Operations Carried on For Accomplishing a Trigonometical Survey of England and Wales; from the Commencemnt in the Year 1784 to the End of the Year 1796 . . . . Volume II . . . 1797 . . . 1799; Volume III 1800, 1801, 1803, 1804, 1806, 1807, 1808 & 1809. London: 1799-1811. V. 41; 46

General Survey of England and Wales Sheets I, II, XLVII and XLVIII. V. 44

General Survey of England and Wales. London: 1805. V. 41

MUDGE, JOHN

A Radical and Expeditious Cure for a Recent Catarrhous Cough . . . . London: 1779. V. 37

MUDIE-COOKE, OLIVE

With the V.A.D. Convoys in France, Flanders, Italy. Cambridge: 1920. V. 45; 46

MUDIE, JAMES

An Historical and Critical Account of a Grand Series of National Medals. London: 1820. V. 42

MUDIE, ROBERT

China and Its Resources, and Peculiarities, Physical, Political, Social and Commercial . . . London: 1840. V. 42

The Feathered Tribes of the British Islands. 1835. V. 46

The Feathered Tribes of the British Islands. London: 1835. V. 37; 38; 39; 45

The Feathered Tribes of the British Islands. London: 1841. V. 37; 38; 39

The Feathered Tribes of the British Islands. London: 1878. V. 42; 43

The Feathered Tribes of the British Islands. London: 1834. V. 37; 39

Hampshire: Its Past and Present Condition, and Future Prospects. Winchester,: 1838. V. 39

Hampshire: Its Past and Present Condition, and Future Prospects. Winchester: 1840. V. 37

The Heavens. London: 1835. V. 45

A Historical Account of His Majesty's Visit to Scotland. Edinburgh: 1822. V. 37; 39

The Modern Athens: A Dissection and Demonstration of Men and Things in the Scotch Capital. London: 1825. V. 37

The Picture of Australia . . . London: 1829. V. 39; 46

Spring: Summer: Autumn: Winter. London: 1837. V. 38

MUDWINKLE, H. J.

A Study of Dionsaurs on the Comparative Method or Comparative Dionsaurs for Students, Amateurs and Breeders. Andoversford and Fullerton: 1988. V. 39

A Study of Dinosaurs on the Comparative Method or Comparative Dinosaurs for Students, Amateurs, Fanciers and Breeders. California: 1988. V. 40

MUELLER, F. VON

Eucalyptographia. Melbourne: 1879-84. V. 43

Iconography of Australian Species of Acacia and Cognate Genera. Melbourne: 1887-88. V. 43; 44; 46

The Vegetation of the Chatham-Islands. Melbourne: 1964. V. 38

MUELLER, HANS ALEXANDER

Woodcuts and Wood Engravings: How I Make Them. New York: 1933. V. 39

Wood Cuts and Engravings How I Make Them. New York: 1939. V. 38; 39; 41; 44

MUELLER, JOHN

A Treatise Containing the Elementary Part of Fortification, Regular and Irregular. London: 1756. V. 46

MUELLER, OTTO FREDERIK

Animalcula Infusoria Fluvia Tilia et Marina, Quae Detexit, Systematice Descripsit ad Vivum Delineari Curavit . . . Havniae: 1786. V. 38

MUELLER, R. VON

The Vegetation of the Chatham-Islands. Melbourne: 1864. V. 37

MUENCH, DAVID

Arizona. N.P.: Portland: 1971. V. 45

MUENSTER, SEBASTIAN 1489-1552

Cosmographey. Basel: 1598. V. 41

Der Horologien, Oder Sonnen Uhren Kunstliche Beschreibung . . . Basel: 1579. V. 45; 46

Horologiographia. Basel: 1533. V. 42

(Hebrew Title) Kalendarium Hebraicum. Basle: 1527. V. 38

MUENSTERBERGER, WARNER

Sculpture of primitive Man. New York: (1955). V. 37

MUENTZ, J. H.

Encaustic; or, Count Caylus's Method of Painting in the Manner of the Ancients. London: 1760. V. 44

MUFFETT, THOMAS 1553-1604

1 Healths Improvement. London: 1655. V. 38; 45

MUFFLY, J. W.

The Story of Our Regiment. Des Moines: 1904. V. 42; 45

MUGGERIDGE, MALCOLM

Autumnal Face. London: 1931. V. 42

Picture Palace. London: 1934. V. 44

MUGLISTON, WILLIAM

A Letter, on the Subject of Wool, Interspersed with Remarks on Cotton, Addressed to the Public at Large . . . Nottingham: 1782. V. 43

A Letter, on the Subject of Wool, Interspersed with Remarks on Cotton, Addressed tot he Public at Large, but More Particularly to the Committee of Merchants and Manufactures at Leeds. Nottingham: 1782 1990. V. 40

A Letter, on the Subject of Wool, Interspersed with Remarks on Cotton, Addressed to the Public at Large. London: 1825. V. 43

MUHLBACH, LOUISA

Historical Romances. New York: & London: 1898. V. 44

MUIR, ALAN

Tumbledown Farm. London: 1889. V. 42; 43

MUIR, D. D. JAMES

An Examination of the Principles Contained in the Age of Reason. Baltimore: 1795. V. 44

MUIR, EDWIN

Chorus of the Newly Dead. 1926. V. 39

Chorus of the Newly Dead: a Poem. London: 1926. V. 37; 40

First Poems. 1925. V. 38

First Poems. London: 1925. V. 40

The Labyrinth - Poems. London: 1949. V. 43

Latitudes. New York: 1924. V. 37

Scottish Journey. London: 1935. V. 38

Social Credit and the Labour Party. London: 1935. V. 41

Transition: Essays. London: 1926. V. 37; 41

We Moderns: Enigmas and Guesses. London: 1918. V. 37; 40

We Moderns: Enigmas and Guesses. New York: 1920. V. 37

MUIR, J. B.

The Olde New-Markitt Calendar of Matches. London: 1892. V. 42

Racinana or Riders' Colours of the Royal Foreign and Principal Patrons of the British Turf from 1762 to 1883 . . . London: 1890. V. 43

MUIR, JAMES

Sermons, by James Muir, A.M. Minister of the Presbyterian Church, Bermuda. Princeton: 1787. V. 39

MUIR, JOHN 1838-1914

Climb the Mountains. Pasadena: 1965. V. 41

The Cruise of the Corwin. Boston: 1917. V. 37; 39; 40; 44; 46

The Cruise of the Corwin. Boston & New York: 1917. V. 37; 40

Cruise of the Revune-Steamer Corwin in Alaska and the Northwest Arctic Ocean in 1881. Notice and Memoranda; Medical and Anthropological, Botanical, Ornithological. Washington: 1883. V. 37

John of the Mountains. The Unpublished Journals of John Muir. Boston: 1938. V. 37

Letters to a Friend Written to Mrs. Ezra S. Carr 1866-1879. Boston: 1915. V. 46

The Mountains of California. New York: 1894. V. 37; 38; 39; 40; 44; 46

The Mountains of California. New York: 1913. V. 43; 46

My First Summer in the Sierra. Boston: 1911. V. 44

My First Summer in the Sierra. Covelo: 1988. V. 39; 40; 46

Our National Parks. Boston: 1901. V. 44

Picturesque California and the Region West of the Rocky Mountains, from Alaska to Mexico. New York & San Francisco: 1887-188. V. 42

Picturesque California and the Region West of the Rocky Mountains, from Alaska to Mexico. San Francisco & New York: 1888. V. 46

Picturesque California: the Rocky Mountains and the Pacific Slope. New York: and: 1894. V. 46

Picturesque California: The Rocky Mountains and the Pacific Slope. New York: and San Francisco: 1894. V. 44

Steep Trails. Boston & New York: 1918. V. 40

The Story of My Boyhood and Youth. Boston: 1913. V. 38; 41; 44

The Story of My Boyhood and Youth. Boston and New York: 1913. V. 46

A Thousand Mile Walk to the Gulf. Boston & New York: 1915. V. 40

A Thousand Mile Walk to the Gulf. Boston: 1916. V. 44; 46

A Thousand Mile Walk to the Gulf. Boston & New York;: 1916. V. 37; 38; 41; 42; 46

Travels in Alaska. Boston: 1915. V. 40; 44

Travels in Alaska. Boston & New York: 1915. V. 40

Travels in Alaska. New York: 1915. V. 37

Two Essays on the Mountains and Meadows of the Sierra Nevada. Palo Alto: 1969. V. 46

The Writings of John Muir. Boston: 1916-24. V. 44

The Writings. Boston: 1917-24. V. 42

The Yosemite. New York: 1912. V. 38

Yosemite and the Sierra Nevada. Boston: 1948. V. 37; 44

MUIR, LEO JOSEPH

A Century of Mormon Activities in California. Salt Lake City: 1952. V. 38; 44

A Century of Mormon Activities in California. Volume I, Historical, Volume II, Biographical. Salt Lake City: (1952). V. 37

MUIR, M.

A Bibliography of Australian Children's Books. New York: 1976. V. 44

MUIR, M. M. PATTISON

A History of Chemical Theories and Laws. New York: 1907. V. 46

MUIR, PERCY H.

A. F. Johnson: Selected Essays on Books and Printing. Amsterdam: 1970. V. 38; 41

Bibliographical Notes and Queries. Edinburgh: 1935-9. V. 41

Catnachery. San Francisco: 1955. V. 40; 42; 46

English Children's Books. London: 1954. V. 38

Points 1874-1930 . . . (with) Points, Second Series 1866-1934. London: 1931-34. V. 39; 41

Points, 1874-1930 with Points, Second Series, 1866-1934. London: 1931 and 1934. V. 38; 42; 44

Points, Second Series. London: 1934. V. 38; 40; 41; 42; 44; 46

Selected Essays on Books and Printing. Amsterdam: 1970/71. V. 46

Victorian Illustrated Books. New York: 1971. V. 39; 40

MUIR, RAMSAY

A History of Municipal Government in Liverpool from the Earliest Times to the Municipal Reform Act of 1835. London: 1906. V. 39

MUIR, THOMAS, PSEUD.

The Telegraph; a Consolatory Epistle . . . N.P., n.d.: 1796. V. 39

The Telegraph . . . Edinburgh: 1825. V. 46

MUIR, W.

Gleanings from the Records of Dysart, from 1545 to 1796. Edinburgh: 1862. V. 40

MUIR, WILLIAM

Records of the Intelligence Department of the Government of the North-West Provinces of India During the Mutiny of 1857 . . . Edinburgh: 1902. V. 40

MUIRHEAD, ARNOLD

Grace Revere Osler. A Brief Memoir. 1931. V. 46

MUIRHEAD, GEORGE

The Birds of Berwickshire, With Remarks on Their Local Distribution, Migration and Habits, and Also on the Folk Lore, Proverbs, Popular Rhymes and Sayings . . . Edinburgh: 1889. V. 41; 46

The Birds of Berwickshire. Edinburgh: 1889-95. V. 37; 38

MUIRHEAD, J. F.

The United States with an Excursion into Mexico. Leipsic: 1893. V. 37

MUIRHEAD, JAMES PATRICK

The Life of James Watt. London: 1858. V. 42

The Origin and Progress of the Mechanical Invention of James Watt Illustrated by His Correspondence with His Friends and the Specifications of His Patents. London: 1854. V. 39; 43

MUIR'S List of Dates Expected Arrival At, and Departure from Malta, of Steamers with Mails and Passengers Together, with the Dates of the Latest Intelligence Received by the Inward, and the Probably Dates of Arrival of the Outward, Mails . . . Valletta: 1843. V. 40

MUJICA, FRANCISCO

History of the Skyscraper. Paris: 1929. V. 38

MUKHERJEE, BHARATI

Wife. Boston: 1975. V. 46

MUKHOPADHYAYA, GIRINDRANATH

History of Indian Medicine. New Delhi: 1974. V. 38

MULAS, UGO

Calder. London: 1971. V. 44

MULDER, G. J.

The Chemistry of Vegetble and Animal Physiology. Edinburgh: 1845-49. V. 38

MULER, NICOLAUS

Tabulae Frisicae Lunae-Solares Quadruplices. Alkmaar: 1611. V. 38; 44

MULFORD, AMI FRANK

Fighting Indians in the 7th United States Cavalry Custer's Favorite Regiment. Corning: 1930. V. 40

MULFORD, PRENTICE

Prentice Mulford's Story. New York: 1889. V. 40

MULGRAVE, CONSTANTINE JOHN PHIPPS, 2ND BARON 1744-1792

A Voyage Towards the North Pole Undertaken by His Majesty's Command. London: 1774. V. 39; 44

MULHALL, MARION MC MURROUGH

Between the Amazon and Andes, or Ten Years of a Lady's Travels in the Pampas, Gran, Chaco, Paraguay and Matto Grosso. London: 1881. V. 38

MULHALL, MICHAEL G.

The English in South America. Buenos Ayres and London: 1878. V. 44

Handbook of the River Plate, comprising the Argentine Republic, Uruguay, an paraguay, with six maps. Buenos Ayres: 1885. V. 37

MULHALL, MICHAEL GEORGE

Handbook of the River Plate Republics. London: 1875. V. 40

MULHOLLAND, ROSA

Puck and Blossom. London. V. 39

Puck and Blossom. London: 1874. V. 43

MULLALY, B. R.

History of the 10th Gurkha Rifles. The First Battalion. 1890-1921. Aldershot: 1924. V. 45

MULLALY, JOHN

A Trip to Newfoundland Its Scenery and Fisheries; with an Account of the Laying of the Submarine Telegraph Cable. New York: 1855. V. 38; 41; 42; 45

MULLAN, JOHN 1830-1909

Military Road Expedition. Washington: 1860. V. 46

Military Road from Fort Benton to Fort Walla-Walla. 1861. V. 46

Military Road from Fort Benton to Fort Walla Walla. Washington: 1861. V. 37; 40; 41; 42; 46

Miners and Travelers' Guide to Oregon, Washington, Idaho, Montana, Wyoming and Colorado Via the Missouri and Columbia Rivers. New York: 1865. V. 38; 40; 41; 43; 45; 46

Report on the Construction of Military Road from Fort Walla-Walla to Fort Benton. Washington: 1863. V. 39; 40; 41; 43; 44; 45

MULLAY, JOHN

The Laying of the Cable, or the Ocean Telegraph. New York: 1858. V. 39

MULLEN, STANLEY

Kinsmen of the Dragon. Chicago: 1951. V. 45

MULLEN, W.

Rambles After Sport; or, Travels and Adventures in the Americas and at Home. London: 1874. V. 43

MULLENS, W. H.

A Bibliography of British Ornithology. London: 1916-17. V. 37; 38

A Bibliography of British Ornithology. London: 1917. V. 39

A Bibliography of British Ornithology. London: 1986. V. 38

MULLER, AEMILIUS

The Swiss Colour Atlas. London: 1946. V. 41

MULLER, BALTHASER

Ein Neuer Nutzlicher und Tractat von Rechtem Wahren Gebrauch Natur, Kraft und Vermogen der Gemeinsten und Gebrachlichtsten als 147 Distilirten Wasser. Rudolstadt: 1670. V. 37

MULLER, CHRISTIAN

Journey through Greece and the Ionian Islands in June, July and August, 1821. London: 1822. V. 37; 39; 40

MULLER, F. MAX

Chips from a German Workshop. London: 1880. V. 41

Lecutres on the Science of Language . . . First Series . . . Second Series. London: 1864. V. 38

Lectures on the Science of Language. London: 1866, 1864. V. 37

MULLER, FREDERICK PALUDAN

The Fountain of Youth. London: 1867. V. 40

MULLER, FREDERIK

Catalogue of Books and Pamphlets Relating to North and South America. Amsterdam: 1877. V. 38

MULLER, FRIEDRICH

Voyages from Asia to America, For Completing the Discoveries of the North West Coast of America. London: 1764. V. 41

MULLER, FRIEDRICH C. G.

Krupp's Steel Works. London: 1898. V. 44

MULLER, GERHARD FRIEDRICH

A Letter from a Russian Sea-Officer, to a Person of Distinction, at the Court of St. Petersburgh . . . London: 1754. V. 43

Voyages et Decouvertes Faites para les Russes le Long des Cotes de la Mer Glaciale & sur l'Ocean Oriental, Tant Vers le Japon que Vers l'Amerique. Amsterdam: 1766. V. 38

MULLER, J.

On Certain Variations in the Vocal Organs of the Passeres. Oxford: 1878. V. 37

MULLER, JOHANN HEINRICH JACOB 1809-1875

Principles of Physics and Meteorology. London: 1847. V. 40

MULLER, JOHANNES

Ueber den Feinem Bau und die Formen der Krankhaften Geschwulste . . . Berlin: 1838. V. 38; 43

Ueber die Phantastischen Gesichtserscheinungen. Coblenz: 1826. V. 37

MULLER, JOHN 1699-1784

The Attack and Defence of Fortified Places. London: 1770. V. 40

The Attack and Defence of Fortified Places. London: 1791. V. 44

Elements of Mathematics. London: 1765. V. 38

A System of Camp-Discipline, Military Honours,Garrison-Duty, and Other Regulations for the Land Forces . . . London: 1757/ V. 46

A Treatise Concerning the Elementary Part of Fortification, Regular and Irregular. London: 1746. V. 37; 46

A Treatise Containing the Practical Part of Fortification. London: 1764. V. 40

A Treatise Containing the Elementary Part of Fortification, Regular and Irregular. London: 1782. V. 39; 42

MULLER, JOSEPH

The Star Spangled Banner. (Frances Scott Key). Words and Music Issued Between 1814-1864. An Annotated Bibliographical List by . . . New York: 1935. V. 44; 45

MULLER, MARGARETHE

Carla Wenckebach Pioneer. Boston: 1908. V. 39

MULLER, O. F.

Zoologia Danica seu Animalium Daniae et Norvegiae Rariorum ac Minus Notarum Descriptiones et Historia. Copenhagen: 1788-1806. V. 41

MULLER, WILLIAM

The Elements of the Science of War. London: 1811. V. 39; 40

MULLER, WILLIAM G.

The Twenty Fourth Infantry Past and Present. N.P.: 1923. V. 45

MULLER, WILLIAM J.

Catalogue of a Loan Collection of Paintings in Oil and Watercolours by William J. Muller. London: 1876. V. 39

MULLIN, ROBERT

The Strange Story of Wayne Brazel. Canyon: 1969. V. 43

MULLINER, H. H.

The Decorative Arts in England 1660-1780. London: 1923. V. 42
The Decorative Arts in England 1660-1780. London: 1924. V. 46

MULLINER, MAY

Stuart's Twins. London: 1912. V. 44

MULLOOLY, JOSEPH

Saint Clement, Pope and Martyr and His Basilica in Rome. Rome: 1873. V. 43

MULLOY, SHEILA

Franco-Irish Correspondence. December 1688-February 1692. Dublin: 1983/4. V. 38

MULOCK, GEORGE F. A.

The Charts of the Discovery Antarctic Expedition. London: 1908. V. 40; 41

MULOCK, MISS

The Little Lame Prince. Racine: 1916. V. 46

MULSANT, M. E.

Histoire Naturelle des Oiseaux-Mouches ou Colibris . . . Lyons: 1877-79. V. 42

MULTATULI

Parables of Authority. 1963. V. 46

MULVANEY, CHARLES PELHAM

The History of the North West Rebellion of 1885 . . . Toronto: 1885. V. 43; 44

MULVANY, C. PELHAM

Toronto: Past and Present. Toronto: 1884. V. 46

MULVANY, THOMAS

The Life of James Gandon, Esq. Dublin: 1846. V. 37; 40

MUMBY, A. N. L.

Phillipps Studies: The Catalogues, The Family Affairs, Formation of the Library of 1840, Formation of the Library from 1841-1872, The Dispersal of the Phillipps Library. Cambridge: 1951-60. V. 37

MUMBY, FRANK A.

The Romance of Bookselling. London: 1910. V. 38

MUMEY, NOLIE

The Art and Activities of John Dare (Jack) Howland . . . Indian Trader and Pioneer. Boulder: 1973. V. 38; 39
Bloody Trails Along the Rio Grande. Denver: 1958. V. 38
Calamity Jane 1852-1903. Denver: 1950. V. 40; 43
Colorado Territorial Scrip. Boulder: 1966. V. 40
Creede - The History of Colorado Silver Mining Town. Denver: 1949. V. 37
The Early Settlement of Denver 1598-1859 from the T. F. Dawson Scrap Books State Historical Society Denver, Colorado. Denver. V. 42
History of Early Settlements Old Denver (1599-1860). Glendale: 1942. V. 37; 41; 45; 46
An Iconographic Sketch of the Life of Rene Theophile Hyacinthe Laennec (1781-1826). Denver: 1932. V. 37; 38; 39
James Pierson Beckwourth, an Enigmatic Figure of the West 1856-1866. Denver: 1957. V. 44
Jim Baker-Trapper, Scout, Guide and Indian Fighter. Denver: 1931. V. 39
John Williams Gunnison (1812-1853). Denver: 1955. V. 38; 40
March of the First Dragoons to the Rocky Mountains in 1835; the Diaries and Maps of Lemuel Ford. Denver: 1957. V. 37; 42
Old Forts and Trading Posts of the West. Denver: 1956. V. 39; 40
Pioneer Denver. Denver: 1948. V. 37; 44
Reverend Thomas Thacher. Denver: 1937. V. 46
Saga of 'Auntie' Stone and Her Cabin; Elizabeth Hickok Robbins Stone (1801-1895), a Pioneer Woman Who Built & Owned the First Dwelling, Operated the First Hotel, Built the First Flour Mill . . . Boudler: 1964. V. 37; 38
A Study of Rare Books with Special Reference to Colophons, Press Devices and Title Pages of Interest to the Bibiliohpile and The Student of Literature. Denver: 1930. V. 37; 38; 39; 42

MUMFORD, ERASMUS

A Letter to the Club at White's. London: 1750. V. 40; 46

MUMFORD, JOHN KIMBERLY

Oriental Rugs. New York: 1900. V. 42

MUMM, ARNOLD LOUIS

Five Months in the Himalya; a record of mountain travel in Garhwal and Kashmir. London: 1909. V. 37

MUMMERY, A. F.

My Climbs in the Alps and Caucasus. London: 1895. V. 40; 41; 42; 44; 46
My Climbs in the Alps and Caucasus. London: 1908. V. 43; 46

MUN, THOMAS

A Discourse of Trade, From England Unto the East-Indies. London: 1621. V. 39; 40

MUNAWAR, M.

Seasonality of Freshwater Plankton: a Global Perspective. London: 1986. V. 38

MUNBY, A. N. L.

The Alabaster Hand and Other Ghost Stories. London: 1949. V. 38; 40
Phillipps Studies. 1951-60. V. 46
Phillipps Studies. London: 1971. V. 39; 45
Phillips Studies. Cambridge: 1951-1960. V. 38; 41
Phillips E. Cambridge: 1951-60. V. 40

MUNBY, ARTHUR JOSEPH

Ann Morgan's Love. London: 1896. V. 43

MUNCHAUSEN

The Adventures of Baron Munchausen. London: 1866. V. 46
The Adventures of Baron Munchausen. London: 1878. V. 42
Baron Munchausen's Remarkable Travels and Adventures by Land and Water. Stockholm: 1899. V. 46
Surprising Adventures of the Renowned Baron Munchausen . . . (with) an Account of A Voyage to the Moon and Dog Star. London: 1809. V. 39
The Surprising Adventures of Baron Munchausen. New York: 1927. V. 43
The Travels and Suprising Adventures of Baron Munchausen. London: 1859. V. 40; 44
The Travels and Surprising Adventures of Baron Munchausen. London: 1870. V. 38

MUNDAY, ANTHONY

The First Part (The Second Part) of the No Lesse Rare, Then Excellent and Stately History of the Famous and Fortunate Prince Palmerin of England. London: 1639. V. 45
The Fishmongers' Pageant on Lord Mayor's Day, 1616 . . . London: 1844. V. 46

MUNDAY, DON

The Unknown Mountains. London: 1948. V. 44

MUNDAY, LURANIA A. H.

Acacian Lyrics and Miscellaneous Poems. St. Louis: 1857. V. 40

MUNDELL, ALEXANDER

The Influence of Interest and Prejudice Upon Proceedings in Parliament Stated, and Illustrated by What Has Been Done in Matters Relative to Education - Religion - The Poor - The Corn Laws - Joint Stock Companies - and Taxes. London: 1825. V. 37

MUNDT, KLARA

Henry VIII and His Court, or Catherine Parr. Mobile: 1865. V. 45
Joseph H. and His Court. Mobile: 1864. V. 45

MUNDY, FRANCIS NOEL CLARKE

Needwood Forest. Lichfield: 1776. V. 40
Poems. Oxford: 1768. V. 37; 39; 42; 44

MUNDY, GODFREY CHARLES d. 1860

Our Antipodes. London: 1852. V. 40; 43; 46
Pen and Pencil Sketches. London: 1832. V. 40; 41; 43; 44; 45
Pen and Pencil Sketches Being the Journal of a Tour in India. London: 1833. V. 41

MUNDY, R. G.

English Delft Pottery. London: 1928. V. 41; 42

MUNDY, RODNEY

Narrative of Events in Borneo and Celebes, Down to the Occupation of Labuan . . . London: 1848. V. 39

MUNDY, T.

C.I.D. 1932. V. 43

MUNDY, TALBOT

Cock O'The North. 1929. V. 46

East and West. 1937. V. 37

Full Moon. 1935. V. 43

Full Moon. New York: 1935. V. 42

The Gunga Sahib. New York: 1934. V. 44

Jimgrim. New York: 1931. V. 38; 39

The King in Check. 1934. V. 44; 46

OM: The Secret of Ahbor Valley. Indianapolis: 1924. V. 37

Queen Cleopatra. 1929. V. 44; 46

Queen Cleopatra. Indianapolis: 1929. V. 39; 41; 42; 46

The Thunder Dragon Gate. New York: 1937. V. 42

MUNGIA, CLEMENTE

Mantifesto . . . Dirige a la Nacion Mejicana. Morelia: 1851. V. 38

MUNGUIA, CLEMENTE

Sermon que en la Solemnisim y Religiosa Funcion Gracias Consagrada el Todopoderson . . . Mexico: 1830. V. 38

MUNIMENTA Gildhallae Londiniensis: Liber Albus, Liber Custumarum, et Liber Horn. London: 1859-62. V. 44

MUNK, J. A.

Arizona Bibliography: a Private Collection of Arizoniana. Los Angeles: 1908. V. 45

MUNK, JOSEPH A.

Activities of a Lifetime. Los Angeles: 1924. V. 43

Arizona Sketches. New York: 1905. V. 42; 43

MUNK, S.

Palestine. Description Geographique, Historique, et Archeologique. Paris: 1860. V. 37

MUNK, WILLIAM

Euthanasia: or, medical Treatment in Aid of an Easy Death. London: 1887. V. 45

The Roll of the Royal College of Physicians of London . . . London: 1878. V. 42

The Roll of the Royal College of Physicians of London. London: 1878-1968. V. 39

The Roll of the Royal College of Physicians of London. 1955/1968/1982. V. 37; 39

MUNKITTRICK, R. K.

The Acrobatic Muse. Chicago: 1897. V. 38

MUNN, B. T.

Love on the Wing. Boston: 1871. V. 41

MUNN, GEOFFREY C.

Castellani and Giuliano; Revivalist Jewelelrs of the 19th Century. New York: 1984. V. 44

MUNNINGS, ALFRED

The Tale of Anthony Bell, a Hunting Ballad. N.P.: 1921. V. 39

MUNNINGS, ALFRED J.

An Artist's Life: The Second Burst; The Finish. London: 1950-52. V. 37; 39; 40; 41

An Artist's Life: the Second Burst: The Finish. (and with) Ballads and Poems or A Rhyming Succession of Rhyming Digression. London: 1950-57. V. 37; 40

The Autobiography of . . . An Artist's Life. London: 1951. V. 39

Ballads and Songs. London: 1957. V. 40; 41

Pictures of Horses and English Life. London: 1927. V. 37; 39; 42

Pictures of Horses and English Life. With an Appreciation by Lionel Lindsay. New York/London: 1927. V. 37

Pictures of Horses and English Life. London: 1939. V. 37; 42

The Tale of Anthony Bell. London: 1921. V. 43

MUNOZ, DON JUAN BAUTISTA

Historia Del Nuevo-Mundo. Madrid: 1793. V. 38; 44

MUNRO ALICE

Dance of Happy Shades. Toronto: 1968. V. 42; 43

Lives of Girls and Women. New York: 1971. V. 45

MUNRO-FRASER, J. P.

History of Marin County California. San Francisco: 1880. V. 45

History of Alameda County, California, Including Its Geology, Topography, Soil and Productions . . . Oakland: 1883. V. 40; 41

MUNRO, HAROLD

Real Property. Real. London: 1922. V. 40

MUNRO, HECTOR HUGH 1870-1916

Beasts and Super-Beasts. London: 1914. V. 38

Reginald. London: 1904. V. 37; 38; 45

Reginald in Russia and Other Sketches. London: 1910. V. 37

The Square Egg and Other Sketches, With Three Plays and Illustrations. London: 1924. V. 39; 40; 45

The Toys of Peace. London: 1919. V. 38; 39; 40; 46

The Unbearable Bassington. London: 1912. V. 45; 46

The Westminster Alice. London: 1901. V. 46

The Westminster Alice. London: 1902. V. 37; 40; 41; 42; 43; 44

The Works of Saki. New York: 1927. V. 38

MUNRO, HENRY

Articles on Reform in Private Asylums. London: 1852. V. 37

MUNRO, HUGH

A Compendious System of the Theory and Practice of Modern Surgery. London: 1792. V. 39; 40; 41

MUNRO, I. S. R.

The Fishes of New Guinea. Port Moresby: 1967. V. 37; 38

The Marine and Freshwater Fishes of Ceylon. Delhi: 1982. V. 37; 38

MUNRO, INNES

A Narrative of the Military Operations on the Coromandel Coast Against the Combined Forces of the French, Dutch and Hyder Ally Cawn from the Year 1780 to the Peace in 1784 in a Series of Letters. London: 1789. V. 39

MUNRO, NEIL

The History of the Royal Bank of Scotland 1727-1927. Edinburgh: 1928. V. 41

The Lost Pibroch and Other Sheiling Stories. Edinburgh: 1896. V. 39

MUNRO, ROBERT

Ancient Scottish Lake Dwellings or Crannogs . . . Edinburgh: 1882. V. 38; 40

The Lake Dwellings of Europe. London: 1890. V. 37; 38; 40; 41; 46

MUNRO, WILLIAM BENNETT

Documents Relating to the Seigniorial Tenure in Canada 1598-1854. Toronto: 1908. V. 37; 39; 44; 45

Documents Relating to the Seigniorial Tenure in Canada, 1598-1854. Toronto: 1908. V. 37

MUNROE, ALICE

Dance of the Happy Shades. Toronto: 1968. V. 41

MUNSELL, A. H.

A Grammar of Color, Arrangements of Strathmore Papers in a Variety of Printed Color Combinations According to the Munsell Color System. Mittineague: 1921. V. 37

MUNSELL, CHARLES

Collection of Songs of the American Press, and Other Poems Relating to the Art of Printing. Albany: 1868. V. 37

MUNSELL, JOEL

A Chronology of Paper and Papermaking. Albany: 1856. V. 38

A Chronology of Paper and Paper-Making. Albany: 1857. V. 44

Chronology of Paper and Paper-Making. Albany: 1870. V. 41

MUNSEY, FRANK A.

Under Fire; or, Fred Worthington's Campaign. New York: 1890. V. 39; 46

MUNSON, GORHAM B.

Robert Frost. New York: 1927. V. 45

MUNSON, JOHN W.

Reminiscences of a Mosby Guerrilla. New York: 1906. V. 43

MUNSTER, GEORGE FITZCLARENCE, 1ST EARL OF

Journal of a Route Across India through Egypt to England . . . London: 1819. V. 39

MUNSTER, SEBASTIAN

Dictionarium Hebraicum, nunc Primum Aeditum & Typis Excusum. Basel: 1523. V. 37

MUNSTERBERG, HUGO

Chinese Buddhist Bronzes. Rutland & Tokyo: 1967. V. 41

MUNTHE, AXEL

The Story of San Michele. London: 1936. V. 37

MUNTING, ABRAHAM 1626-1683

De Vera Antiquorum Herba Britannica . . . ; Aloidarium, sive Alves Mucronato Folio Americanae . . . Amsterdam: 1681/80. V. 37; 42

MUNTING, ABRAHAM 1626-1683 continued

Waare Oeffening der Planten, Waar in de Rechte Aart Natuire, en Verborgene Eigenschappen, der Boomen Heesteren . . . Amsterdam: 1682. V. 41; 42; 43; 45; 46

MUNTZ, J. H.

Encaustic; or, Count Caylus's Method of Painting in the Manner of the Ancients to Which is Added a Sure and Easy Method for Fixing Crayons. London: 1760. V. 38; 40; 41

MUNY, TALBOT

The Mystery of Khufu's Tomb. New York & London: 1935. V. 42

MUNZ, LUDWIG

Bruegel: the Drawings. London: 1961. V. 43; 45

Rembrandt's Etchings. London: 1952. V. 40; 46

MURAI, GENSAI

Hana a Daughter of Japan. 1904. V. 40

Hana a Daughter of Japan. Tokyo: 1904. V. 44

MURAL Painting of the Mexican Revolution 1921-1960. Mexico City: 1960. V. 40

MURALT, BEAT LOUIS DE

Letters Describing the Character and Customs of the English and French Nations . . . London: 1726. V. 37

MURAT, ACHILLE

A Moral and Political Sketch of the United States of North America. London: 1833. V. 39; 40

MURATORI, LODOVICO ANTONIO

Il Cristianesimo Felice nelle Missioni de' Padri Della Compagnia di Gesu nel Paraguai. Venice: 1743. V. 39

MURCH, JEROM

Mrs. Barbauld and Her Contemporaries . . . London: 1877. V. 37; 39; 41; 43; 45

MURCHISON, CHARLES

Clinical Lectures on Diseases of the Liver, Jaundice and Abdominal Dropsy. New York: 1877. V. 42

A Treatise on the Continued Fevers of Great Britain. London: 1873. V. 39; 42

MURCHISON, RODERICK IMPEY

The Geology of Russia in Europe and the Ural Mountains. London: 1845. V. 38; 39

Siluria. London: 1854. V. 38; 40; 42; 46

Siluria. London: 1859. V. 38

Siluria. London: 1867. V. 46

Siluria. London: 1872. V. 44

The Silurian System. London: 1839. V. 37; 38; 46

MURDEN, ELIZA

Miscellaneous Poems. New York: 1827. V. 37; 38; 46

MURDEN, JOSEPH R.

The Art of Memory, Reduced to a Systematic Arrangement, Exemplified Under the Two Leading Principles, Locality and Association. New York: 1818. V. 40

MURDOCH, IRIS

The Bell. London: 1958. V. 38

The Existentialist Political Myth. 1989. V. 42

The Existentialist Political Myth. Birmingham: 1989. V. 44

The Existentialist Political Myth. London: 1989. V. 41

A Fairly Honourable Defeat. London: 1970. V. 37

The Fire and the Sun: Why Plato Banished the Artists. Oxford: 1977. V. 40

The Flight from the Enchanter. London: 1956. V. 38; 40; 42; 46

The Good Apprentice. London: 1985. V. 46

The Philosopher's Pupil. London: 1983. V. 37

The Sandcastle. London: 1957. V. 37; 41

Sartre. Cambridge: 1953. V. 37; 38; 41; 46

Sartre - a Romantic Rationalist. London: 1953. V. 45

The Sea. London: 1978. V. 42

The Servants - Opera in Three Acts. London: 1980. V. 46

A Severed Head. London: 1961. V. 42

The Sovereinty of Good Over Other Concepts: A Lecture. London: 1967. V. 37

Under the Net. London: 1954. V. 39; 40; 46

Under the Net. New York: 1954. V. 45

Dans le Filet. Paris: 1957. V. 46

The Unicorn. London: 1963. V. 42

A Year of Birds. Tisbury: 1978. V. 38; 40; 43; 44

A Year of Birds. Wiltshire: 1978. V. 42; 44

MURDOCH, J.

Classified Catalogue of Tamil printed Books with Introductory Notices. Madras: 1865. V. 44

MURDOCH, J. BURN

Notes and Remarks Made in Jersey, France, Italy and the Mediterranean, in 1843 and 1844. Edinburgh & London: 1846. V. 40

MURDOCH, JAMES

A History of Japan. London: 1925=26. V. 39

MURDOCH, WILLIAM G. BURN

From Edinburgh To The Antarctic; An Artist's Notes & Sketches During the Dundee Antarctic Expedition of 1892-93. London: 1894. V. 37; 38

Modern Whaling & Bear-Hunting: A Record of Present-Day Whaling With Up-to-Date Appliances in Many Parts of the World, and of Bear and Seal Hunting in the Arctic Regions. Philadelphia: 1917. V. 37

MURDOCK, CHARLES A.

A Backward Glance at Eighty. San Francisco: 1921. V. 45

MURDOCK, HAROLD

Early Percy Dines Abroad. Boston: 1924. V. 43

Earl Percy Dines Abroad, a Boswellian Episode. Cambridge: 1924. V. 39

MURDOCK, JOHN

Ethnological Results of the Point Barrow Expedition by John Murdock. (Washington: 1892). V. 37

MURDOCK, KENNETH B.

The Portraits of Increase Mather, with Some Notes on Thomas Johnson, an English Mezzotinter. Cleveland: 1924. V. 39

MURET, MARC ANTOINE

Hymnorvm Sacrovm Liber. Ingolstadt: 1584. V. 40; 45

Variarum Lectionum Libri VIII. Venice: 1559. V. 46

Variarum Lectionum Libri XV. Antwerp: 1586. V. 38

MURET, PIERRE

Rites of Funeral Ancient and Modern, in the Use Through the Known World. London: 1683. V. 38

MURETUS, ANTONIUS

Orationes Eiusdem Interpretatio Quinti Libri Ethicorum Aristotelis ad Nicomachum. Lugduni: 1586. V. 37

MURETUS, MARCUS A.

Oratio Habita. In. Fvnere Pli. V. Pont. Maximi. Franc. Ziletti,: 1572. V. 42

MURILLO, G.

Las Artes Populares en Mexico. Mexico: 1922. V. 41

MURMUR, FRETFUL

More Miseries! Addressed to the Morbid, the melancholy and the Irritable. London: 1806. V. 45

MURPHEY, ARCHIBLAD D.

Report of the Committee of Inland Navigation Submitted to the Legislature of North Carolina, Nov. 30, by . . . Their Chairman. Raleigh: 1815. V. 40

MURPHEY, CHARLES

A Journal of a Whaling Voyage On Board Ship Dauphin of Nantucket. Maatapoisett: 1877. V. 41

MURPHY, ARTHUR

An Essay on the Life and Genius of Samuel Johnson, LL.D. London: 1792. V. 37; 38; 45

An Essay on the Life and Genius of Samuel Johnson. London: 1793. V. 37; 41

The Grecian Daughter. London: 1772. V. 40

The Life of David Garrick, Esq. Dublin: 1801. V. 40

The Life of David Garrick. London: 1801. V. 38; 39; 41; 42

Ranger's Progress: Consisting of a Variety of Poetical Essays, Moral, Serious, Comic and Satyrical. London: 1760. V. 37

The Rival Sisters. London: 1793. V. 40

The Upholsterer, or What News? London: 1758. V. 46

The Upholsterer, or, What News? London: 1765. V. 46

The Works. London: 1786. V. 45

MURPHY, AUDIE

To Hell and Back. New York: 1949. V. 38

MURPHY, BAILEY SCOTT

English and Scottish Wrought Ironwork. Edinburgh: 1904. V. 37; 39

MURPHY, BEATRICE

Negro Voices. An Anthology of Contemporary Verse. New York: 1938. V. 43

MURPHY, DENIS

Cromwell in Ireland. Dublin: 1885. V. 38

The Life of Hue Roe O'Donnell. Prince of Tirconnell 1586-1602. Dublin: 1895. V. 46

MURPHY, DERVLA

A Place Apart. London: 1978. V. 39

MURPHY, HENRY

Journal of a Voyage to New York and a Tour in Several of the Colonies in 1679-80, by Jaspar Dankers and Peter Sluyter. Brooklyn: 1867. V. 37; 38; 43

MURPHY, HENRY C.

Anthology of New Netherland or Translations from the Early Dutch Poets of New York with Memoirs of Their Lives. New York: 1865. V. 46

Catalogue of the Magnificent Library of the Late. hon. Henry C. Murphy of Brooklyn, Long Island . . . New York: 1884. V. 44

MURPHY, JAMES 1760-1814

Plans Elevations Sections and Views of the Church of Batalha, in the Province of Estremadura in Portugal, With the History and Description by Fr. Luis de Sousa. London: 1795. V. 37; 39

Travels in Portugal . . . in the Years 1789 and 1790 . . . London: 1795. V. 39

MURPHY, JAMES B.

The Lymphocyte in Resistance to Tissue Grafting, Malignant Disease, and Tuberculous Infection . . . New York: 1926. V. 44

MURPHY, JOHN

Message. To the Speaker and Members of the House of Representatives (of the State of Alabama). Cahawba: 1825. V. 39

Message. To the Speaker and Members of the House of Representatives (of the State of Alabama). V. 39

A Treatise on the Art of Weaving . . . . Glasgow: 1852. V. 45

A Treatise on the Art of Weaving, With Calculations and Tables for the Use of Manufacturers. Glasgow: 1857. V. 37; 39; 41

MURPHY, JOHN MC LEOD 1827-1871

Nautical Routine and Stowage, with Short Rules in Navigation. New York: 1849. V. 39

MURPHY, JOHN MORTIMER

Rambles in North-Western America, from the Pacific Ocean to the Rocky Mountains. London: 1879. V. 37

Sporting Adventures in the Far West. London: 1879. V. 39; 40

MURPHY, JOHN NICHOLAS

Ireland, Industrial, Political and Social. London: 1870. V. 37; 38; 43; 46

Terra Incognita or the Convents of the United Kingdom. London: 1873. V. 42; 46

MURPHY, LIEUT. COL.

The History of the Suffolk Regiment. 1914-1927. London: 1928. V. 44; 45

MURPHY, P.

The Falling Woman. Toronto: 1988. V. 44

MURPHY, PATRICK

An Inquiry into the Nature and Cause of Miasmata, More Particularly Illustrated in the Former and Present State of the Campagna di Roma. London: 1825. V. 40

MURPHY, RICHARD

The Archaeology of Love. Dublin: 1955. V. 40; 41

The Last Galway Hooker. Dublin: 1961. V. 40

The Price of Stone. Hereford: 1985. V. 37

Sailing to an Island: Poems. London: 1963. V. 39

The Woman of the House. 1959. V. 42

The Woman of the House. Dublin: 1959. V. 38; 40

MURPHY, ROBERT CUSHMAN

Oceanic Birds of South America. New York: 1936. V. 39; 40; 42; 43

Oceanic Birds of South America . . . New York: 1948. V. 37; 38

MURPHY, THOMAS D.

Three Wonderlands of the American West, Being the Notes of a Traveler, Concerning the Yellowstone Park, the Yosemitie National Park and the Grand Canyon of the Colorado River, with a Chapter on Other Wonders of the Great American West. Boston: 1913. V. 46

MURPHY, WILLIAM

A Special Diet for Patients with Pernicious Anemia. 1926. V. 42

MURPHY, WILLIAM S.

The Textile Industries: practical Guide to Fibres, Yarns and Fabrics. London: 1912. V. 46

MURRAY, A. S.

Designs from Greek Vases in the British Museum. London: 1894. V. 44

Greek Bronzes and Greek Terra-Cotta Statuettes. London: 1899. V. 40

Terracotta Sarcophagi: Greek and Etruscan in the British Museum. London: 1898. V. 37; 42; 44

Twelve Hundred Miles on the Murray River. Australia: 1898. V. 39

Twelve Hundred Miles on the River Murray. Sydney: 1898. V. 45

White AThenian Vases in the British Museum. London: 1896. V. 37; 44

MURRAY, ALEXANDER

Account of the Life and Writings of James Bruce of Kinnaird, Esq. F.R.S. Edinburgh: 1808. V. 38

Geological Survey of Newfoundland. London: 1881. V. 37

MURRAY, AMELIA M.

Letters from the United States, Cuba and Canada. New York: 1856. V. 40; 42

MURRAY, ANDREW 1812-1878

The Book of the Royal Horticultural Society, 1862-1863. London: 1863. V. 38

The Geographical Distribution of Mammals. London: 1866. V. 37; 38; 45

MURRAY, ANN

Mentoria: or the Young Ladies Instructor. London: 1800. V. 38

MURRAY, ARCH K.

History of the Scottish Regiments in the British Army. Glasgow: 1862. V. 41

MURRAY, ARTHUR

How to Become a Good Dancer. New York: 1938. V. 46

MURRAY, C. FAIRFAX

Catalogue of a Collection of Early French Books in the Library of C. Fairfax Murray. London: 1961. V. 41

Catalogue of the Pictures Belonging to the Duke of Portland at Welbeck Abbey. London: 1894. V. 38

MURRAY, CHARLES AUGUSTUS 1806-1895

The Prairie Bird. London: 1844. V. 37; 38; 39; 40; 41; 43; 46

The Prairie-Bird. New York: 1844. V. 39

The Prairie-Bird. London: 1845. V. 37; 41

The Prairie-Bird. New York: 1845. V. 39

Travels in North America. London: 1839. V. 38; 42; 43; 44; 45; 46

Travels in North America During the Years 1834, 1835 & 1836. New York: 1839. V. 37; 38; 40; 41; 45

MURRAY, CHARLES FAIRFAX 1849-1919

Catalogue of a Collection of Early German Books in the Library of . . . London: 1962. V. 41; 42; 43

Catalogue of a Collection of Early French Books in the Library of C. Fairfax Murray; London: 1961. V. 39; 41; 42

MURRAY, CHARLOTTE

The British Garden. Bath: 1799. V. 42

The British Garden; A Descriptive Catalogue of Hardy Plants, Indigenous, or Cultivated in the Climate of Great Britain. London: 1808. V. 42

The British Garden. A descriptive catalogue of Hardy plants, indigenous, or cultivated in the climate of Great Britain . . . with introductory remarks. (In two volumes). London: 1799. V. 37

MURRAY, CHRISTOPHER GRIEVE

A Drunk Man Looks at the Thistle. Edinburgh: 1926. V. 37

MURRAY, DAVID

Robert & Andrew-Foulis and the Glasgow Press with some account of the Glasgow Academy of the Fine Arts. Glasgow: 1913. V. 37

Some Letters of Robert Foulis. Glasgow: 1917. V. 40

MURRAY, DAVID CHRISTIE

My Contemporaries in Fiction. London: 1897. V. 39

The Way of the World. London: 1884. V. 45

MURRAY, DAVID K. WOLFE

Birds through the Years. London: 1938. V. 39

MURRAY, EUSTACE CLARE GRENVILLE

From Mayfair to Marathon. London: 1853. V. 46

High Life in France Under the Republic: Social and Satirical Sketches in Paris and Provinces. London: 1885. V. 46

The Member for Paris: a Tale of the Second Empire. London: 1871. V. 46

People I Have Met. London: 1883. V. 46

MURRAY, EUSTACE CLARE GRENVILLE continued

Pictures from the Battle Fields. London: 1855. V. 46

Queer Stories from Truth. London. V. 46

Round About France. London: 1878. V. 46

Strange Tales. Leipzig: 1878. V. 46

That Artful Vicar; the Story of What a Clergyman Tried to Do for Others and Did for Himself. London: 1879. V. 46

Under the Lens: Social Photographs. London: 1885. V. 39; 46

Young Brown or the Law of Inheritance. London: 1874. V. 46

Young Widows. London: 1886. V. 46

MURRAY, FRANCIS EDWIN

From a Lover's Garden. London: 1924. V. 37

MURRAY, FRANCIS J.

Mathematical Machines. Volume I: Didital Computers. Volume II: Analog Devices. New York: 1961. V. 42

MURRAY, G. W.

The Tweedale Shooting Club. Edinburgh: 1945. V. 43

The Tweedale Shooting Club. Edinburgh: 1945. V. 43; 45

MURRAY, GEORGE

A Particular Account of the Battle of Culloden, April 16, 1746. London: 1749. V. 44

MURRAY, GEORGE W.

A History of George W. Murray, and His Long Confinement at Andersonville, Ga. Northampton: 1865. V. 40

A History of George W. Murray and His Long Confinement at Andersonville, Ga. Northampton: 1865? V. 43; 44

MURRAY, GRISELL

Memoirs of the Lives and Characters of . . . George Baillie and of Lady Grisell Baillie. Edinburgh: 1822. V. 40

MURRAY, HENRY

A Man of Genius. London: 1895. V. 41

MURRAY, HUGH

Adventures of British Seamen in the Souther Ocean. Edinburgh: 1827. V. 43

Historical Account of Discoveries and Travels in Africa, by the Late John Leyden . . . Edinburgh: 1817. V. 41; 44

Historical Account of Discoveries and Travels in Asia, from the Earliest Ages to the Present Time. Edinburgh: 1820. V. 41; 42; 44; 45

Historical Account of Discoveries and Travels in North America . . . London: 1829. V. 38; 42; 43; 46

An Historical and Descriptive Account of British America . . . Edinburgh: 1839. V. 38; 42; 43; 45

An Historical and Descriptive Account of British America. New York: 1840. V. 44

Historical Account of Discoveries and Travels in Africa, from the Earliest Ages to the Present Time . . . Edinburgh: 1818. V. 38; 45

An Historical and Descriptive Account of China . . . Edinburgh: 1836. V. 45

The Swiss Emigrants: a Tale. London: 1804. V. 37

The United States of America. Edinburgh: 1844. V. 40

MURRAY, J. A.

The Avifauna of British India. London: 1887-90. V. 43

The Avifauna of British India and Its Dependencies. London: 1888-90. V. 37; 38

MURRAY, J. OGDEN

The Immortal Six Hundred: A Story of Cruelty to Confederate Prisoners of War. Roanoke: 1911. V. 46

MURRAY, JAMES 1865-

Antarctic Days. London: 1913. V. 40; 41

An Impartial History of the Present War in America. Newcastle-upon-Tyne: 1779. V. 40

An Impartial History of the Present War in America. Newcastle Upon Tyne: 1780. V. 43; 46

An Impartial History of the War in America . . . Newcastle-upon-Tyne: 1782. V. 40

Sermons to Asses. London: 1768. V. 37

MURRAY, JAMES A. H. 1837-1915

A New English Dictionary on Historical Principles . . . with A Supplement . . . 1888-1933/1976- V. 43

MURRAY, JAMES A.H. 1837-1915

A New English Dictionary on Historical Principles. Oxford: 1888-1933. V. 37; 46

The Oxford English Dictionary. Oxford: 1933. V. 38

MURRAY, JOHN

Bath-kol. A Voice from the Wilderness. Boston: 1783. V. 37

Experimental Researches on the Light and Luminous Matter of the Glow Worm . . . Glasgow: 1826. V. 43

Handbook for Travellers in Greece. London: 1854. V. 45

A Handbook for Travellers in India Burma and Ceylon . . . London: 1901. V. 39

Handbook for Travellers in Constantinople, Brusa and the Troad. London: 1900. V. 37

Holy-Rood House; an Elegy. Edinburgh: 1780. V. 40; 41; 42

Lord Byron and His Detractors. London: 1906. V. 37

A Memoir on the Diamond. London: 1839. V. 40; 42

The Original Sin Imputed. Newburyport: 1791. V. 40; 41; 43; 44

Practical Remarks on Modern Paper, with an Introductory Account of Its Former Substitutes. Edinburgh: 1829. V. 37

Practical Remarks on Modern Paper. North Hills: 1981. V. 37; 38; 39; 41; 42; 43; 44; 46

A System of Materia Medica and Pharmacy . . . New York: 1828. V. 45

MURRAY, JOHN OGDEN

The Immortal Six Hundred, a Story of Cruelty to Confederate Prisoners of War. Winchester: 1905. V. 43; 46

MURRAY, JOHN V. A.

Treaties and Agreements with and Concerning China 1849-1919. New York: 1912-19, 1921. V. 40

MURRAY, JOHN WILSON

Memoirs of a Great Detective: Incidents in the Life of John Wilson Murray. London: 1904. V. 44

MURRAY, JUDITH SARGENT STEVENS

The Gleaner. A Miscellaneous Production.. Boston: 1798. V. 43

MURRAY, KEITH A.

The Modocs and Their War. Norman: 1959. V. 42

MURRAY, LINDLEY 1745-1826

A Biographical Sketch of Henry Tuke. York: 1815. V. 38

English Grammar, Adapted to the Different Classes of Learners. York: 1798. V. 41

An English Grammar Comprehending the Principles and Rules of the Language. York: 1809. V. 39; 40

An English Grammar. York: 1819. V. 41

The English Reader; or, Pieces in Prose and Verse . . . to Which are Prefixed the Definitions of Inflections and Emphasis, and Rules for Reading Verse with a Key . . . Montreal: 1824? V. 40; 41; 44

MURRAY, LOIS LOVINA

Incidents of Frontier Life. Goshen: 1880. V. 40; 41

MURRAY, LOUISE WELLES

The Story of Some French Refugees and Their Azilum 1793 - 1800. Athens: 1903. V. 41

MURRAY, LT. COL.

Catalogue of British War Medals, Crosses, Badges, Decorations and Miscellaneous Medals, in the collection of Lieut.-Colonel Murray, of Polmaise. London: 1882. V. 37

MURRAY, M.

History of the United States of America. Boston: 1852. V. 41

MURRAY, MARGARET A.

Cambridge Excavations in Minorca. London: 1932-38. V. 40

Saqqara Mastabas Part I. London: 1905. V. 44

Saqqara Mastabas I-II. London: 1905-37. V. 44

A Street in Petra. London: 1940. V. 43

MURRAY, MARISCHAL

Union-Castle Chronicle. London: 1953. V. 39

MURRAY, MUNGO d. 1770

A Treatise on Ship-Building and Navigation. London: 1754. V. 38; 40; 42

A Treatise on Ship-Building and Navigation. London: 1765. V. 37; 38

MURRAY, NICHOLAS

Notes, Historical and Biographical, Concerning Elizabeth-Town, Its Eminent Men, Churches and Ministers. Elizabethtown: 1844. V. 37; 46

MURRAY, NORMAN

Murray's Illustrated Guide to Montreal and Vicinity. Montreal: 1893. V. 40

MURRAY-OLIVER, ANTHONY

Captain Cook's Artists in the Pacific, 1769-1779. Wellington?: 1969. V. 38

MURRAY, PAULI

Dark Testament and Other Poems. Norwalk: 1970. V. 44

Proud Shoes. New York: 1956. V. 45

MURRAY, R. A. F.

Victoria: Geology and Physical Geography. Melbourne: 1887. V. 43

MURRAY, R. W.

South African Reminiscences . . . Juta: 1894. V. 45

MURRAY, RICHARD

A Literal Translation of Murray's Logic . . . Dublin: 1812. V. 43

MURRAY, ROBERT DUNDAS

The Cities and Wilds of Andalucia. London: 1850. V. 42

A Summer at Port Phillip. Edinburgh: 1843. V. 40; 46

MURRAY, ROBERT H.

The History of the VIII King's Royal Irish Hussars 1693-1927. Volume II. Cambridge: 1928. V. 41

Revolutionary Ireland and Its Settlement. London: 1911. V. 38

MURRAY, S., MRS.

A Companion and Useful Guide to the Beauties of Scotland, to the Lakes of Westmorland, Cumberland, and Lancashire . . . London: 1799. V. 38

MURRAY, T. BUTLER

An Alphabet of Emblems. Stony Stratford: 1863. V. 38

MURRAY, T. DOUGLAS

Sir Samuel Baker. A Memoir. London: 1895. V. 45

MURRAY, THOMAS

The Story of the Irish in Argentina. New York: 1919. V. 37

MURRAY, THOMAS H.

Irish Rhode Islanders in the American Revolution. Providence: 1903. V. 37

MURRAY, W. H. G.

Daylight Land. Boston: 1888. V. 42; 43

MURRELL, WILLIAM

A History of American Graphic Humor. New York: 1933-38. V. 37

Nitro-Glycerine as a Remedy for Angina Pectories. London: 1880. V. 37

MURRELL, WILLIAM MEACHAM

Cruise of the Frigate Columbia Around the World, Under the Command of Commodore George C. Read, in 1838, 1839 and 1840. Boston: 1840. V. 40

MURRY, JOHN MIDDLETON

The Critic in Judgment or Belshazzar of Baronscourt. Richmond: 1918. V. 44

The Defence of Democracy. London: 1939. V. 38

The Evolution of an Intellectual. London: 1920. V. 46

The Wanderer. N.P.,: 1933 to 1934. V. 38

MURTADHA IBN AL KHAFIF

L'Egypte de Murtdi, Fils du Graphiphe, ou il est Trait des Pyrmides, du Debordement du Nil, & des Autres Merveilles de cette Province, Selon les Opinions & Traditions des Arabes. Paris: 1666. V. 38

MURTY, A. S.

Toxicity of Pesticides to Fish. Boca Raton: 1986. V. 37

MUSAE ANGLICANE

Musae Anglicane. London: 1741. V. 39

MUSAE Etonenses: Seu Carminium Delectus Nunc Primum im Lucem Editus. Londini: 1795. V. 39

MUSAE Etonenses Sive Poemata in Duos Tomos Distributa. London: 1755. V. 39

MUSAE Seatonianae. London: 1772. V. 42; 45
MUSAE Seatonianae. Cambridge: 1808. V. 42

MUSAE Seatonianae, a Complete Collection of the Cambridge Prize Poems from the First Institution of that Premium . . . in 1750 to the Present Time . . . London: 1771. V. 40

MUSAEUS

Musaei Opusculum de Herone & Leandro. Col: Venetiis in: 1517. V. 38

Hero and Leander. 1949. V. 42

Hero and Leander. London: 1949. V. 41

Hero and Leander. Waltham St. Lawrence: 1949. V. 44; 46

The Loves of Hero and Leander. London: 1797. V. 44

MUSAEUS GRAMMATICUS

Le Avventure di Ero e Leandro . . . Brescia: 1811. V. 45

MUSAEUS, J. C. A.

Popular Tales of the Germans. London: 1791. V. 43

MUSART, CHARLES

Adolescens Academicvx Svb Institvtione Salomonis. Douai: 1633. V. 42

MUSARUM Anglicanarum Analecta . . . Oxon: 1692. V. 39; 42; 44

MUSARUM Cantabrigiensium Concentus Et Congratulatio . . . Cambridge: 1637. V. 38

MUSARUM Cantabrigiensium Luctus & Gratulatio. Cambridge: 1658. V. 38

MUSARUM Deliciae. London: 1728. V. 42

MUSARUM Lachrymae; or, Poems to the Memory of Nicholas Rowe, Esq., by Several Hands. London: 1719. V. 41

MUSCATINE, CHARLES

The Book of Geoffrey Chaucer, an Account of the Publication of Geoffrey Chaucer's Works from the Fifteenth Century to Modern Times. 1963. V. 38; 39

The Book of Geoffrey Chaucer. San Francisco: 1963. V. 42; 46

The Book of Geoffrey Chaucer. (San Francisco): 1963. V. 37

MUSCHLER, R.

Manual Flora of Egypt. London: 1970. V. 39

MUSCULUS, WOLFGANG 1497-1563

In Mosis Genesim Plenissimi Commentarii. Basileae: 1554. V. 38

MUSEE Cosmpolite. Paris: 1850-63. V. 38

MUSEE GUIMET, PARIS

Oriental Ceramics. Tokyo: 1981. V. 42

MUSEI Etrusci quod Gregorius XVI Pon Max in Aedibus Vaticanis Constituit Monimenta Linearis Picturae Exemplis Expressa et in Utilitatem Studiosorum Antiquitatum et Bonarum Artium Publici Iuris Facta. Rome: 1842. V. 39

THE MUSE'S Library. London: 1741. V. 38

MUSES, C. A.

Aspects of the Theory of Artificial Intelligence. New York: 1962. V. 42

THE MUSES Farewel to Popery & Slavery, or, a Collection of Miscellany Poems, Satyrs, Songs &c. London: 1690. V. 39; 42; 43

THE MUSES Library; or a Series of English Poetry, from the Saxons, to the Reign of King Charles II. London: 1737. V. 40

THE MUSES Library; or a Series of English Poetry, from the Saxons, to the Reign of King Charles II . . . London: 1737. V. 40; 45

THE MUSE'S Pocket Companion. Carlisle,: 1782. V. 42

MUSEUM Disneianum, Being a Description of a Collection of Ancient Marbles, Specimens of Ancient Bronze and Various Ancient Fictile Vases . . . at the Hyde, near Ingatestone. London: 1848-49. V. 38

MUSEUM OF FAR EASTERN ANTIQUITIES, STOCKHOLM.

Oriental Ceramics. Tokyo: 1982. V. 42

MUSEUM OF FINE ARTS, BOSTON.

Artist and the Book, 1860-190, in Western Europe and the U.S. Boston: 1963. V. 40

M. & M. Karolik Collection of American Water Colors and Drawings 1800-1875. Boston: 1962. V. 46

Portfolio of Indian Art: Objects Selected from the Collections of the Museum. Boston: 1923. V. 46

MUSEUM OF MODERN ART, NEW YORK.

First Loan Exhibition. New York: 1929. V. 46

MUSEUM Rusticum et Commerciale; or, Select Papers on Agriculture, Commerce, Arts, and Manufactures. London: 1766. V. 43; 46

MUSEUM Rusticum et Commerciale; or, Select Papers on Agriculture, Commerce, Arts and Manufactures, Drawn from Experience and Communicated by Gentlemen Engaged in These Pursuits, Revised and Digested . . . London: 1764-66. V. 39; 42

MUSGRAVE, GEORGE M.

A Pilgrmage Into Dauphine; Comprising a Visit to the Monastery of The Grande Chartreuse . . . London: 1857. V. 37

MUSGRAVE, PERCY

Notes on the Ancient Family of Musgrave, of Musgrave, Westmorland, and Its Various Branches in Cumberland. Leeds: 1911. V. 44; 46

MUSGRAVE, RICHARD

Memoirs of the Different Rebellions in Ireland from the Arrival of the English . . . Dublin: 1801. V. 38; 43; 45

MUSGRAVE, SAMUEL

Dr. Musgrave's Reply to a letter Publisher in the News-Papers by the Chevalier D'Eon. Plymouth: 1769. V. 45

MUSGRAVE, THOMAS

Castaway on the Aukland Isles. Melbourne: 1865. V. 40

Castaway on the Auckland Isles . . . London: 1866. V. 42; 46

MUSGROVE, RICHARD

History of the Town of Bristol, N.H. Bristol: 1904. V. 42

MUSHER, ANDREA

At The Chinese Exhibit. Madison: 1977. V. 42

MUSHET, DAVID

Papers on iron and Steel, Practical and Experimental. London: 1840. V. 44; 45

MUSHET, ROBERT

A Series of Tables, Exhibiting the Gain and Loss to the Fundholder, Arising from the Fluctuations in the Value of the Currency. From 1800 to 1821 . . . London: 1821. V. 38

THE MUSIC Bijou, an Album of Music and Poetry for 1845. London: 1844. V. 42

THE MUSICAL Miscellany; a Select Collection of the Most Approved Scots, English and Irish Songs, set to Music. Perth: 1786. V. 37; 39; 45

THE MUSICAL Miscellany Being a Collelction of Choice Songs Set to the Violin and Flute by the Most Eminent Masters. London: 1729-1731. V. 38; 39; 40; 45

MUSIL, ALOIS

The Middle Euphrates. New York: 1927. V. 45

MUSKOGEE NATION

Constitution and Laws of the Muskogee Nation. Muskogee, Indian: 1893. V. 37

MUSNICKI, L. N. H.

Roxolana, the Podolian; a Tale of the Sixteenth Century. London: 1805? V. 43

MUSOPHILUS

The Little Passion. 1971. V. 44

MUSPRATT, JAMES

The Corporation of Liverpool Against James Muspratt, Esq., Manufacturer of Alkali. Liverpool: 1838. V. 37

A Full Report of the Trial of the Important Indictment Preferred by the Corporation of Liverpool, Against James Muspratt, Esq . . . . Liverpool: 1838. V. 42

MUSPRATT, SHERIDAN

Chemistry, Theoretical, Practical and Analytical, as Applied and Relating to the Arts and Manufactures. London: 1860. V. 46

MUSS, CHARLES

Thirty-Three Original Designs from Gay's Fables, Drawn and Etched by the Late . . . London: 1825. V. 40

MUSSCHENBROEK, PETER VAN

Physicae Experimentales, et Geometricae, de Magnete, Tuborum Capillarium Vitreorumque Speculorum Attractione . . . Leiden: 1729. V. 44

MUSSER, A. MILTON

The Fruits of 'Mormonism'. Salt Lake City: 1878. V. 42

MUSSET, ALFRED DE 1810-1857

The Complete Writings. New York: 1905. V. 42

MUSSO, CORNELIO

Prediche . . . Fatte in Vienna alla Sacra Maesta Cesarea & al Serenissimo Re, & Reina di Bohemia . . . Venice: 1561. V. 45

MUSSON, S. C.

Sicily. London: 1911. V. 38

THE MUSTER Roll of Angus. South African War 1899-1900. A Record and a Tribute. Arbroath,: 1900. V. 42

MUSTERS, GEORGE C.

At Home with Patagonians. London: 1873. V. 39

MUSTIUS, JOSEPHUS ESTENSIS

Theorismata e Trium Principum Disciplinarum Encyclopaedia Delecta Philosophiae, Theologiae, Ivrispvdentiae . . . Perugia: 1658. V. 42

MUSTON, ALEXIS

The Israel of the Alps . . . Glasgow: 1857. V. 37; 42

MUTIO, GIROLAMO

Il Dvello. Venetia: 1565-75. V. 42

MUTIS, J.

Flora de la Real Expedicion Botanica del Nuevo Reino de Granada. Madrid: 1954-87. V. 38; 40

Flora de la Real Expedicion Botanica del Nuevo Reino de Granada (1760-1817). Madrid: 1954-90. V. 46

Flora de la Real Expedicion Botanica del Nuevo Reino de Granada (1760-1817) Volume 6, Liliaceas, Smilacaceas, Haemodoreaceas, Hiposideas, Dioscoreaceas . . . Madrid: 1987. V. 39

MUTTER, THOMAS D.

A Lecture on Loxarthrus, or Club-Foot. Philadelphia: 1839. V. 38; 42

MUTTER, THOMAS DENT 1811-1859

Syllabus on the Course of Lectures on the Principles and Practice of Surgery, Delivered in the Jefferson Medical College, Philadelphia. Philadelphia: 1848. V. 44

MUYBRIDGE, EADWEARD

Animal Locomotion: An Electro-Photographic Investigation of Consecutive Phases of Animal Movements. New York: 1969. V. 40

Animals in Motion, an Electro-Photographic Investigation of Consecutive Phases of Muscular Actions. London: 1899, 1925. V. 37

Animals in Motion. London: 1899,1901. V. 37

Animals in Motion. London: 1902. V. 39

Animals in Motion. London: 1925. V. 38; 39

Animals in Motion. (with) The Human Figure in Motion. London: 1925-31. V. 38

The Human Figure in Motion. London: 1904. V. 46

The Human Figure in Motion. London: 1931. V. 37; 44

Panoramic San Francisco, from California Street Hill, 1877. San Francisco: 1911. V. 46

MUYS, JOHN

A Rational Practice of Chyrurgery. London: 1686. V. 39; 40

MUYS, WIJER WILLEM

Dissertation Sur la Perfection Du Monde Corporel Et Intelligent. Leiden: 1745. V. 37

MUZEL, HEINRICH WILHELM

Verzeichniss Einer Sammlung Haupstachlich zu des Alterthumern, der Historie den Schonen Kunsten . . . Berlin: 1783. V. 44

MUZIO, GIROLAMO 1496-1576

Il Duello . . . con le Riposte Cavalleresche. Di Nuovo dall'Auttore Riveduto, con la Giunta delle Postille in Margine & Una Tavola di Tutte le Cose Notabili. Venice: 1585. V. 40

Il Gentilhvomo. Venice: 1575. V. 37

MUZZY, HARRIET

Poems, Moral and Sentimental. New York: 1821. V. 40

MY Best Story. Second Series. London: 1933. V. 37

MY Dolly. London: 1900. V. 45

MY Dolly's House. London: 1890. V. 39

MY First Publication. San Francisco: 1961. V. 37; 46

MY Illustrated Alphabet. 1986. V. 40

MY Lady's Casket of Jewels and Flowers for Her Adorning. Boston: 1885. V. 43

MY Mother. London: 1870-74. V. 43

MY Mother's Picture Book. London: 1870. V. 39

MY Pets Library: Little Chicks, Merry Legs, Playfellows, Kittie, Miss Mistletoe and Sand Castles. London: 1890. V. 46

MY Trivial Life and Misfortune by a Plain Woman. Edinburgh & London: 1883. V. 41

MYER, ALBERT J.

A Manual of Signals; for the Use of Signal Officers in the Field, and for Military and Naval Students . . . New York: 1874. V. 41

MYER, JESSE S. 1785-1853

Life and Letters of Dr. William Beaumotn, Including Hitherto Unpublished Data Concerning the Case of Alexis St. Martin. St. Louis: 1912. V. 45

MYER, REGINALD

Chats on Old English Tobacco Jars. (with) The Westminster Tobacco Box. London: 1930's. V. 38

MYERS, ARTHUR B. R.

Life with the Hamran Arabs An Account of a Sporting Tour of Some Officers of the Guards in the Soudan During the Winter of 1874-5. London: 1876. V. 40; 43

MYERS, BERNARD S.

Expressionism; a Generation in Revolt. London: 1957. V. 42

The German Experssionists: a Generation in Revolt. New York. V. 43; 46

The German Expressionists: a Generation in Revolt. New York: 1957. V. 41; 46

MYERS, DWIGHT

In Celebration of the Book: Literary New Mexico. Albuquerque: 1982. V. 40

MYERS, FRANCIS

The Coastal Scenery, Harbours, Mountains, and Rivers of New South Wales. Sydney: 1886. V. 39

MYERS, FREDERICK WILLIAM HENRY 1843-1901

Human Personality and Its Survival of Bodily Death. New York: 1903. V. 45; 46

MYERS, H. M.

Life and Nature Under the Tropics, or, Sketches of Travels Among the Andes, and of the Orinoco, Rio Negro and Amazons. New York: 1771. V. 43

MYERS, J. C.

Sketches of a Tour through the Northern and Eastern States, the Canadas & Nova Scotia. Harrisonburg: 1849. V. 39; 40; 46

MYERS, JOSEPHUS HART

Dissertatio Medica Inauguralis De Diabete . . . Edinburgh: 1779. V. 45

MYERS, L. H.

The Orissers. London: 1922. V. 39; 40; 41

MYERS, PETER HAMILTON

The First of the Knickerbockers: A Tale of 1673. New York: 1848. V. 37

MYERS, PETER M., MRS.

The Coming of the White Men. Milwaukee: 1910. V. 46

MYERS, S.

Myer's History of West Virginia. N.P.: 1915. V. 46

MYERS, SARAH A.

Martin's Natural History. New York: 1861. V. 41

Self-Sacrifice, or the Pioneers of Fuegia. Phildelphia: 1861. V. 38

MYERS, THEODORUS BAILEY

Cowpens Papers, Being Correspondence of General Morgan and the Prominent Actors. Charleston: 1881. V. 44

MYERS, VIRGINIA

The Letters and Correspondence of Mrs. Virginia Myers. Philadelphia: 1847. V. 45

MYERS, WILLIAM H.

Sketches of California and Hawaii by William H. Meyers, Gunner, U.S.N., Aboard the United States Sloop-of-War Cyane, 1842-1843. San Francisco: 1970. V. 38

MYERS, WILLIAM STARR

The Story of New Jersey. New York: 1945. V. 46

MYERSCOUGH-WALKER, R.

Stage and Film Decor. London: 1940. V. 45

MYHRMAN, DAVID W.

Sumerian Administrative Documents Dated in the Reigns of the Kings of the Second Dynasty of Ur from the Temple Archives of Nippur. Philadelphia: 1910. V. 40; 42; 44

MYLER VON EHRENBACH, JOHANN NIKOLAS

Metrologia, hoc est, de Jure Statuendi de Mensuris, Ponderibus & Moletrini. Tubingen: 1668. V. 37

MYLES, WILLIAM

A Chronological History of the People Called Methodists. Liverpool: 1799. V. 46

MYLIUS, JOSEPH

De Hortorum Cultura Libri III . . . Brescia: 1574. V. 46

MYLNE, JAMES

Poems, Consisting of Miscellaneous Pieces, and Two Tragedies. Edinburgh: 1790. V. 40; 42

MYLNE, ROBERT SCOTT

The Master Masons to the Crown of Scotland and Their Works. Edinburgh: 1893. V. 37; 38; 39; 40; 42; 44

MYLONAS, GEORGE E.

Aghios Kosmas: an Early Bronze Age Settlement and Cemetery in Attica. Princeton: 1959. V. 40

Excavations at Olynthus. Baltimore: 1929. V. 40

Mycenae Rich in Gold. Athens: 1983. V. 40

MYNSICHT, ADRIAN

Thesavrvs et Armamentarivm Medico-Chymicvm . . . Lvgdvni: 1640. V. 37

MYNSINGER, JOACHIM 1517-1588

Apotelesma Hoc est Scholiorum ad Institutiones Justinian Eas Pertinentium Corpus. Basle: 1584. V. 39

MYNSINGER, JOACHIMUS 1517-1588

Clarissimi Apotelesma, sive Corpus Perfectum Scholiorum . . . Basileae: 1580. V. 40

MYRES, SAMUEL D.

The Permian Basin, Petroleum Empire of the Southwest. 1973. V. 42

MYRHTE, A. T.

Ambrosio de Letinez; or, The First Texian Novel, Embracing a Description . . . With Incidents of the War of Independence. New York: 1842. V. 37

MYRICK, DAVID F.

Railroads of Arizona. Berkeley & San Diego: 1975/80/84. V. 41

Railroads of Nevada and Eastern California. Berkeley: 1962/63. V. 41

Reproductions of Thompson and West's History of Nevada 1881 and Biographical Sketches of Its Prominent Men and Pioneers. Berkeley: 1958. V. 43

MYRICK, HERBERT

Cache La Poudre. New York: 1905. V. 39; 42

Cache la Poudre: The Romance of a Tenderfoot in the Days of Custer. New York & Chicago: 1905. V. 37; 39; 42

How to Cooperate. New York: 1891. V. 43

MYRTHE, A. T.

Ambrosio de Letinez; or, the First Texian Novel Embracing a Descrption . . . New York: 1842. V. 38

MYSINGER VON FRUNDECK, JOACHIM

Clarissimi Apotelesma, Sive Copus Perfectum Scholiorum ad Quatuor Libros Institutionum Juris Civilis . . . additis III. Basileae: 1580. V. 38

MYSTEL, OLE T.

Lost and Found; or Three Months with the Wild Indians. Dallas: 1888. V. 37

LE MYSTERE de Saint Louis Roi de France. Westminster: 1871. V. 40

THE MYSTERIES of Nashua; or Revenge Punished and Constancy Rewarded. Nashua: 1844. V. 39

THE MYSTERIOUS Penitent; or, the Norman Chateau. Dublin: 1801. V. 41

THE MYSTIQUE of Vellum. Boston: 1984. V. 46

MYTTON, JOHN

Memoirs of the Life of the late John Mytton, Esq. With Notices on Hunting, Shooting, Driving, Racing, Eccentric and Extravagant Exploits. London;: 1851. V. 37

N

N., S.

Rawleigh Redivivus; or, The Life and Death of the Right Honourable Anthony, Late Earl of Shaftesbury . . . London: 1683. V. 42

NA Huaolelo a Me Na Olelo Kikeke Ma Ke Olelo Beritania . . . Honolulu: 1884. V. 39; 43

NABBES, THOMAS

The Bride, a Comedie. London: 1640. V. 37

Hannibal and Scipio. London: 1637. V. 45

Microcosmus. London: 1637. V. 37; 40; 42; 44

The Unfortunate Mother. London: 1640. V. 37; 40

NABOKOV, VLADIMIR 1899-1977

Anniversary Notes. N.P.: 1970. V. 44

Bend Sinister. 1947. V. 46

Bend Sinister. New York: 1947. V. 37; 39; 41

The Defence. London: 1964. V. 42

The Defense. New York: 1964. V. 41; 42

La Meprise. Paris: 1939. V. 45

The Eye. New York: 1965. V. 37; 40; 42

The Gift. London: 1963. V. 46

The Gift. New York: 1963. V. 43

Glory. Paris: 1932. V. 39

Invitation to a Beheading. Paris: 1938. V. 39

Invitation to a Beheading. New York: 1959. V. 45

Invitation to a Beheading. London: 1960. V. 39

Laughter in the Dark. Indianapolis: 1938. V. 39; 44

Laughter in the Dark. Indianapolis & New York: 1938. V. 39

Laughter in the Dark. New York: 1950. V. 46

Lectures on Ulysses. Bloomfield Hills/Columbia: 1980. V. 45

Lolita. New York: 1955. V. 43

Lolita. Paris: 1955. V. 37; 38; 39; 42; 45

Lolita. Paris: 1958. V. 39

Lolita. London: 1959. V. 38; 46

Lolita. London: 1961. V. 45

Lolita. New York: 1967. V. 39; 45

The Nabokov-Wilson Letters. London: 1797. V. 40

Nabokov's Dozen. New York: 1958. V. 46

Nabokov's Dozen. London: 1959. V. 42; 43

Nikolai Gogol. Norfolk: 1944. V. 40; 43; 46

Nikolai Gogol. London: 1947. V. 37; 39; 42

Nine Stories. New York: 1947. V. 39; 42; 44

Notes on Prosody - from the Commentary to His Translation of Pushkin's Eugene Onegin. New York: 1963. V. 44

Pale Fire. London: 1962. V. 45

Pale Fire. New York: 1962. V. 43

Pnin. Garden City: 1957. V. 41; 42

Pnin. London: 1957. V. 42

Pnin. Melbourne-London-Toronto: 1957. V. 43

Poems. Garden City: 1959. V. 41; 42; 45; 46

Poems. New York: 1959. V. 46

The Real Life of Sebastian Knight. 1941. V. 44

The Real Life of Sebastian Knight. Norfolk: 1941. V. 40; 42; 43

A Russian Beauty and Other Stories. 1973. V. 46

Speak, Memory. London: 1951. V. 39; 41; 42

Three Russian Poets. 1944. V. 44

Three Russian Poets. Selections from Puskin, Lermontov and Tyutchev in New Translations . . . Norfolk: (1944). V. 37

Trois Courts Poemes. Losne: 1988. V. 44

La Vraie Vie de Sebastian Knight. Paris: 1951. V. 41

NACENTA, RAYMOND

The Painters and the Artistic Climate of Paris Since 1910. Greenwich: 1960. V. 41

NACHTGALL, OTHMAR 1487-1537

Seria Iocique. Strassbourg: 1529. V. 43

NACHTIGAL, GUSTAV

Sahara und Sudan. Berlin: 1889. V. 46

NADEAU, REMIA

The Water Seekers. Garden City: 1950. V. 46

NADELHOFFER, HANS

Cartier: Jewelers Extraordinary. New York: 1984. V. 41

NAEFF, M. A.

Property Atlas of Montgomery County, Pennsylvania. Philadelphia: 1893. V. 42

NAEGELE, FRANZ CARL

The Obliquely Contracted Pelvis . . . New York: 1939. V. 44

NAGEL, CHARLES

Seal Islands of Alaska: Letter from . . . Transmitting . . . Information . . . Washington: 1911. V. 39

NAGEL, OTTO

The Drawings of Kathe Kollwitz. New York: 1972. V. 39; 41; 43

NAGLE, THEODORE M.

Reminiscences of the Civil War by . . . Erie: 1923. V. 44

NAGLEE, HENRY M.

Report of Brigadier-General Henry M. Naglee of His Command of the District of Virginia. Philadelphia: 1863. V. 44

NAGLES, HENRY MORRIS

Love Life of Brig. Gen. Henry M. Naglee, Consisting of a Correspondence on Love, War and Politics. N.P.: 1867. V. 38

NAHL, ARTHUR

Instructions in Gymnastics. San Francisco: 1863. V. 45

NAHUM, PETER

Monograms of Victorian and Edwardian Artists. London: 1976. V. 46

NAIBOD, VALENTIN

Enarratio Elementorum Astrologiae, in qua Praaeter Alcabicii . . . Cologne: 1560. V. 38

NAIPAUL, SHIVA

The Chip-Chip Gatherers. London: 1973. V. 38

Fireflies. 1970. V. 44

Fireflies. London: 1970. V. 38; 45

A Hot Country. London: 1983. V. 42

NAIPAUL, VIDIADHAR SURAJPRASAD

An Area of Darkness. London: 1964. V. 46

A Congo Diary. California: 1980. V. 43; 45

A Congo Diary. Los Angeles: 1980. V. 38; 39; 40; 43; 45

A Flag on the Island. London: 1967. V. 40

A House for Mr. Biswas. 1961. V. 44

A House for Mr. Biswas. London: 1961. V. 38; 39; 42

A House for Mr. Biswas. London: 1973. V. 42

India. London: 1990. V. 43; 45

The Loss of El Dorado - a History. London: 1969. V. 38

The Middle Passage. New York: 1963. V. 44

Miguel Street. London: 1959. V. 41

The Mimic Man. London: 1967. V. 40

Mr. Stone and the Knights Companion. London: 1963. V. 44

The Mystic Masseur. London: 1957. V. 37; 40; 44; 45; 46

the Mystic Masseur. New York: 1959. V. 44

The Overcrowded Barracoon and Other Articles. London: 1972. V. 38; 40; 42

The Return of Eva Peron with the Killings in Trinidad. London: 1980. V. 42

A Turn in the South. 1989. V. 43

NAIPAUL, VIDIADHAR SURAJRASAD

A House for Mr. Biswas. New York: 1961. V. 39

NAIRNE, THOMAS

A Letter from South Carolina Giving an Account of the Soil, Air, Product, Trade, Government, Laws, Religion, People, Military Strength &c of that Province. London: 1732. V. 40

NAISMITH, JOHN

Elements of Agriculture; Being an Essay Towards Establishing the Cultivation of the Soil . . . London: 1807. V. 42

General View of the Agriculture of the County of Cyldesdale. Glasgow: 1798. V. 38

NAISMITH, JOHN continued

General View of the Agriculture of the County of Clydesdale . . . London: 1806. V. 44

Thoughts on Various Objects of Industry Pursued in Scotland, With a View to Enquire by What Means the Labour of the People May Be Directed to Promote the Public Propserity. Edinburgh: 1790. V. 43; 45

NAITO, AKIRA

Katsura: a Princely Retreat. Tokyo: 1977. V. 39

NAITO, TOICHIRO

The Wall Paintings of Horyuji. Baltimore: 1943. V. 41

NAJERA, ANTONIO DE

Suma Astrologica, y Arte Para Ensenar Hazer Pronosticos de las Tiempos . . . el Aire, con Calores, Frios, Humedades . . . Lisbon: 1632. V. 42

NALDRET, PERCY

Collected Magic Series. Numbers 1-8. Portsmouth: 1920-27. V. 46

NALEY, JAMES

Boy. London: 1931. V. 40

NALSON, JOHN

The Common Interest of King and People . . . London: 1678. V. 38; 45

A True Copy of the Journal of the High Coourt of Justice for the Tryal of King Charles I. Dublin: 1731. V. 46

THE NAMES and Descriptions of the Proprietors of unclaimed Dividends on Bank Stock, and on the Public Funds transferable at the Bank of England which become due on and before the 5th July 1797, and remained unpaid . . . London: 1800. V. 37

NAMES of Marshals, Cartmen, &c. N.P.?: 1800-10. V. 45

NANBA MATSUTARO, MUROGA NOBUO

Old Maps in Japan. Osaka: 1973. V. 43

NANCE, R. MORTON

Sailing Ship Models. London: 1924. V. 38; 41; 42; 46

NANCREDE, JOSEPH

Proposals for Publishing, by Subscription, a New System of Geography, Ancient and Modern. Salem: 1802. V. 45

NANCREDE, JOSEPH G.

A General System of Toxicology; or, a Treatise on Poisons . . . with Physiology, Pathology and Medical Jurisprudence. Philadelphia: 1817. V. 38

NANCY, SULLIVAN

The Treasury of American Short Stories. New York: 1981. V. 45

NANGLE, EDWARD

The Apocalypse Explained. London: 1877. V. 38

NANI, GIOVANNI BATTISTA 1616-1678

The History of the Affairs of Europe in This Present Age, but more Particularly of the Republick of Venice. London: 1673. V. 39; 42

NANJUNDAYYA, H. V.

The Mysore Tribes and Castes. Bangalore: 1928-36. V. 40; 42

NANKIVELL, JOHN H.

The History of the Twenty-Fifth Regiment in United States Infantry, 1869-1926. N.P.: 1927. V. 45

History of the Military Organizations of the State of Colorado 1860-1935. Denver: 1935. V. 37

NANNONI, LAURENTI 1749-1812

De Similarium Partium Humanum Corpus Constitutentium Regeneratione . . . Milan: 1782. V. 42

NANSEN, FRIDJTOF 1861-1930

Eskimo Life. London: 1893. V. 40

NANSEN, FRIDTJOF 1861-1930

Eskimo Life. London: 1894. V. 42

Farthest North . . . London: 1893-96. V. 46

'Farthest North'. London: 1897. V. 37; 40; 41; 42; 44; 45; 46

'Farthest North'. New York: 1897. V. 37; 38; 39; 40; 42; 43; 46

Farthest North. Westminster: 1897. V. 37; 45

Farthest North. London: 1898. V. 37; 38; 41; 43; 45

Farthest North. New York: 1898. V. 37; 40; 43

The First Crossing of Greenland. London: 1897. V. 45

The First Crossing of Greenland. London: 1890. V. 37; 38

Hunting and Adventure in the Arctic. New York: 1925. V. 45

Hunting and Adventure in the Arctic. V. 45

In Northern Mists. London: 1911. V. 37; 46

In Northern Mists. New York: 1911. V. 37; 39; 42; 43

The Norwegian North Pole Expedition, 1893-96. London: 1900-06. V. 42

The Norwegian North Pole Expedition, 1893-96. London, New York & Bombay: 1900-06. V. 42

The Norwegian North Polar Expedition 1893-1896. Christiania: 1904. V. 41

Through Siberia - The Land of the Future . . . London: 1914. V. 37; 39; 40

Through Siberia the Land of the Future. New York: 1914. V. 37; 43; 44

NANTES, BERNARD DE

Katecismo Indico da Lingua Kariris, Acrescentado de Varias Praticas Doutrinaes, & Moraes, Adaptadas ao Genio & Capacidade dos Indios do Brasil. Lisbon: 1709. V. 41

NAPA City and County Porfolio and Directory. Napa: 1908. V. 46

NAPEA, OLOFF

Letters from London. London: 1816. V. 39

NAPIER, CHARLES JAMES

The Colonies: Treating of Their Value Generally - of the Ionian Islands in Particular. London: 1833. V. 41

NAPIER, DAVID

David Napier, Engineer, 1790-1869. An Autobiographical Sketch, with Notes. Glasgow: 1912. V. 37

NAPIER, E.

Reminiscences of Syria, and the Holy Land. London: 1847. V. 39

Scenes and Sports in Foreign Lands. London: 1840. V. 39; 42; 43

Wild Sports in Europe, Asia and Africa. London: 1844. V. 43

NAPIER, FRANCIS

Notes of a Voyage from New South Wales to the North Coast of Australia, from the Journal of the Late Francis Napier. Glasgow: 1879. V. 40

NAPIER, GEORGE

The Homes and Haunts of Sir Walter Scott, Bart. Glasgow: 1897. V. 37; 38; 39; 40; 45

NAPIER, GEORGE T.

Passages in the Early Military Life of General Sir George T. Napier. London: 1884. V. 42

NAPIER, HENRY EDWARD

Florentine History from the Earliest Authentic Records to the Accession of Ferdinand the Third, Grand Duke of Tuscany. London: 1846-7. V. 43

NAPIER, J. H.

A Handbook of Living Primates. New York: 1967. V. 37

NAPIER, J. R.

A Handbook of Living Primates. New York: 1967. V. 37

NAPIER, JAMES

A Manual of Dyeing and Dyeing Receipts. London: 1875. V. 38; 40

NAPIER, JOHN

Logarithmorum Canonis Descriptio, Seu Arithmeticarum Supputationum Mirablilis Abbreviatio. Lyon and: 1620. V. 41

Mirifici Logarithmorum Canonis Descriptio, Eiusque Usus, in Utraque Trigonometria . . . Edinburgh: 1614. V. 44

A Plaine Discovery of the Whole Revelation of St. John. Edinburgh: 1645. V. 38; 40

NAPIER, MARK

Memorials and Letters Illustrative of the Life and Times of John Graham of Claverhouse, Viscount Dundee. Edinburgh: 1859. V. 38; 40

NAPIER, ROBERT W.

John Thomson of Duddingston. Landscape Painter. Edinburgh: 1919. V. 46

NAPIER, ROBINA

A Noble Boke off Cookry Ffor a Prynce Houssolde or Eny Other Estately Houssolde. London: 1882. V. 46

NAPIER, W.

The Life and Opinions of General Sir Charles James Napier, G.C.B. London: 1857. V. 41

NAPIER, WILLIAM

History of Sir Charles Napier's Administration of Scinde, and the Cutchee Hills. London: 1851. V. 40

NAPIER, WILLIAM FRANCIS PATRICK

History of the Peninsular War and in the South of France, from the Year 1807 to 1814. London: 1828-1840. V. 39

NAPIER, WILLIAM FRANCIS PATRICK continued

History of the War in the Peninsula and in the South of France, from the Year 1807 to the Year 1814. London: 1832-1840. V. 37; 46

History of the War in the Peninsula and in the South of France, 1807-1814. London: 1860. V. 39; 40

History of the War in the Peninsula and in the South of France from the Year 1807 to the Year 1814. London: 1876. V. 40

History of the War in the Peninsula and in the South of France from the Year 1807 to the Year 1814. London: 1892. V. 40

NAPOLEON

Napoleon's Memoirs. London: 1945. V. 37

Supper at Beaucaire. 1945. V. 45

NAPOLEON I, EMPEROR OF THE FRENCH 1769-1821

The Confidential Correspondence of Napoleon Bonaparte with His Brother Joseph. New York: 1856. V. 40

Historical Memoirs of Napoleon. Book IX. London: 1820. V. 42

Memoirs. London: 1945. V. 40

Napoleon's Memoirs. Waltham St. Lawrence: 1945. V. 46

Napoleon His Own Histories. London: 1818. V. 43

A Selection from the Letters and Despatches of the First Napoleon. London: 1884. V. 42

NAPOLEON'S Book of Fate. Edinburgh: (1900). V. 37

NAPORA, JOE

Scighte. New York: 1987. V. 40; 45

NAPORA, JOSEPH

Scighte. New York: 1987. V. 45

NAPTON, WILLIAM B.

Over the Santa Fe Trail, 1857. Kansas City: 1905. V. 37; 40; 43

NARAHARA, IKKO

Where Time Has Vanished. Tokyo: 1975. V. 39

NARAMORE, R. C.

A Souvenir of the United States Treasury Notes and National Bank Notes . . . Bridgeport: 1866. V. 43

NARAYAN, R. K.

My Days. New York: 1974. V. 46

Mysore. London: 1939. V. 38

Mysore. Mysore: 1939. V. 41

NARBOROUGH, JOHN

An Account of Several Late Voyages and Discoveries to the South and North, Towards the Streights of Magellan, the South Seas . . . London: 1694. V. 42

NARDELLI, F.

The Rhinoceros, a Monograph. London: 1988. V. 40; 41; 42; 43

NARDI, JACOPO

Le Historie Della Citta di Fiorenza. Lyons: 1582. V. 42

NARDINI, FAMIANO

Roma Antica. Rome: 1666. V. 38; 40

NARES, EDWARD

Heraldic Anomalies . . . London: 1823. V. 42; 46

Think's-I-To-Myself. London: 1811. V. 37

NARES, G. S.

Journals and Proceedings of the Arctic Expedition, 1875-76, under the Command of Captain Sir George S. Nares, R.N., K.C.B. London: 1877. V. 45

NARES, GEORGE STRONG

Narrative of a Voyage to the Polar Sea. London: 1878. V. 37; 38; 46

NARES, JOHN

A Summary of the Law of Penal Convictions. London: 1814. V. 40

NARES, ROBERT

Elements of Orthoepy: Containing a Distinct View of the Whole Analogy of the English Language. London: 1784. V. 37; 41

A Glossary; or, Collection of Words, Phrases, Names and Allusions to Customs, Proverbs, etc., Which Have Been Thought to Require Illustration, in the Works of English Authors, Particularly Shakespeare and His Contemporaries . . . London: 1872. V. 41

Principles of Government deduced from Reason, Supported by English Experience, and Opposed to French Errors. London: 1792. V. 38

NARJOUX, FELIX

Notes and Sketches of an Architect Taken During a Journey in the North-West of Europe. London: 1876. V. 44

NARKISS, MORDECHAI

The Hanukkah Lamp. Jerusalem: 1939. V. 41

NARRATIVE and Report of The Causes and Circumstances of the Deplorable Conflagration at Richmond. N.P.: 1812. V. 39

NARRATIVE of a Voyage to the Spanish Main, in the Ship 'Two Friends' . . . London: 1819. V. 45

NARRATIVE of a Voyage to the Spanish Main, in the Ship 'Two Friends': The Occupation of Amelia Island, by M'Gregor &c. Sketches of the Province of East Florida; and Anecdotes Illustrative of the Habits and Manners of the Seminole Indians . . . London: 1819. V. 39

NARRATIVE of a Yacht Voyage in the Mediterranean During the Years 1840-41. London: 1842. V. 45

A NARRATIVE of Capt. Peyton's Proceedings, During the Time He Commanded His Majesty's Ships in the East-Indies. And of What Happen'd Relative Thereto. London: 1750. V. 41

THE NARRATIVE of Captain David Woodard and Four Seamen, Who Lost Their Ship While in a Boat at Sea, and Surrendered Themselves Up to the Malays, in the Island of Celebes . . . London: 1804. V. 40

A NARRATIVE of Events That Have Lately Taken Place in Ireland Among the Society Called Quakers, with Corresponding Documents and General Observations (1792-1803). London, Dublin & Belfast: 1804. V. 43

A NARRATIVE of Five Youth from the Sandwich Islands, Now Receiving an Education in this Country. New York: 1816. V. 37; 40; 42

NARRATIVE of James Williams, an American Slave, Who Was For Several Years a Driver on a Cotton Plantation in Alabama. New York: 1838. V. 45

NARRATIVE of Lord Byron's Voyage to Corsica and Sardinia, During the Summer and Autumn of the Year 1821 . . . Paris: 1825. V. 44

NARRATIVE of Proceedings Regarding the Erection of the Leciester Monument, with a Statement of Account and List of Subscribers. Norwich: 1851. V. 38

A NARRATIVE of the Captivity of Isaac Webster. Metuchen: 1927. V. 42

A NARRATIVE Of the Conjunction of the Two Seas, the Ocean and the Mediterranean, by a Channel Cut through Lanquedoc in France . . . London: 1670. V. 41

A NARRATIVE of the Dreadful Shipwreck of the Vryheid (Late the Melville-Castle), Capt. Scherman, a Dutch Indiaman, Bound to the Cape of Good Hope, Which was Wrecked Off Dymchurch Wall, Near Dover, Nov. 23, 1802, by Whcih Catastrophe, 454 Persons Perished.. London: 1803. V. 39

A NARRATIVE of the Expedition to, and the Storming of Buenos Ayres, by the British Army, Commanded by Lieutenant-General Whitelocke. Bath: 1807. V. 37

NARRATIVE of the Expedition to the Baltic. 1808. V. 40

NARRATIVE of the Expedition to the Baltic, With an Account of the Siege and Capitulation of Copenhagen, Including the Surrender of the Danish Fleet. London: 1808. V. 43

A NARRATIVE of the Facts and Circumstances Relating to the Kidnapping and Presumed Murder of William Morgan. Batavia, New York: 1827. V. 37

NARRATIVE of the French Revolution in 1830. Paris: 1830. V. 40; 42

A NARRATIVE of the Horrid Massacre by the Indians, of the Wife and Children of the Christian Hermit. St. Louis: 1840. V. 46

A NARRATIVE of the Horrid Massacre by the Indians, of the Wife and Children of the Christian Hermit, a Resident of Missouri, with a Full Account of His Life and Sufferings, Never Before Published. St. Louis: 1840. V. 37

NARRATIVE of the Loss of the Hindostan East-Indiamen, Capt. Edw. Balston, Which Was Wrecked on the Wedge-Sand, in the Queen's Channel, Off Margate, January 11, 1803. London: 1803. V. 39

NARRATIVE of the Loss of the Hon. East India Company's Ship Duke of York, in the Bay of Bengal, on the 21st may, 1833. Edinburgh: 1834. V. 46

A NARRATIVE of the Preparations at Hatfield House, the Seat of the Most Noble the Maruqess of Salisbury, for Their Majesties and the Royal Family to Review the Volunteer Corps and Militia of the County of Hartford, on Friday 13th June, 1800. London: 1818. V. 38

A **NARRATIVE** of the Proceedings of His Majesty's Fleet in the Mediterranean, and the Combined Fleets of France and Spain, from the Year 1741 to March 1744. London: 1744. V. 38; 40

NARRATIVE of the Total Loss of the Alexander, East-Indianman, on Her Passage Homeward from Bombay, March, 1815, on the Beach off Portland; When the Captain and All the Crew Perished. London: 1815. V. 46

NARRIEN, JOHN
An Historical Account of the Origin and Progress of Astronomy. London: 1850. V. 42

NASATIR, A. P.
Before Lewis and Clark. Documents Illustrating the History of the Missouri 1785-1804. St. Louis: 1952. V. 37; 40; 41
A French Journalist in the California Gold Rush. Georgetown: 1964. V. 40

NASEWEIS, SEBALDUS
Edinburgh and its Society in 1838. Edinburgh: 1838. V. 39

NASH, CHARLES
History of the War in Affghanistan, From Its Commencement to Its Close . . . London: 1843. V. 43

NASH, ERNEST
Pictorial Dictionary of Ancient Rome. New York: 1916-62. V. 42
Pictorial Dictionary of Ancient Rome. London: 1961. V. 45
Pictorial Dictionary of Ancient Rome. New York: 1961-62. V. 40

NASH, F.
A Series of Views of the Collegiate Chapel of St. George at Windsor with Illustrative Plates. London: 1805. V. 38

NASH, J.
Poisonous Plants, Deadly, Dangerous and Suspect . . . London: 1927. V. 39

NASH, JOHN
Blaise Hamlet. Bristol: 1826. V. 46
English Garden Flowers. London: 1948. V. 38
The Wood Engravings. 1987. V. 43
The Wood Engravings. Liverpool: 1987. V. 40; 46

NASH, JOHN HENRY
California. A History of Upper and Lower California, by Alexander Forbes. With an Introduction by Herbert Ingram Priestley. San Francisco: 1937. V. 37
A Catalogue of Books Printed by John Henry Nash. Compiled and Annotated, Including a Biographical Note, by Nell O'Day. San Francisco: 1937. V. 37
Cobden-Sanderson and the Doves Press. The History of the Press and Story of Its Types Told by Alfred W. Pollard. San Francisco: 1929. V. 43

NASH, JOSEPH 1809-1878
The Mansions of England in the Olden Time. London: 1830. V. 38
the Mansions of England in the Olden Times. (with) Views of the Interior and Exterior of Windsor Castle. London: 1839-52. V. 45; 46
The Mansions of England in Olden Time. London: 1869. V. 37; 38; 40; 45; 46
The Mansions of England in Olden Time. London: 1869. V. 45
Mansions of England and Wales in the Olden Time. London: 1869-71. V. 39; 41
The Mansions of England in the Olden Time. London: 1869-72. V. 41
Views of the Interior and Exterior of Windsor Castle. London: 1848. V. 38; 43

NASH, OGDEN
Free Wheeling. New York: 1931. V. 43
Happy Days. New York: 1933. V. 43
Hard Lines. New York: 1931. V. 37; 40; 42; 44; 46
The Primrose Path. New York: 1935. V. 43; 45

NASH, PAUL
Aerial Flowers. Oxford: 1947. V. 38; 42
Catalogue of a Memorial Exhibition. London: 1948. V. 38
Dear Mercia: Letters to Mercia Oakley 1909-1918. London: 1991. V. 46
Outline. An Autobiography and Other Writings. London: 1949. V. 37; 42; 43
Outline - an Autobiography. 1949. V. 37
Paul Nash: Paintings, Drawings and Illustrations. London: 1948. V. 42
Paul Nash: Ten Coloured Plates. London: 1937. V. 43
Places. London: 1922. V. 44; 45; 46
A Private World. London: 1978. V. 42; 44
The Sun Calendar for the Year 1920. London: 1920. V. 40

NASH, THOMAS
The Choise of Valentines or the Merie Ballad of Nash His Dildo. London: 1899. V. 41
Qvarternio or a Fovrfold Way to a Happie Life . . . London: 1633. V. 46
The Returne of the Renowned Cavaliero Pasquill of England, from the Other Side of the Seas, and His Meeting with Marforius at London Upon the Royall Exchange. N.P.: 1589. V. 40; 42

NASH, WALLIS
Oregon: There and Back in 1877. London: 1878. V. 42; 43; 46
Two Years in Oregon. New York: 1882. V. 44

NASHE, THOMAS
The Complete Works . . . London: 1883-5. V. 45
The Works . . . London: 1904. V. 40
The Works. London: 1904-10. V. 46
The Works. Oxford: 1966. V. 40

NASMITH, JAMES
Proposals for Printing by Subscription, I. Itinerarium, sive Liber Memorabilium Willelmi de Worcestre. II. Itinerarium Simonis Simeonis & Hugonis Illuminatoris . . . Cambridge: 1777. V. 41

NASMYTH, JAMES
James Nasymth, Engineer: an Autobiography. London: 1883. V. 40
The Moon: Considered as a Planet, a World and a Satellite. V. 40
The Moon: Considered as a Planet, a World and a Satellite. London: 1874. V. 37; 38; 40; 41; 45

NASPY, C. J.
At Face Vale. A Biography of Father Louis J. Twomey, S. J. New Orleans: 1978. V. 44

NASR, SEYYED HOSSEIN
Persia. Bridge of Turquoise. Toronto: 1975. V. 38

NAST, THOMAS
Christmas Drawings for the Human Race. New York: 1890. V. 46
The Fight at Dame Europa's School. New York: 1871. V. 38

NASU, N.
Formation of Active Fault Margins. London: 1986. V. 37; 38

NATALIBUS, PETRUS DE
Catalogus Sanctorum et Gestorum Eorum ex Diversis Voluminibus collectus. Vicenza: 1493. V. 37; 44
Catalogus Sanctorum. Strassbourg: 1513. V. 40

NATALIS, HIERONYMUS
Adnotationes et Meditationes in Evangelia Quae in Sacrosancto Missae Sacrificio Toto Anno Leguntur. Antwerp: 1594. V. 40

NATHAN, GEORGE JEAN
The Theatre Book of the Year 1942-1943 to 1950-1952. V. 46

NATHAN, I.
Fugitive Pieces and Reminicences of Lord Byron . . . London: 1829. V. 37; 42; 44

NATHAN, LEONARD
The Matchmaker's Lament and Other Astonishments. Northampton: 1967. V. 42

NATHAN, MAUDE
The Decoration of Leather. London: 1905. V. 45

NATHAN, PSEUD.
Nathan to Lord North. London: 1780. V. 39

NATHAN, ROBERT 1894-
The Bishop's Wife. Indianapolis: 1928. V. 37; 38; 39; 40; 42
Portrait of Jennie. New York: 1940. V. 39
Youth Grow's Old. New York: 1922. V. 37; 38; 39; 40; 42

NATILIS, HIERONYMUS
Evangelicae Historiae Imagines, ex Ordine Euangeliorum. Antwerp: 1596. V. 38

NATIONAL ASSOCIATION FOR THE ADVANCEMENT OF ART
Transactions of the National Association for the Advancement of Art and Its Application to Industry. Liverpool meeting 1888. London: 1888. V. 40; 44; 46

NATIONAL ASSOCIATION FOR THE ADVANCEMNT OF ART
Transactions of the National Association for the Advancement of Art and Its Application to Industry. Edinburgh Meeting 1889. London: 1890. V. 46

NATIONAL ASSOCIATION FOR THE PROMOTION OF SOCIAL SCIENCE

Transactons . . . London: 1871. V. 43

Transactions . . . London: 1872. V. 43

Transactions . . . London: 1873. V. 43

Transactions . . . London: 1876. V. 43

NATIONAL ASSOCIATION FOR THE PROMOTION OF SOCIAL SCIENCES

Transactions . . . London: 1880. V. 43

NATIONAL ASSOCIATION OF VETERANS OF THE MEXICAN WAR

Proceedings of the National Association of Veterans of the Mexican War, Second Annual Reunion, Held in the City of Washington, February 22d and 23d 1875. Washington: 1875. V. 40

NATIONAL Competitions, 1896-97. An Illustrated Record of National Gold, Silver and Bronze Medal Designs, Models, Drawings, Etc. London: 1899. V. 38

NATIONAL CONVENTION OF COLORED MEN, SYRACUSE.

Proceedings of the National Convention of Colored men, Held in the City of Syracuse, N.Y. Oct. 4-7, 1864; with the Bill of Wrongs and Rights, and the Address to the American People. Boston: 1864. V. 42

THE NATIONAL Costumes of Holland. V. 44

THE NATIONAL Encyclopaedia a Dictionary of Universal Knowledge. London: 1800. V. 39

NATIONAL GALLERY OF CANADA

Catalogue of Printing and Sculpture. Volume III. Canadian School. Ottawa: 1960. V. 41

NATIONAL GALLERY OF SCOTLAND

Portfolio of the National Gallery of Scotland. London: 1903. V. 40

NATIONAL Gazeteer of Great Britain and Ireland. London: 1860. V. 44; 46

NATIONAL INSTITUTE OF OCEANORAPHY

Collected Reprints, Volumes 1-21. London: 1953-73. V. 38

NATIONAL LEAGUE OF AMERICAN PEN WOMEN, BIRMINGHAM BRANCH.

Historic Homes of Alabama and Their Traditions. Birmingham: 1935. V. 42

NATIONAL LEAGUE OF PROFESSIONAL BASE BALL CLUBS

Constitution and Playing Rules of the National League of Professional Base Ball Clubs. Chicago: 1882. V. 40

NATIONAL LIBRARY OF MEDICINE

A Catalogue of Sixteenth Century Printed Books in the National Library of Medicine. Bethesda: 1967. V. 40; 46

NATIONAL LIVESTOCK ASSOCIATION

Proceedings of the Sixth Annual Convention and Annual Report of the Nataional Live Stock Association, Kansas City, Missouri, 1903. Denver: 1903. V. 38

NATIONAL MARITIME MUSEUM

National Maritime Museum Catalogue of the Library. London: 1968-76. V. 44

NATIONAL MINING CONGRESS

Report of the Proceedings of the National Mining Congress . . . in the City of Denver, Nov. 18, 19 and 20, 1891. Denver: 1892. V. 42

NATIONAL Nursery Ryhmes and Nursery Songs. London: 1871. V. 44

NATIONAL Oeconomy Recommended, as the Only Means of Retrieving Our Trade and Securing Our Liberties . . . London: 1746. V. 41; 45

NATIONAL Portrait Gallery of Eminent Americans. New York: 1861. V. 39

NATIONAL Portrait Gallery of Eminent Americans, 1862. 1862. V. 39

NATIONAL Prejudice, Opposed to the National Interest, Candidly Considered in the Dentention of Yielding up Gibralter and Cape Briton by the Ensuing Treaty of Peace . . . London: 1748. V. 37

NATIONAL RAILROAD CONVENTION, ST. LOUIS, 1875.

Proceedings of the National Railroad Convention at St. Louis in Regard to the Construction of the Texas and Pacific Railway . . . St. Louis: 1875. V. 39; 43

NATIONAL SHIP CANAL CONVENTION, CHICAGO, 1863.

The Necessity of a Ship-Canal Between the East and the West. Chicago: 1863. V. 38

THE NATIONAL Standard Family and Business Atlas of the World Specially Adapted for Commercial and Library Reference . . . Chicago: 1901. V. 45

NATIONAL Unanimity Recommended, or, the Necessity of a Constitutional Resistance to the Sinister Designs of False Brethern . . . In Answer to a Late Ministerial Pamphlet, Intitled, An Enquiry into the Present State of Our Domestick Affairs. London: 1742. V. 41

NATIONAL WOMAN SUFFRAGE AND EDUCATIONAL COMMITTEE

An Appeal to the Women of the United States by the National Woman Suffrage and Educational Committee. Washington: 1871. V. 43

THE NATIVITY of Napoleon Bonaparte, Emperor of all the French, Calculated by a Professor. High Wycombe: 1805. V. 42

NATTA, MARCUS A.

Volumina Quaedam Nuper Excussa. Venice: 1562. V. 38; 40

NATTER, JOHANN LORENZ

A Treatise on the Ancient Method of Engraving on Precious Stones . . . London: 1754. V. 42

NATTES, J. C.

Guide to Draw from Nature, or Elementary Lessons for Those Who Wish to Attain the Useful and Pleasing Art of Drawing Local Views. London: and Paris: 1803-18. V. 45

Practical Geometry, or an Introduction to Perspective. London: 1805. V. 40

NATURA Brevium Newly Corrected, in Englishe: with Divers Addicions. London: 1557. V. 45

THE NATURAL History of Insects, Compiled from Swammerdam, Brookes, Goldsmith, etc. Perth: 1792. V. 38; 40; 42

NATURAL History of Quadrupeds and Cetaceous Animals from the Works o the Best Authors, Antient and Modern, Embellished with Numerous Plates . . . Bungay: 1811. V. 37

NATURAL HISTORY SOCIETY OF HARTFORD

Transactions of the Natural History Society of Hartford, Number One. Hartford: 1836. V. 41

THE NATURAL Interest of Great-Britain, In Its Present Circumstances, Demonstrated. In a Discourse in Two Parts. London: 1746-48. V. 41; 45

THE NATURAL Resources and Economic Conditions of the State of Texas Report of an Examinaation Made by a Special Committee of the Merchant's Association of New York . . . New York: 1901. V. 37

THE NATURAL Resources and Industrial Development and Condition of Colorado. Denver: 1889. V. 39

NATURE and Art. London: 1866. V. 39

THE NATURE and Making of Papyrus. 1973. V. 40

THE NATURE and Making of Papyrus. Barkston Ash: 1973. V. 38

THE NATURE and Making of Papyrus. Yorkshire: 1973. V. 41

NATURE and Philosophy. New York: 1830. V. 37

THE NATURE, Extent and Province of Human Reason Considered . . . London: 1792. V. 41

NAUBERT, CHRISTIANE BENEDICTE EUGENIE

Alf von Deulmen; or the History of the Emperor Philip and His Daughters. London: 1794. V. 41

NAUCLERUS, JOHN

Tomus Primus. Chronicon D. Iohannis Naucleri. Praepositi Tubingensis Succinctim Compraehendentium res Memorabiles Seculorum Omnium ac Gentium . . . Coloniae apud Haered: 1564. V. 45

NAUDE, GABRIEL

The History of Magick by Way of Apology, For all the Wise Men Who Have Unjustly Been Reputed Magicians . . . London: 1657. V. 42

Instructions Concerning Erecting of a Library. London: 1661. V. 38; 39

Instructions Concerning the Evening of a Library: Presented to My Lord the President De Mesme. Boston: 1903. V. 41

Instructions Concerning Erecting of a Library. Cambridge: 1903. V. 39; 40

Instructions Concerning Erecting of a Library . . . London: 1661. V. 38

NAUMANN, J. A.

Naturgeschichte der Vogel Deutschlands. Gera: 1897-1905. V. 43

NAUMANN, J. F.

Naturgeschichte der Vogel Mitteleuropas . . . Gera-Untermhaus and Leipzig: 1905-09. V. 38

NAUNTON, ROBERT

The Court of Queen Elizabeth. London: 1814. V. 41; 42; 46

Memoirs of Elizabeth, Her Court and Favourites (Fragmentia Regalia). London: 1824. V. 43

NAVAL and Martial Biography. Ormskirk: 1806. V. 38

NAVAL and Military Despatches Relating to Operations in the War, 1914-18. London: 1914-18. V. 45

NAVAL Chronicle. London: 1799-1805. V. 38
THE NAVAL Chronicle. London: 1799-1818. V. 40

THE NAVAL Chronicle . . . London: 1760. V. 38

THE NAVAL Chronicle, or Voyages, Travels and Expeditions, Remarkable Exploits and Achievements of the Most Celebrated English Navigators, Travellers and Sea-Commanders . . . London: 1760. V. 40; 41

NAVAL Documents Related to the Quasi-War Between the U.S. and France. Naval Operations From February 1797 to December 1801. Washington: 1935-38. V. 46

NAVAL HISTORY SOCIETY, NEW YORK. BARNES MEMORIAL LIBRARY

Catalogue of the Books, Manuscripts and Prints and Other Memorabilia in the John S. Barnes Memorial Library of the Naval History Society. New York: 1915. V. 42

NAVAL Operations in World War I. History of the Great War Based on Offical Documents. London: 1920. V. 38

NAVARI, LEONORA

Greece and the Levant. London: 1989. V. 45; 46

NAVARRETE, DOMINGO

The Travels and Controversies of . . . Cambridge: 1962. V. 46

NAVARRETTE, DON MARTIN FERNANDEZ DE

Coleccion de los Viages y Descubrimientos, que Hicieron por Mar Los Espanoles desde Fines del Siglo XV, con Varios Documentos Ineditos Concernientes a la Historia de la Marina Castellana y de los Establecimientos Espanoles en Indias. Madrid: 1825. V. 39

NAVARRO, JUAN SUAREZ DE

Informe Sobre Las Causas Y Caracter de Los Frecuentes Cambios Politicos Ocurridos en el Estado de Yucatan. Mexico City: 1861. V. 38

NAVARRO Y NORIEGA, FERNANDO

Memoria Sobre la Poblacion del Reino de Nueva Espana. Mexico: 1820. V. 41

NAVIER, L. M. H.

Rapport a Monsieur Becquey . . . et Memoire sur les Ponts Suspendus. Paris: 1823. V. 45

THE NAVIGATOR Containing Directions for Navigating the Monogahela, Alleghany, Ohio and Mississippi Rivers . . . Pittsburgh: 1808. V. 42; 45

THE NAVIGATOR, Containing Directions for Navigating the Ohio and the Mississippi Rivers . . . Pittsburgh: 1824. V. 45

NAVILLE, EDOUARD

The Cemeteries of Abydos. London: 1913-14. V. 40; 42; 44
The XIth Dynasty Temple at Deir el-Bahari. Part I. London: 1907. V. 40
The XIth Dynasty Temple at Deit el-Bahari. London: 1907-13. V. 37; 42; 44
The Festival-Hall of Osorkon II in the Great Temple of Bubastis (1887-1889). London: 1892. V. 37
The Temple of Deir el Bahari. London: 1894-1908. V. 42

NAVILLE, EDUOARD

The Temple of Deir el Bahari. London: 1895-98. V. 42

THE NAVY and Army Illustrated. London: 1895-1899. V. 37; 38

THE NAVY in Congress: Being Speeches of Hon. Messrs. Grimes, Doolittle and Nye; of the Senate and the Hon. Messrs. Rice, Pike, Griswold and Blow, of the House . . . Washington: 1865. V. 41

NAVY RECORDS SOCIETY

Publications from Volume I to Volume 121. London: 1894-1980. V. 37

NAWAB, SARABHAI MANILAL

Oldest Rajasthani Paintings from Jain Bhandars. Ahmedabad,: 1959. V. 38; 43

NAYARD, M. P.

Red Data Book of Indian Plants. Calcutta: 1987-88-90. V. 45

NAYLER, GEORGE

A Collection of Coats of Arms Borne by the Nobility and Gentry of the County of Glocester. London: 1792. V. 38; 44
The Coronation of His Most Sacred Majesty King George the Fourth. London: 1839. V. 40; 45

NAYLOR, GEORGE

A Collection of Coats of Arms Borne by the Nobility and Gentry of the County of Glocester. London: 1792. V. 38

NAYLOR, GLORIA

The Women of Brewster Place. New York: 1982. V. 38; 43; 44; 45

NAYLOR, M. J.

The Insanity and Mischief of Vulgar Superstitions. Cambridge: 1795. V. 43; 45

NAYLOR, W. H.

History of the Church in Clarendon. St. Johns: 1919. V. 40

NAZZOLINI, SILVESTRO, DA PRIERIAS

Scala del Sancto Amore Diuotissima e Scientifica. Bologna: 1501. V. 38

NEAGOE, PETER

Americans Abroad: an Anthology. The Hague: 1932. V. 37; 46
Americans Abroad. 1932. V. 37
Storm: A Book of Short Stories. With an introduction by Eugene Jolas. New Riview Publications. Paris: 1932. V. 37; 40; 42

NEAL, ALICE B.

All's Not Gold that Glitters, or The Young Californian. New York: 1853. V. 37; 45

NEAL, AVON

Pigs and Eagles: an Ecological Parable. N. Brookfield: 1978. V. 37; 46

NEAL, DANIEL 1678-1743

The History of New England Containing an Impartial Account of the Civil and Ecclesiastical Affairs of the Country to the Year of Our Lord, 1700. London: 1720. V. 37; 38; 39; 40; 41; 43; 46
The History of the Puritans or Protestant Non-Conformists . . . London: 1732. V. 38
The History of New-England, Containing an Impartial Account of the Civil and Ecclesiastical Affairs of the Country to the Year of Our Lord, 1700 . . . London: 1747. V. 44
The History of the Puritans or Protestant Non-Conformists. London: 1754. V. 40
The History of the Puritans; or, Protestant Non-Conformists . . . London: 1837. V. 42

NEAL, FREDERICK A.

Narrative of a Residence at the Capital of the Kingdom of Siam. London: 1852. V. 38

NEAL, JOHN

Authorship, a Tale. Boston: 1830. V. 43
Battle of Niagara, a Poem, Without Notes . . . Baltimore: 1818. V. 37; 46
Brother Jonathan: or, the New Englanders. Edinburgh & London: 1825. V. 37; 44
The Down-Easters, &c, &c. New York: 1833. V. 43
Portland Illustrated. Portland: 1874. V. 44
Rachel Dyer: a North American Story. Portland: 1828. V. 43; 46
Seventy-Six, by the Author of Logan. Baltimore: 1823. V. 40

NEAL, JOSEPH C.

In Town and About or Pencillings and Pennings. Philadelphia: 1843. V. 45

NEAL, JOSEPH CLAY

Charcoal Sketches; or, Scenes in a Metropolis. Philadelphia: 1838. V. 43

NEAL, TOM

Pretty Pictures, a Fable. Los Angeles: 1967. V. 41
Sixth and Figueroa. Los Angeles: 1965. V. 41

NEALDS, ADELINE MARTHA

Poems. London: 1829. V. 40

NEALE, EDWARD VANSITTART

May I Not Do What I Will With My Own? London: 1852. V. 43

NEALE, GEORGE

Some Observations on the Use of the Agaric, and Its Insufficiency in Stopping Haemorrhages After Capital Operations, in a Letter to a Surgeon in the Country. London: 1757. V. 43

NEALE, J. P.

Views of the Most Interesting Collegiate and Prochial Churches in Great Britain . . . London: 1824. V. 44

NEALE, JAMES

The Abbey Church of Stain Alban, Hertfordshire. London: 1878. V. 38

NEALE, JOHN MASON 1818-1866

Good King Wencelas, a Carol. Birmingham: 1895. V. 37; 41; 42; 46
Good King Wenceslas. 1919. V. 42

NEALE, JOHN PRESTON 1780-1847

The History and Antiquities of the Abbey Church of St. Peter, Westminster... London: 1818. V. 42

The History and Antiquities of the Abbey Church of St. Peter, Westminster. London: 1818-23. V. 42; 43

Views of the Seats of Noblemen and Gentlemen in England, Wales, Scotland and Ireland. London: 1818-24. V. 46

Views of the Seats of Noblemen and Gentlemen in England, Wales, Scotland and Ireland. London: 1818-29. V. 39; 44

Views of the Most Interesting Collegiate and Paraochial Churches in Great Britian. London: 1824. V. 41; 46

Views of the Seats of Nobleman and Gentlemen, in England, Wales, Scotland and Ireland. London: 1824-29. V. 39; 42

NEALE, T. H.

A Proposal for Amending the Silver Coins of England... London: 1696. V. 42

NEALE, WALTER

Autobiographies and Portraits of the President, Cabinet, Supreme Court and Fifty Fifth Congress. Washington: 1899. V. 37

Sovereignty of the States. An Oration Address to the Survivors of the Eighth Virginia Regiment, While They Were Gathered About the Graves of Their Fallen Comrades... New York & Washington: 1910. V. 38

NEALE, WILLIAM JOHNSON

The Flying Dutchman. London: 1840. V. 39

Gentleman Jack. London: 1837. V. 46

Paul Periwinkle; or, the Pressgang. London: 1841. V. 46

Paul Periwinkle; or, the Pressgang. London: 1847. V. 46

The Port Admiral; a Tale of the War. Philadelphia: 1835. V. 40

The Priors of Prague. London: 1836. V. 46

NEALLY, AMY

Baby Days; Our Baby's History. New York. V. 41

Baby Days; Our Baby's History. New York: n.d. V. 37

NEANDER, JOHANN AUGUST 1789-1850

General History of the Christian Religion and Church. London: 1892. V. 39

NEAPOLITAN Captive. Interesting Narrative of the Captivity and Sufferings of Miss Viletta Laranda, a Native of Naples. Middletown: 1831. V. 41

NEASHAM, GEORGE

North Country Sketches. Durham: 1893. V. 45; 46

NEAU, ELIAS

An Account of the Sufferings of the French Protestants, Slaves on Board the French Kings Galleys. London: 1699. V. 46

NEBRASKA. GOVERNOR - 1855

Annual Message of... Governor of the Territory of Nebraska. Addressed to the Legislative Assembly. December 18, 1855. Omaha: 1855. V. 39

NEBRASKA - Her Resources, Advantages and Development. Omaha: 1893. V. 38; 43

NEBRASKA. LEGISLATURE - 1867

Senate Journal of the State Legislature of Nebraska. First, Second and Third Sessions... Omaha: 1867. V. 37; 39

NEBRASKA. LEGISLATURE - 1869

Senate Journal of the Legislative Assembly of Nebraska, Fifth Session and First Regular Session, with Accompanying Documents. Omaha: 1869. V. 37

NEBRASKA LOAN AND TRUST COMPANY

First Mortgage Bonds... by the Nebraska Loan and Trust Co., Hastings Nebraska. Hastings: 1885. V. 39

NEBRASKA STATE HISTORICAL SOCIETY

Transactions and Reports of the... Lindoln: 1885-87. V. 39

NEBRASKA. (TERRITORY). LEGISLATIVE ASSEBMBLY - 1866

Journal of the Council of the Legislative Assembly of the Territory of Nebraska, at Their Regular Session, Begun & Held at Omaha, Jan. 4, 1866. Chicago: 1867. V. 37; 38

NEBRASKA. (TERRITORY). LEGISLATIVE ASSEMBLY - 1861

Council Journal of the Legislative Assembly of the Territory of Nebraska, Seventh Session. Nebraska City: 1861. V. 39

NEBRASKA. (TERRITORY). LEGISLATIVE ASSEMBLY - 1865

Journal of the Council of the Legislative Assembly of the Territory of Nebraska. Tenth Session. Omaha: 1865. V. 37

NEBRIJA, ELIO ANTONIO DE

Opuscula Quae in Hoc Volumine Continentur sunt Haec. Passio Domini Hexametris Versibus Composita. Eiusdem Passionis Threni per Philippum Beroaldum, etc. Logrono: 1528. V. 37

De Peregrinaru Dictionu Accentu. Salmanca: 1506. V. 43

A NECESSARY Abstract of the Laws Relating to the Militia, Reduced into a Practical Method. London: 1691. V. 41

A NECESSARY Doctrine and Erudition for any Chrysten Man, Set Furth by the Kynges Maiestye of Englande. Colophon: 1543. V. 40

A NECESSARY Doctrine and Erudition for Any Chrysten Man, Set Furth by the Kynges Maiestye of Englande &c... London: 1543. V. 40

THE NECESSITY of a Ship-Canal Between the East and West. Chicago: 1863. V. 38

THE NECESSITY of Repealing the American Stamp-Act Demonstrated: or, A Proof that Great Britain Must be Injured in That Act. In a Letter to a Member of the British House of Commons. London: 1766. V. 41

NECK, JACOB VAN

Journael Van de Tweede Reys, Gedaen by den Heer Admirael Jacob van Neck... Amsterdam: 1663. V. 45

NECKER, JACQUES

De l'Administration de Finances de la France. Paris: 1784. V. 38; 41

Compte Rendu au Roi. Paris: 1781. V. 38

Eloge de Jean-Baptiste Colbert, Discours qui a Remporte le Prix de l'Academie Francaise en 1773. Paris: 1773. V. 38

Of the Importance of Religious Opinions. London: 1788. V. 38

Of the Importance of Religious Opinions. Boston: 1796. V. 37; 38; 42; 45

On the French Revolution... London: 1797. V. 37; 39; 40

NECKER, SUZANNE CURCHOD 1739-1794

The Salon of Madame Necker. London: 1882. V. 41

NEDHAM, MARCHAMONT

The Case of the Common Wealth fo England, Stated; or, the Equity, Utility and Necessity, of a Submission to the Present Government; Cleared Out of Monuments Both Sacred and Civill, Agaisnt at the Scruples and Pretences of the Opposite Parties... London: 1650. V. 45

NEED, THOMAS

Six Years in the Bush; or Extracts from the Journal of a Settler in Upper Canada. London: 1838. V. 37; 40

NEEDHAM, E. J.

The First Three Months. The Impressions of an Amateur Infantry Subaltern. Aldershot: 1936. V. 43; 44

NEEDHAM, J.

Studies of Trees in Pencil and in Water Colors. London: 1884. V. 42

NEEDHAM, JOHN

Hymns Devotional and Moral, on Various Subjects. Bristol: 1768. V. 38

NEEDHAM, JOHN TURBEVILLE

An Account of Some New Microscopical Discoveries Founded on an Examiniation of the Calamary... London: 1745. V. 38

NEEDHAM, JOSEPH

Biochemistry and Morphogenesis. Cambridge: 1942. V. 40

A History of Embryology. Cambridge: 1934. V. 40

Science and Civilisation in China. Cambridge: V. 46

Science and Civilization in China. Cambridge: 1954-71. V. 42; 45

Science and Civilisation in China. Cambridge: 1961-62. V. 44

Science and Civilisation in China. Volume 5: Chemistry and Chemical Technology, Part IV: Spagyrical Discovery and Invention: Apparatus, Theories and Gifts. Cambridge: 1980. V. 46

Science and Civilisation in China. Volume VI, Part 2, Agriculture. London: 1984. V. 37

NEEDHAM, MARCHAMONT

Medela Medicinae. A Plea for the Free Profession and a Renovation of the Art of Physick... London: 1665. V. 41

NEEDHAM, P.

William Morris and the Art of the Book. 1976. V. 44

NEEDHAM, PAUL

Twelve Centuries of Bookbinding 400-1600. London: 1979. V. 39; 40

Twelve Centuries of Book Bindings. 400 to 1600 A.D. New York: 1979. V. 40

Twelve Centuries of Bookbindings 400-1600. New York: (1979). V. 37

NEEDLER, HENRY

The Works of Mr. Henry Needler. London: 1728. V. 40; 42

NEEF, JOSEPH

Sketch of a Plan and Method of Education, Founded on an Analysis of the Human Faculties... Philadelphia: 1808. V. 37; 43

NEELE, GEORGE P.

Railway Reminiscences. London: 1904. V. 46

NEELY, RUTH

Women of Ohio, a Record of Their Achievements in the History of the State. N.P.: 1938? V. 44; 45

NEESE, GEORGE MICHAEL

Three Years in the Confederate Horse Artillery. New York: 1911. V. 42

Three Years in the Confederate Horse Artillery. New York & Washington: 1911. V. 41

NEESER, ROBERT WILDEN

Statistical and Chronological History of the United States Navy 1775-1907. New York: 1909. V. 40

NEFF, WALLACE

Architecture of Southern California: a Selection of Photos, Plans and Scale Details from the Work. New York: 1969. V. 46

NEFZAOUI, CHEIKH

The Perfumed Garden of Cheikh Nefzaoui. London: 1886. V. 37

NEGAHBAN, EZAT O.

A Preliminary Report on Marlik Excavation. Gohar Rud Expedition. Iran: 1964. V. 40; 44

THE NEGOTIATIORS. Or, Don Diego Brought to Reason. London: 1738. V. 40; 45

NEGREIROS, ANTONIO THOMAZ DE

Tratado de Operacoes de Banco, ou Directorio de Banqueiros Extrahido dos Melhores Authores, a Dedicado ao Illmo . . . Bahia: 1817. V. 38

NEGRETTI & ZAMBRA. LONDON.

A Treatise on Meteorological Instruments. London: 1864. V. 38; 40

NEGRETTI, ENRICO ANGELO LUDOVICO 1817-1879

A Treatise on Meteorlogical Instruments . . . London: 1864. V. 42

NEGRI, ANGELICA PAULA ANTONIA DI 1508-1555

Lettere Spiritavli de la DEvota Religiosa Angelica Pavla Antonio di Negri. Milan: 1549. V. 44

NEGRI, FRANCESCO

Liberum Arbitrium, Tragoedia. Geneva: 1559. V. 45

NEGRO PROTECTIVE ASSOCIATION OF VIRGINIA

Proceedings of the . . . Held Tuesday, May 18th, 1897. In the True Reformers' Hall, Richmond, Va. Richmond: 1897. V. 38

NEGRO, SALVATORE DAL

Nuovo Metodo di Costruire Macchine Elettriche de Grandezza Illimitata e Nuovi Sperimenti Diretti a Rettificare l'Apparato Elettrico. Venezia: 1799. V. 45

NEGRO Slavery; or, a View of Some of the More Prominent Features of that State of Society, As It Exists in the United States of America and in the Colonies of the West Indies, Especially in Jamaica. London: 1824. V. 40

NEGRONI, GIULIO

Orationes XXV. Nunc Primvm In Gratiam Stvdiosorvm, In Belgio Editae, & ab Auctore Recognitae. Douai: 1614. V. 40

NEHLS, EDWARD

D. H. Lawrence: a Composite Biography. Madison: 1957-58. V. 38

D. H. Lawrence: a Composite Biography Gathered Arranged and Edited by 1885-1919, 1919-1925, 1925-1930. 1957/58/59. V. 46

NEHRU, JAWAHARLAL

The Discovery of India. Calcutta: 1946. V. 46

Nuclear Explosions and Their Affects. Delhi: 1958. V. 44

NEIDECKER, LORINE

My Life by Water - Collected Poems 1936-1968. London: 1970. V. 45

North Central. London: 1968. V. 45

NEIL, J. F.

The New Zealand Family Herb Doctor. Dunedin: 1891. V. 37; 38

NEILD, JAMES 1744-1814

An Account of the Rise, Progress and Present State of the Society for the Discharge and Relief of Persons Imprisoned for Small Debts . . . England and Wales. London: 1802. V. 38; 40

An Account of the Rise, Progress and Present State of the Society for the Discharge and relief of Persons Imprisoned for Small Debts . . . England and Wales. London: 1808. V. 40

State of the Prisons In England, Scotlnd and Wales . . . London: 1812. V. 38

NEILL, CHARLES O'

A Dictionary of Calico Printing and Dyeing. London: 1st edition; V. 40

NEILL, EDWARD D.

Dahkota Land and Dahkota Life With the History of the Fur Traders of the Extreme Northwest During the French and British Dominions. Philadelphia: 1859. V. 41

History of the Virginia Company of London, with Letters to and From the First Colony Never Before Printed. Albany: 1869. V. 38; 45

History of the Minnesota Valley, Including the Explorers and Pioneers of Minnesota and History of the Sioux Massacre. Minneapolis: 1882. V. 41

The History of Minnesota, from the Earliest French Explorations to the Present Time. Minneapolis: 1883. V. 39; 42

Materials for the Future History of Minnesota . . . St. Paul: 1856. V. 46

NEILL, EDWARD DUFFIELD

The History of Minnesota. Philadelphia: 1858. V. 40

NEILL, HECTOR

The Poetical Works. London: 1801. V. 37

NEILL, JOHN

Outlines of the Arteries; with Short Descriptions. Philadelphia: 1852. V. 43

NEILL, JOHN R.

The Scalawagons of Oz. 1941. V. 46

The Scalawagons of Oz. Chicago: 1941. V. 42

The Wonder City of Oz. Chicago: 1940. V. 42

NEILL, PATRICK

Journal of a Horticultural Tour Through Some Parts of Flanders, Holland and the North of France, in the Autumn of 1817 . . . Edinburgh: 1823. V. 37; 38; 39; 40; 46

A Tour through Some of the Islands of Orkney and Shetland . . . Edinburgh: 1806. V. 42; 43

NEILSON, CHARLES

An Original, Compiled and Corrected Account of Burgoyne's Campaign, and the Memorable Battle of Bemis's Heights, Sept. 19 and Oct. 7, 1777, From the Most Authentic Sources of Information . . . Albany: 1844. V. 40; 46

NEILSON, WILLIAM

An Introduction to the Irish Language. Dublin: 1808. V. 38

NELATON, AUGUST

Elemens de Pathologie Chirurgicale . . . Paris: 1844-59. V. 45

NELIGAN, J. MOORE

Atlas of Cutaneous Diseases. Dublin: 1855. V. 43

Atlas of Cutaneous Diseases. Philadelphia: 1856. V. 42

NELLA, PSEUD.

Prince Babillon or the Little White Rabbit. London: 1907. V. 40

NELLES, ANNIE

Annie Nelles: or, The Life of a Book Agent: an Autobiography. Cincinnati: 1868. V. 37

NELLIGAN, EMILE

Je Sens Voler . . . . Montreal: 1977. V. 39

NELLUS DE SANCTO GEMINANO

Tractatus de Bannitis. Venice: 1498. V. 38; 40

NELMES, ERNEST

Curtis's Botanical Magazine Dedications, 1827-1927. London: 1931. V. 44

NELSON, ANSON

Memorials of Sarah Childress Polk, Wife of the Eleventh President. New York: 1892. V. 42

NELSON, COUTTS

What Old Father Said. A Novel. London: 1876. V. 37; 41; 42; 45

NELSON, EDWARD WILLIAM

The Eskimo About Bering Strait. Washington: 1899. V. 37; 43

Lower California and Its Natural Resources. Washington: 1921. V. 38; 39; 43; 44

Report Upon Natural History Collections Made in Alaska Between the Years 1877 and 1881. Washington: 1877. V. 44

Report Upon Natural History Collections Made in Alaska Between the Years 1877 and 1881. Washington: 1887. V. 39; 43; 46

NELSON, HAROLD HAYDEN

The Great Hypostyle Hall at Karnak. Chicago: 1981. V. 40; 44

NELSON, HENRY LOOMIS

   The Army of the United States: Uniforms, 1774-1888. V. 39

NELSON, HORATIO, VISCOUNT 1758-1805

   The Letters of Lord Nelson to Lady Hamilton with a Supplement . . . London: 1814. V. 38

   The Life of Admiral Lord Nelson K.B. from His Lordships Manuscripts. London: 1809. V. 46

   The Life of Admiral Lord Nelson K.B. from His Lordships Manuscripts. London: 1810. V. 46

   Nelson's Letters from the Leeward Islands. London: 1953. V. 37

   Nicolas (Harris), Sir. The Dispatches and Letters. London: 1844. V. 44

NELSON, HORATIOM VISCOUNT 1758-1805

   Nelson's Letters from the Leeward Islands and Other Original Documents in the Public Record Office and the British Museum. 1953. V. 42

NELSON, HORATIO,VISCOUNT 1758-1805

   The Life and Services of Horatio Viscount Nelson, Duke of Bronte, Vice Admiral of the White, K.B., et., from His Lordships Manuscripts. London: 1840. V. 46

NELSON, JAMES 1710-1794

   An Essay on the Government of Children, Under Three General Heads . . . London: 1753. V. 42

   An Essay on the Government of Children, Under Three General Heads, Viz. Health, Manners and Education. London: 1763. V. 41; 45; 46

NELSON, JOHN

   The History, Topography and Antiquities of the Parish of St. Mary Islington in the Country of Middlesex. London: 1811. V. 39

   The History and Antiquities of the Parish of Islington, in the county of Middlesex . . . London: 1823. V. 37

NELSON, PHILIP

   The Coinage of Ireland in Copper, Tin and Pewter 1460-1826. Liverpool: 1905. V. 38

NELSON, R.

   Reminiscences of the Right Rev. William Meade, D.D., Bishop of the Prot. Epis. Church in Virginia. Shanghai: 1873. V. 39; 41

NELSON, ROBERT

   An Address to Persons of Quality and Estate. London: 1715. V. 41; 43; 45

   The Life of Dr. George Bull, Late Lord Bishop of St. David's. London: 1713. V. 46

   The Life of Dr. George Bull. London: 1714. V. 39

NELSON, T.

   Nelson's Pictorial Guide Books. The Union Pacific Railroad: A Tour Across the North American Continent from Omaha to Ogden. New York: 1870. V. 37

   The Union Pacific Railroad: a Trip Across the North American Continent from Omaha to Ogden. New York: 1871. V. 38

NELSON, T. H.

   The Birds of Yorkshire. London: 1907. V. 37; 38; 39; 40; 44; 45; 46

   The Birds of Yorkshire. London: 1907. V. 37

NELSON, THOMAS H.

   The Birds of Yorkshire. London: 1907. V. 46

   The Birds of Yorkshire. 1907. V. 46

NELSON-WHITEHEAD PAPER CORP.

   Oriental Printing, Fantasy and Art Papers. New York: 1959. V. 38; 41

NELSON, WILLIAM

   The Law of Evidence. London: 1717. V. 38

   The Laws of England Concerning the Game of Hunting, Hawking, Fishing and Fowling . . . London: 1736. V. 40

   Lex Maneriorum: or the Law and Customs of England, Relating to Manors and Lords of Manors . . . London: 1726. V. 40; 43

   Observations on the Management of Peruvian Bark . . . Philadelphia: 1802. V. 45

   The Office and Authority of a Justice of Peace. London: 1718. V. 40

   The Office and Authority of a Justice of Peace . . . In the Savoy: 1721. V. 45

   The Office and Authority of a Justice of Peace. London: 1729. V. 39; 40

   The Office and Authority of a Justice of Peace: Collected out of all the Books, whethr of Common or Statute Law, hitherto written on that Subject . . . To which are added English Precedents . . . The Eleventh Edition, Corrected, Amended and . . . In the Savoy: 1736. V. 37

   The Rights of the Clergy of Great Britain. London: 1709. V. 40

NELSON, WOLFRED

   Five Years at Panama: the Trans-Isthmian Canal. London: 1891. V. 44

NELSON'S Pictorial Guide Books for Tourists. Great Salt Lake City and Utah Territory. Salt Lake City: 1870's. V. 39

NELTHORPE, GEORGE

   Julia to Pollio. London: 1770. V. 42

NEMEROV, HOWARD

   The Image and the Law. New York: 1947. V. 38; 39

   The Salt Garden. Boston: 1955. V. 46

   Stories, Fables & Other Diversions. Boston: 1971. V. 38; 40; 44; 46

NEMESIUS

   Nemesis Episcopi et Philosophi, de Natura Hominis. Antverpiae: 1565. V. 46

NEMOGUCE. / *L'Impossible.* Beograd: 1930. V. 42

NENNIUS

   The Historia Brittonum . . . with an English Version, Notes and Illustrations. London: 1819. V. 37

NENTWIG, W.

   Ecophysiology of Spiders. Berlin: 1986. V. 37

THE NEOLITH Number One (of four issues only). London: 1907. V. 37

NEPOS, CORNELIUS

   Aemilii Probi Vitae Excellentium Imperatorum. Colophon: 1506. V. 42

   Liber Aemilii Probi, Sen. Corn. Nepotis, de Vita Excellentium Imperatorum . . . Leyden: 1616. V. 39

   The Life and Death of Pomponius Atticus . . . London: 1677. V. 40

   The Lives of Illustrious Men. Oxon: 1684. V. 46

NEQUATEMA, EDMUND

   Truth of a Hopi. Flagstaff: 1936. V. 42

NERNST, WALTHER

   Experimental and Theoretical Applications of Thermodynamics to Chemistry. London: 1907. V. 45

NERSESSIAN, SIRAPIE DER

   Armenian Manuscripts in the Freer Gallery of Art. Washington: 1963. V. 46

   Armenian Manuscripts in the Walters Art Gallery. Baltimore: 1973. V. 46

   The Chester Beatty Library. Dublin: 1958. V. 44

NERUDA, PABLO 1904-1973

   Bestiary/Bestiario. New York: 1965. V. 44; 45

   Canto General. Mexico: 1950. V. 45

   The Heights of Macchu Picchu. N.P.: 1987. V. 46

   Ode to Typography. Torrance: 1977. V. 39

   Red Bird, Love Poems by Christopher Logue, Based on the Spanish of Pablo Neruda. Guildford, Surrey: 1979. V. 37; 39

   Residence on Earth and Other Poems. Norfolk: 1946. V. 45

   Skystones. Easthampton: 1981. V. 37; 39; 40; 42; 43

   We Are Many. London: 1957. V. 39

   We Are Many. London: 1967. V. 43; 45

   We Are Many. London: 1970. V. 46

NESBIT, E.

   Children's Stories from Shakespeare. London: 1910. V. 42

   Children's Stories from English History. London: 1910. V. 43

   The Literary Sense. London: 1903. V. 43

   Spring Songs and Sketches. London: 1886. V. 40

NESBIT, EDITH

   The Book of Dragons. London: 1901. V. 46

   Harvest Home: Original Poems. 1894. V. 46

   The House of Arden. London: 1908. V. 41

   The Magic City. London: 1910. V. 45; 46

   The Magic World. London: 1912. V. 41

   New Treasure Seekers. London: 1904. V. 45; 46

   Oswald Bastable and Others. London: 1905. V. 46

   A Pomander of Verse. London: 1895. V. 46

   Pub Peter, King of Mouseland . . . His Adventures. London: 1910. V. 45

   The Railway Children. London: 1906. V. 45

   The Rainbow and the Rose. London: 1905. V. 41

   The Story of the Treasure Seekers. London: 1899. V. 45

   The Wonderful Garden or the Three C's. London: 1911. V. 45

   The Would Be Goods. New York: 1901. V. 39

   The Wouldbegoods. 1901. V. 46

   The Wouldbegoods Being the Further Adventures of the Treasure Seekers. London: 1901. V. 46

NESBIT, J. C.

   On Agricultural Chemistry, and on the Nature and properties of Peruvian Guano. London: 1856. V. 40

NESBITT, FRANCES E.

Algeria and Tunis. London: 1906. V. 44

NESBITT, ROBERT

History of the Nesbitt Family Sometime Resident in the Townland of Corglass, Parish of Ematris, Co. Monaghan, Ireland. Belfast: 1930. V. 38

NESFIELD, W. EDEN

Specimens of Medieval Architecture Chiefly Selected from Examples of the 12th and 13th Centuries in France and Italy. V. 38

NESFIELD, WILLIAM EDEN

Specimens of Mediaeval Architecture Chiefly Selected from Examples of the 12th and 13th Centuries in France and Italy . . . . London: 1862. V. 37; 42; 44; 46

NESTOROFF, MARCO

The Oriental Tobaccos. Dresden: 1928. V. 40

NETHERLANDS. (UNITED PROVINCES, 1581-1795). STATEN GENERAAL

A Letter from the States-General of the United Provinces of the Low Countries to the King of Great Britain. The Hague: 1673. V. 40; 42

NETHERSOLE, FRANCIS

Memoriae Sacra . . . Cambridge: 1612. V. 45

NETHERSOLE-THOMPSON, DESMOND

The Greenshank. London: 1951. V. 44

NETHERY, WALLACE

Charles Lamb, Bibliophile. Los Angeles: 1965. V. 41

NETTER, THOMAS d. 1430

Doctrinalis Antiquitatum Ecclesiae . . . de Sacramentis . . . Paris: 1521. V. 46

NETTLE, RICHARD

The Salmon Fisheries of the St. Lawrence and Its Tributaries. Montreal: 1857. V. 44; 45

The Salmon Fisheries of the St. Lawrence and Its Tributaries. Montreal: 1857. V. 44

NETTLEFOLD, FREDERICK JOHN

Catalogue of the Paintings and Drawings in the Collection of . . . London: 1933-38. V. 38; 39; 44

The Collection of Bronzes and Castings in Brass and Ormolu Formed by . . . London: 1934. V. 39; 42; 44

NETTLESHIP, JOHN T.

Robert Browning Essays and Thoughts. London: 1890. V. 42

NETTO, J. F.

Die Kunst zu STricken in Ihrem Ganzen Umfange, Oder Vollstandige und Grundliche Anweisung . . . Leipzig: 1800. V. 44

NEU-EINGERICHTETES Gesangbuch . . . Sammlung Schoener, Lehrreicher und Erbaulicher Lieder, Welche von Langer Zeit her Bei den Bekennern und Liebhabern der Glorien und Wahrheit Jesu Christi in Uebung Gewesen . . . Germantown: 1762. V. 38

NEU, JOHN

Isis Cumulative Bibliography 1966-1975. London: 1980-85. V. 41; 42

NEUBERGER, MAX

History of Medicine. London: 1910-25. V. 40; 41

History of Medicine. London: 1910/25. V. 46

History of Medicine. Translated by Ernest Playfair. London: 1910. V. 37

NEUBURG, FREDERIC

Glass in Antiquity. London: 1949. V. 40

DAS NEUE Und Verbesserte Gesangbuch, Worinnen die Psalmen Davids . . . Alter und Neuer Geistreicher Lieder. Germantown: 1799. V. 39

NEUFELD, E.

the Hittite Laws. London: 1951. V. 44

NEUFFORGE, JEAN FRANOIS DE

Recueil Elementaire d'Architecture Contenant Plusieurs Etudes des Ordres d'Architecture d'Apres l'Opinion des Anciens et le Sentiment des Modernes. Paris: 1757-68/72-80. V. 42

NEUGEBAUER, O.

Astronomical Cuneiform Texts. Princeton. V. 42; 44

Mathematical Cuneiform Texts. New Haven: 1945. V. 44

NEUHAS, E.

The Art of the Exposition . . . The Architecture and Landscape Gardening . . . The Galleries . . . The Sculpture and Mural Decorations . . . The San Dieo Garden Fair. San Francisco: 1915. V. 37

NEUHAUS, EUGENE

William Keith, the Man and the Artist. Berkeley: 1938. V. 46

NEUJAHRS-WUNSCH (New Year's Wish) . . . des Readinger Adlers . . . 1825. Reading: 1825. V. 39

NEUJAHRS-WUNSCH (New Year's Wish) . . . des Readinger Adlers . . . 1838. Reading: 1838. V. 39

NEUKOMM, SIGISMUND VON 1778-1858

David. An Oratorio, in Two Parts. Boston: 1835. V. 40

NEUMANN, ARTHUR H.

Elephant Hunting in East Equatorial Africa. London. V. 39

Elephant Hunting in East Equatorial Africa. London: 1898. V. 39; 43

Elephant Hunting in East Equatorial Africa. London: 1982. V. 40

NEUMANN, CASPAR

The Chemical Works of Caspar Neumann, M.D . . . . London: 1759. V. 38

NEUMANN, M.

Grundsatze und Erfahrungen Uber die Anlegung, Erhaltung und Pflege von Glashausern aller Art . . . Weimar: 1862. V. 45

NEURDENBURG, ELISABETH

Odd Dutch Pottery and Tiles. New York: 1923. V. 39

Old Dutch Pottery and Tiles. London: 1923. V. 37; 41; 42; 46

NEUSTADT, EGON

The Lamps of Tiffany. New York: (1970). V. 37

NEUTRA, RICHARD

Architecture of Social Concern in Regions of Mild Climate. Sao Paulo: 1948. V. 46

Life and Human Habitat/Mensch Und Wohnen. Sao Paulo: 1948. V. 46

Survival Through Design. New York: 1954. V. 46

NEUVIALLE, JEAN SYLVAIN DE

Relacacao da Jornada, que Fez no Imperio da China, e Summaria Noticia da Embaixada . . . Lisbon: 1754. V. 45

NEVADA.

The Journal of the Assembly During the Second Session of the Legislature of the State of Nevada, 1866. Carson City: 1866. V. 37; 43

NEVADA. ASSEMBLY - 1875

The Journal of the Assembly During the Fifth Session of the legislature of the State of Nevada, 1871 . . . Carson City: 1871. V. 37

The Journal of the Assembly of the Seventh Session of the Legislature of the State of Nevada, 1875. Carson City: 1875. V. 37

NEVADA. CONSTITUTION - 1867

Constitution and By-Laws of the Fire Department of Gold Hil, Nevada, Organized May 22D, 1867. San Francisco: 1878. V. 37

NEVADA. LAWS, STATUTES, ETC. - 1864

Statutes of the State of Nevada Passed at the Fist Session of the Legislature, 1846-65. Carson City: 1865. V. 39

NEVADA. LAWS, STATUTES, ETC. - 1877

Rules Governing the Legislature of the State of Nevada, Together with the Constitution of the State, and an Act Concerning the Number of Employees in the Legislature, etc. Carson City: 1877. V. 37

NEVADA. LAWS, STATUTES, ETC. - 1881

Rules Governing the Legislature of the State of Nevada, Together with the constitution of the State and an Act Concerning the Number of Employees (sic) in the Legislature, etc. Carson City: 1881. V. 37

NEVADA. SENATE

Journal of the Senate During the Second Session of the Legislature of the State of Nevada, 1866. Carson City;: 1866. V. 41

NEVADA. SURVEYOR GENERAL - 1866

Annual Report of the Surveyor-General of the State of Nevada, for the Year 1865. (N.P.: 1866). V. 37

NEVE, RICHARD

Arts Improvement; or, Choice Experiments and Observations in Building, Husbandry, Gardening, Mechanicks, Chimistry, Painting, Japanning, Varnishing, Guilding, Inlaying, Embossing, Carving . . . London: 1703. V. 41; 42

The City and Country Purchaser, and Builder's Dictionary. London: 1726. V. 38; 40; 44; 45

The City and Country Purchaser's and Builder's Dictionary. London: 1736. V. 41

NEVE, TIMOTHY

Animadversions Upon Mr. Phillips's History of the Life of Cardinal Pole . . . Oxford: 1766. V. 45

NEVE Y MOLINA, LUIS DE

Reglas de Orthographia, Diccionario, Y Arte del Idioma Othomi, Breve Instruccion Para Los Principiantes . . . Mexico: 1767. V. 37

NEVILE, THOMAS

Imitations of Juvenal and Persius. London: 1769. V. 46

NEVILL, RALPH

British Military Prints. London: 1909. V. 37; 39; 42

Light Come, Light Go. Gambling, Gamesters, Wagers, The Turf. London: 1909. V. 42; 46

Old Cottage and Domestic Architecture in South-West Surrey. Guildford: 1889. V. 38; 40

Old English Sporting Prints. London: 1923. V. 37; 38; 39; 40; 41; 42

Old English Sporting Books. London: 1924. V. 37; 38; 42

Old French Line Engravings. London: 1924. V. 38; 39; 41; 42

Piccadilly to Pall Mall. London: 1908. V. 38

NEVILL, SAMUEL

The Acts of the General Assembly of the Province of new Jersey. V. 41

NEVILLE, A. W.

The History of Lamar County, Texas. Paris: 1937. V. 41; 43

The Red River Valley Then and Now. Paris: 1948. V. 38; 42

NEVILLE, ALEXANDER 1544-1614

De Furoribus Norfolcensium Ketto Duce . . . Eiusdem Norvicus. London: 1575. V. 40; 45

NEVILLE, HENRY

Plato Redivivus; or, a Dialogue Concerning Government. London: 1681. V. 41; 42

Plato Redivivus: or, Dialogues concerning Government . . . The Third Edition. London: 1745. V. 37

NEVILLE, J. E. H.

The Oxfordshire and Buckinghamshire Light Infantry Chronicle. Aldershot: 1949-54. V. 41

NEVILLE, RICHARD CORNWALLIS

Saxon Obsequies Illustrated by Ornaments and Weapons. London: 1852. V. 38; 40

NEVINS, IRIS

Varieties of Spanish Marbling. Newtown: 1991. V. 44

NEVINSON, C. R. W.

Modern War - Paintings by C. R. W. Nevinson. London: 1917. V. 43; 45; 46

NEVINSON, HENRY WOODD

Rough Islanders. London: 1930. V. 42

NEW Remarks of London: or, A Survey of the Cities of Westminster, of Southwark, and part of Middlesex and Surrey, within the circumference of the Bills of Mortality. . . . . Collected by the Company of Parish-Clerks . . . London: 1732. V. 39

THE NEW American Clerk's Magazine, and Complete Practical Conveyancer . . . Hagerstown: 1808. V. 39

THE NEW American Clerk's Magazine and Complete Practical Conveyancer . . . Adapted to the Use of the Citizens of the United States and More Particularly to Those of the State of Maryland . . . Hagerstown: 1806. V. 38; 39; 40

A NEW and Accurate Description of the Present Great Roads and the Principal Cross Roads of England and Wales. London: 1756. V. 39

A NEW and Complete System of Arithmetic, Composed for the Use of the Citizens of the United States. Newburyport: 1788. V. 42

THE NEW and Complete Universal Vermin-Killer: Being an Infallible Directory, for Taking Alive, Destroying and Driving Away All Fourfooted, Creeping & Winged Vermin. London: 1818. V. 39

A NEW and Easy Introduction to the Art of Penmanship, On an Improved Plan of Distance and Proportion, Made Easy and Attainable to the Capacities of Youth of Both Sexes, In Much Less Time Than Any Other in Present Use. Philadelphia: 1819. V. 40; 46

A NEW and Further Narrative of the State of New England. London: 1676. V. 42; 44; 45

A NEW and General Biographical Dictionary . . . London: 1784. V. 38; 45
A NEW and General Biographical Dictionary . . . London: 1795. V. 45

A NEW and General Biographical Dictionary; containing an historical and critical account of the lives and writings of the most eminent persons in every nation . . . to the present period. London: 1798. V. 37; 46

A NEW and Impartial Collection of Interesting Letters, From the Public Papers . . . London: 1767. V. 42

NEW and Improved English Atlas, Divided Into Counties . . . London: 1807. V. 46

A NEW and Present State of England . . . . London: 1750. V. 41

THE NEW Bankers Proved Bankrupts, in a Dialogue Between Themselves and a Free-Citizen. N.P.: 1760. V. 40

THE NEW Biblical Atlas and Scripture Gazetteer. Philadelphia: 1855. V. 45

THE NEW Book Collector. 1952-86. V. 40

A NEW Book of Instruments, Fitted for the Use of Attornies, Ecclesiastical Persons, Scriveners, Merchants, Solicitors, Owners of Ships, Mariners and Generally for all Persons Concerned in Trade and Commerce, Either at Home or Abroad. London: 1680. V. 37; 39

THE NEW Bookbinder, Journal of Designer Bookbinders. Volumes 1-5. London: 1981-85. V. 40

THE NEW Bristol Channel Pilot. London: 1844. V. 46

THE NEW British Jewel, or, Complete Housewife's Best Companion. London: 1788. V. 44

NEW Brunswick Directory for 1877-8. New Brunswick: 1877. V. 41
NEW Brunswick Directory for 1880-81. New Brunswick: 1880. V. 41; 46
NEW Brunswick Directory for 1883-84. New Brunswick: 1883. V. 41; 46

NEW Brunswick City Directory 1886-87. New Brunswick: 1886. V. 46

NEW Brunswick Directory, for 1872-73. New Brunswick: 1872. V. 46

NEW BRUNSWICK HISTORICAL SOCIETY

Collections of the . . . Saint John: 1894-1955. V. 37

Collections of the . . . Saint John: 1896-1909. V. 38

NEW Cambridge Bibliography of English Literature. Cambridge: 1971. V. 46

NEW Cambridge Modern History. Cambridge: 1957. V. 39
THE NEW Cambridge Modern History. Cambridge: 1957-. V. 44

NEW Century Atlas of Cayuga County, New York. Philadelphia: 1904. V. 41

NEW, CHARLES

Life, Wanderings and Labours in Eastern Africa. London: 1873. V. 46

A NEW Child's Play. London: 1879. V. 44

THE NEW Circuit Companion; or a Mirror for Grand-Juries. London: 1769. V. 40

A NEW Collection of Enigmas, Charades, Transpositions &c. London: 1791. V. 42; 46

A NEW Collection of Miscellnies in Prose and Verse. London: 1725. V. 38

A NEW Collection of Poems Relating to State Affairs, from Oliver Cromwel to this Present Time . . . London: 1705. V. 39; 44; 45

THE NEW Colophon, A Book Collector's Quarterly. New York: 1948-50. V. 38

THE NEW Complete Dictionary of Arts and Sciences. London: 1778. V. 40

NEW Cyclopaedia of Botany and Complete Book of Herbs. Huddersfield: 1853. V. 38

THE NEW Decameron. Oxford: 1919. V. 42
THE NEW Decameron. Oxford: 1919-29. V. 39

NEW Directions In Prose and Poetry. Norfolk: 1936. V. 38

NEW Directions in Prose and Poetry 1937. Norfolk: 1937. V. 40

NEW Directions in Prose and Poetry 1939. Norfolk: 1939. V. 40; 46

THE NEW Dispensatory. London: 1770. V. 40

THE NEW Domestic Cookery, or the Housewife's Sure Guide . . . Derby: 1835. V. 46

THE NEW Edinburgh Dispensatory. Edinburgh: 1801. V. 38

A NEW Empire. The Box Butte Country of Nebraska. The Black Hills Region of South Dakota. Sheridan and John Counties Wyoming. Omaha: 1896. V. 39

NEW ENGLAND GUARDS

Constitution of the New-England Guards. Boston: 1813. V. 37; 46

THE NEW England Historical and Genealogical Register. Boston;: 1847-68. V. 45; 46

NEW ENGLAND LAND COMPANY

Opening Sale. New England City, Georgia, Tuesday April 15th, 1890. N.P.: 1890. V. 45

NEW ENGLAND MISSISSIPPI LAND COMPANY

Memoiral of the Directors of the New England Mississippi Land Company, Citizens of the State of Massachusetts. Washington. V. 39

Memoiral of the Directors of the New England Mississippi Land Company, Citizens of the State of Masschusetts. Washington: 1814. V. 39

NEW ENGLAND NON-RESISTANCE SOCIETY

Principles of the Non-Resistance Scoeity. Boston: 1839. V. 37

THE NEW England Primer, Improved. Bennington: 1802. V. 40

THE NEW England Primer Improved, Being an Easy Method to Teach Children the English Language. New York: 1804. V. 44

THE NEW England Primer, Improved, for the More Eeasy Attaining the True Reading of English . . . Hartford: 1802. V. 37

THE NEW England Primer, Improved, for the More Easy Attaining the True Reading of English. Bennington: 1802. V. 37

NEW ENGLAND RAILWAY PUBLISHING CO.

ABC Pathfinder Railway Guide . . . Published on the First of Each Month. Boston: 1880. V. 45

NEW ENGLAND TELEPHONE AND TELEGRAPH CO.

Planning for Home Telephone Conveniences, for the Use of Architects, Engineers, Builders, Owners. ?Boston: 1928. V. 38

A NEW English Dictionary on Historical Principles. Oxford: 1888-1933. V. 41

THE NEW Family Atlas of the World, Containing New Colored Maps of Each State and Territory in the United States. Detroit: 1885. V. 45

A NEW Family Receipt Book, Containing all the truly Valuable Receipts for Various Branches of Cookery Selected from the Best Authorities. Hartford: 1827. V. 39

THE NEW Family Receipt-Book, Containing Eight Hundred Truly Valuable Receipts in Various Branches of Domestic Economy. New Haven: 1819. V. 40

THE NEW Female Instructor; or Young Woman's Guide to Domestic Happiness . . . London: 1834. V. 43
THE NEW Female Instructor; or, Young Woman's Guide to Domestic Happiness . . . London: 1839. V. 37

NEW Flora and Silva. London: 1928-37. V. 37

THE NEW Forest. London: 1863. V. 44

THE NEW Forget-Me-Not: A Calendar. London: 1929. V. 37; 46

THE NEW Fortune-Telling Almanack; or, Entertaining Oracle, for the Year 1775. London: 1774. V. 44

THE NEW Foundling Hospital for Wit. London: 1786. V. 38; 39

A NEW Garden of Bloomers. London: 1967. V. 44

A NEW Gazetteer or Geographical Dictionary, of North America and the West Indies . . . etc. Baltimore: 1833. V. 39

A NEW Guide of Constables, Head-Boroughs, Tythingmen, Churchwardens, Overseers and Collectors for the Poor . . . Collected by J. P. Gent. London: 1709. V. 40

THE NEW Guide to Cheltenham Being a Complete History and Description . . . Cheltenham: 1820. V. 40

NEW HAMPSHIRE. CONSTITUTION - 1805

Constitution and Laws of the State of New Hampshire. Dover: 1805. V. 37

NEW HAMPSHIRE. CONSTITUTION CONVENTION - 1902

Convention to Revise the Constitution, December, 1902. Concord: 1903. V. 37

NEW HAMPSHIRE. CONSTITUTIONAL CONVENTION, 1792.

Articles in Addition to and Amendment of the Constitution of the State of New Hampshire, Agreed to by the Convention of Said State, and Submitted to the People Thereof for Their Approbation. Dover: 1792. V. 41

NEW HAMPSHIRE. LAWS, STATUTES, ETC.

The Perpetual Laws of the State of New Hampshire, from the Session of the General-Court, July 1776 to the Session in December 1788, Continued Into the Present Year 1789 . . . Portsmouth: 1789. V. 45

NEW HAMPSHIRE MISSIONARY SOCIETY

The Constitution of the New Hampshire Missionary Society, with an Address to All Christian People. Concord: 1801. V. 45

THE NEW Handmaid to Arts, Sciences, Agriculture, &c. London: 1790. V. 39

THE NEW Handmaid to Arts, Sciences, Agriculture, etc. in 9 Books. Manchester: 1800. V. 41

NEW Historical Atlas of Muskingum Co. Ohio. 1875. V. 44

NEW Historical Description of Cheltenham and Its Vicinity. Cheltenham: 1826. V. 39; 41

NEW Indexed Family Atlas of the United States, with Maps of the World. New York: 1883. V. 39; 40

NEW Instructions for Playing the Harpsichord, Spinnet or Piano-forte, Wherein the Italian Manner of Fingering is Shewn by a Variety of Examples. London: 1770. V. 37

NEW JERSEY

Archives of the State of New Jersey. Subset: Journal of the Governor and Council, 1682-1775. Trenton: 1890-93. V. 46

Archives of the State of New Jersey. Subset: Calendar of New Jersey Wills, Administrations, Etc. 1670-1817. V.P.: 1901-49. V. 46

Archives of the State of New Jersey. Subset: Extracts from American Newspapers Relating to New Jersey, 1704-1782. 1894-1923. V. 46

Report of the Minority of the Committee of Enquiry, Relative to the Rail Road at Trenton &c. Trenton: 1837. V. 46

Report on the Rail Road Controversy, Made by the Joint Committee of the Legislature of New Jersey, with the Correspondence, Between the Treasurer, Attorney General and the Companies. Read March 8th 1841. Trenton: 1841. V. 46

THE NEW Jersey Almanack for the Year of Our Lord 1795 . . . Trenton: 1794. V. 44

THE NEW Jersey and Pennsylvania Almanac, for the Year 1801. Trenton: 1800. V. 46

NEW JERSEY BAPTIST CONVENTION

Thirty-Second (-Ninety-Seventh) Anniversary . . . 1861-(1926). V.P.: 1861-1926. V. 46

NEW JERSEY. (COLONY).

The Grants, Concessions and Original Constitutions of the Province of New-Jersey. The Acts Passed During the Proprietary Governments . . . Philadelphia: 1758. V. 39; 43; 45

NEW JERSEY. (COLONY). LAWS, STATUTES, ETC.

The Acts of the General Assembly of the Province of New Jersey, from the Time of the Surrender of the Government of the said Province, to the Fourth Year of the Reign of King George the Second . . . Philadelphia: 1732. V. 43; 45

Acts of the General Assembly of the Province of New Jersey from the Surrender of the Government to Queen Anne, on the 17th Day of April, 1702 to the 14th Day of Jan. 1776. To Which is Annexed the Ordinance for Regulating and Establishing the Fees . . . Burlington: 1776. V. 43; 44; 45; 46

NEW JERSEY CONFERENCE OF CHARITIES AND CORRECTION

Proceedings of the Second (-5th, 7th, 17th) Annual Meeting . . . 1903 (-1918). V.P.: 1903-18. V. 46

NEW JERSEY CONFERENCE OF SOCIAL WORK

Proceedings of the Twenty-Third (-Twenty Ninth) Annual Meeting . . . (1924)-1930. N.P.: 1925-31. V. 46

NEW JERSEY. DEPARTMENT OF CONSERVATION & DEVELOPMENT

Annual Report . . . (1915 (-1923). Trenton: 1916-23. V. 46

NEW JERSEY. DEPARTMENT OF HEALTH

Fifty-Third (55th-61st) Annual Report . . . 1930-(1938). Trenton: 1931-39. V. 46

NEW JERSEY EDITORIAL ASSOCIATION

Minutes of the Twenty-Fifth (26th, 28th, 29th, 31st-43rd, 45th, 47th, 49th-52nd) Annual Meeting . . . 1881-(1908). V.P.: 1881-1908. V. 41

NEW JERSEY HISTORICAL SOCIETY

Proceedings of the New Jersey Historical Society. Newark: 1849-67. V. 46

NEW JERSEY. LAWS, STATUTES, ETC.

An Act Securing to Mechanics and Others Payment for Their Labor and Materials in Erecting Any House or Other Building, Within the Townships of Trenton and Nottingham . . . N.P.: 1822. V. 46

NEW JERSEY. LAWS, STATUTES, ETC. continued

Acts Relative to the Delaware and Raritan Canal Company, and Camden and Amboy Rail Road and Transportation Company, Passed by the Legislature of the State of New Jersey. N.P.: 1832. V. 46

Acts of the One Hundred and Twenty-Fifth (-One Hundred and Seventy Third) Legislature of the State of New Jersey . . . Trenton: 1901-1950. V. 38; 41; 46

Laws of the State of New Jersey . . . New Brunswick: 1800. V. 46

Laws of the State of New Jersey. Newark: 1800. V. 46

NEW JERSEY. LAWS, STATUTES, ETC. - 1783

Acts of the General Assembly of the State of New Jersey, from the Establishment of the Present Government, and Declaration of Inpedence to the First Sitting of the Eighth Session . . . 24th Day of December 1783 . . . Trenton: 1784. V. 40; 41

NEW JERSEY. (PROVINCE). LAWS, STATUTES, ETC. - 1752

The Acts of the General Assembly of the Province of New-Jersey . . . (with) Volume the Second. N.P.: 1752, 1761. V. 40

THE NEW Jersey Register, for the Year Eighteen Hundred and Thirty-Seven . . . Trenton: 1837. V. 41; 44

NEW JERSEY SOCIETY

The Constitution of the New Jersey Society, for Promoting the Abolition of Slavery. Burlington: 1793. V. 42

NEW JERSEY. STATE BOARD OF ASSESORS - 1884

Annual Report . . . for the Year 1884-(1890). Trenton: 1884-1891. V. 38

NEW JERSEY. STATE BOARD OF EDUCATION

Annual Report . . . 1910-1920. V.P.: 1911-21. V. 46

NEW JERSEY STATE HORTICULTURAL SOCIETY

Proceedings of the Eleventh (12th, 17th, 18th, 20th, 23rd-45th, 47th-57th) Annual Meeting . . . 1885 (-1931). V.P.: 1886-1932. V. 46

THE NEW Keepsake. London: 1931. V. 44

THE NEW Lion and the Unicorn Fighting for the Crown. London. V. 45; 46

THE NEW Magna Charta or Historical Record of the Debates . . . on the Settlement of the Catholic Claims in 1829. London: 1829. V. 40

A NEW Medicinal, Economical and Domestic Herbal. Blackburn: 1808. V. 37; 40; 42

A NEW Medicinal, Economical, and Domestic Herbal: Containing a familiar and accurate description of upwards of six hundred British Herbs, Shrubs, Trees, etc. Various useful purposes in Domestic . . . 1808. V. 37

NEW MEXICO

Land Claims-New Mexico. Washington: 1857. V. 37

NEW MEXICO. CONSTITUTION - 1911

The Constitution of the State of New Mexico Adopted by the Constitutional Convention Held at Santa Fe, New Mexico from October 3 to November 21, 1920. Washington: 1911. V. 37

NEW MEXICO. CONSTITUTION - 1914

Constitution of the State of New Mexico. Santa Fe: 1914. V. 39

NEW MEXICO. CONSTITUTIONAL CONVENTION - 1910

Proceedings of the Constitutional Convention of the Proposed State of New Mexico, Held at Santa Fe, 1910. Albuquerque: 1910. V. 37

NEW Mexico Historical Review. Albuquerque: 1926-80. V. 40

NEW MEXICO. TERRITORIAL BUREAU OF IMMIGRATION - 1881

Report as to Socorro County. Socorro: 1881. V. 38

NEW MEXICO. (TERRITORY). BUREAU OF INFORMATION

Mines of New Mexico. Santa Fe: 1896. V. 40

NEW Military Dictionary; or, the Field of War. London: 1760. V. 46

A NEW Miscellany. London: 1730. V. 43

A NEW Miscellany of Original Poems, on Several Occasions. London: 1701. V. 39

NEW Naturalist. London: 1945-82. V. 37

THE NEW Newgate Calendar; or, Malefactor's Bloody Register. London: 1800. V. 44; 46

NEW Numbers. Gloucester: 1914. V. 42

NEW ORLEANS. ORDINANCES, ETC. - 1866

The Laws and General Ordinances of the City of New Orleans . . . New Orleans: 1866. V. 39

THE NEW Oxford Guide: or, Companion through the University . . . Oxford: 1770? V. 38

A NEW Parliamentary Register, Being Exact Lists of I. The Lords Spiritual and Temporal II. The Counties, Citites and Burgs in Alphabetical Order and . . . London: 1717 recte 1727. V. 44

THE NEW Peerage; or Ancient and Present State of the Nobility of England, Scotland, and Ireland . . . London: 1778. V. 39

THE NEW Peerless Atlas of the World. Springfield: 1898. V. 45

THE NEW People's Atlas of the World. Springfield: 1898. V. 45
THE NEW People's Atlas of the World. Springfield: 1899. V. 45

NEW Pictorial Atlas of the World . . . Chicago:/New York: 1896. V. 45
NEW Pictorial Atlas of the World . . . Chicago/New York: 1898. V. 45

NEW PLYMOUTH COLONY

A Declaration of the Warrantable Grounds and Proceedings of the First Associates of the Government of New Plymouth . . . Together with Generl Fundamentals of Their Laws. Boston: 1773. V. 38

Records of the Colony of New Plymouth in New England. Boston: 1855-1861. V. 39

A NEW Pocket Companion for Oxford . . . Buildings, Gardens, Statues, Pictures . . . the Buildings, Paintings, Gardens, etc. at Blenheim, Ditchley, Heythrop and Nuneham. Oxford: 1808. V. 37

NEW Poems. New York: 1941. V. 39

THE NEW Present State of Great-Britain . . . London: 1776. V. 42

NEW Puss in Boots or Marquis of Carabas. London: 1845. V. 45

A NEW Remonstrance of Several Matters of Consequence Betweene the Kings Most Excellent Majestie and the High Court of Parliament. London: 1642. V. 43

NEW Rhymes for Nursery Times. London: 1901. V. 41

A NEW Roman History, from the Foundation of Rome to the End of the Common-Wealth. London: 1784. V. 39

A NEW Route from Europe to the Interior of North America With a Description of Hudson's Bay and Straits. Montreal: 1881. V. 37

THE NEW Scottish Group. Glasgow: 1947. V. 45

NEW Series Toy Books: Alphabet House. London: 1880. V. 46

A NEW Song of Old Similes, to Ye Tune of Chevy Chase by Dean Swift (sic). N.P.: 1730. V. 45

NEW Spain and the Anglo-American West. Los Angeles: 1932. V. 46

NEW Spain and the Anglo-American West: Historical Contributions Presented to Herbert Eugene Bolton. Lancaster: 1932. V. 45

NEW Stories from the Chap Book. Chicago: 1898. V. 46

NEW Story About Little Jack Horner. London: 1840. V. 39

NEW Story About Little Tom Thumb and His Mother. London: 1840. V. 39

NEW SYDENHAM SOCIETY

Atlas of Illustrations of Clinical Medicine, Surgery and Pathology. London: 1902. V. 38

A NEW System of Agriculture; or, a Plain, Easy and Demonstrative Method of Speedily Growing Rich. London: 1755. V. 40; 41

A NEW System of Agriculture; or, a Plain, Easy and Demonstrative Method of Speedily Growing Rich . . . Dublin: 1755. V. 45

A NEW System of Practical Domestic Economy; Founded on Modern Discoveries and the Private Communcations of Persons of Experience. London: 1828. V. 43

A NEW System of the Natural History of Quadrupeds, Fishes, and Insects. Edinburgh: 1791-92. V. 38

THE NEW Table Book. London: 1867. V. 44

NEW Training School for Female Teachers Under the Direction of the Ladies' Committee of the British and Foreign School Society. London: 1842. V. 45

THE NEW Universal Parish Officer. London: 1767. V. 40; 46

THE NEW Week's Preparation for a worthy receiving of the Lord's Supper as appointed by the Church of England, etc. Cork: 1801. V. 37

THE NEW Week's Preparation for a Worthy Receiving of the Lord's Supper, as Recommended and Appointed by the Church of England . . . London: 1811. V. 46

A NEW Weymouth Guide, with a Description of Milton Abbey, Sherborne Castle, Lulworth Castle . . . Weymouth: 1815. V. 40

THE NEW Work by the Author of 'The Pickwick Papers' on the Thirty-First of March Will be Published . . . The Life and Adventures of Nicholas Nickleby . . . London: 1838. V. 43

THE NEW World: A Quarterly Review of Religion, Ethics and Theology. Boston: 1892-1900. V. 40

THE NEW World; or, The United Sttaes and Canada, Illustrated & Described. London & New York: 1859. V. 38

THE NEW-YEARS Gift, Complete: in Six Parts. London: 1709. V. 43

THE NEW-YEARS Gift . . . Composed of Meditations and Prayers for Every Day of the Week. London: 1709. V. 45

NEW YORK

An Ordinance for Establishing and Regulating Fees, by His Excellency Robert Hunter.. New York: 1710. V. 44

Remarks upon the Auction System, as Practised in New-York: To which are Added Numerous Facts in Illustration. By a Plain Practical Man. New York: 1828. V. 37

Squadron A: A history of its First Fifty Years 1889-1939. New York: 1939. V. 37

NEW YORK ACADEMY OF SCIENCES. ANNALS

Annals of the Lyceum of Natural History of New York. New York: 1852. V. 39

Annals of the Lyceum of Natural History of New York. New York: 1858. V. 39

Annals of the Lyceum of Natural History of New York. New York: 1862. V. 39

Annals of the Lyceum of Natural History of New York. New York: 1867. V. 39

NEW YORK AND MONTANA SILVER MINING CO.

Prospectus of the New York and Montana Silver Mining Company. New York: 1866. V. 40; 42

NEW York Aristocracy; or, Gems of Japonica-Dom. New York: 1851. V. 39

NEW York As It Is; Containing a General Description of the City of New York . . . New York: 1839. V. 42

THE NEW York Book of Poetry. New York: 1837. V. 37

NEW YORK. BUCHHOLZ GALLERY

Twelve Bronzes by Jacques Lipchitz. 1943. V. 39

THE NEW York Business Directory, for 1841 and 1842. New York: 1841. V. 39

NEW YORK. CANAL COMMISSION - 1824

Annual Report of the Canal Commissioners of the State of New York, Presented to the Legislature. Albany;: 1824. V. 37

NEW YORK. (CITY)

The Charter of the City of New York. New York: 1801. V. 40; 46

Historical Index to the Manuals of the Incoprotation of the City of New York. New York: 1900. V. 46

Manual of the Corporation of the City of New York, for the Year 1847. New York: 1847. V. 46

Manual of the Corporation of the City of New York, for the Year 1848. New York: 1848. V. 46

Manual of the Corporation of the City of New York, for the Year 1849. New York: 1849. V. 46

Manual of the Corporation of the City of New York, for the Year 1851. New York: 1851. V. 46

Manual of the Corporation of the City of New York, for the Year 1852. New York: 1852. V. 46

Manual of the Corporation of the City of New York, for the Year 1853. New York: 1853. V. 46

Manual of the Corporation of the City of New York, for the Year 1854. New York: 1854. V. 46

Manual of the Corporation of the City of New York, for the Year 1855. New York: 1855. V. 46

Manual of the Corporation of the City of New York, for the Year 1856. New York: 1856. V. 46

Manual of the Corporation of the City of New York, for the Year 1857. New York: 1857. V. 46

Manual of the Corporation of the City of New York, for the Year 1858. New York: 1858. V. 46

Manual of the Corporation of the City of New York, for the Year 1859. New York: 1859. V. 46

Manual of the Corporation of the City of New York, for the Year 1860. New York: 1860. V. 46

Manual of the Corporation of the City of New York, for the Year 1861. New York: 1861. V. 46

Manual of the Corporation of the City of New York, for the Year 1863. New York: 1863. V. 46

Manual of the Corporation of the City of New York, for the Year 1864. New York: 1864. V. 46

Manual of the Corporation of the City of New York, for the Year 1865. New York: 1865. V. 46

Manual of the Corporation of the City of New York, for the Year 1866. New York: 1866. V. 46

NEW YORK. (CITY). AQUEDUCT COMMISSION.

Report to the Aqueduct Commissioners . . . 1887 . . . 1895 Including Plans and the Work of Construction of the new Croton Aqueduct . . . 1887-1895. New York. V. 39

NEW YORK. (CITY). COMMON COUNCIL

The Charter of the City of New-York . . . New York: 1801. V. 41

Manual of the Corporation of the City of New York for 1855. V. 38

NEW YORK. (CITY). COMMON COUNCIL - 1862

Manual of the Corportion of the City of New York. 1863. New York: 1862. V. 40

NEW YORK. (CITY). DEPT. OF PUBLIC PARKS

First Annual Report of the Board of Commissioners of the Department of Public Parks for the Year Ending May 1, 1871. New York: 1871. V. 45

NEW York City Guide. New York: 1939. V. 44

NEW YORK. (CITY). MUSEUM OF MODERN ART

Ludwig Mies van der Rohe. Drawings in the Collection of the Museum of Modern Art. New York: 1969. V. 41

NEW YORK. (COLONY). GENERAL ASSEMBLY

Journal of the Votes and Proceedings of the General Assembly of the Colony of New York . . . 1691 to 1765. New York: 1764/66. V. 44

NEW YORK. (COLONY). LAWS, STATUTES, ETC.

The Colonial Laws of New York: from 1664 to the Revolution. Albany: 1894. V. 44

An Ordinance for the Regulating of Deeds and Other Writings. By His Excellency William Burnet . . . New York: 1723. V. 44

NEW YORK. FAR GALLERY

Leonard Baskin: The Graphic Work: 1950-1970. 1970. V. 39

NEW YORK. FOREST, FISH AND GAME COMMISSION - 1902

Seventh Report of the Forest, Fish and Game Commission of the State of New York. London: 1902. V. 37

THE NEW York Gardener, or, Twelve Letters from a Farmer to His Son. Albany: 1824. V. 39

THE NEW York Gardener, or, Twelve Letters from a Farmer to His Son . . . White Creek: 1827. V. 39

THE NEW York Gardener, or, Twelve Letters from a Farmer to His Son, In Which He Describes the Method of Laying Out and Managing the Kitchen Garden. Albany: 1824. V. 42

NEW YORK HISTORICAL SOCIETY

Collections of the New York Historical Society for the Year 1871 (2, 3, 4). New York: 1872-75. V. 40

NEW YORK. JULIEN LEVY GALLERY

Salvador Dali. 1941. New York: 1941. V. 42

NEW YORK. LAWS, STATUTES, ETC.

Laws of New York, from the Year 1691 to 1751, Inclusive, Published Accroding to an Act of the General Assembly. New York: 1752. V. 44

Laws of the State of New York. Comprising the Constitution and the Acts of the Legislature Since the Revolution From the First to the Twelfth Session, Inclusive. New York: 1789. V. 44

Laws of the State of New York, Passed at the Fifty-First Session of the Legislature. Albany: 1828. V. 44

Laws of the State of New York, Passed at the Fifty-Fifth Session of Legislature. Albany: 1832. V. 44

New-York, Laws and Acts of the General Assembly for thie Majesties Province . . . New York: 1894. V. 37

Report of the Commissioners: Apointed by an Act of the Legislature of the State of New York, entitled 'An Act to Provide for the Improvement of the Internal Navigation of the State'. Albany: 1812. V. 37

Laws of the State of New York, Passed at the Fifty-Seventh Session of the Legislature. Albany: 1834. V. 44

NEW YORK. LAWS, STATUTES, ETC. - 1762

Laws of New York from the Year 1691, to 1751, Inclusive . . . (with) Laws of New York, from the 11th Nove. 1752 to 22d May 1762 . . . New York: 1752, 1762. V. 40

Laws of New York, from the 11th Nov. 1752 to 22d May 1762 . . . New York: 1762. V. 40

NEW YORK. LAWS, STATUTES, ETC. - 1784

Laws of the State of 7th-10th Sessions of the State Legislature. New York: 1784-1787. V. 37

NEW YORK. LEGISLATURE

Report of the Joint Committee of the Senate and Assembly of the State of New York, Appointed to Investigate the Affairs of Life Insurance Companies. New York: 1906. V. 43

NEW YORK. METROPOLITAN MUSEUM OF ART

The Architect and the Industrial Arts: An Exhibition of Contemporary Design. New York: 1929. V. 37

NEW YORK MICROSCOPICAL SOCIETY

Journal of the New York Microscopical Society. New York: 1885-1897. V. 38

NEW York Mirror and Ladies' Literary Gazette: being a Repository of Miscellaneous Literary Productions, in Prose and Verse. New York: 1824. V. 42

NEW YORK NAUTICAL INSTITUTIION & SHIPMASTERS' SOCIETY

Constitution and By-Laws, of New York Naturical Inst. and Shipmaster's Society. New York: 1821. V. 44

NEW YORK. (PROVINCE). LAWS, STATES, ETC.

Acts of Assembly Passed in the Province of New York, from 1691 to 1725. 1726. V. 44

NEW YORK. (PROVINCE). LAWS, STATUTES, ETC. - 1762

Laws of New-York from the 11th Nov. 1752 to 22d May 1762 . . . New York: 1762. V. 44

NEW YORK. PUBLIC LIBRARY

Treasures from the New York Public Library. (Catalogue of an Exhibition in 1985). New York: 1985. V. 42

NEW YORK. RAILROAD COMMISSION - 1829

Report of the Commissioners Appointed Under the Act of April 15, 1828, Relative to the Construction of a Railroad from the City of Boston to the Hudson River. N.P.: 1829. V. 37

NEW YORK. (STATE).

Third Annual Report . . . Regents of the University . . . Natural History. Albany: 1850. V. 37

NEW YORK (STATE). FOREST, FISH AND GAME COMMISSION

Seventh Report of the Forest, Fish and Game Commission of the State of New York. 1902. V. 38

NEW YORK. (STATE). LAWS, STATUTES, ETC.

Laws of the State of New York. In Relation to the Erie and Champlain Canals. Together with the Annual Reports of the Canal Commissioners, and Other Documents, Requisite for a Complete Official History of Those Works. Albany: 1825. V. 45

An Ordinance for Regulating the Recording of Deeds and Other Writings. New York: 1723. V. 45

NEW YORK. (STATE). LAWS, STATUTES, ETC. - 1894

Facsimile of the Laws and Acts of the Gen'l. Assembly for Their Majesties Province of New York etc. at New York. New York: 1894. V. 42

NEW YORK. (STATE). LEGISLATURE

Journal of the House of Assembly of the State of New York. The Second Meeting of the Thirteenth Session. New York: 1790. V. 45

NEW York. (State). MONUMENTS COMMISSION FOR THE BATTLEFIELDS OF GETTYSBURG & CHATTANOOGA Final Report on the Battlefield of Gettysburg. Albany: 1900. V. 39

NEW YORK. (STATE). SECRETARY OF STATE

Journals of the Military Expedition of Major John Sullivan Against the Six nations of Indians in 1779 with Records of Centennial Celebrations. Auburn: 1887. V. 39

NEW YORK. (STATE). STATE BOTANIST

Annual Reports of the State Botanist. 1891-1899. V. 39

NEW YORK. (STATE). STATE SURVEY

Special Report of New York State Survey on the Preservation of the Scenery of Niagara Falls. Albany: 1880. V. 39; 45

NEW YORK. (STATE). UNIVERSITY

Third Annual Report of the Regents of the University of the Condition of the State Cabient of Natural History, and the Historical and Antiquarian Collection, Annexed Thereto, Made to the Senate Jan. 11, 1850. Albany: 1850. V. 39

THE NEW York Tribune's History of the United States from the Discovery of America Until the Present Time with a Pocket Atlas of the World . . . Chicago: 1887. V. 45

NEW ZEALAND ASSOCIATION

A Statement of the Objects of the New Zealand Association with Some Particulars Concerning the Position, Extent, Soil and Climate, Natural Productions and Natives of New England. London: 1837. V. 45

NEW Zealand Ferns. Dunedin: 1880? V. 43

NEW Zealand: Letters from Settlers & Labouring Emigrants in the New Zealand Company's Settlement of Wellington, Nelson and New Plymouth. From Feb. 1842 to Jan. 1843. London: 1843. V. 41

NEW ZEALND ASSOCIATION

A Statement of the Objects of the New Zealand Association with Some Particulars Concerning the Position, Extent, Soil and Climate, Natural Productions . . . London: 1837. V. 38

NEWALL, J. T.

Hog-Hunting in the East and Other Sports. London: 1867. V. 38; 40

THE NEWARK Anniversary Poems. New York: 1917. V. 37; 40; 42

NEWARK. BOARD OF EDUCATION

Twenty-Third (27th-29th, 33rd-35th) Annual Report . . . 1879 (-1891). Newark: 1880-1892. V. 46

NEWARK CHARITABLE EYE AND EAR INFIRMARY

First (2nd, 3rd, 7th, 9th) Annual Report . . . 1880 (-1888). Newark: 1881-1888. V. 46

NEWARK, HARRIS

Sixty Years in Southern California 1853-1913. New York: 1916. V. 43

NEWARK. PUBLIC LIBRARY

First (-5th, 7th, 9th-12th) Annual Report . . . 1889 (-1900). Newark: 1891-1901. V. 46

NEWBERRRY, JOHN S.

Reports on the Geology, Botany and Zoology of Norther California and Oregon . . . made to the War Department. Washington: 1857. V. 37

NEWBERRY, ARTHUR ST. JOHN

A Fisherman's Paradise. Cleveland: 1914. V. 39

NEWBERRY, J. S.

The U.S. Sanitary Commission in the Valley of the Mississippi, During the War of the Rebellion, 1861-1866. Cleveland: 1871. V. 41

NEWBERRY, PERCY E.

Beni Hasan. London: 1893-1900. V. 37; 42

El Bersheh with Plans and Measurements of the Tombs by G. Willough Fraser. London: 1895. V. 40; 42; 44

The Life of Rekhamara, Vezir of Upper egypt Under Thothmes III and Amenhetep II. Westminster: 1900. V. 40; 42; 44

Scarabs. An Introduction to the study of Egyptian Seals and Signet Rings. London: 1908. V. 37; 40

NEWBERY, F.

An Historical Account of all the Voyages Round the World Performed by English Navigators. London: 1774-73. V. 40

NEWBERY, JOHN

A Catalogue of Medicines, Sold by Virtue of His Majesty's Royal Letters Patent at the Wholesale Warehouse Kept by John Newbury & Co . . . London: 1750. V. 40

An Historical Account of the Curiosities of London and Westminster, in Three Parts. London: 1767. V. 44

Letters on the Most Common, as Well as Important, Occasions in Life . . . . London: 1757. V. 41; 45

A Spelling Dictionary of the English Language on a New Plan . . . London: 1766. V. 41

NEWBIGGING, THOMAS

King's Treatise on the Science and practice of the Manufacture of and Distribution of Coal Gas. London: 1878-1882. V. 37

NEWBOLD, HARRY BRYANT

House and Cottage Construction. London: 1923. V. 41; 44

NEWBOLT, HENRY

Drakes Drum, and Other Songs of the Sea, with 12 mounted plates by McCormick. London: (ca. 1912). V. 37

NEWBROUGH, JOHN BALLOU

Oahspe: A New Bible in the Words of Jehovih and His Angel Ambassadors. New York & London: 1882. V. 40

Oahspe: a New Bible in the Words of Jehovih and His Angel Embassadors! Boston and London: 1891. V. 45

NEWCASTLE, MARGARET CAVENDISH, DUCHESS OF 1624?-1674

Poems and Fancies. London: 1653. V. 37

NEWCASTLE, MARGARET LUCAS CAVENDISH, DUCHESS OF 1624?-1674

CCVI Sociable Letters. Written by the Thrice Noble, Illustrious, and Excellent Princess, The lady Marchioness of Newcastle. London: 1664. V. 37

Grounds of Natural Philosophy. The Second Edition, much altered from the first. London: 1668. V. 37

The Life of the Thrice Noble, High and Puissant Prince William Cavendishe, Duke, Marquess and Earl of Newcastle. London: 1667. V. 37; 42; 43; 44

Orations of Diver Sorts, Accommodated to Divers Places. London: 1662. V. 37; 40

Plays Never Before Printed. London: 1668. V. 41

CCXI Sociable Letters, Written by the Thrice Noble, Illustrious and Excellent Princess, the Lady Marchioness of Newcastle. London: 1664. V. 40

NEWCASTLE, WILLIAM CAVENDISH, DUKE OF

A General System of Horsemanship in All It's Branches . . . The Hague: 1970s? V. 39

A New Method and Extraordinary Invention, to Dress Horses, and Work Them According to Nature. London: 1667. V. 37; 38; 43

NEWCOMB, FRANC JOHNSON

Saintpaintings of the Navajo Shooting Chant. New York. V. 37; 39

NEWCOMB, FRANC JOHONSON

Navaho Omens and Taboos. Santa Fe: 1941. V. 39

NEWCOMB, HERVEY

The Wyandot Chief; or, the History of Barnet, a Converted Indian; and His Two Sons: with some account of the Wea Mission. Boston: 1835. V. 37

NEWCOMB-MACKLIN CO., CHICAGO & NEW YORK.

Picture Frames, Mouldings, Cornices, Mirrors and Decorative Specialities: Decorative Catalogue. 1930s. V. 45

NEWCOMB, RAYMOND L.

Our Lost Explorers; the Narrative of the Jeanette Arctic Expedition, As Related by the Survivors . . . Hartford & San Francisco: 1882. V. 39; 40

NEWCOMB, REXFORD

Architectural Monographs on Tiles and Tilework. Beaver Falls: 1924-26. V. 46

Architecture of the Old Northwest Territory. Chicago: 1950. V. 39; 42; 46

The Spanish House for America. Philadelphia: 1927. V. 38; 41; 45; 46

NEWCOMB, THOMAS

The Manners of the Age. London: 1733. V. 39; 42

A Miscellaneous Collection of Original Poems, Consisting of Odes, Epistles, Translations &c . . . . London: 1740. V. 45

NEWCOMB, W. W.

The Indians of Texas, from Prehistoric to Modern Times. Austin: 1961. V. 37

The Rock Art of Texas Indians. Austin: 1967. V. 45

NEWCOMBE, C. F.

The First Circumnavigation of Vancouver Island. Victoria: 1914. V. 41; 42; 44; 45; 46

NEWCOMBE, PETER

The History of the Ancient and Royal Foundation, Called the Abbey of St. Alban, in the County of Hertford. London: 1795. V. 38; 39; 40; 43; 45

NEWCOME, RICHARD

An Account of the Castle and Town of Denbigh. Denbigh: 1829. V. 41

NEWCOMEN, MATTHEW

Irenicum; or, an Essay Towards a Brotherly Peace and Union, Between Those of the Congregational and Presbyterian Way . . . London: 1659. V. 46

NEWCOMER, C. ARMOUR

Cole's Cavalry; or Three Years in the Saddle in the Shenandoah Valley. Baltimore: 1895. V. 42; 44

NEWDEGATE, C. N.

A Collection of the Customs' Tariffs of All Nations. London: 1855. V. 38

NEWDIGATE, BERNARD H.

Book Production Notes, Articles Contributed to The London Mercury, 1920-1925. Oxshott, Surrey: 1920-25. V. 39

Book Production Notes. 1986. V. 40

Book Production Notes. Oxshott: 1986. V. 39; 44

Book Production Notes: Articles Contributed to the London Mercury, 1920-1925. Surrey: 1986. V. 37; 40; 42; 43; 45

A NEWE Booke of Copies, 1754. 1959. V. 45

NEWELL, CHESTER

History of the Revolution in Texas, Particularly of the War of 1835-36 . . . 1838. V. 42; 44

History of the Revolution in Texas, Particularly of the War of 1835 & 36. New York: 1838. V. 37; 38; 39; 40; 42; 45

NEWELL, EDWARD THEODORE 1886-1941

Ancient Oriental Seals in the Collection of Mr. Edward T. Newell. Chicago: 1934. V. 40

NEWELL, GORDON

Pacific Tugboats. Seattle: 1957. V. 45

NEWELL, P. S.

Topsys and Turvys. New York: 1893. V. 46

Topsys & Turvys --Number 2. New York: 1894. V. 46

NEWELL, PETER

Creature Songs. Words and Music by Louise Ayres Garnett. Boston: (1921). V. 37

Favorite Fairy Tales. New York: 1907. V. 45

The Hole Book. New York: 1908. V. 41; 42; 45; 46

Pictures and Rhymes. New York: 1900. V. 37

The Rocket Book. New York: 1912. V. 37; 39; 40

The Rocket Book. new York: (1912). V. 37

The Slant Book. New York: 1910. V. 46

NEWELL, PETER S.

A Shadow Show. New York: 1896. V. 38

NEWELL, R. H.

Letters on the Scenery of Wales Including Series of Subjects for the Pencil with Their Stations Determined to a General Principle. London: 1821. V. 37; 40; 41

NEWELL, ROBERT

Robert Newell's memoranda: Travels in the Territory of Missourie . . . Portland: 1959. V. 45

NEWELL, W. W.

The Angel Bride. For Her Friends. Cambridge: 1868. V. 44

NEWELL, WILLIAM WELLS

Games and Songs of American Children. New York: 1883. V. 40; 42

NEWENHAM, THOMAS

A View of the Natural, Political and Commercial Circumstances of Ireland. London: 1809. V. 41; 43

A View of the Natural, Political and Commercial Circumstances of Ireland. London: 1890. V. 45

NEWGATE, BERNARD

The Art of the Book. London: 1938. V. 40

NEWHALL, BEAUMONT

The Daguerreotype in America. New York: 1961. V. 41

The History of Photography from 1839 to the Present Day. New York: (1949). V. 37

The History of Photography from 1839 to the Present Day. New York: 1949. V. 37

NEWHALL, CHARLES L.

The Adventures of Jack; or, a Life on the Wave. Southbridge: 1859. V. 38; 39

The Adventures of Jack. Cambridge: 1859. V. 37

NEWHALL, FREDERIC C.

With General Sheridan in Lee's Last Campaign, by a Staff Officer. Philadelphia: 1866. V. 46

NEWHALL, JAMES ROBINSON

Lin; or, Jewels of the Third Plantation. Lynn: 1862. V. 40

NEWHALL, JOHN B.

Glimpse of Iowa in 1846 . . . Burlington: 1846. V. 37; 38; 46

Sketches of Iowa, or the Emigrant's Guide. New York: 1841. V. 37; 39; 45

NEWHALL, JOHN R.

A Glimpse of Iowa in 1846. Burlington, (i.e. St.: 1846. V. 46

NEWHALL, NANCY

Ansel Adams. The Eloquent Light. San Francisco: 1963. V. 41; 44

Ansel Adams. The Eloquent Light. Millerton: 1980. V. 41

Fiat Lux. The University of California. New York: 1967. V. 41

The Pageant of History and the Panorama of Today in Northern California. San Francisco: 1954. V. 41

The Photographs of Edward Weston. New York: 1946. V. 40; 41

NEWHALL, NANCY continued

This is The American Earth. San Francisco: 1960. V. 41; 46

TIME IN ENGLAND. New York. V. 37; 44; 46

Time in England. New York: 1950. V. 46

NEWHALL, VIRGINIA WHITING

Edwin White Newall. San Francisco: 1915. V. 46

NEWHOUSE, C. B.

The Roadster's Album. London: 1845. V. 44

NEWHOUSE, S.

The Trapper's Guide. Wallingford: 1867. V. 40

NEWINGTON, THOMAS

A Butler's Recipe Book, 1719. Cambridge: 1935. V. 42

NEWLAND, GEORGE

Directions for Cultivating Geo. Newland's Mammoth Alpine Strawberries. V. 43

NEWLAND, HENRY

The Erne. Its Legends and Fishing. London: 1851. V. 40; 43

NEWLANDS, JAMES

The Carpenter and Joiner's Assistant. London. V. 38; 40

The Carpenter and Joiner's Assistant. London: 1860. V. 42; 44

The Carpenter and Joiner's Assistant. Glasgwo: 1865. V. 39

The Carpenter and Joiner's Assistant. London: 1880. V. 37

Carpenter and Joiner's Assistant: Being a Comprehensive Treatise . . . London: 1888. V. 37

NEWLANDS, JOHN ALEXANDER REINA

On the Discovery of the Periodic Law and on Relations Among the Atomic Weights. London: 1884. V. 37; 40; 45; 46

NEWLOVE, JOHN

Sirs. Vancouver: 1962. V. 43

NEWMAN, ARTHUR

Pleasvres Vision; with Deserts Complaint; and a Short Dialogve of a Womans Properties Betweene an old man and a Young. Ryde, Isle of Wight: 1840. V. 46

NEWMAN, BERNARD

Double Menace. London: 1954. V. 42

NEWMAN, CHARLES

The Evolution of Medical Education in the Nineteenth Century. London: 1957. V. 45

NEWMAN, CHESTNUT

Mining in San Juan! A Mineralogy for Miners, Together with The Mining Laws of COlorado. Alamosa, Co.: 1879. V. 37

NEWMAN, EDWARD

A Familiar Introduction to the History of Insects. London: 1841. V. 43

NEWMAN, F. W.

Kabail Vocabulary. London: 1887. V. 38

NEWMAN, FRANCES

Dead Lovers are Faithful Lvoers. New York: 1928. V. 39

The Short Story's Mutations: from Petronius to Paul Morand. New York: 1924. V. 46

NEWMAN, FRANCIS W. 1805-1897

Lectures on Logic. Oxford: 1838. V. 38; 42; 45

Lectures on Political Economy. London: 1851. V. 42

NEWMAN, ISADORA

Fairy Flowers. London. V. 40

Fairy Flowers: Nature Legends of Facts and Fantasy. 1926. V. 46

Fairy Flowers. New York: 1926. V. 43

Fairy Flowers of Fact and Fancy. London: 1929. V. 46

NEWMAN, J. A.

The Autobiography of an Old Fashioned Boy. Oklahoma City: 1923. V. 39; 40; 42

The Autobiography of an Old Fashioned Boy. (Oklahoma City): 1923. V. 37

NEWMAN, JEREMIAH WHITTAKER

The Lounger's Common-Place Book, or, Miscellaneous Anecdotes. London: 1796. V. 41; 43

The Lounger's Common-Place Book, or, Miscellaneous Anecdotes. London: 1796/98/99. V. 45

The Lounger's Common-Place Book or Miscellaneous Collections, in History, Criticism, Biography, Poetry & Romance. London: 1805. V. 42

NEWMAN, JOHN B.

The Home Doctor. Rochester: 1849. V. 39

Texas and Mexico in 1846 . . . New York: 1846. V. 37; 42; 45

NEWMAN, JOHN HENRY, CARDINAL 1801-1890

Achilli vs. Newman. A Full Report of the Most Extraordinary Trial for Seduction and Adultery Charged Against Dr. Achilli, the Apostate Catholic Priest, by the Celebrated Dr. Newman, the Oxford Puseyite. New York: 1852. V. 43

Apologia Pro Vita Sua; Being a Reply to a Pamphlet Entitled 'What, Then, Does Dr. Newman Mean?' London: 1864. V. 37; 38; 39; 40; 41; 42; 43; 44; 45; 46

Discourses on University Education. Addressed to the Catholics of Dublin . . . Dublin: 1852. V. 45

The Dream of Gerontius. London: 1976. V. 37; 39

An Essay on the Development of Christian Doctrine. London: 1845. V. 39

Historical Sketkches. London: 1873. V. 37; 45

History of My Religious Opinions. London: 1865. V. 42

Lectures on he Prophetical Office of the Church, Viewed Relatively to Romanism and Popular Protestation. London: 1837. V. 41

Lectures on Certain Difficulties Felt by Anglicans. London: 1850. V. 38

Lectures on the Present Position of Catholics in England. London: 1851. V. 38

The Office and Work of Universities. London: 1856. V. 41

Remarks on Certain Passages in the Thirty Nine Articles. London: 1841. V. 39; 42

Sermons, Chiefly on the Theory of Religious Belief, Preached Before the University of Oxford. London: 1843. V. 39

Stray Essays on Controversial Points, Variously Illustrated. Birmingham: 1890. V. 38

Verses on Various Occasions. London: 1868. V. 37; 38; 39; 40; 44

NEWMAN, K.

Roadside Birds of South Africa. London: 1969. V. 37

NEWMAN, L. M.

Edward Gordon Craig Black Figures, 105 Reproductions with an Unpublished Essay. Northants: 1989. V. 45

NEWMAN, LOUIS I.

A Leaf from the 1611 King James Bible with 'The Noblest Monument of English Prose' by John Livingstone Lowes & 'The Printing of the King James Bible' by Louis I. Newman. San Francisco: 1937. V. 37

NEWMAN, NEIL

Famous Horses of the American Turf. New York: 1931. V. 42

Famous Horses of the American Turf. New York: 1931-32. V. 41

Famous Horses of the American Turf. New York: 1931-33. V. 39; 41; 43

NEWMAN, RICHARD

The Complaint of English Subjects, Delivered in Two Parts. London: 1700. V. 39

NEWMAN, SAMUEL 1600-1663

A Concordance to the Holy Scriptures; Together with the Books of the Apocrypha. Cambridge;: 1698. V. 39

A Large and Compleat Concordance to the Bible in English. London: 1658. V. 39

NEWMAN, SAMUEL P.

Elements of Political Economy. Andover: 1835. V. 41

NEWMAN, T.

Grandma Keeler's Housekeeper. Los Angeles: 1903. V. 46

NEWMAN, WILLIAM

Rhymes and Pictures, to Illustrate the Histories of a Quartern Loaf &c. London: 1860. V. 39

NEWMARK, HARRIS

Sixty Years in Southern California, 1853-1913. New York: 1926. V. 40

NEWNHAM, WILLIAM 1790-1865

Essay on Superstition . . . London. V. 46

Essay on Superstittion; Being an Inquiry into the Effects of Physical Influence on the Mind in the Production of Dreams, Visions, Ghosts and Other Supernatural Appearances. London: 1830. V. 37; 42; 45

Some Observations on the Medicinal and Dietetic Properties of Green Tea, and Particularly on the Controuling (sic) Influence it Exerts Over Irritation of the Brain. London: 1827. V. 40; 43

THE NEWS-Boy's Address, to the Worthy Patrons of the Cincinnati Emporium. Cincinnati: 1824. V. 40

NEWS from Ireland. London: 1679. V. 42

NEWS from Purgatory. Or, The Jesuits Legacy to All Countries. London: 1679? V. 42

NEWSOM, SAMUEL

Japanese Garden Construction. Tokyo: 1939. V. 44

NEWSON, T. M.

Pen Pictures of St. Paul, Minnesota and Biographical Sketches of Old Settlers, From the Earliest Settlement of the City, Up to . . . 1857. Volume 1. St. Paul: 1896. V. 42

NEWSON, THOMAS M.

Pen Pictures of St. Paul, Minnesota, and Biographical Sketches of Old Settlers from the Earliest Settlement of the City, Up to and Including the Year 1857. St. Paul: 1886. V. 37; 38; 39; 43

NEWSTEAD, ROBERT

Monograph of the Coccidae of the British Isles. London: 1901-03. V. 43

NEWTE, THOMAS

Prospects and Observations on a Tour in England and Scotland . . . London: 1791. V. 44

T Tour in England and Scotland, in 1785. London: 1788. V. 37; 38

NEWTON, A.

Ootheca Wolleyana: an Illustrated Catalogue of the Collection of Birds' Eggs Formed by the Late John Wolley, Part I, Accipitres. London: 1864. V. 37; 38

NEWTON, A. EDWARD

Protection: a Brief Story of the I-T-E Circuit Breaker. Philadelphia: 1910. V. 44

NEWTON, ALFRED

A Dictionary of Birds. London: 1896. V. 42

NEWTON, ALFRED EDWARD 1864-1940

The A. Edward Newton Collection of Books and Manuscripts. New York: 1941. V. 39; 40; 41

The Act of Creation by William Blake. Oak Knoll: 1925. V. 41

The Amenities of Book Collecting. Boston: 1918. V. 39; 42

Derby Day. 1934. V. 43

Derby Day and Other Adventures. Boston: 1934. V. 37; 41; 43

The Format of the English Novel. Cleveland: 1928. V. 37; 43

The Greatest Book in the World and Other Papers. Boston: 1925. V. 39

The Gutenberg Bible. A Noble Fragment. New York: 1921. V. 41

A History of Early Nineteenth Century Drama 1800-1850. Cambridge: 1930. V. 42

A Magnificent Farce and Other Diversions of a Book Collector. Boston: 1921. V. 41

A Magnificent Farce and Other Diversions of a Book-Collector. Boston: 1922. V. 39; 45

Mr. Strahan's Dinner Party. San Francisco: 1930. V. 37; 39; 41; 42

Thomas Hardy, Novelist or Poet? 1920. V. 39

Thomas Hardy, Novelist or Poet? 1928. V. 39

NEWTON, C. T.

The Collection of Ancient Greek Inscriptions in the British Museum. London: 1874 & 1883. V. 39

A History of Discoveries at Halicarnassus, Cnidus and Branchidae. London: 1862-63. V. 37

NEWTON, CHARLES THOMAS 1816-1894

Travels and Discoveries in the Levant. London: 1865. V. 37; 38; 39; 40; 45; 46

NEWTON, G. W.

Rural Spots, and How to Enjoy Them. London: 1867. V. 37

NEWTON, HENRY

Report on the Geology and Resources of the Black Hills of Dakota. Washington: 1880. V. 46

NEWTON, ISAAC 1642-1727

Arithmetica Universalis; sive de Compositione et Resolutione Arithmetica Liber. London: 1707. V. 40

Arithmetica Universalis. Leyden: 1732. V. 38

The Chronology of Ancient Kingdoms Amended. London: 1728. V. 37; 38; 39; 40

The Correspondence (1661-1718). Cambridge: 1959-76. V. 44

The Correspondence. London: 1959-77. V. 45

The Correspondence of Isaac Newton. Cambridge: 1959/60/61/67. V. 37

Lectiones Opticae, Annis MDCLXIV, MDCLXX & MDCLXXI. London: 1729. V. 37; 46

The Mathemtical Papers. Volume I - 1664-1666. Cambridge: 1967. V. 40

The Mathematical Papers 1664-1673. Cambridge: 1967-69. V. 45

Mathematical Papers (1664-1684). Cambridge: 1967-71. V. 44

The Mathematical Principles of Natural Philosophy. London: 1729. V. 38

Mathematical Principles of Natural Philosophy. London: 1777. V. 40

The Mathematical Principles of Natural Philosophy. London: 1803. V. 38; 41; 42

The Mathematical Principles of Natural Philosophy. London: 1819. V. 45

Mathematische Principien der Naturlehre. Berlin: 1872. V. 40

Mathematische Principien der Naturlehre. Berlin: 1872. V. 38; 39; 41

Sir Isaac Newton's Mathematical Principles of Natural Philosophy and His System of the World. Berkeley: 1947. V. 40

Observations Upon the Prophecies of Daniel, and the Apocalypse of St. John. London: 1733. V. 38; 39; 40; 44

Optice: sive de Reflexionibus, Refractionibus, Inflexionibus & Coloribus Lucis Libri tres . . . London: 1706. V. 37; 46

Optice: Sive de Reflexionibus, Refractionibus, Inflexionibus & Coloribus Lucis, Libri Tres. London: 1719. V. 41; 45

Optice; sive de Reflexionibus, Refractionibus, Inflexionibus et Coloribus Lucis, Libri Tres . . . Lausanne & Geneva: 1740. V. 39

Opticks. London: 1704. V. 42

Opticks. London: 1730. V. 40; 41; 45; 46

Optique.. Paris: 1787. V. 40; 42

Opuscula Mathematica, Philosophica Philologica. Lausanne & Geneva: 1744. V. 38

Philosophia Naturalis Principia Mathematica. London: 1726. V. 40

Philosophiae Naturalis Principia Mathematica. London: 1687. V. 38; 42; 44; 45; 46

Philosophiae Naturalis Principia Mathematica. Cambridge: 1713. V. 44

Philosophiae Naturalis Principia Mathematica. Londini: 1726. V. 37; 38; 39; 40

Philosophiae Naturalis Principia Mathematica . . . Genevae: 1739-42. V. 38

Philosophiae Naturalis Principia Mathematica. Glasgow: 1871. V. 39

Philosophiae Naturalis Principia Mathematica. Cambridge: 1972. V. 38

The First Three Sections of Newton's Principia. Cambridge: 1843. V. 40

Principia. Glasgow: 1871. V. 40

Sir Isaac Newton's Theory of Light and Colours, and His Principle of Attraction, Made Familiar to the Ladies in Several Entertainments. London: 1742. V. 41

The System of the World Demonstrated in an Easy and Populara Manner Being a Proper Introduction to the Most Sublime Philosophy . . . London: 1740. V. 37

Thirteen Letters from Sir Isaac Newton, Representative in Parliament of the University of Cambridge to John Covel. Norwich: 1848. V. 38

A Treatise of the System of the World. London: 1728. V. 38; 39; 42; 45

Two Treatises of the Quadrature of Curves and Analysis by Equations of an Infinite Number of Terms. London: 1745. V. 41

NEWTON, JAMES 1670?-1750

A Complete Herbal. London: 1805. V. 38

NEWTON, JOHN

*An Authentic Narrative of Some Remarkable and Interesting Particulars in the Life of *********. Communicated in a Series of Letters, to the Reverend Mr. Haweis.* London: 1786. V. 44

Cardiphonia: or, the Utterance of the Heart: in the Coure of a Real Correspondence. London: 1781. V. 38

The English Academy. London: 1677. V. 38

The Life of John Newton, Once a Sailor, Afterwards Captain of a Slave Ship. New York: 1846. V. 42

NEWTON, JOHN MARSHALL

Memoirs of John Marshall Newton. Cambridge: 1913. V. 42

Memoirs of John Marshall Newton. Cambridge, New York: 1913. V. 40

NEWTON, JOSEPH

The Landscape Gardener. London: 1876. V. 41

NEWTON, RICHARD

The Jewish Tabernacle and its Furniture, in Their Typical Teachings. New York: 1864. V. 39

Rules and Statutes for the Government of Hertford College, in the University of Oxford. London: 1747. V. 45

NEWTON, THOMAS

Dissertations on the Prophecies, which have Remarkably been Fulfilled, and at this Time are Fulfilling the World . . . The Eighth Edition. Elizabeth Town/New York: 1787. V. 37

A Letter to the New Parliament; with Hints of Some Regulations Which the Nation Hopes and Expects from Them. London: 1780. V. 40

On the Imperfect Reception of the Gosepl. London: 1769. V. 40

The Works. London: 1787. V. 38

NEWTON, W.

The Architecture; translated from the original Latin, by W. Newton. London: 1791. V. 37

NEWTON, WILLIAM

The Life of White Kennett, With Several Original letters of the Late Dr. Tennison. London: 1730. V. 38; 39

Twenty Years on the Saskatchewan. London: 1897. V. 45

NEY, MARSHAL

Memoires du Marechal Ney, Duc d'Elchingen, Prince de la Moskowa, Publies par sa Famille. Paris: 1833. V. 37; 39

THE NIAGARA Book, Containing Sketches, Stories and Essays . . . Buffalo: 1893. V. 40

NIBBS, R. H.

Antiquities of Sussex, etched by . . . N.P.. V. 39

Antiquities of Sussex (First Series). Brighton: 1874. V. 37; 40

The Churches of Sussex. London: 1851. V. 44

NIBELUNGENLIED

The Fall of the Niebelungers, Otherwise the Book of Kriemhild. London: 1850. V. 42

The Nibelungenlied. New York: 1960. V. 40

NIBLICK

Hints to Golfers. Salem: 1902. V. 43

NICANDER

Alexipharmaca. Parisiis: 1549. V. 38; 40; 44

NICCOL, ROBERT

Essay on Sugar, and General Treatise on Sugar Refining, as Practised in the Clyde Refineries . . . Greenock: 1864. V. 45

NICELY, WILSON S.

Th Great Southwest; or, Plain Guide for Emigrants and Capitalists, Embracing a Description of the States of Missouri and Kansas . . . St. Louis: 1867. V. 37; 41; 42

NICERON, JEAN FRANCOIS 1613-1646

La Perspective Curieuse ou Magie Artificielle des Effets Merveilleux. Paris: 1638. V. 39

NICETAS, ACOMINATO 1140-1213

La Historia de Gli Imperatori Greci . . . Nella Quale si Contengono le Cose di Constantinopoli . . . Venice: 1562. V. 40

NICHELSON, WILLIAM

A Treatise on Practical Navigation and Seamanship . . . London: 1792. V. 40

NICHOL, B. P.

Craft Dinner, Stories and Texts, 1966-1976. Toronto: 1978. V. 39

NICHOL, J. P.

The Phenomena and Order of the Solar System. Edinburgh: 1838. V. 41

Views of the Architecture of the Heavens. In a Series of Letters to a Lady. New York: 1840. V. 40

NICHOLAS, GEORGE

A Letter from George Nicholas, of Kentucky to His Friend in Virginia Justifying the Conduct of the Citizens of Kentucky. As to Some of the Late Measures of the General Government. Lexington: 1799. V. 46

A Letter from George Nicholas of Kentucky to His Friend in Virginia . . . Philadelphia: 1799. V. 37; 38; 39; 41; 42; 44; 45

NICHOLAS, HILDA R.

The Art of . . . Sydney: 1919. V. 41

NICHOLAS, JOHN L.

Narrative of a Voyage to new Zealand, Performed in the Years 1814 & 1815 . . . London: 1817. V. 38; 41

NICHOLAS, NICHOLAS HARRIS

Privy Purse Expenses of Elizabeth of York . . . London: 1830. V. 44

NICHOLAS, PAUL HARRIS

Historical Record of the Royal Marine Forces. London: 1845. V. 38

NICHOLAS, PHILIP

Sir Francis Drake Revived. London: 1626. V. 38

NICHOLLS, GEORGE 1782-1865

A History of the English Poor Law, in Connexion with the Legislation and Other Circumstances Affecting the Condition of the People. London: 1854. V. 37; 39; 41

A History of the Irish Poor Law In Connection with the Condition of the People. London: 1856. V. 38; 39; 41

A History of the Scotch Poor Law, in Connexion with the Condition of the People. London: 1856. V. 38; 39

A History of the English Poor Law in Connection with the State of the Country and the Condition of the People. London: 1904. V. 38

Second Report to Her Majesty's Principle Secretary of State for the Home Department on Poor Laws. 1837. V. 40

Second Report to Her Majesty's Principal Secretary of State for the Home Department on Poor Laws. London: 1837. V. 41

NICHOLLS, H. G.

The Forest of Dean. London: 1858. V. 40; 43

Iron Making in the Olden Times . . . London: 1866. V. 44

NICHOLLS, J. F.

Bristol, Past and Present. Bristol: 1881. V. 37

NICHOLLS, THOMAS

The Harp of Hermes. Poems. London?: 1797? V. 43

NICHOLLS, W. A.

The National Drawing Master. London: 1865. V. 44

NICHOLLS, W. H.

Orchids of Australia. Melbourne: 1969. V. 39

NICHOLLS, WILLIAM 1664-1712

A Commentary on the Book of Common Prayer and Administration of the Sacraments. London: 1712-11. V. 39

NICHOLS, BEACH

Atlas of Seneca County New York from Actual Surveys by and Under the Direction of . . . Philadelphia: 1874. V. 39

NICHOLS, BEVERLEY

A Book of Old Ballads. 1934. V. 46

A Book of Old Ballads. London: 1934. V. 40

NICHOLS, CHARLES LEMEL

Bibliography of Worcester, A List of Books, Pamphlets, Newspapers and Broadsides Printed in the Town of Worcester, Massachusetts from 1775 to 1848. Worcester: 1918. V. 45

NICHOLS, CHARLES LEMUEL

Isaiah Thomas, Printer, Writer and Collector, a Paper Read April 12, 1911, Before the Club of Odd Volumes. Boston: 1912. V. 37

NICHOLS, DALE

A Philosophy of Esthetics. Chicago: 1938. V. 42

NICHOLS, FRANCIS

Rudiments of Honour; or, the Second Part of the British Compendium . . . the Present Nobility of Scotland. London: 1720. V. 41

NICHOLS, GEORGE C.

Sandusky Of To-Day (Historically Reviewed) Its Facilities and Inducements for the Investment of Capital . . . Sandusky: 1888. V. 38

NICHOLS, GEORGE WARD 1831-1885

The Story of the Great March. New York: 1865. V. 41

The Story of the Great March: From the Diary of a Staff Officer. London: 1865. V. 37

NICHOLS, HENRY W.

Standard Cotton Cloths and Their Construction. Fall River: 1927. V. 39

NICHOLS, ISAAC T.

Historic Days in Cumberland County, New Jersey, 1855-1865. N.P.: 1907. V. 46

NICHOLS, J.

Antiquities in Kent and Sussex . . . London: 1790. V. 44

Antiquities in Leicestershire. London: 1790. V. 44

Antiquities in Lincolnshire. London: 1790. V. 44

Antiquities in Middlesex and Surrey. London: 1790. V. 44; 46

NICHOLS, JAMES L.

Confederate Quartermaster Operations in the Trans-Mississippi Department. Austin: 1947. V. 39

NICHOLS, JAMES WILSON

Now You Hear My Horn: The Journal of James Wilson Nichols. Austin: 1967. V. 37; 39; 42

NICHOLS, JOHN 1745-1826

Biographical Anecdotes of William Hogarth; and a Catalogue of His Works Chronologically Arranged . . . London: 1781. V. 42

Biographical and Literary Anecdotes of William Bowyer, Printer, F.S.A. and of Many of His Learned Friends. London: 1782. V. 38; 39; 40; 44

Biographical Anecdotes of William Hogarth, with a Catalogue of His Works. London: 1785. V. 44

Biographical Anecdotes of William Hogarth. London: 1782. V. 40

Biographical Anecdotes of William Hogarth; with a catalogue of his works . . . London: 1775. V. 37

NICHOLSON, PETER continued

The Carpenter's New Guide. Philadelphia: 1860. V. 42

Carpentry, Joinery and Cabinet-Making. London: 1837. V. 40

Encyclopedia of Architecture. London: 1852. V. 41

The Guide to Railway Masonry . . . London: 1839. V. 46

The New and Improved Practical Builder. London: 1837. V. 38

The New Practical Builder. London: 1823. V. 37

Nicholson's New Carpenter's Guide. London: 1850. V. 40

Practical Carpentry, Joinery and Cabinet-Making . . . London: 1826. V. 44

The Practical Cabinet-Maker, Upholsterer, and Complete Decorator. London: 1827. V. 41

Practical Carpentry, Joinery and Cabinet Making . . . London: 1851. V. 42; 43

The Student's Instructor in Drawing and Working the Five Orders of Architecture. London: 1810. V. 42

The Student's Instructor in Drawing and Working the Five Orders of Architecture Explaining the Method for Striking Mouldings. London: 1845. V. 39

NICHOLSON, RENTON

Dombey and Daughter: a Moral Fiction. London: 1847. V. 46

The Lord Chief Baron Nicholson. London: 1860. V. 38

NICHOLSON, REYNOLD A.

A Literary History of the Arabs. London: 1923. V. 42

NICHOLSON, S.

Twenty-Six Lithographic Drawings in the Vicinity of Liverpool. Liverpool: 1821. V. 42; 45

NICHOLSON, WILLIAM 1872-1949

An Almanac of Twelve Sports. London: 1898. V. 39; 40; 42; 45

An Alamanc of Twelve Sports. New York: 1898. V. 39; 40; 41

An Almanac of Twelve Sports. London: 1898/97. V. 44

An Almanac of Twelve Sports and London Types. 1980. V. 40

An Almanac of Twelve Sports. Andoversford: 1980. V. 39; 41; 46

An Almanac of Twelve Sports and London Types. Gloucestershire: 1980. V. 37; 39; 44

An Alphabet. London: 1898. V. 37; 40; 44; 46

An Alphabet. Andoversford: 1978. V. 44

An Alphabet. Gloucestershire: 1978. V. 39

The Book of Blokes. London. V. 38; 46

Book of Blokes. London: 1929. V. 37; 39; 42; 43; 44; 45

The British Encyclopedia, or Dictionary of Arts and Sciences. London: 1809. V. 39

Characters of Romance. London: 1900. V. 44

Clever Bill. London. V. 40

Clever Bill. London: 1929. V. 41

A Dictionary of Chemistry. London: 1795. V. 40

The English Scotch and Irish Historical Libraries. London: 1736. V. 39

The First Principles of Chemistry. London: 1790. V. 38

The History of the Wars Occasioned by the French Revolution. Including a Sketch of the Early History of France . . . with a History of the Revolution in France, The War in Spain and Portugal . . . Russia & Prussia, etc. By William Nicholson. London: (1816). V. 37

Introduction of Natural Philosophy . . . London: 1782. V. 38

An Introduction to Natural Philosophy. London: 1790. V. 40

The Irish Historical Library. Authors and Records in print or MSS. serviceable to the Compilers of a General History of Ireland. Dublin: 1724. V. 37; 43

A Journal of Natural Philosophy, Chemistry and the Arts. London: 1797-1801. V. 42

A Journal of Natural Philosophy, Chemistry and the Arts. London: 1797-1802. V. 43

A Journal of Natural Philosophy, Chemistry and the Arts. London: 1797-98. V. 42

Letters on Various Subjects, Literary, Political and Ecclesiastical . . . London: 1809. V. 43

London Types. London: 1898. V. 37; 42

The Pirate Twins. London: 1929. V. 40

The Pirate Twins. London: 1930. V. 37

The Square Book of Animals. London: 1900. V. 37; 42

Tales in verse, and Miscellaneous Poems: Discriptive of Rural Life and manners. The Second Edition. To which is prefixed, a Memoir of the author. Edinburgh: 1828. V. 37

The Winter Owl. London: 1923. V. 42

NICHOLSON, WINIFRED

Flower Tales. London: 1976. V. 43

NICHSOLSON, G. W. L.

The Gunners of Canada. The History of the Royal Regiment of Canadian Artillery. Volume I, 1534-1919. Volume II 1919-1967. Toronto & Montreal: 1967-72. V. 40

NICKELSON, B. C.

A Brief Sketch of the Life of an Ex-Confederate Soldier and the Ups and Downs During Pioneer and Indian Warfare in Texas. Dallas: 1928. V. 42

NICKLIN, PHILIP A.

A Pleasant Perigrination Through the Prettiest Parts of Pennsylvania. Philadelphia: 1836. V. 42

NICKLIN, PHILIP H.

Remarks on Literary Property. Philadelphia: 1838. V. 43

NICKOLLS, JOHN

Original Letters and Papers of State Addressed to Oliver Cromwell; Concerning the Affairs of Great Britain. London: 1743. V. 41; 43

NICKOLLS, ROBERT BOUCHER

A Letter to the Treasurer (Samuel Hoare) of the Society Instituted for the Purpose of Effecting the Abolition of the Slave Trade. London: 1787. V. 41

NICKSON, CHARLES

History of Runcorn. London: 1887. V. 38

NICLAES, HENRICK

New Ballade or Songe of the Lambes Feast. Long Crendon: 1927. V. 46

NICOL, J. W.

Brush-Drawing, a Handbook for Teachers and Students. London: 1902. V. 38

NICOL, JOHN

The Life and Adventures of John Nicol, Mariner. Edinburgh: 1822. V. 38; 41; 42

NICOL, WALTER

The Gardener's Kalendar . . . Edinburgh: 1810. V. 42

The Gardener's Kalendar. Edinburgh: 1814. V. 40

The Planter's Kalendar. Edinburgh: 1812. V. 37; 39; 40; 44

The Practical Planter, or, a Treatise on Forest Planting . . . Edinburgh: 1799. V. 40; 44

The Villa Garden Directory, or Monthly Index of Work to be Done in Town and Villa Gardens . . . Edinburgh: 1809. V. 41

The Villa Garden Directory, or Monthly Index of Work. Edinburgh: 1810. V. 38; 40; 44

NICOLAI, NICOLO DE

Le Navigationi et Viaggi Nella Turchia. Antwerp: 1576. V. 39

NICOLAS DE BLONY

Tractatus de Sacramentis. Strasbourg: 1499. V. 38

NICOLAS DE LYRA

Moralia Super Totam Bibliam. Cologne: 1478. V. 37

NICOLAS, HARRIS

Report on the Proceedings on the Claim to the Earldom of Devon. London: 1832. V. 46

NICOLAS, NICHOLAS HARRIS 1799-1848

The Dispatches and Letters of Vice-Admiral Lord Viscount Nelson, with Notes (1771-1805). London: 1845-46. V. 42

The History of the Battle of Agincourt and of the Expedition of Henry the Fifth into France. London: 1827. V. 39; 42

History of the Battle of Agincourt, and of the Expedition of Henry the Fifth into France, in 1415 . . . London: 1832. V. 44

A History of the Royal Navy, from the Earliest Times to the Wars of the French Revolution. London: 1847. V. 39; 46

Notitia Historica. London: 1824. V. 40

The Privy Purse Expenses of King Henry the Eighth, from November, 1529 to Dec. 1532; with Introductory Remarks and Illustrative Notes. London: 1827. V. 38

Privy Purse Expenses of Elizabeth of York: Wardrobe Accounts of Edward the Fourth. London: 1830. V. 38

Public Records. A Description of the Contents, Objects and Uses of the Various Works Printed by the Record Commission. London: 1831. V. 45

Statutes of the Order of the Guelphs. London: 1828. V. 42; 46

NICOLAUS DE AUSMO

Supplementum. Canones Penitentiales, Consilia Alexandri de Nevo Contra Judaeos Foenerantes. Venice: 1482. V. 41

NICOLAUS DE LYRA d. 1349

Postilla Seu Expositio Literalis et Moralis. Venice: 1500. V. 45

NICOLAUS DE LYRA d. 1349 continued

Praeceptorium (Divinae Legis), cum Additionibus et Tractatulis Pulcerrimus Multis. Cologne: 1502. V. 45

NICOLAY, CHARLES GRENFELL

The Oregon Territory. London: 1846. V. 37; 38; 41; 42; 45; 46

NICOLAY, JOHN G.

Abraham Lincoln: a History. New York: 1890. V. 42; 44

NICOLAY, NICOLAS DE

Le Navigationi et Viaggi Nella Turchia, di Nicolo de Nicolai del Definato . . . Antwerp: 1576. V. 42

NICOLE, PIERRE

Discourses; Translated from Nicole's Essays, by John Locke . . . London: 1828. V. 40

Logic; or, the Art of Thinking. London: 1723. V. 42; 44

Moral Essays, Contain'd in Several Treatises on Many Important Duties. London: 1677. V. 40; 43

NICOLL, ALLARADYCE

The Development of the Theatre. London: 1927. V. 37

NICOLL, ALLARDYCE

The Berkshire Series. Waltham St. Lawrence: 1296. V. 45

The Berkshire Series. Waltham St. Lawrence: 1926. V. 41

Shakespeare Survey. Cambridge: 1948-58. V. 42

Stuart Masques and the Renaissance Stage. London: 1937. V. 45

NICOLL, DONALD

Health and Its Appliances. London: 1885. V. 38

Publicity. An Essay on Advertising. London: 1878. V. 42

NICOLL, HENRY J.

C (100) Sonnets by C (100) Authors. Edinburgh: 1883. V. 44

NICOLL, W. ROBERTSON

Literary Anecdotes of the Nineteenth Century. London: 1895. V. 45

Literary Anecdotes of the Nineteenth Century. London: 1895-1896. V. 40

NICOLLET, JOSEPH NICOLAS

Report Intended to Illustrate a Map of the Hydrographical Basin of the Upper Mississippi. Washington: 1843. V. 40; 41; 42; 45; 46

Report Intended to Illustrate a Map of the Hydrographical Basin of the Upper Mississippi River. Washington: 1845. V. 37; 41; 44

NICOLS, ARTHUR

Wild Life and Adventure in the Australian Bush. London: 1887. V. 39

NICOLS, WILLIAM

De Literis Inventis Libri Sex. Ad Illustrissimum Principem Thomam Herbertum. Londini: 1711. V. 45

NICOLSON, BENEDICT

The International Caravaggesque Movement: Lists of Pictures by Caravaggio and His Followers throughout Europe from 1590 to 1650. Oxford: 1979. V. 40; 43

Joseph Wright of Derby, Painter of Light. London: 1968. V. 37; 40; 44; 45

NICOLSON, HAROLD

Diaries and Letters 1930-1962. London: 1966-68. V. 39

The English Sense of Humour - an Essay. London: 1946. V. 43; 44

King George V - His Life and Reign. London: 1952. V. 44

NICOLSON, JOSEPH

The History and Antiquities of the Counties of Westmorland and Cumberland. London: 1777. V. 37; 46

NICOLSON, M.

Voyages to the Moon. 1948. V. 46

Voyages to the Moon. London: 1948. V. 44

NICOLSON, WILLIAM 1655-1727

The English Historical Library. London: 1696-1697. V. 37; 38; 41; 44

The English Historical Library. London: 1696/97/99. V. 38; 42

The English Historical Library. London: 1696-99. V. 38

The English Historical Library. London: 1714. V. 38; 42; 44

The English, Scotch and Irish Historical Libraries. London: 1736. V. 43

The English, Scotch and Irish Historical Libaries. Giving a short view and character of most of our historians, either in printe or manuscript. With an account of our records, law-books, coins, &c. To which is added a letter to . . . London: 1776. V. 37; 39; 46

The English, Scotch and Irish Historical Libraries. Giving a short view and character of most of our historians, either in print or manuscript. With an account of our records, law books, coins &c. To which is added a letter to the . . . 1776. V. 37

The Irish Historical Library. Dublin: 1724. V. 41

Leges Marchiarum, or Border Laws . . . London: 1705. V. 37; 40

Leges Marchiarum or Border Laws. London: 1747. V. 40

NIDER, JOHANNES c.1380-1438

Exposic(i)one(m) Decalogi. Basel: 1474. V. 44

Formicarius. Cologne: 1473. V. 40

Praeceptorium Divinae Legis. Augsburg: 1475. V. 40; 45

Sermones de Tempore et de Sanctis Cum Quadragesimali. Speier: 1479. V. 42

Sermones de Tempore et de Sanctis. Ulm: 1479. V. 37; 38

Sermones Aurei de Tempore et de Sanctis cum Quadragesimali. Ulm: 1480. V. 38; 40

NIEBAUER, ABBY

Three Windows. Woodside: 1980. V. 37

NIEBUHR, CARSTEN

Beschreibung von Arabien Aus Eigenen Beobachtungen und im Lande Selbst Gesammleten Nachrichten. Copenhagen: 1772. V. 40; 45; 46

Description de l'Arabie, Faite sur des Observations Propres et des Avis Recueillis dans les Lieux Memes. (with) Voyage en Arabie . . . Amsterdam: 1774, 1780. V. 39

Travels through Arabia, and Other Countries in the East, Performed by . . . Edinburgh: 1792. V. 38; 39; 41

Travels through Arabia and Other Countries . . . Perth: 1799. V. 43

NIEBUHR, REINHOLD

The Nature and Destiny of Man. Part II. New York: 1943. V. 39

NIEBUHT, BARTHOLD GEORG

Stories of the Gods and Heroes of Greece, told by Berthold (sic) Niebuhr to his son. London: 1843. V. 45

NIEDECKER, LORINE

Blue Chichory. New Rochelle: 1976. V. 45

North Central: Poems. 1968. V. 37; 43

North Central. London: 1968. V. 37; 38; 39; 40

NIEDIECK, PAUL

Cruises in the Bering Sea. London: 1909. V. 43

With Rifle in Five Continents. London: 1908. V. 43

NIEL, P. G. J.

Portraits des Personnages Francais. Paris: 1848-56. V. 43; 45

NIELD, JONATHAN

Illustrations of the County of Somerset. London. V. 44

NIELL, JOHN R.

Lucky Bucky in Oz. 1942. V. 46

NIELSEN, KAY

East of the Sun and West of the Moon. New York: c. 1920. V. 37

NIEREMBERG, JUAN EUSEBIO

Historia Naturae, Maxime Peregrinae Libris XVI Distincta. Antwerp: 1635. V. 44

NIEREMBERG Y OTTIN, JUAN EUSEBIO 1595-1658

Honor del Gran Patriarca San Ignacio de Loyola . . . Madrid: 1649. V. 40

NIERSZESOUICZ, DEODAT

Dictionarium Latino-Armenum. Rome: 1695. V. 46

NIES, JAMES B.

Historical, Religious and Economic Texts and Antiquities. New Haven: 1920. V. 44

Ur Dynasty Tablets . . . Leipzig: 1920. V. 44

NIETZSCHE, FRIEDRICH WILHELM 1844-1900

The Antichrist of Nietzsche. London: 1928. V. 41; 44; 46

The Antichrist of Nietzsche: A New Version in English. London: (1928). V. 37

Die Geburt der Tragodie aus dem Geiste der Musik. Leipzig: 1872. V. 45

Gedichte und Spruche. Leipzig: 1898. V. 46

A Genealogy of Morals (and) Poems. London: 1899. V. 37; 38

The Nietzsche-Wagner Correspondence. London: 1922. V. 40

NIEUWENTIJDT, BERNARD

The Religious Philosopher. London: 1719-20. V. 40

NIGER, ANTONIUS

Consilivm De Tvenda Valetvdine. Leipzig: 1554. V. 40

THE NIGHT-FLYERS. London: 1860. V. 44; 46

THE NIGHT Watch; or, Tales of the Sea. London: 1828. V. 42

NIGHTINGALE, B.

The Ejected of 1662 in Cumberland and Westmorland. Manchester: 1911. V. 44

NIGHTINGALE, BENJAMIN

Lancanshire Nonconformity; or, Sketches Historical and Descriptive of the Congregational and Old Presbyterian Churches in the County. Manchester: 1890-93. V. 37; 40

NIGHTINGALE, FLORENCE 1820-1910

Army Sanitary Administration and Its Reform Under the Late Lord Herbert. London: 1862. V. 42

A Contribution to the Sanitary History of the British Army During the Late War with Russia. London: 1859. V. 45

Introductory Notes on Lying-In Institutions, Together With a Proposal for Organising An Institution for Training Midwives and Midwifery Nurses. London: 1871. V. 42

Notes on Nursing; What It Is, and What It Is Not. London: 1859. V. 37; 42; 45

Notes on Nursing: What It Is and What It Is Not. London: 1859 or 1860? V. 44

Notes on Nursing. Boston: 1860. V. 37; 38; 39; 40; 41; 42; 44

Notes on Nursing; What It Is and What It Is Not. London: 1860. V. 37; 39; 40; 41; 44; 45

Notes on Nursing. New York: 1860. V. 37; 40; 42; 43; 44; 46

Om Sjukskotsel: Hvad den ar och Hvad den Icke ar Ofversattning Fran Engelskan af E.N-n. Goteborg: 1861. V. 41

Organization of Nursing . . . Liverpool: 1865. V. 37

NIGHTINGALE, J.

English Topography . . . London: 1816. V. 41

NIGHTINGALE, JOSEPH

London and Middlesex; or an Historical, Commercial and Descriptive Survey of the Metropolis of Great Britain . . . Volume III. Part II. London: 1819. V. 40

NIJENHUIS, JAN TIBERIUS BODEL

Liste Alphabetique d'une Petite Collection de Portraits d'Imprimeurs . . . Leiden: 1836-68. V. 38

NIKITIN, AFANASY

Voyage Beyond Three Seas 1466-1472. Moscow: 1960. V. 41

NIKLAS, K. J.

Paleobotany and Evolution. London: 1981. V. 37

NILES, AARON

A Controversy Between the Four Elements. Wrentham: 1812. V. 40

NILES, H.

The Weekly Register: Containing Political, Historical, Geographical, Scientific . . . Documents, Essays and Facts . . . Baltimore & Washington: 1845. V. 41

NILES, HEZEKIAH

Journal of the Proceedings of Domestic Industry, in General Convention Met at the City of New York, October 26, 1831. Baltimore: 1831. V. 37; 42

Principles and Acts of the Revolution in America. Baltimore: 1822. V. 38

NILES, JOHN J.

Singing Soldiers. New York: 1927. V. 46

NILES, JOHN MILTON

History of South America and Mexico . . . to Which is Annexed a Geographical and Historical View of Texas . . . Hartford: 1837. V. 37; 40; 42

History of South America and Mexico . . . Hartford: 1838 c. 1837. V. 44

History of South America and Mexico . . . To Which is Annexed, a Geographical and Historical View of Texas, with a Detailed Account of the Texaian Revolution and War. Hartford: 1838. V. 37; 42; 43; 45; 46

The Life of Oliver Hazard Perry . . . to Which is Added a Biography of General Pike and a View of the Leading Events in the Life of General Harrison. Hartford: 1821. V. 42

A View of South America and Mexico, Comprising Their History, The Political Condition, Geography, Agriculture, Commerce &c . . . New York: 1825. V. 40; 42

A View of South America and Mexico Comprising Their History, the Political Condition, Geography, Agriculture and Commerce. New York: 1828. V. 39

NILES, NATHANIEL

The Perfection of God the Fountain of Good. Norwich: 1791. V. 46

NILES Weekly Register. Baltimore: 1811-36. V. 39
NILES' Weekly Register. Baltimore: 1823-1826. V. 37

NILSEN, VLADIMIR

The Cinema as a Graphic Art. N.P.: 1936. V. 38

NILSSON, SVEN

The Primitive Inhabitants of Scandinavia. London: 1868. V. 40

NIMMO, JOSEPH

Letter from the Sec. of the Treasury, Transmitting A Report . . . In Regard to the Range & Ranch Cattle Traffic in The Western States & Territories. Washington: 1885. V. 37

Report to the Secretary of the Treasury In Relation to the Foreign Commerce of the United States . . . Washington: 1871. V. 41

Report on the Internal Commerce of the U.S . . . . The Range and Ranch Cattle Industry of Texas. Washington: 1885. V. 37; 38

Treasury Department Report on the Internal Commerce of the United States. Washington. V. 42

NIMMO, WILLIAM

History of Stirlingshire. London: 1817. V. 40; 46

NIMROD, HARRY

The Fudge Family in Washington. Baltimore: 1820. V. 44

NIN, ANAIS

Anais Nin Reader. Chicago: 1973. V. 46

Celebration. Riverside: 1973. V. 43

A Child Born Out of the Fog. New York: 1946 or 1947. V. 39

A Child Born Out of the Fog. New York: 1947. V. 39; 43

Children of the Albatross. New York: 1947. V. 37; 39; 44

Children of the Albatross. London: 1959. V. 37; 43; 46

Cities of the Interior. New York: 1959. V. 43

Collages. Denver: 1964. V. 37; 42

Collages. London: 1964. V. 37

D. H. Lawrence, an Unprofessional Study. Paris: 1932. V. 37; 39; 42; 43; 46

The Diary of Anais Nin, 1931-1934 (1934-1966). New York: 1966-76. V. 41

The Diary of . . . New York: 1966/80. V. 43

The Four-Chambered Heart. New York: 1950. V. 44

The House of Incest. Paris: 1936. V. 37; 38; 39; 40; 41; 43; 46

House of Incest. New York: 1945. V. 42

House of Incest. N.P.: 1947. V. 46

An Interview with Anais Nin. 1970. V. 46

Ladders to Fire. New York: 1946. V. 37

Nuances. Cambridge: 1970. V. 39; 43

Nuances. N.P.: 1970. V. 39; 46

Seduction of the Minotaur. Denver: 1961. V. 37; 42

A Spy in the House of Love. Paris: 1954. V. 38

This Hunger. New York: 1945. V. 39; 40; 42

This Hunger . . . (New York): (1945). V. 37

Under a Glass Bell. New York: 1944. V. 38; 39; 43

Under a Glass Bell. N.P.: 1948. V. 42

Unpublished Selections from the Diary. 1968. V. 39

Winter of Artifice. N.P. V. 39

Winter of Artifice. 1942. V. 39

Winter of Artifice. New York: 1942. V. 37; 39; 42; 43; 45

1934 Film Daily Year Book. N.P.: 1934. V. 37

UNITED States. Geological AND GEOGRAPHICAL SURVEY OF THE TERRITORIES - 1877 Ninth Annual Report of the United States Geological and Geographical Survey of the Territories . . . Washington: 1877. V. 42

NIPHUS, AUGUSTINUS

De Verissimis Temporum Signis Commentariolus. Venice: 1540. V. 39

NISBET, ALEXANDER 1657-1725

A System of Heraldry, Speculative and Practical. Edinburgh: 1722. V. 38

A System of Heraldry Speculative and Practical. Edinburgh: 1722 & 1742. V. 38; 39; 40

A System of Heraldry. Edinburgh: 1804. V. 39

A System of Heraldry, Speculative and Practical with the True Art of Blazon . . . Edinburgh: 1816. V. 41

NISBET, CHARLES 1736-1804

An Address to the Students of Dickinson College, Carlisle. Edinburgh: 1786. V. 43; 46

NISBET, HUME

A Colonial Tramp Travels and Adventures in Australia and New Guinea. London: 1891. V. 41

NISBET, JOHN

Our Forests and Woodlands. London: 1909. V. 39

NISBETH, HUGO

Tva Ar I Amerika (1872-1874). Stockholm: 1874. V. 39

NISSEN, CLAUS

Herbals of Five Centuries. Munich: 1958. V. 41; 42

Krauterbucher aus funf Jahrhunderten. Munich: 1956. V. 41

NISTER, E.

Playtime Library. London. V. 45

NISTER, ERNEST

Nister's Little Folks Inquire Within. London: 1880. V. 44

NIVEN, L.

Footfall. 1985. V. 39

A Gift from the Earth. 1969. V. 44

Inconstant Moon. 1973. V. 39

Lucifer's Hammer. 1977. V. 39

Neutron Star. 1969. V. 39

Neutron Star. London: 1969. V. 44

World of Ptavvs. 1968. V. 39; 43

NIVEN, LARRY

Dream Park. Huntington Woods: 1981. V. 42

Ringworld. 1972. V. 39

Ringworld Engineers. HW: 1979. V. 46

NIVEN, W.

Monograph of Aston Hall, Warwickshire. London & Birmingham: 1900. V. 40

NIX, EVETT DUMAS

Oklahombres, Particularly the Wilder Ones. St. Louis: 1929. V. 41

NIXON, ANTHONY

The Warres of Swethland. With the Grovnd and Originall of the Said Warres. London: 1609. V. 37

NIXON, FRANCIS H.

Population; or, a Plea for Victoria. Melbourne: 1862. V. 45

NIXON, HOWARD MILLAR 1909-

Broxbourne Library. London: 1956. V. 39; 40; 41; 43; 44

Catalogue of the Pepys Library at Magdalene College, Cambridge. 1984. V. 39

English Restoration Bookbindings, Samuel Mearne and His Contemporaries. London: 1974. V. 39; 40

Sixteenth Century Gold-Tooled Bookbindings in the Pierpont Morgan Library. New York: 1971. V. 39; 40; 41

Styles and Designs of Bookbindings from the Twelfth to the Twentieth Century. London: 1956. V. 39

NIXON, PAT IRELAND 1883-1965

King's Highway, the Great Strategic Military Highway of America, El Camino Real, The Old San Antonio Road. N.P.: 1945. V. 44

The Medical Story of Early Texas, 1528-1853. 1946. V. 45

The Medical Story of Early Texas, 1528-1853. Lancaster: 1946. V. 37; 38

NIXON, PATRICK IRELAND 1883-1965

A Century of Medicine in San Antonio, the Story of Medicine in Bexar County, Texas. San Antonio: 1936. V. 41; 42

NIXON, RICHARD MILHOUS 1913-

The Memoirs of Richard Nixon. New York: 1978. V. 39; 44; 46

1999. Victory Without War. New York: 1988. V. 39; 40; 41

No More Vietnams. New York: 1985. V. 46

The Real War. New York: 1980. V. 39; 44

Real Peace. Boston: 1984. V. 46

Six Crises. New York: 1962. V. 37; 38; 39; 44; 46

NIXON, RICHARD MILHOUSE 1913-

The Memoirs. Illustrated with photographs. New York: (1978). V. 37

NIXON, ROBERT

Nixon's Prophecies. London: 1840. V. 46

NIZAMY

The Poems of . . . London: 1928. V. 46

NIZOLIUS, MARIUS

Nizolius, Siue Thesaurus Ciceronianus . . . Nunc Iterum, Caelij Secundi Curionis Herculeo Labore atq . . . Basiliae: 1568. V. 41

Thesaurus Ciceronianus. Lyons. V. 45

NJALS SAGA

The Story of Burnt Njal or Life in Iceland at the End of the Tenth Century. Edinburgh: 1861. V. 38

NOAH, M. M.

An Address Delivered Before the General Society of Mechanics and Tradesmen of the City of New York, on the Opening of the Mechanic Institution to Which is added, the Remarks Made on Laying the Corner Stone of the Edifice. New York: 1822. V. 45

A Mirror for Politicians. New York?: 1828. V. 45

NOAH, MORDECAI

Travels in England, France, Spain and the Barbary States in the Years 1813-14 and 15. New York, London: 1819. V. 40

NOAILLES, COMTESSE MATHIEU DE NEE PRINCESS ANNA ELIZABETH DE BRANCOVAN

Les Climats. Paris: 1924. V. 45

NOAKES, AUBREY

Ben Marshall 1768-1835. Leigh-on-Sea: 1978. V. 39

NOAKES, GEORGE

Historical Account of the Services of the 34th & 55th Regiments, the Linked Line Battalions in the 2nd or Cumberland and Westmorland Sub-District Brigade, from the Periods of Their Formation to the Present Time. Carlisle: 1875. V. 38

THE NOBILITY of Life, Its Graces and Virtues, Portrayed in Prose and Verse by the Best Writers. London: 1870. V. 43

NOBLE, ALDEN CHARLES

Scott Who Was Nine. Chicago: 1901. V. 40

THE NOBLE and Renowned History of Guy Earl of Warwick. Chiswick: 1821. V. 39

THE NOBLE Cricketers; a Poetical and Familiar Epistle, Address'd to Two of the Idlest Lords in His Majesty's Three Kingdoms. London: 1778. V. 41

NOBLE, EDWARD MOORE

A Treatise on Opthalmy; and Those Diseases Which are Induced by Inflammations of the Eyes. Birmingham: 1800-01. V. 42

A NOBLE Heritage: Two Conjugate Leaves from the First Edition of the Bishops' Bible Printed by Richard Jugge, London, 1568. Dallas: 1973. V. 46

NOBLE, JAMES

The Professional Practice of Architects and that of Measuring Surveyors, and Reference to Builders &c. London: 1836. V. 39; 40; 41

NOBLE, JAMES ASHCROFT

The Sonnet in England and Other Essays. London: 1893. V. 38; 41

NOBLE, JOHN

Letter from . . . Transmitting . . . the Compilation Concerning the Legal Status of the Indians of Indian Territory. Washington: 1890. V. 39

Letter from the Secretary of Interior . . . Giving Information Relative to Certain Contracts Made with Indians and the Relation of Agents or Attorneys to the Same. Washington: 1892. V. 37

The Queen's Taxes: an inquiry into the amount, incidence & economic results, of the Taxation of the United Kingdom, direct and indirect. London: 1870. V. 37

The Voyage to South Africa on Castle Line mail Packet . . . London: 1891. V. 39

NOBLE, JOHN W.

In the Senate of the United States . . . In Relation to the Affairs of the Indians at the Pine Ridge and Rosebud Reservations in South Dakota. Washington: 1892. V. 46

THE NOBLE Knight Paris and the Fair Vienne. Kentfield: 1956. V. 38

NOBLE, LOUIS L.

After Icebergs with a Painter: a Summer Voyage to Labrador and Around Newfoundland. New York: 1861. V. 39

After Icebergs with a Painter. New York: 1861. V. 37; 38; 39; 40; 42

After Icebergs with a Painter. New York & London: 1861. V. 42

After Icebergs with a Painter. London: 1862. V. 40; 44

After Icebergs with a Painter: A Summer to Labrador and Around Newfoundland. New York: 1861. V. 37

NOBLE, MARK 1754-1827

A History of the College of Arms. London: 1805. V. 40

Memoirs of the Protectorate House of Cromwell . . . Birmingham: 1734. V. 46

Memoirs of the Protectorate House of Cromwell. Birmingham: 1784. V. 38; 40; 42

Memoirs of the Protectorate-House of Cromwell. Birmingham: 1784. V. 42

Memoirs of the Protectorate-House of Cromwell . . . Birmingham: 1784. V. 38

NOBLE, OLIVER

Some Strictures Upon the Sacred Story Recorded in the Book of Esther . . . in a Discourse Delivered at Newbury-Port, . . . March 8th, 1775. In Commemoration of the Massacre at Boston. Newbury-Port,: 1775. V. 37

NOBLE, SAMUEL H.

Life and Adventures of Buckskin Sam. Rumford Falls: 1900. V. 37; 40; 42

NOBLE, T.

The Counties of Chester, Derby, Leicester, Lincoln and Rutland Illustrated. London: 1836. V. 46

NOBLE, T. C.

Memorials of Temple Bar: with Some Account of Fleet Street, and the Parishes of St. Dunstan and St. Bride, London. London: 1869. V. 37

NOBLE, THOMAS

Practical Perspective, Exemplified on Landscapes. London: 1809. V. 41

NOBLE, W. B.

A Guide to the Watering Places on the Coast, Between the Exe and the Dart, Including Teignmouth, Dawlish and Torquay . . . Teignmouth: 1817. V. 41

A Guide to the Watering Places, on the Coast Between the Exe and the Dart. 1821. V. 38

NOBLES, WILLIAM H.

Speech of Hon. Wm. H. Nobles, Together with Other Documents, Relative to an Emigrant Route to California and Oregon . . . Saint Paul: 1854. V. 37; 40; 41; 43

NODAL, BARTOLOME G. DE

Relacion Del Viaje Qve por Orden de Sv Magd. Y Acverdo Del Real Consejo De Indias . . . Al Descubrimiento Del Estrecho Nuebo de S. Vicente Y Reconosimio Del de Magallanes . . . Madrid: 1621. V. 40; 41; 43

NODIN, JOHN

The British Duties of Customs, Excise &c., Containing an Account of the Net Sums Payable on all Goods Imported, Exported or Carried Coastwise . . . London: 1792. V. 45

NOE, F.

Viaggio da Venezia al S. Sepolcro ed al Monte Sinai, Col disegno delle citta, Castelli, Ville, Chiese, Monasteri, Isole, Porti e Fiumi, che sin la Si Ritrovano. Bassano: 1791. V. 46

NOEL, AUGUSTUS

Owen Gwyne's Great Work. London: 1875. V. 41

NOEL, BAPTIST WRIOTHESLEY

Freedom and Slavery in the United States of America. London: 1863. V. 40

Notes on a Tour in Switzerland in the Summer of 1847. London: 1848. V. 40

NOEL, E. B.

A History of Tennis. Oxford: 1924. V. 39

NOEL, GERARD THOMAS

Arundel; or, Sketches in Italy and Switzerland. London: 1826. V. 42

NOEL, JOHN BAPTIST LUCIUS

Through Tibet to Everest. London: 1927. V. 43; 45

NOEL, RODEN

My Sea and Other Poems. Chicago: 1896. V. 38

NOEL Ronello. A Tale of the Present Century. Portland: 1840. V. 42

NOEL, THEOPHILUS

Autobiography and Reminiscences. Chicago: 1904. V. 37; 38; 39; 42; 45; 46

A Campaign from Santa Fe to the Mississippi. Raleigh: 1961. V. 37; 38; 42

NOGUCHI, ISAMU

A Sculptor's World. New York: 1968. V. 46

NOGUCHI, YONE

Hiroshige. New York: 1921. V. 44

Seen and Unseen, or, Monologues of a Homeless Snail. San Francisco: 1897. V. 42

Through the Torii. London: 1914. V. 41

NOHL, LUDWIG

Beethoven. Reminiscences of the Artistic and Home Life of the Artist, from the Diay of a Lady in Close Personal Intercourse with Him. London: 1880. V. 37

NOLAN, EDWARD H.

the History of the British Empire in India and the East. London: 1855-57. V. 42

The Illustrated History of the War Against Russia. London: 1857. V. 41; 46

The Illustrated History of the British Empire in India and the East . . . London: 1859. V. 42

The Illustrated History of the British Empire in India and the East, from the Earliest Times to the Suppression of the Sepoy Mutiny in 1859. London: 1859? V. 40; 46

NOLAN, J. BENNETT

Southeastern Pennsylvania. Philadelphia: 1943. V. 41; 42

NOLAN, LOUIS EDWARD

Cavalry: its History and Tactics. London: 1853. V. 41

Cavalry; Its History and Tactics. London: 1854. V. 41

The Training of Cavalry Remount Horses, a New System. London: 1852. V. 41

The Training of Cavalry Remount Horses, by the Late Captain Nolan. London: 1861. V. 41

NOLAN, MICHAEL d. 1827

A Treatise of the Laws for the Relief and Settlement of the Poor. London: 1825. V. 40; 41

NOLAN, WILLIAM F.

Logan's Run. 1967. V. 44

Logan's Run. New York: 1967. V. 42

NOLAND, THOMAS H.

Central Mining District, Jamestown, Boulder County, Colorado. Denver: 1882. V. 45

NOLCINI, EDMUND

The Story of an Ostrich. An Allegory and Humorous Satire in Rhyme, by Judd Isaacs. Boston: (1903). V. 37

NOLL, ARTHUR

Doctor Quintard, Chaplain, C.S.A. and Second Bishop of Tennessee: Being His Story of the Wara (1861-1865). Sewanee: 1905. V. 37

NOLLET, JEAN ANTOINE

Lecons de Physique Experimentale. Paris: 1783-84. V. 41

NOLTE, VINCENT

Fifty Years in Both Hemispheres or Reminiscences of the Life of a Former Merchant. New York: 1854. V. 40

NONA

In Idle Moments. N.P.: 1912. V. 42

THE NONESUCH Century: an Appraisal, A Personal Note and a Bibliography of the First Hundred Books Issued by the Press. London: 1936. V. 46

NONESUCH PRESS

The Nonesuch Century. London: 1936. V. 37; 39; 44

Prospectus and Retrospectus of the Nonesuch Press (5 prospectuses: 1925, 1926, 1930, 1932 (2 copies) and Nonesuch Books for Christmas 1925, for the Spring 19256 with a Hand-List of Books Hitherto Published by the Press. V. 41

NONIUS, TOBIAS d. 1570

Interpretationes in Nonnullos Institutionum Titulos. Venice: 1579. V. 40

NONNIUS, LUDOVICUS

Diaeteticon Sive de Re Cibaria. Libri IV. Antverpiae: 1627. V. 44

NONNUS, LUDOVICUS

Ichtyophagia Sive de Piscium esu Commentarius. Antverpiae: 1616. V. 39

NONNUS PANOPOLITANUS

Dionysiaca. Antwerp: 1569. V. 38; 40

NOONAN, LAURENCE A.

The First Jesuit Mission in Malacca:f the Peiho River. Lisbon: 1974. V. 40

NOORTHOUCK, JOHN 1746?-1816

A New History of London. London: 1773. V. 44

NOOTH, CHARLOTTE

Original Poems and a Play. London: 1815. V. 42; 43

NORBERG-SCHULZ, CHRISTIAN

Late Baroque and Rococo Architecture. New York: 1974. V. 39

NORBURY, JOHN

The Box of Whistles. London: 1877. V. 39; 41

NORDAU, MAX

A Question of Honor. Boston & London: 1907. V. 43

NORDEN, FREDERICK LEWIS

Travels in Egypt and Nubia. London: 1757. V. 39; 40

NORDEN, FREDERICK LEWIS continued

The Travels of Frederick Lewis Norden, through Egypt and Nubia. New Haven: 1814. V. 40

Voyage d'Egypte et de Nubie. Copenhague: 1755. V. 40

NORDEN, JOHN 1548-1626

Speculi Britanniae Pars: a Topographical and Historical Description of Cornwall. London: 1728. V. 45

Speculi Britanniae Pars: an Historical and Chorographical Description of the County of Essex. London: 1840. V. 38

Speculum Britanniae; an Historical and Chorographical Description of Middlesex and Hartfordshire. London: 1723. V. 39; 41; 44

The Surveiors Dialogue. London: 1738. V. 37

NORDENSKIOLD, A. E.

Periplus: an Essay on the Early History of Charts and Sailing Directions. New York: 1967? V. 43

NORDENSKIOLD, ADOLF E.

The Voyage of the Vega Round Asia and Europe... London: 1881. V. 39; 40; 46

Voyage of the Vega Round Asia and Europe with a Historical Review of Previous Journeys Along the North Coast of the Old World. New York: 1882. V. 39; 44; 46

NORDENSKIOLD, ERIK

The History of Biology, a Survey. London: 1929. V. 39

NORDENSKIOLD, G.

The Cliff Dwellers of Mesa Verde. Stockholm & Chicago: 1893. V. 38; 39

Ruiner af Klippboningar i Mesa Verde's Canons. Stockholm: 1893. V. 41; 45

NORDENSKIOLD, NILS A. E.

Lettres de... Racontant la Decouverte du Passage Nord-Est Du Pole Nord. Paris: 1880. V. 38

NORDENSKJOLD, N. OTTO

Antarctica, or Two years Amongst the Ice of the South Pole. New York: 1905. V. 38

NORDEZ, M. LE

Jeanne d'Arc, Racontee par l'Image d'Apres les Sculpeurs, les Graveurs et les Peintre. Paris: 1898. V. 39

NORDHOFF, CHARLES 1830-1901

California for Health, Pleasure and Residence. New York: 1872. V. 44; 46

California for Health, Pleasure, and Residence... London: 1882. V. 42

California: for Health, Pleasure and Residence. New York: 1873. V. 37; 39

The Communistic Societies of the United States. New York: 1875. V. 40; 41; 43; 45; 46

The Cotton States in the Spring and Summer of 1875. New York: 1876. V. 43

Northern California, Oregon and the Sandwich Islands. London: 1874. V. 46

Peninsular California. New York: 1888. V. 46

NORDHOFF, CHARLES BERNARD 1887-1947

Botany Bay. Boston: 1941. V. 45

The Hurricane. 1936. V. 43

The Hurricane. Boston: 1936. V. 43; 45

Mutiny on the Bounty. Boston: 1932. V. 38

Mutiny on the Bounty. 1947. V. 39

Mutiny on the Bounty. New York: 1947. V. 43

NORDHOFF, EVELYN HUNTER

The Doves Bindery... 1964. V. 46

NORDNESS, LEE

Art USA Now. New York: 1963. V. 37; 39; 41

NORES, GIASONE DE

Introdvttione Ridotta Poin in Alcvne Tavole Sopra I Tre Libri Delle Rhetorica di Aristotile. Venice: 1578. V. 42

NORFOLK AND NORWICH SOCIETY FOR THE EDUCATION OF THE POOR

Norfolk and Norwich Society, for the Education of the Poor in the Principles of the Established Church. Norwich: 1812. V. 40

NORFOLK, CHARLES HOWARD, 10TH DUKE OF

Historical Anecdotes of Some of the Howard Family. London: 1769. V. 38; 41; 43

NORIE, J. W.

Directions for Sailing to and From the Coast of Brazil, River Plate, Cape of Good Hope &c... London: 1819. V. 43

New Piloting Directions for the Coasts, Harbours and Islands of North America; from Labrador... Part I (Only of 3)... From Belle Isle to Cape Cod. London: 1827. V. 39

NORIE, JOHN WILLIAM

The Description and Use of Hadley's Quadrant and Sextant. London: 1803. V. 40

New and Extensive Sailing Directions for the Navigation of the North Sea... London: 1846. V. 38; 40; 43; 44

Piloting Directions for the Cattegat and Baltic... London: 1826. V. 38

NORMAN, BENJAMIN M.

Norman's New Orleans and Environs... New Orleans: 1845. V. 42; 44; 46

Rambles in Yucatan, Including a Visit to the Remarkable Ruins of Chi-Chen, Kabah, Zayi, Uxmal &c. 1843. V. 42

Rambles in Yucatan, or, Notes of Travel through the Peninsula, Including a Visit to the Remarkable Ruins of Chi=Chen, Kabah, Zayi and Uxmal. New York: 1843. V. 37; 38; 39; 40; 41

Rambles by Land and Water, or Notes of Travel in Cuba and Mexico... New York: 1845. V. 40

NORMAN, DON CLEVELAND

The 500th Anniversary Pictorial Census of the Gutenberg Bible. Chicago: 1961. V. 41; 45

NORMAN, DOROTHY

Dualities. New York: 1933. V. 45

Stieglitz Memorial Portfolio 1864-1946. New York: 1947. V. 37

NORMAN, GEORGE WARDE 1793-1882

Remarks Upon Some Prevalent Errors, with Respect to Currency and Banking, and Suggestions to the Legislature and the Public as to the Improvement of the Monetary System. London: 1838. V. 38

NORMAN, GURNEY

Crazy Quilt - a Novel in Progress. Monterey: 1990. V. 46

NORMAN, HASKELL F.

The Haskell F. Norman Library of Science and Medicine. San Francisco: 1990. V. 46

NORMAN, MARK WILLIAM

A Popular Guide to the Geology of the Isle of Wight. 1887. V. 38

A Popular Guide to the Geology of the Isle of Wight... Ventnor: 1887. V. 40

NORMAN, ROBERT

The New Attractive. London: 1592. V. 38

NORMAN, SIDNEY

Northwest Mines Handbook. Spokane: 1918. V. 38

NORMAN, SYLVA

Contemporary Essays 1933. London: 1933. V. 37

NORMANBY, CONSTANTINE HENRY PHIPPS, 1ST MARQUIS OF 1797-1863

The Contrast. London: 1832. V. 41

Matilda; a Tale of the Day. London: 1825. V. 39; 42

A Voyage Towards the North Pole Undertaken by His Majesty's Command. London: 1774. V. 42

A Voyage Towards the North Pole Undertaken by His Majesty's Command 1773. Dublin: 1775. V. 42

Yes and No: a Tale of the Day. London: 1828. V. 41

NORMAND, CHARLES

Le Guide de l'Ornemaniste ou de l'Ornament Pour la Decoration des Batimens... Paris: 1826. V. 38

Recueil Varie de Plans et de Facades. Paris: 1815. V. 39

NORMAND, LOUIS MARIE

Paris Moderne, ou Choix de Maisons Construites dans les Nouveaux Quartiers de la Capitale et dans ses Environs. Liege. V. 39

NORMINGTON, THOMAS

The Lancashire and Yorkshire Railway. Manchester & London: 1898. V. 38

NORRIS, CHARLES 1779-1858

An Account of Tenby, Containing an Historical Sketch of the Place... London: 1820. V. 41

Etchings of Tenby... London: 1812. V. 37; 39

NORRIS, CHARLES G.

Seed. A Novel of Birth Control. Garden City & New York: 1930. V. 41

NORRIS, EDWIN

The Ancient Cornish Drama. Oxford: 1859. V. 42; 46

Memoir on the Scythic Version of the Behistun Inscription. London: 1853. V. 37

NORRIS, FRANK 1870-1902

Blix. New York: 1899. V. 43

NORRIS, FRANK 1870-1902 continued

The Epic of the Wheat. The Octopus. A Story of California. New York: 1901. V. 39

Frank Norris: Collected Letters. San Francisco: 1986. V. 42; 45; 46

The Letters of Frank Norris. San Francisco: 1956. V. 38; 42; 46

A Man's Woman. New York: 1900. V. 39

McTeague. New York: 1889. V. 39

McTeague. New York: 1899. V. 38; 39; 40; 44

McTeague a Story of San Francisco. Chicago: 1899. V. 37

Moran of the Lady Letty. New York: 1898. V. 39

The Octopus. New York: 1901. V. 40

The Octopus. New York: 1901. V. 42; 46

Vandover and the Brute. Garden City: 1914. V. 37; 43

Vandover and the Brute. New York: 1914. V. 46

Argonaut Manuscript Limited Edition of Frank Norris's Works. Garden City: 1928. V. 42

Works. Garden City: 1928. V. 42

NORRIS, GEORGE W.

The Early History of Medicine in Philadelphia. Philadelphia: 1886. V. 37

NORRIS, H. F.

Valuable Information About Napa County, California . . . Napa: 1885. V. 41

NORRIS, HENRY HANDLEY 1771-1850

A Respectful Letter to the Earl of Liverpool, K.G. London: 1822. V. 42

NORRIS, ISAAC

The Journal of . . . During a Trip to Albany in 1745, and an Account of a Treaty Held thre in October of that Year. Philadelphia: 1867. V. 40

NORRIS, J. W.

Norris' Chicago Directory for 1848-49. Chicago: 1848. V. 37

NORRIS, JOHN

An Account of Reason and Faith in Relation to the Mysteries of Christianity. London: 1697. V. 39

An Account of Reason and Faith. London: 1728. V. 43

A Collection of Miscellanies; Consisting of Poems, Essays, Discourses and Letters. London: 1692. V. 38; 42; 45

A Collection of Miscellanies: Consisting of Poems, Essays, Discourses and Letters. London: 1706. V. 42

A Collection of Miscellanies: Consisting of Poems, Essays, Discourses and Letters. Occasionally Written . . . Oxford: 1687. V. 37

The Theory and Regulation of Love. Oxford: 1688. V. 37

Treatises Upon Several Subjects: viz. Reason and Religion, or the Grounds and Measures of Devotion. Reflections Upon the Conduct of Human Life. The Charge of Schism Continued. Two Treatises Concerning Divine Light. Spiritual Counsel, or the Fathers . . . London: 1698. V. 41

NORRIS, KATHLEEN

The Works. Garden City: 1920. V. 42

NORRIS, LESLIE

Islands off Maine. (Cranberry Isle: 1977). V. 37

Poems. London: 1946. V. 46

NORRIS, MARIA

Life and Times of Madame de Stael. London: 1853. V. 39; 41; 43; 45

NORRIS, RICHARD

An American Text-Book of Obstetrics. Philadelphia: 1895. V. 42

Minutes Taken At A Court-Martial, Assembled on Board His Majesty's Ship Torbay . . . Being an Enquiry into the Conduct of Captain Richard Norris, in the Engagement Between the English Fleet . . . and the United Fleet . . . (with) Appendix . . . London: 1745. V. 41

NORRIS, ROBERT

Memoirs of the Reign of Bossa Ahadee, King of Dahomy, An Inland Country of Guiney. London: 1789. V. 41

NORRIS, THADDEUS

The American Angler's Book. Philadelphia: 1864. V. 37

NORRIS, THOMAS WAYNE

A Descriptive & Priced Catalogue of Books, Pamphlets and Maps Relating to the History, Literature and Printing of California and the Far West, Formerly the Collection of . . . Oakland: 1948. V. 38; 46

A Descriptive and Priced Catalogue of Books, Pamphlets, and Maps Relating Directly or Indirectly to the History, Literature and Printing of California and the Far West. San Francisco: 1948. V. 38

NORRIS, W.

Modern Steam Wagons. London: 1906. V. 38

NORRIS, WILLIAM

The Hunterian Oration Delivered Before the Royal College of Surgeons on Friday Feb. 14, 1817. London: 1817. V. 44; 45; 46

NORSE Fairy Tales. London: 1910. V. 45

NORSINI, CARLO FILIPPO

Clemente XI. Sonetti Dedicata alla Santita Sua. Florence: 1709. V. 38

NORTH, A. J.

Nests and Eggs of Birds Found Breeding in Australia. Melbourne: 1985. V. 37

THE NORTH-AMERICAN and the West-Indian Gazeteer. London: 1776. V. 38; 40; 42; 46

THE NORTH-AMERICAN and the West-Indian Gazeteer. Containing an Authentic Description of the Colonies and Islands in that part of the Globe, Shewing their Situation, Climate, Soil, Produce, and Trade . . . Illustrated with Maps. London: 1778. V. 37; 38

THE NORTH-AMERICAN and the West-Indian Gazetteer. London: 1778. V. 38

NORTH AMERICAN LAND CO.

Observations on the North-American Land Company, Lately Instituted in Philadelphia. London: 1796. V. 42

Plan of Association of the North American Land Co. Philadelphia: 1795. V. 37; 38

NORTH AMERICAN MINING CO.

For Gold and Silver Mining in Nevada and Other Sections of the United States. Chaprter Perpetual. Capital. $1,000,000 . . . Philadelphia: 1865. V. 42

NORTH American Tourist. New York: 1839. V. 38

NORTH AMERICAN TRANSPORTATION & TRADING COMPANY

Standard Price List of the North American Transportation and Trading Company for the Present Season, 1903. Council City: 1903. V. 39

THE NORTH British Review. Edinburgh: 1844-Aug. 1854. V. 43
THE NORTH British Review. Edinburgh: 1851-71. V. 38

NORTH CAROLINA

Colonial Records of North Carolina. Raleigh: 1963-84. V. 44

James Sprunt: A Tribute from the City of Wilmington. Raleigh: 1925. V. 37

NORTH CAROLINA. CONSTITUTION

Constitution of the State of North Carolina, Together with the Ordinances and Resolutions of the Constitutional Convention. Raleigh: 1868. V. 37; 39; 45

NORTH CAROLINA. GENERAL ASSEMBLY - 1862

Journal of the Senate of the General Assembly of the State of North Carolina, at its Second Extra Session, 1861. (with) The House of Commons of the General Assembly of the State of North Carolina, at its Second Extra Session, 1861. Raleigh: 1862. V. 38

NORTH CAROLINA. GENERAL ASSEMBLY - 1864

Executive and Legislative Documents, Extra Sessions 1863-64. Raleigh: 1864. V. 38

Journal of the Senate and House of Commons or 1863-64. V. 38

NORTH CAROLINA. GENERAL ASSEMBLY. HOUSE OF COMMONS

Journal of the House of Commons of North Carolina, at Its Session 1862-1863. Raleigh: 1862. V. 42

Journal of the House of Commons of the General Assembly of the State of North Carolina, at Its Second Extra Session, 1861. Raleigh: 1862. V. 42

NORTH CAROLINA. GENERAL ASSEMBLY. SENATE

Journal of the Senate of the General Assembly of the State of North Carolina, At Its Second Extra Session, 1861. Raleigh: 1981. V. 42

NORTH CAROLINA LAND COMPANY

A Statistical and Descriptive Account of the Several Counties of the State of North Carolina, United States of America. Raleigh: 1869. V. 45

NORTH CAROLINA. LAWS, STATUTES, ETC.

A Collection of the Statutes of the Parliament of England in Force in the State of North Carolina Published According to a Resolve of the General Assembly by Francois-Xavier Martin, Esq. New Bern: 1792. V. 45

Laws of the State of North Carolina. Published According to Act of Assembly by James Iredell . . . Edenton: 1791. V. 45

The Public Acts of the General Assembly of North Carolina. New Bern: 1804. V. 45

NORTH CAROLINA. LAWS, STATUTES, ETC. - 1863

Laws of the Extra Sessions of the General Assembly of the State of North Carolina 1863-64. Raleigh: 1863-64. V. 38

THE NORTH Country Angler; or, The Art of Angling as Practised in the Northern Countries of England. London: 1817. V. 39; 40; 43; 45

NORTH Dakota. A Few Facts Concerning Its Resources and Advantages. Bismarck: 1892. V. 42

NORTH Dakota, A Guide to the Northern Prairie State. Fargo: 1938. V. 43

NORTH Dakota History. Bismarck: 1926-82. V. 40

NORTH DAKOTA. LAWS, STATUTES, ETC. - 1890

Laws Passed at the First Session of the Legislative Assembly of the State of North Dakota. Bismarck: 1890. V. 40

NORTH DAKOTA STOCK GROWERS' ASSOCIATION

Brand Book of the North Dakota Stock Growers' Association for 1892. Mandan: 1892. V. 40; 45

NORTH, DANBY

The Mildmayes or the Clergyman's Secret. London: 1856. V. 46

NORTH, EDWARD PAYSON

Memoir of Edward Payson North . . . N.P.: 1812. V. 42

NORTH, ELISHA

A Treatise on a Malignant Epidemic, Commonly Called Spotted Fever . . . New York: 1811. V. 41

A NORTH Extraordinary: Written By a Young Scotsman, Now a Volunteer in the Corsican Service. Corte: 1769. V. 41

NORTH, I. W.

A Week in the Isles of Scilly. Penzance: 1850. V. 42; 45

NORTH, J. D.

Richard of Wallingford. Oxford: 1976. V. 38

NORTH, JOHN

Practical Observations on Convulsions of Infants. London: 1826. V. 40

NORTH, JOSEPH

Men in the Ranks. The Story of 12 Americans in Spain. New York: 1919. V. 45

NORTH, MARIANNE

Recollections of a Happy Life: Autobiography. (with) Some Further Recollections . . . London: 1893. V. 38

NORTH Pacific Coast. a Semi-Monthly Journal. New Tacoma: 1879-81. V. 41; 43

NORTH, ROBERT

The Gentleman Accomptant. London: 1721. V. 40

NORTH, ROGER 1653-1734

The Autobiography. London: 1887. V. 37; 39

A Discourse of Fish and Fish-Ponds. London: 1713. V. 38; 39; 40; 43; 44; 45

Examen; or, an Enquiry into the Credit and Veracity of a Pretended Complete History. London: 1740. V. 41

The Lives of Francis North, Baron Guilford . . . Sir Dudley North and John North. London: 1826. V. 41

NORTH, SAMUEL

The Family Physician and Guide to Health, Together with Some Remarks on Surgery . . . Waterloo: 1830. V. 42; 45; 46

NORTH, STERLING

The Pedro Gorino The Adventures of a Negro Sea Captain in Africa and on the Seven Seas in His Attempts to Found an Ethiopian Empire. Boston: 1929. V. 37; 40

NORTH, THOMAS

Five Years in Texas; or, What You Did Not Hear During the War from January 1861 to January 1865. Cincinnati: 1870. V. 45; 46

Five Years in Texas. Cincinnati: 1871. V. 38; 39; 41

NORTH-WEST American Water Boundary. Correspondence Respecting the Award of the Emperor of Germany in the Matter of the Boundary Line (etc.). London: 1873. V. 46

NORTHALL, G. F.

A Warwickshire Word Book Comprising Obsolescent and Dialect Words, Colloquialisms, etc . . . London: 1896. V. 38

NORTHALL, JOHN

Travels through Italy. London: 1766. V. 42

NORTHALL, W. K.

Life and Recollections of Yankee Hill; Together with Anecdotes and Incidents of His Travells. New York: 1850. V. 43

NORTHALL, WILLIAM KNIGHT

Before and Behind the Curtain or Fifteen Years' Observations Among the Theatres of New York. New York: 1851. V. 46

NORTHAMPTON ASSOCIATION OF EDUCATION & INDUSTRY

Social Reform: or an Appeal in Behalf of Association, Based Upon the Principles of a Pure Christianity. Northampton: 1844. V. 44

NORTHAMPTON, HENRY HOWARD, EARL OF 1540-1614

A Defensative Against the Poyson of Supposed Prophecies. London: 1620. V. 43

NORTHAMPTON, MASSACHUSETTS

Memorial to the 27th Congress from Inhabitants of Northampton, Massachusetts. Northhampton: 1842. V. 37

NORTHAMPTON, SPENCER COMPTON, MARQUIS OF

The Tribute: a Collection of Miscellaneous Unpublished Poems by Various Authors. London: 1837. V. 46

NORTHCLIFFE, ALFRED C.

Motors and Motor-Driving. London: 1906. V. 37

NORTHCOTE, J. SPENCER

Roma Sotterranea, or an Account of the Roman Catacombs Especially of the Cemetery of St. Callixtus . . . London: 1879. V. 42

NORTHCOTE, JAMES

The Artist's Book of Fables. London: 1845. V. 40; 41

Memoirs of Sir Joshua Reynolds, Knt. London: 1813-15. V. 40; 43

One Hundred Fables, Original and Selected . . . London. V. 42

One Hundred Fables. London: 1828. V. 38; 39; 42

One Hundred Fables. London: 1828-33. V. 40; 46

One Hundred Fables. London: 1829/33. V. 42; 46

NORTHEAST DRAMA INSTITUTE. RESEARCH STUDIO

Designs on Chinese Opera Costumes. Peking: 1957. V. 40

NORTHEN, WILLIAM J.

Men of Mark in Georgia. Atlanta: 1907. V. 42; 44

NORTHERN California, a Description of Its Soil, Climate, Productions, Markets, Occupied and Unoccupied Lands. Sacramento: 1885. V. 38

NORTHERN Iowa: Containing Hints and Information of Value to Emigrants. By a Pioneer. Dubuque: 1858. V. 38

NORTHERN Lights. V. 42

NORTHERN Numbers - Being Representative Selections from Certain Living Scottish Poets. Edinburgh & London: 1920. V. 45

NORTHERN PACIFIC RAILROAD

Guide to the Northern Pacific Railroad Land's in Minnesota. New York: 1872. V. 42

Land Department of the Northern Pacific Railroad Company Bureau of Immigration for Soldiers and Sailors. New York?: 1871. V. 42

The Northern Pacific Railroad: Its Route, Resources, Progress and Business. The New Northwest and Its Great Thoroughfare. Philadelphia: 1870. V. 42

The Northern Pacific Railroad's Land Grant and the Future Business of the Road. Philadelphia: 1870. V. 42

Northern Pacific Railroad. Its Character and Importance to the Government. Fort Keogh: 1880. V. 42

People's Pacific Railroad Company. Charter, Organization, Address of the President . . . with By-Laws of the Board of Commissioners. Boston: 1860. V. 42

Report of Edwin F. Johnson, Engineer-in-Chief to the Board of Directors Nov. 1867. Hartford: 1867. V. 42

Report of the Chief Engineer on the Unfinished Portion of the Northern Pacific Railroad, Made to the President of the Company April 27, 1874. New York?: 1874. V. 42

Settler's Guide to Oregon and Washington Territory and to the Lands of the Northern Pacific Railroad on the Pacific Slope. N.P.: 1872. V. 42

Special Report of a Reconnoissance of the Route for the Northern Pacific Railroad Between Lake Superior and Puget Sound, Via the Columbia River Made in 1869. Philadelphia: 1869. V. 42

NORTHERN PACIFIC RAILROAD CO.

Alice's Adventures in the New Wonderland, Yellowstone National Park. Chicago: 1884. V. 43

Memorial of the Board of Direction of the Company, Communications from Lieut. Gen'l. Grant, Brevet Maj. Gen'l Meigs, Q.M.G. and Brevet Gen'l. Ingalls, A.Q.M. and Report of the Engineer in Chief. Hartford: 1867. V. 40

The Northern Pacific Railroad; Its Land Grant, Resources, Traffic and Tributary Country. Philadelphia: 1873. V. 43

Northern Pacific Railroad: Opening Excursion (with) List of Guests, August, 1883. Portland: 1883. V. 38

Report of the President and Directors of the Northern Pacific Railroad Co to the Stockholders 27th, 1876. New York: 1876. V. 38

Northern Pacific Railroad: Report of the President. New York: 1883. V. 38

NORTHERN PACIFIC RAILROAD COMPANY

Charter of the Northern Pacific Railroad Co., Organization, Proceedings, By-Laws, and Appendix. Boston: 1865. V. 37

The Northern Pacific Railraod; Its Route, Resources, Progress and Business. Philadelphia: 1871. V. 37

The Northern Pacific Railroad. Sketch of Its History . . . and a Description . . . of the Regions Traversed by It . . . by a Member of the Chicago Press. New York: 1882. V. 37

Saint Paul and the Northern Pacific Railway. Grand Opening, September, 1883. St. Paul: 1883. V. 37

Tacoma, The Pacific Terminus of the Northern Pacific Railroad. Tacoma: 1884. V. 37

NORTHERN Pacific Tour. From the Lakes and Mississippi River to the Pacific Including Puget Sound and Alaska. 1888. V. 38

THE NORTHERN Poetical Keepsake . . . Newcastle-upon-Tyne: 1856. V. 39

NORTHERN Regions; or, a Relation of Uncle Richard's Voyages for the Discovery of a North-West Passage and an Account of the Overland Journies of Other Enterprizing Travellers. London: 1825. V. 45

THE NORTHERN Traveller, Containing the Hudson River Guide and Tour to the Springs, Lake George, and Canada. New York: 1844. V. 41; 45

NORTHLEIGH, JOHN

Topographical Descriptions: with Historico-Political and Medico-Physical Observations . . . London: 1702. V. 44

NORTHMORE, THOMAS

Washington, or Liberty Restored. Baltimore: 1809. V. 44

NORTHROP, CLAUDIAN BIRD

Southern Odes, by the Outcast, a Gentleman of South Carolina. Charleston: 1861. V. 44

NORTHROP, JOHN WORRELL

Chronicles from the Diary of a War Prisoner in Andersonville and Other Military Prisons of the South in 1864. V. 42

Chronicles from the Diary of a War Prisoner in Andersonville and Other Military Prisons of the South in 1864. Wichita: 1904. V. 39; 42; 44

NORTHROP, NIRA B.

Pioneer History of Medina County. Medina: 1861. V. 40; 44

NORTHUMBERLAND, ALGERNON PERCY, 4TH DUKE OF 1792-1865

Descriptive Catalogue of a Cabinent of Roman Family Coins Belonging to His Grace the Duke of Northumberland. London: 1856. V. 40

NORTHUMBERLAND, ELIZABETH PERCY, DUCHESS OF

A Short Tour Made in the Year One Thousand Seven Hundred and Seventy One. London: 1775. V. 37; 38; 39; 40; 45

NORTHWEST Iowa. Fair, Fresh and Fruitful. Fort Dodge: 1895. V. 38

NORTHWOOD, J. D'A.

Familiar Hawaiian British Birds. London: 1920. V. 37

NORTON, A.

Ordeal in Otherwhere. 1964. V. 44

The X Factor. 1965. V. 44

NORTON, A. BANNING

A History of the Western Reserve. Chicago: 1910. V. 45

NORTON, ANDREWS

A Review of the Character and Writings of Lord Byron. London: 1826. V. 44

A Statement of Reasons for Not Believing the Doctrines of Unitarians, Concerning the Nature of God, and the Person of Christ. Cambridge & Boston: 1833. V. 43

NORTON, C. B.

Treasures of Art, Industry and Manufacture Represented in the American Centennial Exhibition at Philadelphia 1876. Buffalo: (1877). V. 37

NORTON, CAROLINE ELIZABETH SARAH SHERIDAN 1808-1877

Aunt Carry's Ballads for Children. London: 1847. V. 38; 42

The Coquette, and Other Tales and Sketches, in Prose and Verse. London: 1835. V. 44

The Dream and Other Poems. London: 1841. V. 46

The Dream and other Poems. London: 1840. V. 37

Lost and Saved. London: 1863. V. 37

Some Unrecorded Letters of Caroline Norton in the Altschul Collection of Yale University. 1934. V. 39

Stuart of Dunleath. A story of modern times. London: 1851. V. 37

NORTON, CHARLES

American Breech Loading Small Arms, a Description of Late Inventions Including Gatling Gun . . . Cartridges. New York: 1872. V. 39

NORTON, CHARLES ELIOT 1827-1908

Considerations on Some Recent Social Theories. Boston: 1853. V. 37; 39; 41

The Poet Gray as a Naturalist. Boston: 1903. V. 44

A Review of a Translation into Italian of the Commentary by Benvenuto da Imola on the Divina Commedia. Cambridge: 1861. V. 44

NORTON, E. F.

The Fight for Everest: 1924. London: 1925. V. 42; 46

The Fight for Everest, 1924. New York: 1925. V. 41; 44; 46

NORTON, FRANCIS L.

Cuba . . . To the Honorable Charles Sumner, United States Senator. New York: 1873. V. 42

NORTON, FRANK

Frank Leslie's Historical Register of the United States Centennial exposition, 1876. New York: 1877. V. 39

NORTON, FREDERICK JOHN

A Descriptive Catalogue of Printing in Spain and Portugal, 1501-1520. Cambridge: 1978. V. 37; 42; 46

A Descriptive catalogue of printing in Spain and Portugal 1501-20. Cambridge: (1978). V. 37

Italian Printers 1501-1520. London: 1958. V. 39

Printing in Spain 1501-1520. London: 1966. V. 39

NORTON, H. W.

Calcutta to Liverpool by China, Japan and America, in MDCCCLXXVII. London: 1881. V. 38

NORTON, HARRY J.

A Bird's-Eye View of the Black Hills Gold Mining Region. New York: 1879. V. 37; 40; 43

NORTON, HERMAN

Record of Facts Concerning the Presecutions at Maderia in 1843 and 1846 . . . New York: 1849. V. 45

NORTON, JOHN

Abel Being Dead Yet Speaketh; or, the Life and Death of that Deservedly Famous Man of God, Mr. John Cotton, Late Teacher of the Church of Christ. London: 1658. V. 42; 44

An Account of Remarkable Cures, Performed by the Use of Maredant's Antiscorbutic Drops, Prepared by John Norton, Suregon, in Golden Square. London: 1774. V. 38

Directions for Taking the Drops. London: 1780. V. 42

The Heart of New England Rent at the Blasphemies of the Present Generation. London: 1660. V. 40

The Journal of Major John Norton, 1816. Toronto: 1970. V. 45

NORTON, LEWIS A.

Life and Adventures of Col. L. A. Norton. Oakland: 1887. V. 37; 39; 40; 41; 43; 45

NORTON, MARY

The Borrowers. The Borrowers Afield. The Borrowers Afloat. The Borrowers Aloft. New York: 1953-61. V. 42

NORTON, OLIVER WILLCOX

The Attack and Defense of Little Round Top, Gettysburg, July 2, 1863. New York: 1913. V. 42; 43

NORTON, RICHARD

Bernini and Other Studies in the History of Art. New York: 1914. V. 43

A History of Gold Snuff Boxes. London: 1938. V. 37; 39

NORTON-SMITH, J.

Bodleian Library MS Fairfax 16. London: 1979. V. 39

NORTON, WILLIS H.

Biographical Sketches of Eminent Persons, Whose Portraits form Part of the Duke of Dorset's Collection at Knole. London: 1795. V. 41

NORTON'S Literary Almanac, . . . 1852 and Norton's Literary Register . . . 1853 & 1854. New York: 1851/53/54. V. 42

NORVELL, LIPSCOMB, MRS.

King's Highway, The Great Strategic Military Highway of America, El Camino Real, the Old San Antonio Road. N.P.: 1945. V. 45

King's Highway: The Great Strategic Military Highway of America, El Camino Real, The Old San Antonio Road. N.P.: 1945. V. 37

NORWOOD, C. W.

Sholes Georgia State Gazetteer and Business Directory for 1879 & 1880. Atlanta: 1879. V. 45

NORWOOD, J. G.

Illinois Geological Survey . . . Chicago: 1857. V. 42

NORWOOD, RICHARD

The Seamans Practice Containing a Fundamental in Navigation, Experimentally Verified . . . London: 1676. V. 46

NORWOOD, THOMAS MANSON

The Texas Pacific Railway Contrasted with a Real Southern Pacific R. R. Along the Thirty Second Parallel of Latitude. N.P.: 1878. V. 38

The Texas Pacific Railway. Washington: 1878. V. 44

NOSHPITZ, JOSEPH D.

Basic Handbook of Child Psychiatry. New York: 1979/87. V. 43

NOSHY, IBRAHIM

The Arts in Ptolemaic Egypt. London: 1937. V. 40; 44

NOSPHPITZ, JOSEPH D.

Basic Handbook of Child Psychiatry. New York: 1979. V. 45

THE NOSTITZ Papers, Notes on Watermarks Found in the German Imperial Archives of the 17th and 18th Centuries and Essays Showing the Evolution of a Number of Watermarks. Hilversum: 1956. V. 38; 41

NOSTRADAMUS, MICHAEL

The True Prophecies or Prognostications of Michael Nostradamus, Physician . . . London: 1672. V. 42

NOSTREDAME, JEAN DE

Le Vite Delli Piv Celebri et Antichi Primi Poeti Provenzali. Lyons: 1575. V. 37

NOTES and Observations on the Bill Supplementary to the 'Act for the Final Adjustment of Land Titles in the State of Louisiana and Territory of Missouri. Washington: 1816. V. 40

NOTES on California. Written for a Class of Young Pupils. San Jose: 1880. V. 39

NOTES on the Surgery of the War in the Crimea, With Remarks on the Treatment of Gunshot Wounds. Philadelphia: 1862. V. 40

NOTHING But Leaves. A Poem. Philadlephia: 1868. V. 45

NOTICE About the Artificial Port of Ponta Delgada. Azores: 1876. V. 40

NOTICES and Illustrations of the Costume, Processional Pagentry &c . . . Norwich: 1850. V. 44

NOTICES of East Florida, with an Account of the Seminole Nation of Indians. Charleston: 1822. V. 45

NOTICIAS e Avisos de Interesse Mercantile, Extrahidos de Documentos Officiaes, Sobre a California e Susas Minas de Ouro . . . Porto: 1849. V. 40

NOTITIA Utraque Cum Orientis Tum Occidentis Ultra Arcadia Honoriique Caesarum Tempora . . . Basle: 1552. V. 38; 40

NOTLE, VINCENT

Fifty Years in Both Hemispheres or, Reminiscences of the Life of a Former Merchant. New York: 1854. V. 46

NOTLEY, FRANCES ELIZA MILLETT

Family Pride. London: 1871. V. 44

NOTMAN, WILLIAM

Portrait of a Period: a Collection of Notman Photographs, 1856-1915. Montreal: 1967. V. 45

NOTT, CHARLES C.

Sketches in Prison Camps . . . New York: 1865. V. 42; 43; 44

NOTT, J. C.

Indigenous Races of the Earth; or New Chapters of Ethnological Inquiry. Philadelphia: 1857. V. 41

Indigenous Races of the Earth; or, New Chapters of Ethnological Enquiry . . . Philadelphia & London: 1857. V. 42

NOTT, J. FORTUNE

Wild Animals in Captivity. New York: 1887. V. 46

NOTT, JOHN

Alonzo; or, the Youthful Solitaire. London: 1772. V. 40; 42

The Cooks and Confectioners Dictionary. London: 1726. V. 42

Of the Hotwell Waters, Near Bristol. Bristol: 1793. V. 46

NOTT, JOSIAH CLARK

Types of Mankind; or, Ethnological Researches . . . Philadelphia: 1854. V. 45

Types of Mankind: or, Ethnological Researches, Based Upon the Ancient Monuments, Paintings, Sculptures and Crania of Races, and Upon their Natural, Geographical, Philological and Biblical History. London: 1854. V. 38

NOTT, SAMUEL

Slavery and the Remedy; or, Principles and Suggestions for a Remedial Code. New York: 1857. V. 44

NOTT, STANLEY CHARLES

A Catalogue of Rare Chinese Jade Carvings. Palm Beach: 1940. V. 38; 41; 43

Chinese Jade Throughout Ages: a Review of Its Characteristics, Decoration, Folklore, and Symbolism. London: 1936. V. 38; 39; 40; 42; 43; 45

Chinese Jade Throughout the Ages. London: 1962. V. 40

Chinese Jade Throughout the Ages. A review of its Characteristices, Decoration, Folklore and Symbolism. With an introduction by Sir Cecil Harcourt-Smith. London: (1936). V. 37

NOTTINGHAM CASTLE MUSEUM AND ART GALLERY

Catalogue of the Special Exhibition of Art Bookbindings. Nottingham: 1891. V. 41

NOTTINGHAM, HENEAGE FINCH, 1ST EARL OF 1621-1682

The Arguments of the Right Honourable, the Late Lord Chancellor Nottingham, Upon Which He Made the Decree in the Cause Between the Honourable Charles Howard . . . (and) Henry Late Duke of Norfolk. London: 1685. V. 45

The Indictment, Arraignment, Tryal and Judgment at Large of Twenty-Nine Regicides, the Murtherers of His Most Sacred Majesty Charles the First of Glorious Memory, Begun at Hick's Hall on Tuesday the Ninth of October 1660. London: 1713. V. 43

NOUET, JACQUES

An Answer to the Provinciall Letters Published by the Jansenists, Under the Name of Lewis Montalt, Against the Doctrine of the Jesuits and School-Divines. Paris: 1659. V. 41

NOURSE, J. E.

American Explorations in the Ice Zones. Boston: 1884. V. 43

Narrative of the Second Arctic Expedition Made by Charles F. Hall . . . During the Years 1864-69. Washington: 1879. V. 37; 38

NOVA SCOTIA. DEPARTMENT OF MINES - 1874

Report of the Department of Mines, Nova Scotia. For the Year 1874. Halifax: 1875. V. 37

NOVA SCOTIA INSTITUTE OF NATURAL SCIENCE

Transactions of . . . Halifax: 1863-66. V. 38

NOVAK, B.

Nineteenth Century American Painting. London: 1986. V. 39

NOVAK, JOSEPH

The Future is Ours, Comrade. New York: 1960. V. 37

THE NOVELIST'S Library. London: 1821-24. V. 38

NOVELLAS Espanolas. Or, Moral and Entertaining Novels . . . London: 1747. V. 44

NOVELLUS, JACOBUS

Volumen Statutorum, Legum, ac Iurium D. Venetorum . . . Venice: 1564. V. 40

NOVERRE, JEAN GEORGES

Letters on Dancing and Ballets . . . London: 1930. V. 39

Lettres sur la Danse, et sur les Ballets. Stutgard: 1760. V. 45; 46

NOVISSIMA Canzone Al Sereniss. Sig. D. Giovanni D'Avstria Generale Dell' Armata Della Santissima Lega Sopra la Vittoria Seguita Contra l'Armata Turchesca, il VII. Giorno di Ottobre MCLXXI. Venice: 1571. V. 37

NOVOTNY, FRITZ

Gustav Klimt, with a Catalogue Raisonne of His Paintings. Boston: 1968. V. 44

Gustav Klimt. With a Catalogue Raisonne of His Paintings. London: 1968. V. 39

Gustav Klimt with a Catalogue Raisonne of His Paintings. Boston: 1975. V. 37; 43; 45; 46

NOWELL, THOMAS

An Answer to a Pamphlet, Entitled Pietas Oxoniensis, or a Full and Impartial Account of the Expulsion of Six Students from St. Edmund-Hall. Oxford: 1768. V. 44

NOWELL-USTICKE, GORDON W.

Rembrandt Etchings. The Distinguished Collection . . . formed by . . . New York: 1967-68. V. 43

NOWLIN, WILLIAM

The Bark Covered House, or Back in The Woods Again . . . Detroit: 1876. V. 42; 46

NOWROJEE, JEHANGEER

Journal of a Residence ot two years and a half in Great Britain. London: 1841. V. 37

NOY, WILLIAM 1577-1634

The Compleat Lawyer. London: 1661. V. 38; 40

The Grounds and Maxims of the English Laws. London: 1757. V. 45

The Grounds and Maxims and also an Analysis of the English Laws (with) A Treatise of Estates . . . London: 1794. V. 38; 40

The Grounds and Maxims and also an Analysis of the English Laws.. London: 1821. V. 40

Reports and Cases Taken in the Time of Queen Elizabeth, King James and King Charles (1559-1649) . . . London: 1656. V. 37; 38; 40

NOYES, ALVA J.

In the Land of the Chinook or the Story of Blaine County. Helena: 1917. V. 39; 42; 43; 44; 45

The Story of Ajax. Life in the Big Hole Basin . . . Helena: 1914. V. 37; 45

NOYES, CHARLES GOODWIN

Redwood and Lumbring in California Forests. San Francisco: 1884. V. 37

NOYES, DAVID

History of Norway; Comprising a Minute Account of Its First Settlement . . . Norway: 1852. V. 46

NOYES, HENRY D.

A Treatise Diseases of the Eye. New York: 1881. V. 41; 43

NOYES, HENRY E.

Genealogical Record of some of the Noyes Descendants of James, Nicholas and Peter Noyes. Boston: 1904. V. 37

NOYES, JOHN H.

Essays on Scientific Propagation. Oneida: 1872. V. 39

Male Continence. Onedida: 1872. V. 39

NOYES, JOHN HUMPHREY 1811-1886

The Berean; a Manual for the Help of Those Who Seek the Faith of the Primitive Church. Putney: 1847. V. 37; 40; 41; 43

History of American Socialisms. Philadlephia: 1870. V. 38; 39; 43

Home Talks. Oneida: 1875. V. 43; 44

NOYES, ROBERT

Distress. a Poem. Canterbury: 1782. V. 42

NOZICK, ROBERT

Philosophical Explanations. Cambridge: 1981. V. 45

NRIPENDRA NARAYANA BHUPA, MAHARAJAH OF COOCH BEHAR 1862-1911

Thirty-Seven Years of Big Game Shooting in Cooch Behar, the Duars, and Assam. A Rough Diary. London: 1908. V. 39

NROMAN, BENJAMIN M.

Rambles in Yucatan . . . New York: 1843. V. 44

NUCK, ANTONIUS

Adenographia Curiosa et Uteri Foeminei Anatome Nova. Lugduni Batavorum: 1691. V. 39

NUCLEAR Explosions and Their Effects. Delhi: 1958. V. 46

NUDELMAN, EDWARD D.

Jessie Willcox Smith: a Bibliography. Gretna: 1989. V. 41

NUGENT, CHRISTOPHER

An Essay on Hydrophobia; to Which is Prefixed the Case of a Person Who Was Bit by a Mad Dog; Had the Hydrophobia and Was Happily Cured. London: 1953. V. 43

NUGENT, ROBERT CRAGGS

Verses Addressed to the Queen with a New Year's Gift of Irish Manufacture. London: 1775. V. 40

NUGENT, ROBERT CRAGGS, LORD

Considerations Upon a Reduction of the Land Tax. London: 1749. V. 41; 42; 45

Farther Considerations Upon a Reduction of the Land-Tax; Together with a State of the Annual Supplies of the Sinking-Fund, and of the National Debt, at Various Future Periods and in Various Suppositions. London: 1751. V. 42

NUGENT, ROBERT NUGENT, EARL OF

An Essay on Happiness. London: 1737. V. 41

NUGENT, THOMAS

The Grand Tour, or a Journey Through the Netherlands, Germany, Italy, and France. London: 1756. V. 43

The Life of Benvenuto Cellini . . . London: 1771. V. 45

The New Pocket Dictionary of the French and English Languages. Lyons: 1781. V. 38

Travels through Germany . . . Observations on Arts and Antiquities. London: 1768. V. 37; 40

NUIX, JUAN

Reflexiones Impaarciales Sobre la Humanidad de Los Espanoles en Las Indias. Madrid: 1782. V. 38

NUMBER One Joy Street - No (sic) Fourteen Joy Street: a Medley of Prose and Verse for Boys and Girls. Oxford: 1923-36. V. 39

NUMBERS One-Four. English Text. With original lighographs by matisse, Leger, Miro, Kandinsky, Masson, Chagall, Klee, etc. Paris: 1937-39. V. 37

NUNES DA SILVA, MANUEL

Arte Minima, que Com Semibreve Prolacam Tratta em Tempo Breve, Os Modos da Maxima & Longa Sciencia da Musica. Lisbon: 1685. V. 38

NUNEZ CABECZA DE VACA, ALVAR, 16th century

The Narrative of Alvar Nunez Cabeca de Vaca. Washington: 1851. V. 44; 46

NUNEZ CABEZA DE VACA, ALVAR, 16th century

La Relacion Y Comentarios Del Gouernador Alvar Nunez Cabeca de Vaca, De Lo Acascido en Las Dos Jornadas Que Hizo a Las Indias. Valladolid: 1555. V. 40; 44

A Relation of Alvaro Nunez called Capo di Vauna . . . London. V. 40

Relation That Alvar Cabeca de Vaca Gave of What Befel the Armament in the Indias. San Francisco: 1929. V. 39; 40; 41; 42; 45; 46

NUNEZ CABEZA DE VACA, ALVAR, 16th century 16TH CENTURY

Relation of Alvar Nunez Cabeca de Vaca. New York: 1871. V. 41

NUNEZ DE CASTRO, ALONSO

Coronica de Los Senores Reyes de Castilla, Don Sancho el Deseado, Don Alonso el Octauo, Y Don Enrique Primo, En Que Se Refiere Todo Lo Sucedido en Los Reynos . . . Madrid: 1665. V. 40

NUNEZ, IGNACIO BENITO

Esquisses Historiques, Politiques et Statistiques, de Buenos-Ayres, des Autres Provinces Unies du Rio de la Plata . . . Paris: 1826. V. 38

NUNEZ, PEDRO JUAN d. 1602

Epitheta M. T. Ciceronis Collecta A. P. Ioanne. Venice: 1570. V. 40

NUNN, GEORGE E.

The Geographical Conceptions of Columbus . . . New York: 1924. V. 39

NUNN, JOHN

Narrative of the Wreck of the 'Favorite' on the Island of Desolation . . . London: 1850. V. 41; 42

NUNN, KENNETH S.

Whales, Dolphins and Porpoises. Berkeley & Los Angeles: 1966. V. 41

NUOVA Raccolta d'Autori, Che Trattano Del Moto Dell'Acque. Parma: 1766-68. V. 40

NUOVA Racolta di Fontane che si Vedano Nel'alms Citta di Roma, Tivoli e Frascati. Rome. V. 44

NUOVI Avisi dell'Indie di Portogallo . . . Venice: 1658. V. 45

NUR EL-DIN, M. A. A.

The Demotic Ostraca in the National Museum of Antiquities at Leiden. Leiden: 1974. V. 42

NURA

Nura's Garden of Betty & Booth. Text and 12 original lithographs by Nura. New York: 1935. V. 37

The Silver Bridge. Written, designed and illustrated with 7 original color lithographs by Nura. New York: (1937). V. 37

NURNBERG, WALTER

Words in Their Hands. London: 1964. V. 39

NURSE Lovechild's Legacy Being a Mighty Fine Collection of the Most Noble, Memorable and Veracious Nursery Rhymes . . . London: 1916. V. 46

THE NURSERY Navy. London: 1910. V. 39

NURSERY Rhymes. London: 1919. V. 46

THE NURSERY Story Book. London: 1864. V. 39

THE NURSERY Zoo. London: 1910. V. 39

NURSIE'S Little Rhyme Book. V. 44
NURSIE'S Little Rhyme Book. London. V. 43

NUSSEY, S. L.

Ye Quaint, An Omnium Gahterum. Potternewton Hall,: 1895. V. 40

NUTT, FREDERIC

The Complete Confectioner; or, The Whole Art of Confectionary . . . London: 1790. V. 42

The Complete Confectioner, or, the Whole Art of Confectionary Made Easy . . . New York: 1807. V. 37

NUTTALL, THOMAS

The Genera of North American Plants, and a Catalogue of the Species. Philadelphia: 1818. V. 38

An Introduction to Systematic and Physiological Botany. Boston & Cambridge: 1827. V. 38

A Journal of Travels into the Arkansas Territory, During the Year 1819. V. 40

A Journal of Travels into the Arkansas Territory during the Year 1819. Philadelphia: 1821. V. 37; 38; 39; 41; 45

A Manual of the Ornithology of the United States and of Canada: the Land Birds. Cambridge: 1832. V. 41

A Manual of the Ornithology of the United States and of Canada . . . the Water Birds. Boston: 1834. V. 40

Manual of the Ornithology of the U.S. and Canada. Boston: 1834-40. V. 39

The North American Sylva; or, a Description of the Forest Trees of the United States, Canada and Nova Scotia . . . Philadelphia: 1849. V. 45

NUTTALL, ZELIA

Codex Nuttall. Facsimile of an Ancient Mexican Codex Belonging to Lord Zouche of Harynworth, England. Cambridge: 1902. V. 42

The Fundamental Principles of Old and New World Civilizations . . . Cambridge: 1901. V. 44

New Light on Drake: a Collection of Documents Relating ot His Voyage of Circumnavigation 1577-1580. London: 1914. V. 45

NUTTER, M. E.

Carlisle in the Olden Time, a Series of Views of Ancient Public Buildings. Carlisle: 1835. V. 41

Carlisle in the Olden Time. London: 1835. V. 41

NUTTING, JUDGE

The History of One Day Out of Seventeen Thousand. Oswego: 1889. V. 45

NUTTING, M. ADELAIDE

A History of Nursing. New York: 1907-12. V. 41; 42

NUTTING, WALLACE

Furniture Treasury (Mostly of American Origin). New York: 1948. V. 40

Furniture of the Pilgrim Century. 1620-1720. Boston: 1921. V. 37

NYBERG, BJORN

The Return of Conan. New York: 1957. V. 41

NYE, EDGAR W.

Nye and Riley's Railway Guide. Chicago: 1888. V. 37

NYE, ELWOOD L.

Marching with Custer. Glendale: 1964. V. 37; 45

NYE, NATHANIEL

The Art of Gunnery. London: 1648. V. 44

NYE, THOMAS

Journal of Thomas Nye Written During a Journey Between Montreal and Chicago in 1837. New York: 1932. V. 38

Two Letters of Thomas Nye. Relating to a Journey from Montreal to Chicago in 1837. New York: 1931. V. 38

NYE, W. B.

The Generic Names of Moths of the World. London: 1957-58. V. 38

The Generic Names of Moths of the World. London: 1975-86. V. 37

NYE, WILLIAM F.

Sonora: Its Extent, Population, Natural Productions, Indian Tribes, Mines, Mineral Lands, etc., etc. San Francisco: 1861. V. 39

NYHOLM, JANET

From a Housewife's Diary. West Burke: 1978. V. 38

NYREN, JOHN

The Young Cricketer's Tutor. London: 1948. V. 38

NYS, JOANNES

Vita-et Miracula S.P. Dominici. Antwerp: 1611. V. 41

NYSTEL, OLE T.

Lost and Found. Or Three Months with the Wild Indians. Dallas: 1888. V. 44; 46

O

OAKES Ames: a Memoir With an Account of the Dedication of the Oakes Memorial Hall . . . Cambridge: 1883. V. 42

OAKES, HENRY

An Authentic Narrative of the Treatment of the English, Who Were Taken Prisoners on the Reduction of Bednore by Tippoo Saib; from the 28th of April 1783, the Day of Capitulation, to Their Englargement on the 25th of April, 1784. London: 1785. V. 39; 42; 44

OAKES, WILLIAM

Scenery of the White Mountains. Boston: 1848. V. 39; 41; 42; 43

Scenery of the White Mountains: with Sixteen Plates, From the Drawings of Isaac Sprague. Cambridge: 1848. V. 46

OAKESHOTT, GEORGE J.

Detail and Ornament of the Italian Renaissance. London: 1888. V. 41

OAKESHOTT, WALTER

Classical Inspiration in Medieval Art. London: 1959. V. 46

The Mosaics of Rome. 1967. V. 46

The Mosaics of Rome from the Third to the Fourteenth Centuries. Greenwich: 1967. V. 38; 42

The Mosaics of Rome from the Third to the Fourteenth Centuries. London: 1967. V. 42

Some Woodcuts by Hans Burgkmair. Oxford: 1960. V. 39; 45

The Two Winchester Bibles. Oxford: 1981. V. 39; 41; 44; 46

OAKEY, A. F.

Building a Home. New York: 1881. V. 42

OAKLAND, CHRISTOPHER

Anglorum Praelia . . . London: 1582. V. 37

OAKLAND COLLEGE

Catalogue of the Officers and Students of Oakland College, 1855-56. Natchez: 1856. V. 37

OAKLEIGH, THOMAS

The Oakleigh Shooting Code. London: 1836. V. 39

OAKLEY, EDWARD

The Magazine of Architectural Perspective and Sculpture in Five Parts. Westminster: 1733. V. 42

OAKLEY, OBADIAH

The Oregon Expedition of Obadiah Oakly (sic). New York: 1914. V. 41; 42

OAKLEY, PETER

Lost Property. London: 1987. V. 39

OAKLEY, VIOLET

The Holy Experiment. Philadelphia: 1922. V. 38; 42

OAKLY, OBADIAH

Expedition to Oregon . . . New York: 1914. V. 40; 45

The Oregon Expedition of Obadiah Oakly. New York: 1914. V. 39

OAKMOTE Hall; or the Adventures of Joe Rattler; with the Extraordinary Lives of Floss, Sharpwrit and a Policeman. London: 1853. V. 43

OAKS, GLADYS

Chinese White: Poems. New York: 1922. V. 41

OARIS, J. A.

A Treatise on Diet: with a view to establish, on practical grounds, a System of Rules for the Prevention and Cure of the Diseases incident to a Disordered State of the Digestive Funtions. London: 1828. V. 37

OASTLER, RICHARD

The Fleet Papers, being Letters to Thomas Thornill, Esq., from his Prisoner in the Fleet. With Occasional Communications from Friends. London: 1841-1843. V. 37

OATES, FRANK

Matebele Land and the Victoria Falls. London: 1881. V. 39; 41

Matebele Land and the Victoria Falls. London: 1889. V. 38; 41

OATES, J. C. T.

Cambridge University Press. A History from the Beginnings to the Copyright Act of Queen Anne. Cambridge: 1986. V. 39

A Catalogue of the Fifteenth Century Printed Books in the University Library Cambridge. Cambridge: 1954. V. 41

OATES, JOYCE CAROL 1938-

The Assassins: A Book of Poems. New York: 1975. V. 41

By the North Gate. New York: 1963. V. 37; 38; 39; 40; 42; 46

Cupid & Psyche. New York: 1970. V. 39

Cybele. Santa Barbara: 1979. V. 46

Daisy. Santa Barbara: 1977. V. 46

Do With Me What You Will. New York: 1973. V. 46

Dreaming America and Other Poems. New York: 1973. V. 39; 40

The Girl. A Short Story. Cambridge: 1974. V. 37

The Lamb of Abyssalia. (Cambridge): 1979. V. 37

Love and Its Derangmenets Poems. Baton Rouge: 1970. V. 46

Nightless Nights. New Hampshire: 1981. V. 40; 41; 42; 43; 44; 46

On Boxing. Garden City: 1987. V. 43

Queen of the Night. California. V. 42

Queen of the Night. 1979. V. 40

Queen of the Night. California: 1979. V. 41

Scenes from American Life: Contemporary Short Fiction. New York: 1973. V. 39

Season of Peril. Santa Barbara: 1977. V. 46

The Seduction and Other Stories. Los Angeles;: 1975. V. 43

Sentimental Education. Los Angeles: 1978. V. 42; 46

Them. New York: 1969. V. 39; 42

The Triumph of the Spider Monkey. Yellow Springs: 1974. V. 39

The Triumph of the Spider Monkey. Santa Barbara: 1976. V. 44

The Wheel of Love. London: 1971. V. 42

With Shuddering Fall. 1964. V. 42

With Shuddering Fall. New York: 1964. V. 44

Woman in the Death of the Soul. Toronto: 1970. V. 46

Women in Love and Other Poems . . . New York: 1968. V. 39

Wonderland. London: 1972. V. 41

OATES, STEPHEN B.

Confederate Cavalry West of the River. Austin: 1961. V. 44

OATES, TITUS

A True Narrative of the Horrid Plot and Conspiracy of the Popish Party Against the Life of His Sacred Majesty . . . London: 1679. V. 39

OATES, WILLIAM CALVIN

The War Between the Union and the Confederacy, and Its Lost Opportunities . . . New York: and Washington: 1905. V. 44

OATTS, L. B.

Proud Heritage. The Story of the Highland Light Infantry. Glasgow: 1952-61. V. 42

OAXACA. CONSTITUTION - 1825

Constitucion Politica del Estado Libre de Oajaca. Mexico: 1825. V. 38

OBAID-E ZAKANI

The Pious Cat. London: 1986. V. 40

O'BEGLEY, CONOR

The English Irish Dictionary . . . Paris: 1732. V. 42

O'BEIRNE, HARRY F.

Indian Territory: Its Chiefs, Legislators and Leading Men. Saint Louis: 1892. V. 42

O'BEIRNE, THOMAS LEWIS

A Short History of the Last Session of Parliament, with Remarks. London: 1780. V. 38

OBER, FREDERICK A.

Camps in the Caribbees: the Adventures of a Naturalist in the Lesser Antilles. Edinburgh: 1880. V. 45

In the Wake of Columbus. Boston: 1893. V. 38; 41; 42; 46

Travels in Mexico and Life Among the Mexicans. Boston: 1884. V. 44; 45

Travels in Mexico and Life Among the Mexicans. San Francisco,: 1884. V. 46

OBERHOLSER, HARRY C.

Bird Life of Texas. 1974. V. 39

The Bird Life of Texas. Austin: 1974. V. 37; 39; 40

The Bird Life of Texas. Austin & London: 1974. V. 42

OBERHOLTZER, ELLIS P.

Jay Cooke, Financier of the Civil War. Philadelphia: 1907. V. 39; 40

Philadelphia: a History of the City and Its People. Philadelphia. V. 41; 42

OBERLIN, JEREMIE JACQUES

Essai d'Annales De la Vie De Jean Gutenberg Inventeur de la Typographie. Strasbourg: 1801. V. 38

OBERSTE, WILLIAM H.

Texas Irish Empresarios and Their Colonies: Power and Hewetson, McMullen & McGloin, Refugio-San Patricio. Austin: 1953. V. 37; 38; 42; 44; 45

OBERSTEINER, HEINRICH

The Anatomy of the Central Nervous Organs in Health and Disease. Philadelphia: 1890. V. 42

OBERTHUR, C.

Etudes de Lepidopterologie Comparee. Rennes: 1904-25. V. 41

OBERVATIONS (sic) On, and Reasons Against Vacating the Bonds Taken by Her Majesty's Collector at Jamaica. London: 1711. V. 42

OBOOKIAH, HENRY

Memoirs of Henry Obookiah, a Native of Owhyhee and a Member of the Foreign Mission School. Elizabethtown: 1819. V. 37; 40; 45

Memoirs of Henry Obookiah, a Nataive of Owhyhee, and a Member of the Foreign Mission School; Who Died at Cornwall, Conn. Feb. 17, 1818, Aged 26 Years. New Haven: 1818. V. 37

OBREGON, BALTASAR DE

Obregon's History of the 16th Century Explorations in Western America Entitled 'Chorinicles, Commentary, or Relation of the Ancient and Modern Discoveries in New Spain and New Mexico, Mexico, 1584.' Los Angeles: 1928. V. 38

O'BRIEN, DILLON

The Dalys of Dalystown. Saint Paul: 1866. V. 39

O'BRIEN, DONOUGH

History of the O'Briens from Brian Boroimhe, A.D. 1000 to A.D. 1945. London: 1949. V. 37

O'BRIEN, EDNA

Girls in Their Married Bliss. London: 1964. V. 40

James and Nora. Northridge: 1981. V. 43

A Scandalous Woman - Stories. London: 1974. V. 45

O'BRIEN, ERIS

The Foundation of Australia, 1786-1800. London: 1937. V. 38

O'BRIEN, FITZ-JAMES

The Poems and Stories of Fitz-James O'Brien. Boston: 1881. V. 40

O'BRIEN, FLANN

An Beal Bocht . . . le Myles na gCopaleen. Dublin: 1941. V. 42; 46

The Dalkey Archive. London: 1964. V. 42; 46

The Hard Life. London: 1961. V. 46

The Poor Mouth. London: 1973. V. 37; 42

The Third Policeman. New York: 1967. V. 39

The Various Lives of Keats and Chapman and Brother. London: 1976. V. 46

O'BRIEN, GEORGE

The Economic History of Ireland in the Seventeenth Century. Dublin: 1919. V. 38

The Economic History of Ireland from the Union to the Famine. London: 1921. V. 37

O'BRIEN, HENRY

The Round Towers of Ireland. London: 1834. V. 38; 43

The Round Towers of Ireland. London: 1834. V. 38

The Round Towers of Ireland, or the History of the Guath-de-Danaans. London: 1898. V. 41; 45

The Round Towers of Ireland. London: 1989. V. 42

O'BRIEN, J.

J. O'Brien's Irish English Dictionary. Dublin: 1832. V. 38

O'BRIEN, JAMES

Hoovers' Millions and How He Made Them. New York: 1932. V. 38

A Irish Celts. A Cyclopedia of Race History. Detroit: 1884. V. 39

O'BRIEN, JOHN

Focaloir Gaoidhilge-Sax-Bhearla, or an Irish-English Dictionary. Paris: 1768. V. 45

O'BRIEN, M. B.

A Manual for Authors, Printers and Publishrs, Being a Guide in All Matters Pertaining or Incidental to Printing and Publishing. London: 1890. V. 38

O'BRIEN, PHILIP

T. E. Lawrence: a Bibliography. London: 1988. V. 40

T. E. Lawrence: A Bibliography. Winchester: 1988. V. 41

O'BRIEN, R. BARRY

Fifty Years of Concessions to Ireland, 1831-1881. London: (1882). V. 37

O'BRIEN, THOMAS, & CO.

Stoves, Chimney Pieces and Ranges. London: 1901-02. V. 37

O'BRIEN, TIM

Going After Cacciato. London: 1978. V. 44

Going After Cacciato. New York: 1978. V. 42; 43; 44; 45; 46

If I Die in a Combat Zone. London: 1973. V. 41; 46

If I Die in a Combat Zone. New York: 1973. V. 42; 43; 44

Northern Lights. New York: 1975. V. 37; 42; 44

The Nuclear Age. New York: 1985. V. 45

The Nuclear Age. Portland: 9181. V. 44

The Things they Carried. Boston: 1990. V. 44; 45

O'BRYEN, DENIS

A View of the Present State of Ireland, with an Account of the Origin and Progress of the Disturbances in that Country; and a Narrative of Facts, Addressed to the People of England. London: 1797. V. 39

O'BRYEN, DENNIS

A Defence of the Right Honourable the Earl of Shelburne, from the Reproaches of His Numerous Enemies . . . London: 1782. V. 46

OBSEQUIES, on the Unexemplar Champion of Chivalrie and Perfect Patern of True Prowesse, Arthur Lord Capell. London: 1649. V. 41

OBSERVATIONS Applying to Such Parts of the Fifth Report of the Commissioners of Military Enquiry, as Relate to the Patent Office of Apothecary-General to the Army. Southwark: 1808. V. 39

THE OBSERVATIONS Of Sir Richard Hawkins, Knt., in His Voyage into the South Sea in the Year 1593. London: 1847. V. 45

OBSERVATIONS on a Late Pamphlet, entitled 'Considerations Upon the Society or Order of the Cincinnati,' Clearly Evincing the Innocence and Propriety of that Honourable and Respectable Institution . . . Philadelphia: 1783. V. 37

OBSERVATIONS On a Letter by John Eardley-Wilmot, Esq. London: 1820. V. 43

OBSERVATIONS on, and Reasons Against Vacating the Bonds taken by Her Majesty's Collector at Jamaica. London: 1713. V. 37

OBSERVATIONS on Several Acts of Parliament, Passed in the 4th, 6th, and 7th Years of His Present Majesty's Reign, and also on the Conduct of the Officers of the Customs, Since Those Acts Were Passed and Board of Commissioners Appointed to Reside in . . . Boston: 1769. V. 37; 39

OBSERVATIONS on the Bedford Charity; in a Series of Letters That Were Signed Justus. London: 1761. V. 43

OBSERVATIONS on the Campaign in the Netherlands, Terminated by the Battle of Waterloos, June 18th, 1815. Hitchin: 1858. V. 41

OBSERVATIONS on the Case of the Northern Colonies. London: 1731. V. 41; 44

OBSERVATIONS on the Conduct of Great-Britain, in Respect to Foreign Affairs. In Which . . . the Measures of the Present Ministry (are) fully Vindicated. London: 1742. V. 41

OBSERVATIONS on the Conduct of Great Britain with Regard to Negociations and Other Transactions Abroad. London: 1729. V. 45

OBSERVATIONS on the Conduct of Mr. Fox, In the Impeachment of Mr. Hastings. London: 173. V. 41

OBSERVATIONS on the Fifth Report of the Commissioners of Military Enquiry and More Particularly on Those Parts of It Which Relate to the Surgeon General. London: 1808. V. 39

OBSERVATIONS on the Importance and Use of Theatres; Their Present Regulation, and Possible Improvements. London: 1759. V. 43

OBSERVATIONS on the Last Session of P--rl--m--nt. In a Letter from a Member to a Nobleman of Distinction. London: 1749. V. 41

OBSERVATIONS on the Late Treaty of Peace with France; so Far As It Relates to the Slave Trade, in a Letter to a Friend. London: 1814. V. 42

OBSERVATIONS on the Present Condition of Louisiana. Washington: 1865. V. 39

OBSERVATIONS on the Present Convention with Spain. London: 1739. V. 38

OBSERVATIONS on the Present State of Denmark, Russia and Switzerland. In a Series of Letters. London: 1784. V. 38; 41; 42; 44

OBSERVATIONS on the Real, Relative and Market Value, of the Turnpike Stock of the State of New York. New York: 1806. V. 42

OBSERVATIONS on the Runious Tendency of the Spitalfields Act to the Silk Manufactures of London: to Which is Added a reply to Mr. Hale's Appeal to the Public in Defence of the Act . . . London: 1822. V. 40

OBSERVATIONS on the Swedish History. London: 1743. V. 41; 43

OBSERVATIONS on the Trail by Jury: With Miscellaneous Remarks Concerning Legislation & Jurisprudence, & The Professors of the law; Also, Shewing the Dangerous Consequences of the Civil Polity of a State . . . By an American. Strasburg, (PA): 1803. V. 37; 38

OBSERVATIONS on the Treatment of Convicts in Ireland. London: 1862. V. 39

OBSERVATIONS on the Wisconsin Territory; Chiefly on the Part Called the 'Wisconsin Land District'. Philadelphia: 1838. V. 42

OBSERVATIONS Upon a Bill Entitled, An Act for Taking Away and Abolishing the Heritable Jurisdictions in that Part of Great Britain, Called Scotland, and for Restoring Such Jurisdictions to the Crown . . . Edinburgh: 1747. V. 39

OBSERVATIONS Upon Certain Passages in Mr. Jefferson's Notes on Virginia. New York: 1804. V. 38; 44

OBSERVATIONS Upon Mr. Budgell's Two Late Pamphlets, Entitled, Liberty and Property, and Upon Mr. Walsingham's Proper Reply; with a Little Secret History . . . London: 1732. V. 42

OBSERVATIONS... Upon the Act for Taxing Income.. Principles and Provisions of the Act . . . Considered . . . with the Act at Large . . . London: 1799. V. 40

OBSERVATIONS Upon the Act for the Redemption of the Land Tax; Shewing the Benefits Likely to Arise from the Measure Both to the Public and to Individuals. London: 1798. V. 40

OBSERVATIONS Upon the Administration of Justice in Bengal; Occasioned by Some Late Proceedings at Dacca. N.P.: 1778. V. 42

OBSERVATIONS Upon the Times. London: 1642. V. 43

OBSOLETE Ideas. In Six Letters, Addressed to Maria, by a Friend. London: 1805. V. 39

THE OBSTETRICAL Journal of Great Britain and Ireland Including Midwifery and the Diseases of Women and Children. London: 1873-79. V. 45

O'BYRNE, M. L.

The Pale and the Septs; or, the Baron of Belgard and the Chiefs of Glenmalure. Dublin: 1876. V. 42; 46

O'BYRNE, WILLIAM R.

A Naval Biographical Dictionary: Comprising the Life and Services of Every Living Officer in His Majesty's navy, from the Rank of Admiral of the Fleet to that of Lieutenant . . . London: 1849. V. 42; 46

O'CALLAGHAN, EDMUND B.

Docments Relative to the Colonial History of the State of New York. Albany: 1856-1887. V. 40; 44

The Documentary History of the State of New York. Albany: 1849. V. 39

The Documentary History of the State of New York. Albany: 1849-51. V. 39

The Documentary History of the State of New York. Albany: 1850-51. V. 37; 39

Documents Relative to the Colonial History of the State of New York . . . Albany: 1856-58. V. 43

O'CALLAGHAN, JEREMIAH 1780-1861

Usury; or, Lending at Interest; also, the Exaction and Payment of Certain Church-Fees, Such as Pew-Rents, Burial Fees and the Like, Together with Forstalling Traffick; all Proved to be Repugnant to the Divine and Ecclesiastical Law . . . London: 1828. V. 38

Usury, Funds and Banks, also Forestalling Traffick and Monopoly, likewise Pew Rent, & Grave Tax . . . Burlington: 1834. V. 42

O'CALLAGHAN, JOHN CORNELIUS

The Green Book or Gleanings from the Writing Desk of a Literary Agiatator. Dublin: 1844. V. 46

John Cornelius: The Green Book, or Gleanings from the Writing Desk. Boston: 1849. V. 46

History of the Irish Brigades in the Service of France, from the revolution in Great Britain and Ireland Under James II to the Revolution in France Under Louis XVI. New York: 1869. V. 39

History of the Irish Brigades in the Service of France from (1688-1793). Glasgow: 1870. V. 38

History of the Irish Brigades in the Service of France, from the Revolution in Great Britain and Ireland Under James II . . . Glasgow: 1880. V. 41

O'CALLAGHAN, O. B.

History of New Netherland; or, New York Under the Dutch. New York: 1846. V. 44

OCAMPO, VICTORIA

338171 T. E. (Lawrence of Arabia). London: 1963. V. 44

O'CASEY, SEAN 1884-1964

Cock-A-Doodle Dandy. London: 1949. V. 37

Drums Under the Windows. London: 1945. V. 37

I Knock at the Door. London: 1939. V. 37

Inishfallen Fare Thee Well. London: 1949. V. 37

Oak Leaves and Lavendar. London: 1946. V. 39

The Plough and the Stars: a Tragedy in Four Acts. London: 1926. V. 44

The Plough and the Stars. New York: 1926. V. 45

Purple Dust. London;: 1940. V. 37

Red Roses for Me. London: 1942. V. 37

The Silver Tassie. London: 1928. V. 39

The Story of the Irish Citizen Army. Dublin: 1919. V. 37; 38; 40; 42

The Story of the Irish Citizen Army. Dublin & London: 1919. V. 37; 38; 39; 41

The Story of the Irish Citizen Army. London: 1919. V. 42

OCCOM, SAMSON

A Sermon Preached at the Execution of Moses Paul, An Indian, Who Was Executed . . . for the Murder of Mr. Moes Cook, of Waterbury . . . Boston: 1773. V. 38

OCCUM, SAMSON

A Sermon Prached at the Execution of Moses Paul, an Indian. London: 1788. V. 40

OCEAN Flowers and Their Teachings: By the Author of 'Wild Flowers and Their Teachings.' Bath: 1847. V. 44

OCHINO, BERNARDINO 1487-1564

Antithesis De Praeclaris Christi et Indignis Papae Facionoribus . . . Geneva: 1558. V. 45

De Purgatorio Dialogus. Zurich: 1555. V. 37

Zwaintzig Predige . . . Neubrug am der Donau: 1545. V. 45

OCHSNER, ALBERT

The Surgery and Pathology of the Thyroid and Parathyroid glands. St. Louis: 1913. V. 42

OCKENGA, STARR

Mirror After Mirror: Reflections on Women. Garden City: 1976. V. 44

OCKLAND, CHRISTOPHER

Anglorum Praelia ab Anno 1327 . . . ad Addum 1558 (etc.). London: 1582. V. 44; 45

OCKLEY, SIMON

The Conquest of Syria, Persia, and Aegypt, by the Saracens . . . London: 1708. V. 44

Introductio Ad Linguas Orientales. Cantabrigiae: 1706. V. 43

O'CLERY, LUGHAIDH

Beatha . . . the Life of Hugh Roe O'Donnell, Prince of Tirconnell (1856-1602). Dublin: 1893. V. 38

Beatha . . . The Life of Hugh Roe O'Donnell, Prince of Tirconnell . . . Dublin: 1895. V. 38

O'CONNELL, DANIEL

The Correspondence of Daniel O'Connell, 1792-(1847). Dublin: 1983-80. V. 37

Observations on Corn Laws, on Political Pravity and Ingratitude, and on Clerical and Personal Slander. Dublin: 1842. V. 43

The Selected Speeches of Daniel O'Connell. Dublin: 1865. V. 39

A Special report of the Proceedings in the Case of the Queen Against Daniel O'Connell, Esq., John O'Connell Esq., Thomas Steele, and others in the Court of the Queens Bench, Ireland, Michaelmas TErm, 1843 and Hilary Term, 1844 on an Indictment . . . Dublin: 1844. V. 39

O'CONNELL, J. J.

Catholicity in the Carolinas and Georgia; Leaves of Its History. New York: 1879. V. 42

Catholicity in the Carolinas and Georgia: Leaves of Its History. A.D. 1820-A.D. 1878. New York: 1979. V. 46

O'CONNELL, JAMES JAY

The Auto Guyed. A Pictorial Alphabet. New York: 1906. V. 41

O'CONNELL, MORGAN J., MRS.

Charles Bianconi: a Biography 1786-1875. London: 1878. V. 45

O'CONNOR, ARTHUR

The Present State of Great Britain. Paris: 1804. V. 44

O'CONNOR, CHARLES

Chronicles of Eiri. London: 1822. V. 46

Dissertations on the Ancient History of Ireland Wherein an Account is Given of the Original Government Letters, Sciences, Religion, Manners and Customs of the Ancient Inhabitants. Dublin: 1753. V. 46

O'CONNOR, FLANNERY 1925-1964

The Artificial Nigger and Other Tales. London: 1957. V. 38; 39; 46

The Complete Short Stories. New York: 1971. V. 37; 38; 39; 40; 42; 45

Everything That Rises Must Converge. 1965. V. 43

Everything That Rises Must Converge. New York: 1965. V. 38; 39; 44; 45; 46

Everything That Rises Must Converge. London: 1966. V. 45

A Good Man is Hard to Find. New York: 1952. V. 45

A Good Man is Hard to Find. 1955. V. 44

A Good Man is Hard to Find. New York: 1955. V. 37; 38; 39; 40; 41; 42; 43; 45; 46

A Good Man is Hard to Find. New York: 1961. V. 39

A Good Man Is Hard to Find and Other Stories. London: 1968. V. 45

The Habit of Being. New York: 1978. V. 42

Mystery and Manners: Occasional prose. New York: 1969. V. 45

Mystery and Manners - Occasional Prose. London: 1972. V. 38

The Violent Bear It Away. London: 1960. V. 38; 39; 40; 42; 46

The Violent Bear It Away. New York: 1960. V. 45

Wise Blood. New York: 1952. V. 37; 38; 39; 41; 42; 43; 44; 45

Wise Blood. London: 1955. V. 39; 44; 45

Wise Blood. New York: (1952). V. 37

O'CONNOR, FLORENCE J.

The Heroine of the Confederacy; or Truth and Justice. New Orleans: 1869. V. 45

O'CONNOR, FRANK 1903-1966

The Big Fellow - a Life of Michael Collins. London: 1937. V. 38

Bones of Contention and Other Stories. London: 1936. V. 38

A Gambler's Throw. Memories of W. B. Yeats. Edinburgh: 1975. V. 38

Guest of the Nation. New York: 1931. V. 38

Guests of the Nation. London: 1931. V. 42

The Little Monasteries. Dublin: 1963. V. 38

Lords and Commons. Dublin: 1938. V. 38; 46

A Picture Book. Dublin: 1943. V. 46

A Picture Book. London: 1943. V. 37

The Saint and Mary Kate. London: 1932. V. 37

Shakespeare's Progress. Cleveland and New York: 1960. V. 38

Shakespeare's Progress. New York: 1960. V. 37; 40

Three Old Brothers and Other Poems. London: 1936. V. 38; 41

Three Tales. Dublin: 1941. V. 38

The Wild Bird's Nest. Poems from the Irish. Dublin: 1932. V. 38; 44

O'CONNOR, JACK

The Big Game Animals of North America. New York: 1978. V. 44

Game in the Desert. New York: 1939. V. 39; 43

O'CONNOR, JEANNIE

The Wood Engravings of John O'Connor. 1989. V. 44

O'CONNOR, JOHN

Dukes Village. 1988. V. 40; 45

Dukes Village: a Suite of Wood Engravings By . . . Biddenden: 1988. V. 42

The Gateway of St. Osyth Priory. V. 46

The Wood-Engravings of John O'Connor. Andoversford: 1989. V. 41

O'CONNOR, M.

Considerations on the Trade to Africa. London: 1749. V. 41

O'CONNOR, MATTHEW

Military History of the Irish nation. Dublin: 1845. V. 38; 46

O'CONNOR, R.

An Introduction to the field Sports of France, Being a Practical View of Hunting, Shooting and fishing on the Continent. London: 1846. V. 41

O'CONNOR, ROGER

Chronicles of Eri; Being the History of the Gaal Sciot Iber; or, the Irish People. London: 1822. V. 38; 46

O'CONNOR, THOMAS

An Impartial and Correct History of the War Between the United States and Great Britain. New York: 1815. V. 39; 41; 42

O'CONNOR, V. C. SCOTT

An Eastern Library. Glasgow: 1920. V. 40

O'CONOR, CHARLES

The O'Conors of Connaught . . . Dublin: 1891. V. 43

O'CONOR, CHARLES CAROLO

Rerum Hibernicarum Scriptores Veteres. Buckingham: 1814. V. 43; 46

O'CONOR, DANIEL PATRICK

The Works . . . Cork: 1798? V. 42

O'CONOR, RODERIC

An Historical and Genealogical Memoir of the O'Connors, Kings of Connaught, and Their Descendants Collected from the Annals of Ireland and Authentic Public Records. Dublin: 1861. V. 39

O'CROULEY, PEDRO ALONSO

A Description of the Kingdom of New Spain. San Francisco: 1972. V. 40; 42

OCTO Autores. Autores Octo Continentes Libros: Videlicet Catonem. Facetum. Theodolum. De Contemptu Mundi. Floretum. Alanum de Parabolis. Fabulas Esopi. Thobiam, etc. Lyon: 1525. V. 37

OCTROY Concede Par les Haults et Puissants Seigneurs les Estats Generaulx a La Compagnie des Indes Occidentales . . . Amsterdam: 1621. V. 44

O'CURRY, EUGENE

Lectures on the Manuscript Materials of Ancient Irish History. Dublin: 1861. V. 39; 44

On the Manners and Customs of the Ancient Irish. London: 1873. V. 39

O'DALY, AENGHUS

The Tribes of Ireland: a Satire, with Poetical Translation . . . Dublin: 1852. V. 38; 39; 40

O'DALY, JOHN

Fenian Poems. Dublin: 1859/61. V. 46

O'DAY, EDWARD F.

An Appreciation of James Wood Coffroth. San Francisco: 1926. V. 39

John Henry Nash: The Aldus San Francisco. San Francisco: 1928. V. 41

O'DAY, NELL

A Catalogue of Books Printed by John Henry Nash. San Francisco: 1937. V. 45

AN ODD Bestiary. 1982. V. 37
AN ODD Bestiary. Easthampton: 1982. V. 39

AN ODD Bestiary. Or, a Compendium of Instructive and Entertaining Descriptions of Animals, Culled from Five Centuries . . . Arranged as an Abecedary. Designed and Illustrated by Alan James Robinson, with 26 original engravings, and initals, hand . . . Easthampton, MA.: 1982. V. 37

THE ODD Fellows. Offering for 1848. New York: 1848. V. 39

ODDI, MARCO DEGLI

Meditationes Doctissimae in Theriacam and Mithridaticam Antidotum . . . Venetiis: 1576. V. 44

ODDI, ODDO DEGLI

In Primam Totam Fen Primi Libri Canonis Avicenne Dilucidissima & Expectatissima Exposito. Venice: 1575. V. 43

ODDI, SFORZA D'

I Morti Vivi. Venice: 1582. V. 37

AN ODE, Sacred to the Memory of a Late Eminently Distinguish'd Placeman, on His Retiring from Business. London: 1763. V. 37

ODE to Lansdown-Hill, with Notes, Mostly Relative to the Granville Family; to Which are added, Two Letters of Advenice from George Lord Lansdown, anno MDCCXI to William Henry Earl of Bath. London: 1785. V. 46

ODE to the Judges. N.P.: 1795? V. 41

O'DEA, AGNEA

Bibliography of Newfoundland. Toronto: 1986. V. 42

ODELL, GEORGE C. D.

Annals of the New York Stage. New York: 1927. V. 44

O'DELL, STACKPOOL E.

Old St. Margaret's. London: 1884. V. 42

ODENHEIMER, W. H.

Jerusalem and Its Vicinity . . . Philadelphia: 1855. V. 38

ODES and Sonnets. London: 1859. V. 39; 42; 44

ODES on Peace and War. London: 1795. V. 43

ODETS, CLIFFORD

Golden Boy. New York: 1937. V. 46

Paradise Lost. New York: 1936. V. 37; 41; 42

Three Plays. New York: 1935. V. 39; 46

ODGEN, PETER SKENE

Traits of American-Indian Life and Character. By A Fur Trader. London: 1853. V. 37

ODIERNA, GIOVANNI BATTISTA 1597-1660

Opuscoli . . . 1 Il Nunzio della Terra. 2. La Nuvola Pendente. 3 L'Occhio della Mosca. 4. Il Sole del Microcosmo. Palermo: 1644. V. 45; 46

Universae Facultatis Directionum Physiotheorica . . . Palermo: 1629. V. 46

ODLE, ALAN

The Gypsy. London: 1915 & May 1916. V. 46

ODO, BP. OF MEUNG

Herbarum Varias qui vis Cognoscere Vires: huc Macer Adest: Quo Duce doctor Eris . . . Paris: 1522. V. 46

O'DONAVAN, JOHN

A Grammar of the Irish Language. Dublin: 1845. V. 39

ODONI, RINALDO

Discorco . . . per via Peripatetica, our si demostra, se l'anima, secondo Aristotele, e mortale, o immortale. Venice: 1557. V. 37

O'DONNELL, CAPTAIN

Historical Records of the 14th Regiment, Now the Prince of Wales's Own (West Yorkshire Regiment) from Its Formation in 1685 to 1892. Devenport: 1893. V. 41

O'DONOGHUE, FREEMAN

Catalogue of Engraved British Portraits Preserved in the Department of Prints and Drawings in the British Museum. London: 1908-14. V. 38; 42

Catalogue of Engraved British Portraits Preserved in the Department of Prints and Drawings in the British Museum. London: 1908-22. V. 38; 39; 41; 44

Catalogue of Engraved British Portraits Preserved in the Department of Prints and Drawings in the British Museum. London: 1908-25. V. 39; 42

O'DONOGHUE, JOHN

Historical Memoir of the O'Briens. Dublin: 1860. V. 39; 42; 44

O'DONOGHUE, NANNIE

The Common Sense of Riding. London: 1887. V. 41

O'DONOVAN, EDMOND

The Merv Oasis. Travels and Adventures East of the Caspian During the Years 1879-80-81. London: 1882. V. 41; 43; 46

The Merv Oasis. Travels and Adventures East of the Caspian During the Years 1879-80-81. New York: 1883. V. 37; 44; 46

O'DONOVAN, JEREMIAH

A Brief Account of the Author's Interview With His Countrymen and of the Parts of The Emeral Isle Whence They Emigrated. Pittsburgh: 1864. V. 40

O'DONOVAN, JOHN

Annals of Ireland. Three Fragments Copied from Ancient Sources . . . Dublin: 1860. V. 38

The Banquet of Dun Na n-Gedh and the Battle of Magh Rath. Dublin: 1842. V. 43

The Economic History of Live Stock in Ireland. Cork: 1940. V. 43

Leabhar na Gceart, or the Book of Rights Now for the First Timed Edited with Translation and Notes. Dublin: 1847. V. 46

Letters Containing Information Relative to the Antiquities of the County of Dublin . . . London: 1927. V. 42

Letters Containing Information Relative to the Antiquities of the County of Down, Collected During the Progress of the Ordnance Survey in 1834. Bray: 1928. V. 38

Letters Containing Information Relative to the Antiquities of the County of Roscommon Collected During the Progress of the Ordnance Survey in 1837. London: 1931. V. 42

The O'Conors of Connaught, Compiled from a Manuscript of the Lte John O'Donovan . . . Dublin: 1891. V. 38

The Topographical Poems of John O Dubhagain and Giolla Na Naomh O Huidhrin. Dublin: 1862. V. 46

Tracts Relating to Ireland. Dublin: 1841. V. 43

O'DRISCOLL, ROBERT

The Untold Story: The Irish in Canada. Toronto: 1988. V. 41

O'DUBHAGAIN, JOHN

The Topographical Poems. Dublin: 1862. V. 44

OECOLAMPADIUS, JOHN d.1531

Quod expediat Epistolae & Evangelii lectionem in Missa. (Strassbourg: 1522). V. 37

OECUMENIUS, BISHOP OF TRICCA

Expositiones Antiquae ac Valde Utiles . . . Ex Diversis Sanctorum Patrum Commentariis ab Oecumenio & Aretha Collectae in Hosce Novi Testamenti Tractatus. Verona: 1532. V. 40

OEHLENSCHLAEGER, ADAM

The Gods of the North. Paris: 1845. V. 38

OEHLENSCHLAGER, ADAM

The Gods of the North, an Epic Poem. London: 1848. V. 43

OEHLER, ANDREW

The Life, Adventures, and Unparalleled Sufferings of Andrew Oehler. Trenton: 1811. V. 37; 38; 43

OEHLER, GOTTLIEB

Description of a Journey and Visit to the Pawnee Indians. New York: 1914. V. 39

OEHLER, J. C.

Cruise to the Orient. Richmond: 1906? V. 42

OESTERLEY, W.

Roses of Sharon. London: 1937. V. 43

OF Beauty. London: 1757. V. 40; 41

OF Beauty. To the Earl of -----. London: 1757. V. 41

OF the Just Shaping of Letters. From the Applied Geometry of Albrecht Durer, Book III. New York: 1917. V. 41

OF the Most Holy Miracle of Saint Francis in Taming the Fierce Wolf of Gubbio. New York: 1949. V. 46

OF the Use of Tobacco, Tea, Coffee, Chocolate and Drams. London: 1722. V. 42; 46

O'FALLON, J.

Memorial of the Ohio and Mississippi Railroad Company . . . to Locate and Construct a Railroad Across the State, Commencing at Illinoistown . . . in The Direction of the City of Vincennes in the State of Indiana . . . St. Louis: 1851. V. 39

O'FAOLAIN, SEAN 1900-

Bird Alone. London: 1936. V. 38

The Born Genius. Detroit: 1936. V. 37; 43; 46

An Irish Journey. London: 1940. V. 38

The Man Who Invented Sin. And Other Stories. New York: 1948. V. 38

A Nest of Simple Folk. London: 1933. V. 40

A Purse of Coppers. Short Stories. London: 1937. V. 38

Teresa, and Other Stories. London: 1947. V. 38

There's a Birdie in the Cage. London: 1935. V. 37; 40; 41; 42

The Vanishing Hero. Studies in Novelists of the Twenties. London: 1956. V. 38

Vive Moi! An Autobiography. Boston: 1964. V. 38

O'FERRALL, CHARLES T.

Forty Years of Active Service. New York: 1904. V. 40

O'FERRALL, S. A.

A Ramble of Six Thousand Miles Through the United States of America. London: 1832. V. 42

L' OFFICE De l'Eglise, a l'Usage de Rome. Paris: 1776. V. 38

OFFICE de la Semaine Sainte. Paris: 1708. V. 40
OFFICE de la Semaine Sainte. Paris: 1728. V. 40; 45
OFFICE de la Semaine Sainte. Paris: 1748. V. 40
L'OFFICE de la Semaine Sainte. Paris: 1757. V. 40

OFFICER, HARVEY

A Baker Street Song Book. New York: 1943. V. 41

THE OFFICER'S Manual in the Field; or, a series of military plans, representing the principal operations of a campaigne. Translated from the German. London: 1798. V. 37

OFFICERS of Our Union Army and Navy. Their Lives, Their Portraits. Boston: 1862. V. 42

OFFICERS of the Army and Navy (Regular and Volunteer) Who Served in the Civil War. Philadelphia: 1894. V. 46

THE OFFICIAL Atlas of the Civil War. New York: 1958. V. 39

AN OFFICIAL Guide to Japan. Tokyo: 1933. V. 44

THE OFFICIAL Guide to the Klondyke Country and the Gold Fields of Alaska with the Official Maps. Chicago: 1897. V. 37

OFFICIAL Guide to the Yellowstone National Park: a Manual for Touristsl . . . St. Paul: 1889. V. 38

OFFICIAL History of the Great War. Mesopotamia Campaign 1914-1918. London: 1923-27. V. 41

OFFICIAL History of the Great War. Military Operations. Gallipoli. London: 1932-36. V. 41

OFFICIAL History of the Great War. Military Operations. Macedonia. London: 1933/35. V. 41

OFFICIAL History of the Great War. The War in the Air. Oxford: 1922-37. V. 41

OFFICIAL Information: a Statement of Facts by the Territorial Board of Immigration. Denver: 1872. V. 46

THE OFFICIAL Pictures of a Century of Progress Exposition, Chicago 1933. Chicago: 1933. V. 37

OFFICIAL Program of the Thirty-Seventh Anniversary of the Emancipation Proclamation (Enforced in Texas June 19th, 1865) at San Pedro Park, San Antonio, Texas, June 19th, 1902. Nashville: 1902. V. 39

OFFICIAL Railway Guide of St. Louis. St. Louis: 1877. V. 37

THE OFFICINA Bodoni, the Operation of a Hand-Press During the First Six Years of Its Work. Paris and New York: 1929. V. 37

OFFICINA BODONI, VERONA.

L'Officina Bondoni: La Regola e la Stampa di Un Torchio Durante I Primi Sei Anni Del Suo Lavoro. Verona: 1929. V. 40

The Officina Bodoni: the Operation of a Hand-Press During the First Six Years. Verona: 1929. V. 40; 44; 45

L'Officina Bodoni. Verona: 1980. V. 40; 41; 42; 44

The Officina Bodoni: An Account of the Work of a Hand Press 1923-1977. 1981. V. 40

The Operation of a Hand-Press During the First Six Years of Its Work. Paris: 1929. V. 38; 45

OFFNER, ELLIOT

The Granjon Arabesque: Thirty Arrangements of the Ornaments With Type and an Introduction. Northampton: 1969. V. 37

O'FLAHERTY, LIAM 1897-1984

The Assassin. 1928. V. 42

The Assassin. London: 1928. V. 37; 39; 40; 41; 43

The Black Soul. London: 1924. V. 38; 41; 42; 43

The Child of God. London: 1926. V. 38; 39

Civil War. 1925. V. 42

Civil War. London: 1925. V. 39; 40

A Cure for Unemployment. London: 1931. V. 39

The Ecstasy of Angus. London: 1931. V. 39; 41; 43

The Fairy Goose and Two Other Stories. New York: 1927. V. 39; 41; 46

The House of Gold. 1929. V. 42

The House of Gold. London: 1929. V. 38

The Life of Tim Healy. London: 1927. V. 39

The Martyr. London: 1933. V. 39

Mr. Gilhooley. London: 1926. V. 39

Mr. Gilhooley. London: 1936. V. 43

The Puritan. London: 1932. V. 40

Red Barbara and Other Stories. New York: 1928. V. 39

Return of the Brute. 1929. V. 42

Return of the Brute. London: 1929. V. 37; 39; 41

Spring Sowing. New York: 1926. V. 39

The Tent and Other Stories. London: 1926. V. 40; 41

The Terrorist. 1926. V. 42

Thy Neighbour's Wife. London: 1923. V. 37; 38

A Tourist's Guide to Ireland. London. V. 42

A Tourist's Guide to Ireland. London: 1943. V. 42

A Tourist's Guide to Ireland. London: (1943). V. 37

O'FLAHERTY, RODERIC

Ogygia or a Chronological Account of Irish Events. Collected from Very Ancient Documents. Dublin: 1793. V. 46

O'FLAHERTY, RODERICK

Ogygia Seu Rerum Hibernicarum Chronologia . . . in Tres Partes . . . London: 1685. V. 38

O'FLANAGAN, J. RODERICK

The Lives of the Lord Chancellors and Keepers of the Great Seal of Ireland, from the Earliest Times to the Reign of Queen Victoria. London: 1870. V. 40

OFRSIUS, SIGFRIDUS ARONUS

Een Berattelse, Och Eenfallight Judicium, Om Then Cometen Som nu I Thetta Aar 1607 i Septembri Och Octobri Manader i 34 Daghar Widh Pass Syntes . . . Colophon: 1607. V. 40

OFWOOD, STEPHEN

A Second Part of the Spanish Practises. London: 1624. V. 44

O'GALLAGHER, JAMES

Sermons in Irish-Gaelic. Dublin: 1877. V. 39

OGAWA, KAZUMASA

The Hakone District, Illustrated . . . in Collotype. Yokohama: 1900. V. 40

A Model Japanese Villa. Tokyo: 1910. V. 42; 44; 45

The Nikko District. 1899. V. 39

A Photographic-Album of the Japan-China War: Army Section. Tokyo: 1896. V. 44

Scenes from the Chiushingura and the Story of the Forty-Seven Ronin. By K. Ogawa, Photographer, Tokyo, Japan. In colotype. With descriptive text by james Murdoch, M.A. Tokyo: (?1900). V. 37

Sights and Scenes on the Tokaido. ?Tokyo: 1900. V. 37

Some Japanes (sic) Flowers. Tokyo: 1890. V. 42

OGBORNE, ELIZABETH

The History of Essex, from the Earliest Period to the Present Time. London: 1814. V. 39; 44

OGDEN, ADELE

The California Sea Otter Trade 1784-1848. Berkeley & Los Angeles: 1941. V. 44

OGDEN, AEDELE

California Sea Otter Trade 1748-1848. Berkeley: 1941. V. 46

OGDEN, GEORGE

Letters from the West Comprising a Tour Through the Western Country. New Bedford: 1823. V. 37; 39

OGDEN, HENRY A.

The Army of the United States. Washington: 1888. V. 40

OGDEN, JAMES

Archery: a Poem. N.P.: Manchester: 1793. V. 39

Ogden on Fly Tying, etc. Cheltenham: 1879. V. 39

OGDEN, JOHN C.

An Excursion into Bethlehem and Nazareth, In Pennsylvania, In the Year 1799. Philadelphia: 1800. V. 38

OGDEN, LEW J. G.

New Century Atlas of Counties of the State of New York. New York & Philadelphia: 1912. V. 39

OGDEN, PETER SKENE

Peter Skene Ogden's Snake Country Journals 1824-25 and 1825-26. London: 1950. V. 37; 39; 40; 42; 44

Peter Skene Ogden's Snake Country Journals 1827-28 and 1828-29. London: 1971. V. 46

Traits of American-Indian Life and Character. London: 1853. V. 41; 42; 45; 46

Traits of American India Life & Character. San Francisco: 1933. V. 37; 39; 40; 44

OGDEN, UZAL

Antidote to Deism. The Deist Unmasked; or an Ample Refutation of all the Objections of Thomas Paine, Against the Christian Religion. Newark: 1795. V. 37; 42

OGHAM. London: 1979. V. 41

OGIER, CHARLES

Caroli Ogerii Ephemerides, sive Iter Danicum Svecicum, Polonicum. 1656. V. 44

OGILBY, JAMES S.

A Pilgrimage in Surrey. London: 1914. V. 42

OGILBY, JOHN

America: Being the Latest, and Most Accurate Description of the New World. London: 1671. V. 39

Britannia. Volume the First. London: 1675. V. 38; 39; 41

Britannia; or, the Kingdom of England and Dominion of Wales . . . London: 1698. V. 44

Britannia Depicta or Ogilby Improv'd. London: 1720. V. 40

OGILBY, JOHN continued

Britannia Depicta. London: 1764. V. 42

A Description and History of the Island of Jamaica. Kingston: 1851. V. 45

Ogilby's Road Maps of England and Wales from Ogilby's 'Britannia' 1675. Reading: 1971. V. 40; 44

The Traveller's Guide or, a Most Exact Description of the Roads of England. London: 1711. V. 39; 42

The Works of Publius Virgilius Maro. Translated by John Ogilby & Adorn'd with Sculptur. London: 1684. V. 37

OGILVIE-GRANT, W. R.

The Gun at Home and Abroad. London: 1912. V. 45

OGILVIE, J. S.

History of the Attempted Assassination of James A. Garfield. New York: 1881. V. 44

OGILVIE, JAMES

The Civil History of the Kingdom of Naples . . . London: 1729-31. V. 46

OGILVIE, JOHN

Providence, an Allegorical Poem in Three Books. Boston: 1766. V. 46

Rona, a Poem, in Seven Books . . . London: 1777. V. 42

OGILVIE, WILLIAM

Early Days in the Yukon. Ottawa: 1913. V. 43

Information Respecting the Yukon District, from the Reports of Wm. Ogilvie, and From Other Sources. Ottawa: 1897. V. 40; 43

The Klondike Official Guide. Toronto: 1898. V. 38

Lecture on the Yukon Gold Fields (Canada). Victoria: 1897. V. 38; 46

OGILVY, DAVID

A General Itinerary of England and Wales, with Part of Scotland . . . London: 1804. V. 43

OGILVY, JAMES

A Pilgrimage in Surrey. London: 1914. V. 42; 44; 46

OGLE, CHALONER

The Tryal of Sir Chaloner Ogle, Kt., Rear Admiral of the Blue. London: 1743. V. 41; 45

OGLE, CHARLES

Speech of Mr. Ogle, of Pennsylvania, on the Regal Splendor of the President's Palace. Delivered in the House of Representatives, April 14, 1840. Colophon: 1840. V. 42

OGLE, GEORGE

Antiquities Explained, Being a Collection of Figured Gems Illustrated by Similar Descriptions Taken from the Classics. Volume I (all published). London: 1737. V. 44

Gualtherus and Griselda; or, the Clerk of Oxford's Tale. London: 1739. V. 42

OGLE, GEORGE A.

Standard Atlas of Allegan County, Michigan. Chicago: 1913. V. 42

OGLE, JOHN

The Harveian Oration - 1880. London: 1881. V. 40; 41

OGLE, NATHANIEL

The Colony of Western Australia. London: 1839. V. 39; 40

OGLETHORPE, PSEUD.

Georgia and the Supreme Court. An Examination of the Opinion of the Supreme Court . . . in the Case of Samuel A. Worcester . . . Verses the State of Georgia. Augusta: 1832. V. 38

OGLETHROPE, JAMES EDWARD 1696-1755

An Impartial Account of the Late Expedition Against St. Augustine Under General Oglethorpe. Occasioned by the Suppression of the Report made by a Committee of the General Assembly in South Carolina . . . London: 1742. V. 37

OGLIVIE, JOHN

Philosophical and Critical Observations on the Nature, Character and Various Species of Composition. London: 1774. V. 37

O'GORMAN, HELEN

Mexican Flowering Trees & Plants. Mexico City: 1961. V. 40

O'GRADY, STANDISH J.

The Queen of the World or Under the Tyranny. London: 1900. V. 40

OGSTON, ALEXANDER

The Prehistoric Antiquities of the Howe of Cromar. Aberdeen: 1921. V. 40

OGSTON, FRANCIS

Lectures on Medical Jurisprudence. Philadelphia: 1878. V. 42

O'HALLORAN, SYLVESTER

A General History of Ireland, from the most authentic records. London: 1778. V. 37

History of Ireland. Dublin: 1819. V. 43

An Introduction to, and an History of Ireland. Dublin: 1803. V. 37; 46

O'HANLEY, J. L. P.

The Political Standing of Irish Catholics in Canada. Ottawa: 1872. V. 41

O'HANLON, JOHN

Canon; The Irish-American History of the U.S. New York: 1907. V. 37

O'HANLON, REDMOND

Into the Heart of Borneo - An Account of a Journey Made in 1983 to the Mountains of Batu Tiban with James Fenton. Edinburgh: 1984. V. 40

O'HANLON, W. M.

The Operative Classes of Great Britain . . . London: 1851. V. 42

O'HANLY, J.

The Intercolonial Railway: Analysis of the Frontier, Central and Bay Chaleurs Routes. Ottawa: 1868. V. 43

O'HARA, DOROTHEA WARREN

The Art of Enameling on Porcelain. 1912. V. 44

The Art of Enameling on Porcelain. N.P.: 1912. V. 38

O'HARA, FRANK

A City in Winter and Other Poems. New York: 1951. V. 45

The Collected Poems. New York: 1971. V. 43

In Memory of My Feelings. New York: 1967. V. 39; 42; 43; 44; 45; 46

Second Avenue. New York: 1960. V. 39

The Selected Poems of Frank O'Hara. New York: 1974. V. 45

O'HARA, JAMES

The History of New South Wales. London: 1817. V. 45

O'HARA, JOHN 1905-1970

And Other Stories. New York: 1968. V. 41; 45; 46

Appointment in Samarra. New York: 1934. V. 37; 39; 46

Appointment in Samarra. New York: (1934). V. 37

Butterfield 8. New York: 1935. V. 38; 39

Butterfield 8. London: 1951. V. 43

Files on Parade. 1939. V. 46

Files on Parade. New York: 1952. V. 45

Hellbox. New York: 1947. V. 37

Here's O'Hara. Cleveland & New York: 1946. V. 37

Hope of Heaven. New York: 1938. V. 39; 42; 44; 46

The Horse Knows the Way. New York: 1964. V. 39; 43

The Instrument. New York: 1967. V. 37; 38; 39; 40; 41; 46

The Lockwood Concern. New York: 1965. V. 43

Lovely Childs: a Philadelphia Story. New York: 1969. V. 40; 41; 42; 45; 46

Meditations in an Emergency. New York: 1957. V. 45

Pal Joey. New York: 1940. V. 37

Pipe Night. New York: 1945. V. 37; 38

A Rage to Live. 1949. V. 46

A Rage to Live. New York: 1949. V. 37; 38; 40; 43; 44; 46

Sermons and Soda Water. 1960. V. 46

Sermons and Soda Water. New York: 1960. V. 42; 43; 45

Sermons and Soda Water. London: 1961. V. 37; 38; 39; 40; 42; 43; 46

Waiting for Winter. 1966. V. 46

O'HARA, JOHN MEYERS

Pagan Sonnets. Portland: 1910. V. 39

O'HARA, KANE

Midas: an English Burletta. London: 1767. V. 41

O'HARA, MELITA

Coast to Coast in a Puddle Jumper. N.P.: 1930. V. 38; 42

O'HARE, KATE RICHARDS

The Sorrows of Cupid. St. Louis: 1912. V. 39

O'HARRA, CLEOPHAS C.

A Bibliography of the Geology and Mining Interests of the Black Hills Region. Rapid City: 1917. V. 42; 44

O'HART, JOHN

Irish Pedigrees . . . Dublin: 1880-1878. V. 43

Irish Pedigrees, or the Origin and Stem of the Irish Nation. Dublin: 1887. V. 43

The Irish and Anglo-Irish Landed Gentry. Dublin: 1892. V. 39

O'HART, JOHN continued

Irish Pedigrees or the Origin and Stem of the Irish Nation. with Second Series. Dublin: 1876. V. 39

OHIO

Comemorative Historical and Biographical Record of Wood County, Ohio; Its Past and Present. Chicago: 1897. V. 37

OHIO. ACTS, STATUTES, ETC. - 1804

Acts of the State of Ohio, Passed and Revised, First Session of the Third General Assembly, Begun and Held at the Town of CHillicothe, December 3, 1804 . . . Chillicothe: 1805. V. 37; 40

OHIO AND MISSISSIPPI RAILROAD

Report of the Present Condition and Prospects of the Ohio and Mississippi Railroad, Uniting the Cities of Cincinnati and St. Louis. Cincinnati: 1852. V. 41

OHIO Annals. Historic Events in the Tuscarawas and Muskingum Valleys, and in Other Portions of the State of Ohio. Dayton: 1876. V. 39

OHIO. LAWS, STATUES, ETC. - 1824

Acts of a General Nature Enacted, Revised and Ordered at the First Session of the 22nd General Assembly of the State of Ohio. Columbus: 1824. V. 37

THE OHIO Railroad Guide. Columbus: 1854. V. 39; 40; 41; 42; 45; 46

OHM, GEORG SIMON 1789-1854

Die Galvanische Kette, Mathematisch Bearbeitet IV. Berlin: 1827. V. 40; 42

OHRWALDER, JOSEPH 1856-1913

Ten Year's Captivity in the Mahdi's Camp 1882-1892. London: 1892. V. 43

OHWI, J.

Flora of Japan. Washington: 1984. V. 37

OKA, HIDEYUKI

How to Wrap 5 Eggs. New York: 1965. V. 41

How To Wrap Five Eggs: Japanese Design in Traditional Packaging. Tokyo: 1969. V. 41

OKE, GEORGE COLWELL 1821-1874

The Magisterial Synopsis: 1860. London: 1861. V. 40

O'KEEFE, ADELAIDE

Zenobia, Queen of Palmyra. London: 1814. V. 44

Zenobia, Queen of Palmyra. London: 1824. V. 38

O'KEEFE, GEORGIA

Georgia O'Keefe. New York: 1975. V. 42; 43

Georgia O'Keefe. New York: 1976. V. 38; 39; 45; 46

Georgia O'Keefe: One Hundred Flowers. New York: 1987. V. 38

Some Memories of Drawings. New York: 1974. V. 37; 38

O'KEEFE, JOHN

Recollections of the Life of John O'Keefe. London: 1826. V. 40; 42; 43

O'KEEFE, THOMAS M.

The Battle of London Life; or, Boz and His Secretary. London: 1849. V. 43

O'KEEFFE, JOHN

O'Keeffe's Legacy to His Daughter, Being the Poetical Works of the Late John O'Keefe, Esq., the Dramatic Author. London: 1834. V. 45

The Son-in-Law, a Comic Opera; in Two Acts. Dublin: 1783. V. 37; 39

OKELL, BENJAMIN

A Short Treatise of the Virtues of Dr. Bateman's Pectoral Drops . . . Published and sold by vertue: 1726. V. 37

O'KELLY, CHARLES

Secret History of the War of the Revolution in Ireland, 1688-1691 . . . Dublin: 1850. V. 38

Secret History of the War of the Revolution in Ireland, 1688-1691, written under the title of 'Destruction of Cyprus:. Edited, from four English copies and a Latin Ms. in the Royal Irish Acaemy, with . . . Dublin: (1850). V. 37

O'KELLY, DENNIS

The Genuine Memoirs of Dennis O'Kelly, Esq. Commonly Caalled Count O'Kelly. London: 1778. V. 37

O'KELLY, PATRICK

The Aonian Kaleidoscope; or, a Collection of Original Poems. Cork: 1824. V. 41

OKEY, C. H.

A Concise Digest of the Law Usage and Custom Affecting the Civil and Commercial Intercourse of the Subjects of Great Britain and France. Paris: 1842. V. 40

OKIGBO, CHRISTOPHER

Heavensgate. Ibadan: 1962. V. 40

OKLAHOMA

Laws of the Choctaw Nation, made and enacted by the General Council, from 1886 to 1890 Inclusive. Atoka, Indian Territory: 1890. V. 37

OKLAHOMA. CONSTITUTION

The Constitution of the State of Oklahoma. Guthrie: 1907. V. 37; 38; 39; 43; 45

OKLAHOMA. CONSTITUTION - 1905

Constitution of the State of Sequoyah. Muskogee: 1905. V. 37

OKLAHOMA. CONSTITUTION - 1907

The Constitution of the State of Oklahoma. Oklahoma City: 1907. V. 37; 42

Constitution and Enabling Act of the State of Oklahoma. Ardmore: 1907. V. 37

The Constitution of the State of Oklahoma. Oklahoma City: (1907). V. 37

OKLAHOMA. CONSTITUTIONAL CONVENTION - 1907

Proceedings of the Constitutional Convention of the Proposed State of Oklahoma, Held at Guthrie, November 20, 1906 to November 16, 1907. Muskogee: 1907. V. 37; 39

OKLAHOMA. (TERRITORY). CONSTITUTIONAL CONVENTION - 1907

Proceedings of the Constitutional Convention of the Proposed State of Oklahoma. Held at Guthrie, Oklahoma, Nov. 20, 1906 to Nov. 16, 1907. 1908. V. 38

OKUDAIRA, HIDEO

Emaki: Japanese Picture Scrolls. Japan: 1962. V. 44

OKUKO, MINE

Citizen 13660. New York: 1946. V. 44

OLAFSSON, EGGERT 1726-1768

Travels in Iceland: Performed by Order of His Danish Majesty. London: 1805. V. 40

OLAFSSON, JON

The Life of the Icelander Jon Olafsson . . . London: 1923. V. 43

O'LAVERTY, JAMES

An Historical Account of the Diocese of Down and Connor, Ancient and Modern. Dublin: 1878. V. 43

An Historical Account of the Diocese of Down and Connor, Ancient and Modern. Dublin: 1878/1895. V. 38

OLCOTT, CHARLES

Two Lectures on the Subjects of Slavery and Abolition, Compiled for the Special Use of Anti-Slavery Lecturers and Debaters. Masillon: 1838. V. 38

OLD ABE's Joker, or, Wit at the White House. New York: 1863. V. 37

THE OLD and New Interest; or a Sequel to the Oxfordshire Contest. London: 1753. V. 45

AN OLD and True Extemporary Anthology, 1939-1941. London: 1942. V. 39

THE OLD BOOK. A Mediaeval Anthology. London: 1930. V. 44

THE OLD Country Houses of the Old Glasgow Century. Glasgow: 1878. V. 38; 45

THE OLD Courtier. London: 1870-74. V. 43

OLD Dutch Nursery Rhymes. London: 1917. V. 45

OLD Edinburgh Characters, Pedlars, Beggards and Criminals with Some Odd Other Characters in Type, the Whole Adorned with Head Pieces and Tail Pieces Curiously Cut in Wood. 1886. V. 38

THE OLD English Drama. London: 1830. V. 45

OLD English Songs and Dances. London: 1902. V. 44

OLD French Nursery Songs. London: 1925. V. 46

OLD Friends. A Remembrancer of Beloved Companions; and Years Bygone. New York: 1835. V. 45

OLD John Brown, a Song for Every Southern Man. Richmond?: 1861. V. 46

THE OLD Lady and her Niece the Fair Incognita, Detected and Brought to Justice. London: 1752. V. 46

THE OLD Lady's Pocket Atlas of the World. Chicago: 1886. V. 45

OLD Mother Hubbard and Her Dog. London: 1830. V. 39
OLD Mother Hubbard and Her Dog. London: 1863. V. 39

THE OLD Nursery Rhymes. London: 1933. V. 46

THE OLD Pack. London: 1710. V. 40
THE OLD Pack. London: 1710? V. 40

OLD Rhymes and New Stories. London. V. 40
OLD Rhymes and New Stories. London: 1930's. V. 40

OLD Rhymes for All Times. London: 1928. V. 46

OLD Testament Miniatures: a Medieval Picture Book with 283 Paintings from the Creation to the Story of David. New York: 1975. V. 46

OLD Things and New; or, Ancient Fables and Modern Men. Baltimore: 1835. V. 46

OLD Time Rhymes. London: 1915. V. 46

THE OLD Water Colour Society's CLUB Annual Volumes 1-12, 14, 15 & 19. London: 1924-41. V. 46

OLDEN, SARAH E.

The People of Tipi Sapa (The Dakotas): Tipi Sapa Mitaoyate Kin. Milwaukee: 1918. V. 39

OLDENBARNEVELD, JAN VAN

Barnevels Apology; or Holland Mysterie, with Marginall Catigations. London: 1618. V. 44

OLDENBERG, HERMANN

Buddha. London: 1904. V. 37

OLDENBURG, CLAES

Injun & Other Histories (1960). New York: 1966. V. 45

Proposals for Monuments and Buildings, 1965-69. Chicago: 1969. V. 42; 43; 46

Store Days. Documents from the Store 91961) and Ray Gun Theater (1962). New York: 1967. V. 41; 45

Store Days. Doceuments from the Store (1961) and Ray Gun Theater (1962). New York: 1967. V. 41

OLDENDORP, C. G. A.

Beschichte der Mission der Evangelischen Bruder auf den Caraibischen Inseln S. Thomas, S. Croix, und S. Jan. Herausgegeben Durch Johann Jakob Bossart. Barby: 1777. V. 42

Geschichte der Mission der Evangelischen Bruder auf den Caraibischen Inselin S. Thomas, S. Croix und S. Jan. Herausgege: 1777. V. 40

Geschichte der Mission der Evangelischen Bruder auf den Caraibischen Inseln S. Thomas, S. Croix und S. Jn. Herusgegeben Durch Johann Bossart... Leipzig: 1777. V. 38

OLDFIELD, CLAUDE 1889-

The Beast. Belfast: 1936. V. 40; 42; 43; 46

Three Fantastic Tales. London: 1934. V. 40; 42

OLDFIELD, OTIS

A Pictorial Journal of A Voyage Aboard the Three Masted Schooner Louise, Last of the Sailing Codfishermen Out of San Francisco, as Recorded in 1931 by the Artist Otis Oldfield. San Francisco: 1969. V. 38; 39; 40; 43; 44

OLDFIELD, THOMAS HINTON BURLEY

An Entire and Complete History, Political and Personal of the Boroughs of Great Britain. London: 1792. V. 39; 40; 43; 45

OLDHAM, J. BASIL

Blind Panels of English Binders. Cambridge: 1958. V. 37; 38; 40; 45; 46

English Blind-Stamped Bindings. Cambridge: 1949. V. 46

English Blind-stamped Bindings. Cambridge: 1952. V. 37; 38; 40; 43; 44; 45; 46

English Blind Stamped Bindings, with Blind Panels of English Binders. (with) Blind Panels of English Binders. Cambridge: 1952/58. V. 41; 43; 45

Shrewsbury School Library Bindings. Oxford: 1943. V. 38; 40

Shrewsbury School Library Bindings. Catalogue Raissone. Shrewsbury: 1943. V. 39

Shrewsbury School Library Binding, Catalogue Raissone. New York: & London: 1990. V. 43

OLDHAM, JOHN 1653-1683

Garnets Ghost, Addressing to the Jesuits, Met in Private Caball, Just After the Murther of Sir Edmund-Bury Godfrey... N.P.: 1679. V. 40; 42

Poems and Translations. London: 1683. V. 38; 40; 44

A Satyr Against Vertue. London: 1679. V. 40

Satyrs (in Verse) Upon the Jesuits... London. V. 44

Satyrs Upon the Jesuits: Written in the Year 1679, and Some Other Pieces by the Same Hand. London: 1682. V. 46

Satyrs Upon the Jesuits; Written in the Year 1679. (with) Some New Pieces Never Before Published. London: 1682, 1681. V. 40; 41

The Works of... Together with His Remains. London: 1684. V. 38

The Works of Mr. John Oldham, together with his Remains. London: 1686. V. 38; 39; 41; 44

The Works of Mr. John Oldham, Together With His Remains. London: 1695. V. 38

The Works. Together with His Remains. London: 1698. V. 37; 38

The Works. (to which) Are Added Memoirs of His Life, and Explanatory Notes Upon Some Obscure Passages of His Writings. London: 1722. V. 38; 40; 41; 42; 44

OLDHAM, W. S.

A Digest of the General Statute Laws... To which are subjoined the Repealed Laws of the Republic of Texas... Also the Colonization Laws of Mexico, Coahuila, and Texas, which were in force before the Declaration of Independence of Texas. Austin: 1859. V. 37

OLDISWORTH, WILLIAM

Callipaedia; or, the Art of Getting Pretty Children. London: 1710. V. 40

OLDMIXON, JOHN

The British Empire in America... London: 1708. V. 40

The British Empire in America. London: 1741. V. 38; 43

The Court of Atlantis. London: 1714. V. 44

The Dutch Barrier Our's. London: 1712. V. 39; 40

The Governour of Cyprus. London: 1703. V. 40

The History of Addresses. London: 1709. V. 39; 40; 41; 46

The History of England, During the Reigns of the Royal House of Stuart, Wherein the Errors of Late Histories are Discover'd and Corrected. London: 1730 for 1729. V. 46

The History of England, During the Reigns of King William and Queen Mary, Queen Anne, King George I. London: 1735. V. 46

Reflections on Dr. Swift's Letter to the Earl of Oxford, About the English Tongue. London: 1712. V. 46

OLDRIGHT, J. C.

Report of the Secretary of State of the State of Texas. Austin: 1870. V. 37

OLDROYD, IDA SHEPARD

Marine Shells of the West Coast of North America. 1924-27. V. 40; 42; 45

OLDROYD, OSBORN H.

The Assassination of Abraham Lincoln... Washington: 1901. V. 42

OLDS, IRVING S.

Bits and Pieces of American History as Told by A Collection of American Naval and Other Historical Prints and Paintings... New York: 1951. V. 37; 38

OLDYS, WILLIAM 1696-1761

The British Librarian. London: 1738. V. 40; 42; 44; 45

A Collection of Epigrams. London: 1735-37. V. 40

The Muses Library... London: 1737. V. 42; 44; 45

A Selection from the Harleian Miscellany of Tracts, Which Principally Regard the English History... London: 1793. V. 38

OLEARIUS, ADAM

Relation du Voyage d'Adam Olearius en Moscovie, Tartarie, et Perse, Augmenteee en Cette Nouvelle Edition de Plus d'un Tiers, & Particulierement d'une Seconde Partie Contenant le Voyage de Jean Albert de Mandelslo aux Indes Orientales. Paris: 1666. V. 38

O'LEARY, ARTHUR

A Defence of the Conduct and Writings of the Rev. Arthur O'Leary, During the Late Disturbances in Munster... London: 1787. V. 39

Miscellaneous Tracts by Rev. Arthur O'Leary... Dublin: 1781. V. 43

Miscellaneous Tracts in Which are Introduced the Rev. John Wesley's Letter and the Defence of the Protestant Associations. New York: 1821. V. 46

The Reverend Arthur O'Leary's Caution to the Common People of Ireland, Against Perjury, so Frequent at Assizes and Elections. Cork: 1783. V. 40

O'LEARY, JOHN

Recollections of Fenians and Feianism. London: 1896. V. 37

O'LEARY, JOSEPH

The Tribute; a Miscellaneous Volume, in Prose and Verse... Cork: 1833. V. 43

O'LEARY, PETER

Travel and Experiences in Canada, the Red River Territory and the United States. London: 1877. V. 38

Travel and Experinces in Canada, the Red River Territory and the United States. London: (1877). V. 37

OLESON, JOHN PETER

The Sources of Innovation in Later Etruscan Tomb Design. (Ca. 350-100 B.C.). Roma: 1982. V. 37

OLIN, STEPHEN

Haifa, or Life in Modern Palestine. Edinburgh: 1897. V. 45

Travels in Egypt, Arabia, Petraea and the Holy Land. New York: 1843. V. 41; 45

OLIN, STEPHEN continued

Travels in Egypt, Arabia Petraea and the Holy Land. New York: 1846. V. 45

OLINA, GIOVANNI PIETRO

Uccelliera Overo Della natura, e Proprieta di Diversi Uccelli e in Particolare di que' che Canano. Rome: 1622. V. 41

Uccelliera Overo Discorso Della Natura . . . Rome: 1684. V. 39

THE OLIO: Collected by a Literary Traveller. Boston: 1833. V. 38

OLIO; Or, Satirical Poetic Hodge Podge with an Illustrative or Explanatory Dialogue in Vindication of the Motive. Philadelphia: 1801. V. 45

OLIPHANT, LAURENCE 1829-1888

Altiora Peto. Edinburgh: 1883. V. 39

Haifa or Life in Modern Palestine. Edinburgh: 1887. V. 46

A Journey to Katmandu. London: 1852. V. 39

A Journey to Katmandu. New York: 1852. V. 39

The Land of Gilead; With Excursions in the Lebanon. Edinburgh: 1880. V. 43

Masollam; a Problem of the Period. Edinburgh & London: 1886. V. 41

Minnesota and the Far West. Edinburgh: 1855. V. 39; 40; 42; 43; 45

Minnesota and the Far West. London: 1855. V. 38; 40; 41

Narrative of the Earl of Elgin's Mission to China and Japan in the Years 1857, '58, '59. Edinburgh: 1859. V. 38; 41; 42; 46

Narrative of the Earl of Elgin's Mission to China and Japan. New York: 1860. V. 42

Narrative of the Earl of Elgin's Mission to China & Japan in the Years 1857, 58', 59'. Edinburgh: 1860. V. 37

Piccadilly. A Fragment of Contemporary Biograpbhy. London;: 1870. V. 39; 43

The Russian Shores of the Black Sea, in the Autumn of 1852, With a Voyage down the Volga, and a Tour through the Country of the Don Cossacks. London: 1853. V. 40

The Russian Shores of the Black Sea in the Autumn of 1852 With a Voyage Down the Volga, and A Tour through the Country of the Don Cossacks. London: 1854. V. 42

OLIPHANT, MARGARET

Agnes Hopetoun's Schools and Holidays. Cambridge & London: 1859. V. 42

A Country Gentleman and His Family. London: 1886. V. 41

The Duke's Daughter and the Fugitives. Edinburgh: 1890. V. 41; 42

OLIPHANT, MARGARET OLIPHANT WILSON 1828-1897

Annals of a Publishing House: William Blackwood and His Sons, Their Magazine and Friends. New York: 1897-98. V. 44

A Beleaguered City. London: 1881. V. 40

Caleb Field. London: 1851. V. 38

Chronicles of Carlingford. The Rector and the Doctor's Family. Edinburgh: 1863. V. 44

Chronicles of Carlingford. The Perpetual Curate. Edinburgh: 1864. V. 44

Cousin Mary. London: 1888. V. 44

The Heir Presumptive and the Heir Apparent. London: 1892. V. 38

John Drayton, Being a History of the Early Life and Devlopment of a Liverpool Engineer. London: 1851. V. 37; 40

Joyce. London: 1888. V. 40

Kirsteen: a Story of a Scotch Family Seventy Years Ago. London: 1890. V. 43

The Laird of Norlaw. London: 1858. V. 40

The Land of Darkness, Along the Some Further Chapters in the Experiences of the Little Pilgrim. London: 1888. V. 40

The Literary History of England. London: 1882. V. 38; 40

The Makers of Venice. London: 1887. V. 43

The Makers of Modern Rome in Four Books. London: & New York: 1895. V. 46

Memoir of Count De Montalembert Peer of France . . . London: 1872. V. 46

Merkland. London: 1851. V. 44

The Railway Man and His Children. London: 1891. V. 38

William Blackwood and His Sons. Their Magazine and Friends. Edinburgh & London: 1897-98. V. 44; 45

Zaidee. Edinburgh & London: 1856. V. 40

OLIPHANT, THOMAS

La Musa Madrigalesca; or a Collection of Madrigals, Ballets, Roundelays, etc. London: 1837. V. 40; 41

OLIVER, A. G.

Entomologie, ou Histoire Naturelle des Insects Avec Leurs Caracteres Generiques et Spefiques . . . Paris: 1808. V. 44

OLIVER & HARRISON

Memoirs of Lady Hamilton . . . London: 1835. V. 46

OLIVER, ANDREW

An Essay on Comets, in Two Parts. Salem: 1772. V. 37

OLIVER, C.

The Winds of Time. New York: 1957. V. 44

OLIVER, D.

Flora of Tropical Africa. London: 1868-1902. V. 37; 38

OLIVER, EDWARD E.

Across the Border or Pathan and Biloch. London: 1890. V. 42; 46

OLIVER, FREDERICK SCOTT 1864-1934

The Endless Adventure. London: 1930-35. V. 41

OLIVER, GEORGE

Monasticon Dioecesis Exoniensis, Being a Collection of Records and Instruments Illustrating the Ancient Conventual Collegiate . . . Exter: 1846. V. 46

Report of the Naval & Military Banquet, Held at Glasgow, 21st June 1849 and Summary of the Peninsular War. Glasgow: 1849. V. 42

OLIVER, GEORGES, BARON 1769-1832

Essay on the Theory of the Earth. Edinburgh & London: 1827. V. 37

OLIVER, ISABELLA

Poems on Various Subjects. Carlisle: 1805. V. 40

OLIVER, J. RUTHERFORD

Upper Teviotdale and the Scotts of Buccleugh; a Local and Family History. Harwick: 1887. V. 37; 39

OLIVER, JAMES

Wreck of the Glide. Boston: 1846. V. 38; 39

OLIVER, JEAN

Architecture of the Kidney in Chronic Bright's Disease. New York: 1939. V. 42; 44

OLIVER, JOHN W.

Songs of the '45. Edinburgh: 1945. V. 41

OLIVER, LEON

The Great Sensation. Chicago: 1873. V. 44

OLIVER, PASFIELD

The Voyage of Francois Leguat of Bresse to Rodriguez, Mauritius, Java and the Cape of Good Hope. London: 1891. V. 45

OLIVER, PETER

A New Chronicle of 'The Compleat Angler'. New York: 1936. V. 39; 40; 42; 43

OLIVER, SAMUEL P.

The True Story of the French Dispute in Madagascar. London: 1885. V. 42; 43

OLIVER, THOMAS

Dangerous Trades: the Historical, Social and Legal Aspects of Industrial Occupations as Affecting Health . . . New York: 1902. V. 45

OLIVER, VERE LANGFORD

The History of the Island of Antigua, one of the Leeward Caribbees in the West Indies, from the First Settlement in 1635 to the Present Time. London: 1894-99. V. 42

The Monumental Inscriptions in the Churches and Churchyards of the Island of Barbados, British West Indies. London: 1915. V. 41

OLIVER, WILLIAM

A Practical Dissertation on Bath-Waters . . . London: 1764. V. 38

OLIVERCRONA, HERBERT

An Experimental Study of the Circulatory Failure in Peritonitis. V. 39

OLIVERS, THOMAS

A Letter to the Reverend Mr. Toplady. London: 1770. V. 44

Thomas Olivers of Tregynon. The Life of an Early Methodist Preacher Written by Himself. 1979. V. 41

OLIVIER DE CASTILLE

The History of Oliver and Arthur. Written in French in 1511 . . . Boston: 1903. V. 41

OLIVIER, E.

Manuel de l'Amateur de Reliures Armoriees Francaises. Paris: 1924-38. V. 41

OLIVIER, EDITH

Night Thoughts of a Country Landlady - Being the Pacific Experiences of Miss Emma Nightingale in Time of War. London: 1943. V. 46

OLIVIER, J.

Fencing Familiarized; or, a New Treatise on the Art of Sword Play. London: 1771. V. 44; 45

Fencing Familiarized; or, a New Treatise on the Art of Sword Play. York: 1771. V. 42

Fencing Familiarized, or a New Treatise on the Art of Sword Play. London: 1771-72. V. 43

Fencing Familiarized: or A New Treatise on the Art of Small Word. London: 1780. V. 37

Memoirs of the Life and Adventures of Signor Rozelli. (with) A Continuation . . . London: 1715/24. V. 45

OLIVIER, LAURENCE

On Acting. London: 1986. V. 44

OLIVIERI, BERNARDINO

Vedute Degli Avanzi Monumenti Antichi delle due Sicilie. Rome: 1795. V. 45

OLIVIERO, ANTONIO FRANCESCO 1520-1580

La Allammana. Venice: 1567. V. 37; 43

OLLA Podrida; or Etchings of Fancy for Grown-up Children. 1831. V. 46

OLLIER, EDMUND

The Dore Gallery. London: and New York: 1870. V. 45

The Life and Works of Gustave Dore. London & New York: 1889. V. 39

OLLIVANT, J. E.

A Breeze from the Great Salt Lake, or New Zealand to New York by the New Mail Route. London: 1871. V. 37; 39; 44

OLLIVER, G. H.

Notes on the Management of the Gardner-Serpollet Steam Motor Car. London: 1903. V. 38

OLLIVIER, WILLIAM

Rules and Articles, or Laws of a Society, Held at the House of Mr. Thomas Hancock . . . in the Borough of Macclesfield and County of Chester . . . Macclesfield: 1862. V. 42

OLMSTEAD, CHARLES H.

The Memoirs of Charles H. Olmstead. Savannah: 1964. V. 44

Reminiscences of Service with the First Volunteer Regiment of Georgia, Charleston Harbor, in 1863. Savannah: 1879. V. 41; 43; 44

OLMSTED, DENISON

An Introduction to Natural Philosophy . . . New Haven: 1831 & 1832. V. 44

OLMSTED, DUNCAN H.

Bartholomeus Zanni, Printer at Venice 1486-1518 and at Portese 1489-90. Berkeley: 1962. V. 39; 41

40 Years - a Chronology of Announcements and Keepsakes The Roxburghe Club of San Francisco. San Francisco: 1968. V. 41; 45

OLMSTED, FREDERICK LAW 1822-1903

The Cotton Kingdom: a Traveller's Observations on Cotton and Slavery in the American Slave States. New York: 1861. V. 42; 46

Frederick Law Olmsted Landscape Artist 1822-1903. Central Park as a Work of Art and as a Great Municipal Enterprise 1853-1895. New York: 1928. V. 39

A Journey in the Seaboard Slave States. New York: 1856. V. 40; 44; 46

A Journey through Texas. New York: 1857. V. 37; 38; 41; 46

A Journey through Texas . . . New York: 1859. V. 39; 46

A Journey in the Back Country. London: 1860. V. 40; 41

A Journey In the Back Country. New York: 1860. V. 40; 44; 45

A Journey in the Seaboard Slave States in the Years 1853-1854, Remarks on Their Economy. New York: 1904. V. 42

A Journey through Texas. London: 1857. V. 40

Walks and Talks of an American Farmer in England. London: 1852. V. 43

Walks and Talks of an American Farmer in England. New York: 1854. V. 40

OLNEY, GEORGE WASHINGTON

A Guide to Florida 'the Land of Flowers.' . . . New York: 1872. V. 41

OLNEY. Hymns in Three Books. London: 1812. V. 42

OLSCHIKI, LEONARDO

Machiavelli the Scientist. Berkeley: 1945. V. 40

OLSEN, O. T.

Fisherman's Epitome of Navigation on Offshore Sailing, the Compass, Methods of Fishing, Signals . . . Hull: 1876. V. 38

OLSEN, TILLIE

Silences. New York: 1977. V. 46

Tell Me a Riddle. Philadelphia: 1961. V. 39; 42

Tell Me a Riddle. Philadelphia/New York: 1961. V. 40; 42

Tell Me a Riddle. New York: 1978. V. 37; 40; 42

OLSHAUSEN, THEODOR

Geschichte der Mormonen Ober Jungsten-Tages-Heiligen in Nordamerika. Gottingen: 1856. V. 45

OLSON, CHARLES

Anecdotes of the Late War. Highlands. V. 37; 38; 40; 42

Archaeologist of Morning. London: 1970. V. 37

Call Me Ishmael. New York: 1947. V. 37; 38; 39; 40; 41; 45; 46

Charles Olson in Connecticut. Iowa City: 1974. V. 42

Charles Olson and Ezra Pound: an Encounter at St. Elizabeths. New York: 1975. V. 40

Charles Olson and Robert Creeley: the Complete Correspondence. 1980-83. V. 42; 44

The Complete Correspondence. Santa Barbara: 1980-83. V. 44

The Maximus Poems 1-10. Stuttgart: 1953. V. 40; 42; 43; 44; 46

The Maximus Poems 1-10 & 11-22. Stuttgart: 1953, 1956. V. 37; 38; 42; 44; 46

The Maximus Poems. 11-22. Stuttgart: 1956. V. 39; 43; 45

The Maximus Poems. New York: 1960. V. 45

Maximus from Dogtown - I. San Francisco: 1961. V. 37

Mayan Letters. Palma de Majorca: 1953. V. 45

Mayan Letters . . . Edited by Robert Creeley. (Palma de Mallorca): 1953. V. 37

Stocking Cap: A Story. N.P.: 1966. V. 45

This. Black Mountain: 1952. V. 39

West. London: 1966. V. 37; 38; 40; 45

OLSON, ERNST W.

History of the Swedes of Illinois. Chicago: 1908. V. 37

OLSON, TOBY

The Brand. Mt. Horeb: 1969. V. 44

Doctor Miriam. Mt. Horeb: 1977. V. 39; 44

Maps. Mt. Horeb: 1969. V. 38

OLUFSEN, O.

Through the Unknown Pamirs. London: 1904. V. 39; 42

OMAHA Illustrated in Albertype. New York: 1888. V. 41

O'MALLEY, BRIAN

The Animals of Saint Gregory. Rhandirmwyn: 1981. V. 37

OMAR KHAYYAM

The Mirror and the Eye. Gloucestershire: 1984. V. 39; 40

The Mirror & the Eye. Rubaiyat of Omar Khayyam. London: 1984. V. 45

Penillion Omar Khayyam Wedi eu Cyfieithu o'r Berseg i'r Gymraeg gan John Morris-Jones. 1928. V. 44

Penillion Omar Khayyam. Wedi eu cyfeithu o'r Berseg i'r Gymraeg gan John Morris Jones. Newtown: 1928. V. 37; 38; 40; 42; 43; 45

The Quatrains of . . . London: 1906. V. 43

The Rubaiyat of Omar Khayyam. V. 38; 39

Rubaiyat of Omar Khayyam. Edinburgh. V. 39

The Rubaiyat of Omar Khayyam. London. V. 38; 40; 43; 45

Rubaiyat of Omar Khayyam. New York. V. 37; 41; 43; 45; 46

The Rubaiyat of Omar Khayyam, the Astronomer-Poet of Persia. London: 1859. V. 46

Rubaiyat of Omar Khayyam. Madras: 1862. V. 38

Rubaiyat of . . . London: 1872. V. 37; 38

The Rubaiyat of . . . Boston: 1878. V. 42

Rubaiyat of Omar Khayyam: and the Salaman and Absal of Jami: Rendered into English Verse. London: 1879. V. 37

Rubaiyat of Omar Khayyam. Boston: 1884. V. 43; 46

Rubaiyat of Omar Khayyam. London: 1887. V. 38

The Rubaiyat. St. Petersburgh: 1888. V. 44

Rubaiyat. Boston: 1894. V. 39

Rubaiyat. Portland: 1895. V. 41

Rubaiyat of Omar Khayyam. Chelsea: 1896. V. 38

The Rubaiyat. London: 1897. V. 37; 38; 45

Rubaiyat of Omar Khayyam: A Paraphrase from Several Literal Translations by Richard Le Gallienne. New York: 1897. V. 37

Rubaiyat of Omar Khayyam. Springfield: 1897. V. 37; 38; 41; 43; 46

The Rubaiyat of Omar Khayyam. New York: 1899. V. 37

Rubaiyat of . . . Portland: 1899. V. 39; 46

Rubaiyat of Omar Khayyam. Boston: 1900. V. 40; 45

The Rubaiyat of . . . East Aurora: 1900. V. 44

Rubaiyat. New York: 1900. V. 41

Rubaiyat of Omar Khayyam. Boston: 1901. V. 45

Rubaiyat of Omar Khayyam. London: 1901. V. 37; 38; 39; 42

OMAR KHAYYAM continued

Rubaiyat of Omar Khayyam. London: 1901. V. 39

The Rubaiyat of . . . New York: 1902. V. 37; 38

The Rubaiyat of Umar Khaiyam. London: 1903. V. 41

The Rubaiyat of Umar Khaiyam Done Into English from the French of J.B. Nicolas . . . With an Introduction by Nathan Haskell Dole. London/New York: 1903. V. 37

So This Then is a Book of the Rubaiyat of Omar Khayyam Done Into English by Edward Fitzgerald. 1904. V. 40

The Rubaiyat of Omar Khayyam. London: 1908. V. 40; 43; 44

Rubaiyat of Omar Khayyam. London: 1909. V. 37; 38; 40; 41; 42; 44; 45; 46

The Rubaiyat of Omar Khayyam. 24 colored plates by Willy Pogany. London: (1909). V. 37

Ruvaiyat of Omar Khayyam. New York: 1909. V. 41

Rubaiyat of Omar Khayyam. London: 1909? V. 41

Rubaiyat. London: 1910. V. 42; 43

Fifty Rubaiyat of Omar Khayyam. Wausau: 1910. V. 41

Rubaiyat of Omar Khayyam. 1911. V. 41

Rubaiyat of Omar Khayyam. London: 1911. V. 46

The Rubaiyat of Omar Khayyam. New York: 1912. V. 37

The Rubaiyat of Omar Khayyam. London: 1913. V. 39; 41; 44; 46

The Rubaiyat. Translated into English Verse by Edward Fitgerald, with Illustrations photographed from Life Studies by Adelaide Hanscom and Blanche Cumming. London: (1914). V. 37

The Rubaiyat of Omar Khayyam. London: 1915. V. 45; 46

Rubaiyat. New York: 1915. V. 38; 45

The Rubaiyat of Omar Khayyam. Edinburgh: 1919. V. 41

Rubaiyat of Omar Khayam. London: & Edinburgh;: 1919. V. 44

The Rubaiyat of Omar Khayyam. London: 1920. V. 40; 41; 42; 43; 46

The Rubaiyat of Omar Khayyam. Singapore: 1920. V. 43

Rubaiyat of . . . Sussex: 1920. V. 39

Rubaiyat of Omar Khayyam. London: 1920's? V. 44

Rubaiyat. London: 1921. V. 41; 46

Rubaiyat of Omar Khayyam. London: 1922. V. 41; 43; 44

Rubaiyat. New York: 1922. V. 43; 45

The Rubaiyat of 'Umar Khaiyam. London: 1924. V. 41; 42; 45

Rubaiyat of . . . San Francisco: 1926. V. 38

Rubaiyat of Omar Khayyam. London: 1927. V. 45; 46

The Rubaiyat of Omar Khayyam. London: 1928. V. 44

Rubaiyat of . . . Garden City: 1930. V. 39; 45

Rubaiyat of Omar Khayyam. London: 1930. V. 42; 44; 46

Rubaiyat of Omar Khayyam. The First and Fourth Renderings in English Verse by Edward Fitzgerald. Introduction by George Saintsbury. New York: (1930). V. 37

Rubaiyat of Omar Khayyam. New York: 1930. V. 39; 42; 46

Rubaiyat of Omar Khayyam. Singapore: 1930. V. 45

From Omar Khayyam. The Andrew Lang Edition of the Rubaiyat. Monroe: 1935. V. 41

Rubaiyat. New York: 1935. V. 45

The Rubaiyat. (New York): 1935. V. 37

The Rubaiyat. N.P.: 1935. V. 45

Rubaiyat. London: 1938. V. 40

Rubaiyat of Omar Khayyam. London: 1940. V. 37; 41; 46

Rubaiyat of Omar Khayyam. New York: 1940. V. 39; 40; 41

The Rubaiyat. London: 1942. V. 37

Rubaiyat of Omar Khayyam. Jamaica: 1943. V. 39; 45

The Rubaiyat. London: 1958. V. 46

The Rubaiyat of Omar Khayyam. Leicester: 1970. V. 40

Rubaiyat of Omar Khayyam. Kent: 1973. V. 39

Rubaiyat of . . . London: 1973. V. 39

The Rubaiyat of Omar Khayyam. London: 1980. V. 40; 41

Rubaiyat. London: 1981. V. 43

Rubaiyat. (Sussex: ca. 1920). V. 37

Rubaiyat of Omar Khayyam. Bombay: (n.d.). V. 37

The Original Rubaiyyat of Omar Khayaam. New York: 1968. V. 43

So this then is a ook of The Rubaiyat of Omar Khayyam, done into English by Edward Fitzgerald with an Introduction by Clarence S. Darrow. East Aurora: 1904. V. 37

OMAR KYAYYAM

Rubaiyat of Omar Khayyam. The first and fourth renderings into English verse by Edward Fitzgerald. London: (1930). V. 37

O'MEARA, BARRY E.

An Exposition of Some of the Transactions, That Have Taken Place at St. Helena, Since the Appointment of Sir Hudson Lowe as Governor of that Island . . . London: 1819. V. 44; 46

Napoleon in Exile: The Opinions and Reflexions of Napoleon on the Most Important Events of His Life and Government in His Own Words. London: 1822. V. 44; 45

O'MEARA, BARRY EDWARD

Napoleon at St. Helena. London: 1888. V. 45

O'MEARA, FREDERICK A.

Shahguhnahshe Ahnuhmeahwine Muzzeneegun Ojibway Anwawaud Azheuhnekenootah Beegahdag. Winnipeg: 1889. V. 44; 45

O'MEARA, JAMES

Broderick and Gwin: the Most Extraordinary Contest for a Seat in the Senate of the United States Ever Known . . . San Francisco: 1881. V. 40; 41; 44

The Vigilance Committee of 1856. San Francisco: 1887. V. 40

OMEGA WORKSHOPS

Original Woodcuts by Various Artists. London: 1918. V. 40

O'MELVENY, HENRY WILLIAM

William G. Kerckhoff, a Memorial. Los Angeles: 1935. V. 41

OMERIQUE, ANTONIO HUGO DE b. 1634

Analysis Geometrica Sive Nova, et Vera Methodus Resolvendi tam Problemata Geometrica, Quam Arithmeticas Quaestiones. Cadiz: 1698. V. 38; 42

Analysis Geometrica sive Nova, et Vera Methodus Resolvendi Tam Problemata Geometrica, Quam Arithmeticas Quaestiones. Gadibus (Cadiz): 1698. V. 38

AN OMITTED Pickwick Paper. Restored by Poz. Reprinted from the Token of 1841. Brooklyn: 1903. V. 40

OMMUNDSEN, HARCOURT d. 1915

Rifles and Ammunition and Rifle Shooting. London: 1915. V. 39

Rifles and Ammunition. New York: 1915. V. 39

OMNIA Comesta a Belo, or, an Answer Out of the West to a Question Out of the North. London?: 1667. V. 38; 39

OMPTEDA, BARON

In the King's German Legion. London: 1894. V. 42

OMWAKE, JOHN

The Conestoga Six-Horse Bell Teams of Eastern Pennsylvania. Cincinnati: 1930. V. 37; 38; 40; 41; 42; 44

ON Monopoly and Reform of Manners. London: 1795. V. 43

ON The Ambitious Projects of Russia in Regard to North West America, with Particular Reference to New Albion and New California. By an Englishman. Kentfield: 1955. V. 38

ON the Ambitious Projects of Russia in Regard to North West Americana, With Particular Refernce to New Albion and New California. San Francisco: 1955. V. 40; 46

ON the Crimes of Those Two Unhappy Brothers, Er and Onan, Judah's Two Sons; Who for Defileing Their Nuptial Bed, and Frustrating the End of Marriage, Were Punished with Immediate Death . . . London: 1724. V. 41

ONANIA Examined, and Detected. London: 1723. V. 41

ONANIA; or, the Heinious Sin of Self-Pollution, and All Its Frightful Consequences, in Both Sexes, Consider'd with Spiritual and Physical Advice to Those Who Have Already Injur'd Themselves by This Abominable Practice. London: 1722. V. 41

ONANIA; or, The Heinous Sin of Self-Pollution, and All Its Frightful Consequences . . . London: 1756. V. 40

ONDERDONK, HENRY

Revolutionary Incidents of Sufolk and Kings Counties. New York: 1849. V. 39

1,000 Quaint Cuts from Books of Other Days, Including Amusing Illustrations from Children's Story Books, Fables, Chap-Books, etc . . . From Original Wooden Blocks Belonging to the Leadenhall Press. London. V. 40

THE ONE-EYED Coronation; or, a Peep into Westminster Abbey. London. V. 38

100 Best Books. London: 1988. V. 45

ONE Hundred Influential American Books Printed Before 1900. 1947. V. 39

ONE Hundred Merrie and Delightsome Stories. U.S.A.: 1924. V. 41

ONE Thousand Valuabe Secrets in the Elegant and Useful Arts . . . Philadelphia: 1795. V. 37; 40; 42

O'NEALL, JOHN BELTON

The Annals of Newberry, Historical, Biographical and Anecdotical. Charleston: 1859. V. 42

The Annals of Newberry in Two Parts. Newberry: 1892. V. 40

O'NEIL, ELIZABETH

The War 1914-1916. A History and an Explanation for Boys and Girls. London: 1914-1917. V. 45; 46

O'NEILL, CHARLES

A Dictionary of Calico Printing and Dyeing. London: 1862. V. 38

A Dictionary of Calico Printing and Dyeing; containing a brief account of all the substances and processes in use in the arts of printing and dyeing textile fabrics; with practical receipts and scientific information. London/Manchester: 1862. V. 37

O'NEILL, EUGENE GLADSTONE 1888-1953

Ah, Wilderness! New York: 1933. V. 39; 42; 44; 45; 46

Ah Wilderness! New York: 1972. V. 43; 44

All God's Chillun Got Wings and Welded. New York: 1924. V. 39; 40; 41; 43

All God's Chillun Got Wings; and Welded. New York: (1924). V. 37

Anna Christie. New York: 1930. V. 39

Beyond the Horizon. New York: 1920. V. 39

Days Without End. 1934. V. 46

Days Without End. New York: 1934. V. 39

Days Without End. New York: 1934. V. 39

Desire Under the Elms. New York: 1925. V. 46

Dynamo. New York: 1929. V. 37; 38; 39; 41; 42; 43; 45; 46

The Emperor Jones. London: 1925. V. 40

The Emperor Jones. New York: 1928. V. 37; 39; 41; 42; 46

George Pierce Baker: A Memorial. New York: 1939. V. 37

Gold. New York: 1920. V. 39; 44

The Great God Brown, Etc. New York: 1926. V. 42; 46

The Hairy Ape and Other Plays. London: 1923. V. 45

The Hairy Ape. New York: 1929. V. 37; 38; 39; 40

The Iceman Cometh. New York: 1946. V. 38; 40; 43

The Iceman Cometh. New York: 1972. V. 38

The Iceman Cometh. 1982. V. 38; 39; 42; 45

The Iceman Cometh. New York: 1982. V. 38; 39; 40; 41; 43; 44; 45; 46

Inscriptions: Eugene O'Neill to Carlott Monterey O'Neill. New Haven: 1960. V. 38; 39; 40; 42

Lazarus Laughed. New York: 1927. V. 38; 39; 40; 41; 42; 43; 45

Lost Plays. 1913-1915. New York: 1950. V. 37

Marco Millions. New York: 1927. V. 39; 41; 43

Mourning Becomes Electra. V. 45

Mourning Becomes Electra. New York: 1931. V. 42; 43; 44; 46

Plays: First Series. London: 1922. V. 44

The Plays. New York: 1927. V. 42; 44

The Plays. New York: 1934. V. 37; 39; 42

Strange Interlude. New York: 1928. V. 37; 39; 40; 41; 43; 45; 46

Thirst. Boston: 1914. V. 39; 41; 42; 43; 45; 46

The Complete Works. New York: 1924. V. 37; 43; 46

O'NEILL, FRANCIS

Irish Folk Music. Chicago: 1910. V. 46

O'NEILL, HENRY

The Fine Arts and Civilization of Ancient Ireland. London: 1862. V. 43

The Fine Arts and Civilization of Ancient Ireland. London: 1863. V. 42; 44

O'NEILL, JAMES

Garrison Tales from Tonquin. Boston: 1895. V. 41; 43

O'NEILL, JOHN

The Horros of Drunkenness. London: 1848. V. 38

O'NEILL, M. J.

The Life, Love and Adventures of Colonel and Chevalier Edgar Daniel Boone, the King of the Beasts, and Mlle. Carlotta, the Lion Queen. New York: 1893. V. 37

O'NEILL, THOMAS

An Address to the People of the United Kingdoms of Great Britain and Ireland Containing An Account of the Sufferings of Thos. O'Neill, a British Officer, While Confined In the Prison of the Conciergerie, at Paris, for Two Years and Ten Moths . . . . London: 1807. V. 38

A Concise and Accurate Account of the Proceedings of the Squadron Under the Command of Rear Admiral Sir Sydney Smith, K.S. &c. in Effecting the Escape of the Royal Family of Portugal to the Brazils, on November 29, 1807 . . . London: 1810. V. 46

O'NEILL, TIP

Man of the House. New York: (1987). V. 37

O'NEILL, W. O.

Hoof and Horn. Prescott: 1888. V. 40

ONGANIA, F.

A Glance at the Grimani Breviary Preserved in S. Mark's Library. Venice: 1906. V. 39

ONGANIA, FERD

Early Venetian Printing Illustrated. Venice: 1895. V. 37; 39; 41

ONGONIA, FERD.

Calli e Canali in Venezia. Venice: 1895. V. 37

O'NIAL, OWEN ROE

Letters. Ireland: 1779. V. 39

ONION, STEPHEN B.

Narrative of the Mutiny on Board the Schooner Plattsburg, William Hackett, Master. Boston: 1819. V. 42

ONIS, LUIS DE

Memoria Sobre Las Negociaciones Entre Espana y Los Estados-Unidos de America . . . Madrid: 1820. V. 40

ONLY a Jap Dollee. London: 1890. V. 39

ONLY Authentic Life of Abraham Lincoln, Alias 'Old Abe.' N.P.: 1864. V. 37

ONO, YOKO

Grapefruit. London: 1970. V. 38; 41

O'NOLAN, BRIAN 1911-1966

At Swim-two-Birds. London: 1939. V. 38

At Swim Two Birds. New York: 1939. V. 41

An Beal boct. 1942. V. 41

The Best of Myles. A Selection from 'Cruiskeen Lawn.' London: 1968. V. 41

The Dalkey Archive. London: 1964. V. 41

The Hard Life. London: 1961. V. 41

The Poor Mouth. London: 1973. V. 41

ONOSANDRO

Dell'Ottimo Capitano Generale, et del Suo Officio. Venice: 1548. V. 38

ONSLOW-FORD, GORDON

Paintings in the Instant. London: 1964. V. 46

ONTARIO. LEGISLATIVE ASSEMBLY

Emigration to Canada. The Province of Ontario; its soil, climate, resources, institutions, free grant lands, &c, &c for the information of intending emigrants. (cover title). Issued by authority of the Government of Ontario. Toronto: 1869. V. 37

ONTYD, COENRAAD GERARD 1776-1844

A Treatise on Mortal Diseases, Containing a Particular View of the Different Ways in Which They Lead to Death and the Best Means of Preventing Them, by Medical Treatment from Proving Fatal. London: 1798. V. 45

ONWHYN, T.

12 Illustrations to the Pickwick Club. Drawn and etched in 1847-now first published. London: 1894. V. 37

ONWHYN, THOMAS

Illustrations to Nicholas Nickleby. London: 1838. V. 43

Illustrations to Nicholas Nickleby, Part II. N.P.: London: 1838. V. 40

Thirty-Two Illustrations to Pickwick. London: 1848. V. 40; 43

O'ORCY, LADISLAS

Airship Manual. New York: 1917. V. 37

OORT, E. D. VAN

Ornithologia Neerlandica. 1922. V. 43

OORT, R. E. D. VAN

Ornithologia Neerlandica; De Vogels van Nederland. 'S Gravenhage: 1922. V. 42

OOSTEN, H. VAN

Dutch Gardener; or, the Compleat Florist, Containing the Most Successful Method of Cultivating All Sorts of Flowers . . . London: 1711. V. 42; 45

THE OPAL. New York: 1847. V. 43

THE OPAL: a Pure Gift for the Holy Days. New York: 1844. V. 38

OPE, ARTHUR

Reproductions of Some of the Important Paintings and of their Details Illustrating the Technique of the Artists. Boston: 1936. V. 46

OPEN COURT PUBLISHING CO.

The Work of the Open Court Publishing Co. Chicago: 1909. V. 40

OPERA at Home. London: 1921. V. 45

THE OPERA Rumpus; or, the Ladies in the Wrong Box! London: 1783. V. 42

THE OPERATIONS of the British and Allied Arms, During the Campaigns of 1743 and 1744. London: 1744. V. 41

OPIE, AMELIA

Adeline Mowbray, or the Mother and Daughter. London: 1805. V. 39
Detraction Displayed. London: 1828. V. 46
Illustrations of Lying in all its Branches. London: 1825. V. 37
New Tales. London: 1818. V. 44
Poems. London: 1802. V. 44
Poems. (with) The Warrior's Return. London: 1808. V. 39
Poems. New York: 1808. V. 38
Simples Tales. London: 1806. V. 37
Tales of the Heart. London: 1820. V. 43
Valentine's Eve. London: 1816. V. 42
The Warrior's Return and Other Poems . . . London: 1808. V. 43
The Warrior's Return and Other Poems. New York: 1808. V. 39

OPIE, EUGENE L.

Disease of the Pancreas. Its Cause and Nature. Philadelphia: 1903. V. 46

OPIE, IONA

Children's Games in Street and Playground. Oxford: 1969. V. 41
The Oxford Nursery Rhyme Book. Oxford: 1955. V. 41

OPIE, JOHN NEWTON

A Rebel Cavalryman with Lee Stuart and Jackson. Chicago: 1899. V. 39; 42

OPITZ, MARTIN

Weltliche Poemata. Frankfurt: 1644. V. 39

OPIUM Eating. An Autobiographical Sketch. By an Habituate. Philadelphia: 1876. V. 38

THE OPIUM Habit, With Suggestions as to the Remedy. New York: 1868. V. 41

OPORINUS, JOHANNES 1536-1567

Dramata Sacra, Comoediae Atquec Tragoediae. Basel: 1547. V. 40; 46

OPPE, ADOLF PAUL 1878-1957

English Drawings, Stuart and Georgian Periods, in the Collection of His Majesty the King at Windsor Castle. London: 1950. V. 39
Raphael. London: 1970. V. 40; 46
Raphael. New York: 1970. V. 44
Thomas Rowlandson. London: 1923. V. 37; 39; 41; 44
The Water-Color Drawings of John Sell Cotman. London: 1923. V. 39
The Watercolours of Turner, Cox and De Wint. London: 1925. V. 39; 42

OPPEN, EDWARD A.

A Catalogue of British and Foreign Postage Stamps. London: 1863. V. 45

OPPEN, GEORGE

Alpine. Mt. Horeb: 1969. V. 44
Primitive. 1978. V. 43; 44

OPPENHEIM, E. C.

New Climbs in Norway. London: 1898. V. 43; 44

OPPENHEIM, LEO

Glass and Glassmaking in Ancient Mesopotamia. Corning: 1970. V. 44

OPPENHEIM, MAX VON

Tell Halaf. A New Culture in Oldest Mesopotamia. London and New York: 1931. V. 40; 42
Tell Halaf: a New Culture in Oldest Mesopotamia. London: 1931. V. 44
Tell Halaf. A New Culture in Oldest Mesopotamia. New York/London: ca. 1931. V. 37

OPPENHEIMER, DAVID

Catalgus der Seit Vielen Jahren Beruhmten Vollstandinge Hebreischen Bibliothek. Hamburg: 1782. V. 46
The Mineral Resources of British Columbia: Practical Hints for Capitalists and Intending Settlers. Vancouver: 1889. V. 42

OPPENHEIMER, LEHMANN J.

The Heart of Lakeland. Manchester: 1908. V. 44

OPPENHEIMER, PAUL

Beyond the Furies. Paris: 1985. V. 42

OPPERT, ERNEST

A Forbidden Land; Voyages to the Corea. London: 1880. V. 43
Forbidden Land: Voyages to the Corea. New York: 1882. V. 44

OPPERT, J.

Grande Inscription du Palais de Khorsabad. Paris: 1863. V. 44

OPPIAN

De Venatione. Libri IIII. Paris: 1555. V. 40; 45
Oppian's Halieuticks of the Nature of Fishes and Fishing of the Ancients. Oxford: 1722. V. 38; 41; 43; 45

OPPRESSION. a Poem. By an American. London: 1765. V. 46

OPSOPAUS, JOHANNES

Sibyllina Oracula ex Vett Codd. Paris: 1599. V. 40; 45

OPZOOMER, ADELE SOPHIA CORNELIA

In Troubled Times. London: 1883. V. 42; 46
Royal Favour. London: 1885. V. 39; 42

ORACIONES et Alia Pulchra ad Sanctam Annam. Heidelberg: 1500. V. 43

THE ORACLE; or, Fortune-Telling Almanack. Newport: 1819. V. 39

ORACLES. Durham: 1977. V. 46

ORACULO de la Europa, Consultado por los Principes de ella, Sobre los Negocios Presentes Politicos, y Militares. Madrid: 1744. V. 38

ORAGE, A. R.

Nietzsche in Outline and Aphorism. Edinburgh & London: 1907. V. 41

ORAM, WILLIAM

Precepts and Observations on the Art of Colouring in Landscape Painting. London: 1810. V. 38; 42; 44

ORANGE, JAMES

The Chater Collection Pictures Relating to China, Hong Kong, Macao, 1655-1860; With Historical and Descriptive Letterpress. London: 1924. V. 39

ORANGE JUDD COMPANY

Barn Plans and Outbuildings. New York: 1884. V. 38

ORATIO Dominica in CLV. Linguas Versa et Exoticis Characteribus . . . Parma: 1806. V. 43

AN ORATION, and Poem, Delivered Before the Government and Students of Harvard University . . . July 31, 1811. Cambridge: 1811. V. 37

AN ORATION Delivered at the State-House, in Philadelphia, to a Very Numerous Audience; on Thursday the 1st of August 1776 . . . . Philadelphia: 1776. V. 46

ORATIONES Horum Rhetorum. Aeschinis. Lysiae. Alcidamantis. Antisthenis (et al). Isocratis Orationes. Alcidamantis Contra Dicendi Magistros (etc.). Colophon. V. 37

ORATIONS Delivered at the Request of the Inhabitants of the Town of Boston to Commemorate the Evening of the 5th of March 1770, When a Number of Citizens Were Killed by a Party of British Troops. Boston: 1807. V. 40

ORATIONS Delivered at the Request of the Inhabitants of the Town of Boston, to Commemorate the Evening of the Fifth of March, 1770; When a Number of Citizens Were Killed by a Party of British Troops, Quatered Among Them, in a Time of Peace. Boston: 1785. V. 37; 40

ORATORES Attici. Ex Recensione Immanuelia Bekkeri. London: 1828. V. 45

ORBELIANI, SULKHAN-SABA

The Book of Wisdom and Lies. Hammersmith: 1894. V. 40
The Book of Wisdom and Lies. London: 1894. V. 43

ORBELLIS, NICOLAUS DE

Summule Philosophie Rationalis: seu Logica. Colophon: 1494. V. 37

ORCHARD, LIZZIE C.

Maj. General Hampton's Quickstep Respectfully Dedicated to the Officers and Privates of His Command. Columbia: 186-. V. 42

ORCHARD Songs. London: 1893. V. 41

THE ORCHID Album. London: 1882. V. 41

THE ORCHID Album. London: 1882-97. V. 39; 42

ORCHID Album, Comprising Coloured Figures and Descriptions of New, Rare and Beautiful Orchidaceous Plants. Tokyo: 1985. V. 38; 46

ORCUTT, WILLIAM DANA

The Book in Italy During the 15th and 16th Centuries Shown in Facsimile reproductions from the Most Famous Printed Volumes. London: 1928. V. 41

The Book in Italy During the Fifteenth and Sixteenth Centuries Shown in Facsimile Reproductions from the Most Famous Printed Volumes. New York: 1928. V. 38; 40; 45

In Quest of the Perfect Book... Boston: 1926. V. 42

ORCZY, BARONESS

The Old Scarecrow; a Story. New York: 1916. V. 37

ORD, CRAVEN

Vain Boastings of Frenchmen. The Same in 1386 as in 1798. London: 1798. V. 39

ORD, E. O. C.

Texas Frontier Troubles. Testimony Taken Before the Committee on Foreign Affairs. Washington: 1878. V. 39

ORD-HUME, A. W. J. G.

Clockwork Music. New York: & London: 1973. V. 44

ORD, MARK

An Essay on the Law of Usury. London: 1809. V. 40

THE ORDER of Chivalry. Hammersmith: 1893. V. 38

ORDER of Services at Faneuil Hall... as a Testimony of Respect to the Memory of John Quincy Adams, by the Legislature of Massachusetts. Boston: 1848. V. 39

ORDINAIRE, CLAUDE NICHOLAS

The Natural History of Volcanoes; Including Submarine Volcanoes, and Other Analogous Phenomena. London: 1801. V. 38; 40; 42; 45

AN ORDINANCE for the Government of the Territory of the United States, Northwest of the River Ohio. Cincinnati: 1795. V. 40

ORDONEZ DE CEVALLOS, PEDRO

Historia y Viage del Mundo... a las Cinco Partes de la Europa, Africa, Asia, America y Magalanica, con el Itinerario de Todo... Madrid: 1691. V. 39

Viage del Mundo. Madrid: 1614. V. 46

ORDONNANCES et Privileges des Foires de Lyon; et Leur Antiquite; Auec Celles de Brie & Champaigne. Lyons: 1560. V. 44

ORDONNANCES, Privileges, Franchises et Assistances Octroyez et Concedez par les... Estats Generaux des Provinces Unies... a La Compagnie des Indes Occidentales (etc.). Paris: 1623. V. 45

ORDWAY, ALBERT

Cycle-Infantry Drill Regulations. Boston: 1892. V. 37; 42; 44

ORDWAY, N. G.

Message of the Governor to the Legislative Assembly. Yankton: 1881. V. 37; 39

Second Biennial Message to the Legislative Assembly. Yankton: 1883. V. 37; 39

OREGON

In the Supreme Court of Oregon... Dowell Vs. Cardwell... Appeal from Jackson County... Suit in Equity to Enforce the Lien of an Attorney and Claim Agent, on $2,580 of the Oregon Indian War Debt, of W.H. Gridley, deceased--Smith Vs. Giswold... Jacksonville: 1877. V. 37

Journal of the Council of the Territory of Oregon, During the Second Session of the Legislative Assembly (With) Journal of the house of Representatives of the Territory of Oregon... Oregon City: 1851. V. 37

Oregon: Facts Regarding Its Climate, Soil, Mineral and Agricultural Resources, Means of Communication, Commerce and Industry With Map. Boston: 1877. V. 37

Proceedings of the First Annual Communication of the Grand Lodge of Odd Fellows of the Territory of Oregon. (Salem: 1867). V. 37

OREGON. CONSTITUTION

Constitution for the State of Oregon Passed by the Convention, Sept. 18, 1857. Salem: 1857. V. 43; 45

OREGON. Facts Regarding Its Climate, Soil, Mineral and Agricultural Resources, Means of Communication, Commerce and Industry... for the Use of Emigrants. Boston: 1876. V. 39; 42

OREGON. LAWS, STATUTES, ETC.

Laws of the A General and Local Nature Passed by the Legislative Committee and Legislative Assembly... Collected and Published Pursuant to an Act of the Legislative Assembly... Salem: 1853. V. 38; 42

The Statutes of Oregon. Enacted and Continued in Force by the Legislative Assembly, at the Session Commencing 5th Dec., 1853. Oregon: 1854. V. 38; 42; 45

OREGON. LAWS, STATUTES, ETC. - 1853

General Laws Passed by the Legislative Assembly of the Territory of Oregon... Fourth Regular Session... December 6, 1852. Oregon: 1853. V. 37

OREGON PIONEER ASSOCIATION

The Oregon Pioneer Association Transactions. Salem: 1875-86. V. 40

Transactions of the Fourth Annual Re-Union of the... for 1876... Salem: 1877. V. 39

Transactions of the Seventh Annual Re-Union of the Oregon Pioneer Association. Salem: 1880. V. 40; 42

Transactions of the Eighth Annual Re-Union of the Oregon Pioneer Association, for 1880. Salem: 1881. V. 42

Transactions of the Nineteenth (and Twenty-First) Annual Reunion of the Oregon Pioneer Association for 1891 (and 1893)... with Biographical Sketches and Other Matters of Historical Interest. Portland: 1893-94. V. 40; 42

OREGON RAILWAY AND NAVIGATION CO.

Annual Report of the Board of Directors of the... to the Stockholders. Boston: 1884. V. 37; 42

OREGON. (TERRITORY). LAWS, STATUTES, ETC. - 1851

Statutes of a General Nature Passed by the Session, Begun and Held at Oregon City, December 2, 1850. Oregon City: 1851. V. 37; 41

OREGON. The Cost, and the Consequences... By A Disciple of the Washington School. Philadelphia: 1846. V. 37; 42

O'REILLY, ALEXANDER

Regulations for the Granting of Land Under the Spanish Government of Louisiana. Washington: 1820. V. 37; 39

O'REILLY, BERNARD

The Adjacent Seas, and the Northwest Passage to the Pacific. New York: 1818. V. 37

The Cause of Ireland. Pleaded Before the Civilized World. New York: 1886. V. 39

Greenland, and Adjacent Seas, and the North-West Passage to the Pacific Ocean. London: 1818. V. 37; 38; 42; 43

Greenland, and the Adjacent Seas, and the Northwest Passage to the Pacific. New York: 1818. V. 37; 44

John MacHale, Archbishop of Tuam. His Life, Times and Correspondence. New York & Cincinnati: 1890. V. 39

Travels Through Denmark and Sweden. London: 1810. V. 40

O'REILLY, E.

An Irish-English Dictionary, with Copious Quotations... Dublin: 1864. V. 41

O'REILLY, EDWARD

An English-Irish Dictionary. Dublin: 1864. V. 46

An Irish-English Dictionary Containing Upwards of Twenty Thousand Words That Never Appeared in Any Former Irish Lexicon with Copious Quotations from the Most Esteemed Ancient and Modern Writers Etc. Dublin. V. 46

O'REILLY, HARRINGTON

Fifty Years on the Trail, a True Story of Western Life. London: 1889. V. 43

50 Years on the Trail. New York: 1889. V. 43

O'REILLY, JOHN BOYLE

In Bohemia. Boston: 1886. V. 37

Songs from the Southern Seas, and Other Poems. Boston: 1873. V. 40

O'REILLY, MONTAGU

Pianos of Sympathy. Norfolk: 1936. V. 44; 46

A Series of Twelve Views from Water-Colour Sketches Made on the Spot, During the Period of Service of H.M.S. Retribution in the Black Sea and the Bosphorus... London: 1856. V. 39

O'REILLY, MYLES

Lives of the Irish Martyrs and Confessors. New York: 1880. V. 39

Lives of the Irish Martyrs and Confessors. Also a Full and Complete History of the Penal Laws by Parnell. New York: 1881. V. 39

O'RELL, MAX

John Bull & Co. The Great Colonial Branches of the Firm. London: 1894. V. 38; 40; 42

OREM, WILLIAM

A Descripion of the Chanonry in Old Aberdeen in the Years 1724 and 1725. London: 1782. V. 38

ORESHIN, POLITRUK

The Diary of Politruk Oreshin. Helsinki: 1941. V. 44

ORFILA, M. P.

Directions for the Treatment of Persons Who Have Taken Poison, and Those in a State of Apparent Death . . . London: 1820. V. 42; 44

ORFORD, ROBERT WALPOLE, 1ST EARL OF 1676-1745

The Last Will and Testament of the Right Honourable . . . London: 1745. V. 38

A Letter on the Genius and Dispositions of the French Government Including a View of the Taxation of the French Empire. Philadelphia: 1810. V. 41

Memoirs of the Reign of King George III. London: 1894. V. 41

A Report from the Committee of Secrecy, Appointed . . . by the House of Commons, to Examine . . . Books and Papers . . . Relating to the Late Negotiations of Peace and Commerce, 9th June 1715 . . . London: 1715. V. 41

ORGEL, STEPHEN

Inigo Jones, the Theatre of the Stuart Court. London: 1973. V. 37; 45

ORIANS, G. H.

Blackbirds of the Americas. Seattle: 1985. V. 39

ORIBASII SARDIANI

Synopseos Ad Evsthivm Vilivm Libri Novem: Qvibus Tota Medicina in Compendivm Redacta Continentvr: Ioanne Baptista Rasario Novariensi Medico Interprete. Venetiis: 1554. V. 39

O'RIELLY, HENRY

Notices of Sullivan's Campaign, or the Revolutionary Warfare in Western New-York . . . Rochester: 1842. V. 46

Origin and Objects of the Slaveholders' Conspiracy Against Democratic Principles, as Well as Against the National Union Illustrated in the Speeches of Andrew Jackson Hamilton . . . New York: 1862. V. 41

Rochester in 1835. Brief Sketches of the Present Condition of the City of Rochester. Rochester: 1835. V. 46

Settlement in the West. Rochester: 1838. V. 43

THE ORIENTAL Annual, or Scenes in India. London: 1835. V. 40

ORIENTAL Ceramics: The World's Great Collections: Volume 12. The Metropolitan Museum of Modern Art. Tokyo: 1977. V. 39

ORIENTAL Ceramics: The World's Great Collections. Volume 7. Percival David Foundation of Chinese Art. Tokyo: 1976. V. 39

ORIENTAL Wanderings; or the Fortunes of Felix. London: 1824. V. 37; 39

ORIGEN, PSEUD.

Contra Celsum Libri octo: Eiusdem Philocalia. Cambridge: 1677. V. 39

THE ORIGIN and Authentic Narrative of the Present Marratta War; and also, the Late Rohilla War, in 1773 and 1774; Whereby the East-Indian Company's Troops (as Mercenaries) Exterminated that Brave Nation, and Openly Drove them for Asylum and Existence . . . London: 1781. V. 37

ORIGIN: First Series I-XX. 1951-57. V. 40

THE ORIGIN of Printing. In Two Essays. I. The Substance of Dr. Middleton's Dissertation on the Origin of Printing in England. II. Mr. Meerman's Account of the Invention of the Art at Harleim, and Its Progress to Mentz . . . London: 1776. V. 39; 42

THE ORIGINAL Bath Guide Considerably Enlarged and Improved. London: 1811. V. 39; 40

ORIGINAL Fables. London: 1810. V. 38

AN ORIGINAL Leaf from Francisco Palou's Life of the Venerable Father Junipero Serra. N.P.: 1958. V. 46

AN ORIGINAL Leaf from the Polycronicon Printed by William Caxton at Westminster in the Year 1482, The Life and Works of William Caxton, with an Historical Reminder of Fifteenth Century England by Benjamin P. Kurtz . . . San Francisco: 1938. V. 45

ORIGINAL Letters and Papers Betwen Adm---l M---ws, and V Adm----l L----k, with Several Letters from Private Hands, Exhibiting Many Particulars Hitehrto Unknown of the Transactions in the Mediterranean. London: 1774. V. 46

ORIGINAL Letters to an Honest Sailor. London: 1746. V. 41; 46

THE ORIGINAL Mr. Jacobs: A Startling Expose. New York: 1888. V. 46

ORIGINAL Papers Relating to the Expedition to the Island of Cuba. London: 1744. V. 37; 38

ORIGINAL Papers Relative to Tanjore: Containing all the Letters Which Passed, and the Conference Which Was Held, Between His Highness the Nabob of Arcot and Lord Pigot, on the Subject of the Restoration of Tanjore . . . London: 1777. V. 44

ORIGINAL Poems and Translations. London: 1714. V. 37

ORIGINAL Poems, Translations and Imitations, from the French, etc., by a Lady. London: 1773. V. 40

ORIOLI, G.

Adventures of a Bookseller. Florence. V. 39; 46

Adventures of a Bookseller. Florence: 1938. V. 38

Adventures of a Bookseller. London: 1938. V. 38; 41; 42; 43

Moving Along: Just a Diary. London: 1934. V. 40

ORLANDI, PELLEGRINO ANTONIO

Repertorium Sculptile-Typicum; or a Complete Collection and Explanation of the Several Marks and Cyphers . . . London: 1730. V. 45

ORLANDINI, NICOLO

Historiae Societatis Iesv. Pars Prima sive Ignativs. (Pars Secvnda, sive Lainivs). Antwerp: 1620. V. 45

ORLEANS, CHARLES, DUKE OF

Poems, Written in English, During His Captivity in Engalnd After the Battle . . . London: 1827. V. 43

ORLEANS, CHARLOTTE ELIZABETH, DUCHESSE D' 1652-1722

Secret Memoirs of the Court of Louis XIV and of the Regency. London: 1824. V. 38

ORLEANS. TERRITORY

Acts Passed at the Second Session of the First Legislatures of the Territory of Orleans. New Orleans: 1807. V. 41

ORLEBAR, F. ST. J.

The Adventures of Her Serene Highness, the Moon Faced Princess, Dulcet and Debonaire. London: 1888. V. 46

ORLICH, LEOPOLD VON

Travels in India, Including Sinde and the Punjab. London: 1845. V. 40

ORLOFSKY, PATSY

Quilts in America. New York: 1974. V. 40

ORLOVSKY, PETER

Dear Allen: Ship Will Land Jan. 23, 58. Buffalo: 1971. V. 41

ORMATHWAITE, JOHN BENN WALSH, 1ST BARON 1798-1881

Poor Laws in Ireland, Considered in Their Probable Effects Upon the Capital, the Prosperity & the Progressive Improvement of that Country. London: 1830. V. 42

ORME, EDWARD

Collection of British Field Sports Illustrated in Twenty Beautifully Colored Engravings from Drawings by S. Howitt. London: 1807. V. 40; 41

An Essay on Transparent Prints and on Transparencies in General. London: 1807. V. 43

Graphic History of the Life, Exploits and Death of Horatio Nelson. London: 1806. V. 43

Historic Military and Naval Anecdotes of Personal Valour, Bravery, and Particular Incidents Which Occured to the Armies of Great Britain and Her Allies . . . London: 1818. V. 38

Historic, Military and Naval Anecdotes . . . London: 1819. V. 40

Orme's Collection of British Field Sports. Guildford: 1955. V. 44; 46

Orme's Collection of British Field Sports Illustrated. London: 1955. V. 38

ORME, ROBERT

A History of the Military Transactions of the British nation in Indostan, from the Year MDCCXLV. London: 1803. V. 39; 40

ORME, WILLIAM

Memoirs, Including Letters and Select Remains of John Urquhart, Late of the University of St. Andrew's. Boston: 1828. V. 46

ORMEROD, GEORGE

History of the County of Palatine and the City of Chester. London: 1819. V. 45

The History of the County Palatine and City of Chester . . . London: 1882. V. 41; 44; 46

ORMEROD, T.

Calderdale. Burnley: 1906. V. 44

ORMOND, JAMES BUTLER, DUKE OF 1610-1688

Memoirs of the Life of His Grace, James, the Late Duke of Ormond . . . London: 1738. V. 39

ORMOND, RICHARD

Dictionary of British Portraiture. The Middle Ages . . . (to) The Twentieth Century. London: 1979-81. V. 39

John Singer Sargent: Paintings, Drawings, Watercolors. New York: 1970. V. 42; 44

John Singer Sargent. Paints, Drawings & Watercolors. London: 1970. V. 39; 46

ORMSBY, ANNE

Memoirs of a Family in Suisserland; Founded on Facts. London: 1802. V. 38

ORMSBY, WATERMAN LILLY

Ormsby's Pentographic Illustrations of the Holy Scriptures . . . New York: 1835. V. 44

ORNDUFF, DONALD R.

Casement of Juniata. As A Man and As A Stockman . . . One of a Kind. Kansas City: 1975. V. 39; 42; 43

ORNITHOLOGIA Nova; or, a New General History of Birds. Birminghma: 1743-45. V. 43

ORNITHOLOGIE Abrege de la France, Contenant les Figures et la Nomenclature en un Grand Nombre de Langues de 134 Especes d'Oiseaux Gravees en Taille-Douce. Neuwied sur le Rhin: 1794. V. 42

ORNITHOPARCUS, VOGELHOFER ANDREAS

Musice Active Micrologus. Leipzig: 1519. V. 41

O'RORKE, T.

History, Antiquities and Present State of the Parishes of Ballysadare and Kilvarnet in the County of Sligo. Dublin. V. 39

The History of Sligo, Town and Country. Sligo: 1986. V. 43

OROSIUS, PAULUS

Adversavs Paganos . . . Historiarvm Libri Septem. Cologne: 1536. V. 42

Historiarum Adversus Paganos Lib. VII. Vicenza: 1480. V. 37

Opus Prestantissimum (Historiarum). 1510. V. 44; 46

Opus Prestantissimum (Historiarum). Paris: 1510. V. 39

Pauli Orosii Historiographi CClarissimi Opus Prestatissimu. colophon: 1510 . . . V. 40

O'ROURKE, JOHN

A Treatise on the Art of War: or, Rules for Conducting an Army in all the Various Operations of Regular Campaigns. London: 1778. V. 37

OROZCO, CRISTOBAL b. 1517

Annotationes in Interpretes Aetii Medici. Basel: 1540. V. 40

OROZCO Y BERRA, MANUEL

Geografia De Las Lenguas y Carta Etnografia de Mexico, Precedidas de un Ensayo de Clasificacion de Las Mismas Lenguas y de Apuntes para Las Immigraciones de Las Tribus. Mexico City: 1864. V. 38

ORPEN, GEORGE

Primitive. 1978. V. 42

ORPEN, GODDARD HENRY

Ireland Under the Normans 1169-1216. Oxford: 1911. V. 39

Ireland Under the Normans, 1169-1216. Oxford: 1911/20. V. 43

ORPEN, WILLIAM

An Onlooker in France. 1917-1919. London: 1921. V. 43; 45

ORPHEUS Caledonicus; or, a Collection of Scots Songs. London: 1733. V. 39

ORR & SONS

Jewellers. Madras: 1890. V. 40

ORR, JOHN

The Theory of Religion, In Its Absolute Internal State . . . London: 1762. V. 45

ORR, THOMAS

Life History Of . . . Pioneer Stories of California and Utah. Placerville: 1930. V. 43

ORRERY, CHARLES BOYLE, 4TH EARL OF 1676-1731

As You Find It. London: 1703. V. 39; 42

Dr. Bentley's Dissertations on the Epistles of Phalaris and the Fables of Aesop Examined. London: 1698. V. 40

Dr. Bentley's Dissertations on the Epistles of Phalaris, and the Fables of Aesop Examin'd. London: 1699. V. 38; 40; 41

ORRERY, JOHN BOYLE, EARL OF

Remarks on the Life and Writings of Dr. Jonathan Swift . . . In a Series of Letters from John Earl of Orrery to his son, the Honourable Hamilton Boyle. London: 1752. V. 37

ORRERY, ROGER BOYLE, 1ST EARL OF 1621-1679

Two New Tragedies: The Black Prince, and Tryphon . . . London: 1669. V. 40

ORRIO, FRANCISCO XAVIER ALEJO DE

Solucion del Gran Problema Acerca de la Poblacion de las Americas, en que Sobre el Fundamento de Los Libros Santos se Descubre Facil Camino a la Transmigracion de los Hombres del Uno al Otro Continente . . . Mexico: 1736. V. 38

ORS, EUGENIO D'

Pablo Picasso. New York: 1930. V. 46

ORTA, G. DA

Aromatum et Simplicium Aliquot Medicamentorum apud Indos Nascentium Historia. Antwerp: 1567. V. 42

ORTEGA, JESUS GONZALES

The Presidency of Mexico. Protest of General . . . President of the Supreme Court of Justice, Against the Decrees of Senor Benito Juarez, Ex-President of the Mexican Republic . . . New York: 1866. V. 41

ORTEGA, JOSE DE

Apostolicas Afanes de la Compania de Jesus Escritos por un Padre de la Misma Sagrada Religion de su Provincia de Mexico. Barcelona: 1754. V. 38; 40

ORTEGA, LOUIS B.

California Stock Horse. Sacramento: 1949. V. 39

ORTELIUS, ABRAHAM 1527-1598

Deorum Dearum Capita ex Antiquis Numismatibus . . . et Historica Naratione Illustrata a Francisco Sweertio. Antwerp: 1602. V. 45

An Epitome of Oretlius. His Theatre of the World . . . London: 1602. V. 42

His Epitome of the Theater of the Worlde. London: 1603. V. 40

Il Theatro Del Mondo . . . Ridotto de la Forma Grande. Brescia: 1598. V. 45

Theatrvm Orbis Terrarvm . . . The Theatre of the Whole World . . . London: 1606. V. 38

The Theatre of the Whole World. Amsterdam: 1968. V. 40

Theatrum Orbis Terrarum. Antwerp 1570. Cleveland & New York: 1964. V. 40

ORTH, SAMUEL P.

A History of Cleveland, Ohio. Chicago: 1910. V. 42; 44

THE ORTHODOX Trinitarian; or an Explication and Assertion of the Doctrine of the Holy Trinity and Unity, According to Scripture, and the Late Act of Parliament. London: 1701. V. 44

ORTHOGRAPHIA de La Lengua Castellana. Madrid: 1792. V. 38

ORTON, J. W.

The Miner's Guide, and Metallurgist's Directory. New York/Cincinnati: 1849. V. 37

ORTON, JOB

Letters to a Young Clergyman. Boston: 1794. V. 44

Memoirs of the Life, Character and Writings of the Late Rev. Philip Doddridge of Northampton. Salop: 1766. V. 39

ORTON, JOE

Head to Toe. London: 1970. V. 45

What the Butler Saw. V. 45

ORTON, JOHN

Turf Annals of York and Doncaster, Together with Particulars of the Derby and Oakes Stakes at Epsom, from the Earliest Period Up to the Close of the Year 1843. London: 1844. V. 42

ORVIS, CHARLES F.

Fishing with the Fly. Manchester: 1883. V. 46

ORWELL, GEORGE 1903-1950

Animal Farm. London: 1945. V. 37; 38; 39; 43; 45; 46

Animal Farm. 1946. V. 43

Animal Farm. New York: 1946. V. 37; 38; 39; 40; 41; 42; 44; 45

Animal Farm. Toronto: 1946. V. 39

Kolgosp Tvarin. (Animal Farm). Munich: 1947. V. 44

Animal Farm. New York: 1954. V. 37; 40; 42

Animal Farm. London: 1954. V. 37

Burmese Days. London: 1935. V. 37; 39; 43; 46

Burmese Days. New York: 1934. V. 37

A Clergyman's Daughter. London: 1935. V. 44

A Clergyman's Daughter. New York: 1936. V. 43

Coming Up for Air. London: 1939. V. 43; 46

Critical Essays. London: 1946. V. 38; 39; 40; 42; 45

Down and Out in Paris and London. 1933. V. 46

Down and Out in Paris and London. London: 1933. V. 40; 43; 46

Down and Out in Paris. New York: 1933. V. 37; 39; 42; 44; 46

England Your England. London: 1953. V. 37; 38; 39; 40; 42; 45

ORWELL, GEORGE 1903-1950 continued

The English People. London: 1947. V. 39; 42; 45

Homage to Catalonia. London: 1938. V. 37; 40; 45

James Burnham and the Managerial Revolution. London: 1946. V. 38; 45

the Lion and the Unicorn. London: 1941. V. 39; 42; 45

1984. 1949. V. 44; 46

Nineteen Eighty-Four. London: 1949. V. 38; 39; 42; 43; 44; 46

Nineteen Eighty-Four. London and Toronto: 1949. V. 42

Nineteen Eight-Four. New York: 1949. V. 37; 39; 42; 45; 46

Nineteen Eighty-Four. Toronto: 1949. V. 39

Nineteen Eighty Four. (The Facsimile). San Diego/New York: (1984). V. 37

1948 and 1984. Edinburgh: 1984. V. 37

Politics and the English Language. N.P.: 1947. V. 38; 40; 42

The Road to Wigan Pier. London: 1937. V. 37; 38; 39; 40; 42

The Road to Wigan Pier. New York: 1958. V. 41

The Road to Wigan Pier. London: 1927. V. 37

Selected Writings. London: 1958. V. 42

Shooting an Elephant and Other Essays. London: 1950. V. 38; 39; 40; 42; 45

Shooting an Elephant and Other Essays. New York: 1950. V. 40

Et Vive l'Aspidistra! Paris: 1960. V. 45

ORY, MATTHAEIUS

Ad Haeresum Redivivas Affectiones Alexipharmacon. Parisiis: 1544. V. 38

O'RYAN, JOHN F.

The Story of the 27th Division. New York: 1921. V. 44

OSAGE NATION

Treaties and Laws of the Osage nation, as Passed to November 26, 1890. Cedar Vale: 1895. V. 37

OSBALDESTON, SQUIRE

His Autobiography. London: 1926. V. 39; 45

OSBALDISTON, WILLIAM AUGUSTUS

The British Sportsman, or, Nobleman, Gentleman and Farmer's Dictionary, of Recreation and Amusement . . . London: 1792. V. 39; 43

OSBECK, PETER

A Voyage to China and the East Indies. London: 1771. V. 39; 42; 43; 45

OSBORN, ALBERT S.

Questioned Documents. A Study of Questioned Documents with an Outline of Methods by Which the Facts May be Discovered and Shown. Rochester: 1910. V. 46

OSBORN, BENJAMIN

Truth Displayed: in a Series of Elementary Principles, Illustrated and Enforced by Practical Observations in Three Parts. Rutland: 1816. V. 44

OSBORN, EMILY F.D.

'Peccavi'. A Novel. London: 1888. V. 44

OSBORN, FRANCIS

The Works of . . . London: 1700. V. 46

OSBORN, H.

Trials and Triumphs, 55th Ohio Vol. Inf. Chicago: 1904. V. 39

OSBORN, HENRY F.

The Titanotheres of Ancient Wyoming, Dakota and Nebraska. Washington: 1929. V. 45

OSBORN, HENRY S.

Plants of the Holy Land with Their Fruits and Flowers. Philadelphia: 1860. V. 42

OSBORN, LAUGHTON

Handbook of Young Artists and Amateurs in Oil Painting, Being Chiefly a Condensed Compilation from the Celebrated Manual of Bouvier . . . New York: 1845. V. 44

Handbook of Young Artists and Amateurs in Oil Painting. New York: 1846. V. 38

OSBORN, MAX

Nathan Altman. Judische Graphik. Reihe: Petropolis,: 1923. V. 41

OSBORN, SARAH

Familiar Letters Written by . . . Late of Newport, Rhode Island. Newport: 1807. V. 45

OSBORN, SELLECK

Poems. Boston: 1823. V. 41

OSBORN, SHERARD

A Cruise in Japanese Waters. Edinburgh: 1859. V. 46

The Discovery of the North West Passage by H.M.S. 'Ivestigator.' Capt. R. M'Clure, 1850, 1851, 1853, 1854. Second Edition. London: 1857. V. 37

The Past and Future of British Relations in China. Edinburgh: 1860. V. 46

Quedah; or, Stray Leaves from a Journal in Malayan Waters. London: 1857. V. 46

Quedah: A Cruise in Japanese Waters: The Fight on the Peiho. Edinburgh: 1865. V. 38

OSBORNE, CHARLES

Poems by Charles Osborne. London: 1968. V. 41

Swansong. 1968. V. 37

Swansong. London: 1968. V. 40

OSBORNE, FRANCIS

Advice to a Son; or, Directions for Your Better Conduct, Through the Various Important Encounters of This Life. London: 1656. V. 44

Advice to a Son; or, Directions for Your Better Conduct, Through the Various and Most Important Encounters of This Life . . . Oxford: 1656. V. 38

Advice to a Son. London: 1658. V. 42

A Miscellany of Sundry Essayes, Paradoxes and Problematicall Discourses from the History of the Earl of Essex . . . London: 1659. V. 41; 42

Political Reflections Upon the Government of the Turks. Nicolas Machiavel. The King of Sweden's Descent into Germany. The Conspiracy. Against Nero. The Greatness & Corruption of the Court of Rome. The Election of Pope Leo XI. Martin Luther. London: 1656. V. 39

The Works. London: 1689. V. 40

OSBORNE, JOHN

Look Back in Anger; a Play. London: 1957. V. 40

OSBORNE, RICHARD

Sir Pelham Wodehouse Old Boy - the Text of an Address at the Opening of the P. G. Wodehouse Corner in the Library of Dulwich College - October 15, 1977. London: 1978. V. 41

OSBORNE, RICHARD B.

Select Plans of Engineering Structures for Railroads and Highways as Actually Constructed. Philadelphia: 1885. V. 46

OSBORNE, ROBERT

50 Golden Years of Oscar . . . La Habra: 1979. V. 45

OSBORNE, SHERARD 1822-1875

Facsimile of the Illustrated Arctic News. Published on Board H.M.S. Resolute: Captn. Horatio T. Austin, C.B. in Search of the Expedition Under Sir John Franklin. London: 1852. V. 39

Stray Leaves from an Arctic Journal; or, Eighteen Months in the Polar Regions, in Search of Sir John Franklin's Expedition, in the Years 1850-51. London: 1852. V. 39

Stray Leaves from an Arctic Journal; or Eighteen Months in the Polar Regions in Search of Sir John Franklin's Expedition, in the Years 1850-51. New York: 1852. V. 38

OSBORNE, SYDNEY GODOLPHIN

Scutari and Its Hospitals. London: 1855. V. 39

OSBORNE, THOMAS

The First Volume of a Catalogue for the Year 1763. London: 1763. V. 41

OSBORNE, W. G.

The Court and Camp of Runject Sing . . . . London: 1840. V. 39; 43

OSBORNE'S Guide to the Grand Junction of Birmingham, Liverpool and Manchester Railway. Birmingham: 1838. V. 39; 40

OSBOURN, JAMES

North Carolina Sonnets, or a Selection of Choice Hymns for the Use of the Old School Baptists. Baltimore: 1844. V. 44

OSBURN, WILLIAM

An Account of an Egyptian Mummy, Presented to the Museum of Leeds Philosophical and Literary Society by the Late John Blayds, Esq. Leeds: 1828. V. 40

THE OSCOTIAN; or Literary Gazette of St. Mary's. Birmingham: 1828-29. V. 42

OSENBRUEGGEN, EDUARD

Das Berner Oberland. Darmstadt: 1880. V. 41

OSGOOD, ERNEST S.

The Field Notes of Captain William Clark 1803-1805. New Haven: 1964. V. 39; 44

OSGOOD, ERNEST STAPLES

The Day of the Cattleman. Minneapolis: 1929. V. 42; 43; 46

OSGOOD, FRANCES S.

The Poetry of Flowers and Flowers of Poetry. New York: 1841. V. 37

OSGOOD, HERBERT L.

The American Colonies in the Seventeenth Century. New York: 1904-07. V. 39

The American Colonies in the Eighteenth Century. New York: 1924. V. 39; 42; 44

OSGOODE, WILLIAM

Remarks on the Laws of Descent. London: 1779. V. 38

O'SHAUGHNESSEY, THOMAS J.

Rambles on Overland Trails. Chicago: 1915. V. 37

O'SHAUGHNESSY, ARTHUR W. E.

An Epic of Women and Other Poems. London: 1870. V. 39

O'SHAUGHNESSY, M. M.

Hetch Hetchy, Its Origin and History. San Francisco: 1934. V. 44

O'SHEA, ELENA ZAMORA

El Mesquite, a Study of the Early Spanish Settlements Between the Nueces and the Rio Grands as Told by 'La Posta del Palo Alto'. Dallas: 1935. V. 44

OSKISON, JOHN M.

Brothers Three. New York: 1935. V. 44

OSLER, E. B.

Catalogue: Pictures of Indians and Indian Life by Paul Kane . . . The Property of E. B. Osler Esq., M.P., Toronto. N.P.: 1890s? V. 44

OSLER, F.

Electric Light Fittings. London: 1900. V. 45

OSLER, VIRGINIA

Principles and Practice of Medicine. New York: 1909. V. 39

OSLER, WILLIAM 1849-1919

Aequanimitas with Other Addresses to Medical Students, Nurses and Practioners of Medicine. London: 1904. V. 45

Aequanimitas with Other Addresses. Philadelphia: 1904. V. 38

Aequanimitas and Other Addresses. Philadelphia: 1906. V. 41

Aequanimitas and Other Addresses. London: 1910. V. 39

An Alabama Student. Baltimore: 1896. V. 39

An Alabama Student and Other Biographical Essays. London: 1908. V. 37; 38; 42; 46

An Alabama Student and Other Biographical Essays. Oxford: 1908. V. 39; 40; 41

An Alabama Student and Other Biographical Addresses. London: 1909. V. 41

An Alabama Sutdent and Other Biographical Addresses. London: 1926. V. 45

An Annotated Bibliography with Illustrations. San Francisco: 1988. V. 43

Bibliotheca Osleriana. Oxford: 1919. V. 38

Bibliotheca Osleriana. Oxford: 1929. V. 38; 40; 41; 44; 45; 46

Bibliotheca Osleriana. Montreal: 1969. V. 37; 38; 41; 42; 44

Bibliotheca Osleriana. Montreal: 1987. V. 39; 40; 41; 44; 45; 46

Cancer of the Stomach. Philadelphia: 1900. V. 44

Case of Aneurism of the Hepatic Artery with Multiple Abcesses of the Liver. Montreal: 1877. V. 39

Case of Progressive Pernicious Anemia. Montreal: 1877. V. 45

The Collected Essays. Birmingham: 1985. V. 42

William Osler's Collected Papers on the Cardiovascular System. Birmingham: 1985. V. 41

Counsels and Ideals: from the Writings of . . . London: 1929. V. 39

The Evolution of Modern Medicine. New Haven: 1921. V. 37; 40; 41; 43; 44; 45; 46

The Evolution of Modern Medicine. New Haven: 1922. V. 39; 43

The Evolution of Modern Medicine. New Haven: 1923. V. 38

The Evolution of Modern Medicine. New Haven: 1943. V. 46

The Growth of Truth as Illustrated in the Discovery of the Circulation of the Blood. London: 1907. V. 40

The Gulstonian Lectures on Malignant Endocarditis. Delivered at the Royal College of Physicians of London, March, 1885. London: 1885. V. 37

Incunabula Medica. London: 1923. V. 42

Incunabula Medica, a Study of the Earliest Printed Medical Books 1467-1480. Oxford: 1923. V. 37

Incunbula Medica. A Study of the Earliest Printed Medical Books 1467-1480. Oxford: 1932. V. 37

Lectures on the Diagnosis of Abdominal Tumors Delivered to the Post-Graduate Class John Hopkins University, 1893. New York: 1895. V. 44

Lectures on Angina Pectoris and Allied States. New York: 1897. V. 42; 44; 45

Lectures on the Diagnosis of Abdominal Tumors. New York: 1901. V. 41

Lehrbuch der Internen Medizine . . . Berlin: 1909. V. 38

Man's Redemption of Man. New York: 1913. V. 38; 45

Men and Books. Pasadena: 1959. V. 42

Modern Medicine. Its Theory and Practice in Original Contributions by American and Foreign Authors. New York: 1907-10. V. 40

Modern Medicine, its Theory and Practice. Philadelphia: 1907-10. V. 37; 42

Modern Medicine, its Theory and Practice. Philadelphia & New York: 1907-10. V. 45

Modern Medicine. Philadelphia: 1925-28. V. 42

The Old Humanities and New Sciences. London: 1919. V. 40; 41

The Old Humanities and New Sciences. Boston: 1920. V. 41; 42; 45

On Some Points in the Etiology and Pathology of Ulcerative Endocarditis. London: 1881. V. 39

On Chorea and Choreiform Affections. Philadelphia: 1894. V. 42; 45

The Opening of the Johns Hopkins Medical School to Women. London: 1891. V. 45

Pasteur: An Introduction to a New Edition of Rene Vallery-Radot's Life. London: 1911. V. 37

The Principles and Practice of Medicine. New York: 1892. V. 37; 38; 39; 40; 41; 42; 43; 44; 45

The Principles and Practice of Medicine. New York: 1893. V. 38; 42; 43; 45

The Principles and Practice of Medicine. Edinburgh: 1894. V. 42

Principles and Practice of Medicine. New York: 1895. V. 39; 41

Principles and Practice of Medicine. New York: 1896. V. 42

Principles and Practice of Medicine. New York: 1897. V. 38; 42; 44

Principles and Practice of Medicine. New York: 1898. V. 38

The Principles and Practice of Medicine. New York: 1899. V. 38; 39; 40; 41; 42; 44

The Principles and Practice of Medicine. London: 1901. V. 38; 39; 40; 41; 44; 45; 46

The Principles and Practice of Medicine. New York: 1902. V. 42

The Principles and Practice of Medicine. London: 1909. V. 38

The Principles and Practice of Medicine. New York: 1909. V. 38; 41; 44; 45

The Principles and Practice of Medicine. New York: 1910. V. 40; 42

Science and Immorality. Boston: 1904. V. 39; 45; 46

Sir Kenelm Digby's Powder of Sympathy. An Unfinished Essay . . . Introduction and notes by K. Garth Huston. Los Angeles: 1972. V. 37

Studies in Typhoid Fever. Nos. I, II, III. Baltimore: 1901. V. 45

Thomas Linacre. Cambridge: 1908. V. 42; 45

A Way of Life. London: 1913. V. 41; 46

A Way of Life. New York: 1914. V. 38; 41; 42

OSLEY, A. S.

Luminario. An Introduction to the Italian Writing Books of the Sixteenth and Seventeenth Centuries. Nieuwkoop: 1972. V. 39

OSMAN, A. H.

Pigeons in the Great War. London: 1929. V. 46

OSMASTON, F. P. B.

The Paradise of Tintoretto. Bognor: 1910. V. 43

OSMER, W.

A Treatise on the Diseases and Lameness of Horses, In Which is Laid Down a Proper Method of Shoeing (in General) and Treating the Different Kinds of Feet. London: 1766. V. 38

OSMOND, R.

John Singer Sargent: Paintings, Drawings, Watercolors. New York: 1970. V. 46

OSMONT, JEAN BAPTISTE LOUIS

Dictionnaire Typographique, Historique et Critique des Livres Rares, Singuliers et Recherches en Tous Genres. Paris: 1768. V. 38; 41

OSORIO, ADRIAN

25 Fotos de Mexico. Mexico: 1934. V. 42

OSORIO, CHRISTOVAO

Pancarpia. Prosas Historicas e Titulares & Versos Differentes . . . Lisbon: 1628. V. 38

OSORIO DA FONSECA, JERONYMO, BP OF SILVES

De Regis Institvtione et Disciplina, Libri Octo . . . Cologne: 1588. V. 45

OSORIO DE CASTRO, ALBERTO

Flores de Coral. Poemetos e Impressoes da Oceania Portugueza. Dilly (Timor): 1908. V. 45

OSORIO, JERONYMO, BP. OF SILVES 1506-1580

Historiae Hieronymi Osorii, Lvsitani, Silvenisis in Algar Biis Episcopi . . . Coloniae: 1580. V. 40

OSORIO, JERONYMO, BP. OF SILVES 1506-1580 continued

Histoire de Portugal, Contenant les Enterprises, Navigations & Gestes Memorables, des Portugallois . . . Geneva: 1581. V. 43

De Rebus, Emmanuelis Regis Lusitaniae Virtute et Auspicio Gestis Libri Duodecim. Lisbon: 1571. V. 40; 43

De Rebus Emmanuelis Regis Lusitaniae Gestis. Cologne: 1574. V. 40; 45

OSORIUS, HIERONYMUS

De Gloria Libri V. De Nobilitate Civili et Christiana. De Iustitia Caelesti. Basle: 1574. V. 39

OSSE, MELCHIOR VON

Testament Gegen Hertzog Augusto Churfursten zu Sachsen . . . 1556. Halle: 1717. V. 42

OSSOLI, SARAH MARGARET FULLER

Conversations with Goethe in the Last Years of His Life . . . Boston: 1839. V. 38

OSSOLI, SARAH MARGARET FULLER, MARCHESA D' 1810-1850

Memoirs of Margaret Fuller Ossoli. Boston: 1852. V. 38; 39; 41

Summer on the Lakes in 1843. Boston: 1844. V. 40

Woman in the Nineteenth Century. Boston: 1855. V. 39; 44

OSSOLINSKY, JERZY, COUNT

A True Copy of the Latine Oration of the Excellent Lord George Ossolinsky, Count Palatine of Tenizyn and Sendomyria, Chamberlain to the Kings Maiestie of Poland and Suethlan . . . London: 1621. V. 41

OSTEN, HANS HENNING VON DER

Ancient Oriental Seals in the Collection of Mrs. Agnes Baldwin Brett. Chicago: 1936. V. 44

OSTERBERG, J. S.

History of the Swedes in Rhode Island . . . Worcester: 1915. V. 46

OSTERLEY Park Ballads. London: 1930. V. 41

OSTERMANN, H.

The Alaskan Eskimos. Copenhagen: 1952. V. 43

OSTERWALD, J. F.

The Nature of Uncleanness Considered. London: 1708. V. 38

OSTRANDER, ALSON B.

After 60 Years: Sequel to a Story of the Plains. Seattle: 1925. V. 38

OSTRANDER, TOBIAS

A Complete System of Mensuration of Superficies and Solids, of All Regular Figures. New York: 1833. V. 43

Key to the Complete System of Mensuration of Superficies and Solids. New York: 1834. V. 43

The Planetarium, and Astronomical Calculator. Lyons: 1832. V. 40

OSTWALD, WILHELM

Individuality and Immorality. Boston: 1906. V. 38

OSTWALD, WOLFGANG 1883-1943

An Introduction to Theoretical and Applied Colloid Chemistry. New York: 1917. V. 42

O'SULLIVAN, FLORENCE

The History of Kinsale. Dublin: 1916. V. 37; 39; 42

O'SULLIVAN, M. D.

Old Galway. The History of a Norman Colony in Ireland. Cambridge: 1942. V. 37

O'SULLIVAN, N.

Captain Rock Detected . . . London: 1824. V. 40; 43

O'SULLIVAN, SAMUEL

College Recollections. London: 1825. V. 43

O'SULLIVAN, SEUMAS

Twenty-Five Lyrics. (Flasham): 1933. V. 37

O'SULLIVAN, T. F.

Romantic Hidden Kerry. Romantic. Tralee: 1931. V. 43

O'SULLIVAN, VINCENT

Ben Ionson His Volpone: or The Fox. A New edition with a critical essay on the author by Vincent O'Sullivan and a frontispice, five initial letters and a cover design illustrative and decorative by Aubrey Beardsley together with an eulogy . . . London: 1898. V. 37

A Book of Bargains. London: 1896. V. 41

The Green Window. London: 1899. V. 41

The Next Room. Edinburgh: 1988. V. 46

Poems. London: 1896. V. 43

OSUMI, TARNEZO

Printed Cottons of Asia. The Romance of Trade Textiles. Tokyo and Rutland: 1963. V. 45

OSVALD, SIREN

China and Gardens of Europe of the Eighteenth Century. New York: 1950. V. 42

OSWALD, ELIZABETH JANE

By Fell and Fjord, or, Scenes and Studies in Iceland. Edinburgh: 1882. V. 43

OSWALD, FELIX

Index of Potters' Stamps on Terra Sigillata 'Samian Ware' with a Supplement. London: 1964. V. 40

An Introduction to the Study of Terra Sigillata, Treated from a Chronological Standpoint. London: 1920. V. 40

OSWALD, FELIX L.

Summerland Sketches, or Rambles in the Backwoods of Mexico and Central America. Philadlephia: 1880. V. 38; 42

OSWALD, JOHN

Poems to Which is Added the Humours of John Bull, an Operatical Farce; (with) A Companion to All the Principal Places of Curiosity and Entertainment in and about Westminster. London: 1789, 1800. V. 41

OSWANDEL, J. JACOB

Notes of the Mexican War, 1846-47-48. Philadelphia: 1885. V. 44; 45

OSWEGO & UTICA RAILROAD CO.

Oswego and Utica Rail Road Co. Report of Joseph D. Allen, Chief Engineer. New York: 1837. V. 43

THE OSWEGO City Residence and Advertising Directory for 1859. Oswego: 1859. V. 39

OSWELL, W. EDWARD

William Cotton Oswell Hunter and Explorer The Story of His Life. London: 1900. V. 39; 40

OTERO, MIGUEL A.

My Nine Years as Governor of New Mexico 1897-1906. Albuquerque: 1940. V. 46

New Mexico Contested Election. Papers and Testimony in the Case of . . . Contesting the Seaat of Jose M. Gallegos, Delegate from the Territory of New Mexico. Washington: 1856. V. 38; 42

The Real Billy the Kid with New Light on the Lincoln County War. New York: 1936. V. 40; 43; 46

Report of the Governor of New Mexico. Washington. V. 44

Report of the Governor of New Mexico . . . Washington: 1901. V. 41

OTHERS. An Anthology of the New Verse (1917). New York: 1917. V. 46

OTHMANSDORFF, MARTIN

Kybeia Antihristiani Accidentis In Integris Natvralibvs Per Lvthervm Ex Domini Templo Eiecti In Locvm Sanctvm Per Qvosdam Neopapistas Restitvti. Germany: 1573. V. 40

OTIS, F. N.

Isthmus of Panama; History of the Panama Railroad. New York: 1867. V. 40; 42; 46

OTIS, GEORGE

A Report of Excisions of the Head of the Femur for Gun-Shot Injury. Washington: 1869. V. 42

A Report to the Surgeon General on the Transport of Sick and Wounded by Pack Animals. Washington: 1877. V. 42

OTIS, JAMES

Toby Tyler or Ten Weeks With a Circus. New York: 1881. V. 42

OTIS, PHILO ADAMS

The Chicago Symphony Orchestra Its Organization, Growth and Development 1891-1924. Chicago: 1924. V. 46

OTLEY, JONATHAN

A Concise Description of the English Lakes, and Adjacent Mountains. London: 1830. V. 39

OTT, ADOLPH

The Art of Manufacturing Soap and Candles, Including the Most Recent Discoveries . . . Philadelphia: 1867. V. 40

OTTANNI, GAETANO

Libro Primo de Cartelle . . . N.P.: 1766. V. 44

OTTAWA BAPTIST ASSOCIATION

Minutes of the Third Anniversary of the Ottawa Baptist Association, Held with the Baptist Church in Harding, Ill. June 25th and 26th 1851. Ottawa: 1851. V. 44

THE OTTAWA Directory, 1875, and Dominion Containing Street, Alphabetical, Business and Miscellaneous Lists, to Which is Added, Directory, City of Hull, also Directories of New Edinburgh, Rochesterville, Aylmer, Buckingham, Chelsea, Gatineau Mills . . . Ottawa: 1875. V. 40

THE OTTAWA Directory, to Which is Added, Directory of the Suburbs, Comprising Archville, Bank St. Road, Billings', Janeville, Mount Sherwood, Richmond Road, Rochesterville, Stewarton and Hull. Ottawa: 1887. V. 38

OTTAWA HYDRAULIC COMPANY

Articles of Agreement of the Ottawa Hydraulic Company, Instituted June 13, 1836. Chicago: 1836. V. 40

OTTER, WILLIAM

The Life and Remains of the Rev. Edward Daniel Clarke, Professor of Mineralogy in the University of Cambridge. London: 1824. V. 39

OTTLEY, DREWRY

The Life of John Hunter, F. R. S. Philadelphia: 1839. V. 42

Observations on Surgical Diseases of the Head and Neck. London: 1848. V. 39; 42

OTTLEY, W. J.

With Mounted Infantry in Tibet. London: 1906. V. 38

OTTLEY, WILLIAM YOUNG

A Collection of Facsimiles of Scarce and Curious Prints, Illustrative of the History of Engraving. London: 1828. V. 45

Engravings of the Most Noble, The Marquis of Stafford's Collection of Pictures . . . London: 1818. V. 40

An Inquiry Into the Origin and Early History of Engraving, Upon Copper and in Wood, with an Account of Engravers and Their Works from the Invention of Calcography by Maso Finiguerra, to the Time of Marc' Antonio Raimondi. London: 1816. V. 41; 42; 45

An Inquiry Concerning the Invention of Printing, In Which the Systems of Meerman, Heinecken, Santander, and Koning are Reviewed . . . London: 1862. V. 44

OTTO, ALEXANDER F.

Mythological Japan or the Symbolisms of Mythology in Relation to Japanese Art. Philadelphia: 1902. V. 37; 43

OTTO, BISHOP OF FREISING 1114-1158

Rerum ab Origine Mundi ad Ipsius Usque Tempora Gestarium, Libri Octo. Strassburg: 1515. V. 43

OTTO, JACOB AUGUST

A Treatise on the Structure and Preservation of the Violin and all Other Bow-Instruments . . . London: 1848. V. 38

OTTO VON PASSAU

Die Vierundzwenzig Alten. Strasbourg: 1500. V. 37; 38

Die Vierundzwenzig Alten. Strasbourg: 1500. V. 37

OTTO, W. T.

Authentic . . . Information on the Origin . . . of the Indian Hostilities on the Frontier. Washington: 1867. V. 41; 42

OTTOLENGUI, RODRIGUES

Methods of Filling Teeth. Philadelphia: 1892. V. 45

OTTONELLI, GIULIO

Discorso Sopra l'Abuso del dire 'Sua Santita, Sua Maesta, Sua Altezza.' Ferrara: 1586. V. 40

OTWAY, CAESAR

Sketches in Erris and Tyrawley. V. 46

Sketches in Erris and Tyrawly. Dublin: 1841. V. 38

A Tour in Connaught, Comprising Sketches of Clonmacnoise, Joyce Country and Achill. Dublin: 1839. V. 38; 43

OTWAY, THOMAS 1652-1685

Alcibiades. London: 1675. V. 40

Alcibiades. London: 1687. V. 45

The Atheist; or, the Second Part of the Souldiers Fortune. London: 1684. V. 44

Don Carlos of Spain. London: 1686. V. 45

Friendship in Fashion. London: 1678. V. 45

The Orphan. London: 1705. V. 38

Titus and Berenice, a Tragedy. London: 1677. V. 45

Windsor Castle. London: 1685. V. 38; 40; 41; 43; 45

The Works. London: 1768. V. 45

Works. London: 1812. V. 41

The Works. London: 1813. V. 37; 38; 46

Complete Works. 1926. V. 37

Complete Works. Bloomsbury: 1926. V. 40; 41; 46

The Complete Works. London: 1926. V. 38; 40; 41; 42; 43; 45; 46

OUDIN, CESAR

Refranes a Proverbios Espanoles Traduzidos en Lengua Francesa. Brussels: 1608. V. 38

OUGHTRED, WILLIAM 1576-1660

Clavis Mathematicae Denuo Limata, Sive Potius Fabricata Cum Aliis Quibusdam Ejusdem Commentationibus . . . Lichfield: 1652. V. 46

Clavis Mathematicae Denuo Limata, Sive Potius Fabricata . . . Oxford: 1652. V. 42

Opuscula Mathematica Hactenus Inedita. Oxford: 1677. V. 41

OULTON, WALLEY CHAMBERLAIN

The History of the Theatres of London . . . London: 1796. V. 38; 41

Poems, Chiefly Comic and Hudibrastic Containing Burlesque Translations . . . London: 1810. V. 43

OUR Exagmination Round His Factification for Incamination of Work in Progress. Paris: 1929. V. 37; 38; 40; 41; 42; 43; 45; 46

OUR Girls. Poems in Praise of the American Girl. New York: 1907. V. 40; 46

OUR Home Population; or, the Voluntary Principle and Lay Agency Sanctioned of God, and Adapted to Promote the Moral and Spiritual Renovation of Those Districts of the Country Still in a State of Moral Degradation and Religious Destitution. London: 1842. V. 40; 43

OUR Lady of the Rosary. Ditchling: 1930? V. 43

OUR Lady's Choir: a Contemporary Anthology of Verse by Catholic Sisters. Boston: 1931. V. 46

OUR Life, Illustrated by Pen and Pencil. London: 1865. V. 38

OUR Living Painters; Their Lives and Their Works. London: 1859. V. 41

OUR National Cathedrals. London: 1887. V. 40

OUR National Cathedrals . . . Their History and Architecture from Their Foundation to Modern Times. London: 1887-88-89. V. 46

OUR Native Land - Its Scenery and Associations. London: 1878. V. 39
OUR Native Land. Its Scenery and Associations. London: 1879. V. 39

OUR Native Land: or, Glances at American Scenery. New York: 1882. V. 39

OUR Old Nursery Rhymes. London: 1911. V. 44

OUR Own Times. London: 1846. V. 41

OUR Picture Book. London: 1890. V. 39

OUR Postal and Revenue Establishments, Considered with a View to Utilising the Former for the Receipt and Payment of Revenue Moneys, the Granting of Licences and Sale of Stamps in all Provincial Towns, and to a Thorough Amalgamation and Consolidation . . . London: 1866. V. 46

OUSLEY, WILLIAM GORE

Oriental Geography of Ebn Haukal, an Arabian Traveller of the Tenth Century. London: 1800. V. 40; 41

Remarks on the Statistics and Political Institutions of the United States. London: 1832. V. 44; 46

Views In South America, from Original Drawings Made in Brazil, the River Plate, the Parana &c. London: 1852. V. 43

OUSPENSKY, P. D.

The Major Arcana of the Tarto as Described by . . . Santa Fe: 1975. V. 38; 46

OUT of the West. Northridge: 1979. V. 39

OUTCAULT, R. F.

Buster Brown's Pranks. New York: 1905. V. 45

OUTERBRIDGE, PAUL

Paul Outerbridge, a Singular Aesthetic: Photographs and Drawings 1921-41. Santa Barbara: 1981. V. 41

OUTHIER, REGINAUD

Journal d'un Voyage au Nord en 1736 and 1737. Paris: 1744. V. 38; 40; 43

OUTHWAITE, GRENBRY

The Enchanted Forest. London: 1925. V. 46

The Little Fairy Sister. London: 1923. V. 42

OUTHWAITE, IDA RENTOUL

Blossom: a Fairy Story. London: 1928. V. 45

Bunny and Brownie: the Adventures of George & Wiggle. London: 1930. V. 45

OUTHWAITE, IDA RENTOUL continued

Bush Songs of Australia for Young and Old. Melbourne: 1924. V. 45

The Little Fairy Sister. London: 1923. V. 46

Sixpence to Spend: Story and Illustrations by Ida Rentoul Outhwaite. Sydney: 1935. V. 41

OUTLINE of a Plan for the Future Management of the Circulation. London: 1838. V. 41

OUTLINE of the Plan for the Proposed Navigation through the Isthumus of Suez. 1850. London: 1850. V. 45

OUTLINES Illustrative of the Journal of F****** A*** K*****. Drawn and etched by Mr. ------. Boston: 1835. V. 37

OUTLINES of a Consular Establishment for the United States of America, in Eastern Asia. New York: 1838. V. 37; 46

OUTRAM, JAMES 1803-1863

The Conquest of Scinde. London: 1846. V. 44

In the Heart of the Canadian Rockies. New York & London: 1906. V. 41

In the Heart of the Canadian Rockies. New York: 1923. V. 44

Lieut. General Sir James Outram's Persian Campaign in 1857. London: 1860. V. 43

Rough Notes of the Campaign in Sinde and Affghanistan in 838-39 . . . London: 1840. V. 38; 46

THE OUTSIDER 1-5. New Orleans & Tucson: 1961-69. V. 39

OUVAROFF, M.

Essay on the Mysteries of Eleusis. London: 1817. V. 41

OVALLE, ALONSO DE

An Historical Relation of the Kingdom of Chile . . . London: 1703. V. 45

Of the Nature and Properties of the Kingdom of Chile. London: 1704. V. 42

OVENDEN, GRAHAM

Satirical Poems and Others. St. Columbs: 1983. V. 44

OVER, CHARLES

Ornamental Architecture in the Gothic, Chinese and Modern Taste . . . for Gardens, Parks, Forests, Woods, Canals, &c. London: 1758. V. 37; 39; 40

OVERALL, JOHN

Bishop Overall's Convocation-Book, 1606, Concerning the Government of God's Catholick Church, and the Kingdoms of the Whole World. London: 1690. V. 40

OVERAN, JOHN

The Genuine Life, &c. of John Overan, Otherwise John Williams, who was Capitally Convicted on Thursday the 8th of December, 1774 for Robbing Mr. Venables in the Tower, of Three Bank Notes and Money . . . London: 1775. V. 38

OVERBEKE, BONAVENTURA

Les Restes de l'Ancienne Rome . . . Amsterdam: 1708. V. 42; 45

OVERBROOK PRESS

A Specimen Book of Types, Ornaments and Miscellany. Stamford: 1948. V. 38; 43

OVERBURY, THOMAS

His Observations on His Travailes Upon the State of the XVII Provinces as They Stood Anno Dom. 1609. N.P.: 1626. V. 40; 44; 46

His Wife. London: 1630. V. 44

Sir Thomas Overbury His Wife. London: 1632. V. 37

OVEREND, CAMPBELL, MRS.

The Noble Printer, a Tale of the First Printed Bible. Edinburgh: 1860. V. 38

OVERFIELD, LOYD J.

The Little Big Horn 1876 - the Official Communications, Documents and Reports with Roster of the Officers and Troops of the Campaign. Glendale: 1971. V. 39

THE OVERLAND Alphabet From Sketches Taken 'En Route' by 'Isabel D---'. London. V. 42

OVERMAN, A. H.

The Overman Wheel Co. Manufactures of Victor Bicycles. Chicopee Falls: 1899. V. 38

OVERMAN, FREDERICK

The Manufacture of Iron, In All Its Various Branches. Philadelphia: 1854. V. 44

OVERS, JOHN

Evenings of a Working Man. London: 1844. V. 40

The True History of the Life and Sudden Death of Old John Overs, the Rich Ferry-Man of London, Shewing How He Lost His Life by His Own Covetousness. London: 1744. V. 45

OVERSTONE, SAMUEL JONES LOYD 1796-1883

The Evidence, given by lord Overstone, before the Select Committee of the House of Commons of 1857, on Bank Acts, with Additions. London: 1858. V. 37

OVERSTONE, SAMUEL JONES LOYD, LORD 1796-1883

The Correspondence. London: 1804-83. V. 38

The Correspondence. Cambridge: 1971. V. 41

Effects of the Administration of the Bank of England. London: 1840. V. 38

Further Reflections on the Stte of the Currency and Action of the Bank of England. London: 1837. V. 38

A Letter to J. B. Smith, Esq., President of the 'Manchester Chamber of Commerce.' London: 1840. V. 38

Questions Communicated by Lord Overstone to the Decimal Coinage Commissioners, with Answers. London: 1857. V. 38; 43

Remarks on the Management of the Circulation; and on the Condition and Conduct of the Bank of England and of the Country Issuers, During the Year 1839. London: 1840. V. 38

OVERTON, RICHARD

Mans Mortallitie or a Treatise Wherein 'Tis Proved, Both Theologically and Phylosophically, that Whole Man (as a RAtionall Creature) . . . Amsterdam: 1643. V. 44

OVID in London; a Ludicrous Poem, in Six Cantos . . . London: 1814. V. 43

OVIDIUS NASO, PUBLIUS 43 BC - AD 17

The Amores. 1932. V. 38; 40

Amores. Qui Fuerant Quinque Libelli sunt Tres. Verona: 1932. V. 42

The Amores of . . . Waltham St. Lawrence: 1932. V. 37; 38; 41; 42; 46

Ovid's Art of Love, in Three Books. London: 1719. V. 42

Ovid's Art of Love. London: 1777. V. 41

Ovid's Art of Love. Together with His Remedy for Love. London: 1795. V. 41

The Art of Love. New York: 1971. V. 38; 43; 46

Commentantibus Ant. Volsco, Ubertino Cres . . . Venetiis: 1535. V. 46

De Arte Amandi Volgare Historiato. Venice: 1542. V. 38

Ovid's Elegies. 1925. V. 38

Ovid's Epistles. London: 1688. V. 39; 44; 46

The Epistles of Ovid Translated into English prose . . . London: 1746. V. 39

Ovid's Epistles; with His Amours. London: 1748. V. 39

Fasti. Venice: 1492. V. 46

The Fasti, Tristia, Pontic Epistles, Ibis and Halieuticon of Ovid. London: 1851. V. 41

Fastorum Libri Sex. Strasbourg: 1515. V. 40

Fastorum Libri Sex. Strassbourg: 1519. V. 40

Fastorum Libri Diligenti Emendatione. Impressum Tusculani: 1527. V. 38; 40

Pub. Ovidii Nasonis Fastorum Lib. VI. Tristium Lib. V De Ponto Lib IIII. Expostrema Iacobi Micylli Recognitione. Francofurti ad Moenum: 1587. V. 46

Ovid's Festivalls. Cambridge: 1640. V. 38

Heroidum Epistolae. Paris: 1585. V. 38; 40; 45

Herodium Epistolae. Paris: 1541. V. 37

Heroides. Commentantibus Ant. Volsco, Ubertino Cres..in Ibin. Domitio Cald. Christ Zaroto . . . Venetiis: 1535. V. 43

Heroides. London: 1789. V. 38; 40

Heroides. Paris: 1938. V. 37

Heroides. Milan: 1953. V. 40; 45

The Love Books of Ovid. London: 1925. V. 45; 46

The Love Books of Ovid. 1930. V. 39

Metamorphoses (with the commentary of Raphael Regius). Venice: 1493. V. 37

Quindecim Metamorphoseos Libri Diligetius Recogniti Cum Familiaribus Comentariis & Indice Alphabetico: ab Ascensio Summa Cura Collecto. Lyon: 1506. V. 39

Metamorphoseon Libri XV. Venice: 1516. V. 37

Metamorphoseon. Venice: 1545. V. 37; 38

Trois Premiers Lives de la Metamorphose. Le Premier & Second par C. L. Marot. Le Tiers par B. Aneau. Lyon: 1556. V. 38

La Metamorphoses. Lyon: 1557. V. 45

La Vita et Metamorfoseo . . . . Figurato & Abbreviato in Forma d'Epigrammi da M. Gabriello Symeoni. Con Altre Stanze Sopra gl'effetti della Luna: il Ritratto d'una Fontana d'Overnia: & un'Apologia Generale . . . Lyon: 1559. V. 38

Metamorphoseon Libri XV. In Singulas Quaesque Fabulas Afgumenta. Ex Postrema Jac. Micylli Recognitione. Frankfurt A.M.: 1567. V. 38

Le Transformation di M. Lodovico Dolce, tratte da Ovido. Venice: 1568. V. 37; 38

The XV Bookes of P. Ouidius Naso . . . Colophon: 1575. V. 46

Le Metamorfosi Ridotte da Giovanni Andrea dellAnguillera in Ottava Rime . . . Venice: 1581. V. 37

La Vita et Metamorfoseo. Lyon: 1584. V. 38; 39; 43

OVIDIUS NASO, PUBLIUS 43 BC - AD 17 continued

Le Metamorfosi, Ridotte da Gia. Andrea dall' Anguillara in Ottava Rima, Nuovamente di Bellissime Figure Adornate . . . Venice: 1592. V. 38; 39

Las Transformaciones . . . en Lengua Espanola. Antwerp: 1595. V. 40

Metamorposewn Ovidianarum Typi Aliquot Artificiosissime Delineati, ac in Gratiam Studiosae Juventutis editi per Crispianum Passaeum Zeelandum Chalcographum. Cologne?: 1602. V. 40

Metamorphoseon Sive Transformationum Ovidianarum Libri . . . Amsterdam: 1606. V. 38

The Fiteen Bookes of P. Ovidivs Naso: Entitled Metamorphosis. London: 1612. V. 46

Ovid's Metamorphosis Englished by G(eorge) S(andys). London: 1626. V. 37

Ovid's Metamorphosis Englished . . . London: 1626. V. 40

Ovid's Metamorphosis. Oxford: 1632. V. 38

Ovid's Metamorphosis Englished . . . London: 1640. V. 38; 39; 44

Metamorphosis. Augsburg: 1681. V. 45

Metamorphoses. London: 1717. V. 38; 46

Les Metomorphoses D'Ovide. Amsterdam: 1732. V. 40

Les Metamorphoses. Paris: (imprint of single: 1767-71. V. 38

Ovid's Metamorphoses in Fifteen Books. London: 1773. V. 41

Metamorphoses, in Fifteen Books. (with) Ovid's Epistles; with his Amours. (with) Ovid's Art of Love, in three books. (with) His Remedy of Love. To which are added, The Court of Love: A Tale from Chaucer: and The History of Love. London: 1773-76. V. 37; 39

Metamorphoseon Libri X. or Ten Select Books of Ovid's Metamorphoses.. Philadelphia: 1790. V. 41; 44

Metamorphoseon Libri X, or Ten Select Books of Ovid's Metamorphoses, with an English Translation. Philadelphia: 1790. V. 42

Ovid's Metamorphoses. London: 1820's or 30's. V. 45

La Vita et Metamorfoseo. Lyon: 1854. V. 42

Hys Booke of Methamorphose. Boston: 1924. V. 44

Ovyde His Booke of Metamorphose. Boston & New York: 1924. V. 37; 38

Ovyde Hys Booke of Metamorphose Books X-XV. Oxford: 1924. V. 44; 46

Metamorphoses. New York: 1950. V. 44

The Metamorphoses of . . . London: 1958. V. 39; 40; 41

Metamorphoses. New York: 1958. V. 38; 39; 41; 46

Metamorphoses. Verona: 1958. V. 38; 42

The Metamorphoses. Waltham St. Lawrence: 1958. V. 44; 46

The Metamorphoses. London: 1968. V. 37

The Metamorphoses. New York: 1968. V. 43

The Metamorphoses. New York & Cambridge: 1968. V. 40

The Metamorphoses of Ovid translated by W. Caxton in 1480. New York/Cambridge: 1968. V. 37

The Metamorphoses of Ovid. New York: 1986. V. 45

Metamorphosis. Lyon: 1497. V. 37

Opera Quae Vocantur Amatoria. Basle: 1549. V. 45

Opera Omnia. Leyden: 1661/1662. V. 40

Opera Omnia. Amstelodami: 1727. V. 38; 43; 44

Opera, e Textu Burmanni; Cum Notis Bentelii Hactenus Inediti, Necnon Harlesii, Gierigii, Burmanni, Lemairii, et Aliorum Selectissimis. Oxonii: 1825-26. V. 39

Phaetons Folly, or, the Downfall of Pride . . . London: 1655. V. 45

Traduction des Fastes d'Ovide, avec des Notes & Recherches de Critique, d'Histoire & de Philosophie . . . Rouen: 1783-8. V. 42

Le Trasformationi di M. Lodovico Dolce Tratte da Ovidio. Venice: 1570. V. 45

A Translation of the First Book of Ovid's Tristia, in Heroic English Verse, with the Original Text. New York: 1821. V. 38; 40

La Vita et Metamorfoseo d'Ovide, Figurato & Abbreviato . . . Lyon: 1559. V. 45

OVIEDO, J. A. DE

La Muger Fuerte, Sermon Panegyrico y Funeral, Que la Casa Professa de la Compania de Jesus de Mexico Celebro a su Insigne Bienhechora, y Patrona de su Iglesia, la Mui Ilustre Senora Marquesa de las Torres de Rada, la Senora a Dona Gertrudis de la Pena . . . Mexico: 1739. V. 41

OVIEDO, JUAN ANTONIO DE

Vida Admirable, Apostolicos Ministerios, Y Heroicas Virtudes Del Venerable Padre Jopseh Vidal . . . Mexico City: 1752. V. 38

OVIEDO Y VALDES, GONZALO FERNANDEZ 1478-1557

La Historia General de las Indias. Seville: 1535. V. 41

OVIEDO Y VALDES, GONZALO FERNANDEZ DE 1478-1557

The Conquest and Settlement of the Island of Boriquen or Puerto Rico. 1975. V. 38; 40

Coronica De Las Indias. La Historia General De las Indias Agora Neuvamente Impressa, Correginda Y Emendada. Salamanca: 1547. V. 37; 40

L'Histoire Naturelle et Generalle des Indes, Isles et Terre Ferme de la Grande mer Oceane. Paris: 1556. V. 37; 38; 39

Historia General y Natural de las Indias, Islas Y Tierra-Firme del Mar Oceano . . . Madrid: 1851-55. V. 39; 42; 43; 46

OVINGTON, MARY WHITE

Portraits in Color. New York: 1927. V. 45

OWEN, AREURIN

Ancient Laws and Institutes of Wales . . . London: 1841. V. 43

OWEN, BESSIE

Aerial Vagabond. New York: 1941. V. 42

OWEN, C. H.

Sketches in the Crimea, Taken During the Late War. London: 1856. V. 40; 43

OWEN, CHARLES

The Danger of the Church and State from Foreigners . . . London: 1750. V. 42

An Essay Towards a Natural History of Serpents. London: 1742. V. 38; 41; 42; 43

OWEN, CORBETT

Carmen Pindaricum in Theatrum Sheldonianum in Solennibus Magnifici Operis Encaeniis Recitatum Julii die 90 Anno 1669. Oxford: 1669. V. 37; 38; 41; 45

OWEN, D. J.

History of Belfast. Belfast: 1921. V. 37

OWEN, DAVID

Herod and Pilate Reconciled . . . Cambridge: 1610. V. 44

OWEN, DAVID DALE 1754-1789

Catalogue of Mineralogical and Geological Specimens, at New Harmony, Indiana. New Harmony: 1840. V. 40

First Report of a Geological Reconnaissance of the Northern Counties of Arkansas, Made During the Years 1857 and 1858. Little Rock: 1858. V. 37; 38; 42

Letter of the Secretary of the Treasury, Communicating a Report of a Geological and Reconnoissance of the Chippewa Land District of Wisconsin and the Northern Part of Iowa. Washington: 1848. V. 37; 46

Mineral Lands of the United States. Message from the President . . . Concerning the Mineral Lands of the United States. Washington: 1840. V. 40

Report of a Geological Reconnoisance of the State of Indiana; Made in the Year 1837. Indianapolis: 1839. V. 45

Report of a Geological Exploration of Part of Iowa, Wisconsin and Illinois. Washington: 1840. V. 42

Report of a Geological Exploration of Part of Iowa, Wiscosin and Illinois, Made in the Autumn of the Year 1839. Washington: 1844. V. 37; 38; 45

Report of a Geological Reconnoisance of the Chippewa Land District of Wisconsin . . . Washington: 1848. V. 39

Report of a Geological Survey of Wisconsin, Iowa & Minnesota, & Incidentally of a Portion of Nebraska Territory. Philadelphia: 1852. V. 38; 42; 43; 44; 46

Second Report of a Geological Reconnoisance of the Middle and Southern Counties of Arkansas. Made During . . . 1859 and 1860. Philadelpia: 1860. V. 40

OWEN, DORA

The Book of Fairy Poetry. London: 1920. V. 40; 41; 46

OWEN, E. A.

Pioneer Sketches of Long Point Settlement; or, Norfolk's Foundation Builders and Their Family Genealogies. Toronto: 1898. V. 43

OWEN, ELIAS

Old Stone Crosses of the Vale of Clwyd and Neighbouring Parishes, Together with Some Account of the Ancient Manners and Customs and Legendary Lore. London: 1886. V. 39

OWEN, FITZ WILLIAM

Narrative of Voyages to Explore the Shores of Africa, Arabia and madagascar, Performed in H. M. Ships Leven and Barracouta. London: 1833. V. 45

OWEN, GUY

Season of Fear. New York: 1960. V. 41

OWEN, HAROLD

Journey from Obscurity: Memoirs of the Owen Family. London: 1963/65. V. 45

Journey from Obscurity: Wilfred Owen 1893-1918. London: 1963-65. V. 46

OWEN, J.

Report by J. Owen, Esq., Supervisor of Metals to the Admiralty, of the Results of Experiments Made at Gospel Oak, Tipton . . . London: 1847. V. 44

OWEN, JOHN 1616-1683

(Greek Title): or, A Discourse Concerning the Holy Spirit . . . London: 1674. V. 39

OWEN, JOHN 1616-1683 continued

The Doctrine of the Saints Preservance, Explained and Confirmed. Oxford: 1654. V. 44

The Doctrine of Justification by Faith through the Imputation of the Righteousness of Christ. London: 1677. V. 39

Exercitations on the Epistle to the Hebrews. London: 1668. V. 39

Joannis Audoeni Cambro-Britanni Epigrammata. Parisiis: 1794. V. 39; 40

The Journals and Letters of Major John Owen, Pioneer of the Northwest, 1850-1871. New York: 1927. V. 37; 38; 39; 40; 45

Meditations and Discourses on the Glory of Christ, in His Person, Office and Grace. London: 1684. V. 39; 42

Meditations and Discourses Concerning the Glory of Christ . . . London: 1691. V. 40

Travels into Different Parts of Europe in the Years 1791 and 1792 . . . London: 1796. V. 42

The Works. Edinburgh: 1850-53. V. 39

OWEN, MARY ALICIA

Folk-Lofe of the Musquakie Indians of North America and Catalogue of Musquakie Beadwork and Other Objects . . . London: 1904. V. 39

Voodoo Tales, as Told Among the Negroes of the Southwest. New York: 1893. V. 43

Voodoo Tales, as Told Among the Negroes of the Southwest. New York & London: 1893. V. 39

OWEN, NARCISSA CHISHOLM

Memoirs . . . 1831-1907. Washington: 1907. V. 37; 43

OWEN, R.

Description of the Skeleton of an Extinct, Gigantic Sloth, Mylodon Robustus, Owen with Observations on the Osteology, Natural Affinities and Probable Habit . . . London: 1842. V. 44; 46

OWEN, RICHARD 1804-1892

Description of the Fossil Repitlia of South Africa in the Collection of the British Museum. London: 1876. V. 37; 38; 41

A History of British Fossil Mammals and Birds. London: 1846. V. 40; 45

A History of British Fossil Reptiles. London: 1849-84. V. 43

Key to the Geology of the Globe: an Essay . . . Nashville: 1857. V. 43

Lectures on the Comparative Anatomy and Physiology of the Invertebrate Animals Delivered at the Royal College of Surgeons. London: 1855. V. 38; 40

The Life of Richard Owen. London: 1894. V. 40; 43

Memoir of the Pearly Nautilus (Nautilus Pompilius, Linn.) With Illustrations of Its External Form and Internal Structure. London: 1832. V. 38; 40; 42

Odontography; or a Treatise on the Comparative Anatomy of the Teeth . . . London: 1840-45. V. 37

On the Archetype and Homologies of the Vertebrate Skeleton. London: 1848. V. 42

On Parthenogenesis . . . London: 1849. V. 42

On the Nature of Limbs. London: 1849. V. 43

On the Anatomy of Vertebrates. London: 1866-68. V. 37; 39; 43

On the Dental Characters of Genera and Species . . . London: 1867. V. 45

On the classification and geographical distribution of the mammalia . . . (with) an appendix 'On the Gorilla', and 'On the extinction and transmutation of species'. London: 1859. V. 37

Researches on the Fossil Remains of the Extinct Mammals of Australia . . . London: 1877. V. 42

Researches on the Fossil Remains of the Extinct Mammals of Australia. London: 1887. V. 37

OWEN, ROBERT

The Book of the New Moral World. London: 1836. V. 37; 39

Debate on the Evidences of Christianity; Containing an Examination of the 'Social System' and of all the Systems of Skepticism of Ancient and Modern Times. Bethany: 1829. V. 41

Debate on the Evidences of Christianity. Cincinnati: 1829. V. 42

Debate on the Evidences of Christianity . . . London: 1839. V. 45

Early Discipline Illustrated; or the Infant System Progressing and Successful. London: 1840. V. 38

Essays on the Formation of the Human Character. Manchester: 1837. V. 39; 41; 43; 45

Marriage: a Lecture. Delivered at the Institution, 14, Charlotte Street, on Sunday Evening, Nov. 30, 1834. London: 1834. V. 40

Report to the County of Lanark, of a Plan for Relieving Public Distresses (sic) and Removing Discontent by Giving Permanent, Productive Employment, to the Poor and Working Classes . . . Glasgow. V. 43

Report to the County of Lanark, of a Plan for Relieving Public Distress, and Removing Discontent, by giving permanent, productive employment, to the poor and working classes; . . . Glasgow: 1821. V. 37

Robert Owen's Manifesto to all the Governments and People of All Nations, on Commencing an Entire New State of Society That it May be Made Gradually and Peacefully to Supercede the Old. Glasgow: 1842. V. 38

Six Lectures on Charity, Delivered at the Institution of New Lamark, Upon the Thirteenth Chapter of the First Epistle to the Corinthians. London: 1834? V. 43

Six Lectures Delivered in Manchester Previously to the Discussion Between Mr. Robert Owen and the Rev. J. H. Roebuck. London: 1837? V. 45

Six Lectures Delivered in Manchester. Manchester: 1839. V. 46

Two Memorials on Behalf of the Working Classes; the First Presented to the Government of Europe and America, the Second to the Allied Powers Assembled in Congress at Aix-la-Chapelle. London: 1818. V. 43

OWEN, ROBERT DALE 1801-1877

Address Touching the Influence and Progress of Literature and the Sciences: Delivered Before the Philomathean Society of the Indiana University, at the Annual Commencement. Richmond: 1838. V. 41

The Debatable Land Between This World and the Next. London: 1871. V. 42

Discussion on the Existence of God and the Authenticity of the Bible. London: 1840. V. 39

Footfalls on the Boundary of Another World. Philadelphia: 1860. V. 37

Hints on Public Architecture Containing, Among Other Illustrations, Views and Plans of the Smithsonian Institution . . . New York: 1849. V. 41; 44

Moral Physiology; or a Brief and Plain Treatise on the Population Question. London: 1848. V. 39

Moral Physiology; or, a Brief and Plain Treatise on the Population Question. New York: 1858. V. 37

Moral Physiology; Or, A Brief and Plain Treatise on the Population Question. London: 1870. V. 37

Neurology. An Account of Some Experiments in Cerebral Physiology. London: 1847. V. 39

Pocahontas. New York: 1837. V. 37; 38; 46

OWEN, T. J. V., MRS

Mrs. Owen's Illinois Cook Book. Springfield: 1871. V. 41

OWEN, WILFRED 1893-1918

Collected Letters. London: 1967. V. 42

Poems. London: 1920. V. 37; 46

Poems. London: 1921. V. 37

Poems. New York: 1921. V. 39; 43

The Poems of Wilfred Owen. London: 1931. V. 37; 43; 45

Poems. Northampton: 1956. V. 41; 44

Selected War Poems. Illustraed by Dale Barnhart. Pasadena: 1983. V. 37; 42; 45

Thirteen Poems. 1956. V. 40; 45

Thirteen Poems. With Drawings by Ben Shahn. Northampton: 1956. V. 37; 41

War Poems. 1983. V. 44

OWEN, WILLIAM

Pictorial Sunday Readings. London: 1862. V. 42

OWEN, WILLIAM F.

Narrative of Voyages to Explore the Shores of Africa, Arabia and madagascar, Performed in H.M. Ships Leven and Barracouta. London: 1833. V. 38

OWENS-ADAIR, B. A.

Dr. Owens-Adair. Some of Her Life Experiences. Portland: 1905? V. 40; 42; 43

Dr. Owens-Adair, Some of Her Life Experiences. Portland: 1906. V. 38

Dr. Owens-Adair. Some of Her Life Experiences. Portland: 1950? V. 37

A Souvenir: Dr. Owens-Adair to Her Friends. Salem: 1922. V. 38

OWENS-ADAIR, B.A.

A Souvenir: Dr. Ownes-Adair to Her Friends. Christmas, 1922. (Salem, OR: 1922). V. 37

OWENS, HARRY J.

Doctor Faust, a Play Based Upon Old German Puppet Versions. Chicago: 1953. V. 38; 40

Doctor Faust. Lexington: 1953-4. V. 44

OWENS, JAMES

Recollections of a Runaway Boy, 1827-1903. Pittsburgh: 1903. V. 42

THE OWL. a Miscellany. London: 1919. V. 38

OXBERRY, WILLIAM

The Actor's Budget of Wit and Merriment . . . London: 1820. V. 41

The Actor's Budget of Wit and Merriment, Consisting of Monologues, Prologues, Epilogues, Tales, Comic Songs . . . London: 1830. V. 44

The Theatrical Banquet; or, the Actor's Budget . . . London: 1809. V. 45

OXENFORD, JOHN

The Illustrated Book of French Songs, From the Sixteenth to the Nineteenth Century. London: 1855. V. 38

OXENHAM & SONS

Catalogue of a Very Valuable and Highly Interesting Collection of British Portraits. London: 1832. V. 38

OXFORD, A. W.

Collecting Small Things in a Small Way. London: 1909. V. 38; 42

OXFORD AND ASQUITH, MARGOT ASQUITH, COUNTESS OF 1864-1945

The Autobiography. London: 1920. V. 39

OXFORD and Cambridge Miscellany Poems. London: 1708. V. 39; 40; 43; 45

OXFORD BIBLIOGRAPHICAL SOCIETY

Proceedings, Volume 1-7, 1917-1946 (continued as) Proceedings, New Series, Volume I-8, 1948-59. London: 1927-59. V. 39

OXFORD Book of English Verse. Oxford: 1926. V. 42

OXFORD Characters. London: 1896. V. 43

OXFORD English Dictionary. Oxford: 1933. V. 41; 44
The OXFORD English Dictionary. London: 1933-86. V. 46
OXFORD English Dictionary. Oxford: 1933-86. V. 37
THE OXFORD English Dictionary. Oxford: 1978-1986. V. 37; 45; 46
OXFORD English Dictionary. (with) Supplement to the Oxford English Dictionary of Vol. I, A-G, (vol. II, H-N, Vol. III O-Sez; Vol. IV Se-Z. Oxford: 1978-86. V. 41
OXFORD English Dictionary. Oxford: 1978-87. V. 40
OXFORD English Dictionary. Oxford: 1982. V. 40
THE OXFORD English Dictionary. Oxford: 1989. V. 40; 41; 43

OXFORD English Dictionary. A New English Dictionary on Historical Principles. Oxford: 1888-9133. V. 46

OXFORD English Prize Poems. Oxford: 1828. V. 37

OXFORD History of English Art. Oxford: 1949-57. V. 39

OXFORD History of English Literature. Oxford: 1948-1979. V. 40

OXFORD Junior Encyclopaedia. London: 1948. V. 46

OXFORD Latin Dictionary. 1982. V. 45
THE OXFORD Latin Dictionary. Oxford: 1982. V. 37
OXFORD Latin Dictionary. Oxford: 1985. V. 40
THE OXFORD Latin Dictionary. Oxford: 1990. V. 44

THE OXFORD Packet. London: 1714. V. 41; 44

OXFORD Poetry 1923. New York: 194. V. 45

OXFORD Poetry. 1927. Oxford: 1927. V. 45

OXFORD, ROBERT HARLEY, 1ST EARL OF 1661-1724

A Catalogue of the Harlean Manuscripts in the British Museum. London: 1808-12. V. 38

Catalogus Bibliothecae Harleianae. London: 1743-45. V. 39

THE OXFORD Sausage: or, Select Poetical Pieces, Written by the Most Celebrated Wits of the University of Oxford. London: 1764. V. 39

OXFORD SOCIETY FOR THE STUDY OF GOTHIC ARCHITECTURE

A Guide to the Archiectural Antiquities in the Neighbourhood of Oxford . . . Oxford: 1860. V. 44

OXFORD UNIVERSITY

Judgment and Decree of the University of Oxford . . . Against Certain Pernicious Books and Damnable Doctrines . . . Oxford: 1683. V. 38; 40; 41

Statutes of the University of Oxford. Oxford: 1729. V. 40

OXFORD UNIVERSITY. BODLEIAN LIBRARY

Catalogue of a Collection of Early Newspapers and Essayists . . . Presented to the Bodleian Library . . . Oxford: 1865. V. 38

A Summary Catalogue of Western Manuscripts in the Bodleian Library Oxford. Oxford: 1953-1897. V. 41

THE OXFORDSHIRE Contest; Or the Whole Controversy Between the Old and New Interest. London: 1753. V. 45

THE OXFORDSHIRE Tragedy, or the Death of Four Lovers. N.P.. V. 42

OXLAD, ROBERT

The Protestant Vindicator; or, a Refutation of the Calumnies Contained in Cobbett's History of the Reformation . . . London: 1826. V. 43

OYEZ Broadsides. San Francisco: 1964. V. 46

OYVED, MOYSHEH

The Book of Affinity. London: 1933. V. 37; 40; 41; 44

OZ, TAHSIN

Turkish Ceramics. N.P.. V. 38; 41

Turkish Ceramics. 1955. V. 41

Turkish Ceramics. 1952. V. 37

Turkish Textiles and Velvets, XIV-XVI Centuries. Ankara: 1950. V. 37

OZANAM, JACQUES

Dictionaire Mathematique, ou Idee Generale des Mathematiques. Amsterdam: 1691. V. 45; 46

Recreations Mathematiques et Physiques, Qui Contiennent Plusieurs Problemes d'Arithmetique . . . d'Optique . . . de Mecanique, de Pyrothechnie & de Physique. Paris: 1694. V. 42

Recreations Mathematical and Physical. London: 1708. V. 39

Recreations in Mathematics and Natural Philosophy. London: 1803. V. 39; 40

OZANNE, NICOLAS

Diverses Maneuvres (sic) Des V. Aux Dessines Sur le Naturel Par Ozanne l'Aine et Gravee par Ozanne Le Cadet. Paris: 1760's. V. 38

OZANNE, T. D.

The South As It Is: or, Twenty One Years Experience in the Southern States of America. London: 1863. V. 41

OZELL, JOHN

Boileau's Lutrin: a Mock-Heroic Poem. London: 1708. V. 42

OZICK, CYNTHIA

Bloodshed and Three Novellas. New York: 1976. V. 45

The Pagan Rabbi and Other Stories. New York: 1971. V. 45

Trust. New York: 1966. V. 40; 42

P

P., J.

A New Guide, for Constables, Headboroughs, Tything-Men, Church-Wardens, Overseers and Collectors for the Poor, Surveyors for Amending the High-Ways and Bridges . . . London: 1700? V. 42

P., P.

Studley Royal; or, the New Guide Book. Knaresborough: 1847. V. 37

P., T.

Witenham-Hill, a Descriptive Poem. London: 1777. V. 40; 42

PAASCH, H.

Dictionary of Naval Terms, From Keel to Truck . . . London: 1885/94/1901/08. V. 42

From Keel to Truck, a Marine Dictionary in English. Antwerp: 1885. V. 39; 45

PAAW, PETRI

Primitiae Anatomicae. De Humani Corporis Ossibus. Leiden: 1615. V. 37

PABOR, WILLIAM E.

Colorado as an Agricultural State. Its Farms, Fields, and Garden Lands. New York: 1883. V. 37; 41

PABST, A. C. S.

Nashes of Ireland . . . and Their Allied Families, 1200-1956. Delaware: 1963. V. 38

PABST, G. F. J.

Orchidaceae Brasilienses. Hildesheim: 1975-77. V. 46

PACATA Hibernia: Ireland Appeased and Reduced or an Histoire of the Late Warres of Ireland Especially Within the Province of Monnster. Dublin: 1810. V. 46

PACCAGNINI, GIOVANNI

Pisanello. London: 1973. V. 46

PACCASSI, JOHANN BAPTISTE, FREIHERR VON

Einleitung in Die Theorie des Mondes . . . Vienna: 1783. V. 45

PACEY, H. B.

Considerations Upon the Present State of the Wool Trade, the Laws Made Concerning that Article, and How Far the Same are Consistent with True Policy, and the Real Interest of the State. London: 1781. V. 39; 46

PACHACAMAC. Report of the William Pepper Peruvian Expedition of 1896. Philadelphia: 1903. V. 37

PACHECO, FRANCISCO

Arte de la Pintura su Antiguedad y Grandezas . . . Seville: 1649. V. 44

PACHECO, JOSE EMILIO

Tree Between Two Walls. Los Angeles: 1969. V. 38

PACHT, O.

Illuminated Manuscripts in the Bodleian Library, Oxford. Oxford: 1966-73. V. 42

PACHT, OTTO

The St. Albans Psalter. London: 1960. V. 46

PACIFIC AGRICULTURAL SOCIETY

Constitution of the Pacific Agricultural Society, Organized August 16th, 1859. Redwood City: 1859. V. 42

PACIFIC AND ATLANTIC RAILROAD

General Railroad Laws, Articles of Association and By-Laws of the Pacific and Atlantic Railroad Company with the Reports of the Chief Engineer and Secretary. San Francisco: 1854. V. 37; 43

THE PACIFIC Coast and the World . . . Chicago: 1893. V. 45

THE PACIFIC Coast Pulpit Containing Sermons by Prominent Preachers of San Francisco and Vicinity. San Francisco: 1875. V. 41

PACIFIC COAST STEAMSHIP CO.

All About Alaska. San Francisco: 1890. V. 42

PACIFIC HOMOEOPATHIC MEDICAL SOCIETY OF THE STATE OF CALIF.

Transactions . . . . from 1874 to 1876. San Francisco: 1876. V. 43

PACIFIC MAIL STEAMSHIP COMPANY

A Sketch of the New Route to China and Japan by the Pacific Mail Steamship Co.'s. Trhough Line of Steamships Between Yew York, Yokohama and Hong Kong, via the Isthmus of Panama and San Francisco. San Francisco: 1867. V. 40

THE PACIFIC Northwest Information for Settlers and Others, Oregon and Washington Territory . . . New York: 1883. V. 37; 42; 43

PACIFIC Northwest, Its Wealth and Resources. Portland: 1893? V. 42

THE PACIFIC Northwest, Its Wealth and Resources . . . Oregon, Washington, Idaho. Portland: 1893? V. 38

PACIFIC RAILROAD

First Annual Report of the Board of Directors, of the Pacific Railroad; and Report of the Chief Engineer Upon the Preliminary Surveys. St. Louis: 1851. V. 45

PACIFIC RAILROAD CO.

Lands of the Central Pacific Railroad Company in California, Nevada, Utah. 1877. V. 38

PACIFIC RAILROAD CONVENTION, LACON, ILLINOIS, 1853.

Proceedings of a Pacific Railroad Convention, at Lacon, Illinois, with the Address of Col. Samuel R. Curtis. Chcinnati: 1853. V. 39

PACIFIC Railroad Report of Explorations & Surveys. Volume II, From the Mississippi River to the Pacific Ocean. Washington, D.C.: 1855. V. 39

PACIFIC WHARF CO. OF SAN FRANCISCO

By-Laws of of the Pacific Wharf Company of San Francisco. San Francisco: 1853. V. 46

PACIFICO DA NOVARA 1420?-1482

Summa Confessionis Intitula Pacifica Conscientia. Venice: 1503. V. 40

PACIOLI, LUCA

De Devine Proportione. Verona: 1956. V. 42

PACIOLI, LUCAS

Ancient Double-Entry Bookkeeping: Lucas Pacioli's Treatise. Denver: 1914. V. 46

PACIUS, JULIUS

L'Art de Raymond Lullius Esclaircy . . . Paris: 1619. V. 46

PACK, GEORGE

Tumors of the Hands and Feet. St. Louis: 1939. V. 42

PACK, RICHARDSON

Miscellanies in Prose and Verse. London;. V. 39

Miscellanies in Verse and Prose. London: 1729. V. 37; 38; 42; 43

A New Collection of Miscellanies in Prose and Verse. London: 1725. V. 41; 45

PACKARD, A. S.

A Monograph of the Geometrid Moths or Phalenidae of the United States. Washington: 1876. V. 41

PACKARD, ALPHEUS SPRING

The Labrador Coast. New York: 1891. V. 44

PACKARD, ELIZABETH PARSONS WARE 1816-1895

Marital Power Exemplified in Mrs. Packard's Trial, and Self Defence from the Charge of Insanity. Hartford: 1866. V. 43

Modern Persecution, or Insane Asylums Unveiled, as Demonstrated by the Report of the Investigating Committee of the Legislature of Illinois. Hartford: 1873. V. 40

PACKARD, FRANCIS

The History of Medicine in the United States. Philadelphia: 1901. V. 40

History of Medicine in the United States. New York: 1931. V. 41

PACKARD, FRANCIS R.

Annals of Medical History. New York: 1917-42. V. 38

PACKARD, SILAS SADLER

My Recollections of Ohio. New York: 1890. V. 46

PACKARD, WELLMAN

Early Emigration to California, 1849-1580. Bloomington: 1928. V. 38

PACKARD, WINTHROP

The Young Ice Whalers. Boston: 1903. V. 46

PACKE, EDMUND

An Historical Record of the Royal Regiment of Horse Guards, or Oxford Blues. Its Services . . . London: 1834. V. 38; 46

An Historical Records of the Royal Regiment of Horse Guards, or Oxford Blues . . . London: 1847. V. 40

PACKER, C.

Paris Furniture by Master Ebenistes. Newport: 1956. V. 37; 44

PACKER, JAMES E.

The Insulae of Imperial Ostia. Rome: 1971. V. 40

PACKER, S. J.

Report of the Committee of the Senate of Pennsylvania, Upon the Subject of the Coal Trade. Harrisburg: 1834. V. 43

PACKMAN, ANA BEGUE DE

Early California Hospitality. The Cookery Customs of Spanish California . . . Glendale: 1938. V. 37; 40; 45

PACKWOOD, GEORGE

Packwood's Whim. London: 1796. V. 42

PADDOCK, B. B.

A History of Central and Western Texas. Chicago: 1911. V. 43

PADDOCK, G. H.

Catalogue of Shropshire Birds. Newport: 1897. V. 43

PADDOCK, JUDAH

A Narrative of the Shipwreck of the Oswego, on the Coast of South Barbary, and of the Sufferings of the Master and the Crew While in Bondage Among the Arabs . . . London: 1818. V. 42

A Narrative of the Shipwreck of the Ship Oswego, on the Coast of south Barbary . . . New York: 1818. V. 43

PADEREWSKI, I. J.

Chopin a Discourse. London: 1911. V. 37

PADERNI, CAMILLO

A Curious Collection of Ancient Paintings, Accurately Engraved from excellent Drawings . . . London: 1741. V. 38

PADGETT, EARL

Plastic and Reconstructive Surgery. Springfield: 1948. V. 42

PADILLA, HERBERTO

Pale Kings and Princes. New York: 1987. V. 44

PADLEY, JAMES SANDBY

The Fens and Floods of Mid-Lincolnshire . . . Lincoln: 1882. V. 44

Selections from the Ancient Monastic, Ecclesiastical and Domestic Edifices of Lincolnshire. 1851. V. 46

Selections from the Ancient Monastic, Ecclesiastical and Domestic Edifices of Lincolnshire. Lincoln: 1851. V. 40

PADMORE, GEORGE

The Gold Coast Revolution - the Struggle of an African People from Slavery to Freedom. London: 1953. V. 45

PADOVANI, FABRIZIO

Tractatus Duo Alter de Ventis Alter Perbrevis de Terraemotu. Bologna: 1601. V. 42

PADUA, ANTONIO DE

Arte de Viver em Paz Com Os Homens . . . *Dedicada aos Vassallos de S. Mag. Fidelissima, Principalmente aos que Habitao a Diocese do Maranhao.* Lisbon: 1783. V. 41

PAE, DAVID

The Coming Struggle Among the Nations of the Earth; or, the Political Events of the Next Thirteen Years . . . Toronto: 1853. V. 43

PAEZ, GASPAR

Lettre Annue di Ethiopia del 1624, 1625 e 1626. Roem: 1628. V. 41

PAGA; a Quarterly Journal for Those in Typography and Printing, Book Design and Production, Print-making and Graphic Arts. Lunenburg: 1953-1965. V. 39

A PAGAN Anthology. New York: 1918. V. 38; 41; 44

PAGAN, BLAISE FRANCOIS DE

An Historical and Geographical Description of the Great Country and River of the Amazones in America. London: 1661. V. 46

Relation Historique et Geographique de la Grande Riviere des Amazones dans l'Amerique . . . Paris: 1655. V. 40

PAGAN, WILLIAM

Road Reform: a Plan for Abolishing Turnpike Tolls and Statute Labour Assessments, and for Providing the Funds Necessary for the Public Roads . . . Edinburgh: 1846. V. 43

PAGANINO, JACINTO JOSE

Roteiro do Neptuno Oriental Para Uso das Cartas de M. M. d'Apres, e d'Alrymple. Lisbon: 1783. V. 41

PAGANO, M.

Il Specchio di Pensieri Delle Belle & Virtuose Donne. Venice: 1549. V. 38

PAGASSE, MR.

The French Preceptor; or, Principles of the French Language . . . Dublin: 1795. V. 42

PAGE & CO.

Illustrated Historical Atlas of the County of Middlesex. Toronto: 1878. V. 42

PAGE, ANTHEA

Egyptian Sculpture, Archaic to Saite, from the Petrie Collection. Warminster: 1976. V. 44

PAGE, CHARLES A.

Letters of a War Correspondent. Boston: 1899. V. 41

PAGE, DAVID P.

Theory and Practice of Teaching, or the Motives and Methods of Good School-Keeping. Syracuse: 1847. V. 43

PAGE, DENYS L.

History and the Homeric Iliad. Berkeley: 1959. V. 44

PAGE, FRANK E.

Homer Watson Artist and Man. Kitchener: 1939. V. 44

PAGE, FREDERICK B.

Prairiedom: Rambles and Scrambles in Texas of New Estremadura. New York: 1845. V. 39; 40; 41; 42; 45

The Principle of the English Poor Laws Illustrated and Defended . . . Bath: 1822. V. 43

PAGE, G. G.

Battle of King's Mountain Fought October 7, 1780. King's Mountain: 1926. V. 42

PAGE, HARRY S.

Between the Flags . . . New York: 1929. V. 41

PAGE, I.

History and Guide for Drawing the Acanthus, and Other Description of Ornamental Foliage. London: 1840. V. 46

PAGE, J.

Guide for Drawing the Acanthus, and Every Description of Ornamental Foliage. London: 1856. V. 38

PAGE, JAMES MADISON

The True Story of Andersonville Prison, a Defense of Major Henry Wirz. New York: 1908. V. 37; 39

The True Story of Andersonville Prison, a Defense of Major Henry Wirz. New York/Washington: 1908. V. 37

PAGE, JAMES RATHWELL

Book of Common Prayer. A Descriptive Catalogue . . . and Related Material in the Collection of James R. Page. Los Angeles: 1955. V. 39; 41; 43; 45; 46

PAGE, JOHN

An Address to the Citizens of the District of York, in Virginia. N.P.: 1796. V. 45

An Address To the Citizens of the District of York, in Virginia, by Their Representative, John Page, of Rosewell. Philadelphia: 1796. V. 42

Receipts for Preparing and Compounding the Principal Medicines Made Use of by the Late Mr. Ward. London: 1763. V. 44

PAGE, P. K.

The Sun and the Moon. Toronto: 1944. V. 43

PAGE, RICHARD CHANNING MOORE

Sketch of Page's Battery, or Morris Artillery, 2d Corps, Army Northern Virginia. New York: 1885. V. 44

PAGE, ROSWELL

Thomas Nelson Page: a Memoir of a Virginia Gentleman. New York: 1923. V. 41

PAGE, THOMAS J.

La Plata, the Argentine Confederation and Paraguay. New York: 1859. V. 37; 40; 41; 44

PAGE, THOMAS NELSON

In Ole Virginia; or, Marse Chan and Other Stories. New York: 1887. V. 39; 46

The Novels, Stories, Sketches and Poems of Thomas Nelson Page. New York: 1906-1912. V. 37

On Newfound River. New York: 1891. V. 39; 41

The Works of Thomas Nelson Page. New York: 1906. V. 39

THE PAGE Volume 2, Number 1. Surrey: 1899. V. 37

PAGE, WILLIAM

Victoria County History. Hertfordshire. London: 1902-23. V. 39

THE PAGEANT. L: 1896. V. 41
THE PAGEANT. London: 1896. V. 42

PAGEANT Of America. New Haven: 1925-29. V. 44

pages;

frontispiece; V. 37

PAGES, PIERRE MARIE FRANCOIS, VICOMTE DE

Travels Round the World in the Years 1767, 1768, 1769, 1770, 1771. London: 1791. V. 41; 42; 43; 46

Travels Round the World , in the Years 1767, 1768, 1768, 1770 and 1771. London: 1792-93. V. 39

Voyages Autour du Monde, et vers les Deux Poles, Par Terre et Par Mer . . . 1767-76. Paris: 1782. V. 38; 39; 40; 42; 45

PAGES, PIERRE MARIE FRANCOIS, VICOMTEDE

Reisen um die Welt und nach den Beiden Polen zu Lande und Zur See in Den Jhren 1767-1777. Frankfurt & Leipzig: 1786. V. 38; 40

PAGET, EDWARD CLARENCE

A memoir of the Honourable Sir Charles Paget, G. C. H. (1778-1839), Vice Admiral of the 'White' and Commander-in-Chief of the North American and West Indian Station . . . Toronto: 1911. V. 45

PAGET, FRANCIS

The Virtue of Simplicity. Oxford: 1898. V. 38

PAGET, GEORGE

The Light Cavalry Brigade in the Crimea. London: 1881. V. 41

PAGET, GUY

The Flying Parson and Dick Christian. Leicester: 1934. V. 37; 39

The History of the Althorp and Pytchley Hunt, 1634-1920. London: 1937. V. 37; 42

The Melton Mowbray of John Ferneley (1782-1860). London:eicester: 1931. V. 46

The Melton Mowbray of John Ferneley (1782-1860). Leicester: 1931. V. 37; 39; 41; 42

PAGET, J. OTHO

Hunting. London: 1900. V. 41; 44

PAGET, JAMES

Lectures on Surgical Pathology, Delivered at the Royal College of Surgeons of England. London: 1853. V. 38; 41

Lectures on Surgical Pathology, Delivered at the Royal College of Surgeons of England . . . Philadelphia: 1854. V. 39; 43; 44

Studies of Old Case-Books. London: 1891. V. 44

PAGET, T.

History of the Althorp and Pytchley Hunt. 1624 to 1920. London: 1937. V. 39

PAGET, THOMAS CATESBY

Miscellanies in Prose and Verse. London: 1741. V. 45

Some Reflections Upon the Administration of Government. London: 1740. V. 42

PAGET, VIOLET 1856-1935

Four Mauric. Five Unlikely Stories. London: 1927. V. 41

PAGETT, THOMAS CATESBY, BARON

An Essay on Human Life. London: 1737. V. 43

PAGINA Tertia de Deluvio Noe. Guildford Surrey: 1986. V. 40

PAGITT, EPHRAIM

Christianographie. London: 1635. V. 40

PAGNINI, SANTE

Kozer Ozar Leshon Ha-Kodesh. Hoc est, Epitome Thesavri Lingvae Sanctae. Antwerp: 1570. V. 38

PAGNINUS, SANTES

Hebraicas Institutiones in Quibus Quicquid est Gram(m)atices Hebraicae Facultatis Edocetur ab Amussim, de Literis, Punctis, Accentibus, Nomine & Nominum Speciebus, de Pronominibus . . . Lyon: 1526. V. 37

PAHER, STANLEY W.

Colorado River Ghost Towns. Las Vegas: 1976. V. 44

Death Valley Ghost Towns. Las Vegas: 1973. V. 38

Nevada: an Annoatated Bibliography. Las Vegas: 1980. V. 40

PAILTHORPE, FREDERICK W.

Twenty-One Illustrations to Oliver Twist. London: 1886. V. 38

24 Illustrations to the Pickwick Club. London: 1882. V. 37

PAIN, WILLIAM

The Builder's Golden Rule, or the Youth's Sure Guide. London: 1782. V. 38

Pain's British Palladio. London: 1786. V. 37

The Practical Builder, or Workman's General Assistant . . . London: 1776. V. 38; 45

The Practical Builder, or Workman's General Assistant. London: 1778. V. 38

The Practical Builder, or Workman's General Assistant . . . London: 1789. V. 42; 43

The Practical Builder, or, Workman's Assistant . . . with Plans and Elevations of Gentlemen's and Farm Houses, Barns, &c. Boston: 1792. V. 40; 45

The Practical House Carpenter; or, Youth's Instructor . . . London: 1792. V. 44

The Practical House Carpenter; or Youth's Instructor . . . Philadelphia: 1797. V. 41; 44

The Practical House Carpenter. London: 1823. V. 39

The Practical House Carpenter, or Youth's Instructor. London: 1805. V. 37; 40; 44

PAINE, ALBERT BIGELOW

Captain Bill McDonald, Texas Ranger: A Story of Frontier Reform. New York: 1909. V. 37; 38; 40; 42; 46

Mark Twain: a Biography. New York: 1912. V. 38; 40; 41; 43; 44

Mark Twain, a Biography. New York: & London: 1912. V. 43

Thomas Nast: His Period and His Pictures. New York: 1904. V. 39; 45

PAINE, BAYARD H.

Pioneers, Indians and Buffaloes. 1935. V. 45

Pioneers, Indians and Buffaloes. Curtis: 1935. V. 38; 45

PAINE, E. S. M.

The Two James's and the Two Stephensons; or, the Earliest History of Passenger Transit on Railways. London: 1861. V. 46

PAINE, JAMES

Plans, Elevations, Sections and Other Ornaments of the Mansion-House Belonging to the Corporation of Doncaster. London: 1751. V. 45

Plans, Elevations and Sections of Noblemen and Gentlemen's Houses..Executed in the Counties of Derby, Durham, Middlesex, Northumberland, Nottingham and York . . . . London: 1783. V. 38; 45

PAINE, JOHN KNOWLES

Composers and Their Works. Boston: 1891. V. 42

PAINE, LEWIS W.

Six Years in a Georgia Prison. New York: 1851. V. 38; 42

PAINE, MARTYN

Letters on the Cholera Asphyxia, as It Has Appeared in the City of New York . . . New York: 1832. V. 40; 45

Physiology of the Soul, an Instinct, as Distinguished from Materialism. New York: 1872. V. 41

PAINE, T. O.

Solomon's Temple; or the Tabernacle; First Temple; House of the King, or House of the Forest of Lebanon . . . Boston: 1861. V. 43

Solomon's Temple. Boston: 1870. V. 37

PAINE, THOMAS 1737-1809

Additions to Common Sense Addressed to the Inhabitants of America. London: 1776. V. 38

Address and Declaration of the Friends of Universal Peace and Liberty, Held at the Thatched House Tavern, St. James's Street, August 20th, 1791 . . . Together with Some Verses, by the Same Author . . . London: 1791. V. 43

Address and Declaration of the Friends of Universal Peace and Liberty, Held at the Thatched House Tavern, St. James's Street, August 20th, 1791 . . . Together with Some Verses, by the Same Author . . . V. 39

Agrarian Justice Opposed to Agrarian Law, and to Agrarian Monopoly. London: 1797? V. 39

The Age of Reason; Being the Investigation of True and Fabulous Theology. Paris: 1795. V. 41

The Age of Reason. London: 1795. V. 37

The Age of Reason. The Age of Reason. Part The Second. Paris: 1794-95. V. 37

PALATINO, GIOVAMBATTISTA fl.1535-1550 continued

Libro Nvovo d'Imparare a Scrivere Tvtte Sorte Lettere Antiche et Moderne di Tvtte Nationi. Rome: 1540. V. 44

Libro Nuovo d'Imparare a Scrivere Tutte Sorte Lettere Antiche, et Moderne di Tutte Nationi, Con Nuove Regole, Misure, et Essempi . . . Rome: 1544. V. 40

PALATIUS, JOANNES

Fasti Ducales ab Anaafesto I ad Silvestrum Valerium, Venetorum Ducem. Venice: 1696. V. 37

PALATY Sanktpeterburgskoi Imperatorskoi Akademii Nauk Biblioteki i Kunstkamery. St. Petersburg: 1741. V. 39; 42

PALAU I FABRE, JOSEPH

Picasso: the Early Years, 1881-1907. New York: 1981. V. 46

PALAU Y DULCET, ANTONIO

Manual del Librero Hispano-Americano . . . Barcelona: 1948-77. V. 40

Manual del Librero Hispano-Americano. Barcelona & Oxford: 1949-87. V. 40

PALAZZO, GIOVANNI

De Dominio Maris, Libri Dvo. Venice: 1663. V. 37

PALEOTTO, ALFONSO

Esplicatione del Sacro Lenzuolo Ove fu Involto il Signore et delle Piaghe in Esso Impresse col Suo Pretioso Sangue . . . Bologna: 1599. V. 38; 39

PALEY, F. A.

Illustrations of Baptismal Fonts. London: 1844. V. 38

A Manual of Gothic Mouldings: With Decorations for Copying Them and Determining their Dates. London: 1865. V. 38

PALEY, GRACE

Leaning Forward: Poems. Penobscot: 1985. V. 46

The Little Disturbances of Man. Garden City: 1959. V. 42; 43; 45

The Little Disturbances of Man. New York: 1959. V. 37

PALEY, MORTON D.

Essays in Honour of Sir Geoffrey Keynes. Oxford: 1973. V. 42

PALEY, WILLIAM 1743-1805

Beauties Selected from the Writings of the Late William Paley, D.D. London: 1810. V. 45

The Law and Practice of Summary Convictions on Penal Statutes by Justices of the Peace . . . London: 1814. V. 40

The Law and Practice of Summary Convictions on Penl Statutes by Justices of the Peace. London: 1838. V. 40

Natural Theology. London: 1817. V. 38

The Principles of Moral and Political Philosophy. Dublin: 1785. V. 41

The Principles of Moral and Political Philosophy. London: 1785. V. 39; 40; 41; 45

The Principles of Moral and Political Philosophy. London: 1786. V. 39; 40; 41; 43; 45; 46

The Principles of Moral and Political Philosophy. Dublin: 1788. V. 37; 45

The Principles of Moral and Political Philosophy. London: 1791. V. 38

The Principles of Moral and Political Philosophy. London: 1806. V. 41

The Principles of Moral and Philosophy. Boston: 1815. V. 45

The Principles of Moral and Political Philosophy. London: 1818. V. 41

The Principles of Moral and Political Philosophy. A New Edition. Philadelphia: 1794. V. 37

Reasons for Contentment: Addressed to the Labouring Part of the British Public. London: 1793. V. 43

Sermons on Various Subjects. London: 1825. V. 45

A View of the Evidences of Christianity. London: 1794. V. 40

Collected Works. London: 1814-18. V. 38

The Works with Extracts from His Correspondence . . . London: 1825. V. 45

Works. London: 1828. V. 37

The Works, with Additional Sermons and a Corrected Account of the Life and Writings of the Author by Edmund Paley. London: 1830. V. 39

The Works. London: 1853. V. 39

PALFREY, JOHN G.

History of New England. Boston: 1882-90. V. 39

PALGRAVE, FRANCIS 1788-1861

Catalogue of the Extensive and Valuable Library (& Collection of manuscripts) of the Late Sir Francis Palgrave. London: 1862. V. 44

An Essay Upon the Original Authority of the King's Council . . . London: 1834. V. 38; 40

Parliamentary Writs and Writs of Military Summons, Together with the Records and Muniments Relating to the Suit and Service Due and Performed to the King's High Courts of Parliament and the Counsels of the Realm or Affording Evidence of Attendance . . . London: 1827-34. V. 38

PALGRAVE, FRANCIS TURNER 1824-1897

The Golden Treasury of the Best Songs and Lyrical Poems in the English Language. London. V. 40

The Golden Treasury of the Best Songs and Lyrical Poems in the English Language. Cambridge: 1861. V. 46

The Golden Treasury of the Best Songs and Lyrical Poems in the English Language. Cambridge: 1863. V. 41; 46

The Golden Treasury of the Best Songs and Lyrical Poems in the English Language. London: 1883. V. 39

The Golden Treasury. London: 1904. V. 38; 41; 42

Palgrave's Golden Treasury. London: 1907. V. 44

The Golden Treasury. London: 1909. V. 44

A Golden Treasury of Songs and Lyrics. New York: 1911. V. 43; 45

The Golden Treasury. London: 1861. V. 37

The Passionate Pilgrim or Eros and Anteros. London: 1858. V. 39

Selected from the Best Songs and Lyrical Poems in the English Language and arragned with notes by Francis T. Palgrave. Revised and Enlarged. London: 1900. V. 37

The Treasury of Sacred Song. Oxford: 1889. V. 46

PALGRAVE, ROBERT HARRY INGLIS

Dictionary of Political Economy. London: 1894. V. 40

Notes on Banking in Great Britain and Ireland, Sweden, Denmark and Hamburg . . . London: 1873. V. 37

PALGRAVE, WILLIAM GIFFORD 1826-1888

Hermann Agha; an Eastern Narrative. London: 1872. V. 43

Narrative of a Year's Journey through Central and Eatern Arabia (1862-63). London: 1865. V. 42; 45; 46

Narrative of a Year's Journey through Central and Eastern Arabia (1862-63). London & Cambridge: 1865. V. 38; 40

Narrative of a Year's Journey through Central and Eastern Arabia (1862-63). London: 1866. V. 40

PALIN, RALPH

Observations On the Influence of Habits and Manners, National and Domestic, Upon the Health and Organization of the Human Race . . . London: 1822. V. 42

PALINGENIUS, MARCELLUS STELLATUS fl.1528

Zodiacus Vitae. Rotterdam: 1698. V. 37

PALINGENIUS, MARCELLUS STELLATUS, PSEUD. fl. 1528

The Zodiake of Life. London: 1588. V. 37; 38; 40

PALL Mall Gazette Book of Racking Colours. London: 1913. V. 40

PALLADINO, LAWRENCE B.

Indian and White in the Northwest, or a History of Catholicity in Montana. Baltimore: 1894. V. 40; 45

Our Friends the Coeur d'Aleine Indians. Montana: 1886. V. 39; 41

Our Friends the Coeur d'Aleine Indians. St. Ignatius' Print: 1886. V. 39; 45

PALLADIO, ANDREA

The Architecture in Four Books . . . London: 1721. V. 42; 44

The Architecture of A. Palladio . . . London: 1742. V. 38

Les Batiments et les Desseins . . . Recueillis et Illustres par Octave Bertotti Scamozzi. (with) Les Thermes des Romains Dessinees par Andre Palladio et Publiees . . . Vicenza: 1796/97. V. 45

Le Fabbriche e i Disegni . . . Raccolti ed Illustrati da Ottavio Bertotti Scamozzi . . . (with) Le Terme dei Romani . . . con la Giunta di Alcune Osservazioni da Ottavio Bertotti Scamozzi. Vicenza: 1776-83/85. V. 41

The First Book of Architecture . . . London: 1724. V. 43; 45

The First Book of Architecture. London: 1676. V. 37

The Four Books of Architecture. London: 1738. V. 38

I Quattro Libri dell'Architettura . . . ne' Quali Dopo un Breve Trattato de' Cinque Ordini & Di Quelli Avertimenti che Sono Piu Necessarii Nell Fabricare . . . Venice: 1768. V. 41

I Quattro Libri Dell'Architettura. Venice: 1570. V. 37

I Quattro Libri Dell'Architettura. Venice: 1581. V. 37

I Quattro Libri di Arachitettura . . . Venice: 1771-80. V. 37

Traicte des Cinq Ordres d'Architecture . . . Augmente de . . . l'Art de Bien Bastir par Le Sr. Le Muet. Paris: 1645. V. 44

PALLADIUS, RUTILIUS TAURUS AEMILIANUS

De Re Rustica. Lyon: 1549. V. 40; 45; 46

PALLADIUS, RUTILLIUS TAURUS AEMIANUS

La Villa . . . Tradotta Nuovamente per Francesco Sansovino. Venice: 1561. V. 40

PALLAS, PETER SIMON 1741-1811

Dierkundig Mengelwerk. Utrecht: 1767-1770. V. 40

Voyages de M.P.S. Pallas, en Differentes Provinces de l'Empire de Russie, et dans l'Asie Septentrionale. Paris: 1789-93. V. 42

PALMER, JULIUS

Mushrooms of America. Boston: 1886. V. 38

PALMER, LOOMIS T.

Gaskell's New and Complete Family Atlas of the World . . . Chicago: 1886. V. 45

New Popular Family Atlas of the World . . . Chicago: 1891. V. 45

The Standard Atlas and Gazetteer of the World. New York: 1892. V. 45

PALMER, MARGARET

The Mapping of Bermuda: a Bibliography of Printed Maps & Charts, 1548-1970. London: 1983. V. 39

PALMER, MARJORIE

1918-1923 German Hyperinflation. New York: 1967. V. 38

PALMER, MARY

A Dialogue in the Devonshire Dialect . . . London: 1837. V. 42

PALMER, PETER S.

History of Lake Champlain, From Its First Exploration by the French in 1609, to the Close of the year 1814. Albany: 1866. V. 40

PALMER, PHOEBE

Promise of the Father; or, a Neglected Speciality of the Last Days. Boston: 1859. V. 39; 45

PALMER, R. M.

Palmer's Pictorial Pittsburgh and Prominent Pittsburghers Past and Present 1758-1905. Pittsburgh: 1905. V. 42

PALMER, R. S.

Handbook of North American Birds. London: 1962/76. V. 42

PALMER, RICHMOND

The Bornu Sahara and Sudan. London: 1936. V. 39; 43; 45

PALMER, ROBIN

Mickey Never Fails. Boston: 1939. V. 45

PALMER, SAMUEL

Catalogue of a Small Exhibition of Water-Colour Drawings and Etchings. N.P.: 1927. V. 44

Catalogue of the Etchings of Samuel Palmer. London: 1937. V. 37; 38

A General History of Printing from the First Invention of It In the City of Mentz . . . London: 1733. V. 41; 44

Moral Essays on some of the most Curious and Significant English, Scotch and Foreign Proverbs. London: 1710. V. 37

The Nonconformist's Memorial. London: 1775. V. 40

St. Pancras. Being Antiquarian, Topographical and Biographical Memoranda Relating to the Extensive Metropolitan Parish of St. Pancras, Middlesex . . . London: 1874. V. 41

Samuel Palmer's Sketch Book. London: 1962. V. 37; 38; 40

PALMER, T. H.

The Historical Register of the United States. Philadelphia: 1814. V. 42

PALMER, THOMAS

An Essay on the Meanes Howvv to Make Our Trauailes, Into Forraine Countries, the More Profitable and Honourable. London: 1606. V. 41; 43

PALMER, THOMAS FYSHE

A Narrative of the Sufferings of T. F. Palmer and W. Skirving, During a Voyage to New South Wales, 1794, on Board the Surprise Transport. Cambridge: 1797. V. 40

The Trial of the Rev. Thomas Fyshe Palmer, Before the Circuit Court of Justiciary; Held at Perth, on the 12th and 13th September 1793, on an Indictment for Seditious Practices. Edinburgh: 1793. V. 45

PALMER, W.

Plain Papers on the Millennium. London: 1865. V. 43; 45

PALMER, WILLIAM

Origines Liturgicae, or Antiquities of the English Ritual and Dissertation on Primitive Liturgies. Oxford: 1839. V. 39

A Short Examination of the Hyderabad Papers, as Far as They Relate to the House of William Palmer & Co. in a Letter Addressed to the Proprietors of East India Stock. London: 1825. V. 42

PALMER, WILLIAM J.

Letters, 1853-1868. Philadelphia: 1906. V. 37

Report of Surveys Across the Continent, in 1867-'68 . . . for a Route Extending the Kansas City Pacific Railway to the Pacific Ocean at San Francisco and San Diego. Philadelphia: 1869. V. 37; 38; 39; 41; 42; 45

PALMGREN, NILS

Selected Chinese Antiquities from the Collection of Gustaf Adolf. Stockhlom: 1948. V. 39; 46

PALMQUIST, PETER E.

Carleton E. Watkins: Photographer of the American West. Albuquerque: 1983. V. 45

Redwood and Lumbering in California Forests: A Reconstruction of the Original Edgar Cherry Edition. San Francisco: 1983. V. 38; 41; 42

PALMSTRUCH, JOHAN WILHELM

Svensk Botanik. Stockholm & Uppsala: 1802-43. V. 38

PALOL, PEDRO

Early Medieval Art in Spain. London: 1967. V. 44

PALOMBA, IGNAZIO

Abrege de la Langue Toscane, ou Nouvelle Methode, Contenant les Principes de l'Italien. Paris & Lyon: 1768. V. 41

PALOU, FRANCISCO

Life of Ven. Padre Junipero Serra. San Francisco: 1884. V. 44

PALOU, FRANCISCO

The Expedition Into California of the Venerable Padre Fray Junipero Serra and His Companions in the Year 1769 . . . San Francisco: 1934. V. 38; 39; 40; 45

Historical Memoirs of New California . . . Berkeley: 1926. V. 37; 38; 42; 44; 45; 46

Life and Apostolic Labors of the Venerable Father Junipero Serra, Founder of the Franciscan Missions of California. Pasedena: 1913. V. 39

Noticias de la Nueva California. San Francisco: 1874. V. 41

Relacion Historica de la Vida y Apostolicas Tareas del Venerable Padre Fray Junipero Serra, y de las Misiones Que Funda en la California Septentrional . . . Mexico: 1787. V. 42

PALTOCK, RICHARD

The Life and Adventures of Peter Wilkins, a Cornish Man . . . London: 1750. V. 46

PALTOCK, ROBERT 1697-1767

The Life and Adventures of Peter Wilkins. London: 1751. V. 37; 40; 43

The Life and Adventures of Peter Wilkins, A Cornish Man. In Two Volumes. By R.S. A. a passenger in the Hector. London: 1783. V. 37

The Life and Adventures of Peter Wilkins, a Cornish Man. Berwick: 1784. V. 41

The Life and Adventures of Peter Wilkins, or the History of the Flying Islanders, taken from His Own Mouth. Boston: 1828. V. 38; 45

The Life and Adventures of Peter Wilkins. London: 1884. V. 46

PALTSITS, VICTOR HUGO

Washington's Farewell Address, in Facsimile, with Transliteration of all the Drafts of Washington, Madison, and Hamilton Together with Their Correspondence and Other Supporting Documents. New York: 1935. V. 41

PAMBOUR, F. M. G. DE

A Practical Treatise on Locomotive Engines . . . London: 1840. V. 38

PAMELA'S Conduct in High Life Publish'd from Her Original Papers to Which are Prefix'd Several Curious Letters Written to the Editor on the Subject. London: 1741. V. 40

PAMPHLET Descriptive of King County, Washington Territory, Showing Its Wonderful Natural Resrouces and Commercial Advantages, with a Short Sketch of Seattle. Seattle;: 1884. V. 40

THE PAMPHLETEER. London: 1813-16. V. 41

PANAMA RAILROAD COMPANY

Capital $1,000,000. With Liberty to Increase to $5,000,000 . . . New York: 1849. V. 38

Letter from the Directors of the Panama Railroad Company, Addressed to the Senate and House of Representatives of the United States, in reply to the Remarks of the Postmaster General Contained in His Report to the President . . . New York: 1856. V. 39

Panama Railroad Company. Capital $1,000,000. With Liberty to Increase to $5,000,000 . . . New York: 1849. V. 39

PANANTI, FILIPPO

Narrative of a Residence in Algiers Comprising a Geographical and Historical Account of the Regency. London: 1818. V. 41

PANANTI, SIGNOR

Narrative of a Residence in Algiers . . . London: 1818. V. 45

PANCAKE, BREECE D'J.

The Stories. Boston: 1982. V. 46

PANCHARIS Queen of Love; or, Woman Unveil'd. London: 1721. V. 40

PANCIROLI, GUIDO

The History of Many Memorable Things Lost, Which Were in Use Among the Ancients: and an Account of Many Excellent Things Found, Now in Use Among the Moderns, Both Natural and Artificial. London: 1715. V. 37

PANCIROLLI, GUIDO

Rerum Memorabilium Sive Deperditarum. Frankfurt: 1629-31. V. 38

PANCOAST, HENRY S.

Impressions of the Sioux Tribes in 1882. With Some Principles of the Indian Question. Philadelphia: 1883. V. 37

PANCOAST, JOSEPH

A Treatise on Operative Surgery . . . Philadelphia: 1846. V. 43

A Treatise on Operative Surgery. Philadelphia: 1844. V. 37; 41; 42

PANDOSKY, M. C.

Grammar and Dictionary of the Yakama Language. New York: 1862. V. 39

PANDOSY, CLES

Grammar and Dictionary of the Yakama Language. New York: 1862. V. 38

A PANEGYRIC on the Town of Paisley. Paisley?. V. 42
A PANEGYRIC on the Town of Paisley. Paisley?: 1765. V. 40

A PANEGYRICK, on the Famous Doctor Duds, Newly arrived from His Travels in Foreign Countries. 1698. V. 43
A PANEGYRICK on the Famous Doctor Duds, Newly Arrived from His Travels in Foreign Countries. 1698. V. 42

PANKHURST, E. SYLVIA

The Suffragette: the History of the Women's Militant Suffrage Movement, 1905-1910. Boston: 1911. V. 40; 42; 43

The Suffragette Movement - an Intimate Account of Persons and Ideals. London: 1931. V. 45

PANKHURST, EMMELINE

My Own Story. New York: 1914. V. 40; 42; 43

PANKHURST, SYLVIA

Writ on Cold Slate. V. 42

PANKRATZ, TERESA

The Wardrobe. Chicago: 1988. V. 44

PANOFSKY, ERWIN

Albrecht Durer. Princeton: 1943. V. 39

Albrecht Durer. London: 1945. V. 44

Albrecht Durer. London: 1948. V. 43

Albrecht Durer. Princeton: 1948. V. 45

Albrecht Durer. Princeton: 1945. V. 37; 40; 43

Early Netherlandish Painting: Its Origin and Character. Cambridge: 1966. V. 42

Tomb Sculpture: Four Lectures on Its Changing Aspects from Ancient Egypt to Gernini. New York. V. 42

Tomb Sculpture, Its Changing Aspects from Ancient Egypt to Bernini. London: 1964. V. 42

THE PANORAMA; or, a Journey to Munster, a Serio Comic Poem. Dublin: 1807. V. 40

PANORMITANUS DE TUDESCHIS, NICOLAUS

Lectura Super V. Libros Decretalium. Volume 1. Basel: 1477. V. 37

PANTER-DOWNES, MOLLIE

At the Pines. Swinburne and Watts-Dunton in Putney. Boston: 1971. V. 39

PANTHOT, JEAN BAPTISTE

Traite des Dragons et des Escarboucles. Lyon: 1691. V. 38

PANTOMIME, a Picture Show for Young. London: 1883. V. 43

PANTON, EDWARD

Speculum Juventutis; or, a True Mirror . . . London: 1671. V. 40; 44

PANTON, J. E.

Nooks and Corners. London: 1891. V. 42

PANTZSCHMANN, HIERONYMUS

Declaratio Praecipuarum Quaestionum Circa Materiam Locationis Conductionis . . . Jena: 1596. V. 40; 44

PANVINIO, ONOFRIO

De Ludis Circensibus, Libri II. De Triumphis, Liber Unus. Quibus Universa fere Romanorum Veterum Sacra Ritusq, Declarantur ac Figuris Aenei Illustrantur. Padua: 1642. V. 37

PANVINIUS, ONOPHRIUS

Romani Pontifices et Cardinales S.R.E. ab Eiusdem a Leone IX ad Paulum IIII per Quingentos Posteriores a Christi Natali annos Creati. Venice: 1557. V. 39

PANVINIUS, ONUPHRIUS

Libri Tres: I. De Ludis Saecularibus. II. De Sibyllis et Carminibus Sibylliniis. III. De Antiquis Romanorum Nominibus. (with) Fastaoarum Libri V a Romulo Rege Usque ad Imp. Caesarem Carolum V Eiusdem Fastorum Libros Commentarii. Heidelberg: 1588. V. 38

PANVINO, ONOFRIO 1529-1568

De Lvdis Saeclaribvs Liber (and) De Sibyllis et Carminibvs Sibyllinis. Venice: 1558. V. 45

PANZANI, G.

The Memoirs of G. Panzani; Giving an Account of His Agency in England 1634-36. Birmingham: 1793. V. 39

PANZER, GEORG WOLFGANG

Aelteste Buchdruckergeschichte Nurnbergs. Nuremberg: 1789. V. 38

PAOLETTI, NICCOLI GASPARI

The Raccolta Dei Disegni Fabriche Regie de Bagni di Montecatini Nella Valdinievole. Firenze: 1787. V. 41

PAPACHRISTOU, T.

Marcel Breuer: New Buildings and Projects. 1970. V. 46

PAPASHVILY, GEORGE

Anything Can Happen. New York: 1945. V. 39; 45

PAPE, AGNES M.

Fair Folk of Many Lands. London: 1920. V. 44

PAPE, FRANK C.

Ruby Fairy Book. London. V. 40

Ruby Fairy Book. London: 1913. V. 42

Stories from the Arabian Nights. London: (ca. 1930). V. 37

PAPENDIEK, CHARLES EDWARD

A Synopsis of Architecture, for the Information of the Student and Amateur. V. 38

THE PAPER Hanger, Painter, Grainer, and Decorator's Assistant. London: 1879. V. 40

THE PAPER of Lending Library Books, With Some Remarks on Their Bindings, Illustrated by Diagrams, and Photomicrographs. Bath. V. 40

PAPERS and Documents Relating to the Bolivian Loan, the National Bolivian Navigation Company and the Madeira and Mamore Railway Company, Ltd. London: 1873. V. 41; 45

PAPERS Appertaining to the Silas Deane Claim. N.P.: 1840. V. 41
PAPERS Appertaining to the Silas Deane Claim. N.P.: 1840. V. 46

PAPERS Connected with the Indian Land Question 1850-1875. Victoria: 1875. V. 37

PAPERS Relating to America. Presented to the House of Commons, 1809. London: 1810. V. 41; 46

PAPERS Relating to Certain Pecuniary Transactions of Messrs. William Palmer & Co. with the Government of His Highness the Nizam. London: 1824. V. 38

PAPERS Relating to the Riot at Canton in July 1846 and to the Proceedings Taken Against Mr. Compton, a British Subject, for His Participation in the Riot. London: 1847. V. 40

PAPERS Relating to the Treaty of Washington. Volume V - Berlin Arbitration. Washington: 1872. V. 45

PAPERS Relative to the Mission of Hon. T. Butler King, to Europe. Milledgeville: 1863. V. 44

PAPERS Relative to the Rupture with Spain, Laid Before Both Houses of Parliament, on Friday the Twenty-Night Day of January 1762. London: 1762. V. 39; 41

THE PAPHIAN Dove. Dublin: 1798. V. 44

PAPILLON, JEAN BAPTISTE MICHAEL

Traite Historique et Pratique de la Gravure en Bois. Paris: 1766. V. 45

PAPIN, DENIS

A New Digester or Engine for Softening Bones . . . (with) A Continuation of the New Digester . . . London: 1681/87. V. 45

A New Digester of Engine for Softening Bones, Containing the Description of Its Make and Use in These Particulars . . . (with) A Continuation of the New Digester . . . London: 1687. V. 41

PAPIN, NICHOLAS

Raisonnemens philosophiques . . . Blois: 1647. V. 37

THE PAPISTS Dream, Concerning What Shall Become of Their Plots, Interests, Persons and Religion. London: 1681. V. 42

PAPPIANI, ALBERTO

Della Sfera Armillare e dell'Uso di Essa Nella Astronomia Nautica e Gnomonica Opera . . . Florence: 1745. V. 45

PAPWORTH, JOHN

An Alphabetical Dictionary of Coats of Arms Belonging to Families in Great Britian and Ireland. London: 1874. V. 43

PAPWORTH, JOHN BUONAROTTI 1775-1847

Hints on Ornamental Gardening . . . London: 1823. V. 37; 39; 41; 42; 44; 45

Poetical Sketches of Scarborough. London: 1813. V. 39; 42; 44; 45; 46

Poetical Sketches of Scaroborough in 1813. Driffield: 1893. V. 39; 44

Rural Residences, Consisting of a Series of Designs for Cottages, Decorated Cottages, Small Villas and Other Ornamental Buildings. London: 1818. V. 37; 38; 39; 44; 45

Rural Residences . . . (with) Hints on Ornamental Gardening. London: 1818, 1823. V. 38

Rural Residences. London: 1832. V. 37

Select Views of London. London: 1816. V. 37; 38; 39; 40; 41; 42; 45; 46

Select Views of London: With Historical and Descriptive Sketches of Some of the Most Interesting of Its Public Buildings. London: 1950. V. 38

PAPWORTH, JOHN W.

An Alphabetical Dictionary of Coats of Arms, Belonging to Families in Great Britian and Ireland. London: 1874. V. 44

PAPYRO Plastics, or, the Art of Modelling in Paper. London: 1825. V. 38

PAPYRO-PLASTICS, Or the Art of Modelling in Paper; Being an Instructive Amusement of Young Persons of Both Sexes. London: 1830. V. 46

PAPYRUS RHIND

Facsimile of the Rhind Mathematical Papyrus in the British Museum. London: 1898. V. 40

PARABALOU. Farmington: 1920. V. 42

THE PARABLES from the Gospels. London: 1903. V. 37

PARABONI, PIETRO

Nuova Raccolta Delle Principali Vedute Antiche e Moderne dell'Alma Citta di Roma e sue Vicinanze. Roma: 1828. V. 38

PARABOSCO, GIROLAMO c. 1524-1557

Comedie . . . Cioe, La Notte, L'Hermafrodito, Il Viluppo, Il Pellegrino, I Contenti, Il Marinaio. Venice: 1560. V. 40

PARACELSUS 1493-1541

Astronomia Magna. Frankfurt. V. 38

Auroram Philosophorum, Thesaurum & Mineralem Oeconomiam Commentaria, cum Quibusdam Argumentis. Frankfurt: 1584. V. 38

Baderbuchlin. Sechs Kostliche Tractat, Armen und Reychen, Mutzlich und Notwendig, Von Wasserbadern. Mulhouse: 1562. V. 43

Centum Quindecim Curationes Experimentaque, e Germanico Idiomate in Latinum Versa. Lyon: 1582. V. 46

Dreyzehen Buecher / des Hoch Gelehrten und Weit Beruempten Herren / D Theophrasti Paracelsi . . . Basle: 1571. V. 38

Fasciculus Paracelsicae Medicinae Veteris . . . Frankfurt am Main: 1581. V. 38

Four Treatises of Theophrastus Von Honeheim Called Paracelsus. Baltimore: 1941. V. 45; 46

Grosse Wundartzney. Frankfurt am. Main: 1563. V. 38

The Hermetic and Alchemical Writings . . . London: 1894. V. 40

Hermetic Waste. London: 1986. V. 41

Medicina Diastatica or Sympatheticall Mumie . . . London: 1653. V. 46

Of the Supreme Mysteries of Nature: of the Spirits of the Planets, Occult Philosophy, the Magical, Sympathetical and Antipathetical Cure of Wounds and Diseases. London: 1656. V. 46

Opera Omnia Medico-Chemico-chirurgica . . . Geneva: 1658. V. 37; 46

Operum Medico-Chimicorum Sive Paradoxorvm . . . Frankfurt: 1605. V. 38; 44

Opus Chyrurgicum. Strassburg: 1564. V. 38; 40; 42; 44

De Peste. Oppenheim: 1613. V. 42; 44

Pharmacandi Modus. Strasbourg: 1578. V. 37; 42

Philosophiae et Medicinae Utriusque Universae, Compendium, Ex Optimis Quibusque Eius Libris . . . Paris: 1567. V. 43

Philosophiae et Medicinae Utriusque Universae Compendium . . . Basel: 1568. V. 38

Philosophy Reformed and Improved in Four Profound Tractates. London: 1657. V. 46

Prognosticatio Eximii Doctoris Theophrasti Paracelsi. N.P.: 1580? V. 38

Sechster Theil der Buecher und Schrifften des Edlen / Hochgelehrten und Vewerten Philosophi & Medici Philippi Theophrasti Bombast von Hohenheim / Paracelsi Genannt. Basle: 1590. V. 38

Von Ersten Dreyen Principiis, Was Jre Formen und Wirckung. N.P.: 1563. V. 38

PARACELSUS, THEOPHRASTUS BOMBASTUS VON HOHENHEIM

La Grande Chirurgie . . . Traduite en francois . . . par M. Claude Dariot. Plus un Discours de la Goutte . . . Traictez de la Preparation des Medicamens . . . Nouvellement mis en Lumiere par ledit Dariot. Lyon: 1603. V. 37

PARADIN, CLAUDE

Devises Heroiques. Paris: 1622-21. V. 46

Devises Heroiques. Lyon: 1557. V. 38; 39; 42

Heroica. Antwerp: 1563. V. 40

Quadrins Historiques de la Bible. Lyon: 1555. V. 45

Quadrins Historiques de la Bible. Lyon: 1558. V. 45

Symbola Heroica. Antwerp: 1567. V. 37

PARADIN, GUILLAUME b. c. 1510

Cronique de Savoie. Lyon: 1552. V. 40

LE PARADIS Musulman. Paris: 1930. V. 45

A PARADOX Against Liberty. Londn (sic).: 1679. V. 44

PARAGRAPHS on Printing. New York: 1943. V. 46

PARAGUAY, a Note As to Its Position and Prospects. London: 1871. V. 40

PARAKER, T. N.

Leaves Out of the Book of a Country Gentleman. Oswestry: 1847. V. 38

PARALLAX. Zetetic Astronomy. Earth Not a Globe. London: 1873. V. 40

THE PARALLEL: An Essay on Friendship, Love and Marriage. London: 1689. V. 41

A PARALLEL of the Ancient Architecture . . . The Second Edition with Large Additions. London: 1707. V. 37

PARAMORE, EDWARD E.

The Ballad of Yukon Jake. New York: 1928. V. 39; 44; 46

THE PARASITE. Dublin: 1765. V. 45

PARBURT, GEORGE R.

Anselmo; a Poem. San Francisco: 1865. V. 44

PARDIES, IGNACE GASTON

Deux Machines Propres a Faire les Quadrans. Paris: 1687. V. 38

Discours du Mouvement Local: La Statique ou la Science des Forces Mouvantes . . . The Hague: 1691. V. 42

PARDIGON, C. F.

The Practice of War: Being a Translation of a French Military Work entitled 'Maxims Counsels and Instructions on the Art of War' . . . to which the Translator has added Marshal Beugeaud's letter of Instruction . . . also, the Second Appendix of Baron Jomini . . . Richmond: 1863. V. 37

PARDOE, E. E.

John Baskerville of Birmingham, Letter-Founder and Printer. London: 1975. V. 41

PARDOE, JULIA

The Beauties of Bosphorus. London: 1838. V. 39; 40; 42; 46

The Beauties of the Bosphorus. London: 1839. V. 39; 40

The Beauties of the Bosphorus: The Danube. London: 1856. V. 39

The Beauties of Bosphorus. London: 1840. V. 37

The Beauties of the Bosphorus . . . London: 1860. V. 37

Memoirs of the French Courts. Courts and Reign of Francis. Louis XIV and the Court of France. The Life of Marie de Medicis. London: 1911. V. 42

The Romance of the Harem. London: 1839. V. 40; 41

The Romance of the Harem. Philadelphia: 1839. V. 46

Traits and Traditions of Portugal, Collected During a Residence in that Country. Philadelphia: 1834. V. 38

PARDON, GEORGE FREDERICK

Boldheart the Warrior and His Adventures in the Haunted Wood . . . London: 1859. V. 44

PARE, AMBROISE

Les Oeuvres . . . Paris: 1614. V. 37

Les Oeuvres. Paris: 1598. V. 40

The Workes of . . . New York: 1968. V. 44

PAREDES, IGNACIO DE

Promptuario Manual Mexicana. Mexico: 1759. V. 40; 45

PAREDES Y ARRILLAGRA, MARIANO

Ultimas Comunicaciones Entre el Gobierno Mexicano y el Enviado Y Ministro Plenipotenciario de Los Estados-Unidos . . . Mexico: 1846. V. 45

PARGETER, SHIRLEY

A Catalogue of the Library at Tatton Park. Chester: 1977. V. 42

PARIAN DE SERRES, JEAN

Inventaire General de l'Histoire de France Depuis Pharamond Iusques a Present. Paris: 1600. V. 46

A PARICULAR Account of Culloden. April 16, 1746. London: 1749. V. 41

PARIS and Its Environs, Displayed in a Series of Two Hundred Picturesque Views, From the Original Drawings, Taken Under the Direction of A. Pugin, Esq. London: 1831. V. 40

PARIS ET VIANA

The Noble Knight Paris & the Fair Vienne. Kentfield: 1956. V. 38; 41; 45; 46

PARIS EXHIBITION, 1889.

Reports of the United States Commissioners to the Universal Expostion of 1889 at Paris. Washington: 1890. V. 44

PARIS, FRANCOIS EDMOND

Souvenirs de Marine: Collections de Plans ou Dessins de Navires et de Bateaux Anciens ou Modernes Existants ou Disparus . . . Paris: 1882-1910. V. 39

PARIS. HOPITAL GENERAL

L'Hospital General de Paris. Paris: 1676-80. V. 40

PARIS Incendie 1871. Album Historique. Paris: 1871. V. 38

PARIS, JOHN AYRTON

A Guide to the Mount's Bay and the Land's End; comprehending the topography, botany, agriculture . . . of Western Cornwall. Second Edition. London: 1824. V. 37; 38; 39; 40; 41; 44; 45; 46

The Life of Sir Humphrey Davy, Bart. LL.D. Late President of the Royal Society, Foreign Associate of the Royal Institute of France. London: 1831. V. 39

Medical Jurisprudence. London: 1823. V. 45

Pharmacologia. London: 1822. V. 38; 42

Pharmacologia. New York: 1822. V. 39

Pharmacologia: Comprehending the Art of Prescribing Upon Fixed and Scientific Principles . . . New York: 1824. V. 45

Pharmacologia. New York: 1844. V. 40

Pharmacologia; comprehending the Art of Prescribing upon Fixed and Scientific Principles; together with the History of Medicinal Substances. Secand American, from the Fifth (enlarged). New York: 1824-23. V. 37

Pharmacologia; Third American, from the Sixth London Edition. Corrected and Extended, in Accordance with the London Pharmacopoeia of 1824 and with the Generally Advanced State of Chemical Science. New York: 1825. V. 37

Pharmacologica. New York: 1828. V. 42

Philosophy in Sport Made Science in Earnest: Being an Attempt to Illustrate the First Principles of Natural Philosophy by the Aid of Popular Toys and Sports. London: 1827. V. 38; 39; 41; 45

Philosophy in Sport Made Science in Earnest . . . London: 1833. V. 39

A Treatise on Diet. London: 1826. V. 40

A Treatise on Diet. London: 1827. V. 39

A Treatise on Diet. New York: 1828. V. 37; 43

PARIS, LOUIS PHILIPPE ALBERT D'ORLEANS, COMTE DE 1838-1894

History of the Civil War in America. Philadelphia: 1876-88. V. 46

The Trader's Unions of England. London: 1869. V. 41

PARIS, MATTHEW 1200-1259

Matthaei Paris Monachi Albanensis Angli Historia Major. London: 1640. V. 41; 45

PARIS. MUSEUM D'HISTOIRE NATURELLE

Annales du Museum National d'Histoire Naturelle, Par Les Professeurs de cet Etablissement. Paris: 1802-03. V. 40

PARIS. UNIVERSITE. FACULTE DE DROIT

Traitte des Veritables et Ivstes Prerogatives De La Faculte De Droit De Paris; et de la Necessite d'y Restablir la Profession du Droit Ciuil. Paris: 1665. V. 39

PARIS, VICE ADMIRAL

Souvenirs de Marine, Collection de Plans ou Dessins de Navires et de Bateau Anciens ou Moderns . . . Paris. V. 41

THE PARISH And the Union; or, the Poor and the Poor Laws Under the Old System and the New. London: 1837. V. 40

THE PARISH Registers of Redruth in Cornwall 1560-1716. Redruth: 1894. V. 40

PARISH, W. D.

A Dictionary of the Sussex Dialect and Collection of Provincialisms in Use in the County of Sussex. Lewes: 1875. V. 41

A Dictionary of the Kentish Dialect and Provincialisms in Use in the County of Kent. Lewes: 1888. V. 45

A Dictionary of the Kentish Dialect and Provincialisms. London: 1888. V. 41

PARISH-WATSON & CO., NEW YORK.

Chinese Pottery of the Han, T'ang and Sung Dynasties; Owned and Exhibited by . . . New York: 1917. V. 39

PARISH, WOODBINE

Buenos Ayres and the Provinces of the Rio de la Plata, Their Present State, Trade and Debt. London. V. 40

Buenos Ayres and the Provinces of the Rio de la Plata: From Their Discovery and Conquest by the Spanish to the Establishment of Their Political Independence. London: 1852. V. 38; 41

PARISOT, P. F.

History of the Catholic Church in the Diocese of San Antonio. San Antonio: 1897. V. 41

PARISOT, R. P.

The Reminiscences of a Texas Missionary. San Antonio: 1899. V. 37; 41; 44; 45; 46

PARIVAL, JEAN NICOLAS

The History of the Iron Age. London: 1656. V. 44

PARK, BENJAMIN

Shakings. Boston: 1867. V. 37

PARK, JAMES ALLAN 1763-1838

A System of the Law of Marine Insurances with Three Chapters on Bottomry, on Insurances on Lives, and on Insurances Against Fire. London: 1790. V. 38; 40

A System of the Law of Marine Insurances . . . London: 1809. V. 40

PARK, JOHN JAMES

The Topography and Natural History of Hampstead, in the County of Middlesex. London: 1814. V. 38

The Topography and Natural History of Hampstead in the County of Middlesex . . . London: 1818. V. 37; 41

PARK, LAWRENCE 1873-1924

Gilbert Stuart. An Illustrated Descriptive List of His Works . . . With an Account of His Life by John Hill Morgan . . . New York: 1926. V. 38; 39

PARK, MUNGO 1771-1806

The Journal of a Mission to the Interior of Africa in the Year 1805 . . . London: 1815. V. 40; 43; 46

Travels in the Interior Districts of Africa: Performed Under the Patronaage of the Africa Association, in the Years 1795, 1796 and 1797. London: 1799. V. 37; 38; 40; 41; 42

Travels in the Interior Districts of Africa: Peformed Under the Direction and Patronage of the African Association in the Years 1795, 1796 and 1797. London: 1800. V. 39

Travels in the Interior Districts of Africa: Performed Under the Direction and Patronage of the African Association, in the Years 1795, 96, 97. New York: 1800. V. 37; 41

Travels and Recent Discoveries, in the Interior Districts of Africa in the Years 1796 & 97. New York: 1801. V. 46

Travels in the Interior Districts of Africa . . . in the Years 1795, 1796 . . . London: 1807. V. 42

Travels in the Interior Districts of Africa; Performed in the Years 1795, 1796 and 1797. London: 1816. V. 44

PARK, ROBERT M.

Sketch of the Twelfth Alabama Infantry of Battle's Brigade, Rodes' Division, Early's Corps, of the Army of Northern Virginia. Richmond: 1906. V. 37; 38

PARK, ROSWELL

An Epitome of the History of Medicine Based Upon a Course of Lectures Delivered in the University of Buffalo. Philadelphia: 1899. V. 44

Selected Papers, Surgical and Scientific. Buffalo: 1914. V. 41; 42; 45

PARK, SAMUEL

Notes of the Early History of Union Township, Licking County, Ohio. Terre-Haute: 1870. V. 40

PARK, THOMAS

Heliconia. Comprising a Selection of English Poetry of the Elizabethan Age. London: 1815. V. 38; 40; 41; 45

Sonnets, and Other Small Poems. London: 1797. V. 38; 43

PARK, W.

The Game of Golf. London: 1896. V. 39

PARK, WILLIAM

The Art of Putting by . . . Open Champion 1887 and 1889. Edinburgh: 1920. V. 38

PARKE, JOHN 1754-1789

The Lyric Works of Horace, translated into English Verse; to Which are Added, a Number of Original Poems. Philadelphia: 1786. V. 40

PARKE, THOMAS HEAZLE

My Personal Experiences in Equatorial Africa as medical Officer of the Emin Pasha Relief Foundation. London: 1891. V. 39; 46

PARKENHAM, PANSY

The Old Expedient. London: 1928. V. 43

PARKER, AMOS A.

Recollections of General Lafayette on His Visit to the United States, 1824 and 1825. Keene: 1879. V. 42; 43

Trip to the West and Texas. Concord: 1836. V. 38; 39; 42; 45

Trip to the West and Texas. Comprising a Journey of Eight Thousand Miles, Through New-York, Michigan, Illinois, Missouri, Louisiana and Texas, in the Autumn and Winter of 1834-5. Concord: 1835. V. 37; 38; 39; 41; 42; 46

PARKER, ARTHUR C.

The Archeological History of New York. Albany: 1922. V. 39

The Life of General Ely S. Parker. Buffalo: 1919. V. 39

PARKER, B.

The Hole and Corner Book. London: 1900. V. 43; 46

PARKER, BARRY

The Art of Building a Home. London: 1901. V. 38

The Art of Building a Home. London: 1910. V. 43

PARKER, BENJAMIN

Philosophical Meditations with Divine Inferences. London: 1734. V. 40

PARKER, CHARLES

Villa Rustica: Selected From Buildings and Scenes in the Vicinity of Rome and Florence. London: 1848. V. 38

PARKER, DOROTHY ROTHSCHILD 1893-1967

Death and Taxes. New York: 1931. V. 37; 38; 39; 40; 42

Enough Rope. New York: 1926. V. 39

Laments for the Living. New York: 1930. V. 41; 42

Men I'm not Married To. Garden City: 1922. V. 44

Men I'm Not Married To. New York: 1922. V. 38

Not So Deep as a Well. The Collected Poems of . . . New York: 1936. V. 39; 41; 42; 43

Not so Deep a Well. Toronto: 1936. V. 39

Sunset Gun. Poems by . . . New York: 1928. V. 39

PARKER, ERIC

The Lonsdale Anthology of Sporting Prose and Verse. London: 1932. V. 39

Shooting by Moor, Field and Shore. London: 1929. V. 39

PARKER, FRANK J.

Washington Territory! The Present and Prospective Future of the Upper Columbia Country . . . Walla Walla: 1881. V. 40; 43

PARKER, G. G.

Piratical Barbarity or the Female Captive. New York: 1826. V. 40

PARKER, GEORGE

Life's Painter of Variegated Characters in Public and Private Life. London: 1789. V. 42; 46

Life's Painter of Variegated Characters in Public and Private Life, by . . . London: 1800. V. 38

PARKER, GEORGE H.

The Elementary Nervous System. Philadelphia: (1919). V. 37; 39; 40; 41

PARKER, H.

Mail and Passenger Steamships of the Nineteenth Century. London: 1928. V. 38; 40; 42; 46

PARKER, HARRY

Naval Battles from Collection of Prints Formed by C. L. Cust Chronologically Arranged. London: 1911. V. 37; 42

PARKER, HENRY 1604-1652

The Case of Shipmony Briefly Discoursed, According to the Grounds of Law, Policy and Conscience. London: 1640. V. 38; 40

The Case of Shipmoney Briefly Discoursed According to the Grounds of Law, Policy and Conscience. N.P.: 1640. V. 41

The Generall Junto, or the Councell of Union, Chosen Equally Out of England, Scotland and Ireland . . . London: 1642. V. 43

PARKER, J. W.

The Textile Designers Plan Book. Leeds: 1879. V. 40

PARKER, JAMES

Conductor Generalis; or, the Office, Duty and Authority of Justices of the Peace, High Sheriffs . . . Constables, Gaolers . . . To Which is Added, A Treatise On the Law of Descents in Fee Simple . . . Woodbridge: 1764. V. 41; 42

The Old Army Memories 1872-1918. Philadelphia: 1929. V. 38; 41; 44

PARKER, JOHN HENRY

A Glossary of Terms Used in Grecian, Roman, Italian and Gothic Architecture. London: 1836. V. 38; 40

A Glossary of Terms Used in Grecian, Roman, Italian and Gothic Architecture. Oxford: 1850. V. 41

A Hand-Book for Visitors to Oxford. Oxford: 1847. V. 38

PARKER, K. LANGLOH

Australian Legendary Tales: Folk Lore of the Noongahburrahs as told to the Piccaninnies. London: 1897. V. 45

The Euahlayi Tribe. London: 1905. V. 40

PARKER, MARY S.

Address to the Free Colored People of the United States. Philadelphia: 1838. V. 45

PARKER, NATHAN HOWE

Iowa As It Is In 1855 . . . Chicago: 1855. V. 40; 42; 43; 45

Iowa As It Is in 1856; A Gazetteer for Citizens, and a Hand-Book for Emigrants, Embracing a Full Description of the State of Iowa. Chicago: 1856. V. 37; 40; 45; 46

The Iowa Handbook, for 1856, with a New and Correct Map. Boston: 1856. V. 37

The Minnesota Handbook, for 1856-7, with a New and Accurate Map. Boston: 1857. V. 37; 38; 40; 41; 44

The Missouri Hand-Book, Embracing a Full Description of the State of Missouri . . . St. Louis: 1865. V. 37; 39

PARKER, RICHARD DUNSCOMBE

Birds of Ireland. Belfast: 1983. V. 43

PARKER, ROBERT B.

A Catskill Eagle. New York: 1985. V. 43

God Save the Child. London: 1975. V. 38; 39; 40; 41; 42; 43

The Godwulf Manuscript. London: 1974. V. 45

The Godwulf Manuscript. Boston: 1973. V. 37

The Godwulf Manuscript. Boston: 1974. V. 37; 38; 39; 41; 42; 43; 45

The Godwulf Manuscript. 1974. V. 46

Mortal Stakes. Boston: 1975. V. 40

Pale Kings and Princes. N: 1987. V. 40

Pale Kings and Princes. New York: 1987. V. 45

Pastime. V. 45

Poodle Springs. London: 1989. V. 43; 46

Promised Land. Boston: 1976. V. 41; 42

Stardust. New York: 1990. V. 43

Surrogate. Northridge: 1982. V. 41; 43

PARKER, SAMUEL 1640-1688

A Demonstration of the Divine Authority. London: 1681. V. 38

A Discourse of Ecclesistical Politie . . . London: 1670. V. 38; 39

History of His Own Time. London: 1727. V. 38

Journal of an Exploring Tour Beyond the Rocky Mountains, Under the Direction of the A.B.C.F.M. Performed in the Years 1835, '36, and '37 . . . . Ithaca: 1838. V. 37; 38; 39; 40; 41; 45

Journal of an Exploring Tour Beyond the Rocky Mountains . . . New York: 1838. V. 38

Journal of an Exploring Tour Beyond the Rocky Mountains . . . with Map of Oregon Territory. Ithaca: 1840. V. 38; 41; 43; 44

Journal of an Exploring Tour Beyond the Rocky Mountains . . . 1842. V. 42

Journal of an Exploring Tour Beyond the Rocky Mountains . . . 1842. V. 42

Journal of an Exploring Tour Beyond the Rocky Mountains . . . 1842. V. 46

Journal of an Exploring Tour Beyond the Rocky Mountains . . . in the Years 1835, 36, 37. Ithaca: 1842. V. 39; 43; 45

Journal of an Exploring Tour Beyond the Rocky Mountains . . . with a Map of Oregon Territory. Ithaca: 1844. V. 40; 42; 43

Journal of an Exploring Tour Beyond the Rocky Mountains . . . New York: 1844. V. 38

Journal of an Exploring Tour Beyond the Rocky Mountains. Auburn: 1846. V. 40; 41

De Rebus Sui Temporis Commentariorum Libri Quatuor. London: 1726. V. 39

PARKER, THEODORE

'The Great Battle Between Slavery and Freedom, Considered in Two Speeches Before the American Anti-Slavery Society, at New York, May 7, 1856. Boston: 1856. V. 42

The Trial of . . . for the 'Misdemeanor' of a Speech in Faneuil Hall Against Kidnapping, Before the Circuit Court of the United States, at Boston, April 3, 1855. with the Defence. Boston: 1855. V. 43

Two Sermons Preached Before the Twenty-Eighth Congregational Society in Boston . . . on Leaving Their Old and Entering a New Place of Worship. Boston: 1853. V. 44

PARKER, THOMAS

Reports of Cases Concerning the Revenue, Argued and Determined in the Court of Exchequer, from Easter Term 1743 to Hilary Term 1767. London: 1776. V. 45

PARKER, THOMAS LISTER

Description of Browsholme Hall. London: 1815. V. 45

PARKER, THOMAS N.

An Essay on the Construction, Hangin and Fastening of Gates; exemplified in six quarto plates. London: 1804. V. 37; 42

PARKER, W. B.

Through Unexplored Texas. Austin: 1984. V. 42

PARKER, W. THORNTON

Personal Experiences Among Our North American Indians . . . 1867 to 1885. Northampton: 1913. V. 39

PARKER, WILLARD 1800-1884

Lectures on Surgery by Willard Parker. New York: 1847. V. 40; 41

PARKER, WILLIAM B.

Notes Taken During the Expedition Commanded by Capt. R. B. Marcy . . . Through Unexplored Texas, in the Summer and Fall of 1854. Philadelphia: 1856. V. 37; 39; 40; 41; 42; 45

PARKER, WILLIAM RILEY

Milton: A Biography. 1968. V. 40

PARKER, WILMOT

An Analysis of the Practice of the Court of Chancery. London: 1794. V. 37; 39

PARKES, HARRY

The Girl Who Wouldn't Mind Getting Married. N.P.: 1887. V. 43

PARKES, HARRY S.

Reports on the Manufacture of Paper in Japan Presented to Both Houses of Parliament by Command of Her Majesty. London: 1871. V. 43

PARKES, KINETON

The Pre-Raphaelite Movement. London: 1889. V. 42

The Pre-Raphaelite Movement. London: & Birmingham: 1889. V. 42

PARKES, M. B.

The Medieval Manuscripts of Keble College, Oxford. London: 1979. V. 39

PARKES, OSCAR

British Battleships, 1860-1950 . . . London: 1970-73. V. 41

British Battleships. London: 1971. V. 39

PARKES, SAMUEL 1759-1825

The Rudiments of Chemistry. London: 1810. V. 40

Thoughts on the Law Relating to Salt. London: 1817. V. 40

PARKES, WILLIAM, MRS.

Domestic Duties; or, Instructions to Young Married Ladies on the Management of Their Households and the Regulation of Their conduct in the Various Relations and Duties of Married Life. New York: 1828. V. 45

Domestic Duties; or, Instruction to Young Married Ladies on the Management of Their Households . . . New York: 1830. V. 45

Domestic Duties; or, Instructions to Young Maried Ladies on the Management of Their Households, and the Regulation of Their Conduct in the Various Relations and Duties of Married Life . . . New York: 1846. V. 37

Domestic Duties, or, Instructions to Young Married Ladies on the management of their Households and the Regulation of their conduct in the various relations and Duties of Married Life. London: 1828. V. 37

PARKGATE IRON & STEEL CO.

List of Sections. Rotherham: 1890's. V. 44

PARKHILL, ROBES

Troopers West. New York: 1945. V. 40

PARKHURST, HENRY M.

The Plowshare, and the American Reporter, Together with the Cosmopolitan 1852 and 1853. Washington: 1843. V. 43

The Plowshare, and the American Reporter, Together with the Cosmopolitan, 1852 and 1853. Washington: 1853. V. 40

PARKHURST, JACOB

Sketches of the Life and Adventures of . . . Knightstown: 1893. V. 42

PARKHURST, JOHN

A Greek and English Lexicon to the New Testament. London: 1769. V. 38

An Hebrew and English Lexicon. London: 1788. V. 44; 45

A Hebrew and English Lexicon, Without Points, In Which the Hebrew and Chaldee Words of the Old Testament are Explained. London: 1829. V. 41

PARKINS, ALMON E.

The Historical Geography of Detroit. Lansing: 1918. V. 46

PARKINS, DR.

The Book of Miracles, or Celestial Museum. London: 1817. V. 42

PARKINSON, JAMES

Hunterian Reminiscences . . . London: 1833. V. 45

PARKINSON, JOHN

Organic Remains of a Former World. London: 1811/08/11. V. 38

Organic Remains of a Former World. London: 1833. V. 41

Outlines of Oryctology. London: 1830. V. 38

Outlines of Oryctology. London: 1831. V. 42

Outlines of Oryctology. London: 1822. V. 38; 40

Paradisi in Sole. London: 1629. V. 37; 39; 40; 42

Paradisi in Sole Paradisus Terrestris . . . London: 1656. V. 44

Paradisi in Sole Paradisius Terrestris. London: 1904. V. 37; 38; 39; 40; 45

Paradisi in Sole Paradisus Terrestris. Amsterdam: 1975. V. 37

Paradisi in sole paradisus terrestris. Faithfully reprined from the edition of 1629. 1904. V. 37

Theatrum Botanicum. London: 1640. V. 37; 38; 39; 42; 43; 45

The Vertues of Salad. Kingston: 1979. V. 37

PARKINSON, P.

Tropical Landshells of the World. Wiesbaden: 1987. V. 38

PARKINSON, RICHARD 1748-1815

The Experienced Farmer, an Entire New Work in Which the Whole System of Agriculture, Husbandry and Breeding of Cattle, is Explained and Copiously Enlarged Upon. London: 1798. V. 38; 40; 41; 46

Poems Sacred and Miscellaneous. London: 1832. V. 43

A Tour in America in 1798, 1799 and 1800. Exhibiting Sketches of Society and Manners, and A Particular Account of the American System of Agriculture . . . etc. By Richard Parkinson. London: 1805. V. 37; 38; 40; 42

PARKINSON, ROGER

Disputatio Medica Inauguralis, De Typho. Edinburgh: 1800. V. 38

PARKINSON, SYDNEY

A Journal of a Voyage to the South Seas, In His Majesty's Ship, the Endeavour. London: 1773. V. 38; 40; 41; 42; 45; 46

PARKINSON, W.

The Knight-Errant of the Nursery. London. V. 43

PARKMAN, DAILEY

'Gentlemen, Be Seated!' A Parade of Old Time Minstrels. New York: 1928. V. 38

PARKMAN, EBENEZER

The Story of the Rice Boys Captured By the Indians August 8, 1704 as Written by May 1769. Westborough: 1906. V. 40

PARKMAN, FRANCIS 1823-1893

The California and Oregon Trail. London: 1849. V. 38

The California and Oregon Trail: Being Sketches of Prairie and Rocky Mountain Life. New York: 1849. V. 38; 39; 40; 41; 42; 43; 44

The California and Oregon Trail . . . New York & London: 1849. V. 38; 40

Count Frontenac and New France Under Louis XIV. Boston: 1877. V. 40

The Discovery of the Great West. Boston: 1869. V. 38

A Half Century of Conflict. Boston: 1892. V. 39; 40

History of the Conspiracy of Pontiac, and the War of the North American Tribes Against the English Colonies After the Conquest of Canada. Boston: 1851. V. 40; 42; 45

History of the Conspiracy of Pontiac and the War of the North American Tribes Against the English Colonies After the Conquest of Canada. London: 1851. V. 45

The Old Regime in Canada. Boston: 1874. V. 38; 44; 46

Oregon Trail: Sketches of Prairie & Rocky-Mountain Life. Boston: 1872. V. 39

The Oregon Trail. London: 1892. V. 40

The Oregon Trail. Boston: 1925. V. 38; 41

The Oregon Trail. Boston: 1925. V. 40

PARKMAN, FRANCIS 1823-1893 continued

The Oregon Trail. New York: 1943. V. 40; 45

The Oregon Trail. New York: 1945. V. 42; 46

The Oregon Trail. Boston: 1892. V. 37; 40; 41; 42; 45

Pioneers of France in the New World (1866): The Jesuits in North America in the 17th Century (1867); The Discovery of Great West (1870); The Old Regime in Canada (1874); Count Frontenac and New France Under Louis IXV (1877). V. 45

Some of The Reasons Against Woman Suffrage. N.P.: 1883. V. 45

Some of the Reasons Against Woman Suffrage. N.P.: 1883. V. 44

The Works of Francis Parkman. Boston: 1897-98. V. 39

Francis Parkman's Works. Toronto: 1898. V. 43

Works. London: 1899. V. 37

The Works of . . . (with) Life of Parkman. Boston: 1899-1901. V. 39

Works. Boston: 1901. V. 37

Parkman's Works. Toronto: 1901. V. 40

The Works. Boston: 1902. V. 42

Collected Works. Boston & New York: 1902. V. 46

The Works. Boston: 1907. V. 38

Works. New York: 1915. V. 42

PARKS, F. S.

Genealogy of the Parke Families of Connecticut. Washington: 1906. V. 38

PARKS, FANNY

Wanderings of a Pilgrim, In Search of the Picturesque, During Four-and-Twenty Years in the East; with Revelations of Life in the Zenana . . . London: 1850. V. 45; 46

PARKS, GORDON

Camera Portraits: the Techniques and Principles of Documentary Portraiture. New York: 1948. V. 44; 45

PARKS, W. A.

Report on the Building and Ornamental Stones of Canada. Volume One. Ottawa: 1912. V. 42; 43

PARKYN, HERBERT A.

Suggestive Therapeutics and Hypnotism. Chicago: 1900. V. 40; 41

PARKYNS, G. J.

Monastic and Baronial Remains. With other interesting fragments of antiquity in England, Wales, and Scotland. London: 1816. V. 37; 39; 41; 44

PARKYNS, GEORGE ISHAM

An Essay on the Different Natural Situations of Gardens. London: 1774. V. 46

PARKYNS, MANSFIELD

Life in Abyssinia. London: 1853. V. 40

Life in Abyssinia: Being Notes Collected During Three Years Residence and Travels in that Country. New York: 1854. V. 42

PARKYNS, THOMAS

The Inn-Play; or, Cornish-Hugg Wrestler. London: 1727. V. 39; 40; 44

Progymnasnata (Greek Title). The Inn-Play . . . London: 1727. V. 39; 42; 44

THE PARLIAMENTARY or Constitutional History of England. London: 1751/61. V. 38

THE PARLIAMENTARY or Constitutional History of England . . . London: 1751/62. V. 43

PARLIAMENTARY PROCEEDINGS. LAWS

The Reasonableness of Parliamentary Proceedings, by attainders, banishments, pains, and penalties, in cases of high treason, shewn by various precendents. From the reign of Edward II to the present time. London: 1723. V. 37

PARLO, MARIA

Miss Parlo's Kitchen Companion. Boston: 1887. V. 38

PARLOA, MARIA

Miss Parloa's New Cook Book, a Guide to Marketing and Cooking. Boston: 1880. V. 38

PARLOUR Magic. A Manual of Amusing Experiments, Transmutations, Sleights and Subtleties, Legerdemain, etc. London: 1861. V. 43

THE PARLOUR Spelling-Book. Philadelphia: 1806. V. 44

PARMELIN, HELENE 1807-1887

Picasso: Women, Cannes and Moughins, 1954-1963. Paris. V. 41

Picasso: Women. Paris and Amsterdam: 1964. V. 38

Picasso: Women, Cannes and Mougins, 1954-1963. Preface by Douglas Cooper. Translated from the French by Humphrey Hare. Paris: n.d. V. 37

PARMENTIER, A. A.

Memoire sur les Avantages que la Province de Languedoe peut Retirer de ses Grains . . . Paris: 1786. V. 39; 40; 44

PARMENTIER, M.

Observations on Such Nutritive Vegetables as May Be Substituted in the Place of Ordinary Food. London: 1783. V. 46

PARMINTER, ANNE

The Votive Wreath and other Poems. London: 1826. V. 42

PARNASSUS Biceps, or Several Choice Pieces of Poetry, 1656. London: 1927. V. 40

PARNELL, EDWARD ANDREW

Dyeing and Calico Printing. London: 1849. V. 43

PARNELL, HENRY

A Treatise on Roads; Wherein the Principles on Which Roads Should be Made are Explained and Illustrated by the Plans, Specifictions and Contracts Made Use of by Thomas Telford . . . London: 1833. V. 40

PARNELL, HENRY BROOKE

On Financial Reform. London: 1830. V. 38; 41; 45

PARNELL, R.

The Grasses of Britain. London: 1842-45. V. 38

PARNELL, THOMAS

An Essay on the Different Stiles of Poetry. London: 1713. V. 37; 39; 40; 42; 43

The Hermit - a Poem. London: 1904. V. 40

Poems on Several Occasions. London: 1726. V. 38; 40; 41; 43

Poems on Several Occasions . . . Dublin: 1735. V. 44

Poems on Several Occasions. London: 1772, 1721. V. 40

Poems on Several Occasions. London: 1722. V. 37; 38; 39; 40; 41; 42; 43; 44; 45

The Poetical Works. Glasgow: 1786. V. 42; 43

PARNELL, WILLIAM

An Enquiry into the Causes of Popular Discontents in Ireland. London: 1805. V. 43

PAROISSIEN Royal. Paris: 1812. V. 42

PARPALEA, GIUSEPPE

Axiomata Pvblicae Patavii Disputata, Per Eximie Spei Adolescentulum Ioseph Parapaleam Legum Tyronem. Padua?: 1550. V. 40

PARR, BARTHOLOMEW 1750-1810

The London Medical Dictionary . . . Philadelphia: 1819. V. 37; 40; 41; 43; 44

PARR, HARRIET 1828-1900

For Richer, for Poorer. London: 1870. V. 44

Legends from Fairyland. London: 1907. V. 40; 43

Mrs. Denys of Cote. London: 1880. V. 44

Mr. Wynard's Ward. London: 1867. V. 44

A Poor Squire. London: 1882. V. 38

The True Pathetic History of Poor Match. London: 1864. V. 44

PARR, LOUISA

Adam and Eve. London: 1880. V. 38

How It all Happened. London: 1871. V. 37

Loyalty George. London: 1888. V. 43

The Squire. London: 1892. V. 43

PARR, RICHARD

The Life of James Ussher . . . London: 1686. V. 39

PARR, SAMUEL

Bibliotheca Parriana, a Catalogue of the Library of the Late Reverend and Learned Samuel Parr, LL.D. London: 1827. V. 39; 45

A Catalogue of the Library of the Late Rev. and Learned Samuel Parr, LL.D. London: 1827. V. 44

Characters of the Late Charles James Fox . . . London: 1809. V. 41

A Discourse on Education and on the Plans Pursued in Charity-Schools. London: 1786. V. 38

A Free Translation of the Preface to Bellendus . . . London: 1788. V. 37; 43

Praefationis ad tres Guliemi Bellendeni Libros, de Statu. London: 1788. V. 44

A Sequel to the Printed Paper Lately Circulated in Warwickshire by the Rev. Charles Curtis, Brother of Alderman Curtis, a Birmingham Rector, &c. London: 1792. V. 43

PARRAMORE, DOCK DILWORTH

Scenes and Stories of Early West Texas: The Parramore Sketches. El Paso: 1975. V. 37

PARRENO, ALBERTO

Spain and Her Colonies in the New World. The Parreno Collection. New York: 1978. V. 37; 42

PARREUDT, JOHANNES

Textus Veteris Artis s. Isagogartu Predicamentorum Aristotelis simul cum Duobus Libris Perihermenias Eiusdem. Nuremberg: 1502. V. 37

PARRISH, EDWARD 1822-1872

A Treatise on Pharmacy. Philadelphia: 1865. V. 45

PARRISH, JOSEPH

Practical Observations on Strangulated Hernia and Some of the Diseases of the Urinary Organs. Philadelphia: 1836. V. 45

PARRISH, LYDIA

Slave Songs of the Georgia Sea Islands. New York: 1942. V. 41

PARRISH, MAXFIELD

A Collection of Colour Prints. New York: 1920. V. 40

PARRISH, MORRIS LONGSTRETH 1867-

Charles Kingsley and Thomas Hughes, Firt Editions (With a few Exceptions) in the Library at Dormy House, Pine Valley, New Jersey, Described with Notes. London: 1936. V. 37; 41

A List of the Writing Of Lewis Carroll, in the Library at Dormy House, Pine Valley, New Jersey. 1928, 1933. V. 40

A Supplementary List of the Writings of Lewis Carroll in the Library at Dormy House, Pine Valley, New Jersey. N.P.: 1933. V. 45

Wilkie Collins and Charles Reade, First Editions (with a Few Exceptions) in the Library At Dormy House, Pine Valley, New Jersey. London: 1940. V. 40; 41

PARRISH, T. MICHAEL

Confederate Imprints: a Bibliography of Southern Publications from Secession to Surrender. Asutin: 1987. V. 39; 40; 41

Confederate Imprints. New York: 1987. V. 41

Confederate Imprints. Austin & New York: 1987. V. 39

PARRISH, THOMAS C.

Colorado Springs Its Climate, Scenery and Society. Colorado Springs: 1889. V. 39

The Pueblo Colony of Southern Colorado. All Who Desire to Join This Colony Can Apply . . . Lancaster, Pa.: 1874. V. 37

PARROT, ANDRE

The Arts of Assyria. New York: 1961. V. 40

Sumer. London: 1960. V. 40; 42; 44

PARROT, GRAY

Some Marbled Papers by Gray Parrot. Northampton: 1988. V. 44

PARROTT, RICHARD

Reflections on Various Subjects Relating to Arts and Commerce . . . London: 1752. V. 41; 42

PARRY, D. H.

'The Death or Glory Boys.' The Story of the 17th Lancers. London: 1889. V. 41

PARRY, E. J.

Parry's Encyclopaedia of Perfumery . . . London: 1925. V. 46

PARRY, EDWARD

The Cambrian Mirror. London: 1850. V. 39

Memoirs of Rear Admiral Sir W. Edward Parry, Kt. London: 1857. V. 46

PARRY, HENRY

The Art of Bookbinding. London: 1818. V. 41

PARRY, I. D.

Select Illustrations, Historical and Topographical, of Bedfordshire. London: 1827. V. 38; 40

PARRY, IDRIS

Stream and Rock: a Talk. 1973. V. 40

PARRY, JOHN

A Selection of Welsh Melodies. London: 1809. V. 40

PARRY, JOHN D.

An Historical and Descriptive Account of the Coast of Sussex. London: 1833. V. 42

History and Description of Woburn and Its Abbey. London: 1831. V. 37

PARRY, JOHN S.

Extra-Uterine Pregnancy: Its Causes, Species, Pathological Anatomy . . . Philadelphia: 1876. V. 38

PARRY, JUDGE

Katawampus Its Treatment and Cure. London: 1895. V. 41

PARRY, MARIAN

Notes on Venice. Cambridge: 1984. V. 38

PARRY, NICHOLAS

In Valleys of Springs of Rivers. Shropshire: 1981. V. 38; 40; 44

PARRY, ROBERT WILLIAMS

Cerddi. Newtown: 1980. V. 37

Cerdi, detholaid Gyda Rhagymadrodd gan Thomas Parry. 1980. V. 39

PARRY, S. H. JONES

My Journey Round the World via Ceylon, New Zealand, Australia Torres Straits, China, Japan and the United States. London: 1881. V. 42

PARRY, THOMAS

The Beauties of Lord Byron: with a Sketch of His Life, and a Dissertation on His Genius and Writings. London: 1823. V. 44

On Diet, With Its Influence On Man. London: 1844. V. 42

PARRY, U. E. S.

Historical Records of the Denbigshire Hussars Imperial Yeomanry, From Their Formation in 1795 till 1906. Wrexham: 1909. V. 38

PARRY, WILLIAM

The Last Days of Lord Byron. London: 1825. V. 37; 38; 44; 46

PARRY, WILLIAM EDWARD 1790-1855

Journal of a Voyage for the Discovery of a North-West Passage from the Atlantic to the Pacific; Performed in the Years 1819-1820. London: 1821. V. 37; 38; 40; 41; 42; 43; 44; 45

Journal of a Second Voyage for the Discovery of a North-West Passage from the Atlantic to the Pacific. London: 1824. V. 37; 38; 40; 42; 43; 44; 45; 46

Journal of a Voyage for the Discovery of a North-West Passage from the Atlantic to the Pacific, Performed in the Yars 1819-20, in His Majesty's Ships Hecla and Griper . . . London: 1824. V. 46

Journal of a Second Voyage for the Discovery of a North-West Passage From the Atlantic to the Pacific, Performed in the Years 1821-22-23. (with) Appendix to Captin Parry's Journal of a Second Voyage . . . London: 1825. V. 43

Journal of a Third Voyage for the Discovery of a North-West Passage from the Atlantic to the Pacific, Peformed in..1824-25. In His Majesty's Ships Hecla and Fury &c.. Philadelphia: 1826. V. 40; 42

Journal of a Second Voyage for the Discovery of a North-West Passage . . . (with) Appendix . . . London: 1824/25. V. 42

Journal of a Second Voyage for the Discovery of a North-West Passage, from the Atlantic to the Pacific . . . New York: 1969. V. 42

Journal of a Third Voyage for the Discovery of a North West Passage from the Atlantic to the Pacific; performed in the eyars 1824-25, in His Majesty's Ships Hecla and Fury . . . London: 1826. V. 37

Journal of a Voyage for the Discovery of a North-West Passage from the Atlantic to the Pacific; Performed in the Years 1819-20 . . . Philadelphia: 1821. V. 37; 38

Journals of the First, Second and Third Voyages for the Discovery of a North West Passage from the Atlantic to the Pacific in 1819-20-21-22-23-24-25 in His Majesty's Ship Hecla, Griper and Fury. London: 1828. V. 45

Journals of the First, Second and Third Voyages for the Discovery of a North-West Passage from the Atlantic . . . London: 1828-1829. V. 42

Letters Written During the Late Voyage of Discvoery in the Western Arctic Sea. London: 1821. V. 42

Memoirs of Rear Admiral Sir William Edward Parry, Kt. London: 1857. V. 43

Narrative of an Attempt to Reach the North Pole, in Boates Fitted for . . . London: 1828. V. 37; 41; 45; 46

Three Voyages for the Discovery of a Northwest Passage from the Atlantic to the Pacific and Narrative of an Attempt to Reach the North Pole . . . New York: 1840. V. 40; 42

Three Voyages for the Discovery of a Northwest Passage from the Atlantic to the Pacific and Narrative of an Attempt to Reach the North Pole. New York: 1842. V. 39; 40; 41

PARSHALL, HORACE FIELD

The Parshall Familly. A.D. 870-1913. A Collection of Historical Records and Notes to Accompany the Parshall Pedigree. London: 1915. V. 41

PARSLEY'S Lyric Repository, for 1790. Containing a Selection of all the Favorite Songs, Duets, Trios, &c. now singing at the Theatres-Royal, and Anacreontic SOciety . . . with a Variety of Ballads, Sonnets . . . London: (1790). V. 37

THE PARSON and His Maid, a Tale (in verse). London: 1722. V. 45

PARSON, GEORGE F.

The Life and Adventures of james W. marshall: The Discoverer of Gold in California. San Francisco: 1935. V. 37; 44

PARSON, THOMAS

A Few Suggestions for Ornamental Decoration in Painters and Decorators at Work. London: 1909. V. 37

PARSONS, ALBERT R.

Anarchism. Its Philosophy and Scientific Basis. Chicago: 1887. V. 46

PARSONS, C. S. M.

China Mending and Restoration. London: 1963. V. 44

PARSONS, EDWARD

The Civil, Ecclesiastical, Literary, Commercial and Miscellaneous History of Leeds, Halifax, Huddersfield, Bradford, Wakefield, Dewsbury, Otley and the Manufacturing District of Yorkshire. Leeds: 1834. V. 42

PARSONS, EDWARD ALEXANDER

The Wonder and the Glory, Confessions of a Southern Bibliophile. New York: 1962. V. 39

PARSONS, ELSIE CLEWS

American Indian Life by Several of Its Students. New York: 1922. V. 46

Taos Pueblo. Menasha: 1936. V. 42; 45

PARSONS, FRANK ALVAH

Interior Decoration Its Principles and Practice. New York & London: 1920. V. 40

PARSONS, GEORGE FREDERIC

The Life and Adventures of James W. Marshall, the Discoverer of Gold in California. Sacramento: 1870. V. 40; 41; 45; 46

The Life and Adventures of James W. Marshall, the Discoverer of Gold in California. San Francisco: 1935. V. 37; 38; 42; 46

PARSONS, HORATIO A.

A Guide to Travelers Visiting the Falls of Nigara . . . Buffalo: 1835. V. 38; 46

PARSONS, J. HERBERT

Elementary Ophthalmic Optics Including Ophthalmoscopy and Retinoscopy. London: 1901. V. 44

An Introduction to the Theory of Perception. Cambridge: 1927. V. 44

PARSONS, JAMES

A Mechanical and Critical Enquiry into the Nature of Hermaphrodites. London: 1741. V. 37

Philosophical Observations on the Analogy Between the Propagation of Animals and that of Vegetables. London: 1752. V. 37; 38; 40; 42; 45

Remains of Japhet, Being Historical Enquiries into the Affinity and Origin of the European Languages . . . London: 1767. V. 45

PARSONS, JOHN HERBERT

An Introduction to the Theory of Perception. Cambridge: 1927. V. 42

PARSONS, PHILIP

Dialogues of the Dead with the Living. London: 1779. V. 38; 40

PARSONS, ROBERT 1546-1610

Andrea Philopater, Elizabethae Reginae Angliae Edictum . . . 29 Nouemb . . . MDXCI. Andreae Philopatri ad idem Edictvm Responsio. Ingolstadt?: 1593. V. 45

An Answere to the Fifth Part of Reportes Lately set Forth by Syr Edward Cooke Knight . . . Concerning the . . . Lawes . . . Which do Apperteyne to Spirituall Power & Jurisdiction. N.P.: 1606. V. 38

An Answere to the Fifth Part of Reportes Lately Set Forth by Syr Edward Co(o)ke, Knight, the Kinges Attorney Generall . . . N.P.: 1606. V. 40

A Christian Directory, Guilding Man to Their Eternal Salvation in Two Parts. Dublin: 1753. V. 38

Conceived, Spoken and Published with Most Earnest Protestation of All Dutifull Good Will and Affection Towards This Realme: . . . London: 1641. V. 45

Leycesters Common-Wealth: Conceived, Spoken and Published with Most Earnest Protestation of all Dutiful Good Will and Affection Towards This Realm . . . London: 1641. V. 38

Parsons His Christian Directory, Being a Treatise of Holy Resolution. London: 1700. V. 40

PARSONS, TALCOTT b. 1902

The Structure of Social Action: A Study in Social Theory with Special Reference to a Group of Recent European Writers. New York: 1937. V. 42

The Structure of Social Action. New York and London: 1937. V. 37

PARSONS, THEODORE

A Forensic Dispute on the Legality of Enslaving the Africans, Held at the Public Commencement in Cambridge, New England, July 21st 1773. Boston: 1773. V. 40; 42

PARSONS, THEOPHILUS 1750-1813

Memoir of the Notices of Some of His Contemoraries by His Son . . . Boston: 1859. V. 40

PARSONS, THOMAS WILLIAM

Poems. Boston: 1854. V. 45

The Shadow of the Obelisk and Other Poems. London: 1872. V. 44

PARSONS, USHER

Boylston Prize Dissertations on 1. Inflammation of the Periostium. 2. Eneursis Irratata. 3. Cutaneous Diseases. 4. Cancer of the Breast. Also Remarks on Malaria. Boston: 1839. V. 39; 42

Physician for Ships: Containing Medical Advice for Seamen and Other Persons at Sea . . . Boston: 1842. V. 38

Physician for Ships: Containing Medical Advice for Seamen and Other Persons at Sea . . . New Bedford: 1877. V. 38

PARSONS, WILLIAM

Chronological Tables of Europe: from the Nativity of Our Saviour to the Year 1703. London: 1707. V. 41; 45

Chronological Tables of Europe . . . to the Year 1714 . . . London: 1714. V. 46

Chronological Tables of Europe, From the Nativity of Our Saviour to the Year 1726. London: 1726. V. 38; 43

A New Book of Cyphers, More Compleat and Regular Than Any Yet Extant, Wherein the Whole Alphabet. London: 1703. V. 38

A Poetical Tour, in the Years 1784, 1785 and 1786. London: 1787. V. 46

Travelling Recreations. London: 1807. V. 43

PARSONS, WILLIAM BARCLAY

Robert Fulton and the Submarine. New York: 1922. V. 46

PARTICULARS and Conditions of Sale of One Undivided Eighth Part of the Stapleton Estate, in the Island of St. Kitt's Commonly Called, The River Plantation. London: 1822. V. 40

PARTICULARS and Recommendations of the Stadium, or, British National Arena. For manly and defensive exercises, equestrian, chivalric, and aquatic games, and skillful and amusing pastimes. London: 1835. V. 37

THE PARTICULARS of all the Late Bloody Fight at Sea on Thursday and Friday Last. London: 1653. V. 43

PARTICULARS of the Piracies; Committed by the Commanders and Crews of the Buenos Ayrean Ship Louisa, and those of the Sloops Mary, of Mobile, and Lawrence, of Charleston; Wheren is Accurately Described the Murder of Capt. Sunley and Four of the Crew . . . Charleston: 1820. V. 37; 45

PARTINGTON, CHARLES FREDERICK

The British Cyclopaedia of the Arts and Sciences. (with) The British Cyclopaedia of Literature, History, etc. (with) The British Cyclopaedi of Natural History. (with) The British Cyclopaedia of Biography. London: 1835-38. V. 38

An Historical and Descriptive Account of the Steam Engine. London: 1822. V. 40

Historical & Descriptive Account of the Steam Engine . . . London: 1826. V. 37

National history and views of London and its environs; embracing their antiquities, modern improvements &c. &c. from original drawings by Eminent artists. In Two Volumes. London: 1834. V. 37; 38; 45; 46

PARTINGTON, J. R.

A History of Chemistry. London: 1961-70. V. 46

Origins and Development of Applied Chemistry. London: 1935. V. 37; 46

PARTINGTON, WILFRED

Thomas J. Wise in the Original Cloth. London: 1946. V. 41; 44

The War Against Malaria and Tropical Diseases. London: 1923. V. 43

PARTON, BENJAMIN

The Life and Times of Benjamin Franklin. New York: 1865. V. 39; 40

PARTON, JAMES

Eminent Women of the Age: Being Narratives of the Lives and Deeds of the Most Prominent Women of the Past Generation. Hartford: 1871. V. 41; 42

Life of Andrew Jackson. New York: 1860. V. 44

Life of Andrew Jackson, Condensed from the Author's 'Life of Andrew Jackson.' New York: 1861. V. 39

Life and Times of Benjamin Franklin. New York: 1865. V. 39

PARTON, JOHN

Some Account of the Hospital and Parish of St. Giles in the Fields, Middlesex. London: 1822. V. 38

PARTONOPEUS DE BLOIS

Partenopex De Blois, a Romance, in Four Cantos. London: 1807. V. 40

PARTRIDGE, EDWARD ALEXANDER

A War on Poverty; The One War That Can End War. Winnipeg: 1926. V. 40; 43

PARTRIDGE, ERIC

Eighteenth Century Romantic Poetry. Paris: 1924. V. 39

An Original Issue of 'The Spectator' Together with the Story of The Famous English Periodical and its Founder Joseph Addison & Richard Steele. (San Francisco): 1939. V. 37; 46

Pirates, Highwaymen and Adventures. London: 1927. V. 43

Slang To-day and Yesterday. London: 1933. V. 41

Songs and Slang of the British Soldier: 1914-1918. London: 1930. V. 40

The Three Wartons - a Choice of Their Verse. London: 1927. V. 43

PARTRIDGE, HENRY M.

The Most Remarkable Echo in the World. New York: 1933. V. 46

PARTRIDGE, JOHN

Opus Reformatum. London: 1693. V. 38

PARTRIDGE, JOSEPH

The Anti-Atheist. Manchester: 1766. V. 41

PARTRIDGE, WILLIAM

A Practical Treatise on Dying of Woolen, Cotton and Skein Silk, the Manufacturing of Broadcloth, and Cassimere . . . New York: 1823. V. 38; 40

A Practical Treatise on Dying Woollen, Cotton and Silk, Including Recipes for Lac Reds and Scarlets . . . New York: 1834. V. 37

PARUTA, PAOLO

Della Perfettione Della Vita Politica . . . Libri Tre . . . Nuovamente con Diligenza Ristampati . . . Venetia: 1586. V. 37

Discorsi Politici. Venice: 1599. V. 40; 45

The History of Venice, Likewise the Wars of Cyprus. London: 1658. V. 39

Perfettione Della Vita Politica. Venice: 1585. V. 38

PARVILLEE, LEON

Architectures et Decoration Turques au XVe Siecle. Paris: 1874. V. 41

PARVIN, THEODORE S.

Report on the Climate of Iowa: Embracing the Result of the Meterological Records of the Year 1856, at Muscantine, Iowa with a Synopsis. Muscantine: 1857. V. 41

PASADENA ART MUSEUM

An Exhibition of Works by Joseph Campbell. 1967. V. 45

Marcel Duchamp. A Retrospective Exhibition. October 8-November 3, 1963. V. 39

PASADENA, California, Illustrated and Described, Showing Its Advantages as a Place for a Desirable Homes. Pasadena: 1886. V. 41

PASADENA, Crown of the Valley. Los Angeles: 1892. V. 40

PASCAL, BLAISE 1623-1662

The Life of Mr. Paschal, with His Letters Relating to the Jesuits. London: 1744. V. 41

Miscellaneous Writings. Consisting of Letters, Essays, Conversations, and Miscellaneous Thoughts. (The Greater part Heretofore unpublished in this country and a large portion from the orignal MSS). Newly translated from the French . . . London: 1849. V. 37; 42

Monsieur's Pascall's Thoughts, Meditations, and Prayers Touching Matters Moral and Divine. London: 1688. V. 37; 39; 43

The Mystery of Jesuitism, Discovered in Certain Letters . . . with Additionals to the Mystery of Jesuitism. London: 1679. V. 39

Pensees . . . sur la Religion et sur Quelques Autres Sujets. Paris: 1670. V. 40

Pensees. Muenchen: 1930. V. 38

Pensees sur la Religion et sur quelques autres sujets. The Hague: 1743. V. 37

Les Provinciales: or, the Mysterie of Jesuitisme . . . London: 1657. V. 38; 45; 46

Provincial Letters, Containing an Exposure of the Reasoning and Morals of the Jesuits. London: 1816. V. 38

Provincial Letters, Containing an Exposure of the Reasoning and Morals of the Jesuits . . . to Which is Added, A View of the History of the Jesuits, and the Late Bull for the Revival of the Order in Europe. New York & Boston: 1828. V. 37

Thoughts on Religion and Other Subjects. Edinburgh: 1825. V. 38; 46

Thoughts on Religion, and Other Curious Subjects. London: 1727. V. 37; 41; 42

Thoughts on Religion and Other Subjects . . . London: 1704. V. 37; 39; 40; 41; 43

Traitez de l'Equilibre les Liqueurs, et de la Pesanteur de la Masse de l'Aire. Paris: 1663. V. 38; 41; 45

Traitez de l'Equilibre de Liqueurs, et de la Pesanteur de la Masse de l'Air. Paris: 1798. V. 42

Traitez de l'Eqvilibre des Liqvevrs, et de la Pesantevr de la Masse de l'Air. Paris: 1664. V. 37

PASCAL Covici 1888-1964. New York: 1964. V. 41

PASCHAL, CHARLES

Legatus. Amsterdam: 1645. V. 37

PASCHAL, GEORGE W.

The Public Printing and the Public Printer. Austin: 1858. V. 37

PASCHALIUS, CAROLUS 1547-1625

Legatus. Accessit Graecarum Dictionum Interpretatio, et Index, Quod Satis Est, Locuples. Rouen: 1598. V. 38; 40

PASCOE, CHARLOTTE CHAMPION

Walks About St. Hilary, Chiefly Among the Poor . . . Penznace: 1879. V. 43

PASCOLI, LIONE

Vite de' Pittori, Scultori, ed Architetti Perugini . . . Rome: 1732. V. 40

PASHA, RUDOLF C. SLATIN

Fire and Sword in the Sudan. London: 1896. V. 41

PASKMAN, DAILEY

Gentlemen, be Seated. Garden City: 1928. V. 45

PASKO, W. W.

American Dictionary of Printing and Bookmaking Containing a History of These Arts in Europe and America. New York: 1894. V. 44

PASLEY, C. W.

Observations on Limes, Calcareous Cements, Mortars, Stuccos and Concrete, and on Puzzolanas, Natural and Artificial; Together with Rules Deduced from Numerous Experiments for Making an Artificial Water Cement, Equal in Efficiency to the Best Natural . . . London: 1838. V. 44

PASLEY, CHARLES WILLIAM 1780-1861

Essay on the Military Policy and Institutions of the British Empire. London: 1811. V. 41

Observations on the Expediency and Practicbility of Simplifying and Improving Measures, Weights and Money, Used in this Country, Without Materially Altering the Present Standards. London: 1834. V. 38

PASOR, GEORG 1570-1637

Lexicon Graeco-Latinum, and Etyma Nominum Propiorum, and Tractatus de Grecis Novi Testmenti Accentibus. London: 1650-49-50. V. 38

PASQUALE, GIUSEPPE ANTONIO

Flora Medica Della Provincia di Napoli. Naples: 1841. V. 39

PASQUIER, ETIENNE

Les Lettres. Paris: 1586. V. 37

PASQUIER, NICOLAS

Les Lettres . . . Contenant divers Discours des Affaires Arrivees en France, Soubs les Regnes de Henry le Grand & Louys XIII. Paris: 1623. V. 37

PASQUIN and Marforio on the Peace; Being A Discussion, by These Celebrated Statues, at Rome, of the General Conduct of England, But Particularly Pending the Late War, and In Negociating the Present Peace. London: 1748. V. 41

PASQUIN Risen from the Dead; or His Own Relation of a Late Voyage He Made to the Other World, in a Discourse with His Friend Manforio. London: 1674. V. 42

PASS, CRISPIN DE

Hortus Floridus. London: 1928-29. V. 37; 39

Hortus Floridus in Quo Rariorum & Minus Vulgarium Florum Icones ad Vivum Veramque Formam Accuratissime Delineatae . . . Impres a Utrecht Ches: 1614-16. V. 37

PASSAGES from Modern English Poets. London: 1862. V. 39
PASSAGES from Modern English Poets. London: 1874. V. 42

PASSARINI, FILIPPO

Nuove Inventioni d'Ornamenti d'Architettura e d'Intagli Diversi, Utili ad Argentieri . . . Rome: 1698. V. 37; 38; 40; 44

PASSAVANT, G.

Verrocchio Sculpture, Paintings and Drawings. London: 1969. V. 44; 46

PASSE, CRIPIJN VAN DE 1593 or 4-1667

Hortus Floridus in Quo Rariorum & Minus Vulgarium Florum Incones ad Vivam Veramque Formam Accuratissime Delineatae. Arnhem: 1617. V. 42

PASSE, CRISPIJN VAN DE 1593 or 4-1667

Hortus Floridus. London: 1928-29. V. 43; 46

Les Planches des Heures. Anvers: 1905. V. 44

La prima Parte Della Luce Del Dipingere et Disegnare . . . Amsterdam: 1663-1665. V. 41

PASSE, CRISPIJN VAN DE 1593 or 4-1667 continued

XII Sibyllarum Icones Elegantissimi . . . N.P.: 1601. V. 46

PASSEMANT, CLAUDE SIMEON

Construction d'un Telescope de Reflexion . . . Paris: 1738. V. 37; 44; 45

PASSERAT, JEAN

Recueil des Oevvres Poetiqves Augmente de Plus de la Moitie, Outre les Precedantes Impressions. Paris: 1606. V. 39

PASSERON, R.

Impressionist Prints. New York: 1974. V. 46

PASSI, D. GIUSEPPE PIETRO

Della Magic'arte Overo Della Magia Naturale . . . Venice: 1614. V. 37

PASSINGHAM, ROBERT

The Whole Trial of Col. Rob. Passingham and John Edwards, for a Conspiracy Against George Townshend Forrester, Esq . . . London: 1805. V. 38

PASSIO Domini Nostri Jesu Christi. Waltham St. Lawrence: 1926. V. 45

THE PASSPORTS Printed by Benjamin Franklin at His Passy Press. Ann Arbor: 1925. V. 45

PASTERNAK, BORIS 1890-1960

Doctor Zhivago. Milan: 1957. V. 40; 46

Doctor Zhivago. London: 1958. V. 38; 44

PASTEUR, LOUIS 1822-1895

Animalcules Infusoires Vivant Sans Gaz Oxygene Libre et Determinant des Fermentations. Paris: 1861. V. 41

Etudes sur la Biere, ses Maladies, Causes qui les Provoquent, Procede Pour la Rendre Inalterable, avec une Theorie Nouvelle de la Fermentation. Paris: 1876. V. 42

Etudes sur le Vin des Maladies Causes qui les Provoquent Procedes Nouveaux Pour le Conserver et Pour le Vieillir. Paris: 1866. V. 37; 42

Les Maladies Virulentes et en Particulier sur la Maladie Appelee Vulgairement Cholera des Poules. Paris: 1880. V. 38

Oeuvres de Pasteur Reunies par Pasteur Vallery-Radot. Paris: 1922-39. V. 41

Studies on Fermentation, the Diseases of Beer, Their Causes and the Means of Preventing Them. London: 1879. V. 38; 41

Studies on Fermentation the Diseases of Beer Their Causes and the Means of Preventing Them. London: 1979. V. 45

PASTIMES Of James Joyce. New York: 1941. V. 38

PASTON, GEORGE

Social Caricature In the Eighteenth Century. With over 200 illustrations. London: 1905. V. 37; 39; 46

PASTON Letters. Original Letters Written During the Reigns of Henry VI, Edward IV, and Richard III, by Various Persons of Rank or Consequence, containing Many Curious Anecdotes, Relative to that Turbulent & Bloody, but hitherto Dark Period of Our History. London: 1787. V. 37

PASTONCHI, FRANCESCO

A Specimen for a New Letter for the Use on the 'Monotype'. London: 1928. V. 46

THE PASTOR, a Poem; or a Caution Against Error and Delusion. London: 1765. V. 46

PASTOR, LUDWIG

The History of the Popes, from the Close of the Middle Ages. London & Liechtenstein: 1938-69. V. 37

PATCHEN, KENNETH

An Astonished Eye Looks Out of the Air. Waldport: 1945. V. 39; 42

Before the Brave. New York: 1936. V. 38; 39; 41; 42; 44

Cloth of the Tempest. New York: 1943. V. 42

Cloth of the Tempest. New York: 1948. V. 44

The Dark Kingdom. New York: 1942. V. 39; 43

The Famous Boating Party. New York: 1954. V. 37; 39; 43

First Will & Testament. New York: 1939. V. 43

First Will and Testament. Norfolk: 1939. V. 39

First Will and Testament. New York: 1948. V. 39; 43

Hallelujah Anyway. Norfolk: 1966. V. 45

Hurrah for Anything Jargon 21. Poems and Drawings. Highlands: 1957. V. 39; 43; 44

The Journal of Albion Moonlight. Mount Vernon: 1941. V. 45

The Journal of Albion Moonlight. New York: 1941. V. 39; 42; 43

The Memoirs of a Shy Pornographer. England: 1948. V. 44

Panels for the Walls of Heaven. Berkeley: 1946. V. 42

Panels for the Walls of Heaven. N.P.: 1946. V. 39

Poem-Scopes. Highlands: 1958. V. 39; 43

Red Wine and Yellow Hair. New York: 1949. V. 37; 39; 40; 43; 44; 46

Sleepers Awake on the Precipice. New York: 1946. V. 43; 44; 46

To Say If You Love Someone and Other Selected Poems. Illinois: 1948. V. 39

To Say If You Love Someone. Prairie City: 1948. V. 44; 45

When We Were Here Together. Norfolk: 1957. V. 39; 40; 41; 43; 46

THE PATENT, a Poem. London: 1776. V. 38

A PATENT for Plymouth in New-England. Boston: 1751. V. 40

PATENT INDENTED STEEL BAR CO.

Indented Steel Bars for Reinforced Concrete Construction. London: 1907. V. 44

PATER, WALTER 1839-1894

Appreciations: with an Essay on Style. London: 1889. V. 38

Gaston de Latour. Portland: 1907. V. 41

Greek Studies: a Series of Essays. London: 1895. V. 38

Greek Studies - a Series of Essays. London: 1928. V. 46

Imaginary Portraits. London: 1887. V. 46

An Imaginary Portrait. Oxford: 1894. V. 37; 40; 43; 46

An Imaginary Portrait. Portland: 1902/1898/1900. V. 44

Marius the Epicurean: His Sensations and Ideas. London: 1892. V. 37; 38; 40

Marius the Epicurean, His Sensations and Ideas. Illustrated with 16 Dry-Point Etchings by Thomas Mackenzie. London: 1929. V. 37; 39; 45

Miscellaneous Studies: a Series of Essays. London: 1895. V. 38

Miscellaneous Studies. New York: 1895. V. 39

Plato and Patonism. New York: 1893. V. 38; 42

The Renaissance. Italy: 1976. V. 43

The Renaissance, Studies in Art and Poetry. New York: 1976. V. 38; 41

Sebastian Van Storck. Vienna: 1924. V. 42; 44

Sebastian van Storck. London & New York: 1927. V. 41

Sebastian von Storck. London: 1927. V. 37

Studies in the History of the Renaissance. London: 1873. V. 37; 38; 40; 42; 44

Works. London: 1900-1901. V. 40; 46

The Works. London: 1910. V. 39

The Works of Walter Pater. London: 1912. V. 41

Works. London: 1913. V. 42

Works. London: 1915. V. 38; 40

Works. London: 1925. V. 43

PATERCULUS, C. VELLEIUS

The Roman History of C. Velleius Paterculus. Edinburgh: 1722. V. 46

PATERSON, DANIEL 1739-1825

British Itinerary. London: 1800. V. 46

An Entirely Original and Accurate Description of all the Direct and Principal Cross-Roads in England and Wales, with Part of the Roads of Scotland. London: 1822. V. 41

A New and Accurate Description of All the Direct and Principal Cross Roads in England and Wales. London: 1789. V. 38; 41

A New and Accurate Description of all the Direct and Principal Cross Roads in Great Britain . . . London: 1799. V. 41

A New and Accurate Description of All the Direct and Principal Cross Roads in England and Wales, and Part of the Roads of Scotland . . . London: 1811. V. 42

Paterson's British Itinerary . . . London: 1785. V. 39; 44; 46

Paterson's British Itinerary. London: 1794. V. 39

Paterson's British Itinerary . . . London: 1796. V. 39

A Travelling Dictionary. London: 1777. V. 38

PATERSON, JAMES

Commentaries on the Liberty of the Subject and the Laws of England Relating to the Security of the Person. London: 1877. V. 40

The Contemporaraies of Burns, and the More Recent Poets of Ayrshire, With Selections from their Writings. Edinburgh: 1840. V. 37

History of the County of Ayr: with a genealogical account of the families of Ayrshire. Ayr: 1847. V. 37

Memoir of the Late James Fillans, Sculptor. Paisley: 1854. V. 40

PATERSON, SAMUEL 1728-1802

Speculation Upon Law and Lawyers; Applicable to the Manifest Hardships, Uncertainty and Abusive Practice of the Common Law. London: 1788. V. 45

PATERSON, WALTER

The Legend of Iona, with Other Poems. Edinburgh: 1814. V. 42

PATERSON, WILLIAM 1658-1719

An Enquiry into the State of the Union of Great Britian, by Wednesday's Club in Friday-Street. London: 1717. V. 39; 41; 43; 45

An Inquiry into the Reasonableness and Consequences of an Union with Scotland. London: 1706. V. 37; 38; 41; 45

A Narrative of Four Journeys into the Country of the Hottentos, and Caffraria. London: 1789. V. 37

PATESHALL, NICHOLAS

A Short Account of a Voyage Round the Globe in H.M.S. Calcutta, 1803-1804. Carlton: 1980. V. 41

PATHOLOGICAL SOCIETY OF LONDON

Transactions of the Pathological Soceity of London. London: 1855-99. V. 42

THE PATHS of Learning Strewed with Flowers; or English Grammar Illustrated. London: 1820. V. 40

A PATHWAY of Flowers. New York: 1890. V. 45

PATINA, CARLA CARTERINA

Pitture Scelte e Dichiarate. Colonia: 1691. V. 38

PATISON, JANE M.

Gleanings Among the British Ferns. London: 1858. V. 39

PATIUS, JOANNES

Fasti Ducales ab Anafesto I ad Silvestrum Valerium, Venetorum Ducem. Venice: 1696. V. 40

PATLOCK, ROBERT 1697-1767

The Life and Adventures of Peter Wilkins, Cornish Man. Dublin: 1751. V. 40

The Life and Adventures of Peter Wilkins, or the History of Flying Islanders, Taken from His Own Mouth, in His Passage to England, from Off Cape Horn in America, in the Hector, by R.S., a Passenger in the Hector. Boston: 1828. V. 46

The Life and Adventures of Peter Wilkins . . . London: 1884. V. 38

PATMORE, COVENTRY KERSEY DIGHTON 1823-1896

The Angel in the House: The Betrothal. (with) The Espousals. London: 1854, 1856. V. 39

The Angel in the House. London: 1860. V. 44

The Angel in the House. London: 1863. V. 46

The Children's Garland from the Best Poets. London: 1862. V. 44

The Child's Purchase. London: 1931. V. 45

Faithful For Ever. London: 1860. V. 46

Poems. London: 1844. V. 37; 41

Poems. London: 1890. V. 43

Two Poems. Maastricht: 1931. V. 37

PATMORE, DEREK

Greek Horizons - Volume 1, Number 1 (all published). Athens: 1946. V. 41

The Star Crescent: Modern Turkish Poetry, an Anthology. V. 46

PATMORE, PETER G.

Finden's Gallery of Beauty, or Court of Victoria. London: 1841. V. 39

PATMORE, PETER GEORGE

British Galleries of Art. London: 1824. V. 38

Mirror of the Months. London: 1826. V. 45

PATON, ALAN

Cry the Beloved County. London: 1948. V. 43; 45; 46

Cry, The Beloved Country. Franklin Center: 1978. V. 44

PATON, ANDREW ARCHIBALD

Highlands and Islands of the Adriatic, Including Dalmatia, Croatia and the Southern Provinces of the Austrian Empire. London: 1849. V. 45

PATON, DAVID

Animals of Ancient Egypt. Princeton: 1925. V. 44

PATON, HUGH

Colour Etching: a Practical Treatise. London: 1909. V. 42

PATON, JAMES

Catalogue Descriptive and Historical of the Pictures and Sculpture in the Corporation Galleries of Art, Glasgow. Glasgow: 1898. V. 44

Scottish History and Life. Glasgow: 1902. V. 39

PATON, JOHN G.

Missionary to the New Hebrides, an Autobiography. London: 1889-90. V. 41

PATON, JOSEPH NOEL 1821-1901

Poems by a Painter. London: 1861. V. 42

Spindrift. London: 1867. V. 42

PATON, LUCY ALLEN

Selected Bindings from the Gennadius Library. Cambridge: 1924. V. 37; 39; 41

PATON, MAGGIE WHITECROSS

Letters and Sketches from the New Hebrides. London: 1894. V. 40; 41

PATON, WILLIAM AGNEW

Down the Islands A Voyage to the Caribees. London: 1888. V. 45

Picturesque Sicily. New York & London: 1898. V. 37

PATOUN, ARCHIBALD

A Complete Treatise of Practical Navigation Demonstrated from Its First Principles . . . London: 1762. V. 42; 45

A Complete Treatise of Practical Navigation, Demonstrated from It's First Principles . . . London: 1770. V. 45

PATRI, GIACOMO

White Collar. San Francisco: 1934. V. 45

White Collar. San Francisco: 1940. V. 38

White Collar. Novel in Linocuts by Giacomo Patri. To the Great Progressive Labor Movement the Congress of Industrial Organizations. (c. 1940). V. 37

WHite Collar: Novel in Linocuts. (N.P.): (ca. 1940). V. 37

PATRIARCHAE, sive Christi Servatoris Genealogia, per Mundi Aetates Traducta A D Emanuele Thesauro . . . Londini: 1657. V. 46

PATRICK, MILLER

The Green Ship. 1936. V. 42

PATRICK, SIMON

Angliae Speculum: a Glass That Flatters Not . . . London: 1678. V. 44

The Pillar and Ground of Truth. London: 1687. V. 42

PATRICK, SYMON

The Parable of the Pilgrim; Written to a Friend. London: 1667. V. 46

The Parable of the Pilgrim. London: 1673. V. 40

The Parable of the Pilgrim: Written to a Friend. London: 1678. V. 43

The Parable of the Pilgrim: Written to a Friend. London: 1687. V. 38

The Parable of the Pilgrim. London: 1787. V. 46

THE PATRIOT Divine to the Female Historian; an Elegiac Epistle to which is added the layd's reply; or a Modest Plea for the Right of Widows. London: 1779. V. 37

THE PATRIOT Poet, a Satire Inscribed to the Reverend Mr. Ch----ll. London: 1764. V. 37; 40; 42

THE PATRIOTIC Songster. Strabane: 1816. V. 38

THE PATRIOTS of North-America: a Sketch. New York: 1775. V. 44

PATRIZI, FRANCESCO 1529-1597

Della Poetica. La Deca Istoriale. Ferrara: 1586. V. 40

Le Livre de Police Humaine . . . Paris: 1544. V. 40; 46

Magia Philosphica hoc est Francisci Patricii Summi Philosophi Zoraster, & Eius 320. Hamburg: 1593. V. 46

La Militia Romana De Polibio, di Tito Livio, E Di Dionigi Alicarnaseo. Ferrara: 1583. V. 38; 41

PATTE, PIERRE

Essai sur l'architecture theatrale. Paris: 1782. V. 37

Memoires sur Les Objets les Plus Importans de l'Architecture. Paris: 1769. V. 44

Monumens Eriges en France a la Gloire de Louis XV . . . et Suivis d'un Choix des Principaux Projets qui ont ete Proposes, Pour Placer la Statue du Roi Dans les Differens Quartiers de Paris. Paris: 1765. V. 38

PATTEE, E. H.

Evaluation of Quality of Fruits and Vegetables. Dordrecht: 1986. V. 38

PATTEN, BRIAN

The Unreliable Nightingale. London: 1973. V. 37; 39

PATTEN, C. J.

The Aquatic Birds of Great Britain and Ireland. 1906. V. 46

PATTEN, GEORGE

Cavalry Drill and Sabre Exercise . . . Richmond: 1862. V. 39

PATTEN, MATTHEW

The Diary of . . . Of Bedford, N.H. from 1754-1788. Concord: 1903. V. 39

PATTEN, ROBERT

The History of the Rebellion in the Year 1715. London: 1745. V. 41

PATTEN, WILLIAM

The Book of Sport. New York: 1901. V. 39; 41

PATTEN, WILLIAM continued

Christianity the True Theology, and Only Perfect Moral System . . . Warren: 1795. V. 43

The New Encyclopedic Atlas and Gazetteer of the World. New York: 1907. V. 45

PATTENSON, MATTHEW

The Image of Bothe Churches, Hierusalem and Babel, Unitie and Confusion, Obedienc and Sedition. 1623. V. 42

PATTERN Book for Jewellers, Gold & Silversmiths. London. V. 41

PATTERSON, A. W.

History of the Backwoods; or, the Region of the Ohio . . . Pittsburgh: 1843. V. 38; 45

PATTERSON, ALEXANDER

A Petition Presented by . . . to the Legislature of Pennsylvania . . . for Compensation fro the Monies He Expended and the Services Rendered in Defense of the Pennsylvania Title Against the Connecticut Claimants . . . Lancaster: 1804. V. 39; 42; 45

PATTERSON, AUGUSTA OWEN

American Homes of To-Day. New York: 1924. V. 41

PATTERSON, J. B.

Life of Ma-Ka-Tai-Me-She-Kia-Klak or Black Hawk, Embracing the Traditions of His Nationa, Indian Wars . . . Boston: 1834. V. 39; 41; 42; 46

PATTERSON, J. H.

In the Grip of the Hyika Further Adventures in British East Africa. London: 1909. V. 41; 42; 45

In the Grip of the Nykia. New York: 1909. V. 37; 42; 45

The Man-Eaters of Tsavo and Other East African Adventures. London: 1907. V. 40; 42; 43; 44

PATTERSON, JAMES

Memoir of the Late James Fillans, Sculptor. Paisley: 1854. V. 38

A Sermon, on the Effects of the Hebrew Slavery as Connected with Slavery in This Country. Philadelphia: 1825. V. 42

PATTERSON, JAMES LAIRD

Journal of a Tour in Egypt, Palestine, Syria and Greece. London: 1852. V. 37; 43

PATTERSON, JOHN

Charles Hopewell; or Society As It Is and As It Should Be. Cincinnati: 1853. V. 42

PATTERSON, LAWSON B.

Twelve Years in the Mines of California: Embracing a General View of the Gold Region, with Practical Observations of Hill, Placer, and Quartz Diggings . . . Cambridge: 1862. V. 37; 39

PATTERSON, PAUL

Brother Jonathan, The Smartest Nation in all Creation. London: 1844. V. 41; 43

The Playfair Papers or Brother Jonathan. London: 1841. V. 40

PATTERSON, R. HOGARTH

The New Golden Age and Influence of the Precious Metals Upon the World. Edinburgh & London: 1882. V. 40; 41; 45

PATTERSON, R. W.

Manual of the Second Presbyterian Church, Chicago, Illinois. Chicago: 1856. V. 41

The Place Where God Records His Name. A Discourse Delivered at the Dedication of the Second Presbyterian Church, on Friday Evening, Jan. 24, 1851, at Chicago, Ill. Chicago: 1851. V. 37

PATTERSON, ROBERT

Letters on the Natural History of the Insects Mentioned in Shakespeare's Plays. London: 1838. V. 45

A Narrative of the Campaign in the Valley of Shenandoah in 1861. Philadelphia: 1865. V. 42

Newtonian System of Philosophy Explained by Familiar Objects, in an Entertaining Manner, for the Use of Young Ladies and Gentlemen. Philadelphia: 1808. V. 40

PATTERSON, ROBERT L.

The Birds, Fishes and Cetacea Commonly Frequenting Belfast Lough. London: 1880. V. 38

PATTERSON, SAMUEL

The Narrative of the Adventures and Sufferings of . . . Experienced in the Pacific Ocean, and Many Other Parts of the World, with An Account of the Feegee and Sandwich Islands. Palmer: 1817. V. 38; 40; 42

PATTERSON, WILLIAM

Charge of Judge Patterson. April Term 1795. Present, Patterson and Peters, Justices. Philadelphia: 1801. V. 42

Observations on the Climate of Ireland and Researches Concerning Its nature from Very Early Periods to the Present Time, with the Thoughts On Some Branches of Rural Economy . . . Dublin: 1804. V. 41

PATTERSON, WILLIAM JOHN

I Am Nature. London: 1949. V. 43

PATTIE, JAMES OHIO b. 1804?

The Hunters of Kentucky; or the Trials and Toils of Trappers and Traders. New York: 1847. V. 42

The Personal Narrative of James O. Pattie, of Kentucky, During an Expedition from St. Louis, Through the Vast Regions Between that Place and the Pacific Ocean . . . Cincinnati: 1833. V. 37; 38; 39; 45

The Personal Narrative of . . . of Kentucky, During an Expedition from St. Louis through the Vast Regions Between that Place and the Pacific Ocean, and Thence Back through the City of Mexico to Vera Cruz . . . Flint: 1833. V. 45

PATTILLO, T. R.

Moose-Hunting, Salmon-Fishing and Other Sketches of Sport. London: 1902. V. 46

PATTISON, EMILIA DILKE

The Renaissance of Art in France. London: 1879. V. 37

PATTISON, FREDERICK HOPE

Personal Recollections of the Waterloo Campaign in a Series of Letters to His Grand-Children. Glasgow: 1873. V. 40; 43

PATTISON, MARK

The Estiennes: A Biographical Essay. 1949. V. 40

The Estiennes: A Biographical Essay . . . 1949. V. 41

The Estiennes: Ai Biographical Essay . . . 1949. V. 39

The Estiennes. A Biographical Essay, illustrated with Original Leaves from Books Printed by the Three Greatest Members of that Distinguished Family. San Francisco: 1949. V. 37; 38; 45; 46

PATTON, JOSEPH

Anaesthesia and Anaesthetics, General and Local. Chicago: 1906. V. 42

PATTON, PHILIP 1739-1815

The Natural Defence of an Insular Empire, Earnestly Recommended; with a Sketch of a Plan to Attach Real Seamen to the Service of Their Country. Southampton: 1810. V. 42

Strictures on Naval Discipline, and the Conduct of a Ship of War . . . London: 1795-1802. V. 38

PAUCTON, ALEXIS JEAN PIERRE

Metrologie, ou Traite des Mesures, Poids et Monnoies des Anciens Peuples & des Modernes. Paris: 1780. V. 38

PAUL A. Bennett Private Press Keepsake (1897-1966), Gathered Together by Friends and Typophiles. New York: 1967. V. 37; 41

PAUL, C. KEGAN

William Godwin: His Friends and Contemporaries. London: 1876. V. 41

PAUL, ELLIOT

All the Brave. New York: 1939. V. 37

PAUL, GEORGE ONESIPHOROUS

Considerations on the Defects of Prisons and Their Present System of Regulation to the Attention of the Gentlemen of the County of Gloster, in the Course of Their Proceedings on a Plan of Reform. London: 1784. V. 41; 42; 45; 46

PAUL, HENRY HOWARD

Dashes of American Humour. London: 1852. V. 41

PAUL, HENRY JOHN DEAN 1802-1868

The Man of Ton, A Satire. London: 1828. V. 42

PAUL III, POPE

Bulla Babstliches ablass-umb Fasten/ Petten/ Almusen/ Unnd Andere Gutte Werck . . . Ingolstadt: 1544. V. 44

Bulla de Auctoritate Libera(n)di, & Extingue(n)di ce(n)sus, Canones Ecclesiarum Monasteriorum & Alios Locorum Pioru(m). Rome: 1540. V. 37

Regula Cancellarjae Ap(osto)licae S. D. N. Pauli Papae III. Super Decreto Processum Gratiarum Expectatiuarum . . . Rome: 1545. V. 45

PAUL, JAMES BALFOUR

The History of the Royal Company of Archers. The Queen's Body-Guard for Scotland. Edinburgh: 1875. V. 37; 39; 41; 46

PAUL, JOHN

The Complete Constable . . . London: 1785. V. 41

A Digest of the Laws Relating to the Game of This Kingdom. London: 1776. V. 38

Every Landlord or Tenant His Own Lawyer . . . London: 1775. V. 43

PAUL, JOHN DEAN

ABC of Fox Hunting. London: 1871. V. 37

PAUL Jones's Victory: and Sterret's Sea Fight. N.P.: 1802. V. 40

PAUL OF AEGINA

The Seven Books of Pauls Aegineta. London: 1844-47. V. 38

PAUL, OF VENICE

Expositio in Libros Posteriorum Aristotelis. Venice: 1481. V. 40

PAUL, RODMAN W.

The California Gold Discovery. Georgetown: 1966. V. 44

Cradle of the West: The Evolution of Mining and Mining Society in California, 1848-1873 . . . 1942. V. 40

PAUL, SAINT

In Epistolam Pauli Ad Romanos Exegesis. Lugduni: 1559. V. 40

PAUL, W.

The Rose Garden. London: 1848. V. 41

PAUL, W. J.

Modern Irish Poets. Belfast: 1894-97. V. 42; 43

PAUL, WILLIAM

Villa Gardening. London: 1890. V. 38

PAULDEN, THOMAS

Pontefract Castle: an Account How It Was Taken and How General Rainsborough was Surprised in His Quarters at Doncaster, October 29, 1648. London: 1804. V. 42

PAULDING, HIRAM

Journal of a Cruise of the United States Schooner Dolphin, Among the Islands of the Pacific Ocean; and a Visit to the Mulgrave Islands, in Pursuit of the Mutineers of the Whale Ship Globe. New York: 1831. V. 37; 41; 43

PAULDING, JAMES KIRKE 1778-1860

The Backwoodsman. A Poem. Philadelphia: 1818. V. 40; 45

The Book of Saint Nicolas. New York: 1836. V. 43

Chronicles of the City of Gotham, from the Papers of a Retired Common Councilman. New York: 1830. V. 45

The Diverting History of John Bull and Brother Jonathan. New York: 1812. V. 38

The Diverting History of John Bull and Brother Jonathan. Philadelphia: 1827. V. 37

The Dutchman's Fireside. New York: 1831. V. 43

John Bull in America; or, the New Munchausen. New York: 1825. V. 39; 43

The Lay of the Scottish Fiddle. London: 1814. V. 40

The Lay of the Scottish Fiddle: A Tale of Haver de Grace . . . New York: 1813. V. 37; 43

Letters from the South, Written During an Excursion in the Summer of 1816. New York: 1817. V. 45

The Merry Tales of the Three Wise Men of Gotham. New York: 1826. V. 43

The New Mirror for Travellers and Guide to the Springs. New York: 1828. V. 43

The Puritan and His Daughter. New York: 1849. V. 43

Sketch of Old England, by a New England Man. New York: 1822. V. 43

Slavery in the United States. New York: 1836. V. 42

Westward Ho! New York: 1832. V. 43; 46

Westward Ho! New York: 1833. V. 39

PAULE, GEORGE

The Life of . . . John Whitgift, Lord Archbishop of Canterbury. London: 1612. V. 40

The Life of John Whitgift. London: 1699. V. 39

PAULHAN, JEAN

Braque le Patron. Geneva & Paris: 1947. V. 39

PAULI, GUSTAV

Zeichnungen Alter Meister in der Kunsthalie zu Hamberg, Niederlander with Zeichnungen Alter Meister in der Kunsthalie . . . Neue Folge. Frankfurt: 1924/26. V. 46

PAULIN, CHARLES O.

Atlas of the Historical Geography of the United States. Washington: 1932. V. 42

PAULIN, M. A.

Traite de'Architecture Theorique et Pratique . . . Paris: 1824. V. 45

PAULIN, TOM

The Book of Juniper - New Poems. Newcastle-Upon-Tyne: 1981. V. 41

PAULINUS, FABIUS

De Graecis Literis Cum Latinis Conjungendis Oratio. Venice: 1586. V. 40

PAULISON, C. M. K.

Arizona: The Wonderful Country. Tuscon its Metropolis. A Comprehensive Review of the Past Progress, Present Condition and Future Prospects of the Territory of Arizona, Showing the Advantages Possessed by Tucson . . . Tucson: 1881. V. 37; 38; 39

PAULLI, SIMON

Commentarius de Abusu Tabaci Americanorum Veteri, et Herbae Thee Asiaticorum in Europa Novo . . . Strasbourg: 1665. V. 38; 41

PAULLIN, CHARLES O.

Atlas of the Historical Geography of the U.S. 1932. V. 39

Atlas of the Historical Geography of the United States. Washington: 1932. V. 40

Atlas of the Historical Geography of the United States. Washington and New York: 1932. V. 40; 43

PAULLINI, CHRISTIAN FRANZ

Cynographica Curisosa seu Canis Descriptio . . . Nuremberg: 1685. V. 43

PAULSON, RONALD

Hogarth: His Life, Art and Times. New Haven: 1971. V. 42; 43

PAULSON TOWNSEND, W. G.

Modern Decorative Art in England Its Development and Characteristics. Volume I. Woven and Printed Fabrics, Wall-Papers, Lace and Embroidery. London: 1922. V. 41

PAULUS DE CASTRO fl. 1400

Prima (and Secunda) Pars Consiliorum. Lugduni: 1522. V. 40

PAULUS DE MIDDLEBURG 1455-1534

De Recta Paschae Celebratione, et de die Passionis Domini Nostri Iesu Christi. Fossombrone: 1513. V. 40

PAULUS DIACONUS

De Gestis Romanorum Libri Octo ad Eutropii Historiam Additi. Paris: 1531. V. 37

L'Historie . . . Seguenti a Quelle d'Eutropio, De i Fatti de'Romani Imperatori. Venice: 1548. V. 43

PAULUS, NICEOLETTI VENETUS

Expositio in Analytica Posteriora Aristotelis. Venice: 1477. V. 46

PAULUS PERGULENSIS

Compendium Perclarum ad Introductionem Iuvenem in Facultate Logice . . . Venice: 1486. V. 43; 45

PAULUS SCRIPTOR

Lectvra . . . Qvam Edidit Declarando Svbtilissimas Doctoris Svbtilis Sententias Circa Magistrvm in Primo Libro. Carpi: 1506. V. 44

PAULUS VENETUS

Habes Fidum Interpretem in Libros Posteriorum Aristotelis, Emendatum per Augustinum Fulginatem. Colphon: 1518. V. 37

Quadratura, Sive Dubia. Venice: 1493. V. 45

PAULY, ALPHONSE

Bibliographie des Sciences Medicales. London: 1954. V. 43

PAUSANIAS

Commentariorum Graeciam Describentitu, Attica & Corinthiaca . . . Quondam Latinitate Donata & Nunc Primum Ex Collatione ad Graecum Exemplar Innumeris Quibus Scatebat Hactenus Mendis Repurgata. Basle: 1541. V. 40

The Description of Greece . . . London: 1824. V. 39

Descrittione Della Grecia . . . Nella Quale si Contiene lOrigine di Essa, Il Sitio, Le Citta, la Religione Antica, i Costumi & Le Guerre Fatte . . . Mantua: 1593. V. 37

Pausaniae De Tota Graecia Libri Decem . . . Basel: 1550. V. 45

PAUSCH, GEORG

Journal of Captain Pausch Chief of the Hanau Artillery During the Burgoyne Campaign. Albany: 1886. V. 40; 43

PAUW, M. CORNEILLE DE

Selections from . . . with Additions by Daniel Webb. Bath: 1795. V. 42

PAVIA. LAWS, STATUTES, ETC.

Statuta de Regimine . . . Civilia & Criminalia Civitatis et Comitatus . . . Pavia: 1505. V. 40

PAVLOV, IVAN PETROVITCH 1849-1936

Conditioned Reflexes. London: 1927. V. 40; 41; 45

Conditioned Reflexes. Oxford: 1927. V. 37; 41; 43

Die Arbeit der Verdauungsdrusen . . . Autorisiete Ubersetzung aus dem Russischen von Dr. A. Walther. Wiesbaden: 1898. V. 39

PAVLOV, IVAN PETROVITCH 1849-1936 continued

Lektsii o Rabote Bol'shikh Polushrii Golovnogo Mazga. (Lectures on the Function of the Cerebral Hemisphere). Moscow & Leningrad: 1927. V. 38

Lectures on Conditioned Reflexes. New York: 1928. V. 42; 43; 44

The Work of the Digestive Glands . . . London: 1902. V. 37; 39; 45

The Work of the Digestive Glands . . . London: 1910. V. 39; 40; 41; 42; 43; 44; 45; 46

PAVY, FREDERICK WILLIAM 1829-1911

On Carbohydrate Metabolism. London: 1906. V. 43

Researches on the Nature and Treatment of Diabetes. London: 1869. V. 43

PAWLOW, J. P.

The Work of the Digestive Glands, Lectures . . . London: 1902. V. 38

PAXTON, ELISHA FRANKLIN

Memoir and Memorials; Elisha Franklin Paxton, Brigadier-General, C.S.A. New York: 1905. V. 45

PAXTON, GEORGE

Illustrations of Scripture, from the Geography, Natural History and Manners and Customs of the East. Edinburgh: 1841-42. V. 43

The Villager, with Other Poems. Edinburgh: 1813. V. 39; 42

PAXTON, JAMES

Illustrations of Paley's Natural Theology. Boston: 1827. V. 41

PAXTON, JOHN

Elisha Franklin Paxton. Memoir and Memorials. New York: 1905. V. 40

PAXTON, JOHN A.

The Stranger's Guide. Philadelphia: 1610. V. 42

PAXTON, JOHN ADAMS

The Philadelphia Directory and Register, for 1819 . . . Philadelphia: 1819. V. 41

PAXTON, JOSEPH

Paxton's Flower Garden. London: 1882. V. 41; 42

Paxton's Flower Garden. London: 1882-84. V. 43

PAYAN, VICOMPTE DE

Les Voyages de Monsieur Payen, Lieutenant General de Meaux Ou Sont Contenues Les Descriptions d'Angleterre, de Flande, de Brabant, d'Holande, de Dennemarc, de Suede, de Pologne, d'Allemagne & d'Italie . . . Paris: 1667. V. 41

PAYEN, NICOLAS

Les Voyages. Paris: 1663. V. 37

PAYER, J. B.

Traite d'Organogenie Comparee de la Fleur. Paris: 1857. V. 38

PAYER, JULIUS

New Lands Within the Arctic Circle. New York: 1877. V. 38; 40; 42

New Lands Within the Arctic Circle Narrative of the Discoveries of the Austrian Ship 'Tegetthoff' in the Years 1872-1874. London: 1876. V. 37; 40; 41; 42; 43

PAYHEMBURY Marbled Papers Sampler with Twenty-Six Samples of Hand-Marbled Paper. Winchester: 1987. V. 38

PAYN, JAMES

The Burnt Million. London: 1890. V. 41

Fallen Fortunes. London: 1876. V. 45; 46

PAYNE, ALBERT HENRY

Illustrated London, or a Series of Views in the British Metropolis and Its Vicinity . . . London. V. 43

PAYNE & FOSS

Catalogue of Printed Books and Manuscripts. London: 1837. V. 39

PAYNE, BUCKER H.

The Negro: What Is His Ethnological Status. Cincinnati: 1867. V. 38; 42

The Negro: What Is His Ethnological Status? Nashville: 1876. V. 42

PAYNE, CHARLES J.

My Sketch Book in the Shiny. London: 1930. V. 46

PAYNE, CHARLES JOHNSON

Osses and Obstacles. London: 1935. V. 46

PAYNE, DANIEL BEAUMONT

An Address to the Proprietors of Bank Stock on the Management of the Governor and Directors of the Bank of England, and on the Laws Relating Thereto. London: 1816. V. 38

PAYNE, EDWARD F.

The Romance of Charles Dickens and Maria Beadnell Winter. Boston: 1929. V. 43

PAYNE, EDWARD J.

Voyages of the Elizabethan Seamen to America. Oxford: 1893. V. 40

PAYNE-GALLWEY, RALPH

The Book of Duck Decoys; Their Construction, Management and History. London: 1886. V. 37; 39

The Fowler in Ireland; or Notes on the Haunts and Habits of Wildfowl and Seafowl. London: 1882. V. 45

High Pheasants in Theory and Practice. London: 1913. V. 45

Letters to Young Shooters. London: 1890/1902/1896. V. 39

Letters to Young Shooters. London: 1895/94/96. V. 39; 45

Projectile-Throwing Engines of the Ancients. London: 1907. V. 42; 46

A Summary of the History, Construction and Effects in Warfare of the Projectile-Throwing Engines of the Ancients. London: 1907. V. 42

PAYNE, GEORGE

Elements of Mental and Moral Science; Designed to Exhibit the Original Susceptibilities of the Mind, and the Rule by Which the Rectitude of Any of Its States or Feelings Should be Judged. New York & Boston: 1829. V. 41

PAYNE, HUMFRY

Archaic Marble Sculpture from the Acropolis. London. V. 46

Archaic Marble Sculpture from the Acropolis. London: 1936. V. 42

Archaic Marble Sculpture from the Acropolis: a Photographic Catalogue. New York: 1950. V. 42; 43; 46

Necrocorinthia: A Study of Corinthian Art in the Archaic Period. Oxford: 1931. V. 40

Perachora: the Sanctuaries of Hera Akraia and Limenia. Oxford: 1940-1962. V. 37; 44

PAYNE, J.

Book of Landscapes. London: 1801. V. 45

PAYNE, JAMES

Herefordshire Song. Hereford: 1785. V. 46

PAYNE, JOHN

The Descent of the Dove and Other Poems. London: 1902. V. 42

Geographical Extracts, Forming a General View of Earth and Nature. London: 1796. V. 42

The Masque of Shadows, and Other Poems. London: 1870. V. 37

A New and Complete System of Universal Geography . . . New York: 1798-1800. V. 39; 45

New Poems. London: 1880. V. 42

Tables for Valuing Labor and Stores, by Weight or by Number. London: 1811. V. 38; 42

Universal Geography Formed in a New and Entire System . . . Dublin: 1792. V. 44

PAYNE, JOHN HOWARD

Accusation; or, the Family of D'Anglade . . . Boston: 1818. V. 43

Brutus; or, The Fall of Tarquin, an Historical Tragedy. London: 1818. V. 39

Brutus; or, the Fall of Tarquin. New York: 1821. V. 45

Clari; or, the Maid of Milan, an Opera, in Three Acts. New York: 1823. V. 43

Clari; or, The Maid of Milan. London: 1823. V. 37

PAYNE, JOSEPH

English Medicine in the Anglo-Saxon Times. Oxford: 1904. V. 41; 42

PAYNE, R. G.

Report to the General Assembly on the Condition of the Railroads in Tennessee. Nashville: 1857. V. 43

PAYNE, W.

Picturesque Views in Devonshire, Cornwall &c. London: 1826. V. 40

PAYNE, W. W.

Little Leaders. Chicago: 1895. V. 38

PAYNE, WILLIAM

Maxims for Playing the Game of Whist . . . London: 1773. V. 38; 42; 44

PAYNE, WYNDHAM

Town and Country. London. V. 41

Town and Country, a Collection of Designs and Decoration. London. V. 44

Town and Country. London: 1926. V. 42

PAYNE'S Royal Dresden Gallery. Dresden & Leipzig: 1860. V. 39

PAYSON, GEORGE

The New Age of Gold; or, The Life and Adventures of Robert Dexter Romaine. Boston: 1856. V. 42; 46

PAYTIAMO, JAMES

Flaming Arrows People by an Acoma Indian. New York: 1932. V. 44

PAZ, OCTAVIO

An Anthology of Mexican Poetry. London: 1958. V. 41
Claude Levi-Strauss. Ithaca: 1970. V. 44
The Four Poplars. 1985. V. 42
The Four Poplars. 1985. V. 44
Homage and Descerations. New York: 1987. V. 42
Sun-Stone. Toronto: 1963. V. 44
Tres Poemas/Three Poems. 1987. V. 42
Three Poems. New York: 1987. V. 46
Three Poems. New York: 1988. V. 44

PEABODY, ELIZABETH PALMER

Aesthetic Papers. Boston: 1849. V. 45
Holiness; or the Legend of St. George . . . Boston: 1836. V. 37; 45
Theory of Teaching, with a Few Practical Illustrations. Boston: 1841. V. 45
To Fathers and Mothers--Letter from Miss Peabody. Boston: 1873. V. 43

PEABODY, GEORGE AUGUSTUS

South American Journals (1858-1859). Salem: 1937. V. 41

PEABODY, JOSEPHINE PRESTON

The Book of the Little Past. Boston: 1908. V. 38
The Wayfarers. Boston: 1898. V. 40

PEABODY, WILLIAM B. O.

Address Delivered at Springfield, Before the Hampden Colonization Society July 4, 1828. Springfield: 1828. V. 42

PEACE. a Poem. London: 1778. V. 37

PEACE, JOHN

Axiomata Pacis. London: 1862. V. 37
A Descant Upon Railroads. London: 1842. V. 42

PEACH, R. E.

Historic Houses in Bath and Their Associations. London: 1883-84. V. 37; 40; 44

PEACHAM, HENRY

Coach and Sedan, Pleasantly Disputing for Place and Precedence, the Brewer's Cart Being Moderator. London: 1925. V. 46
The Compleat Gentleman . . . London: 1661. V. 40; 45
The Complete Gentleman. London: 1627. V. 38; 43
Minerva Britanna, or a Garden of Heroical Devises. London: 1612. V. 40
The Valley of Anetie; or, Discourse Fitting for the Times Containing Passages of Antiquity, Philosophy and History. London: 1638. V. 41

PEACHEY, EMMA

The Royal Guide to Wax Flower Modelling by Mrs. Peachey . . . London: 1851. V. 42

PEACOCK, E. H.

A Game-Book for Burma and Adjoining Territories. London: 1933. V. 38; 40

PEACOCK, EDWARD

Ralf Skirlaugh the Lincolnshire Squire. London: 1870. V. 38

PEACOCK, GEORGE

A Collection of Examples of the Applications of the Differential and Integral Calculus. Cambridge: 1820. V. 40
Handbook of Abyssinia. Exeter: 1867. V. 40
Notes on the Isthmus of Panama and Darien, Also on the River St. Juan, Lakes of Nicaragua &c. Exeter: 1879. V. 43
A Treatise on Algebra. Cambridge: 1830. V. 38
A Treatise on Algebra. Cambridge: 1842-45. V. 38

PEACOCK, JAMES

Oikidia, or Nutshells; Being Ichnographic Distribtuions for Small Villas . . . London: 1785. V. 39; 40; 41; 42

PEACOCK, LUCY

The Adventures of the Six Princesses of Babylon in Their Travels to the Temple of Virtue. London: 1790. V. 40
The Visit for a Week; or, Hints of the Improvement of Time. London: 1795. V. 41
The Visit for a Week; or Hints on the Improvement of time. London: 1802. V. 45; 46

PEACOCK, THOMAS LOVE

Crotchet Castle. London: 1831. V. 42; 43; 44
The Genius of the Thames; a Lyrical Poem, in Two Parts. London: 1810. V. 39; 41; 42
The Genius of the Thames, Palmyra and other Poems. London: 1812. V. 39; 42
The Genius of the Thames. London: 1819. V. 39
Gryll Grange. London: 1899. V. 42
Gryll Grange. London: 1861. V. 37
Headlong Hall. London: 1816. V. 39; 42; 44
Headlong Hall. Nightmare Alley. Maid Marian. Crotchet Castle. London: 1837. V. 39; 40; 42
Headlong Hall and Nightmare Abbey. London: 1896. V. 43
Maid Marian. London: 1822. V. 37; 39; 40; 42; 43
The Misfortunes of Elphin. London: 1829. V. 39; 40; 42; 46
The Misfortunes of Elphin. London: 1928. V. 40
The Misfortunes of Elphin. Newtown: 1928. V. 39; 43; 45
Nightmare Abbey. London: 1818. V. 42; 43; 45
Rhododaphne; or the Thessalian Spell. London: 1818. V. 40; 42
Songs. London: 1904. V. 46
The Works . . . London: 1875. V. 39; 42
The Works. London: 1893. V. 42

PEAKE, JAMES

Rudiments of Naval Architecture . . . London: 1874. V. 42

PEAKE, JOHN

Brown Beer: a Poem. London: 1762. V. 42; 43

PEAKE, MERVYN 1911-1968

Captain Slaughterboard Drops Anchor. 1939. V. 38
Captain Slaughterboard Drops Anchor. London: 1945. V. 42; 46
The Craft of the Lead Pencil. London: 1946. V. 38; 40
The Glassblowers. London: 1950. V. 40; 42; 44; 45
Gormenghast. London: 1950. V. 37; 39; 40
In Sometime Never. 1956. V. 44
Letters from a Lost Uncle. London: 1948. V. 37; 40
Mr. Pye. London: 153. V. 40
Poems and Drawings. London: 1965. V. 44
A Reverie of Bone and Other Poems. London: 1967. V. 38; 40
The Rhyme of the Flying Bomb. London: 1962. V. 40; 43
Rhymes Without Reason. London: 1944. V. 41; 44; 46
Ride a Cock-Horse and Other Nursery Rhymes. London: 1940. V. 40; 45
Shapes and Sounds. London: 1941. V. 46
Titus Groan: a Gothic Novel. New York: 1946. V. 44
Titus Groan; Gormenghast; and Titus Alone. London: 1946-59. V. 38
Titus Alone. London: 1959. V. 39; 40; 41; 45; 46
Titus Groan. 1946. V. 37
Titus Groan. London: 1946. V. 39; 40; 45; 46
Titus Groan; Gormenghast and Titus Alone. London: 1946-59. V. 39; 40
Twelve Poems. 1939-1960. 1975. V. 39

PEAKE, ORA BROOKS

The Colorado Range Cattle Industry. Glendale: 1937. V. 40; 44; 45; 46

PEAKE, R. B.

An Evening's Amusement; or the Adventures of a Cockney Sportsman. London: 1846. V. 44

PEAKE, THOMAS

America; or an Exact Description of the West-Indies . . . London: 1655. V. 44
Cases Determined at Nisi Prius, in the Court of King's Bench. London: 1820. V. 38; 40

PEALE, CHARLES W.

Address Delivered by Charles W. Peale to the Corporation and Citizens of Philadelphia . . . Philadelphia: 1816. V. 38
An Essay to Promote Domestic Happiness. Philadelphia: 1812. V. 38

PEALE, TITIAN RAMSAY

Circular of the Philadelphia Museum: Containing Directions for the Preparation and Preservation of Objects of Natural History. Philadelphia: 1831. V. 46

PEARCE, CHARLES E.

The Amazing Duchess, Being the Romantic History of Elizabeth Chudleigh. London: 1920's. V. 40; 42; 46

PEARCE, NATHANIEL

The Life and Adventures of Nathaniel Pearce, Written by Himself, During a Residence in Abyssinia, from the Years 1810 to 1819. Together with Mr. Coffin's Account of His Visit to Gondr. London: 1831. V. 40

PEARCE, RICHARD

Marooned in the Arctic, Diary of the Dominion Explorers' Expedition to the Arctic August to December 1929. Toronto: 1931. V. 38

PEARCE, ROBERT R.

A Guide to the Inns of Court and Chancery. London: 1855. V. 40

PEARCE, STEWART

Annals of Luzerne County: a Record of Interesting Events, Traditions and Anecdotes. Philadelphia: 1860. V. 41; 42

PEARCE, THOMAS

Addenda to the Justice of the Peace's Pocket Companion. In the Savoy: 1753. V. 41

PEARCE, WALTER J.

Painting and Decorating. London: 1898. V. 42
Painting and Decorating. London: 1902. V. 46

PEARCE, WILLIAM

General View of the Agriculture in Berkshire with Observations on the Means of Its Improvement. London: 1794. V. 40
Ode to memory of the Officers and Men of the Squadron, Under, the Command of the Deeply Revered Lord Nelson . . . N.P.: 1805. V. 42

PEARCE, ZACHARY

The Miracles of Jesus Vindicated . . . London: 1729. V. 45

THE PEARL. San Francisco: 1967. V. 46

PEARL, CYRIL

Remarks on African Colonization and the Abolition of Slavery. Windsor: 1833. V. 42; 43

THE PEARL; or, Affection's Gift. Philadelphia: 1830. V. 38

PEARLS Of American Poetry. New York. V. 44
PEARLS of American Poetry. New York: 1853? V. 38

PEARMAN, D. G.

The Imperial Camel Corps with Colonel Lawrence and Lawrence and the Arab Revolt. London: 1928. V. 46

PEARS, EDWIN

Prisons and Reformatories at Home and Abroad Being the Transactions of the International Penitentiary Congress Held in London July 3-13, 1872 . . . London: 1872. V. 42; 45

PEARSALL, CLARENCE E.

History and Genealogy of the Pearsall Family in England and America. San Francisco: 1928. V. 39

PEARSALL, ROBERT LUCAS DE

A Few Remarks on the Position of the Baronets of Great Britain and Other Branches of the British Gentry, Compared with that of the Continental Lesser Nobility Both a Home and Abroad by a Traveller. Carlsruhe: 1836. V. 45

PEARSALL, WILLIAM BOOTH

Mechanical Practice in Dentistry. London: and New York: 1898. V. 45

PEARSE, G. E.

Eighteenth Century Architecture in South Africa. London: 1933. V. 39; 41; 46

PEARSE, HENRY H. S.

The History of Lumsden's Horse . . . London: 1903. V. 46

PEARSE, JAMES

A Narrative of the Life . . . In Two Parts . . . Rutland: 1825. V. 40; 45; 46

PEARSON, ABEL

An Analysis of the Principles of the Divine Government, In a Series of Conversations . . . Athens: 1833. V. 40
A Analysis of the Principles of the Divine Governemtn, in a Series of Conversations . . . Athens: 1833-1833. V. 40

PEARSON, ALEXANDER

Annals of Kirkby Lonsdale and Lunesdale in Bygone Days. Kendal: 1930. V. 42; 44; 46

PEARSON & CO.

Catalogue of the Well-Known Stock of Valuable Books, Sold in Consequence of the Dissolution of the Partnership of . . . The Collection Comprises Mediaeval Illuminated Manuscripts; French Illustrated Books of the XVII and XVIII Centuries . . . . London: 1924. V. 46

PEARSON, ATNHONY

The Great Case of Tithes Truly Stated, Clearly Open'd and Fully Resolv'd . . . Dublin: 1756. V. 40

PEARSON, E. S.

Studies in the History of Statistics and Probability. London: 1970-77. V. 42

PEARSON, EDWIN

Banbury Chap Books and Nursery Toy Book Literature . . . London: 1890. V. 40

PEARSON, ELLEN CLAIR

A Dream of Garden and Other Poesm. London: 1894. V. 38

PEARSON, GEORGE

Evenings by Eben-Side, or Essays and Poems. Kendal: 1832/37. V. 43

PEARSON, H. H. W.

The Annals of the Bolus Herbarium. 1914-1928. V. 39

PEARSON, HENRY GREENLEAF

Business Man in Uniform. New York: 1923. V. 42

PEARSON, HENRY J.

'Beyond Petsora Eastward' Two Summer Voyages to Novaya Zemlya and the Islands of Barents Sea . . . London: 1899. V. 37; 38; 40; 46
Three Summers Among the Birds of Russian Lapland. London: 1904. V. 40

PEARSON, HESKETH

The Life of Oscar Wilde. London: 1946. V. 43

PEARSON, HUGH

Memoirs of the Life and Writings of REv. Claudius Buchanan. London: 1819. V. 44
Memoirs of the Life and Correspondence of the Reverend Christian Frederick Swartz. London: 1835. V. 40

PEARSON, J. & CO.

Autographs of the Rules of France Charles V Born 1337 to Napoleon III died 1873. London: 1905. V. 44
Catalogue of Coreneille Collection. London: 1905. V. 44
Catalogue of Bossuet Collection. London: 1907. V. 44
Catalogue of Fenelon Collection. London: 1907. V. 44
Catalogue of Le Sage Collection. London: 1907. V. 44
Catalogue of Racine Collection. London: 1907. V. 44
Catalogue of Regnard Collection. London: 1907. V. 44
Catalogue of a Superb Collection of English and Foreign Armorial and Contemporary Bindings of Four Centuries . . . London: 1920. V. 44
Two Hundred Extraordinarily Important Books, Manuscripts and Autograph Letters. London. V. 40

PEARSON, J. P.

Railways and Scenery. London: 1932. V. 37

PEARSON, JOHN

An Exposition of the Creed. London: 1659. V. 38
An Exposition of the Creed. London: 1669. V. 38
An Exposition of the Creed. London: 1715. V. 39
An Exposition of the Creed. London: 1741. V. 42
An Exposition of the Creed. Oxford: 1833. V. 39
An Exposition of the Creed. London: 1723. V. 38
The Life of William Hey. London: 1822. V. 38
Practical Observations on Cancerous Complaints . . . London: 1793. V. 38
Vindiciae Epistolarum S. Ignatii. Accesserunt Isaaci Vossii Epistolae Duae Adversus David Blondellum. Cambridge: 1672. V. 39

PEARSON, KARL

The Grammar of Science. London: 1892. V. 43; 45
The Life, Letters and Labours of Francis Galton. Cambridge: 1914. V. 42; 46
The Life, Letters and Labours of Francis Galton. Cambridge: 1914-1930. V. 39; 41; 42

PEARSON, PAUL M.

Paul Laurence Dunbar: a Tribute. N.P.: 1906. V. 42

PEARSON, ROBERT

Every Man his own Horse, Cattle, and Sheep Doctor; or a Practical Tratis eon the diseases of Horses, Horned Cattle, and Sheep, together with the most simple and effectual Method of curing each disorder, throughout all its various . . . Leicester: 1811. V. 37

PEARSON, T. R.

A Short History of a Small Place. New York: 1985. V. 39

PEARSON, W. H.

Recollections and Records of Toronto of Old. Toronto: 1914. V. 43

PEARSON, WILLIAM

Select Views of the Antiquities of Shropshire. London: 1807. V. 38

PEART, EDWARD

On Electric Atmospheres. 1793. V. 45

On Electric Atmospheres. Gainsborough: 1793. V. 42

PEART, JOSEPH

A Continuation of Hudibras in Two Cantos. London: 1778. V. 40

PEARY, ROBERT EDWIN 1856-1920

Nearest the Pole. London: 1907. V. 37; 40; 41; 42; 46

Nearest the Pole - A Narrative of the Polar Expedition of the Peary Arctic Club in the S.S. Roosevelt, 1905-1906. New York: 1907. V. 37; 39; 40; 42; 43

The North Pole. London: 1910. V. 37; 40; 42

The North Pole ... London: & New York: 1910. V. 42

The North Pole. New York: 1910. V. 37; 39; 40; 45

The North Pole. Toronto: 1910. V. 44

The North Pole: Its Discovery in 1909 under the Auspices of the Peary Arctic Club by Robert Peary, with an Introduction by Theodore Roosevelt. 1910. V. 37

Northward Over the 'Great Ice.' London: 1898. V. 38; 39; 40; 43

Northward Over The 'Great Ice'. New York: 1898. V. 37; 39

PEASE, ALFRED E.

Biskra and the Oases and Desert of the Zibans With Information for Travellers. Stanford: 1893. V. 40

Travel and Sport in Africa. London: 1902. V. 39; 40; 42; 43; 45; 46

PEASE, ALFRED EDWARD

A Dictionary of the Dialect of the North Riding of Yorkshire, with Notes and Comments by John Fairfax-Blakeborough. Whitby: 1928. V. 41

PEASE, BESSIE COLLINS

The Biography of Our Baby. New York: 1906. V. 46

PEASE, E. LLOYD

Scenes from the Saddle, 1921. London: 1921. V. 39; 43

PEASE, ELISHA M.

Message of the Executive in Regard to Mexican Carts. Austin: 1857. V. 43

PEASE, JOHN C.

A Gazetteer of the States of Connecticut and Rhoe Island ... Hartford: 1819. V. 40; 42

PEASE, JOSEPH

The Story of a Three Weeks' Trip to Norway in the Steam Yacht 'Iolanthe', told to Friends at Home in Verse ... N.P.: 1890. V. 40

PEASE, ZEPHANIAH W.

The Catalpa Expediton. New Bedford: 1897. V. 37; 38

PEATTIE, DONALD CULROSS

A Book of Hours. New York: 1937. V. 37

The Bright Lexicon. New York: (1934). V. 37

Immortal Village. Chicago: 1945. V. 39; 45

Immortal Village. (1945). V. 37

The Road of a Naturalist. Boston: 1941. V. 46

PEATTIE, DONALD CURROSS

Immortal Village. (1945). V. 37

PEATTIE, ELIA W.

Castle, Knight and Troubadour. Chicago: 1920. V. 38

Castle Knight and Troubadour in an Aplogy and Three Tableaux. Chicago: 1903. V. 37; 40; 41; 43; 46

A Mountain View. Chicago: 1896. V. 38

A Mountain Woman. Chicago: 1896. V. 37; 41

PECETTIUS, FRANCISCUS

Cheirurgia. Florence: 1616. V. 38

PECHAM, JOHN

Perspectiva Communis. Milan: 1482-83. V. 40

Perspectiva Communis. Venice: 1504. V. 38

PECHELL, SAMUEL JOHN

Observations, Upon the Defective Equipment of Ship Guns; in a Letter Addressed to Vice Admiral Sir Harry Neale, Bart .... Colophon: 1825. V. 40

PECHEY, J.

A Plan and Short Treatise of an Apoplexy, Convulsions, Colick, Twisting of the Guts, Poisons, Bleeding at Nose, Vomiting of Blood, Stone in the Kidneys, Quinsey, Other-Fits, Miscarriage, Hard Labour, Acute Diseases of Women in Childbed. London: 1708. V. 41

PECHEY, JOHN

The Compleat Herbal of Physical Plants. Containing all such English and foreign herbs, shrubs and trees, as used in physick and surgery. And to the virtues of thoses that are now in use, is added one receipt, or more ... London: 1694. V. 37

PECHLIN, JOHANN NICOLAS

Observationum Physico-Medicarum Libri Tres, Quibus Accessit Ephemeris Vulneris Throacici et in Eam Commentaraius. Hamburg: 1691. V. 38

PECHMEJA, JEAN DE 1741-1785

Telephe ... London: & Paris: 1784. V. 43

PECK, ANDREW JAY

'The Date Being-?' A Compendium of Chronological Data. London: 1970. V. 42

PECK, BRADFORD

The World A Department Store. A Story of Life under a Cooperative System. Lewis: 1900. V. 37

PECK, CASSIUS R.

A Vermont Tenderfoot in Oklahoma Territory. La Jolla: 1956. V. 41

PECK, FRANCIS

Academia Tertia Anglicana; or, The Antiquarian Annals of Stanford in Lincoln, Rutland, and Northampton Shires. London: 1727. V. 37

Desiderata Curiosa: or, a Collection of Divers Scarce and Curious Pieces Relating Chiefly to Matters of English History, etc. London: 1779. V. 37; 41

Memoirs of the Life and Actions of Oliver Cromwell as Delivered in Three Panegyrics of Him Written in Latin. London: 1740. V. 38

New Memoirs of the Life and Poetical Works of Mr. John Milton. (with) Memoirs of the Life and Actions of Oliver Cromwell. London: 1740. V. 38

PECK, GEORGE W.

Adventures of One Terence McGrant. New York: 1871. V. 42

PECK, GEORGE WASHINGTON

Aurifodina; or, Adventures in the Gold Region. By Cantell A. Bigly. New York: 1849. V. 37

Melbourne and the Chincha Islands; with Sketches of Lima and a Voyage Round the World. New York: 1854. V. 38; 41; 44

PECK, GEORGE WILBUR

Peck's Bad Boy and His Pa. Chicago: 1883. V. 39; 41

Peck's Bad Boy and His Chums. Chicago: 1907/08. V. 46

PECK, JOHN MASON

A Gazetteer of Illinois, in Three Parts. Jacksonville: 1834. V. 37

Gazetteer of Illinois, in Three Parts: Containing a General View of the State, A General View of Each County, & A Particular Description of Each Town, Settlement, Stream, Prairie, Bottom, Bluff, Etc.; Alphabetically Arranged. Philadelphia: 1837. V. 37; 38

A New Guide for Emigrant's to the West, Containing Sketches of Ohio, Indiana, Illinois, Missouri, Michigan, with the Territories of Wisconsin and Arknsas, and the Adjacent Parts. Boston: 1836. V. 38; 41; 45

PECK, WALTER EDWIN

Shelley. His Life and Work. Boston and New York: 1927. V. 44

PECK, WILLIAM

A Topographical History and Description of Bawtry and Thorne, with the Villages Adjacent. (with) A Supplement ... Doncaster: 1813-14. V. 44

PECK, WILLIAM D.

A Catalogue of American and Foreign Plants, Cultivated in the Botanic Garden, Cambridge, Massachusetts. Cambridge: 1818. V. 45

Catalogue of Books to be Sold at Auction ... Containing a Choice Collection of Works Upon Botany and Natural History, and Comprising the Whole Library of the Late William D. Peck, Professor of Botany and Natural History in the University of Cambridge ... Cambridge: 1823. V. 45

Natural History of the Slug Worm ... Boston: 1799. V. 41

PECKARD, PETER

Memoirs of the Life of Mr. Nicholas Ferrar. Cambridge: 1795. V. 41

PECKHAM, GEORGE

The Poll for Knights and for the Shire to Represent the County of Sussex ... Lewes: 1775. V. 38

PECKHAM, HARRY

A Tour through Holland, Dutch Brabant, the Austrian Netherlands and Part of France. London: 1788. V. 43

PECKHAM, JOHN

Perspectiva Communis. 1482. V. 38

Perspectivae Communis Libri Tres. Cologne: 1580. V. 45

Registrum Epistolarum (17279-92). London: 1882-85. V. 42

PECKHAM, S. F.

Report on the Production, Technology and Uses of Petroleum and Its Products. Washington: 1885. V. 37; 44

PECKTON, T. S.

The Theory and Practice of Gas-Lighting: in Which Is Exhibited an Historical Sketch of the Rise and Progress of the Science ... London: 1819. V. 40

PECQUET, JEAN

Experimenta Nova Anatomica, Quibus Incognitum Hactenus Chyli Receptaculum, & ab Eo per Thoracem in Ramos Usque Subclavios Vasa Lactea Deteguntur. Parisiis: 1651. V. 37

PEDDIE, ALEXANDER

The Linen Manufacturer, Weaver and Warper's Assistant ... Glasgow: 1817. V. 38

The Manufacturer, Weaver and Warper's Assistant, Containing a New and Correct Set of Tables, Drafts, Cordings, Arithmetical Rules and Examples ... Glasgow: 1818. V. 45

THE PEDLARS. Dublin: 1826. V. 37

PEDLEY, CHARLES

The History of Newfoundland: From the Earliest Times to the year, 1860. London: 1863. V. 37; 38; 40

PEDRETTI, C.

Leonardo Da Vinci on Painting: a Lost Book (Libro A) Reassembled from the Codex Vaticanus Urbinas 1270 & from the Codex Leicester. Berkeley: 1964. V. 46

PEDRETTI, CARLO

Leonardo Architetto. Milan: 1981. V. 44

PEDROSA, J. DE LA

Via Lactea, Seu Vita Candissima S. Philippi Nerii ... Mexico: 1698. V. 42

PEEBLES, WILLIAM

The Crisis: or, the Progress of Revolutionary Principles, a Poem. Edinburgh: 1804. V. 43

PEEK, CLIFFORD H.

Five Years - Five Countries - Five Campaigns: an Account of the One-Hundred-Forty-First Infantry in World War II. Munich. V. 41

Five Years -- Five Countries -- Five Campaigns; an Account of the One Hundred Forty First Infantry in World War II. Munich: 1945. V. 42

PEEKE, HEWSON L.

Americana Ebrietatis: The Favorite Tipple of Our Forefathers and the Laws and Customs Relating Thereto. New York: 1917. V. 37; 44

PEEL, C. V. A.

Somaliland. London: 1900. V. 37

PEEL, EDMUND

Judge Not, a Poem, on Christian Charity (and) Minor Poems, Odes &c. London: 1834. V. 40

PEEL, HELEN

Polar Gleams, An Account of a Voyage on the Yacht 'Blencathra'. London: 1894. V. 43

PEEL, ROBERT

An Address to the Electors of the Borough of Tamworth ... London: 1834. V. 37

PEEL, W.

A Ride through the Nubian Desert. London: 1852. V. 43

PEELE, GEORGE

Works. London: 1820-39. V. 37

The Works ... London: 1828. V. 45

The Works ... London: 1829/39. V. 46

PEELE, J.

The Art of Drawing, and Painting in Water Colours. London: 1732. V. 41

A PEEP at Buffalo Bill's Wild West. New York: 1887. V. 39

A PEEP at the Esquimaux or Scenes on the Ice. London: 1833. V. 45

A PEEP-SHOW Alice. Berkeley: 1989. V. 45

THE PEERLESS Atlas of the World. Philadelphia/Springfield: 1889. V. 45

PEET, STEPHEN D.

The Ashtabula Disaster. Chicago: 1877. V. 43

The Cliff Dwellers and Pueblos. Chicago: 1899. V. 46

PEET, T. ERIC

The City of Akhenaten. London: 1923. V. 44

The Stone and Bronze Ages in Italy and Sicily. Oxford: 1909. V. 40; 42

PEETERS, HANS J.

American Hawking, a General Account of Falconry in the New World. Davis: 1970. V. 37

PEGGE, SAMUEL 1704-1796

Anecdotes of the English Language, Chiefly Regarding the Local Dialect of London and Its Environs. London: 1814. V. 38

Curalia: or an Historical Account of the Royal Household. London: 1782-1790. V. 37

Curialia Miscellanea, or Anecdotes of Old Times ... London: 1818. V. 43

An Essay on the Coins of Cunobelin. London: 1766. V. 42

Fitz-Stephen's Description of the City of London. London: 1772. V. 38

The Forme of Cury. London: 1780. V. 42

Sketch of the History of Bolsover and Peak Castles in the County of Derby. London: 1785. V. 42

PEGGS, J.

India's Cries to British Humanity Relative to the Suttee, Infanticide, British Connexion with Idolatry, Ghaut Murders and Slavery in India. London: 1830. V. 42

PEGUY, CHARLES

Le Mystere de la Charite de Jeanne d'Arc. New York: 1943. V. 40

PEICH, MICHAEL

The First Ten. Lincoln: 1978. V. 41; 46

PEILE, W. O.

West of Swardham. London: 1885. V. 41

PEIRCE, AUGUSTUS

The Rebelliard; or Terrible Transactions at the Seat of the Muses. Cambridge: 1863. V. 38

PEIRCE, BENJAMIN

A History of Harvard University, From Its Foundation, in the Year 1636, to the Period of the American Revolution. Cambridge: 1833. V. 43

Ideality in the Physical Sciences. Boston: 1881. V. 42

Physical and Celestial Mechanics: a System of Analytic Mechanics. Boston: 1855. V. 42

PEIRCE, CHARLES

A Meteorological Account of the Weather in Philadelphia, from January 1, 1790 to January 1, 1847. Philadelphia: 1847. V. 46

PEIRCE, CHARLES SANDERS 1839-1914

The New Elements of Mathematics. Edited by Carolyn Eisele. Atlantic Highlands, NJ: 1976. V. 37

PEIRCE, EBENEZER W.

Indian History, Biography and Genealogy, Pertaining to the Good Sachem Massasoit of the Wampanoag Tribe, and His Descendants ... North Abington: 1878. V. 37; 46

PEIRCE, ISAAC

The Narraganset Chief; or, the Adventures of a Wanderer. New York: 1832. V. 40

PEIRCE, JAMES 1674?-1726

The Security of Truth, Without the Assistance of Persecution or Scurrility ... London: 1721. V. 45

A Vindication of the Dissenters. London: 1718. V. 40

PEIRCE, THOMAS

The Odes of Horace in Cincinnati. Cincinnati: 1822. V. 37

PEISSE, J. L. H.

Sketches of the Character and Writings of Eminent Living Surgeons and Physicians of Paris ... Boston: 1831. V. 46

PEIXOTTO, EDGAR D.

Report of the Trial of William Henry Theodore Durrant, Indicted for the Murder of Blanche Lamont. Detroit: 1899. V. 41

PEKIN, HENRY

Poems on Various Subjects. Belfast: 1812. V. 37

PELAGIUS, PORCUPINUS, PSEUD.

Remarkable Satires: the Causidicade, the Triumvirade, the Porpudinade, the Processionade, the 'Piscopade, the Scandalizade and the Pasquinade, with Notes Variorum. London: 1760. V. 40; 44

PELBY, WILLIAM

Letters on the Tremont Theatre, Respectfully Addressed to the Primitive Subscribers . . . Boston: 1830. V. 44

PELETIER DU MANS, JACQUES 1517-1582

L'Arithmetique. Lyon: 1584. V. 38

Les Oeuvres Poetiques. Paris: 1548. V. 40

PELEUS, JULIEN

Les Plaidoyez. Parais: 1614. V. 37

PELHAM, CAMDEN

The Chronicles of Crime. London: 1841. V. 39

The Chronicles of Crime; or, The New Newgate Calendar. London: 1886. V. 42

The Chronicles of Crime. London: 1891. V. 39

PELHAM, DUDLEY

Remarks as to Measures Calculated to Promote the Welfare and Improve the Condition of the Labouring Classes and to Provide for the Maintenance of the Increasing Population . . . London: 1845. V. 43

PELHAM, EDWARD

Gods Power and Providence . . . . London: 1631. V. 42

PELICAN PRESS

Typography, the Written Word and the Printed Word, Some Test for Types, Concerning Printers' Flowers, the Pioneer Work of the Pelican Press . . . Type Specimens, a Display of Borders and Initials. London: 1923. V. 38; 44

PELL, FERRIS

A Review of the Administration and Civil Police of the State of New York, from the Year 1807 to the Year 1819. New York: 1819. V. 42

PELLATT, E.

Western Gleanings. Toronto: 1893. V. 44

PELLEGRIN, SIMON JOSEPH 1663-1745

Pelopee. Paris: 1733. V. 40

PELLEGRINI, MARCO ANTONIO 1530-1616

De Juribus et Privilegiis Fieci Libri VII. Montisbeligardi: 1619. V. 38; 40

PELLEGRINO, CAMILIO 1598-1663

Apparate Alle Antichita di Capua . . . Naples: 1561. V. 43

PELLEPRAT, F. PIERRE

Relation des Missions des PP. De La Compagnie De Jesus Dans Les Isles & Dans la Terre Ferme de l'Amerique Meridionale Divisee en Deux Parties . . . Paris: 1655. V. 41; 42

PELLEPRAT, PIERRE

Introduction a la Langue des Galibis, Sauvages de la ATerre Ferme de l'Amerique Meriodionale. Paris: 1655. V. 37

PELLETAN, EDOUARD

Revue D'Art. Edited by Edouard Pelletan. Paris: 1897-1898. V. 39; 41

PELLETREAU, W. S.

Early New York Houses, With Historical and Genealogical Notes. New York: 1900. V. 38

PELLEW, CLAUGHTON

Claughton Pellew: Five Wood Engravings Printed from the Original Blocks . . . London: 1987. V. 44

PELLHAM, EDWARD

Gods Power and Providence: Shewed, in the Miraculous Preservation and Deliverance of Eight Englishmen, Left by Mischance in Green Land Anno 1630. London: 1631. V. 41

PELLICER, CARLOS

Mural Painting of the Mexican Revolution. Mexico: 1985. V. 38

PELLICER DE OSAU SALAS Y TOVAR, JOSE

El Fenix y su Historia Natural, Escrita en Veinte y dos Exercitaciones, Diatribes, a Capitulos . . . Madrid: 1630. V. 41

PELLICIARI, BARTOLOMMEO

Avertimenti in Fattioni di Gverra. Venice: 1619. V. 37

PELLICO DE SALUZZO, SYLVIO

My Imprisonments: Memoirs. London: 1833. V. 42

PELLICO, SILVIO

Mes Prisons. Paris: 1860. V. 39

PELLING, EDWARD

A Practical discourse Concerning the Redeeming of Time . . . London: 1695. V. 44

PELLISON, PAUL

The History of the French Academy . . . London: 1657. V. 45

PELLISSERY, ANTOINE ROCH DE

Le Caffe Politique d'Amsterdam, ou Entretiens Familiers d'un Francois . . . Amsterdam: 1776. V. 38

PELLOW, THOMAS

The History of the Long Captivity and Adventures of Thomas Pellow, in South Barbary. Sherborne?: 1751? V. 46

PELOUZE, THEOPHILE JULES

Notions Generales de Chimie. Paris: 1853. V. 40

PELTIER, JEAN GABRIEL

The Late Picture of Paris; or, a Faithful Narrative of the Revolution of the Tenth of August. London: 1792-1793. V. 39

Trial of John Peltier, Esq. for a Libel Against Napoleon Buonaparte, First Consul of the French Republic, at the Court of King's Bench, Middlesex, on Monday the 21st of February, 1803. London: 1803. V. 42; 44

PELTON, A. R.

The San Luis Valley with Illustrations of its Public Buildings, Summer Resort and Some of its Residences, Business Blocks, Manufactories and Citizens. (Denver: 1891). V. 37

PELTON, JOHN COTTER

Life's Sunbeams and Shadows Poems and Prose . . . San Francisco: 1893. V. 38; 40; 42; 46

PELZER, LOUIS

The Cattlemen's Frontier. Glendale: 1936. V. 38; 40; 41; 42; 44; 45; 46

Marches of the Dragoons in the Mississippi Valley: An Account of Marches and Activities of the First Regiment United States Dragoons . . . 1833 and 1850. Iowa City: 1917. V. 38; 39; 40; 45

PEMBERTON, CHRISTOPHER ROBERT

A Practical Treatise on Various Diseases of the Abdominal Viscera. London: 1807. V. 38

A Practical Treatise on the Various Diseases of the Abdominal Viscera. Worcester: 1815. V. 37; 38

PEMBERTON, EBENEZER 1671-1717

The Divine Original and Dignity of Government Asserted; and an Advantegous Prospect of the Rulers Mortality Recommended. Boston: 1710. V. 40

Sermons and Discourses on Several Occasions . . . London: 1727. V. 44

A True Servant of His Generation Characterized . . . Boston: 1712. V. 38

PEMBERTON, EDWARD

Travels of His Royal Highness the Duke D'Angouleme, through Several Departments of France in 1817. London: 1819. V. 40

PEMBERTON, ELIZABETH G.

Corinth. Volume XVIII, Part I: The Sanctuary of Demeter and Kore, the Greek Pottery. Princeton: 1989. V. 42

PEMBERTON, HENRY

Observations on Poetry, Especially the Epic . . . London: 1738. V. 41; 42; 44

A View of Sir Isaac Newton's Philosophy. Dublin: 1728. V. 41; 42; 43; 45; 46

A View of Sir Isaac Newton's Philosophy. Dublin: 1758. V. 43

A View of Sir Isaac Newton's Philosophy. London: 1728. V. 38; 41; 46

PEMBERTON, ISRAEL

An Address to the Inhabitants of Pennsylvania, by those Freemen, of the City of Philadelphia, Who Are Now Confined in the Mason's Lodge, by Virtue of General Warrant. Philadelphia: 1777. V. 37; 38; 44; 46

Several Conferences Between Some of the Principal People Amongst the Quakers in Pennsylvania, and the Deputies from the Six Indian Nations . . . Newcastle-upon-Tyne: 1756. V. 45

PEMBERTON, J. C.

Soldiers of the Army, in and Around Vicksburg: The Hour of Trial Has Come! Vicksburg: 1863. V. 40

PEMBERTON, JOSEPH DEPARD

Facts and Figures Relating to Vancouver Island and British Columbia, Showing What to Expect and How to Get There. London: 1860. V. 37; 38; 39; 43

PEMBERTON, OLIVER

Clinical Illustrations of various forms of Cancer, and of other diseases likely to be mistaken for them, with special reference to their Surgical Treatment. London: 1867. V. 37; 38; 39

PENN, WILLIAM 1644-1718 continued

Considerations Moving to a Toleration, and Liberty of Conscience. London: 1685. V. 42

England's Present Interest Discovered With Honour to the Prince and Safety to the People. London: 1675. V. 38; 40; 41; 42

Englands Great Interest in the Choice of this New Parliament . . . N.P.: 1679. V. 44

England's Present Interest Considered, with Honour to the Prince and Safety of People. London: 1698. V. 44

Epicedia Academiae Oxoniensis, in Obitum Celsissimi Principis Henrici Ducis Glocestrensis. Oxoniaee: 1660. V. 37

Good Advice to the Church of England, Roman Catholick and Protestant Dissenter. London: 1687. V. 37

No Cross, No Crown. A Discourse Showing the Nature and Discipline of the Holy Cross of Christ. London: Printed and Sold by: 1762. V. 37

The Peoples Ancient and Just Liberties Asserted, in the Tryal of William Penn and William Mead. London: 1670. V. 42

A Perswasive to Moderation to Church Dissenters, in Prudence and Conscience; Humbly Submitted to the King and His Great Council. London: 1686. V. 38

Primitive Christianity Revived in the Faith and Practice of the People Called Quakers. London: 1696. V. 40; 42

Primitive Christianity Revived: also, Select Essays on Religious Subjects from the Writings of Isaac Penington. Philadelphia: 1783. V. 39; 42

Protestants Remonstrance Against Pope and Presbyter; in a Impartial Essay Upon the Times, or Plea for Moderation by Philanglus. London: 1681. V. 39

Quakerism: a New Nick-Name for Old Christianity . . . London: 1672. V. 40; 41; 42

Select Works of . . . London: 1771. V. 42; 46

Some Fruits of Solitude in Reflections & Maxims. London: 1901. V. 37; 44

Three Treatises in Which the Fundamental Principle, Doctrines . . . of the People Called Quakers, are Plainly Declared. Philadelphia: 1770. V. 39; 42

Three Treatises, in Which the Fundamental Principles . . . of the People Called Quakers, are Plainly Declared . . . Wilmington: 1783. V. 42; 45

Vindicae Britannicae. (with) An Appendix to Vindicae Britanicae. London: 1794. V. 39; 42

A Collection of the Works of . . . To Which is Prefixed a Journal of His Life. London: 1726. V. 44; 45; 46

A Collection of the Works of William Penn . . . London: 1827. V. 44

PENNANT, THOMAS 1726-1788

Antiquities & Scenery of the North of Scotland, in a Series of Letters . . . London: 1780. V. 38

Arctic Zoology. London: 1784-87. V. 41

Arctic Zoology. London: 1792. V. 37; 42; 46

Arctic Zoology. London: 1784/85/87. V. 38

British Zoology. Class I. Quadrupeds. Class II. Birds. London: 1768. V. 40

British Zoology. London & Chester: 1768-70. V. 37; 42

British Zoology. London: 1770. V. 38

British Zoology. Warrington: 1776-77. V. 39; 44

British Zoology. Warrington & London: 1776-77. V. 44

British Zoology. 1812. V. 46

British Zoology. London: 1812. V. 37; 39; 41; 42; 43; 44; 45; 46

The British Zoology. London: 1766. V. 37

Genera of Birds. Edinburgh: 1773. V. 42

Genera of Birds. (with) A General Synposis of Birds. London: 1781. V. 42; 44

The History of the Parishes of Whiteford, and Holywell. London: 1796. V. 37; 38; 41; 46

The History of the Parishes of Whiteford and Holywell. London: 1799. V. 44

The History and Antiquities of London. London: 1813. V. 37

History of Quadrupeds. London: 1781. V. 37

History of Quadrupeds. London: 1793. V. 38

Indian Zoology. London: 1769. V. 41

Indian Zoology. London: 1790-91. V. 42

The Journey from Chester to London. London: 1782. V. 43; 44; 46

The Journey from Chester to London. Dublin: 1783. V. 41; 43

A Journey from London to the Isle of Wight. London: 1801. V. 42

The Journey from Chester to London. London: 1811. V. 40; 44

The Literary Life of the Late Thomas Pennant by Himself. London: 1786. V. 44

The Literary Life of the Lat Thomas Pennant, Esq. By Himself. London: 1793. V. 37; 38; 39; 40; 41; 43

Of London. (with) Additions and Corrections to the First Edition of Mr. Pennant's Account of London. London: 1790. V. 39

Of London. (with) Additions and Corrections to the First Edition of Mr. Pennant's Account of London. London: 1790-91. V. 39

Some Account of London. Dublin: 1791. V. 42; 44; 45

Some Account of London. London: 1791. V. 44; 45

Some Account of London. London: 1793. V. 39

Some Account of London. London: 1805. V. 38

Some Account of London. London: 1813. V. 37; 40; 41; 46

Some Account of London, Westminster, and Southward. London: 1814. V. 37; 39

A Tour from Downing to Alston-Moor. London: 1801. V. 38; 42; 44; 46

A Tour from Downing to Alston Moore. (with) A Tour from Alston-Moore to Harrowgate. London: 1801-1804. V. 46

A Tour in Scotland MDCCLXIX. 1771. V. 46

A Tour in Scotland. Chester: 1771. V. 38

A Tour in Scotland. MCDDLXIX. (with) Supplement to the Tour in Scotland. Chester: 1771/72. V. 43; 44

A Tour in Scotland MDCCLXIX. London: 1772. V. 44

A Tour in Scotland 1769. Warrington: 1774. V. 41; 46

A Tour in Scotland. Dublin: 1775. V. 45

A Tour in Scotland and A Voyage to the Hebrides. London: 1776. V. 44; 46

A Tour in Wales MDCCLXXIII. Dublin: 1779. V. 39; 44

A Tour in Wales. (with) Supplemental Paltes to the Tours in Wales, by Moses Griffiths. London: 1784. V. 42; 46

A Tour in Wales. (with) A Tour in Scotland. London: 1784/69/90. V. 39

A Tour in Wales. (and) A Tour in Scotland. London: 1790. V. 45

A Tour of Scotland MDCCLXIX. (with) A Tour In Scotland and Voyage to the Hebrides, MDCCLXXII. London: 1790. V. 44

A Tour From Alston-Moor to Harrow-gate and Bingham Crags. London: 1804. V. 38; 44

Tours in England, Wales and Scotland. London: 1776-84. V. 38

PENNECUIK, ALEXANDER 1652-1722

Britannia Triumphans, in Four Parts. Edinburgh: 1718. V. 40; 42

A Geographical and Historical Description of the Shire of Tweeddale. Edinburgh: 1715. V. 40; 42

An Historical Account of the Blue Blanket. Edinburgh: 1722. V. 37; 38; 40; 41; 42; 45

Lintoun-Address to His Highness the Prince of Orange. Edinburgh: 1714. V. 45

Streams from the Helicon. Edinburgh: 1720. V. 40

Streams from Helicon. London: 1721. V. 38; 41; 45

PENNEFATHER, FREDERICK WILLIAM

A Handbook for Travellers in New Zealand. London: 1893. V. 39; 40; 46

PENNELL, ELIZABETH ROBINS 1855-1936

The Feasts of Autolycus. The Diary of A Greedy Woman. New York: 1896. V. 40

French Cathedrals: Monasteries and Abbeys and Sacred Sites of France. London: 1909. V. 39

Italy's Garden of Eden. 1927. V. 46

The Life and Letters of Joseph Pennell. Boston: 1929. V. 39; 40

The Life of James McNeill Whistler. London: 1908. V. 39; 40; 42; 43; 46

The Life of James McNeill Whistler. Philadelphia: 1908. V. 40; 44

The Life of James McNeill Whistler. Philadelphia: 1909. V. 37; 41

The Life of James McNeill Whistler. London & Philadelphia: 1908. V. 37

Lithography and Lithographers; Some Chapters in the History of the Art. London: 1915. V. 42

My Cookery Books. Boston: 1903. V. 38; 39

Our Philadelphia. Philadelphia: 1914. V. 37; 39; 40; 41; 42

Our Philadelphia. Philadelphia & London: 1914. V. 39

The Whistler Journal. Philadelphia: 1921. V. 39; 40

PENNELL, H. CHOLMONDELEY

Puck on Pegasus. London: 1861. V. 37

PENNELL, JOSEPH 1857-1926

The Adventures of an Illustrator. 1925. V. 44

The Adventures of an Illustrator, Mostly in Following His Authors in America and Europe. Boston: 1925. V. 39; 41; 42; 44; 46

Aubrey Beardsley and Other Men of the Nineties. Philadlephia: 1924. V. 39; 41

The Glory of New York. New York: 1926. V. 38; 40

The Graphic Arts. Chicago: 1921. V. 40; 41; 44

The Jew at Home. New York: 1892. V. 37

Joseph Pennell. Play in Provence, by Joseph Pennell and Elizabeth Robins Pennell. New York: 1892. V. 37

Lithography & Lithographers. London: 1898. V. 39

Lithography and Lithographers. New York: 1915. V. 38

Pen Drawing and Pen Draughtsmen. London: 1889. V. 38; 40; 42; 43

The Work of Charles Keene. London: 1897. V. 38; 39; 41; 43; 44

PENNIE, JOHN FITZGERALD 1782-1848

The Garland of Wild Roses; a Collection of Original Poems, for Youthful Minds. London: 1822. V. 46

PENNINGTON, B.

The Strange Case of Dr. Richard Kedgway and Other Matters. 1895. V. 46

PENNINGTON, JAMES

The Currency of the British Colonies. London: 1848. V. 42

PENNINGTON, JOHN

Aerostation, or Steam Aerial Navigation. Baltimore: 1836. V. 39

PENNINGTON, JOHN H.

A System of Aerostation, or Steam Aerial Navigation. Washington City: 1842. V. 44

PENNINGTON, MYLES

Railways and Other Ways. Toronto: 1894. V. 44

PENNINGTON, RICHARD

A Descriptive Catalogue of the Etched Work of Wenceslaus Hollar, 1607-1677. 1982. V. 39

A Descriptive Catalogue of the Etched Work of Wenceslaus Hollar 1607-1677. 1982. V. 42

A Descriptive Catalouge of the Etched Work of Wenceslaus Hollar 1607-1677. 1982. V. 44

A Descriptive Catalouge of the Etched Work of Wenceslaus Hollar 1607-1677. Cambridge: 1982. V. 45

Peterley Harvest. The Private Diary of David Peterley. London: 1960. V. 43

PENNINGTON, THOMAS

A Journey Into Various Parts of Europe and a Residence in Them During the Years 1818, 1819, 1820 and 1821. London: 1825. V. 42

PENNINGTON, W. H.

'Left on Six Hundred.' London: 1887. V. 41

Sea Camp and Stage. Bristol: 1906. V. 41

PENNINGTON, WILLIAM S.

A Treatise on the Courts for the Trial of Small Causes, Held by Justices of the Peace, in the State of New Jersey. Containing Useful Information for Justices, Officers, and Suitors of the Court. Newark: 1806. V. 37

PENNOYER, A. SHELDON

This Was California: a Collection of Woodcuts and Engravings Reminiscent of Historical Events, Human Achievements and Trivialities from Pioneer Days to the Gay Nineties. New York: 1938. V. 40

PENNSYLANIA. HIGH COURT

The Resolution of the High Court of Errors and Appeals, for the State of Pennsylvania; in the Case of Silas Talbot . . . Against the Commanders and Owners of the Brigs Achilles, Paty and Hibernia; Jan. 14th, 1785. Philadelphia: 1785. V. 37

PENNSYLVANIA ACADEMY OF THE FINE ARTS

Eighteenth Annual Exhibition of the Pennsylvania Academy of the Fine Arts. Philadelphia: 1829. V. 40

PENNSYLVANIA COMPANY FOR INSURANCES ON LIVES

An Address from the President and Directors of the Pennsylvanaia Company for Insurances on Lives and Granting Annuities, to the Inhabitants of the United States, Upon the Subject of the Beneficial Objects of That Institution. Philadelphia: 1814. V. 41

PENNSYLVANIA. CONSTITUTION - 1838

Amendments to the Constitution of Pennsylvania, Proposed by a Convention to a vote of the People . . . October, 1838. Together with the Existing Constitution. Philadelphia: 1838. V. 41

PENNSYLVANIA. CONSTITUTION - 1871

The Cosntitution of the Common-Wealth of Pennsylvania . . . To which is preficed the (Articles Of) Confederation of the United States. Philadelphia: 1781. V. 37

PENNSYLVANIA. CONSTITUTIONAL CONVENTION

The Constitution of the Commonwealth of Pennsylvania, as Altered and Amended by the Convention for that Purpose Freely Chosen and Assembled, and by Them Proposed for the Consderation of Their Constituents. Philadelphia: 1790. V. 42; 46

PENNSYLVANIA. CONSTITUTIONAL CONVENTION - 1837

Minutes of the Committee of the Whole of the Convention to Propose Amendments to the Constitution, at Harrisburg, May, 1937. Philadelphia: 1837. V. 37

PENNSYLVANIA. GENERAL ASSEMBLY

Votes and Proceedings of the House of Representatives of the Province of Pennsylvania. Philadelphia: 1752/53/54. V. 43

PENNSYLVANIA. GEOLOGICAL SURVEY - 1877

Pennsylvania Second Geological Survey: Oil Region Maps and Charts. Harrisburg: (1877). V. 37

THE PENNSYLVANIA German. Lebanon: 1900-10. V. 41

PENNSYLVANIA. LAWS, STATUTES, ETC. - 1797

Laws of the Commonwealth of Pennsylvania, from the Fourteenth Day of October 1700-Oct. 1, 1781. Philadelphia: 1797. V. 45; 46

PENNSYLVANIA. LAWS, STATUTES, ETC. - 1803

Laws of the Commonwealth. Philadelphia: 1803. V. 42

PENNSYLVANIA. LAWS, STATUTES, ETC. - 1836

A Compilation of the Canal and Railroad Laws of Pennsylvania. Harrisburgh: 1836. V. 37

THE PENNSYLVANIA Magazine of History and Biography. Philadelphia: 1877-81. V. 45

PENNSYLVANIA. (PROVINCE). LAWS, STATUTES, ETC. - 1762

The Charters and Acts of Assembly of the Province of Pennsylvania. Philadelphia: 1762. V. 40

PENNSYLVANIA SOC. FOR THE PROMOTION OF INTERNAL IMPROVEMENTS

The First Annual Report of the Acting Committee of the Society for the Promotion of Internal Improvement in the Commonwealth of Pennsylvania. Philadelphia: 1826. V. 39

PENNSYLVANIA Society for Promoting THE ABOLITION OF SLAVERY, AND RELIEF OF FREE NEGROES, UNLAWFULLY HELD IN BONDAGE
The Constitution of the Pennsylvania Society, for Promoting the Abolition of Slavery, and the Relief of Free Negroes, . . . Philadelphia: 1778. V. 40

PENNSYLVANIA SOCIETY FOR THE PROMOTION OF POLITICAL ECONOMY

Report of the Library Committee . . . Containing a Summary of the Information Communicated by Sundry citizens, in a Reply to the Circular Letter of the Committee of Superintendence of February 21, 1817. Philadelphia: 1817. V. 45

THE PENNSYLVANIA State Trials: Containing the Impeachment, Trial and Acquittal of Francis Hopkinson and John Nicholson . . . the Former Being Judge of the Court of Admiralty . . . Philadelphia: 1794. V. 45

PENNSYLVANIA. UNIVERSITY. BABYLONIAN EXPEDITION

Babylonian Expedition of the University of Pennsylvania. Excavatiions at Nippur. Philadelphia: 1905-06. V. 44

PENNSYLVANIA. UNIVERSITY. PHILOMATHEAN SOCIETY.

Report of the Committee Appointed by the Philomathean Society of the University of Pennsylvania to Translate the Inscription of the Rosetta Stone. Philadelphia: 1859. V. 38

Report of the Committee Appointed by the Philomathean Society of the University of Pennsylvania to Translate the Inscription on the Rosetta Stone. Philadelphia: 1859. V. 38

PENNY, ANNE

Poems, with Dramatic Entertainment. London. V. 45

Poems, with a Dramatic Entertainment. London: 1771. V. 39; 40; 42

PENNY Cyclopaedia of the Society for the Diffusion of Useful Knowledge. London: 1833. V. 40
THE PENNY Cyclopaedia of the Society for the Diffusion of Useful Knowledge. London: 1833-43. V. 39
THE PENNY Cyclopaedia of the Society for the Diffusion of Useful Knowledge. London: 1833-56. V. 37
THE PENNY Cyclopaedia of the Society for the Diffusion of Useful Knowledge. London: 1833-58. V. 39

PENNY, E. B.

Sketch of the Customs and Society of Mexico, in a Series of Familiar Letters . . . London: 1828. V. 45

PENNY, F. E.

Southern India. London: 1914. V. 45

PENNY, FANNY EMILY FARR

Caste and Creed. London: 1890. V. 38; 39

PENNYPACKER, SAMUEL W.

Annals of Phoenixville and Its Vicinity . . . Philadelphia: 1871. V. 42

PENNYSLVANIA. STATE GEOLOGIST

Grand Atlas. Harrisburg: 1884-5. V. 43

THE PENOKEE Iron Range of Lake Superior, with Reports and Statistics. Milwaukee: 1860. V. 44

PENOR, RODOLPHE

Monographie Du Palais de Fontainebleau, Accompagnee d'un Texte Historique et Descriptif. Paris: 1863. V. 44

PENOT, BERNHARD

Georges Tractatus Varii, de Vera Praeparatione et Usu Medicamentorum Chymicorum numc Primum Editi. Frankfurt: 1594. V. 37; 38; 39

PENROSE, BERNARD

An Account of the Late Expedition to Port Egmont, in Falkland's Islands, in the Year 1772. London: 1775. V. 37; 39; 46

PENROSE, ELDER CHARLES W.

The Mountain Meadows Massacre. Who were Guilty of the Crime? The Subject Fully Discussed and Important Documents Introduced in an Address . . . Reported by John Irvine. Salt Lake City: 1884. V. 37

PENROSE, FRANCIS CRANMER

An Investigation of the Principles of Athenian Architecture . . . London: 1851. V. 40

An Investigation of the Principles of Athenian Architecture. London: 1888. V. 45

PENROSE, MATT R.

Pots O Gold. Reno: 1935. V. 46

PENROSE, ROLAND

The Road is Wider than Long . . . London: 1939. V. 45

PENROSE, THOMAS 1742-1779

Address to the Genius of Great Britain. London: 1775. V. 41; 42; 44

Flights of Fancy. London: 1775. V. 41; 44

Poems. London: 1781. V. 40; 42

A Sketch of the Lives and Writings of Dante and Petrach. London: 1790. V. 42

PENS, Inks and Inkstands. London: 1858. V. 38

PENTAGRAM PRESS

The Pentagram Press Commonplace Book. Minneapolis: 1988. V. 40; 42; 45

PENTON, STEPHEN

The Guardian's Instruction, or, The Gentleman's Romance. (with) New Instructions to the Guardian. London. V. 40

The Guardian's Instruction, or the Gentleman's Romance Written for the Diversion and Service of the Gentry. London: 1688. V. 39; 44

PENZER, NORMAN M.

An Annotated Bibliography of Sir Richard Francis Burton. 1923. V. 46

An Annotated bibliography of Sir Richard Francis Burton. 1923. V. 37

An Annotated Bibliography of Sir Richard Francis Burton. London: 1923. V. 37

The Book of the Wine-Label. London: 1947. V. 40

The Most Noble and Famous Travels of Marco Polo, Together with the Travels of Nicolo de' Conti. London: 1929. V. 45

Paul Storr, the Last of the Goldsmiths. London: 1954. V. 37; 42

THE PEOPLE'S Atlas of the World. Philadelphia/Springfield: 1894. V. 45

THE PEOPLE'S Atlas; or the World Displayed in Its Geography, Zoology, Botany, Ethnology . . . Philadelphia: 1896. V. 45

THE PEOPLE'S Freight Railway Co. N.P.: 1873. V. 39

THE PEOPLE'S Illustrated and Descriptive Family Atlas of the World. Chicago: 1884. V. 45
THE PEOPLE'S Illustrated and Descriptive Family Atlas of the World. Chicago: 1886. V. 45

PEOPLE'S Popular Atlas of the World. Chicago: 1904. V. 45

PEOPLE'S PRACIFIC RAILROAD

Charter, Organization, Address of the President . . . With the By-Laws of the Board of Commissioners. Boston: 1860. V. 39

PEPE, GUGLIELMO 1783-1855

Narrative of Scenes and Events in Italy. London: 1850. V. 39; 42

PEPE, LIEUTENANT-GENERAL

Narrative of Scenes and Events in Italy from 1847 to 1849, Including the Siege of Venice. London: 1850. V. 46

PEPLER, HILARY DOUGLAS CLARK d. 1951

Concerning Dragons. Ditchling: 1928. V. 40; 42

Concerning Dragons. Ditchling: 1929. V. 39

The Devil's Devices or Control Versus Service. Ditchling: 1915. V. 37; 42; 43

The Devil's Devices or Control Versus Service. Hammersmith: 1915. V. 37; 39; 40; 45; 46

The Devil's Device or Control Versus Service. London: 1915. V. 38; 42; 46

The Dressmaker. Ditchling: 1917? V. 40

God and the Dragon. Ditchling, Sussex: 1917. V. 40; 46

The Hand Press: An Essay Written and Printed by Hand for the Society of Typographic Arts, Chicago. Ditchling Common, Sussex: 1934. V. 37; 38; 43; 45

The Hand Press. Ditchling: 1952. V. 37

In Petra. Ditchling: 1923. V. 37; 46

Libellus Lapidum. Ditchling: 1924. V. 39; 41; 46

Mimes: Sacred and Profane. Ditchling: 1932. V. 40; 41

Mimes Sacred and Profane. London: 1932. V. 39; 42

Nisi Dominus. Ditchling: 1919. V. 37; 42; 45; 46

Pilate - a Passion Play. Ditchling: 1928. V. 41

Plays for Puppets. Ditchling: 1929. V. 40; 41

St. George and the Dragon: a New Play on an Old Theme. London: 1932. V. 42

PEPPER, D. STEPHEN

Guido Reni. A Complete Catalgoue of His Works . . . Oxford: 1984. V. 46

PEPPER, GEORGE

The History of Ireland from the Colonization of the Country to the Period of the English Invasion Etc. Boston: 1835. V. 46

PEPPER, GEORGE W.

Personal Recollections of Sherman's Campaigns in Georgia and the Carolinas. Zanesville: 1866. V. 45

PEPPER, JOHN HENRY

Cyclopaedic Science Simplified. London: 1869. V. 38

The Playbook of Metals: Including Personal Narratives of Visits to Coal, Lead, Copper and Tin Times. London: 1875. V. 40; 41

PEPPER, WILLIAM

An American Text-Book of the Theory and Practice of Medicine. Philadelphia: 1893. V. 40; 41

An American Text-Book of the Theory and Practice of Medicine. Philadelphia: 1893-94. V. 37

The Medical Side of Benjamin Franklin. Philadelphia: 1911. V. 40

Syllabus of Notes From Lectures on the Theory and Practice of Medicine . . . Philadelphia: 1886. V. 39; 40; 45

A System of Practical Medicine by American Authors. Philadelphia: 1885. V. 38; 42

A System of Practical Medicine by American Authors. Philadelphia: 1885-86. V. 37; 40; 41

PEPPERGRASS, PAUL

Shandy McGuire or Tricks Upon Travellers, Being a Story of the North of Ireland. Boston: 1853. V. 46

PEPPINK, H. J.

100,000 Kilometer, by H.J. Peppink and Piet Maree. s'-Gravenhage: (c. 1940). V. 37

PEPYS, SAMUEL 1633-1703

Bibliotheca Pepysiana. London: 1914-1923. V. 38

The Diary. New York. V. 45

Diary and Correspondence. London: 1854. V. 38

Diary and Correspondence. London: 1858-65. V. 44

Diary and Correspondence. London: 1875. V. 42

Diary and Correspondence. 1876-79. V. 46

Diary and Correspondence. London: 1876-79. V. 44

Diary and Correspondence of Samuel Pepys . . . London: 1887. V. 45

Diary and Correspondence of Samuel Pepys, F.R.S. Philadelphia: 1889. V. 45

The Diary . . . New York: 1892. V. 42

The Diary of . . . London: 1893. V. 38; 46

The Diary of Samuel Pepys. London: 1893-1899. V. 45

The Diary of Samuel Pepys Transcribed from the Shorthand Manuscript in the Pepysian Library Magdalene College Cambridge. London: 1897. V. 41

The Diary of Samuel Pepys . . . New York: 1898. V. 38; 40

The Diary of Samuel Pepys. London: 1902. V. 40; 41; 43

Diary. (with) The Index and Pepysiana: Additional Notes on Pepys Life and on Some Passages in the Diary. London: 1903-04. V. 37

The Diary. London: 1904-17. V. 46

The Diary. London: 1904-29. V. 37

The Diary. London: 1920. V. 46

The Diary of Samuel Pepys. London: 1923. V. 39

The Diary of Samuel Pepys. London: 1926. V. 45

Diary. London: 1928. V. 46

The Diary of . . . London: 1928-1935. V. 38; 40

The Diary of Samuel Pepys. Mount Vernon: 1942. V. 38

The Diary. New York: 1942. V. 38; 44

The Diary of Samuel Pepys. London: 1949. V. 44

The Diary. On the 350th Anniversary of His Birth . . . London: 1970-76, 1983. V. 41

Diary, a New and Complete Translation. London: 1970-83. V. 40; 41; 46

The Diary. London: 1971-76. V. 38

The Diary. London: 1983. V. 44

The Diary of Samuel Pepys. New York: 1898-1900. V. 38

Everybody's Pepys - the Diary of Samuel Pepys 1660-1669. London: 1926. V. 39; 41

Everybody's Pepys. The Diary of Samuel Pepys 1660-1669. London: 1927. V. 44

PEPYS, SAMUEL 1633-1703 continued

Everybody's Pepys. The Diary of Samuel Pepys 1660-1669. Abridged by o.F. Morshead. With 60 illustrations by Ernest H. Shepard. London: 1935. V. 37

Memoires Relating to the State of the Royal Navy of England. London: 1690. V. 37; 46

Memoirs of Samuel Pepys Comprising His Diary from 1659-1669. London: 1825. V. 37; 38; 44; 45; 46

Memoirs. London: 1828. V. 43

Pepys' Diary. New York: 1942. V. 41

A Pepysian Pastorale. Los Angeles: 1945. V. 37

Reliques of Ancient English Poetry. London: 1775. V. 40

Ye Minutes of Ye CLXXVIIth Meeting of Ye Sette of Odd Volumes. Ashendene: 1896. V. 40

Ye Minutes of ye CLXXVIIth Meeting of ye Sette of Odd Volumes. N.P.: 1896. V. 46

PER la Solenne Dedicazione della Statua Equestre Innalzata dal Pubblico di Modena all'Immortale Memoria dell'Altezza Serenissima di Francesco III Gloriosamente Regnante Applausi Poetici . . . Modena: 1774. V. 46

PERAGALLO, H.

Diatomees Marines de France . . . Grez-sur-Loing: 1897-1908. V. 39

PERALTA BARNUEVO ROCHA Y BENAVIDES, PEDRO DE

Historia de Espana Vindicada, en Qve se Haze sv Mas Exacta Descripcion la De Sus Excelencias, Y Antiguas Riquezas se Prueba, su Poblacion, Lengua Y Reyes Verdaderos Primitivos . . . Lima: 1730. V. 40

PERAU, GABRIEL-LOUIS CALABRE

Description Historique de l'hotel Royal des Invalides. Paris: 1756. V. 38

PERCEVAL, E. A.

Panoramic View of Sebastopol. London: 1857. V. 42

PERCEVAL, JOHN

Letters to Sir James Graham and Others, on the Reform of the law affecting the Treatment of Persons alleged to be of Unsound Mind. London;: 1846. V. 37

PERCEVAL OF GALLES

The Romance of Syr Percyvelle of Gales. Hammersmith: 1895. V. 44

PERCIER, CHARLES

Description des Ceremonies et Des Fetes Qui Ont Eu Lieu Pour Le Mariage de S. M. L'Empereur Napoleon . . . Paris: 1810. V. 43

Palais, Maisons, et Autres Edifices Modernes, Dessines a Rome. Paris: 1798. V. 38

Recueil de decorations Interieures, Comprenant Tout ce Qui a Rapport a l'Ameublement. Paris: 1812. V. 38; 39

PERCIVAL, A. BLAYNEY

A Game Ranger on Safari. London: 1928. V. 37; 38

PERCIVAL, J.

The Wheat Plant. London: 1921. V. 37

PERCIVAL, JAMES G.

Clio. No. I. & No. II. Charleston: 1822. V. 41

Clio. No. III. New York: 1827. V. 41

PERCIVAL, MACIVER

The Chintz Book. London: 1923. V. 42

PERCIVAL, ROBERT

An Account of the Island of Ceylon, Containing Its History, Geography, Natural History, with the Manners and Customs of Its Various Inhabitants. London: 1803. V. 40; 42; 43

An Account of the Cape of Good Hope. London: 1804. V. 41

An Account of the Island of Ceylon. London: 1805. V. 38; 43

PERCIVAL, THOMAS

A Father's Instructions . . . Richmond: 1800. V. 45

PERCIVALE, RICHARD

A Dictionary in Spanish and English. London: 1623. V. 45

PERCY, ALGERNON HEBER

Journal of Two Excursions in the British North West Territory of North America by Algernon Heber Percy and Mrs. Heber Percy, 1877 & 1878. Market Drayton: 1878. V. 39

PERCY, CHARLES

A View of the Levant, Particularly of Constantinople, Syria, Egypt and Greece. London: 1743. V. 41

THE PERCY Folio of Old English Ballads and Romances. London: 1905-10. V. 46

PERCY, JOHN

Metallurgy. London: 1861-80. V. 40

Metallurgy: the Art of Extracting Metals from Ores, and Adapting Them to Various Purposes of Manufacture. London: 1864. V. 44

The Metallurgy of Lead Including Desilverization and Cupellation. London: 1870. V. 40; 45

Metallurgy . . . Silver and Gold. London: 1880. V. 40

Metallurgy . . . Fuel, Fire-Clays, Copper, Zinc, Brass, Etc. London: 1861. V. 45

PERCY MacKaye on His 50th Birthday: a Symposium. Hanover: 1928. V. 37; 40

PERCY, SHOLTO

The Percy Anecdotes, Original and Select. London: 1821-23. V. 46

The Percy Anecdotes. London: 1823-6. V. 37

PERCY, THOMAS 1729-1811

Hau Kiou Choaan or the Pleasing History. A Translation from the Chinese Language. London: 1761. V. 37

The Old Ballad of the Boy and the Mantle. Chiswick: 1900. V. 37; 39

The Percy Folio of Old English Ballads & Romances. London: 1905-1910. V. 37

Reliques of Ancient English Poetry. Dublin: 1766. V. 38

Reliques of Ancient English Poetry: Consisting of Old Heroid Ballads, Songs & Other Pieces of our earlier Poets (Chiefly of the Lyric kind). Together with some few of later Date. London: 1967. V. 37

PERCY, THOMAS, BP. OF DROMORE 1729-1811

Bishop Percy's Folio Manuscript. London: 1867. V. 46

PERCY, THOMAS, BP. OF DROPMORE 1729-1811

Five Pieces of Runic Poetry . . . London: 1763. V. 38; 39; 42; 43; 46

The Hermit of Warworth. London: 1771. V. 45

The Hermit of Warkworth. London: 1771. V. 40; 46

The Hermit of Warkworth. Alnwick: 1806. V. 38; 41

Northern Antiquities. London: 1760. V. 41

Reliques of Ancient English Poetry. London: 1765. V. 37; 38; 39; 40; 41; 42; 43; 45; 46

Reliques of Ancient English Poetry. London: 1767. V. 39; 41; 42; 43; 45

Reliques of Ancient English Poetry. London: 1775. V. 37; 38; 39; 42; 43; 46

Reliques of Ancient English Poetry. London: 1794. V. 38; 43; 45

Reliques of Ancient English Poetry. Philadelphia: 1823. V. 43

Reliques of Ancient English Poetry. London: 1839. V. 41

Reliques of Ancient English Poetry. London: 1876. V. 41; 43; 44; 46

PERCY, WALKER 1916-1990

Bourbon. 1979. V. 42

Bourbon. 1979. V. 42

Bourbon. Winston-Salem: 1979. V. 38

Bourbon. 1981. V. 42

Bourbon. 1981. V. 42

Bourbon. 1981. V. 42

Bourbon. 1981. V. 43

Bourbon. North Carolina: 1981. V. 46

Diagnosing the Modern Malaise. New Orleans: 1985. V. 37; 38

Lancelot. New York: 1977. V. 39; 42; 44; 46

The Last Gentleman. 1966. V. 44

The Last Gentleman. New York: 1966. V. 38; 39; 40; 41; 42; 43; 46

The Last Gentleman. London: 1967. V. 41

Lost in Cosmos. New York. V. 45

Lost in the Cosmos. New York: 1983. V. 43; 44; 46

Love in the Ruins. New York: 1971. V. 38

The Message in the Bottle. New York: 1975. V. 43

The Movie-Goer. New York: 1961. V. 37; 38; 39; 42; 43; 44; 46

The Movie-Goer. London: 1963. V. 42

The Movie-Goer. 1963. V. 37

The Moviegoer. Franklin Center: 1980. V. 46

Novel Writing in an Apocalyptic Time. New Orleans: 1986. V. 43; 45; 46

Questions They Never Asked Me. Northridge: 1979. V. 38; 39; 40; 42; 44; 46

The Second Coming. Franklin Center: 1980. V. 44

The Second Coming. New York: 1980. V. 37; 38; 39; 40; 41; 42; 43; 45; 46

The Second Coming. New York: 1980. V. 43

The State of the Novel. New Orleans: 1987. V. 42; 43; 45; 46

Symbol as Need. New York: 1954. V. 46

Symbol as Need. New York: 1954. V. 43

Symbol as Need. V. 38

The Thanatos Syndrome. New York: 1987. V. 43; 45

PERCY, WILLIAM ALEXANDER

The Collected Poems. New York: 1934. V. 37

Lanterns on the Levee: Recollections of a Planter's Son. New York: 1941. V. 39

PERDICARIS, G. A.

The Greece of the Greeks. New York: 1845. V. 39

PERDONNET, AUGUSTE

Nouveau Portefeuille de l'Ingenieur des Chemis de Fer. Paris: 1866. V. 46

PEREFIXE, HARDOUIN DE BEAUMONT DE, ABP.

Histoire du Roy Henry Le Grand. Amsterdam: 1661. V. 38

The History of Henry IV Surnamed the Great King of france and Navarre. London: 1672. V. 44

The Life of Henry the Fourth of France. Paris: 1785. V. 39

PEREGRINUS, PETER

Epistle of Peter Peregrinus of Maricourt to Sygerus of Foncaucourt, Soldier, Concerning the Magnet . . . London: 1902. V. 38; 41

PEREGRINUS PROTEUS

Sermones Peregrini de Tempore et de Sanctis. Strasbourg: 1474-77. V. 39

PEREIRA DA SILVA, MATHIAS

A Fenix Renascida, ou Obras Poeticas dos Melhores Engenhos Portuguzes . . . Segunda vez Impresso, e Accrescentado . . . Lisbon: 1746. V. 39

PEREIRA DE SANTA ANNA, JOSEPH

Vida da Insigne Mestre de Espirito a Virtuosa Madre Maria Perpetua da Luz, Religiosa Carmelita Calcada do Exemplarissimo Convento da Esperanca da Cidade de Beja . . . Lisbon: 1742. V. 39

PEREIRA, JONATHAN

A Treatise on Food and Diet: with Observations on the Dietetical Regimen Suited for Disordered States of the Digestive Organs . . . London: 1843. V. 38; 39; 42; 45

A Treatise on Food and Diet: with observations on the dietetical regimen suited for disordered states of the digestive organs; . . . London: 1848. V. 37

PERELEMAN, S. J.

One Touch of Venus. Boston: 1944. V. 41

PERELMAN, S. J.

Acres and Pains. New York: 1972. V. 41

The Beauty Part. New York: 1963. V. 41

Chicken Inspector No. 23. New York: 1966. V. 41

Dawin Ginsbergh's Revenge. 1929. V. 37

Dawn Ginsburgh's Revenge. New York: 1929. V. 43

Eastward Ha! New York: 1977. V. 41

Look Who's Talking. New York: 1940. V. 37

The Most of . . . New York: 1958. V. 41

One Touch of Venus. Boston: 1944. V. 46

The Rising Gorge. New York: 1961. V. 41

Strictly from Hunger. New York: 1937. V. 45

Vinegar Puss. New York: 1975. V. 43

PERET, BENJAMIN

Au 125 du Boulevard Saint Germain, Conte. Paris: 1923. V. 38

La Brebis Galante. Paris: 1949. V. 42

PEREZ, ANTONIO c. 1540-1611

Cort-Begryp . . . The Hague: 1596. V. 37

PEREZ DE GUZMAN, HERNAN

Mar de Istorias (together with Generaciones y Semblanzas). Valladolid: 1512. V. 40

PEREZ DE LUXAN, DIEGO

Expedition into New Mexico Made by Antonio de Espejo 1582-1583. Los Angeles: 1929. V. 42; 43; 45

PEREZ DE MOYA, JUAN 1513?-1597?

Comparaciones, o Similes Para los Vicios, y Virtudes . . . Alcala: 1584. V. 40

PEREZ ROSALES, VICENTE

California Adventure. San Francisco: 1947. V. 39

PEREZ Y COMOTO, FLORENCIO

Representacion que a Favor del Libre Comercio Dirigieron al Excelentisimo Senor Dan Juan Ruiz de Apodaca . . . Havana: 1818. V. 38

A PERFECT Diurnall of Some Passages and Proceedings of, and in Relation to, the Armies in England, Ireland and Scotland, No. 44, 7 October - 14 October 1650. London: 1650. V. 45

A PERFECT Relation of the Great Fight Between the English and Dutch Fleets on Fryday and Satturday Last, Neer the Coast of Portsmouth . . . N.P.: 1653. V. 43

PERGOLESI, MICHELANGELO

Designs for Various Ornaments. London: 1788-1792. V. 42

Designs for Various Ornaments. London: 1777-1801. V. 37

PERICOT-GARCIA, LUIS

Prehistoric and Primitive Art. London: 1969. V. 46

PERIER, G.

The Life of Mr. Paschal, with His Letters Relating to the Jesuits. London: 1744. V. 38

PERILIUS, AUGUSTIN

Warhafftiger Abriess der Wundergeburt so Unter Eines Ehrenvesten und Hochweisen Rahts der Koniglichen Stadt Zittaw Botmassigkeit zu Drausendorff sich Erenget den 12 Augusti Newes Calenders Anno 1618. Zittau: 1618. V. 45

PERILS of the Ocean, or Disasters of the Seas. New York: 1820. V. 39

PERIM, DAMIAO DE FROES

Theatro Heroino . . . Lisbon: 1736. V. 46

PERING, RICHARD

A Brief Enquiry into the Causes of Premature Decay, in Our Wooden Bulwarks, with an Examination of the Means, Best Calculated to Prolong Their Duration. Plymouth Dock: 1812. V. 41; 43; 45

A Brief Enquiry into the Causes of premature Decay, in our Wooden Bulwarks, with an Examination of the Means, best calculated to Prolong their Duration. London: 1812. V. 37

A Treatise on the Anchor, Shwing How the Component Parts Should be Combined to obtain the Greatest Power, and Most Pefect Holding, with a Table of Dimensions . . . Plymouth Dock: 1819. V. 38

PERINGUEY, L.

Descriptive Catalogue of the Coleoptera of South Africa. Cape Town: 1900. V. 37

PERISH Credit!! Perish Commerce!! Grand Travelling Tory Celebration. ?Haverhill: 1833? V. 39

PERKINS, AUGUSTUS T.

A Sketch of the Life and List of Some of the Works of John Singleton Copley. Boston: 1873. V. 39

PERKINS, BENJAMIN D.

The Efficacy of Perkins's Patent Metallic Tractors, in Topical Diseases, on the Human Body, and Animals . . . London: 1800. V. 43

Experiments with the Metallic Tractos in Rheumatic and Gouty Affections, Inflammations and Various Tropical Diseases . . . London: 1799. V. 42; 43

PERKINS, CHARLES C.

Italian Sculptors: Being a History of Sculpture in Northern, Southern and Eastern Italy. London: 1868. V. 46

Tuscan Sculptors, Their Lives, Works and Times. London: 1864. V. 44

PERKINS, CHARLES ELLIOTT

The Pinto Horse. Santa Barbara: 1927. V. 38; 42; 43

The Pinto Horse . . . Santa Barbara: 1937. V. 38; 44

PERKINS, D. A. W.

History of Osceola County, Iowa. Sioux Falls: 1892. V. 46

History of O'Brien County, Iowa from Its Organization to the Present Time. Sioux Falls: 1897. V. 38

PERKINS, DOUG

Brave Men and Cold Steel: a History of Range Detectives and Their Peacemakers. Fort Worth: 1984. V. 42

PERKINS, EDITH FORBES

Letters and Journals of . . . 1908-1925. Cambridge: 1931. V. 42

Letters and Journal of Edith Forbes Perkins 1908-1925. N.P.: 1931. V. 37

PERKINS, EDWARD T.

Na Motu: or, Reef-Rovings in the South Seas. New York: 1854. V. 37; 38

PERKINS, FRANCIS BEECHER 1828-1899

Scrope; or, the Lost Library. Boston: 1874. V. 37; 42

PERKINS, FREDERIC B.

Scrope; or, the Lost Library, a Novel of New York and Hartford. Boston: 1874. V. 46

PERKINS, GEORGE A.

Early Times on the Susquehanna. Binghampton: 1870. V. 37

PERKINS, HENRY

A Catalogue of the very valuable and important Library formed by the late Henry Perkins, Esq., at the beginning of the present century and comprising many splendid illuminated manuscripts . . . (London): (1873). V. 37

The Perkins Library. A Catalogue of the Very Valuable and Important Library . . . 1873. V. 39

PERKINS, JACOB

Perkins & Fairman's Running Hand Stereographic Copies. 'Patent Steel Plates'. Newburyport: 1810. V. 46

PERKINS, JAMES

A Tour Round the Globe. Letters to the 'City Press'. London: 1891. V. 39; 42

PERKINS, JAMES H.

Annals of the West. St. Louis: 1850. V. 37; 38; 39; 45; 46

PERKINS, JOHN d.1545

A Profitable Booke of Master John Perkins, Fellow of the Inner Temple, Treating of the Lawes of England. Londoni: 1601. V. 46

A Profitable Booke of Master John Perkins, Fellowe of the Inner Temple. London: 1856. V. 46

A Profitable Booke of Mast. John Perkins, Fellow the Inner Temple. London: 1621. V. 40

A Profitable Booke Treating of the Lawes of England. London: 1567. V. 40

A Profitable Booke Treating of the Lawes of England. London: 1642. V. 40

A Profitable Booke Treating of the Lawes of England. London: 1827. V. 40

PERKINS, JOSEPH

An Oration Upon Genius, Pronounced at the Anniversary Commencement of Harvard University, in Cambridge, July 19, 1797. Boston: 1797. V. 37

PERKINS, JULIA ANN SHEPARD 1799-1884

Early Times on the Susquehanna. Binghamton: 1870. V. 39

PERKINS, JUSTIN

A Residence of Eight Years in Persia, Among the Nestorian Christians. Andover: 1843. V. 39

PERKINS, MARY

Old Houses of Ancient Town of Norwich, 1660-1800. Norwich: 1895. V. 46

PERKINS, P. D.

Lafcadio Hearn: A Bibliography of His Writings. Boston: 1934. V. 38

Lafcadio Hearn, a Bibliography . . . Tokyo: 1934. V. 39

PERKINS, SAMUEL

A History of the Political and Military Events of the late War Between the United States and Great Britian. New Haven: 1825. V. 46

A New Alamanack and Prognostication, for the Yeere . . . 1636. London: 1635. V. 39

PERKINS, SIMEON

The Diary of Simeon Perkins. Toronto: 1948. V. 37; 39; 44; 45

The Diary of Simeon Perkins, 1780-89. Toronto: 1958. V. 39; 45

The Diary of Simeon Perkins 1780-1812. Toronto: 1958/61/67/78. V. 44

The Diary of Simeon Perkins, 1790-96. Toronto: 1960. V. 45

The Diary of Simeon Perkins. 1797-1803. Toronto: 1967. V. 45

The Diary of Simeon Perkins 1804-12. Toronto: 1978. V. 41; 44; 45

PERKINS, W. E.

Catalogue of the Walter Frank Perkins Agricultural Library. Southampton: 1961. V. 46

PERKINS, W. T.

Channel Tunnel: Deputation to the Prime Minister. London: 1913. V. 40

PERKOIS and Prins Verzameling van Verschillende Gekleede Mans-en Vrouwenstanded . . . Amsterdam: 1836. V. 44

PERKS, J. HARTLEY, MRS.

From Heather Hills. London: 1887. V. 41

PERLES, ALFRED

My Friend Henry Miller. London: 1955. V. 44

PERLESVAUS

The High History of the Holy Graal. London: 1903. V. 43

PERLEY, JEREMIAH

The Debates, Resolutions and Other Proceedings, of the Convention of Delegates, Assembled at Portland on the 11th and Continued Until the 29th Day of October, 1819 . . . Portland: 1820. V. 41; 42

PERNETY, ANTOINE JOSEPH

The History of a Voyage to the Malouine (or Falkland) Islands, Made in 1763 and 1764 . . . London: 1771. V. 38; 41

Journal fait aux Isles Malouines en 1763 & 1764, Pour les Reconnoitre, & y Former un Etablissement . . . Berlin: 1769. V. 39

THE PERNICIOUS Principles of Tom Paine, Exposed, In an Address to Labourers and Mechanics. London: 1793? V. 39

PERODI, P.

Memoirs of the Reign of Murat, In Which the Circumstances of the Confiscation of the American Vessesl, His Last Campaign and Death, and the Characters of His Generals and Courtiers, are Fully Displayed. Boston: 1818. V. 39

PERON, FRANCOIS

Voyage de Decouvertes aux Terres Australes. Paris: 1807-16. V. 40

PERON, PIERRE F.

Memoires du Capitaine Peron, sur ses Voyages aux Cotes d'Afrique, en Arabie, a l'ile d'Amsteram, aux Iles d'Anjouan et de Mayotte . . . Paris: 1824. V. 38; 41

PEROTTUS, NICOLAUS

In Hoc Uolumine Habentur Haec. Cornucopiae, Siue Linguae Latinae Commentarij Diligentissime Recogniti. Colophon: 1513. V. 37

PEROUSE, J. F. G. DE LA

A Voyage Round the World, in the Years 1785, 1786, 1787 and 1788 . . . London: 1798. V. 38

PERPETUAL Supplies to the State: By Annuities and Eversions . . . London: 1760. V. 41; 42

THE PERQUISITE-MONGER: or the Rise and Fall of Ingratitude. London: 1712. V. 39

PERRAULT, CHARLES 1628-1703

Le Barbe Bleue et la Belle au Bois Dormant. Paris: 1887. V. 41

Cinderella. London;: 1815. V. 37

Les Contes. Paris: 1883. V. 46

Deux Contes de Ma Mere L'Oye: La Belle Au Bois Dormant & Le Petit Chaperon Rouge. 1899. V. 41

Deux Contes de ma Mere Loye. La Belle au Bois Dormant & Le Petit Chaperon Rouge. 1989. V. 45

The Fairy Tales of . . . New York. V. 45

The Fairy Tales. London: 1922. V. 43

Festiva ad Capita Annulumque Decursio, a Rege Ludovico XIV Principibus Summisque Aulae Proceribus Edita Anno MDCLXII. Paris: 1670. V. 37

Histoire de Peau d'Ane. Hammersmith: 1902. V. 44; 45; 46

Histoire de Peau D'ane. London: 1902. V. 43; 46

Les Hommes Illustres qui on Paru en France Pendant ce Siecle, Avec Leurs Portraits au Naturel. Paris: 1696-1700. V. 39; 40; 45

Labyrinte de Versailles. Le Haye: 1724. V. 40

Memoirs for a Natural History of Animals. London: 1688. V. 37

Perrault's Popular Tales. Oxford: 1888. V. 42

Perrault's Tales of Mother Goose. New York: 1956. V. 39

Riquet a La Houppe. Hammersmith: 1907. V. 39; 41

Tales of Passed Times Written for Children by Mr. Perrault. London: 1922. V. 43; 44

Tales of Passed Times Written for Children . . . N.P.: 1922. V. 46

Tom Thumb at the Ogre's House; The Wife of Bluebeard &c. London: 1934. V. 44

PERRAULT, CLAUDE

Essais de Physique, Ou Recueil de Plusieurs Traitez Touchant les Choses Naturelles. Paris: 1680, 1688. V. 37

Memoirs for a Natural History of Animals . . . London: 1701. V. 43

Memoirs from a Natural History of Animals. London: 1702. V. 37; 43

Memoirs for a Natural History of Animals. Containing the Anatomical Descriptions of Several Creatures Dissected by Royal Academy of Sciences at Paris Englished by Alexander Pitfield . . . To which is added an Account of the . . . London: 1688. V. 37

A Treatise of the Five Orders of Columns in Architecture . . . London: 1722. V. 38

PERRAULT, NICHOLAS

The Jesuits Morals. London: 1670. V. 39

PERRAY, BROSSAY DU

Historical Remarks on the Castle of the Bastille. Translated from the French published in 1774. The Second Edition. London: 1784. V. 37

PERRIE, GEORGE W.

Buckskin Mose; or, Life from the Lakes to the Pacific, as Actor, Circus Rider, Detective, Ranger, Gold Digger, Indian Scots, and Guide. New York: 1873. V. 40; 45; 46

PERRIN, ALICE

Into Temptation. London: 1894. V. 37

PERRIN DU LAC, FRANCOIS MARIE 1766-1824

Perrin Du Lac's Reise in die Beyden Louisianen unter die Wilden Volkerschaften am Missouri, Durch die Vereinigten Staaten und die Provinzen am Ohio, in den Jahren 1801, 1802, und 1803. Wien: 1807. V. 43

Reise in Die Beyden Louisianen Unter die Wilden Volkerschaften am Missouri, Durch die Vereinigeten Staaten und die Provinzen am Ohio, in Den Jahren 1801, 1802 und 1803 . . . Leipzig: 1807. V. 38; 41; 43

Travels through the Two Louisianas, and Among the Savage Nations of the Missouri. London: 1807. V. 40; 41

Voyage dans les Deux Louisianes, et Chez les Nations Sauvages du Missouri, par les Etats-Unis, L'Ohio et les Provinces qui le Bordent, en 1801, 1802, et 1803. Paris: 1805. V. 38; 39; 41

PERRIN, FRANCOIS

Cent Et Qvatre Qvatraines de Qvatrains. (with) Petites Prieres a l'Imitation de Celles . . . Lyons: 1587. V. 42

PERRIN, IDA SOUTHWELL ROBINS 1860-

British Flowering Plants. London: 1914. V. 37; 41; 44; 46

PERRIN, JEAN BAPTISTE

The Elements of Conversation in Three Languages, French, Italian and English . . . Leghorn: 1823. V. 37

PERRIN, JEAN PAUL

Luther's Fore-Runners or a Cloud of Witnesses, Deposing for the Protestant Faith. London: 1624. V. 41

PERRIN, JOHN

Instructive and Entertaining Exercises with the Rules of the French Syntax. Philadelphia: 1786. V. 45

PERRIN, WILLIAM HENRY

History of Stark County, with an Outline Sketch of Ohio. Chicago: 1881. V. 46

PERRING, F. H.

Atlas of the British Flora. London: 1962. V. 41

PERRON, JACQUES

The Reply of . . . Cardinal Peron, To the Answeare of the Most Excellent King of Great Britaine the First Tome. 1630. V. 45

PERRONET, JEAN RUDOLPHE

Description des Projets et de la Construction des Ponts de Neuilly de Mantes, d'Orleans & Autres . . . Paris: 1782/83/89. V. 38; 42; 46

PERROT, GEORGES

A History of Art in Ancient Egypt. London: 1883. V. 37; 40; 43; 44

A History of Art in Chaldaea and Assyria. London: 1884. V. 37; 40; 42; 44

History of Art in Phoenicia and Its Dependencies from the French . . . London: 1885. V. 37; 45

History of Art in Sardinia, Judaea, Syria and Asia Minor. London: 1890. V. 40; 44

History of Art in Phrygia, Lydia, Caria and Lycia. London: 1892. V. 44

PERROTT, CHARLOTTE LOUISA EMILY

A Selection of British Birds. London: 1979. V. 40

A Selection of British Birds. Ilkley: 1979. V. 37; 38

PERRY, GEORGE

Conchology, or the Natural History of Shells. London: 1810-11. V. 42

Conchology, or the Natural History of Shells. London: 1811. V. 38; 39; 43; 45

PERRY, GEORGE SESSIONS

Hold Autumn in Your Hand. New York: 1941. V. 40; 41

PERRY, J. R.

The Art of Stair Building, with Original Improvements . . . New York: 1855. V. 43

PERRY, JAMES

The Electric Eel; or, Gymnotus Electricus. London. V. 45

The Electrical Eel; or, Gymnotes Electricus. London: 1777. V. 40

PERRY, JOHN 1670-1732

An Account of the Stopping of Daggenham Breach . . . London: 1721. V. 42

The State of Russia Under the Present Czar . . . London: 1716. V. 38; 39; 40; 42; 43

PERRY, JOHN D.

The Union Pacific Railway (Eastern Division), or (Kansas Pacific Railway). Economy to the Government. Washington: 1868. V. 37

PERRY, JOSEPH

A Sermon Before the General Assembly of the Colony of Connecticut on the Day of Their Anniversary Election May 11, 1775. Hartford: 1775. V. 37; 42; 43; 45

PERRY, M. S.

Message of the Governor of Florida Submitted to the Adjourned Session of the General Assembly November 28, 1859. N.P.: 1859. V. 45

PERRY, MARSDEN J.

A Chronological List of the Books Printed at the Kelmscott Press, etc. Boston: 1928. V. 38

PERRY, MATTHEW CALBRAITH 1794-1858

Narrative of the Expedition of American Squadron to the China Seas and Japan, Performed in the Years 1852, 1853 and 1854. New York: 1856. V. 38; 39; 40; 41; 45; 46

Narrative of the Expedition of an American Squadron to the China Seas and Japan. Washington: 1856. V. 38; 42; 46

Narrative of the Expeditions of an American Squadron to the China Seas and Japan, Performed in the Years 1852, 1853 and 1854 . . . . New York: 1857. V. 40

PERRY, NORA

Another Flock of Girls. Boston: 1890. V. 41

PERRY NURSEY CO.

The Perry Handbook of Choice New Fruits, Ornamentals, Roses, Shrubs, Hardy Perennials, Bulbs, etc. Rochester: 1898. V. 38

PERRY, OLVIER HAZARD

Hunting Expeditions of Oliver Hazard Perry of Cleveland, from His Diaries. Cleveland: 1899. V. 38

PERRY, OTLEY LANE

Rank and Badges, Dates of Formation, Naval and Military Distinctions, Precedence, Salutes, Colours and Small Arms in Her Majesty's Army and Navy and Auxiliary Forces, Including a Record of the Naval and Military Forces in the Different Counties . . . London: 1888. V. 41

PERRY, RICHARD

The Jeannette: and a Complete and Authentic Narrative Encycopedia of All Voyages and Expeditions to the North Polar Region. Chicago: 1882. V. 40

PERRY, SAMPSON 1747-1823

A Disquisition of the Stone and Gravel. London: 1785. V. 40

PERRY, T. M.

Drawings by William Westall. London: 1962. V. 39; 42

PERRY, THOMAS

The Butcher's Boy. New York: 1982. V. 46

PERRY, WIILLIAM

The Royal Standard English Dictionary. Brookfield: 1801. V. 39

PERRY, WILLIAM

The Only Sure Guide to The English Tongue. Brookfield: 179?. V. 38

The Royal Standard English Dictionary. Edinburgh: 1793. V. 38

The Royal Standard English Dictionary. Worcester: 1788. V. 37

PERRY, WILLIAM S.

Historical Collections Relating to the American Colonial Church. Volume 2. Hartford: 1871. V. 42

PERRYMAN, ELISHA

A Sketch of the Life, Labors and Adventures of Elder Elisha Perryman: Prepared From His Own Notes . . . Augusta: 1856. V. 44

PERS, CIRO DI

Poesie. Vicenza: 1666. V. 37

PERS, DIRCK PIERTERSZOON

Bellerophon, of Lust Tot Wysheit, Door Sinne-Beelden Leerlijck Vertoont . . . Waer by Noch Konnen Gebonden Worden . . . Amsterdam: 1669. V. 46

PERSEPOLIS Illustrata; or, the Ancient and Royal Palace of Persepolis in Persia. London: 1739. V. 38

PERSHING, JOHN J.

Final Report of General John J. Pershing Commander-in-Chief American Expeditonary Forces. Washington: 1920. V. 42

My Experiences in the World War. New York: 1931. V. 39; 46

THE PERSIAN and Turkish Tales, Complet. London: 1767. V. 43; 46

PERSIAN Fairy Tales. Mount Vernon: 1930. V. 41

THE PERSIAN Flower: A Memoir of Judith Grant Perkins of Oroomiah, Persia. Boston: 1853. V. 38

PERSIAN Tales, or the Thousand and One Days. London: 1800. V. 40; 45

PERSIUS, AULUS FLACCUS

Aulus Flaccus Persius Cum Glosis Scipionis Ferrarii Georgii filii de Monte Ferrato . . . S.l., s.d., but Venice: 1501. V. 46

A New and Literal Translation of the Satires. Dublin: 1795. V. 37; 42

PERSIUS FLACCUS, AULUS

The Satires of Persius. Dublin: 1827. V. 45

The Satires of Persius. Dublin: 1728. V. 37

A Prosaic Translation of Aulus Persius Flaccus's Six Satyrs. London: 1719. V. 45

PERSON, CLAUDE

Elements of Anatomy and the Animal Oeconomy. London: 1781. V. 41

PERSON, DAVID

Varieties; or, a Surveigh of Rare and Excellent Manners, Necessary and Delectable for All Sorts of Persons. London: 1635. V. 40

PERSON, LUDWIG

Oratio De Witteberga. Wittenberg: 1602. V. 40

A PERSONAL and Confidential Letter to Fanny Hill from the Keeper of the Bedchamber Upon Her Leaving Him to go Under the Care of the Roxburghe Club, December 1929. San Francisco;: 1930. V. 40

THE PERSONAL Philosophers of 23 Eminent Men and Women of Our Time, Entitled 'I Believe'. London: 1940. V. 41

PERSONAL Relics of British Heroes. A Series of Water Colour Drawings by William Gibb. The Descriptive Notes by Richard R. Holmes and an Introduction by F.M. Viscount Wolseley. London: 1896. V. 37

PERSONS, ROBERT

De Persecutione Anglicana Libellus . . . Rome: 1582. V. 37

The Jesuit's memorial, for the Intended Reformation of the Church of England, Under Their First Popish Prince . . . London: 1690. V. 42

PERSOON, C. H.

Icones Pictae Rariorum Fungorum. Paris: 1803-05. V. 38

PERSSON, AXEL W.

New Tombs at Dendra Near Midea. Lund: 1942. V. 40; 44

PERTELOTE. a Sequel to Chanticleer. Being a Bibliography of the Golden Cockerel Press October 1936-1943 April. Waltham St. Lawrence: 1943. V. 45

PERTHIUS, M. DE

Traite d'Architecture Rurale . . . Orne de Vingt-Six Grandes Planches en Taille-Douce. Paris: 1810. V. 42

PERTINENT and Impertinent: an Assortment of Verse. Ditchling: 1926. V. 40; 43
PERTINENT and Impertinent. An Assortment of Verse. London: 1926. V. 37

PERTUSIER, CHARLES

Picturesque Promenades in and Near Constantinople, and on the Waters of the Bosphorus. London: 1820. V. 37

Promenades Pittoresques dans Constantinople et sur les Rives du Bosphore, Suivies d'une Notice sur la Dalmatie. Paris: 1815-17. V. 42

PERUTZ, MAX F.

Some Recent Advances in Molecular Biology. London: 1958. V. 46

PERVIGILIUM Veneris. The Hague: 1712. V. 37
PERVIGILIUM Veneris. Hammersmith: 1910. V. 39; 40; 44; 45; 46
PERVIGILIUM Veneris. London: 1910. V. 37

Pervigilium Veneris. 1910. V. 40

The Vigil of Venus. Waltham St. Lawrence: 1939. V. 41

Vigil of Venus. 1943. V. 42

The Vigil of Venus. Cummington: 1943. V. 38; 40; 41; 44

The Vigil of Venus. Cummington: 1948. V. 39

PERZON, PAUL 1639-1706

Antiquite de la Nation et de la Langue des Celtes. Paris: 1703. V. 38

PESSOA, FERNANDO

Antinous: a Poem. Lisbon: 1918. V. 45

PESTALOZZI, HEINRICH

An Die Unschuld, den ERnst und den Edelmuth Meines Zeitalters und Meines Vaterlandes. 1815. V. 43

An Die Unschuld, den Ernst und den Edelmuth Meines Zeitalters und Meines Vaterlandes. Iserten,: 1815. V. 39; 41

Anschauungslehre der Zahlenverhaltnisse. Erstes (und) Sweytes Heft. Zurich und Bern: 1803. V. 41; 43

Buch der Mutter. Erstes Heft. (all published). Zurich und Bern: 1803. V. 41; 43

PETAU, DENIS 1583-1652

Opus de Doctrina Temproum: Auctius in hac Nova Editione Notis & Emendationibus Quamplurimis . . . Antwerp: 1703. V. 44

Uranologion sive Systema Variorum Authorum, Qui de Sphaera, ac Sideribus, Eorumque Motibus Graece Commentati Sunt . . . Paris: 1630. V. 43

PETAU, DENYS 1588-1652

History of the World or an Account of Time (to 1659). London: 1659. V. 41

PETER, IRMGARD

Silk Ribbons of Basel. Kyoto: 1975. V. 39

PETER Piper's Practical Principles of Plain and Perfect Pronounciation. Brooklyn: 1936. V. 40

PETER Piper's Tales About China. Albany: 1846. V. 39

PETERIUS, BENEDICTUS

De Magia, de Observatione Somniorum, et de Divinatione Astrologica, Libri Tres. Coloniae: 1598. V. 40

PETERKIN, JULIA

Black April. Indianapolis: 1927. V. 39; 42

Bright Skin. Indianapolis: 1932. V. 37; 39; 41; 43; 45

Green Thursday. New York: 1924. V. 39

Roll, Jordan, Roll. New York: 1933. V. 45

Scarlet Sister Mary. Indianapolis: 1928. V. 42

PETERMANN, A.

Geographische Mittheilungen. Gotha: 1860-65. V. 45

PETERMANN, H.

Thesaurus s. Liber Magnus Vulgo 'Liber Adami' Appellatus Opus Mandaeorum Summi Ponderis Descriptisit et . . . Lipsiae: 1867. V. 44

PETERS, CARL

The Eldorado of the Ancients. London: 1902. V. 41

New Light on Dark Africa; Being the Narrative of the German Emin Pasha Expedition. Translated from the German by H.W. Dilcken. London: 1891. V. 37; 39

PETERS, DEWITT C.

Kit Carson's Life and Adventures, from Facts Narrated by Himself. Hartford: 1874. V. 38

The Life and Adventures of Kit Carson. New York: 1858. V. 37; 39; 40; 41

The Life and Adventures of Kit Carson, the Nestor of the Rocky Mountains, from Facts Narrated by Himself. New York: 1859. V. 37

PETERS, E.

Crocodile on the Sandbank. 1975. V. 46

PETERS, ELIZABETH

A Morbid Taste for Bones. London: 1977. V. 45

PETERS, FRED J.

Clipper Ship Prints Including Other Merchant Sailing Ships by N. Currier and Currier and Ives . . . New York: 1930. V. 41; 42; 46

Railroad Indian and Pioneer Prints by Currier & Ives, Being a Pictorial Check List and Collation. New York: 1930. V. 38; 39; 40

PETERS, G. F.

A Treatise on Equitation, or the Art of Horsemanship, Simplified Progressively for Amateurs . . . London: 1835. V. 39

PETERS, HARRY TWYFORD

America on Stone. Garden City: 1931. V. 39; 40; 46

America on Stone. New York: 1931. V. 38; 44; 45

America on Stone . . . A Chronicle of American Lithography Other than That of Currier & Ives. New York & Garden City: 1931. V. 40

America on Stone. New York: 1976. V. 38; 40; 43

California on Stone. Garden City: 1935. V. 37; 38; 39; 43; 46

California on Stone. New York: 1935. V. 37; 41; 44; 46

California on Stone. New York: 1976. V. 37; 38; 40; 41; 42; 43; 44

Currier & Ives: Printemakers to the American People. Garden City: 1929. V. 39

Currier & Ives: Printmakers to the American People. New York: 1976. V. 37; 41; 42; 43; 44; 46

PETERS, HERMANN

Pictorial History of Ancient Pharmacy. Chicago: 1899. V. 38

Pictorial History of Ancient Pharmacy; with Sketches of Early Medical Practice. Chicago: 1902. V. 42

PETERS, HUGH

Dying Fathers Last Legacy to an Onely Child or Mr. Hugh Parker's Advice to His Daughter. London: 1660. V. 38

PETERS, J. L.

Check-List of Birds of the World. Volume 16: Comprehensive Index. Cambridge: 1987. V. 37; 38

Checklist of Birds of the World. Volume XI. Sylviidae to Eopsaltriidae. Cambridge: 1986. V. 37

Check-List of Birds of the World. Cambridge: 1931-70. V. 39

PETERS, JOHN C.

A Treatise on Headaches; Including Acute, Chronic, Nervous, Gastric, Dyspeptic or Sick-Headaches . . . New York: 1853. V. 43

A Treatise on the Origin, Nature, Prevention and Treatment of Asiatic Cholera. New York: 1866. V. 40

PETERS, JOHN PUNNETT

Nippur or Explorations and Adventures on the Euphrates. New York: 1897. V. 39

Nippur, or Explorations and Adventures on the Euphrates. New York: 1898-99. V. 40; 44

Nippur, or Explorations and Adventures on the Euphrates. New York: 1904. V. 45

PETERS, JOHN R.

Guide to, or Descriptive Catalogue of the Chinese Museum, in the Marlboro' Chapel, Boston, with Miscellaneous Remarks Upon the Government, History, Religions, Literature, Agriculture, Arts, Trades, Manners and Customs of the Chinese. Boston: 1845. V. 39

Miscellaneous Remarks Upon the Government, History, Religions, Literature, Agriculture, Arts, Trades, Manners and Customs of the Chinese . . . New York: 1849. V. 40

PETERS, SAMUEL A.

A General History of Connecticut . . . London: 1781. V. 38

PETERS, WILLIAM J.

The Ziegler Polar Expedition 1903-1905. Washington: 1907. V. 45

PETERSEN, CARL

Each in Its Ordered Place: A Faulkner Collector's Notebook. Ann Arbor: 1975. V. 39; 45

PETERSEN, K

The Saga of Norwegian Shipping, an Outline of the History, Growth and Development of a Modern Merchant marine, tracing the activities of Norway's seafarers from early days of sail and Continental Trading, through the age of discovery to . . . Oso: 1955. V. 37

PETERSEN, WILLIAM F.

The Patient and the Weather. Ann Arbor: 1934-38. V. 44

PETERSEN, WILLIAM J.

Steamboating on the Upper Mississippi: The Water Way to Iowa, Some River History. Iowa City: 1937. V. 38; 42; 44

PETERSON, CYRUS A.

Pilot Knob, The Thermopylae of the West. New York: 1914. V. 37

PETERSON, DANIEL H.

The Looking Glass: Being a True Report and Narrative of the Life, Travels and Labors of a Colored Clergyman . . . New York: 1854. V. 43

PETERSON, FREDERICK

A Text-Book of Legal Medicine and Toxicology. Philadelphia: 1903. V. 41

PETERSON, FREDERICK A.

Military Review of the Campaign in Virginia and Maryland Under Gen. Fremont, Banks . . . McClellan and Burnside, in 1862, Part II. New York: 1862. V. 38; 39

Military Review of the Campaign in Virignia and Maryland . . . in 1862. New York: 1862-63. V. 39; 42

PETERSON, JOSEPH

The Raree Show; or, The Fox Trap't. York: 1739. V. 41

PETERSON, MATTIE J.

Little Pansy. Wilmington: 1890. V. 38

PETERSON, ROGER TORY

A Field Guide to the Birds. Boston: 1980. V. 44

A Field Guide to the Birds. Boston: 1981. V. 37

PETERSON, SUSAN

The Living Tradition of Maria Martinez. Tokyo, New York & San: 1977. V. 41

PETHERICK, JOHN

Egypt, the Soudan and Central Africa With Explorations from Khartoum on the White Nile to the Regions of the Equator Being Sketches from Sixteen Years' Travel. London: 1861. V. 40; 43; 45

PETIEVICH, GERALD

Money Men and One Shot Deal. V. 44

PETION DE VILLENEUVE, JEROME

Oeuvres. Paris: 1792-93. V. 39

PETIOT, E. A.

Mascarade a la Grecque. Parma: 1771. V. 37

PETIS DE LA CROIX, FRANCOIS 1653-1713

The History of Genghizcan the Great, First Emperor of the Antient Moguls and Tartars. London: 1722. V. 41; 45

Persian Tales, or the Thousand and One Days. London: 1800. V. 39; 40

Persian and Turkish Tales. From the French of . . . London: 1809. V. 41

PETIT, ARMAND

Projet de Ferme, Offert a la Societe d'Agriculture de Seine-et-Oise. 1849. V. 38

PETIT DE JULLEVILLE, LOUIS 1841-1900

Histoire de la Langue et de la Litterature Francaise des Origines a 1900. Paris: 1896-98. V. 46

PETIT, G.

Lex Parliamentiaria; or, a Treatise of the Law and Custom of the Parliaments of England . . . London: 1698. V. 38; 40

PETIT, GULIELMUS

Historia sive Chronica Rerum Anglicarum, Libris Quinque . . . Oxonii: 1719. V. 39

PETIT, JEAN LOUIS

L'Art de Guerir les Maladies des Os. Paris: 1705. V. 42

PETIT, PETRI PIERRE

De Amazonibus Dissertatio, Qus an vere Exiterint, Necne, Variis Ultro Citroque Conjecturis & Argumentis Disputatur. Parisiorum: 1685. V. 46

PETIT, PIERRE

De Amazonibus Dissertatio. Amsterdam: 1687. V. 37

Selectorvm Poematum Libri Duo: Accessit Dissertation De Furore Poetico. Paris: 1683. V. 37

PETIT, VICTOR

Habitations Champetres Recueil de Maisons, Villas, Chalets, Pavillons, Kiosques, Parcs et Jardins. Paris: 1840. V. 46

PETITOT, E.

Traditions Indiennes du Canada Nord-Quest. Paris: 1886. V. 37

PETITOT, E. A.

Mascarade a la Grecque. Parma: 1771. V. 37

PETIVER, JAMES

Gazophylacii Naturae & Artis Decas Prima. London: 1702. V. 39

PETO, SAMUEL MORTON 1809-1889

The Resources and Prospects of America Acertained During a Visit to the States in the Autumn of 1865. London: 1865. V. 39

The Resources and Prospects of America, Ascertained During a Visit to the States in the Autumn of 1865. London: 1866. V. 38; 40; 41; 42

The Resources and Prospects of America Ascertained During a Visit to the States in the Autumn of 1865. London & New York: 1866. V. 38

PETRAKIS, HARRY MARK

Chapter Seven: From the Hour of the Bell, a Novel Concerning the Greek War of Independence. (Mt. Horeb): 1976. V. 37; 42; 44

PETRARCA, FRANCESCO 1304-1374

The Ascent of Mount Ventoux. A Letter from Petrarch. New York: 1989. V. 46

Chronica delle Vite de Pontefici et Imperatori Romani. Venice: 1507. V. 37

Le Cose Volgari. Venice: 1501. V. 41

Fifteen Sonnets of Petrarch. Boston: 1903. V. 37; 41

Il Petrarca. Lyon: 1545. V. 41

Il Petrarca. Venice: 1546. V. 38; 44

Il Petrarca. Lyon: 1550. V. 45

Il Petrarca. Con la Dichiaratione del Vero Giorno del Suo Innamoramento. Lyon: 1564. V. 45

Il Petrarca Di Nuovo, Ristampato et di Bellisime Figure Adornato, e Diligentemente Corretto, Con Argomenti di Pietro Petracci. Venice: 1638. V. 39

Il Petrarca Nuovamente, Ristampato e Diligentemente Corretto. Venice: 1624. V. 39

Il Petrarcha. Venice: 1521. V. 38

Il Petrarcha. and Il Trionfi. Venice: 1553. V. 38

Il Petrarcha. Con l'Espositione d'Alessandro Vellutello di Novo Ristampato con le Figure a i Triomphi, e con Piu Cose Utili in Varii Luoghi Aggiunte. Venice: 1545. V. 45

Il Petrarcha Con l'Espositione d'Alessandro Velvtello. Venice: 1550. V. 42

PETRARCA, FRANCESCO 1304-1374 continued

Los Sonetos y Canciones del Poeta Francisco Petrarcha que Traduzia Henrique Garces de Lengua Thoscana en Castellana. Madrid: 1591. V. 37

Opera Latina. Librorum Francisci Petrarchae Impressorum Annotatio. Venice: 1503. V. 41

Opera. 1533. V. 44

Opera de Rimedi de l'Una et l'Altra Fortuna. Venice: 1549. V. 40

(Opera) con la Spositione di M. Giovanni Andrea Gesualdo. Venice: 1553. V. 37

Opera. Basel: 1581. V. 39

Opera con l'Espositione di M. Gio. Andrea Gesualdo. Venice: 1582. V. 37

Opvs De Remediis Vtrivsqz Fortvnae. Venice. V. 38

Phisicke Against Fortune, as Well Prosperous, as Adverse. London: 1579. V. 44

De Remediis Utriusque Fortunae. Cremona: 1492. V. 45

Rime. Venice: 1546. V. 37

Le Rime . . . (with) Dissertazione Istorica e Critica sull Vita Di Francesco Petrarca, e su Quella Di Madonna Laura. London: 1811. V. 39

Le Rime del Petrarca con TAvole in rime ed Illustrazione. Firenze: 1821. V. 46

Select Sonnets of Petrarch. Dublin: 1822. V. 40

The Sonnets. New York: 1965. V. 38; 41; 44

The Sonnets of Petrarch. N.P.: 1965. V. 43

The Sonnets of Petrarch. N.P.: 1965. V. 41

The Sonnets of Petrarch. Verona: 1965. V. 37; 39; 43

The Triumphs of Francesco Petrarch. Boston: 1906. V. 46

The Triumphs . . . Florence: 1906. V. 39

The Triumphs of Petrarch. 1928. V. 38

Twenty-Six Sonnets of Ye Divine Poet M. Francesco Petrarca. Shaftesbury: 1929. V. 41

PETRE, HENRY WILLIAM

An Account of the Settlements of New Zealand Company. London: 1841. V. 38; 41

PETREUS, HENRICUS

Carmen de Ioannis Wilhelmi, Ducis Saxoniae Reditu Felici ex Gallia. Jena: 1568. V. 38

PETRIDES, PAUL

L'Oeuvre Complete de Maurice Utrillo. Paris: 1959-74. V. 46

PETRIE, GEORGE

Eccesiastical Architecture of IReland. Dublin: 1845. V. 37; 43; 44; 46

General James Henry Lane, 1833-1907. Auburn: 1946. V. 44

Ireland Illustrated from Original Drawings by G. Petrie and Others . . . London: 1840. V. 43

The Petrie Collection of the Ancient Music of Ireland. Arranged for the piano-forte. Volume I. Dublin: 1855. V. 37; 43; 44; 45

Picturesque Sketches of Some of the Finest Landscape and Coast Scenery of Ireland. Dublin: 1835. V. 41

PETRIE, WILLIAM MATHEW FLINDERS 1853-1942

Stonehenge: Plans, Descriptions, and Theories. London: 1880. V. 37

PETRIE, WILLIAM MATTHEW FLINDERS 1853-1942

Abydos. Parts I-II (only). V. 44

Abydos. London: 1902-03. V. 40; 42

Abydos Parts I-III. London: 1902-04. V. 42; 44

Amulets: Illustrated by the Egyptian Collection in the University College, London. London: 1914. V. 39

Ancient Egypt. London: 1914. V. 46

Ancient Gaza I: Tel el Ajjul. London: 1931. V. 37; 40; 42

Ancient Gaza I-V. London: 1931-52. V. 44

Ancient Gaza II: Tell el Ajjul. London: 1932. V. 37

Ancient Gaza IV, Tell El Ajjul. London: 1934. V. 37

Anthedon, Sinai. London: 1937. V. 44

Athribis. London: 1908. V. 44

Beth-Pelet I (tell Fara) . . . London: 1930. V. 37; 44

Beth-pelet I-II (complete). London: 1930-32. V. 44

Ceremonial Slate Palettes. (and) Corpus of Proto-Dynastic Pottery. London: 1953. V. 42; 44

Corpus of Prehistoric Pottery and Palettes. London: 1921. V. 37; 44

Decorative Patterns of Ancient World. London: 1930. V. 40; 42; 44

Dendereh 1898. London: 1900. V. 40; 42

Descriptive Sociology; or Groups of Sociological Facts, Classified and Arranged by Herbert Spencer. London: 1925. V. 44

Diospolis Parva. The Cemeteries of Abadiyeh and Hu, 1898-9. London: 1901. V. 40; 42

Egyptian Architecture. London: 1938. V. 40; 44

The Formation of the Alphabet. London: 1912. V. 40; 42; 44

The Funeral Furniture of Egypt. (with) Stone and Metal Vases. London: 1937. V. 44

Gerar. London: 1928. V. 37; 40

Gizeh and Rifeh (Double Volumes). London: 1907. V. 37; 40

The Hawara Portfolio: Paintings. London: 1913. V. 37; 40; 44

Heliopolis Kafr Ammar and Shurafa. London: 1915. V. 37; 44

Historical Scarabs: a series of drawings from the principal collections. Arranged chronologically. London: 1889. V. 37

A History of Egypt. London: 1898-1913. V. 40; 42; 44

Hyksos & Israelite Cities. London: 1906. V. 40; 42; 44

Illahun, Kahun and Gurob. 1889-90. London: 1891. V. 42; 44

Inductive Metrology; or, the Recovery of Ancient Measures from the Monuments. London: 1877. V. 42; 44

Kahun, Gurob and Hawara. London: 1890. V. 44

Koptos. London: 1896. V. 37; 42; 44

The Labyrinth, Gerzeh and Mazghuneh. London: 1912. V. 44

Medum. London: 1892. V. 44

Memphis I. London: 1909. V. 40

Memphis I-VI. London: 1909-15. V. 42; 44

Meydum and Memphis (III). London: 1910. V. 40

Naqada and Ballas. London: 1896. V. 40; 44

Naukratis. London: 1886-88. V. 37; 40; 42; 44

Objects of Daily Use. London: 1927. V. 44

The Palace of Apries (Memphis II). London: 1909. V. 40

Prehistoric Egypt Illustrated by Over 1000 Objects in University College, London. London: 1920. V. 37; 40; 42; 44

Qurneh. London: 1909. V. 44

Racial Photographs from the Egyptian Monuments (complete in itself). London: 1887. V. 37

Researches in Sinai. London: 1906. V. 37; 40; 42; 44

Roman Portraits and Memphis (IV). London: 1911. V. 37; 40; 42; 44

The Royal Tombs of the First Dynasty. London: 1900-01. V. 37; 40; 44

Scarabs and Cylinders with Names Illustrated by the Egyptian Collection in University College. London: 1917. V. 37; 40; 42; 44

A Season in Egypt 1887. London: 1887. V. 44

Sedment I-II. London: 1924. V. 37; 40; 42; 44

Tanis. London: 1885-88. V. 40; 42; 44

Tarkhan I and Memphis V. London: 1913. V. 40

Tarkhan I-II. London: 1913-14. V. 37; 40; 42; 44

Tell el Amarna. Warminster: 1974. V. 40; 44

Tombs of the Courtiers and Oxyrhynkhos. London: 1925. V. 37; 40; 42; 44

Tools and Weapons Illustrated by the Egyptian Collection in University College. London: 1917. V. 37; 40; 42; 44

PETROFF, IVAN

Preliminary Report on the Population and Resources of Alaska. Washington: 1881. V. 37

Report on the Population Industries and Resources of Alaska. Washington: 1884. V. 46

Report on the Population, Industries and Resources of Alaska. Washingotn: (1882)> V. 37

PETROFF, P.

Ante-Mortem Depositions of . . . San Francisco: 1895. V. 39; 42

PETRONIO, ALESSANDRO TRAJANO d. 1585

Del Viver delli Romani, et di Conservar la Sanita, Libri Cinque. Doue si Tratta del Sito di Roma, dell'Aria, de'Venti, delle Stagioni, dell'Acque, de'Vini, delle Carni, de'Pesci, de'Frutti, delle Herbe & di Tutte l'Altre Cose Pertinenti . . . Roma: 1592. V. 38; 39

De Victv Romanorvm et de Sanitate Tvenda Libri Qvinqve ad Gregorivm XIII. Romae: 1581. V. 38

PETRONIUS ARBITER

The Satyr of Titus Petronius Arbiter, a Roman Knight. London: 1694. V. 39

The Satyrical Works of Titus Pretronius Arbiter. London: 1708. V. 46

Satyricon. Amsterdam: 1677. V. 39

Satyricon, Johannes Boschius ad Scriptorum Exemplatium Fidem Castigavit & Notus Adjecit. Amsterdam: 1677-76. V. 39

Le Satyricon. Paris: 1951. V. 42; 43; 44

Titi Petronii Arbitri, Equitis Romani, Satyricon . . . Londini: 1711. V. 45

The Complete Works of . . . London. V. 39

The Complete Works of Gaius Petronius. London: 1927. V. 46

The Complete Works of . . . London: 1927. V. 39; 40; 41; 43

PETRONIUS, GAIUS

The Complete works of Gaius Petronius. Done Into English by Jack Lindsay. With one hundred illustrations by Norman Lindsay. London: n.d. V. 37

The Complete Works of . . . London. V. 40

The Complete Works of . . . 1927. V. 41

PETRUCCI, GIOSEFFO

Prodomo Apologetica alli Studi Chircheriani. Amsterdam: 1677. V. 40

PETRUS CHRYSOLOGUS, ST. 406-450

Sermones . . . Bologna: 1534. V. 43

PETRUS COMESTOR

Scholastica Historia Sacre Scripture. Strassburg: 1500. V. 42; 44

PETRUS DE VINEIS

Epistolarum Quibus Res Eius Gestae, Memoria Dignissimae, Historica Fide Describuntur . . . Libri Vi. Nunc Primum . . . Luce Donati, Accessit Hypomnena de Fide, Amicitia & Obsrvantia Pontificum Romanorum Erga Imperatores Germanicos . . . Basle: 1566. V. 37

Querimonia Friderici II Imp. qua se a Romano Pontifice & Caradinalibus Immerito Persecutum & Imperio Dejectum Esse Ostendit. Hagenau: 1529. V. 37

PETRUS RAVENNAS

Alphabetu Aureu Utriusqz Iuris . . . ac in Multis Auctu et Ampliatum per . . . Johanem Thierry . . . Lyon: 1517. V. 37

PETRY, ANN

Harriet Tubman. New York: 1955. V. 39

PETS and Playfellows. London: 1890. V. 40

PETTENGILL, RAY WALDRON 1885-

Letters from America 1776-1779. Being Letters of Brunswick, Hessian and Waldeck Officers with the British Armies During the Revolution. Boston: 1924. V. 40

PETTER, NICOLAES

Klare Onderrichtinge der Voortreffelijcke Worstel-konst, Verhandelende Hoemen in Alle Voorvallen van Twist in Handtgemeenschap, sich Kan Hoeden. Amsterdam: 1674. V. 40; 46

THE PETTICOAT. London: 1716. V. 40

PETTIE, GEORGE

A Petite Pallace of Pettie His Pleasure. London: 1908. V. 41

PETTIGREW, J. BELL

Animal Locomotion . . . New York: 1874. V. 43; 45

Animal Locomotion, or, Walking, Swimming, and Flying, with a Dissertation on Aeronautics. London: 1873. V. 37; 40; 42; 44; 45

Design in Nature Illustrated by Spiral and Other Arrangements. London: 1908. V. 37; 40

PETTIGREW, T. J.

Bibliotheca Sussexiana. London: 1827-39. V. 46

An Eulogy of John Coakley Lettsom . . . Late President of the Philosophical Society of London, Who Died Wednesday, November 1st. London: 1816. V. 42

PETTIGREW, THOMAS

On Supersitions Connected With the History and Practice of Medicine and Surgery. London: 1844. V. 42; 45

PETTIGREW, THOMAS JAMES 1813-1837

Lucien Greville, by a Cornet in the Honourable East India Company's Service. London: 1833. V. 38

PETTIGREW, THOMAS JOSEPH 1791-1865

A History of Egyptian Mummies, and an Account of the Worship and Embalming of the Sacred Animals by the Egyptians. London: 1834. V. 37; 38; 40

Medical Portrait gallery. London: 1838-40. V. 39

Memoirs of the Life and Writings of John Coakley Lettsom, with Selection from His Correspondence. London: 1817. V. 44

PETTIS, OLIVE G.

The Historical Life of Jesus of Nazareth, and Extracts from the Apostolic Age. Providence: 1870-71. V. 37

PETTIT, CHARLES

the Woman Who Commanded 500,000,000 Men. New York: 1929. V. 45

PETTIT, FLORENCE H.

America's Printed and Painted Fabrics 1600-1900. New York: 1970. V. 38; 41

PETTMAN, WILLIAM

An Address to the Members of both Houses of Parliament, on the injury the landholders sustain for the want of a protecting duty on imported corn . . . With a few hints on the expediency of equalizing the poor rates . . . Canterbury: 1823. V. 37

PETTUS, JOHN

Fleta Minor. The Laws of Art and Nature, In . . . Metals. London: 1686. V. 45

Fodinae Regales. Or the History, Laws and Places of the Chief Mines and Mineral Works in England, Wales, and the English Pale in Ireland. London: 1670. V. 37; 43

Volatiles from the History of Adam and Eve . . . London: 1674. V. 42; 44

PETTY, WILLIAM 1623-1687

The Economic Writings of Sir William Petty Together with the Observations Upon the Bills of Mortality More Probably by Captain John Graunt. Cambridge: 1899. V. 39

Political Arithmetick, or a Discourse Concerning the Extent and Value of Lands, People, Buildings . . . London: 1691. V. 41

Political Survey of Ireland, with the Establishment of that Kingdom . . . London: 1719. V. 37; 41; 45

Reflections Upon Some Persons and Things in Ireland, by Letters to and From Dr. Petty . . . London: 1660. V. 39

Several Essays in Political Arithmetick . . . London: 1699. V. 38

Sir William Petty's Political Survey of Ireland, with the Establishment of that Kingdom, When the Late Duke of Ormond was Lord Lieutenant; and also An Exact List of the Present Peers, Members of Parliament and Principal Officers of State . . . London: 1719. V. 37; 38

Tracts Chiefly Relating to Ireland. Containing: 1. A Treatise of Taxes and Contributions. 2. Essays in Political Arithmetic. 3. The Political Anatomy of Ireland. Dublin: 1769. V. 37; 41; 46

PETYT, GEORGE

Lex Parliamentaria: or, a Treatise of the Law and Custom of Parliaments . . . London: 1748. V. 38

PETYT, WILLIAM 1636-1707

Miscellanea Parliamentaria. London: 1681. V. 39

Miscellanea Parliamentaria Containing Presidents 1. Of Freedom from Arrest. 2. of Censures Upon Such as have Wrote Books to the Dishonour of the Lords or Commons, or to Alter the Constitution of the Government; Upon Members of Misdemeanours . . . London: 1680. V. 37

PETZENDORFER, LUDWIG

Schriften-Atlas, eine Sammlung der Wichtigsten Schreib-und Druckschriften aus Alter und Neuer Zeit . . . Stuttgart: 1894. V. 38

PEUCINIAN SOCIETY

Catalogue of the Library of the Peucinian Society, Bowdoin College, January 1829. Brunswick: 1829. V. 37

PEUGNET, EUGENE

The Nature of Gunshot Wounds of the Abdomen and Their Treatment. New York: 1874. V. 40

PEURBACH, GEORG

Tabulae Eclypsium . . . Tabula Primi Mobilis . . . Vienna: 1514. V. 38

Theoricae Novae Planetarum, ab Erasmo Reinholdo Salvedensi Pluribus Figuris Auctae & Illustratae Scholiis . . . Paris: 1557. V. 46

PEVERELLY, CHARLES A.

The Book of American Pastimes . . . New York: 1866. V. 46

PEVSNER, NIKOLAUS

Charles R. Mackintosh. Milan: 1950. V. 40

An Inquiry into Industiral Art in England, by Nikolaus Pevsner. Cambridge: 1937. V. 37; 39

Pioneers of the Modern Movement from William Morris to Walter Gropius. London: 1936. V. 45

Studies in Art, Architecture and Design. London: 1969. V. 42; 44

PEYRE, ANTOINE MARIE 1770-1843

Projets d'Architecture. Paris: 1812. V. 38

Projets de Reconstruction de la Salle de l'Odeon . . . Paris: 1819. V. 37; 38; 42; 44

PEYRE-FERRY, FRANCOIS

The Art of Epistolary Composition, or Models of Letters, Billets, Bills of Exchange, Bills of Lading, Invoices . . . Middletown: 1826. V. 42

PEYRE, MARIE JOSEPH 1730-1785

Oeuvres d'Architecture . . . Paris: 1765. V. 40; 44

Oeuvres d'Architecture. Paris: 1795. V. 38

PEYRERE, ISAAC DE LA

A Theological Systeme Upon Presupposition, That Men Were Before Adam. London: 1655. V. 42

PEYRITSCH, JOHN 1800-1874

Aroideae Maximilinae. Vienna: 1879. V. 39; 41

PEYSSONEL, JEAN DE

De Temporibus Humani Partus, Iuxta Doctrinam Hippocratis, Tractatus. Lyon: 1666. V. 45

PEYSSONNEL, CLAUDE CHARLES DE

An Historical Account of the Present Troubles of Persia and Georgia. London: 1756. V. 41

PEYTON, JOHN L.

The Adventures of My Grandfather . . . London: 1867. V. 37; 38; 40; 43

Memoir of John Howe Peyton. Staunton: 1894. V. 44

PEYTON, JOHN LEWIS

Over the Alleghenies and Across the Prairies. London: 1869. V. 40; 45

PEYTON, JOHN ROWZEE

Three Letters from St. Louis. Denver: 1958. V. 37

PEYTON, PATRICK J.

The Ear of God. Garden City: 1951. V. 45

PEYTY, WILLIAM 1636-1707

The Antient Right of the Commons of England Asserted . . . London: 1680. V. 40

PEZRON, PAUL

The Antiquities of Nations. London: 1706. V. 38

PFAUNDLER, M.

The Diseases of Children. Philadelphia: 1908. V. 42

PFAUNDLER, M. VON

The Diseases of Children. Philadelphia: 1912. V. 38

PFEFFEL, JOHANN ANDREAS

Schweitzerisches Trachten-Cabinet Oder Allerhand Kleidungen, Wie Man Solche in dem Loblichen Schweitzer-Canton Zurch Zutragen Pflegt . . . Le Cabinet de Toutes les Modes . . . Augsburg: 1750. V. 46

PFEFFER, P. E.

Nuclear Magnetic Resonance in Agriculture. Boca Raton,: 1989. V. 46

PFEFFERKORN, IGNAZ

Sonora. A Description of the Province. Albuquerque: 1949. V. 40; 41; 45

PFEIFFER, GUSTAVUS ADOLPHUS

The Philosophical Writings of . . . San Francisco: 1955. V. 38

PFEIFFER, IDA REYER

A Journey to Iceland, and Travels in Sweden and Noray. New York: 1852. V. 43

A Lady's Second Journey Round the World: from London to . . . Borneo, Java, Sumatra, Celebes, Ceram, the Moluccas, etc . . . New York: 1856. V. 45; 46

Visit to Iceland and the Scandinavian North. London: 1852. V. 40; 42; 43; 44

PFEIFFER, ROBERT H.

State Letters of Assyria . . . New Haven: 1935. V. 44

PFISTER, R.

The Textiles. New Haven: 1945. V. 40

PFLUEGER, DONALD

Covina: Sunflowers, Citrus, Subdivisions. Covina: 1964. V. 40

PFORZHEIMER, CARL HOWARD 1879-1957

The Carl H. Pforzheimer Library of English Literature 1475-1700. New York: 1940. V. 38; 42

PFORZHEIMER, WALTER L.

Stocktoniana. Purchase: 1936. V. 44

PFUHL, ERNST

Masterpieces of Greek Drawing and Painting. New York: 1926. V. 42

PHAEDRUS

The Fables . . . London: 1745. V. 42

Fabulae. Glasgow: 1751. V. 38

Fabularum Aesopiarum Libri Quinque. Paris: 1742. V. 39

A Poetical Translation of the Fables of Phaedrus. London: 1765. V. 37; 39; 41; 42; 43; 44; 45

PHAIR, CHARLES

Atlantic Salmon Fishing. New York: 1937. V. 39; 43; 45

PHALARIS

The Epistles . . . London: 1749. V. 42; 44

Epistolae. Florence: 1487. V. 37

PHARAAONIUS, FRANCISCUS

De re Literaria Benemerentis Institutiones Grammaticae. Brescia: 1533. V. 37

PHARETRA Catholice Fidei Sive Ydonea Disputatio Inter Christianos et Judaeos. Landshut: 1514. V. 43

PHARMACOPOEIA Augustana. Madison: 1927. V. 42

PHARMACOPOEIA Londinensis of 1618: Reproduced in Facsimile . . . Madison: 1944. V. 42; 45

THE PHARMACOPOEIA of the United States of America. Boston: 1820. V. 42

THE PHARMACOPOEIA of the United States of America. Boston: 1820. V. 37

THE PHARMACOPOEIA of the United States of America. New York: 1830. V. 41

THE PHARMACOPOEIA of the United States of America. Philadelphia: 1863. V. 42

THE PHARMACOPOEIA of the United States of America. Philadelphia: 1931. V. 38; 41

THE PHARMACOPOEIA of the United States of America. 1820. Boston: 1821. V. 40

THE PHARMACOPOEIA of the Vancouver General Hospital. Vancouver: 1914. V. 39

PHARMACOPOEIAE Collegiae Regalis Londini Remedia Omnia Succincte Descripta . . . London: 1689. V. 42; 44

PHAVORINUS, VARINUS

Dictionarium. Basle: 1538. V. 46

PHAYER, THOMAS

A Treatise on the Plague, Written in English about Two Hundred Years since . . . Republish'd with a Preface, by a Physician. Lonon: 1722. V. 37

PHELAN, WILLIAM 1789-1830

A Digest of the Evidence Taken Before Select Committees of the Two Houses of Parliament, Appointed to Inquire into the State of Ireland: 1824-1825. London: 1826. V. 40

PHELIPS, WILLIAM

The Life of Frederick William I. London: 1750. V. 39

PHELPES, CHARLES

A Caveat Against Drunkenness, Especially in Evil Times. London: 1676. V. 42

PHELPS, ALMIRA H. LINCOLN

Lectures to Young Ladies, Comprising Outlines and Applications of the Different Branches of Female Education for the Use of Female Schools and Private Libraries. Delivered to the Pupils of Troy Female Seminary. Boston: 1833. V. 37; 44

PHELPS, AMOS

A Lecture on Slavery and Its Remedy. Boston: 1834. V. 42

PHELPS and Ensign's Traveller's Guide through the United States. New York: 1839. V. 46

PHELPS, CHARLES

Traumatic Injuries of the Brain and Its Membranes. New York: 1897. V. 42

PHELPS, HUMPHREY

Phelp's Strangers and Citizens Guide to New York City. New York: 1857. V. 37

Phelps's Travellers' Guide Through the United States: Containing Upwards of Seven Hundred Rail-Road, Canal and Stage and Steam Boat Routes. Accompanied with a New Map of the United States. New York: 1847. V. 37; 40; 46

PHELPS, JOHN H.

In the Court of Oyer and Terminer for the County of Albany. Albany: 1855. V. 43

PHELPS, JOHN S.

A Letter from Hon . . . to Citizens of Arkansas in Relation to a Pacific Railroad. St. Louis: 1858. V. 39; 40

PHELPS, NOAH A.

A History of the Copper Mines and Newgate Prison & Granby, Conn. Also of the Captivity of Daniel Hayes, of Granby, by the Indians in 1707. Hartford: 1845. V. 38

PHELPS, STEVEN

Art and Artefacts of the Pacific, Africa and the Americas: The James Hooper Collection by Stevens Phelps. London: 1976. V. 37

PHELPS, SYLVANUS DRYDEN

Holy Land, with Glimpses of Europe and Egypt; a Year's Tour. New York: 1864. V. 46

PHELPS' Travellers' Guide Through the United States; Containing Upwards of Seven Hundred Rail-Road, Canal and Stage and Steamboat Routes Accompanied with a New Map of the United States. New York: 1848. V. 41; 43; 46

PHELP'S Travellers' Guide through the United States. New York: 1850. V. 41; 43; 46

PHELPS, W.

The History and Antiquities of Somersetshire. London: 1839. V. 40

The History and Antiquities of Somersetshire. London: 1836-9. V. 39

PHELPS, WILLIAM D.

Fore and Aft; Or, Leaves from the Life of An Old Sailor. Boston: 1871. V. 37; 39; 42

PHIILIPS, GEORGE

Travels in North America. Dublin: 1824. V. 41

PHILADELPHIA BAPTIST ASSOCIATION

Minutes of the Philadelphia Baptist Association . . . 1812 (-1823, 1827-1830, 1832-1843). Philadelphia: etc.. V. 41

THE PHILADELPHIA Book; or Specimens of Metropolitan Literature. Philadelphia: 1836. V. 46

PHILADELPHIA in 1824; or, a Brief Account of the Various Institutions and Public Objects in this Metropolis . . . Philadelphia: 1824. V. 42

PHILADELPHIA. LAWS, STATUTES, ETC.

The Ordinances of the City of Philadelphia, and the Several Supplements to the Act of Incoporation . . . Philadelphia: 1800. V. 46

PHILADELPHIA. LIBRARY COMPANY

The Charter, Laws and Catalogue of Books, of the Library Company of Philadelphia. Philadelphia: 1764. V. 39; 40; 44

PHILADELPHIA. MUSEUM OF ART

Jasper Johns: Prints 1960-1970. 1970. V. 45

THE PHILADELPHIA National Bank A Century's Record 1803-1903. Philadelphia: 1903. V. 41

PHILADELPHIA Pictorial and Biographical. Steel Plate Supplement. Philadelphia: 1911. V. 41; 42

PHILADELPHIA Public Ledger's Unrivaled Atlas of the World. Chicago/New York: 1897. V. 45
PHILADELPHIA Public Ledger's Unrivaled Atlas of the World. Chicago/New York: 1899. V. 45

PHILADELPHIA SCHOOL OF DESIGN FOR WOMEN

Prospectus of the Philadelphia School of Design for Women: Containing a Programme of the Courses of Study, the Rules and Regulations, Constitution and By-Laws. Philadelphia: 1882. V. 37

PHILADELPHIA. SELECT COUNCIL

Report of a Committee of the Select Council of Philadelphia, Read November 10th, 1796. Philadelphia: 1796. V. 46

PHILAMOUR and Philamena; or Genuine Memoirs of a Late Affecting Transaction. London: 1746. V. 40

PHILANDER, G.

In Decem Libros M. Vitruvii Pollionis de Architectura Annotationes . . . Rome: 1544. V. 38; 40

PHILANDER, JOAKIM

Vitulus Aureus: The Golden Calf. Or, a SUpplement to Apuleuis's Golden Ass. An Enquiry Physico-Critico-Patheologico-Moral in the Nature and Efficacy of GOld . . . The Changes it Causes in the Minds of Men . . . London: 1749. V. 37

PHILBY, HARRY ST. JOHN BRIDGER

Arabia of the Wahhabis. London: 1928. V. 39; 45
Arabia . . . London: 1930. V. 44
Arabian Days. London: 1948. V. 44
Arabian Highlands. Ithaca: 1952. V. 39; 44; 45
Arabian Jubilee. London: 1952. V. 44
The Background of Islam. Alexandria: 1947. V. 39; 46
The Empty Quarter, Being a Description of the Great South Desert of Arabia Known as Rub' al Khali . . . London: 1933. V. 44
Forty Years in the Wilderness. London: 1957. V. 39; 44
The Heart of Arabia. London: 1922. V. 44
The Heart of Arabia. New York & London: 1923. V. 39
The Land of Midian. London: 1957. V. 44
A Pilgrim in Arabia. 1943. V. 45
A Pilgrim in Arabia . . . Waltham St. Lawrence: 1943. V. 42; 44
A Pilgrim in Arabia. London: 1943. V. 37; 45
Sheba's Daughters . . . London: 1939. V. 44

PHILELFUS, FRANCISCUS

Orationes. Paris: 1515. V. 42
Satyrarum. Colophon: 1502. V. 44

PHILEPHUS, FRANCISCUS

Epistolae Elegantiores . . . Strasbourg: 1513. V. 38

PHILES, GEORGE P.

Bibliotheca Curiosa. New York: 1878-79. V. 39

PHILIBERT, PSEUD.

A Poem Compos'd the Second of November, 1747, the Day the Honourable Archibald Stuart, Esq. Was Assoilized from His Second Trial. N.P., n.d.: 1747. V. 40

PHILIDOR, FRANCOIS ANDRE DANICAN

An Amateur. Cheltenham: 1804. V. 46
Chess Analysed; or Instructions by Which a Perfect Knowledge of this Noble Game May In a Short Time be Acquir'd. London: 1791. V. 41
Chess Rendered Familiar by Gabular Demonstrations of the Various Positions and Movements, as Described by Philidor. London: 1819. V. 38
Studies of Chess: Containing a Systematic Introduction to the Game. London. V. 43
Studies of Chess. London: 1808. V. 37; 40
Studies of Chess: Containing Caissa, A Poem, by Sir William Jones, A Systematic Introduction to the Game, and the whole Analysis of Chess . . . with original Critical Remarks. London: 1803. V. 37

PHILIP, A.

The Business of Bookbinding . . . London: 1912. V. 41; 44

PHILIP, A. P. W.

An Inquiry into the Nature of Sleep and Death . . . London: 1834. V. 45
A Treatise on the Nature and Cure of Those Diseases, Either Acute or Chronic . . . Baltimore: 1831. V. 45

PHILIP, ARTHUR

The Voyage of Governor Phillip to Botany Bay. London: 1789. V. 45
A Voyage to Botany Bay . . . London: 1790. V. 41

PHILIP II, KING OF SPAIN

Edictvm De Librorum Prohibitorum Catalogo Obseruando. (with) Index Librorum Prohibitorum. Antwerp: 1570. V. 41
Ordonnantie ende Ghebodt, Aengaende den Reghel die de Crijechsluyden Sullen Moeten Onderhouden . . . Antwerp: 1578. V. 46
Prematica, en que se de la Orden y Forma que se Ha De Tener, y Guardar, en Los Tratamientos y Cortesias de Palabras y por Escrito . . . Mexico: 1600. V. 38

PHILIP III, KING OF SPAIN

Edicto . . . Contra El Tractato della Monarchia de Sicilia Enxerido por Cesar Baronio. N.P.: 1611. V. 37

PHILIP, JOHN

Reminiscences of Gibraltar, Egypt and Egyptian War, 1882. Aberdeen: 1893. V. 41
Researches in South Africa, Illustrating the Civil, Moral and Religious Condition of the Native Trives . . . London: 1828. V. 41; 42; 46

PHILIP, LOTTE BRAND

The Ghent Altarpiece and the Art of Jan Van Eyck. Princeton: 1971. V. 44

PHILIP, PRINCE, DUKE OF EDINBURGH 1921-

Wildlife Crisis. London: 1971. V. 40

PHILIP, ROERT KEMP

The Shopkeeper's Guide . . . London: 1853. V. 38

PHILIP V, KING OF SPAIN

The King of Spain's Declaration of War Against Great Britain. London: 1739. V. 41

PHILIPOT, THOMAS

A Brief Historical Discourse of the Original and Growth of Heraldry, Demonstrating Upon What Rational foundations that Noble and Heroick Science Is Established. London: 1672. V. 39; 41; 44

PHILIPPAKI, BARBARA

The Attic Stamnos. Oxford: 1967. V. 40; 42; 44

PHILIPPI, HENRICUS 1575-1636

Qvaestiones Chronologicae De Annis Nati Et Passi Salvatoris. Cologne: 1630. V. 39

PHILIPPO, JAMES M.

Jamaica: Its Past and Present State. London: 1843. V. 40

PHILIPPOS, N. B., PSEUD.

The Farrier's and Horseman's Dictionary, Being a Compleat System of Horsemanship . . . London: 1726. V. 42

PHILIPPS, FABIAN

Tenenda non Tollenda, or the Necessity of Preserving Tenures in Capite and by Knights-Service, Which According to Their First Institution Were, and Are Yet . . . London: 1660. V. 38; 45

PHILLIPS, HENRY 1775-1838 continued

Floral Emblems. London: 1825. V. 37; 40; 41; 42; 46

Historical Sketches of the Paper Currency of the American Colonies, Prior to the Adoption of the Federal Constitution. First and Second Series. Roxbury: 1865-66. V. 40

History of Cultivated Vegetables . . . London: 1822. V. 37; 38; 39; 40; 42

Pomarium Britannicum: An Historical and Botanic Account of Fruits Known in Great Britain. London: 1820. V. 38

Pomarium Britannicum, an Historical and Botanical Account of Fruits Known in Great Britain. London: 1821. V. 40; 42

Sylvia Florifera; the Shrubbery Historically and Botanically Treated. London: 1823. V. 38; 39; 40; 41

The True Enjoyment of Angling. London: 1843. V. 39; 41; 42; 44; 46

PHILLIPS, HUGH 1886-

The Thames About 1750. London: 1951. V. 39

PHILLIPS, J.

Figures and Descriptions of the Palaeozoic Fossils of Cornwall, Devon and West Somerset. London: 1841. V. 37

PHILLIPS, J. B.

St. Luke's Life of Christ. London: 1956. V. 42; 46

PHILLIPS, J. J.

Architect: A Series of Measured and Sketch Drawings, Details etc. of the Ancient Monastery of Greyabbey, Co. Down (in 1874), with descriptive and historical Letterpress. Belfast: 1874. V. 37

PHILLIPS, J. V.

Report on the Geology of the Mineral Deposits Contiguous to the Iron Mountain Railroad. St. Louis: 1859. V. 39; 42

PHILLIPS, JAMES DUNCAN

Salem in the Seventeenth Century. Boston: 1933. V. 39

Salem and the Indies: the Story of the Great Commercial Era of the City. Boston: 1947. V. 43; 44

PHILLIPS, JAMES JETER

The Drinker's Farm Tragedy. Richmond: 1868. V. 40

PHILLIPS, JAYNE ANNE

Black Tickets. New York: 1979. V. 42; 45

Fast Lanes. N.P.: 1964. V. 42

How Mickey Made It. St. Paul: 1981. V. 42; 43; 45; 46

The Secret Country. N.P.: 1982. V. 42

The Secret Country (Randolph County: Mitch). N.P.: 1982. V. 40

The Secret Country (Randolph County: Mitch). N.P.: 1982. V. 44

The Secret Country. 1982. V. 42

The Secret Country. Winston Salem: 1982. V. 43

Sweethearts. Carboro: 1976. V. 37; 38; 39; 40; 41; 42; 44; 45

PHILLIPS, JOHN

Blenheim, a Poem . . . London: 1705. V. 38

A Comprehensive Synopsis of all the Monetary Systems in the Known World. London: 1842. V. 39

A General History of Inland Navigation, Foreign and Domestic. London: 1792. V. 37; 40; 41

A General History of Inland Navigation, Foreign and Domestic . . . London: 1795. V. 38; 40

A General History of Inland Navigation, Foreign and Domestic. London: 1803. V. 38

Geology of Oxford and the Valley of the Thames. London: 1871. V. 42; 44

Geology of Oxford and the Valley of the Thames. Oxford: 1871. V. 40

Gold-Mining and Assaying: a Scientific Guide for Australian Emigrants. London: 1853. V. 41

Illustrations of the Geology of Yorkshire; or a Description of the Strata and Organic Remains . . . London: 1835-36. V. 44; 46

Illustrations of the Geology of Yorkshire . . . London: 1875. V. 41; 42

Illustrations of the Geology of Yorkshire. London: 1875-1836. V. 38

Illustrations of the Geology of Yorkshire. York: 1829. V. 37; 39

Italian Profiles. London: 1965. V. 37

Manual of Geology: Practical and Theoretical. London: 1855. V. 38; 40

Mexico Illustrated, With Descriptive Letterpress in English and Spanish. London: 1848. V. 39; 45

The Rivers, Mountains and Sea Coast of Yorkshire. London: 1855. V. 38; 40; 43; 44; 45; 46

The Secret History of the Reigns of King Charles II and King James II. London: 1690. V. 37; 44

The Whole Works of John Phillips . . . To Which is Prefixed His Life, by Mr. Sewell. Loldon: (sic) 1720. V. 46

PHILLIPS, JOHN A.

Gold-Mining and Assaying: A Scientific Guide for Australian Emigrants. London: 1853. V. 38

PHILLIPS, JOHN C.

Wenham Great Pond. Salem: 1938. V. 43

PHILLIPS, JOHN CHARLES

John Rowe. An Eighteenth Century Boston Angler. Cambridge: 1929. V. 44

A Natural History of the Ducks. Boston and New York: 1922. V. 44

A Natural History of the Ducks. 1986. V. 38

A Natural History of Ducks. New York;: 1986. V. 39

A Natural History of the Ducks. London: 1922-26. V. 37

Shooting-Stands of Eastern Massachusetts. Cambridge: 1929. V. 39

PHILLIPS, JOHN GOLDSMITH

China Trade Porcelain: An Account of Its Historical Background, Manufacture and Decoration, and a Study of the Helena Woolworth McCann Collections. Cambridge: 1956. V. 41

PHILLIPS, JOSEPH

West India Question. The Outline of a Plan for the Total, Immediate, and Safe Abolition of Slavery Throughout the British Colonies. London: 1833. V. 42

PHILLIPS, KATHERINE

Poems. London: 1664. V. 43

Poems by . . . . Katherine Philips . . . London: 1667. V. 45

Poems by . . . London: 1669. V. 43

Poems by the Most Deservedly Admired Mrs. Katherine Phillips . . . London: 1678. V. 43

PHILLIPS, M.

The Grand Southern Tour of England . . . London. V. 46

PHILLIPS, M. V. B.

Life and Death in Andersonville; or, What I Saw and Experienced During Seven Months in Rebel Prisons. Chicago: 1887. V. 42

PHILLIPS, MICHAEL

An Island in the Moon.. London: 1987. V. 39

PHILLIPS, MORRIS

Abroad and at Home: Practical Hints for Tourists. New York: 1893. V. 43

PHILLIPS, P. LEE

First Map and Description of Ohio, 1787. By Manasseh Cutler: A Bibliographical Account with Reprint of the 'Explanation'. Washington: 1918. V. 40

Notes on the Life and Works of Bernard Romans. Deland, Fla.: 1924. V. 37; 39; 42; 43

PHILLIPS, PAUL C.

The Fur Trade. Norman: 1967. V. 44

PHILLIPS, PAUL CRISLER

The Fur Trade. Norman: 1961. V. 37; 38; 40; 42

PHILLIPS, PEREGRINE

A Diary kept in an Excursion to Little Hampton . . . and Brighthelmston . . . in 1778; and also to the latter place in 1779. London: 1780. V. 37

PHILLIPS, PHILIP

The Forth-Bridge in Its Various Stages of Construction and Compared with the Most Notable Bridges of the World. Edinburgh: 1889. V. 41; 46

The Forth Bridge In Its Various Stages of Construction and Compared with the Most Notable Bridges of the World. Edinburgh: 1890. V. 40

The Forth Bridge In Its Various Stages of Construction, and Compared with the Most Notable Bridges of the World. Edinburgh: 1890 or 1891. V. 38

PHILLIPS, PHILIP A. S.

John Obrisset, Huguenot: Carver, Medallist, Horn & Tortoiseshell Worker & Snuff-Box maker. With Examples of His Work Dated 1705 to 1728. London: 1931. V. 37; 39; 45

Paul de Lamerie, Citizen and Goldsmith of London. London: 1935. V. 42

PHILLIPS, RICHARD

Addisoniana. London: 1803. V. 42

The Explanatory and Pronouncing French Word Book. Boston: 1826. V. 41

A Translation of the Pharmacopoeia of the Royal College of Physicians of London, 1836. With Notes and Illustrations. London: 1838. V. 37

PHILLIPS, ROBERT

A Dissertation Concerning the Present State of the High Roads of England . . . London: 1737. V. 38; 39

PHILLIPS, STEPHEN

Christ in Hades and Other Poems. London: 1896. V. 42

Eremus. A Poem. Fulham: 1890. V. 37

Marpessa. London: & New York: 1900. V. 43

The New Inferno. London: 1911. V. 38; 40; 41; 46

PHILLIPS, STEPHEN continued

Paoloa and Francesca. London: 1900. V. 45

PHILLIPS, TERESIA CONSTANTIA 1709-1765

An Apology for the Conduct of Mrs. Teresia Constantia Phillips, More Particularly that Part of It Which Relates to Her Marriage . . . 1748-9. V. 43

PHILLIPS, TERESIA CONSTANTIA PHILLIPS 1709-1765

A Letter Humbly Address'd to the Right Honourable the Earl of Chesterfield. London: 1750. V. 39; 41

PHILLIPS, THOMAS

The History of the Life of Reginald Pole. Oxford: 1764. V. 38

Londonderry and the London Companies, 1609-1629. Belfast: 1928. V. 38; 43; 45

A Short Catalogue of Sir Thomas Phillips' Privately printed Works. London: 1886. V. 44

PHILLIPS, TOM

Portfolio 2. London: 1975. V. 46

The Sketches of Tom Phillips. Kansas City: 1972. V. 46

PHILLIPS, ULRICH B.

American Negro Slavery: a Survey of the Supply, Employment and Control of Negro Labor as Determined by the Plantation Regime. New York: 1918. V. 42

The Correspondence of Robert Toombs, Alexander H. Stephens, and Howell Cobb. Washington: 1913. V. 42

PHILLIPS, VIVIEN

A Trip to Santa Claus Land, or Ruth's Christmas Eve. London: 1905. V. 46

PHILLIPS, W.

Architectural Iron Construction. London: 1870. V. 44

PHILLIPS, W. ALISON

The War of Greek Independence 1821 to 1833. London: 1897. V. 43

PHILLIPS, W. ALLISON

History of the Church of Ireland, From the Earliest Times to the Present Day. London: 1933. V. 38; 43

PHILLIPS, WALTER J.

The Technique of the Colour Wood-Cut. London: 1926. V. 41

PHILLIPS, WALTER SHELLEY

The Old Timer's Tale. Chicago: 1929. V. 45

PHILLIPS, WATTS

The Hooded Snake. London: 1860. V. 42

PHILLIPS, WENDELL

Freedom for Women, Speech of . . . at the Convention Held at Worcester, October 15, 16, 1851. V. 37

Speech of Wendell Phillips, Esq. The Sims Case . . . Boston: 1852. V. 42

PHILLIPS, WILLARD

The Inventor's Guide. Boston & New York: 1837. V. 43

A Manual of Political Economy, with Particular Reference to the Institutions, Resources and Condition of the United States . . . Boston: 1828. V. 37

PHILLIPS, WILLIAM

An Outline of Mineralogy and Geology. London: 1815. V. 46

An Outline of Mineralogy and Geology, Intended for the Use of Those Who May Desire to Become Acquainted With the Elements of Those Sciences . . . New York: 1816. V. 41

A Selection of Facts from the Best Authorities, Arranged to Form an Outline of the Geology of England and Wales. London: 1818. V. 40

PHILLIPS, WILLIAM W. A.

Manual of the Mammals of Ceylon. Ceylon & London: 1935. V. 40; 42; 43

Manual of the Mammals of Ceylon. Columbia: 1935. V. 43

PHILLPOTT, NICHOLAS

Reasons and Proposalls for a Registry or Remembrancer of All Deeds and Incumbrances of Real Estates, to be Had in Every Country . . . Oxford: 1671. V. 38

PHILLPOTTS, EDEN 1862-1960

Arachne. London: 1927. V. 46

Children of the Mist, a Novel. London: 1898. V. 40

Dartmoor Novels. London: 1927. V. 37; 38; 42

The Dartmoor Novels. London: 1927-28. V. 46

A Dish of Apples. London & New York. V. 41

A Dish of Apples. London: 1921. V. 37; 38; 40; 41; 42

The Girl and the Faun. London: 1916. V. 37; 40; 43

The Grey Room. New York: 1921. V. 38; 40

A Hundred Sonnets. London: 1929. V. 39; 43

The Widecome Edition of Eden Phillpotts' Dartmoor Novels. London: 1927. V. 42

PHILLPS, CONSTANTINE JOHN

A Voyage Towards the North Pole Undertaken by His Majesty's Command. London: 1774. V. 40

PHILLPS, HOWARD

Interiors. Gloucestershire: 1985. V. 40; 45

Interiors: Wood Engravings by Howard Phipps. 1985. V. 44

PHILOBIBLION. New York: 1861-63. V. 39; 42

PHILOLOGICAL SOCIETY

Proposal for the Publication of a New English Dictionary by the Philological Society. London: 1859. V. 38

PHILOPONUS, JOHANNES

In Primos Quatuor Aristotelis de Naturali Auscultatione Libros Comentaria. Venice: 1535. V. 46

PHILOSOPHY of Animal Magnetism Together with the System of Manipulating Adopted to Produce Ecstasy and Somnambulism -- The Effects and Rationale. Philadelphia: 1837. V. 43; 46

PHILOSTRATUS

Les Images ou Tableaux de Platte Peinture des Deux Philostrates . . . mis en Francois par Blaise de Vigenere. Paris: 1629. V. 45

Philostratorum Quae Supersunt Omnia. Leipzig: 1709. V. 41

The Two First Books, of Philostratus, Concerning the Life of Apollonius Tyaneus: Written Originally in Greek, and Now Published in English . . . London: 1680. V. 38

De Vita Pollonii Tyanei . . . Interprete Alemano Rinuccino . . . Venice: 1501. V. 42; 45

De Vita Apollonii. Lyon: 1504. V. 40

PHILP, KENWARD

John Brown's Legs; or, Leaves from a Journal in the Lowlands. New York: 1884. V. 45

PHILP, ROBERT KEMP 1819-1882

The History of Progress in Great Britain. London: 1859. V. 38; 41

PHILPOT, CHARLES

An Introduction to the Literary History of the Fourteenth and Fifteenth Centuries. London: 1798. V. 38

PHIN, JOHN

Open Air Grape Culture . . . New York: 1863. V. 38

PHINNEY, H. F.

The Water Cure in America. New York: 1849. V. 43

PHINNEY, MARY A.

Allen Isham Genealogy: Jiriah Isham Allen Montana Pioneer, Government Scout, Guide Interpretor and Famous Hunter During Four Years of Indian Warfare in Montana and Dakota. Rutland. V. 45

Allen-Isham Genealogy Jirah Isham Allen Montana Pioneer, Government Scout, Guide, Interpreter and Famous Hunter . . . Rutland: 1946. V. 38

PHINNEY, S.

Family Medicine. Dr. S. Phinney's Anti-Dyspeptic Bilious Pills. N.P.: 1827? V. 44

PHIPPEN, GEORGE

The Life of a Cowboy Told through the Drawings, Paintings, and Bronzes of George Phippen. Tucson,: 1969. V. 38; 43

PHIPPS, CONSTANTINE JOHN, 2ND BARON MULGRAVE 1744-1792

A Voyage Towards the North Pole: Undertaken by His Majesty's Command 1773. London: 1774. V. 37; 38; 43; 44; 45; 46

PHIPPS, JOSEPH

The Original and Present State of Man Briefly Considered Wherein Is Shewn the Nature of His Fall and Necessity, Means and Manner of His Restoration through the Sacrifice of Christ and the Sensible Operation of that Divine Principle of Grace & Truth . . . Philadelphia: 1783. V. 41

The Original and Present State of Man, Briefly Considered . . . by the People Called Quakers. New York: 1788. V. 38; 40; 44

The Original and Present State of Man Briefly Considered. Trenton: 1793. V. 38

PHIPPS, MARY

All About Patsy. Garden City: 1930. V. 42

Liza Jane and the Kinkies. New York: 1929. V. 42

PHIPSON, EMMA

Choir Stalls and Their Carvings. London: 1896. V. 44

PHOCYLIDES

The Preceptive Moral Poem of Phocilides.. Chichester: 1780. V. 38

PHOENIX ART MUSEUM

Cowboy Artists of America. Flagstaff: 1973. V. 44

PHOENIX, JOHN

Phoenixiana; or, Sketches and Burlesques. New York: 1856. V. 39

THE PHOENIX Nest. London: 1926. V. 46

PHOONSEN, JOHANNES 1631-1702

Berichten en Vertoogen, Raackende het Bestier van den Omslagh van de Wissel-Banck tot Amsterdam . . . Amsterdam: 1677. V. 38

PHOTIUS

Bibliotheca (in Greek) . . . Librorum Quos . . . Quatuor Mss. Codicibus . . . Augsburg: 1601. V. 40

Lexicon (in Greek). E Codici Gleano Descripsit Richardus Porsonus. Sumptibus Collegii Trinittis Cntabrigiae, veneunt apud J. Mawmn. Londini: 1822. V. 38; 40

PHOTOGRAPHIC View of Hastings. Hastings: 1860. V. 44

PHOTOGRAPHIE 1931. Paris: 1931. V. 37

PHOTOGRAPHS of County Wicklow with Descriptive Letterpress. Glasgow: 1867. V. 41; 45

PHOTOGRAPHS of Plas Newydd. Upper Bangor: 1896. V. 37

PHRENOLOGICAL Journal and Miscellany. Edinburgh: 1824-26. V. 46

PHYS, ERNEST

The Book of Ruth. London: 1896. V. 37

PHYSICK, JOHN

Catalogue of the Engraved Work of Eric Gill. London: 1963. V. 42

PHYSIOLOGICAL PUBLISHING COMPANY

A Special List of Private Medical Works for Those Who Need Them. Bauneg-Beg, York, Co. Maine,: 1880. V. 37

PHYSIOLOGUS de Naturis Duodecim Animalium. Cologne: 1494. V. 38; 40; 42; 44

PHYSIOLOGUS: The Very Ancient Book of Beasts, Plants and Stones. Fairfax: 1953. V. 37
PHYSIOLOGUS The Very Ancient Book of Beasts, Plants and Stones. San Francisco: 1953. V. 37; 38; 46

PIACENZA, FRANCESCO

L'Egeo Redivivo o' sia Chorographia dell' Archipelago, e dello Stato Primiero & Attuale di Quell' Isole, Regni, Citta, Poplationi, Dominii, Costumi, Sito & Imprese, con la Breve Descrittione Particolare si del suo Ambito Littorale . . . Modon: 1688. V. 37

PIAE Aliquot Homiliae Sanctorum Quorundam Patrium Ex Graeco in Latinum Sermonem Translatae, Nunc Recens Editae. Paris: 1535. V. 38

PIAGET, H. F.

The Watch, Its Construction, Its Mertis and Defects, How to Choose It and How to Use It. New York: 1860. V. 46

PIAGET, JEAN 1896-1980

The Child's Conception of Physical Causality. London: 1930. V. 42

PIANKOFF, ALEXANDRE

The Litany of Re. Princeton: 1964. V. 42; 44
Mythological Papyri. New York: 1957. V. 37; 40; 42; 44
The Pyramid of Unas. Princeton: 1968. V. 37; 42
The Shrines of Tut-Ankh-Amon. New York: 1955. V. 42; 44
The Shrines of Tut-Ankh-Amon. New York: 1959. V. 40
The Tomb of Ramesses VI. New York: 1954. V. 40; 41; 42; 44; 46
The Wandering of the Soul. Princeton: 1974. V. 37; 40; 42; 44

PIATIGORSKY, GREGOR

Cellist. Garden City: 1965. V. 45
Cellist. New York: 1976 (1969). V. 45

PIATT, JOHN JAMES

The Hesperian Tree: an Annual of the Ohio Valley - 1903. Columbus: 1903. V. 39
The Nests at Washington, and Other Poems. New York: 1864. V. 40
Poems in Sunshine and Firelight. Cincinnati: 1866. V. 40

PIAZZA, CARLO 1632-1713

La Mendicita Proveduta Nella Citta di Roma coll' Ospizio Publico . . . Rome: 1693. V. 46

PIBRAC, GUY DU FAUR DE

Praecepta Moralia, Heroicis Expressa Ab Avg. Prevotio. Paris: 1584. V. 38
Tetrasticha Graecis & Latinis VErsibus Expressa, Authore Florente Christiano. Paris: 1584. V. 38; 44

THE PICADILLY Annual of Entertaining Literature: Retrospective and Contemporary. London: 1870. V. 38

PICARD, JEAN

De Prisca Celtopaedia, Libri Qvinqve. Quibus Admiranda Priscorum Gallorum Doctrina & Eruditio Ostenditur, nec non Literas Prius in Gallia Fuisse, Quam vel in Graecia vel in Italia. Paris: 1556. V. 38

PICARD, L. B.

The Gil Blas Revolution. London: 1825. V. 41

PICART, BERNARD 1673-1733

Histoire Generale des Cermonies, Moeurs et Coutumes Religieuses de Tous les Peuples du Monde.. Paris: 1741. V. 42
A New Drawing Book of Modes. London: 1764. V. 45
A New Drawing Book of Modes. London: 1766. V. 40
Recueil de Lions, Dessinez d'Apres Nature par Divers Maitres & Grave . . . Amsterdam: 1729. V. 38

PICASSO, PABLO 1881-1973

Le Carmen des Carmens. Paris: 1964. V. 38
Carnet de dessins de Picasso, Reproduits au Format de l'Original. Paris: 1948. V. 41
Les Dejeuners. Paris: 1962. V. 37
Picasso Fifteen Drawings. New York: 1946. V. 43
Picasso. New York: 1955. V. 46
Picasso and the Human Comedy: A Suite of 180 Drawings by Picasso. Text by Michel Leiris. Preface by Teriade. Appreciation by Rebecca West. New York: (1954). V. 37
Picasso - The Recent Years 1939-1946. New York: 1947. V. 39
Picasso 347. New York: 1970. V. 39; 41
Picasso in Antibes. New York: 1960. V. 39
Shakespeare. New York: 1965. V. 39; 46
Variations on Velazquez' Painting 'The Maids of Honor' and Other Recent Works. New York: 1959. V. 41
Women. Cannes and Mougins, 1954-1963. Paris: 1964. V. 41

PICCIOLI, F. M.

Il Ritratto della Gloria Donato all' Eternita. Piazzola,: 1685. V. 37

PICCOLOMINI, ALESSANDRO

Amor Costante. Comedia. Venice: 1586. V. 37
De la Sfera del Mondo; de la STelle Fisse . . . Venice: 1540. V. 37; 38; 42
De la Sfera del Mondo . . . De le Stelle Fisse Libro Uno Con le Sue Figure, e Con le Sue Tavole, Dove Con Maravigliosa Agueolezza Potra Ciascheduno . . . Venice: 1559. V. 43
Della Grandezza Della Terra et Dell'Acqua . . . In Venetia: 1558. V. 38
Della Grandezza Della Terra et Dell'Axqua. Venice: 1561. V. 40
Della sfera del Mondo Libri Quattro in Lingua Toscana . . . Venetia: 1561. V. 38
Dialogo de la Bella Creanza de la Donne. Venice: 1540. V. 41
La Prima Parte Delle Theoriche, Overo Speculationi de i Pianeti. Venice: 1558. V. 38
La Prima Parte delle Theoriche Overo Speculationi de Pianeti. Venice: 1563. V. 45
La Sfera del Mondo . . . Vinegia: 1573. V. 40

PICCOLOMINI, FRANCESCO

Librorum ad Scientiam de Natura Attinentium, Partes Quinque. Francofurti: 1597. V. 46

PICCOLOMINI, GIACOMO AMMANATI

Epistolae & Commentarii. Milan: 1506. V. 43

PICCOLPASSO, CIPRIANO

The Three Books of the Potter's Art in the Original Italian . . . London: 1934. V. 41; 43

PICHARDO, JOSE ANTONIO

Pichardo's Treatise on the Limits of Louisana and Texas . . . Austin: 1934. V. 37

PICHON, JEROME

The Life of Charles Henry County Hoym. New York: 1899. V. 38; 39; 40; 41; 44; 46

PICHON, LEON

The New Book Illustration in France. London: 1924. V. 40; 41

PICHON, THOMAS

Lettres et Memoirs Pour Servir a l'Histoire Naturelle, Civile et Politique du Cap Breton, Depuis son Etablissement Jusqu'a la Reprise de Cette Isle par les Anglois en 1758. Londres: 1760. V. 39

PICHOT, AMEDEE

Vues Pittoresques de l'Ecosse, Dessinees d'Apres Nature par F. A. Pernot . . . Paris: 1826-28. V. 45

PICHOT, PIERRE

De Rheumatismo, Catarrho Variisque a Cerebro Destillationibus, & Horum Curatione Libellus. Bordeaux: 1577. V. 42

PICK, JOHN F.

Surgery of Repair Principles, Problems, Procedures. Philadelhpia: 1949. V. 43

PICKARD-CAMBRIDGE, ARTHUR

The Dramatic Festivals of Athens. Oxford: 1953. V. 44

PICKARD, F. W.

Trout Fishing in Ireland. New York: 1938. V. 39

Trout Fishing in New Zealand in Wartime. New York: 1940. V. 39; 43

Trout Fishing in Ireland. New York: 1940. V. 43

PICKARD, LEONARD

A Catalogue (together with a catalogue, part the second) of the Valuable and Extensive Collection of Prints . . . Etchings, . . . with an Assemblage of Near 1500 English Portraits . . . London: 1802. V. 38; 45

PICKARD, SAMUEL T.

Hawthorne's First Diary With an Account of Its Discovery and Loss. Boston & New York: 1897. V. 37; 40

PICKBOURN, JAMES

A Dissertation on the English Verb. London: 1789. V. 41

PICKELL, JOHN

New Chapter in the Early Life of Washington. New York: 1856. V. 46

PICKEN, ANDREW

The Canadas, as They at Present Commend Themselves to The Enterprize of Emigrants, Colonists and Capitalists. London: 1832. V. 43

PICKEN, EBENEEZER

Miscellaneous Poems, Songs, Etc., Partly in the Scottish Dialect with a Copious Glossary. Edinburgh: 1813. V. 42

PICKENS, FRANCIS WILKINSON

Message No. 1 of His Excellency F. W. Pickens, to the Legislature, at the Annual Session of November 1861. Columbia: 1861. V. 44

Oration Delivered Before the Euphradian and Clariosophic Societies, on the Influence of Government Upon the Nature and Destiny of Man. Columbia: 1855. V. 44

PICKENS, MONROE

Counsin Monroe's History of the Pickens Family. Easley: 1951. V. 42

PICKERELL, ANNIE D.

Pioneer Women in Texas. Austin: 1929. V. 41

PICKERILL, WILLIAM N.

History of the Third Indiana Cavalry. Indianapolis: 1906. V. 42

PICKERING

Catalogue of Biblical, Classical and Historical Manuscripts and of Rare and Curious Books. London: 1834. V. 40

PICKERING, AMELIA

The Sorrows of Werter: a Poem. London: 1788. V. 42

PICKERING & CHATTO

A Catalogue of Old and Rare Books. London: 1893/94/95. V. 38; 42; 44

A Collection of Old and Rare Books of English Literature. London. V. 40

An Illustrated Catalogue of Old and Rare Books . . . London: 1907-09. V. 40

An Illustrated Catalogue of Old and Rare Boosk, Illuminated Manuscripts, Specimens of Fine Old and Modern Bindings. London: 1910. V. 46

PICKERING, ELLEN

The Expectant, a Novel. London: 1842. V. 44

The Prince and the Pedler; or, The Siege of Bristol, by the author of 'The Heiress' etc. New York: 1839. V. 46

The Secret Foe, an Historical Novel. London: 1841. V. 45; 46

PICKERING, HAROLD G.

Angling of the Test, or True Love Under Stress. New York: 1936. V. 39; 40; 43

'Merry Xmas. Mr. Williams 20 Pine St. N.Y.' New York: 1940. V. 43

PICKERING, HENRY

The Ruins of Paestum; and Other Compositions in Verse. (with) Athens; and Other Poems. Massachusetts: 1824. V. 37

PICKERING, JOHN

A Comprehensive Lexicon of the Greek Language. Boston: 1847. V. 38

An Essay on a Uniform Orthography for the Indian Languages of North America. Cambridge: 1820. V. 37; 38; 41; 44

PICKERING, JOSEPH

Emigration or No Emigration; Being the Narrative of the Author . . . from the Year 1824-1830. London: 1830. V. 43

Inquiries of an Emigrant: Being the Narrative of an English Farmer from the Year 1824 to 1830. London: 1832. V. 38

PICKERING, MARY ORNE

Life of John Pickering. Boston: 1887. V. 38

PICKERING, ROGER

Reflections Upon Theatrical Expression in Tragedy. London: 1755. V. 39

PICKERING, TIMOTHY

Instructions to the Envoys Extraordinary from the United States to the French Republic, With Letters and Dispatches. Philadelphia: 1798. V. 39; 43

Letter from the Secretary of War . . . Relative to, I. The Present Military Force of the United States. II. Measures Which Have Been Pursued to Obtain Proper Sites for Arsenals. III. Measures Which Have Been Taken to Replenish . . . Philadelphia: 1796. V. 46

Letter from Mr. Pickering, Secretary of State, to the Dhevalier de Yrujo, Envoy Extraordinary and Minister Plenipotentiary of His Catholic Majesty to the United States of America. August 8, 1797. Trenton;: 1797. V. 37; 46

Recueil de Pieces Relatives a Fievre Jaune d'Amerique. Marseille: 1779. V. 38

Review of the Administration of the Government of the United States of America . . . Boston: 1797. V. 42

PICKERING, WILLIAM

Annual Message of the Governor of the Territory of Washington. Delivered Dec. 17th, 1862. V. 42

Annual Message of the Governor of the Territory of Washington, Delivered Dec. 17th, 1862. Olympia: 1867. V. 42

Annual Message of Governor . . . to the Legislative Assembly of the Territory of Washington, at its Twelfth regular Session . . . Olympia: 1864. V. 37; 42

Annual Message of the Governor of the Territory of Washington, Delivered December 17th, 1862. Olympia: 1862. V. 37

Great Books on Great Subjects. London: 1843-54. V. 40

Veto Message of Governor . . . To the Legislative Assembly of the Territory of Washington, Relative to an Act to Incorporate the Skagit River Log Driving Company. Olympia: 1865. V. 37; 42

PICKETT, ALBERT JAMES

History of Alabama, and Incidentally of Georgia and Mississippi, From the Earliest Period. Charleston: 1851. V. 42; 46

PICKETT, LASALLE CORBELL

The In de Miz Series. Washington: 1900-01. V. 38

PICKETT, WILLIAM VOSE

New System of Architecture, Founded on the Forms of Nature, and Developing the Properties of Metals . . . London: 1845. V. 43

PICKLES, WILKINSON

Reminiscences of Tours: America, 1890 and Palestine, 1894. Halifax: 1895. V. 37; 43

PICKNEY, PAULINE A.

Painting in Texas: The Nineteenth Century. Austin: 1967. V. 37

PICKRELL, ANNIE DOOM

Pioneer Women in Texas. Austin: 1929. V. 37; 38; 43

PICKTHALL, MARJORIE

The Bridge. London: 1922. V. 43

The Wood Carver's Wife. Toronto: 1922. V. 43

PICO DELLA MIRANDOLA, GIOVANNI 1463-1494

Concordia . . . in Disputationes Adversus Astrologos. Bologna: 1496. V. 41

PICO DELLA MIRANDOLA, GIOVANNI FRANCESCO

De Auro Libri Tres. Ferrara,: 1587. V. 37

Dialogo Intitulato la Strega. Pescia: 1555. V. 38

PICO DELLA MIRANDOLA, IOANNES

Omnia Opera. Paris: 1517. V. 37; 42

PICOT, CHARLES

Produit d'une nouvelle machine inventee par C. les Pico, M.d de bois et scieur par mecanique, a Chalons S/M . . . Cette machine permet de tirer 150 feuilles as pouce. 1934. V. 37

PICTON, J. A.

Memorials of Liverpool, Historical and Topographical . . . London: 1873. V. 39

PICTON, THOMAS

A Letter Addressed to the Rt. Hon. Lord Hobart, His Majesty's Late Principal Secretary of State for the Colonial Department . . . London: 1804. V. 43

THE PICTORIAL Album or Cabinet of Painting for the Year 1837. London: 1836. V. 46

PICTORIAL and Biographical Memoirs of Elkhart and St. Joseph Counties, Indiana. Together with Biographies of Many Prominent Men of Northern Indiana and the Whole State . . . Chicago: 1893. V. 43

PICTORIAL Atlas of the Greater United States and the World. Philadelphia: 1899. V. 45
PICTORIAL Atlas of the Greater United States and the World. Philadelphia/Chicago;: 1902. V. 45

PICTORIAL Gallery of Arts. London: 1845. V. 41

A PICTORIAL History of Greece. New York: 1849. V. 44

A PICTORIAL Journal of a Voyage Aboard the Three Mast Schooner Louise . . . San Francisco: 1969. V. 46

THE PICTORIAL Museum of Animated Nature. London: 1870. V. 38

THE PICTORIALIST. Los Angeles: 1931. V. 41; 44; 46
THE PICTORIALIST. Los Angeles: 1932. V. 41

PICTORIUS, GEORG

Physicarvm Qvaestionvm Centvriae Tres. Basle: 1568. V. 43

PICTORUM Effigies Illvstrvm qvos Belgivm Habvit Pictorvm Effigies, ad Vivvm Accvrate Delineate . . . Antwerpen: 1600. V. 43

PICTURE Gallery Annual. London: 1877. V. 40

THE PICTURE Gallery Explored; or, An Account of Various Ancient Customs and Manners . . . London: 1825. V. 45

THE PICTURE of a High-Flyer. Colophon: 1704. V. 42

PICTURE of Hastings; Containing Sketches of the Antiquities and Curiosities of that Interesting Part of the Country. Hastings: 1826. V. 39

THE PICTURE Of India; Geographical, Historical and Descriptive. London: 1830. V. 40

THE PICTURE of Kebes the Theban. Gloucestershire: 1906. V. 46

THE PICTURE of London for 1808. London: 1808. V. 39

A PICTURE of Society, or, the Misanthropist. London: 1813. V. 37

PICTURED A, B, C. Philadelphia: 1840. V. 45

PICTURES And Rhymes of Grandma's Time. New York: 1880's. V. 44

PICTURES and Tales for Little Folk. London: 1880. V. 45

PICTURES Everywhere. London: 1900. V. 41

PICTURES of English Life. London: 1865. V. 39

PICTURES of Society Grave and Gay . . . London: 1866. V. 42

PICTURES of the French: a Series of Literary and Graphic Delineations of French Character. London: 1840. V. 41

PICTURESQUE America; or, the Land We Live In. New York: 1872. V. 39; 40

PICTURESQUE Beauties of Boswell. 1973. V. 40

PICTURESQUE Beauties of Boswell: Part the First Containing Ten Prints. London: 1786. V. 45; 46

A PICTURESQUE Descritpion of North Wales: Embellished with Twenty Select Views from Nature. London: 1823. V. 39; 41; 44

THE PICTURESQUE Drawing Book, Containing Six Beautiful Line Engravings, Arranged and Adapted Expressly for the Use of Amateurs . . . N.P., n.d.. V. 38
THE PICTURESQUE Drawing Book, Containing Six Beautiful Line Engravings, Arranged and Adapted Expressly for the Use of Amateurs . . . N.P.: 1805 or later. V. 40

PICTURESQUE Europe. London. V. 38
PICTURESQUE Europe. London. V. 40

PICTURESQUE Europe. London: 1870. V. 40; 46
PICTURESQUE Europe. London, Paris & New York: 1875. V. 39; 40
PICTURESQUE Europe. London: 1876. V. 46
PICTURESQUE Europe. London: 1876-79. V. 42
PICTURESQUE Europe. London: 1879. V. 44

A PICTURESQUE Guide to the Regent's Park; with Accurate Descriptions of the Colosseum, the Diorama and the Zoological Gardens. London: 1829. V. 45

THE PICTURESQUE Mediterranean. New York: 1880. V. 46

PICTURESQUE Palestine. New York: 1881. V. 39

THE PICTURESQUE Pocket Companion and Visitor's Guide Through Mount Auburn. Boston: 1839. V. 44

PICTURESQUE Remains of Boswell: Part the First Containing Ten Prints, Designed and Etched by Two Capital Artists; Part the Second Containing Ten Prints etc. London: 1786. V. 40

PICTURESQUE Representations of the Dress and Manners of the English. London: 1814. V. 44; 46

PICTURESQUE Representations of the Dress and Manners of the Russians. London: 1814. V. 41

PICTURESQUE Shasta Springs on the Shasta Route of the Southern Pacific Co. Between San Francisco and Portland. San Francisco?: 1895? V. 40

PICTURESQUE Sketches of Rustic Scenery, Including Cottages & Farm Houses. London: 1815. V. 44

PICTURESQUE Tucson and Vicinity. Tucson: 1914. V. 39

PICTURESQUE Views on the River Exe. Tiverton: 1819. V. 39; 45

PIDDINGTON, HENRY

Conversations About Hurricanes: for the Use of Plain Sailors. London: 1853. V. 46

An English Index to the Plants of India. Calcutta: 1832. V. 40

PIDGEON, DANIEL

An Engineer's Holiday or Notes of a Round Trip from Long. O to O. London: 1882. V. 40; 41

PIDGEON, WILLIAM

Traditions of De-Coo-Dah & Antiquarian Researches. New York: 1853. V. 40

PIECHOTKA, MARIA

Wooden Synagogues. Warsaw: 1959. V. 42

THE PIED Printer's Primrose Path. Stamford: 1940. V. 42; 44

PIER, GARRETT CHATFIELD

Egyptian Antiquities in the Pier Collection. Chicago: 1906. V. 37; 40; 42; 44

PIERCE, BENJAMIN

A System of Celestial Mechanics. Boston: 1855. V. 40

PIERCE, BESSIE LOUISE

A History of Chicago. New York: 1937-42. V. 37

PIERCE, CLAY ARTHUR

A Potpourri of Poetry and Prose. Cambridge: 1894. V. 40

PIERCE, F. N.

The Genitalia of the Group Tortricidae of the Lepidoptera of the British Islands. (witth) The Genitalia of the Tineid Families of the Lepidoptera of the British Islands. (witth) The Genitalia of the Pyrales with the Deltoids and Plumes. Oundle, Northants: 1938. V. 45

PIERCE, HENRY H.

Report of an Expedition from Fort Colville to Puget Sound, Washington Territory, by Way of Lake Chelan and Skagit River During the months of August and Septemeber, 1881. Washington: 1883. V. 37; 39; 41; 45

PIERCE, HIRAM DWIGHT

A Forty-Niner Speaks. Oakland: 1930. V. 37; 44

PIERCE, LORNE

The House of Ryerson 1829-1954. Toronto: 1954. V. 45

The Ryerson Canadian History Readers. Toronto: 1926-32. V. 37

PIERCE, N. H.

The Free State of Menard: a History of the County. Menard: 1946. V. 45

PIERCE, RICHARD

A New and Easy Guide to the French Language. London: 1776. V. 45

PIERCE, THOMAS 1622-1691

The Sinner Impleaded in His Own Court . . . to Which is Added the Singal Diagnostick Whereby We are to Judge of Our Own Affections . . . London: 1679. V. 39

The Sinner Impleaded in His Own Court . . . Whereunto is Now Added, The Love of Christ Planted Upon the Very Same Turf . . . London: 1670. V. 37

PIERCE, WILLIAM HENRY

From Potlach to Pulpit; Being the Autobiography of the Rev . . . Native Missionary to the Indian Tribes of the Northwest Coast . . . Vancouver: 1933. V. 37; 42

PIERCY, FREDERICK

Route from Liverpool to Great Salt Lake Valley. Los Angeles: 1959. V. 40

PIERCY, JOHN S.

The History of Retford, in the County of Nottingham. Retford: 1828. V. 42

PIERCY, MARGE

Breaking Camp. Middletown, Conn.: 1968. V. 37

PIERIUS, URBAN

Doctrinae De Peccato Iriginali Explicatio Orthodoxa et Methodica. Wittenburg: 1590. V. 44

PIERMARINI, GIUSEPPE

Teatro della Scala in Milano. Milan: 1789. V. 37

PIEROTTI, ERMETE

Jerusalem Explored, Being a Description of the Ancient and Modern City. London: 1864. V. 44

PIERPONT, JOHN

Airs of Palestine, a Poem. Baltimore: 1816. V. 39

The Anti-Slavery Poems. Boston: 1843. V. 42

Proceedings in the Controversy Between a part of the Proprietors and the Pastor of Hollis Street Church. Boston: 1839. V. 44

PIERPONT MORGAN LIBRARY

Ancient Mesopotamian Art and Selected Texts. New York: 1976. V. 44

Chinese Calligraphy and Painting in the Collection of John M. Crawford, Jr. 1962. V. 38

PIERPONT MORGAN LIBRARY, NEW YORK.

Chinese Calligraphy and Painting in the Collection of John M. Crawford Jr. 1962. V. 41

Central European Manuscripts in the Pierpont Morgan Library. New York: 1958. V. 43

Major Acquisitions of the Pierpont Morgan Library 1924-1974. New York: 1974. V. 43

PIERREPONT, EDWARDS

A Review by Judge Pierrepont of Gen. Butler's Defense, Before the House of Representatives, in Relation to the New Orleans Gold. New York: 1865. V. 37; 39; 42

PIERREVILLE, G.

The Present State of Denmark, and Reflections Upon the Ancient State Thereof. London: 1683. V. 38

PIERS, FRANZ

Orchis of East Africa. 1968. V. 46

PIERS, HARRY

Robert Field: Portrait Painter in Oils, Miniature and Watercolours and Engraver. New York: 1927. V. 44; 45

PIERSON, B. T.

Directory of the City of Newark, for 1840-41. Newark: 1840. V. 42

Directory of the City of Newark, 1843-44. Newark: 1843. V. 42

Directory of the City of Neward, for 1844-45. Newark: 1844. V. 41

Directory of the City of Newark, for 1844-45. Newark: 1849. V. 42

Directory of the City of Newark for 1853-54. Newark: 1853. V. 42

Directory of the City of Newark, for 1854-55. Newark: 1854. V. 41

Directory of the City of Newark: for 1836-7, with an Historical Sketch. Newark: 1836. V. 38

PIERSON, DAVID L.

History of the Oranges (N.J.). New York: 1922. V. 41

PIERSON, E.

The Ramapo Pass . . . Including the Village of Ramapo Works, Founded by the Pierson Brothers in 1795 . . . 1955. V. 38

PIERSON, EMILY CATHARINE

Jamie Parker, the Fugitive. Hartford: 1851. V. 43

PIERSON, HAMILTON W.

In the Brush; or, Old-Time Social, Political and Religious Life in the Southwest. New York: 1881. V. 41

PIERZ, FRANZ

Die Indianer in Nord-Amerika, Ihre Lebenswise, Sitten, Begrauche, U.S.W. Nich Vielhahrigem Aufenthalte und Gesammelten Erfahrungen Unter den Verschiedenen Stammen . . . St. Louis: 1855. V. 46

PIESSE, GEORGE W. SEPTIMUS

The Art of Perfumery. London: 1855. V. 39; 42

Chymical, Natural and Physical Magic . . . for the Instruction and Entertainment of Juveniles . . . London: 1865. V. 42

PIETA Oxoniensis in Memory of Sir Thomas Bodley Kt. 1902. V. 40

PIETAS Academiae Cantabrigiensis in funere Serenissimae Principis Wilhelminae Carolinae et Luctu Augustissimi Georgii II Britanniarum &c Uc. Cantabrigiae: 1738. V. 44

PIETAS Academiae Oxoniensis in Obitum Augustissimae et Desideratissimae Reginae Carolinae. Oxonii: 1738. V. 42

PIETAS et Gratulatio Collegii Cantabrigiensis Apud Novanglos . . . Boston: 1761. V. 38

PIETAS Oxoniensis in Memory of Sir Thomas Bodley, Kt. Oxford: 1902. V. 38

PIETRASANTA, SILVESTRO

De Symbolis Heroicis Libri IX. Antwerp: 1634. V. 41

PIGAFETTA, ANTONIO

Magellans's Voyage. A Narrative Account of the First Circumnavigation. New Haven & London: 1969. V. 39; 43

Premier Voyage Autour du Monde . . . Paris: 1800. V. 39

PIGAGE, NICOLAS DE

La Galerie Electorale de Dusseldorff ou Catalogue Raisonne et Figure de ses Tableaux . . . Basle: 1778. V. 40; 44

PIGANIOL DE LA FORCE, JEAN AYMAR

Description de Paris, de Versailles, de Marly, de Meudon, de S. Cloud, de Fontainebleau et de Toutes les Autres Belles Maisons & Chateaux des Environs de Paris . . . Paris: 1742. V. 40; 44

Nouvelle Description des Chateaux et Parcs de Versailles et de marly. Paris: 1751. V. 40

PIGEONS, a Treatise on Domestic: Comprehending all the Different Species Known in England . . . London: 1765. V. 37

PIGGOT, N.

A Treatise of Common Recoveries, Their Nature and Use. London: 1739. V. 40

PIGGOTT BROS. & CO.

Catalogue of Marquees and Tents (for Sporting, Travelling, Engineering, Surveying & Prospecting); Camp Equipment, Harness and Saddlery, Flags and Banners, Gymnastics and Sports. London: 1886. V. 39

PIGGOTT, G. W.

On the Harrogate Spas, and Change of Air. Harrogate: 1856. V. 37

PIGHIUS, STEPHANUS VINANDO 1520-1604

Hercvles Prodicivs, Sev Principis Ivventvtis Vita et Peregrinatio. Antwerp: 1587. V. 39

PIGMAN, WALTER GRIFFITH

The Journal of Walter Griffith Pigman. Mexico, Missouri: 1942. V. 39; 40; 41; 42; 44

PIGNA, GIOVANNI BATTISTA 1530-1575

Carminvm Lib. Qvatvor . . . His Adiunximus Caelii Calcagnini Carm. Lib. III. Lvdovici Areosti Carm. Lib. II. Venice: 1554. V. 39

Gli Heroici. Venice: 1561. V. 43

De Principibus Atestinis Historiarum Libri VIII. Ferrara: 1585. V. 39

PIGNATTI, TERISIO

Giorgione. Complete Edition. London: 1971. V. 37; 40; 43; 44

Pietro Longhi. London: 1969. V. 44; 45; 46

PIGNOTTI, LORENZO 1739-1812

The History of Tuscany, Interspersed with Essays. Edinburgh: 1823. V. 39

PIGOT, CHARLES

The Jockey Club, or a Sketch of the Manners of the Age. Second edition; The Jockey Club, part the second, First edition and the Female Jockey Club, Second edition. London: 1792/1794. V. 37; 39

PIGOT, R.

Twenty-Five Years Big Game Hunting. London: 1928. V. 39; 42

PIGOT, RICHARD

Moral Emblems with Aphorisms, Adages, and Proverbs of All Edges and Nations, from Jacob Cats and Robert Farlie. New York: 1860. V. 45

PIGOTT, CHARLES

The Female Jockey Club, or a Sketch of the Manners of the Age. London: 1794. V. 41; 42; 45; 46

The Jockey Club: or, a Sketch of the Manners of the Age. London: 1792. V. 38; 42

*The Jockey Club, or a Sketch of the Manners of the Age, Part the Second. *The Female Jockey Club.* London: 1792/94. V. 41

The Jockey Club; or a Sketch of the Manners of the Age. New York: 1793. V. 44

Persecution. The Case of Charles Pigott: Contained in the Defence He Had Prepared, and Which Would Have Been Delivered by Him on His Trial . . . London: 1793. V. 43

PIGOTT, NATHANIEL

A Treatise of Common Recoveries, Their nature and Use to Which is Added the Case of Page and Hayward, More Fully Reported Than in any other Book. London: 1739. V. 38

A Treatise of Common Recoveries, Their Nature and Use. In the Savoy: 1739. V. 37

PIGOU, A. C. 1877-1959

The Economics of Welfare. London: 1920. V. 38

Industrial Fluctuations. London: 1927. V. 46

The Theory of Unemployment. London: 1933. V. 43; 46

PIKE, ALBERT

Ariel. N.P.: 1875. V. 45

Cleopatre. N.P.: 1875. V. 40

Hymns to the Gods. 1872. V. 45

Hymns to the Gods and Other Poems . . . N.P.: 1872. V. 42

Hymns to the Gods and Other Poems. Washington: 1872. V. 39; 45

Hymns To the Gods, and Other Poems. Washington: 1873/1882. V. 45

A Last Farewell. Albert Pike's Touching Letter to a Dying Friend. N.P.: 1885. V. 39

A Letter to the President of the United States. New York: 1865. V. 42

Letters to the People of the Northern States. Washington: 1856. V. 39

The Light of Days Long Past. Washington: 1869. V. 37

Nugae. Philadelphia: 1854. V. 46

Prose Sketches and Poems. Boston: 1834. V. 37; 38; 40; 41; 42; 44; 45; 46

Re-Nnion (Sic). Washington: 1869. V. 40

State or Province! Bond or Free! Little Rock: 1861. V. 42

Thoughts on Certain Political Questions by a Looker On. Washington: 1859. V. 39

PIKE, JAMES

The Scout and Ranger: Being the Personal Adventures . . . as a Texas Ranger, in the Indian Wars, and as scout and spy. Cincinnati: 1865. V. 37; 39; 41; 42; 43; 45

The Scout and Ranger: Being the Personal Adventures of Corporal Pike of the Fourth Ohio Cavalry. Hawley, Cincinnati &: 1865. V. 46

PIKE, JAMES S.

Auid-Carolina Onder Documents Relating to South Carolina, Now Existing In the State Paper Office. London . . . Charleston: 18. V. 46

The Prostrate State: South Carolina Under Negro Government. New York: 1874. V. 42

PIKE, LUKE OWEN

A History of Crime in England Illustrating the Changes of the Laws in the Progress of Civilisation. London: 1873-76. V. 38

PIKE, NICHOLAS

Sub-Tropical Rambles in the Land of the Aphanapteryx. New York: 1873. V. 42

Sub-Tropical Rambles in the Land of the Aphanapteryx. London: 1873. V. 38; 43

PIKE, NICOLAS

A New and Complete System of Arithmetic, Composed for the Use of the Citizens of the U.S. Worcester: 1797. V. 40; 41

A New and Complete System of Arithmetic, for the Use of the Citizens of the U.S. Newburyport: 1788. V. 37; 40; 43

Sub-Tropical Rambles in the Land of the Aphanapteryx: Personal Experiences, Adventures and Wanderings in and Around the Island of Mauritius. New York: 1873. V. 43

PIKE, SAMUEL

A Compendious Hebrew Lexicon Adapted to the English Language. Cambridge: 1802. V. 38

PIKE, WARBURTON

The Barren Ground of Northern Canada. London: 1892. V. 39; 42; 43

Through the Subarctic Forest. London: 1896. V. 42; 44

PIKE, WARBURTON MAYER

The Barren Ground of Northern Canada. London: & New York: 1892. V. 37

Through the Subarctic Forest. A Record of a Canoe Journey from Fort Wrangel to the Pelly Lakes and down the Yukon River to the Behring Sea. London/New York: 1896. V. 37; 42; 43

PIKE, ZEBULON MONTGOMERY 1779-1813

An Account of Expeditions to the Sources of the Mississippi and Through the Western Parts of Louisiana, to the Sources of the Arkansaw . . . V. 45

An Account of a Voyage Up the Mississippi River, from St. Louis to Its Source . . . Philadelphia. V. 46

An Account of a Voyage Up the Mississippi River, from St. Louis to Its Source; Made Under the Orders of the War Department, by Lieut. Pike . . . Waashington: 1807. V. 38

An Account of Expeditions to the Source of the Mississippi . . . and a Tour through the Interior Parts of New Spain. Philadelphia: 1810. V. 37; 38; 39; 40; 41; 42; 43; 45; 46

An Account of a Voyage Up the Mississippi River from St. Louis to Its Source. Washington?: 1807? V. 40

The Expeditions of Zebulon Mongomery Pike . . . New York: 1895. V. 39

The Expeditions . . . to Headwaters of the Mississippi River, Through Louisiana Territory, and in New Spain During the Years 1805-7 . . . New York: 1895. V. 39; 40; 41; 42; 44; 45; 46

Exploratory Travels through the Western Territories of North America . . . Performed in the Years 1805, 1806, 1807. London: 1811. V. 38; 39; 40; 41; 42; 43; 45; 46

Exploratory Travels through the Western Territories of North America. Denver: 1889. V. 40

The Journals of Zebulon Montgomery Pike with Letters and Related Documents. Norman: 1966. V. 39; 43; 46

Pike's Explorations by Order of the U. S. Government to the Source of the Mississippi in 1805 through the Territory of Louisiana and Provinces of New Spain in 1806-07. Denver: 1889. V. 37; 39

Voyage au Nouveau-Mexique . . . Pour Reconnoitre Les Sources des Rivieres Arkansas, Kansas, La Plate et Pierre-Jaune. Paris: 1812. V. 40

PIKE'S Illustrated Catalogue of Scientific and Medical Instruments. Dracut: 1984. V. 45
PIKE'S Illustrated Catalogue of Scientific and Medical Instruments. Dracut and San Francisco: 1984. V. 42

THE PIKE'S Peak Region: Picturesque and Descriptive Including Colorado Springs, Manitou, and Colorado City. Neehah: 1889. V. 42

PILADE, GIOVANNI FRANCESCO BOCCARDO

Vocabvlarivm. Brescia: 1567. V. 42

PILATE, PONTIUS

Thresor Admirable de la Sentence Prononce par Ponce Pilate . . . Paris: 1581. V. 46

PILCHER, LEWIS

The Treatment of Wounds, Its Principles and Practice, General and Special. New York: 1883. V. 42

PILCHER, LEWIS STEPHEN

A List of Books by Some of the Old Masters of Medicine and Surgery Together with Books on the History of Medicine and On Medical Biography in the Possession of Lewis Stephen Pilcher With Biographical and Bibliographical Notes and Reproductions . . . Brooklyn: 1918. V. 41; 42; 45

PILCHER, VELONA

The Searcher. Garden City: 1929. V. 45

PILCHER, VERONA

The Searcher. London: 1929. V. 37; 40

PILES, ROGER DE

The Art of Painting with the Lives and Characters of Above 300 of the Most Eminent Painters . . . London: 1744. V. 38

The Art of Painting, with the Lives and Characters of Above 300 of the Most Eminent Painters. London: 1750? V. 42; 44

The Principles of Painting . . . London: 1743. V. 42

THE PILGRIM Fathers: a Journal of their Coming in the Mayflower to New Engladn and their Life and Adventures There. London: 1939. V. 43; 46

PILGRIM, THOMAS

Live Boys; or, Charley and Nasho in Texas . . . Boston: 1878. V. 37; 46

PILKINGTON, H. W.

A Musical Dictionary, Comprising the Etymology and Different Meanings of all the Terms that Most Frequently Occur in Modern Composition. Boston: 1812. V. 46

PILKINGTON, JOHN CARTERET

The Real Story of John Carteret Pilkington. London: 1760. V. 42

PILKINGTON, MARY HOPKINS

The Calendar; or, Monthly Recreations . . . London: 1807. V. 42; 44; 45

Celebrity: or the Unfortunate Choice. London: 1815. V. 38

A Mirror for the Female Sex. Hartford: 1799. V. 37; 44; 45

PILKINGTON, MARY S.

Edward Barnard; or, Merit Exalted, Containing the History of the Edgerton Family. London: 1797. V. 45; 46

PILKINGTON, MATTHEW

A Dictionary of Painters . . . London: 1805. V. 39; 40

A General Dictionary of Painters. London: 1824. V. 37

The Gentleman's and Connoisseur's Dictionary of Painters. L: 1798. V. 38

The Gentlemen's and Connoisseur's Dictionary of Painters. London: 1770. V. 44

Poems on Several Occasions. Dublin: 1730. V. 45

Poems on Several Occasions. London: 1731. V. 40

Poems on Several Occasions. London: 1731. V. 39; 40; 42; 45

A PILL to Purge State-Melancholy; or, a Collection of Excellent New Ballads. London: 1715. V. 45

PILLANS, JAMES 1778-1864

Three Lectures on the Proper Objects and Methods of Education in Reference to the Different Orders of Society . . . Edinburgh: 1836. V. 45

PILLAY, P. STREENEVASSA

A Manual for Youth and Students. N.P.: 1846. V. 41

PILLERI, G.

Investigations on Beavers. Ostermundigen: 1983-86. V. 37

Investigations on Cetacea. Ostermundigen: 1969-86. V. 37; 38

PILLING, JAMES CONSTANTINE

Bibliography of the Algonquian Languages. Washington: 1891. V. 38; 39

Proof-Sheets of a Bibliography of the Language of the North American Indians. Washington: 1885. V. 45

Proof-Sheets of a Bibliography of the Languages of the North America Indians. Brooklyn: 1970. V. 40; 42; 43

Proof-Sheets of a Bibliography of the Languages of the North American Indians. Brooklyn: 1975. V. 44

PILLING, WILLIAM

Near the Lagunas; or, Scenes in the States of La Plata. London: 1878. V. 39; 42

PILON, FREDERICK

Aerostation; or, the Templar's Stratagem. London: 1784. V. 39

PILSBRY, H. A.

Land Mollusca of North America. Philadelphia: 1939-48. V. 37

PIM, BEDFORD

Dottings on the Roadside, in Panama, Nicaragua, and Mosquito. London: 1869. V. 39

The Gate of the Pacific. London: 1863. V. 37; 39

PIM, JAMES

The Atmospheric Railway. A Letter to the Right Hon. the Earl of Ripon, President of the Board of Trade. London: 1841. V. 46

PIMENTA, NICOLAU

Epistola Partis Nicolai Pimentae Visitatoris Societatis Jesu in India Orientali. Rome: 1601. V. 38

PINAMONTI, F.

Hell Opened to Christians, to Caution Them from Entering Into It. Dublin: 1836. V. 46

PINCHARD, ELIZABETH SIBTHORPE

The Blind Child, or Anecdotes of the Wyndham Family. London: 1791. V. 41; 42; 45

The Blind Child, or Anecdotes of the Wyndham Family Written for the Use of Young People. London: 1795. V. 40

The Two Cousins, a Moral Story, for the Use of Young Persons. London: 1794. V. 40; 45; 46

PINCKARD, GEORGE

Notes on the West Indies. London: 1806. V. 40

PINCKNEY, CHARLES

Three Letters, Writeen & Originally Published, Under the Signature of a South Carolina Planter. The first, on the case of Jonathan Robbins . . . the second, on the recent captures of American vessels by British cruisers, contrary to the . . . Philadelphia: 1799. V. 37; 38; 46

PINCKNEY, CHARLES COATESWORTH

Nebuchadnezzar's Fault and Fall. A Sermon Preached at Grace Church, Charleston, S.C. On the 17th of February, 1861. Charleston: 1861. V. 44

PINCKNEY, GUSTAVUS M.

Life of John C. Calhoun Being a View of the Principal Events of His Career and an Account of His Contributions . . . Charleston;: 1903. V. 42

PINCKNEY, HENRY L.

Address to the Electors of Charleston District, South Carolina, on the Subject of the Abolition of Slavery. Washington: 1836. V. 42

PINCKNEY, JOSEPHINE

Sea-Drinking Cities. New York: 1927. V. 39

PINCKNEY, PAULINE A.

Painting in Texas: The Nineteenth Century. Austin: 1967. V. 38; 42; 45

PINCOCK, JENNY O'HARA

The Trails of Truth. Los Angeles: 1930. V. 43

PINCOT, DANIEL

An Essay on the Origin, Nature, Uses and Properties of Artificial Stone. London: 1770. V. 44; 45

PINDAR

Carmina. Notae Heynianae: Paraphrasis Benedictina: & Lexicon Pindaricum. London: 1814. V. 40

Pindar's Odes of Victory: The Olympian and Pythian Odes. Stratford-on-Avon: 1928. V. 41; 46

Odes: With Several Other Pieces in Prose and Verse. London: 1753. V. 40; 46

Odes of Victory. Boston: 1929-30. V. 46

Olympia, Pythia, Nemea, Isthmia. Caeterorum Octo Lyricorum Carmina. Geneva: 1560. V. 37

Olympia . Pythia. Nemea. Isthmia. Geneva: 1599. V. 38; 40; 41; 43; 45

Olympia, Pythia, Nemea, Isthmia. Samur: 1620. V. 40

Olympia, Nemea, Pythia, Istmia. Oxford: 1697. V. 43

Pindari Olympia Nemea, Pythia, Isthmia. Oxonii: 1697. V. 38

(Greek & Latin) Pindari Lyricoru Principis . . . Wittenberg: 1616. V. 44

The Pythian, Nemean and Isthmian Odes of Pindar Translated into English Verse. London: 1778. V. 42; 46

Pythian Odes. London: 1928. V. 41

Pythian Odes. London: 1928. V. 38; 39; 41; 42; 44

Opera. Rome: 1515. V. 45

Opera. (In Greek). Glasguae: 1754-58. V. 37

PINDAR, PETER

The Works. London: 1794-1801. V. 43

PINDAR, PETER, JR., PSEUD.

The Hop-boy; or Idalia's Grove. London: 1804. V. 38

PINDARUS

Hoc est Pindari Lyricorum Principis, plus Quam Sexcentis in Locis Emaculati; ut Jam Legi & Intelli Possit . . . Wittenberg: 1616. V. 39

Olympia. Geneva: 1599. V. 38

PINDBORG, J. J.

The Dentist in Art. Copenhagen: 1961. V. 39

The Dentist in Art. London: 1961. V. 38; 40

PINDEMONTE, MARCO ANTONIO

Orazione Funebre in Morte del Marchese Scipione Maffei detta Nella Cattedrale di Verona . . . Verona: 1755. V. 46

PINDER, ULRICH

Speculum Passionis Domini Nostri Ihesu Christi. Nuremberg: 1507. V. 38

PINE, GEORGE W.

Beyond the West: . . . Two Years' Travel in . . . The Rocky Mountains, and Picturesque Parks of Colorado . . . Utica: 1870. V. 40; 45

PINE, JOHN

The Procession and Ceremonies Observed at the Time of the Installation of the Knights Companions of the Most Honourable Military Order of the Bath, Upon Thursday, June 17, 1725. London: 1730. V. 38

PINEDA, JUAN DE ?1515-1597

Commentariorum in Iob Libri Tredecim. Cologne: 1600, 1603. V. 40

PINEDA, PEDRO

A Short and Compendious Method for the Learning to Speak, Read and Write the Spanish Language. London: 1726. V. 40; 42; 44

A Short and Compendious Method for Learning to Speak, Read and Write, the English and Spanish Languages . . . London: 1762. V. 42

PINEDA, PEDRO continued

A Synopsis of the Genealogy of the Most Antient and Most Noble Family of the Brigantes or Douglas. London: 1754. V. 38

PINEDA, PETER

A Dictionary of Spanish and English. London: 1740. V. 45

PINEL, PHILLIPE 1745-1826

Traite Medico-Philosophique sur l'Alienation Mentale, ou la Manie. Paris: 1801. V. 37; 45

A Treatise on Insanity, In Which are Contained the Principles of a New and More Practical Nosology of Maniacal Disorders . . . Sheffield: 1806. V. 45

PINELLI, BARTOLOMEO

Raccolta di Cinquante Costumi Pittoreschi. Rome: 1809. V. 46

PINELLI, MAFFEI

A Catalogue of the Magnificent and Celebrated Library of Maffei Pinelli . . . Will be Sold at Auction. London: 1789. V. 38

PINERO, ARTHUR WING

The Amazons. London: 1895. V. 45

Dr. Harmer's Holidays. London: 1924. V. 46

The Gay Lord Quex: a Comedy in Four Acts. London: 1900. V. 37; 45

The Notorious Mrs. Ebbsmith. London: 1895. V. 45

The Second Mrs. Tanqueray. London: 1895. V. 45

PINESVILLE LAND & LUMBER CO.

A Glimpse of Pinesville Kentucky. Louisville: 1888. V. 45

PINGENOT, BEN

Paso Del Aguila: A Chronicle of Frontier Days on the Texas Border Recorded in the Memoirs of Jesse Sumpter. Austin: 1969. V. 37

PINGONIUS, PHILIBERTUS

Inclytorum Saxoniae Sabaudiaeque Principium Arbor Gentilitia. Augustae Taurinorum: 1581. V. 38

PINGRE, ALEXANDRE GUI

Cometographie ou Traite Historique et Ehtorique des Cometes . . . Paris: 1783-84. V. 44

PINGRET, EDOUARD

Voyage de S. M. Louis-Philippe Ier Roi des Francais au Chateau de Windsor dedie a S.M. Victoria . . . Paris: 1846. V. 39; 44

PINHEY, E. C. G.

Moths of Southern Africa. Cape Town: 1975. V. 38; 40

Moths of Southern Africa. Rotterdam: 1979. V. 37

PINKEMAN, WILLIAM

The Last New Prologue and Epilogue Spoken by the Famous Commedian Mr. William Pinkeman. London: 1701. V. 39

PINKERTON, ALLAN

Claude Melnotte as a Detective and Other Stories. Toronto: 1875. V. 46

Strikers, Communists, Tramps and Detectives. New York: 1878. V. 38

PINKERTON, JOHN

Ancient Scotish Poems, Never Before in Print. London: 1786. V. 37; 39; 45; 46

An Enquiry into the History of Scotland Preceding the Reign of Malcolm III or the Year 1056. London: 1789. V. 45

An Essay on Medals. London: 1784. V. 38; 45

A General Collection of the Best and Most Interesting Voyages and Travels in All Parts of the World . . . London: 1808-14. V. 42; 46

The History of Scotland from the Accession of the House of Stuart to that of Mary. London: 1797. V. 38; 39; 44

Modern Geography. London: 1807. V. 45

Modern Geography a Description of the Empires, Kingdoms, States and Colonies with the Oceans, Seas and Isles; In all Parts of the World. London: 1802. V. 37

Petralogy. A Treatise on Rocks. London: 1811. V. 40

Recollections of Paris, in the Years 1802-3-4-5. London: 1806. V. 45

Rimes. London: 1781. V. 45; 46

Rimes . . . London: 1782. V. 41; 45

PINKERTON, ROBERT

Russia: or, Miscellaneous Observations on the Past and Present State of that Country and Its Inhabitants . . . London: 1833. V. 38; 40; 45; 46

PINKERTON, THOMAS A.

Amy Wynter. London: 1880. V. 46

PINKEY, MILES

Sweete Thoughts of Jesus and Marie. Paris: 1665. V. 37

PINKHAM, DANIEL

Symphony No. 1 for Orchestra. New York: 1961. V. 45

PINKNEY, EDWARD COOTE

Look Out Upon the Stars My Love. Baltimore: 1823. V. 37

PINKNEY, NINIAN 1776-1825

Travels through the South of France, and in the Interior of the Provicnes of provence and Languedoc . . . by a Route . . . along the Banks of the Loire, the Isere and the Garonne. London: 1809. V. 39

PINKNEY, WILLIAM

Message from the President of the United States, Transmitting Extracts from the Correspondence of . . . Agreeably to a Resolution of the House . . . Washington: 1809. V. 37

Speech of . . . in the House of Delegates of Maryland, at Their Session in November 1789. Philadelphia: 1790. V. 46

PINKS, WILLIAM J.

The History of Clerkenwell. London: 1881. V. 41

PINNEY, H.

The Family Receipt Book . . . Philadelphia: 1847. V. 43

PINNINGTON, E.

George Paul Chalmers and the Art of His Time. Glasgow: 1896. V. 39

PINNOCK, W.

A Guide to Knowledge. London: 1833-34. V. 46

PINNOCK, WILLIAM

Pinnock's Catechisms. London: 1825? V. 37

PINO, P. B.

Three New Mexico Chronicles . . . Albuqueruque: 1942. V. 37

PINO, PEDRO BAPTISTA

Exposicion Sucinta y Sencilla de la Provincia del Nuevo Mexico . . . Cadiz: 1812. V. 40; 41; 42

Noticias Historicas Y Estadisticas de la Antigua Provincia de Nuevo-Mexico . . . Mexico: 1849. V. 38; 40

PINSENT, JOSEPH

Conversations on Political Economy: or, A Series of Dialaogues with Remarks on Our Present Distresses, Their Causes and the Remedies Applicable to Them. London: 1821. V. 37

PINTER, HAROLD 1930-

The Birthday Party. London: 1959. V. 40

The Birthday Party and the Room. New York: 1961. V. 43

The Caretaker. London: 1960. V. 41

The Caretaker. A Play in Three Acts. (1960). V. 37

Five Screenplays. London: 1971. V. 37

The French Lieutenant's Woman. A Screenplay. Boston: 1981. V. 39; 40; 41; 42; 43; 44; 46

The Homecoming. London: 1968. V. 46

Monologue. London: 1973. V. 39; 42; 46

No Man's Land. London: 1975. V. 37; 40; 42; 43

Poems. London: 1968. V. 39; 40; 43; 45

Poems. London: 1971. V. 39; 44

The Servant. V. 46

PINTO DE AZEREDO, JOSE

Ensaios Sobre Algumas Enfermedades d'Angola. Lisbon: 1799. V. 39

PINTO, PEDRO DE SAO JOAO

Vida Espiritual do Homem, Conferida com as 6. Idades da Vida Temporal. Lisbon: 1633. V. 38

PINTO PIZARRO DE ALMEIDA CARVALHAES, RODRIGO

Noticias Biographicas de Francisco Homem de Magalhaes Pizarro . . . Rio de Janeiro: 1819. V. 39

PINTO RIBEIRO, J.

Elogio do Muy Valeroso e de Rares Virtudes Dom Joao de Castro Illustrissimo Governador & Visorrey da India. Lisbon: 1642. V. 45

PINTURA del Gobernador, Alcades y Regidores de Mexico. Madrid: 1878. V. 45

PINU, JOSEPHUS

Carmen Continens Narrationem Non Qvidem Historicam Sed Conflictam Admontendae Adolescentiae Causa. Wittenberg?: 1564? V. 39; 40; 45

PINWELL, G. J.

A Catalogue of Pictures and Sketches Exhibited at the Royal Society of Artists, Birmingham, March 1895. London. V. 39

PIO, GIOVANNI MICHELE

Della Nobile et Generosa Progenie del P. S. Domenico in Italia. Bologna: 1615. V. 37

PIONEER LAW-MAKERS ASSOCIATION OF IOWA

A Brief History of the Organization and Proceeding of the Reunions of 1886 and 1890-(1902). Des Moines: 1890-1902. V. 38

THE PIONEER Press Standard Atlas of the World. St. Paul/Indianapolis: 1888. V. 45

PIONEERS of the Sacramento. San Francisco: 1953. V. 42

PIORRY, PIERRE ADOLPHE 1794-1879

De la Percussion Mediate et des Signes Obtenus a l'Aide de ce Nouveau Moyen d'Exploration, dans les Maladies des Organes Thoraciques et Abdominaux. Paris: 1828. V. 42

PIOZZI, HESTER LYNCH SALUSBURY THRALE 1741-1821

Anecdotes of the Late Samuel Johnson, LL.D. During the Last Twenty Years of His Life. Dublin: 1786. V. 38; 40; 41

Anecdotes of the Late Samuel Johnson, LL.D. London: 1826. V. 46

Anecdotes of the late Samuel Johnson, LL.D. during the last Twenty Years of his Life. London: 1786. V. 37; 39; 40; 41; 42; 43; 44; 45; 46

Autobiography, Letters and Literary Remains of . . . Boston: 1861. V. 39; 40

Autobiography: Letters and Literary Remains of . . . London: 1861. V. 37; 38; 39; 40; 41; 42; 45; 46

British Synonymy. Dublin: 1794. V. 38

Johnsoniana, Anecdotes of the Late Samuel Johnson, by Mrs. Piozzi, Richard Cumberland, Bishop Percy and others. London: 1884. V. 39

Letters to and from the late Samuel Johnson, to which are added some Poems never before printed. Published from the original Mss. in her possession. London: 1788. V. 37; 45

Observations and Reflections Made in the Course of a Journey through France, Italy and Germany. Dublin: 1789. V. 40; 43; 44; 45; 46

Observations & Reflections Made in the Course of a Journey through France, Italy and Germany. London: 1789. V. 37; 38; 39; 41; 42; 44; 45; 46

Piozzi Marginalia. Cambridge: 1927. V. 40

Piozzi Marginalia . . . Cambridge: 195. V. 46

Piozzi Marginalia. Comprising Some Extracts from Manuscripts, and Annotations from her book. Cambridge: 1925. V. 37; 39; 40; 41; 45

Piozziana Thraliana, the Diary of Mrs. Hester Lynch Thrale (later Mrs. Piozzi) 1776-1809. Oxford: 1942. V. 40

Piozziana Thraliana, the Diary of Mrs. Hester Lynch Thrale (later Mrs. Piozzi) 1776-1809. Oxford: 1951. V. 40

Piozziana; or, Recollections of the late Mrs. Piozzi, with remarks. By a friend. London: 1833. V. 37; 42

Retrospection: or a Review of the Most Striking Important Events, Characters, Situations and Their Consequences, Which the Last Eighteen Hundred Years Have Presented to the View of Mankind. London: 1801. V. 37; 38; 39; 40; 42; 45; 46

Thraliana, the Diary of . . . Oxford: 1942. V. 39; 45; 46

Thraliana. The Diary of Mrs. Hester Lynch Thrale . . . 1951. V. 42

Thrailiana. The Diary of Mrs. Hester Lynch Thrale . . . 1951. V. 45

Thraliana, the Diary of Mrs. Hester Lynch Thrale. Oxford: 1951. V. 39; 45; 46

PIOZZI, HESTER LYNCY SALUSBURY THRALE 1741-1821

Mrs. Thrale Afterwards Mrs. Piozzi Edited L.B. Seeley. A Sketch of Her Life and Passages from Her Diaries, Letters and Other Writings. With nine illustrations (ans numerous extra engravings tipped in). London: 1891. V. 37

PIPER, H. BEAM

Four Day Planet. 1961. V. 39

Murder in the Gun Room. New York: 1953. V. 39; 42

PIPER, JOHN

Buildings and Prospects. London: 1948. V. 40; 43

Catalogue to an Exhibition of Paintings, Drawings, Prints and Illustrated Books. 1973. V. 37

Elizabethan Love Songs. Barham Manor, Suffolk: 1955. V. 37; 41

The Gaudy Saint and Other Poems. Bristol: 1924. V. 38

John Piper. Paintings, Drawings, and Theatre Designs 1932-1954. New York: 1955. V. 46

Oxon. London: 1930's. V. 44

Piper's Places - John Piper in England and Wales. London: 1983. V. 40

PIPER, MYFANWY

The Wood-Engravings of Reynolds Stone. London: 1951. V. 45

PIPER, WATTY

The Little Engine That Could. New York: 1930. V. 45

PIPPET, GABRIEL

A Little Rosary. Sussex: 1930. V. 45

A Little Rosary. (Flansham: 1930). V. 37

PIRANESI, FRANCESCO

Il Teatro d'Ercolano. Rome: 1783. V. 37

Il Treatro d'Ercolano. Paris: 1800. V. 37

PIRANESI, GIAMBATTISTA

Le Antichita Romane Divisa in Quattro Tomi. Rome: 1756-57. V. 37

Campus Martius Antiquae Urbis. Rome: 1762. V. 37

Della Magnificenza ed Architettura de 'Romani. (with) Osservazioni . . . Sopra la Lettre de M. Mariette aux Auteurs de la Gazette Litteraire de l'Europe . . . Rome: 1761. 1765. V. 37

Diverse Maniere d'Adornare i Cammini . . . Diverse Mannrs of Ornamenting Chimneys and all Other Parts of Houses Taken from the Egyptian, Tuscan, and Grecian Architecture with an Apologetic Essay in Defence of Egyptian and Tuscan Architecture. Rome: 1769. V. 37; 45

Pianta delle Fabriche Esistenti Nella Villa Adriana. Rome: 1781. V. 37

PIRANESI, GIOVANNI BATTISTA

Campus Martius Antique Urbis. Rome: 1762. V. 42

EL PIRATA. N.P.,: 1855. V. 39

PIRCKHEIMER, WILIBALD 1470-1530

Bilibaldi Pirckheymeri de Convitiis Monachi illius, Qui Grecolatine Caecolmpadius, Germanice Uero Ausshin Nuncupa tur, ad Eleutherium suum Epistola. Nurebergae: 1527. V. 38

PIRES CARVALHO, LOURENCO

Epitome das Indulgencias, e Privilegios da Bulla da Santa Cruzada . . . Lisbon: 1697. V. 41

PIRIE, W. R.

An Inquiry into the Constitution, Powers and Processes of the Human Mind, with a View to the Determination of the Fundamental Principles of Religious, Moral and Political Science. Aberdeen: 1858. V. 38; 40

PIRO, HENRICUS DE

Super Institutionibus. Louvain: 1488. V. 40

PIROLI, THOMAS & SONS

Sculture del Palazzo Della Vigna Borghese Detta Pinciana. Rome: 1796. V. 39

PIRON, ALEXIS

Oeuvres Complettes . . . Paris: 1776. V. 41

L'Origine des Puces. London - Paris: 1761. V. 39

PIRRIE, WILLIAM

The Principles and Practice of Surgery. London: 1852. V. 42

PIRSIG, ROBERT M.

Zen and the Art of Mortorcycle Maintenance. New York: 1974. V. 39

PIRSSON, LOUIS V.

Fly-Fishing Days, or, the Reminiscences of an Angler. Washington: 1946. V. 39; 43

PIRSTINGER, BERTHOLD, BP. OF CHIEMSEE

Theologia Germanica. (with) Tewtsch Rational. (with) Keligpuchel. Augsburg: 1531-35. V. 44

PISANELLI, BALDASSAR

Balthasaris Pisanelli Doctoris Medici Bononiensis; de Alimentorum Facultatibus Libellus Aureus. Bruxelles: 1662. V. 38

Trattato Della Natvra de' Cibi et del Bere. Nel Quale Non Solo Tutte le Virtu, & I Vitij di Quelli Minutamente si Palesano, ma Anco I Rimedii Per Correggere I Loro Difetti Copiosamente s'Insegnano . . . Venetia: 1593. V. 39

PISANI, MADAME

Vendeleur; or, Animal Magnetism. London: 1836. V. 46

PISO, NICOLAS

De Cognoscendis et Curandis Praecipue Internis Humani Corporis Morbis Libri Tres . . . Frankfurt: 1580. V. 38

PISO, WILLEM c.1611-1678

Guilielmi Pisonis Medici Amstelaedamensis de Indiae Utriusque Re Naturali et Medica Libri Quatuordecim . . . Amsterdam: 1658. V. 40; 41

De Indiae Utriusque re Naturali et Medica Libri Quatuordecim . . . Amsterdam: 1658. V. 43

Indiae Utriusque re Naturali et Medica . . . Leyden: 1658. V. 45

PISSARO, LUCIEN

Travaux des Champs. (First Series). 1893. V. 37

PISSARRI, CAROLO ANTONIO

Dialoghi Tra Claro, E Sarpiri per Istruire Chi Desidera d'Essere un Eccellente Pittore Figurista. Bologna: 1778. V. 42

PISSARRO, LUCIEN 1863-1944

De la Typographie et d'Harmonie de la Page Imprimee. Paris: 1898. V. 37

Notes on the Eragny Press, and a Letter to J. B. Manson. Cambridge: 1957. V. 37; 38; 39; 40; 41; 45

Notes on a Selection of Wood-Blocks Held at the Ashmolean Museum, Oxford. Oxford: 1981. V. 40

Rossetti. London. V. 38

Twelve Woodcuts in Black and Colors by Lucien Pissarro. Chelsea: 1891. V. 37

Vachere Au Bords de L'Eau. London: 1905. V. 46

Wood Engravings by Lucien Pissaro. With notes on a selection of wood blocks held at the Ashmolean Museum by David Chambers. Oxford: 1981. V. 37; 39; 40; 43; 45

PISSISS, PEDRO J. A.

Geografia Fisica de la Republica de Chile. aris: 1875. V. 39; 40

PISTOLESI, ERASMO

Il Vaticano. Rome: 1829, 1838. V. 37; 39

PISTORIUS, JOHANN

De Vara Curandae Pestis Ratione, Liber Unus. Frankfurt am Main: 1568. V. 38

PITATI, PIETRO

Almanach Noveum . . . ad Annos Quinque Supra Ultimas Hactenus in Luceum Editas Ioannis Stoefleri Ephemeridas Sese Extendens, ab Anno Scilicet 1552 ad Annum 1556 . . . Tubingen: 1552. V. 44

PITCAIRN, ARCHIBALD 1652-1710

Elementa Medicinae Physico-Mathematica . . . The Hague: 1718. V. 41; 46

Selecta Poemata. (with) Poems in English and Latin on the Archers and Royal Company of Archers. Edinburgh: 1727/26. V. 43

The Whole Works of Dr. Archibald Pitcairn, Published by Himself. London: 1727. V. 41

PITCAIRN, ROBERT 1793-1855

Criminal Trials in Scotland, from 1488 to 1624 Embracing the Entire Regins of James IV and V., Mary Queen of Scots and James VI. Edinburgh: 1833. V. 38; 40

PITCAIRN: the Island, the People and the Pastor, to Which is Added a Short Notice of the Original Settlement and Present Condition of Norfolk Island. London: 1860s. V. 45

PITCHER, DONALD EDGAR

An Historical Geography of the Ottoman Empire . . . from the Earliest Times to the End of the Sixteenth Century. Leiden: 1972. V. 39

An Historical geography of the Ottoman empire from earliest times to the end of the sixteenth century. 1972. V. 37

PITCHLYNN, PETER P.

Remonstrance, Appeal and Solemn Portest of the Choctaw Nation. Addressed to the Congress of the United States. Washington: 1870. V. 43

To His Excellency the Principal Chief and General Council of the Choctaw Nation. Washington: 1868. V. 43

PITFIELD, A.

The Natural History of Animals . . . London: 1702. V. 42

PITHOU, PIERRE 1539-1596

Epigrammata et Poemata Vetera. Quorum Pleraque Nunc Primum ex Antiquis Codicibus & Lapidibus. Lyon: 1596. V. 44; 46

Prevves des Libertez de l'Eglise Gallicane. Rouen?: 1639. V. 40

PITISCUS, BARTHOLOMAEUS

Canon Manvel des Sinvs, Tovchantes et Covppantes . . . Paris: 1619. V. 45

PITKIN, TIMOTHY 1766-1847

A Political and Civil History of the Unites States of America From the Years 1763 to the Close of the Administration of President Washington in March 1797 . . . New Haven: 1828. V. 38; 39; 40; 42; 46

A Statistical View of the Commerce of the United States of America . . . Hartford: 1816. V. 42; 43; 46

A Statistical View of the Commerce of the United States . . . Also an Account of Banks, Manufactures and Internal Trade. New Haven: 1835. V. 38

PITMAN, ALMIRA

After Fifty Years. Norwood: 1931. V. 38

PITMAN, BENN

The Assassination of President Lincoln and the Trial of the Conspirators David E. Herold, Mary E. Surratt, Lewis Payne, George A. Atzerodt, Edward Spangler, Samuel A. Mudd, Samuel Arnold, Michael O'Laughlin. Cincinnati and New York: 1865. V. 45

Sir Isaac Pitman, His Life and Labors. Cincinnati: 1902. V. 38

The Trials for Treason at Indianapolis, Discoling the Plans for Establishing a North-Western Confederacy. Cincinnati: 1865. V. 37

PITMAN, EMMA RAYMOND

Lady Hymn Writers. London: 1892. V. 43

PITMAN, ISAAC

A General Specimen of Printing Types in Use by Isaac Pitman, Phonetic and General Printer and Publisher. Bath: 1850. V. 43; 44

PITMAN, PHILIP

The Present State of the European Settlements on the Mississippi; with a Geographical Description of that River. London: 1770. V. 40

PITOT, ALLAIN

L'Automate De Longitude Nouveau Systeme d'Hydrometrie . . . London: 1716. V. 43

PITROU, ROBERT

Recueil de Differents Projets d'Architecture de Charpente et Autres Concernant la Construction des Ponts. Paris: 1756. V. 38; 42

PITT, CHRISTOPHER

The Plague of Marseilles: a Poem. London: 1721. V. 45

Vida's Art of Poetry. London: 1742. V. 40

PITT, JOHN

How to Brew Good Beer. London: 1859. V. 40

PITT-RIVERS, AUGUSTUS HENRY LANE FOX 1827-1900

Antique Works of Art from Benin. London: 1900. V. 39

Excavations in Cranborne Chase, Near Rushmore, on the Borders of Dorset and Wiltshire. London: 1887-1905. V. 45

Excavations in Cranborne Chase, near Rushmore, on the Borders of Dorset and Wilts. London: 1887-8-92. V. 38

King John's House. London: 1890. V. 39; 45

PITT, W.

General View of the Agriculture of the County of Stafford; with Observations on the Means of Its Improvement. London: 1794. V. 41

PITT, WILLIAM

Anecdotes of the Life of the Right Honourable William Pitt, Earl of Chatham; and of the Principal Events of his Time, with his Speeches in Parliament, from the year 1736 to the Year 1778. The Fifth Edition. London: 1796. V. 37

An Inquiry into the conduct of a Late Right Honourable Commoner. London: 1766. V. 46

Pitt Versus Prince. Prince Versus Pitt. Dublin: 1789. V. 43

The Speech of the Right Honourable William Pitt, in the House of Commons, on Friday Feb. 21, 1783. London: 1783. V. 38

The Speech of the Right Honourable William Pitt, on a Motion for the Abolition of the Slave Trade, in the House of Commons, on Monday the Second of April, 1792. London: 1792. V. 38

Speeches . . . in the House of Commons. London: 1808. V. 39

PITTER, RUTH

First Poems. London: 1920. V. 38

PITTILOCH, ROBERT

Oppression Under the Colour of the Law, or, My Lord Hercarse His New Praticks . . . Edinburgh: 1827. V. 42; 46

PITTINGER, WILLIAM

The Great Locomotive Chase. New York: 1893. V. 46

PITTIS, W.

Dr. Radcliffe's Life and Letters. The Fourth Edition. London: 1736. V. 37

PITTONI, BATTISTA b. 1520

Imprese Nobili, et Ingeniose di Diversi Prencipi, et d'Altri Personaggi Illustri nell' Arme et Nelle Lettere . . . Venice: 1583. V. 40; 43

PITTS, J. MARTIN

Gymnopaediae. Near Monmouth: 1989. V. 45

PITTS, JOHN W.

Eleven Numbers Against Lawyer Legislation and Fees at the Bar . . . N.P.: 1843. V. 44

PITTS, JOSEPH

A True and Faithful Account of the Religion and Manners of the Mohammetans. Exeter: 1704. V. 41

PITTS, WILLIAM

Some Memoirs of the Life of John Radcliffe, M.D. London: 1715. V. 39

THE PITTSBURGH Dispatch Universal Atlas of the World. Chicago/New York: 1899. V. 45

PITY'S Gift: A Collection of Interesting Tales, to excite the Compassion of Youth for the Animal Creation . . . From the Writings of Mr. (Samuel Jackson) Pratt. Selected by a Lady (?Laetitia Pilkington). London: 1798. V. 37

PIUS II, POPE

Asiae Europaeque Elegantissima Descriptio . . . Parisijs: 1534. V. 44

Costumi et Successi della Nobilissima Provincia delli Boemi . . . Venice: 1545. V. 44

La Discrittione de l'Asia et Europa . . . con l'Aggionta de l'Africa. Venice: 1544. V. 41

Epistolae. Nuremberg: 1496. V. 40

Pii Secundi Pontificis Max. Commentarii Rerum, Quae Temporis Suis Contigerunt, a R. D. Ioanne Gobellino . . . Rome: 1584. V. 40

PIUS IV, POPE

Bulla . . . Super Confirmatione, ac Innouatione Prohibitionis Duellorum. Rome: 1560. V. 45

Literae Apostolicae sev Bullae Santissmorum Pii et Pii V. Pontif. Max ad Observationem & Declarationem Sacrosncti Oecumenici Concilij Tridentini Pertinentes. Dilingae: 1566. V. 38

PIUS VI, POPE

Ritus in Clausure Portae Sanctae Vaticanade Servandus. Rome: 1775. V. 43

PIUS XI, POPE

Pius XI on Christian Marriage. New York: 1931. V. 39

PIX, MARY

The Deceiver Deceived . . . London: 1698. V. 44

PIZZAGALLI, FELICE

Dell'arte Pratica del Carpentiere. Milan: 1827. V. 44

PLACCAET ende Ordinantie ons Heeren des Coninks Daerby Wordt Geboden . . . dat die Placcaten Hiervoormaels Gepubliceert Opt Stuck Vande Calmynen Wel . . . Brussels: 1590. V. 41

PLACCAET Ende Ordinentie Ons Heeren des Conincx, om die Plunderinghe, Pillerye, Scheynidinghe ende Bederfenisse van den Kercken, Cloisters ende Gods-huysen te Verhoeden ende Remedieren . . . Brussel: 1566. V. 43

PLACE, FRANCIS

Proposals for Establishing in the Metropolis, a Day School, in Which an Example May be Set of the Application of the Methods of Dr. Bell, Mr. Lancaster and Others, to the Higher Branches of Education. London: 1816. V. 40

PLACENTINUS, CALISTUS

Piisimae Simul Ac Eruditissimae in Evangelia . . . . Venice: 1574. V. 40; 45

PLACER County Business and Official Directory. Auburn: 1875. V. 40

PLACER County, California. Its Resources and Advantages . . . A Region Little Advertised but Full of Merit . . . N.P.: Auburn?: 1886. V. 42

PLACER Mining. A Hand-Book for Klondike and Other Miners and Prospectors. Scranton: 1897. V. 38

PLACERVILLE & SACRAMENTO VALLEY RAILROAD CO.

Report of the Chief Engineer on the Survey and Cost of Construction of the San Francisco & Washoe Railroad of California . . . San Francisco: 1865. V. 42

PLACZEK, A. K.

Macmillan Encyclopedia of Architects. London: 1982. V. 41

A PLAIN and Concise Treatise on the Properties of Apples and Pears, and Quality of Their Liquors. Bridgwater: 1780. V. 39; 40

A PLAIN and Succinct Discourse on Convulsions in General; but More Particularly in Children. London: 1721. V. 41

PLAIN Facts About Dakota: Its Fertile Lands, Its Wonderful Crops and Its Inexhuastible Resources. Milwaukee: 1888. V. 44

THE PLAIN Question Upon the Present Dispute with Our American Colonies. London: 1776. V. 45

THE PLAIN Reasoner. London: 1745. V. 45

PLAIN Reasons Addressed to the People of Great Britain, Against the (Intended) Petition to Parliament from the Owners and Occupiers of Land in the County of Lincoln, for Leaves to Export Wool. Leeds: 1782. V. 40; 43

THE PLAINS Farm. Catalogue of the Herd of Pure Bred Improved Short-Horned CAttle, the Property of David Christie. Ottawa: 1868. V. 46

PLAISTED, BARTHOLOMEW

A Journey from Calcutta in Bengal, by Sea to Busserah. London: 1757. V. 41

PLAIX, CESAR DE

Le Passe-Par-Tovt Des Peres Iesvites. N.P.: 1607. V. 37

PLAKE, KATE

The Southern Husband Outwitted by His Union Wife. Philadelphia: 1867. V. 38

PLAN by the Commissioners and Trustees for Improving Fisheries and Manufactures in Scotland, for the Application of Their Funds. Edinburgh: 1734. V. 42

PLAN de Ensenanza Para Escuelas de Primeras Letras, o Edicion Compuesta del Plan Publicado en Frances en 1815 por el Sr. Conde de Laborde . . . y del Manual Pratico del Metodo de Mutua Ensenanza, Publicado en Cadiz en 1818 Por la Sociedad Economica de . . . Buenos Aires: 1823. V. 41

PLAN de la Constitucion Politica de la Nacion Mexicana. Mexico: 1823. V. 40

PLAN de Paris, Commence l'annee 1734. Dessine et Grave Sous les Ordres de Messire Michel Etienne Turgot . . . Leve et Dessine par Louis Bretez, Grave par Claude Lucas et Ecrit par Aubin. Paris: 1739. V. 39

PLAN for Shortening the Time of Passage Between New York and London, with Documents Relating Thereto Including the Proceedings of the Railway Convention at Portland, Maine . . . Portland: 1850. V. 45

PLAN of an Universal Fishing Company, in Ireland. Dublin: 1773. V. 41

PLANAT, P.

Habitations Particulieres, Premiere Serie: Hotels Prives. Paris. V. 40

PLANCHE, J. R.

A Corner of Kent; or, Some Account of the Parish of Ash-Nex-Sandwich, Its Historical Sites and Existing Antiquites. London: 1864. V. 44

Descent of the Danube, from Ratisbon to Vienna, During the Autum of 1827. London: 1828. V. 39

PLANCHE, JAMES ROBINSON

A Cyclopaedia of Costume or Dictionary of Dress . . . London: 1876-79. V. 43

A Cyclopaedia of Costume, or Dictionary of Dress . . . London: 1879. V. 42

An Old Fairy Tale Told Anew in Pictures and Verse . . . London: 1865. V. 42

PLANCK, CHARLES E.

Women with Wings. New York: 1942. V. 44; 45

PLANCK, MAX

Theory of Light. London: 1932. V. 44; 45

PLANIS CAMPY, DAVID DE

L'Hydrope Morbifique Exterminee Par l'Hercule Chimique. Paris: 1628. V. 38; 45

PLANNCK, STEPHEN

The Letter of Columbus on His Discovery of the New World. Los Angeles: 1989. V. 45

PLANS des Hopitaux et Hospices Civils de la Ville de Paris, Leves par Ordre du Conseil General d'Adminsitration des Ces Etablissemens. Paris: 1820. V. 44

LES PLANS, Profils et Elevations des Ville et Chateau de Versailles, avec les Bosquets et Bosquets et Fontaines, tels quils Sont a Present . . . en 1714 et 1715. Paris. V. 44

LES PLANS, Profils, et Elevations, des Ville, et Chateau de Versailles, avec les Bosquets, et Fontaines, tels Quils sont a Present. Paris: 1716. V. 38

PLANTA, JOSEPH 1744-1827

The History of the Helvetic Confederacy. London: 1800. V. 39

The History of the Helvetic Confederacy. London: 1807. V. 37; 39

PLANTAGENET-HARRISON, MARSHALL GENERAL

The History of Yorkshire - Wapentake of Gilling West. London: 1885. V. 38

PLANTE, DAVID

The Ghost of Henry James. 1970. V. 43

PLANTIN, CHRISTOPHER

An Account of Calligraphy and Printing in the Sixteenth Century. Cambridge: 1940. V. 40

PLANTIN'S Index Characterum of 1567. New York: 1924. V. 44

PLANUS, AMANDUS

the Substance of Christian Religion . . . London: 1608. V. 46

PLARR, VICTOR

In the Dorian Mood. Title page design by Patten Wilson. London: 1896. V. 37

PLASSIUS, HERMANNUS

Euterpe, sive Epigrammatum Liber. Thalia, sive Carminum Liber. Clio, sive Elegiarum Liber. Helmstedt: 1590. V. 38

PLAT, HUGH

The Jewel House of Art and Nature. London: 1653. V. 37; 40; 43

PLATAES Illustrative of Natural History: Parts 3-5. London: 1842-50. V. 37

THE PLATE-GLASS Book, Consisting of the Following Authentic Tables . . . Looking-Glass . . . , Glass-House Table . . . , Grinding, Polishing, Silvering . . . . (with, as issued) The Complete Appraiser . . . fro the Valuing of brass, Copper, Pewter, Iron . . . London: 1757/56. V. 38; 44

A PLATFORM of Church-Discipline. Boston: 1772. V. 46

PLATH, SYLVIA 1932-1963

Above the Oxbow. Northampton: 1985. V. 39

Ariel. 1965. V. 37

Ariel. London: 1965. V. 37; 38; 39; 40; 43; 44; 45; 46

Ariel. New York: 1966. V. 43

The Bell Jar. London: 1963. V. 37; 41

The Bell Jar. London: 1964. V. 41

The Bell Jar. New York: 1971. V. 40; 41

Child. Exeter: 1971. V. 38; 42

The Colossus and Other Poems. London: 1960. V. 38; 39; 41

The Colossus. New York: 1962. V. 37; 43

The Colossus and Other Poems. New York: 1962. V. 44

The Colossus and Other Poems. New York: 1962. V. 45

The Colossus and Other Poems. New York: 1962. V. 46

The Colossus and Other Poems. New York: 1962. V. 40

The Colossus. London: 1967. V. 37; 40

Crystal Gazer. 1971. V. 44

Crystal Gazer and Other Poems. 1971. V. 40

Crystal Gazer & Other Poems. London: 1971. V. 39; 40; 41; 45; 46

Dialogue Over a Ouija Board. Cambridge: 1981. V. 38; 40

Dialogue Over a Ouija Board. London: 1981. V. 42

Fiesta Melons. Exeter: 1971. V. 38; 45

The Green Rock Embers. Ely: 1982. V. 41; 46

Johnny Panic and the Bible of Dreams. London: 1977. V. 38; 46

Lyonnesse. 1971. V. 40

Lyonnesse, Poems by . . . London: 1971. V. 39; 42; 43; 44; 45; 46

The Magic Mirror. Rhiwargor, Llangynog, Powys: 1989. V. 42

Million Dollar Month. Surrey: 1971. V. 44

Pursuit: Poems. London: 1973. V. 41

Sculptor: to Leonard Baskin. N.P.. V. 41

Sculptor: To Leonard Baskin. N.P.. V. 42

The Surgeon at 2 A.M. & Other Poems. Portland: 1971. V. 44; 46

Three Women - a Monologue for Three Voices. London: 1968. V. 38; 43

Two Poems. Knotting, Bedfordshire: 1980. V. 42

Uncollected Poems. London: 1965. V. 41

Winter Trees. London: 1971. V. 38

PLATINA, BARTOLOMEO 1421-1481

The Lives of the Popes. London: 1685. V. 41

The Lives of the Popes from the Time of Our Saviour Jesus Christ to the Reign of Sixtus IV. London: 1688. V. 38; 45

Vitae Pontificum. Trevisol?: 1485. V. 39

Vitae Pontificum. Nuremberg: 1481. V. 37

De Vitis Pontificum Romanorum. Cologne: 1600. V. 37; 40

PLATO

The Banquet of Plato. Chicago: 1895. V. 37; 40

The Banquet of Plato. Boston: 1908. V. 39

The Banquet of Plato. Cambridge: 1908. V. 45

The Cratylus, Phaedo, Parmenides, and Timaeus of Plato. London: 1793. V. 38

Crito. A Socratic Dialogue. Montagnola: 1926. V. 42

Crito: a Socratic Dialogue. Paris: 1926. V. 40; 41; 42; 44; 45

The Dialogues Translated into English with Analyses and Introductions by B. Jowett. Oxford: 1885. V. 41

The Dialogues. 1892. V. 45

The Dialogues. Oxford: 1892. V. 37; 38; 39; 42; 46

The Dialogues of Plato Translated Into English with Analyses and Introductions by B. Jowett. London: 1924. V. 46

The Dialogues of Plato. London: 1931. V. 42

Dialogues. Oxford: 1931. V. 37; 42; 44

The Dialogues. 1953. V. 45

Divini Platonis operum a Marsilio Ficino Tralatorum tomus primus (-tomus quintus). Lyons: 1550. V. 37

Lysis. 1930. V. 45

Lysis. 1930. V. 42

Lysis, or Friendship: The Symposium and Phaedrus. New York: 1968. V. 44; 46

Minos, sive De Lege. De Legibus . . . Louvain: 1531. V. 40

Phaedon; or Dialogue on the Immortality of the Soul. New York: 1833. V. 38; 40

Phaedrus. San Francisco: 1976. V. 39; 45

Phedon: or a Dialogue of the Immortality of the Soul. London: 1777. V. 43

Plato His Apology of Socrates, and Phaedo or Dialogue Concerning the Immortality of Mans Soul . . . London: 1675. V. 37; 38; 42; 44

Platonos Epta Eklektoi Dialogi. (translit. from Gr.). Plaontis Septem Selecti Dailogi. Juxta Editionem Serrani. Dublinii: 1738. V. 45

La Republique divisee en dix Livres, ou Dialogues . . . Pllus, Quelques Autres Traictez Platoniques. Paris: 1600. V. 38

The Republic of Plato. Glasgow: 1763. V. 40; 46

Plato's Republic. New York: 1944. V. 38; 40; 43; 44; 45

Scripta Graece Omnia ad Codices Manuscriptos Recensuit Variasque Inde Lectiones . . . London: 1826. V. 39; 40; 41

The Symposium. 1986. V. 40

Symposium. 1986. V. 38

Symposium. 1986. V. 38

Symposium of Plato. 1986. V. 44

The Symposium. Marlborough: 1986. V. 37; 39

Symposium. Wiltshire: 1986. V. 37; 39; 42; 45; 46

The Trial and Death of Socrates. 1962. V. 40

The Trial and Death of Scorates. New York: 1962. V. 41; 44

The Trial and Death of Socrates. Verona: 1962. V. 42; 46

The Trial and Death of Socrates. New York: 1963. V. 44

The Trial and Execution of Socrates. London: 1972. V. 40

Opera. Venice: 1491. V. 38

(Greek title, then): Opera Omnia. Frankfurt: 1602. V. 40

The Works of Plato. London: 1804. V. 41; 44; 45

The Works of Plato. London: 1883-5. V. 41

PLATT, A. E.

The History of the Parish and Grammar School of Sedbergh. London: 1876. V. 44

PLATT, CHARLES A.

Monograph of the Work of Charles A. Platt. New York: 1925. V. 45

PLATT, ELIZA

Journal of a Tour through Egypt, the Peninsula of Sinai and the Holy Land in 1838, 1839 . . . London: 1841-42. V. 41; 45

PLATT, HUGH

Delights for Ladies, to Adorne Their Persons, Tables, Closets and Distillatories, with Beauties, Banquests, Perfumes and Waters. London: 1632. V. 45

The Garden of Eden. London: 1653 (1652). V. 40

The Garden of Eden, or an Accurate Description of All Flowers and Fruits Now Growing in England . . . London: 1655. V. 37; 41; 43

The Garden of Eden. London: 1660. V. 38; 39; 40; 41; 44

The Garden of Eden, or, An Accurate Description of all Flowers and Fruits Now Growing in England. London: 1675. V. 38; 40

The Garden of Eden. Printed for William Lake,: 1653, 1652. V. 38

The Jewel House of Arat and Nature. London: 1653. V. 38

PLATT, P. L.

Travelers' Guide Across the Plains Upon the Overland Route to California. 1963. V. 45

Traveler's Guide Across the Plains Upon the Overland Route to California. San Francisco: 1963. V. 39; 41; 42; 44

PLATT, S. H.

The Martyrs and the Fugitive; or, a Narrative of the Captivity, Sufferings and Death of an African Family . . . New York: 1859. V. 46

PLATTES, GABRIEL

A Discovery of Subterrancal Treasure. London: 1653. V. 43; 46

A Discovery of Subterranean Treasure. London: 1679. V. 38; 40

PLATUS, HIERONYMUS

The Happiness of a Religious State. Rouen: 1632. V. 44

PLAUT, JAMES S.

Oskar Kokoschka. London: 1948. V. 44

PLAUTUS, TITUS MACCIUS

M. Accii Plauti Comoediae Viginti, ilim a Ioachimo Camerario Emendatae . . . 1566. V. 39

Plautus's Comedies, Amphitryon, Epicidus, and Rudens, Made English . . . London: 1694. V. 39; 45

Comoediae. Milan: 1500. V. 40

Comoediae Sex. Paris: 1530. V. 39

Comoediae XX, Ex Antiqvis, Recentrioribusque Exemplaribus . . . Paris: 1530. V. 43

Comoediae Viginti, Olim a Joachimo Camerario Emendatae . . . Opera et Diligentia Ioannis Sambvci. Antverpiae: 1566. V. 46

Comoediae. Amsterdam: 1629. V. 38

Comoediae et Tragoediae Selectae ex Plauto, Terentio, et Seneca . . . Florence: 1748. V. 38

Marci Accii Plauti Comoediae Quae Supersunt. Parisiis: 1759. V. 43

Comoediae VI. Leipzig: 1549. V. 37

Ex Comoediis XX . . . Venice: 1522. V. 37; 40; 42

PLAW, JOHN 1745-1820

Ferme Ornee; or Rural Improvements. London: 1795. V. 39; 40

Ferme Ornee; or Rural Improvements. London: 1800. V. 38

Ferme Ornee: or Rural Improvements. London: 1803. V. 37; 44

Rural Architecture. London: 1794. V. 38; 41

Rural Architecture; or Designs, from the Simple Cottage to the Decorated Villa . . . London: 1802. V. 38; 42

Rural Architecture. London: 1802. V. 38

Sketches for Country Houses, Villas and Rural Dwellings . . . London: 1800. V. 38; 42

Sketches for Country Houses, Villas and Rural Dwellings. London: 1803. V. 38

Sketches for Country Houses, Villas and Rural Dwllings . . . London: 1812. V. 38; 40; 45

PLAYFAIR, G. M. H.

The Cities and Towns of China. Hong Kong: 1879. V. 42

PLAYFAIR, HUGO, R.N., PSEUD.

Brother Jonathan, the Smartest Nation in all Creation. London: 1844. V. 39; 41; 42; 44

PLAYFAIR, JAMES 1738-1819

A Geographical and Statistical Description of Scotland . . . Edinburgh: 1819. V. 41; 44

PLAYFAIR, JOHN

Biographical Account of the Late Dr. Matthew Stewart. 1786. V. 38

Elements of Geometry . . . Edinburgh: 1814. V. 43; 46

Illustrations of the Huttonian Theory of the Earth. Edinburgh: 1802. V. 37; 38

The Works . . . with a Memoir of the author. Edinburgh: 1822. V. 45; 46

PLAYFAIR, R. L.

A Bibliography of Morocco from the Earliest Times to the End of 1891. London: 1892. V. 38

PLAYFAIR, R. LAMBERT

Travels in the Footsteps of Bruce in Algeria and Tunis . . . London: 1877. V. 39; 46

PLAYFAIR, R. T.

Fishes of Zanzibar. California: 1971. V. 39

PLAYFAIR, WILLIAM

The History of Jacobinism, Its Crimes, Cruelties and Perfidies . . . Philadelphia: 1796. V. 39

Inevitable Consequences of a Reform in Parliament. London: 1792. V. 37; 42

PLAYFORD, HENRY 1657-1706

The Divine Companion. London: 1722. V. 40

PLAYFORD, JOHN

An Introduction to the Skill of Musick. London: 1674. V. 40

PLAZZONUS, FRANCISCUS

De Partibus Generationi Inservientibus Libri Duo . . . Leyden: 1644. V. 38

A PLEA for the Dumb Creation. Philadelphia: 1876. V. 38

PLEADWELL, FRANK L.

The Life and Works of Joseph Rodman Drake (1795-1820). Boston: 1935. V. 46

PLEAS, ELWOOD

Henry County: Past and Present: a Brief History of the County from 1821 to 1871. New Castle: 1871. V. 46

A PLEASANT Funeral-Oration, at the Interment of the Three (Lately Deceased) Tower Lyons. London: 1681. V. 42

PLEASANTON, AUGUSTUS JAMES

The Influence of the Blue Ray of the Sunlight and the Blue Colour of the Sky, in Developing Animal and Vegetable Life, in Arresting Disease . . . Philadelphia: 1877. V. 39; 42

The Influence of the Blue Ray of the Sunlight. Philadelphia: 1876. V. 37

PLEASANTS J. HALL

Maryland Silversmiths 1715-1830 with Illustrations of Their Silver and Their Marks with a Facsimile of the Design Book of William Faris. Baltimore: 1930. V. 37; 41

THE PLEASE of the Colonies, on the Charge Brought Against Them by Lord M-------d, and Others, in a Letter to His Lordship. London: 1775. V. 37

THE PLEASING Companion; a Collection of Fairy Tales, Calculated to Improve the Heart. London: 1794. V. 39

THE PLEASING Instructor; or Entertaining Moralist. London: 1768. V. 39

THE PLEASURES of a Single Life, or, the Miseries of Matrimony. London: 1708. V. 44

THE PLEASURES of Friendship. London: 1823. V. 39; 42

THE PLEASURES of Human Life, etc. London: 1807. V. 38

PLENCIZ, MARC ANTONY

Opera Medico Physica, in Quatuor Tractatus Digesta . . . Vienna: 1762. V. 41; 45

PLESCH, ARPAD

The Magnificent Botanical Library of the Stiftung fur botanik Vaduz Liechtenstein Collected by the Late Arpad Plesch. London: 1975. V. 41

The Magnificent Botanical ibrary of the Stiftung fur Botanik. 1975-76. V. 39

The Magnificient Botanical Library of the Stiftung fur Botanik VAduz Lichtenstein . . . London: 1975-76. V. 39; 41; 42

PLESCHEEF, SERGEY

Survey of the Russian Empire, According to Its Present Newly Regulated State . . . London: 1792. V. 46

PLESKE, THEODORE

Birds of the Eurasian Tundra. Boston: 1928. V. 40; 45

PLETSCH, OSCAR

Buds and Flowers of Childish Life. London: 1870. V. 44

Chimes and Rhymes for Youthful Times! London: 1871. V. 45

PLEUNUS, ARRIGO

A Nevv, Plain, Methodical and Compleat Italian Grammar Whereby Who May Very Soon Attain to The Perfection of the Italian Tongue. Leghorn: 1715? V. 40

PLIES, M. DE

The Art of Painting, and the Lives of the Painters. London: 1706. V. 38

PLIMPTON, GEORGE ARTHUR

Rara Arithmetica: A Catalogue of the Arithmetics Written Before the Year MCDI with a Description of those in the Library of George Arthur Plimpton of New York. By David Eugene Smith. Boston: 1908. V. 37

PLIMPTON PRESS

Year Book; an Exhibit of Versatility. Norwood: 1911. V. 38; 40

PLIMSOLL, SAMUEL

Cattle Ships: Being the Fifth Chapter of Mr. Plimsoll's Second Appeal for Our Seamen. London: 1890. V. 39

Our Seaman. An Appeal. London: 1873. V. 38; 39; 40; 41; 42; 43; 46

PLINIUS CAECILIUS SECUNDUS, C. 61-112

An Address of Thanks to a Good Prince, Presented in the Panegyrick of Pliny Upon Trajan, the Best of Roman Emperors. London: 1686. V. 40

De Viris Illustribus Liber. Paris: 1539. V. 42

The Epistles. Boston: 1925. V. 42

Epistolae. Milan: 1478. V. 46

Epistolae per Philippum Beroaldum Correcte. Bologna: 1498. V. 46

Epistolae et Panegyricus. Oxonii: 1677. V. 40

Epistolae et Panegyricus Trajano Dictus. Parisiis: 1769. V. 38

Epistolae, Panegyricus. Florence: 1515. V. 37

Epistolarum Librix. (with) De Viris Illustribus Liber. Paris: 1529. V. 40

C. Plinii Secundi Novocomensis, Epistolarum Libri X . . . Eiusdem Panegyrius Traiano Principi Dictus. Parisiis: 1529. V. 46

Epistolarum Libri X . . . . (with) De Viris in Re Militari et Administranda Republica Illustribus Liber. Basel: 1552. V. 39

PLINIUS CAECILIUS SECUNDUS, C. 61-112 continued

Epistolarum Libri Decem (Panegyricus, De Viris Illustribus, Suetonii Tranquilli de Claris Grammaticis. Julii Obsequentis Prodigiorum Liber). Lyon: 1539. V. 37

Epistolarum Libri X. Venice: 1518. V. 37

Pliny's Epistles and Panegyrick. London: 1724. V. 38

The Letters of Pliny the Younger. With Observations on Each Letter; and an Essay on Pliny's Life. London: 1751. V. 38; 41

The Letters of Pliny the Consul: With Occasional Remarks. London: 1777. V. 45

The Letters of Pliny. London: 1796. V. 38

Panegyricus Caesari Imp. Nervae Triano Avg. Nuremberg: 1746. V. 42

Works. Glasgow: 1751. V. 39

PLINIUS SECUNDUS, C. 23-79

De Mundi Historia, cum Commentario Iacobi Milichius . . . Lipsiae: 1573. V. 38

Historia Naturale Tradocta di Lingua Latina in Fiorentina per Christoforo Landino . . . Venice: 1489. V. 46

Historia Naturale di Caio Plinio Secondo di Lingua Latina in Florentina Tradocta per il Doctissimo Homo Misser Christophero Landino Florentino Nouamete Correcta e da Infiniti Errori Purgada . . . Venice: 1516. V. 44; 46

Historia Mundi, Denuo Emendata. Basle: 1535. V. 45

Historia Mundi Naturalis. Frankfurt: 1582. V. 40

Historiae Naturlais Libri XXXVII ab Alexandro Benedicto Ve. Physico Emendatio res Redditi. Colophon: 1507. V. 45

Naturalis Historiae. Index in C. Plinii Naturalis Historiae Libros. Venice: 1535-40. V. 40

Historiae Mundi Libri XXXVII Ex Postrema Ad Vetvstos Codices Collatione . . . Parisiis: 1543. V. 44; 45

Secundii Historiae Mundi Libri XXXVII Opus Omni Quidem Commendatione Maivs, sed Nullis ad Hunc Diem Editionibus Nulla Cuius-etc. Geneva: 1631. V. 46

Historiae Naturalis Libri XXXVII. Leiden: 1635. V. 40

Historiae Naturalis Libri XXXVII. Quos Interpretatione et Notis Illustravit Joannes Harduinus . . . Paris: 1723. V. 40

Historiae Naturalis Libri XXXVII Quos Recensuit & Notis Illustravii. Paris: 1779. V. 45

The Historie of the World. Colophon: 1601. V. 45

The Historie of the World. London: 1634. V. 38; 41; 42

The Historie of the World, Commonly Called the Naturall History of . . . London: 1601. V. 38; 40

Naturae Historiam Libri XXXVII. Hagenau: 1518. V. 46

Historia Naturalis Libri XXXVII. Venice: 1507. V. 39

Naturalis Historiae Lib-LXXXVII Diligenti Studio ex Multorum Obseruationibus Auctorum in Varietate Lectionis. Paris: 1516. V. 39

Naturae Historiarum Libri XXXVII. Venetiis: 1519. V. 39

Naturalis Historiae Opus . . . Cologne: 1524. V. 43

In C. Plinii Naturalis Historiae Libros Castigationes. Basileae: 1534. V. 42

Naturalis Historiae Libri Trigintaseptem. Venice: 1559. V. 39

The Historie of the World: Commonly Called the Natural Historie of . . . London: 1635-34. V. 39; 41

Naturalis Historiae Libri Trigintaseptem. Venice: 1558. V. 37

PLIPTON, GEORGE ARTHUR

Rara Arithmetica; a Catalogue of the Arithmetics Written Befofe the Year MDCI with a Description of Those in the Library George Arthur Plimpton of New York. Boston: 1908. V. 38

PLOMER, HENRY R.

A Dictionary of the Printers and Booksellers Who Were at Work In England, Scotland and Ireland from 1668-1775. Oxford: 1922, 1932. V. 38

English Printers' Ornaments. London: 1706. V. 38

English Printers' Ornaments. London: 1924. V. 37; 40; 46

Wynkyn de Worde & His Contemoraries from the Death of Caxton to 1535 . . . London: 1925. V. 37; 39; 42; 44; 46

PLOMER, WILLIAM

Address Given at the Memorial Service for Ian Fleming. London: 1964. V. 42; 46

The Dorking Thigh and Other Satires: Poems. London: 1945. V. 40

The Family Tree. London: 1929. V. 37

The Fivefold Screen. London: 1923. V. 41

The Fivefold Screen. London: 1932. V. 38; 41; 46

The Fivefold Screen. New York: 1932. V. 37

I Speak of Africa. London: 1927. V. 40; 45

Museum Pieces. London: 1952. V. 46

Notes for Poems. London: 1927. V. 40

Paper Houses. New York: 1929. V. 45

Remarks When Opening the George Gissing Exhibition at the National Book League London 23 July 1971 (in fact 23rd, June 1971). London: 1971. V. 44

Sado. London: 1931. V. 38

A Shot in the Park: Poems. London: 1955. V. 39

Turbott Wolfe. 1925. V. 39

Turbott Wolfe. London: 1925. V. 37

PLOOIJ, D.

Leyden Documents Relating to the Pilgrim Fathers. Leyden: 1920. V. 38; 44

PLOSS, H. H.

Woman: An Historical Gynaecological and Anthropological Compendium. Edited by E.J. Dingwall. London: 1935. V. 37

PLOT, RICHARD

The Natural History of Oxfordshire, Being an Essay Towards the Natural History of England. Oxford: 1705. V. 41; 45

PLOT, ROBERT

The Natural History of Oxford-Shire, Being an Essay Toward the Natural History of England. Oxford: 1677. V. 38; 41

The Natural History of Stafford-shire. Oxford: 1686. V. 46

The Natural History of Stafford-shire. Manchester: 1973. V. 38; 39

PLOTINUS

The Ethical Treaties/ Psychic & Physical Treatises/ On the Nature of the Soul/ The Divine Mind/ On the One and Good. London: 1917-30. V. 46

Opera. Florence: 1492. V. 40

PLOUGH PRESS

The Plough Press 1967-1981: Fifteen Years of Printing in a Loughborough Garage. Oxford: 1982. V. 39

PLOUGHMAN, WILLIAM

Oeconomy in Brewing. Romsey: 1798. V. 42

PLOVRUS, NICOLAUS

Tractatus Sacerdotalis . . . Parisiis: 1551. V. 38

PLOWDEN, FRANCIS

The Constitution of the United Kingdom of Great Britain and Ireland, Civil and Ecclesiastical. London: 1802. V. 42

An Historical Review of the State of Ireland, from the Invasion of that Country Under Henry II to Its Union with Great Britain on the 1st of January 1801. London: 1803. V. 39; 44

An Historical Review of the STate of Ireland from the Invasion of That Country Under Henry II to Its Union with Great Britain on the First of January 1801. Philadelphia: 1805. V. 46

Jura Anglorum. The Rights of Englishmen. London: 1792. V. 38

A Short History of the British Empire during the last twenty months; viz, from May 1792 to the close fo the year 1793. London: 1794. V. 37; 43

PLOWDEN, WALTER CHICHELE

Travels in Abyssinia and the Galla Country with an Account of a Mission to Ras Ali in 1848. London: 1868. V. 40

PLOWMAN, GEORGE T.

Etching and Other Graphic Arts . . . New York: 1922. V. 46

PLOWMAN, MAX

A Subaltern on the Somme in 1916. London: 1927. V. 46

PLUCHE, NOEL ANTOINE

Histoire du Ciel . . . Paris: 1739. V. 38

The History of the Heavens. London: 1743. V. 40

PLUMB, R. HUDSON

The Log of Amka. London: 1928. V. 45

PLUMBE, JOHN

Memorial Against Mr. Asa Whitney's Railroad Scheme. Washington: 1850. V. 41

Memorial Against Mr. Asa Whitney's Railroad Scheme . . . Washington: 1851. V. 37; 39; 46

Sketches of Iowa & Wisconsin, taken During a Residence of Three Years in Those Territories. St. Louis: 1839. V. 37; 38

PLUMER, HERBERT

An Irregular Corps in Matabeleland. London & New York: 1897. V. 41

PLUMER, THOMAS

The Speech . . . at the Bar of the House of Lords, on the Second Reading of the Bill for the Abolition of the Slave-Trade. London: 1807. V. 37

PLUMER, WILLIAM

Youth, or Scenes from the Past and Other Poems. Boston: 1841. V. 44

PLUMIER, CHARLES

L'Art de Tourner. Lyon: 1701. V. 40

L'Art de Tourner, ou de Faire en Perfection Toutes Sortes d'Ouvrages au Tour. Paris: 1706. V. 41; 45

THE POACHER'S Progress. Edinburgh: 1826. V. 40
THE POACHER'S Progress. Edinburgh: 1981. V. 45

POCCIANTI, MICHELE

Catalogus Scriptorum Florentinorum Omnis Generis. Florence: 1589. V. 37

A POCKET Map and Visitor's Guide to the Central Park in the City of New York . . . New York: 1859. V. 44

A POCKET Companion for Oxford. Oxford: 1744. V. 46
A POCKET Companion for Oxford. London: 1756. V. 40; 43

A POCKET Companion to the Royal Palaces of Kensington, Kew and Hampton Court . . . Windsor: 1785. V. 37

THE POCKET Conveyancer. Dublin: 1783. V. 38

THE POCKET Courier or Traveller's Directory Through France, the Netherlands, the Rhenish Countries, the South of Germany, Switzerland and Italy . . . Brussells: 1830. V. 42

A POCKET Dictionary; or Complete English Expositor . . . London: 1758. V. 41

POCOCK, J. G.

The Spirit of a Regiment, Being the History of 19th King George V's Own Lancers, 1921-1947. London: 1962. V. 46

POCOCK, LEWIS

A Chronological List of Books and Pamphlets, Relating to the Doctrine of Chances and the Rate of Mortality, Annuities, Reversions, Marine and Fire Insurances . . . London: 1842. V. 44

POCOCK, MRS. R. R.

The Longleat Views. Bristol: 1840. V. 40

POCOCK, NICHOLAS

Records of the Reformation: The Divorce 1527-1533. 1870. V. 39
Records of the Reformation: the Divorce 1527-1533. Oxford: 1879. V. 42

POCOCK, R. R.

Views of Longleat House. Bristol: 1840. V. 38

POCOCK, RICHARD

Memorials of the Family of Tufton, Earls of Thanet. Gravesend: 1800. V. 37; 39; 42

POCOCK, ROGER

Following the Frontier. New York: 1903. V. 38

POCOCK, W. INNES

Five Views of the Island of St. Helena. London: 1815. V. 40

POCOCK, WILLIAM FULLER 1779-1849

Architectural Designs for Rustic Cottages, Picturesque Dwellings, Villas, etc. London: 1807. V. 38; 42
Designs for Churches and Chapels . . . . London: 1824. V. 39
Modern Furnishings for Rooms. London: 1811. V. 39
Modern Finishings For Rooms . . . London: 1823. V. 42; 44

POCOCKE, RICHARD

Beschreibung des Morgenlandes und Einiger Andern Laender. Erlangen: 1791-92. V. 41
A Description of the East and Some Other Countries. London: 1743-45. V. 37; 43

PODESCHI, JOHN B.

Books on the Horse and Horsemanship. 1981. V. 46
Dickens and Dickensiana, a Catalogue of the Richard Gimbel Colllection in the Yale University Library. New Haven: 1980. V. 43; 45; 46

PODMORE, FRANK 1856-1910

Modern Spiritualism . . . London: 1902. V. 46

POE, DAVID

Personal Reminiscences of the Civil War. Charleston: 1908. V. 44

POE, EDGAR ALLAN 1809-1849

Anastatic Printing. Northampton: 1971. V. 45
The Bell and Other Poems. London, New York & Toronto. V. 38
The Bells an Other Poems. London. V. 43
The Bells and Other Poems. London. V. 37; 39; 40; 42; 44; 45; 46
The Bells. Philadelphia: 1881. V. 46
The Bells and Other Poems. London: 1912. V. 46
The Bells and Other Poems. New York: 1912. V. 39; 41
The Black Cat. 1984. V. 45
The Black Cat. Easthampton: 1984. V. 39; 46
The Black Cat. West Hatfield: 1984. V. 42
The Black Cat. Williamsburg: 1984. V. 37

The Black Cat. Illustrated with 11 wood engravings by Alan James Robinson. Williamsburh, MA.: 1985. V. 37
The Cask of Amontillado. Chicago: 1904. V. 41
The Centenary Poe: Tales, Poems, Criticism, Marginalia and Eureka. London: 1949. V. 39
The Complete Poems of Edgar Allan Poe . . . Boston & New York: 1911. V. 38
The Conchologist's First Book. Philadelphia: 1840. V. 39
A Descent into the Maelstrom. Paris: 1920. V. 42
Edgar Allan Poe Letters Till Now Unpublished. Philadelphia: 1925. V. 39; 40; 41; 42
Edgar Allan Poe Letters, Till Now Unpublished, In the Valentine Museum, Richmond, Virginia. Philadelphia & London: 1925. V. 42
Eureka. A Prose Poem. New York: 1848. V. 39; 43
The Fall of the House of Usher. 1928. V. 41
The Fall of the House of Usher. Paris: 1928. V. 37; 41; 44; 46
The Fall of the House of Usher. Maastricht: 1930. V. 41; 43; 44
The Fall of the House of Usher. New York: 1931. V. 41
The Fall of the House of Usher. 1985. V. 41
The Fall of the House of Usher. 1985. V. 39
The Fall of the House of Usher. New York: 1985. V. 37; 38; 40; 41; 42; 43; 45; 46
The Fall of the House of Usher. New York: 1921. V. 37
The Gold Bug. New York: 1928. V. 40
Histoires Extraordinaries. Paris: 1856. V. 40
The Journal of Julius Rodman. San Francisco: 1947. V. 39; 41; 42
The Life of Edgar Allan Poe. New York/London: 1878. V. 37
The Literati. New York: 1850. V. 45
The Mask of the Red Death. Baltimore: 1960. V. 39
The Mask of the Red Death. Baltimore: 1969. V. 39
The Masque of the Red Death and Other Tales. Maastrich and London: 1932. V. 43
The Masque of Red Death and Other Tales. Maastricht: 1932. V. 41; 44; 45
Mesmerism 'In Articulo Mortis.' London: 1846. V. 37; 45; 46
The Murders in the Rue Morgue. Philadelphia: 1895. V. 46
Murders in the Rue Morgue. Antibes: 1958. V. 41
Mystery and Imagination. London: 1915. V. 44
The Narrative of Arthur Gordon Pym. London: 1838. V. 37; 40; 42; 45
The Narrative of Arthur Gordon Pym. New York: 1838. V. 37; 42; 46
The Narrative of Arthur Gordon Pym. London: 1930. V. 41
Nouvelles Choisies d'Edgard Poe. Paris: 1853. V. 43
Les Poemes d'Edgar Poe. Paris: 1889. V. 39
The Poems of Edgar Allan Poe. London: 1900. V. 38
Poems. East Aurora: 1901. V. 46
Poems. New York: 1929. V. 43; 45
The Poems of . . . New York: 1943. V. 46
the Poetical Works. London: 1853. V. 42; 46
The Poetical Works. London: 1858. V. 40; 41
The Poetical Works of Edgar Allan Poem. Melbourne: 1868. V. 40
Poetical Works. London: 1912. V. 45
Politician. An Unfinished Tragedy. Richmond: 1923. V. 39
The Purloined Letter. London: 1931. V. 46
The Raven and Other Poems. New York: 1845. V. 37; 40; 43; 44
The Raven and Other Poems. London: 1846. V. 46
The Raven. New York: 1884. V. 39; 46
The Raven: and, The Philosophy of Composition. San Francisco: 1907. V. 39
The Raven. New York: 1926. V. 41
The Raven and Other Poems. Detroit: 1936. V. 40
The Raven and Other Poems. New York: 1945. V. 38
The Raven. The Hague: 1951. V. 43
The Raven. New York: 1978. V. 46
The Raven. Easthampton: 1985. V. 46
The Raven. Easthampton: 1986. V. 39
The Raven and Other Poems. 1989. V. 45
The Raven and Other Poems. Brighton: 1989. V. 45
Selected Tales of Mystery. London: 1909. V. 41
Some Poems With Drawings by James J. Guthrie and edited with a prefatory biographical notes of the poet by J.C. Wright. Kent: 1901. V. 37
Tales of the Grotesque and Arabesque. Philadelphia: 1840. V. 38; 39; 40; 42; 43; 46
Tales. London: 1845. V. 42
Tales. New York: 1845. V. 37; 38; 42; 44
Tales and Poems. New York: 1850. V. 42
Tales and Poems of Edgar Allan Poe. New York: 1900. V. 42
Tales and Poems of Edgar Allan Poe. Philadelphia: 1900. V. 40; 42
Tales of Mystery and Imagination. London: 1919. V. 37; 40; 41; 42; 44; 45

POLE, REGINALD continued

Libri Duo D. Reginaldi Poli Laudatissimi Cardinalis . . . Colophon: 1562. V. 40

Pro Ecclesiasticae Unitatis Defensione, Libri Quatuor. Rome: 1538. V. 40; 42; 43

Testamentum vere Christianum, Pium ac Prudentissimum . . . Dillingen: 1559. V. 41

THE POLE Star. London: 1858-61 (sic). V. 39

POLE, THOMAS 1753-1829

The Anatomical Instructor; or, an Illustration of the Modern and Most Approved Way of Preparing and Preserving the Different Parts of the Human Body . . . London: 1790. V. 39; 40; 41; 43; 44

POLEHAMPTON, EDWARD T. W.

The Gallery of Nature and Art. London: 1821. V. 38

POLEMON

Declamationes. Geneva: 1567. V. 40

POLENI, GIOVANNI

Epistolarum Mathematicarum Fasciculus. Padua: 1729. V. 44

Exercitationes Vitruuianae Primae - (Tertiae) . . . Patavii: 1739. V. 44

Exercitationes Vitruvianae Primae (-Tertiae). Padua: 1739-41. V. 40; 44

Memorie Istroiche della Gran Cupola del Templo Vaticano, e de'Danni di Essa, e De'Ristoramenti Loro, Divise in Libri Cinque. Padua: 1748. V. 37; 42

POLES and Tails; or English Vagabondism in Switzerland in the Summer of 1854. London: 1855. V. 37; 43

POLETIKA, PETR IVANIVICHE

A Sketch of the Internal Condition of the United States of America, and of Their Political Relations with Europe. Baltimore: 1826. V. 38; 39; 40; 45; 46

POLHILL, CHARLES

The Chronicle of the Kingdom of the Cassiterides, Under the Reign of the House of Lunen. London: 1783. V. 37

POLICE Regulations for Establishing a System of Morality and Good Order in Rural Districts, Under the New Poor Law Act. London: 1836. V. 37

THE POLICY and Interest of Great Britain with Respect to Malta, Summarily Considered. London: 1805. V. 41

POLIDORI, JOHN WILLIAM 1795-1821

Ernestus Berchtold; or, the Modern Oedipus. London: 1819. V. 43

Sketches Illustrative of the Manners and Costumes of France, Switzerland, and Italy. Text by John William Polidori. London: 1821. V. 37

The Vampyre. London: 1819. V. 37; 38; 40; 41; 42; 43

Il Vampiro, Novella di Lord Byron tradotta dall'inglese. Udine: 1831. V. 43

Ximenes, the Wreath and Other Poems. London: 1719. V. 45

POLIGNAC, MELCHIOR DE

Anti Lucretius, sive de Deo et Natura, Libri Novem . . . Opus Posthumum . . . Parisiis: 1749. V. 46

POLIIANO, ANGELO 1454-1494

Opera. Colophon: 1498. V. 43

THE POLITE Repository. London: 1786. V. 45; 46

POLITI, LEO

Juanita. New York: 1948. V. 46

The Nicest Gift. New York: 1973. V. 39

POLITIAN, ANGELO AMBROGINI 1454-1494

Angeli Politiani, et Aliorum Virorum Illustrium Epistolarum Libri Duodecim. Basel: 1522. V. 37

Conjurationis Pactianae Anni MCCCCLXXVII Commentarium. Naples: 1769. V. 37

Stanze Cominciate per la Giostra del Magnifico Giuliano di Piero de Medici. Venice: 1541. V. 37

POLITIANUS, ANGELUS

Omnia Opera. Venice: 1498. V. 38

THE POLITICAL Cabient. Boston: 1806-07. V. 38

A POLITICAL Essay Upon the English and French Colonies in Northern and Southern America, Considered in a New Light. London: 1760. V. 41; 42

THE POLITICAL History of England. London: 1906-07. V. 42

POLITICAL History of Jackson County. Kansas City: 1902. V. 45

THE POLITICAL Magnet; or, an Essay in Defence of the Late Revolution, and of the Settlement of the Crown in the Protestant Line. London: 1745. V. 41; 46

POLITICAL Merriment; or, Truths Told to Some Tune . . . London: 1714-15. V. 45

THE POLITICAL Mirror, or, a Review of Jacksonism. New York: 1835. V. 42

THE POLITICAL Padlock, and the English Key, a Fable (in verse). London: 1742. V. 40; 41; 46

POLITICAL Sketches, in a Letter to a Friend; Containing the Characters of the King, the Constitution, the Church, the Minister, the Opposition, the National Assembly of France, etc. London: 1792? V. 43

THE POLITICKS of the French King, Lewis the XIV. Discovered: with Respect to Rome . . . Spain, England, United Provinces, Northern Provinces . . . London: 1689. V. 42

POLITUS, AMBROSIUS CATHARINUS, ABP. OF CONZA

Oratio Habita . . . in Secunda Sessione Synodi Tridentini. Rome?: 1546. V. 45

POLITZER, ADAM

History of Otology. Phoenix: 1981. V. 43

The Membrana Tympani in Health and Disease . . . . New York: 1869. V. 42

A Text-Book of the Diseases of the Ear and Adjacent Organs. Philadelphia: 1894. V. 41; 43

POLIZIANO, ANGELO 1454-1494

Illustrium Virorum Epistolae . . . Paris: 1520. V. 40

Miscellaneorum Centuria Prima. Florence: 1489. V. 40

Opera Omnia. Venice: 1498. V. 43

POLK, BURR H.

The Big American Caravan in Europe . . . Evansville: 1879. V. 40

POLK, JAMES KNOX

Diary of . . . During His Presidency, 1845 to 1849. Chicago: 1910. V. 37; 40; 41

Message from the President . . . in Relation to California and New Mexico. Washington: 1850. V. 37

Message from the President of the United States to the Two Houses of Congress at the Commencement of the First Session of the Thirtieth Congress. December 7, 1847 . . . Washington: 1847. V. 37

Message of the President . . . Communicating the Proceedings of the Court Martial in the Trail of Lieutenant Colonel Fremont. Washington: 1848. V. 37

Message of the President of the United States, December 1845. Washington?: 1845. V. 37

POLK, R. L.

California State Gazetteer and Business Directory 1888. San Francisco: 1880. V. 46

POLK, WILLIAM M.

Leonidad Polk, Bishop and General. New York: 1915. V. 39

POLK, WILLIS

A Matter of Taste. San Francisco: 1979. V. 41

POLK'S Medical Register and Directory of North America . . . an Index to the Physicians of the United States Arranged Alphabetically. Detroit: 1906. V. 41

THE POLL-PARROT Picture Book. London: 1870. V. 40

A POLL Taken Before Edward Leeds, Esq., High Sheriff of the County of Huntingdon, March 29th, 30th, 31st, April 1st, 1768. Cambridge: 1768. V. 42

POLLARD, ALFRED WILLIAM 1859-1944

Catalogue of Books, Mostly from the Presses of the First Printers . . . . Collected by Rush C. Hawkins. Oxford: 1910. V. 42

Cobden-Sanderson and the Doves Press. San Francisco: 1929. V. 37; 41; 45; 46

Early Illustrated Books. London: 1893. V. 41; 45

An Essay on Colophons, with Specimens and Translations. Chicago: 1905. V. 37; 39

Fine Books. London: 1912. V. 37; 40

Fine Books. New York: 1912. V. 38

Fine Books. The Connoisseurs Library. (1912). V. 37

Last Words on the History of the Title-page with Notes on Some Colophon and Twenty Seven Facsimiles of Title-pages. London: 1891. V. 38; 44

Last Words on the History of the Titlepage. London: 1981. V. 38; 40

POLLARD, ALFRED WILLIAM 1859-1944 continued

Odes from the Greek Dramatists. London: 1890. V. 40

The Romance of King Arthur. London: 1917. V. 42; 43

The Romance of King Arthur and His Knights of the Round Table. New York: 1917. V. 45

A Short Title Catalogue of Books Printed In England, Scotland and Ireland and of English Books Printed Abroad, 1475-1640. London: 1926. V. 37; 39; 40; 41; 46

A Short Title Catalogue of Books Printed in England, Scotland and Ireland 1475-1640. London: 1950. V. 40

A Short Title Catalogue of Books Printed in England, Scotland and Ireland and of English Books Printed Abroad 1475-1640. London: 1969. V. 43; 45

A Short-Title Catalogue of Books Printed in England, Scotland and Ireland, and of English Books Printed Abroad, 1475-1640. London: 1976. V. 38; 39; 44

A Short-Title Catalogue of Books Printed in England, Scotland & Ireland and of English Books printed Abroad 1475-1640 . . . London: 1986. V. 39

Short-Title Catalogue of Books Printed in England, Scotland and Ireland and of English Books Printed Abroad 1475-1640. London: 1986 & 1976. V. 37; 42

The Trained Printer and the Amateur and the Pleausre of Small Books. London: 1929. V. 39

POLLARD, EDWARD A.

Black Diamonds Gathered in the Darkey Homes of the South. New York: 1856. V. 39

Southern History of the War. The First Year of the War. New York: 1864. V. 46

Southern History of the War. The Last Year of the War. New York: 1866. V. 46

Southern History of the War. The Second Year of the War. New York: 1865. V. 46

Southern History of the War. The Third Year of the War. New York: 1865. V. 46

POLLARD, EDWARD ALBERT

Lee and His Lieutenants . . . New York: 1867. V. 42

The Second Year of the War. Richmond: 1863. V. 42

The Second Year of the War. New York: 1864. V. 46

The Seven Days' Battles in Front of Richmond. Charleston: 1862. V. 42

POLLARD, EDWARD ALFRED

The First Year of the War. Richmond: 1862. V. 44; 46

The First Year of the War. New York: 1863. V. 46

Observations in the North: Eight Months in Prison and on Parole. Richmond: 1865. V. 38; 39; 40; 43; 46

The Second Battle of Manasas: With Sketches of the Recent Campaign in Northern Virginia and On the Upper Potomac . . . Richmond: 1862. V. 44

POLLARD, GRAHAM

Bibliogrphica: Papers on Books, Their History and Art. London: 1895-97. V. 39; 44

POLLARD, HUGH B. C.

British and American Game Birds. New York: 1939. V. 39; 43; 45

British and American Game Birds. London: 1945. V. 39

Game Birds. Rearing, Preservation and Shooting. London: 1929. V. 39; 43; 45

The Gun Room Guide. London: 1930. V. 39; 45

A History of Firearms. London: 1926. V. 39

A History of Firearms. With Forty-One Half-Tone and Line Plates. London: 1930. V. 37

Wildfowl and Waders. London: 1928. V. 39; 40

POLLARD, JOSEPHINE

Elfinland. New York: 1882. V. 41

Flowers from Field and Woodland. New York: 1890. V. 43

POLLARD, LANCASTER

A History of he State of Washington. New York: 1937. V. 39

POLLARD, W. C.

Life on the Frontier. London: 1930. V. 43

POLLEFXFEN, HENRY

The Arguments and Reports of Sir Hen. Pollexfen, Kt . . . In Some Special Cases, by Him Argued During the Time of His Practice at the Barr . . . London: 1702. V. 45

POLLEN, JOHN HUNGERFORD

Gold and Silver Smith's Work. London: 1879. V. 42

POLLEN, MARGARET MARIA LA PRIMAUDAYE d. 1919

Seven Centuries of Lace. London: 1908. V. 38; 40; 44

POLLER, HENRY A.

Among the Indians . . . Eight Years in the Far West: 1858-1866. Philadelphia: 1868. V. 42

POLLEXFEN, JOHN

England and East India Inconsistent in their Manufactures. London: 1697. V. 37

Of Trade 1. In General. 2. In Particular. 3. Domestick. 4. Foreign. 5. The East Indies. 6. The African. 7. The Turky . . . 20. The French &c. London: 1700. V. 44

POLLEY, JOSEPH BENJAMIN

Hood's Texas Brigade: Its Marches, Its Battles, Its Achievements. New York: 1910. V. 42

Hood's Texas Brigade, Its Marches, Its Battles, Its Achievements. New York: & Washington: 1910. V. 37; 38; 39; 46

A Soldier's Letters to Charming Nellie. New York: 1908. V. 37; 38; 39; 42; 44

A Soldier's Letters to Charming Nellie. New York: & Washington: 1908. V. 41; 46

POLLITT, ROBERT

The Great Pickwick Case, Arranged as a Comic Opera. Manchester: 1884? V. 40

POLLOCK, A. J. O.

Sporting Days in Southern India, Reminiscences of twenty trips in Pursuit of Big Game. London: 1894. V. 37

POLLOCK, CHANNING

The Enemy: a Play in Four Acts. New York: 1925. V. 45

The Enemy: a Play in Four Acts. New York: 1926. V. 46

POLLOCK, FREDERICK 1845-1937

The History of English Law Before the Time of Edward I. Cambridge: 1911. V. 40; 43

Spinoza, His Life and Philosophy. London: 1880. V. 38; 41; 42

POLLOCK, ROBERT

The Course of Time, a Poem. Blackwood: 1857. V. 37

POLLOCK, W. H.

Amateur Theatricals. By Walter Herries Pollock and Lady Pollock. London: 1879. V. 37

He, by the Author of 'It' . . . London: 1887. V. 42

POLLOK, FITZWILLIAM THOMAS

Wild Sports of Burma and Assam. London: 1900. V. 45

POLLOK, ROBERT

The Course of Time: a Poem in Ten Books . . . New York: 1827. V. 39

The Course of Time. New York: 1830. V. 46

The Course of Time: a Poem in Ten Books. Edinburgh and London: 1840. V. 45

POLLUX, JULIUS

Onomasticon (Graece). Vocabularius. Venice: 1502. V. 41

POLO, MARCO 1254-1323?

The Book of Ser Marco Polo, the Venetian. London: 1871. V. 38

The Book of Ser Marco Polo the Venetian Concerning the Kingdoms and Marvels of the East. New York: 1926. V. 40

The Most Noble and Famous Travels of Marco Polo togehter with the Travels of Nicolo de' Conti. Edited from the Elizabethan Translation of John Frampton, with Introduction, Notes and Appendixes by N.M. Penzer. London: 1929. V. 37; 41; 45

The Travels. New York: 1934. V. 40

POLSON, JOHN

Monaco and Its Gaming Tables. London: 1881. V. 39

POLUNIN, OLEG

Flowers of Greece and the Blakans, a Field Guide. Oxford: 1980. V. 38

POLWHELE, RICHARD 1760-1838

Biographical Sketches in Cornwall. Truro: 1831. V. 38

An Essay on Marriage, Adultery and Divorce (Now First Printed) with an Essay on the State of the Soul Between Death and the Resurrection. London: 1823. V. 38; 46

Essays, by a Society of Gentlemen, at Exeter. Exeter: 1796. V. 41

The Follies of Oxford, or Curosry Sketches on a Unviersity Education from an Undergraduate to His Friend in the Country. London: 1785. V. 40; 41; 42

The History of Cornwall: Civil, Military, Religious, Architectural, Agricultural, Commercial, Biographical and Miscellaneous. London: 1803-06. V. 38

The History of Cornwall, Civil, Military, Religious, Architectural, etc. London: 1816. V. 39

The Influence of Local attachment with respect ot Home. London: 1796. V. 37

POLWHELE, RICHARD 1760-1838 continued

The Old English Gentleman, a poem. London: 1797. V. 37

Traditions and Recollections. London: 1826. V. 39; 46

POLYAENUS

Polyaeni Stratagematvm Libri Octo. Is. Casavbonvs Graece Nunc Primum Edidit. Lvgdvni: 1598. V. 46

POLYBIUS

Dell'Imprese de Greci, de gli Asiatici, de Romani, et d'Altri, con due Fragment delle Republiche . . . Venice: 1563. V. 45

The General History of the Wars of the Romans. London: 1812. V. 37

Historiarum Libri Quinque. Haganoae: 1530. V. 46

Historiarum Libri Priores V, Nicolao Perotto . . . Basel: 1549. V. 45

Historiarum Libri Priores Quinque, Nicolao Perotto Sipontino Interprete. Lugduni: 1554. V. 39

Polybii . . . Historiarum Libri Qui Supersunt . . . Paris: 1609. V. 44

Historiarum Quidquid Superest. Oxford: 1823. V. 45

The History of Polybius, The Megalopolitan . . . London: 1698. V. 38; 45

De Legationibus. Antwerp: 1582. V. 38; 45

Undici Libri di Polibio, Nuovamente Trovati et Tradotti per M. Lodovico Domenichi. Vinegia: 1553. V. 40

POLYCARP, SAINT, BISHOP OF SMYRNA

Polycarpi et Ignatii Epistolae. Oxoniae: 1644. V. 39

POLYGRAPHIA Curiosa; The Book of Inital Letters and Ancient Alphabets. London: 1847. V. 38

POMERANZ, HERMAN

Medicine in the Shakespearean Plays and Dickens's Doctors. New York: 1936. V. 41; 42; 45

POMERIUS, JULIANUS

De Uita Coteplatiua de Uita Actuali. Speyer: 1486. V. 44

POMEROY, HIRAM STERLING

The Ethics of Marriage, with a Prefatory Note by Thomas A. Emmet, M.D. New York: 1885. V. 37

POMEROY, JOHN

The Scandanavian Ring. London: 1871. V. 39; 42

POMEROY, RALPH

Stamos. New York. V. 46

POMET, M.

A Complete History of Drugs . . . London: 1743. V. 37

POMET, PIERRE

A Compleat History of Druggs, Written in French by . . . , Chief Druggist to the Present French King . . . London: 1712. V. 39

A Compleat History of Drugs . . . London: 1737. V. 37; 39; 45

Histoire Generale des Drogues, Traitant des Plantes, des Animaux & des Mineraux. Paris: 1694. V. 40

Histoire Generale des Drogues, Simples et Composees. Paris: 1735. V. 38; 40

Neu-Eroffnetes Materialien und Naturalien Magazin, Darinnen Nicht Allein die Materialien, Specereyen und Handelswahren, Sondern Auch die sur Artzney . . . Leipzig: 1727. V. 42

POMEY, FRANCOIS ANTOINE

Panthevm Mythicvm, sev Fabvlosa Deorvm Historia. Lipsiae: 1771. V. 44

POMFRET, JOHN

Miscellany Poems on Several Occasions. London: 1702. V. 42; 45

Miscellany Poems on Several Occasions . . . London: 1707. V. 37; 43

Poems Upon Several Occasions. London: 1716. V. 42

POMODORO, GIOVANNI

Geometrica Pratica Cavata da gl'Elementi d'Euclide e d'altri Famosi Autori. Rome: 1624. V. 40; 44

POMPADOUR, JEANNE ANTOINETTE POISSON, MARQUIS DE

Catalogue des Livres de la Bibliotheque de Feue Madame La Marquise de Pompadour, Dame du Palais de la Reine. Paris: 1765. V. 40

Memoirs of the . . . Wherein are Displayed the Motives of the Wars, Treaties of Peace, Embassies and Negotiations, in Several Courts of Europe. London: 1766. V. 37

POMPONIUS MELA

Pomponius Mela; Julius Solinus; Itinerarium Antonini Aug; Vibius Sequester; P. Victor de Regionibus Urbis Rome; Dionysius Afer de Situ Orbis Prisciano Interprete. Toscolano: colophon: 1521. V. 40

PONCE, N.

Collection des Tableaux et Arabesques Antiques, Trouves a Rome, dans les Ruines des Thermes de Titus. (with) *Araabesques Antiques des Bains de Livie et de la Ville Adrienne, avec les Plafonds de la Ville-madame, Peints d'Apres les Dessins de Raphael.* Paris: 1789. V. 38

PONCINS, GONTRAN DE

Kabloona. New York: 1941. V. 41

POND, JOHN

The Sporting Kalendar. London: 1754. V. 45

POND, MAJOR JAMES B.

Eccentricities of Genius. New York: 1900. V. 43; 44

PONET, JOHN

An Apologie Fully Answering by Scriptures and Aunceant Doctors a Blasphomose Book Gatherid by D. Steph. Gardiner of Late Lord Chancelar D. Smyth of Oxford . . . Strassburg: 1556. V. 42

PONGE, FRANCOIS

Braque. New York: 1971. V. 41

PONS, FRANCOIS RAIMOND J.

Recollections of a Service of Three Years During the War of Extermination in the Republics of Venezuela and Columbia. London: 1828. V. 43

PONS, FRANCOIS RAYMOND JOSEPH DE

Travels in Parts of South America, During the Years 1801, 1802, 1803 and 1804, Containing a description of the Captain-Generalship of Carraccas, with an Account of the Laws, Commerce, and Natural Productions of that Country.. London: 1806. V. 38

PONSONBY. London: 1817. V. 39

PONSONBY, EMILY

Clare Abbey; or, The Trials of Youth. London: 1851. V. 37

PONSONBY, EMILY CHARLOTTE MARY, LADY

The Discipline of Life. London: 1848. V. 43

PONSONBY, FREDERICK

The Grenadier Guards in the Great War of 1914-1918. London: 1920. V. 37

PONT, TIMOTHY

Cuninghame, Topographized 1604-1608. Glasgow: 1876. V. 38

PONTANO, GIVOANNI GIOVANO

Liber de Meteoris. Cum Interpretatione Viti Amerbachij. Strasbourg: 1539. V. 44

PONTANUS, GIOVANNI GIOVIANO

De Bello Neapolitano et de Sermone. Naples: 1509. V. 43

Opera Omnia Soluta Ordine Composita. Venice: 1518/19/19. V. 43

Qvae In Hoc Enchyridio Continneantvr . . . Vrania . . . Meteororum . . . De Hortis Hesperidum . . . Pompae Septem . . . (with Volume II:) Amorum . . . de Amore Coniugali . . . Tumulorum . . . de Diuinis Laudibus . . . Florence: 1514. V. 43; 45

PONTANUS, JOANNES JOVIANNUS

Opera. Venetiis: 1513. V. 37; 44

PONTANUS, JOANNES JOVIANUS 1429-1503

Ioannis Ioviani Potani Amorum Libri II. De Amore Coniugali III. Tumulorum II, qui in Superiore Aliorum Poematon Editione Desyderabantur. Lyrici I. Eridanorum II(and other works). (col:) Venetiis in: 1518. V. 38

Opera. Venice: 1501. V. 39

PONTECOULANT, PHILIPPE GUSTAVE LE DOULCET, COMTE DE 1795-1874

A History of Hailey's Comet. London: 1835. V. 39; 41

PONTEDERA, GIULIO

Compendium Tabularum Botanicarum, in quo Plantae CCLXXI ab eo in Italia Nuper Detectae Recensentur. Padua: 1718. V. 46

PONTEY, WILLIAM

The Forest Pruner; or, Timber Owner's Assistant. London: 1808. V. 40; 42

The Forest Pruner; or, Timber Owner's Assistant; a Treatise on the Training and Management of British Timber Trees . . . Leeds: 1826. V. 39

The Profitable Planter. London: 1809. V. 39

The Profitable Planter: A Treatise on the Theory and Practice of Planting Forest Trees, in every description of soil and situation . . . 4th edition, enlarged. With an appendix. London: 1814. V. 37; 39; 42; 43; 46

PONTICUS, LUDOVICUS VIRUNIUS

Pontici Virunni Viri Doctissimi Britannicae Historiae Libri Sex, Magna et Fide et Diligentia Conscripti . . . Londini: 1585. V. 40; 42

PONTIFICALE Romanum . . . Nuper Summa Diligentia Revisum, Emendatum et Impressum. Venice: 1572. V. 41

PONTING, HERBERT G.

The Great White South, Being an Account of Experiences with Captain Scott's South Pole Expedition of the Natural Life of the Antarctic . . . London: 1921. V. 46

In Lotus-Land Japan. London: 1910. V. 42

PONTIO, FRANCESCO

Problemata ex Omnibus Prope Scientiis . . . Publice Disputanda Proponuntur. Venice: 1559. V. 40

PONTOPPIDAN, ERIK 1698-1764

The Natural History of Norway. London: 1755. V. 37; 38; 39; 40; 42; 43; 44

PONY Express Courier. Placerville: 1934. V. 39

PONY Express Courier: Telling the Story of California and the Old Trails. Placerville: 1934-47. V. 40

POOL, BENJAMIN

Conventry: Its History and Antiquities . . . London: and Coventry: 1870. V. 44

POOL, EUGENE H.

Surgery at the New York Hospital One Hundred Years Ago. New York: 1929. V. 40

POOL, ROBERT

Views of the Most Remarkable Public Buildings, Monuments and Other Edifices in the City of Dublin. Dublin: 1780. V. 37; 39; 46

POOLE, BENJAMIN

Coventry; its History and Antiquities Compiled from Authentic Publications, Ancient Manuscripts and Charters, Corporation Records, Original Contributions, etc. London: 1870. V. 41

POOLE, CAROLINE

A Modern Prairie Schooner on the Transcontinental Trail the Story of a Mother Trip. San Francisco: 1919. V. 37; 38; 40; 41; 43

POOLE, DEWITT C.

Among the Sioux of Dakota Eighteen Months Experience as in Indian Agent. New York: 1881. V. 37; 40; 45

POOLE, EDWARD R.

The Bibliographical and Retrospective Miscellany, Containing Notices Of, and Extracts from Rare, Curious and Useful Books, In All Languages. London: 1830. V. 41; 44

POOLE, FRANCIS

Queen Charlotte Islands a Narrative of Discovery and Adventure in the North Pacific. London: 1872. V. 39; 40; 42; 43

POOLE, G. A.

An Historical and Descriptive Guide to York Cathedral and Its Antiquities. York: 1850. V. 39; 40

POOLE, JOHN

Crochets of the Air; or, an (Un)Scientific Account of a Balloon Trip. London: 1838. V. 39

Lessons in Scripture Chronology. Oxford: 1819. V. 39; 41

Little Pedlington and the Pedlingtons. London: 1939. V. 39; 42

Pry: Oddities of London Life. London: 1838. V. 43

Sketches and Recollections. London: 1835. V. 38

POOLE, JOSHUA

The English Parnassus, or a Helpe to English Poesie . . . London: 1657. V. 39; 42

The English Parnassus; or, a Help to English Poesie. London: 1677. V. 45

The English Parnassus . . . London: 1677. V. 38; 45; 46

POOLE, MARGARET ELIZABETH

Thomas Poole and His Friends. London: 1888. V. 45

POOLE, MATTHEW

Synopsis Criticorum Aliorumque S. Scripturae Interpretum, Opera Matthaei Poli, Londiensis. London: 1669-76. V. 39

POOLE, MONICA

The Wood Engravings of John Farleigh. London: 1985. V. 43; 45

POOLE, REGINALD STUART

Horae Aegyptiacae; or, the Chronology of Ancient Egypt Discovered from Astronomical and Hieroglyphic Records Upon Its Monuments . . . London: 1851. V. 42

POOLE, SOPHIA

The Englishwoman in Egypt: Letters from Cairo, Written During a Residence There in 1842, 3 & 4 . . . London: 1844. V. 38

POOLE, T. W.

Some Late Words About Louisiana By . . . . Commissioner of Immigration of the State of Louisiana . . . New Orleans: 1891. V. 39; 44

POOLE, THOMAS EYRE

Life, Scenery and Customs in Sierra Leone and the Gambia. London: 1850. V. 40; 43

POOLE, WATKIN

The Female's Best Friend. Manchester: 1826. V. 38

POOR, CHARLES LANE

Men Against the Rule: a Century of Progress in Yacht Design. New York: 1937. V. 39; 42; 44

POOR, HENRY V. 1812-1905

Money and Its Laws: Embracing a History of Monetary Theories, and a History of the Currencies of the United States. New York: 1877. V. 45

POOR, HENRY VARNUM 1812-1905

Manual of the Railroads of the United States, for 1872-73 . . . New York: 1872. V. 38

Manual of the Railroads of the United States for 1876-77. Showing their Mileage, Stocks, Bonds, Cost, Traffice, Earnings, Ezpenses and Organizations: with a Sketch of their Rise, Progress, Influence, Etc . . . New York: 1876. V. 37

Money and Its Laws: Embracing a History of Monetary Theories, and a History of the Currencies of the United States. London: 1877. V. 38

POOR, HENRY WILLIAM

American Bookbindings in the Library of Henry William Poor. New York: 1903. V. 41; 44

Catalogue of the Library of Henry W. Poor. New York: 1908. V. 39; 40; 41

Catalogue of the Library of Henry W. Poor. New York: 1908-09. V. 40

THE POOR Law Bill Explained. Wakefield: 1837. V. 43

POOR, M. C.

Denver South Park & Pacific. A History of the Denver South Park & Pacific Railroad and Allied Narrow Gauge Lines of the Colorado & Southern Railway Co. Denver: 1949. V. 37; 40; 42; 45

THE POOR Man's Posey of Prayers; or the Key of Heaven. London: 1783. V. 45

POOR Robin, 1690. An Almanack of the Old and New Fashion . . . London: 1690. V. 40

POOR Robin, 1694. An Almanack of the Old and New Fashion. London: 1694. V. 40

POOR Sarah; or the Indian Woman. New York: 1859's. V. 44

POOR Will's Pocket Almanack, for the year 1774; Fitted to the Use of Pennsylvania, and the neighbouring Provinces. Philadelphia: 1773. V. 40

POORE, BENJAMIN PERLEY

Biographical Sketch of John Stuart Skinner. New York: 1924. V. 39

The Life and Public Services of Ambrose E. Burnside, Soldier-Citizen-Statesman. Providence: 1882. V. 44

Perley's Reminiscences of Sixty Years in the National Metropolis . . . Intrigues of Brillant Statesmen, Ladies, Officers, Diplomats . . . Philadelphia: 1886. V. 37; 39; 42

POORTENAAR, JAN

The Art of the Book and Its Illustration . . . Philadelphia. V. 44

The Art of the Book and Its Illustrations. London: 1935. V. 39; 41

POORTENAR, JAN

The Art of the Book and Its Illustration. London/Bombay/Sydney: 1935. V. 37

The Art of the Book and Its Illustrations. Philadelphia: 1935. V. 37

POPE, ALEXANDER 1688-1744

Additions to the Works of Alexander Pope, Esq. London: 1776. V. 38; 44

The Beauties of Pope, or Useful and Entertaining Passages Selected from the Works of That Admired Author. London: 1796. V. 41; 42; 45

Carmen Cl. Alexandri Pope in S. Caeciliam . . . Cambridge: 1743. V. 41

The Correspondence. Oxford: 1956. V. 40

Court Poems. London: 1726. V. 41

The Duncaid. With Notes Variourm, and the Prolegomena of Scriblerus. Written in the Year, 1727. London: (1735). V. 37; 38; 40; 44

The Dunciad. London: 1728. V. 43

The Dunciad, Variorum. 1729. V. 43

The Dunciad. London: 1729. V. 38; 39; 40; 41; 42; 43; 44; 46

The Dunciad. London: 1736/35. V. 44

The Dunciad: Book the Fourth . . . London: 1742. V. 38

The Dunciad, in Four Books. London: 1743. V. 40

POPE, ALEXANDER 1688-1744 continued

The Dunciad, in Four Books. (with) The New Dunciad: As It Was Found in the Year MDCCXLI. London: 1743, 1742. V. 38

The Dunciad. London: 1953. V. 40

Eloge Historique et Critque d'Homere. Paris: 1749. V. 45

Eloisa to Abelard. London: 1720. V. 38

An Epistle to the Right Honourable Richard Lord Visct. Cobham. London: 1733. V. 40; 42; 45

An Epistle from Mr. Pope to Dr. Arbuthnot. London: 1734. V. 38; 40; 43; 44

An Epistle from Mr. Pope, to Dr. Arbuthnot. London: 1734-5. V. 41; 45

An Epistle to the Right Honourable Richard Lord Vist. Cobham. London: 1773. V. 37

An Essay on Criticism. San Francisco: 1928. V. 37; 38; 40; 42; 43; 44; 45; 46

Essai sur l'Homme . . . Avec l'Original Anglois; Ornee de Figures en Taille-Douce. Lausanne: 1745. V. 44

Essai sur l'Homme. Lausanne: 1762. V. 41; 42; 46

An Essay on Criticism. London: 1719. V. 42

An Essay on Man Address'd to a Friend. Part I. Dublin: 1733. V. 38

An Essay on Man. Philadelphia: 1760. V. 44

Essai Sur l'Homme, Poeme Philosophique en Cinc Languages, Savoir: Anglois, Latin . . . Strasbourg: 1762. V. 45

An Essay on Man. London: 1767. V. 45; 46

An Essay on Man . . . Preston: 1780. V. 41

An Essay on Man. 1927. V. 45

An Essay on Man. Oxford: 1962. V. 37; 38; 44

An Essay on Man. I nEpistles to a Friend. Epistle I. Corrected by the Author. The Second Edition. (Epistle II) (Epistle III) (Epistle IV). London: 1735. V. 37

The First Satire of the Second Book of Horace. London: 1733. V. 38; 39; 40; 43

The First Epistle of the First Book of Horace Imitated. London: 1737. V. 38; 46

The First Epistle of the Second Book of Horace, Imitated. London: 1737. V. 40

The First Satire of the Second Book of Horace Imitated in Dialogue Between Alexander Pope of Twickenham . . . and His Learned Council. To Which is added the Second Satire of the Same Book by the Same Hand, Never Before Printed. London: 1734. V. 37

Imitations of English Poets. Wiltshire: 1987. V. 45

A Key to the Lock. London: 1715. V. 39; 45

Letters of . . . and Several of His Friends. London: 1737. V. 42

Letters of Mr. Alexander Pope, and Several of His Friends. (and) The Works of Alexander Pope. London: 1737/41. V. 45

Letters of the Late Alexander Pope, Esq. to a Lady. London: 1769. V. 38; 39

Memoirs of the Extraordinary Life, Works and Discoveries of Martinus Scriblerus. Dublin: 1741. V. 40; 41; 45

Miscellaneous Poems and Translations. London: 1712. V. 41; 42; 45

Miscellaneous Poems and Translations by Several Hands. London: 1722. V. 38; 39; 40; 46

Miscellaney Poems . . . London: 1726. V. 38; 41

Miscellany Poems. London: 1726-27. V. 45

Miscellany Poems. London: 1732. V. 45

Mr. Pope's Worms to the Igenious Mr. Moore. London: 1720-30? V. 45

The New Dunciad: as It Was Found in the Year 1741. Dublin: 1742. V. 38

The New Dunciad. London: 1742. V. 40; 42; 43; 45

Ode for Musick on St. Cecilia's Day. London: 1719. V. 45

Of False Taste. London: 1731. V. 38; 39; 40; 43

Of the Character of Women. London: 1735. V. 38; 40; 41; 42

Of the Knowledge and Character of Man. An Epistle to the Right Honourable the Lord Viscount Cobham. London: 1733. V. 40

Of the Knowledge and Characters of Men. London: 1733, 1734. V. 40

Of the Use of Riches, an Epistle. London: 1732. V. 39; 40; 41; 43

Of the Use of Riches, an Epistle to the Right Honorable Allen Lord Bathurst. London: 1732, 1733. V. 40

One Thousand Seven Hundred and Thirty Eight. Dialogue II. London: 1738. V. 40

A Select Collection of Poems. New London: 1796. V. 40; 44

A Select Collection of Poems. Hartford: 1804. V. 39; 42

The Poems. London: 1939-61. V. 40

Poetical Miscellanies: the Sixth Part. London: 1709. V. 44

The Poetical Works. Glasgow: 1785. V. 37; 42; 43; 44

The Poetical Works. London: 1787. V. 43

The Poetical Works. London: 1821. V. 45; 46

The Poetical Works of Alexander Pope. London: 1853. V. 39; 40; 41

The Poetical Works of . . . London: 1853/54. V. 38

Pope's Own Miscellany. London: 1935. V. 44; 45

The Rape of the Lock. London: 1714. V. 37; 38; 40; 41; 42; 43; 45

The Rape of the Lock. London: 1715. V. 45

The Rape of the Lock. London: 1798. V. 38; 40; 41

The Rape of the Lock . . . London: 1798/99. V. 45

The Rape of the Lock. 1896. V. 37

The Rape of the Lock. 1896. V. 37; 39; 40; 42; 43; 45

The Rape of the Lock. London: 1897. V. 37; 38; 42; 44

The Rape of the Lock. New Rochelle: 1902. V. 37; 38; 40; 41; 43

Der Lockenraub. (The Rape of the Lock). Leipzig: 1908. V. 41

The Rape of the Lock. London: 1912. V. 41; 44

The Rape of the Lock. Vienna: 1930. V. 43

The Second Epistle of the Second Book of Horace, Imitated. London: 1737. V. 41; 45

The Second Epistle of the Second Book of Horace. N.P.: 1737. V. 41

The Sixth Epistle of the First Book of Horace Imitated. London: 1737. V. 38; 40

Sober Advice from Horarce, to the Young Gentlemen about Town . . . London: (1734). V. 37

The Temple of Fame. London: 1715. V. 37; 40; 42; 45

The Universal Prayer by the Author of the Essay on Man. London: 1738. V. 38

Upland Game Birds and Waterfowl of United States. 1877. V. 37

Verses Upon the Late D---ss of M------. London: 1746. V. 37; 42

Windsor Forest. London: 1713. V. 37; 40; 43

Windsor Forest. London: 1720, 1792. V. 41

The Works. London: 1717. V. 40; 41; 42; 45; 46

The Works . . . London: 1717/35. V. 42

The Works. London: 1717/35/37/41. V. 44

The Works. London: 1736-42. V. 38; 44

The Works. London: 1740. V. 40

The Works of Alexander Pope. Volume I, Parts I & II. Consisting of Fables, Translations & Imitations, etc. London: 1740-1741. V. 37

The Works. London: 1751. V. 39; 40; 43; 44

The Works. London: 1752. V. 37; 38; 40; 42; 44

Oeuvres Diverses de M. Pope. Amsterdam & Leipzig: 1753. V. 46

The Works . . . In Nine Volumes, Complete. With his last corrections, additions, and improvements . . . Together with the commentary and notes of Mr. Warburton. London: 1753. V. 37

The Works in Nine Volumes, Complete. London: 1757. V. 38; 39; 41

Oeuvres Diverses de Pope. Amsterdam and Leipzig: 1763. V. 40; 45

The Works of Alexander Pope, Esq. London: 1766. V. 40; 44; 46

Oeuvres Diverses . . . Amsterdam: 1767. V. 45

The Works. London: 1769. V. 42

The Works. London: 1769-1807. V. 43

Works. Edinburgh: 1770. V. 38; 40

The Works. In Six Volumes Complete. With His Last Corrections, Additions and Improvements; Together with: All his notes, as they were delivered to the Editor a little before his Death: Printed Verbatim from the Octavo Edition of . . . London: 1776. V. 37; 42

Oeuvres Complette. Paris: 1779. V. 38

Oeuvres Complettes . . . Paris: 1780. V. 42

The Works. London: 1797. V. 39; 42

The Works, In Verse and Prose. London: 1806. V. 37; 41

The Works. London: 1822. V. 38; 39; 42

Pope's Works. London: 1835. V. 40; 41; 42; 44

The Works. London: 1847. V. 37; 40; 41; 44; 46

The Works. London: 1871-86. V. 39; 42; 46

The Works. London: 1871-89. V. 38; 40; 43

The Works. London: 1879/89. V. 39

Works. London: 1935. V. 37

POPE, ALEXNDER 1688-1744

An Epistle from Mr. Pope, to dr. Arbuthnot. London: 1734(/5). V. 38

POPE, ARTHUR

Reproductions of Some of the Important Paintings and Of Their Details Illustrating Technique of the Artists. Boston: 1936. V. 43

POPE, ARTHUR UPHAM

A Survey of Persian Art. London: 1938-39. V. 45

A Survey of Persian Art from Prehistoric Times to the Present. London & New York: 1938. V. 37

POPE, C. H.

Reptiles in China. New York: 1935. V. 37; 39

POPE, CHARLES

The Merchant, Ship-Owner, and Ship Master's Import and Export Guide . . . London: 1825. V. 38

The Merchant, Ship-Owner, and Ship-Master's Custom and Excise Guide. London: 1822. V. 38

POPE, FRANKLIN LEONARD

Evolution of the Electric Incandescent Lamp. V. 38

Evolution of the Electric Incandescent Lamp. Elizabeth: 1889. V. 42

POPE-HENNESSEY, JAMES

History Under Fire - 52 Photographs of Air Raid Damage to London Buildings, 1940-1941. London: 1941. V. 40

POPE-HENNESSY, JOHN

Catalogue of Italian Sculpture in the Victoria and Albert Museum. London: 1964. V. 42; 44

The Drawings of Domenichino in the Collection of His Majesty the King at Windsor Castle. London: 1948. V. 43

Fra Angelico. Ithaca: 1874. V. 43; 45

Fra Angelico. London: 1974. V. 42; 44

An Introduction to Italian Sculpture. Italian Renaissance Sculpture. (with) Italian High Renaissance and Baroque Sculpture. London: 1958-63. V. 39

Luca Della Robbia. Oxford: 1890. V. 42

Sassetta. London: 1939. V. 37; 40

POPE-HENNESSY, UNA

Early Chinese Jades. London: 1923. V. 39; 42; 46

POPE, JESSIE

Three Jolly Huntsmen. London: 1912. V. 46

War Poems. London: 1915. V. 43

POPE, JOHN

The Report of An Exploration of the Territory of Minnesota. Washington: 1850. V. 41

Report of the Secretary of War . . . an Exploration of the Territory of Minnesota by Brevet Capt. Pope. Washington: 1850. V. 42

POPE, JOHN ALEXANDER

Chinese Porcelains from the Ardebil Shrine. Washington: 1956. V. 42

Chinese Porcelain from the Ardebil Shrine. London: 1981. V. 38; 41

The Freer Chinese Bronzies. Washington: 1967-69. V. 42

POPE, JOHN RUSSELL

The Architecture of . . . New York: 1926-30. V. 44

The Architecture of John Russell Pope. New York: 1930. V. 39; 43

POPE, RICHARD

Authenticated Report of the Discussion Which Took Place Between Pope and Maguire in the Lecture Room of the Dublin Institution from the 19th-25th of April, 1827. Dublin: 1827. V. 46

POPE, SIMEON

Interesting Suggestions to Proprietors and Trustees of Estates, Respecting the Land-Tax Sale and Redemption Act. London: 1798. V. 40

POPE, THOMAS

A Treatise on Bridge Architecture . . . New York: 1811. V. 37; 43

POPE, WALTER

The Memoires of Monsieur Du Vall . . . London: 1670. V. 43

The Wish. London: 1710. V. 41

POPE, WILLIAM

The Triumphal Chariot of Friction, or a Familiar Elucidation of the Origin of Magnetic Attraction. London: 1829. V. 45

POPE, WILLIAM F.

Early Days in Arkansas Being for the Most Part the Personal Recollections of an Old Settler. Little Rock: 1895. V. 37; 38; 39; 41

POPHAM, A. E.

Catalogue of the Drawings of Parmigianino. New Haven & London: 1971. V. 42

Correggio's Drawings. London: 1957. V. 37; 43

Drawings. London: 1957. V. 44; 46

The Drawings of Leonardo Da Vinci. With an Introduction and notes by A.E. Popham. London: 1946. V. 37

The Italian Drawings of the XV and XVI Centuries in the Royal Library at Windsor Castle. London: 1949. V. 44

Italian Drawings in the Department of Prints and Drawings in the British Museum. The Fourteenth and Fifteenth Centuries. London: 1950. V. 46

POPHAM, HOME

Telegraphic Signals or Marine Vocabulary. London: 1812. V. 38

POPHAM, HUGH

Three Cantos From: To the Unborn-Greetings. London: (1945). V. 37

POPHAM, JOHN

Reports and Cases, Collected by the Learned Sir John Popham, Knight, Late Lord Chief-Justice of England. London: 1656. V. 41; 42

Reports and Cases Collected by the Learned Sir John Popham Kt . . . London: 1682. V. 45

POPHAM, M. R.

Lefkandi I: The Iron Age. London: 1980-79. V. 44

The Minoan Unexplored Mansion at Knossos. London: 1984. V. 44

POPPER, FRANK

Agam. New York: 1980. V. 44

POPPETT'S Delight. London: 1850-1900. V. 44

POPPING, J. F.

Orbis Illustratus seu Nova Historico-Politico-Geographica, Imperiourum Rerumque Publicarum per Totum Terrarum Orbem, Descriptio. Razeburg: 1668. V. 46

POPPLE, WILLIAM

The Lady's Revenge: or, the Rover Reclaim'ed. London: 1734. V. 37

A Rational Catechism or, an Instructive Conference Between a Father and His Son. London: 1687. V. 38; 42

THE POPULAR Atlas of the World . . . Philadelphia/Springfield: 1892. V. 45

POPULAR Encyclopaedia; or Conversations Lexicon. London: 1890-93. V. 46

POPULAR Flowers. (name of flower); Its Propogation, Cultivation and General Treatment, In all Seaons. London: 1843. V. 39

POPULAR Prejudices Against the Convention and Treaty with Spain, Examin'd and Answer'd. With Remarks on a Pamphlet, Entitled, Considerations Upon the Present State of Our Affair at Home and Abroad. London: 1739. V. 38; 41; 42; 45

POPULAR Romances: Consisting of Imaginary Voyages and Travels. Edinburgh: 1812. V. 40

POPULAR Tales and Romances of the Northern Nations. London: 1823. V. 46

POPULAR Topics; or, the Grand Question Discussed. In Which the Following Subjects are Considered. Viz. The King's Perogative, the Privileges of Parliament, Secret Influence, and a System of Reform for the East-India Company. London: 1784. V. 39; 42

POR la Religion de Santo Domingo de la Provincia de Filipinas, Colegio de Santo Tomas, y Universidad de la Cuidad de Manila. Manilla: 1655. V. 45

PORADA, EDITH

Corpus of Ancient Near Eastern Seals in North American Collections: the Collection of the Pierpont Morgan Library. Washington: 1948. V. 38; 40; 42

Seal Impressions of Nuzi. New Haven: 1947. V. 40

PORCACCHI, THOMASO b. 1530

Funerali Antichi di Diversi Popoli et Nationi; Forma, Ordine et Pompa di Sepolture. Venice: 1574. V. 45

PORCACCHI, TOMMASO b.1530

Le Attioni d'Arrigo Terzo re di Francia et Quarto di Polonia . . . Venice: 1574. V. 38

L'Isole Piu Famose Del Mondo Descritte Da Thomaso Poracchi DaCastiglione Arretino E Intagliate da Girolamo Porro Pdovano Al Sereniss Principe et Sigre Il S. Don Giovanni d'Austria . . . Venice: 1572. V. 38; 39

L'Isole Piu Famose Del Mondo . . . Con L'Aggiunta di Molte Isole. Venice: 1590. V. 38

L'Isole Piu Famose Del Mondo. Venice: 1686. V. 38

PORCHER, FRANCES PEYRE

Resources of the Southern Fields and Forests, Medical, Economical and Agricultural . . . Charleston: 1869. V. 45

PORCHER, FRANCIS PEYRE

Resources of the Southern Fields and Forests, Medical, Economical, and Agricultural. Being also a Medical Botany of the Confederate States . . . Charleston, SC: 1863. V. 37

PORCHER, JEAN

French Miniatures from Illuminated Manuscripts. London: 1960. V. 41

Medieval French Miniatures. New York. V. 43

PORCHIA, ANTONIO

Voices. 1977. V. 39

Voices. Concigny: 1978. V. 41

THE PORCUPINE: a Journal of Current Events. Liverpool: 1878-79. V. 39

PORDAGE, SAMUEL

The Siege of Babylon; As It is Acted at the Dukes Theatre. London: 1678. V. 42; 44

PORNY, MARK ANTHONY

The Elements of Heraldry. London: 1765. V. 37; 38; 40

The Elements of Heraldry . . . London: 1771. V. 40

The Elements of Heraldry, Containing The Definition . . . The Divers Sorts of Coats-of-Arms . . . The Different Kinds of Ornaments Used . . . The Laws of Heraldry . . . London: 1795. V. 37

PORPHYRIUS

Homericaru(m) Quaestionu(m) Liber. Et de Nympharu(m) antro in Odyssea: Opusculum Leonis Decimi Pon. Max. Benefitio e Tenebris Erutum. Rome: 1518. V. 37

PORPHYRIUS, PUBLILIUS OPTATIANUS

Panegyricus Dictus Constantino Augusto. Augsburg: 1595. V. 37

PORRALIUS, CLAUDIUS

In Hippocratis Librum de Vulneribus Capitis Commentarius Brevis. Lyon: 1580. V. 38

PORRO, GIROLAMO

Statue antiche Che Sono Poste in Deversi Luoghi Nella Citta di Roma . . . Venice: 1576. V. 37; 40

PORSON, RICHARD 1759-1808

The Devil's Walk. London: 1830. V. 38; 39; 40; 42; 44

The Devil's Walk: a Poem. London: & Edinburgh: 1830. V. 45

Letters to mr. Archdeacon Travis, In Answer to His Defence of the Three Heavenly Witnesses. London: 1790. V. 37; 38

Tracts and Miscellaneous Criticisms. London: 1815. V. 38

PORT Darwin: Its Soil, Climate and Resources and Prospects as a Goldfield . . . Melbourne: 1872. V. 41

PORTA, COSTANZO

Missarum Liber Primus. Venice: 1578. V. 40

PORTA, GIOVANNI BATTISTA DELLA 1535-1615

De Humana Physiognomonia Libri IV. Rothomagi: (i.e. Rouen): 1650. V. 37

Della Fisonomia dell'Huomo . . . Libri Sei. Tradotta de Latino in volgare e dall'Istesso Autore . . . Naples: 1610. V. 43

Della Celeste Fisonomia . . . Libri Sei. Padua: 1616. V. 37

Della Fisionomia dell'Hvomo . . . Libri Sei . . . Venice: 1644. V. 37

Io. Bap. Portae Nepolitni De Distillatione Lib. IX. Quibus Certa Methodo, Multipliciq . . . Romae: 1608. V. 38

La Fisonomia dell'Huomo, et la Celeste. Venetia: 1668. V. 41

De Humana Physiognomonia . . . Hanovae: 1593. V. 45

De Humana Physiognomonia Libri IV. Frankfurt: 1618. V. 38

De I Miracoliet Mara Vigliosi Effetti Dalla Natura Prodotti, Libri IIII. Venice: 1560. V. 46

De I Miracoliet Mara Vigliosi Affetti dalla Ntura Prodotti Libri Quatro . . . Venice: 1611. V. 46

Magia naturalis Libri Viginti . . . Leyden: 1644. V. 46

Magia naturalis Libri Viginti. Leyden: 1651. V. 46

Magiae Naturalis sive De Miraculis Rerum Naturalium Libri IIIII. Antverpaie: 1564. V. 42

Magiae Naturalis Libri XX. Neapoli: 1589. V. 38

Natural Magick In Twenty Books . . . London: 1658. V. 46

Phytognomonica. Frankfurt: 1591. V. 37; 41

PORTA GREGORIANA

Al Monumento Dell'Acqua Claudia Aperta Il VI. Rome: 1840. V. 41

THE PORTABLE Atlas, Consisting of Maps of . . . New York: 1870. V. 45

PORTAL, ABRAHAM

Poems. London: 1781. V. 41; 42; 46

PORTAL, GERALD H.

The British Mission to Uganda in 1893. London: 1894. V. 46

My Mission to Abyssinia. London: 1892. V. 46

PORTAL, PAUL 1630-1703

The Compleat Practice of men and Women Midwives or the True Manner of Assisting a Woman in Child-Bearing . . . London: 1705. V. 45

La Pratique des Accouchemens Soutenue d'un Grand Nombre d'Observations. Paris: 1685. V. 42

PORTAL, ROBERT

Letters from the Crimea. 1854-55. Winchester: 1900. V. 41

PORTALIS, ROGER

Researches Concerning Jean Grolier, His Life and His Library. New York: 1907. V. 41

PORTANO, GIOVANNI GIOVANO

Amorum Libri II. De Amore Coniugali III. Venice: 1518. V. 37

Opera Omnia. Venice: 1519. V. 37

PORTER, A. KINGSLEY

Medieval aRchitecture. Its Origin and Development. New York: 1909. V. 39

Romanesque Sculpture of the Pilgrimage Roads. Boston: 1923. V. 37; 40; 42; 44

PORTER, ANNA MARIA

Ballad Romances, and Other Poems. London: 1811. V. 39; 44

The Barony. London: 1830. V. 46

Don Sebastian; or, the House of Braganza. London: 1809. V. 37; 42; 46

The Hungarian Brothers. London: 1807. V. 37

The Recluse of Norway. London: 1814. V. 37; 42; 43; 44

PORTER, ARTHUR L.

The Chemistry of the Arts. Philadelphia: 1830. V. 39

PORTER, BERTHA

Topographical Bibliography of Ancient Egyptian Hieroglyphic Texts, Reliefs and Paintings. Oxford: 1927-51. V. 44

Topographical Bibliography of Ancient Egyptian Hieroglyphic Texts. Oxford: 1972. V. 41

PORTER, BRUCE

Art in California. San Francisco: 1916. V. 38; 39; 40

Art in California. Irvine: 1988. V. 46

To Remember Willis Polk, Archiect. San Francisco: 1926. V. 39

PORTER, BURTON B.

One of the People: His Own Story. Colton: 1907. V. 39; 44

PORTER, CHARLES T.

Review of the Mexican War, Embracing the Causes of the War. Auburn: 1849. V. 46

PORTER, COLE

Red, Hot and Blue. New York: 1936. V. 37; 41; 46

PORTER, DAVID

A Dissertation on Christian Baptism. Catskill: 1809. V. 46

An Exposition of the Facts and Circumstances Which Justified the Expedition to Foxardo, and the Consequences Thereof . . . Washington: 1825. V. 41; 42; 46

Journal of a Cruise Made to the Pacific Ocean by Captain David Porter, in the United States Frigate Essex, in the Years 1812, 1813 and 1814 . . . Philadelphia: 1815. V. 46

Journal of a Cruise Made to the Pacific Ocean by . . . New York: 1822. V. 42

PORTER, DAVID D.

The Naval History of the Civil War. New York: 1886. V. 41; 42

PORTER, DOROTHY B.

North American Negro Poets: a Bibliographical Checklist of Their Writings 1760-1944. Hattiesburg: 1945. V. 45

PORTER, EBENEZER

The Fatal Effects of Ardent Spirits . . . New York: 1813. V. 44

PORTER, EDNA

Double Blossoms: Helen Keller Anthology. New York: 1931. V. 37

PORTER, EDWIN H.

The Fall River Tragedy. A History of the Borden Murders. Fall River: 1893. V. 37

PORTER, ELIOT

All Under heaven: the Chinese World. New York: 1983. V. 46

All Under Heaven: the Chinese World. New York: 1983. V. 46

Galapagos: The Flow of Wildness: Discovery, Prospect. San Francisco: 1968. V. 44

In Wilderness is the Preservation of the World. San Francisco: 1962. V. 37

The Place No One Knew. Glen Canyon the Colorado. San Francisco: 1963. V. 37

PORTER, EUGENE

San Elizario. Austin: 1973. V. 37; 38; 40; 42

PORTER, FRANK

Postal Directory of the Cycle Trades of Great Britain and Ireland. Liverpool: 1896. V. 40

PORTER, G. R.

The Progress of the Nation, In Its Various Social and Economic Relations, from the Beginning of the Nineteenth Century to the Present Time. London: 1836-38-43. V. 42; 46

PORTER, GENE STRATTON 1863-1924

After the Flood. Indianapolis: 1911. V. 39

A Daughter of the Land. Garden City: 1918. V. 44

Homing with the Birds: the History of a Lifetime of Personal Experience with the Birds. Garden City: 1919. V. 41

Homing with the Birds. Garden City: 1920. V. 43

Homing with the Birds. New York: 1920. V. 46

Keeper of the Bees. Garden City: 1925. V. 39; 45

The Keeper of the Bees. New York: 1925. V. 46

Laddie: a True Blue Story. Garden City: 1913. V. 39

Michael O'Halloran. New York: 1915. V. 46

Moths of the Limberlost. London: 1912. V. 46

The Song of the Cardinal. Indianapolis: 1903. V. 38; 40; 42; 46

The Song of the Cardinal. New York: 1915. V. 46

Tales You Won't Believe. New York: 1925. V. 46

PORTER, GEORGE RICHARDSON

The Nature and Properties of the Sugar Cane . . . London: 1843. V. 43

The Progress of the Nation, In Its Various Social and Economic Relations, from the Beginning of the Nineteenth Century to the Present Time. London: 1836-38-43. V. 39

The Progress of the Nation, In Its Various Social and Concomic Relations, From the Beginning of the Nineteenth Century. London: 1847. V. 38

The Progress of the Nation, In Its Various Social and Economical Relations, From the Beginning of the 19th Century. London: 1851. V. 41; 42

A Treatise on the Origin, Progressive Improvement and Present State of the Silk Manufacture. Philadelphia: 1832. V. 39; 42

PORTER, J.

Under the Maltese Cross, Antietam to Appomatox. Pittsburgh: 1910. V. 39

PORTER, J. L.

Five Years in Damascus . . . London: 1855. V. 40; 45

Five Years in Damascus . . . London: 1870. V. 45

PORTER, JACOB

Topographical Description and Historical Sketch of Plainfield in Hampshire County, Massachusetts May 1834. Greenfield: 1834. V. 39

PORTER, JAMES 1710-1786

Observations on the Religion, Law, Government and Manners Is Added, The State of the Turkey Trade, From Its Origin to the Present Time. London: 1771. V. 42; 45

Thaddeus of Warsaw. London: 1831. V. 41

PORTER, JAMES PORTER

The operative's Friend, and Defence: or, Hints to Young Ladies Who are Dependent on Their Own Exertions. Boston: 1850. V. 37

PORTER, JANE 1776-1850

Duke Christian of Luneburg; or, Tradition from the Hartz. London: 1824. V. 37; 44

the Pastor's Fire-Side, a Novel. London: 1817. V. 37; 39; 42; 45

The Scottish Chiefs. London: 1810. V. 40; 41; 46

The Scottish Chiefs, a Romance. London: 1816. V. 44

The Scottish Chiefs, revised, corrected, and illustrated with a New Retrospective Introduction, Notes, etc. London: (c. 1840). V. 37

Thaddeus of Warsaw. Boston: 1809. V. 38

Thaddeus of Warsaw. London: 1816. V. 38

Thaddeus of Warsaw. London: 1819. V. 45

PORTER, JOHN

Kingsclere. London: 1896. V. 46

The Riddles from the Exeter Book. (Market Drayton): 1978. V. 37

PORTER, JOHN SHERMAN

Moody's Manual of Investments, American and Foreign. New York: 1933. V. 39; 45

PORTER, JOHN W. H.

A Record of Events in Norfolk County, Virginia, from April 19th, 1861 to May 10th 1862 . . . Portsmouth: 1892. V. 45

PORTER, KATHERINE ANNE 1890-1980

A Christmas Story. N.P.: 1958. V. 39

A Christmas Story. New York: 1967. V. 39; 40; 44; 45; 46

Collected Essays and Occasional Writings. New York: 1970. V. 39; 43

The Days Before. New York: 1952. V. 45

A Defense of Circe. New York: 1954. V. 44

Flowering Judas. New York: 1930. V. 37; 39; 40; 42; 43; 46

Flowering Judas and Other Stories. New York: 1935. V. 37; 38; 39; 41; 44; 46

French Song-Book. 1913. V. 40

French Song Book. New York: 1933. V. 38; 39; 40; 41

French Song Book. Paris: 1933. V. 37; 39; 41; 43; 44; 45; 46

French Song-Book. 1933. V. 37

Hacienda. New York. V. 45

Hacienda. New York: 1934. V. 38; 40; 41; 42

Hacienda. Paris: 1934. V. 39; 43; 44; 46

Hacienda. Paris: 1934. V. 38; 40; 42

My Chinese Marriage. 1921. V. 46

My Chinese Marriage. New York: 1921. V. 37; 41; 43

My Chinese Marriage. New York: 1922. V. 37

Noon Wine. Detroit: 1937. V. 39; 40; 44; 45; 46

Pale Horse, Pale Rider. New York: 1939. V. 40; 43

Ship of Fools. Boston: 1962. V. 37; 39; 40; 43

PORTER, KENNETH W.

The Jacksons and the Lees: Two Generations of Massachusetts Merchants, 1765-1844. Cambridge: 1937. V. 42

PORTER, KENNETH WIGGINS

John Jacob Astor, Business Man. Cambridge: 1931. V. 37; 46

PORTER, MILLIE JONES

Memory Cups of Panhandle Pioneers. 1945. V. 42

Memory Cups of Panhandle Pioneers. Clarendon: 1945. V. 44

PORTER, NOAH

Evangeline: the Place, the Story and the Poem. New York: 1882. V. 41

The Human Intellect; with an Introduction Upon Psychology and the Soul. New York: 1868. V. 43

PORTER, P. B.

Indian Affairs. Letter from . . . in Relation to Our Indian Affairs Generally. Washington: 1829. V. 39; 44

PORTER, PETER

Once Bitten Twice Bitten. Northwood: 1961. V. 40

Poems Ancient and Modern. 1964. V. 40

PORTER, ROBERT KER 1777-1842

Anacreon (Illustrations to the Odes). London: 1803-05. V. 38; 39

Traveling Sketches in Russia and Sweden During the Years 1805, 1806, 1807, 1808. London: 1813. V. 41; 42; 43; 46

Travelling Sketches in Russia and Sweden. London: 1809. V. 45

Travelling Sketches in Russia and Sweden During the Years 1805, 1806, 1808. Philadelphia: 1809. V. 42; 43

Travels in Georgia, Persia, Armenia, Ancient Babylonia &c. &c. During the Years 1817, 1818, 1819 and 1820. London: 1821. V. 38; 39; 45

PORTER, ROBERT P.

Report of Indians Taxed and Not Taxed in the United States. Census of 1890. Washington: 1894. V. 45

PORTER, RUFUS

Aerial navigation: the Practicability of Traveling Pleasantly and Safely from New York to California in Three Days . . . San Francisco: 1935. V. 39; 44

A New Collection of Genuine Receipts, for the Preparation and Execution of Curious Arts . . . Boston: 1831. V. 43

PORTER, S. C.

Late-Quaternary Environments of the United States. London: 1984. V. 37

PORTER, T. P.

The Railroad Handbook and Guide to the Isthmus 1888-89. Colon-Panama: 1888. V. 39

PORTER, THOMAS

The Mail Robbers, or evils Attendant on a Sinful Life . . . Philadelphia: 1830. V. 44

The Villain, a Tragedy. London: 1670. V. 39; 44

PORTER, THOMAS CUNNINGHAM

Impressions of America. London: 1899. V. 37; 38; 42; 43; 46

PORTER, WHITWORTH

History of the Corps of Royal Engineers. London: 1889. V. 38; 41

History of the Corps of Royal Engineers. London: 1889-1915. V. 38; 40

A History of the Knights of Malta, or the Order of the Hospital of St. John of Jerusalem. London: 1858. V. 40

PORTER, WILLIAM D.

State Sovereignty and the Doctrine of Coercion . . . Charleston: 1860. V. 46

PORTER, WILLIAM SIDNEY 1862-1910

The Hiding of Black Bill. New York: 1908. V. 37

PORTER, WILLIAM SYDNEY 1862-1910

Cabbages and Kings. New York: 1904. V. 37; 38

Cabbages and Kings. New York: 1904. V. 39; 46

The Gift of the Magi. London: 1939. V. 37; 39; 40; 41

Heart of the West. New York: 1907. V. 39

Let Me Feel Your Pulse. New York: 1910. V. 43

Postscripts. New York & London: 1923. V. 39

The Stories of O. Henry. New York: 1965. V. 41

The Voice of the City. Further Stories of the Four Million. New York: 1908. V. 45

The Voice of the City and Other Stories. 1935. V. 39

The Voice of the City and Other Stories. New York: 1935. V. 38; 40; 41; 42; 43; 44; 45; 46

Waif's and Strays: Twelve Stories by O. Henry. Garden City: 1917. V. 46

Waifs and Strays. New York: 1917. V. 46

Complete Works. Garden City: 1912. V. 37; 39

The Complete Writings. Garden City: 1917. V. 42

PORTER, WILLIAM T.

A Quarter Race in Kentucky, and Other Sketches Illustrative of Scenes, Characters and Incidents . . . Philadelphia: 1847. V. 45

PORTEUS, BEILBY

A Letter to the Governors, Legislatures, and Proprietors of Plantations, in the British West India Islands. London: 1808. V. 40; 44

Sermons on Several Subjects. London: 1794. V. 44

Sermons on Several Subjects. London: 1797, 1799. V. 40

PORTFOLIO: a Magazine for the Graphic Arts. Volume 1, Number 1 and 2. (With): 'Portfolio: The Annual of the Graphic Arts.' Number 1. Cincinnati: 1950-1951. V. 37

THE PORTFOLIO; Containing Essays, Letters and Narratives. London: 1814. V. 40

A PORTFOLIO Honoring Harold for His Contribution to Scholarly Printing. N.P.: 1978. V. 41

A PORTFOLIO Honoring Harold Hugo for His Contribution to Scholarly Printing. 1978. V. 44
A PORTFOLIO Honoring Harold Hugo for His Contribution to Scholarly Printing. N.P.: 1978. V. 40

A PORTFOLIO Honoring Harold Hugo for His Contribution to Scholary Printing. N.P.: 1978. V. 40

THE PORTFOLIO of Fine Comic Art. 1978. V. 43
THE PORTFOLIO of Fine Comic Art. 1978. V. 45

PORTFOLIO of Santa Rosa and Vicinity . . . Santa Rosa: 1909. V. 38

PORTFOLIO of the National Galerie of Scotland. London: 1903. V. 41

PORTFOLIO One/1983: Ten Illustrated Broadsides. Roslyn Harbor: 1983. V. 41

PORTFOLIO Three, a Further Collection of Resettings, Specimen Settings and Display Settings printed by Will and Sebastian Carter at the Rampant Lions Press. Cambridge: 1982. V. 42

PORTIUS, SIMON

De Coloribus Libellus. Florence: 1548. V. 38

De Dolore. De Coloribus Oculorum. An Homo Bonus Vel Malus Volens Fiat. Florence: 1551/50/51. V. 39

De Pvella Germanica, Qvae Fere Biennivm Vixerat Sine Cibo, Potvque. Florentiae: 1551. V. 39

PORTLAND MUSEUM

A Catalogue of the Portland Museum, Lately the Property of the Duchess Dowager of Portland, Deceased . . . London: 1786. V. 38

PORTLAND, NATHANIEL

A Voyage Around the World; But more Particularly to the North-West Coast of America: Performed in 1785, 1786, 1787 and 1788, in the King George and Queen Charlotte, Captains Portlock and Dixon. London: 1789. V. 37

PORTLAND, Oregon, The Metropolis of the Pacific Northwest. Portland: 1888. V. 37

PORTLAND, WILLIAM JOHN ARTHUR CHARLES CAVENDISH, 6TH DUKE OF 1857-1943

Catalogue of the Pictures Belonging to the Duke of Portland at Welbeck Abbey. London: 1894. V. 40; 44

Catalogue of the Pictures Belonging to the Duke of Portland at Welbeck Abbey. Cambridge: 1936. V. 40

PORTLOCK, J. E.

Report on the Geology of the County of Londonderry and of Parts of Tyrone and Fermanagh. Dublin: 1843. V. 37; 38; 40; 43; 46

PORTLOCK, NATHANIEL

A Voyage Round the World; but More Particularly to the North-West Coast of America; Performed in 1785, 1786, 1787 and 1788 in the King George and Queen Charlotte. Amsterdam: 1968. V. 43; 45

A Voyage Round the World, but More Particularly to the North-West Coast of America, Performed in 1785, 1786, 1787 and 1788 . . . New York: & Amseterdam: 1968. V. 43

A Voyage Round the World; but More Particularly to the North-West Coast of America; Performed in 1785, 1786, 1787 and 1788 in the King George and Queen Charalotte, Captains Portlock and Dixon. London: 1789. V. 37; 38; 39; 40; 41; 42; 44; 45

PORTMAN, EDWARD BERKELEY, 1ST VISCOUNT

Rules, Regulations and Tables of Contributions and Allowances, Recommended for the Constitution of a Friendly Society in the County of Dorset, Upon Legal and Scientific Principles, on the Plan of the Rev. John Thomas Becher. Blandford: 1825. V. 39

PORTMAN, LOUISA MARY

Catalogue of the Pictures at Sherborne Castle. London: 1862. V. 38

PORTMAN, MAURICE V.

A History of Our Relations with the Andamanese. Calcutta: 1899. V. 40

PORTOGHESI, PAOLO

The Rome of Borromini: Architecture as Language. New York: 1968. V. 40; 43

Rome of Renaissance. London: 1972. V. 42; 46

PORTRAIT and Biographical Record of Denver & Vicinity. Chicago: 1898. V. 37; 38; 43; 45

PORTRAIT and Biographical Album of Gratiot County, Michigan. Chicago: 1884. V. 40; 46

PORTRAIT and Biographical Album of Lenawee County, Michigan, containing Full Page Portraits and Biographical Sketches of Prominent and Representative Citizens of the County . . . Chicago: 1888. V. 46

PORTRAIT and Biographical Album of Peoria County, Illinois. Chicago: 1890. V. 37; 38; 46

PORTRAIT and Biographical Album of Wapello County, Iowa, Containing Full Page Portraits and Biographical Sketches of Prominent and Representative Citizens of the County. Chicago: 1887. V. 39

PORTRAIT and Biographical Record of Allen & Van Wert Counties, Ohio . . . Chicago: 1896. V. 46

PORTRAIT and Biographical Record of Hunterdon and Warren Counties, New Jersey. New York: 1898. V. 41

PORTRAIT and Biographical Record of Lancaster County, Pennsylvania. Chicago: 1894. V. 41; 42

PORTRAIT and Biographical Record of the State of Colorado. Chicago: 1899. V. 38; 39; 43; 45

THE PORTRAIT Monthly: Containing Sketches of Departed Heroes and Prominent Personages of the Present Time . . . Volume I. New York: 1864. V. 39

PORTRAIT of a Publisher, 1915-1965. New York: 1965. V. 40

PORTRAITS and Lives of Remarkable and Eccentric Characters. London: 1819. V. 39

PORTRAL, GERALD H.

An Account of the English Mission to King Johannis of Abyssinia in 1887. Winchester: 1888. V. 45

PORTSMOUTH ANTHENAEUM

Catalogue of Books in the Portsmouth Anthenaeum. Portsmouth: 1862. V. 38

PORTSMOUTH, ENGLAND.

Extracts from Records in the Possession of the Municipal Corporation of the Borough of Portsmouth, and from Other Documents. Portsmouth: 1891. V. 39

PORTUGAL, D. FRANCISCO DE 1585-1632

Arte de Galanteria . . . Lisbon: 1670. V. 45

PORTUGAL. LAWS, STATUTES, ETC. - 1539

Ley Sobre o Pam Que se Vende Fiado. E Sobre o que se Empresta a Pagar em Pam. Lisbon: 1539. V. 41

Ordenacam Pera os Estudantes da Universidade de Coymbra Sobre os Criados Bestas, e Trajos e Outras Cousas. Lisbon: 1539. V. 41

PORTUGAL. LAWS, STATUTES, ETC. - 1651

Dom Ioam por Graca de Deos Rey de Portugual . . . Que eu Passey Ora Huma ley por my Assinada, & Passada por Minha Chancellaria da Qual o Treslado he o Seguinte . . . Lisbon: 1651. V. 41

PORTUGAL. TREATIES, ETC. - 1642

D. Joam IV de Portugal, & os Poderosos Estados das Provincias Unidas. Lisbon: 1642. V. 45

PORTUGAL. TREATIES, ETC. - 1810

Tratado de Commercio, e Navegacao Entre os Muito Altos, e Muito Poderosos Senhores o Principe Regente de Portugal, e ElRey do Reino Unido da Grande Bretanha e Irlanda Assinado no Rio de Janeiro . . . Rio de Janeiro: 1810. V. 45

PORTULANO de la America Setentrional. Construido en la Direccion de Trabajos Hidrograficos. Madrid: 1809. V. 43

PORTUS, FRANCISCUS

Commentarii in Pindari Olympia, Pythia, Nemea, Isthmia. Lausanne?: 1583. V. 44

PORTY, JAMES

What Michael Said to the Census Taker. (San Francisco: 1922). V. 37

PORZINARIO, GIUSEPPE BONETTA

Clamori Delle Anime del Purgatorio e Modo d'Acquietarli. Roma: 1741. V. 37

PORZIO, SIMONE 1497-1554

De Coloribus Libellus. (with) *An Homo Bonus vel Malus Volens Fiat . . .* Florence: 1548/51. V. 45

De Coloribus Ocuforum. Florence: 1550. V. 41

De Conflagratione Agri Puteolani . . . Florence: 1551. V. 40

Se l'Hvomo Diventa Bvono o Cattivo Volontariamente. Florence: 1551. V. 44

POSADA, JOSE GUADALUPE

Las Obras de Jose Guadalupe Posada, Grabador Mexicano, Con Introduccion de Diego Rivera. Mexico: 1930. V. 45

POSENER-KRIEGER, PAULE

Hieratic Papyri in the British Museum. London: 1968. V. 40; 42

POSITIVE Medical Agents: Being a Treatise On the New Alkaloid, Resinoid and Concentrated Preparations of Indiginous and Foreign Medical Plants. New York: 1855. V. 42

POSNANSKY, ARTHUR

Tihuanacu, the Cradle of Ancient Man. New York: 1945. V. 42

Tihuanacu, the Cradle of American Man. New York and Le Paz: 1945-57. V. 42

POSNER, DAVID

A Rake's Progress, a Poem in Five Sections. 1967. V. 40

A Rake's Progress. London: 1967. V. 39

POSSEVINUS, ANTONIUS

Apparavts Ad Omnivm Gentivm Historiam . . . Venice: 1597. V. 37

POSSIBLE Progenitor to Lincoln Steffens. Sanmateo: 1938. V. 46

POST, ALFRED

Report on Military Hygiene and Therapeutics. Washington: 1863. V. 42

POST, AUSTIN

Glacier Ice. Toronto: 1971. V. 44; 45

THE POST-CHAISE Companion . . . Dublin: 1786. V. 42

THE POST Chaise Companion: or Traveller's Directory through Ireland. Dublin: 1803. V. 46

POST, CHARLES C.

Ten Years a Cowboy. Chicago: 1889. V. 44; 46

POST, CHARLES CLEMENT

Phil. Johnson's Life on the Plains. Chicago: 1888. V. 38

POST, EMILY

Etiquette . . . New York: 1922. V. 41

Woven in Tapestry. New York: 1908. V. 39

POST, HENRY A. V.

A Visit to Greece and Constantinople, in the Year 1827-8. New York: 1830. V. 37

POST, KARL

Life in the New World or Sketches of American Society. New York: 1842. V. 39

POST, MELVILLE DAVISSON

Uncle Abner. New York: 1918. V. 37

THE POST Office - a Review of the Activities of the Post Office. London: 1934. V. 45

POST, PIETER

Alle de Wercken. s'Gravenhage,: 1665. V. 43

Begraffenisse van syne Hoogheyt Frederick Henrick . . . Prince van Orange . . . Amsterdam: 1651. V. 46

Swanenburch. Gemeenlants Huys van Rynlant. Amsterdam: 1654. V. 40

POSTAN, ALEXANDER

The Complete Graphic Work of Paul Nash. London: 1973. V. 38; 39

POSTEL, GUILLAUME

De Magistratibvs Atheniensium Liber, ad Intelligendam non Solum Graecorum, sed & Romanorum Politiam, ac Ömnem Ueterum Historiam . . . Basle: 1551. V. 37

De Originibus, seu, de Varia et Potissimum Orbi Latino d hanc diem Incognita . . . Basel: 1553. V. 38

POSTELLUS, GULIELMUS

De Orbis Terrae Concordia Libri Quatuor . . . Basle: 1544. V. 38

POSTELTHWAITE, JOHN

Mines and Mining in the English Lake District. Whitehaven: 1913. V. 38

POSTER Art in Vienna. Chicago: 1925. V. 43

THE POSTER Book. London: 1912. V. 42

POSTERITAS, PSEUD.

The Siege of London. London: 1885. V. 40

POSTERS In Miniature. New York: 1896. V. 44

POSTGATE, RAYMOND

How to Make a Revolution. London: 1934. V. 41; 42

POSTL, KARL

The Americans as They Are: Described in a Tour through the Valley of the Mississippi. London: 1828. V. 38

The Cabin Book; or, Sketches of Life in Texas. New York: 1844. V. 37; 45

POSTLEHWAYT, JAMES

The History of the Public Revenue, from the Revolution in 1688 to Christmas 1758. London: 1759. V. 41; 46

POSTLETHWAITE, JOHN

Mines and Mining in the (English) Lake District. Whitehaven: 1913. V. 40

POSTLETHWAYT, MALACHY

Britain's Commercial Interest Explained and Improved . . . London: 1757. V. 39

Britain's Commercial Interest Explained and Improved . . . Dublin: 1767. V. 41

Considerations on the Revival of the Royal-British-Assiento; Between His Catholick-Majesty, and the Honourable the South-Sea Company. London: 1749. V. 41

Great Britain's True System. London: 1757. V. 39; 45; 46

The Merchant's Advocate. London: 1749. V. 42

The Merchant's Advocate: or, an Enquiry, Whether the Merchants are not Intitled to a Discount of 5 p per cent, Given to the King by Act of Parliament Made in the Year 1747. London: 1759. V. 41

The Universal Dictionary of Trade and Commerce. London: 1751-55. V. 39

The Universal Dictionary of Trade and Commerce. London: 1774. V. 39

POSTON, CHARLES D.

Apache-Land. San Francisco: 1878. V. 37; 38; 39; 41; 43; 45

The Parsees: a Lecture . . . Ex Delegate in the Congress of the U.S. From The Territory of Arizona. London: 1870. V. 42

Speech of Hon. Charles D. Poston, of Arizona on Indian Affairs. New York: 1865. V. 43; 45

POSTSCRIPT to the Pennsylvania Journal . . . Thursday Evening, Seven O'Clock, December 9, 1773 . . . Reporting the Resolves of the Citizens of Boston to Prevent the Unloading of the Tea in Boston Harbor, Followed by the News that a Ship Carrying Tea . . . Philadelphia: 1773. V. 40

POSTSCRIPTS on Dwiggins. New York: 1960. V. 41

POTE, B. E.

Abbassah, an Arabian Tale. London: 1826. V. 43

POTE, JOSEPH

Les Delices de Windsore; or, a Description of Windsor Castle, and the Country Adjacent . . . Eton: 1755. V. 41

POTE, JOSEPH continued

The History and Anqtiquities of Windsor Castle, and the Royal College, and Chapel of St. George . . . Eton: 1749. V. 37; 40; 42; 44; 46

POTE, THOMAS

Le Delices de Windsore; or a Description of Windsor Castle and the Country Adjacent. Eton: 1755. V. 37

POTE, WILLIAM

The Journal of Captain William Pote, Jr. During His Captivity in the French and Indian War from May 1745 to August 1747. New York: 1896. V. 39; 40

POTIER, PIERRE

Opera Omnia Practica et Chymica, cum Annotationibus et Additamentis Utilissimis Parter ac Curiosis Friderici Hoffmanni . . . Francofurti: 1698. V. 42

POTIER, ROBERT JOSEPH

A Treatise on Obligations, Considered in a Moral and Legal View. Newbern: 1802. V. 37; 39

POTONNIEE, GEORGES

The History of the Discovery of Photography. New York: 1936. V. 41

POTT, JOSEPH HOLDEN

An Essay on the Landscape Painting. London: 1782. V. 42

POTT, PERCIVAL

An Account of the Method of Obtaining a Perfect or Radical Cure of the Hydrocele, or Wary Rupture, By Means of a Section. London: 1772. V. 43

Chirurgical Observations Relative to the Cataract, the Polypus of the Nose, the Cancer of the Scrotum, the Different Kinds of Ruptures and the Mortifications of Toes and Feet. (with) Essays, Medical and Experimental. Volume II. London: 1775, 1773. V. 38

The Chirurgical works of Percivall Pott, F.R.S., and Surgeon to St. Bartholomew's Hospital. London: 1779. V. 41

A Treatise on the Hydrocele,or Warty Rupture and Other Diseases of the Testicle, Its Coats and Vessels. London: 1773. V. 43

POTTER, ALONZO

The School and the Schoolmaster. New York: 1846. V. 39

POTTER, BEATRIX 1866-1943

Appley Dapley's Nursey Rhymes. London: 1917. V. 38; 45; 46

Cecily Parsley's Nursery Rhymes. London: 1922. V. 38; 41; 42

Ginger and Pickles. London: 1909. V. 42

The Journal of, from 1881 to 1897. London: 1974. V. 40

Panorama - the Story of Miss Moppet. London: 1906. V. 43

Peter Rabbit's Painting Book. London: 1917. V. 43

The Pie and the Patty-Pan. London. V. 45

The Pie and the Patty-Pan. n.d. V. 40

The Pie and the Patty Pan. London: 1905. V. 38; 40; 41; 44; 45

The Roly-Poly Pudding. London: 1908. V. 38; 45; 46

The Roly-Poly Pudding. London & New York: 1908. V. 38

The Songs of Peter Rabbit. London: 1951. V. 42

The Story of a Fierce Bad Rabbitt. London. V. 38

The Story of a Fierce Bad Rabbit. London: 1906. V. 40; 41; 46

The Story of Miss Moppet. London: 1906. V. 42

The Story of Miss Moppet. London: & New York: 1906. V. 44

The Story of a Fierce Bad Rabbit. New York & London: 1906. V. 41

The Tailor of Gloucester. London: 1903. V. 37; 45

The Tailor of Gloucester. London: 1930. V. 45

The Tale of Benjamin Bunny. London: 1904. V. 44; 45; 46

The Tale of Flopsy Bunnies. London: 1909. V. 38; 41; 44

The Tale of Jemima Puddle Duck. London: 1908. V. 44; 45; 46

The Tale of Little Pig Robinson. London: 1930. V. 41; 45

The Tale of Mrs. Tiggy-Winkle. London: 1905. V. 40; 45

The Tale of Mrs. Tittlemouse. London: 1910. V. 45; 46

The Tale of Mr. Tod. London: 1912. V. 38; 40; 41; 42; 43; 44

The Tale of Little Pig Robinson. 1930. V. 46

The Tale of Peter Rabbit. London: 1902. V. 46

The Tale of Peter Rabbit. (N.P.: 1902. V. 37

The Tale of Pigling Bland. London: 1913. V. 38; 41; 46

The Tale of Squirrel Nutkin. London: 1903. V. 45

The Tale of Samuel Whiskers. London: 1943? V. 46

The Tale of Two Bad Mice. London: 1904. V. 41

The Tale of Tom Kitten. London: 1907. V. 38; 39; 40; 42; 44

The Tale of Timmy Tiptoes. London: 1911. V. 38; 45

Tom Kitten's Painting Book. London: 1917. V. 41

Wag-By-Wall. Boston: 1944. V. 45

POTTER, CHRISTOPHER

Want of Charitie Justly Charged, on all Such Romanists, as Darae (without Truth or Modesty) aaffirme, the Protestancie Destroyeth Salvation. Oxford: 1633. V. 38

POTTER, DENIS

The Glittering Coffin. London: 1960. V. 40; 43

POTTER, DENNIS

Son of Man - a Play. London: 1970. V. 45

POTTER, ELI

Remarks . . . at the Trial of Two Individuals, for a Breach of the Peace in Disturbing a Meeting, In Which a Female Was Lecturing Upon the Subject of Abolition. Litchfield: 1840. V. 41; 44

POTTER, FRANCIS

An Interpretation of the Number 666. Oxford: 1642. V. 45

An Interpretation of the Number 666. Oxford: 1647. V. 38

POTTER, HELEN

Helen Potter's Impersonations. New York: 1891. V. 40

POTTER, ISRAEL RALPH 1744-1826?

Life and Remarkable Adventures of Israel R. Potter. Providence: 1824. V. 37; 40; 42; 44

POTTER, J. H.

Across the Continent and Back Again. Cincinnati: 1893. V. 43

POTTER, JACK MYERS

Cattle Trails of the Old West. Clayton: 1935. V. 43

Cattle Trails of the Old West. Clayton: 1939. V. 37; 38; 43; 44; 46

POTTER, JOHN 1674-1747

Archaelogia Graeca, Sive Veterum Graecorum, Praecipve Vero Atheniensium, Ritus Civiles, Religiosi, Militares et Domestici . . . Lugduni Batavorum: 1702. V. 46

Archaeologia Graeca, or, the Antiquities of Greece. London: 1715. V. 40

The Curate of Coventry: a Tale. London: 1771. V. 41; 43

Festivious Notes on the History and Adventures of the Renowned Don Quixote. London: 1771. V. 42; 43; 46

Musick in Mourning; or, Fiddlestick in the Suds. London: 1780. V. 37; 38; 39; 42; 43

The Theatrical Review, or New Companion to the Playhouse. London: 1772. V. 41

POTTER, JOHN STEPHEN

An Historical Developement (sic) of the Present Political Constitution of the Germanic Empire. London: 1790. V. 38; 40

POTTER, JOSEPH

Remains of Ancient Monastic Architecture in England; Represented by a Series of Views, Plans, Elevations, Sections and Details. London: 1847-51. V. 38

POTTER, PARACLETE

Every Man His Own Lawyer, or The Clerk and Magistrate's Assistant. Poughkeepsie: 1831. V. 37

POTTER, REUBEN

A Lecture of Mexico, Delivered at San Antonio, Texas in September, 1860. New York: 1863. V. 37

POTTER, ROBERT

An Inquiry into Some Passages in Dr. Johnson's Lives of the Poets; Particularly His Observations on Lyric Poetry, and the Odes of Gray. London: 1783. V. 38; 41; 42

Observations on the Poor Laws, on the Present State of the Poor and on Houses of Industry. London: 1775. V. 42; 43

POTTER, T. R.

Charnwood Forest with Illustrations. London: 1842. V. 45; 46

POTTER, THEODORE EDGAR

The Autobiography of . . . Concord: 1913. V. 37; 40

POTTER, THOMAS

Concrete: Its Use in Building and the Construction of Concrete Walls, Floors, Etc. London: 1877. V. 44

Concrete: Its Use in Building and the Construction of Concrete Walls, Floors, etc. Winchester: 1891. V. 44

Concrete: Its Uses in Building From Foundations to Finish. London: 1908. V. 44

POTTER, THOMAS R.

The History and Antiquities of Charnwood Forest. London: 1842. V. 42

The History and Antiquities of Charnwood Forest. London, Nottingham &: 1842. V. 39

POTTER, THOMAS R. continued

The History and Antiquities of Charnwood Forest. Nottingham: 1842. V. 42

POTTER, WOODBURNE

The War in Florida . . . Campaigns of Generals Clinch, Gaines and Scott. Baltimore: 1836. V. 42; 45

POTTIER DE LA HESTROYE, M.

Reflexions sur le Traite de la Dime Royale de Mr. Le Mareschal de Vauban. N.P.: 1716. V. 41

POTTINGER, HENRY

Flood, Fell and Forest. London: 1905. V. 42; 46

POTTLE, FREDERICK A.

Boswell and the Girl from Botany Bay. New York: 1937. V. 40

Boswell in Holland 1763-1764. V. 37

Boswell in Holland. 1763-1764. New York: 1952. V. 37

The Literary Career of James Boswell, Esq. 1929. V. 39

The Literary Career of James Boswell, Esq. Being the Biographical Materials for a Life of Boswell. Oxford: 1967. V. 46

POTTS, JOSEPH C.

The New Jersey Register, for the Year 1837. Trenton: 1837. V. 41

POTTS, STACY GARDNER

Village Tales, or Recollections of By-Past Times. Trenton: 1827. V. 43

POTTS, THOMAS

The British Farmer's Cyclopaedia . . . London: 1807. V. 44

A Compendious Law Dictionary. London: 1813. V. 40

POUCHER, W. A.

Perfumes, Cosmetics and Soaps with Especial Reference to Synthetics. New York: 1936-36-36. V. 45; 46

POUCHET, F. A.

The Universe; or, the Infinitely Great and the Infinitely Little. London: 1874. V. 45

POULAIN, ROGER

Batiments: Civils, Industriels, Commerciaux. Paris: 1931. V. 43

POULET, SIR AMIAS 1536?-1588

Copy Book of Sir Amias Poulet's Letters, Written During His Embassy to France (A.D. 1577) from a Ms in the Bodleian Library. London: 1866. V. 40

POULET, W.

Atlas on the History of Spectacles. Bonn-Bad Godesberg: 1978. V. 37

POULSEN, FREDERIK

Delphi. L: 1920. V. 42

Delphi. London: 1920. V. 44

Greek and Roman Portraits in English Country Houses. Oxford: 1923. V. 37; 40; 42; 44

POULSON, GEORGE

The History and Antiquites of the Seignory of Holderness, in the East-Riding of the County of York . . . Hull: 1840. V. 39; 42; 43; 46

POUNCEY, PHILIP

Italian Drawings in the Department of Prints and Drawings in the British Museum. London: 1962. V. 38; 42

POUNCY, JOHN

Dorsetshire Photographically Illustrated, the Detail and Touch of Nature Faithfully Reproduced. London: 1857. V. 40

POUND, EZRA 1885-1972

Papillon Quattuor Epigrammata. Milan: 1957. V. 37

POUND, EZRA LOOMIS 1885-1972

A B C of Economics. London: 1933. V. 43

ABC of Reading. London: 1934. V. 37; 39; 40

Active Anthology. London: 1923. V. 46

Active Anthology. London: 1933. V. 39; 41

Active Anthology. 1933. V. 37

America, Roosevelt and the Causes of the Present War. London: 1951. V. 43

Antheil and the Treatise on Harmony. Chicago: 1927. V. 41

Antheil and the Treatise on Harmony. Paris: 1924. V. 37

An Autobiographical Outline. New York: 1980. V. 41

Canto CX. Paris: 1967. V. 43

The Cantos of Ezra Pound - Some Testimonies. New York: 1933. V. 40; 46

Cantos LII-LXXI. London: 1940. V. 41; 43

Cantos LII-LXXI. Norfolk: 1940. V. 37; 41; 42

The Cantos of Ezra Pound. New York: 1948. V. 39; 41; 46

The Cantos of Ezra Pound. New York: 1951. V. 39

The Cantos (1-95). New York: 1956. V. 45

Cantos 110-116. New York: 1967. V. 42

The Cantos of Ezra Pound. New York: 1972. V. 42

I Cantos. Milano: 1985. V. 39; 41

Cantos LXXII & LXXIII. Washington: 1973. V. 42

Canzoni. London: 1911. V. 37; 41; 45

Cathay. London: 1915. V. 37; 38; 39; 41; 42; 43; 46

Cavalcanti Poems: Sonnets, Ballate, Canzone. 1966. V. 40

Cavalcanti Poems: Sonnets. 1966. V. 45

Cavalcanti Poems. 1966. V. 41

Cavalcanti Poems. Colophon: printed in Dante: 1966. V. 43

Cavalcanti Poems. London: 1966. V. 44

Cavalcanti Poems. New York: 1966. V. 38

The Classic Anthology Defined by Confucius. London: 1955. V. 39

Confucio: Ta S'eu Dai Gaku Studio Integrale. Rapallo: 1942. V. 40

Confucius: the Unwobbling Pivot and The Great Digest. Norfolk: 1947. V. 40

Dialogues of Fontenelle. London: 1917. V. 37

Diptych Rome-London: Homage to Sextus Propertius & Hugh Selwyn Mauberley Contacts and Life. London: 1958. V. 40

A Draft of XVI Cantos. Paris: 1925. V. 37; 40; 42

A Draft of the Cantos 17-27 of Ezra Pound. London: 1928. V. 42

A Draft of XXX Cantos. London: 1930. V. 37; 43

A Draft of XXX Cantos. Paris: 1930. V. 38

A Draft of XXX Cantos. London: 1933. V. 37; 39; 40; 43

A Draft of XXX Cantos. New York: 1933. V. 43; 46

A Draft of Cantos XXXL-XLI. London: 1935. V. 39; 41; 42; 44

Drafts & Fragments of Cantos CX-CXVII. Iowa: 1968. V. 43

Drafts and Fragments of Cantos CX-CXVII. New York: 1968. V. 38; 39; 44; 46

Drafts and Fragments of Cantos CX-XVII . . . London: 1969. V. 41

Drafts & Fragments of Cantos CX-CXVII. New York: 1969. V. 40

Drafts and Fragments of Cantos CX-CXVII. New York & Iowa City: 1969. V. 37; 40

Drafts and Fragments of Cantos CX-CXVII. London: 1970. V. 40

Drafts & Fragments of Cantos CX-CXVII. London: 1967. V. 37

Eleven New Cantos XXXI-XLI. New York: 1934. V. 43; 46

Etre Citoyan Romain Etait un Privilege Etre Citoyen Moderne est une Calamite. Liege: 1965. V. 46

The Exile - Numbers 1 and 2. Dijon and Chicago: 1927. V. 38

The Exile. Paris & Chicago: 1927-28. V. 41; 42

The Exile. Chicago: 1928. V. 41

The Exile. Paris and Chicago: 1928. V. 44

Exultations. London: 1909. V. 38; 40; 41; 42; 43; 44; 46

The Fifth Decade of Cantos. London: 1937. V. 38; 45; 46

The Fifth Decad of Cantos. New York: 1937. V. 37; 38; 39

Forked Branches. Iowa City: 1985. V. 37; 42; 44; 46

Gaudier-Breska: a Memoir. London: 1916. V. 37; 39; 41; 46

Gaudier Brzeska - a Memoir. New York: 1916. V. 37

Gists & Piths. Iowa City: 1982. V. 46

Gold and Work. London: 1951. V. 43

Guide to Kulchur. London: 1938. V. 37; 40; 42

Guido Cavalcanti Rime. Genova: 1932. V. 37; 38; 39; 40

Homage to Sextus Propertius. London: 1934. V. 37; 40; 43

Hugh Selwyn Mauberley. London: 1920. V. 44; 46

I Cantos. Milano: 1985. V. 37; 38; 40; 42

'If This Be Treason.' Siena: 1948. V. 38; 39; 40; 41

Imaginary Letters. Paris: 1930. V. 37; 44; 46

Des Imagistes. London: 1914. V. 42

An Immorality. 1923. V. 42

An Immortality. 1980. V. 42

Indiscretions. Paris: 1923. V. 39; 43; 45; 46

Introduzione Alla Natura Economica Degli S. U. A. Venezia: 1944. V. 40

Jefferson and/or Mussolini. London: 1935. V. 39

Jefferson and/or Mussolini L'Idea Statale Fascism as I Have Seen It. New York: 1935. V. 46

Jefferson and/or Mussolini. New York: 1936. V. 37; 39; 40; 41; 42; 43

Jefferson and/or Mussolini. New York: 1939. V. 42

The Literary Essays of Ezra Pound. Norfolk: 1954. V. 41; 42

Lustra. London: 1916. V. 38

Lustra. New York: 1917. V. 39; 40

Mr. Houseman's Message. Palo Alto: 1931. V. 44

POUND, EZRA LOOMIS 1885-1972 continued

'Noh' or Accomplisment - a Study of the Classical Stage of Japan. London: 1916. V. 37; 41

'Noh' or Accomplishment. London: 1917. V. 37

Oro E Lavora. Rapallo: 1944. V. 40

Pavannes and Divisions. New York: 1918. V. 41

Pavannes and Divisions. New York: 1928. V. 43

Personae. London: 1909. V. 37; 40; 42; 43; 46

Personae & Exultations. London: 1913. V. 45

Personae the Collected Poems of Ezra Pound . . . New York: 1925. V. 45

Personae. New York: 1926. V. 39; 40; 44

The Pisan Cantos. New York: 1948. V. 37; 39; 46

The Pisan Cantos. Norfolk: 1948. V. 40

Poems 1918-1921. New York: 1921. V. 37; 39; 40; 43; 46

Polite Essays. Norfolk: 1940. V. 37; 40; 42

Provenca. Boston: 1910. V. 38; 39; 40; 42

Provenca. Boston: 1917. V. 44

Quia Pauper Amavi. 1919. V. 42

Quia Papuper Amavi. London: 1919. V. 37; 38; 40; 41; 44; 45

A Quinzane for this Yule. London: 1908. V. 39; 40

Ripostes. London: 1912. V. 40

Section: Rock Drill 85-95 de Los Canates. 1956. V. 46

Selected Poems. London: 1928. V. 37; 44

Selected Cantos of Ezra Pound. London: 1967. V. 43

Seventy Cantos. London: 1950. V. 41; 43

Sonnets and Ballate of Guido Cavalcanti. London: 1912. V. 42

The Spirit of Romance. London: 1910. V. 40

The Spirit of Romance. London & New York: 1910. V. 38; 40

The Spirit of Romance. New York: 1910. V. 37; 38; 40

The Spirit of Romance. Norfolk: 1952. V. 43

Thrones 96 - 109 de Los Cantares. Milan: 1959. V. 41

The Tomb at Akr Caar. Helsinki: 1965. V. 46

Versi Prosaici. Rome: 1959. V. 37

POUND, ROSCOE

New Paths of the Law. Lincoln: 1950. V. 44

POUNTNEY, W. J.

Old Bristol Potteries. Bristol: 1920. V. 37; 38; 41; 43

POUQUEVILLE, F. C. H. L.

Travels through the Morea, Albania, and Several Other Parts of the Ottoman Empire to Constantinople During the Years 1798, 1799, 1800 and 1801. London: 1806. V. 40

Voyage dans la Grece. Paris: 1820-21. V. 39

POUSETTE-DART, NATHANIEL

Ernest Haskell, His Life and Work. Boston: 1934. V. 41; 44

POVEY, CHARLES

The Virgin in Eden; or, The State of Innocency. London: 1741. V. 44; 46

POW-KEY, SOHN

Early Korean Typography. N.P.: 1982. V. 44

Early Korean Typography. N.P.: 1982. V. 37

POWDER RIVER CATTLE COMPANY LTD.

Report of the General Manager, Mr. Moreton Frewen, to the Shareholders at the First Annual Meeting Held February 26th, 1884. London: 1884. V. 42

POWE, JOHN HARRINGTON

Reminiscences and Sketches of Confederate Times. Columbia: 1909. V. 44

POWEL, DANIEL

The Love of Wales to Their Soveraigne Prince. London: 1837. V. 40

POWEL, GABRIEL 1576-1611

The Catholikes Svpplication vnto the Kings Maiestie; for Toleration of Catholike Religion in England. London: 1603. V. 40

POWELL, AARON MACY

Personal Reminiscences of the Anti-Slavery and Other Reforms and Reformers. New York: 1899. V. 45

POWELL, ANTHONY DYMOKE 1905-

The Acceptance World. London. V. 42

The Acceptance World. London: 1955. V. 38; 39; 41; 46

The Acceptance World. New York: 1955. V. 45

Agents and Patients. London: 1936. V. 38

At Lady Molly's. Boston: 1957. V. 39; 44

At Lady Molly's. London: 1957. V. 40; 41; 46

Books Do Furnish a Room. London: 1971. V. 41

A Buyer's Market. London: 1952. V. 39; 42; 46

A Buyer's Market. New York: 1953. V. 45

Casanova's Chinese Restaurant. Boston: 1960. V. 46

Casanova's Chinese Restaurant. London: 1960. V. 38; 41; 42; 46

A Dance to the Music of Time. London: 1951-75. V. 38; 44

A Dance to the Music of Time. London: 1957-75. V. 44

A Dance to the Music of Time. London: 1962. V. 42

From a View to a Death. London: 1933. V. 37

John Aubrey and His Friends. London: 1948. V. 37; 40; 45

the Kindly Ones. London: 1962. V. 38; 39; 42

The Military Philosophers. London: 1968. V. 39

Mr. Zouch Superman (from a View to a Death in England). New York. V. 38

A Question of Upbringing. London: 1950. V. 42

A Question of Upbringing. London: 1951. V. 40; 42

A Question of Upbringing. New York: 1951. V. 37; 38; 40; 44; 45

The Soldier's Art. London: 1966. V. 46

Temporary Kings. London: 1973. V. 37

To Keep the Ball Rolling. London: 1976-82. V. 45; 46

Two Plays. London: 1971. V. 46

The Valley of Bones. London: 1964. V. 41

Venusberg. London: 1932. V. 37; 40

POWELL, C. FRANK

Life of Major-General Zachary Taylor. New York: 1846. V. 40; 42

POWELL, CHARLES

The Poets in the Nursery. London: 1920. V. 38; 40

POWELL, CLAYTON

The Aftermath of the Civil War, in Arkansas. New York: 1915. V. 37; 39

POWELL-COTTON, P. H. G.

A Sporting Tour through Abyssinia. London: 1902. V. 38; 40; 43

POWELL, GABRIEL

The Catholikes Supplication unto the kins maiestie; for toleration of catholike religion in England: with short notes or animaduersions in the margine. Whereunto is annexed parallel-wise, a supplicatorie . . . London: 1603. V. 37

POWELL, GEORGE

Alphonso, King of Naples. London: 1691. V. 46

A Very good Wife. London: 1693. V. 38; 45

POWELL, H. M. T.

The Santa Fe Trail to California, 1849-1852: The Journal and Drawings of H. M. T. Powell. New York: 1918. V. 41

The Santa Fe Trail to California 1849-1852. San Francisco: 1931. V. 38; 41; 42; 43; 44; 45; 46

The Santa Fe Trail to California 1849 - 1852. New York: 1981. V. 38; 39; 40; 42; 44

POWELL, HARRY

Recollections of a Young Soldier During the Crimean War. Oxford: 1876. V. 41

POWELL, HENRY J.

Glass-Making in England. Cambridge: 1923. V. 42

POWELL, J. GILES

The Narrative of a Voyage to the Swan River . . . London: 1831. V. 39

POWELL, J. W. DAMER

Bristol Privateers and Ships of War . . . London: 1930. V. 42

POWELL, JOHN JOSEPH

Essay Upon the Law of Contracts and Agreements. Dublin,: 1796. V. 38

POWELL, JOHN WESLEY 1834-1902

Atlas Accompanying the Report on the Geology of a Portion of the Unita Mountains. Washington: 1875. V. 41

Canyons of the Colorado. Meadville: 1895. V. 39

Down the Colorado. V. 44

Down the Colorado - Diary of the First Trip through the Grand Canyon. New York: 1969. V. 38

Exploration of the Colorado River of the West and Its Territories. Washington: 1875. V. 37; 40; 41; 42; 43

Introduction to the Study of Indian Languages. Washington: 1880. V. 38; 39; 42

Outlines of the Philosophy of the North American Indians. New York: 1877. V. 37

POWELL, JOHN WESLEY 1834-1902 continued

Report of the Lands of the Arid Region of the United States, with a More Detailed Account of the Lands of Utah. Washington: 1879. V. 37; 38; 39; 42; 46

POWELL, LAWRENCE CLARK

Book Shops by L.C.P. Los Angeles: 1965. V. 41

The Desert as Dwelled on by L.C.P. Los Angeles: 1973. V. 41

From the Heartland. Flagstaff: 1976. V. 38; 42

Heart of the Southwest. Los Angeles: 1955. V. 42; 46

My New Mexico Literary Friends. Santa Fe: 1986. V. 44

Profiles of People and Places of the Southwest and Beyond. Flagstaff: 1976. V. 43

Robinson Jeffers; The Man and His Work. Los Angeles: 1934. V. 42; 45; 46

Robinson Jeffers: the Man and His Work. Pasadena: 1940. V. 39

Robinson Jeffers: The Man and His Work. Pasadena: 1940/34. V. 44

The Sea As Seen By El Sea Powell. Malibu: 1962. V. 41

A Southwestern Century. Van Nuys: 1958. V. 43

POWELL, PETER JOHN

People of the Sacred Mountain. New York: 1981. V. 44

People of the Sacred Mountain. A History of the Northern Cheyenne Chiefs and Warrior Societies 1830-1879. San Francisco: 1981. V. 39; 45

Sweet Medicine. Norman: 1969. V. 44; 45

POWELL, RICHARD

Proceedings of a General Court Martial Held at the Horse-Guards, on the 24th of March, 1792, for the Trial of Capt. Richard Powell, Lieut. Christopher Seton and Lieut. John Hall, of the 54th Regiment of Foot . . . London: 1809. V. 40

POWELL, ROBERT fl. 1634-1652

A Treatise of the Antiquity, Authority, Uses and Jurisdiction of the Ancient Courts of Leet . . . London: 1641. V. 40

A Treatise of the Antiquity, Authority, Uses and Jurisdiction of the Ancient Courts of Leet, or View of Franck-Pledge . . . Together with Additions and Alterataions of the Moderne Lawes and Statutes Inquirable at those Courts, Until this Present Yeare, 1642. London: 1642. V. 37

POWELL, THOMAS 1572-1635

The Attornies Almanacke. London: 1627. V. 38

The Attourney's Academy or the Manner and Forme of Proceeding In any Court of Record. London: 1630. V. 37; 38; 40

Humane Industry: or, a History of Most Manual Arts, Deducing the Original Progress and Improvement of Them. London: 1601. V. 37

The Living Authors of America. New York: 1850. V. 39; 46

POWELL, WILLIAM H.

Records of Living Officers of the United States Army. Philadelphia: 1890. V. 45

POWELL, WILLIAM SAMUEL

A Defence of the Observations on the First Chapter of a Book Called Miscellanea Analytica. London: 1760. V. 38

POWELL, WILLIS J.

Tachyhippodamia, or Art of Quieting Wild Horses in a Few Hours, as Discovered by the author, in the Year 1814. New Orleans: 1838. V. 43; 45

POWER, BERTHA KNIGHT

William Henry Knight: California Pioneer. 1932. V. 44

William Henry Knight: California Pioneer. 1932. V. 41

William Henry Knight California Pioneer. N.P.: 1932. V. 40

William Henry Knight California Pioneer. N.P.: 1932. V. 39

POWER, D'ARCY

Portraits of Dr. William Harvey. Oxford: 1913. V. 37; 38; 40; 41; 45

POWER, HENRY 1623-1668

Experimental Philosophy. London: 1664. V. 37; 38; 40; 42

POWER, M.

A Recollection of an Indian Battle and the Story of Time Doolan the Deserter. Darjeeling: 1890. V. 45

POWER, MARGUERITE A.

The Keepsake for 1857. London: 1857/56. V. 42

POWER, P.

The Place Names of Decies. London: 1907. V. 46

POWER, RHODA

How It Happened. Cambridge: 1930. V. 42

POWER, WILLAIM GRATTAN TYRONE 1797-1841

Impressions of America, During the Years 1833, 1834, and 1835. London: 1836. V. 37; 38; 40; 41; 42; 44; 45

POWER, WILLIAM GRATTAN TYRONE 1797-1841

Sketches in New Zealand, with Pen and Pencil. London: 1849. V. 38; 41; 43

POWERLL, LAWRENCE FITZROY

Johnson, Boswell and their Circle. Oxford: 1965. V. 45

POWERS, ALAN

The English Tivoli. 1988. V. 40

The Marches: A Picturesque Tour. 1989. V. 45

POWERS, GRANT

Historical Sketches of the Discovery, Settlement, and Progress of Events in the Coos Country and Vicinity . . . Between . . . 1754 and 1785. Haverhill: 1841. V. 38

POWERS, J. F.

The Old Bird: a Love Story. Minneapolis: 1991. V. 46

POWERS, PERRY F.

History of Northern Michigan and Its People. Chicago: 1912. V. 39

POWERS, STEPHEN

Afoot and Alone; a Walk from Sea to Sea by the Southern Route. Hartford: 1872. V. 37; 39; 40; 45

Tribes of California. Washington: 1877. V. 39

Tribes of California. Washington: 1887. V. 39

POWERS, TIM

The Anubis Gates. New York: 1983. V. 42

On Stranger Tides. 1987. V. 44

On Stranger Tides. New York: 1987. V. 45

The Way Down the Hill and the Pink of Fading Neon. 1986. V. 39

POWERS, W. P.

Some Annals of the Powers Family. Los Angeles: 1924. V. 37; 44; 45

POWHELE, RICHARD

The History of Cornwall: Civil, Military, Religious, Architectural, Agricultural, Commercial, Biographical and Miscellaneous. London: 1803-36. V. 43

POWIS, EDWARD HERBERT, 2ND EARL OF 1785-1848

Speech by the Earl of Powis in the House of Lords May 23, 1843, on Moving the Second Reading of a Bill for Preventing the Union of the Sses of St. Asaph and Bangor. London: 1843. V. 40

POWLES, C. G.

the New Zealanders in Sinai and Palestine. Auckland: 1922. V. 44

POWLES, L. D.

The Land of the Pink Pearl, or Recollections of Life in the Bahamas. London: 1888. V. 38; 39

POWNALL, CHARLES A. W.

Thomas Pownall, M.P., F.R.S., Governor of Massachusetts Bay . . . London: 1908. V. 38; 39; 40

POWNALL, THOMAS

The Administration of the Colonies. London: 1765. V. 38

The Administration of the Colonies. London: 1768. V. 39

Considerations on the Scarcity and High Prices of Bread-Corn and Bread at the Market . . . Cambridge: 1795. V. 38

The Measure of Regulating the Assize and of the Due Making of Bread Explained . . . London: 1795. V. 45

The Present State of the British Interest in India: with a Plan for Establishing a regular System of Government in that Country. London: 1772. V. 42

The Right, Interest and Duty of the State as Concerned in the Affairs of the East Indies. London: 1773. V. 37; 38; 46

Two Speeches of an Honourable Gentleman, on the Late Negociation and convetion with Spain. London: 1771. V. 46

Two Memorials, Not Originally Intended for Publication, now published. London: 1782. V. 37

POWNEY, RICHARD

The Stag in Windsor Forest. London: 1739. V. 43

POWNOLL, NATHANIEL

The Young Divine's Apology for His Continuance in the University. Oxford: 1658. V. 42

POWYS, E. MATHERS

Procreant Hymn. 1926. V. 41

Procreant Hymn. Waltham St. Lawrence: 1926. V. 41; 45

POWYS, ELIZABETH

A Ballad Upon the Popish Plot. N.P.: 1679. V. 42

POWYS, JOHN COWPER 1872-1964

The Brazen Head. London: 1925. V. 41

Confessions of Two Brothers. Rochester: 1916. V. 37; 38

Homer and the Aether. London: 1959. V. 44

Lucifer. London: 1956. V. 38; 41; 42; 43; 44; 45

Odes and Other Poems. London: 1896. V. 40

The Owl, the Duck and - Miss Rowe! Miss Rowe! Chicago: 1930. V. 38

Poems. London: 1899. V. 40

Porius. A Romance of the Dark Ages. London: 1951. V. 39

Rodmoor. New York: 1916. V. 37; 42

Samphire. New York: 1922. V. 42; 45

Suspended Judgments. New York: 1916. V. 37; 40; 42; 43

The War and Culture. New York: 1914. V. 37; 40

Wolf Solent. London: 1929. V. 41

Wood and Stone. New York: 1915. V. 37; 38; 41; 43

Wood and Stone. London: 1917. V. 40

POWYS, LLEWELYN 1884-1939

A Baker's Dozen. Herrin: 1939. V. 40

Black Laughter. New York: 1924. V. 38

The Book of Days. London: 1937. V. 37; 38; 42

The Book of Days of Llewelyn Powys - Thoughts from His Philosophy. Waltham St. Lawrence: 1937. V. 46

Ebony and Ivory. London: 1923. V. 38

Impassioned Clay. New York & London: 1931. V. 41

Now That the Gods are Dead by Llewelyn Powys. New York: 1932. V. 37

Out of the past. Pasadena: 1928. V. 39

Somerset Essays. London: 1937. V. 39

The Twelve Months. London: 1936. V. 41; 42

POWYS, LLWELYN 1884-1939

Now That the Gods Are Dead. New York: 1932. V. 45

POWYS, MARIAN

Lace and Lace Making. Boston: 1953. V. 41

POWYS, PHILIPPA

Some Poems. Sidmouth: 1937. V. 42

POWYS, THEODORE FRANCIS 1875-1953

Black Bryony. London: 1923. V. 42; 44

A Christmas Story. Bristol: 1930. V. 40

The Dewpond. London: 1928. V. 41; 42

Fables. London: 1928. V. 45

Fables. London: 1929. V. 39; 42

Goat Green, or the Better Gift. London: 1937. V. 40

Innocent Birds. London: 1926. V. 42

An Interpretation of Genesis. London: 1929. V. 41; 42

An Interpretation of Genesis. New York: 1929. V. 39; 45; 46

An Interpretation of Gensis. New York: 1929. V. 45

An Interpretation of Genesis. 1929. V. 37

The Key of the Field. London: 1930. V. 41; 42

Kindness in a Corner. London: 1930. V. 38; 40

Kindness in a Corner. New York: 1930. V. 46

Mr. Weston's Good Wine. London: 1927. V. 38; 40; 42; 46

The Only Penitent. London: 1931. V. 38

The Rival Pastors. London: 1927. V. 42

Rosie Plum and Other Stories. London. V. 41

Soliloquies of a Hermit. 1918. V. 41

Soliloquies of a Hermit. London: 1918. V. 37; 38; 40; 41; 42; 44; 46

The Soliloquy of a Hermit. New York: 1916. V. 39

Three Short Stories. Loughton: 1971. V. 39

Two Stories: Come and Dine and Tadnol. Hastings: 1967. V. 42

Two Stories: Come and Dine and Tadnol. London: 1967. V. 43

Unclay. London: 1931. V. 41; 42

Uncle Dottery. Bristol: 1930. V. 37; 42; 45; 46

When Thou Wast Naked. Berkshire: 1931. V. 46

When Thou Was Naked. Waltham St. Lawrence: 1931. V. 37; 39; 40; 42; 44

POYARES, F. PEDRO DE

Diccionario Lusitanico-Latino de Nomes Proprios de Regioens; Reinos; Provincias; Cidades, Villas; Castellos . . . Lisbon: 1667. V. 45

POYAS, CATHARINE G.

Year of Grief, and Other Poems. Charleston: 1869. V. 38; 46

POYAS, ELIZABETH A.

The Olden Time of Carolina. Charleston: 1855. V. 44

POYNDER, F. S.

The 9th Gurkha Rifles 1817-1936. London: 1937. V. 41

POYNDER, JOHN 1779-1849

A History of the Jesuits, to Which is Prefixed a Reply to Mr. Dallas's Defence of that Order. London: 1816. V. 46

Observations Upon Sunday Newspapers . . . London: 1820. V. 42

POYNET, JOHN 1516-1556

Diallacticon, c'est a Dire, Reconciliatoire d'un bon & Sainct Personnage Touchant la Verite, Nature & Substance du Corps & Sang de Iesus Christ en l'Eucharistie. ?Frankfurt. V. 40

POYNTER, F. N. L.

A Bibliography of Gervase Markham 1568?-1637. Oxford: 1962. V. 37; 42

POYNTING, FRANK

Eggs of British Birds With an Account of Their Breeding Habits: Limicolae. London: 1895-96. V. 37; 38; 40; 42; 43

POYNTON, F. J.

Researches on Rheumatism. New York: 1914. V. 42

POYNTZ, JOHN

The Present Prospect of the Famous and Fertile Island of Tobago . . . London: 1683. V. 43

POYNTZ, STEPHEN

The Barrier-Treaty Vindicated. London: 1712. V. 40

POYNTZ, SYNDHAM

The Vindication of Colonel General Poyntz, Against the False and Malicious Slanders Secretly Cast Forth Again Him; as in a Letter to a Friend of His, and a Servant to the State, Doth Appear. London: 1645/6. V. 41

POZZI, S.

Treatise on Gynaecology, Medical and Surgical. New York: 1891-92. V. 42

POZZO, ANDREA 1642-1709

Der mahler und Baumeister Perspectiv, Erster Theil . . . (Zweyter Theil . . .). Augsburg: 1708-09. V. 45

Perspectiva Pictorum et Architectorum . . . Pars Prima. (Pars Secunda) -in Qua Docetur Modux Expeditissimus Delineandi Optice Omnia Quae Pertinent ad Architecturam. Rome: 1693-1700. V. 37; 45

Prospettiva de'Pittori et Architetti. Rome: 1700. V. 37

Prospettiva d'Pittori et Architetti. Rome: 1717. V. 37

Rules and Examples of Perspective Proper for Painters and Architects. London: 1707. V. 38; 42; 44

Rules and Examples of Perspective Proper for Painters and Architects . . . London: 1720's. V. 42

Rules and Examples of Perspective Proper for Painters and Architects, etc. London: 1720's. V. 37

Rules and Examples of Perspective Proper for Painters and Architects, etc. London: 1720's? V. 37

PRACTICAL American Cook Book; or, Practical and Scientific Cookery. (with) Complete Confectioner, Pastray-Cook, and Baker. New York: 1848. V. 37

PRACTICAL Carpentry, Joinery and Cabinet Making . . . London: 1826. V. 43; 44

A PRACTICAL Manual of Appropriate Ornamentation. New York: 1876. V. 38

PRACTICAL Masonry, Bricklaying, and Plastering, Both Plain and Ornamental . . . London: 1830. V. 44

THE PRACTICAL Reigster in Chancery. London: 1714. V. 40

PRACTICAL Treatise on Painting in Oil-Colours. London: 1795. V. 45

PRAED, ROSA CAROLINE MURRAY-PRIOR 1851-1935

Mrs. Tegaskiss: a Novel of Anglo Australian Life. New York: 1895. V. 45

The Romance of a Chalet. London: 1892. V. 39

PRAED, WINTHROP MACKWORTH

Australasia. Cambridge: 1823. V. 42

Birds of the Southern Third of Arica. London: 1962. V. 45

Lillian. London: 1823. V. 37; 39

PRAEGER, ROBERT L.

Irish Topographical Botany. Dublin: 1901. V. 39; 42; 43

A Tourist's Flora of the West of Ireland. Dublin: 1909. V. 39; 42; 43

The Way That I Went. An Irishman in Ireland. Dublin: 1937. V. 38

PRAETORIUS, PAUL

Caesares Romani . . . in Institutione Propositi. Frankfurt a.O.: 1559. V. 38

PRAGAY, JOHANN

Der Krieg in Ungarn . . . New York: 1850. V. 39

LA PRAGMATIQUE Sanction, Contenant les Decrets du Concile National de l'Eglise Gallicane Assemblee en la Ville de Bourges au Regne du Roy Charles Septieme. Paris: 1561. V. 40

PRAIN, DAVID

On the Morphology, Teratology, and Diclinism of the Flowers of Cannabis. Calcutta: 1904. V. 38

THE PRAISES of Isis; a Poem. London: 1755. V. 37

PRAKTISCHE Anleitung . . . Zweyte Auflage. Munchen: 1823. V. 41

PRANDO, P. P.

History of the Old Testament. Montana: 1890's. V. 42

PRANESI, FRANCESCO

Il Teatro d'Ercolano. Rome: 1783. V. 42

PRANG, LOUIS

Officers of Our Union Army and Navy, Their Lives and Portraits. Volume I. Boston: 1862. V. 41

Suggestions for a Course of Instruction in Color for Public Schools. Boston: New York: &: 1893. V. 46

PRANG'S Standard Alphabets. Boston: 1878. V. 37; 39

PRASSE, LEONA E.

Lyonel Felininger: a Definitive Catalogue of His Graphic Work: Etchings, Lithographs, Woodcuts. Cleveland: 1972. V. 39; 41

PRATHER, J. B.

The Gold Fields of the Klondike. Douglas: 1898. V. 39

PRATT, A. E.

To the Snows of Tibet through China. London: 1892. V. 40

PRATT, ANNE

The Flowering Plants, Grasses, Sedges and Ferns of Great Britain and Their Allies the Club Mosses, Pepperworts and Horsetails. London: 1860. V. 45

The Flowering Plants and Ferns of Great Britian: The British Grasses and Sedges. London: 1870. V. 43

The Flowering Plants, Grasses, Sedges, & Ferns of Great Britain, and Their Allies, the Club Mosses, Horsetails &c . . . London: 1899. V. 38

The Flowering Plants, Grasses, Sedges and Ferns of Great Britain and their Allies, the Club Mosses, Horsetails &c. London: 1899-1900. V. 42

The Flowering Plants, Grasses, Sedges & Ferns of Great Britain. London: 1905. V. 40

The Flowering Plants, Grasses, Sedges and Ferns of Great Britain. London: 1873. V. 37

The Flowering Plants, Grasses, Sedges and Ferns of Great Britain. London: 1874. V. 37

The Flowering Plants, Grasses, Sedges and Ferns of Great Britain. London: 1899-1905. V. 37

Our Native Songsters. London: 1852. V. 43

Our Native Songsters. London: 1857. V. 38

Poisonous, Noxious, and Suspected Plants of Our Fields and Woods. London: 1860. V. 45

Wild Flowers. London: 1853. V. 41

Wild Flowers. London: 1857. V. 40; 46

PRATT, CHARLES E.

The American Bicycler; a Manual for the Observer, the Learner and the Expert. Boston: 1879. V. 42

PRATT, CHARLES STUART

Baby's Lullaby Book. Boston: 1888. V. 38; 46

Bye-O-Baby Ballads. Boston: 1886. V. 38

PRATT, CHRISTOPHER

Christopher Pratt. Toronto: 1981. V. 39

PRATT, E. J.

The Fable of Goats. Toronto: 1937. V. 43

The Iron Door. Toronto: 1927. V. 44

Titans. London: 1926. V. 43

The Wtiches' Brew. Toronto: 1926. V. 43

PRATT, EDWIN

British Railways and the Great War. London: 1921. V. 43; 44; 45; 46

PRATT, F. M.

California Gold Regions, with a Full Account of their Mineral Resources . . . New York: 1849. V. 38

PRATT, FRANCES

Ceramic Figures of Ancient Mexico. Graz: 1979. V. 37; 42; 44

PRATT, FRANCES HAMMOND

La Belle Zoa; or the Insurrection of Hayti. Albany: 1854. V. 37; 39

PRATT, FREDERIC THOMAS

Law of Contraband of War. London: 1856. V. 40

PRATT, HARVEY H.

The Early Planters of Scituate: a History of the Town of Scituate, Massachusetts . . . Scituate: 1929. V. 46

PRATT, IDA A.

Ancient Egypt: Sources of Information in the New York Public Library. (with) Ancient Egypt 1925-1941: a Supplement. New York: 1942. V. 44

PRATT, JOHN HENRY

The Mathematical Principles of Mechanical Philosophy, and their Application to the Theory of Universal Gravitation. Cambridge: 1836. V. 37

PRATT, JULIUS HOWARD

Reminiscences Personal and Otherwise. 1910. V. 44

Reminiscences Personal and Otherwise. 1910. V. 42

Reminiscences Personal and Otherwise. 1910. V. 41

Reminiscences Personal and Otherwise. N.P.: 1910. V. 42

Reminiscences Personal and Otherwise. N.P.: 1910. V. 43

PRATT, ORSON

The Bible & Polygamy. Salt Lake City: 1877. V. 42

Great First Cause, or the Self-Moving Forces of the Universe. Liverpool: 1851. V. 42

New and Easy Method of Solution of the Cubic and Biquadratic Equations . . . London & Liverpool: 1866. V. 42

A Series of Pamphlets, by . . . , One of the Twelve Apostles of the Church of Jesus Christ of Latter-Day Saints . . . Liverpool: 1851. V. 42; 45

A Series of Pamphlets on the Doctrines of the Gospel . . . Salt Lake City: 1884. V. 42

PRATT, PARLEY PARKER 1807-1857

The Autobiography of Parley Parker Pratt . . . Chicago: 1888. V. 42

History of the Late Persecution Inflicted by the State of Missouri Upon the Mormons, in Which Ten Thousand American Citizens Were Robbed, Plundered, and Driven from the State, and Many Others Imprisoned . . . Detroit: 1839. V. 40; 41; 42

Key to the Science of Theology. Liverpool: 1855. V. 41; 45

Key to the Science of Theology . . . Liverpool & London: 1855. V. 42

Proclamation of the Twelve Apostles of the Church of Jesus Christ of Latter-Day Saints to All the Kings of the World, to the President of the United States of America . . . Liverpool: 1845. V. 42

A Voice of Warning and Instruction to All People . . . New York: 1837. V. 37; 42

A Voice of Warning and Instruction to All People . . . to the Faith and Doctrine of the Church and Jesus Christ of Latter-Day Saints. Liverpool: 1854. V. 38

A Voice of Warning and Instruction to All People . . . Plano: 1863. V. 39; 45

PRATT, SAMUEL JACKSON

Emma Corbett. London: 1789. V. 40; 45

Family Secrets, Literary and Domestic. London: 1797. V. 38

Garrick's Looking-Glass: or, the Art of Rising on the Stage. A Poem. In Three Cantos. Decorated with dramatic characters by the author of*****. London: 1776. V. 37

Gleanings through Wales, Holland and Westphalia, with Views of Peace and War at Home and Abroad. London: 1794. V. 45

Gleanings in England. London: 1801. V. 40; 46

Gleanings through Wales, Holland and Westphalia, with Views of Peace and War . . . London: 1802. V. 38

Humanity, or The Rights of Nature, A Poem: In Two Books. London: 1788. V. 37; 43

PRATT, T. A. B.

Travels in Lycia, Milyas and the Cibyratis, in Company with the Late Rev. E. T. Daniell. London: 1847. V. 39

PRATT, ZADOCK

Lecture of Hon. Zadock Pratt, of Prattsville, N.Y. on the Subject of the Horse. Prattsville: 1869. V. 45

PRAUSNITZ, M. W.

From Hunter to Farmer and Trader . . . Jerusalem: 1970. V. 40; 42

THE PRAYER Book of King Edward VII. 1904. V. 39

THE PRAYER Book of King Edward VII. Norwood: 1904. V. 41

PRAYERS and Thanksgiuing to be Vsed by all the Kings Maiesties Louing Subjects, for the Happy Deliuerance of His Maiestie, the Queene, Prince and States of Parliament, From the Most Tratierous and Bloody Intended Massacre by Gunpowder, 5 Nouember 1605. London: 1606? V. 38; 41

PRAYERS in the Crow Indian Language Composed by the Missionaries of the Society of Jesus. Idaho: 1891. V. 39

PRAZ, MARIO
Studies in Seventeenth-Century Imagery. Roma: 1964. V. 43

PREBLE, GEORGE HENRY
A Chronological History of the Origin and Development of Steam Navigation. 1543-1882. Philadelphia: 1883. V. 39
A Chronological History of the Origin and Development of Steam Navigation. Philadelphia: 1895. V. 39
History of the Flag of the United States of America, and of the Naval and Yacht-club Signals, Seals and Arms, and Principal National Songs of the United States . . . Boston: 1880. V. 41; 42
Notes for a History of Steam Navigation. Philadelphia: 1881. V. 45
Origin and History of the American Flag and of the Naval and Yacht Club Signals, Seals and Arms and Municipal National Songs of the United States. Philadlephia: 1917. V. 44

PRECHAC, JEAN DE
Le Voyage de La Reine D'Espagne. Paris: 1680. V. 37

PRECIOUS Promises Relating to a Holy Life. Boston: 1857. V. 41

PRECISO dos Sucessos, que Tiverao Lugar em Pernambuco, Desde a Faustissima e Gloriozissima Revolucao Operada Felismente na Praca do Recife . . . Pernambuco: 1817. V. 45

PREECE, WILLIAM HENRY 1834-1913
The Telephone. London: 1889. V. 40

PREFONTAINE, M. DE
Maison Rustique, a l'Usage des Habitants de la Partie de la France Equinoxiale . . . Followed by Dictionnaire Galibi . . . Paris: 1763. V. 43

PREHISTORIC Proverbs. London. V. 40

PREISLER, JOHANN DANIEL
Orthogrpahia. Nuremberg: 1720. V. 46

PREISSLER, JOHANN JUSTIN
Der Beruhmten Kunstler. Nuremberg: 1735. V. 40

PREITO, GUILLERMO
San Francisco in the Seventies. San Francisco;: 1938. V. 39
Viaje a los Estados-Unidos. Mexico: 1877-78. V. 45

PREMIUM, BARTON, PSEUD
Eight Years in British Guiana; . . . Edited by his Friend. London: 1850. V. 39

PRENDERGAST, JOHN P.
The Cromwellian Settlement of Ireland. London: 1865. V. 39
The Cromwellian Settlement of Ireland. Dublin: 1875. V. 38; 44
The Cromwellian Settlement of Ireland. Dublin: 1922. V. 38; 43
Ireland from the Restoration to the Revolution. London: 1887. V. 38

PRENDERGAST, MAURICE
Water-color Sketchbook, 1899. Cambridge: 1960. V. 41

PRENDEVILLE, J.
Photographic Facsimiles of the Antique Gem Formerly Possessed by the Late Prince Poniatowski . . . First Series. London: 1859. V. 37

PRENNER, GIORGIO GASPARO DE
Illusri Fatti Farnesiani Coloriti nel Real Palazzo di Caprarola dai Fratelli Taddeo Federico e Ottaviano Zuccari. Rome: 1748. V. 37

PRENTICE, ANDREW N.
Renaissance Architecture and Ornament in Spain . . . London. V. 42
Renaissance Architecture and Ornament in Spain. New York. V. 44
Renaissance Architecture and Ornament in Spain. London: 1893. V. 38; 39
Renaissance Architecture and Ornament in Spain . . . New York. 1920's. V. 44

PRENTICE, ARCHIBALD
A Tour in the United States with Two Lectures on Emigration, Del'd in the Mechanics Institution Manchester. London: 1849. V. 40

PRENTICE, ARCHIBLAD
History of the Anti-Corn-Law League by . . . one of its Executive Council. London: 1853. V. 37

PRENTICE, DAVID
Some Philological Remarks Concerning Beauty. Glasgow: 1817. V. 44
Thoughts on the Repeal of the Bnk Restriction Law. London: 1811. V. 38; 41

PRENTICE, GEORGE D.
Biography of Henry Clay. Hartford: 1831. V. 40

PRENTICE, H. W.
The Beagle in America and England. Dekalb: 1920. V. 37

PRENTIES, S. W.
Narrative of a Shipwreck on the Island of Cape Breton, in a Voyage from Quebec in 1780. London: 1783. V. 43

PRENTISS, CHARLES
The Life of Gen. William Eaton . . . Principally Collected from His Correspondence and Other Manuscripts. Brookfield: 1813. V. 38; 40; 44; 45

PREPOSITIONS: Fifteen Relief Prints in Colour. 1987. V. 45

THE PREROGATIVE of Man or His Soule's Immortality and High Perfection Defended, and Explained Against the Rash and Rude Conceptions of a Late Author Who Hath Inconsiderably Adventured to Impugne It. Oxford: 1645. V. 40

PRESBREY, FRANK
The History and Development of Advertising. With More than three hundred and fifty illustrations. New York: 1929. V. 37
The Land of the Sky and Beyond. New York;: 1894. V. 39

PRESBYTERIAN CHURCH
The Constitution of the Presbyterian Church in the U.S. of America, containing the Confession of Faith, the Catechisms, the Government and Discipline. Philadelphia: 1797. V. 37

PRESCOTT, ANNE M.
Makapala-by-the-Sea. Honolulu: 1899. V. 42

PRESCOTT, BENJAMIN
A Letter to the Reverend Mr. Joshua Gee, in Answer to His of June 3, 1743. Boston: 1743. V. 43; 44

PRESCOTT, G. B.
Electricity and the Electric Telegraph. New York: 1877. V. 38

PRESCOTT, GEORGE BARTLETT
History, Theory and Practice of the Electric Telegraph. Boston: 1860. V. 37; 39

PRESCOTT, ISAAC
The Trial of Isaac Prescott, Esq. A Captain in the Royal Navy, Late Commander of His Majesty's Ship the Seaford . . . London: 1785. V. 42
The Trial of Isaac Prescott, Esq. London: 1786. V. 40

PRESCOTT, K. W.
The Complete Graphic Works . . . New York: 1973. V. 46

PRESCOTT, OLIVER
A Dissertation on the Natural History and Medicinal Effects of the Secale Cornutum, or Ergot. Boston: 1813. V. 39

PRESCOTT, WILLIAM HICKLING 1796-1859
Conquest of Peru; Ferdinand and Isabella; and Conquest of Mexico. New York: 1849-50. V. 40
Histoire de la Conquete Du Mexique, et La Vie de Fernand Cortes. Paris: 1863. V. 42
History of the Conquest of Mexico. New York: 1843. V. 37; 40; 41; 43; 44
History of the Conquest of Peru. New York: 1847. V. 37; 39; 40; 42; 43; 44; 45
History of the Conquest of Peru with a Preliminary View of the Civilization of the Incas. New York: 1848. V. 45
History of the reign of Philip the Second, King of Spain. Boston: 1855. V. 45
History of the Reign of Philip the Second King of Spain. London: 1855/59. V. 38
History of the Conquest of Peru. Mexico City: 1957. V. 38; 39; 43; 45
History of the Conquest of Mexico. London: 1843. V. 39
History of the Conquest of Mexico, with a Preliminary View of the Ancient Mexican Civilization, and Life of the Conqueror, Hernando Cortes. London: 1865. V. 39
History of the Reign of Ferdinand and Isabella, the Catholic, of Spain. London: 1838. V. 39
Memoir of the Honorable Abbott Lawrence. 1856. V. 38
Memoir of the Honorable Abbott Lawrence. 1856. V. 44
Memoir of the Honorable Abbott Lawrence. 1856. V. 41
Memoir of the Honorable Abbott Lawrence. 1856. V. 40
Memoir of the the Honorable Abbott Lawrence. London: 1856. V. 43

PRESCOTT, WILLIAM HICKLING 1796-1859 continued

The Complete Works. London. V. 44

Complete Works. London: 1849-64. V. 37

Works. New York: 1851. V. 42

Works. Philadelphia: 1865. V. 42

Works. Philadelphia: 1871. V. 46

The Complete Works of William Hickling Prescott. London: 1875. V. 41

Works. London: 1878. V. 42

Prescott's Works. Philadelphia: 1882-83. V. 38; 40; 41

The Complete Works. London: 1896. V. 37; 42

The Works. Philadelphia: 1904. V. 40; 41; 42; 45

The Complete Works. London: 1907. V. 38; 42

THE PRESENT Condition of France, In Reference to Her Revenues, Comparint Them with the Infinite Expences. London: 1692. V. 37

THE PRESENT Conduct of the War. London: 1746. V. 41

A PRESENT for a Good Child. The Christian Alphabet, or Parents' and Children's Guide and Instructor. London: 1830. V. 43

THE PRESENT Hour. London: 1782. V. 38; 42

THE PRESENT Influence and Conduct of Great Britain Impartially Considered. In a Letter from a Foreign Minister at the Hague, to Count Residing at the Court of London. London: 1741. V. 41

THE PRESENT Ruinous Land-War, Proved to be a H(anove)r War, by Facts As Well As Arguments; or the Opposition Fully Vindicated. London: 1745. V. 41

THE PRESENT State of British Influence in Holland, Exemplified by the States-General's Answer of the 23/11 May, 1742 . . . In a Letter to the Right Honourable the Lord V(iscount) C(obham). London: 1742. V. 41

THE PRESENT State of Colombia: Containing an Account of the Principal Events Of Its Revolutionary War; the Expeditions Fitted Out in England to Assist in Its Emancipation . . . London: 1827. V. 39; 43

THE PRESENT State of Europe, or the Historical and Political Monthly Mercury Giving an Account of all the Publick and Private Occurrences . . . That are Most Considerable in Every Court. London: 1694-1697. V. 41

THE PRESENT State of Fairy-Land. (with) The Testimonies of Several Citizens of Fickleborough, in the Kingdom of Fairy-Land. London: 1713. V. 41

THE PRESENT State of Germany. London: 1738. V. 42

THE PRESENT State of Holland, or a Description of the United Provinces. London: 1745. V. 43

THE PRESENT State of Ireland: Together with Some Remarques Upon the Ancient State Thereof. London: 1673. V. 40

THE PRESENT State of the British Interest in India. London: 1773. V. 38

THE PRESENT State of the West-Indies . . . London: 1778. V. 38; 40; 42; 43

THE PRESENT State of the West-Indies; Containing An Accurate Description of What Pare are Possessed by the Several Powers in Europe . . . London: 1778. V. 46

PRESENT Taxes Compared to the Payment Made to the Publick Within the Memory of Man. With Some Thoghts on the Possible Consequences That May Ensue from the National Debts. London: 1749. V. 41

A PRESENTATION of Flower Composition. Milan: 1979. V. 37

A PRESERVATIVE Against Popery, in Several Select Discourses Upon the Principal Heads of Controversy Between Protestants and Papists. London: 1738. V. 39

PRESERVATIVO Contra Las Revoluciones Que Atacan la Indepencia de America. Mexico City: 1827. V. 38

PRESIDENT Lincoln's Views. An Important Letter on the Principle Involved in the Vallandigham Case. Correspondence in Relation to the Democratic Meeting, at Albany, New York. Philadelphia: 1863. V. 46

THE PRESIDENTIAL Election. Appeal of the National Union Committee to the People of the United States. New YorK;: 1864. V. 39

PREST, THOMAS PECKETT

Gallant Tom; or, the Perils of a Sailor, Ashore and Afloat. London: 1841. V. 43

The Life and Adventures of Oliver Twiss, the Workhouse Boy. London: 1838-39. V. 40

Nickelas Nicelberry. N.P.: 1838? V. 43

Pickwick in America. N.P.: 1838-39. V. 43

The Post-Humorous Notes of the Pickwickian Club. London: 1838-39. V. 40; 43

Posthumous Papers of the Cadger's Club . . . London: 1838. V. 43

Schamyl; or, the Wild Woman of Circassia. London: 1856. V. 39

The Sketch Book by 'Bos'. London: 1837? V. 43

PRESTON, CHOLE

The Peek-A-Boos in Winter. London: 1916. V. 46

PRESTON, EDGAR

Metropolitan Drinking Fountain and Cattle Trough Association. Half a Century of Good Work (1859-1909). A Jubilee History. London: 1909. V. 40

PRESTON, JAMES

The History of the World, from the Creation to the Birth of Abraham, containing the space of 1948 years; into Two Books: the first, from the Creation to the Flood; and the Second, from the Flood, to the . . . Edinburgh: 1701. V. 37

PRESTON, JOHN

The Breast-Plate of Faith and Love . . . Delivered in 18 Sermons Upon Three Severall Texts . . . London: 1634. V. 40

Sermons Preached Before His Maiestie. London: 1637. V. 37

Sins Overthrow; or, a Godly and Learned Treatise of Mortification . . . (with) Remains of . . . John Preston . . . London: 1633/1634. V. 39

PRESTON, LIONEL

Sea and River Paitners of the Netherlands in the Seventeenth Century. 1937. V. 46

Sea and River Painters of the Netherlands in the Seventeenth Century. Oxford: 1937. V. 42

PRESTON, MARGARET JUNKIN

A Handful of Monographs, Continental and English. New York: 1886. V. 37; 46

Silverwood: Book of Memories. New York: 1856. V. 46

PRESTON, R.

A Succinct View of the Rule in Shelley's Case; Exhibiting, by Negative and Affirmative Propositions, the Instances in Which Several Limitations, One to the Ancestor, the Other to the Heirs, - the Heirs of the Body, - or Issue of the Body of that Person . . . Exeter: 1794. V. 37

PRESTON, R. A.

Kingston Before the War of 1812. A Collection of Documents. Toronto: 1959. V. 44

PRESTON, R. M. P.

The Deserted Mounted Corps, an Account of the Cavalry Operations in Palestine and Syria, 1917-1918. London: 1921. V. 38

PRESTON, THOMAS W.

Historical Sketches of the Holston Valleys. Kingsport: 1926. V. 44

PRESTON, WILLIAM

Illustrations of Masonry . . . London: 1788. V. 42

Illustrations of Masonry. Portsmouth: 1804. V. 39

Illustrations of Masonry . . . London: 1812. V. 46

Journal in Mexico. By . . . of the Fourth Kentucky Regiment of Volunteers Dating from November 1, 1847 to May 25, 1848. Paris: 1930. V. 39

The Poetical Works. Dublin: 1793. V. 38

Seventeen-Hundred and Seventy-Seven; or, a Picture of the Manners and Character of the Age. Dublin: 1777. V. 41

PRESTONGRANGE, WILLIAM GRANT, LORD 1701?-1764

The Occasional Writer. London: 1745. V. 39

PRESTWICH, JOHN d. 1795

Prestwich's Respublica; or a Display of the Honors, Ceremonies and Ensigns of the Commonwealth, Under the Protectorship of Oliver Cromwell . . . London: 1787. V. 41

PRESTWICH, JOSEPH

A Geological Inquiry Respecting the Water-Bearing Strata of the Country Around London . . . London: 1851. V. 37; 39

PRETTY, EDWARD

A Practical Essay on Flower Painting in Water Colours. London: 1810. V. 41

THE PRETTY Little Coronet and Great Big B! London: 1878? V. 38

THE PRETTY Page Scrap Book, with Pictures and Rhymes, to Amuse Little People at All Sorts of Times. London: (n.d.). V. 37

PRETTY Stories About the Camel. London: 1845. V. 45; 46

THE PRETTY Women of Paris; Their Names and Addresses, Qualities and Faults, Being a Complete Directory. Paris?: 1883. V. 40

PREUSCHOFT, H.

The Lesser Apes, Evolutionary and Behavioural Biology. Edinburgh: 1984. V. 37; 38

PREUSS, WOLFGANG

American Rhapsody. Harrisburg: 1941. V. 39

PREVERT, JACQUES

Fetes. Paris: 1971. V. 38; 39

PREVOST, ANTOINE FRANCOIS, CALLED PREVOST D'EXILES 1697-1763

En Fri-Murares Lefwernes Beskrifning, Utgifwen af et Fruntimmer, N:1(-72). Stockholm: 1754. V. 39

Histoire Generale des Voyages ou Nouvelle Collection de Toutes les Relations de Voyages par Mer et Par Terre. Paris: 1749-80. V. 39

Histoire du Chevalier des Grieux et de Manon Lescaut. Stamford: 1958. V. 42

The History of the Chevalier des Grieux. London: 1767. V. 39

The Life and Entertaining Adventures of Mr. Cleveland, Natural Son of Oliver Cromwell, Written by Himself. London: 1734/35. V. 42

Manon Lescaut. London: 1928. V. 39; 42; 43; 44; 45; 46

Manon Lescaut. New York: 1928. V. 45

Manon Lescaut. Paris: 1941. V. 44

Voyages du Capitaine Robert Lade en Differentes Parties d l'Afrique de l'Asie et de l'Amerique . . . Paris: 1744. V. 44

PREVOST, JEAN LOUIS

Bouquets. London: 1960. V. 37

PREVOST, LOUIS

California Silk Grower's Manual. San Francisco: 1867. V. 39

PREWETT, FRANK

Poems. Richmond: 1921. V. 40

The Rural Scene. London: 1924. V. 46

PRIAPEA

Sive Diversorum Poetarum in Priapum Lusus. Pavia: (Amsterdam): 1664. V. 37

PRICE, ANTHONY

The Alamat Ambush. London: 1971. V. 41

For the Good of the State. New York: 1986. V. 38

Here Be Monsters. New York: 1985. V. 38

The Labyrinth Makers. London: 1970. V. 42

War Game. London: 1976. V. 44

PRICE, BONAMY 1807-1888

Chapters on Practical Political Economy Being the Substance of Lectures Delivered in the University of Oxford. London: 1878. V. 43

The Principles of Currency. Oxford & London: 1859. V. 42

PRICE, BYRON

Roll Call on the Little Big Horn, June 28, 1876. Ft. Collins: 1974. V. 45

PRICE, CHARLES

The Eventful Life, and Wonderful History of that Most Notorious Character, Swindler and Forger, Charles Price, Commonly Called Old Patch . . . London: 1810. V. 43; 44

PRICE, CHESTER B.

Portraits of Ten Country Houses Designed by Delano & Aldrich. Drawn by Chester B. Price. Garden City - New York: 1924. V. 42

PRICE, CON

Trails I Rode. Pasadena: 1947. V. 42

PRICE, EBENEZER

A Chronological Register of Boscawen, in the County Of Merrimack and State of New-Hampshire . . . Concord: 1823. V. 37

PRICE, EDMUND E.

The Science of Self Defence. New York: 1867. V. 43

PRICE, EDWARD

Sketches in Norway. N.P.? London: 1836. V. 38

Views of Wild Scenery; and Journal. London: 1834. V. 39

PRICE, ELEANOR C.

Constantia. London: 1876. V. 40

Red Towers. London: 1889. V. 41

PRICE, F. G. HILTON

A Handbook of London Bankers, with Some Account of Their Predecessors the Early Goldsmiths, Together with Lists of Bankers from 1670 . . . London: 1890-91. V. 40

PRICE, FRANCIS

The British Carpenter; or, a Treatise on Carpentry. London: 1735. V. 44

The British Carpenter, or Treatise on Carpentry . . . Dublin: 1768. V. 38

A Description of that admirable structure, the Cathedral Church of Salisbury. With the chapels, monuments, grave-stones, and their inscriptions . . . (with) an account of old Sarum. London: 1774. V. 37

A Series of Particular and Useful Observations . . . (on) the Cathedral-Church of Salisbury. London: 1753. V. 37; 38

PRICE, GEORGE

Across the Continent with the Fifth Cavalry. New York: 1883. V. 41

A Treatise on Fire and Thief-Proof Depositories and Locks and Keys. London: 1856. V. 38; 40

PRICE, HENRY

Poems on Several Subjects. London: 1741. V. 41

PRICE, HENRY CLAY

How to Make Pictures. New York: 1886. V. 41

PRICE, HOLLAND

The Horrors of Invasion, a Poem. Wrexham: 1804. V. 40

PRICE, HOWELL

A Genuine Account of the Life and Transactions of . . . London: 1752. V. 44

PRICE, I.

History of 97th Regt. Penna. Vol . . . . Philadelphia: 1875. V. 39; 42; 46

PRICE, J.

The Buyers' Manual and Business Guide. San Francisco: 1872. V. 42; 43; 45

PRICE, J. COOPER

'Wild Oats' and Later and Better Experiences. Toledo: 1879. V. 41

PRICE, JAMES P.

Seven Years of Prairie Life. Hereford: 1891. V. 37; 40

Seven Years of Prairie Life. Hereford: 1981. V. 42

PRICE, JOHN

Historiae Brytannicae Defensio, . . . London: 1573. V. 45

An Historical and Topographical Account of Leominster and It's Vicinity . . . Ludlow: 1795. V. 41

An Historical Account of the City of Hereford. Hereford: 1796. V. 42

L. Apulei Madaurensis Philosophi Platonici Apologia. Paris: 1635. V. 38

PRICE, JOHN EDWARD

A Descriptive Account of the Guildhall of the City of London. London: 1886. V. 37; 40; 44

PRICE, JOHN G.

Debates and Proceedings of the Convention Which Assembled at Little Rock Jan. 7, 1868 . . . Little Rock: 1868. V. 38

PRICE, JONATHAN

Oxford Poetry, 1954. Swinford: 1954. V. 44

PRICE, JOSEPH

Some Observations and Remarks on a Late Publication Intitled, Travels in Europe, Asia and Africa . . . London: 1782. V. 42

PRICE, JULIUS M.

From Euston to Klondike. The Narrative of a Journey through British Columbi and the North-West Territory in the Summer of 1898. London: 1898. V. 37; 38

From the Arctic Ocean to the Yellow Sea. The Narrative of a Journey . . . New York: 1892. V. 37

The Land of Gold, the Narrative of a Journey through the West Australian Goldfields in the Autumn of 1895. London: 1896. V. 46

PRICE, L. L. F. R.

Industrial Peace Its Advantages, Methods and Difficulties. London: 1887. V. 43

PRICE, REYNOLDS 1933-

The Dream of a House. 1977. V. 42

A Generous Man. New York: 1966. V. 39; 46

A Generous Man. New York: 1975. V. 43

Home Made. Rocky Mount: 1990. V. 46

Late Warning. New York: 1968. V. 39

A Long and Happy Life. New York: 1961. V. 45

A Long and Happy Life. New York: 1962. V. 37; 39; 41; 44; 46

The Names and Faces of Heroes. New York: 1963. V. 38; 39; 44

Nine Mysteries. N.P.: 1979. V. 38

Oracles. Durham: 1977. V. 46

PRICE, REYNOLDS 1933- continued

Pure Boys and Girls. 1978. V. 42

The Source of Light. New York: 1981. V. 39

A Start. 1981. V. 42

A Start. N.P.: 1981. V. 44

The Thing Itself. Durham: 1966. V. 39; 41

The Tongues of Angels. New York: 1990. V. 46

Torso of an Archaic Apollo. New York: 1969. V. 39

PRICE, RICHARD 1723-1791

Additional Observations on the Nature and Value of Civil Liberty, and the War with America . . . London: 1776. V. 42; 46

Additional Observations on the Nature and Value of Civil Liberty, and the War with America. London: 1777. V. 40

An Appeal to the Public, on the Subject of the National Debt. London: 1774. V. 43

A Discourse on the Love of Our Country. London: 1789. V. 38

A Discourse on the Love of Our Country, Delivered on Nov. 4, 1789, at the Meeting House in the Old Jewry. London: 1790. V. 39; 40

An Essay on the Population of England, from the Revolution to the Present Time. London: 1780. V. 43; 46

Four Dissertations. I. On Providence. II. On Prayer. III. On the Reasons for Expecting That Virtuous Men Shall Meet After Death in a State of Happiness. IV. On the Importance of Christianity, the Nature of Historical Evidence and Miracles. London: 1777. V. 40; 41

Four Dissertations. London: 1778. V. 42

Four Dissertations. I. On Providence. II. On Prayer. III. On the Reasons for expecting that virtuous men shall meet death in a state of happiness. IV. On the importance of Christianity . . . London: 1767. V. 37

A Free Discussion of the Doctrines of Materialism, and Philosophical Necessity, in a Correspondence Between Dr. Price, and Dr. Priestley. London: 1778. V. 45

The General Introduction and Supplement to the Two Tracts on Civil Liberty, the War with America, and the Finances of the Kingdom. London: 1778. V. 37

Observations on the Nature of Civil Liberty, The Principles of Government, and the Justice and Policy of the War with America. Boston: 1776. V. 40

Observations on the Nature of Civil Liberty, the Principles of Government, and the Justice & Policy of the War with America. (with) An Appendix . . . London: 1776. V. 37; 38; 40; 45

Observations on the Nature of Civil Liberty, the Principles of Government, and the Justice and Policy of the War with America. Philadelphia: 1776. V. 42; 43; 45; 46

Observations on the Nature of Civil Liberty. (with) Additional Observations on the Nature and Value of Civil Liberty, and the War with America. London: 1776, 1777. V. 40

Observations on Reversionary Payments; on Schemes for Providing Annuities for Widows and for Persons in Old Age. London: 1783. V. 40; 41

Observations on the Importance of the American Revolution, and the Means of Making It a Benefit to the World. Trenton: 1785. V. 41; 43

Observations on the Nature of Civil Libery, the Principles of Government and the Justice and Policy of the War with America. To which is added an Appendix . . . Dublin: 1776. V. 37

Postscript to a Pamphlet by Dr. Price on the State of the Public Debts, and Finances at Signing the Preliminary Articles of Peace in January 1783. London: 1784. V. 46

A Review of the Principal Questions and Difficulties in Morals . . . London: 1758. V. 41; 43; 46

A Review of the Principal Questions and Difficulties in Morals . . . London: 1769. V. 40

The State of the Public Debts and Finances. London: 1783. V. 38

The Wanderers. Boston: 1974. V. 44

PRICE, ROSE LAMBART

A Summer on the Rockies. London: 1898. V. 39

The Two Americas; an Account of Sport and Travel. London: 1877. V. 37; 41; 42; 45

PRICE, RUTH CLAY

A Pagan Anthology. New York: 1918. V. 42

PRICE, SARAH

Illustrations of the Fungi of Our Fields and Woods. London: 1864-65. V. 45

PRICE, THOMAS

Wisdom and Genius of Shakespeare . . . with Select and Original Notes. London: 1838. V. 46

PRICE, UVEDALE

An Essay on the Picturesque, as Compared with the Sublime and the Beautiful . . . London: 1794. V. 40; 41; 45; 46

Essays on the Picturesque, as Compared with the Sublime and the Beautiful . . . London: 1810. V. 41; 45

On the Picturesque; with an Essay on the Origin of Taste and Much Original Matter by Sir Thomas Dick Lauder. Edinburgh: 1842. V. 46

PRICE, WARREN ELBRIDGE

Paper Covered Books: a Catalogue. San Francisco: 1894. V. 41

PRICE, WESTON A.

Dental Infections Oral and Systemic. Cleveland: 1923. V. 38

PRICE, WILLIAM

A Dissertation upon the Antiquities of Persepolis. London: (1825). V. 37

A Grammar of the Three Principal Oriental Languages, Hindoostanee, Persian and Arabic . . . London: 1823. V. 44

Journal of the British Embassy to Persia . . . London: 1825. V. 43

PRICE WOOD, J. N.

Travel and Sport in Turkestan. London: 1910. V. 42

PRICHARD, A.

A History of Infusoria, Including the Desmidiaceae and Diatomaceae, British and Foreign. London: 1861. V. 37

PRICHARD, H. HESKETH

Hunting Camps in Woods and Wilderness. London: 1910. V. 42

Through the Heart of Patagonia. London: 1902. V. 39

Through the Heart of Patagonia. New York: 1902. V. 44; 46

Through Trackless Labrador. London: 1911. V. 43

Through Trackless Labrador. New York: 1911. V. 45

PRICHARD, JAMES COWLES 1786-1848

The Natural History of Man: Comprising Inquiries into the Modifying Influence of Physical and Moral Agencies on the Different Tribes of the Human Family. London: 1843. V. 38; 46

The Natural History of Man. London: 1848. V. 39; 41

The Natural History of Man . . . London: 1855. V. 37; 38; 40

The Natural History of Man. Paris: 1843. V. 37

The Natural History of Man. London: 1845. V. 37

Researches into the Physical History of Man. London: 1813. V. 39

Researches into the Physical History of Mankind. London: 1836-47. V. 38

Researches into the Early History of Mankind. London: 1826. V. 37

Researches into the Physical History of Man. London: 1813. V. 37

Researches into the Physical History of Mankind. London: 1837/44. V. 37

Researches into the Physical History of Mankind. London: 1851, 1841-4-7. V. 38

A Treatise on Insanity and Other Disorders Affecting the Mind. London: 1835. V. 41

A Treatise on Insanity and Other Disorders Affecting the Mind. Sherwood: 1835. V. 38

A Treatise on Insanity and Other Disorders Affecting the Mind. Philadelphia: 1837. V. 41

PRICHARD, JOHN

Practical Observations on Hysteria, especially relating to its Organic Character. Leamington: 1838. V. 37

PRICHARD, REES

The Welshman's Candle; or the Divine Poems . . . Carmarthen: 1771. V. 41

PRICHARD, THOMAS JEFFERY LLEWELLYN

The Adventures and Vagaries of Twm Shon Catti, Descriptive of Life in Wales . . . Aberystwyth: 1828. V. 40; 42

PRICHARD, THOMAS JEFFERY LLEWELYN

Welsh Minstrelsy . . . London: 1825. V. 42

PRICKETT, FREDERICK

The History and Antiquities of Highgate, Middlesex. London: 1842. V. 40

PRICKETT, MISS

Warwick Castle, an Historical Novel. London: 1815. V. 38; 46

PRIDEAU, MATHIAS

An Easy and Compendious Introduction for Reading All Sorts of Histories . . . Oxford: 1682. V. 40

PRIDEAUX, FREDERICK 1817-1891

The Hand-Book of Precedents in Conveyancing Adapted to the Modern Law and Practice. London: 1852. V. 40

PRIDEAUX, HUMPHREY 1648-1724

Directions to Church-Wardens for the Faithful Discharge of Their New Office. Norwich: 1704. V. 43

Marmoru, Arundellianorum, Seldenianorum, Aliorumque Academiae Oxoniensi Donatorum cum Variis Commentariis & Indice. London: 1732. V. 40

The Old and New Testament Connected in the History of the Jews and Neighbouring Nations from the Declension of the Kingdoms of Israel and Judah to the Time of Christ. London: 1717. V. 39

The Old and New Testament Connected in the History of the Jews and Neighbouring Nations, from the Declension of the Kingdoms of Israel and Judah to the Time of Christ. London: 1749. V. 38; 43

PRIESTLEY, JOSEPH 1733-1804 continued

Letters to the Right Honourable Edmund Burke Occasioned by His Reflections on the Revolution in France, &c. Dublin: 1791. V. 39

Letters to Occasioned by His Reflections on the Revolution in France. New York: 1791. V. 43

Letters to the Inhabitants of Northumberland and Its Neighborhood . . . To which is added a Letter to a Friend in Paris, Relating to Mr. Liancourt's Travels in North American States. Philadelphia: 1801. V. 37

Lettres au Tres-Honorable Edmund Burke, au Sujet de Ses Reflexions sur la Revolution de France . . . Paris: 1791. V. 40

Memoirs of the Rev. Dr. Joseph Priestley. London: 1809. V. 39

Memoirs of . . . to the Year 1795; with a Continuation . . . by his Son . . . and Observations on his Writings by Thomas Cooper President Judge of the 4th District of Pennsylvania; and the Reverend William Christie. London: 1806. V. 37

Miscellaneous Observations Relating to Education. Bath: 1778. V. 45

Miscellaneous Observations Relating to Education. Cork: 1780. V. 38

Miscellaneous Observations Relating to Education. New London: 1796. V. 39

Observations on the Increase of Infidelity. London: 1796. V. 40

The Present State of Europe Compared With Antient Prophecies; a Sermon Preached at the Gravel Pit Meeting in Hackney, Feb. 28, 1794 . . . London: 1794. V. 39

Reflections on Death; a Sermon on Occasion of the Death of the Rev. Robert Robinson of Cambridge, delivered at the New Meeting in Birmingham, June 13, 1790. Birmingham: 1790. V. 39; 40

The Rudiments of English Grammar, adopted to the sue of schools; with notes and observations for the use of those who made some proficiency in the language. The Fourth edition. Dublin: 1784. V. 37

Thoughts on the Late Riot at Birmingham. London: 1791. V. 38

Three Tracts . . . I. An Appeal to the Serious and Candid Professors of Christianity . . . II. A Familiar Illustration of Certain Passages of Scripture. III. A General View of the Arguments for the Unity of God. London: 1791. V. 40

Vorlesungen uber Redekunst und Kritik. Leipzig: 1779. V. 38

PRIESTLEY, MARY

A Book of Birds. London: 1937. V. 38; 40

PRIESTLEY, RAYMOND E.

Antarctic Adventure. London: 1914. V. 38; 40; 46

Antarctic Adventure: Scott's Northern Party. New York: 1915. V. 38

PRIESTLY, H. I.

Jose de Galvez Visitor-General of New Spain 1765-1771. Berkeley: 1916. V. 39

PRIETO, G.

Viaje a Los Estados-Unidos . . . Mexico: 1877-8. V. 42

PRIETO, GUILLERMO

Viaje a Los Estados-Unidos . . . Mexico: 1877-78. V. 39

PRIEZAC, SALOMON DE

L'Histoire des Elephants. Paris: 1650. V. 39

PRIMARY Bible Questions for Young Children. Atlanta: 1864. V. 37; 43

PRIME, ALFRED COXE

The Arts and Crafts in Philadelphia, Maryland and South Carolina 1721-1785 . . . N.P.: 1929-32. V. 40

The Arts & Crafts in Philadelphia, Maryland and South Carolina. 1721-1785, with . . . Second Series. 1786-1800. Topsfield: 1929/32. V. 38; 39; 41; 44

PRIME, NATHANIEL SCUDDER

Mount Pleasant Female Seminary in the Village of Sing-Sing, Westchester County, N.Y. Mount Pleasant: 1831. V. 38; 45

PRIME, SAMUEL IREANEUS

The Life of Samuel F. B. Morse, Inventor of the Electromagnetic Recording Telegraph. New York: 1875. V. 39

PRIME, W. C.

I Go A-Fishing. New York: 1873. V. 43

PRIME, WENDELL

Fifteenth Century Bibles, a Study in Bibliography. New York: 1888. V. 45

PRIME, WILLIAM C.

Pottery and Porcelain of all Times and Nations. New York: 1879. V. 39

THE PRIMER, or Office of the Blessed Virgin Marie, in Latin and English. Antwerp: 1650. V. 46

THE PRIMER, Set Furth by the Kinges Maiestie. London: 1710. V. 38

PRIMEVAL Gods. Manaton: Devon: 1934. V. 37

PRIMITIVE Christian Discipline not to be Slighted . . . London?: 1658. V. 44

PRIMM, W.

Report of the Celebration of the Anniversary of the Founding of St. Louis. St. Louis: 1847. V. 37; 40

PRIMROSE, JAMES

Popular Errours of the People in Physick. London: 1651. V. 40; 44

PRIN, ALICE 1901-

Kiki's Memoirs. Paris: 1930. V. 37; 40; 41; 42; 43; 46

PRINCE, JOHN

Danmonii Orientales Illustres: or, the Worthies of Devon . . . London: 1810. V. 39

A Wreath for St. Crispin: Being Sketches of Eminent Shoemakers. Boston: 1848. V. 45

PRINCE, L. BRADFORD

Historical Sketches of New Mexico from the Earliest Records to the American Occupation. Kansas City: 1883. V. 43; 44

Historical Sketches of New Mexico from the Earliest Recors, to the American Occupation. New York & Kansas City: 1883. V. 38; 40

New Mexico, Its Wonderful Resources and Products, Past and Present. Albuquerque: 1883. V. 41

New Mexico's Claims Ex-Gov. Prince Pleas for Statehood. Santa Fe: 1903. V. 45

New Mexico's Struggle for Statehood. Santa Fe: 1910. V. 37; 38

PRINCE, MORTON 1854-1929

The Nature of Mind and Human Automatism. Philadelphia/London: 1885. V. 45

PRINCE, NANCY

A Narrative of the Life and Travels. Boston: 1850. V. 42; 44

THE PRINCE of Nursey Playmates. London: 1880. V. 40

THE PRINCE of Peace. Christmas Canticles. Flemington: 1965. V. 37

PRINCE, OLIVER

A Digest of the Laws of the State of Georgia . . . With a Copious Index. Milledgeville: 1822. V. 37; 39

PRINCE PHILIP, DUKE OF EDINBURGH

Wildlife Crisis. London: 1971. V. 37

PRINCE, THOMAS

Bibliotheca Curiosa. Edinburgh: 1887. V. 40

Bibliotheca Curiosa. Edinburgh: 1887/88. V. 46

A Chronological History of New England. Edinburgh: 1887-88. V. 39

Earthquakes the Works of God and Tokens of His Just Displeasure. Boston: 1727. V. 45

Extraordinary Events the Doings of God, and Marvellous in Pious Eyes. Boston: 1746. V. 41

The Vade Mecum for America: or a Companion for Traders and Travellers. Boston: 1732. V. 44

The Vade Mecum for America; or a Companion for Traders and Travellers . . . Boston: 1732. V. 41; 43; 44

PRINCE, WILLIAM

A Short Treatise on Horticulture . . . New York: 1828. V. 37; 41

PRINCE, WILLIAM ROBERT

The Pomological Manual. New York: 1831. V. 44

PRINCESS Elizabeth Gift Book. London. V. 41

PRINCIPLES of English Grammar and Idiomatic Sentences in English and Marathi. Bombay: 1851. V. 43

PRINCIPLES of Virtue and Morality or Essays and Meditations on Various Subjects. Dublin: 1783. V. 38

PRINGLE, CAPTAIN

Remarks on the Campaign of 1815, in the Netherlands. Hitchen: 1861. V. 42

PRINGLE, J. F.

Lunenburgh or the Old Eastern District . . . . Cornwall: 1890. V. 42; 44

PRINGLE, J. J.

An Atlas of Skin Diseases. New York: 1900. V. 38

PRINGLE, JOHN

A Discourse on the Torpedo, delivered at the Anniversary Meeting of the Royal Society, 1775. V. 37

A Discourse on the Attraction of Mountains, Delivered at the Anniversary Meeting of the Royal Society, November 30, 1775. London: 1775. V. 37; 39; 40; 43

A Discourse on the Theory of Gunnery Delivered at the Anniversary Meeting of the Royal Society, Nov. 30, 1778. London: 1778. V. 39; 42; 44

PRINGLE, JOHN continued

A Garland for the Laureate - Poems Presented to Sir John Betjeman on His 75th Birthday. Stratford-upon-Avon: 1981. V. 42

Observations on the Diseases of the Army in Camp and Garrison, in Three Parts . . . London: 1753. V. 40

Observations on the Diseases of the Army. Philadelphia: 1810. V. 41

Observations on the Diseases of the Army. Philadelphia: 1812. V. 40

Observations on the Diseases of the Army. London: 1761. V. 37

Six Discourses, Delivered by John Pringle, Bart. London: 1783. V. 40; 44

PRINGLE, M. A.

A Journey in East Africa Towards the Mountains of the Moon. London: 1886. V. 43

PRINGLE, ROGER

A Garland for the Laureate - Poems Presented to Sir John Betjeman on His 75th Birthday. Stratford-upon-Avon: 1981. V. 38

Poems for Shakespeare 6. London: 1977. V. 38; 41

PRINGLE, THOMAS

African Sketches. London: 1834. V. 46

PRINT, a Quarterly Journal of the Graphic Arts. New Haven. V. 41

THE PRINT Connoisseur. New York: 1920-24. V. 41

PRINTED Pages from English Literature. A Portfolio of Original Leaves Taken from Rare and Notable Printed Books . . . New York: 1925. V. 41

THE PRINTER. London: 1833. V. 44

PRINTER'S Valhalla Series. Rochester: 1947-50. V. 40

PRINTING and the Mind of Man. London: 1967. V. 37
PRINTING and the Mind of Man. London & New York: 1967. V. 37
PRINTING and the Mind of Man. New York: (1967). V. 37

PRINTING HISTORICAL SOCIETY

Journal of the Printing Historical Society. London: 1965-83. V. 39; 40

Journal of the Printing Historical Society. London: 1965-84. V. 37

PRINTING in the Twentieth Century: A Survey. Reprinted from the Special Number of the TImes, October 29, 1919. London: 1930. V. 37

PRINZ, JOHANNES

John Wilmot Earl of Rochester, His Life and Writings. Leipzig: 1927. V. 40

PRINZMETAL, MYRON

The Auricular Arrhythmias. Springfield: 1952. V. 42

PRIOLO, BENJAMIN

The History of France Under the Ministry of Cardinal Mazarine. London: 1671. V. 42

PRION, ALEXIS

Oeuvres Complettes . . . Paris: 1776. V. 42

PRIOR, JAMES

The Life of Oliver Goldsmith, from a Variety of Original Sources. London: 1837. V. 39; 40

Life of Edmund Malone. London: 1860. V. 39

Memoir of the Life and Character of the Right Hon. Edmund Burke, with Specimens of His Poetry and Letters, and an Estimate of His Genius and Talents . . . London: 1824. V. 39

Memoir of the Life and Character of the Right Hon. Edmund Burke, With Specimens of His Poetry and Letters . . . London: 1826. V. 39; 42; 43

Narrative of a Voyage in the Indian Seas in the Nisus Frigate, to the Cape of Good Hope, Isles of Bourbon, France and Scychelles: to Madras and the Isles of Java, St. Paul and Amsterdam During the Years 1810 and 1811. London: 1811. V. 45

Voyage Along the Eastern Coast of Africa, to Mosambique, Johanna and Quiloa; to St. Helena; to Rio de Janeiro, Bahia, and Pernambuco in Brazil, in the Nisus Frigate. London: 1819. V. 37; 40; 43; 44; 45

PRIOR, MATHEW

Poems on Several Occasions. London: 1718. V. 37

PRIOR, MATTHEW 1664-1721

An English Ballad: In Answer to Mr. Despreaux's Ode on the Taking of Namure. London: 1695. V. 41; 45

The Hind and the Panther Transvers'd to the Story of the Country Mouse and the City Mouse. London: 1687. V. 37; 42; 44; 46

Miscellaneous Works. London: 1740. V. 37; 39; 40; 42; 45

An Ode Humbly Inscrib'd to the Queen on the Late Glorious Success of Her Majesty's Arms. London: 1706. V. 37

Poems on Several Occasions. London: 1709. V. 38; 40; 41; 42; 43

Poems on Several Occasions. London: 1718. V. 38; 39; 40; 41; 42; 43; 44; 45; 46

Poems on Several Occasions . . . London: actually The Hague: 1720. V. 41

Poems on Several Occasions. Glasgow: 1751. V. 41

Poems on Several Occasions. London: 1754. V. 38; 41

Poems on Several Occasions. Glasgow: 1759. V. 41

Poems. London: 1825. V. 39

The Poetical Works. London: 1779. V. 37; 43; 44

Some Memoirs of the Life and Publick Employments of Matthew Prior, Esq. London: 1722. V. 40

PRIOR, R.

Lusus Westmonasterienses, Sive Epigrammatum et Poematum Minorum Delectus. Londini: 1740. V. 40

PRIOR, S.

Illustrations of the Fungi of Our Fields and Woods, Drawn from Natural Specimens. London: 1864-65. V. 38

PRIOR, SAMUEL

The Universal Traveller . . . Popular Features . . . of the Best Standard Modern Travels . . . 46 accounts compiled from the 1809 and 1822 editions of Phillips 'Voyages and Travels'. London: 1822. V. 37

PRIOR, THOMAS

An Authentic Narrative of the Success of Tar-Water in Curing a Great Number and Variety of Distempers. Dublin: 1746. V. 40; 44

An Authentic Narrative of the Success of Tar-Water, In Curing a Great Number and VAriety of Distempers . . . London: 1746. V. 37; 42

Instructions for Planting and Managing Hogs, and for Raising Hop-Poles. Dublin: 1733. V. 38

A List of the Absentees of Ireland, and the Yearly Value of Their Estates and Incomes Spent Abroad . . . Dublin printed: 1730. V. 43

Observations on Coin in General. Dublin: 1729. V. 38; 41

PRIP-MOLLER, J.

Chinese Buddhist Monasteries. Hong Kong: 1967. V. 39

Chinese Buddhist Monasteries. Copenhagen/London: 1937. V. 37

PRISCIANUS, THEODORUS

Octavii Horatiani Rerum Medicarum lib. Quatuor . . . Albucasis Chirurgicorum . . . Lib. res . . . Strasbourg: 1532. V. 38; 42

PRISON ASSOCIATION OF NEW YORK

24th Annual Report for 1868. Albany: 1869. V. 38

PRISON Etiquette. The Convict's Compendium of Useful Information. Bearsville: 1950. V. 45

PRITCHARD, ALAN

Alchemy: a Bibliography of English-Language Writings. London: 1980. V. 45

PRITCHARD, ANDREW

A History of Infusoria . . . London: 1861. V. 38; 40

The Microscopic Cabinet of Select Animated Objects. London: 1832. V. 42

The Natural History of Animalcules. London: 1834. V. 38; 40; 41

PRITCHARD, H. BADEN

Dangerfield. London: 1878. V. 42

PRITCHARD, H. HESKETH

Hunting Camps in Wood and Wilderness. London: 1910. V. 38; 40; 46

Through Trackless Labrador. London: 1911. V. 38; 40; 46

PRITCHARD, JAMES A.

The Overland Diary and James A. Pritchard from Kentucky to California in 1849. Denver: 1959. V. 38; 39; 40; 41; 43; 46

PRITCHARD, JAMES COWLES

On the Different Forms of Insanity, in relations to Jurisprudence. London;: 1842. V. 37

A Treatise on Insanity and Other Disorders Affecting the Mind. London: 1835. V. 43

PRITCHARD, W. T.

Polynesian Reminiscences; or, Life in the South Pacific Islands. London: 1866. V. 40; 43

PRITCHARD, WILLIAM A.

W. A. Pritchard's Address to the Jury in the Crown vs. Armstrong, Heaps, Bray, Ivens, Johns, Pritchard and Queen (R.B. Russell was previously tried), Indicted for Seditious Conspiracy and Common Nuisance; Fall Assizes. Winnipeg: 1919-20. V. 40

W. A. Pritchard's Address to the Jury in the Crown vs. Armstrong, Heaps, Bray, Ivens, Johns, Pritchard and Queen . . . Winnipeg: 1920. V. 39; 41

PRITCHETT, V. S.

Clare Drummer. London: 1929. V. 41

Dead Man Leading. London: 1937. V. 46

The Spanish Virgin and Other Stories. London: 1930. V. 41

The Turn of the Years. Great Britain: 1982. V. 41; 42

PRITT, T. E.

North Country Flies. London: 1886. V. 40

North Country Flies. London: 1886. V. 39

PRITTS, JOSEPH

Incidents of Border Life, Illustrative of the Times and Condition of the First Settlements in Parts of the Middle and Western States . . . Chambersburg: 1839. V. 45

Incidents of Border Life, Illustrative of the Times and Condition of the First Settlements in Parts of the Middle and Western States . . . Lancaster: 1841. V. 40

Mirror of Olden Time Border Life. Abingdon: 1849. V. 39; 45

PRITZEL, G. A.

Thesaurus Literaturae Botanicae Omnium Gentium . . . Milano: 1950. V. 46

PRIULI, GIROLAMO 1579-1625

La Galatea Poema Lirico con l'Allegorie . . . Venice: 1625. V. 39; 46

PRIVATE Land Claims in Missouri. Washington: 1834. V. 37

PRIVATE LIBRARIES ASSOCIATION

Private Press Books 1959 (-1979). Pinner: 1960-84. V. 41

PRIVATE Tombs at Thebes. Volume I. Four Eighteenth Dynasty Tombs. Oxford: 1957. V. 41

PRIVATE Worth the Basis of Public Decency. An Address to People of Rank and Forutne, Dedicated to the Bishop of London. London: 1789. V. 42; 46

THE PRIVILEDGES and Practice of Parliaments in England. London: 1641. V. 38; 40

THE PRIVILEGED Islands, Being a Companion to the Islands of Guernsey, Jersey, Alderney, Serk, Herm and Jethou, With a Memo of Burhou . . . Jersey: 1840. V. 40

THE PRIVILEGES and Practice of Parliaments in England. London: 1680. V. 42

LES PRIVILEGES de Cocouage, Ouvrage Necessaire Tant Aux Cornards Actuels, Qu'aux Cocus eu Herbe. Holland: 1682. V. 43

PRIVILEGIA et Indulgentie Fratrum Mendicantium. Leipzig: 1498. V. 44

PRO-SLAVERY Ball, to be Given at the Skillman House, Platte City, Mo. Platte City. V. 41

PROBATIONARY Odes, by the Various Candidates for the Office of Poet Laureate to His Majesty, in the Room of William Whitehead, Esq. Deceased; To Perpetuate Whose Memory the Following Epitaph is Intended. London: 1785. V. 39

PROBERT, JOHN

Catalogue of Miniatures, Enamels, Pastels and Waxes at 112 Gloucester Place, Portman Square. London: 1890. V. 38

PROBST, GERHARD F.

The Kikkuli Text on the Training of Horses. Lexington: 1977. V. 37

PROBUS, M. VALERIUS

De Interpretandi Romanorum Litteris (etc.). Venice: 1499. V. 40

PROBY, DOUGLAS JAMES

A Catalogue of the Pictures at Elton Hall in Huntingdonshire in the Possession of Col. Douglas James Proby. London: 1924. V. 44

PROCEEDINGS And Speeches at a Meeting for the Promotion of the Cause of Temperance in the United States, Held at the Capitol, in Washington City, February 24, 1833. Washington: 1833. V. 39

THE PROCEEDINGS and Tryal in the Case of the Most Reverend Father in God William, Lord Archbishop of Canterbury, and the Right Reverend Fathers in God, William Lord Bishop of St. Asaph, Francis Lord Bishop of Ely, John Bishop of Chichester . . . London: 1689. V. 37; 41

PROCEEDINGS At the Reception and Dinner in Honor of Mr. Geo. Peabody . . . Boston: 1856. V. 38

PROCEEDINGS in Behalf of the Morton Testimonial. Boston: 1861. V. 37; 39; 45

PROCEEDINGS of a Meeting of Representatives of the Several Railroad Companies . . . Cleveland: 1854. V. 38

PROCEEDINGS of the Friends of a Rail-Road To San Francisco, at Their Public Meeting . . . Including an Address to the People of the U. States. Boston: 1849. V. 39

PROCEEDINGS of the Friends of the Liberty of the Press; on December, the 22nd, 1792 and January 19th and March 9th, 1793. London: 1793. V. 39

PROCEEDINGS of the Meeting in Charleston, S.C. May 13-15, 1845 on the Religious Instruction of the Negroes . . . Charleston: 1845. V. 43

PROCEEDINGS of the Morton Testimonial. Boston: 1868. V. 39

PROCEEDINGS of the Public Meeting Held at Freemason's Hall, on the 18th June, 1824 for Erecting a Monument to the Late James Watt. London: 1824. V. 43

THE PROCESSION and Ceremonies Observed at the Time of the Installation of the Knights of Companions of the Most Honourable Military Order of the Bath; upon Thursday, June 17, 1725. London: 1730. V. 45

PROCESSUS Juris Clarissumi Viri . . . Lipsi: 1512. V. 40

PROCHASKA, GEORGE

The Principles of Physiology . . . and a Dissertation on the Functions of the Nervous System. London: 1851. V. 37

PROCHASKA, GEORGIUS

Disquisitio Anatomico-Physiologica Organismi Corporis Humani Eiusque Processus Vitalis. Vienna: 1812. V. 43

PROCLAMATION of the Twelve Apostles of the Church of Jesus Christ of Latter Day Saints. To All the Kings of the World; to the President of the United States of America; to the Governors of the Several States . . . New York: 1845. V. 38

PROCLUS

De Sphaera Liber. Cleomedis De Mundo, Sive Circularis Inspectionis Meteororum Libri Duo. Basle: 1547. V. 44

La Sfera . . . Tradotta da Maestro Egnatio Danti . . . Florence: 1573. V. 40

The Treatises of Proclus, The Platonic Successor. London: 1833. V. 38; 41

PROCOPIUS

Historiarum Procopii Caesariensis Libri VIII, Nunc Primum Graece editi. Augsburg: 1607. V. 45

The History of the Warres of . . . Justinian in Eight Books. London: 1653. V. 45

PROCOPIUS CAESARIENSIS 500-565

De Rebus Gothorum, Persarum ac Vandalorum Libri VI, una Cum Aliis Mediorum Temporum Historicis. Basle: 1531. V. 40; 45

PROCOPIUS, CESARIENSE

De Gli Edifici di Giustiniano Imperatore. Di Greco in Volgare Tradotti per Benedetto Egio da Sploeti. 1547. V. 42

PROCOPIUS OF CAESAREA

Historiarum Nun Primum Graece Editi. Accessit Liber de Aedificiis Justiniani fere duplo quam antea auctior. Opera Davidis Hoeschelli Avg. Augsburg: 1607. V. 37; 38

The History of the Warres of the Empeorer Justinian in Eight Books. London: 1653. V. 39

PROCTER, ADELAIDE

Legends and Lyrics - A Book of Verses - Second Series. London: 1892. V. 38

PROCTER, ADELAIDE ANNE

Legends and Lyrics. Second Volume. London: 1861. V. 42

PROCTER, BRYAN WALLER 1787-1874

Charles Lamb, a Memoir. London: 1866. V. 39; 40

Dramatic Scenes. London: 1857. V. 39

English Songs, and Other Small Poems. London: 1832. V. 39

The Flood of Thessaly and Other Poems. London: 1823. V. 37; 39; 40; 42

Marcian Colonna, an Italian Tale. London: 1820. V. 41; 44; 46

Mirandola. London: 1821. V. 43

The Poetical Works. London: 1822. V. 39

A Sicilian Story, with Diego de Montilla and other Poems. London: 1820. V. 39; 46

PROCTER, E. H.

The Rabbits Day in Town. London: 1910. V. 45

PROCTER, RICHARD WRIGHT 1816-1881

The Barber's Shop. Manchester: 1883. V. 40

The Barber's Shop. Manchester and London: 1883. V. 39

PROCTOR, ADELAIDE ANNE

Legends and Lyrics, a Book of Verses. London: 1812. V. 41

Legends and Lyrics. London: 1866. V. 40; 43; 46

PROCTOR, C. H.

The Life of James Williams, Better Known as Professor Jim . . . Hartford: 1873. V. 43

PROCTOR, EDNA DEAN

The Song of the Ancient People. Boston: 1903. V. 38; 39

PROCTOR, EDWARD K.

Belfast Scenery, in Thirty Views. London: 1832. V. 43

PROCTOR, G.

*The Lucubrations of Humphrey Ravelin, Esq. Late major in the ** Regiment of Infantry.* London: 1823. V. 46

PROCTOR, JOHN CLAGETT

Washington Past and Present, a History. New York: 1930. V. 38

PROCTOR, PERCIVAL

The Modern Dictionary of Arts and Sciences. Birmingham: 1790. V. 38

PROCTOR, R.

Bibliographical Essays Printed at the Chiswick Press. London: 1905. V. 45

PROCTOR, REDFIELD

Irrigation and Water Storage in the Arid Regions. Letter from . . . Transmitting a Report of the Chief Signal Officer of the Army . . . Washington: 1891. V. 37

PROCTOR, RICHARD A.

Old and New Astronomy. London: 1892. V. 46

Watched by the Dead, a Loving Study of Charles Dickens' Half Told Tales. London: 1887. V. 40; 41; 44

PROCTOR, ROBERT

Jan Van Doesborgh, Printer at Antwerp. London: 1894. V. 39

Narrative of a Journey Across the Cordillera of the Andes and of a Residence in Lima, and Other Parts of Peru, in the Years 1823 and 1824. Edinburgh: 1825. V. 39; 42

Narrative of a Journey Across the Cordillera of the Andes, and of a Residence in Lima and Other Parts of Peru . . . London: 1825. V. 42

The Printing of Greek in the 15th Century. London: 1900. V. 45

The Printing of Greek in the Fifteenth Century. Oxford: 1900. V. 37

LES PRODIGIEVSES et Admirables Visions Apparues a Acmeth Grand Seigneur des Turcs, le 3. d'Aoust Mil Six Cents Quatorze. Paris: 1614. V. 37

PROEF Van Letteren, Welke Gegooten Worden in De Nieuwe Haarlemsche Lettergietery Van J. Enschede. 1768. Haarlem: 1768. V. 44

PROEMS. London: 1938. V. 38

PROFECIA Politica, Verificada en lo Que Esta Sucediendo a los Portugueses por su Ciega Aficion a Los Ingleses. Madrid: 1762. V. 45

PROFESSIONAL Knowledge 'The Art of Cookery' for the Hotel, Restaurant, and Catering Trade. London: 1951/51/52. V. 46

PROFFATT, JOHN

The Law of Private Corporations. San Francisco: 1876. V. 37

PROFIT and Loss of Great Britain and Spain, from the Commencement of the Present War, to the Time, Impartially Stated . . . London: 1742. V. 41; 45

THE PROGRESS of Her Majesty Queen Victoria and His Royal Highness Prince Albert in France, Belgiuma nd England. London. V. 44

THE PROGRESS of a Rake; or, the Templar's Exit. In Ten Cantos, in Hudibrastic Verse . . . London: 1732. V. 38

THE PROGRESS of Her Majesty Queen Victoria and His Royal Highness Prince Albert, to Burghley House, Northamptonshire . . . London: 1845. V. 39

THE PROGRESS of the Rake; or, the Templar's Exit, In Ten Cantos, in Hudibrastic Verse . . . London: 1732. V. 42

PROGRESSIVE Drawing Book; Containing a Series of Easy and Comprehensive Lessons for Drawing Landscape, Architecture, the Human Figure, Shipping, Animals &c. London: 1853. V. 44

PROGRESSIVE Men of Northern Ohio. Cleveland: 1906. V. 46

PROGRESSIVE Men of the State of Montana. Chicago: 1902. V. 43; 45

PROGRESSIVE Men of the State of Wyoming. Chicago: 1903. V. 37
PROGRESSIVE Men of the State of Wyoming. Chicago: 1903. V. 39

PROGRESSIVE Men of Western Colorado. Chicago: 1905. V. 37; 38

PROIX, ROBERT

Albert Camus and the Men of the Stone. San Francisco: 1971. V. 45

PROKOSCH, FREDERIC

Banquet Song. Barcelona: 1953. V. 38; 40

Storm and Echo. New York: 1948. V. 39; 43

Three Sorrows. New Haven: 1932. V. 41; 42

Three Mysteries. New Haven: 1932. V. 37

PROLUSIONES Praemiis Anniversariis Dignatae et in Auditorio Recitatae Scholae Harroviensis. Harrow: 1841-98. V. 40

PROMINENT People of the Maritime Provinces. St. John: 1922. V. 37; 39; 40; 42; 44

THE PROMPTER. London: 1789. V. 39

PROMPTUARIUM Iconum. Lyon: 1553. V. 45

PROMPTUARIUM Medicinae. 1483. V. 46

A PRONOUNCING Gazetteer and Geographical Dictionary of the Philippine Islands, United States of America . . . Washington: 1902. V. 38

PROPAGANDA Fide. Oratio Dominica, in CCL Linguas Versa. Rome: 1870. V. 38

A PROPEHSIE, Which Hath Been in Manuscript, in the Lord Powis's Family Sixty Years. N.P.: 1679. V. 44

PROPER Lessons to Be Read at Morning and Evening Prayer. Oxford: 1835. V. 39

A PROPER Memorial for the 29th of May, The Glorious Day Which Bless'd These Nations with the Reutrn of King Charles the IId, Their Rightful Monarch . . . London: 1715. V. 42

PROPERT, J. L.

A History of Miniature Art. London: 1887. V. 38; 40; 44

PROPERT, W. A.

The Russian Ballet In Western Europe 1909-1920. London: 1921. V. 38; 40

The Russian Ballet in Western Europe 1909-1920. New York: 1921. V. 44

The Russian Ballet, 1921-1929. London: 1931. V. 41

The Russian Ballet in Western Europe 1909-1920. London/New York: 1921. V. 37

PROPHECIES Delivered by a Descendant from the Oracle of Delphos, of the Future Lives and Deaths of the Following Distinguished Personages. Dublin: 1791. V. 42; 46

THE PROPHECIES of the Times: a Satire. London: 1795. V. 39

THE PROPHECY of Liberty: a Poem. London: 1768. V. 46

A PROPOSAL for Humbling Spain. London: 1739. V. 45

PROPOSALS for a Regulation or an Entire Suppression of Pawn-Brokers. With a Detection of Their Fraudulent Practices, and a Recommendation of the Methods Used by the States of Holland, for the Relief of the Necessitous, by Lending on Pledges. London: 1733. V. 46

PROPOSALS For a Regulation, or an Entire Suppression, of Pawnbrokers. London: 1732. V. 42

PROPOSALS for Enriching the Principality of Wales . . . Glocester: 1762. V. 46

PROPOSALS for Establishing a Clearing-House, at the Stock-Exchange to be Used on all Settling Days, Upon the Plan of Each Member Giving Memorandums for His Differences Instead of Checks and Settling Those Memorandums by a Balance-Draft . . . N.P.: 1827. V. 43

PROPOSALS for Establishing a Number of Farms, Like Those of New England, New York, New Jersey, Pennsylvania and Delaware. N.P.: 1816. V. 40
PROPOSALS for Establishing a Number of Farms, Like Those of New England, New York, New Jersey, Pennsylvania, and Delaware. Raleigh: 1816. V. 45

PROPOSALS for Establishing a Number of Farms, like those of New England . . . on the South side of the Western Districts of North Carolina, for the Mutual benefit of the Settlers and of the Trade of Charleston, Wilimington . . . and of the Planters on . . . (Raleigh): 1816. V. 37

PROPOSALS for Printing a New Weekly Paper, Called the Boston Chronicle. Boston: 1767. V. 42

PROPOSALS For Publishing by Subscription, the Following Works of Purcell. N.P.: 1790. V. 43

PROPOSALS for Raising a Million of Money Out of the Forfeited Estates in IReland; Together with the Anwers of the Irish to the Same and a Reply Thereto. Dublin: 1704. V. 44

PROPOSED Regulations for the Instruction, Formations and Movements of the Cavalry. London: 1832. V. 41

PROPPER, G. R.

Gold and Copper are Kings. Basin City: 1890s. V. 44

THE PROPRIETY of Retaining Gibraltar Impartially Considered. London: 1783. V. 38; 42

PROPYLAEN. Eine Periodische Schrift. Tubingen: 1798-1800. V. 38

PROSCH, CHARLES

Reminiscences of Washington Territory. Scenes and Incidents and Reflections of the Pioneer Period on Puget Sound. Seattle: 1904. V. 39; 41; 43; 45

PROSCH, THOMAS W.

The Conkling-Prosch family, with Some Refernece to the Dotter, Roe, Reynolds, Brooks, Mapes, Elder, McCArver and Other Connections. Seattle: 1909. V. 46

McCarver and Tacoma. Seattle: 1906. V. 40; 41; 45

PROSE and Poetry of the Live Stock Industry of the United States. New York: 1959. V. 40

PROSE, e Versi per Onorare la Memoria di Livia Doria Caraffa . . . Parma: 1784. V. 45

PROSE, e Versi Per Onorare la Memoria di Livia Doria Caraffa Principessa del S. R. Imp. e della Rocella di Alcuni Rinomati Autori. Parma: 1784. V. 40; 41; 45

PROSKOURIAKOFF, TATIANA

An Album of Maya Architecture. Washington: 1946. V. 39; 44; 45

An Album of Maya Architecture. Merida: 1958. V. 44

A Study of Classic Maya Sculpture. Washington, DC: 1950. V. 37

A PROSPECTUS of Wrangel (sic), Alaska. San Francisco: 1901. V. 40

PROSPER, MERIMEE

Carmen and Letters from Spain. New York: 1931. V. 45

Mateo Falcone. Paris: 1906. V. 46

PROSSER, GEORGE FREDERICK

Select Illustrations of Hampshire. London & Winchester: 1833. V. 38

PROSSER, WILLIAM FARRAND

A History of the Puget Sound Country. New York: 1903. V. 45

THE PROTEST. London. V. 46

A PROTEST Against the Admission of Dakota as a State . . . N.P.: 1881. V. 42; 45

PROTESTANT EPISCOPAL CHURCH

Constitution of the Protestant Episcopal Church in the Confederate States of America and Digest of the Canons Adopted in General Council, in Augusta, Georgia, November, 1862. Augusta: 1863. V. 44

Hymnal of the Protestant Episcopal Church in the United States of America. Buffalo: 1872. V. 38

Journal of Proceedings of an Adjourned Convention of Bishops, Clergymen and Laymen . . . Montgomery: 1861. V. 41

Okodakiciye-Wakan Odowan Qa Okna Ahity Ay Api Kta Ho Kin. New York: 1896. V. 40

PROTESTANT EPISCOPAL CHURCH. BOOK OF COMMON PRAYER

The Army and Navy Prayer Book. Richmond: 1864. V. 44

The Book of Common Prayer: and Administration of the Sacraments and Other Rites and Ceremonies of the Church. According to the Use of the Protestant Episcopal Church in the United States of America. Together with the Psalter or Psalms of David. Boston: 1930. V. 45

PROTESTANT EPISCOPAL CHURCH. DAKOTA (MISSIONARY DISTRICT).

First Triennial Convocation of the Missionary District of South Dakota. Journal and Bishop's Address. Sioux Falls: 1885. V. 39

Missionary District of South Dakota. Annual Address of the Bishop with Journals of the Eastern and Western Deaneries. Sioux Falls: 1884. V. 39

PROTESTANT Episcopal Church in the U. S. A. BOOK OF COMMON PRAYER The Book of Common Prayer, and Administration of the Sacraments; and Other Rites & Ceremonies of the Church . . . Use of the Protestant Episcopal Church in the U.S.A. N: 1843. V. 40

PROTHERO, G. W.

Armenia and Kurdistan. London: 1920. V. 40

THE PROTICAL Son; A Welch Preachment, by the Parson of Llangtyddre. London: 1750. V. 44

PROUD, J. A.

A Candid and Impartial Reply to the Rev. Dr. Priestley's Letters, Addressed by Him to the Members of the New Jerusalem. Birmingham: 1791. V. 40

PROUD, ROBERT 1728-1813

The History of Pennsylvania in North America, From the Original Institution and Settlement of that Province, Under the First Proprietor and Governor William Penn in 1681. Philadelphia: 1797-98. V. 40; 41; 42; 43

PROUDHON, P. J.

Les Confessions d'un Revolutionnaire, pour servir a l'Histoire de la Revolution de Fevrier. Bruxelles: 1850. V. 39

PROUDLOCK, LEWIS

The Posthumous Poetical Works. Jedburgh: 1826. V. 37

PROUST DE LA GIRONIERE, PAUL

Twenty Years in the Philippines. New York: 1854. V. 44

PROUST, MARCEL 1871-1922

Cities of the Plain. London: 1929. V. 40

47 Unpublished Letters from Marcel Proust to Walter Berry. Paris: 1930. V. 37; 43; 45

Jean Santeuil. Paris: 1952. V. 41; 43

Quelques Lettres de Marcel Proust Precedees de Remarques sur les Derniers Mois de sa Vie Par Leon Pierre Quint. Paris: 1928. V. 41

A La Recherche du Temps Perdu. Paris: 1968-69. V. 43

Remembrance of Things Past. London: 1922-31. V. 38

Remembrance of Things Past. New York: 1925/1927-32. V. 46

Remembrance of Things Past. London: 1981. V. 43

Swann's Way. New York: 1954. V. 44

A Vision of Paris. New York: 1963. V. 41

The Works . . . London: 1941. V. 39

Works. London: 1960. V. 37

PROUSTEAU, GUILLAUME

Catalogue des Livres de la Bibliotheque Publique Fondee par M. Prousteau . . . Paris: 1777. V. 38

PROUT, JOHN W.

A Sketch of Mining, and Its Commercial Possibilities. Liverpool: 1903. V. 40

PROUT, SAMUEL 1783-1852

Hints on Light and Shadow, Composition, etc., as Applicable to Landscape Painting . . . London: 1838. V. 44

Hints on Light and Shadow, Composition, etc. as Applicable to Landscape Painting. London: 1848. V. 38; 42

Hints on Light and Shadow. London: 1876. V. 44

Hints on Light and Shadow, Compositions, etc., as Applicable to Landscape Painting. London: 1898. V. 46

Progressive Fragments . . . London: 1817. V. 42

Prout's Microcosm. London: 1841. V. 37; 43; 44

Prout's Microcosm. London: 1881. V. 38; 40

Rudiments of Landscape . . . London: 1814. V. 42

A Series of 10 Hand Coloured Etchings by Samuel Prout. London: 1814. V. 42

Studies of Boats and Coast Scenery, for Landscape and Marine Painters, Drawn and Etched in Imitation of Chalk. London: 1816. V. 44

Studies of Cottages and Rural Scenery, Drawn and Etched in Imitation of Chalk. London: 1816. V. 41

PROUT, T.

Bob Norberry. Dublin: 1844. V. 38

PROUT, TIMOTHY

Diana's Shrines Turned Into Ready Money, By Priestly Magic; or, Virtue Given Up . . . New York: 1773. V. 37; 40; 44

PROUT, WILLIAM

Chemistry, Meteorology, and the Function of Digestion Considered with Reference to Natural Theology. Philadelphia: 1834. V. 40; 42; 43; 45

An Inquiry Into the Nature and Treatment of Gravel, Calculus, and Other Diseases Connected with A Deranged Operation Of the Urinary Organs. London: 1821. V. 42

An Inquiry into the Nature and Treatment of Diabetes, Calculus, and Other Affections of the Urinary Organs. London: 1825. V. 39

An Inquiry inot the Nature and Treatment of Diabetes, Calculus and Other Affections of the Urinary Organs . . . Philadelphia: 1826. V. 38; 42; 43

On the Nature and Treatment of Stomach and Renal Diseases . . . London: 1848. V. 43

On the Nature and Treatment of Stomach and Renal Diseases; being an inquiry into the Connexion of Diabetes, Calculus, and Other Affections of the Kidney and Bladder, with Indigestion. Philadelphia: 1843. V. 37

PROUTY, OLIVE HIGGINS

Now, Voyager. Boston: 1941. V. 40; 41; 42; 43; 44

PROVENCE, HARRY

Lyndon Johnson: A Biography. New York: 1964. V. 39

THE PROVIDENCE Directory. Providence: 1830. V. 40

THE PROVIDENCE Directory. Providence: 1832. V. 38

PROVINCE of Manitoba; and North West Territory of the Dominion of Canada. Ottawa: 1876. V. 42

PROVIS, WILLIAM

An Historical and Descriptive Account of the Suspension Bridge Constructed Over the Menai Straits in North Wales. London: 1828. V. 39

PROWELL, GEORGE R.

The History of Camden County, New Jersey. Philadelphia: 1886. V. 41

History of the Eighty-Seventh Regiment, Pennsylvania Volunteers . . . York: 1903. V. 42; 46

History of York County, Pennsylvania. Chicago: 1907. V. 41; 42

PROWN, JULES DAVID

American Painting: From Its Beginnings to the Armory Show: the 20th Century. Geneva: 1969. V. 42

American Painting. Cleveland: 1970. V. 41

American Painting From the Colonial Period to the Present. London: 1977. V. 41

John Singleton Copley: in America, 1738-1774. In England 1774-1815. Cambridge: 1966. V. 44; 45

PROWSE, D. W.

A History of Newfoundland, from the English, Colonial and Foreign Records. New York: 1895. V. 41

A History of Newfoundland, from the English Colonial and Revised & Corrected. London: 1896. V. 40

PRUDEN, DUNSTAN

Silversmithing Its Principles and Practice in Small Workshops. Ditchling: 1933. V. 43

PRUDENTIUS, AURELIUS CLEMENS 348-410

Opera. Antwerp: 1564. V. 45

Opera. Paris: 1687. V. 46

Opera Omnia. Parma: 1788. V. 45

Opera . . . Parma: 1789. V. 37

Theodori Pulmanni Cranenburgii Et Victoris Giselini Opera, Ex Fide Decem Librorum Manuscriptorum, Emendatus, et In Eum, Eiusdem Victoris Giselini Commentarius. Antwerp: 1564. V. 45; 46

PRUEN, S. TRISTRAM

The Arab and the African. Experiences in Eastern Equatorial Africa During a Residence of Three Years. London: 1891. V. 41

PRUITT, MOMAN

Moman Pruitt: Criminal Lawyer. Oklahoma City: 1945. V. 42

PRUYN, JOHN V. L.

Catalogue of Books Relating to the Literature of the Law Collected by John V. L. Pruyn of Albany, New York. Albany: 1901. V. 43

PRY, PAUL

Oddities of London Life. London: 1838. V. 40

PRYCE, F. N.

Catalogue of Sculpture in the Department of Greek and Roman Antiquities in the British Museum. London: 1928. V. 44

PRYCE, WILLIAM 1725-1790

Archaeologia Cornu-Britannica. Sherborne: 1790. V. 37; 40; 41; 42; 43; 46

Bibliotheca Cornu-Britannica; or, an Essay to Preserve the Ancient Cornish Language . . . Sherborne: 1790. V. 42

Mineralogia Cornubiensis: a Treatise on Minerals, Mines and Mining. London: 1773. V. 46

Mineralogia Cornubiensis; a Treatise on Minerals, Mines and Mining . . . London: 1778. V. 37; 41; 42; 46

PRYDE, DAVID

The Genius and Writings of Charles Dickens; a Lecture. Edinburgh: 1869. V. 43

PRYNNE, WILLIAM 1600-1669

Brevia Parliamentaria Rediviva in XIII Sections . . . London: 1662. V. 42

A Breviate of the Life of William Laud Arch-bishop of Canterbury . . . . London: 1644. V. 39

Brief Animadversions on Amendments of an Additional Explanatory Records the Fourth Part of the Institutes of the Lawes of England, Concerning the Jurisdiction of Courts. London: 1669. V. 38; 40

Canterburies Doome. London: 1646. V. 44

A Counter-Plea to the Cowards Apologie, Manifesting by an Ancient Record and Law . . . N.P.: 1647. V. 43

Demophilos, or the Assertor of the Peoples Liberty . . . London: 1658. V. 45

The First (to Fourth) Part(s) of a Brief Register, Kalendar and Survey of the Several Kinds, Forms of all Parliamentary Writs. London: 1659-64. V. 46

The Fourth Part of a Brief Register, Kalender and Survey of the Kinds, Forms of Parliamentary Writs . . . London: 1664. V. 40

Histrio-Mastix. The Players Scourge, or, Actors Tragaedie. London: 1633. V. 37; 39; 45

An Humble Remonstrance to His Maiesty, Against the Tax of Ship-Money Imposed, Laying Open the Illegalitie, Abuse and Inconvenience Thereof. London: 1641. V. 41; 45

An Humble Remonstrance to His Majesty, Against the Tax of Ship-money Imposed, Laying Open the Illegalitie, Abuse and Inconvenience Thereof. N.P.: 1641. V. 38

An Humble Remonstrance Against the Tax of Ship-Money Lately Imposed . . . London: 1643. V. 38; 40

A Legal Vindication of the Liberties of England Against Illegal Taxes and Pretended Acts of Parliament Lately Enforced on the People. London: 1649. V. 37; 38

A New Discovery of the Prelates Tyranny . . . London: 1641. V. 44

Newes from Ipswich: Discovering Certaine Late Detestable Practices of Some Domineering Lordly Prelates . . . Ipswich: 1636. V. 45

A Plea for the Lords; or, A Short yet Full and Necessary Vindication of the Judiciary and Legislative Power of the House of Peeres . . . London: 1648. V. 44

A Plea for the Lords, and House of Peers. London: 1658. V. 42

Romes Master-Peece, or, the Grand Conspiracy of the Pope and His Jesuited Instruments to Extripate the Protestant Religion, Re-Establish Popery, Subvert Lawes, Liberties, Peace, Parliaments by Kindling a Civil War in Scotland. V. 46

A Seasonable Vindication of the Supream Authority and Jurisdiction of Christian Kings, Lords, Parliaments, as well over the Possessions, as Persons of Delinquent Prelates and Churchmen; or An Antient Disputation of the Famous . . . London: 1660. V. 37

The Second Tome of an Exact Chronological Vindication and Historial Demonstration of Our British, Roman, Saxon . . . London: 1665. V. 40

A Short, Legal Medicinal Useful Safe Easie Prescription to Recover Our Kingdom, Church, Nation, from Their Present Dangerous, Distractive, Destructive Confusion . . . London: 1659. V. 39; 44

The Treachery and Disloyalty of Papists to Their Soveraignes, in Doctrine and Practice. London: 1643. V. 38; 40

A True and perfect Narrative of What was done, spoken by and between Mr. Prynne, the old and newly Forcibly secluded Members, the Army Officers and those now sitting, both in the Commons Lobby, House, and elsewhere; on Saturday . . . London: 1659. V. 37

A Vindication of the Imprisoned and Secluded members of the House of Commons, from the Apsersions Cast Upon Them, and the Majority of the House . . . London: 1649. V. 44

PRYOR, ABRAHAM

An Interesting Description of British America, from Personal Knowledge and Observation . . . Providence: 1819. V. 38

PRZEZSZIEKI, A.

Monuments de Moyen Age et de la Renaissance Dans l'Ancienne Pologne . . . jusqu' a la Fin du XVIIe Siecle. Warsaw and Paris: 1853-58. V. 37

PSALMANAZAAR, GEORGE 1679-1763

Memoirs of ****. Commonly known by the Name of George Psalmanazaar; A Reputed Native of Formosa. Written by himself in order to be published after his Death. Containing an Account of his Education, Travels, Adventures, Connections . . . London: 1764. V. 37; 38; 39; 40; 41; 42; 45; 46

PSALMANAZAR, GEORGE 1679-1763

An Historical and Geographical Description of Formosa, an Island Subject to the Emperor of Japan Giving an Account of the Religion, Custom, Manners, etc. of the Inhabitants. London: 1704. V. 38; 41; 46

An Historical and Geographical Description of Formosa, An Island Subject tot he Emperor of Japan. London: 1705. V. 41; 46

Memoirs of . . . London: 1765. V. 38; 42

PSAUME, ETIENNE

Lives of Remarkable Characters Who Have Distinguished Themselves From the Commencement of the French Revolution to the Present Time. London: 1814. V. 42

PSELLUS, MICHAEL

De Operatione Daemonum Dialogus, Graece et Latine. Paris: 1615. V. 37

De Victus Ratione. Basileae: 1529. V. 37; 42; 44

Sapientissimi Pselli Opus Dilucidum in Quattuor Mathematicas Disciplinas, Arithmeticam, Musicam, Geometriam & Astronomiam . . . Venice: 1532. V. 40

PSEUDO-AMMONIUS, ALEXANDRINUS

Evangelicae Historiae Ex Qvatvor Evangelistis Perpetvo Tenore Continuato Narratio . . . Augsburg: 1523. V. 40

PSYCHOUNDAKIS, GEORGE

The Cretan Runner - His Story of the German Occupation. London: 1955. V. 46

PTOLOMAEUS, CLAUDIUS

Almagestum . . . Opus Ingens ac Nobile Omnes Ceolorum Motus Continens . . . Venice: 1515. V. 43

PTOLOMAEUS, CLAUDIUS continued

Geografia di Claudio Ptolemeo Alessandrino, Con Alcuni Comenti & Aggiunte Fatteui da Sebastiano Munstero Alamanno . . . Venice: 1547. V. 45

Geografia Cio e Descrittione Universale Della Terra. Venice: 1598. V. 40

Geografia. Venice: 1598-99. V. 39; 41; 42

Geographia. Venice: 1562. V. 37

Geographicae Enarrationis Libri Octo. Strasbourg: 1525. V. 38; 40

Geography. New York: 1932. V. 40

Harmonicorum Libri Tres. Oxford: 1682. V. 41; 44; 46

Liber de Analemmte, a Federico Commandino Insturatus & Commentariis Illustratus . . . Venice: 1562. V. 38

Vier de Annalemmate, a Federico Commandino Instauratus, & Commentariis Illustratus, qui nunc primum eius opera . . . in Lucem Prodit. Rome: 1562. V. 42

Sexta Asiae Tabula. A double page map of Arabia, from the Red Sea across Arabia to the Persian Gulf and the coast of Persia. Rome: 1507. V. 37

Tabulae Geographicae Orbis Terrarum. Veteris Cogniti. Trajecti ad Rhenum Apud: 1598. V. 39

Trattato de la Descittione Della Sfera Celeste in Piano . . . Bologna: 1572. V. 37

PUAUX, RENE

Marshall Foch. His Life, His Work, His Faith. London: 1918. V. 43

PUBLIC and Private Life of Animals. London: 1877. V. 39

THE PUBLIC Buildings of Westminster Described. London: 1831. V. 37

PUBLIC Discussion of the Issues Between the Reorganized Church of Jesus Christ of Latter Day Saints and the Church of Christ (Disciples), Held in Kirtland, Ohio, Beginning February 12th, and Clsoing March 8th, 1884 . . . St. Louis: 1884. V. 37

THE PUBLIC Domain. Its History, With Statistics . . . Washington: 1880. V. 39

THE PUBLIC Edifices of the British Metropolis with Historical and Descriptive Accounts of the Different Buildings. London: 1820. V. 38

THE PUBLIC-HOUSE-KEEPER'S Monitor; Being a Serious Admonition to the Masters and Mistresses of Those, Commonly Called Publick-Houses, of What Kind of Denomination So-Ever. London: 1730. V. 41; 43

PUBLIC Records: Reports from the Commissioners . . . Respecting the Public Records of Ireland. London: 1810-20. V. 40

PUBLIC School Verse: an Anthology: Volume V, 1924-1925. London: 1925. V. 44

PUBLICIUS, JACOBUS

Oratoriae Artis Epitoma . . . Venice: 1485. V. 39

PUCKETT, JAMES L.

History of Oklahoma and Indian Territory and Homeseeker's Guide. Vinita: 1906. V. 39; 42

PUCKETT, R. CAMPBELL

Sciography, or Radial Projection of Shadows. London: 1868. V. 40

PUCKLE, JAMES

The Club; or, a Grey-Cap for a Green-Head. London: 1733. V. 39; 45

The Club, a Dialogue Between Father and Son. London: 1817. V. 37; 39; 41

The Club; in a Dialogue Between Father and Son. London: 1842. V. 38

England's Path to Wealth and Honour: in a Dialogue Between an Englishman and a Dutchman. London: 1750. V. 41

PUCKLE, JOHN

The Church and Fortress of Dover Castle. Oxford: 1864. V. 40

PUDDICOMBE, JOHN NEWELL

The British Hero in Captivity. London: 1782. V. 37; 40

PUDNEY, JOHN

Almanack of Hope. London: 1944. V. 42

PUEBLO Indian Painting. Santa Fe: 1979. V. 38

PUECKLER-MUSKAU, HERMANN LUDWIG HEINRICH, PRINZ VON

Hints on Landscape Gardening . . . Boston: 1917. V. 38; 40

Hints on Landscape Gardening. Boston: 1971. V. 37

Tour in England, Ireland and France in the Years 1828 and 1829. London: 1832. V. 38; 43

Tutti Frutti. New York: 1834. V. 43

PUENTE Y GOMEZ, FREDERICO FERNANDEZ

Condecoraciones Espnolas. Madrid: 1964. V. 38

PUEYO, RAYMUNDO DEL

A New Spanish Grammar. London: 1792. V. 39

PUFENDORF, SAMEL, FREIHERR VON 1632-1694

The Whole Duty of man According to the Law of Nature. Dublin,: 1754. V. 38

PUFENDORF, SAMUEL, FREIHERR VON 1632-1694

Dissertationes Academicae Selectiores. Londini: 1675. V. 40

The Divine Feudal Law. London: 1703. V. 40

Le Droit de la Nature et des Gens, Ou Systeme General des Principes les Plus Importans de la Morale . . . Amsterdam: 1706. V. 38; 41

An Introduction to the History of the Principal Kingdoms and States of Europe. London: 1695. V. 39

An Introduction to the History of the Kingdoms and State of Asia, Africa and America, Both Ancient and Modern, According to the Method of Samuel Puffendorf . . . London: 1705. V. 42

An Introduction to the History of the Principal Kingdoms and States of Europe. (with) A Continuation of Samuel Puffendorf's Introduction to the . . . Brought to the Present Year. London: 1705. V. 40

An Introduction to the History of the Principal Kingdoms and States of Europe. Venice, Modena, manuta,: 1728. V. 40

An Introduction to the Principal Kingdoms and States of Europe. (with) a Supplement . . . London: 1728, 1726. V. 38; 40

De Jure Naturae et Gentium, Libri VIII. Frankfurt & Leipzig: 1744. V. 40

Of the Law of Nature and Nations. Oxford: 1710. V. 39

Of the Law of Nature and Nations. Oxford: 1703. V. 38

De Officio Hominis & Civis Juxta Legem Naturalem. Cambridge: 1735. V. 40

De Officio Hominis & Civis Juxta Legem Naturalem. London: 1737. V. 40

The Whole Duty of man According to the Law of nature. London: 1698. V. 38

The Whole Duty of Man According to the Law of Nature. London: 1716. V. 40

PUFFENDORE, BARON

Of the Law of Nature and Nations, Eight Books. London: 1717. V. 44

PUGH, E.

Cambria Depicta: A Tour through North Wales . . . London: 1816. V. 39; 40; 41; 42; 44

PUGH, EDWARD

Cambria Depicta: a Series of Fifty Piecturesque Views in Wales . . . London: 1827. V. 45

PUGH, EDWIN

Tony Drum, a Cockney Boy. London: 1898. V. 37; 41

PUGH, JOHN

Remarkable Occurences in the Life of Jonas Hanway . . . London: 1787. V. 37; 39; 41; 42; 43; 46

Remarkable Occurrences in the Life of Jonas Hanway, Esq. London: 1798. V. 39

A Treatise on the Science of Muscular Action . . . N.P.. V. 42; 45

PUGHE, WILLIAM OWEN

Geiriadur Cynmraeg a Saesoneg. London: 1793. V. 42; 43

PUGIN, AUGUSTUS CHARLES
V. 44

Examples of Gothic Architecture. London: 1850. V. 38; 41

Examples of Gothic Architecture Selected from Various Ancient Edifices in England. Edinburgh: 1895. V. 39

Examples of Gothic Architecture selected from various Ancient Edificesin England: consisting of Plans, Elevations, Sections . . . the Various Styles and the Practical Constuction . . . Edinburgh: 1895. V. 37

Gothic Ornaments Selected from Various Ancient Buildings . . . London: 1854. V. 38; 42

The Microcosm of London. London: 1808-10. V. 41

Paris and Its Environs. London: 1829. V. 37; 41; 42; 44

Paris and Its Environs, Displayed in a Series of Picturesque Views. London: 1829-31. V. 39; 41

Paris and Its Environs. London: 1831. V. 42; 46

Paris and Its Environs, Displayed in a Series of Two Hundred Picturesque Views, from Original Drawings . . . London: 1833. V. 40

Pugin's Gothic Furniture. London: 1828? V. 41

A Series of Ornamental Timber Gables. London: 1839. V. 38; 40; 44

A Series of Ornamental Timber Gables, From Existing Examples in England and France, of the Sixteenth Century. London: 1854. V. 45; 46

Specimens of Gothic Architecture . . . London: 1821-23. V. 42; 44

Specimens of the Architectural Antiquities of Normandy. London: 1829. V. 41

Specimens of the Architecture of Normandy from the XIth to the XVIth Century. London: 1874. V. 38

PUGIN, AUGUSTUS WELBY NORTHMORE 1812-1852

An Apology for the Revival of Christian Architecture in England. London: 1843. V. 38; 39; 41; 42; 44

Contrasts; or, a Parallel Between the Noble Edifices of the Fourteenth and Fifteenth Centuries . . . London: 1836. V. 45

Contrasts; or, a Parallel Between the Noble Edifices of the Middle Ages . . . London: 1841. V. 42

Designs for Iron and Brass Work in the Style of the XV and XVI Centuries. London: 1836. V. 45; 46

Designs for Gold and Silver-Smiths. London: 1836. V. 38

Floriated Ornament: a Series of Thirty-One Designs. London: 1849. V. 43

Glossary of Ecclesiastical Ornament and Costume . . . London: 1846. V. 37; 45

Gothic Furniture in the Style of the 15th Century. London: 1835. V. 37

Ornaments of the XVth and XVIth Centuries. London. V. 44

Photographs from Sketches by Augustus Welby N. Pugin by Stephen Ayling. London: 1865. V. 44

The Present State of Ecclesiastical Architecture in England. London: 1843. V. 38

A Treatise on Chancel Screens and Rood Lofts, Their Antiquity, Use and Sumbolic Significance. London: 1851. V. 37; 38; 39; 44; 45; 46

The True Principles of Pointed or Christian Architecture: Set forth in two lectures at S. Marie's Oscott. London: 1841. V. 37

PUKETT, R CAMPBELL

Sciography; or Radial Projection of Shadows. London: 1868. V. 39

PULA, J.

Ke Kumu Mua Ano Hou, I Hoonania I Na Kii Maikai. Bosetona: 1862. V. 43

PULCRA Historia Marie Egypciace. Basel?: 1490-95? V. 44

PULITZER, ALBERT

Romance of Prince Eugene. New York: 1895. V. 38

PULITZER, JOSEPH

A Tradition of Conscience, Proposals for Journalism. St. Louis: 1965. V. 40

PULLAN, MATILDA MARIAN CHESNEY

The Lady's Manual of Fancy-Work. New York: 1859. V. 38; 39; 44

PULLEIN, SAMUEL

The Eleventh Epistle of the First Book of Horace, Imitated, and Addressed to a Young Physician Then on His Travels. Dublin: 1749. V. 38

The Silkworn: a Poem. Dublin: 1750. V. 38

PULLEN, H. W.

The Fight at Dame Europa's School Shewing How the German Boy Thrased the French Boy . . . London: 1871. V. 41

PULLEN, SAMUEL

The Culture of Silk: or, an Essay on Its Rational Practice and Improvement . . . London: 1758. V. 46

PULLER, TIMOTHY

The Moderation of the Church of England, Considered as Useful for Allaying the Present Distempers Which the Indisposition of the Time Has Contracted. London: 1679. V. 46

PULLING, ALEXANDER 1813-1895

The Order of the Goif. London: 1884. V. 37; 40

A Practical Treatise on the Laws, Customs, and Regulations of the City and Port of London, as settled by charter, usage, by-law, or statute. London: 1842. V. 37

PULLING, WILLIAM

Sonnets: Written Strictly in the Italian Style. To which is prefixed and Essay on Sonnet-Writing. London: 1840. V. 37

PULMAN, G. P. R.

The Book of the Axe, Containing Piscatorial Description of that Stream and Historical Sketches of all the Parishes. London: 1875. V. 40; 45

Rustic Sketches: Being Rhymes and 'Skits' On Angling, and Other Subjects, In One of the South-Western Dialects . . . London: 1871. V. 42

The Vade-Mecum of Fly-Fishing for Trout . . . London: 1846. V. 43; 45

The Vade Mecum of Fly-Fishing for Trout. London: 1851. V. 39; 40; 43

PULSZKY, FRANCIS

The Tricolor on the Atlas; or, Algeria and the French Conquest. London: 1854. V. 45

White, Red, Black Sketches of American Society in the United States. New York: 1853. V. 40

PULTENEY, R.

Catalogues of the Birds, Shells and Some of the More Rare Plants of Dorsetshire from the New and Enlarged Edition of Mr. Hutchin's History of that County . . . London: 1813. V. 43

PULTENEY, RICHARD

A General View of the Writings of Linnaeus. London: 1781. V. 37

Historical and Biographical Sketches of the Progress of Botany in England from Its Origin to the Introduction of the Linnaean System. London: 1790. V. 37; 38; 42; 44; 46

PULTENEY, WILLIAM

The Budget Opened. London: 1733. V. 42

Considerations on the Present of Public Affairs and the Means of Raising the Necessary Supplies. London: 1779. V. 38; 39; 42; 43; 44

A Short View of the State of Affairs, with Relation to Great Britain, for Four Years Past. London: 1730. V. 38; 43; 45

Thoughts on the Present State of Affairs with America, and the Means of Conciliation. London: 1778. V. 37; 39; 42; 44; 45

PULTON, FERDINANDO

De Pace Regis et Regni, viz. A Treatise Declaring Which be the Great and Generall Offences of the Relame . . . London: 1615. V. 37

PUMPELLY, RAPHAEL 1837-1923

Across America and Asia. New York: 1870. V. 38; 42; 44

Explorations in Turkestan with an Account of the Basin of Eastern Persia and Sistan. Expedition of 1903 . . . (with) Explorations in Turkestan. Expedition of 1904. Washington: 1905/08. V. 46

Explorations in Turkestan, Expedition of 1904; Prehistoric Civilizations of Anau . . . Washington: 1908. V. 44

PUMPHREY, STANLEY

Indian Civilization: a Lecture. Philadelphia: 1877. V. 37; 38; 40; 42; 43

PUNCH'S Almanack for 1848. London: 1848. V. 39

PUNCH'S Merry Pranks: a Little Play for Little People. London. V. 46

PUNGILEONI, P. L.

Memorie Istoriche di Antonio Allegri Detto il Correggio . . . Parma: 1817-21. V. 45

PUPIN, MICHAEL

From Immigrant to Inventor. New York & London: 1923. V. 38

PUPPI, LIONELLO

Andrea Palladio. London: 1975. V. 46

PURCELL and Handel in Bickham's Musical Entertainer. London: 1942. V. 46

PURCELL, HENRY

Dido and Aeneas. An Opera Perform'd at Mr. Josias priest's Boarding-School at Chelsey by Young Gentlewomen. Newark: 1989. V. 41

Orpheus Britannicus . . . London: 1698/1702. V. 44

Orpheus Britannicus. London: 1702. V. 42

Orpheus Britannicus. London: 1706-12. V. 38

The Vocal and Instrumental Musick of the Prophetess, or the History of Dioclesian. London: 1691. V. 40; 42

PURCHAS, SAMUEL 1575?-1626

Hakluytus Posthumus or Purchas His Pilgrimes Contayning a History of the World in Sea Voyages and Lande Travells by Englishmen and Others. Glagow: 1905-07. V. 42

Purchas His Pilgrimage. London: 1613. V. 38; 40; 41; 43; 45

Purchas His Pilgrimage or Relations of the World and the Religions Observed in Al (sic) Ages and Places Discovered from the Creation Unto This Present . . . London: 1614. V. 38; 40

His Pilgrim. Microcosmus, or the Historie of Man. London: 1619. V. 40

His Pilgrimes. (with) His Pilgrimage. London: 1625-26. V. 41

His Pilgrims, or Relations of the World and the Religions Observed in All Age and Places Discoverd from the Creation unto this Present . . . etc. London: 1617. V. 37

Purchas His Pilgrimage or Relations of the World . . . London: 1617. V. 41

Purchas His Pilgrimes . . . London: 1625. V. 45

A Theatre of Politicall Flying-Insects. London: 1657. V. 41

PURDON, H. G.

Memoirs of the Services of the 64th Regt. 1758 to 1881. London: 1881. V. 43

PURDON, WILLIAM

Report of the Secretary of State for India on the Navigation of the Punjab Rivers. London: 1860. V. 38

PURDY, J.

Memoir Descriptive and Explanatory . . . the Northern Atlantic Ocean . . . London: 1845. V. 41

PURDY, JAMES

The Candles of Your Eyes. New York: 1985. V. 41; 42; 46

Color of Darkness. New York: 1956. V. 41; 42

A Day After the Fair. New York: 1977. V. 37; 41; 42; 43

PUTNAM, GEORGE PALMER continued

The Home Book of Picturesque; or American Scenery, Art and Literature . . . New York: 1852. V. 39

The Tourist in Europe; or a Concise Summary of the Various Routes, Objects of Interest, &c. in Great Britain, France, Switzerland, Italy, Germany, Belgium and Holland . . . New York: 1838. V. 46

PUTNAM, H. PHELPS

Trinc - A Book of Poems. New York: 1927. V. 38; 41

PUTNAM, SAMUEL

The World of Jean De Bosschere. London. V. 45

The World of Jean De Bosschere. 1932. V. 43

The World of Jean de Bosschere. London: 1932. V. 37

The World of Jean de Bosschere with a letter by Paul Valery. The Fortune Press. V. 37

PUTNAM'S Library of Choice Stories. Sea Stories. New York: 1858. V. 45

PUTNAM'S Monthly Magazine. New York: July 1857. V. 40

PUTSCHE, CARL WILHELM ERNST

Versuch Einer Monographieder Kartoffeln. Weimer: 1819. V. 40

PUTTE, JOACHIM VAN DEN

Eene(n) Claren Spiegel Der Warachticher Christelijker Maedchen. Antwerp: 1551. V. 44

PUTTENHAM, GEORGE

The Arte of English Poesie. London: 1589. V. 38; 42

PUTTER, JOHN STEPHEN

An Historical Development of the Present Political Constitution of the Germanic Empire. London: 1790. V. 38

PUYVELDE, LEO VAN

Flemish Painting from the Van Eycks to Metsys. New York: 1970. V. 39

PUZO, MARIO

The Dark Arena. New York: 1955. V. 43

PYCROFT, JAMES

The Cricket Field: or, The History and the Science of Cricket. London: 1851. V. 39

PYE, CHARLES

A New Dictionary of Ancient Geography . . . London: 1803. V. 42

PYE, HENRY JAMES

Beauty, a Poetical Essay. London: 1766. V. 42; 45; 46

The Democrat. New York: 1795. V. 40

Faringdon Hill. Oxford: 1774. V. 38

Naucratia; or Naval Dominion. London: 1798. V. 40

Poems on Various Subjects. London: 1787. V. 39

Shooting, a Poem. London: 1784. V. 40; 42

Sportsman Dictionary . . . Riding . . . Hunting . . . etc. London: 1807. V. 38; 45

Summary of the Duties of a Justice of the Peace. London: 1808. V. 43; 45

Summary of the Duties of a Justice of the Peace Out of Sessions, with Some Preliminary Observations. London: 1810. V. 38

PYE, THOMAS

Candian Scenery: District of Gaspe . . . Beautifully Illustrated with Tinted Lithographs, tinted Lithographs, from Photographs by the Author. Montreal: 1866. V. 37

PYKE, E. J.

A Biographical Dictionary of Wax Modellers. Oxford: 1973. V. 42

PYLE, HOWARD

Howard Pyle's Book of Pirates. New York: 1921. V. 42

The Book of Pirates. 1930. V. 46

Howard Pyle's Book of Pirates. Fiction, Fact & Fancy Concerning the Buccaneers & Marooners of the Spanish main . . . Compiled by Merle Johnson. New York/London: 1921. V. 37

Howard Pyle's Book of the American Spirit. New York: 1923. V. 39

Men of Iron. New York: 1892. V. 41

The Merry Adventures of Robin Hood. New York: 1933. V. 41

A Modern Aladdin. New York: 1892. V. 37; 39; 41

Otto of the Silver Hand. New York: 1888. V. 37; 42; 43; 44; 46

Otto of the Silver Hand. New York: 1888. V. 44

Pepper & Salt or Seasoning for Young Folk. New York: 1886. V. 38; 44; 46

The Ruby of Kishmoor. New York: 1908. V. 44; 46

Saint Joan of Arc. New York: (1919). V. 37

The Story of the Champions of the Round TAble. New York: 1905. V. 44

The Wonder Clock or Four and Twenty Marvelous Tales. New York: 1888. V. 46

Yankee Doodle, an Old Friend in a New Dress. New York: 1881. V. 44; 46

PYLE, HOWARDA

The Price of Blood. Boston: 1899. V. 37

PYLE, J. G.

Picturesque St. Paul. St. Paul: 1888. V. 43

PYM, BARBARA 1913-1980

Excellent Women. London: 1952. V. 41; 43

A Glass of Blessings. London: 1958. V. 40; 42

Jane and Prudence. London: 1953. V. 41; 43; 45

Less than Angels. New York. V. 42

Less Than Angels. London: 1955. V. 38; 41; 43; 45

Less than Angels. 1955. V. 37

No Fond Return of Love. London: 1961. V. 40

Quartet in Autumn. London: 1977. V. 40; 41

Quartet in Autumn. London: 1978. V. 42

Some Tame Gazelle. London: 1950. V. 46

PYM, HORACE N.

Odds and Ends at Foxwold. A Guide for the Inquiring Guest. London: 1887. V. 40

A Tour Round My Book-Shelves. London: 1891. V. 42

PYM, JOHN

The Churche's Lamentation for the Good Man His Loose. London: 1644. V. 37; 40; 41; 43; 44

A Discovery of the Great Plot for the Utter Ruine of the City of London, and the Parliament. London: 1643. V. 40

PYNCHON, THOMAS 1937-

The Crying of Lot 49. 1965. V. 44

The Crying of Lot 49. London: 1965. V. 41

The Crying of Lot 49. Philadlephia: 1965. V. 42; 45

The Crying of Lot 49. 1966. V. 46

The Crying of Lot 49. Philadelphia: 1966. V. 37; 38; 39; 41; 42; 43; 44; 45; 46

The Crying of Lot 49. Philadlephia and New York: 1966. V. 39; 40

The Crying of Lot 49. London: 1967. V. 41; 42; 45

Gavity's Rainbow. New York: 1973. V. 37; 38; 39; 40; 42; 43; 44; 45; 46

Gravity's Rainbow. London: 1973. V. 41; 44

V. Philadelphia: 1961. V. 40

V. 1963. V. 43

V. London: 1963. V. 37; 41; 42

V. Philadelphia: 1963. V. 37; 38; 41; 42; 44; 45; 46

V. Philadelphia and New York: 1963. V. 39

Vineland. Boston: 1990. V. 43

PYNE, HENRY R.

The History of the First New Jersey Cavalry. Trenton: 1871. V. 38; 43

PYNE, JAMES BAKER 1800-1870

Lake Scenery of England. London: 1859. V. 37; 40; 41; 43; 45

Mountain, River, Lake and Landscape Scenery of Great Britain. Leeds. V. 40

Windsor, with Its Surrounding Scenery, The Parks, The Thames, Eton College . . . London: 1839. V. 38; 40

PYNE, PERCY R

A Catalogue of Engraved Views Plans &c of New York City. New York: 1912. V. 37

PYNE, THOMAS

Judaca Libera; or, the Eligibility of the Jews. London: 1850. V. 43; 45

PYNE, WILLIAM HENRY 1769-1843

The Costume of Great Britain. London: 1804. V. 39

The Costume of Great Britain. London: 1808. V. 37; 38; 39

The History of the Royal Residence of Windsor Castle, St. James Palace, Carlton House, Kensington Palace, Hampton Court, Buckingham House and Frogmore. London: 1819. V. 39; 40; 41; 42; 43; 44; 45

Lancashire Illustrated, in a Series of Views, Towns, Public Buildings, Streets, Docks, Churches, Antiquities, Abbeys, Castles, Seats of the Nobility &c . . . V. 42; 44; 46

Microcosm; or a Picturesque Delineation of the Arts, Agriculture, Manufactures &c. of Great Britain . . . London: 1806-08. V. 40

Microcosm: or, a Picturesque Delineation of the Arts, Agriculture, Manufactures &c. of Great Britain . . . London: 1822-24. V. 39

On Rustic Figures in Imitation of Chalk. London: 1817. V. 37; 44; 45

Wine and Walnuts; or, After Dinner Chit-Chat. London: 1823. V. 41

PYRARD, FRANCOIS

Voyage . . . Contenant sa Navigation aux Indes Orientales, Maldives, Molques, & au Bresil . . . Paris: 1679. V. 45

Voyages de . . . Contenant sa Navigation Aux Indes Occidentales, Maldives, Moluques, Bresil.. Paris: 1619. V. 40

PYRON DU MARTRE, ANTOINE

The Elements of Heraldry . . . London: 1765. V. 38

PYSENT'S Ghost. London: 1766. V. 37

PYTHAGORAS

The Golden Verses of Pythagoras. N.P.: 1740. V. 41

The Golden Verses of Pythagoras. N.P.: Edinburgh,: 1740. V. 40; 45

Q

QUACKENBOS, JOHN D.

Geological Ancestors of the Brook Trout and Recent Saibling Forms from Which It Evolved. New York: 1916. V. 39; 40; 43

QUAD, M.

Brother Gardner's Lime - Kiln Club: Being the Regular Proceedings of the Regular Club for the Last Three years With Some Philosophy, Considerable Music. 1882. V. 43

Brother Gardner's Lime Kiln Club. Chicago: 1892. V. 39

QUAD, MATTHIAS

Chronica, Oder Zeitregister/ aller Furnemsten Historien und Geschicht/ vom Anfange der Welt/ bis auf das M.D.LXXVI. Jahr. Erfurt: ?1587. V. 39; 40

QUAIFE, MILO MILTON

The Attainment of Statehood. Madison: 1928. V. 46

The Convention of 1846. Madison: 1916. V. 46

The Convention of 1846. Madison: 1919. V. 43

The Development of Chicago 1674-1914 . . . Chicago: 1916. V. 46

The John Askin Papers. Detroit: 1928. V. 44

The Movement for Statehood, 1845-1846. Madison: 1918. V. 46

The Struggle Over Ratification. 1846-1847. Madison: 1920. V. 46

QUAIN, JONES

A Series of Anatomical Plates in Lithography with References and Physiological Comments, Illustrating the Structure of the Different Parts of the Human Body. London: 1836-42. V. 43

QUAIN, RICHARD

A Dictionary of Medicine Including General Pathology, General Therapeutics, Hygiene, and the Diseases Peculiar to Woman and Children. New York: 1884. V. 40; 41; 45; 46

The Diseases of the Rectum. London: 1854. V. 42

QUAKENBOS, JOHN D.

Geological Ancestors of the Brook Trout. 1916. V. 39

THE QUAKER Queries: New England Queries in Past and Present Forms. Boston: 1969. V. 38; 44

QUALE, ERIC

The Collector's Book of Detective Fiction. V. 39

QUARENGHI, GIACOMO 1744-1817

Fabbriche e Disegni di Giacomo Quarenghi Architetto dei S. M. l'Imperatore di Russia . . . Milan: 1821. V. 45

Fabbriche e Disegni . . . Illustrate dal cav. Giulio suo Figlio. Mantua Negretti: 1843-44. V. 37

QUARETTE, The Christmas Annual of the Civil and Military Gazette, by Four Anglo Indian Writers. Lahore: 1885. V. 40

QUARITCH, BERNARD 1819-1899

A Catalogue of Fifteen Hundred Books Remarkable for The Beauty or the Age of Their Bindings or as Bearing Indications of Former ownership by Great Book Collectors and Famous Historical Personages. London: 1889. V. 41; 44

A Catalogue of English and Foreign Bookbindings. London: 1921. V. 39; 40; 41; 44

Contributions Towards a Dictionary of English Book-Collectors. London: 1892-1921. V. 39; 40; 44

Contributions Towards a Dictionary of English Book-Collectors As Also of Some Foreign Collectors Whose Libraries Were Incoporated in English Collections. London: 1892-99. V. 45

Examples of the Art of Book-Illumination Reproduced in Facsimile. (with) Facsimiles of Illustrations in Biblical and Liturgical Manuscripts. (with) Mexican Picture-Chronicle. London: 1889-92-90. V. 38

Facsimiles of Illustrations in Biblical and Liturgical Manuscripts Executed in Various Countries During the XI-XVI Centuries Now in the Possession of Bernard Quaritch. London: 1892. V. 46

Facsimiles of Some Examples of the Art of Book-Ornamentation During the Middle Ages. London: 1900. V. 41

Facsimiles of Some Examples of the Art of Book-Ornamentation During the Middle Ages. London: 1990. V. 44

A General Catalogue of Books, Offered to the Public for Sale at the Affixed Prices. London: 1874. V. 37

Mediaeval Ornamental Alphabets. London: 1900. V. 45

QUARLES' Emblems. London: 1861. V. 45

QUARLES, FRANCES

Divine Poems . . . London: 1633. V. 45

QUARLES, FRANCIS

Argalus and Parthenia . . . London: 1656. V. 45; 46

Boanerges and Barnabas: Judgement and Mercy, Or, Wine and Oil for Wounded and Afflicted Souls. London: 1664. V. 39

Boanerges and Barnabas: Judgment and Mercy or Wine and Oil for Wounded and Afflicted Souls. London: 1674. V. 42

Divine Poems . . . London: 1633. V. 45; 46

Divine Poems. London: 1638. V. 42; 44; 45

Divine Fancies Digested Into Epigrams, Meditations & Observations. London: 1660. V. 38; 41

Divine Poems, Containing the History . . . London: 1674. V. 42

Divine Fancies, Digested Into Epigrams, Meditations, and Observations. London: 1675. V. 42; 44; 46

Divine Poems, Containing the History of Jonah, Esther, Job, Sampson, Together with Sion's Sonnets, Elegies . . . London: 1717. V. 41

Divine Poems. London: 1632. V. 38

Emblemes. London: 1696. V. 39

Emblems. London: 1861. V. 43

Emblems Divine and Moral; Together with Hieroglyphicks of the Life of man. In the Savory: 1718. V. 38

Emblems, Divine and Moral; together with Hieroglyphicks of the Life of Man. London: 1736. V. 37; 39

A Feast for Wormes. London: 1626. V. 40; 43

Institutions, Essays and Maxims, Political, Moral and Divine. London: 1695. V. 46

Judgment and Mercy for Afflicted Souls; or, Meditations, Soliloquies and Prayers. London: 1807. V. 40

The Shepheards Oracle. London: 1646. V. 39

QUARLES, JOHN

Divine Meditations Upon Several Subjects. London: 1679. V. 46

Regale Lectum Miseriae; or, a Kingly Bed of Miserie. London: 1658. V. 37

QUARLL, PHILIP

The Hermit; or the Unparalleled Sufferings and Surprising Adventures of Philip Quarll. London: 1807. V. 43

THE QUARTERLY Review. London: 1809-1840. V. 38

THE QUARTO. An Artistic and Musical Quarterly for 1896. London: 1896. V. 37; 40

QUATERMAIN, L. B.

South to the Pole: the Early History of the Ross Sea Sector, Antarctica. London: 1967. V. 43

QUATREFAGES, A. DE

The Pygmies. London: 1895. V. 46

QUATREMERE, ETIENNE

Catalogue d'une Collection de Livres . . . Paris: 1858-59. V. 38

QUATUOR Sermones. London: 1883. V. 45; 46

QUAYLE, BASIL

General View of the Agriculture of the Isle of Man. London: 1794. V. 40

QUE Meyo se Podera Tomar Pera Extinguir o Iudaismo de Portugal. N.P.: 1630-40. V. 45

QUEBEC, ADELA

The Girls of Radcliff Hall. N.P.. V. 38

QUEBEC and Lower St. Lawrence Tourist's Guide. Quebec: 1875. V. 42

QUEBEC Guide, Comprising an Historical and Descriptive Account of the City and Every Place of Note in the Vicinity . . . Quebec: 1844. V. 44; 45

QUEBEC. LEGISLATIVE ASSEMBLY

Return in Part to An Address from the Legislative Assembly of the 21st Instant, for Certain Papers Relative to Affairs of the Grand Trunk Railway Company; and for a List of the Stockholders of the Grand Trunk Railway Co . . . . Quebec: 1855. V. 45

THE QUEEN City of the South. Natchez Mississippi on Top, Not 'Under the Hill'. Natchez: 1880. V. 44

QUEEN, ELLERY

The Chinese Orange Mystery. 1934. V. 46

The Detective Short Story: a Bibliography. Boston: 1942. V. 38; 40; 46

The Detective Short Story. A Bibliography. New York: 1969. V. 37; 46

The Dragon's Teeth. London: 1939. V. 39

Half Way House. London: 1936. V. 46

QUEEN, ELLERY continued

The Misadventures of Sherlock Holmes. Boston: 1944. V. 37; 41; 42; 43; 44

The Roman Hat Mystery. 1929. V. 46

The Roman Hat Mystery. New York: 1979. V. 39

There Was an Old Woman. Boston: 1943. V. 45

THE QUEEN in the Moon. London: 1820. V. 39

QUEEN Mab's Fairy Realm. Illustrated by H. Cole, A. Garth Jones, H.R. Millar, A. Rackham & R. Savage. London: 1901. V. 37; 40

QUEEN Victoria's Diamond Jubilee at Shanghai. Shanghai: 1897. V. 38; 40

QUEEN Victoria's Dolls. London: 1894. V. 45

THE QUEEN'S Book of the Red Cross. London: 1939. V. 41

THE QUEENS Leying in State Who Departed This Life the 28 Day of December 1694 to the Great Greefe of all Good Subjects . . . London: 1694-5. V. 39

QUEENSBURY, JAMES, DUKE OF

The Articles of the Union as They Pass'd with Amendments in the Parliament of Scotland and Ratify'd by the Touch of the Royal Scepter at Edinburgh, Jan. 16, 1707. London: 1707. V. 43

QUEENY, EDGAR M.

Cheechako. The Story of an Alaskan Bear Hunt. New York: 1941. V. 39; 43; 44

Praire Wings. Pen and Camera Flight Studies. New York: 1946. V. 37; 39; 40; 43; 44; 46

Prairie Wings. Phiadelphia: 1947. V. 38; 41; 43; 45

Prairie Wings: Pen and Camera Flight Studies. Alhambra: 1962. V. 38

QUEER Stories About Animals Told in Rhymes and Jingles. Philadelphia: 1905. V. 39

QUEKETT, ARTHUR S.

The Constitution of Northern Ireland. The origin and Development of the Constitution, Belfast, H.M.S.O., 1928. The Government of Ireland Act, 1920 and subsequent Enactments. Belfast, H.M.S.O., 1933. A Revies of Operations under . . . Belfast: 1946. V. 37

QUENARD

Appercu d'un Plan d'Education Publique. Paris: 1797. V. 38

QUENEAU, RAYMOND

Miro Lithographs II. New York: 1975. V. 44

QUENELL, NANCY

Lovers Progress; Seventeenth Century Lyrics. London: 1938. V. 46

QUENNELL, NANCY

The Epicure's Anthology. London: 1936. V. 37

A Lovers Progress. Waltham St. Lawrence: 1938. V. 41; 46

QUENNELL, PETER

Masques and Poems. Waltham St. Laurence: (1922). V. 37; 38

Poems. London: 1926. V. 37

QUENSTEDT, JOHANN ANDREAS

Dialogue de Patriss Illustrium Doctrina et Scriptis Virorum, Omnium Ordinum Ac Facultatum . . . Wittebergae: 1691. V. 42

QUENTIN, CHARLES, PSEUD.

So Young, My Lord, and True. London: 1878. V. 41

QUERINI, ANGELO MARIA

Primordia Corcyrae. Brescia: 1738. V. 39

THE QUEST. Birmingham: 1894. V. 37

THE QUEST. Volume 1, Nos. 1 to 3 1894/5. Birmingham: Printed at the: 1894/95. V. 41

QUESNAY, FRANCOIS 1694-1774

Traite de la Suppuration. Paris: 1749. V. 44

THE QUESTION about Septennial, or, Frequent New Parliaments, Impartially Explained. Dublin: 1761. V. 41

QUESTION the Beauty . . . Worcester: 1957. V. 44

QUETELET, ADOLPHE

Letters Addressed to H.R.H. the Grand Duke of Saxe Coburg and Gotha, on the Theory of Probabilities, as Applied to the Moral and Political Sciences . . . London: 1849. V. 37

Sur l'Homme, et le Developpement de ses Facultes, our Essai de Physique Sociale. Paris: 1835. V. 38; 41

QUEVEDO, FRANCIESCO

The Dog and the Fever. Hamden: 1954. V. 46

QUEVEDO Y VILLEGAS, FRANCISCO GOMEZ DE

The Life and Adventures of Buscon, the Witty Spaniard. London: 1670. V. 39; 42; 44

Virtud Militante Contra las Quaatro Pestes del Mundo. Saragossa: 1651. V. 37

The Visions. London: 1673. V. 38; 41; 42

The Visions of . . . London: 1678/67. V. 44

QUIBELL, J. E.

Hierakonpolis Parts I-II. London: 1900-02. V. 44

The Ramesseum. London: 1898. V. 44

Teti Pyramid, North Side (Excavations at Saqqara). Le Caire: 1927. V. 42

The Tomb of Hesy. Le Caire: 1913. V. 44

QUICK, ROBERT

A Portfolio of Birds. San Francisco: 1958. V. 44

QUICKENS, QUARLES, PSEUD.

English Notes: Intended for Very Extensive Circulation. Boston: 1842. V. 43

THE QUICKSILVER Mining Company. Charter and By Laws. Reports of the Proceedings at the Annual Meeting of the Stockholders . . . New York: 1864. V. 37

QUIGGIN, E. C.

A Dialect of Donegal, Being the Speech of Meenwannia in the Parish of Glenties. Cambridge: 1906. V. 38

QUIGLEY, HUGH

The Irish Race in California, and on the Pacific Coast. San Francisco: 1878. V. 37; 38; 43

QUILLER-COUCH, ARTHUR THOMAS

Book of Pictures. London: 1913. V. 44

In Powder and Crinoline. London. V. 40

In Powder & Crinoline. London: 1913. V. 37; 38; 39; 40; 44; 45; 46

In Powder and Crinoline. London. V. 37

My Best Book. N.P.: 1912. V. 44

On the Art of Reading. (with) On the Art of Writing. (and) Studies in Literature, First and Second Series. Cambridge: 1921/23/24/23. V. 40

The Oxford Book of English Verse, 1250-1918. Oxford: 1961. V. 44

The Oxford Book of English Verse 1250 - 1900. Oxford: 1919. V. 37

The Sleeping Beauty and Other Fairy Tales from the Old French. London. V. 38

Sleeping Beauty. London: 1910. V. 37; 39; 44; 45; 46

The Sleeping Beauty and Other Fairy Tales From the Old French. Retold by Arthur Quiller-Couch. London: n.d. V. 37

The Twelve Dancing Princesses. New York. V. 43

The Twelve Dancing Princesses and Other Fairy Tales Retold by . . . New York. V. 42

The Tewlve Dancing Princesses and Other Fairy Tales Retold by . . . New York: 1920. V. 41

QUILLER-COUCH, MABEL

A Book of Children's Verse. London: 1911. V. 44; 45; 46

QUILLET, CLAUDE

Callipaediae, or, an Art How to Have Handsome Children . . . London: 1710. V. 39; 40; 43; 46

Callipaedia, seu De Pulchrae Prolis Habendae Ratione, Poema Didacticon. Paris: 1656. V. 45

Callipaedia, &c. et Scaevolae Sammarthani Paedotrophia. Londini: 1709. V. 40

Callipaedia or The Art of Getting Beautiful Children. London: 1733. V. 41; 42

Callipaedia. Los Angeles: 1963. V. 41

QUILLINAN, DOROTHY WORDSWORTH

Journals of a few Months' Residence in Portugal and Glimpses of the South of Spain. London: 1847. V. 45

QUILLINAN, EDWARD

Ball Room Votaries; or, Canterbury and Its Vicinity. London: 1810. V. 45

The Conspirators. London: 1841. V. 37

New Canterbury Tales; or the Glories of the Garrison. London: 1811. V. 37; 40

Poems. London: 1853. V. 39; 42; 46

QUILTER, HARRY

The Photographic Art Journal. Volume 1 March, 1901 to February, 1902. Leicester: 1901. V. 46

Preferences in Art, Life and Literature. London: 1892. V. 38; 40; 42

QUIN, EDWARD

An Historical Atlas, In a Series of Maps as Known at Different Periods . . . London: 1830. V. 39

QUIN, MICHAEL J.

Nourmahal, an Oriental Romance. London: 1838. V. 40; 42; 46

A Steam Voyage Down the Danube. London: 1835. V. 37; 39

A Vist to Spain. London: 1824. V. 38

QUINCEY, THOMAS

A Short Tour in the Midland Counties of England; performed in the summer of 1772. Together with an account of a similar excursion undertaken September 1774. London: 1775. V. 37; 42

QUINCY, JOHN d. 1722

The Dispensatory of the Royal College of Physicians in London. London: 1721. V. 41; 45

Lexicon Physico Medicum; or, a New Physical Dictionary . . . London: 1719. V. 38; 40; 42; 45

Lexicon Physico-Medicum; or, a New Medicinal Dictionary . . . London: 1730. V. 44

Lexicon Physico-Medicum; or, a New Medicinal Dictionary. London: 1757. V. 40

Pharmacopoeia Officinalis & Extemporanea. London: 1736. V. 38; 39; 40; 42

Pharmacoepia Officinalis and Extemporanea . . . London: 1728. V. 42

Pharmacopoeia Officinalis Extemporanea, or . . . London: 1724. V. 41; 46

Pharmacopoeia Officinalis & Extemporanea. London: 1730. V. 40; 41

Pharmacopoeia Officinalis . . . or a Compleat English Dispensatory . . . London: 1749. V. 39

QUINCY, JOSIAH 1772-1864

An Address to the Citizens of Boston, on the XVIIth of September 1830, the Close of the Second Century from the First Settlement of the City. Boston: 1830. V. 38; 40; 41

The History of Harvard University. Cambridge: 1840. V. 40

Memoir of the Life of Josiah Quincy, Jun. of Massachusetts by His Son . . . Boston: 1825. V. 45

Observations on the Act of Parliament, Commonly Called the Boston Port Bill: with Thoughts on Civil Society and STanding Armies. Boston: 1774. V. 40; 41; 43

Observations on the Act of Parliament, Commonly Called the Boston Port-Bill; with Thoughts on Civil Society and Standing Armies. London: 1774. V. 42

Observations on the Act of Parliament Commonly Called the Boston Port-Bill; with Thoughts on Civil Society and Standing Armies. Philadelphia: 1774. V. 37; 38

Speech of . . . on the Passage of the Bill to Enable the People of the Territory of Orleans, to form a Constitution and State Government. Baltimore: 1811. V. 39

QUINCY, SAMUEL

Twenty Sermons . . . Preached in the Parish of St. Philip, Charles Town, South Carolina. Boston: 1750. V. 41

QUINE, W. V. O.

Methods of Logic. New York: 1959. V. 45

QUINER, E. B.

The Military History of Wisconsin a Record of Civil and Military Patriotism of the State, in the War of the Union. Chicago: 1866. V. 39

QUINN, DAVID

The Roanoke Voyages 1584-1590: Documents to Illustrate the English Voyages to North America Under the Patent Granated to Walter Raleigh in 1584. London: 1955. V. 37

QUINN, DAVID BEERS

The Voyages and Colonising Enterprises of Sir Humphrey Gilbert. London: 1940. V. 44

QUINN, EDWARD

Max Ernst. 1977. V. 41

Max Ernst. 1977. V. 45

Max Ernst. Boston: 1977. V. 37; 39

Max Ernst. London: 1977. V. 42

QUINN, ERNST

Max ERnest. London: 1978. V. 44

QUINN, J. M.

Historical and Biographical Record of Southern California. Chicago: 1902. V. 43

QUINN, JOHN

The Library of John Quinn. New York. V. 43

The Library of John Quinn. New York: 1923. V. 38; 40

The Library of John Quinn. New York: 1923-24. V. 38; 41

The Library of John Quinn: Parts I-V. New York: 1924. V. 40; 42

QUINN, JOHN PHILIP

Fools of Fortune or Gambling and Gamblers. Chicago: 1892. V. 43

Gambling and Gambling Devices. Canton: 1912. V. 40; 46

QUINNEY, THOMAS

Sketches of a Soldier's Life in India. Glasgow: 1853. V. 45

QUINTANA, AGUSTIN DE

Doctrina Christiana, y Declaracion de los Principales Mysterios de Nuestra Santa Fee Catholica . . . Puebla: 1729. V. 45

QUINTANA, FRANCISCO DE

The Most Entertaining History of Hippolyto and Aminta . . . London: 1729. V. 39

QUINTANILLA, LUIS

All the Brave. New York: 1939. V. 42

QUINTARD, C. T.

Doctor Quintard: Chaplain C.S.A. and Second Bishop of Tennessee; being His story of the war (1861-1865). 1905. V. 37

QUINTILIAN

Declamationes C.XXXVII . . . Nunc Demum P. Aerodii . . . Studio & Diligentia Castigatae, Scholiis Illustratae, ac in Lucem Postliminio Reuocatae. Paris: 1563. V. 39

The Declamations of . . . Being an Exercitation or Praxis Upon His XII Books . . . London: 1686. V. 42

De Institutione Oratoria Libri Duodecim. Oxford: 1693. V. 45

Institutionum Oratoriarum Libri XII. Venice: 1521. V. 43

Institutionum Oratoriarum, Libri XII. Parisiis: 1542. V. 37; 42; 44

Institutionum Oratoriarum Libri XII. Venice: 1522. V. 45

Oratorum Institutionum Libri XII. (with) Oratoris Eloquentissimi Declamationum Liber. Basle: 1549. V. 41

QUINTILIANUS

The Declamationes . . . London: 1686. V. 37

Institutionum Oratoriarum Libri XII. Paris: 1541. V. 38

QUINTINIE, JEAN DE LA

Instruction Pour les Jardins Fruitiers et Potagers, avec un Traite des Orangers, Suivi de Quelques Reflexions sur l'Agriculture . . . Amsterdam: 1697. V. 39

QUINTINYE, J. DE

The Compleat Gard'ner; or, Directions for Cultivating and Right Ordering of Fruit Gardens and Kitchen Gardens . . . London: 1699. V. 42

QUIRINI, ANGELO MARIA

Liber Singularis de Optimorum Scriptorum Editionibus Quae Romae Primum Prodierunt . . . Lindau: 1761. V. 38

QUIRINO, CARLOS

Philippine Cartography (1320-1899). Amsterdam: 1969. V. 43

QUIROS, PEDRO FERNANDEZ DE

The Voyages of Pedro Fernandez De Quiros, 1595 to 1606. London: 1904. V. 42

QUISENBERRY, ANDERSON C.

Lopez's Expeditions to Cuba 1850 and 1851. Louisville: 1906. V. 39; 40

THE QUIVER of Love: a Collection of Valentines, Ancient and Modern. London: 1876. V. 44
THE QUIVER of Love: a Collection of Valentines Ancient and Modern. London: 1976. V. 42

THE QUIVER of Love. A Collection of Valentines Ancient and Modern. With Illustrations in Colors From Drawings by Walter Crane and K. Greenaway. London/Belfast: 1876. V. 37

QUIZ, JEREMIAH

The Ass of Parnassus and From Scotland, Ge Ho!!. London: 1815. V. 42

QUIZEM, CALEB, PSEUD.

Annals of Sporting. London: 1809. V. 37

QUOID, KATHARINE S.

Maisie Derrick. London: 1892. V. 38

QVEVEDO Y VILLEGAS, FRANCISCO GOMEZ DE

The Comical Works . . . London: 1709. V. 40

QVEVEDO Y VILLEGAS, FRANCISCO GOMEZ DE

Visions Translated from the Spanish of . . . London: 1774. V. 46

R

R., A.

Designs for Church Embroidery. London: 1894. V. 43

Designs for Church Embroidery. London: 1894. V. 45

R., H.

Figures in Rhymes; or, Metrical Computations. Newcastle upon Tyne: 1814. V. 40

R. H. D. Appreciations of Richard Harding Davis. New York: 1917. V. 41; 46

R, J. H.

British Melodies, Containing Some of the Minor Pices, and Other Extracts, From the Works of the Modern Poets . . . Norwich: 1820. V. 39

R., N.

Proverbs, English, French, Dutch, Italian and Spanish . . . London: 1659. V. 43

R., R. H.

Rambles in Istria, Dalmatia and Montenegro. London: 1875. V. 43; 46

R., S.

A Brief and Perfect Relation, of the Answers and Replies of Thomas EArle of Strafford. London: 1647. V. 46

R., W.

A Concise History of Worcester. Worcester: 1808. V. 37; 40

RABAIOTTI, RENATO

Horae Bibliographicae Cantabrigienses. New Castle: 1989. V. 43

RABAN, JONATHAN

Old Glory. London: 1981. V. 38

RABASCO, OTTAVIANO

Il Convito Overo Discorsi di Quelle Materie Che al Convito s'Appartengono . . . V. 43

RABEL, DANIEL

Cartouches de Differantes Inventions, Utiles a Plusieurs Sortes de Persones. Paris. V. 45

Theatrum Florae in Quo Ex toto Orbe Selecti Mirabiles Venustiores ac Praecipui Flores Tanquam Ab Ipsius Deae sinu Proferuntur Lutetiae Parisiorum Apud Nicolaum de Mathoniere . . . V. 42

RABELAIS CLUB

Recreations of the Rabelais Club. 1880-1881 (with 1882-1885 and 1885-1888). Colophon: 1881-8. V. 45

RABELAIS, FRANCOIS 1494?-1553

All the Extant Works. New York: 1929. V. 43

Catalogue of the Choice Books Found by Pantagruel in the Abbey of Saint Victor. Burlingame: 1952. V. 41; 42; 46

Catalogue of The Choice Books Found by Pntagruel in the Abbey of Saint Victor. San Francisco: 1952. V. 38

Les Epistres de Maistre Francois Rabelais . . . Paris: 1651. V. 40

Five Books of the Lives, Heroic Deeds and Sayings of Gargantua and His Son Pantagruel. London: 1892. V. 42; 44; 45

Five Books of the Lives, Heroic Deeds, and Sayings of Gargantua and His Son Pantagruel. London: 1904. V. 40

Gargantua and Pantagruel. New York: 1936. V. 37; 38; 39; 41; 44

Les Horribles et Espovantables Faictz et Prousses du Tres Renomme Pantagruel . . . Paris: 1943. V. 38

The Works of Mr. Francis Rabelais. London. V. 46

Oeuvres. Lyon: 1600. V. 44

Les Oeuvres de Maistre Francois Rabelais . . . Contenant Cinq Livres de Vie, Faicts et Dicts Heroiques de Gargantua & de Son Fils Pantagruel. Paris: 1626. V. 39

The Works of the Famous Mr. Frances Rabelais . . . London: 1644. V. 38

The Works of the Famous Mr. Francis Rabelais . . . London: 1664. V. 43

The Works of F. Rabelais, M.D. or the Lives, Heroic Deeds and Syings of Gargantua and Pantagruel . . . (with) The Second Book of the Works of Mr. Francis Rabelais. Treating of the Heroic Deeds and Sayings of the Good Panatagruel. London: 1694. V. 37

The Works . . . London: 1750. V. 42; 44

Works. London: 1845. V. 42

The Works. London: 1904. V. 41; 42; 46

The Works of . . . Philadlephia: 1920. V. 42

The Works of . . . London: 1921. V. 43

Works. London: 1925. V. 42

The Complete Works of Doctor Francois Rabelais . . . London: 1927. V. 37; 39; 43

The Works . . . London: 1927. V. 43

The Complete Works of Doctor Francois Rabelais. Rendered into English by Sir Thomas Urquhart and Peter Motteux a new introduction by J. Lewis May, and many illustrations by Frank Pape. London/New York: 1927. V. 37

All the Extant Works. New York: 1929. V. 38; 39; 43; 45

The Works . . . London: 1784. V. 38

RABINAL: An Ancient Play of the Quiche Indians of Guatemala. Lexington: 1977. V. 45

RACCOLTA d'Autori Che Trattano del Moto dell'Acque. Florence: 1723. V. 37

RACCOLTA D'Autori Italiani Che Trattano Del Moto Dell'Acque. (with) Nuova Raccolta. Bologna: 1821-29. V. 40

RACCOLTA Di Varii Poemi Latini, e Volgari; Fatti da Diuersi Belissimi Ingegni Nella Felice Vittoria Reportata da Christiani Contra Turchi. Venice: 1572. V. 37

RACCONTO delle Sontuose Esequie Fatte alla Serenissima Isabella, Reina de Spana, nella Chiesa Maggiore della Citta di Milano . . . Milan: 1644. V. 38

RACHFORD, BENJAMIN KNOX 1857-1929

Neurotic Disorders of Childhood . . . New York: 1905. V. 43

RACINE, JEAN 1639-1699

Andromache. A Tragedy as It is Acted at the Duke's Theatre. London: 1675. V. 39

Andromache. Lexington: 1971. V. 38

Andromache: a Tragedy. 1986. V. 40

Andromache: a Tragedy. 1986. V. 45

Andromache: a Tragedy. Lexington: 1986. V. 46

Andromaque. Lexington: 1985-86. V. 44

Oeuvres. Amsterdam: 1690. V. 40

Oeuvres. Paris: 1885-1890. V. 44

RACINE, JEAN BAPTISTE 1639-1699

Oeuvres. Paris: 1807. V. 39

RACINET, ALBERT

Polychromatic Ornament . . . London: 1877. V. 40; 44

RACINET, AUGUSTE

Le Costume Historique. Paris: 1888. V. 45

L'Ornement Polychrome. Paris: 1869-87. V. 45

RACINET, M. A.

Le Costume Historique. Paris: 1888. V. 43

L'Ornement Polychrome Cent Planches en Couleurs Or et Argent Contenant Environ 2000 Motifs do Tous les Styles Art Ancient et Asiatique Moyen Age Renaissance XVIIe et XVIIIe Siecle. Paris. V. 41

RACING at Home and Abroad. London: 1923/27/31. V. 39
RACING at Home and Abroad. London: 1923-31. V. 42

RACK, EDMUND

Essays, Letters and Poems. (bound with) Mentor's Letters, Addressed to Youth. Bath: 1781, 1778. V. 38

RACKHAM, ARTHUR 1867-1939

The Allies' Fairy Book. London: 1916. V. 40; 41

Arthur Rackham's Book of Pictures. London: 1913. V. 37; 38; 40; 41; 44; 46

Arthur Rackham's Book of Pictures. London: 1927. V. 43

The Arthur Rackham Fairy Book. 1933. V. 40

The Arthur Rackham Fairy Book. London: 1933. V. 38; 40; 44

The Arthur Rackham Fairy Book. Philadelphia: 1933. V. 46

The Arthur Rackham Fairy Book. London: 1933. V. 37; 41

Catalog of the First American Exhibition of Water Colour Drawings by Arthur Rackham. New York: 1919. V. 42

Cinderella. Retold by C.S. Evans. London: (1919). V. 37

Costume through the Ages. London: 1938. V. 41

A Fairy Book. New York: 1923. V. 40

Land of Enchantment. London: 1907. V. 37

Mother Goose, The Old Nursery Rhymes. London: 1913. V. 43

Mother Goose. The Old Nursery Rhymes. New York: 1913. V. 37

Peter Pan Pictures from Peter Pan In Kensington Gardens. London: 1907. V. 46

RACKHAM, ARTHUR 1867-1939 continued

Some British Ballads. London: 1919. V. 37; 40; 41; 44

Some British Ballads. London: (1918). V. 37

Three Drawings by Arthur Rackham from Peter Pan in Kensington Gardens. London?: 1906. V. 39

L'Oeuvre de Arthur Rackham. Paris: 1913. V. 41

RACKHAM, BERNARD

The Ancient Glass of Canterbury Cathedral. 1949. V. 42

The Ancient Glass of Canterbury Cathedral. London: 1949. V. 41; 43; 46

A Book of Porcelain. London: 1905. V. 42

Catalogue of the Herbert Allen Collection of English Porcelain. London: 1917. V. 38

Early Netherlands Maiolica with Special Reference to the Tiles at the Vyne in Hampshire. London: 1926. V. 37; 41

English Pottery. Its Development from Early Times to the End of the Eighteenth Century. London: 1924. V. 46

RACKSTROW, BENJAMIN

An Explanation of the Figure of Anatomy, Wherein the Circulation of the Blood is Made Visible thro' Glass Veins and Arteries. London: 1747. V. 43; 44

RADAU, HUGO

Letter to Cassite kings from the Temple Archives of Nippur. Philadelphia: 1908. V. 37; 40; 42; 44

RADCLIFF, T.

Authentic Letters from Upper Canada . . . Dublin: 1833. V. 42

RADCLIFFE, ALEXANDER

Ovid Travestie, a Burlusque upon Several of Ovid's Epistles. London: 1680. V. 38; 41

Ovid Travesty, a Burlesque upon Ovid's Epistles. Dublin: 1760. V. 44

Ovid Travestie - a Burlesque Upon Ovid's Epistles. 1889. V. 38

The Ramble; an Anti-Heroick Poem. London: 1682. V. 38; 39; 42; 44; 46

RADCLIFFE, ANN 1764-1823

The Castles of Athlin and Dunbayne. London: 1793. V. 37; 39; 40; 41; 42; 43; 45; 46

Gaston de Blondeville, or the Court of Henry III. London: 1826. V. 38; 41; 42; 44

Gaston de Blondeville, or, the Court of Henry III. London: 1839. V. 46

The Italian, or, the Confessional of the Black Penitents. Dublin: 1797. V. 40

The Italian. London: 1797. V. 37; 39; 41; 42; 44; 45; 46

A Journey Made in the Summer of 1794, Through Holland and the Western Frontier of Germany . . . Dublin: 1795. V. 44

The Mysteries of Udolpho. London: 1794. V. 37; 38; 39; 40; 42; 45; 46

The Mysteries of Udolpho. London: 1803. V. 39

The Mysteries of Udolpho, a Romance. London: 1823. V. 45; 46

The Romance of the Forest. London: 1791. V. 43; 44

The Romance of the Forest: Interspersed with Some Pieces of Poetry. Dublin: 1792. V. 38; 45

The Romance of the Forest. London: 1794. V. 40; 42

The Romance of the Forest. London: 1796. V. 46

The Romance of the Forest . . . London: 1799. V. 41

A Sicilian Romance. London: 1792. V. 40

The Southern Tower; or, Conjugal Sacrifice and Retribution. London: 1802. V. 43

RADCLIFFE, CHARLES

Genuine and Impartial Memoirs of the Life and Character of Charles Ratcliffe, Esq. Who Was Beheaded on Tower Hill, Monday, December 8, 1746. With an Account of His Family, and How Far He was Concerned in the Rebellion in 1715 . . . London: 1746. V. 38

RADCLIFFE, F. P. DELME 1804-1875

The Noble Science: A Few General Ideas on Fox-Hunting, for the Use of the Rising Generation of Sportsmen. London: 1875. V. 39

The Noble Science. London: 1893. V. 38; 39

The Noble Science. London: 1911. V. 37; 38; 39; 40; 44

The Noble Science: a Few General Ideas on Fox-Hunting. London: 1839. V. 37; 38; 41

RADCLIFFE, JOANNES

Bibliotheca Chethamensis, Sive Bibliothecae Publicae mancuniensis Catalogus. Manchester: 1791. V. 40

RADCLIFFE, JOHN

Dr. RAdcliffe's Life and Letters . . . London: 1716. V. 44

Dr. Radcliffe's Life, and Letters, with a True Copy of His Last Will and Testament. Dublin: 1724. V. 44

Pharmacopoeia Radcliffeana; or, Dr. Radcliff's Prescriptions, Faithfully Gather'd from His Original Recipe's. London: 1716. V. 42

RADCLIFFE, MARY ANNE

Manfrone; or, the One Handed Monk. London: 1809. V. 42

Radzivil. London: 1790. V. 45

RADCLIFFE, RICHARD

The President's Tour. New Ipswich: 1822. V. 44

RADCLYFFE, C. R. E.

Big Game Shooting in Alaska. London: 1904. V. 38; 43

RADCLYFFE, C. W.

Memorials of Charterhouse, a Series of Original Views Taken and Drawn on Stone. London: 1844. V. 41

Memorials of Rugby, Drawn from Nature and on Stone . . . Rugby, Cambridge, Oxford: 1843. V. 41

RADCLYFFE-HALL, MARGUERITE

Poems of the Past and Present. London: 1910. V. 38

RADEMAKER, ABRAHAM

Hollands Arcadia, of de Vermaarde River Den Amstel. Amsterdam: 1730. V. 42

RADER, J. L.

South of Forty from the Mississippi to the Rio Grande. Norman: 1947. V. 37; 40; 41

RADER, MATTHAEUS 1561-1634

Petri Siceli Historia ex Codice Bibliothecae Vaticanae. Ingolstadt: 1604. V. 43

RADFORD, CYRUS S.

Handbook of Naval Gunnery . . . New York: 1898. V. 42

RADFORD, DOLLIE

Songs for Somebody. London: 1893. V. 43

RADFORD, ERNEST

Old and New. London: 1895. V. 42; 43

RADFORD, GEORGE

Yorkshire by the Sea. Leeds: 1891. V. 41

RADFORD, W.

On the Construction of the Ark, as Adapted to the Naval Architecture of the Present Day. London: 1840. V. 37; 39; 42; 45

RADI, BERNARDINO

Varie Inventione per Depositi. Rome: 1625. V. 45

THE RADICAL Review. London: 1877. V. 41

RADICAL Rule: Military Outrage in Georgia. Louisville: 1868. V. 44

RADISSON, PIERRE ESPRIT

Voyages of Peter Esprit Radisson, Being an Account of His Travels and Experiences Among the North American Indians from 1652 to 1684. Boston: 1885. V. 43

RADIUS, J. S. C. DE

Condensed Historical Notice of the Languages of the Slavic Nations. London: 1853. V. 43

RADSTOCK, WILLIAM WALDEGRAVE, 1ST BARON

The British Flag Triumphant! London: 1806. V. 44

RAE, COLIN

Malaboch, or Notes from My Diary on the Boer Campaign of 1894 Against the Chief Malaboch of Blaauwberg, District Zoutpansberg, South African Republic. London: 1898. V. 41

RAE, EDWARD

The Country of the Moors. London: 1877. V. 46

The White Sea Peninsula, a Journey in Russian Lapland and Karelia. London: 1881. V. 37; 44

RAE, GEORGE 1817-1902

The Country Banker: His Clients, Cares and Work . . . London: 1885. V. 41

RAE, JOHN

John Rae's Correspondence with the Hudson's Bay Company on Arctic Exploration 1844-1855. London: 1953. V. 43; 45

New Adventures of 'Alice'. Chicago: 1917. V. 45

Rae's Arctic Correspondence 1844-55. London: 1953. V. 43

RAE, JULIO H.

Rae's Philadelphia Pictorial Directory and Panormaic Advertiser. Philadelphia: 1851. V. 42

RAE, PETER

The History of the Late Rebellion: Rais'd Against His Majesty King George. Dumfries: 1718. V. 43

RAE, WILLIAM FRASER 1835-1905

Newfoundland to Manitoba. London: 1881. V. 39

Newfoundland to Manitoba through Canada's Maritime, Mining and Prairie Provinces. New York: 1881. V. 46

Westward by Rail: a Journey to San Francisco and Back and a Visit to the Mormons. London: 1871. V. 39

RAEL, JOHANNES DE

Clavis Philosophiae Naturalis, seu Introductio ad Naturae Contemplationem, Aristotelico-Cartesiana. Leiden: 1654. V. 46

RAEMAEKER, LOUIS

The Century Edition Deluxe of Raemaekers' War Cartoons. New York: 1917. V. 44

RAEMAEKERS, LOUIS

The Great War: A Neutral's Indictment. (With) The Great War: Victory Volume. London: 1916-19. V. 38

RAEMAKERS, LOUIS

The Great War. London: 1916. V. 40

RAFFALD, ELIZABETH 1733-1781

The Experienced English Housekeeper, for the Use and Ease of Ladies, Housekeepers, Cooks & Etc. London: 1773. V. 39

Experienced English Housekeeper, For the Use and Ease of Ladies, Housekeepers, Cooks &c. . . . . Consisting of near Nine Hundred Original Receipts, most of which never appeared in Print. London: 1776. V. 39

The Experienced English Housekeeper for the Use and Ease of Ladies, Housekeepers, Cooks &c. London: 1780. V. 42; 45

The Experienced English Housekeeper. London: 1786. V. 38

The Experienced English Housekeeper, for the Use and Ease of Ladies, Housekeepers, Cooks &c. London: 1789. V. 41

The Experienced English Housekeeper . . . for the Use and Ease of Ladies, Housekeepers, Cooks, etc. Dedicated to the Hon. Lady Elizabeth Warburton, whom the Author lately served as Housekeeper. Consisting of Several Hundred . . . London: 1806. V. 37

The Experienced English Housekeeper for the Use and Ease of Ladies . . . . London: 1791. V. 46

RAFFALOVICH, MARK ANDRE

Tuberose and Meadowsweet. London: 1885. V. 37

RAFFLES, SOPHIA

Memoir of the Life and Public Services of Sir Thomas Stamford Raffles, F.R.S. &c. London: 1830. V. 41

RAFFLES, THOMAS STAMFORD

Antiquarian, Architectural and Landscape Illustrations of the History of Java. London: 1844. V. 39

The History of Java. London: 1817. V. 40

The History of Java. (with) Atlas, Antiquarian, Architectural and Lanscape Illustrations of the History of Java. London: 1830/1844. V. 39

RAFINESQUE, CONSTANTINE SAMUEL

The American Nations; or, Outlines of Their General History, Ancient and Modern. Philadelphia: 1836. V. 38

Ancient History, or Annals of Kentucky. Frankfort: 1824. V. 37; 40; 45

The Complete Writings . . . on Recent & Fossil Conchology. New York: London: 1864. V. 43

Medical Flora; or, Manual of the Medical Botany of the United States of North America. Philadelphia: 1828-30. V. 37; 38

RAFIULLAH, MOHAMMAD

Gwailor's Part in the War. 1920. V. 44

RAFN, C. C.

Antiquitates Americanae Sive Scriptores Septentrionales Rerum Ante-Columbianarum in America . . . Copenhagen: 1387. V. 41

Antiquitates Americanae Sive Scriptores Septentrionales Rerum Ante-columbianarum in America . . . Hafnie: 1837. V. 41; 44

Antiqvitates Americanae Sive Scriptores Septentrionales Rerum Ante-Columbianarum in America . . . Copenhagen: 1837. V. 41

R.A.G., 1900-1973. San Francisco: 1973. V. 46

RAGAN, ROBERT H.

Escape From East Tennessee to the Federal Lines. The History, Given as Nearly as Possible by Captain R.A. Ragan of His Indivdual Experiences During the War of the Rebellion from 1861 to 1864. Washington: 1910. V. 38

RAGGETT, JOHN JAMES

A Series of Plans for Single-Fronted Residences with Quantities for Estimating Their Approximate Cost . . . (and) Plans for Intermediate and Double-Fronted Residences . . . Birmingham: 1900. V. 38; 44

RAGSDALE, FRANCIS A.

Pictorial Roster of Camp Barrett and Vancouver Barracks. Vancouver: 1898. V. 42

RAGUET, CONDY

An Inquiry Into the Causes of the Present State of the Circulating Medium of the United States. Phidelphia: 1815. V. 42

RAHT, CARLYSLE GRAHAM

The Romance of Davis Mountains and Big Bend Country. El Paso: 1919. V. 37; 38; 39; 41; 42; 43; 44; 46

RAHTER, ETHEL ZIVLEY

Dewitt's Colony. Austin: 1905. V. 37

RAIKES, CHARLES

Notes on the Revolt of the North Western Provinces of India. London: 1858. V. 40

RAIKES, G. A.

The Ancient Vellum Book of the Honourable Artillery Company. London: 1890. V. 41

The History of the Honourable Artillery Company. London: 1878. V. 46

RAIKES, RICHARD

Considerations on the Alliance Between Christianity and Commerce, Applied to the Present State of This Country. London: 1806. V. 46

RAIKES, THOMAS

A Portion of the Journal, 1831 to 1847; Comprising Reminiscences of Social and Political Life in London and Paris During that Period. London: 1856-57. V. 38; 39

A Portion of the Journal Kept by Thomas Raikes, Esq. from 1831 to 1847 . . . London: 1856-58. V. 37; 42

RAILEY, WILLIAM EDWARD

History of Woodford County. Frankfort: 1938. V. 43

THE RAILROAD and Steam-Packet Guide; Containing the Times of Departure of the Trains on the London and Birmingham, the Great Western, the Eastern Counties, the Northern and Eastern, the London and Brighton, the London and Croydon, the London and Greenwich . . . London: 1842. V. 38

RAILROAD Communication with the Pacific. With an Account of the Central Pacific Railroad of California . . . New York: 1867. V. 37; 40

RAILROAD Ribaldry being 96 Pages of Railway Humour. London: 1935. V. 41

RAILROADS Through the Indian Territory. Washington: 1870. V. 37

RAILWAY AGE

Recent Locomotives. New York: 1883. V. 39

RAILWAY Posters and the War Reprinted from the Railway Gazette, Nos. 1-6. London: 1939-43. V. 37

RAIMBACH, ABRAHAM

Memoirs and Recollections of the Late Abraham Raimbach, Esq., . . . London: 1843. V. 38; 39; 40; 44

RAIMO, JOHN W.

A Guide to Manuscripts Relating to America in Great Britain and Ireland. London: 1979. V. 40

RAIMONDI, EVGENIO

Delle Caccie Di . . . Bresciano Libri Quattro Aggiuntovi 'n Questa Nuova 'Mpressione Il Quinto Libro della Villa. Napoli: 1626. V. 38

RAINBIRD, GEORGE

An Illustrated Guide to Wine. London: 1983. V. 43

THE RAINBOW. Albany & New York: 1848. V. 43

RAINE, CRAIG

The Prophetic Book: Ksiega Proroctw; a Poem in Seven Parts. Lodz: 1989. V. 45

RAINE, JAMES

A Brief Historical Account of the Epsicopal Castle, or Palace, of Auckland. Durham: 1852. V. 38

Catterick Church, in the County of York. London: 1834. V. 45

Saint Cuthbert. Durham: 1828. V. 37; 38; 40

RAINE, KATHLEEN

Blake and Tradition. Princeton: 1968. V. 42

Blake and Tradition. The A. W. Mellon Lectures in the Fine Arts. Washington: 1968. V. 42

Blake and Traditions. London: 1969. V. 39

The Lost Country. Dublin & London: 1971. V. 41

RAINE, KATHLEEN continued

The Lost Country. London: 1971. V. 39

A Place, a Sate - a Suite of Drawings by Julian Trevelyan with Commentary By Kathleen Raine. London: 1974. V. 44

Selected Poems. New York: 1952. V. 41; 42; 46

Six Dreams and Other Poems. London: 1968. V. 41

Stone and Flower. Poems 1935-43. London: 1945. V. 42

RAINE, WALTER

Bird-Nesting in North-West Canada. Toronto: 1892. V. 44

RAINE, WILLIAM MAC LEOD

A Daughter of Raasay. New York: 1902. V. 37

RAINES, C. W.

An Analysis of C. W. Raines' Bibliography of Texas. Waco: 1962. V. 45

A Bibliography of Texas. Austin: 1896. V. 38; 39; 40; 42; 44; 45

Speeches and State Papers of James Stephen Hogg. Austin: 1905. V. 44

RAINEY, GEORGE

The Cherokee Strip. Guthrie: 1933. V. 42; 43; 45

RAINOLDES, JOHN

Th'overthrow of Stage-Playes . . . Middelburg: 1599. V. 45

RAINOLDS, JOHN

De Romanae Ecclesiae. Oxford: 1596. V. 37

The Overthrow of Stage Plays. Oxford: 1629. V. 37

RAINOLDS, WILLIAM

Calvino-Tvrcismvs: Id Est, Calvinisticae Perfidiae Cvm Mahvmetana Collatio, et Dilvcida Vtrivsqve Sectae Confvtatio. Antverpiae: 1597. V. 40

De Ivsta Reipbv. Christianae in Reges Impios et Haereticos Avthoritate . . . Antwerp: 1592. V. 42

RAINSFORD, MARCUS

An Historical Account of the Black Empire of Hayti. London: 1805. V. 37; 39; 40

RAISTRICK, ARTHUR

Quakers in Science and Industry. London: 1950. V. 45

Two Centuries of Industrial Welfare. London: 1938. V. 45

RAITHBONE, HANNAH MARY

So Much of the Diary of Lady Willoughby as Relates to Her Domestic History, and to the Eventful Period of the Reign of Charles the First. London: 1844. V. 38

RAITHBY, JOHN 1766-1826

The Law and Principle of Money Considered in a Letter to W. Huskisson, Esq. M.P. London: 1811. V. 38; 41

The Study and Practice of the Law Considered in Their Various Relations to Society. Portland: 1806. V. 40; 41

THE RAKE'S Progress; Giving an Account of a Wealth Farmer's Son Who was ruined in a Noted Bad-House. London: 1830. V. 46

RAKOWSKY, MARTIN d. 1579

Libellus, de Partiobus Reipub(licae); et Clavis Mutationum Regnorum Imperiorumq(ue) . . . Vienna: 1560. V. 40

RALEIGH & GASTON RAILROAD CO.

Proceedings of the Fourteenth Annual Meeting of the Stockholders of the Raleigh & Gaston Railroad Company, With the Repots (sic) of the President, Treasurer, &c. Raleigh: 1864. V. 44

RALEIGH, WALTER 1552-1618

An Abridgement of Sir Walter Raleigh's History of the World. London: 1698. V. 45

An Abridgement of Sir Walter Raleigh's History of the World. London: 1702. V. 46

The Cabinet Council. London: 1658. V. 37

A Declaration of the Demeanor and Carriage of Sir Walter Raleigh, Knight, as Well in His Voyage, As In and Since, His Return . . . London: 1618. V. 44; 46

The Discoverie of the Large and Beautiful Empire of Guiana. London: 1928. V. 37; 44; 45

Discoverie of the Large, Rich and Beautiful Empyre of Guiana, with a Relation of the Great and Golden Citie of Manoa . . . London: 1596. V. 38

The Discovery of the . . . Empire of Guiana, with a Relation of the Great and Golden City of Manoa . . . Performed in the Year 1595. London: 1848. V. 45; 46

The Historie of the World. Colophon: 1644. V. 43

The Historie of the World. London: (1934). V. 37

The History of the World. London: 1614. V. 46

The History of the World. London: 1621. V. 42

The History of the World. London: 1652. V. 45

The History of the World, in Five Books. London: 1677. V. 38; 40; 43; 44

The History of the World in Five Books. London: 1697. V. 46

The History of the World. London: 1736. V. 38; 40; 43; 44

Instructions for Youth, Gentlemen and Noblemen. London: 1722. V. 40

Instructions for Youth, Gentlemen and Noblemen. London: 1722. V. 39

Judicious and Select Essayes and Observations, by the Renowned and Learned Knight, Sir Walter Raleigh. London: 1650. V. 40; 42

The Marrow of Historie, or an Epitome of all Historical Passages from the Creation to the End of the Last Macedonian War. London: 1650. V. 38

Maxims of State. London: 1650. V. 42

Maxims of State. Whereunto is Added His Instructions to His Sonne. London: 1751. V. 38

The Ocean to Cynthia, His Autographic Poems. Omaha: 1984. V. 37; 39

Papers Relating to the Claims of Francisco De Avila of Seville AGainst Sir Walter Raleigh for the Loss of His Merchandise in Guiana. London: or Seville: 1618-21. V. 44

The Perogative of Parliaments in England. London: 1640. V. 38; 42

The Poems of Sir Walter Raleigh. Kent: 1813. V. 40

The Poems. London: 1814. V. 38; 40

The Prerogative of Parliaments in England; Proved in a Dialogue (Pro & Contra) Betweene a Councellour of State and a Justice of Peace. Hamburgh: 1628. V. 43

The Prerogative of Parliaments in England. Midelburge: 1628. V. 40

The Prerogative of Parliaments in England. Middleburg: 1628 and 1640. V. 41

The Prince, or maxims of state. Written by Sir Walter Rawley and presented to Prince Henry. London: 1642. V. 37

Reliquiae Raleighianae, Being Discourses and Sermons on Several Subjects. London: 1679. V. 45

A Report of the Truth Concerning the Last Sea Fight of the Revenge. Cambridge: 1902. V. 37; 42; 45

Six Essays on Johnson. Oxford: 1910. V. 40

Three Discourses of Sr. Walter Ralegh. I. Of a War with Spain, and Our Protecting the Netherlands. II. Of the Original, and fundamental cause of Natural, Arbitrary and Civil War. III. Of Ecclesiastical Power. London: 1702. V. 39; 43; 46

The Works . . . Political, Commercial and Philosophical; Together with His Letters and Poems. London: 1751. V. 42

RALEIGH, WALTER A.

The War in the Air. Oxford: 1922-1931. V. 38

RALEY, DOROTHY

A Century of Progress Homes and Furnishings. Chicago: 1934. V. 45

RALFE, JAMES

The Battle of Navarin, Compared with Other Important Naval Events. London: 1829. V. 37

The Naval Chronology of Great Britain; or, an Historical Account of Naval and Maritime events . . . London: 1820. V. 39; 45; 46

RALFE, P. G.

The Birds of the Isle Of Man. Edinburgh: 1903. V. 46

The Birds of the Isle of Man. Edinburgh: 1905. V. 40

The Birds of the Isle of Man. (with) Supplementary Notes to The Birds . . . Edinburgh: 1905/1923. V. 44

RALFS, J.

The British Desmidieae. London: 1848. V. 37; 46

RALLING, JOHN

Miscellanies, viz. I. The Time-Piece; or, an Honest Servant's Advice to His Master. II. Verses on the Month of May. III. An Affectionate Father's Dying Advice. Philadelphia: 1790. V. 37

RALPH, BENJAMIN

The School of Raphael . . . London: 1782. V. 42

RALPH, JAMES 1705?-1762

The Case of Authors by Profession or Trade Stated. London: 1758. V. 43; 45; 46

The Case of Our Present Theatrical Disputes, Fairly Stated. London: 1743. V. 37

The Conduct of the Late Administration With Regard to Foreign Affairs from 1722 to 1742, Wherein the Right Honble. the Earl of Orford (Late Sir Robert Walpole) is Particularly Vindicated: In a Letter to a Certain . . . Member of the Present Parliament. London: 1742. V. 41; 46

A Critical Review of the Public Buildings, Statues and Ornaments in and About London and Westminster. London: 1734. V. 37; 41

The Muses' Address to the King: an Ode. London: 1728. V. 38; 45; 46

Night: a Poem. London: 1728. V. 38; 41; 45

Of the Use and Abuse of Parliaments; in Two Discourses, viz. I: A General View of Government in Europe. II: A Detection of the Parliaments of England from the Year 1660. London: 1744. V. 38

The Other Side of the Question. London: 1742. V. 39; 41; 42; 46

The Taste of the Town. London: 1731. V. 37; 38; 46

RALPH, JAMES 1705?-1762 continued

The Touch-Stone; or, Historical, Critical, Political, Philosophical and Theological Essays on the Reigning Diversions of the Town . . . London: 1728. V. 42

Zeuma: or the Love of Liberty. London: 1729. V. 38

RALPH, JOSEPH

A Domestic Guide to Medicine. New York: 1835. V. 37

RALPH, JULIAN

On Canada's Frontier. New York: 1892. V. 39; 40; 41; 45

RALPH; or I Wish He Wasn't Black. Hopedale: 1855. V. 39

RALPH Webster Yarborough at 80. A Gathering of Tributes from Several of His Book Loving Friends. Austin: 1984. V. 37

RALSTON, W.

North Again. Golfing this Time. London: 1894. V. 38; 45

Tippoo: A Tale of a Tiger. London. V. 43

RALSTON, WILLIAM

Tibetan Tales devired from Indian Sources. Translated from the Tibetan of the Kay-Gyur (by) F. Anton von Schiefner. London: 1882. V. 37

RALSTON, WILLIAM CHAPMAN

Ralston (cover title). Memorial of William C. Ralston. San Francisco: 1875. V. 45

RAMADGE, FRANCIS HOPKINS

Consumptuion Curable; and the Manner in Which Nature as Well as Remedial Art Operates in Effecting a Healing Process in Cases of Consumption. New York: 1839. V. 46

Consumption Curable; and the Manner in Which Nature as Well as Remedial Art operates in Effecting a Healing Process in Cases of Consumption. London: 1836. V. 38

RAMALHO ORTIGAO, JOSE DUARTE

Notas de Viagem 1878-1879. Rio de Janeiro: 1879. V. 38

RAMAN, C. V.

Molecular Diffraction of Light. Calcutta: 1922. V. 38

RAMAZZINI, BERNARDINO

A Treatise on the Diseases of Tradesmen Shewing the Various Influence of Particular Trades Upon the State of Health . . . London: 1705. V. 45; 46

RAMBAUD, ALFRED

History of Russia; From earliest Times to 1880. Translated by L.B. Lang. Boston: (1879). V. 37

A RAMBLE Thro' Hyde-Park; or, the Humours of the Camp, a Poem. London: 1722. V. 38; 42

RAMBLES in the Deserts of Syria and Among the Turkomans and Bedaweens. London: 1864. V. 46

RAMBLES through Our Country. An Instructive Geographical Game for the Young. Hartford: 1881. V. 41

RAMEAU, JEAN PHILIPPE

Generation Harmonique, ou Traite de Musique Theorique et Pratique. Paris: 1737. V. 40

RAMEAU, JEAN PHILLIPPE

Les Fetes d'Hebe ou les Talents Liriques. Paris: 1739. V. 40; 43

RAMEL, JEAN PIERRE

Memoirs of Adj. Gen. Ramel . . . Norwich: 1805. V. 42

Relation de la Deportation a Cayenne des Citoyens Barthelemy, Pichegru, Willot, La Rue, &c. Hambourg: 1799. V. 37; 38

RAMELLI, AGOSTINO

Le Diverse et Artificiose Machine.. Paris: 1588. V. 37; 38; 40

The Various and Ingenious Machines (1588). London: 1979. V. 37

RAMESAY, WILLIAM

The Gentlemans Companion. London: 1672. V. 39

The Gentleman's Companion. London: 1676. V. 40; 41

The Gentleman's Companion; or, a Character of True Nobility, and Gentility . . . London: 1719. V. 41

RAMEY, EARL

The Beginnings of Marysville. San Francisco: 1936. V. 40; 46

RAMIE, GEORGES

Picasso's Ceramics. New York. V. 43; 45; 46

RAMIREZ DE PRADO, LORENZO

Pentakontarchos, Sive Quinquaginta Militum Ductor. Antwerp: 1612. V. 40

RAMON, THOMAS

Nueva Prematica de Reformacion, Contra los Abusos de los Afeytes, Calcado, Guedejas, Guarda-Infantes, Lenguage Critico, Monos, Trajes: y excesso en el uso del Tabaco. Saragossa: 1635. V. 37

RAMON Y CAJAL, S.

Degeneration and Regeneration of the Nervous System. New York: 1959. V. 42

Histology. Baltimore: 1933. V. 42

Studies on the Cerebral Cortex. Springfield: 1955. V. 42

RAMON Y CAJAL, SANTIAGO

Les Nouvelles Idees sur la Structure du Systeme Nerveux Chez l'Homme et Chez les Vertebres. Paris: 1894. V. 43

Textura del Sistem a Nervioso del Hombre s de los Vertebrados . . . Madrid: 1899-1904. V. 45

RAMOND DE CARBONNIERRES, LOUIS FRANCOIS ELISABETH, BARON

Travels in the Pyrenees. London: 1813. V. 42

RAMOS ARIZPE, JOSE MIGUEL

Memoria que el Doctor D. Miguel Ramos de Arispe . . . *Sobre el Estado Natural, Politico, y Civil de su Dicha Provincia* . . . Cadiz: 1812. V. 42

RAMPA, T. LOBSANG

The Third Eye. London: 1945. V. 39

RAMPANT LIONS PRESS

The Rampant Lions Press Miscellany. Cambridge: 1988. V. 42; 45

THE RAMPANT Lions Press: A Printing Workshop Through Five Decades. Cambridge: 1982. V. 40; 41

RAMPEGOLIIS, ANTONIUS DE

Biblia Aurea. Ulm: 1475. V. 39

RAMSAY, A. C.

The Geology of the Island of Arran, from Original Survey. Glasgow: 1841. V. 38

RAMSAY, A. MAITLAND

Eye Injuries and Their Treatment. Glasgow: 1907. V. 42

RAMSAY, ALEXANDER

Anatomy of the Heart, Cranium and Brain . . . *(with) A Series of Plates of the Heart, Cranium and Brain* . . . Edinburgh: 1813. V. 43

RAMSAY, ALLAN 1686-1758

The Ever Green. Edinburgh: 1724. V. 38; 39; 41; 42; 43; 45

The Ever Green, Being a Collection of Scots Poems, Wrote by the Ingenious Before 1600. Edinburgh: 1761. V. 40; 42; 45

The Ever Green. Glasgow: 1874. V. 39

The Gentle Shepherd: A Scots Pastoral Comedy. Edinburgh: 1764. V. 39

The Gentle Shepherd: a Scots Pastoral Comedy Adorn'd with Cuts . . . Edinburgh: 1776. V. 45

The Gentle Shepherd. Glasgow: 1788. V. 37; 38; 42; 44; 45

The Gentle Shepherd, a Scotch Pastoral. London: 1790. V. 43

The Gentle Shepherd. Glasgow: 1796. V. 40; 42

The Gentle Shepherd, a Pastoral Comedy . . . Edinburgh: 1808. V. 37; 42

The Gentle Shepherd. Edinburgh: 1880. V. 41; 43

The Gentle Shepherd. Edinburgh: 1814. V. 37

The Great Shepherd, a Pastoral Comedy. Glasgow: 1796. V. 41

A Letter to the Right Honourable the Earl of ----- Concerning the Affair of Elizabeth Canning. London: 1753. V. 46

Letters on the Present Disturbances in Great Britain and Her American Provinces. London: 1777. V. 40

A Poem on the South-Sea. To which is prefix'd, A familiar epistle to Anthony Hammond Esq; by a friend. London: 1720. V. 37

Poems. Edinburgh: 1721. V. 40; 43

Poems by Allan Ramsay. London: 1731. V. 38; 41; 45

Poems by Allan Ramsay. Dublin: 1733. V. 38

Poems. Glasgow: 1770. V. 38

The Poems of Allan Ramsay. London: 1800. V. 46

Poetical Works. London: 1870. V. 37; 42

The Select Songs of the Gentle Shepherd. London: 1781. V. 42

Tales from Turkey Collected and Done into English. London: 1914. V. 41

The Tea-Table Miscellany: a Collection of Choice Songs, Scots and English. Edinburgh: 1775. V. 44

Wealth, or the Woody: a poem on the South-Sea. To which is prefex'd, A familiar epistle to Anthony Hammond Esq.; by Mr. Sewell. The second edition, corrected. London: 1720. V. 37

RAMSAY, ANDREW MAITLAND

Atlas of the External Diseases of the Eye . . . New York: 1898. V. 45

RAMSAY, ANDREW MICHAEL 1686-1743

An Essay Upon Civil Government. London: 1722. V. 37

The History of Henri De La Tour D'Auvergne, Viscount de Turenne, Marshal-General of France. London: 1735. V. 43

The Travels of Cyrus . . . London: 1727. V. 40

The Travels of Cyrus. London: 1727-28. V. 45; 46

The Travels of Cyrus. London: 1730. V. 45

The Travels of Cyrus . . . Dublin: 1763. V. 44

The Travels of Cyrus. Boston: 1795. V. 37; 40; 41; 43; 44

RAMSAY, DAVID 1749-1815

Histoire de la Revolution d'Amerique, Par Rapport a la Caroline Meridionale. London: & Paris: 1797. V. 45

The History of the Revolution of South Carolina, from a British Province to an Independent State. Trenton: 1785. V. 39; 44; 45

The History of the American Revolution. Philadelphia: 1789. V. 40; 41; 44

The History of the American Revolution. London: 1791. V. 41

The History of the American Revolution. Dublin: 1793. V. 40; 42

The History of the American Revolution. Dublin: 1795. V. 41; 46

The History of South Carolina, from Its First Settlement in 1670 to the Year 1808. Charleston: 1809. V. 38; 40; 41; 43; 44

The History of the American Revolution . . . Trenton: 1811. V. 37

The History of the American Revolution. Lexington: 1815. V. 37

History of the United States from Their First Settlement as English Colonies in 1607 to the Year 1808. Philadelphia: 1816. V. 40

History of the United States, From Their First Settlement as English Colonies, in 1607 to the Year 1608 . . . Philadelphia: 1816-17. V. 42; 45

The Life of George Washington, Commander in Chief of the Armies of the United States in the War Which Established Their Indepdendence, and First President of the United States . . . London: 1807. V. 42; 43; 46

The Life of George Washington, Commander in Chief of the Armies of the United States of America. New York: 1807. V. 41

Memoirs of the Life of Martha Laurens Ramsay. Charlestown: 1812. V. 40

Memoirs of the Life of Martha Laurens Ramsay . . . Lexington: 1813. V. 38

Military Memoirs of Great Britain; or, a History of the War, 1755-1763. Edinburgh: 1779. V. 42; 43; 44

An Oration, Delivered on the Anniversary of American Independence July 4, 1794 . . . to the Inhabitants of Charleston, South Carolina. London: 1795. V. 41

RAMSAY, GEORGE

An Enquiry into the Principles of Human Happiness and Human Duty. London: 1843. V. 41

A New Dictionary of Anecotes, Illustrative of Character and Events. London: 1822. V. 37; 41

RAMSAY, HUGH

The Art of Hugh Ramsay. Melbourne. V. 41

RAMSAY, JAMES

An Essay on the Treatment and Conversion of African Slaves in the British Sugar Colonies. London: 1784. V. 37; 43

Objections to the Abolition of the Slave Trade, with Answers. London: 1788. V. 41; 42; 43

RAMSAY, L.

Ornithology of the Scottish Nationa Antarctic Expedition. London: 1902-04. V. 43

RAMSAY, T. W.

Costumes on the West African Coast of Africa. London: 1833. V. 39; 40

RAMSAY, W. M.

Studies in the History and Art of the Eastern Province of the Roman Empire. Aberdeen: 1906. V. 44

Studies in the History of the Art of the Eastern Provinces of the Roman Empire. Aberdeen: 1906. V. 42

The Thousand and One Churches. London: 1909. V. 39; 42; 45

RAMSAYE, TERRY

A Million and One Nights. New York: 1926. V. 42; 44; 45

RAMSBOTHAM, FRANCIS H.

The Principles and Practice of Obstetric Medicine and Surgery, in Reference to the Process of Parturition. London: 1844. V. 39

The Principles and Practice of Obstetric Medicine and Surgery, in Reference to the Process of Parturition. Philadelphia: 1843. V. 37

RAMSDELL, CHARLES

Laws and Joints Resolutions of the Last Session of the Confederate Congress (1864-65) . . . with the Secret Acts of Previous Congresses. Durham: 1941. V. 45

RAMSDELL, CHARLES W.

Behind the Lines in the Southern Confederacy. Baton Roughe: 1944. V. 46

Reconstruction in Texas. New York: 1910. V. 37; 38; 43

RAMSDEN, CHARLES

Bookbinders of the United Kingdom (Outside London), 1780-1840. 1954. V. 38

Bookbinders of the United Kingdom (Outside London) 1780-1840. London: 1954. V. 43

French Bookbinders 1789-1848. London: 1950. V. 39; 40; 42; 46

London Bookbinders, 1780-1840. London: 1956. V. 38; 39

RAMSEY, ALEX

Address Delivered by Ex-Gov. Ramsey, President of the Minnesota Territorial Agricultural Society at the Annual Territorial Fair. St. Paul: 1857. V. 41

Message of the Governor of Minnesota. To the Legislative Assembly, Jan. 7, 1851. Saint Paul: 1851. V. 41

Message of the Governor of Minnesota, to the Legislative Assembly Delivered January 13, 1852. St. Anthony: 1852. V. 37; 39

RAMSEY, ALEXANDER

Annual Message of Governor Ramsey to the Senate and House of Representatives of the State of Minnesota. St. Paul: 1861. V. 37; 42; 46

Memorial, &c. Northern Pacific Railroad. Washington: 1867. V. 38

RAMSEY, DAVID 1749-1815

An Oration, Delivered on the Anniversary of American Independence, July 4, 1794 . . . to the Inhabitants of Charleston, South Carolina. London: 1795. V. 38

RAMSEY, J. G. M.

The Annals of Tennessee to the End of the Eighteenth Century. Charleston: 1853. V. 42

The Annals of Tennessee to the End of the Eighteenth Century; Comprising Its Settlement . . . Philadelphia: 1860. V. 43

RAMSEY, JAMES

Examination of the Rev. Mr. Harris's Scriptural Researches on the Licitness of the Slave Trade. London: 1788. V. 43

RAMSEY, MILTON C.

Ramsey and Brother, Dealers in Watches, Clocks & Jewelry, No. 83, Fourth Street, . . . Louisville, Ky . . . Louisville: 1855-56. V. 40

RAMSEY, STANLEY C.

Small Houses of the Late Georgian Period, 1750-1820. (with) Details & Interiors. London: 1919/23. V. 39; 46

Small Houses of the Later Georgian Period. London: 1924, 1923. V. 43; 46

RAMSEY, WILLIAM

Astrologia Restaurata; or, Astrologie Restored. London: 1653. V. 38

Conjugium Conjurgium; or, Some Serious Considerations on Marriage. London: 1675. V. 43

RAMUS, PETRUS

Arithmetices Libri Duo, et Algebrae Totidem: a Lazaro Schonero Emendati & Explicati. Frankfurt: 1592. V. 37

RAMUSIO, GIOVANNI BATTISTA 1485-1557

Delle Navigationi et Viaggi . . . Volume Primo (Second, Terzo). Venice: 1563/1606/1556. V. 43; 44

Delle Navigatione et Viaggi . . . Venice: 1563/83/56. V. 41

Delle Navigationi et Viaggi . . . Volume Primo - Volume Terzo . . . Venice: 1606. V. 37; 38; 40; 42; 43

RANBY, JOHN

The Method of Treating Gunshot Wounds. London: 1744. V. 40

RAND, AUSTIN L.

Handbook of New Guinea Birds. London: 1967. V. 38; 39; 40

RAND, AVERY & CO.

The ABC Pathfinder Railway Guide, . . . Published on the First Monday of Each Month. Boston: 1876. V. 45

RAND, AYN

Anthem. Los Angeles: 1946. V. 41; 42; 44

Atlas Shrugged. New York: 1928. V. 44

Atlas Shrugged. New York: 1957. V. 37; 39; 40; 41; 42; 43; 45; 46

The Cashing-In: The Student 'Rebellion'. New York: 1965. V. 41

The Cashing-In: the Student 'Rebellion'. New York: 1965. V. 42

For the New Intellectual. New York: 1961. V. 37

The Fountain Head. 1943. V. 46

The Fountain Head. (1943). V. 37

The Fountainhead. 1943. V. 46

The Fountainhead. Indianapolis/New York: 1943. V. 41; 42

The Fountainhead. Indianpolis: 1943. V. 39; 46

The Fountain Head. New York: 1943. V. 39

Night of January 16th. New York & Toronto: 1936. V. 39

The Virtue of Selfishness. New York: 1964. V. 43

RANDOLPH, THOMAS continued

Poems with the Muses Looking Glasse; and Amyntas. Oxford: 1638. V. 37; 42; 45

Poems. With the Muses Looking Glasse. Amyntas. Jealous Lovers. Arystippus. London: 1652. V. 39

Poems and Play. London: 1652. V. 46

Poems. London: 1652. V. 44

Poems: With the Muse's Looking Glasse, Amyntas, Jealous Lovers. London: 1652. V. 43

Poems with the Muses Looking Glass and Amyntas; Whereunto is Added the Jealous Lovers. Oxford: 1668. V. 40

RANDOLPH, VANCE

Ozark Mountain Folks. New York: 1932. V. 46

RANDOLPH, WILLIAM FITZHUGH

With Stonewall Jackson, at Chancellorsville. N.P.: 1905. V. 44

RANDOM DE BERENGER, CHARLES, BARON DE

Helps and Hints How to Protect Life and Property. London: 1835. V. 37; 39

RANDS, W. B.

Lilliput Revels and Innocents' Island. London. V. 43

RANDS, WILLIAM B.

Lilliput Levee. London: 1864. V. 39

THE RANELEAN Religion Displayed. London: 1750. V. 37

RANFOLDI, LATTANZIO

Misteriosi Significati Delle Parole, Gesti, Cerimonie & Altre Cose Appartenenti . . . Della Messa. Venice: 1581. V. 38; 44

RANGER'S Progress; Consisting of a Variety of Poetical Essays, Moral Serious, Comic, Satyrical by Honest Ranger, of Bedford Row. London: 1760. V. 40

RANHOFER, CHARLES

Epicurean. New York: 1894. V. 39; 45

The Epicurean. Chicago: 1920. V. 38

The Epicurean. Evanston: 1920. V. 38

The Epicurean. New York: 1920. V. 46

Epicurean. Analytical and Practical Studies on the Culinary Art. New York: 1916. V. 37

RANKE, HERMANN

Babylonian Legal and Business Documents from the Time of the First Dynasty of Babylon, Chiefly from Sippar. Philadelphia: 1906. V. 42; 44

RANKE, LEOPOLD

The Ecclesiastical and Political history of the Popes of Rome. London: 1841. V. 38

A History of Servia and the Servian revoluiton from Original Mss. and Documents. London: 1847. V. 46

A History of the Papacy, Political and Ecclesiastical, in the Sixteenth and Seventeenth Centuries. Edinburgh: 1851. V. 46

RANKE, LEOPOLD VON 1795-1886

A History of England, Principally in the 17th century. Oxford: 1875. V. 39; 41

RANKEN, ALEXANDER 1755-1827

The History of France from the Time of Its Conquest by Clovis A.D. 486 (to 1793). London: 1801. V. 39

RANKEN, W. H. L.

The Dominion of Australia: an Account of Its Foundations. London: 1874. V. 39; 45

RANKIN, ADAM

Dialogues, Pleasant and Interesting, Upon the All-Important Question in Church Government, What are the Legitimate Terms of Admission to Visible Church Communion? Lexington: 1819. V. 44

RANKIN, D. J.

A History of the County of Antigonish. Toronto: 1929. V. 44

RANKIN, DANIEL J.

The Zambesi Basin and Nyassaland. London: 1893. V. 41

RANKIN, M. WILSON

Reminiscences of Frontier Days. Denver: 1935. V. 37; 42; 45

Reminiscences of Frontier Days Including an Authentic Account of the Thornburg and Meeker Massacre. Denver: 1938. V. 45

RANKIN, MELINDA

Texas in 1850. Boston: 1850. V. 41; 43

Twenty Years Among the Mexicans, a Narrative of Missionary Labor. Cincinnati: 1875. V. 37; 42

RANKINE, DAVID

A Popular Exposition of the Effect of Forces Applied to Draught. Glasgow: 1828. V. 46

A Popular Exposition of the Effect of Forces Applied to Draught. With Illustrations of the Principles of Action, and Tables of the Performance of Horses and Locomotive Engines on Railways. And an Appendix . . . Glasgow/Edinburgh: 1828. V. 37

RANKINE, W. J.

Miscellaneous Scientific Papers . . . London: 1881. V. 45

RANKINE, W. J. MACQUORN

On the Thermal Energy of Molecular Vortices. Edinburgh: 1869. V. 40

RANLETT, WILLIAM H.

The Architect, a Series of Original Designs, for Domestic and Ornamental Cottages and Villas, Connected with Landscape Gardening. New York: 1847, 1849. V. 40

The Architect, a Series of Original Designs for Domestic and Ornamental Cottages and Villas . . . New York: 1849. V. 43

The Architect, a Series of Original Designs for Domestic and Ornamental Cottages and Villas Connected with Landscape Gardening Adapted to the United States. New York: 1847. V. 37; 46

RANNEY, THOMAS STOWE

Pocket Companion of the Student of the Burmese Language . . . Rangoon: 1858. V. 43

RANNIE, DOUGLAS

My Adventures Among South Sea Cannibals an Account of the Experiences and Adventures of a Government Official Among the Natives of Oceania. Philadelphia: 1912. V. 43

RANNIE, JOHN

Poems. London: 1791. V. 37

RANNISS, RUTH S.

A Descriptive Catalogue of the First Editions in Book Form of the Writings of Percy Bysshe Shelley. New York: 1923. V. 37

RANSOM, CAROLINE L.

Couches and Beds of the Greeks, Etruscans and Romans. Chicago: 1905. V. 42; 44

RANSOM, JOHN CROWE 1888-1974

Armageddon. Charleston: 1923. V. 37; 42

Chills and Fever. New York: 1924. V. 37; 38; 39; 40; 42; 45

Grace After Meat. London: 1924. V. 39; 41; 44

Poems About God. 1919. V. 46

Poems About God. New York: 1919. V. 37

Selected Poems. New York: 1945. V. 38

Selected Poems. New York: 1963. V. 40

Two Gentlemen in Bonds. New York: 1927. V. 37

The World's Body. New York: 1938. V. 39; 41

RANSOM, JOHN L.

Andersonville Diary. Escape, and List of the Dead, with Name, Co., Regiment, Date of Death and No. of Grave in Cemetary. Auburn: 1881. V. 44

RANSOM, WILL

The Ashendene Press. Meriden: 1939. V. 37

Private Presses and Their Books. New York: 1929. V. 37; 38; 39; 41; 43; 45; 46

Private Presses and Their Books. With Selective Checklists of Press Books . . . New York: 1963. V. 40

Selective Check Lists of Press Books. New York: 1945-50. V. 38; 45

Selective Check Lists of Press Books, A Compiltation of All Important and Significant Private Dresses . . . New York: 1963. V. 38; 43

RANSOME, ARTHUR

Aladdin and His Wonderful Lamp in Rhyme. London. V. 41

Aladdin and His Wonderful Lamp in Rhyme. London. V. 44

Aladdin and His Wonderful Lamp in Rhyme. London. V. 43

Aladdin and His Wonderful Lamp. London: 1919. V. 46

A Collection of Letters from Arthur Ransome to Morley Kennerley, His Editor at Faber & Faber, the Publishers Comprisng 14 Lett. V. 39

Edgar Allen Poe - a Critical Study. London: 1910. V. 40

Oscar Wilde. A Critical Study. London: 1912. V. 43

Rod and Line; Essays, Together with Aksakov on Fishing. London: 1929. V. 40

A Selection of Works. London: 1930-47. V. 44; 46

The Souls of the Streets and Other Little Papers. London: 1904. V. 38

Winter Holiday. London: 1933. V. 44

RANSOMES & RAPIER

Catalogue of Railway Materials No. 133. (and) Catalogue of Little Railways No. 139. London: 1877/80. V. 46

RANTLETT, WILLIAM H.

The Architect, a Series of Original Designs for Domestic and Ornamental Cottages and Villas, Connected with Landscape Gardening, Adpated to the United States . . . New York: 1847. V. 41; 44

RANTOUL, ROBERT

Letter to Robert Schuyler, Esq., President of the Illinois Central Railroad on the Value of the Public Lands of Illinois. Boston: 1851. V. 37; 43; 44

RANYARD, ELLEN H. WHITE

The Missing Link; or, Bible women in the Homes of the London Poor. New York: 1860. V. 44; 45

RAO, T. A. GOPINATHA

Elements of Hindu Iconography. Madras: 1914-16. V. 43

RAOUL-ROCHETTE, DESIRE

Lettres sur la Suisse. Paris: 1823. V. 39

RAPER, ELIZABETH

Receipt Book of Elizabeth Raper and a Portion of Her Cipher Journal. London: 1924. V. 37; 40; 44

RAPER, HENRY

The Practice of Navigation of Ships or with the Determination of Latitude and Longitude on Shore by Means of the Sextant or Reflecting Circle. London: 1849. V. 42

RAPHAEL 1483-1520

An Analysis of the Picture of the Transfiguration of Raffaello Sanzio d'Urbino. London: 1817. V. 40

The Cartons (sic) of Raphael D'Urbino. London: 1809. V. 40; 45

RAPHALL, M. J.

Bible View of Slavery. New York: 1861. V. 42

Devotional Exercises, for the Use of the Daughters of Israel, Intended for Public and Private Worship . . . New York: 1852. V. 44

RAPIER, RICHARD C.

Renumerative Railways for New Countries. London: 1878. V. 40

RAPIN, RENE 1621-1687

The Comparison of Plato and Aristotle. London: 1673. V. 45

Hortorum Libri IV. Cum Disputatione de Cultura Hortensi. Ioan. Meursii Fil. Arboretum Sacrum. Angeli Politiani Rusticus. Adhaec Lipsii Leges Hortenses, & Lazari Bonamici Carmen de Vita Rustica. Utrecht: 1672. V. 37

Hortorvm Libri IV. Parisiis: 1665. V. 37; 46

The Modest Critick. London: 1689. V. 38

Observations on the Poems of Homer and Virgil. London: 1672? V. 37

Of Gardens. London: 1673. V. 46

Of Gardens. London: 1706. V. 38; 40; 41; 43

Of Gardens. London: 1728. V. 46

Rapin of Gardens. London: 1718. V. 38; 46

Reflections Upon the Eloquence of These Time; Particularly of the Barr and Pulpit. London: 1672. V. 39; 46

The Whole Critical Works of Monsieur Rapin . . . London: 1716. V. 45

The Whole Critical Works. London: 1706. V. 41

RAPIN-THOYRAS, PAUL DE

Acta Regia Being the Account Which Mr. Rapin de Thoyras publised of the History of England . . . London: 1734. V. 38

Atlas..for the History of England. (together with) The Metallick History of the Reigns of King William III and Queen Mary, Queen Anne, and King George I . . . London: 1747. V. 40

The History of England. London: 1757-59. V. 39

RAPINE, RENE 1621-1687

Reflections Upon the Eloquence of These Times; Particularly of the Barr and Pulpit. London: 1672. V. 43

Reflections on Aristotle's Treatise on Poesie. London: 1674. V. 43

RAPPORT, LEONARD

Rendezvous with Destiny, a History of the 101st Airborne Division. Washington: 1948. V. 45

RAREKES, HENDRIK

Algemeene Ophelderende Verklaring van het oud Letterschrift, in Steenplaatdruk . . . Leyden: 1818. V. 38

RAREY, JOHN SOLOMON

The Arabian Art of Taming and Training Wild and Vicious Horses. Cincinnati: 1856. V. 45

The Modern Art of Taming Wild Horses. Columbus: 1857. V. 39

RASCH, HEINZ

Gefesselter Blick. 25 Kurze Monografien und Beitrage Uber Die Neue Werbegestaltung. Stuttgart: 1930. V. 42

RASCOE, B.

The Smart Set Anthology. 1934. V. 45

RASHDALL, HASTINGS

The Universities of Europe in the Middle Ages. (1942). V. 46

The Universities of Europe in the Middle Ages. London: 1987. V. 42

The Universities of Europe in the Middle Ages. Oxford: 1987. V. 38

The Universities of Europe in the Middle Ages . . . London: 1969. V. 37

RASHLEIGH, PHILIP

Specimens of British Minerals Selected from the Cabinet of Philip Rashleigh, of Menabilly, in the County of Cornwall, Esq. M.P. F.R.S. and F.A.S. with General Descriptions of Each Article. London: 1797-1802. V. 37

RASK, ERASMUS

A Grammar of the Anglo-Saxon Tonge. Copenhagen: 1830. V. 46

A Grammar of the Danish Language for the Use of Englishmen Together with Extracts in Prose and Verse. Copenhagen: 1830. V. 40

RASKIN, SAUL

The New Face of Israel. New York: 1960. V. 38

RASMUSSEN, KNUD

Across Arctic America. Narrative of the Fifth Thule Expedition. New York/London: 1927. V. 37

Greenland by the Polar Sea. London: 1921. V. 37; 43; 44; 46

The People of the Polar North. a Record. Philadelphia/London: 1908. V. 43

RASPE, RUDOLF ERIC H. 1737-1794

The Surprising Adventures of Baron Munchausen, Abridged. London: 1809. V. 37; 39

RASPE, RUDOLF ERICH 1737-1794

An Account of Some German Volcanos, and Their Productions. London: 1776. V. 37; 42; 44

RASPE, RUDOLPH ERICH 1737-1794

The Travels of Baron Munchausen. New York: 1929. V. 45

RASSAM, HORMUNDZ

Narrative of the British Mission to Theodore, King of Abyssinia. London: 1869. V. 41

RASSAM, HORMUZD

Asshur and the Land of Nimrod Being an Account of the Discoveries Made in the Ancient Ruins of Nineveh, Asshur, Sepharvaim, Calah, Babylon, Borsippa, Cuthah, and Van . . . New York: 1897. V. 40

RASTALL, WILLIAM DICKINSON

A Practical Guide to the Quarter, and Other Sessions of the Peace. London: 1815. V. 40

RASTELL, JOHN

An Exposition of Certaine Difficult and Obscure Wordes and Termes of the Lawes of this Relame . . . London: 1598. V. 46

Pastime of People, or, The Chronicles of Divers Realms: and Most Especially of the Realm of England. London: 1811. V. 40

The Pastime of People, or the Chronicles of Diverse Realms, and most especially of the Realm of England. Compiled by John Rastell. London: 1801. V. 37

Les Termes de la Ley: or, Certain Difficult and Obscure Words and Terms of the Common and Statute Laws of this Realm, Now in Use . . . 1721. V. 39; 40

RASTELL, WILLIAM 1508-1565

A Collection of Entrees, of Declaracions, Barres, Replicacions, Rejoinders, Issues, Verdicts and Divers other Matters . . . London: 1596. V. 40

Les Termes de la Ley; or, Certaine Difficult and Obscure Words and Termes of the Common Lawes and Statutes of this Realme Now in Use Expounded and Explained. London: 1641. V. 40

Les Termes de la Ley; or, Certaine Difficult and Obscure Words and Termes of the Common Lawes and Statutes of this Realme Now in Use Expounded. London: 1671. V. 40

RATAHBUN, JONATHAN

Narrative of . . . with Accurate Accounts of the Capture of Groton Fort, the Massacre that Followed, and the Sacking and Burning of New London, Sept. 6, 17811 . . . New London?: 1840. V. 37

RATCHFORD, FANNIE E.

Legends of Angria. New Haven: 1933. V. 46

A Review of Reviews. Austin: 1946. V. 38

The Story of Champ D'Asile, as Told by Two of the Colonists. Dallas: 1937. V. 37; 42

The Story of Champ D'Asile as Told by Two of the Colonists . . . Dallas: 1937. V. 42

RATCLIFF, S. C.

Elton Manorial Records 1279-1351. Cambridge: at the: 1944. V. 37

RATCLIFFE, D.

A Nature Conservation Review, the Selection of Biological Sites of National Importance to nature Conservation in Britain. London: 1977. V. 37

RATCLIFFE, DOROTHY UNA

Hoops of Steel. London: 1935. V. 40

To the Blue Canadian Hills. Leeds: 1928. V. 43

RATCLIFFE, HENRY

Observations on the Rate of Mortality and Sickness Exisiting Amongst Friendly Societies . . . Colchester: 1862. V. 46

RATHBONE, AMBROSE B.

Camping and Tramping in Malaya Fifteen Years' Pioneering in the Native States of the Malay Peninsula. London: 1898. V. 40

RATHBONE, BASIL

In and Out of Character. Garden City: 1962. V. 46

RATHBONE, FREDERICK

Old Wedgwood, the Decorative or Artistic Ceramic Work, in Colour and Relief, Invented and Produced by Josiah Wedgwood, F.R.S. &c. at Etruria, in Staffordshire, 1760-1794. London: 1898. V. 41

RATHBONE, HANNAH MARY REYNOLDS

The Poetry of Birds Selected From Various Authors . . . Liverpool: 1833. V. 38

The Poetry of Birds Selected from Various Authors. Liverpool & London: 1833. V. 40

So Much of the Diary of Lady Willoghby as Relates to Her Domestic History. London: 1844-48. V. 42

RATHBONE, ST. GEORGE

A Texas Thoroughbred, or the Strange Adventures of Colonel Rocket. Cleveland: 1912. V. 45

RATHBONE, WILLIAM 1757-1809

A Narrative of Events That Have Lately Taken Place in Ireland, Among the Society Called Quakers. (with) A Memoir . . . 1804; V. 41

RATHBUN, VALENTINE WIGHTMAN

Some Brief Hints of a Religious Scheme, Taught and Propagated by a Number of Europeans, Living in a Place Called Nisqueunia, in the State of New York. New York: 1783. V. 38; 40

RATHENAU, ERNEST

Kokoschka: Drawings. V. 39

RATHER, ETHEL ZIVLEY

Dewitt's Colony. Austin: 1904. V. 41; 42; 45

Recognition of the Republic of Texas by the United States. Austin: 1901. V. 42

Recognition of the Republic of Texas by the United States. Austin: 1911. V. 37; 38; 39; 45

RATHER, LOIS

Gertrude Stein and California. Oakland: 1974. V. 46

RATIOCINATIO et Fabrica. ?Rome or Florence: 1797. V. 38

THE RATIONAL Humourist; Being a Choice Collection of Bon Mots and Pleasing Witticisms . . . Beverley: 1815. V. 41; 42

RATIONAL Sports or Entertaining Questions and Answers in Trades. Gainsborough: 1790. V. 45

RATTI, ABATE ACHILLE

The Climbs on Alpine Peaks. London: 1923. V. 41

RATTIGAN, TERENCE

In Praise of Love - Two Plays; After Lydia and Before Dawn. London: 1973. V. 42

Ross. A Dramatic Portrait. London: 1960. V. 41

The Sleeping Prince. London: 1954. V. 45

RATTLEHEAD, DAVID

The Life and Adventures of an Arkansaw Doctor. Washington: 1879. V. 37

RATTRAY, ALEXANDER

Vancouver Island and British Columbia. London: 1862. V. 37; 45

RATTRAY, JAMES

The Costumes of the Various Tribes, Portraits of Ladies of Rank, Celebrated Princes and Chiefs, Views of the Principal Fortresses and Cities and Interior of the Cities and Temples of Afghaunistan. London: 1847-48. V. 42

RATZEL, FRIEDRICH

The History of Mankind. London: 1896. V. 39

RAU, CHARLES

Prehistoric Fishing in Europe and North America. Washington City: 1884. V. 39

RAUCOURT DE CHARLEVILLE, A.

A Manual of Lithography, or Memoir on the Lithographic Experiments Made in Paris, at the Royal School of the Roads and Bridges . . . London: 1821. V. 44

A Manual of Lithography . . . London: 1832. V. 38; 44

Traite sur l'art de Faire de Bons Mortiers et d'en Bien Diriger l'Emploi, ou Methode Generale Pratique Pour Fabriquer en Tous Pays la Chaux, Les Cimens et les Mortiers les Meilleurs et les Plus Economiques. Paris: 1828. V. 44

RAUE, CHRISTIAN

A Generall Grammer for the Ready Attaining of the Ebrew, Samaritan, Calde, Syriac, Arabic and the Ethiopic Languages . . . London: 1650. V. 46

RAULET, SYLVIE

Jewelry of the 1940s and 1950s. New York: 1988. V. 45

RAULIN, JEAN

Doctrinale Mortis. Paris: 1519. V. 37

Itinerarium Paradisi. Paris: 1524. V. 37

RAULSTN, MARION CHURCHILL

Memories of Owen Humphrey Churchill and His Family. N.P.;: 1950. V. 44

RAULSTON, MARION CHURCHILL

Memories of Owen Humphrey Churchill and His Family. Los Angeles: 1950. V. 42

Memories of Owen Humphrey Churchill & His Family. N.P.: 1950. V. 38

RAUMER, FREDERICK VON

America and the American People. New York: 1846. V. 39; 40; 42; 45

England in 1835: A Series of Letters Written to Friends in Germany. London: 1836. V. 39

RAUMER, FRIEDRICH VON

England in 1841; Being a Series of Letters Written to Friends in Germany . . . London: 1842. V. 43

RAUSKOLB, F. W.

History of Gold Leaf, and Its Uses . . . Boston: 1915. V. 40

RAUTHMEL, RICHARD

Antiquitates Bremetonacenses; or the Roman Antiquities of Overborough. London: 1824. V. 41

RAUWOLF, LEONHARD

Aigentliche Beschreibung der Raiss so er Vor Diser Zeit Gegen Auffgang Inn Die Morgenlander Furnemlich Syriam, Judaeam, Arabiam, Mesopotamiam Babyloniam, Assyriam, Armenian . . . colophon: 1582. V. 39

Aigentliche Beschreibung der Rais, so er vor Diserzeit Gegen Auffgang inn die Morganlander, Furnemlich Syriam, Judaeam, Arabiam, Mesopotamiam, Babyloniam, Assyriam, Armeniam, etc. Lauingen: 1582. V. 39

RAVEN, HENRY CUSHIER

The Anatomy of the Gorilla . . . New York: 1950. V. 42

The Anatomy of the Gorilla. Colorado University Press;: 1950. V. 37

RAVEN, MATHILDE

The Two Brothers; or, the Family that Lived in the First Society. London: 1850. V. 42

RAVEN, SIMON

Captain Raven's Sporting Tours. London. V. 45

Doctors Wear Scarlet - a Romantic Tale. London: 1960. V. 44

RAVENS Creek-M.CM.LX. Lexington, KY: 1960. V. 37

RAVENSCROFT, B. C.

Greenhouse Construction and Heating. London: 1901. V. 38

RAVENSCROFT, EDWARD

The Italian Husband. London: 1698. V. 41; 43

RAVENSTEIN, E. G.

Martin Behaim, His Life and His Globe. London: 1908. V. 40; 44; 45

Official Guide the Inman Line. London: 1886. V. 42

RAVERAT, GWEN

Modern Woodcutters Number 1 - Gwendolen Raverat. London: 1920. V. 44

Period Piece. A Cambridge Childhood. London: 1953. V. 37

The Wood Engravings of Gwen Raverat. London: 1959. V. 46

RAVESIES, PAUL

Scenes and Settlers of Alabama. Mobile: 1886. V. 37

RAVIGLIO ROSSO, GIULIO

Historia Delle Cose Occorse Nel Regno d'Inghilterra, in Materia del Duca di Nortomberlan Dopo la Morte di Odoardo VI. Venice: 1558. V. 38

Historia d'Inghilterra, Dopo la Morte di Odoardo Sesto. Ferrara: 1591. V. 39

I Successi d'Inghilterra Dopo la Morte di Odoardo Sesto. Ferrara: 1560. V. 41; 44

RAVILIOUS, ERIC

Almanack 1929. London: 1929. V. 37; 41

A Memorial Exhibition (Catalogue) of Water-Colours Wood-Engravings, Illustrations, Designs, etc. London: 1948/49. V. 42

The Wood Engravings of Eric Ravilious. London: 1972. V. 37; 40; 42; 43; 45

RAVISIUS TEXTOR, JOANNES

De Memorabilibus et Claris Mulieribus. Paris: 1521. V. 41

RAVITCH, MARK M.

A Century of Surgery. Philadelphia: 1981. V. 40

RAVOUX, A.

Reminiscences, Memoirs and Lectures Of . . . St. Paul: 1890. V. 46

RAVOUX, AUGUSTIN 1815-1906

Wakantanka Ti Ki Canku. Prairie du Chien: 1843. V. 40

RAWES, WILLIAM

The Gospel Ministry of Women, Under the Christian Dispensation, Defended from Scripture and from the Writings of John Locke, Josiah Martin &c. London: 1801. V. 45

RAWLE, WILLIAM B.

History of the Third Pennsylvania Cavalry, 60th Regiment Pennsylvania Volunteers . . . 1861-1865. Philadelphia: 1905. V. 42

RAWLEIGH Rediviuus; or, The Life and Death of the Right Honourable Anthony, Late Earl of Shaftesbury. London: 1683. V. 40

RAWLET, JOHN

Poetick Miscellanies of Mr. John Rawlet, B.D. and Late Lecturer of S. Nicholas Church in the Town and County of New-castle upon Tine. London: 1687. V. 40; 46

RAWLING, C. J.

History of the First Regiment Virginia Infantry. Philadelphia: 1887. V. 41

RAWLING, CECIL GODFREY

The Great Plateau: Being an Account of Exploration in Central Tibet, 1903 and the Gartok Expedition, 1904-05. London: 1905. V. 46

RAWLINGS, CHARLES

An Olla Podrida. London: 1862. V. 42

RAWLINGS, MARJORIE KINNAN

Cross Creek. New York: 1942. V. 41; 42; 43; 45

Cross Creek. New York: 1945. V. 37

Jacob's Ladder. Coral Gables: 1950. V. 44; 46

The Sojourner. New York: 1953. V. 37

The Sojourner. New York: 1953. V. 39; 40; 44

The Yearling. New York: 1938. V. 45

The Yearling. New York: 1938. V. 45

The Yearling. New York: 1938. V. 41

The Yearling. New York: 1938. V. 42

The Yearling. New York: 1938. V. 42

The Yearling. New York: 1939. V. 41

The Yearling. New York: 1939. V. 39; 40; 46

The Yearling. New York: 1940. V. 40; 46

RAWLINGS, NATHAN J.

War Time Stories. McCauley: 1909. V. 38

RAWLINSON, GEORGE

The Five Great Monarchies of the Ancient Eastern World. London: 1862-67. V. 42

History of Ancient Egypt. London: 1881. V. 46

History of Ancient Egypt. Boston & New York: 1882. V. 40; 42

History of Ancient Egypt. London: 1881. V. 37

Works of . . . London: 1862-89. V. 46

RAWLINSON, RICHARD

The Deed of Trust and Will of Richard Rawlinson, of St. John Baptist College, Oxford, Doctor of Laws. London: 1755. V. 41

The English Topographer. London: 1720. V. 38; 40; 42; 44

The English Topographer. London: 1770. V. 44

RAWLINSON, ROBERT

Designs for Factory Furance and Other Tall Chimney Shafts. London: 1858. V. 38; 40; 45; 46

RAWLINSON, WILLIAM GEORGE 1840-

The Engraved Work of J. M. W. Turner. London: 1908. V. 39

The Engraved Work of J. M. W. Turner, RA. London: 1908/13. V. 42

RAWLS, JOHN

A Theory of Justice. Cambridge: 1971. V. 45

RAWLS, WALTON

The Great Book of Currier & Ives' America. New York: 1979. V. 40

RAWORTH, TOM

The Big Green Day. London: 1968. V. 41

Logbook. Berkeley: 1977. V. 38; 39; 42

RAWSON, GEOFFREY

Nelson's Letters from the Leeward Islands and Other Original Documents in the Public Record Office and the British Museum. London: 1953. V. 44

RAWSON, JONATHAN

A Compendium of Military Duty, Adapted for the Militia of the United States. Dover: 1793. V. 37; 39

RAWSTORNE, J. G.

An Account of the Regiments and Royal Lancashire Militia, 1759 to 1870. Lancaster: 1814. V. 38

RAWSTORNE, JAMES

A Descriptive and Explanatory Key to the View of the Sailing of the British Portion of the Allied Expedition from Baljik to the Crimea . . . London: 1859. V. 42

RAWSTORNE, LAWRENCE

Gamonia; or, The Art of Preserving Game. London: 1837. V. 39; 40; 43; 45

Gamonia. London: 1929. V. 38; 39; 40; 42; 44; 46

RAY, GORDON N.

The Art of the French Illustrated Book 1700 to 1914. 1982. V. 40

The Art of the French Illustrated Book 1700 to 1914. 1982. V. 42

The Art of the French Illustrated Book 1700 to 1914. 1982. V. 46

The Art of the French Illustrated Book, 1700 to 1914. New York: 1982. V. 39; 41

H. G. Wells and Rebecca West. London: 1974. V. 39; 41

RAY, ISAAC 1807-1881

Contributions to Mental Pathology. Boston: 1873. V. 43; 45

Insanity of King George III. Read Before the Association of Superintendents of Insane Hospitals, May 22, 1855. Utica: 1855. V. 43

Medical Jurisprudence of Insanity. A Treatise. Boston: 1853. V. 40

Mental Hygiene. Boston: 1863. V. 39; 43; 44; 45

A Treatise on the Medical Jurisprudence of Insanity. Boston: 1838. V. 45

A Treatise on the Medical Jurisprudence of Insanity. Boston: 1853. V. 43; 45

RAY, JOHN

Catalogue Plantarum Circa Cantabrigiam . . . (with) Index Plantarum Agri Cantabrigiensis. Cambridge: 1660. V. 37; 45

A Collection of English Proverbs. Cambridge: 1670. V. 45

A Collection of English Words Not Generally Used, With Their Significations and Original, in Two Alphabetical Catalogues . . . London: 1691. V. 37; 39; 41; 42; 43

A Collection of English Proverbs Digested into a Convenient Method for the Speedy Finding Any One Upon Occasion . . . Cambridge: 1678. V. 37

Historia Plantarum. London: 1686-1704. V. 38; 40

Historia Plantarum Species Hactenus Edditas Aliasque Insuper Multas Noviter Inventas & Descriptas. London: 1686-88. V. 38; 40; 42; 44; 46

Historia Plantarum, Species Hactenus Editas Aliasque Insuper Multas Noviter Inventas et Descriptas Complectens . . . London: 1686-88/1704. V. 42

Mehtodus Plantarum Emendata et Aucta. London: 1733. V. 37

Miscellaneous Discourses Concerning the Dissolution and Changes of the World. London: 1692. V. 38; 40

Observations Topographical, Moral & Physiological Made in a Journey through Part of the Low-Countries, Germany, Italy and France. London: 1673. V. 38; 39; 40; 42; 43

Philosophical Letters Between the Late Learned Mr. Ray and Several of His Ingenious Correspondents, Natives and Foreigners. London: 1718. V. 40

Select Remains of the Learned John Ray, M.A. and F.R.S. with His Life by the Late William Derham. London: 1760. V. 41; 43; 45

Stirpium Europaearum Extra Britannias Nascentium Sylloge . . . London: 1694. V. 40

Synopsis Methodica Stirpium Britannicarum . . . London: 1690/1689. V. 42

RAY, JOHN continued

Synopsis Methodica Animalium Quadrupedum et Serpentini Generis. London: 1693. V. 39

Synopsis Methodica Stirpium Britannicarum . . . London: 1689, 1690. V. 37

Three Physico-Theological Discourses . . . London: 1713. V. 37; 42

Travels through the Low Countries, Germany, Italy and France. The Travels of Francis Willoughby through a Great Part of Spain. Rauwolf's Journey into the Eastern Countries. London: 1738. V. 46

The Wisdom of God, Manifested in the Works of the Creation. London: 1701. V. 42

The Wisdom of God Manifested in the Works of the Creation. Glasgow: 1750. V. 41

The Wisdom of God manifested in the Works of Creation. London: 1762. V. 37

RAY, MAN

An Alphabet. New York: 1974. V. 38; 44; 45

Les Mains Libres. Illustres Parles Poemes. Paris: 1937. V. 39

Man Ray. Photographs 1929-1934, Paris. Hartford & New York: 1934. V. 41

The Photographic Image. Woodbury: 1980. V. 39

Revolving Doors. Torino: 1972. V. 39

Self Portrait. Boston: 1963. V. 39; 42; 43; 44

RAY, MARCEL

George Grosz. Paris: 1927. V. 45

RAY, MILTON

The Farallones, The Painted World and Other Poems of California. San Francisco;: 1934. V. 43

RAY, NICOLAS

The Importance of the Colonies of North America, and the Interest of Great Britain, with Regard to them Considered. London: 1781. V. 37

RAY, OPHELIA

Daughter of the Tejas. Greenwich: 1965. V. 39; 41; 42; 44

RAY, P. H.

Report of the International Polar Expedition to Point Barrow, Alaska. Washington: 1885. V. 38; 39; 43; 45

RAY, P. ORMAN

The Repeal of the Missouri Compromise. Cleveland: 1909. V. 40

RAY, PATRICK HENRY

Report of the International Polar Expedition to Point Barrow, Alaska, in Response to the Resolution of the House of Representatives of December 11, 1884. Washington: 1885. V. 46

RAY, WILLIAM

Horrors of Slavery; or, the American Tars in Tripoli. Troy: 1808. V. 40

Sophia, or the Girl of the Pine Woods; and the Golden Eagle. Paterson: 1834. V. 39

RAYER, P. F.

A Theoretical and Practical Treatise on the Diseases of the Skin . . . Philadelphia: 1845. V. 42; 45

RAYITCH, MARK

The Papers of Alfred Blalock. Baltimore: 1966. V. 38

RAYLEIGH, JOHN WILLIAM STRUTT, BARON 1842-1919

Argon. Washington: 1896. V. 38; 39; 42; 43; 45

Scientific Papers. Cambridge: 1899-1900-1920. V. 37; 38; 39; 41

Scientific Papers. Cambridge: 1899-1903. V. 40

Scientific Papers. New York: 1964. V. 45

The Theory of sound. London: 1877. V. 41

The Theory of Sound. London: 1894-1896. V. 39

The Theory of Sound. New York: 1945. V. 42

RAYLEIGH, R. J. STRUTT,

The Becquerel Rays and the Proprieties of Radium. London: 1904. V. 38

RAYMOND, ALEX

Flash Gordon, the Tournament of Death. Chicago: 1935. V. 45

Flash Gordon in the Caverns of Mongo. New York: 1938. V. 46

RAYMOND, ANTONIN

Antonin Raymond, an Autobiography. Rutland: 1973. V. 44

RAYMOND, DANIEL

Thoughts on Political Economy. Baltimore: 1820. V. 38; 39; 44

RAYMOND, DORA N.

Captain Lee Hall of Texas. Norman: 1940. V. 37

RAYMOND, ELEANOR

Early Domestic Architecture of Pennsylvania. New York: 1931. V. 42

RAYMOND, GEORGE

Memoirs of Robert William Elliston, Comedian. London: 1846. V. 45

RAYMOND, HENRY J.

History of the Administration of Pres. Lincoln . . . New York: 1864. V. 39

The Life and Public Services of Abraham Lincoln . . . His State Papers, Including His Speeches, Addresses, Messages, Letters and Proclamations . . . New York: 1865. V. 39

RAYMOND, I. H.

Santa Cruz Country. Resources, Advantages, Objects of Interest. Santa Cruz: 1887. V. 41

RAYMOND, JEAN PAUL

Beyond the Threshold. N.P.: 1927. V. 45

Oscar Wilde: Recollections. Bloomsbury: 1932. V. 41; 45

RAYMOND, ROSSITER W.

Statistics of Mines and Mining in the States and Territories West of the Rocky Mountains . . . Washington: 1877. V. 42

Statistics of Mines and Mining in the States and Territories West of the Rocky Mountains; Being the Fifth Annual Report of . . . Washington: 1873. V. 37

RAYMOND, THOMAS

Reports of Divers Special Cases, Adjudged in the Courts of King's Bench, Common Pleas, and Exchequer, in the Reign of King Charles II. Dublin: 1793. V. 39

RAYMUNDUS DE SABUNDE

Theologia Naturalis. Strassburg: 1501. V. 38

Theologia Naturalis Sive Liber Creaturam et Specialiter de Homine & de Natura Eius. Nuremberg: 1502. V. 43

RAYNAL, GUILAUME THOMAS FRANCOIS 1713-1796

The Revolution of America. London: 1781. V. 45

RAYNAL, GUILLAUME THOMAS FRANCOIS 1713-1796

Histoire Philosophique et Politique des Etablissemens et Du Commerce Des Europeans dans les Deux Indes. Geneve: 1781. V. 46

Historia Politica de los Establecimientos Ultramarinos de las Naciones Europeas pour Eduardo Malo de Lugue. Madrid: 1784-1790. V. 41

A Philosohical and Political History of the British Settlements and Trade in North America. Edinburgh: 1776. V. 42

A Philosophical and Political History of the Settlements and Trade of the Europeans in the East and West Indies. London: 1776. V. 38; 42

A Philosophical and Political History of the Settlement and Trade of the Europeans in the East and West Indies. Dublin: 1779. V. 42; 43

A Philosophical and Political History of the British Settlements and Trade in North America. Edinburgh: 1779. V. 40; 41; 43

A Philosophical and Political History of the Settlements and Trade of the Europeans in the East and West Indies. London: 1783. V. 38; 40

A Philosophical and Political History of the Settlements and Trade of the Europeans in the East and West Indies. Dublin: 1784. V. 40

The Revolution in America. London: 1781. V. 37; 40; 45

RAYNAL, MAURICE

History of Modern Painting. Geneva: 1949-50. V. 41

RAYNAUD, MAURICE

On Local Asphyxia and Symmetrical Gangrene of the Extremities. London: 1888. V. 42

RAYNBIRD, WILLIAM

An Old Man's Legacy; or the Labour of Many Years Devoted to Biblical, Artistic and Historical Literature . . . London: 1867. V. 43

RAYNER, S.

The History and Antiquities of Haddon Hall . . . Derby: 1836. V. 39; 44

RAYNER, WILLIAM

Miscellanies in Prose and Verse. Ipswich: 1767. V. 40; 41; 42

RAYNES, FRANCIS

An Appeal to the Public . . . London: 1817. V. 39; 42

RAYNOLDS, W. F.

Report of the Secretary of War - Report by . . . on the Exploration of the Yellowstone River. 1868. V. 37

Report of . . . On the Exploration of the Yellowstone and the Country Drained by that River. Washington: 1868. V. 37; 40; 43

RAYNOR, TED

Old Timers Talk in Southwestern New Mexico. El Paso: 1960. V. 46

THE RE-REPRESENTATION: or, a Modest Search After the Great Plunderers of the Nation. London: 1711. V. 38

RE, VINCENZO

Narrazione delle Solenni Reali Feste Fatte Celebrare in Napoli da Sua Maesta il Re Delle Due Sicile Carlo Infante di Spagna . . . Naples: 1749. V. 37

REA, ALICE

Dalefolk. London: 1895. V. 38; 41; 43

REA, JOHN

Flora seu, De Florum Cultura. London: 1665. V. 38; 41; 43

Flora: Seu De Florum Cultura. London: 1676. V. 42; 45

REA, SAMUEL

The Railways Terminating in London, with a Description of the Terminal Stations, nd the Underground Railways. New York: 1888. V. 38

REACH, ANGUS B.

Clement Lorimer; or, the Book with the Iron Clasps. London: 1849. V. 37; 40; 44

READ, ALEXANDER

The Workes of that Famous Physitian (sic) Dr. Alexander Read. London: 1659. V. 44

READ, BENJAMIN M.

Illustrated History of New Mexico. (Santa Fe): 1912. V. 37

READ, C. RUDSTON

What I Heard, Saw and Did at the Australian Gold Fields. London: 1853. V. 46

READ, CHARLES HERCULES

Antiquities from the City of Benin and From Other Parts of West Africa in the British Museum. London: 1899. V. 41

READ, CHARLES R.

Squash Rackets. London: 1929. V. 43

READ, COLLINSON

Precedents in the Office of a Justice of Peace. Phiadelphia: 1794. V. 43

READ, D. D.

The Bergen County Democrats' History of Hackensack, N.J . . . . Hackensack: 1898. V. 41

READ, DANIEL

Oration on the Life and Character of Stephen A. Douglas. Madison: 1861. V. 45

READ, DAVID

Nathan Read: His Invention of the Multi-Boiler and Portable High Pressure Engine . . . New York: 1870. V. 46

READ, GEORGE H.

The Last Cruise of the Saginaw. Boston & New York: 1912. V. 40

READ, H.

Catalogue of the Silver Plate. Mediaeval and Later. Bequeathed to the British Mueum by Sir Augustus Wollaston Franks. London: 1928. V. 37

READ, HENRY

Pursuits and Verdicts. Edinburgh: 1983. V. 38

READ, HERBERT

Design and Tradition. Huntingdon: 1962. V. 40

Eclogues: a Book of Poems. Westminster: 1919. V. 39; 44

English Stained Glass. London: 1926. V. 39; 42

Eric Gill an Essay. 1963. V. 46

Henry Moore Sculptor. London: 1934. V. 40

Henry Moore - a Study of His Life and Work. London: 1965. V. 45

In Retreat. London: 1925. V. 46

Marino Marini: Complete Works. New York: 1970. V. 39

The Modern Movement in English Architecture, Painting and Sculpture. London: 1934. V. 42

Naked Warriors. London: 1919. V. 37; 40; 42; 46

The Parliament of Women: a Drama in Three Acts. 1960. V. 45

The Parilament of Women: a Drama in Three Acts. Huntingdton: 1960. V. 40; 42; 46

Pursuits and Verdicts. Edinburgh: 1983. V. 40; 46

Sculptures and Drawings. London: 1944-77. V. 42

Staffordshire Pottery Figures. London: 1929. V. 38; 42

Surrealism. London: 1936. V. 39; 42; 45

Unit One - the Modern Movement in English Architecture Painting and Sculpture. London: 1934. V. 37; 41

A World Within a War. London: 1943. V. 42

READ, HOLLIS

The Christian Brahmun; or, Memoirs of the Life, Writings and Character of the Converted Brahmun, Babajee. New York: 1836. V. 44

READ, J. A.

Journey to the Gold Diggins (sic) by Jeremiah Saddlebags. Burlingame: 1950. V. 45

READ, JOHN E.

Nansen in the Frozen World. Philadelphia: 1897. V. 46

READ, JOHN MERDITH

A Historical Inquiry concerning Henry Hudson . . . and the Discovery of Delaware Bay. Albany: 1866. V. 37

READ, MARION J.

A History of the California Academy of Medicine 1870-1930. San Francisco: 1930. V. 38; 40; 46

READ, OPIE

Arkansas Planter. Chicago: 1896. V. 37

Bolanyo a Novel. Chicago: 1897. V. 38; 39; 44; 46

Len Gansett. Boston: 1888. V. 41

READ, OPIE P.

A Kentucky Colonel. Chicago: 1890. V. 43

READ, ROBERT

Modern Leicester . . . London: 1881. V. 44

READ, THOMAS BUCHANAN

Poems. Philadelphia: 1853. V. 44

READE, A. ARTHUR

Study and Stimulants; or the Use of Intoxicants and Narcotis in Relation to Intellectual Life . . . Manchester & London: 1883. V. 39

READE, ALEYN LYELL

Johnsonian Gleanings. London: 1901, 1912, V. 43

Johnsonian Gleanings. London: 1909-1935. V. 42

Johnsonian Gleanings. London: 1909-52. V. 38; 41

Johnsonian Gleanings. By Alyne Lyell Reade. New York: 1968. V. 37

The Reades of Blackwood Hill in the Parish of Horton. London: 1906. V. 37; 40; 42; 45

READE, BRIAN

Aubrey Beardsley. London: 1967. V. 39; 44

READE, CHARLES

Charles Reade, Dramatist, Novelist, Journalist . . . London: 1887. V. 46

Christie Johnstone. London: 1853. V. 43

The Cloister and the Hearth. London & Philadelphia. V. 39

The Cloister and the Hearth. 1861. V. 37

The Cloister and the Hearth. London: 1861. V. 37; 38; 39; 41

The Cloister and the Hearth. New York: 1861. V. 45

The Cloister and the Hearth. New York: 1932. V. 40; 41; 43

Come Over and Stay Till Domesday. From the Cloister and the Hearth. Meriden: 1937. V. 41; 42; 46

The Course of True Love Never Did Run Smooth. London: 1857. V. 39; 43; 46

Cream Contains Jack of All Trades . . . and the Autobiography of a Thief. London: 1858. V. 43; 46

The Eighth Commandment. London: 1860. V. 46

Foul Play. London: 1868. V. 43

Griffith Gaunt, or Jealousy. London: 1866. V. 43

Griffith Gaunt or, Jealousy. London: 1867. V. 39

Hard Cash. London: 1863. V. 38; 43

A Hero and a Martyr. New York: 1875. V. 46

'It Is Never Too Late to Mend.' London: 1856. V. 40; 43

Love Me Little, Love Me Long. London: 1859. V. 43

Peg Woffington. London: 1853. V. 43

Peg Woffington. London: 1899. V. 45; 46

Peg Woffington. New York: 1887. V. 38

A Perilous Secret. London: 1884. V. 43

Put Yourself in His Place. London: 1870. V. 43; 46

A Simpleton. London: 1873. V. 43

A Terrible Temptation. London: 1871. V. 43

Trade Malice. London: 1875. V. 43

Two Loves and a Life. London: 1854. V. 41

White Lies. London: 1857. V. 43; 46

A Woman Hater. Edinburgh & London: 1877. V. 39; 46

READE, CHARLES continued

A Woman-Hater. London: 1877. V. 43

The Works. London. V. 42

The Works. London: 1895. V. 38

READE, ROLF S.

Registrum Librorum Eroticorum. London: 1936. V. 39

READE, WINWOOD

The African Sketch Book. London: 1873. V. 39; 46

Savage Africa. New York: 1864. V. 40

READER, A.

The Bradley Bibliography, a Guide to the Literature of the Woody Plants of the World. London: 1911-18. V. 37

READER, FRANK S.

History of the Fifth West Virginia Cavalry, Formerly the Second Virginia Infantry, and Battery G, First West V. Light Artillery. New Brighton: 1890. V. 39; 40

Some Pioneers of Washington County, Pennsylvania. New Brighton: 1902. V. 42

READING, DANIEL

The English Clerk's Instructor, in the Practice of the Court of King's Bench and Common Pleas ... London: 1733. V. 40

READING, JOSEPH H.

The Ogowee Band: a Narrative of African Travel. Philadelphia: 1890. V. 39

The Ogowe Band. Philadelphia: 1901. V. 43; 44; 45

READING Made Quite Easy and Diverting. London: 1788. V. 43

READING, PETER

For the Municipality's Elderly. London: 1974. V. 40

Water and Waste. Walton-on-Thomas: 1970. V. 40; 43; 44

READ'S Characteristic National Dances, Including a Series of Tales by Popular Authors. London: 1853. V. 40

REAGAN, JOHN H.

Bound Volume of Court Cases Involving John H. Reagan as Texas Railroad Commissioner. N.P.: 1892-94. V. 37

Memoirs, with Special Reference to Secession and Civil War. New York: 1906. V. 37; 38; 42

Memoirs, With Special Reference to Secession and the Civil War. New York: 1906. V. 37

REAGAN, OLIVER

American Architecture of the Twentieth Century. New York: 1927-29. V. 42

REAGAN, RONALD

House of the Oireachtas Joint Sitting. Dublin: 1984. V. 41; 42

Where's the Rest of Me? New York: 1965. V. 46

REAL Cedula de Ereccion de la Compania de Filipinas ... Madrid: 1785. V. 40

REAL COMPANIA GUIPUZCOANA DE CARACAS

Noticias Historiales Practicas de los Sucessos y Adelantamientos de Esta Compania Desde su Fundacion Ano de 1728, Hasta el de 1764 ... Madrid: 1765. V. 40

THE REAL Devil's Walk. London: 1830. V. 38

THE REAL Issue. Facts for Northern Laboring Men. N.P.: 1856. V. 45

REAL Life in London; or the Rambles and Adventures of Bob Tallyho, and His Counsin the Hon. Tom Dashall Through the Metropolis ... London: 1823-29. V. 41

REAL Life in London; or, the Rambles and Adventures of Bob Tallyho, Esq. and His Cousin, the Hon. Tom. Dashall &c ... London: 1824. V. 45

THE REAL or Moral Cause of her Royal Highness the Princess Charlotte's Death ... London: 1817. V. 44; 45

REAL Pen Work, Self-Instructor in Penmanship. Pittsfield: 1884. V. 40

REALITIES of Life: Sketches Designed for the Improvement of The Head and Heart. New Haven: 1839. V. 43

R'EAMUR, RENE ANTOINE FERCHAULT

The Art of Hatching and Bringing Up Domestic Flowls of All Kinds ... London: 1750. V. 41

REANEY, JAMES

The Dance of Death at London. London: 1963. V. 44

REARDEN, T. H.

Petrarch and Other Essays. San Francisco: 1893. V. 39; 46

REARICK, JANET COX

The Drawings of Pontormo. Cambridge: 1964. V. 46

REASONER, CALVIN

The Late Manifesto in Politics: Practical Working of 'Counsel' in Relation to Civil and Religious Liberty in Utah. Salt Lake City: 1896. V. 46

REASONS for Registry; Shewing Briefly the Great Benefits and Advantages that My Accrew to this Nation Thereby. London: 1678. V. 38; 42

REASONS Against a Registry for Lands, Etc. Shewing Briefly the Great Disadvantages, Charges, and Inconveniences That May Accrue to the Whole Nation in General Thereby, Much Overbalancing the Particular Advantages That are Imagined ... London: 1678. V. 42

REASONS Against National Despondency, in Refutation of Mr. Erskine's View of the Causes and Consequences of the Present War with Some Remarks Upon the Supposed Scarcity of Specie. London: 1797. V. 39; 42

REASONS Demonstrating that the Breach in the Levels of Havering and Dagenham, Hath Already Done Very Great Damage to the Navigation of the River Thomaes and Will (if not speedily stopp'd) be more and More Prejudicial to It. N.P.: 1716. V. 41

REASONS for a Generall Assemblie. Edinburgh: 1638. V. 37

REASONS for a War; From the Imminent Danger With Which Europe is Threatened, by the Exorbitant Power of the House of Bourbon ... London: 1734. V. 45

REASONS for Giving Up Gibralatar ... With an Appendix ... London: 1749. V. 41; 45; 46

REASONS Grounded on Facts. I. That a New Duty on Sugar Must Fall on the Planter ... IV. That It Will Probably Occasion the Desertion of Our Sugar Islands. London: 1748. V. 46

REASONS Humbly Offered for the Bill to Prevent the Mischief Which May Happen by Keeping Too Great Quantities of Gun-Powder in or Near the Cities of London and Westminster; and the Suburbs Thereof. N.P.: 1719. V. 42

REASONS Humbly Offered to Prove that the Letter Printed at the End of the French Memorial of Justification Is a French Forgery, and Falsely Ascribed to His R--- H---ss. London: 1756. V. 45

REASONS Shewing the Necessity of Reducing the Army, and Proving That the Navy of England Is Her Only, and Natural Strength. London: 1732. V. 41

REASONS Why the Present System of Auctions Ought to be Abolished. New York: 1828. V. 39; 40; 44
REASONS Why the Present System of Auctions Ought to be Abolished. New York: 1828. V. 44

REASONS Why the Swamp and Overflowed Land in Arkansas Should Not be Taxed. Memphis: 1858. V. 40

REAU, LOUIS

Inedited Works of Bakst, Essays on Bakst by Louis Reau, Denis Roche, V. Svietlov, A. Tessier. New York: 1927. V. 40

REAUGH, FRANK

Paintings of the Southwest; by Frank Reaugh. Dallas. V. 42

REAUMUR, R. A. F. DE

The Art of Hatching and Brining Up Domestick Fowls of all Kinds at any Time of the Year. London: 1750. V. 37; 45; 46

The Natural History of Bees. London: 1744. V. 38

REAUMUR, R.A.F. DE

L'Art de Convertir Le Fer Forge Acier ... Paris: 1722. V. 40; 42; 45

REAVEY, GEORGE

The Colours of Memory. New York: 1955. V. 39

Nostradam - a Sequence of Poems. Paris: 1935. V. 38

REAVIS, L. U.

A Change of National Empire; or Arguments in Favor of the Removal of the National Capital from Washington City to the Mississippi Valley. St. Louis: 1869. V. 39

REAVIS, LOGAN URIAH

Railway and River Systems of the City of St. Louis ... Designed to Demonstrate that St. Louis is Rapidly Becoming the Food Distributing Center of the North American Continent ... St. Louis: 1879. V. 45

Saint Louis, the Commercial Metropolis of the Mississippi Valley. St. Louis: 1874. V. 45

REAY, HENRY UTRICK

A Treatise on that Useful Invention Called the Sportsman's friend; or, the Farmer's Footman. London: 1801. V. 45

THE REBELLION of 1895. A Complete and Concise Account . . . Honolulu: 1895. V. 44

REBELLO DA COSTA, AGOSTINHO

Descripcao Topografica e Historica da Cidade do Porto . . . Oporto: 1789. V. 40

REBOK, HORACE M.

Last of the Mus-Qua-Kies and the Indian Congress, 1898. Dayton: 1900. V. 46

RECEPTION and Entertainemnt of the Chinese Embassy, by the City of Boston. Boston: 1868. V. 39; 40

RECHINGER, K. H.

Flora of Lowland Iraq. 1964. V. 39

RECKITT, HAROLD

The Adventures of Ann and The White Seals. London: 1940. V. 44

RECLUS, ELISEE

The Earth. London: 1871. V. 43

The Ocean, Atmosphere and Life . . . New York: 1873. V. 41

The Ocean, Atmosphere and Life. London: 1873. V. 37

RECOPILACION de Les Leyes Destos Reynos, Hecha Por Mandado . . . Del Rey Don Felipe Segundo . . . ; Que se Ha Mandado Imprimir, Con Las Leyes Que Despues De La Ultima Impression se Han Publicado, Por . . . El Rey Don Felipe . . . Madrid: 1640. V. 40

THE RECORD of Crimes in the United States . . . Buffalo: 1833. V. 43

A RECORD of Some Worthie Proceedings in the Honorable Wise and Faithfull House of Commons in the Parliament Holden in the Yeare 1611. London: 1641. V. 40

RECORD of the 94th Regiment Ohio Volunteer Infantry in the War of the Rebellion. Cincinnati. V. 45

A RECORD of the Black Prince. London: 1849. V. 43

THE RECORD of the Celebration of the Two Hundredth Anniversary of the Birth of Benjamin Franklin, Under the Auspices of the American Philosophical Society held at Philadelphia for Promoting Useful Knowledge, April the Twentieth, A.D. Nineteen Hundred & Six. Philadelphia: 1906-08. V. 45

RECORD of the Confederate Sailors Devoted to the History of the Confederate Navy and Those Who Served In It. Richmond: 1925. V. 46

RECORD Of the Fedeeral Dead Buried from Libby, Belle Isle, Danville & Camp Lawton Prisons and at City Point, and in the Field Before Petersburg and Richmond. Philadelphia: 1865. V. 44

RECORDE, ROBERT 1510?-1558

The Castle of Knowledge. Colophon: 1556. V. 40

The Castle of Knowledge. London: 1556. V. 37

Record's Arithmetick; or, the Ground of Arts . . . London: 1654. V. 45

Record's Arithmetick; or, The Ground of Arts . . . London: 1673. V. 40

The Urinall of Phisicke. London: 1599. V. 44

The Urinal of Physick. London: 1651. V. 40

RECORDS of the Borough of Nottingham. Nottingham: 1882-1956. V. 46

RECORDS of the Court of New Castle on Delaware, 1676-1691 . . . Lancaster: 1904. V. 46

RECORDS of the General Conference of the Protestant Missionaris of China, held at Shanghai May 10-24, 1877. Shanghai: 1878. V. 37

RECORDS of the Lives of Ellen Free Pickton and Featherstone Lake Osler. Oxford: 1915. V. 42

RECORDS of the Past, Being English Translations of the Assyrian and Egyptian Monuments of Egypt and Western Asia. London: 1889-1892. V. 37

RECORDS of the Past, Being English Translations of the Assyrian and Egyptian Monuments Published Under the Sanction of the Society of Biblical Archeology. London: 1873=81. V. 37

RECORDS of the Town of Brookhaven. Brook B, 1679-1756. New York: 1932. V. 39

RECREATIONS in Natural History, or Popular Sketches of British Quadrupeds . . . London: 1815. V. 45; 46

RECTOR, MARGARET L.

Cowboy Life on the Texas Plains; The Photographs of Ray Rector. College Station: 1982. V. 42

RECUEIL de Diverses Pieces Concernant la Quietisme et le Quietistes, ou Lolinos ses Sentiments et ses Disciples . . . Amsterdam: 1688. V. 37

RECUEIL des Loix Constitutives des Colonies Angloises, Confederees Sous La Denomination D'Etats-Unis de L'Amerique-Septentrionale, Auquel on a Joint Les Actes du Congres General, Traduit de L'Anglois . . . Philadelphia: 1778. V. 44

RECUEIL d'Estampes Representant les Differents Envenemens de la Guerre Qui a Procure l'Independance aux Etats-Unis l'Amerique. Paris;: 1784. V. 39; 40; 44; 45

RECVEIL de Qvelqves Pieces Cvrievses, Servant a l'Esclaircissement de l'Histoire de la Vie de la Reyne Christine. Cologne: 1669. V. 37

RED, GEORGE PLUNKETT

The Medicine Man in Texas. 1930. V. 42

The Medicine Man in Texas. 1930. V. 44

The Medicine Man in Texas. Houston: 1930. V. 38; 45

RED Riding Hood. Boston: 1863. V. 45; 46
RED Riding Hood. London: 1890. V. 45

REDDING, CYRUS

Fifty Years' Recollections, Literary and Personal, with Observations on Men and Things. London: 1858. V. 39

A History and Description of Modern Wines. London: 1833. V. 38

An Illustrated Itinerary of the County of Lancaster. London: 1842. V. 41

The Pictorial History of the County of Lancaster. London: 1894. V. 38

REDDING, ISABELLA REMSHART

Life and Times of Jonathan Bryan, 1708-1788. Savannah: 1901. V. 39

REDE, LEMAN THOMAS

The Art of Money Getting . . . London: 1828. V. 46

Bibliotheca Americana; or, a Catalogue of the Most Curious and Interesting Books, Pamphlets, State Papers, Etc . . . . London: 1689. V. 46

Bibliotheca Americana; or, a Catalogue of the Most Curious and Interesting Books, Pamphlets, State Papers, Etc. Upon the Subject of North and South America, from the Earliest Period to the Present . . . London: 1789. V. 41; 45

REDE, WILLIAM LEMAN

The Royal Rake, and the Adventures of Alfred Chesterton. London: 1842. V. 46

REDEKER, CONRAD

Brevis Descriptio Initio Julii Anni MDCLXVI Detecti, Saluberrimi Bilfeldiani Fontis & Usus Ejusdem, Quam, Cum, Subjunctis Selectioribus Sanaatorum Exemplis . . . Amsterdam: 1668. V. 38

REDEL, CARL ADOLPH

Das Sehenswurdige Prag Worinnen alle Sehens-Merck- und Wunderwurdige Begenbenheiten, Denckmahle und Autiqiutaten. Nuremberg and Prag: 1720. V. 38

REDESDALE, JOHN MITFORD, 1ST BARON 1748-1830

A Treatise on the Pleadings in Suits in the Court of Chancery by English Bill. London: 1787. V. 40

A Treatise on the Pleadings in Suits in the Court of Chancery by English Bill. Dublin: 1795. V. 40

A Treatise on the Pleadings in Suits in the Court of Chancery by English Bill. London: 1814. V. 40

A Treatise on the Pleadings in Suits in the Court of Chancery by English Bill. London: 1847. V. 40

REDFERN GALLERY, LONDON.

Lithographies de l'Atelier Mourlot, Paris. London: 1965. V. 41

REDFERN, W. B.

Royal and Historic Gloves and Shoes. London: 1904. V. 38; 45

REDFIELD, WILLIAM C.

Sketch of the Geographical Rout (sic) of a Great railway By Which It Is Proposed to Connect the Canals and Navigable Waters . . . New York: 1829. V. 44

Sketch of the Geographical Route of a Great Railway to Connect the Canals and Navigable Waters of Ohio, Indiana, Illinois, Michigan. New York: 1830. V. 38

REDFORD, A. H.

The History of Methodism in Kentucky (to 1832). Nashville: 1868-70. V. 43

REDGRAVE, R.

A Century of Painters of the English School with Critical Notes, and an Account of the Progress of Art in England. London: 1866. V. 39

On the Necessity of Principles in Teaching Design. London: 1853. V. 45

REDGRAVE, SAMUEL

A Descriptive Catalogue of the Historical Collection of Water Colour Painting in the South Kensington Museum. London: 1877. V. 39; 44

Water-Colour Paintings in the South Kensington Museum - a Descriptive Catalogue of the Historical Collection . . . London: 1877. V. 39; 43

REDGROVE, PETER

Happiness. Berkhamsted: 1978. V. 38

Work in Progress. London: 1969. V. 38

REDHEAD, WILLIAM

Observations on the Different Breeds of Sheep, and the State of Sheep Farming In Some of the Principal Counties of England. Edinburgh: 1792. V. 42

REDHOUSE, JAMES W.

An English and Turkish Dictionary. London: 1856-57. V. 38

REDI, FRANCESCO

Bacchus in Tuscany, a Dithyrambic Poem . . . London: 1825. V. 43

Bacco in Toscana. Ditirambo di Franceso Redi Accademico Della Crvsca con Le Annotazioni. Firenze: 1685. V. 39

Opera. Venice: 1712-45. V. 37

Opere. Milan: 1809-11. V. 38

Opere di Francesco Redi. Venezia: 1742/28/45. V. 37

REDIVIVUS, LUDLOW

Aesop at Amsterdam, Balancing the Aesops at Tunbridg, Bathe, Whitehal, etc. Amsterdam: 1698. V. 45; 46

REDMAN, JOHN

The Emporium of Arts and Sciences. Philadelphia: 1812-14. V. 40

REDMOND'S Bride, a Fragment and Other Poems. Pembroke: 1824. V. 39

REDON, ODILON

Le Jure. Brussels: 1887. V. 37

L'Oeuvre Graphique de Odilon Redon. The Hague: 1913. V. 44

REDOUTE, PIERRE JOSEPH

Album de Redoute. London: 1954. V. 39

Facsimile Prints Made from Mostly Unpublished Original Paintings from the Collection of the Hunt Institute for Botanical Documentation. Regensburg & Pittsburgh: 1972. V. 37

Facsimile Prints Made from Mostly Unpublished Original Paintings from the Collection of the Hunt Institute for Botanical Documentation, Pittsburgh, Pa. Regensburg & Pittsburgh: 1972. V. 37

Les Roses. Paris: 1824. V. 39

REDPATH, GEORGE

The Stage Condemned, and the Encouragement Given to the Immoralities and Profanes of the Theatre. London: 1698. V. 43

REDPATH, JAMES 1833-1891

A Guide to Hayti. Boston: 1861. V. 40

A Guide to Hayti. New York: 1861. V. 46

The Public Life of Capt. John Brown. Boston: 1860. V. 44; 46

The Roving Editor; or, Talks with Slaves in the Southern States. New York: 1859. V. 42; 43

REDSHAW, T. D.

Hill Field: Poems and Memoirs for John Montague on His Sixtieth Birthday. Minneapolis: 1989. V. 41

REDSHAW, THOMAS DILLON

Hill Field - Poems and Memoirs for John Montague on His Sixtieth Birthday, 28 February 1989. Minneapolis & Oldcastle: 1989. V. 44

REDWOOD and Lumbering in California Forests. San Francisco: 1884. V. 37

REDWOOD County, Minnesota, Its Advantages to Settlers. St. Paul: 1879. V. 42

REDWOOD LIBRARY COMPANY

Charter of the Redwood Library Company, Grant(ed) A.D. 1747. Newport: 1816. V. 40

REECE, RICHARD

A Narrative of Circumstances that Attended the Last Illness and Death of Mrs. Southcott . . . London: 1815. V. 43

REED, ALMA

Jose Clemente Orozco. New York: 1932. V. 45

REED and Brett's Auckland Alamanac. Auckland: 1874. V. 40

REED, ANDREW

Memoirs of the Life and Philanthropic Labours of Andrew Reed, D.D. with Selections from His Journals. London: 1863. V. 42

A Narrative of the Visit to the American Churches by the Deputation from the Congregational Union of England and Wales. London: 1835. V. 37; 44

A Narrative of the Visit to the American Churches. New York: 1835. V. 37; 38; 39; 40; 44; 46

REED, EARL H.

Sketches in Jacobia. Chicago: 1919. V. 42

REED, EDWARD J.

Japan Its History, Traditions and Religions. London: 1880. V. 43

Modern Ships of War. New York: 1888. V. 39

Our Iron-Clad Ships: Their Qualities, Performances, and Cost. London: 1869. V. 42

Shipbuilding in Iron and Steel. London: 1869. V. 44

A Treatise on the Stability of Ships. London: 1885. V. 46

REED, ELIOT, PSEUD.

Skhytip. London: 1951. V. 46

REED, FRED H.

Illustrations of Tattershall Castle, Lincolnshire, from Measured Drawings Made by Fred H. Reed, to Whom was Awarded the Silver Medal of the Royal Institute of British Architects. London: 1872. V. 38; 42

REED, HENRY

Bigamy and Polygamy. New York: 1879. V. 42

Lessons of the War. 1970. V. 42

Lessons of the War. New York: 1970. V. 41

REED, HENRY A.

Topographical Drawing and Sketching, Including Applications of Photography. New York: 1906. V. 42

REED, ISAAC

The Repository: a Select Collection of Fugitive Pieces of Wit and Humour, in Prose and Verse. London: 1790. V. 42

REED, ISHAMEL

The Free Lance Pallbearers. New York: 1967. V. 40; 46

REED, ISHMAEL

The Free Lance Pallbearers. 1967. V. 42

The Free-Lance Pallbearers. Garden City: 1967. V. 37; 38; 39; 46

REED, J. T. A.

Cow Pock Inoculation . . . Respecting the Efficacy and Success of Vaccine Inoculation; and to Confirm Others In Their Good Opinion . . . Buckingham: 1810. V. 37; 38; 39; 40; 41; 45; 46

REED, JEREMY

The Lipstick Boys. V. 41

Target: Preliminary Poems. La Haule: 1972. V. 44

REED, JOHN

The Day in Bohemia. New York: 1913. V. 39; 45

Sangar: the mad Recreant Knight of the West (Lincoln Steffens). Riverside: 1913. V. 45

Sangar to Lincoln Steffens. Riverside: 1913. V. 45

The War in Eastern Europe. New York: 1916. V. 41

REED, JOHN A.

History of the 101st Regiment, Pennsylvania Veteran Volunteer Infantry, 1861-1865. Chicago: 1910. V. 42; 46

REED, JOHN E.

History of Erie County, Pennsylvania. Indianapolis: 1925. V. 42

REED, JONAS

A History of Rutland; Worcester County, Massachusetts, from Its Earliest Settlement, With a Biography of Its First Settlers. Worcester: 1836. V. 40; 46

REED, JOSEPH

Madrigal and Trulletta. London: 1758. V. 38

Remarks on a Late Publication in the Independent Gazetteer . . . Philadelphia: 1783. V. 45

Tom Jones, a Comic Opera . . . London: 1769. V. 46

REED, NATHANIEL

The Life of Texas Jack. Tulsa: 1936. V. 43

REED, P. FISHE

Incidents of the War, or, the Romance and Realities of Soldier Life. Indianapolis: 1862. V. 41

REED, RONALD

The Nature and Making of Parchment. 1975. V. 40

The Nature and Making of Parchment. Leeds: 1975. V. 38; 41; 42

REED, S. B.

House-Plans for Everybody. For Village and Country Residences Costing from $250 to $8000 ... New York: 1883. V. 44

REED, S. G.

A History of the Texas Railroads. Houston: 1941. V. 38; 39

REED, ST. CLAIR GRIFFIN

History of the Texas Railroads. Houston: 1941. V. 45

REED, SAMUEL R.

Offthoughts About Women and Other Things. Chicago: 1888. V. 40

REED, TALBOT BAINES

A History of Old English Letter Foundries ... London: 1887. V. 40; 46

A History of the Old English Letter Foundries. London: 1937. V. 40

A History of the Old English Letter Foundries. London: 1952. V. 37; 38; 40; 44; 46

REED, THOMAS BENTON

A Private in Gray. Camden: 1905. V. 43; 46

REED, WALT

Harold Von Schmidt. Flagstaff: 1972. V. 45; 46

The Illustrator in America. New York: 1966. V. 38

REED, WALTER

An Investigation into the So-called Lymphoid Nodules of the Liver in Abdominal Typhus. 1895. V. 37

Report on the Origin and Spread of Typhoid Fever in the U.S. Military Camps During the Spanish War of 1898. Washington: 1901. V. 40

Report on the Origin and Spread of Typhoid Fever In U.S. Military Camps During the Spanish War of 1898. Washington: 1904. V. 40

REED, WILLIAM

Olaf Wieghorst. Flagstaff: 1969. V. 41; 45

REED, WILLIAM B.

Life and Correspondence of Joseph Reed, Military Secretary of Washington, at Cambridge; Adjutant General of the Continental Army; Member of the Congress of the United States ... Philadelphia: 1847. V. 40

A Rejoinder to Mr. Bancroft's Historical Essay on President Reed. Philadelphia: 1867. V. 42

REED, WILLIAM BRADFORD

The Life of Esther de Berdt, Afterwards Esther Reed of Pennsylvania. Philadelphia: 1853. V. 39

REEMELIN, CHARLES

The Vine-Dresser's Manual, an Illustrated Treatise on Vineyards and Wine-Making. New York: 1856. V. 37; 43

REES, ABRAHAM

The Cyclopaedia; or, Universal Dictionary of Arts, Sciences and Literature. Philadelphia: 1810-24. V. 39

The Cyclopaedia; or, Universal Dictionary of Arts, Sciences and Literature. London: 1819-20. V. 45

The Cyclopaedia; or, Universal Dictionary of Arts, Sciences and Literature. Philadelphia: 1820. V. 45

REES, GEORGE OWEN 1813-1889

On the Analysis of the Blood and Urine, in Health and Disease. London: 1836. V. 40

REES, IOAN BOWEN

The Mountains of Wales. Newtown: 1987. V. 38; 44

REES, JAMES

The Life of Edwin Forrest. Philadelphia: 1874. V. 46

REES, THOMAS

A New System of Stenography, or Short Hand. Philadelphia: 1800. V. 45

The Racovian Cathecism, with Notes and Illustrations ... London: 1818. V. 46

REESE, DAVID MEREDITH

Letters to the Hon. William Jay, Being a Reply to His 'Inquiry Into the American Colonization and American Anti-Slavery Societies.' New York: 1835. V. 42

REESE, GEORGE H.

Proceedings of the Virginia State Convention of 1861. Richmond: 1965. V. 37; 40

REESE, HARRY

The Sandragraph: Between Printing and Painting. Los Angeles: 1987. V. 38

REESE, LIZETTE WORDWORTH

A Branch of May. Poems. Baltimore: 1887. V. 45

REESE, WILLIAM S.

Six Score: the 120 Best Books on the Range Cattle Industry. Austin: 1976. V. 37; 38; 39

REEVE, ARTHUR B.

Enter Craig Kennedy. New York: 1935. V. 42

REEVE, CLARA

Fatherless Fanny. Manchester: 1820. V. 40

Fatherless Fanny or a Young Lady's First Entrance into Life ... London: 1821. V. 45

The Old English Baron: a Gothic Story. London: 1778. V. 43

The Old English Baron. London: 1789. V. 40

The Old English Baron: a Gothic Story. London: 1797. V. 42

REEVE, CLARE

The Old English Baron: a Gothic Story. London: 1798. V. 40

REEVE, F. D.

Nightway. 1987. V. 39

REEVE, J. ARTHUR

Monograph of Fountains Abbey, Yorkshire. London: 1892. V. 40

REEVE, JAMES

Arcadian Ballads. Andoversford: 1977. V. 44

REEVE, JOHN 1608-1658

A General Epistle from the Holy Spirit, Unto all Prophets, Ministers, or Speakers in the World. London: 1653. V. 45

REEVE, JOSEPH

Ugbrooke Park: a Poem. London: 1776. V. 42; 45

REEVE, L.

Elements of Conchology. London: 1860. V. 37

REEVE, LOVELL AUGUSTUS 1814-1865

Conchologia Iconica. Berlin: 1843-78. V. 39

Letter to the Right Honourable the Earl of Derby ... on the Management, Character and Progress of the Zoological Society of London. London: 1846. V. 39

REEVE, SOPHIA

The Flowers at Court. London: 1809. V. 46

REEVE, TAPPING 1744-1823

The Law of Baron and Femme; of Parent and Child; of Guard and Ward; of Master and Servant; and of the Powers of Courts of Chancery. New Haven: 1816. V. 40

The Law of Baron and Femme; or Parent and Child ... New Haven: 1816. V. 38

REEVES, ARTHUR MIDDLETON

The Finding of Wineland the Good. London: 1890. V. 46

REEVES, EDWARD

Brown Men and Women or the South Sea Islands in 1895 and 1896. London: 1898. V. 40; 41

REEVES, FRANK

Hacienda de Atoton Ilco. Yerbanis: 1936. V. 46

REEVES, J.

History of the English Law, from the Time of the Saxons to the End of the Reign of Philip and Mary. London: 1787. V. 37

REEVES, JAMES

Arcadian Ballads. 1977. V. 45

Arcadian Ballads. 1977. V. 44

Arcadian Ballads. 1977. V. 43

Arcadian Ballads. 1977. V. 46

Arcadian Ballads. Gloucestershire: 1977. V. 37; 45

Arcadian Ballads. London: 1977. V. 42

Arcadian Ballads. (Anderversford): (1977). V. 37

The Natural Reed. Deya, Majorca & London: 1935. V. 40

The Natural Need. Majorca: 1935. V. 39

The Natural Need. Deya, Majorca: 1935. V. 37

Prefabulous Animals. London: 1957. V. 41

REEVES, JAMES EDMUND

A Hand-Book of Medical Microscopy . . . Philadelphia: 1894. V. 43

REEVES, JAMES J.

History of the Twenty-Fourth Regiment, New Jersey Volunteers. Camden: 1889. V. 38; 41

REEVES, JESSE

American Diplomacy Under Tyler and Polk. Baltimore: 1907. V. 37; 38; 39

REEVES, JOHN

The Art of Farriery Both in Theory and in Practice, Containing the Causes, Symptoms, and Cure of all Diseases Incident to Horses. Salisbury: 1763. V. 38

History of the English Law, from the Time of the Saxons, to the End of the Reign of Philip and Mary. London: 1787. V. 43

History of the English Law. London: 1787, 1829. V. 40

History of the Government of the Island of Newfoundland. London: 1793. V. 42; 43; 44

Reeve's History of the English Law . . . Philadelphia: 1880. V. 40

History of the English Law. London: 1787. V. 38

REEVES, RICHARD STONE

Classic Lines. A Gallery of the Great Thoroughbreds. Birmingham: 1975. V. 37; 42

Decade of Champions. London: 1980. V. 42

Thoroughbreds I Have Known. Cranbury: 1973. V. 37

REEVES, WILLIAM

Ecclesiastical Antiquities of Down, Connor and Dromore, Consisting of a Taxation of Those Dioceses . . . Dublin: 1847. V. 38

The Life of St. Columba Founder of HY. Dublin: 1857. V. 46

REEVES, WILLIAM PEMBER

New Zealand. London: 1908. V. 45; 46

REFF, THEODORE

The Hotebooks of Edgar Degas. Oxford: 1976. V. 46

REFLECTIONS and Considerations Occasioned by the Petition Presented to the Honourable House of Commons for Taking off the Drawback on Foreign Linens &c. London: 1738. V. 45; 46

REFLECTIONS and Suggestions on the Present State of Parties. Nashville: 1856. V. 44

REFLECTIONS on a Paper, Pretending to be an Apology for the Failures Charged on Mr. Walker's Account of the Siege of London-Derry. London: 1689. V. 41; 45

REFLECTIONS on the Case of Mr. Wilkes, and on the Right of the People to Elect Their Own Representatives. London. V. 38

REFLECTIONS on the Importation of Bar-Iron, From Our Own Colonies of North America. London: 1757. V. 39

REFLECTIONS on the Pernicious Custom of Recruiting by Crimps; and on Various Other Modes now Practiced in the British Army. London: 1795. V. 38

REFLECTIONS Upon Naturalization, Corporations and Companies, Supported by the Authorities of Both Ancient and Modern Writers. London: 1753. V. 46

REFLECTIONS Upon the Opinions of Some Modern Divines, Concerning the Nature of Government in General, and That of England in Particular. London: 1689. V. 39

REFLEXIONS on Courtship and Marriage in Two Letters to a Friend. London: 1759. V. 45

REFLEXIONS upon the Controversy About the Oath of Allegiance, Occasion'd by the Letter in Answer to English Loyalty. London: 1682. V. 42

REFORM CLUB

Catalogue of the Library of the Reform Club (printed for the members) and Revised Historical Introduction. London: 1894. V. 44

REFORM or Ruin: Take Your Choice! In Which the Conduct of the King, the Lord Lieutenant, the Parliament, the Ministry . . . the Lower Classes &c. is Considered . . . Dublin: 1798. V. 39

REFORMATIO Legum Ecclesiasticarum, Ex Authoritate Primum Regis Henrici 8. Londini: 1640. V. 38

REFORMED DUTCH CHURCH OF NORTH AMERICA

The Constitution of the Reformed Dutch Church in America. Philadelphia: 1840. V. 40

THE REFUGE. London: 1815. V. 41; 42

THE REFUGE by the Author of The Guide to Domestic Happiness. London: 1801. V. 46

A REFUTATION of Sir Crisp Gascoyne's Account of His Conduct, in the Cases of Elizabeth Canning and Mary Squires. London: 1754. V. 46

REGAN, C. T.

Biologia Centrali-Americana: Pisces. London: 1906-08. V. 37

REGAN, JOHN

The Emigrant's Guide to the Western States of America . . . Edinburgh: 1852. V. 45

The Western Wilds of America or Backwoods and Prairies, and Scenes in the valley of the Mississippi. Second Edition. Edinburgh: 1859. V. 37

REGEMORTE, LOUIS DE

Description du Nouveau Pont de Pierre Construit sur la Riviere d'Allier a Moulins. Paris: 1771. V. 38

REGEMORTER, B. VAN

Some Oriental Bindings in the Chester Beatty Library. Dublin: 1961. V. 38; 41

REGIMEN SANITATIS SALERNITANUM

Code of Health of the School of Salernum. Philadelphia: 1870. V. 37; 38; 39; 40; 41

Regimen Sanitatis . . . N.P., n.d.: 1500? V. 37

Regimen Sanitatis cum Expositione Magistri Arnaldi de Villanoua Cathellano Nouiter Impressus. s.l.s.a.: 1500? V. 37

Regimen Sanitatis Salerni. This Booke Teachyng All People to Gouerne the in Health. London: 1575. V. 37

REGIMENTAL Orders of the Second Ohio Artillery, From Its First Organization, September 23, 1863. N.P.: 1864. V. 44

REGINALD, HALLWARD

The Religion of Art. London: 1899? V. 40

REGINO, ABBOT OF PRUEM

Reginoni Monarachi Pruemonsis Annales non tam de Augustorum Vitis, quam Aliorum Germanorum Gestis. Mainz: 1521. V. 37

REGIOMONTANUS, JOANNES

Fundamenta Operationum, Quae Fiunt per Tabulam Generalem. Neuburgi ad Danubium: 1557. V. 37

REGIOMONTANUS, JOHANNES

Calendarium. Nuremberg: 1474. V. 44

THE REGISTER of Folly; or, Characters and Incidents at Bath and the Hot-Wells, in a Series of Poetical Epistles, by an Invalid. London: 1773. V. 38; 40

REGISTER of the Commissioned Officers and Privates of the New Jersey Volunteers, in the Service of the United States. Jersey City: 1863. V. 41

REGISTRUM Malmesburiense. The Register of Malmesbury Abbey, Preserved in the Public Record Office. London: 1879-80. V. 44

REGISTRUM Vocabularii Sequentis. Augsburg: 1478. V. 37

REGLAMENTO Para el Ejercicio y Maniobras de la Infanteria. Mexico: 1821. V. 45

REGLAMENTO Para La Milicia Civica Del Estado de Coahuila Y Texas. Monclova: 1834. V. 45

REGLEMENT de la Confrerie de l'Adoration-Perpetuelle du S. Sacrement et de la Bonne Mort. Erigee dans l'Eglise Paroissiale de Ville-Marie, en l'Isle de Montreal, en Canada. Montreal: 1776. V. 46

REGLER, GUSTAV

The Great Crusade. New York: 1940. V. 46

REGNAULT, NOEL

Philosophical Conversations; or, a New System of Physics, by Way of Dialogue. London: 1731. V. 41; 42; 46

REGNIER, HENRI DE

La Sandale Ailee. Paris: 1914. V. 41

REGNIER, M.

Recueil des Loix Constitutives des Colonies Angloises, Confederees Sous la Denomination d'Etats-Unis de l'Amerique Septentrionale. Philadelphia, i.e. Paris: 1778. V. 41

REGULAMENTO Dos Portos da Provincia de Mozambique. 1854. Mozambique: 1854. V. 41

REGULATIONS for the Instruction, Formations and Movements of the Cavalry. London: 1844. V. 41

REHBERG, FREDERICK

Drawings Faithfully Copied from Nature at Naples, and With Permission Dedicated to the Right Honorable Sir William Hamilton . . . Rome or London: 1794. V. 37; 43; 44

REHDER, A.

Bibligraphy of Cultivated Trees and Shrubs, Hardy in the Cooler Temperate Regions of the Northern Hemisphere. Jamaica Plain: 1949. V. 43; 44; 45; 46

The Bradley Bibliography. Cambridge: 1911-18. V. 43; 44; 45; 46

REI *Agrariae Auctores Legesque Variae. Quaedam Nunc Primum Caetera Emendatiora Prodeunt Cura Wilelmi Goesii, Cujus Accedunt Indices, Antiquitates Agrariae & Notae . . .* Amstelredami: 1674. V. 39

REICH, SHELDON

John Marin: a Stylistic Analysis and a Catalogue Raisonne. Tucson: 1970. V. 39; 41; 42; 45; 46

REICH, WILHELM 1897-1957

The Cancer Biopathy. 1948. V. 43

Character Analysis: Principles and Technique for Psychoanalysts in Practice and in Training. New York: 1945. V. 43; 45

The Function of the Orgasm . . . New York: 1942. V. 45

The Function of the Orgasm: Sex-Economic Problems of Biological Energy. New York: 1948. V. 43

The Murder of Christ. Rangeley: 1953. V. 43

People in Trouble. Orgonon: 1953. V. 43

The Sexual Revolution: Toward a Self Governing Character Structure. New York: 1945. V. 43; 45

REICHARD, GLADYS

Melanesian Design: A Study in Style in Wood and Tortoise Shell Carving. New York: 1933. V. 37; 39

Navaho Religion: a Study of Symbolism. New York: 1950. V. 39

REICHARD, GLADYS A.

Navjo Shepherd and Weaver. New York: 1936. V. 38

Navajo Medicine Man: Sandpaintings and Legends of Miguelito. New York: 1939. V. 37; 41; 45

REICHARD, HEINRICH

An Intinerary of France and Belgium, or, an Account of the Post and Cross Roads, Rivers, Canals . . . London: 1816. V. 39

REICHARDT, JOHANN FRIEDRICH 1752-1814

Neue Lieder Geselliger Freude. Leipzig: 1799-1804. V. 40

REICHE, CHARLES CHRISTOPHER

Fifteen Discourses on the Marvellous Works in Nature, Delivered by a Father to His Children. Philadelphia: 1791. V. 37

REICHENBACH, CHARLES VON

Physico-Physiological Researches on the Dynamcis of Magnetism, Electricity, Heat, Light, Crystallization and Chemism, In Their Relations to Vital Force. London: 1851. V. 39

REICHENBACH, KARL, BARON VON

Researches on Magnetism, Electricity, Heat, Light, Cyrstallization and Chemical Attraction, in Their Reltions to the Vital Force.. London: 1850. V. 38; 39

REICHENTHAL, ULRICH VON

Das Concilium so Zu Constanz Gehalten ist Worden des Jars. Augsburg: 1536. V. 38; 45

REICHERT, IRVING FREDERICK

Judaism and the American Jew. San Francisco: 1953. V. 39; 41; 46

Judaism and the American Jew, Selected Sermons and Addresses. San Francisco: 1953. V. 39

REICHHELM, GUSTAVUS

Chess in Philadelphia. Philadelphia: 1898. V. 40; 43

REID, A. J.

Illustrated Annual Review of the Appleton Post, Devoted to the City of Appleton Wisconsin . . . Appleton: 1879. V. 42

REID, ALASTAIR

Ounce, Dice, Trice. Boston: 1958. V. 44

The Printed Poem/The Poem as Print. Colorado Springs: 1985. V. 37

REID, C. MC. G.

A Revision of African Species of Labeo (Pisces: Cyprinidae) and a Redefinition of the Genus. London: 1985. V. 37

REID, DAVID BOSWELL

Illustrations of the Theory and Practice of Ventilation, With Remarks on Warming, Lighting . . . London: 1844. V. 37; 39

REID, ELIZABETH

Mayne Reid. A Memoir of His Life. London: 1890. V. 42

REID, F. A. S.

Comic Insects. London: 1870. V. 39

REID, FORREST

Brian Westby. London: 1934. V. 40

Illustrators of the Sixties. London: 1928. V. 37; 38; 39; 42; 43; 46

Pender Among the Residents. London: 1922. V. 45

REID, G. H.

An Essay on New South Wales. Sydney: 1876. V. 41

REID, GEORGE WILLIAM

Designs for Goldsmiths, Jewellers, etc. London: 1869. V. 38

Works of the Italian Engravers of the Fifteenth Century. London: 1884. V. 38; 40

REID, HENRY

A Practical Treatise on Concrete, and How to Make It; With Observations on the Uses of Cements, Limes and Mortars. London: 1869. V. 44

The Science and Art of the Manufacture of Portland Cement. With Observations on Some of Its Constructive Applications. London: 1877. V. 44

REID, JAMES

The Evolution of Horse-Drawn Vehicles with Historical Notes . . . London: 1933. V. 37; 42

The Life of Christ in Woodcuts. London: 1930. V. 44

REID, JAMES D.

The Telegraph in America: Morse Memorial. New York: 1886. V. 37

REID, JESSE WALTON

History of the Fourth Regiment of S.C. Volunteers, from the Commencement of the War Until Lee's Surrender . . . Greenville: 1892. V. 44

REID, JOHN

Bibliotheca Scoto-Celtica . . . Glasgow: 1832. V. 40

Essays on Hypochondriasis, and Other Nervous Affections. London: 1821. V. 45

Physiological, Anatomical and Pathological Researches. Edinburgh: 1848. V. 38; 45

The Scots Gard'ner in Two Parts . . . Edinburgh: 1683. V. 39

The Young Surveyor's Preceptor, a Clear and Comprehensive Analysis of the Art of Architectural Mensuration. London: 1858. V. 38; 40

REID, JOHN COLEMAN

Reid's Tramp; or a Journal of the Incidents of Ten Months Travel through Texas, New Mexico, Arizona, Sonora and California. Selma: 1858. V. 38; 39; 42; 44

REID, K. E. J.

The Book of Wedding Days. London: 1889. V. 38

REID, MAYNE 1818-1883

The Bandolero; or, a Marriage Among the Mountains. London: 1866. V. 40; 46

The Chase of Leviathan or, Adventures of the Ocean. London & New York: 1885. V. 39

The Child Wife: A Tale of the Two Worlds. London: 1868. V. 44; 46

The Child Wife: a Tale of two Worlds. New York: 1869. V. 46

Croquet. London: 1863. V. 40; 45

The Desert Home; or, the Adventures of a Lost Family in the Wilderness. London: 1852. V. 44; 46

The Free Lances. London: 1881. V. 43

The Headless Horseman; a Strange Tale of Texas. London: 1866. V. 40; 44; 46

The Lone Ranche: a Tale of the Staked Plain. London: 1871. V. 44

The Maroon. London: 1862. V. 40; 44

The Plant Hunters; or, Adventures Among the Himalaya Mountains. Boston: 1858. V. 44

The Plant Hunters or Adventures Among the Himalaya Mountains. London: 1858. V. 40

The Quadroon; or a Lover's Adventures in Louisiana. London: 1856. V. 41; 46

The Scalp Hunters . . . London: 1851. V. 44

The Scalp Hunters; or Adventures Among the Trappers. New York: 1856. V. 40

The White Chief; a Legend of Northern Mexico. London: 1855. V. 44; 46

REID, ROBERT

Observations on the Structure of Hospitals for the Treatment of Lunatics . . . Edinburgh. V. 40

REID, SAM C.

International Law: the Case of the Private Armed Brig. of War Gen. Armstrong. New York: 1857. V. 37; 44

REID, SAMUEL C.

The Scouting Expeditions of McCulloch's Texas Rangers; or, the Summer and Fall Campaign of the Army of the United States in Mexico - 1846. Philiadelphia: 1847. V. 41; 43

The Scouting Expeditions of McCulloch's Texas Rangers. Philadelphia: 1859. V. 37; 38

REID, STUART J.

Life and Letters of the First Earl of Durham 1792-1840. London: 1906-07. V. 38

REID, THOMAS

Account of the Life and Writings of Thomas Reid . . . late Professor of Moral Philosophy in the University of Glasgow. Edinburgh: 1803. V. 37

An Essay on the Nature and Cure of the Phithisis Pulmonalis; or Consumption of the Lungs . . . Philadelhia: 1785. V. 43

Essays on the Intellectual Powers of Man. Edinburgh: 1785. V. 38; 42

Essays on the Active Powers of Man. London: 1788. V. 42

Essays on the Intellectual and Active Powers of Man. Dublin: 1790. V. 42; 43; 45

Essays on the Powers of the Human Mind. Edinburgh: 1812. V. 41

Essays on the Powers of the Human Mind; to Which are Added, An Essay on Qeulity, and an Analysis of Aristotle's Logic. London: 1822. V. 43

Essays on the Powers of the Human Mind; to Which are Added an Essay on Quantity, and an Analysis of Aristotle's. London: 1827. V. 38; 41

Essays on the Intellectual Powers of Man. London: 1843. V. 41

Essays on the Active Powers of Man. Edinburgh: 1788. V. 40

Essays on the Intellectual Powers of Man. Edinburgh: 1785. V. 40

Essays on the Powers of the Human Mind. London: 1819. V. 40

An Inquiry into the Human Mind, on the Principles of Common Sense. Edinburgh: 1764. V. 42; 43

An Inquiry into the Human Mind, on the Principles of Common Sense. London: 1764. V. 38

An Inquiry Into the Human Mind, on the Principles of Common Sense. Edinburgh: 1765. V. 44

An Inquiry into the Human Mind on the Principles of Common Sense . . . London: 1769. V. 37; 38

An Inquiry into the Human Mind, on the Principles of Common Sense. Edinburgh: 1801. V. 38

An Inquiry into the Human Mind on the Principles of Common Sense. London: 1818. V. 41

An Inquiry into the Human Mind on the Principles of Common Sense. Glasgow: 1819. V. 42

An Inquiry into the Human Mind on the Principles of Common Sense. Glasgow: 1819. V. 45

Treatise on Clock and Watch Making, Theoretical and Practical. Philadelphia: 1821. V. 40

REID, THOMAS MAYNE 1818-1883

The Headless Horseman, a Strange Tale of Texas. London: 1866. V. 37; 38

No Quarter. London: 1888. V. 41

Oceola. London: 1859. V. 38

The Plant Hunters or Adventures Among the Himalaya Mountains. London: 1859. V. 38

The Queen of the Lakes. London: 1880. V. 38

The Scalp Hunters. London: 1851. V. 38

The Scalp Hunters: a Romance of Northern Mexico. London & New York: 1889. V. 38

REID, WILLIAM

An Attempt to Develop the Law of Storms By Means of Facts. London: 1838. V. 40

An Attempt to Develop the Law of Storms . . . to Point Out a Cause for the Variable Winds with the View to Practical Use in Navigation. London: 1850. V. 40; 46

Nuevo Tratado de la Ley de las Tormentas y Vientos Variables, Para el Uso Practico de la Navegacion . . . Cadiz;: 1853. V. 45

The Progress of the Development of the Law of Storms, and of the Variable Winds, with the Practical Application of the Subject to Navigation. London: 1849. V. 38

REID, WILLIAM HAMILTON

Memoirs of the Life of Colonel Wardle . . . London: 1809. V. 46

REID, WILLIAM JAMESON

Through Unexplored Asia. Boston: 1899. V. 39; 43

THE REIGN of Terror in Carlow, Comprising an Authentic Detail of the Proceedings of Mr. O'Connell and His Followers, from the Period of His Invading That Country, Down to the First of September. London: 1841. V. 38; 45

REIK, THEODOR

The Temptation. New York: 1961. V. 46

REIL, LOUIS

The Queen vs. Louis Riel, Accused and Convicted of the Crime of High Treason. Ottawa: 1886. V. 41

REILL, JOHANN CHRISTIAN

Rhapsodieen Uber Die Anwendung der Psychischen Kurmethode auf Geisterzeruttungen. Halle: 1818. V. 38

REILLY, EMILY G. S.

Historical Anecdotes of the Families of the Boleyns, Careys, Hamiltons and Joycelyna . . . 1839. V. 38

REILLY, HUGH

Genuine History of Ireland. Boston: 1838. V. 39

REILLY, ROBERT THOMAS

Facets of the Diamond. Ashfield: 1990. V. 45

REILY, JOHN T.

Conewago: a Collection of Catholic Local History Gathered From the Fields of Catholic Missionary Labor Within Our Reach . . . Martinsburg: 1885. V. 42

REINBECK, G.

Travels from St. Petersburgh through Moscow, Grodno, Warsaw, Breslaw &c. to Germany in the year 1805; in a Series of Letters. London: 1807. V. 40; 42

REINHARD, JOSEPH

A Collection of Swiss Costumes in Miniature Designed by Reinhardt. London: 1828. V. 39; 45

REINHARDT, VICTOR

A Drummer Boy of Shiloh. Terrell: 1910. V. 44

REINHOLD, KARL LEONARD

Beytrage zur Berichtigung Bisheriger Missverstandnisse der Philosophen. Jena: 1790-94. V. 45

Versuch Einer Neuen Theorie des Menschlichen Vorstellunsvermogens. Prag und Jena: 1789. V. 45

REINICK, ROBERT

Lieder Eines Malers Mit Randzeichnungen Seiner Freunde. Deutsche Dichtungen Mit Randzeichnungen Deutscher Kuenstler I & II. Duesseldorf: 1838/43/46. V. 38

REISCHAUER, ROBERT KARL

Early Japanese History. Princeton: 1937. V. 39

REISNER, GEORGE A.

The Hearst Medical Papyrus. Leipzig: 1905. V. 39

Mycerinus: the Temples of the Third Pyramid at Giza. Cambridge: 1931. V. 42

A Provincial Cemetery of the Pyramid Age. Berkeley & Los Angeles: 1932. V. 40; 42; 44

REISNER, GEORGE ANDREW

Canopics. Le Caire: 1967. V. 37

The Development of the Egyptian Tomb Down to the Accession of Cheops. Cambridge: 1936. V. 44

Harvard Excavations at Samaria 1908-1910. Cambridge: 1924. V. 40

REITLINGER, HENRY SCIPIO

Old Master Drawings. London: 1922. V. 38; 40; 46

RELACAO Curiosa, E Descripcam Geographica Das Terras De Mocambique, Rios de Sena. Lisbon: 1760. V. 40

RELACION de la Batalla que Nuno Albarez Botello, General de la Armada de Altobordo, del Mar de la India, Tuuo con Las Armadas de Orlando, y Ingalaterra en el Estrecho de Ormuz. Madrid: 1626. V. 41

RELACION de la Valerosa Defensa de los Naturales Bisayas del Pueblo de Palompong en la Isla de Leyte, de la Provincia de Cathalogan en las Yslas Philipinas, que Hicieron Contra las Armas Mahometanas de Ylanos . . . Manila: 1754. V. 40

RELACION de lo Sucedido en los Galeones y Flota de Terra Firme. N.P., n.d.: 1622. V. 45

RELACION del Temblor, Y Terromoto Que Dios Nuestro Senor Fue Servido de Embiar a La Ciudad Del Cuzco a 31 March Este Ano Passado de 1650. Madrid: 1651. V. 40

RELACION Publicada en Roma del Principio, y Estado Presente de la Mission del Dilatado Reyno del Gran Tibet, Y Otros Renos Confinantes, Recomendada a la Vigilancia, y Zelo de Los Padres Capuchinos de la Provincia de la Marca, en el Estado Eclesiastico. Cervera: 1743. V. 40

RELAND, ADRIAN

Hadriani Relandi Palestina, ex Monumentis Veteribus Illustrata . . . Nuremberg: 1716. V. 42

RELAND, HADRIAN

Palaestine Ex Monumentis Veteribus Illustrata. Utrecht: 1714. V. 37

A RELATION Concerning the Particulars of the Rebellion Lately Raised in Muscovy by Stenko Razin. London: 1672. V. 37

RELATION de l'Inauguration Solonelle de . . . Marie Therese, Reine de Hongrie et de Boheme, Comme Duchesse de Flandres. Ghent: 1744. V. 38; 40

RELATION du Voyage de Sa Majeste Britannique en Hollande, et de la Reception qui luy a ete Faite . . . La Haye: 1692. V. 40

RELATION en Forme de Journal du Voyage et Sejour que . . . Charles II a Fait en Hollande. Hague: 1660. V. 40; 46

A RELATION of Maryland. New York: 1865. V. 46

A RELATION Of Several Hundreds of Children and Others that Propesie and Preach in Their Sleep. London: 1689. V. 40

A RELATION of the Defeating Card. London: 1666. V. 45

A RELATION of the Engagement of His Majesty's Fleet with the Eneimies, on the 11th of August, 1673. London: 1673. V. 38

A RELATION of the Siege of Candia, from the First Expedition of the French Forces Under the Command of M. de la Fueillade, Duke of Roannez, to Its Surender, the 27th of September 1669. London: 1670. V. 39

RELATION Officielle des Fetes Organisees par la Ville de Paris Pour la Visite des Officiers et Marines de l'Escadre Russe de la Mediterranee les 17–24 Octobre 1893. Paris: 1896. V. 46

A RELATION To the Adventures of a Christian Ship at Alexandria in Egypt. N.P.: 1680. V. 42

RELATIONE del Successo Nell'Isola Della Terzera. Naples: 1583. V. 45

RELCAO da Viagem e Successos da Armada do Estrito de Ormus e Batalha do Congo. Lisbon: 1670. V. 41

RELHAN, RICHARD

Flora Cantabrigiensis, Exhibens Plantas Agro Cantabrigiensi Indigenas . . . Cambridge: 1785. V. 37; 39

RELIGIOUS Courtship: Being Historical Discourses on the Necessity of Marrying Religious Husbands and Wives Only, as Also, of Husbands and Wives Being of the Same Opinions in Religion with One Another. New York: 1793. V. 44

RELIGIOUS Instructions for the Susoos. Edinburgh: 1801. V. 39; 41

THE RELIQUES of Father Prout, late P.P. of Watergrasshill in the County of Cork, Ireland. Collected and Arranged by Oliver York. Illustrated with Engravings by Alfred Croquis. London: 1836. V. 37

RELPH, JOSEPH

Poems . . . Carlisle: 1798. V. 41; 42; 44; 46

RELPH, JOSIAH

Poems, Humourous and Sentimental . . . London: 1805. V. 45

RELTON, H. E.

Sketches of Churches, with Short Descriptions. London: 1843. V. 39

THE REMAINS of Robert Bloomfield. Volume One. London: 1824. V. 37

REMAINS of St. Mary's Abbey, Dublin. Their Explorations and Researches A.D. 1886. Dublin: 1887. V. 43; 44; 45

REMAK, ROBERT

Observations Anatomicae et Microscopicae de Systematis Nervosi Structura. Berloni: 1838. V. 40

REMARKABLE Story of Chicken Little. Boston: 1843. V. 41

A REMARKABLE Cause on a Note of Hand Try'd in the Court of Conscience, Anno 1741. London: 1742. V. 45

REMARKABLE Insects. London: 1860. V. 40

REMARKABLE Shipwrecks; or, a Collection of Interesting Accounts of Naval Disasters . . . Hartford: 1813. V. 40; 45

REMARKS on a Pamphlet, Intitled, a Inquiry in to the Revenue, Credit and Commerce of France, Exposing the False Quotations and False Reasoning of the Author, and the Evil Tendency of His Pamphlet. London: 1742. V. 41; 45

REMARKS on a Pamphlet Intitled, Considerations on the Late Bill for Paying the National Debt, etc. Number IV. Dublin: 1754. V. 41

REMARKS on a Voyage to the Hebrides, in a Letter to Samuel Johnson, LL.D. London: 1775. V. 40

REMARKS on African Colonization and the Abolition of Slavery. Winsor: 1833. V. 46

REMARKS On Dr. Price's Observations on the Nature of Civil Liberty &c. London: 1776. V. 44; 45

REMARKS on Dr. Priestley's Letter to the Right Honourable William Pitt (on the Repeal of the Test Acts); in a Second Address to the Candidates for Orders, in Both Universities. London: 1787. V. 39

REMARKS on Mr. Rousseau's Emilius; in Which the Celebrated Profession of Faith of a Savoyard Curate is Particularly Considered. London: 1783. V. 41

REMARKS on Several Late Publications relative to the Dissenters; in a Letter to Dr. Priestley. London: 1770. V. 37

REMARKS on Some Recent Publications Respecting Free Trade and Retaliation. London: 1844. V. 43

REMARKS on the Climate, Produce, and Natural Advantages of Nova Scotia. In a Letter to the Right Hon. the Earl of Macclesfield. London: 1782. V. 38

REMARKS on the Conduct of the B*** M*** Through the Course of the War, Together with Political Conjectures as To What May be Expected From a Peace. London: 1748. V. 41

REMARKS on the Demoralizing Influence of Slavery. London: 1828. V. 42

REMARKS on the French Memorials Concerning the Limit of Acadia, Printed at the Royal Printing House At Paris, and Distributed by the French Ministers At All the Foreign Courts of Europe. London: 1756. V. 40

REMARKS on the Morality of Dramatic Compositions; with Particular Reference to 'La Traviata', etc. London: 1856. V. 39

REMARKS on the New Sugar-Bill, and on the National Compacts Respecting the Sugar-Trade and Slave Trade. London: 1792. V. 46

REMARKS on the Novel of Reginald Dalton with Extracts from the Work, Illustrative of Life in Oxford. Oxford: 1824. V. 42

REMARKS on the Proposed Railway Between Birmingham and London, Proving by Facts and Arguments That the Work Would Cost Seven Millions and a Half; That It Would be a Burden Upon the Trade of the Country and Would Never Pay. London: 1831. V. 44

REMARKS on the Rights of Inventors, and the Influence of Their Studies in Promoting the Enjoyments of Life and Public Prosperity. Boston: 1807. V. 43

REMARKS on the Sentence Given in Favour of E. W. M. and T. T., Esqs. by the Lt. C-l at Paris. London: 1752. V. 46

REMARKS on the Trial of John Peter Zenger, Printer of the New York Weekly Journal, Who Was Lately Try'd and Acquitted for Printing and Publishing Two Libels Against the Government of that Province. London: 1738. V. 40

REMARKS Upon a Pamphlet, Intitled, The Considerations in Relation to Trade Considered, and a Short View of Our Present Trade and Taxes Reviewed. London: 1706. V. 41

REMARKS Upon Mr. Webber's Scheme and the Draper's Pamphlet. London: 1741. V. 39; 42
REMARKS Upon Mr. Webber's Scheme and the Draper's Pamphlet. London: 1741. V. 39

REMARKS Upon the Trial of William Sutton, Esq. London: 1761. V. 43

REMARKS with Reference to the Land-Laws of England, on Some Passages in Mr. John Sguart Mill's 'Principles of Political economy and M. Louis Blanc's 'Letters on England'. London: 1867. V. 42; 46

REMARKS, with Reference to the Land-Laws of England, On Some Passages in Mr. John Stuart Mill's 'Principles of Political Economy.' and M. Louis Blanc's 'Letters on England'. London: 1867. V. 42

REMARQUE, ERICH MARIA

All Quiet on the Western Front. 1929. V. 44

Im Westen Nichts Neues. (All Quiet on the Western Front). Berlin: 1929. V. 42

All Quiet on the Western Front. Boston: 1929. V. 45

All Quiet on the Western Front. Boston: 1929. V. 44

All Quiet on the Western Front. London: 1929. V. 43

All Quiet on the Western Front. London: 1929. V. 37; 43; 44

The Road Back. Boston: 1931. V. 42

The Road Back. London: 1931. V. 37

Shadows in Paradise. New York: 1972. V. 45

REMARQUES on the Humours and Conversations of the Town. London: 1673. V. 37

REMBERT, W. R.

The Georgia Bequest. Augusta: 1854. V. 42; 43

Manolia; or, the Vale of Tallulah. Augusta: 1854. V. 38

REMBRANDT

Operum Rembrandt Quibus Bibliorum Sac-Rorum Diversae Partes . . . e Veteri e Novo Testamento . . . Amsterdam: 1906-10. V. 44

THE REMEMBRANCER, or Impartial Repository of Public Events. London: 1775-80. V. 44

REMIGIO, FIORENTINO 1518-1580

Epistole d'Ovidio Divise in Due Libri. Con la Tavola. Venice: 1555. V. 40

REMINGTON, FREDERIC 1861-1909

Crooked Trails. New York: 1898. V. 37; 40; 42; 45

Crooked Trails. New York & London: 1898. V. 39

Done in the Open. New York: 1902. V. 37; 40; 41; 43; 45

Done in the Open. New York: 1903. V. 39; 41

Drawings. New York: 1897. V. 37; 38; 39

Drawings. New York: 1898. V. 44

Frederic Remington 4 Pictures in Color. V. 39

Frontier Sketches. Chicago: 1898. V. 39

Frontier Sketches. New York: 1898. V. 38; 46

John Ermine of the Yellowstone. New York: 1902. V. 38; 40; 45

Men with the Bark On. New York: 1900. V. 37; 38; 39; 41; 43; 44; 45; 46

Men with the Bark On. New York: 1909. V. 40

Pony Tracks. New York: 1895. V. 37; 38; 39; 40; 41; 44; 45

Remington's Frontier Sketches. Akron: 1898. V. 40

Remington's Frontier Sketches. Chicago: 1898. V. 39; 42

Remington's Frontier Sketches. 1898. V. 37

Sundown Leflare. New York: 1889. V. 39; 41

Sundown Leflare. New York: 1899. V. 37; 40; 41; 42; 43; 44; 45

The Way of an Indian. London: 1906. V. 38

Way of an Indian. New York: 1906. V. 39; 42

REMINISCENCES of Chicago During the Civil War. Chicago: 1914. V. 44

REMINISCENCES of the Cleveland Light Artillery. Cleveland: 1906. V. 45

REMISE, J.

The Golden Age of Toys. Lausanne: 1967. V. 46

REMOND DES COURS, NICOLAS

The True Conduct of Persons of Quality. London: 1694. V. 44

REMONDINI, JOSEPH

Catalogus Recens in VArias Classes Disbributus Librorum . . . Venice: 1785-84. V. 45

REMONDINO, P. C.

History of Circumcision From the Earliest Times to the Present With a History of Eunuchism, Hermaphorodism, etc. Philadelphia: 1891. V. 38; 42; 45

The Mediterranean Shores of America, Southern California: Its Climatic, Physical and Meteorological Conditions. Philadelphia: 1892. V. 44

REMSBURG, JOHN

Charlie Reynolds, Soldier, Hunter, Scout and Guide. Kansas City: 1931. V. 45

REMY, JULES

A Journal to Great Salt Lake City . . . with a Sketch of the History, Religion and Customs of the Mormons . . . London: 1861. V. 38; 40; 41; 42; 43; 45

Voyage au Pays des Mormons; Relation, Geographie, Histoire Naturelle, Histoire, Theologie, Moeurs et Costumes. Paris: 1860. V. 46

REMY, NICHOLAS

Daemonolatreiae Libri Tres. Francofurti: 1596. V. 39

REMY, NICOLAS 1530-1612

Demonolatry. London: 1930. V. 38; 44; 45; 46

RENAN, ERNEST

The Life of Jesus. London: 1864. V. 37

RENARD, JULES

Histoires Naturelles. Lausanne: 1953. V. 41

Natural History. Cambridge: 1960. V. 39; 40; 42; 46

RENAU D'ELICARGARAY, BERNARD

Memoire ou Est Demonstre un Principe de la Mechanique des Liqueurs . . . N.P.: 1700. V. 45

RENAUDOT, EUSEBE

A General Collection of Discourses of the Virtuosi of France, Upon Questions of all Sorts of Philosophy, and Other Natural Knowledge. London: 1664. V. 37

RENAUDOT, EUSEBIUS

Ancient Accounts of India and China. London: 1733. V. 44

RENAULT, MARY

Kind Are Her Answers. London: 1940. V. 46

Purposes of Love. London: 1939. V. 46

RENDALL, MONTAGUE JOHN

The Winchester Charts: Paitners of North Italy. London: 1905? V. 42

RENDELL, RUTH

A Guilty Thing Surprised. London: 1970. V. 41

Matters of Suspense. Helsinki: 1986. V. 44; 45

A New Lease of Death. London: 1967. V. 43

RENDELL, WILLIAM EDGCUMBE

Rendle's Patent System of Glazing Railway Stations, Winter Gardens, Exhibition Buildings, Skating Rinks, Railway Sheds, Markets, Public Buildings . . . London: 1876. V. 43

RENDER, WILHELM

A Concise Practical grammar of the German Tongue . . . London: 1799. V. 41

RENEAULME, PAUL DE

Specimen Historiae Plantarum. Paris: 1611. V. 45; 46

RENFROE, JOHN J. D.

The Battle is God's. Richmond: 1863. V. 44

RENIER, G. J.

Oscar Wilde. London: 1933. V. 46

RENLOW, H.

The Human Eye and Its Auxiliary Organs, Anatomically Represented, with Explanatory Text. London: 1896. V. 42

RENN, LUDWIG

War. London: 1929. V. 44; 45

RENNEFORT, SOUCHU DE

Histoire des Indes Orientales. Leiden: 1688. V. 39

RENNELL, JAMES

The Geographical System of Herodotus Examined and Explained . . . London: 1800. V. 37; 44

Memoir of a Map of Hindoostan; or the Mogul's Empire. London: 1783. V. 40

Observations on a Current that Often Prevails to the Westward of Scilly . . . London: 1793. V. 37; 43

On the Rate of Travelling as Performed by Camels; and Its Application, as a Scale to the Purposes of Geography. London: 1791. V. 45

RENNEMANN, ALEXANDER

Neu Aufgelegtes Gluecks - Raedlein, Darinnen Manns - und Weibs - Personen, Junggesellen und Jungfrauen, Durch Einen Wuerfel . . . Germany: 1680. V. 42

RENNER, FREDERIC

Charles M. Russell. Paintings, Drawings and Sculpture in the Amon Carter Museum. New York: 1974. V. 44

RENNER, GINGER

A Limitless Sky. Flagstaff: 1986. V. 46

RENNEVILLE, RENE AUGUSTIN CONSTANTIN DE

The French Inquisition; or, the History of the Bastille of Paris, the State Prison of France . . . London: 1715. V. 46

RENNIE, D. F.

The British Army in North China and Japan: Peking 1860; Kagosima 1862. London: 1864. V. 41

Peking and the Pekingese During the First Year of the British Embassy at Peking. London: 1865. V. 45

RENNIE, DAVID FIELD

Bhotan and the Story of the Dooar War Including the Sketches of a Three Months' Residence in the Himalayas, and Narrative of a Visit to Bhotan in May 1865. London: 1866. V. 39

RENNIE, ELIZABETH

Traits of Character; being twenty-five years' literary and personal recollections. By a Contemporary. London: 1860. V. 37

RENNIE, GEORGE 1749-1828

General View of the Agriculture of the West Riding of Yorkshire, Surveyed by Messrs Rennie, Brown and Shirreff. London: 1793. V. 46

General View of the Agriculture of the West Riding of Yorkshire, Surveyed by Messrs. Rennie & shirreff 1793. Edinburgh: 1799. V. 41

Views of the Old and New London Bridges Drawn and Etched by Edward William Cooke with Scientific and Historical Notices of the Two Bridges . . . London: 1833. V. 38

RENNIE, JOHN

Autobiography. London: 1875. V. 39

Plans and Sections of the Shrewsbury & Birmingham Railway Extension, from Shrewsbury to Newtown. London: 1844. V. 46

The Theory, Formation and Construction of British and Foreign Harbours. London: 1854. V. 38; 41; 45

RENNIE, R.

Essays on the Natural History and Origin of Peat Moss . . . Edinburgh: 1807. V. 44

Essays on the Natural History and Origin of Peat Moss. Edinburgh: 1807-10. V. 38

RENNO'S Raiders. Nappanee: 1966. V. 38

RENNY, ROBERT

History of Jamaica with Observations on the Climate, Scenery, Trade, Productions, Negroes, Slave Trade, diseases of Europeans, Customs, Manners . . . London: 1807. V. 37; 38

RENODEUS, JOANNES

A Medicinal Dispensatory, Containing the Whole Body of Physick. London: 1657. V. 38

RENOLDS, GEORGE

The State of the Greatest King, Set Forth in the Greatness of Solomon, and the Glory of His Reign . . . Bristol: 1721. V. 38

RENOUARD, ANTOINE AUGUSTIN

Annales de l'Imprimerie des Alde, ou Histoire des Trois Maunce et de Leurs Editions. Paris: 1803/1812. V. 37

RENOUARD, P. V.

History of Medicine, from Its Origin to the Nineteenth Century. Cincinnati: 1856. V. 37; 40; 41; 42; 44; 45

RENOUF, P. LE PAGE

The Egyptian Book of the Dead. London: 1904. V. 40

THE RENOWNED History of Goody Two-Shoes. London: 1881. V. 42

RENSHAW, WALTER CHARLES

Searches into the History of the Family of Byne or Bine of Sussex. London: 1913. V. 39

RENTON, EDWARD

Intaglio Engraving of Gems. London: 1896. V. 40

RENTOUL, ANNIE R.

The Little Green Road to Fairyland. London: 1925. V. 44

The Little Green Road to Fairyland. London: 1947. V. 42

RENWICK, JAMES

Treatise on the Steam Engine. New York: 1839. V. 42

REPINGTON, CHARLES A'COURT

The War in the Far East 1904-1905 by the Military Correspondent of The Times. London: 1905. V. 46

REPLOGLE, CHARLES

Among the Indians of Alaska. London: 1904. V. 43

A REPLY to a Letter Addressed to the Right Hon. George Grenville, Etc. In Which the Truth of the Facts is Examined and the Propriety of the motto Fully Considered. London: 1763. V. 38

A REPLY To a Pamphlet Intitled Popular Prejudices Against the Convention and Treaty with Spain, Examind'd and Answered. London: 1739. V. 41; 45

A REPLY to John Stuart Mill on the Subjection of Women. Philadelphia: 1870. V. 38

A REPLY to Some Financial Misstatements, in and Out of Parliament. London: 1803. V. 38

A REPLY to the Answer to a Short Essay on the Modes of Defence Best Adapted to the Situation and Circumstances of this Island, Etc. In a Letter to His Grace the Duke of Richmond. London: 1785. V. 42

A REPLY to the Treasury Pamphlet, entitled 'The Proposed System of Trade with Ireland Explained.' London: 1785. V. 39

UNITED States. Commission APPOINTED BY THE PRESIDENT TO INVESTIGATE THE CONDUCT OF THE WAR DEPARTMENT IN THE WAR WITH SPAIN Report of the Commission Appointed by the President to Investigate the Conduct of the War Department in the War with Spain. Washington: 1900. V. 39

A REPORT from the Committee Appointed to Enquire into the State of Gaols of this Kingdom: Relating to the Fleet Prison. London: 1729. V. 45

A REPORT From the Committee Appointed to View The Cottonian Library, and Such of the Public Records of This Kingdom, As They Think Proper, and to Report to the House the Condition Thereof . . . London: 1732. V. 37

REPORT of a Trial for Bigamy . . . at the Assizes Held at Mold, in the county of Flint . . . with a Preface and Notes by a Student of the Inner Temple, London. London: 1807. V. 45

THE REPORT of an Action of Assault, Battery and Wounding, Tried in the Supreme Court of Judicature for the Province of New York, in the Term of October 1764, Between Thomas Forsey, Plantiff and Waddel Cunningham, Defendant. New York: 1765. V. 44

REPORT of the Case of John Dorrance Against Arthur Fenner, with the Proceedings in the Case of Fenner Vs. Dorrance. Providence: 1802. V. 37

REPORT of the Commissioner-General for the United States to the International Universal Expostion, Paris, 1900. Washington: 1901. V. 37

REPORT of the Committee Appointed to Examine into the Rise, Progress, and Present State of the Society of Artists of the United States. Read April 15, 1812. Philadelphia: 1812. V. 37

REPORT of the Committee . . . to Enquire What Compensation Ought to be Made to Captain Zebulon M. Pike and His Companions. Washington City: 1808. V. 41

A REPORT of the Decisions of the Supreme Court . . . in the Case of Dred Scott vs. John F. A. Sanford. New York: 1857. V. 41

REPORT of the Great Railroad Conspiracy Case. Detroit: 1851. V. 42

A REPORT of the Proceedings in Relation to the Contested Election for Delegate to the Nineteenth Congress from the Territory of Michigan, Between Austin E. Wing, Gabriel Richard and John Biddle . . . Detroit: 1825. V. 44

REPORT of the Special Commission Appointed to Investigage the Affairs of the Red Cloud Indian Agency, July, 1875; Together with the Testimony and Accompanying Documents. Washington: 1875. V. 37

REPORT of the Trial Had Before the Rt. Hon. ARthur, Lord Kilwarden . . . on Tuesday, the 2nd Day of December 1800, Between Robert Tighe, Esq. M.P. Plaintiff and Dive Jones, Esq. Captain in the 54th Regiment of Foot, Defendant, for Crime . . . N.P.: 1782. V. 46

REPORT of the Trial of an Action, Wherein the Honourable Frederick Cavendish was Plantiff, and the Hope Insurance Company of London were Defendants. Dublin: 1813. V. 40

A REPORT of the Trial of Pedro Gilbert, Bernardo de Soto, Francisco Ruiz, Nicola Costa, Antonio Ferrer, Manuel Boyga, Domingo de Guzman, Juan Montenegro alias Jose Basilio de Castro, Before the United States Circuit Court . . . Boston: 1834. V. 42

REPORT on the Condition of the Real Estate Within the Limits of the City of San Francisco, and the Property Beyond, Within the Bounds of the Old Mission Delores . . . San Francisco: 1851. V. 40

REPORT on the Typography of the Cambridge University Press, Prepared in 1917 at the Request of the Syndics by Bruce Rogers and Now Printed in Honour of His Eightieth Birthday. N.P.: 1950. V. 37

REPORT Upon the Claims of Mr. George Stephenson Relative to the Invention of His Safety Lamp. By the Committee Appointed at a Meeting Holden in Newcastle, on the First of November, 1817. Newcastle: 1817. V. 38

REPORTS from the Commissioners. Appointed by His Majesty to Execute the Measures Recommended in an Address of the House of Commons, Respecting the Public Records of Ireland. With Supplements and Appendices 1810-1815. 1815. V. 40

REPORTS of the Committee of Investigation Sent in 1873 by the Mexican Government to the Frontier of Texas. New York: 1875. V. 39; 42; 45; 46

THE REPOSITORY of Arts, Literature, Commerce, Manufactures, Fashions and Poltiics. London: 1809-28. V. 42

REPPLIER, AGNES

If the Unresponsive Gods . . . Yselta: 1943. V. 44

REPRESENTATION au Naturel e Fontainebleau. Amsterdam: 1660. V. 45

REPRESENTATION of the Embossed, Chased, & Engraved Subjects and Inscriptions, which Decorate the Tobacco Box and Cases, belonging to the Past Overseers Society, of the Parishes of St. Margaret and St. John the Evangelist, in the City of Westminster. London: 1824. V. 37

THE REPRESENTATION of the Leaseholders and Contractors Interested in the Houses and Buildings in Pickett Street, Fleet Market; and Snow Hill . . . London: 1807. V. 38

A REPRESENTATION to Congress by the Morton Testimonial Association . . . Urging Compensation for the Use of Anaesthetics in the Army and Navy Submitted to the 38th Congress, and Printed for the Use of Its Members. Washington: 1864. V. 39

REPRESENTATIVE Men of Colorado in the Nineteenth Century. New York: 1892. V. 39

REPRESENTATIVE Men of Colorado in the Nineteenth Century: A Portrait Gallery of Men who Have Been Instrumental in Upbuilding of Colorado. New York/Denver: 1902. V. 37

REPS, J. W.

Cities of the American West. A History of Frontier Urban Planning. Princeton: 1979. V. 39; 40; 43

REPS, JOHN W.

The Making of Urban America: a History of City Planning in the United States. Princeton: 1965. V. 42

REPS, PAUL

Gold Fish Signatures. San Francisco: 1962. V. 46

REPTON, HUMPHREY 1752-1818

The Art of Landscape Gardening. Boston: 1907. V. 37; 39

The Art of Landscape Gardening. Boston & New York: 1907. V. 37; 38; 43

Designs for the Pavilion at Brighton. London: 1808. V. 38; 42

An Enquiry into the Changes of Taste In Landscape Gardening . . . London: 1806. V. 38; 39; 40

Fragments . . . London: 1816. V. 41; 44

The Landscape Gardening and Landscape Architecture . . . London: 1840. V. 40; 44

Observations on the Theory and Practice of Landscape Gardening. London. V. 42

Observations on the Theory and Practice of Landscape Gardening. London: 1803. V. 38; 39; 41; 42; 44; 45

Observations on the Theory and Practice of Landscape Gardening. London: 1805. V. 37; 40; 42; 44; 45

Observations on the Theory and Practice of Landscape Gardening. Oxford: 1981. V. 38

Odd Whims and Miscellanies. London: 1804. V. 39; 43

The Red Books of Humphry Repton. London: 1976. V. 38; 39; 40; 41; 42; 45; 46

Sketches and Hints on Landscape Gardening, Collected from the Designs and Observations Now in the Possession of the Different Noblemen and Gentlemen, For Whose Use They Were Originally Made. London: 1794. V. 43

THE REPUBLICAN Mountain Silver Mines, Limited. London: 1882. V. 39

THE REPUBLICK Rescued from Danger: in a Letter from My Lord G----m to a Man of Quality, of the Province of Utrecht. London: 1747. V. 41

REQUA, RICHARD S.

Architectural Details: Spain and the Mediterranean . . . Los Angeles: 1926. V. 46

Old World Inspiration for American Architecture. Los Angeles: 1929. V. 46

RERESBY, JOHN

The Memoirs of . . . London: 1734. V. 46

The Memoirs of the Honourable Sir John Reresby, Bart and Last Governor of York . . . London: 1735. V. 38

The Travels and Memoirs of Sir John Reresby, Bart . . . London: 1813. V. 42; 46

RERESBY, TAMWORTH

A Miscellany of Ingenious Thoughts and Reflections, In Verse and Prose . . . London: 1721. V. 38; 42

RERUM Britannicarum . . . Scriptores Vetustiores ac Praecipui . . . Heidelberg: 1587. V. 45

RERUM Bohemicarum Antiqui Scriptores Insignes, Partim Hactenus Incogniti. Accedunt Joh. Dubr. Episcopi Olmucensis Historiae Bohemicae Commentarii. Hanau: 1602. V. 37

RERUM Germanicarum Libri Tres . . . Quibus Praemissa est Vita Beati Rhenani, a Ioanne Sturmio Eleganter Conscripta. Basle: 1551. V. 40

RESANOV, NIKOLAI PETROVICH

Rezanov Reconnoiters California, 1806. San Francisco: 1972. V. 39

RESE, FRIEDRICH

Arbriss Der Geschichte des Bisthumus Cincinnati in Nord Amerika. Wein: 1829. V. 39

RESEN, PEDER HANSEN

Inscriptiones Haffnienses Latinae, Danicae et Germanicae . . . Haffniae: 1668. V. 43; 44

RESENDE, ANDRE DE 1498-1573

Sententiae et Exempla ex Probatissimis Scriptoribus Collecta . . . Venice: 1586. V. 40

RESENDE, LUCIO ANDREA

Libri Quatuor de Antiquitatibus Lusitaniae . . . a Jacobo Menoetio Vasconcello Recogniti Atque Absoluti. Evora: 1593. V. 37; 44

THE RESIGNATION Discusses. In Which Many of the False Facts are Detected and Sophistical Reasoning Refuted, in a Pamphlet, Intitled, An Apology for a Late Resignation &c. London: 1748. V. 41

RESNAL, ABBE

A Philosophical and Political History of the Settlements and Trade of the Europeans in the East and West Indies. Dublin: 1776. V. 40

A RESOLUTION to Act, the Only Way Left us to Be Free. Paris: 1795. V. 39

RESOLUTIONS and a Declaration, Adopted Unanimously by a Convention of Delegates from the States and Territories of the West, and South West; Held in the City of Cincinnati, on the Third, Fourth and Fifth Days of July, 1843. Cincinnati: 1843. V. 39; 40

RESOLUTIONS of the Associated Architects, with the Report of a Committee by Them Appointed to Consider the Causes of Frequent Fires, and the Best Mens of Preventing the Like in the Future. N.P.: 1793. V. 42

THE RESOLUTIONS of Virginia and Kentucky; Penned by Madison and Jefferson in Relation to the Alien and Sedition Laws. Richmond: 1826. V. 41

RESOURCES and Advantages of Colorado. Denver: 1873. V. 41

THE RESOURCES and Attractions of the Territory of Utah. Omaha: 1979. V. 39

RESOURCES of he State of Oregon, Revised; a Book of Statistical Information Treating Upon Oregon as a Whole and By Counties. Salem: 1892. V. 42

RESOURCES of Wyoming, 1889. Cheyenne: 1889. V. 37

THE RESPONSE of the Judges of the Court of Appeals to the Preamble, Resolutions and Address, Proposed by a Joint Committee of the Senate and House of Representatives, for the Purpose of Removing Them from Office of the House of Representatives, Dec. 9, 1824. Frankfort: 1824. V. 44

RESPUBLICA Siue Status Regni Poloniae, Lituaniae, Prussiae, Livoniae, etc. Lvgdvni Batavorvm: 1627. V. 45

RESPUESTA Documentada a la Imputacion Hecha a la Asamblea Electoral de Popayan con Motivo de la Peticion que Dio Sobre la Ley de Manumision. Popayan: 1823. V. 41

RESTA, SEBASTIANO

The True Effigies of the Most Eminent Painters . . . Antwerp: 1694. V. 45

The True Effigies of the Most Eminent Painters and Other Famous Artists that Have Flourished in Europe. London: 1694. V. 42; 43

RESTIF DE LA BRETONNE, NICHOLAS EDME 1734-1806

Monsieur Nicolas, or the Human Heart Unveiled. London: 1930. V. 37; 38; 43; 44

Monsieur Nicolas or the Human Heart Unveiled. London: 1930-31. V. 38

RESTORATION Love Songs. Hitchin: 1950. V. 37

THE RESTORATIONIST. Boston: 1837-38. V. 41

RESTOUT, JEAN BERNARD

Galerie Francoise, ou Portraits des Hommes et des Femmes Celebres qui ont Paru en France . . . avec un Abrege de Leur Vie . . . Paris: 1771. V. 38

THE RETFORD Centenary Exhibition. London: 1975. V. 37

RETROPROGRESSION. Being a Short Account of a Short Residence in the Celebrated Town of Jumbleborough. Boston: 1839. V. 37; 39

A RETROSPECT of Andrew Jackson's Administration. N.P.: 1832. V. 43

THE RETROSPECT of Practical Medicine and Surgery. New York: 1840-73. V. 44

A RETURN of Departed Spirits of the Highest Characters of Distinction, as Well as the Indiscriminate of All Nations, Into the Bodies of the 'Shakers', or 'United Society of Believers in the Second Advent of the Messiah.' Philadelphia: 1843. V. 42

THE RETURNS for the West Riding of the County of York of the Poll Tax Laid in the Second Year of the Reign of King Richard the Second. London: 1882. V. 45

RETZIUS, GUSTAF 1842-1919

Das Menschenhirn Studien in der Makroskopischen Morphologie. Stockholm: 1896. V. 42

Studien in der Anatomie des Nervensystems und des Bindegewebes. Stockholm: 1875-76. V. 37; 39; 42

RETZIUS, GUSTAV 1842-1919

Das Gehororgan der Wirbelthiere Morphologisch-Histologische Studien. Stockholm: 1881-84. V. 39

REUCHLIN, JOHANNES 1455-1522

De Arte Cabalistica Libri Tres Leoni X Dicati. Hagenau: 1517. V. 40

REUILLY, J.

Travels in the Crimea, and Along the Shores of the Black Sea, Performed During the Year 1803. London: 1807. V. 40

REUNERT, THEODORE

Diamonds and Gold in South Africa. Cape Town: 1893. V. 40

REUS, CONDE DE

Mejicanos. Veracruz: 1862. V. 45

REUSNER, NICOLAUS

Emblemata Nicolai Feusneri. Francoforti ad Moenum: 1581. V. 37; 42

Icones Sive Imagines Virorum Literis Illustrium. Strasbourg: 1590. V. 38; 41

REUSS, W. F.

Calculations and Statements Relative in the Trade Between Great Britain and the United States of America . . . London: 1833. V. 46

REUTER, FRITZ

An Old Story of My Farming Days. London. V. 40

An Old Story of My Arming Days. London. V. 41

REVEIL, ACHILLE

Museum of Painting and Sculpture, or Collection of the Principal Figures, Statues and Bas Reliefs in the Public and Private Galleries of Europe. London and Paris: 1828-34. V. 40; 44

REVEILLE: Devoted to the Disabled Sailor & Soldier. All published. August 1918-February 1919. V. 37

REVELATIO Admirabilis de Statu Alterius Seculi, Diuini Apprime Timoris Erudiotira. Paris: 1530. V. 43

The Revelation of Saint John the Divine. London. V. 40

REVELATIONS of a Slave Smuggler Being the Autobiography of Capt. Rich'd Drake, an African Trader for Fifty Years -- From 1807 to 1857 . . . New York: 1860. V. 38

REVELEY, HENRY

Notices Illustrative of the Drawing and Sketches of Some of the Most Distinguished Masters in all the Principle Schools of Design. London: 1820. V. 44

REVELL, J.

A Complete Guide to the Ornamental Leather Work. London: 1853. V. 41

REVERDY, PIERRE

Selected Poems. New York: 1969. V. 46

Une Aventure Methodique. Georges Braque. Paris: 1949-50. V. 42

Une Aventure Methodique: Braque. Paris: 1950. V. 41

REVERE, JOSEPH WARREN 1812-1880

Keel and Saddle: a Retrospect. Boston: 1873. V. 39; 42

A Tour of Duty in California. New York: 1849. V. 38; 40; 42; 44

A Tour of Duty in California. New York & Boston: 1849. V. 39

REV. George Morris and the Directors of the London Missionary Society. Papeete: 1870. V. 38

REVEREND, D.

Letters to Monsieur H*** (i.e. Herinch) Concerning the Most Antient Gods or Kings Of Egypt, and the Antiquity of the First Monarchs of Babylon and China. London: 1734. V. 38

REVESI BRUTI, OTTAVIO

Archisesto per Formar con Facilita li Cinque Ordini d'Architettura, con Altri Particolari Intorno la Medesima Professione. Vicenza: 1627. V. 37

THE REVIEW of Modern Art. Mexico: 1942-44. V. 41

A REVIEW of Some of the Arguments Which Are Commonly Advanced Against Parliamentary Interference on Behalf of the Negro Slaves. Manchester: 1824. V. 42; 46

A REVIEW of the Late Engagement at Sea, Being a Collection of Private Letters, Never BEfore Printed . . . London: 1704. V. 43

A REVIEW of the Late Motion for an Address to His Majesty and a Certain Great Minister (Robert Walpole), and the Reasons For It . . . . London: 1741. V. 42

A REVIEW of the Prosecution Against Abner Kneeland for Blasphemy. Boston: 1835. V. 41

REVILLE, F. DOUGLAS

History of the County of Brant. Brantford: 1920. V. 38; 42

THE REVIVAL of Printing. A Bibliographical Catalogue of Works Issued by the Chief Modern Presses with an introduction by Robert Steele. London: 1912. V. 40; 41; 43; 46

REVOIL, B. H.

Shooting and Fishing in the Rivers, Prairies and Backwoods of North America. London: 1865. V. 39; 43

REVOIL, BENEDICT HENRY

Chasses Dans l'Amerique du Nord . . . Tours: 1886. V. 37

THE REVOLTER. London: 1686. V. 41

REVOLUTION Politicks: Being a Compleat Collection of all the Reports, Lyes and Stories, Which Were the Forerunners of the Great Revolution in 1688 . . . London: 1733. V. 43

A REVOLUTION-WHIG the Best Subject. Seriously Recommending the Choice of Such Men for the Magistracy of Edinburgh, as Were Whigs at Michaelmas 1745. Edinburgh: 1746. V. 39

REVOLUTIONARY Radicalism, Its History, Purpose and Tactics with an Exposition and Discussion of the Steps Being Taken and Required to Curb It . . . Albany: 1920. V. 44

REVUE de l'Hypnotisme Experimental & Therapeutique. Paris: 1887-1911. V. 46

REWALD, JOHN

Degas Works in Sculpture. A Complete Catalogue. London: 1944. V. 43; 46

Degas Sculpture. The Complete Works. London: 1957. V. 37; 43; 45

Paul Cezanne: The Watercolours. London: 1984. V. 44

THE REWARD of Virtue, or, the History of Miss Polly Graham. London: 1769. V. 40

REXROTH, KENNETH

The Art of Worldly Wisdom. Prairie City: 1949. V. 37

Between Two Wars. Athens: 1982. V. 37; 41; 42; 43; 44; 46

Between Two Wars. Athens & San Francisco: 1982. V. 44

Between Two Wars. Selected Poems. San Francisco: 1982. V. 44

In What Hour. New York: 1940. V. 37; 40; 42

Lovers Who Feed Goldfish in the Fontaine de Medicis Will Always Be True to One Another. Cambridge: 1972. V. 45

The New British Poets. Verona: 1948. V. 46

The Phoenix and the Tortoise. 1944. V. 39

The Phoenix and the Tortoise. 1944. V. 46

The Signature of All Things. New York: 1949. V. 41

The Signature of all Things. Norfolk: 1949. V. 38; 40

The Spark in the Tinder of Knowing. 1968. V. 39

The Spark in the Tinder of Knowing. 1968. V. 40

REY DEPLANAZU, FRANCOIS JOSEPH

Oeuvres d'Agriculture et d'Economie Rurale, Nouvelle Edition, Revue, Corrigee et Augmentee. Paris: 1801. V. 39

REY, GUIDO

The Matterhorn. London: 1907. V. 43

The Matterhorn. London: 1908. V. 40

REY, JEAN

Essays sur la Recherche de la Cause Pour Laquelle l'Estain & le Plomb Augmentent de Poids Quand on les Calcine. Paris: 1777. V. 38

REYMONT, W. S.

The Peasants: Autumn, Winter, Spring, Summer. London: 1925. V. 38

REYMOUR, H. D.

Russia on the Black Sea and Sea of Azof. London: 1855. V. 39

REYNAL, EUGENE S.

Thoughts Upon a Hunting Kit in a Series of Nine Letters to a Friend . . . Milbrook: 1934. V. 39; 43; 44

REYNARD THE FOX

The History of Reynard Foxe. Hammersmith: 1892. V. 39; 45

The History of Reynard the Foxe . . . Hammersmith: 1893. V. 37; 41

The History of Reynard the Foxe. London: 1893. V. 41; 46

The History of Reynard the Fox. London: 1894. V. 39

The History of Reynard the Fox. London: 1897. V. 41

The History of Reynard the Foxe. 1892. V. 37

The Most Delectable History of Reynard the Fox. London: 1846. V. 43

Reynard the Fox. London: 1840's. V. 38

Reynard the Fox. Dresden & Leipzig: 1852. V. 45

REYNARDSON, C. T. S. BIRCH

Down the Road. London: 1875. V. 40

Down the Road or the Reminiscenses of a Gentleman Coachman. London: 1887. V. 43

Sports & Anecdotes of Bygone Days in England, Scotland, Ireland, Italy and Sunny South. London: 1887. V. 43

REYNARDSON, FRANCIS

An Ode to the Pretender. London: 1713. V. 41

The Stage: a Poem. London: 1713. V. 37; 40; 43

REYNAUD, LEONCE

Memoir Upon the Lighting, Beaconage and Buoyage of the Coasts of France. Washington: 1871. V. 40

Les Travaux Publics de la France. Paris: 1876-83. V. 38

REYNELL, CAREW

The True English Interest. London: 1674. V. 38

REYNIER, JEAN LOUIS EBENAZER

State of Egypt, After the Battle of Heliopolis, Preceded by General Observations on the Physical and Political Character of the Country. London: 1802. V. 38; 41

REYNOLDES, EDWARD

A Treatise of the Passions and Faculties of the Soule of Man. London: 1640. V. 42

REYNOLDS, CHARLES B.

Old Saint Augustine: a Story of Three Centuries. St. Augustine: 1888. V. 41

REYNOLDS, EDWARD

A Further Manifestation of the Progress of the Gospel, Among the Indians of New England. New York: 1865. V. 39

Hints to Students on the Use of the Eyes. Edinburgh: 1835. V. 44

Three Treatises of the Vanity of the Creature. The Sinfulnesse of Sinne. The Life of Christ. London. V. 44

REYNOLDS, F.

The Millenium Seaside ABC for Children. Liverpool. V. 41

REYNOLDS, FRANCIS J.

The New Encyclopedic Atlas and Gazeteer of the World. New York: 1914. V. 45

The Story of the Great War: the Complete Historical Records of Events to Date. New York: 1916-17. V. 42

The United States Navy, from the Revolution to Date . . . New York: 1915-17. V. 41

REYNOLDS, FRANK

Mr. Pickwick. London: 1910. V. 38; 42; 43

Mr. Pickwick. London: 1930. V. 44

REYNOLDS, FREDERIC MANSEL

The Keepsake for MDCCCXXXI. London: 1830. V. 38

REYNOLDS, FREDERICK

The Life and Times . . . Written by Himself. London: 1827. V. 38

A Playwright's Adventures. London: 1831. V. 43

REYNOLDS, FREDERICK MANSEL

'Miserrimus'. London: 1833. V. 37; 41

REYNOLDS, G.

The Later Paintings and Drawings of John Constable. New Haven: 1984. V. 39

REYNOLDS, G. W.

The Aloes of South Africa. Johannesburg: 1950. V. 38; 46

The Aloes of Tropical Africa and Madagascar. Mbabane: 1966. V. 38

REYNOLDS, GEORGE

The Book of Abraham. Its Authenticity Established as a Divine and Ancient Record . . . Salt Lake City: 1879. V. 42

REYNOLDS, GEORGE W. M.

A Sequel to Don Juan. London: 1843. V. 39

REYNOLDS, GEORGE WILLIAM MACARTHUR

Master Timothy's Book-Case. London: 1844. V. 40

The Mysteries of London. London: 1845-50. V. 42

The Mysteries of the Court of London. London: 1849-56. V. 40

Pickwick Abroad; or, the Tour in France. Glasgow: 1839. V. 44

Pickwick Abroad; or, the Tour in France. London: 1839. V. 38; 40; 43

Pickwick Abroad, or the Tour in France. London: 1864. V. 40; 43

REYNOLDS, GILBERT WESTACOTT

The Aloes of South Africa. Johannesburg: 1950. V. 39; 40

REYNOLDS, GRAHAM

John Constable's Sketchbooks of 1813 and 1814. London: 1973. V. 46

REYNOLDS, H. E.

Wells Cathedral: Its Foundation, Constitutional History and Statutes. Leeds: 1881. V. 39; 42

REYNOLDS, HELEN WILKINSON

Dutch Houses in the Hudson Valley Before 1776. New York: 1929. V. 39; 44

Dutchess County (N.Y.) Doorways and Other Examples of Period-Work in Wood, 1730-1830. New York: 1931. V. 39

REYNOLDS, HENRY REVELL

An Address to the Ladies from a Young Man. London: 1796. V. 38; 40; 45

REYNOLDS, HUGHES

The Coosa River Valley, From De Soto to Hydroelectric Power. Cynthiana: 1944. V. 45

REYNOLDS, J. H.

Case of John C. Watrous: Report of the Committee on the Judiciary. Washington: 1860. V. 37

REYNOLDS, J. N.

Explore Pacific Ocean . . . Report . . . Praying That an Exploring Expedition to the Pacific Ocean and South Seas May Be Authorized by Congress . . . Washington: 1835. V. 41

REYNOLDS, J. RUSSELL

A System of Medicine. Philadelphia: 1880. V. 42

REYNOLDS, JAN

William Callow RWS. London: 1980. V. 46

REYNOLDS, JEREMIAH

Voyage of the United States Frigate Potomac . . . During the Circumnavigation of the Globe, in the Years 1831, 1832, 1833 and 1834. New York: 1835. V. 37; 40; 42; 43; 46

REYNOLDS, JOHN 1788-1865

Friendship's Offering. A Sketch of the Life of Dr. John Mason Peck. Belleville: 1858. V. 40; 41

My Own Times, Embracing Also, the History of My Life. Belleville: 1855. V. 37; 40; 42

Pioneer History of Illinois. Belleville: 1852. V. 37; 38; 39; 40; 42; 43; 46

Practical and Philosophical Principles of Making Malt . . . London: 1809. V. 39

Recollections of Windsor Prison . . . Boston: 1834. V. 46

Sketches of the Country, on the Northern Route from Belleville, Illinois, to the City of New York. Belleville: 1854. V. 37; 38; 39; 40

The Triumphs of Gods Revenge Against the Crying Sin of Murther, in Thirty Several Tragical Histories. London: 1662. V. 39

The Triumphs of Gods Revenge Against the Crying and Exercrable Sinne of Wilful and Premeditated Murther . . . London: 1663. V. 43

Vox Coeli, or Newes from Heaven. 1624. V. 39

Vox Coeli, or, Newes from Heaven. 1624. V. 40

REYNOLDS, JOHN C.

History of the M.W. Grand Lodge of Illinois. Springfield: 1869. V. 42

REYNOLDS, JOHN HAMILTON 1794-1852

The Fancy. London: 1905. V. 41

The Garden of Florence; and Other Poems. London: 1821. V. 43

REYNOLDS, JOHN N.

A Kansas Hell, or Life in the Kansas Penitentiary. Atchison: 1889. V. 41

REYNOLDS, JOSHUA 1723-1792

A Discourse Delivered to the Students of the Royal Academy, on the Distribution of the Prizes, December 10, 1778. London: 1779. V. 40

A Discourse Delivered to the Students of the Royal Academy, on the Distribution of the Prizes, Dec. the 10th, 1774. V. 40

REYNOLDS, JOSHUA 1723-1792 continued

A Discourse, Delivered to the Students of the Royal Academy, on the Distribution of the Prizes, December 11, 1769, by the President. London: 1769. V. 38; 40; 41

A Discourse Delivered at the Royal Academy, January 2, 1769 - Dec. 10, 1790 by the President. London: 1769-90. V. 45

A Discourse, Delivered to the Students of The Royal Academy, on the Distribution of the Prizes, Dec. 10, 1790. By the President. London: 1791. V. 38

Johnson and Garrick. London: 1816. V. 45

The Letters. Cambridge: 1929. V. 39

Letters of Joshua Reynolds. London: 1929. V. 39; 43

Life and Times of Sir Joshua Reynolds with Notices of Some of His Contemporaries. London: 1865. V. 40

Portraits by Sir Joshua Reynolds . . . New York: 1952. V. 43

Seven Discourses Delivered in the Royal Academy by the President. London: 1778. V. 37; 38; 40; 43; 44; 45; 46

The Works of Sir Joshua Reynolds. London: 1797. V. 37; 39

The Works . . . London: 1798. V. 45; 46

The Works . . . London: 1801. V. 39

The Works. London: 1809. V. 39; 40; 45; 46

The Complete Works. London: 1824. V. 38; 40; 41

REYNOLDS, MICHAEL

Engine-Driving Life. London: 1894. V. 46

Locomotive Engine Driving. London: 1877. V. 39; 40; 45

REYNOLDS, PERCY

Military A.B.C. London: 1895. V. 41

REYNOLDS, R. E.

County and City of Kingman, Kansas. Illustrated Southern Kansas, An Industrial Publication Devoted to the History of Kingman. Kingman: 1887. V. 39

REYNOLDS, ROBERT

Thirty Years on the Frontier. Colorado Springs: 1906. V. 38

REYNOLDS, SAMUEL WILLIAM

Engravings from the Pictures and Sketches Painted by Sir Joshua Reynolds . . . London: 1820-1865. V. 40

REYNOLDS Stone. His Early Development as an Engraver on Wood. Cambridge: 1947. V. 44

REYNOLDS, THOMAS C.

Circular. Sir: . . . Each County and Parish Should Form a Voluntary Confederate Association to Cooperate with the Trans-Mississippi Committee of Public Safety, and the Corresponding Committees . . . Marshall: 1863. V. 39

REYNOLDS, TIM

Poems 1962-4. N.P.. V. 40

Poems 1962-64. N.P.. V. 42

Poems 1962-4. N.P.. V. 37

REYNOLDS, WILLIAM D.

Miss Martha Brownlow; or the Heroine of Tennessee. Philadelphia: 1863. V. 44

REYNOLDSON, JOHN

Practical and Philosophical Principles of Making Malt. Newark: 1809. V. 41

REYNOLDS'S Geological Atlas of Great Britain, Comprising a Series of Maps Geologically Coloured . . . London. V. 46

REZANOV, NICOLAI P.

Rezanov Reconnoiters California, 1806. San Francisco: 1972. V. 37; 42; 43

REZNIKOFF, CHARLES

By the Waters of Manhattan an Annual. New York: 1929. V. 38

Early History of a Sewing-Machine Operator. New York: 1936. V. 38; 40

Nine Plays. New York: 1927. V. 46

THE RHAPSODY. London: 1750. V. 40

RHAZES

A Treatise on the Small-pox and Measles. London: 1848. V. 38

De Variolis et Morbilis, Arabice et Latine; Cvm Aliis Nonnvllis Eivsdem Argvmenti. Londiensis. V. 39

RHAZES, ABU BAKR MUHAMMAD IBN ZAKARIYA

A Treatise on the Small-Pox and Measles. London: 1848. V. 42

RHEAD, G. WOLLISCROFT

History of the Fan. London: 1910. V. 38

RHEAD, LOUIS

American Trout Stream Insects; a Guide to Angling Flies and Other Aquatic Insects Alluring to the Trout. New York: 1916. V. 44

RHEEDE TOT DRAAKESTEIN, ADRIAAN VON

Hortus Indicus Malabaricus, Continens Regni Malabarici Apud Indos Celeberrimis Generis Plantae Rariori . . . 1979-83. V. 46

RHEES, WILLIAM

The Smithsonian Institution Documents Relative to its Origin and History. 1835-1899. Washington: 1901. V. 37; 38; 41; 42; 45

RHEGIUS, URBANS

Ain Kurtze Erklaerung Etlicher Leyffiger Punktenn der Gschryfft. Augsburg: 1523. V. 38; 41

RHEIMS, MAURICE

The Age of Art Nouveau. London: 1966. V. 46

The Flowering of Art Nouveau. London. V. 42

The Flowering of Art Nouveau. New York: 1966. V. 41

THE RHENISH Album; or Scraps from the Rhine. London: 1836. V. 43

RHENIUS, CARL THEOPHILUS EWALD

A Grammar of the Tamil Language, with an Appendix. Madras: 1836. V. 41

RHETORES Graeci In Aphthonii Progymnasmata Commentarii Innominati Autoris, Syriani, Sopatri, Marcellini Commentari in Hermogenes Rhetorica. Venice: 1509. V. 43

RHIND, ALEXANDER HENRY 1833-1863

Facsimiles of Two Papyri Found in a Tomb at Thebes. London: 1863. V. 42

Thebes, Its Tombs and Their Tenants, Ancient and Present . . . London: 1862. V. 44

RHIND, W. G.

The Holy Vessels and Furniture of the Tabernacle of Israel. London: 1845. V. 39

RHIND, WILLIAM

A History of the Vegetable Kingdom . . . Glasgow: 1862. V. 46

A History of the Vegetable Kingdom. London: 1868. V. 42; 43; 44; 46

A History of the Vegetable Kingdom . . . London: 1872. V. 46

RHO, GIOVANNI

Assemblea Celeste. Fadunata Novam(en)te in Parnasso Sopra la Nova Cometa. Dall' Academico Danico Il Riposato Descritta in Una Lettera all'Academico . . . Milan: 1619. V. 43

RHOAD, ALBERT O.

Santa Gertrudis, Breeders International Recorded Herds. Kingsville: 1953. V. 44

RHOADS, ASA

The New Instructor, Being the Second Part of the American Spelling Book. Stanford: 1804. V. 38

RHODE, ELEANOR SINCLAIR

The Old English Herbals. London: 1922. V. 43

The Old English Herbals. London: 1922. V. 38; 42; 45

The Old English Gardening Books. London: 1924. V. 38

RHODE, INGLES

The Pickletons, Their Astonishing Adventures. London: 1905. V. 40

RHODE ISLAND. CONSTITUTIONAL CONVENTION - 1834

An Address to the People of Rhode Island, from the Convention Assembled at Providence, on the 22nd day of February, and Again on the 12th Day of March, 1834 to Promote the Establishment of a State Consitition. Providence: 1834. V. 37

RHODE ISLAND. CONVENTION CONVENTION - 1859

Journal of the Convention Assembled to Frame a Constitution for the State of Rhode Island, at Newport, Sept. 12, 1842. Providence: 1859. V. 37

RHODE ISLAND. GENERAL ASSEMBLY

Report of the Committee Appointed by the General Assembly of Rhode Island to Investigate the Charges Against Freemasonry and Masons in Said State . . . Providence: 1832. V. 46

RHODE ISLAND. LAWS, STATUTES, ETC. - 1798

The Public Laws of the State of . . . and Providence Plantations . . . Jan. 1798. (with) The Charter, Declaration, ARticles of Confederation, Constitution and Pres. Washington's Address of Sept. 1796. Providence: 1798. V. 42

RHODE, JOHN

The Venner Crime. London: 1933. V. 44

RHODES, ALESSANDRO DI

Relazione De'Felici Successi Della Santa Fede Predicata da Padri Della Compagnia di Gesu Nel Regno Di Tunchino, Alla Santita Di S. PP. Rome: 1650. V. 40

RHODES, BENJAMIN

A Concise English Grammar, Rendered Easy to Every Capacity . . . Birmingham: 1795. V. 46

A New Book of Cyphers . . . London: 1695. V. 46

To the Methodist Preachers in Particular; and to the Methodists in General. Birmingham: 1795. V. 44

RHODES, CECIL J.

A Chronicle of the Funeral Ceremonies from Muizenberg to the Matopos, March-April 1902. Cape Town: 1905. V. 44

RHODES, CHARLES D.

History of the Cavalry of the Army of the Potomac, Including That of the Army of Virginia (Pope's) and Also Virginia During the War. Kansas City: 1900. V. 41; 45

RHODES, D. E.

Catalogue of Seventeenth Century Italian Books in the British Library. London: 1988. V. 43

RHODES, E.

Peak Scenery, or the Derbyshire Tourist. London: 1824. V. 37

Yorkshire Scenery; or, Excursions in Yorkshire. London: 1826. V. 38

RHODES, EUGENE MANLOVE

Little World Waddies. 1946. V. 42

The Little World Waddies. Chico: 1946. V. 37; 38; 42

The Little World Waddies. Pass of the Rio Bravo: 1946. V. 38

Penalosa. 1934. V. 42

Say Now Shibboleth. Chicago: 1921. V. 43

The Trusty Knaves. Boston: 1933. V. 43

West is West. New York: 1917. V. 39

RHODES, GODFREY

Tents and Tent Life, from the Earliest Ages to the Present Time. London: 1858. V. 39

RHODES, HENREITTA

Rosalie; or the Castle of Montalabretti. Richmond: 1811. V. 40

RHODES, JAMES MONTAGUE

A Descriptive Catalogue of the Latin Manuscripts in the John Rylands Library at Manchester. 1921. V. 42

RHODES, JOHN

The Sufferings and Adventures of . . . , *a Seaman of Workington.* New York: 1798. V. 37; 39; 40

The Surprising Adventures and Sufferings of John Rhodes, a Seaman of Workington. Newark: 1799. V. 43; 45; 46

The Surprising Adventues and Sufferings of John Rhodes, a Seaman of Workington. Containing an Account of his Captivity and Cruel Treatment during Eight years with the Indians, and Five Years in Different Prisons . . . New York: 1799. V. 37

RHODES, JOHN W.

Melini, or the Victim of Guilt. Boston: 1844. V. 45

RHODES, W. H.

The Case of Summerfield. San Francisco: 1907. V. 42

RHODES, WILLIAM BARNES

Bibliotheca Dramtica. A Catalogue of the Entire, Curious and Extensive Dramatic Library of William Barnes Rhodes. London: 1825. V. 38; 41; 46

Bombastes Furioso: a Burlesque Tragic Opera. London: 1830. V. 38

A Catalogue of the Entire, Curious and Extensive Dramatic Library of William Barnes Rhodes. London: 1825. V. 44

RHODIUS, AMBROSIUS

Optica. Wittenberg: 16111. V. 46

RHYGYFARCH

The Life of Saint David. Montgomeryshire: 1927. V. 45

RHYMER'S CLUB

The Second Book of the Rhymers' Club. London: 1894. V. 37; 38; 40

The Second Book of Rhymers' Club. London: and New York: 1894. V. 41; 42

RHYMES and Roundelayes in Praise of a Country Life. London: 1857. V. 39

RHYMES for the Times by a Bingley Tallow Chandler. Keighley: 1849. V. 46

RHYMES on Matrimony by an University Bachelor. London: 1829. V. 45

RHYS, ERNEST

Frederic Lord Leighton, Late President of the Royal Academy of Arts. London: 1898. V. 40

Sir Frederic Leighton, Pra. London: 1895. V. 39; 41; 42

RHYS, HEDLEY HOWELL

Maurice Prendergast, 1859-1924. Cambridge: 1960. V. 44

RHYS, HORTON

A Theatrical Trip for a Wager! Through Canada and the United States. London: 1861. V. 43; 45; 46

A Theatrical Trip for a Wager! Through Canada and the United States . . . Vancouver: 1966. V. 38; 46

RHYS, JEAN 1894-1979

After Leaving Mr. Mackenzie. London: 1931. V. 38

After Leaving Mr. MacKenzie. New York: 1931. V. 41

After Leaving Mr. Mackenzie. London: 1969. V. 40

Good Morning Midnight. London: 1939. V. 38

Good Morning, Midnight. London: 1967. V. 40

Good Morning, Midnight. New York: 1970. V. 40

The Left Bank. London: 1927. V. 37; 38; 41; 45

The Left Bank and Other Stories. New York: 1927. V. 42

The Left Bank & Other Stories. New York & London: V. 37

Postures. London: 1928. V. 38

Quartet. London: 1969. V. 40

Sleep It Off Lady; Stories. London: 1976. V. 40; 43

Tigers Are Better Looking with a Selection From the Left Bank. Harmondsworth: 1972. V. 41

Les Tigres Sont Plus Beaux Voir. Paris: 1968. V. 46

Voyage in the Dark. London: 1934. V. 38; 40; 42; 44

Voyage in the Dark. New York: 1935. V. 41

Wide Sargasso Sea. London: 1966. V. 40; 43; 45; 46

RHYS, JOHN DAVID 1534-1609

Cambrobrytannicae Cyraecaeve Linguae Institutiones et Rudimenta . . . London: 1592. V. 37; 38; 40

RHYTHM. London: 1911-12. V. 40

RIBADENEIRA, PEDRO

Illvstrivm Scriptorvm Religionis. Lyons: 1609. V. 38

Vita del P. Ignatio Loisola, Fondatore Della Religione della Compagnia di Giesu Descritta . . . *Prima in Lingua Latina, e Dopo* . . . *Ridutta Nella Castigliana and Ampliata* . . . Venetia: 1586. V. 38

RIBADENEIRA, PEDRO A.

The Lives of Saints, with Other Feasts of the Year, According to the Roman Calendar . . . Dublin: 1763. V. 44; 45

RIBADENEYRA, PEDRO DE

Historia . . . *del Scisma* . . . *di Inglaterra.* Antwerp: 1594. V. 41

Vida del P. Ignacio de Loyola, Fundador de la Religion de la Compania de Iesus: y de los Padres Maestro Diego Laynez, y Francisco de Borja, Segundo y Tercero Preposito General de la Misma Compania. Madrid: 1594. V. 40

RIBAUT, JEAN

The Whole and True Discouerye of Terra Florida. Deland: 1927. V. 40; 46

RIBERA, FRANCISCO DE

In Librum Duodecim Prophetarum Commentarij, Sensum Eorundem Prophetarum Historicum, & Moralem, Persaepe Etiam Allegoricum Complectentes. Cologne: 1610. V. 37

RIBERA, JUAN DE

Lettera Annua Della Vice-Provincia delle Filippine. Venice: 1605. V. 45

RIBERA, JUSEPE DE

Livre de Portraitvre Receuily des Oeures de Ioseph de Rivera dit l'Espagnolet. Paris: 1640's. V. 37

RIBOUD, KRISHNA

In Quest of Themes and Skills: Asian Textiles. Bombay: 1990. V. 43

RIBTON-TURNER, C. J.

A History of Vagrants and Vagrancy and Beggars and Begging. London: 1887. V. 38; 41; 42

RICARD, JEAN PIERRE

Le Negoce d'Amsterdam, Contenant tout ce que Doivent Savoir les Marchands & Bnqulers, Tant Ceux qui sont Etablis a Amsterdam, que Ceux des Pays Etrangers. Amsterdam: 1722. V. 38

RICARD, SAMUEL

Traite Generale du Commerce. Amsterdam: 1781. V. 39

RICARDO, DAVID 1772-1823

Letters of David Ricardo to Thomas Robert Malthus 1810-1823. Oxford: 1887. V. 39

Letters of David Ricardo to Hutches Trower and Others 1811-1823. Oxford: 1899. V. 38

On the Principles of Political Economy and Taxation. London: 1817. V. 43

On the Principles of Political Economy, and Taxation. London: 1819. V. 42; 46

On the Principles of Political Economy and Taxation. London: 1821. V. 37; 38; 39; 41; 45

On Protective Agriculture. London: 1822. V. 42

Principles of Political Economy and Taxation. London: 1891. V. 38

Proposals for an Economical and Secure Currency. London: 1816. V. 37; 38

The Works of . . . London: 1846. V. 37

The Works . . . London: 1852. V. 37; 41

The Works.. London: 1852. V. 38

The Works of David Ricardo. London: 1888. V. 40; 41

The Works and Correspondence of . . . Cambridge: 1951. V. 42

The Works and Correspondence of David Ricardo. Cambridge: 1951-55. V. 41; 42

The Works . . . with a notice of the life and writings of the author, by J.R. McCulloch. London: 1871. V. 37

RICARDO, DAVOD 1772-1823

The Works and Correspondence of David Ricardo. Cambridge: 1951-73. V. 37; 46

RICARDO, JOHN LEWIS 1812-1862

Mr. Ricardo's Speech on the Subject of Commercial Treaties, in the House of Commons on the 25th April, 1843. London: 1843. V. 41

RICARDO, SAMSON 1792-1862

Observations on the Recent Pamphlet of J. Horsley Palmer, Esq. on the Causes and Consequences of the Pressure on the Money Market. London: 1837. V. 38

RICARDUS DE MEDIA VILLA

Clarissimi Theologici Magistri Reciardi de Media Villa . . . Super Quatuor Libros Sententiarum Petri Lombardi Quaestiones Subtilissimae . . . Frankfurt am Main,: 1963. V. 40

RICAUTI, T. J.

Sketches for Rustic Work. London: 1842. V. 38

Sketches for Rustic Work: Including Bridges, Park and Garden Buildings, Seats and Furniture. London: 1848. V. 41

RICCARDI, P.

Biblioteca Matematica Italiana Dalla Origine Della Stampa ai Primi Anni del Secolo XIX. Modena: 1870-1928. V. 38

RICCHIERI, LODOVICO

Sicuti Antiquarum Lectionum Commentarios Concinnarat Olim Vindex Ceselius . . . Venice: 1516. V. 44

RICCHIERI, LODOVICO, KNOWN AS LODOVICUS CAELIUS RHODIGINUS 1450-1525

Lectionum Antiquarum. Lyon: 1562. V. 39

RICCHIERI, LODOVICO, KNOWN AS LODOVICUS CAELIUS RHODIGNUS 1450-1520

Lectionum Antiquarum Libri XVI. Venice: 1516. V. 38

RICCHIERI, LODOVICO, KNOWN AS LODOVICUS CAELIUS RHODOGINUS 1450-1520

Lectionum Antiquarum Libri XXX. Lvgdvni: 1560. V. 44

Sicuti Antiquarum Lectionum Commentarios Concinnarat olim Vindex Ceselius, Ita Nunc Eosdem per Incuriam Interceptos Reparavit Lodovicus Caelius Rhodiginus. Venice: 1516. V. 40; 41

RICCI, BARTHOLOMEO

Apparatus Latinae Locutionis . . . Lyon: 1534. V. 41; 45

RICCI, CORRADO

Antonio Allegri da Correggio: His Life, His Friends and His Time. London: 1896. V. 41

Vatican. Its History - Its Treasures. New York: 1914. V. 39

RICCI, ELISA

Old Italian Lace. London: 1913. V. 38; 39; 45; 46

RICCI, JAMES V.

The Genealogy of Gynaecology. Philadelphia: 1943. V. 44; 45

One Hundred Years of Gynaecology, 1800-1900. Philadelphia: 1945. V. 38

RICCI, MATTEO 1552-1610

De Christiana Expeditione apud Sinas Suscepta ab Societate Jesu, ex P. Matthaei Ricii Eiusdem Societatis Commentariis Libri V . . . in Quibus Sinensis Regni Mores, Leges Atque Instituta . . . Augsburg: 1615. V. 40

De Christiana Expeditione, Apud Sinas Suscepta ab Societate Iesu . . . Lyon: 1616. V. 41; 45

RICCI, MICHELE

Oratio Elegantissima . . . Dudu Romae Habita ad Iulium Secudum Pontificem Maximu in Obedientia Pro Ludouico, Duodecimo Francorum Rege . . . Paris: 1505. V. 40

RICCI, ROBERT H. DE

Rambles in Istria, Dalmatia and Montenegro. London: 1875. V. 45

RICCI, SEYMOUR DE 1881-1942

Catalogue of a Collection of Mounted Porcelain Belonging to E. M. Hodgkins. Paris: 1911. V. 40

A Catalogue of Early English Books in the Library of John L. Clawson. Philadelphia: 1924. V. 38; 43

A Catalogue of Early English Books in the Library of John L. Clawson, Buffalo. Philadelphia & New York: 1924. V. 46

A Census of Caxtons. 1909. V. 39

A Census of Caxtons. London: 1909. V. 45

A Census of Caxtons. Oxford: 1909. V. 40; 43; 46

A Handlist of a Collection of Books and Manuscripts Belonging to the Right Hon. Lord Amherst of Hackney at Didlington Hall, Norfolk. Cambridge: 1906. V. 38

Louis XVI Furniture. London & New York: 1910. V. 41

Louis XIV and Regency Furniture and Decoration. New York: 1929. V. 42

RICCIARDI, GIUSEPPE, COUNT

The Autobiography of an Italian Rebel. London: 1860. V. 44

RICCIO, BARTHOLOMEO

Apparatus Latinae Locutionis. Argentorati: 1535. V. 40

RICCIO, FRANCESCO

Conclusiones Philosophicae Publice Propugnate in Collegio Romano Sub Auspiciis . . . Innocentii Duodecimi. Rome: 1697. V. 42

RICCIOLI, GIAMBATTISTA

Astronomiae Reformatae Tomi Duo, Quorum Prior Observationes, Hypotheses, et Fundamenta Tabularum, Posterior Praecepta Pro Usu Tabularum Astronomicarum . . . Bologna: 1665. V. 43

Geographiae et Hydrographiae Reformatae Libri Duodecim Quorum Argumentum Sequens Pagina Explicabit . . . Bologna: 1661. V. 45

RICCIOLI, GIOVANNI BATTISTA

Chronologiae Reformatae . . . Bologna: 1669. V. 38; 44

RICCIUS, BARTHOLOMAEUS 1490-1569

De Imitatione Libri Tres. Venice: 1545. V. 45

RICCO, DANIEL

Ristretto Anotomico, o Sia Aleanza Degl'astri con l'Huomo, e Vegetabili . . . Venice: 1690. V. 42

RICCOBONI, L.

An Historical and Critical Account of the Theatres in Europe. London: 1741. V. 42; 45

RICCOBONI, MARIE JEANNE

Letters from Juliet Lady Catesby, to Her Friend Henrietta Campley. Dublin: 1763. V. 37; 39; 43

Letters from Elizabeth Sophia de Valiere to Her Friend Louisa Hortensia de Canteleu . . . London: 1772. V. 43

Letters from Juliet Lady Catesby to Her Friend Lady Henrietta Campley. London: 1780. V. 40

letters of Adelaide de Sancerre to Count de Nance. Newbern: 1801. V. 37; 45

Letters of Adelaide de Sancerre to Count De Nance. Newbern: 1901. V. 41

RICE, ANNE

Beauty's Punishment. New York: 1984. V. 39; 43; 45

Beauty's Release. New York: 1985. V. 39; 42

The Claiming of Sleeping Beauty. New York: 1983. V. 39; 42; 43

Interview with a Vampire. New York: 1975. V. 42

Interview with a Vampire. New York: 1976. V. 39; 42; 43; 44; 45; 46

The Mummy. New York: 1989. V. 42; 43

The Queen of the Damned. 1988. V. 46

The Queen of the Damned. New York: 1988. V. 39; 42; 43; 44; 45; 46

The Vampire Lestat. New York: 1985. V. 42; 44; 45

The Vampire Chronicles. New York: 1990. V. 45

The Witching Hour. New York: 1990. V. 45

RICE, D. G.

Rockingham Ornamental Porcelain. London: 1965. V. 37

RICE, DAVID

Slavery Inconsistent with Justice and Good Policy; Proved by a Speech Delivered In the Convention Held at Danville, Kentucky. London: 1793. V. 41; 45

RICE, DAVID TALBOT

The Church of Haghia Sophia at Trebizond. Edinburgh: 1968. V. 44; 45; 46

The Icons of Cyprus. London: 1937. V. 39

RICE, GEORGE

Southern California Illustrated. Los Angeles: (1883). V. 37

RICE, GEORGE E.

Ephemera. Boston: 1852. V. 44

RICE, HARVEY

Letters from the Pacific Slope; or First Impressions. New York: 1870. V. 45

RICE, HOWARD C.

American Campaigns of Rochambeau's Army 1780, 1781, 1782, 1783. Princeton: 1972. V. 37; 39; 42; 43

Barthelemi Tardiveau, a French Trader in the West. Baltimore: 1938. V. 46

RICE, JOHN

An Introduction to the Art of Reading with Energy and Propriety. London: 1765. V. 46

Review of the 'Doctrines of the Church Vindicated from the Misrepresentations of Dr. John Rice . . . Richmond: 1827. V. 43

RICE, JOHN A.

Catalogue of Mr. John A. Rice's Library to Be Sold at Auction . . . by Bangs, Merwin & Co . . . . New York: 1870. V. 37; 39; 40

RICE, JOHNSTON

Photographic Supplies. Catalogues of Camera Kodaks, Plates, Films, Apparatus. Montreal: (1907). V. 37

RICE, NATHAN

Trials of a Public Benafactor, as Illustrated in the Discovery of Etherization. New York: 1859. V. 37; 38

Trials of a Public Benefactor, as Illustrated in the Discovery of Etherization. New York: 1850. V. 37

RICE, NATHAN LEWIS

An Account of the Lawsuit Instituted by Rev. G.A.M. Elder, President of ST. Joseph's College, Against Rev. N. L. Rice, Presbyterian Minister, for a Pretended Libel on the Character of Rev. David Duparque. Louisville: 1837. V. 44

Ten Letters on the Subject of Slavery: Addressed to the Delegates from the Congregational Associations to the Last General Assembly of the Presbyterian Church. St. Louis: 1855. V. 41

RICE, WALLACE

Under the Stars and Other Songs of the Sea. Chicago: 1898. V. 38

RICE, WILLIAM

'Indian Game' (From Quail to Tiger). London: 1884. V. 43

Tiger Shooting in India Being an Account of Hunting Experiences on Foot in Rajpootana During the Hot Seasons from 1850 to 1854. London: 1857. V. 38; 43

RICE, WOODFORD

The Rutland Volunteer Influenza'd; or, a Receipt to a Patriot, a Soldier or a Poet. London: 1783. V. 43

The Rutland Volunteer Influenza'd; or, a Receipt to Make a Patriot, a Soldier, or a Poet. London: 1783. V. 42

RICETTARIO Fiorentino. Fiorenza: 1574. V. 37

RICETTARIO Fiorentino di Nvovo Illvstrato. Firenze: 1670. V. 39

RICH, ADRIENNE

The Fantasy Poets No. 12. Swinford, Eynsham: 1952 V. 40

The Knight. San Francisco: 1957. V. 44

Poems. Eynsham: 1952. V. 41

Snapshots of a Daughter-in-Law. New York: 1963. V. 39

Sources. Woodside: 1983. V. 37; 39

Twenty-One Love Poems. 1976. V. 39

RICH, CLAUDIUS

Narrative of a Journey to the Site of Babylon in 1811, Now First Published . . . London: 1839. V. 39

RICH, CLAUDIUS JAMES

Memoir (-Second Memoir) on the Ruins of Babylon. London: 1818. V. 37; 40

Narrataive of a Journey to the Site of Babylon in 1811, Now First Published. London: 1839. V. 37; 40; 42; 45

Narrative of a Residence in Koordistan . . . an Account of a Visit to Shiraux and Persepolis . . . London: 1836. V. 45

RICH, E. E.

Cumberland and Hudson House Journals, 1775-1782. London: 1951-52. V. 42

The History of the Hudson's Bay Co., 1670-1870. London: 1958-59. V. 44

The History of the Hudson's Bay Company, 1670-1870. 1763-1870. London: 1959. V. 46

Hudson's Bay Copy Booke of Letters, Commissions, Instructions Outward, 1688-1696. London: 1957. V. 46

Hudson's Bay Company, 1670-1870. Toronto: 1960. V. 38

Hudson's Bay Company, 1670-1870. New York: 1961. V. 40

Peter Skene Ogden's Snake County Journals 1824-25 and 1825-26. London: 1950. V. 39

RICH, EDWARD PICKERING

A Sermon Preach'd at Cheltenham, Before a Polite Audience, on Sunday August 5, 1750. London: 1750. V. 39

RICH, EDWARD R.

Comrades Four. New York/Washington: 1907. V. 37

RICH, EDWIN ERNEST

Copy-Book of Letters Outward Etc. Begins 29th May 1680 Ends July 1687. London: 1948. V. 43

RICH, GREGORY

The Mutiny in Sialkot. Sialkot: 1924. V. 42

RICH, JEREMIAH

The Pen's Dexterity; or, the Ingenious and Useful Art of Writing Short-Hand . . . Leeds: 1792. V. 45

RICH, OBADIAH

Bibliotheca Americana Nova; or a Catalogue of Books in Various Languages Relating to America, printed Since the Year 1700. (with) Volume II. 1801-1844. London: 1835-46. V. 45

Catalogue of Books Relating Principally to America. London: 1832. V. 38

RICH, ROBERT

A Letter . . . to the Right Honourable Lord Viscount Barrington, His Majesty's Secretary at War. London: 1775. V. 44

A Letter . . . to the Right Honourable Lord Viscount Barrington, His Majesty's S. V. 44

RICH, SHEBNAH

Truro-Cape Cod or Land Marks and Sea Marks. Boston: 1883. V. 46

RICHARD Bentley & Son. London: 1886. V. 38; 39

RICHARD Bentley & Son, Reprinted from 'Le Livre' of October 1885 with some Additional Notes. N.P.: 1886. V. 37

RICHARD, C. A.

The Demonstration of the Atmospheric Conditions. Columbus: 1858. V. 39

RICHARD DE FOURNIVAL

Master Richard's Bestiary of Love, and Response. Northampton: 1985. V. 37

RICHARD, EDOUARD

Acadia. Missing Links of a Lost Chapter in American History. New York: 1895. V. 38

RICHARD, JOHN

A Tour from London & Petersburgh, from Thence to Moscow, and Return to London by Way of Courland, Poland, Germany and Holland. London: 1778. V. 43

A Tour from London to Petersburgh, and from Thence to Moscow. Dublin: 1781. V. 37; 45

RICHARD, LOUIS CLAUDE

A Botanical Dictionary, Being a Translation from the French . . . New Haven: 1817. V. 45

Observations on the Structure of Fruits and Seeds. London: 1819. V. 39; 42

RICHARD Meier, Architect: Buildings & Projects, 1966-76. New York: 1976. V. 46

RICHARD OF CIRENCESTER

Speculum Historiale de Gestis Regum Angliae. London: 1863-69. V. 44

RICHARD OF ST. VICTOR

Opera Venerabilis & Eximii Doctoris Ricardi de Sancto Victore. Venice: 1506. V. 38

Richardus de Duodecim Patriarchis . . . Richardus de Arca Mystica. Basel: 1494. V. 38

RICHARD OF WALLINGFORD 1292?-1335

An Edition of His Writings with Introductions, English Translation and Commentary. Oxford: 1976. V. 39

RICHARD, W.

His Majesty's Territorial Army. A Descriptive account of the Yeomanry, Artillery, Engineers and Infantry with the Army Service and Medical Corps Comprising 'The King's Imperial Army of the Second Line'. London: (c. 1910). V. 37

RICHARD, WILLIAM P.

To the Freedmen of Davidson County: Fellow Citizens It Is Well Known to Most of You That I Am a Candidate to Represent You in Part of the House of Commons of the Next Legislature. Science Grove: 1846. V. 39

RICHARDS, A.

Zilla Fitz James, The Female Bandit of the South-West, or The Horrible, Mysterious and Awful Disclosures in the Life of the Creole Murderess, Zilla Fitz James, Paramour and Accomplice of Green H. Long, the Treble Murder . . . Little Rock: 1852. V. 44

RICHARDS, ALFRED B.

A Sketch of the Career of Richard F. Burton. London: 1886. V. 46

RICHARDS, ALFRED BATE

Croesus. London: 1845. V. 38

RICHARDS, CERI

Drawings to Poems by Dylan Thomas. London: 1980. V. 41

The Magic Horse. London: 1930. V. 42

RICHARDS, E. F., MRS.

My Mother's Cook Book. Woodward: 1875. V. 40

RICHARDS, EUGENE

Eugene Richards Portfolio. Great Barrington: 1978. V. 45

RICHARDS, FRANK

Old Soldiers Never Die. London: 1933. V. 44

Old Soldier Sahib. London: 1936. V. 40

Old Soldier Sahib. New York: 1936. V. 37

Old Soldiers Never Die. London: 1933. V. 37

RICHARDS, FRANKLIN D.

A Compendium of the Faith and Doctrines of the Church of Jesus Christ of Latter Day Saints . . . Liverpool: 1857. V. 42

A Compendium of the Doctrines of the Gosepl. Salt Lake City: 1882. V. 42

A Compendium of the Doctrines of the Gospel. Salt Lake City: 1898. V. 42

RICHARDS, G. H.

Report on the Maritime Canal Connecting the Mediterranean at Port Said with Red Sea at Suez. London: 1870. V. 40

RICHARDS, GEORGE

The Declaration of Independence; a Poem Accompanied by Odes, Songs, &c. Boston: 1793. V. 44

Modern France; a Poem. Oxford: 1793. V. 41; 42

Songs of the Aboriginal Bards of Britain. Oxford: 1792. V. 43

RICHARDS, GRANT

Author Hunting - by an Old Literary Sportsman - Memories of Years Spent Mainly in Publishing 1897-1925. London: 1934. V. 45

Every Wife. London: 1924. V. 41

RICHARDS, J.

A Treatise on the Construction and Operation of Wood-Working Machines. London: 1872. V. 40; 46

RICHARDS, J. M.

The Castles on the Ground - the Anatomy of Suburbia. London: 1973. V. 40

High Street. London: 1938. V. 37; 41; 42; 43; 44

RICHARDS, JOHN

The Gentleman's Steward and Tenants of manors Instructed . . . London: 1730. V. 38; 41

Sermons and Letters, To Which is Prefixed a memoir of the Author. Bath: 1827. V. 43

RICHARDS, LAURA E. 1783-1859

Acting Charades. Boston: 1924. V. 40; 41; 43; 44

Camp Merryweather Songs. Maine: 1930. V. 44

Fairy Operettas. Boston: 1916. V. 40; 41; 43; 44

Five Minute Stories. Boston: 1895. V. 41; 44

I Have a Song to Sing You. New York: 1938. V. 40; 41; 43; 44

Joan of Arc. New York: 1919. V. 40; 41

The Joyous Story of Toto. Boston: 1886. V. 40

Julia Ward Howe 1819-1910. Boston: 1915. V. 37; 39; 41; 42; 44; 45; 46

L.E.R., 1886. Gardiner: 1886. V. 40; 41; 42; 43; 44; 46

Margaret Montfort. Boston: 1898. V. 40

Melody: the Story of a Child. Boston: 1893. V. 40

Merry Go Round. New York: 1935. V. 40; 41; 43; 44

More Five Minute Stories. Boston: 1903. V. 40; 41; 43; 44

Please! Rhymes of Protest. Gardiner: 1936. V. 40; 41; 43; 44

Queen Hildegarde. Boston: 1889. V. 40

St. Nicholas Songs. New York: 1885. V. 41

Seven Oriental Operettas. Boston: 1924. V. 40; 41; 43; 44

The Silver Crown. Boston: 1906. V. 40; 41; 43; 44

Sketches & Scraps. Boston: 1881. V. 41

What Shall the Children Read? New York: 1939. V. 40; 41; 43; 44

RICHARDS, LOUIS

Eleven Days in the Militia During the War of the Rebellion . . . Philadelhia: 1883. V. 43; 44

RICHARDS, MARIA T.

Life in Israel; or, Portraitures of Hebrew Character. New York: and Chicago: 1857. V. 44

RICHARDS, RAYMOND

Old Cheshire Churches. London: 1947. V. 41

RICHARDS, RICHARD BRINSLEY

Prince Roderick. London: 1889. V. 43

RICHARDS, ROBERT

Californian Crusoe; or the Lost Treasure Found. London: 1854. V. 39

RICHARDS, THOMAS

Antiquae-Linguae Britannicae Thesaurus . . . Dolgelley: 1815. V. 41

Antiquae Linguae Britannicae Thesaurus A Welsh and English Dictinary . . . Trefriw: 1815. V. 45

Antiquae Linguae Britannicae Thesaurus, Being a British, or Welsh-English Dictionary . . . Bristol: 1753. V. 45

Cambriae Suspiria in Obitum Reginae Carolinae. London: 1738. V. 42

The Latin Description of Hogland. London: 1711. V. 37; 43

RICHARDS, THOMAS ADDISON

American Scenery, Illustrated. New York: 1854. V. 39; 40

Appleton's Illustrated Hand-Book of American Travel. Part II. The Southern and Western States, and the Territories. New York: 1857. V. 41

Appleton's Companion Hand-Book of Travel . . . New York: 1866. V. 41

RICHARDS, VYVYAN

T. E. Lawrence; Book Designer. London: 1985. V. 44; 46

RICHARDS, WALTER

Her Majesty's Army. London. V. 42

Her Majesty's Army. London. V. 46

Her Majesty's Army: Indian and Colonial Forces, A Descriptive Account of the Various Regiments Now Comprising the Queen's Forces in India and the Colonies. London: 1880's. V. 38

Her Majesty's Army. New York: 1889. V. 39

Her Majesty's Army. A Descriptive Account of the Various Regiments Now Comprising the Queen's Forces . . . London: 1889-91. V. 46

Her Majesty's Army. London: 1890. V. 44

RICHARDS, WILLIAM

Memoir of Keopuolani, Late Queen of the Sandwich Islands. Boston: 1825. V. 38; 44

RICHARDS, WILLIAM C.

Georgia Illustrated in a Series of Views, Embracing Natural Scenery and Public Edifices. Penfield: 1842. V. 38

The Last Billionaire. Henry Ford. New York: 1948. V. 45

RICHARDSON, A. E.

Regional Architecture of the West of England. London: 1924. V. 39

RICHARDSON, ALBERT D.

Beyond the Mississippi! N.P.: 1866-75. V. 39

Beyond the Mississippi: From the Great River to the Great Ocean. Hartford: 1867. V. 42

Our New States and Territories, Being Notes of a Recent Tour of Observation through Colorado, Idaho, Nevada, Oregon, Montana, Washington Territory and California . . . New York: 1866. V. 39

RICHARDSON, ALEX

Vickers Sons and Maxim Limited. Their Works and Manufactures. London: 1902. V. 37; 40

RICHARDSON & CO.

Texas Almanac for 1870 and Emigrants Guide to Texas. Galveston News. V. 44

Texas Almanac for 1872 and Emigrant's Guide to Texas. Galveston: 1871. V. 44

RICHARDSON, CHARLES

British Steeplechasing. London: 1927. V. 42

A New Dictionary of the English Language. London: 1836-37. V. 46

A New Dictionary of the English Language. London: 1844. V. 41; 46

A New Dictionary of the English Language, Combining Explanation with Etymology . . . London: 1856. V. 38

A New Dictionary of the English Language . . . London: 1867. V. 41

The New Book of the Horse. London: 1911. V. 39

Tales of a Warrior. New York: & Washington: 1907. V. 46

RICHARDSON, CHARLES F.

The College Book. Boston: 1878. V. 38; 40

RICHARDSON, CHARLES JAMES 1806-1871

Architectural Remains of the Reigns of Elizabeth and James I. London: 1840. V. 38

The Englishman's House from a Cottage to a Mansion. London: 1871. V. 41

The Englishman's House, a Practical Guide for Selecting and Building a House. London: 1898. V. 38; 40

Observations on the Architecture of England and Reigns of Queen Elizabeth and King James. London: 1837. V. 38; 41

Picturesque Designs for Mansions, Villas, Lodges &c . . . . London: 1870. V. 44

Studies of Ornamental Design. London: 1851. V. 38; 44

RICHARDSON, DOROTHY

Dawn's Left Hand. London: 1931. V. 42; 44

Deadlock. London: 1921. V. 46

Honeycomb. London: 1917. V. 37; 46

Interim. London: 1919. V. 37; 40

John Austen and the Inseparables. London: 1930. V. 37; 43; 45

Oberland. London: 1927. V. 45

Pointed Roofs. London: 1915. V. 40; 42

Revolving Lights. London: 1923. V. 46

The Trap. London: 1925. V. 40; 41

RICHARDSON, EMELINE

Etruscan Votive Bronzes, Geometric, Orientalizing, Archaic. Mainz am Rhein: 1983. V. 39; 44

RICHARDSON, FRANK

From Sunrise to Sunset: Reminiscence. Bristol: 1910. V. 42

RICHARDSON, G. B.

A Descriptive Catalogue of the Charters, Deeds and Records of Trinity House, Newcastle-upon-Tyne. Newcastle-upon-Tyne: 1854-55. V. 38

RICHARDSON, GEORGE

Iconology; or a Collection of Emblematical Figures; London: 1779. V. 38; 40

The New Vitruvius Britannicus. London: 1810, 1808. V. 38

RICHARDSON, GEORGE W.

Speech of . . . of Hanover, in Committee of the Whole, on the Report of (sic) The Committee on Federal Relations in the Convention of Virginia, April 4, 1861. Richmond: 1862. V. 38; 40; 44

RICHARDSON, HENRY

The Loss of the Tigris. London: 1840. V. 40; 43; 46

RICHARDSON, HENRY HANDEL, PSEUD. 1870-1946

Christkinleina Wiegenlied - an Old German Carol Set to Music by Henry Handel Richardson. London: 1931. V. 41

The Fortunes of Richard Mahony. London: 1930. V. 40

The Getting of Wisdom. London: 1931. V. 39; 41; 43; 45

Richard Mahonys Skaebne. Copenhagen: 1931. V. 39; 41; 43; 45

Two Studies. 1931. V. 40; 41; 46

Ultima Thule Being the Third Part of The Chronicles of the Fortunes of Richard Mahony. London: 1929. V. 39; 41; 43; 45

The Young Cosima. London: 1939. V. 40; 41

RICHARDSON, HENRY HOBSON

Austin Hall, Harvard Law School, Cambridge, Mass. Boston: 1886. V. 39

RICHARDSON, HESTER D.

Side-Lights on Maryland History, With Sketches of Early Maryland Families. Baltimore: 1913. V. 46

RICHARDSON, J.

Furness Past and Present. Barrow-in-Furness: 1880. V. 38

The Museum of Natural History. London. V. 42

The Museum of Natural History. London: 1859-62. V. 38

RICHARDSON, JAMES

Narrative of a Mission to Central Africa Performed in the Years 1850-51. London: 1853. V. 46

Travels in the Great Desert of Sahara, in the Years 1845 and 1846. London: 1848. V. 38; 44

RICHARDSON, JAMES CHARLES

Architectural Remains of the Reigns of Elizabeth and James 1st. London: 1838. V. 44

RICHARDSON, JAMES D.

A Compilation of the Messages and Papers of the Presidents, 1789-1897. Washington: 1896. V. 42

A Compilation of the Messages and Papers of the Confederacy. Nashville: 1905. V. 42

RICHARDSON, JOHN

An Account of the Life of that Ancient Servant of Jesus Christ. London: 1757. V. 38

An Account of the Life of that Ancient Servant of Jesus Christ, John Richardson, Giving a Relation of . . . His Services in the Work of the Ministry, in England, Ireland, America, &c. London: 1758. V. 45

An Account of the Life of that Ancient Servant of Jesus Christ, John Richardson, Giving a Relation of . . . His Services in the Work of the Ministry, in England, Ireland, America, &c. London: 1758. V. 40

An Account of the Life of . . . Services in the Work of the Ministry, in England, Ireland, America, etc. Philadelphia: 1773. V. 40

An Account of that Ancient Servant of Jesus Christ John Richardson . . . London: 1774. V. 44

An Account of the Life of that Ancient Servant of Jesus Christ, John Richardson. Philadelphia: 1783. V. 39

An Account of the Life of that Ancient Servant of Jesus Christ, John Richardson, Giving a Relation of Many of His Trials and Exercises in His Youth . . . Philadlelphia: 1783. V. 38; 44

Arctic Searching Expedition: a Journal of a Boat Voyage through Rupert's Land and the Arctic Sea. London: 1851. V. 38; 39; 41; 43; 44; 45

The Canon of the New Testament Vindicated: In Answer to the Objections of J.T. In His Amyntor. London: 1700. V. 44

Fauna Boreali - Americana; (Mammalia, Part 1). London: 1829. V. 37; 39; 41; 42; 43; 44

A Grammar of the Arabick Language. London: 1776. V. 45

A Grammar of the Arabic Language. London: 1801. V. 42

Journal of the Movements of the British Legion. London: 1836. V. 41

Movements of the British Legion, with Strictures on the Course of Conduct Pursued by Lieutenant-General Evans. London: 1837. V. 37

The Museum of Natural History. London: 1860. V. 46

Museum of Natural History . . . London: 1869. V. 46

The Museum of Natural History. London: 1859-62. V. 37

The Museum of Natural History. London: 1868. V. 37

The Polar Regions. Edinburgh: 1861. V. 37; 38; 39; 41

Richardson's War of 1812 with Notes and a Life of the Author by Alexander Clark Casselman. Toronto: 1902. V. 42

RICHARDSON, JOHN MAUNSEL

Gentlemen Riders, Past and Present. London: 1909. V. 39

RICHARDSON, JONATHAN

An Account of Some of the Statues, Bas-Reliefs, Drawings and Pictures in Italy, etc. with Remarks. London: 1722. V. 37

An Essay on the Theory of Painting. London: 1715. V. 38; 41; 45

An Essay on the Theory of Painting. London: 1725. V. 44

Explanatory Notes and Remarks on Milton's Paradise Lost. London: 1734. V. 40; 42

Two Discourses. I. An Essay on the Whole Art of Criticism as It Relates to Painting. . . . II. An Argument in Behalf of the Science of a Connoisseur . . . London: 1719. V. 41

The Works. London: 1773. V. 45

The Works of Jonathan Richardson. London: 1773. V. 38; 44

The Works Containing I. Theory of Painting. II. Essay on the Art of Criticism. III. The Science of Connoisseur . . . Strawberry Hill: 1792. V. 44

RICHARDSON, JOSEPH

Jekyll: a Political Eclogue. London: 1788. V. 38; 43

Literary Relics. London: 1807. V. 40; 43; 46

A Practical Treatise on Mechanical Dentistry . . . Philadelphia: 1860. V. 45

The Rolliad in Two Parts: Probationary Odes for the Laureatship and Political Miscellanies. Dublin: 1796. V. 43; 46

RICHARDSON, JOSHUA

Observations on the Proposed Railway from Newcastle Upon Tyne to North Shields and Tynemouth. Newcastle upon Tyne: 1831. V. 46

RICHARDSON, L. J. D.

Studies in Mycenaean Inscriptions and Dialect. .London: 1965-77. V. 40; 42; 44

RICHARDSON, M. A.

Etchings of Antiquities in Newcastle-Upon-Tyne. Newcastle: 1827. V. 37

The Lost Historian's Table Book of Remarkable Occurrences, Historical Facts, Traditions, Legendary and Descriptive Ballads, Etc. Newcastle upon Tyne: 1841-46. V. 42

RICHARDSON, M. T.

Practical Blacksmithing, a Collection of Articles Contributed by Skilled Workmen to the Columns of 'The Blacksmith and Wheelwright'. New York: 1889-95. V. 45

Practical Carriage Building. New York: 1903, 1905. V. 39

RICHARDSON, R. H.

'Wickedness in High Places.' Chicago: 1854. V. 42

RICHARDSON, ROBERT

A State of the Evidence in the Cause Between His Grace the Duke of Hamilton and Others . . . London: 1769. V. 38

Travels Along the Mediterranean, and Parts Adjacent, in Company with the Earl of Belmore, During the years 1816-17-18. London: 1822. V. 37; 40

RICHARDSON, RUPERT N.

The Comanche Barrier to South Plains Settlement. Glendale: 1933. V. 37; 40; 42

The Comanche Barrier to South Plains Settlement. Abilene: 1991. V. 46

The Frontier of Northwest Texas 1846 to 1876. Glendale: 1963. V. 38; 46

The Greater Southwest: the Economic, Social and Cultural Development of Kansas, Oklahoma, Texas, Utah, Colorado, Nevada, New Mexico, Arizona and California from the Spanish Conquest to the Twentieth Century. Glendale: 1934. V. 37; 41; 46

The Greater Southwest: the Economic, Social and Cultural Development of Kansas, Oklahoma, Texas, Utah, Colorado, Nevada, New Mexico, Arizona and California from the Spanish Conquest to the Twentieth Century. Glendale: 1935. V. 45

Texas, the Lone Star State. New York: 1943. V. 37

RICHARDSON, SAMUEL 1689-1761

Clarissa. London: 1741. V. 38; 40; 41

Clarissa. London: 1748. V. 38; 41; 42; 45

Clarissa. London: 1751. V. 39; 43

Clarissa. London: 1764. V. 37

Clarissa, or, the History of a Young Lady. London: 1774. V. 39; 41

Clarisse Harlowe. Geneve: 1785-86. V. 42

Clarissa, or the History of a Young Lady. Dublin: 1792. V. 40

Clarissa; or the History of a Young Lady. London: 1795. V. 43

Clarissa. Or, the History of a Young Lady: Comprehending the Most Important Concerns of private life. London: 1747-48. V. 37

A Collection of the Moral and Instructive Sentiments, Maxims, Cautions and Reflections . . . London: 1755. V. 43

A Collection of the Moral and Instructive Sentiments, Maxims, Cautions and Reflexions, Contained in the Histories of Pamela, Clarissa and Sir Charles Grandison. London: 1755. V. 37; 38; 39; 41; 43; 44; 45

The Correspodence of . . . Selected from the Original Manuscript, Bequeathed by Him to His Family. London: 1804. V. 38; 40; 41; 42; 43

The History of Sir Charles Grandisons. London. V. 40

The History of Sir Charles Grandison. London: 1753-54. V. 40

The History of Charles Grandison. London: 1754. V. 37; 38; 39; 40; 41; 43; 45

The History of Sir Charles Grandison. London: 1762. V. 38; 40

The History of Sir Charles Grandison. London: 1766. V. 45

The History of Sir Charles Grandison. London: 1770. V. 46

The History of Sir Charles Grandison. London: 1774. V. 39; 45

The History of Sir Charles Grandison. (with) Clarissa. Suffield: 1798. V. 43; 44

The History of Sir Charles Grandison in a series of letters. Formerly published in seven volumes. Now comprised in two large volumes, octavo. London: 1795. V. 37

The Novels. New York: 1901. V. 37; 38; 39; 40; 42; 44

The Novels. New York: 1901-02. V. 39

The Novels. London: 1902. V. 37; 42

The Novels. Oxford: 1929-31. V. 44

The Novels. Oxford: 1931. V. 37

Pamela. London. V. 40

Pamela; or, Virtue Rewarded. London: 1741. V. 43

Pamela. London: 1741, 1742. V. 40

Pamela. London: 1741-42. V. 40; 43; 45

Pamela; ou La Vertu Recompensee. Londres: i.e. Paris,: 1742. V. 41

Pamela. London: 1742 (1741). V. 45

Pamela, ou la Vertu Recompensee. Amsterdam: 1743. V. 39; 40

Pamela. Amsterdam: 1765. V. 45

Pamela's Conduct in High Life. London: 1741. V. 45

Works. London: 1811. V. 37; 38; 42; 43; 46

The Works. London: 1883. V. 39; 40

RICHARDSON, STEPHEN J.

Catalogue of an Extensive and Valuable Collection of Books Relating to Ireland, Fromed by S. J. Richardson . . . 1913. V. 43

RICHARDSON, T. A.

The Art of Architectural Modelling in Paper. London: 1859. V. 37; 40; 44

RICHARDSON, T. M.

The Castles of the English and Scottish Border, from Original Drawings . . . Newcastle: 1834. V. 38

The Castles of the English and Scottish Border, from Original Drawings. Newcastle: 1854. V. 39

Memorials of Old Newcastle Upon Tyne. Edinburgh: 1880. V. 41; 45

RICHARDSON, W.

Dr. Zell and the Princess Charlotte. 1892. V. 44

A General Collection of Voyages and Discoveries Made by the Portuguese and Spaniards, During the Fifteenth and Sixteenth Centuries. London: 1789. V. 41

RICHARDSON, W. H.

The Boot and Shoe Manufacturers Assistant and Guide. Boston: 1858. V. 37

RICHARDSON, W. R.

A Brief Sketch of the History of the Protestant Episcopal Church in the Missionary District of Western Texas. San Antonio: 1902. V. 37; 44

RICHARDSON, WILLARD

The Texas Almanac for 1860. Galveston: 1859. V. 41

The Texas Almanac for 1867. Galveston: 1866. V. 43

RICHARDSON, WILLIAM

Anecdotes of the Russian Empire. London: 1784. V. 38; 41; 44

Cursory Remarks on Tragedy, on Shakespear, and on Certain French and Italian Poets, Principally Tragedians. London: 1774. V. 41; 42; 43

Essays on Shakespeare's Dramatic Character of Sir John Falstaff . . . London. V. 42

Essays on Shakespeare's Dramatic Characters of Richrd the Third, King Lear and Timon of Athens. London: 1784. V. 43

Essays on Shakespeare's Dramatic Characters of Richard the Third, King Lear and Timon of Athens. London: 1784. V. 42

Essays on Shakespeare's Dramatic Characters of Richard the Third, King Lear and Timon of Athens. London: 1785. V. 39

Essays on Some of Shakespeare' Dramatic Characters to Which is Added, an Essay on the Faults of Shakespeare. London: 1798. V. 38

Essays on Shakespeare's Dramatic Character of Sir John Falstaff, and on His Imitation of Female Characters . . . London: 1788. V. 46

Essays on Shakespeare's Dramatic Characters of Richard the Third, King Lear and Timon of Athens. London: 1784. V. 46

The Monasteries of Yorkshire. York: 1843. V. 37

The Monastic Ruins of Yorkshire. York: 1843. V. 38; 40; 41; 44; 45

A Philosophical Analysis and Illustration of Some of Shakespeare's Remarkable Characters. Edinburgh: 1774. V. 44

A Philosophical Analysis and Illustration of Some of Shakespeare's Remarkable Characters. Philadelphia: 1788. V. 39

Poems Chiefly Rural. Glasgow: 1776. V. 42

Simple Measures, by Which the Recurrence of Famines May Be Prevented, and the Pressure of the Poor Laws Greatly Abated . . . London: 1816. V. 41

RICHARDSON, WILLIAM H.

Journal of William H. Richardson, a Private Soldier in Col. Doniphan's Command. Baltimore: 1847. V. 41

Journal of William H. Richardson, a Private Soldier in the Campaign of New and Old Mexico Under the Command of Colonel Doniphan. Baltimore: 1848. V. 40; 42

Journal of William H. Richardson, a Private Soldier in the Campaign of New and Old Mexico Under the Command of Colonel Doniphan. New York: 1848. V. 37; 38

RICHARDSON, WILLIS

Plays and Pageants from the Life of the Negro. Washington: 1930. V. 42

RICHARDSON'S Virginia and North Carolina Almanac, for the Year of Our Lord 1862 . . . Richmond: 1861. V. 42

RICHARDSON'S Virginia and North Carolina Almanac for the Year of Our Lord 1863 . . . Richmond: 1862. V. 44

RICHEL, DIONISIO

Este es Un Copedio Breue Que Tracta Dla Manera De Comose Ha de Hazer Las Pcessiones . . . (caption title). Mexico City: 1544. V. 41

RICHELIEU, ARMAND JEAN DU PLESSIS, CARDINAL DE

Letters of the Cardinal Duke de Richelieu, Great Minister of State to Lewis XIII . . . London: 1697. V. 44

RICHELIEU, JEAN ARMAND DU PLESSIS

Instrvction Dv Chrestien. Rouen: 1629. V. 37

Traitte Qvi Contient La Plvs Facile . . . Povr Convertir Cevx Qvi Se Sont Separez de l'Eglise. Paris: 1663. V. 37

RICHEOME, LOUIS

Expostvlatio Apologetica Ad Henricvm IV. Francorum . . . Pro Societate Jesv. Lyons: 1606. V. 37

RICHER, ADRIEN

Great Events from Little Causes. London: 1767. V. 38; 43

RICHERS, THOMAS

The History of the Royal Genealogy of Spain . . . London: 1724. V. 44

RICHET, CHARLES

Physiology and Histology of the Cerebral Convolutions, Also, Poisons of the Intellect. New York: 1879. V. 42

RICHEY, J. E.

The Geology of Ardnamurchan, North-West Mull and Coll. London: 1930. V. 46

RICHIE, DONALD

The Masters' Book of Ikebana; Background & Principles of Japanese Flower Arrangement. Tokyo: 1966. V. 38; 39; 41; 46

The Masters' Book fo Ikebana: Background & Principles of Japanese Flower Arrangement. Tokyo: 1966. V. 40

RICHIE, LEITCH

Wanderings by the Seine. London: 1834. V. 39

RICHMAN, IRVING BERDINE

California Under Spain and Mexico 1535-1847. Boston & New York: 1911. V. 45

California Under Spain and Mexico 1535-1847. V. 37

RICHMOND, ALEXANDER BAILEY fl. 1809-1834

Narrative of te Condition of the Manufacturing Population; and the Proceedings of Government Which Led to the State Trials in Scotland, for Administering Unlawful Oaths, and the Suspension of the Habeas Corpus Act in 1817 . . . London: 1824. V. 38; 41; 43

Narrataive of the Condition of the Manufacturing Population . . . London: 1825. V. 41

RICHMOND AND LENNOX, CHARLES LENNOX, 3RD DUKE OF 1735-1806

A Letter from His Grace, the Duke of Richmond, to Lt. Col. Sharman, Chairman of the Committee of Correspondence . . . London: 1794. V. 43

RICHMOND, CHARLES LENNOX, 3RD DUKE OF

An Answer to 'A Short Essay on the Modes of Defence Best Adapted to the Situation and Circumstances of this Island.' London: 1785. V. 38

RICHMOND, IAN A.

The City Wall of Imperial Rome. Oxford: 1930. V. 40

RICHMOND, LEONARD

The Technique of the Poster. London: 1933. V. 42

RICHTER, CONRAD 1890-

Brothers of No Kin. New York: 1924. V. 38; 40; 41; 42; 43; 44

The Trees. The Fields. The Town. New York: 1940/46/50. V. 41

RICHTER, GEORGE MARTIN

Giorgio da Castelfranco called Giorgione. Chicago: 1937. V. 46

RICHTER, GISELA M. A.

Animals in Greek Sculpture: a Survey. London: 1930. V. 44

The Archaic Gravestones of Attica. London: 1961. V. 44

Catalogue of Engraved Gems in the Classical Style. New York: 1920. V. 40

Catalogue of Engraved Gems: Greek, Etruscan and Roman. Roma: 1956. V. 40

Engraved Gems of the Greeks, Etruscans and Romans. London: 1968-71. V. 40; 42; 44

Greek Portraits. Bruxelles-Berchem: 1955-62. V. 44

Kouroi: Archaic Greek Youths: A Study of the Development of the Kouros Type in Greek Sculpture. London: 1960. V. 38

Kouroi, Archaic Greek Youths. London: 1970. V. 40; 46

The Portraits of the Greeks. London: 1965. V. 40; 42

Red-Figured Athenian Vases in the Metropolitan Museum of Art. New Haven: 1935. V. 37

Red-Figures Athenian Vases in the Metropolitan Museum of Art. New Haven: 1936. V. 37

The Sculpture and Sculptors of the Greeks. New Haven: & London: 1929. V. 42

Shapes and Names of Athenian Vases. New York: 1935. V. 42

Three Critical Periods in Greek Sculpture. Oxford: 1951. V. 38

RICHTER, GISELA M.A.

Animals in Greek Sculpture. New York: 1930. V. 41

Kouroi: a Study of the Development of the greek Kouros from the Late Seventh to the Early Fifth Century BC. New York: 1942. V. 46

RICHTER, H. DAVIS

Floral Art: Decoration and Design. South Benfleet: 1932. V. 44

RICHTER, HANS

Hans Richter. Neuchatel: 1965. V. 38; 41

RICHTER, JEAN PAUL

Catalogue of Pictures at Locko Park. London: & Derby: 1901. V. 44

The Golden Age of Classic Christian Art. London: 1904. V. 42; 44

The Literary Works of Leonardo Da Vinci. London: 1939. V. 46

The Literary Works of Leonardo da Vinci. London: 1970. V. 46

RICHTHOFEN, WALTER BARON VON

Cattle Raising on the Plains of North America. New York: 1885. V. 37; 38; 39

RICHTOFEN, FERDINAND

Baron Richthofen's Letters, 1870-1872. Shanghai: 1872. V. 40

RICKARD, GEORGE

Practical Mining; fully and Familiarly Described. London: 1869. V. 41

RICKARD, T. A.

Across the San Juan Mountains, Engineering and Mining Journal. New York: 1903. V. 46

Journeys of Observation. San Francisco: 1907. V. 38

RICKARDS, CONSTANTINE GEORGE

The Ruins of Mexico. London: 1910. V. 37; 42

RICKEMEYER, RUDOLF

Down South. New York: 1900. V. 44

RICKENBACKER, EDWARD

Fighting the Flying Circus. New York: 1919. V. 38

RICKERT, MARGARET

The Reconstructed Carmelite Missal: an English Manuscript of the Late XIV Century in the British Museum. London: 1952. V. 39

RICKETSON, ANNA

Daniel Ricketson and His Friends. Boston & New York: 1902. V. 40; 46

RICKETSON, DANIEL

The History of New Bedford, Bristol County, Massachusetts: . . . The Old Township of Dartmouth and the Present Townships of Westport, Dartmoutn and Fairhaven . . . New Bedford: 1858. V. 37

RICKETSON, OLIVER G.

Uaxactun, Guatemala. Group E 1926-1931. Washington: 1937. V. 42

RICKETSON, SHADRACH

Means of Preserving Health and Preventing Diseases Founded Principally on Attention to Air and Climates . . . Austin: 1608. V. 45

Means of Preserving Health. New York: 1806. V. 37; 38; 39; 40; 41; 42; 43; 44; 45

RICKETT, ARTHUR

Lost Chords. Some Emotions About Morals. London: 1895. V. 43

RICKETT, H. W.

Wild Flowers of the United States: The Northeastern States. New York: 1966. V. 40; 45

Wild Flowers of the United States: The Southwestern States. New York: 1970. V. 45

Wild Flowers of the United States. Volume 1. Northeastern States. New York: 1973. V. 46

Wild Flowers of the United States. Volume 2. The Southeastern States. New York: 1967. V. 46

Wild Flowers of the United States. Volume 5. The Northwestern States. New York: 1971. V. 46

Wild Flowers of the United States. Volume 6. The Central Mountains and Plains. New York: 1973. V. 46

RICKETT, HAROLD W.

Wild Flowers of the United States . . . Texas. New York: 1969. V. 38; 39; 42; 43; 44

RICKETT, HAROLD W. continued

Wild Flowers of the United States; The Southeastern States. New York: 1966. V. 40

RICKETTS, BENJAMIN

The Surgery of the Heart and Lungs. New York: 1904. V. 41; 45

RICKETTS, CHARLES

Beyond the Threshold. N.P.: 1927. V. 43

Beyond the Threshold. London: 1929. V. 40

Charles Ricketts R. A. - Sixty-Five Illustrations. London: 1933. V. 41

De la Typographie et de l'Harmonie de la Page Imprimee. London: 1898. V. 39; 44

A Defence of the Revival of Printing. London: 1899. V. 37; 38; 39; 44; 45; 46

Pages on Art. London: 1913. V. 37; 38

The Parables from the Gospels. With 10 Original Woodcuts Designed and Engraved on the Wood by Charles Ricketts. London: 1903. V. 37

Recollections of Oscar Wilde. London: 1932. V. 41; 45

Self-Portrait Taken from the Letters and Journals of Charles Ricketts. London: 1939. V. 41; 45

Sixty-Five Illustrations Introduced by T. Sturge Moore. London: 1933. V. 46

De La Typographie et de l'Harmonie de la Page Imprimee. London: 1898. V. 42; 43

Unrecorded Histories. London: 1933. V. 37; 40; 41; 42; 45

RICKETTS, W. P.

50 years in the Saddle. Sheridan: 1942. V. 42; 44

RICKIUS, JACOBUS

Tractatus de Unione Prolium. V. 40

RICKMAN, EDWIN

Madness, or the Maniacs' Hall; a Poem, in Seven Cantos. London: 1841. V. 46

RICKMAN, JOHN

Journal of Captain Cook's Last Voyage to the Pacific Ocean, on Discovery, Performe din the Years 1776, 1777, 1778, 1779. Dublin: 1781. V. 43

Journal of Captain Cook's Last Voyage to the Pacific Ocean, on Discovery . . . London: 1781. V. 42

RICKMAN, PHILIP

A Bird Painter's Sketch Book. London: 1935. V. 45

Bird Sketches and Some Field Observations. 1938. V. 40; 43; 46

A Selection of Bird Paintings and Sketches. 1979. V. 40

A Selection of Bird Paintings and Sketches. 1979. V. 46

A Selection of Bird Paintings and Sketches. London: 1979. V. 37; 45; 46

A Selection of Bird Paintings and Sketches. Written and Illustrated by . . . with a Foreword by H.R.H. The Duke of Edinburgh. 1979. V. 37

RICKMAN, THOMAS

An Attempt to Discriminate the Styles of Architecture in England from the Conquest to the Reformation. London: 1825. V. 45

An Attempt to Discriminate the Styles of Archiecture . . . London: 1848. V. 42; 46

An Attempt to Discriminate the Styles of Architecture in England, from the Conquest to the Reformation . . . Oxford and London: 1862. V. 41

RICO, UL DE

The Rainbow Goblins. New York: 1978. V. 44

RICORD, FREDERICK W.

History of Union County, New Jersey. Newark: 1897. V. 41

RICORD, PHILIPPE

Illustrations of Syphilitic Disease. Philadelphia: 1852. V. 39; 42

A Practical Treatise on Venereal Diseases; or, Critic and Experimental Researches on Inoculation, Applied to the Study of These Affections. New York: 1842. V. 42

RICORDATTO, FRANCESCO

Prediche Sopra il Sacramento Dell' Altare da lui Predicate Quando Incominciaarono l'Heresie nella Flandra. Con un Predica Sopra Le Imagini Delle Chiese in Difese Della Fede Cattolica Tradotte Della Francese Nella Lingua Toscana da M. Piero Spinelli. Florence: 1576. V. 38

RICRAFT, JOSIAH

A Survey of Englands Champions and Truths Faithful Patriots or a Chronological Recitement of the Principall Proceedings of the Most Worthy Commanders of the Prosperous Armies Raised for the Preservation of Religion . . . London: 1649. V. 46

RIDABOCK & CO.

Military Goods. New York: 1880? V. 44

RIDDELL, CHARLOTTE

Phemie Keller. London: 1866. V. 44

RIDDELL, J. L.

A Monograph of the Silver Dollar, Good and Bad. New Orleans: 1845. V. 37

RIDDELL, JOHN

Architectural Designs for Model Country Residences . . . Philadelphia: 1864. V. 39

RIDDELL, MARIA

The Metrical Miscellany Consisting Chiefly of Poems Hitherto Unpublished. London: 1803. V. 42

Voyages to the Madeira, and Leeward and Caribbean Isles; With Sketches of the Natural History of These Islands. Edinburgh: 1792. V. 41

Voyages to the Madeira and Leeward Caribbean Isles . . . Salem: 1802. V. 42

RIDDELL, ROBERT

The Carpenter and Joiner. London: 1860? V. 42

The Carpenter and Joiner, Stair Builder and Hand-Railer . . . Edinburgh: 1870. V. 44

The Carpenter and Joiner Stair Builder and Hand Railer. London: 1870. V. 37; 43

The New Elements of HandRailing. Philadelphia: 1871. V. 43

The Scientific Stair Builder. Philadelphia: 1854. V. 46

RIDDELL, WILLIAM RENWICK

The Bar and the Courts of the Province of Upper Canada, or Ontario. Toronto: 1928. V. 42

The Legal Profession in Upper Canada in Its Early Periods. Toronto: 1916. V. 42

The Life of William Dummer Powell. Lansing: 1924. V. 40

RIDDLE, EDWARD

Treatise on Navigation, and Nautical Astronomy, Adapted to Practice, and to the Purposes of Elementary Instruction . . . London: 1824. V. 42

RIDDLE, JEFF C.

The History of the Modoc War and the Causes that Led to It. San Francisco: 1914. V. 38

The Indian History of the Modoc War and the Causes that Led To It. N.P.: 1914. V. 40

Indian History of the Modoc War and Causes That Led to It. N.P.: 1914. V. 39

Indian History of the Modoc Indian War and the Causes that Led to It. San Francisco: 1914. V. 40

A RIDE with Father Christmas. London: 1918. V. 42

RIDEING, WILLIAM

A Saddle in Wild West A Glimpse of Travel Among the Mountains, Lava Beds, San Deserts, Adobe Towns, Indian Reservations . . . Of Southern Colorado, New Mexico and Arizona: London: 1879. V. 37; 40

RIDEING, WILLIAM H.

A Saddle in the Wild West. New York: 1879. V. 38; 40

RIDEOUT, H. M.

The Fool-Path Way. New York: 1920. V. 46

RIDEOUT, JACOB BARZILLA, MRS.

Camping Out in California. San Francisco: 1889. V. 40; 42

RIDER, CARDANUS

Rider's (1737) British Merlin: Adorn'd With Many Delightful Varities and Useful Verities . . . London. V. 44

RIDER, FREMONT

Rider's California: a Guide-Book for Travelers . . . New York: 1925. V. 46

RIDER, JOHN

Rider's Dictionarie, Corrected and Augmented with the Addition of Many Hundred Words . . . V. 43

RIDER, WILLIAM

Views in Stratford-Upon-Avon and Its Vicinity, Illustrative of the Biography of Shakespeare . . . London: 1828. V. 46

RIDER'S British Almanac . . . 1780. London: 1780. V. 38

RIDER'S British Merlin, for the Year of 1780 (1782-1784). London: 1780-82-84. V. 38

RIDER'S British Merlin. For the year of Our Lord 1782 . . . London: 1782. V. 39

RIDER'S British Merlin: for the Year of Our Lord God 1754 . . . London: 1754. V. 44

RIDER'S British Merlin: for the Year of Our Lord God 1766 . . . . London: 1765. V. 46

RIDGE, J. D.

Annotated Bibliographies of Mineral deposits in europe, Including Selected Deposits in the U.S.S.R. London: 1987. V. 37; 38

RIDGE, JOHN R.

Poems. San Francisco: 1868. V. 45

RIDGE, LOLA

Dance of Fire. New York: 1935. V. 39; 41

Firehead. New York: 1929. V. 40

RIDGELY, DAVID

Annals of Annapolis, Comprising Sundry Notices of that Old City from 1649 Until the War of 1812. Baltimore: 1841. V. 37; 39

RIDGELY-NEVITT, CEDRIC

American Steamships on the Atlantic . . . Newark: 1981. V. 39

RIDGWAY, BRUNILDE SISMONDO

The Archaic Style in Greek Sculpture. Princeton: 1970. V. 42

Fifth Century Styles in Greek Sculpture. Princeton: 1981. V. 42; 44

The Severe Style in Greek Sculpture. Princeton: 1970. V. 44

RIDGWAY, R.

Color Standards and Color Nomenclature. Washington: 1912. V. 42; 44

A Nomenclature of Colors for Naturalists. Boston: 1886. V. 37; 43

RIDGWAY, ROBERT 1850-1929

The Birds of North and Middle America. Washington: 1901-50. V. 38

United States Geological Exploration of the Fortieth Parallel . . . *Part III. Ornithology.* Washington: 1876. V. 42

RIDGWAY, S. H.

Handbook of Marine Mammals, Volume 3. The Sirenians and Baleen Whales. London: 1985. V. 37

RIDING, LAURA 1901-

Anarchism is Not Enough. London: 1928. V. 38

The Close Chaplet. New York: 1926. V. 37

Collected Poems. London: 1938. V. 40; 45

The Collected Poems. New York: 1938. V. 39; 40; 43

Contemporaries and Snobs. London: 1928. V. 43

Description of Life. New York: 1980. V. 43

Epilogue - A Critical Summary - Volume I. Deya & London: 1935. V. 40

Four Unposted Letters to Catherine. Paris. V. 39

Four Unposted Letters to Catherine. Paris: 1930. V. 37

Laura and Francisca. Deja: 1931. V. 37; 39; 41; 46

The Left Hersy - in Literature and Life. 1939. V. 37

The Life of the Dead. London. V. 39

The Life of the Dead. London: 1933. V. 39

Lives of Wives. New York: 1939. V. 42; 43

Love as Love, Death as Death. London: 1928. V. 37; 41; 43; 45

Poems: A Joking Word. London: 1930. V. 37

Poet: a Lying Word. London: 1933. V. 38

Progress of Stories. Deya: 1935. V. 39

Progress of Stories. Deya, Majorca, and London: 1935. V. 41

Progress of Stories. London: 1935. V. 45

Selected Poems. New York: 1973. V. 42

Some Communications of Broad Reference. Northridge: 1983. V. 40; 43

Though Gently. Deya: 1930. V. 37; 39; 42

Twenty Poems Less. Paris: 1930. V. 37; 39

Voltaire: A Biographical Fantasy: a Poem. London: 1927. V. 37; 41

RIDINGER, JOHANN ELIAS

Enswurf Einiger Thiere . . . Augsburg: 1738-55. V. 41; 43

RIDINGS, SAM P.

The Chisholm Trail. Guthrie: 1936. V. 38; 40; 42; 43; 45; 46

RIDLER, ANNE

The Jesse Tree. London: 1972. V. 37; 41; 42; 44

The Jesse Tree. London: 1977. V. 37

Poems. London;: 1939. V. 37

RIDLER, WILLIAM

British Modern Press Books. London: 1971. V. 45

RIDLEY, GLOCESTER

Juvi Eleutheric; or, an Offering to Liberty. London: 1745. V. 40

The Life of Dr. Nicholas Ridley . . . London: 1763. V. 39

A Sermon Preached before the Honourable Trustees for Establishing the Colony of Georgia in America and the Associates of the Late Reverend Dr. Bray . . . London: 1746. V. 46

RIDLEY, HUMPHREY 1653-1708

The Anatomy of the Brain . . . London: 1695. V. 37

Observationes Quaedam Medico-Practicae & Physiologicae . . . London: 1703. V. 45; 46

RIDLEY, JAMES 1736-1765

The Tales of the Genii. London: 1764. V. 42; 43

The Tales of the Genii. London: 1764-1765. V. 40

The Tales of the Genii; or, the Delightful Lessons of Horam, the Son of Asmar. London: 1786. V. 43

The Tales of the Genii; or, the Delightful Lessons of Horam, the Son of Asmar. London: 1793. V. 43

The Tales of the Genii. London: 1805. V. 43

The Tales of the Genii. London: 1820. V. 38

The Tales of the Genii. London: 1820. V. 46

RIDLEY, THOMAS

A View of the Civile and Ecclesiasticall Law . . . Oxford: 1634. V. 42

A View of the Civile and Ecclesiasticall Law. Oxford: 1662. V. 41

RIDLEY, W.

Snapshots from the North Pacific. Letters Written by Bishop Ridley of Caledonia. London: 1904. V. 38

RIDLON, GIDEON TIBBETTS

Saco Valley Settlements and Families. Portland: 1895. V. 42

RIDNER, JOHN P.

The Artist's Chromatic Hand-Book. New York: 1850. V. 40

RIDOLFI, BERNARDINO

In Funere Caroli III Hispaniar. Regis Catholici Oratio Habita in Sacello Pontificio a Bernardino Ridolfi Sanctissimi D. N. Pii Sexti Intimo Cubiculario . . . Parma: 1789. V. 38

RIDOLFI, CARLO 1594-1658

Vita di Giacopo Robusti detto Il Tintoretto, Celebre Pittore . . . Venice: 1642. V. 46

RIDOUT, THOMAS

Ten Years of Upper Canada in Peace and War. Toronto: 1890. V. 40

RIDOUT, WILLIAM

A Catalogue of the Collection of Italian and Other Majolica, Mediaeval English Poetry, Dutch, Spanish and French, Faience, and Other Ceramic Wares, Formed by William Ridout. London: 1934. V. 38

RIDPATH, GEORGE 1717-1772

The Border History of England and Scotland, Deduced from the Earliest Times to the Union of the Two Crowns. London, Edinburgh & Berwick: 1776. V. 39

An Enquiry Into the Causes of the Miscarriage of the Scots Colony at Darien. Glasgow: 1700. V. 40; 43

Parliamentary Right Maintain'd or the Hanover Succession Justify'd, Wherein the Hereditary Right to the Crown of England Asserted etc. is Consider'd. N.P.: Edinburgh: 1714. V. 40

The Reducing of Scotland by Arms, and Annexing it to England as a Province Considered. London: 1705. V. 38

Reflections on a Late Speech by the Lord Haversham, in so Far as It Relates to the Affairs of Scotland. Edinburgh: 1704. V. 38

RIDSDALE, B.

Scenes and Adventures in Great Namaqualand. London: 1883. V. 40; 42

RIEDER, HERMAN

Atlas of Urinary Sediments: With Special Reference to Their Clinical Significance. London: 1899. V. 42

RIEDESEL, FRIEDRICH A.

Memoirs, Letters and Journals of . . . *During His Residence in America.* Albany: 1868. V. 40

RIEFSTAHL, ELIZABETH

Ancient Egyptian Glass and Glazes in the Brooklyn Museum. Brooklyn: 1968. V. 44

RIEFSTAHL, R. MEYER

The Parish-Watson Collection of Mohammadan Potteries. New York: 1922. V. 38; 41; 42; 43

RIEGER, CHRISTIAN

Elementos da Toda la Architectura Civil. Madrid: 1763. V. 44

RIEGER, CHRISTIAN continued

*Vniversae Architectvrae Civilis Elementa Brevibus Recentiorum
Observationibus Illustrata Conscripta a Christiano Rieger. (with) Universae
Architecturae Militaris Elementa, Brevibus Recentiorum Observationibus
Illustrata Conscripta a Christiano Rieger.* Vienna, Prague, Trieste: 1756,
1758. V. 39

RIEMANN, GEORG FRIEDRICH BERNHARD

Oeuvres Mathematiques . . . Paris: 1898. V. 38

RIENAECKER, VICTOR

John Sell Cotman 1782-1842. Leigh-on-Sea: 1953. V. 39; 46

RIERA, JUAN

Transumtum Memorialis in Causa Pii Eremitae, et Martyris Raimundi Lulli.
Palma, Majorca: 1627. V. 37

RIESENBERG, FELIX

Early Steamships. New York: 1933. V. 41

RIEU, C.

Catalogue of the Persian Manuscripts in the British Museum. 1966-1883.
V. 38

*Supplement to the Catalogue of the Arabic Manuscripts in the British
Museum.* London: 1894. V. 39

RIEZLER, WALTER

Weissgrundige Attische Lekythen nach Furtwanglers Auswahl. Munchen:
1914. V. 44

RIGAUD & BARON

*Stowe Gardens in Buckinghamshire, Belonging to the Right Honourable the
Lord Viscount Cobham; Laid Out by Mr. Bridgeman . . . Drawn on the Spot
by Mons. Rigaud and engraved by Him and Mons. Bernard Baron.*
London: 1746. V. 39; 40

RIGAUD, JACQUES

*Recueil Choisi des Plus Belles Vues des Palais, Chateaux et Maisons
Royales de Paris et des Environs.* Paris: 1730. V. 38; 41

*Stowe Gardens in Buckinghamshire, Belonging to the Right Honourable the
Lord Viscount Cobham; Laid Out by Mr. Bridgeman . . . Drawn on the Spot
by Mons. Rigaud, and Engraved by Him and Mons. Bernard Baron.*
London: 1746. V. 38

RIGAUD, STEPHEN PETER

Historical Essay on the First Publication of Sir Isaac Newton's Principia.
Oxford: 1838. V. 38

RIGAULT, NICOLAS

Hierakosophion. Rei Accipitrariae Scriptores. Paris: 1612. V. 37

RIGBY, EDWARD

Chemical Observations on Sugar . . . London: 1788. V. 45

holkham in Agriculture etc. Norwich: 1817. V. 46

A System of Midwifery. Philadelphia: 1841. V. 43; 45

RIGG, R.

The nature Lesson Series of Brush-Drawing Exercises. London: 1905. V. 38

RIGG, ROBERT

*Experimental Researches; Chemical and Agricultural, Shewing Carbon to be
a Compound Body . . .* London: 1844. V. 39

RIGGE, AMBROSE

*A Brief and Serious Warning to Such as Are Concerned in Commerce and
Trading . . .* London: 1771. V. 45

RIGGS, LYNN

Green Grow the Lilacs. 1954. V. 41

Green Grow the Lilacs. New York: 1954. V. 45

Green Grow the Lilacs. Norman: 1954. V. 40; 41; 44

Russet Mantle and the Cherokee Night: Two Plays. New York: 1936. V. 39

RIGGS, STEPHEN R.

Dakota Odowan. Hymns in the Dakota Language. New York: 1864. V. 40

Dakota Odowan. Hymns in the Dakota Language. New York: 1865. V. 39

Dakota Grammar. Texts and Ethnography. Washington: 1893. V. 46

Grammar and Dictionary of the Dakota Language . . . New York: 1851.
V. 45

*Grammar and Dictionary of the Dakota Language, Collected by Members of
the Dakota Mission.* Washington: 1852. V. 37; 38; 39; 40; 43

Mary and I: Forty Years with the Sioux. Boston: 1887. V. 46

Mary and I. Forty Years with the Sioux. Chicago: 1880. V. 37

Tah-Koo Wah-Kan; or, the Gosepl Among the Dakotas. Boston: 1869. V. 39

THE RIGHT of British Subjects to Petition and Apply To Their
Representatives Asserted and Vindicated. London: 1733. V. 41

THE RIGHT of the Governor and Company, of the Colony of
Connecticut, to Claim and Hold the Lands Within the Limits of Their
Charter, Lying West of the Province of New York, Stated and
Considered, in a Letter to J. H. Esquire. Hartford: 1773. V. 37; 39; 44;
45; 46

THE RIGHT Review. London: 1936-47. V. 40

RIGHTS of Citizens: Being an Inquiry Into Some of the Consequences of
Social Union, and an Examination of Mr. Paine's Principles Touching
Government. London: 1791. V. 39

THE RIGHTS Of Parliament Vindicated, on Occasion of the Stamp Act.
London: 1766. V. 38

RIGOLEY DE JUVIGNY, JEAN ANTOINE

*Les Bibliotheques Francoises De La Croix Du Maine et De Du Verdier Sieur
de Vauprivas.* Paris: 1772-73. V. 45; 46

RIHAKU

*Cathay. Translations . . . for the Most Part from the Chinse Rihaku, from the
Notes of the Late Ernest Fenollosa . . .* London: 1915. V. 37

RIKER, JAMES

The Annals of Newtown, in Queens County, New York . . . New York:
1852. V. 44

RILAND, JOHN

Memoirs of a West-India Planter. London: 1827. V. 37; 43

RILDEN, BRYANT P.

*Notes on the Upper Rio Grande, Explored in the Months of October and
November, 1846 on Board the U.S. Steamer Major-Brown . . .* Philadelphia:
1847. V. 39

RILEY, ATHELSTAN

Athos or the Mountain of the Monka. London: 1887. V. 37; 45

RILEY, CHARLES V.

The Locust Plague in the United States . . . Chicago: 1877. V. 46

RILEY, HENRY A.

An Atlas of the BAsal Ganglia, Brain Stem and Spinal Cord. Baltimore:
1943. V. 38; 39; 40; 41; 44

RILEY, J. H.

*Birds from Siam and the Malay Peninsula in the United States National
Museum Collected by Drs. Hugh M. Smith and William L. Abbott.*
Washington: 1938. V. 40

RILEY, JAMES

*Loss of the American Brig Commerce, Wrecked on the Western Coast of
Africa, in the Month of August, 1815.* London: 1817. V. 40; 46

RILEY, JAMES FRANCIS

Recollections of James Francis Riley 1838-1918. Independence: 1959. V. 41

RILEY, JAMES WHITCOMB 1849-1916

Afterwhiles. Indianapolis: 1888. V. 37

All the Year Round. Indianapolis: 1912. V. 37; 41; 46

Armazindy. Indianapolis: 1894. V. 43

The Book of Joyous Children. New York: 1902. V. 44

A Child-World. Indianapolis & Kansas City: 1897. V. 38; 39; 40

A Defective Santa Claus. Indianapolis: 1904. V. 38; 40

The Flying Islands of the Night. Inianapolis: 1892. V. 39; 43

The Flying Islands of the Night. Indianapolis: 1913. V. 43; 45

Fun, Wit and Poetry. New York: & Chicago: 1890. V. 40; 41; 43; 44

Green Fields and Running Brooks. Indianapolis: 1893. V. 45; 46

Home Again With Me. 1908. V. 46

A Host of Children. Indianapolis: 1920. V. 41

'Kissing the Rod.' Indianapolis: 1885. V. 43

Neighborly Poems: On Friendship, Grief, and Farm-Life. Indianapolis: 1891.
V. 41

The Old Swimmin' Hole and 'Leven More Poems. Indianpolis: 1883.
V. 41; 44; 45

An Old Sweetheart of Mine. Indianpolis: 1902. V. 46

The Orphant Annie Book. Indianapolis: 1908. V. 41; 46

Poems Here at Home. 1893. V. 43

The Raggedy Man. Indianapolis: 1907. V. 42

Rhymes of Childhood. Indianapolis: 1891. V. 39

Riley Farm-Rhymes. Indianapolis: 1901. V. 39

Riley Child Verse. Indianapolis: 1906. V. 41

Riley's Roses. Indianapolis: 1909. V. 40; 41; 43; 44

The Runaway Boy. Indianapolis: 1906. V. 41; 43

While the Heart Beats Young. Indianapolis: 1906. V. 41; 43

The Complete Works. Indianapolis: 1913. V. 43

The Complete Works. New Castle: 1913. V. 42

RILEY, JAMES WHITCOMB 1849-1916 continued

The Complete Works of . . . New York: 1916. V. 45

RILING, R.

Guns and Shooting, A Bibliography. Philadelphia: 1951. V. 38

RILING, RAY

Guns and Shooting. New York: 1951. V. 40; 46

The Powder Flask Book. V. 45

The Powder Flask Book. New Hope: 1953. V. 37; 38; 45

RILKE, RAINER MARIA 1875-1926

Das Buch der Bilder. Berlin: 1906. V. 41

Die Dritte Elegie. 1986. V. 45

Duineser Elegien. Leipzig: 1923. V. 46

Duineser Elegien. Elegies from the Castle of Duino. 1931. V. 45

Duineser Elegien. London: 1931. V. 38; 40; 41; 42; 43

Duino Elegies. New York: 1987. V. 40; 41; 46

Five Prose Pieces. Cummington: 1947. V. 37; 39; 40

Larenopfer. Prague: 1896. V. 41

The Lay of Love and Death of Cornet Christopher Rilke. San Francisco: 1983. V. 39; 42; 43; 46

The Notebooks of Malte Laurids Brigge. New York: 1987. V. 39; 45; 46

The Notebooks of Malte Laurids Brigge . . . Translated by John Linton. London: 1930. V. 37

Poems. New York: 1918. V. 37

Primal Sound and Other Prose Pieces. Cummington: 1943. V. 41

Rainer Maria Rilke: Last Poems. Oakland: 1989. V. 41; 42

Selected Poems. New York: 1981. V. 43; 46

Sonnets to Orpheus Duino Elegies. New York: 1945. V. 41

RIMBAUD, ARTHUR

Drunken Boat. Reading: 1976. V. 37

Les Illuminations. Paris: 1973. V. 39

A Season in Hell. London: 1949. V. 38; 39; 40

A Season in Hell. Cambridge: 1976. V. 41; 45

A Season in Hell. 1986. V. 42

A Season in Hell. 1986. V. 45

A Season in Hell. 1986. V. 45

A Season in Hell. New York: 1986. V. 38; 39; 44

A Season in Hell. N.P.: 1986. V. 41

Ten Poems. Of Type. New York: 1982. V. 46

Une Saison En Enfer. Paris: 1951. V. 37

RIMBAULT, EDWARD F.

Bibliotheca Madrigaliana. London: 1847. V. 44

RIMBAULT, EDWARD FRANCIS

Cathedral Chants of the XVI, XVII and XVIII Centuries. London: 1844. V. 42

RIME di Diversi Antichi Autori Toscani in Dieci Libri Raccolte. Venice: 1532. V. 40

RIMIUS, HENRY

A Candid Narrative of the Rise and Progress of the Hernhunters, Commonly Call'd Moravians of United Fratrum . . . London: 1753. V. 37; 46

A Candid Narrative of the Rise and Progress of the Herrnhuters, Commonly Called Moravians, or Unitas Fratrum . . . Philadelphia: 1753. V. 43; 45

RIMMER, WILLIAM

Art Anatomy. Boston and New York: 1893. V. 41

Elements of Design. Book First. Boston: 1864. V. 40

RIMON. a Hebrew Magazine of Art and Letters. Berlin & London: 1922-24. V. 41

RINALDIS, ALDO DE

Neapolitan Painting. Florence: 1929. V. 42

RINCKES, WILLIAM

The Christian Synagogue; or the Original, Use and Benefit of Parochial Churches . . . London: 1710. V. 42

RINCON, ANTONIO

Arte Mexicana . . . Mexico: 1885. V. 42

RINDER,

D. Y. Cameron. An Illustrated Catalogue of His Etched Work with Introductory Essay and Descriptive Notes on Each Plate. Glasgow: 1912. V. 40; 44

RINDER, FRANK

D. Y. Cameron: an Illustrated Catalogue of His Etched Work . . . Glasgow: 1912. V. 42

Old World Japan. Legends of the Land of the Gods. London: 1895. V. 43

RINDFLEISCH, EDUARD

A Manual of Pathological Histology to Serve as an Introduction to the Study of Morbid Anatomy. London: 1872. V. 41

RINEHART, F. A.

Rinehart's Indians. Omaha: 1899. V. 37; 41; 42

RINEHART, MARY ROBERTS

The After House: A Story of Love, Mystery and a Private Yacht. Boston: 1914. V. 38

The Circular Staircase. Indianapolis: 1908. V. 39; 42; 46

The Red Lamp. New York: 1925. V. 42

Temperamental People. New York: 1924. V. 43

Through Glacier Park. Seeing America First with Howard Eaton. Boston & New York: 1916. V. 39

Tish. Boston & New York: 1916. V. 43

RINERUS DE PISIS

Pantheologia: sive, Summ Universae Theologiae. Nuernberg: 1477. V. 38

RING, JOHN

An Answer to Dr. Moseley, Containing a Defence of Vaccination. London: 1805. V. 43; 46

Treatise on the Cow Pox . . . Part 1. London: 1801. V. 43

RINGELBERG, JOACHIM FORTIUS

Institutiones Astronomicae Ternis Libris Contentae. Venice: 1535. V. 44

RINGGOLD, CADWALADER

Memorial of Commander Cadwalader Ringgold. United States Navy, to the Congress . . . Praying to be Reinstated on the Active List of the Service. Washington: 1856. V. 42

A Series of Charts, with Sailing Directions, Embracing Surveys of the Farallones, Entrance to the Bay of San Francisco . . . State of California . . . Washington: 1852. V. 39; 43

RINGHIERI, INNOCENZIO

Cento Giuochi Liberali, et d'Ingegno . . . in Dieci Libri Descritti. Bologna: 1551. V. 40

RINGWALT, JOHN LUTHER

American Encyclopaedia of Printing. Philadelphia: 1871. V. 37; 38; 39; 44

Development of Transportation Systems in the United States . . . Philadelphia: 1888. V. 44

RINK, HENRY

Danish Greenland Its People and Its Products. London: 1877. V. 37; 40; 42; 43; 46

Tales and Traditions of the Eskimo. Edinburgh: and London: 1875. V. 37; 43; 44; 46

Tales and Traditions of the Eskimo. London: 1875. V. 37

RINUCCINI, OTTAVIO

La Dafne . . . Rappresentata alla Sereniss. Florence: 1600. V. 40

RIO, ANDRES MANUEL DEL

Delementos ed Orictognosia, o del Conocimiento de Los Fosiles, Dispuestos . . . Mexico: 1795. V. 42

RIO, ANTONIO DEL

Description of the Ruins of an Ancient City, Discovered Near Palenquae, in the Kingdom of Guatemala . . . London: 1822. V. 38; 39; 40; 42; 43

RIOLAN, JEAN

Opera Omnia. Tam Hactenvs Edita, Quam Postuma, Authoris Postrema Manu Exarata & Exornato . . . Paris: 1610. V. 46

Opuscula Anatomica Nova Quae Nunc Primum in Lucem Prodeunt. Londini: 1649. V. 37

A Sure Guide; or the Best and Nearest Way to Physick and Chyrurgery . . . London: 1657. V. 39; 43

A Sure Guide; or the Best and Nearest Way to Physick and Chyrurgery. London: 1671. V. 40; 42; 43

RION, MARY C.

Ladies Southern Florist. Columbia: 1860. V. 38

RIOT in Barbados, and Destruction of the Wesleyan Chapel and Mission House. London: 1823. V. 40

RIPA, CESARE

Iconologia. Venetia: 1645. V. 42

Iconologie Ou La Science des Emblemes Devises, &c . . . Amsterdam: 1698. V. 46

RIPA, JOANNES FRANCISCUS DE SANCTO NAZARIO DE

De Peste Libri Tres. Avignon: 1522. V. 38

RIPALDA, GERONIMO DE 1535-1618

Catecismo Mexicano . . . Christianoyotl Mexicanemachtiloni . . . Mexico: 1758. V. 46

RIPLEY, A. LASSELL

Sporting Etchings. Barre: 1970. V. 39

RIPLEY, DOROTHY

The Bank of Faith and Works United. Philadelphia: 1819. V. 38; 39

RIPLEY, EZRA

A History of the Fight at Concord on the 19th of April, 1775. Concord: 1827. V. 42; 46

RIPLEY, GEORGE

A Farewell Discourse, Delivered to the Congregational Church in Purchase Street, March 28, 1841. Boston: 1841. V. 44

Philosophical Miscellanies. Boston: 1838. V. 43; 44

RIPLEY, HENRY

Hand-Clasp of the East and West. Denver: 1914. V. 37; 39; 42

RIPLEY, JAMES

Select Original Letters on Various Subjects by James Ripley. London: 1781. V. 38; 42; 46

RIPLEY, R. S.

The War with Mexico. New York: 1849. V. 37; 38; 42; 43

The War With Mexico. London: 1850. V. 40

RIPLEY, ROBERT L.

Believe It Or Not! Omnibus. New York: 1934. V. 46

RIPLEY, S. DILLON

Rails of the World. 1977. V. 46

Rails of the World. Boston: 1977. V. 37; 39; 46

Rails of the World. London: 1977. V. 37; 38; 39

Rails of the World. Toronto: 1977. V. 38

Rails of the World. U.S.A.: 1977. V. 45

RIPPERDA, JOAN WILLEM VAN, DUQUE d. 1737

Memoirs of the Duke de Ripperda. London: 1740. V. 39; 40; 41; 42; 43; 46

Memoirs of the Duke of Ripperda . . . London: 1740. V. 42

RIPPINGHAM, JOHN

The Art of Public Speaking, Ex-Tempore, Including a Course of Discipline, for Obtaining the Faculties of Discrimination, Arrangement and Oral Discussion. London: 1814. V. 46

RIPPON, JOHN

The Gentle Dismission of Saints from Earth to Heaven: a Sermon Occasioned by the Decease of the Rev. John Ryland, Senior, A.M. Who Departed This Life at Enfield, July 24, 1792, in the 69th Year of His Age. London: 1792. V. 45

RIQUEL, HERNANDO

Relacio Muy Cierta y Verdrada . . . Seville: 1574. V. 40

RISCHBIETER, HENNING

Art and the Stage in the 20th Century. Greenwich: 1968. V. 42

RISK, T. F.

Western Journal and Civilian. St. Louis: 1848-56. V. 38

RIIS, JACOB A.

The Children of the Poor. New York: 1893. V. 46

RIST, JOHANN

Neuer Teutscher Parnasss, Auff Welchem Befindlich Ehr - und Lehr / Schertz und Schmertz / Leid-und Freuden-Gewaechse zu Untershiedlichen Zeiten Gepflanzet . . . Luneburg: 1652. V. 39; 41

RISTER, CARL COKE

Border Captives. The Traffic in Prisoners by Southern Plains 1835-1875. Norman: 1940. V. 39; 44

Comanche Bondage. Glendale: 1955. V. 37; 40; 41; 44; 45; 46

Southern Plainsmen. Norman: 1938. V. 46

The Southeastern Frontier, 1865-1881. Cleveland: 1928. V. 37; 39; 43; 45

RITCH, JOHN W.

The American Architect . . . Designs of . . . Country and Village Residences. New York: 1849-56. V. 37

RITCH, W. G.

Inaugural Address of Hon. W. G. Ritch. Santa Fe: 1881. V. 46

The Legislative Blue-Book, of the Territory of New Mexico. Santa Fe: 1882. V. 45

RITCH, WILLIAM G.

Aztlan: the History, Resources and Attractions of New Mexico. Boston: 1885. V. 37; 38

Illustrated New Mexico, Historical and Industrial. Santa Fe: 1885. V. 38

The Legislative Blue Book, of the Territory of New Mexico . . . Santa Fe;: 1882. V. 37

RITCHER, M. A.

The Engraved Gems of the Greeks, Etruscans and Romans. Part I. London: 1968. V. 42

RITCHIE, ANNA CORA MOWATT

Mimic Life; or, Before and Behind the Curtain. Boston: 1856. V. 43

RITCHIE, ANNE ISABELLA THACKERAY, LADY 1837-1919

A Book of Sibyls. London: 1883. V. 42; 43

A Book of Sibyls: Mrs. Barbauld, Mrs. Opie, Miss Edgeworth, Miss Austen. London: 1883. V. 40

A Book of Sibyls. London: 1883. V. 45

Little Red Riding Hood. Boston: 1867. V. 42

Mrs. Dymond. London: 1885. V. 41

Old Kensington by Miss Thackeray. London: 1873. V. 38

Records of Tennyson, Ruskin and Browning. London: 1892. V. 38; 40

The Story of Elizabeth. London: 1863. V. 46

To Esther, and other sketches. London: 1869. V. 37

The Village on the Cliff. London: 1867. V. 40; 44

Works. London: 1886. V. 38

RITCHIE, D. G.

Darwinism and Politics. London: 1889. V. 46

RITCHIE, G. S.

The Admiralty Chart. British Naval Hydrography in the Nineteenth Century. London: 1967. V. 40; 41

RITCHIE, J. EWING

To Canada with Emigrants. London: 1885. V. 44

RITCHIE, JAMES EWING

An Australian Ramble or a Summer in Australia. London: 1890. V. 43

The Life and Discoveries of David Livingstone. London: 1870. V. 39

The Pictorial Edition of the Life and Discoveries of David Livingstone. London: 1920. V. 38

The Night Side of London. London: 1857. V. 38

RITCHIE, JAMES S.

Wisconsin and Its Resources; with Lake Superior . . . Philadelphia: 1857. V. 46

Wisconsin and Its Resources: With Lake Superior, Its Commerce and Navigation . . . Philadelphia: 1860. V. 37; 40

RITCHIE, LEITCH

Ireland, Picturesque and Romantic. London: 1838, 1837. V. 41

A Journey to St. Petersburg and Moscow through Courland and Livonia. London: 1836. V. 40; 43

Scott and Scotland. London: 1835. V. 45

Travelling Sketches in the North of Italy, and on the Rhine. London: 1832. V. 46

Travelling Sketches on the Rhine and in Belgium and Holland. London: 1833. V. 46

Travelling Sketches on the Sea-Coasts of France. London: 1834. V. 40

Wanderings by the Liore. London: 1833. V. 39

Wanderings by the Loire. (with) Wanderings by the Seine. (with) Wanderings by the Seine from Rouen to the Source. London: 1833-4-5-. V. 41

Wanderings by the Seine. London: 1834. V. 43

Wanderings by the Seine from Rouen to the Source. London: 1835. V. 39; 46

Windsor Castle, and Its Environs. London: 1840. V. 43

The Wye and Its Associations, a Picturesque Ramble. London: 1841. V. 39

RITCHIE, ROBERT

Railways; Their Rise, Progress and Construction: with Remarks on Railway Accidetns and Proposals for Their Prevention. London: 1846. V. 46

RITCHIE, THOMAS

A Full Report, Embracing All the Evidence and Arguments in the Case of the Commonwealth of Virginia vs. Thomas Ritchie Jr. New York: 1846. V. 40

RITCHIE, W. M.

The Pre-Iroquoian Occupations of New York State. 1944. V. 37

RITCHIE, WARD

Art Deco, the Books of Francois-Louis Schmied, Artist/Engraver/Printer. San Francisco: 1987. V. 43

RITCHIE, WARD continued

The Books of Francois-Louis Schmied. San Francisco: 1987. V. 46

Job Printing in California. Los Angeles: 1955. V. 38

A Late Offering of Quince. Laguna Beach: 1990. V. 45

Laguna Verde 1975-1987. Laguna Beach: 1988. V. 40

Merle Armitage: His Loves and His Many Lives. Laguna Verde Imprenta: 1982. V. 37

RITCHIE, WILLIAM A.

The Pre-Iroquian Occupations of New York State. 1944. V. 39

RITHEIMER, GEORG

Epitome Peri Ton Octo Tou Logou Meron, Kai Skematismoi Ton Kronon. Cologne: 1536. V. 42

RITNER, WILLIAM D.

Juan the White Slave; and the Rebel Planter's Daughter. Philadelphia: 1865. V. 44

RITRATTO di Roma Antica. Rome: 1645. V. 40

RITSON, JOSEPH

Ancient English Metrical Romances. London: 1802. V. 39; 44

Ancient Songs and Ballads, from the Reign of King Henry the Second to the Revolution. London: 1829. V. 39; 45

Annals of the Caledonians, Picts and Scots. Edinburgh: 1828. V. 37; 42

Bibliographia Poetica. London: 1802. V. 37; 39; 43

The English Anthology. London: 1793-4. V. 39

An Essay on Abstience from Animal Food as a Moral Duty. London: 1802. V. 39; 40

Fairy Tales, Now First Collected . . . London: 1831. V. 39; 46

The Jurisdiction of the Court Leet. London: 1816. V. 38

The Life of King Arthur: from Ancient Historians and Authentic Documents. London: 1825. V. 39; 45

Memoirs of the Celts or Gauls. London: 1827. V. 39

Northern Garlands. London: 1810. V. 38; 39; 42

Observations on the Three First Volumes of the History of English Poetry. London: 1782. V. 37; 38

Piece of Ancient Popular Poetry. London: 1833. V. 39; 40; 46

Pieces of Ancient Popular Poetry from Authentic Manuscripts and Old Printed Copies. London: 1791. V. 38; 45

Poems on Interesting Events in the Regin of King Edward III. London: 1795. V. 45

The Quip Modest. London: 1788. V. 37

Robin Hood. London: 1820. V. 39; 46

Scotish Song. London: 1794. V. 39

A Select Collection of English Songs. London: 1783. V. 41

A Select Collection of English Songs, with their Original Airs. London: 1813. V. 38

RITSOS, YANNIS

Manifestation of Emptiness. Cambridge: 1979. V. 45

The Return and Other Poems. 1983. V. 40

Return and Other Poems. Tuscalossa: 1983. V. 39; 42; 44

RITTANGEL, JOHANN STEPHAN 1606-1652

(Title in Hebrew) Id Est, Liber Iezirah Qui Abrahamo Patriarchae Adscribitur, Una Cum Commentario Rabi Abrahamo Patriarchae . . . Amstelodami: 1642. V. 46

RITTENHOUSE, DAVID

An Oration, Delivered February 24, 1775, Before the American Philosophical Society, Held at Philadelphia, for Promoting Useful Knowledge. Philadelphia: 1775. V. 37

RITTENHOUSE, JACK D.

American Horse Drawn Vehicles. Los Angeles: 1948. V. 46

RITTER, AUGUST GOTTFRIED 1811-1885

Die Erhaltung und Stimmung der Orgel Durch den Organisten. Erfurt & Leipzig: 1861. V. 38

RITTNER, HEINRICH

Dresden mit Seinen Prachtgebauden und Schonsten Umgebungen. Dresden: 1807-08. V. 40

RITUAL of the Methodist Episcopal Church South. Richmond: 1851. V. 43

RITUALE Abbatum, Sub Regula Sancti Patris Benedicti in Congregatione Anglicana. Wigorniae: 1963. V. 46

RITUALE Monasticum ad Usum Congregationis S. Mauri Ordinis S. Benedicti. Paris: 1666. V. 40

RITZ, PHILIP

Letter Upon the Agricultural and Mineral Resources of the North-Western Territories, on the Route of the Northern Pacific Rail Road. Washington: 1868. V. 37; 38

RIVA PALACIO, VICENTE

memoria Presentada al Congreso de la Union par el Secretario de Estado y del Despacho de Fomento, Colonizacion, Industria y Comercia de la Republica Mexicana . . . Mexico City: 1877. V. 45

RIVADENEIRA, PEDRO DE

Vita Ignatii Loiolae, Qui Religionem Clericorum Societatis Iesu . . . Ingolstadt: 1590. V. 44

THE RIVAL Brothers: a Tragedy. London: 1704. V. 38

THE RIVAL Roses of York and Lancaster. London: 1813. V. 42

THE RIVAL Sisters; with Other Poems. London: 1834. V. 41; 42

THE RIVAL Wives Answer'd: or, Skirra to Clarissa. London: 1738. V. 38

RIVAROL, ANTOINE

De l'Universalite de la Langue Francaise; Qui a Remporte Le prix a l'Academie de Berlin. Berlin & Paris: 1784. V. 39

RIVERA, DIEGO

Acuarelas (1935-1945) Coleccion Frieda Kahlo. Atlante: 1948. V. 46

Frescoes. New York: 1933. V. 39

Portrait of America. New York: 1934. V. 44

RIVERIUS, LAZARUS

The Secrets of the Famous Lazarvs Riverius . . . Professor of Physick in the University of Montpelier Newly translated from the Latin, by E.P. M.D. London: 1685. V. 37

RIVERO, M .E.

Peruvian Antiquities, by M.E. Rivero and J.J. Von Tschudi. New York: 1853. V. 37

RIVEROLL, ROBERTO

Mexican Dances. Mexico City: 1947. V. 40; 45

RIVERS, ELIZABETH

Stranger in Aran. 1946. V. 42

Stranger in Aran. Dublin: 1946. V. 41; 45

This Man - a Sequence of Wood Engravings. London: 1939. V. 40

RIVERS, HENRY J.

The Tale of Two Cities: A Drama in Three Acts, and a Prologue, Adapted from Mr. Charles Dickens' Story. London: 1862? V. 40

RIVERS, LARRY

Drawings and Digressions. New York: 1979. V. 39; 41

RIVERS of Great Britian. The Thames, from Source to Sea: Rivers of the East Coast. London: 1891-1892. V. 41

RIVERS, R. H.

The Life of Robert Pains, D.D., Bishop of the Methodist Episopal Church, South. Nashville: 1884. V. 44

RIVERS, W. H. R.

Psychology and Ethnology. London: 1926. V. 43; 44

RIVERS, WILLIAM JAMES

Rivers' Account of the Raising of Troops in South Carolina for State and Confederate Service, 1861-65. Columbia: 1899. V. 44

A Sketch of the History of South Carolina to the Close of the Proprietary Government by the Revolution of 1719, with an Appendix Containing many Valuable Records Hitherto Unpublished. Charleston: 1856. V. 37

RIVERSIDE County, California: Its Productions, Resources and Advantages as a Place of Residence and of Profitable Investment. Riverside: 1894. V. 39; 42

RIVES, AMELIE

Athelwold. New York: 1893. V. 43

RIVES, BRUNO

Angliae Ruina; or, Englands Ruine . . . London: 1648. V. 46

RIVES, GEORGE LOCKHART

The United States and Mexico, 1821-1848. New York: 1913. V. 38; 39; 40; 44; 45

RIVES, JUDITH PAGE

Tales and Souvenirs of a Residence in Europe. Philadelphia: 1842. V. 43

RIVES, REGINALD W.

The Coaching Club, Its History, Records and Activities. New York: 1935. V. 39

RIVES, WILLIAM CABELL

Correspondence. Albemarle County, Jan. 12, 1861 . . . N.P.: 1861. V. 46
Correspondence. Albemarle County Jan. 12, 1861 . . . N.P.: 1861. V. 42

RIVETT-CARNAC, M.

Fairies, Elves and Flower-Babies. London: 1899. V. 37

THE RIVIERA: Pen and Pencil Sketches from Cannes to Genoa. London: 1870. V. 41; 43; 44

RIVIERE, LAZARE

Arcana. Utrecht: 1680. V. 44
Four Books of that Learned and Renowned Doctor, Lazarus Riverius. London: 1658. V. 37; 41; 44
Opera Medica Universa. Lyons: 1679. V. 38
The Practice of Physick. London: 1668. V. 41
The Practice of Physick . . . London: 1678. V. 41
The Practice of Physick. London: 1688. V. 38
The Practice of Physick. London: 1658. V. 37; 40

RIVIERE, LOUIS

Poh-Deng. Scenes de la Vie Siamoise. Paris: 1913. V. 41

RIVIERE, R.

Examples of Modern Bookbinding. London: 1919. V. 41

RIVIERE (ROBERT) & SON, LONDON

Illustrated Trade Catalogue of Miscellaneous Books in Various Leather Bindings. London: 1909. V. 39; 41

RIVIERE (ROBERT) & SON, LONDON

Examples of Modern Bookbinding, Designed and Executed by Robt. Riviere & Son. London: 1919. V. 39; 44

RIVOIRA, GIOVANNI TERESIO

Lombardic Architecture - Its Origin, Development and Derivatives. London: 1910. V. 38; 40; 46
Moslem Architecture. Its Origina and Development. London;: 1918. V. 37; 46
Roman Architecture and Its Principles of Construction Under the Empire. Oxford: 1925. V. 44

RIVOLA, FRANCISCO

Dictionarium Armeno-Latinum. Paris: 1633. V. 46

RIX, M.

The Art of the Plant World. Woodstock: 1981. V. 45; 46

RIZZETTI, JOHN

The Knowledge of Play, Written for Publick Benefit, and the Entertainment of All Fair Players. London: 1732. V. 41

RIZZI, ALDO

The Etchings of the Tiepolos. London: 1971. V. 37; 44; 45

RIZZO, TANIA

The Herbert Clark Hoover Collection of Mining and Metallurgy. Claremont: 1980. V. 37; 44

ROACH, JOHN

Letter to the Hon. Samuel Shellabarger. Iron Steamships: Shall We Build Them of Our Own Material or Buy Them, or the Material to Build Them, Abroad? Washington: 1872. V. 46

ROADKILLS. Easthampton: 1981. V. 40
ROADKILLS. Williamsburg: 1981. V. 41

THE ROADS and Railroads, Vehicles and Modes of Travelling, of Ancient and Modern Countries . . . London: 1839. V. 42

ROARK, GARLAND

Drill a Crooked Hole. New York: 1968. V. 40; 41

ROBAUT, A.

Catholic Prayers and Hymns in Innuit. Holy Cross: 1899. V. 42

ROBB, F. H. H.

The Negro in Chicago 1779 to 1929. Chicago: 1929. V. 37

ROBB, HUNTER

Aseptic Surgical Technique: With Especial Reference to Gynaecological Operations, Together With Notes on the Technique Employed in Certain Supplementary Procedures. Philadelphia: 1894. V. 42

ROBB, ISABEL HAMPTON

Nursing: its Principles and Practice for Hospital and Private Use. Cleveland: 1906. V. 42

ROBB, JAMES

A Southern Confederacy. A Letter By Jas. Robb, Late a Citizen of New Orleans, to Hon. Alexander H. STephens of Georgia. Chicago: 1863. V. 44

ROBB, JOHN S.

Streaks of Squatter Life, and Far West Scenes. Philadelphia: 1847. V. 45

ROBB, THOMAS P.

Depredations on the Frontiers of Texas . . . Washington: 1872. V. 43

ROBBE-GRILLET, ALAIN

Jealousy: Rhymthmic Themes. 1971. V. 38
Jealousy: Rhythmic Themes. 1971. V. 39
Jealousy. 1971. V. 44
Jealousy. Kentfield: 1971. V. 38; 40; 44
Jealousy: Rhythmic Themes. 1971. V. 37
The Voyeur. New York: 1958. V. 41; 46

THE ROBBER of the Wood; and the Russian Pirate . . . London: 1820. V. 39

ROBBERDS, J. W.

Geological and Historical Observations on the Eastern Vallies of Norfolk. Norwich: 1826. V. 43; 45

ROBBINS, AMMI R.

Journal of the Rev. Ammi R. Robbins, A Chaplain in the American Army, in the Northern Campaign of 1776. New Haven: 1850. V. 41

ROBBINS, ARCHIBALD

A Journal, Comprising an Account of the Loss of the Brig Commerce, of Hartford, (con.) James Riley, Master, Upon the Western Coast of Africa, August 28th, 1815 . . . Rochester: 1818. V. 41

ROBBINS, CHANDLER

A Sermon Preached Before John Hancock . . . Being the Day of General Election. Boston: 1791. V. 45

ROBBINS, THOMAS

Diary. 1796-1854. Boston: 1886. V. 40
A View of all Religions; and the religious Ceremonies of all Nations at the Present Day . . . Hartford: 1824. V. 40

ROBBINS, TOM

Another Roadside Attraction. Garden City: 1971. V. 42; 44
Another Roadside Attraction. New York: 1971. V. 37; 41
Another Roadside Attraction. New York: 1971. V. 37
Even Cowgirls Get the Blues. Boston: 1976. V. 39; 41; 42; 43; 44; 45
Still Life with Woodpecker. New York: 1980. V. 39

ROBBINS, WALTER RALEIGH

War Record and Personal Experiences of Walter Raleigh Robbins . . . N.P.: 1923. V. 43

ROBBINS, WARREN

African Art in American Collections. New York: (1966). V. 37

ROBERSTON, BRYAN

Jackson Pollock. London: 1960. V. 39

ROBERT, CHARLES EDWIN

Negro Civilization in the South; Educational, Social and Religious Advancement of the Colored People. Nashville: 1880. V. 39

ROBERT Dawson Evans 1843-1909. 1910. V. 42

ROBERT DE VAUGONDY, GILLES

Atlas Portaif, Universel. Compose d'Apres les Meilleures, Cartes, tant Gravees que Manuscrites des plus Celebres Geographes et Ingenieurs. Paris: 1774? V. 44

ROBERT Frost: A Chronological Survey. Middletown: 1936. V. 37

ROBERT Granjon: Sixteenth Century Type Founder and Printer. Brooklyn: 1931. V. 37; 39; 40; 43
ROBERT Granjon: Sixteenth Century Type Founder and Printer. New York: 1931. V. 38; 44

THE ROBERT GRAVES CO., NEW YORK. The Robert Graves Co. Wallpapers. 1916. V. 45

ROBERT-HOUDIN, JEAN EUGENE

Memoirs of Robert-Houdin, Ambassador, Author and Conjuror. London: 1859. V. 38
Robert Houdin, the Great Wizard, Celebrated French Conjurer, Author, Ambassador. Philadelphia: 1865. V. 46

ROBERT-HOUDIN, JEAN F.

Card Sharpers . . . London: 1891. V. 42

Memoirs of Robert Houdin. Philadelphia: 1859. V. 42; 43

ROBERT LA DIABLE

Roberte the Deuyil. London: 1798. V. 42; 44

Robert the Devil. Iowa City: 1981. V. 39; 41; 46

ROBERT, N.

Diverses Fleurs. London: 1975. V. 39

ROBERT, NICOLAS

Variae ac Multiformes Florum Species Expressae ad Civum et Aeneis Tabluis Incisae . . . Rome: 1665. V. 42

ROBERT, OF GLOUCESTER

Chronicle. Oxford: 1724. V. 39

Robert of Gloucester's Chronicle. Transcrib'd and Now First Published from a MS in the Harleyan Library by Thomas Hearne . . . Oxford: 1724. V. 42

ROBERT of Gloucester, the Metrical Chronicle. London: 1887. V. 44

ROBERT THE DEVIL

Robert the Devyll. A Metrical Romance, from an Ancient Illuminated manuscript. London: 1798. V. 37

ROBERT, WILLEM C. H.

Contributions to a Bibliography of Australia and the South Sea Islands. Amsterdam: 1968-72. V. 40; 43

ROBERTI, ANTONIUS

Clavis Homerica, sive Lexicon Vocabulorum Omnium, Quae Continentur in Homeri Iliade et Postissima Parte Odysseae. London: 1741. V. 46

ROBERTON, JOHN

Critical Remarks on certain recently published opinions concerning Life and Mind. London: 1836. V. 39

ROBERTS, A.

The Mammals of South Africa. Cape Town: 1954. V. 38

The Mammals of South Africa. London: 1954. V. 38

ROBERTS, B. H.

A Comprehensive History of the Church of Jesus Christ of Latter-Day Saints Century I. Salt Lake City: 1930. V. 42

The Mormon Battalion. Its History and Achievements. Salt Lake City: 1919. V. 42

ROBERTS, BARRE CHARLES

Letters and Miscellaneous Papers by Barre Charles Roberts, Student of Christ Church, Oxford; with a Memoir of His Life. London: 1814. V. 45

ROBERTS, BENJAMIN T.

Ordaining Women. Rochester: 1891. V. 37

ROBERTS, BRIGHAM HENRY

The Mormon Battlion. Its History and Acievements. Salt Lake City: 1919. V. 37

ROBERTS, CHARLES

Bibliotheca Quakeriana. The Private Library of the Late Charles Roberts of Philadelphia, Comprising and Extensive Collection of Quakeriana. To be sold on Wednesday, April 10, 1918. New York: 1918. V. 44

ROBERTS, CHARLES G. D.

The Book of the Native. Boston: 1896. V. 41

The Forge in the Forest. Boston: 1896. V. 38; 41

A Standard Dictionary of Canadian Biography: The Candian Who Was Who. Toronto: 1934/38. V. 44

ROBERTS, DAN W.

Ranger and Sovereignty. San Antonio: 1914. V. 37; 38; 42; 43; 46

Rangers Sovereignty. Sant Antonio: 1914. V. 46

ROBERTS, DAN W. MRS.

A Woman's Reminiscences of Six Years with the Texas Rangers. Austin: (1928). V. 37

ROBERTS, DAVID

Egypt and Nubia From Drawings Made on the Spot . . . London: 1846-49. V. 37; 43

The Holy Land, Syria, Idumea, Arabia . . . London: 1842-49. V. 39

The Holy Land, Syria, Idumea, Arabia, Egypt and Nubia. London: 1855. V. 44

The Holy Land, Syria, Indumea, Arabia, Egypt and Nubia . . . London: & New York: 1855-56. V. 44

The Holy Land, Syria, Idumea, Arabia, Egypt & Nubia. New York: 1855-56. V. 46

The Holy Land. London: Paris & New York: 1879-84. V. 44

The Holy Land, Syria, Idumea, Arabia, Egypt and Nubia. London: 1855-56. V. 37; 39

The Military Adventures of Johnny Newcome, with Account of His Campaign on the Peninsula and In Pall Mall. London: 1816. V. 37

The Town of Cambridge As It Ought to Be Reformed. Cambridge: 1955. V. 45

ROBERTS, E. M.

A Flying Fighter, an American Above the Lines in France. New York: 1918. V. 46

ROBERTS, EDWARD

With the Invader: Glimpses of the Southwest. San Francisco: 1885. V. 41

ROBERTS, ELIZABETH MADOX

A Buried Treasure. New York: 1931. V. 44

The Great Meadow. New York: 1930. V. 37; 41; 44; 46

Song in the Meadow. New York: 1940. V. 41

ROBERTS, ELLWOOD

Biographical Annals of Montgomery County, Pennsylvania. New York: 1904. V. 42

ROBERTS, EMMA

The East India Voyager, or Ten Minutes Advice to Outward Bound. London: 1839. V. 39

Indostan Its Landscapes, Palaces, Temples, Tombs. London: 1845. V. 40; 43

Scenes and Characteristics of Hindostan, with Sketches of Anglo-Indian Society. London: 1835. V. 45

Views in India, China and on the Shores of the Red Sea. London. V. 40

Views in India, China and on the Shores of the Red Sea. London: 1835. V. 38; 44

ROBERTS, GEORGE C. M.

Centenary Pictorial Album, Being Contributions of the Early History of Methodism in the State of Maryland. Baltimore: 1866. V. 43; 44

ROBERTS, HENRY

Calliope or English Harmony, a Collection of the Most Celebrated English and Scots Songs. London: 1737-46. V. 44

The Dwellings of the Labouring Classes, Their Arrangement and Construction. London: 1850. V. 37; 42

The Dwellings of the Labouring Classes, their Arrangement and Construction . . . London: 1867. V. 43

ROBERTS, ISAAC

A Selection of Photographs of Stars, Star-Clusters and Nebulae, Together with Information Concerning the Instruments and the Methods Employed in the Pursuit of Celestial Photography. London: 1893-99. V. 40; 41

ROBERTS, JAMES

Introductory Lessons, with Familiar Examples in Landscape . . . London: 1808. V. 44

The Sportsman's Pocket Companion. London: 1760. V. 42

ROBERTS, JANE

Lowenstein: King of the Forests: a Tale. London: 1836. V. 43

Two Years at Sea, Being the Narrative of a Voyage to Swan River, Van Diemen's Land, Thence through the Torres Straits, to the Burman Empire. London: 1837. V. 46

ROBERTS, JOB

The Pennsylvania Farmer; Being a Selection and the Settlement of the Township. Philadelphia: 1804. V. 38; 40; 41; 42; 45

ROBERTS, JOHN

The Belloniad, an Heroick Poem. London: 1785. V. 37

Roberts on Billiards. London: 1869. V. 42

Surgical Delusions and Follies. Philadelphia: 1844. V. 41

The Surgical Treatment of Disfigurements and Deformities of the Face. Philadelphia: 1901. V. 42

ROBERTS, K.

Anita. 1976. V. 39

Kaeti and Company. 1986. V. 39

ROBERTS, KATE

Two Old Men and Other Stories. 1981. V. 45

Two Old Men and Other Stories. 1981. V. 40

Two Old Men and Other Stories. Newtown: 1981. V. 39; 45

ROBERTS, KEITH

The Boat of Fire. London: 1971. V. 38

The Chalk Giants. London: 1974. V. 38

The Grain Kings - Science Fiction Stories. London: 1976. V. 38

The Inner Wheel. London: 1970. V. 38

ROBERTS, KEITH continued

Machines and Men - Science Fiction Stories. London: 1973. V. 38

Pavane. London: 1968. V. 38; 46

ROBERTS, KENNETH

Antiquamania. New York: 1928. V. 46

Arundel. Maine: 1985. V. 37; 41; 44

Black Is the Color of My True Love's Hair. New York: 1938. V. 44

Boon Island. New York: 1956. V. 46

Captain Caution. Garden City: 1934. V. 43

The Collector's What Not. 1923. V. 46

Concentrated New England: a Sketch of Calvin Coolidge. Indianapolis: 1924. V. 41; 42; 43; 44

Cowpens: The Great Morale-Builder. 1957. V. 46

Don't Say That About Maine! 1951. V. 46

Europe's Morning After. New York: 1921. V. 46

Florida Loafing. Indianapolis: 1925. V. 46

Lydia Bailey. Garden City: 1947. V. 43

Lydia Bailey. New York: 1947. V. 37; 39; 45; 46

Northwest Passage. Garden City: 1937. V. 39; 42; 44; 46

Northwest Passage. New York: 1937. V. 41

Oliver Wisell. 1940. V. 46

Oliver Wiswell. Garden City: 1940. V. 43

Oliver Wiswell. New York: 1940. V. 39; 41; 42

Sun Hunting. Indianapolis: 1922. V. 45; 46

Trending into Maine. 1938. V. 46

Trending Into Maine. 1938. V. 43

Trending Into Maine. Boston: 1938. V. 37; 38; 41; 42; 44

Why Europe Leaves Home. 1922. V. 46

Why Europe Leaves Home. 1922. V. 46

ROBERTS, LEWES

The Merchants Map of Commerce. London: 1677. V. 40

ROBERTS, LORD

Forty-One Years in India. London: 1897. V. 43; 45

ROBERTS, LOU CONWAY

A Woman's Reminiscences of Six Years in Camp with the Texas Rangers. Austin: 1928. V. 38

ROBERTS, M. J.

The Spiders of Great Britain and Ireland. Colchester: 1984-87. V. 37; 38

ROBERTS, MARY 1789-1864

The Conchologist's Companion, Comprising the Instincts and Constructions of Testaceous Animals. London: 1824. V. 39

The Royal Exile; or Poetical Epistles of Mary, Queen of Scots . . . London: 1822; V. 42

Voices from the Woodlands, Descriptive of Forest Trees, Ferns, Mosses, and Lichens. London: 1850. V. 46

ROBERTS, MICHAEL

New Country: Prose and Poetry by the Authors of New Signatures. London: 1933. V. 41

New Signatures. Poems by Several Hands. London: 1932. V. 37

ROBERTS, MIRANDA S.

Genealogy of the Descendants of John Kirk, Born 1660 at Alfreton . . . England. Died 1705 in Darby Township, Chester (now Delaware County, Pennsylvania. Doylestown: 1912-13. V. 46

ROBERTS, MORLEY

The Western Avernus. London: 1887. V. 38

The Western Avernus. London: 1904. V. 46

ROBERTS, O. M.

A Description of Texas, Its Advantages and Resources, with Some Account of Their Development. St. Louis: 1881. V. 39; 41; 42; 43; 44

Our Federal Relations, from a Southern View of Them. Austin: 1892. V. 37; 39

Speech of Judge O.M. Roberts of the Supreme Court of Texas, at the Capitol, on the 1st December, 1869, Upon the 'Impending Crisis'. (Austin: 1860). V. 37

Texas (Confederate Military History). Atlanta: 1905. V. 37; 38; 39

ROBERTS, ORLANDO W.

Narrative of Voyages and Excursions on the East Coast and in the Interior of Central America. Edinburgh: 1827. V. 39; 42; 45

ROBERTS, PETER

Anthracite Coal Communities . . . New York: 1904. V. 42

The Cambrian Popular Antiquities. London: 1815. V. 38; 39; 41

ROBERTS, RANDAL

The River's Side; or, the Trout and the Grayling, and How to Take Them. London: 1866. V. 41

ROBERTS, RICHARD

Hanes Taith Drwy Unol Daleithiau yr America . . . Wales: 1842. V. 42

ROBERTS, ROBERT

The House Servant's Directory, or a Monitor for Private Families. Boston: 1827. V. 37; 39; 42; 45

The House Servant's Directory, or a Monitor for Private Families. Boston: 1828. V. 44

ROBERTS, ROBERT E.

Sketches of the City of Detroit, State of Michigan, Past and Present. Detroit: 1855. V. 38; 39; 42

ROBERTS, ROBERT W.

A Tramp to the Klondike; or How I Reached the Gold Fields of Alaska. Vaughnsville: 1898? V. 45

ROBERTS, S. C.

An Address Delivered at the Unveilling and Dedication of the Memorial to Sir Max Beerbohm in Saint Paul's Cathedral on 12 April 1962. Cambridge: 1962. V. 38

An Address Delivered at the Unveiling and Dedication of the Memorial to Sir Max Beerbohm in Saint Paul's Cathedral. London: 1962. V. 46

S. C. R. Distinguished Visitors. Essays in Imitation. Cambridge: 1937. V. 38

ROBERTS, SAMUEL

Chimney Sweepers' Boys. Sheffield: 1817. V. 42

The Gypsies: Their Origin, Continuance and Destination. London: 1836. V. 42

ROBERTS, THOMAS

The English Bowman, or Tracts on Archery. London: 1801. V. 38; 39; 41; 46

ROBERTS, THOMAS S.

Birds of Minnesota. Minneapolis: 1932. V. 39; 40

The Birds of Minnesota. 1936. V. 39

The Birds of Minnesota. Minneapolis: 1936. V. 39

ROBERTS, VERNE L.

Bibliotheca Mechanica. New York: 1991. V. 46

ROBERTS, W.

The Book-Hunter in London. Chicago: 1895. V. 44

Memorials of Christie's. London: 1897. V. 41; 42

Printers Marks - a Chapter in History of Typography. London: 1893. V. 39

ROBERTS, W. H.

The British Wine-Maker and Domestic Brewer. Edinburgh: 1847. V. 43

The British Wine-Maker and Domestic Brewer. London: 1847. V. 37

ROBERTS, WALTER

An Answer to Mr. Fords Booke, Entituled A Designe for Bringing a Navigable River, From Rickmanaworth in Hartfordshire to St. Giles in the Fields. London: 1641. V. 43

ROBERTS, WARREN

A Bibliography of D. H. Lawrence. London: 1963. V. 40; 41

ROBERTS, WILLIAM

An Account of the First Discovery and Natural History of Florida. London: 1763. V. 38; 39; 40; 41

Marmorum Oxoniensium Inscriptiones Graecae ed Chandleri Exemplar . . . Oxford: 1791. V. 44

Memoirs of the Life and Correspondence of Mrs. Hannah More. London: 1834. V. 41

A Treatise Upon Wills and Codicils, with an Appendix of the Statutes, and a Copious Collection of Useful Precedents . . . London: 1809. V. 39

ROBERTS, WILLIAM HAYWARD

Poems. London: 1774. V. 39; 42; 43; 45

A Poetical Essays on the Esixtence of God . . . London: 1771. V. 42

A Poetical Epistle, to Christopher Anstey, Esq . . . London: 1773. V. 42

ROBERTSON, A. W.

Catalogue of the Royal Library . . . Aberdeen: 1901. V. 45

ROBERTSON, ABRAHAM

Sectionum Conicarum Libri Septem . . . Oxford: 1792. V. 42

ROBERTSON, ALEC

Contrasts: the Arts & Religion. Worcester: 1980. V. 38

In the Little Things. With a Tribute by Gerald Moore. Worcester: 1969. V. 38

ROBERTSON, ALEXANDER

The Laws of Thought, Objective and Subjective. London: 1864. V. 42

Poems on Various Subjects and Occasions . . . Edinburgh: 1751? V. 40; 42

ROBERTSON, ARCHIBALD

Archibald Robertson His Diaries and Sketches in America 1762-1780. New York: 1930. V. 40; 43; 46

A Topographical Survey of the Great Road from London to Bath and Bristol. London: 1792. V. 38; 41; 44; 46

ROBERTSON, C. LOCKHART

Notes on the Prognosis in Cases of Mental Disease. Exeter: 1859. V. 46

ROBERTSON, DAVID

Poems. Edinburgh: 1784. V. 40; 42

Reports of the Trials of Col. Aaron Burr . . . for Treason in Preparing the Means of a Military Expedition Against Mexico. Philadelphia: 1808. V. 37; 38; 39; 43; 45; 46

Sir Charles Eastlake and the Victorian World. Princeton: 1978. V. 39

A Tour through the Isle of Man. London: 1794. V. 40; 41; 46

ROBERTSON, DAVID HENDERSON

The Sculptured Stones of Leith with Historical and Antiquarian Notices. Edinburgh: 1851. V. 38

ROBERTSON, DON

The Ideal Genuine Man. Bangor: 1987. V. 42; 46

ROBERTSON, E. GRAEME

Early Buildings of Southern Tasmania. Melbourne: 1970. V. 41

Early Houses of Northern Tasmania. Melbourne: 1966. V. 41

Sydney Lace: Ornamental Cast Iron in Architecture in Sydney. Melbourne: 1962. V. 41

ROBERTSON, EMILY

Letters and Papers of Andrew Robertson . . . London: 1897. V. 39

ROBERTSON, F. K.

The Book of Health, Thomsonian Theory and Practice of Medicine, Including the Latest Views of Physiology, Pathology and Therapeutics . . . Bennington: 1843. V. 41

ROBERTSON, FRED L.

Soldiers of Florida in the Seminole Indian-Civil and Spanish American Wars. Live Oak: 1903. V. 44

ROBERTSON, GEORGE

Chitral. The Story of a Minor Siege. London: 1899. V. 40

General View of the Agriculture of the County of Mid-Lothian; with Observtions on the Means of its Improvement. Edinburgh: 1795. V. 38; 45

Outline of the Life of George Robertson, Written by Himself. Lexington: 1876. V. 42

Speech of the Hon. George Robertson, Delivered in Committe of the Whole in the Legislature of Kentucky on the Fourth Day of December, 1823 . . . In Relation to the Court of Appeals, for Their Late Decision Against the Two Years Replevin and . . . Frankfort?: 1823. V. 44

ROBERTSON, GRAHAM

A Masque of May Morning. London: 1904. V. 44

ROBERTSON, HENRY

Natural History of the Atmosphere - Volumes I & II. Edinburgh: 1808. V. 41

ROBERTSON, J.

Michigan in the Civil War. Lansing: 1882. V. 45

ROBERTSON, J. B.

Texas the Home for the Emigrant, from Everywhere. Houston: 1875. V. 43

ROBERTSON, J. M.

A History of Freethought in the 19th Century. London: 1929. V. 40

ROBERTSON, JAMES

A Few Months in America. London: 1855. V. 37

General View of the Agriculture in the County of Perth. Perth: 1799. V. 41

General View of the Agriculture in the County of Inverness; with Observations on the Means of Its Improvement. London: 1808. V. 41

The Heroine of Love, a Musical Piece of Three Acts. York: 1778. V. 37

ROBERTSON, JAMES A.

Louisiana Under the Rule of Spain, France and the United States, 1785-1807. Cleveland. V. 39

Louisiana Under the Rule of Spain, France and the United States 1785-1807 . . . Cleveland: 1911. V. 37; 39; 42; 43; 45

ROBERTSON, JOHN 1712-1776

The Elements of Navigation: the Theory and Practice with the Necessary Tables . . . For Finding the Latitude and Longitude at Sea . . . London: 1786. V. 39

Michigan in the War. Lansing: 1882. V. 44

Rusticus ad Clericum or, the Plow-Man Rebuking the Priest, In Answer to Verus Patroclus, Wherein The False-hoods . . . of William Jamison are Detected. Edinburgh: 1694. V. 45

A Treatise of Such Mathematical Instruments as are Usually Put Into a Portable Case . . . London: 1775. V. 43

A Treatise of Such Mathematical Instruments as Are Usually Put into a Portable Case, Containing Their Various Uses in Arithmetic, Geometry, Trigonometry, Architecture, Surveying, Gunnery, &c. London: 1757. V. 37

The Universal Penman, Containing Rules for Acquiring the Knowledge and Practice of Penmanship, and the Principles of Current Hand Writing. Edinburgh: 1810. V. 40

ROBERTSON, JOHN DRUMMOND 1857-1934

The Evolution of Clockwork, with a Sepecial Section on the Clocks of Japan . . . London: 1931. V. 39

ROBERTSON, JOHN PARISH

Letters on Paraguay: Comprising an Account of a Four Years' Residence in that republic, Under the Government of the Dictator Francia. London: 1838. V. 41

Letters on Paraguay. London: 1839. V. 38

Letters on South America . . . London: 1843. V. 38

ROBERTSON, JOHN ROSS

Robertson's Landmarks of Toronto. Toronto: 1894-1914. V. 40

ROBERTSON, JOHN W.

Bibliography of the Writings of Edgar A. Poe. With Commentary on the Bibliography of Edgar A. Poe. San Francisco: 1934. V. 41; 42

Commentary on the Bibliography of Edgar Allan Poe. San Francisco: 1934. V. 40

Francis Drake and Other Early Explorers Along the Pacific Coast. San Francisco;: 1927. V. 37; 38; 42; 45; 46

The Harbor of St. Francis. San Francisco: 1926. V. 46

ROBERTSON, JOSEPH

An Essay on Culinary Poisons. London: 1781. V. 38

An Essay on Punctuation. London: 1785. V. 42; 46

An Essay on the Nature of the English Verses, with Directions for Reading Poetry. London: 1799. V. 38

ROBERTSON, KIRK

West Nevada Waltz. A Suite of Poems. Isla Vista: 1981. V. 38

ROBERTSON, MARTIN

A History of Greek Art. Cambridge: 1975. V. 37; 40; 42

ROBERTSON, MERLE GREEN

The Sculpture of Palenque. Volume III. The Late Buildings of the Palace. Princeton: 1985. V. 42

ROBERTSON, MERLE GREENE

The Sculpture of Paneque. Princeton: 1983. V. 44

The Sculpture of Palenque. Princeton: 1985. V. 44

The Sculpture of Palenque. Volume I. The Temple of the Inscription. Princeton: 1983. V. 42

The Scultpure of Palenque. Volume II. The Early Buildings of the Palace and the Wall Paintings. Princeton: 1985. V. 42

ROBERTSON, PARISH

Visit to Mexico, by the West India Islands Yucatan and United States, With Observations and Adventures on the Way. Volumes I and II. London: 1853. V. 39

ROBERTSON, ROBERT 1742-1829

Directions for Administering Peruvian Bark, in a Fermenting State, in Fever, and Other Diseases in Which Peruvian Bark is Proper . . . London: 1799. V. 46

An Essay on Fevers; Wherein Their Theoretic Genera, Species and Various Denominations, Are, From Observation and Experience For Thirty Years in Europe, Africa and America and On the Intermediate Seas, Reduced Under Their Characteristic Genus . . . London: 1790. V. 42

ROBERTSON, THOMAS WILLIAM

W. S. Woodin's New Entertainment. London: 1866. V. 42

ROBERTSON, W. GRAHAM

Gold, Frankincense and Myrrh and Other Pageants for a Baby Girl. London: 1907. V. 46

Old English Songs and Dances. London: 1902. V. 41; 46

Pinkie and the Fairies. London: 1909. V. 44; 46

ROBERTSON, WILLAIM 1721-1793

The History of America; Containing the History of Virginia, to the Year 1688 and of New England to the Year 1652. London: 1822. V. 46

ROBERTSON, WILLIAM

A Collection of Various Forms of Stoves, Used for Forcing Pine Plants, Fruit Trees and Preserving Tender Exotics . . . London: 1798. V. 46

An Historical Disquisition Concerning Knowledge Which the Ancients Had of India . . . London: 1791. V. 37; 38; 39; 40; 42; 43; 44; 45

An Historical Disquisition Concerning the Knowledge Which the Ancients Had of India. Basil: 1792. V. 44

An Historical Disquisition Concerning the Knowledge Which the Ancients Had of India. London: 1804. V. 42

The History of the Reign of the Emperor Charles V. London: 1769. V. 38; 39; 40

The History of Scotland. London: 1776. V. 42

The History of America. London: 1777. V. 38; 40; 41; 45

Histoire de l'Amerique. Paris: 1778. V. 42

L'Histoire de l'Amerique. Paris: 1780. V. 44

The History of the Reign of the Emperor Charles V. with a View of the Progress of Society in Europe . . . London: 1792. V. 44

The History of America, with the Posthumous Volume (of) The History of Virginia to 1688; and New England to 1652. London: 1800. V. 42

The History of America. London: 1803. V. 40; 42; 44

The History of America . . . London: 1808. V. 39

The History of the Reign of the Emperor Charles the Fifth . . . Workington: 1809. V. 42

The History of America. London: 1778. V. 40

The History of America. Philadelphia: 1812. V. 40

The History of America, with the Posthumous volume (of) the History of Virginia to 1688; and New England to 1652. London: 1800. V. 37

The History of Scotland during the Reigns of Queen Mary and of King James VI . . . London: 1759. V. 37

History of the Reign of Charles the Fifth. London: 1857. V. 40

(Hebrew Title) Manipulus Lingae Sanctae & Eruditorum, in Quo, Quasi, Manipulatim . . . Cantabrigiae: 1683. V. 43

Phraseologia Generalis . . . Cambridge: 1681. V. 40; 42; 44

Phraseologia Generalis . . . Cambridge: 1693. V. 38; 41; 42; 43; 46

Proceedings Relating to the Peerage of Scotland, from January 16 1707 to April 29 1788. Edinburgh: 1790. V. 39

Proceedings Relating to the Peerage of Scotland, from January 16, 1708 to April 29, 1788. Edinburgh: 1790. V. 39

Thesaurus Graecae Linguae, Inepitomen, Sive Compendium . . . Cantabrigiae: 1676. V. 45

Thesaurus Graecae Linguae, in Epitomen, Sive Compendium, Redactus, et Alphabetice, Secundum Constantini Methodum et Schrevelli . . . London: 1676. V. 46

Thesaurus Linguae Sanctae . . . Sive, Concordantiale Lexicon Hebraeo-Latino-Biblicum . . . London: 1686. V. 43

Works. London: 1820. V. 46

The Works of William Robertson. London: 1821. V. 41

The Works. Chiswick: 1824. V. 46

The Works. London: 1840. V. 45

The Works of William Robertson. London: 1851. V. 38

The Works of William Robertson with an Account of His Life and Writings. London: 1824. V. 37

ROBERTSON, WILLIAM PARISH

A Visit to Mexico by the West India Islands, yucatan and the United States with Observations and Adventures on the Way. London: 1853. V. 40; 45

ROBERTSON, WILLIAM SCHENCK 1820-1881

Nakcokv es Kerrtv Enhvteceskv. Muskokee or Creek First Reader. Philadelphia: 1913. V. 39

ROBERTSTON, DON

The Ideal, Genuine Man. Bangor: 1987. V. 41

ROBERTSTON, GEORGE

Scrap Book of Law and Politics, Men and Times. Lexington: 1855. V. 40

ROBES of Thespis. Costume Design by Modern Artists. London: 1928. V. 44

ROBESON, KENNETH

The Man of Bronze. New York: 1933. V. 40; 44; 46

ROBESON, PAUL

Here I Stand. New York: 1958. V. 43

ROBETS, BRIGHAM HENRY

A Comprehensive History of the Church of Jesus Christ of Latter Day Saints. Salt Lake City: 1930. V. 39

ROBICSEK, FRANCIS

Copan, Home of the Mayan Gods. New York: 1972. V. 37; 42; 45

ROBIDOUX, ORRAL MESSMORE

Memorial to the Robidoux Brothers; a History of the Robidouxs in America. Kansas City: 1924. V. 40

ROBIN, ABBE

New Travels through North America . . . Boston: 1784. V. 44; 45

ROBIN HOOD

A Collection of All the Ancient Poems, Songs and Ballads now Extant . . . to which are prefixed Historical Anecdotes of His Life. London: 1820. V. 44

A Lytell Geste of Robyn Hode and His Meiny. San Francisco: 1931. V. 46

A Lytell Geste of Robyn Hode and His Meiny. 1932. V. 41

A Lytell Geste of Robyn Hode and His Meiny. 1932. V. 40

A Lytell Geste of Robin Hode and His Meiny. San Francisco: 1932. V. 37; 39; 40; 42; 45; 46

A Lytell Geste of Robin Hood, With other Ancient & modern Ballads and Songs Relating to this Celebrated Yeoman . . . To which is prefixed his History and Character . . . Grounded upon other documents than those made use by his former biographer . . . London: 1847. V. 37

The Merry Adventures of Robin Hood. New York: 1883. V. 41; 42

Robin Hood, His Deeds and Adventures. London. V. 40

Robin Hood's Garland. Nottingham: 1794. V. 39; 41; 44

Robin Hood: a Collection of all the Ancient Poems, Songs and Ballads, Now Extant Relative to that Celebrated English Outlaw . . . London: 1795. V. 41; 44

Robin Hood: A Collection of al the Ancient Poems, Songs and Ballads, Now extant, Relative to that Celebrated English Outlaw. London: 1820. V. 39; 44

Robin Hood and Little John or the Merry Men of Sherwood Forest. London: 1850. V. 45

A Collection of all the Ancient Poems, Songs and Ballads Now Extant Relative to that Celebrated English Outlaw. London: 1885. V. 38

Five Ballads About Robin Hood. Birmingham: 1899. V. 39

Robin Hood. London: 1912. V. 41

Robin Hood. 1917. V. 46

Robin Hood. Philadelphia: 1917. V. 45

ROBIN, ISAAC

Letters of Isaac Robin, Esq., Private Secretary to Hon. George Clarke, Secretary of the Province of New York 1718-1730. Albany: 1872. V. 43

ROBIN, JEAN

Histoire des Plantes. Paris: 1620. V. 40

THE ROBIN Redbreast: a New Song Book, Being Choice Collection of 25 Popular Songs . . . Newcastle: 1810. V. 38

THE ROBINS at Home. London: 1890's. V. 45

ROBINS, BENJAMIN

An Address to the Electors, and Other Free Subjects of Great Britain. London: 1739. V. 41; 45

New Principles of Gunnery . . . London: 1805. V. 40

Observations on the Present Convention with Spain. London: 1739. V. 41; 45

A Proposal for Increasing the Strength of the British Navy, by Changing all the Guns, from the Eighteen Pounders Downwards into others of Equal Weight but of a agreat Bore. London: 1747. V. 37

ROBINS, ELIZABETH

Ibsen & the Actress. London: 1928. V. 45

ROBINS, F. W.

The Story of the Lamp (and the Candle). London: 1939. V. 42

ROBIN'S Last Shift: or, Weekly Remarks and Political Reflections Upon the Most Material News Foreign and Domestick. London: 1717. V. 45

ROBINS, W. P.

Etching Craft. London: 1922. V. 38; 40

ROBINSON, A. H. W.

Marine Cartography in Britain; a History of the Seat Chart to 1855. Leicester: 1962. V. 42

Marine Cartography in Britain. Oxford: 1962. V. 40

ROBINSON, ALAN JAMES

Atlantic Salmon. Easthampton: 1988. V. 46

The Banging Rocks, a Dissertation on the Origins of a Species of Rock Descended with Modification from the Ancient Piroboli . . . Easthampton: 1990. V. 46

Cetacea. Easthampton: 1981. V. 37

Cheloniidae - Sea Turtles. Easthampton: 1987. V. 46

F Fowl Alphabet. Northampton: 1986. V. 46

Game Animals. Easthampton: 1982. V. 42; 45

Game Fishes. Easthampton: 1982. V. 42

Game Fishes. Easthampton: 1980. V. 45

ROBINSON, ALAN JAMES continued

Gamebirds & Waterfowl. Easthampton: 1980. V. 42; 45

HPM. A Celebration of Fifty Years of Printing. Easthampton: 1991. V. 46

Leda or In Praise of the Blessings of Darkness. Easthampton: 1985. V. 46

An Odd Bestiary. 1982. V. 46

An Odd Bestiary. Easthampton: 1982. V. 46

An Odd Bestiary, or, a Compendium of Instructive and Entertaining Descriptions of Animals . . . N.P.: 1982. V. 39

An Odd Bestiary. Williamsburg: 1982. V. 41

Songbirds. Williamsburg. V. 39

Songbirds. Williamsburg: 1983. V. 38

Trout and Bass. Easthampton: 1992. V. 46

ROBINSON, ALBERT

Account of Some Recent Improvements in the System of Navigating the Ganges by Iron Steam Vessels. London: 1848. V. 40

ROBINSON, ALFRED

Life in California: During a Residence of Several Years in that Territory, Comprising a Description of the Country, and the Missionary Establishments . . . New York: 1846. V. 44

Life in California. New York: 1846. V. 38; 42

Life in California: During a Residence of Several Years in that Territory, Comprising a Description of the Country and the Missionary Establishments, with Incidents, Observations, etc. London: 1851. V. 40; 45

Life in California During a Residence of Several years in That Territory. San Francisco: 1891. V. 44; 45

ROBINSON, B. W.

A Descriptive Catalogue of the Persian Paintings in the Bodleian Library. 1958. V. 46

Islamic Painting and the Arts of the Book. London: 1976. V. 42

ROBINSON, C. W.

Lectures Upon the British Campaigns in the Peninsula, 1808-14. London: 1871. V. 38

ROBINSON, CHANDLER A.

J. Evetts Haley: Cowman-Historian. El Paso: 1967. V. 44

ROBINSON, CHARLES

The Big Book of Fables. London. V. 37

Jack of All Trades. London: 1900/1899. V. 45

Navy and Army Illustrated. London: 1895-1903. V. 38

Nebraska and Kansas. Report of the Committee of the Massachusetts Emigrant Aid Co. with Act of Incorporation and Other Documents. Boston: 1854. V. 43

New South Wales, the Oldest and Richest of the Australian Colonies. Sydney: 1873. V. 43

Rule Britannia. London. V. 45

Rule Britannia. London. V. 46

The Silly Submarine. London. V. 45

Very Short Stories for Very Short People. London: 1st edition; V. 44

ROBINSON, CHARLES H.

Hausaland, or, Fifteen Hundred Miles thorugh the Central Soudan. London: 1896. V. 42

ROBINSON, CHARLES HENRY

Specimens of Hausa Literature. Cambridge: 1896. V. 45

ROBINSON, CHARLES N.

Old Naval Prints and Engravers. London: 1924. V. 38; 42; 44; 46

ROBINSON, CLOUGH

The Dialect of Leeds. London: 1862. V. 38; 40

ROBINSON, CONWAY

An Account of Discoveries in the West Until 1519 and of Voyages to and Along the Atlantic Coast of North America, from 1520 to 1573. Richmond: 1848. V. 40; 45

ROBINSON, CORINNE ROOSEVELT

The Poems of Corinne Roosevelt Robinson. New York: 1924. V. 42

ROBINSON, CRESCENS & CO.

Ornamental designs for Tea Papers. London: 1870. V. 40

ROBINSON, DAVID M.

A Catalogue of the Greek Vases in the Royal Ontario Museum of Archaeology, Toronto. Toronto: 1930. V. 37; 38; 42; 44

Excavations at Olynthus, Part X (only). Baltimore: 1941. V. 44

ROBINSON, DOANE

History of South Dakota. Aberdeen: 1904. V. 40; 45

History of South Dakota. N.P.: 1904. V. 38

History of South Dakota. N.P.: 1904. V. 39

History of South Dakota. N.P.: 1904. V. 37

South Dakota Stressing the Unique and Dramatic in South Dakota History. Chicago: 1930. V. 45

ROBINSON, DUNCAN

William Morris, Edward Burne-Jones and the Kelmscott Chaucer. London: 1982. V. 40

ROBINSON, EDWARD

Biblical Researches in Palestine. London: 1841. V. 39; 44

ROBINSON, EDWIN ARLINGTON 1869-1935

Avon's Harvest. New York: 1921. V. 37; 38; 40; 41; 42

Captain Craig. New York: 1915. V. 41; 42

Cavender's House. New York: 1929. V. 37; 41; 42; 44

The Children of the Night. Boston: 1897. V. 37; 38; 41; 42; 43; 44; 46

The Children of the Night. Boston: 1907. V. 44

The Children of the Night. A Book of Poems. New York: 1905. V. 37

Collected Poems. Cambridge: 1915. V. 38

The Collected Poems. New York: 1921. V. 40

Collected Poems. New York: 1929. V. 41; 42; 43; 44

Dionysus in Doubt. New York: 1925. V. 40; 41; 42; 43; 44

Fortunatus. Reno: 1928. V. 37; 40

The Man Who Died Twice. New York: 1924. V. 41

Modred. Colophon: 1929. V. 40

Roman Bartholomew. New York: 1923. V. 40

Sonnets: 1889-1927. New York: 1928. V. 40

Tilbury Town: Selected Poems. New York: 1953. V. 41; 42

The Torrent and the Night Before. Cambridge: 1896. V. 44

The Torrent and the Night Before. Gardiner: 1896. V. 37; 40

The Torrent and the Night Before. Colophon: 1928. V. 40

The Torrent and the Night Before. New York: 1928. V. 37

Tristram. New York: 1927. V. 39; 40

Van Zorn: a Comedy in Three Acts. New York: 1914. V. 41; 42

ROBINSON, EMMA

Caesar Borgia. London: 1846. V. 39; 46

Dorothy Firebrace or the Armourer's Daughter of Birmingham. London: 1865. V. 40; 41

The Merry Wives of Stamboul . . . London: 1846. V. 42

Whitehall; or, The Days of Charles I. London: 1845. V. 39

ROBINSON, F. J. G.

Eighteenth Century British Books: an Author Union Catalogue Extracted from the British Museum General Catalogue of Printed Books, the Catalogues of the Bodleian Library and of the University Library. Cambridge: 1981. V. 39

ROBINSON, F. W.

The Wrong That Was Done. London: 1892. V. 41

ROBINSON, FAYETTE

An Account of the Organization of the Army of the United States. Philadelphia: 1848. V. 40

Mexico and her Military Chieftains, from the REvolution of Hidalgo to the Present Time . . . Philadelphia: 1847. V. 40; 46

ROBINSON, FRANCIS

Refutation of Lieut. Wellstead's Attack on Lord Valentia's Work Upon the Red Sea. London: 1840. V. 45

A Selection of Irish Melodies. Dublin: 1869. V. 38

ROBINSON, FRANCIS KILDALE

A Glossary of Yorkshire Words and Phrases, Collected in Whitby and the Neighbourhood. London: 1855. V. 41

ROBINSON, FREDERICK

Diary of the Crimean War. London: 1856. V. 41

ROBINSON, FREDERICK WILLIAM

Church and Chapel. London: 1863. V. 38

Prison Characters Drawn from Life. London: 1866. V. 43

ROBINSON, GEORGE

Contributions to the Physiology and Pathology of the Circulation of the Blood. London: 1857. V. 43

On the Prevention and Treatment of Mental Disorders. London: 1859. V. 38

Three Years in the East. London: 1837. V. 40; 45

The Travels in Palestine and Syria. Paris & London: 1837. V. 39

ROBINSON, GEORGE F.

History of Greene County, Ohio. Chicago: 1902. V. 39; 46

ROBINSON-GIVVINGS, T. H.

Furniture of Classical Greece. New York: 1963. V. 44

ROBINSON, H. B.

Memoirs of Lieutenant-General Sir Thomas Picton, G.C.B. &c. London: 1935. V. 41

ROBINSON, H. C.

The Birds of the Malay Peninsula. London: 1927-39. V. 38

The Birds of the Malay Peninsula. London: 1927-76. V. 43

The Birds of Malay Peninsula. London: 1927-28. V. 37

The Birds of the Malay Peninsula. Volume 3: Sporting Birds; Birds of the Shore and Estuaries. London: 1936. V. 38

The Birds of the Malay Peninsula. Volume 4: The Birds of the Low-country, Jungle and Scrub. London: 1939. V. 38

On Birds from South Annam and Cochin China. London: 1919. V. 43

ROBINSON, H. E.

Chronology of Printing. Maryville: 1877. V. 44

ROBINSON, H. M.

The Great Fur Land or Sketches of Life in the Hudson's Bay Territory. New York: 1879. V. 43

ROBINSON, HARRIET

Loom and Spindle or Life Among the Early Mill Girls with a Sketch of 'The Lowell Offering' and some of Its Contributers. New York: 1898. V. 44; 45

ROBINSON, HENRY CRABB

The Correspondence . . . Oxford: 1927. V. 45

Diary, Reminiscences, and Correspondence. London: 1869. V. 39; 40; 46

ROBINSON, HENRY S.

Pottery of the Roman Period, Chronology. Princeton: 1959. V. 40

ROBINSON, HUGH

Scholae Wintoniensi Phrases Latinae. London: 1664. V. 38; 41

Scholae Wintoniensis Phrases Latinae. London: 1667. V. 42; 46

Scholae Wintoniensis Phrases Latinae. The Latine Phrases of Winchester-School. Corrected and much augmented with poeticals added; and these foru tracts . . . the foruth edition; with many additions. Published for . . . 1664. V. 37

ROBINSON, J.

Canaries, Hybrids and British Birds in Cage and Aviary. London: 1911. V. 38

Sailing Ships of New England . . . Salem: 1922-24-28. V. 41

ROBINSON, J. B.

Designs from Monuments, Tombs, Gravestones &c. London: 1856. V. 44

ROBINSON, J. C.

The Treasury of Ornamental Art . . . London: 1857. V. 46

ROBINSON, J. H.

Journal of an Expedition 1400 Miles Up the Orinoco and 300 Up the Arauca; with an Account of the Country, the Manners of the People, Military Operations, &c. London: 1822. V. 39; 45

ROBINSON, J. W.

Railroad and Steamboat Sketches, Between New York and Kansas. Philadelphia: 1857. V. 38; 40; 41; 43

ROBINSON, JAMES

The Philadelphia Directory for 1809. V. 41

The Philadelphia Directory of 1816 . . . . V. 41

The Whole Art of Making British Wines, Cordials and Liquers . . . London: 1848. V. 40

ROBINSON Jeffers. Vale: 1962. V. 39

ROBINSON, JOAN

Essays in the Theory of Employment. London: 1937. V. 46

ROBINSON, JOHN

A Account of Sueden: Together with an Extract of the History of that Kingdom. London: 1694. V. 37; 39

An Account of Sveden: Together with an Extract of the History of the Kingdom. London: 1711. V. 40; 42; 43

A Guide to the Lakes, in Cumberland, Westmorland and Lancashire Illustrated . . . London: 1819. V. 45; 46

Proofs of a Conspiracy Against All the Religions and Governments of Europe, Carried On in the Secret Meetings of Free Masons, Illuminati and Reading Societies . . . Edinburgh: 1797. V. 40

The Sailing Ships of New England. Salem: 1922-28. V. 46

The Sailing Ships of New England. Series Two. Salem: 1924. V. 39

The Savage. Knoxville: 1833. V. 44

A System of Mechanical Philosophy. Edinburgh: 1822. V. 43

ROBINSON, JOHN BEVERLY

Canada and the Canada Bill . . . London: 1840. V. 42

ROBINSON, JOHN CHARLES

Catalogue of the Various Works of Art, Forming the Collection of Matthew Uzielli of Hanover Lodge, London. London: 1860. V. 38

A Critical Account of the Drawings by Michel Angelo and Raffaello in the University Galleries, Oxford. Oxford: 1870. V. 38; 39; 44

Descriptive Catalogue of the Drawings by the Old Masters, Forming the Collection of John Malcolm of Poltalloch. London: 1869. V. 38

Italian Sculpture of the Middle Ages . . . a Descriptive Catalogue of the Works Forming the Above Section of the Museum. London: 1862. V. 38

The Treasury of Ornamental Art. London: 1857. V. 42; 44

The Treasury of Ornamental Art. London: 1858. V. 45

ROBINSON, JOHN HOVEY

The Life and Adventures of Wm. Harvard Stinchfield, or the Wanderings of a Traveling Merchant. Portland: 1851. V. 37

Silver Knife; or, the Hunters of the Rocky Mountains. Boston: 1854. V. 38; 46

ROBINSON, LENOX

A Young Man from the South. Dublin: 1917. V. 42

ROBINSON, M. S.

A Pageant of the Sea. The Macpherson Collection of Maritime Prints and Drawings in the National Gallery Museum Greenwich. London: 1950. V. 38; 39; 42; 46

Van de Velde Drawings: A Catalogue of the Drawings in the national Maritime Museum Made by the Elder and the Younger Willem Van de Velde. Cambridge: 1973-74. V. 41

ROBINSON, MARIA ELIZABETH

The Wild Wreath. London: 1804. V. 39; 42

ROBINSON, MARILYNNE

Housekeeping. New York: 1980. V. 45

ROBINSON, MARIUS R.

The Anti-Slavery Bugle. Salem: 1859. V. 42

ROBINSON, MARK H.

La Crosse. (The National Game of Canada). London: 1868. V. 39

ROBINSON, MARY 1758-1800

Life and Works of Mrs. Robinson. Written by Herself. London: 1801. V. 39

Memoirs of the Late Mrs. Robinson, Written by Herself. London: 1801. V. 39

Memoirs of the Late Mrs. Robinson. London: 1801/03. V. 42

Memoirs of the Late Mrs. Robinson, Written by Herself. London: 1803. V. 38

Memoirs of the Late Mrs. Robinson, Written by Herself. London: 1803. V. 37; 41

Poems. London: 1775. V. 40

Poems. London: 1791. V. 38; 40; 45

ROBINSON, MATTHEW

Considerations on the Meausres Carrying on With Respect to the British Colonies in North America. Boston: 1774. V. 41

Peace the Best Policy or Reflections Upon the Appearance of a Foreign War, the Present State of Affairs at Home and the Commission for Granting Pardons in America. London: 1777. V. 37

ROBINSON, MERLE GREENE

The Sculpture of Palenque. Princeton: 1983-85. V. 45

ROBINSON, NICHOLAS

A Compleat Treatise of the Gravel and Stone, with all their Causes, Symptoms and Cures, Accounted For. London: 1723. V. 41

The Heroick Christian; or, the Man of Honour. London: 1721. V. 44

ROBINSON, NOEL

Blazing the Trail through the Rockies. Vancouver: 1914. V. 43

ROBINSON, P. F.

An Attempt to Ascertain the Age of the Church of Mickelham in Surrey with Remarks on the Architecture of that Building. London: 1824. V. 41

ROBINSON, PATRICK

Classic Lines. Birmingham: 1975. V. 43

Decade of Champions. The Greatest Years in the History of Thoroughbred Racing 1970-1980. New York: 1980. V. 39

ROBINSON, PEDITA

Memoirs of the Late Mrs. Robinson. L: 1801. V. 41

ROBINSON, PERCY J.

Toronto During the French Regime. Toronto: 1933. V. 44

ROBINSON, PETER FREDERICK 1776-1858

Designs for Farm Buildings, with a View to Prove that the Simplest Forms May be Rendered Pleasing and Ornamental . . . Bohn: 1837. V. 42

Designs for Farm Buildings, with a View to Prove That the Simplest Forms May be Rendered Pleasing and Ornamental by a Proper Disposition of the Rudest Materials. London: 1837. V. 38; 45

Designs for Gate Cottages, Lodges and Park Entrances, in Various Styles, from the Humblest to the Castellated. London: 1837. V. 38; 45

Designs for Farm Buildings. London: 1830. V. 37

Designs for Lodges and Park Entrances. London: 1833. V. 38

Domestic Architecture in the Tudor Style, Selected from Buildings Erected After the Designs and Under the Superintendence of P. F. Robinson. London: 1837. V. 38

Rural Architecture, or a Series of Designs for Ornamental Cottages. London: 1823. V. 38; 42; 45

Rural Architecture, Being a Series of Designs for Ornamental Cottages. London: 1826. V. 44

Rural Architecture, Being a Series of Designs for Ornamental Cottages. London: 1828. V. 38

ROBINSON, PHIL

Sinners and Saints. London: 1883. V. 42

ROBINSON, POLLINGROVE

Cometilia; or Views of Nature. London: 1789. V. 40

ROBINSON, R. W.

Los Angeles, Little History of a Big City. Los Angeles: 1963. V. 44

ROBINSON, ROBERT 1735-1790

The History of Baptism. London: 1790. V. 39

A Political Catechism. London: 1782. V. 38; 41; 42

Thomas Bewick, His Life and Times. Newcastle: 1877. V. 40

Thomas Bewick, His Life and Times. Newcastle: 1887. V. 37; 45

ROBINSON, ROWLAND EVANS

Forest and Stream Fables. New York: 1886. V. 37

ROBINSON, S.

Callahan and Company. 1988. V. 43

ROBINSON, S. F. H.

Celtic Illuminative Art in the Gospel Books of Durrow, Lindisfarne, and Kells. Dublin: 1908. V. 37; 38

ROBINSON, SAMUEL

Catalogue of American Minerals, With Their Localities Including All Which Are Known to Exist in the United States and British Provinces . . . Boston: 1825. V. 46

A Course of Fifteen Lectures on Medical Botany, Denominated Thomson's New Theory of Medical Practice. Columbus: 1830. V. 39

A Course of Fifteen Lectures, on Medical Botany, Denominated Thomson's New Theory of Medical Practice . . . Columbus: 1832. V. 37; 46

ROBINSON, SARA T. L.

Kansas: Its Interior and Exterior Life. Boston: 1856. V. 38; 40; 41

ROBINSON, SELMA

City Child. New York: 1931. V. 42

ROBINSON, SUSANNE ANTROBUS

The Resources and Natural Advantages of Florida . . . Tallahassee: 1882. V. 41

ROBINSON, TANCRED

An Account of Several Late Voyages and Discoveries to the South and North. London: 1694. V. 40

ROBINSON, THERESE L. VON J.

Talvi's History of the Colonization of America. London: 1851. V. 40

ROBINSON, THOMAS d. 1719

The Anatomy of the Earth. London: 1694. V. 38; 40

The Common Law of Kent; or, the Customs of Gavelkind with an Appendix Concerning Borough-English by Thomas Robinson. London: 1788. V. 40

The Common-Law of Kent. London: 1822. V. 39

The Common Law of Kent: or, the Customs of Gavelkind. In the Savoy: 1741. V. 37

An Essay Towards a Natural History of Westmorland and cumberland . . . thier several Mineral and Surface Productions . . . how to discover Minerals by the External and Adjacent Strata and Upper Covers . . . A VIndication of the Philosophical . . . London: 1709. V. 37

Scripture Characters: or, a Practical Improvement of the Principal Histories in the Old and New Testament. London: 1793. V. 39

The Tyrolese Villagers; or, a Prospect of War. London: 1810. V. 37; 38; 42; 43

ROBINSON, VICTOR

An Essay on Hasheesh. New York: 1930. V. 37; 45

ROBINSON, W.

The Parks, Promenades and Gardens of Paris. London: 1869. V. 44

ROBINSON, W. G.

Head-Quarters District of Pamlico, Office of the Provost Marshal, Newbern, Jan. 31st, 1862. Newbern: 1862. V. 44

ROBINSON, W. HEATH 1872-1944

Some 'Frightful' War Pictures. London: 1915. V. 37; 41

ROBINSON, W. J.

West Country Churches. 1914. V. 46

ROBINSON, W. W.

Little History of a Big City, Los Angeles. Los Angeles: 1963. V. 41

Maps of Los Angeles. Los Angeles: 1966. V. 38; 40; 43; 46

Ranches Become Cities. Pasadena: 1939. V. 38

ROBINSON, WILLIAM

The English Flower Garden and Home Grounds. London: 1911. V. 37

Flora and Sylva. London: 1903-05. V. 38; 46

Gleanings form French Gardens . . . London: 1868. V. 41

Gravetye Manor or Twenty Years' Work Round an Old Manor House. London: 1911. V. 38; 39

Gravetye Manor: Or Twenty Years' Work Round an Old Manor House. New York: 1984. V. 37

The History and Antiquities of the Parish of Tottenham, in the County of Middlesex. London: 1840. V. 41

Home Landscapes. London: 1920. V. 39; 42

The Magistrate's Pocket Book; or an Epitome of the Duties and Practice of a Justice of the Peace, Out of Sessions. London: 1825. V. 40

Nautical Economy; or, Forecastle Recollections of Events During the Last War. London: 1836. V. 44

The Parks, Promenades and Gardens of Paris Described and Considered in Relation to the Wants of Our Own Cities. London: 1869. V. 41; 46

The Parks, Promenades and Gardens of Paris. London: 1860. V. 37

The Virgin's Bower. London: 1912. V. 46

The Wild Garden or the Naturalization and Natural Grouping of Hardy Exotic Plants. London: 1894. V. 39

The Wild Garden or the Naturalization and Natural Grouping of Hardy Exotic Plants. London: 1895. V. 42

ROBINSON, WILLIAM DAVIS

Memoirs of the Mexican Revolution . . . Philadelphia: 1820. V. 41; 45

Memoirs of the Mexican Revolution; Including a Narrative of the Expedition of General Xavier Mina. London: 1821. V. 38; 39

ROBINSON, WILLIAM HEATH 1872-1944

Absurdities. London: 1934. V. 41

The Adventures of Uncle Lubin. London: 1902. V. 44

Behind the Scenes at Moss Bross. London: n.d. V. 37

Bill the Minder. New York. V. 41

Bill the Minder. London: 1912. V. 37; 38; 40; 41; 42; 43; 44; 45; 46

Bill the Minder. New York: 1912. V. 43

Book of Goblins. London. V. 45

The Dream of Maxen Wledig. 1910. V. 42

Heath Robinson's Book of Goblins. London: 1934. V. 43

Heath Robinson on Leather. London: 1950. V. 40

How to Build a New World. London: 1942. V. 41

Hunlikely! London: 1916. V. 44; 45; 46

A Jamboree of Laughter. London: (ca. 1920). V. 37

My Line of Life. London: 1938. V. 40; 41; 45

Railway Ribaldry. 1935. V. 45

Railway Ribaldry. London: 1935. V. 41

Railway Ribaldry. Paddington: 1935. V. 40

Some 'Frightful' War Pictures. London: 1915. V. 42

Technical Talks. London: 1920. V. 42

The W. Heath Robinson Calendar. London: 1935. V. 42

The Wonders of Wilmington. Wilmington. V. 46

The Wonders of Wilmington. Wilmington: 1930. V. 45

ROBINSON, WILLIAM HENRY

Her Navajo Lover. Phoenix: 1903. V. 37

ROBINSON, WILLIAM WILCOX 1891-

Maps of Los Angeles from Ord's Survey of 1849 to the End of the Boom of the Eighties. Los Angeles: 1966. V. 39

Ranchos become Cities. With Illustrations by Irene Robinson. Pasadena: 1939. V. 37

ROBINSON, WIRT

A Flying Trip to the Tropics. Cambridge: 1895. V. 39

ROBINSON'S Atlas of Morris County, New Jersey. New York: 1887. V. 46

ROBISON, JOHN

Proofs of Conspiracy Against All the Religions and Governments of Europe, Carried On in the Secret Meetings of Free Masons, Illuminati and Reading Societies. London: 1797. V. 42

Proofs of Conspiracy Against All the Religions and Governments of Europe . . . Dublin: 1798. V. 45

Proofs of a Conspiracy Against All the Religions and Governments of Europe, Carried on In the Secret Meetings of Free Masons, Illuminati, and Reading Societies. London: 1798. V. 44

Proofs of a Conspiracy against all the Religions and Governments of Europe, carried on in the secret meetings of Free Masons, Illuminati, and Reading Societies. Collected from Good Authorities . . . Edinburgh: 1797. V. 37

ROBOTTOM, ARTHUR

Travels to the Far West in Search of Borax. (Birmingham): 1876. V. 37

ROBSJOHN-GIBBINGS, T. H.

Furniture of Classical Greece. New York: 1963. V. 40; 42

ROBSON, ALBERT H.

Canadian Landscape Painters. London: 1932. V. 46

Canadian Landscape Painters. Toronto: 1932. V. 44

Tom Thomson. Toronto: 1937. V. 43

ROBSON' Classification of Trades, London Commercial Directory, Street Guide and Carrier's List, for 1821. London: 1821. V. 40

ROBSON, EDWARD ROBERT

School Architecture. London: 1877. V. 38; 41

ROBSON, G. F.

Scenery of Grampion Mountains . . . London: 1819. V. 38

ROBSON, GEORGE FENNELL

Scenery of the Grampian Mountains; London: 1814. V. 44; 46

ROBSON, HENRY

Figures in Rhymes. Newcastle-upon-Tyne: 1814. V. 40; 44

ROBSON, J. P.

Summer Excursions in the North of England . . . Newcastle: 1851. V. 46

ROBSON, JAMES

A Catalogue, etc. Books of Prints, From the Galleries and Cabinets of the Curious, in Various Languages. N.P.: 1775. V. 42

ROBSON, JOHN S.

How a One-Legged Rebel Lives. Charlottesville: 1888. V. 44

ROBSON, JOSEPH

An Account of Six Years Residence in Hudson's Bay, from 1733 to 1736 and 1744 to 1747. London: 1752. V. 39; 42

An Account of Six Years Residence in Hudson's Bay, from 1733 to 1736, and from 1744 to 1747. London: 1759. V. 37; 38; 40; 42

The British Mars. London: 1763. V. 41; 42

ROBSON, JOSEPH PHILIP

The Life and Adventures of the Far-Famed Billy Purvis. Newcastle-upon-Tyne: 1849. V. 42

ROBSON, STEPHEN

The British Flora, Containing the Select Names, Chracters, Places of Growth, Duration and Time of Flowering of the Plants Growing Wild in Great Britain . . . York: 1777. V. 44

The British Flora. York: 1778. V. 45

ROBUCK, J. E.

Archie McDonald of South Carolina, a Victim of Circumstantial Evidence Under the Pressure of Negro Slavery Abolition Prejudice. Fifty Years 1850-1900 a White Slave. Brimingham: 1909. V. 44

ROBY, J.

Traditions of Lancashire. First & Second Series. London: 1829. V. 38

Traditions of Lancashire. First and Second Series. London: 1829, 1831. V. 38; 40

Traditions of Lancashire. London: 1829-31. V. 40

ROBY, JOHN

Jokeby, a Burlesque of Rokeby: a Poem in Six Cantos. Boston: 1813. V. 40

Jokeby, a Burlesque of Rokeby. London: 1813. V. 39; 41; 42

ROCA, PAUL M.

Paths of the Padres Through Sonora. Tucson: 1967. V. 40

ROCAFUERTE, VICENTE

Cartas de un Americano Sobre las Ventajas de Los Gobiernos Republicanos Federativos. London: 1826. V. 45

Ideas Necesarias a Todo Pueblo Americano Independiente, que Quiera ser Libre. Philadelphia: 1821. V. 38

ROCCA, ANGELO

De Sacrosancto Christi Corpore Romanis. Romae: 1599. V. 38

ROCCHIETTI, JOSEPH

Lorenzo and Oonalaska. Winchester: 1835. V. 40; 43

ROCCO, ANTONIO

Esercitationi Filosofiche di D. Antonio Rocco filosofo Peripatetico. Venice: 1633. V. 43

ROCCUS, FRANCESCO

A Manual of Maritime Law, Consisting of a Treatise on Ships and Freight and a Treatise on Insurance. Philadelphia: 1809. V. 40

ROCHA PEREIRA, M. HELENA

Greek Vases in Portugal. Coimbra: 1962. V. 42

ROCHA PITTA, SEBASTIAO DA

Breve Compendio e Narracam do Funebre Espectaculo, Que na Insigne Cidade de Bahia . . . Lisbon: 1709. V. 41

Historia da America Portugueza, Desde o Anno de Mil e Quinhentos . . . Lisboa Occidental: 1730. V. 41

ROCHAMBEAU, JEAN B. D. DE VIMEUR, COMTE DE

Memoires Militaires, Historiques et Politiques de Rochambeau, Ancient Marechal de France et Grand Officier de la Legion d'Honneur. Paris: 1809. V. 41

ROCHAS, HENRY DE

La Physique Demonstrative, Divisee en Trois Livres. Paris: 1643. V. 45

ROCHE, EMMA LANGDON

Historic Sketches of the South. New York: 1914. V. 45

ROCHE, H.

Pastels a la Gerbe. Paris: 1911. V. 41

ROCHE, HAMILTON

Waterloo; a Heroic Poems. London: 1815. V. 43

ROCHE, JAMES JEFFREY 1847-1908

The Story of Filibusters. London: 1891. V. 37; 38

The Story of the Filibusters to which is added the life of Colonel David Crockett. New York: 1891. V. 38

ROCHE, PAUL

Enigma Variations And. London: 1974. V. 40

The Kiss. 1974. V. 46

ROCHE, S.

Mirrors. London: 1957. V. 37

ROCHEFORT, CHARLES DE

Histoire Naturelle et Morale des Iles Antilles de l'Amerique. Roterdam: 1665. V. 40

Histoire Naturelle et Morale des Iles Antilles de L'Amerique . . . Rotterdam: 1675. V. 40; 42

The History of Barbados, St. Christophers, Mevis St. Vincents, Antego, Martinico, Monserrata dn the Rest of the Caribby-Islands. London: 1666. V. 40; 42

Natuurlijke en Zedelijke Historie der Voor-Eylanden van Amerika . . . Rotterdam: 1662. V. 39; 40; 43

ROCHEFORT, EDITH

The Lloyds of Ballymore. London: 1890. V. 41

ROCHEFOUCAULD-LIANCOURT, FRANCOIS ALEXANDRE FREDERIC

Voyages dans les Etatis-Unis d'Amerique, fait en 1795, 1796 et 1797. Paris: 1799. V. 39

ROCHESTER, JOHN WILMOT, 2ND EARL OF 1647-1680

Collected Works. London: 1926. V. 45; 46

Familiar Letters. London: 1697. V. 42

The Poetical Works of the Earls of Rochester, Roscommon, and Dorset, the Dukes of Deonshire, Buckinghamshire &c. With Memoirs of Their Lives. London: 1739. V. 38

The Poetical Works. Manchester: 1933. V. 38

The Poetical Works of John Wilmot, Earl of Rochester. N.P.: 1933. V. 42

A Satyr Against Mankind. N.P.: 1679. V. 40

ROCHESTER, JOHN WILMOT, 2ND EARL OF 1647-1680 continued

Valentinian . . . V. 45

Valentinian. London: 1685. V. 38

The Works of the Right Honourable the Late Earls of Rochester and Roscommon . . . London: 1707. V. 38

The Works of . . . (with Roscommon, Dorset, etc.). London: 1774. V. 38

ROCHFORT, EDITH

The Lloyds of Ballymore: a story of Irish Life. London: 1890. V. 37

ROCHFORT, JOHN A.

Business and General Directory of Newfoundland, 1877. Montreal: 1877. V. 44

ROCHON, ABBE ALEXIS DE

A Voyage to Madagascar, and the East Indies . . . to which is Added a Memoir on the Chinese Trade. London: 1792. V. 41

ROCK & CO.

England Under Victoria: Lancashire and Cheshire. London: 1850. V. 45

ROCK, DANIEL

Textile Fabrics in the South Kensington Museum. London: 1870. V. 42

ROCK, JAMES L.

Southern and Western Texas Guide for 1878. St. Louis: 1878. V. 40

ROCK LIFE ASSURANCE COMPANY

The Deed of Settlement of the Rock Life Assurance Company. London: 1834. V. 40

ROCK, WILLIAM FREDERICK

Jim and Nell: a Dramatic Poem in the Dialect of North Devon. London: 1867. V. 42

ROCKAFIELD, H. A.

The Manheim Tragedy. Lancaster: 1858. V. 45

ROCKER SILVER MINING CO.

Prospectus of the Rocker Silver Mining Co., Jefferson Co. Montana . . . New York: 1879. V. 43

ROCKFELLOW, JOHN A.

IOG OF AN aRIZONA TRAIL bLAZER. tUCSON. V. 46

Log of an Arizona Trail Blazer. Tucson: 1933. V. 37; 38; 39; 42; 44; 46

ROCKHILL, WILLIAM WOODVILLE

Diary of a Journey through Mongolia and Tibet in 1891 and 1892. Washington: 1894. V. 45

ROCKLEY, ALICIA MARGARET TYSSEN-AMHERST CECIL, BARONESS

A History of Gardening in England. London: 1896. V. 38

A History of Gardening in England. London: 1910. V. 37; 38; 40

ROCKWELL, CHARLES

Sketches of Foreign Travel and Life at Sea. Boston: 1842. V. 37; 39; 42; 45

ROCKWELL, IRVIN ELMER

Saga of the American Falls Dam. New York: 1947. V. 42

ROCKWELL, JOHN A.

A Compilation of Spanish and Mexican Law in Relation to Mines and Titles to Real Estate, in Force in California, Texas and New Mexico and in the Territories Acquired Under the Louisiana and Florida Treaties . . . New York: 1851. V. 39; 43

ROCKWELL, KENT

Resolutions and Memorial of a Meeting of the Mechanics, Manufacturers and Labouring Men of the Second WArd of the City of New York, on the Subject of the Removal of the Public Deposites from the United States Bank. N.P.: 1833. V. 44

ROCKWELL, NORMAN

My Adventures as an Illustrator. Garden City: 1960. V. 46

Norman Rockwell Album. New York: 1955. V. 44

THE ROCKY Mountain Directory and Colorado Gazeteer for 1871. Denver: 1870. V. 37; 40; 43

ROCKY MOUNTAIN MEDICAL ASSOCIATION

By Laws of the Rocky Mountain Medical Association. New Mexico. Territorial Medical Society. Trinidad, Col.: 1875. V. 37

ROCKY Mountain Scenery: A Brief Description of Prominent Places of Interest Along the Line of the Denver & Rio Grande Railroad . . . N.P.: 1888? V. 38

ROCKY Mountain Song Book, Published for the Use of the Fremont Flying Artillery of Providence. Providence: 1856. V. 39

THE ROCKY Mountains Directory and Colorado Gazetteer for 1871 . . . Denver: 1870. V. 41

ROCQUE, JOHN

A Collection of Plans of the Principal Cities of Great Britain and Ireland; with Maps of the Coast of the Said Kingdoms . . . . London: 1764. V. 41

A Topographical Survey of the County of Berks . . . London: 1761. V. 39

A ROD in Brine, or a Tickler for Tom Paine, in Answer to His First Pamphlet Entitled The Rights of Man. Canterbury: 1792. V. 39

RODA, JOSEPH

Bows for Musical Instruments of the Violin Family. Chicago: 1959. V. 37; 38

RODD, RENNELL

Bulletin of the Keats-Shelley Memorial Rome. V. 46

Newdigate Prize Poem. Raleigh. Recited in the Theatre, June 9, 1880. Oxford: 1880. V. 39

The Princes of Achaia and the Chronicles of Morea. London: 1907. V. 45

Rose Leaf and Apple leaf. Philadelphia: 1882. V. 38; 41; 42; 43; 44

Rose Leaf and Apple Leaf. 1906. V. 46

RODD, THOMAS

History of Charles the Great and Orlando. London: 1812. V. 38; 39; 40

RODDENBERRY, G.

Star Trek. 1979. V. 44

Star Trek. 1979. V. 46

RODEN, EARL OF

Progress of the Reformation in Ireland . . . From a Series of Letters from the West of Ireland . . . in September 1851. London: 1851. V. 38

RODENBAUGH, THEO F. 1838-1912

From Everglade to Canon with the Second Dragoons . . . New York: 1875. V. 39; 40; 42; 45

History of the 18th Regiment of Cavalry, Pennsylvania Volunteers (163rd REgiment of the Line). 1862-1865. New York: 1909. V. 42; 46

RODENBERG, JULIUS

King 'By the Grace of God.' London: 1871. V. 40

RODEUR, PSEUD.

Unobtrusive Observations in Rhyme and Prose on the Horse, Turf Gambling, the Game Laws, Hunting in Warwickshire, etc., etc. Leamington: 1866. V. 43

RODGER, ALEXANDER

Peter Cornclips, a Tale of Real Life. Glasgow: 1827. V. 39; 41

RODGERS, JOSEPH

The Scenery of Sherwood Forest. 1898. V. 44

RODGERS, RICHARD

Carousel. New York: 1946. V. 40; 46

Oklahoma! New York: 1943. V. 39; 40

RODGERS, ROBERT L.

Report of Robert L. Rodgers, Historian to Atlanta Camp No. 159, U.C.V. On the Capture of the DeGress Battery and Battery A, 1st Ill. Light Artillery, in the Battle of Atlanta, July 22D, 1864, With Other Papers Relating Thereon. Atlanta: 1896. V. 44

RODGERS, VINCENTIA

Cluthan and malvina. An Ancient Legend and Other Poems. Belfast: 1923. V. 37

RODGERS, WILLIAM LEDYARD

Greek and Roman Naval Warfare. Annapolis: 1937. V. 44

RODITI, EDOUARD

Emperor of Midnight. Los Angeles: 1974. V. 37; 42

Meetings with Conrad. Los Angeles: 1977. V. 42

Poems 1928-1948. 1949. V. 40

RODKER, JOHN

Adolphe 1920. 1929. V. 38

Adolphe 1920. London: 1929. V. 37

Hymns. London: 1920. V. 37; 39; 40; 46

Memoirs of Other Fronts. London: 1932. V. 37

Poems. London: 1914. V. 39; 43; 44

Poems. White-chapel: 1914. V. 37; 40; 46

RODLICH, H. F.

Praktische Anweisung zur Verfertigung der Venezianischen Estriche. Berlin: 1810. V. 42

RODMAN, SELDEN

Horace Pippin. New York: 1947. V. 39; 43

RODNEY, C. A.

The Reports on the Present State of the United Provinces ofSouth America; Drawn Up By Messrs. Rodney and Graham, Commissioners Sent to Buenos Ayres by the Government of North America. London: 1819. V. 40

RODNEY, GEORGE

Letter-Books and Order-Book fo George, Lord Rodney, Admiral of the White Squadron, 1780-1782. New York: 1932. V. 46

RODNEY, RICHARD S.

Colonial Finances in Delaware. Wilmington: 1928. V. 41

RODOREDA, MERCE

Two Tales. New York: 1983. V. 42

RODRIGUES DE SOUZA, GENTIL

Compilacao das Leis Provinciaes do Amazonas 1852-1883. Manaus: 1883. V. 38

RODRIGUES, J. B.

Sertum Palmarum Brasiliensium ou Relation des Palmiers Nouveaux du Bresil. Brussels,: 1903. V. 38

RODRIGUES, JOSE FRANCISCO

Espingarda Perfeyta, & Regras Para a Sua Operacam Com Circunstancias Necessarias Para o Seu Artificio . . . Lisbon: 1718. V. 40

RODRIGUEZ, MANUEL

Explicacion de la Bulla de la Sancta Cruzada (etc.). Barcelona: 1591. V. 41

RODRIGUEZ, V. F. ALONSUS

The Practice of Christian and Religious Perfection. Kilkenny: 1806. V. 43

RODULPHIUS, PETRUS

Dictionarvm Pavpervm, Ordine Alphabetico de Virtutib. & Vitijs. Bologna: 1580. V. 40

RODWELL, C. HERBERT

The Memoirs of An Umbrella. By C. Herbert Rodwell. Illustrated with 68 Engravings by landells from Designs by Phiz. London: 1850. V. 37

RODWELL, JAMES

Queen Cora; or Slavery and Its Downfall. London: 1856. V. 37

The Rat: it's History and Destructive Character, with Numerous Anecdotes. 1860. V. 46

ROE, C. H.

Historical Record of the 2nd 'Queen Victoria's Own' Sappers and Miners. From 1780 to 1910. From 1910 to 1914. Bangalore: 1921. V. 42

ROE, CHARLES F.

Custer's Last Battle. New York: 1927. V. 45

ROE, F. CORDON

Cox the Master The Life and Art of David Cox 1783-1859. Leigh on Sea: 1946. V. 43

ROE, F. G.

Sea Painters of Britian from Van de Velde to Turner (and) From Constable to Brangwyn. Leigh-on-Sea: 1947-48. V. 39

ROE, FRANCIS M., MRS.

Army Letters from an Officer's Wife. New York: 1909. V. 37; 44; 46

ROE, FRANK GILBERT

The North American Buffalo: A Critical Study of the Species in Its Wild State. Toronto: 1951. V. 40

ROE, JOHN

The Deformity Termed 'Pug-Nose' and Its Correction, By a Simple Operation, 1887. 1887. V. 42

Pickwickian Quadrilles. London: 1840? V. 40

ROE, NORMAN

Sonnets of Old Things and Other Verses. Liverpool: 1919. V. 43

ROE, THOMAS

A Discourse Upon the Reasons of the Resolution in the Valte-Line Against the Tyranny of the grisons and Heretiques to the Most Mighty Catholique King of Spaine, D. Phillip the Third. London: 1628. V. 40

Sir Thomas Rowe His Speech at the Councell-Table Touching Brasse Money, or Against Brasse Money; with many notable Observations thereupon, Iuly 1640. London: 1641. V. 38

Sir Thomas Rowe's Speech at the Councel Table about the alteration of the Coyn, in July 1640. With Some Observations thereon. London: 1695. V. 38

A Speech Delivered in Parliament by a Person of Honour, Wherein is Shewn the Cause and Cure of the Decay of Trade and Merchandise. London: 1739. V. 42

ROEBLING, JOHN A.

Long and Short Span Railway Bridges. New York: 1869. V. 39

ROEBUCK, JOHN A.

The Colonies of England: a Plan for the Government of Some Portion of Our Colonial Possessions. London: 1849. V. 46

ROELANDS, DAVID

Magazin Oft Pac-Huys der Loffelycker Penn-Const . . . 1617. V. 43

ROEMER, FERDINAND

Die Kreiderbildungen von Texas und Ihre Organischen Einschlusse. Bonn: 1852. V. 37

Texas, Mit Besonder Rucksicht auf Deutsche Auswanderung. Bonn: 1849. V. 41; 43; 45

Texas, with Particular Reference to German Immigration and the Physical Appearance of the Country, Described through Personal Observation. San Antonio: 1935. V. 37; 40; 41; 44

ROENIGK, ADOLPH

Pioneer History of Kansas. N.P.: 1933. V. 37

ROENTGEN, WILHELM

Eine Neue Art Von Strahlen. Wurzburg: 1896. V. 41; 44; 45; 46

Ueber Eine Neue Art Von Strahlen. Wurzburg: 1895. V. 45

ROERGAS DE SERVIEZ, JACQUES

The Lives and Amours of the Empresses, Consorts to the First Twelve Caesars of Rome . . . London: 1723. V. 44

ROESCH, KURT

Sprig and Turfy. New York: 1938. V. 39

ROESLER, HUGO

Atlas of Cardio-Roentgenology. Springfield: 1940. V. 42

ROESSLIN, EUCHARIUS d. 1526

The Birth of Mankynde, Otherwyse Named the Womans Booke. London: 1565. V. 42

The Birth of Man-Kinde; Otherwise Named the Womans Booke . . . London: 1626. V. 37

ROETHEL, H. K.

Catalogue Raisonne of the Oil Paintings. V. 43

Kandinsky Catalogue Raisonne of the Oil Paintings. V. 42

ROETHEL, HANS KONRAD

Kandinsky: Das Graphische Werk. Cologne: 1970. V. 44

Kandinsky Catalogue Raisonne of the Oil Paintings. London: 1982. V. 41; 44

ROETHER, SUSAN

Reflections on Color. San Francisco: 1982. V. 39

ROETHKE, THEODORE

The Collected Poems of . . . London: 1968. V. 39

The Exorcism. N.P.. V. 39

The Exorcism. San Francisco: 1957. V. 46

The Lost Son and Other Poems. Garden City: 1946. V. 39

Lost Son and Other Poems. Garden City: 1948. V. 38; 40; 43

The Lost Son and Other Poems. London: 1949. V. 40; 43

Open House. New York: 1941. V. 37; 38; 39; 40; 42; 43; 46

Praise to the End! Garden City: 1951. V. 40

The Waking. Poems 1933-1953. 1953. V. 39

The Waking. Poems: 1933-1953. New York: 1953. V. 45

Words for the Wind. London: 1957. V. 39; 41; 43; 44; 46

Words for the Wind. New York: 1958. V. 41; 42; 43; 44; 46

ROETHLISBERGER, M.

Claude Lorrain. The Drawings. Berkeley: 1968. V. 46

ROFFIGNAC, J.

Memorial of the Mayor, Aldermen and Inhabitants of New Orleans. Washington: 1828. V. 37; 39

ROGANUS, LEO

In Galeni Libellum de Pulsibus ad Tyrones Commenatarius. Neapoli: 1556. V. 42

ROGER, EUGENE

*La Terre Sainte, ou Description Topographique Tresparticuliere des Saints Lieux, * de la Terre de Promission.* Paris: 1664. V. 37

ROGER-MARX, CLAUDE

Bonnard Lithographe. Monte Carlo: 1952. V. 41; 42

L'Oeuvre Grave de Vuillard. Monte Carlo: 1948. V. 46

Yvette Guilbert, vue par Toulouse-Lautrec. Paris: 1950. V. 41

ROGER OF WENDOVER

Rogeri de Wendover Chronica . . . London: 1841-44. V. 44

ROGER WILLIAMS BANK, PROVIDENCE.

The Charter of the Roger Williams Bank, in Providence. Providence: 1803. V. 39

ROGERS, A. N.

Communication Relative to the Location of the U. P. R. R. Across the Rocky Mountains Through Colorado Territory. Central City: 1867. V. 37; 38; 41; 42; 45

ROGERS, ALBERT G. MRS.

A Winter in Algeria. London: 1865. V. 37

ROGERS, AMMI

Memoirs of . . . Clergyman of the Episcopal Church . . . Persecuted in the State of Connecticut . . . and Finally Falsely Accused and Imprisoned. Schenectady: 1826. V. 46

Memoirs of the Rev. Ammi Rogers, A. M., A Clergyman of the Episcopal Church . . . Johnstown: 1837. V. 40

ROGERS, ARTEMAS

Trial of Daniel Davis Farmer, for the Murder of the Widow Anna Ayer, at Goffstown on the 4th of April 1821. Concord: 1821. V. 44

ROGERS, BRUCE

An Account of the Making of the Oxford Lectern Bible. London: 1936. V. 43

Bruce Rogers, Selected Letters: 1915-1918. 1988. V. 43

Bruce Rogers Selected Letters, 1915-1918. N.P.: 1988. V. 40

The Centaur Types. Chicago: 1949. V. 45

The Last Letter: a Story of the Museum Press. 1975. V. 43

The Last Letter: a Story of the Museum Press. 1975. V. 41

The Last Letter: A Story of the Museum Press. 1975. V. 37

Of the Just Shaping of Letters. New York: 1917. V. 42

Paragraphs on Printing. New York: 1943. V. 37; 38; 39; 41; 43; 44; 45

Report on the Typography of the Cambridge University Press. 1950. V. 46

Report on the Typography of the Cambridge University Press Prepared in 1917 at the Request of the Syndics by Bruce Rogers . . . 1950. V. 38

Report on the Typography of the Cambridge University Press. Cambridge: 1950. V. 38; 39; 40; 41; 42; 45

Typographical Partnership: Ten Letters Between Bruce Rogers and Emery Walker, 1907-31. Cambridge: 1971. V. 45

Typographical Partnership; Ten Letters Between Bruce Rogers and Emery Walker, 1907-31, Together with an Unpublished Fragment of Bruce Rogers' 'Bye Ways of Bookmaking.' New York: 1971. V. 38; 41

The Work of Bruce Rogers. New York: 1939. V. 40

The Work of Bruce Rogers: A Catalogue. 1939. V. 39

The Works of Bruce Rogers - a Definitive Catalog. New York: 1939. V. 39

ROGERS, CHARLES

Catalogue of the Capital and Extensive Collection of Prints and Books of Prints, of Charles Rogers, Esq. F.R.S.S.A. deceased . . . Which Will Be Sold by Auction Under the Direction of Mr. Thomas Philipe . . . Monday, the 18th of March, 1799 and Twenty . . . London: 1799. V. 46

Ottawa Past and Present, or a Brief Account of the First Opening Up of the Ottawa Country and Incidents in Connection with the Rise and Progress of Ottawa City, and Parts Adjacent Thereto. Ottawa: 1871. V. 40

ROGERS, DAVID B.

Prehistoric man of the Santa Barbara Coast . . . Santa Barbara: 1929. V. 46

ROGERS, EBENEZER

A Modern Sphinx. N.P.: 1895. V. 37

ROGERS, EDWARD

A Catalogue of a Capital Collection of Valuable Pictures by Much Esteemed Masters . . . also a Collection of Prints, Drawings and Books of Prints . . . Liverpool: 1797. V. 38; 40

A Record of the City of Armagh, from the Earliest Period to the Present Time . . . Armagh: 1861. V. 38

ROGERS, FAIRMAN

A Manual of Coaching. London: 1900. V. 37; 39; 40; 42

A Manual of Coaching. New York: 1900. V. 44

ROGERS, FRANCIS M.

List of Editions of the Libro del Infante Don Pedro de Portugal. Lisbon: 1959. V. 42

ROGERS, FRED B.

Soldiers of the Overland. San Francisco: 1938. V. 38; 39; 40; 42; 45

ROGERS, HESTER ANN

Short Account of the Experience of mrs. Hester Ann Rogers . . . New York: 1813. V. 40

ROGERS, J.

Modern English Furniture. London: 1930. V. 37

ROGERS, J. E.

Ridicula Rediviva. London: 1869. V. 39; 44

ROGERS, J. SMYTH

Catalogue of a Cabinet of Materia Medica. New York: 1826. V. 43

ROGERS, JAMES EDWIN THOROLD 1823-1890

Education in Oxford: Its Method, Its Aids and Its Rewards. London: 1861. V. 45

The First Nine Years of the Bank of England. Oxford: 1887. V. 39

A History of Agriculture and Prices in England. Oxford: 1866-87. V. 41

The Industrial and Commercial History of England. London: 1892. V. 41

Six Centuries of Work and Wages. London: 1884. V. 37; 38; 39; 46

ROGERS, JASPER W.

Facts for the Kind-Hearted of England! As to the Wretchedness of the Irish Peasantry, and the Means for Their Regeneration . . . 1847. (with) The Potato Truck System of Ireland . . . London: 1847. V. 44

ROGERS, JOHN

A Mid-Night Cry from the Temple of God to the Ten Virgins Slumbering and Sleeping. New London: 1722. V. 38; 40

Rogers Groups: Thought and Wrought by John Rogers. Boston: 1934. V. 37; 39

ROGERS, JOHN WILLIAM

Finding Literature on the Texas Plains. Dallas: 1931. V. 42; 44

ROGERS, JUSTUS H.

Colusa County: Its History Traced From a State of Nature through the Early Period of Settlement and Development to the Present Day. Orland: 1891. V. 39

ROGERS, MEYRIC REYNOLD 1893-

Carl Milles: An Interpretation of His Work. New Haven: 1940. V. 39; 46

Carl Milles: an Interpretation of His Work. New Haven: 1940. V. 39

ROGERS, PATRICK

The Irish Volunteers and Catholic Emancipation 1778-1793. London: 1934. V. 38

ROGERS, ROBERT

A Concise Account of North America. London: 1765. V. 37; 38; 40; 41; 42; 45

A Concise Account of North America . . . to which is Subjoined an Account of the Several Nations and Tibes (sic) Residing . . . Dublin: 1769. V. 38

Journals of Major Robert Rogers. London: 1765. V. 40; 45

Journals of Major Robert Rogers: Containing an Account of Several Excursions He Made Under the Generals Who Commanded Upon the Continent of North America During the Late War. Dublin: 1769. V. 38

Ponteach or the Savages of America, a Tragedy. Chicago: 1914. V. 37; 38; 45

ROGERS, SAMUEL

Catalogue of the . . . Works of Art the Property of Samuel Rogers, Esq., Deceased . . . London: 1856. V. 39

Fifty-Six Engravings Illustrative of Italy, a Poem. London: 1829-30. V. 39

Human Life, a Poem. London: 1819. V. 37; 39; 40

Human Life, a Poem. Cambridge: 1820. V. 42

Italy. London: 1823. V. 39; 40; 42; 43

Italy. London: 1830. V. 39; 40

italy, a Poem. (and) Poems. London: 1830-34. V. 40; 45

Italy: a Poem. London: 1836. V. 44

Italy (a Poem) & Poems. London: 1838. V. 39; 42; 45

Italy, a Poem. London: 1842. V. 42

Italy, a Poem. London: 1844. V. 42

Italy, a Poems. London: 1859. V. 40

The Pleasures of Memory . . . London: 1875. V. 45

Poems. London: 1822. V. 40; 43

Poems. London: 1834. V. 37; 39; 40; 41; 45

Poems. (with) Italy, a Poem. London: 1834-35. V. 38

Poems. London: 1838. V. 42

Poems. London: 1839. V. 39; 42

Poems. (with) Italy. London: 1839, 1840. V. 42

The Poetical Works. London: 1848. V. 46

ROGERS, SAMUEL continued

The Poetical Works. London: 1869. V. 38

Recollections of the Table-Talk of Samuel Rogers to which is added Porsonina. London: 1856. V. 38; 46

Recollections. London: 1859. V. 37

ROGERS, TIMOTHY

Early Religion; or a Discourse of the Duty and Interest of Youth. London: 1691. V. 42

ROGERS, W. H.

Records of the Cheriton Otter Hounds. Taunton: 1925. V. 42

ROGERS, W. S.

A Book of the Poster. London: 1901. V. 46

ROGERS, WOODES

A Cruising Voyage Round the World . . . London: 1712. V. 38; 43

A Cruising Voyage Round the World: First to the South Sea, Thence to the East Indies, and Homewards by the Cape of Good Hope. London: 1718. V. 42

ROGERSON, IAN

Agnes Miller Parker, Wood-Engraver and Book Illustrator, 1895-1980. 1990. V. 45

Agnes Miller Parker: Wood Engraver and Book Illustrator 1895-1980. Wakefield: 1990. V. 44; 45

ROGET, JOHN LEWIS

Outlines of Portions of the Life of Trelawny Spoon, Gent. Cambridge: 1847-48. V. 40

ROGET, PETER M.

An Introductory Lecture on Human and Comparative Physiology. London: 1826. V. 41

ROH, FRANZ

German Art in the 20th Century. Greenwich: 1968. V. 46

ROHAULT, JACQUES

System of Natural Philosophy . . . London: 1729-28. V. 45

ROHDE, ELEANOR SINCLAIR

The Old English Gardening Books. London: 1924. V. 38; 39; 40; 44

The Old English Herbals. London: 1922. V. 37; 38; 39; 40; 46

Shakespeare's Wildflowers: Fairy Lore, Gardens, Herbs, Gatherers Simples and Bee Lofe. London: 1935. V. 41

ROHLFS, ANNA KATHARINE GREEN

Marked 'Personal'. New York: 1893. V. 45

ROHMER, SAX

The Bat Flies flow. 1935. V. 46

The Bat Flies Low. 1935. V. 44

Bim-Bash Baruk. 1944. V. 44

Bim-Bash Baruk. 1944. V. 46

The Book of Fu-Manchu. 1930. V. 43

Brood of the Witch - Queen. 1924. V. 43

Daughter of Fu Manchu. New York: 1931. V. 43

The Insidious Dr. Fu Manchu. New York: 1913. V. 42

The Mask of Fu Manchu. Garden City: 1932. V. 45; 46

Seven Sins. New York: 1943. V. 40

She Who Sleeps. Garden City: 1928. V. 37

The Sins of Several Bablon. London: 1914. V. 46

Tales of East and West. Garden City: 1933. V. 46

The Yellow Claw. New York: 1915. V. 43; 44; 46

ROHR, JULIUS BERNARD

Einleitung zur Ceremoniel Wissenschafft der . . . Herren . . . Berlin: 1729. V. 38

ROIAS, J. DE

Commentariorum in Astrolabium Quod Planisphaerium vocant, Libri Sex Nunc Primum in Lucem Editi. Paris: 1550. V. 45

ROIRK, DONATUS

Hibernia Resvrgens. Sive Refrigerium Antidotale. Rouen: 1621. V. 44

ROISECCO, GREGORIO

Roma Antica, e Moderna o Sia Nuova Descrizone di Tutti gl' Edifici Antichi, e Moderni, Tanto Sangri, Quanto Profani Della Citta' di Roma . . . Rome: 1750. V. 43; 46

ROKEBY, MATTHEW ROBINSON MORRIS, 2ND BARON 1713-1780

Considerations on the Measures Carrying on with Respect to the British Colonies in North America. London: 1774. V. 39; 42

A Further Examination of Our Present American Measures and of the Reasons and the Principles on Which they are Founded. Bath: 1776. V. 44

ROKEBY, MORRIS ROBINSON-MORRIS, 3RD BARON

An Essay on Bank-Tokens, Bullion &c. 1811. V. 38

ROKITANSKY, CARL

A Manual of Pathological Anatomy. London: 1854. V. 37; 41; 44

A Manual of Pathological Anatomy. Philadelphia: 1855. V. 37; 42

ROKITANSKY, CARL VON

A Manual of Pathology Anatomy. London: 1849-54. V. 46

ROLAND DE LA PATIERE, MARIE JEANNE PHILIPON

An Appeal to Impartial Posterity . . . or, a Collection of Tracts. London: 1796. V. 37; 38; 39

ROLAND, GEORGE

An Introductory Course of Fencing. Edinburgh: 1840? V. 40; 42; 43

An Introductory Coure of Fencing. Edinburgh: 1837. V. 38

A Treatise on the Theory and Practice of the Art of Fencing . . . Edinburgh: 1823. V. 39

A Treatise on the Theory and Practice of the Art of fencing . . . London: 1824. V. 46

ROLAND, JEANNE-MARIE PHILPON

Works. London: 1796-1800. V. 42; 44

ROLAND LE VIRLOYS, C. F.

Dictionnaire d'Architecture, Civile, Militaire et Navale (etc.). Paris: 1770. V. 37; 38

ROLAND, WALPOLE

Algoma West: Its Mines, Scenery and Industrial Resources . . . Toronto: 1887. V. 37; 38; 39

ROLANDO, LUIGI

Inductions Physiologiques et Pathalogiques sur les Differentes Especes d'Excitabilite et d'Excitment . . . Paris: 1822. V. 41; 44

ROLEWINCK WERNER

Fasciculus Temporum. Utrecht: 1480. V. 46

Fasciculus Temporum. Venice: 1485. V. 37; 38; 40

Fasciculus Temporum Omnes Antiquorum Cronicas Complectens. Strassburg: 1490. V. 41; 42

ROLFE, FREDERICK

Tarcissus; the Boy Martyr of Rome, in the Diocletian Persecution. Saffron Walden: 1880. V. 43

ROLFE, FREDERICK WILLIAM 1860-1913

Amici Di Sandro: a Fragment of a Novel. London: 1951. V. 41; 45

The Armed Hand and Other Stories and Pieces. London: 1974. V. 41

The Bull Against the Enemy of the Anglican Race. London: 1929. V. 40

The Cardinal Perfect of Propaganda and Other Stories. London: 1957. V. 40; 41; 43; 46

Chronicles of the House of Borgia. London: 1901. V. 41

Chronicles of the House of Borgia. London: 1901. V. 37

Collected Poems. London: 1974. V. 42

The Desire and Pursuit of the Whole. London: 1934. V. 39; 40; 41; 43; 45

Don Tarquinio. London: 1905. V. 37; 40; 41

Don Renato. London: 1963. V. 41; 42; 46

Hadrian The Seventh. London: 1904. V. 41

Hadrian the Seventh. New York: 1925. V. 44

Hubert's Arthur. London: 1935. V. 43

Hubert's Arthur. London: 1935. V. 37; 39; 40; 41; 43; 46

In His Own Image. London: 1901. V. 41; 43; 45

In His Own Image. London: & New York: 1901. V. 43

In His Own Image. London: 1924. V. 38

In His Own Image. New York: 1925. V. 39

Letters to Grant Richards. London. V. 41

Letters to Grant Richards. London: 1952. V. 45

Letters to C. H. C. Pirie Gordon . . . to Leonard Moore . . . to R. M. Dawkins. London: 1959-62. V. 40; 43

Letters to Leonard Moore. London: 1960. V. 41

The Letters of Baron Corvo to Kenneth Grahame. London: 1962. V. 42

Letters to R. M. Dawkins. London: 1962. V. 40; 43

Nicholas Crabbe or the One and the Many. London: 1958. V. 44

Nicholas Crabbe. London: 1960. V. 38; 39; 41; 43

Stories Toto Told Me. London. V. 43

Stories Toto Told Me. London and New York: 1898. V. 37; 38; 46

Tarcissus: the Boy Martyr of Rome, in the iocletian Persecution, A.D.CCCIII. Saffron Walden: 1880. V. 46

ROLFE, FREDERICK WILLIAM 1860-1913 continued

Tarcissus, The Boy Martyr of Rome, in the Diocletian Persecution, A.D. CCCIII. (wrapper title); Éssex: 1880. V. 37

Three Tales of Venice. London: 1950. V. 41

The Venice Letters. London: 1974. V. 41

The Weird of the Wanderer, Being the papyrus Records of Some Incidents In One of the Previous Lives of Mr. Nicholas Crabbe. London: 1912. V. 41

Without Prejudice: One Hundred Letters from Frederick William Rolfe (Baron Corvo) to John Lane. Kent: 1963. V. 41

'Without Prejudice.' One Hundred Letters from . . . to John Lane. London: 1963. V. 37; 38; 40; 41; 42; 44; 46

THE ROLIAD in Two Parts; Probatory Odes for the Laureatship; and Political Miscellanies: with Criticisms and Illustrations. London: 1795. V. 46

ROLLE, HENRY

Les Reports de Henry Rolle Serjent del' Ley, De Divers Cases en le Court del' Banke le Roy. London: 1675. V. 38

Un Abridgment des Plusieurs Cases et Resolutions del Common Ley; Alphabeticalment Digest Desouth Severall Titles. London: 1668. V. 39

ROLLENHAGEN, GABRIEL

Vier Buecher Wunderbarlicher bisz Daher Unerhoerter und Unglaublicher Indianischer Reisen . . . 1614. V. 41

ROLLENHAGEN, GEORG

Froschmeuseler. Duncker: 1600. V. 39

Froschmeuseler Der Froesch und Meuse Wunderbare Hoffhaltunge. Magdeburgk: 1600. V. 41

ROLLER Rink Attractions. Chicago: 1937. V. 44

ROLLER Skating Made Easy. Portland: 1884. V. 44

ROLLESTON, C. W.

Parsifal. With acknowledgement to the 'Parsifal' of Richard Wagner by C.W. Rolleston. London: (n.d.). V. 37

ROLLESTON, HUMPHRY

Cardio-Vascular Diseases Since Harvey's Discovery. Cambridge: 1928. V. 45

ROLLESTON, T. W.

Parsifal or the Legend of the Holy Grail. London: 1912. V. 40; 43; 44

Parsifal; or the Legend of the Holy Grail retold from Antient Sources with acknowledgement to the 'Parsifal' of Richard Wagner, by T.W. Rolleston. Presented by Willy Pogany. New York: (1912). V. 37; 43

The Tale of Lohengrin, Knight of the Swan . . . London. V. 40

The Tale of Lohengrin. London: 1913. V. 42; 43

The Tale of Lohengrin. Crowell, New York: 1913. V. 37

Tannhauser, a Dramatic Poem. London: 1911. V. 40; 43

ROLLI, PAOLO

Aristodemo Tiranno di Cuma. London: 1744. V. 40

ROLLI, PAOLO ANTONIO

Di Anzonette e di Cantae Libri due. Londra: 1727. V. 44

ROLLIN, CHARLES

The Ancient History of the Egyptians, Carthaginians, Assyrians, Babylonians, Medes and Persians, Macedonians and Grecians. London: 1734-39. V. 41

The Ancient History of the Egyptians, Carthaginians, Assyrians, Babylonians, Medes, and Persians, Macedonians and Grecians. Boston: 1823. V. 40

The Method of Teaching and Studying the Belles Lettres; or, an Introdcution to Languages, Poetry, Rhetoric, History, Moral Philosophy . . . London: 1810. V. 41

New Thoughts Concerning Education. London. V. 46

New Thoughts Concerning Education. London: 1735. V. 42

Taste, an Essay. London: 1732. V. 44

ROLLIN, M.

The Method of Teaching and Studying the Belles Lettres . . . London: 1734. V. 46

ROLLINS, ALICE W.

From Palm to Glacier with an Interlude. New York & London: 1892. V. 39

ROLLINS, CARL PURINGTON

A Leaf from the Kelmscott Chaucer. New York: 1941. V. 43

ROLLINS, HYDER E.

The Keats Circle: Letters and Papers. (1816-1878. Incorporating) More Letters and Poems of the Keats Circle. Cambridge: 1965. V. 46

ROLLINS, PHILIP ASHTON

Gone Haywire. New York: 1939. V. 39

ROLLINS, PHILLIP ASHTON

Jinglebob. 1930. V. 46

ROLLINSON, JOHN K.

Pony Trails in Wyoming, Hoofprints of a Cowboy and the U.S. Ranger. Caldwell: 1941. V. 45

Wyoming Cattle Trails, History of the Migration of Oregon Raised Herds to Mid Western Markets. Caldwell: 1948. V. 37; 42; 43

ROLLO, JOHN

Observations on the Diseases which appeared in the Army on St. Lucia, in 1778 and 1779. To which are prefixed, Remarks calculated to assist in ascertaining the causes, and in explaining the treatment . . . London: 1781. V. 37

ROLLOCK, ROBERT 1555?-1599

In Epistolam Pavli Apostoli Ad Ephesios. Edinbvrgi: 1590. V. 37; 38

In Epistolam Pavli Apostoli ad Thessalonicenses, Priorem (et secundam) Commentarius. Edinbvrgi: 1598. V. 38

In Librvm Danielis Prophetae. Edinbvrgi: 1591. V. 38

Lectures Upon the Epistle of Paul to the Colossians. London: 1603. V. 41

Tractatus de Vocatione Efficaci. Edinburgh: 1597. V. 38

ROLLS, HENRY, MRS.

The Home of Love, A Poem. London: 1817. V. 41; 42

Legends of the North, or, the Feudal Christmas; a Poem. London: 1825. V. 42

ROLLS, S. C.

Steel Chariots in the Desert - the Story of an Armoured-Car Driver with the Duke of Westminster in Libya and in Arabia with T. E. Lawrence. London: 1937. V. 46

ROLO, CHARLES

The World of Evelyn Waugh. Boston: 1958. V. 43

ROLPH, J. ALEXANDER

Dylan Thomas: A Bibliography. New York: 1956. V. 39

ROLPH, THOMAS

A Brief Account, Together with Observations Made During a Visit in the West Indies, and a Tour Through the United States of America . . . Dundas: 1836. V. 44

Emigration and Colonization: Emboodying the Results of a Mission to Great Britain and Ireland, During the Years 1839, 1840, 1841 and 1842. London: 1844. V. 38

ROLT, RICHARD

The Lives of the Principal Reformers. London: 1759. V. 38; 39; 41; 46

Memoirs of the Life of the Late Right Honourable John Lindesay, Earl of Craufourd and Lindesay . . . London: 1753. V. 41

Memoirs of the Life of the Late Right Honourable John Earl of Craufurd. London: 1769. V. 40

ROLVAAG, OLE EDVART 1876-1931

Giants in the Earth. New York: 1927. V. 37; 38

Peder Victorious; a Novel. New York: 1929. V. 39

ROMA Antica e Moderna o Sia Nuova Descrizione. Rome: 1750. V. 45

ROMA Antica (Moderna) Distinta per Regioni. Rome: 1741. V. 37

ROMAIN, HENRI

Compendium Hystorical des Polices des Empires/Royaulmes et Choses Publiques. Paris: 1528. V. 40

ROMAN, ALFRED

The Military Operations of General Beauregard in the War Between the States 1861 to 1865. New York: 1884. V. 41; 46

ROMAN DE LA ROSE

The Romaunt of the Rose. London: 1974. V. 39; 46

THE ROMAN History, from the Foundations of Rome to the End of the Common-Wealth. London: 1784. V. 43

THE ROMAN Martyrologe set Forth by the Command of Pope Gregory XIII and Revived by the Authority of Urban VIII. London: 1667. V. 42

ROMAN Stories: or, the History of the Seven Wise Masters of Rome . . . Berwick: 1785. V. 45

ROMANCE of Commerce Calendar. Iowa: 1941. V. 41

THE ROMANCE Of El Camino Real with Authentic Kaloprints Attesting to the Period of Construction (1769-1830) The Period of Depletion (1835) and Partial Preservation of the Historic California Missions. Los Angeles: 1390. V. 39

THE ROMANCIST, and Novelist's Library. London: 1839-40. V. 39

ROMANES, GEORGE JOHN

Jelly-Fish, Star-Fish and Sea-Urchins Being a Research On Primitive Nervous Systems. London: 1885. V. 42

The Life and Letters of George John Romanes. London: 1896. V. 42

ROMANES, GEORGE JOHN continued

Mental Evolution in Animals. London: 1885. V. 39; 42

ROMANET, JEAN

Voyage a La Martinique. Paris: 1804. V. 37

ROMANO, DAMIANO 1708-1776

Apologia Sopra il . . . Principio Della Scienza Nuova del . . . Vico, . . . Naples: 1749. V. 46

ROMANOF, P.

Three Pairs of Silk Stockings . . . New York: 1931. V. 43

ROMANS, BERNARD

The Complete Pilot for the Gulf Passage . . . (with) The Complete Pilot for the Windward Passage . . . London: 1789, 1789. V. 37

A Concise Natural History of East and West Florida, Containing an Account of the Natural Produce of all the Southern Part of British America. New York: 1775. V. 37; 38

ROMANUS, A.

Parvum Theatrum Urbium Sive Urbium Praecipuarum Totius Orbis Brevis et Methodica Descriptio. Frankfurt: 1595. V. 39

ROMANUS, WILHELM

Epainos Siue Oratio, Vt Vocant, Commentatitia, Pro . . . Vldarico, Haerede Norvegiae . . . Leipzig: 1595. V. 40

ROMAS, JACQUES DE

Memoire . . . Suivi d'une Lettre sur l'Invention du Cerf-Volant Electrique. Bordeaux: 1776. V. 46

ROMAYNE, NICHOLAS

An Address Delivered at the Commencement of the Lectures, in the College of Physicians and Surgeons in the City of New York. New York: 1808. V. 41

ROMBAUER, IRMA S.

The Joy of Cooking. St. Louis: 1931. V. 37; 45

The Joy of Cooking. Indianapolis: 1936. V. 37; 45; 46

Streamlined Cooking. Indianapolis, New York: 1939. V. 41

ROMBERG, ANDREAS 1767-1821

The Harmony of the Spheres. Boston: 1839. V. 40

ROMBLESON'S Views of the Rhine, edited by W.G. Fearnside. 1832. V. 37

ROME. (CITY). CALCOGRAFIA NAZIONALE.

Indice Delle Stampe Intagliate in Rame a Bulino, ed in Acqua forte Esistententi Nella Calcografia Della Rev. Camera Apostolica . . . Con Nuove Aggiunte, e co' Loro Prezzi Secondo Corrono al Presente, Valutati a Moneta Romana di Scudi . . . Rome: 1776. V. 39

ROME DELISLE, JEAN BAPTISTE LOUIS

Des Caracteres Exterieurs des Mineraux ou Reponse a Cette Question. Paris: 1784. V. 38

ROME in an Uproar, and the Pope in Armour. London: 1706 and 1720. V. 41

ROME. LAWS, STATUTES, ETC.

Statuta Nobilis Artis Agriculturae Urbis Romae. Rome: 1566. V. 41

ROMEI, ANNIBALE

Discorsi . . . Divisi in Sette Giornate Nelle Quale fra Dame e Cavaglieri Regionando . . . Pavia: 1591. V. 39

ROMER, F.

The Bone Caves of Ojcow in Poland. London: 1884. V. 45

ROMERO, CARLOS OROZCO

13 Mexican Painters. Mexico: 1929. V. 44

13 Mexican Painters. Mexico: 1939. V. 39

ROMERO, JOSE MARIANO

Tablas Para los Ninos Que Empiezan a Contar. Los Angeles: 1976. V. 46

ROMEYN DE HOOGHE

To the Burgermasters of Haarlem. Northampton: 1971. V. 37; 42; 44

ROMILLY, SAMUEL 1757-1818

Memoirs of the Life Written by Himself with a Selection from His Correspondence. London: 1840. V. 37; 38; 41

The Speeches of Sir Samuel Romilly in the House of Commons. London: 1820. V. 38; 45

ROMNALL, THOMAS

A Treatise of Specters. London: 1658. V. 39

ROMNEY, GEORGE

Catalogue of the Select and Reserved Collection of Paintings . . . London: 1807. V. 38; 40

ROMNEY, HUGH

Song of Alive and Other Poems. N.P.: 1959? V. 45

ROMNEY, THOMAS C.

The Mormon Colonies in Mexico. Salt Lake City: 1938. V. 42

ROMSPERT, GEORGE W.

The Western Echo. Dayton: 1881. V. 37

RONALD, MARY

The Century Book with a New Supplement of One Hundred Receipts of Especial Excellence. New York: 1920. V. 39

RONALDS, ALFRED

Companion (Wallet) to Alfred Ronalds' Fly Fisher's Entomology. London: n.d. V. 39

The Fly-Fisher's Entomology. London: 1836. V. 40; 41

The Fly-Fisher's Entomology. London: 1839. V. 39; 40; 41; 42

The Fly-Fisher's Entomology, Illustrated by Coloured Representations of the Natural and Artificial Insect. London: 1844. V. 42

The Fly-Fisher's Entomology. London: 1856. V. 37; 39

The Fly-Fisher's Entomolgy. London: 1883. V. 44

The Fly-Fisher's Entomology. London: 1901. V. 38; 42

The Fly-Fisher's Entomology. Liverpool: 1913. V. 40

Fly Fishers Entomology. London;: 1849. V. 37

RONALDS, HUGH

Pyrus Malus Brenfordiensis; or, a Concise Description of Selected Apples. London: 1831. V. 38; 41

RONAN, MYLES V.

The Reformation in Ireland Under Elizabeth 1558-1580; from Original Sources. London: 1930. V. 38

The Reformtion in Dublin, 1536-1558, from Original Sources. London: 1926. V. 38

RONAN, PETER

Historical Sketch of the Flathead Indian Nation from the Year 1813 to 1890. Helena: 1890. V. 40; 43; 45; 46

RONAYNE, PHILIP

A Treatise of Algebra in Two Books. London: 1727. V. 39

RONCA, ANTONIO

Modo e Regola di Fare le Colonne a Spiria. Rome: 1773. V. 38

RONCIERE, C. DE LA

La Decouverte de l'Afrique au Moyen Age. Le Caire: 1924-27. V. 44

RONDELET, GUILLAUME

Libri de Piscibus Marinis, in Quibus Verae Piscium Effigies Expressae sunt.-Universae Acquatilium Historiae pars Altera, Cum Veris Ipsorum Imaginibus. Lugduni: 1554-55. V. 39

Methodus Curandorum Omnium Morborum Corporis Humani. Lyons: 1586. V. 37; 42; 44

RONEY, FRANK

Frank Roney, Irish Rebel and California Labor Leader. An Autobiography. Edited by Ira. B. Cross. Berkeley: 1931. V. 37

RONGE, JOHANN

A Practical Guide to the English Kinder-Garten . . . London: 1878. V. 45

RONQUILLO, PEDRO

The Political Views of the Court of France Delineated. London: 1744. V. 41

RONSARD, PIERRE DE

Abrege de l'Art Poetique. London: 1903. V. 46

Abrege de l'Art Poetique. London: 1930. V. 43

Choix de Sonnets. 1902. V. 40

Choix De Sonnets. 1902. V. 39

Choix de Sonnets. 1902. V. 38

Choix de Sonnets. Hammersmith: 1902. V. 40; 43

Choix De Sonnets. London: 1902. V. 41

Livret de Folastries. Paris: 1938. V. 39

Livret de Folastries. Paris: 1940. V. 39

Les Oeuvres. Paris: 1560. V. 40

Les Oeuvres . . . Paris: 1571-73. V. 40

Les Oeuvres. Paris: 1573. V. 40

Les Oeuvres. Paris: 1578. V. 40

Les Oeuvres . . . Revues Corrigees et Augmentees par l'Auteur. Paris: 1584. V. 40; 41; 42; 43

RONSARD, PIERRE DE continued

Les Oeuvres. Paris: 1587. V. 40

Les Oeuvres. Lyon: 1592. V. 40

Les Oeuvres. Paris: 1597. V. 40

Songs and Sonnets of . . . Boston: 1903. V. 40

Songs and Sonnets. Boston & New York: 1903. V. 38; 45

RONSHEIM, MILTON

The Life of General Custer. Cadiz: 1929. V. 38; 45

ROO, GERARD DE

Annales Rerum Belli Domique ab Austriacis Habspurgicae Gentis Principibus, a Rdolpho Primo, Usque ad Carolum V Gestarum: ex Optimis Quibusque cum Typo Excusis Tum Manuscriptis, Authoribus . . . in Libris XII. Insbruck: 1592. V. 38; 40; 45

ROOIJ, NELLY DE

Reptiles of the Indo-Australian Archipelago. 1915-17. V. 38

ROOKE, HAYMAN

Descriptions and Sketches of Some Remarkable Oaks in the Park at Welbeck . . . Seat of His Grace the Duke of Portland. London: 1790. V. 43

ROOKWOOD, AMBROSE

The Arraignment, Tryal, and Condemnation of Ambrose Rookwood. For his horrid and execrable Conspiracy to Assassinate his Sacred Majesty King William, in Order to a French Invasion of this Kingdom. London: 1696. V. 37

ROOME, EDWARD

The Jovial Crew. London: 1731. V. 44

ROOME, JOHN

Laws of the Legislature of the State of New York in Force Against the Loyalists and Affecting the Trade of Great Britain, and British Merchants, and Others Having Property in that State. London: 1786. V. 40

ROOPER, GEORGE

Flood, Field and Forest. London: 1869. V. 43

Thames and Tweed. London & New York: 1870. V. 39; 41

ROORBACH, ORVILLE AUGUSTUS

Bibliotheca Americana. Catalogue of American Publications . . . 1820 to 1852. (bound with) Supplement. New York: 1852-55. V. 38; 46

ROOSES, MAX

Rubens. London: 1904. V. 40

ROOSEVELT, ELEANOR

Christmas, a Story. New York: 1940. V. 42

India and the Awakening East. New York: 1953. V. 42

On My Own. New York: 1958. V. 39; 46

This I Remember. New York: 1949. V. 37; 38; 43

ROOSEVELT, FRANKLIN DELANO

The Happy Warrier: Alfred E. Smith. New York: 1928. V. 39

Looking Forward. New York: 1933. V. 40; 42

On Our Way. New York: 1934. V. 39

Public Papers and Addresses, 1928-40. New York: 1938-41. V. 44

Whither Bound, a Lecture at Milton Academy. Boston: 1926. V. 41

ROOSEVELT, R. BARNWELL

Fish Hatching, and Fish Catching. Rochester: 1879. V. 43

ROOSEVELT, ROBERT

Game Fish of the Northern States of America, and British Provinces. New York: 1862. V. 44

The Game Fish of the Northern States of America, and British Provinces. New York: 1869. V. 44

ROOSEVELT, THEODORE 1858-1919

African Game Trails. London: 1910. V. 40; 46

African Game Trails. New York: 1910. V. 39; 43; 45

African Game Trails, an Account of the African Wanderings of an American Hunter Naturalist. London: 1926. V. 44; 45

American Big Game Hunting. Edinburgh: 1893. V. 39

American Big Game Hunting. New York: 1893. V. 37; 39; 43; 44; 46

American Ideals and Other Essays Social and Political. New York: & London: 1897. V. 45

Americanism and Preparedness. New York: 1917. V. 45

Big Game Hunting in the Rockies and on the Great Plains. New York: 1899. V. 38; 39; 40; 41; 43; 45

A Book Lover's Holiday in Open. New York: 1916. V. 46

The Conservation of Childhood. New York: 1911. V. 41

The Deer Family. New York: 1902. V. 37

The Great Adventure. New York: 1918. V. 41

Hunting Trips of a Ranchman; Sketches of a Sport on the Northern Cattle Plains. New York & London: 1855. V. 38

Hunting Trips of a Ranchman. New York: 1885. V. 38

Hunting Trips of a Ranchman; Sketches of a Sport on the Northern Cattle Plains. New York & London: 1885. V. 39

Hunting Trips of a Ranchman. Sketches of Sport on the Northern Cattle Plains. New York: 1886. V. 39; 46

Hunting in Many Lands. New York: 1893. V. 40

Hunting in Many Lands; the Book of the Boone and Crockett Club. New York: 1895. V. 44; 46

Life Histories of African Game Animals. New York: 1914. V. 39

Message of the Governor of the State of New York. Albany: 1900. V. 41; 43

Outdoor Pastimes of an American Hunter. London: 1905. V. 39; 40

Outdoor Pastimes of an American Hunter. New York: 1905. V. 39; 40; 42; 43; 45; 46

Ranch Life and the Hunting Trail. London: 1888. V. 40; 46

Ranch Life and Hunting Trail. New York: 1888. V. 37; 38; 39; 46

Ranch Life and the Hunting-Trail . . . New York: 1899. V. 37

The Rough Riders. New York: 1899. V. 40; 45

The Summer Birds of the Adirondacks in Franklin County, New York. Salem: 1877. V. 46

Through the Brazilian Wilderness. London: 1914. V. 37; 42; 43

Through the Brazilian Wilderness. New York: 1914. V. 38; 40; 41; 42; 45; 46

Trail and Campfire; the Book of the Boon and Crockett Club. New York: 1897. V. 44; 46

Trailing the Giant Panda. New York: 1929. V. 40

The Wilderness Hunter. New York: 1893. V. 41; 45

The Winning of the West. New York: 1900. V. 37; 38; 40; 41; 43; 44; 46

The Winning of the West. New York/London: 1889-1896. V. 37

The Works of . . . New York: 1906-20. V. 46

Works. New York: 1923. V. 42

The Works of Theodore Roosevelt. 1923-1926. V. 39; 46

The Works of Theodore Roosevelt. 1910. V. 37

ROOT, DAVID

Liberty of Speech and of the Press. A Thanksgiving Sermon. Delivered 26, 1835, to the Congregational Church and Society in Dover, N.H. Dover: 1835. V. 42

ROOT, EDWARD W.

Philip Hooker. A Contribution to the Study of the Renaissance in America. New York: 1929. V. 44

ROOT, FRANK A.

The Overland Stage of California. Topeka: 1901. V. 37; 40; 41; 42; 43

The Overland Stage to California . . . Columbus: 1950. V. 44

ROOT, HENRY

Henry Root, Surveyor, Engineer and Inventor. Personal History and Reminiscences. San Francisco: 1921. V. 41; 45

Personal History and Reminiscences With Personal Opinions on Contemporary Events 1845-1921. San Francisco: 1921. V. 40; 42

ROOT, RALPH RODNEY

Contourscaping. Chicago: 1941. V. 44

ROOT, RILEY

Journal of Travels from St. Josephs to Oregon, with Observations of that Country, Together with a Description of California, Its Agricultural Interests . . . Galesburg: 1850. V. 37; 38; 39

Musical Philosophy . . . Galesburg: 1866. V. 42; 46

ROPER, IDA M.

The Monumental Effigies of Gloucestershire and Bristol. Gloucester: 1931. V. 41

ROPER, MOSES

Narrative of the Adventures and Escape of Moses Roper, From American Slavery. Berwick-Upon-Tweed: 1848. V. 43

ROPER, R. S. DONNISON 1771-1823

A Treatise on the Law of Legacies. Philadelphia: 1829. V. 38; 40

ROPER, WILLIAM

Guilielmi Roperi Vita d. Thomae Morie Equitis Aurati, Lingua Anglicana Contexta. Oxford: 1716. V. 46

ROPES, HANNAH

Six Months in Kansas. Boston: 1856. V. 41; 43; 45

ROPS, FELICIEN

Das Erotische Werk. N.P.: 1905. V. 39

ROQUEFEUIL, C. DE

A Voyage Round the World Between the Years 1816-1819. London: 1823. V. 39

ROQUES, JOSEPH

Histoire des Champignons Comestibles et Veneneux . . . Paris: 1832. V. 38; 45

ROQUET, ANTOINE E.

Le Relieurs Francais (1500-1800). Biographie Critique et Ancedotique . . . Paris: 1893. V. 44

ROREM, NED

Paul's Blues. New York: 1984. V. 39; 42

RORIE, DAVID

A Medico's Luck in the War. Aberdeen: 1929. V. 46

RORTY, JAMES

What Michael Said to the Cenus-Taker. San Fransisco: 1922. V. 38

ROS, AMANDA M.

Donald Dudley The Bastard Critic. London: 1954. V. 39
Fumes of Formation. Belfast: 1933. V. 39

ROS, AMANDA MC KITTRICK

Irene Iddesleigh, a Novel. London: 1926. V. 40
Irene Iddesleigh. Belfast: 1897. V. 37; 39; 40; 41
A Little Belgian Orphan. London: 1916. V. 42

ROSA Bonheur's Horse Fair. N.P.. V. 46

ROSA, SALVATORE

The Life and Times of Salvator Rosa. London: 1824. V. 46
Satire . . . con le Notte d Anton Maria Sal. Londra: 1787. V. 46

ROSA, THOMAS

Idaea, Sive de Iacobi Magnae Britanniae, Galliae et Hyberniae, Praestantissimi & Augustissimi Regis . . . Londini: 1608. V. 41; 46

ROSACCIO, GIOSEPPE

Il Medico del Dottore in Filosofia, et Medicina & Osservatore de' Motti Celesti Gioseppe Rosaccio. Venetia: 1621. V. 39

ROSACCIO, GIUSEPPI

Treatro Del Cielo, e Della Terra. Bologna: 1620. V. 45

ROSALES, VICENTE PEREZ

California Adventure. San Francisco: 1947. V. 38; 40; 41; 46

ROSAMUND, Countess of Clarenstein. London: 1812. V. 39

ROSCHER, WILHELM 1817-1894

Principles of Political Economy . . . New York: 1878. V. 43

ROSCIUS in London. Biographical Memoirs of William Hen. West Betty, from the Earliest Period of His Infancy. London: 1805. V. 39

ROSCIUS, JULIUS

Triumphus Martyrum . . . Rome: 1589. V. 38; 39

ROSCOE, HENRY

Radioactive Substances and Their Radiations. Cambridge: 1913. V. 38
Westminster Hall; or Professional Relics and Anecdotes of the Bar Bench and Woolsack. London: 1825. V. 38

ROSCOE, MARGARET LACE

Floral Illustrations of the Seasons . . . London: 1829-31. V. 38

ROSCOE, MR.

The Butterfly's Ball and the Grasshopper's Feast. London: 1816. V. 45

ROSCOE, ROBERT

Chevy Chase, a Poem Founded on the Ancient Ballad. London: 1813. V. 42

ROSCOE, THOMAS

The Book of Grand Junction Railway . . . London: 1839. V. 41
German Novelists: Tales Selected from Ancient and Modern Authors . . . to the Close of the Eighteenth Century. London: 1826. V. 42
The German Novelists. (with) The Italian Novelists. (with) The Spanish Novelists. London: 1826-32. V. 38
Italian Tales: Tales of Humour, Gallantry, and Romance . . . London: 1824. V. 45
The Italian Novelists. London: 1825. V. 37; 40; 44
The London and Birmingham Railway . . . London: 1839. V. 39; 43; 46
The London and Birmingham Railway . . . London: 1839? V. 45
Memoirs of Scipio de Ricci, Late Bishop of Pistoia and Praato, Reformer of Catholicism in Tuscany Under the Reigh of Leopold. London: 1829. V. 38

The Pleasant History of Reynard the Fox. London: 1873. V. 45
Rambles in France and Switzerland. London. V. 46
Roscoe's Novelist's Library. London: 1831-32. V. 46
Summer Tour in the Isle of Wight . . . London: 1843. V. 44
Summer Tour in the Isle of Wight . . . . London: 1843. V. 44
The Tourist in Switzerland and Italy. London: 1830. V. 37; 39; 42; 44
The Tourist in Switzerland and Italy. London: 1830-39. V. 39
The Tourist in Italy. London: 1831. V. 44; 45; 46
The Tourist in Spain. London: 1835. V. 45
The Tourist in Spain . . . London: 1836. V. 41
The Tourist in Switzerland. London: 1830. V. 46
Wanderings and Excursions in South Wales; Including the Scenery of the River Wye. London. V. 43
Wanderings and Excursions in South Wales; Including the Scenery of the River Wye. London. V. 44
Wanderings and Excursions in South Wales . . . London. V. 39
Wanderings and Excursions in North Wales. London: 1836. V. 42; 43; 44; 46
Wanderings and Excursions in North Wales. Birmingham: 1836-39. V. 39
Wanderings and Excursions in South Wales . . . London: 1837. V. 46
Wanderings and Excursions in South Wales, Including the Scenery of the River Wye. London: 1840. V. 39
Wanderings and Excursions in South Wales, with the Scenry of the River Wye. London: 1850. V. 44
Wanderings and Excursions in South Wales; Including the Scenery of the River Wye. (with) Wanderings and Excursions in North Wales. London: 1836-37. V. 37

ROSCOE, WILLIAM

A Brief Statement of the Causes Which Have Led to the Abadonment of the Celebrated System of Penitentiary Discipline, In Some of the United States of America. Liverpool: 1827. V. 40
Catalogue of the Very Select and Valuable Library. Liverpool: 1816. V. 38; 40; 41; 46
Catalogue of the Very Select and Valuable Library of William Roscoe, Esq. which will be sold by auction by Mr. Winstanely, at his rooms in Marble Street, Liverpool. London: 1816. V. 38
The Life of Lorenzo De' Medici, Called The Magnificent. Liverpool: 1795. V. 42
The Life of Lorenzo de' Medici. London: 1797. V. 38; 41; 46
The Life of Lorenzo de Medici, Called the Magnificent. London;: 1800. V. 39
The Life and Pontificate of Leo the Tenth. Liverpool: 1805. V. 39
The Life and Pontificate of Leo the Tenth. London: 1827. V. 39
Mount Pleasant; a Descriptive Poem. Warrington: 1777. V. 40
Poems for Youth. London: 1820. V. 45

ROSCOMMON, WENTWORTH DILLON, 4TH EARL OF

An Essay on Translated Verse. (In verse. With laudatory verses by John Dryden and others). London: 1685. V. 37
Poems . . . To Which is dded an Essay on Poetry by the Earl of Mulgrave, now Duke of Buckingham, Together with Poems by Mr. Richard Duke. London: 1711. V. 38
Poems. London: 1717. V. 37; 38; 39; 40; 42; 43; 45

ROSE, ALFRED

Register of Erotic Books. New York: 1965. V. 46

ROSE, ALGERNON SIDNEY

The Spirit of Oisin. London: 1902. V. 38; 40

ROSE, BARBARA

American Painting: the 20th Century. Skira,: 1970. V. 46
Frankenthaler. New York. V. 44
Frankenthaler. New York: 1979. V. 39; 46

THE ROSE: Being a Detection of the Pernicious Tendency of Two Libels Lately Published, viz, in the Old England Journal, and a Pamphlet Entitled, The Thistle, Together with Some Considerations for Repealing the Heretable Jurisdictons Reserved . . . London: 1747. V. 41

ROSE, COWPER

Four Years in Southern Africa. London: 1829. V. 45

ROSE, DAN

The Ancient Mines of Ajo. Ajo: 1936. V. 46

ROSE, FRANCIS

Francis Rose. New York: 1947. V. 44

ROSE, GEORGE 1744-1818

A Brief Examination into the Increase of the Revenue, Commerce and Navigation of G. B. Since the Peace . . . in 1783. London: 1792. V. 41
A Brief Examination Into the Increase of the Revenue, Commerce and Manufactures of G. B. from 1792-9. London: 1799. V. 37; 39; 41

ROSE, GEORGE 1744-1818 continued

A Brief Examination Into the Increase of the Revenue, Commerce and Navigation of G. B. During the Administration of . . . William Pitt . . . London: 1806. V. 41

Observations on the Historical Work of the Late Rt. Hon. Charles James Fox . . . London: 1809. V. 40

The Proposed System of Trade with Ireland Explained. London: 1785. V. 37; 38; 39; 42; 43; 46

The Speech in the House of Commons, on the 5th of May 1814 on the Subject of the Corn Laws. London: 1814. V. 38; 41

ROSE, GEORGE B.

Art Work of the State of Arkansas. Racine: 1905. V. 37; 38; 39; 42

ROSE, HILDA

The Stump Farm. A Chronicle of Pioneering. Boston: 1928. V. 43

ROSE Hill; a Tale of the Old Dominion. Philadelphia: 1835. V. 40

ROSE, HUGH JAMES 1795-1838

A New General Biographical Dictionary. London: 1857. V. 39

ROSE, JAMES ANDERSON

A Collection of Engraved Portraits: Catalogued and Exhibited by . . . (with) A Collection of Engraved Portraits (Further Selection) Exhibited by . . . London: 1874-94. V. 39

A Collection of Engraved Portraits Exhibited by the Late . . . London: 1894. V. 38; 41

ROSE, JOHN

The English Vineyard Vindicated, with an Address, Where the Best Plants are to Be Had at Easie Rates. London: 1672. V. 45

A Reply to a Bridge Trustee, author of a Letter to Mr. Pine in the Bristol Gazette, of October 24, Respecting 'an Impartial History of the Late Disturbances in Bristol', lately published. Bristol: 1793. V. 42

Strictures on a Pamphlet, Entitled 'An Impartial History of the Late Riots At Bristol.' . . . Bristol: 1793. V. 42

The United States Arithmetician . . . Bridgeton: 1830. V. 46

The United States' Arithmetician: or the Science of Arthmetic Simplified. Adapted to the Commerce of the United States . . . By John Rose. Bridgeton/Philadelphia: 1830. V. 37

ROSE, JOHN AUGUSTUS

An Impartial History of the Late Disturbances in Bristol . . . Bristol: 1793. V. 42

ROSE, JOHN HOLLAND

The Life of Napoleon I . . . London: 1902. V. 38

THE ROSE of Sharon. Boston: 1843-48. V. 41

THE ROSE of Sharon; a Religious Souvenir for MDCCCXLII. Boston: 1842. V. 40

ROSE, R. SELDEN

Winemaking for the Amateur. New Haven: 1930. V. 39; 40; 41; 42; 43; 44

ROSE, ROBERT H.

Sketches in Verse. Philadelphia: 1810. V. 38; 40; 45

ROSE, THOMAS

Cumberland, Its Lake and Mountain Scenery etc. London: 1860. V. 45

Picturesque Rambles in Westmorland. 1847. V. 44

Picturesque Rambles in Westmorland, Cumberland, Durham and Northumberland. London: 1847. V. 39

Westmoreland, Cumberland, Durham and Northumberland Illustrated. London: 1832. V. 41; 42; 44

Westmorland, Cumberland, Durham and Northumberland. London: 1832-35. V. 40

Westmorland, Cumberland, Durham and Northumberland. London: 1833. V. 38

ROSE, VICTOR

M. Ross' Texas Brigade, Being a Narrative of Events Connected With Its Service in the Late War Between the States. Louisville: 1881. V. 38; 44; 45

ROSE, VICTOR M.

Some Historical Facts in Regard to the Settlement of Victoria, Texas; Its Progress and Present Status. Laredo: 1883. V. 37

ROSE, WILLIAM

The Surgical Treatment of Neuralagia of the Fifth Nerve. London: 1892. V. 41; 44; 45; 46

ROSE, WILLIAM STEWART 1775-1843

Letters from the North of Italy, Addressed to Henry Hallam. London: 1819. V. 38; 39; 42

ROSEFIELD, MRS.

The Domestic Economist and Family Physician. New York: 1855. V. 45

ROSELLINI, IPPOLITO 1800-1843

Elementa Linguae Aegyptiacae Vulgo Copticae . . . Rome: 1837. V. 46

ROSELLIS, ANTONIUS DE

Tractatus de Potestate Imperatoris: ac Pape . . . Et de Materia . . . 1487. V. 42

ROSELLIUS, COSMAS

Thesaurus Artificiosae memoriae. Venice: 1579. V. 38

ROSEMAY Lodge; or, Domestic Vicissitudes. London: 1823. V. 42
ROSEMAY Lodge; or, Domestic Vicissitudes. London: 1823. V. 40

ROSEMONDT, GODSCHALCK 1483-1526

Liber Perpotim(um) . . . Cuilibet Confessori Recte Co(n)fiteri Volenti Admodu(m) Utilis Ac Necesssari(um). Antwerp: 1518. V. 44

ROSEN, ERIC VON

Popular Account of Archaeological Research During the Swedish Chaco-Cordilera-Expedition. Stockholm: 1924. V. 42; 44

ROSEN, GEORGE

The History of Miners' Diseases, a Medical and Social Interpretation. New York: 1943. V. 37; 45

ROSEN VON ROSENSTEIN, NILS

Underraettelser Om Barn-Sjukdomar Och deras Bote-Wedel. Stockholm: 1764. V. 37; 40

ROSENBACH, ABRAHAM SIMON WOLF 1876-1952

The All Embracing Doctor Franklin. Philadelphia: 1932. V. 37; 39; 40; 42

An American Jewish Bibliography. Baltimore: 1926. V. 38; 41; 44

A Book Hunter's Holiday. Boston: 1936. V. 37; 39; 40; 42; 43; 44; 45

Books and Bidders. Boston: 1927. V. 37; 39; 41; 42

Books and Bidders. London: 1928. V. 40

The Collected Catalogues of Dr A. S. W. Rosenbach 1904-1951. New York: 1967. V. 41

Early American Children's Books. V. 43

Early American Children's Books. Portland: 1933. V. 37; 38; 39; 41; 44; 46

Early American Children's Books. New York: 1966. V. 39

An Introduction to Herman Melville's Moby Dick. New York: 1924. V. 38; 39; 41; 42

Neuverejniteline Memoary. Praze: 1925. V. 41

Samuel Johnson's Prologue. New York: 1902. V. 38; 41

The Unpublishable Memoirs. London: 1917. V. 42

The Unpublishable Memoirs. New York: 1917. V. 44; 46

ROSENBAUM, ELISABETH

A Catalogue of Cyrenaican Portrait Sculpture. London: 1960. V. 42; 44

ROSENBAUM, J. W.

Myer Myers, Goldsmith 1723-1795. Philadelphia: 1954. V. 37

ROSENBERG, C. G.

Jenny Lind in America. New York: 1851. V. 38; 39

ROSENBERG, FRANTZ

Big Game Shooting in British Columbia and Norway. London: 1928. V. 37

ROSENBERG, GIUSTINIANA WYNNE, CONTESSA DI

Alticchiero. Padua: 1787. V. 37

ROSENBERG, HAROLD

Artworks and Packages. New York: 1969. V. 44

ROSENBERG, ISAAC

Collected Works. London: 1937. V. 45

Moses a Play. London: 1916. V. 39; 40; 41; 42; 46

Poems. London: 1922. V. 37

Youth. London: 1915. V. 39; 41; 42; 44

ROSENBERG, JOHANN CARL WILHELM

Alt-Berliner Ausrufer. Leipzig: 1920's. V. 46

ROSENBERG, JUSTINA WYNNE, COMTESSE DE

Alticchiero. Padua: 1787. V. 44

ROSENBERG, LOUIS

Canada's Jews. A Social and Economic Study of the Jews in Canada. Montreal. V. 40

Canada's Jews. Montreal: 1939. V. 42

ROSENBERG, LOUIS C.

American Etchers; New York: 1930. V. 45

ROSENBERG, M. E.

The Museum of Flowers. London and Bath: 1856. V. 37

ROSENBERG, MOSES

Poems. London: 1922. V. 42

ROSENBERG-ORSINI, JUSTINE

Moral and Sentimental Essays, on Miscellaneous Subjects, Written in Retirement on the Banks of the Grenta, in the Venetian State. London: 1785. V. 46

ROSENBERG, PETER CARL JOHANN VON

Von Rosenberg Family of Texas. Boerne: 1949. V. 44

ROSENBLATT, ALBERT

The Sherlock Holmes Crossword. St. Paul: 1985. V. 40

ROSENE, WALTER

The Bobwhite Quail, Its Life and Management. New Brunswick: 1969. V. 39

ROSENFELD, PAUL

The Boy in the Sun. 1928. V. 42

Musical Chronicle (1917-1923). New York: 1923. V. 38

Port of New York: Essays on Fourteen American Moderns. New York: 1924. V. 38; 45

ROSENMUELLER, E. F. C.

Views of Interesting Places in the Holy Land. Philadephia: 1832. V. 40; 43

ROSENTHAL, JACQUES

Incunabula Typographica . . . Munich: 1900-06. V. 43; 44

ROSENTHAL, LEONARD

The Kingdom of the Pearl. 1920. V. 39

The Kingdom of the Pearl. London: 1920. V. 37; 41

The Kingdom of the Pearl. New York: 1920. V. 37; 38; 39

The Kingdom of the Pearl. London: (n.d.). V. 37

ROSENWALD, LESSING J.

Recollections of a Collector. Jenkintown: 1976. V. 37

ROSES of Sharon. 1937. V. 45

ROSES of Sharon, Poems Chosen from the Flower of Ancient Hebrew Literature. Waltham St. Lawrence: 1937. V. 40

ROSETTA STONE INSCRIPTION

Report of the Committee Appointed by the Philomathean Society of the University of Pennsylvania to Translate the Inscription on the Rosetta Stone. Philadelphia: 1858. V. 41

Report of the Committee Appointed by the Philomathean Society of the University of Pennsylvania to Translate the Inscription on the Rosetta Stone. Philadelphia: 1859. V. 39; 41; 43

ROSETTI, DOMENICO

Il Sepolcro di Winckelmann in Trieste. Venezia: 1823. V. 44

ROSEVEARE, HENRY

Markets and Merchants of the Late Seventeenth Century. The Marescoe-David Letters 1668-1680. London: 1987. V. 41

ROSEY, GUY

Drapeau Negre. Tout un Poeme. Paris: 1933. V. 42

ROSICKY, ROSE

History of Czechs (Bohemians) in Nebraska. Omaha: 1929. V. 46

ROSINI, JOHANNIS

Romanarum Antiquitatum Corpus Absolutis Simum Cum Notes Doctissimis Thomae Dempsteri I.C. et Aneis Figuris Accuratissmis. Amstelodami: 1685. V. 46

ROSINSKI, HERBERT

The German Army. London: 1939. V. 46

ROSKELL, ARTHUR H.

Six Years of a Tramp's Life in South Africa. Cape Town: 1886. V. 39; 40; 42

ROSKILL, S. W.

History of the Second World War. The War at Sea 1939-45. London: 1954-61. V. 42

The War at Sea 1930-1945. London: 1954-1961. V. 46

ROSNY, JOSEPH DE

Discours Sur l'Influence Que les Femmes ont Exerce en France sur le Gout et la Litterature, Depuis le XV Siecle Jusqu'a nos Jours. Valenciennes: 1810. V. 39

ROSNY, LEON DE

Codex Peresianus. Manuscrit Hieratique des Anciens Indiens de l'Amerique Centrale Conserve a Bibliotheque Nationale de Paris . . . Paris: 1887. V. 42

Manuscrit Hieratique des Anciens Indiens de l'Amerique Central Conserve a la Bibliotheque Nationale de Paris. Paris: 1887. V. 45

ROSS, ALEXANDER 1783-1856

Adventures of the First Settlers on the Oregon or Columbia River. London: 1849. V. 37; 39; 41; 42; 43

Adventures of the First Settlers on the Oregon or Columbia River. Cleveland: 1904. V. 38; 44

Arcana Microcosmi . . . London: 1652. V. 39; 40; 41

Fur Hunters of the Far West. London: 1855. V. 37; 39; 40; 41; 42; 43; 44; 45; 46

Mel Heliconium; or, Poeticall Honey, Gathered Out of the Weeds of Parnassus. London: 1642. V. 41

Mystagogus Poeticus, or the Muses Interpreter . . . London: 1648. V. 42

Pansebeia. London: 1653. V. 38; 40; 46

Pansebeia or, A View of All Religions in the World. London: 1675. V. 37

Panzebeia (Graece)or, A View of all Religions in the World; With the Several Church Governments . . . London: 1672. V. 42; 45

The Red River Settlement: its Rise, Progress and Present State. London: 1856. V. 37; 39; 40; 41; 42; 45

Virgilii Evangelisantis Christiados Libri XIII. London: 1638. V. 46

Virgilius Triumphans, una cum Psychomachia Virgiliana. Rotterdam: 1661. V. 37

ROSS, ANDREW

Old Scottish Regimental Colours. Edinburgh: 1885. V. 38

ROSS, C. D.

The Cartulary of Cirencester Abbey, Gloucestershire. London: 1964-77. V. 39

ROSS, C. P.

Early Day History of Wilbarger County. Vernon: 1933. V. 37

ROSS, CHARLES H.

Rummical Rhymes with Peicturs to Match Set Forth in Fayre Prospect Alphabetically. London: 1863. V. 39

ROSS, CHRISTIAN K.

The Father's Story of Charley Ross, the Kidnapped Child . . . Philadelphia: 1876. V. 45

ROSS-CRAIG, S.

Drawings of British Plants. London: 1948-74. V. 37

Drawings of British Plants. London: 1948-79. V. 37

ROSS-CRAIG, STELLA

Drawings of British Plants, Being Illustrations of the Species of Flowering Plants Growning Naturally in the British Isles. London: 1948-73. V. 39

Drawings of British Plants Being Illustrations of the Species of Flowering Plants Growing Naturally in the British Isles. London: 1979. V. 39; 45

ROSS, DAVID

The Land of the Rive Rivers and Sindh. London: 1883. V. 45

ROSS, E. C.

Annals of 'Oman. Calcutta: 1874. V. 39

ROSS, EDMUND G.

History of the Impeachment of Andrew Jackson. Santa Fe: 1896. V. 37; 42

ROSS, FREDERICK

The Ruined Abbeys of Britain. London. V. 42

The Ruined Abbeys of Britain. London. V. 40

The Ruined Abbeys of Britain. London: 1880. V. 43; 44

The Ruined Abbeys of Britain. London: 1882. V. 39; 40; 41; 43; 44; 46

Ruined Abbeys of Britain. Lonon: (1889). V. 37

ROSS, J.

A Treatise on Navigation by Steam . . . London: 1828. V. 42

ROSS, JAMES

From Wisconsin to California, and Return, as Reported from the 'Wisconsin State Journal' . . . Madison: 1869. V. 38; 42

Hobart Town Almanack and Van Diemen's Land Annual for 1836. Hobart: 1836. V. 39

Ross's Hobart Town Almanack, and Van Diemen's Land Annual for 1835. Hobart: 1835. V. 38

ROSS, JAMES CLARK

Narrative of a Second Voyage in Search of a North-West Passage, and of a Residence in the Arctic Regions During the Years 1829, 1830, 1831, 1832, 1833. London: 1835. V. 43; 45; 46

A Voyage of Discovery and Researach in the Southern and Antarctic Regions During the Years 1839-43. London: 1847. V. 37; 38; 41; 43; 45; 46

ROSS, JANET

Florentine Villas. London: 1901. V. 38

Florentine Villas. New York: 1901. V. 38

Three Generations of Englishwomen. London: 1888. V. 38; 42

Three Generations of English Women: Memoirs and Correspondence of Susannah Taylor, Sarah Austin and Lady Duff Gordon. London: 1893. V. 40; 41

ROSS, JOHN 1777-1856

Appendix to the Narrative of a Second Voyage in Search of a North-West Passage. London: 1835. V. 43

An Authentic and Highly Interesting Narrative of the Perilous Voyage of Capt. Ross to Discover a North West Passage, Giving a Heart-Rending Account of the Unparalleled Hardships and Privations of Capt. Ross and His Intrepid Crew . . . London: 1830. V. 43

The Book of the Red Deer and Empire Big Game. London: 1925. V. 39

British North Borneo: an Account of the History Resources and Native Tribes. London: 1922. V. 40

Historia Regum Angliae. E. Codice MS in Bibliotheca Bodlejana Descripsit, Notisuqe & Indice Adornavit Tho. Hearnius, A.M. Oxoniensis. Oxonii: 1716. V. 38

Interesting Particulars of Captain Ross's Voyage to the North Pole. London: 1833. V. 46

Letter from John Ross, the Principal Chief of the Cherokee Nataion to a Gentleman of Philadelphia. Philadelphia: 1837. V. 38

Memoirs and Correspondence of Admiral Lord de Saumarez. London: 1838. V. 41

Narrative of a Second Voyage in Search of a North-West Passage. London: 1835. V. 40

Narrative of a Second Voyage in Search of a North-West Passage and of a Residence in the Arctic regions During the Years 1826, 1830, 1831, 1832, 1833 . . . London: 1835. V. 37; 38; 39; 40; 42; 43; 44; 45; 46

Narrative of a Second Voyage in Search of a North-West Passage, and of a Residence in the Arctic Regions, During the Years 1829, 1830, 1831, 1832, 1833. Philadelphia: 1835. V. 40

A Treatise on Navigation by Steam. London: 1828. V. 38

A Voyage of Discovery Made Under the Orders of Admiralty, in His Majesty's Ships, Isabella and Alexander, for the Purpose of Exploring Baffin's Bay and Inquiring into the Probability of a North West Passage. London: 1819. V. 37; 38; 40; 41; 42; 43; 46

ROSS, JOHNNY

The Biggin Hill Frescoes. 1975. V. 45

ROSS, LILLIAN

Big Sur. Paris: 1949. V. 44

ROSS, LT. COL.

A History of the Coldstream Guards from 1815 to 1895. London: 1896. V. 37

ROSS, MARVIN C.

The Art of Karl Faberge and His Contemporaries . . . Norman: 1965. V. 44

Russian Porcelains . . . The Collections of Marjorie Merriweather Post, Hillwood, Washington, D.C. Norman: 1968. V. 40; 45

ROSS, MRS.

The Bachelor and the Married Man, or the Equilibrium of the 'Balance of Comfort.' London: 1817. V. 38; 46

The Balance of Comfort; or the Old Maid and the Married Woman. London: 1817. V. 37; 41; 46

ROSS, PETER

A History of Long Island From Its Earliest Settlement to the Present Time. New York: 1903. V. 46

ROSS, ROBERT

The American Latin Grammar; or a Compleat Introduction to the Latin Tongue. Providence: 1780. V. 41

The American Latin Grammar; or, a Complete Introduction to the Latin Tongue . . . Newburyport: 1780? V. 45

Aubrey Beardsley. London: 1909. V. 40; 41; 43

Forty-Three Drawings. With a Note of Exclamation by Robert Ross. London: 1914. V. 37

ROSS, VICTOR

A History of the Canadian Bank of Commerce . . . Toronto: 1920. V. 44

The History of the Canadian Bank of Commerce, with an Account of the Other Banks Which Now Form Part of the Organization. Toronto: 1920-34. V. 37; 42; 43

ROSS, VICTOR M.

Ross' Texas Brigade, Being a Narrative of Events Connected with Its Service in the Latae War Between the States. Louisville: 1881. V. 38

ROSS, WALTER

Lectures on the History and Practice of the Law of Scotland, Relative to Conveyancing and Legal Diligence. (with) A Discourse on the Removing of Tenants; Edinburgh: 1822. V. 38; 40

ROSS, WILLAIM

The French Scholar's Guide. Glasgow: 1772. V. 40

ROSS, WILLIAM P.

Indian Territory. Remarks in Opposition to the Bill to Organize the Territory of Oklahoma. Washington: 1874. V. 39; 42; 45

ROSS, WILLIAM P., MRS.

The Life and Times of Hon. William P. Ross. Ft. Smith: 1893. V. 37; 38; 39; 40

ROSS, WILLIAM POTTER, MRS.

The Life and Times of Hon. William P. Ross. Fort Smith. V. 45

ROSSE, ALEXANDER

Mel Heliconium: or, Poeticall Honey, Gathered Out of the Weeds of Parnassus. London: 1642. V. 42

ROSSE, HERMAN

Designs and Impressions. Chicago: (1920). V. 37

ROSSE, WILLIAM PARSONS, 3RD EARL OF

The Scientific Papers, Collected and Republished by the Hon. Sir Charles Parsons. London: 1926. V. 45

ROSSELLI, TIMOTEO

Della Summa de' Secreti Universali in Ogni Materia. Venice: 1565. V. 46

Della Summa de I Secreti Universali in Ogni Materia. Venice: 1619. V. 46

ROSSELLIUS, COSMAS

Thesaurus Artificiosae Memoriae . . . Venice: 1579. V. 37

ROSSER, W. H.

The Navigation of the Three Oceans, The Atlantic, Indian and Pacific Including the China Sea. London: 1876. V. 42

ROSSER, WILLIAM HENRY

Sailing Directions for the South Part of Japan and the Islands to the Southward. London: 1871. V. 40

ROSSET, PIERRE FULCRAND DE

L'Agriculture. Poeme. Paris: 1774/82. V. 46

ROSSETTI, CHRISTINA 1830-1894

Commonplace and Other Short Stories. London: 1870. V. 40; 44

Goblin Market and Other Poems. Cambridge & London: 1862. V. 40; 41; 42

Goblin Market and Other Poems. London: 1862. V. 45

Goblin Market and Other Prose. Boston: 1866. V. 38

Goblin Market. London: 1893. V. 37; 38; 40; 41; 42; 44; 46

Goblin Market. Chicago: 1905. V. 38; 41; 43; 46

Goblin Market. London: 1933. V. 40; 41

Goblin Market. London: 1939. V. 44

Goblin Market. London: 1933. V. 37; 38

Letter and Spirit. London: 1883. V. 46

Maude: Prose and Verse. Chicago;: 1897. V. 42

Maude a Story for Girls. London: 1897. V. 44

New Poems. London: 1896. V. 38; 42

A Pageant and Other Poems. Boston: 1881. V. 44; 46

A Pageant and Other Poems. London: 1881. V. 37; 38; 40; 41; 42; 43; 44; 45; 46

Poems by . . . London, Glasgow & Bombay. V. 41

Poems. London: 1891. V. 44

Poems. London: 1910. V. 38

Poems by Christina Rossetti. London: 1910. V. 37; 40

Poems, Chosen by Walter de la Mare. London: 1930. V. 38; 42

Poems. Newtown: 1930. V. 40; 42; 44; 46

Poems of Christina Rossetti. London: 1923. V. 37

The Poetical Works of Christina G. Rossetti. Boston: 1902. V. 44

The Poetical Works of Christina Georgina Rossetti. London: 1904. V. 38; 39; 41

The Prince's Progress and Other Poems. London: 1866. V. 37; 40; 41; 43; 44; 45

The Prince's Progress. London: 1900. V. 41; 44

Sing Song. London: 1872. V. 44; 46

Sing-Song a Nursery Rhyme Book. London: 1893. V. 41; 43; 44; 46

ROSSETTI, CHRISTINA 1830-1894 continued

Speaking Likenesses. London: 1874. V. 37; 39; 42; 44; 46

Verses. Hammersmith: 1906. V. 37

Verses by Christina Rossetti. London: 1906. V. 43

ROSSETTI, DANTE GABRIEL 1828-1882

The Ballad of Jan Hunks. London: 1929. V. 39; 43

Ballads and Sonnets. London: 1881. V. 37; 44; 46

Ballads and Narrative Poems. Hammersmith: 1893. V. 37; 45; 46

Ballads and Narrative Poems. London: 1893. V. 41

The Blessed Damozel. New York: 1886. V. 41

The Blessed Damozel. A Poem by Dante Gabriel Rossetti. (Park Ridge: 1903). V. 37

Chimes. London: 1969. V. 40; 41; 42

Dante and His Circle, London: 1874. V. 37; 38

Dante Gabriel Rossetti His Family Letters with a Memoir. Boston: 1895. V. 39; 41

Dante Gabriel Rossetti His Family-Letters. London: 1895. V. 40

The Early Italian Poets . . . London: 1861. V. 37; 42

Hand and Soul. 1895. V. 44

Hand and Soul. Hammersmith: 1895. V. 37; 46

Hand and Soul. London: 1895. V. 41; 42

Hand and Soul. 1899. V. 38

Hand and Soul. Maastricht: 1928. V. 43; 45

Hand and Soul. Hilversum: 1929. V. 38

Henry the Leper. Boston: 1905. V. 38; 40

The House of Life. Boston: 1894. V. 37; 38; 40; 41; 43; 46

The House of Life. East Aurora: 1899. V. 39; 45

The House of Life. New Rochelle: 1901. V. 39

The House of Life. Edinburgh: 1904. V. 38; 41

The House of Life. Portland: 1908. V. 41

Letters of Dante Gabriel Rossetti to William Allingham 1854-1870. London: 1897. V. 39

The New Life. London. V. 37

Poems. London: 1870. V. 37

Poems. London: 1870. V. 40; 42; 44; 45; 46

Poems. (with) Ballads and Sonnets. London: 1870/81. V. 41; 46

Poems. Leipzig: 1873. V. 39

Poems. London: 1881. V. 41

Poems. London: 1900. V. 40; 41; 44

The Poems of . . . Troy: 1903. V. 39

The Poems of . . . London: 1904. V. 42

Sister Helen. Oxford: 1857. V. 39; 42

Rossetti's 'Sister Helen'. New Haven: 1939. V. 39

Sonnets and Lyrical Poems. Hammersmith: 1894. V. 39; 46

Sonnets and Lyrical Poems. London: 1894. V. 41

The Stone Beloved: Six Poems. Austin: 1986. V. 40

The White Ship. A Little Book of Poems. Boston: 1896. V. 41

The Collected Works. London: 1886. V. 40; 42; 43; 46

The Collected Works of Dante Gabriel Rossetti. London: 1887. V. 42

The Collected Works of . . . London: 1897. V. 37; 38; 40; 41; 43; 44; 45

The Works. London: 1911. V. 38; 39; 41

ROSSETTI, GABRIEL E. 1783-1854

Disquisitions on the Anti-Papal Spirit which Produced the Reformation; its Secret Influence on the Literature of Europe in General and of Italy in Particular. London: 1834. V. 37; 42

ROSSETTI, GABRIELE

Sullo Spirito Antipapale Che Produsse la Riforma, e Sulla Segreta Influenza ch'Esercito Nella Lettertatura d'Europa, e Specialmente d'Italia. Londra: 1832. V. 42

ROSSETTI, MARIA FRANCESCA

Aneddoti Italiani. London: 1867. V. 40

A Shadow of Dante. London: 1872. V. 46

A Shadow of Dante. London: 1894. V. 38; 40; 41

ROSSETTI, WILLIAM MICHAEL

Bibliography of the Works of Dante Gabriel Rossetti. London: 1905. V. 43

Dante Gabriel Rossetti as Designer and Writer. London: 1889. V. 39

Dante Gabriel Rossetti, His Family Letters with a Memoir. Boston: 1895. V. 37

Dante Gabriel Rossetti His Family Letters, with a Memoir. London: 1895. V. 37

Democratic Sonnets. London: 1907. V. 37

Fine Art, Chiefly Contemporary. London: 1867. V. 40

Fine Art, Chiefly Contemporary. London & Cambridge: 1867. V. 39

The Germ. London: 1850. V. 46

Life of John Keats. London: 1887. V. 44

A Memoir of Shelley. London: 1886. V. 39

Ruskin: Rossetti: Preraphaelitism. London: 1889. V. 43

Ruskin: Rossetti: Pre-Raphaelitism. Papers 1854 to 1862. London: 1899. V. 42; 43

Swinburne's Poems and Ballads. London: 1866. V. 37; 40; 41; 44; 46

ROSSI, DOMENICO DE

Studio d'Architettura Civile - Opera de Piu Celebri Architetti. Roma: 1702/11/21. V. 46

Studio d'Architettura Civile Sopra gli Ornament di Porte e Finestre Tratti da Alcune Fabgriche Insigni di Roma . . . Rome: 1702-21. V. 37; 42

ROSSI, FILIPPO

Italian Jeweled Arts. New York: 1954. V. 43; 46

Ritratto di Roma Antica. Rome: 1654. V. 38

ROSSI, FILIPPO DE

Ritratto di Roma Moderna. Rome: 1645. V. 40

ROSSI, G. B. DE

La Roma Sotterranea Christiana. Roma: 1864-77. V. 45

ROSSI, GERONIMO DE

De Destillatione Sive de Stillatitiorvm Liqvorvm. Venetiis: 1604. V. 37

ROSSI, GIAN BERNARDO DE

Iscrizione Esotiche a Caratteri Novellamente Incisi e Fusi. Colophon: 1774. V. 41

ROSSI, GIO GIACOMO DE

Disegni di Vari Altari e Capelle Nelle Chiese di Roma con Loro Facciate Fianchi Piante e Misure de Piu Celebri Architetti. Rome: 1695. V. 37

ROSSI, GIOVANNI BERN DE 1742-1831

Variae Lectiones Veteris Testamenti . . . Parma: 1784-8. V. 40

ROSSI, GIOVANNI GIACOMO

Insignum Romae Templorum. (with) Disegni di Vari Altari e Cappelle nelle Chiese di Roma. Rome: 1684. V. 42

ROSSI, GIOVANNI GIACOPO

Effigies Insignia Nomina Cognomina Patriae et Dies Promotionis ac Obitus Summorum Pontificum et S.R.E. Cardinalium Defunctorum ab anno MDCLVIII. Rome: 1691. V. 45

ROSSI, PAUL A.

The Art of the Old West; From the Gilcrease Institute. New York: 1971. V. 37

ROSSI, SALAMON

Hashirim Asher Lish'lomo. New York: 1967-73. V. 40

ROSSIG, CARL G.

Die Nelken Nach Ihren Arten, Besonders Nach der J. C. Etlers in Schneeberg und Andem Beruhmten Sammlungen, in Blattern Nach der Natur Gezeichnet und Ausgemahlt. Leipzig: 1800-08. V. 45

ROSSIO, GIOVANNI GIACOMO

Insignium Romae Templorum Prospectus Exteriores Interioresque a Celebrioribus Architectis Inventi Nunc Tandem Suis Cum Plantis Ac Mensuris A Io Iacobo de Rubeis Romano. (with) Disegni Vari Altari e Capelle nelle Chiese di Roma con le Loro Facciate . . . Rome: 1648, n.d. V. 38

ROSSLYN, ALEXANDER WEDDERBURN, 1ST EARL OF 1733-1805

Observations on the State of English Prisons, and the Means of Improving Them . . . Wakefield: 1800. V. 46

ROSSLYN, EARL OF

The Gram. London: 1901. V. 42

ROSSMAN, C.

Enchanted Rock: Views of a Texas Batholith . . . Austin: 1985. V. 41; 44; 45

ROST, JOHANN LEONHARD

Atlas Portatalis Coelestis. Nuremberg: 1723. V. 45

ROSTAND, EDMOND

L'Aiglon. New York: 1900. V. 39

Cyrano de Bergerac. Paris: 1898. V. 44; 45

ROSTEN, LEO

'Hope and Honor and High Resolve.' New York: 1961. V. 40

People I Have Loved, Known or Admired. New York: 1970. V. 45

ROSTINIO, PIETRO

Trattato di Mal Francese . . . Venice: 1623. V. 44

ROSTOVTZEFF, M.

Dura-Europos and Its Art. Oxford: 1938. V. 40

Iranians and Greeks in South Russia. Oxford: 1922. V. 40; 45

The Social and Economic History of the Hellenistic World. Oxford: 1986. V. 44

The Social and Economical History of the Hellenistic World. Oxford: 1941. V. 37

ROSTOVTZEFF, M. I.

The Excavations at Dura Europos. Preliminary Report of the Ninth Season of Work, 1935-1936. New Haven: 1944-1946. V. 37

The Social and Economic History of the Hellenistic World. Oxford: 1941. V. 39

ROTA, GIOVANNI FRANCESCO d. 1558

De Tormentariorum Pulnerum Natura, et Curatione Liber. Bologna: 1555. V. 37; 42

ROTCH, T. M.

Medical and Surgical Report of the Children's Hospital 1869-1894. Boston: 1895. V. 38

ROTCH, THOMAS

Pediatrics: the Hygienic and Medical Treatment of Children. Philadelphia: 1896. V. 42

ROTCH, WILLIAM

Memorandum Written by William Rotch in the Eightieth Year of His Age. Boston & New York: 1916. V. 41

ROTH, DIETER

Collected Works: Volume 40: Books and Graphics. Stuttgart: 1979. V. 40

96 Piccadillies. London: 1977. V. 46

ROTH, DR.

Reise Handbuch fur Auswanderer nach Nordamerika. Zurich: 1851. V. 45

ROTH, H. LING

Oriental Silverwork, Malay and Chinese. London: 1910. V. 39; 42; 44; 46

Oriental Silverwork: Malay and Chinese. Kuala Lumpur: 1966. V. 38; 41

ROTH, HENRY

Call It Sleep. 1934. V. 46

Call It Sleep. New York: 1934. V. 37; 41; 42; 46

Call It Sleep. New York: 1935. V. 37; 38; 39; 40; 42; 45

Call It Sleep. London: 1963. V. 46

Nature's First Green. New York: 1979. V. 45

ROTH, HENRY LING

The Natives of Sarawak and British North Borneo. London: 1896. V. 45

ROTH, IRVING

Cardiac Arrhythmias, Clinical Features and Mechanism of the Irregular Heart. New York: 1928. V. 42

ROTH, LOTTIE ROEDER

History of Whatcom County. Chicago, Seattle: 1926. V. 45

ROTH, M.

The Prevention and Cure of Many Chronic Diseases By Movements. London: 1851. V. 42

ROTH, PHILIP

The Anatomy Lesson. New York: 1983. V. 38

Goodbye Columbus and Five Short Stories. 1959. V. 43

Goodbye Columbus. Boston: 1959. V. 39; 42; 44; 45

Goodbye, Columbus. London: 1959. V. 37; 45

The Great American Novel. New York: 1973. V. 38

Letting Go. London: 1962. V. 46

On the Air, a Long Story. New York: 1970. V. 46

On the Air. 1970. V. 37

Our Gang (Starring Tricky and His Friends). New York: 1971. V. 40

Portnoy's Complaint. New York: 1969. V. 39; 42; 45; 46

Portnoy's Complaint. 1969. V. 37

Zuckerman Unbound. New York: 1981. V. 41

Zuckerman Bound. New York: 1985. V. 45

ROTH, SAMUEL

Stone Walls Do Not. The Chronicle of a Captivity. New York: 1930. V. 45

ROTH, WALTER E.

Ethnological Studies Among the North-West-Central Queensland Aborigines. Brisbane: 1897. V. 39; 46

ROTHA, PAUL

Celluloid - the Film Today. London: 1931. V. 41

The Film Till Now. London: 1930. V. 41

Movie Parade. London: 1936. V. 45

ROTHENBERG, JEROME

B R M TZ V H. Mt. Horeb: 1979. V. 39

A Mertz Sonata. Rosendale: 1985. V. 41; 45

A Merz Sonata. 1985. V. 39

A Merz Sonata. 1985. V. 40

A Poem to Celebrate the Spring and Diane Rothenberg's Birthday. Mt. Horeb: 1975. V. 39

Sightings I-IX and Red Easy a Colour. London: 1968. V. 39

ROTHENSTEIN, JOHN

British Artists and the War. London: 1931. V. 37; 43

Contemporary British Artists: Eric Gill. London: 1927. V. 43

Francis Bacon. London: 1964. V. 41

The Life and Death of Conder. London: 1938. V. 41

The Portrait Drawings of William Rothenstein 1889-1925. London: 1926. V. 37; 38; 40; 42; 44

Victor Hammer. Artist and Craftsman. Boston & Lexington: 1978-81. V. 44

ROTHENSTEIN, WILLIAM

Goya. London: 1900. V. 45

Men and Memories. London: 1931/32/39. V. 42

Twenty-Four Portraits. London: 1920. V. 41

Twenty-Four Portraits. First and Second Series. London: 1920 & 1923. V. 40

ROTHERAM, JOHN

An Essay on the Distinction Between the Soul and Body of Man. Newcastle-upon-Tyne: 1781. V. 42

ROTHERY, CHARLES WILLIAM

Notes on a Yacht Voyage to Hardanger Fjord, and Adjacent Estuaries. London: 1850. V. 38

Notes on a Yacht Voyage to Hardanger Fjord, and the Adjacent Estuaries . . . London: 1855. V. 43

ROTHERY, G. A.

A Diary of the Wreck of His Majesty's Ship Challenger, on the Western Coast of south America in May 1835. London: 1836. V. 46

ROTHSCHILD, FERDINAND DE, BARON

Livre d'Or. Cambridge: 1957. V. 44

ROTHSCHILD, JAMES A. DE

The James A. De Rothschild Collection at Waddesdon Manor. Fribourg: 1967-82. V. 41

ROTHSCHILD LIBRARY

The Rothschild Library. A Catalogue of the Collection of Eighteenth Century Printed Books and Manuscripts Formed by Lord Rothschild. London: 1969. V. 37

ROTHSCHILD, LORD

The History of Tom Jones, a Changeling. Cambridge: 1951. V. 37

ROTHSCHILD, MIRIAM

Fleas, Flukes and Cuckoos. London: 1952. V. 44

ROTHSCHILD, NATHANIEL MAYER VICTOR, BARON 1910-

A Catalogue of the Collection of Eighteenth Century Printed Books and Manuscripts Formed by Lord Rothschild. Cambridge: 1954. V. 40; 42

The Rothschild Library. A Catalogue of the Collection of Eighteenth Century Printed Books and Manuscripts Formed by Lord Rothschild. 1954. V. 39

The Rothschild Library, a Catalogue of the Collection of Eighteenth Century Printed Books and Manuscripts formed by Lord Rothschild. London: 1979. V. 39

ROTHSCHILD, W.

Avifauna of Laysan and the Neighboring Islands. London: 1892-1900. V. 39

The Avifauna of Laysan and the Neighbourging Islands . . . London: 1893-1900. V. 42

ROTHSCHILD, WALTER

Extinct Birds, an Attempt to Unite in One Volume a Short Account of Those Birds Which Have Become Extinct in Historical Times. London: 1907. V. 44

ROTHSTEIN, WILLIAM

Twenty-Four Portraits . . . London: 1923. V. 42

ROTHWAY, JOSEPH

Mechanical Improvements . . . Royal Navy . . . London & Davenport: 1831-30. V. 42

ROTHWELL, C. F. SEYMOUR

The Printing of Textile Fabrics. London: 1897. V. 38; 39

ROTHWELL, RICHARD P.

The Mineral Industry, Its Statistics, Technology and Trade, In the United States and Other Countries from the Earliest Times to the End of 1894. Washington. V. 41

The Mineral Industry, Its Statistics, Technolgy and Trade, In the United States and Other Countries, from the Earliest Time to the End of 1892. New York: 1893. V. 41

ROTONCHAMP, JEAN DE

Paul Gauguin 1848-1903. Paris: 1906. V. 41

ROTTIERS, BERNARD EUGENE ANTOINE 1771-1858

Description des Monumens de Rhodes. Bruxelles: 1828/30. V. 42

ROTZ, JEAN

The Maps and Text of the Boke of Idrography Presented by Jean Rotz to Henry VIII . . . 1981. V. 44

The Maps and Text of the Boke of Idrography Presented by Jean Rotz to Henry VIII Now in the British Library. Oxford: 1981. V. 43

ROUART, DENIS

Degas: Monotypes. Paris: 1948. V. 37

E. Degas: Monotypes. Paris/New York: 1948. V. 40; 43

ROUART, HENRI

Catalogue . . . Composant La Collection de Feu M. Henri Rouart e Dont la Vente . . . Paris: 1912. V. 44

ROUART, R.

Edouard Manet. Paris: 1986. V. 44

ROUAULT, GEORGES

Divertissement. Paris: 1943. V. 42

ROUGEMONT, FRANCOIS DE

Relacam do Estado Politico e Espiritual do Imperio da China, Pellos Annos de 1659, ate o de 1666. Lisbon: 1672. V. 41

THE ROUGH and Ready Songster . . . by An American Officer. New York: 1847. V. 38

ROUGH, JAMES

The Conspiracy of Gowrie, a Tragedy. London: 1800. V. 41

ROUGHTON, ROGER

Contemporary Poetry and Prose. London. V. 44

ROUGUETTE, A. E.

Critical Dialogue Between Aboo and Caboo on a New Book or a Grandissime Ascension. Mingo City: 1880. V. 43

ROUHAULT, JACQUES 1620-1673

A Treatise of Mechanicks . . . London: 1716. V. 42

ROUHAULT, PIERRE SIMON

Traite des Playes de Tete . . . Turin: 1720. V. 45

ROUILLE D'ORFEUIL, AUGUSTE

L'Ami des Francois. Constantinople: 1771. V. 41

ROUILLE, GUILLAUME 1518?-1589

La Premiere (-Seconde) Partie du Promptuaire des Medalles des Plus Renommees Personnes qui Ont Este Depuise le Commencment du Monde. Lyons: 1553. V. 40; 45

THE ROUND Guide from New York to Montreal Via the Hudson, Connecticut, Harlem, Lebanon and Vermont Valleys. New York: 1871. V. 45

A ROUND of Days Described in Original Poems by Some of Our Most Celebrated Poets. London: 1866. V. 38

A ROUND of Days Described in Original Poems by Some of Our Most Celebrated Poets and in Pictures by Eminent Artists. London: 1866. V. 38; 39

ROUNDELL, CHARLES, MRS.

Ham House. Its History and Art Treasures. London: 1904. V. 46

ROUPELL, ARABELLA E.

More Cape Flowers, by a Lady. Johannesburg: 1964. V. 44

Specimen of the Flora of South Africa. London: 1849. V. 39; 41; 43; 45; 46

ROUQUET, ANDRE

L'Art Nouveau de la Peinture en Fromage, ou en Ramequin, Inventee Pour Suivre le Louable Projet de Trouver Graduellement des Facons de Peindre . . . Paris: 1755. V. 44

ROUQUETTE, L. F.

Le Grand Silence Blanc. Paris: 1928. V. 40; 43

ROURKE, CONSTANCE

Charles Sheeler. Artist in the American Tradition. New York: 1938. V. 41; 46

ROURKE, J.

Memetes. Rondebosch: 1983. V. 37

The Proteas of Southern Africa. Cape Town: 1980. V. 39; 41

ROURKE, J. P.

Mimetes, an Illustrated Account of Mimetes Salisbury and Orothamnus Pappe, Two Notable Cape Genera of the Proteaceae. Cape Town. V. 41

Mimetes, an Illustrated Account of Mimetes Salisbury and Orothamnus Pappe . . . Cape Town: 1982. V. 42

ROUS, FRANCIS

Archaeologiae Atticae Libri Septem. Oxford: 1649. V. 39; 42

Archaeologiae Atticae Liber Septem. Oxford: 1671. V. 43

Archaeologie Atticae Libri Septem. Oxford: 1658. V. 44

ROUS, GEORGE

The Restoration of the King of Tanjore Considered. N.P.: 1777. V. 45

ROUS, HENRY JOHN

On the Laws and Practice of Horse Racing, etc., etc. London: 1866. V. 43

ROUS, THOMAS BATES

Observations on the Communtation Project. London: 1786. V. 41

ROUSE, J.

Rouse's Beauties and Antiquities of the County of Sussex . . . London: 1827. V. 38

ROUSE, T.

Poems by Miss T. Rouse of Cley. Holt: 1840. V. 41

ROUSE, W. H. D.

The Giant Crab and Other Tales from Old India. London: 1900. V. 37

ROUSE, WILLIAM

The Doctrine of Chances, or the Theory of Gaming. London: 1814. V. 37; 40; 42; 43

ROUSIERS, PAUL DE

American Life . . . New York: 1892. V. 44

ROUSO D'ERES, CHARLES DENNIS b. 1761

Memoirs of . . . a Native of Canada . . . . Exeter: 1800. V. 41

ROUSPEAU, YVES c. 1540-1601

Traitte de la Preparation a la Saincte Cene de Nostre Seul Sauveur et Redempteur Iesus Christ. La Rochelle: 1570. V. 40

ROUSSAT, RICHARD

Livre de l'Estaat et Mutation des Temps, Prouvant . . . Par Raisons Astrologales, la Fin du Monde estre Prochaine. Lyon: 1550. V. 37

ROUSSEAU, JEAN JACQUES 1712-1778

Aphorisms on Education; Selected from the Works of the Most Celebrated English, French, and Latin Writers. London: 1800. V. 43

The Confessions of J. J. Rousseau. London: 1746. V. 39

The Confessions . . . with the Reveries of the Solitary Walker. London: 1783. V. 40

The Confessions. Part the Second. To Which is Added, a New Collection of Letters from the Author. London: 1790. V. 39

Confessions . . . Philadelphia: 1902. V. 38; 42

THE CONFESSIONS of J.J. Rousseau. Anonymous English Version First Published in Two parts in 1783-1790. Revised and completed by A.S. Glover. Wood-Engravings by Reynolds Stone. London: 1938. V. 37

Discours sur l'Origine et les Fondemens de l'Inegalite Parmi Les Hommes. Amsterdam: 1755. V. 39; 41; 44; 45

A Discourse Upon the Origin and Foundation of the Inequality Among Mankind. London: 1761. V. 39

The Discourse which carried the Praemium at the Academy of Dijon, in MDCCL. London: 1751. V. 39

A Dissertation on Political Economy; To Which is Added, a Treatise on the Social Compact, or, The Principles of Political Law. Albany: 1797. V. 42

Eloisa. London: 1761. V. 37; 40

Eloisa; or, a Series of Original Letters. London: 1769. V. 41

Eloisa; or, a Series of Original Letters . . . Dublin: 1795. V. 39

Eloisa: Or, a Series of Original Letters Collected and Published by Mr. J.J. Rousseau, Citizen of Geneva. Translated from the French. A New Edition: To which is now first added . . . London;: 1784. V. 37

Emile, ou de l'Education. Amsterdam: 1762. V. 38; 40; 41

Emile, ou De l'Education. Francfort: 1762. V. 41

ROUSSEAU, JEAN JACQUES 1712-1778 continued

Emilius: or, a Treatise of Education. Edinburgh: 1763. V. 46

Emilius; or, an Essay on Education. London: 1763. V. 42; 43; 45

An Inquiry into the Nature of the Social Contract... London: 1791. V. 43

Letters on the Elements of Botany. London: 1791. V. 39; 41

The Miscellaneous Works. London: 1767. V. 41; 44

The Miscellaneous Works of Mr. J.J. Rousseau. 1767. V. 37

A Treatise on the Social Compact; or the Principles of Politic Law. London: 1764. V. 39

A Treatise on the Social Compact. London: 1795. V. 42

Oeuvres. Amsterdam: 1762-69. V. 41

ROUSSEAU, SAMUEL

The Flowers of Persian Literature. London: 1801. V. 40

ROUSSEAU, V.

The Messiah of the Cylinder. 1917. V. 44

ROUSSEL, MICHEL

L' Antimariana Ov Refvtation des Propositions de Mariana. Paris: 1610. V. 37

ROUSSEL, RAYMOND

La Doublure. 1897. V. 44

Locus Solus. Paris: 1914. V. 46

ROUSSELET, L.

India and Its Native Princes. London: 1882. V. 44

ROUSSELOT DE SURGY, JACQUES PHILIBERT

Histoire Naturelle et Politique de la Pensylvanie... Paris: 1768. V. 38

ROUTLEDGE, SCORESBY MRS.

The Mystery of Easter Island; The Story of an Expedition. London: (1920). V. 37

ROUTLEDGE, WILLIAM

The Children's Musical Cinderalla, Told in Familiar Words to Familiar Tunes. London: 1879. V. 46

ROUTLEDGE'S Book of Alphabets Containing The Good Boys' and Girls' Alphabet. London: 1890. V. 45

ROUTLEDGE'S Handbook of Fishing. London: 1867. V. 40

ROUTSONG, ALMA

Round Shape. Boston: 1959. V. 39

ROUX, ANTOINE

Ships and Shipping; a Collection of Pictures Including Many American Vessels Painted by Antoine Roux and His Sons. Salem: 1925. V. 37

ROUX DE ROCHELLE, JEAN B.

Etats-Unis d'Amerique. Paris: 1837. V. 38

ROUX, PHILIBERT JOSEPH

Memoire sur la Staphyloraphie, ou Suture du Voile du Palais. Paris: 1825. V. 43

ROVEN, PHILIP

Tractatus de Missionibus... et Conversionem Infidelium et Haereticonum... Louvain: 1626. V. 40

ROVILLE, GUILLAUME

Promptvarii Iconvm Insigniorvm a Secvlo Hominum. Lyon: 1553. V. 38; 44

ROVINSKII, DMITRII ALEKSANDROVICH

Russkiia Narodnyia Kartinki. St. Petersburg: 1900-01. V. 38; 40

ROWAN, ALISTAIR

Designs for Castles and Country Villas by Robert and James Adam. Oxford: 1985. V. 38; 39

ROWAN, ARCHIBALD HAMILTON

Autobiography. Dublin: 1840. V. 38

ROWAN, JOHN J.

The Emigrant and Sportsman in Canada. Some Experience of an Old Country Settler. London: 1876. V. 37; 40

ROWBOTHAM, FRANCIS JAMESON

A Trip to Prairie-Land Being a Glance at the Shady Side of Emigration. London: 1885. V. 37; 38; 42

ROWE, ALAN

A Catalogue of Egyptian Scarabs, Scaraboids, Seals and Amulets in the Palestine Archaeological Museum. Le Caire: 1936. V. 37; 40; 42; 44

The Topography and History of Beth-shan with Details of Egyptian and Other Inscriptions Found on the Site. Philadelphia: 1930. V. 40

ROWE, ELIZABETH

Devout Exercise of the Heart, in Meditation and Soliloquy... Newry: 1762. V. 41

Devout Exercises of the Heart, In Meditation and Soliloquy, Prayer and Praise. Dedham: 1796. V. 38; 40

Friendship in Death; In Twenty Letters, to Which are Added, Letters, Moral and Entertaining. London: 1745. V. 43

Friendship in Death. In Twenty Letters from the Dead to the living... With: Letters Moral and Entertaining, in Prose and Verse. In Three Parts. London: 1740. V. 37

ROWE, ELIZABETH SINGER

Philomela; or, Poems by Mrs. Elizabeth Singer. Dublin: 1738. V. 38

ROWE, HENRY d. 1819

Fables in Verse. London: 1810. V. 42; 43

ROWE, JOHN

Letters and Diary of... Boston Merchant 1759-1762, 1764-1779. Boston: 1903. V. 42

ROWE, NICHOLAS

The Ambitious Step-Mother. London: 1701. V. 41; 42

Callipaedia. A Poem. London: 1712. V. 41

The Fair Penitent. London: 1703. V. 38

Ode for the New Year MDCCXVI. London: 1716. V. 37

The Poetical Works. London: 1715. V. 45

The Royal Convert. London: 1708. V. 45

Tamerlane. London: 1702. V. 40; 45

Tamerlane. London: 1703. V. 38; 40; 45

Three Plays: Tamerlane; The Fair Penitent; Jane Shore. London: 1929. V. 46

The Tragedy of Jane Shore. London: 1714. V. 40; 45

The Tragedy of the Lady Jane Grey. London: 1715. V. 37; 43; 45

Ulysses: a Tragedy... London: 1706. V. 42

The Works. London: 1766. V. 40; 45; 46

The Works. London: 1792. V. 38

ROWE, RICHARD

Friends and Acquaintances. London: 1871. V. 37

ROWE, SAMUEL

A Preambulation of the Antient and Royal Forest of Dartmoor and the Venville Precints or a Topographical Survey of the Antiquities and Scenery. Exeter, London: 1896. V. 45

ROWE, THEOPHILUS

The Life of Elizabeth Rowe. (with Friendship in Death in Twenty Letters from the Dead to the Living. London: 1747. V. 46

ROWE, WILLIAM CARPENTER

The Act for the Amendment of the Representation of the People in England and Wales. London: 1832. V. 42

ROWELL, EARLE ALBERT

On the Trail of Marihuana: The Weed of Madness. Mountainview: 1939. V. 43

ROWELL, HOPKINS

The Great Resources and Superior Advantages of the City of Joliet, Illinois. Joliet: 1871. V. 43

ROWELL, MARGIT

Miro. New York: 1970. V. 39; 46

ROWETT, W.

The Ocean Telgraph Cable... London: 1856. V. 42

ROWFANT CLUB

Auction Prices of American Book Club Publications 1857-1901. Cleveland: 1904. V. 39; 42

The Code of Regulations of the Rowfant Club. Cleveland: 1896. V. 41

Rowfant Rhymes by Frederick Locker. With an Introduction by Austin Dobson. Cleveland: 1895. V. 37

ROWLAND, ALEXANDER

The Human Hair, Popularly and Physiologically Considered with Special Reference to Its Preservation, Improvement and Adornment... London: 1853. V. 45

ROWLAND, BENJAMIN

The Wall-Paintings of India, Central Asia and Ceylon. Boston: 1938. V. 43

ROWLAND, DAVID L.

An Epitome of Ecclesiastical History. New Haven: 1806. V. 44

ROWLAND, DUNBAR

History of Mississippi, the Heart of the Old South. Chicago: 1925. V. 37; 39; 42

Jefferson Davis, Constitutionalist: His Letters, Papers and Speeches. Jackson: 1923. V. 38

Mississippi Provincial Archives, 1701-1743. Jackson: 1927. V. 37; 39

Mississippi Provincial Archives. French Dominion 1701-1743 French-English-Indian Relations. Wars with the Natchez and Chickasan Indians. Jackson: 1927/29/32. V. 39

ROWLAND, KATE MASON

Life of George Mason 1725-1792. New York: 1892. V. 41

The Life of Charles Carroll of Carrollton, 1737-1832. New York: 1898. V. 41

ROWLAND, ORAN W.

History of Van Buren County, Michigan. Chicago & New York: 1912. V. 42

ROWLAND, W. ORLANDO

Original Sketchbook of This English Artist. V. 41

ROWLANDS, HENRY

Mona Antiqua Restaurata. London: 1766. V. 37; 38; 39; 41; 42

ROWLANDS, RICHARD

A Restitution of Decayed Intelligence: in Antiquities. London: 1634. V. 39

The Restitution of Decayed Intelligence. London: 1628. V. 37

ROWLANDS, WILLIAM

Cambrian Bibliography . . . Llanidloes: 1869. V. 44

ROWLANDSON, MARY

Narrative of the Captivity, Sufferings . . . Clinton: 1853. V. 45

The Narrative of the Captivity and Restoration of Mrs. Mary Rowlandson, First Printed in 1682 at Cambridge, Massachusetts and London, England . . . Lancaster: 1903. V. 44

A True History of the Captivity and Restoration of Mrs. Mary Rowlandson. London: 1682. V. 42

ROWLANDSON, THOMAS

The Adventures of Doctor Comicus or the Frolicks of Fortune. London: 1815. V. 43

The Beauties of Boswell. San Francisco: 1942. V. 41; 43

The English Dance of Death, from the Designs of Thomas Rowlandson . . . London: 1815-16. V. 41; 45

The English Dance of Death from the Designs of Thomas Rowlandson. (and) The Dance of Life. London: 1815-17. V. 37

An Essay on the Art of Ingeniously Tormenting. A New Edition, Corrected, Revised and Illustrated . . . London: 1808. V. 37

The History of Johnny Quae Genus, the little foundling of the late Doctor Syntax: A Poem . . . London: 1822. V. 37

Hugarian & Highland Broad Sword. London: 1799. V. 40; 46

Journal of Sentimental Travels in the Southern Provinces of France, Shortly Before the Revolution . . . London: 1821. V. 41; 45

Loyal Volunteers of London and Environs, Infantry & Cavalry in Their Respective Uniforms. London: 1798-99. V. 45

Medical Caricatures. New York: 1971. V. 46

Naples and the Campagna Felice. London: 1815. V. 45

A Selection from His works, with Adnecdotal Descriptions of His famous Caricatures and a sketch of His Life, Times, and Contemporarires. London: 1880. V. 37

The Sheep Breeder's Guide. San Francisco: 1861. V. 43

A Treatise on Earthquake Dangers, Earthquake Dynamics and Palliatives . . . San Francisco: 1868. V. 44

ROWLES, W. P.

The Life and Character of Capt. William B. Allen, of Lawrence County, Tenn. Who Fell at the Storming of Monterey on the 21st of September, 1846. Columbia: 1853. V. 39

ROWLETT'S Tables of Discount, or Interest on Every Dollar, from Unit, or One , to Two Thousand. Philadelphia: 1802. V. 38

ROWLEY, G. D.

Ornithological Miscellany. London: 1876-78. V. 38

ROWLEY, HUGH

Gamosagammon; or Hints on Hymen for the Use of Parties About to Connubialize. London: 1870. V. 38

Gamosagammon; or, Hints on Hymen. London: 1871. V. 44

More Puniana; or, Thoughts Wise and Other-Why's. London: 1875. V. 44

ROWLEY, J. DE LA MARE

The Passage in Park Lane - Being a Singular Episode in the Life of Mr. Jonathan Merryman. London: 1928. V. 43

ROWLEY, WILLIAM

The Causes of the Great Number of Deaths Amongst Adults and Children, in Putrid, Scarlet Fevers, and Ulcerated Sore Throats, Explained . . . London: 1793. V. 38

The Rational Practice of Physic. London: 1793. V. 42; 45

ROWNING, J.

A Compendious System of Natural Philosophy . . . London: 1744. V. 41; 42

A Compendious System of Natural Philosophy. London: 1758. V. 40

A Compendious System of Natural Philosophy. London: 1759. V. 40

ROWSE, A. L.

A Cornishman Abroad. London: 1976. V. 39

ROWSON, DREW, & CO.

Illustrated Catalogue of Constructional Iron Work. London: 1870's. V. 44

ROWSON, SUSANNA HASWELL 1762-1824

An Abridgment of Universal Geography, Together with Sketches of History, Designed for the Use of Schools and Academies in the United States. Boston: 1806. V. 39

Biblical Dialogues Between a Father and His Family . . . Boston: 1822. V. 42

Charlotte Temple. Philadelphia: 1794. V. 40

Charlotte Temple. Alexandria: 1802. V. 40

Charlotte Temple. Harrisburgh: 1802. V. 40

Miscellaneous Poems. Boston: 1804. V. 40

Reuben and Rachel. Boston: 1798. V. 38; 41; 43

A Spelling Dictionary, Divided into Short Lessons for the Easier Committing to Memory by Children and Young Persons . . . Boston: 1807. V. 42

Trials of the Human Heart, a Novel. Philaldelphia: 1795. V. 38

ROX, RICHARD

A Letter . . . to Thomas Prior, Esq; Showing, From Experience, a Sure Method to Establish the Linen Manufacture . . . Dublin printed: London: 1749. V. 43

ROXBURGHE CLUB

Chronology of Twenty-five Years: The Roxburghe Club of San Francisco, 1928-1953. San Francisco: 1954. V. 41; 45

Chronology of Twenty-Five Years. San Francisco: 1953. V. 38; 44

The Gardyners Passetaunce c. 1512. Edited with an introduction and transcript by F.B. Williams Jr. With notes on the two unique editions in Westminster Library, descriptions of the bindings in which they were preserve . . . 1985. V. 37

Keepsake from the Roxburghe Club of San Francisco. San Francisco: 1965. V. 40

THE ROXBURGHE Club of San Francisco. San Francisco: 1978. V. 45

ROXBURGHE, JOHN, DUKE OF

A Catalogue of the Library of the Late John Duke of Roxburghe. London: 1812. V. 38; 39

ROXBY, ROBERT

The Lay of the Reedwater Minstrel, Illustrated with Notes Historical and Explantory, Addressed to Matthew Forster, of Broomyholme, Esq. Newcastle: 1809. V. 41; 42

ROY, ANDREW

Recollections of a Prisoner of War. Columbus: 1909. V. 42

ROY, CLAUDE

Hans Erni. Geneva: 1955. V. 46

ROY, J. EDMOND

In and Around Tadousac . . . Levis,: 1891. V. 44

ROY, JULES

Chants & Prieres Pour Des Pilotes. Algiers: 1943. V. 38

ROY, JUST J. E.

The Adventures of a French Captain, at Present a Planter in Texas. New York: 1878. V. 40

ROY, RAMMOHUM

Translation of Several Principal Books, Passages and Texts of the Veds, and of Some Controversial Works on Brahmunical Theology. London: 1832. V. 45

ROY, WILLIAM

The Military Antiquities of the Romans in (North) Britain (and particularly Their Ancient System of Castramentation, Illustrated from Vestiges of the Camps of Agricola Existing There . . . London: 1793. V. 41

ROYAL ACADEMY

The Exhibition of the Royal Academy, 1823. London: 1823. V. 38; 40

ROYAL AFRICAN COMPANY

A Detection of the Proceedings and Practices of the Directors ... from 1672 to 1748 ... with Remarks on the Use and Importance of the British Forts and Settlements on the Coast of Guiney ... London: 1749. V. 39

ROYAL AFRICAN COMPANY OF ENGLAND

Answer of the Company of Royal Adventurers of England Trading Into Africa, to the Petition and Paper of Certain Heads and Particulars Thereunto Relating and Annexed Exhibited to the Honourable House of Commons ... Concerned in His Majesty's Plantations ... London: 1667. V. 40

The Several Declarations of the Company of Royal Adventurers of England Trading to Africa, Inviting His Majesty's Native Subects in General to Subscribe, and Become Sharers in Their Joynt-Stock. London: 1667. V. 40

ROYAL ARGRICULTURAL SOCIETY

The Journal of the Royal Agricultural Society of England. Volumes 1 - 12. London: 1840-51. V. 37

THE ROYAL Artillery Commemoration Book 1939-1945. 1950. V. 38

ROYAL Artillery War Commemoration Book. London: 1920. V. 46

ROYAL ASIATIC SOCIETY LIBRARY

Catalogue of Printed Books Published Before 1932 in the Library of the Royal Asiatic Society. London: 1940. V. 46

THE ROYAL Charter of Confirmation Granted by King Charles II to the City of London. (with) An Index ... London: 1680. V. 40

ROYAL COLLEGE OF PHYSICIANS OF LONDON

International Conference of Physicians ... London 8th to 13th September, 1947. London: 1947. V. 37

ROYAL COLLEGE OF SURGEONS IN LONDON

A Descriptive and Illustrated Catalogue of the Calculi and Other Animal Concretions Contained in the Museum of the Royal College of Surgeons in London. London: 1842-45. V. 43

ROYAL COLLEGE OF SURGEONS OF ENGLAND

Catalogue of the Hunterian Collection in the Museum. London: 1830-31. V. 37; 38

Descriptive Catalogue of the Osteological Series Contained in the Museum. London: 1853. V. 37

ROYAL COMMISSION ON HISTORICAL MONUMENTS

An Inventory of the Historical Monuments in the City of Cambridge. London: 1959. V. 46

An Inventory of the Historical Monuments in the City of Oxford. London: 1966. V. 46

An Inventory of the Historical Monuments in the County of Dorset. London: 1970-75. V. 40

London. London: 1924-30. V. 46

ROYAL EDINBURGH LIGHT DRAGOONS

Rules and Regulations of the Royal Edinburgh Light Dragoons 1798. Edinburgh: 1799. V. 43

THE ROYAL French Grammar; by Which One May in a Short Time Attain the French Tongue in Perfection. London. V. 41

ROYAL GEOGRAPHICAL SOCIETY

A Selection of Papers on Arctic Geography and Ethnology ... London: 1875. V. 46

ROYAL GEOGRAPHICAL SOCIETY. LONDON

The Journal of the Royal Geographical Society. Volume the Forty-Ninth. London: 1879. V. 38

The Lands of Cazembe. Lacerda's Journey to Cazembe in 1798. London: 1873. V. 38

ROYAL GEOLOGICAL SOCIETY OF CORNWALL

Transactions of the Royal Geological Society of Cornwall. London: 1871. V. 38; 40

A ROYAL Guest. Oxford: 1908. V. 45

ROYAL HOLLOWAY COLLEGE

Catalogue of Pictures. London: 1890. V. 40

ROYAL HORTICULTURAL SOCIETY

Dictionary of Gardening. 1951. V. 38

Dictionary of Gardening. Oxford: 1951. V. 39

Dictionary of Gardening. London: 1951-69. V. 42

Dictionary of Gardening. London: 1956. V. 37; 38; 42

Dictionary of Gardening, a Practical and Scientific Encyclopedia of Horticulture. Oxford: 1956. V. 38; 45

Dictionary of Gardening. London: 1976. V. 40

Dictionary of Gardening. Oxford: 1981. V. 40

Dictionary of Gardening. London: 1974, 1984. V. 37

Report on the Third International Conference 1906 on Genetics. London: 1907. V. 40

THE ROYAL Inniskilling Fusiliers. Being the History of the Regiment From Dec. 1688 to July 1914. London: 1928. V. 41

ROYAL INSTITUTE OF BRITISH ARCHITECTS

Catalogue of the Drawings Collection. Farnborough: 1959 onwards. V. 45

Catalogue of the Drawings Collection. Farnborough: 1969 onwards. V. 46

International Architecture 1924-34. Catalogue to the Centenary Exhibition. London: 1934. V. 45

ROYAL INSTITUTION OF GREAT BRITAIN

The Prospectus, Charter, Ordinances and Bye-Laws, of the Royal Institution of Great Britain. London: 1800. V. 38

ROYAL INSTITUTION OF GREAT BRITAIN. LONDON. LIBRARY

A Catalogue of the Library of the Royal Institution of Great Britain, Including a complete List of all the Greek Writers ... London: 1821. V. 39; 40

THE ROYAL Legacies of Charles the First of that Name, of Great Britaine, France, and Ireland, King and Martyr; to His Persecutors and Murderers. London: 1649. V. 41

ROYAL MEDICO-CHIRURGICAL SOCIETY

Scient Omnes Praesidem, Concilium et Sodales ... Virum Doctissimum et Spectatissimum Carolum Darwin in Sodalitium Suum, Inter Socios Honorarios Cooptasse ... Londoni: 1868. V. 39

ROYAL Natural History. London: 1893-96. V. 37
ROYAL Natural History. London: 1894. V. 46

THE ROYAL Repository; or Picturesque Pocket Diary. London: 1817. V. 40; 42

ROYAL SOCIETY

An Account of the Late Proceedings in the Council of the Royal Society in Order to Remove From Grensham College into Crane-Court, in Fleet Street. London: 1710. V. 41

Biographical Memoirs of fellows of the Royal Society. London: 1955-76. V. 39

Philosophical Transactions. London: 1667. V. 41

The Philosophical Transactions 1700-1720. London: 1721. V. 39

ROYAL SOCIETY LIBRARY

Catalogue of a Collection of Early Printed Books in the Library of the Royal Society. London: 1910. V. 46

ROYAL SOCIETY OF ARTS

Transactions of the Society ... for the Encouragement of Arts, Manufactures and Commerce. London: 1799-1812. V. 39

ROYAL SOCIETY OF EDINBURGH

Transactions of ... 1788. V. 45

Transactions. Edinburgh: 1788-1900. V. 38

Transactions ... Edinburgh: 1814. V. 40

ROYAL SOCIETY OF LONDON

Notes and Records of the Royal Society. London: 1938-62. V. 42

The Philosophical Transactions (and Collections). London: 1734-56. V. 38

ROYAL TOXOPHILITE SOCIETY

Year Books 1876-86. 1877-86. V. 46

ROYALL, ANNE

The Black Book; or Continuation of Travels in the United States. Washington City: 1828. V. 45

Sketches of History, Life and Manners in the United States. New Haven: 1826. V. 40

Sketches of History, Life and Manners, in the United States. New Haven: 1832. V. 38

ROYALL, ANNE NEWPORT

Mrs. Royall's Pennsylvania or Travels Continued in the United States. Washington: 1829. V. 46

The Tennessean. New Haven: 1827. V. 37; 43; 46

ROYALL, WILLIAM L.

Some Reminiscences. New York: 1909. V. 44

ROYCE, JOSIAH

California from the Conquest in 1846 to the Second Vigilance Committee in San Francisco. Boston & New York: 1886. V. 38

ROYCE, WILLIAM HOBART

A Balzac Bibliography. Chicago: 1929. V. 39

THE ROYCROFT Books. A Catalogue and Some Comment Concerning the Shop and Workers at East Aurora, New York. East Aurora: 1900. V. 39; 40

ROYDE-SMITH, NAOMI

The Housemaid. London: 1926. V. 46

ROYEN, VAN P.

Alpine Flora of New Guinea. 1979-1983. V. 39

ROYIDIS, EMMANUEL

Pope Joan. London: 1954. V. 37; 38

ROYLE, J. F.

An Essay on the Antiquity of Hindoo Medicine . . . London: 1837. V. 37

Illustrations of the Botany and Other Branches of the Natural History of the Himalayan Mountains and of the Flora of Cashmere. London: 1839. V. 37

Illustrations of the Botany and Other Branches of the Natural History of the Himalayan Mountains and the Flora of Cashmere; London & New Delhi: 1839-1970. V. 37

ROYLE, J. FORBES

The Fibrous Plants of India Fitted for Cordage, Clothing and Paper. London: 1855. V. 45

ROYLE, JOHN FORBES 1799-1858

On the Culture and Commerce of Cotton in India, and Elsewhere with an Account of the Experiments Made by the Hon. East India Company Up to the Present Time. London: 1851. V. 46

ROYS, RALPH L.

The Book of Chilam Balsam of Chumayel. Washington: 1933. V. 42; 44

The Titles of Ebtun. Washington: 1939. V. 40; 42; 44; 45

ROYSTON, VISCOUNT

Cassandra. Cambridge: 1806. V. 46

ROZIER, FIRMIN A.

Rozier's History of the Early Settlement of the Mississippi Valley. St. Louis: 1890. V. 40

RPW 24.IV.80. N.P.: 1980. V. 44

RUARK, ROBERT

Horn of the Hunter: the Story of an African Safari. Garden City: 1953. V. 37

The Old Man's Boy Grows Older. New York: 1961. V. 37

Something of Value. N.P.. V. 45

Uhuru. New York: 1962. V. 39

Women. 1967. V. 46

RUBENS, PETER PAUL

La Gallerie du Palais du Luxembourg . . . Paris: 1710. V. 40

RUBENS, PHILIP

Electorvm Libri II. Antwerp: 1608. V. 37

RUBEUS, THEODOSIUS PRIVERNAS

Tabulae XII Ad Elevationem Poli Graduum 42. Rome: 1593. V. 40

RUBIE, G.

The British Celestial Atlas . . . London: 1830. V. 45

RUBIN, I. C.

Uterotubal Insufftation. St. Louis: 1947. V. 44

RUBIN, WILLIAM

Anthony Caro. New York: 1975. V. 46

Dada and Surrealist Art. New York: 1969. V. 42

RUBIN, WILLIAM S.

Dada and Surrealist Art. New York: 1968? V. 45

RUBINSTEIN, ARTUR

My Young Years. New York: 1973. V. 39; 41

RUBOVITS, FRANK

Doggerel Exchanges. Mt. Horeb: 1978. V. 44

THE RUBY Fairy Book. London. V. 46

RUCCO, JULIUS

Introduction to the Science of the Pulse as Applied to the Practice of Medicine. London: 1827. V. 38

RUCELLAI, GIOVANNI 1475-1525

Tragedia . . . Intitolata Rosmunds. Venice: 1528. V. 40

RUCKER, MAUDE A.

The Oregon Trail and Some of Its Makers. New York: 1930. V. 37

RUDBECK, OLOF

Book of Birds. (with) Commentary. Stockholm: 1986. V. 37; 38; 40

RUDD, RENNELL

Rose Leaf and Apple Leaf. Philadelphia: 1882. V. 42

RUDD, ROSWELL

Rose Leaf and Apple Leaf. Philadelphia: 1882. V. 40

RUDD, SAYER

The Certain Method to Know the Disease. London: 1742. V. 41; 43; 45

RUDDER, SAMUEL

A New History of Gloucestershire, Comprising the Topography, Antiquities, Curiosities, Produce, Trade and Manufactures of that County . . . Cirencester: 1779. V. 41; 43

RUDDIMAN, THOMAS

A Collection of Scarce, Curious and Valuable Pieces, Both in Verse and Prose . . . Edinburgh: 1785. V. 42

A Dissertation Concerning the Competition for the Crown of Scotland, Betwixt Lord Robert Bruce and Lord John Baliol, in the Year 1291. Edinburgh: 1748. V. 38

A Letter to the Reverend Mr. G. Logan, A.M. One of the Ministers of Edinburgh. Edinburgh: 1747. V. 41

A Vindication of Mr. George Buchanan's Paraphrase of the Book of Psalms from the Objections Raised Against it By William Benson, Esq. Edinburgh: 1745. V. 38

RUDENKO, SERGEI I.

Frozen Tombs of Siberia; The Pazyryk Burials of Iron-Age Horsemen. London: 1970. V. 39

RUDGE, EDWARD

An Introduction to the Study of Painting, Arranged Under Three Heads . . . London: 1828. V. 44

RUDGE, THOMAS

The History of the County of Gloucester . . . London: 1803. V. 45

RUDIGER, JOHANN CHRISTOPH

Sachsische Merckwurdigkeiten Oder Vollstandige Alte, Mittle und Neue Historie von Sachsen und dem Durchlauchtigsten Chur und Furstlichen Hause. Leipzig: 1714. V. 39

RUDIMENTS of the Italian Language. London: 1781. V. 45

RUDING, WALT

An Evil Motherhood. London: 1896. V. 37; 41; 43; 44

RUDISILL, RICHARD

Mirror Image: the Influence of the Daguerreotype on American Society. Albuquerque: 1971. V. 46

RUDLAND, E. M.

Selection from Ballads of Old Birmingham. 1945. V. 42

RUDMOSE BROWN, R. N.

The Voyage of the 'Scotia' Being the Record of a Voyage of Exploration in Antarctic Seas. London: 1906. V. 40

RUDOLF, CROWN PRINCE OF AUSTRIA 1858-1889

Travels in the East Including a Visit to Egypt and the Holy Land. London: 1884. V. 40

RUEFF, JACOB

Ein Schon Lustig Trostbuchel . . . Zurich: 1554. V. 40

Libellus de Tumoribus Quibusdam Phlegmaticis non Naturalibus . . . ex Ueteribus & Recentioribus Chiurgis Collectus. Zurich: 1556. V. 37

RUEFF, JACOBUS 1500-1558

De Conceptu et Generatione Hominis: De Maurice et Eius Partibus, Nec Non de conditione Infantis in Utero, et Gravidarum Cura et Officio . . . Francoforti ad Moenum: 1580. V. 37; 45

The Expert Midwife, or an Excellent and Most Necessary Treatise of the Generation and Birth of Man . . . London: 1637. V. 45

RUEL, JEAN 1474-1537

Veterinariae Medicinae Libri Duo Primum in Lucem Aediti. Basle: 1537. V. 40; 45

Veterinariae Medicinae Libri II. Paris: 1530. V. 38

RUEL, JOANNES

De Natura Stirpium Libri Tres. Basileae: 1537. V. 37; 41

RUEMANN, ARTHUR

Alte Deutsche Kinderbucher. Wein, Leipzig, Zurich: 1937. V. 37

RUEPPEL, WILHELM PETER EDUARD SIMON

Atlas zu der Reise im Nordlichen Afrika. Frankfurt: 1826-28. V. 42

RUEPPEL, WILHELM PETER EDUARD SIMON continued

Neue Wirbelthiere zu der Fauna von Abyssinien Gehorig, Entdekt und Beschrieben. Frankfurt: 1835-40. V. 42

RUESS, EVERETT 1914-1935?

On the Desert Trails with Everett Ruess. El Centro: 1940. V. 43

RUFFHEAD, OWEN

The Life of Alexander Pope, Esq. London: 1769. V. 37; 38; 39; 40; 41; 42; 44

RUFFIN, EDMUND

Agricultural, Geological, and Descriptive Sketches of Lower North Carolina. Raleigh: 1861. V. 45

Anticipations of the Future, to Serve as Lessons for the Present Time, in the Form of Extracts of Letters from an English Resident in the United States, to the London Times, from 1864 to 1870. Richmond: 1860. V. 42

An Essay on Calcareous manures. Shellbanks: 1835. V. 44

RUFFIN, FRANK G.

The Negro as a Political and Social Factor. Richmond: 1888. V. 42

RUFFNER, E. H.

Report Lines of Communication Between Souther Colorado and Northern New Mexico. Washington: 1876. V. 37

RUFFNER, WILLIAM HENRY

A Report on Washington Territory. New York: 1889. V. 37; 40; 44; 45

RUFUS, SEXTUS

Le Dignita de' Consoli, e de gl'Imperadori, e I Fatti de' Romani . . . Venice: 1561. V. 45

RUGELEY, ROWLAND

Miscellaneous Poems, and Translations from La Fontaine and Others. Cambridge: 1763. V. 42; 45

RUGGIE, CATHIE

Crackerjack Harry and His Box of Magic. Madison: 1974. V. 46

RUGGIERI, FERDINANDO

Studio d'Architettura Civile . . . Florence: 1755. V. 37

RUGGLE, GEORGE

Ignoramus. London: 1630. V. 37; 39; 40

Ignoramus. London: 1700. V. 39

Ignoramus, Comoedia . . . London: 1787. V. 38

RUGGLES, DAVID

A Brief Review of the First Annual Report of the American Anti-Slavery Society, By David M. Reese, M.D. of New York. Boston: 1834. V. 42

RUGINELLUS, JULIUS CAESAR

De Arboribus Controversis Resolutionum Liver Singularis . . . Milan: 1624. V. 43

RUHEMANN, HELMUT

The Cleaning of Paintings: Problems and Potentialities. 1968. V. 46

The Cleaning of Paintings: Probelms and Potentialities. New York: 1968. V. 37

RUHLAND, W.

Encyclopaedia of Plant Physiology. Berlin: 1955-67. V. 45

RUHMER, EBERHARD

Tura Paintings and Drawings. London: 1958. V. 46

RUHRAH, JOHN

Pediatrics of the past. An anthology compiled & edited by . . . with a foreword by F.H. Garrison. New York: 1925. V. 37; 39

THE RUINED City; or, the Horrors of Ghicago (sic). New York: 1871. V. 41

RUINI, CARLO 1530-1598

Anatomia & Medicina Equorum Noua. Frankfurt: 1603. V. 41

Anatomia del Cavallo, Infirmita et Suoi Rimedii. Venice: 1618. V. 41; 43; 44; 45; 46

Anatomia del Cavallo, Infirmita, e Suoi Remedii. Venetia: 1707, 1706. V. 38

THE RUINOUS Condition of the Tobacco-Trade, and the Causes Thereof Mathematically Demonstrated. London: 1752. V. 41

RUIZ DE LEON, FRANCISCO

Hernandia Triumphos e la fe, y Gloria de las Armas Espanolas Poema Heroyco . . . Madrid: 1755. V. 42

RUIZ DE MONOYA, ANTONIO

Conquista Espiritual Hecha por los Religiosos de la Compania de Iesus, en las Provincias del Paraguay, Parana, Urguay, y Tape. Madrid: 1639. V. 38

RUIZ DE VIRUES, ALONSO

Philippicae Disputationes Viginti Adversus Lutherana Dogmata, per Philippum Melanchthonem Defensa. Cologne: 1542. V. 38

RUIZ LOPEZ, H.

Prodromus Flora Peruviana et Chilensis. 1966. V. 39

RUIZ NAUFAL, V. M.

El Territorio Mexicano (withO Planos y Mapas . . . Mexico: 1982. V. 39

RUKEYSER, MURIEL

Body of Waking. New York: 1958. V. 42

Elegies. N.P.: 1949. V. 44

Elegies. Stuttgart: 1949. V. 40; 41; 42

The Green Wave. Garden City: 1948. V. 39

The Outer Banks. 1965. V. 39

Theory of Flight. New Haven: 1935. V. 37; 39; 40; 41; 44

U.S. 1. New York: 1938. V. 39; 41

Wake Island. Garden City: 1942. V. 37

RULE, JANE

The Desert of the Heart. Canada: 1964. V. 43

RULES and Articles for the Government of the Armies of the United States. Washington: 1861. V. 45

RULES and Regulations for the Formation, Exercise and Movements of the Militia of Lower Canada. Quebec: 1812. V. 37

RULES and Regulations for the Government of the Common Gaol and Bridewell of the County of Oxford. Oxford: 1810. V. 46

RULES and Regulations for the Sword Exercise of the Cavalry. London: 1796. V. 39; 40

RULES and Regulations for the Sword Exercise of the Cavalry. War Office: 1796. V. 37

RULES for the Management and Cleaning of the Rifle Musket, Model 1863, for the Use of Soldiers . . . Washington: 1863. V. 40

RULHIERE, CLAUDE

A History, or Anecdotes of the Revolution in Russa, in the Year 1762. Boston: 1798. V. 37; 39

RUMBAUGH, JACOB

Reminiscences of Jacob Rumbaugh. N.P.: 1910. V. 39; 40; 45

RUMBOLD, THOMAS

An Answer to the Charges Exhibited Against Sir Thomas Rumbold, in the Reports of the Secret Committee of the House of Commons, and in the General Letter from the Court of Directors of the 10th of Jan. 1781. N.P.: 1782. V. 42

RUMFORD, SIR BENJAMIN THOMPSON, COUNT 1753-1814

Essays, Political, Economical and Philosophical. London: 1798-1802. V. 38; 40; 42

Essays, Political, Economical and Philosophical. London: 1798/98/1802. V. 46

The Complete Works. Boston: 1870. V. 43

The Complete Works. London: 1875-76. V. 45

RUMI

The Parrot and the Merchant. New York: 1981. V. 46

RUMMY. Waltham St. Lawrence: 1932. V. 40

THE RUMP, or a Collection of Songs and Ballads, Made Upon Those Who Would be a Parliament, and Were but the Rump of an House of Commons, Five Times Dissolv'd. London: 1660. V. 41

RUMP; or an Exact Collection of the Choycest Poems and Songs Relating to the Late Times. London: 1662. V. 43; 45

RUMPEL, O.

Cystoscopy as Adjuvant in Surgery With an Atlas of Cystoscopic Views and Concomitant Text for Physicians and Students. New York: 1910. V. 42

RUMPF, G. E.

Herbarii Amboinense Auctarium. Amsterdam: 1755. V. 38

RUMSEY, JAMES

A Short Treatise on the Application of Steam. Philadelphia: 1788. V. 40; 43; 45

RUN Yank Or Die. Tune---Root Hog Or Die! N.P.: 186-? V. 40

THE RUNAWAY - a Victorian Story for the Young. London: 1936. V. 45

RUNDALL, THOMAS

Narratives of Voyages Towards the Northwest, in Search of a Passage to Cathay and India 1496 to 1631 . . . . London: 1849. V. 37; 40

RUNDELL, MARIA ELIZA

The Experienced American Housekepper, or Domestic Cookery. New York: 1823. V. 40

The Experienced American Housekeeper, or Domestic Cookery Formed on Principles of Economy, for the Use of Private Families. Hartford: 1829. V. 40

A New System of Domestic Cookery, Formed Upon Principles of Economy and Adapted to the Use of Private Families. Boston: 1807. V. 41

A New System of Domestic Cookery. London: 1808. V. 41

The New Family Receipt-Book. London: 1810. V. 40

A New System of Domestic Cookery, Formed Upon Principles of Economy, and Adapted to the Use of Private Families Throughout the United States. New York: 1814. V. 37; 40; 44; 45

A New System of Domestic Cookery, Formed Upon Principles of Economy, and Adapted to the Use of Private Families Throughout the United States. New York: 1815. V. 41

A New System of Domestic Cookery . . . London: 1819. V. 42

A New System of Domestic Cookery. London: 1827. V. 42

A New System of Domestic Cookery . . . London: 1831. V. 38

A New System of Domestic Cookery; Formed Upon Principles of Economy . . . London: 1839. V. 42; 43

RUNDELL, MARY ELIZA

A New System of Domestic Cookery; Formed Upon Principles of Economy. London: 1808. V. 39

A New System of Domestic Cookery. London: 1836. V. 39

RUNNELS, HARDIN R.

Message of the Governor of Texas. Austin: 1859. V. 41; 45

RUNYON, DAMON

Furthermore. London: 1938. V. 46

Honey from Home. New York: 1935. V. 38

In Our Town: Twenty Seven Slices of Life. Illustrated by Garth Williams. New York: 1946. V. 37

Take It Easy. 1938. V. 46

Take It Easy. New York: 1938. V. 45; 46

The Tents of Trouble. New York: 1911. V. 39; 40; 42; 46

RUOFF, HENRY W.

Biographical and Portrait Cyclopedia of Montgomery County, Pennsylvania. Philadelphia: 1895. V. 41; 42

RUPERT Brooke's Death and Burial. New Haven: 1917. V. 37; 38; 40; 42

RUPERT, C.

Apostle Spoons, Their Evolution from Earlier Types and the Embelms Used by the Silversmiths for the Apostles. Oxford: 1929. V. 37

RUPERT, MILAN

Chinese Bronze Mirrors: a Study Base on the Todd Collection of 1000 Bronze Mirrors Found in the Five Northern Provinces of Suiyuan, Shensi, Shansi, Honan and Hopel, China. Peiping: 1935. V. 38; 41

RUPERT, PRINCE, COUNT PALATINE 1619-1682

A Brief Relation of His Majesties, and the French Kings Forces Under My Command, with the Dutch, the 11th of August, 1673, Near the Texel. London?: 1673. V. 38

RUPERT'S LAND. NORTHERN DEPT. COUNCIL

Minutes of Council Northern Department of Rupert Land 1821-1831. London: 1940. V. 43

RUPIN, ERNEST

L'Oeuvre de Limoges. Paris: 1890-91. V. 46

RUPP, I. DANIEL

He Pasa Ekklesia. Philadelphia: 1844. V. 43; 45

History of Northampton, Lehigh, Monroe, Carbon and Schuylkill Countries . . . First Settlers. Harrisburgh: 1845. V. 37

RUPP, ISRAEL DANIEL

Collection of Upwards 30,000 Names of German, Swiss, Dutch, French & Other Imigrants in Pennsyvlania, from 1727 to 1776 . . . Philadelphia: 1876. V. 38

Early History of Western Pennsylvania and of the West and of Western Expeditions and Campaigns from 1754 to 1833. Pittsburgh: 1846. V. 40

Early History of Western Pennsylvania, and of the West, and of Western Expeditions and Campaigns From 1754 to 1833. Pittsburg: 1850. V. 38

The History and Topography of Dauphin, Cumberland, Franklin, Bedford, Adams and Perry Counties . . . Lancaster: 1846. V. 41; 42

History of Lancaster County. Lancaster: 1844. V. 41; 42

History of Northampton, Lehigh, Monroe, Carbon and Schuylkill Counties . . . Harrisburg: 1845. V. 42

RUPPERT, KARL

Archaeological Reconnaissance in Campeche, Quintana Roe, and Peten. Washington: 1943. V. 42

Bonampak, Chiapas, Mexico. Washington: 1955. V. 42

The Caracol at Chichen Itza, Yucatan, Mexico. Washington: 1935. V. 42; 44

THE RURAL Socrates: or an Account of a Celebrated Philosophical Farmer, Lately Living in Switzerland, and Known by the Name of Kliyogg. Hallowel: 1800. V. 45

RURAL Tales for Youth. London: 1845. V. 39

RUSCELLI, GIROLAMO d. 1566

I Fiori Delle Rime de' Poeti Illustri . . . Venice: 1586. V. 37

Le Imprese Illustri Con Espositioni, et Discorsi del Sor Ieronimo Ruscelli. Con la Giunta di altre Imprese Tutto Riordinato e Corretto da Fran. Patritio. Venice: 1572. V. 39; 45

Le Impresi Illustri . . . Aggiuntovi Nuovamte, il Qudro Libro da Vicenzo Ruscelli da Viterbo, Al Serenissimo Principe Guglielmo Gonzaga Duca di Mantova et Monferato. Venice: 1584. V. 43

Lettere di Principi, le Quali o' si Scrivono de Principi, o' a Principi, o' Ragionano di Principi. Venice: 1564-81. V. 40

Lettura Sopra un Sonetto dell' Illustriss. Signor Marchese della Terza alla Divina Signora Marchesa del Vasto. Venice: 1552. V. 37

Precetti Della Militia Moderna, Tanto per Mare Quanto per Terra. Venice: 1583. V. 40

Precetti della Militia Moderna, Tanto per Mare Qvanto per Terra. 1595. V. 42

The Secretes of the Reuerende Maister Alexis of Piemount . . . London: 1563-66-68. V. 42

The Secretes of the Reuerend Maister Alexis of Piemont . . . 1580-n.d.-1578. V. 46

De Secretis Libri Septem. BAsle: 1568. V. 46

Tre Discorsi a M. Lodovico Dolce. Venice: 1553. V. 38; 39; 40; 41; 43

Tre Discorsi a M. Lodovico Dolce. 1553. V. 42

RUSCHA, EDWARD

Crackers. Hollywood: 1969. V. 45

RUSCHENBERG, WILLIAM SAMUEL WAITHMAN

Three Years in the Pacific; Including Notices of Brazil, Chile, Bolivia and Peru. Philadelphia: 1834. V. 40

RUSCHENBERGER, WILLIAM SAMUEL WAITHMAN

Narrative of a Voyage Round the World, During the Years 1835, 36 and 37. London: 1838. V. 41

A Voyage Round the World Including an Embassy to Muscat and Siam in 1835, 1836 and 1837. Philadelphia: 1838. V. 38

A Voyage Round the World. Philadelphia: 1838. V. 37; 40

RUSCHENBURGER, WILLIAM SAMUEL WAITHMAN

Three Years in the Pacific . . . London: 1835. V. 43

RUSCHI, A.

Aves do Brasil (Birds of Brazil). Volumes 4 and 5: Beija-Flores (Humming Birds). Rio de Janeiro: 1986. V. 38

Orquideas do Estado do Espirito Santo. Rio de Janeiro: 1986. V. 38

RUSDEN, GEORGE W.

History of Australia. London: 1883. V. 38

RUSH, BENJAMIN 1745-1813

An Account of the Bilious Remitting Yellow Fever, as It Appeared in the City of Philadelphia in the year 1793. Philadelphia: 1794. V. 37; 39; 42; 44

An Account of the Life and Character of Christopher Ludwick. Philadelphia: 1831. V. 40; 44

An Account of the Manners of the German Inhabitants of Pennsylvania. Lancaster: 1910. V. 42

Essays, Literary, Moral and Philosophical. Philadelphia: 1806. V. 37; 40; 45

An Eulogium, Intended to Perpetuate the Memory of David Rittenhouse, Late President of the American Philosophical Society, Delivered Before the Society in the First Presbyterian Church, in High Street, Philadelphia, on the 17th Dec. 1796. Philadelphia: 1796. V. 40; 41; 42; 43; 44

An Inquiry Into the Influence of Physical Causes Upon the Moral Vaculty. 1786. V. 42

An Inquiry Into the Effects of Public Punishments, and Especially on the Punishment of Murder by Death . . . New York: 1816. V. 44

Letters of Benjamin Rush. Princeton: 1951. V. 41; 42; 43; 45; 46

Medical Inquiries and Observations. Volume 2. Philadelphia: 1793. V. 42

Medical Inquiries and Observations. Philadelphia: 1794. V. 42

Medical Inquiries and Observations. Volume I. Philadelphia: 1794. V. 40

Medical Inquiries and Observations . . . Volume 4. Philadelphia: 1796. V. 42

Medical Inquiries and Observations . . . Philadelphia: 1796. V. 44

Medical Inquiries and Observations . . . Philadelphia: 1798. V. 45

Medical Inquiries and Observations Containing an Account of the Yellow Fever, As It Appeared in Philadelphia in 1797 and Observations Upon the Nature and Cure of the Gout, and Hydrophobia. Volume 5. Philadelphia: 1798. V. 42

Medical Inquiries and Observations. Philadelphia: 1809. V. 40; 41; 42; 44

Medical Inqiuiries and Observations Upon the Diseases of the Mind. Philadelphia: 1812. V. 45

RUSH, BENJAMIN 1745-1813 continued

Medical Inquiries and Observations Upon Diseases of the Mind. Philadelphia: 1812. V. 40; 44; 45

Medical Inquiries and Observations. Philadelphia: 1815. V. 41; 43

Medical Inquiries and Observations. Philadelphia: 1818. V. 38; 41; 42

Medical Inquiries and Observations. Medical. Philadelphia: 1818. V. 45

Medical Inquiries and Observations. Philadelphia: 1830. V. 41; 43

Medical Inquiries and Observations Upon the Diseases of the Mind. Philadelphia: 1830. V. 39; 44; 45

Medical Inquiries and Observations Upon the Diseases of the Mind. Philadelphia: 1835. V. 43

Medical Inquiries and Observations. Philadelphia: 1818. V. 37

Medical Inquiries and Observations Upon the Diseases of the Mind. Philadelphia: 1827. V. 37

Medical Inquiries and Observations Upon the Diseases of the Mind. Philadelphia: 1830. V. 37

Medical Inquiries and Observations. Volume II. Philadelphia: 1805. V. 38

Medical Inquiries and Observations. Volume III. Philadelphia: 1805. V. 38

Medical Inquiries and Observations. Volumes I-IV. Philadelphia: 1809. V. 38

Sermons to the Rich and Studious on Temperance and Exercise. London: 1772. V. 40

Six Introductory Lectures, to Courses of Lectures, Upon the Institutes and Practice of Medicine, Delivered in the University Of Pennsylvania. Philadelphia: 1801. V. 38

Sixteen Introductory Lectures, to Courses of Lectures Upon the Institutes and Practice of Medicine . . . to which are added, Two Lectures Upon the Pleasures of the Senses and of the Mind . . . Philadelphia: 1811. V. 40; 41; 42

A Syllabus of a Course of Lectures on the Institutes and Practice of Medicine. Philadelphia: 1798. V. 43; 45; 46

The Works of Thomas Sydenham, M.D., on Acute and Chronic Diseases: With Their Histories and Modes of Cure. With Notes, Intended to Accomodate them to the Present State of Medicine, and to the Climate and Diseases of the U.S. by Benjamin Rush, M.D. Philadelphia: 1809. V. 38

RUSH, CAROLINE E.

The Dew-Drop of the Sunny South . . . Philadelphia: 1851. V. 44

The North and South; or, Slavery and Contrasts. Philadelphia: 1852. V. 42

RUSH, JAMES

The Ingenious Beilbys. London: 1973. V. 37; 44

The Philosophy of the Human Voice. Philadelphia: 1833. V. 40

RUSH, NORMAN

Whites. New York: 1986. V. 46

RUSH, R.

Growth and Manufacture of Silk . . . Washington: 1828. V. 46

RUSH, REBECCA

Kelroy, a Novel. Philadelphia: 1812. V. 45

RUSH, RICHARD

American Jurisprudence, Written and Published at Washington, Being a Few Reflections Suggested on Reading 'Wheaton on Captures'. Washington: 1815. V. 45

Land Claims in East Florida. Letter from . . . In Relation to Claims to Land in East Florida, with the General Report of the Commissioners of that District. Washington: 1826. V. 39

Letter and Accompanying Documents from Richard Rush to Joseph Gales, Mayor of Washington. Washington: 1830. V. 37; 39; 42

Memoranda of a Residence at the Court of London. Philadelphia: 1833. V. 40

Memoranda of a Residence at the Court of London, Comprising Incidents Official and personal from 1819 to 1825. Philadelphia: 1845. V. 40

Report of . . . With a Letter from the Register and Receiver of Public Moneys for the District of East Florida. Transmitting Their Report and Decisions Upon Private Land Claims. Washington: 1828. V. 39

A Residence at the Court of London. London: 1833. V. 38

A Residence at the Court of London, Comprising Incidents, Official and Personal, from 1819 to 1825 . . . London: 1845. V. 42

RUSHDIE, SALMAN

Grimus. London: 1975. V. 39; 40; 44; 45

Haroun and the Sea of Stories. London: 1990. V. 44; 45; 46

Haroun and the Sea of Stories. London: 1990. V. 46

The Jaguar Smile. New York: 1987. V. 46

Midnight's Children. V. 42

Midnight's Children. New York: 1980. V. 42

Midnight's Children. London: 1981. V. 42; 45; 46

Midnight's Children. New York: 1981. V. 42; 43; 44; 46

Midnight's Children. 1981. V. 37

The Satanic Verses. London: 1988. V. 40; 43; 44; 45; 46

The Satanic Verses. New York: 1988. V. 42; 43

The Satanic Verses. New York: 1989. V. 42; 44

Shame. London: 1983. V. 44; 46

RUSHFORTH, G.

Medieval Christian Imagery as Illustrated by the Painted Windows of Great Malvern Priory Church, Worcestershire, Together with a Description and Explanation of All the Ancient Glass in the Church. 1936. V. 39

Medieval Christian Imagery as Illustrated by the Painted Windows of Great Malvern Priory Church Worcestershire . . . Oxford: 1936. V. 42

RUSHO, W. L.

Everett Ruess. A Vagabond for Beauty. Salt Lake City: 1983. V. 44

RUSHTON, EDWARD

The Dismember'd Empire. Liverpool: 1782. V. 40

Expostulatory Letter to George Washington, of Mount Vernon in Virginia on His Continuing to be a Proprietor of Slaves. Liverpool: 1797. V. 40

Poems. London: 1806. V. 42

RUSHWORTH, JOHN

The Case of the Late James Keil, Dr. of Physick. Oxford: 1719. V. 42

Historical Collections of Private Passages of State; Weighty Matters in Law; Remarkable Proceedings in Five Parliaments. London: 1659. V. 40

Historical Collections . . . Beginning the Sixteenth Year of King James. London: 1659. V. 39

Historical Collections. The Second Part. London: 1680. V. 41

Historical Collections. London: 1680. V. 45

Historical Collections of Private Passages of State, Weighty Matters in Law, Remarkable Proceedings in Five Parliaments. London: 1721. V. 37; 40; 44

Historical Collections of Private Passages of State, Wieghty Matters in Law, Remarkable Proceedings in Five Parliaments . . . 1618-1648. London: 1659-1701. V. 38

Mr. Rushworth's Historical Collections Abridg'd and Improved. London: 1703/06/08. V. 42

RUSIN, JOHN

The Storm Cloud of the Nineteenth Century. Orpington: 1884. V. 37

RUSINOW, IRVING

Middle Rio Grande Valley. A Photographic Record of the Middle Rio Grande Conservancy District New Mexico. Albuquerque: 1939. V. 37

RUSK, J. M.

Letter from . . . Transmitting a Report on the Preliminary Investigation to Determine the Proper Location of Artesian wells Within the Area of the Ninety Seventh Meridian and East of the Foot Hills of the Rocky Mountains. Washington: 1890. V. 42

Letter from . . . Transmitting . . . A Report on the Progress of Irrigation Investigation Under the Deficiency Appropriation Act of 1890. Washington: 1891. V. 37; 42

RUSKIN, ARTHUR

Classics in Arterial Hypertension. Springfield: 1956. V. 41; 42; 45

RUSKIN, JOHN 1819-1900

Alexander Francesca, Nee Esther Frances Alexander. New York: 1883. V. 46

Ariadne Florentina. Six Lectures on Wood and Metal Engraving. London: 1890. V. 41

Arrows of the Chace Being a Collection of Scattered Letters Published Chiefly in the Daily Newspapers, 1840-1880. London: 1880. V. 38; 39; 46

Arrows of the Chace Being a Collection of Scattered Letters Published Chiefly in the Daily Newspapers 1840-1880. Orpington: 1880. V. 39; 41; 43; 44

The Art of England. Orpington: 1884. V. 37; 44; 45; 46

A Collection of Criticisms by John Ruskin Not Heretofore Reprinted and Now Re-Edited and Rearranged. London: 1902. V. 46

The Contemptible Horse. Harper Woods: 1962. V. 41; 42; 44

The Contemptible Horse. Harper Woods: 1962. V. 44

Dame Wiggins of Lee and Her Seven Wonderful Cats. London: 1885. V. 40; 41

Dame Wiggins of Lee, and her Seven Wonderful Cats: A Humerous Tale Written Principally by a Lady of Ninety. Edited, With Additional Verses, by John Ruskin, LL.D. And With New Illustrations by Kate Greenaway. Sunnyside, Orphington, Kent: 1885. V. 37

The Eagle's Nest. Ten Lectures on the Relation of Natural Science to Art, given before the University of Oxford in Lent Term, 1872. Orpington: 1880. V. 37

The Elements of Drawing. London: 1857. V. 38; 40; 42; 44; 46

The Elements of Drawing in Three Letters to Beginners. London: 1898. V. 45

An Endeavour Towards the Teaching of John Ruskin and William Morris. London: 1901. V. 37

Ethics of the Dust. London: 1866. V. 39; 40

Ethics of the Dust. London: 1883. V. 46

Fors Clavigera. London: 1871. V. 40

Fors Clavigera. London: 1871-77. V. 46

Fors Clavigera. Kent: 1871-84. V. 42

RUSLING, JAMES F.

Across America: or, The Great West and the Pacific Coast. New York: 1874. V. 39

Across America; or, the Great West and the Pacific Coast. New York: 1875. V. 37; 38

RUSO D'ERES, CHARLES DENNIS

Memoir of . . . A Native of Canada, who was with the . . . Indinas Eleven Years, with a Particular Account of His Sufferings. Exeter, N.H.: 1800. V. 37; 38

RUSPINI, BARTHOLMEW

A Concise Relation of the Effects of an Extraordinary Styptic, Lately discovered . . . London: 1787. V. 38

RUSS, HORACE

The Headsman: a Sketch. New York: 1840. V. 39

RUSS, KARL

The Speaking Parrots: a Scientific Manual. London: 1884. V. 38

RUSS, KURT

The Speaking Parrots: a Scientific Manual. London: 1885. V. 41

RUSSEL, RICHARD

A Dissertation on the Use of Sea-Water in the Diseases of the Glands. London: 1752. V. 44

Oeconomy of Nature in Acute and Chronical Diseases of the Glands. London: 1755. V. 42

RUSSELL, ALEX J.

The Red River Country, Hudson's Bay and North-West Territories . . . Ottawa: 1869. V. 38; 42

RUSSELL, ALEXANDER

The Natural History of Aleppo . . . London: 1756. V. 42

RUSSELL, ARCHIBALD G. B.

The Engravings of William Blake. London: 1912. V. 40

RUSSELL, BERTRAND RUSSELL, 3RD EARL OF 1872-1970

The Amberley Papers: The Letters and Diaries of Bertrand Russell's Parents. New York: 1937. V. 44

The Analysis of Matter. London: 1927. V. 45

Autobiography. London: 1967. V. 40

Bolshevism and the West. London: 1924. V. 46

A Critical Exposition of the Philosophy of Leibniz. 1900. V. 45

A Critical Exposition of the Philosophy of Leibniz. Cambridge: 1900. V. 41; 43; 45

An Essay on the Foundation of Geometry. Cambridge: 1897. V. 39; 41; 42; 45

An Essay on the Foundations of Geometry. Paris: 1901. V. 41

German Social Democracy. London: 1896. V. 39; 41; 43; 45

History of the World. London: 1962. V. 39

Introduction to Mathematical Philosophy. London: 1919. V. 39; 40; 41

Justice in War-Time. Manchester & London: 1915. V. 41; 43; 45

Memoirs of the Affairs of Europe from the Peace of Utrecht. London: 1824-29. V. 41

My Philosophical Development. London: 1959. V. 41

Mysticism and Logic, and Other Essays. London: 1918. V. 43

Mysticism and Logic. New York: 1929. V. 41; 44; 46

Our Knowledge of the External World: as a Field for Scientific Method in Philosophy. Chicago: 1914. V. 44

Our Knowledge of the External World. Chicago/London: 1914. V. 42

Our Knowledge of the External World. As a Field for Scientific Method in Philosophy. London: 1914. V. 38; 39; 41

Our Knowledge of the External World. Open Court: 1914. V. 45

Philosophical Essays. London: 1910. V. 41; 42; 45

Political Ideas. London: 1916. V. 39

Political Ideas. New York: 1917. V. 41

Power: a New Social Analysis. New York: 1938. V. 40; 41; 46

Principia Mathematica. Cambridge: 1910. V. 41

Principia Mathematica. Cambridge: 1910-13. V. 41

Principia Mathematica. Cambridge: 1925-27. V. 41

Principia Mathematica. Cambridge: 1950. V. 41

The Principles of Mathematics. 1903. V. 45

The Principles of Mathematics. Cambridge: 1903. V. 40; 41; 45

Principles of Social Reconstruction. London: 1916. V. 40; 46

The Problem of China. London: 1922. V. 40

The Prospects of Industrial Civilization. London: 1923. V. 43

Roads to Freedom, Socialism, Anarchism and Syndicalism. London: 1918. V. 41; 45; 46

Satan in the Suburbs. London: 1953. V. 41; 42; 43; 44; 45; 46

War. The Offspring of Fear. London: 1914. V. 40; 41; 45

Why I Am Not a Christian. 1927. V. 43

RUSSELL, BERTRAND RUSSELL, THIRD EARL OF 1872-1970

A Critical Exposition of the Philosophy of Leibnitz with an Appendix of Leading Passages. Cambridge: 1900. V. 45

RUSSELL, C. E. M.

Bullet and Shot in Indian Forest, Plain and Hill. London: 1900. V. 42

RUSSELL, C. W.

The Life of Cardinal Mezzofanti . . . London: 1858. V. 38

RUSSELL, CARL P.

Firearms, Traps and Tools of the Mountain Men. New York: 1967. V. 46

RUSSELL, CAROLINE

The English Captive. Lincoln: 1823. V. 37

RUSSELL, CHARLES

Diary of a Visit to the United States in the Year 1883. New York: 1910. V. 39

RUSSELL, CHARLES E.

English Mezzotint Portraits and Their States. London: 1926. V. 39; 45

RUSSELL, CHARLES MARION 1864-1926

Back Trailing on the Old Frontiers. Great Falls: 1922. V. 37; 39

Back Trailing on the Old Frontiers. Great Falls: 1922. V. 42

Good Medicine. Garden City: 1930. V. 37; 38; 39; 40

Hope Hathaway. Boston: 1904. V. 39

How the Buffalo Lost His Crown. N.P.: 1894. V. 40

More Rawhides. Great Falls: 1925. V. 39; 42; 45; 46

Pen Sketches. Great Falls: 1899. V. 42

Pen Sketches. Alhambra: 1964. V. 39

Pen and Ink Drawings. Pasadena: 1946. V. 38

Pen Sketches. Great Falls: 1899. V. 37

Rawhide Rawlins Stories. Great Falls: 1921. V. 39; 46

Rawhide Rawlins Rides Again . . . Pasadena: 1948. V. 37; 44

Seven Drawings by . . . With an Additional Drawing by Tom Lea . . . and an Essay on These Pictures: 'The Conservatism of Charles M. Russell' By J. Frank Dobie. El Paso: 1950. V. 39

Studies of Western Life. Cascade: 1890. V. 39

Studies of Western Life By . . . The Cowboy Artist, With Descriptions by Granville Stuart. New York: 1890. V. 39; 42

Trails Plowed Under. Garden City: 1927. V. 38; 45

RUSSELL, CHARLES THEODORE

The History of Princeton, Worcester County, Mass. Boston: 1838. V. 39

RUSSELL, DAVID

Letters, Chiefly Practical and Consolatory: Designed to Illustrate the Nature and Tendency of the Gospel. Edinburgh: 1846. V. 45

The Secret Carnival. London: 1988. V. 42

RUSSELL, DON

One Hundred and Three Fights and Scrimmages. The Story of General Reuben F. Bernard. Washington: 1936. V. 37; 43; 44

RUSSELL, DORA

A Hidden Chain. London: 1894. V. 39

RUSSELL, E. F.

Dreadful Sanctuary. 1951. V. 43

Dreadful Sanctuary. 1951. V. 43

Sinister Barrier. 1948. V. 43

RUSSELL, F. S.

The Medusae of the British Isles. Cambridge: 1953-70. V. 37

RUSSELL, FRANK

Explorations in the Far North, Being the Report of an Expedition Under the Auspices of the University of Iowa 1892-95. Iowa City: 1898. V. 37

RUSSELL, GEORGE

A Tour through Sicily in the Year 1815. London: 1819. V. 43

RUSSELL, GEORGE WILLIAM 1867-1935

The Earth Breath and Other Poems. New York: & London: 1897. V. 37

Gods of War with Other Poems. Dublin: 1915. V. 42

The Hero in Man. London: 1909. V. 43

The House of the Titans and Other Poems. London: 1934. V. 40

Imaginations and Reveries. Dublin & London: 1915. V. 46

Midsummer Eve. New York: 1928. V. 37; 38; 40; 42

RUSSELL, GEORGE WILLIAM 1867-1935 continued

Some Passages from the Letters of A.E. to W. B. Yeats. Dublin: 1936. V. 42; 45; 46

Voices of the Stones. London: 1925. V. 41

RUSSELL, H. R.

A Memorial of the Marriage of H.R.H. Albert Edward Prince of Wales and H.R.H. Alexandrina Princess of Denmark. London: 1864. V. 41

RUSSELL, ISRAEL C.

Volcanoes of North America. New York: 1897. V. 40

RUSSELL, J. RUTHERFURD

Homoeopathy in 1851. London: 1852. V. 46

A Treatise of Epidemic Cholera. London: 1849. V. 42

RUSSELL, JAMES

Remarks Concerning the Professorship of Surgery, and Private Lectures; Addressed to the President and Fellows of the Royal College of Surgeons of Edinburgh. Edinburgh: 1827. V. 39

Reports of Cases Argued and Determined in the High Court of Chancery, During the Time of Lord Chancellor Eldon, in 1826 (1823)-1828. London: 1827-30. V. 38

A Treatise on Scrufula. Edinburgh: 1808. V. 38

RUSSELL-JEAFFRESON, JOSEPH

The Faroe Islands. London: 1898. V. 42

RUSSELL, JOHN

An Address Presented to the Members of the Faustus Association, in Boston, at Their Annual Celebration, Oct. 4, 1808. Boston: 1808. V. 40

Adventures in the Moon and Other Worlds. London: 1841. V. 39

Ben Nicholson: Drawings, Paintings and Reliefs 1911-1968. New York: 1969. V. 39

A Complete and Useful Book of Cyphers. London. V. 42

A Complete and Useful Book of Cyphers. London. V. 44

A Complete and Useful Book of Cyphers. London: n.d. V. 38

An Essay on the History of the English Government and Constitution, from the Reign of Henry VII to the Present Time. London: 1821. V. 37; 39; 45

An Essay on the History fo the English Government and Constitution, from the Reign of Henry VII. To the Present Time. London: 1823. V. 46

Francis Bacon. Greenwich: 1971. V. 39; 43; 46

In Dark Places. New York: 1923. V. 38; 40

Instructions for the Drill, and the Method of Performing the Eighteen Manoeuvres. Philadelphia: 1814. V. 44

The Life and Times of Charles James Fox. London: 1859-66. V. 46

Max Ernst: Life and Work. New York. V. 46

Max Ernst: Life and Work. New York. V. 39

Max Ernst: Life and Work. London: 1967. V. 43; 46

The Meanings of Modern Art. New York: 1974-75. V. 46

Memoirs of the Affairs of Europe from the Peace of Utrecht. London: 1824-1829. V. 39

The Speech . . . in the House of Commons, Feb. 8, 1850 on Colonial Policy. London: 1850. V. 45

Theory of Conveyancing. Edinburgh: 1791. V. 38

A Tour in Germany, and Some of the Southern Provinces of the Australian Empire, in the Years 1820, 1821, 1822. Edinburgh: 1825. V. 39

RUSSELL, JOHN, EARL

The Nun of Arrouca. London: 1822. V. 40

RUSSELL, JOHN RUTHERFORD

The History and Heroes of the Art of Medicine. London: 1861. V. 45

RUSSELL, JOSEPH

A Treatise on Practical and Chemical Agriculture . . . Warwick: 1831. V. 40; 43; 46

RUSSELL, K. F.

British Anatomy, 1525-1800, a Bibliography. Melbourne: 1963. V. 37; 39; 42

Catalogue of the Historical Books in the Library of the Royal Australasian College of Surgeons. Melbourne: 1979. V. 41

RUSSELL, LADY RACHEL WRIOTHESLEY VAUGHAN 1636-1723

Letters from the Manuscript in the Library at Woburn Abbey. London: 1773. V. 38; 39; 41; 42; 43; 45; 46

Letters . . . From the Manuscript in the Library of Woburn Abbey . . . London: 1774. V. 42; 46

Letters of Lady Rachael Russell . . . London: 1793. V. 42

RUSSELL, LADY RACHEL WRIOTHESLEY VAUGHN 1636-1723

Letters of Lady Rachel Russell . . . London: 1801. V. 37

RUSSELL, LEONARD

The Saturday Book 4. London: 1944. V. 46

RUSSELL, LORIS S.

A Heritage of Light. Toronto: 1968. V. 43

RUSSELL, MARIAN SLOAN

Land of Enchantment: Memoirs of Marian Russell Along the Santa Fe Trail. Evanston: 1954. V. 43

RUSSELL, MARY ANNETTE BEAUCHAMP RUSSELL, COUNTESS 1866-

The April Baby's Book of Tunes. London: 1900. V. 38; 42

Elizabeth and Her German Garden. London: 1899. V. 41; 43; 44

The Solitary Summer. New York: & London: 1899. V. 41; 43; 44

RUSSELL, MICHAEL

History and Present Condition of the Barbary States. Edinburgh: 1835. V. 38; 41; 44

Polynesia: a History of the South Sea Islands, Including New Zealand. London: 1849. V. 38

Polynesia: a History of the South Sea Islands. London: 1852. V. 39

RUSSELL, OSBORNE

Journal of a Trapper or Nine Years in the Rocky Mountains 1834-1843. Boise: 1921. V. 37; 40; 41; 44; 45; 46

Osborne Russell's Journal of a Trapper. 1955. V. 39

Osborne Russell's Journal of a trapper . . . Portland: 1955. V. 37; 38

RUSSELL, P.

Russell's Adventures. N.P.: 1812. V. 40

Russell's Adventures . . . N.P.: 1812? V. 40

Russell's Adventures . . . N.P.: 1812? V. 45

RUSSELL, PATRICK

A Treatise of the Plague. London: 1791. V. 38

RUSSELL, PERCY

A Journey to Lake Taupo, and Australian and New Zealand Tales and Sketches. London: 1889. V. 37; 41

RUSSELL, PETER

The Correspondence of the Honourable Peter Russell. With Allied Documents relating to His Adminstration of the Government of Upper Canada during the Official Term of Lieut.-Governor J.G. Simcoe while on Leave of Absence. Collected and Edited . . . Toronto: 1932-1936. V. 37

Picnic to the Moon - Poems. London: 1944. V. 38; 44

RUSSELL, R. O.

The History of the 11th (Lewisham) Battalion. The Queen's Own Royal West Kent Regiment. 1934. V. 46

The History of the 11th (Lewisham) Battalion. The Queen's Own, Royal West Kent Reiment. 1934. V. 45

RUSSELL, RICHARD

A Dissertation on the Use of Sea-Water in the Diseases of the Glands. London: 1752. V. 43

Dissertation Concerning the Use of Sea Water in Diseases of the Glands, Etc. Oxford: 1753. V. 37; 38; 44; 45; 46

A Dissertation on the Use of Sea-Water in the Diseases of the Glands. London: 1755. V. 43

De Tabe Glandulari, sive de Usu Aquae Marinae in Morbis Glandularum Dissertatio. Oxford: 1750. V. 41; 43

RUSSELL, ROBERT

North America. Its Agriculture and Climate. Edinburgh: 1857. V. 39

RUSSELL, ROBERT VANE

The Tribes and Castes of the Central Provinces of India. London: 1916. V. 37

RUSSELL, ROLLO

On Hail. London: 1893. V. 42

RUSSELL, THOMAS C.

Narrative of a Voyage to California Ports in 1841 - Together with Voyages to Sitka, the Sandwhich Islands and okhotsk to which are added Sketches of Journeys Across America, Asia and Europe from the Narrative of a Voyage Round the World . . . San Francisco: 1930. V. 38

The Shirley Letters from California Mines in 1851-52. With Synopses of the Letters, Foreword, and Many Typographical Corrections by Thomas C. Russell. Illustrated with 8 Hand-Colored Engravings after old prints. San Francisco: 1922. V. 37

RUSSELL, W.

Eccentric Personages. London: 1864. V. 39

RUSSELL, W. CLARK

The British Seas: Picturesque Notes by . . . . and Other Writers. New York & London: 1892. V. 41

The Convict Ship. London: 1895. V. 43

The Frozen Pirate. London: 1887. V. 43

RUSSELL, W. CLARK continued

Heart of Oak. London: 1895. V. 43

Marooned. London: 1889. V. 37; 43

A Marriage at Sea. London: 1891. V. 41

My Shipmate Louise. London: 1890. V. 41; 43

The Tale of Ten. London: 1896. V. 41

What Cheer! London: 1897. V. 41

RUSSELL, WILLIAM

The History of Modern Europe. Philadelphia: 1802. V. 37; 40; 46

The History of Modern Europe . . . and a View of the Progress of Society . . . London: 1837. V. 43

Leaves from the Diary of a Law-Clerk. London: 1857. V. 42

Recollections of a Detective Police-Officer. London: 1856. V. 38; 42

RUSSELL, WILLIAM CLARK

The Hunchback's Charge. London: 1867. V. 44

A Sea Queen. London: 1883. V. 38

The Ship Her Story. New York: 1899. V. 46

RUSSELL, WILLIAM H.

The Atlantic Telegraph. London: 1866. V. 40; 42

RUSSELL, WILLIAM H. C.

Traditions of London, Historical and Legendary. London: 1859. V. 40

RUSSELL, WILLIAM HOWARD

The Atlantic Telegraph. London: 1865. V. 37; 40; 44

The British Expedition to the Crimea. London: 1858. V. 46

A Diary in the East. London: 1869. V. 37; 40; 43; 46

A Memorial of the Marriage of H.R.H. Albert Edward Prince of Wales and H.R.H. Alexandra, Princess of Denmark. London: 1864. V. 44

My Diary in India, in the Year 1858-59. London: 1860. V. 46

My Diary North and South. London: 1863. V. 37; 40; 42; 43

My Diary North and South. New York: 1863. V. 39

RUSSELL, WILLIS

Quebec: As It Was, and As It Is, or a brief History of the Oldest City in Canada, From Its Foundation to the Present Time . . . Quebec: 1864. V. 37; 42; 43

RUSSIAN Missions into the Interior of Asia . . . London: 1823. V. 37

RUSSIANS in California. San Francisco;: 1933. V. 37; 44

RUSSO, DOROTHY RITTER

A Bibliography of Booth Tarkington, 1869-1946. Indianapolis: 1949. V. 41

THE RUSSO-JAPANESE War. Medical and Sanitary Reports from Officers Attached to the Japanese and Russian Forces in the Field. London: 1908. V. 40

THE RUSSO-Japanese War: Naval. Tokyo: 1904. V. 39

RUSSOLI, FRANCO

Modigliani. London: 1959. V. 46

RUST, GEORGE d. 1670

A Letter of Resolution Concerning Origen and Chief of His Opinions. London: 1661. V. 39

RUST, MARGARET

The Queen of the Fishes. Essex: 1894. V. 44

RUSTON, ARTHUR G.

Hooton Pagnell. London: 1934. V. 45

RUSTON, THOMAS

An Essay in Inoculation for the Small Pox. London: 1767. V. 38

RUTHERFORD, ERNEST

Bakerian Lecture. Nuclear Constiution of Atoms. London: 1920. V. 37

The Collected Papers of Lord Rutherford of Nelson. London: 1962-65. V. 39; 40; 46

Radiation from Radioactive Substances. Cambridge: 1930. V. 38

Radio-Activity. Cambridge: 1904. V. 37; 46

Radio-Activity. Cambridge: 1905. V. 44

Radioactive Substances and Their Radiations. Cambridge: 1913. V. 38

RUTHERFORD, MARK

The Revolution in Tanner's Lane. London: 1887. V. 46

RUTHERFORD, SAMUEL

The Due Right of the Presbyteries or a Peacable Plea for the Government of the Church of Scotland, 1. The Way of the Church of Christ in New England. London: 1644. V. 38

Joshua Redivivus, or Mr. Rutherfoord's Letters. Edinburgh?: 1671. V. 42

Letters. Waterford: 1857. V. 40

RUTHERFORD, WILLIAM

A View of Antient History Including the Progress of Literature and the Fine Arts. London: 1788-9. V. 40

A View of Antient History. London: 1788-91. V. 40

RUTHERFORTH, THOMAS 1712-1771

Ordo Institutionum Physicarum in Privatius Lectionibus. Cambridge: 1756. V. 40

A System of Natural Philosophy, Being a Course of Lectures in Mechanics, Optics and Astronomy . . . Cambridge: 1748. V. 38; 40; 41; 42; 44

RUTHERFURD, LIVINGSTON

John Peter Zenger. His Press, His Trial and a Bibliography of Zenger Imprints . . . New York: 1904. V. 44

RUTHERSTON, ALBERT

Sixteen Designs for the Theatre. London: 1928. V. 39; 43; 45

RUTHVEN, PATRICK 1615-1662

Letters and Papers. 1868. V. 45

RUTHVEN, PATRICK, 3RD BARON 1520?-1566

Letters and Papers of Patrick Ruthven, Earl of Forth and Brentford and of His Family A.D. 1615-A.D. 1662. London: 1868. V. 38

RUTKOW, IRA M.

The History of Surgery in the United States, 1775-1900. Volume 1. San Francisco: 1988. V. 40; 41; 42; 44; 45; 46

RUTLAND, JOHN HENRY, 5TH DUKE OF

A Tour through Part of Belgium and the Rhenish Provinces. London: 1822. V. 37

RUTLAND, JOHN HENRY MANNERS, 5TH DUKE OF

A Tour through Part of Belgium and Rhenish Provinces. London: 1822. V. 40; 43; 46

Travels in Great Britain. London: 1805-13. V. 38; 40

RUTLAND, W. R.

The Becoming of God. London: 1971. V. 40

RUTLEDGE, ARCHIBALD

Brimming Chalice. New York: 1936. V. 46

Home by the River. Indianapolis & New York: 1941. V. 39

Hunter's Choice. New York: 1946. V. 40

Under the Pines and Other Poems. Winchester and New Yonk: 1906. V. 46

RUTLEDGE, DICK

Brief Sketches in the Life of Col. Dick Rutledge the Last Living Indian Scout. N.P.. V. 46

RUTLEDGE, HUGH

Everest; The Unfinished Adventure. London: 1937. V. 41

RUTLEDGE, JEAN JACQUES

The Englishman's Fortnight in Paris; or the Art of Ruining Himself There in a Few Days. London: 1777. V. 46

RUTTENBER, EDWARD M.

History of the Indian Tribes of Hudson's River; Their Origin, Manners and Customs. Albany: 1872. V. 38; 39; 40; 45

RUTTENBERG, EDWARD M.

Obstructions to the Navigation of Hudson's River; Embracing the Minutes of the Secret Committee Appointed by the Provincial Convetion of New York, July 16, 1776 and Other Original Documents Relating to the Subject. Albany: 1860. V. 40

RUTTER, ELDON

The Holy Cities of Arabia. London: 1928. V. 39; 45

RUTTER, FRANK

The British Empire Panels Designed for the House of Lords by Frank Brangwyn, R. A. Descriptive Text by Frank Rutter. Foreword by the Earl of Iveagh. Benfleet: 1933. V. 37

RUTTER, JOAN

Here's Flowers, an Anthology of Flower Poems. London: 1937. V. 38

Here's Flowers: an Anthology of Flower Poems. Waltham St. Lawrence: 1937. V. 40; 44

RUTTER, JOHN

Delineations of Fonthill and Its Abbey. London: 1823. V. 37; 39; 41; 44

Delineations of Fonthill and Its Abbey. Shaftesbury: 1823. V. 38; 39; 41; 46

Delineations of the North Western Division of the County of Somerset, and Of Its Antediluvian Bone Caverns . . . London: 1829. V. 43

RUTTER, OWEN

We Happy Few: an Anthology. London: 1946. V. 46

We Happy Few: An Anthology. (Waltham St. Lawrence): 1946. V. 37

RUTTLEDGE, HUGH

Everest 1933. London: 1934. V. 43; 44

Everest: the Unfinished Adventure. London: 1937. V. 42; 44

RUTTY, JOHN 1698-1775

An Account of Some New Experiments and Observations of Joanna Stephen's Medicine for the Stone. London: 1745. V. 38

The Argument of sulphur or no sulphur in waters discussed: with a comparison of the waters of Aix-la-Chapelle, Bath and Bristol . . . Being the subjects of a correspondence between the author of the Methodical Synopsis of Mineral Waters . . . Dublin: 1762. V. 37

An Essay Towards a Natural History of the County of Dublin. Dublin: 1772. V. 43

A History of the Rise and Progress of the People Called Quakers in Ireland from the Year 1653-1700. London: 1800. V. 46

The Liberty of the Spirit and the Flesh Distinguished. Dublin: 1756. V. 38

Observations on the London and Edinburgh Dispensatories. London: 1776. V. 45; 46

A Second Dissertation on the Liberty of Preaching Granted to Women by the People Called Quakers . . . Dublin: 1739. V. 38

A Spiritual Diary and Soliloquies. London: 1776. V. 40

RUUSCHER, MELCHIOR DE

Natuerlyke Historie van der Couchenille . . . Histoire Naturelle de la Couchenille . . . Amsterdam: 1729. V. 42

RUXTON, GEORGE FREDERICK

Adventures in Mexico and the Rocky Mountains. London: 1847. V. 38; 39; 41; 43

Adventures in Mexico and the Rocky Mountains. London: 1847. V. 38; 45

Adventures in Mexico and the Rocky Mountains. New York: 1848. V. 37; 38; 41; 42; 43

Life in the Far West. Edinburgh: 1849. V. 37; 38; 46

Life in the Far West. Edinburgh and London: 1849. V. 40

Life in the Far West. New York: 1849. V. 41

Life in the Far West. Edinburgh & London: 1851. V. 42

RUXTON, GEORGE FREDERICK AUGUSTUS

Life in the Far West. New York: 1849. V. 43

RUYSCH, FRIEDRICH 1638-1731

Thesaurus Animalium Primus. Het Eerste Cabinet der Dieren. Amsterdam: 1710. V. 42

RUYSDALE, PHILIP

The Fortunes of a Colonist. London: 1854. V. 42

RUYTER, MICHAEL ADRIAANZOON 1607-1676

The Life of Michael Adrian de Ruyter, Admiral of Holland. London: 1677. V. 39

RUYTER, MICHIEL DE

Journael Gehouden Op's Lants Schip de Spiegel, Van 'Tgene Gepasseert en Verricht is Op de Custen Van Africa en America. Amsterdam: 1665. V. 40

RUZICKA, RUDOLPH

The Engraved and Typographic Work of Rudolph Ruzicka: an Exhibition. New York: 1948. V. 41

Newark. A Series of Engravings on Wood by Rudolph Ruzicka, with an Appreciation of the Town by Walter Prichard Eaton. Newark: 1917. V. 41

Studies in Type Design. Hanover: 1968. V. 40; 41; 42; 44

RVSSIA seu Moscovia Itemque Tartaria Commentario Topographico Atque Politico Illustratae. Leyden: 1630. V. 37

RYALL, LYDIA J.

Sketches and Stories of the Lake Erie Islands. Norwalk: 1913. V. 37; 38; 39

RYALS, J. V.

Yankee Doodle Dixie. Richmond: 1890. V. 40

RYAN, ABRAM J.

Father Ryan's Poems. Mobile: 1879. V. 41

RYAN, EDWARD

Analysis of Words, Errator of the Protestant Bible . . . Dublin: 1808. V. 46

RYAN, GEORGE

Was Lord Cardigan a Hero at Balaklava? London: 1855. V. 41

RYAN, HENRY

Rough Sketches from Nature. New York: 1885. V. 46

RYAN, JAMES

A Letter from Mr. James Ryan . . . On His Method of Ventilating Coal Mines . . . London: 1816. V. 45

RYAN, JAMES T.

Specifications of a Revolving Iron Fort, Mounting Eight XV-Inch Guns. New York: 1867. V. 37

RYAN, MARAH ELLIS

The Flute of Gods . . . New York: 1909. V. 37; 41; 42

RYAN, MICHAEL

Prostitution in London, With a Comparative View of That of Paris and New York, As Illustrative of the Capitals and Large Towns of All Countries . . . London: 1839. V. 42

RYAN, RICHARD

Biographia Hibernica. London: 1821. V. 46

Dramatic Table Talk or Scenes, Situations and Adventures, Serious and Comic . . . London: 1825 and 1830. V. 42

RYAN, THOMAS FORTUNE

Gothic and Renaissance Art. Collection of the Late Thomas Fortune Ryan. Sold by Order of the Guaranty Trust Company of New York. New York: 1963. V. 40

RYAN, THOMAS H.

Open Door to a Magnificent Country. New York: 1890. V. 43

RYAN, VINCENT W.

Mauritius and Madagascar. London: 1864. V. 39

RYAN, WILLIAM REDMOND

Personal Adventures in Upper and Lower California in 1848-49, with Author's Experience at the Mines. London: 1850. V. 37; 38; 39; 40; 43; 45; 46

Personal Adventures in Upper and Lower California in 184-9; With the Author's Experiences at the Mines. London: 1850-51. V. 40

Personal Adventures in Upper and Lower California, in 1848-9. London: 1851. V. 37; 40; 41; 43

RYBACK, ISSACHAR

Issachar Ryback. Zein Leben und Shafen. Paris: 1937. V. 41

On the Jewish Fields of the Ukraina. Paris: 1926. V. 41

RYBACK, ISSACHAR BER

Shtetl, Mayn Khoyever Heym, A Gedenknish. (Small Town, My Destroyed Home, a Recollection). Berlin: 1923. V. 39

RYBERG, INEZ SCOTT

Panel Reliefs of Marcus Aurelius. New York: 1967. V. 40

RYCAUT, PAUL

The History of the Turkish Empire, from the Year 1623 to the Year 1677, Containing the Reigns of the Three Last Emerours. London: 1680. V. 37; 39

The History of the Turks. London: 1700. V. 37; 39

The Present State of the Ottoman Empire, Containing the Maxims of the Turkish Politie. London: 1658. V. 39

The Present State of the Ottoman Empire. London: 1668. V. 37; 43; 45

The Present State of the Greek and Armenian Churches, Anno Christi, 1678. London: 1679. V. 37

RYCE, JOHN

The Rector of Amnesty. London: 1891. V. 41

RYCQUUS, JUSTUS 1587-1627

De Capitolo Romano Commentarius. Ghent: 1617. V. 40

RYDBERG, P. A.

A Monograph of the North American Potentilleae. London: 1898. V. 46

RYDEN, STIG

Andean Excavations I-II. Stockholm: 1957-59. V. 44

RYDER, JAMES F.

Voigtlander and I in Pursuit of Shadow Catching. Cleveland: 1902. V. 41

RYE, E. C.

British Beetles: an Introduction to Our Indigenous Coleoptera. London: 1866. V. 42; 43; 44

RYE, EDGAR

The Quirt and the Spur. Chicago: 1909. V. 38; 39; 43; 45; 46

RYE, REGINALD ARTHUR

Catalogue of the Printed Books and Manuscripts Forming the Library of David Mocatta. London: 1904. V. 45

RYE, WALTER

A Glossary of Words Used in East Anglia. London: 1895. V. 41

RYECROFT, HENRY

The Private Papers of Henry Ryecroft. London: 1903. V. 39

The Private Papers of Henry Ryecroft. Portland: 1928. V. 37

RYERSON, FLORENCE

Fear of Fear. New York: 1931. V. 45

Shadows. New York: 1934. V. 45

RYERSON, JOHN

Hudson's Bay; or, a Missionary Tour in the Territory of the Hon. Hudson's Bay company. Toronto: 1855. V. 45

RYERSON PRESS

Type Book, Borders, Ornaments, Rules (spine title: Specimens of The Ryerson Press Type Faces). (1950s?). V. 37

RYFF, WALTHER

Kurtz Handbuechlein und Experiment Viler rtzneyen . . . Nuernberg: 1551. V. 38

RYFF, WALTHER HERMANN fl. 1540-1570

Enchiridion Remediorum Facile Parabilium . . . Francofurti: 1610. V. 44

RYLAND, JOHN

An Address to the Ingenious Youth of Great Britain. London: 1792. V. 40; 42

Serious Essays on the Truths of the Glorious Gospel, and the Various Branches of Vital Experience. London: 1771. V. 41

RYLAND, R. H.

The History, Topography and Antiquities of the County and City of Waterford, with an Account of the Present State of the Peasantry of that Part of the South of Ireland. London: 1824. V. 43

RYLANDS, GEORGE

Distraction of Wits, Nurtured in Elizabethan Cambridge, an Anthology Selected and Introduced by George Rylands. Cambridge: 1958. V. 39

Poems. London: 1931. V. 39; 41; 43; 44; 45

RYLANDS, W. H.

Book of the Fundamental constitutions and Orders of the Philo-Musicae et Architecturae Societas. London: 1900. V. 46

RYLEY, SAMUEL WILLIAM

The Adventures of an Actor; or, Life of a Strolling Player. London: 1840. V. 42

The Itinerant, or Memoirs of an Actor. London: 1808. V. 38

RYLEY, WILLIAM

The Visitation of Middlesex Begain in the Year 1663. Salisbury: 1820. V. 39; 41; 42

RYMER, THOMAS

Edgar, or the English Monarch; an Heroick Tragedy. London: 1677. V. 42; 43

Edgar, or the English Monarch. London: 1678. V. 38

Foedera. Conventiones, Literae, et Cujuscunque Generis Acta Publica, Inter Reges Angliae et Alios Quosvis Imperatores . . . London: 1704-35. V. 39

A Short View of Tragedy; It's Original, Excellency and Corruption. London: 1693. V. 37; 42; 44; 45

The Tragedies of the Last Age Consider'd and Examin'd by the Practice of the Ancients, and by the Common Sense of All Ages. London: 1678. V. 38

RYMILL, J.

Southern Lights. New York: 1939. V. 38

Southern Lights. The Narrative of the British Graham Land Expedition 1934-37. London: 1939. V. 37; 43

RYMSDYK, JAN VAN

Museum Britannicum; or, a Display in Thirty Two Plates, in Antiquities and Natural Curiosities . . . V. 43

Museum Britanicum; or a Display in thirty-Two Plates . . . London: 1791. V. 43

RYMSDYK, JOHN

Museum Britannicum, Being an Exhibition of a Great VAriety of Antiquities and Natural Curiosities, Belonging to the Noble and Magniificent CAbinet, the British Museum. London: 1778. V. 46

RYND, EVELYNE E.

Otherland. London: 1907. V. 40

RYVES, BRUNO

Mercurius Rusticus; or, the Countries Complaint of the Barbarous Outrages Comitted by the Sectaries of the Late Flourishing Kingdom . . . London: 1685. V. 42; 45

RYVES, LAVINIA J. H. DE SERRES

An Appeal for Royalty: A Letter to Her Most Gracious Majesty Queen Victoria From Lavinia Princess of Cumberland. London: 1858. V. 38

RYVES, THOMAS

Historia Navalis Antiqua, Libris Quatuor. London: 1633. V. 41

S

S., A.

The Husbandman's Instructor, or Countryman's Guide. London: 1710. V. 41

S., A., GENT.

The Gentleman's Compleat Jockey . . . London: 1696. V. 43

S., E.

The Godmother's Tales. London: 1808. V. 44

S., J.

A Brief History of the Pious & Glorious Life of . . . Mary, Queen of England. London: 1695. V. 37

A View of the Cotton Manufactories of France, with the Several Progresses They Have Made, and the State in Which They Remained at the Close of the Year 1802 . . . Manchester: 1803. V. 44

S., J. W.

Wild Achievements, and Romantic Voyages, of Captain John Francis Knapp . . . Boston: 1830. V. 40; 42

S., N.

Flying Sketches of the Battle of Waterloo, Brussels, Holland, etc. in June 1815. London: 1852. V. 43

S., P.

The Hungarian Exile, and His Adventures. Portland: 1855. V. 40

S., T.

Horkstow Village. Hull: 1802. V. 39

S., W.

An Answer to a Letter of Enquiry into the Grounds and Occasions of the Contempt of the Clergy. London: 1671. V. 39

SA DE MIRANDA, FRANCISCO DE

As Obras. Lisbon: 1614. V. 41

SAABYE, HANS EGEDE

Greenland. London: 1818. V. 41; 44; 45

SAAD, ZAKI YOUSSEF

Royal Excavations at Helwan (1945-1947). Le Caire: 1951. V. 37; 40; 42; 44

SAAR, JOHANN JACOB

Ost-Indianische Funfzehen-Jahrige Kriegs Dienste und Wahrhafftige Beschreibung . . . von 1644 bis 1659, zur . . . Nuremberg: 1672. V. 38; 41

SAARINEN, EERO

Eero Saarinen on His Work. New Haven: 1962. V. 40; 41

Eero Saarinen on His Work. New Haven: 1963. V. 40

On His Work. A Selection of Buildings Dating from 1947 to 1964, with Statements by the Architect. New Haven: 1962. V. 39

SAAVEDRA, FAJARDO, DIEGO DE

Idea de un Principe Politico Christiano Representada en Cien Empresas. Munich: 1640. V. 37

Idea de un Principe Politico Christiano, Representada en Cien Empressas. Va Emmendada en esta Sexta Impression de Todos los Yerros que Avia en las Otras. Valencia: 1675. V. 37; 40

The Royal Politician. London: 1700. V. 38; 41

SABARTES, JAIME

Picasso: Variations on Velazquez painting 'The Maids of Honour' and Other Recent Works. New York: 1959. V. 42

Picasso: Toreros. New York: 1961. V. 41

SABATINI, RAFAEL

The Novels of . . . London: 1926-28. V. 46

Novels. London: 1926-32. V. 41; 44

SABBA DA CASTIGLIO, FRA

Riccordi Overo Ammaestramenti. Venice: 1578. V. 40

SABBATH Bells Chimed by the Poets. London: 1856. V. 44
SABBATH Bells Chimed by the Poets. London: 1865. V. 39; 43
SABBATH Bells Chimed by the Poets. London: 1870. V. 39

SABBATINI, NICOLA

Practica di Fabricar Scene e machine ne' Teatri . . . Ristampata di Novo Coll' Aggiunta del Secondo Libro. Ravenna: 1638. V. 37

SABELLICO, MARCO ANTONIO 1436-1506

Annotationes Veteres & Recentes ex Plinio, Livio & Pluribus Authoribus (and other works . . .). Venice: 1508. V. 45

Rerum Venetarum Decades. Venice: 1487. V. 40

SABELLICUS, MARCUS ANTONIUS

Decades Rerum Venetarum. Venice: 1487. V. 39

De Omnium Gentium Omniumque Seculorum Insignibus Memoriaq . . . Basiliae: 1563. V. 41

SABER, CLIFFORD

Desert Rat Sketch Book. New York: 1959. V. 37; 42

SABIN, EDWIN LEGRAND

Kit Carson Days 1809-1868. New York: 1935. V. 38; 39; 40; 43; 45; 46

SABIN, ELIJAH ROBINSON

A Discourse, Preached on Tuesday, Feb. 11, 1812, in Presence of the Supreme Executive of Massachusetts, by Request of the Young Men of Boston. Boston: 1812. V. 44

The Life and Reflections of Charles Observator: In Which are Displayed the Real Characters of Human Life. Boston: 1816. V. 38; 43

SABIN, JOSEPH

The American Bibliopolist. New York: 1869-74. V. 44; 45

The American Bibliopolist. New York: 1869-77. V. 45

A Bibliography of Bibliography or a Handy Book About Books Which Relate to Books . . . New York: 1877. V. 46

Bibliotheca Americana: A Dictionary of Books Relating to America From Its Discovery to the Present Time. New York: n.d. V. 44

Bibliotheca Americana: A Dictionary of Books Relating to America From Its Discovery to the Present Time. Amsterdam: 1961-62. V. 38

Catalogue of the Library Collected by the Late Professor Amos Dean of Albany, New York . . . New York: 1868. V. 44

A Dictionary of Books Relating to America, From Its Discovery to the Present Time. New York. V. 41; 43

A Dictionary of Books Relating to America From Its Discovery to the Present Time. Amsterdam: 1961. V. 43

A Dictionary of Books Relating to America, From Its Discovery to the Present Time. Amsterdam: 1961-62. V. 40; 42; 44

A Dictionary of Books Relating to America From Its Discovery to the Present Time. New York: 1967. V. 40

SABINE, EDWARD

The North Georgia Gazette and Winter Chronicle. London: 1821. V. 42

Report on the Variations of the Magnetic Intensity Observed at Different Points of the Earth's Surface . . . London: 1838. V. 44

SABINE, H.

The Publican's Sure Guide, or, Every Man His Own Cellerman. London: 1807. V. 39

SABINE, JAMES

The Demise of the President Improved in a Sermon, Delivered on Fast Day, May 14, 1841 as Recommended by the Government. Vermont: 1841. V. 43

SABINE, LORENZO

An Address Before the New Engalnd Historic Genealogical Society . . . Tuesday Sept. 13th, 1859. Boston: 1859. V. 41; 43

The American Loyalists. Boston: 1847. V. 38

Biographical Sketches of Loyalists of the American Revolution. Boston: 1864. V. 37; 40; 42

SACCARDO, P. A.

Fungi Italici Autographice Delineati. Patavii: 1877-86. V. 38

SACCO di Roma Del MDXXVII: Narrazioni di Contemporanei; Scelte per Cura id Carlo Milanesi. Florence: 1867. V. 39

SACCO, LUIGI

Trattato di Vaccinazione con Osservasioni sul Giavardo e Vajuolo Pecornio. Milan: 1809. V. 38; 41; 45

Trattato di Vaccinazione con Osservazioni sul Ciavardo e Vajuolo Pecorino. Milano: 1809. V. 42; 43

SACCONI, SIMONE F.

The Secrets of Stradivari. Cremona: 1980. V. 38

SACHER-MASOCH, LEOPOLD

Seraph, a Tale of Hungary. New York: 1893. V. 39

SACHEVERELL, HENRY

The New Association. Part II. With Father Improvements, As Another and Later Scots Presbyterian-Covenant . . . 1703. V. 39

SACHEVERELL, HENRY continued

The Trial of . . . Before the House of Peers, for High Crimes and Misdemeanors. Dublin: 1710. V. 40

The Tryal of Dr. Henry Sacheverell, Before the House of Peers, for High Crimes and Misdemeanors . . . London: 1710. V. 39; 40; 46

SACHEVERELL, WILLIAM

An Account of the Isle of Man, Its Inhabitants, Language, Soil, Remarkable Curiosities, the Succession of Its Kings and Bishops, Down to the Present Time. London: 1702. V. 38; 42; 43

SACHS, EDWIN O.

Facts on Fire Prevention; the Results of Fire Tests Conducted by the British Fire Prevention Committee. London: 1902. V. 45

Fires and Public Entertainments. London: 1897. V. 37

Modern Opera Houses and Theatres. London: 1897-98. V. 41

Modern Opera Houses and Theatres. London: 1896-98. V. 37

Modern Opera Houses and Theatres. New York: 1968. V. 37

Stage Construction. Examples of Modern Stages Selected from Playhouses Recently Erected in Europe with Descriptive and Critical Text . . . London: 1898. V. 37

SACHS, HANS

Hans Sachs in Gewande Seiner Zeit Oder Gedichte Dieses Meistersangers in Derselben Gestalt, Wie sie Zuerst auf Cinzelne . . . Gotha: 1821. V. 45

SACHSE, JULIUS F.

Falckner's Curieuse Nachricht von Pensylvania . . . Philadelphia: 1905. V. 41; 42

The Fatherland: (1450-1700). Philadelphia: 1897. V. 42

The Wayside Inss of the Lancaster Roadside Between Philadelphia and Lancaster. Lancaster: 1912. V. 41

SACKET, DELOS BENNET

Manual for Sharps' Carbine. Fort Smith: 1859. V. 40

SACKETT, FRANCES R.

Dick Dowling. Houston: 1937. V. 38

SACKVILLE, GEORGE

The Proceedings of a General Court Martial Held . . . upon the Trial of Lord George Sackville. London: 1760. V. 38; 40

The Trial of the Right Honourable Lord George Sackville, at a Court-Martial . . . February 29, 1760 for an Enquiry into His Conduct. London: 1760. V. 39; 43; 45

SACKVILLE, MARGARET

The Dream-Pedlar. London: 1914. V. 46

Poems. London: 1923. V. 42

SACKVILLE-WEST, EDWARD

Graham Sutherland. Harmondsworth: 1943. V. 43

The Rescue: a Melodrama for Broadcasting Based on Homer's Odyssey. London: 1945. V. 44

The Ruin. London: 1926. V. 37

Simpson - a Life. London: 1931. V. 46

SACKVILLE-WEST, LIONEL

Knole House: Its State Rooms, Pictures and Antiquities. Sevenoaks: 1906. V. 37; 45

SACKVILLE-WEST, VICTORIA MARY 1892-1962

All Passion Spent. London: 1931. V. 42; 43

Andrew Marvell. London: 1929. V. 38; 40

Andrew Marvell. London: 1939. V. 37

Collected Poems. London: 1933. V. 40; 44; 46

Constantinople. London: 1915. V. 37; 39; 40; 42; 45

The Dark Island. London: 1934. V. 38; 40; 41; 42

The Dark Island. New York: 1934. V. 44

A Democrat's Chapbook. London: 1942. V. 37; 40; 42

The Edwardians. London. V. 41

The Edwardians. London: 1929. V. 44

The Edwardians. London: 1930. V. 37; 39; 40; 41; 43

Family History. London: 1932. V. 37; 38; 41

The Garden. London: 1946. V. 39; 40; 43; 44; 45

The Heir. London: 1922. V. 38; 43; 45; 46

Heritage. 1919. V. 44

Invitation to Cast Out Care. London: 1931. V. 42

King's Daughter. London: 1929. V. 44

Knole and the Sackvilles. London: 1922. V. 39; 43; 45

Knole and the Sackvilles. New York: 1922? V. 41

Knole and the Sackvilles. London: 1931. V. 46

The Land. London: 1926. V. 38; 40; 43

Nursery Rhymes. London: 1947. V. 37; 39; 40; 42; 45

The Old Chorister to Himself As A Boy. London: 1946. V. 39; 42; 44

Orchard and Vineyard. London: 1921. V. 38; 39; 41; 42; 43

Passenger to Teheran. London: 1926. V. 40; 45

Pepita. London: 1933. V. 39

Pepita. London: 1937. V. 40; 41; 42

Poems of East and West. London: 1917. V. 38; 43

Saint Joan of Arc. London: 1936. V. 38; 39; 41; 42

Seducers in Ecuador. London: 1924. V. 37; 38; 39

Sissinghurst. London: 1931. V. 37; 38; 42

Sissinghurst. Warlingham: 1933. V. 45

Solitude - a Poem. London: 1938. V. 40

Solitude. New York: 1939. V. 40

Timgad. London: 1944? V. 41

Twelve Days. London: 1928. V. 40

The Women's Land Army. London: 1944. V. 41; 42

THE SACRAL Art in Poland: Architecture. Translated from the Polish by Krystyna Dobrowolska. Warsaw: 1956. V. 37

SACRAMENTO County and Its Resources; Our Capital City Past and Present. A Souvenir of the Bee, 1894. Sacramento: 1895. V. 41

LA SACRE et Couronnement de Louis XVI. Paris: 1775. V. 44

SACRE, JOSSE

Les Mysteres des Bandes Noires. Bruxelles: 1866. V. 38

SACRED HARMONIC SOCIETY

Catalogue of the Library . . . London: 1872. V. 45

THE SACRED Treasury, a Literary and Religious Souvenir. London: 1845. V. 39

SACROBOSCO, JOHANNES DE d. 1244

De Anni Ratione, seu . . . Computus Ecclesiasticus. Paris: 1551. V. 45

Annotationi Sopra la Lettione Della Spera (sic) del Sacro Bosco Dove si Dichiarono Tutti e Principii Mathematici & Naturali che in Quella si Possan'Desiderare. Firenze: 1550. V. 38

In Sphaeram Ioannis de Sacro Bosco Commentarius nunc Iteram ab Ipso Auctore Recognitus & Multis ac Varijs Locis Locupletatus. Dominico Basa: 1581. V. 46

Libellus de Sphaera. Wittenberg: 1558. V. 38

Opuscula Johannis de Sacrobusto Spericum cu Figuris Optimis et Novis Textu in se. Sine Ambiguitate Declarantibus. Leipzig: 1494. V. 44

Sfera . . . Sienna: 1604. V. 45

Sphaera Mundi; Regiomontanus; Disputationes Contra Cremonensia Deliramenta, Georgius Purbachius, Theoricae Novae Planetarum. Venice: 1482. V. 42; 45

Sphaera. Venice: 1557. V. 44

Sphaera . . . Emendata. Paris: 1577. V. 46

Sphera Volgare Novamente Tradotta con Molte Notande Additioni di Geometria, Cosmographia, Arte Naviatoria, et Steremetria, Proportioni, et Qvantita delli Elementi, Distanze, Grandeze, et Movimenti dv tvtti li Corpi . . . Venice: 1537. V. 38

Uberrimum Sphere Mundi Commentum Inersertis Etiam questionibus Domini Petri de Aliaco Nuper Magna cum Diligentia Castigatum. Paris: 1508. V. 38; 44

SACRORUM Bibliorum Vulgatae Editionis Concordantiae. Lyons: 1726. V. 39

SACROSANCTI Concilii Tridentini Canones et Decreta. Antwerp: 1586. V. 38

SACY, LOUIS DE

A Discourse on Friendship. London: 1707. V. 40

THE SAD Case of Mrs. Kate Southern! Philadelphia: 1878. V. 38

SADE, DONATIEN ALPHONSE FRANCOIS, COMTE, CALLED MARQUIS DE 1740-1814

Histoire de Justine ou Les Malheurs de la Vertu . . . (with) Histoire de Juliette ou Les Prosperites du Vice . . . Amsterdam?. V. 41

Histoire de Justine ou Les Malheurs de la Vertu . . . century. V. 42

Justine. Paris: 1889. V. 45

Zoloe et ses Deux Acolythes; ou Quelques Decades de la Vie de Trois Jolies Femmes . . . Turin: 1800. V. 42; 43

SADE, JACQUES FRANCOIS PAUL ALPHONSE DE

The Life of Petrarch. London: 1775. V. 37

SADELER, IAN

Planetarum Effectus et Eorum in Signis Zodiaci Super Provincias, Regiones et Civitates Dominia. Antwerp: 1585. V. 38

SADELER, JUSTUS

Septem Artium Liberalium Icones. Venice: 1609. V. 40

SADELER, MARCO

Vestigi Delle Antichita di Roma, Tivoli, Possuolo et Altri Luochi. Prague: 1606. V. 38; 42; 45

SA'DI

The Gulistan or Rose Garden of Sa'di. Benares: 1888. V. 45

SADI, MOSHARREF OD-DIN IBN MOSLEH OB-DIN SADI

V. 41

SADLEIR, MICHAEL

Daumier. The Man and the Artist. London: 1924. V. 42

Desolate Splendour. London: 1923. V. 38

The Evolution of Publisher's Binding Styles 1770-1900. London: 1930. V. 39; 41

Excursions in Victorian Bibliography. London: 1922. V. 38; 39; 41; 42

Fanny by Gaslight. London: 1940. V. 38

Forlorn Sunset. London: 1947. V. 44

XIX Century Fiction; A Bibliographical Record Based on His Own Collection. Cambridge: 1951. V. 37; 38; 39

XIX Century Fiction. London: 1951. V. 39; 42

XIX Century Fiction. New York: 1969. V. 40; 42

XIX Century Fiction. London & Berkeley: 1951. V. 38

Trollope, a Commentary. London: 1927. V. 39

Trollope - a Bibliography - an Analysis of the History and Structure of the Works of Anthony Trollope, and a General Survey of the Effect of Original Publishing Conditions on a Book's Subsequent Rarity. London: 1928. V. 40

SADLER, BARRY

The Moi. Nashville: 1977. V. 44

SADLER, JOHN

Rights of the Kingdom; or Customs of Our Ancestours: Touching the Duty, Power, Election or Succession of Our Kings and Parliaments . . . London: 1649. V. 38

SADLER, MICHAEL THOMAS

Ireland; Its Evils, and Their Remedies; Being a Refutation of the Errors of the Emigration Committtee and Others, Touching that Country. London: 1828. V. 41; 42; 43

Ireland: Its Evils, and Their Remedies. London: 1830. V. 43

The Law of Population: a Treatise, in Six Books . . . London: 1830. V. 39

The Speech of Michael Thomas Sadler, M.P. for Newark, in the House of Commons on Thursday the Third of June, on Proposing Poor Laws for Ireland . . . . London: 1830. V. 43

SADOLETO, JACOPO, CARDINAL 1477-1547

Epistolarum Libri XVI. Eiusdem ad Paulum Sadoletum Epistolarum Liber Unus. Vita Eiusdem Autoris per Antonium Florabellum. Cologne: 1564. V. 39

In Pavli Epistolam Ad Romanos Commentariorvm Libri Tres. Lyon: 1535. V. 43

De Laudibus Philosophiae. Venice: 1539. V. 38; 39

De Liberis Recte Instituendis, Liber. Colophon: Venetiis: 1533. V. 39

De Liberis Recte Institvendis, Liber. Venice: 1533. V. 42

SADOLETUS, JACOBUS

Epistolarum Libri Sex Decim. Lvgdvni: 1560. V. 44

SADOVNIKOV, VLADIMIR

Souvenir de St. Petersbourg. St. Petersburg: 1833. V. 39

SAEL, G.

Mental Amusement; or, the Juvenile Moralist . . . London: 1798. V. 37; 41

SAEL, GEORGE

Mental Amusement: Consisting of Moral Essays, Allegories and Tales. London: 1797. V. 46

SAENGER, PAUL

A Catalogue of the Pre-1500 Western Manuscript Books at the Newberry Library. Chicago: 1989. V. 46

SAFA, Z.

A History of Iranian Literature, from the Beginning of the Islamic Period to the Middle of the 12th Century A.H. Teheran: 1956-85. V. 39

THE SAFETY of France to Monsieur the Dauphin. London: 1690. V. 45

SAFFELL, W. T. R.

Records of the Revolutionary War. Baltimore: 1894. V. 39

SAFFORD, A. P. K.

Resources of Arizona Territory with a Description of the Indian Tribes . . . . San Francisco: 1871. V. 39

SAFFORD, JAMES M.

A Geological Reconnoissance of the State of Tennessee . . . Nashville: 1856. V. 43

SAFFORD, WILLIAM H.

Blennerhassett Papers. Cincinnati: 1861. V. 42

The Blennerhassett Papers, Embodying the Private Journal of Harman Blennerhassett, etc. Cincinnati: 1864. V. 40

The Life of Harman Blennerhassett. Chillicothe: 1850. V. 40; 42; 46

SAFIAN, JOSEPH

Corrective Rhinoplastic Surgery. New York: 1935. V. 42

THE SAGA of Llywarch the Old. London: 1955. V. 44

SAGA of the All American. Chicago: 1946. V. 38

SAGAN, FRANCOISE

New York. Paris: 1956. V. 46

SAGARD, GABRIEL

The Long Journey to the Country of the Hurons. Toronto: 1939. V. 37

SAGATOO, MARY A.

Wah Sash Kah Moqua; or, Thirty-Three Years Among the Indians. Boston: 1897. V. 43

SAGE, BETTY

Rhymes of Real Children. London: 1905. V. 46

SAGE, DEAN

The Ristigouche and Its Salmon Fishing. Edinburgh: 1888. V. 43; 44

SAGE, JOHN

An Account of the Late Establishment of Presbyterian Government by the Parliament of Scotland in Anno 1690. London: 1693. V. 45

The Case of the Present Afflicted Clergy in Scotland Truly Represented. London: 1690. V. 38

Presbytery, Untwisted from the Bottom. London: 1709. V. 45

SAGE, RUFUS B.

Scenes in the Rocky Mountains, Oregon, California, New Mexico, Texas and Grand Prairies . . . Philadelphia: 1846. V. 42

Wild Scenes in Kansas and Nebraska, The Rocky Mountains, Oregon, California, New Mexico, Texas and the Grand Prairies . . . Philadelphia: 1855. V. 40; 41

SAGE, WALTER N.

Sir James Douglas and British Columbia. Toronto: 1930. V. 46

SAGERUS, GASPAR 1463-1527

De Sanctorum Imploratione et Eorum Suffrgiis Scriptum. Ex Monaco: 1524. V. 38

SAGRA, RAMON DE LA

Historia Economico-Politca Y Estadistica de la Isla de Cuba o Sea de Sus Progresos en la Poblacion, La Griacultura, el Comercio y Las Rentas. Havana: 1831. V. 40

SAGREDO, GIOVANNI

Memorie Istoriche de Monarchi Ottomani. Venetia: 1673. V. 39

SAHAGUN, B. DE

Historia General de Las Cosas de Nueva Espana . . . Mexico: 1829. V. 38

Historia General de Las Cosas de Nueva Espana . . . Mexico: 1829-30. V. 39

SAHAGUN, BERNARDINO DE

Florentine Codex: General History of the Things of New Spain. Salt Lake City: 1953-81. V. 37

Historia General de las Cosas de Nueva Espana. Mexico: 1982. V. 38

SAHAGUN, LUIS

Historia General de las Cosas de Nueva Espana. Mexico: 1938. V. 45

SAIA, NONIO MARCELLO

Ragionamenti Sopra la Celste Sfera in Lingua Italiana Comune. Paris: 1552. V. 45

THE SAILOR'S Happiness, a Scheme to Prevent the Impressing of Seamen in Time of War. London: 1751. V. 41

SAINBEL, CHARLES VIAL DE

Elements of Veterinary Art . . . London: 1797. V. 46

Lectures on the Elements of Farriery; or, the Art of Horse-Shoeing, and on the Diseases of the Foot. London: 1793. V. 46

SAINCTES, CLAUDE DE

liturgiae, Sive Missae Sanctorum Patrum: Iacobi Apostoli & Fratris Domini . . . De Ritu Missae et Eucharistia. Antwerp: 1562. V. 45

SAINE, U. C.

The Legend of Ermengarde. Paris: 1929. V. 41

SAINSBURY, MARIA TUKE

Henry Scott Tuke, RA, RWS. A Memoir. London: 1933. V. 46

SAINSBURY, W. NOEL

Original Unpublished Papers Illustrative of the Life of Sir Peter Paul Rubens as an Artist and a Diplomatist, Preserved in HM State Paper Office . . . London: 1859. V. 46

SAINT James's: A Satirical Poem in Six Epistles to Mr. Crockford. London: 1827. V. 38
SAINT Augustine, Florida. Sketches of Its History . . . New York: 1871. V. 41

THE ST. ALBAN'S Abbey Guide . . . The Decline of Verulam . . . Account of the Churches of St. Michael, St. Stephen and St. Peter . . . London: 1824. V. 40

SAINT ALBANS ABBEY

Chronica Monasterii S. Albani. London: 1863-76. V. 44

SAINT-AMANT, MARC ANTOINE GERARD, SIEUR DE 1594-1660

Les Oeuvres Reueues, Corrigees, et de Beaucoup Augmentees. Paris: 1665. V. 38

ST. AUBIN; or the Infidel. Edinburgh: 1821. V. 43

SAINT AUBIN, CHARLES GERMAIN DE

Premier (-IIme) Receuil de Chiffres . . . Paris: 1770. V. 46

SAINT AUGUSTINE, PSEUDO.

Sermones ad Heremitas. Strassburg: 1487. V. 43

SAINT BRIDE FOUNDATION

Catalogue of the Technical Reference Librarry of Works on Printing and the Allied Arts. London: 1919. V. 38; 42; 43; 44

SAINT CHRISTOPHER. LAWS, STATUTES, ETC. - 1832

The Laws of Saint Christopher. From 1711 to 1831 Inclusive. Saint Christopher: 1832. V. 40

SAINT CLAIR, ARTHUR

A Narrative of the Manner in Which the Campaign Against the Indians, in the Year 1791, Was Conducted, Under the Command of Major General St. Clair, Together With His Observations on the Statements of the Secretary of War . . . Philadelphia: 1812. V. 37; 40; 41; 43; 45

A Narrative of the Manner in Which the Campaign Against the Indians . . . Philadelphia: 1812. V. 38

The St. Clair Papers. Cincinnati: 1882. V. 40; 41; 46

SAINT CLAIR, THOMAS STAUNTON

A Residence in the West Indies and America, with a Narrative of the Expedition to the Island of Walcheren. London: 1834. V. 42; 46

SAINT-CRICQ, LAURENT

A Journey Across South America from the Pacific to the Atlantic . . . London: 1873-74. V. 45

SAINT CUTHBERT: Life, Written Anonymously About the Year A.D. 700. Edinburgh: 1888. V. 40

SAINT EVREMOND, CHARLES DE MARGUETEL ST. DENIS, SIGNEUR DE 1613?-1703

The Works. London: 1728. V. 40

SAINT EXUPERY, ANTOINE DE

Flight to Arras. New York: 1942. V. 39; 41

The Little Prince. New York: 1943. V. 38; 40; 42; 43; 46

Le Petit Prince. New York: 1943. V. 42; 45

Night Flight. Paris: 1932. V. 46

SAINT-FOIX, GERMAIN FRANCOIS DE

Historical Essays Upon Paris. London: 1767. V. 38

SAINT GERMAIN, CHRISTOPHER ?1460-1540

The Dialogue in English, Betweene a Doctor of Divinity and a Student in the Laws of England. London: 1638. V. 37; 40

Two Dialogues in English, Between a Doctour of Divinity and a Student in the Lawes of England, of the Grounds of the Said Laws and of Conscience. London: 1668. V. 41

Two Dialogues in English, Between a Doctor of Divinity, and A Student in the Laws of England . . . London: 1687. V. 37

SAINT GERMAINE, CHRISTOPHER ?1460-1540

The Dialogues in English, Betwene a Doctor of Divinity and a Student in the Lawes of England. Londini: 1580. V. 40

The Dialogues in English, Betwene a Doctor of Divinity, and a Student in the Lawes of England. London: 1607. V. 40

The Dialogues in English, Betwene a Doctor of Divinity and a Student in the Lawes of England. London: 1673. V. 40; 44

The Dialogues in English, Betwene a Doctor of Divinity, and a Student in the Lawes of England. London: 1721. V. 40

SAINT-GERMAN, CHRISTOPHER

The Dialogue in English, Between a Doctor of Divinitie, and a Student in the Lawes of England. London: 1613. V. 38

The Dialogue in English, Betweene a Doctor of Divinitie and a Student in the Lawes of England. London: 1623. V. 45

Doctor and Student; or Dialouges Between a Doctor of Divinity and a Student in the Laws of England . . . London: 1761. V. 46

THE SAINT HELENA Calendar and Directory of 1832. St. Helena: 1832. V. 46
THE SAINT HELENA Almanac and Annual Register. St. Helena: 1856. V. 40

ST. JAMES': a Satirical Poem in Six Epistles to Mr. Crockford. London: 1827. V. 43; 46

THE ST. JAMES'S Magazine and Heraldic and Historical Register. London: 1849-50. V. 41

SAINT-JOHN, BAYLE

The Memoirs of the Duke of Saint Simon: on the Reign of Louis XIV, and the Regency, First and Second Series, Complete. London: 1857. V. 38

The Subalpine Kigndom; or, Experiences and Studies in Savoy, Piedmont and Genoa. London: 1856. V. 45

Village Life in Egypt: With Sketches of the Said. Boston: 1853. V. 40; 42; 44

SAINT JOHN, CHARLES

Short Sketches on the Wild Sports and Natural History of the Highlands . . . London: 1893. V. 44

A Tour in Sutherlandshire. London: 1849. V. 43

A Tour In Sutherlandshire, with Extracts from the Field Books of a Sportsman and Naturalist. London: 1849. V. 43

A Tour in Sutherlandshire, with Extracts from the Field-Books of a Sportsman and Naturalist. London: 1849. V. 46

A Tour in Sutherland . . . London: 1884. V. 38

Wild Sports & Natural History of the Highlands. London: 1919. V. 40

SAINT JOHN, F. E. M.

the Sea or Mountains. London: 1877. V. 44

SAINT JOHN, H. C.

Notes and Sketches from the Wild Coasts of Nipon with Chapters on Cruising After Pirates in Chinese Waters. Edinburgh: 1880. V. 43

Notes and Sketches from the Wild Coasts of Nippon, With Chapters on Crusing After Pirates in Chinese Waters. Edinburgh: 1880. V. 43

SAINT JOHN, HENRY CRAVEN

Notes and Sketches from the Wild Coasts of Nipon . . . Edinburgh: 1880. V. 45

SAINT JOHN HOPE, W.

Cowdray and Eastbourne Priory in the County of Sussex. London: 1919. V. 42

SAINT-JOHN, J.

The Californian Tourist's Guide Book. San Francisco: 1886. V. 38

SAINT JOHN, J. A.

Egypt and Nubia. London: 1845. V. 45

SAINT JOHN, JAMES AUGUSTUS

Oriental Album. Characters, Costumes and Modes of Life in the Valley of the Nile, Illustrated from Designs Taken on the Spot by E. Prisse. London: 1851. V. 46

SAINT JOHN, JOHN 1746-1793

Observations on the Land Revenue of the Crown. London: 1787. V. 41

SAINT JOHN, JUDITH

The Osborne Collection of Early Children's Books 1566-1910. (Volume 2 covering the years 1476-1910). Toronto: 1958/75. V. 42; 46

SAINT JOHN, MOLYNEUX

The Province of British Columbia, Canada. Montreal?: 1886. V. 45

SAINT JOHN, OLIVER

Mr. St. Johns Speech, or Argument in Parliament; Shewing Whether a Man May be a Judge and a Witness in the Same Cause. London: 1641. V. 45; 46

SAINT JOHN, PERCY BOLINGBROKE

The Texas Rifle-Hunter, or Field Sports on the Prairie by Captain Flack ('The Ranger') Late of the Texan Rangers. London: 1866. V. 37

The Trapper's Bride: A Tale of the Rocky Mountains. London: 1845. V. 40; 41; 45

SAINT JOHN, S.

Life in the Forests of the Far East. London: 1862. V. 37

SAINT JOHN, SPENSER

Hayti or the Black Republic. London: 1889. V. 44

The Life of Sir James Brooke Rajah of Sarawak from His Personal Papers and Correspondence. Edinburgh: 1879. V. 46

SAINT JOHNSTON, ALFRED

A South Sea Lover: a Romance. London: 1890. V. 44

SAINT LAWRENCE & ATLANTIC RAIL-ROAD CO.

Proceedings of the Fifth Annual General Meeting of the Proprietors of the . . . Held in Montreal, on the 16th January 1850; with the Report of the Directords. Montreal: 1850. V. 45

SAINT LEGER, FRANCIS BARRY BOYLE 1799-1829

Mr. Blount's Mss. Being Selections from the Papers of a Man of the World . . . London: 1826. V. 45

Mr. Blount's MSS being Selections from the Papers of a Man of the World . . . London: 1826. V. 38

SAINT LO, GEORGE

England's Interest; or, a Discipline for Seamen. London: 1694. V. 43

SAINT LOUIS

Manual of the Metropolitan Police Department of the City of St. Louis. St. Louis: 1902. V. 44

SAINT LOUIS & St. Joseph Railroad. Its Business Importance and Value of Its First Mortgage Bonds. St. Louis: 1870. V. 42

SAINT LOUIS, IRON MOUNTAIN AND SOUTHERN RAILWAY

Importnat To All! Bound for the Happy Lands! Low Rates to Arkansas and Missouri Via Saint Louis Over the Popular St. Louis, Iron Mountain and Southern Railway. St. Louis: 1878. V. 44

SAINT LOUIS, IRON MT. & SOTHERN RAILROAD COMPANY

Eastern Missouri and Arkansas. St. Louis. V. 45

SAINT MARC, JEAN PAUL ANDRE DE 1728-1818

Oeuvres. Paris: 1785. V. 40

SAINT MAUR, ALGERNON, MRS.

Impressions of a Tenderfoot During a Journey in Search of Sport in the Far West. London: 1890. V. 42; 45

ST. NICHOLAS Songs. New York: 1885. V. 40

SAINT PAUL City Directory for 1856-57. Saint Paul: 1857. V. 45
SAINT PAUL, Minneapolis & Manitoba RY 3024 Miles of Steel Track in Minnesota, Dakota and Montana . . . St. Paul,: 1888. V. 38

ST. PAUL & CHICAGO RAILWAY COMPANY

Revised Statutes of the Territory of Minnesota, Passed at the Second Session of the Legislative Assembly. St. Paul: 1851. V. 37

SAINT PAUL, HENRY

Our Home and Foreign Policy . . . Novemeber, 1863. Mobile: 1863. V. 42
Our Home and Foreign Police, by . . . November, 1863. Mobile: 1863. V. 37

SAINT PAUL'S ECCLESIOLOGICAL SOCIETY

Transactions. London: 1881-1920. V. 45; 46

SAINT PHALE, MM. DE

The History of Mademoiselle De St. Phale. London: 1787. V. 45

SAINT PIERRE, J. H.

Paul and Virginia. Philadelphia: 1808. V. 44
Paul and Virgina, and the Indian Cottage. London: 1848. V. 44

SAINT-PIERRE, JACQUES HENRI BERNARDIN DE

Beauties of the Studies of Nature: selected from the Works of Saint Pierre. London & New York: 1799. V. 37

Botanical Harmony Delineated: or, Applications of Some General Laws of Nature to Plants. Worcester: 1797. V. 37

Harmonies of nature. London: 1815. V. 38

The Indian Cottage. To Which is added the Coffee-House of Surat. London: 1802. V. 37

Paul and Virginia. London: 1796. V. 38; 45

Paul and Virginia. London: 1839. V. 38; 39

Studies of Nature . . . London: 1796. V. 40

The Studies of Nature, To Which are Added the Indian Cottage, and Paul and Virginia. London: 1836. V. 39

Studies of Nature. Worcester: 1797. V. 37

A Vindication of Divine Providence; Derived from a Philosopic and Moral Survey of Nature and of Man. Worcester: 1797. V. 37

a Voyage to the Island of Mauritius . . . London: 1775. V. 41; 44; 45

Voyages of Amasis. In French and English. Translated by M.M.*****. Boston: 1795. V. 37

SAINT-PRIEST

Malta, par un Voyageur Francois. Malta: 1791. V. 46

SAINT QUENTIN, DOMINIQUE DE

A Poetical Chronology of the Kings of England . . . Reading: 1792. V. 45

SAINT REAL, CAESAR VISCHARD DE

The Memoirs of the Duchess Mazarine. London: 1676. V. 43; 45

SAINT-REAL, CESAR VICHARD DE

Conspiracy of the Spaniards Against Venice, and of John Lewis Fiesco Against Genoa. Boston: 1828. V. 44

De L'Usage de l'Histoire. Paris: 1671. V. 37

Dom Carlos Novvelle Historiqve. Amsterdam: 1673. V. 37

Frantzoesischer Sack-Spiegel Denen Jenigen So sich Selbsten Gerne Kennen Moechten zu Liebe. Augsburg: 1691. V. 37

SAINT ROBERT'S Chapel at Knaresborough Near Harrowgate Spaw in Yorkshire. London: 1778. V. 45

SAINT SAUVEUR, A. G. DE

Travels through the Balearic and Pithiusian Islands Performed Between the Years 1801 and 1806. London: 1808. V. 40

SAINT-SIMON, DUC DE

Memoires, Complets et Authentiques. Paris: 1856. V. 46

SAINT-SIMON, DUKE OF

Memoirs on the Reign of Louis XIV and the Regency. London: 1891. V. 37

SAINT VINCENT, J. B. G. M. BORY DE

Voyage to, and Travels through the Four Principal Islands of the African Seas, Performed by Order of the French Government, During the Years 1801 and 1802. London: 1805. V. 40

ST.CLAIR, ARTHUR

A Narrative of the Manner in Which the Campaign Against the Indians, in the Year 1791, Was Conducted, Under the Command of Major General St. Clair . . . Philadelphia: 1812. V. 38

SAINT CLAIR, PHILIP R.

Frederic Remington: The American West. Kent: 1978. V. 39

SAINTE MARTHE, SCAEVOLE DE

Gallorvm Doctrina Illvstrivm, Qvi Nostra Patrumque Memoria Flouerunt, Elogia. Poitiers: 1602. V. 40

SAINTE-MARTHE, SCEVOLE DE

Carmen de Victoria Apud Evriacum Parta Pridie Eid. Martieae anno clc. lc. xc. ad Christianias Regem Henricum IIII. Leyden: 1592. V. 37

Les Oevvres. Poitiers: 1559. V. 42

Paedotrophia; or, the Art of Nursing and Rearing Children. London: 1787. V. 39; 41

Paedotrophia: or the Art of Nursing and Rearing Children, in a Poem in Three Books . . . London: 1797. V. 45

LE SAINTE Messe ou Sont Representees par les Actions du Pretre Les Misteres de la Passion de Notre Seigneur Jesus Christ Avec les Oraisons Applique a Chacun Mistere. Paris: 1650. V. 41

SAINT GEORGE, HENRY

The Cambridgeshire Visitation. Middle Hill: 1840. V. 39

SAINT JOHN, CHARLES

Natural History and Sport in Moray. Collected from His Journals and Letters . . . Edinburgh: 1882. V. 39

Short Sketches of the Wild Sports and Natural History of the Highlands. London: 1849. V. 39

A Tour in Sutherlandshire, with Extracts from the Field-Books of a Sportsman and Naturalist. London: 1849. V. 39

SAINT JOHN HOPE, W. H.

The Stall Plates of the Knights of the Order of the Garter 1348-1485. Westminster: 1901. V. 39

ST.JOHN, S.

Life in the Forests of the Far East. London: 1862. V. 37

SAINT LOUIS AND IRON MOUNTAIN RAILROAD COMPANY

Second Annual Report of the Board of Directors of the St. Louis and Iron Mountain Railroad Company, and the Report of the Engineers. Saint Louis: 1854. V. 39

SAINT LOUIS AND ST. PAUL PACKET COMPANY

Tourists' Summer Guide, Containing Points of Interest Along the Upper Mississippi from St. Louis to St. Paul, and the Famous Summer Resorts of the Golden North-West. St. Louis: 1882. V. 39

SAINT LOUIS. POLICE DEPT.

Manual of the Metropolitan Police Department of the City of St. Louis. St. Louis: 1902. V. 39

SAINTONGE, LOUISE GENEVIEVE GILLOT DE

Histoire Secrete de Dom Antoine Roy de Portugal. Paris: 1696. V. 37

SAINT PAUL & CHICAGO RAILWAY COMPANY

Statement of the St. Paul & Chcicago Railway Co., Respecting the Issuance of Its First Mortgage Land Grant Skinking Fund Bonds, Amounting to Four Millions of Dollars. Saint Paul: 1867. V. 39

SAINTSBURY, GEORGE

Minor Poets of the Caroline Period. Oxford: 1905-21. V. 46

A Primer of French Literature. Oxford: 1880. V. 42

A Scrap Book. A Second Scrap Book. A Last Scrap Book. London: 1922-24. V. 45

A Scrap Book; A Second Scrap Book; A Last Scrap Book. London: 1922/1923/1924. V. 37

SAINT VALLIER, JEAN BAPTISTE DE LA CROIX CHEVRIERES DE

Estat Present de l'eglise et de la Colonie Francoise dans la Nouvelle France, Par M. l'Eveque de Quebec. Paris: 1688. V. 39

SAISSY, JEAN ANTOINE

An Essay on the Diseases of the Internal Ear . . . With a Supplement on Diseases of the External Ear . . . Baltimore: 1829. V. 42

SAJOUS, CHARLES

The Internal Secretions and the Principles of Medicine. Philadelphia: 1903-07. V. 42

SAKEL, MANFRED JOSHUA 1900-1957

The Pharmacological Shock Treatment of Schizophrenia. New York: 1938. V. 43; 45

THE SAKKARAH Expedition. The Mastaba of Mereruka. Chicago: 1938. V. 40

SALA, GEORGE AUGUSTUS

America Revisited. London: 1883. V. 40

The Baddington Peerage: Who Won It, and Who Wore It. London: 1860. V. 39

Charles Dickens. London: 1870. V. 40

The Hats of Humanity, Historically, Humorously and Aesthetically Considered, a Homily. Manchester: 1868. V. 37

Under the Sun. London: 1886. V. 41

SALAMAN, MALCOLM

The Etchings of James McBey. London: 1929. V. 37; 39; 40; 42; 44

The New Woodcut. London: 1930. V. 37; 40; 41

SALAMAN, MALCOLM C.

The Etchings of Francis Seymour Haden. London: 1923. V. 41; 44

The Woodcut of Today: at Home and Abroad. London: 1927. V. 41

SALAME, A.

A Narrative of the Expedition to Algiers in the Year 1816, Under the Command of the Right Hon. Admiral Lord Viscount Exmouth. London: 1819. V. 39

SALAMON, GEORGE

Atlas of the Arteries of the Human Brain. Paris: 1971. V. 42

SALANDRI, ENRICO

Architectural and Decorative Designs, for the Use of Those Engagaed in Architecture, Sculpture, Working in Metals, Cabient Work . . . London: 1869. V. 38

SALAS BARBADILLO, ALONSO JERONIMO DE

The Lucky Idiot; or, Fools Have Fortune. London: 1710. V. 45

SALAZAR, AMBROSIO DE

Espexo General de la Gramatica en Dialogos, para Saber la natural y Perfecta Pronunciation de la Lengua Castellana . . . Rouen: 1614. V. 37

SALAZAR Y CASTRO, LUIS DE

Jornada de Los Coches de Madrid a Alcala, o Sataisfacion al Palacio de Momo, y a las Apuntaciones a la Carta del Maestro de Ninos. Zaragoza: 1714. V. 38

SALAZAR Y LARREGUI, JOSE

Datos de Los Trbajos Astronomicos y Topograficos, Dispuestos en Forma de Diario. Mexico: 1850. V. 38; 40; 41

SALDANHA DA GAMA, JOSE DE

Coup-d'oeil Philosophique et Historique sur les Affaires Bresiliennes Avant, Pendant et Apres la Regeneration. Rio de Janeiro: 1831. V. 39

SALE Catalaogues of Eminent Persons. London: 1971-75. V. 40

SALE, EDITH TUNIS

Historic Gardens of Virginia. Richmond: 1930. V. 42

Manors of Virginia in Colonial Times. Philadelphia: 1909. V. 41; 46

Old Time Belles and Cavaliers. Philadelphia: 1912. V. 44

SALE, FLORENTIA WYNCH, LADY 1790-1853

A Journal of the Disasters in Afghanistan, 1841-42. London: 1843. V. 40; 43; 46

SALE, G.

A Comprehensive commentary on the Quran: comprising G. Sale's translation and preliminary discourse, with additional notes. Together with a complete index to the text. By E.M. Wherry. 1882-1886. V. 37

SALE, WILLIAM MERRITT

Samuel Richardson. A Bibliographical Record of His Literary Career . . . New Haven: 1936. V. 45

THE SALEM Belle: a Tale of 1692. Boston: 1842. V. 43

SALES, FRANCIS

An Introduction to a Devoute Life . . . Paris: 1637. V. 45

SALGADO DE ARAUJO, JOAO

Carta que un Cavaallero Biscaino Escrivio en Discursos Polyticos y Militares, a Otro del Reino de Navarra, en Repuesta de Auerle Consultado Sobre la Justificacion de las Armas Auxiliares . . . Lisbon: 1643. V. 38

SALI, S. A.

Daimabad 1976-79. New Delhi: 1986. V. 38

SALICETI, NATALE

Catalogo della Biblioteca. Rome: 1789. V. 46

SALINAS, PORFIRIO

Bluebonnets & Cactus, an Album of Southwestern Paintings. Austin: 1967. V. 37

SALINGER, JEROME DAVID 1919-

The Catcher in the Rye. Boston: 1951. V. 37; 39; 40; 45; 46

The Catcher in the Rye. London: 1951. V. 40; 41; 43; 44

For Esme - With Love and Squalor. London: 1953. V. 38; 39; 41; 42; 46

The Hang of It. Chicago: 1943. V. 46

Nine Stories. Boston: 1953. V. 43; 44

Raise High the Roof Beam, Carpenters. 1963. V. 44

Uncollected Short Stories. N.P.. V. 40; 42; 43

The Complete Uncollected Short Stories. N.P.. V. 38; 41

The Complete Uncollected Stories. N.P.: n.d.. V. 42

The Complete Uncollected Short Stories. 1974. V. 39

SALIS, BAPTISTA DE

Summa Casuum Conscientiae Quae Baptistiana Nuncupatur. Nuremberg: 1488. V. 46

SALIS, WILLIAM FANE DE

Reminiscences of Travel in China and India in 1848. London: 1892. V. 45

SALISBURY, EDWARD

Weeds and Aliens. London: 1961. V. 44

SALISBURY, JESSE

A Glossary of Words and Phrases Used in S. E. Worcesterhsire. London: 1893. V. 38; 40

SALISBURY, R. A.

The Paradisus Londinensis. London: 1805-08. V. 37; 38

The Paradisus Londinensis . . . London: 1806. V. 43

SALISBURY, THOMAS

Mathematical Collections and Translations. London & Los Angeles: 1967. V. 40

SALISBURY, W.

Hortus Siccus Gramineus . . . London: 1802. V. 39; 41

SALISBURY, WILLIAM

Hints Addressed to Proprietors of Orchards and to Growers of Fruit, in General . . . London: 1816. V. 43

SALIUS DIVERSUS, PETRUS

De Febre Pestilenti Tractatus, et Curationes Quorundam Particularium Morborum . . . Frankfurt: 1586. V. 39

SALKELD, WILLIAM

Reports of Cases Adjudged in the Court of King's Bench; with Some Special Cases in the Courts of Chancery, Common Pleas and Exchequer (etc.). Dublin: 1791. V. 45

Reports of Cases Adjudged in the Court of King's Bench: with Some Special Cases in the Courts of Chancery, Common Pleas. London: 1795. V. 38; 39; 46

SALLER, S. J.

Excavations at Bethany (1949-1953). Jerusalem: 1957. V. 44

The Memorial of Moses on Mount Nebo. Jerusalem: 1941-50. V. 44

SALLEY, A. S.

The History of Orangeburg County, South Carolina. Orangeburg: 1898. V. 40; 46

SALLEY, ALEXANDER SAMUEL

Tentative Roster of the Third Regiment, South Carolina Volunteers, Confederate States Provisional Army. Columbia: 1908. V. 44

SALLEY, H. E.

History of California Post Offices 1849-1976. La Mesa: 1976. V. 38

History of California Post Offices 1849-1976. La Mesa: 1977. V. 39

SALLUST, HUGH

The Cataline and Jugurthine Wars. Dublin: 1772. V. 40

SALLUSTE DU BARTAS, GUILLAUME DE

Bartas His Devine Weekes & Workes. London: 1605-06. V. 45

SALLUSTIUS CRISPUS, C.

All the Works of that Famous Historian Sallust. London: 1692. V. 46

Catalinae Contra Romanum Senatorum Coniuratio. Paris: 1536. V. 38

The Catiline and Jugurthine Wars. Dublin: 1772. V. 42

De Coniuratione Catilnae. Eiusdem, De Bello Iugurthino. Schlettstadt: 1521. V. 38

La Conjuracion de Catalina y la Guerra de Jugurta por Cayo Salustio Crispo. Madrid: 1772. V. 40; 41; 45

La Historia . . . Venice: 1564/1563. V. 44

Opera cum Plusculis Additamentis Noviter & Diligenter. Venundantur Parisius a: 1521. V. 40

Opera Omnia, Quae Extant, Inerpretatione et Notis Illustravit Daniel Crispinus, in Usum Serenissimi Delphini. Londini: 1735. V. 43

Opera. Birminghamiae: 1773. V. 45

Opera. Birmingham: 1774. V. 38; 40

Opera. Paris: 1823. V. 38

Opera . . . cum Jodici Badii Asce(n)sii Expositione . . . que . . . sunt Adiectis Aliquot Historiis Immoverius Figuris tota Quibus Aperitur rei Series Venustate. Lyon: 1517. V. 37

Salluste Aucteur Romain. Paris: 1539. V. 40; 43

L Sergii Catalinae Contra Romanum Senatum Coniuratio seu Ballum Catilinarium. Parisiis: 1534. V. 42

The Works of Sallust. London: 1744. V. 46

The Works. London: 1744. V. 38

The Works of Sallust. London: 1746. V. 40

The Works of Sallust . . . London: 1806. V. 42

The Works. London: 1806. V. 38

SALLUSTIUS, Neoplatonist

Sallust on the Gods and the World; and the Pythagoric Sentences of Demophilus. London: 1793. V. 42

SALM, ABRAHAM

Java. Na Schilderijen en Teekeningen. Amsterdam: 1872. V. 39

SALMASIUS, CLAUDE

Defensio Regia pro Carlo I. Leiden: 1649. V. 37

SALMERON, MARCOS

Recuerdos Historicos y Politicos de los Servicios Que los Generales, y Varones Ilustres de la Religion de Nuestra Senora de la Merced, Redencion de Cautivos hand Echo a Los Reyes de Espana Desde . . . 1218 Hasta . . . 1640. . . . Valencia: 1646. V. 41

SALMI, MARIO

The Complete Work of Raphael (Sanzio). New York: 1969. V. 39

Italian Miniatures. London: 1957. V. 41

SALMON ANDRE

Correspondances. Paris: 1929. V. 39

SALMON, BERNARD

The Sea Curry. Brixton: 1983. V. 39

SALMON, J.

An Historical Description of Ancient and Modern Rome. London: 1816. V. 40

SALMON JOSEPH WHITTINGHAM

The Beauties of Booths, the Seat of Willoughby Legh, Esq., with It's Surrounding, Picturesque Scenery, a Poem . . . Nantwich: 1820. V. 46

SALMON, MR.

Dictionnaire Hermetique, Contenant l'Explication des Termes, Fables, Enigmes, Emblemes & manieres de Parler des Vrais Philosophes . . . Paris: 1695. V. 46

The Modern Gazetteer; or, a Short View of the Several Nations of the World . . . London: 1758. V. 46

SALMON, NATHANIEL 1675-1742

The History of Hertfordshire. London: 1728. V. 39

A New Survey of England. London: 1731. V. 39; 44

Roman Stations in Britain, According to the Imperial Itinerary. London: 1726. V. 38; 40

SALMON, RICHARD

Fly Fishing for Trout. New York: 1952. V. 39

SALMON, THOMAS 1679-1767

The Chronological Historian; Containing a Regular Account of All Material Transactions and Occurrences . . . London: 1747. V. 41

A Critical Essay Concerning Marriage. London: 1724. V. 37; 43; 46

The Foreigner's Companion through the Universities of Cambridge and Oxford, and the Adjacent Counties. London: 1748. V. 41

Hedendaagsche Historie . . . Amsterdam: 1763. V. 45

New Abridgment and critical Review of the State Trials. London: 1735. V. 38

A New Geographical and Historical Grammar. London: 1766. V. 39

SALMON, WILLIAM

Ars Chirurgica. A Compendium of the Theory and Practice of Chirurgery, in Seven Books. London: 1699. V. 39

Botanologia. The English Herbal. London: 1710. V. 37

The Builder's Guide, and Gentleman and Trader's Assistant. London: 1736. V. 37

The Compleat English Physician. London: 1693. V. 38; 40; 46

The London and Country Builder's Vade Mecum; or, the Complete and Universal Architect's Assistant. London: 1748. V. 45

The London and Country Builder's Vade Mecum. London: 1755. V. 39

Medicina Practica; or Practical Physick . . . London: 1692. V. 41

Palladio Londinensis; or, The London Art of Building. London: 1755. V. 41

Palladio Londinensis; or, the London Art of Building. London: 1767. V. 46

Palladio Londinensis; or, the London Art of Building. London: 1773. V. 38; 41

Palladio Londinensis: or the London Art of bulding . . . To which is annexed, the Builder's Dictionary . . . The second edition . . . by E. Hoppus. London: 1738. V. 37; 42

Pharmacoepia Londinensis. London: 1685. V. 40; 41; 42

Pharmacopoeia Londienensis; or, the New London Dispensatory. London: 1682. V. 42

Pharmacopoeia Bateana; or Bate's Dispensatory. London: 1694. V. 40

Pharmacopoeia Londinensis, or the New London Dispensatory in VI Books. London: 1696. V. 43

Polygraphice; or the Art of Drawing, Engraving, Etching, Limning, Painting, Washing . . . London: 1673. V. 41; 43; 45

Polygraphice; or The Arts of Drawing, Engraving, Etching, Linning, Painting . . . London: 1675. V. 44

Polygraphice. London: 1685. V. 40

Polygraphice: or, the Arts of Drawing, Engraving, Etching, Limning, Painting, Varnishing, Japaning, Gilding, &c. London: 1701. V. 43

Praxis Medica. London: 1707. V. 40

SALMONS, C. H.

The Burlington Railway Strike. Aurora: 1889. V. 42

SALMONY, ALFRED

Carved Jade of Ancient China. Berkeley: 1938. V. 42

SALOMONS, D. L.

Breguet (1747-1823). London: 1921. V. 37

SALOMONS, DAVID

Catalogue of the Library at Broomhill, Tunbridge Wells . . . London: 1916-20. V. 40

A Defence of the Joint-Stock Banks: An Examination of the Causes of the Present Monetary Difficulties, and Hints for the Future Management of the Circulation. London: 1837. V. 38

SALOMONS, DAVID LIONEL

Catalogue of the Library at Broomhill, Tunbridge Wells, The Property of . . . N.P.: 1916-20. V. 39

SALOMONS, VERA

Choffard. London: 1911. V. 46

Gravelot. London: 1911. V. 46

SALOMONSEN, FINN

The Birds of Greenland; Gronlands Fugle. 3 VOlumes. With 52 full page colour plates by Gitz-Johansen. Preface by Hans Hedtoft. Kobenhavn: (1950-51). V. 37

Gronlands Fugle. The Birds of Greenland. Kobenhavn: 1950. V. 39; 46

SALOMONSKY, VERNA COOK

Masterpieces of Furniture Design. Grand Rapids: 1931. V. 39

SALPOINTE, JEAN BAPTISTE

Soldiers of the Cross. Notes on the Ecclesiastical History of New Mexico, Arizona and Colorado. Banning: 1898. V. 39; 40; 43; 44

SALT, HENRY

CVM Grano: Verses and Epigrams. Berkeley Heights: 1931. V. 40; 41

CVM Granp: Verses and Epigrams. By Henry Salt. Berkely Heights, N.J.: 1931. V. 37

A Descriptive Poem with Notes by a Traveller. Alexandria: 1824. V. 40

Egypt a Descriptive Poem with Notes by a Traveller. Alexandria: 1824. V. 43

Essay on Dr. Young's and M. Champollion's Phonetic System of Hieroglyphics . . . London: 1825. V. 44

Facsimile of an Ancient Greek Inscription on a Gold Plate Found in the Ruins of the Ancient City of Canopus . . . and Sent to Sir Sidney Smith. Paris: 1800. V. 45

A Voyage to Abyssinia, and Travels into the Interior of that Country. London: 1814. V. 38; 43; 45

SALT, HENRY S.

A Group of Unpublished Letters, by Henry S. Salt to Joseph Ishill, with an Appreciation by Henry W. Nevinson. 1942. V. 46

Percy Bysshe Shelley, Poet and Pioneer. A Biographical Study. London: & New York: 1896. V. 43; 46

SALT, HENRY STEPHENS

Animals' Rights Considered in Relation to Social Progress. London: 1892. V. 39

SALT LAKE CITY, UTAH. CITY COUNCIL

Investigation by the City Council of Salt Lake City of Rumors Affecting the Peace, Reputation and Welfare of the City and Its Inhabitants. Salt Lake City: 1885. V. 40

SALT River Valley. Its Attractions for the Immigrant, the Capitalist, the Invalid. Phoenix: 1888. V. 46

SALTEN, FELIX

Bambi: a Life in the Woods. New York: 1928. V. 40

Walt Disney's Bambi. New York: 1941. V. 44

Walt Disney's Bambi. New York: 1942. V. 45

SALTER, EDWIN

History of Monmouth and Ocean Counties . . . Bayonne: 1890. V. 46

History of Monmouth and Ocean Counties, Embracing a Genealogical Record of Earliest Settlers in Monmouth and Ocean Counties and Their Descendants. Bayonne, 1890, i.e.: 1980. V. 46

Old Times in Old Monmouth. Freehold: 1887. V. 44

SALTER, HENRY

On Asthma: Its Pathology and Treatment. New York: 1882. V. 42

SALTER, J. W.

A Catalogue of the Collection of Cambrian and Silurian Fossils Contained in the Geological Museum of the University of Cambridge. Cambridge: 1873. V. 37

SALTER, JAMES

The Arm of Flesh. New York: 1961. V. 42

The Hunters. New York: 1956. V. 42

Light Years. New York: 1975. V. 45

Solo Faces. Boston: 1979. V. 44

A Sport and a Pastime. London: 1987. V. 45

SALTER, JOSEPH

The East in the West: or, Work Among the Asiatics and the Africans in London. London: 1896. V. 40

SALTER, T. F.

The Troller's Guide. London: 1820. V. 44

SALTER, THOMAS FREDERICK

The Angler's Guide. London: 1825. V. 39

The Angler's Guide . . . London: 1841. V. 39

The Troller's Guide. London: 1820. V. 39

SALTONSTALL, WINTHROP

An Augural Dissertation on the Chemical and Medical History of Septon, Azote, or Nitrogene . . . New York: 1796. V. 45

SALTUS, EDGAR

The Gardens of Aphrodite. Philadelphia: 1920. V. 37; 40

The Paliser Case. New York: 1919. V. 43

SALTUS, EDGAR EVERTSON

The Philosophy of Disenchantment. Boston: 1885. V. 44

Victor Hugo and Golgotha. Chicago: 1925. V. 46

SALUS, PETER H.

For Auden February 21st, 1972. New York: 1972. V. 45

SALUSBURY, THOMAS

Mathematical Collections and Translations in Two Tomes . . . London: 1967. V. 38; 40; 41

Mathematical Collections and Translations. London: & Los Angeles: 1967. V. 42

Mathematical Collections and Translations in Two Tomes . . . London: 1661/1665. V. 37

SALUSTIO Con Alcune Belle Cose, Volgareggiato per Agostino Ortica de la Porta Genovese. Venice: 1518. V. 40

SALVATOR, L. L.

Los Angeles in the Sunny Seventies. Los Angeles: 1929. V. 43

SALVATOR, LUDWIG 1847-1915

Die Liparischen Inseln. Vulcano; Salina; Lipari; Panaria; Alicuri, STromboli; Allgemeiner Theil; Ustica. Prague: 1893-98. V. 42

SALVATORE, C.

Italian Architecture, Furniture and Interiors During the 14th, 15th and 16th Centuries. Boston: 1904. V. 37

SALVERTE, EUSEBE

The Occult Sciences. London: 1846. V. 43

SALVIAN, SAINT

De Gubernatione Dei. Oxford: 1633. V. 37

SALVIATI, GIUSEPPE

The World Turned Upside Down. London: 1822. V. 38

SALVIATI, LIONARDO 1539-1589

Il Primo Libro delle Orazioni. Nuovamente Raccolte. Firenze: 1575. V. 39

SALVIN, F. H.

Falconry in the British Isles. London: 1855. V. 38

SALVIN, FRANCIS HENRY

Falconry in the British Isles. London: 1873. V. 39

SALVIN, HUGH

Journal Written on Board of His Majesty's Ship Cambridge. From January 1824 to May 1827. Newcastle: 1829. V. 39

SALVIO, ALESSANDRO fl. 1604-1634

Trattato dell' Inventione et Arte Liberale de Giuoco di Scacchi. Naples: 1604. V. 40

SALVO, CARLO, MARQUIS DE

Travels in the Year 1806, From Italy to England, through the Tyrol, Styria, Bohemia, Gallicia (sic), Poland and Livonia . . . Troy: 1808. V. 46

SALWAY, CHARLOTTE M.

Fans of japan. London: 1894. V. 38; 41; 42; 43

SALWEY, REGINALD E.

Ventured in Vain. London: 1894. V. 46

SALZMANN, CHRISTIAN GOTTHILF

Elements of Morality, for the Use of Children. London: 1792. V. 40

SALZMANN, MAXIMILIAN

The Anatomy and Histology of the Human Eyeball in the Normal State, Its Development and Senescence. Chicago: 1912. V. 43; 44

SAMAAN-HANNA, A.

Moods that Endure: Poems. Worcester: 1978. V. 46

SAMARAS, LUCAS

Samaras Album: . . . New York: 1971. V. 46

SAMBER, ROBERT

Eunuchism Disply'd. Describing all the Different Sorts of Eunuchs: The Esteem They Have Met with in the World, nd How They Came to Be Made so . . . London: 1718. V. 38

SAMBIN, HUGUES

Oeuvre de la Diversite des Termes, Dont on Use en Architecture, Reduict en Ordre. Lyon: 1572. V. 37

SAMBUCUS, JOANNES 1531-1584

Emblemata et Aliquot Nummi Antiqui Operis . . . Antwerp: 1566. V. 38; 40

Emblemata Aliquot * Nummi Antiqui Operis * Epigrammata. Leyden: 1599. V. 38

SAMBUCUS, JOHANNES 1531-1584

Emblemata, cum Aliquot Nummis Antiqui Operis. Antwerp: 1564. V. 38; 39

SAMLER, ROBERT

Ebrietatis Encomium; or, the Praise of Drunkenness . . . London: 1812. V. 45

SAMMES, AYLETT

Britannia Antiqua Illustrata. London: 1676. V. 40; 44; 46

Britannia Antiqua Illustrata . . . . London: 1676. V. 42

SAMOUELLE, G.

The Entomological Cabinet; Being a Natural History of British Insects . . . London: 1841. V. 43

SAMOUELLE, GEORGE

The Entomologist's Useful Compendium . . . London: 1819. V. 39; 42; 43

The Entomologist's Useful Compendium . . . London: 1824. V. 44; 46

SAMPLE, H.

Art of Tranining Animals. New York: 1869. V. 39

SAMPSON, ALONZO D.

Three Times Around the World, Life and Adventures of Alonzo D. Sampson. Buffao: 1867. V. 42

SAMPSON, EZRA

Brief Remarks on the Ways of Man; Or, Compendious Dissertations, Respecting Social and Domestic Relations and Concerns, and the Various Economy of Life . . . Hudson: 1818. V. 42

The Youth's Companion, or an Historical Dictionary. Hudson: 1807. V. 38

SAMPSON, GEORGE V.

A Memoir Explanatory of the Chart and Survey of the County of London-Derry, Ireland. London: 1814. V. 43

Statistical Survey of the County of Londonderry, with Observations on the Means of Improvement . . . Dublin: 1802. V. 42; 43

SAMPSON, H. C.

The Coconut Palm. London: 1923. V. 45

SAMPSON, HENRY

A History of Advertising from the Earliest Times. London: 1875. V. 40; 42; 46

A History of Advertising from the Earliest Times. Illustrated by Anecdotes, Curious Specimens, and Biographical Notes. With Illustrations and Facsimiles. London: 1874. V. 37

SAMPSON, JOHN

The Dialect of the Gypsies of Wales, Being the Older Form of British Romani Preserved in the Speech of the Clan of Abram Wood. Oxford: 1926. V. 40

XXI Welsh Gypsy Folk Tales. Newtown: 1933. V. 43

SAMPSON, JOHN PHILPOT CURRAN

An Oration, Delivered Before the Members of the Law Institution, at Litchfield, on the Fourth of July, 1818. New York: 1818. V. 45

SAMPSON, MARMADUKE B.

Central American and the Transit Between the Oceans. New York: 1850. V. 43

SAMPSON, WILLIAM

Memoirs . . . of His Adventures in Various Parts of Europe. New York: 1807. V. 37

Sampson Against the Philistines; or, the Reformation of Lawsuits . . . Philadelphia: 1808. V. 42

Speech . . . on the Trial of James Cheetham, for Libelling Madame Bonneville, in His Life of Thomas Paine . . . New York: 1810. V. 43

Trial of Mr. William Parkinson, Pastor of the First Baptist Church in the City of New York, on an Indictment for Assault and Battery Upon Mrs. Eliza Wintringham. New York: 1811. V. 41

SAMS, JOSEPH 1784-1860

Ancient Egypt, Objects of Antiquity, Forming Part of the Extensive and Rich Collections from Ancient Egypt . . . London: 1839. V. 44

SAMS, SAMUEL

A Complete and Universal System of Stenography, or Short-Hand . . . Bath: 1812. V. 42

SAMS, WILLIAM

A Tour through Paris Illustrated with Twenty-One Colored Plates Accompanied with Descriptive Letterpress. London: 1822-24. V. 39; 45

A Tour Through Paris. London: 1825 or 1828? V. 44

SAMUDA, JOSEPH D'AGUILAR

A Treatise on the Adaptation of Atmospheric Pressure to the Purposes of Locomotion on Railways. London: 1841. V. 46

SAMUEL Beckett: an Exhibition. 1971. V. 43

SAMUEL, BUNFORD

Secession and Constitutional Liberty, in which is shown the Right of a Nation to Secede from a Compact of Federation and that such right is Necessary to Constitutional Liberty and a Surety of Union. New York: 1920. V. 37

SAMUEL, L.

Portland and Vicinity. Willamette Valley, Columbia River, Puget Sound. Portland: 1887. V. 37; 44

SAMUEL, SIGMUND

The Seven Years War in Canada 1756-1763. London: 1934. V. 44

SAMUELS, EDWARD A.

The Birds of New England and Adjacent States. Boston: 1872. V. 44

SAMUELS, FREDERICK K.

Ports of An Francisco, San Diego, Puget Sound, Portland and Honolulu. San Francisco: 1889. V. 46

SAMUELS, LEE

A Hemingway Check List. New York: 1951. V. 41; 43

SAMUELS, MARUICE VICTOR

The Florentines: a Play. New York: 1904. V. 39; 45

SAMWAIES, RICHARD

England's Faithfull Reprover and Monitour. London: 1653. V. 40

SAMWELL, DAVID

Captain Cook and Hawaii. San Francisco: 1957. V. 37; 39

SAN Angelo and the Concho Country. San Angelo: 1910. V. 38

SAN BERNARDINO OF SIENA

True Charity. Bronxville: 1979. V. 45

SAN DIEGO E VILLALON, F. GIOAN

Discorsi Apologetici, In Che Si Da Relatione Delle Persecutioni e Travagi Patiti dal Revrendissimo Padre D. Fr. Bernadino de Cardenas, Vescovo del Paraguay, nelle Indie Occidentali.. Madrid: 1658. V. 41

SAN Francisco. San Francisco: 1900. V. 40

The Laws of the Town of San Frnacisco, 1847. San Francisco: 1854. V. 37

Manual of the Corporation of the City of San Francisco . . . San Francisco: 1852. V. 40

Ordinances and Joint Resolutions of the City of San Francisco. San Francisco: 1854. V. 37

SAN Francisco Blue Book and Pacific Coast Directory. Season 1892-93. San Francisco: 1893. V. 38; 40

SAN FRANCISCO. BOARD OF ENGINEERS

Report of the Board of Engineers Upon the City Grades, San Francisco, May 12, 1854. San Francisco: 1854. V. 40

SAN Francisco, California. Site of the Proposed Panama-Pacific International Exposition, 1915, Celebrating the Completion of the Panama Canal. San Francisco: 1915. V. 41

SAN FRANCISCO. PARK COMMISSIONERS

Third Biennial Report of the San Francisco Park Commissioners 1874-5. San Francisco: 1875. V. 44

SAN Joaquin County, California, Its Favorable Location, Rich, Soil, Healthy Climate, Varied Productions and General Prosperity. City of Stockton: Its Industries, Trade, Commercial Importance and Business Advantages. Stockton: 1887. V. 46

SAN Jose Directory, Including Santa Clara, San Mateo, Santa Cruz, San Benito and Monterey Counties . . . San Francisco: 1889. V. 40

SAN JUAN CONSOLIDATED MINING & MILLING COMPANY

Prospectus of the San Juan Consolidated Mining and Milling Co., of Madison, Wisconsin. Chicago: 1878. V. 37; 40; 43

SAN PEDRO, DIEGO DE

Carcer d'Amore, Tradotto del Magn. Messer Lelio de Ma(n)fredi, Ferrarese, de Idioma Spagnolo in Lingua Materna. Venice: 1533. V 37

SAN YU LOW

San-Yu-Low; or the Three Dedicated Rooms. Canton: 1815. V. 40

SAN ALBERTO, JOSE ANTONIO DE

Carta Circular, o Edicto Dirigida a Todos Sus Amados Hijos, y Diocesanos, que Desean y Solicitan y en un Adelante Solicitaren ser Promovidos a los Sagrados Ordenes. Buenos Aires: 1781. V. 38

Prevenciones del Pastor en su Vista, Que Dirige a Todos Los Curas, Y Tenientes de su Diocesi . . . Buenos Aires: 1788. V. 40

SANBORN, F. B.

The Personality of Emerson. Boston: 1903. V. 38

SANBORN, F. T.

A. Bronson Alcott, His Life and Philosophy. Boston: 1893. V. 41; 44

SANBORN, FRANK

Recollections of Seventy Years. Boston: 1909. V. 39

SANBORN, FRANKLIN B.

Emancipation in the West Indies. Concord: 1862. V. 42

SANBORN, MARGARET

Robert E. Lee: a Portrait, 1806-1861. (and) The Complete Man, 1861-1870. Philadelphia: 1966. V. 44

SANCHEZ, FRANCISCUS

De Multum Nobili & Prima Universali Scientia Quod Nihil Scitur; Deque Literarum Pereuntium Agone, Eiusque Causis, Libelli Singulares Duo . . . Francofurti: 1618. V. 39

De Multum Nobili & Prima Universali Scientia Quod Nihil Scitur: Deque Literarum Pereuntium Agone, Eiusque Causis, Libelli Singulares Duo . . . Frankfurt: 1618. V. 40

SANCHEZ, MARTIN

Conspicua & Adprime Frugifera Diuidui et Individui Arbor. Toulouse: 1519. V. 40

SANCHEZ, THOMAS

Native Notes from the Land of Earthquake and Fire. Iverness: 1979. V. 44

Rabbit Boss. New York: 1973. V. 42; 45

De Sancto Matrimonii . . . Leyden: 1590. V. 44

Starman and the Two Sisters. Santa Barbara: 1974. V. 45

SANCHO, IGNATIUS

Letters of the Late Ignatius Sancho, an African. London: 1782. V. 37; 38; 42; 43

Letters of the Late Ignatius Sancho, an African. London: 1784. V. 44

Letters. To Which are Prefixed, Memoirs of His Life. London: 1784. V. 41

SANCROFT, WILLIAM

Lex Ignea; or The School of Righteousness. London: 1666. V. 42

Modern Policies, Taken from Machiavel, Borgia and Other Choice Authors, by an Eyewitnesse. London: 1652. V. 38

Modern Policies Taken from Machiavel, Borgia and Other Choice Authors, by an Eye-Witness. London: 1653. V. 39; 40

The Proceedings and Tryal in the Case of the Most Reverend Father in God William (Sancroft) Lord Archbishop of Canterbury, and the Right Reverend Fathers in God, William Lord Bishop of St. Asaph (& others) London: 1689. V. 40

The Proceedings and Tryal in the Case of . . . William (Sancroft), Lord Archbishop of Canterbury . . . Anno Dom. 1688. London: 1716. V. 46

SANCTO GEORGIO, JOHANNES ANTONIUS DE

Tractatus Appellationum. Venezia: 1497. V. 44

SANCTORIUS

Medica Statica: Being the Aphorisms of Sanctorius. London: 1723. V. 38

SAND, GEORGE, PSEUD. OF MME. DUDEVANT 1804-1876

Consuelo. London: 1847. V. 39

The Devil's Pool. New York: 1894. V. 41; 43; 45

Francis the Waif. London: 1889. V. 39; 41; 42; 43

Francois the Waif. Boston: 1894. V. 40

Indiana. Paris: 1847. V. 41

Letters. London: 1886. V. 46

The Master Mosaic Workers. Boston: 1895. V. 39; 41; 43; 45

The Masterpieces. Philadelphia: 1900. V. 45

The Masterpieces of George Sand . . . Philadelphia: 1900-02. V. 46

The Masterpieces . . . Philadelphia: 1902. V. 42

The Mosaic Workers; A Tale to Which is Added the Orco; A Tradition. London: 1844. V. 39

La Petite Fadette. Paris: 1930. V. 46

Valentine. Paris: 1832. V. 39

Winter in Majorca. London: 1956. V. 41

SAND, MAURICE

The History of the Harlequinade. London: 1915. V. 45

SANDARS, JOSEPH

A Letter on the Subject of the Projected Rail Road Between Liverpool and Manchester. Liverpool: 1824. V. 46

SANDARS, MARY F.

The Life of Christina Rossetti. London. V. 38

SANDBURG, CARL 1878-1967

Abraham Lincoln. The Prairie Years. New York: 1926. V. 40; 46

Abraham Lincoln, The Prairie Years. The War Years. New York: 1926/36. V. 39

Abraham Lincoln, the Prairie Years: Abraham Lincoln, the War Years. New York: 1926-39. V. 46

Abraham Lincoln: The War Years. New York: 1939. V. 38; 44

Abraham Lincoln - the War Years. New York: 1941. V. 39

Address of Carl Sandburg - Abraham Lincoln's One Hundredth Inaugural Anniversary. Chicago and Skokie: 1961. V. 41

Always the Young Strangers. New York: 1952. V. 39

Always the Young Strangers. New York: 1953. V. 37; 42; 44

The American Songbag. New York: 1927. V. 44

Bronze Wood. San Francisco: 1941. V. 38; 40; 42; 43; 46

Bronze Wood. San Francisco: 1942. V. 41; 43

Chicago Poems. New York: 1916. V. 38; 41; 43; 44

Chicago Poems. New York: 1936. V. 37

Cornhuskers. New York: 1918. V. 39; 43

Early Moon. New York: 1930. V. 39

Good Morning America. New York: 1928. V. 39; 43; 45

Home from Memo. New York: 1943. V. 42; 46

Lincoln Collector. New York: 1949. V. 38; 44

Lincoln Collector. The Story of Oliver R. Barrett's Great Private Collection. New York: 1949. V. 38; 39; 46

M'Liss and Louie. Los Angeles: 1929. V. 41

The People, Yes. New York: 1936. V. 39; 41; 46

The People Yes. New York: 1942. V. 43

Poems of the Midwest. Cleveland: 1946. V. 39; 44

Complete Poems. New York: 1950. V. 39

Potato Face. New York: 1930. V. 38; 41

Potato Face. New York: (1930). V. 37

Rembrance Rock. New York: 1948. V. 38; 39; 40; 41; 42; 43; 45; 46

Seven Poems. New York: 1970. V. 40; 43

Slabs of the Sunburnt West. New York: 1922. V. 39

Slabs of the Sunburnt West. New York: (1922). V. 37

Smoke and Steel . . . Slabs of Sunburnt West . . . Good Morning, America. New York. V. 44; 46

Smoke and Steel. New York: 1920. V. 38; 39; 41; 43

Steichen the Photographer. New York: 1929. V. 37; 38; 40; 43; 44

SANDBY, GEORGE 1799-1880

Mesmerism and Its Opponents: With a Narrative of Cases. London: 1844. V. 46

SANDBY, PAUL

A Collection of One Hundred and Fifty Select Views in England, Wales, Scotland and Ireland. London: 1782-83. V. 45

A Collection of One Hundred and Fifty Select Views in England, Wales, Scotland, and Ireland. London: 1783. V. 39

SANDBY, WILLIAM

The History of the Royal Academy of Arts from Its Foundation in 1768 to the Present Time. London: 1862. V. 42; 46

SANDEMAN, CHRISTOPHER

Thyme and Bergamot. London: 1947. V. 38; 39; 40; 41

SANDEMAN, FRASER

Angling Travels in Norway. London: 1895. V. 40

SANDEMAN, ROBERT

The Honour of Marriage Opposed to all Impurities: an Essay. London: 1777. V. 37

SANDER, FREDERICK

Reichenbachia. Orhicds Illustrated and Described. London: 1888-94. V. 39

SANDERS, ALVIN H.

Short-Horn Cattle. Chicago: 1900. V. 42

Short Horn Cattle. Chicago: 1909. V. 46

SANDERS, CHARLOTTE

The Little Family. Bath: 1797. V. 40

SANDERS, CONES AND CO.

The Rail and Its Localities; or, a Guide to Places Along the Railway Line from Howrath to Raneegunj . . . Calcutta: 1855. V. 46

SANDERS, DANIEL C.

A History of the Indian Wars With the United States to the Commencement of the Late War . . . Rochester: 1828. V. 45

SANDERS, DANIEL CLARK

A History of the Indian Wars With the First Settlers of the United States, Particularly in New England. Montpelier: 1812. V. 37; 38; 40; 44; 45

SANDERS, DORI

Clover. Chapel Hill: 1990. V. 45

SANDERS, EDWARD

The Hymenoptera Aculeata of the British Islands. London: 1896. V. 43

SANDERS, ELIZABETH ELKINS

Reviews of a Part of Prescott's 'History of Ferdinand and Isabella' and of Campbell's 'Lectures on Poetry'. Boston: 1841. V. 43

SANDERS, FRANCIS

An Abridgement of the Life of James II, King of Great Britain, &c. London: 1704. V. 44

SANDERS, HELEN F.

A History of Montana. Chicago: 1913. V. 45

SANDERS, JAMES

The Compleat Fisherman. London: 1724. V. 43

A Comprehensive View of the Small Pox, Cow Pox and Chicken Pox. Edinburgh: 1813. V. 45

SANDERS, JOHN

Memoirs on the Military Resources of the Valley of the Ohio, as Applicable to Operations on the Gulf of Mexico and Common Defense. Pittsburgh: 1845. V. 37; 38; 39; 42

Memoirs on the Military Resources of the Valley of the Ohio . . . Washington: 1845. V. 39; 42

SANDERS, JONATHAN

A New Narrative of a Fiery Apparition Seen on Several Days About Tower Hill or a Just Relation of Unjust Proceedings. London: 1681. V. 42

SANDERS, LESLIE

A Soldier of England. Dumfries: 1920. V. 45; 46

SANDERS, MARK

Poems on Occasional subjects. Dublin: 1778. V. 42; 46

Poems on Occasional Subjects. Dublin: 1788. V. 43

SANDERS, NICOLAS

De Origine et Progressu Schismatis Anglicani Libri Tres. Ingolstadt: 1587. V. 38

SANDERS, SUE A.

A Journey to and From the Golden Shore. Delavan: 1887. V. 46

SANDERSON, A.

A Catalogue of a Collection of Plaques, Medallions, Vases, Figures, etc. in Coloured Jasper and Basalte: Produced by Josiah Wedgwood, F.R.S. at Eturia in the County of Stafford, the Property of Arthur Sanderson. Edinburgh: 1901. V. 37

SANDERSON, G. P.

Thirteen Years Among the Wild Beasts of India. London: 1890. V. 38

SANDERSON, GEORGE P.

Thirteen Years Among the Wild Beasts of India . . . London: 1882. V. 40

SANDERSON, GORDON

Architectural Features of the Settle District. London: 1911. V. 45

SANDERSON, JAMES M.

Camp Fires and Camp Cooking . . . Washington: 1862. V. 45

My Record in Rebeldom. New York: 1865. V. 46

SANDERSON, JOHN

A Gift of Fortune. Edinburgh: 1980. V. 46

SANDERSON, ROBERT 1587-1663

De Juramenti Promissorii Obligatione Praelectiones Septem Habitae in Schola Tehologica Oxon. 1646. London: 1647. V. 38

Logicae Artis Compendium. Oxford: 1640. V. 45

Logicae Artis Compendium. Oxford: 1664. V. 45

Logicae Artis Compendium. Oxford: 1680. V. 43; 45

XXXIV Sermons. (and) XXI Sermons. London: 1671. V. 39

SANDERSON, THOMAS W.

20th Century History of Youngstown and Mahoning County, Ohio and Representative Citizens. Chicago: 1907. V. 46

SANDERSON, WILLIAM

Aulicus Coquinariae; or a Vindication in Answere to a Pamphlet, Entitvled The Court and Character of King James . . . London: 1650. V. 43

A Compleat History of the Life and Raigne of King Charles from His Cradle to His Grave. London: 1658. V. 44

Graphice, or, the Use of Pen and Pensill . . . London: 1658. V. 38; 40

SANDES, E. W. C.

In Kut and Captivity with the Sixth Indian Division. London: 1919. V. 42

The Royal Engineers in Egypt and the Sudan. Chatham: 1937. V. 42

SANDFORD, CHRISTOPHER

Heart's Desire. V. 41

Primeval Gods. London: 1934. V. 39

SANDFORD, FRANCIS

A Genealogical History of the Kings of England and Monarchs of Great Britian. London: 1707. V. 40

SANDFORD, JOHN

Parochialia; or, Church, School and Parish. London: 1845. V. 45

SANDFORD, JOHN, MRS.

Woman, in Her Social and Domestic Character, from the London Edition. Boston: 1833. V. 37; 44; 45

SANDFORD, L. C.

The Water Fowl Family. New York: 1903. V. 37

SANDFORD, LETTICE

Wood Engravings. Pinner: 1985. V. 42

Wood Engravings. 1988. V. 40

Wood Engravings. 1988. V. 45

SANDFORD, MR. fl. 1720

The Female Fop; or, The False One Fitted. London: 1724. V. 38

SANDHAM, ALFRED

Coins and Tokens and Medals of the Dominion of Canada . . . Montreal: 1869. V. 45

Ville-Marie, or, Sketches of Montreal Past and Present. Montreal: 1870. V. 43

SANDHAM, ELIZABETH

The School-Fellows, a Moral Tale. London: 1819. V. 44; 46

SAN DIEGO Y VILLALON, JUAN DE

Memorial y Defensorio al Rey Nuestro Senor por el Credito, Opinion, y Derechos Episcopales de al Persona . . . Madrid?: 1652? V. 38

SANDIFORT, EDUARD

Observations Anatomico-Pathologicae. Leyden: 1777. V. 42

SANDILANDS, J.

Western Canadian Dictionary and Phrase Book. Winnipeg: 1912. V. 43

SANDLER, IRVING

Al Held. New York: 1984. V. 45

SANDOLINI, CHERUBINO

Thaumalemma Cherubicum Catholicum, Universlia, et Particularia Continens Instrumenta . . . Venice: 1598. V. 38

SANDOVAL, PRUDENCIO

Chronica del Inclito Emperador de Espana, Don Alonso VII. Madrid: 1600. V. 40

SANDOZ, MARI 1901-1966

The Beaver Men. Spearheads of Empire. New York: 1964. V. 38; 40; 42; 44; 45

The Beaver Men: Spearhead of Empire. New York: (1964). V. 37

The Cattleman. New York: 1958. V. 37; 40; 42; 44

Love Song to the Plains. New York: 1961. V. 45

Old Jules Country. New York: 1965. V. 37; 38

Slogum House. Boston: 1937. V. 42

Son of Gamblin' Man: the Youth of an Artist. New York: 1960. V. 39; 42; 45

The Tom Walker. New York: 1947. V. 40; 45

SANDOZ, MAURICE

Fantastic Memories. Garden City: 1945. V. 41

The Maze. Garden City: 1945. V. 42; 44; 46

The Maze. London: 1945. V. 44

SANDOZ, MAURICE continued

The Pleasures of Mexico. New York: 1957. V. 45

SANDRART, JOACHIM VON

Academia Nobilissimae Artis Pictoriae . . . Furemberg and Frankfurt: 1683. V. 46

SANDS, BENJAMIN

Metamorphosis; or, a Transformation of Pictures, with Poetical Explanations, for the Amusement of Young Persons. Philadelphia: 1810. V. 45

Metamorphosis; or, a Transformation of Pictures, with Poetical Explanations, for the Amusement of Young Persons. Philadelphia: 1811. V. 38

SANDS, FRANK

A Pastoral Prince. The History and Reminiscences of J. W. Cooper. Santa Barbara: 1893. V. 43; 46

SANDS, HAROLD

The Dashing Sally Duel, and Other Stories. New York: 1905. V. 37; 41

SANDS, ROBERT

Life and Correspondence of John Paul Jones, Including His Narrative of the Campaign of the Liman, from Original Letters and Manuscripts in the Possession of Miss Janette Taylor. New York: 1830. V. 38

SANDS, ROBERT C.

The Writings of Robert C. Sands, in Prose and Verse. With a Memoir of the Author. New York: 1834. V. 42

SANDS, ROBERT CHARLES

The Bridal of Vaumond. New York: 1817. V. 37

SANDWEISS, M. A.

Pictures from an Expedition . . . Early Views of the American West. New Haven: 1978. V. 40

SANDWEISS, MARTHA A.

Laura Gilpin, an Enduring Grace. Ft. Worth: 1986. V. 37

Masterworks of American Photography: The Amon Carter Museum Collection. Birmingham: 1982. V. 41

SANDWICH, JOHN MONTAGU, EARL OF 1718-1792

A Voyage Round the Mediterranean in the Years 1738 and 1739. London: 1799. V. 39

SANDWITH, HUMPHREY

A Narrative of the Siege of Kars, and of the Six Month's Resistance by the Turkish Garrison Under General Williams to the Russian Army. London: 1856. V. 39; 42

SANDWITH, HUMPHRY

The Hekim Bashi; or, the Adventures of Giuseppe Antonelli . . . London: 1864. V. 37; 43

SANDWITH, THOMAS

On the Different Style of Pottery found in Ancient Tombs in the Island of Cyprus. London: 1877. V. 37

SANDYS, E. W.

Fishing and Shooting on the Canadian Pacific Railway. Montreal: 1891. V. 42

SANDYS, EDWIN 1561-1629

Europae Speculum; or a View or Survey of the State of Religion in the Westerne Parts of the World. The Hague: 1629. V. 40

SANDYS, EDWYN

Upland Game Birds. New York: 1902. V. 37; 39

SANDYS, GEORGE

Anglorum Speculum, or the Worthies of England, in Church and State. London: 1684. V. 38; 44

A Paraphrase Upon the Divine Poems. London: 1637. V. 43

A Paraphrase Upon the Divine Poems. N.P.: 1648. V. 40

A Relation of a Journey Begun An Dom. 1610. Foure Bookes. London: 1610. V. 39

A Relation of a Journey Begun in An: Dom: 1610. London: 1615. V. 38

A Relation of a Journey Begun An Dom 1610. London: 1621. V. 40

Sandy's Travels. London: 1673. V. 39

Travels, Containing a History of the Original and Present State of the Turkish Empire. London: 1673. V. 41

SANDYS, JOHN

The Salopian Zealot; or, the Good Vicar in a Bad Mood. Bristol? London?: 1778. V. 46

SANDYS, WILLIAM

Christmas Carols, Ancient and Modern. London: 1833. V. 37; 40

Christmastide: its History, Festivities and Carols. London: 1855. V. 41

Specimens of Macaronic Poetry. London: 1831. V. 38

Transactions of the Loggerville Literary Society. London: 1867. V. 37

SANFORD, ELIZABETH d. 1853

Woman, in Her Social and Domestic Character. London: 1837. V. 45

SANFORD, EZEKIEL

A History of the United States Before the Revolution. Philadelphia: 1819. V. 40

SANFORD, J. L.

The Great Governing Families of England. Edinburgh: 1865. V. 39

SANFORD, JOHN

A Man Without Shoes. Los Angeles: 1951. V. 42

The Winters of that Country: Tales of the Man Made Seasons. Santa Barbara: 1984. V. 37

SANFORD, L. C.

The Water-Fowl Family. New York: 1903. V. 37; 39

SANGER, GEORGE P.

Public Laws of the United States of America Passed at the First Session of the Fortieth Congress, 1867 and Treaties, Carefully Collated with the Originals at Washington. Boston: 1868. V. 38; 39

SANGER, MARGARET

An Autobiography. New York: 1938. V. 45

SANGINETO, DOMENICO

Dialoghi . . . ove si Ragiona Della Struttura, e Del Moto Del Cuore, Della Circolazione Delle Sangue, Delle Sostanze Nutrichevoli, e Della Natura Delle Febbri. Naples: 1724. V. 41

SANGRINUS, ANGELUS

Speculum & Exemplar Christicolarum, Vita Beatissimi Partis Benedicti. Rome: 1587. V. 37

SANGSTER, CHARLES

Hesperus and Other Poems and Lyrics. Montreal: 1860. V. 39; 43

THE SANITARIUM Of the World. Colorado in 1875. Hotels, Railroads, Distances, Altitudes, &c. Denver: 1875. V. 37

SANKEY, JOHN

Diary of a Trip . . . by the Cunard Company's Steam-ship 'Tarifa' from Liverpool, to the Mediterranean and Adriatic. Manchester: 1888. V. 40

SAN MARTINO, MATTEO, CONTI DI 1495-1556

Pescatoria et Ecloghe. Venezia: 1566. V. 39

SANNAZARO, JACOB

Opera Omnia. Venice: 1570. V. 40

SANNAZARO, JACOBO 1458-1530

Arcadia. Venice: 1524. V. 39; 40; 44

Arcadia. Colophon: 1534. V. 41

Arcadia . . . Nvovamente Corretta & Ornata di Figure & di Annotationi da M. Francesco Sansouino. Colophon: 1586. V. 41

Opera Omnia. Cologne: 1587. V. 39

SANNAZARO, JACOPO

De Partu Virginis (and Other Poems). Naples: 1526. V. 37

SANNE, A.

A Treatise on Diphtheria Historically and Practically Considered . . . St. Louis: 1887. V. 38

SANQUIRICO, ALESSANDRO 1780-1849

Scene Teatrali. Milan: 1865. V. 40

SANS, L'ABBE

Guerison de la Paralysie, Par l'Electricite . . . Paris: 1778. V. 45

SANSAY, LEONORA

Secret History; or, the Horrors of St. Domingo, in a Series of Letters . . . Philadelphia: 1808. V. 39

SANSOM, JOSEPH

Letters from Europe, During a Tour through Switzerland and Italy, in the Years 1801, and 1802. Philadelphia: 1805. V. 38; 40; 43

Sketches of Lower Canada, Historical and Descriptive . . . New York: 1817. V. 37; 38; 40; 42

Travels in Lower Canada. London: 1820. V. 37; 38; 44; 46

SANSOM, WILLIAM

Fire Over London. London: 1941. V. 38; 39; 40

SANSON D'ABBEVILLE, NICHOLAS

L'Afrique en Plusieurs CArtes Nouvelles et Exactes; en en Divers Traittez de Geographie & d'Histoire. Paris: 1652. V. 43

SANSON, HENRY

Memoirs of the Sansons from Private Notes and Documents. London: 1876. V. 43

SANSON, N.

The Present State of Persia. London: 1695. V. 40

SANSONE, ANTONIO

The Printing of Cotton Fabrics. Manchester: 1887. V. 40

SANSOUINO, FRANCISCO

The Quintesence of Wit. London: 1590. V. 38; 44

SANSOVINO, FRANCESCO

Dell'Historia Universale dell'Origine et Imperio de Turchi. Venice: 1560-61. V. 40

Venetia Citta Nobilissima et Singolare. Venice: 1604. V. 40

SANSOVINO, FRANCISCO

Le Osservationi della Lingua Volgare. Venice: 1565. V. 41

SANTA ANA, CALIFORNIA

Santa Ana Chamber of Commerce. Souther California, N.P.: n.d. V. 37

SANTA ANNA, ANTONIO LOPEZ DE

The Eagle: the Autobiography of Santa Anna. Austin: 1967. V. 37; 38

SANTA ANNA NERY, FREDERICO JOSE DE 1849-1902

The Land of the Amazons. London: 1901. V. 40

SANTA Catalina Island: Winter and Summer. Los Angeles: 1895. V. 46

SANTA Clara County and Its Resources: Historical, Descriptive, Statistical. A Souvenir of the San Jose Mercury, 1895. (San Jose: 1895). V. 37

SANTA Clara County California. San Francisco: 1887. V. 37

SANTA Claus ABC Speller. Chicago: 1890. V. 46

LA SANTA Missa de los Caldeos y de Los Maronitas, del Monte Libano, Traducida de Siriaco en Francez, y de Frances, en Castillano . . . Bayonne: 1679. V. 37

SANTA RITA COPPER AND IRON COMPANY OF NEW MEXICO

The Santa Rita Cooper and Iron Company of New Mexico. 1881. New York: 1881. V. 39

THE SANTA Rita Copper and Iron Company of New Mexico. 1881. (New York: 1881). V. 37

SANTA RITA DURAO, JOSE DE

Caramaru. Poema Epico do Descubrimento da Bahia. Lisbon: 1781. V. 39

SANTA TERESA DE AVILA 1515-1582

Los Libros de la Santa Madre Teresa de Jesus . . . de Nuevo Corregidos cun su Original, y Anadido Tablas Muy Copiosas en Esta Ultima Impression. Valencia: 1649. V. 40; 46

SANTA TERSA DE AVILA OR JESUS 1515-1582

Las Obras. Antwerp: 1649. V. 40

SANTANDER, CHARLES ANTOINE DE LA SERNA

An Historical Essay on the Origin of Printing. Newcastle: 1819. V. 45

SANTANGELO, A.

The Development of Italian Textile Design from the 12th to the 18th Century. London: 1964. V. 37

SANTANGELO, ANTONIO

A Treasury of Great Italian Textiles. New York: 1964. V. 41

SANTAREM, PEDRO DE

Tractatus de Assecurationibus, et Sponsionibus Mercatorum . . . Nunc Primum in Germania in Lucem Editus. Coloniae: 1599. V. 45

SANTAYANA, GEORGE 1863-1952

A Hermit of Carmel and Other Poems. New York: 1901. V. 46

The Life of Reason. London: 1905. V. 46

Lucifer. Chicago: 1899. V. 46

Lucifer, or the Heavenly Truce . . . Cambridge: 1924. V. 37; 38; 42

Persons and Places. Memories of Childhood and Youth. New York: 1943. V. 42

Platonism in the Italian Poets. Buffalo: 1896. V. 45

Platonism and the Spiritual Life. New York: 1927. V. 46

Poems. London: 1922. V. 41; 42; 44

Sonnets and Other Verses. Cambridge: 1894. V. 41

Sonnets and Lucifer. Chicago: 1906. V. 44

Sonnets and Other Verses. New York: 1906. V. 46

Works. New York: 1936-37. V. 37; 42; 45; 46

SANTEE, ROSS

Apache Land. New York: 1947. V. 39; 41; 42; 44; 46

The Bubbling Spring. New York: 1949. V. 45; 46

Hardrock and Silver Sage. New York: 1951. V. 41; 42; 44; 46

Men and Horses. New York & London: 1926. V. 39; 42

SANTI, SOLINORI

Le Cose Maravigliose dell'alma Citta di Roma. (and) Stationi delle Chiese di Roma. Venice: 1588. V. 45

SANTLEBEN, AUGUST

A Texas Pioneer: Early Staging and Overland Freighting Days on the Frontiers of Texas and Mexico. New York: 1910. V. 37; 38; 40; 42

A Texas Pioneer: Early Staging and Overland Freighting Days on the Frontiers of Texas and Mexico. New York & Washington: 1910. V. 39

SANTO-DOMINGO, JOSEPH HIPPOLYTE DE, COMTE

Roman Tablets . . . London: 1826. V. 44

SANTON, ELIZABETH CADY

The Slave's Appeal. Albany: 1860. V. 42

SANTORINI, J. DOMINICI

Septemdecim Tabulae Quas Nunc Primum Edit Atque Explicat Iisque Alias Addit de Structura Mammarum et de Tunica Vestis Vaginali Michael Girardi . . . Parma: 1775. V. 37; 39

SANTORIO, SANTORIO 1561-1636

Commentaria in Artem Medicinalem Galeni. Venice: 1630. V. 42

Medicina Statica; Being the Aphorisms . . . London: 1712. V. 42

Medicina Statica: Being the Aphorisms of Sanctorius. London: 1723. V. 43; 46

Medicina Statica . . . London: 1737. V. 41; 42; 43; 45

Medicina Statica: Being the Aphorisms of Sanctorius. Washington: 1896. V. 39

Methodi Vitandorum Errorum Omnium Qui in Arte Medica Contingunt . . . Geneve: 1631. V. 42

SANTOS-DUMONT, ALBERTO

My Airships: the Story of My Life. London: 1904. V. 45

SANTOS, FRANCISCO DE LOS

Descripcion Breve del Monasterio de S. Lorenzo et Real del Escorial. Madrid: 1657. V. 37

SANTUCCI, LUIGI

La Donna con la Bocca Aperita; The Woman with Her Mouth Open . . . 1980. V. 38; 40; 45

La Donna Con la Bocca Aperta. The Woman with Her Mouth Open. Verona: 1980. V. 38; 39

SAO THOMAS DE AQUINO, PAULO DE

Oracao Funebre da Muito Alta, e Muito Poderoza Senhora D. Maria . . . N.P.,: 1817. V. 38

SAPHIRE, LAWRENCE

Fernand Leger: The Complete Graphic Work. New York: 1978. V. 43; 44

SAPHO to Phaon: an Epistle from a Lady of Quality to a Noble Lord (i.e. John, Lord Hervey), occasion'd by the Late publication of His Miscellaneous Thoughts. London: 1743. V. 40; 41; 45

SAPPER, H. C. MC NEILE

The Island of Terror: a Jim Maitland Novel. London: 1931. V. 42

SAPPER'S War Stories. London: 1930. V. 44

SAPPHO

Fragmenta Nova. Brookston: 1981. V. 40

Fragments from Sappho. 1973. V. 45

Poems. Manaton, Devon: 1932. V. 42

SAPPINGTON, JOE

Joe Sap's Tales. Belton: 1908. V. 37

SAPPINGTON, JOHN 1776-1856

The Theory and Treatment of Fevers. Arrow Rock: 1844. V. 37; 38; 39; 41; 42; 45

THE SARAH-AD; or, A Flight for Fame. London: 1742. V. 42

SARBADHICARY, S. B.

Sojourn in the West; with Its Brief Ancient History. Alahabad: 1900. V. 40

SARDI, ALESSANDRO 1520-1588.

De moribus ac ritibus gentium. Venice: 1557. V. 37

Discorsi. Della Bellezza. Della Nobilita. Della Poesia di Dante. De i Precetti Historici. Della Qualita del Generale. Del Terremoto. Venice: 1586. V. 38

SARDI, PIETRO

Corono Imperiale dell'Architettura Militare. Venice: 1618. V. 44

SARGANT, JANE ALICE

An Address to the Females of Great Britain. London: 1832. V. 45

SARGEANT, EPES

Philip in Search of Wife. New York: 1843. V. 37

SARGEANT, WALDO

Old London. London: 1900. V. 44

SARGEANT, WINTHROP

Jazz: Hot & Hybrid. New York: 1938. V. 45

SARGENT, ANGELA M.

Notes of Travel and Mementos of Friendship. Rochester: 1894. V. 40

SARGENT, C. S.

The Silva of North America . . . Boston: 1891-1902. V. 43

SARGENT, EPES

Songs of the Sea, with Other Poems. Boston: 1847. V. 44

Wealth and Worth; or, Which Makes the Man? New York: 1842. V. 43

SARGENT, F. W.

On Bandaging and Other Operations of Minor Surgery. Philadelphia: 1848. V. 41; 43

On Bandaging, and Other Operations of Minor Surgery. Philadelphia: 1859. V. 42

SARGENT, GEORGE

The Writings of A. E. Newton - a Bibliography. Philadelphia: 1927. V. 39

SARGENT, GEORGE ETELL

Frank Layton, Eene Australische Geschiedenis. Amsterdam: 1856. V. 44

Frank Layton: an Australian Story. London: 1865. V. 44

SARGENT, HERBERT H.

Napoleon Bonaparte's First Campaign. Chicago: 1895. V. 37; 44

SARGENT, JOHN

The Mine: a Dramatic Poem. London: 1775. V. 42

The Mine. London: 1785. V. 37; 38; 40; 43; 45

The Mine. London: 1788. V. 40

The Mine: a Dramatic Poem. London: 1796. V. 37

SARGENT, JOHN O.

A Lecture on the Late Improvements in Steam Navigation and the Arts of Naval Warfare. New York: 1844. V. 43

Major-General Hazen, on His Post of Duty in the Great American Desert, Reviewed. New York: 1874. V. 37; 38

SARGENT, JOHN SINGER

The Work of John S. Sargent. With Introductions by J.B. Manson and Mrs. Meynell (1903). London/New York: 1927. V. 37

SARGENT, MARTIN P.

Pioneer Sketches; Scenes and Incidents of Former Days . . . Erie: 1891. V. 41

SARGENT, WINTHROP

Diary of Col. Winthrop Sargent, Adjutant General of the United States Army, During the Campaign of MDCCXCI (1791). Wormsloe: 1851. V. 44; 45

The History of an Expedition Against Fort Du Quesne, in 1755 Under Major-General Edward Braddock. Philadelphia: 1855. V. 42; 45

The Life and Career of Major John Andre, Adjutant-General of the British Army in America. Boston: 1861. V. 40; 45

Papers in Relation to the Official Conduct of Governour Sargent. Boston: 1801. V. 40

SARIANDI, VICTOR

Bactrian Gold from the Excavtions of the Tillya-Tepe Necropolis in Northern Afghanistan. Leningrad: 1985. V. 40

SARIS, JOHN

Agtste Oost-Indiesche Reys, Op Kosten van d'Engelsche Maatschappy, Gedaan met Drie Scheepen, Onder Capitain Joan Saris in't Jaar 1611 . . . Leiden: 1727. V. 45

SARLANDIERE, JEAN BAPTISTE

Systematized Anatomy, or Human Organography. New York: 1835. V. 42

SARMA, P.

The Feshwater Chaetophorales of New Zealand. 1986. V. 37

SARMIENTO, DOMINGO F.

Life in the Argentine Republic in the Days of the Tyrants. London: 1868. V. 40

SAROYAN, WILLIAM

An Act or Two of Foolish Kindness. 1977. V. 39

An Act or Two of Foolish Kindness. Lincoln: 1977. V. 46

The Adventures of Wesley Jackson. New York: 1946. V. 39

Asssassinations, and Jim, Sam and Anna. Northridge: 1979. V. 46

The Beautiful People. New York: 1941. V. 39

The Beautiful People. New York: (1941). V. 37

The Daring Young Man on the Flying Trapeze, and Other Stories. New York: 1934. V. 37; 39; 40; 46

The Daring Young Man on the Flying Trapeze and Other Stories. London: 1935. V. 39

The Daring Young Man on the Flying Trapeze: and Other Stories. Covelo: 1984. V. 37; 46

Farewell Speech of King Edward the Eighth. San Francisco: 1938. V. 41

The Fiscal Hoboes. Bronxville. V. 44

The Fiscal Hoboes. New York: 1949. V. 39; 45

Harlem As Seen by Hirschfeld. New York: 1941. V. 43

Hilltop Russians in San Francisco. San Francisco: 1941. V. 38

Hilltop Russians of San Francisco. Stanford: 1941. V. 41

Inhale and Exhale. New York: 1936. V. 40

Jim Dandy. New York: 1947. V. 39

Little Children. New York: 1937. V. 43

My Heart's in the Highlands. New York: 1939. V. 39

My Name is Aram. New York: (1940). V. 37

A Native American. San Francisco: 1938. V. 39; 42; 43

A New Chapter in the Human Comedy. V. 46

Razzle Dazzle. New York: 1942. V. 39

The Saroyan Special: Selected Short Stories. New York: 1948. V. 46

Saroyan's Fables. New York: 1941. V. 39; 43; 45; 46

A Special Announcement. New York: 1940. V. 39; 42; 43; 45

Those Who Write Them and Those Who Collect Them. Chicago: 1936. V. 39

Three Plays. New York: 1940. V. 39; 45

Three Times Three. Los Angeles: 1936. V. 39

The Time of Your Life. New York: 1939. V. 39

The Trouble with Tigers. New York: 1938. V. 39; 43

SARPI, PAOLO 1552-1623

The Historie of the Councel of Trent. London: 1629. V. 38

The Historie of the Council of Trent. London: 1640. V. 40

The History of the Inquisition . . . London: 1655. V. 45

The History of the Council of Trent. London: 1676. V. 37; 39; 40; 41; 44

Historie du Concile de Trente, Ecrite en Italien Par Fra-Paolo Sarpi . . . Et Traduite de Nouveau en Francois . . . Londres: 1736. V. 40

The Maxims of the Government of Venice. London: 1707. V. 37

The Opinion of Padre Paolo, of the Order of the Servites, Consultor of State, Given to the Lords the Inquisitors of State. London: 1689. V. 43

SARPI, PIETRO

The Free Schoole of Warre, or a Treatise, Whether it be Lawfull to Beare Armes for the Service of a Prince that is of a Divers Religion. London: 1625. V. 37

SARRANS, B.

Memoirs of General Lafayette, and of the French Revolution of 1830. New York: 1833. V. 38

SARRATT, LIEUT.

Life of Buonaparte . . . London: 1803? V. 42

SARRAZIN, GENERAL

History of the War in Spain and Portugal from 1807 to 1814. London: 1815. V. 41

SARRE, FRIEDRICH

Islamic Bookbindings. London: 1923. V. 37; 38

SARS, G. O.

An Account of the Crustacea of Norway, With Short Descriptions and Figures of all the Species. Bergen: 1893-1928. V. 37

SARTAIN, J. 1808-1897

The American Gallery of Art, From the Works of the Best Artists . . . Philadelphia: 1848. V. 39; 40; 41

SARTON, GEORGE

A History of Science: Ancient Science through the Golden Age of Greece and Hellenistic Science and Culture in the Last Three Centuries B.C. Cambridge: 1952-59. V. 42

A History of Science. Cambridge: 1959. V. 40

Introduction to the History of Science. N.P.: 1927. V. 45

Introduction to the History of Science. Baltimore: 1927-48. V. 37; 38; 46

Introduction to the History of Science. Baltimore: 1927-50. V. 39; 40; 46

Introduction to the History of Science. Baltimore: 1953. V. 42

Introduction to the History of Science. Volume II. From Rabbi Ben Ezra to Roger Bacon in Two Parts. Baltimore: 1931. V. 37

SARTON, MAY

Joanna and Ulysses. New York. V. 42

Journal of Solitude. New York: 1972. V. 42

Mrs. Stevens Hears the Mermaids Singing. New York: 1965. V. 42

Plant Dreaming Deep. New York. V. 42

The Poet and the Donkey. New York: 1969. V. 42

The Single Hound. Boston: 1938. V. 39; 44

SARTORIO, BERNARDO

Considerationi Christiane, E Civili, Proposte da Salomone alla Gioventv Nobile. Venice: 1675. V. 42

SARTORIS, ADELAIDE KEMBLE

Past Hours. London: 1880. V. 40

A Week in a French County-Home. London: 1867. V. 40

SARTORIS, RAMON

Three Plays. Washington: 1944. V. 46

SARTORIUS, CHRISTIAN 1796-1872

Importancia De Mexico Para La Emigracion Alemana . . . Traducida del Aleman Por Agustin S. de Tagle. Mexico: 1852. V. 39

Mexico Landscapes and Popular Sketches by Dr. Gaspey . . . Darmstadt: 1858. V. 42

Mexico. Landscapes and Popular Sketches. London: 1859. V. 40

SARTORIUS, PAUL

Neue Teutsche Liedlein, Mit Vier Stimmen, Nach der Art der Welschen Canzonette . . . Nuernberg: 1601. V. 40

SARTRE, JEAN PAUL

Kean. London: 1954. V. 41

Reflexions sur la Question Juive. Paris: 1946. V. 46

SARTRE, JOHN PAUL

Five Plays. Franklin Center: 1978. V. 43

SARTYSCHEW, GAWRILA

Account of a Voyage of Discovery to the North-East of Siberia, the Frozen Ocean and the North-East Sea. London: 1806. V. 44

SARYCHEV, GAVRILA A.

Puteshestvie Flota Kapitana Sarycheva . . . St. Petersburg: 1802. V. 43

SARYTSCHEW, GAWRILA

Account of a Voyage of Discovery to the North-East of Siberia, the Frozen Ocean, and the Northeast Sea. London: 1806-06. V. 40

SASOWSKY, NORMAN

The Prints of Reginald Marsh: an Essay and Definitive Catalog of His Linoleum Cuts, Etchings, Engravings and Lithographs. New York: 1976. V. 41

SASSI, GIUSEPPI ANTONIO

Historia Literario-Typographica Mediolanensis . . . Mediolani: 1745. V. 38

SASSOON, SIEGFRIED LORRAINE 1886-1967

Ave Atque Vale. The Last Four Poems of Siegfried Sassoon. Leicester: 1967. V. 37

Awaitment. Worcester: 1960. V. 41

Collected Poems. London: 1947. V. 38; 40

Collected Poems. London: 1957. V. 41

Common Chords. 1950. V. 45

Common Chords. Stanford Dingley: 1950. V. 44

Counter - Attack, and Other Poems. London: 1918. V. 37; 41; 42; 45

The Counter-Attack and Other Poems. London: 1917. V. 37

The Daffodil Murderer . . . 1913. V. 42

The Daffodil Murder. London: 1913. V. 40; 41

Diaries 1915-1925. London: 1981/85. V. 45

Diaries 1915-1925. London: 1981-85. V. 43

Doctor Dunne and Gargantua - the First Six Cantos. London: and New York: 1930. V. 45

Four Poems. Cambridge: 1918. V. 45

The Heart's Journey. New York: 1927. V. 37; 38; 39; 40; 42; 46

The Heart's Journey: Poems. New York: & London: 1927. V. 39; 43

The Heart's Journey. London: 1928. V. 38; 40; 46

Lingual Exercises for Advanced Vocabularians: Poems. Cambridge: 1925. V. 37

Memoirs of a Fox Hunting Man. London: 1928. V. 37; 39; 40; 43; 45; 46

Memoirs of a Fox-Hunting Man; Memoirs of an Infantry Officer; Sherston's Progress. London: 1928/30-36. V. 37; 39; 40

Memoirs of a Fox-Hunting Man; Memoirs of an Infantry Officer. London: 1928/30/36. V. 44

Memoirs of a Fox-Hunting Man; Memoirs of an Infantry Officer; Sherston's Progress. London: 1928-36. V. 43

Memoirs of a Fox Hunting Man. London: 1929. V. 37; 38; 39; 40; 41; 43; 44

Memoirs of an Infantry Officer. London: 1930. V. 37; 38; 39; 41

Memoirs of an Infantry Officer. London: 1931. V. 37; 41; 42

Memoirs of An Infantry Officer. New York: 1981. V. 38; 42; 44; 45; 46

Memoirs of an Infantry Officer. Portland: 1981. V. 40

Memoirs of a Fox-Hunting Man. New York: 1977. V. 38; 39

Memoirs of an Infantry Captain. London: 1930. V. 45

Memoris of an Infantry Officer . . . 1930. V. 37

Nativity. London: 1927. V. 41

Nativity. New York: 1927. V. 37; 46

An Octave. London: 1966. V. 37; 39; 43; 45

The Old Huntsman and Other Poems. London: 1917. V. 37; 43; 45; 46

The Old Huntsman and Other Poems. New York: 1918. V. 39

The Old Century. London: 1938. V. 41

The Old Century. London: 1938. V. 37

The Old Century and Seven More Years. The Weald of Youth. Siegfried's Journey, 1916-1920. London: 1938/1942/1945. V. 37

The Path to Peace. Worcester: 1960. V. 41; 45

Picture Show. 1919. V. 39

Picture Show: Poems. Cambridge: 1919. V. 43

Picture Show. Cambridge: 1919. V. 39; 40

Poems. London: 1931. V. 40; 41; 42; 44

Poems from Italy. London: 1945. V. 45

The Redeemer. 1916. V. 37

The Redeemer. Cambridge: 1916. V. 41

Rhymed Ruminations: Poems. London: 1940. V. 39

The Road to Ruin. London: 1935. V. 42

Satirical Poems. London: 1926. V. 37; 38; 39; 40; 41

Selected Poems. London: 1925. V. 42

Sequences. 1956. V. 37

Sequences: Poems. London: 1956. V. 39

Sherston's Progress. London: 1936. V. 37; 39; 43

Something About Myself. 1966. V. 43

Something About Myself. London: 1966. V. 46

Something About Myself. Worcester: 1966. V. 38; 41; 43; 46

A Suppressed Poem. N.P.: 1919. V. 39; 41

The Tasking. Cambridge: 1954. V. 37

To My Mother. London. V. 40

To My Father. London. V. 38

To Any Dead Officer. Cambridge: 1917. V. 45

To My Mother. London: 1928. V. 42; 46

To the Red Rose. London: 1931. V. 38

Vigils. Bristol: 1934. V. 37; 42

Vigils: Poems. London: 1934. V. 40

Vigils. London: 1935. V. 41

War Poems. London: 1919. V. 37; 43; 45

The Weald of Youth. New York: 1942. V. 37

SASTRI, PANDIT S. M.

Folklore in Southern India. Bombay: 1884/86/88. V. 42

SATAN'S Harvest Home; or the Present State of Whorecraft, Adultery, Fornication, Procuring, Pimping, Sodomy and the Game of Flatts. London: 1749. V. 43

SATCHELL, THOMAS

The Bibliography of Izaak Walton's Compleat Angler. London: 1882. V. 39

SATIE, ERIK

Sports and Divertissements. Paris: 1919. V. 45

SATO, SHOZO

The Art of Arranging Flowers: a Complete Guide to Japanese Ikebana. New York: 1965. V. 42; 46

SATOW, ERNEST

The Jesuit Mission Press in Japan 1591-1610. London?: 1888. V. 39

SATTER, GUSTAVE

The Life and Works of Gustave Satter. Macon: 1879. V. 40

SATTERLEE, M. P.

The Court Proceedings in the Trial of Dakota Indians Following the Massacre in Minnesota in August 1862. Minneapolis: 1927. V. 38

SATTERLEE, MARION P.

A Detailed Account of the Massacre by the Dakota Indians of Minnesota in 1862. Minneapolis: 1923. V. 42

SATYRA Manneiana in Jejunos Quosdam Philologos qui Limites suos Egressi Literas & Mores and Novam Disciplinam Revocare . . . N.P: 1650. V. 38

SATYRE Menippee De la Vertv Dv Catholicon d'Espagne, et de la Tenve des Estatz de Paris. Paris: 1594. V. 42

SAUER, GORDON C.

John Gould the Bird Man. 1982. V. 46
John Gould the Bird Man. Australia: 1982. V. 45

SAUER, MARTIN

An Account of a Geographical and Astronomical Expedition to the Northern Parts of Russia. London: 1802. V. 46
An Account of a Geographical and Astronomical Expedition to the Northern Parts of Russia. London: 1802. V. 37; 38; 40; 41; 46

SAUERLANDER, WILLIBALD

Gothic Sculpture in France, 1140-1270. New York. V. 38

SAUGRAIN, CLAUDE-MARIN

Code de La Librairie et Imprimerie de Paris . . . Paris: 1744. V. 46

SAUL, EDWARD

An Historical and Philosophical Account of the Barometer', or Weather-Glass. London: 1735. V. 38; 40

SAULCY, F. DE

Narrative of the Journey round the Dead Sea and an Account of the Discovery of the Sites of Sodom and Gomorrah. London: 1854. V. 37; 42; 46

SAUMAISE, CLAUDE DE

Claudii Salmasii ad Johannem Miltonum Repsonsio, Opus Posthumum. London: 1660. V. 45
De Manna et Saccharo, Commentarius. Paris: 1663. V. 45

SAUMAREZ, RICHARD

A Dissertation on the Universe in General, and on the Procession of the Elements in Particular. London: 1795. V. 45

SAUNDERS, BOYD

The Etchings of James Fowler Cooper. Columbia: 1982. V. 40

SAUNDERS, CHARLES

Tamerlane the Great. London: 1681. V. 41

SAUNDERS, EDWARD

The Hemiptera Heteroptera of the British Islands. London: 1892. V. 37; 43
The Hymenoptera Aculeata of the British Islands. London: 1896. V. 37; 38

SAUNDERS, EDWARD MANNING

History of the Baptists of the Maritime Provinces. Halifax: 1902. V. 44

SAUNDERS, FREDERIC

The Author's Printing and Publishing Assistant. London: 1839. V. 40; 45

SAUNDERS, FREDERICK

The Author's Printing and Publishing Assistant. New York: 1839. V. 38
Festival of Song: a Series of Evenings with the Poets. New York: 1866. V. 44
Salad for the Solitary. New York: 1853. V. 39
Salad for the Solitary. New York: 1853. V. 38

SAUNDERS, GEORGE

A Treatise on Theatres. London: 1790. V. 38; 41
A Treatise on Theatres. London: 1968. V. 37

SAUNDERS, HENRY MARTIN

The Crimps, or the Death of Poor Howe. London: 1794. V. 39

SAUNDERS, HENRY S.

Whitman Portraits. Toronto: 1923. V. 38

SAUNDERS, J. B. DE C. M.

The Illustrations from the Works of Andreas Vesalius of Brussels, With Annotations and Translations . . . Cleveland: 1950. V. 41; 45

The Illustrations from the Work of Andreas Vesalius of Brussels, with Annotations and Translations. Cleveland & New York: 1950. V. 42
The Illustrations from the Works of Andreas Vesalius of Brussels, With Annotations and Translations, a Discussion of the Plates and Their Background, Authorship and Influence, and a Biographical Sketch of Vesalius. New York: 1982. V. 42

SAUNDERS, J. E.

Early Settlers of Alabama. New Orleans: 1899. V. 42

SAUNDERS, JAMES

The Compleat Fisherman. London: 1724. V. 39; 40; 41; 42; 43

SAUNDERS, JAMES E.

Early Settlers of Alabama. New Orleans: 1899. V. 37; 38

SAUNDERS, JAMES EDMOND

Early Settlers of Alabama . . . With notes and Genealogies . . . Part I (All Published). New Orleans. V. 37

SAUNDERS, JOHN

The Lion in the Path. London: 1875. V. 38
Miss Vandeleur; or, Robbing Peter to Pay Paul. London: 1884. V. 41

SAUNDERS, JOHN CUNNINGHAM

A Treatise on Some Practical Points relating to the Diseaes of the Eye . . . London: 1811. V. 43; 45

SAUNDERS, LOUISE

The Knave of Hearts. London: 1925. V. 40; 41
The Knave of Hearts. New York: 1925. V. 37; 39; 44; 46
The Knave of Hearts. Racine: 1925. V. 40

SAUNDERS, LYLE

A Guide to Materials Bearing on Cultural Relations in New Mexico. Albuquerque: 1944. V. 38

SAUNDERS, MARGARET

Beautiful Joe: an Autobiography. Philadelphia: 1894. V. 41

SAUNDERS, MONTAGU

The Mystery in the Drood Family. Cambridge: 1914. V. 42

SAUNDERS, O.

Elfrida. Paris: 1928. V. 44

SAUNDERS, O. ELFRIDA

English Illumination. Firenze: 1928. V. 42
English Illumination. Paris: 1928. V. 45

SAUNDERS, RICHARD

Angelographia Sive Pneumata Leiturgia Pneumatalogia. London: 1701. V. 40
Angelographia Sive Pneumata Leiturgia Pneumatalogia . . . London: 1701. V. 46

SAUNDERS, RICHARD L.

Eloquence from a Silent World. Salt Lake City: 1990. V. 45; 46

SAUNDERS, W. W.

Refugium Botanicum . . . London: 1869-70. V. 43

SAUNDERS, WILLIAM

Observations on the Superior Efficacy of the Red Peruvian Bark in the Cure of Fevers. London: 1783. V. 38
Through the Life Continent; or, the United States in 1877-8. London: 1879. V. 46
Through the Light Continent; or, The United States in 1877-8. London and New York: 1879. V. 39
A Treatise on the Structure, Economy and Diseaes of the Liver . . . London: 1793. V. 42; 44
A Treatise on the Structure, Economy and Diseases of the Liver . . . Walpole: 1810. V. 44

SAUNDERSON, NICHOLAS

The Elements of Algebra in Ten Books. Cambridge: 1740. V. 38; 40; 46
The Method of Fluxions Applied to a Select Number of Useful Problems . . . London: 1756. V. 38; 41; 45

SAUNDERSON, THOMAS

A Royall Loyall Poem. London: 1660. V. 45

SAUNER, CLAUDIUS

Treatise on Modern Horology in Theory and practice. London: 1878-81. V. 39

SAUNIER, CLAUDIUS

Treatise on Modern Horology in Theory and Practice. London: 1882. V. 42

SAUNTER, SOLOMON

Literary Leisure, ot The Recreations of Solomon Saunter. London: 1802. V. 37

SAUSSURE, FERDINAND DE

Cours de Linguistique Generale. Lausanne & Paris: 1916. V. 39

SAUSSURE, H. B. DE

Voyages dans les Alpes, Precedes d'un Essai sur l'Histoire Naturelle des Environs de Geneve. Neuchatel,: 1779-96. V. 39

SAUSSURE, HORACE BENEDICT DE

Essais Sur l'Hygrometrie . . . (with) Defense de l'Hygrometre a Cheveu . . . Neuchatel: 1788. V. 38

Voyage dans les Alpes, Precedes d'un Essai sur l'Histoire Naturelle des Environs de Geneve. Neuchatel: 1779/86/96. V. 43

Voyages Dans Les Alpes, Precedes d'un Essai sur l'Histoire Naturelle des Environs De Geneve. Neuchatel & Geneva: 1780-96. V. 43

SAUSSURE, NICOLAS THEODORE DE

Recherches Chimiques sur la Vegetation . . . Paris: 1804. V. 37

SAUTER, DANIEL

Practica der Bancarottierer das ist: Eigentliche, Lebhaffte Entwerffung der Wunderlichen Practicen der Bancarottierer und Fallicen zu Disen Unsern Zeiten. Augsburg: 1615. V. 45

SAUVAGE, DENIS

Croniqve de Flandres, Ancienement Composee par Avtevr Incertain, et Nouvvellement Mise en Lvmiere . . . Continvation de l'Histoire et Croniqve de Flandres, Extraitte de Plvsievrs bons Auteurs . . . Lyon: 1562. V. 39

SAUVAN, JEAN BAPTISTE BALTHAZAR

Picturesque Tour of the Seine from Paris to the Sea. London: 1821. V. 45

SAUZAY, ALEXANDRE

Monographie de l'Oeuvre de Bernard Pallissy Suivie d'un Choix de ses Continuateurs ou Imitaeurs Dessinee par MM. Carle Dealgne, et C. Borneman et Accompagnee d'un texte par M. Sauzay Conservateur adjoint du Musee du Louvre et M. Henri Delange. Paris: 1862. V. 44

SAVAGE, C. R.

The Reflex of Salt Lake City and Vicinity . . . Salt Lake City: 1893. V. 40

THE SAVAGE Club Papers. London: 1897. V. 46

SAVAGE, EDWARD H.

A Chronological History of the Boston Watch and Police, from 1631 to 1865 . . . Boston: 1865. V. 42

SAVAGE, G.

The American Birds of Dorothy Doughty. A Critical Appreciation by G. Savage. Worcester: (1962). V. 37

SAVAGE, GEORGE

The Catholick Question at Boston; or an Attempt to Prove that a Calvinist is a Christian. Boston: 1815. V. 45

SAVAGE, HENRY

Balliofergus, or a Commentary Upon the Foundation, Founders, and Affaires, of Balliol Colledge, Gathered Out of the Records Thereof . . . Oxford: 1668. V. 43

The Surgery, Surgical Pathology and Surgical Anatomy of the Female Pelvic Organs. New York: 1880. V. 42; 44

SAVAGE, J.

A Full View of Popery, in a Satyrical account of the Lives of the Popes &c . . . London: 1704. V. 39

SAVAGE, JAMES

A Genealogical Dictionary fo the First Settlers of New England. Boston: 1860-62. V. 46

History of the Hundred of Carhampton, in the County of Somerset, from the Best Authorities. Bristol: 1830. V. 42

The Librarian. London: 1808/09. V. 46

The Librarian. London: 1808-10. V. 37

SAVAGE, JAMES W.

The Discovery of Nebraska . . . Omaha: 1880. V. 44

SAVAGE, JOHN

Fenian Heroes and Martyrs. Boston: 1868. V. 39

Horace to Scaeva. London: 1730. V. 37; 40; 42; 45

Picturesque Ireland. New York: n.d. V. 37

SAVAGE-LANDOR, A. HENRY

Across the Unknown South America. London: 1913. V. 38

SAVAGE, MARIMION W.

The Falcon Family; or, Young Ireland. London: 1845. V. 37

SAVAGE MINING COMPANY

Annual Report of the Savage Mining Company, for the Fiscal Year Ending July 11th, 1873. San Francisco: 1873. V. 39

SAVAGE, RICHARD

The Life of Mr. Richard Savage. London: 1727. V. 43

Miscellaneous Poems and Translations. London: 1726. V. 38; 41; 45

A Nonsensical Song, or the Charms of Nonsence. N.P.: 1720. V. 45

A Nonsensical Song or the Charms of Nonsence. London: 1725-30. V. 45

A Poem to the Memory of Mrs. Oldfield. London: 1730. V. 38

Various Poems. London: 1761. V. 42; 45; 46

The Wanderer. London: 1729. V. 37; 39; 40; 41; 42

The Works of Richard Savage, Esq., Son of Earl Rivers. London: 1775. V. 42

The Works. London: 1777. V. 38; 41

The Works of Richard Savage, Esq., Son of the Earl of Rivers. London: 1777. V. 39; 43; 46

SAVAGE, SARAH

Trial and Self-Discipline. Boston and Cambridge: 1835. V. 43

SAVAGE, TIMOTHY

The Amazonian Republic, Recently Discovered in the Interior of Peru. New York: 1842. V. 40

SAVAGE, WILLIAM

A Dictionary of the Art of Printing. London: 1841. V. 44; 45; 46

Practical Hints on Decorative Printing. London: 1818. V. 44

Practical Hints on Decorative Printing With Illustrations Engraved in Wood and Printed in Colours at the Type Press. London: 1822. V. 41; 44

SAVANNAH. Commercial Relations Between the West and Savannah. Commercial History of Savannah. Savannah: 1891. V. 41

SAVARY, CLAUDE

Letters on Egypt with a Parallel Between the Manners of Its Ancient and Modern Inhabitants, the Present State, the Commerce, Agriculture and Government of that Country. London: 1786. V. 41

SAVARY, CLAUDE ETIENNE

Letters on Egypt. Dublin: 1787. V. 43

Letters on Egypt . . . and an Account of the Descent of St. Lewis at Damietta . . . (with) Letters on Greece: Being a Sequel to Letters on Egypt. Dublin: 1787, 1788. V. 37

SAVARY DES BRUONS

The Universal Dictionary of Trade and Commerce . . . London: 1757. V. 41

SAVE-SODERBERGH, TORGNY

Private Tombs at Thebes. Oxford: 1957-63. V. 44

SAVIARD, BARTHELEMY

Observations in Surgery. London: 1740. V. 38

SAVIGNY, J. B.

Narrative of a Voyage to Senegal in 1816 . . . Comprising an Account of the Shipwreck of the Medusa . . . & the Various Occurrences on Board the Raft, in the Desert of Zaara . . . to which are subjoined observations respecting the . . . London: 1818. V. 37; 45

SAVILE, ALBANY

Thirty-Six Hints to Sportsmen. Okehampton: 1825. V. 44

SAVILE, HENRY

Advice to a Painter &c. 1679. V. 44

Advice to a Painter, &c. caption: 1679. V. 45

Advice to a Painter, &c. N.P.: 1679. V. 43

Rerum Anglicanarum Scriptores Post Bedam Praecipui . . . London: 1596. V. 38

SAVILE, SARAH

William and Marian. London: 1842. V. 40

SAVILLE, HENRY 1549-1622

Commentarius DE Militia Romana. Heidelbergae: 1601. V. 46

SAVILLE-KENT, W.

A Manual of the Infusoria. London: 1881-82. V. 37; 38

The Naturalist in Australia. London: 1897. V. 37

SAVILLE-KENT, WILLIAM

The Great Barrier Reef of Australia. London: 1893. V. 37; 38

Manual of the Infusoria. London: 1880-82. V. 40

SAVILLE, MARSHALL H.

Turquois Mosaic Art in Ancient Mexico. New York: 1922. V. 42

The Wood Carver's Art in Ancient Mexico. New York: 1925. V. 42

SAVIN, F. H.

Falconry in the British Isles. London: 1873. V. 37

SAVIOLI, LODOVICO 1729-1804

Amori. Crisopoli: 1795. V. 40

SAVONAROLA, GIROLAMO

Compendium Totius Philosophiae tam Naturalis Quam Moralis, nunc Primum in Lucem Editum. De Ultimo Fine Humanae Vitae. De Divisione. Ordine & Utilitate Omnium Scientiarum. Compendium Logices. Venice: 1534. V. 39

Epistola de Contemptu Mundi di Frate Hieronymo da Ferrara dellordine de Frat Predicatori la Quale Manda ad Elena Buonaccorsi sua Madre, per Consolarla Della Morte del Fratello, Suo Zio. Hammersmith: 1894. V. 46

Epistola de Contemptu Mundi di Frate Hieronymo da Ferrara . . . Londra: 1894. V. 44

Expositione del Reverendissimo in Christo Padre Frate Hieronymo da Ferrara . . . Florence: 1485. V. 45

Expositiones in Psalmos . . . Item Regulae Quedam Fructuossimae ad Omnes Religiosos Attinentes. Venice: 1517. V. 37

Operette Molto Divota Sopra e Dieci Comandamenti Didio. Florence: 1598. V. 37

Opuscula De Simplicitate Vitae Christianae. Alcala: 1529. V. 37

Prediche del Rev. P. F. Hieronymo Sauonaruola . . . Sopra Aiquanti Salmi & Sopra Aggeo Profeta . . . colophon: 1544. V. 45

Prediche . . . Sopra Alquanti Salmi & Sopra Aggeo Profeta Fatte . . . Venice: 1544. V. 45

Tractato o Uero Sermone della Oratione . . . Florence: 1495. V. 45

Triumphus Crucis de Fidei Veritate. Venice: 1521. V. 40

Triompho della Croce di Christo . . . Venice: 1547. V. 40

SAVONAROLA, H.

Molti Devotissimi Trattati . . . 1538. V. 42

De Simplicitate Vite Xr(ist)iane. 1512. V. 42

SAVONAROLA, HIERONYMUS

Aurea Expositio Psalmi Miserere Mei Deus. Paris: 1505-10. V. 38

SAVORY, ISABEL

A Sportswoman in India. London: 1900. V. 42

SAVOT, LOUIS

L'Architecture Francoise des Bastimens Particuliers . . . avec des Figures et des Notes de M. Blondel. Paris: 1673. V. 44

THE SAVOY. London: 1896. V. 37; 38; 40; 41; 44
THE SAVOY. London: 1896-Dec. 1896. V. 44

THE SAVOY Cocktail Book. London: 1930. V. 46
THE SAVOY Cocktail Book. New York: 1930. V. 41

SAVVA, MONK 1659-1725

The Book of Wisdom and Lies. Hammersmith: 1894. V. 39; 46

The Book of Wisdom and Lies. London: 1894. V. 40; 41; 44

SAWARD, B. C.

Decorative Painting. London: 1883. V. 38; 41

SAWARD, BLANCHE

Decorative Painting. London: 1885. V. 38

SAWER, J. C.

Odorographia, a Natural History of Raw Materials and Drugs Used in the Perfume Industry . . . (and) . . . Second Series. London: & Brighton: 1892-94. V. 40

SAWKINS, JAMES GAY

A Pictorial Tour of Hawaii 1850-1852. San Francisco: 1991. V. 46

SAWYER, ALVAN L.

History of the Northern Peninsula of Michigan, & Its People. Chicago: 1911. V. 39

SAWYER, ARTHUR ROBERT

Accidents in Mines, in the North Staffordshire Coalfield.. Hanley: 1886. V. 40

Miscellaneous Accidents in Mines, with Special Reference to the North Staffordshire Coalfield; their Causes, and the Means of Diminishing their Frequency. Manchester/London: 1889. V. 37

SAWYER, CAROLINE MEHETABEL

The History of the Blind Vocalists. New York: 1853. V. 43

SAWYER, CAROLINE MEHETABEL FISHER

The Merchant Widow, and Other Tales. New York: 1841. V. 43

SAWYER, CHALRES J.

English Books 1475-1900. London: 1927. V. 45

SAWYER, CHARLES

Way Sketches, Containing Incidents of Travel Across the Plains from St. Joseph to California in 1850, with Letters Describing Life and Conditions in the Gold Region . . . New York: 1926. V. 37

SAWYER, CHARLES C.

When This Cruel War is Over: Ballad. Richmond: 1863. V. 39; 40

SAWYER, CHARLES CARROLL

When This Cruel War is Over; Ballad: Words by Charles C. Sawyer: Music by Henry Tucker. Richmond: 186-. V. 40

SAWYER, CHARLES J.

English Books 1475-1900. London: 1927. V. 38; 42; 46

English Books 1475-1900. New York: 1927. V. 46

English Books 1475-1900. Westmisnter: 1927. V. 37; 38; 40; 46

SAWYER, EDMUND

Memorials of Affairs of State in the Regins of Q. Elizabeth and K. James I . . . . London: 1725. V. 44

SAWYER, EUGENE T.

The Life and Career of Tiburcio Vasquez, the California Stage Robber. Oakland: 1944. V. 38; 45

SAWYER, GEORGE S.

Southern Institutes; or, an Inquiry Into the Origin and Early Prevalence of Slavery and the Slave-Trade. Philadelphia: 1859. V. 42; 45

SAWYER, JAMES A.

Wagon Road from Niobra to Virginia City. Washington: 1866. V. 40; 41

SAWYER, LORENZO

Way Sketches. New York: 1926. V. 37; 38; 39; 40; 41; 43; 46

SAWYER, R. H.

The Truth About the Invisible Empire Knights of the Ku Klux Klan. Portland: 1922. V. 39

SAWYER, R. T.

Leech Biology and Behaviour. London: 1985. V. 37; 38

Leech Biology and Behaviour. Oxford: 1986. V. 37

SAWYER, RUTH

The Long Christmas. New York: 1941. V. 44

This Way to Christmas. 1924. V. 46

SAWYER, WALTER LEON

An Outland Journey. Boston: 1896. V. 38

SAXBY, HENRY L.

The Birds of Shetland with Observations on Their Habit, Migration and Occasional Appearance. Edinburgh: 1874. V. 46

The British Customs: Containing an Historical and Practical Account of Each Branch of the Revenue . . . London: 1757. V. 38; 46

SAXBY, JESSIE M. E.

Shetland Traditional Lore. Edinburgh: 1932. V. 46

SAXE, JOHN

The Money-King and Other Poems. Boston: 1860. V. 45

SAXE, JOHN G.

Progress: a Satire. New York: 1847. V. 42

SAXE, MAURICE, COMTE DE

Reveries, or Memoirs Upon the Art of War . . . to which are added some original letters, upon various military Subjects . . . newver before made Publick: together with his Reflections upon the Propagation of the Human Species. London: 1757. V. 37; 38; 39; 40; 45

SAXI, F.

England and the Mediterranean Tradition. Oxford: 1945. V. 46

SAXL, F.

Lectures. London: 1957. V. 42

SAXO

Danica Historia Libris XVI . . . Cum Indice Rerum Memorabilium Locupletismo. Frankfurt: 1576. V. 41

The History of Amleth Prince of Denmark. Copenhagen: 1954. V. 45

Saxonis Grammatici Historia Danicae Libri XVI. 1644-45. V. 43

Saxonis Grammatici Historiae Danicae Libri XVI. Sorae: typis et sumptibus: 1644-45. V. 44

THE SAXON and the Gael; or, the Northern Metropolis: Including a View of the Lowland and Highland Character. London: 1814. V. 38

SAYWER, LORENZO 1820-1891.

Way Sketches Containing Incidents of Travel across the Plains from St. Joseph to California in 1850. With Letters Describing Life and Conditions in the Gold Region. With Historical notes compiled from rare sources and an . . . New York: 1926. V. 37

SCADDING, HENRY

Toronto of Old: Collections and Recollections. Toronto: 1878. V. 44

SCAFE, JOHN

A Geological Primer in Verse; with a Poetical Geognosy, or Feasting and Fighting . . . London: 1820. V. 43

SCAINO, ANTONIO DA SALO

Trattato del Giuoco Della Palla di Messer . . . Venegia: 1555. V. 38

LA SCALA, a Historical Digest 1778-1946. Milano: 1946. V. 43

SCALA, A. VON

Illustrations of Turkish, Arabian, Persian, Central Asiatic and Indian Metal Ware . . . Vienna: 1895. V. 38

SCALAPINO, LESLIE

Instead of an Animal. N.P.: 1977. V. 46

SCALE, BERNARD

Directions for Navigating into the Bay of Dublin from Wicklow Head, and from Balbriggen. Dublin: 1765. V. 42

An Hiberian Atlas; or General Description of the Kingdom of Ireland . . . London: 1776. V. 42; 43

An Hibernian Atlas; or General Description of the Kingdom of Ireland. London: 1798. V. 39; 43

SCALES, JOHN

History of Dover, New Hampshire. 1923. V. 42

SCALI, PIETRO PAOLO

Catalogus Omnium Animalium Testaceorum Quae in Celeberrimo Musaeo Petri Pauli Scali Liburnensis Adservantur. colophon: 1752. V. 43

SCALIGER, JOSEPH J.

Proverbiorum Arabicorum Centuriae Duae, ab Anonymo Quodam Arabe Collectae et Explicatae. Leiden: 1614. V. 37

Scaligeriana sive Exerpta ex Ore . . . Lugduni: 1668. V. 40

SCALIGER, JOSEPH JUSTE

(Greek) Paroimiai Emmetroi. Proverbiales Graecorum Versus. Paris: 1594. V. 38

SCALIGER, JOSEPH JUSTUS

Ios. Iusti Scaligeri Iulii Caesaris a Burden Filii Opuscula Varia . . . Paris: 1610. V. 45

SCALIGER, JULIUS CAESAR

Adversus Desid. Erasmum Orationes Duae. Toulouse: 1622-1620. V. 38

Animadversiones in Historias Theophrasti. Lyon: 1584. V. 38

De Causis Lingue Latinae Libri Tredecim. Lyon: 1540. V. 38

Exotericarum Exercitationum Liber Exercitationum Liber Quintus Decimus de Subtilitate, ad Hieronymum Cardanum. Paris: 1557. V. 38; 40; 45

Poemata. Heidelberg: 1591. V. 40

SCALZO OF PALERMO

Idea Del Cavalier Gierosolimitano Mostrata nella Vita Di Fra D. Agostino Grimaldo, E. Rosso. Messina: 1662. V. 37

SCAMMON, CHARLES M.

The Marine Mammals of the North Western Coast of North America Described and Illustrated, Together with an Account of the American Whale Fishery. San Francisco: 1874. V. 37; 38; 39; 41; 45

The Marine Mammals of the North-Western Coast of North America and the American Whale Fishery. Riverside: 1969. V. 43

SCAMMON, L. N.

Spanish Missions California. San Francisco: 1926. V. 38

SCAMOZZI, VICENZO

L'Idea della Architettura Universale, Divisa in X Libri. Venice: 1714. V. 37

SCAMOZZI, VINCENT

The Mirror of Architecture; or the Ground-Rules of the Art of Building, Exactly Laid Down by Vincent Scamozzi, Master-Builder of Venice . . . London: 1708. V. 41

Oeuvres d'Architecture de Vincent Scamozzi Vicentin, Architecte de la Republique de Venise . . . Leide: 1713. V. 38

SCAMOZZI, VINCENZO

Les Cinq Ordres d'Architecture de Vincent Scamozzi, Vicentin, Architecte de la Republique de Venise . . . Paris: 1685. V. 39

Dell'Idea della Architectura Vniuersale. Venetia: 1615. V. 37

Discorsi Sopra l'Antichita di Roma . . . Venice: 1583. V. 37; 40; 44

Oeuvres d'Architecture . . . Traduites en Francois par Mr. Augustin Charles D'Aviler & Samuel Du Ry. Leiden: 1713. V. 37

SCAMUI, ERNESTO

Egyptian Art in the Egyptian Museum of Turin, Paintings, Sculpture, Furniture, Textiles, Ceramics, Papyri. New York: 1965. V. 42

SCAMUZZI, ERNESTO

Egyptian Art in the Egyptian Museum of Turin. New York: 1956. V. 40; 44

Egyptian Art in the Egyptian Museum of Turin: Paintings, Sculpture, Furniture, Textiles, Cermaics, Papyri. New York: (1965). V. 37

SCANLAN, CHARLES M.

Indian Massacre and Captivityof Hall Girls. Milwaukee: 1915. V. 37

SCANZONI, F. W. VON 1821-1891

A Practical Treatise on the Diseases of the Sexual Organs of Women. New York: 1861. V. 43

SCAPPI, BARROLOMEO

Opera Di M. Bartolomeo Scappi Cuoco Secreto di Papa Pio Quinto, Divisa in Sei Libri. Venetia: 1570. V. 38

SCAPPI, BARTOLOMEO

Opera Di M. Bartolomeo Scappi, Cuoco Secreto di Papa Pio Quinto. Venetai: 1598. V. 38

Opera . . . dell'Arte del Cvcinae, Con Laquale si Puo Ammaestrare Qual si Voglia Cuoco, Scalco, Trinciante, o Masestro di Casa . . . Venetia: 1610. V. 39

SCAPULA, JOHANN

Lexicon Graeco-Latinum Novum . . . Basel: 1600. V. 46

SCARANUS, LUCIUS

Scenophylax Dialouge, in Quo Tragaedijs, & Comeadijs Antiquus Carminum . . . Venice: 1601. V. 43

SCARARON, PAUL

The Comic Romance of Monsieur Scarron . . . London: 1775. V. 38

THE SCARBOROUGH Album of History and Poetry. Scarborough: 1825. V. 46

SCARBOROUGH, DOROTHY

The Wind. New York: 1925. V. 45

THE SCARBOROUGH Guide. Hull: 1796. V. 44

THE SCARBOROUGH Tragedy: from 'Curiosities of Street Literature'. 1975. V. 45

SCARBOROUGH'S New Standard Atlas of the World. Indianapolis/Boston/: 1910. V. 45

THE SCARED Treasury, a Literary & Religious Souvenir . . . London: 1845. V. 43

SCARGILL, WILLIAM PITT

Blue-Stocking Hall. London: 1827. V. 46

The Puritan's Grave. London: 1833. V. 46

Tales of a Briefless Barrister. London: 1829. V. 41

SCARISBRICK, EDWARD

The Life of the Lady Warner . . . in Religion Call'd Sister Clare of Jesus. London: 1692. V. 37

SCARPA, ANTONIO

Engravings of the Cardiac Nerves, The Nerves of the Ninth Pair, The Glosso-Pharyngeal . . . Edinburgh: 1829. V. 40

A Treatise on the Principal Diseases of the Eyes. London: 1818. V. 44

SCARRON, PAUL

Le Roman Comique de M. Scarron. Paris: 1727. V. 38

Le Roman Comique de Scarron. Paris: 1883. V. 38

The Comical Romance, and Other Tales. London: 1892. V. 38; 42

The Comical Romance and Other Tales. London: 1902. V. 46

The Whole Comical Works of Monsr. Scarron . . . London: 1703. V. 46

The Whole Comical Works of . . . London: 1712. V. 45

The Whole Comical Works of Mons. London: 1759. V. 43

SCARUFFI, GASPARO

L'Alitinonfo di M. Gasparo Scaruffi Regiano . . . (with) Part 2: Breve Instruttione Sopra il Discorso Fatto dal Mag. M. Gasparo Scaruffi . . . Reggio: 1582. V. 38

SCATTERGOOD, DAVID

Scattergood's Delaware River From Trenton to the Sea . . . Philadelphia: 1878. V. 42

SCELTA di Facezie, Tratti, Buffonerie, Motti e Burle. Florence: 1586. V. 40

SCELTA id Poesie Italiane D'Autori Moderni. Parigi: 1822. V. 39

SCENECAE Tragoedaie. Venice: 1517. V. 40

SCENES and Adventures in Spain from 1835 to 1840. London: 1845. V. 38

SCENES and Life in the Transvaal. Johannesburg: 1898. V. 42

SCENES from the Life of Nickleby Married. London: 1840. V. 40; 43

SCENES in Paris. London: 1830. V. 45

SCENES in Washington; a Story of the Last Generation. New York: 1848. V. 37

SCHAARSCHMIDT-RICHTER, IRMTRAUD

Japanese Gardens. New York: 1979. V. 37; 41

SCHACHNER, AUGUST

Ephraim McDowell: 'Rather of Ovariotomy' and Founder of Abdominal Surgery. Philadelphia: 1921. V. 42

Ephraim McDowell 'Father of Ovariotomy' and Founder of Abdominal Surgery. Philadelphia & London: 1921. V. 45

SCHAD, CHRISTIAN

Christian Schad-Mappe. N.P.: 1915. V. 42

SCHADE, WERNER

Cranach: a Family of Master Painters. New York: 1980. V. 43

SCHAEFER, JACK

Conversations with a Pocket Gopher. Santa Barbara: 1978. V. 41

First Blood. Boston: 1953. V. 38; 40

First Blood. 1954. V. 43

Monte Walsh. Boston: 1963. V. 45

Shane. Boston: 1954. V. 39

SCHAEFFER, CASPER

Memoirs and Reminiscences Together with Sketches of the Early History of Sussex County, New Jersey. Hackensack: 1907. V. 41

SCHAEFFER, J. C.

Elements Entomologica . . . Ratisbon: 1766. V. 42

SCHAEFFER, LUTHER M.

Sketches of Travels in South America, Mexico and California. New York: 1860. V. 38; 40; 41; 43; 45

SCHAEFFER, MARY T. S.

Old Indian Trails: Incidents of Camp and Trail Life, Covering Two Years' Exploration through the Rocky Mountains of Canada. Toronto: 1911. V. 46

SCHAFER, E. A.

Text-Book of Physiology. Edinburgh: 1898-1900. V. 41

SCHAFFER, JACOB

C. Proefnemingen en Monster-Bladen, Om Papier te Maaken Zonder Lompen. Amsterdam: 1770. V. 38

SCHAFFER, MARY T. S.

Old Indian Trails. London: 1911. V. 39

SCHALDACH, WILLIAM J.

Carl Rungius, Big Game Painter. West Hartford: 1945. V. 42; 46

Coverts and Casts. New York: 1943. V. 43

Fish. Collected Etchings, Drawings and Watercolors of Trout and Salmon. Philaelphia: 1937. V. 37; 40; 43; 46

SCHALLING, JACOB

Opthalmia Sive Disquisitio Hermetico-Galenica de Natura Oculorum Eorumque Visibilibus Characteribus Morbis & Remediis. Erffurdt: 1615. V. 40

SCHANGE, J. M. ALEXIS b. 1807

Precis sur le Redressement des dents, ou expose des Moyens Rationaels de Prevenir et de Corriger les Deviations des Dents. Paris: 1841. V. 42

SCHANILEC, CLAYTON

Farmers. Stockholm: 1989. V. 43; 45

SCHARDT, HERMANN

Paris 1900: Masterworks of French Poster Art. New York: 1970. V. 39; 41; 42

SCHARF, J. THOMAS

History of the Confederate States Navy, from its Organization to the Surrender of its Last Vessel. New York: 1887. V. 37; 38; 41; 42

SCHARF, JOHN THOMAS

History of Philadelphia, 1609-1884. Philadelphia: 1884. V. 39; 40; 42

History of Westchester County, New York, Including Morrisania, Kings Bridge & West Farms, Which Have Been Annexed to New York City. Philadelphia: 1886. V. 38

History of the Confederate States Navy. New York: 1887. V. 41

History of Baltimore City and County, from the Earliest Period to the Present. Philadelphia: 1881. V. 37; 39; 46

History of Philadelphia, 1609-1884. Philadelphia: 1884. V. 46

History of Saint Louis City and County, from the Earliest Periods to the Present Day . . . Philadelphia: 1883. V. 46

History of the Confederate States Navy. Albany: 1894. V. 38

History of the Confederate States Navy from Its Organization to the Surrender of Its Last Vessel. New York: 1887. V. 40; 46

SCHARL, JOSEF

Josef Scharl. New York: 1945. V. 46

SCHARMANN, HERMAN B.

Scharmann's Landreise Nach Californien . . . (New York: 1905). V. 37

SCHARMANN, HERMANN B.

Scharmann's Overland Journey to California from the Pages of a Pioneer's Diary. New York: 1918. V. 38; 41

SCHARNHORST, GENERAL

Military Field Pocket Book. London: 1811. V. 42

SCHATZ, A. H.

Opening a Cow Country. Ann Arbor: 1939. V. 44

SCHATZ, BEZALEL

Exhibition of Oil Paintings, San Francisco Museum of Art, August 16 through September 11, 1949. Berkeley. V. 39

SCHATZ, OLGA

Juval Sings into the Spirit of Art. Berkeley: 1949. V. 44

SCHATZKI, WALTER

Children's Books, Old and Rare, Offered for Sale. Catalogue Number One. New York: 1930's. V. 37

SCHAUDINN, FRITZ

Vorlaufiger Bericht Uber das Vorkommen von Spirochaeten in Syphilitischen Krankheitsprodukten und bei Papillom. Berlin: 1905. V. 39

SCHAUENSEE, R. M.

The Birds of Columbia, and Adjacent Areas of South and Central America. USA: 1964. V. 45

SCHEBE, CHINUA

The Sacrificial Egg and Other Short Stories. Onitsha: 1962. V. 41

SCHEDEL, HARTMANN 1440-1514

Liber Chronicarum. Nuremberg: 1493. V. 38; 39; 40; 42; 43; 46

Nuremberg Chronicle. New York: 1979. V. 38

SCHEDEL, HARTMANO

Chronicon Nurembergense, V. 44

SCHEDULE of the French and Dutch Loans, Shewing the Periods of Their Redemption with the Annual Interest Payable Thereone Until Their Final Extinction, for Which Provision Is Yet to Be Made. New York: 1786. V. 46

A SCHEDULE of the Net Duties Payable on the Importation of Certain Goods, Ware, and Merchandize . . . Imported From any Other Country than Great Britian, and Afterwards Exported to Any of the British Planations in America or the West Indies . . . London: 1793. V. 46

SCHEELE, CARL WILHELM

Memoires de Chymie Tires des Memoires de l'Academie Royale des Sciences de Stockholm Traduits du Suedois et de l'Allemand. Dijon: 1785. V. 40

SCHEFFER, JOHANNES

The History of Lapland. At the Theater in Oxford: 1674. V. 45

The History of Lapland. Oxford: 1674. V. 38; 40; 41; 42; 43; 44; 46

Lapponia, id est, Regionis Lapponum et Gentis Nova et Verissima Descriptio. Francofurti: 1673. V. 40; 44

SCHEFFER, JOHN

The History of Lapland. 1674. V. 45

SCHEFFERI, JOANNIS

De Militia Navali Veterum, Libri Quatuor. Ad Historian Gracam Latinamque Utiles. Sweden: 1654. V. 44

SCHEIBLER, CHRISTOPH

Philosophia Compendiosa, seu Philosophia Exhibens Logicae, Physicae, Astronomiae, Ethicae, Metaphysicae, Geometriae, Opticae, Politicae et Oeconomicae. N.P.: 1628. V. 40

SCHEINER, CHRISTOPH

De Maculis in Sole Animadversis & Tanquam ab Apelle in Tabula Spectandum in Publica Luce Expositis, Batavi Dissertatiununclia . . . Antwerp: 1612. V. 46

Selected Works. Moscow & Leningrad: 1935. V. 39

SCHELE DE VERE, MAXIMILIAN

The Great Empress: a Portrait. Philadelphia: 1870. V. 41

SCHELL, JAMES PEERY

In the Ojibway Country, a Story of Early Missions on the Minnesota Frontier. Walhalla: 1911. V. 38; 42; 45

SCHELL, MARY L.

The Love Life of Brig. Gen. Henry M. Naglee . . . San Francisco: 1867. V. 38

SCHELLING, FRIEDRICH WILHELM JOSEF

Neue Zeitschrift fur Speculative Physik. Tubingen: 1802-1803. V. 41

Sammtliche Werke. Stuttgart und Augsburg: 1856-61. V. 38

Ueber die Moglichkeit Einer Form der Philosophie Uberhaupt. Tubingen: 1795. V. 41; 45

A SCHEME for Establishing a Militia, etc. Eton: 1749. V. 39

A SCHEME for Uniting the Two Kingdoms of England and Scotland, Different from Any Tht Has Been Hitherto Laid Down. Edinburgh?: 1705/06? V. 38

A SCHEME to Secure and Extend the Credit and Strength of the British Nation. London: 1747. V. 40

SCHENCK, DAVID

North Carolina 1780-1. Raleigh: 1889. V. 40; 46

SCHENCK, FRANKLIN L.

Paintings by Franklin L. Schenck 1856 - 1927. Feburary 28th to March 12th 1928. New York City: 1928. V. 37

SCHENCK, J. S.

History of Warren County, Pennsylvania. Syracuse: 1887. V. 41; 42

SCHENCK, JOHN S.

History of Ionia and Montcalm Counties, Michigan. Philadelphia: 1881. V. 46

SCHENCK VON GRAFENBERG, JOHANN GEORG

Monstrorum Historia Memorabilis, Monstrosa Humanorum Partuum Miracula . . . Frankfurt: 1609. V. 38

SCHENCK VON GRAFENBERG, JOHANNES

Observationum Medicarum, Rararum, Novarum, Admirabilium & Monstrosarum. Frankfurt: 1609. V. 45

SCHERCK, MICHAEL G.

Pen Pictures of Early Pioneer Life in Upper Canada. Toronto: 1905. V. 46

SCHERER, HEINRICH

Atlas Novus Exhibens Orbem Terraqueum . . . Augsburg: 1702-10. V. 42; 43

SCHERPF, G. A.

Entstehungsgeschichte und Gegenwartiger Zustand des Neuen, Unabhangigen, Amerikanischen Staates Texas. Augsburg: 1841. V. 43; 45

SCHERZER, CARL

Travels in the Free States of Central America, Nicaragua, Honduras and San Salvador. London: 1857. V. 43

Travels in the Free States of Central America . . . London: 1857. V. 45

SCHETKY, J. C.

Reminiscences of the Veterans of the Sea. London: 1867. V. 38

SCHETKY, JOHN C.

Illustrations of Walter Scott's Lay of the Last Minstrel, Consisting of Twelve Views . . . with Anecdotes and Descriptions. London: 1808. V. 38; 39

SCHETKY, S. F. L.

Sketches from the Public and Private Career of John Schristian Schetky, Late Marine Painter in Ordinary to Her Majesty. London: 1877. V. 38

SCHEUCHZER, JOHANN JACOB

Kupfer-Bibel in Welcher die Physica Sacra Oder Geheiligte Natur-Wissenschafft derer in Heil. Augsburg & Ulm: 1731-35. V. 38

SCHEUCHZER, JOHN GASPAR

An Account of the Success of Inoculating the Small Pox in Great Britain for the Years 1727 and 1728. London: 1729. V. 42; 44

SCHEVILL, JAMES

Ghost Names . . . Ghost Numbers. Providence: 1985. V. 41; 45

Ghost Names . . . Ghost Numbers. Rhode Island: 1985. V. 40

SCHEVILL, MARGARET ERWIN

In the Garden of the Home God. Santa Fe: 1943. V. 38

SCHEYB, FRANZ CHRISTOPHER DE 1704-1777

Peutingeriana Tabula Itineraria. Vienna: 1753. V. 44

SCHHOLCRAFT, HENRY ROWE

Oneota, or the Red Face of America: Their History, Traditions, Customs, Poetry, Picture-Writing, &c. New York: 1844-45. V. 37

SCHIEFER, JOHN FREDERIC

An Explanation of the Practice of Law; Containing the Elements of Special Pleading, Reduced to the Comprhension of Every One . . . Dublin: 1793. V. 45

SCHIEFLER, GUSTAV

Verzeichnis des Graphischen Werks Edvard Munchs bis 1906. Berlin: 1907. V. 42

SCHIELE, EGON

Egon Schiele: Aquarelle und Zeichnungen. Salzburg: 1968. V. 41

SCHIERSTAB, JOHANN PHILIPP

Speculum Coniugale das ist Christlicher Ehe-Unnd Hausspiegel. Nuremberg: 1615. V. 44

SCHIFF, MORTIMER L.

Catalogue of a Selected Portion of the Famous Library Formed by the Late Mortimer L. Schiff. London: 1938. V. 41

SCHIFF, SYDNEY

Concessons. London: 1913. V. 37; 40

Richard Kurt. (with) Elinor Colhouse. (with) Prince Hempseed. London: 1919/21/23. V. 37

SCHIFFMAN, C.

Pictorial and Historical History of the 347th Fighter Squadron, 350th Fighter Group, 12th Air Force 1942-1945. N.P.: 1948? V. 37

SCHILLER, FRIEDRICH

Demetrius. Munich: 1922. V. 45

SCHILLER, JOHANN CHRISTOPH FRIEDRICH VON 1759-1805

The Bride of Messina. London: 1837. V. 40; 42

Geschichte des Dreyssigjahrigen Krieges. Leipzig: 1793. V. 38

*The Ghost-Seer; or, Apparitionist: an Interesting Fragment, Found Among the Papers of Count O****.* New York: 1796. V. 39

The History of the Thirty Years War in Germany. London: 1799. V. 38; 40; 42

Kleinere Prosaische Schriften. Leipzig: 1792-1802. V. 40; 44

Mary Stuart, a Tragedy. The Maid of Orleans, a Tragedy. London: 1824. V. 38

The Piccolomini, or the First Part of Wallenstein, a Drama. London: 1800. V. 43

The Poems and Ballads. London: 1844. V. 38

The Robbers. London: 1792. V. 38; 40; 45

Sammtliche Werke. Stuttgart: 1869. V. 40; 41; 44; 45

Wallenstein. London: 1800. V. 39; 40; 42; 45

Wallenstein. Edinburgh: 1827. V. 39; 42

SCHILLER, JOHANN FRIEDRICH VON 1759-1805

The Fight with the Dragon. London: 1825. V. 39

SCHILLER, JULIUS

Coelum Stellatum Cristianum Concavum . . . Augsburg: 1627. V. 38

SCHILLINGS, C. G.

Flashlights in the Jungle - a Record of Hunting Adventures . . . New York: 1906. V. 42; 45

In Wildest Africa. London: 1907. V. 37; 40; 42; 45

With Flashlight and Rifle. London: 1906. V. 45

SCHILPP, ARTHUR

Albert Einstein: Philosopher-Scientist . . . Evanston: 1949. V. 45

SCHIMMELPENNINCK, MARY ANNE

The Principles of Beauty as Manifested in Nature, Art and Human Character, with a Classification of Deformities. London: 1859. V. 46

Theory on the Classification of Beauty and Deformity. London: 1815. V. 40; 42; 45

SCHIMPER, A. F. W.

Plant Geography Upon a Physiological Basis. Oxford: 1903. V. 37; 38

SCHINDLER, SOLOMON

Young West, a Sequel to Edward Bellamy's Celebrated Novel Looking Backward. Boston: 1894. V. 39

SCHINDLER, VALENTIN

Lexicon Pentaglottum. London: 1635. V. 46

Lexicon Pentaglotton Hebraicum Chaldaicum Syriacum, Talmudico Rabbinicum & Arabicum. London: 1637. V. 40

Lexicon Pentaglotton, Hebraicum, Chaldeicum, Syriacum, Talmudico-Rabbinicum, & Arabicum. Frankfurt: 1612. V. 37

SCHINKEL, CARL FRIEDRICH

Sammlung Aarachitektonisher Entwurfe Enthaltend Theils Werke, Welche usgefurht sind, Theils Gegenstande deren Ausfuhrung Beaabsichtigt Wurde. Berlin: 1858. V. 37; 38

SCHINKEL, KARL

Collection of Architectural Designs, Including Designs which have been executed and objects whos execution was intended. Chiago: 1981. V. 37

SCHINKEL, KARL FRIEDRICH

Collection of Archiectural Designs. Chicago: 1981. V. 46

SCHINZ, HEINRICH RUDOLF

Naturgeschichte und Abbildung des Menschen der Verschiedenen Rassen und Stamme . . . Dritte Vermehrte Auflage. Zurich: 1845. V. 40

SCHIODTE, J.

Zoologica Danica. Copenhagen: 1878-1907. V. 43

SCHIOLER, E. L. T. L.

Danmarks Fugle . . . Copenhagen: 1925. V. 40

SCHLAGINTWEIT, ROBERT VON 1833-1885.

Californien. Leipzig: 1871. V. 37

Die Santa Fe und Sudpacifichahn in Nord-Amerika. Koln: 1884. V. 38; 40

SCHLECHTER, R.

The Orchidaceae of German New Guinea. (with) Figure Atlas. Leiden: 1982. V. 37

SCHLEGAL, AUGUSTUS WILLIAM

A Course of Lectures on Dramatic Art and Literature. London: 1815. V. 39; 42; 44; 46

SCHLEGEL, FREDERICK VON

The Philosophy of History in a Course of Lectures Delivered at Vienna. London: 1848. V. 41

SCHLEGEL, H.

Essay on the Physiognomy of Serpents. Edinburgh: 1843. V. 40

Traite de Fauconnerie. Leyden & Dusseldorf,: 1844-53. V. 37

SCHLEGEL, HERMAN

De Vogels van Nederlandsch Indie, Beschreven en Afgebeeld. Leiden and Amsterdam: 1863-66. V. 42

SCHLEGEL, J. F. W.

Upon the Visitation of Netural Vessels Under Convoy or an Impartial Examination of a Judgement Pronounced by the English Court of Admiralty the 11th June 1799 in the Case of the Swedish Convoy . . . London: 1801. V. 46

SCHLEGEL, JOHAN FRIEDRICH WILHELM

Neutral Rights; or, an Impartial Examination of the Right of Search of Neutral Vessels Under Convoy . . . Philadelphia: 1801. V. 44

SCHLEIDEN, J. M.

Principles of Scientific Botany; or Botany as an Inductive Science. London: 1849. V. 39

SCHLEIDEN, MATTHIAS JAKOB

Grundzuge der Wissenschaftlichen Botanik Nebst Einer Methodolgischen Einleitung als Anleitung zum Studium der Pflanze. Leipzig: 1842-43. V. 42; 46

SCHLESINGER, ARTHUR M.

The Colonial Merchants and the American Revolution. New York: 1918. V. 39

SCHLETZER, D.

Old Silver Jewellery of the Turkoman. A contribution to the research on symbols in the culture of the nomads of Inner Asia. Translator P. Knight. 1983. V. 37

SCHLEY, W. S.

The Rescue of Greely. London: 1885. V. 44

SCHLEY, WINFIELD S.

Report of Winfield S. Schley, Commander, U.S. Navy, Commanding Greely Relief Expedition of 1884. Washingtaon: 1887. V. 37; 38; 41

SCHLICK, MORITZ

Space and Time in Contemporary Physics. New York: 1920. V. 38; 42

SCHLIEMANN, HEINRICH

Atlas des Antiquites Troyennes. Leipzig: 1874. V. 44

Mycenae; a Narrative of Researches and Discoveries Made on the Site of Ilium and in the Trojan Plain. London: 1875. V. 44

Troy and Its Remains: A Narrative of Researches and Discoveries Made on the Site of Ilium and In the Trojan Plain. New York: 1875. V. 44

SCHLIEMANN, HENRY

Ilios: the City and Country of the Trojans. London: 1880. V. 37; 42; 44; 45

Ithaque, le Peloponnese, Troie: Recherches Archeologiques. Paris: 1869. V. 42

Mycenae; a Narrative of Researches and Discoveries at Myceane and Tiryns. London: 1878. V. 40; 42; 43

Mycenae: a Narrative of Researches and Discoveries at Mycenae and Tiryns. New York: 1880. V. 39

Tiryns. New York: 1885. V. 39; 40; 42

Tiryns. The Prehistoric Palace of the Kings of Tiryns. London: 1886. V. 37

Troja. Results of the Latest Researches and Discoveries on the Site of Homer's Troy and in the Heroic Tumuli and Other Sites Made in the Year 1882 . . . New York: 1884. V. 37; 40

Troy and Its Remains; a Narrative of Researches and Discoveries Made on the Site of Ilium, and in the Trojan Plain. London: 1875. V. 39; 40; 45

SCHLOSS, DAVID FREDERICK

Methods of Industrial Renumeration. London: 1892. V. 46

SCHLOSSER, L. B.

An Exhibition of 71 Books on Papermaking at the Free Library of Philadelphia. From the Collection of . . . . 1968. V. 44

A Pair on Paper. Two Essays by L. B. Schlosser and Henry Morris. 1976. V. 44

SCHLOSSER, LEONARD B.

An Exhibition of Books on Papermaking. V. 41

An Exhibition of Books on Papermaking. A Selection of Books from the Collection of Leonard B. Schlosser. Philadelphia: 1968. V. 40; 43

An Exhibition of Books on Papermaking. A Selection of Books from the Collection of Leonard B. Schlosser. (Cover title). (North Hills: 1968). V. 37

A Pair on paper. By Leonard B. Schlosser and Henry Morris. North Hills, Pa.: 1976. V. 37

A Pair on Paper: Two Essays on Paper History and Related Matters, by Leonard B. Schlosser and Henry Morris. North Hills: 1976. V. 37

SCHLOSS'S English Bijou Almanac for 1839. London: 1839. V. 39

SCHLOTEL, A. E.

Still a Wife's Sister. London: 1886. V. 41

SCHLUTER, CHRISTOPH ANDREAS

Grundlicher Unterricht von Hutte-Werken . . . Braunschweig: 1738. V. 45

SCHMALENBACH, WERNER

Kurt Schwitters. New York: 1967. V. 43

Kurt Schwitters. London: 1970. V. 45

Kurt Schwitters. New York: 1970. V. 46

SCHMAUK, THEODORE E.

A History of the Lutheran Church in Pennsylvania (1638-1820). Philadelphia: 1903. V. 41; 42

SCHMEISSER, J. G. 1767-1837

A System of Mineralogy, formed Chiefly on the Plan of Cronstedt. London: 1795. V. 38; 43

SCHMID, GEORG LUDWIG

Principes de l Legislation Universelle . . . Amsterdam: 1776. V. 38; 41

SCHMID, JOHANN CHRISTOPH VON

The Basket of Flowers; or, Piety and Truth Triumphant. London: 1868. V. 44

SCHMID, R.

Dictionary of Biotechnology in English-Japanese German. Berlin: 1986. V. 37; 38

SCHMIDT, ADOLF

Bucheinbande Aus Dem XIV-XIX Jahrhundert in der Landesbibliothek zu Darmstadt. Leipzig: 1921. V. 45

SCHMIDT, ALEXANDER

Shakespeare-Lexicon. A Complete Dictionary of All the English Words, Phrases, and Constructions in the Works of the Poet. Berlin & London: 1886. V. 41

SCHMIDT, ARNO

Evening Edged in Gold. New York: 1980. V. 45

SCHMIDT, CARL E.

A Western Trip. Detroit: 1904. V. 39; 44

SCHMIDT, CARL E. continued

A Western Trip. Detroit: 1906. V. 41; 45

SCHMIDT, E. F.

Persepolis. I. Structures. Reliefs. Inscriptions. Chicago: 1953. V. 37

Persepolis, III. The Royal Tombs and Other Monuments. Chicago;: 1970. V. 37

SCHMIDT, EDUARD OSCAR

The Anatomy of the Human Head and Neck, Graphically Illustrated by Means of Superimposed Plates. London: 1895. V. 42; 44

SCHMIDT, ERICH F.

The Alishar Huyuk Seasons of 1928 and 1929. Chicago: 1932-33. V. 40

The Alishar Huyik Seasons of 1928 and 1929. Chicago: 1933. V. 40; 44

Excavations at Tepe Hissar Damghan with an Additional Chapter on the Sasanian Building at Tepe Hissar by Fiske Kimball. Philadelphia: 1937. V. 40; 44

Flights over ancient cities of Iran. Chicago: (1940). V. 37

Persepolis III: The Royal Tombs and Other Monuments. Chicago: 1970. V. 40

Persepolis I: structures, reliefs, inscriptions. Chicago: (1953). V. 37

Persepolis III: the Royal Tombs and other monuments. Chicago: (1970). V. 37

the Treasury of Persepolis and Other Discoveries in the Homeland of the Achaemenians. Chicago: 1939. V. 40; 44

SCHMIDT, GEORG

Ten Reproductions in Facsimile of Paintings by Paul Klee. New York: 1946. V. 39; 46

SCHMIDT, GEORGE

Psaligraphy. Boston: 1870. V. 44

SCHMIDT-KUNSEMULLER, F.

T. J. Cobden-Sanderson as Bookbinder. Esher: 1966. V. 37; 41

SCHMIDT, MINNA MOSCHEROSCH

400 Outstanding Women of the World and Costumology of Their Fine. Chicago: 1933. V. 45

SCHMIDT, OSCAR C.

Practical Treatise on Automobiles . . . Philadelphia: 1909. V. 46

SCHMIDT, ROBERT

Early European Porcelain as Collected by Otto Blohm. Munchen: 1953. V. 42

SCHMIED, FRANCOIS LOUIS

Art Deco: The Books of Francois-Louis Schmied, Artist/Engraver/Printer. San Francisco: 1987. V. 37; 40; 45; 46

Art Deco. 1987. V. 45

Le Paradis Musulman. Paris: 1930. V. 44

Ruth et Booz. Paris: 1930. V. 46

SCHMIED, WIELAND

Alfred Kubin . . . Catalogue by Alfred Marks. New York & Washington: 1969. V. 41

SCHMIEDEL, CASIMIRUS CHRISTOPHORUS

Fossilium Metalla et Res Metallicas . . . Descriptsit et Digessit . . . 1753. V. 46

SCHMITZ, E. E.

Proclamation by the Mayor. San Francisco: 1906. V. 41

SCHMITZ, HERMANN

The Encyclopaedia of Furniture, an Outline History. New York: 1926. V. 44

SCHMITZ, JOSEPH W.

Texan Statecraft, 1836-1845. San Antonio: 1941. V. 37; 38

Thus They Lived: Social Life in the Republic of Texas. San Antonio: 1936. V. 37; 39

SCHMOLDER, BRUNO

Neuer Praktischer Wegweiser fur Auswanderer Nach Nord-Amerika in Drei Abtheilungen . . . Mainz: 1849. V. 41

SCHMOLLER, HANS 1916-1985

Chinese Decorated Papers. Newtown: 1987. V. 38; 39; 42; 44

Chinese Decorated Papers. By Hans Schmoller. Newtown, Pa.: 1987. V. 37

Gladstone's Washi, a Survey of Reports on the Manufacture of Paper in Japan. Newtown: 1984. V. 39

Mr. Gladstone's Washi. Netown: 1983. V. 39; 41

Mr. Gladstone's Washi. 1984. V. 38; 44

Mr. Gladstone's Washi. Newtown: 1984. V. 37; 38; 39; 42; 43; 44

Mr. Gladstone's Washi: A Survey of Report on the Manufacture of Paper in Japan , the Parkes Report of 1871. By Hans Schmoller. Newtown, Pa.: 1984. V. 37

SCHMOLLER, TANYA

Remondini and Rizzi. A Chapter in Italian Decorated Paper History. New Castle: 1990. V. 45; 46

SCHMUCK, MARTIN

Secretorum Naturalium, & Medicorum, Thesauriolus. Nurnberg: 1642. V. 37

SCHMUCKER, SAMUEL 1799-1873

Psychology, or, Elements of a New System of Mental Philosophy on the Basis of Consciousness and Common Sense. New York: 1842. V. 42

SCHMUTZLER, ROBERT

Art Nouveau. New York: 1962. V. 38; 42; 46

Art Nouveau. New York: 1964. V. 41

SCHNAPPER, E. B.

The British Union Catalogue of Early Music Printed Before the Year 1801. London: 1957. V. 39

The British Union Catalogue of Early Music printed before the year 1801. 1957. V. 37

SCHNEE, EMIL

Diabetes, its Cause and Permanent Cure, from the Standpoint of Experiences and Acientific Investigation. Translated from the Germany by R.L. Tafel, English edition revised and enlarged by the author. London: 1889. V. 37

SCHNEIDER, G.

The Book of Choice Ferns for the Garden, Conservatory and Stove. London: 1892-94. V. 38

SCHNEIDER-HERRMANN, G.

Red Figured Lucanian and Apulian Nestorides and Their Ancestors. Amsterdam: 1980. V. 40

Red-figured Lucanian and Apulian Nestorides and their ancestors. Amsterdam: 1980. V. 37

SCHNEIDER, I.

Doctor Transit. 1925. V. 43

SCHNEIDER, ISADORE

Doctor Transit. New York: 1925. V. 39

SCHNEIDER, ISIDOR

Comrade: Mister: Poems. New York: 1934. V. 39

SCHNEIDER, PIERRE

Matisse. New York: 1984. V. 45

SCHNITZLER, ARTHUR

Casanova's Homecoming. New York: 1947. V. 40

SCHNIZ, HEINRICH RUDOLF

Naturgeschichte und Abbildung des Menschen der Verschiedenen Rassen und Stamme . . . Zurich: 1845. V. 40

SCHOBERL, FREDERICK

The World in Miniature. London: 1821-28. V. 44

SCHODDE, R.

The Fairy Wrens, a Monograph of the Maluridae. Melbourne: 1982. V. 42

Noctural Birds of Australia. Melbourne: 1980. V. 37

Nocturnal Birds of Australia. Melbourne: 1980. V. 38; 42

SCHOEN, HAROLD

Monuments Erected by the State of Texas to Commemorate the Centenary of Texas Independence. 1939. V. 42

Monuments Erected by the State of Texas to Commeorate the Centenary of Texas Independence. Steck: 1939. V. 44

SCHOENER, ALLAN

Harlem on my Mind. Cultural Capital of Black America 1900-1968. New York: 1968. V. 37; 46

SCHOENER, JOHANNES

Luculentissima Quaedam Terrae Totius Descripto . . . Nuremberg: 1515. V. 37; 40; 43

SCHOENER, REINHOLD

Rome Condensed and Edited by Mrs. ARthur Bell. London: 1898. V. 45

SCHOENRICH, OTTO

The Legacy of Christopher Columbus. Glendale: 1949. V. 40

The Legacy of Christopher Columbus; The Historic Litigations Involving His Discoveries, His Will, His Family and His Descendants. Glendale: 1949-50. V. 43

SCHOEPF, JOHANN DAVID

Historia Testudinum Iconibus Illustrata. Erlangen: 1792-1801. V. 40

Travels in Confederation 1783-1784. Philadelphia: 1911. V. 40; 42; 43; 45

SCHOEPFF, JOHANN DAVID 1752-1800

Historia Testudinum Iconibus Illustrata. Erlangen: 1792. V. 43

SCHOEPFLIN, JOHANN DANIEL

Vindiciae Typographicae. Strasbourg: 1760. V. 41

SCHOFIELD, ANNE

Austrian Jewellery 19th and Early 20th Century. Woodbridge,: 1990. V. 46

SCHOFIELD, F. H.

The Story of Manitoba. Winnipeg: 1913. V. 41

The Story of Manitoba. Winnipeg, Vancouver,: 1913. V. 38

SCHOFIELD, JAMES

An Historical and Descriptive Guide to Scarborough and its Environs. London: 1787. V. 39; 40; 43

An Historical and Descriptive Guide to Scarborough and Its Environs. York: 1787. V. 39

An Historical and Descriptive Guide to Scarbrough and Its Environs. York: 1787? V. 45

SCHOFIELD, JOHN M.

Forty Six Years in the Army. New York: 1897. V. 43

SCHOLDERER, V.

Fifty Essays in Fifteenth, and Sixteenth Century Bibliography. Amsterdam: 1966. V. 38; 39; 40

Greek Printing Types 1465-1927. London: 1927. V. 45

SCHOLDERER, VICTOR

Women of Troy: Poems. Cambridge: 1965. V. 40

SCHOLEFIELD, E. O. S.

British Columbia. From the Earliest Times to the Present. Vancouver: 1913. V. 45

SCHOLES, JAMES CHRISTOPHER

History of Bolton. Bolton: 1892. V. 40

SCHOLES, PERCY

The Great Dr. Burney, His Life, His Travels, His Works, His Family and Friends. Oxford: 1948. V. 39

SCHOLES, PERCY A.

The Life and Activities of Sir John Hawkins . . . Oxford: 1953. V. 40; 43

SCHOLIER, PETER

Diogenes Cynicus Sive Sermonum Familiarium. Antwerp: 1635. V. 42

SCHOLIRIUS, PETRUS

Sermones Familiares. Antverpiae: 1623. V. 46

SCHOLZ, JANOS

Baroque and Romantic Stage Design. New York: 1955. V. 37

SCHOMBERG, ALEXANDER

Bagley; a Descriptive Poem. Oxford: 1787. V. 45

SCHOMBERG, ALEXANDER CROWCHER

Bagley; a Descriptive Poem. Oxford: 1777. V. 43

SCHOMBURG, ROBERT H.

The History of Barbadoes . . . London: 1848. V. 40; 41; 46

SCHOMBURGK, R. H.

The Fishes of British Fuiana. Edinburgh. V. 37

SCHOMBURGK, ROBERT

Twelve Views on the Interior of Guiana: From Drawings Executed after . . . Sketches During the Expedition Carried on in the Years 1835 to 1839. London: 1841. V. 39

SCHOMBURGK, ROBERT H.

Remarks to Accompany a Comparative Vocabulary of Eighteen Langues and Dialects of Indian Tribes Inhabiting Guiana. London: 1848. V. 38

SCHON, JAMES FREDERICK

Journals . . . Who, with the Sanction of Her Majesty's Government, Accompanied the Expedition up the Niger in 1841 . . . London: 1842. V. 45

SCHONBERG'S Standard Atlas of the World. New York: San Francisco: 1867. V. 45

SCHONER, JOHANNES

Opusculum Astrologicum, ex Diversorum Libris, Summa Cura Pro Studiosorum Utilitate Collectum, Subnotata Continens. Nuremberg: 1539. V. 38

SCHONFIELD, H.

The New Hebrew Typography. London: 1932. V. 44

SCHONFIELD, HUGH J.

For the Train - Five Poems and a Tale - Being Contributions to 'The Train' 1856-1857. London: 1932. V. 40

SCHONHEINTZ, JACOB

Apologia Astrologiae. Nuremberg: 1502. V. 40; 45

SCHONICHEN, GEORG

Den Achtbarn und Hochgelerten zu Leypssck, Petro Mosellano Rector, Oschsenfart Prediger zu S. Nicolao, Andree Camiciano, Meynen Gunstigen Herrn und Lieben Brudern in Christo Jhesu &c. Eilenburg: 1523. V. 37

SCHOOCK, MARTINUS

Admiranda Methodvs Novae Philosophiae Renati Des Cartes. Maastricht: 1643. V. 46

THE SCHOOL: a Poem. Leeds: 1830. V. 46

THE SCHOOL for Scandal. London: 1779. V. 46

THE SCHOOL of Arts Improv'd; or Companion for the Ingenious. Gainsborough: 1776. V. 44; 46

THE SCHOOL of Raphael; or the Student's Guide to Expression in Historical Painting. London: 1759. V. 38

SCHOOLCRAFT, HENRY ROWE 1793-1864

Algic Researches, Comprising . . . the Mental Characteristics of the North American Indians. New York: 1839. V. 38; 39; 44; 45

The American Indians, Their History, Condition and Prospects . . . Buffalo: 1851. V. 45

The American Indians, Their History, Condition and Prospects, From Original Notes and Manuscripts. Rochester: 1851. V. 40

Historical and Statistical Information Respecting the History, Condition and Prospects of the Indian Tribes of the United States . . . Philadelphia: 1851-57. V. 39; 40

Historical and Statistical Information, Respecting the History, Condition and Prospects of the Indian Tribes of the United States. Philadelphia: 1851-7. V. 38

The Indian in His Wigwam, or, Characteristics of the Red Race of America. From orignal notes and manuscripts. New York: 1848. V. 37

Information Respecting the History, Condition and Prospects of the Indian Tribes of the United States. Philadelphia: 1853-56. V. 38; 39

Information, Respecting the History, Condition and Prospects of the Indian Tribes of the United States. Philadelphia: 1853-57. V. 42

Information Respecting the History, Condition and Prospectus of the Indian Tribes of the U.S. Philadelphia: 1855. V. 37

Inquires, Respecting the History, Present Condition and Future Prospects of the Indian Tribes of the United States. Washington: 1847. V. 38

Journal of a Tour in the Interior of Missouri and Arkansas. London: 1821. V. 37; 38; 40; 41; 43; 44

Journal of a Tour Into the Interior of Missouri and Arkansaw, From Potosi, or Mine a Burton, in Missouri Territory . . . London: 1831. V. 44

The Myth of Hiawatha, and Other Oral Legends, Mythologic and Allegoric, of the North American Indians. Philadelphia: 1856. V. 38; 39

The Myth of Hiawatha, and Other Oral Legends, Mythologic and Allegoric. Philadelphia & London: 1856. V. 40; 45

Narrative of an Expedition through the Upper Mississippi to Itasca Lake, the Actual Source of the River . . . in 1832. New York: 1834. V. 37; 38; 40; 41; 43; 45

Narrative Journal of Travels Through the Northwestern Regions of the United States Extending from Detroit through the Great Chain of American Lakes to the Sources of the Mississippi River . . . Albany: 1821. V. 37; 38; 40; 41; 45

Notes on the Iroquios; or, Contributions to the Statistics, Aboriginal, Antiquities and General Ethnology of Western New York. New York: 1846. V. 40

Notes on the Iroquois: or Contributions to American History, Antiquities and General Ethnology. Albany: 1847. V. 38; 43

Oneota, or Characteristics of the Red Race of America. New York: 1845. V. 43

Personal Memoirs of a Residence of Thirty Years with the Indian Tribes on the American Frontiers . . . Philadlephia: 1851. V. 38; 42; 43; 45

Report of Mr. Schoolcraft, to the Secretary of State, Transmitting the Census Returns in Relation to the Indians. Albany: 1846. V. 38

Scenes and Adventures in the Semi-Alpine Region of the Ozark Mountains of Missouri and Arkansas, Which Were First Traversed by DeSoto in 1541. Philadelphia: 1853. V. 39; 40

Schoolcraft and Allen - Expedition to North-West Indians. Washington: 1834. V. 38; 39

Summary Narrative of an Exploratory Expedition to the Sources of the Mississippi River in 1820. Philadelphia: 1855. V. 43

SCHOOLCRAFT, HENRY ROWE 1793-1864 continued

Travels in the Central Portions of the Mississippi Valley. New York: 1825. V. 40; 46

SCHOOLING, WILLIAM

The Hudson's Bay Comapny 1670-1920. London: 1920. V. 39

SCHOONEBEEK, ADRIEN

Histoire de Tours Les Ordres Militaires ou de Chevalerie . . . Amsterdam: 1699. V. 38

SCHOONHOVIUS, FLORENTINUS

Emblemata . . . V. 46

SCHOONHOVIUS, FLORENTIUS

Emblemata . . . Partim Moralia, Partim Etiam Civilia. Gouda: 1618. V. 39

SCHOONMAKER, MARIUS

The History of Kingston. New York: 1888. V. 46

SCHOOTEN, FRANZ VON

De Organica Conicarum Sectionum in Plano Descriptione, Tractatus. Leiden: 1646. V. 37

SCHOPENHAUER, ARTHUR

Die Welt als Wille und Vorstellung. Leipzig: 1819. V. 38; 39; 41; 43; 45

Select Essays . . . Milwaukee: 1881. V. 39

Ueber die Vierfache Wurzel des Satzes von Zureichenden Grunde. Rodolfstadt: 1813. V. 40

SCHOPF, J. W.

Earth's Earliest Biosphere, Its Origin and Evolution. London: 1984. V. 37

SCHORLEMMER, CARL

The Rise and Development of Organic Chemistry . . . London: 1894. V. 40

SCHOTT, FRANCOIS

Italy, In Its Original Glory, Ruine and Revival, Being an Exact Survey of the Whole Geography and History of that Famous Country. London: 1660. V. 39; 45; 46

SCHOTT, GASPAR

Anatomia Physico-Hydrostatica Fontium ac Fluminum, Libris VI Explicata & Figuris Aeri Incisis Exornata. Wurzburg: 1663. V. 40; 42; 45

Organon Mathematicarum Libris ix Explicatum. Wurzburg: 1668. V. 41

Pantometrum Kircherianum, Hoc Est, Instrumentum Geometricum Novum, a Celeberrimo Viro P. Athanasio Kirchero ante hac Inventum . . . Wurzburg: 1669. V. 38

Technica Curiosa. Nurnberg: 1664. V. 38

SCHOTT, KASPAR S. J. 1608-1666

Pantometrium Kircherianum. Wurzburgh: 1660. V. 37

SCHOTTUS, FRANCISCUS

Itinerari Italiae Rerumque Romanorum. Antwerp: 1600. V. 45

SCHOULER, WILLIAM

A History of Massachusetts in the Civil War. Boston: 1868. V. 46

SCHOUTEN, WOUTER

Oost Indische Voyagie . . . Een Curieuse Beschrijving der Voornaemste Landed . . . Amsterdam: 1676. V. 46

SCHRADER, PAUL

Waldo. Boston: 1967. V. 43

SCHRANTZ, WARD L.

Jaspar County, Missouri, in the Civil War. Carthage: 1923. V. 39; 42

Jaspar County, Missouri, in the Civil War. Carthage, Missouri: 1923. V. 37

SCHREBER, DANIEL PAUL 1842-1911

Denkwurdigkeiten Eines Nervenranken Nebst Nachtragen und Einem Anhang . . . Leipzig: 1903. V. 43; 45

Medical Indoor Gymnastics or a Share of Hygienic Exercises for Home Use to be Practised Anywhere Without Apparatus or Assistance by Young and Old . . . London/Edinburgh/Oxford: 1899. V. 43; 45

SCHREGER, ODILO

Speismeister. Augsburg: 1778. V. 38; 42

SCHREIBER & SON

Portraits of Noted Horses of America. New York: 1875. V. 37

SCHREIBER, C.

Fans and Fan Leaves: English, Foreign. London: 1888. V. 37

SCHREIBER, CHARLOTTE

Lady Schreiber's Journals. Confidences of a Collector of Ceramics and Antiquities. London: 1911. V. 38

SCHREIBER, EMMANUEL

Reformed Judaism and Its Pioneers . . . Spokane: 1892. V. 46

SCHREIBER, FRED

The Estiennes: an Annotated Catalogue of 300 Highlights from the Various Presses. New York: 1982. V. 41

SCHREIBERS, CARL FRANZ ANTON

Beytrage zur Geschichte und Kenntniss Meteorischer Steine und metall-Massen, und Deren Erscheinungen, Welche Deren Niederfallen zu Begleiten Pflegen. Wien: 1820. V. 38

SCHREIER, JOSEPH

Theoria Solis et Lunae. Una Cum Parergis ex Universa Mathesi Depromptis . . . Ingolstadt: 1728. V. 43

SCHREINER, OLIVE 1855-1920

Dreams. London: 1891. V. 38; 41; 43

Dreams. East Aurora: 1901. V. 41

Dreams. Portland, Maine: 1917. V. 37

So Here Then Are Dreams. East Aurora: 1901. V. 39; 41

So Here Then are Dreams, by Olive Schreiner. (East Aurora: 1901). V. 37

The Story of an African Farm. London: 1883. V. 38

The Story of An African Farm. 1961. V. 40

Trooper Peter Halket of Mashonaland. London: 1897. V. 40; 44; 45; 46

Undine. London: 1929. V. 38

SCHRETLEN, M. J.

Dutch and Flemish Woodcuts of the Fifteenth Century. London: 1925. V. 41; 43; 46

SCHREYVOGEL, CHARLES

My Bunkie and Others. New York: 1909. V. 39; 40; 41; 42

My Bunkie and Others. V. 38

SCHRIBER, FRITZ

The Complete Carriage and Wagon Painter. New York: 1903. V. 41

The Complete Carriage and Wagon Painter. New York: 1910. V. 38; 40

SCHRICK, MICHAEL PUFF VON

Von Den Uszgeprenten Wassern. Strassburg: 1505. V. 37

SCHRODER, JOHN

Catalogue of Books and Manuscripts by Rupert Brooke. Cambridge: 1970. V. 41; 42

Catalogue of Books and Manuscripts by Rupert Brooke, Edward Marsh and Christopher Hassall. London: 1970. V. 41

The Compleat Chymical Dispensatory. London: 1669. V. 38

The Compleat Chymical Dispensatory, in five books: Treating of all sorts of Metals, Precious Stones, and Minerals . . . Written in Latin . . . And Englished by William Rowland . . . 1669. V. 37

SCHROEDER, FRANCIS

Shores of the Mediterranean, with Sketches of Travel. New York: 1846. V. 40

SCHROEDER, JOHN FREDERICK

The Life and Times of Washington Revised, Enlarged and Enriched. Albany: 1903. V. 46

SCHROEDER VAN DE KOLK, JACOB LUDWIG CONRAD

Minute Structure and Functions of the Spinal Cord and Medulla Oblongata and . . . Elipepsy. London: 1859. V. 37

SCHROETER, JOHANN F.

Allgemeine Geschichte der Laender und Voelker von America. Halle: 1752. V. 38

SCHROTER, JOHANN SAMUEL

Vollstandige Einleitung in Die Kenntniss und Geschichte der Steine und Versteinerungen. Altenburg: 1774-84. V. 43

SCHUBERT, CLEMENT

Libri Qvatuor De Scrvpvlis Chronologoru In Qvibvs Non Solvm Calculus Sacrae Scripturae cum Series Quatuor Monarchiarum & Olympiadibus Graecorum, atq Annis Primvm Editi. Strassburg: 1575. V. 40

SCHUBERT, GREGORY KENT

Compilation and Evaluation of Selected Positive and Negative Reactions to the Three and One Half Day Television News Coverage Which Followed the Assassination of President John F. Kennedy. V. 42

SCHUBLER, JOHANN JACOB

Nutzliche Anweisung zur Unentbehrlichen zu Zimmermanns-Kunst. Nuremberg: 1749. V. 45

SCHUCHARDT, C.

Schliemann's Excavations . . . London: 1891. V. 37; 40; 42; 43; 44; 46

SCHUCK, H.

Alfred Nobel. London: 1929. V. 44; 46

SCHUCK, OSCAR T.

The California Scrap-Book: A Repository of Useful Information and Select Reading . . . San Francisco: 1869. V. 40

SCHUENEMANN-POTT, FRIEDRICH

The Story of My Life. San Francisco: 1937. V. 43; 44

SCHULL, JOSEPH

The Legend of Ghost Lagoon. Toronto: 1937. V. 44

SCHULLIAN, DOROTHY

A Catalogue of Incunabula and manuscripts in the Army Medical Library. New York: (1950). V. 37

SCHULLIAN, DOROTHY M.

The Baglivi Correspondence from the Library of Sir William Osler. Ithaca: 1974. V. 40

SCHULT, FRIEDRICH

Ernst Barlach. Das Plastische Werk/Das Graphische Werk/Werkkatalog der Zeichnungen . . . Hamburg: 1958-71. V. 42

SCHULTENS, ALBERT

Institutiones ad Fundamenta Linguae Hebraeae . . . In Usum Collegii Domestici. Leyden: 1737. V. 44

SCHULTES, HENRY

An Essay on Aquatic Rights. London: 1811. V. 39; 40; 45

SCHULTZ, BENJAMIN

An Inaugural Botanico-Medical Dissertation, on the Phytolacca Decandra of Linnaeus. Philadelphia: 1795. V. 42

SCHULTZ, CHRISTIAN

Travels on an Inland Voyage through the States of New York, Pennsylvania, Virginia, Ohio, Kentucky and Tennessee and through the Territories of Indiana, Louisiana, Mississippi and New Orleans. New York: 1810. V. 39; 40; 41; 42; 43; 44; 45

SCHULTZ, JAMES WILLARD

My Life as an Indian. New York: 1907. V. 37; 42

My Life as an Indian: The Story of a Red Woman and a White in the Lodges of the Blackfeet. Boston: 1907. V. 37

Plumed Snake Medicine. 1924. V. 46

The Quest of the Fish-Dog Skin. Boston: 1913. V. 44

Questers of the Desert. Boston: 1925. V. 44

Signposts of Adventure. Boston: 1926. V. 44

Skull Head the Terrible. Boston: 1929. V. 41; 44

A Son of the Navahos. Boston: 1927. V. 41; 44

A Son of the Navahos. Boston & New York: 1927. V. 41

Stained Gold. Boston: 1937. V. 44

William Jackson Indian Scout. Boston: 1926. V. 44; 46

SCHULTZ, JOHANN

Prufung der Kantischen Critik der Reinen Vernunft. Frankfrut & Leipzig/: 1791/2. V. 41

Prufung der Kantischen Critik der Reinen Vernunft. Frankfurt & Leipzig: 1791/92. V. 45

SCHULTZE-MOTEL, W.

Advances in Bryology. 1981. V. 39

SCHULZ, BRUNO

Birds. Madison: 1980. V. 38

SCHULZ, CHARLES M.

Peanuts Jubilee: My Life and Art with Charlie Brown and Others. New York: 1975. V. 39; 41; 42

SCHULZ, ERNST

The Study of Incunables. Philadelphia: 1977. V. 42; 44

SCHULZ, H. C.

French Illuminated Manuscripts. San Francisco: 1958. V. 38; 41; 46

The Gothic Script of the Middle Ages. San Francisco: 1939. V. 38; 46

A Monograph on the Italian Choir Book. San Francisco: 1941. V. 37; 38; 46

A Monograph on the Italian Choir Book. San Francisco: 1941. V. 37

SCHUMACHER, GOTTLIEB

Across the Jordan: Being an Exploration and Survey of Part of Hauran and Jaulan . . . London: 1886. V. 45

SCHUMAN, FREDERICK

The Council of Europe. 1951. V. 46

The Council of Europe. London: 1951. V. 40

SCHUMANN Album of Children's Pieces for Piano. London. V. 40

SCHUMANN, AUGUST

Versuch Eines Allgeminen Handlungs- und Fabrikenaddressbuches von Deutschland . . . Ronneburg and Leipzig: 1798. V. 46

SCHUMANN, PETER

White Horse Butcher. West Burke: 1977. V. 40

SCHURHAMMER, G.

Shin-To the Way of the Gods in Japan. Bonn & Leipzig,: 1923. V. 38

SCHURICHT, HERMANN

History of the German Element in Virginia. Baltimore: 1897-8. V. 42

SCHURIG, MARTIN

Gynaecologia Historico-Medica Hoc Est Congressus Muliebris Consideratio Physico- Medico- Forensis Qua Utriusque Sexus Salacitas . . . Dresden & Leipzig: 1730. V. 43

SCHURZ, CARL

Henry Clay. Boston: & New York: 1899. V. 46

White River Ute Commission Investigation. Washington;: 1880. V. 38

SCHUSTER, R. M.

The Hepaticae and Anthocerotae of North America East of the Hundredth Meridian. New York: 1966-69-74. V. 46

SCHUSTER, T. E.

Printed by Kate Greenaway: a Catalogue Raisonne. London: 1987. V. 40

SCHUTZ, ALEXANDER

Die Renaissance in Italien. Eine Sammlung der Werthvollsten Erhaltenen Monumente. Hamburg: 1896, 1907-08. V. 46

SCHUYLER, EUGENE

Turkistan, Notes of a Journey in Russian Turkistan, Khokand, Bukhara, and Kuldja. New York: 1876. V. 44; 45

SCHUYLER, HARTLEY & GRAHAM

Illustrated Catalogue of Arms and Military Goods. New York: 1864. V. 41

SCHUYLER, JAMES

The Crystal Lithium. New York: 1972. V. 44

SCHUYLKILL MINING COMPANY

The Schuylkill Mining Co., Creed, Colorado . . . Pottsville, Pa.: 1890. V. 37

SCHWAAB, EUGENE L.

Travels in the Old South, 1783-1860. Louisville: 1973. V. 41; 42; 44

SCHWABACHER, FRANK

Verses. San Francisco: 1943. V. 40

SCHWANN, THEODOR

Mikroskopische Untersuchungen Uber die Uebereinstimmung in der Struktur und dem Wachsthum der Thiere und Pflanzen. Berlin: 1839. V. 39

Microscopical Researches Into the Accordance in The Structure and Growth of Animals and Plants. London: 1847. V. 37; 39; 42; 43; 44; 46

SCHWARTZ, DELMORE 1886-1967

The Heart's Journey. New York: 1927. V. 39

In Dreams Begin Responsibilities. 1938. V. 39

In Dreams Begin Responsibilities. Norfolk: 1938. V. 37; 38; 41; 44; 45

Shanendoah. 1941. V. 44

Shenandoah. (1941). V. 37

Shenandoah. Norfolk: 1941. V. 45

Summer Knowledge. Garden City: 1959. V. 43; 45

Vaudeville for a Princess and Other Poems. Nofolk: 1950. V. 43

The World is a Wedding. Norfolk: 1948. V. 46

SCHWARTZ, EDWARD

Katherine Anne Porter: A Critical Bibliography. New York: 1953. V. 43

SCHWARTZ, JOHANN CASPAR

Klystiren Als Ein Allgemeines Hausmittel . . . Inngleichen von Wasser-Und Tobaks-Gebrauch. Hamburg: 1723. V. 38

SCHWARTZ, JOZUA MARIUS WILLEM 1858-1915

An Old Maid's Love. London: 1891. V. 46

SCHWARTZ, SEYMORE

The Mapping of America. New York: 1980. V. 39; 40

SCHWARZ, ARTURO

The Complete Works of Marcel Duchamp. New York: 1970. V. 39; 43; 45

SCHWARZ, ARTURO continued

Marcel Duchamp. Ready-Mades etc. (1913-1964). Milano/Paris: 1964. V. 39

SCHWARZ, GEORG

Almost Forgotten Germany. Deya and London: 1936. V. 41

Almost Forgotten Germany. Deya, Majorca and London: 1936. V. 38; 41

SCHWARZ, HEINRICH

David Octavius Hill, Master of Photography. New York: 1931. V. 37

SCHWARZ, HERBERT F.

Stingless Bees (meliponidae) of the Western Hemisphere. New York: 1948. V. 41; 43; 45

SCHWARZ, KARL

Das Graphische Werk von Lovis Corinth. Berlin: 1917. V. 45

SCHWARZ, S. I.

The Mapping of America. New York: 1980. V. 38

SCHWARZWALD, EUGENIE

The Homecoming of the Lost Book. Chicago: 1961. V. 38

SCHWATKA, FREDERICK

Along Alaksa's Great River. New York: 1885. V. 46

Report of Military Reconnaissance in Alaska, made in 1833. Washington: 1885. V. 38; 39; 45

A Summer in Alaska. Philadelphia: 1891. V. 39

A Summer in Alaksa. St. Louis: 1893. V. 43; 44

SCHWEINFURTH, GEORG

The Heart of Africa. New York: 1874. V. 42

The Heart of Africa. New York: 1896. V. 42; 45

SCHWEITZER, ALBERT

The Decay and Restoration of Civilization. London: 1932. V. 45

On the Edge of the Primeval Forest . . . London: 1951. V. 37

SCHWEITZER, JEAN

La Juive: Grand Opera en 5 Actes . . . the Jewess: A Grand Opera in Five Acts. Napoleonville: 1860. V. 39

SCHWENCKFELD, KASPAR

Stirpium & Fossilium Silesiae Catalogus. Leipzig: 1600. V. 43

SCHWENTER, DANIEL 1585-1636

Deliciae Physico-Mathematicae . . . Nuremberg: 1651. V. 42

Geometriae Practicae Novae et Auctae I (-IV). Nuremberg: 1641. V. 42

SCHWERDT, C. F. G. R.

The Hampshire Hunt in a Series of Five Plates. London: 1929. V. 42

Hunting, Hawking, Shooting. London: 1928-37. V. 39; 40; 42; 45

Hunting, Hawking and Shooting Illustrated in a Catalogue of Books, Manuscripts, Prints and Drawings. 1985. V. 41; 45

Hunting, Hawking, Shooting. Hildesheim: 1985-86. V. 42

Hunting, Hawking, Shooting. London: 1985-87. V. 37

Hunting, Hawking, Shooting. Illustrated in a Catalogue of Books, Manuscripts, Prints and Drawings. Collected by . . . . London: 1986. V. 37

A Panorama of the Progress of Human Life Fashionably Displayed Illustrating 'Shakespeare's Ages' and Exhibiting the Manners, Costume, Character and Field Sports of the English People. London: 1930. V. 37

SCHWERDT, CARL FRANZ GEORG R.

Hunting, Hawking, Shooting. Hildesheim: 1985. V. 39; 40

SCHWERDT, CARL FRANZ GEORG RICHARD

The Schwerdt Collection. London: 1939. V. 40

SCHWERNER, ARMAND

Sounds of the River Naranjana and the Tablets I-XXIV. Barrytown: 1983. V. 39

The Tablets I-VIII Presented by the Scholar-Trnaslator . . . . West Branch: 1968. V. 39

SCHWETTMANN, CARL

Santa Rita: the University of Texas Oil Discovery. Austin: 1943. V. 44

SCHWIMMER, JOHANN MICHAEL

Academia Prisca Graeciae h.e. Tractatvs Historicvs De Graeciae Priscis Professoribvs, Socraticis, Platonicius seu Academicis, Peripateticis & Stoicis Aliisque. Rudolstadt (but Jena),: 1674. V. 37

SCHWOB, MARCEL

La Porte des Reves. Paris: 1899. V. 39; 45

SCICLUNA, HANNIBAL P.

The Church of St. John in Valletta. San Martin: 1955. V. 42

SCIDMORE, E. R.

Alaska: its Southern Coast and the Sitkan Archipelago. Boston: 1885. V. 46

SCIDMORE, E. RUHAMAH

Appleton's Guide-Book to Alaska - and the Northwest Coast . . . New York: 1896. V. 42

LA SCIENCE des Medailles pour L'Instruction de Ceux Quis s'Appliquent a la Connoissance des Medailles Antiques & Modernes. Amsterdam: 1693. V. 45

SCILLA, AGOSTINO

La Vana Speculazione Disingannata dal Senso. Naples: 1670. V. 38; 39; 46

SCIPIO'S Reflections on Monroe's View of the Conduct of the Executive on the Foreign Affairs of the United States. Boston: 1798. V. 45

SCLATER, P. L.

A Monograph of the Jacamars and Puff Birds. London: 1882. V. 37

On Certain Species of Deer Now or ately Living in the Society's Menagerie. London: 1871. V. 37

SCLATER, W. L.

A History of the Birds of Colorado. London: 192. V. 38

SCLATER, W. S.

A Complete and Authentic History of Libby Prison. Richmond: 1897. V. 37

SCLATER, WILLIAM L.

A History of the Birds of Colorado. London: 1912. V. 37; 39

SCOBELL, HENRY

Memorials of the Method and Manner of the Proceedings in Parliament in Passing Bills. London: 1670. V. 37; 39; 41; 42; 46

Remembrances of Methods, Orders and Proceedings . . . in the House of Lords . . . to which is added, The Priviledges of the Baronage of England . . . London: 1689. V. 46

SCOBIE, I. H. MACKAY

An Old Highland Fencible Corps. The History of the Reay Fencible Highland Regiment of Foot, or Mckay's Highlanders, 1794-1802 . . . Edinburgh: 1914. V. 38

SCOFFERN, JOHN

The Manufacture of Sugar, in the Colonies and at Home, Chemically Considered. London: 1849. V. 45

SCOFIELD, SAMUEL

A Practical Treatise on Vaccina or Cowpock . . . New York: 1810. V. 42; 43

SCOGGAN, HOMER J.

Flora of Canada. 1979. V. 38

SCOPPA, LUCIO GIOVANNI

In Varios Authores Collectanea. Naples: 1507. V. 38

SCORESBY, W.

The Whaleman's Adventures in the Southern Ocean . . . London: 1850-62. V. 42

SCORESBY, WILLIAM

An Account of the Arctic Regions, with a History and Description of the Northern Wale-Fishery. Edinburgh: 1820. V. 37; 40; 42; 43

The Arctic Regions and the Northern Whale-Fishery. London: 1849. V. 40; 42

The Arctic Regions and the Northern Whale-Fishery. London: (1849). V. 37

Journal of a Voyage to the Northern Whale-Fishery, Including Researches and Discoveries on the Eastern Coast of West Greenland Made in the Summer of 1822 in the Ship 'Baffin' of Liverpool. Edinburgh: 1823. V. 37; 38; 41; 42; 44; 46

Journal of a Voyage to Australia and Round the World, for Magnetical Research. London: 1859. V. 38; 41

Journal of a Voyage to the Northern Whale Fishery; including researches and discoveries on the Eastern Coast of Greenland, made in the summer of 1822, in the Ship Baffin of Liverpool. London: 1823. V. 37

Memorials of the Sea. London: 1835. V. 42; 46

Seven Log Books Concerning the Arctic Voyages of Captain . . . Issued in Facsimile by the Explorer's Club of New York. New York: 1917. V. 37; 38

SCOT, ALEXANDER

Rudiments and Practical Exercises, for Learning the French Language, by an Easy Method. Edinburgh: 1794. V. 43

SCOT, ELIZABETH

Alonzo and Cora, with Other Original Poems. London: 1801. V. 39; 42

SCOT, JOHN

An Enquiry into the Origin of the Gout, Wherein Its Various Symptoms and Appearances, and Those of All Bilious and Nervous Disorders . . . London: 1783. V. 44

SCOT, REGINALD

The Discoverie of Witchcraft. London: 1930. V. 41; 42; 44

The Discoverie of Witchcraft. Imprinted at London: 1548. V. 37

A Perfite Platforme of a Hoppe Garden, and Necessarie Instructions for the Making and Mayntenance thereof, With Notes and Rules for Reformation of all Abuses . . . London: 1578. V. 39; 41

Scot's Discovery of Witchcraft . . . London: 1651. V. 43

SCOT, WALTER

A True History of Several Honourable Families of the Right Honourable Name of Scot. Edinburgh: 1776. V. 41; 45

SCOT, WILLIAM

No Necessity to Alter the Common-Prayer . . . London: 1718. V. 39

THE SCOTCH House Wife, Containing the Inward and Outward Virtues Which is Proper and Pertinent to Every Good Wife and Mistres of a Family. N.P.: 1720. V. 45

THE SCOTCH Hut, a Poem, Addressed to Euphorbus; or the Earl of Grove. London: 1779. V. 40; 42

THE SCOTCH Medal Decipher'd, and the New Hereditary-Right Men Display'd: or, Remrks on the Late Proceedings of the Faculty of Advocates at Edinburgh, Upon Receiving the Pretender's Medal. London: 1711. V. 38

SCOTCHER, GEORGE

The Fly Fisher's Legacy. London: 1974. V. 39; 43

THE SCOTIAD, or Wise Men of the North!!! London: 1809. V. 40

SCOTISH Descriptive Poems; with Some Illustrations of Scotish Literary Antiquities. Edinburgh: 1803. V. 39

SCOTLAND

In the Parliament of The Richt Excellent, Richt Heigh, and Michtie Prince, lames the sext, be the Grace of God King of Socttis . . . Lawis. 1575. V. 37

SCOTLAND. CENSUS OFFICE - 1872

Eighth Decennial Cenus of the Population of Scotland, Taken 3d April Á871.. Edinburgh: 1872-71. V. 42

SCOTLAND. COURT OF SESSION

The Decision of the Court of Session, Upon the Question of Literary Property . . . Edinburgh: 1774. V. 43

SCOTLAND. COURT OF SESSIONS c.1574-1644

The Decisions of the Lords of Council and Session, from July 1621-July 1642. Edinburgh: 1690. V. 40

SCOTLAND. LAWS, STATUTES, ETC.

The Acts of Robert I, 1306-1329. Edinburgh: 1988. V. 44

SCOTLAND. LAWS, STATUTES, ETC. - 1609

Regiam Majestatem, the Ancient Laws and Constitutions of Scotland . . . Edinburgh: 1609. V. 40

SCOTLAND. LAWS, STATUTES, ETC. - 1661

The Laws and Acts of the First Parliament of Our Most High and Dread Sovereign Charles II . . . Holden at Edinburgh the First of January 1661. Edinburgh: 1661. V. 40

SCOTLAND. LAWS, STATUTES, ETC. - 1662

Laws and Acts Past in the Second Session of the First Parliament, Or Our Most High and Dread Soveraign, Charles the Second . . . Holden at Edinburgh by the Noble Lord, John Earl of Middleton . . . Edinburgh: 1662. V. 40

SCOTLAND. LAWS, STATUTES, ETC. - 1681

The Laws and Acts of the (Scottish) Parliament 1424-1681. Edinburgh: 1681. V. 40

SCOTLAND. LAWS, STATUTES, ETC. - 1682

Laws and Acts of Parliament by King James I and His Royal Successors. Edinburgh: 1682. V. 40

SCOTLAND. LAWS, STATUTES, ETC. - 1740

Acts of Sederunt of the Lords of Council and Session. Edinburgh: 1740. V. 40

SCOTLAND. ROYAL COMM. ON ANCIENT & HISTORICAL MONUMENTS & CONSTRUCTIONS

Royal Commission on the Ancient Monuments of Scotland. An Inventory of the Ancient and Historical Monuments of the City of Edinburgh . . . Edinburgh: 1951. V. 44

SCOTLAND'S Opposition to the Popish Bill. Edinburgh: 1780. V. 38

SCOTO, ANDREA

Itinerario Overa Nova Descrittione de' Viaggi Principali d'Italia. Rome: 1650. V. 40; 44

SCOTT, A.

Plain Reasons for Adopting the Plan of the Societies Calling Themselves the Friends of the People, and Their Convention of Delegates, as Coppied From the Works of Mr. Thos. Paine. Edinburgh: 1793. V. 41

SCOTT, ANNA MILLER

The Flower Babies' Book. Chicago: 1914. V. 45

SCOTT, BENJAMIN

The Description and Use of an Universal and Perpetual Mathematical Instrument. Shewing the most Expeditious and Exact Method of solving all practical Questions in Arithmetick, Trigonomentry, Navigation, Dyalling, Astromony, &c . . . London: 1733. V. 37

SCOTT, BERESFORD

An Account of the Destruction of the Fleets of the Celebrated Pirate Chieftains Chui-Apoo and Shap-Ng-Tsai on the Coast of China, in Sept. and Oct. 1849 . . . N.P.: 1851. V. 43

SCOTT, CAROLINE LUCY

A Marriage in High Life. London: 1828. V. 44

SCOTT, CHARLES ROCHEFORT

Excursions in the Mountains of Ronda and Granada, with Characteristic Sketches of the Inhabitants of the South of Spain. London: 1838. V. 38

Rambles in Egypt and Candia, with Details of the Military Power and Resources of those Countries . . . London: 1837. V. 43

SCOTT, D. GAVIN

History of the Rise and Progress of Joint Stock Banks in England with a Statement of the Law Relating to Them, also an Analysis of the Evidence Before the Select Committee Appointed to Inquire Into Their Affairs, and Suggestions . . . London: 1837. V. 38

SCOTT, DAVID

Selections from the Works of Etched by William Bell Scott. Glasgow: 1866-7. V. 42

Selections from the Works of . . . Glasgow: 1866/7. V. 43

SCOTT, DRED

The Case . . . in the United States Supreme Court . . . New York: 1857. V. 42

SCOTT, DUNCAN CAMPBELL

The Poems of Duncan Campbell Scott. Toronto: 1926. V. 41

W. J. Phillips. Toronto: 1947. V. 43

SCOTT, EDMUND

Proceedings of the Sussex Agricultural Society, From Its Institution (in 1796) to 1798, Inclusive. Lewes: 1800. V. 39

SCOTT, EDWARD B.

The Saga of the Sandwich Islands. Crystal Bay, Lake Tahoe: 1968. V. 38

Squaw Valley. Crystal Bay: 1960. V. 46

SCOTT ELLIOTT, G. F.

A Naturalist in Mid-Africa Being an Account of a Journey to the Mountains of the Moon and Tanganyika. London: 1896. V. 39

SCOTT, EVELYN

Ideals. New York: 1927. V. 39

On William Faulkner's 'The Sound and the Fury'. New York: 1929. V. 37; 39

The Wave. New York: 1929. V. 39; 45

SCOTT, FLORENCE J.

Historical Heritage of the Lower Rio Grande. San Antonio: 1937. V. 38

SCOTT, FRANK J.

The Art of Beautifying Suburban Home Grounds of Small Extent . . . and the Best Modes of Laying Out Planting, and Keeping Decorated Grounds. New York: 1870. V. 44

SCOTT-GATTY, ALFRED

I Wonder Why, Sixteen Songs for the Children. London: 1920. V. 46

SCOTT, GENIO C.

Fishing in American Waters. New York: 1869. V. 39

SCOTT, GEOFFREY

A Box of Paints. 1923. V. 43

A Box of Paints. London: 1923. V. 46

The Portrait of Zelide. London: 1925. V. 40

SCOTT, GEORGE

The Memoirs of Sir James Melvil . . . London: 1683. V. 46

SCOTT, GEORGE GILBERT

An Essay on the History of English Church Architecture Prior to the Separation of England from the Roman Obedience. London: 1881. V. 37; 39; 45

Gleanings from Westminster Abbey . . . Oxford: 1863. V. 38

Lectures on the Rise and Development of Medieval Architecture Delivered at the Royal Academy. London: 1879. V. 38

A Plea for the Faithful Restoration of Our Ancient Chambers. London: 1850. V. 38

Remarks On Secular and Domestic Architecture, Present and Future. London: 1857. V. 42

Remarks on Secular and Domestic Architecture, Present & Future. London: 1858. V. 37

SCOTT, GILBERT

Personal and Professional Recollections by the Late Sir Gilbert Scott. London: 1879. V. 45

SCOTT, H. L.

Military Dictionary. New York: 1864. V. 39

SCOTT, HAROLD

A History of Tropical Medicine. Baltimore: 1939. V. 41

SCOTT, HELENUS

The Adventures of a Rupee. Dublin: 1782. V. 37

SCOTT, HENRY THOMAS

A Guide to the Collector of Historical Documents, Literary Manuscripts and Autograph Letters Etc. London: 1891. V. 38

SCOTT, HUGH LENOX

Some Memories of a Soldier. New York: 1928. V. 37; 44

SCOTT, HUGH STOWELL 1862-1903

From One Generation to Another. London: 1892. V. 38; 41; 42; 43

The Grey Lady. London: 1897. V. 40; 43

The Money Spinner and Other Character Notes. London: 1896. V. 40

The Phantom Furture. London: 1888. V. 41

Prisoners and Captives. London: 1891. V. 42

The Slave of the Lamp. London: 1892. V. 38; 41; 42

Suspense. London: 1890. V. 41; 43

With Edged Tools. London: 1894. V. 40; 41; 43

Young Mistley. London: 1888. V. 43

SCOTT, J.

The Pocket Companion and History of Free-Masons. London: 1759. V. 37; 38

SCOTT, J. D.

Combination Atlas Map of Montgomery County, Pennsylvania. Philadelphia: 1877. V. 42

SCOTT, J. E.

A Bibliography of the Works of Sir Henry Rider Haggard, 1856-1925. Takely,: 1947. V. 45

SCOTT, J. W.

A Presentation of Causes Tending to Fix the Position of the Future Great City of the World in the Central Plain of North America. Toledo: 1876. V. 46

SCOTT, JAMES

Odes on Several Subjects. Cambridge: 1761. V. 38

The Perils of Poetry. 1766. V. 40; 42

SCOTT, JAMES L.

A Journal of a Missionary Tour through Pennsylvania, Ohio, Indiana, Illinois, Iowa, Wiskonson and Michigan. Providence: 1843. V. 38; 42

SCOTT, JOB

Journal of the Life, Travels and Gospel Labours of that Faithful Servant and Minister of Christ, Job Scott. New York: 1797. V. 38; 39; 40; 42

A Letter from a Friend in America, to Luke Howard, of Tottenham, Near London, In Which the Character of Our Late Friend Job Scott, Is Vindicated and Defended and His Doctrines Shown to be Consistent with Scripture and Sound Reason. Philadelphia: 1826. V. 44

SCOTT, JOHN

Amwell. A Descriptive Poem. Dublin: 1776. V. 43; 44

Amwell. London: 1776. V. 38; 45

Berwick-Upon-Tweed. The History of the Town and Guild . . . London: 1888. V. 41

A Brochure, During the War and After the War. Warrenton: 1900. V. 44

Catalogue of the Valuable and Extensive Library of the Late John Scott, Esq. C.B. London: 1905. V. 39

The Christian Life, from Its Beginning to Its Consummation in Glory. London: 1729. V. 39

Critical Essays on Some of the Poems, of Sevral English Poets. London: 1785. V. 37

Digests of the General Highway and Turnpike Laws . . . London: 1778. V. 42

Four Elegies: Descriptive and Moral. London: 1760. V. 37

The Indiana Gazetteer, or Topographical Dictionary. Indianapolis: 1833. V. 38; 40

The Indiana Gazetteer, or Topographical Dictionary of the State of Indiana. Indianapolis: 1849. V. 41

The Life of the Rev. Thomas Scott . . . Including a Narrative Drawn Up by Himself, and Copious Extracts of His Letters. Lexington: 1826. V. 44

Paris Revisited, in 1815. London: 1816. V. 44; 46

Partisan Life with Col. John S. Mosby. New York: 1867. V. 44

The Poetical Works of John Scott, Esq. London: 1782. V. 44

SCOTT, JOHN ROBERT

A Dissertation on the Progress of the Fine Arts. London: 1800. V. 46

SCOTT, JONATHAN

Tales and Anecdotes and Letters. Shrewsbury: 1800. V. 42; 43

SCOTT, JOSEPH

A Geographical Dictionary; or the United States of North America. Philadelphia: 1805. V. 40; 43; 45

SCOTT, JULIA H. KINNEY

Prize Tale. The Sacrifice; a Clergyman's Story. Hudson: 1837. V. 43

SCOTT, LYDIA

Trevelyan. London: 1833. V. 37

SCOTT, M. LE BARON

Aerostat Dirigeable a Volonte. Paris: 1789. V. 38

SCOTT, MARY

Abbotsford: The Personal Relics and Antiquarian Treasures of Sir Walter Scott. London: 1893. V. 37; 38

SCOTT, MARY H.

The Oregon Trail through Wyoming. Aurora: 1958. V. 46

SCOTT, MICHAEL 1175?-1234?

Phisionomia . . . . Si Prudentiam. Paris: 1520. V. 45

Specification of Michael Scott. London: 1877/78. V. 44

Tom Cringle's Log. Edinburgh: 1833. V. 39; 43

Tom Cringle's Log. Edinburgh: 1833. V. 42

SCOTT-MITCHELL, FREDERICK

Practical Gilding, Bronzing, Lacquering and Glass Embossing. London: 1945. V. 46

SCOTT-MONCRIEFF, CHARLES KENNETH 1889-1930

The Strange and Striking Adventures of Four Authors in Search of A Character. Kensington: 1926. V. 41

SCOTT, NANCY

A Memoir of Hugh Lawson White, Jude of the Supreme Court of Tennessee. Philadelphia: 1856. V. 42

SCOTT, ORANGE

The Grounds of Secession from M.E. Church, or, Book for the Times. New York: 1848. V. 40

SCOTT, PAUL

After the Funeral. 1979. V. 40

The Alien Sky. London: 1953. V. 38

The Jewel in the Crown. London: 1966. V. 38; 41

Johnnie Sahib. London: 1952. V. 37; 38; 41

Johnnie Sahib. London: 1968. V. 40

A Male Child. London: 1956. V. 40

The Mark of the Warrior. London: 1958. V. 43

SCOTT, PETER

Morning Flight. London: 1935. V. 39; 41; 42; 45; 46

Wild Chorus. London: 1935. V. 41

Wild Chorus. London: 1938. V. 39; 40; 42; 44; 46

Wild Chorus. London & New York: 1938. V. 39

SCOTT, QUINTA

Route 66: the Highway and Its People. Norman: 1988. V. 41

SCOTT, REGINALD

A Perfite Platforme of a Hoppe Garden, and Necessarie Instructions for the Making and Mayntenance Thereof . . . London: 1578. V. 40

SCOTT, RICHARD

A Topographical and Historical Account of Hayling Island, Hants. Havent: 1826. V. 43

SCOTT, ROBERT EDEN 1770-1811

Elements of Intellectual Philosophy . . . Edinburgh: 1805. V. 45

SCOTT, ROBERT FALCON 1868-1912

Capt. Scott's Last Expedition. London: 1913. V. 41; 45

'Scott's Last Expedition.' London: 1913. V. 37; 38; 39; 40; 41; 42; 43; 46

Scott's Last Expedition . . . London: 1914. V. 44

Scott's Last Expedition. New York: 1913. V. 37; 43; 44

The Voyage of 'The Discovery.' London: 1905. V. 38; 41; 42; 46

SCOTT, SARAH

A Description of Millenium Hall, and the Country Adjacent. London: 1762. V. 38; 45

The History of Sir George Ellison. London: 1766. V. 40

The Test of Filial Duty. London: 1772. V. 38; 45

SCOTT, TEMPLE

Oliver Goldsmith Bibliographically and Biographically Considered, Based on the Collection of Material in the Library of W. M. Elkins. Esq. New York: 1928. V. 39; 42; 46

Oliver Goldsmith Bibliographically and Biographically Considered. New York: 198. V. 46

SCOTT, THOMAS

A Choice Narrative of Count Gondamor's Transactions During His Embassy in England . . . London;: 1659. V. 43

An Experimental Discoverie of Spanish Practices or the Counsell of a well wishing Souldier, for the good of His Prince and State. Wherein is Manifested from the Known experience, both the Cruelty, and Policy of the Spaniard, to effect . . . (London?): 1623. V. 37

The Mock-Marriage. London: 1696. V. 41

A Tongue-Combat. Lately Happening Between Two English Souldiers . . . London: 1623. V. 41

Vox Populi. London: 1620. V. 40

SCOTT, W. A.

The Bible and Politics; or, an Humble Plea for Equal, Perfect, Absolute Religious Freedom . . . San Francisco: 1859. V. 46

Esther: The Hebrew Persian Queen. San Francisco: 1859. V. 38

The Wedge of Gold; or, Achan in El Dorado . . . San Francisco: 1855. V. 37; 39

SCOTT, W. H.

The Sportsman's Calendar. London: 1818. V. 40; 43

SCOTT, WALTER 1771-1832

The Abbot. Edinburgh: 1820. V. 37; 40; 41; 43; 44; 45

The Abbot: by the Author of 'Waverley'. Edinburgh: 1821. V. 44

An Account of the First Edinburgh Theatrical Fund Dinner, Held at Edinburgh, on Friday 23d February, 1827. Edinburgh: 1827. V. 37

Hermetica: the Ancient Greek and Latin Writings Which Contain Religious or Philosophic Teachings Ascribed to Hermes Trismegistus. Oxford: 1924. V. 46

Anne of Geierstein; or, the Maiden of the Mist. Edinburgh: 1829. V. 37; 42; 43; 44

The Antiquary. Edinburgh: 1816. V. 37; 42; 43

Ballads and Lyrical Pieces. Edinburgh: 1806. V. 43; 44; 45

The Border Antiquities of England and Scotland. London: 1814. V. 37; 39; 40; 42; 43

The Border Antiquities of England and Scotland. London: 1814-17. V. 38; 39; 40; 41; 43; 45

The Border Antiquities of England and Scotland; comprising specimens of Architecture . . . together with Illustrations of Remarkable Incidents in Border History and Tradition and Original Poetry. 1814-1817. V. 37

The Bridal of Triermain, Harold the Dauntless, Field of Waterloos and Other Poems. Edinburgh: 1836. V. 45

Catalogue of the Library at Abbotsford. Edinburgh: 1838. V. 39; 40; 43; 46

Chronicles of the Canongate. Edinburgh: 1827. V. 37; 40; 41; 42; 43; 44; 46

Chronicles of the Canongate. Edinburgh: 1826. V. 43

Chronicles of the Canongate. Philadelphia: 1827. V. 45

Chronicles of Canongate. Edinburgh: 1827-28. V. 39

Chronicles of the Canongate (Second Series). Edinburgh: 1828. V. 37; 43; 46

Der Astrolog. Leipzig: 1817. V. 39

The Doom of Devorgoil, a Melo-Drama. Auchindrane; or, The Ayrshire Tragedy. Edinburgh: 1830. V. 42

The Field of Waterloo. Boston: 1815. V. 45

The Field of Waterloo; a Poem. Edinburgh: 1815. V. 39; 43

The Fortunes of Nigel. Edinburgh: 1822. V. 37; 39; 40; 41; 42; 43; 44; 45; 46

The Fortunes of Nigel. Edinburgh and London: 1822. V. 46

The Fortune of Nigel. London: 1822. V. 39

Guy Mannering. Edinburgh: 1815. V. 37; 39; 40; 42; 43; 44

Guy Mannering; or, the Astrologer. Edinburgh: 1815. V. 37

Halidon Hill. Edinburgh: 1822. V. 43; 46

Harold the Dauntless; a Poem, in Six Cantos. Edinburgh: 1817. V. 39

Harold the Dauntless; a Poem, in Six Cantos. Edinburgh/London: 1817. V. 37

The Heart of Midlothian. Edinburgh: 1818. V. 38; 40

Het Lied van den Laatsten Meistreel. Dordrecht: 1840. V. 39

Hints Addressed to the Inhabitants of Edinburgh, and Others.. Edinburgh: 1822. V. 37; 38

The History of Scotland. Philadelphia: 1830. V. 45

Introductions and Notes and Illustrations, to the Novels, Tales and Romances, of the Author of Waverley. Edinburgh: 1833. V. 37

Ivanhoe. Edinburgh: 1819. V. 43

Ivanhoe. Edinburgh: 1820. V. 37; 39; 40; 42

Ivanhoe. Edinburgh & London: 1820. V. 40

Ivanhoe. Philadelphia: 1820. V. 39

Ivanhoe. Edinburgh: 1870. V. 43

Ivanhoe. New York: 1922. V. 38

Ivanhoe. New York: 1940. V. 41; 43

The Journal of Sir Walter Scott . . . Edinburgh: 1890. V. 44

Kenilworth; a Romance. Edinburgh: 1821. V. 37; 42; 43; 44

Kenilworth. New York. 1966. V. 39

The Lady of the Lake. Edinburgh: 1810. V. 40; 42

The Lady of the Lake. London: 1869. V. 43

The Lady of the Lake. Edinburgh: 1870. V. 38

The Lady of the Lake. Edinburgh: 1871. V. 39; 43

The Lady of the Lake. Indianapolis: 1910. V. 42

The Lady of the lake. London: 1863. V. 37

Landscape Illustrations of the Waverley Novels, with descriptions of the views. 1832. V. 37

The Lay of the Last Minstrel, a Poem. London: 1805. V. 46

The Lay of the Last Minstrel. London: 1807. V. 45

Lay of the Last Minstrel. London: 1809. V. 37; 39

The Lay of the Last Minstrel. London: 1811. V. 41

The Lay of the Last Minstrel. Edinburgh: 1854. V. 45

The Lay of the Last Minstrel: A Poem. V. 37

The Lay of the Last Minstrel, a Poem. Savannah: 1811. V. 37

Letters on Demonology and Witchcraft Addressed to J. G. Lockhart. London: 1830. V. 37; 38; 43; 45; 46

Letters on Demonology and Witchcraft. New York: 1830. V. 46

Letters on Demonology and Witchcraft, Addressed to J. G. Lockhart, Esq. (etc.). London: 1831. V. 45

Letters of Sir Walter Scott; Addressed to the Rev. R. Polwhele; D. Gilbert, Esq.; Francis Douce, Esq. &c Uc. London: 1832. V. 43

The Life of Napleon Buonaparte, Emperor of the French. Edinburgh: 1827. V. 39; 41; 42; 43; 44; 45

The Life of Napoleon Bonaparte, Emperor of the French . . . Philadelphia: 1827. V. 41

The Life of Napoleon Buonaparte, Emperor of the French. With a preliminary view of the French Revolution. Edinburgh/London: 1827. V. 37

Lives of the Novelists. Paris: 1825. V. 42

Lives of the Novelists. Boston: 1826. V. 39; 40

The Lord of the Isles, a Poem. Edinburgh: 1815. V. 37; 39; 42; 43

The Lord of the Isles. Edinburgh: 1857. V. 39

Marmion. Edinburgh: 1808. V. 39; 42; 43

Marmion. London: 1809. V. 37

Marmion. Edinburgh: 1811. V. 37

Marmion: a Tale of Flodden Field. Edinburgh: 1815. V. 46

Marmion, a Tale of Flodden field. Edinburgh: 1821. V. 42

Marmion. Edinburgh: 1866. V. 37; 38; 42; 45

Memoirs of the Life of Sir Walter Scott, Bart. Edinburgh: 1837-38. V. 37

Memorials of the Haliburtons. Edinburgh: 1820. V. 43

Memorials of the Haliburtons. Edinburgh: 1824. V. 37

Minstrelsy of the Scottish Border. Kelso: (Volume III: 1802-03. V. 39; 46

Minstrelsy of the Scottish Border. Edinburgh: 1803. V. 39

Minstrelsy of the Scottish Border. London: 1902. V. 37

Miscellaneous Poems. Edinburgh: 1820. V. 37; 42; 43; 46

The Monastery. Edinburgh: 1820. V. 37; 42; 43; 46

The Novels of . . . Paris: 1838. V. 42

Paul's Letters to His Kinsfolk. Edinburgh & London: 1816. V. 38; 40; 43

Peveril of the Peak. Edinburgh: 1822. V. 37; 39; 40; 41; 42

Peveril of the Peak. Philadelphia: 1823. V. 43; 45

The Pirate. Edinburgh: 1822. V. 39; 41; 42; 43; 44; 45; 46

The Pirate. Edinburgh: 1825. V. 46

Poems. Edinburgh: 1873. V. 38

SCOTT, WALTER 1771-1832 continued

Poetical Works. New York: 1811. V. 40

(Poetical) Works. Edinburgh: 1812-13. V. 38

The Poetical Works. Edinburgh: 1820. V. 39; 42

The Poetical Works. Francofort: 1826. V. 39

The Poetical Works of Sir Walter Scott. Edinburgh: 1830. V. 39; 41

The Poetical Works of Sir Walter Scott, Bart. Edinburgh: 1833-34. V. 43

The Poetical Works of Sir Walter Scott, Bart. Edinburgh: 1841. V. 45

The Poetical Works. Edinburgh: 1848. V. 42

The Poetical Works. Edinburgh: 1848. V. 39

Poetical Works. Edinburgh: 1851-57. V. 40

The Poetical Works. Edinburgh: 1853. V. 39

The Poetical Works of Sir Walter Scott. Edinburgh: 1868. V. 38

The Poetical Works. London: 1871. V. 46

Poetical Works. London: 1892. V. 40

Poetical Works. Oxford: 1904. V. 42

The Private Letter-Book of Sir Walter Scott. London: 1930. V. 43

Provincial Antiquities and Picturesque Scenery of Scotland, with Descriptive Illustrations by Sir Walter Scott, Bart. London: 1826. V. 43

Quentin Durward. Edinburgh: 1823. V. 37; 39; 42; 43

Red Gauntlet. Edinburgh: 1824. V. 37; 39; 42; 43; 45

Redgauntlet, a Tale of the Eighteenth Century. London: 1824. V. 39

Religious Discourses. London: 1828. V. 38

Rob Roy. Edinburgh: 1818. V. 40; 41; 42; 43

Rob Roy. 1818. V. 37

Rokeby. Edinburgh: 1813. V. 44

Rokeby. Edinburgh: 1813. V. 39; 40; 41; 42; 43; 44; 45

Rokey: a Poem. London: 1813. V. 46

Rules and Regulations of the Royal Edinburgh Light Dragoons. Edinburgh: 1798. V. 40; 43

St. Ronan's Well. Edinburgh: 1824. V. 37; 41; 42; 43

St. Ronan's Well. Edinburgh & London: 1824. V. 42

St. Valentine's Day. Edinburgh: 1828. V. 38; 46

St. Ronan's Well. Edinburgh: Dec. 1823. V. 43

A Second Letter to the Editor of the Edinbrugh Weekly Journal, from Malachi Malagrowther, Esq. on the Proposed Change of Currency, and other Late Alterations as they Affect or are Intended to Affect, the Kingdom of Scotland. Edinburgh: 1826. V. 43

Tales of a Grandfather: Being Stories Taken from the History of France. Edinburgh: 1830. V. 43

Marmion: A Tale of Flodden Field. London: 1866. V. 44

Tales of My Landlord. First Series. Edinburgh: 1816. V. 43

Tales of My Landlord. Edinburgh: 1817-1832. V. 38

Tales of My Landlord, Second Series. Edinburgh: 1818. V. 39; 41; 42; 43

Tales of My Landlord. Third Series. Edinburgh: 1819. V. 40; 41; 42; 43; 44

Tales of the Crusaders. Edinburgh: 1825. V. 37; 40; 43; 45

Tales of Crusaders. Edinburgh: 1825. V. 43

Tales of a Grandfather, Being Stories from Scottish History. Edinburgh: 1827. V. 43

Tales of My Landlord. Fourth and Last Series. Edinburgh: 1832. V. 41

Tales and Romances of the Author of Waverley. Edinburgh: 1827. V. 42

Tales of a Grandfather . . . Edinburgh: 1828/29/30. V. 44

Tales of My Landlord, collected and arranged by Jedediah Cleishbotham, schoolmaster and parish-clerk of Goandercleugh. Edinburgh: 1816. V. 37

Tales of My Landlord. Fourth and Last Series. Edinburgh: 1832. V. 37; 41; 42

Tales of the Crusaders. Paris: 1825. V. 42

A Third Letter to the Editor of the Edinburgh Weekly Journal, from Malachi Malagrowther, Esq . . . . Edinburgh: 1826. V. 43

A True History of Several Honourable Families of the Right Honourable Name of Roxburgh and Selkirk. Hawick: 1786. V. 40

The Vision of Don Roderick. 1811. V. 46

The Vision of Don Roderick. Edinburgh: 1811. V. 37; 38; 40; 43

The Waverley Novels. New York. V. 46

Waverley. Edinburgh: 1814. V. 37; 38; 40; 41; 42; 43; 45

Waverley; or, 'Tis Sixty Years Since. Edinburgh: 1817. V. 42

The Waverley Novels. Edinburgh: 1829. V. 40; 42; 46

Waverley Novels. Edinburgh: 1829-33. V. 37; 39; 45; 46

Waverley Novels, Poetical Works, Prose Works and Memoirs of the Life of Sir Walter Scott. Edinburgh: 1830-1855. V. 43

The Waverley Novels. Edinburgh: 1842. V. 41

Waverley Novels. London: 1842-47. V. 40

Waverley Novels. Edinburgh: 1842-7. V. 46

The Waverley Novels. Edinburgh: 1865. V. 42

The Waverley Novels. Edinburgh: 1865-68. V. 39

Waverley Novels. Edinburgh: 1871. V. 38; 40; 42

The Waverley Novels. Edinburgh: 1877. V. 42

Waverley Novels. Philadelphia: 1879. V. 39

The Waverley Novels. Edinburgh,: 1886. V. 38

The Waverley Novels. Edinburgh: 1890. V. 42

The Waverley Novels. Boston: 1892. V. 45

The Waverley Novels. Boston: 1893. V. 39

The Waverly Novels. New York: 1900. V. 40; 41

The Waverley Novels. Edinburgh: 1901. V. 38; 39; 42

Waverley Novels. Edinburgh: 1901-03. V. 37; 39; 40

Waverley. Edinburgh: 1914. V. 42

Waverley Novels. Edinburgh/London. V. 37

Waverley Novels. Edinburgh: 1879-1881. V. 37

Waverley Novels. 'Abbotsford Edition'. Edinburgh/London: 1842-7. V. 37

The Waverly Novels. Philadelphia: 1854. V. 38; 40

The Waverly Novels by Sir Walter Scott. 1892. V. 37

Woodstock; or, The Cavalier. Edinburgh: 1822. V. 41

Woodstock; or, the Cavalier. Edinburgh: 1826. V. 37; 42; 43; 44; 46

Woodstock. Edinburgh: 1826. V. 40

Woodstock, or the Cavalier. Philadelphia: 1826. V. 40; 41; 43; 44; 46

Works. London: 1852. V. 44

Works . . . London: 1900. V. 40; 46

SCOTT, WALTER SIDNEY

The Athenians: Harriet and Mary; Shelley at Oxford. London: 1943-44. V. 37

Harriet and Mary Being the Relations Between Percy Bysshe Shelley, Harriet Shelley, Mary Shelley and Thomas Jefferson Hogg as Shown in Letters Betweeen Them Now Published for the First Time. (with) Shelley at Oxford. 1944. V. 41

Harriet and Mary. London: 1944. V. 42; 46

Harriet and Mary. Waltham St. Lawrence: 1944. V. 46

SCOTT-WARING, JOHN

An Epistle from Oberea, Queen of Otaheite, to Joseph Banks, Esq. London: 1774. V. 40

SCOTT, WILLIAM

Lessons in Elocution: or, a Selection of Pieces, in Prose and Verse, for the Inprovement (sic) of Youth in Reading and Speaking. Leicester: 1815. V. 46

O Tempora. Mores. Or The Best New Year's Gift for a Prime Minister. London: 1774. V. 39; 42

SCOTT, WILLIAM BELL 1811-1890

Antiquarian Gleanings in the North of England . . . London: 1849. V. 42

Antiquarian Gleanings in the North of England, Being Examples of Antique Furniture, Plate, Church Decoration, Objects of Historical Interest, etc. London: 1851. V. 39; 42; 44

Autobiographial Notes . . . and Notices of His Artistic and Poetic Circle of Friends 1830 to 1882. London: 1892. V. 39; 42

Gems of Modern French Art. London: 1871. V. 39

Gems of Modern Belgian Art. London: 1872. V. 39

Illustrations to Chorea Sancti Viti: or Steps in the Journey of Prince Legion. London: 1851. V. 42

Poems. London: 1854. V. 37; 39

Poems. Ballads, Studies from Nature, Sonnets, Etc. London: 1875. V. 39

William Blake, Etchings from His Works. London: 1878. V. 38; 42; 43

SCOTT, WILLIAM F.

The Story of a Cavalry Regiment: the Career of the Fourth Iowa Veteran Volunteers, from Kansas to Georgia, 1861-65. New York: 1893. V. 42

SCOTT, WILLIAM FORSE

Philander P. Lane Colonel of Volunteers in the Civil War Eleventh Ohio Infantry. New York: 1920. V. 43

SCOTT, WILLIAM HENRY

British Field Sports: Embracing Practical Instructions in Shooting . . . London: 1820. V. 39; 43

The Sportsman's Calendar; or, Monthly Remembrance of Field Diversions. London: 1818. V. 39

SCOTT, WILLIAM ROBERT

Francis Hutcheson. His Life, Teaching and Position in the History of Philosophy. Cambridge: 1900. V. 42

SCOTT, WINFIELD

V. 45

Contestaciones Habidas Anoche Entre el Senor General en Gefe del Ejercito de los Estados-Unidos y el Supremo Gobierno de la Republica Mexicana. Mexico: 1847. V. 39

Headquarters of the Army . . . General Orders . . . No. 294. Mexico. V. 45

Headquarters of the Army . . . General Orders . . . no. 281 (and) General Orders no. 282 (and) General Orders . . . no. 283. Tacubaya: 1847. V. 42

Headquarters of the Army . . . General Orders - No. 190. Mexico: 1848. V. 41; 42

Life of General Scott. N.P.. V. 37

SCOTT, WINFIELD continued

Memoirs of Lieut. General Scott, LL.D. Written by Himself. New York: 1864. V. 39; 40; 43

SCOTT, WINFIELD TOWNLEY

Biography for Traman. New York: 1937. V. 39

Elegy for Robinson. New York: 1936. V. 37

SCOTT, ZACHARY

John Emery. New York: 1964. V. 45

SCOTTISH Art and National Encouragement. Edinburgh: 1846. V. 38

THE SCOTTISH Tourist, and Itinerary; or, a Guide to the Scenery and Antiquities of Scotland. Edinburgh: 1832. V. 41

SCOTT MONCRIEFF, CHARLES KENNETH 1889-1930

Evensong and Morwe Song. London: 1908. V. 40

SCOTTO, GIACOMO

Alfabeto di Iniziali Tratte dai Libri corali di Siena de Quelli del Duomo, e Della Chiesa di S. Marco di Firenze. Firenze: 1844. V. 38; 40

SCOTTOWE, JOHN

John Scottowe's Alphabet Books. 1974. V. 38; 44

THE SCOURGE in Vindication of the Church of England. London: 1717. V. 41

SCOUTETTEN, RAOUL HENRI JOSEPH

Memoir of the Radical Cure of Club-Foot. Philadelphia: 1840. V. 40

SCRAFTON, LUKE

Reflections on the Government of Indostan. London: 1770. V. 42; 43

SCRANTON STOVE WORKS

Dockash Stoves. Catalog No. 46. 1866-1911. Scranton: 1911. V. 38

SCRAPS About Petroleum. Philadelphia: 1865. V. 46
SCRAPS About Petroleum. Philadelphia: 1866. V. 43

SCRATCHLEY, ARTHUR

Industrial Investment and Emigration, Being a Treatise on Benefit Building Socieites, and on the General Principals of Associations for Land Investment and Colonization. London: 1851. V. 40

Industrial Investment and Emigration, Being a Treatise on Benefit Building Societies, and on the General Principals of Associations for Land Investment and Colonization. London: 1851. V. 40

SCRATTON, BRIDE

England. Paris: 1923. V. 38; 40; 42

SCRAYON, PORTE

Virginia Illustrated: Containing a Visit to the Virginian Canaan and the Adventures of Portre Crayon and His Cousins. New York: 1871. V. 43

SCRIBNER, HENRY S.

A Catalogue of the Spang Collection of Greek and Italian Vases and Etruscan Urns in the Carnegie Museum. Pittsburgh: 1937. V. 40

SCRIPPS, JOHN L.

The Undeveloped Northern Portion of the American Continent. Chicago: 1856. V. 45

SCRIPPS, JOHN LOCKE

The First Published Life of Abraham Lincoln Written in the Year MDCCCLX. Detroit: 1900. V. 41; 42; 46

SCRIPTORES de Re Rustica. Libri de Re Rustica a Nicolao Angelio . . . Recogniti & Typis Excusi . . . Catonis, Varronis, Columellae, Palladij . . . Florentiae: 1521. V. 38

SCRIPTORES Rei Resticae. Paris: 1543. V. 46

SCRIPTORES REI RUSTICAE

Libri de re Rustica. Florence: 1515. V. 40

Libri De Re Rustica. Venice: 1533. V. 41

Libri de re Rustica. M. Catonis Lib. I.M. Tenrentii Varronis Lib. III. I. Junii Moderati Columellae Lib XII. Venice: 1533. V. 39

Scriptores Rei Rustica. 1492. V. 39

Scriptores Rei Rusticae. Florentiae: 1521. V. 39

Scriptores Rei Rusticae. Paris: 1543. V. 40

Scriptores Rei Rvsticae Veteres Latini Cato, Varro, Colvmella, Palladivs Qvibvs Nvnc Accedit Vegetivs de Mvlo . . . Lipsiae: 1735. V. 39

SCRIPTORES Rei Rusticae. Libri de re Rustica M. Catonis Lib. I. M. Terentii Varoonis Lib. III. L. Iunii Moderati Columellae Lib. XII . . . Palladii Lib. XIIII. Venice: 1514. V. 38

SCRIPTURAL History Versified, from the Creation to the Flood. Columbia: 1863. V. 44

SCRIPTURAL Stories, for Very Young Persons. Philadelphia: 1814. V. 40

SCRIPTURE the Friend of Freedom: Exemplified by a Refutation of the Arguments Offered in Defence of Slavery, in a Tract Entitled Scriptural Researches on the Licitness of the Slave Trade. London: 1789. V. 42

SCROGGS, WILLIAM

The Practice of Courts-Leet, and Courts-Baron. London: 1714. V. 38

SCROLLS, Monographs, Ornaments, Crests, Etc. for the Use of Artists, Designers, Engravers & Art Workmen. N.P.: 1876. V. 46

SCROPE, G. P.

Volcanos . The Character of Their Phenomena, Their share in the Structure and Composition of the Surface of the Globe and their Relation to Its Internal Forces. London: 1862. V. 38; 41; 43; 45; 46

SCROPE, GEORGE

The Geology and Extinct Volcanoes of Central of Sussex. London: 1858. V. 43

SCROPE, GEORGE JULIUS DUNCOMBE POULETT

History of the Manor and Ancient Barony of Castle Combe, in the County of Wilts. London: 1852. V. 39

Memoir of the Life of Lord Sydenham, with a Narrative of His Administration in Canada. London: 1843. V. 39

SCROPE, JOHN

Reflections Upon Tithes, Seriously Addressed, in Behalf of the Clergy, to the Gentlemen Associated for the Purpose of Considering an Equivalent for the Payment of Tithes in Kind. Salisbury: 1773. V. 46

SCROPE, JOHN CLERK, BARON

Historical View of the Forms and Powers of the Court of Exchequer in Scotland; to which is added an Appendix containing the Rules of Procedure and certain Minutes of Court relating there. Edinburgh: 1820. V. 37

SCROPE, RICHARD

A Letter to - -, Esq. Occasioned by a Late Misrepresentation of the Circumstances of a Prosecuion Commenced A.D. 1763, by the Proctors of the University of Oxford, Against W. C. -, B.A . . . . Salisbury: 1773. V. 42

SCROPE, WILLIAM

The Art of Deer Stalking. London: 1838. V. 39; 40; 46

The Art of Deer Stalking. London: 1839. V. 38; 39; 43

Days and Nights of Salmon Fishing in the Tweed. London: 1843. V. 38; 39; 40; 41; 43; 46

Days of Deer Stalking in the Scottish Highlands. London: 1883. V. 39

Days of Deer-Stalking in the Scottish Highlands. Glasgow: 1894. V. 39

SCRUTATOR, PSEUD.

The Impractibility of a North-West Passage for Ships, Impartially Considered. London: 1824. V. 40

SCRUTINY. a Quarterly Review. London: 1963. V. 38

SCRYMGEOUR, DANIEL

The Poetry and Poets of Britain from Chaucer to Tennyson . . . Edinburgh: 1860. V. 42

SCUDAMORE, CHARLES

Cases Illustrating and Confirming the Remedial Power of the Inhalation of Iodine and Conium in Tubercular Phthisis and Various Disordered States of the Lungs and Air-Passages. London: 1834. V. 43

A Treatise on the Nature and Cure of Gout . . . London: 1816. V. 42; 46

SCUDAMORE, JAMES

Homer A la Mode. Oxford: 1665. V. 45

SCUDDER, M. L.

American Methodism. Hartford: 1867. V. 44

SCUDDER, S. H.

The Butterflies of the Eastern U.S. and Canada. Cambridge: 1889. V. 38

The Winnipeg Country, or, Roughing It with an Eclipse Party. Boston: 1886. V. 39; 43; 45

SCUDERY, GEORGE DE

Curia Politiae; or, the Apologies of Severall Princes. London: 1654. V. 37; 42

SCUDERY, MADELEINE DE

Almahide; or, the Captive Queen. London: 1677. V. 40; 43

Clelia. London: 1655. V. 38; 40

An Essay Upon Glory. London: 1708. V. 38

Ibrahim. Or the Illustrious Bassa. London: 1652. V. 41

Ibrahim. London: 1652. V. 38

A Triumphant Arch, Erected and Consecrated to the Feminine Sexe . . . London: 1656. V. 42

SCULL, G. D.

The Montressor Journals in Collections of the New York Historical Society for the Year 1881. New York: 1882. V. 44

SCULLY, DENIS

A Statement of the Penal Laws which Aggrieve the Catholics of Ireland with Commentaries. Dublin: 1812. V. 46

SCULLY, W.

A Statement of the Penal Laws Which Aggrieve the Catholics of Ireland, with Commentaries. Dublin: 1812. V. 38

SCULPTURA Historico-Technica; or the History and Art of Engraving. London: 1747. V. 38
SCULPTURA Historico-Technica; or, The History and Art of Engraving. London: 1770. V. 38; 44

SCULPTURE and Architecture. Szukalski: Projects in Design. Chicago: 1929. V. 46

SCULTETUS, BARTHOLOMEAUS

Gnomice de Solariis, Sive Doctrina Practica Tertiae Partis Astronomicae. Gorlitz: 1572. V. 37

SCULTETUS, JOHANN

(Greek text) Armanentarium Chiruvgicum XLIII. Hagae-Comitum: 1656. V. 40

SCUPHAM, PETER

The Gift - Love Poems. Richmond: 1973. V. 38
Under the Barrage: Twenty-Two Poems. 1988. V. 40

SCURFIELD, GEORGE

Cambridge Christmas. Stickful of Nonpareil. Cambridge: 1956. V. 40
A Stickful of Nonpareil. Cambridge: 1956. V. 40; 41; 45

SCURLOCK, DAVID

Thoughts on the Influence of Religion in Civil Government, and Its Tendency to Promote and Preserve the Social Liberty and Rights of Man. London: 1792. V. 42

SEA, Forest and Prairie: Being Stories of Life and Adventure in Canada Past and Present by Boys and Girls in Canada's Schools. Montreal: 1893. V. 45

SEABORG, GLENN T.

Man-Made Transuranium Elements. Englewood Cliffs: 1963. V. 38

SEABRIGHT, THOMAS B.

The Old Pike. A History of the National Road, With Incidents, Accidents, and Anecdotes Thereon. Uniontown: 1894. V. 38

SEABROOK, WILLIAM B.

Jungle Ways. New York: 1931. V. 46

SEABURY, GEORGE J.

An Ode to Lake Bass. New York: 1890. V. 39

SEABURY, JOSEPH STOWE

Reflections of a Moose Hunter. Boston: 1921. V. 39

SEABURY, SAMUEL

A Discourse Delivered in St. James Church, in New-London, On Tuesday the 23rd of December, 1794 . . . New-London: 1795. V. 45
Free Thoughts on the Proceedings of the Continental Congress, Held at Philadelphia Sept. 5, 1774. 1774. V. 40
Free Thoughts on the Proceedings of the Continental Congress, Held at Philadelphia Sept. 5, 1774. New York: 1774. V. 38

SEACOMBE, JOHN

Memoirs: Containing a Genealogical and Historical Account of the . . . House of Stanley, from the Conquest to the Death of James, the Earl of Derby in the Year 1735 . . . . Liverpool: 1741. V. 38; 39; 46
Memoirs, Containing a Genealogical and Historical Account of the Antient and Honourable House of Stanley . . . Manchester: 1767. V. 37; 39

THE SEAFARER. Bangor: 1991. V. 46

SEAFIELD, FRANK

Literature and Curiosities of Dreams . . . London: 1877. V. 45

SEAGREN, ANA MAE

A Day In Fairyland. Printed in Sweden: 1940. V. 42

SEALSFIELD, CHARLES

The Americans as They are, Described in a Tour through the Valley of the Mississippi. London: 1828. V. 42; 46
The Cabin-Book; or, National Characteristics. London: 1852. V. 38; 40; 43
Das Cajutenbuch oder Nationale Charakteristiken. Zurich: 1841. V. 39
Die Vereinigten Staaten von Nordamerika, Nach Ihrem Politischen, Religiosen und Gesellschaftlichen Verhaltnisse Betrachtet. Stuttgart & Tubingen: 1827. V. 38; 40

Life in the New World; or Sketches of American Society. New York: 1844. V. 37; 39; 40

SEALY, GEORGE

A Brief History of the Galveston Wharf Co. Established 1854 . . . N.P.: 1927. V. 38

SEALY, HOWARD

A Lone Sar Bo-Beep and Other Tales. New York: 1885. V. 43

SEALY, THOMAS HENRY

The Porcelain Tower; or, Nine Stories of China. London: 1841. V. 40; 46

SEAMAN, EZRA C.

Essays on the Progress of Nations . . . New York: 1852. V. 43

SEAMAN'S Lyceum of Philadelphia. Philadelphia: 1836. V. 41

SEAMEN, L.

What Miscegenation Is! And What We Are to Expect Now That Mr. Lincoln is Re-Elected. New York: 1865? V. 41

SEARCH for an Albion. Nappanee: 1963. V. 38

SEARCH, SIMON

The Spirit of the Times. London: 1790. V. 38

SEARIGHT, THOMAS B.

The Old Pike: a History of the National Road, with Incidents, and Anecdotes Thereon. Uniontown: 1894. V. 38; 42

SEARLE, AMBROSE

Americans Against Liberty; or an Essay on the Nature and Principles of True Freedom, Shewing that the Decisions and Conduct of the Americans Tend Only to Tyranny and Slavery. London: 1785. V. 39

SEARLE, HENRY

A Treatise on the Tonic System of Treating Affections of the Stomach and Brain. London: 1843. V. 39; 42

SEARLE, JOHN

A New and Improved Method of Constructing Bee-Houses and Bee-Hives, and the Management of the Same. Concord: 1839. V. 42

SEARLE, M.

Turnpikes and Toll-Bars. London: 1930. V. 39; 40

SEARLE, RONALD

Slightly Foxed - but Still Desirable. Ronald Searle's Wicked World of Book Collecting. 1989. V. 45
Slightly Foxed - But Still Desirable Ronald Searle's Wicked World of Book Collecting. London: 1989. V. 42
Slightly Foxed - But Still Desirable. London: 1989. V. 43; 46

SEARLS, NILES

The Diary of a Pioneer and Other Papers. San Francisco: 1940. V. 40

SEARS, EDWARD S.

Faxon's Illustrated Hand-Book of Summer Travel to the Lakes, Springs and Mountains of New Eland and New York. Boston: 1875. V. 39; 40

SEARS, JOSEPH HAMBLEN

Tennessee Printers 1791-1945. Kingsport: 1945. V. 42

SEARS, REUBEN

A Poem, on the Mineral Waters of Ballston and Saratoga. Ballston Spa: 1819. V. 40

SEARS, ROBERT

An Illustrated Description of the Russian Empire. New York: 1855. V. 42
An Illustrated Description of the Russian Empire. New York: 1856. V. 42; 43

SEARSON, JOHN

Mount Vernon, a Poem . . . Philadelphia: 1800. V. 42

A SEASONABLE Recapitulation of Enormous National Crimes and Grievances to Help the Memory, and for the Use and Consideration of All Honest Men and True Britons. London: 1749. V. 41

SEASS, HERBERT RAVENAL

A Carolina Rice Plantation of the Fifties. New York: 1936. V. 37

THE SEATS of the Nobility and Gentry in Great Britain and Wales. Islington: 1787. V. 44; 46

SEAVER, GEORGE

Albert Schweitzer the Man and His Mind. 1947. V. 37
History of the Seaver Family, Formerly of Heath Hall in the County of Armagh, and Their Connections. Dundalk: 1950. V. 38

SEAVER, JAMES E.

Deh-He-Wa-Mis; or a Narrative of the Life of Mary Jemison: Otherwise Called the White Woman . . . Batavia: 1842. V. 38

A Narrative of the Life of Mrs. Mary Jemison, Who Was Taken by the Indians in the Year 1755, and Has Continued to Reside Amongst Them to the Present Time. Canandalgua: 1824. V. 42; 44

A Narrative of the Life of Mrs. Mary Jemison, who Was Taken by the Indians, in the Year 1755 When Only About Twelve Years of Age. Howden: 1826. V. 42; 45

SEAVER, JESSE

The Holcomb(e) Genealogy . . . Philadelphia: 1925. V. 46

SEAWELL, MARY WRIGHT

Our Father's Care. Richmond: 1864. V. 44

SEBASTIAN I, KING OF PORTUGAL

Provisam Sobre as Ordenancas. Colophon: 1574. V. 41

SEBASTIAN, KING OF PORTUGAL

Oratio Habita in Concillio Tridentino. Riva: 1562. V. 38

SEBASTIANI, CLAUDI

Bellum Musicale, Inter Plani et Mensuralis Cantus Reges de Principatu in Musicae Provincia Obtiendo Contendentes. Strasbourg: 1563. V. 40

SEBER, WOLFGANG 1573-1634

Index Vocabulorum in Homeri . . . Heidelberg: 1604. V. 37; 40

SEBISCH, MELCHIOR 1578-1674

Dissertatio de Senectutis et Senum Statu ac Conditione. Argentorati: 1645. V. 40

SEBRIGHT, GEORGIANA MARY MUIR MAC KENZIE, LADY

Travels in the Slavonic Provinces of Turkey in Europe. London: & New York: 1866. V. 46

SEBRIGHT, JOHN SAUNDERS

The Art of Improving the Breeds of Domestic Animals. In a letter addressed to the Right Hon. Sir Joseph Banks, K. B. London: 1809. V. 37

Observations Upon Hawking . . . London: 1828. V. 39

SECCHI, NICCOLO

Gli Inganni. Comedia del Signor N. S. Recitata in Milano lAnno 1547, Dinanzi alla Maesta del Re Filippo. Venice: 1587. V. 37

SECCOMBE, CAPTAIN

Army and Navy Drolleries. Printed in Colours by Kronheim. London: (c. 1870). V. 37

SECCOMBE, JOHN

A Sermon Occasioned by the Death of the Honorable Abigail Belcher, Late Consrot of Jonathan Belcher, Esq., Late Lieutenant Governor and Commander in Chief, and His Majesty's Chief Justice of His Province of Nova-Scotia, delivered at Halifax . . . Boston: 1772. V. 40

SECCOMBE, JOSEPH

Some Occasional Thoughts on the Influence of the Spirit. Boston: 1742. V. 43; 44

A Specimen of the Harmony of Wisdom and Felicity, in Relation to Our Civil, Moral and Spiritual Behaviour. Boston: 1743. V. 40

SECCOMBE, MAJOR

Military Misreadings of Shakspeare (sic). London. V. 46

SECCOMBE, THOMAS STRONG 1840-1899

Army and Navy Birthday Book for Children. Routledge: 1880. V. 40

SECHSICH Weychbild und Lehenrecht itzt Auffs Naw Nach den Warhafften Alden Exemplarn and Texten mit Vleis Corrigirt Sampt eim Nawen Register Oder Remissorio Uber Diese Swey Bucher und den Sachsenspiegel Gemacht. Leipzig: 1537. V. 40

SECKEL, DIETRICH

Emakimono. New York: 1959. V. 38; 39; 41; 44

SECKENDORF, VEIT LUDWIG VON 1626-1692

Ausfuhrliche Historie des Lutherthums Und der Heilsamen Reformation, Welche der Theure Martin Luther Binnen Dreyfzig Jahren Glucklich Ausgefuhret. Leipzig: 1714. V. 38

SECKENDORF, VEIT LUDWING VON 1626-1692

Compendium Seckendorfianum oder Kurzgefaszte Reformations-Geschichte aus des Hern Veit Ludwigs on Seckendorf Historia Lutheranismi zur Allgemeinen Ebauung Zusammen Gezogen . . . Franckfurt & Leipzig: 1755. V. 38

SECKENDORFF, BARON DE

(Caption title) Discours Prononce a l'Assemblee Generale du 29 Mai 1787. V. 39

SECKER, THOMAS

An Answer to Dr. Mayhew's Observations on the Charter and Conduct of the Society for the Propagation of the Gospel in Foreign Parts. Boston: 1764. V. 38

A Sermon Preached Before the Incorporated Society for the Propagation of the Gospel in Foreign parts; at Their Anniversary Meeting . . . London: 1741. V. 38

A SECOND Book of Bookplates. Muscatine: 1942. V. 39

THE SECOND Book of the Authors Club Liber Scriptorum. New York: 1921. V. 37

A SECOND Letter to the Right Honourable the Earl of B****. London: 1761. V. 45

THE SECOND Mystery Book. New York: (1940). V. 37
THE SECOND Mystery Book. New York: 1940. V. 42

A SECOND Pagan Anthology. New York: 1919. V. 41; 42; 43; 44

SECOND Political Dialogue Between the Celebrated Statues of Pasquin and Masorio at Rome . . . London: 1737. V. 45

A SECOND Postscript to a Late Pamphlet, Entitled, a Letter to Mr. Almon, in Matter of Libel. London: 1770. V. 38

THE SECRET History of Persia. London: 1745. V. 43; 46

THE SECRET History of the Court and Cabinet of St. Cloud in a Series of Letters from a Gentleman at Paris to a Nobleman in London. London: 1895. V. 46

SECRET History of the Court of James the First . . . Edinburgh: 1811. V. 43

THE SECRET History of the Green Room; Containing Authentic and Entertaining Memoirs of the Actors and Actresses in the Three Theatres Royal. London: 1793. V. 42

THE SECRET History of the Green Rooms. London: 1792. V. 38

THE SECRET History of the Jubilee, Celebrated at Rome in the Year 1750. London: 1753. V. 39

THE SECRET History of the Most Renowned Q. Elizabeth & the E. of Essex. London: 1708. V. 37; 42; 44

SECRET Memoirs of the Late Mr. Duncan Campbel, the Famous Deaf and Dumb Gentleman. London: 1732. V. 41

SECRETAN, E.

Catalogue of the Celebrated Collection of Paintings by Modern and Old Masters and of Water-Colors and Drawings Formed by Mr. E. Secretan, Which Will be Sold by Auction . . . On Monday, first of July 1889 . . . Paris: 1889. V. 41; 46

SECRETS of the Courts of Europe from the 16th to the 19th Century. Philadelphia: 1900. V. 46

SECRETS Pour Teindre la Fleur d'Immortelle en Diverses Couleurs, Avec la maniere de La Cultiver. Paris: 1690. V. 39

SECUNDUS, JOANNES NICOLAI 1511-1536

Basia, or the Kisses of Joannes SEcundus Nicolaius of the Hague. London: 1731. V. 46

Kisses. London: 1778. V. 40

SECUNDUS, JOHANNES NICOLAI 1511-1536

Kisses. London: 1803. V. 46

Kisses. London: 1804. V. 40

SECURE a Home! A Lot for Nothing. A Perfect Deed to Every Man, Woman and Child that Will Apply for It in Golden City . . . Cincinnati: 1860's. V. 39

SEDBERRY, WILLIAM R.

Fellow Citizen of the Sixtieth Representative District, Composed of the Counties of McLennan and Bosque. Waco?: 1861. V. 39

SEDDON, JOHN

The Penman's Paradise, Both Pleasant and Profitable. Stuttgart: 1966. V. 46

Penmans Paradis both Pleasant and Profitable. London: 1694-95. V. 37

SEDDON, JOHN P.

King Rene's Honeymoon Cabinet. London: 1898. V. 42

SEDGWICK, ADAM

A Memorial by the Trustees of Cowgill Chapel . . . (with) Supplement . . . Cambridge: 1868-70. V. 45

Preface to the Catalogue of the Cambrian and Silurian Fossils in the Geological Museum of the University of Cambridge . . . Cambridge: 1872. V. 39; 40

SEDGWICK, ANNE DOUGLAS

The Little French Girl. Boston: 1924. V. 42; 44

The Little French Girl. London: 1924. V. 42

SEDGWICK, CATHERINE MARIA

Clarence: or a Tale of Our Times. New York: 1848. V. 38

Hope Leslie; or Early Times in the Massachusetts. New York: 1827. V. 39; 40; 44; 45

Letters From Abroad to Kindred at Home. London: 1841. V. 41

Letters From Abroad to Kindred at Home. New York: 1841. V. 45

The Linwoods' or 'Sixty Years Since' in America . . . New York: 1835. V. 40; 41; 43; 44

Live and Let Live; or, Domestic Service Illustrated. New York: 1837. V. 45

A Love Token for Children . . . New York: 1838. V. 44

A New England Tale. New York: 1822. V. 46

SEDGWICK, JAMES

Remarks, Critical and Miscellaneous, on the Commentaries of Sir William Blackstone. London: 1800. V. 45

SEDGWICK, JOHN

Correspondence of John Sedgwick, Major-General. N.P.: 1902, 1903. V. 40

SEDGWICK, SUSAN ANNE LIVINGSTON RIDLEY

Allen Prescott: or, the Fortunes of a New England Boy. New York: 1834. V. 43

SEDGWICK, THEODORE

A Memoir of the Life of William Livingston, Member of Congress in 1774, 1775 and 1776 . . . New York: 1833. V. 46

Thoughts on the Proposed Annexation of Texas to the United States. New York: 1844. V. 37; 38; 40; 42

SEDGWICK, WILLIAM

Animadversions Upon a Letter and paper, First Sent to His Highness by Certain Gentlemen and Others in Wales . . . London: 1656. V. 42; 44

SEDGWICKE, WILLIAM

Zions Deliverance and Her Friends Duty . . . London: 1642. V. 41; 44

SEDLEY, CHARLES

Asmodeus; or, the Deveil in London: a Sketch. London: 1808. V. 46

Bellamira, or the Mistress. London: 1687. V. 38; 42; 44; 45; 46

The Miscellaneous Works . . . London: 1702. V. 45

The Mulberry-Garden. London: 1668. V. 38

The Mulberry-Garden, a Comedy. London: 1675. V. 45

The Poetical Works of the Honourable Sir Charles Sedley Baronet, and His Speeches in Parliament . . . London: 1707. V. 45

The Works in Prose and Verse. With Memoirs of the Author's Life writ by an Eminent Hand. London: 1722. V. 37

SEDULIUS

Mirabilium Divinorum Libri. Paschale Carmen et Hymni Duo. Halle: 1704. V. 40

SEDWICK, B. F.

Baptist Pretentions . . . Met and Confuted. Nashville: 1876. V. 38

SEE, R. R. M.

English Pastels, 1750-1830. London: 1911. V. 42

SEEBOHM, H.

The Geographical Distribution of the Family Charadriidae, or the Plovers, Sand-Pipers, Snipes and Their Allies. London: 1888. V. 41

SEEBOHM, HENRY

The Birds of Siberia. London: 1901. V. 40; 43; 45

Coloured Figures of the Eggs of British Birds. Sheffield. V. 43

The Geographical Distribution of the Family Charadriidae . . . London. V. 42

The Geographical Distribution of the Family Charadriidae, or the Plovers, Sandpipers, Snipes and Their Allies. London: 1887. V. 38; 40

The Geographical Distribution of all the Family Charadriidae, or the Plovers, Sandpipers, Snipes and Their Allies. London: 1887-88. V. 37; 39; 42

The Geographical Distribution of the Family Charadriidae, or the Plovers, Sand-Pipers, Snipes and their Allies. London: 1888. V. 37; 38; 40

A History of British Birds. London: 1883-85. V. 37; 39; 42; 46

A History of British Birds. London: 1896. V. 38

A History of British Birds. London: 1883-85, 1896. V. 37

A Monograph of the Turdidae, or Family of Thrushes. London: 1898-1902. V. 39

A Monograph of the Turdidae, or Family of Thrushes. London: 1902. V. 38; 39

Siberia In Europe: a Visit to the Valley of the Petchora in North-East Russia with Descriptions of the Natural History. London: 1880. V. 45; 46

Siberia in Asia. London: 1882. V. 42; 43

Siberia in Asia: A Visit to the Valley of the Yenesay in East Siberia. London: 1901. V. 45

SEEBOHM, HUGH E.

On the Structure of Greek Tribal Society. London: 1895. V. 43

The Picture of Kebes the Theban. London: 1906. V. 41

SEECHI, GIAMPETRO

Monumenti Inediti d'un Antico Sepolcro Greco Scoperto in Roma. Rome: 1843. V. 45

SEEGER, ALAN

Letters and Diary. New York: 1917. V. 37

Poems. New York: 1916. V. 37

SEEGER, EUGEN

Chicago. Entwickelung, Zerstorung und Wideraufban der Bunderstadt . . . Chicago: 1872. V. 43

THE SEEKERS. Worcester: 1969. V. 46

SEELEY, B.

Stowe: a Description of the Magnificent House and GArdens of the Right Honourable Richard Grenville Temple . . . Embellished with a General Plan of the Gardens . . . London: 1769. V. 45; 46

Stowe: a Description of the Magnificent Gardens. London: 1756. V. 45

Stowe: a Description of the Magnificent House and Gardens with the Description of the Inside of the House. London: 1766. V. 45

SEELEY, CHARLES SUMNER

The Lost Canyon of the Toltecs. Chicago: 1893. V. 46

SEELEY, L. B.

Mrs. Thrale, Afterwards Mrs. Piozzi. London: 1891. V. 38

SEELEY, ROBERT BENTON

Remedies Suggested for Some of the Evils Which Constitute 'The Perils of the Nation'. London: 1844. V. 43

SEELY, HOWARD

A Lone Star Bo-Peep and Other Tales of Texas Ranch Life. New York: 1885. V. 43

SEELY, JOHN B.

The Wonders of Elora. London: 1824. V. 37; 44

SEEMAN, BERTHOLD

History of the Isthmus of Panama. Panama: 1867. V. 38; 39; 46

Viti: an Account of a Government Mission to the Vitian or Fijian Islands in the Years 1860-61. Cambridge: 1862. V. 41

SEEMANN, B. 1825-1870

Flora Vitiensis. London: 1865-73. V. 41

Flora Vitiensis, a Description of the Plants of the Viti or Fiji Islands. London: 1977. V. 37

SEEMANN, BERTHOLD

Flora Vitiensis, a Description of the Plants of the Viti or Fijii Islands. London: 1865-73, 1977. V. 38

Narrative of the Voyage of the H.M.S. Herald During the Years 1845-51 . . . London: 1853. V. 45

Viti: an Account of a Government Mission to the Vitian or Fijian Islands in the Years 1860-61. Cambridge: 1862. V. 46

SEFERIS, GEORGE

(Title in Greek). Poems. Athens: 1964. V. 46

SEGAL, LORE

Other People's Houses. New York: 1964. V. 44

SEGAR, JOSEPH EGGLESTON

Speech of Joseph Segar, Esq., of the York District in the House of Delegates of Virginia, March 30th, 1861, on the Resolution of the Senate Directing the Governor of Virginia to Seize . . . Richmond?: 1861. V. 42

SEGAR, NATHANIEL

A Brief Narrative of the Captivity and Sufferings of . . . New York: 1940. V. 45

SEGARD, W.

Picturesque Views of Public Edifices in Paris. London: 1814. V. 38; 44; 46

SEGER, JOHN H.

Tradition of the Cheyenne Indians. 1905. V. 42

Tradition of the Cheyenne Indians. Darlington: 1905. V. 38

SEGNERI, PAOLO

Eposicion del Miserere Dado a Considerar con Cuydado a Toda Alma Devota, Practica de interior Union con Dios, Sacada de los Psalmos, y Apologia por la Concordia entre la quietud . . . Madrid: 1699. V. 37

SEGNERI, PAULO

Incredulus Non Excusatus, Opus . . . Cologne: 1894. V. 46

SEGUIER, JEAN FRANCOIS

Bibliotheca Botanica, Sive Catalogus Auctorum et Librorum Omnium Qui de Re Botanica, de Medicamentis ex Vegetabilibus Paratis . . . The Hague: 1740. V. 43

SEGUIN, E. C.

Medical Thermometry and Human Temperature. New York: 1876. V. 42

SEGUIN, EDWARD

Idiocy: and Its Treatment by the Physiological Method. New York: 1866. V. 42

Medical Thermometry and Human Temperature. New York: 1876. V. 43

SEGUIN, L. G.

A Picturesque Tour in Picturesque Lands: France, Spain, Germany, Switzerland, Holland, Belgium, Tyrol, Italy, Scandanavia. London: 1881. V. 44

SEGUIN, LISBETH GOOCH

Mr. Caroli. London: 1881. V. 39; 40

SEGUR, PHILIP DE, COUNT

History of the Expedition to Russia, Undertaken by the Emperor Napoleon, in the Year 1812. London: 1825. V. 40; 42

SEGUR, SOPHIE ROSTOPCHINE, COMTESSEE DE 1799-1874

Old French Fairy Tales. Philadelhpia: 1920. V. 43

SEIDEL, MAX

Bruegel. New York: 1971. V. 41

SEIDEL, WOLFGANG 1492-1562

Ob der Abgestorben Seelen so Bey Christo sein Aigentlich Einander Erkennen . . . Ingolstadt: 1551. V. 45

SEIDELIUS, BRUNO

Commentarius Didascalicus, Valde Eruditus et Perspicuus de Corpore Animato . . . Hanover: 1594. V. 40

SEIDLITZ, W. VON

A History of Japanese Colour-Prints. London: 1910. V. 39

A History of Japanese Color-Prints. Philadelphia: 1920. V. 44

SEIDMANN-FREUD, TOM

The Magic Boat. Berlin: 1929. V. 41

SEIKISHIRO, GOTO

Kami-o-Suku-Mura: Villages of Paper Making. 1973. V. 42

SEILHAMER, GEORGE O.

History of the American Theatre, 1749-1797. Philadelphia: 1888-91. V. 40; 41

SEILLER, HIERONYMUS

Von Den Flussen Des Haupts und Dero Vrsachen Wie Sich Dafur Zu Hutten Auch Wie Solchen . . . Lignitz: 1612. V. 40; 44

SEIROKU, NOMA

The Arts of Japan. Tokyo: 1966-67. V. 39; 41

SEITZ, A.

Die Gross-Schmetterlinge der Erde, Band 6. Die Amerikanischen Spinner und Schwarmer. Stuttgart,: 1940. V. 39

Macrolepidoptera of the World, Volume 3, Palaearctic Noctuae. Stuttgart: 1914. V. 37; 39

The Macrolepidoptera of the World. Stuttgart: 1906-44. V. 38

The Macrolepidoptera of the World. Supplement to Volume 2, Palaearctic Bombydies and Sphingides. Stuttgart: 1934. V. 37

Macrolepidoptera of the World. Volume 14: African Bombyces and Sphinges. Stuttgart: 1930. V. 37

Macrolepidoptera of the World, Volume 4, Palaearctic Geometrae. Stuttgart: 1912. V. 37; 39

SEITZ, DON C.

A Chapter on Autography. New York: 1926. V. 39

Paul Jones, His Exploits in English Seas During 1778-1780. New York: 1917. V. 46

SEKIGAWA, SAKIO

The Kelmscott Press and Japan: an Illustrated Bibliography. Tokyo: 1982. V. 41

SELBY, CHARLES

Barnaby Rudge. A Domestic Drama in Three Acts. London: 1875. V. 40

Maximums and Speciments of William Muggins, Natural Philosopher and Citizen of the World. London: 1841. V. 38

SELBY, HUBERT

Last Exit to Brooklyn. N: 1964. V. 45

Last Exit to Brooklyn. New York: 1964. V. 42

SELBY LOWNDES, M. W.

Two Month's Leave: a Shoot in the Himalayas, May & June 1924. London: 1924. V. 39

SELBY, P. J.

A History of British Forest Trees, Indigenous and Introduced. London: 1842. V. 46

SELBY, PRIDEAUX JOHN

The Natural History of Pigeons. Edinburgh. V. 38

The Natural History of Parrots. Edinburgh: 1836. V. 37

The Natural History of Pigeons. Edinburgh: 1835. V. 37

SELDEN, ALMIRA

Effusions of the Heart, Contained in a Number of Original Poetical Pieces, on Various Subjects. Bennington: 1820. V. 40

Effusions of the Hert, Contained in a Number of Original Poetical Pieces, on Various Subjects. Bennington: 1820. V. 41

SELDEN, AMBROSE

Love and Folly. London: 1749. V. 41; 42

Love and Folly. London: 1749. V. 43

SELDEN, HENRY R.

Rights of Women Under the Late Constitutional Amendments. New York: 1873. V. 44

SELDEN, JOHN 1584-1654

De Dis Syris Syntagmanta II. Adversaria Nempe de Numinibus Commentitijs in Vetere Instrvmento Memoratis . . . London: 1617. V. 45

Fleta, Seu Commentarius Juris Anglicani Sic Nuncupatus, Sub Edwardo Rege Primo. London: 1685. V. 39

The Historie of Tithes. London: 1618. V. 41; 42; 45

The Historie of Tithes. N.P.: 1618. V. 40

De Jure Naturali et Gentium, Juxta Disciplinam Ebraeorum, Libri Septem. Lipsiae & Francofurti: 1695. V. 43

Mare Clausum seu Dominio Maris. London: 1635. V. 38; 40

Mare Clausem seu de Dominio Maris Libri Duo. Londini: 1636. V. 46

Mare Clausum; The Right and Dominion of the Sea in Two Books . . . London: 1663. V. 42

Of the Dominion, or, Ownership of the Sea. (bound with) Dominium Maris . . . Expressing the Title Which the Venetians Pretend . . . London: 1652. V. 39; 46

Of the Judicature in Parliaments, a Posthumous Treatise. London: 1681? V. 40

Of Judicature in Parliaments, a Posthumous Treatise . . . London: 1689? V. 42

Opera Omnia, tam Edita Quam Inedita. London: 1726. V. 40

The Priviledges of the Baronage of England, When they Sit in Parliament. London: 1642. V. 38; 40; 46

De Synedriis & Praefecturis Juridicis Veterum Ebraecorum Liber Secundus. Londini: 1653. V. 40

Table-Talk; Being the Discourses of John Selden, Esq . . . London: 1689. V. 37; 40; 46

Table Talk: Being Discourses of John Selden, Esq. London: 1696. V. 38; 40

Table Talk: Being the Discourses; or His Sense of Various Matters of Weight and High Consequence; Relating Especially to Religion and State. London: 1716. V. 39

Table Talk: Being the Discourses of . . . etc. London: 1797. V. 41

The Table Talk of John Selden. Chiswick;: 1818. V. 43

The Table-Talk of John Selden, Esq. London: 1847. V. 39

Theanthrop(o)s, or, God Made Man. London: 1661. V. 38; 40

Titles of Honor. London: 1614. V. 40; 41

Titles of Honor. London: 1631. V. 38; 41; 45

Titles of Honor. London: 1672. V. 41

Tituli Honorum . . . Francofurti: 1696. V. 45

Tracts: I: Jani Anglorum Facies Altera . . . II: England's Epinomis. III: Of the Original of Ecclesiastical Jurisdictions of Testaments. IV: Of the Disposition or Administration of Intestates Goods. London: 1683. V. 38

SELDEN, PERRY

History of Washington County. Address by Hon. Perry Selden, Delivered July 4, 1876, Blair, Nebraska. Nebraska: 1876. V. 41

SELDEN, RICHARD E.

The Newest Keepsake for 1840. Norwich: 1840. V. 40

SELDER, EDUARD F.

Josef Hoffman: the Architectural Work. Princeton: 1985. V. 46

SELDES, GILBERT

The Seven Lively Arts. New York: 1924. V. 45

SELDIS, HENRY J.

The Sculpture of Jack Zajac. Los Angeles: 1960. V. 41

SELDON, JOHN 1584-1654

Tracts ... the First Entituled, Jani Anglorum Facies Altera, Rendered into English, with Large Notes Thereupon by Redman Westcot, Gent. The Second England's Epinomis. The Third, of the Original of Ecclesiastical Jurisdcitions . . . The Fourth, of the . . . London: 1683. V. 42

SELDON, RICHARD E.

The Newest Keep-Sake for Eighteen Hundred and Thirty-Nine. Boston: 1839. V. 37; 40

A **SELECT** and Impartial Account of the Lives, Behaviour and Dying Words of the Most Remarkable Convicts, from the Year 1700, Down to the Present Time. London: 1745. V. 39

A **SELECT** Collection of Novels and Histories. London: 1729. V. 44

SELECT Collection of Old Plays. London: 1825. V. 40

A **SELECT** Collection of Original Scottish Airs for the Voice with Introductory and Concluding Symphonies & Accompaniments for the Piano Forte, Violin and Violincello . . . Edinburgh: 1801-02. V. 37

A **SELECT** Collection of Poems . . . Edinburgh: 1768. V. 39; 40; 42; 45

A **SELECT** Collection of the Most Interesting Letters on the Government, Liberty and Constitution of England. London: 1763/1765. V. 38

SELECT Criminal Trials at Justice-Hall in the Old Bailey. Edinburgh: 1803. V. 38

SELECT Essays from the Encyclopedy, Being the Most Curious, Entertaining and Instructive Parts of that Very Extensive Work. London: 1772. V. 40

SELECT Essays in Anglo-American Legal History. Boston: 1907. V. 43

SELECT Essays on Commerce, Mines, Agriculture, Fisheries, and Other Useful Subjects. London: 1754. V. 38

SELECT Essays on Husbandry. Edinburgh: 1767. V. 37; 38; 40; 42; 44

SELECT Letters Taken from Fog's Weekly Journal. London: 1732. V. 39

SELECT Pieces on Commerce, Natural Philosophy, Morality, Antiquities, History, etc. London: 1754. V. 37

SELECT Portions of Psalms and Hymns for the Use of Fitz Roy Chapel. London: 1822. V. 44

SELECT Portions of Psalms, Taken from the Old and New Versions, and that of Mr. Merrick; to Which are Added a Few Hymns from Approved Authors . . . Halifax: 1798. V. 43

SELECT Tales and Fables with Prudential Maxims and Other Little Lessons of Morality in Prose and Verse Equally Instructive and Entertaining for the Use of Both Sexes . . . London: 1780. V. 41; 42

SELECT Tracts relating to the Colonies . . . London: 1732. V. 39; 43

SELECT Views in Italy, with Topographical and Historical Descriptions in English and French. London: 1796. V. 43

SELECTA Epigrammata Ex Florilegio Et Alia Qvaedam Ex Veteribvs Poetis Comicis Potissimum, Latino Item Carmine Conuersa. Rome: 1608. V. 40

SELECTA Poemata Italorum Qui Latine Scripserunt. Londini: 1740. V. 39

THE **SELECTED** Poetry Which Appeared in the 'Shieffield Mercury' for the Year 1825. Sheffield: 1826. V. 44

A **SELECTION** from the Harleian Miscellany of Tracts Which Principally Regard the English History Many Referred to by Hume. London: 1793. V. 39; 40

A **SELECTION** of Anancy Stories. Kingston: 1899. V. 37

A **SELECTION** of Curious Articles from the Gentleman's Magazine. London: 1809. V. 40
A SELECTION of Curious Articles from the Gentleman's Magazine. London: 1814. V. 40

A **SELECTION** of Sacred Poetry, etc. With Specimens of Music, Used in Teaching the Blind. Glasgow: 1840. V. 40

A **SELECTION** of the Most Favorite Scots Songs, Chiefly Pastoral. London: 1772-79. V. 40

A **SELECTION** of War Lyrics. New York: 1866. V. 37; 38; 40

SELER, EDUARD

Mexican and Central American Antiquities, Calendar, Systems and History. Washington: 1904. V. 42; 44

SELF-DELUSION; or, Adelaide d'Hauteroche: a Tale. London: 1823. V. 38

SELFRIDGE, THOMAS O.

Reports and Explorations and Surveys to Ascertain the Practicabilty of a Ship-Canal Between the Atlantic and Pacific Oceans by the Way of the Isthmus of Darien. Washington: 1874. V. 37; 39; 40; 42; 43

Trial of Thomas O. Selfridge, Attorney at Law Before the Hon. Isaac Parker, Esquire for Killing Charles Austin, on the PUblic Exchange, in Boston, August 4th, 1806. Boston: 1806. V. 38; 46

SELIGMAN, G. SAVILLE

Domestic Needlework. London: 1926. V. 43

SELIGMAN, GERMAIN

The Drawings of Georges Seurat. New York: 1947. V. 46

SELIGMAN, JOHANN MICHAEL

Verzameling van Uitlandsche en Zeldzaame Vogelen, Benevens Eenige Vreemde Dieren en Plantgewassen . . . Amsterdam: 1772-81. V. 39

SELIGMANN, HERBERT J.

D. H. Lawrence: an American Inerpretation. New York: 1924. V. 41; 42; 43

SELKIRK, LORD

Lord Selkirk's Diary, 1803-04. Toronto: 1958. V. 37; 45

SELKIRK, THOMAS DOUGLAS, 5TH EARL OF

Observations on the Present State of the Highlands of Scotland. London: 1805. V. 37; 39; 41; 42; 43

On the Necessity of a More Effectual System of National Defence, and the Means of Establishing the Permanent Security of the Kingdom . . . London: 1808. V. 43; 46

SELKIRK, THOMAS DOUGLAS, EARL OF

A Narrative of Occurrences in the Indian Countries of North America, Since the Connexion of the Right Hon. the Earl of Selkirk with the Hudson's Bay Company . . . London: 1817. V. 46

SELLARS, WILFRED

Philosophical Perspectives. Springfield: 1967. V. 45

SELLER, ABEDNEGO

The Antiquities of Palmyra. London: 1696. V. 37; 40; 45

SELLER, JOHN

A Pocket Book. Containing Several Choice Collections in Arethmetick, Astronomy, Geometry, Surveying, Dialling, Navigation, Astrology . . . London: 1706? V. 41

SELLERS, CHARLES COLEMAN

Benjamin Franklin in Portraiture. New Haven: 1962. V. 46

SELLERS, W. W.

A History of Marion County, South Carolina, from Its Earliest Time to the Present, 1901. Columbia: 1902. V. 42

SELLEY, JOHN B.

The Wonders of Elora. London: 1824. V. 46

SELLHEIM, HUGO 1871-1936

Topographischer Atlas zur Normalen und Pathologischen Anatomie des Weiblichen Beckens . . . Leipzig: 1900. V. 43

SELLON, BAKER JOHN 1762-1835

An Analysis of the Practice of the Courts of King's Bench and Common Pleas. London: 1789. V. 40

SELOUS, EDMUND

Bird Watching. London: 1901. V. 44; 45

SELOUS, FREDERICK COURTENEY 1851-1917

African Nature Notes and Reminiscences. London: 1908. V. 37; 38; 39; 45; 46

A Hunter's Wanderings in Africa . . . London: 1881. V. 45

A Hunter's Wanderings in Africa. London: 1893. V. 38

A Hunter's Wanderings in Africa. London: 1907. V. 37; 43

Recent Hunting Trips in British North America. London: 1907. V. 37; 38; 40; 43

Sport and Travel, East and West. London: 1901. V. 37; 38; 43

Sunshine and Storm in Rhodesia. London: 1896. V. 38; 39; 40; 42; 43

Travel and Adventure in South East Africa. London: 1890. V. 39

Travel and Adventure in South East Africa. London: 1893. V. 38; 39; 40; 41; 43; 44; 45; 46

SELOUS, FREDERICK COURTNEY 1851-1917

A Hunter's Wanderings in Africa. London: 1890. V. 46

SELOUS, PERCY

Travel and Big Game. London: 1897. V. 42

SELTZER, C. A.

The Ranchman. 1919. V. 46

SELVA, LORENZO 1530-1591

Della Metamorfosi Cioe Trasformatione del Virtuso. Orvieto: 1582. V. 43

SELWAY, G. UPTON

A Mid-Lothian Village. Edinburgh: 1890. V. 38

SELWAY, N. C.

The Golden Age of Coaching and Sport as Depicted by James Pollard. Leigh-on-Sea: 1972. V. 39

James Pollard 1792-1867. Leigh-on-Sea: 1965. V. 39; 42

The Regency Road, the Coaching Prints of James Pollard. London: 1957. V. 37; 42

SELWOOD, SAMUEL

A Narrative of the Proceedings of the Committee for Preservation of the Customes in the Case of Mr. George Cony, Merchant. London: 1655. V. 41

SELWYN-BROWN, ARTHUR

The Physician throughout the Ages. New York: 1938. V. 39; 45

SELWYN, CECIL EDWARD

Prairie Patchwork, or, Western Poems for Western People. Winnipeg: 1910. V. 43; 45

SELWYN, JOHN RICHARDSON

Melanesian Mission. Ludlow: 1877. V. 39

SELWYN, WILLIAM

An Abridgement of the Law of Nisi Prius. Philadelphia: 1807-8. V. 39

SELYE, HANS

The Physiology and Pathology of Exposure to Stress. Montreal: 1950. V. 43

SELZ, JEAN

XIX Century Drawings and Watercolours. Milan: 1960. V. 41

SEMEDO, ALVAREZ

The History of that Great and Renowned Monarchy of China. London: 1655. V. 45

SEMEDO, P. ALVAREZ

Histoire Universell de la Chine, Avec l'Histoire de la Guerre des Tartares... Lyon: 1667. V. 39

SEMI-CENTENNIAL Memoir of the Harlan and Hollingsworth Company, 1836-1886. Wilmington: 1886. V. 39

THE SEMI-CENTENNIAL of Anaesthesia, October 16, 1846, October 16, 1896. Boston: 1897. V. 41

SEMMEDO, ALVARO

The History of that Great and Renowned Monarchy of China. London: 1655. V. 44

SEMMEDO, F. ALVAREZ

The History of that Great and Renowned Monarchy of China... London: 1655. V. 41

SEMMELWEIS, I. P.

Offener Brief an Sammtliche Professoren der Geburtshilfe. Ofen. Budapest: 1862. V. 44; 45

SEMMES, RAPHAEL

The Campaign of General Scott in the Valley of Mexico. Cincinnati: 1852, V. 37

Captains and Mariners of Early Maryland. Baltimore: 1937. V. 46

The Cruise of the Alabama and the Sumter. New York: 1864. V. 45

Memoirs of Service Afloat, During the War Between the States. Baltimore: 1869. V. 42

Memoirs of Service Afloat During the War Between the States. Baltimore: 1869. V. 38; 42

My Adventures Afloat. London: 1869. V. 42; 46

Service Afloat; or, the Remarkable Career of the Confederate Cruisers Sumter and Alabama, During the War Between the States. Baltimore: 1887. V. 38

Service Afloat Sumter and Alabama During the War Between the States. London: 1887. V. 37

SEMON, RICHARD

In the Australian Bush and on the Coast of the Coral Sea. London: 1899. V. 44; 46

SEMONIDES OF AMORGOS

Women: a Poem. 1983. V. 40

Women: a Poem. Brisbane: 1983. V. 39; 45

SEMPER, GOTTFRIED

Der Stil in den Technischen und Tektonischen Kunsten, Oder Praktische Aesthetik. Ein Handbuch fur Techniker, Kunstler und Kunstfreunde. Vol. 1: Die Textile Kunst fur Sich Betrachtet und in Beziehung zur Kaukunst. Vol. 2: Keramik, Tektonik, Stereotomie... Frankfurt: Verlag fur Kunst: 1863. V. 41

SEMPLE, AGNES SOPHIA

Thoughts on Education. London: 1812. V. 45

SEMPLE, GEORGE

A Treatise on Building In Water. Dublin: 1776. V. 42; 44

SEMPLE, MISS

The Costume of the Netherlands, Displayed in Thirty Coloured Engravings after Drawings from nature... London: 1817. V. 39

SEMPLE, ROBERT

A Journey through Spain and Italy to Naples; and Thence to Smyrna and Constantinople... London: 1807. V. 45

Observations on a Journey through Spain and Italy to Naples... London: 1807. V. 44

Sketch of the Present State of Caracas. London: 1811. V. 40

SEMPLE, ROBERT B.

A History of the Rise and Progress of the Baptists in Virginia. Richmond: 1810. V. 40

SEN, SANSAR CHANDER

A Short Account of His Highness the Maharajah of Jaipur and His Country. Ajmer: 1902. V. 40

SENAC DE MEILHAN, GABRIEL

Considerations sur les Richesses et le Luxe. Amsterdam, Paris: 1787. V. 38

SENAULT, JEAN FRANCOIS 1601-1672

The Use of the Passions. London: 1649. V. 42

SENAULT, L.

Heures Nouvelles Tirees de la Sainte Ecriture... Paris: 1670. V. 38

SENAULT, LOUIS

Livre d'Ecriture Representant Naivement la Beaute de Tous les Caracteres Financieres... Paris: 1670. V. 40

Petit Office de la Ste. Vierge, Elevations Durant la Ste. Messe et Autres Prieres Tirees de la Ste. Paris & Versailles: 1670. V. 40

SENDAK, MAURICE

Atomics for Millions. New York: 1947. V. 46

The Cunning Little Vixen. New York: 1985. V. 37; 40

In the Night Kitchen. London: 1971. V. 44

Nutcracker. New York: 1984. V. 42

Pictures by Maurice Sendak. New York: 1971. V. 39; 44

Pictures by Maurice Sendak. (New York: 1971). V. 37

SENDEL, NATHANIEL

Historia Succinorum Corpora Aliena Involventium et Naturae Opere Pictorum et Caelatorum ex Regiis Augustorum Cimeliis Dresdae Conditis... Leipzig: 1742. V. 43

SENDER, RAMON

Counter-Attack in Spain. 1937. V. 43

SENDIVOGIUS, MICHAEL

A New Light of Alchymie... London: 1650. V. 41

SENEBIER, JEAN

Ueber die Vorhemsten Mikroskopischen Entdeckungen in den Drey Naturreichen, Nebst ihrem Einfluss aud die Vervollkommnung des Menschlichen Geistes. Leipzig: 1795. V. 37

SENECA Canoe and Camp Cookery: a Practical Cook Book for Canoeists, Corinthian Sailors and Outers. New York: 1885. V. 39

SENECA, LUCIUS ANNAEUS 5 BC - AD 65

De Benefeizii... Florence: 1554). V. 37

The Epistles... London: 1786. V. 42

The Epistles of... London: 1786. V. 37

Hippolitus Translated Out of Seneca. London: 1651. V. 39

His Tenne Tragedies. London: 1927. V. 45

Seneca's Morals by Way of Abstract. London: 1685. V. 39

Les Oeuvres de Seneque. Paris: 1659-1658. V. 40

Opera Philosophica. Treviso: 1478. V. 40

(Opera Philosophica). Seneca Moralis. Venice: 1490. V. 45

Opera. Basileae: 1529. V. 38; 40

Opera Quae Exstant Omnia. Antwerp: 1652. V. 45

Opera. Quae Exstant... Amsterdam: 1672. V. 39

SENECA, LUCIUS ANNAEUS 5 BC - AD 65 continued

Opuscula Philosophica Selecta minora. Leyden: 1650. V. 39

Philosophi Scripta . . . Paris. V. 44

Philosophi Opera, Quae Exstant Omnia. Antwerp: 1652. V. 37

Pistole Del Moralissimo Seneca Nvovamente Fatte Volgare. Venice: 1494. V. 37

Seneca His Tenne Tragedies. London: 1927. V. 46

Seneca's Morals by Way of Abstract. London: 1685. V. 40

Sittliche Zuchtbucher, des Hochberumpten Philosophi end Lerers Lucii Annei Senece. Strassburg: 1536. V. 38

Tragedie Senece cum Commento. Venice: 1492. V. 37

Tragodiae. Florence: 1513. V. 37

Senecae Tragoediae. Venetiis: 1517. V. 44

Tragoediae. Venice: 1517. V. 37

Tragoediae cum Commento. Lyon: 1491. V. 37

The Workes. London: 1614. V. 39; 40; 42; 44

The Works. Colophon: 1620. V. 45

The Workes of . . . London: 1620. V. 39; 44

SENEFELDER, ALOIS 1771-1834

A Complete Course of Lithography. London: 1819. V. 38; 44

The Invention of Lithography. New York. V. 44

The Invention of Lithography. New York: 1911. V. 41; 42

SENESE, ALESSANDRO

Il Vero Maneggio Di Spada Di . . . Gentil'Huomo Bolognese. Bologna: 1660. V. 38

SENEX, J.

An Actual Survey of all the Principal Roads of England and Wales. London. V. 40

SENIOR, JOSEPH

Smithy Rhymes and Stithy Chimes . . . Sheffield: 1882/84. V. 42

SENIOR, NASSAU W.

Four Introductory Lectures on Political Economy, Delivered Before the University of Oxford. London: 1852. V. 40

SENIOR, NASSAU WILLIAM 1790-1864

American Slavery . . . London: 1856. V. 42

American Slavery. London: 1862. V. 46

Conversations with Distinguished Persons During the Second Empire from 1860 to 1863 . . . London: 1880. V. 37

Essays on Fiction. London: 1864. V. 37

An Introductory Lecture on Politicl Economy, Delivered Before the University of Oxford, on the 6th of December, 1826. London: 1831. V. 38

A Journal Kept in Turkey and Greece in the Autumn of 1857 and the Beginning of 1858. London: 1859. V. 37; 39; 41; 42; 45

Journals, Conversations and Essays Relating to Ireland. London: 1868. V. 37; 38; 42; 43

Journals Keep in France and Italy from 1848 to 1852. With a Sketch of the Revolution of 1848. London: 1871. V. 37

Letters on the Factory Act, As It Affects the Cotton Manufacture, Addressed to the Right Honourable the President of the Board of Trade. London: 1837. V. 42

Political Economy. London: 1858. V. 39

Report from His Majesty's Commissioners for Inquiring into the Administration and Practical Operation of the Poor Laws. London: 1834. V. 41

Three Lectures on the Value of Money, Delivered Before the University of Oxford, in 1829 (Unpublished). London: 1840. V. 41; 45

Two Lectures on Population, Delivered Before the University of Oxford, in Easter Term, 1828 . . . to which is added a correspondence between the author and the Rev. T. R. Malthus. London: 1831. V. 38

SENIOR, NASSU WILLIAM 1790-1864

Three Lectures on the Cost of Obtaining Money, and on Some Effects of Private and Govnerment Paper Money; Delivered Before the University of Oxford, in Trinity Term, 1829. London: 1830. V. 38

SENIOR, WILLIAM

Pike and Perch. London: 1900. V. 39

Travel and Trout in the Antipodes. London: 1880. V. 43

SENN, NICHOLAS

Intestinal Surgery. Chicago: 1889. V. 42

A Nurse's Guide for the Operating Room. Chicago: 1932. V. 42

The Pathology and Surgical Treatment of Tumors. Philadelphia: 1895. V. 38

Principles of Surgery. Philadelhpia: 1891. V. 42

Principles of Surgery. Philadelphia: 1895. V. 43; 46

SENNERT, DANIEL

Epitome Naturalis Scientiae Editio Ultima. (with) Auctarium Epitomes Physicae. Amsterdam: 1651. V. 37

Institutionum Medicinae Libri V. Institutionum. Wittenberg. V. 44

Institutionum Medicinae Libri V. Wittenberg: 1667. V. 42

SENNETT, A. R.

Carriages Without Horses Shall Go . . . London: 1896. V. 42

Garden Cities in theory and Practice, Being an Amplification of a Paper on the Potentialites of Applied Science in a Garden City . . . London: 1905. V. 46

SENS. LAWS, STATUTES, ETC.

Coustume du Bassillage de Sens . . . Sens: 1556. V. 40

THE SENSE of the Court and Parliaments of England, As to the Dissenters, Ever Since the Restoration. London: 1712. V. 39

THE SENSE of the nation, Concerning the Duke of Marlborough, as It Is Express'd in Several Acts of Parliament in the Votes and Joint Addresses of Both Houses . . . London: 1702/1710. V. 44

SENTENTIAE et Proverbia ex Poetis Latinis. Venice: 1550. V. 45

SENTENTIAE Uberiores ex Scriptis Beati Thomae et Venerabilis Alberti Super Octo Libros Physicorum Aristotelis. Leipzig: 1498-1500. V. 38

THE SENTIMENTS of a Great Man Upon Proposals for the General Reduction of Interest to Three Per Cent. London: 1751. V. 40; 41

THE SENTIMENTS of a Tory, in Respect to a Late Important Transaction, and in Regard to the Present Situation of Affairs. London: 1741. V. 41

SEPHORA; a Hebrew Tale, Descriptive of the Country of Palestine, and of the Manners and Customs of the Ancient Israelites. Worcester: 1835. V. 42

SEPP, JAN CHRISTIAAN

Houtkunde, Behelzendde de Afbeelidingen van Meest Alle Bekende, Inen Uitlandsche Houten. Amsterdam: 1791. V. 46

SEPTALIUS, LUDOVICUS

De Naevis Liber . . . Patavii: 1628. V. 37

SEQUEIRA, I.

A New Merchant's Guide; containing a concise system of information for the Port and City of London: together with some observations particularly useful to commercial men and their clerks. London: 1798. V. 37

A SEQUEL to Common Sense: or, The American Controversy Considered in Two Points of View Hitherto Unnoticed. Dublin: 1777. V. 37

A SEQUEL to Sir William Jones's Pamphlet on the Principles of Government in a Dialogue Between a Freeholder in the County of Denbigh, and the Dean of Gloucester. Gloucester: 1784. V. 38

A SEQUEL to the Congress of the Beasts; or, the Northern Election . . . London: 1749. V. 41

SERAFINI, MICHELANGELO

Sopra un'Sonetto Della Geolsia Di M. Giovanbatista Strozzi. Fiorenza: 1550. V. 40

SERANTONI, G. M.

Dialogo Intorno Alla Cagione Della Celebre Aurora Boreale Vedutasi in Cielo Nella Notte Susseguente Alli 16 Decembre Del' Anno 1737. Lucca: 1740. V. 44

SERARIUS, NICOLAUS

Rabbini, et Herodes, seu de Tota Rabbinorum Gente, Partitione, Creatione, Auctoritate, Pluribusque . . . Mainz: 1607. V. 46

SERENDIPITY PRESS

Folio of Private Presses. N.P.: 1978. V. 45

SERGEANT, ADELINE

A Broken Idol. London: 1893. V. 38

The Story of a Penitent Soul. London: 1892. V. 39; 42

SERGEANT, EMILY FRANCES

Esther Denison: a Novel. London: 1889. V. 41

SERGEANT, JOHN 1622-1707

Solid Philosophy Asserted, Against the Fancies of the Ideists; or, the method to Science Farther Illustrated. London: 1697. V. 45

Sure-Footing in Christianity, or, Rational Discourses on the Rule of Faith with Short Animadversions on Dr. Pierce's Sermon . . . London: 1665. V. 37; 41

SERGEAUNT, B. E.

The Royal Monmouthshire Militia. London: 1910. V. 38

SERGEEVICH 1818-1883

THE TURF Register, and Sportsman and Breeder's Stud-Book. York: 1803-05-22. V. 39

A **SERIES** of Letters on Courtship and Marriage. Hudson: 1804. V. 44

A **SERIES** of Progressive Lessons Intended to Elucidate the Art of Flower Painting in Water Colours. London: 1815. V. 42; 44

A **SERIES** of Textbooks . . . Scranton: 1905. V. 40

SERIMAN, ZACCARIA 1708-1784

Storia Dei Regni Delle Scimie e Dei Cinocefali, Ossia i Viaggi Straordinari di un Inglese in Vari Paesi Ignoli Agli Europei . . . Bassano: 1764-1780. V. 45

Storia dei Regni delle Scimie e Dei Cinocefali . . . Bern: 1764-80. V. 46

Viaggi di Enrico Wanton Alle Terre Incognito Austali . . . Berna: i.e. Venice: 1764. V. 39

SERINGE, NICOLAS CHARLES

Essai de Formules Botaniques Representant les Caracteres des Plantes par des Signes Analytiques qui Remplacent les Phrases Descriptives . . . Paris: 1835. V. 39

THE SERIO-COMIC Drama of Punch and Judy. London: 1840. V. 39

SERIONNE, JACQUES

Les Interets des Nations de l'Europe, Developpes Relativement au Commerce. Leyden: 1766. V. 45

A **SERIOUS** and Faithfull Representation of the Judgements of Ministers of the Gospell Within the Province of London. London: 1649. V. 45

SERIOUS Considerations on a Late Very Important Decision of the House of Commons. London: 1769. V. 37; 39

SERIOUS Reflections On the Present Condition of Great Britain. In an Address to the Electors of Members to Represent Them in the Next Parliament. London: 1733. V. 41

SERJEANTSON, R. M.

The Serjeantsons of Hanlith. N.P.. V. 45

SERLE, AMBROSE

Americans Against Liberty; or an Essay on the Nature and Principles of the True Freedom, Shewing that the Designs and Conduct of the Americans Tend Only to Tyranny and Slavery. London: 1775. V. 40

SERLE, PERCIVAL

A Bibliography of Australasian Poetry and Verse. 1925. V. 38

SERLIO, SEBASTIANO

Architettura di Sebastiano Serlio Bolognese, in Sei Libri Divisa. Venice: 1663. V. 37

De Architectura Libri Quinque. Venice: 1568-69. V. 37

Die Gemaynen Reglen von der Architectur Uber die Funf Manieren der Gebeu (etc.). Antwerp: 1542. V. 39

Extraordinario Libro di Architettura . . . Nel Quale si Dimonstrano Trenta Porte di Opere Rustica Mista con Diversi Ordini & Venti di Opera Dilicata di Diverse Specie, con la Scrittura Davanti, che Narra il Tutto. Venice: 1566. V. 37

The First (-Firft) Booke of Architecture, Made by . . . 1611. V. 45

The First (-Fift) Booke of Architecture, Made by . . . London: 1611. V. 38; 40; 46

Il Terzo Libro Nel Qval Si Figvrano, E Descrivono Le Antiqvita Di Roma, E Le Altre Che Sono In Italia . . . (with) Regole Generali Di Architettvra Sopra Le Cinqve Maniere De Gli Edifici . . . (with) Qvinto Libro D'Architettvra. Venice: 1551. V. 41

Il Primo Libro d'Architettura (il secondo libro di perspettiva); il Terzo Libro; Regole Generali di Architettura; Quinto Libro d'Architettura. Venice: Books 1-2 -Cornellio: 1551. V. 37

Il Primo Libro d'Architettura. Paris: 1545. V. 41

SERLIO, SEBASTINO

The First (Second-Fifth) Book of Architecture. London: 1611. V. 45

A **SERMON**, Addressed to the Honorable De Witt Clinton . . . New York: 1804. V. 45

A **SERMON** Preached to the Society in Brattle Street, Boston, October 20, 1793; and Occasioned by the Death of His Excellency John Hancock, Governor of Massachusetts. Boston: 1793. V. 44

A **SERMON** to be Preach'd at the Interment of the Renowned Observator. London: 1682. V. 40

SERMONES Dormi Secure de Sanctis. Sermones Dominicales cum Expositionibus Evangeliorum. Basle: 1489. V. 41

SERMONES Exquisiti Super Epistolis Per Anni Circulum. Strasbourg: 1489. V. 38

SERMONES Sancti Augustini ad Heremitas. Strasbourg: 1485? V. 37

SERMONS by Artists. London: 1934. V. 37; 38; 42
SERMONS by Artists. Waltham St. Lawrence: 1934. V. 46

SERRA, JUNIPERO

Writings of . . . Washington: 1955-66. V. 38

SERRAO, ELIA

De Tremuoti e Della Nuova Filadelfia in Calabria. Naples: 1785. V. 37

SERRES, JEAN DE 1540?-1598

A General Historie of France. London: 1624. V. 41

SERRES, JEAN PUGET DE LA

The Mirrour Which Flatters Not. London: 1639. V. 37

SERT, JOSE LUIS

Can Our Cities Survive? Cambridge: 1942. V. 42

Can Our Cities Survive? An ABC of Urban Problems, Their Analysis, Their Solutions. Cambridge: 1944. V. 41

SERVEN, JAMES E.

Colt Firearms: 1836-1958. Santa Ana: 1959. V. 45

SERVERINUS, M. A.

Vipera Pythia, id Est de Viperae Natura, Veneno, Medicina, Demonstrationes et Experimenta Nova. Padua: 1651. V. 37

SERVICE, JAMES

Metrical Legends of Northumberland . . . Alnwick: 1834. V. 41

SERVICE, JOHN PATERSON

Recreation for Youth. London: 1787. V. 37

SERVICE, ROBERT

Bar-Room Ballads: a Book of Verse. New York: 1940. V. 44

Lyrics of a Low Brow. New York: 1951. V. 44

Ploughman of the Moon/Harper of Heaven. New York: 1945/48. V. 44; 46

Songs of the Yukon. Toronto: 1913. V. 44

SERVICE, ROBERT W.

The Complete Poems. New York: 1940. V. 39

Rhymes of a Rolling Stone. Toronto: 1912. V. 39

SERVICE, ROBERT WILLIAM 1874-1958

Ballads of Cheechako. Toronto: 1933. V. 38; 43

The Complete Poems of Robert Service. New York: 1945. V. 43

Ploughman of the Moon: An Adventure into Memory. New York: 1945. V. 41; 46

Rhymes of a Red Cross Man. Toronto: 1916. V. 43; 46

Rhymes of a Red Cross Man. New York: 1916. V. 38

Rhymes of a Red Cross Man. Toronto: 1933. V. 38

Songs of a Sourdough. Toronto: 1933. V. 38; 43

SERVIEZ, M. DE

The Lives and Amours of the Empresses, Consorts to the Twelve Caesars of Rome . . . London: 1723. V. 41

SERVISS, G.

The Moon Metal. New York: 1900. V. 43

THE SERVITOUR: a Poem. London: 1709. V. 40; 45

SESS, J. HENEAGE

London: Its Celebrated Characters and Remarkable Places. London: 1871. V. 37

SESSE Y PINOL, IOSEPE

Libro de la Cosmographia Universal del Mundo y Particular Descripcion de la Syria y Tierra Santa. Zaragoza,: 1619. V. 40

SESSIONS, ROGER

Idyll of Theocritus: for Soprano and Orchestra. New York: 1957. V. 45

SETH-SMITH, D.

Parrakeets, a Handbook to the Imported Species. London: 1903. V. 37; 38; 39

SETON, ALEXANDER

A Treatise of Mutilation and Demembration. London: 1699. V. 45

SETON, ERNEST THOMPSON 1860-1946

Animal Heroes. New York: 1905. V. 39; 46

The Arctic Prairies. New York: 1911. V. 44

The Arctic Prairies. London: 1912. V. 39

The Biography of a Grizzly. New York: 1900. V. 42; 43; 45

The Buffalo Wind. Put Forth from the Seton. V. 39

The Buffalo Wind. Santa Fe: 1938. V. 40

Fauna of Manitoba. Winnipeg,: 1909. V. 44

The Gospel of the Red Man; an Indian Bible. Garden City: 1941. V. 43

Life Histories of Northern animals. New York: 1909. V. 37; 40; 42

Life Histories of Northern Animals. London: 1910. V. 46

SETON, ERNEST THOMPSON 1860-1946 continued

Lives of the Hunted. London: 1901. V. 39; 46

Lives of Game Animals. Garden City: 1925. V. 40; 41

Lives of Game Animals. 1937. V. 39

Santana. The Hero Dog of France. Los Angeles: 1945. V. 40

Studies in the Art Anatomy of Animals. London: 1896. V. 38; 40; 41; 42; 43

Studies in the Art of Anatomy of Familiar Mammals and Birds, Designed for the Use of Sculptures, Painters, Illustrators, Naturalists and TAxidermists. Toronto: 1924. V. 40

The Youth's Companion Bird Folio. Boston & Cincinnati: 1901. V. 42

SETON, JULIA M.

The Indian Costume Book. Santa Fe: 1938. V. 37; 39

SETON-KARR, H.

My Sporting Holidays. London: 1904. V. 38

SETON-KARR, H. W.

Bear-Hunting in the White Mountains or Alaska and British Columbi Revisited . . . London: 1891. V. 37; 38; 42

Ten Years Wild Sports in Foreign Lands. London: 1889. V. 38

SETON, WALTER

William Howard Lister. London: 1919. V. 46

SETOUN, GABRIEL

The Child World. London: 1896. V. 40; 41; 43; 45

SETTERWALL, A.

The Chinese Pavilion at Drottningholm. Malmo: 1974. V. 37

SETTLE, DIONYSUS

I.N.J. Historia Navigationis Martini for Bisseri Angli Praetoris Sive Capitanei, A. C. 1577. Majo, Junio, Julio, Augusto & Septembri Mensibus, Jussu Reginae Elisabethae . . . Hamburg: 1675. V. 37; 39

SETTLE, ELKANAH

Absalom Senior; or, Achitophel Transpos'd. London: 1682. V. 39; 40; 42; 45; 46

Carmen Irenicum. London: 1707. V. 39; 40

The Character of a Popish Successor, and What England may Expect from Such a One Humbly Offered to the Consideration of Both Houses of Parliament, Appointed to Meet at Oxford, on the One and Twentieth of March, 1680/1. London: 1681. V. 45

The City-Ramble; or, a Play-House Wedding. London: 1711. V. 45

A Defence of Dramatick Poetry. London: 1698. V. 42

Eusebia Triumphans. London: 1702. V. 39; 40; 44; 45

Eusebia Triumphans. London: 1702 i.e. 1703. V. 43

Fears and Dangers, Fairly Display'd . . . London: 1706. V. 42

The Female Prelate: Being the History of the Life and Death of Pope Joan. London: 1680. V. 38; 45

Ibrahim the Illustrious Bassa. London: 1677. V. 42

Reflections on Several of Mr. Dryden's Plays. London: 1687. V. 39

SETTLE LITERARY SOCIETY

Catalogue of Books Belonging to the Society. Settle, Yorkshire: 1864. V. 38

SETTLE, MARY LEE

The Killing Ground. New York: 1982. V. 44

The Kiss of Kin. London: 1955. V. 41

The Kiss of Kin. New York: 1955. V. 41; 46

The Love Eaters. London: 1953. V. 45

The Love Eaters. London: 1954. V. 42; 44

The Love Eaters. New York: 1954. V. 41; 42; 44; 46

SETTLE, RAYMOND

The March of the Mounted Riflemen First United States Military Expedition to Travel the Full Length of the Oregon Trail . . . Glendale: 1940. V. 42; 45

SETWER, A. CHARLES

The Stained Glass of William Morris and His Circle. New Haven: 1974. V. 37

SEUME, J. G.

A Tour through Part of Germany, Poland, Russia, Sweden, Denmark &c. During the Summer of 1805. London: 1807. V. 40

SEUPHOR, MICHEL

L'Autre Cote des Choses. N.P.: 1976. V. 42

Piet Mondrian: Life and Work. New York. V. 39; 43

Piet Mondrian: Life and Work. New York: 1956. V. 45; 46

Piet Mondrian: Life and Work. New York: 1958. V. 39; 41

Piet Mondrian: Life and Work. New York: 1968. V. 39

The Sculpture of This Century. New York: 1960. V. 42

SEUSS, DR.

The 500 Hats of Bartholomew Cubbins. New York: 1938. V. 46

SEUTONIUS TRANQUILLUS, CAIUS

The Historie of Twelve Ceasars, Emperors of Rome . . . London: 1931. V. 39; 43

Vitae XII Caesares. Milan: 1480. V. 46

SEVEN Days in Chicago. 1878. V. 38

SEVEN SAGES

Dicta Septem Sapientium et Eorum qui Cum Iis Numerantur. Paris: 1569-70. V. 44

The Sayings of the Seven Sages of Greece. Verona: 1976. V. 39; 40; 41; 42; 44; 45; 46

The Seven Sages, in Scottish Metre. Edinburgh: 1837. V. 43

The Seven Sages of Greece. 1976. V. 44

THE SEVEN Voyages of Sinbad the Sailor. New York: 1949. V. 46

THE SEVEN Wonders of the World; and Other Magnificent Buildings &c. New York: 1811. V. 38

1789 History of Wyange County, New York. Philadelphia: 1877. V. 39

SEVENTH-DAY Baptist Missionary and Bible Society of the County of Cumberland The Constitution of the Seventh-Day Baptist Missionary and Bible Society of the County of Cumberland . . . Adopted November 10, 1816. Bridgeton: 1823. V. 41

THE SEVENTY-SEVENTH Pennsylvania at Shiloh. Harrisburg: 1905. V. 42; 46

SEVENTY Years of Life in the Victorian Era by a Physician. London: 1893. V. 45

SEVERAL Conferences Between Some of the Principal People Amongst the Quakers in Pennsylvania, and the Deputies from the Six Indian Nations, in Alliance with Britain . . . Newcastle-upon-Tyne: 1756. V. 44

THE SEVERAL Depositions Concerning the Late Riot in Oxford. London: 1716. V. 40

SEVERANCE, F. H.

Peace Episodes on the Niagara. Buffalo: 1914. V. 42

SEVERANCE, FRANK H.

An Old Frontier of France: the Niagara Region and Adjacent Lakes Under French Control. New York: 1917. V. 44

SEVERIM DE FARIA, MANOEL

Discursos Varios Politicos. Evora: 1624. V. 41

Promptuario Espiritual, e Exemplar de Virtudes . . . Lisbon: 1651. V. 38

SEVERIN, MARK

Engraved Bookplates: European Ex-Libris 1950-70. Pinner: 1972. V. 41

SEVERINO, MARCO AURELLO

Re Recondita Abscessum Natura Libri VIII. Frankfurt: 1643. V. 37; 41

SEVERINUS, MARCUS AURELIUS

Vipera Pythia, id est de Viperae, Natura, Veneno, Medicina, Demonstrationes et Experimenta Nova. Padua: 1651. V. 37

SEVERINUS, PETRUS

Idea Medicinae Philosohicae . . . Basel: 1571. V. 37; 39; 40; 41; 44; 45; 46

SEVERN, an Elegiac Poem. To the Memory of a Lady. Worcester: 1767. V. 40

SEVERN, MARK

Background. London: 1931. V. 45

SEVERN, WALTER

Good Night and Good Morning. London: 1870. V. 44

SEVERSON, D. R.

Specimens of Hawaiian Kapa Together with Specimens of Polynesian Tapa . . . Hawaii: 1978/83. V. 46

SEVIGNE, MARIE DE RABUTIN-CHANTAL, MARQUISE DE 1626-1696

The Letters. London: 1927. V. 45

The Letters. Philadelphia: 1927. V. 42; 43

SEWALL, JONATHAN MITCHELL

Miscellaneous Poems, with Several Specimens from the Author's Manuscript Version of the Poems of Ossian. Portsmouth: 1801. V. 39

SEWALL, JOSEPH

The Holy Spirit Convincing the World of Sin, of Righteousness and of Judgment, Considered in Four Sermons. Boston: 1741. V. 40

Precious Treasure in Earthen Vessels. A Sermon Occasion'd By the Death of the Reverend & Learned Mr. Ebenezer Pemberton . . . Who Expired Wednesday, Febr. 13th 1716. Boston: 1717. V. 38

SEWALL, R. K.

Sketches of St. Augustine. New York: 1848. V. 42; 44; 45

SEWALL, SAMUEL 1652-1730

Diary of . . . 1674-1729. Boston: 1878-82. V. 40

Phaenomena Quaedam Apocalyptica ad Aspectum Novi Orbis Configurata. Boston: 1727. V. 41

The Selling of Joseph/A Memorial. Northampton: 1968. V. 41

SEWALL, THOMAS 1786-1845

An Examination of Phrenology. Washington City: 1837. V. 46

SEWALL, WILLIAM B.

The Trial of Charles Stevens, for the Murder of Charles Henry C. Stevens. 1823. V. 42

SEWARD, ANNA

Elegy on Captain Cook. To Which is Added an Ode to the Sun. The Fourth Edition, with Additions. Lichfield: 1784. V. 37

Letters, Written Between the Years 1784 and 1807. Edinburgh: 1811. V. 38; 40

Louisa. London: 1792. V. 41; 42

Memoirs of the Life of Dr. Darwin. London: 1804. V. 37; 39; 40; 41; 42; 46

Monody on Major Andre. Lichfield: 1781. V. 38; 40; 42; 44

Monody on Major Andre. Lichfield: printed and sold: 1781. V. 45

Poem to the Memory of Lady Miller. London: 1782. V. 39; 40; 42; 43

SEWARD, JOHN

Observations on the Re-building of London Bridge . . . London: 1824. V. 40

The Spirit of Anecdote and Wit. London: 1823. V. 38

SEWARD, WILLIAM

Anecdotes of Some Distinguished Persons, Chiefly of the Present and Two Preceding Centuries. London: 1795-97. V. 40

Anecdotes of Distinguished Persons, Chiefly of the Present and Preceding Two Centuries. London: 1798. V. 41; 42; 43; 45

Anecdotes of Distinguished Persons, Chiefly of the Last and Two Preceding Centuries. London: 1804. V. 39

Biographiana. London: 1799. V. 43

Journal of a Voyage from Savannah to Philadelphia, and From Philadelphia to England 1740. 1740. V. 46

SEWARD, WILLIAM H.

The Whale Fishery, and American Commerce in the Pacific Ocean. Washington: 1852. V. 42

SEWARD, WILLIAM HENRY

Argument of . . . In Defence of Abel F. Fitch and Others, Under an Indictment for Arson, Delivered at Detroit on the 11th, 12th and 14th of September, 1851. Detroit: 1851. V. 37

Communication of Hon. William H. Seward, Secretary of State, Upon the Subject of an Intercontinental Telegraph Connecting the Eastern and Western Hemispheres by way of Behring's Strait . . . Washington: 1864. V. 37

SEWARD, WILLIAM WENMAN

Collectanea Politica, or the Political Transactions of Ireland . . . from 1760 to 1801. Dublin: 1801. V. 38

Topographia Hibernica; or the Topography of Ireland, Antient and Modern. Dublin: 1795. V. 37; 43

SEWEL, WILLIAM 1653-1720

The History of the Rise, Increase an Progress of the Christian People Called Quakers. London: 1722. V. 42; 46

The History of the Rise, Increase, and Progress, of the Christian People Called Quakers . . . Philadelphia: 1728. V. 42

The History of the Rise, Increase and Progress of the Christian People Called Quakers. Burlington: 1774. V. 37; 38; 42; 43

SEWELL, ALFRED L.

The Great Calamity. Chicago: 1871. V. 42

SEWELL, ANNA

Black Beauty. London: 1877. V. 39

Black Beauty. Boston: 1890. V. 42; 43; 45

Black Beauty . . . Boston: 1980. V. 42

Black Beauty. His Grooms and Companions. Boston: (1890). V. 37

SEWELL, BROACARD

Frances Horovitz: Poet. Aylesford: 1987. V. 42

SEWELL, BROCARD

Olive Custance: Her Life and Work. London: 1975. V. 41

SEWELL, ELIZABETH MISSING

Laneton Parsonage; a Tale for Children . . . London: 1848. V. 43

Ursula. A Tale of Country Life. London: 1858. V. 41

SEWELL, GEORGE

A New Collection of Original Poems, Never Printed in Any Miscellany. London: 1720. V. 40; 45

Observations Upon Cato, a Tragedy. Edinburgh: 1713. V. 39

SEWELL, HENRY

A Letter to Lord Worsley, on the Burthens Affecting Real Property Arising from the Present State of the Law . . . London: 1846. V. 37

SEWELL, MARY

Poems. Egham & Chertsey: 1803. V. 39

The Poor Brother. London: 1863. V. 43

SEWELL, MARY W.

'Our Father's Care'. A Ballad. Richmond: 1864. V. 46

SEWELL, ROBERT

An Essay in Rhyme, in two parts; with Miscellaneous Poetry. Halstead. V. 37

SEWELL, ROCARD

Three Privatae Presses. Saint Dominic's Press. The Press of Edward Walters. Saint Albert's Press. Wellingborough: 1979. V. 38

SEWELL, SARAH ANN

Woman and the Times We Live In. Manchester: 1869. V. 44

SEWELL, WILLIAM

The History of the Rise, Increase and Progress of the Christian People called Quakers, Intermixed with several Remarkable Occurences. London: 1722. V. 37

SEWELL, WILLIAM G.

The Ordeal of Free Labor in the British West Indies. New York: 1861. V. 42

The Ordeal of Free Labor in the British West Indies. New York: 1862. V. 39

SEWTER, A. CHARLES

The Stained Glass of William Morris and His Circle. New Haven: 1974. V. 41

SEX Linguarum Latinae, Gallicae, Hispanicae, Italicae, Anglicae, & Teutonicae Dilucidissimum Dictionarium . . . Zurich: 1579. V. 38

SEXE, MARCEL

Two Centuries of Fur Trading, 1723-1923. Paris: 1923. V. 39; 43

SEXTON, ANNE

All My Pretty Ones. Boston: 1962. V. 42

The Book of Folly. Boston: 1972. V. 41

To Bedlam and Part Way Back. Boston: 1960. V. 42; 43

SEXTON, FRANKLIN BARLOW

Diary of a Confederate Congressman, 1862-1863. Austin. V. 46

SEXTON, GROVER F.

The Arizona Sheriff. 1925. V. 38

SEXTON, LUCY A. FOSTER

The Foster Family, California Pioneers. Santa Barbara: 1925. V. 37

SEXTON, R. W.

American Apartment Houses of To-day. New York: 1926. V. 41; 42

American Theatres of Today. New York: 1927. V. 44

American Theatres of Today. New York: 1930. V. 39

SEXTUS EMPIRICUS

Adversus maathematicos. Pyrrhoniarum Hypotyposeon Libri Tres. Paris: 1569. V. 37

SEYBERT, ADAM

Statistical Annals; Embracing Views of the Population, Commerce, Navigation, Fisheries, Public Lands, Post Office Establishment, Revenues, Mint, Military and Naval Establishments, Expenditures, Public Debt and Sinking Fund of the United States of America. Philadelphia: 1818. V. 37; 38; 39; 40; 42

SEYBOLT, PAUL S.

A Catalogue of the First Editions of First Books in the Collection of Paul S. Seybolt. Boston: 1946. V. 43; 46

SEYD, ERNEST

California and Its Resources. London: 1858. V. 37; 38

SEYFERT, C. K.

The Encyclopedia of Structural Geology and Plate Tectonics. London: 1987. V. 38

SEYFFERT, OSCAR

A Dictionary of Classical Antiquities. London & New York: 1891. V. 40

SEYMOUR, CHARLES CROSSLEY

How I won the Indian Mutiny Medal; and How Things Went Afterwards. Benares: 1888. V. 41

SEYMOUR, E. H.

Remarks, Critical, Conjectural and Explanatory Upon the Plays of Shakespare. London: 1805. V. 37; 38; 39; 43; 45

SEYMOUR, E. S.

Sketches of Minnesota, the New England of the West . . . New York: 1850. V. 37; 43; 45

SEYMOUR, EDWARD

The Complete History of England. London: 1764. V. 39

SEYMOUR, H. D.

Russia on the Black Sea and Sea of Azof . . . London: 1855. V. 40

SEYMOUR, RICHARD

The Compleat Gamester . . . London: 1739. V. 43

The Compleat Gamester. London: 1750. V. 43; 46

SEYMOUR, ROBERT

The Book of Christmas. London: 1836. V. 42

Humorous Sketches. London. V. 39

The March of Intellect. London: 1829. V. 38

Maxims and Hints for an Angler, and Miseries of Fishing. London: 1833. V. 40

New Readings of Old Authors. London. V. 43

Seymour's Sketches. London: 1840. V. 44

Seymour's Humorous Sketches . . . London: 1843. V. 43

Seymour's Humorous Sketches, Comprising Ninety-Two Characters Etchings. London: 1846. V. 43

Seymour's Humorous Sketches, Comprising Eighty-Six Caricature Etchings. London: 1866. V. 42

Sketches by Seymour. London: (1867). V. 37

SEYMOUR, SAMUEL

War Dances in the Interior of a Kanza Lodge. Philadelphia: 1832. V. 39

SEYMOUR, SILAS

Incidents of a Trip through the Great Platte Valley, to the Rocky Mountains and Laramie Plains, in the Fall of 1866 . . . New York: 1867. V. 38; 40

Incidents of a Trip through the Great Platte Valley to the Rocky Mountains and Laramine Plains, in the Fall of 1866. New York: 1867. V. 45

A Reminiscence of the Union Pacific Railroad. Quebec: 1873. V. 37

SEYSSEL, CLAUDE DE

Moralis Explicatio Evangelii Lucae. Paris: 1514. V. 37

SFONDRATI, CELESTINUS

Innocentia Vindicata, in Quae Gravissimis Argumentis. St. Gallen: 1695. V. 45

SFONDRATO, PANDULPHO

Causa Aestus Maris. Ferrara: 1590. V. 43

SFORTUNATI, GIOVANNI

Nuovo Lume. Libro di Arithmetica . . . Venice: 1545. V. 37

SGAI, FRANCESCO

Riflessioni . . . Danzig: 1779. V. 46

SGOBBIS, ANTONIO DE

Vniversale Theatro Farmacevtico Fondato Sopra le Preparationi Farmaceutiche Scritte da'Medici Antichi, Greci, & Arabi, Principalmente da Galeno . . . Venetia: 1682. V. 39

SHAARA, MICHAEL

The Broken Place. New York: 1968. V. 44

The Killer Angels. New York: 1974. V. 37; 40; 42; 44; 46

SHAARP, GRANVILLE

The Law of Passive Obedience. London: 1776. V. 37

SHABISTARI, MAHMUD IBN ABD AL-KARIM

Mahmud Schebisteri's Rosenflor des Geheimnisses. Pesth und Leipzig: 1838. V. 43; 45

SHACKELTON, ERNEST HENRY 1874-1922

Aurora Australis Published at the Winter Quarters of the British Antarctic Expedition, 1907, During the Winter Months of April, May, June, July, 1908 . . . Auckland: 1988. V. 46

SHACKETON, ERNEST HENRY 1874-1922

South Polar Times. London: 1907-1911. V. 37

SHACKLETON, ERNEST HENRY 1874-1922

Adventure. London: 1928. V. 43

Heart of the Antarctic. Philadelphia: 1901. V. 43

The Heart of the Antarctic: Being the Story of the British Antarctic Expedition 1907-1909. London: 1908. V. 46

The Heart of the Antarctic. London: 1909. V. 37; 38; 39; 41; 42; 46

The Heart of Antarctic . . . Philadelphia: 1909. V. 37; 38; 41; 43; 44; 46

The Imperial Trans-anarctic Expedition. London: 1914. V. 41

South Polar Times. London: 1907-14. V. 41

South. The Story of Shackleton's Last Expedition 1914-1917. London: 1920. V. 45

South: The Story of Shackleton's Last Expedition 1914-1917. New York: 1920. V. 37; 38; 43; 44; 45

SHADBOLT, SYDNEY H.

The Afghan Campaign of 1878-1880 . . . Comprising Historical and Biographical Divisions. London: 1882. V. 38

SHADWELL, THOMAS

Bury-Fair. London: 1689. V. 38; 40

The Dramatick Works of Thomas Shadwell. London: 1720. V. 40; 41; 43; 44

Epsom Wells. London: 1642?-1692. V. 42

Epsom-Wells. London: 1673. V. 40

Epsom-Wells: A Comedy. London: 1693. V. 38

The History of Timon of Athens, the Man-Hater. London: 1678. V. 45

Psyche: a Tragedy. London: 1675. V. 42

The Scowrers. London: 1691. V. 38; 39; 44

The Squire of Alsatia. London: 1688. V. 44

The Sullen Lovers. London: 1670. V. 39

A True Widow. London: 1689. V. 42

The Virtuoso. London: 1676. V. 38; 40; 42; 44

The Virtuoso; a Comedy. London: 1691. V. 43

The Woman-Captain. London: 1680. V. 38; 39; 44

The Complete Works. London: 1927. V. 40; 41; 42; 43; 44; 46

SHAEFF, NORMAN B.

Western Stories. N.P.: 1949. V. 39

SHAFFER, ANTONY

The Woman in the Wardrobe. London: 1951. V. 41

SHAFFER, ELLEN

Fray Maturino Gilberti & His Books. Los Angeles: 1963. V. 37

The Garden of Health. An Account of Two Herbals. The Gart der Gesundheit and the Hortus Sanitatis. San Francisco: 1957. V. 37; 38; 39; 42; 43; 45

The Garden of Health an Account of Two Herbals: The Gart der Gesundheit an the Hortus Sanitatis. San Francisco: 1947. V. 37

The Nuremberg Chronicle. Los Angeles: 1950. V. 38; 39; 41; 42; 46

SHAFFER, NEWTON

Pott's Disease, Its Pathology and Mechanical Treatment with Remarks on Rotary Lateral Curavture. New York: 1879. V. 42

SHAFFER, PETER

Five Finger Exercise. New York: 1959. V. 45

Five Finger Exercise: A Paly in Two Acts and Four Scenes. New York: (1959). V. 37

SHAFFNER, TALIAFERRO P.

The War in America: Being an Historical and Political Account of the Southern and Northern States . . . London: 1862. V. 46

SHAFFORD, JOHN CONRAD

Narrative of the Extraordinary Life of John Conrad Shafford . . . New York: 1841. V. 37

SHAFTESBURY, ANTHONY AHSLEY COOPER, 3RD EARL OF

Characteristics . . . Colophon: London: 1727. V. 39

Characteristicks &c. London: 1733. V. 38; 39; 45

SHAFTESBURY, ANTHONY ASHLEY COOPER, 3RD EARL OF 1671-1713

A Brief Account of the Designs Which the Papists Have Been Against the Earl of Shaftesbury, Occasioned by His Commitment, July 2, 1681. Whitehall: 1681. V. 40

SHAFTESBURY, ANTHONY ASHLEY COOPER, 3RD EARL OF 1671-1713 continued

Characteristicks of Men, Manners, Opinions, Times. London: 1732. V. 38; 41

Characteristicks of Men, Manners, Opinions, Times. Birmingham: 1773. V. 37; 38; 39; 43; 44; 45; 46

Characteristicks of Men, Manners, Opinions, Times. N.P.: 1711. V. 37

Characteristics of Men, Manners, Opinions, Times. London. V. 40

Characteristics of Men, Manners, Opinions, Times. London: 1711. V. 38

Characteristics of Men, Manners, Opinions and Times . . . (together with) Several Letters Written by a Noble Lord to a Young Man at the University. London: 1711/14/14/16. V. 41

Characteristics of Men, Manners, Opinions, Times. London: 1714. V. 38

Characteristicks of Men, Manners, Opinions, Times . . . Colophon: London: 1715. V. 39

An Essay on Painting, Being a Notion of the Historical Draught or Tablature of the Judgment of Hercules. London: 1714. V. 38

*A Letter Concerning Enthusiasm to My Lord****.* Somers: 1708. V. 38

SHAFTESBURY, ANTHONY ASHLEY COPPER, 3RD EARL OF 1671-1713

Characteristicks of Men, Manners, Opinions, Times. London: 1732-7. V. 40

SHAFTESBURY, ARTHUR ASHLEY COOPER, 3RD EARL OF

*A Letter Concerning Enthusiasm to My Lord *****(Somers).* London: 1708. V. 39

SHAFTOE, FRANCES

Narrative Containing an Account of Her Being in Sir Theophilus Oglethorpe's Family. London: 1708. V. 41; 42

SHAH, IDRIES

Tale of the Sands. Del mar: 1980. V. 37; 45

SHAHN, BEN

The Alphabet of Creation. New York: 1954. V. 43

Ben Shahn. New York. V. 39

The Complete Graphic Works. New York: 1973. V. 39; 46

Hallelujah. New York: 1970. V. 46

Love and Joy About Letters. New York: 1963. V. 37; 38; 41; 45

SHAHN, BERNARDA BRYSON

Ben Shahn. New York. V. 43; 46

Ben Shahn. New York: 1972. V. 41; 42; 45

SHAKER Heights Then and Now. Cleveland: 1938. V. 37

SHAKESPEARE, EDWARD O.

Report on Cholera in Europe and India. Washington: 1890. V. 38; 42

THE SHAKESPEARE Head Press Booklets, I-VI. Stratford-on-Avon: 1906. V. 46

SHAKESPEARE, HENRY

The Wild Sports of India: With Detailed Instructions from the Sportsman, To which is added Remarks on the Breeding and Rearing of Horses, and the Formation of Light Irregular Cavalry. London: 1862. V. 39

SHAKESPEARE, L. W.

History of the 2nd King Edward's Own Goorkhas (The Sirmoor Rifles). Volume II 1911-1921. Aldershot: 1924. V. 41

History of the Assam Rifles. London: 1929. V. 42

SHAKESPEARE SOCIETY

Shakespeare Society's Papers. London: 1844-49. V. 44

SHAKESPEARE, WILLIAM 1564-1616

The Tragedie of Anthony and Cleopatra. Hammersmith: 1912. V. 38; 39; 40; 44

Antony and Cleopatra. Guildfor, Surrey: 1979. V. 39

The Tragedie of Antony and Cleopatra. San Francisco: 1960. V. 38; 39

Antony and Cleopatra. Guildford: 1979. V. 37

Antony & Cleopatra. William Shakespeare. Designed and produced (with screen images) by Ronald King. With notes and an introductory essay by Keith Please. Surrey: 1979. V. 37

As You Like It. London. V. 40

As You Like It. London: 1799. V. 46

As You Like It. London: 1811. V. 42; 45

The Comedy of As You Like It. East Aurora: 1903. V. 39

As You Like It. London: 1909. V. 38; 42

As You Like It. London & New York: 1909. V. 39

Shakespeare's Comedy Of As You Like It. London: 1910. V. 46

As You Like It. London: 1930. V. 37; 39; 40; 43; 45

As You Like It. Toronto: 1909. V. 37; 38

The Beauties of Shakspear. London: 1752. V. 44

The Beauties of Shakespere; Selected from His Plays and Poems. London: 1783. V. 37; 45

The Beauties of Shakespear. New York: 1971. V. 40

Cassells' Illustrated Shakespeare. London: 1886. V. 46

A Collection of Poems. viz. 1. Venus and Adonis. II. The Rape of Lucrece. III. The Passionate Pilgrim. IV. Sonnets to Sundry Notes of Musick. London: 1709? V. 45

Mr. William Shakespeare Comedies, Histories and Tragedies. London: 1632. V. 38; 46

Comedies, Histories and Tragedies . . . London: 1632. V. 44

Comedies, Histories and Tragedies. London: 1632. V. 40; 44; 46

Comedies, Histories and Tragedies. London: 1663. V. 43

Comedies, Histories and Tragedies. London: 1664. V. 46

Comedies, Histories and Tragedies. London: 1685. V. 42; 44; 45

Mr. William Shakespeare His Comedies, Histories and Tragedies, Set Out by Himself in Quarto. London: 1767-68. V. 42

Comedies, Histories and Tragedies. London: 1807. V. 44

Comedies, Histories, Tragedies and Poems. London: 1858. V. 38; 46

The Comedies, Histories, & Tragedies as Presented at the Globe's Blackfriars Theatres, Circa 1591-1623. New York: 1888-92. V. 42

The Comedies. New York: 1896. V. 42

The Comedies of William Shakespeare. New York: 1899. V. 39; 41; 44; 46

Comedies, Histories and Tragedies. 1902. V. 40

Shakespeare's Comedies, Histories and Tragedies. Being a Reproduction in Facsimile of the First Folio Edition 1623 From the Chatsworth Copy in the Possession of the Duke of Devonshire. Oxford: 1902. V. 39; 42; 44

Comedies, Histories and Tragedies. London: 1909. V. 46

Comedies, Histories and Tragedies. London: 1910. V. 46

Shakespeare's Comedies. London: 1925. V. 46

The Comedies, Histories and Tragedies of William Shakespeare. New York: 1939-40. V. 45

The Comedies, Histories and Tragedies of William Shakespeare. (with the Two Volumes of Poems). New York: 1939-40/1941. V. 44

The Comedies, Histories and Tragedies of William Shakespeare. Also The Poems and a Prospectus. New York: 1939-41. V. 41; 43; 46

Comedies, Histories and Tragedies. New Haven: 1955. V. 44

Mr. William Shakespeare's Comedies, Histories and Tragedies. Cambridge: 1985. V. 46

Mr. William Shakespeares Comedies, Histories and Tragedies. Published According to the True Orignall Copies. London: 1623. V. 38

The Comedy of Errors - the Text of the First Folio. New York: 1939. V. 41

Coriolanus . . . London: 1755. V. 42

Coriolanus, as Arranged for Stage in Three Parts. London: 1901. V. 44

The Tragedy of Coriolanus. Hammersmith: 1914. V. 37; 39; 45; 46

The Tragedy of Coriolanus. London: 1914. V. 37

The Tragedie of Cymbeline. 1923. V. 42; 44

The Tragedie of Cymbeline. London: 1923. V. 38; 40

Cymbeline. Stratford-upon-Avon: 1923. V. 41

The Dramatic Works of William Shakespeare . . . also, an Inquiry Into the Authenticity of the Shakespeare Portraits . . . London. V. 44

Stockdale's Edition of Shakespeare . . . the Whole of His Dramatic Works . . . London: 1784. V. 42

Dramatic Works. London: 1785. V. 46

Dramtic Works. London: 1785. V. 41

The Dramatick Writings. London: 1786. V. 38; 39; 42

The Dramatic Works. Oxford: 1786. V. 38; 39; 43

The Dramatic Works of Shakespeare. Oxford: 1786-91. V. 38; 40

The Dramatick Writings. London: 1788. V. 38

Prolegomean to the Dramatick Writings. (with) The Dramatick Writings of Will. Shakespeare. London: 1788-1801. V. 39

Dramatic Works; with Explanatory Notes. London: 1790. V. 41; 42

The Dramatic Works of Shakespeare. London: 1791-1802. V. 41

The Dramatic Writings . . . Perth: Ptd. by R. Morison: 1798. V. 43

Dramatic Works. London: 1802. V. 39; 41; 42; 46

The Dramatic Works. London: 1802, 1803. V. 40

Boydell's Graphic Illustrations of the Dramatic Works of Shakespeare. London: 1807. V. 38

The Dramatick Works of William Shakespeare. Boston: 1807-08. V. 44

The Dramatic Works of . . . London: 1812-15. V. 44

The Dramatic Works. London: 1825. V. 46

The Dramatic Works . . . Chiswick: 1826. V. 41; 46

Dramatic Works. London: 1827. V. 38

The Dramatic Works. London: 1837. V. 39

The Dramatic Works of William Shakespeare . . . Boston: 1841. V. 44

Dramatic Works. London: 1856. V. 38

Dramatic Works. London: 1885. V. 44

Dramatische Werke. Berlin: 1889. V. 40

The Family Shakespeare. London: 1827. V. 38; 42

The First Part of Henry the Fourth. San Francisco: 1961. V. 46

SHAKESPEARE, WILLIAM 1564-1616 continued

First Folio Shakespeare. New York: 1968. V. 38

XIV Shakespeare Sonnets, XIV Original Woodcuts. Providence: 1987. V. 40; 45

Guliemi Shakespeare Carmina Quae Sonnets Nuncupantur Latine Reddita ab Alvredo Thoma Barton Edenda Curavit Joannes Harrower. London: 1913. V. 43

The Tragicall Historie of Hamlet Prince of Denmark. V. 42

The Tragedie of Hamlet, Prince of Denmark. London: 1623. V. 44

Hamlet, Prince of Denmark . . . Boston: 1794. V. 38

Hamlet. Tragedia . . . traducida e ilustrada con la vida del autor y notas criticas por Inarco Celenio P.A. Madrid: 1798. V. 37

Hamlet. and As You Like It. London: 1820. V. 38

Hamlet. Philadelphia: 1877. V. 37

Shakespeare's Tragedy of Hamlet Prince of Denmark. East Aurora: 1902. V. 38; 41

Shakespeare's Tragedy of Hamlet, Prince of Denmark. New York: 1902. V. 46

The Tragic Historie of Hamlet. Hammersmith: 1909. V. 44; 46

The Tragicall Historie of Hamlet Prince of Denmarke. London: 1909. V. 38

Hamlet. Philadelphia: 1918. V. 45

Shakespeare's Tragedy of Hamlet. London: 1920. V. 41; 42

Hamlet, Prince of Denmark. London: 1922. V. 42; 45; 46

Shakespeare's Hamlet. London: 1922. V. 44

Die Tragishe Geschichte von Hamlet Prinzen von Daenemark. Weimar: 1928. V. 43; 45

The Tragedie of Hamlet of Denmarke. Weimar: 1930. V. 37; 38; 39; 42; 43; 46

The Tragedy of Hamlet, Prince of Denmark. 1933. V. 40

The Tragedy of Hamlet, Prince of Denmark. Great Britain: 1933. V. 43

The Tragedy of Hamlet, Prince of Denmark. High Wycombe: 1933. V. 37; 43

The Tragedy of Hamlet, Prince of Denmark. New York: 1933. V. 38; 41; 42

Hamlet. New York: 1933. V. 37; 41

Hamlet. London: 1934. V. 41

The Tragic History of Hamlet, Prince of Denmark. New York: 1972. V. 44

Hamlet. 1978. V. 40; 45

Hamlet, Prince of Denmark. Torino: 1978. V. 38

Henry VI. London: 1903. V. 41

Henry the Fourth Part 1. New York: 1939. V. 37; 41

The First Part of the Henry the Fourth. San Francisco: 1961. V. 38; 41; 43

Henry the Fifth. New York: 1940. V. 41

Henry the Sixth. New York: 1940. V. 41

Henry the Eighth. New York: 1939. V. 41

King Henry IV. Glasgow/London: 1904. V. 37

King Henry the Eighth. 1903. V. 41

The Illustrated Shakespeare. London: 1843. V. 43

Julius Caesar. London: 1684. V. 40; 43

Julius Caesar. London: 1691. V. 45

The Tragedie of Julius Caesar. Hammersmith: 1913. V. 38; 39; 40

Julius Caesar. New York: 1939. V. 41

The Tragedie of Julius Caesar. San Francisco;: 1954. V. 38; 45; 46

King Henry IV, First Part. (with) The Merchant of Venice. London: 1934, 1935. V. 39

King Henry the Eighth. (with) The Coronation of Anne Bullen. London: 1762. V. 40; 43; 46

King Henry the Eighth. London: 1903; V. 40

The Life of King Henry VIII. London: 1948. V. 40

King Henry the Eighth. London: 1762. V. 43

King Lear, Othello and Anthony and Cleopatra. London: 1631. V. 44

The Tragedie of King Lear. London: 1927. V. 37; 38; 40; 41; 42; 44; 45; 46

King Lear, by William Shakespeare. With an Introduction by G.K. Chesterton. (London: 1930). V. 37

King Lear. San Francisco: 1930. V. 45

The Tragedie of King Lear. San Francisco: 1959. V. 38; 43; 44

King Lear. With Nine Original Etchings by Christopher Kent. Guildford: 1973. V. 37

The Tragedie of King Lear. Austin: 1986. V. 38; 40; 44; 45

The Tragedie of King Lear. Bangor: 1986. V. 37; 38; 40; 43; 45

The Tragedie of King Lear. Newark: 1986. V. 39

The Tragedie of King Lear. Newark, Vermont: 1986. V. 37

The Library Shakespeare. London: 1840. V. 46

The Life and Death of John Falstaff. London: 1923. V. 43

The Life of King Henry V. New York: 1951. V. 42; 43

The Life of Timon of Athens. London: 1900. V. 38

The Love and Friendship Sonnets. Philadelphia: 1901. V. 43

Loves Labour's Lost. London: 1924. V. 40

Shakespeare's Loves Labour's Lost. London: 1924. V. 38

Lucrece. Oxford: 1905. V. 46

Lucrece. Hammersmith: 1915. V. 44; 46

Macbeth. Tubingen: 1801. V. 40

Macbeth. Tubingen: 1801. V. 46

Macbeth. New York: 1903. V. 38

Shakespeare's The Tragedie of MacBeth. London: 1923. V. 38; 40; 43; 45

Macbeth. New York: 1939. V. 41

Macbeth. Garden City: 1946. V. 39

Macbeth. New York: 1946. V. 40

Macbeth. Guildford, Surrey: 1970. V. 39

Macbeth. Surrey: 1970. V. 37; 40

Measure for Measure. London: 1685. V. 39

The Merchant of Venice. London: 1909. V. 42; 46

The Merchant of Venice. London: 1920. V. 39

The Merchant of Venice. London: 1923. V. 38

The Merchant of Venice. Stratford-on-Avon: 1923. V. 41

The Merchant of Venice. London: 1924. V. 40

The Merchant of Venice. London: 1930. V. 41

The Merchant of Venice. New York: 1939. V. 41

The Merry Wives of Windsor. London: 1910. V. 37; 38; 41; 42; 43; 44

A Mid-Summer Night's Dream. London: 1908. V. 37; 39; 40; 41; 43; 44; 45; 46

Shakespeare's Midsummer-Night's Dream. Boston: 1870. V. 40

A Midsummer's Night Dream. London: 1895. V. 40

A Midsummer Night's Dream. London: and New York: 1908. V. 45

A Midsummer Night's Dream. New York: 1912. V. 38

Shakespeare's Comedy of a Midsummer-Night's Dream. London: 1914. V. 37

Shakespeare's Comedy of a Midsummer Night's Dream. New York: 1914. V. 37

A Midsummer Night's Dream. London: 1924. V. 37; 38; 40; 42; 44; 46

A Midsummer Night's Dream. Avalun Press at Hellerau: 1926. V. 43

A Midsummer Night's Dream. New York: 1939. V. 41

A Midsummer Night's Dream. San Francisco: 1955. V. 37; 38; 45; 46

A Midsummer Night's Dream. London: 1977. V. 41

Mr. William Shakespear's Comedies, Histories, and Tragedies. London: 1685. V. 41

The National Shakespeare. London: 1888-89. V. 39; 42

The National Shakespeare. London: 1904. V. 46

The Norton Facsimile of the First Folio. New York: 1968. V. 43

Of Imagination All Compact: a Suite of Four Sonnets. San Francisco: 1971. V. 46

Original Leaves from the Shakespeare Folios. 1623-1632-1663-1685. V. 45

Original Leaves from the Shakespeare Folios. 1623-1632, 1663-1685. San Francisco: 1938. V. 43

Othello. London: 1926. V. 44

Othello. New York: 1939. V. 41

The Tragedie of Othello. San Francisco: 1956. V. 37; 38; 39; 44

Othello. Northampton: 1973. V. 37

The Passionate Pilgrim. London: 1896. V. 37; 43; 44; 45

The Passionate Pilgrim & The Songs in Shakespeare's Plays, edited by T. Sturge Moore. (London: 1896). V. 37

The Passionate Pilgrim. Oxford: 1905. V. 46

Pericles Prince of Tyre. London: 1900. V. 39

Pericles. Oxford: 1905. V. 43; 46

The Plays of William Shakespeare. London: 1765. V. 38; 44

Comedies, Histories and Tragedies . . . London: 1767. V. 37

The Plays . . . With the Corrections & Illustrations of Various Commentators; to Which aare Added Notes by Sam. Johnson. London: 1768. V. 38

The Plays, from the Text of Dr. Johnson . . . . (with) Shakespeare's Poems. Dublin: 1771. V. 42

The Plays of William Shakespeare. London: 1773. V. 38; 39; 42; 46

The Plays, With the Corrections and Illustrations of Various Commentators: to which are added Notes by Samuel Johnson and George Steevens. London: 1778-80; V. 37

The Plays. London: 1785. V. 38

The Plays and Poems . . . London: 1790. V. 40

The Plays. London: 1791. V. 37

The Plays of William Shakespeare. London: 1793. V. 37; 38; 39; 42; 45

The Plays and Poems. Dublin: 1794. V. 38

The Plays of William Shakespeare. London: 1798. V. 42; 43

The Plays. London: 1800. V. 41

The Dramtic Works. London: 1802. V. 37

The Plays of William Shakespeare. London: 1803. V. 43

The Plays of William Shakespeare. London: 1803-05. V. 37; 40; 46

The Plays of William Shakespeare. London: 1805. V. 37; 38; 45

The Plays of William Shakespeare. London: 1807. V. 37; 42

SHAKESPEARE, WILLIAM 1564-1616 continued

Plays. London: 1811. V. 38; 42

The Plays of William Shakespeare. London: 1812. V. 38

Plays. London: 1813. V. 37; 42

The Plays, Accurately Printed from the Text of the Corrected Copies Left by . . . London: 1823. V. 42

The Plays. London: 1825. V. 37; 41; 42

The Plays. Accurately Reprinted from the Text of the Corrected Copies Left by the Lte George Steevens and Edmond Malone. London: 1826. V. 38; 43

The Plays and Poems of William Shakespeare. London: 1831. V. 38

The Plays and Poems. London: 1832. V. 38; 40; 44

The Plays and Poems. Leipsic: 1833. V. 40

The Plays. London: 1845. V. 39

Shakespeare's Plays . . . New York: 1847. V. 42; 46

The Plays of . . . Carefully Revised from the Best Authorities . . . London: 1853. V. 38

The Plays of . . . London: 1858. V. 39

The Plays of William Shakespeare. Together with The Poems of William Shakespeare. New York: 1939-40. V. 37

The Plays. 1939-41. V. 38

Plays, Poems and Commentary. Mount Vernon: 1939-41. V. 40

The First Folio. The Norton Facsimile. New York: 1968. V. 37

Poems. London: 1640. V. 38; 39

Poems. London: 1775. V. 43

The Poems. Boston: 1807. V. 38; 40; 43

The Poems. London: 1832. V. 38

The Poems. London: 1842. V. 38; 39

The Poems After the Original Copies. Venus and Adonis 1593. The Rape of Lucerece 1594. Sonnets 1609. The Lover's Complaint. Hammersmith: 1893. V. 43; 44; 45

The Poems. London: 1893. V. 41; 42

Poems. London: 1899. V. 37; 39; 41; 43; 45; 46

The Poems of Shakespare. London: 1900. V. 38; 46

The Poems of . . . Venus and Adonis, The Rape of Lucrece, The Sonnets, a Lover's Complaint, The Passionate Pilgrim, the Phoenix and Turtle. Stamford: 1939. V. 41; 43

The Poems of William Shakespeare. New York: 1941. V. 45

The Poems and Sonnets. 1960. V. 45

The Poems and Sonnets. London: 1960. V. 37; 39; 40; 42

Poems. New York: 1967. V. 37

Poems for Shakespeare. London: 1972. V. 37

The Rape of Lucrece. Hammersmith: 1915. V. 37; 41; 43

The Rape of Lucrece. London: 1915. V. 37

The Rape of Lucrece. 1925. V. 39

Richard the Second. New York: 1940. V. 41

The Tragedy of Richard the Third. San Francisco: 1953. V. 38; 40; 44; 46

Romeo e Giulietta Tragedia . . . Firenze: 1814. V. 40

Romeo and Juliet: Parallel Texts of the First Two Quartos. London: 1874. V. 45

Romeo and Juliet. London: Paris & New York: 1880. V. 44

Shakespeare's Tragedy of Romeo and Juliet. New York & London: 1912. V. 41

The Tragedy of Romeo and Juliet. London: 1920. V. 44

Romeo and Juliet. London: 1936. V. 41

Romeo (and) Juliet. 1988. V. 40; 44; 45

Romeo and Juliet. Greenbrae: 1988. V. 42; 43

The Royal Shakespeare. London. V. 38

The Seven Ages of Man. London: 1864. V. 44

Shakespeare's Sonnets - Reconsidered and In Part Rearranged . . . London: 1899. V. 43

Shakespeare's Sonnets. Hammersmith: 1909. V. 44

The Songs and Sonnets of William Shakespeare. London. V. 45

The Songs and Ballads of Shakespeare. New York. V. 44

Songs of . . . London: 1865. V. 39

Songs from the Plays. London: 1899. V. 37; 38

The Songs and Sonnets. London: 1915. V. 40; 41

Songs from Shakespeare. London: 1961. V. 43

Songs From Shakespeare's Plays. Verona: 1973. V. 45

Songs from Shakespeare's Plays. 1974. V. 37; 38; 39

Songs from Shakespeares Plays. Verona: 1974. V. 38; 40; 42; 46

Sonnet XXIX. N.P.: 1919. V. 44

The Sonnets of Shakespeare and Milton. London: 1830. V. 44

The Sonnets. London: 1881. V. 40

The Sonnets of William Shakespeare. London: 1893. V. 38; 43

The Sonnets of Shakespeare. East Aurora, NY: 1899. V. 37

Shakespeare's Sonnets. Cambridge: 1901. V. 44

The Sonnets. New Rochelle: 1901. V. 39; 40; 46

The Sonnets of Shakespare. New York: 1901. V. 39; 41; 44

Shakespeare's Sonnets and a Lover's Complaint. Oxford: 1907. V. 37

Shake-speares Sonnets; Tercentenary Edition. Hammersmith: 1909. V. 45

The Sonnets. London: 1913. V. 39

Sonette. Meunchen: 1921. V. 41

The Sonnets of . . . London: 1923. V. 46

The Sonnets. London: 1928. V. 40

The Sonnets of William Shakespear. London: 1933. V. 46

The Sonnets of William Shakespeare & Henry Wriothesley, Third Earl of Southampton . . . Oxford: 1938. V. 44

Sonnets. Lexington: 1956. V. 43; 44

Shakespeare's Sonnets. Lexington: 1956. V. 37

The Sonnets of . . . London: 1974. V. 42

Shakespeare's Sonnets. London: 1979. V. 37

Sonnets. 1988. V. 40; 45

The Sonnets of William Shakespeare. New York: 1990. V. 45

The Sonnets of William Shakespeare. New York City: 1990. V. 39; 45

Tales from Shakespeare. London: 1909. V. 45

The Taming of the Shrew. New York: 1940. V. 41

The Taming of the Shrew. Palo Alto: 1967. V. 40

The Taming of the Shrew. (Palo Alton): 1967. V. 37

The Taming of the Shrew. San Francisco: 1967. V. 41

The Taming of the Shrew. San Francisco: 1967. V. 38

The Tempest. London. V. 40; 43

The Tempest. London: 1860. V. 39

Shakespeare's Tempest. London: 1893. V. 44

The Tempest. London: 1901. V. 44; 45

The Tempest. Glasgow: 1904. V. 44

Shakespeare's Comedy of the Tempest. London: 1908. V. 41; 42; 43; 44

Shakespeare's Comedy of the Tempest. London: (1908). V. 37

The Tempest. New York: 1910. V. 44

The Tempest. 1924. V. 42

The Tempest. Montagonola: 1924. V. 38; 39; 40; 45

The Tempest. London: 1926. V. 37; 38; 40; 42; 43; 44; 45; 46

The Tempest. New York: 1926. V. 40

The Tempest. San Francisco: 1951. V. 37; 38; 39; 40; 46

The Tempest. London: 1982. V. 45

Shakespeare's Comedy of the Tempest. London: (n.d.). V. 37

The Temple Shakespeare, A Complete Set, Including the Sonnets. London: 1914-19. V. 46

Timon of Athens. New York: 1940. V. 41

Titus Andronicus. 1973. V. 44; 46

Titus Andronicus. Northampton: 1973. V. 37; 38; 39; 42

The Lamentable Tragedy of Titus Andronicus. (Edited by T. Sturge Moore). 1901. V. 37

Tragedies, Comedies, Historical Plays, Poems and Sonnets. London: 1907. V. 45

The Tragedy of Romeo and Juliet. London: 1685. V. 42

Trolius and Cressida. London: 1695. V. 38

Shakespeare's Comedy of Twelfth Night or What You Will. London: 1908. V. 41; 42; 43; 46

Twelfth Night, or, What You Will. Waltham St. Lawrence: 1932. V. 46

Shakespeare's Comedy of Twelfth Night. London: (n.d.). V. 37

Two gentlemen of Verona. London: 1894. V. 44

Venus and Adonis. London: 1912. V. 37; 39; 40; 43

Venus and Adonis. 1905. V. 45

Venus and Adonis. Stratford-on-Avon: 1905. V. 46

Venus and Adonis. Hammersmith: 1912. V. 38; 39; 40; 42; 45

Shakespeare's Venus and Adonis. Paris: 1930. V. 37; 41; 44; 46

Venus & Adonis. Rochester: 1931. V. 37; 39; 40; 41; 42; 43; 44; 45; 46

Venus and Adonis. San Francisco: 1975. V. 39; 40; 43

Venus and Adonis. Tempe: 1984. V. 46

Venus and Adonis. New York: 1930. V. 38

Venus and Adonis. Harrow Weald: 1931. V. 37

The Winter's Tale. London: 1735. V. 42

The Winter's Tale. London: 1756. V. 42

The Winter's Tale. London: 1888. V. 42

The Winter's Tale. New York: 1940. V. 41

Works. Glasgow. V. 38

The Works. London. V. 38; 40; 46

The Works of Mr. William Shakespeare; in six (i.e. seven) volumes. Adorn'd with Cuts. Revis'd ane Corrected, with an Account of the Life and Writings of the Author. By N. Rowe, Esq. London: 1709-10. V. 37

The Works of Mr. William Shakespeare . . . London: 1710. V. 41

The Works. London: 1723-25. V. 37; 40; 42

The Works of Shakespeare. London: 1725. V. 38

SHAKESPEARE, WILLIAM 1564-1616 continued

The Works in Eight volumes. London: 1740. V. 45

The Works. Oxford: 1744. V. 41

The Works of . . . Oxford: 1744-43-44. V. 38

The Works. London: 1747. V. 42; 45

The Works of Shakespear in Nine Volumes. London: 1747-60. V. 41

The Works of Shakespeare; in Seven Volumes. London: 1753. V. 46

The Foulis Press Edition of the Works. Glasgow: 1766. V. 39

The Works. London: 1767. V. 37; 38

The Works. Oxford: 1770-71. V. 38

The Works of Shakespeare. London: 1773. V. 38; 46

The Dramatic Works of Shakespeare. Oxford: 1786-91. V. 37

The Works, Containing His Plays and Poems . . . London: 1797. V. 42; 46

The Dramatic Works of Shakespeare, Revised by George Steevens. London: 1802. V. 37

The Works of . . . London: 1803-04. V. 46

The Complete Works. Leipzig: 1837. V. 43

The Works. London: 1842-44. V. 39; 42; 45

The Works . . . London: 1844. V. 38

Works. London: 1850. V. 46

The Works of . . . London: 1857. V. 46

The Works. London: 1860. V. 39; 45

Works. The Pictorial Edition (Extra illustrated) Edited by Charles Knight. Lonon: (1860's). V. 37

The Works of . . . London: 1862. V. 42

Works. Cambridge: 1863. V. 42

The Works of William Shakespeare. Cambridge & London: 1863-66. V. 38

The Works of . . . . London: 1863-66. V. 46

The Works. London: 1864. V. 44; 46

The Library Shakespeare. London: 1865? V. 37

The Works of . . . Cambridge & London: 1866. V. 44

The Works. London: 1866-67. V. 42

The Works of Shakespeare (sic). New York: 1868-70. V. 46

The Works. London: 1870. V. 37; 43

Works. Boston: 1871. V. 42

The Library Shakespeare. London: (1873). V. 37

The Works. London: 1874. V. 37; 46

The Works . . . The Text revised by the Rev. Alexander Dyce. In Nine Volumes. Third Edition. London: 1874-7. V. 37; 38

The Works. London: 1875. V. 38; 42

The Works of William Shakespeare. London: 1875-76. V. 43

The Works of Shakespeare. London: 1876. V. 39; 40

The Complete Works of William Shakespeare. 1878. V. 46

The Works of . . . London: 1878. V. 44

Works. London: 1880-81. V. 37; 40; 42

The Works of Shakspeare . . . London: 1880? V. 42

The Works. London: 1881. V. 38; 42

The Works. London: 1881. V. 42

The Works. London: 1881-82. V. 37; 39

Works. London: 1886. V. 42; 43

The National Shakespeare. A Fac-simile of the text of the first folio of 1623. London: (1888-89). V. 37

The Works. London: 1888-90. V. 45

The Works. London: 1890. V. 39

Works. London: 1890. V. 39

The Pictorial Edition of the Works of Shakepeare. London: 1890. V. 39

The Works of . . . London: 1891. V. 46

The Works. London: 1893. V. 38; 42; 44

Works. London: 1894. V. 44

The Works. London: 1895. V. 37

The Works. London: 1895-1904. V. 46

The Works. London: 1897. V. 38; 40

The 'Pocket Falstaff' Edition of the Complete Works. London: 1897. V. 39

The Works.. London & New York: 1898. V. 41

Works. London: 1900. V. 40

The Works of . . . London: 1900-1903. V. 37

The Complete Works. London: 1901. V. 42

The Works. London: 1901-03. V. 42

The Works of Shakespeare. Edinburgh: 1901-04. V. 37; 42

The Works. London: 1902. V. 38

Works. New York: 1902. V. 46

The Works. London: 1903-04. V. 44

Works. London: 1904. V. 39

The Works . . . Stratford-on-Avon: 1904. V. 40

The Works. Stratford-on-Avon: 1904-07. V. 38; 42; 44; 46

The Complete Works. London: 1905. V. 42

The Works of. London: 1905. V. 38; 40

The Works. London: 1906. V. 39

Complete Works . . . New York: 1907-09. V. 44

Works of . . . London: 1911. V. 45

The Comedies, Histories, Tragedies and Poems of . . . Boston: 1912. V. 38

Works. London: 1919. V. 45

The Works . . . London: 1920's. V. 42

Works. New York: 1920's. V. 42

Works. London: 1922. V. 42

Shakespeare's the Tragedia of Macbeth Printed from the Folio fo 1623. (With the introduction by Harley Granville-Barker. Illustrations by Charles Ricketts. Under the editorship of Ibert Rutherston). London: 1923. V. 37

The Works. Oxford: 1928-29. V. 42

The Works. London: 1929. V. 37; 38; 41; 42; 44; 45

Works. New York: 1929. V. 42

The Works of . . . London: 1929-32. V. 41

The Works of Shakespeare. London: 1929-33. V. 37; 39; 41; 46

The Works. New York: 1929-33. V. 41; 44; 45; 46

The Works. London: 1930. V. 38; 42

The New Temple Shakespeare. London: 1935-39. V. 37

The Complete Works. Garden City: 1936. V. 38; 42; 46

The Complete Works. New York: 1936. V. 43

Complete Works. New York: 1940-41. V. 46

Complete Works. New York: 1946. V. 37

Complete Works. London: 1953. V. 37; 40; 42; 43; 46

Works. London: 1953. V. 40

The Yale Shakespare (Works). New Haven & London: 1963. V. 41

The Works of Shakespeare. New York: 1969. V. 43

The Complete Works. Oxford: 1986. V. 40

SHAKESPEARE'S England. An Account of the Life and Manners of His Age. London: 1916. V. 46

SHAKESPEAR'S Seven Stages of Man's Life, From the Cradle to the Grave . . . N.P.: 1840? V. 44

SHAKSPEAR, JOHN

A Grammar of the Industani Language. London: 1826. V. 39

SHAKU, SOYEN

Sermons of a Buddhist Abbot. 1906. V. 44

SHALDACH, WILLIAM J.

Carl Rungius: Big Game Painter. West Hartford: 1945. V. 46

SHALER, NATHANIEL SOUTHGATE

Glaciers. Boston: 1881. V. 40

SHALER, WILLIAM

Journal of a Voyage Between China and the North Western Coast of America (and California) Made in 1804. Philadelphia: 1808. V. 39

Journal of a Voyage Between China and the North-Western Coast of America Made in 1804 By . . . Claremont: 1935. V. 44

SHALLENBERGER, ELIZA JANE

Stark County and Its Pioneers. Cambridge: 1876. V. 42

THE SHANACHIE: An Illustrated Irish Miscellany. Dublin: 1906-07. V. 39; 40

SHAND, ALEXANDER INNES

Fortune's Wheel. London: 1886. V. 41

Shooting the Rapids. London: 1872. V. 42; 43

SHAND, MASON & CO.

Manual Fire Engines, Fire Escapes, Hydrants, Pumps &c. London: 1885. V. 38

SHAND, P. MORTON

Modern Theatres and Cinemas. London: 1930. V. 37

SHANE, BRIAN DE

De Sade. London: 1929. V. 46

SHANGE, NTOSAKE

For Colored Girls Who Have Considered Sucide, When the Rainbow is Enuf. San Lorenzo: 1975. V. 42; 45

SHANKLAND, H.

Messer Pietro Mio. The Letters Between Lucrezia Borgia and Pietro Bembo. Marlborough: 1986. V. 39

SHANKLAND, HUGH

Messer Pietro Mio: Letters Between Lucrezia Borgia and Pietro Bembo. 1985. V. 44

SHANKS, EDWARD

The Universal War and the Universal State. London: 1946. V. 38; 40

SHANNON, CHARLESHAZELWOOD

The Pageant. London: 1896/97. V. 41; 42

SHANNON, FRANCIS BOYLE, VISCOUNT

Discourses Useful for the Vain Modish Ladies and Their Gallants. London: 1696. V. 46

Several Discourses and Characters Address'd to the Ladies of the Age. London: 1689. V. 41; 42

SHANNON, FRED A.

The Organization and Administration of the Union Army 1861-1865. Cleveland: 1928. V. 40; 44; 45

SHANNON, JAMES

An Address Delivered Before the Pro-Slavery Covnention of the State of Missouri . . . July 13, 1855, on Domestic Slavery. St. Louis: 1855, 1855. V. 39

SHANNON, S. D.

Resources of Wyoming: The Soil, Climate, Productions, Advantages, and Development . . . Cheyenne: 1889. V. 37

SHAPED Poetry. San Francisco: 1981. V. 44

SHAPIRO, DAVID

January. New York: 1965. V. 42; 43; 45

SHAPIRO, HARVEY

The Book and Other Poems. Rowe: 1955. V. 37

SHAPIRO, KARL

Adam and Eve. Lewisburg: 1986. V. 43

Trial of a Poet and Other Poems. New York: 1947. V. 39

SHAPIRO, KARL JAY

Person, Place and Thing. New York: 1942. V. 46

Poems. Baltimore: 1935. V. 43

SHAPLAND, H. P.

The Practical Decoration of Furniture. London: 1927. V. 42

SHARE, F. A. C.

The Registers of the Parish Church of Linton-In-Craven, Co. York. 1562-1812. 1900-03. V. 45

SHARIF, W. I.

Oil and Dvelopment in the Arab Gulf States. London: 1985. V. 44

SHARKEY, P. A.

The Heart of Ireland. Boyle: 1927. V. 39

SHARMAN, JULIAN

The Library of Mary, Queen of Scots. London: 1889. V. 39; 40

SHARP, A.

Bicycles & Tricycles. An elementary treatise on their Design and Construction . . . London: 1896. V. 37

SHARP & SMITH

Catalog of General Surgical Supplies. Chicago: 1926. V. 42

SHARP, CECIL J.

The Dance. An Historical Survey of Dancing in Europe. London: 1924. V. 45

SHARP, CUTHBERT

Catalogue of Rare and Curious Books, Copperplates and Woodcuts and Valuable Literary Copyrights . . . Newcastle: 1849. V. 45

SHARP, D.

Fauna Hawaiiensis or the Zoology of the Sandwich (Hawaiaan) Isles. Cambridge: 1899-1913. V. 43

SHARP, ELIZABETH A.

Lyra Celtica. Edinburgh: 1896. V. 46

SHARP, EVELYN

The Story of the Weather Cock. New York & Bosotn: 1907. V. 40

SHARP, EVLEYN

The Story of the Weathercock. London: 1907. V. 46

SHARP, GRANVILLE 1734-1813

An Account of the Ancient Division of the English Nation into Hundreds and Tithings . . . London: 1784. V. 38; 39

A General Plan for Laying Out Towns and Townships on the New Acquired Lands in the West Indies, America, or Elsewhere. London: 1794. V. 46

The Gilbart Prize Essay on the Adaptation of Recent Discoveries and Inventions in Science and Art to the Purposed of Practical Banking. London: 1854. V. 38; 41

The Law of Retribution; or, a Serious Warning to Great Britain and Her Colonies. London: 1776. V. 38; 46

Remarks Concerning the Encroachments on the River Thames Near Durham Yard Addressed to the Right Honourable the Lord Mayor . . . London: 1771. V. 42

Remarks On the Opinions of Some of the Most Celebrated Writers on Crown Law, Respecting the Due Distinction Between Manslaughter and Murder . . . London: 1773. V. 38; 42

Remarks on the Opinions of Some of the Most Celebrated Writers on Crown Law, Respecting the Due Distinction Between Manslaughter and Murder . . . London: 1773. V. 39

A Tract on the Law of Nature and Principles of Action in Man. London: 1777. V. 39

SHARP, HENRY

Modern Sporting Gunnery. London: 1906. V. 37; 39; 40

Practical Wildfowling. London: 1895. V. 39

SHARP, J. F. MAINWARING

The Thoroughbred Mares' Record. London: 1929. V. 37

SHARP, JOHN

A Sermon Preached at Trinity Church in New York. America. August 13, 1706. At the Funeral of the Right Honourable Katherine Lady Cornbuny . . . Wife to . . . Her Majesty's Captain General, and Governor in Chief of the Provinces of New Jersey and Territories . . . . London: 1706. V. 41; 44

A Sermon Preached at Trinity Church in New York, in America, August 13, 1706. At the Funereal of the Right Honourable Katherine Lady Cornbury. London: 1708. V. 41

SHARP, JONATHAN

Jonathan Sharp; or, The Adventures of a Kentuckian. London: 1845. V. 39; 41

SHARP, RICHARD

Epistles in Verse. London: 1828. V. 40

Letters and Essays in Prose and Verse. London: 1834. V. 40

SHARP, SAMUEL

A Critical Enquiry into the Present State of Surgery. London: 1750. V. 41; 44; 45; 46

A Description of a New Method of Opening the Cornea, In Order to Extract the Crystalline Humour. 1753. V. 42

Letters from Italy . . . The Years 1765, and 1766. London: 1766. V. 43

Letters from Italy, Describing the Customs and Manners of that Country. London: 1767. V. 41; 42; 44; 45

A Treatise on the Operations of Surgery, with a Description and Representation of the Instruments Used in Performing Them . . . London: 1739. V. 39

A Treatise on the Operations of Surgery, with a Description and Representation of the Instruments Used in Performing Them . . . London: 1740. V. 41; 42; 45

A Treatise On the Operations of Surgery, with a Description and Representation of the Instruments Used in Performing Them . . . London: 1761. V. 42

SHARP, THOMAS 1770-1841

A Dissertation on the Pageants or Dramatic Mysteries Anciently Performed at Coventry . . . Coventry: 1825. V. 39; 42

A Dissertation on the Pageants of Dramatic Mysteries Anciently Performed at Coventry . . . Coventry: 1825. V. 38

SHARP, WILLIAM

An Account of a New Method of Treating Fractured Legs, Read Before the Royal Society of London . . . London: 1767. V. 37

Dante Gabriel Rossetti: A Record and a Study. London: 1882. V. 40; 41; 43

Deirdre and the Sons of the USNA. Portland: 1903. V. 43

Sante Gabriel Rossetti: A Record and a Study. By William Sharp. London: 1882. V. 37

Sospira di Roma. Roma: 1891. V. 39

The Works. London: 1910. V. 38

The Works. London: 1910-19. V. 38

SHARPE, CHARES KIRKPATRICK

Etchings. Edinburgh: 1869. V. 38; 39

SHARPE, CHARLES KIRKPATRICK

Metrical Legends and Other Poems. Oxford: 1807. V. 43; 45

Surgundo. Edinburgh: 1837. V. 43

SHARPE, DANIEL

Description of the Fossil Remains of Mollusca Found in the Chalk of England. Parts I, II and III (complete). London: 1853-54-56. V. 40

SHARPE, EDMUND

An Account of the Churches Visited During the Lincoln Excursion. London: 1871. V. 37

Architectural Parallels, or the Progress of Ecclesiastical Architecture in England through the Twelfth and Thirteenth Centuries . . . London: 1848. V. 38

The Seven Periods of English Architecture Defined and Illustrated. London: 1851. V. 42

Supplement to 'Architectural Parallels' Containing the Full Sized Mouldings. London: 1848. V. 38

A Visit to the Domed Chruches of Charente . . . London: 1875. V. 37; 40; 44

SHARPE, GREGORY

A Second Argument in Defence of Christianity, Taken from the Ancient Prophesies, Applied to the Most Remarkable Events in the Life and Character of Jesus Christ. London: 1762. V. 38

A Short Dissertation Upon that Species of Misgovernment Called Oligarchy. London: 1748. V. 41

SHARPE, JAMES BIRCH

Elements of Anatomy, Designed for the Use of Students in the Fine Arts. London: 1818. V. 40; 44

SHARPE, JOHN

British Classics. London: 1803-10. V. 37

The Church. a Poem. London: 1797. V. 41

A Sermon Preached at Trinity-Church in New York, in America, August 13, 1706. London: 1706? V. 37; 45; 46

SHARPE, LEWIS

The Noble Stranger. London: 1640. V. 37; 40

SHARPE, R. B.

Monograph of the Paradiseidae or Birds of Paradise and Ptilonorhynchidae or Bower Birds. London: 1891-98. V. 42

SHARPE, R. BOWDLER

An Analytical Index to the Works of the Late John Gould. London: 1893. V. 42; 43

SHARPE, R. S.

Dame Wiggins of Lee and Her Seven Wonderful Cats. Orpington: 1885. V. 42

SHARPE, REGINALD R.

Calendar of Wills Proved and Enrolled in the Court of Husting, London, A.D. 1258 - A.D. 1688. London: 1889. V. 42

SHARPE, RICHARD BOWDLER

A Hand-List of the Genera and Species of Birds. London: 1899-1912. V. 37; 38

Lloyd's Natural History. London: 1896-97. V. 37; 38

A Monograph of the Alcedinidae: or, Family of Kingfishers. London: 1868-71. V. 37; 38

On the Birds Collected by Professor J. B. Steere in the Philippine Archipelago. London: 1877. V. 37; 38

SHARPE, RICHARD SCRAFTON

The Margate New Guide; or Memoirs of Five Families Out of Six. London: 1799. V. 42

Matilda, or the Welch Cottage. London: 1801. V. 43

Theodore, or, the Gamester's Progress. London: 1824. V. 43

SHARPE, SAMUEL

The Alabaster Sarcophagus of Oimenetah I. King of Egypt, now in Sir John Soane's Musem, Lincoln's Inn Fields. Drawn by Joseph Bonomi. London: 1864. V. 37

The Early History of Egypt, from the Old Testament, Herodotus, Manetho and the Hieroglyphical Inscriptions. London: 1836. V. 44

The Triple Mummy Case of Aroeri-ao an egyptian Priest, in Dr. Lee's Museum at Hartwell House, Buckinghamshire. Drawn by Joseph Bonomi. London: 1858. V. 40

SHARPE, TOM

The Indecent Exposure. London: 1973. V. 38

Porterhouse Blue. London: 1974. V. 44; 45; 46

Riotous Assembly. London: 1971. V. 40

SHARPE, WILLIAM

Diagnosis and Treatment of Brain Injuries with and Without a Fracture of the Skull. Philadelphia 7 London: 1920. V. 45

SHARROCK, R.

The History of the Propagation and Improvement of Vegetables by the Concurrence of Art and Nature. Oxford: 1660. V. 37

SHARSTEN, M. O.

George Drouillard, Hunter and Interpreter for Lewis and Clark and Fur Trader, 1807-10. Glendale: 1964. V. 45

SHARTS, JOHN

Eulogy on the Death of Capt. Abram Van Olinda, Who Fell at the Battle of Chapultepec, September 13, 1847 . . . Albany: 1848. V. 46

SHASKY, FLORIAN J.

Letters to Elizabeth: a Selection of Letters from John Steinbeck to Elizabeth Otis. Los Angeles: 1978. V. 38

SHASTREE, TREVANGADACHARYA

Essays on Chess Adapted to the European Mode of Play. Bombay: 1814. V. 40

SHATTUCK, LEMUEL

A History of the Town of Concord. Concord: 1835. V. 38

Letter to the Secretary of State on the Registration of Births, Marriages and Deaths in Massachusetts. Boston: 1845. V. 44

SHAVER, LEWELLYN A.

A History of the Sixtieth Alabama Regiment, Gracie's Alabama Brigade. Montgomery: 1867. V. 45

SHAVER, RUTH M.

Kabuki Costume. Rutland: 1966. V. 44

SHAVIN, NORMAN

The Atlanta Century: a Non Partisan Account . . . (1860-1865). Atlanta: 1975. V. 43

SHAVING Ambassadors Beards the Delight of the Ammonites; or, a Further Mite of Testimony. N.P.: Edinburgh?: 1739. V. 44

SHAW, ALBERT

Abraham Lincoln: His Path to the Presidency. New York: 1929. V. 44

SHAW, ALEXANDER

Narrative of the Discoveries of Sir Charles Bell in the Nervous System. London: 1839. V. 44; 45; 46

SHAW, BARNABAS

Memorials of Southern Africa. London: 1841. V. 45

Memorials of South Africa. New York: 1841. V. 40

SHAW, BYAM

India's Love Lyrics Including the Garden of Kara. Arranged in verse by Laurence Hope. New York: 1921. V. 37

Life's Ironies. London: 1912. V. 45

Old King Cole's Book of Nursery Rhymes. London: (1901). V. 37

SHAW, CHARLES

The Trials of Shaw, for Murdering John Oldcroft, Tomlinson for Murdering Mary Evans, His Sweetheart, Smith, for Drowning Her Infant Child . . . London: 1834. V. 42

SHAW, D. A.

El Dorado of California as Seen by a Pioneer 1850-1900. Los Angeles: 1900. V. 40; 44; 45

SHAW, EDWARD

Civil Architecture; or a Complete Theoretical and Practical System of Building . . . Boston: 1832. V. 39

SHAW, FLORA L.

A Tropical Dependency . . . London: 1905. V. 44

SHAW, FRED

Fred Shaw's Dime American Comic Songster . . . New York: 1858? V. 46

SHAW, FRED G.

The Complete Science of Fly Fishing and Spinning. New York: 1915. V. 44

SHAW, GEORGE 1751-1813

General Zoology, or Systematic Natural History. London: 1800-27. V. 40

The Naturalist's Miscellany. London: 1789-1790. V. 39

The Naturalist's Miscellany. London: 1789-1813. V. 39

Zoological Lectures Delivered at the Royal Institution in the Years 1806 and 1807. London: 1809. V. 39

SHAW, GEORGE A.

Madagascar and France With Some Account of the Island . . . London: 1885. V. 43

SHAW, GEORGE BERNARD 1856-1950

Androcles and the Lion, Overuled Pygmalion. London: 1916. V. 40

Androcles and the Lion. London: 1924. V. 44

The Apple Cart. London: 1930. V. 41

SHAW, GEORGE BERNARD 1856-1950 continued

Augustus does His Bit. London. V. 41

Augustus Does His Bit. 1916. V. 38

Back to Methuselah. London: 1921. V. 40; 41

Bernard Shaw on Capital Punishment. London: 1949. V. 40

The Case for Equality. London: 1913. V. 40

Cashel Byron's Profession. London: 1886. V. 37; 39; 41; 43

Cashel Byron's Profession. Chicago: 1901. V. 39

Cashel Byron's Profession. 1886. V. 38

Collected Works. New York: 1930-32. V. 38; 39

The Copyright Act, 1911. London: 1950. V. 40

The Doctor's Dilemma, Getting Married, & The Shewing-Up of Blanco Posnet. London: 1911. V. 38; 39

Don Juan in Hell. London: 1907. V. 39

Ellen Terry and Bernard Shaw a Correspondence. London: 1931. V. 39

Fabian Essays In Socialism. London: 1889. V. 38; 41

Flyleaves. 1977. V. 39

Flyleaves. Austin: 1977. V. 40

Flyleaves. North Hills: 1977. V. 38

Geneva. London: 1939. V. 38

The Great Flight. London: 1921. V. 37

Heartbreak House, Great Catherine and Playlets of the War. London: 1919. V. 41

In Good King Charles's Golden Days; a history lesson. Illustrated by Feliks Topolski. London: (1939). V. 37

The Intelligent Woman's Guide to Socialism. 1928. V. 43

The Illigent Woman's Guide to Socialism and Capitalism. London: 1928. V. 38; 46

Is Free Trade Alive or Dead? London: 1906. V. 45

John Bull's Other Island and Major Barbara: Also How He Lied to Her Husband. London: 1907. V. 38; 39

Man and Superman and The Revolutionist's Handbook & Pocket Companion. 1962. V. 40

Man and Superman. New York: 1962. V. 41; 44; 46

Misalliance. London: 1914. V. 37; 38; 39; 40

Mrs. Warren's Profession. London: 1902. V. 40

Mr. Bernard Shaw's Appeal for a British Alphabet. London: 1944. V. 40

Nine Answers, as Privately Printed for Jerome Kern in 1923 . . . Lewisbury: 1988. V. 40; 45

Nine Answers. London: 1923. V. 37

O'Flaherty V.C. An Interlude in the Great War of 1914. London. V. 41

On Going to Church. East Aurora: 1896. V. 38

Passion Play. 1971. V. 40

Passion Play. A Dramatic Fragment, 1878. London: 1971. V. 38; 44; 45

The Perfect Wagnerite. Chicago: 1899. V. 39

Playboy and Prophet. New York: 1932. V. 44

Plays; Pleasant and Unpleasant. London: 1898. V. 37; 45; 46

Plays: Pleasant and Unpleasant. London: 1901. V. 38

The Plays of . . . London: 1927-29. V. 38

The Plays. London: 1929. V. 42

Plays and Perfaces. London: 1931-34. V. 43

The Plays of George Bernard Shaw. London: 1926. V. 37

Prefaces. London: 1934. V. 37; 41; 44

Press Cuttings: A Topical Sketch. New York: 1909. V. 43

Pygmalion. London: 1913. V. 38

Pygmalion. Harmondsworth: 1941. V. 40

Pygmalion; and Candida. Avon: 1974. V. 45

The Quintessence of Ibsenism. London: 1891. V. 37; 38; 44; 46

The Quintessence of Ibsenism. Chicago: 1899. V. 39

Saint Joan. London: 1923. V. 41

Saint Joan. London: 1924. V. 37; 38; 39; 40; 41; 42

Saint Joan. New York: 1924. V. 46

Saint Joan: A Chronicl Play. London: (1942). V. 37

Selected Plays. New York: 1948. V. 46

Shaw Gives Himself Away. London: 1939. V. 40

Shaw Gives Himself Away. Newtown: 1939. V. 37; 38; 39; 40; 42; 43; 45; 46

Shaw Gives Himself Away. An Autobiographical Miscellany. (Newton, Montgomeryshire): 1939. V. 37

The Shewing Up of Blanco Posnet. New York: 1909. V. 43

The Simpleton, The Six, and the Millinairess. London: 1936. V. 39

Sixteen Self Sketches by Bernard Shaw. London: 1949. V. 39; 41

This Time the Preachment on Going to Church . . . New York: MDCCCXCVI. V. 41

Three Plays for Puritans. Chicago: 1901. V. 40; 42

Translations and Tomfooleries. London: 1926. V. 39

An Unsocial Socialist. London: 1887. V. 44

Vote! Vote!! Vote!!! London: 1892. V. 40

Widowers' Houses. London: 1893. V. 42

Works. London: 1930. V. 39; 40; 46

The Collected Works. New York: 1930. V. 38

Collected works. New York: 1930. V. 37; 42; 45

The Works. London: 1930-32. V. 40; 43

The Works of . . . London: 1930-34. V. 37

Works. London: 1930-38. V. 37; 38; 42

Standard Edition of the Works of Bernard Shaw. London: 1949. V. 39

SHAW, GEORGE C.

The Chinook Jargon and How to Use It. Seattle: 1909. V. 45

SHAW, H.

Observations on the Origin and Nature of Comets. London: 1832. V. 39

SHAW, HENRY 1800-1873

Alphabets Numerals and Devices of the Middle Ages. London: 1845. V. 38

Alphabets Numerals and Devices of the Middle Ages. Pickering: 1845. V. 37

The Arms of the Colleges of Oxford. Oxford: 1855, 1857. V. 38

Booke of Sundry Draughtes. London: 1848. V. 38; 41; 43

The Decorative Arts of the Middle Ages. London: 1850. V. 38

The Decorative Arts Eccclesiastical and Civil of the Middle Ages. London: 1851. V. 37; 39; 41; 46

Details of Elizabethan Architecture. London: 1839. V. 38; 39; 41

Details of Elizabethan Architecture. Edinburgh: 1898. V. 38

Dresses and Decorations of the Middle Ages. London: 1843. V. 37; 38; 39; 40; 41; 43; 44; 46

Dresses and Decorations of the Middle AGes from the Seventh to the Seventeenth Centuries. London: 1858. V. 39; 43

The Encyclopaedia of Ornament. London: 1842. V. 38; 43

The Encyclopaedia of Ornament. Edinburgh: 1898. V. 38

Examples of Ornamental Metal Work. London: 1836. V. 42; 45

The Hand Book of Medieval Alphabets and Devices. London: 1856. V. 39

The Handbook of Mediaeval Alphabets and Devices. London: 1853. V. 37; 40

A Handbook of the Art of Illumination as Practised During the Middle Ages. London: 1866. V. 39

The History and Antiquities of the Chapel at Lutton Park Seat of . . . the Marquess of Bute. London: 1829. V. 44

The History and Antiquities of the Chapel at Luton Park, a Seat of the Most Honourable the Marquess of Bute. London: 1930. V. 38

illuminated Ornaments Selected from Manuscripts and Early Printed Books from the Sixth to the Seventeenth Centuries. London: 1833. V. 38; 40; 41; 43; 44; 46

Illuminated Ornaments Selected from Manuscripts and Early Printed Books from the Sixth to the Seventeenth Centuries. London: 1933. V. 38

Specimens of Ancient Furniture. London: 1836. V. 38; 39; 44

The Vine and Civilisation. St. Louis: 1884. V. 40

SHAW, HENRY WHEELER 1818-1885

Old Probability, Perhaps Rain-Perhaps Not. New York: 1879. V. 39; 41

SHAW, HORACE H.

The First Maine Heavy Artillery 1862-1865. Portland: 1903. V. 42

SHAW, IRWIN

Bury the Dead. New York: 1936. V. 46

The Young Lions. New York: 1948. V. 46

SHAW, J.

The Practical Justice of the Peace. In the Savoy: 1751. V. 37

SHAW, JAMES

Early Reminiscences of Pioneer Life in Kansas. Atchison: 1886. V. 42

Our Last Campaign and Subsequent Service in Texas. Providence: 1905. V. 39

The Scotch-Irish in History. Springfield/Bloomington: 1899. V. 43

Sketches of the History of the Austrian Netherlands . . . London: 1786. V. 43

SHAW, JAMES BYAM

Drawings by Old Masters at Christ Church, Oxford. 1976. V. 44

Drawings by Old Masters at Christ Church Oxford. Oxford: 1976. V. 43

SHAW, JOHN 1559-1625

The Divine Art of Memory; or, the Sum of the Holy Scriptures Delivered in Acrostick Verses. London: 1683. V. 38

Experimental Observations on the Development and growth of Salmon-Fry from the Exclusion of the Ova to the Age of Two Years. Edinburgh: 1840. V. 45

A Tramp to the Diggings; Being Notes of a Ramble in Austalia and New Zealand 1852. London: 1852. V. 41; 46

SHAW, JOHN BENNETT

The Whole Art of Detection by Sherlock Holmes. Chicago and Skokie: 1968. V. 41

SHAW, JOHN HOLBROOK

Vacation Journeys: An Account of Holiday Trips to the Pacific Coast, Florida, and Scotland, Including Some Observations of Bird-Life by the Way. N.P.: 1912. V. 39

SHAW, JOSEPH

The Lakes of Scotland: a Series of Views, From Paintings Taken Expressly for the Work by John Fleming . . . Glasgow: 1834. V. 46

Parish Law; or, a Guide to Justices of the Peace, Ministers, Church-Wardens, Overseers of the Poor, Constables, Surveyors of the Highways, Vestry Clerks. London: 1734. V. 41

Parish Law; or, a Guide to Justices of the Peace, Ministers, Church-wardens, Overseers of the Poor . . . In the Savoy: 1743. V. 44

Parish Law; or, a Guide to the Justices of the Peace, Ministers, Churchwardens, Overseers of the Poor, Constables, Surveyors of the Highways, Vestry-Clerks, and All Others Concern'd in Parish Business. In the Savoy: 1748. V. 39

Parish Law: or Guide to Justices of the Peace, Ministers, Churchwardens, Overseers of the Poor, Constables, Surveyors of the Highways, Vestry Clerks and All Others Concerned in Parish Business. London: 1763. V. 46

SHAW, JOSEPH W.

Minoan Architecture: Materials and Techniques. Roma: 1973. V. 42

SHAW, LACHLAN

The History of the Province of Moray: Extending from the Mouth of the River Spey, to the Borders of Lochaber in Length . . . Edinburgh: 1775. V. 39; 44

The History of the Province of Moray. Elgin: 1827. V. 38

SHAW-LAWRENCE, BETTY

An Herbarium for the Fair. London: 1949. V. 38

SHAW, LUELLA

The History of Some of the Pioneers of Colorado. Hotchkiss: 1909. V. 38; 40; 42; 43; 45

True History of Some of the Pioneers of Colorado. 1909. V. 37

SHAW, OLIVER

A Favourite Selection of Music. Dedham: 1806. V. 37; 39; 40

SHAW, PETER

Chemical Lectures Publickly Read at London in the Years 1731 and 1732 and Since at Scarborough in 1733, for the Improvement of Arts, Trades and Natural Philosophy. London: 1734. V. 40; 46

An Enquiry into the Contents, Virtues and Uses of the Scarborough Spaw-Waters. London: 1734. V. 37; 40; 44; 46

An Enquiry into the Contents, Virtues and Uses, of the Scarborough Spaw-Waters . . . Scarborough: 1734. V. 44

The Juice of the Grape; or, Wine Preferable to Water . . . London: 1724. V. 42; 46

A New Practice of Physic; Wherein the Various Diseases Incident to the Human Body are Orderly Described . . . London: 1728. V. 39

A New Practice of Physic. London: 1753. V. 41

The Tablet, or Picture of Real Life. London: 1762. V. 38; 42; 46

SHAW, PRINGLE

Ramblings in California: Containing a description of the Country, Life at the Mines, State of Society &c . . . Toronto: 1856-60. V. 40

Ramblings in California. Toronto: 1860. V. 40

SHAW, R. C.

Across the Plains in Forty-Nine. Farmland: 1896. V. 38; 40; 42; 45

SHAW, R. CUNLIFFE

Across the Plains in Forty-Nine. Farmland: 1895. V. 46

Kirkham in Amounderness. Preston: 1949. V. 46

SHAW, R. NORMAN

Architecture, a Profession or an Art. London: 1892. V. 42

SHAW, R. R.

American Bibliography. A Preliminary Checklist for 1801 (through) 1832. New York: 1958-77. V. 40

SHAW, RALPH R.

American Bibliography, a Preliminary Checklist for 1801-1830. New York: 1958-72. V. 42

American Bibliography: a Preliminary Check-list. New York: 1958-89. V. 42

American Bibliography, a Preliminary Checklist, 1801-1837. (with) Title Index, Author's Index, and Corrections . . . through 1829. (with) Index to Printers, Publishers, Booksellers and Geographical Index. New York. V. 37

SHAW, RICHARD NORMAN

Architectural Sketches from the Continent. London: 1858. V. 38; 40; 44; 45

Architectural Sketches from the Continent. London: 1865. V. 39

Architectural Sketches from the Continent. London: 1872. V. 45

SHAW, ROBERT

Visits to High Tartary, Yarkand and Kashghar (Formerly Chinese Tartary) and a Return Journey Over the Karakoram Pass. London: 1871. V. 40; 41

SHAW, SAMUEL

(Greek Letter): or, the Different Humours of Men; Represented in an Interlude at a Country-School Dec. 15, 1691. London: 1692. V. 43

The Journals of Major Samuel Shaw, the First American Consul at Canton. Boston: 1847. V. 45

SHAW, SIMEON

History of the Staffordshire Potteries: And the Rise and Progress of the Manufacture of Pottery and Porcelain. Hanley: 1829. V. 42

SHAW, STEBBING

A Tour to the West of England, in 1788. London: 1789. V. 39; 42

SHAW, T. E.

Letters from T. E. Shaw to Bruce Rogers. 1933. V. 40

SHAW, THOMAS

A Mournfull Soung, on the Death of the Wife and Child of Mr. nathaniel Knights, of Windham, Who Fell off the Bridge at the Falls Above Horse-Beef Mills, on Presumpscutt River, February 22, 1807. N.P.: 1807. V. 40

Travels, or Observations Relating to Several Parts of Barbary and the Levant. Oxford: 1738. V. 37; 38; 39

Travels . . . London: 1757. V. 37; 39; 42

Travels, or Observations Relating to Several Parts of Barbary and the Levant. Edinburgh: 1808. V. 45

SHAW, THOMAS B.

Outlines of English: for the Use of the Imperial Alexander Lyceum. St. Petersburg: 1847. V. 41

SHAW, THURSTAN

Igbo-Ukwu - an Account of Archaeological Discoveries in Eastern Nigeria. Evanston: 1970. V. 39; 42

SHAW, VERO

British Horses Illustrated. London: 1899. V. 39

SHAW, W. A.

The History of Currency 1252 to 1894. New York: 1896. V. 46

SHAW, WILLIAM

An Analysis of the Galic Language. Edinburgh: 1778. V. 37; 38; 43; 45; 46

An Analysis of the Galic Language. (with) A Galic and English Dictionary. London: 1778, 1780. V. 40

An Enquiry into the Authenticity of the Poems Ascribed to Ossian. London: 1781. V. 38

A Galic and English Dictionary. London: 1780. V. 38

Golden Dreams and Waking Realities. London: 1851. V. 38

The Land of Promise; or, My Impressions of Australia. London: 1854. V. 46

Memoirs of the Life and Writings of the Late Dr. Samuel Johnson. London: 1785. V. 37; 39

SHAW, WILLIAM H.

History of Essex and Hudson Counties, New Jersey. Philadelphia: 1884. V. 38; 41; 46

SHAWE, JOHN

Memoirs of the Life of Master John Shawe . . . Hull: 1824. V. 39

SHAWN, TED

Gods Who Dance. New York: 1929. V. 46

SHAY, FELIX

Elbert Hubbard of East Aurora. New York: 1926. V. 41

SHAY, FRANK

Drawn from the Wood. New York: 1929. V. 38

Iron Men and Wooden Ships. New York: 1924. V. 44; 46

My Pious Friends and Drunken Companions. New York: 1930. V. 40

Pious Friends and Drunken Companions. New York: 1927. V. 38

SHE Ventures, and He Wins. London: 1696. V. 38

SHE Woke Me Up So I Killed Her. San Francisco: 1985. V. 43

SHEA, GEORGE

Jefferson Davis: a Statement Concerning the Imputed Special Causes of His Long Imprisonment By the Government of the United States, and of His Tardy Release by Due Process of Law; Contained in a Letter From . . . London: 1877. V. 42

SHEA, JOHN G.

A French-Onondaga Dictionary . . . New York: 1860. V. 37

SHEA, JOHN GILMARY 1824-1892

Catholic Missions Among the Indian Tribes of the United States 1529-1854. New York: 1855. V. 45

Discovery and Exploration of the Mississippi Valley . . . Clinton Hall: 1852. V. 42; 43

Discovery and Exploration of the Mississippi. New York: 1852. V. 38; 40; 42; 44

Discovery and Exploration of the Mississippi Valley. New York: 1853. V. 39

Discovery and Exploration of the Mississippi Valley with the Original Narratives of Marquette, Allouez, Membre, Hennepin, and Anastase Douay. Albany: 1903. V. 39; 43; 45

Early Voyages Up and Down the Mississippi by Cavelier. St. Cosme, Le Suer, Gravier and Guignas. Albany: 1861. V. 38; 43

A French-Onondaga Dictionary. New York: 1860. V. 38

History of the Catholic Missions Among the Indian Tribes of the United States, 1529-1854. New York: 1855. V. 38

History of the Catholic Church in the United States 1521-1866. New York: 1866-1892. V. 42

History of the Catholic Church in the United States (1521-1866). New York: 1886-92. V. 45

SHEABBARE, JOHN

A Letter to the People of England, on Foreign Subsidies, Subsidiary Armies, and Their Consequences to This Nation. London: 1755. V. 40

SHEALE, RICHARD

The Hounting of the Chivyat. (Market Drayton): 1981. V. 37

SHEAR, THEODORE LESLIE

Sardis. Cambridge: 1926. V. 40

SHEARDOWN, WILLIAM

Doncaster Races. Doncaster: 1861. V. 42

SHEARER, FREDERICK E.

The Pacific Tourist. New York: 1884. V. 38; 39; 45

The Pacific Tourist. New York: 1886. V. 40

SHEARMAN, ABRAHAM

Directions for Buzzard's Bay and New Bedford. (New Bedford): 1821. V. 37

SHEARMAN, WILLIAM

Essay on the Nature, Causes and Treatment of Water in the Brain. London: 1825. V. 44; 45

SHEBBEARE, JOHN 1709-1788

Fourth Letter to the People of England. London: 1756. V. 39; 40; 41; 44

The History of the Excellence and Decline of the Constitution, Religion, Laws, Manners and Genius of the Sumatrans. London: 1760? V. 45

Letters on the English Nation. London: 1755. V. 39; 40

SHECKLEY, R.

Journey Beyond Tomorrow. London: 1964. V. 44

SHECKLEY, ROBERT

Immortality Delivered. Avalon: 1958. V. 43

Untouched by Human Hands: Stories. London: 1955. V. 45

SHEE, MARTIN ARCHER

Elements of Art, a Poem. London: 1809. V. 41

Rhymes on Art, Or, the Remonstrance of a Painter, in Two Parts, with Notes . . . Philadelphia: 1811. V. 41

SHEEHAN, J. EASTMAN

General and Plastic Surgery with Emphasis on War Injuries. New York: 1945. V. 42

A Manual of Reparative Plastic Surgery. New York: 1938. V. 42

SHEEHAN, NEIL

A Bright Shining Lie. New York: 1988. V. 45

A Bright Shining Lie. New York: 1989. V. 44

SHEEHY, MAURICE P.

Pontificia Hibernica. Medieval Papal Chancery Documents Concerning Ireland. Dublin: 1962. V. 38

SHEEN, JAMES RICHMOND

Wines and Other Fermented Liquors; from the Earliest AGes to the Present Time . . . London: 1864. V. 39

SHEERES, HENRY

A Discourse Touching Tanger; on the Heads . . . London: 1680. V. 42

An Essay on the Certainty and Causes of the Earth's Motion on Its Axis &c. London: 1698. V. 46

SHEFELDT, ROBERT W.

Reports of Explorations and Surveys, to Ascertain the Practicability of a Ship-Canal. Washington: 1872. V. 44

SHEFFEY, DANIEL

Mr. Sheffey's Motion Concerning the Batture of New Orleans. City of Washington: 1809. V. 39

SHEFFIELD & MANCHESTER RAILWAY

Appendix to the Report of the Provisional Committee of the Sheffield & Manchester Railway to the Company of Proprietors, at Their First General Assembly, to Be Held Oct. 20, 1831, at the Albion Inn, Manchester, by Appointment of the Act of Parliament. Liverpool: 1831. V. 46

Report of the Provisional Committee of the Sheffield & Manchester Railway, Appointed for Obtaining the Act of Parliament. (with) Appendix to the Report . . . Liverpool: 1831. V. 46

SHEFFIELD Directory and Guide. London: 1828. V. 40

SHEFFIELD, JOHN

Poems on Several Occasions. To which are added, the Tragedies of Julius Caesar, and Marcus Brutus. Glasgow: 1752. V. 37

SHEFFIELD, JOHN BAKER HOLROYD, 1ST EARL OF 1735-1821

Observations on the Commerce of the American States. London: 1784. V. 38; 41; 43; 44; 45; 46

Observations on the Manufactures, Trade and Present State of Ireland. London: 1785. V. 39; 40; 41; 43

Observations on the Impolicy, Abuses and False Inerpretation of the Poor Laws; and on the Reports of the Two Houses of Parliament. London: 1818. V. 43

Strictures on the Necessity of Inviolably Maintaining the Navigation and Colonial System of Great Britain. London: 1804. V. 46

SHEFFIELD, JOHN BAKER HOLROYD, EARL OF

A Letter on the Corn Laws, and on the Means of Obviating the Mischiefs and Distress, Which are Rapidly Increasing. London: 1815. V. 37

SHEIL, JOHN B.

Observations on the Salmon Fisheries of Ulster; Urging Their Claims to Legislative Protection. London: 1842. V. 39

SHEIL, M. L.

Glimpses of Life and Manners in Persia. London: 1856. V. 45

SHEIL, TERESA

Poems by . . . Dublin: 1930. V. 42

SHEILD, A. MARMADUKE

A Clinical Treatise on Diseases of the Brest. London: 1898. V. 42

SHELDEN, JOHN

Of the Judicature in Parliaments, A Post-humous Treatise. London: (1681). V. 37

SHELDON, A. E.

Official Report of the Debates and proceedings in the Nebraska Constitutional Convention, Assembled in Lincoln, 1871. York, Neb.: 1906. V. 37

SHELDON, CHARLES

The Wilderness of the Upper Yukon. New York: 1911. V. 37; 39; 43; 45

The Wilderness of the North Pacific Coast. New York: 1912. V. 39; 43; 44; 45; 46

The Wilderness of the Upper Yukon . . . New York: 1913. V. 43; 44

The Wilderness of Denali; Explorations of a Hunter-Naturalist in Northern Alaska. New York: 1930. V. 38

The Wilderness of Denali: Explorations of a Hunter-Naturalist in Northern Alaska. New York: 1930. V. 37

SHELDON, D.

The Wilderness of Denali. New York: 1930. V. 39

SHELDON, ELECTRA M.

The Early History of Michigan, from the First Settlement to 1815. New York: 1856. V. 37; 39

SHELDON, GEORGE

History of Deerfield, Massachusetts . . . Deerfield: 1895. V. 46

SHELDON, GEORGE WILLIAM

American Painters: With Eighty-Three Examples of their Work Engraved on Wood. New York: 1879. V. 41; 44; 46

SHELDON, H. H.

Television: Present Methods of Picture Transmission. New York: 1930. V. 38

SHELDON, H. P.

Tranquility. Tranquility Revisited. Tranquility Regained. 1945. V. 46

SHELDON, HAROLD P.

Tranquility. New York: 1936. V. 39; 43

Tranquility Revisited. New York: 1940. V. 39; 43

Tranquility Revisited. By Col. Harold P. Sheldon. Illustrated with 7 mounted color plates by A. Lassell Ripley. New York: (1940). V. 37

SHELDON, WILLIAM

Mormonism Examined; or Was Joseph Smith a Divinely Inspired Prophet? Brodhead: 1876? V. 43

SHELDON, WILLIAM H. b. 1899

Atlas of Men: A Guide for Somatotyping the Adult Male at All Ages. New York: 1954. V. 45

SHELE, RICHARD

The Battle of Chevy Chase. Newcastle: 1830. V. 45

SHELEKHOV, GRIGORI

Erste und Zweite Reise von Ochotsk . . . nach den Kusten von Amerika in den Jahren 1783 bis 1789. St. Petersburg: 1793. V. 40

SHELFORD, ROBERT WALTER CAMPBELL

A Naturalist in Borneo . . . London: 1916. V. 45; 46

SHELLENBERGER, JOHN K.

The Battle of Spring Hill, Tennessee, Nov. 29, 1864. Cleveland: 1913. V. 44

SHELLEY, DONALD A.

The Fraktur-Writings of Illuminated Manuscripts of the Pennsylvania Germans. Allentwon: 1961. V. 43

SHELLEY, E. M.

Hunting Big Game with Dogs in Africa. Columbus: 1924. V. 43; 45

SHELLEY, G. E.

A Handbook to the Birds of Egypt. London: 1872. V. 37; 38; 40; 42; 45

SHELLEY, GEORGE

The Second Part of Natural Writing Containing the Breaks of Letters and Their Dependence on Each Other. London: 1714. V. 41

SHELLEY, GEORGE ERNEST

The Birds of Africa. London: 1896-1912. V. 38

A Monograph of the Nectariniidae, or Family of Sun-Birds. London: 1876-80. V. 37; 38; 42

SHELLEY, HENRY C.

The Homes and Haunts of Thomas Carlyle. London: 1895. V. 40

SHELLEY, MARY WOLLSTONECRAFT 1797-1851

Frankenstein; or, the Modern Prometheus. By Mary Shelley. From the 1818 text in 3 volumes. Illustrated by Barry Moser. With Essays by William St. Clair, Emily Sunstein, Joyce Carol Oates, and Ruth Mortimer. Northampton, Mass.. V. 37

Valperga: or the Life and Adventures of Castruccio, Prince of Lucca. London: 1823. V. 37; 38

SHELLEY, MARY WOLLSTONECRAFT GODWIN 1797-1851

The Choice: A Poem of Shelley's Death . . . London: 1876. V. 42

Essays, Letters from Abroad. Philadephia: 1840. V. 42

The Fortunes of Perkin Warbeck, a Romance. London: 1830. V. 43

Frankenstein. Northampton. V. 39

Frankenstein; or, the Modern Prometheus. London: 1818. V. 43; 44

Frankenstein; or the Modern Prometheus. London: 1823. V. 44

Frankenstein. London: 1831. V. 38; 40; 41; 42; 43; 44

Frankenstein; or, the Modern Promethus. Philadelphia: 1833. V. 45

Frankenstein. London: 1839. V. 40

Frankenstein; or, the Modern Prometheus. London: 1849. V. 37

Frankenstein; or, the Modern Prometheus. Boston & Cambridge: 1869. V. 39

Frankenstein. London: 1880. V. 42

Frankenstein. Introduction by Edmund Lester Pearson. Illustrations by Everet Henry. 1934. V. 37

Frankenstein. New York: 1934. V. 38; 40; 41; 43; 46

Frankenstein or the Modern Prometheus. New York: 1938. V. 44

Frankenstein. Hartfield: 1983. V. 40

Frankenstein; or the Modern Prometheus. West Hatfield: 1983. V. 43; 44; 46

Frankenstein, or the Modern Prometheus. 1984. V. 38

Frankenstein; or the Modern Prometheus. Northampton: 1984. V. 38; 39; 42

History of a Six Weeks' Tour through a Part of France, Switzerland, Germany and Holland. With Letters . . . London: 1817. V. 42

The Last Man. London: 1826. V. 38; 39; 41

The Last Man. Philadelphia: 1833. V. 44

The Last Man. Philadelphia: 1833. V. 45

The Life & Letters of Mary Wollstonecraft Shelley. Edited by Mrs. Julian Marshall. London: 1889. V. 37

Lodore. London: 1835. V. 40; 45

Mounseer Nontongpaw: a New Version. London: 1808. V. 38

Tales and Stories. London: 1891. V. 41

SHELLEY Memorials. Boston: 1859. V. 39

SHELLEY Memorials from Authentic Sources. London: 1859. V. 42
SHELLEY Memorials: from Authentic Sources. London: 1859. V. 39

SHELLEY, PERCY BYSSHE 1792-1822

An Account of Shelley's Visits to France, Switzerland and Savoy, in the Years 1814 and 1816. London: 1894. V. 42

Adonais An Elegy on the Death of John Keats. London: 1935. V. 42; 46

Alastor, or The Spirit of Solitude. London: 1876. V. 42

The Beauties of Percy Bysshe Shelley . . . London: 1832. V. 42

The Beauties of Percy Bysshe Shelley, Consisting of Miscellaneous Selections from His Poetical Works. London: 1830. V. 37

The Celandine. Winchester: 1927. V. 40

The Cenci. Italy: 1819. V. 37; 43; 44

The Cenci. Livorno: 1819. V. 42

The Cenci. London: 1821. V. 37; 38; 39; 42

The Cenci. London: 1827. V. 38

The Cenci. New Rochelle: 1903. V. 42

The Daemon of the World . . . London: 1876. V. 42

The Divinity of Poetry (Fragment). 1966. V. 46

The Dramatic Poems of Percy Bysshe Shelley. London: 1922. V. 46

Dramatic Poems, Lyrical Poems and Translations. London: 1922-27. V. 44

Epipsychidion . . . A Type Fac-Simile Reprint of the Original Edition, First Published in 1821. London: 1887. V. 42

Epipsychidion. London: 1921. V. 42

Epipsychidion. Montagnola: 1923. V. 40; 42; 44; 45

Epipsychidion. (Montagnola: 1923). V. 37

Epipsychidion: Verses Addressed to the Nobel and Unfortunate Lady Emilia V(ivian) Now Imprisoned in the Convent of (St. Anne). London: 1821. V. 46

Essays, Letters from Abroad. London: 1840. V. 38; 40; 45

Essays, Letters from Abroad, Translations and Fragments. London: 1852. V. 39

Harriet and Mary: Being the Relations Between Percy Bysshe Shelley, Harriet Shelley, Mary Shelley and Thomas Jefferson Hogg. London: 1944. V. 37; 40; 43

Harriet and Mary, Being the Relations Between Percy Bysshe Shelley, Harriet Shelley, Mary Shelley and Thomas Jefferson Hogg . . . Waltham St. Lawrence: 1944. V. 40

Hellas. London: 1822. V. 43

Hellas, a Lyrical Drama. London: 1886. V. 40

History of a Six Weeks' Tour through a Part of France, Switzerland, Germany and Holland. London: 1817. V. 39; 41; 43; 45; 46

Laon and Cythna; or, the Revolution fo the Golden City: A Vision of the Nineteenth Century. In the Stanza of Spenser. London: 1818. V. 37

A Letter from Percy B. Shelley to T. Peacock, July MDCCCXVI. London: 1901. V. 38

Letters. London: 1852. V. 40; 42

Letters . . . to J. H. Leigh Hunt. London: 1894. V. 39

Letters from Percy Bysshe Shelley to Elizabeth Hitchener Now First Published. London: & New York: 1908. V. 46

Letters from Percy Bysshe Shelley to Elizabeth Hitchener Now First Published. New York: 1908. V. 43

The Letters. Oxford: 1964. V. 40

The Lyrical (Dramatic, Narrative) Poems and Translations. London: 1918-27. V. 40

Lyrical Poems and Translations. (with) Narrative Poems. 1924-27. V. 46

The Mask of Anarchy. London: 1887. V. 39

The Masque of Anarchy. London: 1832. V. 37; 40; 42; 45; 46

Miscellaneous and Posthumous Poems. London: 1826. V. 39; 42

The Notebooks of Percy Bysshe Shelley. Boston: 1911. V. 37

Notes on Sculptures in Rome and Florence Together with a Lucianic Fragment and a Criticism of Peacock's Poem 'Rhododaphne.' London: 1879. V. 39

Ode to the West Wind. Florence: 1951. V. 38

Poems and Sonnets. Philadelphia: 1887. V. 39

The Poems of Percy Bysshe Shelley. 1901-02. V. 39; 41; 44

The Poems of Percy Bysshe Shelley. London: 1901-02. V. 39; 41

Poems. London: 1902. V. 38

Poems. London: 1906. V. 41

The Poems. Cambridge: 1971. V. 45

The Poems. New York: 1971. V. 38

Poetical Pieces . . . (together with) Posthumous Poems . . . London: 1824. V. 46

Poetical Works. Edited by Mrs. Shelley. London: 1839. V. 37

SHELLEY, PERCY BYSSHE 1792-1822 continued

The Poetical Works. London: 1839. V. 38; 39; 40; 41; 42; 43; 44; 46

The Poetical Works. London: 1840. V. 39; 40

Poetical Works. 1845-5. V. 41

Poetical Works. London: 1847. V. 42

The Poetical Works. London: 1853. V. 42

The Poetical Works of Percy Pysshe Shelley. Edited by Mrs. Shelley. With a Memoir. Boston: 1855. V. 37

The Poetical Works. London: 1857. V. 39; 43

The Poetical Works . . . London: 1870. V. 39

The Poetical Works. London: 1876. V. 39

The Poetical Works. Edited by Henry Buxton Forman. London: 1876-77. V. 38; 39; 40

The Poetical Works. London: 1876-77. V. 37

The Poetical Works. (with) The Prose Works. London: 1876-80. V. 39

The Complete Poetical Works. London: 1878. V. 39

The Complete Poetical Works. London: 1878. V. 42

The Poetical Works. London: 1882. V. 39

The Complete Poetical Works. London: 1885. V. 38

The Complete Poetical Works. London: 1885. V. 42

The Poetical Works of . . . given from His Own editions and other Authentic Sources. Collated with many manuscripts and with all editions of authority. Together with his Prefaces and Notes, his Poetical Translations and Fragments and an Appendix . . . London: 1886. V. 37

The Poetical Works . . . (The Prose Works). London: 1888. V. 42

The Poetical Works. 1889. V. 42

The Complete Poetical Works. Cambridge: 1892. V. 42

The Poetical Works of Percy Bysshe. London: 1892. V. 44

The Complete Poetical Works. London: 1893. V. 39

The Poetical Works. Hammersmith: 1894-95. V. 38; 39; 41; 42; 43; 44

The Poetical Works of Percy Bysshe Shelley. London: 1894-95. V. 41

The Poetical Works. Hammersmith: 1895. V. 40

Complete Poetical Works. London: 1927. V. 41

The Complete Poetical Works of Percy Bysshe Shelley. London: 1934. V. 46

The Complete Poetical Works. Oxford: 1972 & 1975. V. 39

Posthumous Poems. London: 1824. V. 37; 40; 42; 43; 44; 45; 46

Posthumous Fragments of Margaret Nicholson. Oxford: 1870. V. 40

Prometheus Unbound. London: 1820. V. 37; 38; 39; 42; 43; 44

Prometheus Unbound. Campden: 1904. V. 43; 44; 46

Prometheus Unbound. Gloucestershire: 1904. V. 38; 40; 41

Prometheus Unbound. London: 1904. V. 40; 43; 45; 46

A Proposal for Putting Reform to the Vote throughout the Kingdom. London: 1887. V. 40; 42

The Prose Works. London: 1880. V. 42

Queen Mab. London: 1821. V. 38; 39; 40; 42; 43

Queen Mab. New York: 1821. V. 39; 42; 45

Queen Mab. London: 1822. V. 37; 45

Queen Mab. London: 1829. V. 38; 42; 46

Queen Mab. London: 1832. V. 40

Queen Mab, with Notes. London: 1834. V. 46

Review of Hogg's Memoirs of prince Alexy Haimatoff . . . Together with an Extract from Some Early Writings of . . . London: 1887. V. 39

Relics of Shelley. London: 1862. V. 37; 38; 40; 41; 44; 46

Reproductions and Transcriptions of Letters, 1810-16 . . . London. V. 42; 45

The Revolt of Islam; a Poem . . . London: 1818. V. 37; 42; 43

The Revolt of Islam; a Poem . . . London: 1829. V. 37; 46

Rosalind and Helen, a Modern Eclogue. London: 1819. V. 37; 39; 40; 43; 45; 46

The Sensitive Plant. New York. V. 42

The Sensitive Plant. Philadelphia. V. 45

The Sensitive Plant. London: 1898. V. 41; 46

The Sensitive Plant. London: 1911. V. 40; 41; 42; 43; 46

The Sensitive Plant. By Percy Bysshe Shelley. Introduction by Edmund Gosse. London: (c. 1911). V. 37

The Sensitive Plant. Introduction by Edmund Gosse. Illustrations by Charles Robinson. London: (1911). V. 37

The Shelley Papers. London: 1833. V. 39

Shellley Memorials; from Authentic Sources. London: 1875. V. 41

Shelley. Hammersmith: 1914. V. 46

Shelley at Oxford: The Early Correspondence of P. B. Shelley with His Friend T. Hogg. London: 1944. V. 37; 40; 43; 46

The Shelley Library. London: 1886. V. 40

Shelley Memorials; from Authentic Sources. Boston: 1859. V. 40

Shelley Memorials: from Authentic Sources . . . London: 1859. V. 37; 39; 40

Shelley's Preface to Promethus Unbound. London. V. 39

Shelley's Declaration of Rights. N.P.: 1870. V. 42

Shelley's Declaration of Rights. London: 1868. V. 37

To a Skylark. Evanston: 1962. V. 38

Verse and Prose from the Manuscripts of Percy Bysshe Shelley . . . London: 1934. V. 44

Verse and Prose from the Manuscripts of . . . London: 1934. V. 40; 44

The Wandering Jew. London: 1877. V. 44

The Wandering Jew. London: 1887. V. 38; 41; 45; 46

The Wandering Jew, a Poem. London: 1888. V. 45

We Pity the Plumage, But Foget the Dying Bird. An Address to the People on the Death of the Princess Charlotte. London: 1835. V. 39; 40; 46

'We Pity the Plumage, But Forget the Dying Bird.' colophon: London: 1843. V. 41

'We Pity the Plumage, but Forget the Dying Bird'. London: 1843. V. 39; 44

We pity the plumage, but forget the dying bird. An Address to the People on the death of the Princess Charlotte. By the Hermit of Marlow. London;: (ca. 1838). V. 37

The Works, edited by Mrs. Shelley. London: 1817. V. 37

The Works. (with) Miscellaneous Poems. London: 1826. V. 39

The Works. London: 1834. V. 39; 42; 45

The Works . . . London: 1847. V. 38

The Works in Verse and Prose. London: 1876-80. V. 39; 42

Works of Percy Bysshe Shelley in Verse and Prose. London: 1880. V. 40; 42; 46

The Complete Works and Life of . . . London and Boston: 1904. V. 41; 42; 43

The Complete Works of . . . London: 1904-06. V. 46

The Complete Works. London: 1906. V. 42

Works. Hammersmith: 1914. V. 38

The Complete Works of Percy Bysshe Shelley. Newly edited by Roger Ingpen and Walter E. Peck. The Julian Edition. London/New York: 1926-1930. V. 37

The Complete Works of . . . London: 1926-30. V. 37

The Complete Works. London: 1927. V. 38; 42

The Complete Works . . . London: 1927. V. 41; 46

The Complete Works. London & New York: 1927. V. 42

The Complete Works . . . New York: 1965. V. 38; 41

The Complete Works. New York: 1965. V. 44

Complete Works. New York: & London: 1965. V. 42; 46

Zastrozzi, a Romance . . . London: 1810. V. 46

Zastrozzi: a Romance. 1955. V. 38; 43

Zastrozzi. London: 1955. V. 37; 40; 41; 42

SHELTON, FREDERICK WILLIAM

The Trollopiad; or Travelling Gentlemen in America. New York and Providence: 1837. V. 41

SHELTON, LOUISE

Beautiful Gardens in American. New York: 1916. V. 44

SHELTON, PERRY W.

Personal Letters Written by Lawrence Sullivan Ross (Sept. 1861-May 1894). Waco: 1938. V. 41

SHELTON, WILLIAM HENRY

The Salmagundi Club. Boston & New York: 1918. V. 37; 45

SHELVOCKE, GEORGE

A Voyage Round the World by the Way of the Great South Sea, Peform'd in the Years 1719, 20, 21, 22. London: 1726. V. 37; 38; 40; 41; 42; 44; 45; 46

A Voyage Round the World, by Way of the Great South Sea; Performed in a Private Expedition During the War, Which Broke Out with Spain in the Year 1718. London: 1757. V. 39

SHENSTONE, WILLIAM 1714-1763

The Judgment of Hercules. London: 1741. V. 38; 41; 44

Letters Written by the Right Hon. Lady Luxborough (Henrietta Knight) to William Shenstone, Esq. London: 1775. V. 42

Men and Manners. London: 1927. V. 41

The School-Mistress. London: 1742. V. 38; 40; 41; 45

The Works in Prose and Verse of . . . London: 1764. V. 37; 39; 40; 41; 43; 45

The Works. London: 1764, 1769. V. 38; 40

The Works in Verse and Prose . . . London: 1764-66. V. 45

The Works. London: 1764-69. V. 38; 40; 41; 42; 45

The Works in Verse and Prose. London: 1765. V. 40; 41

The Works in Verse and Prose. London: 1765/69. V. 38

The Works in Verse and Prose. London: 1768. V. 37; 43

The Works, in Verse and Prose of William Shenstone. London: 1768 & 1769. V. 41

The Works in Verse and Prose. London: 1769. V. 42

SHEPARD, ANNA O.

Plumbate - a Mesoamerican Trade Ware. Washington: 1948. V. 42

SHEPARD, ELIHU H.

The Autobiography of Elihu H. Shepard. St. Louis: 1869. V. 41

The Early History of St. Louis and Missouri from Its First Exploration by White Men in 1673 and 1843. St. Louis: 1870. V. 39; 42

SHEPARD, ERNEST H.

Fun & Fantasy: a Book of Drawings. London: 1927. V. 38; 39; 42; 44; 46

SHEPARD, ISABEL S.

The Cruise of the U.S. Steamer 'Rush' in the Behring Sea; Summer of 1889. San Francisco: 1889. V. 43

SHEPARD, ODELL

The Lore of the Unicorn. London: 1930. V. 37

SHEPARD, SAM

Five Plays. 1967. V. 46

Five Plays. Indianapolis: 1967. V. 42; 45; 46

Hawk Moon. Los Angeles: 1973. V. 42; 43

Hawk Moon. Santa Barbara: 1973. V. 42

Hawk Moon. New York: 1981. V. 43

Operation Sidewinder. Indianapolis: 1970. V. 42; 44

La Turista. Indianapolis: 1968. V. 42; 44

The Unseen Hand and Other Plays. Indianpaolis: 1972. V. 42

SHEPARD, THOMAS

The Clear Sunshine of the Gospel Breaking Forth Upon the Indians in New England. New York: 1865. V. 39

The Parable of the Ten Virgin Opened and Applied . . . London: 1660. V. 42; 44

The Parable of the Ten Virgins, Opened and Applied. London: 1660. V. 44

The Parable of the Ten Virgins Opened and Applied. London: 1695. V. 38; 44

SHEPARD, WILLIAM

The Life of Poggio Bracciolini. Liverpool: 1802. V. 44

SHEPARD, WILLIAM B.

An Address Delivered before the Two Literary Societies of the University of North-Carolina. Raleigh, NC: 1838. V. 37

SHEPHARD, CHARLES

Historical Account of the Island of Saint Vincent. London: 1831. V. 38; 43

SHEPHARD, RUPERT

Passing Scene. London: 1966. V. 37

SHEPHEARD, H.

A Vindication of the Clergy Daughters' School and of the Rev. Carus Wilson, From Remarks in The Life of Charlotte Bronte. London: 1857. V. 43

SHEPHERD, CHARLES WILLIAM

The North-West Peninsula of Iceland . . . London: 1867. V. 42; 43

SHEPHERD, DAVID

Paintings of Africa and India. London: 1978. V. 37; 38; 43; 44; 45

SHEPHERD, HENRY

The Orphans; or, Generous Lovers. London: 1800. V. 42

SHEPHERD, HENRY E.

Life of Robert Edward Lee. New York: and Washington: 1906. V. 45

SHEPHERD, J. C.

Gardens and Design. London: 1927. V. 39; 45

Italian Gardens of the Renaissance. London: 1925. V. 39

SHEPHERD, JOSEPH S.

Journal of Travel Across the Plains to California, and Guide to the Future Emigrant. Placerville?: 1945. V. 43

SHEPHERD, MICHAEL

The Road to Gandolfo. New York: 1975. V. 46

SHEPHERD, RICHARD HERNE

The Bibliography of Thackeray. London: 1881. V. 42; 45

Poetical Sketches now first reprinted from the Original Edition of 1783. Edited and Prefaced by Richard Herne Shepherd. London: 1868. V. 37

Tennysoniana. London: 1866. V. 39

Waltoniana. London: 1878. V. 39

SHEPHERD, T. H.

Remembrances of the Great Exhibition, a Series of Views Beautifully Engraved on Steel . . . Paris: 1854. V. 39; 41

SHEPHERD, THOMAS

London: Metropolitan Improvements; or London in the Nineteenth Century. London: 1827/29. V. 45

Metropolitan Improvements; or London in the Nineteenth Century. London: 1828. V. 39

SHEPHERD, THOMAS H.

Bath and Bristol: with the Counties of Somerset and Gloucester, Displayed in a Series of Views. London: 1829. V. 46

London and Its Environs in the Nineteenth Century . . . London: 1829-30. V. 40

London and Its Environs in the Nineteenth Century . . . London: 1831? V. 40

Metropolitan Improvements; or London in the Nineteenth Century . . . London: 1827. V. 42; 45

Metropolitan Improvements; or London in the Nineteenth Century . . . London: 1827-29. V. 46

Metropolitan Improvements or London in the Nineteenth Century. (with) London and Its Environs in the Nineteenth Century. London: 1828-29-29-31. V. 42

Metropolitan Improvements; or London in the Nineteenth Century. London: 1829-30. V. 40

Metropolitan Improvements: or, London in the Nineteenth Century . . . London: 1830. V. 42

Metropolitan Improvements; or, London in the Nineteenth century. London and its Environs in the Nineteenth century. London: 1828-1831. V. 37

Modern Athens! London: 1829. V. 42

Modern Athens! London: 1829. V. 40

SHEPHERD, W.

Systematic Education: or, Elementary Instruction in the Various Departments of Literature and Science. London: 1817. V. 41

SHEPHERD, WILLIAM

The Life of Poggio Bracciolini. Liverpool: 1802. V. 37; 39

Prairie Experiences in Handling Cattle and Sheep. London: 1884. V. 40

Prairie Experiences in Handling Cattle and Sheep. 1885. V. 42

Prairie Experiences in Handling Cattle and Sheep. New York: 1885. V. 38; 39; 42; 46

Prairie Experiences in Handling Cattle and Sheep. London: 1884. V. 38

Systematic Education: or, Elementary Instruction in the Various Departments of Literature and Science . . . London: 1815. V. 46

THE SHEPHERDESS of the Alps, an Interesting Tale; Being a Narrative of the Singular Adventures of Adelaide de Valmont, Daughter of a Nobelman in France, in Love with Count Orestan . . . London: 1810. V. 44

SHEPPARD, EDGAR

Lectures on Madness in Its Medical, Legal and Social Aspects. London: 1873. V. 42

SHEPPARD, ERIC WILLIAM

Bedford Forrest, the Confederacy's Greatest Cavalryman. New York: 1930. V. 44

SHEPPARD, ISSAC A.

Excelsior Stove Works: Illustrated Trade Catalogue and Price List No. 45. Philadelphia: 1914. V. 38

SHEPPARD, J. BRIGSTOCKE

Literae Cantuarienses. The Letter Books of the Monastery of Christ Church, Canterbury. London: 1887-89. V. 44

SHEPPARD, JAMES

Hints to the Landlord and Tenant . . . Doncaster: 1833. V. 46

SHEPPARD, SAMUEL T.

The Bombay Volunteer Rifles, a History. Bombay: 1919. V. 46

SHEPPARD, SARAH

Illustrations of Scripture, the Hebrew Converts, and Other Poems. London: 1837. V. 39

SHEPPARD, THOMAS

The Evolution of Kingston-Upon-Hull, as Shewn By Its Plans. Hull: 1911. V. 45

SHEPPARD, W.

The Parson's Guide; or the Law of Tythes. London: 1671. V. 39

SHEPPARD, WILLIAM d. 1675

Actions Upon the Case for Slander or, a Methodical Collection Under Heads, of Thousands of Cases, Dispersed in the Many Great Volumes of the Law, of What Words are Actionable and What Not. London: 1674. V. 38; 40

SHEPPARD, WILLIAM d. 1675 continued

The Court-Keepers Guide. L: 1656. V. 40

The Court-Keepers Guide. London: 1662. V. 40

The Court-Keepers Guide. London: 1656. V. 38

Englands Balme; or, Proposals by Way of Grievance & Remedy; Humbly Presented to His Highness and the Parliament . . . London: 1657. V. 46

A Grand Abridgment of the Common and Statute Law of England. London: 1675. V. 40

The Justice of the Peace His Clerks Cabinet. London: 1660. V. 38

A New Survey of the Justice of Peace His Office, with the Names, or Times of the Statutes, Acts and Ordinances Themselves . . . London: 1659. V. 38

The Office of a Justice of Peace. London: 1662-61. V. 46

The Practical Counsellor in the Law. London: 1671. V. 38

The President of Presidents. London: 1684. V. 45

The Second Part of the Faithfull Councellour; or, the Marrow of the Law in English. London: 1654. V. 46

The Touch-Stone of Common Assurance. London: 1651. V. 38; 40; 43

The Touchstone of Common Assurances: or, a Plain and Familiar treatise, Opening the Learning of the Common Assurances, or Conveyances of the Kingdom. New York: 1808. V. 39

Touchstone of Common Assurances; or a Plain and Familiar Treatise, Opening the Learning of the Common Assurances, or Conveyances of the Kingdom. London: 1820. V. 40; 46

SHEPPERD, TAD

Pack and Paddock. New York: 1938. V. 39

SHERARD, ROBERT HARBOROUGH

A Bartered Honour. London: 1883. V. 40

Oscar Wilde, the Story of an Unhappy Friendship. London: 1902. V. 37

SHERATON, THOMAS

The Cabinet Dictionary. London;: 1803. V. 39; 40

The Cabinet-Maker and upholsterer's Drawing-Book . . . London: 1802. V. 37

SHERBORN, CHARLES DAVIES

Index Animalium, Sive Index Nominum Quae ab A.D. MDCCLVIII . . . London: 1880. V. 45

Index Animalium, Sive Index Nominum Quae ab A.D. MDCCLondon:III Generibus et Speciebus Animalium Imposita Sunt. Cantabrigiae/London: 1902. V. 43

SHERBOW, BENJAMIN

Sherbow's Type Charts for Advertising. New York: 1921. V. 38

SHERBURNE, ANDREW

Memoirs of Andrew Sherburne: a Pensioner of the Navy of the Revolution, Written by Himself. Utica: 1828. V. 41; 42

Memoirs of Andrew Sherburne: A Pensioner of the Navy of the Revolution . . . William Williams;: 1828. V. 37

SHERBURNE, HENRY

The Oriental Philanthropist, or True Republican. Portsmouth: 1800. V. 41; 43; 44

SHERBURNE, JOHN HENRY

Life and Character of the Chevalier John Paul Jones, A Captain in the Navy of the United States, During the Revolutionary War . . . Washington: 1825. V. 41; 42

SHERER, JOHN

The Classic Lands of Europe, Embracing Italy, Sicily and Greece . . . London: 1879-81. V. 42

Europe Illustrated: Its Picturesque Scenes and Places of Note. London: 1876-79. V. 42

The Gold Finder of Australia . . . . London: 1853. V. 39; 45; 46

SHERER, JOSEPH MOYLE

Notes and reflections during a Ramble in Germany. London: 1827. V. 37

Recollections of the Peninsula. London: 1824. V. 38

SHERER, MOYLE 1789-1869

The Broken Font. London: 1836. V. 43

Military Memoirs of Field Marshall the Duke of Wellington. London: 1830. V. 39

Notes and Reflections During a Ramble in Germany. London: 1826. V. 40

Recollections of the Penninsula. London: 1825. V. 40; 44

Sketches of India. London: 1824. V. 40

Tales of the Wars of Our Times. London: 1829. V. 42

SHERIDAN and His Times. By an Octongenarian, who Stood by His Knee in Youth and Sat at his Table in Manhood. London: 1859. V. 38

SHERIDAN, CHARLES FRANCIS

A History of the Late Revolution in Sweden. Dublin: 1778. V. 40

A History of the Late Revolution in Sweden. London: 1778. V. 40

A History of the Late Revolution in Sweden . . . London: 1788. V. 44

SHERIDAN, FRANCES

La Decouverte, Comedie . . . 1764? V. 45

The Dupe, a Comedy as It Is Now Acting at . . . *Drury Lane.* London: 1764. V. 43

The History of Nourjahad. London: 1767. V. 40; 41; 42; 46

Memoirs of Miss Sidney Bidulph . . . London: 1796. V. 41

Memoirs of the Life and Writings of Mrs. Frances Sheridan, Mother of the Late Richard Brinsley Sheridan. etc . . . London: 1824. V. 46

SHERIDAN, FRANCES CHAMBERLAINE

Memoirs of Miss Sidney Bidulph, Extracted from Her Own Journals, Now First Published. Conclusion of the Memoirs of Miss Sidney Bidulph . . . London: 1761/67. V. 42

Memoirs of Miss Sidney Bidulph. (with) Conclusion of the Memoirs of Miss Sidney Bidulph. London: 1767. V. 42

SHERIDAN, J. R.

A Full and Genuine Account of the Revolution in the Kingdom of Sweden. London: 1782. V. 38

SHERIDAN, LOUISE H.

The Diadem: A Book for the Boudoir. London: 1838. V. 38

SHERIDAN, NIAL

Twenty Poems. Dublin: 1934. V. 38

SHERIDAN, PHIL

Regulations Governing Military Transportation Over Land-Grant and Bonded Railroads. Washington: 1885. V. 39

SHERIDAN, PHILIP H.

Outline Descriptions of the Posts in the Military Division of the Missouri . . . Chicago: 1872. V. 41; 42

Personal Memoirs. New York: 1888. V. 42; 46

Record of Engagements with Hostile Indians Within the Military Division of the Missouri, from 1868 to 1882 . . . Chicago: 1882. V. 41; 45

SHERIDAN, PHILIP HENRY 1831-1888

Outline Descriptions of the Posts in the Military Division of the Missouri . . . Chicago: 1872. V. 37; 39; 43

Personal Memoirs. New York: 1888. V. 39; 46

Record of Engagements with Hostile Indians within Military Division of the Missouri from 1868-1882. Chicago: 1882. V. 37

Report of Lieut. General P.H. Sheridan dated September 20, 1881, of His Expedition through the Big Horn Mountains, Yellowstone National Park, etc . . . Washington: 1882. V. 37

Reports of the Inspection Made in the Summer of 1877 by . . . *of Country North of the Union Pacific Railroad.* Washington: 1878. V. 37; 39; 42

SHERIDAN, RICHARD BRINSLEY BUTLER 1751-1816

The Camp, a Musical Entertainment. London: 1795. V. 42

A Comparative Statement of the Two Bills, for the Better Government of the British Possessions in India, Brought into Parliament by Mr. Fox and Mr. Pitt. London: 1806. V. 37; 38

The Critic. London: 1781. V. 37; 38; 40; 41; 42; 43; 45

Dramatic Works. London: 1804. V. 42

The Duenna. Dublin: 1794. V. 38

The Duenna: a Comic Opera . . . London: 1794. V. 42; 45

Memoirs of the Life of the Right Honourable Richard Brinsley Sheridan. London: 1825. V. 45

An Ode to Scandal. London: 1819. V. 39

Pizarro. London: 1799. V. 38; 42; 43; 45

The Rivals . . . Dublin: 1775. V. 43

The Rivals. London: 1775. V. 37; 40; 41

The Rivals. New York: 1953. V. 38

The School for Scandal. London & New York. V. 39; 43

The School for Scandal. Dublin: 1780. V. 38; 41; 45

The School for Scandal and The Rivals. London: 1896. V. 42

The School for Scandal: a Comedy. London: 1900. V. 44

The School for Scandal. and The Rivals. London: 1902. V. 45

The School for Scandal. 1930. V. 44; 46

The School for Scandal. London: 1934. V. 40

School for Scandal. New York: 1934. V. 41

The School for Scandal. London. V. 37; 40

The School for Scandal. London: 1911. V. 37; 40; 41; 45

The School for Scandal. By Richard Brinsley Sheridan. Illustrated by Hugh Thomson. London: (c. 1911). V. 37

A Trip to Scarborough, a Comedy. Dublin: 1781. V. 41

A Trip to Scarborough. London: 1781. V. 37; 41; 42

Verses to the Memory of Garrick. London: 1779. V. 40; 42; 45

The Works. London: 1821. V. 38; 40; 46

SHERIDAN, RICHRD BRINSLEY 1751-1816

A Comparative Statement of the Two Bills for the Better Government of the British Possessions in India, Brought into Parliament by Mr. Fox and Mr. Pitt. London: 1806. V. 38

SHERIDAN, THOMAS

British Education: or, the Source of the Disorders of Great Britain. London: 1756. V. 41

A Complete Dictionary of the English Language. Both with Regard to Sound and Meaning. London: 1789. V. 37; 45

A Complete Dictionary of the English Language . . . . London: 1790. V. 41; 43

A Course of Lectures on Elocution; Together with Two Dissertations on Language; and Some Other Tracts Relative to Those Subjects. London: 1762. V. 37; 40; 41; 43

A Course of Lectures on Elocution; Together with Two Dissertations on Language . . . London: 1781. V. 41; 43

A Course of Lectures on Elocution; Together with Two Diessertations on Language. London: 1798. V. 41; 45

A Discourse of the Rise and Power of Parliaments, of Law's, of Courts of Judicature, of Liberty, Property, and Religion, of the Interest of England in Reference to the Dessines of France . . . N.P.: 1677. V. 39

A Discourse of the Rise and Power of Parlaments of Law's, of Courts of Judicature, of Liberty, Property and Religion, of the Interest of England in Reference to the Desines of France . . . London: 1677. V. 37

A General Dictionary of the English Language. Dublin: 1784. V. 41

Lectures on the Art of Reading. Dublin: 1775. V. 46

Lectures on the Art of Reading. London: 1775. V. 37; 38

Lectures on the Art of Reading. London: 1787. V. 37; 41; 45

The Life of the Rev. Dr. Jonathan Swift. London: 1787. V. 38; 40; 41

A Rhetorical Grammar of the English Language. Dublin: 1781. V. 37; 41

Sheridan's and Henderson's Practical Method of Reading and Reciting English Poetry, Elucidated by a Variety of Examples Taken from Some of Our Most Popular Poets . . . London: 1796. V. 43; 46

A State of the Case in Regard to the Point in Dispute Between Mr. Mosse and Mr. Sheridan. Dublin: 1750. V. 46

The Trial of Thomas Sheridan, Esq. for Criminal Conversation with the Lady of Peter Campbell, Esquire . . . On July the 7th, 1807. London: 1807. V. 38

SHERIFF, R. C.

Journey's End. London: 1929. V. 39

SHERINGHAM, GEORGE

Design in the Theatre. London: 1927. V. 37

Robes of Thespis. London: 1928. V. 41

SHERINGHAM, HUGH

The Book of the Fly Rod. Illustrated by George Sheringham. London: 1931. V. 37; 39

SHERINGHAM, ROBERT

De Anglorum Gentis Origine Disceptatio. Cambridge: 1670. V. 37

SHERLEY, ANTHONY

Sir Anthony Sherley His Relation of His Travels Into Persia. London: 1613. V. 43

SHERLOCK, JOHN

A Practical Discourse concerning a Future Judgement. London: 1692. V. 39

SHERLOCK, MARTIN

Letters from an English Traveller. (with) New Letters from an English Traveller. London: 1780, 1781. V. 38

SHERLOCK, THOMAS

A Letter from the Lord Bishop of London to the Clergy and People of London and Westmisnter; on Occasion of the Late Earthquakes. London: 1750. V. 45

The Tryal of the Witnesses of the Resurrection Jesus. London: 1729. V. 45

SHERLOCK, W.

A Practical Discourse of Religious Assemblies. London: 1681. V. 46

SHERLOCK, WILLIAM

A Practical Discourse Concerning Death. London: 1689. V. 38; 45

Reflexions sur la Mort . . . Londres: 1693. V. 40

A Vindication of Both Parts of the Preservative Against Popery: in Answer to the Cavils of Lewis Sabran, Jesuit. London: 1688. V. 45

A Vindication of the Doctrine of the Holy and Ever Blessed Trinity, and the Incarnation of the Son of God. London: 1694. V. 39

SHERMAN, E. HELENE

Pearls of Wisdom. 1965. V. 41

SHERMAN, EDWIN A.

The Life of the Late Rear Admiral John Drake Sloat of the United States Navy, Who Took Possession of California . . . July 7th 1846. Oakland: 1902. V. 41; 42; 43

SHERMAN, ELEAZER

the Narrative of Eleazer Sherman, Giving an Account of His Life, Experience, Call to the Ministry of the Gospel, and Travels as Such to the Present Time . . . Providence: 1832. V. 45

SHERMAN, FREDERIC FAIRCHILD

Landscape and Figure Painters of America. New York: 1917. V. 41

SHERMAN, JOHN

John Sherman's Recollections of Forty Years in the House, Senate and Cabinet. Chicago: 1895. V. 44; 46

The Philosophy of Language Illustrated . . . Trenton Falls: 1826. V. 41

Trenton Falls, Picturesque and Descriptive. New York: 1868. V. 38

SHERMAN, JOHN H.

A General Account of Miranda's Expedition, Including the Trial and Execution of Ten of His Officers, and an Account of the Imprisonment and Sufferings of the Remainder of His Officers and men Who Were Taken Prisoners. New York: 1808. V. 38; 42; 44; 45

SHERMAN, MATT

You Must Run the World. N.P.: 1959. V. 46

SHERMAN, S. M.

History of the 133rd Regiment O.V.I. Columbus: 1896. V. 45

SHERMAN, WILLIAM TECUMSEH

Protection Across the Continent. Washington: 1866. V. 42

Report of Journey Made by Genl. W. T. Sherman in the Northwest and Middle Part of the United States in 1883. Washington: 1884. V. 37

Two Letters from General William Tecumseh Sherman to General Ulysses S. Grant and William T. McPherson . . . Boston: 1919. V. 43

SHERRIF, R. C.

The Hopkins Manuscript. 1939. V. 37

SHERRIFF, R. C.

Journey's End. A Novel. London: 1930. V. 43; 46

SHERRILL, HUNTING

A Review of the Diseases of Dutchess County, from 1809 to 1825. New York: 1826. V. 41

SHERRIN, A. A.

Brett's Historical Series. Early History of New Zealand. Auckland: 1890. V. 42

SHERRIN, R. A. A.

Handbook of the Fishes of New Zealand. Auckland: 1886. V. 39

SHERRING, CHARLES A.

Western Tibet and the British Borderland the Sacred Country of Hindus and Buddhists . . . London: 1906. V. 43

SHERRINGTON, C. S.

Inhibition as a Coordinative Factor. Stockholm: 1933. V. 46

Interaction Between Ipsilateral Spinal Reflexes Acting on the Flexor Muscles of the Hind. Limb. 1927. V. 44

Reflex Activity of the Spinal Cord. London: 1932. V. 45

Reflex Activity of the Spinal Cord. London: 1938. V. 41; 44

SHERRINGTON, CHARLES

The Integrative Action of the Nervous System. London: 1911. V. 40; 41; 44; 45; 46

The Integrative Action of the Nervous System. Cambridge: 1947. V. 42

The Integrative Action of the Nervous System. New Haven: 1911. V. 37

Man On His Nature. New York: 1941. V. 42

Selected Writings of Sir Charles Sherrington. London: 1939. V. 41

Selected Writings of Sir Charles Sherrington. New York: 1940. V. 42; 45

Water-Cure for Ladies . . . New York: 1844. V. 46

SHERRY, LAURA

Old Prairie du Chien. Paris: 1931. V. 44

SHERWELL, SAMUEL

Old Recollections of an Old Boy. New York: 1923. V. 38; 39; 40; 42; 43; 44

SHERWIN, HENRY

Mathematical Tables, Contrived After a Most Comprehensive Method. London: 1726. V. 40; 41

SHERWIN, HENRY ALDEN

Bibliotheca Piscatoria. The Library of the Late Henry Alden Sherwin. Cleveland, Ohio. New York: 1946. V. 45

SHIPHERD, JACOB R.

History of the Oberlin-Wellington Rescue. Boston: 1859. V. 38; 45

SHIPLEY, JONATHAN 1714-1788

A Sermon Preached Before the Incorporated Society for the Propagation of the Gospel in Foreign Parts . . . Newport: 1773. V. 41; 44

SHIPLEY, MALCOLM A.

Artificial Flies and How to Make Them. Philadelphia: 1888. V. 43

SHIPLEY, MARY E.

Cousin Deborah's Whim. London: 1878. V. 42

SHIPLEY, WILLIAM

A True Treatise on the Art of Fly-Fishing, Trolling, Etc . . . . London: 1838. V. 41; 43

SHIPLEY, WILLIAM DAVIES 1745-1826

The Whole Proceedings at the Assizes at Shrewsbury, on Friday August the Sixth, 1784, in the Case of the King on the Prosecution of William Jones . . . Against the Rev. William Davis Shipley, Dean of St. Asaph. For Libel . . . London: 1784. V. 39; 44

SHIPMAN, ALICE JACK

Letters Past and Present to My Nephews and Nieces. N.P.: 1930's. V. 38

THE SHIPMODELER: Official Organ of the Ship Model Makers Club. Brookyln: 1929-33. V. 39

SHIPP, BARNARD

History of Hernando De Soto and Florida; or, Record of the Events of Fifty Six Years from 1512 to 1568. Philadelphia: 1881. V. 39; 40; 44; 45

The Indian and Antiquities of America. Philadelphia: 1896. V. 42

SHIPP, HORACE

The English Review of Short Stories. London: 1932. V. 41

SHIPP, JOHN

Cases in Farriery: in Which the Diseases of the Horse Are Treated on the Principles of the Veterinary School of Medicine. Leeds: 1808? V. 39

SHIPP, M. BARD

The Salt Lake Sanitarian. Salt Lake City, Utah: 1882. V. 37

SHIPPAM, AUDREY FORFAR

Feet We Meet. N.P.: 1924. V. 42

SHIPPEN, WILLIAM

Faction Display'd. London: 1704. V. 38; 40; 41; 45

Faction Display'd. (with) Moderation Display'd. London: 1705. V. 38

Faction Display'd. A Poem . . . London: 1709. V. 39

Moderation Display'd. A Poem. London: 1704. V. 40

SHIPPEY, LEE

Folks Ushud Know. Sierra Madre: 1930. V. 39

THE SHIP'S Bell. Baltimore: 1927. V. 45

SHIPTON, ERIC

Mountains of Tartary. London: 1951. V. 39

SHIPTON, HELEN

Alston Crucis. London: 1893. V. 41

Dagmar. London: 1888. V. 39

SHIPTON, URSULA

Mother Shipton's Prophesie. London: 1678. V. 45

SHIPWAY, WILLIAM

The Campanalogia; or, Universal Instructor in the Art of Ringing. London: 1813/16. V. 46

SHIRAI, A.

Ecological Encyclopaedia of the Marine Animals of the Indo-Pacific, Volume I: Vertebrate. Tokyo: 1986. V. 37

SHIRAI, S.

Ecological Encyclopaedia of the Marine Animals of the Indo-Pacific. Volume I, Vertebrata 1 (Mammals, Reptiles, Fishes). Tokyo: 1986. V. 37

SHIRAKAWA, YOSHIKAZU

Himalayas. New York: 1986. V. 44

SHIRASU, MASAKO

Noh-Men. 1963. V. 40; 45

SHIRK, DAVID

The Cattle Drives of David Shirk, from Texas to the Idaho Mines, 1871 and 1873 . . . His Later Experiences . . . Portland: 1956. V. 44

SHIRLEY, ALFRED H.

H.M.S. Fox in the East Indies 1908-1910. Oxford: 1910. V. 43

SHIRLEY, ANDREW

Bonington. London: 1941. V. 39

Bonnington. London: 1940. V. 46

SHIRLEY, E. P.

Some Account of English Deer Parks, with Notes on the Management of Deer. London: 1867. V. 46

SHIRLEY, EVELYN PHILIP

Catalogue of the Library at Lough Fea in Illustration of the History and Antiquities of Ireland. 1872. V. 38

Catalogue of the Library at Lough Fea, in Illustration of the History and Antiquities of Ireland. London: 1872. V. 40; 43

Catalogue of the Library at Lough Fea in Illustration of the History and Antiquities of Ireland. London: 1872. V. 40

Lower Eatington: Its Manor House and Church. London: 1869. V. 42

Some Account of the Territory of Dominion of Farney (Monaghan) in the Province and Earldom of Ulster. London: 1845. V. 38; 43

Some Account of English Deer Parks. London: 1867. V. 38; 39; 40

Stemmata Shirleiana; or, the Annals of the Shirley Family. London: 1873. V. 37

SHIRLEY, JAMES

The Bird in a Cage. A Comedie. London: 1633. V. 37

The Corporation, a Comedy, As it Was Presented by Her Majesties Servants at the Private House in Drury Lane. London: 1640. V. 37

The Court Secret. London: 1653. V. 46

The Doubtful Heir. London: 1652. V. 46

The Dramatic Works and Poems of How First Collected. London: 1833. V. 37; 38; 39; 44; 45

The Grateful Servant. London: 1662. V. 39; 44

The Imposture. London: 1652. V. 46

The Maides Revenge. London: 1639. V. 37

The Tragedie of Chabot, Admirall of France . . . London: 1639. V. 46

The Wife's Relief; or, the Husband's Cure. London: 1712. V. 39; 42; 45

SHIRLEY, JOHN fl. 1680-1702

The Accomplished Ladies Rich Closet of Rarities; or, the Ingenious Gentlewoman and Servant Maids Delightful Companion. London: 1691. V. 40; 42

Ecclesiastical History Epitomized. London: 1682. V. 40

The Honour of Chivalry, or the Famous and Delectable History of Don Bellianis of Greece. London: 1683-83. V. 38

The Life of the Valiant & Learned Sir Walter Raleigh, Knight. London: 1677. V. 37; 38; 42; 45

SHIRLEY, R. W.

The Mapping of the World. London: 1983. V. 40; 43

SHIRLEY, RODNEY W.

The Mapping of the World, Early Printed World Maps 1472-1700. London: 1987. V. 46

SHIRLEY, THOMAS

The Angler's Museum; or, The Whole Art of Float and Fly Fishing . . . V. 39; 45

The Angler's Museum, or, The Whole Art of Float and Fly Fishing . . . London: 1790's. V. 41

SHIRLEY, WILLIAM

Edward the Black Prince . . . London: 1750. V. 42

A Letter from William Shirley, Esq; Governor of Massachusetts Bay, to His Grace the Duke of Newcastle. London: 1746. V. 40

SHIRREFF, PATRICK

A Tour through North America; Together with a Comprehensive View of the Canadas and United States . . . Edinburgh: 1835. V. 37; 40

SHIRREFS, ANDREW

Jamie and Bess or the Laird in Disguise, A Scots Pastoral Comedy . . . Aberdeen: 1787. V. 43

Poems, Chiefly in the Scottish Dialect. Edinburgh: 1790. V. 37; 39; 42

SHIRTCLIFFE, ROBERT

The Theory and Practice of Gauging, Demonstrated in a Short and Easy Method. London: 1740. V. 40; 43

SHITE, CHRISTOPHER

Rembrandt's Etchings. Amsterdam: 1969. V. 38

SHKLOVSKY, I. W.

In Far North-East Siberia. London: 1916. V. 40

SHLOMO Ibn Melch Michol Yofi (Grammar). Constantinople: 1549. V. 45

SHOBERL, FREDERIC 1775-1853

Austria; Containing a Description of the Manners, Customs, Character and Costumes of the People of that Empire. Philadelphia: 1828. V. 46

Foget-me-not for 1830. London: 1830. V. 38; 40

Frederick the Great and His Times. Philadelphia: 1842. V. 40

Narrative of the Most Remarkable Events Which Occurred In and near Leipzig. London: 1814. V. 46

Persia; Containing a Description of the Country, with an Account of its Government, Laws & Religion & of the Character, Manners & Customs. Philadelphia: 1828. V. 46

Persia: Containing a Description of the Country, with an Account of Its Government, Laws and Religiion, and of the Character, Manners and Customs, Arts, Amusements &c. of Its Inhabitants. Philadelphia: 1834. V. 39

Suffolk, Surrey and Sussex. London: 1813. V. 40

Turkey, Being a Description of the Manners, Customs, Dresses and Other Peculiarities Characteristic of the Inhabitants of the Turkish Empire . . . Philadelphia: 1829. V. 39

The World in Miniature: Africa. London: 1821. V. 38; 40; 41; 42; 43; 45; 46

The World in Miniature: the Asiatic Islands. London: 1824. V. 38

SHOBERL, FREDERICK

Austria: Containing a Description of the Manners, Customs, Character and Costumes of the People of That Empire. Philadelphia: 1828. V. 42

The World in Miniature; England, Scotland and Ireland. Edited by W.H. Pyne. London: 1827. V. 37

The World in Miniature . . . Tibet, and India Beyound the Ganges; Containing a Description of the Character, Manners, Customs, Dress, Religion and Amusements . . . London: (c. 1822). V. 37

SHOBERL, FREDRICK

Persia . . . Philadelphia: 1828. V. 42

SHOBERL, MR.

A Topographical and Historical Description of the County of Suffolk. London: 1820. V. 37

SHOCK, NATHAN

A Classified Bibliography of Gerontology and Geriatrics. Stanford: 1951. V. 45

SHOE, LUCY T.

Profiles of Western Greek Mouldings. Roma: 1952. V. 40; 42; 44

SHOEMAKER, ABRAHAM

The New-Jersey and Pennsylvania Almanac for the Year 1800 . . . Trenton: 1799. V. 41

The New-Jersey and Pennsylvania Almanac for the Year 1801. Trenton: 1800. V. 41

SHOEMAKER, BENJAMIN H.

Genealogy of the Shoemaker Family of Cheltenham, Pennsylvania. Philadelphia: 1903. V. 46

SHOEMAKER, WILLIAM L.

La Santa Yerba. Boston: 1898. V. 40; 43

SHOEMAN, CHARLES HENRY

A Dream and Other Poems. Ann Arbor: 1899. V. 38

SHOLES, A. E.

Chronological History of Savannah . . . to December 31, 1899.., and Savannah's roll of Honor, a Roster of Soldiers . . . Savannah: 1900. V. 43; 45

SHONE, A. B.

A Century and a Half of Amateur Driving. London: 1955. V. 42

SHONE, RICHARD

Bloomsbury. London: 1976. V. 41

SHOOTER, JOSEPH

The Kafirs of Natal and the Zulu Country. London: 1857. V. 38

THE SHOP Signs of Peking. Peking: 1931. V. 44

SHOPPELL, ROBERT W.

How to Build, Furnish and Decorate. New York: 1883. V. 42

Modern Houses: Beautiful Homes. New York: 1887. V. 46

SHORE, HENRY NOEL

The Flight of the Lapwing. A Naval Officer's Jotting in China, Formosa and Japan. London: 1881. V. 37

A SHORT Account of the Administration, During the Summer Recess of Parliament. London: 1779. V. 37

SHORT Account of the Ancient and Modern State of the City and Close of Lichfield; also the Cathedral. Lichfield: 1819-1821. V. 40

SHORT Account of the Ancient and Modern State of the City and Close of Lichfield; also the Cathedral. (and) A Supplement to the Short Account. Lichfield: 1819-18-21. V. 37

A SHORT Account of the Late Application to Parliament Made by the Merchants of London Upon the Neglect of Their Trade; with the Substance of the Evidence Thereupon . . . London: 1742. V. 41; 45

A SHORT Account of the Life and Work of Wynken de Worde with an Original Leaf from the Golden Legend, Printed by Him at the Sign of the Sun in Fleet Street, London, the Year 1527. San Francisco: 1968. V. 42; 45

A SHORT Account of the Life and Work of Wynkyn De Worder, with a Leaf from the Golden Legend Printed by him at The Sign of the Sun in Fleet Street, London, the Year 1527. San Francisco: 1949. V. 37

A SHORT Account of the Naval Actions of the Last War; In Order to Prove That the French Nation Never Gave Such Slender Proofs of Maritime Greatness as During that Period . . . London: 1788. V. 37; 43

A SHORT Account of the Part of Africa Inhabited by the Negroes. Philadelphia: 1762. V. 43

A SHORT Account of the Resignation of Warren Hastings, Esq. Governor General of Bengal, in the Year MDCCCLXXV with Remarks. London: 1781. V. 42

A SHORT Account of the Two Charitable Foundations at King's Cliffe in the County of Northampton. Stamford: 1755. V. 43

A SHORT Account of Vessels used in the British Service. London: 1833. V. 38

A SHORT Address to the Public; Containing Some Thoughts How the National Debt May be Reduced, Some of the Internal Taxes Diminished, or Perhaps Abolished and the Supplies Raised within the Year. Oxford: 1798. V. 39

A SHORT and True Relation Concerning the Soap-Business. London: 1641. V. 38; 46

A SHORT Answer to Earl Stanhope's Observations of Mr. Pitt's Plan for the Reduction of the National Debt. London: 1786. V. 41

SHORT, CHARLES W.

A Biographical Memoir of H. Hulbert Eaton, A. M., Late Assistant Professor of Chemistry, in the Medical Department of Transylvania University. Lexington: 1832-33? V. 43

A SHORT Essay on the Modes of Defence Best Adapted to the Situation and Circumstances of This Island. London: 1785. V. 42

A SHORT History of the Highland Regiment; Interspersed with Some Occasional Observations as to the Present State of the Country, Inhabitants, and Government of Scotland. London: 1743. V. 45

SHORT, L.

Woodpeckers of the World. Delaware: 1982. V. 37; 38

A SHORT Narrative of the Horrid Massacre in Boston. Perpetrated in the Evening of the Fifth Day of March, 1770. By Soldiers of the XXIXth Regiment . . . Boston: 1700. V. 42

A SHORT Narrative of the Wonderful and Providential Preservation of Charles the Second . . . London: 1806. V. 46

SHORT Reflections Upon Patents, Relating to the Abuses of the Noble Priviledge, and Proposing the Means to Reform Them. London: 1760. V. 45; 46

SHORT, RICHARD

Peri Psychroposias (Greek) of Drinking Water, Against Our Novelists, That Prescribed it in England . . . whereunto is added, Peri Thermoposias (Greek) of Warm Drink, and is an Answer to a Treatise of Warm Drink. London: 1646. V. 37

A SHORT State of the War and the Peace. London: 1715. V. 40

A SHORT Survey or History of the Kingdome of Sveden. London: 1632. V. 40; 43; 44

SHORT, THOMAS

Discourses on Tea, Sugar, Milk, Made-Wines, Spirits, Punch, Tobacco &c. London: 1750. V. 44; 46

A Dissertation Upon Tea . . . London: 1730. V. 40

A General Chronological History of the Air, Weather, Seasons, Meteors, Etc. London: 1749. V. 37; 38; 40; 42

A General Treatise on the Different Sorts of Cold Mineral Waters in England, with a Variety of Experiments and a Discourse on the nature and Effects of Milk. London: 1766. V. 37

The Natural, Experimental and Medicinal History of the Mineral Waters. London: 1734. V. 42

A SHORT View of the Continual Sufferings and Heavy Oppressions of the Episcopal Reformed Churches, Formerly in Bohemia and Now in Great Poland and Polish Prussia. London: 1716. V. 46

A SHORT View of the Encroachments of France in America; and the British Commerce with Spain. London: 1750. V. 40

A SHORT View of the Inconveniences of War; With Some Observations on the Expediency of Peace. London: 1796. V. 40; 42

A SHORT View of the Proposals Lately Made for the Final Adjustment of the Commercial System Between Great-Britain and Ireland. London: 1785. V. 39

A SHORT Way to Know the World; or the Rudiments of Geography; Being a New Familiar Method of Teaching Youth the Knowledge of the Globe, and the Four Quarters of the World. 1712. V. 40

SHORTER, ALFRED H.

Paper Mills and Paper Makers in England, 1495-1800. Hilversum: 1957. V. 38; 39; 41

SHORTER, CLEMENT

The Brontes: Life and Letters... London: 1908. V. 44

SHORTHOUSE, JOSEPH HENRY

Blanche, Lady Falaise, a Tale. London: 1891. V. 40

John Inglesant; a Romance. Birmingham: 1880. V. 40

John Inglesant; a Romance. Birmingham: 1881. V. 40

Sir Percival. A Story of the Past and of the Present. London: 1886. V. 46

SHORTLAND, EDWARD

Traditions and Superstitions of the New Zealanders. London: 1854. V. 39

SHORTRIDGE, C. G.

The Mammals of South West Africa. London: 1934. V. 39; 42; 43; 44; 45; 46

SHORTT, ADAM

Canada and Its Provinces. Toronto: 1913-14. V. 42

Canada and Its Provinces: A History of the Canadian People and Their Institutions by One Hundred Associates. Toronto: 1914-17. V. 37

A History of the Canadian People and Their Institutions by One Hundred Associates. General Editors: Adam Shortt and Arthur G. Doughty. (Archives Edition). Toronto: 1914-1917. V. 37

SHOSTAKOVICH, DMITRI

Concerto for Piano and Orchestra. Moscow: 1935. V. 46

SHOTEN, KADOKAWA

A Pictorial Encyclopedia of the Oriental Arts: China. New York: 1969. V. 39

SHOTTEREL, ROBERT

Archerie Reviv'd; or, the Bow-Man's Excellence. London: 1676. V. 39

SHOTWELL, S. R.

Report on the Influence and Efficiency of the Press in Promoting the Cause of Missions. N.P.. V. 45

SHOURDS, THOMAS

History and Genealogy of Fenwick's Colony. Bridgeton: 1876. V. 41

SHOVE, CARRIE L.

Wedded and Saved! Spreading the Toils, Cruelly Wronged, The Sport of Fortune, Her Mistake, A Secret Engagement. Chicago: 1882. V. 44

SHOWER, BARTHOLOMEW 1658-1701

Cases in Parliament Resolved and Adjudged, Upon Petitions, and Writs of Error. London: 1698. V. 39; 40

The Reports of Sir Bartholomew Shower, Kt. of Cases Adjudg'd in the Court of King's Bench, in the Reign of His Late Majesty King William III. London: 1708. V. 45

Reports and Cases and Special Arguments, Arued and Adjudged in the Court of King's Bench. London: 1720. V. 40

SHOWER, JOHN

Practical Reflections on the Earthquakes That Have Happened in Europe and America, But Chiefly in the Islands of Jamaica, England, Sicily, Malta, &c... London: 1750. V. 41

SHRADY, GEORGE F.

General Grant's Last Days. New York: 1908. V. 37

SHREVE, FORREST

Vegetation and Flora of the Sonoran Desert. 1964. V. 40

Vegetation and Flora of the Sonoran Desert. Stanford: 1964. V. 37; 38; 39; 45

SHREWSBERRY, EARL OF

Letter from the Earl of Shrewsbury to Ambrose Lisle Phillips, Esq. Descriptive of the Elastatica of Caldara and the Addolarata of Capriana. New York: 1843. V. 45

SHREWSBURY, CHARLES JOHN CHETWYND TALBOT, 19TH EARL OF 1830-

Meliora; or, Better Times to Come. London: 1852. V. 43

SHRIMPTON, CHARLES

The Crimean War. Paris: 1864. V. 40; 43

SHRINER, CHARLES A.

Paterson, New Jersey: Its Advantages for Manufacturing and Residence... Paterson: 1890. V. 37; 41

SHRUBSOLE, EDGAR S.

The Chronicles of the Old Cronies' Angling Club. Scarborough. V. 39

SHUCK, J. LEWIS

Portfolio Chinensis; or a Collection of Authentic Chinese State Papers. Macao: 1840. V. 40; 45

SHUCK, OSCAR T.

Bench and Bar in California. San Francisco: 1887-89. V. 40; 45

Bench and Bar in California. San Francisco: 1889. V. 45

The California Scrap-Book. San Francisco: 1869. V. 39

History of the Bench and Bar of California, Being Biographies of Many Remarkable Men... Los Angeles: 1901. V. 40; 45

SHUCKBURGH-EVELYN, GEORGE

An Account of the Equatorial Instrument. London: 1793. V. 40

SHUCKFORD, SAMUEL c. 1694-1754

The Sacred and Prophane History of the World Connected. The Creation and Fall of Man. London: 1743-40-53. V. 39

The Sacred and Profane History of the World Connected, from the Creation of the World to the Dissolution of the Assyrian Empire at the Death of Saradanapalus... Oxford: 1848. V. 42; 43; 46

SHUFELDT, R. W.

Studies of the Human Form for Artists, Sculptors and Scientists. Philadelphia: 1908. V. 42

SHUFELDT, ROBERT W.

Reports of Explorataions and Surveys to Ascertain the Practicability of a Ship-Canal Between the Atlantic and Pacific Oceans by the Way of the Isthmus of Tehuantepec. Washington: 1872. V. 37

SHULDHAM, MOLYNEUX

The Despatches of Molyneux Shuldham... New York: 1913. V. 41; 42

SHULTZ, BENJAMIN

An Inaugural Botanico-Medical Dissertation, on the Phytolacca Decandra of Linnaeus. Philadelphia: 1795. V. 41

SHUMWAY, JOHN

Sheridan's Raid. Washington: 1865. V. 39

SHUNK, HARRY

Christo: Wrapped Walk Ways, Loose Park, Kansas City, Missouri, 1977-78. New York: 1973. V. 43

SHURE, DAVID S.

Hester Bateman: Queen of English Silversmiths. Garden City: (1959). V. 37

SHURTLEFF, NATHANIEL B.

A Decimal System for the Arrangement and Administration of Libraries. Boston: 1856. V. 45

SHURTLEFF, ROSWELL

A Discourse Delivered at the Funeral of Mrs. Mary Woodward, Consort of the Late Hon. Professor Woodward, in the Meeting-House Near Dartmouth College, March 29, 1807. Hanover: 1807. V. 38

SHUTE, E. L.

Fancies Free. London. V. 45

Jappie Chappie and How He Loved a Dollie. London. V. 43

SHUTE, HENRY

The Country Band. Boston: 1910. V. 37; 41; 42; 43; 44

SHUTE, HENRY A.

The Real Diary of a Real Boy. Boston: 1902. V. 41; 43

'Sequil' or Things Which Aint Finished in the First. Boston: 1904. V. 43

SHUTE, JOHN

The First and Chief Groundes of Architecture. London: 1912. V. 42; 44

SHUTE, NEVIL

In the Wet. London: 1953. V. 38

On the Beach. New York: 1957. V. 41

The Rainbow and the Rose. London: 1958. V. 45

A Town Like Alice. London: 1950. V. 45

SHUTE, NEVIL continued

Trustee from the Toolroom. London: 1960. V. 45

SHUTTLEWORTH, E. B.

The Windmill and Its Times. Toronto: 1924. V. 37; 38; 41

SHUTTLEWORTH, NINA L. KAY

A Life of Sir Woodbine Parish K.C.H., F.R.S., (1796-1882), Sometime Secretary to Lord Castlereagh; Charge d'Affaires and Minister Plenipotentiary to the Provinces of the River Plate . . . London: 1910. V. 39

THE SIAMESE Tales. Baltimore: 1797. V. 40

SIBBALD, GEORGE

Notes and Observations, on the Pine Lands of Georgia, Showing the Advantages They Possess, Particularly in the Culture of Cotton. Augusta: 1801. V. 37

SIBBALD, ROBERT

The History Ancient and Modern of the Sheriffdoms of Fife and Kinross, with a Description of Both, and the Firths of Forth and Tay, and the Islands of Them. London: 1803. V. 39

Scotia Illustrata Sive Prodromus Historiae Naturalis in Quo Regionis Natura . . . Edinburgh: 1683-84. V. 40

Scotia Illustrata Sive Prodromus Historiae Naturalis. Edinburgh: 1684. V. 37; 39; 43

SIBBES, RICHARD 1577-1635

Evangelical Sacrifices in XIX Sermons. 1640. V. 38

A Fountain Sealed. London: 1638. V. 38

the Saints Safetie in Evil Times. London: 1633. V. 42; 45

SIBBETT, R. M.

Orangeism in Ireland and Throughout the Empire, 1688-1938. London: 1939. V. 38

SIBBS, RICHARD 1577-1635

Soules Conflict with It Selfe, and Victory over It Selfe by Faith. London: 1635. V. 45

SIBER, ADAM 1515-1583

Lvdvs Literarvm Apvd Cheminicvm Misniae, Qva Ratione Administretur, Adami Siberi. Strassburg: 1549. V. 39; 40

SIBLEY, EBENEZER

The Medical Mirror. London: 1794? V. 42

SIBLEY, H. H.

Address Delivered Before the Minnesota Historical Society . . . Saint Paul: 1856. V. 37; 39

SIBLEY, HENRY H.

Minnesota Territory: Its Present Condition and Prospects. Washington: 1852. V. 42; 45

SIBLEY, JOHN

Louisiana: an Account of the Red River and Country Adjacent, to General Henry Dearborn, Secretary of War. V. 46

Louisiana: an Account of the Red River and Country Adjacent to General Henry Dearborn, Secretary of War. Philadelphia. V. 39

Travels in the Interior Parts of America. London: 1807. V. 38; 40

SIBLEY, JOHN LANGDON

History of the Town of Union, in the County of Lincoln, Maine, to the Middle of the Nineteenth Century. Boston: 1851. V. 41

SIBLY, EBENEEZER

The Celestial Science of Aastarology. London: 1784-88. V. 38

SIBLY, EBENEZER

A New and Complete Illustration of the Celestial Science of Astrology. London: 1784-1788. V. 41; 42

SIBORNE, H. T.

Waterloo Letters. London: 1891. V. 42

SIBORNE, W.

History of the War in France and Belgium in 1815 . . . London: 1844. V. 42

SIBSON, THOMAS

Racy Sketches of Expeditions, from the Pickwick Club. London: 1838. V. 40

Sketches of Expeditions from the Pickwick Club. London: 1838. V. 43

SIBYLLA, BARTHOLOMAEUS

Speulum Peregrinarum Questionum . . . Tres Decades Complectens in Quibus Varie Questiones de Animabus Rationalibus in Coniuncto & Separatis . . . Lugduni: 1534. V. 40

SIBYLLINA Oracula ex Uett. Codd. Aucta, Renovata et Notis Illustrata a D. Iohanne Opsopaeo Brettano.M i. Paris: 1599. V. 43

SIBYLLINA Oracula, ex Veteris Codicibus Emendata, cum Notis Variorum. Amsterdam: 1689. V. 37

SIBYLLINE Leaves, or Anonymous Papers. London: 1755. V. 38; 43

SICHEL, JULES

Iconographie Opthalmologique ou Description . . . Paris: 1852-59. V. 42

SICKELMORE'S Descriptive Views of Brighton. Brighton: 1830. V. 45

SICKLER, FREDERICK C. L.

Herculaneum Rolls. London: 1817. V. 40

SICKLER, JOSEPH

The History of Salem County, New Jersey. Salem: 1937. V. 41; 46

SIDDONS, HENRY

Practical Illustrations of Rhetorical Gesture and Action, Adapted to the English Drama. London: 1807. V. 45; 46

Practical Illustrations of Rhetorical Gesture and Action. London: 1822. V. 39; 46

SIDERFIN, THOMAS

Les Reports des Divers Special Cases Argue & Adjudge en le Court del Bnk Le Roy et Auxy en le Co. Ba. & L'Echequer en les Premier dix ans Apres le Restauration del son Tres-Excellent Majesty Le Roy Charles le II. London: 1683. V. 38

SIDGWICK, HENRY

The Elements of Politics. London: 1891. V. 40

The Methods of Ethics. London: 1874. V. 39

The Principles of Political Economy. London: 1883. V. 41

The Principles of Political Economy. London: 1901. V. 42

SIDIS, BORIS 1867-1923

Psyhopathological Researches. Studies in Mental Dissociation. New York: 1902. V. 46

SIDNEY, ALGERNON

The Arraignment, Tryal & Condemnation of Algernon Sidney, Esq. for High Treason. For Conspiring the Death of the King, and Intending to Raise a Rebellion in This Kingdom. London: 1684. V. 44

Discourses Concerning Government. London: 1692. V. 45

Discourses Concerning Government. London: 1698. V. 37; 38; 39

Discourses Concerning Government . . . London: 1704. V. 40

Discourses Concerning Government, to Which are Added, Memoirs of His Life and an Aplogy for Himself. London: 1751. V. 37; 40; 41; 43; 44

Discourses Concerning Government. London: 1763. V. 40

Discourses on Government. New York: 1805. V. 39

Letters of the Honourable Algernon Sydney, to the Honourable Henry Savile, Ambassador in France. London: 1742. V. 45

The Very Copy of a Paper Delivered to the Sheriffs Upon the Scaffold on Tower-Hill on Friday Dec. 7, 1683, By Algernon Sidney, Esq., Before His Execution There. London: 1683. V. 40

SIDNEY JANIS GALLERY, NEW YORK.

Dada 1916-1923. 1953. V. 39

SIDNEY, JOSEPH

An Oration, Commemorative of the Abolition of the Slave Trade in the United States: Delivered Before the Wilberforce Philanthropic Association in the City of New York. New York: 1809. V. 42

SIDNEY Lawton Smith, Designer, Etcher, Engraver, with Extracts from His Diary and a Check-List of His Bookplates. Boston: 1931. V. 41

SIDNEY, PHILIP 1554-1586

Astrophel & Stella. N.P.: 1931. V. 38; 46

Astrophel and Stella. V. 44

Astrophel and Stella. London: 1931. V. 44

Certain Sonnets from the Countess of Pembroke's Arcadia. V. 43

Certaine Sonnets. Boston: 1904. V. 44

Certaine Sonets. Cambridge: 1904. V. 39

The Countess of Pembrokes Arcadia. London: 1605. V. 41; 42

The Covntesse of Pembrokes Arcadia. London: 1627-28. V. 46

The Countess of Pembroke's Arcadia. 1638. V. 42

The Countess of Pembroke's Arcadia. London: 1638. V. 39; 40; 41; 43; 44; 45

The Countess of Pembroke's Arcadia . . . London: 1674. V. 38

The Countesse of Pembrokes Arcadia . . . London: 1613. V. 40; 44; 46

The Countesse of Pembrokes Arcadia . . . Now the Sixth Time Published, with Some New Additions. London: 1627. V. 37; 38

The Defence of Poesy. London: 1810. V. 42; 46

The Defence of Poesie. Boston: 1908. V. 43

SIDNEY, PHILIP 1554-1586 continued

The Lad Philisides, Being a Selection of Songs, Pastoral Eclogues & Elegies . . . 1988. V. 40

The Lad Philisides Being a Selection of Songs, Pastroal Eclogues & Elegies from the Countess of Pembroke's Arcadia. Monmouth: 1988. V. 45

Sir Philip Sydney's Defence of Poetry. And, Observations on Poetry and Eloquence, from the Discoveries of Ben Johnson. (Edited by Joseph Warton). London: 1787. V. 37

The Sonnets. 1898. V. 40

The Works . . . London: 1725-1724. V. 39

The Complete Works of Sir Philip Sidney. Cambridge: 1922-26. V. 41

SIDNEY, RICHARD J.

In British Malay To-Day. London: 1927. V. 40

SIDNEY, S.

The Book of the Horse. London. V. 38

The Book of the Horse . . . London: 1884-86. V. 42

SIDNEY, SAMUEL

Gauge Evidence. The History and Prospects of the Railway System . . . London: 1846. V. 46

The Three Colonies of Australia. London: 1852. V. 41; 45

SIDONIUS APOLLINARIS, C. SOLLIUS

Lucubrationes, Liberalium Literarum Studiosis Cognoscendae. Basle: 1542. V. 40

SIDONIUS APOLLINARIS, GAIUS SOLLIUS

Opera. Paris: 1599. V. 45

SIDONIUS, CAIUS SOLLIUS APOLLINARIS

Opera. Paris: 1609. V. 37

SIDOROVA, N. A.

Antique Painted Pottery in the Pushkin State Museum of Fine Arts, Moscow. Moscow: 1985. V. 44

SIEBEL, J. E.

One Hundred Years of Brewing. Chicago: 1903. V. 44

SIEBER, F. W.

Travels in the Island of Crete in the Year 1817. London: 1823. V. 37; 39; 45

SIEBERT, WILBUR HENRY

Loyalists in East Florida 1774-1785. Deland: 1929. V. 40; 46

The Underground Railroad from Slavery to Freedom. New York: 1899. V. 40

SIEBMACHER, JOHANN

Das Erneuerte and Vermehrte Teutsche Wappenbuch . . . Erster(-Vierdte) Theil . . . Nuremberg: 1657. V. 39

SIEBOLD, P. F. VON

Flora Japonica sive Plantae, Quas in Imperio Japonico Collegit . . . Leiden: 1835-70. V. 42

THE SIEGE of Quebec and Conquest of Canada; in 1759. Quebec: 185?. V. 37

THE SIEGE of the Castle of Aesculapius, an Heroic Comedy. London: 1768. V. 42

SIEGEL, HENRY A.

The Derrydale Press. A Bibliography. Goshen: 1981. V. 43

SIEGEL, PAUL

Neuzeitliche Ornamentik. Dresden: 1925. V. 46

SIEGEMUNDIN, JUSTINE

Die Chur-Brandenburgische Hoff-Wehe-Mutter. 1690. V. 44

Die Chur-Brandenburgische Hoff-Wehe-Mutter. Coelln an der Spree,: 1690. V. 41; 45; 46

SIEGENTHALER, FRED

Strange Papers, a Collection of the World's Rarest Handmade Paper. Muttenz: 1987. V. 38; 41; 45

SIEGFRIED, W. R.

Antarctic Nutrient Cycles and Food Webs. Berlin: 1985. V. 37

SIEMENS, C. WILLIAM

On the Conservation of Solar Energy. London: 1883. V. 42; 43; 45

SIEMER, J.

Josiah C. Marshall's Nord Amerikanischen Farmers und Auswanderers Handbuch . . . Hamburg: 1854. V. 42

SIEMIENOWITZ, KAZIMIERZ

Grand Art d'Artillerie. Ars Magna Artilleriae . . . Amsterdam: 1651. V. 39; 45

SIENKIEWICZ, HENRY

Quo Vadis? Verona: 1959. V. 38; 39

SIENKIEWICZ, HENRYK

Quo Vadis? New York: 1959. V. 41

Quo Vadis. Boston: 1897. V. 37

SIERRA CLUB

Sierra Club Bulletin. San Francisco: 1928-38. V. 41

SIERRA LEONE

Constitution of the Colony of Sierra Leone, and Its Dependencies from the 20th Deg. North to the 20th Deg. South Latitude, As Established by Charter . . . London: 1835. V. 39; 42

SIEVEKING, L. DE G.

Dressing Gowns and Glue. London: 1919. V. 38

SIEVEKING, LANCE

Smite and Spare Not. London: 1933. V. 45

SIEVER, R. W.

Sculpture Illustrations, with a Dissertation on Sculpture and Sculptures. London: 1850. V. 38; 40

SIFFERARTH, N. L.

A Short Compendium of the Cathechism for the Indians, with the Approbation of the Rt. Rev. Frederic Baraga, Bishop Saut Sainte Marie, 1864. Buffalo;: 1869. V. 38; 42

SIFTON, CLIFFORD

Descriptive Atlas of Western Canada Showing Maps of Manitoba and British Columbia and Districts of Assinboia, Alberta, and Saskatchewan. Ottawa: 1899. V. 42

SIGAL, CLANCY

Going Away. 1961. V. 44

SIGAUD DE LA FOND, JOSEPH AIGNAN

Essai sur Differentes Especes d'Air . . . Paris: 1779. V. 38

SIGEBERT OF GEMBLOUX

Chronicon ab Anno 381 ad 1113 cum Insertionibus ex Historia Galfridi & Additionibus Roberti Abbatis Monti. Paris: 1513. V. 37; 45

SIGEL, GUSTAV A.

Germany's Army and Navy by Pen and Picture. Akron: 1900. V. 40

SIGERIST, HENRY

American Medicine. New York: 1934. V. 41

American Review of Soviet Medicine. London: 1943-47. V. 45

The Great Doctors. New York: 1933. V. 37; 41; 42; 45

SIGERIST, HENRY E.

Man and Medicine: an Introduction to Medical Knowledge. New York: 1932. V. 41

SIGERSON, GEORGE

History of the Land Tenures and Land Classes of Ireland . . . London: 1871. V. 38

SIGMOND, G.

Tea: Its Effects, Medicinal and Moral. London: 1839. V. 42

SIGNAL Fires on the Trail of the Pathfinder. New York: 1856. V. 45

SIGNATURE. a Quadrimestrial of Typography and the Graphic Arts. London: 1946-1954. V. 40; 41

SIGNOT, JACQUES

La Totale et Vraye Description de Tous les Passaiges, Lieux et Destroitz . . . Paris: 1522. V. 38

SIGONIUS, CARLO

Fasti Consulaares, ac Triumphi Acti. Venetiis: 1556. V. 38

SIGONIUS, CAROLUS

De Antiquo Iure Civium Romanorum Libri Duo Eiusdem De Antiquo Iure Italiae Libri Tres. (with) Orationes. Paris: 1573. V. 40

Fasti Consulares, Ac Triumphi Acti a Romulo Rege Usque ad Ti. Caesarem. Hanover: 1609. V. 45

Historiarum de Regno Italiae Libri Viginti. Francofurti: 1591. V. 40

Scholia Quibus T. Livii Patavini Hitoriae et Earum Epitome Paratim Emendantur Partim Etiam Explanatur Multis in Locisaucta. Venetiis: 1572. V. 37

SIGORGNE, PIERRE

Institutions Newtoniennes, ou Introduction a la Philosophie de M. Newton . . . Paris: 1747. V. 45

SIGOURNEY, L. H.

Select Poems. Philadelphia: 1845. V. 41

SIGOURNEY, LYDIA H.

Sketch of Connecticut, Forty Years Since. Hartford: 1824. V. 44

SIGOURNEY, LYDIA HOWARD HUNTLEY

Letters to Mothers. Hartford: 1838. V. 46

Past Meridian. New York: 1854. V. 46

Sketches. Philadelphia: 1834. V. 38; 46

Traits of the Aborigines of America. Cambridge: 1822. V. 38

SIGOURNEY, LYDIA HUNTLEY

Myrtis, with Other Etchings and Sketches. New York: 1846. V. 43

SIGSBY, WILLIAM

Life and Adventures of Timothy Murphy the Benefactor of Schoharie, Including His History from the Commencement of the Revolution . . . . 1839. V. 41

Life and Adventures of Timothy Murphy . . . from the Commencement of the Revolution. New York: 1839. V. 41; 45

Life and Adventures of Timothy Murphy . . . from the Commencement of the Revolution. Schoharie: 1839. V. 39

SIGUENZA Y GONGORA, CARLOS DE

Glorias de Queretaro . . . Mexico: 1803. V. 42

The Merucrio Volante . . . an Account of the First Expedition of Don Diego de Vargas into New Mexico in 1692. London: 1932. V. 42

The Mercurio Volante of Don Carlos de Siguenza y Gongora: an Account of the First Expedition of Don Diego de Vargas into New Mexico i 1692. Los Angeles: 1932. V. 39; 40; 41; 45

SIKELIANOS, ANGELOS

The Dithyrambe of the Rose. N.P.: 1939. V. 46

SILBER & FLEMING

Illustrated Pattern-Book of Furniture, Carpets, Rugs, Linoleums, Floor Cloths, Curtains, Window Blinds, Table Linen, Towellings, Blankets, etc . . . Section 1. London: 1870. V. 45

SILBER, EVELYN

The Sculpture of Epstein with a Complete Catalouge. Oxford: 1986. V. 44

SILBERTEIN, AUGUST

Album der Kronprinz Rudolfs-Bahn. I. Section. Leoben-Villach. Vienna: 1868. V. 45

SILIUS ITALICUS

De Bello Punico Secundo XVII Libri. Venetiis: 1523. V. 37

Punica. Venice: 1483. V. 46

Punica. Venice: 1492. V. 37; 43

Punica. Venice: 1493. V. 46

Punica. London: 1792. V. 38; 39; 42

SILIUS ITALICUS, CAIUS

Silii Italici, Poetae Clarissimi, de Bello PUnico Libri Septemdecim. 1551. V. 45

SILIUS ITALICUS, TIBERIUS CATIUS

De Bello Punico Secundo VII Libri. Venetiis: 1523. V. 38

SILKIN, JON

The Peaceable Kingdom: Poems Newly Revised. Boston: 1975. V. 45

The Peaceable Kingdom. Williamsburg: 1975. V. 41; 44

SILKO, LESLIE HARMON

The Man to Send Rain Clouds. New York: 1973. V. 42

SILKO, LESLIE MARMON

Ceremony. New York: 1977. V. 44; 45

Five Broadsides from Fusions: a Sense of Place. N.P.: 1985. V. 43

Stories Southwest. Prescott: 1973. V. 43

SILL, EDWARD R.

The Hermitage, and Other Poems. San Francisco: 1868. V. 40

SILL, EDWARD ROWLAND

Field Notes. Berkeley: 1882. V. 39

The Prose of Edward Rowland Sill. Boston & New York: 1900. V. 46

SILLAR, DAVID

Poems. Kilmarnock: 1789. V. 37; 40; 41; 42; 43

SILLETT, J.

Grammar to Flower-Painting. Norwich: 1826. V. 42; 45

SILLIMAN, AUGUSTUS E.

A Gallop Among American Scenery; or, Sketches of American Scenes and Military Adventure. New York: 1843. V. 40

SILLIMAN, B.

On Some of the Mining Districts of Arizona Near the Rio Colorado, with Remarks on the Climate &c. N.P.: 1866. V. 39

Remarks, Made on a Short Tour Between Hartford and Quebec, in the Autumn of 1819. New Haven: 1820. V. 39

SILLIMAN, BENJAMIN

The American Journal of Science . . . New York: 1818. V. 44

A Description of the Recently Discovered Petroleum Region in California. New York: 1865. V. 38

Elements of Chemistry, in the Order of the Lectures Given in Yale College. New Haven: 1830. V. 40

Elements of Chemistry. New Haven: 1830-31. V. 37

A Journal of Travels in England, Holland and Scotland, and of Two Passages Over the Atlantic in the Years 1805 and 1806. Boston: 1812. V. 40

An Oration Delivered at Hartford on the 6th of July, A.D., 1802. Hartford: 1802. V. 43

Remarks, Made On a Short Tour, Between Hartford and Quebec. New Haven: 1820. V. 37; 38; 42

Review of the Nature, Resources and Plan of Development (Now in Progress) Of the Northern Division of the Mariposa Estate. New York: 1873. V. 45

A Visit to Europe in 1851. New York: 1854. V. 44

SILLIMAN, H.

Report on the Influence and Efficiency of the Press in Promoting the Cause of Missions. V. 43

SILLITOE, ALAN

Barbarians and Other Poems. London: 1973. V. 41

Day-Dream Communique. 1977. V. 39

The Death of William Posters. London: 1965. V. 43

The Loneliness of the Long Distance Runner. London: 1959. V. 40; 42; 46

The Ragman's Daughter. London: 1963. V. 43

The Rats and Other Poems. London: 1960. V. 43

Saturday Night and Sunday Morning. New York: 1959. V. 45

Saturday Night & Sunday Morning. London: 1958. V. 37

Somme. London. V. 45

SILSBURY MANUFACTURING CO.

Ctalogue of the Silsby Steam Fire Engine, Hose Carriages, Carts and Reels. Seneca Falls: 1881. V. 38

SILTZER, FRANK

The Story of British Sporting Prints. London. V. 39

The Story of British Sporting Prints. London: 1925. V. 39; 42

The Story of British Sporting Prints. New York: 1925. V. 38; 41; 42

The Story of British Sporting Prints. London: 1929. V. 37; 39; 42; 46

SILURIST, HENRY VAUGHAN

Sacred Poems of . . . London: 1897. V. 37

SILVA ALVARENGA, MANOEL IGNACIO

O Desertor. Poema Heroicomico . . . Coimbra: 1774. V. 45

SILVA COUTINHO, JOAO MARTINS DA

Relatorio. Apresentado ao Illm e Exm Snr. Dr. Manoel Clementino Carniero de Cunha, Residente da provincia do Amazonas . . . Manaos: 1861. V. 45

SILVA DE ECA, MATHIAS AIRES RAMOS DA

Problema de Architectura Civil, a Saber . . . Lisbon: 1770. V. 45

SILVA E SOUSA, ANTONIO DA

Instruccam Politica de Legados: ao Serenissimo Principe Dom Alfonso: Nosso Senhor. Hamburg: 1656. V. 38

SILVA, ERCOLE

Dell'Arte dei Giardini Inglesi. Milan: 1801. V. 37; 45

SILVA LISBOA, JOSE DA

Agradecimento do Povo ao Salvador da Patria o Senhor Principe Regente do Reino do Brasil. Rio de Janeiro: 1822. V. 39

SILVAGIUS, MATTHEUS

Opus Pulchrum et Studiosis Viris Satis Iucu(n)dum de Tribus Peregrinis seu de Colloquiis Trium Peregrinorum, de Divinis Perfectionibus . . . Venice: 1542. V. 37

SILVE, CLAUDE

Benediction. New York: 1936. V. 46

SILVEIRA DE BRAGANZA, RONALD LOUIS

The Hill Collection of Pacific Voyagaes . . . San Diego: 1974. V. 38

SILVEIRA, LUIS

Ensai de Iconografia das Cidades Portuguesas do Ultramar. Lisbon: 1955. V. 39; 40

SILVEIRA, MIGUEL

El Macabeo. Poema Heroico. Naples: 1638. V. 38

SILVER, JACOB MORTIMER WIER

Sketches of Japanese Manners and Customs . . . London: 1867. V. 41

THE SILVER Mines of Nevada. New York: 1864. V. 41

SILVER, ROLLO G.

Nicolas Jensen. Boston: 1966. V. 39

SILVER, S. W., & CO.

Handbook for Australia & New Zealand (Including also the Fiji Islands) with New Map of the Colonies. London: 1884. V. 46

SILVER, S. WILLIAM

Catalogue of the York Gate Library formed by Mr. S. William Silver. London: 1886. V. 40

SILVERBERG, R.

Lord Valentine's Castle. 1980. V. 39

SILVERBERG, ROBERT

Lord Valentine's Castle. New York: 1980. V. 39; 41; 43

SILVERHEELS, HENRY

Proclamation! Seneca Nation New York Indians! Cattaraugus and Allegany Reservations, Executive Department, Nov. 3d, 1864. N.P.: 1864. V. 39

SILVERS, ASH

The Land of the O-O. Facts, Figures, Fables and Fancies. Cleveland: 1892. V. 40

SILVERSPARRE, AXEL

Appendix to New map of COlorado Containing Alphabetical Register and Indexed Location of All Peaks, Passes, Watercourses and Plats of All Patented Mines, Etc. Chicago: 1882. V. 37; 40

SILVERTOP, CHARLES

A Geological Sketch of the Teritary Formation in the Provinces of Granada and Murcia, Spain, with Notices Respecting Primary, Secondaray and Volcanic Rocks in the Same District and Sections. London: 1836. V. 37; 38

SILVESTRE, ISRAEL

Les Plaisirs del'Isle Enchantee, ou Les Fetes et Divertissements du Roy, a Versailles. 1664. V. 38

SILVESTRE, M. J. B.

Universal Palaeography; or, Facsimiles of Writings of All Nations and Periods . . . London: 1850. V. 41; 43; 45

SILVESTRI, GIUESEPPE MARIA

Ragionamento Sopra l'Uso ed Abuso del Tabacco. Rome: 1773. V. 46

SIM, T. R.

Forest Flora and Forest Resources of Portuguese East Africa. Aberdeen: 1909. V. 37

SIMAK, C.

All Flesh is Grass. 1965. V. 43

City. 1952. V. 43

They Walked Like Men. 1962. V. 43

SIMAK, CLIFFORD D. 1904-1988

Best Science Fiction Stories of . . . . 1967. V. 39

The Fellowship of the Talisman. New York: 1978. V. 44

Way Station. 1963. V. 39

SIMAKOFF, N.

L'Art de L'Asie Centrale Recueil de l'Art Decoratif de L'Asie Centrale. St. Petersburg: 1883. V. 45

SIMCOE and Norfolk County. In Commemoration of the Simcoe Reunion of Norfolk County Old Boys, August 2nd to 7th, 1924. Simcoe: 1924. V. 38; 42

SIMCOE COUNTY PIONEER & HISTORICAL SOCIETY

Pioneer Papers. No. 1. Barrie: 1908. V. 42

SIMCOE, ELIZABETH P.

The Diary of Mrs. John Graves Simcoe. Toronto: 1911. V. 42

SIMCOE, JOHN GRAVES

Simcoe's Military Journal. New York: 1844. V. 41; 45

SIME, S. H.

Bogey Beasts. London: 1924? V. 38

SIME, SIDNEY H.

Bogey Beasts. Jingles &c by S. H. Sime. Music by Holbrooke. (Cover title). London: (1923). V. 37

The Book of Bogey Beasts. London: 1923. V. 46

The Butterfly. London: 1893-94. V. 42

SIMENON, GEORGE

Maigret in Society. London: 1962. V. 41

SIMENON, GEORGES

The Patience of Maigret. New York: 1940. V. 39; 44

SIMEON, CORNWALL

Stray Notes on Fishing and Natural History. Cambridge & London: 1860. V. 40

SIMEONI, GABRIEL

Dialogo Pio et Speculativo . . . Lyon: 1560. V. 37

SIMEONI, GABRIELLE

Illustratione de gli Epitaffi et Medaglie Antiche. Lyon: 1558. V. 43

SIMES, THOMAS

The Military Guide for Young Offiers. London: 1772. V. 37; 39

A Military Course for the Government and Conduct of a Battalion, Designed for Their Regulations in Quarter Camp, or Garrison . . . London: 1777. V. 43

The Military Guide for Young Officers, Containing a System of the Art of War . . . London: 1781. V. 42; 44

A Military Course for the Government and Conduct of a Battalion . . . London: 1777. V. 37

New Military, Historical and Explanatory Dictionary . . . Philadelphia: 1776. V. 42

SIMIC, CHARLES

Pyramids and Sphinxes. New York: 1989. V. 42; 46

Weather Forecasts for Utopia and Vicinity. Poems 1967-1982. Barrytown: 1983. V. 46

What the Grass Says. San Francisco. V. 46

White. New York: 1972. V. 46

SIMIENOWICZ, CASIMIR

The Great Art of Artilllery. London: 1729. V. 37

SIMKIN, R.

Life in the Army. London: 1886/1890. V. 42

SIMKIN, RICHARD

Military Types. London: 1888-1902. V. 41

Our Armies Illustrated and Described. London: 1890. V. 41

The War in Egypt. London: 1883. V. 42

SIMLER, GEORG

Obseruationes de Arte Grammatica. De Literis Gr(a)ecis ac Dipthongis . . . Abbreuiatones Quibus Frequentissime Graecu Utuntur . . . Tubingen: 1512. V. 44

SIMMONDS, J. H.

Trees from Other Lands for Shelter and Timber in New Zealand: Eucalypts. Auckland: 1927. V. 38

SIMMONDS, PETER LUND

Sir John Franklin and the Arctic Regions . . . Buffalo: 1852. V. 37; 40; 42; 45

SIMMONS, ALBERT DIXON

Wing Shots: a Series of Camera Studies of American Game Birds and Other Birds of Field and Stream on the Wing. New York: 1936. V. 37; 40; 43; 45

simmons, amelia

American Cookery, or the Art of Dressing Viands, Fish, Poultry and Vegetables and the Best Modes of Making Pastes, Puffs, Pies, Tarts, Pudding, Custads and Preserves and All Kinds of Cakes . . . Hartford: 1798. V. 40; 45

American Cookery . . . Albany: 1804. V. 45

American Cookery. New York: 1822. V. 39

American Cookery . . . New York: 1958. V. 45

American Cookery . . . Hartford: Hudson & Goodwin,: 1798. V. 37

SIMMONS, D.

The Fall of Hyperion. 1990. V. 43

SIMMONS, DAN

Summer of Night. New York: 1991. V. 44

SIMMONS, FRANK E.

History of Coryell County. Coryell County News: 1936. V. 37

SIMMONS, G.

A British Rifle Man. London: 1899. V. 42

SIMMONS, J. W.

An Inquiry into the Moral Character of Lord Byron. London: 1826. V. 42

SIMMONS, JAMES

The Diaries of James Simmons, Paper Baker of haslemere, 1831-1868. 1990. V. 44; 45

The Diaries of James Simmons, Paper Maker of Haslemere 1831-1868. Oxshott: 1990. V. 45

Out on the Edge. Leeds: 1958. V. 40

SIMMONS, NOAH

Heroes and Heroines of the Fort Dearborn Massacre . . . Lawrence: 1896. V. 43

SIMMONS, OWEN

The Book of Bread. London. V. 38

The Book of Bread. London: 1903. V. 45

The Book of Bread. London: 1904. V. 42

SIMMONS, THOMAS FREDERICK

Remarks on the Constitution and Practice of Courts Martial. 1830. V. 40

SIMMS, FREDERIC WALTER

Public Works of Great Britain Consisting of Railways . . . Cast Iron Bridges, Iron and Gas Works. London: 1838. V. 38; 46

SIMMS, FREDERICK W.

A Treatise on the Principal Mathematical Instruments Employed in Surveying, Levelling and Astronomy . . . Baltimore: 1844. V. 41

SIMMS, FREDERICK WALTER

Practical Tunnelling. London: 1896. V. 38; 45

Practical Tunnelling. London: 1896. V. 38

The Public Works of Great Britain . . . London: 1853. V. 39

SIMMS, JAMES M.

The First Colored Baptist Church in North America. Philadelphia: 1888. V. 43

SIMMS, JEPTHA

The Frontiersmen of New York. Albany: 1882. V. 40

SIMMS, JEPTHA R.

History of Schoharie County, and Border Wars of New York . . . Albany: 1845. V. 45

SIMMS, JOSEPH

Nature's Revelations of Character. London: 1873. V. 39

The Past, Present and Future of Woman. San Francisco: 1889. V. 42

SIMMS, W. G.

Pelayo; a Story of the Goth. New York: 1838. V. 44

SIMMS, WILLIAM

The Achromatic Telescope, and Its Various Mountings Especially the Equatorial. London: 1852. V. 40; 44

SIMMS, WILLIAM GILMORE 1806-1870

Atalantis: a Story of the Sea. New York: 1832. V. 38

Border Beagles: a Tale of Mississippi. Philadelphia: 1840. V. 45

Carl Werner, an Imaginative Story. New York: 1838. V. 45; 46

Charlemont or the Pride of the Village. New York: 1856. V. 43

Count Julian; or, the Last Days of the Goth. Baltimore: 1845. V. 45; 46

The Damsel of Darien. Philadelphia: 1839. V. 43

Early Lays. Charleston: 1827. V. 45; 46

Egeria; or, Voices of Thought and Counsel, for the Woods and Wayside. Philadelphia: 1853. V. 43

Eutaw, a Sequel to the Forayers; or the Raid of the Dog-Days. New York: 1856. V. 43; 46

The Golden Christmas: a Chronicle of St. John's, Berkeley. Charleston: 1852. V. 42; 43

Guy Rivers. New York: 1834. V. 37; 40; 43; 45; 46

Katharine Walton; or, the Rebel of Dorchester, an Historical Romance of the Revolution in Carolina. Philadelphia: 1851. V. 42

The Life of Francis Marion. New York: 1844. V. 37

The Lily and the Totem, or, the Huguenots in Florida. New York: 1850. V. 43; 45; 46

Marie De Berniere. Philadelphia: 1853. V. 45; 46

The Maroon: a Legend of the Caribees and Other Tales. Philadelphia: 1855. V. 43

Martin Faber, the Story of a Criminal and Other Tales. New York: 1837. V. 39; 40; 43

Mellichampe. New York: 1836. V. 41

Mellichampe. New York: 1836. V. 43; 46

The Partisan; a Tale of the Revolution. New York: 1835. V. 40; 41; 43; 44

Pelayo. New York: 1838. V. 38; 41; 43; 45; 46

Poems, Descriptive, Dramatic, Legendary and Contemplative. New York: 1853. V. 38; 43; 46

Richard Hurdis; or the Avenger of Blood. Philadelphia: 1838. V. 40; 43

Sabbath Lyrics; or Songs from Scripture. Charleston: 1849. V. 43

Sack and Destruction of the City of Columbia, S.C. to Which is Added a List of the Property Destroyed. Columbia: 1865. V. 40; 42

The Scout, or the Black Riders of Congaree. New York: 1854. V. 43

South Carolina in the Revolutionary War . . . Charleston: 1853. V. 43

Southern Passages and Pictures. New York: 1839. V. 41; 44; 45; 46

Southward Ho! New York: 1854. V. 43; 46

Views and Reviews in American History, Literature and Fiction. First Series. New York: 1845. V. 37; 42

War Poetry of the South. New York: 1866. V. 39; 43; 45

The Wigwam and the Cabin. First (and Second) Series. New York: 1845. V. 42; 43; 45

The Yemassee. New York: 1835. V. 39; 43; 45; 46

SIMON, ANDRE

Bibliotheca Gastronomica A Catalogue of Books and Documents on Gastronomy. London: 1953. V. 37

Tea and Tea Cakes. London: 1940's. V. 43

A Wine Primer. London: 1956. V. 41

SIMON, ANDRE L.

Bibliotheca Gastronomica. London: 1953. V. 39

Bibliotheca Bacchica. London: 1972. V. 39; 42; 44

Bibliotheca Gastronomica. A Catalogue of Books and documents on Gastronomy . . . London: 1978. V. 40

Bibliotheca Vinaria. London: 1979. V. 39

Bottlescrew Days. London: 1926. V. 40; 42

Clarets and Sauternes. London: 1920. V. 41

The History of the Wine Trade in England. London: 1906-09. V. 44

Star Chamber Revels, or the Fountayne of Justice. Peekskill: 1937. V. 40

Star Chamber Dinner Accounts Being Some Hitherto Unpublished Accounts of Dinners Provided for the Lords of the Privy Council in Star Chamber . . . London: 1959. V. 40

Tables of Content. London: 1933. V. 44

Wine in Shakespeare's Days and Shakespeare's Plays. London: 1931. V. 46

SIMON, BARBARA ANNE

The Ten Tribes of Israel Historically Identified with the Aborigines of the Western Hemisphere. London: 1836. V. 40

SIMON, CLAUDE

Femmes. Paris: 1965. V. 41

SIMON, HENRY

Modern Flour Mill Machinery. Manchester: 1898. V. 40

The Present Position of Roller Flour Milling. Manchester: 1892. V. 42

SIMON, HUGO F.

In Memoriam: Walther Rathenau, 24 Juni 1922. Weimar: 1925. V. 45

SIMON, JAMES

An Essay Towards an Historical Account of Irish Coins and of Currency of Foreign (!) Monies in Ireland. Dublin: 1749. V. 41

Simon's Essay on Irish Coins, and of the Currency of Foreign Monies in Ireland. Dublin: 1810. V. 42

SIMON, JOHN

English Sanitary Institutions, Reviewed in Their Course of Development . . . London: 1890. V. 37; 45

SIMON, KATHLEEN HARVEY

Slavery. London: (1929). V. 37

SIMON, M. J.

Your Solar House. New York: 1947. V. 38; 46

SIMON, OLIVER

The Curwen Press Miscellany. Curwen: 1931. V. 43

The Curwen Press Miscellany. London: 1931. V. 42

SIMON, OLIVER continued

The Curwen Press Miscellany. Plaistow: 1931. V. 45

Printing of Today. London: 1928. V. 39; 40; 41; 43

Printing of Today: An Illustrated Survey of Post War Typography in Europe and the United States. With a general introduction by Aldous Huxley. London/New York: 1928. V. 37; 40

SIMON, RICHARD

A Critical History of the Old Testament, In Three Books. London: 1682. V. 42; 46

SIMOND, L.

A Tour in Italy and Sicily. London: 1828. V. 45

SIMOND, LOUIS 1767-1831

Journal of a Tour and Residence in Great Britain During the Years 1810 and 1811. Edinburgh: 1815. V. 38; 42; 44; 46

Switzerland; or, a Journal of a Tour and Residence . . . in the years 1817, 1818 and 1819. Boston: 1822. V. 38

SIMONDE DE SISMONDI, JEAN CHARLES LEON

De La Condition Dans Laquelle Il Convient de Placer Les Negres en les Affranchissant . . . Paris: 1833. V. 38

SIMONDE DE SISMONDI, JEAN CHARLES LEONARD 1773-1842

Histoire des Republiques Italiennes du Moyen Age. Bruxelles: 1838-39. V. 46

Historical View of the Literature of the South of Europe. London: 1823. V. 43

Nouveaux Principes d'Economie Politique . . . Paris: 1819. V. 41; 45

Political Economy, and the Philosophy of Government. London: 1847. V. 41

SIMONDS, BARNABAS

A Treatise on Field Diversions. Norwich: 1776. V. 40

SIMONDS, WILLIAM EDGAR

Manual of Patent Law. Hartford: 1874. V. 40

Practical Suggestions on the Sale of Patents, with Forms of Assingment, License, Contract, Power of Attorney to Sell Rights . . . Hartford: 1871. V. 40

SIMONIN, L.

Mines and Miners; or Underground Life. London: 1868. V. 38

SIMONIUS, SIMON

Poematia Avrea. Leyden: 1619. V. 37

SIMONS, C. J., MRS.

The Child's Wreath of Hymns and Songs. Maulmain: 1840. V. 43

SIMONS, J.

Jerusalem in the Old Testament. Leiden: 1952. V. 44

SIMONSON, GEORGE A.

Francesco Guardi, 1712-1793. London: 1904. V. 43

Francesco Guardi, 1712-1793. London: 1940. V. 40

SIMONSON, LEE

The Art of Scenic Design. New York: 1950. V. 37; 44

SIMPLE Stories, in Words of One Syllable, for Little Boys and Girls. London: 1825. V. 39

SIMPLICIO MARIA DAS NECESSIDADES

Carta Escripta Pelo Sachristaeo da Freguezia, de S. Joao de Itaboray ao Reverendo Vigario da Mesma Freguezia . . . Rio de Janeiro: 1822. V. 39

SIMPSON, A. CARSON

Simpson's Sherlockian Studies. Volumes 1-8. Philadelphia: 1953-1960. V. 43

SIMPSON, A. L.

Selections from the Works of Sir George Harvey, P.R.S.A. Edinburgh: 1870. V. 39

SIMPSON, ANNA PATT

Problems Women Solved. Prtd. for the Women's Board: 1916. V. 38

SIMPSON, ANNA PRATT

Problems Women Solved. San Francisco: 1915. V. 45

SIMPSON, ARTHUR

Secret Memoirs of Madame Catalani. Bath: 1811. V. 43; 45

Southwest Texas. 1952. V. 42

SIMPSON, C. H.

Life in the Far West: or, a Detective's Thrilling Adventures Among the Indians and Outlaws of Montana. Chicago: 1901. V. 44

SIMPSON, CHARLES

The Harvoro' Country. London: 1927. V. 39; 43

Trencher and Kennel. Some Famous Yorkshire Packs, Including the Bramham Moor, the York and Ainsty, Lord Middleton's Hunt, the Sinnington, the Bilsdale and the Farmdale . . . London: 1927. V. 39; 44

SIMPSON, CHARLES TORREY

Synposis of the Naiades, or Pearly Fresh-Water Mussels. Washington: 1900. V. 40

SIMPSON, CHRISTOPHER 1605?-1669

A Compendium. London: 1732. V. 40

SIMPSON, DAVID

A Discourse on Stage Entertainments. Manchester: 1823. V. 39

SIMPSON, EDWARD

Report of Ice and Ice Movements in the Bering Sea and the Arctic Basin. Washington: 1890. V. 43

SIMPSON, F. B.

Letters on Sport in Eastern Bengal. London: 1886. V. 39

SIMPSON, GEORGE, lecturer on anatomy

The Anatomy of the Bones and Muscles Exhibiting the Parts as They Appear on Dissection . . . London: 1825. V. 37; 39; 40

Journal of Occurrences in the Athabasca Department. Toronto: 1938. V. 37; 42

London Correspondence Inward from Sir George Simpson 1841-42. London: 1973. V. 46

Narrative of a Journey Round the World During the Years 1841 and 1842. London: 1847. V. 37; 38; 40; 41; 42; 44; 45; 46

Narrative of a Voyage to California Ports in 1841-42. San Francisco: 1930. V. 38; 39; 40; 42; 44; 46

An Overland Journey Round the World, During the Years 1841 and 1842. Philadelphia: 1847. V. 38

Part of Dispatch from George Simpson, Esqr., Governor of Ruperts Land; to the Governor & Committee of the Hudson's Bay company, London, March 1, 1829, Continued and Completed March 24th and June 5, 1829. London: 1947. V. 37; 42; 45

SIMPSON, GEORGE, lecturer on anatomy

The Anatomy of the Bones and Muscles Exhibiting the Parts as They Appear on Dissection . . . for the Use of Artist . . . London: 1825. V. 41

SIMPSON, HENRY I.

The Emigrant's Guide to the Gold Mines. New York: 1848. V. 38; 40

Emigrant's Guide to the Gold Fields. Haverford: 1978. V. 38; 39; 40; 42; 43; 44; 45; 46

The Emigrant's Guide to the Gold Mines . . . August, 1848. Haverford, Pa.: 1978. V. 37

SIMPSON, HIRAM K.

From the Stage Coach to the Pulpit. St. Louis: 1874. V. 46

SIMPSON, JAMES 1781-1853

Letters to Sir Walter Scott, Bart. on the Moral and Political Character and Effects of the Visit to Scotland in August 1822 of His Majesty King George IV. Edinburgh: 1822. V. 43

Necessity of Popular Education, as a National Object; with Hints on the Treatment of Criminals and Observations on Homicidal Insanity. Edinburgh: 1834. V. 43; 46

SIMPSON, JAMES E.

Report of Explorations Across the Great Basin of the Territory of Utah. Washington: 1876. V. 40; 44

SIMPSON, JAMES H.

Journal of a Military Reconnaissance from Santa Fe, New Mexico, to the Navajo Country. Philadelphia: 1852. V. 38; 39; 43; 45

. . . Report and Map of the Route from Fort Smith, Arkansas, to Santa Fe New Mexico, Made by . . . Washington: 1850. V. 41

Report of the Secretary of War. Communicting . . . Captain Simpson's Report and Map of Wagon Road Routes in Utah Territory. Washington: 1859. V. 43

Report of Lieut. Col. James H. Simpson, Corps of Engineers, U.S.A., on the Change of Route West from Omaha, Nebraska Territory . . . Washington: 1865. V. 38

Report of . . . on the Union Pacific Railraod and Branches, Central Pacific Railroad of California, Northern Pacific Railroad . . . Washington: 1866. V. 39; 42; 43

Report of Explorations Across the Great Basin of the Territory of Utah for a Direct Wagon Route from Camp Floyd to Genoa, In Carson Valley in 1859. Washington: 1876. V. 38; 40; 41; 44

Report of Explorations Across the Great Basin of the Territory of Utah, for a Direct Wagon-Route from Camp Floyd to Genoa, in Carson Valley, in 1859. Washington: 1876. V. 37

Route from Fort Smith to Santa Fe. Washington: 1850. V. 41; 42

A Visit to Flanders, in July, 1815, Being Chiefly an Account of the Field of Waterloo. Edinburgh: 1816. V. 41

SIMPSON, JAMES HERVEY

Report of . . . on th Union Pacific Railroad and Branches, Central Pacific Railroad of California, Northern Pacific Railroad, Wagon Road in the Territories of Idaho, Montana, Dakota and Nebraska . . . with Lasw Relating to the Pacific Railroad. Washington: 1865. V. 37

The Shortest Route to California. Philadelphia: 1869. V. 37; 40; 42; 43

SIMPSON, JAMES Y.

Acupressure a New Method of Arresting Surgical Haemorrhage and of Accelerating the Healing of Wounds. Edinburgh: 1864. V. 37; 38

Archaeological Essays. Edinburgh: 1872. V. 42

The Obstetric Memoirs and Contributions of James Y. Simpson, M.D. Philadelphia: 1855. V. 41

Remarks on the Superinduction of Anaesthesia in Natural and Morbid Parturition. Boston: 1848. V. 37

SIMPSON, JAMES YOUNG

Archaic Sculpturings of Cups, Circles &c. Upon Stones and Rocks in Scotland, England and Other Countries. Edinburgh: 1867. V. 37

The Modern Advancement of Practical Medicine and Surgery, an Inaugural Address to the Medico-Chirurgical Society of Edinburgh. Edinburgh: 1853. V. 43

SIMPSON, JOHN

A Complete System of Cookery, on a Plan Entirely New. London: 1815? V. 46

SIMPSON, JOHN PALGRAVE

Letters from the Danube. London: 1847. V. 40; 42

SIMPSON, LOUIS

The Arrivistes. Poems 1940-1949. New York: 1949. V. 39

SIMPSON, M. O.

Hunting and Shooting Incidents in the Life of Bill Purdee. Boston: 1904. V. 37

SIMPSON, PERCY

Proof-Reading in the Sixteenth, Seventeenth and Eighteenth Centuries. London: 1970. V. 40

SIMPSON, ROBERT

The Annals of Derry, Showing the Rise and Progress of the Town From the Earliest Accounts on Record to the Plantation Under King James I. Londonderry: 1847. V. 42; 44

A Collection of Fragments llustrative of the History and Antiquites of Derby. Derby: 1826. V. 41

The History and Antiquities of the Town of Lancaster . . . Lancaster: 1852. V. 46

SIMPSON, STEPHEN

The Author's Jewel. Philadelphia: 1823. V. 43

SIMPSON, T. L.

The Cell Biology of Sponges. Berlin: 1984. V. 37

SIMPSON, THOMAS

The Doctrine and Application of Fluxions. London: 1776. V. 40; 42

Essays on Several Curious and Useful Subjects, in Speculative and Mix'd Mathematicks. London: 1740. V. 42; 45

Mathematical Dissertations on a Variety of Physical and Analytical Subjects. London: 1743. V. 41

Miscellaneous Tracts on Some Curious and Very Interesting Subjects in Mechanics, Physical-Astronomy and Speculative Mathematics . . . London: 1757. V. 44

Modern Etchings and Their Collectors. London: 1919. V. 40; 42

Narrative of the Discoveries on the North Coast of America, Effected by the Officers of the Hudson's Bay Company During 1836, 39. London: 1843. V. 42

SIMPSON, WILLIAM

Meeting the Sun: a Journey All Round the World, Through Egypt, China, Japan, and California, Including an Account of the Marriage Ceremonies of the Emperor of China. London: 1874. V. 37; 38; 40

A Private Journal Kept During the Niger Expedition. London: 1843. V. 42

The Seat of War in the East. London: 1855-56. V. 45; 46

SIMPSON, WILLIAM KELLY

Papyrus Reisner II (only): Accounts of the Dockyard Workshop at This Reign of Sesostris I. Boston: 1965. V. 40; 42; 44

SIMS, F. MARION

Clinical Notes on Uterine Surgery. New York: 1866. V. 45; 46

SIMS, GEORGE

last of the Rare Book Game. Philadelphia: 1990. V. 46

More of the Rare Book Game. Philadelphia: 1988. V. 46

The Rare Book Game: More of the Rare Book Game: Last of the Rare Book Game. Philadelphia: 1985-90. V. 46

SIMS, GEORGE R.

Living London: Its Work and Its Play, Its Humour and Its Pathos, Its Sights and Its Scenes. London: 1903-1906. V. 40

SIMS, JAMES MARION 1813-1883

Clinical Notes on Uterine Surgery. New York: 1866. V. 42

Clinical Notes on Uterine Surgery. New York: 1873. V. 41; 42

On Intra-Uterine Fibroids. New York: 1874. V. 42

SIMS, ORLAND L.

Cowpokes, Nesters and So Forth. Austin: 1970. V. 38; 46

SIMS, RICHARD

A Manual for the Genealogist, Topographer, Antiquary and Legal Professor, Consisting of Descriptions of Public Records . . . London: 1856. V. 45

SIMS, WILLIAM

Kansas: Information Concerning Its Agriculture, Horticulture and Live Stock, Together with Statements Relating to Vacant Lands, Schools, Churches, Manufactures, Wealth, Mineral Resources, Etc. Topeka: 1884. V. 38

SIMSIR, BILAL N.

British Documents on Ottoman Armeinas. 1856-1895. Ankara: 1989. V. 45

SIMSON, ALFRED

Travels in the Wilds of Ecuador and the Exploration of the Putumayo River. London: 1886. V. 37

SIMSON, F. B.

Letters on Sport in Eastern Bengal. London: 1886. V. 38

SIMSON, ROBERT

Sectionum Conicarum Libri V. Edinburgh: 1735. V. 38; 40; 41; 45

SIMSON, THOMAS 1730-1806

An Inquiry How Far the Vital and Animal Actions of the More Perfect Animals Can be Accounted for Independent of the Brain. Edinburgh: 1752. V. 42

SINCE Man Began to Eat Himself. 1986. V. 40; 45
SINCE Man Began to Eat Himself. N.P.: 1986. V. 39

SINCE Man began to Eat Himself. Four Poems, Two Stories: Lawrence Ferlinghetti; Kenneth Barnard; Allen Ginsburg; Toby Olson; Jerome Rothenberg and Joel Oppenheimer, with six etched illuminations and one composite drawing provisioned . . . (Mt. Horeb): 1986. V. 37

SINCLAIR, CATHERINE

Modern Flirtations. Edinburgh: 1841. V. 39; 41

SINCLAIR, DONALD

The History of the Aberdeen Volunteers, Embracing Also Some Account of the Early Volunteers of the Counties of Aberdeen, Banff and Kincardine. Aberdeen: 1907. V. 38

SINCLAIR, FRANCIS, MRS.

indigenous Flowers of the Hawaiian Islands. London: 1885. V. 37

SINCLAIR, GEORGE 1786-1834

Hortus Gramineus Woburnensis. London: 1816. V. 38

Hortus Gramineus Woburnensis. London: 1824. V. 39

Hortus Gramineus Woburnensis. London: 1825. V. 39

Hortu Gramineus woburnensis. London: 1826. V. 37; 41

The Hydrostaticks. Edinburgh: 1672. V. 38; 41

SINCLAIR, GEORGE V.

Roosevelt in the Jungle, by George V. Sinclair. Chicago/New York: (1912). V. 37

SINCLAIR, IAN

White Chappell. Scarlet Tracings. Upplingham: 1987. V. 38

SINCLAIR, J. D.

An Autumn in Italy: Being a personal narrative of a tour in the Austraian, Tuscan, Roman and Sardinian States in 1827. V. 37

SINCLAIR, JAMES

History of Shorthorn Cattle. London: 1908. V. 43

SINCLAIR, JOHN

An Account of the Systems of Husbandry Adopted in the More Improved Districts of Scotland . . . Edinburgh: 1812. V. 40; 45; 46

Account of the Origin of the Board of Agriculture, and Its Progress for Three Years After Its Establishment. London: 1796. V. 37

Address to the Society for the Improvement of British Wool; Constituted at Edinburgh, on Monday, January 31, 1791. London: 1791. V. 45

The Code of Health and Longevity; or, a Concise View of the Principles of Health and Attainment of Long Life. Edinburgh: 1807. V. 37; 38; 40

The Code of Agriculture, Including Observations on Gardens, orchards, Woods and Plantations. Hartford: 1818. V. 45

SINCLAIR, JOHN continued

The Code of Health and Longevity. London: 1818. V. 38

The Code of Agriculture; including observations on gardens, orchards, woods and plantations. Third edition, enriched by the remarks of a number of the ablest practical farmers, in England, Scotland and Ireland. London: 1821. V. 37; 39

Considerations on Militias and Standing Armies. London: 1782. V. 38

The History of the Public Revenue of the British Empire. London: 1785. V. 42

The History of the Public Revenue of the British Empire. London: 1785-90. V. 39

The History of the Public Revenue of the British Empire. London: 1803-04. V. 38; 41; 43; 46

Observations of the Scottish Dialect. London: 1782. V. 41; 43; 46

Remarks on a Pamphlet intitled 'The Question Concerning the Depreciation of the Currency States and Examined' by William Huskisson . . . London: 1810. V. 38

Specimen of the Statistical Account of Scotland. Edinburgh: 1791. V. 37

The Statistical Account of Scotland. Edinburgh: 1791-99. V. 37; 39

SINCLAIR, L.

The Art of Norval Morrisseau. Toronto: 1979. V. 37

SINCLAIR, MAY

Fame. London: 1929. V. 41

SINCLAIR, UPTON 1878-1968

Affectionately Eve. New York: 1961. V. 39

Boston, a Contemporary Historical Novel. N.P.: 1928. V. 39

Cliff Faraday in Comman or The Fight of His Life by Ensign Clarke Fitch, U.S. N. No. 39 in the True Blue Series . . . New York: 1899. V. 46

Dragon's Teeth. Pasadena: 1942. V. 46

The Goose-Step: a Study of American Education. California: 1923. V. 37; 40

The Jungle. 1906. V. 46

The Jungle. New York: 1906. V. 37; 38; 39; 40; 41; 44; 46

The Jungle. Toronto: 1906. V. 46

King Midas. New York: 1901. V. 39

Theirs be the Guilt. New York: 1959. V. 46

Upton Sinclair Presents William Fox. Los Angeles: 1933. V. 44; 45

A West Point Treasure, or Mark Mallory's Strange Find. Philadelphia: 1903. V. 46

A World to Win. Monrovia: (1946). V. 37

SINCLAIR, W. J.

Semmelweis. His Life and His Doctrine. Manchester: 1909. V. 40; 41

SINDEREN, ADRIAN VAN

The Other Half of the Earth, Record of the Author's Eleven Voyages in the Pacific, 1928-1959. New Haven: 1959. V. 39

SINDONA, ENIO

Pisanello. New York. V. 40; 44

Pisanello. New York: (n.d.). V. 37

SINEL, JOSEPH

A Book of American Trade Marks & Devices. New York: 1924. V. 41

SINGER, CHARLES

The Earliest Chemical Industry. London: 1948. V. 39; 42; 46

The Earliest Chemical Industry. An Essay in the Historical Relations of Economics & Technology illustrated from the Alum Trade. London: 1948. V. 37

Essays on the History of Medicine Presented to Karl Sudhoff on the Occasion of His Seventieth Birthday, November 26th, 1923. London: 1924. V. 41

The Evolution of Anatomy. New York: 1925. V. 41; 42

The Evolution of Anatomy. A Short history of anatomical and physiological discovery to Harvey . . . London: 1925. V. 37

From Magic to Science: Essays on the Scientific Twilight. London: 1928. V. 38; 41; 42; 45

A History of Technology. New York: & London: 1954. V. 46

A History of Technology. New York: 1954-58. V. 40

A History of Technology. New York: & London: 1954-58. V. 45

A History of Technology. Oxford: 1954-58. V. 40

A History of Technology. 1955-58. V. 42; 46

A History of Technology. Oxford: 1957-59. V. 37; 39; 40; 41

A History of Technology. Oxford: 1978-80. V. 42

A History of Technology. Volumes I-V. Oxford: 1957-58. V. 37

A Prelude to Modern Science. Cambridge: 1946. V. 39; 41; 42; 45

A Prelude to Modern Science. London: 1946. V. 39; 40; 41

Science, Medicine and History. 1953. V. 40

Science Medicine and History. London: 1953. V. 39; 44; 45

Science, Medicine and History. Oxford: 1953. V. 37; 39; 46

A Short History of Medicine. Oxford: 1928. V. 42

Studies in the History and Method of Science. Oxford: 1917-21. V. 45

Studies in the History and Method of Science. Oxford: 1917/55/21. V. 44

Studies in the History and Method of Science. Oxford: 1921. V. 46

Studies in the History and Method of Science. 1975. V. 46

Vesalius on the Human Brain. London: 1952. V. 41

Vesalius on the Human Brain. Oxford: 1952. V. 39; 41; 45

SINGER, D. J.

Big Game Fields of America North and South. London: 1914. V. 38

SINGER, DOROTHEA WALEY

Catalogue of Latin and Vernacular Alchemical Manuscripts in Great Britain and Ireland Dating from Before the XVI Century. Brussels: 1928-31. V. 46

SINGER, I. J.

The Brothers Ashkenzai. London: 1936. V. 38; 46

The Brothers Ashkenazi. New York: 1936. V. 38

East of Eden. London: 1939. V. 38

The Sinner (Yoshe Kalb). New York: 1933. V. 45

SINGER, ISAAC BASHEVIS

The Collected Stories. New York: 1982. V. 37; 38; 39; 41; 42; 43

The Family Moskat. New York: 1950. V. 37; 44; 45

The Gentleman from Cracow. New York: 1979. V. 37; 38; 39; 40; 41; 43; 45

Gimpel the Fool and Other Stories. New York: 1957. V. 46

The Golem. New York: 1982. V. 43

The Image and Other Stories. New York: 1985. V. 43

Lost in America. Garden City: 1981. V. 39; 41; 42; 43; 44; 45

Love and Exile. Garden City: 1984. V. 43

The Magician of Lublin. New York: 1960. V. 38; 39; 40; 41

The Magician of Lublin. 1984. V. 38; 39

The Magician of Lublin. New York: 1984. V. 37; 38

One Day of Happiness. New York: 1982. V. 39; 42

Satan in Goray. New York: 1981. V. 39

Satan in Goray. New York: 1982. V. 46

Shosha. New York: 1978. V. 40

The Slave. New York: 1962. V. 42

Satan in Goray. New York: 1955. V. 44

Yentil the Yeshiva Boy. New York: 1983. V. 43

A Young Man in Search of Love. Garden City: 1978. V. 39

SINGER, R.

The Agaricales in Modern Taxonomy. Koenigstein: 1986. V. 37

SINGER, SAMUEL WELLER

Researches into the History of Playing Cards. London: 1816. V. 40; 46

Shakespeare's Jest Book. Whittingham: 1814. V. 46

SINGER, WILLIAM d. 1840

General View of the Agriculture, State of Property and Improvements in the County of Dumfries. Edinburgh: 1812. V. 39

SINGH, CHANDRAMANI

Woollen Textiles and Costumes from Bharat Kala Bhavan. Banaras: 1981. V. 43

SINGH, D. P.

Breeding for Resistance to Diseases and Insect Pests. Berlin: 1986. V. 37

SINGH, FREDERICK DULEEP

Portraits in Norfolk Houses. Norwich: 1927. V. 38; 40

SINGH, MADANJEET

Himalayan Art. Greenwich: 1968. V. 42

SINGLETON, ESTHER

The Furniture of Our Forefathers. New York: 1901. V. 41

Japan as Seen and Described by Famous Writers. New York: 1904. V. 46

The Wild Flower Fairy Book. New York: 1905. V. 46

SINGLETON-GATES, PETER

The Black Diaries. Paris: 1959. V. 38

SINGULAR Sufferings of Two Friends, Who Had Lost Themselves in an American Forest. York: 1825. V. 44

SINIGAGLIA, LEONE

Climbing Reminiscences in the Dolomites. London: 1896. V. 43; 45; 46

SINISTRARI, LOUIS MARIE

Demoniality or Incubi and Succubi . . . Paris: 1879. V. 45

SINISTRARI, LUDOVICO MARIA

Demoniality. London: 1927. V. 46

THE SINK of Solitude. London: 1928. V. 44

SINKER, ROBERT

The Library of Trinity College, Cambridge. Cambridge: 1891. V. 38; 40

SINN Fein Rebellion Handbook. Dublin: 1917. V. 39

SINNER'S Redemption. A New Christmas Carol. London: 1788. V. 42

SINNETT, ALFRED PERCY

Karma. London: 1885. V. 43

SINNETT, C.

The Emigrant Soldier's Gazette and Cape Horn Chronicle. Victoria: 1907. V. 41; 43

SINNETT, FREDERICK

An Account of the Colony of South Australia Prepared for Distribution at the International Exhibition of 1862 . . . London: 1862. V. 41

SINNETT, JANE

A Story About a Christmas in the Seventeenth Century. London: 1846. V. 39; 41

SINOBALDO, GIOVANNI BENEDETTO

Hippocratis Coi Medicorum Principis Antiphona. Romae: 1650. V. 40

SINOPOULOS, TAKIS

(title in Greek) Acquaintanceship with Max. Athens: 1956. V. 44

SIOLI, H.

The Amazon, Limnology and Landscape, Ecology of a Mighty Tropical River and Its Basin. The Hague: 1984. V. 37

SIORDET, I. M.

A Letter to the Rt Hon. Sir John Sinclair . . . Supporting His Arguments in Refutation of those Advanced by Mr Huskisson . . . London: 1811. V. 38

SIPE, C. HALE

The Indian Wars of Pennsylvania. Harrisburg: 1929. V. 41; 42

SIPES, WILLIAM B.

The Pennsylvania Railroad. Philadelphia: 1875. V. 38; 42

The Seventh Pennsylvania Veteran Volunteer Cavalry. Its Record, Reminiscences and Roster. Pottsville: 1905. V. 38; 46

SIPLE, PAUL

A Boy Scout with Byrd. New York: & London: 1931. V. 45

SIR *** Speech Upon the Peace. To the Tune of the Abbot of Canterbury. London: 1739. V. 38

SIR Christopher Wren A.D. 1632-1723. London: 1923. V. 37; 39

SIR DEGREVAUNT

Sire Degrevaunt. Hammersmith: 1896. V. 46

SIR Francis Drake Crowned King of Nova Albion: a Prelude for Roxburghers' Welcome of Zamoranos in Nineteen Fifty-Six. Kentfield: 1956. V. 46

SIR Frantic the Reformer; or, the Humours of the Crown and Anchor . . . London: 1809. V. 43; 46

SIR Giddy Whim, or, the Lucky Amour. London: 1703. V. 38

SIR Richard Steele's Recantation: Prov'd in a Letter of Thanks from His Holiness Pope Clement XI for the Service Done the Catholick Church, by the Dedication and Preface of a Late Book, Intitul'd, An Account of the State of the Roman Catholick Religion.. London: 1715. V. 38

SIR Robert Brass; or, the Intrigues, Serious and Amorous, of the Knight of the Blazing Star. London: i.e. Dublin: 1731. V. 38

SIRAT BANI HILAL

The Celebrated Romance of the Stealing of the Mare. 1930. V. 43

The Celebrated Romance of the Stealing of the Mare. London: 1930. V. 40

The Stealing of the Mare. Newtown: 1930. V. 44

SIREN, OSVALD

Early Chinese Paintings form A. W. Bahr Collection. London: 1938. V. 39; 45; 46

Gardens of China. New York: 1949. V. 39; 44; 45

A History of Early Chinese Paintings. London: 1933. V. 46

Leonardo Da Vinci: L'Artiste et l'Homme. Paris: 1928. V. 37

La Sculpture Chinoise du V au XIV Siecle. Paris: 1926. V. 44

The Walls and Gates of Peking. London: 1924. V. 40; 41

SIREN, OSWALD

Chinese and Japanese Sculptures and Paintings in the National Museum, Stockholm. London: 1931. V. 38; 41

SIRIGATTI, LORENZO

La Pratica di Prospettiva. Venetia: 1596. V. 41

SIRINGO, CHARLES ANGELO 1855-1928

A Cowboy Detective. Chicago: 1912. V. 37; 39; 41; 43; 46

A Lone Star Cowboy. Sante Fe: 1919. V. 38; 39; 42; 43; 44

Riata and Spurs. Boston: 1927. V. 37

Riata and Spurs. Boston: 1927. V. 40; 43; 46

Riata and Spurs. Boston and New York: 1927. V. 37

Riata and Spurs. Boston and New York: 1927. V. 46

Riata and Spurs. New York: 1927. V. 39; 43

A Texas Cow Boy or, Fifteen Years on the Hurricane Deck of a Spanish Pony. Chicago: 1885. V. 40; 41

A Texas Cow-Boy; or, Fifteen Years on the Hurricane Deck of a Spanish Pony. Chicago: (1886). V. 37

A Texas Cow-Boy; or, Fifteen Years on the Hurricane Deck of a Spanish Pony. Chicago: 1886. V. 39

A Texas Cowboy or Fifteen Years on the Hurricane Deck of a Spanish Pony. Chicago and New York: 1886. V. 37

A Texas Cow Boy or, Fifteen Years on the Hurricane Deck of a Spanish Pony . . . New York: 1886. V. 42

A Texas Cow Boy. New York: 1914? V. 40

Two Evil Isms Pinkertonism and Anarchism. Chicago: 1915. V. 42

SIRMOND, JACQUES

Censvra Coniectvrae Anonymi Scriptoris De Suburbicariis Regionibus et Ecclesiis. Paris: 1618. V. 37

SIRR, HENRY CHARLES

China and the Chinese: Their Religion, Character, Customs and Manufactures . . . London: 1859. V. 46

SISMONDE DE SISMONDI, JEAN CHARLES LEONARD 1773-1842

Hisotrical View of the Literature of the South of Europe. London: 1823. V. 37; 40

Nouveaux Principes d'Economie Politique ou de la Richesse dans ses Rapports avec la Population. Paris: 1819. V. 40

Political economy, and the Philosophy of Government. London: 1847. V. 40; 43; 44

SISSON, C. H.

Essays. London: 1967. V. 38

Versions and Perversions of Heine. London: 1955. V. 40

SISSON, MARJORIE

The Cave. Huntingdon: 1957. V. 40

THE SISTERS of Orleans: a Tale of Race and Social Conflict. New York: 1871. V. 44

SITGREAVES, LORENZO

Northern and Western Boundary Line of the Creek Country. Washington: 1858. V. 38; 40; 41; 42; 43; 45

Report of an Expedition Down the Zuni and Colorado Rivers. 1853. V. 41

Report of an Expedition Down the Zuni & Colorado Rivers. Washington: 1853. V. 37; 38; 40; 41; 42; 43; 45

Report of an Expedition Down the Zuni and Colorado Rivers. Washington: 1854. V. 39; 40

SITJAR, BONAVENTURE

Vocabulary of the Language of San Antonio Mission, California. New York: 1861. V. 38; 40; 43; 45

SITTENBERG UNIVERSITY

Leges Academiae VVitebergensis De Studiis Et Moribvs Auditorvm. Item Artickel Etlicher Notwendiger ordnung und Satzung/ zu Erhaltung Guter Policey/ Rhue/ Friede und Einigkeit/ im Schul und Stadregiment/ Auch Guter Zucht und Erbarkeit in Hochzeiten . . . Wittenberg: 1573. V. 38

SITWELL, EDITH 1887-1964

Alexander Pope. London: 1930. V. 37; 40; 43; 44

Auction Catalogue of a Collection of Works by Pavel Tchelitchew, the Property of Dame Edith Sitwell. London: 1961. V. 41

A Book of the Winter. London: 1950. V. 37

Buccolic Comedies. London: 1923. V. 44; 46

The Canticle of the Rose: Selected Poems 1920-1947. London: 1949. V. 40

The Canticle of the Rose - Poems 1917-1949. New York: 1949. V. 41

Children's Tales. London: 1920. V. 39

The Death of Venus. New York: 1983. V. 46

Elegy on Dead Fashion. London: 1926. V. 39; 40; 45; 46

SKARSTEN, M. O.

George Drouillard, Hunter and Interpreter for Lewis and Clark and Fur Trader 1807-10. Glendale: 1964. V. 40; 46

SKEAT, WALTER W.

An Etymological Dictionary of the English Language. Oxford: 1888. V. 41

The Tale of Gamelyn. New Rochelle: 1901. V. 43; 44; 46

SKEAT, WALTER WILLIAM

Malay Magic. London: 1900. V. 40; 43

SKEEN, WILLIAM

Adam's Peak. Ceylon: 1870. V. 42

SKEETERS, PAUL W.

Maxfield Parrish: the Early Years, 1893-1930. Secaucus: 1973. V. 46

SKELDING, SUSIE BARSTOW

Flowers from Hill and Dale. New York: 1883. V. 38; 39

Flowers from Glade and Garden. New York: 1884. V. 45

SKELTON, JOHN 1460-1529

Charles I. London: 1898. V. 40; 46

Charles I. Edinburgh: 1898. V. 37; 40

John Skelton: a Sculptor's Work 1950-1975. London: 1977. V. 41

Mary Stuart. New York: 1893. V. 44

Mary Stuart. London: 1893. V. 40

Pithy Pleasant and Profitable Workes of Maister Skelton, . . . London: 1736. V. 38

A Poem Called the Tunning of Elynour Rummynge the Famouse Ale-Wife of England. Worcester: 1953. V. 39; 45

SKELTON, JOSEPH

Engraved Illustrations of the Principal Antiquities of Oxfordshire, from Original Drawings by F. Mackenzie. Oxford: 1823. V. 45

Engraved Illustrations of Antient Armour, from the Collection of Goodrich Court, Herefordshire, from Drawings and with the Descriptions of Dr. Meyrick. London and Oxford: 1854. V. 38

Engraved Illustrations of Antient Armour, from the Collection at Goodrich Court, Herefordshire. Drawings and Descriptions of Dr. Meyrick now Published by Joseph Skelton. London/Oxford: 1830. V. 37

Pietas Oxoniensis; or, Records of Oxford Founders. London: 1828. V. 42

Pietas Oxoniensis, or, Records of Oxford Founders. Oxford: 1828. V. 45

Skelton's Engraved Illustrations of the Principal Antiquities of Oxfordshire. Oxford: 1823. V. 44

Skelton's Engraved Illustrations of the Principal Antiquities of Oxfordshire from Original Drawings by F. Mackenzie. London: 1823. V. 37

SKELTON, PHILIP

The Candid Reader; or, a Modest, Yet Unanswerable Apology For All Books That Ever Were, or Possibly Can Be Wrote. Dublin: printed: 1744. V. 43

A Letter to the Writer of a Certain Historical Cathechism Printed in the Name of One Watson, a Yorkshire Vicar. Dublin: 1786. V. 40

Truth in a Mask. London: 1744. V. 38; 42

Truth in a Mask. Dublin: 1744. V. 37

SKELTON, PHILLIP

Truth in a Mask. Dublin printed: 1744. V. 43

SKELTON, R. A.

Decorative Printed Maps of the 15th to 18th Centuries. New York & London: 1952. V. 39

A Description of Maps and Architectural Drawings in the Collection Made by William Cecil, First Baron Burghley, now at Hatfield House. Oxford: 1971. V. 38; 40; 41; 44; 45

SKELTON, ROBIN

John Ruskin: the Final Years. Manchester: 1955. V. 37; 40; 41

SKEMPTON, MARY

The Wood Engravings of . . . Marlborough: 1989. V. 44

SKENE, A.

Memorials for the Government of the Royal Brughs in Scotland. London: 1685. V. 46

SKENE, ALEXANDER

Electro-Haemostasis in Operative Surgery. New York: 1899. V. 39

Memorials for the Government of the Royalburghs in Scotland. Aberdeen: 1685. V. 38

SKENE, FELICIA MARY FRANCES

Use and Abuse, a Tale. London: 1849. V. 43; 45

SKENE, JAMES

Rambles in the Deserts of Syria Among the Turkomans and Bedaweens. London: 1864. V. 45

SKENE, JAMES HENRY

Anadol; the Last Home of the Faithful. 1853. V. 39

The Frontier Lands of the Christian and the Turk. London: 1853. V. 39

SKENE, M. JOHN

The Exposition of the Termes and Difficill Wordes, Contened in the Foure Buikes of Regiam Majestatem, and Others . . . Edinburgh: 1597. V. 38

SKENE, WILLIAM F.

Celtic Scotland; a History of Ancient Alban. Edinburgh: 1876-80. V. 42

The Highlanders of Scotland, their Origin, History, and Antiquities . . . London: 1837. V. 37

A SKETCH from Public Life: a Poem, Founded Upon Recent Domestic Circumstances. London: 1816. V. 39

A SKETCH of a Plan for Reducing the Present High Price of Corn and Other Provisions, and for Securing Plenty of Both for the Time to Come. London: 1772. V. 42

SKETCH Of a Tour through Swisserland. London: 1787. V. 41

SKETCH of St. Anthony and Minneapolis, Minnesota Territory. St. Anthony: 1857. V. 40; 41

SKETCH of the Alaskan Missions, with an Account of the Death of the Late Most Rev. Charles J. Seghers, Archbishop of Vancouver Island B.C. N.P.: 1887. V. 43

A SKETCH of the Further Proceedings of the Committees Appointed by the Yearly Meetings of Friends of Pennsylvania, &c. and Maryland, for Promoting the Improvement and Gradual Civilization of the Indian Natives in Some Parts of North America. London: 1812. V. 37

A SKETCH of the Internal Condition of the United States of America, and of the Historical Relation with Europe. Baltimore: 1826. V. 37

A SKETCH of the Life and Character of Gen. Taylor the American Hero and People's Man . . . New York & Boston: 1847. V. 39

A SKETCH of the Life and Character of Gen. Taylor . . . Together with a Concise History of the Mexican War . . . Boston: 1847. V. 40

SKETCH of the Life of Marquis de Lafayette . . . Keene: 1836. V. 38

SKETCH of the Life, Personal Appearance, Character, and Manners of Charles S. Stratton . . . Known as General Tom Thumb. New York: 1860. V. 37

A SKETCH of the Organization, Objects and Membership of the Old Settlers' Association of Minnesota . . . St. Paul: 1872. V. 39

SKETCH of the Resources of the City of New York. New York: 1827. V. 39

SKETCH of the System of Education, Moral and Intellectual, in Practice to the Schools of Bruce Astle, Tottenham and Hazelwood, Near Birmingham. 1833. V. 42

SKETCH, SALLY

An Alphabetical Arrangement of Animals for Little Naturalists. London: 1821. V. 39

SKETCHES and Eccentricites of David Crockett of West Tennessee. New York: 1833. V. 39; 40; 44; 45

SKETCHES and Eccentricities of Col. David Crockett, of West Tennessee. London: 1834. V. 44

SKETCHES and Memoranda of te Works for the Tunnel Under the Thames, from Rotherhithe to Wapping. Rotherhithe: 1828. V. 39

SKETCHES and Memoranda of the Works for the Tunnel Under the Thames from Rotherhithe to Wapping. London: 1827. V. 38

SKETCHES at Malvern. London: 1855. V. 37

SKETCHES Illustrative of the History of Browseholme Hall, in the County of York. London: 1814. V. 42

SKETCHES Illustrative of the Topography and History of New and Old Sleaford, in the County of Lincoln, and of Several Places in the Surrounding Neighbourhood. Sleaford: 1825. V. 44

SKETCHES of Character, or Specimens of Real Life. London: 1813. V. 42

SKETCHES of Obscure Poets, with Specimens of Their Writings. London: 1833. V. 39

SKETCHES of the Inter-Mountain States, Together with Biographies of the many Prominent and Progressive Citizens Who Have Helped in the Development and History-Making of this Marvelous Region, 1847-1909. Utah, Idaho, Nevada. Salt Lake City: 1909. V. 37

SKETCHES Of the Life and Indian Adventures of Captain Samuel Brady, a Native of Cumberland County, Born 1758, a Few Miles Above Northumberland. Lancaster: 1891. V. 44

SKETCHES of the North River. New York: 1838. V. 46

SKETCHES of the Works of the Tunnel Under the Thames from Rotherhithe to Wapping. London: 1829. V. 38

SKETCHES of Trojan Life. Troy: 1847. V. 43

SKETCHES of Washingtonians. Washington: 1907. V. 45

SKETCHES on Political Economy, Illustrative of the Interests of Great Britain. London: 1809. V. 38

SKETCHLEY, R. E. D.

English Book Illustration of Today. New York: 1897. V. 43

English Book Illustration of To-Day. London: 1903. V. 37; 40; 41

SKETCHLEY, W.

The Cocker, Containing Every Information to the Breeders and Amateurs of that Noble Bird, The Game Cock . . . Burton on Trent: 1814. V. 40

SKEY, FREDERIC CARPENTER

Hysteria. London: 1867. V. 42

SKIDMORE, P.

The Biology of the Muscidae of the World. The Hague: 1985. V. 37

SKIFF, F. W.

Adventures in Ameicana. Portland: 1935. V. 40

SKILLMAN, DAVID BISHOP

Biography of a College . . . Easton: 1930. V. 43

SKILLMAN, JOHN

Squash Rackets. New York: 1937. V. 43

SKINNER, ADA

A Child's Book of Modern Stories. New York: 1920. V. 42

A Very Little Child's Book of Stories. New York: 1923. V. 41; 44

SKINNER, ADA M.

A Child's Book of Country Stories. New York: 1935. V. 45

SKINNER, B. F.

About Behaviorism. New York: 1974. V. 43

The Behavior of Organisms. An Experimental Analysis. New York: 1938. V. 46

Beyond Freedom and Dignity. New York: 1971. V. 43

Walden Two. London: 1948. V. 43; 44

SKINNER, CHARLES M.

Do Nothing Days. Philadelphia: 1899. V. 43; 46

With Feet to the earth. Philadelphia: 1899. V. 43; 46

SKINNER, HENRY

the Origin of Medical Terms. Baltimore: 1949. V. 45

SKINNER, J. E. H.

Roughing It in Crete. London: 1868. V. 39

SKINNER, J. S.

The General Stud Book, Containing Pedigrees of English Race Horses &c. Baltimore: 1834. V. 39

SKINNER, JOHN

Amusements of Leisure Hours; or Poetical Pieces, Chiefly in the Scottish Dialect . . . Edinburgh: 1809. V. 45

The Office for the Sacrament of the Lord's Supper, or Holy Communion . . . Aberdeen: 1807. V. 41

Songs and Poems, with Sketch of His Life by H. G. Reid. London: 1859. V. 38

SKINNER, JOHN EDWIN HILARY

After the Storm; or, Jonathan and His Neighbours in 1865-6. London: 1866. V. 37

SKINNER, JOSEPH

The Present State of Peru: Comprising Its Geography, Topography, Naatural History . . . London: 1805. V. 38; 41

SKINNER, ROBERT

Reports of Cases Adjudged in the Court of King's Bench from the Thirty-Third Year of King Charles the Second to the Ninth Year of King William the Third. In the Savoy: 1728. V. 45

SKINNER, ROBERT T.

A Notable family of Scots Printers. Edinburgh: 1927. V. 38; 40

SKINNER, STEPHEN 1623-1667

Etymologicon Linguae Anglicanae, Seu Explicationem Vocum Anglicarum Etymologica ex Propriis Fontibus . . . London: 1671. V. 39; 40

SKINNER, THOMAS

Adventures During a Journey Overland to India, by Way of Egypt, Syria and the Holy Land. London: 1836. V. 42

Adventures During a Journey Overland to India, by Way of Egypt, Syria and the Holy Land. London: 1837. V. 45

Excursions in India. London: 1832. V. 37; 40; 41; 44

The Life of General Monk: Late Duke of Albemarle . . . London: 1723. V. 42

SKODA, JOSEPH

Ausculation and Percussion. Philadelphia: 1854. V. 42

SKOGMAN, CARL JOHAN ALFRED 1820-1907

Fregatten Eugenies resa Omkring Jorden Aren 1851-1853 Under Befal af C. A. Virgin. Stockholm: 1854-55. V. 38; 46

SKORY, EDMUND

An Extract Out of the Historie of the Last French King Henry the Fourth. London: 1610. V. 44

SKOTTOWE, AUGUSTINE

The Life of Shakespeare . . . London: 1824. V. 45

SKOTTSBERG, CARL

The Wilds of Patagonia. London: 1911. V. 41

SKREBNESKI, VICTOR

Skrebneski. New York: 1969. V. 42

SKRESLET, S.

The Role of Freshwater Outflow in Coastal Marine Ecosystems. Berlin: 1986. V. 37

SKUES, G. E. M.

Minor Tactics of the Chalk Stream, and Kindred Studies. London: 1910. V. 40

Side-Lines. Side Lights and Reflections. Fugitive Papers of a Chalk Stream Angler. London: 1932. V. 39; 40

Silk, Fur and Feather: the Trout-Fly Dresser's Year. Beckenham, Kent: 1950. V. 46

Silk, Fur and Feather; the Trout Dresser's Year. London: 1950. V. 40

The Way of a Trout with a Fly. London: 1921. V. 39; 40

The Way of a Man with a Trout. London: 1977. V. 40

SKURRAY, FRANCIS

Bidcombe Hill, a Rural and Descriptive Poem . . . London: 1824. V. 39; 43; 46

SKUTCH, ALEXANDER F.

The Life of the Woodpecker. 1985. V. 46

The Life of the Woodpecker. California: 1985. V. 45

Life of the Woodpecker. Santa Monica: 1985. V. 37; 39

SLADE, ADOLPHUS

Records of Travel in Turkey, Greece &c and of a Cruise in the Black Sea, with Capitan Pasha, in the Years 1829, 1830 & 1831. Philadelphia: 1833. V. 39

SLADE, HIPP & MELOY, INC.

Catalogue and Price List. Chicago: 1901. V. 46

SLADE, WILLIAM

Vermont State Papers; being a collection of Records and Documents, Connected with the Assumption and Establishment of Government by the People of Vermont; Together with the Journal of the Council of Safety . . . And the Laws from the Year 1779 to 1786 . . . Middlebury, Vt.: 1823. V. 37

SLADEK, JOHN

The Reproductive System. London: 1968. V. 41

SLADEN, DOUGLAS

On the Cars and Off. London: 1898, 1895. V. 41

SLAFTER, CARLOS 1825-1909

Sir Humfrey Gylberte and His Enterprise of Colonization in America. Boston: 1903. V. 38; 39; 40; 41; 44

SLAFTER, EDMUND F.

John Checkley; or, the Evolution of Religious Tolerance in Massachusetts Bay. Boston: 1897. V. 42; 44

Sir William Alexander and American Colonization. Boston: 1873. V. 44

Voyages of the Northmen to America Including Extracts from Icelandic Sagas Relating to Western Voyages by Northmen in the Tenth and Eleventh Centuries . . . Boston: 1877. V. 40

SLANEY, ROBERT A.

Essay on the Beneficial Direction of Rural Expenditure. London: 1824. V. 37; 42

SLANEY, ROBERT A. continued

A Few Verses from Shropshire. (with) A Few More Verses from Shropshire. London: 1846, 1855. V. 40

A Few Verses from Shropshire. (with) A Few More Verses from Shropshire. London: 1846/55. V. 42

SLANGE, NIELS PEDERSEN 1657-1737

Den Stolmaegtigste Konges Christian den Fierdes Konges til Danmark og Norge . . . Historie. Copenhagen: 1749. V. 43

SLARE, FREDERICK

Experiments and Observations Upon Oriental and Other Bezoar-Stones, Which Prove them to be of No Use in Physick. London: 1715. V. 39; 41; 43

SLATER, CHARLES

An Atlas of Bacteriology. London: 1898. V. 42

SLATER, HENRY H.

Manual of the Birds of Iceland. Edinburgh: 1901. V. 44

SLATER, J. HERBERT

Engravings and Their Value: A Guide for the Print Collector. London: 1912. V. 41

Illustrated Sporting Books. London: 1899. V. 46

SLATER, JOHN HERBERT

Engravings and Their Value. London: 1929. V. 42

SLATER, JOHN M.

El Morro: Inscription Rock, New Mexico. Los Angeles: 1961. V. 37; 39; 42

SLATER, JOHN ROTHWELL

Printing and the Renaissance. New York: 1921. V. 45

SLATER, NELSON

Fruits of Mormonism. Coloma: 1851. V. 38

SLATER, P. L.

Exotic Ornithology, Containing Figures and Descriptions of New or Rare Species of American Birds. London: 1866-69. V. 41

A Monograph of the Jacamars and Puff-Birds, or Families Galbulidae and Bucconidae. London: 1879-82. V. 41

SLATER, ROBERT

An Inquiry into the Principles Involved in the Decimilization of the Weights, Measures and Monies of the United Kingdom. London: 1855. V. 41

SLATIN, RUDOLPH CARL, FREIHERR VON 1857-1932

Fire and Sword in the Sudan. London: 1896. V. 40; 42; 43; 44; 45

SLATTERY, MARY

Woman and Rome, a Book for Ladies Only by . . . Boston: 1891. V. 44

SLATYER, WILLIAM

The History of Great Britanie from the first peopling of this Island to this present Raigne of or peacefull Monarke K. James. London: (1621). V. 37

SLAUGHTER, FRANCES E.

The Sportswoman's Library. London: 1898. V. 40

SLAUGHTER, JAMES

A Treatise on Consumption, Dropsy, Insanity, Dyspepsia and Asthma. Philadelphia: 1831. V. 37

SLAUGHTER, PEREGRINE 1827-1905

Lock, Stock and Barrel: Forty Years of Dogged Hunting. London: 1904. V. 42

SLAUGHTER, PHILIP

A Sketch of the Life of Randolph Fairfax. Richmond: 1864. V. 40; 42; 44

THE SLAVE of Passion: or, the Fruits of Werter. Philadelphia: 1802. V. 37

SLAVERY: a Treatise, Showing that Slavery is Neither a Moral, Political, Nor Social Evil. Penfield: 1844. V. 43

SLAVIN, F. H.

Falconry in the British Isles. London: 1873. V. 37

SLAYTON, STEVEN

This is just a data check. V. 38

SLEATH, FREDERICK

The Seventh Vial. London: 1920. V. 44

Sniper Jackson. London: 1919. V. 44

SLEDIANUS, JOHANNES 1506-1556

The General History of the Reformtion of the Church . . . London: 1689. V. 38

SLEEMAN, C.

Torpedoes and Torpedo Warfare. Porstmouth: 1880. V. 39

Torpedoes and Torpedo Warfare. Portsmouth: 1889. V. 42

SLEEMAN, J. H.

Lexicon Plotinianum. 1980. V. 37

SLEEMAN, W. H.

A Journey through the Kingdom of Oude in 1849-1850. London: 1858. V. 40

Ramasseeana, or a Vocabulary of the Peculiar Language Used by the Thugs, with an Introduction and Appendix . . . Calcutta: 1836. V. 41

SLEEMAN, WILLIAM HENRY

A Report on the System of Megpunnaism, or the Murder of Indigent Parents for Their Young Children (Who are Sold as Slaves) as It Prevails in the Delhie Territories, and the Native States of Rajpootana, Ulwar and Bhurtpore. Serampore: 1839. V. 39

The Thugs or Phansigars of India. Philadelphia: 1839. V. 39

THE SLEEPING Beauty. London: 1920. V. 37

THE SLEEPY Song Book. London: 1918. V. 46

SLEIDANUS, JOHANNES 1506-1556

The General History of the Reformation of the Chruch from the Errors and Corruptions of the Church of Rome, Begun in Germany . . . to the Year 1556. To Which is added a Continuation . . . to 1562 . . . London: 1689. V. 39

SLEIDEN, JOHANN

Commentariorum de Statu Religionis & Reipublicae Carolo Caesare, Libri XXVI . . . Strasburg: 1555-56. V. 44

SLEIGH, BERNARD

The Faery Calendar. London: 1920. V. 43

SLEVIN, JOSEPH R.

Log of the Schooner 'Academy' on a Voyage of Scientific Research to the Galapagos Islands 1905-1906. San Francisco: 1931. V. 45

SLEZER, JOHN

Theatrum Scotiae . . . Aberdeenshire: 1979. V. 39

SLIDER, THOMAS P.

Memoirs of General William Butler . . . Atlanta: 1885. V. 44

SLIGH, CHARLES R.

History of the Services of the First Regiment Michigan Engineers and Mechanics During the Civil War 1861-1865. Grand Rapids: 1921. V. 44

SLIGHT, BENJAMIN

Indian Researches; or, Facts Concerning the North American Indians . . . Montreal: 1844. V. 38

A SLIGHT Review of the Transactions of the Late Long Parliament, With Some Observations on the Rise and Progress of the Septennial Bill. Dublin: 1762. V. 41

SLIGO, PETER HOWE, MARQUIS OF

Jamaica Under the Apprenticeship System by a Proprietor. London: 1838. V. 40

SLINGSBY, F. WILLIAM

The Registers of the Parish Church of Grinton in Swaledale Co. York. 1905. V. 45

SLINGSBY, HENRY 1602-1658

A Journal of the Most Remarkable Events Which Occurred During the Life of Sir Henry Slingsby, Bart. V. 43

SLINGSBY, WILLIAM CECIL

Norway, The Northern Playground. Edinburgh: 1904. V. 40

SLIVERS, ASH

The Land of the O-O. Facts, Figures, Fables and Fancies. Cleveland: 1892. V. 40

SLIVERS, D. D.

Fables of the Nexhaco. Vancouver: (1912?). V. 37

SLKCIEI

V. 45

SLOAN, E. L.

The Salt Lake City Directory and Business Guide . . . Salt Lake City: 1869. V. 37; 38

SLOAN, HANS

An Account of a Most Efficacious Medicine for Soreness, Weakness and Several Other Distempers of the Eye. London: 1745. V. 39

SLOAN, JOHN ALEXANDER

North Carolina in the War Between the States. Washington: 1883. V. 44

Reminiscences of the Guilford Grays, Co. B, 27th N.C. Reiment. Washington: 1883. V. 37; 38

SLOAN, JULIE

Women in the Cattle Country. Austin: 1986. V. 37

SLOAN, MARGY

Infiltration; Poems. Mexico: 1989. V. 45

SLOAN, MAURICE M.

The Concrete House and Its Construction. Philadlephia: 1912. V. 44

SLOAN, RICHARD E.

History of Arizona. Phoenix: 1930. V. 39

SLOAN, ROBERT W.

The Great Contest. Salt Lake City: 1887. V. 42

The Meears Prize Essay. Utah: Her Attractions and Resources. Salt Lake City: 1861. V. 42

Utah Gazetteer and Directory of Logan, Ogden, Provo and Salt Lake Cities, for 1864. Salt Lake City: 1884. V. 42; 44

SLOAN, SAMUEL

City and Surburban Architecture . . . Philadelphia: 1859. V. 43

The Model Architect. Philadelphia: 1852. V. 38; 40; 42

Sloan's Constructive Architecture: a Guide to the Practical Builder and Mechanic . . . Philadelphia: 1859. V. 37; 41; 46

Sloan's Homestead Architecture Containing Forty Designs for Villas, Cottages and Farm Houses, with Essays on Style. Philadlephia: 1861. V. 44

Sloan's Constructive Architecture: a Guide to the Practical Builder and Mechanic . . . Philadelphia: 1866. V. 43

Sloan's Homestead Architecture. Philadelphia: 1867. V. 41

Some Reminiscences in the Life of Samuel Sloan. Rochester: 1899. V. 46

SLOAN, TOD

Tod Sloan, by Himself. London: 1915. V. 37

SLOANE, ERIC

Almanac and Weather Forecater. New York: 1955. V. 46

SLOANE, HANS

An Account of a Most Effcacious Medicine for Soreness, Weakness, and Several Other Distempers of the Eyes. London: 1745. V. 37

A Voyage to the Islands Madera, Barbados, Nieves, S. Christophers and Jamaica, with the Natural History of the Herbs and Trees . . . London: 1707. V. 41; 45

A Voyage to the Islands Madera, Barbados, Nieves, S. Christopher's and Jamaica. London: 1707-25. V. 37; 39; 40; 41; 42

SLOANE, WILLIAM M.

Life of Napoleon Bonaparte. London: 1896. V. 46

SLOANE, WILLIAM MILLIGAN

Life of Napoleon Bonaparte. New York: 1896. V. 42; 44

SLOCUM, CHARLES E.

History of the Maumee River Basin from the Earliest Account to Its Organization into Counties. Defiance: 1905. V. 40

The Life and Services of Major General Henry Warner Slocum . . . Toledo: 1913. V. 43

SLOCUM, JOHN J.

A Bibliography of James Joyce. New Haven: 1953. V. 38; 39; 40; 42; 46

The Youth of Hamlet: an Interpretation. South Pasadena: 1932. V. 44

SLOCUM, JOSHUA

Sailing Alone Around the World. New York: 1900. V. 38; 44

Sailing Alone Around the World. New York: 1901. V. 45

Sloop Spray Souvenir. Arranged and supplied with notes by Henrietta E. Slocum. N.P.: (1905). V. 37

Voyage of the Liberdade, Description of a Voyage 'Down to the Sea.' Boston: 1890. V. 40; 41

Voyage of the Liberdade. Boston: 1894. V. 40; 41; 43

SLOMANN, VILHELM

Bizarre Designs in Silks, Trade and Traditions. Copenhagen: 1953. V. 37; 38; 40

SLY, COSTARD, PSEUD.

Sayings and Doings at the Tremont House. Boston: 1833. V. 43

SMALL Books on Great Subjects. London: 1843-54. V. 38

A **SMALL** Collection of Valuable Tracts, Relating to the Herring Fishery. London: 1751. V. 40; 41

SMALL, H. B.

The Canadian Handbook and Tourist's Guide Giving a Description of Canadian Lake and River Scenery and Places of Historical Interest with the Best Spots for Fishing and Shooting. Montreal: 1866. V. 37; 39; 43; 45

The Canadian Handbook and Tourist's Guide. Montreal: 1886. V. 40

Mineral Resources of the Dominon of Canada; Comprising the Provinces of Prince Edward Island, Nova Scotia, New Brunswick, Quebec, Ontario, Manitoba, British Columbia, North-West Territories. Specially Adapted for Emigrants, Capitalists and Settlers. Ottawa: 1882. V. 37; 42

SMALL, H. BEAUMONT

The Animals of North America. Montreal: 1864. V. 41; 44

SMALL, HAROLD A.

Adventures of Joseph-Alexandre de Chabrier de Peloubet, at the Time of the French Revolution. San Francisco: 1953. V. 42

SMALL, HENRY B.

The Canadian Handbook and Tourist's Guide Giving a Description of Canadian Lake and River Scenery and Places of Historical Interest with the Best Spots for Fishing and Shooting. Montreal: 1867. V. 37; 38; 39; 42

SMALL, JAMES

A Treatise on Ploughs and Wheel Carriages. Edinburgh: 1784. V. 40

SMALL, JOHN

The Castles and Mansions of the Lothians Illustrated in One Hundred and Three Views with Historical and Descriptive Accounts. Edinburgh: 1883. V. 38

Historical Sketch of Newry, by 'Newryensis'. Newry: 1876. V. 37

SMALL, JOHN W.

Ancient and Modern Furniture. Stirling: 1903. V. 40

Scottish Woodwork of the 16th and 17th Centuries. New York: 1878. V. 41

SMALL Rain. London: 1832. V. 38

SMALL Rain Upon the Tender Herb. London: 1830. V. 38; 39; 40; 42; 43; 45

SMALL, ROBERT

An Account of the Astronomical Discoveries of Kepler . . . London: 1804. V. 38

THE SMALLEST English Dictionay in the World. Glasgow: 1898. V. 37

THE SMALLEST French and English Dictionary in the World. Glasgow: 1898. V. 38

SMALLEY, DAN S.

The American Phonetic Dictionary of the English Language. Cincinnati: 1855. V. 43

SMALLEY, EUGENE V.

History of the Northern Pacific Railroad. New York: 1883. V. 37; 42

SMALLEY, JOHN

Fragments of Mythology Poems and Etchings. London: 1979. V. 37

SMALLFIELD, W. E.

The Story of Renfrew, from the Coming of the First Settlers about 1820. Renfrew: 1919. V. 38

SMALL'S Guide to Jedburgh and Vicinity and Angler's Guide to the Teviot and Its Tributaries. Jedburgh: 1871. V. 40

SMALLWOOD, J. H.

The Book of Newfoundland. St. Johns: 1937. V. 37; 38; 43

SMALRIDGE, GEORGE

A Poem on the Death of . . . Queen Anne; and the Succession of . . . London: 1715. V. 40; 45

Sixty Sermons Preach'd on Several Occasions. London: 1727. V. 39

SMART, BENJAMIN HUMPHREY

Sequel to Sematology . . . V. 45

SMART, CHRISTOPHER 1722-1771

The Hilliad; an Epic Poem . . . London: 1753. V. 38; 40

The Horatian Canons of Friendship. London: 1750. V. 38; 42

Musae Seatonianae. London: 1772. V. 37; 39; 42

The Nonpareil. London: 1757. V. 38; 41

On the Immensity of the Supreme Being. Cambridge: 1751. V. 38; 41

Poems on Several Occasions. London: 1752. V. 37; 38; 41; 42; 45

Poems on Several Occasions. London: 1752. V. 44

SMART, CHRISTOPHER 1722-1771 continued

Poems by Mr. Smart . . . London: 1763. V. 46

The Poems of the Late Christopher Smart. Reading: 1791. V. 38; 41; 43

A Song to David and Other Poems. London: 1924. V. 46

A Song to David. London: 1960. V. 38; 43

A Translation of the Psalms of David. London: 1765. V. 38; 40; 42

SMART, ELIZABETH

A Bonus. London: 1977. V. 39; 41

By Grand Central Station I Sat Down and Wept. London: 1945. V. 40

Grand Central Station I Sat Down and Wept. London: 1945. V. 42

SMART, HAWLEY

Beatrice and Benedick. A Romance of the Crimea. London: 1891. V. 37

Cecile; or, Modern Idolaters. London: 1871. V. 38

Cecile; or, Modern Idolaters. In Three Volumes. London: 1811. V. 37

From Post to Finish. London: 1884. V. 38

SMART, JAMES H.

A Manual of Free Gymnastic and Dumb-Bell Exercises. Cincinnati: 1864. V. 38

SMART, JOHN

Tables of Interest, Discount, Annuities, &c. London: 1726. V. 42; 45; 46

SMART, STEPHEN F.

Colorado Tourist and Illustraed Guide via the 'Golden Belt Route' . . . Kansas City: 1879. V. 39

SMART, THOMAS

The Cottage Treat; or, Selections for the Curious: containing an account of the Holy Wars - The Assassins - Old man of the Mountains Earthquakes in Clabria, Jamaica, and Sicily, Destruction of Carthage, singular distress of an aged prisoner in the . . . Huddersfield: (c. 1810). V. 37

SMART, WILLIAM

The Return to Protection. London: 1904. V. 43

SMEATON, JOHN

An Experimental Enquiry Concerning the Natural Powers of Water and Wind to Turn Mills, and Other Machines, Depending on a Circular Motion. London: 1760. V. 40

Experimental Enquiry Concerning the Natural Powers of Wind and Water to Turn Mills and Other Machines Depending on a Circular Motion. London: 1794. V. 38; 41; 42; 46

Experimental Enquiry Concerning the Natural Powers of Wind and Water to Turn Mills and Other Machines Depending on a Circular Motion. London: 1796. V. 43; 46

Experimental Enquiry Concerning the Natural Powers of Wind and Water to Turn Mills and Other Machines . . . London: 1813. V. 39

An Experimental Enquiry Concerning the Natural Powers of Water and Wind to Turn Mills and Other Machines. London: 1755. V. 37

A Narrative of the Building and a Description of the Construction of the Eddystone Lighthouse with Stone; To Which is Subjoined an Appendix Giving Some Account of the Lighthouse on the Spurn Point, Built Upon a Sand. London: 1791. V. 41; 44

A Narrative of the Building and Description of the Construction of the Eddystone Lighthouse with Stone: to which is subjoined, An Appendix, Giving Some Account of the Lighthouse on the Spurn Point, Built Upon a Sand. London: 1793. V. 38

A Narrative of the Building and a Description of the Construction of the Eddystone Lighthouse with Stone to Which is Subjoined, an Appendix . . . London: 1813. V. 41

The Report of John Smeaton, Engineer, Concerning the Drainage of the North Level of the Fens, and the Outfall of the Wisbeach River. N.P.: 1768. V. 42

Report Concerning the Drainage of the North Level of the Fens and the Outfall of Wisbeach River. 1770. V. 38

Report . . . Concerning the Drainage of the North Level of the Fens and the Outfall of Wisbeach River. London: 1770. V. 40

Reports of the Late John Smeaton, F. R. S. Made on Various Occasions, in the Course of His Employment as a Civil Engineer. (with) The Miscellaneous Papers of John Smeaton . . . London: 1812-14. V. 38; 39; 45

SMEDES, SUSAN DABNEY

Memorials of a Southern Planter. Baltimore: 1887. V. 44

A Southern Planter. London: 1889. V. 43

SMEDLEY, CONSTANCE

Crusaders - the Reminiscences of Constance Smedley. London: 1929. V. 42

SMEDLEY, EDWARD 1788-1836

Erin. A Geographical and Descriptive Poem. London: 1810. V. 42; 44

SMEDLEY, FRANCIS EDWARD 1818-1864

The Fortunes of the Colville Family; or, a Cloud and Its Silver Lining a Christmas Story. London: 1853. V. 46

Frank Fairlegh; or, Scenes from the Life of a Private Pupil. London: 1850. V. 38; 46

Lewis Arundel: or the Railroad of Life. London: 1899. V. 39

SMEDLEY, FRANK E.

Frank Fairlegh or Scenes from the Life of a Private Pupil. Harry Coverdale's Courtship. Lewis Arundel, or the Railroad of Life. London. V. 41

Harry Coverdale's Courtship and All That Came of It. London. V. 40

Harry Coverdale's Courtship, and All That Came of It. London: 1854. V. 40; 43

Harry Coverdales Courtship, and All That Came of It. London: 1855. V. 39

Harry Coverdale's Courtship, and All That Came of It. With Illustrations by Phiz. London: (1855). V. 37

Lewis Arundel . . . London: 1852. V. 42

SMEDLEY, JONATHAN

Gulliveriana; or, a Fourth Volume of Miscellanies . . . London: 1728. V. 40; 41; 45; 46

SMEDLEY, R. C.

History of the Underground Railroad in Chester and the Neighboring Counties of Pennsylvania. Lancaster: 1883. V. 41; 42

SMEDLEY, WILLIAM

Across the Plains in '62. Denver: 1916. V. 38

Across the Plains in '62. (Denver: 1916). V. 37

SMEE, ALFRED

Elements of Electro-Metallurgy. London: 1843. V. 40

Instinct and Reason: Deduced from Electro-Biology. London: 1850. V. 42

The Mind of Man: Being a natural System of mental Philosophy. London: 1875. V. 42

Principles of the Human Mind Deduced from Physical Laws . . . London: 1849. V. 43

The Process of Thought Adapted to Words and Language. London: 1851. V. 41; 42; 43

SMEE, JOHN

A Complete Collection of Abstracts of Acts of Parliament and Cases With Opinions of the Judges Upon the Following Taxes . . . London: 1797. V. 43

SMEETON, GEORGE

Biographia Curiosa: or Memoirs of Remarkable Characters of the Regin of George III. London: 1822. V. 39

SMELLEY, WILLIAM

The Man in the Moon. London: 1804. V. 37

SMELLIE, WILLIAM 1740-1795

An Abridgement of the Practice of Midwifery . . . Boston: 1786. V. 40

Anatomical Tables, with Explanations and an Abridgement of the Practice of Midwifery . . . Edinburgh: 1787. V. 43; 45

The Philosophy of Natural History. Edinburgh: 1790. V. 38; 40; 41; 43

The Philosophy of Natural History. Edinburgh: 1790-99. V. 37; 38; 41; 42; 45

The Philosophy of Natural History. Edinburgh: 1790/99. V. 42

The Philosophy of Natural History. Philadelphia: 1791. V. 45

The Philosophy of Natural History. Boston: 1827. V. 40

A Sett of Anatomical Tables, with Explanations and an Abridgement, of the Practice of Midwifery. London: 1754. V. 37; 38; 39

A Set of Anatomical Tables with Explanations and an Abridgement of the Practice of Midwifery. Worcester: 1793. V. 37; 39; 40; 41

A Sett of Anatomical Tables . . . . and of the Practice of Midwifery. Auckland: 1971. V. 39

Smellie's Treatise on the Theory and Practice of Midwifery. London: 1876-77-78. V. 39; 40

SMELT, LEONARD

An Account of Some Particulars Relative to the Meeting Held at York, on Thursday the 30th of December, 1779. London: 1780. V. 39; 42

SMET, HEINRICH

Prosodia . . . Quae Syllabarum Positione & Dipthongis Carentium . . . Cantabrigiae: 1654. V. 45

SMET, PIERRE JEAN DE 1801-1873

Cinquante Nouvelles Lettres . . . Paris: 1858. V. 40; 41; 42

Letters and Sketches with a Narrative of a Year's Residence Among the Indian Tribes of the Rocky Mountains. Philadelphia: 1843. V. 38; 39; 40; 41; 42; 43; 45

Life, Letters and Travels . . . Among the Wild Tribes of the North American Indians. New York: 1905. V. 43

Missions de L'Oregon et Voyages Aux Montagnes Rocheuses, Aux Sources de la Colombie, De l'Athabasca et du Sascatshawin, en 1845-46. Gand: 1848. V. 41; 42

SMET, PIERRE JEAN DE 1801-1873 continued

Missions de l'Oregon et Voyages aux Montagnes Rocheuses aux Sources de la Colombie, de l'Athabasca, et du Sscatshawin, en 1845-46. Ghent: 1848. V. 38

New Indian Sketches. New York: 1863. V. 38

New Indian Sketches. New York: & Montreal: 1863. V. 43

Oregon Missions and Travels Over the Rocky Mountains in 1845-46. New York: 1847. V. 37; 38; 40; 42; 44; 45

Voyages aux Montagnes Rocheuses, et une Annee de Sejour chez les Tribus Indiennes du Vasate Territoire de l'Oregon. Malines;: 1844. V. 37

Western Missions and Missionaries: a Series of Letters. New York: 1859. V. 42

Western Missions and Missionaries: a Series of Letters. New York: 1863. V. 38

SMETHURST, THOMAS

Hydrotherapia, or, The Water Cure. London: 1843. V. 40

SMIALOWSKI, ARTHUR

Photography in Medicine. Springfield: 1960. V. 42

SMIDIUS, MELCHIOR

Programma in Funere Hermanni Conringii, Primum Physicae, Deinde Medicinae & Politicae Professoris Optime Meriti, Regum & Plurium Imperii Principum Consiliarii Academiae Juliae Senioris qui d. XII. December. MDCLXXXI pie placideque obitt. Helmestadii: 1681. V. 37

SMIDS, LUDOLF

Pictura Loquens, sive Heroicarum Tabularum Hadriani Schoonebeeck, Enarratio et Explicatio. Amsterdam: 1695. V. 37

SMILES, LEONARD

Lives of the Engineers . . . Comprising Also a History of Inland Communication in Britain. London: 1861-62. V. 40

SMILES, ROBERT

Memoir of the Late Henry Booth, of the Liverpool and Manchester, and Afterwards of the London and North-Western Railway. London: 1869. V. 46

SMILES, SAMUEL

The Autobiography. London: 1905. V. 40

The Huguenots: Their Settlements, Churches & Industries in England and Ireland. London: 1867. V. 40; 45

James Nasmyth, Engineer: An Autobiography . . . London: 1883. V. 45

Jasmin: Barber, Poet, Philanthropist. London: 1891. V. 40

Josiah Wedgwood F.R.S. His Personal History. London: 1894. V. 40

The Life of George Stephenson, Railway Engineer. London: 1857. V. 37; 45

Life of A Scotch Naturalist: Thomas Edward. London: 1876. V. 44

Lives of the Engineers, with an Account of Their Principal Works. London: 1861-62. V. 40; 43; 44; 45

Lives of the Engineers . . . Their Principal Works . . . London: 1861-62-62. V. 42; 43

Lives of the Engineeers and with an Account of Their Principal Works . . . (with) Lives of Boulton and Watt . . . London: 1861-65. V. 46

Lives of the Engineers, with an Account of Their Principal Works . . . London: 1862. V. 38; 42; 45

Lives of the Engineers. London: 1862-68. V. 41; 46

Lives of the Engineers. London: 1874. V. 40

A Publisher and His Friends. London: 1891. V. 40

Robert Dick, Baker, of Thurso, Geologist and Botanist. London: 1878. V. 40

Round the World . . . New York: 1872. V. 42

Self-Help; With Illustrations of Character and Conduct. London: 1859. V. 38; 40; 43

Self-Help. London: 1860. V. 40

Thrift. London: 1875. V. 40; 43; 46

SMILEY, JANE

A Thousand Acres. New York: 1991. V. 46

SMILEY, THOMAS T.

Sacred Geography, or a Description of the Places Mentioned in the Old and New Testament . . . Philadelphia: 1824. V. 45

SMILLIE, JAMES

A Panoramic View from Bunker Hill Monument. Boston: 1848. V. 39

SMIRDIN, A.

(Russian title) Rospis' Rossijskim Knigam . . . St. Petersburg: 1828-29-32. V. 45

SMIRKE, EDWARD

The Case of Vice Against Thomas, Determined on Appeal before the Lord Warden of the Stannaries of Cornwall . . . London: 1843. V. 40

SMIRKE, R.

Review of a Battalion of Infantry Including Eighteen Maneuvers Illustrated by a Series of Engraved Diagrams Together with the Word of Command. New York: 1811. V. 38

SMIRKE, ROBERT

A Catalogue Raisonne of the Pictures Now Exhibiting in Pall Mall. London: 1816. V. 45

The Cession of the District of Matavai in the Island of Otaheite to Captain James Wilson for the Use of the Missioanries Sent Thither by that Society in the Ship Duff. London. V. 41

Proofs from Pictures Painted by Robert Smirke, R.A. and Engraved by A. Raimbach, the Subjects Taken from the Rasselas of Dr. Johnson . . . London: 1805. V. 39

SMIT, PIETER

History of the Life Sciences: an Annotated Bibliography. Amsterdam: 1974. V. 41; 42; 45; 46

SMITH, A.

Illustrations of the Zoology of South Africa. London: 1838-49. V. 38

SMITH, A. A.

List of Attorneys for the United States Traders' Commission. Rochester: 1873. V. 45

SMITH, A. C.

Guide to the British and Roman Antiquities of the North Wiltshire Downs in a Hundred Square Miles Round Abury. 1885. V. 37

SMITH, A. CROXTON

Tail-Waggers. London: 1935. V. 40; 45

SMITH, A. DONALDSON

Through Unknown African Countries. London: 1897. V. 39; 40; 44

SMITH, A. H.

A Catalogue of Engraved Gems in the British Museum (Department of Greek and Roman Antiquities). London: 1888. V. 44

A Catalogue of Sculpture in the Department of Greek and Roman Antiqutites, British Museum. London: 1892-1904. V. 37

Marbles and Bronzes: Fifty Plates from Selected Subjects in the Department of Greek and Roman Antiquities. London: 1914. V. 44

Marbles and Bronzes. London: 1922. V. 37; 40

The Place Names of the West Riding of Yorkshire. 1961. V. 38

The Place-Names of the West Riding of Yorkshire. Cambridge: 1961-63. V. 37; 41

The Place-Names of . . . (E.P.N.S.). Cambridge: 1964/5. V. 39

SMITH, A. J. E.

The Moss Flora of Britain and Ireland. Cambridge: 1977. V. 39

SMITH, A. J. M.

News of the Phoenix. Toronto: 1943. V. 43; 44

SMITH, A. L.

A Monograph of the British Lichens. London: 1918-26. V. 37; 38

SMITH, A. LEDYARD

Excavation at Nebaj, Guatamala. Washington: 1951. V. 42; 44

Excavations at Nebaj, Guatamala with notes on the skeletal material by T.D. Steward. Washington, DC: 1951. V. 37

SMITH, A. M.

Visitor's Guide and History of the United States Mint, Philadelphia, Pa . . . Current Coins of the World, Colonial and Continental Currency, Ancient Greece and Rome. Philadelphia: 1885. V. 38

SMITH, A. MORTON

Twelve Years of Trooping. Gainesville: 1944. V. 46

SMITH, AARON

The Atrocities of the Pirates . . . London: 1824. V. 42

The Atrocities of the Pirates, or, a Faithful Narrative of the Unparalleled Sufferings Endured by the author. New York: 1824. V. 44

The Atrocities of the Pirates . . . 1929. V. 42

The Atrocities of the Pirates; Being a Faithful Narrative of the Unparalleled Sufferings Endured by the Author During His Captivity Among the Pirates of the Island of Cuba; with an Account of the Excesses and Barbarities of those Inhuman Freebooters. Waltham St. Lawrence: 1929. V. 37; 38; 41

SMITH, ADAM 1723-1790

An Inquiry into the Nature and Causes of Wealth of Nations. Oxford: 1880. V. 39

A Catalogue of the Library of Adam Smith. London: 1894. V. 41

Essays on Philosophical Subjects . . . Dublin: 1795. V. 38; 41

Essays on Philosophical Subjects. London: 1795. V. 37; 40; 43

Essays on Philosophical Subjects. London & Edinburgh: 1795. V. 38

SMITH, ADAM 1723-1790 continued

An Inquiry into the Nature and Causes of the Wealth of Nations. Dublin: 1776. V. 37

An Inquiry into the Nature and Causes of the Wealth of Nations. London: 1776. V. 37; 38; 41; 43; 46

An Inquiry into the Nature and Causes of the Wealth of Nations. London: 1778. V. 41; 45

An Inquiry into the Nature and Causes of the Wealth of Nations . . . London: 1784. V. 45

An Inquiry into the Nature and Causes of the Wealth of Nations. Dublin: 1785. V. 37; 38; 41; 42

An Inquiry into the Nature and Causes of the Wealth of Nations. London: 1786. V. 38; 39; 40; 41; 43

An Inquiry into the Nature and Causes of the Wealth of Nations . . . London: 1789. V. 37

Recherches sur la Nature et les Causes de la Richese des Nations . . . Paris: 1790-91. V. 43

An Inquiry Into the Nature and Causes of the Wealth of Nations. London: 1791. V. 39; 40; 42

An Inquiry into the Nature and Causes of the Wealth of Nations. Dublin: 1793. V. 38; 40; 43

An Inquiry Into the Nature and Causes of the Wealth of Nations. London: 1793. V. 38; 39; 41; 43; 44

An Inquiry into the Nature and Causes of the Wealth of nations. London: 1796. V. 39; 41; 42; 44

An Inquiry into the Nature and Causes of the Wealth of Nations. London: 1799. V. 38

An Inquiry into the Nature and Causes of the Wealth of Nations. Dublin: 1801. V. 44; 45

An Inquiry into the Nature and Causes of the Wealth of nations. London: 1802. V. 38; 42; 46

Recherches sur la Nature et Causes de la Richesse des Nations. Paris: 1802. V. 38; 41; 45

An Inquiry Into the Nature and Causes of the Wealth of Nations. Glasgow: 1805. V. 45

An Inquiry into the Nature and Causes of the Wealth of nations. London: 1805. V. 37; 38; 39; 40; 41; 45

An Inquiry Into the Nature and Causes of the Wealth of nations. London: 1811. V. 39; 40; 41; 42; 43; 46

An Inquiry into the Nature and Cuases of the Wealth of Nations, With a Life of the Author. Edinburgh: 1817. V. 38; 41

An Inquiry into the Nature and Causes of the Wealth of Nations. Hartford: 1818. V. 40

An Inquiry Into the Nature and Causes of the Wealth of Nations. London: 1819. V. 38; 40

An Inquiry into the Nature and Causes of the Wealth of Nations. With a Life of the Author. Also, a view of the Doctrine of Smith . . . from the French of M. Garnier. London/Edinburgh: 1819. V. 37

An Inquiry into the Nature and Causes of the Wealth of Nations . . . London: 1826. V. 42

An Inquiry into the Nature and Causes of the Wealth of Nations. Edinburgh: 1828. V. 37

An Inquiry Into the Nature and Causes of the Wealth of Nations . . . Edinburgh & London: 1828. V. 41

An Inquiry into the Nature and Causes of the Wealth of nations . . . London: 1843. V. 43

An Inquiry Into the Nature and Causes of the Wealth of Nations. Edinburgh: 1847. V. 37

An Inquiry Into the Nature and Causes of the Wealth of Nations. Oxford: 1880. V. 41

An Inquiry Into the Nature and Causes of the Wealth of Nations . . . Oxford: 1880. V. 43

An Inquiry Into the Nature and Causes of the Wealth of Nations. London: 1904. V. 42

An Inquiry Into the Nature and Cause of the Wealth of Nations. London: 1976. V. 38; 40

An Inquiry into the Nature and Cause of the Wealth of Nations. Tokyo: 1976. V. 40

Lectures on Justice, Police, Revenue and Arms. Oxford: 1896. V. 42

Lectures on Rhetoric and Belles Lettres. London: 1963. V. 40; 41

Recherches sur la Nature et Les Causes de la Richesse des Nations . . . Paris: 1802. V. 38

Recherches sur la Nature et les Causes de la Richesse des nations . . . Traduction nouvelle, avec des notes et observations; par Germain Garnier, de l'Institut Nation. Paris: 1802. V. 37

Theorie der Sittlichen Gefuhle. Leipzig: 1791/95. V. 41

The Theory of Moral Sentiments . . . London: 1749. V. 45

The Theory of Moral Sentiments. London: 1759. V. 37; 40; 41; 42; 46

The Theory of Moral Sentiments. London: 1761. V. 42; 43

The Theory of Moral Sentiments. London: 1792. V. 40

The Theory of Moral Sentiments. (with) A Dissertation on the Origin of Languages. Basil: 1793. V. 38

The Theory of Moral Sentiments; or, An Essay towards an Analysis of the Principles by which Men naturally judge concerning the Conduct and, Character, first of their Neighbors, and afterwards of themselves. To which is added, a dissertation . . . London: 1797. V. 37; 39; 42

The Theory of Moral Sentiments . . . Glasgow: 1809. V. 46

The Theory of Moral Sentiments . . . Boston: 1817. V. 39

The Theory of Moral Sentiments; or, an Essay Towards an Analysis of the Principles by Which Men Naturally Judge Concerning the Conduct and Character . . . Philadelphia: 1817. V. 42; 43

The Works of Adam Smith. London: 1812, 1811. V. 38

The Works of Adam Smith, LL.D. London: 1812-1811. V. 37; 38; 39

The Glasgow Edition of the Works and Correspondence. London: 1976-1986. V. 41

Works and Correspondence. Oxford: 1977-83. V. 42

SMITH, AGNES

Glimpses of Greek Life and Scenery. London: 1884. V. 37

SMITH, ALBERT

The Adventures of Mr. Ledbury and his friend Jack Johnson. London: 1844. V. 37

The Drama Founded on the New Christmas Annual of Charles Dickens, Esq. London: 1846? V. 40; 43

The English Hotel Nuisance. London: 1855/56. V. 42

Gavarni in London. London: 1849. V. 44

A Hand-Book to Mr. Albert Smith's Entertainment, Entitled Overland Mail. London: 1850. V. 39

The Man in the Moon. London: 1845. V. 40

The man in the Moon. London: 1847-1849. V. 46

The Pottleton Legacy . . . London: 1849. V. 37; 42; 44

The Story of Mont Blanc. London: 1853. V. 42; 43

The Story of Mount Blanc. New York: 1853. V. 43

The Story of Mont Blanc. London: 1854. V. 41

The Struggles and Adventures of Christopher Tadpole at Home and Abroad. London: 1848. V. 38

The Wassail Bowl. London: 1843. V. 39; 41

SMITH, ALBERT RICHARD

The Cricket on the Hearth . . . A Drama, in Three Acts. London: 1883. V. 40

To China and Back: Being a Diary Kept, Out and Home. London: 1859. V. 42

To China and Back. N.P.: 1859. V. 40

SMITH, ALEXANDER

The Comical and Tragical History of the Lives and Adventures of the Most Noted Bayliffs in and About London and Westminster . . . London: 1723. V. 45

Dreamthorp. London: 1863. V. 39; 40; 41; 46

Nobody, and Some-Body. 1877. V. 38

SMITH, ALICE R. HUGER

The Dwelling Houses of Charleston, South Carolina. Philadelphia: 1917. V. 40

SMITH AND PARMELEE GOLD COMPANY

The Smith & Parmelee Gold Company. New York: 1864. V. 37

SMITH, ANDREW M.

Up and Down in the World, or Paddle Your Own Canoe. Minneapolis: 1891. V. 38

SMITH, ANN ELIZA BRAINERD 1818-1905

Notes of Travel in Mexico and California. St. Albans: 1886. V. 43

SMITH, AQUILA

On the Irish Coins of Edward the Fourth. Dublin: 1839. V. 38

SMITH, ARCHIBALD

Peru As It Is; a Residence in Lima and Other Parts of the Peruvian Repulic . . . London: 1839. V. 42

SMITH, ARNOLD C.

The Architecture of Chios. London: 1962. V. 45

SMITH, ARTHUR H.

China in Convulsion. New York: 1901. V. 40

SMITH, ASHBEL

An Address Delivered in the City of Galveston on the 22nd of February, 1848, the Anniversary of the Birth of Washington, and of the Battle of Buena Vista. Galveston: 1848. V. 45; 46

Reminiscences of the Texas Republic. Annual Address Delivered Before the Historical Society of Galveston, December 15, 1875 with Preliminary Notice of the Historical Society of Galveston. Austin: 1876. V. 39

Reminiscences of the Texas Republic. Galveston: 1876. V. 40; 45

SMITH, ASHER L.

How to Be Rich . . . New York: 1856. V. 42

SMITH, BERNARD

Australian Painting 1788-1960. Melbourne: 1962. V. 41

SMITH, BERNARD E.

Designs and Sketches for Furniture in the Neo-Jacobean and Other Styles. London: 1876. V. 43

SMITH, BERTHA

Yosemite Legends. San Francisco: 1904. V. 38; 44

SMITH, BETTY

A Tree Grows in Brooklyn. New York: 1943. V. 42

SMITH, BRADLEY

Mexico: A History in Art By Bradley Smith. 1968. V. 37

SMITH, BUCKINGHAM

A Grammatical Sketch of the Heve Language. N: 1861. V. 44

A Grammatical Sketch of the Heve Language. New York: 1861. V. 38; 40; 41; 44

Rudo Ensayo . . . Albany: 1863. V. 42

Rudo Ensayo, Tenative de Una Prevencional Description Geographica de la Provincia de Sonora . . . St. Augustine: 1863. V. 39

SMITH, C.

City. 1952. V. 44

SMITH, C. A.

Lost Worlds. Sauk City: 1944. V. 44

SMITH, C. FOX

Here and There in England with the Painter Brangwyn. Leigh-on-Sea: 1945. V. 42

SMITH, C. R.

Catalogue of the Museum of London Antiquities Collected by, and the Property of.. London: 1854. V. 38

SMITH, CAPTAIN

Asiatic Costumes: a Series of Forty-four Coloured Engravings, from Designs Taken from Life . . . London: 1828. V. 46

SMITH, CATHERINE GRANT FURLEY

Quixote, the Weaver. London: 1892. V. 41

SMITH, CECIL

The Birds of Somersetshire. London: 1869. V. 43

SMITH, CECIL H.

Catalogue of the Antiquities (Greek, Etruscan and Roman) in the Collection of the Late Wyndham Francis Cook, Esq. London: 1908. V. 44

SMITH, CHARD POWERS

Prelude to Man. Mount Vernon: 1936. V. 46

SMITH, CHARLES

The American War, from 1775 to 1783, With Plans. New York: 1797. V. 44

The Ancient and Present State of the County and City of Waterford . . . Dublin: 1774. V. 43; 44; 45

The Ancient and present state of the county and city of Cork. Containing a natural, civil, ecclesiastical, historical and topographical description thereof. A new edition. Cork: 1815. V. 37

The Antient and Present State of the County and City of Waterford . . . Dublin: 1746. V. 38

The Antient and Present State of the County of Kerry. Dublin: 1756. V. 38; 41

The Antient and Present State of the County of Down. A Chorographical Description, with the natural and Civil History of the same . . . with a survey of the new Canal, etc. Dublin: 1757. V. 37

The Emigrants, a Poem. London: 1793. V. 45

Smith's new general atlas . . . arranged according to the general treaty signed . . . at Vienna, June 1815. London: 1827. V. 37

Three Tracts on the Corn Trade and Corn Laws. 1. A Short Essay on the Corn Trade . . . 2. Considerations on the Laws . . . 3. A Collection of Papers Relative to the Price, Exporatation . . . London: 1766. V. 39; 40; 42; 43; 44

SMITH, CHARLES H. J.

Landscape Gardening. New York: 1856. V. 39

SMITH, CHARLES HAMILTON

Costume of the Army of the British Empire. London: 1812-15. V. 44; 45

The Natural History of Dogs. Bohn: n.d. V. 38

The Natural History of Horses. Edinburgh: 1841. V. 43

The Natural History of the Human Species, Its Typical Forms, Primaevil Distribution, Filiztions and Migrations. Edinburgh. V. 38

Selections of the Ancient Costume of Great Britain and Ireland, from the Seventh to the Sixteenth Centuries. London: 1814. V. 38; 39; 42; 46

SMITH, CHARLES JOHN

Autographs of Royal, Noble, Learned and Remarkable Persoanges Conspicuous in English History, From the Reign of Richard the Second to that of Charles the Second. London: 1829. V. 40

Historical and Literary Curiosities . . . London: 1840. V. 37; 38; 40; 43; 45

Historical and Literary Curiosities . . . London: 1847. V. 43

Historical and Literary Curiosities, Consisting of Fac-Similes of Original Documents . . . London: 1852. V. 46

Historical and Literary Curiosities . . . London: 1875. V. 46

SMITH, CHARLES LYMAN

Notes by the Way. Boston: 1900-07. V. 40; 43

SMITH, CHARLES MANBY

The Working Man's Way in the World. New York: 1854. V. 39

SMITH, CHARLES MANLY

The Working-Man's Way in the World. London: 1854. V. 41

SMITH, CHARLES ROACH

The Antiquities of Richborough, Reculver and Lymne in Kent. London: 1850. V. 39

Collectanea Antiqua. London: 1848-80. V. 40

SMITH, CHARLES W.

Check-List of Books and Pamphlets Relating to the History of the Pacific Northwest. Olympia: 1909. V. 45

Old Charleston: Twenty-Four Woodcuts by Charles W. Smith. Richmond: 1933. V. 40

SMITH, CHARLIE

Red Roads. New York: 1987. V. 46

SMITH, CHARLOTTE

Beachy Head: with Other Poems, Now First Published. London: 1807. V. 39

Celestina. London: 1791. V. 40; 41; 42

Conversations Introducing Poetry. London: 1804. V. 45

Desmond. London: 1792. V. 37; 40; 43

Disbound. A Novel. London: 1792. V. 37

Elegiac Sonnets. London: 1795. V. 42; 46

Elegiac Sonnets, and Other Poems. London: 1797. V. 38

Elegiac Sonnets and Other Poems. London: 1800. V. 40

The Emigrants. London: 1793. V. 42; 43; 46

Emmeline, the Orphan of the Castle. London: 1788. V. 42

Ethelinde, or the Recluse of the Lake. London: 1789. V. 37; 40

Ethelinde, or the Recluse of the Lake. London: 1790. V. 40; 42

Marchmont: A Novel. London: 1796. V. 37

Montalbert. London: 1795. V. 40; 42

A Narrative of the Loss of the Catharine, Venus and Piedmont Transports, and the Thomas Golden Grove and Aeolus Merchant Ships Near Weymouth on Wednesday the 18th of November Last. London: 1796. V. 45

The Old Manor House. London: 1793. V. 37; 40; 42; 45

Rambles Farther . . . London: 1800. V. 43

Rural Walks; in Dialogues. London: 1795. V. 42

The Wanderings of Warwick. London: 1794. V. 45

Woman's Rescue League. Boston: 1893. V. 41

The Young Philosopher . . . London: 1798. V. 42

SMITH, CHARLOTTE TURNER

Rambles Farther: a Continuation of Rural Walks in Dialogues. Dublin: 1796. V. 44

SMITH, CHETWOOD

Rogers Groups. Though and Wrought by John Rogers. Boston: 1934. V. 37; 38

SMITH, CLARA A.

Narratives of Captivity Among the Indians of North America. Chicago: 1928. V. 40

SMITH, CLARK ASHTON

Ebony and Crystal. Auburn: 1922. V. 37

Ebony and Crystal. Poems in Verse and Prose. (Auburn, Ca.: 1922). V. 37

Genius Loci and Other Tales. 1948. V. 45

Genius Loci and Other Tales. Sauk City: 1948. V. 42; 43; 45; 46

The Immortals of Mercury. 1932. V. 43

Lost Worlds. 1944. V. 45; 46

Lost World. Sauk City: 1944. V. 39; 42; 43; 45

Lost Worlds. S.C.: 1944. V. 37

Nero and Other Poems. Lakeport, CA: 1937. V. 37

Odes and Sonnets. San Francisco: 1918. V. 40

Out of Space and Time. Sauk City: 1942. V. 39; 42; 43; 45

SMITH, CLARK ASHTON continued

Poems in Prose. Sauk City: 1964. V. 45

Spells and Philtres. Sauk City: 1958. V. 42; 43

The Star-Treader and Other Poems. San Francisco: 1912. V. 37; 38; 39

Tales of Science and Sorcery. Sauk City: 1964. V. 44

SMITH, D. E.

Rara arithmetica: A catalogue of the arithmetics written before the year MDCI with a description of those in the library of George Arthur Plimpton on New York; Addenda . . . Boston: 1908-39. V. 37

SMITH, D. MURRAY

Arctic Expeditions from British and Foreign Shores From the Earliest Times to the Expedition of 1875-76. London: 1877. V. 40

SMITH, DAVE

Gray Soldiers. 1983. V. 42

Gray Soldiers. N.P.: 1983. V. 41

Gray Soldiers. Winston Salem: 1983. V. 46

SMITH, DAVID

Rara Arithmetica: a Catalogue of the Arithmetics Written Before the Year MDCI . . . Boston: 1908. V. 40; 42; 45

SMITH, DAVID R.

Conrad's Manifesto, Preface to a Career, the History of the Preface to the Nigger of the 'Narcissus' with Facsimiles of the Manuscripts. Philadelphia: 1966. V. 44

SMITH, DODIE

The Hundred and One Dalmatians. London: 1956. V. 42

SMITH-DORRIEN, HORACE

General Sir Horace Smith-Dorrien's Statement with Regard to the First Edition of Lord French's Book '1914'. London: 1919. V. 46

SMITH, DUNCAN

The Academical Instructor. London: 1794. V. 39

SMITH, DWIGHT

Ralph Smyth of Hingham and Eastham, Mass. and His Descendants. New York: 1913. V. 46

SMITH, E.

Researches of . . . in Armenia: Including a Journey through Asia Minor, and into Georgia and Persia. Boston: 1833. V. 45

Roller Skating Made Easy. Portland: 1884. V. 39

SMITH, E. B.

Architectural Symbolism of Imperial Rome and the Middle Ages. 1956. V. 37

SMITH, E. BALDWIN

Egyptian Architecture as Cultural Expression. New York: 1938. V. 40; 42; 44

SMITH, E. BOYD

After they Came Out of the Ark. New York: 1918. V. 42

The Early Life of Mr. Man Before Noah. Boston: 1914. V. 42

The Early Life of Mr. Man Before Noah. Boston & New York: 1914. V. 40

My Village. New York: 1896. V. 44

The Railroad Book. Boston: 1913. V. 42

Fun in the Radio World. New York: 1923. V. 45

The Story of Noah's Ark. New York: 1905. V. 43

The Story of Noah's Ark. 1913. V. 43

SMITH, E. E.

Children of the Lens. 1954. V. 43

First Lensman. 1950. V. 43

The Skylark of Space. 1947. V. 44

The Skylark of Valeron. 1949. V. 44

Spacehounds of IPC. 1947. V. 44

SMITH, E. QUINCY

Travels at Home and Abroad. New York: 1911. V. 38; 40

SMITH, E. VALE, MRS.

History of Newburyport: from the Earliest Settlement. Newburyport: 1854. V. 42

SMITH, E. W.

A Tomato Can Chronicle. New York: 1937. V. 38

SMITH, EDGAR C.

A Short History of Marine Engineering from the Earliest Efforts of Steam Navigation by Hull in 1736 to the Diesel Electric Engines of Today. Cambridge: 1937. V. 41

SMITH, EDGAR NEWBOLD

American Naval Broadsides. Philadelphia: 1974. V. 46

SMITH, EDGAR W.

Appointment in Baker Streeter. 1938. V. 39

Appointment in Baker Street. New York: 1938. V. 43

A Baker Street Four-Wheeler. New York: 1944. V. 39; 41

Baker Street Inventory. New Jersey: 1945. V. 42

Baker Street and Beyond. Together with Some Trifling Monographs. Morristown: 1957. V. 44

Baker Street and Beyond. N.P.: 1940. V. 43

Baker Street and Beyond, Together with Some Trifling Monographs. Morristown: 1957. V. 43

Baker Street Inventory. 1945. V. 43

The Baker Street Journal. New York: 1946-47. V. 43

Letters from Baker Street . . . Together with the Stories in Which These Letters are Quoted . . . New York: 1942. V. 43

The Long Road from Maiwand. New York: 1940. V. 42

Profile by Gaslight. 1944. V. 39; 46

Profile by Gaslight. New York: 1944. V. 42; 46

SMITH, EDMOND REUEL

The Araucanians; or, Notes of a Tour Among the Indian Tribes of Southern Childe. New York: 1855. V. 37; 40; 46

SMITH, EDMUND

Oratio in Publicis Academiae Oxoniensis Scholis, in laudem . . . . Thomae Bodleii, equitis aurati Publicae ibidem Bibliothecae Fundatoris . . . . London: 1711. V. 39; 40

Phaedra and Hippolitus. London: 1707. V. 37; 42; 45

Phaedra and Hippolitus. London: 1709. V. 38

SMITH, EDMUND WARE

The Further Adventures of the One-Eyed Poachers. New York: 1947. V. 39

The One-Eyed Poacher of Privilege. New York: 1941. V. 44

Tall Tales and Short. New York: 1938. V. 39

A Tomato Can Chronicle and Other Stories of Fishing and Shooting. New York: 1937. V. 43

SMITH, EDWARD

Account of a Journey through North-Eastern Texas, Undertaken in 1849, for the Purpose of Emigration. London & Birmingham: 1849. V. 39; 40

A Dialogue Between the Pulpit and Reading-Desk. Albany: 1793. V. 42

William Cobbett, a Biography. London: 1878. V. 39

SMITH, EDWARD E.

Second Stage Lensmen. Reading: 1953. V. 39

SMITH, EDWIN W.

The Ila-Speaking Peoples of Northern Rhodesia. London: 1920. V. 39

SMITH, ELBERT

Ma-Ka-Tai-Me-She-Kia-Kiak; or, Black Hawk. New York: 1848. V. 38; 39

SMITH, ELBERT H.

Black Hawk and Scenes in the West. New York: 1848. V. 41

SMITH, ELIAS

The American Physician, and Family Assistant. Boston: 1837. V. 39

The Life, Conversion, Preaching, Travels and Sufferings of Elias Smith. Portsmouth: 1816. V. 45

The Peoples' Book. Boston: 1836. V. 43

SMITH, ELIZA

The Compleat Housewife; or, Accomplish'd Gentlewoman's Companion . . . London: 1732. V. 41

The Compleat Housewife . . . London: 1736. V. 46

The Compleat Housewife. London: 1737. V. 41; 42

SMITH, ELIZABETH

Fragments, in Prose and Verse. Burlington: 1811. V. 46

SMITH, ELIZABETH OAKES

Bertha and Lily: the Parsonage of Beech Glen. New York: 1854. V. 45

The Salamander: Found Amongst the Papers of the Late Ernest Helfenstein. New York: 1849. V. 39

SMITH, ELIZABETH OAKES PRINCE 1806-1893

The Salamander: a Legend for Christmas. New York: 1848. V. 43

The Sinless Child and Other Poems. New York: 1843. V. 43

The Western Captive; or, the Times of tecumseh. New York: 1842. V. 46

SMITH, EMMA

Sacred Hymns and Spiritual Songs, for the Church of Jesus Christ of Latter Day Saints. Liverpool: 1854. V. 41

SMITH, EPHRAIM K.

To Mexico with Scott: Letters of Captain E. Kirby Smith to His Wife. Cambridge: 1917. V. 37

SMITH, ERNEST BRAHAM 1867-1942

The Wallet of Kai Lung. New York: n.d. V. 37

SMITH, ERNEST BRAMAH 1867-1942

Call of the Blood by George Owen Baxter. New York: (1934). V. 37

English Farming and Why I Turned It Up. London: 1894. V. 37; 39; 41; 42; 45

The Eyes of Max Carrados. London: 1923. V. 46

The Eyes of Max Carrados. 1924. V. 39

A Guide to the Varieties and Rarity of English Regal Coins. London: 1929. V. 39

Kai Lung's Golden Hours. London: 1924. V. 37; 39; 40; 41

Kai Lung Unrolls His Mat. London: 1928. V. 44; 46

Kai Lung Beneath the Mulberry Tree. 1940. V. 43

Kai Lung Unrolls the Mat. New York: 1928. V. 41; 42; 43; 45

Kai Lung's Golden Hours. London: 1922. V. 42; 43

The Mirror of Kong Ho. New York: 1930. V. 37; 39; 45

The Specimen Case. London: 1924. V. 44; 46

The Wallet of Kai Lung. London: 1903. V. 41; 42

SMITH, ERWIN E.

Life on the Texas Range. Austin: 1952. V. 38

SMITH, ETHAN

View of the Hebrews. Poultney: 1825. V. 39

SMITH, FAY JACKSON

Father Kino in Arizona. Phoenix: 1966. V. 39

SMITH, FRANCIS

The Canary: Its Varieties, Management and Breeding . . . London: 1868. V. 44

SMITH, FRANCIS HOPKINSON 1838-1915

American Illustrators. New York: 1893. V. 42

Colonel Carter of Cartersville. Boston: 1891. V. 37

In Dicken's London. New York: 1914. V. 43

Venice of To-day. New York: 1896. V. 41

SMITH, FRANK MERIWEATHER

San Francisco Vigilance Committee of '56, with Some Interesting Sketches of Events Succeeding 1846. San Francisco: 1883. V. 37; 39; 44

SMITH, FRANKLIN WEBSTER

Designs, Plans and Suggestions for the Aggarandizemnt of Washington. Washington: 1900. V. 40

SMITH, FREDERIC

Report of Lieut.-Colonel Sir Frederic Smith, Royal Engineers and Professor BArlow, to the Right Honourable the Earl of Ripon, President of the Board of Trade, on the Atmospheric Railway. London: 1842. V. 46

SMITH, FREDERICK

A History of the Royal Army Veterinary Corps 1796-1919. London: 1927. V. 41

Some Friends of Dr. Johnson. London: 1934. V. 39

SMITH, G.

The Oldest London Bookshop, a History of Two Hundred Years. London: 1928. V. 41

SMITH, G. E. KIDDER

A Pictorial History of Architecture in America. New York: 1976. V. 41

SMITH, G. ELLIOT

Egyptian Mummies. London: 1924. V. 40; 42; 44

SMITH, GEORGE

Alden of Aldenholme. London: 1873. V. 42

Assyrian Discoveries; an Account of Explorations and Discoveries on the Site of Nineveh, During 1873 and 1874. London: 1875. V. 40

Assyrian Discoveries; an Account of Explorations and Discoveries on the Site of Nineveh, During 1873 and 1874. New York: 1875. V. 40; 42

The Cabinet-Maker and Upholsterer's Guide . . . London: 1836. V. 42; 46

The Cassiterides; an Inquiry into the Commercial Operations of the Phoenicians in Western Europe, With Particular Reference to the British Tin Trade. London: 1863. V. 40; 43; 46

The Chaldean Account of Genesis. London: 1880. V. 44

A Collection of Designs for Household Furniture and Interior Decoration, in the Most Approved and Elegant Taste . . . London: 1808. V. 39

A Compleat Body of Distilling, Explaining the Mysteries of That Science, in a Most Easy and Familiar Manner. London: 1725. V. 39; 45; 46

A Compleat Body of Distilling . . . London: 1738. V. 45

Essay on the Construction of Cottages Suited for the Dwellings of the Labouring Classes . . . Glasgow: 1834. V. 37; 40; 42; 44

Essay on the Construction of Cottages Suited for the Dwellings of the Labouring Classes, for Which the Premium was Voted by the Highland Society of Scotland. Glasgow (etc.): 1834. V. 38

Essay on the Construction of Cottages Suited for the Dwellings on the Labouring Classes . . . Glasgow: (1834). V. 37

Gipsy Life. London: 1880. V. 42

I've Been a Gipsying, or Rambles Among Our Gipsies and Their Children in Their Tents and Vans. London: 1883. V. 42

A Narrative of an Exploratory Visit to Each of the Consular Cities of China, and to the Islands of Hong Kong and Chusan, in Behalf of the Church Missionary Society in the Years 1844, 1845, 1846. New York: 1847. V. 40; 41

The Oldest London Bookshop: a History of Two Hundred Years. London: 1928. V. 46

An Universal Military Dictionary. London: 1779. V. 42

SMITH, GEORGE, 18th century

A Compleat Body of Distilling, Explaining the Mysteries of that Science. London: 1731. V. 43

The Laboratory; or, School of Arts . . . London: 1810. V. 41

SMITH, GEORGE A.

The Rise, Progress and Travels of the Church of Jesus Christ of Latter Day Saints Being a Series of Answers to Questions . . . Salt Lake City: 1869. V. 40

The Rise, Progress and Travels of the Church of Jesus Christ of Latter Day Saints. Salt Lake City: 1872. V. 42

SMITH, GEORGE D.

The Life and Times of George Foster Pierce, D.D., LL.D., Bishop of the Methodist Episcopal Church, South. Sparta: 1888. V. 45

SMITH, GEORGE EVERARD KIDDER

A Pictorial History of Architecture in America. New York: 1976. V. 42

SMITH, GEORGE G.

The Story of Georgia and The Georgia People, 1732-1860. Atlanta: 1900. V. 37; 39

SMITH, GEORGE GILLMAN

The Story of Georgia and the Georgia People 1732-1860. Macon: 1900. V. 44

SMITH, GEORGE PUTNAM

The Law of Field-Sports: A Summary of the Rules of Law Affecting American Sportsmen. New York: 1886. V. 37

SMITH, GERALD C.

All at Sea. New York: 1939. V. 43

SMITH, GERIT

The True Office of Civil Government. New York: 1851. V. 41

SMITH, GERRIT

Gerrit Smith's Land Auction. Peterboro: 1846. V. 45

SMITH, GERTRUDE

The Arabella and Araminta Stories. Boston: 1903. V. 37

SMITH, GODFREY

The Laboratory; or, School of Arts. London: 1755. V. 38; 43

the Laboratory; or, School of Arts. London: 1770-56. V. 39

SMITH, GOLDIE CAPERS

The Creative Arts in Texas: a Handbook of Biography. Nashville and Dallas: 1926. V. 40; 45

SMITH, GREENE

Catalogue of Birds, Eggs and Nests. Morrisville: 1881. V. 43

SMITH, GREGORY G.

The Spectator. The Text Edited and Annotated by G. Gregory Smith. With an Introductory Essay by Austin Dobson. Eight Volumes. New York: 1897. V. 37

SMITH, GUSTAVUS WOODSON

The Battle of Seven Pines. New York: 1891. V. 43

Confederate War Papers. Fairfax Court House, New Orleans, Seven Pines, Richmond and North Carolina. New York: 1884. V. 42; 46

SMITH, GYLES

Serious Reflections on the Dangerous Tendency of the Common Practice of Card-playing . . . London: 1754? V. 37

SMITH, H. ALLEN

The Great Chili Confrontation. New York: 1969. V. 46

SMITH, H. CLIFFORD

Buckingham Palace, Its Furniture, Decoration and History. London: 1931. V. 38; 39

The Complete History of Buckingham Palace. London: 1930. V. 40

Jewellery. New York: 1908. V. 40; 46

Sulgrave and the Washingtons. London: 1933. V. 38; 40

SMITH, H. P.

Syracuse and its Surroundings. Syracuse: 1878. V. 39

SMITH, H. S.

Saqqara Demotic Papyri I. London: 1983. V. 40; 42; 44

SMITH, HANNAH WHITALL

The Christian Secret to a Happy Life. Chicago: 1883. V. 37

SMITH, HARRY

Harry Smith: Magic Moments. Los Angeles: 1981. V. 41; 44

SMITH, HARRY B.

First Nights and First Editions. Boston: 1931. V. 42

A Sentimental Library. New York: 1914. V. 39

A Sentimental Library; Comprising Books Formerly Owned by Famous Writers, Presentation Copies, Manuscripts and Drawings Collected and Described by Harry B. Smith. N.P.: 1914. V. 43

A Sentimental Library. Comprising Books Formerly Owned by Famous Writers, Presentation Copies, Manuscripts, and Drawings. 1914. V. 37

SMITH, HARRY WORCESTER

Life and Sport in Aiken and Those Who Made It. New York: 1935. V. 37

A Sporting Tour Through Ireland, England, Wales and France. London: 1925. V. 39

A Sporting Tour Through Ireland, England, Wales and France, in the Years 1912-1913. Worcester: 1925. V. 39

SMITH, HELEN ZENNA

'Not So Quiet . . . ' Stepdaughters of War. London: 1930. V. 46

'Not So Quiet . . . ' Stepdaughters of War. London: 1930. V. 45

SMITH, HENRY

Anatomical Atlas Illustrative of the Structure of the Human Body. Philadelphia: 1859. V. 42

Specimens of Nature Printing from Unprepared Plants, Etc., Etc. Madras: 1857. V. 43

SMITH, HENRY ECROYD

The History of Conisborough Castle with Glimpses of Ivanhoe-Land. Worksop: 1887. V. 44

Reliquia Isuriane: The Remains of the Roman Isurium . . . London: 1852. V. 39

SMITH, HERBERT H.

Brazil. New York: 1879. V. 45

Brazil, the Amazons and the Coast. New York: 1879. V. 42; 45

SMITH, HOMER

Medicamentorum Formulae: Ad Varias Medendi Intentiones Concinnatae. London: 1760. V. 38

SMITH, HOMER W.

The Kidney, Structure and Function in Health and Disease. New York: 1951. V. 43

SMITH, HORACE

Arthur Arundel, a Tale of the English Revolution. London: 1844. V. 39

Brambletye House; or, Cavaliers and Roundheads. London: 1826. V. 46

Gaieties and Gravities; a Series of Essays, Comic Tales and Fugitive Vagaries. London: 1825. V. 38; 46

Horace in London. London: 1813. V. 38; 40

Rejected Addresses. London: 1833. V. 38

Reuben Apsley. London: 1827. V. 38

The Tor Hill. London: 1826. V. 38; 39; 40

Zillah: a Tale of the Holy City. London: 1828. V. 38

SMITH, HORACE WEMYSS

Life and Correspondence of the Rev. William Smith. Philadelphia: 1879-80. V. 40; 42

SMITH, HORATIO

Amarynthus, the Nympholept. London: 1821. V. 37; 40; 46

Festivals, Games and Amusements. New York: 1831. V. 43

SMITH, HUGH

Formulae Medicamentorum Concinnatae; or, Elegant Medical Prescriptions for Various Disorders . . . London: 1791. V. 41

Formulae Medicamentorum: or, A Compendium of the Modern Practice of Physic. To Which is Prefixed an Essay on the Effects of Blood-Letting. V. 37

Letters to Married Women. London: 1774. V. 38; 42; 46

Letters to Married Women on Nursing and the Management of Children. Philadelphia: 1796. V. 37

Medicamentorum Formulae: ad Varias Medendi Intentiones Concinnatae. London: 1760. V. 39; 41; 44; 45; 46

SMITH, J.

Sixteen Views of the Lakes in Cumberland and Westmorland. London. V. 39; 44

SMITH, J. CALVIN

Guide Through Ohio, Michigan, Indiana, Illinois, Missouri, Wisconsin, and Iowa Showing the Township Lines of the United States Surveys . . . New York: 1850. V. 44

The Illustrated Hand-Book, a New Guide for Travelers through the United States of America. New York: 1848. V. 37; 38; 42

The Illustrated Hand-Book: A New Guide for Travelers through the United States of America . . . New York: 1850. V. 37

The Western Tourist. New York: 1846. V. 38

SMITH, J. E.

A Sketch of a Tour on the Continent. London: 1807. V. 38

SMITH, J. FREDERICK

Frederick Swanwick. 1888. V. 46

SMITH, J. GRAY

Brief Historical and Descriptive Review of East Tennessee, United States of America . . . London: 1842. V. 37; 43

SMITH, J. L.

History of the 118th Pennsylvania Volunteers Corn Exchange Regiment . . . Philadelphia: 1905. V. 42

SMITH, J., MISS

Studies of Flowers from Nature. Adwick Hall near Doncaster: 1818. V. 44

SMITH, J. T.

Lives of Famous London Beggars . . . London. V. 45

SMITH, J. V.

Report of the Debates and Proceedings of the Convention for the Revision of the Cinstitition of the State of Ohio. Columbus: 1851. V. 37; 43

SMITH, J. VICTOR

Trial of Oscar T. Caldwell, Late a Conductor on the Chicago an Burlington Railroad Line, for Embezzlement: Before the Recorder's Court of the City of Chicago . . . Chicago: 1855. V. 37

SMITH, JAMES 1737-1812

An Account of the Remarkable Occurrences in the Life and Travels of Col. James Smith . . . Philadelphia: 1831. V. 40

An Account of the Remarkable Occurrences in the Life and Travels of Col. James Smith. Cincinnati: 1870. V. 38

The Art of Living in London. London: 1768. V. 38

The Art of Living in London: a Poem, in Two Cantos. London: 1768. V. 37

The Carpenter's Companion. London: 1733. V. 40; 44

The Panorama of Science and Art . . . Liverpool: 1815. V. 42; 43

Rejected Addresses; or the New Theatrum Postarum. London: 1812. V. 39; 40

The Winter of 1840 in St. Croix, with an Excrusion to Tortola and St. Thomas. New York: 1840. V. 41

SMITH, JAMES E.

A Famous Battery and its Campaigns 1861-64. Washington: 1892. V. 41

An Introduction to Physiological and Systematical Botany. Philadelphia: 1814. V. 40

SMITH, JAMES EDWARD

The English Flora. London: 1830. V. 44

English Botany; Or, Coloured Figures of British Plants . . . London: 1832-1846. V. 37

Exotic Botany . . . . London: 1804-05. V. 43

Fifteen Views Illustrative of a Tour to Hafod in Cardiganshire, the Seat of Thomas Johnes, Esq. London: 1810. V. 39

Fifteen Views Illustrative of a Tour to Hafod. London: 1815. V. 38

Flora Britannica. London: 1804. V. 37

A Grammar of Botany Illustrative of Artificial, as Well as Natural Classification with an Explanation of Jessieu's System. New York: 1822. V. 41; 43; 45

An Introduction to Physiological and Systematical Botany. Philadelphia: 1814. V. 38; 39

An Introduction to Physiological and Systematical Botany . . . London: 1819. V. 46

SMITH, JAMES EDWARD continued

An Introduction to Physiological and Systematical Botany. London: 1825. V. 38; 40

An Introduction to Physiological & Systematical Botany. First American from the Secon London Edition, with notes by Jacob Bigelow. Philadelphia: 1814. V. 37

A Sketch of a Tour on the Continent. London: 1807. V. 44

Spicilegium Botanicum: Gleanings of Botany. London: 1791-92. V. 37

SMITH, JAMES F.

The Cherokee Land Lottery, Containing a Numerical List of the Names of the Fortunate Drawers in Said Lottery. New York: 1838. V. 37; 42; 44; 45

SMITH, JAMES P.

General Lee at Gettysburg. Richmond: 1905. V. 42; 44

Stonewall Jackson and Chancellorsville. Richmond: 1904. V. 39

SMITH, JAMES WALTER

A Handy-Book on the Law of Master and Servant, Employer and Employed, As Regards Their Civil Rights. London: 1872. V. 45

SMITH, JEDIDIAH 1819-1894

The Southwest Expedition of Jedidiah S. Smith . . . Glendale: 1977. V. 40; 43; 44

SMITH, JEROME VAN CROWNINSHEILD

Natural History of the Fishes of Massachusetts, Embracing a Practical Essay on Angling. Boston: 1833. V. 44

SMITH, JEROME VAN CROWNINSHIELD 1800-1879

Memoirs of Andrew Jackson, Late Major-General and Commander in Chief of the Southern Division of the Army of the United States. Boston: 1828. V. 40

Trout and Angling. New York: 1929. V. 39; 43; 44

SMITH, JESSIE WILCOX

A Child's Book of Old Verses. New York: 1910. V. 42

A Child's Book of Old Verses. New York: 1935. V. 45

SMITH, JOHN 1580-1631

Advertisements for the Unexperienced Planters of New England, or Anywhere; or, the Pathway to Erect a Plantation. Boston: 1865. V. 38; 42

Advertisements for the Unexperienced Planters of New England, or Anywhere . . . Boston: 1875. V. 39

A Catalogue Raisonee of the Works of the Most Eminent Dutch, Flemish and French Painters; In Which is Included a Short Biographical Notive of the Artists . . . London: 1829-42. V. 39; 46

Chronicon Rusticum - Commerciale; or, Memoirs of Wool &c . . . London: 1747. V. 40

Chronicon Rusticum - Commerciale; or, Memoirs of Wool . . . London: 1757. V. 43

Condemned at Stanley. Falkland Islands: 1969. V. 40

A Description of New England; or, Observations and Discoveries in the North of America in the Year of Our Lord 1614. Boston: 1865. V. 41; 42; 44; 45

England's Improvement Reviv'd: . . . London: 1670. V. 42

England's Improvement Reviv'd . . . London: 1673. V. 39; 43

The Excellency and Nobleness of True Religion, in Its Original, Nature, Propertys, Opertaions, Progress and End. Glasgow: 1745. V. 38

Fruits and Farinacea the Proper Food of Man. London: 1845. V. 40

Galic Antiquities . . . Edinburgh: 1780. V. 42

The Generall Histories of Virginia. London: 1632. V. 37

The General Histories of Virginia, New England, and the Summer Isles. London: 1632. V. 38; 40

Twee Scheeps-Togten van Capiteyn Johan Smith, Beyde Gedaan na Nieuw-Engeland. Leyden: 1707. V. 38

General View of the Agriculture of the County of Argyle . . . London: 1805. V. 44

The General Historie of Virginia. New England and the Summer Isles . . . Together With the True Travels, Adventures and the Observations and A Sea Grammr. Glasgow: 1907. V. 41; 45

The Generall Historie of Virginia, New England and The Summer Isles. Glasgow: 1907. V. 46

The Generall Historie of Virginia, New England and the Summer Isles. Cleveland: 1966. V. 37; 43; 44

The Generall Historie of Virginia, New England and the Summer Isles . . . London: 1966. V. 38

The Generall Historie of Virginia, New England and the Summer Isles. London: 1624. V. 44

Handbook of Old Scottish Clockmakers. Edinburgh: 1903. V. 40

A Hebrew Grammar . . . Boston: 1803. V. 42

A Hebrew Grammr, Without Points . . . Boston: 1810. V. 43

Irish Diamonds. London: 1847. V. 40

Memoirs of Wool, Woolen Manufacture, and Trade (Particularly in England) from the Earliest to the Present Times. London: 1757-56. V. 40

The Missionary Smith. London: 1824. V. 40

the Mysterie of Rhetorique Unvail'd. London: 1657. V. 46

The Narrative of Mr. John Smith, of Walworth, in the County-Palatine of Durham, Gent. London: 1679. V. 40

On the Origin of Colour and the Theory of Light. Manchester: 1860. V. 37; 41

Poems Upon Several Occasions. London: 1713. V. 42; 43

The Portrait of Old Age. London: 1752. V. 40

The Printer's Grammar . . . London: 1755. V. 44

Scheeps-Togt . . . Na Virginia . . . 1606. Amsterdam: 1706. V. 41

Select Views in Italy with Topographical Descriptions in English and French. London: 1792. V. 37

Sketches of Cantabs. London: 1850. V. 40

Speeches Delivered in the House of Commons, on June 1st and 11th, 1824, Regarding the Proceedings at Demerara, Relative to the Late Mr. John Smith, Missionary at that Place . . . Edinburgh: 1824. V. 45

A System of Modern Geography; or, The Natural and Political History of the Present State of the World. London: 1810. V. 37; 38

The True Travels, Adventures and Observations of Captain John Smith, in Europe, Asia, Africa and America, from Anno Domini 1593 to 1629. London: 1630. V. 40; 41

The True Travels, Adventures and Observations of Captaine John Smith in Europe, Asia, Africke and America. Richmond: 1819. V. 37; 38; 39; 40; 41; 42; 43; 45

The True Travels, Adventures and Observations of Captain John Smith. New York: 1930. V. 39

Wayfaring Notes. Sydney: 1865. V. 39

Works. Birmingham: 1884. V. 38

SMITH, JOHN CALVIN

The Illustrated Hand-Book, a New Guide for Travelers Through the United States of America . . . New York: 1847. V. 38; 39

The Illustrated Hand-Book, A New Guide for Travelers Through the United States of America . . . New York: 1848. V. 43

The Illustrated Hand-Book, a New Guide for Travelers through the United States of America . . . New York: 1850. V. 41

Western Tourist and Emigrant's Guide. New York: 1839. V. 42

The Western Tourist and Emigrant's Guide. New York: 1845. V. 41

The Western Toursit and Emigrant's Guide . . . New York: 1846. V. 41

The Western Tourist of Emigrant's Guide Through the States of Ohio, Michigan, Indiana, Illinois and Missouri, and the Territories of Wisconsin and Iowa. New York: 1849. V. 41

The Western Tourist and Emigrant's Guide through the States of Ohio, Michigan, Indiana, Illinois, Missouri, Iowa and Wisconsin, and the Territories of Minnesota, Missouri and Nebraska . . . New York: 1850. V. 41

Western Tourist and Emigrant's Guide through the States of Ohio, Michigan, Indiana, Illinois, Missouri, Iowa and Wisconsin . . . New York: 1851. V. 45

The Western Tourist and Emigrant's Guide through the States of Ohio, Michigan, Indiana, Illinois, Missouri, Iowa and Wisconsin, and the Territories of Minnesota, Missouri and Nebraska. New York: 1853. V. 41

SMITH, JOHN COTTON

Smith Papers: papers of John Cotton Smith While Lieutenant Governor. Hartford: 1948-1965. V. 37; 40; 42; 44

SMITH, JOHN GORDON

The English Army in France. London: 1831. V. 42

Santarem or Sketches of Society and Manners in the Interior of Portugal. London: 1832. V. 45

SMITH, JOHN JAY

American Historical and Literary Curiosities . . . Philadelphia: 1861. V. 46

SMITH, JOHN RUSSELL 1810-1894

A Bibliographical Catalogue of English Writers on Angling and Ichtyology. London: 1856. V. 39; 40

Bibliotheca Cantiana: a Bibliographical Account of What Has Been Published On the History, Topography, Antiquities, Customs . . . (with) Bibliotheca Cantiana. A Catalogue of a Valuable and Interesting Collection of Books . . . London: 1837/37. V. 44

Bibliotheca Cantiana; a Bibliographical Account of What Has Been Published on the History, Topography, Antiquities, Customs and Family History . . . London: 1837. V. 42; 43

A Biographical Catalogue of English Writers on Angling and Ichthyology. London: 1856. V. 41

Bookish Quotations. Oxfordshire: 1985. V. 39

SMITH, JOHN THOMAS

Ancient Topography of London . . . London: 1815. V. 44

An Antiquarian Ramble in the Streets of London, with Anecdotes of Their More Celebrated Residents. London: 1846. V. 39

Antiquities of London and Its Environs . . . London: 1791. V. 39; 43

Antiquities of London and Its Environs. London: 1791-1800. V. 39; 44

Antiquities of Westminster. London: 1807. V. 37; 38; 40; 42; 45; 46

Etchings of Remarkable Beggars and Other Persons of Notoriety in London and Its Environs. London: 1815. V. 39; 45

Lives of Famous London Beggars, with Forty Portraits of the Most Remarkable . . . London: 1850's. V. 41

Lives of Famous London Beggars, with Forty Portraits of the Most Remarkable . . . London: 1880. V. 40

SMITH, JOHN THOMAS continued

Nollekens and His Times. London: 1829. V. 39; 40; 45; 46

Nollekens and His Times: comprehending a Life of that Celebraed Sculptor; and Memoirs of Several Contemporary Artists from the time of Roubillac, Hogarth, and Reynolds, to that of Fuseli, Flaxman, and Blake. By John Thomas Smith. London: 1828. V. 37; 39

Remarks on Rural Scenery . . . London: 1797. V. 44

Vagabondiana; or, Anecdotes of Mendicant Wanderers through the Streets of London . . . London: 1817. V. 40

SMITH, JOSEPH

The V. 45

Bibliotheca Smithiana Seu Catalogus Librorum Josephi Smithii Angli per Cognomina Authorum Dispositus. Venice: 1755. V. 39

Bibliotheca Anti-quateriana: or a Catlaogue of Books Adverse to the Society of Friends, Alphabetically Arranged . . . London: 1873. V. 44

The Book of Mormon: An Account written by the Hand of Mormon . . . Part I. New York: 1869. V. 37

Dactyliotheca Smithiana . . . Venice: 1767. V. 40

A Descriptive Catalogue of Friends' Books, or Books Written by Members of the Society of Friends . . . London: 1867. V. 42

Doctrine and Covenants of the Church of the Latter Days Saints . . . Kirtland: 1835. V. 42

The Doctrine and Covenants of the Church of Jesus Christ of Latter Day Saints. Nauvoo: 1846. V. 41

History of the Church of Jesus Christ of Latter-Day Stains. Period I. History of Joseph Smith, The Prophet, by Himself. Salt Lake City: 1902-12/32. V. 42

Not of God. Lamoni: 1883. V. 44

Old Redstone; or, Historical Sketches of Western Presbyterianism, Its Early Ministers, Its Perilous Times and Its First Records. Philadelphia: 1854. V. 37; 38; 44

The Pearl of Great Price; Being a Choice Selection from the Revelations, Translations and Narrations of Joseph Smith . . . Liverpool: 1851. V. 42

Trade and Travels in the Gulph of Guinea, Western Africa with an Account of the Manners, Habits . . . of the Inhabitants. London: 1851. V. 46

SMITH, JOSEPH R.

Observations on Texas Cattle. Concord: 1884. V. 42

SMITH, JOSEPH W.

Visits to Brunswick, Georgia and Travels South. Boston: 1907. V. 40; 44

SMITH, JOSHUA HETT 1736-1818

Authentic Narrative of the Causes Which Led to the Death of Major Andre, Adjutant-General of His Majesty's Forces in North America. London: 1808. V. 38; 42; 43

An Authentic Account of the Causes that Led to the Death of Major Andre. New York: 1809. V. 38

SMITH, JOSHUA TOULMIN

The Northmen in New England, or America in the Tenth Century. Boston: 1839. V. 38

SMITH, JOSIAH

The Character, Preaching & of the Reverend Mr. George Whitefield . . . Preached in Charlestown, South Carolina . . . 1740 . . . Boston: 1740. V. 46

SMITH, JULIA

Letters of the Swedish Court, Written Chiefly in the Early Part of the Reign of Gustavus III. London: 1809. V. 40

SMITH, JUSTIN H.

The Annexation of Texas. New York: 1911. V. 41; 42

The Annexation of Texas. New York: 1919. V. 44; 45

The Historie Booke: Done to Keep in Lasting Remebrance the Joyous Meeting of the Honourable Artillery Company of London and the Ancient and Honorable Artillery Company of the Massachusetts in the Towne of Boston, A.D. 1903. N.P.: 1903. V. 38

Our Struggle for the Fourteenth Colony: Canada and the American Revolution. New York: 1907. V. 44; 46

The War With Mexico. New York: 1919. V. 37; 39; 42

SMITH, JUSTIN HARVEY

Annexation of Texas. Corrected Edition. New York: 1941. V. 37; 38; 41

The Historie Book. Done to keep in lasting remembrance the joyous meeting of the Honourable Artillery Cornpany of London and the Ancient and Honorable Artillery Company of the Massachusetts in the Towne of Boston . . . London: 1903. V. 37

SMITH, KENNETH M.

Mumps Measles and Mosaics. London: 1954. V. 44

SMITH, LANGDON

Evolution. Wassau. V. 46

Evolution. Wausau: 1905? V. 37

SMITH, LAURA ALEXANDRINE

Music of the Waters. London: 1888. V. 39

SMITH, LEE

Bob, a Dog. Chapel Hill: 1988. V. 46

Cakewalk. New York: 1981. V. 46

Fancy Strut. New York: 1973. V. 42; 43

The Last Day the Dogbushes Bloomed. New York: 1968. V. 39; 42

The Last Day the Dogbushes Bloomed. New York: (1968). V. 37

Oral History. New York: 1983. V. 38

SMITH, LILLIAN

Killers of the Dream. London: 1950. V. 44

Strange Fruit. New York: 1944. V. 44

SMITH, LOGAN PEARSALL

Afterthoughts. London: 1931. V. 40

A Portrait Drawn From His Letters and Diaries. London: 1950. V. 44; 45

Trivia. London: 1902. V. 43

The Youth of Parnassus. London: 1895. V. 41; 43; 45

SMITH, LUCY

Biographical Sketches of Joseph Smith the Prophet, and His Progenitors for Many Generations. Liverpool: 1853. V. 42

SMITH, M.

Studies in Early Mysticism in the Near and Middle East. London: 1931. V. 44

SMITH, M. A.

The Reptilia and Amphibia Fauna of British India, Ceylon: Reptilia and Amphibia. London: 1931-43. V. 38

SMITH, MARGARET

A Winter in Washington; or, Memoirs of the Seymour Family. New York: 1824. V. 43

SMITH, MARGARET B.

What is Gentility? City of Washington: 1828. V. 39

SMITH, MARSHALL

The Vision, or a Prospect of Death, Heav'n and Hell. London: 1702. V. 40

SMITH, MARY

An Affecting Narrative of the Captivity and Sufferings of Mrs. Mary Smith, Who with Her Husband and Three Daughters Was Taken Prisoner by the Indians, in August 1814 . . . N.P.: 1818. V. 43

An Affecting Narrative of the Captivity and Sufferings of Mrs. Mary Smith, Who, With Her Husband and Three Daughters, Were Taken Prisoner by the Indians, in August 1814 and Rescued by a Detached Party of the Army . . . Williamsburgh: 1818. V. 42

Complete Housekeeper, and Professed Cook. . . . . Containing upwards of Seven Hundred practical and approved Receipts. Newcastle: 1803. V. 39

SMITH, MATTHEW

52 Colored Plates. London: 1962. V. 37

A Declaration and Remonstrance of the Distressed and Bleeding Frontier Inhabitants of the Province of Pennsylvania, Presented by Them to the Honourable the Governor and Assembly of the Province, Shewing the Causes of Their Late Discontents and Uneasiness. Philadelphia: 1764. V. 40; 42; 44; 45

Memoirs of Secret Service. London: 1699. V. 42; 43

SMITH, MICHAEL

A Geographical View of the Province of Upper Canada . . . New York: 1813. V. 40; 43

A Geographical View of the Province of Upper Canada; and Promiscuous Remarks on the Government. Philadelphia: 1813. V. 38

A Geographical View of te Province of Upper Canada. Trenton: 1813. V. 40

A Geographical View of the British Possessions in North America: Comprehending Nova Scotia, New Brunswick, New Britain, Lower and Upper Canada, With all the Country in the Frozen Sea on the North, and Pacific Ocean on the West. With an . . . Baltimore: 1814. V. 37; 44

SMITH, MISS

Studies of flowers from Nature . . . This Work Will Consist Chiefly of a Selection of Subjects from the Choicest Exotics . . . 1820. V. 46

Studies of Flowers from Nature. Doncaster: 1820. V. 46

SMITH, MOSES

History of the Adventures and Sufferings of Moses Smith, During Five Years of His Life. Brooklyn: 1812. V. 40

History of the Adventures and Sufferings of Moses Smith, During Five Years of His Life . . . Albany: 1814. V. 43

SMITH, NATHAN

Address of the Association of Mechanics and Other Working Men, of the City of Washington, to the Operatives Throughout the United States. Washington: 1830. V. 41

SMITH, NATHAN RYNE

A Discourse on the Influence of Diseases on the Intellectual and Moral Powers Delivered as an Introductory Lecture at the College of Physicians and Surgeons in the City of New York. Baltimore: 1831. V. 45

Medical and Surgical Memoirs. Baltimore: 1831. V. 38; 41; 44; 45; 46

Practical Essay on Typhous Fever. New York: 1824. V. 38; 44

Surgical Anatomy of the Arteries. Baltimore: 1830. V. 46

Surgical Anatomy of the Arteries. Baltimore: 1832. V. 39

Surgical Anatomy of the Arteries. Baltimore: 1835. V. 42

Treatment of Fractures of the Lower Extremity By the Use of the Anterior Suspensory Apparatus. Baltimore: 1867. V. 42

SMITH, NOBEL

The Surgery of Deformities. London: 1882. V. 42

SMITH, NORA ARCHIALD

Boys and Girls of Bookland. New York: 1923. V. 42; 46

SMITH, NORA ARCHIBALD

Boys and Girls of Bookland. Philadelphia: 1923. V. 42

Under the Cactus Flag a Story of Life in Mexico. Boston: 1899. V. 45

SMITH, OLIVER HAMPTON

Early Indiana Trails and Sketches. Cincinnati: 1858. V. 37

SMITH, OLIVER P.

The Domestic Architect . . . Buffalo: 1854. V. 37; 44

SMITH, PAT

The World of Sport. New York: 1970. V. 37; 41

SMITH, PAUL JORDAN

A Key to the Ulysses of James Joyce. Chicago: 1927. V. 37; 38; 40; 42; 46

smith, percy

Sixteen Drypoints and Etchings. London: 1930. V. 44

SMITH, PETER

The Indian Doctor's Dispensatory, Being Father Smith's Advice Respecting Diseases and Their Cure. Cincinnati: 1813. V. 37; 40; 42

SMITH, PHILIP

The Book: Art and Object. Merstham: 1982. V. 40

Letter to Mrs Gardner, Narrating the Proceedings of the Meeting, Held at the hequers Inn, Fordham . . . to Investigate the Imputations of Mr Evans, of Ely. Bury St. Edmund's: 1837. V. 39

New Directions in Bookbinding. London: 1974. V. 38; 41

New Directions in Bookbinding. N.P.: 1974. V. 37; 45

SMITH, R.

Notes Made During a Tour in Denmark, Holstein, Mecklenburg-Schwerin, Pomerania, the Isle of Rugen, Prussia, Poland, Saxony, Brunswick, Hannover, the Hanseatic Territories, Oldenburg, Friesland, Holland, Brabant, the Rhine Country and France . . . London: 1827. V. 39

SMITH, R. A.

History of Dickinson County, Iowa. Des Moines: 1902. V. 46

Philadelphia As It Is in 1852 . . . Philadelphia: 1852. V. 42

SMITH, R. ANGUS

To Iceland in a Yacht. Edinburgh: 1873. V. 37

SMITH, R. MURDOCH

History of the Recent Discoveries at Cyrene. London: 1864. V. 45

SMITH, R. R. R.

Hellenistic Royal Portraits. Oxford: 1988. V. 44

SMITH, R. S.

A Manual of Topographical Drawing . . . New York: 1885. V. 40; 44

SMITH, RAY WINFIELD

The Akhenaten Temple Project. Warminster & Toronto: 1976-88. V. 42

SMITH, REEDER

Importance and Claims of Lawrence University of Wisconsin, Founded in 1848 by Hon. A. A. Lawrence and the Late Samuel Appleton . . . Boston: 1860. V. 46

SMITH, REGINALD A.

The Sturge Collection: an Illustrated Selection of Flints from Britain, Bequeathed in 1919 by William Allen Sturge. (and) An Illustrated Selection of Foreign Stone Impelements. London: 1931-37. V. 45

SMITH, RICHARD

The Confederate Spelling Book, with Reading Lessons for the Young, Adopted for the Use of Schools or for Private Instruction. Richmond: 1865. V. 37

List of Plants of the Fir Tribe, Suitable for the Climate of Great Britain. Worcester: 1864. V. 38

Notes Made During a Tour in Denmark, Holstein, Mecklenburg-Schwerin, Pomerania, the Isle of Rugen, Prussia, Poland, Saxony, Brunswick, Hannover and Hansetic Territories . . . London: 1827. V. 43; 44; 46

A Tour of Four Great Rivers: The Hudson, Mohawk, Susquehanna and Delaware in 1769 Being the Journal of . . . New York: 1906. V. 37; 38; 39

SMITH, RICHARD PENN

The Miscellaneous Works of the Late Richard Penn Smith. Philaelphia: 1856. V. 42

SMITH, ROBERT 1689-1768

A Compleat System of Opticks. Cambridge: 1738. V. 38; 39; 40; 41; 44; 45; 46

Cours Complet d'Optique . . . Avec des Additions Considerables sur Toutes les Nouvelles Decouvertes qu'on a faites en Cette Matiere Depuis la Publciation de l'Ouvrage Anglois. Avignon: 1767. V. 44

Court Cookery. London: 1723. V. 40

The Elementary Parts of Dr. Smith's Compleat System of Opticks, Slected and Arranged for the Use of Students at the Universities. Cambridge: 1778. V. 39

Harmonics, or the Philosophy of Musical Sounds. Cambridge: 1749. V. 39; 42; 46

Harmonics, or the Philosophy of Musical Sounds. Cambridge: 1759. V. 43

Harmonics of the Philosophy of Musical Sounds . . . London: 1759. V. 41; 45; 46

Robert Smith's Address to the People of the United States. Baltimore: 1812. V. 44

The Universal Directory for Taking Alive and destroying Rats, and all Other Kinds of Four-Footed and Winged Vermin, in Method Hitherto Unattempted . . . Dublin: 1772. V. 39

The Universal Directory for Taking Alive and Destroying Rats, and all Other Kinds of Four Footed and Winged Vermin, in a Method Hitherto Unattempted. London: 1768. V. 38; 40

SMITH, ROBERT ANGUS

Memoir of John Dalton, and History of the Atomic Theory Up to His Time. London: 1856. V. 42

SMITH, ROBERT E.

Ceramic Sequence at Uaxactun, Guatemala. New Orleans. V. 43

Ceramic Sequence at Uaxactun, Guatemala. New Orleans: 1955. V. 42; 44

SMITH, ROBERT HOUSTON

Pella of the Decapolis. Wooster: 1973. V. 37; 40; 42; 44

SMITH, ROBERT PERCY

Early Writings . . . London: 1850. V. 37; 40

SMITH, ROBERT, rat catcher

The Complete Rat-Catcher. London: 1790. V. 41; 42

SMITH, ROBERT W.

History of Armstrong County, Pennsylvania. Chicago: 1883. V. 41

SMITH, RODERICK A.

History of Dickinson County, Iowa, Together with an Account of the Spirit Lake Massacre and the Indian Troubles on the North Western Frontier. Des Moines: 1902. V. 38; 46

SMITH, ROSS

Reminiscences of an Old Timer. Johnson City: 1930. V. 39; 42; 43

SMITH, S. COMPTON

Chile Con Carne; or, the Camp and the Field. New York: 1857. V. 37; 38; 42

SMITH, SAMUEL

Aditus ad Logicam. Oxonii: 1684. V. 45

The History of the Colony of Nova-Caesaria, or New Jersey. Burlington: 1765. V. 37; 41; 42; 43; 45

SMITH, SAMUEL J.

Siamese Domestic Institutions. Bangkok: 1880. V. 40

SMITH, SAMUEL STANHOPE

An Essay on the Causes of the Variety of Complexion and Figure in the Human Species. Philadelphia: 1787. V. 37; 40; 42; 43; 44; 45

An Essay on the Causes of the Variety of Complexion and Figure in the Human Species. New Brunswick: 1810. V. 37; 40; 42

A Funeral Sermon, on the Death of the Hon. Richard Stockton, Esq. Princeton, March 2, 1781 . . . Trenton: 1781. V. 37

The Lectures, Corrected and Improved, Which Have Been Delivered for a Series of Years, in the College of New Jersey . . . Trenton: 1812. V. 37

SMITH, SAMUEL STANHOPE continued

An Oration, Upon the Death of General George Washington . . . Trenton: 1800. V. 37; 46

SMITH, SARAH

The Clives of Burcot. London: 1867. V. 44

SMITH, SEBA

John Smith's Letters, with 'Picters' to Match. New York: 1839. V. 41

the Life and Writings of Major Jack Downing of Downingsville, Away Down East in the State of Maine. Boston: 1833. V. 39; 41; 42

The Life and Writings of Major Jack Downing, of Downingville, Away Down East in the State of Maine. Boston: 1834. V. 38

SMITH, SIDNEY LAWTON

Sidney Lawton Smith, Designer, Etcher, Engraver with Extracts from His Diary and a Check List of His Bookplates. Boston: 1931. V. 39

SMITH, SIDNEY URE

The Art of William Dobell. Sydney: 1946. V. 42

SMITH, SIMON

The Golden Fleece: or, the Trade, Interest and Well Being of Great Britain Considered. London: 1736. V. 45

SMITH, SOL

Theatrical Journey-Work and Anecdotal Recollection of Sol Smith, Comedian, Attorney at Law. Philadelphia: 1854. V. 46

Theatrical management in the West and South for Thirty Years. New York: 1868. V. 42

SMITH, SOLOMON F.

The Theatrical Apprenticeship and Anecdotal Recollections of Sol. Smith, Comedian, Attorney at Law . . . Philadelphia: 1847. V. 41; 45

SMITH, SOUTHWOOD

A Lecture Delivered Over the Remains of Jeremy Benthan, Esq., in the Webb Street School of Anatomy and Medicine, on the 9th of June, 1832. London: 1832. V. 39

A Treatise on Fever. Philadelphia: 1830. V. 44

SMITH, STEVIE

Francesca in Winter. London: 1970. V. 45

The Frog Prince and Other Poems. London: 1966. V. 38

A Good Time Was Had by All. London: 1937. V. 38; 42; 45

Harold's Leap. London: 1950. V. 40; 42; 44

The Holiday. London: 1949. V. 44

Not Waving But Drowning. London: 1957. V. 42

Novel on Yellow Paper - Or Work It Out for Yourself. London: 1936. V. 37; 38; 40

Novel on Yellow Paper. New York: 1937. V. 41; 42; 45

Over the Frontier. London: 1938. V. 40

SMITH, STROTHER A.

The Tiber and Its Tributaries, Their Natural History and Classical Assocations. London: 1877. V. 45

SMITH, SYDNEY

Bon Monts. London: 1893. V. 40

Elementary Sketches of Moral Philosophy, Delivered at the Royal Institution in the Years 1804, 1805 and 1806. London: 1849. V. 38; 42; 43

Elementary Sketches of Moral Philosophy, Delivered at the Royal Institution in the Years 1804, 1805 and 1806. London: 1850. V. 40

The Works. London: 1839-40. V. 37

The Works. (with) Elementary Sketches of Moral Philosophy. (with) A Memoir of Sydney Smith.. London: 1840-55. V. 38

The Works. London: 1845. V. 42; 44

Works. London: 1848. V. 38

SMITH, SYDNEY H.

Snowden Slights, Wilfowler. York: 1912. V. 39

SMITH, T.

Rambling Recollections of a Trip to America. Edinburgh: 1875. V. 46

SMITH, T. MARSHALL

Legends of the War of Independence and of the Earlier Settlements. Louisville: 1855. V. 38

SMITH, T. R.

Poetica Erotica. New York: 1921. V. 38

SMITH, THEOPHILUS

Animadversions on the Fellows of Trinity College. Dublin: 1794. V. 38

SMITH, THOMAS

Catalogue of the Manuscripts in the Cottonian Library 1696 . . . Cambridge: 1984. V. 38

Catalogus Librorum Manuscriptorum Bibliothecae Cottonianae. Oxoni: 1696. V. 46

The Common-Vvelth of England, and Maner of Government Thereof. London: 1633. V. 43; 46

The Common-Wealth of England. London: 1633. V. 45

A Compendious or Briefe Examination of Certayne Ordinary Complaints of Divers of Our Countrymen in These Our Dayes. London: 1751. V. 37

The Cricket Match. London: 1859. V. 44

Extracts from the Diary of a Huntsman. London: 1838. V. 43; 44

A Gagg of the Quakers, with an Answer to Mr. Denn's Quaker no Papist. London: 1659. V. 39

Journals of the Rev. Thomas Smith, & The Rev. Samuel Daane, Pastors of the First Church in Portland: With Notes & Biographical Notices: And a Summary History Of Portland. By William Willis. Portland: 1849. V. 37

Poems. Manchester: 1797. V. 37

De Republica Anglorum. London: 1583. V. 41; 45

De Republica Anglorum . . . Leiden: 1630. V. 46

De Repvblica Anglovrm. Leiden: 1625. V. 42

The Shepherd's Sons . . . London: 1800. V. 41

Vitae Quorumdam Eruditissimorum et Illustrium Virorum. London: 1707. V. 46

The Young Artist's Assistant in the Art of Drawing in Water Colours Exemplified in a Course of Twenty-Nine Progressive Lessons. London. V. 44

The Young Artist's Assistant in the Art of Drawing in Water Colours Exemplified in a Course of Twenty-Nine Progressive Lessons. London: 1824. V. 42

SMITH, THOMAS CHARLTON

27th; or, Enniskillen Regiment. Rude Rhymes. Dublin: 1817. V. 37

SMITH, THOMAS LACEY

Chronicles of Turkeytown; or, The Works of Jeremy Peters. Philadelphia: 1829. V. 43; 46

SMITH, THOMS

Extracts from the Diary of a Huntsman . . . London: 1852. V. 45

SMITH, THORNE 1893-1934

Biltmore Oswald. New York: 1918. V. 42

The Passionate Witch. Garden City: 1941. V. 46

Topper. New York: 1926. V. 37; 40; 42

SMITH, TOM

Sporting Incidents in the Life of Another Tom Smith. London: 1867. V. 39; 43

SMITH, TOM C.

Records of the Parish Church of Preston in Amounderness. Preston: 1892. V. 44

SMITH, TRUMAN

An Examination of the Question of Anaesthesia, arising on the Memorial of Charles Thomas Wells, presented in the United States Senate. New York: 1858. V. 37

An Examination of the Question of Anaesthesia, arising on the Memorial of Charles Thomas Wells, presented in the United States Senate. New York: 1859. V. 37

An Examination of the Question of Anaesthesia, on the Memorial of Charles Thomas Wells, Referred to a Select Committee of the Senate of the United States, of Which Hon. Isaac P. Walker is Chairman. Washington: 1853. V. 37

Speech of . . . on the Physical Charter of the Northern States of Mexico. Washington: 1848. V. 39; 43

SMITH, URIAH

The State of the Dead and the Destiny of the Wicked. Battle Creek: 1873. V. 43

The United States in the Light of Prophecy; or, an Exposition of Rev. 13:17. Battle Creek: 1874. V. 42

SMITH, VINCENT A.

A History of Fine Art in India and Ceylon from the Earliest Times to the Present Day. Oxford: 1911. V. 42

SMITH, W.

Examples of Household Taste. New York: 1875. V. 37

A Synopsis of the British Diaatomaceae. London: 1853-56. V. 37

SMITH, W. A.

The Anson Guards: Company C, Fourteenth Regiment, North Carolina Volunteers 1861-1865. Charlotte: 1914. V. 38

SMITH, W. EUGENE

Minamata. New York: 1975. V. 41

SMITH, W. G.

A Report on the Route of General Patterson's Division from matamoras to Victoria. Washington: 1850. V. 42

A Study in Canadian Immigration. Toronto: 1920. V. 43

SMITH, W. H.

The Life and Services of Captain Philip Beaver, Late of H.M.S. Nisus. London: 1829. V. 38

The Sailors Word-Book: An Alphabetical Digest of Nautical Terms . . . London: 1867. V. 46

Smith's Family Physician comprising the Nature, Causes, Symptoms and Treatment of Diseases; with Instructions for Nursing the Sick; List of Poisons: Animal, Vegetable and Mineral . . . Verified by Many Years; Experience. Montreal: 1873. V. 37

SMITH, W. H., MRS.

The Children's Japan. Tokyo. V. 45

SMITH, W. RAMSAY

Myths and Legends of the Australian Aboriginals. London: 1930. V. 40

SMITH, W. W.

Genus Primula. 1977. V. 38

The Genus Primula. London: 1977 (1929-50). V. 46

SMITH, WADDELL F.

The Story of the Pony Express. San Rafael: 1964. V. 40

SMITH, WALLACE

Garden of the Sun. Los Angeles: 1939. V. 40

SMITH, WALTER

The Bronte Sisters, a Bibliographical Catalogue. Los Angeles: 1991. V. 46

Charles Dickens in the Original Cloth. Los Angeles: 1982-83. V. 46

Examples of Household Taste. New York: 1875. V. 40; 44

SMITH, WALTER H. B.

Pistols & Revolvers Rifles. Compiled by the National Rifle Association. Washington: (1948). V. 37

SMITH, WILLIAM

An Answer to Mr. Franklin's Remarks, on a Late Protest. Philadelphia: 1764. V. 46

An Assistant to the Evangelical Psalmodist, in Setting Forth the Most Worthy Praise of Almightly God. New Haven: 1816. V. 45

An Authentic Journal of the Expedition to Belleisle, and of the Siege of the Citadel of Palais. London: 1761. V. 39

An Authentic Account of the Life and Memoirs of Mr. William Smith, an unfortunate convict, executed at Tyburn, on the 3rd of October, 1750, for forgery. In which are inserted some original letters, and an ode, never yet published . . . London: 1750. V. 37; 41

A Brief State of the Province of Pennsylvania. London: 1755. V. 39; 42

A Brief State of the Province of Pennsylvania. London: 1756. V. 38; 39

Diary of William Smith, 1784-1793. Toronto: 1963-65. V. 45

The Diary and Selected Papers of Chief Justice William Smith, 1784-1793. Toronto: 1965. V. 44

A Dictionary of the Bible. London: 1863. V. 46

A Discourse Concerning the Conversion of the Heathen Americans . . . Philadelphia: 1760. V. 40

Discourses on Public Occasions in America. London: 1762. V. 43

Dr. William Smith's Ancient Atlas. Boston: 1874. V. 45

Etat Present de la Pensilvanie, ou l'On Trouve le Detail de ce Qui s'y Est Passe Depuis la Defaite du General Braddock Jusqu'a la Prise d'Oswego, Avec Une Carte Praticuliere de Cette Colonie. France: 1756. V. 44; 46

Eulogium on Benjamin Franklin . . . Delivered March 1, 1791 . . . Before the American Philosophical Society . . . Philadelphia: 1792. V. 41; 46

An Examination of the Connecticut Claim to Lands in Pennsylvania. Philadelphia: 1774. V. 43

A Geographical View of the British Possesions in North America . . . Baltimore: 1814. V. 42

Historical Account of Bouquet's Expedition Against the Ohio Indians in 1764. Cincinnati: 1868. V. 43

An Historical Account of the Expedition Against the Ohio Indians, in the Year 1764. Under the Command of Henry Bouquet, Esq . . . Including His Transactions With the Indians, Realtive to the Delivery of Their Prisoners . . . Philadelphia: 1765. V. 37

History of Canada . . . Quebec. V. 44

The History of the Province of New York, from the First Discovery to the Year 1732. London: 1757. V. 37; 38; 39; 40; 41; 42

The History of the Province of New York. London: 1776. V. 37; 38; 41; 42; 43; 44

The History of the Province of New-York, from the First Discovery to the Year 1732. Philadelphia: 1792. V. 42

History of the Province of New York, from the Discovery to the Year MDCCXXII. Albany: 1814. V. 37; 43

History of Canada; From Its First Discovery to the Peace of 1763. Quebec: 1815. V. 37; 38; 40

The History of the Post Office in British North America, 1639-1870. Cambridge: 1920. V. 40

Lectures on the Philosophy and Practice of Slavery, as Exhibited in the Institution of Domestic Slavery in the United States . . . Nashville: 1857. V. 42

Nouveau Voyage de Guinee . . . Paris: 1751. V. 38

Observations on the Utility, Form and Management of Water Meadows. Norwich: 1806. V. 43

Old Yorkshire. London: 1881-84. V. 38

Old Yorkshire. London: 1881-85. V. 37

An Oration in Memory of General Montgomery, and of the Officers and Soldiers, Who Fell with Him, December 31, 1775, Before Quebec. Philadelphia: 1776. V. 37

Plain Truth: Addressed to the Inhabitants of America. London: 1776. V. 38

The Poetic Works . . . Chester: 1782. V. 42

The Poetical Works of the Reverend William Smith, D.D. Late Dean of Chester . . . Chester: 1788. V. 38

Proposals for Printing by Subscription, a Body of Sermons Upon the Most Important Branches of Practical Christianity. Philadelphia: 1789. V. 46

Relation Historique de l'Expedition Contre les Indiens de l'Ohio en MDCCLXIV. Amsterdam;: 1769. V. 40; 45

Relation Historique de lExpedition Contres Les Indiens de l'Ohio en MDCCLXIV. Amsterdam: 1769. V. 38

A Sermon on the Present Situation of American Affairs, Preached in Christ-Church June 23, 1775. Philadelphia: 1775. V. 40

The Student's Vade Mecum. London: 1770. V. 38

Tracts on the Subject of Legislative Union . . . Dublin: 1800. V. 42

Xenephon's History of the Affairs of Greece. By the Translator of Thucydides. London: 1760. V. 37

A Yorkshireman's Trip to Rome in 1866. London: 1868. V. 44

A Yorkshireman's Trip to the United States and Canada. London: 1892. V. 38; 39

SMITH, WILLIAM ALEXANDER

The Anderson Guards Company C. Fourteenth Regiment North Carolina Volunteers 1861-1865. Charlotte: 1914. V. 42

SMITH, WILLIAM BENJAMIN

James Sidney Rollins. Memoir by . . . . New York: 1891. V. 39

SMITH, WILLIAM C.

Indiana Miscellany; Consisting of Sketches of Indian Life, The Early Settlement, Customs and Hardships of the People . . . Cincinnati: 1867. V. 42

SMITH, WILLIAM CUSACK

The Goblins of Neapolis. Dublin: 1836. V. 45

SMITH, WILLIAM, F.S.A.S.

A Yorkshireman's Trip to the United States and Canada. London: 1892. V. 42

SMITH, WILLIAM H.

Canada: Past, Present and Future. Toronto: 1851. V. 37

Smith's Canadian Gazetteer . . . Toronto: 1846. V. 37; 38; 42; 43; 44

SMITH, WILLIAM HAWKES

Essays in Design. Birmingham: 1818. V. 40

Kenilworth, in the 16th, 18th and 19th Centuries . . . 1821. V. 45

Kenilworth Castle in the 16th, 18th and 19th Centuries. Birmingham: 1821. V. 40

SMITH, WILLIAM HENRY

Bacon and Shakespeare. London: 1857. V. 40; 43; 44

The St. Clair Papers . . . Cincinnati: 1882. V. 41; 45

SMITH, WILLIAM J.

A Synopsis of the Origin and Progress of Architecture; To Which is Added, a Dictionary of General Terms. London: 1831. V. 46

SMITH, WILLIAM JAY

Journey to the Dead Sea. Omaha: 1979. V. 37; 42

Poems. New York: 1947. V. 38; 40

SMITH, WILLIAM L.

American Arguments for British Rights; Being a Republication of the Celebrated Letters of Phocion, on the Subject of Neutral Trade. London: 1806. V. 46

SMITH, WILLIAM MOORE

Poems on Several Occasions. Philadelphia: 1786. V. 37

SMITH, WILLIAM O'BRIEN

Report of the Trail of William Smith O'Brien for High Treason. At the Special Commission of for the Co. Tipperary, held at Clonmel, Sept. & Oct. 1848 as reported by John George Hodges. Dublin: 1849. V. 37

SMITH, WILLIAM PRESCOTT

A History and Description of the Baltimore and Ohio Rail Road . . . Batlimore: 1853. V. 37; 42

SMITH, WILLIAM PROVOST

A Brief View of the Conduct of Pennsylvania, for the Year 1755. London: 1756. V. 41

An Historical Account of the Expedition Against the Ohio Indians, in the Year MDCCLXIV. Under the Command of Henry Bouquet, Esq. London: 1766. V. 41; 46

SMITH, WILLIAM RUDOLPH

The History of Wisconsin, in Three Parts . . . Madison: 1854. V. 42

Incidents of a Journey from Pennsylvania to Wisconsin Territory, in 1837 Being the Journal of Gen. William Rudolph Smith, U.S . . . Chicago: 1927. V. 39; 42

Incidents of a Journey from Pennsylvania to Wisconsin Territory, in 1837. Wooster: 1927. V. 42

SMITH, WILLIAM S.

The Trials of William S. Smith, and Samuel G. Ogden, for Misdemeanors, Had in the Circuit Court of the United States for the New York District, in July 1806. New York: 1807. V. 37; 40; 42

SMITH, WILLIAM STEVENSON

A History of Egyptian Sculpture and Painting in the Old Kingdom. London: 1946. V. 41

A History of Egyptian Sculpture and Painting in the Old Kingdom. Oxford: 1946. V. 44

A History of Egyptian Sculpture and Painting in the Old Kingdom. London: 1949. V. 40; 42; 44

Interconnections in the Ancient Near East: a Study of the Relationships Between the Arts of Egypt, the Aegean and Western Asia. New Haven: 1965. V. 40

SMITHERS, HENRY

Observations Made During a Tour in 1816 and 1817 Through . . . Brussels: 1817/18. V. 43

Observations Made During a Residence in Brussels and Several Tours throuh the Netherlands . . . Brussels: 1820? V. 38

SMITHERS, LEONARD C.

The Thousand and One Quarters of an Hour (Tartarian Tales). Edited by Leonard C. Smithers. London: 1893. V. 37

SMITH'S New English Atlas. London: 1804. V. 38

SMITHSON, WILLIAM T.

The Methodist Pulpit South. Washington: 1858. V. 38; 42

SMITHSONIAN INSTITUTION

Tenth Annual Report of the . . . Smithsonian Insitution. Washington: 1856. V. 38

SMITHSONIAN INSTITUTION. NATIONAL COLLECTION OF FINE ARTS

Prints from the Mourlot Press: Exhibition Sponsored by the French Embassy, Circulated . . . 1964-65. Paris: 1964. V. 41

SMITHURST, BENJAMIN

Britain's Glory, and Englands Bravery. London: 1689. V. 46

SMITHWICK, NOAH

The Evolution of a State: or, Recollections of Old Texas Days. 1900. V. 42

The Evolution of a State or Recollections of Old Texas Days. Austin: 1900. V. 39; 41; 42

The Evolution of a State; or, Recollections of Old Texas Days. Gammel: 1900. V. 44

SMOLL, J. P.

Diatoms and Lake Acidity, Recosntructing pH from Siliceous Algal Remains in Lake Sediments. Dordecht: 1986. V. 37

SMOLLETT, TOBIAS GEORGE 1721-1771

The Adventures of Ferdinand Count Fathom. London: 1753. V. 37; 42; 43; 45; 46

The Adventures of Ferdinand Count Fathom. London: 1771. V. 37; 40

The Adventures of Ferdinand Count Fathom. London: 1789. V. 43

The Adventures of Gil Blas de Santillane. London: 1819. V. 46

The Adventures of Peregrine Pickle; In which are Included, Memoirs of a Lady of Quality. London: 1751. V. 37; 38; 40; 41; 43; 45

The Adventures of Peregrine Pickle. In which are included, memoirs of a Lady of Quality. London: 1773. V. 37

The Adventures of Peregrine Pickle. London: 1769. V. 44

The Adventures of Peregrine Pickle. London: 1776. V. 40

The Adventures of Peregrine Pickle. London: 1784. V. 41; 42; 46

The Adventures of Peregrine Pickle. Harrisburgh: 1807. V. 43

The Adventures of Peregrine Pickle. London: 1831. V. 41; 42

The Adventures of Peregrine Pickle. New York: 1929. V. 43

The Adventures of Peregrine Pickle. London: 1936. V. 43

The Adventures of Peregrine Pickle. New York: 1936. V. 38

The Adventures of Peregrine Pickle. Oxford: 1936. V. 40; 41

The Adventures of Peregrine Pickle in Which is Included Memoirs of a Lady of Quality. New York. V. 43

The Adventures of Roderick Random. London: 1748. V. 37; 38; 45; 46

The Adventures of Roderick Random. London: 1770. V. 40

The Adventures of Sir Launcelot Greaves. Dublin: 1763. V. 37; 40; 41

The Exhibition of Humphrey Clinker. London: 1771. V. 37; 39; 40; 41; 42; 44; 45; 46

The Expedition of Humphrey Clinker. London: 1671. V. 41

The Expedition of Humphry Clinker. London: 1671/1771. V. 43

The Expedition of Humphry Clinker. Dublin: 1771. V. 40; 42; 45

The Expedition of Humphrey Clinker. London: 1772. V. 39; 40

The Expedition of Humphry Clinker. Altenbourg;: 1785. V. 40

Travels through France and Italy. London: 1766. V. 44

The History and Adventures of an Atom. London: 1769. V. 40

The History of England, from the Revolution to the Death of George the Second. London: 1793. V. 40

The History of England from the Revolution in 1688 to the Death of George II. London: 1805. V. 38

The History of England from the Revolution to 1688 to the Death of George II. Designed as a Continuation of Hume. London: 1822. V. 40; 46

The History of England. London: 1848. V. 37; 40; 41; 43; 44

The History and Adventures of an Atom. London: 1769. V. 37; 39; 41

A Journal of the Expedition to Carthagena, with Notes. London: 1744. V. 40

The Miscellaneous Works. Edinburgh: 1790. V. 37; 38; 40

The Miscellaneous Works . . . With Memoirs of His Life and Writings . . . Edinburgh: 1817. V. 46

The Miscellaneous Works . . . London: 1850. V. 44

The Miscellaneous Works. London: 1853. V. 38

Miscellaneous Works, to which is Prefixed Memoirs of His Life and Writings. Edinburgh: 1809. V. 37

The Miscellaneous Works . . . with Memoirs of His Life and Writings, by Robert Anderson. Edinburgh: 1820. V. 37; 43

Novels. London: 1895. V. 38; 42

Novels. Oxford: 1925. V. 38

The Novels. Boston: 1926. V. 39; 41; 43; 44; 46

The Novels. Boston & New York: 1926. V. 45

Plays and Poems. London: 1777. V. 41; 42; 46

The Regicide. London: 1749. V. 37; 38; 42; 43

Samlede Skrivter. Copenhagen: 1833-34. V. 46

Select Essays on Commerce, Agriculture, Mines, Fisheries and Other Useful Subject. London: 1754. V. 41

Travels through France and Italy. London: 1766. V. 38; 41

Travels through France and Italy. London: 1778. V. 40

The Works. London: 1797. V. 42

Miscellaneous Works. With Memoirs of His Life and Writings by Robert Anderson. Edinburgh: 1806. V. 38

The Miscellaneous Works of . . . London: 1856. V. 39

The Works. London: 1884. V. 37

The Works. London: 1899. V. 38; 42

The Works. London: 1899-1901. V. 38; 39; 42

Works. New York: 1902. V. 38; 41

The Works. New York: 1905. V. 42

SMTIH, BRADLEY

Japan. A History of Art. New York: 1964. V. 37

SMUTS, M. M. S.

Anatomy of the Dromedary. Oxford: 1986. V. 37

SMYRL, FRANK H.

Unionism, Abolitionism and Vigilantism in Texas, 1856-1865. Houston. V. 39

SMYTH, ALBERT H.

The Writings of Benjamin Franklin. Collected and Edited with a Life and Introduction . . . New York: 1905-07. V. 37

SMYTH, ALEXANDER

Regulations for the Field Ercise, Manoeuvres and Conduct of the Infantry of the United States. Philadlephia: 1812. V. 37; 38; 42; 46

SMYTH, C. PIAZZI

Madeira Spectroscopic. Edingurgh: 1882. V. 38

Teneriffe, an Astronomer's Experiment. London: 1858. V. 37; 38; 40; 41; 42

Teneriffe, an Asatronomer's Experiment. London: 1858. V. 37

SMYTH, CHARLES PIAZZI

Life and Works at the Great Pyramid During the Months of January, February, March and April, 1865. Edinburgh: 1867. V. 46

SMYTH, CHARLES PIAZZI continued

Micrometrical Measures of Gaseos Spectra Under High Dispersion. Edinburgh: 1886. V. 40

Our Inheritance the Great Pyramid. London: 1864. V. 46

Report on the Teneriffe Astronomical Experiment of 1856. London: and Edinburgh: 1858. V. 45

SMYTH, COKE

Sketches in the Canada. Toronto: 1968. V. 45

SMYTH, ETHEL

Inordinate (?) Affection: a Story for Dog Lovers. London. V. 42

SMYTH, EUGENE LESLIE

The Missions of California. Chicago: 1899. V. 46

SMYTH, GEORGE LEWIS

Ireland, Historical and Statistical. London: 1844/1849. V. 37

SMYTH, HENRY DE WOLF

Atomic Energy for Military Purposes . . . Princeton: 1945. V. 43; 44

A General Account of the Development of Methods of Using Atomic Energy for Military Purposes Under the Auspices of the United States Government 1940-1945. London: 1945. V. 40

A General Account of the Development of Methods of Using Atomic Energy for Military Purposes Under the Auspcies of the United States Government 1940-1945. Washington: 1945. V. 38; 39; 40; 42; 43; 45

SMYTH, JAMES CARMICHAEL

A Description of the Jail Distemper, As It Appeared Amongs the Spanish Prisoners at Winchester in the Year 1780. London: 1795. V. 40; 42; 46

The Effect of the Nitrous Vapour in Preventing and Destroying Contagion . . . Philadelphia: 1799. V. 41; 44; 45; 46

SMYTH, JOHN FERDINAND DALZIEL

A Tour in the United States of North America. London: 1784. V. 38; 40; 42

SMYTH, PAUL

Thistles and Thorns: Abraham and Sarah at Bethel. Omaha: 1977. V. 44; 45

SMYTH, R. BROUGH

The Aborigines of Victoria. Melbourne: 1878. V. 41; 46

The Gold Fields and Mineral Districts of Victoria, with Notes on the Modes of Occurence of Gold and other Metals and Minerals. Melbourne;: 1869. V. 37

SMYTH, SAMUEL GORDON

A Genealogy of the Duke-Shepherd-Van Metre Family from Civil, Military, Church and Family Records and Documents. Lancaster: 1909. V. 42

SMYTH, THOMAS

The Character of the Late Thomas Chalmers, D.D., L.D. and the Lessons of His Life. Charleston: 1848. V. 46

SMYTH, WARINGTON W.

A Year with the Turks or Sketches of Travel in the European and Asiatic Dominions of the Sultan. New York: 1854. V. 40

SMYTH, WILLIAM

English Lyricks. Liverpool: 1798-1805. V. 43

Lectures on Modern History from the Irruption of the Northern Nations to the Close of the American Revolution . . . On the French Revolution. London: 1848. V. 38

Narrative of a Journey from Lima to Parma, Across the Andes and Down the Amazon . . . London: 1836. V. 38; 40; 42; 45

The New American Clerk's Instructor, Containing a Variety of Useful Precedents . . . and Many Other Instruments of Writing (etc.). Philadelphia: 1810. V. 45

SMYTH, WILLIAM HENRY

Aedes Hartwellianae, or Notices of the manor and Mansion of Hartwell. (with) Addenda. London: 1851, 1864. V. 37

The Cycle of Clestial Objects Coninued at the Hartwell Observatory to 1859 . . . London: 1860. V. 44

Descriptive Catalogue of a Cabinet of Roman Family Coins Belonging to His Grace the Duke of Northumberland. 1856. V. 38

Description of an Astrological Clock Belonging to the Society of Antiquaries. London: 1848. V. 40

Memoir Descriptive of the Resources, Inhabitants and Hydrography of Sicily and Its Islands. London: 1824. V. 39; 40; 42; 43

A Cycle of Celestial Objects . . . Observed, Reduced and Discussed. London: 1844. V. 40; 45

The Sailor's Word-Book: an Alphabetical Digest of Nautical Terms, Including Some More Especially Military and Scientific . . . London: 1867. V. 41

Sidereal Chromataics; Being a Re-print, with additions, from the 'Bedford Cycle of Celestial Objects,' and its 'Hartwell continuation' on the Colours of Multiple Stars. London: 1864. V. 37

SMYTHE, A. T., MRS.

South Carolina Women in the Confederacy. Columbia: 1903, 1907. V. 42

SMYTHE, CHARLES W.

Our Own Primary Grammar for the Use of Beginners. Greensborough, NC: 1861. V. 37

SMYTHE, CHARLES WINSLOW

Our Own School Grammar. Greensborough: 1862. V. 44

SMYTHE, F. S.

Over Tyrolese Hills. London: 1936. V. 39

The Valley of Flowers. London: 1938. V. 43

SMYTHE, G. W.

Views and Descriptions of the Late Volcanic Island Off the Coast of Sicily. London: 1831. V. 38; 40

SMYTHE, GLADYS

The Fairy Scales and Other Stories. London: 1915. V. 44; 46

SMYTHE, GONZALVO

Medical Heresies Historically Considered. Philadelphia: 1880. V. 42; 45

SMYTHE, HENRY

Historical Sketch of Parker County and Weatherford. St. Louis: 1877. V. 37; 43; 44

SMYTHE, SARAH M.

Ten Months in the Fiji Islands. Oxford: 1864. V. 41

SMYTHE, SARAH MARIA BLAND

Ten Months in the Fiji Islands. Oxford and London: 1864. V. 38; 39; 42; 46

SMYTHE, W. J.

Ten Months in the Fifi Islands. Oxford: 1864. V. 37

SMYTHE, WILLIAM E.

The Conquest of Arid America. New York: 1900. V. 39

SMYTHIES, B. E.

The Birds of Burma. London: 1953. V. 37; 38; 42; 43; 45

The Birds of Borneo. London: 1960. V. 37; 38; 42

SMYTHIES, BERTRAM E.

The Birds of Burma. Edinburgh: 1953. V. 39; 43

SMYTHIES, BERTRAM EVELYN

The Birds of Borneo. Edinburgh: 1968. V. 39; 46

The Birds of Borneo. London: 1968. V. 37

Birds of Burma. Rangoon: 1940. V. 43; 46

The Birds of Burma. 1953. V. 46

SMYTHIES, GORDON, MRS.

Left to Themselves. London: 1863. V. 41

SMYTHIES, MISS

Lucy Wellers Histoire. The Hague: 1766. V. 45

SMYTHIES, RAYMOND

Historical Records of the 40th (2nd Somersetshire) Regiment, now 1st Battalion The Prince of Wale's Volunteers (South Lancashire Regiment). From its Formation, in 1717 to 1893. Devonport: 1894. V. 37

SMYTHSON, HUGH

The Compleat Family Physician. London: 1781. V. 38

SNAFFLES

My Sketch Book in the Shiny. London. V. 37

SNAPE, ANDREW

The Anatomy of an Horse. London: 1683. V. 43

The Anatomy of an Horse. London: 1686. V. 43

SNEED, ACHILLES

To the People of Kentucky. Frankfort: 1825. V. 44

SNEL, WILLEBRORD

Descriptio Cometae, qui Anno 1618 Mense Novembri Primum Effulsit. Leiden: 1619. V. 46

SNELGROVE, DUDLEY

The Paul Mellon Collection: British Sporting and Animal Prints 1658-1874. 1981. V. 42

SNELL, GEORGE

The Right Teaching of Useful Knowledg, to Fit Scholars for Some Honest Profession . . . London: 1649. V. 40

SNELL, H. SAXON

Charitable and Parochial Establishments. London: 1881. V. 38

SNELL, HENRY JAMES

Practical Instructions in Enamel Painting on Glass, China Tiles, etc. London: 1890. V. 46

SNELL, JAMES P.

History of Hunterdon & Somerset Counties, N.J. Philadelphia: 1881. V. 41

History of Sussex and Warren Counties, N.J. Philadelphia: 1881. V. 41

SNELL, WILEBROD

Tiphys Batavus, Sive Histiodromice de Navium Cursibus . . . Leyden: 1624. V. 41

SNELL, WILLEBROD

De Re Nummaria. Liber Singularis. Leyden: 1613. V. 41

SNELL, WILLEBRORD

Tiphys Batavus, Sive Histiodromice, de Navium Cursibus, et re Navali. Leiden: 1624. V. 44

SNELLENBERG, TARQUIN

Practica auff das Jhar (sic) M.D. xli. Zu Ehren unnd wolfardt der lobelichen freihen keyserlichen Stadt Northusen . . . Erfurt: 1541. V. 44

SNELLING, THOMAS 1712-1773

The Doctrine of Gold and Silver Computations; in Which is included tht of the Par of Money . . . London: 1766. V. 38; 41

A View of the Silver Coin and Coinage of England, from the Norman Conquest to the Present Time. London: 1763. V. 43

SNELLING, W. J.

A Brief and Impartial History of the Life and Actions of Andrew Jackson. Boston: 1831. V. 41

The Polar Regions of the Western Continent Explored . . . Boston: 1831. V. 44

SNELLING, WILLIAM J.

Expose of the Vice of Gaming, As It Lately Existed in Massachusetts. Boston: 1833. V. 42

SNELLING, WILLIAM JOSEPH

Tales of the Northwest. Boston: 1830. V. 38; 40

SNEYD, PAMELA

Jac Urquhart's Daughter. London: 1882. V. 41

SNEYD, WALTER

Portraits of the Sprugins Family, Arranged by Richard Sucklethumkin Sprugins, Esq. s.l., s.n.: 1829. V. 38

SNEYD, WILLIAM

The Trials of the Rev. William Sneyd, for Seducing, Debauching, and Carrying off Mrs. Cecil . . . and Samuel Hawker, Esq. for Seducing and Debauching The Wife of Hooker Barrtealot, Esq. London: 1790? V. 37

SNIFT OF BRAZEN-NOSE, DEAN

A Pinch of Snuff. London: 1840. V. 37

SNODGRASS, ANTHONY

Early Greek Armour and Weapons from the End of the Bronze Age to 600 B.C. Edinburgh: 1964. V. 40; 42

SNODGRASS, W. D.

The Boy Made of Meat. Concord: 1983. V. 37; 40; 43

The Boy Made of Meat. Concord, N.H.: 1983. V. 37

Heart's Needle. New York: 1959. V. 37; 39; 40; 42; 45

If Birds Build with Your Hair. New York: 1979. V. 39; 41

Kinder Capers. New York: 1986. V. 41; 42; 46

To Shape a Song. New York: 1988. V. 41; 42

SNORRI STURLASON 1178-1241

Heims Kringla, Eller Snorre Sturlusons Nordlandske Konunga Sagor. Stockholm: 1697-1700. V. 40; 42

Heimskringla edr Noregs Konunga-Sogur . . . Havniae: 1777-78. V. 42

The Heimskringla, or, Chronicle of the Kings of Norway. London: 1844. V. 40

SNOUCK HURGRONJE, C.

Mekka. The Hague: 1888-89. V. 39

SNOW, BONNIE E.

The Theory and Practice of Color. New York: 1918. V. 38; 40

SNOW, C. P.

A Coat of Varnish. London: 1979. V. 46

Death Under Sail. London: 1931. V. 45

Last Things. London: 1970. V. 46

The Malcontents. London: 1972. V. 39; 46

The Sleep of Reason. London: 1968. V. 46

SNOW, EDGAR

Red Star Over China. London: 1937. V. 43

SNOW, ELIZA R.

Poems: Religious, Historical and Political. Volume I. Liverpool/London: 1856. V. 37

SNOW, ELLIOT

The Sea, The Ship and the Sailor. Salem: 1925. V. 44

SNOW, ERASTUS

One Year in Scandinavia: Results of The Gospel in Denmark and Sweden - Sketches and Observations on the Country and People - Remarkable Events - Late Persecutions and Present Aspect of Affairs. Liverpool: 1851. V. 37

SNOW, FLORENCE I.

The Lamp of Gold. Chicago: 1896. V. 38

SNOW, H. J.

In Forbidden Seas. Recollections of Sea-Other Hunting in the Kurils. New York/London: 1910. V. 37

SNOW, HEBERT

The Proclivity of Women to Cancerous Diseases and to Certain Benign Tumors. London: 1891. V. 45

SNOW, J.

The Shaggy Man of Oz. 1949. V. 37; 39

SNOW, LORENZO

The Italian Mission. London: 1851. V. 37; 42

The Voice of Joseph. Liverpool & London: 1852. V. 42

SNOW White and The Seven Dwarfs. Philadelphia: 1937. V. 37

SNOW, WILBERT

Before the Wind. New York: 1938. V. 39

SNOW, WILLIAM P.

Southern Generals, Their Lives and Campaigns. New York: 1866. V. 46

SNOW, WILLIAM PARKER

A Two Year's Cruise off Tierra Del Fuego, the Falkland Islands, Patagonia and in the River Plate. London: 1857. V. 38; 39; 40; 45; 46

SNOW, ZERUBBABEL

Communication of Attorney General Z. Snow in Response to a Vote of the House of Representatives of the Territorial Legislature. Salt Lake City: 1874. V. 42

SNOWDEN, JAMES ROSS

A Description of Anicent and Modern Coins in the Cabinet Collection of the Mint of the United States. Philadelphia: 1860. V. 43

SNOWDEN, RALPH LECONBY

The Magistrate's Assistant and Police Officer and Constable's Guide. London: 1846. V. 43

SNOWDEN, RICHARD

The American Revolution Written in Scriptural or Ancient Historical Style. (with) The Columbiad; or a Poem of the American War in Thirteen Cantos. Baltimore: 1802. V. 40; 46

The History of North and South America. Philadelphia: 1819. V. 40

SNOWDEN, YATES

History of South Carolina. Chicago: 1920. V. 40

SNOWMAN, A. K.

The Art of Carl Faberge. Greenwich: 1964. V. 37

SNOWMAN, A. KENNETH

The Art of Carl Faberge. Boston. V. 42

The Art of Carl Faberge. London: 1953. V. 45

Eighteenth Century Gold Boxes of Europe. Boston: 1966. V. 39; 41; 42

Eighteenth century Gold Boxes of Europe. London: 1966. V. 38; 40; 42; 46

SNYDER, GARY

All In the Family. 1975. V. 39

The Back Country. London: 1967. V. 41; 45

The Blue Sky. New York: 1969. V. 39; 46

The Fates of Rocks and Trees. San Francisco: 1986. V. 39; 42; 44

The Fudo Trilogy. 1973. V. 39

The Fudo Trilogy. Berkeley: 1973. V. 42

SNYDER, GARY continued

Good Wild Sacred. Madley: 1984. V. 40; 42

Myths and Texts. New York: 1960. V. 45

Rip Rap. Ashland: 1959. V. 37; 39; 42

Riprap. 1959. V. 42

Six Sections from Mountains and Rivers Without End. London: 1967. V. 45

Tree Song. San Francisco: 1986. V. 39; 42

True Night. N. San Juan: 1980. V. 38

SNYDER, JOSEPH B.

Supplement to Ezra E. Eby's Biographical History of Early Settlers and Their Descendants in Waterloo County. Waterloo: 1931. V. 42

SOAMES, HENRY 1785-1860

The History of the Reformation of the Church of England. London: 1826-28. V. 39

SOANE, GEORGE

Rob Roy, the Gregarach. London: 1818. V. 39

SOANE, JOHN

Description of the House and Museum on the North Side of Lincoln's Inn Fields, the Residence of Sir John Soane. (with) Description de la Maison et du Musee . . . London. V. 38

Description of the House and Museum on the North Side of Lincoln's Inn Fields, the Residence of Sir John Soane. London: 1830. V. 38

Description of the House and Museum on the North Side of Lincoln's Inn Fields, the Residence of Sir John Soane. London: 1835. V. 38

Designs in Architecture; Consisting of Plans, Elevantions and Sections, for Temples, Baths, Cassines, Pavilions, Garden-Seats, Obelisks and Other Buildings (etc.). London: 1778. V. 38

Designs for Public and Private Buildings. London: 1828. V. 41

Lectures on Architecture as Delivered from 1809 to 1836 . . . London: 1929. V. 42

Plans, Elevations and Sections of Buildings Executed in the Counties of Norfolk Suffolk Yorkshire Staffordshire Warwickshire Hertfordshire at Cetera. London: 1788. V. 38; 42

Sketches in Architecture Containing Plans and Elevations of Cottages-Villa and Other Useful Buildings with Characteristic Scenery. London: 1798. V. 42

Sketches in Architecture . . . London: 1798. V. 41

SOAR, C. D.

The British Hydracarina. London: 1925-29. V. 37; 38

SOARES, GUSTAVE DE MIRELLES

Sketches on the Wing. London: 1870. V. 42

SOAVE, FRANCESCO

Novelle Morali . . . Colla Spiegazione Inglese di Vari Idiomi e Frasi Che in Esse s'Incontranto. Chelsea, London: 1799. V. 45

SOBIESKI, JOHN

Lays of the Deer Forest. Edinburgh: 1848. V. 39; 40; 43; 46

The Life Story and Personal Reminiscences of . . . Shelbyville: 1900. V. 44

The Life Story and Personal Reminiscences of Col. John Sobieski. Los Angeles: 1907. V. 40; 42

SOBY, JAMES THRALL

Ben Shahn: Paintings: His Graphic Work. New York: 1963. V. 39

The Early Chirico. New York: 1941. V. 46

Giorgio de Chirico. New York: 1955. V. 39

The Prints of Paul Klee. New York: 1945. V. 42

Salvador Dali. 1946. V. 46

SOCCINO, FAUSTO

Amicos Apistolae. In Quibus Variae de Rebus Divinis Quastiones Expediuntur, Multaque Sacrarum Litterarum Loca Explanatur. Rakow: 1618. V. 39

THE SOCIALISTS, a Society of Beasts . . . Important and Interesting Proposal: Addressed to Robert Owen, Esq . . . Edinburgh: 1840? V. 41

SOCIETE DE LA GRAVURE SUR BOIS ORIGINALE

Imagier de la Societe de la Gravure sur Bois Originale. Pris: 1920-29. V. 38

SOCIETY FOR BETTERING THE CONDITION OF THE POOR

Of the Education of the Poor; Being the First Part of a Digest of the Reports of the Society for Bettering the Condition of the Poor . . . London: 1809. V. 43

Report of the Society for Bettering and Condition of the Poor in the Hundred of Oswestry, and Parishes of Chirk and Llansilin. Oswestry: 1813. V. 38

SOCIETY FOR CONSTITUTIONAL INFORMATION

Tracts Published and Distributed by the Society . . . with a Design to Convey to the Minds of the People a Knowledge of Their Rights. London: 1783. V. 39

SOCIETY FOR PHILOSOPHICAL EXPERIMENTS AND CONVERSATIONS

Minutes of . . . London: 1795. V. 41

SOCIETY FOR PURE ENGLISH

Tracts I-XL. Oxford: 1919-34. V. 41; 45

SOCIETY FOR THE PROPAGATION OF CHRISTIAN KNOWLEDGE

State of the Society . . . in Scotland . . . Giving a brief Account of the Condition of the Highlands and Islands of Scotland. V. 40

SOCIETY FOR THE PROTECTION OF ANCIENT BUILDINGS

Six Annual Reports of the Committee. London: 1878-1914. V. 38

First, Second and Third Annual Reports. London: 1878-80. V. 45

SOCIETY OF ARTISTS OF GREAT BRITAIN

A Catalogue of the Pictures, Sculptures, Models, Drawings, Prints & Exhibited by the Society of Artists in Great Britain, at the Great Room in Spring Garden, Charing Cross, May the 9th 1761. London: 1761. V. 46

SOCIETY OF BEAUX-ARTS

Winning Designs 1904-1927 Paris Prize in Architecture. New York: 1928. V. 39

SOCIETY OF CALIFORNIA PIONEERS

Cermonies at the Laying of the Corner Stone of the New Pioneer Hall, July 7th, 1862. San Francisco: 1862. V. 37; 45

Quarterly. San Francisco: 1924-1933. V. 41

SOCIETY OF CONSTABLES OF EDINBURGH

Instructions and Regulations . . . N.P.,: 1786. V. 38

SOCIETY OF DILETTANTI

Historical Notices of the . . . London: 1855. V. 45

Ionian Antiquities. London: 1769. V. 39

The Unedited Antiquities of Attica. London: 1817. V. 39; 44

SOCIETY OF FRIENDS

A Brief Account of the Proceedings of the Committee Appointed in the Year 1795 by the Yearling Meeting of Friends of Pennsylvania, New Jersey, &c. for Promoting the Improvement and Gradual Civilization of the Indian Natives. Philadelphia: 1805. V. 45

SOCIETY OF GENTLEMEN

The Complete Farmer; or, a General Dictionary of Husbandry. London: 1766. V. 38; 41

SOCIETY OF GUARDIANS FOR THE PROTECTION OF TRADE

A List of the Members of the Society of Guardians, for the Protection of Trade, Against Swindlers and Sharpers. Established, March 25th, 1776. London: 1814. V. 39

SOCIETY OF ICONOPHILES

Catalogue of the Engravings Issued by the Society of Iconophiles of the City of New York. New York: 1908. V. 40

SOCIETY OF MAYFLOWER DESCENDANTS IN THE STATE OF CALIFORNIA

Register of the . . . : a Record of Descent from Passengers on the Good Ship 'Mayflower'. San Francisco: 1917. V. 43

SOCIETY OF PRIVATE PRINTERS

Chap-Books, 1982-1986. V.P.: 1982-86. V. 38

SOCIETY of Sherwood Archers, Established in June, 1838. Mansfield: 1848. V. 39

SOCIVIZCA, STANISLAO

The Life and Extraordinary Adventures of . . . London: 1779. V. 40

SODDY, FREDERICK

The Evolution of Mattaer as Revealed by the Radio-Active Elements. Manchester: 1904. V. 37

The Interpretation of Radium. London: 1909. V. 43; 44; 45

SOEMMERING, SAMUEL THOMAS

Abbildungen des Menschlichen Auges. Frankfurt a.M.: 1801. V. 40

De Basi Encephali et Originibus Nervorum Cranio Egredientium . . . Gottingen: 1778. V. 40

SOEMMERING, DETMAR WILHELM 1793-1871

Beobachtungen uber die Organischen Veranderungen im Auge nach Staaroperationen. Frankfurt: 1828. V. 42

SOEMMERING, SAMUEL THOMAS VON

Description Figuree de l'Oeil Humain . . . Paris: 1818. V. 45

Icones Oculi Humani. V. 44

Icones Organorum Humanorum Gustus et Vocis. Frankfurt: 1808. V. 45

SOESKI, MUSO

Sun at Midnight. 1985. V. 40

SOESMAN, ELEASAR

(Hebrew title, then) De Bruidschat Israels of Onderwys der Hebreeuwsche Spraak-Kunst. Amsterdam: 1741. V. 46

SOLA, A. E.

Ironmonger. Klondyke: Truth and Facts of the New El Dorado. London: 1897. V. 37; 40

SOLA, A. E. IRONMONGER

Ironmonger. Klondyke: Truth and Facts of the New El Dorado. London: (c. 1897). V. 37

THE SOLDIER'S Wife. Atlanta: 1862. V. 44

SOLDINI, FRANCESCO MARIA

De Anima Brutorum Commentaria. Florence: 1776. V. 45

SOLE, WILLIAM

Menthae Britanicae. Bath: 1798. V. 38; 40; 46

SOLEM, A.

Endodontoid Land Snails from Pacific Islands. Chicago: 1976-86. V. 37
Endodontoid Land Snails from Pacific Islands. Chicago: 1976-86. V. 37

A SOLEMN Exhortation Made and Published to the Several Churches of Christ Within This Province of Lanceaster . . . London: 1649. V. 42

THE SOLEMN Mock Procession of the Pope Cardinalls Jesuits Fryers &c. Through the City of London November the 17th 1680. London: 1680. V. 41

SOLERI, PAOLO

Arcology: the City in the Image of Man. Cambridge: 1969. V. 39; 42; 43; 46
Arcology: the City in the Image of Man. Cambridge: London: 1969. V. 41

SOLEY, JAMES RUSSELL

The Blockade and the Cruisers. New York: 1883. V. 45

SOLIDAY, GEORGE W.

A Descriptive List & Title Index of 7500 Items of Western Americana of the Library of George W. Soliday. New York: 1960. V. 37; 39

THE SOLIDER'S Hymn Book. Charleston: 1863. V. 44

SOLIER, CHARLES

Chagall's Posters: a Catalogue Raisonne. New York: 1975. V. 46

SOLINGEN, CORNELIS

Alle de Medicinale en Chirurgicale Werken Mitsgaders Embryulcia Vera . . . Amsterdam: 1698. V. 37

SOLINUS, GAIUS JULIUS

De Memoralibus mundi; De Mirabilia Romae. Venetiis: 1491. V. 38

SOLIS-COHEN, J.

Diseases of the Throat: a Guide to the Diagnois and Treatment of Affections of the Pharaynx, Esophagus, Trachea, Larynx and Nares. New York: 1872. V. 42
Inhalation in the Treatment of Disease: Its Therapeutics and Practice. Philadelphia: 1876. V. 42

SOLIS, VIRGIL

Drinking-Cups Vases Ewers and Ornaments Designed for the Use of Gold and Silversmiths. London: 1862. V. 38

SOLIS Y RIBADENEYRA, ANTONIO DE

Histoire de la Conquete du Mexique, ou la Nouvelle Espagne, par Fernand Cortez. Paris: 1759. V. 39
Historia De La Conquista de Mexico, Poblacion Y Pr Gressos de la America Septentrional, Conocida por el Nombre de Nueva Espana. Barcelona: 1691. V. 38
Historia de la Conquista de Mexico. Madrid: 1684. V. 42
The Conquest of Mexico by the Spaniards. London: 1724. V. 38; 41; 42; 45
The History of the Conquest of Mexico by the Spaniards. Dublin: 1727. V. 42
The History of the Conquest of Mexico by the Spaniards. London: 1738. V. 39
The History of the Conquest of Mexico by the Spaniards. London: 1753. V. 42

THE SOLITARY Frenchman on the Banks of the Thames, to a Friend in Switzerland. London: 1794. V. 41

SOLL, IVAN

Carpe Diem. Madison: 1989. V. 41; 45
Tryangulations. Madison: 1991. V. 46

SOLLE, HENRI FRANCOIS DE LA

Memoirs of a Man of Pleasure, or the Adventures of Versorand . . . London: 1751. V. 42

SOLLEYSELL, JACQUES DE

The Compleat Horseman. London: 1702. V. 38

SOLLEYSELL, SIEUR DE

The Compleat Horseman, or Perfect Farrier. London: 1729. V. 42

SOLLY, HENRY

James Woodford, Carpenter and Chartist. London: 1881. V. 41
Lady Stella and Her Lover. London: 1888. V. 42

SOLLY, N. NEAL

Memoir of the Life of David Cox. London: 1873. V. 40; 46
Memoir of the Life of William James Muller, a Native of Birstol, Landscape and Figure Painter, with Original Letters and an Account of His Travels of His Principal Works. London: 1875. V. 39; 45

SOLLY, S. EDWIN

Manitou, Colorado, U.S.A., Its Mineral Waters and Climate. St. Louis: 1875. V. 37

SOLLY, SAMUEL

The Human Brain, Its Configuration, Structure, Development and Physiology. London: 1836. V. 42
Surgical Experiences. London: 1865. V. 37; 38; 39

SOLMS-BRAUNFELS, CARL, PRINCE OF

Texas 1844-1845. 1936. V. 42; 44

SOLMS-BRAUNFELS, PRINCE CARL OF

Texas 1844-1845. Houston: 1936. V. 37

SOLOMON, ALAN

New York: The Art Scene. New York: 1967. V. 46

SOLOMON, S. J.

Strategic Camouflage. London: 1920. V. 44

SOLOMON, SIMEON

A Vision of Love Revealed in Sleep. London: 1871. V. 42

SOLOMON, SOLOMON J.

Strategic Camoflage. London: 1920. V. 46

SOLON, L. M.

The Art of the Old English Potter. London: 1883. V. 45
The Art of the Old English Potter. London: 1885. V. 37

SOLON, LOUIS MARC EMMANUEL 1835-1913

The Art of the Old English Potter. London: 1855. V. 42
A Brief History of Old English Porcelain. London: 1903. V. 38; 40; 42
Ceramic Literature: an Analytical Index to the Works . . . London: 1910. V. 42
A History and Description of Italian Magolica. London: 1907. V. 41; 42

SOLON, M. L.

A History and Description of the Old French Faience . . . London: 1903. V. 41

SOLORZANO PEREIRA, JUAN DE 1575-1655

Disputationum de Indiarum Iure sive de Justa Indiarum Occidentalium Inquisitione, Acquisitione et Retentione Tribus Libris. Madrid: 1629. V. 40
Emblemata Centum, Regio Politica. Madrid: 1653. V. 37
Obras Posthumas. Zaragoza: 1676. V. 38
Politica Indiana, Sacada en Legnus Castellana de los dos Tomos del Derecho 1 Govierno Municipal de las Indias Occidentales . . . Madrid: 1647. V. 40

SOLORZANO Y PEREIRA, JUAN DE

Politica Indiana. Madrid: 1776. V. 38

SOLTAU, G. W.

Trout Flies of Devon and Cornwall. London: 1847. V. 39

SOLVYNS, FRANS BALTASAR

A Collection of Two Hundred and Fifty Colored Etchings: Descriptive of the Manners, Customs and Dresses of the Hindoos. Calcutta: 1799. V. 39

SOLZHENITSYN, ALEKSANDER

August 1914. Paris: 1971. V. 39
August 1914. New York: 1987. V. 37; 43
August 1914. 1989. V. 42
From Under the Rubble. Boston: 1975. V. 42; 43
The Gulag Archipelago. Paris: 1973. V. 39

SOLZHENITSYN, ALEKSANDER continued

Stories and Prose Poems. New York: 1971. V. 43

SOLZHENITSYN, ALEKSANDR

August 1914: the Red Wheel/Knot I. New York: 1989. V. 41; 42; 46
A World Split Apart. New York: 1978. V. 45

SOMADEVA BAHATTA

The Ocean of Story. London: 1924-28. V. 42; 44; 46

SOMADEVA BHATTA

The Ocean of Story. London: 1924. V. 38; 40

SOMASCHO, GIOCAMO ANTONIO

Nova Esposizione de Recami et Dessegni. Venice: 1600. V. 41

SOME Account of Belair, Also of the City of Sanford, Florida, with a Brief Sketch of Their Founder. Sanford: 1889. V. 41

SOME Account of London. London: 1791. V. 41

SOME Account of Suffragan Bishops in England. London: 1785. V. 41

SOME Account of the Ancient Monuments in the Priory Church Abergavenny. Newport: 1872. V. 46

SOME Account of the Ancient Priory of Grosmont, in the Vale of Esk, Near Whitby. N.P.: 1839. V. 41

SOME Account of the Antiquities of Hawkstone. Shrewsbury: 1835. V. 37

SOME Account of the Blackmoe Museum Salisbury. The Opening Meeting. Devizes & London: 1868. V. 37

SOME Account of the Conduct of the Religious Society of Friends towards the Indian Tribes in the Settlement of the Colonies of East and West Jersey and Pennsylvania; with a Brief Narrative of their Labours; for the . . . London: 1844. V. 37; 38; 41; 43; 46

SOME Account of the Family of the Butlers, But More Particularly of the Late Duke of Ormond, the Earl of Offory His Father, and James Duke of Ormond His Grandfather. London: 1716. V. 44; 46

SOME Account of the Life and Religious Labours of Sarah Grubb . . . Wilmington: 1795. V. 41

SOME Account of the Medical School in Boston and of the Massachusetts General Hospital. Boston: 1824. V. 45

SOME Account of Thomas Paine, In His Last Sickness. New York: 1820. V. 38

SOME Brief Particulars Regarding the Arrival of the Marquis of Douglas and His Illustrious Bridge . . . at Hamilton Place. Glasgow: 1843. V. 40

SOME British Ballads. New York. V. 43
SOME British Ballads. London: 1919. V. 39; 40; 42; 44

SOME Considerations Humbly Offered to the Publick, Concerning the Revenue of the Customs. London: 1752. V. 41

SOME Considerations on the Game Laws, and the Present Practice in Exercising Them. London: 1754. V. 39

SOME Doubts Occasioned by the Second Volume of an Estimate of the Manners and Principles of the Times. London: 1758. V. 42

SOME Early American Hunters. New York: 1928. V. 39; 41

SOME Examples of the Work of American Designers. Philadelphia: (1918). V. 37

SOME Favorites. San Francisco: 1926. V. 39

SOME Further Considerations on the Trade of Scotland with France. In Three Lettes from the Most Considerable Merchants in Scotland. To which is added, the French King's Edict 1701, Which Now Must Be the Rule of Trade. Edinburgh: 1713. V. 38

SOME Like Them Dead. London: 1960. V. 40

SOME New Light on the Genesis of the Ampersand. New York: 1936. V. 45

SOME Observations on the Assiento Trade, As It Has Been Exercised by the South-Sea Company; Proving the Damage, Which Will Accrue Thereby to the British Commerce and Plantations in America and Particularly to Jamaica. London: 1728. V. 37; 41

SOME Observations Relating to the Establishment of Schools. Philadelphia: 1778. V. 42

SOME Observations Upon the Late Tryals of Sir George Wakeman, Corker and Marshall &c. London: 1679. V. 41; 42

SOME Particulars of the Royal Indisposition of 1788-1789 and Of Its Effects Upon Illustrious Personages and Opposite Parties Interested by It. London: 1804. V. 39

SOME Queries, Which May Deserve Consideration. London: 1701. V. 46

SOME Remarks on a Society, Called the Prctical Society, Lately Established in Edinburgh. Edinburgh?: 1821. V. 38

SOME Replies to the Letter of the Committee in Commemoration of A. Growoll's Fifty Years of Service to the American Book Trade. N.P.: 1908. V. 39

SOME Rules for Speaking and Action; To Be Observed at the Bar, in the Pulpit, and the Senate, and by Every One that Speaks in Publick. London: 1716. V. 39

SOME Rules for the Conduct of Life: to which are added, a few cautions, for use of such Freemen of London, as take apprentices. (London: c. 1775). V. 37

SOME Saunterings in the Land of Lakes . . . St. Paul: 1882. V. 37

SOME Seasonable and Important Queries Earnestly Recommended to the Serious Consideration of Divines and Lawyers. London: 1718-19. V. 45

SOME Southwestern Trails. El Paso: 1948. V. 42

SOME Thoughts Humbly Submitted to the Consideration of the Barons, Freeholders and Burgesses of Scotland: Before they Proceed to the Election of Members to Represent Them in the Ensuing Parliament. Edinburgh?: 1722. V. 45

SOME Thoughts on the Constitution; Particularly with Respect to the Power of Making Peace and War . . . London: 1748. V. 41

SOME Thoughts on the Land Forces, Kept in this Kingdom. London: 1739. V. 43

SOME Thoughts on the Nature of Paper Credit, Relative to the Late Failures of Bankers and Receivers in Ireland. Dublin: 1759. V. 40

SOME Thoughts on the Present State of Our Trade to India. London: 1754. V. 43

SOME Transactions Between the Indians and Friends in Pennsylvania in 1791 & 1792. London: 1792. V. 37; 38; 42

SOMERS, JOHN

A collection of Scarce and Valuable Tracts, of the Most Interesting and Entertaining Subjects. London: 1810-14. V. 39; 42

Jura Populi Anglicani; or the Subject's Right of Petitioning Set Forth. London: 1701. V. 46

Jus Regium: or, the King's Right to Grant Forfeitures, and Other Revenues of the Crown . . . London: 1701. V. 45

SOMERS, JOHN, 1ST BARON 1651-1716

A Collection of Scarce and Valuable Tracts, on the Most Interesting and Entertaiing Subjects. London: 1809-1815. V. 40

Jura Populi Anglicani; or the Subject's Right of Petitioning Set Forth. London: 1701. V. 40

The True Secret History of the Lives and Regins of all the Kings and Queens of England, from King William the First, Called the Conquerour. London: 1702. V. 37; 41

SOMERTON, WILLIAM HENRY

A Narrative of the Bristol Riots, on the 29th, 30th and 31st of October, 1831. Bristol: 1831. V. 46

SOMERVELL, JOHN

Water-Power Mills of South Westmorland on the Kent, Bela and Gilpin and Their Tributaries. Kendal: 1930. V. 41

Water-Power Mills of South Westmorland, on the Kent, Bela and Gilpin and Their Tributaries. London: 1930. V. 38

SOMERVILE, WILLIAM

The Chase. London: 1735. V. 37

SOMERVILLE, ALEXANDER 1811-1885

The Autobiography of a Working Man, by 'One Who Has Whistled at the Plough.' London: 1848. V. 39

The Whistler at the Plough. Manchester: 1852. V. 39; 42

SOMERVILLE, EDITH OE.

ABC of Fox Hunting. London: 1903. V. 37

Beggars on Horseback. Edinburgh: 1895. V. 38; 44

Beggars on Horseback. (With numerous illustrations by E. OE. SOmerville). Edinburgh/London: 1895. V. 37

Dan Russell the Fox. London: 1911. V. 37; 41

Dan Russell the Fox: an Episode in the Life of Miss Rowan. London: 1911. V. 44

An Enthusiast. London: 1921. V. 42

Further Experiences of an Irish R.M. London: 1908. V. 40; 41; 43

SOMERVILLE, EDITH OE. continued

In the Vine Country. London: 1893. V. 38; 44

Irish Memories. London: 1917. V. 38; 46

Mount Music. London: 1919. V. 44

A Patrick's Day Hunt. Westminster. V. 38

A Patrick's Day Hunt. London: 1902. V. 42

The Real Charlotte. London: 1894. V. 38

Slipper's ABC of Fox Hunting. London: 1903. V. 38

Some Experiences of an Irish R.M. London: 1899. V. 44

Some Irish Yesterdays. London: 1906. V. 44

The States through Eyes . . . Boston: 1930. V. 39

Through Connemara in Governess Cart. London: 1893. V. 38

Through Connemara in a Governess Cart. London: 1893/1892. V. 44

SOMERVILLE, H.

Madness in Shakesperian Tragedy. London: 1929. V. 43

SOMERVILLE, ROBERT

General View of the Agriculture of East Lothian. London: 1805. V. 44

SOMERVILLE, THOMAS 1741-1830

The History of Political Transactions and of Parties from the Restoration of King Charles Ii to the Death of King William. London: 1792. V. 37; 38; 41; 43

SOMERVILLE, WILLIAM 1675-1742

The Chace. London: 1735. V. 37; 38; 39; 40; 41; 42; 43; 45; 46

The Chace. a Poem. Hobbino, or the Rural Games. London: 1757. V. 43

The Chace. London: 1767. V. 43

The Chase, a Pome. London: 1800. V. 41

The Chase. London: 1802. V. 38; 39; 40; 41; 43; 44; 45

The Chace: a Poem. New York: 1929. V. 40

The Chase, a Poem. To Which is added Hobbinol, or the Rural Games. Birmingham: 1767. V. 38; 39; 40; 46

The Chase. London: 1796. V. 37; 38

The Chase, a Poem. London: 1804. V. 46

Field Sports. A Poem. London: 1742. V. 38; 40; 43; 45

Hobbinol, or Rural Games. London: 1740. V. 38; 46

Hobbinol, or Rural Games. (with) The Chace. London: 1740; 1743. V. 39

Hobbinol, Field Sports, and the Bowling Green. London: 1813. V. 38; 44

Occasional Poems, Translations, Fables, Tales. London: 1727. V. 38; 39; 41; 45; 46

SOMES, JOHN J.

The Gloucester Fire Department. Its History and Work from 1793-1893. Gloucester: 1892. V. 38

SOMETHING for the Children, or Uncle John's Story of His First Visit to the Centennial. Philadelphia: 1876. V. 40

SOMIS, IGNAZIO

An Historical Narrative of a Most Extraordinary Event Which Happened at the Village of Bergemoletto in Italy . . . London: 1765. V. 42

SOMMERFELDT, HAKON A.

Atals to the Elementary and Practical Principles of the Construction of Ships for Ocean and River Service. London: 1861. V. 37

SOMMERFIELD, ARNOLD

Lectures on Theoretical Physics. New York: 1950-56. V. 40

SOMMERO, FABIANO

De Inventione, Descriptione, Temperie, Viribus, et in Primis Usu, Thermarum D. Caroli III. Imperatoris. Lipsie: 1571. V. 38

SOMMERS, JOHN S., BARON

The Judgment of Whole Kingdoms and Nations, Concerning the Rights, Power and Prerogative of Kings, and the Rights, Privileges and Properties of the People . . . Philadelphia: 1773. V. 38; 44

SOMMERVILLE, MAXWELL

Engraved Gems: Their History and an Elaborate View of Their Place in Art. Philadelphia: 1889. V. 40; 44

SOMMIERES, L. C. VIALLE DE

Travels in Montenegro. London: 1820. V. 39

SOMNER, W.

The Antiquities of Canterbury. London: 1703. V. 42

SOMNER, WILLIAM

Julii Caesaris Portus Iccius Illustratus. Oxonii: 1694. V. 46

A Treatise of Gavelkind, Both Name and Thing . . . London: 1660. V. 38

A Treatise of the Roman Ports and Forts in Kent. Oxford: 1693. V. 38; 46

A Treatise of Gavelkind, Both Name and Thing. London: 1726. V. 40; 42

SONDES, GEORGE

Authentic Memorials of Remarkable Occurences and Affecting Calamtities in the Family of Sir George Sondes, Bart. Evesham: 1790. V. 43

Authentic Memorials of Remarkable Occurences and Affecting Calamities in the Family of Sir George Sondes, Bart. London: 1790. V. 46

SONDHEIM, STEPHEN

Sunday in the Park. New York: 1986. V. 46

SONETTI E Canzoni di Diversi Antichi Aautori Toscani. Florence: 1527. V. 37; 38

A SONG for the Ladies. New Orleans: 1863. V. 39

A SONG in Favor of Bundling. Leicester: 1960-61. V. 37
A SONG in Favor of Bundling. Leicester: 1961. V. 46

A SONG in Favour of Bundling. Leicester: 1916. V. 44

THE SONG of Roland. Translated by Isabel Butler. Cambridge: (1906). V. 37

A SONG to the Tune of Auld Lang Syne. Edinburgh?: 1746? V. 41
A SONG to the Tune of Auld Lang Syne. N.P.: 1746? V. 40

SONGBIRDS I. Williamsburg: 1983. V. 44

SONGS, Duets and Choruses, in the Pantomimical Drama of Obi, or, Three Fingered Jack: Invented by Mr. Fawcett, and Perform'd at the Theatre Royal, Crow Street. Dublin: 1800. V. 46

SONGS from Shakespeare's Plays. Verona: 1974. V. 41; 43

SONGS In the New Opera of Tit for Tat; or, the Cadi Gull'd. Dublin: 1766. V. 45

THE SONGS, Italian and English, Together with a Catalogue of the Instrumental Music; Performed at the Musical Festival at Salisbury, on Friday 25, 1769. Salisbury: 1769. V. 43

SONGS of the Chace, &c . . . . London: 1811. V. 46

SONGS to Our Lady of Silence. London: 1921. V. 37

SONN, ALBERT H.

Early American Wrough Iron. New York: 1928. V. 38; 42

SONNERAT, PIERRE

Voyage a la Nouvelle Guince, Dans Lequel on Trouve la Description des Lieux, des Observations Physiques & Morales & des Details Relatifs a l'Histoire Naturelle deans le Regne Animal & la Regne Vegetal . . . Paris: 1776. V. 44

Voyage Aux Indes Orientales et a La Chine. Paris: 1782. V. 41; 45

SONNETS. Munich: 1931. V. 45

SONNICHSEN, C. L.

Billy King's Tombstone. The Private Life of an Arizona Boom Town. Caldwell: 1942. V. 41

The El Paso Salt War of 1877. El Paso: 1961. V. 39

El Paso Salt War (1877). Pass of the North: 1961. V. 45

Pass of the North: Four Centuries on the Rio Grande. El Paso: 1968. V. 37

SONNINI, C. S.

Travels in Upper and Lower Egypt: Undertaken by Order of the Old Government of France. London: 1799. V. 40; 42; 46

Travels in Upper and Lower Egypt, Undertaken by Order of the Old Government of France . . . London: 1800. V. 37; 41; 45

THE SONS of Liberty, in 1776, and in 1856. New York: 1856. V. 40

SONTE, WILLIAM LEETE

Ups and Downs in the Life of a Distressed Gentleman. New York: 1836. V. 43

SOPHOCLES 496-406 BC

Antigone. Marseilles: 1935. V. 45

Antigone. Haarlem: 1975. V. 43

Antigone. 1978. V. 45

Antigone. Greenbrae: 1978. V. 41; 46

(Greek) Tragodiai . . . Demetriou tou Trikliniou Peri Metron hois Echresato Sophokles . . . Scholia. Paris: 1552. V. 37

King Oedipus. New York: 1968. V. 38

Oedipus. Berlin: 1919. V. 37

Oedipus the King. New York: 1955. V. 38; 44; 46

The Plays and Fragments, with Critical Notes. Cambridge: 1873-94. V. 39

Sochoclis Tragaediae Septem cum Commentariis. (Greek). Venetiis: 1502. V. 38

Sophoclis Trageodiae Septem . . . Oxford: 1836. V. 41

The Tragedies of Sophocles, Translated from the Greek. London: 1729. V. 41

SOPHOCLES 496-406 BC continued

Tragedies. Glasgow: 1745. V. 39

The Tragedies of Sophocles. London: 1759. V. 38

The Tragedies. London: 1766. V. 41

The Tragedies of Sophocles. London: 1788. V. 41

Tragoediae Omnes, Nvnc Primum Latinae ad Uerbum Factae, ac Scholijs Quibusdam, Illustratae, Ioanne Baptista Gabia Interprete. Venice: 1543. V. 40

Tragoediae Septem. Frankfurt: 1544. V. 40

(Greek title: then) Tragoediae Septem. Geneva: 1568. V. 43

Tragoediae, Nova Versione Donatae, Scholiisque Veteribus. London: 1737/46. V. 43

Tragedies. Glasgow: 1745. V. 40

Tragoediae Superstites. (Greek). London: 1846. V. 40

SOPHRONIA or Letters to the Ladies. Dublin: 1762. V. 40

SOPRANI, RAFFAELE

Le Vite de Pittori, Scoltori, et Architetti Genovesi, e de Forastieri, che in Genoua Operarono . . . Genova: 1674. V. 40

SOPWITH, THOMAS

An Account of the Mining Districts of Alston Moor, Weardale and Teesdale, in Cumberland and Durham. Alnwick: 1833. V. 45

A Treatise on Isometrical Drawing, as Applicable to Geological and Mining Plans . . . Ornamental Grounds . . . Buildings and Machinery . . . London: 1838. V. 40; 43

SORANZO, LAZARO

L'Ottomano . . . Ferrra: 1598. V. 38

SORBIERE, SAMUEL

Relations, Lettres, Discovrs svr Diverses Matieres Curieux. Paris: 1660. V. 37

SORBY, H. CLIFTON

Papers and Monographs. London: 1851-1908. V. 44

SORCHO, LEWIS

Captain Lewis Sorcho's Great Deep Sea Divers, the Most Scientific, Instructive and Interesting Entertainment on Earth. Cincinnati: 1899. V. 41

SORCHO, LOUIS

Life and Adventures of Frances Namon Sorcho. The Only Woman Deep Sea Diver in the World. Philadelphia: 1888. V. 37

SOREDD, CURTIUS

One Hundred and Thirty Quatrains by . . . Pasadena: 1928. V. 39

SOREL, CHARLES

La Bibliotheque Francoise . . . ou Le Choix et l'Examen des Livres Francois qui Traitent de l'Eloquence, de la Philosophie, de la Devotion, et de la Conduite des Moeurs . . . Paris: 1667. V. 37; 38; 45

The Comical History of Francion. London: 1703. V. 40

The Extravagant Shepherd . . . London: 1660. V. 38

The Extravagant Shepherd: or, the History of the Shepherd Lysis. An Anti-Romance; written originally in French, and now made English. London: 1654. V. 37

SORELL, WALTER

The Story of the Human Mind. Indianapolis: 1967. V. 42

SORELLI, GUIDO

La Peste, Poema . . . The Plague a Poem. London: 1834. V. 40

SORENSON, AL

Hands Up, the History of a Crime. College Station: 1982. V. 42

SORENSON, THEODORE C.

Kennedy. New York: 1965. V. 37

SORGE, ERNST

With 'Plane, Boat and Camera in Greenland. London: 1936. V. 40

With 'Plane, Boat and Camera in Greenland. New York: 1936. V. 42

With 'Plane, Boat and Camera in Greenland. New York & London: 1936. V. 42

SORIA, BONAVENTURA

Abrege de la Vie de . . . Marie Terese D'Austriche, Reyne de France & de Navarre. Paris: 1683. V. 37

SORIA, MARTIN S.

The Paintings of Zurbaran. London: 1953. V. 40

The Paintings of Zurbaran. London: 1955. V. 45

SORIA VELASQUEZ, GERONIMO DE

Los Capitanes D. Miguel Diez de la Mora . . . y Don Juan de Larrea . . . Mexico: 1696. V. 38

SORLIER, CHARLES

The Ceramics and Sculptures of Chagall. 1972. V. 42

The Ceramics and Sculpture of Chagall. Monaco: 1972. V. 39; 44

Chagall's Posters: A Catalogue Raisonne. New York: 1975. V. 39; 43; 46

The Lithographs of Chagall. New York: 1974. V. 42

SORNAUS

Soranus' Gynecology. Baltimore: 1956. V. 45

SORREL, G. MOXLEY

Recollections of a Confederate Staff Officer. New York & Washington: 1905. V. 37

Recollections of a Confederate State Officer. New York: 1905. V. 37

SORRENTINO, GILBERT

Corrosive Sublimate. Santa Barbara: 1971. V. 40; 42

The Darkness Surrounds Us. Highlands: 1960. V. 42

Elegiacs of Sulpicia. Mt. Horeb: 1977. V. 44

Mulligan Stew. New York: 1979. V. 44

White Sail. Santa Barbara: 1977. V. 40; 42

SORRENTIO, GILBERT

Corrosive Sublimate. Santa Barbara: 1971. V. 37

SORTAIN, JOSEPH

Count Arensberg; or, the Days of Martin Luther. Brighton: 1853. V. 40

SORTORE, ABRAM

Biography and Early Life Sketch of teh late . . . Including His Trip to California and Back. Alexandria: 1909. V. 45

SOSEKI, MUSO

The Sun At Midnight. London: 1985. V. 42

The Sun at Midnight: 23 Poems. New York: 1985. V. 41; 46

THE SOT. a Burletta in Two Parts. London: 1775. V. 46

SOTBENE, OSWOLD

The Shrine of Aesculapius. Cleveland: 1905. V. 41; 45

The Shrine of Aesculapius. Cleveland: 1905. V. 42

SOTHEBY & CO.

The Dyson Perrins Collection. London: 1958-60. V. 39

The Magnificent Botanical Library of the Stiftung Fur Botanik. London: 1975-76. V. 37

SOTHEBY, S. L.

Principia Typographica. London: 1858. V. 45

Principia Typographica. The Block-books, or zylographic delineations of scripture history, issued in Holland, Flanders, and Germany, during the 15th century. Exemplified and Considered in connextion with the origin of printing. To which is . . . 1858. V. 37

Specimen of Mr. S. Leigh Sotheby's Principia Typographica . . . London: 1858. V. 45

SOTHEBY, SAMUEL LEIGH

Ramblings in the Elucidation of the Autograph of Milton. London: 1861. V. 38; 41

Unpublished Documents, Marginal Notes and Memoranda. London: 1840. V. 38; 40

SOTHEBY, WILKINSON & HODGE

A Complete Set of the Illustrated Editions of the Britwell Sales; Together with a Copy of the Britwell Handlist, a Useful but Still Imperfect Index to the Set. London: 1916-71/1933. V. 39

SOTHEBY, WILKINSON & HODGE, LONDON.

Catalogue of the Cabinet of Old Fans, the Property of Mr. Robert Walker, of Uffington, Berkshire and the Marvelous Work by W. Holman Hunt: 'Strayed Sheep,' Painted in 1852 for the Late Charles Theobald Maud. 1882. V. 43

SOTHEBY, WILLIAM

Constance de Castile. A Poem. London: 1810. V. 37; 42; 46

Farewell to Italy, and Other Occasional Poems. London. V. 39

Poems. London: 1825. V. 40; 43; 44; 46

Saul, a Poem, in Two Parts. Boston: 1808. V. 42

To the Memory of Sir Henry Englefield. London: 1822. V. 44

To the Memory of Sir Henry Charles Englefield, Baronet. V. 38

A Tour through Parts of Wales, Sonnetes, Odes and Other Poems. London: 1794. V. 37; 39; 41; 45; 46

SOTHERAN, HENRY

Bibliotheca Chemico-Mathematica: Catalogue of the Works in Many tongues on Exact and Applied Science, with Subject Index . . . (with) First Supplement. London: 1921. V. 39

SOTHERAN, HENRY, LTD.

Annotated Catalogues of Works on Chemistry, Pure and Applied. (Catalogues 839, 357, 894 and 907). London: 1934-54. V. 46

SOTHERN, JOHN RUSSELL

Zephyrus, and Other Poems. Melbourne: 1862. V. 41

SOTHERON, CHARLES

Genealogical Memoranda Relating to the Family of Sotheron, of Counties Durham, Northumberland, York, etc. and to the Sept of MacManus. London: 1871. V. 39

SOTO AVILES Y VILLAVICENCIO, JUAN IGNACIO

Memoria, Que la Muy Noble, Ciudad de Cadiz Consagra . . . La Reyna N.S. Dona Mariana de Austria . . . Cadiz: 1668. V. 37; 40

SOTO, HERNANDO DE

The Discovery of Florida. San Francisco: 1946. V. 38; 39; 41; 45

True Relation of the Hardships Suffered by Governor . . . and Certain Portuguese Gentlemen During the Discovery of the Province of Florida. Deland: 1932. V. 42; 45

SOTO, PETRUS DE

Methodus Confessionis . . . Accessit Evangelica Historia . . . Dilingae: 1576. V. 42

SOUBEIRAN, JEAN LEON

La Matiere Medicale chez les Chinois. Paris: 1874. V. 45

SOUCHAL, FRANCOIS

French Sculpture of the 17th and 18th Centuries. The Reign of Louis XIV. London: 1977/81/87. V. 46

THE SOUL of Harmony: Being a Collection of the Most Admired Glees, Catches, Duets and Songs, Ancient and Modern, in the English Language, as Sung at the Harmonic and Anacreontic Societies of London, Norwich, Bath, etc. Norwich: 1804. V. 40

SOULAS D'ALLAINVAL, LEON JEAN CHRISTINE

Le Temple du Goust, Comedie. A La Haye: 1733. V. 38

SOULBY, W. H.

The Hoax Art Album. London: 1897. V. 41

SOULE, F.

The Annals of San Francisco. New York: 1855. V. 37; 38; 39; 40; 44; 45

SOULE, FRANK

The Annals of San Francisco . . . New York, San Francisco &: 1855. V. 39

Annals of San Francisco . . . Together with the Continuation, through 1855. Palo Alto: 1966. V. 38

Annals of San Francisco . . . Palo Alto: 1968. V. 38; 44

SOULE, WINSOR

Spanish Farm Houses and Minor Public Buildings. New York: 1924. V. 38

SOULES, FRANCOIS

Histoire des Troubles de l'Amerique Angalise, Ecrite Sur Les Memoires Les Plus Authentiques. Paris: 1787. V. 39; 42; 44

SOULIGNE,

The Desolation of France Demonstrated. London: 1697. V. 45

SOULSBY, B. H.

A Catalogue of the Works of Linnaeus . . . . London: 1933-36. V. 39

SOURY, JULES

Le Systeme Nerveux Central structure et fonctions. Histoire Critque Des Theories et Des Doctrines. Paris: 1899. V. 37; 44

SOUSA DE MACEDO, ANTONIO

Lusitania Liberata ab Injusto Castellarnorum Domino . . . London: 1645. V. 45

SOUSA DE MACEDO, ANTONIO DE

Armonia Politica Dos Documentos Divinos com as Conveniencias d'Estado. The Hague: 1651. V. 41

Dominio Sobre a Fortuna, e Tribunal da Razao. Em que se Examinaum as Felicades, & se Beatifica a Vida no Patrocinio da Virgem May da Graca . . . Lisbon: 1682. V. 41

SOUSA, JOHN PHILIP

The Fifth String. London: 1903. V. 46

SOUSA, MANUEL DE FARIA Y

Imperio de La China, Y Cultura Evangelica en el, por los Religiosos de la Compania de Jesus. Lisbon: 1731. V. 46

SOUSTER, RAYMOND

As Is. Toronto: 1967. V. 38

Crepe-Hanger's Carnival: Selected Poems 1955-58. Toronto: 1958. V. 38

A Dream That is Dying: Poems. Toronto: 1954. V. 38

For What Time Slays: Poems. Toronto: 1955. V. 38

A Local Pride: Poems. Toronto: 1962. V. 38; 44

Place of Meeting. Poems 1958-1960. Toronto: 1961. V. 44

Place of Meeting: Poems 1958-1960. Toronto: 1962. V. 38

The Selected Poems. Chosen by Louis Dudek. Toronto: 1956. V. 38

Shake Hands with the Hangman: Poems 1940-1952. Toronto: 1953. V. 38

Walking Death: Poems. Toronto: 1954. V. 38

When We Are Young. Montreal: 1946. V. 38

SOUTER, DANIEL d. 1634

Paedagogvs Divitvm, De Luxu, Et Vero Opum Usu. Leiden: 1622. V. 39; 40

SOUTH CAROLINA

A Compilation of all the Acts, Resolucitons, Reports and Documents in Relation to the bank of the State of South Carolina. Columbia: 1848. V. 37

The Debate in the South Carolina Legislature in December 1830, on the Reports of the Committee of Both Houses in Favor of Convention. Columbia: 1831. V. 46

Journal of the Provincial Congress of South Carolina. 1776. Published by Order of the Congress. Charles-Town: 1776. V. 44

Journal of the Convention of the People of South Carolina Assembled at Columbia on the 19th November, 1832 and Again on the 11th March 1833. Columbiia: 1833. V. 46

Journal of the State Convention of South Carolina, Together with the Resolution and Ordinance. Columbia: 1852. V. 40; 42

Journal of the Convention of the People of South Carolinia Held in 1860-61. Charleston: 1861. V. 40

Speeches Delivered in the Convention, of the State of South Carolina, Held in Columbia in March 1833. To Which is Prefixed the Journal of Proceedings. Charleston: 1833. V. 46

SOUTH CAROLINA. CONSTITUTION

The Constitution of the State of the State of South Carolina, with the Ordinances Thereunto Appended. Charleston: 1868. V. 39; 42; 45

SOUTH CAROLINA. CONVENTION

Report on the Address of the Portion of the Members of the General Assembly of Georgia. Charleston: 1860. V. 45

The State of South Carolina. At a Convention of the People of the State . . . Begun and Holden at Columbia, the 17th of Dec., 1860 . . . An Ordinance to Dissolve the Union Between the State of South Carolina and Other States . . . Michigan: 1865. V. 45

SOUTH CAROLINA. CONVENTION, 1832-1833.

The Report, Ordinance and Addresses of the Convention of the People of South Carolina. Adopted Nov. 24, 1832. Columbia: 1832. V. 44

SOUTH CAROLINA. CONVENTION, 1860-1862

Declaration of the Immediate Causes Which Induce and Justify the Secession of South Carolina from the Federal Union; and the Ordinance of Secession. Printed by Order of the Convention. Charleston: 1860. V. 39

SOUTH CAROLINA. HOUSE OF REPRESENTATIVES - 1842

Journal of the House of Representatives of the State of South Carolina Being the Annual Session of 1842. Columbia: 1842. V. 39

SOUTH CAROLINA. LAWS, STATUTES, ETC.

Acts and Resolutions of the General Assembly of the State of South Carolina, Passed in December 1792. Charleston: 1793. V. 46

Acts and Resolutions of the General Assembly of the State of South Carolina, Passed in Dec. 1793. Charleston: 1794. V. 46

Acts and Resolutions of the Gen. Assembly of the State of South Carolina Passed in Dec. 1794. Charleston: 1795. V. 46

Acts and Resoltuions of the Gen. Assem. of the State of South Carolina Passed in Nov. and DEc. 1795. Charleston: 1796. V. 46

Acts and Resolutions of the General Assembly of the State of South Carolina Passed in Dec. 1796. Charleston: 1797. V. 46

Acts and Resolutions of the Gen. Assembly of the State of South Carolina, Passed in Dec. 1797. Charleston: 1798. V. 46

Acts and Resolutions of the Gen. Assembly of the State of South Carolina, Passed in Dec., 1798. Charleston: 1799. V. 46

Acts and Resolutions of the Gen. Assembly of the State of South Carolina Passed in Dec., 1799. Charleston: 1800. V. 46

Acts and Resolutions of the General Assembly of the State of South Carolina, Passed Dec. 1800. Columbia: 1801. V. 46

Acts of the General Assembly of the State of South Carolina Passed in December, 1861 . . . Columbia;: 1862. V. 45

Acts of the General Assembly of the State of South Carolina, Passed in December 1864 . . . Columbia: 1865. V. 44

SOUTH CAROLINA. LEGISLATURE - 1842

Journal of the House of Representatives of the State of South Carolina. Being te Annual Session of 1842. Columbia: 1842. V. 37

SOUTH Dakota Brand Book. 1898-9. Fort Pierre: 1899. V. 45

SOUTHEY, ROBERT 1774-1843 continued

The Life and Correspondence of... London: 1849. V. 40

The Life and Correspondence of Robert Southey. New York: 1851. V. 39

The Life of Nelson. Hartford: 1814. V. 37

The Life of Nelson. London: 1814. V. 39

The Life of Nelson. London: 1878. V. 38

Lives of the British Admirals. London: 1833-1840. V. 39

Madoc. London: 1805. V. 42

Madoc. London: 1812. V. 39

Madoc. London: 1825. V. 40

Metrical Tales and Other Poems. London: 1805. V. 42

Nelson's Leben. Stuttgart: 1837. V. 42

Omnia, or Horae Otiosiores. London: 1812. V. 40; 42; 45

Poems: Containing the Retrospect, Odes, Elegies, Sonnets, etc. Bath: 1795. V. 46

Poems. Bristol: 1797. V. 40; 45

Poems. (with) Poems. The Second Volume. Bristol: 1797/99. V. 43

Poems... Bristol: 1799. V. 41

Poems. London: 1801/1800. V. 39

The Poetical Works of... London: 1837. V. 46

The Poetical Works... Collected by Himself. London: 1837-38. V. 37; 42

The Poetical Works... Collected by Himself. London: 1845-50. V. 39

Poetical Works of Robert Southey. London: 1847. V. 46

The Poetical Works. London: 1977. V. 39

Poetry of the Anti-Jacobin. London: 1799. V. 37

The Poet's Pilgrimage to Waterloo. London: 1816. V. 37; 39; 40

The Remains of henry Kirke White of Nottingham, Late of St. John's College, Cambridge, with an Account of His Life... London: 1822. V. 44

Robin Hood, a Fragment. Edinburgh: 1847. V. 39; 42

Roderick, the Last of the Goths. Philadelphia: 1815. V. 38

Sir Thomas More; or Colloquies on the Progress and Prospects of Society... London: 1831. V. 43

Sir Thomas More; or, Colloquies on the Progress and Prospects of Society. London: 1829. V. 37

Southey's Common-Place Book. London: 1849-51. V. 39

Specimens of the Later English Poets. London: 1807. V. 37; 41; 45

A Tale of Paraguay. London: 1825. V. 42

A Tale of Paraguay. Boston: 1827. V. 43; 45

Thalaba the Destroyer. London: 1801. V. 39; 42; 45

A Vision of Judgement. London: 1821. V. 42

Wat Tyler. London: 1817. V. 37; 38; 39

SOUTHEY, THOMAS

Chronological History of the West Indies. London: 1827. V. 40; 44

A Treatise on Sheep, Addressed to the Flock-Masters of Australia, Tasmania and Southern Africa... London: 1840. V. 41

SOUTHGATE, FRANK

Wildfowl and Waders. London: 1928. V. 37; 38; 39; 43; 45

SOUTHGATE, H.

Narrative of a Tour through Armenia, Kurdistan, Persia and Mesopotamia... New York: 1840. V. 37

SOUTHGATE, HORATIO

Narrative of a Tour Through Armenia, Kurdistan, Persia and Mesopotamia With Observations on the condition of Mohammendanism and Christianity in those Countries. London: 1840. V. 45

SOUTHGATE, RICHARD

Bibliotheca Southgatiana. London: 1795. V. 46

SOUTHMAYD, F. R.

Digest of the Ordinances and Resolutions of the Second Municipality; and of the General Council of the City of New Orleans, Applicable. New Orleans: 1848. V. 39

SOUTHWARD, JOHN

Practical Printing: a Handbook of the Art of Typography. London: 1900. V. 38; 42

Progress in Printing and the Graphic Arts During the Victorian Era. London: 1897. V. 44

SOUTHWART, ELIZABETH

Bronte Moors & Villages from Thornton in Haworth. London: 1923. V. 41; 43

SOUTHWELL, ROBERT

St. Peters Complaite. Mary Magdal(ene's) Teares. With Other Workes of the Author. London: 1636-34. V. 46

St. Peter's Complaint, and Other Poems... London: 1817. V. 44

SOUTHWESTERN Lore. V. 37

SOUTHWOOD, MARION

Tit for Tat: a Novel. New York: 1856. V. 38

SOUTHWORTH, ALVAN S.

Four Thousand Miles of African Travel. New York: 1875. V. 38; 41; 42; 46

SOUTHWORTH, JOHN

The Last Speech and Confession. London: 1679. V. 37

SOUTHWORTH, SYLVESTER S.

Trial, Life and Confession of Amos Miner, Who Was Executed on Friday, Dec. 27, 1833 for the Murder of John Smith, Late Town Sergeant of Foster. Providence: 1834. V. 45

A SOUVENIR of the Anchor Line Agents Excursion on the Steamer California, August 14, 1872. New York: 1872. V. 41; 45

SOUVENIR Of Scotland, Its Cities and Mountains. London: 1890. V. 40; 46

SOUVENIR of Scotland Its Cities, Lakes and Mountains. London: 1897. V. 45

SOUVENIR of Tacoma Washington. Tacoma: 1892. V. 45

SOUVENIR of the Island of Jersey. Its Towns, Antiquities, and Objects of Interest. London: 1892. V. 40

A SOUVENIR of the Trans-Continental Excursion of Railroad Agents, 1870. By One of the Party. Albany: 1871. V. 40

SOUVENIR Of Toronto. Toronto: 1915. V. 42

A SOVERIGN Remedy for the Dropsy. London: 1805. V. 44

SOWDEN, WILLIAM

The Northern Territory As It Is. Adelaide: 1882. V. 41

SOWDONE OF BABYLONE

The Romance of the Sowdone of Babylone and of Ferumbras His Sone Who Conquerede Rome. London: 1854. V. 40; 45; 46

SOWELL, ANDREW J.

Early Settlers nd Indian Fighters of Southwest Texas. Austin: 1900. V. 37; 38; 39; 41; 42; 43; 45; 46

Rangers and Pioneers of Texas. San Antonio: 1884. V. 37; 45

SOWERBY, ARTHUR DE CARLE

The Naturalist in Manchuria. Tientsin: 1922-23-30. V. 42

Sport and Science on the Sino-Mongolian Frontier. London: 1918. V. 46

SOWERBY, E. MILLICENT

Catalogue of the Library of Thomas Jefferson. Washington;: 1952-59. V. 42

SOWERBY, G. B.

A Chonchological Manual. London: 1852. V. 44; 46

Illustrated Index of British Shells... London: 1875. V. 43

Illustrated Index of British Shells... London: 1887. V. 37; 42

SOWERBY, GEORGE BRETTINGHAM 1812-1884

A Conchological Manual. London: 1839. V. 38

SOWERBY, GITHA

The Gay Book. London. V. 38

SOWERBY, J. E.

British Poisonous Plants. London: 1861. V. 44

SOWERBY, JAMES 1757-1822

The British Miscellany. London: 1804-06-1875. V. 43; 45

The British Miscellany. London: 1806. V. 43

Coloured Figures of English Fungi or Mushrooms. London: 1797-1803. V. 43

Coloured Figures of English Fungi, or Mushrooms. London: 1797-1803-1815. V. 39

Coloured Figures of English Fungi. London: 1797-99. V. 43

English Botany. London: 1790-1814. V. 37; 38; 39

English Botany. London: 1790-1866. V. 39

English Botany. Supplement, Volume I. London: 1831. V. 38

English Botany; or, Coloured Figures of British Plants. London: 1832-46. V. 42

English Botany. London: 1841-42. V. 37; 38; 39

English Botany. London: 1847-54. V. 43

English Botany; or, Coloured Figures of British Plants. London: 1863-92. V. 46

English Botany. London: 1863-99. V. 39

English Botany. London: 1866-92. V. 37; 38; 40

SOWERBY, JAMES 1757-1822 continued

English Botany or Coloured Figures of British Plants. London: 1899. V. 43; 45

English Botany. London: 1913. V. 39; 41

English Botany. Volume 12, Algae. London: 1846. V. 37

English Botany. Volumes 8 & 9: Ferns and Fern Allies and the Mosses. London: 1841-42. V. 37

A New Elucidation of Colours . . . London: 1809. V. 45

Supplement to English Botany. London: 1849-66. V. 38

SOWERBY, JAMES DE CARLE

Tortoises, Terrapins and Turtles. London: 1872. V. 43

SOWERBY, JOHN EDWARD 1825-1870

British Wild Flowers. London: 1863. V. 38; 40; 41

British Wild Flowers. London: 1876. V. 41

British Wild Flowers. London: 1882. V. 40; 44; 45

British Wild Flowers. London: 1860. V. 37; 38

British Wild Flowers. London: 1894. V. 37

British Wild Flowers. London: 1902. V. 37; 46

The Ferns of Great Britain. (with) The Fern Allies: A Supplement. London: 1855, 1856. V. 39

The Ferns of Great Britain. (with) The Fern Allies: A Supplement to the Ferns of Great Britain. London: 1855-56. V. 43

The Ferns of Great Britain. London: 1859. V. 37; 42

The Grasses of Great Britain. London: 1857-61. V. 38

SOWERBY, MILLICENT

The Bumbletoes. London: 1907. V. 46

SOYER, ALEXIS

Modern Housewife or, Menagere. New York: 1850. V. 40; 45

The Modern Housewife or Menagere. London: 1861. V. 38

Soyer's Culinary Campaign. London: 1857. V. 40

SOYER, RAPHAEL

A Painter's Pilgrimage. By Raphael Soyer. An Account of a Journey with drawings by the Author. New York: 1962. V. 37

SOYINKA, WOLE

Three Plays. Swamp Dwellers, Trials of Brother Jero, The Strong Breed. Ibadan: 1963. V. 42

SPACH, E.

Histoire Naturelle des Vegetaux Phanerogames. London: 1834-48. V. 43

SPACKMAN, W. H.

Trout in New Zealand: Where to Go and How to Catch Them; Wellington: 1892. V. 39

SPACKMAN, WILLIAM FREDERICK

An Analysis of the Occupations of the People, Showing the Relative Importance of the Agricultural, Manufacturing, Shipping, Colonial, Commercial and Mining Interests . . . London: 1847. V. 43

SPADA, GIOVANNI GIACOMO

Corporum Lapidefactorum Agri Veronensis Catalogus Quae apud J. J. Spadam.. Verona: 1744. V. 39; 42

SPAENDONCK, G. VAN

Flowers Drawn from Nature. London: 1957. V. 37

SPAETH, SIGMUND

Barber Shop Ballads: a Book of Close Harmony. New York: 1925. V. 39

SPAFFORD, HORATIO GATES

A Gazetteer of the State of New York . . . Albany: 1813. V. 42; 45

A Gazetteer of the State of New York. Albany: 1824. V. 40

The Mother-in-Law; or Memoirs of Madam de Morville. Boston: 1817. V. 40

SPAFFORD, JAMES M.

A Geological Reconnoissance of the State of Tennessee; Being the Author's First Biennial Report . . . Nashville: 1845. V. 37

SPAIGHT, ASHLEY W.

The Resources, Soil and Climate of Texas. Galveston: 1882. V. 38; 39; 41

SPAIN

Constitution of the Spanish Monarchy, Promulgated at Cadiz on the 19th of March, 1812. Philadelphia: 1814. V. 37

The Political Constitution of the Spanish Monarchy . . . 1812. Translated from the Castillian, By Daniel Robinson, Esq., Lieutenant of His Majesty's Royal Marine Force, and Captain in the Armies of Spain. London: 1813. V. 37

SPAIN. LAWS, STATUTES, ETC. - 1793

Ordenanzas Generales de la Armada Naval. PArte Primera. Sobre La Governacion Militar y Marinera de la Armada en General, Y Uso de Sus Fuerzas en La Mar. Madrid: 1793. V. 40

SPAIN. SOVERIGNS, ETC. 1759-1788 (CHARLES II)

REGLAMENTO E Instruccion Para Los Presidios Que se Han de Formar en La Linea de Frontera ne La Nueva Espana. Resuelto Por el Rey Nuestro Senor en Cedula de 10 de Setiembre de 1772. Mexico: 1834. V. 39

SPAIN. TREATIES, ETC.

Tratado de paz, Ajustado Entre la Corona de Espafna, y la de Portugal. Madrid: 1715. V. 45

Tratado Definitivo de Paz Concluido Entre el Rey Nuestro Senor Y El Rey De La Gran Bretana Firmado en Versailles A 3 de Setiembre de 1783 . . . Madrid: 1783. V. 45

SPAIN. TREATIES, ETC. - 1796

Real Cedula de S. M. y Senores del Consejo, en que se Manda Observar y Guardar el Tratado de Amistad, Limites de Navegacion Concluido y Ratificado Entre su Real Persona y Los Estados Unidos de America. Madrid: 1796. V. 39

SPALDING, A. G.

Catalogue A: Summer Sports. Chicago, etc.,: 1892. V. 37

SPALDING, ALBERT G.

America's National Game: Baseball: Historic Facts Concerning the Begining, Evolution, Development and Popularity of Baseball. New York: 1911. V. 44

SPALDING & HODGE

A Specimen Book of Printing Papers Designed Chiefly for the Use of Printers. London: 1906. V. 41

SPALDING, CHARLES C.

Annals of the City of Kansas. Kansas City: 1858. V. 37; 38; 40; 42; 43; 45

SPALDING, H. H.

Earl Labors of the Missionaries of the American Board of Foreign Missions in Oregon . . . Washington: 1871. V. 39

SPALDING, J. A.

From New England to the Pacific. Notes of a Vacation Trips Across the Continent in April, May and June, 1884. Hartford: 1884. V. 42

From New England to the Pacific. Notes of a Vacation Trip Across the Continent in April, May and June, 1884. Hartford, Conn.: 1884. V. 37

SPALDING, JOHN

The History of the Troubles and Memorable Transactions in Scotland, from the Year 1624 to 1645. Aberdeen: 1792. V. 39

SPALDING, JOHN F.

The Cathedral and Cathedral System. A Sermon Preached in St. John's Church, Denver. Denver: 1880. V. 39; 44

SPALDING, JOSHUA

Sentiments, Concerning the Coming and Kingdom of Christ . . . Salem: 1796. V. 39

SPALDING, LYMAN

An Inaugural Dissertation on the Production of Animal Heat: Read and Defended at a Public Examination, Held by the Medical Professors, Before The Rev. Joseph Willard . . . President and the Governors of Harvard College . . . July 10, 1797. Walpole: 1797. V. 38

SPALDING, PHEBE ESTELLE

Womanhood in Art. San Francisco: 1905. V. 39; 42

SPALDING, WILLIAM

Italy and the Italian Islands from the Earliest Ages to the Present Time. Edinburgh: 1841. V. 46

SPALDING'S Official Base Ball Guide 1902. New York: 1902. V. 39

SPALDING'S Official Base Ball Guide for 1879. Chicago: 1879. V. 39

SPALLANZANI, A.

Dissertations Relative to the Natural History of Animals and Vegetables . . . London: 1884. V. 39; 40

SPALLANZANI, LAZARO

Dissertations Relative to the Natural History of Animals and Vegetables. London: 1784. V. 40

SPALLANZANI, LAZZARO

Dissertations Relative to the Natural History of Animals and Vegetables. London: 1789. V. 38; 40

Opuscules de Physique, Animale et Vegetale . . . A Pavie: 1787. V. 42

Tracts on the Natural History of Animals and Vegetables. Edinburgh: 1803. V. 42

Travels in the Two Sicilies and Some Parts of the Apennines. London: 1798. V. 38; 39; 40; 42

SPALLANZANI, LAZZARO continued

Viaggi alle Due Sicile e in Alcune Parti Dell' Apprennino. Tomo Primo (- Sesto, ed Ultimo). Pavia: 1792-97. V. 39

SPALLANZI, LAZZARO

Dissertations Relative to the Natural History of Animals and Vegetables. London: 1789. V. 43

SPANG, WILLIAM

Motuum Britannicorum Verax Cushi ex Ipsis Joabi & Oculati Testis Prototypis Totus Translatus . . . Rotterdam: 1647. V. 42

SPANGENBERG, AUGUST GOTTLIEB 1704-1792

A Concise Historical Account of the Present Constitution of the Unitas Fratrum. London: 1775. V. 39

An Exposition of Christian Doctrine, as Taught in the Protestant Church of the United Brethren, or, Unitas Fratrum. London: 1784. V. 39

SPANGLER, EDWARD W.

The Annals of the Families of Caspar, Henry, Baltzer and George Spengler Who Settled in York County, Respectively in 1729, 1732, 1732, 1751. York: 1896. V. 42

SPANISH America and the United States . . . Philadelphia: 1818. V. 42

SPANISH Approach to Pensacola, 1689-1693. Albuquerque: 1939. V. 45

THE SPANISH History; or, a Relation of the Differences That Happened in the Court of Spain, Between Don John of Austria, and Cardinal Nitard . . . London: 1678. V. 40

THE SPANISH Occupation of California: Plan for the Establishment of a Government Junta or Council Held at San Blas, May 16, 1768. San Francisco: 1934. V. 42; 45

SPARAGO, JOHN

Anthony Haswell, Printer, Patriot, Ballader . . . Rutland: 1925. V. 38

SPARAKS, JARED

The Life of Gouverneur Morris, with Selections from His Correspondence and Miscellaneous Papers. Boston: 1832. V. 38

SPARCK, R.

The Zoology of the Faroes. Copenhagen: 1928-71. V. 43

SPARE, AUSTIN O.

Darling, the Honourable Mr. Justice. On the Oxford Circuit and Other Verses. London: 1909. V. 46

SPARE, AUSTIN OSMAN

A Book of Satyrs. London: 1907. V. 45

A Book of Automatic Drawings. London: 1972. V. 39; 41

The Focus of Life. London: 1921. V. 40; 45

SPARE Your God. Cambridge: 1919. V. 44; 45

SPARGO, JOHN

Anthony Haswell Printer-Patriot-Ballader. Rutland: 1925. V. 42

SPARK, MURIEL

The Bachelors. London: 1960. V. 40; 42

Child of Light; a Reassessment of Mary Wollstonecraft Shelley. Essex: 1951. V. 37; 44; 46

Child of Light. Hadleigh: 1951. V. 37; 39; 40; 41

Collected Poems 1. London: 1967. V. 42

The Comforters. London: 1957. V. 38

The Comforters. Philadelphia: 1957. V. 45

The Fanfarlo. Aldington: 1952. V. 37; 40; 42

The Fanfarlo and other Verse. Ashford, Kent: 1952. V. 37

A Far Cry From Kensington. London: 1988. V. 46

Memento Mori. Philadelphia & New York: 1959. V. 39

Memento Mori. London: 1959. V. 40

Not to Disturb. London: 1971. V. 44

The Prime of Miss Jean Brodie. London: 1961. V. 38; 40; 45

The Public Image. London: 1968. V. 46

Robinson. London: 1958. V. 42

Selected Poems of Emily Bronte. 1952. V. 37

The Seraph and the Zambesi. Philadelphia & New York: 1960. V. 43

Tribute to Wordsworth. London: 1950. V. 37

SPARKE, EDWARD

Scintilla-Altaris. London: 1660. V. 46

SPARKE, MICHAEL

A Catalogue of Printed Books Written by William Prynne of Lincolnes-Inne, Esquire, Before, During, Since His Imprisonment. London: 1643. V. 41

A Narrative History of King James for the First Fourteen Years. London: 1651. V. 46

Truth Brought to Light and Discovered by Time or a Discourse and Historical Narration of the First XIIII Years of King James Reigne. London: 1651. V. 46

SPARKES, BRIAN A.

Black and Plain Pottery of the 6th, 5th and 4th Centuries B.C. Princeton: 1970. V. 37

SPARKMAN, ANDERS

A Voyage to the Cape of Good Hope, Towards the Arctic Polar Circle, and Round the World. London: 1786. V. 40

SPARKMAN, R. S.

The Texas Surgical Society. The First Fifty Years. Dallas: 1965. V. 41

SPARKMAN, ROBERT

Minutes of the American Surgical Association, 1880-1968. Dallas: 1972. V. 41

SPARKMAN, ROBERT S.

A Day in the Life of Lon Tinkle. Dallas: 1981. V. 44

SPARKS, EDWIN ERLE

English Settlement in the Illinois. London & Cedar Rapids: 1907. V. 38

SPARKS, JARED

Catalogue of the Library of Jared Sparks. Cambridge: 1871. V. 40

Correspondence of the American Revolution: Being Letters of Eminent Men to George Washington, from the Time of His Taking Command of the Army to the End of His Presidency. Boston: 1853. V. 39; 42; 46

The Life of John Ledyard, the American Traveller. Cambridge: 1828. V. 37; 38; 43; 46

The Life of John Ledyard, the American Traveller. Cambridge: 1829. V. 38

The Life of Gouverneur Morris, with Selections from His Correspondence and Miscellaneous Papers. Boston: 1832. V. 40; 42

Memoirs of the Life and Travels of John Ledyard, from His Journals and Correspondence. London: 1828. V. 38; 39; 40; 41; 42; 43

SPARKS, MICHAEL

Verses on Man's Mortality. Long Crendon: 1925. V. 46

SPARKS, W. H.

The Memories of Fifty Years. Philadelphia: 1870. V. 38; 42

SPARLING, H. H.

The Kelmscott Press and William Morris, Master Craftsman. 1924. V. 46

SPARLING, H. HALLADAY

The Kelmscott Press and William Morris, Master Craftsman. London: 1924. V. 37; 38; 39; 40; 41; 42; 43; 44; 45

SPARLING, HALLIDAY

The History of Godefrey of Boloyne and the Conquest of Iherusalem. Reprinted from Caxton's edition of 1481. Edited by H. Halliday Sparling. (Hammersmith: 1893). V. 37

SPARLING, HENRY HALLIDAY

The Kelmscott Press and William Morris, Master Craftsman. Bologna: 1929. V. 39

SPARRMAN, ANDERS 1748-1820

A Voyage to the Cape of Good Hope, Towards the Antarctic Polar Circle, and Round the World, but Chiefly into the Country of the Hottentos and Cafres, from the Year 1772 to 1776. London: 1785. V. 38; 41; 43; 44

A Voyage to the Cape of Good Hope, Towards the Anarctic Polar Circle, and Round the World . . . London: 1786. V. 38; 43

A Voyage Round the World with Captain James Cook. London: 1944. V. 41

SPARRMAN, ANDREW

A Voyage to the Cape of Good Hope, Towards the Antarctic Polar Circle, and Round the World. Perth: 1789. V. 39

SPARRMANN, ANDERS

A Voyage Round the World with Captain James Cook in H.M.S. Resolution. London: 1944. V. 37

SPARROW 37-48. Santa Barbara: 1976. V. 46

SPARROW, ANTHONY

A Collection of Articles. London: 1674. V. 44

A Rationale Upon the Book of Common Prayer of the Church of England. London: 1657. V. 39

SPARROW, JOHN

Lapidaria; Lapidaria Altera; Lapidaria Tertia; Lapidaria Quarta; Lapidaria Quinta; Lapidaria Sexta; Lapidaria Septima. Cambridge: 1943-1976. V. 41

Lapidaria Tertia. 1954. V. 45

Line Upon Line. Cambridge: 1967. V. 38; 39; 40; 41; 45

SPEED, JOHN continued

The History of Great Britaine Under the Conquests of Ye Romans, Saxons, Danes and Normans. London: 1623. V. 42

The History of Great Britaine . . . from Julius Caesar, to our most gracious soveraigne King James. London: 1611. V. 37

John Speed's England. London: 1953-54. V. 40

What Europe Knew of China Three Hundred Years Ago, an Early Seventeenth Century Map of China . . . San Francisco: 1936. V. 46

SPEED, JOSHUA F.

Reminiscences of Abraham Lincoln and Notes of a Visit to California. Louisville: 1884. V. 45

SPEED, KELLOGG

Traumatic Injuries of the Carpus Including Colles' Fracture. New York: 1925. V. 42

SPEED, ROBERT

The Counter-Scuffle. Where Unto is Added The Counter-Rat. London: 1670. V. 38

The Counter-Scuffle. London: 1680. V. 40; 42; 44

SPEED, SAMUEL

Fragmenta Carceris; or, the Kings-Bench Scuffle . . . London: 1675. V. 42; 44

SPEER, JOHN

Life of Gen. James H. Lane 'the Liberator of Kansas' With Corroborative Incidents of Pioneer History. Garden City: 1896. V. 40

SPEER, JOSEPH SMITH

The West India Pilot. London: 1771. V. 37; 38; 39; 41

SPEER, WILLIAM

An Humble Plea, Addressed to the Legislature of California, in Behalf of the Immigrants from the Empire of China to This State. San Francisco: 1856. V. 39

The Oldest and the Newest Empire: China and the United States. Hartford: 1870. V. 46

SPEERT, HAROLD

Iconographia Gyniatrica. Philadelphia: 1973. V. 40; 41

Obstetric and Gynecologic Milestones: Essays and Eponymy. New York: 1958. V. 41

SPEIDELL, JOHN

A Breefe Treatise of Sphaericall Triangles, Wherein is Handled the Sixteene Cases of a Right Angled Triangle, Being all Extracted Out of One Diagram, and Reduced Into Theorems With the Totall Sine in the First Place . . . London: 1627. V. 39; 42

SPEIGHT, HARRY

Chronicles and Stories of Old Bingley. London: 1898. V. 45

The Craven and North West Yorkshire Highlands. London: 1892. V. 45; 46

Lower Wharfedale. London: 1902. V. 46

Nidderdale and the Garden of the Nidd . . . London: 1894. V. 41

Romantic Richmondshire. London: 1897. V. 44

Upper Wharfdale. London: 1900. V. 44; 46

Upper Nidderdale, with the Forest of Knaresborough. London: 1906. V. 41

SPEILBERGEN, JORIS VAN

The East and West Indian Mirror, Being an Account of . . . London: 1906. V. 45

SPEISER, E. A.

Excavations at Tepe Gawra. Philadelphia: 1935. V. 40

SPEISER, WERNER

Chinese Art: Painting, Calligraphy, Stone Rubbing, Wood Engraving. 1964. V. 42

Chinese Art: Painting, Calligraphy, Some Rubbing, Wood Engraving. New York: 1964. V. 41

SPEKE, HUGH

The Secret History of the Happy Revolution, in 1688. London: 1715. V. 37

SPEKE, JOHN HANNING

Journal of the Discovery of the Source of the Nile. Edinburgh: 1863. V. 45

Journal of the Discovery of the Source of the Nile. London: 1863. V. 39; 42; 43

Journal of the Discovery of the Source of the Nile. Edinburgh: 1864. V. 41

Journal of the Discovery of the Source of the Nile. Edinburgh & London: 1864. V. 43; 45

Journal of the Discovery of the Source of the Nile. London: 1864. V. 46

Journal of the Discovery of the Source of the Nile. New York: 1864. V. 42

SPELL, LOTA M.

Music in Texas. Austin: 1936. V. 37; 41

SPELLMAN, HENRY

Villare Anglicum; or a View of All the Cities. London. V. 46

SPELLMAN, JOHN 1594-1643

The Case of Our Affaires in Law, Religion and Other Circumstances Briefly Examined . . . Oxford: 1643. V. 39; 43

SPELMA, W. W. R.

Lowestoft China. Norwich: 1905. V. 38

SPELMAN, HENRY

De non Temerandis Ecclefis, Churches Not to be Violated. Oxford: 1668. V. 44

The English Works . . . London: 1727. V. 42

The English Works of Sir Henry Spelman, Kt. Pub. in His Life-Time, Together with His Posthumous Works Relating to the Laws and Antiquities of England. 1727-1723. V. 42

Glossarium Archaiologicum Continens Latino-Barbara, Peregrina, Obsoleta & Novate Significationis Vocabula . . . London: 1664. V. 45

Glossarium Archaiologicum: Continens Latino-Barbara . . . 1687. V. 39

Glossarium Archaiologicum. Londini: 1687. V. 39; 40

Glossarium Archaeologicum. London: 1687. V. 37; 38; 39; 40

The History and Fate of Sacrilege, Discover'd by Examples of Scripture, of Heathens and of Christians . . . London: 1698. V. 45

Of the Law Terms: a Discourse . . . Wherein the Laws of the Jews, Grecians, Romans, Saxons and Normans, Relating to the Subject are Fully Explained. London: 1684. V. 45

Relation of Virginia. London: 1872. V. 43; 45

Villare Anglicum; or a View of the Townes of England. London: 1656. V. 37; 42

Villare Anglicum; or a View of all the Cities, Towns and Villages in England . . . London: 1678. V. 39; 41; 44

SPELMAN, JOHN

Aelfredi Magni Anglorum Regis. Oxford: 1678. V. 40; 41

The Life of Aelfred the Great. Oxford: 1709. V. 38

SPELMAN, W. W. R.

Lowestoft China. Norwich: 1905. V. 40; 46

SPELMAN, WILLIAM

A Dialoge or Confabulation Between Two Travellers Which Treateth of Civile and Pollitike Gouvernement in Dyvers Kingdomes & Countries. London: 1896. V. 40

A Dialogue or Confabulation Between Two Travellers, Written c. 1580. 1896. V. 45

SPELTZ, ALEXANDER

The Colored Ornament of All Historical Styles. Leipzig: 1914-1915. V. 40

The Colored Ornament of all Historical Styles. With Colored Plates from own Paintings in Water Colours. Three Parts Containing Sixty Coloured Plates Each, with Text. Sixty Plates in Three Colour and Four Colour and Five Colour Printing . . . Leipzig: (1914-15). V. 37

SPENCE, ELIZABETH ISABELLA

The Wedding Day. London: 1807. V. 42; 43

SPENCE, GEORGE

The Equitable Jurisdiction of the Court of Chancery, Comprising Its Rise, Progress and Final Establishment. London: 1846-49. V. 43

SPENCE, JAMES

The American Union; Its Effect on National Character and Policy, with an Inquiry into Secession as a Constitutional Right, and the Causes of the Disruption. London: 1861. V. 46

SPENCE, JOSEPH

An Account of the Life, Character, and Poems of Mr. Blacklock, Student of Philosophy, in the University of Edinburgh. London: 1754. V. 45

Anecdotes, Observations and Characters, of Books and Men. London: 1820. V. 38; 41; 42; 45

Anecdotes, Observations and Characters, of Books and Men. London & Edinburgh: 1820. V. 38

Anecdotes, Observations and Characters, of Books and Men. London: 1858. V. 38; 43

Crito, or a Dialogue on Beauty. London: 1752. V. 39; 40; 44

Essay on Pope's Odyssey . . . London: 1726. V. 38

Miscellaneous Antiquities; or a Collection of Curious Papers. Strawberry Hill: 1772. V. 45

Observations, Anecdotes and Characters of Books and Men . . . London: 1820. V. 38; 40; 46

A Parallel in the Manner of Plutarch Between a Most Celebrated Man of Florence and One Scarce Ever Heard of In England. 1758. V. 38; 43

A Parallel; in the Manner of Plutarch: Between a Most Celebrated Man of Florence. London: 1758. V. 40; 44

A Parallel: In the Manner of Plutarch: Between a Most Celebrated Man of Florence: and . . . Printed at Strawberry Hill,: 1758. V. 44

SPENCE, JOSEPH continued

A Parallel; in the Manner of Plutarch; Between A Most Celebrated Man of Florence . . . Twickenham: 1758. V. 42

A Parallel; in the Manner of Plutarch, Between a Most Celebrated Man of Florence; and One, Scarce Ever Heard Of, in England . . . Strawberry-Hill,: 1758. V. 37

Polymetis. London: 1747. V. 37; 38; 39; 44; 46

Polymetis, or an Enquiry Concerning the Agreement Between the Works of the Roman Poets and the Remains of the Ancient Artists . . . London: 1755. V. 43

Polymetis: or, an Enquiry Concerning the Agreement Between Works of the Roman Poets and the Remains of the Antient Artists . . . London: 1774. V. 45

SPENCE, THOMAS

Manitoba, and the North-West of the dominion, Its Resources and Advantages to the Emigrant and Captialist, as Compared with the Western States of America . . . Toronto: 1871. V. 39

The Prairie Lands of Canada; Presented to the World as a New and Inviting Field of Enterprise . . . Montreal: 1879. V. 37; 39; 43

SPENCE-WATSON, ROBERT

A Visit to Wazan, the Sacred City of Morocco. London: 1880. V. 45; 46

SPENCE, WILLIAM

Agriculture the Source of the Wealth of Great Britain . . . London: 1808. V. 43

Britain Independent of Commerce . . . London: 1808. V. 41

The Radical Cause of the Present Distresses of the West-India Planters Pointed Out . . . London: 1807. V. 42

Tracts on Political Economy. London: 1822. V. 41; 45

SPENCER, BALDWIN

Across Australia. London: 1912. V. 42

The Arunta a Study of a Stone Age People. London: 1927. V. 43

The Native Tribes of Central Australia. London: 1938. V. 46

Native Tribes of Central Australia. London: 1899. V. 37

Native Tribes of the Northern Territory of Australia. London: 1914. V. 37

Wanderings in Wild Australia. London: 1928. V. 40

SPENCER, BENJAMIN

Chrysomeson, a Golden Meane. London: 1659. V. 42

SPENCER, CAPTAIN

Turkey, Russia, the Black Sea, and Circassia. London: 1854. V. 42

SPENCER, CORNELIA P.

The Last Ninety Days of the War in North Carolina. New York: 1866. V. 43

SPENCER, EDMUND

Travels in Circassia, Krim, Tartary &c. London: 1837. V. 37; 39; 40; 45

Travels in the Western Caucasus, Including a Tour through Imeritia, Mingrelia, Turkey, Moldavia, Galicia, Silesia, and Moravia, in 1836. London: 1838. V. 41

Travels in Circassia, Krim-Tartary &c. London: 1839. V. 40; 43

Travels in European Turkey, in 1850, through Bosnia Servia, Bulgaria, Macedonia, Thrace, Albania and Epirus. London: 1851. V. 37; 39

SPENCER, EDWARD

The King's Racehorses. London: 1902. V. 37; 42; 43

SPENCER, ELIZABETH

Fire in the Morning. New York: 1948. V. 38

The Legacy. Chapel Hill: 1988. V. 39

On the Gulf. Jackson. V. 45

On the Gulf. Jackson: 1991. V. 46

The Stories of Elizabeth Spencer. New York: 1980. V. 46

The Stories of Elizabeth Spencer. Garden City: 1981. V. 46

This Crooked Way. London: 1952. V. 39

This Crooked Day. New York: 1952. V. 39; 40; 43; 44

SPENCER Farm, With Some Account of Its Owners. Sudbury: 1845. V. 43; 45

SPENCER, GILBERT

British Artists of Today Number III. London: 1926. V. 38

The Ten Commandments. Stanford Dingley: 1934. V. 39

SPENCER, HERBERT 1820-1902

An Autobiography. London: 1904. V. 38; 43; 45

Descriptive Sociology. New York: 1873-81. V. 37

Education, Intellectual, Moral and Physical. London: 1861. V. 42; 45

The Principles of Psychology. London: 1870-72. V. 41

Railway Morals and Railway Policy. London: 1855. V. 45

SPENCER, J. A.

The History of the United States, from Its Earliest Period to the Administration of James Buchanan. New York: 1858. V. 40

SPENCER, JOHN

A Discourse Concerning Prodigies. London: 1665. V. 38; 40; 41; 42; 45; 46

Hermes or the Acarian Shepherds. Newcastle upon Tyne: 1782. V. 38

Kaina Kaiaaia. Things New and Old. London: 1658. V. 41; 42; 44

De Legibus Hebraeorum Ritualibus et Earum Rationibus Libri Tres. Cambridge: 1685. V. 38; 41; 45

Things New and Old. London: 1658. V. 40

SPENCER, JOHN R.

Filarete's Treatise on Architecture . . . New Haven: 1965. V. 44

SPENCER, NATHAN F.

A Narrative of the Cruelties Inflicted Upon Friends of North Carolina Yearly Meeting During the Years 1861 to 1865, in Consequence of Their Faithfulness to the Christian View of the Unlawfulness of War. London: 1868. V. 40; 42

SPENCER, O. M.

Indian Captivity: A True narrative of the Capture of the Rev. O.M. Spencer by the Indians, in the Neighborhood of Cincinnati, written by Himself. New York: 1842. V. 37

SPENCER, ORSON

The Prussian Mission of the Church of Jesus Christ of Latter-Day Stains. Liverpool: 1853. V. 42; 43

SPENCER, PLATT ROGERS

Spencerian or Semi-Angular Exercise Principle in Penmanship Book 13. Buffalo: 1857. V. 44

SPENCER, SPENCE

Scenery of Ithaca and the Head Waters of the Cayuga Lake, as Portrayed by Different Wirters . . . Ithaca: 1866. V. 39

SPENCER, THOMAS

Vital Chemistry: Lectures on Animal Heat. Geneva: 1845. V. 38

SPENDER, J. A.

Life of Herbert Henry Asquith, Lord Oxford and Asquith. London: 1932. V. 39

SPENDER, LILY HEADLAND

Her Brother's Keeper. London: 1888. V. 42

SPENDER, STEPHEN 1909-

Cyril Connolly - a Memoir. Edinburgh: 1978. V. 42

The Edge of Being. London: (1949). V. 37

The Edge of Being. London: 1949. V. 37

The Generous Days. London: 1971. V. 38

Letters to Christopher. Santa Barbara: 1980. V. 39

Poems. London: 1933. V. 37; 42; 45

Poems. London: 1935. V. 40

Poems. London: 1938. V. 41

Poems for Spain. London: 1939. V. 40

Poems of Dedication. London: 1947. V. 44

Poems of Dedication. New York: 1947. V. 45

Poems of Dedication. London: (1947). V. 37

Returning to Vienna 1947, Nine Sketches; Poems. Pawlet: 1947. V. 45

Ruins and Visions. Poems. London: (1941). V. 37

Spiritual Exercises. London: 1943. V. 38; 39; 42; 46

The Still Centre. London: 1939. V. 38

The Still Centre. London: (1939). V. 37

The Temple. London: 1988. V. 41

Three Versions from the German. 1955. V. 38

Three Versions from the German. 1955. V. 44

Trial of a Judge: a Tragedy. London: 1938. V. 39

Twenty Poems. London: 1930. V. 42

Twenty Poems. Oxford: 1930. V. 37; 38

Vienna. London: 1934. V. 37; 41

Vienna. London: (1934). V. 37

W. H. Auden: a Memorial Address. London: 1973. V. 38; 40; 45

W. H. Auden: a Tribute. London: 1975. V. 45

SPENDLOVE, F. ST. GEORGE

The Face of Early Canada. Toronto: 1958. V. 37; 43; 44; 45

SPENER, PHILIP JACOB 1635-1705

Die Allgemeine Gottesgelahrtheit Aller Glaeubigen Christen aus Gottes Wort Erwiesen . . . Frankfurt: 1680. V. 38; 41

SPENGLER, OSWALD

The Decline of the West. New York: 1926/28. V. 44

SPENSER, EDMUND 1552-1599

Amoretti Written Not Long Since. New York: 1901. V. 39

Colin Clouts Come Home Againe. London: 1595. V. 40; 44; 45

Epithalamion. New York: 1895. V. 41

Epithalamion. London: 1901. V. 37; 40; 46

Epithalamion. New Rochelle: 1902. V. 41; 43; 46

Epithalamion and Amoretti. London: 1903. V. 44

The Faerie Qveene Disposed into Twelue Books. (with) The Second Part . . . London: 1590, 1596. V. 38

The Faerie Queene. London: 1596. V. 37; 41

The Faerie Queen; The Shepherds Calendar; Together with the Other Works. 1611. V. 41

The Faerie Queen; The Shepheards Calendar; Together with Other Works of England's ARch-Poet. London: 1611. V. 37; 40; 42; 44; 46

The Faerie Queen; the Shepheards Calendar. Together with the Other Works of England's Arch-Poet . . . London: 1617. V. 45

The Faerie Queene. London: 1751. V. 37; 40; 44

The Faerie Queene . . . London: printed for J.: 1751. V. 37

Faerie Queene. London: 1758. V. 39; 46

The Faerie Queene. London: 1758-59. V. 41

Spenser's Faerie Queene. London: 1892. V. 38

Faerie Queene. London: 1894-1897. V. 40; 41; 42

The Faierie Queen. London: 1894-96. V. 42

The Faerie Queen. London: 1894-96. V. 39

Spencer's Faerie Queene. London: 1894-97. V. 38; 41; 42; 44

The Faerie Queene. London: 1897. V. 37; 39; 41; 46

Spenser's Faerie Queene. London: 1897. V. 41

The Faerie Queene. Cambridge: 1909. V. 44; 46

The Faerie Queene Disposed into Twelve Bookes Fashioning XII Morall Vertues. 1923. V. 39; 40

The Faerie Queene. Chelsea: 1923. V. 39; 40; 44

The Faerie Queene Disposed into Twelve Bookes Fashioning XII Morall Vertues. London: 1923. V. 37; 38; 44

The Faerie Queene . . . Chelsea: 1923/25. V. 39; 45

Faerie Queene. 1953. V. 45

The Faerie Queene. Oxford: 1953. V. 40; 44

Spenser's Minor Poems. Chelsea: 1925. V. 44

Minor Poems. London: 1925. V. 37; 44

Poems. Edinburgh: (1906). V. 37

Poems of . . . Edinburgh: 1906. V. 39

Poems. London: 1906. V. 39

The Poetical Works. London: 1825. V. 39

The Poetical Works. Boston: 1839. V. 40

The Poetical Works. London: 1839. V. 42; 46

The Poetical Works. London: 1852. V. 37

Prothalamion: Epithalamion. Boston: 1902. V. 40

The Shepherd's Calendar, Containing Twelve Aeglogues . . . Calendarium Pastorum, si Aeglogae XII . . . London: 1732. V. 39

The Shepheardes Calendar . . . Hammersmith: 1896. V. 37; 42

The Shepheardes Calendar. 1930. V. 38; 39; 43

The Shepheardes Calendar. London: 1930. V. 37; 41; 44; 46

The Shepheard's Calendar. 1898. V. 42

The Shepheard's Calender. New York: 1898. V. 43

The Shepherd's Calendar. London: 1732. V. 37; 38; 41; 44

The Shepheardes Calender: Conteyning Twelve Aeglogues, Proportionable to the Twelve Months. Edited by F.S. Ellis. Hammersmith: 1896. V. 37

The Shepheardes Calender . . . . London: 1896. V. 40; 41

The Shepheard's Calender. London: 1898. V. 38; 41

Spenser's Minor Poems. Chelsea: 1925. V. 45

Spenser's Minor Poems. London: 1925. V. 45; 46

Thalamos, or the Brydall Boure. London: 1932. V. 46

A View of the State of Ireland As It Was in the Reign of Queen Elizabeth. Dublin: 1763. V. 38

The Works of that Famous English Poet, Mr. Edmond Spenfer . . . London: 1679. V. 38; 41; 42; 43; 44; 46

The Works. London: 1679. V. 37

Collected Works. London: 1679. V. 37

.he Works. In Six Volumes. With a Glossary Explaining the Old & Obsure Words. Published by Mr. Huges. London: 1715. V. 37; 39

The Works. London: 1805. V. 38; 41; 43; 46

The Works. London: 1862. V. 46

The Works of . . . London: 1873. V. 38

The Complete Works in Verse and Prose. London: 1882-84. V. 38; 40; 42

The Works. Oxford: 1930. V. 38; 41; 42; 43; 45; 46

The Works of . . . Stratford-on-Avon: 1930. V. 41

SPENSER SOCIETY

A Complete Set of the Publications of this Famous Society. London: 1867-88. V. 37

SPERONI, SPERON 1500-1588

Dialoghi . . . da Nuovo Ricorretti a Quali Sons Aggiunti Molti Altri non Piu Stampati. Venice: 1596. V. 39

SPERONI, SPERONE 1500-1588

Canace Tragedia . . . alla Quale Sono Aggiunte Alcune Altre sue Compositioni, & Una Apologia & Alcune Lettioni in Difesa Della Tragedia. Venice: 1597. V. 37; 40; 45

Nuovamente Ristampati & Con Molta Diligenza Reveduti & Corretti. Venice: 1543. V. 40

SPERRY, I. J.

Family Medical Adviser. Hartford: 1847. V. 46

SPICE Islands Passed in the Sea of Reading. Bradford: 1859. V. 42

SPICE, R. P.

The Wanderings of the Hermit of Westminster Between New York and San Francisco in the Autumn of 1881. London: 1882. V. 38; 39; 42

SPICER, A. DYKES

The Paper Trade, a Descriptive and Historical Survey of the Paper Trade from the Commencement of the Nineteenth Century. London: 1907. V. 38

SPICER, DOROTHY GLADYS

Latin American Costumes. New York: 1941. V. 44

SPICER, JACK

A Lost Poem. Verona: 1974. V. 46

SPICER, JOHN

Tables of Interest . . . Computed and Carefully Examined by John Spicer, Gent at the Exchequer. London: 1693. V. 46

SPICER-SIMPSON, THEODORE

Men of Letters of the British Isles. New York: 1924. V. 37

SPICER, W. W.

A Handbook of the Plants of Tasmania. Hobart: 1878. V. 37

SPICER, WILLIAM A.

History of the Ninth and Tenth Regiments Rhode Island Volunteers. Providence: 1892. V. 46

SPIE, C. HALE

The Indian Chiefs of Pennsylvania. Butler: 1927. V. 41

The Indian Wars of Pennsylvania. Harrisburg: 1929. V. 38

SPIEGELBERG, WILHELM

Report on Some Excavations in the Theban Necropolis During the Winter of 1898-9. London: 1908. V. 44

SPIEGHEL, ADRIAAN VAN DEN

Isagoges in Rem Herbariam Libri Duo. Leiden: 1633. V. 43

SPIELMAN, M. H.

Kate Greenaway. London: 1905. V. 38; 39; 40; 41; 43; 44; 45; 46

Littledom Castle and Other Tales. London: 1903. V. 42

Littledom Castle and Other Tales. London: 1912. V. 43

SPIELMANN, ISIDORE

International Fine Arts Exhibition Rome 1911 - Souvenir of the British Section. V. 41

International Fine Arts Exhibitions. Souvenir of the British Section. London: 1911. V. 37

SPIELMANN, M. H.

British Sculpture and Sculptures of Today. London: 1900. V. 40

British Portrait Painting to the Opening of the Nineteenth Century. London: 1910. V. 46

The History of 'Punch'. London: 1895. V. 46

The Hitherto Unidentified Contributions of W. H. Thackeray to 'Punch' With a Complete and Authoritative Bibliography from 1843 to 1848. London: 1899. V. 42

Kate Greenaway. New York: 1905. V. 37

SPIELMANN, MARION H.

Hugh Thomson - His Art, His Letters, His Humour & His Charm. London: 1931. V. 40; 41; 45; 46

SPIELMANN, PERCY EDWIN

Catalogue of (His) Library of Miniature Books . . . Together with some Descriptive Summaries. London: 1961. V. 38; 39; 42; 44; 46

SPIER, LESLIE

Yuman Tribes of the Gila River. Chicago: 1933. V. 39

SPIES, AUGUST

Attention Workingmen! Great Mass Meeting Tonight, at 7:30 O'Clock at the Haymarket . . . Chicago: 1886. V. 39; 45

SPIES, WERNER

Max Ernst - Collagen: Inventar und Widerspruch. Cologne: 1975. V. 43

Max Ernst Oeuvre-Katalog. Houston: 1975-87. V. 42

The Return of La Belle Jardiniere: Max Ernst 1950-70. New York: 1971. V. 46

Sculpture by Picasso with a Catalogue of the Works. New York: 1971. V. 43; 45; 46

Victor Vasarely. New York: 1971. V. 41; 43; 44; 46

SPIES, WILLIAM B.

The Seventh Pennsylvania Veteran Volunteer Cavalry, Its Record, Reminiscences and Roster. Pottsville: 1905. V. 42

SPIESS, GUSTAV

Die Preussische Expedition nach Ostasien Wahrend der Jahre 1860-62. Berlin: 1864. V. 43

SPIKER, SAMUEL HEINRICH

Travels through England, Wales & Scotland, in the year 1816. Translated from the German. London: 1820. V. 37

SPILBERGEN, JORIS VAN

Jouranel vn de Voyagie Gedaen mit Drie Schepen Uyt Elandt, Naer Oost-Indien, Onder het Beleydt van den Commandeur Joris van Spilbergen, Zijjn eerst Reyse, Uytghevaren in den Jare 1601. 1602. 1603 en 1604. Amsterdam: 1663. V. 45

SPILIMBERGO, IRENE DE

Rime di Diversi Nobilissimi et Eccellentissimi Autori, in Morte Della Signora Irene Delle Signore di Spilimbergo . . . Diversorum Poetarum Carmina in Obitu Irenes Spilimbergiae. Venice: 1561. V. 38

SPILLANE, MICKEY

Tomorrow I Die. 1984. V. 46

SPILLER, BURTON L.

Firelight. New York: 1937. V. 39; 43; 44; 45; 46

Grouse Feathers. New York: 1935. V. 39; 44

Grouse Feathers. By Burton L. Spiller. New York: (1935). V. 37

More Grouse Feathers. New York: 1938. V. 39; 43; 44

More Grouse Feathers. By Burton L. Spiller. New York: (1938). V. 37

Thoroughbred. New York: 1936. V. 39; 44

SPILLER, GEORGE

Observations on certain branches of the Commissariat System, particularly connected withthe present Military State of the Country. London: 1806. V. 37

SPILLER, ROBERT E.

A Descriptive Bibliography of the Writings of James Fenimore Cooper. New York: 1934. V. 39; 42; 43

Literary History of the United States. New York: 1948 & 1959. V. 39

The Philobiblon Club of Philadelphia, 1893-1973. North Hills: 1973. V. 38; 42; 43; 44

The Philobiblon Club of Philadelphia: The First Eighty Years 1893-1973. Philadelphia: 1973. V. 37; 41

The Philobiblon Club of Philadelphia. The First Eighty Years. (Philadelphia): 1973. V. 37

The Philobiblon Club of Philadelphia. The First Eighty Years, 1893-1973, by Robert E. Spiller. (North Hills): 1973. V. 37

SPILSBURY, FRANCIS B.

Account of a Voyage to the Western coast of Africa; Performed by H.M.S. Favourite, in the Year 1805. London: 1807. V. 38; 40

Picturesque Scenery in the Holy Land and Syria, Delineated During the Campaigns of 1799 and 1800. London: 1823. V. 38

SPILSBURY, JOHN

A Journal of the Siege of Gibralter, 1779-1783. Gibralter: 1908. V. 39

SPILSBURY, WILLIAM HOLDEN

Lincoln's Inn, Its Ancient and Modern Buildings, with an Account of the Library. London: 1850. V. 40; 41

SPINCKES, NATHANIEL

No Reason for Restoring the Prayers and Directions of Edward VI's Liturgy. London: 1717. V. 39

No Sufficient Reason for Restoring the Prayers and Directions of King Edward the Sixth's First Liturgy. London: 1718. V. 39

SPINDEN, HERBERT J.

A Study of Maya Art. Cambridge: 1913. V. 37; 44

SPINDLER, CARL

The Natural Son. London: 1835. V. 40

SPINELLI, GIOVANNI PAULO DE

Lectiones Aureae, in Omni Quod Pertinet ad Artem Pharmasopaaeam Lucubrate. Bari: 1633. V. 38

SPINKS, THOMAS

The Ecclesiastical and Admiralaty Reports. London: 1855. V. 38; 40

THE SPINNERS' Book of Fiction. San Francisco: 1907. V. 38; 46
THE SPINNERS' Book of Fiction. San Francisco and New York: 1907. V. 38

SPINO, P.

Historia Della Vita et Fatti Dell'Eccellentissimo Capitano di Guerra Bartolomeo Coglione. Venice: 1569. V. 38

SPINO, PIETRO

Historia Della Vita, et Fatti dell'eccellentissimo Caapitano di Guerra Barolomeo Coglione. Vinetia: 1569. V. 37

SPINOZA, BENEDICT

Opera Posthuma, Quorum Series Post Praefationem Exhibetur. Amsterdam: 1677. V. 38; 39; 41; 43; 45; 46

SPINOZA, BENEDICT DE

La Clef du Santuaire Par un Scavant Homme de Notre Siecle. A Leyde: 1678. V. 42

La Clef du Santuaire Par Un Scavant Homme de Notre Siecle. Leyde: 1678. V. 41

De Rechtzinnige Theologant, of Godgeleerde Staatkundige Verhandelinge. Hamburg (Amsterdam): 1693. V. 41; 45

Renati des Cartes. Amsterdam: 1663. V. 41

Tractatus Theologicus-Politicus. Continens Dissertationes Aliquot, Quibus Ostenditur Libertatem Philosophandi non Tantum Salva Piete & Reipublicae Pace Posse Concedi . . . Hamburgi: 1670. V. 41

Tractatus Theologico-Politicus: A Critical Inquiry into the History, Purpose and Authenticity of the Hebrew Scriptures . . . London: 1862. V. 41

Tractatus Theologicao-Politicus . . . (with) Opera Posthuma. Hamburg: Apud Henricum: 1677. V. 37

Tractatus Theologico-Politicus, Cui Adjunctus est Philosophia S. Scripturae Interpres. N.P.: 1674. V. 37

THE SPIRIT of Canada Dominion and Provinces 1939: a Souvenir of Welcome to H. M. King George VI and H. M. Queen Elizabeth. N.P.: 1939. V. 44

THE SPIRIT of France and the Politick Maxims of Lewis XIV, Laid Open to the World. London: 1689. V. 40

THE SPIRIT of Praise. London: 1867. V. 44
THE SPIRIT of Praise. London: 1871. V. 42

SPIRIT of the Metropolitan Conservative Press. London: 1840. V. 39

SPITTA, PHILIP

Johann Sebastian Bach: His Work and Influence on the Music of Germany 1685-1750. London: 1899. V. 41

SPITTAL, JOHN KER

Contemporary Criticisms of Dr. Samuel Johnson, His Works and His Biographies. New York: 1923. V. 41

SPITZKA, E. C.

Insanity: Its Classification, Diagnosis and Treatment. New York: 1893. V. 40

SPIX, JOHANN BAPTIST VON

Delectus Animalium Articulatorum, Quae in Itinere per Brasiliam Annis MDCCCXVII - MDCCCXX . . . 1830-4. V. 41

Dellectus Animalium Articulatorum . . . Monachii: 1830-4. V. 44

Travels in Brazil in the Years 1817-1820. London: 1824. V. 38

SPLATT, CYNTHIA

Isadora Duncan and Gordon Craig. 1988. V. 41

Isadora Duncan and Gordon Craig. San Francisco: 1988. V. 42

SPLAWN, A. J.

Ka-Mi-a Kin. Last Hero of the Yakimas. Portland: 1917. V. 43

SPLENDID Shackles. London. V. 43

SPOCK, BENJAMIN

Avoiding Behavior Problems. New York: 1945. V. 46

SPOFFORD, HARRIET PRESCOTT

Art Decoration Applied to Furnitue. New York: 1878. V. 37

Art Decoration Applied to Furniture, by Harriet Prescott Spofford. New York: 1877. V. 37

The Maid He Married. Chicago: 1899. V. 43

Poems. Boston: 1882. V. 41; 43

SPOFFORD, HARRY

The Mysteries of Worcester; or, Charley Temple and His First Glass of Liquor. Worcester: 1846. V. 39; 44

SPOFFORD, THOMAS

Astronomical Diary and Pocket Almanack for 1845. Boston: 1844. V. 38

SPOFFORD'S Cabinet Cyclopaedia Atlas of the World. Philadelphia: 1900. V. 45

SPOFFORD'S new Cabient Cyclopaedia. Philadelphia: 1899. V. 45

SPOKESFIELD, WALTER E.

The History of Wells County, North Dakota, and Its Pioneers with a Sketch of North Dakota and the Oregin (sic!) of the Place Names. Jamestown: 1929. V. 39

The History of Wells County, North Dakota and Its Prioneers, with a Sketch of North Dakota and the Oregon (sic) of the Place Names. Jamestown, North Dakota: 1929. V. 37

SPOKESFIELD, WALTER ERNEST

History of Wells County, North Dakota, and Its Pioneers, with a Sketch of North Dakota History and the Oregin (sic) of the Place Names. Jamestown. V. 42

SPOLLEN, JAMES

Trial of James Spollen, for the Murder of Mr. George . . . Saamuel Little, at the Brodstone Terminus of the Midland Great Western Railway, Ireland . . . Dublin: 1857. V. 38

SPON, ERNEST

Workshop Receipts, for the Use of Manufacturers, Mechanics, and Scientific Amateurs, First and Second Series. London: 1884, 1885. V. 40

Workshop Receipts for the Use of Manufacturers, Mechanics and Scientific Amateurs. London: 1895-97. V. 39

SPON, ISAAC

The History of the City and State of Geneva, From Its first Foundation to this Present Time . . . London: 1687. V. 38

SPON, JACOB

The History of Geneva. London: 1687. V. 37

Recherches des Antiquites et Curiosites de la Ville de Lyon . . . Lyon. V. 44

Voyage d'Italie de Dalmatie, De Grece, et du Levant Fait Aux Annees 1675 & 1676. Amsterdam: 1679. V. 41

SPOONER, C. E.

Narrow Gauge Railways. London: 1871. V. 37; 42; 46

SPOONER, ELLA B.

The Brown Family History. Laurel: 1929. V. 40; 41

SPOONER, LYSANDER

Address to the Free Constituionalists to the People of the United States. Boston: 1860. V. 42

A Defence for Fugitive Slaves, Against the Acts of Congress of Feb. 12, 1793 and Sept. 18, 1850. Boston: 1850. V. 42

The Unconstitutionality of Slavery. Boston: 1845. V. 42

SPORANI, RAFFAELE

Vite de Pittori, Scultori, ed Architetti Genovesi . . . Genova: 1768-69. V. 40

SPORTING Anecdotes: Original and Select . . . London: 1804. V. 45

SPORTING Anecdotes; Original and Select; Including Characteristic Sketches of Eminent Persons Who Have Appeared on the Turf . . . London: 1808. V. 39; 40

SPORTING Anecdotes; Original and Select; Including Chracteristic Sketches of Eminent Prsons Who Have Appeared on the Turf . . . London: 1804. V. 37; 39; 40; 45

THE SPORTING Fishes of the British Isles. Tiverton: 1986. V. 45

THE SPORTING Repository, Containing Horse-Racing, Hunting, Coursing, Shooting, Aarchery, Trotting and Tandem Matches, Cocking, Pedestrianism, Pugilism. London: 1822. V. 37

SPORTMAN'S Dicitonary, or the Gentleman's Companion for Town and Country. London: 1792. V. 46

THE SPORTSMAN'S Dictionary. London: 1778. V. 42; 43
THE SPORTSMAN'S Dictionary. London: 1792. V. 38; 40; 42

THE SPORTSMAN'S Dictionary; Containing Instructions for Various Methods to Be Observed in Riding, Hunting, Fowling, Setting, Fishing, Racing, Farriery, Hawking, Breeding and Feeding Horses for the Road and Turf . . . London: 1807. V. 39

THE SPORTSMAN'S Dictionary; or, the Country Gentleman's Companion, In All Rural Recreations. London: 1735. V. 39
THE SPORTSMAN'S Dictionary; or, The Country Gentleman's Companion, in All Rural Recreations. London: 1744. V. 39; 40; 45

THE SPORTSMAN'S Dictionary; or, The Gentleman's Companion: for Town and Country. London: 1800. V. 39

THE SPORTSMAN'S Dictionary; or, the Gentleman's Companion: for Town and Country. Containing full and particular Instructions for Riding, Hunting, Fowling, Setting, Fishing, Racing, Farriery, Cocking, Hawking, &c with the various . . . 1785. V. 37

THE SPORTSMAN'S Porfolio of American Field Sports. New York: 1930. V. 39

THE SPORTSMAN'S Portfolio of American Field Sports. Boston: 1855. V. 43

SPOTSWOOD, JOHN

The History of the Church of Scotland, Beginning the Year of Our Lord 203 and Continued to the End of the Reign of King James the VI . . . London: 1655. V. 44

SPOTTISWOOD, JOHN 1565-1639

The History of the Church of Scotland, Beginning the Year of Our Lord 203 . . . London: 1666. V. 44

An Introduction to the Knowledge of the Stile of Writs, Simple and Compound, Made Use of in Scotland . . . V. 46

An Introduction to the Knowledge of the Stile of Writs . . . (with) A Treatise Concerning the Origin and Progress of Fees . . . Edinburgh: 1761. V. 43

SPOTTISWOODE, JOHN 1646-1728

A Discourse Shewing the Necessary Qualifications of a Student of the Laws. Edinburgh: 1704. V. 40

The History of the Church of Scotland. London: 1655. V. 39

SPOTTS, DAIVD L.

Campaigning with Custer and the Nineteenth Kansas Volunteer Cavalry on the Washita Campaign 1868-69. Los Angeles: 1928. V. 45

THE SPOUTER'S Companion; Containing Favourite Recitations, Comic and Serious . . . London: 1823? V. 43

THE SPOUTER'S Companion; or Theatrical Remembrancer . . . London: 1770? V. 45; 46

SPRAGUE, CARLTON

The Mission of Beauty. A Poem. Buffalo: 1905. V. 46

SPRAGUE, HOSEA

Hosea Sprague's Register of the Weather, in Hingham, Massachusetts, on the Plain, One Mile from the Sea. 1837. V. 37

SPRAGUE, J. T.

The Treachery in Texas, the Secession of Texas, and the Arrest of the United States Officers and Soldiers Serving in Texas. New York: 1862. V. 40

SPRAGUE, JOHN T.

The Origin, Progress, an Conclusion of the Florida War . . . New York: 1848. V. 42

SPRAGUE, KURTH

Promise Kept. Austin: 1975. V. 42

SPRAGUE, WILLIAM

Alphabet: the Alderman's Feast. Albany: 1855. V. 41

SPRAGUE, WILLIAM B.

Annals of the American Pulpit; or, Commemorative Notices of Distinguished American Clergymen of VArious Denominations, from the Early Settlement of the Country to the Close of the Year 1855. New York: 1866-77. V. 42

SPRANGE, J.

The Tunbridge Wells Guide . . . to which is added a Particular Description of the Towns and Villages, Remains of Antiquities, Gentlemens Seats . . . Tunbridge Wells: 1797. V. 37; 40

SPRAT, THOMAS 1635-1713

The History of the Royal Society of London. London: 1667. V. 37; 38; 42

The History of the Royal Society of London, for the Improving of Natural Knowledge. London: 1702. V. 37; 38; 42; 44

The History of the Royal Society of London, for Improving of Natural Knowledge. London: 172-. V. 46

The History of the Royal Society of London. London: 1722. V. 38; 39; 40; 42; 43; 44

The History of the Royal Society of London, for the Improving of Natural Knowledge. London: 1734. V. 43

Observations on Monsieur de Sorbier's Voyage into England. London: 1665. V. 41; 45

A Relation of the Late Wicked Contrivance of Stephen Blackhead and Robert Young, Against the Lives of Several Persons, by Forging an Association Under Their Hands. In the Savoy: 1693. V. 45

A True Account and Declaration of the Horrid Conspiracy Against the Late King, His Present Majesty and the Government . . . In the Savoy: 1685. V. 44

SPRAT, THOMAS 1635-1713 continued

A True Account and Declaration of the Horrid Conspiracy Against the Late King, His Present Majesty and the Government. London: 1685. V. 42; 43

A True Account and Declaration of the Horrid Conspiracy Against the Late King, His Present Majesty, and the Government. London, in the Savoy: 1685. V. 45

SPRATT, G.

Obstetric TAbles . . . London: 1833. V. 43

Obstetric Tables: Comprising Graphic Illustrations, With Descriptions and Practical Remarks . . . Philadelphia: 1847. V. 42

SPRATT, G., MRS.

The Language of Birds. London: 1837. V. 43

SPRATT, GEORGE

Obstetric Tables. London: 1843. V. 44

Obstetric Tables: Comprising Graphic Illustrations, with Descriptions and Practical Remarks . . . Philadelphia: 1848. V. 45

SPRATT, T. A. B.

Travels and Researches in Crete. London: 1865. V. 37; 40

SPRATT, THOMAS A. B.

On the Geology of Malta and Gozo. London: 1854. V. 40

SPRATT, THOMAS ABEL BRIMAGE

Travels in Lycia, Milyas and the Cibyratis, in Company with Late Rev. E. T. Daniell. London: 1847. V. 40; 46

SPRECCHIUS, POMPEIUS

Antabsinthium Clavanae id est quod Absinthium Umbelliferum, in Monte Servae Belluni, et aliis Italiae Montibus ortum fit idem cum Absinthio Alpino Umbellifero Caroli Clusii . . . Venice: 1611. V. 37

SPRENGEL, CHRISTIAN KONRAD 1750-1816

Das Entdeckte Geheimniss der Natur im Bau und in der Befruchtung der Blumen. Berlin: 1793. V. 46

SPRENGEL, KURT

Versuch Einer Pragmatischen Geschichte der Arzneykunde. Halle: 1821/23/1/1/3/. V. 38

SPRENGER, GEORGE F.

Concise History of the Camp and Field Life of the 122nd Regiment, Pennsylvania Volunteers . . . Lancaster: 1885. V. 46

SPREULL, JOHN

An Accompt Current Betwixt Scotland and Englnd Balanced. Edinburgh?: 1705. V. 38

SPRIG and Turfy. Mt. Vernon. V. 40

SPRING, AGNES WRIGHT

The Cheyenne and Black Hills Stage and Express Routes. Glendale: 1949. V. 37; 40; 42; 43; 44

The Cheyenne Club, Mecca of the Aristocrats of the Old-Time Cattle Range. Kansas City: 1961. V. 37; 43

The Cheyenne Club. Kansas City: 1976. V. 43

70 Years a Panoramic History of the Wyoming Stock Growers Association. 1942. V. 37; 43

Seventy Years: a Panoramic History of the Wyoming Stock Growers Association Interwoven with Data Relative to the Cattle Industry in Wyoming. Cheyenne: 1942. V. 39; 44

Seventy Years, a Panoramic History of the Wyoming Stock Growers Association, Interwoven with Data Relative to the Cattle Industry in Wyoming. 1943. V. 38

William Chapman Deming of Wyoming. Glendale: 1944. V. 40; 45

SPRING, GARDINER

Memoirs of the Rev. Samuel J. Mills, Late Missionary to the South Western Section of the United States, and Agent of the American Colonization Society, Deputed to Explore the Coast of Africa. New York: 1820. V. 38; 40; 42; 45

SPRING, HOWARD

Shabby Tiger. London: 1934. V. 37

SPRING, MAURICE

Quattrocentisteria. How Sandro Botticelli Saw Simonetta in the Spring. New York: 1937. V. 44

SPRING, SAMUEL

A Sermon, Delivered Before the Massachusetts Missionary Society. Newburyport: 1802. V. 38; 40

SPRINGER, ANTON

Albrect Durer. Mit Tafeln und Ullustrationem im Text. Berlin: 1892. V. 44

SPRINGER, FERDINAND

Plato. The Symposium of Socrates. (Stuttgart): 1937. V. 37

SPRINGER, JOHN S.

Forest Life and Forest Trees . . . New York: 1851. V. 42; 44

SPRINGS, ELLIOTT WHITE

The Rise and Fall of Carol Banks. Garden City: 1931. V. 42

SPRINGSTEED, ANNE FRANCES

The Expert Waitress. New York: 1894. V. 44

SPROAT, GILBERT MALCOLM

Scenes and Studies of Savage Life. London: 1868. V. 37; 42

SPROAT, NANCY

Village Poems. New York: 1825? V. 40

SPROGLE, HOWARD

The Philadelphia Police. Philadelphia: 1887. V. 42

SPROT, LIEUT. GENERAL

Incidents and Anecdotes in the Life of Lieut. Gen. Sprot, Honorary Colonel of the Princess Louise's Argyll and Sutherland Highlanders . . . Edinburgh: 1906-07. V. 42

SPROULE, JOHN

Elements of Practical Agriculture, Comprehending the Nature, Properties, and Improvement of Soils. London: 1844. V. 40

SPRUCE, RICHARD

Notes of a Botanist on the Amazon and Andes. London: 1908. V. 43; 46

SPRUNGER, S.

Orchids from Curtis's Botanical Magazine. London: 1987. V. 43; 44; 46

SPRUNT, ALEXANDER

South Carolina Bird Life. Columbia: 1949. V. 40

SPRUNT, JAMES

Chronicles of the Cape Fear River . . . Raleigh: 1914. V. 45

Derelicts. Wilmington: 1920. V. 45; 46

Tales of the Cape Fear Blockade. Wilmington: 1960. V. 46

SPRY, IRENE M.

The Papers of the Palliser Expedition, 1857-1960. Toronto: 1968. V. 45

SPRY, W.

The British Coleoptera Delineated, Consisting of Figures of all the Genera of British Beetles. London: 1861. V. 40

SPRY, W. J. J.

The Cruise of Her Majesty's Ship Challenger. London: 1876. V. 41

SPRY, WILLIAM J.

Life on the Bosophorus. London: 1895. V. 37

SPUHLER, FRIEDRICH

Islamic Carpets and Textiles in the Keir Collection. London: 1978. V. 46

SPUNT, JAMES

Chronicles of the Cape Fear River Being Some Account of Historic Events on the cape Fear River. Raleigh: 1914. V. 37

SPURLING, HALLIDAY

The Kelmscott Press and William Morris Master-Craftsman. London: 1924. V. 41

SPURNT, JAMES

Tales and Traditions of the Lower Cape Fear, 1661-1896. Wilmington, NC: 1896. V. 37

SPURR, HARRY A.

Bachelor Ballads. London: 1899. V. 41

SPURR, JOSIAH

The Times. Boston: 1820. V. 42

SPURR, JOSIAH E.

Through the Yukon Gold Diggings: a Narrative of Personal Travel. Boston: 1900. V. 45; 46

SPURR, JOSIAH EDWARD

Geology of the Aspen Mining District, Colorado with Atlas. Washington: 1898. V. 38; 41; 45

Geology of the Tonopah Mining District, Nevada. Washington: 1905. V. 38

SPURRIER, JOHN

The Practical Farmer, Being a New and Compendious System of Husbandry, Adopted to the Different soils and Climates of America. Wilmington: 1793. V. 46

SPURZHEIM, JOHANN GASPAR 1776-1832

The Anatomy of the Brain with a General View of the Nervous System. London: 1826. V. 46

Examination of the Objections Made in Britain Against the Doctrines of Gall and Spurzheim. Edinburgh: 1817. V. 39; 40; 42

Observations on the Deranged Manifestations of the Mind, or Insanity. London: 1817. V. 38

Observations on the Deranged Manifestations of the Mind, or Insanity. Boston: 1833. V. 38; 42; 46

Observations on the Deranged Manifestations of the Mind or, Insanity. Boston: 1835. V. 43; 45; 46

Observations on the Deranged Manifestations of the Human Mind; or, Insanity . . . Boston: 1836. V. 42

Outlines of the Physiognomical System of Drs. Gall and Spurzheim. London: 1815. V. 40; 42

Phrenology, or, the Doctrine of the Mind; and of the Relations Between Its Manifestations and the Body. London: 1825. V. 39

Phrenology in Connexion with the Study of Physiognomy: Part 1. London: 1826. V. 43; 46

Phrenology in Connexion with the Study of Physiognomy. Boston: 1833. V. 40; 44

The Physiognomical System of Drs. Gall and Spurzheim. London: 1815. V. 37; 38

The Physiognomical System of Drs. Gall and Spurzheim . . . London: 1815. V. 43

A Sketch of the Natural Laws of Man. London: 1828. V. 42

A View of the Elementary Principles of Education, Founded on the Study of the Nature of Man . . . Boston: 1832. V. 42

A View of the Elementary Principles of Education, Founded on the Study of the nature of man. Edinburgh: 1821. V. 37

A SPY Upon the Spectator. London: 1711. V. 39

SPYRI, JOHANNA

Gritli's Children. Philadelphia: 1924. V. 41

Heidi. Boston: 1885. V. 37; 38; 41; 42

Heidi. Philadelphia: 1922. V. 38; 39

SQUADRON A: a History of its First Fifty Years 1889-1939. New York: 1939. V. 37; 42

SQUAIR, JOHN

The Townships of Darlington and Clarke. Including Bowmanville and Newcastle, Province of Ontario, Canada. Toronto: 1927. V. 37

SQUARE, JOHN

Cheddar Gorge. London: 1937. V. 41

SQUIBB, ROBERT

The Gardener's Calendar for the States of North Carolina, South Carolina and Georgia. Charleston: 1827. V. 38; 39; 40

SQUIER, EPHRAIM GEORGE 1821-1888

Antiquities of the State of New York. Buffalo: 1851. V. 42

Honduras Interoceanic Railway. Preliminary Report. New York: 1854. V. 41; 44

Honduras: Descriptive, Historical and Statistical. London: 1870. V. 45

Monograph of Authors Who Have Written on the Languages of Central America, and Collected Vocabularies or Composed Works in the Native Dialects of that Country. London: 1861. V. 37

Nicaragua; Its People, Scenery, Monuments, and the Propsoed Ineteroceanic Canal . . . New York: 1852. V. 37; 39; 45

Nicaragua; Its People, Scenery, Monuments, and the Proposed Interoceanic Canal. New York: 1856. V. 38; 39

Nicaragua; Its People, Scenery, Monuments, Resources, Condition & Proposed Canal. Revised Edition. New York: 1860. V. 37

Notes on Central America; Particularly the States of Honduras and San Salvador . . . New York: 1855. V. 37; 43; 46

Observations on the Aboriginal Monuments of the Mississippi Valley . . . New York: 1847. V. 37; 46

Peru. Incidents of Travel and Exploration in the Land of the Incas. London: 1877. V. 44

Peru: Indicents of Travel and Exploration in the Land of the Incas. New York: 1877. V. 38; 41

The Serpent Symbol, and the Worship of the Reciprocal Principles of Nature in America. New York: 1851. V. 44

Travel in Central America Particularly in Nicaragua . . . New York: 1853. V. 38; 40; 42

Tropical Fibres: Their Production and Economic Extraction. New York: 1861. V. 46

Tropical Fibres: Their Production and Economic Extraction. London: & New York: 1863. V. 44

Tropical Fibres: Their Production and Exonomic Extraction. London/New York: 1863. V. 37

Waikna: Adventures on the Mosquito Shore by Samuel A. Bard. New York: 1855. V. 38; 43

SQUIER, LOUISE SMITH

Sketches of Southern Scenes. New York: 1885. V. 39

SQUINTS Through an Opera Glass. New York: 1850. V. 45

SQUIRE Bickerstaff Detected; or, the Astrological Impostor Convicted . . . London: 1708. V. 38; 41

SQUIRE Bickerstaff Detected; or, the Astrological Impostor Convincted, by John Partridge, Student in Physick and Astrology. N.P.: 1708. V. 40

SQUIRE, J. C.

If It Happened Otherwise. 1931. V. 43

SQUIRE, JACK COLLINGS

Poems and Baudelaire Flowers. London: 1909. V. 37

SQUIRE, JANE

A Proposal for Discovering Our Longitude . . . Proposition Pour La Decouverte de Notre Longitude . . . London: 1742. V. 40; 41

SQUIRE, JOHN

Cheddar Gorge. London: 1937. V. 39; 40; 41; 43; 44; 46

SQUIRE, LORENE

Wildfowling with a Camera. Philadelphia & New York: 1938. V. 37

SQUIRE, M. C.

The Beggar and His Benafactor! London: 1809. V. 39

SQUIRE, SAMUEL 1713-1766

An Enquiry into the Foundation of the English Constitution. London: 1745. V. 40; 42

The Important Question Discussed; or, a Serious and Impartial Inquiry into the True Interest of England, with Respect to the Continent. London: 1746. V. 39

SQUIRE, WATSON

Resources and Development of Washington Territory. Seattle: 1886. V. 37; 42; 43

SQUIRES, FREDERICK

Architectonics: The Tales of Tom Thumbtack, Architect. Volume One. New York: 1914. V. 42

The Tales of Tom Thumtack, Architect. New York: 1914. V. 38

SQUIRES, J. DUANE

The Granite State of the United States. New York: 1956. V. 42

SQUIRES, RADCLIFFE

Waiting in the Bone and Other Poems. Omaha: 1973. V. 40

SRACHEY, LYTTON

Books and Characters. London: 1922. V. 40

STAAL DE LAUNAY, MARGUERITE JEANNE CORDIER DE LAUNAY 1684-1750

Memoires . . . Londres: 1755. V. 43

STAATS, WILLIAM

A Tight Squeeze. Boston & New York: 1879. V. 43

STABLES, GORDON

A Boy's Book of Battleships. London: 1914. V. 44

STABLES, W. GORDON

Turkish and Other Baths. London: 1883. V. 41

STACE, MACHELL

John Bon and Mast Person. London: 1808. V. 45

Merrie Conceited Iests of George Peele Gentleman . . . London: 1809. V. 45

STACEY, C. P.

Records of the Nile Voyageurs 1884-1885 . . . Gordon Relief Expedition. Toronto: 1959. V. 39; 42; 45

STACK, RICHARD

An Introduction to the Study of Chemistry, Explaining Its Principles and Their Application to Arts, Manufactures &c. &c. Dublin: 1802. V. 37; 39; 41; 43; 46

STACKE, H. F.

The Worcestershire Regiment in the Great War . . . Kidderminster: 1929. V. 42

STACKHOUSE, JOHN

Nereis Britannica: Containing All the Species of Fuci, Natives of the British Coasts; with Description in English and Latin, and Plates Coloured from Nature. Bath: 1795-1801. V. 37; 42; 43

STACKHOUSE, JOHN continued

Nereis Britannica. Bath: 1795. V. 37

STACKHOUSE, T.

A New History of the Bible from the Beginning of the World to the Establishment of Christianity . . . London: 1742-44. V. 38

STACKHOUSE, THOMAS

Memoirs of the Life, Character, Conduct and Writings of Dr. Francis Atterbury, Late Bishop of Rochester, From His Birth to His Banishment. London: 1727. V. 40

STACKPOLE, EVERETT

history of Durham New Hampshire (Oyster River Plantation) with Generalogical Notes. 1913. V. 42

STACPOOLE, ALBERIC

The Seven Words from the Cross: a Meditation in Poetic Idion. Worcester: 1974. V. 46

STACPOOLE, FLORENCE

Our Babies and How to take Care of Them. London: 1890. V. 40

STACPOOLE, HENRY DE VERE

The Blue Lagoon. 1910. V. 44; 46

The City in the Sea. New York: 1925. V. 40

Pierrette. London: 1900. V. 46

STACTON, DAVID

An Unfamiliar Country. (1953). V. 37

STACY, EDMUND

The Black Bird's Tale. London: 1710. V. 40; 42

STACY-JUDD, ROBERT B.

Atlantis - Mother of Empires. Los Angeles: 1939. V. 37; 41

STADEN, HANS

America Tertia Pars. Frankfort: 1592. V. 40; 43

The Captivity of Hans Stade of Hesse, in A.D. 1547-1555, Among the Wild Tribes of Eastern Brazil. London: 1874. V. 41; 45

STADEN, JOHANNES 1581-1634

Neue Teutsche Lieder, mit Poetischen Neuen Texten, so Zu Taentzen Bequem. Nuernberg: 1609. V. 40

STAEL-HOLSTEIN, ANNE LOUISE GERMAINE NECKER, BARONNE DE 1766-1817

Considerations of the Principal Events of the French Revolution. New York: 1818. V. 45

Corinne ou l'Italie. Paris: 1807. V. 45

Delphine: a Novel. London: 1803. V. 44

Delphine: a Novel. London: 1805. V. 44

Germany . . . London: 1813. V. 41; 43; 45

De l'Influence des Passions sur le Bonheur des Individus et des Nations. Lausanne: 1796. V. 45

The Influence of the Passions Upon Happiness of Individuals and of Nations. London: 1813. V. 44; 45

Letters and Reflections of the Austrian field-Marshall Prince de Ligne . . . Philadelphia: 1809. V. 45; 46

A Treatise on the Influence of the Passions, Upon the Happiness of Individuals and of Nations . . . London: 1798. V. 38; 42

Zulma, and Other Tales: To Which is Prefixed an Essay on Fictions. London: 1813. V. 44

STAEL-HOLSTEIN, ANNE LOUISE GERMAINE NECKER DE 1766-1817

Corinna. London: 1807. V. 37

STAEL-HOLSTEIN, AUGUSTE-LOUIS DE

Letters on England. London: 1825. V. 37

STAFFORD, CORNELIUS WILLIAM

The Philadelphia Directory for 1798. Philadelphia: 1798. V. 41; 42

STAFFORD, JEAN

Boston Adventure. New York: 1944. V. 37; 44

STAFFORD, MALLIE

The March of Empire Through Three Decades. San Francisco: 1884. V. 38; 42

STAFFORD, RICHARD

To the Representatives of the People and Nation of England, at What Time or Place Soever They Shall be Assembled. London: 1695. V. 45

STAFFORD, RICHARD ANTHONY

A Series of Observations on Strictures of the Urethra. London: 1829. V. 39

STAFFORD, THOMAS

Pacata Hibernia. Ireland Appeased and Reduced. London: 1633. V. 41

Pacata Hibernia. London: 1821. V. 46

Pacta Hibernia, or a History of the Wars of Ireland During the Reing of Queen Elizabeth . . . Dublin: 1820. V. 38

STAFFORD, W. COOKE

History of the War in Russia and Turkey . . . London: 1855-56. V. 39

STAFFORD, WILLIAM

Listening Deep. 1984. V. 39

The Quiet of the Land. New York: 1979. V. 40; 42

Smoke's Ways: Poems from Limited Editions 1968-1981. Port Townsend: 1983. V. 44

Sometimes Like a Legend. 1981. V. 37; 40

Sometimes Like a Legend. Copper Canyon Press: 1981. V. 38

Things that Happen. New York: 1980. V. 41

Tuft by Puff. Mt. Horeb: 1978. V. 38

Weather. 1969. V. 39

West of Your City. Los Gatos: 1960. V. 39

STAFILEO, GIOVANNI, BP. d. 1528

Tractatus Non Minus Utilis Quam Necessarius de Literis Gratiae. Paris: 1557. V. 40

STAFLEU, F. A.

Taxonomic Literature, a Selective Guide to Botanical Publications and Collections with Dates, Commentaries and Types, Volume 6, Sti-Vuy. Utrecht,: 1986. V. 37; 38

Taxonomic Literature: Volumes 1-4, A-Sak. Utrecht and the Hague: 1976-84. V. 37

THE STAGE in 1816. A Satirical Poem in three Parts. London: 1816. V. 39; 42

STAGE Register. Supplement to the American Traveler. Boston: 1825. V. 46

STAGG, JOHN

The Cumbrian Minstrel. Manchester: 1821. V. 39

The Minstrel of the North; or, Cumbrian Legends. London: 1810. V. 42; 43

STAHLBERG, GEORGE

An History of the Late Revolution in Sweden, Which Happened on the 19th of August 1772. Edinburgh: 1776. V. 46

STAHLE, WILLIAM

The Description of the Borough of Reading . . . Reading: 1841. V. 42

STAIKOS, KONSTANTINOS S.

'Charts' of Greek Typography. Athens: 1989. V. 45

STAINED Windows and Painted Glass Initiated by the Beautiful Process. Diaphanie: a Description of the Best Methods with Concise Directions for Transparency Paitnings. London: 1860. V. 41

STAINFORTH, MARTIN

Racehorses in Australia. Sydney: 1922. V. 37; 42

STAIR, JOHN DALRYMPLE, 5TH EARL OF 1720-1789

An Argument to Prove That It Is the Indispensable Duty of the Creditors of the Public to Insist, That Overnment do Forthwith Bring Forward the Considerations of the State of the nation; in Order to Ascertain, As Near as May be the Annual Receipts . . . London: 1783. V. 41

An Attempt to Balance the Income and Expenditure of the State . . . London: 1783. V. 42

Considerations Preliminary to the Fixing the Supplies, the Ways and Means and the Taxes for the Year 1781. London: 1781. V. 41

Facts and Their Consequences Submitted to the Consideration of the Public at Large, but More Particularly to that of the Finance Minsiter, and of Those Who Are Or Mean to Become Creditors of the State. London: 1782. V. 41

STALEY, EDGCUMBE

The Guilds of Florence. London: 1906. V. 42

STALKARTT, MARMADUKE

Naval ARchtiecture or the Rudiments of Ship Bilding Exemplified in a Series of Draughts and Plans. London: 1787. V. 37; 46

STALLARD, J. H.

London Pauperism Amongst Jews and Christians. London: 1867. V. 40

STALLWORTHY, JON

Wilfred Owen - a Biography. London: 1975. V. 40; 41

STALPART VANDER WIEL, CORNELIS

Hondert Seldzame Aanmerkingen, so Inde Geneesals Heel-en Sny-konst. Amsterdam: 1686. V. 43

STAMFORD, THOMAS GREY, 2ND EARL OF

The Case of the Earl of Stamford, Relating to the Wood Lately Cut in Enfield Chace. London: 1701. V. 39

STAMP ACT CONGRESS, NEW YORK, 1765.

Authentic Account of the Proceedings of the Congress Held at New York in MDCCLXV, on the Subject of the American Stamp Act. London: 1767. V. 40

STAMP, GAVIN

Temples of Power. Burford: 1979. V. 37; 39; 43

STAMP, JOSIAH

The Fundamental Principles of Taxation in the Light of Modern Developments. London: 1921. V. 37

STAMPIGLIA, SILVINO

Camilla. An Opera. London: 1706. V. 38

STANBROOK ABBEY PRESS

The Stanbrook Abbey Press. Ninety-Two Years of Its History. Written and Illustrated by the Benedictines of Stanbrook. Worcester: 1970. V. 38

STANBURY, HOWARD

Exploration and Survey of the Valley of the Great Salt Lake of Utah . . . Philadelphia: 1852. V. 44

STAND, PAUL

Time in New England. New York: 1950. V. 45

STANDARD Atlas of Livingston County, Michigan Including a Plat Book of the Villages, Cities and Townships . . . Chicago: 1895. V. 39

STANDARD Atlas of Macomb County, Michigan, Including a Plat Book of the Villages, Cities and Townships. Chicago: 1916. V. 39

STANDARD Atlas of Stutsman County North Dakota Including a Plat Book . . . Chicago: 1930. V. 40

STANDARD Blue Book Texas Edition Featuring West Texas and the Panhandle Plains Section. San Antonio: 1921. V. 44

A STANDARD Dictionary of the English Language Upon Original Plans . . . New York & London: 1900. V. 40

STANDARD, HENRIETTA ELIZA VAUGHAN PALMER 1856-1911

Beautiful Jim, of the Blankshire Regiment. London: 1888. V. 41

Mrs. Bob. London: 1889. V. 41

The Soul of the Bishop. London: 1893. V. 41

THE STANDARD Library Cyclopaedia of Political, Constitutional, Statistical and Forensic Knowledge. London: 1853. V. 39; 42; 45

THE STANDARD Medical Directory of North America, 1902. Chicago: 1902. V. 38

STANDEN, E. A.

European Post-Medieval Tapestries and Related Hangings in the Metropolitan Museum of Art. New York: 1985. V. 37

STANDING BEAR, CHIEF

My People the Sioux. New York: 1928. V. 45

STANDING BEAR, CHIEF, OF THE OGLALA SIOUX

My People the Sioux. 1928. V. 41

STANDING, JULIET

Exordium: Daedalus Press 1968-1983. Wymondham: 1983. V. 42

STANDING Orders and Regulations for the Royal Fusiliers. Malta: 1834. V. 41

STANDING Orders. XXIII Regiment, or, Royal Welsh Fusiliers . . . Montreal: 1841. V. 37

STANDING, PERCY CROSS

Cricket of Today and Yesterday. London: 1902. V. 42; 44

STANDISH, FRANK HALL

The Life of Voltaire, with Interesting Particulars Repsecting His Death and Anecdotes and Characters of His Contemporaries. London: 1821. V. 41; 43; 45

STANDLEY, P. C.

Trees and Shrubs of Mexico. 1982. V. 39

Trees and Shrubs of Mexico. London: 1982. V. 37; 38

STANELY, THOMAS

The History of Philosophy. London: 1687. V. 38

STANESBY, SAMUEL

The Bridal Souvenir. London: 1857. V. 43

Light for the Path of Life. London: 1860. V. 42

STANFIELD, CLARKSON

Stanfield's Coast Scenery, a Series of Views in the British Channel . . . 1836. V. 44

Stanfield's Coast Scenery. London: 1836. V. 45; 46

Stanfield's Coast Scenery. London: 1847. V. 44; 45

STANFIELD, J. A.

Central Gaulish Potters. London: 1958. V. 40

STANFORD, DON

The Traveler; Allegorical Lyrics. Rowe: 1955. V. 37

STANFORD, JOHN

The Winters of that Country. 1984. V. 46

STANFORD, P. THOMAS

The Tragedy of the Negro in America. Boston: 1898. V. 42

STANFORD UNIVERSITY

A Memorial Library of Music at Stanford University. Stanford: 1950. V. 40

STANFORD, WILLIAM 1509-1558

An Exposition of the Kinges Praerogative Collected Out of the Great Abridgement of Justice Fitzherbert, and Other Old Writers of the Lawes of England. London: 1590. V. 40

Les Plees del Coron, Divisees in Plusors Titles and Common Lieux. London: 1607. V. 40

STANHOPE, CHARLES, EARL

A Letter from Earl Stanhope, to the Right Honourable Edmund Burke, Containing a Short Answer to His Late Speech on the French Revolution. London: 1790. V. 39; 42

Principles of the Science of Tuning. London: 1806. V. 41

The Rights of Juries Defended Together with Authorities of Law in Support of Those Rights. London: 1792. V. 41

STANHOPE, EARL OF

Life of the Right Honourable William Pitt. London: 1862. V. 38

STANHOPE, EUGENIA

The Deportment of a Married Life: Laid Down in a Series of Letters, Written by the Honourable E----- S-----, Few Years Since, to a Youn Lady, Her Relation, Then Lately Married. London: 1790. V. 38

The Deportment of a Married Life: laid down in a series of letters, written by the Honorable E--S-- a few years since, to a young lady, her relation, then lately married. London: 1798. V. 37; 40; 45

STANHOPE, GEORGE

A Paraphrase and Comment upon the epistles and gospels appointed to be used in the Church of England on all saints and holy days throughout the year. The Second Edition, corrected. London: 1706/9. V. 37

Parsons, His Christian Directory, Being a Treatise of Holy Resolution. London: 1709. V. 45

STANHOPE, HESTER

The Life and Letters of Lady Hester Stanhope. London: 1897. V. 46

Memoirs of the Lady Hester Stanhope, as Related by Herself in Conversations with Her Physician . . . London: 1845. V. 44

STANHOPE, JOHN SPENCER

Olympia; or, Topography illustrative of the actual state of the plain of Olympia and the ruins of the city of Elis. London: 1824. V. 37

STANHOPE, LOUISA SIDNEY

The Crusaders. London: 1820. V. 39

STANHOPE MOLYNEUX, HERBERT, 5TH EARL OF 1866-1923

Catalogue of Books Selected from the Library of an English Amateur. London: 1893. V. 40

STANHOPE, PHILIP DORMER, of the 1st Dragoon Guards

Genuine Memoirs of Asiaticus, in a Series of Letters to a friend, During Five Years Residence in Different Parts of India, Three of Which Were in the Service of the Nahob of Arcot. London: 1784. V. 41

STANHOPE, PHILIP HENRY, 5TH EARL OF 1805-1875

History of England from the Peace of Utrecht to the Peace of Aix-La°Chapelle. London: 1836-54. V. 39

History of England from the Peace of Utrecht to the Peace of Versailles 1713-1783 . . . London: 1858. V. 37; 40

Notes of Conversations with the Duke of Wellington 1831-1851. London: 1888. V. 42

STANIHURST, RICHARD

De Rebus in Hibernia Gestis. Antwerp: 1584. V. 40; 42

STANISLAVSKY, CONSTANTIN

My Life in Art. Boston: 1924. V. 37

STANLEY, ARTHUR PENRHYN

The Gipsies: A Prize Poem Recited In the Theatre Oxford. Oxford: 1837. V. 37

Historical Memorials of Westminster Abbey. London: 1896. V. 38; 39

Sermon Preached by Arthur Penrhyn Stanley, Dean of Westminster in Westminster Abbey June 19, 1870 . . . London: 1870. V. 43

Sinai and Palestine in Connection With Their History. London: 1856. V. 39; 40; 45

Sinai and Palestine in Connection with Their History. London: 1860. V. 42

STANLEY, CLARK

The Life and Adventures of the American Cowboy . . . Providence. V. 39

The Life and Adventures of the American Cow-Boy. Life in the Far West. Providence: 1897. V. 39

True Life in the Far West by an American Cowboy. Worcester: 1898. V. 43

STANLEY, D. S.

Personal Memoirs of . . . Cambridge: 1917. V. 45

Report on the Yellowstone Expedition of 1873. Washington: 1874. V. 37

STANLEY, EDWARD

Before and After Waterloo. London: 1908. V. 42

Elmira, a Dramatick Poem: With Thoughts on Tragedy. Norwich: 1790. V. 37

The Young Horsewoman's Compendium of the Modern Art of Riding. London: 1827. V. 39

STANLEY, EDWIN J.

Life of Rev. L. B. Stateler or 65 Years on the Frontier. Dallas: 1907. V. 38

Life of Rev. L. B. Stateler or Sixty Five Years on the Frontier. Nashville: 1907. V. 39; 40; 42; 43; 45

Rambles in Wonderland. New York: 1878. V. 37; 39

STANLEY, F.

The Apaches of New Mexico, 1540-1940. Pampa Texas: 1962. V. 40

Ciudad Santa Fe: Spanish Domination (1610-1821). (with) Ciudad (sic) Santa Fe: Mexican Rule, 1821-1846. (with) Ciudad Santa Fe: Territorial Days, 1846-1912. Denver and Pampa: 1958/62/65. V. 40

Desperadoes of New Mexico. Denver: 1953. V. 40

Fort Bascom: Comanche-Kiowa Barrier. Pampa: 1961. V. 40

The Grant that Maxwell Bought. Denver: 1952. V. 38

Ike Stockton. Denver: 1959. V. 40

Jim Courtright: Two Gun Marshal of Fort Worth. Denver: 1957. V. 40; 41

The Las Vegas, New Mexico Story. Denver: 1951. V. 39; 43

Raton Chronicle. Denver: 1948. V. 43

Rodeo Town (Canadian, Texas). Denver: 1953. V. 40

Santanta and the Kiowas. Borger: 1968. V. 37; 45

Socorro, the Oasis. Denver: 1950. V. 43

STANLEY, GEORGE F. G.

In the Face of Danger. The History of the Lake Superior Regiment. Port Aruthur: 1960. V. 39

STANLEY, HENRY MORTON

The American Testimonial Banquet to Henry M. Stanley, in Recognition of His Heroic Achievements in the Cause of Humanity, Science & Civilization and a Greeting to His Chief Officers. V. 46

The Autobiography of Sir Henry Morton Stanley. London: 1909. V. 46

The Congo and the Founding of Its Free State. London: 1885. V. 40; 41; 42; 43; 44; 45

The Congo and the Founding of Its Free State. New York: 1885. V. 42; 45; 46

The Congo and the Founding of Its Free State. London: 1886. V. 44; 45

Coomassie and Magdala: The Story of Two British Campaigns in Africa. New York: 1874. V. 42

Coomassie. The Story of the Campaign in Africa 1873-4. London: 1896. V. 41

How I Found Livingstone. London: 1872. V. 38; 40

In Darkest Africa . . . V. 44

In Darkest Africa. London: 1890. V. 38; 39; 40; 41; 42; 44; 45; 46

In Darkest Africa. New York: 1890. V. 38; 40; 42; 43; 44; 45

In Darkest Africa. New York: 1891. V. 38; 39

Magdala. The Story of the Abyssinian Campaign of 1866-67. London: 1896. V. 41

My Dark Companions and Their Strange Stories. London: 1813. V. 42

My Early Travels and Adventures in America and Asia. New York: 1905. V. 38

Through the Dark Continent, or the Sources of the Nile Around the Great Lakes of Equitorial Africa and Down the Livingstone River to the Atlantic Ocean. London. V. 46

Through the Dark Continent or the Sources of the Nile Around the Great Lakes of Equatorial Africa and Down the Livingstone River to the Atlantic Ocean. London: 1878. V. 40; 42

Through the Dark Continent. New York: 1878. V. 37; 40; 44

Through the Dark Continent, or The Source of the Nile, Around the Great Lakes of Equatorial Africa and Down the Livingstone River to the Atlantic Ocean. Toronto: 1878. V. 42

Through the Dark Continent, or, the Sources of the Nile Around the Great Lakes of Equatorial Africa and Down the Livingstone River to the Atlantic Ocean. London: 1899. V. 46

STANLEY, JOHN THOMAS

An Account of the Hot Springs in Iceland . . . Edinburgh?: 1793. V. 46

An Account of the Hot Springs in Iceland with an Analysis of Their Waters. n.p.: 1795. V. 45

STANLEY, THOMAS 1625-1678

The History of Philosophy. London: 1655. V. 39; 41

The History of Philosophy. London: 1656. V. 40

The History of Philosophy . . . 1687. V. 45

The History of Philosophy. London: 1687. V. 39; 41; 42

Historia Philosophiae. Vitas, Opiniones, Resque Gestas, et Dicta Philosophorum Sectae . . . Venice: 1731. V. 40; 41

The History of Philosophy. London: 1743. V. 39; 42

STANLEY, W. B.

Elephant Hunting in West Africa. London. V. 43

STANLY, EDWARD

Report to the House of Representatives of the United States of America, Vindicating the Rights of Charles T. Jackson to the Discovery of the Anaesthetic Effects of Ether Vapor, and Disproving the Claims of W. T. G. Morton. Boston: 1852. V. 39

Report to the House of Representatives of the United States of America, Vindicating the Rights of Charles T. Jackson to the Discovery of Etherization. Washington: 1852. V. 41; 42

STANNUS, HUGH

Alfred Stevens and His Work. London: 1891. V. 39

STANSBERRY, LON R.

The Passing of the 3D Ranch. N.P.: 1930. V. 38

STANSBERY, LON R.

The Passing of 3D Ranch. Tulsa: 1930. V. 40; 43

STANSBURY, CAROLINE M. KIRKLAND

Montacute; or, a New Home - Who'll Follow. London: 1840. V. 42

STANSBURY, HOWARD

An Expedition to the Valley of the Great Salt Lake of Utah . . . Philadelphia: 1855. V. 37; 40

Exploration and Survey of the Valley of the Great Salt Lake of Utch Including a Reconnoissance of a New Route Through the Rocky Mountains. Philadelphia: 1852. V. 38; 39; 40; 41; 42; 43; 46

Exploration and Survey of the Valley of the Great Salt Lake of Utah. Washington: 1853. V. 38; 41; 44; 45

Survey of the Cumberland River. 1835. V. 41

STANTON, DANIEL

A Journal of the Life, Travels and Gospel Labours of a Faithful Minister of Jesus Christ. Philadelphia: 1772. V. 37; 39; 42; 46

STANTON, EDWIN M.

Letter of . . . the Official Reports, Papers and Other Facts in Relation to the Causes and Extent of the Late Massacre of United States Troops by Indians at Fort Phil Kearney. Washington: 1867. V. 43

STANTON, ELIZABETH CADY

Address to the Legislature of New York, Adopted by the State Woman's Rights Convention, Held at Albany . . . Albany: 1854. V. 40

Eighty Years and More (1815-1897). Reminiscences of . . . New York: 1898. V. 37

STANTON, G. SMITH

'When the Wildwood Was In Flower'. New York: 1909. V. 43; 45

STANTON, IRVING

Sixty Years in Colorado Reminiscences and Reflections of a Pioneer of 1860. Denver: 1922. V. 37; 40

STANTON, SAMUEL WARD

American Steam Vessels. New York: 1895. V. 45

American Steam Vessels Series. Upper Montclair: 1962-89. V. 45

STANTON, THEODORE

Rosa Bonheur, Reminiscences. London: 1910. V. 39

Reminiscences of Rosa Bonheur. New York: 1910. V. 43

STANYAN, ABRAHAM

An Account of Switzerland. London: 1714. V. 39; 40; 43; 45

STANYAN, TEMPLE

The Grecian History. London: 1781. V. 45

STANYHURST, RICHARD 1547-1618

Richardi Stanihurst Dubliniensis de Rebus Hibernia Gestis . . . Antwerp: 1584. V. 45

STANYON, ELLIS

Magic. London: 1900-20. V. 39

STANZANI

Arsinoe, Queen of Cyprus. An Opera. London: 1705. V. 38

STANZAS for the King's Landing. N.P.: 1822? V. 42

STAPHILEO, GIOVANNI

Tractatus de Gratiis Expectativis ac Aliis Litteris Gratie et Iustitie . . . Venetiis: 1539-40. V. 37

THE STAPLE Contract, Betwixt the Royal Burrows of Scotland, and the City of Campvere in Zealand (1697). (with) An Historical Account of the Staple, by a Private Gentleman (Charles Stewart). Edinburgh: 1749. V. 41

STAPLEDON, OLAF 1886-1950

Last and First Men - a Story of the Near and Far Future. London: 1930. V. 40

Last Men in London. 1932. V. 39

Last and First Men. London: 1934. V. 44; 46

Quadratic. 1949. V. 44

Star Maker. London: 1937. V. 42

Waking World. London: 1934. V. 41

STAPLETON, AUGUSTUS G.

The Affair at Grey Town. London: 1857. V. 43; 46

STAPLETON, J. W.

The Great Crime of 1860 . . . London: 1861. V. 42

STAPLETON, THOMAS

Promptuarium Morale, Das ist/ Sittliche Speisskam(m)er Darinnen Heylsame Lehren . . . Ingolstadt: 1597. V. 43

Tres Thomae: Seu De S. Thomae Apostoli Rebus Gestis, De S. Thoma Archiepiscopo Cantaurriensi & martyre, d. Thomae Mori Angliae Quondam Cancellarij Vita. Duaci: 1588. V. 38

STAPLETON, WALTER HENRY

Comparative Handbook of Congo Languages. Yakusu: 1930. V. 39

STAPLEY, MILDRED

Popular Weaving and Embroidery in Spain. New York: 1924. V. 38; 43

STAPP, WILLIAM P.

The Prisoners of Perote. Philadelphia: 1845. V. 37; 39; 40; 42; 43; 45

STAPYLTON, ROBERT

Juvenal's Sixteen Satyrs or, A Survey of the Manners and Actions of Mankind. Withe Arguments, Marginall Notes, and Annotations. By Sir Robert Staypylton, Knight. London: 1647. V. 37

STAR Science Fiction Stories No. 2. New York: 1953. V. 45

THE STAR Spangled Banner. Baltimore: 1825. V. 37

STARBUCK, ALEXANDER

History of the American Whale Fishery. Washington: 1878. V. 38; 39; 41

History of the American Whale Fishery. New York: 1964. V. 37; 41

STARBUCK, EDITH

Crossing the Plains. Nashville: 1927. V. 40; 42

STARBUCK, LUCY COFFIN

Seaweed from the Shores of Nantucket. Boston: 1853. V. 42

STARFORTH, JOHN

The Architecture of the Farm, a Series of Designs for Farm-Houses and Farm-Steadings, Factor's Houses and Labourers' Cottages. Edinburgh: 1853. V. 39

Villa Residences and Farm Architecture. Edinburgh & London: 1865. V. 38

STARING, A.

Jacob De Wit 1695-1754. Amsterdam: 1958. V. 37; 40; 44

STARK, A. C.

The Fauna of South Africa: The Birds of South Africa. London: 1900-06. V. 43

STARK, A. W.

Instruction for Field Artillery; Compiled from Standard Military Authority . . . Richmond, VA: 1864. V. 37

STARK, CALEB

History of the Town of Dunbarton, Merrimac County, New Hampshire . . . 1751 to 1860. Concord: 1860. V. 39

STARK, CORDELIA

The Female Wanderer. Wells' River (Vt.): 1826. V. 37

STARK, FREYA

Baghdad Sketches. Baghdad: 1932. V. 38; 44

Beyond Euphrates - Autobiography 1928-1933. London: 1951. V. 45

Space, Time and Movement in Landscape. London: 1969. V. 40

STARK, GLADYS

The Old Ship Meeting House of Hingham, Massachusetts. Boston: 1951. V. 44; 46

STARK, JAMES 1794-1859

Scenery of the Rivers of Norfolk Comprising the Yare-The Waveney and the Bure. Norwich & London: 1834. V. 42

Stark's History and Guide to Barbados and the Caribee Islands, Containing a description of Everything on or About These Islands . . . Boston: 1893. V. 40

STARK, JAMES A.

The Loyalists of Massachusetts and the Other Side of the American Revolution. Boston: 1907. V. 43

STARK, WILLIAM

Remarks on the Construction of Public Hospitals for the Cure of Mental Derangement. Glasgwo: 1810. V. 41

STARKE, AUBREY HARRISON

Sidney Lanier: a Biographical and Critical Study. Chapel Hill: 1933. V. 46

STARKE, JAMES

Picturesque Views on and Near the Eastern Coast of England, Comprising the Romantic Scenery of the Yare, the Waveney and the Bure . . . London: 1834. V. 46

STARKE, MARIAN

The Widow of Malabar. London: 1791. V. 43

STARKE, MARIANA

Travels in Europe, for the Use of Travellers on the Continent and Likewise in the Island of Sicily. Paris: 1836. V. 43

STARKEY, GEORGE d. 1666

Chymie Oder Erklaerung der Natur und Verthedigung Helmonts. Nuremberg: 1722. V. 38

Liquor Alcahest, or a Discourse of that Immortal Dissolvent of Paracelsus & Helmont . . . London: 1675. V. 46

STARKEY, WILLIAM

Poems and Translations. Dublin: 1875. V. 44

STARKMAN, S. B.

The Contemplative Man's Recreation. Vancouver: 1970. V. 37

STARKWEATHER, GEORGE B.

The Secret Wings: The Principles of Their Inimitably Exquisite Mechanism Clearly Set Forth . . . Washington: 1882. V. 38

STARLING, ERNEST H.

Mercer's Company Lectures on Recent Advances in the Physiology of Digestion. Chicago: 1906. V. 38

STARLING, THOMAS

Family Cabinet Atlas. London: 1831. V. 37

STARR, DILLWYN PARRISH

The War Story by His Father. New York: 1917. V. 45; 46

STARR EMMET

History of the Cherokee Indians and Their Legends and Folk Lore. Oklahoma City: 1921. V. 39; 41; 42

STARR, FREDERICK

Catalogue of a Collection of Objects Illustrating Folklore of Mexico. London: 1899. V. 45

Congo Natives: an Ethnographic Album. Chicago: 1912. V. 43; 46

In Indian Mexico. 1908. V. 42

In Indian Mexico. Chicago: 1908. V. 37; 38; 43

Indians of Southern Mexico. Chicago: 1899. V. 37; 38; 39; 43

STARR, JIMMY

365 Nights in Hollywood. Hollywood: 1926. V. 44; 45

Three Short Biers. Hollywood: 1945. V. 44; 45

STARR, LOUIS

An American Textbook of the Diseases of Children . . . London & Philadelphia: 1895. V. 39

STARR, M. ALLEN

Familiar Forms of Nervous Diseaes. New York: 1890. V. 45; 46

STARRETT, VINCENT

Ambrose Bierce. Chicago: 1920. V. 37; 43

Arthur Machen A Novelist of Ecstasy and Sin. Chicago: 1918. V. 37; 42

Ballad of Brobdingnag. N.P.. V. 46

Brillig Sonnets and Other Verse. Chicago: 1949. V. 46

Ebony Flame. Chicago: 1922. V. 39; 42; 43; 44

Et Cetera, a Collector's Scrap Book. Chicago: 1924. V. 46

Flame and Dust. Chicago: 1924. V. 44

Oriental Encounters. Chicago: 1938. V. 45

Oriental Encounters. Chicago and Skokie: 1975. V. 41

Penny Wise and Book Foolish. New York: 1929. V. 45

Persons from Porlock and Other Interruptions. Chicago: 1938. V. 44

The Private Life of Sherlock Holmes. New York: 1923. V. 46

The Private Life of Sherlock Holmes. New York: 1933. V. 42; 45

The Private Life of Sherlock Holmes. 1934. V. 39

The Private Life of Sherlock Holmes. London: 1934. V. 42; 43

The Private Life of Sherlock Holmes. Missouri: 1979. V. 42

Stephen Crane - a Bibliography. Philadelphia: 1923. V. 38; 43; 44

221B Studies in Sherlock Holmes. 1940. V. 39

221b: Studies in Sherlock Holmes. New York: 1940. V. 43

Sherlock Holmes 221B: Studies in Sherlock Holmes. 1956. V. 39

221B Studies in Sherlock Holmes by Various Hands. Morristown: 1956. V. 43; 44

STARRETT, W. A.

Empire State. A Pictorial Record of Its Construction. New York: 1931. V. 41

START Making Paper Everyone! (Santa Cruz: 1987. V. 37

STATE Atlas of New Jersey . . . New York: 1872. V. 41; 46

STATE HISTORICAL SOCIETY OF IOWA

First Annual Report of the State Historical Society of Iowa. Des Moines: 1857. V. 39

STATE HISTORICAL SOCIETY OF WISCONSIN

First Annual Report and Collections of the . . . for the Year 1854. Madison: 1855. V. 42

THE STATE in the Year 1900, a Souvenir being a Collection of Photogravure Plates Portraying the leading Players and Playwrights . . . and a History of the Stage during the Victorian Era. Compiled by W. Eden Hooper and Joseph Knight. 1901. V. 37

STATE of Facts Relative to Greenwich Hospital. N.P.: 1779. V. 39

STATE of Facts Shewing the Right of Certain Companies to the Lands Lately Purchased by Them from the State of Georgia. Philadelphia: 1795. V. 45

THE STATE of Indina Delineated: Geographical, Historical, Statistical and Commercial and a Brief View of the Internal Improvements, Geology, Eduction, Tavelling Routes &c. New York: 1838. V. 38

STATE of Ireland Considered, with an Enquiry into the History and Operation of Tithe, and a Plan for Modifying the System and Providing Adequate Maintenance for the Catholic and Presbyterian Clergy. Dublin: 1810. V. 38

THE STATE of Representation of England and Wales, Delivered to the Society, the Friends of the People, Associated for the Purpose of Obtaining a Parliamentary Reform on Saturday the 9th of Febrary 1793. London: 1793. V. 40; 46

THE STATE of the Charity for the Relief of Widows and Orphans of Poor Clergymen in Wiltshire for the Year 1770. London: 1770? V. 40

THE STATE of the Nation. Cincinnati: 1940. V. 40

THE STATE of the Nation, at the Commencement of the Year 1822 . . . Considered Under the Four Departments of the Finance, Foreign Relations, Home Department, Colonies and Board of Trade. London: 1822. V. 41

THE STATE Of the Nation, with a General Balance of the Public Accounts. London: 1748. V. 41; 45

THE STATE of the Silk and Woollen Manufacture, Considered: in Relation to a French Trade. London: 1713. V. 46

THE STATE of the Trade and Manufactory of Iron in Great Britain Considered. London: 1750. V. 37; 40; 46

STATE Papers and Publick Documents of the United States 1789-96. Boston: 1815. V. 44

STATE Papers and Publick Documents of the United States from the Accession of George Washington to the Presidency, Exhibiting a Complete View of Our Foreign Relatiaons Since That Day. 1789-96. Boston: 1815-17-19. V. 37

STATE-POEMS: Continued from the Time of O. Cromwel, to This Present Year 1696. London: 1697. V. 44

THE STATE Preferable to the Church; or, Reasons for Making Sale of the Whole Present Property of the Church, in England and Ireland, for the Use of the State . . . London: 1748. V. 41

THE STATE Register and Year Book of Facts: For the Year 1859. San Francisco: 1859. V. 37; 40

STATE Tracts: Being a Collection of Several Treatises Relating to the Government. London: 1689. V. 39

STATE Tracts Being a Collection of Several Treatises Relating to the Government. London: 1693. V. 40

A STATEMENT of Claims of the West India Colonies to a Protecting Duty Against East India Sugar. London: 1823. V. 43

STATEMENT and Remarks Upon the Affidavits Filed by Lieut. Col. Calthorpe in the Court of Queen's Bench; with Some Further Evidence in Contradiction of Some of the Statements Contained in Them. London: 1864. V. 41

A STATEMENT, Explanatory of the Resignation of the Officers of the Regiment of Artillery, of the City & County of New York. New York: 1797. V. 37

STATEMENT of the Oregon and Washington Delegation, In Regard to the War Claims of Oregon and Washington. Washington: 1860. V. 40

STATEMENT Presented to the Meeting of the Holders of Colombian Bonds, Held at the City of London Tavern, 11th January, 1823. London: 1823. V. 40

STATEMENT Respecting the Prevalence of Certain Immoral Practices in His Majesty's Navy Addressed to the Right Honourable the Lord Commissioners of the Admiralty. London: 1821. V. 38; 39; 40; 42

STATEMENTS of the Loss of His Majesty's New Ship the Bounty, W. Bligh, Esq. Commander, By a Conspiracy of the Crew . . . London: 1809. V. 41

THE STATISTICAL Account of Scotland 1791-1799. Wakefield: 1983. V. 39

A STATISTICAL Account of the Schuylkill Permanent Bridge, Communicated to the Philadelphia Society of Agriculture, 1806. Philadelphia: 1815. V. 43

STATISTICAL Account of the Shetland Isles, by the Ministers, by the Ministers of the Respective Parishes. London: 1841. V. 40; 46

A STATISTICAL and Chronological View of the United States and Territories, and Traveler's Guide through the United States . . . Utica: 1842. V. 39

A STATISTICAL Inquiry Into the Condition of the People of Colour, of the City and Districts of Philadelphia. Philadelphia: 1849. V. 42

STATISTICS and Information Concerning the Indian Territory, Oklahoma, and the Cherokee Strip, with Its Missions of Acres of Unoccupied Lands, for the Farmer and Stock Raiser . . . St. Louis: 1897. V. 42

STATISTICS and Information Concerning the State of Texas, With its millions of Acres of Unoccupied Lands, for Farmer and Stock Raiser . . . Great Inducements for the Investment of Captial, Health for the Invalid . . . St. Louis: 1889. V. 37

STATISTICS of Dane County, Wisconsin; With a Business Directory in Part, of the Village of Madison. Madison: 1851. V. 42

STATISTICS of Madison and Dane County Wisconsin. Madison: 1853. V. 42

STATIUS

La Thebaide . . . Ridotta dal Sig. ERasmo di Valvasone in Ottava Rime. Venice: 1570. V. 41

STATIUS, PUBLIUS PAPINIUS

Sylvarum Libri Quinque. Thebaidos Libri Duodecim. Achilleidos. With the Orthographia et Flexus Dictionum Graecarum Onmium. Venice: 1502. V. 38; 40; 42; 45

Sylvarum Libri V. Cambridge: 1651. V. 46

Sylvarum, Lib. V. Thebaidos, Lib. XII. Achilleidos, Lib. II. Warringtoniae: 1788. V. 40

Sylvarum Libri V. Achilleidos Libri XII. Orthographia et Flexus Dictionum Graecarum Omnium. Venice: 1519. V. 37

Sylvarvm Libi V. Thebaidos Lib XII. Ascilleidos Lib. II. Lvgdvni: 1559. V. 44

STATIUS, PUBLIUS PAPINUS

The Thebaid. Oxford: 1767. V. 45

STATON, FRANCES M.

A Bibliography of Canadiana. Toronto: 1934. V. 37; 43

A Bibliography of Canadiana. Toronto: 1965-69. V. 40; 42; 43

A Bibliography of Canadiana: being items in the Public Library of Totonto, Canada, relating to the early history and development of Canada. Edited by Frances M. Staton and Marie Tremaine with an introduction by George H. Locke. Toronto: 1965. V. 37

STATUTS de l'Ordre de St. Michel. Paris: 1725. V. 38

LES STATUTS de l'Ordre du St. Esprit. Paris: 1788. V. 40

STAUFER, DAVID MC NEELEY

American Engravers Upon Copper and Steel. New York: 1907. V. 41

STAUFFACHER, JACK

Janson: A Definitive Collection. San Francisco: 1954. V. 38

STAUFFER, DAVID MCNELLEY

American Engravers Upon Copper and Steel. New York: 1907. V. 39

STAUNFORD, WILLIAM 1509-1558

An Exposicion of the Kinges Prerogatiue Collected Out of the Great Abridgement of Iustice Fitzherbert and Other Olde Writers of the Lawes of Englande (etc). London: 1568. V. 45

Les Plees de Coron; and An Exposicioun of the Kinges Prerogtive. London: 1560, 1568. V. 40

Les Plees de Coron. (and) An Exposicioun of the Kinges Prerogative. London: 1560 & 1658. V. 38

STAUNTON, GEORGE LEONARD, BART 1737-1801

An Authentic Account of an Embassy from King of Great Britain to the Emperor of China. London: 1797. V. 42

An Authentic Account of an Embassy from the King of Great Britain to the Emperor of China . . . London: 1797. V. 37; 41; 42; 43

STAUNTON, GEORGE THOMAS 1781-1859

An Authentic Account of an Embassy from the King of Great Britain to the Emperor of China. Philadelphia: 1799. V. 38; 39

The Fundamental Laws, and a Selection from the Supplementary Statutes, of the Penal Code of China. London: 1810. V. 40

Memoir of the Life and Family of the Lat Sir George Leonard Staunton, Bart . . . Havant: 1823. V. 39

Miscellaneous Notices Relating to China, and Other Commercial Intercouse . . . London: 1822. V. 45

Miscellaneous Notices Relating to China and Our Commercial Intercourse, Including a Few Translations from the Chinese Language. London: 1822-50. V. 41

Miscellaneous Notices Relating to China and the Commercial Intercourse with that Country. Part the Second. Havant: 1828. V. 40

Notes of Proceedings and Occurrences During the British Embassy to Pekin in 1816. London: 1824. V. 41

STAVELEY, THOMAS

The Romish Horseleech. London: 1674. V. 40

STAVELY, S. W.

The New Whole Art of Confectionary, Sugar Boiling, Iceing, Candying, Wines, Jelly Making &c. &c. Derby: 1827. V. 41

STAVERT, W. J.

The Churchwarden's Accounts of the Parish of Burnsall-in-Craven, 1704-1769. Skipton: 1899. V. 45

STAVORINUS, JOHN SPLINTER

Voyages to the East Indies. London: 1798. V. 42

STAWELL, MAUD MARGARET KEY

FABRE'S Book of Insects, Retold by Mrs. Rodolph Stawell. New York: 1936. V. 38

The Fairy of Old Spain and Other Important People. London: 1912. V. 42

My Day with the Fairies. London. V. 40

My Days with the Fairies. London: 1913. V. 44; 45

My Days with the Fairies. London: 1914. V. 38

My Days with the Fairies. London: (1910). V. 37

STAYNER, RICHARD

A True Narrative of the Late Success Which It Has Pleased God to Five Some Parte of the Flete of this Common-Wealth Upon the Spanish Coast . . . London: 1656. V. 45

STCHUDI, J. J. VON

Travels in Peru, During the Years 1838-1842, on the Coast in the Sierra Across the Condilleras and the Andes, into the Primeval Forests . . . London: 1847. V. 46

STEAD, CHRISTINA

The Man Who Love Children. New York: 1940. V. 43; 44

The Salzburg Tales. London: 1934. V. 38; 42

The Salzburg Tales. New York. V. 45

The Salzburg Tales. New York & London: 1934. V. 40

The Salzburg Tales. New York: 1934. V. 37

STEAD, JOHN

A Picture of Jersey; or, Stranger's Companion through that Island. Jersey: 1809. V. 41

STEAD, WILLIAM THOMAS

The Maiden Tribute of Modern Babylon. London: 1885. V. 37

STEADMAN, J. G.

Narrative of a Five Years' Expedition Against the Revolted Negroes of Surinam. London: 1806. V. 42

STEADMAN, RALPH

Sigmund Freud. London: 1979. V. 40; 43

Steam Press Portfolio No. 3. London: 1976. V. 40

STEALINGWORTH, SLIM

Tom Sesselmann. New York: 1980. V. 43

STEARN, WILLIAM T.

The Australian Flower Paintings of Ferdinand Bauer. 1976. V. 46

The Australian Flower Paintings of Ferdinand Bauer. London: 1976. V. 39; 40; 41

STEARNS, CHARLES

The Black Man of the South and the Rebels. New York: 1872. V. 42; 44; 45

Facts in the Life of General Taylor. Boston: 1848. V. 38

The Ladies Philosophy of Love. Leonminster: 1797. V. 37; 38; 40; 42; 43

The Ladies' Philosophy of Love, a Poem. Leonminster: 1777. V. 37

STEARNS, EZRA S.

History of Ashburnham Massachusetts from the Grant of Dorchester Canada to the Present Time 1734-1886. Ashburnham: 1887. V. 44

STEARNS, JOHN B.

Reliefs from the Palace of Ashurnasirpal II. Graz: 1961. V. 40

STEARNS, SAMUEL

The American Oracle. London: 1791. V. 42; 46

STEAVENSON, W. E.

Electricity and Its Manner of Working in the Treatment of Disease. London: 1884. V. 38; 39

STEBBING, EDWARD PERCY

The Diary of a Sportsman Naturalist in India. London: 1920. V. 42

Indian Forest Insects of Economic Importance. London: 1914. V. 37; 41

Jungle By-Ways in India. London: 1911. V. 42

A Manual of Elementary Forest Zoology for India. Calcutta: 1908. V. 43

Stalks in the Himalaya. London: 1912. V. 37; 42

STEBBING, HENRY

The Christian in Palestine. London: 1847. V. 37; 40

An Essay Concerning Civil Government. London: 1724. V. 37

STEBBING, WILLIAM

Outlines. Oxford: 1899. V. 42

STEBBINS, G. B.

Facts and Opinions Touching the Real Origin, Character and Influence of the American Colonization Society . . . Boston: 1853. V. 46

STEBBINS, GEORGE STANFORD

My Satchel and I, or Literature on Foot. By Ikabod Izax. Springfield: 1873. V. 39

STEBBINS, JAMES H.

Catalogue of the Private Collection of Paintings and Sculpture Belonging to Mr. James H. Stebbins New York. New York: 1889. V. 46

STEBBINS, THEODORE E.

The Life and Works of Martin Johnson Heade. New Haven: 1975. V. 45

STECHOW, WOLFGANG

Dutch Landscape Painting of the Seventeenth Century. London: 1966. V. 44

STEDMAN, CHARLES

The History of the Origin, Progress, and Termination of the American War. London: 1794. V. 41; 43; 44

STEELE, RICHARD 1672-1729 continued

The State of the Case Between the Lord Chamberlain of His Majesty's Household, and the Governor of the Royal Company of Comedians. London: 1720. V. 37; 38; 39; 42; 43; 45

The Tatler. London: 1806. V. 41

The Tender Husband. London: 1705. V. 40; 42

The Theatre; to Which are Added, the Anti-Theatre; . . . London: 1791. V. 37; 42

Town-Talk. London: 1716. V. 45

STEELE, ROBERT

A Bibliography of Royal Proclamations of the Tudor and Stuart Sovereigns and of Others Published Under Authority 1485-1714, with an Historical Essay on Their Origin and use. New York: 1967. V. 46

A Bibliography of Royal Proclamations of the Tudor and Stuart Sovereigns, etc, 1485-1714. Volume I. England and Wales. Volume II. Ireland. New York: 1957. V. 37

The Earliest English Music Printing, a Description and Bibliography of English Printed Music to the Close of the Sixteenth Century. London: 1903. V. 39

The Revival of Printing. London: 1912. V. 37; 38

Some Old French and English Ballads. Hammersmith: 1905. V. 39; 43; 44

Some Old French and English Ballads. London: 1905. V. 37; 38; 39; 41; 43

The Story of Alexander. London: 1894. V. 40

STEELE, S. B.

Forty Years in Canada. Toronto: 1915. V. 41

STEELE, W. J.

Meat. 1928. V. 37

STEELE, WILLIAM

A Catalogue of the Freehold Estate of William Steele, Esq.; Late of Lamaby in the County of Kent, Deceased . . . London: 1761. V. 46

STEELE, ZADOCK

Captivity. The Indian Captive; or, A Narrative of the aptivity and Sufferings of Zadock Steele. Related by Himself. To which is prefixed an account of the Burning of Royalton. V. 37

The Indian Captive. Montpelier;: 1818. V. 38; 40; 42; 45

The Indian Captive; or a Narrative of the Captivity and Sufferings of Zadock Steele. Montpelier: 1818. V. 38

STEELL, ROBERT

A Treatise of Conic Sections. Dublin printed: 1745. V. 38

STEEN, JAMES ELDER

Illustrated Souvenir of Winnipeg. Winnipeg: 1903. V. 42

STEER, GEORGE

The Compleat Mineral Laws of Derbyshire, taken from the Originals. I. The High Peak Laws, with their Customs. II. Stony Middleton and Eame, with a new Article made 1733. III. The Laws of . . . London: 1734. V. 37

STEER, VINCENT

Printing Design and Layout. The Manual for Printers, Typographers and all Designers and Users of Printing and Advertising. London. V. 39

STEERE, RICHARD

The History of the Babylonish Cabal. London: 1682. V. 39

STEERE, W. C.

The Mosses of Arctic Alaska. 1978. V. 39

STEEVENS, GEORGE 1736-1800

Bibliotheca Steevensiana . . . the Curious and Valuable Library of George Steevens. London: 1800. V. 39

Six Old Plays, On Which Shakespeare Founded His Measure for Measure, Comedy of Errors, Taming of the Shrew, King John, Henry IV and Henry V. London: 1779. V. 40

STEFANI, BARTOLOMEO

L'Arte di Ben Cucinare & Istruire i men Periti in Questa Lodevole Professione. Milano: 1671. V. 38

STEFANSSON, VILHAJALMUR

Arctic Manual. Volume 1. Washington: 1940. V. 44

STEFANSSON, VILHJALMUR

The Adventure of Wrangel Island. New York: 1925. V. 44; 45; 46

The Friendly Arctic. New York: 1921. V. 44

My Life with the Eskimo. New York: 1913. V. 37

The Problem of Meighen Island. New York: 1939. V. 38; 44

Ultima Thule: Further Mysteries of the Arctic. New York: 1940. V. 45

Unsolved Mysteries of the Arctic. New York: 1938. V. 42; 43

STEFFEN, RANDY

The Horse Soldier, 1776-1943; the United States Cavalryman; His Uniforms, Arms, Accoutrements, and Equipments. Norman: 1977. V. 42

STEFFENS, HEINRICH

Anthropologie. Breslau: 1822. V. 38

STEFFENS, JONES & CO.

Imported Stock Bands, Private Bands Our Speciality. New York. V. 38; 46

STEFFENS, LINCOLN

John Reed under the Kremlin. Introduction by Clarence Darrow. Chicago: (1922). V. 37

The Shame of the Cities. New York: 1904. V. 45

Upbuilders . . . New York: 1909. V. 45

STEGGALL, JOHN

An Essay on Mineral, Vegetable, Animal and Aerial Poisons. London: 1833. V. 44

STEGNER, WALLACE

All the Little Live Things. New York: 1967. V. 46

Angle of Repose. Garden City: 1971. V. 43; 46

Beyond the 100th Meridian, John Wesley Powell and the Second Opening of the West. Boston: 1954. V. 46

Beyond the 100th Meridian, John Wesley Powell and the Second Opening of the West. Lincoln: 1982. V. 46

The Big Rock Candy Mountain. New York: 1943. V. 43; 44; 46

The Big Rock Candy Mountain. London: 1950. V. 46

The Big Rock Candy Mountain. Franklin Center: 1978. V. 45

The City of the Living. Boston: 1955. V. 45

The City of the Living and Other Stories. Boston: 1956. V. 46

Collected Stories of Wallace Stegner. New York: 1990. V. 46

Fire and Ice. New York: 1941. V. 46

Look at America: The Central Northwest. Boston: 1947. V. 44

Mormon Country. New York: 1942. V. 46

On a Darkling Plain. New York: 1940. V. 46

On the Writing of History. N.P.: 1989. V. 46

The Potter's House. Muscatine: 1938. V. 46

The Preacher and the Slave. Boston: 1950. V. 39; 45; 46

Remembering Laughter. Boston: 1937. V. 42; 44; 46

Remembering Laughter. London: 1937. V. 46

A Shooting Star. New York: 1961. V. 46

A Shooting Star. N.P.: 1961. V. 42

This is Dinosaur, Echo Park County and its Magic Rivers. New York: 1955. V. 44

Two Rivers. Covelo: 1989. V. 46

Wolf Willow, a History, a Story and a Memory of the Last Plains Frontier. London: 1963. V. 46

The Women on the Wall. Boston: 1950. V. 45; 46

STEICHEN, EDWARD

The Blue Ghost. New York: 1947. V. 42

The Early Years 1900-1927. New York: 1981. V. 45

Edward Steichen - His Photographs and Achievements. New York: 1956. V. 37

Memorable Life Photographs. New York: 1951. V. 46

Sandburg: Photographers View Carl Sandburg. New York: 1966. V. 45

Steichen - a Life in Photography. New York: 1963. V. 37

STEIN, A. H.

History of the Thirty-Seventh U.S. C(olored) Infantry. From Its Organization in the Winter of 1863 and '64. Philadelphia: 1866. V. 39

STEIN, ALBERT

Letter to Samuel J. Peters, Esq . . . . in Relation to the Improvement of the Navigation of the Mississippi River. Philadelphia: 1841. V. 41

STEIN, AUREL 1862-1943.

Ancient Kotan. Detailed Report of Archaeological Explorations in Chinese Turkestan . . . 2 Volumes in One. New York: 1975. V. 37

Archaeological Reconnaissances in North Western India and south Eastern Iran. London: 1937. V. 45

Les Documents Chinois de la Troisieme Expedition. London: 1953. V. 46

Old Routes of Western Iran. Narrative of an Archaeological Journey Carried Out and Recorded. Antiquities Examined, Described and Illustrated with the Assistance of Fred H. Andrews. London: 1940. V. 37; 43

On Alexander's Track to the Indus. London: 1929. V. 38; 40; 45; 46

On Ancient Central Asian Tracks. London: 1933. V. 38; 40; 42; 44; 46

Ruins of Desert Cathay. London: 1912. V. 37; 40; 43; 46

Sand-Buried Ruins of Khotan. Personal Narrative of a Journey of Archaeological & Geographical Exploration in Chinese Turkestan. London: 1903. V. 40

STEIN, GERTRUDE 1874-1946

Absolutely Bob Brown, or Bobberd Brown. Pawlet: 1955. V. 39

An Acquaintance with Description. Hammersmith: 1929. V. 40

An Acquaintance with Description. London: 1929. V. 37; 43; 45

Americains d'Amerique. Paris: 1933. V. 39

The Autobiography of Alice B. Toklas. New York: 1933. V. 39; 41; 44; 45; 46

Before the Flowers of Friendship Faded. Paris: 1931. V. 37

Blood on the Dining Room Floor. 1948. V. 39; 44

Blood on the Dining Room Floor. New York: 1948. V. 42

Blood on the Dining Room Floor. N.P.: 1948. V. 37; 40

Composition as Explanation. London: 1926. V. 37

Dix Portraits. Paris: 1930. V. 37

An Elucidation: Printed in 'Transition' 1927. N.P.: 1927. V. 39; 40

An Elucidation. Paris: 1927. V. 39; 41; 42; 43; 44; 46

Everybody's Autobiography. New York: 1937. V. 39; 42; 44; 45

Everybody's Autobiography. London: 1938. V. 40

Four Saints in Three Acts. New York: 1934. V. 39; 42

The Geographical Mind of America or the Relation of Human Nature to the Human Mind. New York: 1936. V. 39

Geography and Plays. Boston: 1922. V. 37; 38; 39; 40; 41; 42; 45

Have they Attacked Mary. He Giggled. Westchester: 1917. V. 41

How to Write. Paris: 1931. V. 37; 38; 39; 40; 42; 45

How Writing is Written. Los Angeles: 1974. V. 39

How to Write. Paris: (1931). V. 37

Ida: a Novel. New York: 1941. V. 45

In Savoy or 'Yes' Is for a Very Young Man. London: 1946. V. 46

Last Operas and Plays. New York: 1949. V. 37; 41; 42; 43; 44; 46

Lectures in America. New York: 1935. V. 38

Lectures in America. New York: (1935). V. 37

Literally True. Tujunga: 1947. V. 41

Lucy Church Amiably. Paris: 1930. V. 37; 38; 40; 42; 46

The Making of Americans. Dijon: 1925. V. 38; 39; 40

The Making of Americans. New York: 1925. V. 38

The Making of Americans. New York: 1926. V. 39; 40; 42; 44

Matisse, Picasso and Gertrude Stein, with Two Shorter Studies. Paris: 1933. V. 37; 38; 39; 40; 42; 43; 45

Money. Los Angeles: 1973. V. 39; 42

Money. Santa Barbara: 1973. V. 37; 40

Morceaux Choisis de La Fabrication des Americains. Paris: 1949. V. 37

The Mother Of Us All: an Opera. New York: 1947. V. 45

Narration. Chicago: 1935. V. 37; 38; 39; 42; 46

Operas and Plays. Paris: 1932. V. 37; 43

Paris France. New York: 1940. V. 44

Picasso. Paris: 1938. V. 44; 45; 46

Portrait of Mabel Dodge a the Villa Curonia. Florence: 1912. V. 37; 40

Portraits and Prayers. New York: 1934. V. 37; 40; 42; 45; 46

A Primer for the Gradual Understainding of Gertrude. Los Angeles: 1971. V. 39

Reflections on the Atomic Bomb. Los Angeles: 1974. V. 39

Tender Buttons. New York: 1914. V. 37; 39; 40

Things as They Are. 1950. V. 39

Things as they Are. Pawlet: 1950. V. 37; 38; 40; 42; 46

Three Lives. New York: 1909. V. 37; 39

Three Lives. New York: 1915. V. 39; 45

Three Lives. London: 1927. V. 45

Three Lives. Norfolk;: 1941. V. 42

The Unpublished Work of Gertrude Stein. New Haven: 1951-58. V. 37

Useful Knowledge. New York: 1928. V. 42

Useful Knowledge. London: 1929. V. 40

A Village Are You Ready Yet Not Yet. Paris: 1928. V. 43

Wars I Have Seen. London: 1945. V. 42; 43

What are Masterpieces. Los Angeles: 1940. V. 42

Why are There Whites to Console, a Portrait of Janet. New York: 1973. V. 39

The World is Round. New York: 1939. V. 39; 42; 43

The World is Round. San Francisco: 1986. V. 42; 44

STEIN, HENRI

Manuel de Bibliographie Generale. Paris: 1897. V. 38

STEIN, M. A.

Memoir on Maps Illustrating the Ancient Geography of kashmir. Calcutta;: 1899. V. 41

STEINBECK, CARL

The Collected Poems of Amnesia Glasscock. San Francisco: 1976. V. 43

STEINBECK, JOHN ERNEST 1902-1968

America and Americans. New York: 1966. V. 42

Bombs Away. New York: 1942. V. 40; 44; 45

Burning Bright. New York: 1950. V. 37; 39; 41; 42; 43; 44; 45

Cannery Row. London: 1945. V. 39; 45

Cannery Row. New York: 1945. V. 38; 39; 40; 43; 45

Chapter Thirty-Four from the Novel East of Eden. Bronxville: 1952. V. 45

The Collected Poems. 1976. V. 42

The Collected Poems of Amnesia Glasscock. San Francisco: 1976. V. 39

Cup of Gold. 1929. V. 46

Cup of Gold. New York: 1929. V. 39; 43; 45

Cup of Gold. New York: 1936. V. 39; 41; 42; 44; 45; 46

East of Eden. London: 1952. V. 41; 45

East of Eden. New York: 1952. V. 37; 38; 39; 40; 41; 43; 44; 45; 46

The First Watch. New York: 1947. V. 37; 42; 46

Flight. Covelo: 1984. V. 37; 42; 46

The Forgotten Village. New York: 1941. V. 39; 42; 43; 46

The Grapes of Wrath. New York: 1030/ V. 41

The Grapes of Wrath. London: 1939. V. 39; 45

The Grapes of Wrath. New York: 1939. V. 37; 38; 39; 40; 41; 42; 43; 44; 45; 46

The Grapes of Wrath. Toronto: 1939. V. 39

The Grapes of Wrath. New York: 1940. V. 37; 39; 40; 43; 45

The Grapes of Wrath. 1939. V. 37

In Dubious Battle. New York: 1936. V. 37; 41; 43; 44; 45

In Dubious Battle. 1936. V. 37

John Emery. New York: 1964. V. 37

John Steinbeck, His Language. Aptos: 1970. V. 37

Journal of a Novel. New York: 1969. V. 39; 44; 45; 46

A Letter From John Steinbeck. N.P.: 1964. V. 42

Letters to Elizabeth. San Francisco: 1978. V. 40; 45; 46

The Log from the Sea of Cortez. New York: 1951. V. 37; 45

The Log from the Sea of Cortez. London: 1958. V. 38; 39; 44; 45; 46

The Long Valley. New York: 1938. V. 38; 39; 40; 42; 43; 44; 45

Love Poems to Gwyn Conger Steinbeck. Austin. V. 43

The Moon is Down. London: 1942. V. 38; 43

The Moon is Down. New York: 1942. V. 38; 39; 40; 41; 43; 44; 45; 46

Nothing So Monstrous. New York: 1936. V. 37; 39; 43; 44; 45

Of Mice and Men. London: 1937. V. 44; 45

Of Mice and Men. New York: 1937. V. 37; 38; 39; 40; 41; 42; 43; 44; 45; 46

Of Mice and Men. New York: 1970. V. 41; 45

Of Mice and Men. London & Toronto: 1937. V. 38

Of Mice and Men. New York: (1937). V. 37

Once There Was a War. New York: 1958. V. 45

Once There Was a War. London: 1959. V. 43

The Pastures of Heaven. New York: 1932. V. 39; 40; 45

The Pastures of Heaven. London: 1933. V. 45

The Pastures of Heaven. New York: 1935. V. 42

The Pastures of Heaven. New York: (ca. 1935). V. 37

The Pearl. New York: 1947. V. 39; 41; 42; 43; 45

Pipe Dream. New York: 1956. V. 45

Plan Tortilla. Praha: 1960. V. 45

Positano. Salerno: 1954. V. 43; 45

Positano. Salerno: 1959. V. 41; 43; 46

The Red Pony. New York: 1937. V. 37; 38; 39; 40; 41; 44; 45

The Red Pony. New York: (1937). V. 37

A Russian Journal. New York: 1948. V. 38; 44; 45; 46

Saint Katy the Virgin. Mount Vernon: 1936. V. 46

Saint Katy and the Virgin. New York: 1936. V. 39; 40; 41; 45

Sea of Cortez. New York: 1941. V. 39; 41; 43; 44; 45

The Short Reign of Pippin IV. New York. V. 41

Speech Accepting the Nobel Prize for Literature. Stockholm, Dec. 10, 1962. New York. V. 45

Speech Accepting the Nobel Prize for Literature. New York: 1962. V. 43; 45

Steinbeck: a Life in Letters. New York: 1975. V. 44

Sweet Thursday. London: 1954. V. 45

Sweet Thursday. New York: 1954. V. 39; 45

To a God Unknown. 1933. V. 37; 43

To a God Unknown. New York: 1933. V. 37; 41; 42; 43; 45; 46

Tortilla Flat. London: 1935. V. 42; 46

Tortilla Flat. New York: 1935. V. 38; 42; 43; 44; 45

Tortilla Flat. New York: 1947. V. 39; 41; 43; 45

Tortilla Flat. Illustrated by Ruth Gannett. New York: (1935). V. 37

STEINBECK, JOHN ERNEST 1902-1968 continued

Tortilla Flat. With seventeen paintings by Peggy Worghington. New York: (1947). V. 37

Un Americain a New-York et a Paris. 1956. V. 44

Vanderbilt Clinic. N.P.: 1947. V. 43

The Wayward Bus. New York: 1947. V. 41

The Winter of Our Discontent. New York: 1961. V. 40; 41; 44

The Winter of Our Discontent. Taipei: 1961. V. 45

Working Days. New York: 1989. V. 43

STEINBERG, ISAAC

Why We Are Against the Brest-Litovsk Peace. Geneva: 1918. V. 44

STEINDLER, ARTHUR

Diseases and Deformities of the Spine and Thorax. St. Louis: 1929. V. 42

Orthopedic Operations: Indications, Technique and End Results. Springfield: 1940. V. 42

Reconstructive Surgery of the Upper Extremity. New York: 1923. V. 42

STEINDORFF, GEORGE

Catalogue of the Egyptian Sculpture in the Walters Art Gallery. Baltimore: 1946. V. 43; 44

STEINER, F. GEORGE

Poems. Oxford: 1952. V. 37; 40; 42

STEINER, GEORGE

Malice - Chancellor's English Prize Essay. Oxford: 1952. V. 44

STEINER, WILLIAM

German Process Cigar Bands. New York: century. V. 46

STEINKOPFF, KARL FRIEDRICH ADOLF

Letters Relative to a tour on the Continent, Undertaken at the Request of the Committee of the British and Foreign Bible Society, in the year 1812. London: 1813. V. 37

STEINMAN, EMMA C. C.

Our Little Gipsy. London: 1881. V. 45

STEINMAN, G.

A Memoir of Barbara Duchess of Cleveland. London?: 1871. V. 42

STEINMANN, J.

Souvenirs de Rio de Janeiro Dessines d'Apres Nature . . . Paris: 1837. V. 40

STEINMETZ, ANDREW

The Gaming Table: Its Votaries and Victims, in all Times and Countries, Especially in Englnd and in France. London: 1870. V. 38

Japan and Her People. London: 1859. V. 41

The Romance of Duelling in all Times and Countries. London: 1868. V. 46

STEINMETZ, CHARLES PROTEUS 1865-1923

Radiation, Light and Illumination. New York: 1909. V. 40

Theory and Calculation of Transient Electric Phenomena and Oscillations. New York: 1909. V. 40

STELL, CHARLES

Aleck Hormby. New York: 1898. V. 38; 40

STELL, I.

The Hastings Guide: or, A Description of that Ancient Town and Port and Its Environs. London: 1794. V. 39

STELLA, ANTONIO

Descrizione de; Funerali a Monsignor Giambattista STella. Bologna: 1760. V. 46

STELLA, BENEDETTO

Il Tabacco. Opera . . . Nella Quale si Tratta dell'Origine, Historia, Coltura, Preparatione, Qualita, Natura, Virtu & Uso in Fumo, in Polvere, in Foglia, in Lambitivo . . . Rome: 1669. V. 42; 44; 46

STELLA, JOANNES

A Vewayling of the Peace of Germany. London: 1637. V. 44

STELLE, J. P.

The Gunsmith's Manual: a Complete Handbook for the American Gunsmith. New York: 1883. V. 40

STELLIOLA, NICOLO ANTONIO

Il Telescopio over Ispecillo Celeste. Naples: 1627. V. 38

STELLMANN, LOUIS

The Vanished Ruin Era. San Francisco: 1910. V. 44

THE STENCIL Process at the Curwen Press. London: 1928. V. 37

STENGEL, JOANES PETERSON

Gnomonica Universalis, sive Praxis Amplissima Geometrice describendi Horologia Solaria, Stabilia Quidem Juxta Omnes Species in Quacunque Superficie Plana Intra Sphaeram Rectam & Obliquam . . . Ulm: 1680. V. 40

STENGER, ERICH

The March of Photography. London: 1958. V. 37; 42

STENHOUSE, T. B. H., MRS.

An Englishwoman in Utah: The Story of a Life's Experiences in Mormonism . . . London: 1880. V. 45

STENHOUSE, WILLIAM

Tables of Simple Interest, and of Commission, Brokerage or Exchange. Edinburgh: 1806. V. 38

STENNET, R.

Aidiborontiphoskyphormiostikos: a Round Game for Merry Parties. London: 1822. V. 45

STENNETT, SAMUEL

Discourses on Domestick Duties. London: 1783. V. 41

STENO, NICOLAUS

Elementorum Myologiae Specimen, seu Musculi Descriptio Geometrica. Florentiae: 1667. V. 41; 45

De Musculis et Glandulis Observationum Specimen cum Epistolis Duabus Anatomicis. Copenhagen: 1664. V. 41

STEPENS, WILLIAM

A State of the Province of Georgia, Attested Upon Oath in the Court of Savannah, November 10, 1724. London: 1742. V. 37

STEPHAN, JOHN

A Treatise on the Manufacture, Imitation, Adulteration and Reduction of Foreign Wines, Brandies, Gins, Rums, Etc. Philadelphia: 1860. V. 40

STEPHANINI, J.

The Narrative of . . . a Native of Arta, in Greece. Charleston: 1829. V. 40

The Personal Narrative of the Sufferings of . . . A Native of Arta, in Greece . . . New York: 1829. V. 37; 45

STEPHANUS, BYZANTINUS

De Urbibus. Venice: 1502. V. 46

STEPHANUS, CAROLUS

Dictionarium Historicum ac Poeticum. Lyon: 1581. V. 38

Dictionarium Historicum, Geographicum, Poeticum. Geneva: 1660. V. 37

STEPHANUS, HENRICUS

Conciones Sive Orationes ex Graecis Latinisque Historicis Excerptae. N.P.: Geneva,: 1570. V. 40

Francofordiense Emporium, sive Francofordienses Nundinae. Geneva: 1574. V. 38

Parodiae Morales H. Stephani, In Poetarum vet. Sententias Celebriores. Geneva: 1575. V. 45

STEPHEN, ADRIAN

The 'Dreadnought' Hoax. London: 1936. V. 37; 42; 44

STEPHEN, GEORGE 1794-1879

A Letter to the Rt. Hon. Lord John Russell &c. &c. on the Probable Increase of Rural Crime, in Consequence of the Introduction of the New Poor-Law and Railroad Systems. London: 1836. V. 40

STEPHEN, JAMES

An Inquiry Into the Right and Duty of Compelling Spain to Relinquish Her Slave Trade in Northern Africa. London: 1816. V. 40

New Reasons for Abolishing the Slave Trade . . . London: 1807. V. 42; 46

War in Disguise; or, the Frauds of the Neutral Flags. London: 1806. V. 42

STEPHEN, JAMES FITZJAMES 1829-1894

Liberty, Equality, Fraternity. London: 1873. V. 41

Liberty, Equality, Fraternity. London: 1874. V. 37

The Story of Nuncomar and the Impeachment of Sir Elijah Impey. London: 1885. V. 43

STEPHEN, LESLIE

An Agnostic's Apology and Other Essays. London: 1893. V. 37

American Humour. V. 46

The English Utilitarians. London: 1900. V. 41; 42

The English Utilitarians. London: 1912/ V. 41

History of English Thought in the Eighteenth Century. London: 1881. V. 39; 41

Hours in a Library. London: 1877-81-79. V. 46

Hours in a Library. London: 1892. V. 37; 39; 40; 41; 43; 44; 45

Hours in a Library. London: 1899. V. 46

Hours in a Library. London: 1909. V. 41; 42

STEPHEN, LESLIE continued

The Playground of Europe. London: 1894. V. 45

Sketches from Cambridge. London & Cambridge: 1865. V. 39

Social Rights and Duties. Addresses to Ethical Societies. London: 1896. V. 39

Studies of a Biographer. London: 1898-1902. V. 43; 45

STEPHEN, OF BYZANTIUM

(Greek title, then): De Urbibus . . . Integro Commentario Illustravit Abrahamus Berkelius. Leyden: 1694. V. 40

STEPHENS, ALEXANDER H.

A Constitutional View of the Late War Between the States . . . Philadelphia: 1868-70. V. 42

STEPHENS, ANN S.

High Life in New York: Philadelphia: 1854. V. 45

Malaeska: the Indian Wife of the White Hunter. New York: 1860. V. 43

Mary Derwent. Philadelphia: 1858. V. 45

Palaces and Prisons. Philadelphia: 1871. V. 45

STEPHENS, FREDERIC G. 1828-1907

Flemish Relics; Architectural, Legendary and Pictorial as Connected with Public Buildings in Belgium. London: 1866. V. 39; 42; 43; 44

STEPHENS, FREDERIC GEORGE 1828-1907

Frederick George Stephens and the Pre-Raphaelite Brothers. London: 1920. V. 42

Memoirs of Sir Edwin Landseer. London: 1874. V. 39

Sir L. Alma-Tadema, R. A. A Sketch of His Life and Work . . . London: 1880. V. 42

STEPHENS, FREDERICK GEORGE

William Holman Hunt and His Works. London: 1860. V. 45

STEPHENS, GEORGE

Gertrude and Beatrice; or the Queen of Hungary. London: 1839. V. 43; 45; 46

The Manuscripts of Erdely. London: 1836. V. 38

STEPHENS, HENRY

The Book of the Farms: London: 1844. V. 38

STEPHENS, HIRAM B.

Jacques Cartier and His Four Voyages to Canada. An Essay with Historical, Explantory and Philological Notes. Montreal: 1890. V. 37; 39; 42; 43

STEPHENS, JAMES 1882-1950

The Charwoman's Daughter. London: 1912. V. 38

Collected Poems. London: 1926. V. 38; 43

The Crock of Gold. London: 1912. V. 38; 39; 40; 41; 42; 43

The Crock of Gold. London: 1926. V. 37; 38; 39; 40; 41; 42; 43; 44; 45; 46

The Crock of Gold. New York: 1942. V. 44

Etched in Moonlight. New York: 1928. V. 45

Five New Poems. Westminster: 1913. V. 45

Green Branches. Dublin & London: 1916. V. 38

Here are Ladies. London: 1913. V. 38

The Hill of Vision. New York: 1912. V. 39

Hunger - a Dublin Story. Dublin: 1918. V. 37; 38; 39; 40; 41; 42; 43; 44; 46

In the Land of Youth. London: 1924. V. 38

Insurrections. Dublin: 1909. V. 37; 38; 39; 40; 46

Irish Fairy Tales. London: 1920. V. 37; 38; 39; 40; 41; 42

Julia Elizabeth. A Comedy in One Act. New York: 1929. V. 38; 46

Kings and the Moon. London: 1938. V. 43

Little Things. Freelands: 1924. V. 37

Optimist. Gaylordsville: 1929. V. 38; 39

Reincarnations. London: 1918. V. 38

Stars Do Not Make a Noise. Los Angeles: 1931. V. 40

Theme and Variations. New York: 1930. V. 38; 43

STEPHENS, JAMES FRANCIS

Illustrations of British Entomology. Mandibulata Volume 1-6 (of 7) & Haustellata Volume 1-3 (of 4), together with the supplement to both parts. London: 1828-46. V. 43

STEPHENS, JOHN H.

History of Miami County Illustrated. Peru: 1896. V. 41

STEPHENS, JOHN LLOYD 1805-1852

Incidents of Travel in Eygpt, Arabia Petraea and the Holy Land by an American. New York: 1837. V. 43

Incident of Travel in Central America, Chiapas and Yucatan. 1841. V. 37

Incidents of Travel in Central America, Chiapas and Yucatan. New York: 1841. V. 37; 38; 39; 40; 41; 42; 44

Incidents of Travel in Central America, Chiapas and Yucatan . . . (and) Incidents of Travel in Yucatan . . . New York: 1841-3. V. 42

Incidents of Travel in Central America, Chiapas and Yucatan. London: 1846. V. 39

Incidents of Travel in Central America, Chiapas, and Yucatan. New York: 1852. V. 38

Incidents of Travel in Central America, Chiapas and Yucatan. London: 1854. V. 42; 43

Incidents of Travel in Central America, Chiapas and Yucatan. London: 1861. V. 38

Incidents of Travel in Central America, Chiapas and Yucatan. New York: 1863. V. 39

Incidents of Travel in Egypt, Arabia Petraea and the Holy Land. New York: 1849. V. 40

Incidents of Travel in Greece, Turkey, Russia and Poland. New York: 1838. V. 40

Incidents of Travel in Yucatan. London: 1843. V. 39; 42; 45; 46

Incidents of Travel in Yucatan. New York: 1843. V. 37; 38; 41; 42

Incidents of Travel in Yucatan. New York: 1848. V. 38

Incidents of Travel in Yucatan. New York: 1860. V. 39

Incidents of Travel in Yucatan. Norman: 1962. V. 39

STEPHENS, L. DOW

Life Sketches of a Jayhawker of '49. San Jose: 1916. V. 39

STEPHENS, PETER

Racolta di Alcune delle Piu Belle Vedute d'Italia. London: 1767. V. 39

STEPHENS, STEPHEN DE WITT

The Mavericks. New Brunswick: 1950. V. 44

STEPHENS, THOMAS

A Brief Account of the Causes that Have Retarded the Progress of the Colony of Georgia. London: 1743. V. 40; 41; 42; 43; 44

STEPHENS, W. P.

Canoe and Boat Building. A Complete Manual for Amateurs . . . New York: 1889. V. 38

STEPHENS, W. R. W.

A History of the English Chruch. London: 1901-10. V. 39; 42

A History of the English Church; from Its Foundation to the End of the 19th Century. London: 1907-10. V. 39; 40

STEPHENS, WILLIAM

A Journal of the Proceedings in Georgia, Beginning Oct. 20, 1737. London: 1742. V. 42

A Letter to (John Toland) the Author of the Memorial of the State of England. London: 1705. V. 42

A State of the Province of Georgia, Attested Upon Oath in the Court of Savannah, November 10, 1740. London: 1742. V. 38; 39; 42; 44

STEPHENSON, BLAKE

Specimens of Wood Letter, Borders, Ornaments &c. Sheffield & London: 1934. V. 40

STEPHENSON, BLAKE & CO.

Select Specimens of Modern Printing Types, Plain and Ornamental. Sheffield: 1860. V. 38

STEPHENSON, C.

A Text Book Dealing with Ornamental Design for Woven Fabrics. London: 1897. V. 42

STEPHENSON, ELIZA TABOR

Nature's Nobleman. London: 1869. V. 46

STEPHENSON, GEORGE

A Description of the Safety Lamp, Invented by George Stephenson and Now in Use in Killingworth Colliery. London: 1817. V. 38; 40

A Report on the Practicability and Utility of the Limerick and Waterford Railway . . . Edinburgh: 1827. V. 46

STEPHENSON, ISAAC

Recollections of a Long Life 1829-1915. chicago: 1915. V. 46

STEPHENSON, J.

Medical Botany. London: 1834-36. V. 37

STEPHENSON, JOHN

Medical Zoology, and Mineralogy; or Illustrations and Descriptions . . . London: 1838. V. 43

STEPHENSON, JOHN W.

Drapery Cutting and Making. New York: 1934. V. 39; 44

STEPHENSON, MARMADUKE

A Call from Death to Life, and Out of the Dark Wayes and Worships of the World . . . London: 1660. V. 42

STEPHENSON, ROBERT

Observations on the Comparative Merits of Locomotive and Fixed Engines, as Applied to Railways . . . Liverpool: 1830. V. 38; 40; 46

Report on the Atmospheric Railway System. London: 1844. V. 46

STEPHENSON, S. M.

A Historical Essay on the Parish and Congregtion of Templepatrick . . . Belfast: 1825. V. 38

STEPHENSON, SIMON

Representations of the Embossed, Chased and Engraved Subjects and Inscriptions Which Decorate the Tobacco Box and Cases Belonging to the Past Overseers Society, of the Parishes of St. Margaret and St. John the Evangelist in the City of Westminster. London: 1824. V. 42

STEPHENSON, T. A.

The British Sea Anemones. London: 1928/1935. V. 37; 40

The British Sea Anemones. London: 1928-35. V. 37; 38

STEPHENSON, TERRY E.

Caminos Viejos: Tales Found in the History of California of Especial Interest to Those Who Love the Valleys, the Hills and the Canyons of Orange County, Its Traditions and Landmarks. Santa Ana: 1930. V. 40; 44

STEPHNUS, CAROLUS

Dictionarium Historicum, Geographicum, Poeticum. Geneva: 1633. V. 38

STEPNEY, CATHERINE MANNERS

Poems. London: 1793. V. 42

STEPNEY, GEORGE

An Epistle (in verse) to Charles Montague Esq; on His Majesty's Voyage to Holland. London: 1691. V. 40; 42; 43; 44

An Essay Upon the Interest of England, in the Present Circumstances of Affairs . . . Dublin: 1701. V. 43

A Poem Dedicated to the Blessed Memory of Her Late Gracious Majesty Queen Mary. London: 1695. V. 41; 45

STEPNIAK

King Stork and King Log. A Study of Modern Russia. London: 1895. V. 37

STERLING, CHARLES

Still Life Paintings from Antiquity to the Present Time. New York: 1959. V. 42

STERLING, GEORGE

Beyond the Breakers and Other Poems. San Francisco: 1914. V. 45

The Caged Eagle and Other Poems. San Francisco: 1916. V. 45

Continent's End. San Francisco: 1925. V. 44; 45

The House of Orchids and Other Poems. San Francisco: 1911. V. 45

Lilith, a Dramatic Poem. San Francisco: 1919. V. 38; 40

Robinson Jeffers. New York: 1926. V. 38; 45

Rosamund: A Dramatic Poem by George Sterling. 1920. V. 37

Sonnets to Craig. Long Beach: 1928. V. 37

The Testimony of the Suns. San Francisco: 1903. V. 37; 41; 44

Thirty-Five Sonnets. San Francisco: 1917. V. 38

Truth. Chicago: 1923. V. 46

A Wine of Wizardry, and Other Poems. San Francisco: 1909. V. 40; 43

Yosemite: an Ode. San Francisco: 1918. V. 46

STERLING, JAMES

A Sermon Preached Before His Excellency the Governor of Maryland and Both Houses of Assembly, at Annapolis, December 13, 1754. Annapolis: 1755. V. 38

STERLING, JOHN

Essays and Tales. London: 1848. V. 39; 46

Fitz-George. Philadelphia: 1833. V. 45

Poems. (and) Strafford: a Tragedy. London: 1839-43. V. 38; 40

A System of Rhetorick, in a Method Entirely New . . . Dublin: 1786. V. 41; 42

STERLING, JOSEPH

Bombarino, a Romance with Poems on the Four Sister Arts . . . Dublin: 1768. V. 44

Poems. London: 1789. V. 38; 39; 42; 45; 46

STERLING, LOUIS

Catalogue of the Sterling Library. A Catalogue of the printed books and literary manuscripts. Collected by Sir Louis Sterling. (Oxford): 1954. V. 37

The Sterling Library. Cambridge: 1954. V. 39; 40

The Sterling Library. A Catalogue of the Printed Books and Literary Manuscripts collected by Sir Louis Sterling. London: 1954. V. 39

STERLING, RICHARD

Our Own Fourth Reader: for the Use of Schools and Families. Greensboro: 1865. V. 38

Our Own Third Reader; for the Use of Schools and Families. Greensboro: 1862. V. 37; 38

STERLING, WILLIAM

Annals of the Artists of Spain. London: 1848. V. 37

STERLING, WILLIAM ALEXNDER, EARL OF

Recreations with the Muses. London: 1637. V. 38

STERMANN, C. VON

Architecture of the Renaissance in Tuscany. New York: 1924. V. 46

STERN, EDGAR

A Sentimental Journey through France and Italy (and other Countries). Philadelphia: 1938. V. 46

STERN, F. C.

A Study of the Fenus Paeonia. London: 1946. V. 38; 43; 44; 46

STERN, GIOVANNI

Piante, Elevazione, Profili e Spaccati Degli Edifici della Villa Surburbana di Giulio III. Rome: 1784. V. 37

STERN, HAROLD P.

Master Prints of Japan: Ukiyo-e Hanga. New York: 1969. V. 41

STERN, HENRY

The Captive Missionary. London: 1868. V. 40

Wanderings Among the Falashas in Abyssinia. London: 1862. V. 40; 45

Wanderings Among the Falashas in Abyssinia. Together with a Description of the Country and Its Various Inhabitants. Wrtheim: 1862. V. 41

STERN, JAMES

The Heartless Land. London: 1932. V. 38

STERNDALE, ROBERT ARMITAGE

Denizens of the Jungles: a Series of Sketches of Wild Animals Illustrating their Forms and Natural Attitudes. Calcutta: 1886. V. 37

Seonee; or, Camp Life on the Satpura Range. Calcutta: 1887. V. 46

STERNE, ADOLPHUS

Hurrah for Texas! The Diary of Adolphus Sterne. Waco: 1969. V. 37

STERNE, HAROLD E.

Catalogue of Nineteenth Century Bindery Equipment and Catalogue of Nineteenth Century Printing Presses. Cincinnati: 1978. V. 38; 40

STERNE, HENRY

A Statement of Facts, Submitted to the Right Hon. Lord Gleneig, His Majesty's Principal Secretary of State for the Colonies, Preparatory to An Appeal About to Be Made by the Author, to the Commons of Great Britain . . . London: 1837. V. 40; 43; 46

STERNE, L.

A Concordance to the Prose Works of John Milton. London: 1987. V. 39

STERNE, LAURENCE 1713-1768

The Beauties of Sterne . . . London: 1782. V. 42

The Beauties of Sterne. London: 1793. V. 38; 41

The Beauties of Sterne. London: 1799. V. 39

Letters of the Late Rev. Mr. Laurence Sterne. London: 1775. V. 37; 38; 39; 40; 41; 42; 45

Letters of the Late Rev. Mr. Laurence Sterne, to His Most Intimate Friends. Dublin: 1776. V. 37; 39; 42

Letters of the Late Rev. Mr. Laurence Sterne, to His Most Intimate Friends. London: 1776. V. 37; 40; 45

Lettres de Sterne a ses Amis, Traduites sur les Originaux Nouvellement Publies a Londres. The Hague: 1789. V. 46

Letters from Yorick to Eliza and Sterne's Letters to His Friends on Various Occasions. Dublin: 1776. V. 43

Lettres d'Yorick a Eliza, et d'Eliza a Yorick. Geneva: 1779. V. 46

The Life and Opinions of Tristram Shandy, Gentleman. London: 1760. V. 40

Life and Opinions of Tristram Shandy, Gentleman. London: 1760-67. V. 38; 39; 40; 41; 45

The Life and Opinions of Tristram Shandy, Gentleman. N.P. York: 1760; Volumes 8-4: 1760-67. V. 37

The Life and Opinions of Tristram Shandy, Gentleman. York and London: 1760-67. V. 37; 38; 44; 46

The Life and Opinions of Tristram Shandy, Gentleman. York & London: 1760-69. V. 41; 42; 45

The Life and Opinions of Tristram Shandy, Gentleman. (with) The Sermons of Mr. Yorick. (with) The Letters to His Most Intimate Friends; London: 1760-76. V. 41

The Life and Opinions of Tristram Shandy, Gentleman. London: 1769. V. 41; 44

STERNE, LAURENCE 1713-1768 continued

The Life and Opinions of Tristram Shandy, Gentleman. London: 1777. V. 40

The Life and Opinions of Tristram Shandy. London: 1779. V. 40

La Vie et les Opinions de Tristram Shandy. London: 1784. V. 42

Tristram Shandy. London: 1832. V. 45

The Life and Opinions of Tristram Shandy, Gentleman. London & New York: 1900. V. 40

The Life and Opinions of Tristram Shandy, Gentleman. Waltham St. Lawrence: 1929. V. 39

The Life and Opinions of Tristram Shandy, Gentleman ... Berkshire: 1929-30. V. 46

The Life and Opinions of Tristam Shandy, Gentleman. Waltham St. Lawrence: 1929-30. V. 37

The Life and Opinions of Tristram Shandy, Gentleman. Waltham St. Lawrence: 1930. V. 40

The Life and Opinions of Tristram Shandy, Gentleman. New York: 1935. V. 44

Original Letters of the Late Rev. Laurence Sterne; Never Before Published. Dublin: 1788. V. 38; 41

Original Letters Never Before Published. London: 1788. V. 39; 40; 45

A Political Romance, by Laurence Sterne. An Exact Reprint of the First Edition of 1759 with an Introduction by Wilbur L. Cross. Boston: 1914. V. 37

A Sentimental Journey. V. 45; 46

A Sentimental Journey through France and Italy. Dublin: 1767. V. 38

A Sentimental Journey through France and Italy. London: 1768. V. 37; 38; 39; 40; 41; 42; 43; 44; 45; 46

A Sentimental Journey through France and Italy. London: 1769. V. 37; 44

A Sentimental Journey. London: 1770. V. 40

A Sentimental Journey. London: 1771. V. 39

A Sentimental Journey through France and Italy. London: 1774. V. 40; 41

A Sentimental Journey through France and Italy. London: 1780. V. 38; 41; 45

A Sentimental Journey, through France and Italy, by Mr. Yorick. Paris: 1783. V. 41

A Sentimental Journey through France and Italy. London: 1790. V. 41; 46

Voyage Sentimental ... Strasbourg: 1790. V. 42

A Sentimental Journey through France and Italy. London: 1794. V. 41; 42; 46

A Sentimental Journey through France and Italy. New York: 1796. V. 41

Voyage Sentimental, suivi des Lettres d'Yorick a Eliza. Paris et a: 1799. V. 38

Voyage Sentimental, Suivi les Letrres d'Yorick a Eliza ... Paris et a Amsterdam: 1799. V. 40

Yorick's Sentimentale Reise Giennem Frankfrig Og Italien. Copenhagen: 1841. V. 40

A Sentimental Journey through France and Italy. New York: 1884. V. 37; 45

A Sentimental Journey through France and Italy. Boston: 1905. V. 44

A Sentimental Journey through France and Italy. London: 1910. V. 40; 43

Voyage Sentimental en France & en Italie. Paris: 1920. V. 46

A Sentimental Journey through France and Italy. London: 1928. V. 42; 44; 46

A Sentimental Journey through France and Italy. Reading, Berkshire: 1928. V. 41

A Sentimental Journey through France and Italy. Waltham St. Lawrence: 1928. V. 40; 41; 42; 44

A Sentimental Journey through France and Italy. Paris: 1929. V. 38; 46

A Sentimental Journey through France and Italy. 1936. V. 37; 44

A Sentimental Journey Through France and Italy. High Wycombe: 1936. V. 40; 43; 44; 45; 46

A Sentimental Journey. New York: 1936. V. 39; 40; 41; 42; 43

A Sentimental Journey. Stamford: 1936. V. 41

The Sermons of Mr. Yorick. London: 1760. V. 38; 43

The Sermons of Mr. Yorick. London: 1760/64/66. V. 45

The Sermons of Mr. Yorick. London: 1760-66-69. V. 40

The Sermons of Mr. Yorick. London: 1769. V. 40

The Sermons of Mr. Yorick. London: 1784. V. 44

Sermons by the Late Laurence Sterne, A.M. Prebendary of York, and Vicar of Sutton on the Forest, and of Stillington, Near York. London: 1787. V. 45

Seven Letters Written by Sterne and His Friends, Hitherto Unpublished. London: 1844. V. 37

The Works. Dublin: 1774. V. 41; 42; 45; 46

Works. With a Life of the Author. Philadelphia: 1774. V. 41

The Works of Laurence Sterne. London: 1780. V. 41; 42

The Works of Laurence Sterne M.A. London: 1783. V. 38; 42

The Works. London: 1788. V. 46

The Works. London: 1793. V. 38; 41; 45

The Works. Harrisburgh: 1804. V. 45

The Works of ... Harrisburgh: 1804-05. V. 39

The Works of ... London: 1808. V. 41

Works of Laurence Sterne ... Baltimore: 1816. V. 46

The Works. London: 1819. V. 37; 38; 46

The Works of Laurence Sterne in Six Volumes. London: 1823. V. 46

The Works of Laurence Sterne. London: 1873. V. 46

The Works of ... London: 1900. V. 43

The Works. Stratford-upon-Avon: 1925. V. 38

The Works of ... London: 1926. V. 46

Works. Oxford: 1926. V. 42

The Works. Stratford-upon-Avon,: 1926. V. 42

The Works of Laurence Sterne. Oxford: 1926-27. V. 46

The Works (Including Sermons and Letters) with a Life of the Author, written by Himself. London: 1815. V. 37

STERNE, LOUIS

Seventy Years on an Active Life. London: 1912. V. 40

STERNHOLD, THOMAS, PSEUD.

The Daily Advertiser in Metre. London: 1781. V. 39

STERRE, JOANNES CHRYSOTOMUS VAN DER

Vita S. Norberti, Canonicorum Praemonstratensium Patriarachae. Antwerp: 1622. V. 37

STERRY, CONSIDER

The American Youth. Providence: 1790. V. 40; 44

STETSON, CHARLOTTE PERKINS

In This Our World and Other Poems. San Francisco: 1895. V. 44

STETSON, JAMES B.

San Francisco During the Eventful Days of April, 1906. San Francisco: 1906. V. 44

STEUART, HENRY

The Planter's Guide. Edinburgh: 1828. V. 38; 40; 41; 44; 46

The Planter's Guide. Edinburgh & London: 1828. V. 37; 38; 41; 42; 43

The Planter's Guide; or, a Practical Essay on the Best Method of Giving Immediate Effect to Wood by the Removal of Large Trees and Underwood ... New York: 1832. V. 41; 44; 46

STEUART, JAMES 1635-1715

Dirleton's Doubts and Questions in the Law of Scotland, Resolved and Answered. Edinburgh: 1715. V. 40

Dirleton's Doubts and Questions in the Law of Scotland, Resolved and Answered. Edinburgh: 1762. V. 40

An Inquiry into the Principles of Political Oeconomy: Being an Essay on the Science of Domestic Policy in Free Nations. Dublin: 1770. V. 41

An Inquiry into the Principles of Political Economy. Basil (Basle): 1796. V. 38

A Plan for Introducing an Uniformity of Weights and Measures Within the Limits of the British Empire. London: 1790. V. 42

The Principles of Money Applied to the Present State of the Coin of Bengal. London: 1772. V. 38

The Works, Political, Metaphisical and Chronological ... London: 1805. V. 39; 43

STEUART, JOHN R.

A Description of Some Ancient Monuments, With Inscriptions, Still Existing in Lydia and Phrygia ... London: 1842. V. 37; 39; 42; 43

STEUART, R. H. J.

March, Kind Comrade. London: 1931. V. 37

STEUBEN, FRIEDRICH WILHELM LUDOLF VON

A Letter on the Subject of an Established Militia, and Military Arrangements, Addressed to the Inhabitants of the United States. New York: 1784. V. 37

Regulations for the Order and Discipline of the Troops of the United States. Hartford: 1782. V. 37

Regulations for the Order and Discipline of the Troops of the United States ... Bennington: 1794. V. 37

Regulations for the Order and Discipline of the Troops of the United States. Halifax: 1794. V. 45

Regulations for the Order and Discipline of the Troops of the United States. Philadelphia: 1800. V. 42

Regulations for the Order and Discipline of the Troops of the United States ... To which is Added, An Appendix Containing the United States Militia; Together with the Law Organizing the militia of the State of New York, now Amended. Albany: 1803. V. 37

Regulations for the Order and Discipline of the Troops of the United States. Hartford: 1779 or 1783. V. 37

STEUCHUS, AUGUSTINUS, BP. OF CISAMUS

Veteris Testamenti ad Veritatem Hebraicam Recognito. Lyons: 1531. V. 40; 45

STEVENS, ALEXANDER

Public Characters of 1799-1800. London: 1799. V. 41

STEVENSON, ROBERT LOUIS BALFOUR 1850-1894 continued

A Child's Garden of Verses. New York: 1927. V. 43

A Child's Garden of Verses. London: 1931. V. 44

A Child's Garden of Verses. Edinburgh: 1947. V. 42; 43; 45

A Child's Garden of Verses. San Francicso: 1978. V. 40; 44

A Child's Garden of Verses. Chicago, New York: 1981. V. 41

Confessions of a Unionist. 1921. V. 39

David Balfour . . . New York: 1893. V. 40; 44; 46

David Balfour. New York: 1924. V. 44

Deacon Brodie or the Double Life. Edinburgh: 1888. V. 46

Diogenes at the Savile Club. Chicago: 1921. V. 38; 43

Diogenes in London. San Francisco: 1920. V. 38

The Dynamiter. London: 1885. V. 38; 43; 45; 46

The Ebb Tide . . . Chicago & Cambridge: 1894. V. 46

The Ebb-Tide. London: 1894. V. 39; 45; 46

Edinburgh. Picturesque Notes . . . London: 1879. V. 38; 40; 43

Familiar Studies of Men and Books. London: 1882. V. 37; 39; 40; 41; 42; 46

Father Damien. London: 1890. V. 41

. . . Father Damien; an Open Letter to the Reverend Dr. Hyde of Honolulu . . . Sydney: 1890. V. 41

Father Damien. San Francisco: 1930. V. 40; 43; 44

A Footnote to History. London: 1892. V. 39; 41

The Graver & the Pen. Or, Scenes from Nature with Appropriate Verse. Edinburgh: (1882). V. 37

Guinea. Edinburgh: 1884. V. 46

The Hanging Judge. London: 1914. V. 45

An Inland Voyage. London: 1878. V. 37; 41; 43; 45

An Inland Voyage. Boston: 1883. V. 39; 46

An Inland Voyage. London: 1912. V. 39

An Inland Voyage. Stamford: 1938. V. 41; 42; 43; 44; 45

An Inland Journey. Along the Escaut River, the Willebroek Canal, the Sambre and the Oise. Stamford: 1938. V. 42

Island Nights' Entertainments. London: 183. V. 41

Island Nights' Entertainments. London: 1893. V. 38; 39; 40; 43; 46

Island Night's Entertainments. London: Paris and: 1893. V. 45

Island Nights' Entertainment. London: 1895. V. 42

Kidnapped. London: 1886. V. 37; 38; 41; 42; 43; 45

Kidnapped. (London): 1886. V. 37

Kidnapped. New York: 1886. V. 43

Kidnapped. N.P.: 1886. V. 40

Kidnapped. New York: 1887. V. 40; 41

Kidnapped. London: 1930. V. 45

Kidnapped, the Adventrues of David Balfour, by Robert Louis Stevenson. New York: 1913. V. 37

The Letters of Robert Louis Stevenson. 1900. V. 41

A Lodging for the Night. East Aurora: 1902. V. 37; 44

A Lowden Sabbath Morn. New York: 1898. V. 40

The Master of Ballantrae. London: 1889. V. 38; 46

Memories & Portraits. London: 1887. V. 37

The Merry Men and Other Tales and Fables. London: 1887. V. 40; 41; 45

Moral Emblems. A Second Collection of Cuts and Verses. Davos-Platz: 1882. V. 40

More Arabian Nights. The Dynamiter. London: 1885. V. 38; 40; 41; 45; 46

New Arabian Nights. London;: 1882. V. 37

The Novels and the Tales of Robert Louis Stevenson. New York: 1901. V. 45

The Novels and Tales. New York: 1902. V. 42

The Novels and Tales. New York: 1905. V. 42

The Novels and Tales . . . New York: 1907. V. 41

The Novels and Tales. New York: 1909. V. 42

The Novels and Tales. New York: 1911. V. 42

Plain John Wiltshire on the Situation. Midland: 1989. V. 41; 43

La Porte De Maletroit. Cagnes-sur-Mer: 1952. V. 39; 40; 41; 43

La Porte at the Maletroit. San Francisco: 1952. V. 46

Prayers Written at Valima. London: 1910. V. 41; 46

Prayers Written at Vailima. London: 1922. V. 40

Prince Otto. London: 1885. V. 37; 39; 45

Providence and the Guitar. N.P.: 1985. V. 45

Recollections of Robert Louis Stevenson in the Pacific. London: 1905. V. 41

Records of a Family of Engineers. London: 1912. V. 43

Robert Louis Stevenson to His Good Friend M. Donat. San Francisco: 1925. V. 38; 43; 44

Robert Louis Stevenson to His Good Friend M. Donat. San Francisco: 1926. V. 42

St. Ives, Being the Adventures of a French Prisoner in England. London: 1897. V. 44

St. Ives Being the Adventures of a French Prisoner in England. New York: 1897. V. 39

The Silverado Squatters. London: 1883. V. 40

The Silverado Squatters. London: 1893. V. 39

A Stevenson Medley. London: 1899. V. 41

Stevenson's Workshop. Boston: 1921. V. 44

The Story of a Lie and Other Tales. Boston: 1904. V. 46

The Strange Case of Dr. Jekyll and Mr. Hyde. London: 1886. V. 37; 38; 39; 40; 41; 42; 43; 44; 45; 46

Strange Case of Dr. Jekyll and Mr. Hyde. New York: 1886. V. 39; 44

Strange Case of Dr. Jekyll and Mr. Hyde. New York: 1887. V. 40

Strange Case of Dr. Jekyll and Mr. Hyde. New York: 1888. V. 46

Doktoro Jekyll Kaj Sinjoro Hyde. London: 1909. V. 39; 40

Strange Case of Dr. Jekyll and Mr. Hyde. New York: 1929. V. 39; 44

Strange Case of Dr. Jekyll and Mr. Hyde. New York: 1952. V. 41

Three Plays. London: 1892. V. 39

Three Letters From Robert Louis Stevenson. London: 1902. V. 41

Travels With a Donkey in the Cevennes. Boston: 1879. V. 39; 42

Travels with a Donkey in the Devennes. London: 1879. V. 40

Treasure Island. London. V. 41

Treasure Island. London: 1882. V. 40; 43; 46

Treasure Island. London: 1883. V. 37; 39; 42

Treasure Island. London: 1885. V. 46

Treasure Island. New York: 1911. V. 37; 38; 43

Treasure Island. New York: 1924. V. 40

Treasure Island. London: 1927. V. 37

Treasure Island. London: 1929. V. 43; 44; 45

Treasure Island. Philadelphia: 1930. V. 45

Treasure Island. New York: 1941. V. 41

Treasure Island. London: 1947. V. 38; 41

Treasure Island. London: 1949. V. 38; 46

Treasure Island. London: (1985). V. 37

Underwoods. London: 1887. V. 41; 44

Virginibus Puerisque. London: 1881. V. 37; 39; 40; 44; 45; 46

Virginibus Puerisque and Other Papers. London: 1887. V. 46

Virginibus Puerisque. East Aurora;: 1903. V. 37; 40

Weir of Hermiston. London: 1896. V. 41; 44; 46

The Weir of Hermiston. London: 1986. V. 41

When the Devil Was Well. Boston: 1921. V. 44; 46

When the Devil Was Well. New York: 1921. V. 39

Will o' the Mill. East Aurora: 1901. V. 43; 46

Collection of Works . . . V. 45

The Works of . . . 1894-1898. V. 40

The Works. Edinburgh: 1894-1901. V. 43

Works. Edinburgh: 1894-98. V. 37; 42

The Edinburgh Edition of the Works. Edinburgh: 1894-99. V. 38

The Works. Edinburgh: 1895. V. 37

The Works of Robert Louis Stevenson . . . Volume XXII: The Misadventures of John Nicholson; The Wrong Box; (and) Fables. Edinburgh: 1897. V. 38

The Works of . . . New York: 1904. V. 46

Works of . . . New York: 1905. V. 42

Works of . . . New York: 1905/12. V. 46

The Works. London: 1906. V. 44

The Works of Robert Louis Stevenson. New York: 1906. V. 40

Works. London: 1906-07. V. 37; 39; 42; 46

The Works of Robert Louis Stevenson. 1907. V. 37

Works. London: 1909-1914. V. 37

Works. London: 1911. V. 38; 39

The Works. New York: 1921. V. 38; 42; 44

Works. London: 1921/23. V. 42

The Works. New York: 1921-23. V. 37; 38; 40

Works. London: 1921/33. V. 38

Works. New York: 1922. V. 45

Works. London: 1922-23. V. 37; 40; 41; 42; 43; 44

The Works . . . London: 1924. V. 37

Works. London: 1924-26. V. 42

The Wrecker. London: 1892. V. 39; 40; 41; 43; 44

The Wrong Box. London: 1889. V. 39; 40; 46

The Wrong Box. New York: 1889. V. 46

STEVENSON, ROGER

Military Instructions for Officers Detached in the Field . . . Philadelphia: 1775. V. 45

Military Instructions for Officers Detached in the Field: Containing a Scheme for Forming a Corps of Partisan. Philadelphia: 1775. V. 37

STEVENSON, THOMAS

The Design and Construction of Harbours, the Civil and Marine Engineering Involved. Edinburgh: 1864. V. 39

The Design and Construction of Harbours. Edinburgh: 1874. V. 38

STEVENSON, W. F.

Wounds in War: the Mechanism of Their Production and Their Treatment. London: 1910. V. 45

STEVENSON, WILLIAM

Historical Sketch of the Progress of Discovery, Navigation and Commerce . . . to the Beginning of the Nineteenth Century. Edinburgh & London: 1824. V. 39; 41; 44

Some Account of the Religious Institutions of Old Nottingham . . . Nottingham: 1895-99. V. 39

A Supplement to the First Edition of Mr. Bentham's History and Antiquities of the Cathedral and Conventual Church of Ely. Norwich: 1817. V. 38

STEVENSON, WILLIAM B.

A Historical and Descriptive Narrative of Twenty Years' Residence in South America, Containing Travels in Arauco, Chile, Peru and Colombia; with an Account of the Revolution, Its Rise, Progress and Results. London: 1825. V. 41

STEWARD, ISABELLA

The Mascarenhas. London: 1836. V. 46

STEWARD, JULIAN H.

Handbook of South American Indians. Washington: 1946-59. V. 42

STEWARD, RICHARD

Catholique Divinity. London: 1657. V. 39

STEWARD, WILLIAM

The First Edition of Steward's Healing Art, Corrected and Improved by the Original Hand. V. 39

The First Edition of Steward's Healing Art, Corrected and Improved by the Original Hand. Saco: 1827. V. 40

STEWART, A. M.

A Historical Sermon. Chicago: 1850. V. 41

STEWART, A. T.

Catalogue of the . . . Collection of Paintings, Sculptures, and Other Objects of Art . . . New York: 1887. V. 37

STEWART, ALVAN

A Legal Argument Before the Supreme Court of . . . New Jersey . . . for the Deliverance of 4,000 Persons from Bondage. New York: 1845. V. 42

Writings and Speeches of Alvan Stewart, on Salvery. New York: 1860. V. 46

STEWART, ANGUS

Sense and Inconsequence. London: 1972. V. 38

STEWART, ARCHIBALD

The Trial of Archibald Stewart Esq; Late Lord Provost of Edinburgh . . . For Neglect of Duty, and Misbehaviour in the the Execution of His Office . . . Before and at the Time the Rebels Got Possession of the City In . . . September 1745 . . . Edinburgh: 1747. V. 41

STEWART, B.

Subjects Portrayed in Japanese Colour Prints. London: 1922. V. 42

STEWART, C.

Report of Arbitration Between the Bookbinding Trade Section of the London Chamber of Commerce and the London Societies of Journeymen Bookbinders. London: 1903. V. 41

STEWART, CAROL

Poems of Sleep and Dream. London: 1947. V. 40

STEWART, CECIL

Topiary. London. V. 37

Topiary. 1954. V. 42

Topiary. London: 1954. V. 40; 41

Topiary. By Cecil Stewart. An historical diversion with colour engravings by Peter Barker-Mill. London: (1954). V. 37

STEWART, CHARLES

Two Sermons on Family Prayer, with Extracts from Various Authors; and a Collection of Prayers, Selected and Compiled by the Hon. and Rev. Charles Stewart, Minster of St. Armand, Lower Canada and Chaplain to the Lord Bishop of Quebec. Montreal: 1814. V. 37; 38

STEWART, CHARLES S.

Journal of a Residence in the Sandwich Islands, During the Years 1823, 1824 and 1825. London: 1828. V. 41

Private Journal of a Voyage to the Pacific Ocean and Residence at the Sandwich Islands in the Years 1822, 1823, 1824 and 1825. New York: 1828. V. 42

The Private Journal of the Rev. C. S. Stewart, Late Missionary to the Sandwich Islands . . . Dublin: 1830. V. 44

A Visit to the South Seas, in the U.S. Ship Vincennes, During the Years 1829 and 1830; with Scenes in Brazil, Peru, Manilla, the Cape of Good Hop and St. Helena. New York: 1831. V. 37

A Visit to the South Seas, in the U.S. Ship Vincennes, During the Years 1829 and 1830 . . . London: 1832. V. 46

A Visit to the South Seas in the U. States Ship Vincennes, During the Years 1829 and 1830; Including Notices of Brazil, Peru, Manila, the Cape of Good Hope and St. Helena. New York: 1833. V. 37; 38; 40; 43; 46

STEWART, D. J.

A Geography for Beginners. Richmond: 1864. V. 37

STEWART, DAVID

Sketches of the Character, Manners and Present State of the Highlanders of Scotland. Edinburgh: 1825. V. 45

STEWART, DUGALD 1753-1828

Account of the Life and Writings of Thomas Reid, D.D., F.R.S. Edinburgh: 1803. V. 42; 43

Account of the Life and Writings of William Robertson, D.D. London: 1801. V. 42; 43

Biographical Memoirs of Adam Smith, LL.D., of William Robertson, D.D. and of Thomas Reid, D.D., Read Before the Royal Society of Edinburgh. Edinburgh: 1811. V. 40

Dissertations on the History of Metaphysical and Ethical, and of Mathematical and Physical Science. Edinburgh: 1835. V. 38; 42

Dissertations onthe History of Metaphysical and Ethical and of Mathematical and Physical Science. London: 1835. V. 40

Elements of the Philosophy of the Human Mind. London: 1792. V. 42

Elements of Philosophy of the Human Mind. Edinburgh: 1802. V. 42

Elements of Philosophy of the Human Mind. London: 1802. V. 38

Elements of Philosophy of the Human Mind. London: 1808. V. 42

Elements of the Philosophy of the Human Mind. Edinburgh: 1814. V. 45

Elements of the Philosophy of the Human Mind. London: A. Strahan & T.: 1814. V. 37

Elements of the Philosophy of the Human Mind. London: 1814-16. V. 43

Elements of the Philosophy of the Human Mind. Boston: 1818. V. 43

Elements of Philosophy of the Human Mind . . . London: 1818. V. 39

Elements of the Philosophy of the Human Mind. London: 1818/16. V. 43

Outlines of Moral Philosophy. Edinburgh: 1793. V. 42

Outlines of Moral Philosophy. Edinburgh: 1801. V. 42; 43

Outlines of Moral Philosophy. For the Use of Students in the University of Edinburgh. Edinburgh/London: 1793. V. 37

Philosophical Essays. Edinburgh: 1810. V. 37; 38; 39; 41; 42; 43; 45

Philosophical Essays. Philadelphia: 1811. V. 42; 45

Philosophical Essays. Edinburgh: 1818. V. 38; 40; 42

Some Account of a Boy Born Blind and Deaf, Collected from Authentic Sources of Information. Edinburgh: 1815. V. 37

STEWART, ELEANOR

Vounous 1937-38: Field Report on the Excavations Sponsored by the British School of Archaeology at Athens. Lund: 1950. V. 40

STEWART, ELINORE P.

Letters of Woman Homesteader. London: 1914. V. 38

STEWART, F. CAMPBELL

Eminent French Surgeons, with a historical and statistical account of the Hospitals of Paris; together with Miscellanous information and biographical notices. Buffalo: ca. 1845. V. 37

STEWART, FRANK A.

Hunting Countries. London: 1935. V. 39

STEWART, FRANK H.

History of the First United States Mint. Camden: 1924. V. 42

History of the First United States Mint. Its People and Its Operation. N.P.: 1924. V. 44

Notes on Old Gloucester County, New Jersey. Camden: Woodbury,: 1917, 1934-37. V. 41

STEWART, GILBERT

A View of Society in Europe, In Its Progress from Rudeness to Refinement. Edinburgh. V. 39

STEWART, IOANNES

De Adventu Henrici Valesii Christianissimi Francorum Regis in Metroplim . . . Paris: 1549. V. 46

STEWART, JAMES

An Accompt of Scotlands Grievances by Reason of all the D. of Lauderdales Ministrie, Humbly Tendred to His Sacred Majesty. Edinburgh: 1672. V. 39

STEWART, JAMES continued

Index or Abridgement, of the Acts of Parliament and Convention, from the First Parliament of King James 1 Holden the 26 Maii, anno 1424 to the Fourth Session of the First Parliament of Her Majesty's Queen Anne . . . Edinburgh: 1707. V. 43

Plocacosmos; or, the Whole Art of Hair Dressing. London: 1782. V. 46

The Principles of the Law of Real and Personal Property. London: 1840. V. 40

Rudyard Kipling. A Bibliographical Catalogue. Toronto: 1959. V. 38

STEWART, JAMES HERVEY

Recollections of the Early Settlement of Carroll County, Indiana. Cincinnati: 1872. V. 46

STEWART, JAMES INNES MACKINTOSH 1906-

'Stop Press'. London: 1939. V. 40

STEWART, JOHN

An Account of Prince Edward Island. London: 1806. V. 39; 40

An Account of Prince Edward Island, in the Gulph of St. Lawrence, North America. London: 1806. V. 43

An Account of Jamaica and Its Inhabitants. London: 1808. V. 42; 46

At a Numerous and Respectable Meeting of Inhabitants, Held (by Adjournment) at the King's Head this Evening . . . n.p.: 1791. V. 43

Genevieve; or the Spirit of the Drave. London: 1810. V. 43

Genevieve; or the Spirit of the Drave. London: 1810. V. 45

The Moral State of Nations, or Travels Over the Most Interesting Parts of the Globe . . . Granville, Middletown: 1837. V. 46

The Moral State of Nations, or Travels Over the Most Interesting Nations, or Travels Over the Most Interesting Parts of the Globe, to Discover the Source of Moral Motion . . . Middletown: 1837. V. 43

The Pleasures of Love. London: 1806. V. 37

The Revelation of Nature, with the prophesy of Reason. New York: 1796. V. 37

Roll of a Tennis Ball, through the Moral World, in a Series of Contemplations Religious, Historical and Sentimental, by a Solitary Traveller. Dublin: 1812. V. 38; 39

The Royal Highland Regiment. The Black Watch Formerly 42nd and 73rd Foot. Medal Roll 1801-1911. Edinburgh: 1913. V. 37

Stable Economy: a Treatise on the Management of Horses, in Relation to Stabling, Grooming, Feeding, Watering and Working. Edinburgh: 1838. V. 39

A View of the Past and Present State of the Island of Jamaica with Remarks on the Moral and Physical Condition of the Slaves and on the Abolition of Slavery in the Colonies. Edinburgh: 1823. V. 41; 42; 46

STEWART, K. J.

The Freemason's Manual . . . Philadelphia: 1855. V. 45

A Geography for Beginners. Richmond: 1864. V. 42

STEWART, MARY

The Way to Wonderland. London. V. 45

STEWART, MATTHEW

The Distance of the Sun from the Earth Determined. Edinburgh: 1763. V. 38

STEWART, OLIVER

Aelous, or the Future of the Flying Machine. New York: 1928. V. 46

STEWART, ROBERT LAIRD

Sheldon Jackson: Pathfinder and Prospector of the Missionary Vanguard in the Rocky Mountains and Alaska. New York: 1908. V. 43

STEWART, ROBERT WALTER

The Tent and the Khan: a Journey to Sinai and Palestine. Edinburgh: 1857. V. 37; 46

STEWART, SARAH FRANCES COWLES

Cowles-Hutchinson Letters. N.P.: 1943. V. 39

STEWART, W. C.

The Practical Angler, or the Art of Trout-Fishing. Edinburgh: 1857. V. 46

STEWART, W. FRANK

Pleasant Hours in an Eventful Life. San Francisco: 1869. V. 46

STEWART, W. M.

The Policy of Extending Government Aid to Additional Railroad to the Pacific. Washington: 1869. V. 38; 39

STEWART, WILLIAM

Forms of Practical Proceedings in the Courts of King's Bench. London: 1825. V. 43

STEWART, WILLIAM DRUMMOND 1796-1871

Altowan; or, Incidents of Life and Adventure in the Rocky Mountains. New York: 1846. V. 37; 39; 40; 41; 42; 43

STEWART, WILLIAM M.

Reminiscences of Senator Wm. M. Stewart of Nevada. New York: 1908. V. 43

Reminiscences of Senator William M. Stewart of Nevada. New York & Washington: 1908. V. 39

STEWARTON,

The Female Revolutionary Plutarch, Containing Biographical, Historical and Revolutionary Sketches, Characters and Anecdotes by the Author of the Revolutionary Plutarch and Memoirs of Talleyrand. London: 1805-06. V. 41; 43; 45

The Secret History of the Court and Cabient of St. Cloud. London: 1806. V. 38; 39; 40; 41; 42

The Secret History of the Court and Cabinet of St. Cloud . . . from a Resident in Paris to a Nobleman in London. New York: 1807. V. 44

STEWART'S Cotton Planter. Patented July 1, 1856. Louisville: 1866? V. 44

STEYN, PETER

Hunters of the African Sky. V. 45

STICKLAND, REX W.

El Paso in 1854. El Paso: 1969. V. 38

STICKLAND, SAMUEL

Twenty-Seven Years in Canada West; or, the Experience of an Early Settler. London: 1853. V. 43

STICKLEY, GUSTAV

Craftsman Homes. New York: 1909. V. 37

More Craftsman Homes. New York: 1912. V. 38

STICKNEY, WILLIAM SOULE

Memorial Sketch of William Soule Stickney by His Father. Washington: 1881. V. 37

STIEGLITZ, ALFRED 1864-1946

America and Alfred Stieglitz: A Collective Portrait. Garden City: 1934. V. 44; 46

America and Alfred Steiglitz. New York: 1934. V. 39

Camera Work. New York: 1912. V. 44

Camera Work #44. New York: 1913. V. 40

Georgia O'Keefe: a Portrait. New York: 1978. V. 39; 41

Steiglitz Memorial Portfolio, 1864-1946. New York: 1947. V. 46

STIEGLITZ, C. L.

Archaeologie der Baukunst der Griechen und Romer. Weimar: 1801. V. 40; 44

STIEGLITZ, CHARLES LUDWIG

Descriptions Pittoresques de Jardins du Gout le Plus Moderne. Leipzig: 1802. V. 41

STIEHL, HENRY

Autobiography of . . . The Life of a Frontier Builder. Salt Lake City: 1941. V. 43

STIFF, DEAN

The Milk and Honey Route. A Handbook for Hobos. Illustrations by Ernie Bushmiller. New York: 1931. V. 37

STIFF, EDWARD

A New History of Texas . . . Cincinnati: 1848. V. 42

The Texan Emigrant; Being a Narration of the Adventures of the Author in Texas, and a Description of the Soil, Climate, Productions, Minerals . . . Cincinnati: 1840. V. 37; 41; 43

STIGAND, C. H.

Central African Game and Its Spoor. London: 1906. V. 38

The Game of British East Africa. London: 1909. V. 43; 45

The Game of British East Africa. London: 1913. V. 39

Hunting the Elephant in Africa and Other Recollections of Thirteen Years' Wanderings. London: 1913. V. 45

Hunting the Elephant in Africa. New York: 1913. V. 39; 40; 43; 44

The Land of Zinj Being an Account of British East Africa, Its Ancient History and Present Inhabitants. London: 1913. V. 39; 40; 45

To Abyssinia through an Unknown Land. London: 1910. V. 42

STIGEL, JOHANN

Tabvla de Speciebvs Continuae Quantitatis, ex Euclide & Alijs Bonis Autoribus Collecta. Wittenberg: 1537. V. 39

STILES, EZRA 1727-1795

A History of Three of the Judges of King Charles I . . . Who, at the Restoration, 1660, Fled to America, and Were Secreted and Concealed, in Massachusetts and Connecticut, for Near Thirty Years . . . Hartford: 1794. V. 38; 39; 40; 43

The Literary Diary of Ezra Stiles, D.D . . . New York: 1901. V. 42

STILES, H. M.

Who's Who in Smith Falls. Smith Falls: 1924. V. 38

STILES, HENRY R.

Civil, Political . . . History and Commercial and Industrial Record of the County of Kings and the City of Brooklyn. New York: 1884. V. 46

The History of Ancient Wethersfield, Connecticut. New York: 1904. V. 46

STILES, HENRY REED

Bundling Its Origin, Progress and Decline in America. Albany: 1871. V. 40

Joutel's Journal of La Salle's Last Voyage 1684-87. Albany: 1906. V. 45

STILES, JOSEPH C.

Modern Reform Examined; or, the Union of North and South on the Subject of Slavery. Philadelphia: 1857. V. 43

STILES, JOSEPH CLAY

National Rectitude, the Only True Basis of National Prosperity: an Appeal to the Confederate States. Petersburg: 1863. V. 44

STILES, WILLIAM H.

An Address, Delivered Before the Georgia Democratic State Convention, Held at Milledgeville, July 4th, 1856. Atlanta: 1856. V. 45

Austria in 1848-49; Being a History of the Late Political Movements in Vienna Milan, Venice and Prague . . . London: 1852. V. 39

STILL, GEORGE

The History of Pediatrics: The Progress of the Study of Diseases of Children Up to the End of the 18th Century. London: 1965. V. 45

STILL, GEORGE F.

Common Disorders and Diseases of Childhood. London: 1909. V. 45

STILL, I.

The Hastings Guide . . . Hastings: 1804. V. 44

STILL, JAMES

Early Recollections and Life of Dr. James Still. N.P.: 1827. V. 41

Hounds on the Mountain: Poems. New York: 1937. V. 44

River of Earth. New York: 1940. V. 39; 41; 44

STILL, WILLIAM

The Underground Rail Road. Philadelphia: 1872. V. 39; 40; 42; 45

STILL, WILLIAM GRANT

Troubled Island: an Opera in Three Acts. New York: 1949. V. 39

STILLE, ALFRED

Epidemic Meningitis, or Cerebro-Spinal Meningitis. Philadelphia: 1867. V. 42

STILLE, CHARLES

Memorial of the Great Central Fair for the U.S. Sanitary Commission, Held at Philadelphia, June 1864. Philadelphia: 1864. V. 42

STILLE, CHARLES J.

The Life and Times of John Dickinson, 1732-1808. Philadelphia: 1891-1895. V. 46

Major General Anthony Wayne and the Pennsylvania Line in the Continental Army. Philadelphia: 1893. V. 42; 46

STILLINGFLEET, BENJAMIN 1702-1771

An Essay on Conversation. London: 1737. V. 37; 38; 40; 43; 45; 46

Miscellaneous Tracts Relating to Natural History, Husbandry and Physick . . . London: 1762. V. 37; 38; 39; 40; 41; 44; 45; 46

Miscellaneous Tracts Relatin to Natural History, Husbandry, and Physick. London: 1775. V. 37; 38

STILLINGFLEET, EDWARD

The Council of Trent Examin'd and Disprov'd by Catholick Tradition, in the Main Points in Controversie Between Us and the Church of Rome. London: 1688. V. 39

The Grand Question, Concering the Bishops Right to Vote in Parliament in Cases Capital, Stated and Argued . . . London: 1680. V. 44

Origines Britannicae, or, the Antiquities of the British Churches. With a preface Concerning some pretended Antiquities Ralating to Britain, in Vindication of the Bishop of St. Asaph. London: 1685. V. 37; 38; 39

Protestant Charity, a Sermon Preached at S. Sepulchres Church, on Tuesday in Easter Wekk, A.D. MDCLXXXI. London: 1681. V. 45

STILLMAN, JACOB DAVIS BABCOCK

The Horse in Motion. Boston: 1882. V. 37; 38; 39; 41; 43; 44

The Horse in Motion . . . London: 1882. V. 42

Seeking the Golden Fleece; a Record of Pioneer Life in California. San Francisco: 1877. V. 37; 38; 39; 40

STILLMAN, SAMUEL

Death, the Last Enemy, Destroyed by Christ. A Sermon, Preached March 27, 1776, Before the Continental Congress, on the death of . . . Samuel Ward, Esq. One of the Delegates from the Colony of Rhode Island . . . Philadelphia: 1776. V. 45

An Oration Delivered July 4th, 1789, at the Request of the Inhabitants of the Town of Boston, in Celebration of the Anniversary of American Independence. Boston: 1789. V. 45

A Sermon Preached Before the Honorable Council, and the Honorable House of Representatives of the State of Massachusetts Bay, in New England, at Boston, May 26, 1779. Boston: 1779. V. 39

STILLMAN, W. J.

Poetic Localitites of Cambridge. Boston: 1876. V. 37

STILLWELL, JOHN E.

The History of the Burr Portraits, Their Origin, Their Dispersal and Their Reassemlage. New York: 1928. V. 46

The History of the Burr Portraits. Their Origin, Their Dispersal and Their Reassemlage. N.P.: 1928. V. 44

STILLWELL, LEANDER

The Story of a Common Soldier of Army Life in the Civil War 1861-1865. Erie: 1920. V. 46

STILLWELL, LUCILLE

John Cabell Breckinridge. Caldwell: 1936. V. 44

STILLWELL, MARGARET

The Awakening Interest in Science During the First Century of Printing 1450-1550. New York: 1970. V. 40; 45

STILLWELL, MARGARET BINGHAM

Gutenberg and the Catholicon of 1460. New York: 1936. V. 37; 38; 44

STIMSON, A. L.

Express Office Hand-Book and Directory for the Use of 1200 Express Agents and Their Customers . . . New York: 1860. V. 39; 40; 46

History of the Express Companies; and the Origin of American Railroads. Together with Some Reminiscences of the Latter Days of the Mail Coach and Baggage Wagon. New York: 1858. V. 37; 45

STINE, THOMAS OSTENSON

Scandinavians on the Pacific, Puget Sound. Seattle: 1900. V. 39; 42

THE STING of the Wasp. San Francisco: 1967. V. 37; 38; 46

STINSON, ALVAH L.

Woman Under the Law. Boston: 1924. V. 44

STINSON, JOHN HARRISON

Organon of Science. Eureka: 1879. V. 41; 44

STIPP, GEORGE WASHINGTON

John Bradford's Historical &c. Notes on Kentucky, from the Western Miscellany . . . . San Francisco: 1932. V. 40; 42

STIRLIING-MAXWELL, JOHN

An Essay Towards a Collection of Books Relating to Proverbs, Embelms, Apopthegms (sic) . . . London: 1860. V. 40

STIRLING, A. M. W.

Coke of Norfolk and His Friends. London: 1908. V. 44; 46

STIRLING, EDWARD

The Battle of Life, A Drama in Three Acts. London: 1847? V. 40

The Cricket on the Hearth . . . As Peformed at the Theatre Royal, Adelphi. London: 1846. V. 40

The Fortunes of Smike, or a Sequel to Nicholas Nickleby. London: 1840? V. 40

Martin Chuzzlewit: a Drama in Three Acts. London: 1844. V. 40

Mrs. Harris! London: 1846? V. 40; 43

Nicholas Nicleby: a Farce in Two Acts. London: 1838? V. 40

The Old Curiosity Shop. London: 1868? V. 40

Old Drury Lane. London: 1881. V. 42

STIRLING, JAMES

Letters from the Slave States. London: 1857. V. 42; 45

Naphtali, or the Wrestlings of the Church of Scotland for the Kingdom of Christ. Edinburgh: 1667. V. 42; 44

STIRLING, JAMES HUTCHINSON

Philosophy and Theology, Being the First Edinburgh University Gifford Lectures. Edinburgh: 1890. V. 40

STIRLING, JAMES HUTCHISON

Lectures on the Philosohy of Law. Together with Whewell and hegel, and Hegel and Mr. W. R. Smith . . . London: 1873. V. 43; 45

STIRLING, JAMES HUTCHISON continued

The Secret of Hegel: Being the Hegelian System in Origin, Principle, Form and Matter. London: 1865. V. 41; 43; 45

The Secret of Hegel, Being the Hegelian System in Origin, Principle, Form and Matter. Edinburgh: 1898. V. 42

Text-Book to Kant. Edinburgh: 1881. V. 43; 45

STIRLING, JOHN

Fifty Years with Rod: With Essays on What We Know of the Salmon and the Scottish Seatrout. London: 1929. V. 41

Our Regiments in South Africa 1899-1902. Edinburgh and London: 1903. V. 41

A System of Rhetorick, in a Method Entirely New . . . Dublin: 1786. V. 43

STIRLING-MAXWELL, WILLIAM, BART 1818-1878

Don John of Austria or Passages from the History of the Sixteenth Century. London: 1883. V. 39

An Essay Towards a Collection of Books Relating to Proverbs, Emblems, Apophtegms, Epitaphs and . . . London: 1860. V. 44

Examples of the Ornamental Heraldry of the Sixteenth Century. London: 1868. V. 38; 40; 44

Works, Comprising Annals of the Artists of Spain. London: 1891. V. 39; 40

STIRLING, PATRICK JAMES

Australian and Californian Gold Discoveries. Edinburgh: 1853. V. 43; 46

STIRLING, WILLIAM

An Essay Towards a Collection of Books Relating to Proverbs, Emblems . . . London: 1860. V. 45

Some Apostles of Physiology. London: 1902. V. 37; 38; 39

Velazquez and His Works. London: 1855. V. 41

STIRLING, WILLIAM ALEXANDER, 1ST EARL OF 1567?-1640

Aurora. London: 1604. V. 39

Recreation with the Muses. London: 1637. V. 38; 39; 40; 42; 45

STIRNER, MAX

Der Einzige und Sein Eigenthum. Leipzig: 1845. V. 45

STIRRUP, THOMAS

Horometria; or, The Compleat Diallist. London: 1659. V. 42

STISTED, GEORGIANA

The True Life of Capt. Sir Richard F. Burton. London: 1896. V. 43

STISTED, HENRY, MRS.

Letters from the Bye-Ways of Italy. London: 1845. V. 46

STITH, WILLIAM 1707-1755

The History of the First Discovery and Settlement of Virginia . . . Williamsburg: 1747. V. 43; 45

The History of the First Discovery and Settlement of Virginia. New York: 1865. V. 38; 42; 43; 45

STOBAEUS, JOANNES

Eclogarum Libri Duo: Quorum Prior Physicas, Posterior Ethicas Complectur nunc Primum Graece editi . . . Antwerp: 1575. V. 37; 46

STOBAEUS, JOHANNES

(Greek title, then:) Collectiones Sententiarum. Venice: 1535, 1536. V. 43

STOBO, ROBERT

Memoirs of Major Robert Stobo, of the Virginia Regiment. Pittsburgh: 1854. V. 40

STOCK, ALFRED 1876-1946

Hydrides of Boron and Silicon. Ithaca: 1933. V. 42

STOCK, EUGENE

The History of the Church Missionary Society, Its Environment, Its Men and Its Work. London: 1899-1916. V. 39; 42

STOCK, J.

A Narrative of What Passed at Killala in Co. Mayo . . . During the French Invasion of Summer 1798. Dublin: 1800. V. 43

STOCK, JOHN SHAPLAND 1804?-1867

A Practical Treatise on the Law of Non Compotes Mentis, or Persons of Unsound Mind. London: 1838. V. 45

STOCK, JOSEPH

A Reply to Dr. Campbell's Vindication of the Principles and Character of the Presbyterians of Ireland . . . Dublin: 1787. V. 38

STOCKDALE, F. W. L.

Excursions in the County of Cornwall, Comprising a Concise Historical and Topographical Delineations . . . London: 1821. V. 44

Excursions in the County of Cornwall. London: 1824. V. 39; 40

STOCKDALE, JAMES

Annales Caermoelenses: or, Annals of Cartmel. Ulverston: 1872. V. 38

STOCKDALE, JOHN

Sketches Civil and Military of the Island of Java and Its Immediate Dependencies. London: 1811. V. 39

Sketches Civili and Military of the Island of Java and Its Immediate Dependencies . . . London: 1812. V. 39

The Whole Proceedings on the Trial of an Information Exhibited ex Officio, by the King's Attorney General, Against John Stockdale, for a libel on the House of Commons . . . December 1789 . . . Dublin: 1790. V. 38; 43

The Whole Proceedings on the Trial of an Information Exhibited ex Officio, by the King's Attorney General, Against John Stockdale, for a Libel on the House of Commons, Tried in the Court of King's-Bench Westmisnter, on Wednesday, the Ninth of Dec. 1789 . . . London: 1790. V. 38; 46

STOCKER, JOHANN

Empirica, Sive Medicamenta Varia, Experienta . . . Frankfurt: 1601. V. 38

Praxis Aurea, as Corporis Humani Morbos Omnes. Leiden: 1634. V. 38

STOCKER, RHAMANTHUS M.

Centennial History of Susquehanna County, Pennsylvanai. Philadelphia: 1887. V. 41; 42

STOCKLEIN, JOSEPH

Allerhand so Lehr-Als Geistreiche Beief, Scrifften und Reis-Beschreibungen, Welche von Denen Missionariis der Gebellschafft Jesu Aus Beyden Indien . . . Augsburg & Gratz: 1726-30. V. 43

STOCKLEY, C. H.

Big Game Shooting in the Indian Empire. Bombay: 1928. V. 46

Big Game Shooting in the Indian Empire. London: 1928. V. 39; 40; 43

Stalking in the Himalayas and Northern India. London: 1936. V. 42

STOCKLEY, V. M.

Big Game Shooting in India, Burma, and Somalilnd. London: 1913. V. 38

STOCKMANS, BERNARDUS

Aritmetica . . . van Nieuws Ghecorigeert Ende Verbetert met Lustighe Gheometrische Questien Door Cornelis van Nienrode . . . Antwerpen: 1676. V. 38

STOCKTON & DARLINGTON RAILWAY

Jubilee Memorial of the Railway System. A History of the Stockton and Darlington Railway and a Record of Its Results. London: 1875. V. 46

STOCKTON, FRANK R.

The Bee-Man of Orn. New York: 1964. V. 45

The Queen's Museum and Other Fanciful Tales. New York: 1906. V. 45

STOCKTON, FRANK RICHARD

The Captain's Toll Gate. New York: 1903. V. 46

The Casting Away of Mrs. Lecks and Mrs. Aleshine. New York: 1886. V. 39; 40; 41; 46

The Novels and Stories. New York: 1899. V. 42

The Novels and Stories of . . . New York: 1899-1904. V. 39

Round-About Rambles in Lands of Fact and Fancy. New York: 1872. V. 40; 41

The Squirrel Inn. New York: 1891. V. 41; 44; 46

Ting-a-Ling. New York: 1870. V. 41

STOCKTON, HAROLD MACMILLAN

The Middle Way. London: 1938. V. 45

STOCKTON, THOMAS

Prayer at the Dedication of the National Cemetery at Gettysburg, Thursday, November 19th, 1863. Philadelphia: 1863. V. 44

STOCQUELER, J. H.

The British Soldier: an Anecdotal History of the British Army, from Its Earliest Formation to the Present Time. London: 1856. V. 44

The Hand Book of India, a Guide to the Stranger and Traveller, and a Companion to the Resident. London: 1844. V. 39

STOCQUELER, JOACHIM HAYWARD

The Canadian Volunteers' Hand-Book. Toronto: 1863. V. 37

The Life of Field Marshal the Duke of Wellington. London: 1852. V. 37

STODART, ROBERT R.

Memorials of the Browns of Fordell, Finmount and Vicarsgrange. Edinburgh: 1887. V. 37

STODDARD, AMOS

Sketches, Historical and Descriptive of Louisiana. Philadelphia: 1812. V. 38; 39; 40; 41; 42; 43

STODDARD, CHARLES WARREN

Over the Rocky Mountains to Alaska. St. Louis: 1899. V. 39

STODDARD, CHARLES WARREN continued

Poems. San Francisco: 1867. V. 43; 45

STODDARD, HERBERT L.

The Bobwhite Quail: Its Habits, Preservation and Increase. New York: 1931. V. 39

STODDARD, JOHN L.

Glimpses of the World . . . Containing a Rare and Elaborate Collection of Photographic Views of the Entire World of Nature and Art, Presenting and Describing the Choicest Treasures of Europe, Asia, Africa, Australia, North and South America. New York, Akron & Chicago: 1901. V. 37

STODDARD, JOHN LAWSON

Portfolio of Photographs of Famous Cities . . . Scenes and Paintings . . . Chicago: 1893. V. 44

STODDARD, SOLOMON

An Appeal to the Learned Being a Vindication of the Right of Visible Saints to the Lords Supper . . . Boston: 1709. V. 42

A Guide to Christ. Boston: 1735. V. 43

STODDARD, THOMAS TOD

Angling Reminiscences. London: 1837. V. 40

The Art of Angling as Practiced in Scotland. Edinburgh: 1835. V. 39

STODDARD, W. O.

The Great Union Pacific Railroad Excursion to the Hundredth Meridian, From New York to Platte City. Chicago: 1867. V. 37; 41

STODDARD, WHITNEY S.

The West Portals of Saint-Denis and Chartres. Cambridge: 1952. V. 44

STODDART, D. R.

Biogeography and Ecology of the Seychelles Islands. The Hague: 1984. V. 38

STODDART, JOHN

A Brief Journal of the Life, Travels, and Labours of Love in the Work of the Ministry . . . Dublin: 1728. V. 43

An Journal of the Life, Travels, Sufferings and Labour of Love . . . of William Edmundson . . . London: 1774. V. 45

Remarks on Local Scenery and Manners in Scotland During the Years 1799 and 1800. London: 1801. V. 37; 38; 41

STODDART, THOMAS T.

The Death-Wake or Lunacy, a Necromaunt in three Chimeras. Chicago: 1895. V. 38

STODDART, THOMAS TOD

Abel Massinger; or the Aeronaut. Edinburgh: 1846. V. 42

The Angler's Companion to the Rivers and Lochs of Scotland. Edinburgh: 1847. V. 41; 43

The Angler's Companion to the Rivers and Lochs of Scotland. London: 1847. V. 40

Songs and Poems: In Three Parts. Edinburgh: 1839. V. 39

STOEFFLER, JOHANN 1452-1531

Elvcidatio Fabricae Vsvsqve Astrolabii . . . Paris: 1564. V. 40

In Procli Diadochi, Authoris Gravissimi Sphaeram Mundi, Omnibus Numeris Longe Absolutissimus Commentarius. Tubingen: 1534. V. 43

STOERCK, ANTHONY

An Essay on the Use and Effects of the Root of the Colchicum Autumnale or Meadow Saffron. London: 1764. V. 41; 42

STOEVER, DIETRICH HEINRICH

The Life of Sir Charles Linnaeus . . . London: 1794. V. 39; 40

STOKER, BRAM 1847-1912

Dracula. London: 1897. V. 42; 46

Dracula. Westminster: 1897. V. 37; 40; 41; 45; 46

Dracula. Westminster: 1904. V. 40

Dracula. New York: 1965. V. 37; 39

The Jewel of Seven Stars. London: 1903. V. 42

The Lair of the White Worm. 1911. V. 37; 39; 44

The Mystery of the Sea. London: 1902. V. 37; 39; 44

The Mystery of the Sea. London: 1903. V. 43

Personal Reminiscences of Henry Irving. London: 1906. V. 44

Personal Reminiscences of Henry Irving. New York: 1906. V. 44

Personal Reminiscences of Henry Irving. London: 1908. V. 45

The Snake's Pass. London: 1892. V. 38

Under the Sunset. London: 1882. V. 37; 38; 41; 43

The Watter's Mou'. 1895. V. 37; 39

The Watter's Mou'. London: 1895. V. 46

The Watter's Mou'. Westminster: 1895. V. 42

STOKER, WILLIAM

Pathological Observations, Part I. On dropsy, purpura, and the influenza of the latter end of the year 1822, and beginning of that of 1823; and particularly on the morbid changes of the blood and their influence on the production and course of these . . . Dublin: 1823. V. 37

STOKES, ANSON PHELPS

Stokes Records; Notes regarding the Ancestry and Lives of Anson Phelps Stokes and Helen Louisa (Phelps) Stokes. New York: 1910-15. V. 37

STOKES, GEORGE GABRIEL

Mathematical and Physical Papers. Cambridge: 1880-1905. V. 45

Memoir and Scientific Correspondence . . . Cambridge: 1907. V. 45

STOKES, HENRY SEWELL

The Gate of Heaven, the Plaint of Morwenstow and Other Verses. Bodmin: 1876. V. 43

STOKES, HUGH

Belgium. London: 1916. V. 40

Belgium. New York: 1916. V. 41

STOKES, I. N. PHELPS

American Historical Prints, Early Views of American Cities, Etc. New York: 1932. V. 38; 39; 40; 43

American Historical Prints, Early Views of American Cities, Etc. New York: 1933. V. 39; 40; 41; 42

The Iconography of Manahattan Island, 1498-1909. New York: 1915-28. V. 40

STOKES, J.

The Cabinet-Maker and Upholster's Companion. Philadelphia: 1869. V. 38

The Complete Cabinet-Maker, and Upholster's Guide . . . London: 1841. V. 45

STOKES, J. LORT

Discoveries in Australia with an Account of the Coasts and Rivers Explored and Surveyed During the Voyage of HMS Beagle in the Years 1837-43 . . . London: 1846. V. 40

STOKES, MARGARET

Three Months in the Forests of France. A Pilgrimage in Search of Vestiges of the Irish Saints in France. London: 1895. V. 38

STOKES, RALPH

A Text Book of Rand Metallurgical Practice . . . London: 1913-12. V. 40

A Text-Book of Rand Metallurgical Practice. London: 1926-? V. 40

STOKES, SEWELL

Without Veils: the Intimate Biography of Gladys Cooper. London: 1953. V. 43; 45

STOKES, WHITLEY

Beunans Meriasek. Dublin: 1872. V. 42

Gwreans an Bys. The Creation of the World, a Cornish Mystery. Berlin: 1864. V. 43

The Tripartite Life of Patrick, with other Documents relating to that Saint . . . edited with translations and indexes. London: 1887. V. 37

STOKES, WILLIAM

The Diseases of the Heart and Aorta. Dublin: 1854. V. 37; 39; 41

The Diseases of the Heart and the Aorta. Philadlephia: 1854. V. 45

The Diseases of the Heart and Aorta. Philadelphia: 1855. V. 42

An Introduction to the Use of the Stethoscope With Its Application to the Diagnosis in Diseases of the Thoracic Viscera . . . Edinburgh: 1825. V. 37; 41

The Life and Labours in Art and Archaeology of George Petrie, LL.D. London: 1868. V. 39

Medicine in Modern Times or Discourses Delivered at a Meeting of the British Medical Association at Oxford. London: 1869. V. 42; 45

A Treatise on New Diagnosis and Treatment of Diseases of the Chest. Philadelphia: & New Orleans: 1839. V. 43

A Treatise on the Diagnosis and Treatment of Diseases of the Chest. London: 1882. V. 40; 41; 42; 43

STOLBERG, FREDERIC LEOPOLD 1750-1819

Travels through Germany, Switzerland, Italy and Sicily. London: 1797. V. 39

STOLBERG, FREDERICK LEOPOLD 1750-1819

Travels through Germany, Switzerland, Italy and Sicily. London: 1796-97. V. 41; 45

STOLBERG, JOHN SOBIESKI

The Costume of the Clans. Edinburgh: 1845. V. 44

STOLI, H.

The Amazon, Limnology and Landscape, Ecology of a Mighty Tropical River and Its Basin. The Hague: 1984. V. 38

STOLICKA, FERDINAND

Scientific Results of the Second Yarkand Mission . . . Calcutta & London: 1879-86. V. 43

STOLICZKA, FERDINAND

Scientific Results of the Second Yarkand Mission; Based Upon the Collections and Notes of the Late Ferdinand Stoliczka. Calcutta & London: 1878-86. V. 43

STOLL, JOHN B.

History of Indiana Democracy, 1816-1916. Indianapolis: 1917. V. 42

STONE & KIMBALL

The Green Tree Library. Chicago: 1895. V. 40

STONE, ARTHUR L.

Following Old Trails. Missoula: 1913. V. 37; 40; 42; 43; 44; 45

STONE, BENJAMIN

Sir Benjamin Stone's Pictures: Records of National Life and History. London: 1910. V. 46

STONE, DORIS

The Archaeology of Central and Southern Honduras. Cambridge: 1957. V. 38

STONE, E.

An Analytick Treatise of Conick Sections, and Their Use for Resolving of Equations in Determinate and Indeterminate Problems. London: 1723. V. 38; 40; 46

STONE, E. HERBERT

The Stones of Stonehenge: A Full Description of the Structure and of Its Outworks. London: 1924. V. 37

STONE, EDWARD DURRELL

Recent and Future Architecture. New York: 1967. V. 40

STONE, EDWIN MARTIN

The Invasion of Canada in 1775 . . . Providence: 1867. V. 42; 43

Our French Allies. Providence: 1884. V. 42

STONE, ELIZABETH

Uinta County: Its Place in History. Laramie: 1924. V. 44

Unita County Its Place in History. (Laramie: 1924). V. 37

William Langshawe, the Cotton Lord. London: 1842. V. 44

STONE, FRANCIS 1775-1835

Picturesque Views of all the Bridges Belonging to the County of Norfolk. Norwich?: 1830. V. 38

Picturesque Views of all the Bridges Belonging to the County of Norfolk. 1840. V. 39

STONE, G. F.

Bristol: As It Was and As It Is. Bristol: 1909. V. 39

STONE, GEORGE CAMERON

A Glossary of the Construction Decoration and Use of ARms and Armor In All Countries and In all Times. New York: 1961. V. 44

A Glossary of the Construction Decoration and Use of Arms and Armor in All Countries and in All Times. Portland: 1934. V. 38

STONE, HENRY DICKINSON

Personal Recollections of the Drama, or Theatrical Reminiscences. Albany: 1873. V. 40; 46

STONE, HENRY LANE

'Morgan's Men,' A Narrative of Personal Experiences . . . Louisville: 1919. V. 44

STONE, HERBERT L.

Millions for Defense. A Pictorial History of the Races for the America's Cup. New York: 1934. V. 39

STONE, HERBERT S., & CO.

Essays from the Chap-Book: Being a Miscellany of Curious and Interesting Tales . . . Chicago: 1896. V. 46

STONE, HERBERT STUART

First Editions of American Authors. Cambridge: 1893. V. 37; 38; 39; 40; 41; 44; 45

STONE, IRVING

Adversary in the House. Garden City: 1947. V. 43

Lust for Life, a Novel of Vincent Van Gogh. New York: 1936. V. 41

Men to Match My Mountains. Garden City: 1956. V. 45

Men to Match My Mountains. New York: 1956. V. 46

Sailor on Horseback. Boston: 1938. V. 43

Sailor on Horseback. Cambridge: 1938. V. 38

Those Who Love. Garden City: 1965. V. 43

STONE, J. HARRIS

Connemara and the Neighbouring Spots of Beauty, Being Notes on Achill Island, CAshel, Clifden, Galway, Kylemore, Maam, Renvyle, Sligo . . . London: 1906. V. 43

STONE, JOHN A.

Put's Golden Songster Containing the Largest and Most Popular Collection of California Songs Ever Published. San Francisco: 1858. V. 46

STONE, JOHN BENJAMIN

Children in Norway, or a Holiday on the Ekeberg. London: 1884. V. 40; 43

STONE, JOHN HURFORD

Copies of Original Letters Recently Written by Persons in Paris to Dr. Priestley in America. London: 1798. V. 39

STONE, MRS.

Chronicles of Fashion, from the Time of Elizabeth to the Early Part of the 19th Century, in Manners, Amusements, Banquets, Costume &c. London: 1845. V. 38

STONE, R. FRENCH

Biography of Eminent American Physicians and Surgeons Illustrated with Fine Photo-Engraved Portraits. Indianapolis: 1894. V. 41

STONE, REYNOLDS

A Book of Lettering. London: 1935. V. 40; 41; 45

Boxwood and Graver: a Miscellany of Blocks. London: 1958. V. 37; 41

Reynolds Stone Engravings. Brattleboro: 1977. V. 45

Engravings. London: 1977. V. 37; 39; 40; 41; 42

The Old Rectory. London: 1976. V. 40

The Wood Engravings of Gwen Raverat. London: 1959. V. 40; 46

Woodcut Designs by Reynolds Stone for Scribners 1933-1940. London: 1946. V. 41

STONE, ROBERT

Children of Light. 1986. V. 45

Children of Light. New York: 1986. V. 38; 39; 42; 45

The Day of the Locust. A New Introduction. N.P.: 1989. V. 43

Dog Soldiers. 1974. V. 43

Dog Soldiers. Boston: 1974. V. 42; 44; 45; 46

Dog Soldiers. New York: 1974. V. 38; 39; 41

A Flag for Sunrise. New York: 1981. V. 39; 41; 44; 45

A Hall of Mirrors. 1967. V. 46

A Hall of Mirrors. Boston: 1967. V. 37; 38; 39; 40; 42; 43; 44; 45; 46

A Hall of Mirrors. Boston & Cambridge: 1967. V. 46

A Hall of Mirrors. New York: 1967. V. 38; 39; 41

A Hall of Mirrors. Boston: 1968. V. 46

A Hall of Mirrors. London: 1968. V. 44; 45

Outerbridge Reach. New York: 1992. V. 46

STONE, THOMAS

An Essay on Agriculture, with a View to Inform Gentlemen of Landed Property, Whether Their Estates are Managed to the Greatest Advantage. Lynn: 1785. V. 42

General View of the Agriculture of the County of Lincoln, With Observations on the Means of Its Improvement, Drawn Up for the Consideration of the Board of Agriculture and Internal Improvement. London. V. 40

General View of the Agriculture of the County of Lincoln Drawn Up for the Consideration of the Board of Agriculture and Internal Improvement. London: 1799. V. 39; 44

STONE, WILBUR FISK

History of Colorado. Chicago: 1918. V. 37; 39; 46

History of Colorado. Chicago: 1918-1919. V. 39

STONE, WILBUR M.

The Gigantick Histories of Thomas Boreman. Maine: 1933. V. 45

STONE, WILBUR MACEY

Bookplates of Today. New York: 1902. V. 42

A Snuff-Boxful of Bibles. Newark: 1926. V. 39

The Thumb Bible of John Taylor. Brookline: 1928. V. 39; 44

STONE, WILLIAM L.

The Campaign of Lieut. Gen. John Burgoyne and the Expedition of Lieut. Col. Barry St. Leger. Albany: 1877. V. 42

History of New York City from the Discovery to the Present Day. New York: 1872. V. 42

Letters on Masonry and Anti-Masonry, Addressed to the Hon. John Quincy Adams. New York: 1832. V. 41

Life of Joseph Brant - Thayendanegea. New York: 1838. V. 38; 39; 41; 42; 44; 46

STONE, WILLIAM L. continued

The Life and Times of Sa-go-ye-wat-ha, or Red Jacket. New York: 1841. V. 40; 42

The Life and Times of Sa-go-Ye-Wat-Ha, or Red Jacket. Albany: 1866. V. 42; 45

The Life and Times of Sir William Johnson, Bart. Albany: 1865. V. 42

The Mysterious Bridal, and Other Tales. London: 1835. V. 41

Tales and Sketches, -- Such as they Are. New York: 1834. V. 40

STONE, WITMER

Bird Studies at Old Cape May. Philadelphia: 1937. V. 37; 38; 39; 41; 46

STONEBACH, H. R.

Cartographers of the Deus Loci: The Mill House. North Hills: 1982. V. 38; 39; 40; 42; 43; 44

STONEBACK, H. R.

Cartographers of the Deus Loci: The Mill House. Newtown: 1982. V. 38

Cartographers of the Deus Loci. The Mill House, North Hills: 1982. V. 39

STONEBECK, H. R.

Cartographer of the 'Deus Loci': The Mill House. 1982. V. 39; 41

STONEBRAKER, JOSEPH R.

A Rebel of '61. New York: 1899. V. 44

STONEHILL, CHARLES A.

Anonyma and Pseudonyma. London: 1926. V. 42

Anonyma and Pseudonyma. New York: 1927. V. 41; 43

STONEHOUSE, JOHN HARRISON

The Story of the Great Omar Bound by Francis Longinus Sangorski and its Romantic Loss. London: 1933. V. 46

STONEMAN, V.

John and Thomas Seymour. Cabinetmakers in Boston 1794-1816. Boston: 1959. V. 37

STONER, FRANK

Chelsea, Bow and Derby Porcelain Figures: Their Distinguishing Characteristics. Newport: 1955. V. 40; 41; 42

Chelsea Bow and Derby Porcelain Figures, their Distinguishing Characteristics. Newport: (1955). V. 37

STONES, M.

The Endemic Flora of Tasmania. London: 1967-78. V. 37

STONEY, H. BUTLER

A Residence in Tasmania. London: 1856. V. 38; 39

STONEY, P. S.

A History of the 26th Punjabis 1857-1923. Aldershot: 1924. V. 42

STONEY, SAMUEL GAILLARD

Charleston: Azaleas and Old Bricks. Boston: 1937. V. 40

Plantations of the Carolina Low Country. Charleston: 1938. V. 44

Plantations of the Carolina Low Country. Charleston: 1945. V. 40

STONG, PHIL

Horses and Americans. New York: 1939. V. 39

STONHAM, CHARLES

The Birds of the British Islands. London: 1906. V. 39; 43

The Birds of the British Isles. London: 1906-11. V. 37; 39

STOOKEY, BYRON

Surgical and Mechanical Treatment of Peripheral Nerves. Philadelphia: 1922. V. 42; 44; 45; 46

STOOKS-SMITH, HENRY

An Alphabetical List of the Officers of the Yorkshire Hussars, from the Formation of the Regiment to the Present Time. London: 1853. V. 38

STOPES, H.

Malt and Malting, an Historical, Scientific and Practical Treatise, Showing..What Malt is and How to Make It . . . London: 1885. V. 37; 38; 42

STOPES, MARIE

Contraception (Birth Control). Its Theory, History and Practice. London: 1924. V. 45

STOPFORD, FRANCIS

The Romance of the Jewel. London: 1920. V. 45

STOPFORD, JOSHUA

Pagano-Papismus; Or, an Exact Parallel Between Rome-Pagan and Rome-Christian, In Their Doctrines and Ceremonies . . . . London: 1675. V. 42

STOPPARD, TOM

Albert's Bridge and If You're Glad I'll be Frank - Two Plays for Radio. London: 1969. V. 40

Artist Descending a Staircase and Where Are They Now? London: 1973. V. 41

Dirty Linen and New-Found-Land. London: 1976. V. 42

Jumpers. London: 1972. V. 44

Lord Malquist & Mr. Moon. London: 1966. V. 37; 38; 39; 40; 42; 43; 44; 46

Lord Malquist and Mr. Moon. New York: 1966. V. 43

The Real Inspector Hound. London: 1968. V. 39; 40; 42; 43

Rosencrantz and Guildenstern Are Dead. London: 1967. V. 41; 46

Rosencrantz and Guildenstern are Dead. New York: 1967. V. 46

STOR, NIKOLAUS

Expositio Officii Misaae Sacrique Canonis. Strassburg: 1474. V. 46

STORCH, HEINRICH FRIEDRICH VON

Cours d'Economie Politique, ou Exposition des Principes qui Determinent la Prosperite des Nations. St. Petersbourg: 1815. V. 38

Cours D'Economie Politique ou Exposition des Principes qui Determinent la Prosperite des Nations. Paris: 1823. V. 38

STORCH, HENRY

The Picture of Petersburg. London: 1801. V. 45

STORCK, ANTON

Annus Medicus, Quo Sistuntur Observationes Circa Morbos Acutos et Cronicos . . . Neapoli: 1761. V. 46

An Essay on the Medicinal Nature of Hemlock . . . Edinburgh: 1762. V. 41; 43

Libellus, Quo Demonstratur . . . Vindobonae: 1763. V. 46

STORER, CLOUSTON J.

Carrington's Cases. 1920. V. 39

STORER, D. HUMPHREYS

Reports on the Fishes, Reptiles and Birds of Massachusetts. Boston: 1839. V. 40

STORER, HORATIO ROBINSON

Why Not! Boston: 1868. V. 44

STORER, J.

Views in Edinburgh and Its Vicinity; Drawn and Engraved by J. & H. S. Storer, Exhibiting Remains of Antiquity, Public Buildings and Picturesque Scenery. Edinburgh: 1820. V. 41; 46

STORER, JAMES

The Wild White Cattle of Great Britain. London: 1880. V. 37; 38

STORER, JAMES S.

Antiquarian and Topographical Cabinet, Containing a Series of Elegant Views of the Most Interesting Objects of Curiosity in Great Britain. London: 1807. V. 43

The Antiquarian and Topographical Cabinet; Containing a Series of Elegant Views . . . London: 1817-19. V. 40; 42

Cowper Illustrated by a Series of Views in or Near the Park of Weston Underwood, Bucks . . . London: 1803. V. 37; 40

Delineations, Graphical and Descriptive, of Fountains Abbey, in the West Riding of the County of York . . . Ripon. V. 38

Delineations of Fountains Abbey. Ripon: 1820. V. 38

Delineations, Graphical and Descriptive, of Fountains' Abbey, in the West Riding of the County of York. London: 1840. V. 41

Delineations, Graphical and Descriptive of Fountains Abbey in the West Riding of the County of York. Ripon: 1840. V. 45

History and Antiquities of the Cathedral Churches of Great Britain. London: 1814-19. V. 38

Views in North Britain. London: 1805. V. 43

Views in North Britain, Illustrative of the Works of Robert Burns. London: 1811. V. 44

STORER, MALCOLM

Numismatics of Massachusetts. Cambridge: 1923. V. 43; 46

STOREY, DAVID

Flight into Camden. London: 1960. V. 38; 40; 42

This Sporting Life. London: 1959. V. 38; 46

This Sporting Life. London: 1960. V. 38; 41; 44

STOREY, H.

Hunting and Shooting Ceylon. London: 1907. V. 40

STOREY, HENRY W.

History of Cambria County, Pennsylvania. New York: 1907. V. 41

STOREY, SAMUEL

To the Golden Land: Sketches of a Trip to Southern California. London: 1889. V. 42

STORHAUG, GLENN

The Kilpeck Anthology. Near Madley: 1981. V. 42

STORIE of Faire Landgartha, Queene of Norway, Wherein Honest Gentlemen Shall Receive Some Taste of Virtue, and a Gentlewomen Shall Have Means to See and Consider, How to Make Choyse of Virtue in Loving . . . London: 1827. V. 41; 43

STORIES About Mortimer A Present for Little Boys and Girls Four Years Old. London. V. 41

STORIES About the Alphabet. N.P.: (c. 1830). V. 37

STORIES by an Archaeologist and His Friends. London: 1856. V. 42

STORIES from the Chap-Book. Chicago: 1896. V. 46

STORIES of Chivalry and Romance. London: 1827. V. 46

STORIES of New York. New York: 1893. V. 40

STORIES of the War of 1812, and the Mexican War with Numerous Engravings. Philadelphia: 1859. V. 40

STORIES Southwest. Prescott: 1973. V. 44

STORK, WILLIAM

An Account of East-florida, with a Journal, Kept by John Bartram of Philadelphia, Botanist to His Majesty for the Floridas . . . London: 1766. V. 45

A Description of East Florida, with a Journal, Kept by John Bartram of Philadelphia, Botanist to His Majesty for the Floridas . . . London: 1769. V. 38; 41; 43; 44

STORKE, ELLIOT

A Complete History of the Great American Rebellion Embracing Its Causes, Events and Consequences. Auburn: 1865. V. 42

STORRS, AUGUSTUS

Answers of Augustus Storrs, of Missouri, to Certain Queries Upon the Origin, Present State and Future Prospect of Trade and Intercourse Between Missouri and the Internal Provinces of Mexico. Washington: 1825. V. 39; 40; 41; 43; 45

STORRS, RONALD

Orientations. London: 1937. V. 41

STORY, ALFRED T.

William Blake: His Life Character and Genius. London: 1893. V. 39

STORY, DAVID

This Sporting Life. 1960. V. 37

STORY, ISAAC

A Parnassian Shop, Opened in the Pindaric Stile. Boston: 1801. V. 37; 40

STORY, JOSEPH

Commentaries on the Law of Agency as a Branch of Commercial and Maritime Jurisprudence, with Occasional Illustrations from the Civil and Foreign Law. Boston: 1857. V. 39

A Discourse Pronounced at the Request of the Essex Historical Society, on the 18th of September 1828, in Commemoration of the First Settlement of Salem, in the State of Massachusetts. Boston: 1828. V. 42

A Discourse Pronounced Before the Phi Beta Kappa Society, at the Anniversary Celebration on the Thirty-Fisrt (sic) day of August, 1826. Boston: 1826. V. 37

An Eulogy on General George Washington; Written at the Request of the Inhabitants of Marblehead and Delivered Before Them on the Second Day of January, A.D. 1800. Salem: 1800. V. 45

The Miscellaneous Writings of Joseph Story. Boston: 1852. V. 43

The Power of Solitude. Boston: 1800. V. 42

A Selection of Pleadings in Civil Actions, Subsequent to the Declaration. Salem: 1805. V. 39; 43

STORY-MASKELYNE, MERVYN HERBERT 1823-1911

Crystallography: a Treatise on the Morphology of Crystals. Oxford: 1895. V. 40

A STORY of Active Service in Foreign Lands. Edinburgh: 1886. V. 41

THE STORY of Blue Beard. London: 1890. V. 39

THE STORY of Champ D'Asile, as Told by Two of the Colonists. Dallas: 1937. V. 42

THE STORY of Klondike. (Portland, Maine): ca. 1896). V. 37

THE STORY of the 1st and 2nd Battalions, 41st Dogras. Volume 1. October 1900 to December 1923 & October 1917 to March 9122. Bombay: 1924. V. 42

THE STORY of the 5th Bombardment Group (Healy). Raleigh: 1946. V. 37

THE STORY of Tom Restless: with an Account of His Voyages and Travels and His Imprisonment in the Bastille at Paris. London: 1820. V. 39

STORY, ROBERT

The Poetical Works. London: 1857. V. 37

STORY, THOMAS 1670-1742

A Journal of the Life of Thomas Story. Newcastle-upon-Tyne: 1747. V. 38; 40; 44

STORY, WILLIAM W.

A Treatise on the Law of Sales of Personal Property, With Illustrations from Foreign Law. London & Boston: 1847. V. 39

STOTHARD, CHARLES ALFRED

The Monumental Effigies of Great Britain. London: 1817. V. 41

The Monumental Effigies of Great Britain . . . London: 1817-32. V. 39; 44

STOTHARD, THOMAS 1755-1834

Illustrations of the Deacmeron of Boccacio. London: 1825. V. 38

STOTT, RAYMOND TOOLE

A Bibliography fo English Conjuring, 1581-1876. Derby: 1976. V. 40; 42

Circus and Allied Arts. A World Bibliography 1500-1957. Derby: 1858-1971. V. 46

Circus and Allied Arts; a World Bibliography 1500-1970. Derby: 1958-71. V. 37; 39

STOTZ, CHARLES MORSE

The Early Architecture of Western Pennsylvania. New York: 1936. V. 42

STOURTON, WILLIAM JOSEPH 1776-1846

Two Letters to the Right Honourable the Earl of Liverpool . . . On the Distresses of Agriculture, and Their Influence on the Manufactures, Trade and Commerce of the United Kingdom; with Observations on Cash Payments and a Free Trade. London: 1821. V. 42

STOUT, BENJAMIN

Narrative of the Loss of the Ship Hercules, Commanded by Captain Benjamin Stout, on the Coast of Caffraria, the 16th of June, 1796 . . . London: 1798. V. 42

Narrative of the Loss of the Ship Hercules . . . on the Coast of Caffraria, the 16th of June 1796; . . . Hudson: 1800. V. 45

Narrative of the Loss of the Ship Hercules, Commanded by Captain Benjamin Stout, on the Coast of Caffraria, the 16th of June, 1796. New Bedford: 1800. V. 40

STOUT, D. G.

The Shorebirds of North America. New York: 1967, 1968. V. 37

STOUT, PETER F.

Nicaragua: Past, Present and Future: A Description of Its Inhabitants, Customs, Mines, Minerals, Early History . . . Philadelphia: 1859. V. 46

STOUT, REX

Alphabet Hicks. 1941. V. 46

Black Orchids. 1942. V. 46

The Broken Vase. 1941. V. 46

Corsage. Bloomington: 1977. V. 37; 40

Double for Death. New York: 1939. V. 44; 46

Forest Fire. London: 1934. V. 40

The President Vanishes. New York: 1934. V. 40

The President Vanishes. 1968. V. 46

The Second Confession. New York: 1949. V. 46

The Silent Speaker. New York: 1946. V. 45

Three Trumps. New York: 1973. V. 41; 42

Too Many Cooks. 1938. V. 41

Trouble in Triplicate. London: 1949. V. 41

STOUT, SAMUEL H.

An Address on Education, Delivered in Pulaski, Tenn., at the Close of the Examination of the Students of Wurtemburg Academy . . . Pulaski: 1851. V. 44

STOUT, TOM

Montana, Its Story and Biography A History of Aboriginal and Territorial Montana and Three Decades of Statehood. Chicago: 1921. V. 44

STOVALL, PLEASANT A.

Fruits of Industry: Points and Pictures Along the Central Railroad of Georgia. Buffalo: 1895. V. 43

Robert Toombs, Statesman, speaker, Solider, Sage, His Career in Congress and on the Hustings - His Work in the Courts - His Record with the Army - His Life at Home. New York: 1892. V. 46

STOW, J. W.

Probate Confiscation, and the Unjust Laws Which Govern Women. San Francisco: 1876. V. 39

STOW, JOHN

The Abridgement or Summarie of the English Chronicle . . . London: 1607. V. 37; 44

The Annales of England, Faithfully Collected Out of the Most Authenticall Authors . . . London: 1592. V. 43

The Annales, or Generall Chronicle of England, Begun First by Maister John Stow, and After Him Continued and Augmented with Matters Forreyne, and Doemstic . . . London: 1615. V. 38; 43

Annales, or, a General Chronicle of England. London: 1631. V. 43

A Summarie of the Chronicles of England. London: 1598. V. 46

A Summarie of the Chronicles of England. London: 1604. V. 46

A Survay of London. London: 1603. V. 40; 43

The Survey of London. London: 1633. V. 39

A Survey of the Cities of London and Westminster . . . London: 1720. V. 40

A Survey of London. Oxford: 1908. V. 46

STOW, MARIETTA LOIS BEERS

Probate Chaff; or, Beautiful Probate; or Three Years Porbating in San Francisco. Boston: 1879. V. 46

STOW, RANDOLPH

Outrider - Poems 1936-1962. London: 1962. V. 40

STOW, W., MRS.

Probate Confiscation. Unjust Laws Which Govern Women. N.P.: 1877. V. 43

Probate Confiscation, Junjust Laws Which Govern Women. N.P. Boston?: 1877. V. 45

STOWE, HARRIET ELIZABETH BEECHER 1811-1896

The American Woman's Home. New York: 1869. V. 38; 46

Dred; a Tale of the Great Dismal Swamp. Boston: 1856. V. 37; 38; 40; 43; 44; 45; 46

Dred: A Tale of the Great Dismal Swamp. London: 1856. V. 41

The Edmundson Family, and the Capture of the Schooner Pearl. Cincinnati: 1854. V. 42

Herinneringen uit Vreemde Landen. Amsterdam: 1855. V. 46

The Key to Uncle Tom's Cabin. London. V. 45

A Key to Uncle Tom's Cabin. Boston: 1853. V. 38; 45

The Key to Uncle Tom. Leipzig: 1853. V. 40

A Key to Uncle Tom's Cabin. London: 1853. V. 37; 39; 40; 43

Lady Byron Vindicated. Boston: 1870. V. 41; 43

Little Foxes. Boston: 1866. V. 44

The Mayflower; or, Sketches of Scenes and Characters Among the Descendants of the Pilgrims. New York: 1843. V. 39; 43; 44

The Mayflower. London: 1852. V. 43

Men of Our Times. Hartford: 1868. V. 43

The Minister's Wooing. New York: 1859. V. 37; 39; 40

Oldtown og dets Beboere. Et Tidsbillede of Livet i Amerika i Gamle Dage. Copenhagen: 1876. V. 45

Palmetto Leaves. Boston: 1873. V. 41; 46

Pink and White Tyranny. Boston: 1871. V. 41; 43; 44; 45; 46

Sunny Memories of Foreign Lands. Boston: 1854. V. 42; 44

Uncle Sam's Emancipation; Earthly Care, a Heavenly Discipline and Other Sketches. Philadelphia: 1853. V. 42

Uncle Tom's Cabin. V. 43

Uncle Tom's Cabin. London. V. 45

Uncle Tom's Cabin. 1852. V. 37

An Edition for the Million! Uncle Tom's Cabin or Life Among the Lowly. Boston: 1852. V. 45

Uncle Tom's Cabin. Boston: 1852. V. 37; 38; 39; 40; 41; 42; 43; 44; 46

Uncle Tom's Cabin. Boston & Cleveland: 1852. V. 37; 39; 40

Uncle Tom's Cabin. Leipzig: 1852. V. 43

Uncle Tom's Cabin. London: 1852. V. 37; 38; 42; 43; 44; 45; 46

Onkel Toms Stuga Eller Negerlifvet I Amerikanska Slafstaterna. Stockholm: 1852. V. 40; 43

Uncle Tom's Cabin; or, Life Among the Lowly. (with) A Key to Uncle Tom's Cabin. Boston: 1852, 1853. V. 40

Uncle Tom's Cabin. Edinburgh: 1853. V. 41; 42

Uncle Tom's Cabin. Introduction by Raymond Weaver. Illustrations by Miguel Covarrubias. 1938. V. 37

Uncle Tom's Cabin. New York: 1938. V. 39; 43; 44; 46

Woman in Sacred History. New York: 1873. V. 38

The Writings of Harriet Beecher Stowe. Boston: 1896. V. 45; 46

STOWELL, JOHN

Don Coronado through Kansas 1541 Then Known as Quivira. Seneca: 1908. V. 45

STOWELL, MYRON R.

'Fort Frick', or the Siege of Homestead. Pittsburg: 1893. V. 45

STOWELL, T.

The Statutes and Ordinances of the Isle of Man, Now in Force . . . . Douglas: 1792. V. 42; 46

STOWER, CALEB

The Compositor's and Pressman's Guide to the Art of Printing. London: 1812. V. 40

The Printer's Grammar. London: 1787. V. 40

The Printer's Grammar; or, Introduction to the Art of Printing. London: 1808. V. 44

The Printer's Grammar . . . London: 1827. V. 39

STRABO

Geographia. Venice: 1494. V. 38; 44

Geographia. Venice: 14949. V. 37

Geographicorum Lib. XVII. Olim ut Putatur a Guarino Veronensi ac Gregorio Trifernate Latinitate Donati, iam Denuo a Conrado Heresbachio . . . Basle: 1539. V. 40

De Situ Orbis. Venice: 1494. V. 40

Strabonis De Situ Orbis Libri XVII . . . Amsterdam: 1652. V. 43

STRABO, WALAFRID

Hortulus, of the Little Garden. A Ninth-Century Poem by Walafrid Strabo. Middlesex: 1924. V. 37

STRACHAN, JAMES

A Visit to the Province of Upper Canada in 1819. Aberdeen: 1820. V. 39

STRACHEY, G. L.

Landmarks in French Literature. (1912). V. 37

STRACHEY, LYTTON 1880-1932

Books and Characters. French and English. London: 1922. V. 38; 46

Books and Characters - French & English. London: 1924. V. 41

Elizabeth and Essex. New York: 1928. V. 37; 38; 40; 41; 42

Ermyntrude and Esmeralda. London: 1969. V. 44

Ermyntrude and Esmeralda: An Entertainment. (London): (1969). V. 37

Portraits in Miniature and other Essays. London: 1931. V. 41; 43

STRADA, FAMIANO

The History of the Low-Countrey Warres . . . London: 1667. V. 46

STRADA, JACOBUS DE

Epitome du Thresor des Antiquitez, c'est a Dire, Pourtraits des Vrayes Medailles des Empp . . . Lyon: 1553. V. 37; 41; 43

Epitome Thesauri Antiquitatum . . . Iconum, Ex Antiquis Numismatibus. Tiguri: 1557. V. 40; 45

STRADANUS, JOANNES

Mediceae Familiae Rerum Feliciter Gestarum Victoriae et Triumphi. (with) Venationes Ferarum, Avium, Piscium . . . Antwerp: 1583/1578. V. 42

STRAET, JAN VAN 1523-1605

Passio, Mors, et Resurrectio dn. Nostri Iesu Christi. N.P.: 15--? V. 41

STRAETEN, EDMUND S. J. VAN DER

History of the Violoncello, The Viol Da Gamba, Their Percursors and Collateral Instruments with Biographies of all the Most Eminent Players of Every Country. London: 1915. V. 39

The History of the Violin. London: 1933. V. 39

STRAFFORD, THOMAS WENTWORTH, 1ST EARL OF 1593-1641

The Earl of Strafforde's Letters and Despatches, with An Essay Towards His Life by Sir George Radcliffe. London: 1739. V. 39

The Tryal of Thomas Earl of Strafford . . . Upon an Indictment of High Treason by the Commons then Assembled in Parliament. London: 1680. V. 39

STRAHAN, EDWARD

A Century After: Picturesque Glimpses of Philadlephia and Pennsylvania . . . Philadelphia: 1875. V. 42

Etudes in Modern French Art . . . New York: 1882. V. 41

STRAHLENBERG, PHILIP JOHN VON

An Historico-Geographical Description of the North and Eastern Parts of Europe and Asia . . . London: 1738. V. 38

STRAHORN, CARRIE ADELL

Fifteen Thousand Miles by Stage, A Woman's Unique Experience During Thirty Years . . . New York: 1911. V. 43

Fifteen Thousand Miles by Stage: a Woman's Unique Experience During Thirty Years of Path Finding and Pioneering from the Missouri to the Pacific and from Alaska to Mexico. New York & London: 1911. V. 37; 38; 39; 44

Fifteen Thousand Miles by Stage. New York: 1915. V. 43

STRAHORN, ROBERT EDMUND

The Hand-Book of Wyoming and Guide to the Black Hills and Big Horn Regions for Citizen, Emigrant and Tourist. Cheyenne: 1877. V. 37; 38; 39; 42; 43; 45

The Hand Book of Wyoming and Guide to the Black Hills and Big Horn Regions for Citizen, Emigrant and Tourist. Chicago: 1879. V. 39

Montana and Yellowstone National Park. Facts and Experiences on the Farming, Stock Raising, Mining, Lumbering and other Industries of Montana. Kansas City: 1881. V. 37; 38

The Resources and Attractions of Idaho Territory. Boise City: 1881. V. 38; 39; 42; 45

To the Rockies and Beyond, or a Summer on the Union Pacific Railway and Branches . . . Nebraska, Dakota, Wyoming, Colorado, New Mexico, Utah, Montana and Idaho . . . Omaha: 1878. V. 38; 39; 42

To the Rockies and Beyond. Omaha: 1879. V. 37; 38; 39

STRAKER, C.

Instructions in the Art of Lithography. London: 1867. V. 38; 40

STRALEY, WILLIAM W.

Pioneer Sketches Nebraska and Texas. Hico: 1915. V. 38; 39

STRANAHAN, C. H.

A History of French Painting from Its Earliest to Its Latest Practice. New York: 1893. V. 40

STRAND, A. E.

History of the Swedish-Americans of Minnesota; a Concise Record of the Struggles and Achievements of the Early Settlers . . . Chicago: 1910. V. 37; 38

THE STRAND Magazine. London: 1891-94. V. 38; 39

STRAND, MARK

The Garden. 1981. V. 42

STRAND, PAUL

Living in Egypt. New York: 1969. V. 41

A Retrospective Monograph. The Years 1915-1968. Millerton: 1971. V. 41

Time in New England. New York: 1950. V. 40; 41

STRANG, JAMES J.

Ancient and Modern Michilimackinac. Burlington: 1894? V. 39; 42

The Book of the Law of the Lord. Beaver Island: 1856. V. 42

STRANG, JESSE

The Confessions of Jesse Strang, Who Was Executed at Albany August 24, 1827, for the Murder of John Whipple. Albany: 1827. V. 41

The Trial and Confession of Jesse Strang, for the Murder of John Whipple at Albany on the 7th of May, 1827. New York: 1827. V. 44

STRANG, JOHN

The Cruise: with Other Poems. London: 1812. V. 46

STRANG, LEWIS C.

Famous Actresses of the Day in America. Boston: 1899. V. 39

STRANG, WILLIAM

A Book of Giants, Drawn, Engraved and Written by Edward Strang. London: 1898. V. 45

The Doings of Death. London: 1901. V. 44

The Earth Fiend. London: 1892. V. 39; 41; 42

A Series of Thirty Etchings . . . Illustrating Subjects from the Writings of Rudyard Kipling. London: 1901. V. 44

STRANGE, CALTHORPE

Two Worlds of Fashion. London: 1872. V. 37

STRANGE, CHARLES

Ponds in the Parlour; or, How to Form and Manage an Aquarium. Manchester: 1861. V. 39

STRANGE, EDWARD F.

Alphabets-A Handbook of Lettering. London: 1895. V. 39

Chinese Lacquer. London: 1926. V. 41

The Colour-Prints of Hiroshige. London: 1925. V. 38; 40; 44; 45; 46

STRANGE, J.

The Tunbridge Wells Guide . . . to Which is added, a Particular Description of the Towns and Villages, Reamins of Antiquities, Gentlemens Seats . . . Tunbridge Wells: 1786. V. 44

STRANGE, JAMES

Journal and Narrative of the Commercial Expedition from Bombay to the North-West Coast of America. Madras: 1928. V. 37

STRANGE, JOHN

Reports of Adjudged Cases in the Courts of Chancery, King's Bench, Common Pleas, and Exchequer, from Trinity Term in the 2d Year of K. Geo. II to Trinity Term in the 21st Year of K. Geo. II. Dublin: 1792. V. 39

STRANGE, T. A.

An Historical Guide to French Interiors, Furniture, Decoration, Woodwook & Allied Arts During the last Half of the Seventeenth Cenutry, the whole ot the Eighteenth Century, and the Earlier part of the Nineteenth. New York: (1903). V. 37

STRANGE Visitors: a Series of Original Papers, Embracing Philosophy, Science, Government, Religion, Poetry, Art, Fiction, Satire, Humour, Narrative and Prophecy . . . Boston: 1871. V. 43

THE STRANGER'S Guide in Philadelphia to All Public Buildings, Places of Amusement . . . Philadelphia: 1866. V. 42

THE STRANGER'S Guide in Philadelphia to all Public Buildings, Places of Amusement, Commercial, Benevolent and Religious Institutions, etc. Philadelphia: 1862. V. 41; 42

THE STRANGER'S Guide through London and Westmisnter. London: 1800. V. 37

STRANGE'S Case, Strangly Altered. Or a Hue and Cry After a Strange Old Yorkshire Tike. London: 1680. V. 41

STRANGEWAYS, THOMAS

Sketch of the Mosquito Shore. Edinburgh: 1822. V. 42; 43

STRANGFORD, EMILY ANNE BEAUFORT SMYTHE, VISCOUNTESS 1826-1887

The Eastern Shores of the Adriatic in 1863. London: 1864. V. 37; 40; 45

STRANGFORD, GEORGE AUGUSTUS FREDERICK PERCY, 7TH VISCOUNT 1818-1857

Angela Pisani: a Novel. London: 1875. V. 42; 45; 46

STRANGFORD, GEORGE AUGUSTUS FREDERICK PERCY SYDNEY SMYTHE, 1818-1857

Historic Fancies. London: 1844. V. 39

STRANGFORD, PERCY CLINTON SYDNEY, 6TH VISCOUNT

Poems, by the Honorable Percy Clinton Smythe. Dublin: 1796. V. 41; 46

STRAPAROLA, GIOVANNI FRANCESCO

The Most Delectable Nights. Paris: 1906. V. 40; 41

STRASBERG, LEE

Strasberg at the Actor's Studio. Tape Recorded Sessions. Edited by Robert H. Hethmon. New York: 1965. V. 37

STRASSBURGER, RALPH B.

Pennsylvania German Pioneers. Norristown: 1934. V. 41

STRATHMORE, MARY ELEANOR LYON BOWES, COUNTESS OF 1749-1800

The Confessions of the Countess of Strathmore, Written by Herself. London: 1793. V. 39; 41

STRATMAN, CARL J.

Bibliography of English Printed Tragedy 1565-1900. S. Illinois University: 1965. V. 46

STRATMAN, FRANCIS HENRY

A Middle-English Dictionary Containing Words Used by English Writers from the Twelfth to the Fifteenth Century. Oxford: 1891. V. 41

STRATTON, ARTHUR

The Life, Work and Influence of Sir Christopher Wren. Liverpool: 1897. V. 38; 45; 46

STRATTON, CHARLES S.

Sketch of the Life, Personal Appearance, Character and Manners of Charles S. Stratton, Known as General Tom Thumb. New York: 1860. V. 42

STRATTON, LILYAN

Reno. A Book of Short Stories and Information. Newark: 1921. V. 38

STRATTON-PORTER, GENE

Laddie: A True Blue Story. Garden City: 1913. V. 37

Music of the Wild. Cincinnati: 1910. V. 37

The Song of the Cardinal. Indianapolis: 1903. V. 37

STRATTON, ROBERT BURCHER

The Heroes in Gray. Lynchburgh: 1894. V. 44

STRATTON, ROYAL B. d.1875

Captivity of the Oatman Girls. Chicago: 1857. V. 37; 41

Captivity of the Oatman Girls. San Francisco: 1857. V. 37; 38; 39; 40; 41; 43; 44; 45; 46

STRATTON, ROYAL B. d.1875 continued

Captivity of the Oatman Girls; Being an Interesting Narrative of Life Among the Apache and Mohave Indians. New York: 1859. V. 38

Life Among the Indians; or, The Captivity of the Oatman Girls Among the Apache and Mohave Indians. San Francisco: 1935. V. 37; 38; 42; 45; 46

STRAUB, PETER

If You Could See Me Now. 1977. V. 37; 43

If You Could See Me Now. New York: 1977. V. 39; 42; 46

Ishamel. 1972. V. 39; 46

Ishmael. London: 1972. V. 42; 43; 45

STRAUS, RALPH

Carriages and Coaches. Their History and Their Evolution. London: 1912. V. 37

John Baskerville. Cambridge: 1907. V. 42; 46

Pengard Awake. New York: 1920. V. 38

The Unspeakable Curll. London: 1927. V. 41; 42; 46

The Unspeakable Curll, Being Some Account of Edmund Curll, Bookseller. New York: 1928. V. 39

STRAUSS, DAVID FRIEDRICH

The Life of Jesus, Critically Examined. London: 1846. V. 37; 42; 43; 44; 45

A New Life of Jesus. London: 1865. V. 43; 46

STRAUSS, WALTER L.

Chiaroscuro. The Clair-Obscur Woodcuts by the German and Netherlandish Masters of the XVIth and XVIIIth Centuries. New York: 1973. V. 46

The Complete Drawings of Albrecht Durer (a Catalogue Raisonne). New York: 1974. V. 40

STREAMER, VOLNEY

The World Awheel. London & New York: 1896. V. 41

STREATFEILD, THOMAS

Exerpta Cantiana: Being the Prospectus of a History of Kent Preparing for Publication. London: 1836. V. 39

STREET, A. G.

Farmer's Glory. London: 1934. V. 44

STREET, ARTHUR EDMUND

Memoir of George Edmund Street, R.A. 1824-1881. London: 1888. V. 39; 45

STREET, G. S.

The Autobiography of a Boy. London & Philadelphia: 1894. V. 38; 41

STREET, GEORGE

Che! Wah! Wah! or, The Modern Montezumas in Mexico. Rochester: 1838. V. 38

Che! Wah! or, the Modern Montezumas in Mexico. Rochester: 1883. V. 38; 39; 40; 41; 43; 44; 45

STREET, GEORGE E.

Brick and Marble in the Middle Ages: notes of a tour in the North of Italy. London: 1855. V. 37

Brick and Marble in the Middle Ages; Notes of Tours in the North of Italy. London: 1874. V. 37

STREET, GEORGE EDMUND

The Cathedral of the Holy Trinity, Commonly Called Christ Church Cathedral, Dublin. London: 1882. V. 38; 39; 40; 45; 46

STREET, GEORGE EDWARD

Some Account of Gothic Architecture in Spain. London: 1865. V. 40

STREET Sketches of London Life. London: 1895? V. 40

STREET, WILLIAM B.

Gentlemen-Up. New York: 1930. V. 39

STREETE, THOMAS

Astronomia Carolina, Nova Theoria Motuum Coelestium, Secundum Optimas Observationes & Rationi Maxime Consentania Fundamenta Artis . . . Nuremberg: 1705. V. 38

STREETER, EDWIN

Precious Stones and Gems. London: 1879. V. 39

STREETER, EDWIN W.

Precious Stones and Gems. London: 1882. V. 40; 41

Precious Stones and Gems, Their History and Distinguishing Characteristics. London: 1884. V. 38

Precious Stones and Gems, Their History and Distinguishing Characteristics. London: 1877. V. 38

STREETER, FLOYD BENJAMIN

Michigan Bibliography, a Partial Catalogue of Books, Maps, Manuscripts and Miscellaneous Materials Relating to the Resources, Development and History of Michigan from Earliest Times to July 1, 1917. Lansing: 1921. V. 44; 45

Prairie Trails and Cow Towns. Boston: 1936. V. 44

STREETER, RUSSELL

Mirror of Calvinistic Fanaticism, or Jedediah Burchard & Co. During a protracted Meeting of Twenty-Six Days in Woodstock, Vermont. Woodstock: 1835. V. 45

STREETER, THOMAS WINTHROP

Americana-Beginnings. A Selection from the Library of Thomas W. Streeter. Morristown: 1952. V. 40

Americana-Beginnings. Portland: 1952. V. 42

Americana-Beginnings. (Portland, Maine: 1952). V. 37

Bibliography of Texas, 1795-1845. Cambridge: 1955. V. 42; 46

Bibliography of Texas, 1795-1845. Cambridge: 1955-1960. V. 37; 38; 40; 42; 44; 45

Bibliography of Texas, 1795-1845. Part III, United States and European Imprints Relating to Texas. Cambridge: 1960. V. 40

Bibliography of Texas 1795-1845. Woodbridge: 1983. V. 39; 45

The Celebrated Collection of Americana Formed by the Late Thomas Winthrop Streeter. New York: 1966. V. 41

The Celebrated Collection of Americana Formed by the Late Thomas Winthrop Streeter. New York: 1966-1969. V. 37; 39; 40; 42; 45; 46

The Celebrated Collection of Americana Formed by the Late Thomas Winthrop Streeter. New York: 1966-1970. V. 37; 38

The Celebrated Collection of Americana Formed by the Late Thomas Winthrop Streeter. London: 1966-70. V. 44

The Celebrated Collection of Americana Formed by the Late Thomas Winthrop Streeter. Morristown: 1966-70. V. 46

The Celebrated Collection Formed by the Late Thomas W. Streeter. New York: 1966-71. V. 42; 44

The Celebrated Collection of Americana Formed by the Late Thomas Winthrop Streeter. New York: 1970. V. 40

Notes on North American Regional Bibliographies. N.P.: 1942. V. 43

STREETON, ARTHUR

Arthur Streeton Memorial Exhibition. National Gallery of Victoria. Melbourne: 1944. V. 41

STREETT, WILLIAM B.

Gentleman Up. New York: 1930. V. 43

Gentlemen Up. 1930. V. 38

STREHLNEEK, E. A.

Chinese Pictorial Art. Shanghai: 1914. V. 42; 46

STRETCH, RICHARD H.

Annual Report of the State Mineralogist of the State of Nevada for 1866. Carson City: 1867. V. 37

Illustrations of the Zygaenidae and Bambycidae of North America. San Francisco: 1873. V. 40

Illustrations of the Zygaenidae and Bombycidae of North America. San Francisco: 1872-73. V. 37

STRETE, CRAIG KEE

Paint Your Face on a Drowning in the River. New York: 1978. V. 46

STRETSER, THOMAS

A New Description of Merryland. Bath, Printed: 1741. V. 38

A New Description of Merryland . . . London: 1742. V. 43

STRETTON, CHARLES

Sport and Sportsmen: a Book of Recollections. London: 1866. V. 43

STRETTON, JULIA CELIA

The Queen of the County. London: 1865. V. 44

STREVELL, CHARLES N.

As I Recall Them. N.P.: 1943. V. 37; 42; 46

STRIBLING, ROBERT M.

Gettysburg Campaign and Campaigns of 1864 and 1865 in Virginia. Petersburg: 1905. V. 42

STRIBLING, T. S.

The Cruise of the Dry Dock. Chicago: 1917. V. 46

The Sound Wagon. New York: 1935. V. 41; 42

STRICKER, LOUIS

The Crystalline Lens System. N.P.: 1899. V. 42

STRICKER, SOLOMON

Manual of Human and Comparative Histology. London: 1870. V. 38; 39; 40; 41; 42

STRICKLAND, AGNES

Alda, the British Captive. London: 1841. V. 38

Demetrius: Tale of Modern Greece. London: 1833. V. 42

The Little Tradesman. London: 1825. V. 43

Lives of the Queens of England, from the Norman Conquest. London: 1841-48. V. 42

Lives of the Queens of England, from the Norman Conquest. London: 1852. V. 37

Lives of the Queens of England, from the Norman Conquest. London: 1864. V. 42; 46

Lives of the Queens of England, from the Norman Conquest. London: 1882. V. 37

Lives of the Queens of England from the Norman Conquest. London: 1885. V. 38; 40; 42

Lives of the Queens of England from the Norman Conquest . . . Philadelphia: 1902. V. 37

Lives of the Queens of Scotland and English Princesses Connected with the Regal Succession of Great Britain. Edinburgh: 1850. V. 42

Lives of the Queens of Scotland and English Princesses. Edinburgh: 1852-59. V. 42

Queen Victoria from Her Birth to Her Bridal. London: 1840. V. 44

Worcester Field; or, the Cavalier. London: 1826. V. 45

STRICKLAND, EDWARD D.

The Fabulous Wilson Mizner. New York: 1935. V. 46

STRICKLAND, H. E.

Dodo and Its Kindred; or, the History, Affinities and Osteology of the Dodo, Solitaire and Other Extinct Birds. London: 1848. V. 38; 39; 41

Ornithological Synonyms . . . Volume 1 Accipitres. London: 1855. V. 43

STRICKLAND, MAJOR

Twenty-Seven Years in Canada West; or, the Experiences of an Early Settler. London: 1853. V. 44

STRICKLAND, REX

El Paso in 1854. El Paso: 1969. V. 37; 38; 40; 41; 42; 44

STRICKLAND, SAMUEL

Twenty Seven years in Canada West; Or, the Experience of an Early Settler. London: 1853. V. 37; 38; 41; 42; 45

STRICKLAND, WALTER G.

A Dictionary of Irish Artists. Dublin: 1913. V. 37; 43

A Dictionary of Irish Artists. Dublin & London: 1913. V. 39

STRICKLAND WILLIAM

Address Upon a Proposed Rail Road from Wilmington to the Susquehanna. Philadelphia: 1835. V. 46

Reports on Canals, Railways, Roads, and Other Subjects Made to 'The Pennsylvania Society for the Promotion of Internal Movement.' Philadelphia: 1826. V. 42

STRICTURAE Breves in Epistolas D. D. Genevensium & Oxoniensium Nuper Editas, Iterumque Juxta Exemplar Oxoniense Typis Mandatas. London: 1707. V. 39

STRICTURES on the Army Interspersed with Interesting Anecdotes and Illustrative Facts. Dublin: 1809. V. 42

STRID, A.

The Mountain Flora of Greece. Cambridge: 1986. V. 37; 38

Wild Flowers of Mount Olympus. Kifissia: 1980. V. 37; 38

STRIDER, D. L.

Diseases of Floral Crops. London: 1985. V. 37

STRIGELIUS, VICTORINUS

In Rhetoricen Domini Philippi Melanchtonis Breues & ad Vsum Accomodatae Commentationes Propositae in Academia Ienensi . . . Jena: 1588. V. 42

STRINGA, GIOVANNI

La Chiesa di San Marco. Venice: 1610. V. 38; 40; 44

STRINGER, MOSES

Opera Mineralia Explicata; or, the Mineral Kingdom Within the Dominions of Great Britain Display'd. London: 1713. V. 41; 43

Opera Mineralia Explicata; or, the Mineral Kingd. V. 43

STRINGFELLOW, THORNTON

Slavery; Its Origin, Nature and History. Alexandria: 1860. V. 42

STRNADT, ANTON

Beschreibung der Beruhmten Uhr-Und Kunstwerke am Altstadter Rathhause und auf der Konigl. Prague and Dresden: 1791. V. 45

STROCK, DANIEL

Pictorial History of King Philip's War; . . . Containing an Account of the Indian Tribes, their manners and customs. Boston: 1851. V. 37

STRODE, HUDSON

Jefferson Davis. New York: 1955-64. V. 42

STRODE, MURIEL

My Litte Book of Prayer. Chicago: 1906. V. 39

STRODE, WILLIAM

Four Poems. Sussex: 1934. V. 42; 45

STROM, INGRID

Problems Concerning the Origin and Early Development of the Etruscan Orientalizing Style. Odense: 1971. V. 37

STROMER, HEINRICH DE AUERBACH

Saluberrime Adversus Pestilentiam Observationes. Strassburg: 1518. V. 37

STROMMENGER, EVA

The Art of Mesopotamia. London: 1964. V. 46

STRONG, A. B.

The American Floral. The Montly Flora, or Botanical Magazine . . . New York: 1846-8. V. 37

STRONG, ANNA LOUISE

One-Fifth of Mankind. New York: 1938. V. 44

STRONG, D. E.

Catalogue of the Carved Amber in the Department of Greek and Roman Antiquities. London: 1966. V. 37; 44

STRONG, EUGENIE

Catalogue of the Greek and Roman Antiques in the Possession of the Right Honourable Lord Melchett. Oxford: 1928. V. 37; 40

Catalogue of the Greek and Roman Antiquities in the Possession of the Right Honourable Lord Melchett . . . Oxford/London: 1928. V. 38; 40

Catalogue ofo the Greek and Roman Antiquities in the Possession of the Right Honourable the Lord Melchett . . . 1928. V. 38

STRONG, GEORGE TEMPLETON

Diary of . . . 1835-1875. New York: 1974. V. 46

STRONG, JAMES CLARK

Biographical Sketch of . . . Los Gatos: 1910. V. 37; 42

Wah-Kee-Nah and Her People, the Curious Customs, Traditions and Legends of North American Indians. New York: 1893. V. 46

Wah-Kee-Nah and Her People, The Curious Customs, Traditions, and Legends of the North American Indians. New York & London: 1893. V. 38

STRONG, LEONARD ALFRED GEORGE

A Defence of Ignorance. New York: 1932. V. 42

Dublin Days. Oxford: 1921. V. 38

The Hansom Cab and the Pigeons. Waltham St. Lawrence: 1935. V. 42

The Sacred River. London: 1949. V. 37; 38; 40; 42

Sixteen Portraits - of People Whose Houses Have Been Preserved by the National Trust. London: 1951. V. 40; 42

Two Stories: Coming to Tea and While the Going is Good. 1936. V. 41

STRONG, NATHANIEL T.

Appeal to the Christian Community on the Condition and Prospects of the New York Indians, in Answer to a Book, Entitled the Case of the New York Indians, and other Publications of the Society of Friends. New York: 1841. V. 37

A Further Illustration of the Case of the Seneca Indians in the State of New York. Philadelphia: 1841. V. 38; 41; 44

STRONG, NEHEMIAH

Astronomy Improved; or, a New Theory of the Harmonious Regularity Observable in the Mechanism or Movements of the Planetary System in Three Lectures . . . In New Haven, Begun Feb. 17, 1781. New Haven: 1784. V. 40; 45

STRONG, ROY

The English Icon - Elizabethan and Jacobean Portraiture. London: 1969. V. 39; 42; 46

Tudor & Jacobean Portraits. London: 1969. V. 39; 46

STRONG, S. ARTHUR

A Catalogue of Letters and Other Historical Documents Exhibited at the Library at Wellbeck. London: 1903. V. 38; 40

Reproductions of Drawings by Old Masters in the Collection of the Duke of Devonshire at Chatsworth . . . London: 1902. V. 38

STRONG, TITUS

The Tears of Columbia; a Poem, to the memory of American Heroes and Statesmen. Dedham: 1812. V. 44

STRONG, W. K.

General Orders, Nos. 12 through 55, Headquarters, ST. Louis District, August 11-December 31, 1863. St. Louis: 1863. V. 39

STRONG, WILLIAM DUNCAN

Archaeological Studies in Peru 1941-1942. New York: 1943. V. 42

STRONG, WILLIAM E.

A Trip to the Yellowstone National Park in July, August and September 1875. Washington: 1876. V. 37; 38; 39; 41; 44

STROTHER, DAVID H.

The Blackwater Chronicle. New York: 1853. V. 43

Virginia Illustrated: Containing a Visit to the Virginia Canaan. New York: 1857. V. 37; 39; 42

STROTHER, EDWARD

Criticon Febrium; or, a Critical Essay on Fevers . . . London: 1716. V. 45; 46

Dissertations Upon the Ingraftment of the Small Pox, According to the Method of Turky. London: 1722. V. 43

Dr. Radcliff'e Practical Dispensatory. London: 1721. V. 42; 45; 46

STROUD, DOROTHY

Humphry Repton. London: 1962. V. 45

STROUND, DOROTHY

Capability Brown. London: 1950. V. 40

STROUSE, NORMAN H.

C-S The Master Craftsman. An Account of the Work of T. J. Cobden-Sanerson. Harper Woods: 1969. V. 37; 40; 43

How to Build a Poor Man's Morgan Library. Detroit: 1959. V. 39

The Passionate Pirate. North Hills: 1964. V. 37

STROZII Poetae, Pater et Filius. Venice: 1513. V. 39

STROZZI, GIOVANBATTISTA 1505-1571

Madrigali. Florence: 1593. V. 39

STROZZI, GIOVANNI

Oratio Habita Illustra. Cosimi Ducis Florentiae & Senarum in Eius Comparitione. Riva: 1562. V. 38

STROZZI, TITO VESPASIANO

Strozii Poetae Pater et Filius. Venice: 1513/14. V. 41

Strozzii Poetae Pater et Filius. Venice: 1513. V. 37

STRUBBERG, FRIEDRICH ARMAND

The Backwoodsman. Boston: 1866. V. 38

STRUBERG, FRIEDRICH ARMAND

The Backwoodsman; or, Life on the Indian Frontier. London: 1880. V. 37

STRUENSEE, COUNT

The Trial of Count Struensee, Late Prime Minister to the King of Denmark, Before the Royal Commission of Inquisition, at Copenhagen. London: 1775. V. 37

STRUMPFELL, ADOLF

A Textbook of Medicine . . . New York: 1891. V. 37; 39; 40; 41

STRUTHER, JAN

Sycamore Square and Other Verses. London: 1932. V. 43

STRUTHERS, JOHN

Anatomical and Physiological Observations. Edinburgh: 1854. V. 42; 44

The History of Scotland from the Union to the Abolition of the Heritable Jurisdictions in 1748. Glasgow: 1927. V. 38

STRUTT, BENJAMIN

The History and Description of Colchester . . . Colchester: 1803. V. 42

STRUTT, DAPHNE H.

Fashion in South Africa, 1652-1900. Cape Town: 1975. V. 41

STRUTT, JACOB GEORGE fl. 1820-1850

Bury St. Edmunds Illustrated in Twelve Etchings. London: 1821. V. 44

Sylva Britannica, or Portraits of Forest Trees. London: 1830-36. V. 44; 46

Sylva Britannica or, Portraits of Forest Trees, distinguished by their Antiquity, Magnitude, or Beauty. London: 1830. V. 37; 42; 43; 45

STRUTT, JOHN WILLIAM

Argon, a New Constituent of the Atmosphere. Washington: 1896. V. 38; 40

STRUTT, JOSEPH

A Biographical Dictonary . . . London: 1785. V. 46

The Chronicle of England. London: 1777-78. V. 39

A Complete View of the Dress and Habits of the People of England, from the Establishment of the Saxons in Britain to the Present Time . . . London: 1842. V. 39; 44

A Complete View of the Dress and habits of the People of England, from the Establishment of the Saxons in Britain to the Present Time. London: 1796-1799. V. 37

Glig-Gamena Angel-Deod. London: 1801. V. 39; 44

Gling-Gamena Angel-Deod: or, The Sports and Pastimes of the People of England. London: 1810. V. 37

Honda Angel-cynnan; or a Complete view of the Manners, Customs, Arms, Habits, etc. of the Inhabitants of England from the Arrival of the Saxons to the Present Time. London: 1775-76. V. 46

Queenhoo-Hall, a Romance. Edinburgh: 1808. V. 39; 42

The Regal and Ecclesiastical Antiquities of England. London: 1773. V. 42

The Regal and Ecclesiastical Antiquities of England. London: 1777. V. 41; 43

The Regal and Ecclesiastical Antiquities of England. London: 1793. V. 46

The Regal and Ecclesiastical Aantiquities of England. London: 1842. V. 38

The Sports and Pastimes of the People of England. London: 1810. V. 39; 40

The Sports and Pastimes of the People of England. London: 1830. V. 40; 41

The Sport and Pastimes of the People of England. Including the Rural and Domestic Recreations . . . London: 1831. V. 37; 43

The Sports and Pastimes of the People of England. London: 1833. V. 39; 40; 43

The Sports and Pastimes of the People of England. London: 1834. V. 46

The Sports and Pastimes of the People of England . . . London: 1841. V. 43

The Sports and Pastimes of the People in England. London: 1845. V. 39

The Sports and Pastimes of the People of England. London: 1868. V. 38

The Sports and Pastimes of the People of England. London: 1876. V. 39; 40; 45

The Sports and Pastimes of the People of England. London: 1903. V. 39

The Test of Guilt; or Traits of Antient Superstition . . . Together with the Bumpkin's Disaster. London: 1808. V. 40

STRUTT, R. J.

Becquerel Rays and the Properties of Radium. London: 1904. V. 38; 44

STRUVE, CHRISTIAN AUGUST

A Practical Essay on the Art of Recovering Suspended Aniamtion; Together with a Review of the . . . Albany: 1803. V. 41; 45; 46

STRUVE, CHRISTIAN AUGUSTUS

Asthenology: or, the Art of Preserving Feeble Life. London: 1801. V. 38

STRUVE, FRIEDRICH GEORG WILHELM

Beobachtungen des Halleyschen Cometen bei Seinem Erscheinen im Jahre 1835 auf der Dorpater Sternwarte Angestellt. St. Petersburg: 1839. V. 43

Catalogus Novus Stelarum Duplicium et Multiplicium Maxima ex Parte in Specula Universitatis Caesareae . . . Dorpat: 1827. V. 38; 45

Catalogus Novus Stellarum Duplicium et Multiplicium Maxima ex Parte in Specula Universitatis Caesareae Dorpatensis per Magnum Telescopium Achromaticum Fraunhoferi Detectarum. Tehrpata: 1827. V. 41

Description de l'Observatoire Astronomique Central de Poulkova. St. Petersburg: 1845. V. 45

Stellarum Duplicium et Multiplicium Mensurae Micrometriciae per Magnum Fraunhoferi Tubum Annis a 1824 ad 1837 in Specula Dorpatensi Institutae . . . St. Petersburg: 1837. V. 44

STRUVE, JOHANN CHRISTIAN VON

Travels in the Crimea. London;: 1802. V. 40; 43

STRYKER, ROY EMERSON

In This Proud Land: America 1935-1943 As Seen in the FSA Photographs. Greenwich: 1973. V. 41

STRYKER, WILLIAM S.

Official Register of the Officers and Men of New Jersey in the Revolutionary War. Trenton: 1872. V. 41

Record of Officers and Men of New Jersey in the Civil War, 1861-1865. Trenton: 1876. V. 41; 46

STRYPE, JOHN 1643-1737

Ecclesiastical Memorials . . . London: 1721. V. 39; 44

The History of the Life and Acts of the Most Reverend Father in God, Edmund Grindal . . . London: 1710. V. 45

The Life of the Learned Sir John Cheke, Kt . . . . London: 1705. V. 45

Memorials of the Most Reverend Father in God Thomas Cranmer, Sometime Lord Archbishop of Canterbury, Wherein the History of the Church and the Reformation of It . . . . Oxford: 1812. V. 38

STRZELECKI, PAUL E. DE

Physical Description of a New South Wales and Van Diemen's Land . . . London: 1845. V. 46

STUART, A. A.

Iowa Colonels and Regiments: Being a History of Iowa Regiments in the War of the Rebellion. Des Moines: 1865. V. 37; 39; 42

STUART, ANDREW d. 1801

Considerations on the Present State of East-India Affairs and Examination of Mr. Fox's Bill; Suggesting Certain Material Alterations for Averting Dangers and Preserving the Benefits of that Bill. London: 1784. V. 41

Genealogical History of the Stewarts, from the Earliest Period of Their Authentic History to the Present Times. (with) Supplement . . . London: 1798/99. V. 42

Letters to the Right Honorable Lord Mansfield, from Andrew Stuart, Esq. London: 1773. V. 38; 39; 40; 41; 42

STUART, CHARLES

Two Expeditions into the Interior of Southern Australia During the Years 1828, 1829, 1830 and 1831. London: 1834. V. 46

The West India Question. Immediate Emancipation Would Be Safe for the Masters . . . New Haven: 1833. V. 42

The West India Question. Newburyport: 1835. V. 43

STUART, CHARLES A.

Memoir of Indian Wars, and Other Occurences . . . Richmond. V. 45

STUART, CHARLES B.

The Naval Dry Docks of the United States. New York: 1852. V. 37; 38; 42; 43; 45

STUART, ESME AMELIE CLAIRE LE ROY

Married to Order. London: 1895. V. 40

A Mine of Wealth. London: 1896. V. 40

STUART, FRANCIS 1902-

The Bridge. London: 1937. V. 38

The Coloured Dome. London: 1932. V. 38

Glory. London: 1933. V. 38; 41

In Search of Love. London: 1935. V. 38; 46

Pigeon Irish. London: 1932. V. 38

Try the Sky. London: 1933. V. 37; 38

We Have Kept the Faith. Dublin: 1923. V. 41

We Have Kept the Faith - New and Selecte Poems. Dublin: 1982. V. 43

The White Hare. London: 1936. V. 38; 46

Women and God. London: 1931. V. 38

STUART, GILBERT

The History of Scotland from the Establishment of the Reformation, Till the Death of Queen Mary. London: 1784. V. 41

Lectures on the Constitution and Laws of England . . . London: 1776. V. 46

A View of Society in Europe, In Its Progress from Rudeness to Refinement; or, Inquiries Concerning the History of Law, Government and Manners. Edinburgh: 1778. V. 37; 39; 46

STUART, GLORIA

The Inscriptions at Tor House and Hawk Tower. N.P.: 1989. V. 42

Writing a Poem About Flying a Kite. Los Angeles: 1987. V. 39

STUART, GRANVILLE

Forty Years on the Frontier. Cleveland: 1925. V. 40; 41; 42; 43; 45

Forty Years on the Frontier as Seen in the Journals and Reminiscences of Granville Stuart, Gold Miner, Trader. Glendale: 1957. V. 38

Montana As It Is. N.P.: 1865. V. 42

STUART, H. A.

A Pilgrimage in the South Seas. San Francisco: 1871. V. 41

STUART, I. W.

Life of Captain Nathan Hale the Martyr-Spy of the American Revolution. Hartford: 1856. V. 38

STUART, JAMES 1713-1788

Les Antiquites d'Athenes, Mesurees et Dessinees, Ouvrage Traduit de l'Anglais . . . Paris: 1808-22, 1832. V. 38; 40

The Antiquities of Athens, Measured and Delineated by James Stuart, FRS and FSA and Nicholas Revett, Painters and Architects. London: 1762-1830. V. 38

The Antiquities of Athens Measured and Delineated by James Stuart FRS, FSA, and Nicholas Revett, Painters and Architects. London: 1762-1830. V. 45

The Antiquities of Athens and Other Monuments of Greece. London: 1858. V. 42

The Antiquities of Athens. London: 1881. V. 42

Critical Observations on the Buildings and Improvements of London. London: 1771. V. 38

Etchings from Scott & Byron. London: 1821. V. 43

Historical Memoirs of the City of Armagh. Newry: 1819. V. 37; 38; 39; 43

Historical Memoirs of the City of Armagh for a Period of 1373 Years. Newry: 1819. V. 43

Historical Memoirs of the City of Armagh for a Period of 1373 Years . . . Newry: 1819. V. 39

Historical Memoirs of the City of Armagh for a period of 1373 years, etc. Newry: 1819. V. 37

Historical Memoirs of the City of Armagh for a period of 1373 years etc. etc. Newry: 1819. V. 37

Poems on Various Subjects. Belfast: 1811. V. 38

Refutation of Aspersions on 'Stuart's Three Years in North America.' London: 1834. V. 42

Three Years in North America. Edinburgh: 1832. V. 38; 43

Three Years in North America. Edinburgh: 1833. V. 38; 40; 41; 44; 45

Three Years in North America. New York: 1833. V. 39; 42

STUART, JESSE

Beyond Dark Hills. New York: 1938. V. 37; 39; 41

Man with a Bull-tongue Plow. New York: 1934. V. 39

Mongrel Mette. The Autobiography of a Dog. New York: 1944. V. 41

Tales from the Plum Grove Hills. Tales. New York: 1946. V. 39

Tree of Heaven. New York: 1940. V. 41; 42; 43; 44

STUART, JOHN MC DOUALL

Explorations in Australia. London: 1864. V. 43

STUART, JOSEPH A.

My Roving Life, a Diary of Travels and Adventures by Sea and Land During Peace and War. Auburn: 1895. V. 40; 43

STUART, LOUISA

Notes on George Selwyn and His Contemporaries. London: 1928. V. 46

Notes on George Selwyn and His Contemporaries. London & New York: 1928. V. 42

STUART, M.

Conscience and the Constitution with Remarks on the Recent Speech of the Hon. Daniel Webster in the Senate of the United States on the Subject of Slavery. Boston: 1850. V. 45

STUART, MOSES

A Hebrew Grammar with a Praxis on Select Portions of Genesis and the Psalms. Andover: 1823. V. 43

STUART, ROBERT 1812-1848

Caledonia Romana. Edinburgh: 1845. V. 40

Descriptive History of the Steam Engine. London: 1829. V. 37

The Discovery of the Oregon Trail. New York: 1935. V. 37; 40; 41; 42; 45

STUART, RUTH MC ENERY

The Story of Babette, a Little Creole Girl. New York: and London: 1898. V. 45

STUART, VILLIERS

Egypt After the War. London: 1883. V. 40; 42

The Funeral Tent of an Egyptian Queen. London: 1882. V. 37; 40; 42

Nile Gleanings Concerning the Ethnology, History and Art of Ancient Egypt as Revealed by Egyptian Paintings and Bas Reliefs . . . London;: 1879. V. 40; 43

STUART, W. J.

Forbidden Planet. 1956. V. 43

STUART, WILLIAM

Stuartiana, or Bubbles blow by and to some of the Family of Stuart. London: 1857. V. 37

STUART-WORTLEY, LADY EMMELINE CHARLOTTE ELIZABETH MANNERS 1806-1855

Travels in the United States, Etc. During 1849 and 1850. London: 1851. V. 42

Travels in the United States, etc. During 1849 and 1850. New York: 1851. V. 40; 42; 43

STUART-YOUNG, JOHN MORAY

Osrac the Self-Sufficient and Other Poems, With a Memoir of the Late Oscar Wilde. London: 1905. V. 41; 46

The Soul-Slayer. London: 1920. V. 41

An Urning's Love. London: 1905. V. 41; 44

STUBBE, EDMUND

Fraus Honesta. Comoedia Cantabrigiae Olim Acta. London: 1632. V. 37; 38; 44

STUBBE, H.

An Account of the Rise and Progress of Mahometanism . . . London: 1911. V. 44

STUBBE, HENRY

Medice Cura Teipsum! or, the Apothecaries Plea in some short and Modest Animadversions, upon a late Tract Entituled A short view of the Frauds and Abuses of the Apothecaries, and the only Remedy by Physicians making their own Medicines . . . London: 1671. V. 37

STUBBE, HENRY continued

The Miraculous Conformist. Oxford: 1666. V. 40; 41

STUBBES, GEORGE

A Dialogue on Beauty. London: 1731. V. 40

A New Adventure of Telemachus. London: 1731. V. 42; 45

STUBBES, PHILIP

The Anatomie of Abuses. London: 1836. V. 46

STUBBING, FRANK H.

Mycenaean Pottery from the Levant. Cambridge: 1951. V. 44

STUBBS, GEORGE

The Anatomy of the Horse . . . London: 1766. V. 43

The Anatomy of the Horse. London: 1899. V. 37

STUBBS, HENRY

A Justification of the Present War Against the United Netherlands. London: 1673. V. 38

STUBBS, STEPHEN

Agnes; or the Power of Love. Boston: 1825. V. 45

STUBBS, W.

The Crown Circuit Companion . . . Dublin: 1766. V. 45

The Crown Circuit Companion. Dublin: 1791. V. 39

STUBBS, WILLIAM

Chronicles and Memorials of the reign of Richard I. London: 1864-65. V. 44

The Constitutional History of England . . . Oxford: 1880. V. 43

STUBENRAUCH, PHILIPP VON

Darstellung der k.k. Osterr. Armee Nach der Neuesten Adjustirung . . . Vienna: 1821. V. 40

STUBER, ROSE R.

William G. Stuber: a Biography. Rochester: 1951. V. 46

STUCK, HUDSON

Voyages on the Yukon and Its Tributaries: a Narrative of Summer Travel on the Interior of Alaska. New York: 1917. V. 43

A Winter Circuit of Our Arctic Coast: a Narrative of a Journey with Dog-Sleds ARound the Enire Arctic Coast of Alaska. New York: 1920. V. 44

STUCKEY, VINCENT 1771-1845

Thoughts on the Improvement of the System of Country Banking. London: 1836. V. 41

STUCKI, JOHN S.

Family History Journal of John S. Stucki. Salt Lake City: 1932. V. 42

STUCKIUS, JOHANN WILHELM

Antiquitatum Convivialium Libri III. In Quibus Hebraeorum, Graecorum, Romanorum Aliarumque Nationum Antiqua . . . 1582. V. 39

THE STUDENT'S Companion; Being a Collection of Historical Quotations From the Best Ancient and Modern Authors, On all Sorts of Subjects. London: 1748. V. 41

STUDER, JACOB H.

The Birds of North America. New York: 1881. V. 38

The Birds of North America. New York: 1897. V. 40

Columbus, Ohio: Its History, Resources and Progress. N.P.: 1873. V. 46

Studer's Popular Ornithology. Montreal: 1881. V. 45

Studer's Popular Ornithology. The Birds of North America. New York & Columbus: 1881. V. 40; 41

STUDIES in History and Philosophy of Science. London: 1970-81. V. 46

STUDIES in Jewish Bibliography and Related Subjects in Memory of Abraham Solomon Freidus (1867-1923). New York: 1929. V. 38

STUDIES in Renaissance & Baroque Art Presented to Anthony Blunt of His 60th Birthday. London: 1967. V. 42; 44

STUDIES Presented to F.Ll. Griffith. London: 1932. V. 37

THE STUDIO. London: 1894/6/7/8. V. 40

THE STUDIO. Special Winter-Number 1898-9. London: 1899. V. 46

THE STUDIO Year-Book of Decorative Art 1907. London: 1907. V. 37

STUDION, SIMON

Carmen in Nvptias Honesti, et Ervditi Viri M. Iacobi Mercatoris Sindel-Fingensis, Vtiliter Docentis Iuuentutem in Monasterio Albano & Pudicae Virginis Margaritae Strolingae Grieningensis . . . Tubingen?: 1564. V. 44

STUDLEY, VANCE

Specimens of Handmade Botanical papers. Los Angeles: 1979. V. 46

THE STUDY and Practice of the Law, Considered in Their Various Relations to Society, in a Series of Letters. Portland: 1806. V. 39

STUKELEY, WILLIAM

An Account of a Large Silver Plate, of Antique Basso Relievo, Roman Workmanship, Found (at Risley Park) in Derbyshire, 1729. Read Before the Antiquarian Society of London, 8 April, 1736. London: 1736. V. 37

Itinerarium Curiosum; or, Account of the Antiquities, and Remarkable Curiosities in Nature or Art, Observed in Travels through Great Britain Illustrated with Copper-Plates. London: 1776. V. 41

A Letter . . . to Mr. Macpherson, On His Publication of Fingal and Temora. London: 1763. V. 41

Of the Spleen . . . Some Anatomical Observations in the Dissection of an Elephant . . . London: 1723. V. 37

Palaeographia Britannica; or, Discourses on Antiquities in Britain. London: for R. Manby, 1743.: 1746. V. 45

Paleographia Britannica. Stamford: 1746. V. 38; 40

Paleographica Britannica; or, Discourses on Antiquities in Britain. London: 1743. V. 41

Stonehenge. London: 1740. V. 40

STULLKEN, GERHARD

My Experiences on the Plains. Wichita: 1913. V. 41; 43

STUMPF, FRANZ, MRS.

San Antonio's Menger. N.P.: 1953. V. 45

STUMPFF, DAVID

Institutio Conjugalis. Das ist/ Handtbuchlein von H. Ehestandt/ wie mann unnd Weib Denselben Anfangen unnd Fuhren Sollen . . . Marburg: 1606. V. 42

STURGE, JOSEPH

A Visit to the United States in 1841. London: 1842. V. 42

The West Indies in 1837. London: 1838. V. 38; 41

STURGEON, A. G.

Bulldogdom. Altrincham: 1926. V. 40

STURGEON, MARY

Westminster Abbey, Its Memories and Its Message. London. V. 39

STURGEON, T.

Caviar. 1955. V. 43

The Joyous Invasions. London: 1965. V. 43

The Joyous Invasions. 1966. V. 44

More Than Human. 1953. V. 44

A Way Home. 1955. V. 43

STURGEON, THEODORE

E. Pluribus Unicorn. New York: (1953). V. 37

I, Libertine. 1956. V. 44

I, Libertine. New York: 1956. V. 41

Without Sorcery. 1948. V. 39; 42; 46

Without Sorcery. London: 1948. V. 45

STURGES, LEE

Salmon Fishing on Cain River, New Brunswick. Chicago: 1919. V. 43

STURGESS, H. A. C.

Register of Admissions to the Honourable Society of the Middle Temple, from the 15th Century to the Year 1944. London: 1949. V. 38; 42

STURGESS, R. W.

The Life and Work of R. W. Sturgess. Melbourne: 1938. V. 41

STURGIS, RUSSELL

A History of Architecture. Garden City: 1915-17. V. 46

STURGIS, WILLIAM

The Oregon Question. Boston: 1845. V. 43

STURGIS, WILLIAM BAYARD

New Lines for Flyfishers. New York: 1936. V. 39; 44; 45

STURKIE, P. D.

Avian Physiology. London: 1986. V. 37

STURLUSON, SNORRI

Heims Kringla. Stockholm: 1697-1700. V. 38

Heimskringla . . . Havniae: 1777-78. V. 38

STURM, JUSTIN

The Bad Samaritan. New York: 1926. V. 38; 40; 46

STURM, LEONARD CHRISTOPH

Project de la Resolution du Fameux Probleme Touchant la Longitude sur Mer. Nuremberg: 1720. V. 38

STURT, CHARLES

Two Expeditions into the Interior of Southern Australia, During the Years 1828, 1829, 1830 and 1831. London: 1833. V. 41; 45

STURT, JOHN

The Orthodox Communicant. London: 1721. V. 37; 38; 40; 45

STUTTERHEIM, KARL FREIHERR VON

A Detailed Account of the Battle of Austerlitz . . . London: 1807. V. 46

STYFFE, KNUT

The Elasticity, Extensibility and Tensile Strength of Iron and Steel. London: 1869. V. 44

STYLE, WILLIAM 1603-1679

Narrationes Modernae, or Modern Reports Begun in the Now Upper Bench Court at Westminster (1646-55) as Well as on the Criminall, as on the Pleas Side. London: 1658. V. 40

STYLES, JOHN

An Essay on the Character and Influence of the Stage on Morals and Happiness. London: 1806. V. 43

STYRON, WILLIAM 1925-

Admiral Robert Penn Warren and the Snows of Winter. 1978. V. 42

Admiral Robert Penn Warren and the Snows of Winter? Winston-Salem: 1978. V. 38; 39; 45

Admiral Robert Penn Warren and the Snows of Winter. 1981. V. 42

Admiral Robert Penn Warren and the Snows of Winter. N.P.: 1981. V. 43

Against Fear. 1981. V. 45

Against Fear. London: 1981. V. 42

As He Lay Dead, a Bitter Grief. New York: 1981. V. 44; 46

The Confessions of Nat Turner. New York: 1967. V. 38; 39; 40; 41; 42; 43; 44; 46

The Confessions of Nat Turner. 1968. V. 44

Darkness Visible: a Memoir of Madness. New York: 1990. V. 45

In the Clap Shack. New York: 1973. V. 37

Lie Down in Darkness. 1951. V. 46

Lie Down in Darkness. Indianapolis/New York: 1951. V. 38; 42; 45; 46

Lie Down in Darkness. Indianpolis: 1951. V. 38; 39; 41; 42; 44; 45; 46

Lie Down in Darkness. New York: 1951. V. 39; 42

Lie Down in Darkness. Indianapolis: (1951). V. 37

The Long March. London: 1952. V. 41

The Long March. New York: 1952. V. 39

The Long March. London: 1962. V. 38; 45

Mr. Jefferson and Out Times. 1984. V. 42

One and Twenty: Duke Narrative and Verse, 1924-1925. Durham: 1945. V. 46

Set This House on Fire. New York: 1960. V. 39; 41; 43; 45

Shadrach. Los Angeles: 1979. V. 37; 46

Sophie's Choice. 1979. V. 46

Sophie's Choice. New York: 1979. V. 37; 39; 44; 45; 46

This Quiet Dust. New York: 1965. V. 39

This Quiet Dust. New York: 1967. V. 37; 39

This Quiet Dust and Other Writings. New York: 1982. V. 37; 39; 40; 42; 43; 44; 45; 46

SUAREZ DE SALAZAR, JUAN BAUTISTA

Grandezas Y Antiguedades De La Isla Y Ciudad de Cadiz. Cadiz: 1610. V. 40

SUAREZ, FRANCIS 1548-1615

Metaphysicarum Disputationem, in Quibus et Universa naturalis Theologia Ordinate Traditur . . . Geneva: 1614. V. 40

THE SUBALTERN'S Log Book. London: 1828. V. 39; 42; 46

SUBIRA, ORIOL VALLIS I.

Paper and Watermarks in Catalonia. Amsterdam: 1970. V. 38

SUBIRA, ORIOL VALLS I

A Lively Look at Papermaking. North Hills: 1980. V. 43

SUBMISSION Exemplified; or, the Amiable Stranger. London: 1818. V. 45

SUBSTANCE o the Charge of Mismanageent in His Majesty's Naval Affairs, in the Year 1781, Compared with Authentic Papers Laid Before the House, on Mr. Fox's Motion, in the Month of February 1782. London: 1782. V. 38; 43

SUBSTANCE of the Examination of Thomas Jones, a Bankrupt; Late a Partner in the Wear Bank, at Sunderland. 1816. V. 45

THE SUCCESSION of Spain Discussed. Dublin: 1701. V. 43

A SUCCINCT Description of France . . . Dedicated to the Eminent and Learned Physician, Dr. Martin Lister; and May Serve as a Supplement to His Journey to Paris. London: 1700. V. 40

SUCHTEN, ALEXANDER VON

De Secretis Antimoni Liber Unus . . . Basle: 1757. V. 46

SUCKLEY, GEORGE

The Natural History of Washington Territory and Oregon, With Much Relating to Minnesota, Nebraska, Kansas, Utah and California . . . New York: 1860. V. 39; 40; 41; 42

SUCKLING, ALFRED

Memorials of the Antiquities and Architecture, Family History and Heraldry of the County of Essex. London: 1845. V. 39

SUCKLING, GEORGE

An Historical Account of the Virgin Islands, in the West Indies. London: 1780. V. 46

SUCKLING, JOHN

A Ballad Upon a Wedding. Waltham St. Lawrence: 1927. V. 37

Fragmenta Aurea. London: 1646. V. 37; 38; 40; 42; 43; 44; 45

Fragmenta Aurea. London: 1696. V. 45

The Poems of Sir John Suckling. London: 1896. V. 46

The Works . . . London: 1696. V. 42; 43

The Works of . . . London: 1719. V. 43; 44; 45

The Works. Dublin: 1766. V. 38; 41

SUCKOV, LORENZ JOHANN DANIEL

Erste Grunde der Burgerlichen Baukunst in Einem Zusammenhange Entworfen . . . Jena: 1781. V. 44

SUCKOW, RUTH

The Bonney Family. New York: 1928. V. 45

SUDAN

The Anglo-Egyptian Sudan: a Compendium Prepared by Officers of the Sudan Government. London: 1905. V. 40

SUDAN Campaign 1896-1899. London: 1899. V. 41

SUDHOFF, KARL

The Earliest Printed Literature on Syphilis, being Ten Tractates from the Years 1495-1498, in Complete Facsimile. Florence: 1925. V. 37

Essays in the History of Medicine. New York: 1926. V. 44

SUE, EUGENE 1804-1857

The Mysteries of Paris. London: 1845. V. 37; 39; 40; 43

The Mysteries of Paris. London: 1845-46. V. 37; 39; 40; 43

Paula Monti; or, the Hotel Lambert. London: 1845. V. 46

The Rival Races. London: 1863. V. 38

The Wandering Jew. Boston. V. 39

The Wandering Jew. London: 1844. V. 40; 46

The Wandering Jew. London: 1844-45. V. 38

Works. London: and Boston. V. 44

Complete Works in French. Brussels: 1838-52. V. 42

The Works. Boston: 1900. V. 40; 46

The Works. London & Boston: 1900. V. 37

The Works. Boston: (ca. 1900). V. 37

SUE, JEAN JOSEPH 1760-1830

Elemens d'Anatomie, a l'Usage des Peintres, des Sculpteurs, et des Amateurs . . . Paris: 1805. V. 38; 42

A Series of Engravings, Representing Bones of the Human Skeleton; with the Skeletons of Some of the Lower Animals. London: 1819-1820. V. 39; 42; 41; 46

SUE, LOUIS 1875-1968

Architectures. Paris: 1921. V. 38; 41; 44

SUEDERICUS, JAKOB

De religiosorum origine . . . (Dresden: 1525). V. 37

SUES, OTTO L.

Grigsby's Cowboys. Salem: 1900. V. 38; 41

SUESS, DOCTOR

The Seven Lady Godivas. New York: 1939. V. 37

SUESS, E.

The Face of the Earth. Oxford: 1904-24. V. 38

SUETONIUS TRANQUILLUS, GAIUS 75-160

De vita XII Caesarum. (Florence: 1510). V. 37

SUETONIUS TRANQUILLUS, GAIUS 75-160 continued

Commentationes Condite a Philippo Beroaldo in Suetonium Trnquillum. Paris: 1512. V. 37; 38

XII Caesares. Sexti Aurelii Victoris a. d. Caesare Augusto usq(ue) ad Theodosium Excerptae. Eutropius de Gestis Romanorum Lib. X, Pauli Diaconi Lbri VIII ad Eutropii Historiam Additi. Venice: 1516. V. 45

In Hoc Uolumine Haec Continentur. C. Suetonii Tranquilli XII Caesares. Colophon: 1521. V. 37

La Tresillustre et Memorable Vie . . . des Douze Cesars. Paris: 1530. V. 46

Des Faictz et Gestes des Douze Caesars. Paris: 1540. V. 37

Duodecim Caesares ex Erasmi Recognitione. Paris: 1543. V. 37

Le Vite di Dodici Cesari di Gaio Suetonio Tranquillo. Venice: 1550. V. 40

XII Caesares. Lyons: 1565. V. 37

The Lives of the XII Caesars, or the First Twelve Roman Emperors. London: 1717. V. 38

The Lives of the Twelve Caesars. London: 1796. V. 41

Suetonius Lives of the Twelve Caesars. N.P.: 1930. V. 46

The Historie of the Twelve Ceasars, Emperors of Rome. London: 1931. V. 37; 41; 44

Lives of the Twelve Caesars. New York: 1963. V. 38

The Lives of the Twelve Caesars. Verona: 1963. V. 39; 42

History of the Twelve Caesars. By Suetonius. Translated by Philemon Holland (Anno 1606). Edited with Introduction & Notes by J.H. Freese. London: (ca.1950). V. 37

SUFFOLK, EDWARD HOWARD, EARL OF

Musarum Deliciae . . . London: 1728. V. 45

THE SUFFOLK Garland: or, a Collection of Poems, Songs, Tales, Ballads, Sonnets and Elegies . . . Ipswich: 1818. V. 44

SUFFOLK, HENRY CHARLES HOWARD, 18TH EARL OF 1833-1898

The Encyclopaedia of Sport. London: 1903. V. 44

SUGAR AND MUTINY BILLS

Considerations upon the Sugar and Mutiny Bills, adressed to the People of Ireland in General and the Citizens of Dublin in particular. Dublin: 1780. V. 37

a Dispassionate Examen of the most popular objections against the Sugar and Mutiny Acts, with some conclusive arguments . . . Second Edition. Dublin: 1782. V. 37

SUGDEN, ALAN VICTOR

A History of English Wallpaper, 1509-1914. London: 1925. V. 39; 43

A History of English Wallpaper 1509-1914. New York: 1925. V. 45

A History of English Wallpapers 1509-1914. London: 1914. V. 37

Potters of Darwen 1839: 1939 - a Century of Wallpaper Printing by Machinery. Manchester: 1939. V. 44

SUGDEN, EDWARD BURTENSHAW, BARON ST. LEONARDS 1781-1875

A Letter to James Humphreys, Esq. on His Proposal to Repeal the Laws of Real Property and Substitute a New Code. London: 1826. V. 40

A Practical Treatise of the Law of Vendors and Purchasers of Estates. London: 1806. V. 40

A Practical Treatise of the Law of Vendors and Purchasers of Estates. Philadelphia: 1820. V. 40

A Series of Letters to a Man of Property on the Sale, Purchase, Mortgaging, Leasing, Settling and Devising of Estates . . . London: 1815. V. 37; 40

SUIDAE Historica, Caeteraque Omnia Quae Ulla Ex Parte ad Lognitionen Rerum Spectant . . . Basel: 1581. V. 37

A SUIT of Armour for Youth. London: 1824. V. 37; 38

SUKENIK, ELEAZAR L.

The Ancient Synagogue of Beth Alpha. Jerusalem: 1932. V. 37; 40; 42

The Ancient Synagogue of El-Hammeh. Jerusalem: 1935. V. 44

The Dead Sea Scrolls of the Hebrew University. Jerusalem: 1955. V. 40; 42

The Third Wall of Jerusalem: an account of excavations. Jeruslaem: 1930. V. 37

SUKURAI, TADAYOSHI

Human Bullets, a Soldier's Story of Port Arthur . . . London: 1907. V. 46

SULLIVAN, ARABELLA

Recollections of a Chaperon. Edited by Lady Dacre. London: 1833. V. 37

Tales of the Peerage and the Peasantry. London: 1835. V. 39; 42; 45; 46

SULLIVAN, C. A.

A Full Description of the Aervolant, or Flying Machine, Invented by C. A. Sullivan, of Mississippi. Patented November 30, 1880. Starkville: 1881. V. 37

SULLIVAN, DENNIS

A Picturesque Tour Through Ireland. London: 1824. V. 39; 41; 45

SULLIVAN, EDWARD

Rambles and Scrambles in North and South America. London: 1852. V. 37; 38; 39; 40; 41; 42; 43

Yachting. London: 1894. V. 38; 43

SULLIVAN, EDWARD, BART 1852-1928

Book of Kells. London: 1914. V. 39

SULLIVAN, ELEANOR

Whodunit: A Biblio-Bio-Anecotal Memoir of Frederic Dannay. New York: 1984. V. 46

SULLIVAN, FRANCIS STOUGHTON

An Historical Treatise on the Feudal Law and On the Constitution and Laws of England; with a Commentary on Magna Carta. Dublin: 1772. V. 40; 41

Lectures on the Constitution and Laws of England. London: 1776. V. 39

SULLIVAN, G. L.

Dhow Chasing in Zanzibar Waters and on the Eatern Coast of Africa. London: 1873. V. 39

SULLIVAN, JAMES

Biographical Sketch of the Life and Character of His Late Excellency Governor Hancock. Boston: 1793. V. 37

The History of the District of Maine. Boston: 1795. V. 43

Observations Upon the Government of the United States of America. Boston: 1791. V. 37; 38

The Path to Riches. Boston: 1792. V. 43

SULLIVAN, JOHN

Journals of the Military Expedition of Major General John Sullivan Against the Six Nations of Indians in 1779. Auburn: 1887. V. 39

Letters and Papers of Major-General John Sullivan. Concord: 1930-31-39. V. 46

Letters and Papers of Major-General John Sullivan. Concord: 1930-39. V. 39

SULLIVAN, JOHN L.

A Description of the American Marine Rail-Way, as Constructed at New York, by Mr. John Thomas, Naval Architect. Philadelphia: 1827. V. 39

The Modern Gladiator. St. Louis: 1889. V. 40

SULLIVAN, JOHN T.

Report of Historical and Technical Information Relating to the Problem of Interoceanic Communication by Way of the American Isthmus. Washington: 1883. V. 43

SULLIVAN, LOUIS HENRI 1856-1924

Kindergarten Chats on Architecture, Education and Democracy. Washington: 1934. V. 38

SULLIVAN, LOUIS HENRY 1856-1924

Kindergarten Chats on Architecture, Education and Democracy. N.P.: 1934. V. 43

SULLIVAN, M. J.

The Internationa Blue Book, 1912-1914: A Deluxe Issue of Southeast Texas. Houston: 1912. V. 37

SULLIVAN, MARK

Our Times. New York: 1926-35. V. 42

SULLIVAN, MAURICE S.

Jedediah Smith, Trader and Trail Breaker. New York: 1936. V. 37; 39; 44

The Travels of Jedediah Smith. Santa Ana: 1934. V. 37; 38; 39; 40; 41; 42; 45

SULLIVAN, MAY KELLOGG

The Trail of a Sourdough Life in Alaska. Boston: 1910. V. 42

SULLIVAN, MICHAEL

Chinese Ceramics, Bronzes and Jades in the Collection of Sir Alan and Lady Barlow. London: 1963. V. 42

SULLIVAN, RICHARD JOSEPH

Observations Made During a Tour through Parts of England, Scotland and Wales. London: 1780. V. 43; 46

SULLIVAN, STEPHEN

An Epistle to a Friend at Rome. London: 1772. V. 40

SULLIVAN, T. D.

Bantry, Berehaven and the O'Sullivan Sept. Dublin: 1908. V. 43

SULLIVAN, W. J. L.

Twelve Years in the Saddle for Law and Order on the Frontiers of Texas. Austin: 1909. V. 37; 38

SULLIVAN, WILLIAM L.

Dunne: Judge, Mayor, Governor. Chicago: 1916. V. 38

SULLIVANT, WILLIAM S.

The Musci and Hepaticae of the United States East of the Mississippi River. New York: 1856. V. 44

SULLY, MAXIMILIAM DE BETHUNE, DUC DE 1559-1641

Memoirs of Maximilian de Bethune, Duke of Sully. Edinburgh: 1770. V. 39; 40; 45; 46

SULLY, MAXIMILIEN DE BETHUNE, DUC DE 1559-1641

Memoires des Sages et Royalles Oeconomies d'Estat . . . de Henry Le Grand. Amsterdam: 1638. V. 42

Memoires des Sages et Royalles Oeconomies D'Estat . . . de Henry Le Grand. Amsterdam: Paris: 1638-62. V. 37

Memoires de Maximilien de Bethune duc De Sully, Principal Ministre de Henry Le Grand . . . London: 1747. V. 41

Memoirs of Maximilian de Bethune, Duke of Sully, Prime Minister to Henry the Great. London: 1756. V. 44

Memoirs of Maximilien de Bethune, Duke of Sully . . . London: 1761. V. 39; 41

Memoires. London: 1778. V. 39

SULPITIUS VERULANIS, JOHANNES

De Arte Grammatica, sive de Octo Partibus Orationis. Regulae Sulpitii. Venice: 1495? V. 37

SULZBERGER, CYRUS

The Resistentialists. New York: 1962. V. 43

A SUMMARY Account of the Viceroyalty of Buenos-Ayres, or La Plata. London: 1805. V. 41

A SUMMARY and Philosophic View of the Genius, Character, Manners, Government, and Politics of the Dutch. London: 1788. V. 46

A SUMMARY View of the Millennial Church, or United Society of Believers (Commonly Called Shakers). Albany: 1823. V. 40; 41

SUMMER, CHARLES

Speech of Hon. Charles Summer, of Massachusetts, on the Cession of Russian America to the United States. Washington: 1867. V. 37

A SUMMER in Thanet, in the year 1817. A Farce, intended for three acts. Deal: (1817). V. 37

SUMMER Saunterings in the Land of Lakes. St. Paul: 1882. V. 42

SUMMERFIELD, CHARLES

Rangers and Regulations of the Tanaha . . . New York: 1856. V. 38; 43; 44

SUMMERHAYES, MARTH

Vanished Arizona: Recollections of the Army Life of a New England Woman. Philadelphia: 1908. V. 37; 39

SUMMERHAYES, MARTHA

Vanished Arizona: Recollections of My Army Life. Salem: 1911. V. 37; 39; 41; 46

Vanished Arizona: Recollections of My Army Life. Tucson: 1960. V. 39; 44

SUMMERING in Colorado. Denver: 1874. V. 37; 42; 45

SUMMERS, JAMES

The Rudiments of the Chinese Language. London: 1864. V. 40

SUMMERS, JOHN

A Short Account of the Success of Warm Bathing in Paralytic Disorders. London: 1751. V. 38; 42

SUMMERS, MONTAGUE

Covent Garden Drollery. London: 1927. V. 43

The Discovery of Witches - a Study of Master Matthew Hopkins Commonly Call'd Witch Finder Generall. London: 1928. V. 38

Essays in Petto. London: 1928. V. 38

The Geography of Witchcraft. London: 1927. V. 46

A Gothic Bibliography. London. V. 39

The Gothic Quest: a History of the Gothic Novel. London: 1938. V. 37; 44

The History of Witchcraft and Demonology. London: 1926. V. 46

Malleus Maleficarum. London: 1928. V. 38

The Werewolf. London: 1933. V. 40; 41

SUMMERS, ROGER

Prehistoric Rock Art of the Rederation of Rhodesia & Nyasaland. Rhodesia: 1959. V. 39

SUMMONTE, ANTONIO

Dell-Historia Della Citta e Regno di Napoli. Napoli: 1675. V. 38

SUMNER, CHARLES

Argument of Charles Sumner, Esq. Against the Constitutionaility of Separate Colored Schools, in the Case of Sarah C. Roberts vs. the City of Boston. Boston: 1849. V. 45

The Crime Against Kansas. Boston: 1856. V. 42

'Cross the Plains. The Overland Trip. San Francisco: 1869. V. 38; 42

Last Three Speeches of Kansas and Freedom. Boston: 1856. V. 39

Speech of Hon. Charles Sumner, of Massachusetts, on the Cession of Russian America to the United States. Washington: 1867. V. 38; 40; 41; 42

SUMNER, CHARLES A.

Fact and Need. A Statement as to Prevailing Repute and Appropriate Vindication. Address By . . . Delivered Before the Territorial Pioneers, at Pacific Hall, San Francisco, on the 27th Anniversary of the Admission of California into the Union. San Francisco: 1877. V. 40; 42

Popular Use and Benefits of Standard Phonography. San Francisco: 1873. V. 46

SUMNER, CHARLES PINCKNEY

The Compass. A Poetical Performance at the Literary Exhibition in September, 1795 at Harvard University. Boston: 1795. V. 45

SUMNER, E. V.

Tactics for the Gatling Gun, Cal. 45, Proposed by Captain E. V. Sumner, 1st Cavalry. San Francisco: 1876. V. 45

SUMNER, GEORGE HEYWOOD MAUNOIR

The Ancient Earthworks of Cranborne Chase. London: 1913. V. 45

The Ancient Earthworks of the New Forest. London: 1917. V. 45

The Book of Gorley. London: 1910. V. 45

SUMNER, HEYWOOD

The Ancient Earthworks of Cranborne Chase. London: 1913. V. 46

The Avon, from Naseby to Twekesbury. London: 1882. V. 41

The Besom Maker and Other Country Folk Songs. London: 1888. V. 41

The Itchen Valley from Titchborne to Southampton. London: 1881. V. 37

SUMNER, JAMES

The Mysterious Marbler. North Hills: 1976. V. 37; 39; 40; 41; 42; 43

SUMNER, LOWELL

Birds and Mammals of the Sierra Nevada. Berkeley: 1953. V. 38; 45

THE SUN Princess Fairy Stories. London. V. 40

SUN, Sea and Earth. Gloucestershire: 1989. V. 42; 43

SUNDAY in London. London: 1833. V. 46

SUNDAY School Songs. Brookhaven: 1846. V. 41

SUNDERLAND, CHARLES SPENCER

Bibliotheca Sunderlandiana. Catalogue of the Sunderland Library removed from Blenheim Palace. With bibliographical notes. Compiled by J. Lawler. (1881-3). V. 37

SUNDERLAND, LA ROY 1804-1885

Pathetism: with Practical Instructions. New York: 1843. V. 46

SUNDRY Papers, in Relation to Claims, Commonly called the Yaoo Claims. City of Washington: 1809. V. 46

THE SUNLIGHT Year-Book for 1898. Port Sunlight: 1898. V. 39; 43

SUNNY Days and Children's Ways. London: 1867. V. 41; 45

SUNNY Florida: A Compendium of Information Regarding 'The State of Orange Groves.' London: 1885. V. 41

SUNNY Hours Nursery Rhyme Book. London: 1894. V. 44

A SUPPLEMENT to the Onania; or, the Heinious Sin of Self Pollution, and All Its Frightful Consequences in Both Sexes . . . London: 1728? V. 41

SUPREME Duck Shooting Stories. Chicago: 1944. V. 43

SURAEZ DE ALARCON, JUAN

La Iffanta Coronada, por El Rey Don Pedro, Dona Ines de Castro . . . Lisbon: 1606. V. 38

SURBY, R. W.

Grierson Raids and Hatch's Sixty Four Days March . . . also the Life and Adventures of Chickasaw the Scout. Chicago: 1865. V. 37; 38; 39; 42; 43; 46

SURGANT, JOHANN ULRICH

Manuale Curatorum Predicandi Prebens Modum: Tam Latino Quam Vulgari Sermone. Basel: 1506. V. 37

SURIA, TOMAS DE

Journal of Tomas de Suria of His Voyage with Malaspina to the Northwest Coast of America in 1791. Glendale: 1936. V. 42

SURIUS, LAURENTIUS

Commentarius Brevis Rerum in Orbe Gestarum, Ab Anno Salutis M.D.LXXIIII . . . Coloniae: 1586. V. 46

THE SURPRISING Adventures and Sufferings of John Rhodes, a Seaman of Workington . . . New York: 1798. V. 38

THE SURPRISING Adventures and Sufferings of John Rhodes. A Sermon of Workington. Newark: 1799. V. 45

SURR, THOMAS SKINNER

The Magic of Wealth. A novel. London: 1815. V. 37

Richmond; or Scenes in the Life of a Bow Street Officer, Drawn Up From His Private Memoranda. London: 1827. V. 42

A Winter in London; or Sketches of Fashion. London: 1806. V. 37; 38; 42; 45

SURREY, HENRY HOWARD, EARL OF 1517?-1547

The Original Poems of Henry Howard, Earl of Surrey. 1929. V. 41

The Original Poems of Henry Howard, Earl of Surrey. London: 1929. V. 43

The Works. London: 1815. V. 37; 40

SURREY, HOWARD HENRY, EARL OF 1517-1547

Poems . . . printed from a Correct Copy. London: 1717. V. 42

SURREY Tourist or Excrusions through Surrey. London: 1819. V. 46

SURTEES, ROBERT SMITH 1803-1864

Analysis of the Hunting Field. London: 1845-6. V. 37; 41

The Analysis of the Hunting Field. London: 1846. V. 40

Analysis of the Hunting Field . . . London: 1847. V. 42

The Analysis of the Hunting Field. London: 1923. V. 39

Ask Mama, or the Richest Commoner in England. London. V. 40; 43

'Ask Mama', or, The Richest Commoner in England. London: 1858. V. 37; 39; 44

'Ask Mamma'. London: 1878. V. 46

Ask Mamma. London: 1880. V. 38

Collected Works. London: & New York: 1888-1929. V. 46

Handley Cross. London. V. 38; 40; 41; 45

Handley Cross. London: 1843. V. 38; 39; 46

Handley Cross. London: 1853-54. V. 44

Handley Cross. London: 1854. V. 37; 38; 39; 40; 46

Handley Cross; Plain or Ringlets; Mr. Facey Romford's Hounds; Hillingdon Hall; Ask Mamma; Mr. Sponge's Sporting Tour; Hawbuck Grange. London: 1847-88. V. 37

Hawbuck Grange. London. V. 38

Hawbuck Grange. London: 1847. V. 38; 40

Hawbuck Grange: or the Sporting Adventures of Thomas Scott, Esq. London: (ca. 1890). V. 37

Hillingdon Hall; or, The Cockney Squire. London: 1845. V. 42

Hillingdon Hall or The Cockney Squire. London: 1888. V. 38

The History and Antiquites of the County Palatine of Durham . . . London: 1816-40. V. 38; 43; 44; 46

The Horseman's Manual. London: 1831. V. 37; 39; 42

Hunting Tours. London: 1949-56. V. 46

The Hunting Tours of Surtees. Edinburgh: 1927. V. 37

Hunts with Jorrocks from Handley Cross. London: 1908. V. 42; 46

Jorrocks' Jaunts & Jollities. London. V. 37; 38

Jorrock's Jaunts and Jollities. Philadelphia: 1838. V. 39

Jorrock's Jaunts and Jollities. London: 1843. V. 37; 42

Jorrocks' Jaunts and Jollities. London: 1869. V. 37; 43

Jorrock's Jaunts and Jollities . . . London: 1893. V. 40

Jorrocks Jaunts & jollities. London: 1900. V. 39

Jorrock's Jaunts and Jolities . . . London: 1901. V. 37; 42

Jorrock's Jaunts and Jollities . . . London: 1920. V. 44

Jorrock's Jaunts and Jollities. London: 1838. V. 37

Jorrock's Jaunts and Jollities. London: 1880. V. 37

Jorrock's Jaunts and Jollities. London: 1924. V. 37

Mr. Sponge's Sporting Tour. London. V. 45

Mr. Sponge's Sporting Tour. London: 1852. V. 40

Mr. Sponge's Sporting Tour. London: 1852-53. V. 42

Mr. Sponge's Sporting Tour. London: 1853. V. 37; 38; 39; 40; 43; 44

Mr. Sponge's Sporting Tour. Handley Cross. Ask Mama. Plain or Ringlets? Mr. FAcey Romford's Hounds. Hillingdon Hall. London: 1853-88. V. 43

Mr. Sponge's Sporting Tour. New York: 1856. V. 40

Mr. Sponge's Sporting Tour. New York: 1859. V. 39

Mr. Facey Romford's Hounds. London: 1865. V. 37; 42; 44; 45; 46

Mr. Sponge's Sporting Tour. London: 1865. V. 40

Mr. Sponge's Sporting Tour; Hawbuck Grange; Ask Mama; Plain or Ringlets; Handley Cross; Mr. Romford's Hounds. London: 1870. V. 40

Mr. Sponge's Sporting Tour, Hawbuck Grange, Ask Mama, Plain or Ringlets, Handley Cross, mr. Facey Romford's Hounds. London: 1892. V. 45

Mr. Facey Romford's Hounds. London: 1892? V. 45

Mr. Jorrock's Lectors from Handley Cross. London: 1910. V. 37; 39

Mr. Romford's Hounds. London: 1876. V. 46

Mr. Sponge's Sporting Tour. London: 1860. V. 37; 46

Mr. Sponge's Sporting Tour. London: 1876. V. 46

Novels. London. V. 37; 38; 42

Novels. London: 1847-65. V. 42

Novels: Handley Cross; Mr. Sponge's Sporting Tour; Ask Mamma; Hawbuck Grange; Plain or Ringlets; Hillingdon Hall. London: 1929. V. 37

Novels. London: 1929-30. V. 46

The Novels of R. S. Surtees. London: 1929-31. V. 43

Plain or Ringlets? London: 1859-60. V. 44

'Plain or Ringlets'. London: 1860. V. 37; 38; 40; 42; 46

'Plain or Ringlets?' London: 1878. V. 46

Plain or Ringlets? London: 1880. V. 38

Shooting with Surtees, Including the Shooting Exploits of Mssrs. John Jorrocks, Jogglebury Crowdey, Facey Romford, and Other Famous Sportsmen. London: 1927. V. 39

Sponge's Sporting Tour. London: 1875? V. 45

Sponge's Sporting Tour. London: 1852-53. V. 37

The Sporting Novels. London: 1847-88. V. 42

Sporting Novels. London: 1880. V. 37; 42; 44; 46

Sporting Novels. London: 1890. V. 37; 42

Sporting Novels. London: 1920. V. 41

The Sporting Novels. London: 1926. V. 37; 39

Works of . . . London. V. 43

Works; Handley Cross; Ask Mamma; Plain or Ringlets; Mr. Facey Romford's Hounds; Mr. Sponge's Sporint Tour; Hawbuck Grange; Hillingdon Hall; Jorrock's Jaunts and Jollities. London: 1949-56. V. 37

SURUGUE, LOUIS

Grand Escalaier du Chateau de Versailles dit Escalier des Ambassadeurs Ordonne et Peint par Charles le Brun Ecuyer Premier Peintre du Roy. Paris: 1725. V. 38

SURVEY of London. London: 1896-1986. V. 45

SURVEY of the Fauna of Iraq. Mammals, Birds, Reptiles, etc., Made by Members of the Mesopotamia Expeditionary Force 'D' 1915-19. Bombay: 1923. V. 37

A SURVEY of the National Debts. The Civil Fund, the Civil List and the Annual Supplies. London: 1745. V. 40; 41

SUSIO, GIOVAN BATTISTA

I Tre Libri Della Ingivstitia del Dvello, et di Coloro, Che lo Permettono. Venetia: 1555. V. 42

SUSO, HEINRICH 1295-1366

Horologium Sapientie. Venice: 1492/3. V. 40

SUSSEX AGRICULTURAL SOCIETY

Proceedings of the Sussex Agricultural Society From Its Institution to 1798. Lewes: 1800. V. 40

SUSSEX Archaeological Collections: Volumes 1-124. 1848-1896. V. 38

SUSSEX: Excursions in the County of Sussex . . . Historical and Topographical Delineations . . . London: 1822. V. 37

SUSSNER, G. W.

Fabric of Creta Polycolor (Coloured Oil-Chalk-Pencils) and Crayons Mecaniques (Mechanical Pencils) in Nuremberg. Greiz: 1859. V. 41

SUTART, ROBERT

Views and Notices of Glasgow in Former Times. 27 Full page Lithographs, drawn by several artists, lighos by Allan & Gerguson. Text by Robert Sutart. Glasgow: 1848. V. 37

SUTCLIFF, ROBERT

Travels in Some Parts of North America, in the Years 1804, 1805 and 1806. York: 1811. V. 38; 40

Travels in Some Parts of North America in . . . 1804, 1805 and 1806. Philadelphia: 1812. V. 38; 42; 45

Travels in Some Parts of North America, in the Years 1804, 1805 and 1806. York: 1815. V. 38; 46

SUTCLIFFE, G. LISTER

The Modern Carpenter Joiner and Cabinet-Maker. London: 1902-04. V. 44

SUTCLIFFE, JOHN H.

British Optical Association Library and Museum Catalogue. London: 1932-35-37. V. 37

SUTCLIFFE, JOSEPH

The Geology of the Avon. Bristol: 1822. V. 42

A Grammar of the English Language. London: 1815. V. 43

SUTCLIFFE, THOMAS

Crusoniana; or, Truth Versus Fiction, Elucidated in a History of the Islands of Juan Fernandez. Manchester: 1843. V. 37; 46

The Earthquake that Occured on the Island of Juan Fernandez and Talcahuana in the Year 1835 . . . Manchester: 1835. V. 38; 45

The Earthquake of Juan Fernandez, as it Occurred in the Year 1835. Manchester: 1839. V. 38; 42

Sixteen Years in Chile and Peru from 1822 to 1839. London: 1841. V. 38; 40; 43; 46

Sixteen Years in Chile and Peru, from 1822 to 1839, by the Retired Governor of Juan Fernandez. London: app. 1841. V. 39

SUTHERLAND, A.

A Summer in Prairie-Land: Notes of a Tour through the North-West Territory. Toronto: 1881. V. 38; 44

SUTHERLAND, ALEXANDER

Attempts to Revive Antient Medical Doctrines. London: 1763. V. 43

SUTHERLAND, DAVID

A Tour Up the Straits, from Gibraltar to Constantinople . . . . London: 1790. V. 37; 38; 41; 44

SUTHERLAND, DUCHESS OF

Wayfarer's Love. Westminster: 1904. V. 41

SUTHERLAND, G. A.

The Heart in Early Life. London: 1914. V. 42

A System of Diet and Dietetics. London: 1908. V. 42

SUTHERLAND, GEORGE

A Manual of the Geography and Natural and Civil History of Prince Edward Island. Charlottetown: 1861. V. 44

SUTHERLAND, GEORGE GRANVILLE LEVESON GOWER, 1ST DUKE OF 1758-1833

Catalogue Raisonne of the Pictures..in the Gallery of Cleveland House, Comprising a List of the Pictures . . . London: 1808. V. 44

SUTHERLAND, GILBERT D.

The Victorian Era 1837-1897. London: 1897. V. 39

SUTHERLAND, GRAHAM VIVIAN 1903-

Catalogue of an Exhibition. Turin: 1965. V. 41

Sutherland. London: 1950. V. 45

The Work of Graham Sutherland. London: 1961. V. 38; 40

SUTHERLAND, H. J.

The City of Scranton and Vicinity. Scranton: 1894. V. 42

SUTHERLAND HARRIS, ANN

Andrea Sacchi, Complete Edition of the Paintings with a Critical Catalogue. London: 1977. V. 42

SUTHERLAND, J. G.

At Sea with Joseph Conrad. London: 1922. V. 43

SUTHERLAND, J. R.

The Narrative of Jasper Weepie - Being an Account of His Strange Journey to the Land of Midanglia, and All that Happened to Him in that Strange Country. London: 1930. V. 43

SUTHERLAND, JAMES

The Adventures of an Elephant Hunter. London. V. 39; 40

The Adventures of an Elephant Hunter. London: 1912. V. 39; 40; 42; 43; 44

Essays on the 18th Century, Presented to David Nichol Smith, in Honour of His 70th Birthday. Oxford: 1945. V. 45; 46

Hortus Medicus Edinburgensis, or a Catalogue of the Plants in the Physical Garden at Edinburgh. Edinburgh: by the Heir of: 1683. V. 37

SUTHERLAND, JOHN

The Fall of the Alamo. 1936. V. 44

The Fall of the Alamo. San Antonio: 1936. V. 42

SUTHERLAND, PETER CORMACK

Journal of a Voyage in Baffin's Bay and Barrow Straits, in the Years 1850-1851, Peformed by H.M. Ships 'Lady Franklin' and 'Sophia.' London: 1852. V. 38; 45

SUTHERLAND, REDDING, MRS.

Five Years Within the Golden Gate. London: 1868. V. 41

SUTHERLAND, S.

Australian Animal Toxins, the Creatures, Their Toxins and Care of the Poisoned. Melbourne: 1983. V. 37; 38

SUTHERLAND, T. W.

Aces and Kings. Aces. London: 1936. V. 44

SUTHERLAND, WILLIAM

Late News of the Excursion and Ravages of the King's Troops on the Nineteenth of April, 1775 as set Forth in the Narratives of . . . Cambridge: 1927. V. 38; 46

The Ship Builder's Assistant; or, Marine Architecture . . . London: 1755. V. 41

SUTHERLIN, R. N.

Legends - Historic, or Smith River in Verse. Sulphur Springs: 1900. V. 39

SUTNAR, LADISLAV

Catalog Design Progress, by K. Lonberg-Holm and Ladislav Sutnar. New York: 1950. V. 37

SUTRO, ADOLPH

Closing Argument of Adolph Sutro, on the Bill Before Congress to Aid the Sutro Tunnel. Washington: 1872. V. 38; 40

Report of the Commissioners and Evidence Taken by the Committee on Mines and Mining . . . in Regard to the Sutro Tunnel. Washington: 1872. V. 40

Sutro Tunnel Company. Virginia City: 1869. V. 43

The Sutro Tunnel to the Comstock Lode in the State of Nevada. New York: 1866. V. 41

SUTRO, ALFRED

The Batheaston Parnasssus Fairs. A Manuscript Identified. San Francisco: 1936. V. 39

SUTRO, OSCAR

Shakespeare and Some Commentators: an Address . . . San Francisco: 1933. V. 39

Some Remarks on Shakepeare Before the Roxburghe Club . . . San Francisco: 1933. V. 38; 42; 43; 46

SUTRO, THEODORE

The Sutro Tunnel Company and the Sutro Tunnel . . . New York: 1887. V. 38

SUTSKEVER, ABRAHAM

In the Sinai Desert. Rhode Island: 1987. V. 40

SUTTER, JEAN

The Neo Impressionists. Greenwich: 1970. V. 38; 42

SUTTER, JOHANN AUGUSTUS

The Diary of Johann August Sutter. San Francisco: 1932. V. 40; 42

The Diary of Johann August Sutter. Introduction by D. S. Watson. San Francisco: 1832. V. 37

New Helvetia Diary, a Record of Events Kept by John A. Sutter and His Clerks at New Helvitia, California, from September 9, 1845 to May 25, 1848. San Francisco: 1939. V. 37; 38; 40; 45

Pioneers of Sacramento. San Francisco: 1953. V. 40

SUTTON, ADA LOUIS

Teddy Bears by Ada Louis Sutton. Akron: (1907). V. 37

SUTTON, ALFRED G.

The Midland Florist and Suburban Horticulturist: a Handbook for the Amateur and Florist. London: 1860. V. 38

SUTTON, DAVID A.

Revision of the Tribe Antirrhineae (Scrophularlaceae). Oxford: 1988. V. 39

SUTTON, E. GRIGGS

Unfettered. Nashville: 1902. V. 42

SUTTON, FREDERICK HEATHCOTE

A Short Account of Organs Built in England from the Reign of King Charles the Second to the Present Time. London: 1847. V. 38; 40

SUTTON, G. M.

Mexican Birds. Norman: 1951. V. 39

SUTTON, R. L.

An Arctic Safari. London: 1933. V. 38

Tiger Trails in Southern Asia. London: 1926. V. 37; 38

SUTTON, ROBERT

A Complee Guide to Landlords, Tenants, and Lodgers . . . London: 1799. V. 42

A Complete Guide to Landlords, Tennants, and Lodgers . . . London: 1800. V. 40

SUTTON, THOMAS

A Practical Account of a Remittent Fever. Canterbury: 1806. V. 39

A Practical Account of a Remittent Fever, frequently occuring among the troops in this climate. Canterbury/London: 1806. V. 37

SUTTON, WAIN

Utah. A Centennial History. New York: 1949. V. 37; 42

SUTTOR, H. M.

Australian Milestones and Stories of the Past 1770-1914. Sydney: 1925. V. 46

SUTTOR, WILLIAM

Dialogue Between a Nobleman and Farmer, Upon the Reduction of the National Debt, and Other Affairs of State. Edinburgh: 1788. V. 38

SUTZKEVER, ABRAHAM

Siberia a Poem. London: 1961. V. 44

SUVATTI, CHOTE

Fauna of Thailand. Thailand: 1950. V. 39

SUYIN, HAN

From One China to the Other. New York: 1956. V. 37

SUYS, F. T.

Palais Massimi a Rome, Plans, Coupes, Elevations, Profiles, Voutes, Plafonds, etc. Paris: 1818. V. 45

SUZUKI, D. T.

Mysticism: Christian and Buddhist. New York: 1957. V. 43

SUZUKI, MAKOTO

Wooden Houses. New York: 1979. V. 44

SUZY, MADEMOISELLE

My Most Beautiful Nights of Love. Paris: 1938. V. 46

SVEDMAN, KARL VILLHELM

Costume of Sweden Illustrated by Twenty Two Engravings. London: 1823. V. 41

SVEVO, ITALO

As a Man Grows Older. London: 1932. V. 41; 42

The Confessions of Zeno. New York: 1930. V. 42; 44

The Nice Old Man and Pretty Girl and Other Stories. London: 1930. V. 40

SVININE, PAUL

Sketches of Russia . . . London: 1814. V. 41

Some Details Concerning General Moreau and His Last Moments. Boston: 1814. V. 40

SVOBODA, ANTONIN

Computing Mechanisms and Linkages. New York: 1948. V. 45

THE SVVEDISH Discipline, Religious, Ciuile, and Military. London: 1632. V. 41

SWAGGERING Farmers. (and) Susannah Don't You Cry. Durham: 1850. V. 45

SWAIM, WILLIAM

A Treatise on Swaim's Panacea. Philadelphia: 1824. V. 38

SWAIN, CHARLES

Beauties of the Midn, a Poetical Sketch; with Lays, Historical and Romantic. London: 1831. V. 45

Letter of Laura D'Auverne. London: 1853. V. 45

The Mind and Other Poems. London: 1841. V. 41

SWAIN, DAVID L.

Early Times in Raleigh: Addresses . . . Raleigh: 1867. V. 37

Report of . . . On the Historical Agency for Procuring Documentary Evidence of the History of North Carolina. Raleigh: 1857. V. 39

SWAIN, JOSEPH

Redemption, a Poem in Five Books. London: 1789. V. 40

SWAIN, LYDIA

Verses from the Island Book. Cambridge: 1865. V. 43

SWAINE, ROBERT T.

The Cravath Firm and Its Predecessors 1819-1947. New York: 1946-48. V. 46

SWAINSON, C. A.

The Greek Liturgies, chiefly from original authorities. Cambridge: 1884. V. 37

SWAINSON, ISAAC

An Account of Cures, By Velnos' Vegetable Syrup, in Disorders Deriving Their Origin of Malignity from Scorbutic Impurities . . . London: 1798. V. 38

SWAINSON, WILLIAM

Fauna Boreali-Americana; or the Zoology of the Northern Parts of British America . . . London: 1831. V. 42

Zoological Illustrations or Original Figures and Descriptions of New, Rare or Interesting Animals. London: 1820-33. V. 46

SWALES, FRANK

Driving As I Found It. London: 1891. V. 43

SWALLOW, GEORGE CLINTON 1817-1899

The First and Second Annual Reports of the Geological Survey of Missouri. Jefferson City: 1855. V. 37

Geological Report of the Country Along the Line of the South-Western Branch of the Pacific Railroad, State of Missouri. St. Louis: 1859. V. 37; 38

Report of the Geological Survey of Miami County, Kansas. Kansas City: 1865. V. 39; 40; 41

Report on the Mineral Lands of Messrs. Woods Christy & Co., In Franklin County, Missouri. Saint Louis: 1866. V. 39

SWALLOW, R. W.

Ancient Chinese Bronze Mirrors. Peiping: 1937. V. 37; 39; 45

Ancient Chinese Bronze Mirrors. Peiping: 1937. V. 37

Sidelights on Peking Life. Peking: 1927. V. 38

SWALVE, BERNHARD

Querelae & Opprobia Ventriculi; Sive Prosopopolia Eiusdem natralia sua Sibi Vendicantis, & Abusus tam Diateticos, Quam . . . Amsterdam: 1664. V. 43

SWAMMDERDAM, J.

The Book or Nature of the History of Insects. London: 1758. V. 37; 41

SWAN, ABRAHAM

The British Architect; or the Builder's Treasury of Stair-Cases. London: 1758. V. 44

A Collection of Designs in Architecture, Containing New Plans and Elevations of Houses, for General Use. London: 1757. V. 38

A Collection of Designs in Architecture. London: 1770. V. 46

SWAN, ALONZO M.

Canton: Its Pioneers and History. Canton: 1871. V. 38

SWAN, CHARLES

Journal of a Voyage up the Mediterranean Principally Among the Islands of the Archipelago, and in Asia Minor. London: 1826. V. 37; 39; 43

SWAN, JAMES G.

The Amoor River. Seattle: 1885. V. 42

The Haidah Indians of Queen Charlotte's Islands, British Columbia. Washington: 1874. V. 43

The Haidah Indians of Queen Charlotte's Islands, British Columbia, with a Brief Description.. Washington: 1879. V. 38

The Northwest Coast; or, Three Years' Residence in Washington Territory. New York: 1857. V. 37; 38; 39; 42; 45

SWAN, JOHN

Speculum Mundi, or, a Glasse Representing the Face of the World. London: 1665. V. 38

The Standard of Time. London: 1656, 1653. V. 39

SWAN, JOSEPH

A Demonstration of the Nerves of the Human Body. London: 1834. V. 42

Illustrations of the Comparative Anatomy of the Nervous System. London: 1835. V. 37

A Treatise on the Law Relating to the Powers and Duties of Justices of the Peace and Constables in the State of Ohio with Practical Forms. Columbus: 1837. V. 45

SWAN, MYRA

Shallows. London: 1894. V. 42; 46

SWAN, TIMOTHY

New England Harmony. Northampton: 1801. V. 41

SWAN, WILLIAM

Letters on Missions. Boston: 1831. V. 40

SWAN, WILLIAM DRAPER

The Critic Criticised, and Worcester Vindicated . . . Boston: 1859. V. 38

SWANK, W.

African Antelopes. London: 1971. V. 38

SWANN, H. KIRKE

A Monograph of the Birds of Prey; Accipitres. London: 1924-25. V. 37; 38; 39

A Monograph of the Birds of Prey. London: 1930-45. V. 39; 42; 44; 46

SWANN, J. C.

The Citizen Soldiers of Buckinghamshire, 1795-1926. London: 1930. V. 38

SWANN, JOHN

The Whole Tryal of John Swann, and Elizabeth Jeffries, for the Murder of Her Uncle Mr. Joseph Jeffryes, at Walthamstow, in Essex . . . July 1751 . . . London: 1752. V. 43

SWANN, THOMAS BURNETT

Alas, in Lilliput. Worcester: 1964. V. 44

SWANZY, HENRY R.

A Handbook of the Diseases of the Eye and Their Treatment. New York: 1884. V. 44

A Handbook of the Diseases of the Eye and Their Treatment. London: 1888. V. 44

SWARBRECK, SAMUEL D.

Sketches in Scotland. L: 1839. V. 40

Sketches in Scotland Drawn from Nature and on Stone by S. D. Swarbreck. London: 1839. V. 40; 42; 43

Sketches in Scotland. London: 1845. V. 44

SWARBRICK, JOHN

Robert Adam and His Brothers. London: 1915. V. 38; 42

Robert Adam and His Brothers, Their Lives, Work and Influence on English Architecture, Decoration and Furniture. London: 1915? V. 42

SWASEY, WILLIAM F.

The Early Days and Men of California. Oakland: 1891. V. 39; 44

SWAYNE, FRANCES

A Woman's Pleasure Trip in Somaliland. Bristol: 1907. V. 40

SWAYNE, GEORGE

Gramina Pascua; or, a Collection of Specimens of the Common Pasture Grasses, Arranged in the Order of Their Flowering . . . Bristol: 1790. V. 38; 42

Gramina Pascua; or, a Collection of Specimens of the Common Pastures Grasses . . . London: 1790. V. 45

SWAYNE, H. G. C.

Seventeen Trips through Somaliland. London: 1895. V. 38; 39

SWAYSLAND, EDWARD J. C.

Boot and Shoe Design and Manufacture. Northampton: 1905. V. 45

SWAYSLAND, WALTER

Familiar Wild Birds. London: 1883. V. 37; 41

Familiar Wild Birds. London: 1894-1899. V. 39; 42; 44

THE SWEARING Master; or, a Conference Between Two Country-Fellows Concerning the Times, Ned and Will. London: 1681. V. 42

SWEDBURG, JOHAN

Dissertatio Gradualis de Sveonum in America Colonia. Uppsala: 1709. V. 38; 40; 44

SWEDENBORG, EMANUEL 1688-1772

Concerning the Earths in Our Solar System, Which Are Called Planets . . . London: 1787. V. 40; 42

Concerning the White Horse Mentioned in the Revelation, Chap. XIX. With Extracts from the Arcana Coelestia, Concerning the Word and It's (sic) Spiritual or Internal Sense. London: 1788. V. 45

Concerning the Earths in Our Solar System, Which are Called Planets. London: 1797. V. 45

The Delights of Wisdom Concerning Conjugal Love; After Which Follow the Pleasures of Insanity . . . London: 1794. V. 37; 42; 45

The Delights of Wisdom Concerning Conjugial Love. Philadelphia: 1796. V. 39

The Generative Organs, Considered Anatomically, Physically and Philosophically. London: 1852. V. 38; 40

Heavenly Arcana. Boston: 1837-47. V. 45; 46

The Heavenly Secrets Which are in the Holy Scripture . . . London: 1858. V. 42

Les Merveilles du Ciel et de l'Enfrer et des Terres Planetaires et Astrales . . . Berlin: 1782. V. 41; 45

A Treatise Concerning Heaven and Hell. London: 1778. V. 38; 45

The True Christian Religion, Containing the Universal Theology of the New Church. Boston: 1833. V. 42

The Wisdom of Angels, Concerning Divine Love and Divine Wisdom. Boston: 1794. V. 39

Works. Boston: 1900. V. 42

SWEDIAUR, FRANCOIS XAVIER 1748-1824

Complete Treatise on the Symptoms, Effects, Nature and Treatment of Syphillis. Philadelphia: 1815. V. 37

The Philosophical Dictionary . . . London: 1786. V. 43

Practical Observations on Venereal Complaints. New York: 1788. V. 40

SWEDISH Peasant Costumes. Stockholm: 1872? V. 40

SWEENEY, J. J.

Marc Chagall. V. 46

SWEENEY, JAMES JOHNSON 1900-

Soulanges. Greenwich: 1972. V. 39

Three Young Rats; and Other Rhymes. New York: 1944. V. 39

SWEERTS, E. M.

Florilegium, Tractans de Variis Floribus et Aliis Indicis Plantis, ad Vivum Delineatum, in Duabus Partibus et Quatuor Linguis Concinnatum. Francofurti A. M.: 1612. V. 37

SWEET, ALEXANDER E.

On a Mexican Mustang, Through Texas, From the Gulf to the Rio Grande. London: 1884. V. 41; 44

On a Mexican Mustang Through Texas, From the Gulf to the Rio Grande. Hartford: 1883. V. 37; 45

Sketches from Texas Siftings. New York: 1882. V. 37; 38; 40

SWEET, FREDERICK A.

Miss Mary Cassatt Impressionist from Pennsylvania. Norman: 1966. V. 39

SWEET, H.

The Epinal Glossary, Latin and Old-English of the Eighth Century. London: 1883. V. 38

SWEET, HOMER D.

Sweet's New Atlas of Onondaga Co., New York. New York: 1874. V. 39

SWEET, MELISSA

Flowers in My Time. 1986. V. 37

SWEET, ROBERT

Flora Australasica; or, a Selection of Handsome or Curious Plants, Natives of New Holland and the South Sea Islands. London: 1827-28. V. 42; 45

The Florist's Guide and Cultivator's Directory . . . London: 1827-32. V. 42

Geraniaceae. The Natural Order of Gerania . . . London: 1820-30. V. 37; 42

the Hot-House and Greenhouse Manual, or Botanical Cultivator. London: 1825. V. 45

The Natural Order of Cistus, or Rock Rose. London: 1825-30. V. 39

The Trial of Robert Sweet, at the Old Bailey, Before Mr. Justice Best. London: 1824. V. 46

SWEETMAN, GEORGE

The History of Wincanton, Somerset, from the Earliest Times to the Year 1903. Wincanton: 1903. V. 44

SWEETSER, M. F.

King's Handbook of Newton, Massachusetts. Boston: 1889. V. 38

SWEETSER, N. F.

King's Handbook of Boston Harbor. Cambridge: 1882. V. 39

SWEETSER, WILLIAM

A Treatise on Consumption; Embracing an Inquiry into the Influence Exerted Upon It by Journeys, Voyages and Changes of Climate. Boston: 1836. V. 40

A Treatise on Digestion and the Disorders Incident to it Which are Comprehended Under the Term Dyspepsia. Boston: 1837. V. 42

SWEM, E. G.

Brothers of the Spade, Correspondence of Peter Collinson, of London and of John Custis of Williamsburg, Virginia, 1734-1746. Worcester: 1949. V. 45; 46

SWEM, EARL GREGG

A Bibliography of Virginia. Richmond: 1916-17. V. 42

SWETE, HORACE

Handy Book of Cottage Hospitals. Weston-Super-Mare: 1870. V. 41

SWETT, CHARLES

A Trip to British Honduras, and to San Pedro, Republic of Honduras. New Orleans: 1868. V. 38; 39; 42

SWETTENHAM, FRANK

Arabella in Africa. London: 1925. V. 40; 41

SWETZOFF, HYMAN

Ins/Outs. Berkeley: 1947. V. 44

SWIFT, JONATHAN 1667-1745 continued

Select Works. London: 1825. V. 38

Selected Essays. London: 1925. V. 42

Selected Essays. Volume One. 1925. V. 37

A Sermon Preached at the Ordination of the Rev. Mr. Joseph Lee at Roylastown, October 19, 1768. Boston: 1769. V. 40

Some Remarks on the Barrier Treaty. London: 1712. V. 41; 42; 45

T----L----nd's Invitation to Dismal, to Dine with the Calves-Head Club. Dublin?: 1712. V. 45

A Tale of a Tub. London: 1704. V. 37; 38; 39; 40; 41; 42; 43; 44; 45

A Tale of a Tub. London: 1710. V. 37; 38; 40; 41; 43; 45; 46

A Tale of a Tub. 1711. V. 37

A Tale of a Tub. (with) A Complete Key to the Tale of a Tub. London: 1714. V. 38

A Tale of the Tub. (with) A Discourse Concerning the Mechanical Operation of the Spirit in a Letter to a Friend. London: 1727. V. 39

A Tale of a Tub. London: 1760. V. 43

A Tale of a Tub. London: 1811. V. 37; 38; 41; 42

Three Sermons: I. On Mutual Subjection. II. On Conscience. III. On the Trinity. Dublin: 1744. V. 42

Three Sermons. I. On Mutal Subjection. II. On Conscience. III. On the Trinity. London: 1744. V. 37; 46

Travels Into Severall Remote Nations of the World. London: 1725. V. 40

Travels into Several Remote Nations of the World. London: 1726. V. 37; 38; 43; 45; 46

Travels into Several Remote Nations of the World by Lemuel Gulliver. London: 1726/27. V. 44

Travels into Several Remote Nations of the World. London: 1727. V. 37; 40; 42

Travels into Several Remote Nations of the World. London: 1751. V. 38

Travels into Several Remote Nations of the World . . . By Captain Lemuel Gulliver. London: 1766. V. 37

Travels into Several Remote Nations of the World by Lemuel Gulliver. London: 1777/76. V. 42

The Travels of Lemuel Gulliver into Several Remote Nations of the World . . . Edinburgh: 1797. V. 45

Travels into Several Remote Nations of the World by Lemuel Guillver. London: 1894. V. 38; 39

Travels into Several Remote Nations of the World. 1925. V. 37; 38; 39; 41

Travels into Several Remote Nations of the World by Lemuel Gulliver. Berkshire: 1925. V. 41

Travels into Several Remote Nations of the World. Waltham St. Lawrence: 1925. V. 43; 45; 46

The Travels of Lemuel Gulliver by Jonathan Swift. 1929. V. 37

The Travels of Lemuel Gulliver. Baltimore: 1929. V. 40; 42

The Travels of Lemuel Gulliver. New York: 1929. V. 37; 40

Unpublished Letters of Dean Swift. London: 1899. V. 46

Verse on the Death of Doctor Swift. London: 1739. V. 40; 42

A Vindication of Isaac Bickerstaff, Esq . . . London: 1709. V. 38; 41; 45

A Voyage to Brobdingnang Made by Lemuel Gulliver in MDCCII. (and) A Voyage to Lilliput by Lemuel Gulliver MDCIC. 1950. V. 40

A Voyage to Lilliput. New York: 1950. V. 41

Voayges du Capitaine Lemuel Gulliver, en Divers Pays Eloignez . . . The Hague: 1727. V. 41; 45; 46

Voyages du Capitaine Gulliver. La ·haye: 1765. V. 40; 44

Voyages de Gulliver. Paris: 1838. V. 45

The Works . . . Dublin: 1735. V. 42

The Works of J.S., D.D., D.S.P.D. Dublin: 1735/38/41. V. 38; 45

The Works. Dublin: 1735-46. V. 37

The Works . . . Comprising: Miscellanies (11 volumes), Travels into Several Remote Nations of the World, (1 volume) The Works (5 volumes) and A Tale of a Tub . . . London: 1751-65. V. 37

The Works. London: 1755-65. V. 40

The Works of Dr. Jonathan Swift. Edinburgh & Glasgow: 1756. V. 41; 42

The Works . . . (with) Letters written by the Late Jonathan Swift, D.D. and Several of His friends from the Year 1703 to 1740. London: 1765-75. V. 37

The Works . . . London: 1768. V. 40; 43

The Works of Dr. Jonathan Swift . . . London: 1768/75/69/8/76. V. 46

The Works.. London: 1768-79. V. 40

The Works of the Rev. Jonathan Swift, D.D . . . London: 1801. V. 41; 46

The Works . . . London: 1803. V. 39

Works. London: 1808. V. 38

The Works. Edinburgh: 1824. V. 37; 46

Works. With Notes and a Life of the Author by Sir Walter Scott. London: 1883. V. 38

SWIFT, LINDSAY

Brook Farm, Its Members, Scholars and Visitors. New York: 1900. V. 43

SWIFT, THEOPHILUS

Animadversions on the Fellows of Trinity College. Dublin: 1794. V. 40

SWILDENS, JOHAN HENDRIK

Vaderlandsch A-B Boek Voor de Nederlandsche Jeugd. Amsterdam: 1781. V. 42

THE SWIMMER'S and Skater's Guide, Containing Rules, Founded on Experience for Acquring a Perfect Knowledge. Derby: 1838? V. 46

SWINBURNE, ALGERNON CHARLES 1837-1909

Astrophel and Other Poems. London: 1894. V. 37; 38; 41; 43; 44; 46

Atalanta in Calydon. London: 1865. V. 38; 39; 43; 44; 46

Atalanta in Calydon. Boston: 1866. V. 39; 44

Atalanta in Calydon. London: 1866. V. 44; 46

Atalanta in Calydon. Hammersmith: 1894. V. 38; 39; 42; 46

Atalanta in Calydon. London: 1894. V. 37; 45

Atalanta in Calydon. Portland: 1897. V. 44

Atalanta in Calydon. London: 1923. V. 41; 42

Bothwell: a Tragedy. London: 1874. V. 40

A Century of Roundels. London: 1883. V. 38; 42; 46

Charles Dickens. London: 1913. V. 46

Chastelard. London: 1865. V. 37; 39; 42; 43; 46

Chastelard. London: 1866. V. 44; 46

Dead Love. London: 1890. V. 42

Dolores. Maastricht: 1933. V. 42

Erechteus: A Tragedy. London: 1876. V. 37

Essays and Studies. London: 1876. V. 45

Grace Darling. London: 1893. V. 38; 40; 46

Hymn to Prosperine. 1944. V. 43

Hymn to Proserpine. London: 1944. V. 37; 39; 40; 41

Hymn to Prosperpine. Waltham St. Lawrence: 1944. V. 46

Laus Veneris and Other Poems and Ballads. New York: 1866. V. 45

Laus Veneris. Waltham St. Lawrence: 1921. V. 45

Laus Veneris. 1948. V. 42

Laus Veneris. London: 1948. V. 37; 38; 39; 40; 42

Laus Veneris. Waltham St. Lawrence: 1948. V. 46

Laus Veneris. Paris: 1956. V. 43

Locrine, a Tragedy. London: 1887. V. 40; 41; 42

Lucretia Borgia. London: 1942. V. 37; 43

Lucretia Borgia. Waltham St. Lawrence: 1942. V. 40; 44; 45; 46

Lucretia Borgia. London: 1947. V. 41

Marino Faliero. London: 1885. V. 41; 43

Note of an English Republican on the Muscovite Crusade. London: 1867. V. 40

Note of an English Republican on the Muscovite Crusade. London: 1876. V. 43

A Note on Charlotte Bronte. London: 1877. V. 37; 45; 46

Notes on Poems and Reviews. London: 1866. V. 38; 40; 41; 46

Ode on the Proclamation of the French Republic. London: 1870. V. 41

On the Cliffs. Lexington: 1980. V. 42; 43; 44; 46

Pasiphae. 1950. V. 43

Pasiphae, a Poem. London: 1950. V. 38; 39; 41; 43

Pasiphae a Poem. Waltham St. Lawrence: 1950. V. 44

Poems and Ballads. London: 1866. V. 43; 44; 46

Poems and Ballads. Second Series. London: 1878. V. 43; 45

Poems. London: 1904. V. 39

The Poems of Algernon Charles Swinburne. New York: 1904. V. 37; 40; 41; 44; 46

The Poems and Tragedies. London: 1904-06. V. 46

The Poems of . . . London: 1904/1905-06. V. 38; 41; 46

The Poems. London: 1909. V. 46

The Poems of . . . London: 1909. V. 39

The Poems of Swinburne. London: 1928. V. 41

Poems et Ballades. Paris. V. 43; 44

Poems and Ballads. (with) Poems and Ballads Second Series. London: 1866 & 1878. V. 37

The Queen Mother. Rosamond. Two Plays. London: 1860. V. 45

The Queen Mother and Rosamond. London: 1866. V. 40; 41

The Queen Mother and Rosamund . . . London: 1868. V. 41

A Record of Friendship. London: 1910. V. 40

Rondeaux Parisiens. London: 1917. V. 46

Rosamund, Queen of the Lombards a Tragedy. London: 1899. V. 44

Sea Song and River Rhyme from Chaucer to Tennyson. London: 1887. V. 38

Selected Poems. London: 1928. V. 37; 40; 41; 42; 43; 45; 46

A Sequence of Sonnets on the Death of Robert Browning. London: 1890. V. 37

Shelley. Worcester: 1973. V. 43

A Song of Italy. London: 1867. V. 38; 39; 41

SWINBURNE, ALGERNON CHARLES 1837-1909 continued

A Song of Italy. Portland: 1904. V. 40; 43

Songs Before Sunrise. London: 1871. V. 37; 38; 39; 40; 41; 44; 46

Songs of the Springtides. New York: 1880. V. 41

Songs Before Sunrise. 1901. V. 45

Songs Before Sunrise. Portland: 1901. V. 43

Songs Before Sunrise. 1909. V. 46

Songs Before Sunrise. London: 1909. V. 46

Songs Before Sunrise. New York: 1909. V. 42

The Spring-Tide of Life. Poems of Childhood. London: 1918. V. 37; 38; 39; 40; 41; 44; 45

The Springtide of Life. Philadelphia: 19128. V. 45

The Springtide of Life; Peoms of Childhood. Preface by Edmund Gosse. London: (1918). V. 37

The Springtide of Life. Philadelphia: 1918. V. 37; 41; 42; 46

Studies in Prose and Poetry. London: 1894. V. 46

Studies in Song. London: 1880. V. 37

A Study of Ben Johnson. London: 1889. V. 46

Tristram of Lyonesse and other Poems. London: 1882. V. 37

The Two Knights and Other Poems. London: 1918. V. 46

Two Unpublished Manuscripts, De Monumentis Epilaphiisque Mortuorum and Limits of Experience, Written During His College Years at Oxford (1857-58). San Francisco: 1927. V. 39; 41; 46

Under the Microscope. London: 1872. V. 37

Unpublished Verses. V. 39

Unpublished Verses. London. V. 42

Unpublished Verses (1866). London: 1888. V. 44

Wearieswa': a Ballad. London: 1917. V. 46

William Blake. London: 1868. V. 41; 45

A Word for the Navy. London: 1887. V. 37; 38; 40

Works. London: 1905-13. V. 46

The Complete Works. London: 1925. V. 38

SWINBURNE, CHARLES ALFRED

A Descriptive Catalogue of a Collection of Water-Colour Pictures and Painter-Etchers' Art at Beech-Hurst, Andover. London: 1900. V. 42; 43

SWINBURNE, HENRY

Travels Through Spain, in the Years 1775 and 1776. London;: 1779. V. 43

Travels in the Two Sicilies, in the Years 1777, 1778, 1779 and 1780. London: 1790. V. 42

Travels in Two Sicilies . . . in the Years 1777, 1778, 1779 and 1780. London: 1783-85. V. 37

A Briefe Treatise of Testaments and Last Wills . . . London: 1635. V. 38; 40

A Treatise of Testaments and Last Wills, Compiled Out of the Laws Ecclesiastical, Civil and Canon . . . In the Savoy: 1743. V. 45

SWINBURNE, LAWRENCE

The Royal Navy. London: 1907. V. 44

SWINDELLS, RUPERT

A Summer Trip to the Island of Saint Michael, the Azores. London: 1877. V. 39

THE SWINDLER Detected: or Necessary Cautions to the Public: Giving a Minute Account of the Various Frauds and Impositions Practiced on the Honest and Industrious Tradesmen of this Metropolis. London: 1781. V. 46

SWINDLER, MARY HAMILTON

Ancient Painting. New Haven: 1929. V. 42; 44

SWINDLING Exposed from the Diary of William B. Moreau King of Fakirs. Methods of the Crooks Explained. History of the Worst Gang That Ever Infested This Country . . . A Volume of Intense Interest. Truth Stranger than Fiction. Syracuse: 1907. V. 40

SWINEFORD, A. P.

Alaska Its History, Climate and Natural Resources. Chicago: 1898. V. 39

SWINFEN, CAROLINE

Helmet and Shako, or the Miseries of Living in a Garrison Town. London: 1865. V. 37

SWING, GILBERT S.

Events in the Life and History of the Swing Family. Camden: 1889. V. 46

SWINHOE, ROBERT

Narrative of the North China Campaign of 1860 . . . London: 1861. V. 45

SWINNERTON, JIMMY

Hosteen Crotchetty or 'How a Good Heart Was Born.' Palm Desert: 1965. V. 45

SWINNEY, SIDNEY

The Battle of Minden, a Poem. London: 1769. V. 39

SWINSTEAD, JOHN HOWARD

A Parish on Wheels. London: 1897. V. 39; 45

SWINSTEAD, MARGARET HONOR

The Affectionate Parent's Gift. Ditchling: 1928. V. 40; 41

SWINTON, ANDREW

Travels into Norway, Denmark and Russia. Dublin: 1792. V. 42

SWINTON, ERNEST

Twenty Years After: the Battlefields of 1914-18 Then and Now. London: 1936-38. V. 46

SWINTON, ERNEST DUNLOP

The Defence of Duffer's Drift. London: 1904. V. 42

SWINTON, GEORGE

Eskimo Sculpture. By George Swinton. Toronto: (1965). V. 37

SWINTON, JOHN d. 1799

A Proposal for Uniformity of Weights and Measures in Scotland by Execution of the Laws Now in Force with Tables of the English Standards. Edinburgh: 1789. V. 41

A Proposal for Uniformity of Weights and Measures in Scotland, by Execution of the Laws Now in Force. Edinburgh: 1779. V. 37; 42

SWIRDOFF, PAUL

Portraits from German Intellectual Life: Portraits from German Economic Life. Pfullingen: 1966-7. V. 39

SWIRE, HERBERT

The Voyage of the 'Challenger'. N.P.: 1938. V. 41

The Voyage of the Challenger. Waltham St. Lawrence: 1938. V. 42; 46

The Voyage of the Challenger. London;: 1938. V. 37; 42

SWISHER, JAMES

How I Know, or Sixteen Years Eventful Experience. Cincinnati: 1880. V. 37; 43

How I Know or 16 Years' Eventful Experience. Cincinnati: 1881. V. 45

SWISHER, JOHN M.

The Swisher Memoirs. San Antonio: 1932. V. 37; 43; 45; 46

SWISSHELM, JANE GREY

Half a Century. Chicago: 1880. V. 41

SWITZER, STEPHEN

A Compedious Method for raising of the Italian Brocoli, Spanish Cardoon, Celeriac, Finochi, and other Foreign Kitchen-Vegetables. As Also an Account of the La Lucerne, ... and of Mr. Liveing's Manure; . . . . London: 1731. V. 39

A Compendious Method for the Raising of the Italian Brocoli, Spanish Cardoon, Celeriac, Fenochi . . . London: 1728. V. 42

An Introduction to a General System of Hydrostaticks and Hydraulicks, Philosophical and Practical. London: 1729. V. 38; 40; 44

The Nobleman, Gentleman and Gardener's Recreation. London: 1715. V. 38

The Practical Fruit Gardener . . . London: 1724. V. 37; 41; 45

The Practical Kitchen Gardiner, or a New and Entire System of Directions for His Employment in the Melonry . . . London: 1727. V. 41; 42; 45

The Practical Fruit-Gardener. London: 1731. V. 37; 38

SWITZLER, WILLIAM F.

Switzler's Illustrated History of Missouri, from 1541 to 1877. St. Louis: 1879. V. 42

SWOOPE, ROLAND D.

Twentieth Century History of Clearfield County, Pennsylvania and Representative Citizens. Chicago: 1911. V. 41

SYDENHAM, CHARLES LORD

Memoirs, With a Narrative of His Administration in Canada. London: 1843. V. 42

SYDENHAM, G. F.

The History of the Sydenham Family. London: 1928. V. 38

SYDENHAM, HUMPHREY

Sermons Upon Solemne Occasions. London: 1637. V. 38

SYDENHAM, THOMAS 1624-1689

Epistolae Responsoriae Duae . . . London: 1680. V. 46

Medecine Pratique, Avec des Notes. Paris: 1784. V. 44

Observationes Medicae Circa Morborum Acutorum Historiam et Curationem. London: 1676. V. 42

Opera Omnia Medica. Padua: 1700. V. 40

SYDENHAM, THOMAS 1624-1689 continued

Opera Universa. Leyden: 1726. V. 38; 45

Opera Universa. Lugduni Batavorum: 1726. V. 44

Opera Medica, in Tomos Duos Divisa. Genevae: 1749. V. 39

Opera Universa . . . Leiden: 1754. V. 45

Opera Medica. Geneva: 1757. V. 44

Opera Omnia. London: 1844. V. 42

Dr. Sydenham's Practice of Physick. London: 1695. V. 38

Praxis Medica Experimentalis. Lipsiae: 1695. V. 38; 44

Praxis Medica Experimentalis, sive Opuscula Universa . . . Lipsiae: 1711. V. 40

Praxis Medica Experimentalis with Opuscula Universa. Leipsic: 1695. V. 37

Processus Integri In Morbis Fere Omnibus Curandis. London: 1726. V. 38; 41; 45; 46

Tractatus de Podagra et Hydrope. London: 1683. V. 41; 45; 46

The Whole Works. London: 1696. V. 42

The Whole Works of that Excellent Practical Physician, Dr. Thomas Sydenham . . . London: 1719. V. 42

The Whole Works . . . London: 1740. V. 40

The Whole Works . . . Wherein not only the History and Cure of acute Diseases are treated of, after a new and accurate Method; but also the shortest and safest way of curing most Chronical Diseases. London: 1734. V. 37; 40

The Entire Works of Dr. Thomas Sydenham. London: 1742. V. 39

The Entire Works of . . . London: 1753. V. 42

The Works of Thomas Sydenham, M.D., on Acute and Chronic Diseases. Philadelphia: 1809. V. 37; 40

The Works of Thomas Sydenham. London: 1848. V. 41

The Works of Thomas Sydenham. London: 1848-50. V. 41; 42; 45

SYDNEY

Catalogue of the Sydney Collection at Frognal, Chislehurst, Kent . . . London: 1915. V. 40

SYDNEY, ALGERNON

Discourses Concerning Government . . . with His Letters. Trial, Apology and Some Memoirs of His Life. London: 1763. V. 46

The Letters of Algernon Sydney, In Defence of Civil Liberty and Against Encroachments of Military Despotism . . . Richmond: 1830. V. 38

SYDNEY, PHILIP

The Sonnets. London: 1898. V. 40

SYEDS, STEPHEN

Mohammed Aben Alamar or the Invention of the Morrish Arch. London: 1905. V. 41

SYERS, ROBERT

The History of Everton. Liverpool: 1830. V. 39

SYKES, ARTHUR ASHLEY

An Essay on the Nature, Design and Origin of Sacrifices. London: 1748. V. 44

SYKES, CHRISTOPHER

Dates and Parties. London: 1955. V. 38

Evelyn Waugh: a Biography. London: 1975. V. 38; 40

Strange Wonders - Tales of Travel. London: 1937. V. 38

Troubled Loyalty. London: 1968. V. 37

SYKES DAVIES, HUGH

Petron. London: 1935. V. 42

SYKES, HENRY

Manual of Penmanship. Manchester: 1897. V. 40

SYKES, MARK MASTERMAN

Catalogue of the Splendid Curious and Extensive Library (Parts I-III). London: 1824. V. 45

SYKES, PERCY

A History of Persia. London: 1921. V. 37; 43; 46

A History of Persia. London: 1930. V. 39; 45

SYLBURGIUS, FRIDERICUS 1536-1596

Etymologicum Magnum. Heidelberg: 1594. V. 38; 45

SYLVESTER, CHARLES

The Philosophy of Domestic Economy. Nottingham: 1819. V. 37; 38

Report on Rail Roads and Locomotive Engines, Addressed to the Chairman of the Committee of the Liverpool and Manchester Projected Rail-Road. Liverpool: 1825. V. 46

SYLVESTER, HERBERT M.

Indian Wars of New England. Boston: 1910. V. 38; 42; 45

Indian Wars of New England. Cleveland: 1910. V. 38

SYLVIUS AMBIANUS, F.

Lucubrationes in M. Tullii Ciceronis Orationes Aliquot Pars Prima. Venice: 1537. V. 38

SYLVIUS, FRANCISCUS DE LE BOE, called 1614-1672

Institvtionvm in Artem Oratoriam Centvriae Tres . . . Cologne: 1589. V. 42

Opera Medica. Amsterdam: 1679. V. 42; 44

SYLVIUS, JACQUES DUBOIS

Ordo et Ordinis RAtio in Legendis Hippocratis et Galeni Libris. Paris: 1541. V. 44

SYM, JOHN 1581?-1637

Lifes Preservative Against Self-Killing. London: 1637. V. 45

SYMBOLUM Apostolicum. Paris: 1927. V. 38; 40

SYMBOLUM Duodecim Apostolorum Domini Nostri Jesu Christi Secundum Unam Quamaque Ipsius Symboli Dictionem Eleganter Metriceque Compositum Atque Prosaice Expositum. 1510? V. 40

SYME, JAMES

Observations in Clinical Surgery. Edinburgh: 1862. V. 42

SYME, PATRICK

A Treatise on British Song Birds. Edinburgh: 1823. V. 37; 38; 40

Werners Nomenclature of Colours. Edinburgh: 1814. V. 37; 44

SYMEONI, GABRIEL 1509-1575.

Dialogo pio et speculativo. Lyon: 1560. V. 37

SYMEONOGLOU, SARANTIS

The Topography of Theoloes from the Bronze Age to Modern Times. Princeton: 1985. V. 40; 42; 44

SYMES, MICHAEL

An Account of an Embassy to the Kingdom of Ava, Sent by the Governor-General of India, in the Year 1795. London: 1800. V. 43; 44; 45

SYMMES, JOHN CLEVES

Symme's Theory of Concentric Spheres. Cincinnati: 1826. V. 38

SYMMES, THOMAS

A Brief History of the Battle Which Was Fought on the 8th of May, 1725 Between Capt. John Lovell, with His Associates, and a Body of Indians Under the Command of Paugus, Sachem of the Pigwacket Tribe. Portland: 1818. V. 40

Lovewell Lamented. Or, a Sermon Occason'd By the Fall of the Brave Capt. John Lovewell and Several of His Valiant Company, in the Late Heroic Action at Piggwackett . . . Boston: 1725. V. 44

SYMMONS, CHARLES

The Life of John Milton. London: 1810. V. 38; 41

The Life of John Milton. London: 1822. V. 37

SYMMONS, EDWARD

A Vindication of King Charles. London: 1648. V. 39; 46

SYMON, BISHOP OF ELY

A Commentary Upon the Third Book of Moses, Called Leviticus. London: 1698. V. 39

SYMONDS, ARTHUR

Frederick Baron Corvo. London: 1927. V. 40

SYMONDS, B.

A Treatise on Field Diversions. Norwich: 1776. V. 40; 43

A Treatise on Field Diversions. Yarmouth;: 1824. V. 43

A Treatise on Field Diversions. Yarmouth: 1924. V. 39

SYMONDS, EMILY MORSE d. 1936

Mrs. Delany, a Memoir, 1700-1788. London: 1900. V. 41

Social Caricature in the Eighteenth Century. London: 1905. V. 42; 45

Social Caricature in the Eighteenth Century. By George Paston (pseud). London: (1905). V. 37

SYMONDS, HENRY

Runs and Sporting Notes from Dorsetshire. Blandford: 1899. V. 39

SYMONDS, JOHN

Remarks Upon an Essay, intituled, The History of the Colonization of the Free States of Antiquity, Applied to the Present Contest Between Great Britain and her American Colonies. London: 1778. V. 38

SYMONDS, JOHN ADDINGTON 1840-1893

Animi Figura. London: 1882. V. 37; 39

The Escorial. A Prize Poem, Recited in the Theatre, Oxford. Oxford: 1860. V. 37; 39; 40; 44

SYMONDS, JOHN ADDINGTON 1840-1893 continued

Essays Speculative and Suggestive. London: 1890. V. 39; 41; 44; 46

In the Key of Blue and Other Prose Verse. London: 1893. V. 37; 41; 44; 45; 46

The Letters of . . . Detroit: 1967/9. V. 41

The Life of Michelangelo Buonarroti. London: 1893. V. 37; 39; 42; 45

Mediaeval Latin Student Songs, Rendered into English Verse . . . 1928. V. 38

Medieval Latin Students. San Francisco: 1928. V. 41

Miscellanies. London: 1871. V. 46

Our Life in the Swiss Highlands. London: 1892. V. 39

The Principles of Beauty. London: 1857. V. 41; 42; 44

The Principles of Beauty. London: 1857. V. 42

A Problem in Modern Ethics, Being an Enquiry into the Phenomenon of Sexual Inversion. N.P.: n.d.,. V. 41

A Problem in Greek Ethics. London: 1901. V. 37; 39; 45

A Problem in Modern Ethics. London: 1896. V. 39; 45

The Renaissance in Italy. London: 1871-72. V. 39

Renaissance in Italy. London: 1875-86. V. 39

Renaissance in Italy. London: 1877-86. V. 38

Renaissance in Italy. Italian Literature. The Fine Arts. The Revival of Learning. Age of the Despots. The Catholic Reaction. New York: 1881-1887. V. 37

Renaissance in Italy. London: 1897-98. V. 38

Renaissance in Italy. London: 1898-1902. V. 46

Sketches in Italy. Leipzig: 1883. V. 40

Verses. Bristol: 1871. V. 46

Verses. London: 1871. V. 37; 40; 42; 46

Walt Whitman. A Study. London: 1893. V. 41

Wine Women and Song. Portland: 1889. V. 45

SYMONDS, MARY

Needle-Work through the Ages. London: 1928. V. 38; 42; 44

SYMONDS, R. W.

English Furniture from Charles II to George II. London: 1929. V. 46

Furniture Making in Seventeenth and Eighteenth Century England. London: 1955. V. 37; 42

Masterpieces of English Furniture and Clocks. London: 1940. V. 37; 42

Thomas Tompion, His Life and Work. Batsford: 1951. V. 41

Thomas Tompion. His Life and Work. London: 1951. V. 39; 40

Thomas Tompion His Life and Work. 1951. V. 37

Victorian Furniture. London: 1965. V. 39

SYMONDS, THOMAS W.

Report of an Examination of the Upper Columbia River and the Territory In Its Vicinity in September and October 1771. Washington: 1882. V. 39

SYMONS, ALPHONSE JAMES ALBERT

Emin the Governor of Equatoria. London: 1928. V. 39; 43

An Episode in the Life of the Queen of Sheba. N.P.: 1929. V. 39; 43

H. M. Stanley. London: 1933. V. 44

The Nonesuch Century. London: 1936. V. 38; 40; 41; 46

The Quest for Corvo. London: 1934. V. 38; 41; 43; 45; 46

SYMONS, ARTHUR 1865-1945.

Amoris Victima. London: 1897. V. 37

Aubrey Beardsley. London: 1898. V. 37; 38; 43; 44

Confessions a Study in Pathology. New York: 1930. V. 38; 39; 41

Days and Nights. London: 1889. V. 37

Figures of Several Centuries. London: 1916. V. 45

London. A Book of Aspects. Minneapolis: 1908. V. 45

London. A Book of Aspects. 1909. V. 40

London. A Book of Aspects. London: 1909. V. 42

Mes Souvenirs. Chapelle-Reanville: 1929. V. 39

Notes on Joseph Conrad. London: 1926. V. 39; 43

Notes on Joseph Conrad with Some Unpublished Letters. London: 1925. V. 38

Persian Nights - A Book of Essays. London: 1926. V. 38

Poems. New York: 1927. V. 41

The Romantic Movement in English Poetry. London: 1909. V. 44

The Romantic Movement in English Poetry. New York: 1909. V. 44

Silhouettes; Poems. London: 1896. V. 40

Spiritual Adventures. London: 1905. V. 41; 42

Studies in Modern Painters. New York: 1925. V. 41

Studies in Strange Souls: Rossetti & Swinburne. London: 1929. V. 42

William Blake. London: 1907. V. 43

SYMONS, G. J.

The Eruption of Krakatoa, and Subsequent Phenomena. London: 1888. V. 40; 44

SYMONS, JELLINGER C.

Arts and Artisans at Home and Abroad; with Sketches of the Progress of Foreign Manufactures. Edinburgh: 1839. V. 39; 42; 46

SYMONS, JOHN

Observations on Vapor-Bathing and Its Effects . . . Bristol: 1766. V. 39

SYMONS, JULIAN

Confusions About X. London: 1940. V. 38

The Immaterial Murder Case. London: 1945. V. 38

A Man Called Jones. London: 1947. V. 38

SYMONS, R.

A Geographical Dictionary or Gazetteer of the County of Cornwall. Penzance: 1884. V. 40

SYMONS, THOMAS W.

Annual Report Upon the Improvement of Certain Rivers and Harbors in Oregon and Washington . . . Washington: 1892. V. 45

Report of an Examination of the Upper Columbia River and the Territory In Its Vicinity in September and October 1771. Washington: 1882. V. 42; 43

SYMONS, W. CHRISTIAN

The British Navy Past and Present. London: 1905. V. 41

SYMONS, WILLIAM

The Practical Gager; or The Young Gager's Assistant. London: 1758. V. 42

SYMPHOSIUS

Aenigmata Symposii Poetae Cvm Scholis Iosephi Castalionis. Rome: 1581. V. 38

SYMPOSIUM Incolniana. Patriotic Speeches by Abraham Lincoln and Poems by Victor Hugo in French & English. Various Display Prints in Denby Types. New York: 1942. V. 39

SYMPSON, JOSEPH

Science Revived or the Vision of Alfred. Philadelphia: 1810. V. 39

SYMPSON, SAMUEL

A New Book of Cyphers, More Compleat and Regular than any Ever Publish'd. London: 1736. V. 39

SYMSON, ANDREW

Unio Politico-Poetico-Joco-Serie. Edinburgh: 1706. V. 41

SYMSON, ARCHIBALD 1564-1628

A Sacred Septenarie or, a Godly and Fruitful Exposition on the Seven Psalmes of Repentance. London: 1638. V. 38

SYNESIUS, BISHOP OF CYRENE

Opera Quae Extant Omnia. Paris: 1612. V. 44

SYNESIUS CYRENAEUS, BP. OF PTOLEMAIS

De Dono, ad Paeonium. Concio Secunda. Constitutio . . . Hymni. Basel: 1567. V. 37

(Greek title, Hymnoi). Paris;: 1570. V. 37

SYNGE, H.

Biological Aspects of Rare Plant Conservation. 1981. V. 39

SYNGE, JOHN MILLINGTON 1871-1909

The Aran Islands. Dublin: 1907. V. 43

The Aran Islands. London: 1907. V. 42

In Wicklow West Kerry and Connemara. Dublin: 1911. V. 41

The Playboy of the Western World. Dublin: 1907. V. 42

The Playboy of the Western World. Boston: 1911. V. 40

The Playboy of the Western World. London: 1927. V. 37

Poems and Translations. Dundrum: 1909. V. 40

Poems and Translations. New York: 1909. V. 44; 46

Poems and Translations. Churchtown, Dundrum: 1909. V. 37; 39

The Shadow of the Glen and Riders to the Sea. London: 1905. V. 45

The Tinker's Wedding. Dublin: 1907. V. 38

The Well of the Saints. New York: 1905. V. 37; 40; 41

The Works. Dublin: 1910. V. 37; 44

Works. Boston: 1912. V. 40; 42

SYNGRAPHEUS, POLYONIMUS

Schola Apiciana. Frankfurt: 1534. V. 38

SYNODO Diocesana, Que Celebro el Ilustrissimo Senor Doctor Don Manual de Alday Y Aspee, Obispo de Santiago de Chile . . . Con Licencia, en Lima: 1764. V. 40

SYNOPSIS Of the Military Career of Gen. Joseph Wheeler, Commander of the Cavalry Corps, Army of the West. New York: 1865. V. 44

SYPHER, J. R.

History of the Pennsylvania Reserve Corps. Lancaster: 1865. V. 42

SYR Isambrace. Hammersmith: 1897. V. 37

SYR Percecyvelle of Gales. Hammersmith: 1895. V. 40

SYR YSAMBRACE

Syr Ysambrace. Hammersmith: 1897. V. 45

SYRIACAE Linguae Prima Elementa. Antwerp: 1572. V. 41

A SYSTEM of Anatomy and Physiology with the Comparative Anatomy of Animals compiled from the Latest and Best Authors . . . The Lectures Delivered in the University of Edinburgh . . . A New Edition, with Additions . . . illustrated with Twenty . . . Edinburgh: 1795. V. 37; 38

A SYSTEM of Education for the Infant Kin of Rome, and Other French Princes of the Blood, Drawn up by the Emperial Council of State . . . London: 1820. V. 38; 39

A SYSTEM of Electrotherapeutics. Scranton: 1899-1900. V. 42

A SYSTEM of Punctuation, Prepared for the Students of East Tennessee University, April 1840. Knoxville: 1840. V. 39

SZARKOWSKI, JOHN

The Idea of Lewis Sullivan. Minneapolis: 1956. V. 45

SZECHENYI, ZSIGMOND, COUNT

Land of Elephants. London: 1935. V. 37; 38; 43; 44; 45

SZWEDZICKI, C.

Sioux Indian Painting . . . Nice: 1938. V. 44; 45

SZYK, ARTHUR

Ink and Blood. New York: 1946. V. 38; 39; 40; 41

The New Order. New York: 1941. V. 40; 41; 45; 46

SZYMONOWICZ, SZYMOND BENDONSKI

Poematia Avrea cum Antiquitate Comparanda Edita ex Bibliotheca Ioachim Morsi Accedit Vita et Obitvs Magni Ioannis Samoschi Patroni Simonidis. Leiden: 1619. V. 39

T

T., D.

Hieraginisticon; or, Corah's Doom, being an Answer to Two Letters of Enquiry Into the Grounds and Occasions of the Contempor of the Clergy and Religion . . . London: 1672. V. 44

T. EATON COMPANY, TORONTO

Special Gun Catalog 1906-1907. Toronto: 1906. V. 42

T., F.

The Wonders of a Week at Bath; in a Doggerel Address to the Hon. T. S----, from F. T-----, Esq. of that City. London: 1811. V. 41

T., H.

A Short Way to Know the World; or The Rudiments of Geography. London: 1712. V. 39

T. S. ELIOT: a Symposium for His Seventieth Birthday. London: 1958. V. 45

TA Hir Grace Her Majesties High Commissioner, an te Honorable Estates of Parlment. Te Address far te Fishers on te Highland Coasts, on All Uthers Inhapiting te Highlands, wha it ma Concern. Edinburgh: 1706. V. 41

TA Hir Grace Her Majesties High Commissioner, an te Honourable Estates of Parlment. Te Address far to Fisherson te Highland Coasts, an all Utters Inhabiting te Highlands, what it ma Concern. N.P.: 1706? V. 45

TABB, JOHN BANISTER 1845-1909.

Child Verse Poems Grave & Gay. Boston: 1899. V. 37

Lyrics. Boston: 1897. V. 37; 41

Poems by . . . Boston: 1894. V. 37; 42

TABBY, A., PSEUD.

The Fishes' Feast, with a Mermaid's Song, Dedicated to the Author of the 'Peacock at Home' with a Poetical Address. London: 1808. V. 39

TABER, CHARLES

New Bedford Fairhaven and Dartmouth Signal Book, 1853. New Bedford: 1853. V. 41

TABERNAEMONTANUS, JACOBUS THEODORUS, called d. 1590

Gewisse und Erfahren Practick, Wie Man Sich mit Goettlicher Hulfe vor der Pestilentz Hueten und Bewaren . . . Heydelberg: 1564. V. 37; 42; 44

Neuw Kreuterbuch Mit Schonen, Kunstlichen und Leblichen Figuren und Konterfeyten Aller Gewachss der Kreuter. Frankfurt a.M.: 1588. V. 41

LE TABLEAU de la Croix Represente dans Les Ceremonies de la Ste. Messe, Ensemble le Tresor de la Devotion aux Soufrances de N.S.J.C. Le Tout Enrichi de Belles Figures. Paris: 1651. V. 38; 39; 40; 45

TABLEAU Historique de la Revolution Francaise. Paris: 1791-1804. V. 40

TABLES for Renewing and Purchasing of the Leases of Cathedral-Churches and Colleges. (and) The Value of Church and College Leases Considered. London: 1722. V. 37

TABLES of the Value of Gold and Silver Per Troy Ouce, at Different Degrees of Fineness . . . Prepared by the San Francisco Assaying and Refining Works. San Francisco: 1867. V. 40

THE TABLET of Memory; Shewing Every Memorable Event in History, From the Earliest Period to the Year 1774, Classed Under Distinct Heads, With Their Dates . . . London: 1774. V. 43; 46

TABOR, ELIZA

Hester's Sacrifice. London: 1866. V. 44

TABOR, J. A.

On the Improvement of the Colne Navigation . . . Colchester: 1840. V. 45

TABOR, SILVER

Star of Blood. Denver. V. 43

TABULA Cebetis Graece, Arabice, Latine, Item Aurea Carmine Pythagorae, cum Paraphrasi Arabica, auctore Joh. Elichmann. Leiden: 1640. V. 37

TACHE, ALEXANDRE ANTONIN

Sketch of the North-West of America. Montreal: 1870. V. 44

TACITUS, CAIUS CORNELIUS

Opera, Recognavit, Emendavit, Supplementis Explevit, Notis, Dissertationibus, Tabulis Geographicis Illustravit Gabriel Brotier. Paris: 1771. V. 45

TACITUS, CORNELIUS

The Annales of Corenlius Tacitus, the Description of Germaine. London: 1605. V. 41

The Annales of Cornelius Tactitus. (with) The End of Nero and the Beginning of Galba . . . London: 1640. V. 46

Cornelii Taciti Historiae Augustae. Venice: 1497. V. 41

Cornelii Taciti de Vita et Moribus Julii Agricolae Liber. Hammersmith: 1900. V. 41

Cornelii Taciti De Vita et Moribus Iulii Agricolae Liber. London: 1900. V. 46

Historiae Augustae. Venice: 1497. V. 46

De Moribus Germanorum et De Vita Agricolae. Cantabrigiae: 1813. V. 43

(Opera). Cornelius Tacitus Exacta Cura Recognitus et Emendatus. Venice: 1534. V. 44

Opera. Paris: 1682. V. 40

Opera Omnia. London: 1790. V. 40

Opera. London: 1825. V. 40; 43

De Vita et Moribus Iulii Agricolae Liber. Hammersmith: 1900. V. 39; 42; 44

The Works . . . to Which are Prefixed Political Discourses Upon the author. London: 1728-31. V. 46

The Works of Cornelius Tacitus. London: 1793. V. 45

The Works of Cornelius Tacitus. London: 1805. V. 41

TACITUS, GAIUS CORNELIUS

The Annales of Cornelius Tacitus . . . The Life of Agricola. London: 1604-05. V. 38

The Ende of Nero and Beginning of Galba. London: 1591. V. 39

Historiarum Libri Quinque, ex I. Lipsii Editione cum not. et emend. H. Grotius. Leiden: 1640. V. 37

Opera Quae Exstant. Dublin: 1730. V. 37

Tacito Espanol, Ilustrado con Aforismos, por Don Baltasar Alamos de Barrientos. Madrid: 1614. V. 37; 38

TACITUS, PUBLIUS CORNELIUS

Opera Quae Extant. Paris: 1771. V. 45

TACKE, JOHANN

Academia Gissena Restavrata . Giessen: 1652. V. 40

TACKHOLM, V.

Flora of Egypt. 1973. V. 39

TACOMA And Vicinity. Tacoma: 1888. V. 39; 42; 45

TACOMA Illustrated . . . Chicago: 1889. V. 37; 42

TACOMA. The Pacific Terminus of the Northern Pacific Railroad. Tacoma: 1884. V. 37; 39; 42

TACOMA: The Western Terminus of the Northern Pacific Railroad. Tacoma: 1885. V. 46
TACOMA the Western Terminus of the Northern Pacific Railroad. Tacoma: 1889. V. 37

TACQUET, ANDREAS

Opera Mathematica. Antwerp: 1669. V. 38; 45

TACTITUS, CORNELIUS

De Vita et Moribus Iulii Agricolae Liber. London: 1900. V. 43

TAFEREEL, of Beschrying Van den Prachtigen. Tempel der Zang-Godinnen. Amsterdam: 1733. V. 45

TAFFRAIL, DORLING

Swept Channels. London: 1935. V. 44

TAFT, ALPHONSO

A Lecture on Cincinnati and Her Railroads. Cincinnati: 1850. V. 37

TAFT, LORADO

Modern Tendencies in Sculpture. Chicago: 1921. V. 46

TAFT, ROBERT

Artists and Illustrators of the Old West, 1850-1900. New York: 1953. V. 42; 44

Artists and Illustrators of the Old West: 1850-1900. New York & London: 1953. V. 41

TAFT, ROBERT A.

A Foreign Policy for Americans. New York: 1951. V. 38

TAGART, EDWARD

A Memoir of the Late Captain Peter Heywood, with Extracts from His Diaries and Correspondence. London: 1832. V. 40

TAGEWOOD, R.

Report of the Naval Advisory Board on the Mild steel Used in the Construction of he Hull, Boilers and Machinery of the Dolphin, Atlanta, Boston and Chicago . . . Washington: 1886. V. 44

TAGGARD, G.

May Days - An Anthology of Masses - Liberator Verse - 1912-1924. 1925. V. 43

TAGGARD, GENEVIEVE

For Eager Lovers. New York: 1922. V. 37; 40; 42

TAGGART, WILLIAM

Sermons by William Taggart, M.A. Strabane: 1788. V. 38

TAGLIENTE, GIOVANANTIO

Lo Presente Libro Insegna Le Vera Arte Delo Excelle te Scrivere de Diverse VArie Sorte di Litere Lequali se Fano '' Geometrica Ragione. Venice: 1546. V. 44

TAGLIENTE, GIOVANANTONIO

Lo Presente Libro Insegna La Vera Arte declo Excellente Scrivere . . . Venice: 1539. V. 40; 42; 46

Lo Presente Libro Insegna la Vera Arte Delo Exclele(n)te Scrivere de Diverse Varie Sorti di Litere. Venice: 1550. V. 45; 46

TAGLIENTI, GIOVANNI ANTONIO fl. 1540

Componimento di Parlamenti, Nuovamente Stamapto. Vineggia: 1537. V. 43

TAGORE, RABINDRANATH

Fruit Gathering. London: 1916. V. 44

Gitanjali. London: 1912. V. 42

The Post Office: a Play. 1914. V. 44

TAGORE, SIR RABINDRANATH 1861-

Fireflies. New York: 1922. V. 41

TAGORE, SOURINDRO MOHUN

The Orders of Knighthood, British and Foreign, with a Brief Review of the Titles of Rank and Merit in Ancient Hindusthan. Calcutta: 1884. V. 39

A TAHITIAN and English Dictionary, with Introductory Remarks on the Polynesian Language, and a Short Grammar of the Tahitian Dialect. Tahiti: 1851. V. 40

TAILFER, PATRICK

A New Voyage to Georgia. London: 1737. V. 45

A True and Historical Narrative of the Colony of Georgia in America, from the First Settlement Thereof Until this Present Period . . . Charles-Town: 1741. V. 37; 38; 40; 45

TAILLANDIER, ALPHONSE HONORE

Traite de la Legislation Concernant les manufactures et Ateliers Dangereux, Insalubres et Incommodes. Paris: 1827. V. 45

TAILLANDIER, YVON

Indelible Miro. New York: 1962. V. 46

Indelible Miro: Aquatints, Drawings, Drypoints, Etchings, Lithographs, Book Illustrations, Posters. New York: 1972. V. 41

TAILLEPIED, NOEL

A Treatise of Ghosts. (1933). V. 37

TAINE, J.

Seeds of Life. 1951. V. 43

TAISNIER, JEAN

Opusculum Perpetua Memoria Dignissimum, de Magnete, de Natura Magnetis, et Eius Effectibus. Cologne: 1562. V. 38; 41

TAIT, GEORGE

A Summary of the Powers and Duties of a Justice of the Peace of Scotland . . . Edinburgh: 1816. V. 40

TAIT, STEPHEN

A Room with a View. A Play . . . London: 1951. V. 41

TAIT, THOMAS

Bamburgh Castle; a Poem, in two parts. Edinburgh: 1818. V. 41; 42

TAKANO, S.

Birds of Japn in Photographs. Tokyo: 1981. V. 37; 38

TAKI, SEIICHI

Japanese Fine Art. Tokyo: 1931. V. 44

TALAMANTEZ, INES

Tse-Gihi. Del Mar: 1975. V. 45

TALBERT, BRUCE J.

Examples of Ancient and Modern Furniture, Metal Work, Tapestries, Decorations, &c. Birmingham: 1876. V. 37

TALBOT, B.

The New Art of Land Measuring; or, a Turnpike Road to Practical Surveying . . . Wolverhampton: 1779. V. 42

TALBOT-BOOTH, E. C.

Merchant Ships, 1942. London: 1942. V. 38

TALBOT, CATHERINE

The Works of the Late Miss Catherine Talbot. London: 1812. V. 38

TALBOT, CHARLES 1685-1737

Cases in Equity During the Time of the Late Lord Chancellor Talbot (1730-1737). London: 1741. V. 40

TALBOT, CLARE RYAN

Historic California in Bookplates. Los Angeles: 1936. V. 46

TALBOT, EDWARD ALLEN

Five Years' Residence in the Canadas. London: 1824. V. 37; 38; 40; 41; 44; 46

Five Years Residence in the Canadas: Including a Tour through Part of the United States of America, in the Year 1823. London: 1824. V. 41

TALBOT, ELEANOR W.

My Lady's Casket of Jewels and Flowers for Her Adorning. Boston: 1885. V. 38; 40; 41

TALBOT, FREDERICK A.

Making Good in Canada. London: 1912. V. 46

The Making of a Great Canadian Railway. London: 1912. V. 43

TALBOT, GILBERT WALTER LYTTELTON

Born September 1 1891. Killed in Action at Hooge, July 30, 1915. London: 1916. V. 46

TALBOT, H. F.

The Process of Calotype Photogenic Drawing, Communicated to the Royal Society, June 10th, 1841. London: 1841? V. 40

TALBOT, J. H.

A Biographical History of Medicine. New York: 1970. V. 41

TALBOT, JAMES

Instructions to a Painter, Upon the Death and Funeral of Her Late Majesty Q. Mary of Blessed Memory. London: 1695. V. 40; 43

TALBOT, MARY ELIZABETH

Rurality. Providence: 1830. V. 44

TALBOT, THEODORE

The Journals of . . . 1843 and 1849-52 with the Fremont Expedition of 1843 and with the First Military Company in Oregon Territory 1849-1852. Portland: 1931. V. 46

TALBOT, THOMAS

Granvilles. London: 1882. V. 40; 41

TALBOT, WILLIAM

Narrative of the Whole of His Proceedings Relative to Jonthan Britain. Bristol: 1772. V. 38

TALBOT, WILLIAM HENRY FOX

English Etymologies. London: 1847. V. 41

The Pencil of Nature. New York: 1969. V. 40

THE TALE of Ali Baba and the Forty Thieves. New York: 1949. V. 46

A TALE of the West, or, Life with a Sister. Providence: 1846. V. 45

TALES for Youth; in Thirty Poems; to Which are Annexed, Historical Remarks and Moral Applications in Prose. London: 1794. V. 44

TALES for Youth, or the High Road to Renown, through the Paths of Pleasure. London: 1797. V. 40

TALES from Blackwood. London: 1860. V. 37
TALES from Blackwood. London: 1885. V. 43

TALES From Switzerland. London: 1827. V. 40

TALES of Adventure and Stories of Travel of Fifty Years Ago. London: 1893. V. 37

TALES of Frontier Life as Told by Those Who Remember the Days of the Territory and Early Statehood of Washington. Washington: 1937-38. V. 44

TALES of Gauber-Spa by Several American Authors. New York: 1832. V. 39

TALES of Our Coast. London: 1896. V. 46

TALES of Terror: with an Introductory Dialogue. Dublin: 1801. V. 37

TALES of the Cordelier Metamorphosed, as Narrated in a Manuscript from the Borromeo Collection . . . London: 1821. V. 45

TALES of the Wars; or Naval and Military Chronicle. London: 1836/8/8/9/40. V. 46

TALES of the Wonder Club. London. V. 43

TALES Of Truth, by a Lady Under the Patronage of the Duchess of York. London: 1800. V. 37

TALFOURD, THOMAS NOON
Final Memoirs of Charles Lamb . . . London: 1848. V. 40; 44; 46
Ion: a Tragedy. London: 1835. V. 40; 41; 43; 44; 45
Ion. London: 1836. V. 45
Ion: A Tragedy. To which are added a few Sonnets. London: (1835). V. 37

TALIAFERRO, HARDEN E.
Fisher's River (North Carolina) Scenes and Characters. New York: 1859. V. 38

TALIESIN
The Poems of Taliesin. 1989. V. 41

THE TALISMAN; Or, Boquet of Literature and the Fine Arts (for 1831). London: 1831. V. 42

TALLACK, WILLIAM
The California Overland Express: The Longest Stage-Ride in the World. London: 1865. V. 37
Friendly Sketches in America. London: 1861. V. 38; 42

TALLAPOOSA LAND, MINING AND MANUFACTURING CO.
Prospectus of the Tallapoosa Land, Mining and Manufacturing Co., Tallapoosa, Haralson Co., Georgia. Tallapoosa: 1887. V. 42

TALLEMANT, GEDEON, SIEUR DES REAUX 1619-1692
Love-Tales from Tallemant. London: 1925. V. 39

TALLENT, ANNIE DONNA
The Black Hills; or, the Last Hunting Ground of the Dakotahs. St. Louis: 1899. V. 39; 41; 42; 45

TALLENTS, FRANCIS
A View of Universal History, From the Creation, to the Destruction of Jerusalem by Adrian, in the Year of the World 4084, and of Christ 135. (with) A View of Universal History, From the Birth of Jesus Christ our Lord, to the Year 1680. N.P.,: 1685). V. 38

TALLENTYRE, S. G.
The Friends of Voltaire. London: 1906. V. 45
The Life of Voltaire. London: 1903. V. 37; 38

TALLEY, MANSFIELD KIRBY
Portrait Painting in England . . . 1981. V. 44

TALLEY, W.
The New Windsor Comic Songster. Windsor: 1872. V. 39

TALLEYRAND-PERIGORD, CHARLES MAURICE DE, PRINCE DE BENEVENT 1754-1838
Memoir Concerning the Commercial Relations of the United States with England. London: 1806. V. 37; 39; 44
Memoir Concerning the Commercial Relations of the United States With England . . . Boston: 1809. V. 41; 42
Memoirs. London: 1891-92. V. 39
Memoirs of the Prince de Talleyrand. Paris: 1895. V. 46

TALLEYRAND-PERIGORD, DOROTHEE VON BIRON, DUCHESSE DE 1793-1863
Memoirs of the Duchesse de Dino (Duchesse de Talleyrand) . . . London: 1909-10. V. 42

TALLIS, JOHN & CO.
Tallis's History and Description of the Crystal Palace and the Exhibition of the World's Industry in 1851. London: 1851. V. 38

TALLIS'S History and Description of the Crystal Palace, and the Exhibition of the World's Industry in 1851; illustrated by beautiful steel engravings, from original drawings and daguerreotypes, by Beard, Mayal, etc., etc. New York/London: (ca. 1851). V. 37

TALLMADGE, BENJAMIN
Memoir of Colonel Benjamin Talmadge. New York: 1904. V. 39; 46

TALLY-HO Back! London: 1931. V. 41

A TALLY of Types Cut for Machine Composition & Introduced at the University Press Cambridge 1922-1932. Cambridge: 1953. V. 40

TALMAN, JAMES J.
Loyalist Narratives from Upper Canada. Toronto: 1946. V. 37; 41; 45

TALMUD
The Living Talmud. New York: 1960. V. 40
New Edition of the Babylonian Talmud. Boston: 1903. V. 40

TALWAR, K.
Indian Pigment Paintings on Cloth. (Volume III Historic Textiles of India at the Calico Museum). Ahmedabad: 1979. V. 37

TAM, H. T.
Saigon 7. Vietnam: 1968. V. 45

TAMANUKI, K.
Beautiful Beetles of the World. Tokyo: 1970. V. 37

TAMAYO DE VARGAS, THOMAS
Restauracion de la Ciudad del Salvador, i Baia de Todos-Sanctos, en la Provincia del Brasil . . . Madrid: 1628. V. 45

TAMAYO, RUFINO
Apocalypse de Saint Jean. Monaco: 1959. V. 37; 39

TAMPLIN, J. M. A.
The Lambeth and Southwark Volunteers. London: 1965. V. 42

TAN, AMY
The Joy Luck Club. New York: 1989. V. 43
The Kitchen God's Wife. New York: 1991. V. 46

TANAKA, S.
Figures and Descriptions of the Fishes of Japan. Tokyo: 1911-58. V. 42; 43

TANARA, VICENZO
L'Economia del Cittadino in Villa. Libri VII. Bologna: 1651. V. 37

TANARA, VINCENZO
L'Economia Del Cittadino in Villa Di . . . Bologna: 1644. V. 38

TANARON, PIETRO PAOLO
L'Oestericia Ovvero l'Arte di Raccogliere i Parti . . . Florence: 1768. V. 42

TANAVOLI, PARVIZ
Shahsavan: Iranian Rugs and Textiles. New York: 1985. V. 40

TANCOCK, JOHN L.
The Sculpture of Auguste Rodin: The Collection of the Rodin Museum of Philadelphia. Philadelphia: 1976. V. 40

TANCOIGNE, J. M.
A Narrative of a Journey into Persia, and Residence at Teheran . . . London: 1820. V. 37; 38; 41

TANEY, ROGER BROOKE
The Dred Scott Decision. New York: 1859. V. 45

TANGE, KENZO
Ise, Prototype of Japanese Architecture. Cambridge: 1965. V. 41; 46
Katsura: Tradition and Creation in Japanese Architecture. New Haven: 1960. V. 41

TANGUAY DE LA BOISSIERE, C. C.
Observations On the Dispatch Written the 16th January 1797. By Mr. Pickering, Secretary of State of the United States of America. Philadelphia: 1797. V. 38; 40; 42; 46

TANGYE, H. LINCOLN
In New South Africa: Travels in the Transvaal and Rhodesia. London: 1896. V. 39; 40; 42; 43

TANGYE, RICHARD
Notes of My Fourth Voyage to the Australian Colonies, Including Australia, Tasmania and New Zealand. Birmingham: 1886. V. 40
Reminiscences of Travel in Australia, America and Egypt. London: 1884. V. 38

TANINDI, ZEREN
The Topkapi Saray Museum: the Albums and Illustrated Manuscripts. London: 1986. V. 39

TANKERVILLE, LOUISA WATERFORD, MARCHIONESS, & COUNTESS OF
Life Songs. London: 1884. V. 42

TANNAHILL, ROBERT

Poems and Songs Chiefly in the Scottish Dialect. London: 1815. V. 37; 46

TANNEHILL, WILKINS

Sketches of the History of Literature, from the Earliest Period to the Revival of Letters in the Fifteenth Century. Nashville: 1827. V. 41

TANNENBAUM, S. A.

Shakspere Forgeries in the Revels Accounts. New York: 1928. V. 43

TANNER, CLARA LEE

Southwest Indian Painting. Tucson: 1957. V. 41

TANNER, H. S.

The American Traveller, or Tourists' and Emigrants' Guide through the United States . . . New York: 1844. V. 43

Memoir on the Recent Surveys, Observations and Internal Improvements, in the United States . . . Philadelphia: 1829. V. 43

TANNER, HEATHER

A Country Alphabet. London: 1984. V. 43

A Country Book of Days. London: 1986. V. 38; 44; 46

Wiltshire Village. London: 1939. V. 38; 46

TANNER, HENRY S.

The American Traveller, or Tourists' and Emigrants' Guide through the United States. New York: 1844. V. 38

The American Traaveller; or, Guide through the United States. Philadelphia: 1842. V. 37

A Description of the Canals and Rail Roads of the United States . . . New York: 1840. V. 42

Memoir on the Recent Surveys, Observations and Internal Improvements, in the United States . . . Philadelphia: 1829. V. 41; 42

Memoir on the Recent Surveys, Observations and Internal Improvements in the United States . . . Philadelphia: 1830. V. 38

Ohio and Indiana. Phi. V. 46

TANNER, J. M.

A Biographical Sketch of James Jensen. Salt Lake City: 1911. V. 42; 45

TANNER, JOHN

The Hidden Treasures of the Art of Physick; Fully Discovered: in Four Books. I. COntaining a Physical Description of Man. 2. The Causes, Signes, and Cures of all Diseases, incident to the Body. 3. The general Cure of Wounds, Tumours, and Ulcers . . . London: 1659. V. 37

TANNER, ROBIN

Robin Tanner: The Memorial Portfolio. London: 1989. V. 45

The More Angels Shall I Paint. London: 1991. V. 45

TANNER, THOMAS

Biblioteca Britannico-Hibernica . . . London: 1748. V. 44

Bibliotheca Britannico-Hibernica. Londini: 1748. V. 38

Notitia Monastica or A Short History of the Religious Houses in England and Wales. London: 1695. V. 38

Notitia Monastica or a Short History of the Religious Houses in England and Wales. Oxford: 1695. V. 38; 44

Notitia Monastica; or, An Account of All the Abbies, Priories and Houses of Friers, Formerly in England and Wales . . . Cambridge: 1787. V. 39

TANNER, V.

Outlines of the Geography, Life and Customs of Newfoundland-Labrador. Helsingfors (Helsinki): 1944. V. 38

Outlines of the Geography, Life and Customs of Newfoundland-Labrador. Helsinki: 1944, 1947. V. 40

TANSELLE, G. THOMAS

Guide to the Study of United States Imprints. Cambridge: 1971. V. 43

TANSER, H. A.

The Settlement of Negroes in Kent County, Ontario . . . Chatham: 1939. V. 41

TANSILL, ROBERT

A Free and Impartial Exposition of he Causes Which Led to the Failure of the Confederate States. Washington: 1865. V. 39; 42

TANSILLO, LUIGI

The Nurse, a Poem. Liverpool: 1798. V. 40

TANSLEY, A. G.

The British Islands and Their Vegetation. London: 1949. V. 45

TANS'UR, WILLIAM

A Compleat Melody; or the Harmony of the Sion. London: 1735. V. 42

The Elements of Musick Display'd . . . Rudimental, Practical, Philosophical, Historical and Technical. London: 1772. V. 37

Heaven on Earth . . . London: 1738. V. 42

The Royal Melody Compleat. London: 1764. V. 40

Sacred Mirth; or, the Pious Soul's Daily Delight. London: 1739. V. 40

TAPLEY, HARRIET SILVESTER

Salem Imprints 1768-1825: A History of the First Fifty Years of Printing in Salem, Massachusetts . . . Salem: 1927. V. 37; 45

TAPLIN, GEORGE

The Folklore, Manners, Customs and Languages of the South Australian Aborigines. Adelaide: 1879. V. 40

TAPLIN, WILLIAM

The Gentleman's Stable Directory; or, Modern System of Farriery. London: 1788/91. V. 37; 43

The Sporting Dictionary and Rural Repository of General Information Upon Every Subject Appertaining to the Sports of the Field. 1803. V. 43

The Sporting Dictionary, and Rural Repository of General Information Upon Every Subject Appertaining to the Sports of the Field. London: 1803. V. 37; 39; 40; 46

The Sportsman's Cabinet. London: 1803-04. V. 39; 40; 43

TAPPAN, WILLIAM B.

Poems. Philadelphia: 1822. V. 41

TAPPEN, GEORGE

Professional Observations on the Architecture of the Principle Ancient and Modern Buildings in France and Italy. London: 1806. V. 37

TAPPING, THOMAS

A Treatise on the Derbyshire Mining Customs and Mineral Court Act 1852 . . . London: 1854. V. 45

TARASCON, LEWIS ANASTASIUS

Petition of Lewis A. Tarascon (and others Praying the Opening of a Wagon Road from the River Missouri to the River Columbia. Washington: 1824. V. 37; 39; 40; 43; 46

TARAVAL, SIGISMUNDO

The Indian Uprising in Lower California 1734-1737. Los Angeles: 1931. V. 37; 38; 39; 41; 42; 43; 44; 45

TARBELL, HARLAN

The Tarbell Course in Magic. New York: 1946. V. 43

TARBELL, IDA MINERVA

The Florida Architecture of Addison Mizner. New York: 1928. V. 37; 38

The Life of Abraham Lincoln Drawn from Original Sources and Containin Many Speeches, Letters and Telegrams Hitherto Unpublished . . . New York: 1909. V. 38; 39

TARBUCK, EDWARD LANCE

The Builder's Practical Director. Leipzig & Dresden: 1855-58. V. 38; 40

The Encyclopaedia of Practical Carpentry and Joinery. Leipzig & Dresden: 1860s? V. 39

TARG, WILLIAM

Bibliophile in the Nursery, a Bookman's Treasury of Collector's Lore on Old and Rare Children's Books. Cleveland & New York: 1957. V. 37

TARKINGTON, BOOTH 1869-1946

Beasley's Christmas Party. New York: 1909. V. 37; 41; 42; 43; 44

Clarence: a Comedy in Four Acts. New York & London: 1921. V. 39

The Conquest of Canaan. New York: 1905. V. 37; 41; 42; 43; 44

The Fascinating Stranger and Other Stories. Garden City: 1923. V. 42; 46

The Fascinating Stranger and Other Stories. New York: 1923. V. 42

Gentle Julia. Garden City: 1922. V. 43

The Gentleman from Indiana. New York: 1899. V. 38; 39; 42; 43; 46

Lady Hamilton and Her Nelson. New York: 1945. V. 39; 42; 45

The Midlander. Garden City: 1923. V. 46

Monsieur Beaucaire. New York: 1900. V. 38

Monsieur Beaucaire. London: 1903. V. 46

Monsieur Beaucaire. New York: 1920. V. 39

Penrod. Garden City: 1914. V. 40; 41; 43; 44

Penrod. New York: 1914. V. 38; 39; 46

Penrod Jashber. Garden City: 1929. V. 37; 41; 42

Some Old Portraits. New York: 1939. V. 38; 39; 40; 42

The Turmoil. New York: 1915. V. 46

The Two Vanrevels. New York: 1902. V. 39; 41; 43

Wanton Mally. Garden City: 1932. V. 46

Works. New York: 1918-29. V. 40; 42; 44

TARLETON, BANASTRE 1754-1833

A History of the Campaigns of 1780 and 1781 in the Southern Provinces of North America. London: 1786. V. 46

A History of the Campaigns of 1780 and 1781, in the Provinces of North America. Dublin: 1787. V. 37; 38; 42; 44; 45

TARLETON, BANASTRE 1754-1833 continued

A History of the Campaigns of 1780 and 1781 in the Southern Provinces of North America. London: 1787. V. 37; 38; 41; 42; 43; 44; 45; 46

TARLING, ALAN

Will Carter, Printer; anaa Illustrated Study. London: 1968. V. 37

TARR, RALPH

Alaskan Glacier Studies of the National Geographic Society in the Yukatat Bay, Prince William Sound and Lower Copper River Regions. Washington: 1914. V. 37; 38; 46

The Yakutat Bay Region, Alaska. Washington: 1909. V. 45

TARRANT, EASTHAM

The Wild Riders of the First Kentucky Cavalry . . . Louisville: 1894. V. 42

TART, HENRY JAMES

The Muses Duty or a World's Thanksgiving and a Wish. London: 1800. V. 43

TARTAGLIA, NICCOLO

Ragionamenti . . . Sopra la Sua Travagliata Inventione. Venice: 1551. V. 45

TARTAGLIA, NICOLO

La Noua Scientia con Una Gionta al Terzo Libro. 1550. V. 42

Qvesiti et Inventioni Diverse, di Novo Restampati con vna Gionta al Sesto Libro, Nella Quale si Mostra Duoi Modi di Redur Una Citta Inespugnabile. 1554. V. 42

Ragionamenti Sopra la Sva Travagliata Inventione. 1551. V. 42

Regola Generale da Svlevare con Ragione e Misvra Non Solamente Ogni Affondata Naue . . . 1551. V. 42

TASISTRO, LOUIS F.

Random Shots and Southern Breezes . . . The Southern States and Southern Institutions, with Semi-Serious Observations of Men and Manners. New York: 1842. V. 37; 44

TASMAN, ABEL JANSZOON

Abel Janzoon Tasman's Journal of His Discovery of Van Diemen's Land and New Zealand in 1642 . . . Los Angeles: 1965. V. 43

TASSE, JOSEPH

Les Canadiens de l'Ouest. Montreal: 1882. V. 42

TASSER, T.

Five Hundred Points of Good Husbandry. London: 1931. V. 37

TASSI, ROBERTO

Graham Sutherland Complete Graphic Work. London: 1978. V. 42; 44

TASSIS Y PERALTA, JUAN DE, CONDE DE VILLAMEDIANA

Obras . . . Anadido en Esta Secunda Impression. Madrid: 1635. V. 40

TASSO, BERNARDO 1493-1569

L'Amadigi. Nuouamente Ristampato & Dalla Prima Impressione da Molti Errori Espurgato. Venetia: 1581. V. 40; 44

I Tre Libri Delle Lettere . . . alle Quali Novamente s'e' Aggiunto il Quarto Libro. Venice: 1564. V. 40

Rime. Salmi. Ode. Venice: 1560. V. 41

TASSO, TORQUATO 1544-1595

Aminta; Favola Boscareccia. Glasgua: 1753. V. 42

Aminta. Favola Boscareccia. Glasgua: 1755. V. 40

Aminta. Crisopoli: 1789. V. 38

Aminta, Favola, Boschereccia. Crisopoli: 1796. V. 37

Apologia in Difesa Della Sua Gierusalemme Liberata a Gli Accademici Della Crusca. Ferrara: 1586. V. 39

Delle Rime . . . Parte Prima (-Seconda). Brescia: 1592-93. V. 41; 45

Di Gerusalemme Conquistata . . . . Libri XXIIII. Paris: 1595. V. 41

Discorso Della Virtu Heroica et Della Charita. Venice: 1582. V. 39

Ein Schauspiel. V. 44

La Gerusalemme Liberata con le Annotationi di Scipion Gentili e di Grulio Guastavini. Genoa: 1617. V. 46

La Gerusalemme Liberata con le Figure di Giambattista Piazzetta . . . Venice: 1745. V. 45

La Gerusalemme Liberata. In Parigi: 1771. V. 38

La Gerusalemme Liberta. Paris: 1771. V. 42

La Gerusalemme Liberata. Florence: 1818. V. 38

Il Godfredo . . . Novamente Corretto, et Ristampato . . . Venetia: 1583. V. 45

Godfrey of Bulloigne, or the Recovery of Ierusalem. London: 1600. V. 40

Godfrey of Boulogne; or The Recoverie of Ierusalem. London: 1624. V. 37; 40

Godfrey of Bulloigne. London: 1687. V. 37; 38; 43

Godfrey of Bulloigne . . . London: 1687. V. 44

Godfrey Bulloigne, or Jerusalem Delivered. London: 1817. V. 41; 43

Godfrey of Bulloigne, or Jerusalme Delivered. London: 1865. V. 37

Il Gonzaga Secondo. Venice: 1582. V. 39

Il Messaggiero. Venice: 1582. V. 39

Jerusalem Delivered: an Heroic Poem. London: 1797. V. 38; 41

Jerusalem Delivered: an Heroic Poem. London: 1803. V. 37; 39; 45

Jerusalem Delivered. London: 1811. V. 39

Jerusalem Delivered . . . London: 1824. V. 42

Jerusalem Delivered; and heroick poem: translated from the Italian of Torquato Tasso, by John Hoole. London: 1763. V. 37

Rinaldo a Poem: Translated from the Italian by John Hoole. London: 1792. V. 37

THE TASTE of the Town; or A Guide to All Publick Diversions. London: 1731. V. 41

TATE, ALEXANDER NORMAN

Petroleum and Its Products. London: 1863. V. 40

TATE, ALLEN

All is Brillig (Or Ought to Be). 1978. V. 42

Christ and the Unicorn. West Branch: 1966. V. 44

Fathers. New York: 1933. V. 45

The Fathers. New York: 1938. V. 39; 40; 42

The Forlorn Demon: Didactic and Critical Essays. Chicago: 1953. V. 46

Jefferson Davis - His Rise and Fall. New York: 1929. V. 39

The Mediterranean and Other Poems. New York: 1936. V. 37; 39; 45; 46

Mr. Pope and Other Poems. New York: 1928. V. 39

Ode to the Confederate Dead. V. 41

Ode to the Confederate Dead. 1952. V. 39

On the Limits of Poetry. New York: 1948. V. 39

Poems 1928-1931. New York: 1932. V. 39

Poems 1922-1927. New York: 1949. V. 38; 40

Poems 1920 - 1945. London: 1947. V. 37

Reactionary Essays on Poetry and Ideas. New York: 1936. V. 44

Reason in Madness: Critical Essays. New York: 1940. V. 46

A Southern Vanguard. New York: 1947. V. 46

Stonewall Jackson. New York: 1928. V. 38; 39; 40; 45

Stonewall Jackson - the Good Soldier - a Narrative. London: 1930. V. 40

Two Conceits (For the Eye to Sing, If Possible). 1950. V. 39

Two Conceits. Cummington: 1950. V. 39

Two Conceits. N.P.: 1950. V. 38

The Vigil of Venus: Perviglium Veneris. The Latin Texas with an Introduction and English Translation by Allen Tate. Cummington: 1943. V. 37

Who Owns America? Boston: 1936. V. 45

The Winter Sea, A Book of Poems. Cummington: 1944. V. 42

The Winter Sea, a Book of Poems. N.P.: 1944. V. 38

TATE, C. M.

Chinook as Spoken by the Indians of Washington Territory, British Columbia and Alaska; for the Use of Traders, Tourists and Others Who Have Business Intercourse with the Indians, Chinook-English, English-Chinook; Victoria: 1889. V. 46

TATE, CHARLES S.

Pickway, a True Narrative. Chicago: 1905. V. 43

TATE, GEORGE

The History of the Borough, Castle and Barony of Alnwick. Alnwick: 1866. V. 44

TATE, JAMES

Betwitched: Twenty-Five Poems. 1989. V. 45

The Destination. (1967). V. 37

The Destination. 1967. V. 39; 40; 41; 42; 43; 44

Hottentot Ossuary. Boston: 1974. V. 39

Just Shades. Tuscaloosa: 1985. V. 42; 44

The Lost Pilot. New Haven: 1967. V. 38

The Torches. Santa Barbara: 1968. V. 40

Viper Jazz. Middletown: 1976. V. 38; 40

TATE, JAMES RODDAM

Madeira; or, the Spirit of Anti-Christ in 1846, as Exhibited in a Series of Outrages Perpetrated in August Last, on British Subjects and Portuguese Protestant Christians. London: 1847. V. 46

TATE, JOSEPH

A Digest of the Laws of Virginia . . . and Judicial Decisions. Richmond: 1823. V. 37; 39

TATE, NAHUM

Brutus of Alba; or, the Enchanted Lovers. London: 1678. V. 37; 38; 44

A Duke and No Duke. A Farce. As it is Acted by Their Majesties Servants. With the several Songs set to Music, with thorow Basses for the Theorbo, or Basse Viol. London: 1685. V. 37

TATE, NAHUM continued

On the Sacred Memory of Our Late Sovereign (Charles II, in verse) . . . London: 1685. V. 37; 40; 44

Poems by Several Hands and on Several Occasions. London: 1685. V. 45

A Poem Upon Tea; With a Discourse on Its Sov'rain Virtues; and Directions in the Use of It for Health. London: 1702. V. 42; 43

A Poem, Occasioned by His Majestys Voyage to Holland, the Congress at the Hague, and Present Seige of Mons. London: 1691. V. 37

Poems Written on Several Occasions . . . London: 1684. V. 45

TATE, WILLIAM

The Modern Cambist, Forming a Manual of Foreign Exchanges . . . London: 1842. V. 43

TATEM, JAMES G.

A Short Account of the Several Charities Belonging to the Parish of Edmonton, in the County of Middlesex . . . High Wycombe: 1846. V. 43

TATHAM, EDWARD

Oxonia Explicata and Ornata. London: 1773. V. 45

TATHAM, JOHN

The Dramatic Works. Edinburgh & London: 1879. V. 46

TATHAM, WILLIAM

An Historical and Practical Essay on the Culture and Commerce of Tobacco. London: 1800. V. 39

TATIANUS

Oratio Ad Graecos. Hermiae Irrisio Gentilim Philosophorum . . . Oxoniae: 1700. V. 46

TATIUS, ACHILLES

The Loves of Clitophon & Leucippe. Stratfrod-upon-Avon: 1923. V. 43

THE TATLER. The Lucubrations of Isaac Bickerstaff, Esq. London: 1710-11. V. 38; 45
THE TATLER. The Lucubrations of Isaac Bickerstaff, Esq. London: 1720. V. 37
THE TATLER. Dublin: 1777. V. 37

The Lucubrations of Isaac Bickerstaff, Esq. Glasgow: 1747. V. 39

The Tatlers. London: 1710. V. 38

The Lucubrations of Isaac Bickerstaff, Esq. London: 1710-12. V. 38

TATLOCK, ELEANOR

Poems. London: 1811. V. 42

TATLOCK, ROBERT R.

English Painting of the XVIIIth-XXth Centuries. London: 1928. V. 41

TATLOW, JOSEPH

Fifty Years of Railway Life. London: 1948. V. 46

TATON, R.

A General History of the Sciences. London: 1963-66. V. 42

TATSCH, J. HUGO

Masonic Bookplates. Cedar Rapids: 1928. V. 38

TATTAM, HENRY

A Compendious Grammar of the Egyptian Language . . . London: 1863. V. 43

TATTEN, GEORGE OAKLEY

Maya Architecture. Washington: 1928. V. 46

TATTERSALL, C. E. C.

A History of British Carpets, from the Introduction of the Craft Until the Present Day. 1934. V. 42

A History of British Carpets, from the Introduction of the Craft Until the Present Day. London: 1966. V. 45

TATTERSALL, GEORGE

The Cracks of the Day. London: 1843. V. 42

The Lakes of England (Tablets of an Itinerant). London: 1836. V. 42

The Pictorial Gallery of English Race Horses. London: 1850. V. 42

Sporting Architecture. London: 1841. V. 44

TATTERSALL, W. M.

Glamorgan County History. Volume I: Natural History. 1936. V. 40

TATUM, LAWRIE

Our Red Brothers and the Peace Policy of President Ulysses S. Grant. Philadelphia: 1899. V. 42; 45

TAUBERT, S.

Bibliopola. Hamburg & London: 1966. V. 38; 40; 44

TAUBERT, SIGFRED

Bibliopola. Pictures and Texts About the Book Trade. Hamburg: 1966. V. 37; 42

Bibliopola. London: 1966. V. 39

TAUBERT, SIGFRIED

Bibliopola. Pictures and Text about the Book Trade. Hamburg/London: 1966. V. 37

Bibliopola: Pictures and Texts about the Book Trade. Hamburg/New York: 1966. V. 37

TAUBMAN, MATTHEW

Loyal Poems and Satyrs Upon the Times, Since the Beginning of the Salamanca Plot. London: 1685. V. 40

TAULER, JOHANNES

Homiliae seu sermones in Evangelia, tam de Tempore quam de Sanctis. Lyon: 1557. V. 38

Sermon des Gross Gelarten . . . Doctoris Johannis Thauleri Prediger Ordens. Leipzig: 1498. V. 38; 41

Sermon des Gross Gelarten . . . London:eipzig: 1498. V. 40

TAUNT, HENRY

A New Map of the River Thames from Oxford to London From Entirely New Surveys, Taken During the Summer of 1871 . . . London: 1873. V. 44

TAUNTON, HENRY

Australind. Wanderings in Western & the Malay East. London: 1903. V. 37

TAUNTON, T. H.

Portraits of Celebrated Racehorses of the Past and Present Centuries . . . London: 1887-88. V. 40; 42; 46

TAUNTON, THEO

Famous Horses, with Portraits, Pedigrees, Principal Performances, Descriptions of Races . . . London: 1895. V. 37; 42

TAUNTON, THOMAS HENRY

Portraits of Celebrated Racehorses of the Past and Present Centuries in Strictly Chronological Order, Commencing in 1702 and ending in 1870, together with their respective pedigrees and performances recorded. London: 1887. V. 37

Some Celebrated Racehorses of the Past Centuries, with their Respective Pedigrees and Performances Recorded in Full. London: 1901. V. 42

TAURELLUS, NICOLAS 1547-1606

De Rerum Aeternitate . . . Marburg: 1604. V. 43

TAURELLUS, NICOLAUS

Medicae Praedictionis Methodus. Frankfurt: 1581. V. 38

TAURINIUS, ZACHARIAS

Travels through the Interiors of Africa, from the Cape of Good Hope to Morocco . . . and Thence through the Desert of Sahara and The North of Barbary to Morocco, Between the Years 1781 and 1797. Charlestown: 1801. V. 40

TAUSSIG, F. W.

Principles of Economics. New York: 1911. V. 43

TAUSSIG, FRANK W.

Protection to Young Industries as Applied in the United States. Cambridge, Mass.: (1883). V. 37

TAUSSIG, HELEN

Congenital Malformations of the Heart. 1947. V. 42

TAUSSIG, HELEN B.

Congential Malformations of the Heart. London: 1960. V. 39

TAUT, BRUNO

Alpine Architektur. Berlin: 1919. V. 44

Houses and People of Japan. London: 1938. V. 42; 43

Modern Architecture. London: 1929. V. 46

TAUVRY, DANIEL

A New Rational Anatomy, Containing an Explication of the Uses of the Structure of the Body of man and Some Other Animals, According to the Rules of Mechanics. London: 1701. V. 41

TAVENOR-PERRY, J.

Dinanderie: A History and Description of Mediaeval Art Work in Copper, Brass and Bronze. London: 1910. V. 40

TAVERNER, ANGUS

The Marlburian. London: 1975. V. 41

TAVERNER, ERIC

The Angler's Weekend Book. London: 1935. V. 39

TAYLOR, DREW KIRKSEY

Taylor's Thrilling Tales of Texas, Being the Experiences of . . . N.P.: 1920. V. 42

TAYLOR, EDWARD ROBINSON

Into the Light. San Francisco: 1902. V. 41

TAYLOR, ELIZABETH

Authentic Memoirs of Mrs. Clarke . . . London: 1809. V. 39

The Daisy, or Cautionary Stories in Verse, adapted to the Ideas of Children from 4 to 8 Years Old. Philadelphia: 1808. V. 37

A Dedicated Man and Other Stories. London: 1965. V. 45

Nibbles and Me. New York: 1946. V. 37

Palladian. London: 1946. V. 44

A Wreath of Roses. New York: 1949. V. 46

TAYLOR, EMILY

The Boy and the Birds. London: 1848. V. 40

Historical Prints, Representing Some of the Most Memorable Events in English History. London: 1821. V. 46

TAYLOR, F. J. R.

The Biology of the Dinoflagellates. London: 1986. V. 37

TAYLOR, FENNINGS

Portraits of British Americans. Montreal: 1865-68. V. 37; 41; 44

TAYLOR, FITCH W.

The Broad Pennant. New York: 1848. V. 39

TAYLOR, FREDERICK WINSLOW 1856-1915

The Principles of Scientific Management. New York: 1911. V. 38; 40; 41; 42; 44

The Principles of Scientific Management. New York & London: 1911. V. 37; 40; 42; 44; 45; 46

The Principles of Scientific Management. New York/London: 1911. V. 41

TAYLOR, GEORGE

An Exposition of the Swedish Movement - Cure, Embracing the History of Philosophy of This System of Medical Treatment, With Examples of Single Movements, and Directions For Their Use in VArious Forms of Chronic Diseases . . . New York: 1860. V. 42

Maps of the Roads of Ireland Surveyed 1777. London: 1778. V. 42; 43

TAYLOR, GEORGE LEDWELL

The Architectural Antiquities of Rome, Measured and Delineated. London: 1821-22. V. 37

Autobiography of an Octogenarian Architect. London: 1870-72. V. 37; 40; 44

TAYLOR, GEORGE WATSON

Catalogue of the Choice, Curious and Splendid London Library of George Watson Taylor. London: 1823. V. 39

TAYLOR, GRIFFITH

With Scott: the Silver Lining. London: 1916. V. 42

TAYLOR, HARRIET OSGOOD

Japanese Gardens. London: 1928. V. 39; 43

Japanese Fine Art. Tokyo: 1931. V. 44

TAYLOR, HENRY

The Apology of Benjamin Ben Moredecai to His Friends, for Embracing Christianity . . . London: 1771. V. 44

An Attempt to Form a System of the Creation of Our Globe, of the Planets and the Sun of Our System. Toronto: 1836. V. 40

Poetical Works . . . London: 1864. V. 42

The Statesman. London: 1836. V. 42

A System of the Creation of Our Globe, of the Planets and the Sun of Our System . . . Quebec: 1855? V. 40

TAYLOR, I.

Catalogue of Modern Books on Architecture. London: 1790. V. 40

TAYLOR, I. T.

The Cavalcade of Jackson County. San Antonio: 1938. V. 39; 44; 45

TAYLOR, ISAAC

African Scenes for Tarry-at-Home Travellers. London: 1820. V. 45

The Alphabet: An Account of the Origin and Development of Letters. London: 1833. V. 38

Ancient Christianity and the Doctrines of the Oxford Tracts for the Times. London: 1839-42. V. 40

Copper Plate Engravings to the Old Testament. London: 1813-15. V. 43

History of the Transmission of Ancient Books to Modern Times . . . London: 1827. V. 42; 43

Home Education. London: 1838. V. 39

Natural History of Enthusiam. London: 1829. V. 38

Natural History of Enthusiasm. London: 1831. V. 42

Scenes in Asia, for the Amusement and Instruction of Little Tarry-at-Home Travellers. London: 1819. V. 45

Scenes of Commerce, by Land and Sea . . . London: 1830. V. 45

Scenes in Africa, for the Amusement and Instruction of Little Tarry-at-Home Travellers. London: 1821. V. 42; 43

Scenes in America. For the Amusement and Instruction of Little TArry-at-Home Travellers. London: 1821. V. 39; 42

Scenes in Asia, for the Amusement and Instruction of Little Tarry-At-Home Travellers. London: 1821. V. 42

Scenes in Europe for the Amuseument and Instruction of Little Tarry-at-Home Travellers. London: 1823. V. 39

Scenes of British Wealth, in Produce, Manufactures, and Commerce, for the Amusement and Instruction of Little Tarry-at-Home Travellers. London: 1823. V. 39

Scenes of Commerce by Land and Sea. London: 1845. V. 42

Scenes of Wealth, or Views and Illustrations of Trades - Manufactures - Produce and Commerce, for the Amusement and Instruction of Tarry-at-Home Travellers. Hartford: 1826. V. 38

The Ship. London: 1831. V. 46

Specimens of Gothic Ornaments Selected from the Parish Church of Lavenham in Suffolk. London: 1796. V. 38

TAYLOR, ISSAC 1787-1865

Physical Theory of Another Life. London: 1836. V. 38

TAYLOR, J.

The Universal Instructor, and Economist. Edinburgh. V. 40

TAYLOR, J. C.

Lights and Shadows in the Recollections of a Youthful Volunteer in the Civil War. Ionia: 1915. V. 43

TAYLOR, J. C. & SON

Patent Improved Ice Caskets for Preserving the Dead by Cold Air. Trenton: ?1881. V. 37

TAYLOR, J. H.

Kaleidoscopic Lives, a Companion Book to Frontier and Indian Life. Washburgn: 1902. V. 37; 43

Taylor on Golf: Impressions, Comments and Hints. London: 1902. V. 38

TAYLOR, J. J.

The Physician as a Businessman; or, How to Obtain the Best Financial Results in the Practice of Medicine. Philadelphia: 1892. V. 45

TAYLOR, J. M.

Bench Show and Field Trial Records and Standards of Dogs in America and Valuable Statistics 1874-1891. New York: 1892. V. 46

TAYLOR, J. W.

Monograph of the Land and Freshwater Mollusca of the British Isles. Leeds: 1894-1921. V. 37

TAYLOR, JAMES

The Great Historic Families of Scotland. London. V. 43

The Pictorial History of Scotland, from the Roman Invasion to the Close of the Jacobite Rebellion A.D. 79-1746. London. V. 40

Narrative of a Voyage to, and Travels in Upper Canada With Accounts of the Customs, Character and Dialect of the Country, also Remarks on Emigration, Agriculture &c. Hull: 1846. V. 40

Remarks on the German Empire. London: 1745. V. 44

Three Panoramic Views of Port Jackson in New South Wales, with the Town of Sydney and the Adjacent Scenery After Original Drawings. London: 1988. V. 45

Wayzgoose Press. Sydney: 1985. V. 37; 39

TAYLOR, JAMES B.

Lives of Virgina Baptist Ministers. Richmond: 1837. V. 40; 44

TAYLOR, JAMES BAYARD

Ximena; or the Battle of the Sierra Morena and Other Poems. Philaldelphia: 1844. V. 43

TAYLOR, JAMES W.

Alleghania: a Geographical and Statistical Memoir. Saint Paul: 1862. V. 42

Gold Mines East of the Rocky Mountains. Washington: 1867. V. 41; 45

The Railroad System of the State of Minnesota, with Its Connections. St. Paul: 1859. V. 37; 38

Relations Between the United States and Northwest British America. Washington: 1862. V. 37; 40; 41; 43

TAYLOR, JANE 1783-1824

The Children's Mirror. London: 1859. V. 46

City Scenes or a Peep Into London. London: 1814. V. 42

City Scenes or a Peep Into London for children. London: 1818. V. 45

City Scenes, or a Peep Into London. London: 1828. V. 45

TAYLOR, JANE 1783-1824 continued

The Contributions of Q. Q. to a Periodical Work: With Some Pieces not Before Published. London: 1826. V. 39

Display. A Tale for Young People. London: 1815. V. 42

Essays in Rhyme, on Morals and Manners. London: 1816. V. 38; 39; 46

Little Ann and Other Poems. London: and New York: 1882. V. 41

Little Ann and Other Poems. London: 1883. V. 38; 39; 41; 43; 46

Little Ann and Other Poems. London & New York: 1883? V. 38; 39; 40

Little Ann and Other Poems. London and New York: 1893? V. 37

Little Ann and other Poems. Illustrated by Kate Greenaway. Printed in Colours by Edmund Evans. London/New York: n.d. (1882). V. 37

TAYLOR, JANETTE

Life and Correspondence of John Paul Jones, Including His Narrative of the Campaign of the Liman. New York: 1830. V. 38

TAYLOR, JEFFERYS

Old English Sayings Newly Expounded, In Prose and Verse. London: 1827. V. 40; 42

TAYLOR, JEREMY 1613-1667

An Answer to a Letter Written by the R.R. the Ld Bp of Rochester. London: 1656. V. 45

Antiquitates Christianae: or, The History of the Life and Death of the Holy Jesus. London: 1675. V. 39

Antiquitates Christianae: Or the History of the Life and Death of the Holy Jesus. London: 1684. V. 39

Antiquitates Christianae: or, the History of the Life and Death of Holy Jesus. London: 1703. V. 43

(Greek title) or a Collection of Polemical and Moral Discourses. London: 1657. V. 39

A Collection of Offices or Forms of Prayer. London: 1658. V. 39

A Discourse of the Liberty of Prophesying. London: 1647. V. 37; 38; 41

A Dissuasive from Popery. London: 1664. V. 38

Ductor Dubitantium, or the Rule of Conscience in all Her General Measures . . . London: 1676. V. 46

Ductor Dubitantium. London: 1696. V. 38

The Great Exemplar of Sanctity and Holy Life According to the Christian Institution. London: 1649. V. 37; 38; 40; 42; 43; 44; 45

The Great Exemplar of Sanctity and Holy Life According to the Christian Institution. London: 1653. V. 39

The Great Exemplar of Sanctity and Holy Life According to the Christian Institution. London: 1657. V. 39

The Great Exemplar of Sanctity and Holy Life. London: 1667. V. 37; 43

Jeremy Taylor: A Selection from His Work, made by Martin Armstrong, from the Early Editions. Waltham Saint Lawrence: (1923). V. 37

Opuscula, the Measure of Friendship . . . London: 1678. V. 40

The Rule and Exercise of Holy Living. London: 1847. V. 37; 38; 40

The Rule and Exercises of Holy Living and Dying. London: 1850-52. V. 39

A Selection from His Works. 1923. V. 42

Symbolon Theologikon (graece) . . . London: 1674. V. 45

Theologia Eklektike. London: 1647. V. 38; 43; 45

XXVIII Sermons Preached at Golden Grove . . . Together with A Discourse of the Divine Institution, Necessity, Sacredness & Separation of the Office Ministerial. London: 1651. V. 38

Unum Necessarium. Or, the Doctrine and Practice of Repentance. London: 1655. V. 37; 44

The Whole Works . . . with a Life of the author, and a critical examination of his writings, by the Right Rev. Reginald Heber . . . In Fifteen VOlumes. London: 1828. V. 37; 40

The Whole Works of the Right Rev. Jeremy Taylor . . . London: 1822. V. 43

The Works. London: 1831. V. 42

The Whole Works of the Right Rev. Jeremy Taylor, D.D. Lord Bishop of Down, Connor and Dromore; with a Life of the Author, and a Critical Examination of His Writings, by the Right Rev. Reginald Heber. London: 1839. V. 39

The Whole Works . . . with a Life of the Author, and a Critical Examination of His Writings by the Right Rev. Reginald Heber . . . London: 1855-6. V. 38

The Whole Works. London, Oxford, Cambridge: 1969-70. V. 39

The Worthy Communicant; or, a Discourse of the Nature, Effects and Blessings Consequent to the Worthy Receiving of the Lords Supper. London: 1674. V. 39

The Worthy Communicant; or, a Discourse of the Nature, Effects and Blessings, Consequent to the Worthy Receiving of the Lords Supper. London: 1678. V. 40

TAYLOR, JOHN

African Rifles and Cartridges. Georgetown: 1948. V. 44; 45

A Defence of the Measures of the Administration of Thomas Jefferson. Washington: 1804. V. 45

The Devil Turn'd Round-Head. London: 1642. V. 45

A Dog of War. London: 1927. V. 42; 44

The Government of God. Liverpool: 1852. V. 37; 39

The Government of God. Liverpool & London: 1852. V. 42

Jane's All the World's Aircraft, 1978-79: The Sixty-Ninth Annual Record of Aviation Development and Progress. Edited by John Taylor. 1978. V. 37

The Life and Extraordinary History of the Chevalier John Taylor . . . Dublin: 1761. V. 38

The Music Speech at the Public Commencement in Cambridge, July 6, 1730. London: 1730. V. 42; 43; 46

Poems on Various Subjects. London: 1827. V. 39

Records of My Life. London: 1832. V. 42

St. Hillaries Teares. London: 1642. V. 46

Sermons on Different Subjects Left for Publication by John Taylor, LL.D. London: 1789. V. 41

Sermons on Different Subjects Left for Publication by John Taylor, LL.D. London: 1790, 1789. V. 42

Sermons on Different Subjects Left for Publication by John Taylor, LL.D. London: 1790/89. V. 46

Sermons, On Different Subjects, Left for Publication by John Taylor, LL.D. Late Prebendary of Westminster. London: 1800. V. 42

Tyranny Unmasked. Washington, DC: 1822. V. 37

All the Workes. London: 1630. V. 43; 45

Works of John Taylor, the Water Poet. London: 1872. V. 40

TAYLOR, JOHN BROUGH

The Legend of St. Cuthbert, with the Antiquities of the Church of Durham . . . Sunderland: 1816. V. 39

TAYLOR, JOHN GLANVILLE

The United States and Cuba; Eight Years of Change and Travel. London: 1851. V. 42

TAYLOR, JOHN HENRY

Taylor on Golf. London: 1902. V. 44

TAYLOR, JOHN LOUIS

Cases Determined in the Superior Courts of Law and Equity of the State of North Carolina. Newbern: 1802. V. 40

TAYLOR, JOSEPH

Apparitions: Or, the Mystery of Ghosts, Hobgoblins, and Haunted Houses. London: 1815. V. 38

The Complete Weather Guide. London: 1812. V. 38

Curiousities for the Ingenious: Selected from the Most Authentic Treasures of Nature, Science and Art . . . London: 1821. V. 43

The General Character of the Dog. London: 1804. V. 39

The General Character of the Dog . . . Philadelphia: 1807. V. 42

Nature the Best Physician, or, a Complete Domestic Herbal. London: 1818. V. 43

The Wonders of Nature and Art. London: 1831. V. 43

TAYLOR, JOSEPH H.

Sketches of Frontier and Indian Life on the Upper Missouri and Great Plains . . . Twenty Five Years . . . in the Two Dakotas and other Territories. Pottstown: 1889. V. 41

TAYLOR, JOSEPH HENRY b. 1845

Beavers Their Ways and Other Sketches. Washburn: 1904. V. 37; 42

Beavers Their Ways and Other Sketches. Washburn: 1906. V. 40

Beavers Their Ways and Other Sketches. Washburn, North Dakota: 1906. V. 37

Kaleidoscopic Lives. A Companion Book to Frontier and Indian Life. Washburn: 1902. V. 37; 38; 45

Sketches of Frontier and Indian Life on the Upper Missouri and Great Plains. Pottstown: 1889. V. 37; 38; 39; 42; 43; 45

Sketches of Frontier and Indian Life on the Upper Missouri and Great Plains. Bismarck: 1897. V. 42

Twenty Years on the Trap Line. Bismarck: 1891. V. 42

TAYLOR, JUDSON R.

Macon Moore, the Southern Detective. New York: 1881. V. 40

TAYLOR, KATHERINE AMES

Lights and Shadows of Yosemite, Being a Collection of Favorite Views . . . San Francisco: 1926. V. 40

Yosemite Tales and Trails. San Francisco: 1934. V. 44

TAYLOR, L. J. ORR

Life History of Thomas Orr, Jr. Pioneer of California and Utah. N.P.: 1930. V. 40

TAYLOR, LANDON

The Battle Field Reviewed. Chicago: 1881. V. 37; 41; 44

Battle Field Reviewed. Chicago: 1883. V. 37; 42

TAYLOR, LESLIE B.

A Brief History of the Westley Richards Firm 1812-1913. Stratford-upon-Avon: 1913. V. 43

TAYLOR, LYTTON

Alaska and the Yukon Valley. Nashville: 1897. V. 45

TAYLOR, M. W.

The Old Manorial Halls of Westmorland and Cumberland. Kendal: 1892. V. 41; 46

TAYLOR, MARSHALL W.

The Fastest Bicycle Rider in the World. Worcester: 1928. V. 39

TAYLOR, MEADOWS

Ralph Darnell. Edinburgh & London: 1865. V. 37

TAYLOR, MICHAEL

A Sexagesimal Table, Exhibiting at Sight the Result of any Proportion, Where the Terms do not Exceed Sixty Minutes . . . London: 1780. V. 38

Tables of Logarithms of All Numbers, from 1 to 101000 and of the Sides and Tangents to Every Second of the Quadrant . . . London: 1792. V. 37; 44; 45; 46

TAYLOR, NANCY M.

Early Travellers in New Zealand. Oxford: 1959. V. 46

TAYLOR, NAT M.

A Brief History of Rogers Mills County. N.P.: 1947. V. 43

TAYLOR, NATHANIEL A.

The Coming Empire. New York: 1877. V. 38

TAYLOR, NATHANIEL W.

Life on a Whaler, or Antarctic Adventures in the Isle of Desolation . . . New London: 1929. V. 42

TAYLOR, NEVILLE

Ibex Shooting on the Himalayas. London: 1903. V. 39

TAYLOR, OWEN M.

The History of Annapolis. Baltimore: 1872. V. 46

TAYLOR, P. A.

Some Account of the Taylor Family (Originally Taylard). London: 1875. V. 38

TAYLOR, P. MEADOWS

Seeta. Seeta. Henry S. King & Co.,: 1872. V. 40

TAYLOR, PETER

The Collected Stories. New York: 1969. V. 41; 46

The Early Guest. 1982. V. 42; 43; 46

The Early Guest. N.P.: 1982. V. 41; 42

The Early Guest. U.S.A.: 1982. V. 45

Happy Families are All Alike. New York: 1959. V. 39; 42

In the Miro District and Other Stories. New York: 1977. V. 41; 46

A Long Fourth. New York: 1947. V. 42

A Long Fourth and Other Stories. New York: 1948. V. 39; 42; 43

A Long Fourth & Other Stories. New York: (1948). V. 37

Miss Lenora When Last Seen and Fifteen Other Stories. New York: 1963. V. 39; 43; 45; 46

The Old Forest. 1985. V. 44

The Old Forest and Other Stories. Garden City: 1985. V. 44; 45

The Old Forest. London: 1985. V. 43

The Old Forest. New York: 1985. V. 42

Presences: Seven One Act Plays. Boston: 1972. V. 41

A Stand in the Mountains. New York: 1986. V. 42

A Stand in the Mountains. New York: (1986). V. 37

A Summons to Memphis. New York: 1986. V. 41; 42; 44

Tennessee Day in St. Louis. New York: 1957. V. 44

The Widows of Thornton. 1954. V. 44

The Widows of Thornton. New York: 1954. V. 44; 45; 46

Woman of Andros. London: 1950. V. 38

A Woman of Means. New York: 1950. V. 39; 41; 43; 44

TAYLOR, PETER ALFRED 1647-1707

Some Account of the Taylor Family. London: 1875. V. 37; 39; 42; 45

TAYLOR, PHILIP MEADOWS

A Noble Queen; a Romance of Indian History. London: 1878. V. 43

Ralph Darnell. Edinburgh & London: 1865. V. 43

The Story of My Life. Edinburgh: 1877. V. 46

TAYLOR, PHOEBE ATWOOD

The Tinkling Symbol. New York: 1935. V. 39

TAYLOR, R. WHATELY COOKE

Introduction to a History of the Factory System. London: 1886. V. 46

The Modern Factory System. London: 1891. V. 42; 43

TAYLOR, RICHARD

Head-Quarters Dept. Ala., Miss. & E. La . . . General Orders No. 15. Meridan: 1865. V. 39

Index Monasticus; or The Abbeys and Other Monasteries . . . Formerly Established in the Diocese of Norwich and the Ancient Kingdom of East Anglia. London: 1821. V. 41

The Past and Present of New Zealand . . . 1868. V. 44

The Past and Present of New Zealand: With its Prospects for the Future. London: 1868. V. 46

Te Ika a Maui, or New Zealand and Its Inhabitants. London: 1855. V. 43

TAYLOR, RICHARD COWLING

Statistics of Coal. London: 1848. V. 38; 39; 40

Statistics of Coal. Philadelphia: 1848. V. 37; 41; 42; 43

Two Reports: on the Coal Lands, Mines and Improvements of the Dauphin and Susquehanna Coal co. and of the . . . Stony Creek Coal Estate, in the . . . County of Lebanon, Pennsylvania. Philadelphia: 1840. V. 41

TAYLOR, ROBERT

Swing; or, Who are the Incendiaries? London: 1831. V. 38; 45

TAYLOR, SAMUEL

Angling in all Its Branches. London: 1800. V. 39; 40; 41; 44; 46

An Essay Intended to Establish a Standard for an universal System of Stenography or Short Hand Wirting. London: 1786. V. 38; 40

An Essay Intended to Establish a Standard for an Universl System of Stenogoraphy, or Short-Hand Writing. London: 1801. V. 39

TAYLOR, SILAS

The History and Antiquities of Harwich and Dovercourt, in the County of Essex. London: 1737. V. 39

TAYLOR, SIMON WATSON

Free Unions - Unions Libres. London: 1946. V. 46

TAYLOR, T. U.

Jesse Chisolm. Bandera: 1939. V. 37; 43

TAYLOR, THEODORE

Thackeray the Humourist and the Man of Letters. London: 1864. V. 43

TAYLOR, THOMAS 1758-1835

A Dissertation on the Philosophy of Aristotle. London: 1812. V. 38

A Dissertation on the Eleusinian and Bacchic Mysteries. Amsterdam: 1790. V. 37

The Elements of New Arithmetical Notation, and of a New Arithmetic of Infinities. London: 1823. V. 42

The Eleusinian and Bacchic Mysteries. London: 1875. V. 38

The History of Wakefield, in the County of York . . . Wakefield: 1886. V. 39

Iamblichus On the Mysteries of the Egyptians, Chaldeans and Assyrians. London: 1821. V. 38

The Metamorphosis, or Golden Ass, and Philosophical Works of Apuleuis. Translated from the original Latin . . . London: 1822. V. 37

Mystical Initiations. London: 1787. V. 37

Select Works of Porphyry. London: 1823. V. 37

Twenty-One Years of Bird and Bull: A Bibliography 1958-1979. 1980. V. 40

The Works of Plato . . . translated from the Greek . . . by Thomas Taylor: with occasional annotation . . . and copious notes . . . LondonL: 1804. V. 37

TAYLOR, THOMAS ULVAN 1858-1941

The Chisholm Trail and Other Routes. San Antonio: 1936. V. 37; 38; 39; 42

Jesse Chisholm. Bandera: 1939. V. 42

TAYLOR, TOM

Ballads and Songs of Brittany. London: 1865. V. 42

Leicester Square: Its Associations and Its Worthies. London: 1874. V. 38

The Railway Station Painted by W. P. Frith. London: 1862. V. 41

Texfake, an Account of the Theft and Forgery of Early Texas Printed Documents. Austin: 1991. V. 46

TAYLOR, W.

Hetch Hetchy. The Story of San Francisco's Struggle to Provide a Water Supply for Her Future Needs. San Francisco: 1926. V. 39

TAYLOR, W. A.

Intermere. 1901. V. 44

TAYLOR, W. C.

the History of Mahommedanism and Its Sects . . . London: 1834. V. 44

TEICHMANN, EMIL

A Journey to Alaska in the Year 1868. Kensington: London: 1925. V. 43

TEIGNMOUTH, HENRY NOEL SHORE, BARON 1847-1926

Memoirs of the Life, Writings and Correspondence of Sir William Jones. London: 1804. V. 42; 43

TEIGNMOUTH, LORD

Sketches of the Coasts and Islands of Scotland, and the Isle of Man . . . London: 1836. V. 46

TEISER, RUTH

Lawton Kennedy, Printer. San Francisco: 1988. V. 42; 43; 45; 46

TEITARO, SUZUKI DAISETZ

Manual of Zen Buddhism. Kyoto: 1935. V. 39

Zen Buddhism and Its Influence on Japanese Culture. Kyoto: 1938. V. 39

TEIXEIRA FEO, BENTO

Relacaco do Naufragio que Fizeram as Naos . . . Lisbon: 1650. V. 38

TEIXEIRA, JOSE

A Treatise Paraenetical . . . Wherein is Shewed . . . the Right Way and True Meanes to Resist the Violence of the Castilian King . . . London: 1598. V. 44; 45

TEJEDA, GASPAR DE

Suma de Arithmetica Pratica y de Todas Mercaderias con la Horden de Contadores. Valladolid: 1546. V. 41

TELESCOPE, TOM, PSEUD.

The Newtonian System of Philosophy . . . London: 1798. V. 37; 44

TELESIO, ANTONIO

Libellus de Coloribus, ubi Multi Leguntur, Praetur Aliorum Opinionem. Paris: ?1529. V. 38

TELESIO, BERNARDINO

De His, quae in Aere Fiunt; & de Terrae Motibus, Liber unicus. Naples: 1570. V. 38

TELESIUS, BERNARDINUS

De Colorum Generatione Opusculum. Neapoli: 1570. V. 37

TELEVISION. Collected Addresses and Papers on the Future of the new Art and Its Recent Technical Developments. New York: 1936-50. V. 40

TELFER, J. BUCHAN

The Crimea and Transcaucasia Being the Narrative of a Journey in the Kouban in Gouria, Georgia, Armenia, Ossety, Imeritia, Swannety and Mingrelia . . . London: 1876. V. 46

TELFER, JAMES

Border Ballads, and Other Miscellaneous Pieces. Jedburgh: 1824. V. 44

TELFORD, THOMAS

Life of Thomas Telford, Civil Engineer, Written by Himself. London: 1838. V. 38

Liverpool and Manchester Rail-Way. Mr. Telford's Report to the Commissioners for the Loan of Exchequer Bills. Liverpool: 1829. V. 40; 46

THE TELL-TALE; or, Anecdotes Expressive of Characters of Persons Eminent for Rank, Learning, Wit or Humour. London: 1756. V. 43; 45

THE TELL-TALE; or Universal Museum, Consisting of a Series of Interesting Adventures, Voyages, Histories, Lives, Tales and Romances. London: 1803? V. 41

TELL-TRUTH'S Answer to Tell Truth's Letter to the Right Honourable the Earl of Shaftesbury, in Vindication of His Lordship . . . N.P.: 1681. V. 38

TELLER, H. M.

Letter from . . . Transmitting . . . Copies of Documents and Correspondence Relating to Leases of Lands in Indian Territory to Citizens of the U.S. for Cattle Grazing and Other Purposes. Washington: 1884. V. 39

TELLES, BALTHAZAR

Chronica da Companhia de Iesu, na Provincia de Portugal, e do Gue Fizeram, nas Conquistas d'este Reyno, os Religiosos . . . Lisbon: 1645-47. V. 39

TELLEZ, BALTHAZAR

The Travels of the Jesuits in Ethiopia . . . London: 1710. V. 38

TELLIER, JULES

Abd-Er-Rhaman in Paradise. Waltham St. Lawrence: 1928. V. 39; 40; 41; 42; 43; 45

TEMANZA, TOMASSO

Vite dei Piu Celebri Architetti, e Scultori Veneziani che Fiorirono ne Secolo Decimosesto. Venice: 1778. V. 37

TEMANZA, TOMMASO

Vita di Andrea Palladio Vicentino Egregio Architetto . . . Aggiuntevi in fine Due Scritture Dello Stesso Palladio finora Inedite. Venice: 1762. V. 38; 39

TEMKIN, OWSEI

The Falling Sickness: a History of Epilepsy From the Greeks to the Beginnings of Modern Neurology. Baltimore: 1945. V. 42

TEMMINCK, C. J.

Manuel d'Ornithologie . . . Paris: 1820-40. V. 43

TEMMINCK, COENRAAD J.

Les Oiseaux d'Europe. Paris: 1848. V. 44

TEMMINCK, CONRAD JACOB

Nouveau Recueil de Planches Coloriees d'Oiseaux, Pour Servir de Suite et de Complement aux Planches Enluminees de Buffon. Paris & Strasbourg: 1820-38-39. V. 37

TEMPERANCE Cook Book; Being a Collection of Receipts for Cooking, From Which All Intoxicating Liquids are Excluded. Philadelphia: 1841. V. 43

TEMPLE, A. G.

Modern English Art. London: 1895. V. 42

Sir John Gilbert. London: 1893. V. 39

TEMPLE, ANNA CHAMBERS GRENVILLE TEMPLE, COUNTESS d. 1777

Poems by . . . . Strawberry Hill: 1764. V. 40

THE TEMPLE Beau; or the Town Coquets. London: 1754. V. 39

LE TEMPLE des Muses, Orne de LX. Tableaux ou Sont Representes les Evenemens Les Plus Remrquables de l'Antiquite Fabuleuse. Amsterdam: 1742. V. 38

TEMPLE, EDMOND

Travels in Various Parts of Peru, Including a Years' Residence in Potosi. London: 1830. V. 38; 41; 45

Travels in Various Parts of Peru, Including a year of residence in Potosi. Philadelphia: 1833. V. 39

TEMPLE, HENRY JOHN 1784-1865

The New Whig Guide. London: 1819. V. 41

TEMPLE, JOHN

The Irish Rebellion or a History of the Beginnings and First Progress of the Great Rebellion Raised Within the Kingdom of Ireland, Upon the Three and Twentieth Day of October in the Year 1641 etc. Dublin: 1713. V. 46

The Irish Rebellion. London: 1812. V. 38

The Irish Rebellion: or, an History of the . . . General Rebellion raised within the Kingdom of Ireland . . . October, 1641 . . . The Sixth Edition . . . To which is added Sir Henry Tichborne's History of the Siege of Drogheda . . . Dublin: 1724. V. 37

TEMPLE, LAUNCELOT

Sketches or Essays on Various Subjects. London: 1758. V. 39

THE TEMPLE of Death, a Poem. London: 1695. V. 46

THE TEMPLE of the Fairies. London: 1804. V. 39

TEMPLE, RICHARD

Journals Kept in Hyderabad, Kasmir, Sikkim and Nepal. London: 1887. V. 40

Oriental Experience: a Selection of Essays and Adddresses Delivered on Various Occasions. London: 1883. V. 46

TEMPLE, RICHARD C.

The Itinerary of Ludovico di Varthema of Bologna from 1502 to 1508. London: 1928. V. 37; 45

The World Encompassed, and Analogous Contemporary Documents Concerning Sir Francis Drake's Circumnavigation of the World. London: 1926. V. 37; 44; 45

TEMPLE, RICHARD GRENVILLE-TEMPLE, EARL OF 1711-1779

Grenville Papers. Being Correspondence of Richard Grenville Earl Temple & the Rt. Hon. George Grenville, Their Friends & Contemporaries. London: 1852-53. V. 39

The Grenville Papers: Being the Correspondence of Richard . . . and George, Their Friends and Contemporaries. London: 1852. V. 39

TEMPLE, WILLIAM

An Introduction to the History of England. London: 1695. V. 40

An Introduction to the History of England. London: 1699. V. 37; 44

Letters Written by Sir W. Temple, Bart . . . London: 1700. V. 37; 39

Memoirs of What Past in Christendom, from the War Begun 1672. London: 1692. V. 37; 41; 46

Miscellanea . . . London: 1681. V. 42

Miscellanea. London: 1696. V. 43

Miscellanea, the Third Part. London: 1701. V. 43

TEMPLE, WILLIAM continued

Miscellanea. In Two Parts. The Fifth Edition. London: 1697. V. 37

Nouveaux Memoires du Chevalier Guillaume Temple . . . The Hague: 1729. V. 41

Observations Upon the United Provinces of the Netherlands. London: 1673. V. 37; 41

Observations Upon the United Provinces of the Netherlands. London: 1680. V. 38; 42; 44

The Works. London: 1720. V. 39; 43

The Works of William Temple, Bart. London: 1731. V. 38; 40; 41

The Works . . . London: 1740. V. 38; 43

The Works of Sir William Temple, Bart. London: 1750. V. 39

TEMPLETON, W.

The Operative Mechanic's Workshop Companion. London: 1845. V. 38; 40

TEMPLIN, HUGH

Fergus: The Story of a Little Town. Fergus: 1933. V. 42

TEMPSKY, GUSTAVUS FERDINAND VON

Mitla. A Narrative of Incidents and Personal Adventures on a Journey in Mexico, Guatemala and Salvador in the years 1853-55. London: 1858. V. 39; 40; 42; 45

TEN Lithographed Drawings, of Scenery in the Vicinity of the Lakes, Taken from Nature. London: 1826. V. 45

TEN Little Nigger Boys (with Music). London. V. 46

TEN Little Niggers. New York: 1870's. V. 45
THE TEN Little Niggers. New York: 1875. V. 45
THE TEN Little Niggers. London: 1880. V. 39
TEN Little Niggers. London: 1910. V. 46

TENANTS Law; or, the Laws Concerning Landlords Tenants and Farmers . . . London: 1760. V. 42

TENCH, WATKIN

Relation d'une Expedition a la Baye Botanique, Situee dans la Nouvelle Hollande, sur la Cote Meridionale, Nommee par le Capitaine Cook, Nouvelle Galles Meridionale. Paris: 1789. V. 39

Voyage a la Baie Botanique; Avec une Description du Nouveau Pays de Galles Meridional, de ses Habitans, de ses Productions, &c, & Quelques Details Relatifs a M. de la Peyrouse . . . Paris: 1789. V. 39; 41

TENCHE, NATHANIEL

Reasons Humbly Offered by the Governor, Assistants and Fellowship of Eastland-Merhants. London: 1689. V. 41

TENDE, GASPARD DE

An Account of Poland. London: 1698. V. 37

Relation Historique de la Pologne . . . Par le Sieur de Hauteville. Paris: 1697. V. 37

TENFOLD: Poems for frances Horovitz. London: 1983. V. 37

TENN, W.

Of All Possible Worlds. 1955. V. 43

TENNANT, CHARLES

A Tour through Parts of the Netherlands, Holland, Germany, Switzerland, Savoy and France in the Year 1821-22. London: 1824. V. 39

TENNANT, EMMA

The Time of the Crack. London: 1973. V. 43

TENNANT, JOSEPH F.

Rough Times 1870-1920. Winnipeg: 1920. V. 44

Rough Times, 1870-1920. Winnpieg?: 1920. V. 43

TENNANT, STEPHEN

Leaves from a Missionary's Notebook. Bavaria: 1920. V. 38

TENNANT, WILLIAM

Indian Recreactions . . . London: 1804. V. 42; 43

TENNENT, JAMES EMERSON

Ceylon. An Account of the Island, Physical, Historical and Topographical. London: 1859. V. 39; 42

Ceylon. An Account of the Island. London: 1860. V. 38; 40

The Story of the Guns. London: 1864. V. 43; 45

TENNENT, WILLIAM

An Address, Occasioned by the Late Invasion of the Liberties of the Americana Colonies by the British Parliament. Philadelphia: 1774. V. 37

TENNESSEE

Check List of Tennessee Imprints, 1841-1850. Nashville: 1941. V. 37

TENNESSEE AND PACIFIC RAILROAD CO.

Charter of the Tennessee and Pacific Railroad Company, and the Various Acts Amendatory Thereof; Together with the General Railroad Laws of the State and the By-Laws of the Board of Directors. Lebanon: 1870. V. 39

TENNESSEE. COSNTITUTION - 1834

The Constitution of the State of Tennessee . . . Nashville: 1834. V. 42

THE TENNESSEE Farmer, or Farmer Jackson in New York. New York:?: 1824? V. 44

TENNESSEE. GOVERNOR - 1847

Message of Governor Aaron V. Brown to the Tennessee Legislature at its October Session 1847. Nashville: 1847. V. 39

TENNESSEE. LAWS, STATUTES, ETC.

Public Acts of the State of Tennessee Passed at the Extra Session of the Thirty-Third General Assembly, April, 1861. Nashville: 1861. V. 44

Regulations Adopted for the Provisional Force of the Tennessee Volunteers, Together with the Act of Tennessee Legislature of 1861, Organizing Said Provisional Force. Nashville: 1861. V. 44

TENNESSEE. LAWS, STATUTES, ETC. - 1803

Laws of the State of Tennessee. Knoxville: 1803. V. 40; 42

TENNEY, E. P.

The New West as Related to the Christian College and Home Missionary. Cambridge: 1878. V. 39

TENNEY, EDWARD P.

Colorado; and Homes in the New West. Boston: 1880. V. 40

Colorado and Homes in the New West. New York: 1880. V. 42

TENNEY, W. J.

The Military and Naval History of the Rebellion in the United States. New York: 1865. V. 45

TENNIEL, JOHN

Sir John Tenniel's Illustrations to Lewis Carroll's Alice's Adventures in Wonderland and Through the Looking Glass. London: 1988. V. 44

TENNYSON, AFLRED TENNYSON, 1ST BARON 1809-1892

The Idylls of the King. London: 1912. V. 41

TENNYSON, ALFRED TENNYSON, 1ST BARON 1809-1892

The Charge of the Light Brigade. London: 1855. V. 40

Demeter and Other Poems. London: 1889. V. 38

The Devil and the Lady. London: 1930. V. 40; 41

Elaine. London: 1867. V. 39

Enid. (and) Vivien. London: 1868/67. V. 42

Enoch Arden. Boston: 1864. V. 43

Enoch Arden. London: 1864. V. 37; 40; 41; 42; 44; 45; 46

Enoch Arden, Etc. London: 1865. V. 45

Enoch Arden. London: 1866. V. 39; 41; 42

Enoch Arden, Etc. London: 1874. V. 37

Gareth and Lynette, etc. London: 1872. V. 39; 40

Geraint and Enid. London. V. 38

Guinevere. New York: 1868. V. 45

Harold. A Drama. London: 1876. V. 37

Harold. London: 1877. V. 39

Helen's Tower, Clandeboye. London: 1861. V. 40

Helen's Tower, Clandeboye. N.P.: 1861. V. 46

Idylls of the King. London: 1859. V. 39; 41; 42

Idylls of the King. London: 1862. V. 41

Idylls of the King. London: 1864. V. 45

Idylls of the King. New York: 1898. V. 44

Idylls of the King. New York: 1952. V. 45

Idyls of the King. Boston: 1859. V. 43

In Memoriam. Boston: 1850. V. 45

In Memoriam. London: 1850. V. 37; 41; 42; 45; 46

In Memoriam. London: 1851. V. 38; 41

In Memoriam and Idylls of the King. London: 1866/67. V. 43

In Memoriam. London: 1880. V. 44

In Memoriam. London: 1894. V. 40

In Memoriam. London & New York: 1894. V. 40

In Memoriam. London: 1899. V. 38; 45

In Memoriam. London: 1900. V. 37; 40; 41; 45

In Memoriam. Portland: 1920. V. 38

In Memoriam. London: 1933. V. 40; 41; 44; 45; 46

In Memoriam. London: 1866. V. 37

The Lady of Shalott. New York: 1881. V. 38; 40; 45

The Lady of Shalott. New York: 1958. V. 42

TENNYSON, ALFRED TENNYSON, 1ST BARON 1809-1892 continued

The Life and Works of . . . London: 1898-99. V. 39

Life and Works of . . . London: 1899. V. 40

The Life and Works, with a Memoir. London: 1898. V. 37

The Lotos Eater. London: 1901. V. 43

The Lover's Tale. London: 1879. V. 41

Lyrical Poems. London: 1885. V. 37

Maud. Boston: 1855. V. 43

Maud, and Other Poems. London: 1855. V. 43

Maud. 1893. V. 37; 42; 44

Maud. Hammersmith: 1893. V. 39; 43

Maud. London: 1893. V. 38; 40; 41; 44

Maud. East Aurora: 1900. V. 46

Maud. London: 1905. V. 44; 46

Maud. London: 1922. V. 42; 43

The May Queen. London: 1861. V. 44

The May Queen. London: 1861. V. 38; 39; 41

The May Queen. London: 1870. V. 39

The May Queen. London: 1872. V. 45

The Miller's Daughter. London: 1858. V. 39

Ode on the Death of the Duke of Wellington. London: 1852. V. 37; 40; 46

Ode on the Death of the Duke of Wellington. London: 1852, 1853. V. 41

Ode on the Death of the Duke of Wellington. (with) A Welcome (to Her Royal Highness Alexandra, Princess of Wales). London: 1852, 1863. V. 39

Poems, Chiefly Lyrical. London. V. 40

Poems by Two Brothers. London: 1827. V. 42; 45

Poems, Chiefly Lyrical. London: 1830. V. 37; 42; 44; 45

Poems. Boston: 1842. V. 45

Poems. London: 1842. V. 37; 40; 42; 46

Poems. London: 1843. V. 42

Poems. London: 1845. V. 42

Poems. London: 1857. V. 37; 38; 42

Poems. London: 1859. V. 43

Poems. N.P.: 1862. V. 40; 41; 43

Poems. MDCCCXXX. MDCCCXXXIII. (Toronto: 1862. V. 37

Poems. London: 1863. V. 40

Poems. London: 1864. V. 39

Poems. London: 1865. V. 40

Poems. London: 1866. V. 39; 42

Poems. London: 1868. V. 44

Poems. London: 1878. V. 43

Poems of Alfred Lord Tennyson. London: 1900. V. 38; 40; 43

The Poems of Alfred Lord Tennyson. Cambridge: 1974. V. 41

The Poems. New York: 1974. V. 38

Poems and Plays of . . . Oxford: 1975. V. 46

The Poetical Works. New York: 1871. V. 46

The (Poetical) Works. London: 1872-73. V. 46

The Poetical Works. London: 1895/96. V. 42

Poetical Works. London: 1899. V. 40; 42

Poetical Works. London: 1905. V. 37

The Poetical Works. London: 1907. V. 46

The Princess: a Medley. London: 1847. V. 46

The Princess, a Medley. London: 1867. V. 38

The Princess: a Medley. London: 1880. V. 42; 45

The Princess, a Medley. Boston: 1884. V. 44

The Princess. N.P.: 1911. V. 46

Prolusiones Academicae . . . Cantabrigiae: 1829. V. 46

The Promise of May. London: 1883. V. 46

Queen Mary, a Drama. Boston: 1875. V. 43

Queen Mary. London: 1875. V. 39; 40; 41; 42; 46

A Selection from the Works. London: 1865. V. 43

Seven Poems and Two Translations. Hammersmith: 1902. V. 37; 40; 43; 44; 45; 46

Some Poems By. London: 1901. V. 39; 42; 43

Song of the Brook. Bronxville: 1959. V. 45

The Story of Elaine. London: 1871. V. 39

The Story of the Idylls of the King. New York: 1912. V. 43

Timbuctoo. Cambridge: 1829. V. 46

Tiresias and Other Poems. London: 1885. V. 42

Tiresias. Northampton: 1970. V. 46

To Virgil. Written at the Request of the Mantuans for the Nineteenth Centenary of Virgil's Death. San Francisco: 1930. V. 46

A Welcome. London: 1863. V. 39; 46

The Works of Alfred Tennyson. London: 1870. V. 46

The Works. London: 1872. V. 37; 42

The Works of Alfred Tennyson. London: 1872/73. V. 43

The Works. London: 1872-73. V. 46

The Works. London: 1879. V. 37

The Works of Alfred Lord Tennyson. London: 1884. V. 41

Collection of Works by . . . London: 1888/91. V. 44

The Works of . . . London: 1892. V. 46

The Works of Alfred Lord Tennyson. London: 1892-1903. V. 46

The Works of Alfred Lord Tennyson. London: 1898. V. 37; 46

Works. London: 1906-11. V. 46

The Works of . . . New York: & London: 1909. V. 40

TENNYSON, CHARLES

Sonnets and Fugitive Pieces. Cambridge: 1830. V. 37; 40; 42; 44

TENNYSON, FREDERICK

Daphne and Other Poems. London: 1891. V. 46

Days and Hours. London: 1854. V. 37

TENNYSON, HALLAM

Alfred Lord Tennyson. A memoir by His Son. London: 1897. V. 46

Jack and the Bean-Stalk. London: 1886. V. 41; 43; 45; 46

TENNYSON, JESSE F.

The City Curious. London: 1920. V. 46

TENSINI, AGOSTINO

La Vera Regola Dello Scrivere. Bassano: 1680. V. 37

TENTZEL, ANDREAS

Medicina Diastatica . . . In Tractatum Tertium de Tempore Seu Philosop. D. Theoph. Raracel. Jena: 1629. V. 42

Secreti Rariora Chymico-Medica, Oder Sammlung Auserlesener Medicinisch-Chymischer Geheimnisse . . . Nuremburg: 17--. V. 46

TEONGE, HENRY

The Diary of Henry Teonge, Chaplain on Board His Majesty's Ships Assistance, Bristol & Royal Oak: Ano 1675 to 1679. London: 1825. V. 43

THE TEPEE Book - Custer Battle Number, June 1916. Sheridan: 1916. V. 37

TERASSE, ANTOINE

Pierre Bonnard. Paris: 1967. V. 42

TERENTIANUS MAURUS

De Literis, Syllabis, Pedibvs et Metris, Tractatus Insignis, Suspiciendus Antiquitate Etiam Reuerenda, Nicolao Brissaeo Montiuillario Commentatore & Emendatore. Paris: 1531. V. 39; 40

TERENTIUS AFER, PUBLIUS 190-159 BC

Andria Commedia.. Verona: 1971. V. 39; 42

A Comedy Called Andria. Verona: 1971. V. 38; 39; 40; 42; 44; 45; 46

Andria. A Comedy. Verona: 1971. V. 37

The Brothers. 1968. V. 44

Les Six Comedies . . . Paris: 1574. V. 37

Les Comedies de Terence, Traduites en Francois, Avec des Remarques par Madame D(acier). Paris: 1688. V. 37

Terence's Comedies: Made English. London: 1699. V. 41

Publii Terentii Afri Comoediae Ad Optimorum Exemplarium Fidem Recensitae. Cantabrigiae: 1701. V. 37

Terence's Comedies. London: 1745. V. 38

Comoediae. Edinburgh: 1758. V. 37; 39

The Comedies of Terence. London: 1765. V. 39

Afri Comoediae. Birmingham: 1772. V. 39

Comoediae Sex. Paris: 1536. V. 38; 40; 45

P. Terentii Comoediae sex, tum ex Doanti Commentariis. Parisiis: 1541. V. 46

P. Terenti Afri . . . Comoediae, Andria, Eunuchus, Heautontimorumenos, Adelphia, Hecyra, Phormio. Venetiis: 1545. V. 40

Comoedia. Lyon: 1546. V. 40

Comoediae . . . Ex Emendatissimis ac Fide Dignissimis Codicibus Summa Diligentia Castigatae. Parisiis: 1552. V. 38

Comoediae Omnes. Venetiis: 1567. V. 44

Comoediae Sex . . . Lyons: 1581. V. 44

Comoediae Sex Elegantissimae. Coloniae Allobrogum: 1614. V. 45

Comoediae Sex. Leiden: 1635. V. 37; 40

Pub. Terentii Comoediae Sex, Ex Recensione Heinsiana. Lugd. Batavorum: i.e.: 1635. V. 44

Comoediae. Paris: 1642. V. 40

Terence's Comedies . . . London: 1694. V. 42

Comoediae Sex. Cantabrigiae: 1701. V. 45

Comoediae Sex. Amsterdami: 1703? V. 38

TERENTIUS AFER, PUBLIUS 190-159 BC continued

Comoediae, Phaedri Fabulae Aesopiae, Publii Syrii et Aliorum Veterum Sententiae, Ex Recensione et cum Notis Richardi Bentleii. Cambridge: 1726. V. 44

Comoediae. Dublin: 1727. V. 45

Comoediae Sex, Cum Interpretatione Donati et Calphurnii et Commentario Perpetuo. Hague: 1732. V. 44; 45

Comoediae Sex. Glasguae: 1742. V. 38

Publii Terentii Afri comoediae Sex. London: 1744. V. 45

Comoediae. Edinburgi: 1758. V. 42

Comoediae Sex. Hamilton: 1758. V. 45

Comoediae. Rome: 1767. V. 40

Comedies of Terence. London: 1768. V. 46

Comoediae. Birmingham: 1772. V. 38; 39; 40; 44; 45; 46

Publii Terentii Afri Comoediae. Birmingham: 1772. V. 38; 44; 45

Comoediae VI. Basle: 1797. V. 45

Comoediae. London: 1823. V. 45

Publii Terentii Afri Comoediae Sex . . . Londini: 1825. V. 45

Comoediae. Londini: 1854. V. 42; 45

A Comedy. 1971. V. 44

Comoediae. Phaedri Fabulae, Publii Syri Sententiae. Recensuit Richardus Bentleius. Amsterdam: 1727. V. 38

Dictionibus Hyperdisyllabis a P. Antesignano . . . Affixi sunt in Puerorum Gratiam Natiui Accentvs . . . Lyon: 1556. V. 42

Le Grant Therece on Francoys Tate en Rime Que en Prose Nouvelellement Imprimee a Paris. Paris: 1539. V. 46

In Quem Triplex Edita Est P. Antesignani Rapistagnensis Commentatio. Lugduni: 1560. V. 44

(Opera) In Singulas Scenas Argumenta . . . Paris: 1534. V. 38

Terenti cum Directorio Vocabulorum, Glossa Interlineari, et Commentariis Donato, Guidonis, et Ascensii. Strassburg: 1499. V. 41; 42; 43

Terentivs, In Quem Triplex Edita est P. Antesignani Rapistagnensis Commentatio . . . Tertivm Exemplar Ex Omnium Interpretum Commentariis Compediosam Expositionem, Omneque Primi Exemplaris Argumentum . . . Lyon: 1560. V. 40

TERESA, OF AVILA, SAINT

the Works of the Holy Mother St. Teresa of Jesus, Foundress of the Reformation of Discalced Carmelites . . . London. V. 46

TERHUNE, ALBERT PAYSON

My Friend the Dog. New York: 1926. V. 45

TERHUNE, MARY VIRGINIA HAWES 1830-1922

Eve's Daughters or Common Sense for Maid, Wife and Mother. New York: 1882. V. 43

TERLON, HUGH

Memoires . . . de ses Negociations, Depuis l'Annee 1656. Jusqu'en 1661. Suivant Paris: 1682-1681. V. 37

TERRA ROSSA, VITALE

Riflessioni Geografiche Circa le Terre Incognite Distese in Ossequio Perpetuo della Nobilta Veneziana. Padua: 1686. V. 40

TERRACE, EDWARD L. B.

Egyptian Paintings of the Middle Kingdom. London: 1968. V. 40; 46

TERRAE-FILIUS, or, the Secret History of the University of Oxford: In Several Essays. London: 1726. V. 42

TERRELL, ALEXANDER WATKINS 1827-1912

From Texas to Mexico and the Court of Maximilian in 1865. Dallas. V. 44

From Texas to Mexico and the Court of Maximilian in 1865. Dallas: 1933. V. 42; 44

TERRELL, J. C.

Reminiscences of Early Days of Fort Worth. Fort Worth: 1906. V. 39; 41

TERRELL, WILLIAMSON

A Debate on Baptism and the Witness of the Holy Spirit Held in Fairview, IA. November 1847, Between Rev. Williamson Terrell, Circuit Preacher of the Methodist Episcopal Church and Henry R. Pritchard, Evangelist of the Christian Church . . . 1848. V. 43

TERREROS Y PANDO, ESTEVAN

Paleografia Espanola, Que Contiene Todos los Modos Conocidos, que ha Habido de Escribir en Espana, desde su Principio . . . Madrid: 1758. V. 38

THE TERRIBLE Tragedy at Wasington. Assassination of President Lincoln . . . Great National Calamity. Philadelphia: (1865). V. 37

TERRIL, ISRAEL

Vocal Harmony, No. 1: Calculated for the Use of Singing Schools, and Worshiping Assemblies. Newhaven: 1805. V. 44

TERRILL, FREDERICK WILLIAM

A Chronology of Montreal and of Canada, from A.D. 1752 to A.D. 1893 . . . Montreal: 1893. V. 45

TERRILL, J. NEWTON

Campaign of the 14th Regiment, New Jersey Volunteers . . . New Brunswick: 1884. V. 39

TERRINK, HERMAN

A Bibliography of the Writings of Jonathan Swift. Philadelphia: (1963). V. 37

TERRY, A. H.

Diary: the Field Diary of General Alfred H. Terry - the Yellowstone Expedition, 1876. V. 39

TERRY, ALFRED H.

Diary. The Field Diary of General Alfred H. Terry. The Yellowstone Expedition. Bellevue: 1969. V. 45

TERRY, CHARLES

New Zealand, Its Advantages and Prospects, as a British Colony, With a Full Account of the Land Claims, Sales of Crown Lands, Aborigines, etc. London: 1842. V. 37

TERRY, D. L.

An Essay on the Theory and Treatment of Fever and Inflammation, According to the Botanical or Reformed System of Physic and Surgery . . . Dayton: 1834. V. 45

TERRY, DANIEL

The Heart of Mid-Lothian, a Musical Drama, in Three Acts, First Produced at the Theatre Royal, Covent Garden, Saturday 17th April 1819. London: 1819. V. 43

TERRY, DAVID S.

Trial of David S. Terry by the Committee of Vigilance. San Francisco: 1856. V. 37

TERRY, ELLEN

The Russian Ballet. With Drawings by Pamela Colman Smith. London: 1913. V. 37

The Story of My Life. London: 1908. V. 38; 40; 42; 44

TERRY, G. W.

The Alphabet Annotated, for Youth and Adults in Doggerel Verse, by an old Etonian. London: 1853. V. 40

TERRY, GEORGE W.

The Alphabet Annotated for Youth and Adults in Doggerel Verse by an Old Etonian. London: 1830. V. 42

TERRY, MICHAEL

Untold Miles. London: 1932. V. 46

TERRY, MILTON SPENSER

Rambles in the Old World. Cincinnati: 1894. V. 45

TERRY, T. PHILIP

Terry's Guide to Cuba Including the Isle of Pines with A Chapter on the Ocean Routes to the Island. Boston: 1926. V. 38; 40; 42

TERRY, THEODORE L.

Extreme Prematurity and Fibroblastic Overgrowth of Persistent Vascular Sheath Behind Each Crystalline Lens. 1942. V. 44

TERTULLIAN, QUINTUS SEPTIMUS FLORENS

Q. Septimii Florentis Tertulliani . . . Scripta & Plura Quam Ante & Diligentius per Industriam bene Literatorum Aliquot . . . Basileae: 1550. V. 40

TERTULLIANUS, QUINTUS SEPTIMUS FLORENS

Opera. Basel: 1521. V. 40

TERTZ, ABRAM

A Voice from the Chorus. London: 1976. V. 40

TERZAGO, PAOLO MARIA

Museum Septalianum Manfredi Septalae . . . Constructum . . . Tortona: 1664. V. 40

TERZIO, FRANCESCO

Austriacae Gentis Imaginum Pars Prima (- Quinta) . . . Innsbruck: 1569-73. V. 38; 39

TESNOHLIDEK, RUDOLF

The Cunning Little Vixen. New York: 1985. V. 45

The Cunning Little Vixen. New York: (1985). V. 37

TESSIER, THOMAS

How We Died. Dublin: 1970. V. 44

The Nightwalker. New York: 1980. V. 45

TESSIMOND, A. S. J.

The Collected Poems. Reading: 1985. V. 38

The Walls of Glass. 1934. V. 37

THE TESTAMENT of Charlotte B. 1988. V. 45

A TESTAMENT of Faith. A Leaf from a Copy of the First American Bible. Boston: 1979. V. 37

TESTAMENT Politique De Charles Duc de Lorraine et de Bar. Leipzig: 1697. V. 37

TESTE, ALPHONSE b. 1814.

A Practical Manual of Animal Magnetism. London: 1843. V. 46

TESTELIN, HENRI

Sentimens des plus Habiles Peintres sur la Pratique de Peinture . . . Paris: 1696. V. 44

TESTIMONY on the Alleged Election Outrages in Texas. Washington: 1889. V. 38

TESTS of the National Wealth and Finances of Great Britian in December 1798. London: 1799. V. 39

TESUARO, EMMANUALE 1591-1677

Elogia and Epigrammata in Duodecim Caesaris Suetonii . . . Milan: 1619. V. 40

TESUKIWASHI Taikan. Tokyo: 1974. V. 43

TEVIS, A. H.

Beyond the Sierras; or, Observations on the Pacific Coast. Philadelphia: 1877. V. 42

TEVIS, WALTER

The Hustler. New York: 1959. V. 41; 42

TEW, DAVID

The Oakham Canal, with a Section on Topography by Trevor Hickman and Rigby Graham. Wymondham: 1968. V. 40

TEWKSBURY, G. E.

The Kansas Picture Book. Topeka: 1883. V. 37

THE TEXARKANA Gateway to Texas and the Southwest. St. Louis: 1896. V. 38

TEXAS

Constitution of the State of West Texas. Austin: 1868. V. 41

TEXAS Almanac and State Industrial Guide for 1904. Galveston: 1904. V. 37

TEXAS Almanac for 1870 and Emigrants Guide to Texas. V. 45

TEXAS Almanac for 1872 and Emigrant's Guide to Texas. Galveston: 1871. V. 45

TEXAS. (caption title, text commences): The Vast Importance of Correct Views, as to the Various Questions of Policy Involved in the Proposed Annexation of Texas . . . N.P.: 1844. V. 45

TEXAS. CONSTITUTION

Constitution of the State of Texas, Adopted by the Constitutional Covention Convened Under the Reconstruction Acts. Austin: 1869. V. 37; 39; 42; 45

TEXAS. CONSTITUTION - 1845

The Constitution of the State of Texas. Washington: 1845. V. 37

TEXAS. CONSTITUTION - 1861

The Constitution of the State of Texas, as Amended in 1861, the Constitution of the Confederate States of America, the Ordinances of the Texas Convention and an Address to the People of Texas. Austin: 1861. V. 41; 45

TEXAS. CONSTITUTION - 1868

Constitution of the State of West Texas. (Asutin?): 1868. V. 37

TEXAS. CONSTITUTION - 1869

Constitution of the State of Texas. Washington: 1870. V. 37

TEXAS. CONSTITUTION - 1875

Journal of the Constitutional Convention of the State of Texas. Austin: 1875. V. 37

TEXAS. CONSTITUTIONAL CONVENTION, 1866.

The Constitution, as Amended, and Ordiannces of the Convention of 1866 . . . Austin: 1866. V. 37; 39; 41; 42

THE TEXAS Cook Book . . . Houston: 1883. V. 45

TEXAS Frontier Troubles. Washington: 1876. V. 38; 41; 42

TEXAS. LAWS, STATUES, ETC. - 1860

General Laws of the Eighth Legislature of the State of Texas. Austin: 1860. V. 37

TEXAS. LAWS, STATUTES, ETC.

Laws Passed by the Sixth Congress of the Republic of Texas. Austin: 1842. V. 45

Laws Passed by the Seventh Congress of the Republic of Texas. Washington: 1843. V. 45

Laws Passed by the Eighth Congress of the Republic of Texas. Houston: 1844. V. 45

TEXAS. LAWS, STATUTES, ETC. - 1835

Laws of the Republic of Texas. Houston, Texas: 1838-1845. V. 37

TEXAS. LAWS, STATUTES, ETC. - 1841

Laws of the Republic of Texas, Passed at the Session of the Fifth Congress. Houston: 1841. V. 37

TEXAS. LAWS, STATUTES, ETC. - 1842

Laws Passed by the Sixth Congress of the Republic of Texas. Austin: 1842. V. 37

TEXAS. LAWS, STATUTES, ETC. - 1845

Laws Passed by the Ninth Congress of The Republic of Texas. Washington, Texas: 1845. V. 37; 45

TEXAS. LAWS, STATUTES, ETC. - 1861

Laws of the Eighth Legislature of the State of Texas. Extra Session. Austin: 1861. V. 38

Special Laws Passed by the Extra Session of the Eighth Legislature, Convened Jan. 21st, 1861. Austin: 1861. V. 39

TEXAS. LAWS, STATUTES, ETC. - 1862

General Laws of the Ninth Legislature of the State of Texas. Houston: 1862. V. 38; 42; 45

TEXAS. LAWS, STATUTES, ETC. - 1863

General Laws of the Extra Session of the Ninth Legislature, of the State of Texas. Austin: 1863. V. 38

TEXAS. LAWS, STATUTES, ETC. - 1864

General Laws of The Tenth Legislature, (Called Session), with the Provisionall and Permanent Constitutions of the Confederate States . . . Houston: 1864. V. 38

Special Laws of the State of Texas. Houston: 1864. V. 38

TEXAS. LAWS, STATUTES, ETC. - 1865

General Laws of the Tenth Legislature (Second Extra Session) Of the State of Texas. Austin: 1865. V. 38

TEXAS. (PROVISIONAL GOVERNMENT). LAWS, STATUTES, ETC.

Ordinances and Decrees of the Consultation, Provisional Government of Texas and the Convention, Which Assembled at Washington March I, 1836. Houston: 1838. V. 42

TEXAS Rangers Sesquicentennial Anniversary 1823-1973. Forth Worth: 1973. V. 42

TEXAS. (REPUBLIC)

Unanimous Declaration of Independence, by the Delegates of the People of Texas, in General Convention, at the Town of Washington, on the Second Day of March, 1836. San Felipe de Austin: 1836. V. 40

TEXAS. (REPUBLIC). LAWS, STATUTES, ETC. - 1838

Laws of the Republic of Texas, in Two Volumes. (with) Laws of the Republic of Texas Volume the Third. Houston: 1838. V. 42; 44

Laws Passed at the 2d Session of the 2d Congress of the Republic of Texas. April and May, 1838. Houston: 1838. V. 39; 40

TEXAS. (REPUBLIC). LAWS, STATUTES, ETC. - 1841

Laws of the Republic of Texas, Passed at the Session of the Fifth Congress. Houston: 1841. V. 40

TEXAS. (STATE). CONSTITUTION - 1869

Constitution of the State of Texas. Washington: 1870. V. 39

TEXAS. (STATE). CONSTITUTION - 1870

Constitution of the State of Texas. Washington: 1870. V. 42

TEXAS. (STATE). CONSTITUTIONAL CONVENTION - 1876

Journal of the Constitutional Convention of the State of Texas. Austin: 1875. V. 39

TEXAS. (STATE). GOVERNOR - 1857

Message of the Governor of the State of Texas to the Seventh Legislature. Austin: 1857. V. 39

TEXAS. (STATE). HOUSE OF REPRESENTATIVES - 1882

Journal of the House of Representatives of the State of Texas: Being A Called Session of the Seventeenth Legislature, Begun . . . April 6, 1882. Los Angeles: 1930. V. 42

TEXAS. (STATE). LAWS, STATUTES, ETC. - 1862

General Laws of the Ninth Legislature of the State of Texas. Houston: 1862. V. 42

TEXAS. (STATE). LAWS, STATUTES, ETC. - 1873

General Laws of the State of Texas: Passed at the Session of the Thirteenth Legislature Begun and Held at the City of Austin, January 14, 1873. Austin: 1873. V. 40

TEXAS. (STATE). LAWS, STATUTUES, ETC. - 1846

Laws Passed by the First Legislature of the State of Texas. Austin: 1846. V. 39; 45

TEXAS, TOPOLOBAMPO & PACIFIC RAILROAD & TELEGRAPH COMPANY

Text of Contract and Concession for the Construction and Operation of a Railroad and Telegraph Line from Piedras Negras to Topolobampo . . . Boston: 1881. V. 37; 39

TEXAS VETERANS ASSOCIATION

'Remember the Alamo.' San Antonio: 1900. V. 38

TEXAS WESTERN RAILROAD

Charter of the Texas Western Railroad Company, and Extracts from the Reports of Col. A. B. Gray and Secretary of War, on the Survey of Route from Eastern Borders of Texas to California. Cincinnati: 1855. V. 38; 39; 40; 42; 43; 45

TEXEIRA, PEDRO

Persia. Antwerp: 1610. V. 46

TEXT Book for the Annual Sermons . . . in the English Reformed Church at Amsterdam. Haarlem: 1819. V. 38; 40

TEXT Book of Small Arms. London: 1909. V. 45

TEXTBOOK of Small Arms, 1929. London: 1929. V. 43

TEXTILE Colorist. Fiftieth Anniversary 1879-1928. New York: 1928. V. 40

TEXTILE Designs of Japan: Volume III. Designs of Ryukyu, Ainu & Foreign Textitles. Osaka: 1961. V. 39

TEYLER, JOHANNES

Architectura Militaris. Rotterdam: 1697. V. 37

TEZCAN, HULYE

The Topkapi Saray Museum: Costume, Embroideries and Other Textiles. Boston: 1986. V. 39

THACHER, AMOS BATEMAN

Turkoman Rugs. New York: 1940. V. 41

THACHER, JAMES 1754-1844

The American New Dispensatory. Boston: 1813. V. 38; 43

The American New Dispensatory. Boston: 1815. V. 42

American Medical Practice. Boston: 1817. V. 41; 44

American Medical Biography. Boston: 1828. V. 37; 40; 41; 44

The American Revolution, from the Commencement to the Disbanding of the American Army. New York: 1857. V. 46

American Modern Practice; or, a Simple Method of Prevention and Cure of Diseases . . . Boston: 1817. V. 37; 43

The American New Dispensatory . . . Boston: (1813). V. 37

The American Orchardist. Plymouth: 1825. V. 40

History of the Town of Plymouth; from Its First Settlement in 1620, to the Year 1832. Boston: 1832. V. 46

A Military Journal During the American Revolutionary War, from 1775 to 1783. Boston: 1823. V. 41; 42

A Military Journal during the American Revolutionary War, from 1775 to 1783 . . . Boston: 1827. V. 37

Observations on Hydrophobia, Produced by the Bite of a Mad Dog, or Other Rabid Animals. Plymouth: 1812. V. 37; 38; 42; 43; 45

A Practical Treatise on the Management of Bees. Boston: 1829. V. 40

THACHER, JOHN BOYD

Catalogues of the John Boyd Thacher Collection of Incunabula. Washington: 1915-31. V. 43

Christopher Columbus His Life, His Work, His Remains as Revealed by Original Printed and Manuscript Records Together with an Essay on Peter Martyr of Angbera and Bartolome De Las Cases, the First Historians of America. New York: 1903. V. 41

THACHER, MOSES

An Address to the Church and Congregation, Under the Care of the Author, on His Seceding from the Masonic Institution Delivered May 24, 1829. Boston: 1829. V. 43

THACHER, PETER

A Sermon Preached to the Society in Brattle Street, Boston, October 20, 1793. Boston: 1793. V. 43

THACKER, T. W.

The Relationship of the Semitic and Eyptian Verbal Systems. Oxford: 1954. V. 38

THACKERAY, WILLIAM MAKEPEACE 1811-1863

The Adventures of Philip on His Way through the World . . . V. 41

The Adventures of Philip on His Way Through the World. London: 1862. V. 37; 38; 39; 40; 41; 42; 44; 45; 46

The Adventures of Philip. New York: 1862. V. 39

Ballads. London. V. 39; 43

Ballads. London: 1855. V. 39; 40; 41

Ballads. Boston: 1856. V. 40

Ballads. London: 1879. V. 41; 42; 46

The Book of Snobs. London: 1848. V. 40; 41; 46

A Book of Drawings. A Series of Metamorphoses Made in Philadelphia, 1853, for the Children of William B. Reed. Philadelphia: 1925. V. 37

Christmas Books. Mrs. Perkins' Ball. Our Street. Dr. Birch. London: 1857. V. 39

The Christmas Books of Mr. M. A. Titmarsh. London: 1872. V. 46

The Chronicle of the Drum. New York: 1882. V. 41

Comic Tales and Sketches. London: 1841. V. 39; 41; 44; 45; 46

The Complete Poems. New York: 1884. V. 46

Denis Duval. London: 1867. V. 39; 44

Doctor Birch and His Young Friends. London: 1849. V. 39; 40; 42

Doctor Birch and His Young Friends. London: 1849, 1848. V. 40

Dr. Brown's Letters. New York: 1853. V. 39

Early and Late Papers, Hitherto Uncollected. Boston: 1867. V. 39; 41; 46

The English Humorists of the Eighteenth Century, a Series of Lectures Delivered in England, Scotland and America. London: 1853. V. 37; 38; 40; 41; 42

The English Humourists of the Eighteenth Century. New York: 1853. V. 39; 43

An Essay on the Genius of George Cruikshank. London: 1840. V. 38; 39; 41; 44; 46

An Essay on the Genius of George Cruikshank. London: 1849. V. 39

An Essay on the Genius of George Cruikshank . . . London: 1884. V. 39

Etchings by the Late William Makepeace Thackeray While at Cambridge, Illustrative of University Life . . . London: 1878. V. 39; 44

The Fatal Boots and Cox's Diary. London: 1855. V. 39

The Fitz-Boodle Papers and Men's Wives. London: 1857. V. 40

The Four Georges. New York: 1860. V. 40

The Four Georges. London: 1861. V. 37; 39; 40; 46

The History of Pendennis. London: 1848-50. V. 42

The History of Pendennis. London: 1849-50. V. 37; 39; 40; 41; 42; 46

The History of Henry Esmond, Esq. London: 1852. V. 37; 39; 40; 41; 45; 46

The History of Pendennis. Ipswich: 1961. V. 43

The History of Pendennis. New York: 1961. V. 44

The History of Henry Esmond, Esq. London: 1853. V. 40; 45

The History of Henry Esmond, Esq. London: 1956. V. 44

The History of Pendennis. London: 1849. V. 37; 45

The History of Pendennis. 1961. V. 40

The History of Samuel Titmarsh and the Great Hoggarty Diamond. London: 1849. V. 41

The History of Samuel Titmarsh and the Great Hoggarty Diamond. London: 1857. V. 40; 45

Illustrations to the Surprising Adventures of Three Men. London: 1850. V. 45

An Interesting Event. London: 1849. V. 40

The Irish Sketch-Book. London: 1843. V. 39; 42; 44

The Irish Sketch-Book. London: 1845. V. 40; 46

The Irish Sketch-Book. London: 1857. V. 40

The Kickleburys on the Rhine. Frankfut: 1851. V. 39

The Kickleburys on the Rhine. London: 1850. V. 40

Kickleburys on the Rhine. New York: 1851. V. 40

The Letters and Private Papers. 1945-46. V. 39; 46

Letters and Private Papers. Cambridge: 1945-46. V. 38; 40

Letters and Private Papers. Cambridge;: 1945/46. V. 42

A Little Dinner at Timmins's; and The Bedford-Row Conspiracy. London: 1856. V. 41; 42

Loose Sketches. London: 1894. V. 40

Lovel the Widower. London: 1861. V. 37; 42

Memoirs of a Most Respectable Family. London: 1853-Aug. 1855. V. 40

The Memoirs of Barry Lyndon. London: 1856. V. 38; 40

Miscellanies, Prose and Verse. London: 1856/57. V. 40

Miscellanies, Prose and Verse. London: 1857/56/57. V. 46

Mrs. Perkins Ball. London: 1847. V. 39; 40

The Newcombes. London: 1854. V. 37; 39; 40; 41; 42; 45; 46

THACKERAY, WILLIAM MAKEPEACE 1811-1863 continued

The Newcombes. Memoirs of a most Respectable Family. Edited by Arthur Pendennis, Esqre. Illustrated with both steel and wood engravings by Richard Doyle. London: 1853-55. V. 37; 39; 41; 44; 45; 46

The Newcomes. London: 1854. V. 39

The Newcomes. London: 1854-55. V. 37; 38; 39; 40; 46

The Newcomes: Memoirs of a Most Respectable Family. Cambridge: 1954. V. 40; 41

The Newcomes. Memoirs of a Most Respectable Family. Edited by Aruthur Pendennis, Esq. London: 1855. V. 37

Notes of a Journey from Cornhill to Grand Cairo. London: 1846. V. 37; 39; 40; 42; 46

Novels. London: 1848-59. V. 37

Novels by Eminent Hands and Character Sketches. London: 1856. V. 46

The Orphan of Pimlico and Other Sketches, Fragments and Drawings. London: 1876. V. 37; 46

Our Street. London: 1848. V. 39; 40

The Paris Sketch Book. London: 1840. V. 39; 40

Punch's Prize Novelists, the Fat Contributor and Travels in London. New York: 1853. V. 39; 41; 46

Reading a Poem. London: 1891. V. 41

Rebecca and Rowena. London: 1850. V. 38; 41; 42; 46

The Rose and the Ring. London: 1855. V. 38; 39; 42; 44; 46

The Rose and the Ring. New York: 1855. V. 43

The Rose and the Ring. New York: 1942. V. 44; 46

Roundabout Papers. London: 1863. V. 38; 39; 40; 44

Roundabout Papers. New York: 1863. V. 39; 40

Roundabout Papers. London: 1868. V. 39

The Second Funeral of Napoleon in Three Letters to Miss Smith of London. London: 1880. V. 40

Sketches and Travels in London. London: 1856. V. 39; 40

The Snob: a Literary and Scientific Journal. (with) The Gownsman, (formerly called) 'The Snob', a Literary nd Scientific Journal, Now Conducted by Members of the University. Cambridge: 1829. V. 38

The Student's Quarter or Paris Five and Thirty Years Since. London: 1874. V. 39; 41

Sultan Stork and Other Stories and Sketches Now First Collected. London: 1887. V. 38; 39; 40; 43; 44

Thackerayana. Notes & Anecdotes, Illustrated by nearly Six Hundred Sketches. (By Joseph Grego). London: 1875. V. 37; 39; 43

Vanity Fair . . . London: 1847-48. V. 44

Vanity Fair. Leipzig: 1848. V. 46

Vanity Fair. London: 1848. V. 37; 38; 39; 41; 42; 44; 45; 46

Vanity Fair. London: 1848-49. V. 40

Vanity Fair. London: 1849. V. 38; 40; 41; 43

La Foire Aux Vanites. Paris: 1855. V. 42

Vanity Fair. A Novel Without a Hero. New York: 1865. V. 37

Vanity Fair. London: 1882. V. 46

Vanity Fair. New York: 1931. V. 38; 41; 45

Vanity Fair. Oxford: 1931. V. 41

The Virginians. London: 1857-59. V. 38; 41; 42; 45; 46

The Virginians. London: 1858. V. 37; 39; 42; 45; 46

The Virginians. London: 1858-59. V. 37; 39; 40; 41; 43; 44; 45; 46

The Virginians. London: 1859. V. 39; 41; 44

Works. London: 1867-69. V. 46

The Works. London: 1869. V. 37; 39; 42; 46

The Works. London: 1869-86. V. 37; 43

The Works. London: 1878-86. V. 40

The Works. London: 1879. V. 40; 42

The Works. London: 1881-82. V. 40

The Works of . . . London: 1883-85. V. 39

The Works of William Makepeace Thackeray. London: 1883-86. V. 46

The Works. London: 1886-88. V. 39

Works. London: 1888. V. 46

Complete Works. Boston & New York: 1889. V. 40

The Works. London: 1894. V. 38

Works. New York: 1897. V. 37

The Works. London: 1898. V. 41

Works. London: 1898-99. V. 38

The Works. London: 1899. V. 38; 42

Works. London: 1899-1900. V. 46

Works. London: 1899-1906. V. 37

The Works. London: 1901. V. 42

The Works. New York: 1903. V. 38; 39

The Works of William Makepeace Thackeray. New York: 1903-04. V. 38; 46

The Complete Works. New York: 1904. V. 42

The Works of . . . London: 1910. V. 40; 46

The Works. New York: & London: 1910. V. 43

The Works. London: 1911. V. 37

THACKRAH, C. TURNER

The Effects of the Principal Arts, Trades and Professions and of Civic States and Habits of Living on Health and Longevity . . . Philadelphia: 1831. V. 39; 44

THACKWELL, EDWARD JOSEPH

Narrative of a Second Seikh War, in 1848-49. London: 1851. V. 42

THALATTA: a Book for the Sea-Side. Boston: 1853. V. 45

THANE, J.

British Autography. A Collection of Fac-Similes of the Handwriting of Royal and Illustrious Personages with their authentic Portraits. 1788-1839. V. 37

THANE, JOHN

British Autography. London: 1788-93? V. 45

THANET, OCTAVE

A Book of True Lovers. Chicago: 1897. V. 37; 38; 44

THARAUD, JEROME

Un Royaume de Dieu. Paris: 1925. V. 41

THATCHER, BENJAMIN B.

A Retrospect of the Boston Tea-Party . . . New York: 1834. V. 41

Traits of the Tea Party. New York: 1835. V. 40

THATCHER, JAMES

A Military Journal During the American Revolutionary War, from 1775 to 1783 . . . Boston: 1827. V. 41

THATCHER, PETER

Observations Upon the Present State of the Clergy of New-England with Strictures Upon the Power of Dismissing Them . . . Boston: 1783. V. 45

THATCHER, W. S.

The Fourth Battalion Duke of Connaught's Own Tenth Baluch Regiment in the Great War. 19th D.C.O. Baluchis. Cambridge: 1932. V. 42

THAULON, GUSTAV

Hegel's Ansichten uber Erziehung und Unterricht. In Drei Theilen. Kiel: 1853-54. V. 41

THAXTER, CELIA

An Island Garden. Boston: 1894. V. 43; 46

An Island Garden. Boston & New York: 1894. V. 39; 43

Poems. New York: 1872. V. 43; 46

THAYE, JOHN

The Catholic Controversy, Maintained in the Periodical Publications of Boston, New Salem, and Other Towns of the United States . . . Dublin: 1809. V. 44

THAYER, ALEXANDER WHEELOCK

The Life of Ludwig Van Beethoven. New York: 1921. V. 46

THAYER, B. W.

List of Cheap and Elegant Music Published By E. Ferrett & Co . . . . Boston?: 1845. V. 44

THAYER, E.

Catalogue of a Collection of Books on Ornithology in the Library of John E. Thayer. London: 1913. V. 43

THAYER, ELI

A History of the Kansas Crusade Its Friends and Foes. New York: 1889. V. 45

THAYER, EMMA HOMAN

Wild Flowers of Colorado. New York: 1885. V. 39; 43; 45

Wild Flowers of the Rocky Mountains. New York: 1887. V. 37; 38; 40; 44; 46

THAYER, ENREST L.

Casey at the Bat. New York: 1901. V. 44

THAYER, GEORGE B.

Ancestors of Adelbert P. Thayer, Florine Thayer McCray and George Burton Thayer, Children of John W. Thayer and Adaline Burton . . . Hartford: 1894. V. 46

THAYER, GERALD H.

Concealing-Coloration in the Animal Kingdom. New York: 1909. V. 37; 38; 39; 41; 43; 44; 45

Concealing-Coloration in the Animal Kingdom. New York: 1918. V. 38

THAYER, HENRY & CO.

Descriptive Catalogue of Fluid and Solid Extracts in Vacuo, also Concentrations and Officinal Pills, Prepared by Henry Tahyer and Co. with Formulas and Receipts. Cambridgeport: 1874. V. 41

Descriptive Catalogue of Fluid and Solid Extracts, Also Pills, Resinoids and Alkaloids, Prepeared by . . . with Formulas and Receipts. Cambridgeport: 1879. V. 41

THAYER, HENRY O.

The Sagadahoc Colony, Comprising the Relation of a Voyage Into New England. Portland: 1892. V. 42

THAYER, JAMES BRADLEY

Legal Essays. Boston: 1908. V. 43

A Preliminary Treatise on Evidence at the Common Law, Part I, Development of Trial by Jury. Boston: 1896. V. 43

A Western Journey with Mr. Emerson. Boston: 1884. V. 38; 41

THAYER, JOHN M.

General Orders No. 43. Fort Smith: 1864. V. 41

General Orders No. 49. Fort Smith: 1864. V. 41

THAYER, WILLIAM SYDNEY

Osler and Other Papers. Baltimore: 1931. V. 45; 46

THEAKSON, M.

British Angling Flies. London: 1862. V. 43

A List of Natural Flies That Are Taken by Trout, Grayling, and Smelt, in the Streams of Ripon. Ripon: 1853. V. 43

THEAKSTON, LUCY E. LLOYD

Some Family Records and Pedigrees of the Lloyds of Allt yr Odyn, Castell Hywel, Ffos y Bleiddiaid . . . Oxford: 1913. V. 40

THEARLE, SAMUEL J. P.

The Modern Practice of Shipbuilding in Iron and Steel. London: 1886. V. 46

The Modern Practice of Shipbuilding in Iron and Steel. London: 1910. V. 41

THEATRES and Cinemas. London: 1933-38. V. 37

THEATRICAL Biography or, Memoirs of the Principal Performers of the Three Theatres Royal. London: 1772. V. 38

THE THEATRICAL Bouquet . . . London: 1778. V. 42

THE THEATRICAL Bouquet: Containing an Alphabetical Arrangement of the Prologues and Epilogues . . . London: 1778. V. 43

THEATRICAL Records: or, an Account of English Dramatic Authors, and Their Works. London: 1756. V. 38

THE THEATRICAL Remembrancer, Containing a Complete List of all the Dramatic Performances in the English Language. London: 1788. V. 37

THE THEATRICAL Review: for the Year 1757, nd Beginnin of 1758. London: 1758. V. 38

THEGLIATIUS, STEPHANUS

Oratio Coram Innocentio VIII pro die Pentecostes Habita. Rome: 1487. V. 44

THELWALL, A. S.

The Inequities of the Opium Trade with China . . . London: 1839. V. 46

THELWALL, JOHN

An Appeal to Popular Opinion, Against Kidnapping & Murder. London: 1796. V. 39; 40; 41

The Rights of Nature, Against the Usurpations of Establishments. London: 1796. V. 39

Sober Reflections on the Seditious and Inflammatory Letter of the Right Hon. Edmund Burke, to a Noble Lord. London: 1796. V. 39

THENARD, L. J.

A Treatise on the General Principles of Chemical Analysis. London: 1818. V. 39; 40

THEO, PSEUD.

Visit of a London Exquisite to His Maiden Aunts in the Country. London: 1859. V. 39

THEOBALD, JOHN

Albion, a Poem. Oxford: 1720. V. 42; 45

Medulla Medicinae Universae; or, a New Compendious Dispensatory. London: 1748. V. 42

Medulla Medicinae Universae; or, a New Compendious Dispensatory. London: 1749. V. 41

A Second Light. NewarK;: 1977. V. 41; 44

THEOBALD, LEWIS

The Cave of Poverty. London: 1714. V. 41

The Cave of Poverty, a Poem. London: 1715. V. 43

The Censor. London: 1717. V. 38

Double Falshood; or, the Distrest Lovers. London: 1728. V. 42; 45

the Life and Character of Marcus Portius Cato Uticensis . . . London: 1713. V. 45

Orestes: a Dramatic Opera. London: 1731. V. 46

The Perfidious Brother, a Tragedy. London: 1715. V. 41

THEOCHARIS, DEMETRIOS R.

Neolithic Greece. Athens: 1973. V. 40

THEOCHARIS, EMETRIOS R.

Neolithic Greece. Athens: (1973). V. 37

THEOCRITOS

The Complete Poems. London: 1930. V. 39

THEOCRITUS c. 308 - c. 240 BC

Bion & Moschus. London: 1922. V. 43; 46

The Complete Poems. London: 1929. V. 39; 40; 44; 45

The Complete Poems. 1929. V. 37; 38; 41; 42

Eclogae Triginta, with Other Pieces, Including Hesiod. Venice: 1495. V. 37; 38

Idyllia (Graece). Rome: 1516. V. 40

Idyllia. Hoc est Poemata XXXV. Epigrammata. Frankfurt: 1545. V. 40

The Idyllia, Epigrams and Fragments of Theocritus. Exeter: 1786. V. 42

Idyllia Triginta-Sex, Recens e Graeco in Latinum Translata. Venice: 1539. V. 37

The Idylliums. London: 1767. V. 38; 40; 41; 44; 46

The Idylls of . . . London: 1922. V. 38; 46

The Idyls of, Rendered into English Prose by Andrew Lang. 1922. V. 39

Sixe Idillia. 1883. V. 45

Sixe Idylla Chosen out of the Sicilian Poet . . . New York: 1971. V. 39; 41

Theocriti Quae Extant. Cum Graecis Scholiis. Oxoniae: 1699. V. 40

Theocritus, Bion and Moschus. London: 1922. V. 41

The Complete Works of Theocritus. London: 1929. V. 46

THEODAT, SAGARD

Le Grand Voyage du Pays des Hurons Situe en l'Amerique vers la Mer Douce . . . Paris: 1865. V. 43

THEODORE Low De Vinne. New York: 1968. V. 40

THEODORETI Episcopi Cyri de Providentia Sermones X. Rome: 1545. V. 43

THEODORETUS c. 390-458

Dialogi tres Contra . . . Haereseos . . . Rome: 1547. V. 40

THEODORETUS Cyrensis Episcopi. In Quatuordecim Sancti Pauli Epistolas Commentarius Nunc Primum Latine Versus Gentiano Herveto Aurelio Interprete. Florentia: 1552. V. 38

THEODORIC, BP. OF CERVIA

The Surgery of Theodoric ca. A.D. 1267. New York: 1955-60. V. 42

THEODORUS GAZA

In Hoc Uolumine Haec Insunt. Theodori Introductiuae Grammatices Libri Quatuor. Eiusdem de Mensibus Opusculum Sane Quam Pulchtum (sic). Apolonii Grammatici de Constructione Libri Quatuor. Colophon: 1495. V. 37

THEODOSIUS

Sphaericorum, Libri Tres. Paris: 1558. V. 44

Sphaericorum Libri III. A Christophoro Clavio . . . Rome: 1585-86. V. 44

THEOGNIS

Theognis Restitutus. The Personal History of the Poet Thognis, Deduced from an Analysis of His Existing Fragments. Malta: 1842. V. 39; 46

THEOLBALD, LEWIS

The Mausoleum. London: 1714. V. 41

THE THEOPHILANTHROPIST. New York: 1810. V. 39

THEOPHILUS

An Essay Upon Various Arts . . . Forming an Encyclopedia of Christian Art of the Eleventh Century. London: 1847. V. 38

THEOPHILUS, PATRIARCH OF ALEXANDRIA

(Greek title: then) Singularis & Pia Dissertatio, Cuius rei Homo Similis Sit, Simulacrumque Habeat. Paris: 1608. V. 43

THEOPHRASTUS

Characteres (Greek text). (with) Capita Duo Hactenus Anecdota Quae ex Cod. London: 1790. V. 38

De Historia Plantarium. Amsterdam: 1644. V. 40; 44

Theophrastus's History of Stones, with an English Version and Critical and Philosophical Notes . . . London: 1746. V. 46

THEOPHRASTUS continued

(Greek & Latin), Notationes Morum. Isaacus Cassaubonus Recensuit in Latinum Sermonem Vertit & Libro Commentario Illustravit. Lyon: 1599. V. 44; 46

Notationes Morvm. Isaacvs Casavbonvs Recensuit, in Latinum Sermonem Vertit, Libri Commentario Illvstravit. Lyon: 1599. V. 38

THEOPHYLACTUS

Ennarationes in Quatuor Evangelica. Rome: 1542. V. 40; 45

Enarrationes in Epistolas S. Pauli. Trans. by Chrisophorus Persona. Rome: 1477. V. 39

THEOPHYLACTUS, ARCHBISHOP OF OKHRID

(In Greek) Hermeneia eis ta Tessara Euangelia. Rome: 1542. V. 37

THEOPHYLACTUS, BULGARIAE EPISCOPUS

In Quatuor Evangelia Enarrationes. Basle: 1525. V. 38; 43

Enarrationes in Quatuor Evangelia. (with) In Omnes Divi Pauli Epistolas Enrrationes . . . Basle: 1531. V. 38

A THEORETICAL and Practical Treatise on the Five Orders of Architecture . . . an Historical Description of Gothic Architecture . . . Treatises on Projection, Perspective . . . Index and Glossary. London: 1834. V. 37

THEORETICAL, Practical, and Analytical, as Applied to the Arts and Manufactures. London. V. 39

THEROUX, ALEANDER

Three Wogs. Boston: 1972. V. 42; 44; 46

THEROUX, ALEXANDER

An Adultery. London: 1988. V. 43

Darconville's Cat. Garden City: 1981. V. 46

Three Wogs. 1972. V. 42

Three Wogs. London: 1973. V. 46

THEROUX, PAUL 1941-

Fong and the Indians. Boston: 1968. V. 44

Girls at Play. Boston: 1969. V. 37; 40; 41; 42

Girls at Play. London: 1969. V. 40; 41

Jungle Lovers. Boston: 1971. V. 45

Jungle Lovers. London: 1971. V. 42

London Snow. Croton-on-Hudson: 1979. V. 44

London Snow Announcement. New York: 1979. V. 43

London Snow. Salisbury: 1979. V. 41; 42; 43; 44; 45; 46

London Snow: a Christmas Story. The Chantry, Wilton,: 1979. V. 43

London Snow. Wiltshire: 1979. V. 41; 42

London Snow - a Christmas Story. London: 1980. V. 45

The Mosquito Coast. Boston: 1982. V. 42; 43; 45

My Secret History. London: 1989. V. 41; 42

The Old Patagonian Express. Boston: 1979. V. 42

The Old Patagoinan Express. London: 1979. V. 37

Patagonia Revisited. Great Britain: 1985. V. 37; 40

Patagonia Revisited. Salisbury: 1985. V. 43

Sailing Through China. 1983. V. 42

Sailing through China. Great Britain: 1983. V. 40

Sailing through China. Salisbury: 1983. V. 41

Sailing Through China. Boston: 1984. V. 42

Saint Jack. Boston: 1973. V. 37; 44

Saint Jack. London: 1973. V. 42; 45

The Shortest Day of the Year . . . Leamington: 1986. V. 45

The Shortest Day of the Year. Leamington Spa: 1986. V. 37; 38; 39; 40; 41; 42; 43; 46

The Shortest Day of the Year. London: 1986. V. 42

The Shortest Day of the Year. A Christmas Fantasy. Ptd. by Sebastian Carter at: 1986. V. 38

Singing with Annie and Other Stories. London: 1975. V. 42

Sinning with Annie. Boston: 1972. V. 41; 42; 44; 45

V. S. Naipaul - an Introduction to His Work. London: 1972. V. 41

Waldo. London. V. 45

Waldo. 1967. V. 44; 46

Waldo. Boston: 1967. V. 37; 39; 41; 42; 43; 44; 45; 46

Waldo. London: 1968. V. 40; 41; 43; 45

Waldo. Boston: 1971. V. 45

Waldo. Boston: 1987. V. 38

White Man's Burden - a Play. London: 1987. V. 40

THERRY, ROGER

Reminiscences of Thirty Years' Residence in New South Wales and Victoria. London: 1863. V. 38

THERSNER, ULRIC

Fordna Och Naharvarande . . . Stockholm: 1816-30. V. 44

THESAURUS Aenigmaticus; or, a Collection of the Most Ingenious and Diverting Aenigma's or Riddles . . . London: 1725-26. V. 45

THESAURUS Cornucopiae & Horti Adonidis. Colophon: Venice: 1496. V. 40

THESAURUS Geographicus. London: 1695. V. 45

THESE Things the Poets Said (of Edward Thomas). Flansham: 1935. V. 45

THE THESPIAN Preceptor; or, a Full Display of the Scenic Art . . . Boston: 1810. V. 40

THETORES Graeci. Venice: 1508-09. V. 37

THEVENOT,

The Art of Swimming. London: 1764. V. 44; 46

THEVENOT, JEAN

Relation d'un Voyage Fait au Levant Dans Laquelle Il Est Curieusement Traite des Estats Sujects au Grand Seigneur, des Moeurs . . . Paris: 1663. V. 43

THEVENOT, JEAN DE

Gedenkwaardige en Zeer Naauwkeurige Reizen Van Den . . . Amsterdam: 1681-82-88. V. 39; 42; 45

The Travels of Monsieur de Thevenot into the Levant. London: 1687. V. 40; 42

THEVENOT, MELCHISEDEC

Relations de Divers Voyages Curieux qui n'ont Point Este Publiees . . . Paris: 1696. V. 39

THEVET, ANDRE

Historia Dell'India America Detta Altramente Francia Antartica. Venice: 1561. V. 45

Les Singularitez De La France Antarctique Autrement Nommee L'Amerique . . . Antwerp: 1558. V. 41; 42

THEY Still Draw Pictures. New York: 1938. V. 38; 41

THICKNESSE, ANN

Sketches of the Lives and Writings of the Ladies of France. London: 1780. V. 44

THICKNESSE, PHILIP

Memoirs and Anecdotes of Philip Thicknesse . . . London?: 1788. V. 43

Memoirs and Anecdotes of Philip Thicknesse, Late Lieutenant Governor of Land Guard Fort, and Unfortunate Father to George Touchet, Baron Audley. N.P.: 1788. V. 37; 40

Memoirs and Anecdotes of Philip Thicknesse, Late Lieut. Governor of Land Guard Fort. Dublin: 1790. V. 37; 38; 39; 42

Observations on the Customs and Manners of the French Nation in a Series of letters in Which that Nation is Vindicated from the Misrepresentations of Some Late Writers. Dublin: 1767. V. 38; 43

Sketches and Characters of the Most Eminent and Most Singular Persons Now Living. Bristol: 1770. V. 38

A Year's Journey through France, and Part of Spain. Bath: 1777. V. 40

A Year's Journey through France and Part of Spain. London: 1778. V. 45; 46

A Year's Journey through the Pais Bas; or, Austrian Netherlands. London: 1786. V. 37; 40; 45

THIEBAUD, J.

Bibliographie des Ouvrages Francais sur la Chasse. London: 1934. V. 39

THIEBAULT, PAUL, BARON

The Memoirs. London: 1896. V. 41; 45

THIEL, PEITER J. VAN

All the Paintings of the Rijksmuseum in Amsterdam. Amsterdam: and Maarssen: 1976. V. 46

THIELE, FRIEDRICH, LEOPOLD

Laub-Moose der Mittelmarki. Berlin: 1832. V. 38

THIERMAIR, FRANZ IGNAZ

Scholia Medica ad Totidem & Ante Nunquam Vulgatas Consultationes et Responsiones, Quas Partim Author, Partim Alii . . . Munich: 1673. V. 46

THIERRY, AUGUSTIN

History of the Conquest of England by the Normans. London: 1825. V. 38

THIERS, JEAN BAPTISTE 1636-1703

Histoire des Perruques ou l'on Fait Voir Leur Origine, Leur Usage, Leur Forme, l'Abus et l'Irregularite de Celles des Ecclesiastiques. Paris: 1690. V. 41

THIERS, LOUIS ADOLPHE

Histoire de la Revolution Francaise. (with) Histoire du Consuault et de l'Empire. (with) Atlas de l'Histoire du Consulat et de l'Empire. Paris: 1845-84. V. 39

THIERS, M. A.

The History of the French Revolution. London: 1838. V. 46

History of the Consulate and the Empire of France Under Napoleon. London: 1845-62. V. 38

THIGPEN, CORBETT H.

The Three Faces of Eve. London: 1957. V. 39; 43

THIMM, CARL A.

A Complete Bibliography of Fencing and Duelling. London: 1896. V. 42; 44

THIMME, JURGEN

Art and Culture of the Cyclades: handbook of an Ancient Civilisation. Karlsruhe: 1977. V. 40

THINGS That A Child Ought to Know. Our Vegetable Food. London: (1890's). V. 37

THIOUT, ANTOINE 1692-1767

Traite de l'Horlogerie, Mechanique et Pratique . . . Paris: 1741. V. 42

THIRA; or, the Cairn Braich. London: 1879. V. 39; 42

THE THIRD American Chess Congress, Held at Chicago, Ill., 1874. Hannibal: 1876. V. 40

THIRKELL, ANGELA

The Brandons. London: 1939. V. 45

Pomfret Towers. London: 1938. V. 39

13 California Towns from the Original Drawings. San Francisco: 1947. V. 38; 39; 41; 46

THIRTY Old-Time Nursery Songs. London: 1907. V. 46

THIRTY-THIRD BATTALION

History and Memoir of the 33rd Battalion Machine Gun Corps and of the 19th, 98th, 100th and 248th. London: 1919. V. 37

32 Counties: Photographs of Ireland. London: 1989. V. 46

THIRTY Years of Bird and Bull. A Bibliography 1958-1988. Newtown: 1988. V. 42; 44

THIRY, PAUL

Eskimo Artifacts Designed for Use. Seattle: 1977. V. 46

THIS Little Pig Went to Market. London: 1870-74.. V. 43

THISTLEWOOD, ARTHUR

An Interesting Correspondence Between Thistlewood and Sidmouth, Concerning the Property Detained in Consequence of an Arrest On, a Charge of High Treason. London: 1817. V. 39; 42

The Trial of Arthur Thistlewood, on a Charge of High Treason. Tried at the Old Baily, April 17th 1820 Before the Lord Chief Justice Abbott. London: 1820. V. 46

THITCHELL, RALPH E.

Old Santa Fe: The Story of New Mexico's Ancient Capital. Santa Fe: 1925. V. 45

THOBURN, JOSEPH B.

A Standard History of Oklahoma . . . Chicago: 1916. V. 44

THOM, ADAM 1802-1890

The Claims of the Oregon Territory Considered. London: 1844. V. 37; 38; 39; 40; 41; 42; 45

THOM, ALEX, & CO.

Thom's Official Directory of the United Kingdom of Great Britain and Ireland, for 19808. Dublin: 1908. V. 44

THOM, ROBERT

Chinese and English Vocabulary. Canton: 1843. V. 41

The Chinese Speaker, or Extracts from Works Written in the Mandarin Language, as Spoken at Peking. Ningpo: 1846. V. 41

THOMA, KURT

Oral Roentgenology, A Roentgen Study of the Anatomy and Pathology of the Oral Cavity. Boston: 1917. V. 42

THOMA, KURT H.

Oral Rosentgenology: a Roentgen Study of the Anatomy and Pathology of the Oral Cavity. Boston: 1922. V. 44

THOMAS, ABEL

A Brief Memoir Concerning Abel Thomas, a Minister of the Gospel of Christ in the Society of Friends. Compiled from Authentic Documents. Philadelphia: 1824. V. 37

Facts for the People. Lowell: 1841. V. 45

THOMAS A'KEMPIS 1830-1471

The Followinc (sic) of Christ. London: 1673. V. 44

Meditations on Our Lady. Ditchling: 1929. V. 41; 42

THOMAS, ALFRED BARNABY

The Plains Indians and New Mexico, 1751-1778. Albuquerque: 1940. V. 42

THOMAS, ANTOINE

A Short Account of the Declaration, Given by the Chinese Emperour Kam Hi, in the Year 1700. London: 1703. V. 43

THOMAS, ANTOINE LEONARD

An Essay on the Character, the Manners, and the Understanding of Women, in Different Ages. London: 1781. V. 46

Essay on the Character, Manners and Genius of Women in Different Ages. London: 1773. V. 37

THOMAS AQUINAS, SAINT 1225?-1274

Catena Aurea Super Quattuor Evangelistas. Venice: 1493. V. 44

Cathena Auera in Q(ua)ttuor Evan(n)ngelia. Lyon: 1520. V. 46

Commerce. Being Extracts from the Summa Theologica of St. Thomas Aquinas. Ditchling: 1919. V. 40; 41

Expositio Divi Thomae Aquinatis Doctoris Angelici Super Octo Libros Physicorum Aristotelis cum Duplici Translatione Antiqua Videlicet . . . Colophon: 1517. V. 41

In Libros de Anima Aristotelis Exposito et cum tex(t) Jo. Argyropyli Ubiq(ue) Primo Loco Addito. Venice: 1507. V. 40

In Libris de Generatione & Corruptione Aristotelis Clarissima Expositio. Venice: 1539. V. 44

Prima Pars Summe Sacre Theologie Angelici Doctoris Sancti Thome de Quino. (with) Prima Seconde Sancti Thome de Quino . . . Colophon: Venice: 1495. V. 43

Quaestiones de Duodecim Quodlibet. Venice: 1476. V. 37; 38; 44

Quaestiones de Duodecim Quodlibet. Cologne: 1485. V. 37

Quaestiones Disputae. Lyon: 1569. V. 43

Saint Thomas Aquinas. Selections From His Works. Chatham: 1969. V. 46

Selections from His Works. Chatham: 1969. V. 37

Summa Theologiae. Basel: 1485. V. 45

Summa Theologica. Rome: 1886. V. 44

Summa Contra Gentiles Sive de Veritate Catholicae Fidei. Venice: 1480. V. 37

Super Primo Libro Sententiarum. Venice: 1486. V. 45

THOMAS, B.

Arabia Felix: Across the Empty Quarter of Arabia . . . London: 1932. V. 44

The Arabs. London: 1937. V. 44

The Shooter's Guide; or, Complete Sportsman's Companion.. London: 1814. V. 45

THOMAS, BARTRAM

Alarms and Excursions in Arabia. Indianapolis: 1930. V. 45

THOMAS, BERTHA

Sundorne. London: 1890. V. 40

THOMAS, BERTRAM

Alarms and Excursions in Arabia. London: 1931. V. 43

Arabia Felix: Across the Empty Quarter of Arabia. V. 40

Arabia Felix; Across the Empty Quarter of Arabia. London: 1932. V. 41; 43

Arabia Felix. New York: 1932. V. 38

THOMAS, BOB

Astaire the Man, the Dancer. New York: 1984. V. 46

THOMAS, C.

Contributions to the History of the Eastern Townships . . . St. Armand, Dunham, Sutton, Brome, Potton and Bolton . . . Montreal: 1866. V. 44

THOMAS, CHARLES ANTOINE

Exposition Retrospective Militaire de Ministere de la Guerre en 1889. 1890. V. 46

THOMAS, CLARENCE

General Turner Ashby, The Centaur of the South. Winchester: 1907. V. 37

THOMAS, CYRUS

The Cherokees in Pre-Columbian Times. New York: 1890. V. 43

Contributions to the History of the Eastern Townships: A Work containing an Account of the Early Settlement of St. Armand, Dunham, Sutton, Brome, Potton, and Bolton; with a history of the principal events that have transpired in each . . . Montreal: 1866. V. 37

THOMAS, P. J.

Our Centennial Memoir. Founding of the Missions. San Francisco de Assis in its Hundredth year. San Francisco: 1877. V. 37

THOMAS, PASCOE

A True and Impartial Journal of a Voyage to the South Seas, and Round the Globe, in His Majesty's Ship the Centurion Under the Command of Commodore George Anson... London: 1745. V. 41; 42; 45

THOMAS, PATRICK J.

Our Centennial Memoir. San Francisco: 1877. V. 46

THOMAS, PETER

Beater Time Tests. Santa Cruz: 1987. V. 38; 39

Papermaking in Seventeenth Century England... Santa Cruz: 1990. V. 45

THOMAS, PETER PERRING

A Dissertation on the Ancient Chinese Vases of the Shang Dynasty, from 1743 to 1496, B.C. London: 1851. V. 41

THOMAS, R. S.

An Acre of Land. Newtown: 1952. V. 42; 44

Babel I: Being a Special R. S. Thomas Number. V. 45

The Bread of Truth. London: 1963. V. 39

The Minister. Newtown: 1953. V. 42

The Mountains. New York: 1968. V. 44

Poetry for Supper. London: 1958. V. 46

Poets' Meeting. Stratford-upon-Avon: 1983. V. 40

The Stones of the Field. Carmarthen: 1946. V. 40

The Stones of the Field. Carmarthen and Dublin: 1946. V. 38

The Stones of the Field; Poems. London: 1946. V. 40

Tares. London: 1961. V. 41

Welsh Airs. 1987. V. 42; 45

Words and the Poet - the W. D. Thomas Memorial Lecture. Cardiff: 1964. V. 41

THOMAS, RALPH

Serjeant Thomas and Sir J. E. Millais. London: 1901. V. 42

THOMAS, RICHARD

Report on a Survey of the Mining District of Cornwall from Chasewater to Camborne. London: 1819. V. 40

THOMAS, ROBERT

The Cause of Truth, Containing, Besides a Great Variety of Other Matters, a Refutation of Errors in the Political Works of Thomas Paine, and Other Publications of a Similar Kind. Edinburgh: 1797. V. 41

Medical Advice to the Inhabitants of Warm Climates, on the Domestic Treatment of All the Diseases Incidental Therein... Nassau: 1794. V. 41

The Modern Practice of Physic, Exhibiting the Characters, Causes, Symptoms, Prognostic, Morbid Appearances and Improved Method of Treating, the Diseases of all Climates. New York: 1811. V. 42

The Modern Practice of Physic, Exhibiting the Characters, Causes, Symptoms, Prognostics, Morbid Appearances and Improved Method of Treating Diseases of All Climates... New York: 1820. V. 39; 42

Modern Domestic Medicine; Being a Treatise Divested of Professional Terms on the Nature, Causes, Symptoms and Treatment of the Diseases of Men, Women and Children. New York: 1829. V. 41

The Modern Practice of Physic, Exhibiting the Characaters, Causes, Symptoms, Prognostic, Morbid, Appearances and Improved Method of Treating the Diseases of all Climates. New York: 1813. V. 37

THOMAS, ROBERT B.

The Farmer's Almanac. Boston: 1801-1900. V. 43

THOMAS, ROBERT M. B.

My Reasons for Leaving the Church of England and Joining the Church of Jesus Christ of Latter-Day Saints. Liverpool: 1897. V. 41

THOMAS, RONALD STUART

Destinations. Shipston-on-Stour: 1985. V. 37; 40

Laboratories of the Spirit. London: 1975. V. 42

Laboratories of the Spirit. London: 1976. V. 42

Laboratories of the Spirit. Cardiff: 1976. V. 37

Song at the Year's Turning. London: 1955. V. 41

Song at the Year's Turning - Poems 1942-1954. Introduced by John Betjeman. 1955. V. 37

THOMAS, ROSE HAIG

Stone Gardens. London: 1905. V. 44

THOMAS, ROSS

Briarpatch. New York: 1984. V. 44

Cast a Yellow Shadow. New York: 1967. V. 44; 46

The Cold War Swap. 1966. V. 46

The Cold War Swap. New York: 1966. V. 41; 46

The Fools in Town are On Our Side. New York: 1971. V. 46

The Highbinders. 1973. V. 43

If You Can't Be Good. New York: 1973. V. 39

The Money Harvest. New York: 1975. V. 37

No Questions Asked. New York: 1976. V. 43

Protocol for a Kidnapping. 1971. V. 46

Protocol for a Kidnapping. New York: 1971. V. 40

The Seersucker Whipsaw. New York: 1967. V. 41; 42

Spy in the Vodka. London: 1967. V. 44

THOMAS, S.

Britannicus Estimator; or, The Trader's Complete Guide. London: 1764. V. 45

THOMAS-STANFORD, C.

Early editions of Euclid's Elements. 1926. V. 37

THOMAS-STANFORD, CHARLES

Early Editions of Euclid's Elements. London: 1926. V. 40; 42; 46

A River of Norway... London: 1903. V. 43; 44

THOMAS, T. GAILLARD

Abortion and Its Treatment, From the Stand-Point of Practical Experience. New York: 1890. V. 42

THOMAS, THEODORE

Correspondence Connected with the Withdrawal of Mr. Theodore Thomas from the College of Music Cincinnati. Cincinnati: 1880. V. 40

THOMAS, THOMAS E.

Letters of... Cincinnati: 1913. V. 43

THOMAS, THOMAS MORGAN

Eleven Years in Central South Africa: a Journey into the Interior... London: 1872. V. 46

Un-Mylnedd-ar-Degg yn Nghanolbarth Dehueol Affrica... London: 1873. V. 39

THOMAS, TREVOR

Sylvia Plath: Last Encounters. Bedford: 1989. V. 45

THOMAS, VAUGHAN

On the Authenticity of the Designs of Raffaele and M. Angelo. Oxford: 1842. V. 38

THOMAS, W. J.

The Old Story Books of England... London: 1845. V. 42

THOMAS, WILLIAM

Hints for Establishing an Office in Newcastle, for Collecting and Recording Authentic Information Relative to the State of the Colleries... Newcastle: 1815. V. 42; 46

Letters from Scandinavia, on the Past and Present State of the Northern Nations of Europe. London: 1796. V. 37

Original Designs in Architecture... London: 1783. V. 38

The Pilgrim: a Dialogue on the Life and Actions of King Henry the Eighth. London: 1861. V. 37

A Survey of the Cathedral Church of Worcester. London: 1737. V. 46

THOMAS, WILLIAM HANNIBAL

Negro Problems. Land and Education. Boston: 1890. V. 42

THOMAS, WILLIAM I.

The Polish Peasant in Europe and America. Boston: 1918-20. V. 46

THOMAS, WILLIAM S.

Hunting Big Game with Gun and with Kodak. New York: 1906. V. 39; 43

THOMASON, GEORGE

Catalogue of the Pamphlets, Books, Newspapers and Manuscripts Relating to the Civil War, the Commonwealth and Restoration. London: 1908. V. 42; 44; 45

THOMASON, JOHN W.

Fix Bayonets! New York: 1926. V. 37

Jeb Stuart. New York: 1930. V. 44

Lone Star Preacher, Being a Chronicle of the Acts of Praxitles Swan, M.E. Church South, Sometime Captain, 5th Texas REgiment, Confederate. New York: 1941. V. 46

THOMASSIN, SIMON

Recueil des Figures, Groupes, Thermes, Fontaines, Vases et Autres Ornemens, Tels qu'ils se Voyent a Present Dans le Chateau et Parc de Versailles. Paris: 1694. V. 39

Recueil des Figures, Groupes, Thermes, Fontaines, Vases, et Autres Ornemens... Dans le Chateau et Parc de Versailles... Amsterdam: 1695. V. 42

THOMASSY, RAYMOND

Cartographie de la Louisiane. New Orleans: 1859. V. 40

THOME DE JESUS, F.

Trabalhos de Jesus, Primeira & Segunda Parte . . . Vao Acrescentados a Margem em Esta Impressam . . . Lisbon: 1666. V. 45

THOME, JAMES

Emancipation in the West Indies. New York: 1838. V. 39; 42

THOMES, WILLIAM H.

The Bushrangers. Boston: 1866. V. 46

On Land and Sea, or California in the Years 1843, 44, 45. Boston: 1884. V. 38

The Whaleman's Adventure in the Sandwich Islands and California. Boston: 1875. V. 38

THOMIN, MARC MITOUFLET

Traite d'Optique Mechanique . . . Paris: 1749. V. 38

THOMLINSON, M. H.

The Garrison of Fort Bliss 1849-1916. El Paso: 1945. V. 37; 38; 42; 46

THOMOND, DOWAGER MARCHIONESS OF

Catalogue of the very Valuable and Highly Important Collection of Ancient and Modern Pictures . . . V. 44

THOMPSON, A. H.

Report Upon the Location and Survey Reservoir Sites During the Fiscal Year Ending June 30, 1891. Washington: 1892. V. 44

THOMPSON, ALBERT W.

They Were Open Range Days - Annals of a Western Frontier. Denver: 1946. V. 37; 39; 43

THOMPSON, ALFRED

The Mask: a Humorous and Fantastic Review of the Month. London: 1868. V. 38

THOMPSON, AMIRA

The Lyre of Tioga. Geneva: 1829. V. 41

THOMPSON, BENJAMIN

Inventions, Improvements and Practice of Benjamin Thompson . . . Newcastle: 1847. V. 45

THOMPSON, BENJAMIN F.

History of Long Island, Containing an Account of the Discovery and Settlement . . . New York: 1839. V. 42

THOMPSON, BLANCHE

Silver Pennies: a Collection of Modern Poems for Boys and Girls. 1950. V. 46

THOMPSON, C.

A Sentimental Tour, collected from a variety of occurrences, from Newbiggin, near Penrith, Cumberland, to London, by way of Cambridge; and from London, to Newbiggin, by way of Oxford, &c. Penrith: 1798. V. 39

THOMPSON, C. W.

Records of the Dorset Yeomanry ('Queen's Own'). Dorchester: 1894. V. 38

THOMPSON, CHARLES

Message of the Principal Chief to the Senate and Council of the Cherokee Nation in National Council Assembled. Tahlequah: 1878. V. 42

Rules for Bad Horsemen. London: 1763. V. 46

Rules for Bad Horseman. London: 1765. V. 42

Rules for Bad Horsemen, or Those Who Depend Upon Practice Without Principles. London: 1787. V. 37; 39; 42; 43

The Travels of the Late Charles Thompson. Reading: 1744. V. 40

THOMPSON, CLARA M.

Reconstruction in Georgia: Economic, Social, Political. New York: 1915. V. 44

THOMPSON, CLARENCE BERTRAND

Scientific Management. A Collection of the More Significant Articles Describing the Taylor System of Management. Cambridge: 1914. V. 37

THOMPSON, D.

The Adventures of Timothy Peacock, Esquire . . . Middlebury: 1865. V. 45

THOMPSON, D' A. W.

On Growth and Form. Cambridge: 1968. V. 38

THOMPSON, D'A. W.

On Growth and Form. Cambridge: 1942, 1968. V. 37

THOMPSON, DANIEL PIERCE

The Green Mountain Boys: a Historical Tale of the Early Settlement of Vermont. Montpelier: 1839. V. 43

The Green Mountain Boys. New York: 1839. V. 42

May Martin; or the Money Diggers. Montpelier: 1835. V. 44

THOMPSON, DAVID

David Thompson's Narrative of His Explorations in Western America 1784-1812. Toronto: 1916. V. 37; 38; 39; 42; 43; 44; 45

David Thompson's Narrative, 1784-1812. Toronto: 1962. V. 37; 38; 45

History of the Late War, Between Great Britain and the United States of America. Niagara: 1832. V. 39; 42; 44

Journals of David Thompson. Missoula: 1950. V. 44

THOMPSON, DOROTHY BURR

Ptolemaic Oinochoai and Portraits in Faience. Oxford: 1973. V. 44

THOMPSON, EBEN FRANCIS

The Rose Garden of Omar Khayyam. Worcester: 1932. V. 45

THOMPSON, ED PORTER

History of the First Kentucky Brigade. Cincinnati: 1868. V. 37; 44

THOMPSON, EDMUND

Maps of Connecticut Before the Year 1800. Windham: 1940-42. V. 42

Maps of Connecticut Before the Year 1800, A Descriptive List (and) Maps of Connecticut . . . 1801-1860. Windham: 1940 & 1942. V. 37

THOMPSON, EDWARD

Cooper's Well. London: 1767. V. 40

The Court of Cupid. London: 1770. V. 43

The Demi-Rep. London: 1766. V. 40; 42

The Meretriciad. London: 1761. V. 42

The Meretriciad. London: 1765. V. 40; 42

The Other Side of the Medal. London: 1925. V. 41

The Thracian Stranger. London: 1929. V. 42; 44

THOMPSON, EDWARD H.

Cave of Loltun, Yucatan. Report of Explorations by the Museum, 1888-89 and 1890-1891. Cambridge: 1897. V. 37; 42; 44

The Chultunes of Labna, Yucatan. Cambridge: 1897. V. 42; 44

THOMPSON, EDWARD M.

An Introduction to Greek and Latin Palaeography. Oxford: 1912. V. 46

THOMPSON, EDWARD MAUNDE

English Illuminated Manuscripts. London: 1895. V. 39; 42

An Introduction to Greek and Latin Paleography. Oxford: 1912. V. 37; 40; 41

THOMPSON, EDWARD P.

Life in Russia; or, the Discipline of Despotism. London: 1848. V. 41

Roentgen Rays and Phenomena of the Anode and Cathode. New York: 1896. V. 38; 39; 40; 42

THOMPSON, EDWIN PORTER

History of the First Kentucky Brigade. Cincinnati: 1868. V. 38; 39; 40

THOMPSON, ELIZABETH

Kindegarten Homes. New York: 1882. V. 43

THOMPSON, ELIZABETH MARIA LLOYD

Exercises in the Gospel Narrative of the Life of Our Lord (Chronologically Arranged) in a Series of Questions and Answers. London: 1833. V. 38; 45

THOMPSON, ERNEST

On Golden Pond. New York: 1979. V. 39; 45

THOMPSON, F. P.

Ceralvo, Mexico Mining and Beneficiating Syndicate. Philadelphia: 1883. V. 46

THOMPSON, FLORA

Lark Rise. London: 1939. V. 41; 42

THOMPSON, FRANCES

Sister Songs, an Offering to Two Sisters. London: & Boston: 1985. V. 44

THOMPSON, FRANCIS 1859-1907

The Collected Poetry. London: 1913. V. 38; 41

The Mistress of Vision. Ditchling: 1918. V. 42; 43

The Mistress of Vision. With a commentary by the Reverened John O'Connor and a Preface by Fr. Vincent McNabb. Ditchling: 1918. V. 37

New Poems. London: 1897. V. 38

Poems. London: 1893. V. 38; 46

Poems. London: Boston: 1894. V. 41

THOMPSON, FRANCIS 1859-1907 continued

Shelley. London: 1909. V. 41; 42

Sister Songs. London: 1895. V. 38; 40; 41

Works. London: (1913). V. 37

The Works. London: 1913. V. 38; 42

THOMPSON, FRANCIS BENJAMIN

The Universal Decorator, a Complete Guide to Ornamental Design Including Designs for Cabinet Makers, Wood Carvers, Metal Workers, Birmingham, Sheffield, and the Potteries. London: 1858-59. V. 41

THOMPSON, G. A.

The Geographical and Historical Dictionary of America and the West Indies ... New York: 1970. V. 39

THOMPSON, GEORGE

Catharine and Clara, or the Double Suicide ... Boston: 1854. V. 45

A Description of the Royal Palace, and the Monastery of St. Laurence, Called the Escurial; and the Chapel Royal of the Pantheon. London: 1760. V. 40

Letters and Addresses ... Boston: 1837. V. 42

Prison Life and Reflections; or a Narrative of the Arrest, Trial, Conviction, Imprisonment, Treatment, Observations, Reflections and Deliverance of Work, Burr and Thompson ... Oberlin: 1847. V. 42

The Prison Bard, or Poems on Various Subjects. Hartford: 1848. V. 44

Prison Life and Reflections: or, a Narrative of the Arrest, Trial, Conviction, Imprisonment, Observations, Reflections and Deliverance of Work, Burr and Thompson ... Hartford: 1850. V. 45

Prison Life and Reflections or, a Narrative of the Arrest, Trial, Conviction, Imprisonment, Treatment, Observations and Deliverance of Work, Burr & Thompson, who Suffered an Unjust & Cruel Imprisonment in Missouri Penitentiary ... Hartford: 1851. V. 38

The Prison Bard; or, Poems on Various Subjects. Dayton: 1858. V. 42

Slavery and Famine. London: 1794. V. 38; 40

The Substance of a Speech Delivered in the Wesleyan Methodist Chapel, Irwell-Street, Salford, Manchester, on Monday August 13th 1832. London: 1832. V. 42

Substance of an Address to the Ladies of Glasgow and Its Vicinity Upon the Present Aspect of the Great Question of Negro Emancipation. Glasgow: 1833. V. 42

Thompson in Africa, or an Account of the Missionary Labors, Sufferings, Travels, Observations &c ... Cleveland: 1852. V. 40

The Tradesman's Law Library: ... Familiar Treatises on the Laws Which Tradesmen in General for Their..Ordinary Affairs of Business Ought to be Conversant with ... London: 1830. V. 41

Travels and Adventures in Southern Africa. London: 1827. V. 38; 41; 46

THOMPSON, HARRY V.

The Rabbit. London: 1956. V. 44

THOMPSON, HENRY

A Catalogue of Blue and White Nankin Porcelain. Forming the Collection of Sir Henry Thompson. London: 1878. V. 42

The Diseases of the Prostate, the Pathology and Treatment. London: 1861. V. 42

THOMPSON, HENRY YATES

Facsimiles in Photogravure of Six Pages from a Psalter, Written and Illuminated about 1325 A.D. for a Member of the St. Omer Family in Norfolk ... London: 1900. V. 44

Illustrations from the Bertrand Duguesclin by Jean Cuvelier from a Manuscript of About 1400 A.D. in the Library of Henry Yates Thompson. London: 1909. V. 44

Illustrations from One Hundred Manuscripts from the Library of ... London: 1916. V. 39

Lord Howard of Effingham and the Spanish Armada. London: 1919. V. 44

THOMPSON, HERBERT

A Family Archive from Siut, from Papyri in the British Museum ... Oxford: 1934. V. 44

THOMPSON, HOLLAND

The Book of Texas. Dallas: 1929. V. 37

THOMPSON, HOMER A.

The Athenian Agora: Results of Excavations Conducted by the American School of Classical Studies at Athens. Princeton: 1972. V. 40

THOMPSON, HOWARD

Fred Astaire. Hollywood's Magic People. New York: 1970. V. 46

THOMPSON, HUNTER S.

The Curse of Lono. New York: 1983. V. 44

Fear and Loathing in Las Vegas. New York: 1971. V. 42; 43; 44

Fear and Loathing: On the Campaign Trail '72. San Francisco;: 1973. V. 42

The Great Shark Hunt. New York: 1979. V. 39

Hell's Angels. New York: 1967. V. 39; 41; 42; 44; 46

THOMPSON, ISAAC

A Collection of Poems, Occasionally Writ on Several Subjects. Newcastle upon Tyne: 1731. V. 42; 43

THOMPSON, J. ERIC

A Commentary on the Dresden Codex: a Maya Hieroglyphic Book. Philadelphia: 1972. V. 39; 42

Excavations at San Jose, British Honduras. Washington: 1939. V. 37; 42

THOMPSON, J. ERIC S.

A Commentary on the Dresden Codex. Philadelphia: 1972. V. 38

Maya Hieroglyphic Writing. Washington: 1950. V. 40; 42; 44

THOMPSON, J. HARRY

Report of Columbia Hospital for Women and Lying-In Asylum, Washington, D.C. Washington: 1873. V. 37; 42

THOMPSON, J., of Clifton, in Yorkshire

The Modern Practice of Farriery; or, Complete Horse-Doctor. New York: 1793. V. 45

The Modern Practice of Farriery; or, Complete Horse-Doctor. Philadelphia: 1807. V. 45

THOMPSON, J. P.

British New Guinea. London: 1892. V. 39

THOMPSON, J. V.

A Catalogue of Plants Growing in the Vicinity of Berwick Upon Tweed. 1807. V. 46

A Catalogue of Plants Growing in the Vicinity of Berwick upon Tweed. London: 1807. V. 37

THOMPSON, JAMES

Poems, in the Scottish Dialect. Edinburgh: 1801. V. 42; 46

THOMPSON, JAMES J.

A History of the Feud Between the Hill and Evans Parties of Garrard County, Ky. Cincinnati: 1854. V. 45

THOMPSON, JAMES WESTFALL

The Frankfort Book Fair. Chicago: 1911. V. 37; 38; 39; 41; 42

THOMPSON, JERRY

Vaqueros in Blue and Gray. 1976. V. 42

THOMPSON, JERRY DON

Vaqueros in Blue and Gray. Austin: 1976. V. 42

THOMPSON, JIM

Bad Boy. New York: 1953. V. 46

The Getaway. New York: 1959. V. 46

A Hell of a Woman. New York: 1954. V. 44; 45

The Killer Inside Me. Los Angeles: 1989. V. 44; 46

Pop. 1280. New York: 1964. V. 46

Wild Town. New York: 1957. V. 44

THOMPSON, JOHN

Francis Thompson, the Preston-Born Poet. Preston: 1912. V. 38

The Life of John Thompson, a Fugitive Slave; Containing His History of 25 Years in Bondaged and His Prudential Escape. Worcester: 1856. V. 37; 41; 42; 44

THOMPSON, JONATHAN R.

Education and Literature in Virginia. Richmond: 1850. V. 43

THOMPSON, JOSEPH JOHN

The Corpuscular Theory of Matter. London: 1907. V. 38

THOMPSON, KAY

Eloise. New York: 1955. V. 46

Eloise at Christmastime. New York: 1958. V. 41; 45; 46

Eloise in Moscow. New York: 1959. V. 41

Eloise in Paris. New York: 1957. V. 41; 46

THOMPSON, M. AGNES

Metaiare and Other Old Aunt Tilda of New Orleans Sketches. New Orleans: 1892. V. 37

THOMPSON, MARTIN

West Australian Bird Folio. Perth: 1981. V. 44

THOMPSON, MAURICE

The Witchery of Archery: A Complete Manual of Archery. New York: 1878. V. 45

THOMPSON, MORTIMER

Doesticks. What He Says. New York: 1855. V. 38

THOMPSON, MORTIMER M.

Plu-Ri-Bus-Tah. A Song That's-by-no-Author. New York: 1856. V. 41; 43

THOMPSON, PISHEY

Collections for a Topograpahical and Historical Account of Boston, and the Hundred of Skirbeck, in the County of Lincoln. Boston: 1820. V. 37

The History and Antiquities of Boston and the Villages of Skirbeck, Fishtoft . . . Leake and Wrangle . . . Boston: 1856. V. 39

THOMPSON, R. CAMPBELL

A Dictionary of Assyrian Chemistry and Geology. Oxford: 1936. V. 40

The Epic of Gilgamish. Oxford: 1930. V. 40; 42

Late Babylonian Letters, Transliterations and Translations of a Series of Letters Written in Babylonian Cuneiform . . . London: 1906. V. 44

The Prisms of Esarhaddon and Ashurbanipal Found at Nineveh, 1927-28. London: 1931. V. 40

THOMPSON, R. R.

The Fifty-Second (Lowland) Division. 1914-1918. Glasgow: 1923. V. 43

THOMPSON, RALPH

An Artist's Safari. London: 1970. V. 45

THOMPSON, REGINALD CAMPBELL

Assyrian Medical Texts. London: 1923. V. 40; 42; 46

THOMPSON, ROBERT

The Gardener's Assistant. London. V. 40

The Gardener's Assistant. London: 1846. V. 40

The Gardener's Assistant. London: 1859. V. 37; 38; 40; 41; 42; 43; 45; 46

The Gardener's Assistant: Practical and Scientific . . . London: 1881. V. 46

The Gardener's Assistant. London: 1908. V. 42

Statistical Survey of the County of Meath, with Observation on the Means and Improvement . . . Dublin: 1802. V. 39; 43

THOMPSON, ROBERT A.

Central Sonoma. Santa Rosa: 1884. V. 38; 42; 45

The Russian Settlement in California Known as Fort Ross, Founded 1812, Abandoned 1841. Santa Rosa: 1896. V. 37; 40; 43

THOMPSON, ROBERT MEANS

Confidential Correspondence of Gustavus Vasa Fox, Assistant Secretary of the navy 1861-1865. New York: 1918/19. V. 46

THOMPSON, RUTH PLUMLEY

The Gnome King of Oz. Chicago: 1927. V. 38; 40

THOMPSON, RUTH PLUMLY

The Cowardly Lion of Oz. Chicago: 1923. V. 38

The Giant Horse of Oz. Chicago: 1928. V. 38; 40; 42

Grampa in Oz. Chicago: 1924. V. 38

Handy Mandy in Oz. Chicago: 1937. V. 41

The Hungry Tiger of Oz. Toronto: 1926. V. 46

The Hungry Tiger of Oz. Chicago: 1926. V. 38

Jack Pumpkinhead of Oz. Chicago: 1929. V. 38

Kabumpo in Oz. Chicago: 1922. V. 38; 40; 41

The Lost King of Oz. Chicago: 1925. V. 38; 39; 40; 42

The Lost King of Oz. Chicago: 1930-35. V. 39

Ozoplaning with the Wizard of Oz. Chicago: 1939. V. 39; 45; 46

Pirates in Oz. 1960. V. 46

The Princess of Cozytown. 1922. V. 46

The Princess of Cozytown. Chicago: 1923. V. 45

Speedy in Oz. Chicago: 1934. V. 39

The Wishing Horse of Oz. Chicago: 1935. V. 39

The Yellow Knight of Oz. Chicago: 1930. V. 38; 39

THOMPSON, S.

Swiss Scenery. London: 1868. V. 42

THOMPSON, SILVANUS P.

Cantor Lectures on Dynamo-Electric Machinery. London: 1883. V. 37

The Life of William Thomson, Baron Kelvin of Largs. London: 1910. V. 39

Light, Visible and Invisible. London: 1897. V. 38

Treatise on Light in Which are Explained the Causes of that Which Occur in Reflexion & in Refraction. London: 1912. V. 37

THOMPSON, T. E.

Biology of Opisthobranch Molluscs. London: 1976-84. V. 37

THOMPSON, THEOPHILUS

Annals of Influenza or Epidemic Catarrhal Fever in Great Britain from 1510 to 1837. London: 1852. V. 41; 42; 45

THOMPSON, THOMAS

An Account of Two Missionary Voyages by the Appointment of the Society for the Propagation of the Gospel in Foreign Parts. London: 1758. V. 40; 41; 42; 43; 44; 45; 46

An Enquiry into the Origin, Nature and Cure of the Small-pox to which is added, A Prefatory Address to Dr. Mead, Concerning the Present Discipline in the General Administration of Physic in this Kingdom. London: 1752. V. 37; 38

THOMPSON, THOMAS D.

Facts for the People, Relating to the Teeth. Boston;: 1854. V. 40

THOMPSON, THOMAS H.

History of Sacramento County California. Berkeley: 1960. V. 39

THOMPSON, THOMAS PERRONET 1783-1869

The True Theory of Rent, in Opposition to Mr. Ricardo and others. London: 1828. V. 41

THOMPSON, W. C.

A Bibliography of Literature Relating to the Assassination of President John F. Kennedy. San Antonio: 1968. V. 40

THOMPSON, W. H.

Sicily and Its Inhabitants. London: 1813. V. 39; 42

THOMPSON, WADDY

Letter of General Waddy Thompson Upon the Annexation of Texas . . . Washington: 1844. V. 42

Recollections of Mexico. New York: 1846. V. 37; 38; 40

Recollections of Mexico. New York: & London: 1846. V. 43

Recollections of Mexico. New York/London: 1846. V. 37

THOMPSON, WILBUR B.

The S. S. Tacoma of Port Towsend, Washington. Seattle: 1948. V. 45

THOMPSON, WILLIAM

Appeal of One Half of the Human Race, Women, Against the Pretentions of the Other Half, men . . . London: 1825. V. 44; 45

An Hymn to May. London: 1746. V. 45

Memoirs of the Life and Gallant Exploits of the Old Highlander, Serjeant Donald MacLeod who Having Returned Wounded with the Corpse of General Wolfe, from Quebec, was Admitted an Out-Pensioner of Chelsea Hospital in 1759 . . . London: 1791. V. 39

The Natural History of Ireland. London: 1849. V. 43

The Natural History of Ireland. London: 1849-56. V. 38

Reminiscences of a Pioneer. San Francisco: 1912. V. 37; 40; 42; 45

Sedbergh Garsdale and Dent. Leeds: 1892. V. 45; 46

Sedbergh Garsdale and Dent. Leeds: 1910. V. 41; 46

Sickness. A Poem. London: 1745-45-46. V. 46

Sickness. London: 1745-6. V. 41

THOMPSON, WILLIAM, floriculturist

The English Flower Garden. London: 1852-53. V. 39; 41

THOMPSON, Z.

The Green Mountain Repository for the Year 1832.. Burlington: 1832. V. 41

THOMPSON, ZADOCK

History of Vermont, Natural, Civil and Statistical. (with) Appendix to the History of Vermont. Burlington: 1842/53. V. 45

THOMPSON,G EORGE

Prison Life and Reflections . . . Oberlin: 1847. V. 44

THOMS, HERBERT

Classical Contributions to Obstetrics and Gynecology. Springfield: 1935. V. 41; 45

THOMS, P. P.

A Dissertation on the Ancient Chinese Vases . . . from 1743 to 1496 B.C. London: 1851. V. 38; 44

THOMS, PETER PERRING

Chinese Courtship. Macao: 1824. V. 40

THOMS, WILLIAM J.

Early English Prose Romances. London: 1858. V. 43

THOMSON, A. T.

Memoirs of Sarah Duchess of Marlborough and of the Court of Queen Anne. London: 1839. V. 40

THOMSON, ADAM

Time and Timekeepers. London: 1842. V. 39

THOMSON, ALEXANDER

Letters of a Traveller, on the VArious Countries of Europe, Asia and Africa . . . London: 1798. V. 42; 44

Pictures of Poetry: Historical, Biographical and Critical. Edinburgh: 1799. V. 42

Sonnets, Odes and Elegies. Edinburgh: 1801. V. 46

Whist; a Poem, in Twleve Cantos. London: 1791. V. 43

THOMSON, ALEXIS

On Neuroma and Neuro-Fibromatiosis. Edinburgh: 1900. V. 42; 44

THOMSON, ANDREW

The Hendersonian Testimony, Being Five Essays by Working Men of Glasgow on the Advantages of the Sabbath to the Working Classes. Edinburgh; London: and: 1849. V. 46

THOMSON, ANTHONY TODD

The London Dispensatory. London: 1831. V. 44

THOMSON, ARTHUR

A Handbook for Art Students. Oxford: 1915. V. 42

THOMSON, ARTHUR S.

The Story of New Zealand: Past and Present - Savage and Civilized. London: 1859. V. 39

THOMSON, BASIL

The Fijians. A Study of the Decay of Custom. London: 1908. V. 37

THOMSON, CHARLES

Causes of the Alienation of the Delaware and Shawnese Indians from the British Interest. Philadelphia: 1867. V. 45

Causes of the Alienation of the Delaware and Shawnese Indians from the British Interest. Philaelphia: 1867. V. 38; 42; 45

THOMSON, CHARLES WYVILLE

The Atlantic. Philadelphia: 1873. V. 37

The Atlantic, the Voyage of the 'Challenger' a Preliminary Account of the General Results of the Exploring Voyage of HMS 'Challenger' during the year 1873 and the Early Part of the Year 1876. London: 1877. V. 46

The Depth of the Sea, an Account of the General Results of the Dredging Cruises of H.M.SS. 'Porcupine' and 'Lightning'. London: 1868. V. 37

The Depths of the Sea. London: 1873. V. 37; 38

The Depths of the Sea. London: 1874. V. 42; 45

Report of the Scientific Results of the Voyage of H. M. S. Challenger 1873-76 . . . London: 1889. V. 41

Voyage of the 'Challenger' The Atlantic. London: 1877. V. 38; 42; 43; 45

The Voyage of the 'Challenger'. New York: 1878. V. 39; 42; 43; 44

THOMSON, DAVID CROAL

Life and Labours of Hablot Knight Browne. London: 1884. V. 37; 40; 42

Life and Labours of Hablot Knight Browne, 'Phiz.' London: 1846. V. 37

The Water Colour Drawings of Thomas Bewick. London: 1930. V. 40

THOMSON, EDWARD

The Adventures of a Carpet Bag. London: 1853. V. 38

THOMSON-GREGG, W.

A Desperate Character. London: 1873. V. 39

THOMSON, H. C.

Rhodesia and Its Government. London: 1898. V. 39

THOMSON, J.

The Straits of Malacca, Indo-China, and China . . . New York: 1875. V. 42

THOMSON, J. B.

Joseph Thomson, African Explora, a Biography by His Brother. London: 1896. V. 41

THOMSON, J. C.

Bibliography of the Writings of Tennyson. Wimbledon: 1905. V. 45

THOMSON, J. J.

Conduction of Electricity through Gases. Cambridge: 1903. V. 46

THOMSON, J. P.

British New Guinea. London: 1892. V. 38

THOMSON, JAMES 1834-1882

Address on the Opening of the New Hall of the Leicester Secular Society Sunday March 6th 1881 . . . N.P.: 1881? V. 39

Ancient and Modern Italy Compared Being the First Part of 'Liberty' a Poem. London: 1735. V. 38

The Castle of Indolence. London: 1748. V. 37; 39; 46

The Castle of Indolence: an Allegorical Poem. London: 1845. V. 39

The City of Dreadful Night and Other Poems. London: 1880. V. 39; 42

Colonial and Indian Exhibition, London, 1886. Illustrated Handbook of Victoria, Australia. Melbourne: 1886. V. 46

A Defence of the New Sophonisba, a Tragedy. London: 1730. V. 38; 43

Edward and Eleonora. London: 1739. V. 37; 40; 41; 45

Essays and Phantasies . . . London: 1881. V. 39

A Great Free City, the Book of Silchester. London: 1924. V. 46

Illustrated Handbook of Victoria, Australia. Melbourne: 1886. V. 41

Illustrations of Shakespeare. London: 1830. V. 37

The Poetical Works. Glasgow: 1784. V. 38; 39; 42; 44

Poetical Works. Edinburgh: 1853. V. 46

The Poetical Works of. Edinburgh: 1869. V. 39

The Poetical Works. London: 1895. V. 42

The Poetical Works of. London: 1830. V. 37

Retreats: A Series of Designs, Consisting of Plans and Elevations for Cottages, Villas and Ornamental Buildings. London: 1833. V. 38; 42

The Four Seasons and Other Poems. London: 1726-30. V. 38

The Seaons. London: 1729/30/28/28. V. 42

The Seasons. London: 1730. V. 37; 38; 39; 40; 41; 43; 45

The Seasons. London: 1746. V. 41

The Seasons. London: 1778. V. 40

The Seasons . . . London: 1779. V. 40

The Seasons. London: 1793. V. 40

The Seasons. Perth: 1793. V. 37; 40; 45

Les Saisons. Paris: 1796. V. 46

The Seasons. London: 1797. V. 38; 43

The Seasons. London: 1802. V. 45

The Seasons. Dundee: 1803. V. 40

The Seasons. London: 1805. V. 37; 38; 41; 44; 46

The Seasons. London: 1807. V. 46

The Seasons. London: 1807/08. V. 44

The Seasons. To which is Prefixed the Life of the Author by P. Murdock and an Essay on the Plan and Character of the poem by J. Aikin. London: 1811. V. 37; 42

The Seasons. Chiswick: 1820. V. 37

The Seasons and the Castle of Indolence. London: 1841. V. 37; 42

The Seasons and the Castle of Indolence. London: 1841. V. 37

The Seasons. London: 1842. V. 42

The Seasons. New York: 1842. V. 38

The Seasons and Castle of Indolence. London: 1845. V. 37; 42

The Seasons. London: 1847. V. 38

The Seasons. London: 1852. V. 46

The Seasons. London: 1859. V. 39; 44

The Seasons. Glasgow: 1889. V. 39

The Seasons. London: 1927. V. 43; 44; 45; 46

The Seasons. London: 1950. V. 43

Shelley a Poem. London: 1884. V. 37; 42

Spring. A Poem. London: 1728. V. 38; 41

The Tragedy of Sophonisba . . . London: 1730. V. 37; 40

The Value and Importance of Scottish Fisheries . . . London: 1849. V. 40

Vane's Story, Weddah and Om-El-Bonain . . . London: 1881. V. 39

Winnifred, a Tale of Wonder. London: 1803. V. 41

Winter. London: 1726. V. 38; 43

The Works of Mr. Thomson. London: 1744-9. V. 37

The Works . . . London: 1762. V. 38

The Works. With His Last Corrections and Improvements. London: 1766. V. 39

The Works. London: 1788. V. 38

Works. London: 1788. V. 38

The Works . . . London: 1802. V. 39

THOMSON, JOHN

Etymons of English Words. Edinburgh: 1826. V. 40; 46

Hints Respecting the Improvement of the Literary and Scientific Education of Candidtates for the Degee of Doctor of Medicine in the University of Edinburgh. Edinburgh: 1824. V. 40

Historical Sketch of the Opinions Entertained by medical men Respecting the Varieties and the Secondary Occurence of Small Pox; With Observations on the Nature and Extet of the Security Afforded by Vaccination Against Attacks of that Disease. London: 1822. V. 37; 38; 41

Illustrations of China and Its People. London: 1873. V. 45

Letters of Curtius, Written by the Late John Thomson of Petersburg. Richmond: 1804. V. 40; 42; 46

Memoir of the Late Rev. John Thomson of Duddington. Edinburgh: 1884. V. 42

Narrative of John Thomson, One of the Persons Intended to be Massacred with General Lingan and Others, in the Jail of Baltimoe, on Tuesday, the 28th of July, 1812. Salem: 1812. V. 37

Observations on Preparatory Education of Candidates for the Degree of Doctor of Medicine, in Scottish Universities. N.P.: 1826. V. 40

THOMSON, JOHN continued

Tables of Interest . . . and Tables Shewing the Exchange on Bills or Commissions . . . to Which is Prefixed, a Table of Discount on Bills at a Certain Number of Days or Months. Edinburgh: 1788. V. 43

Tables of Interest . . . Edinburgh: 1794. V. 38

THOMSON, JOHN COCKBURN

The Wits and Beaux of Society. London. V. 46

THOMSON, JOHN, F.R.G.S.

Illustrations of China and Its People. London: 1873. V. 41

Through China with a Camera. London: 1898. V. 41

THOMSON, JOSEPH

Through Masai Land: a Journey of Exploration Among the Snow Clad Volcanic Mountains and Strange Tribes of Eastern Equatorial Africa. London: 1885. V. 41

To the Central African Lakes and Back: the Narrative of the Royal Geographical Society's East Central African Expedition, 1878-80. London: 1881. V. 40

Travels in the Atlas and Southern Morocco. London: 1889. V. 46

THOMSON, JOSEPH JOHN

Conduction of Electricity Through Gases. Cambridge: 1903. V. 38

Notes on Recent Researches in Electricity and Magnetism Intended as a Sequel to Professsor Clerk-Maxwell's Treatise on Electricity and Magnetism. Oxford: 1893. V. 38

Rays of Positive Electricity and Their Application to Chemical Analyses. London: 1913. V. 38

A Treatise on the Motion of Vortex Rings. London: 1883. V. 38; 41

THOMSON, KATHERINE

The Literature of of Society. London: 1862. V. 40

THOMSON, KATHERINE BYERLEY

Memoirs of the Jacobites of 1715 and 1745. London: 1845-46. V. 42

THOMSON, MATT

Early History of Wabaunsee County, Kansas with Stories of Pioneer Days. Alma: 1901. V. 40; 41

THOMSON, O. R. HOWARD

History of the 'Bucktails', Kane Rifle Regiment of the Pennsylvania Reserve Corps. Philadelphia: 1906. V. 42

THOMSON, PETER G.

A Bibliography of the State of Ohio. Cincinnati: 1880. V. 43

THOMSON, R. H. C.

The Outgoing Turk. Impressions of a Journey through the Western Balkans. London: 1897. V. 40

THOMSON, RICHARD

Chronicles of London Bridge: by an Antiquary. London: 1827. V. 43

A Garland for the New Royal Exchange. London: 1845. V. 39; 42

An Historical Essay on the Magna Charta of King John. London: 1829. V. 38; 39; 42

THOMSON, S. HARRISON

Latin Bookhands of the Later Middle Ages. 1100-1500. Cambridge: 1969. V. 44; 46

THOMSON, SAMUEL

The Law of Libel. Boston: 1839. V. 43

A Narrative of the Life and Discoveries of Samuel Thomson . . . St. Clairsville: 1829. V. 43

New Guide to Health, or, Botanic Family Physician. Boston: 1822. V. 41

New Guide to Health; or Botanic Family Physician . . . Boston: 1825. V. 37; 43

New Guide for Health; or, Botanic Family Physician . . . Boston: 1825-1825. V. 44

New Guide to Health . . . Boston: 1831-32. V. 42

New Guide to Health, or, Botanic Family Physician. N.P.: 1838. V. 42

THOMSON, SPENCER

Health Resorts of Britain; and How to Profit by Them. London: 1860. V. 42

The Structure and Functions of the Eye, Illustrative of the Power, Wisdom and Goodness of God. London: 1857. V. 44

THOMSON, T.

Travels in Sweden, During the Autumn of 1812. London: 1813. V. 40

THOMSON, THOMAS

Chemistry of Animal Bodies. Edinburgh: 1843. V. 38; 46

History of the Royal Society, from its Institution to the End of the 18th Century. London: 1812. V. 37; 40

The History of Chemistry. London: 1830-31. V. 46

The History of Chemistry. London: 1835. V. 37; 42; 46

A History of Scottish People. London: 1894. V. 42

System of Chemistry. Philadelphia: 1818. V. 39; 44

Travels in Sweden, During the Autumn of 1812. London: 1813. V. 37; 38; 41

THOMSON, VIRGIL

Eighteen Portraits. New York: 1985. V. 46

THOMSON, W. G.

A History of Tapestry from the Earliest Times Until ahd Present Day. London: 1906. V. 41

THOMSON, WILLIAM

Letters from Scandinavia, on the Past and Present State of the Northern Nations of Europe. London: 1796. V. 38; 39; 40; 42

Memoirs of the Life and Gallant Exploits of the Old Highlander, Serjeant Donald Macleod, who, Having Returned, Wounded, with the Corpse of General Wolfe, from Quebec, Was Admitted an Out-pensioner of Chelsea Hospital, in 1759 . . . London: 1791. V. 38

Orpheus Caledonius. London: 1733. V. 37

Travels into Norway, Denmark and Russia, in the Years 1788, 1789, 1790 and 1791. 1792. V. 40

Travels Into Norway, Denmark and Russia, in the Years 1788, 1789, 1790 and 1791. London: 1792. V. 38; 43; 45

Travels in Europe, Asia, Africa, Describing the Characters, Customs, Manners, Laws and Productions of Nature and Art. London: 1782. V. 37

THOMSON, WILLIAM G.

A History of Tapestry. London: 1930. V. 39; 46

THOMSON, WILLIAM M.

The Land and the Book, or Biblical Illustrations drawn from the Manners and Customs, the Scene and Scenery of the Holy Land. New York: 1880. V. 38; 41

THONNER, F.

Flowering Plants of Africa: an Analytical Key to the Genera. 1962. V. 39

THORBURN, A.

Birds of Prey. Bures: 1985. V. 41; 42

British Birds. London: 1915-18. V. 41

THORBURN, ARCHIBALD

British Birds. London: 1925-26. V. 37; 38; 39; 42; 45

British Birds. London: 1931, 1925-26. V. 38

British Birds. London: 1915-16, 1918. V. 37

British Birds. London: 1915-18. V. 37; 39; 42

British Birds. London: 1916. V. 43

British Birds. London: 1917. V. 42

British Birds. London: 1925. V. 43

British Mammals. London: 1920. V. 42; 43

British Mammals. London: 1920-21. V. 39; 42

Game Birds and Wild Fowl of Great Britain and Ireland. London: 1923. V. 37; 39; 42; 43; 45; 46

A Naturalist's Sketch Book. London: 1919. V. 37; 39; 42; 45

Thorburn's Birds of Prey. London: 1985. V. 37; 38

THORBURN, GRANT

Forty Years' Residence in America. or, the Doctrine of a Particular Providence Exemplified in the life of Grant Thorburn. With an Introduction by John Galt. London: 1824. V. 37

Life and Writings of Grant Thorburn. New York: 1852. V. 42

Men and Manners in Britain. Glasgwo: 1833-4. V. 39

THORBURN, W. STEWART

A Guide to the Coins of Great Britain and Ireland, In Gold, Silver, and Copper . . . London: 1888. V. 41

THORD-GRAY, I.

Tarahumara - English. English - Tarahumara Dictionary, and an Introduction to Tarahumara Grammar. Coral Gables: 1955. V. 40

THORDEMAN, BENGT

Armour from the Battle of Wisby 1361. Stockholm: 1939. V. 37

THORDINARY of Crysten Men. London: 1506. V. 40

THOREAU, HENRY DAVID 1817-1862

Autumn from the Journal of Henry David Thoreau. Cambridge: 1894. V. 46

Cape Cod. Boston: 1864. V. 43

Cape Cod. Boston: 1865. V. 37; 39; 41; 42; 43; 44; 45

Cape Cod. Boston & New York: 1896. V. 39; 42

Cape Cod. Cambridge: 1896. V. 44

Cape Cod. Boston: 1902. V. 39; 40; 41

Cape Cod. Boston: 1896. V. 37; 38

Civil Disobedience. Boston: 1969. V. 37; 46

THORNTON, BONNELL continued

An Ode on Saint Caecilia's Day, Adapted to the Ancient British Musick. London: 1749. V. 38

THORNTON, CATHERINE

The Fothergills of Ravenstronedale. Their Lives and Letters. London: 1905. V. 44

THORNTON, EDWARD

The History of the British Empire in India. London: 1841-45. V. 39; 45

Illustrations of the History and Practices of the Thugs. London: 1637. V. 42

India, Its State and Prospects. 1835. V. 41

India, Its State and Prospects. London: 1835. V. 46

THORNTON, HENRY

On the Probable Effects of the Peace, with Respect to the Commercial Interests of Great Britain . . . London: 1802. V. 43

THORNTON, JESSE QUINN

Memorial of J. Quinn Thornton, Praying the Establishment of a Territorial Government in Oregon . . . Washington: 1848. V. 39; 42

Oregon and California in 1848. New York: 1855. V. 41; 42; 45

THORNTON, JESSY QUINN

Oregon and California in 1848 . . . Including Recent and Authentic Information on the Subject of the Gold Mines of California. New York: 1849. V. 37; 38; 39; 41

THORNTON, MILDRED VALLEY

Indian Lives and Legends. Vancouver: 1966. V. 41

THORNTON, PETER

Authentic Decor. The Domestic Interior 1620-1920. New York: 1984. V. 40

Baroque and Rococo Silks. London: 1965. V. 41

THORNTON, PHINEAS

The Southern Gardener and Receipt Book. Camden: 1840. V. 40

THORNTON, ROBERT JOHN 1768?-1837

The British Flora. London: 1812. V. 38

Elements of Botany. London: 1812. V. 37; 38; 39; 40; 41; 42; 43; 44; 46

A Family Herbal. London: 1814. V. 37; 38; 39

Medical Extracts on the Nature of Health and the Laws of the Nervous and Fibrous Systems. London: 1798. V. 43

Medical Extracts: On the Nature of Health, With Practical Observations. London: 1796-97. V. 38

New Illustrations of the Sexual System of Linnaeus. London: 1799-1801. V. 43

A New Family Herbal. London: 1810. V. 40; 42; 43; 44; 46

The Philosophy of Medicine; or, Medical Extracts on the Nature of Health and Disease . . . London: 1799-1800. V. 42

Temple of Flora. London: 1812. V. 41; 42; 43; 44; 45; 46

Temple of Flora. London: 1951. V. 46

Thornton's Temple of Flora. London: 1951. V. 37; 39; 40; 43

THORNTON, T. C.

An Inquiry into the History of Slavery. Washington: 1841. V. 37; 38; 39; 42

An Inquiry Into the History of Slavery; Its Introduction Into the United States; Causes of its Continuance; and Remarks Upon the Abolition Tracts of William E. Channing, D.D. Washington City: 1841. V. 42

THORNTON, THOMAS

A Sporting Tour Through the Northern Parts of England and a Great Part of the Highlands of Scotland. London: 1804. V. 39; 40; 41; 46

A Sporting Tour through Various Part of France in the Year 1802. London: 1806. V. 38; 45

A Sporting Tour Through the Northern Parts of England and Great Part of the Highlands of Scotland. London: 1896. V. 40; 45

THORNTON, WILLIAM

The Counterpoise. Being Thoughts on a Military and a Standing, Army. London: 1752. V. 41; 45

Political Economy: Founded in Justice and Humanity, In a Letter to a Friend. Washington City: 1804. V. 42

THORNTON, WILLIAM THOMAS

On Labour: Its Wrongful Claims and Rightful Dues . . . London: 1869. V. 38; 41

On Labour, Its Wrongful Claims and Rightful Dues . . . London: 1870. V. 42; 46

On Labour: its wrongful claims and rightful dues, its actual present and possible future. Macmillan: 1869. V. 37

THORNWELL, J. H.

The State of the Country. Columbia: 1861. V. 38

THOROTON, ROBERT

The Antiquities of Nottinghamshire, Extracted Out of Records . . . London: 1677. V. 41

THOROWGOOD, THOMAS

Jewes in America, or, Probabilities that the Americans are of that Race. London: 1650. V. 42; 44; 45

THORP, JOSEPH

A Diary of 1745. Bristol: 1922. V. 46

Early Days in the West Along The Missouri One Hundred Years Ago. Liberty: 1924. V. 38; 41

Eric Gill . . . London: 1929. V. 42; 44

Eric Gill. New York: 1929. V. 42; 43; 44; 45

THORP, N. HOWARD

Songs of the Cowboy. Estancia: 1908. V. 40; 41; 46

THORPE, HALL

Hall Thorpe Coloured Woodcuts. Woolloomooloo: 1980. V. 41

THORPE, JAMES

English Illustration: the Nineties. London: 1935. V. 41

THORPE, T. B.

The Hive of 'the Bee Hunter,' a Repository of Sketches . . . New York: 1854. V. 38

THORPE, THOMAS

Catalogue of the Charters, Grants and Doantaions . . . Constituting the Muniments of Battle Abbey. London: 1835. V. 38; 40

THORPE, THOMAS B.

Our Army on the Rio Grande. Philadelphia: 1846. V. 45

Our Army at Monterey. Philadelphia: 1847. V. 42

THORPE, THOMAS BANGS

The Mysteries of the Backwoods; or Sketches of the Southwest . . . Philadelphia: 1846. V. 43

Our Army at Monterey. Philadelphia: 1847. V. 38

Our Army on the Rio Grande . . . from Corpus Christi to the Surrender of Matamoros. Philadelphia: 1846. V. 38

THORPE, W. A.

A History of English and Irish Glass. London: 1929. V. 42

THOU, JACQUES AUGUSTE DE

Hieracosophioy, Sive de re Accipiatria. Paris: 1587. V. 46

THOUGHTS of a Citizen of London on the Conduct of Dr. Dodd, in His Life and Death. London: 1767, i.e. 1777. V. 38
THOUGHTS of a Citizen of London on the Conduct of Dr. Dodd, in His Life and Death. London: 1777. V. 42

THOUGHTS Of a Parent on Education. London: 1823. V. 37; 38

THOUGHTS on Civilization and the Gradual Abolition of slavey in Africa and the West Indies. London?: 1790? V. 41; 46

THOUGHTS on Happiness, a poem, in four books. Kidderminster: 1802. V. 37; 39

THOUGHTS on the Commercial Arrangement with Ireland; Addressed to the People of Great Britain. London: 1785. V. 39; 42

THOUGHTS on the Constitution of the State of South Carolina. Georgetown: 1819. V. 46

THOUGHTS on the Propriety of Preventing Marriages Founded on Adultery. London: 1800. V. 42

THOUGHTS on What Has Been Called Sensibility of the Imagination, with Practical Illustrations from the Lives of Petrarch, Sterne and Byron . . . London: 1839. V. 42

THOUIN, GABRIEL

Plans Raisonnes de Toutes les Especes de Jardins. Paris: 1838. V. 44

THOULIER D'OLIVET, PIERRE JOSEPH

Thoughts of Cicero . . . London: 1751. V. 38

THOURET, MICHAEL AUGUSTIN 1748-1810

Recherches et Doutes sur le Magnetisme Animal. Paris: 1784. V. 42

THE THOUSAND and One Days: Persian Tales. London: 1765. V. 46

THRAPP, DAN L.

Encyclopedia of Frontier Biography. Spokane: 1990. V. 46

Encyopedia of Frontier Biography. Glendale: 1988. V. 39; 40; 41

Encyclopedia of Frontier Biography. Glendale: 1990. V. 45

THE THREE Blind Mice: Aunt Jenny's Series. New York: 1860. V. 46

THREE Brothers; or, the Travels and Adventures of Sir Anthony, Sir Robert & Sir Thomas Sherley, in Persia, Russia, Turkey, Spain, etc. London: 1825. V. 43; 45

THREE Early French Essays on Paper Marbling 1642-1675. Newtown: 1987. V. 39; 42; 44

THREE Early French Essays on Paper Marbling 1642-1765. 1987. V. 45

THREE Erfurt Tales, 1497-1498. North Hills: 1962. V. 37; 41; 46

THREE Erfurt Tales, 1497-1498. Translated into English by Dr. Arnold H. Price with an Introduction by Lessing J. Rosenwald. (North Hills): 1962. V. 37

THREE Hundred Masterpieces of Chinese Painting in the Palace Museum. Taichung: Taiwan: 1959. V. 41

THREE Hundred Notable Books Added to the Library of the British Museum Under the Keepership of Richard Garnett 1809-1899. Edinburgh: 1899. V. 40
THREE Hundred Notable Books Added to the Library of the British Museum Under the Keepership of Richard Garnett 1809-1899. London: 1899. V. 42; 44

THREE Irish Poets - John Montague, Thomas Kinsella, Richard Murphy - a Poetry Reading Presented by the Dolmen Press at the Royal Hibernian Hotel, Dublin, February 3, 1961. Dublin: 1961. V. 40

THREE Letters of Thanks to the Protestant Reconciler. 1. From the Anabaptists at Munster. 2. From the Congregations in New-England. 3. From the Quakers in Pensilvania. London: 1683. V. 38

THE THREE Little Kittens. London: 1875. V. 39

THREE Months in York: Containing Among Other Matter, Remarks and Strictures on the Construction and Peculiar Mode of Making a Weekly Newspaper . . . York: 1821. V. 38

THREE Views of the Segregation Decisions: William Faulkner, Benjamin E. Mays, Cecil Sims. Atlanta: 1956. V. 37

THREE Years 1924 to 1927: the Story of a New Idea and Its Successful Adaptation. New York: 1927. V. 44

THRENODIA. a Funeral Poem, to the Memory of the Late, Learned, Pious and Reverend, Mr. James Webster. Edinburgh: 1720. V. 41

THRENODIA; or, an Elegy on the Unexpected and Unlamented Death of the M- of B- . . . Oxford: 1753. V. 42; 45

THRESOR Des Recreations, Contenant Histoires Facetievses et Honnestes, Propos Plaisans & Pleins de Gaillardises, Faicts & Touts Ioyeux . . . Douai: 1625. V. 40

THRIFT, TIM
Modern Methods in Marbling Paper. Winchester: 1945. V. 38

THRILLING Narrative! Of the Indian Massacre at Spirit Lake, Iowa, March 1857. And Capture of Miss Abigail Gardner as Given by Herself. V. 40

THROCKMORTON, JAMES W.
Speech of James W. Throckmorton, of M'Kinney, Texas, at a Soldier's Re-Union at Waco, Texas, June 27, 1889. McKinney: 1889. V. 42

THROPE, T. B.
Our Army on the Rio Grande . . . from Corpus Christi to the Surrender of Matamoros. Philadelphia: 1846. V. 37; 42

THROSBY, JOHN
Select Views in Leicestershire from Original Drawings. London: 1789-90. V. 45
Thoroton's History of Nottinghamshire . . . London: 1797. V. 45

THROWER, NORMAN J. W.
A Leaf from the Mercator-Hondius World Atlas. Edition of 1619. Fullerton: 1985. V. 39; 40

THRUM, THOMAS G.
Hawaiian Almanac and Annual for 1876. Honolulu: 1875. V. 38
Hawaiian Almanac and Annual for 1876. Honolulu: 1876. V. 39
Hawaiian Almanac and Annual for 1898. Honolulu: 1898. V. 43
Hawaiian Almanac and Annual for 1876: A Handbook of Valuable and Statistical Information Relating to the Hawaiian Islands. Honolulu: 1876. V. 37

THRUPP, G. A.
The History of Coaches. London: 1877. V. 40; 42; 46

THE THRUSH: a choice selection of the most Admired Popular Songs, Heroic, Plaintive, Sentimental, Humourous, and Bacchanalian. Arranged for the Violin, Flute, and Voice. London: 1827. V. 37

THUBRON, COLIN
The Hills of Adonis. London: 1968. V. 41
Jerusalem. London: 1969. V. 41
Mirror to Damascus. London: 1967. V. 41
Mirror to Damascus. 1967. V. 37

THUCYDIDES
Greek title: then) De Bello Peloponesiaco Libri VIII. Geneva: 1588. V. 43
Cum Commentariis Antique. Florence: 1526. V. 45
De Bello Peloponnesiaco. Venice: 1502. V. 40
Eight Bookes of the Peloponnesian Warre . . . London: 1634. V. 42; 46
Gli otto Libri di Thucydide Atheniese . . . Venice: 1545. V. 37
Histoire de la Guerre des Peloponesiens et Atheniens . . . Paris: 1600. V. 43
Historia de Thucydides . . . Traduzida de Lengua Griega en Castellana . . . por el Secretario Diego Gracian . . . Salamanca: 1564. V. 41
Historia Belli Peloponnesiaci. Treviso: 1483. V. 37
The History of the Grecian War. London: 1676. V. 38; 44
History of Peloponnesian War. 1930. V. 45
History of the Peloponesian War. Chelsea: 1930. V. 41; 43; 44; 46
The History of the Peloponesian War . . . Colophon: 1930. V. 43
The History of the Peloponesian War. London: 1930. V. 41
Thuchdidis Atheniensis De Bello Peloponnesiaco Libri Octo, e Graeco Sermone in Latinum Nova Interpretatione Converse. Tubingae: 1596. V. 37
Thucydides. Chelsea: 1930. V. 40
Thucydides. Translated into English by Benjamin Jowett. London: 1930. V. 45
Thucydides translated into English by Benjamin Jowett. Shelley House, Chelsea: 1930. V. 37
Works in Greek. Venice: 1502. V. 38

THUDICHUM, J. L. W.
A Treatise on the Pathology of the Urine. London: 1877. V. 37; 38
A Treatise on Wines. London: 1894. V. 37; 38; 39

THUDICHUM, JOHN LOUIS WILLIAM
A Treatise on the Origin, Nature and Varieties of Wine. London & New York: 1872. V. 38

THUILLIER, JACQUES
Ruben's Life of Marie de'Medici. New York: 1967. V. 37

THE THUMB Autograph Book, with Gems of Thought from Classical Authors. Glasgow: 1895. V. 45

THE THUMB Book of Bible Promises. Glasgow: 1890's. V. 37

THUNBERG, C. P.
Travels in Europe, Africa and Asia, Made Between the Years 1770 and 1779. London: 1795-96. V. 43

THUNBERG, CHARLES PIERRE
Voyage en Afrique et en Asie, Principalement au Japon Pendant les Annees 1770-1779. Paris: 1794. V. 41

THUNBERG, KARL PETER 1743-1822
Travels in Europe, Africa, and Asia, Performed Between the Years 1770 and 1779. London: 1793-95. V. 37; 40
Voyages au Japon . . . Paris: 1796. V. 40

THURAH, LAURITZ VON
Den Danske Vitruvius . . . Le Vitruve Danois Contient les Plans, Les Elevations et Les Profils des Principaux Batimens du Roiaume de Dannermarc . . . Copenhagen: 1746-49. V. 39
Hafnia Hodierna, Eller Udforlig Beskrivelse om den Kongelige Residentz-og Hoved-Stad Kiobenhavn . . . Copenahgen: 1748. V. 42; 43

THURBER, FRANCIS B.
Coffee: from Plantation to Cup. New York: 1886. V. 46

THURBER, JAMES
Alarms and Diversions. New York: 1957. V. 39
Alarms and Diversions. New York: (c. 1957). V. 37
The Beast in Me and Other Animals. New York: 1948. V. 39
Further Fables of Our Time. New York: 1956. V. 39
Many Moons. New York: 1943. V. 46
The Middle Aged Man on the Flying Trapeze. New York: 1935. V. 41; 46

THURBER, JAMES GROVER 1894-1961
Fables for Our Time. New York: 1940. V. 42
Further Fables for Our Times. New York: 1956. V. 40
The Last Flower. New York: 1939. V. 45
The Last Flower. A Parable in Pictures. New York: 1962. V. 40
Let Your Mind Alone! London: 1937. V. 40

THURBER, JAMES GROVER 1894-1961 continued

Let Your Mind Alone. New York: 1944. V. 42

The Male Animal. New York: 1941. V. 45

Many Moons. New York: 1943. V. 38

The Middle Aged Man on the Flying Trapeze. New York: 1935. V. 40; 45

The Middle-Aged Man on the Flying Trapeze. New York & London: 1935. V. 38

The Middle Aged Man on the Flying Trapeze. New York/London: 1935. V. 40

The Middle Aged Man on the Flying Trapeze. New York: London: 1935. V. 42

The Seal in the Bedroom and Other Predicaments. New York: 1950. V. 37; 39

The 13 Clocks. New York: 1950. V. 38

Thurber Country. A New Collection of Pieces about Males and Females Mainly of Our Own Species. London: 1953. V. 40

The Wonderful O. London: 1958. V. 40

The Years with Ross. Boston: 1959. V. 38; 39; 40

THURLOE, JOHN 1616-1668

A Collection of the State Papers of John Thurloe . . . London: 1742. V. 39; 45

THURLOW, EDWARD, LORD

An Appendix to Poems on Several Occasions; Being a Continuation of the Sylva. London: 1813. V. 43

Moonlight, a Poem; with Several Copies of Verses. London: 1814. V. 40

THURLOW, T. J. HOVELL

Trade Unions Abroad and Hints for Home Legislation . . . London: 1870. V. 43; 46

THURMAN, HOWARD

Deep River. Oakland: 1945. V. 45

THURMAN, WALLACE

The Blacker the Berry. New York: 1929. V. 44

Negro Life in New York's Harlem. Girard. V. 43

THURNEISSER, LEONHARD 1530-1596

Prognosticon Eller Practica, Paa det Aar . . . MDXCI . . . Copenhagen: 1591. V. 46

THURNEISSER, LEONHART

Megale Chymia (Graece), vel Magna Alchymia. Berlin: 1583. V. 42

THURNEISSER ZUM THURN, LEONHARD

Historia Sive Descriptio Plantarum Omnium, Tam Domesticarum Quam Exoticarum . . . Berlin: 1578. V. 39

THURSTON, A. B.

African Incidents Personal Experiences in Egypt and Unyoro . . . and an Account of Major Thurston's Last Stay in 1897 in the Protectorate, His Death and the Mutiny of the Uganda Rifles. London: 1900. V. 39

THURSTON, ALBERT P.

Elmentary Aeronautics, or the Science and Practice of Aerial Machines. London: 1911. V. 45

THURSTON, CLARA BELL

The Jingle of a Jap. Boston: 1906. V. 46

The Jingle of a Jap. Boston: 1908. V. 41; 44

THURSTON, E. TEMPLE

The Open Window. London: 1913. V. 43

THURSTON, EDGAR

Castes and Tribes of Southern India. Madras: 1909. V. 40; 42; 46

THURSTON, GEORGE H.

Pittsbrugh As It Is: or, Facts and Figures, Exhibiting the Past and Present of Pittsburgh, Its Advantages . . . Pittsburgh: 1857. V. 42

THURSTON, JOHN

Religious Emblems, Being a Series of Engravings on Wood, Executed by the Fine Artists in that Line, From Designs Drawn on the Blocks Themselves. London: 1809. V. 39; 41; 43

THURSTON, JOSEPH

The Toilette. London: 1730. V. 41; 42; 45; 46

THURSTON, LORRIN A.

A Hand-Book of the Annexation of Hawaii. N.P.: 1897? V. 38

A Hand-Book on the Annexation of Hawaii. St. Joseph: 1897? V. 38

A Hand Book on the Annexation of Hawaii. St. Joseph, Mich.: ca. 1895. V. 37

A Handbook on the Annexation of Hawaii. St. Joseph: 1895. V. 39

THURSTON, ROBERT H.

A Manual of the Steam-Engine for Engineers and Technical Schools' Advanced Courses. New York:ew York: 1907. V. 40

THWAITE, ANTHONY

Larkin at Sixty. London: 1982. V. 38

THWAITE, LEO

Alberta: An Aacount of Its Wealth and Progress. Chicago/New York: 1912. V. 43

THWAITES, REUBEN GOLD 1853-1913

Afloat on the Ohio. Chicago: 1897. V. 42

Early Western Travels 1748-1846. John Long's Journal 1768-1782. Cleveland: 1904. V. 38; 39

Early Western Travels, 1748-1846. Cleveland: 1904-07. V. 38; 39; 44; 46

Early Western Travels, 1748-1846. Glendale: 1904-07. V. 40

Jesuit relations and Allied Documents. Cleveland: 1896-1901. V. 39; 40; 41; 42; 44; 45

The Jesuit Relations and Allied Documents, Travels and Explorations of the Jesuit Missionaires in New France, 1610-1791. Cleveland: 1896-1904. V. 41; 42; 44; 46

The Jesuit Relations and Allied Documents. New York: 1959. V. 38

The Jesuit Relations and Allied Documents: Travels and Explorations of the Jesuit Missionaires in New France, 1610-1791. The Original French, Latin and Italian texts, with English translations and notes; Illustrations by portraits, maps . . . Cleveland: 1909. V. 37

THE THYOPHILES Whodunit: a Private Revelation of the Hitherto Most Mysterious Origin, Development, Practices and Works of the Typophiles. New York: 1938. V. 41

TIBBITS, GEORGE

Essay on the Expediency and Practicability of Improving or Creating Home Markets for the Sale of Agricultural Productions, and Raw Materials by the Introduction of Growth of Artisans and Manufacturers . . . Philadelphia: 1829. V. 41; 44

TIBBS, THOMAS

A Ballad. N.P.: 1780. V. 42

TIBULLI, ALBIUS

Elegiae. Tolz: 1920. V. 38; 45

TIBULLUS, ALBIUS

A Poetical Translation of the Elegies . . . London: 1759. V. 42

The Works . . . London: 1720. V. 40; 42

TICE, CLARA

One Hundred Merrie and Delightsome Stories. U.S.A.: 1924. V. 40

TICE, JOHN H.

Over the Plains, on the Mountains; or Kansas, Colorado, and the Rocky Mountains. St. Louis: 1872. V. 37; 38; 39; 40

TICEHURST, CLAUD B.

A History of the Birds of Suffolk. 1932. V. 46

A History of the Birds of Suffolk. London: 1932. V. 40; 45

TICHENOR, ISAAC TAYLOR

Fast-Day Sermon, by Rev. I.T. Tichenor, Pastor of the First Baptist Church of Montgomery . . . Montgomery: 1863. V. 44

TICKELL, JOHN

The History of the Town and County of Kingston Upon Hull, from Its Foundation in the Reign of Edward the First to the Present Time. Hull: 1798. V. 38

TICKELL, RICHARD 1751-1793

Anticipation: Containing the Substance of His M . . . Y's Most Gracious Speech to Booth H . . . s of P . . . L . . . T, on the Opening of the Approaching Season . . . London: 1778. V. 38; 42

Anticipation: Containing the Substance of His M---y's Most Gracious Speech to Both H---s of P-·l-·t, on the Opening of the Approaching Session . . . London: 1788. V. 45

Epistle from the Honourable Charles Fox, Partridge-Shooting, to the Honourable John Townshend, Cruising. London: 1779. V. 38; 46

The Project. London: 1788. V. 39

A Woollen Draper's Letter on the French Treaty, to His Friends and Fellow Tradesmen all Over England. London: 1786. V. 38

TICKELL, THOMAS

Kensington Garden. London: 1722. V. 45

Kensington Garden. London: 1722, 1721. V. 40

Oxford. London: 1707. V. 37

TICKNOR, FRANK O.

Poems of F. O. Ticknor, M.D. Philadelphia: 1879. V. 37

TICKNOR, GEORGE

History fo Spanish Literature. New York: 1849. V. 42

Life of William Hickling Prescott. Boston: 1864. V. 46

Life of William Hickling Prescott. London: 1864. V. 38

TIDCOMBE, MARIANNE

The Bookbindings of T. J. Cobden-Sanderson. London: 1984. V. 38; 39; 40; 42; 43; 44; 45

TIDD, THOMAS

Considerations on the Use and Properties of the Aeolus, a New Invented Portable Machine, for Exchanging and Refreshing the Air of Rooms, etc. London: 1755. V. 38

TIDDEMAN, MARK

A Draught of New York from the Hook to New York Town. (and) A Draught of Virginia from the Capes to York in York River and to Kuiquotan or Hamton in James River. V. 45

TIDEWELL, RICHARD T.

The Innkeeper's Legal Guide. London: 1864. V. 39

TIEDEMAN, CHRISTOPHER G.

An Elementary Treatise on the American Law of Real Property. St. Louis: 1885. V. 43

TIELKE, J. A.

An Account of Some of the Most Remarkable Events of the War Between the Prussians, Austrians and Russians, from 1756 to 1763 . . . London: 1787. V. 41

TIEMANN, GEORGE, & CO.

The American Armamentarium Chirurgicum. New York: 1879. V. 40

TIERNAN, CHARLES B.

The Tiernan and Other Families. Baltimore: 1901. V. 38

TIERNEY, MARK A. 1795-1862

The History and Antiquities of the Castle and Tcwn of Arundel. London: 1834. V. 38; 39; 40

TIETJENS, EUNICE

Body and Raiment. New York: 1919. V. 40; 42

TIETZE, HANS

The Drawings of the Venetian Painters in the 15th and 16th Centuries. New York: 1944. V. 46

Titian: the Paintings and Drawings. London: 1950. V. 40

TIFFANY, JOEL

A Treatise on the Unconstitutionality of American Slavery . . . Cleveland: 1849. V. 44

TIFFANY, LOUIS COMFORT

The Art Work of Louis C. Tiffany. Garden City: 1914. V. 38

TIFFANY, OSMOND

The Canton Chinese, or the American's Sojourn in the Celestial Empire. Boston: 1849. V. 40

TIFFANY STUDIOS

Ecclesiastical Department . . . published as an advertising medium . . . to convey in text and illustrationsl some idea of the scope of work in indoor and outdoor memorials of both glass and stone. New York: 1922. V. 37

Memorials in Glass & Stone. Tiffany Favril Galss. Tiffany Windows. Tiffany Mosaics. Tiffany Monuments. Tiffany Granite. New York: 1913. V. 37

The Tiffany Studios Collection of Antique Chinese Ruggs. New York: 1908. V. 39

TIGHE, HUGH USHER

An Historical Account of Cumner; with Some Particulars . . . Oxford: 1821. V. 45

TIGHE, MARY

Psyche; or, the Legend of Love. London: 1805. V. 46

Psyche, with Other Poems. London: 1811. V. 39; 40; 41; 45; 46

TIGHE, ROBERT RICHARD

Annals of Windsor, Being a History of Castle and Town . . . London: 1858. V. 41

A Letter to the Earl of Lincoln on the Present State and Direction of the Roads Intersecting the Parks and Grounds of Windsor Castle and on the Thoroughfares of the Town of Windsor . . . London: 1845. V. 45

TIGHT Lines and a Happy Landing. Anticosti: 1937. V. 39

TIJOU, JOHN

A New Booke of Drawings Invented and Designed by John Tijou. London: 1723. V. 41

TILBY, A. WYATT

The English People Overseas. Boston and New York: 1912-14. V. 39

TILDEN, BRYANT P.

Notes on the Upper Rio Grande, Explored in the Months of October and November 1846 on Board the U.S. Steamer Major Brown. Philadelphia: 1847. V. 40

TILDEN, JOE

Joe Tilden's Recipes for Epicures. San Francisco: 1907. V. 38

TILDEN, LEN ELLSWORTH

The Emigrant's Daughter, a Border Drama. Clyde: 1884. V. 37

TILDEN, WILLIAM P.

Shall the Sword Devour Freedom. A Discourse Suggested by the Death of Lt. Edward Eastman of the U.S. Army . . . Concord: 1847. V. 44

TILDESLEY, MIRIAM

Sir Thomas Browne: His Skull, Portraits and Ancestry. London: 1927. V. 42

TILEMANN, PAUL HEINRICH

De Eo Qvod Justum Est Circa Nuditatem, Von Dem was Nacketer Leute Halber Rechtens. Jena: 1692. V. 39

TILESIUS VON TILENAU, WILHELM GOTTLIEB

Naturhistorische Abbhandlungen und Erlauterungen Besonders die Petrefactenkunde Betreffend. Kassel: 1826. V. 43

TILFORD, OLIVE DARGAN

The Welsh Pony. Boston: 1913. V. 43

TILGHMAN, CHRISTOPHER

In a Father's Place. New York: 1990. V. 44

TILGHMAN, ZOE A.

Marshal of the Last Frontier, Life and Services of William Matthew (Bill) Tilghman. Glendale: 1949. V. 42; 46

TILIA, ANN BRITT

Studies and Restorations at Persepolis and other Sites of Fars. Rome: 1972. V. 37

TILING, M. P. G.

History of the German Element in Texas . . . Houston: 1912. V. 41

TILING, MATTHIAS

Anchora Sacra, Seu de Laudano Opiato, Medicamine isto Divino ac Coelitus Demisso Liber Singularis. Frankfurt: 1671. V. 37

TILING, MORITZ

History of the German Element in Texas, from 1820-1850 and Historical Sketches of the German Texas Singers' League and Houston Turnerein Form 1853-1913. Houston: 1913. V. 37; 38; 39; 42

TILKE, MAX

The Costumes of Eastern Europe. London: 1926. V. 40

Oriental Costumes: Their Designs and Colors. Berlin: 1922. V. 43

Oriental Costumes Their Designs and Colors. London: 1923. V. 40; 46

TILKE, S. W.

An Autobiographical Memoir With . . . London: 1840. V. 38; 44

TILLEY, F.

Teapots and Tea. Newport: 1957. V. 39

TILLEY, FRANK

Teapots and Tea. Newport: 1957. V. 41

Teapots and Tea. Newport: 1947. V. 37

TILLEY, HENRY ARTHUR

Eastern Europe and Western Asia. London: 1864. V. 37; 39; 40

TILLICH, PAUL

The Courage to Be. 1952. V. 42

Dynamics of Faith. New York: 1957. V. 44

TILLIER, CLAUDE

My Uncle Benjamin. New York: 1917. V. 40

TILLMAN, B. R.

The Struggles of 1876: How South Carolina Was Delivered from Carpet-bag and Negro Rule. Speech at the Red-Shirt Re-Union at Anderson. N.P.. V. 46

TILLMAN, SAMUEL

An Oration Delivered July 4th, 1789 at the Request of the Inhabitants of the Town of Boston, in Celebration of the Anniversary of American Independence. Boston: 1789. V. 44

TILLOTSON, JOHN

The Golden Americas. London. V. 38

The Works. London: 1752. V. 38

TILLSON, CHRISTIANA H.

Reminiscences of Early Life in Illinois. Amherst: 1872. V. 39

TILLYARD, E. M. W.

The Hope Vases: a Catalogue and Discussion of the Hope Collection of Greek Vases . . . Cambridge: 1923. V. 42; 44

TILMAN, H. W.

The Ascent of Nanda Devi. New York: Cambridge: 1937. V. 43

TILNEY, F.

The Forms and Functions of the Central Nervous System. New York: 1921. V. 38; 39; 40; 41

TILNEY, F. C.

Robin Hood and His Merry Outlaws. London. V. 46

TILNEY, FREDERICK

The Form and Functions of the Central Nervous System. New York: 1938. V. 37

TILT, CHARLES

Landscape Illustrations of the Waverley Novels, with Descriptions and Views. V. 43

Landscape Illustrations of the Prose and Poetical Works of Sir Walter Scott, Bart. London: 1832-33. V. 43

TILT, EDWARD JOHN

On Diseases of Menstruation and Ovarian Inflammation In Connexion with Sterility, Pelvic Tumours and Affections of the womb. New York: 1851. V. 42

TILTON, CECIL G.

William Chapman Ralston, Builder. Boston: 1935. V. 45

TILTON, THEODORE

Victoria C. Woodhull. New York: 1871. V. 43; 44

Victoria C. Woodhull. New York: 1871. V. 44

TILY, JOSEPH

Select Orations Upon the Liberty and Peace of Europe. London: 1704. V. 39

TIMBERLAKE, HENRY

The Memoirs of Lieut. Henry Timberlake (Who Accompanied the Three Cherokee Indians to England in the Year 1762). London: 1765. V. 44

Voyages du Lieutenant Henry Timberlake . . . Paris: 1797. V. 38

TIMBERLAND, EBENEZER

The History and Proceedings of the House of Lords (from 1660-1742). London: 1737-38/41-42. V. 38

TIMBS, JOHN

Abbeys, Castles and Ancient Halls of England and Wales. Their Legendary Lore and Popular History . . . London: 1872. V. 39

English Eccentrics and Eccentricities. London: 1866. V. 39

Hints for the Table; or, The Economy of Good Living. London: 1859. V. 37; 41; 45

Lives of Wits and Humourists. London: 1862. V. 38

Nooks and Corners of English Life Past and Present. London: 1867. V. 40

A Picturesque Promenade Round Dorking, in Surrey. London: 1823. V. 45

A Picturesque Promenade Round Dorking in Surrey. London: 1824. V. 43

Walks and Talks about London. London: 1865. V. 37

THE TIME-LIFE Encyclopedia of Gardening. Alexandria & New York: 1971-79. V. 45

THE TIMES Atlas. London: 1895. V. 45

THE TIMES Atlas of the World. London: 1955-59. V. 39

THE TIMES History of the War. London: 1914-21. V. 42

TIMES History of the War in South Africa, 1899-1900. London: 1900-09. V. 38

THE TIMES on Sanitary Misrule, Corporate and Parochial; on the London Water Monopoly . . . London: 1851. V. 37; 40

TIMKOVSKI, M. G.

Voyage a Peking, a Travers la Mongolie en 1820 et 1821. Paris: 1827. V. 40

TIMLIN, WILLIAM

The Ship That Sailed to Mars. 1923. V. 45

The Ship that Sailed to Mars. London: 1923. V. 42; 44; 45; 46

TIMLIN, WILLIAM M. 1893-1943

The Ship That Sailed to Mars. New York: 1923. V. 46

TIMM, WERNER

The Graphic Art of Edvard Munch. Greenwich: 1969. V. 43; 46

TIMMONS, WILBERT H.

Morelos, Priest, Soldier, Statesman of Mexico. El Paso: 1963. V. 38; 44

TIMMS, W. H.

The Thirty-Five Styles of Furniture. London: 1904. V. 40

To the Nobility, Gentry and Residents in the County of Berkshire. Reading: 1823. V. 46

Twelve Coloured Views of Reading, Gentlemen's Seats, etc. Reading: 1823. V. 40

TIMOSHENKO, STEPHEN P.

History of Strength of Materials with a Brief Account of the History of Theory of Elasticity and Theory of Structures. New York: 1953. V. 44

TIMOTHY Touchstone His Reply to Mr. Christian's Letter, Written in Vindication of the Great Worth and Innocence of the Earl of Danby. London: 1679. V. 42

TIMPERLAKE, J.

Illustrated Toronto: Past and Present, Being an Historical and Descriptive Guide-Book. Toronto: 1877. V. 44

TIMPERLEY, C. H.

Encyclopaedia of Literary and Typographical Anecdote. Garland: 1977. V. 37

TIMPERLEY, CHARLES H.

A Dictionary of Printers and Printing, with the Progress of Literature, Ancient and Modern, Bibliographical Illustrations, etc., etc. (with) The Printers' Manual. London: 1838-39. V. 39

A Dictionary of Printers and Printing. London: 1839. V. 39

The Printer's Manual. London: 1938. V. 38

Songs of the Press, and Other Poems, Relative to the Art of Printing. London: 1833. V. 38

Songs of the Press, and Other Poems Relative to the Art of Printing. London: 1835. V. 40

TIMPERLEY, CHARLES HENRY

Encyclopaedia of Literary and Typographical Anecdote . . . London: 1842. V. 42

TIMPERLEY, H. W.

A Cotswold Book. London: 1931. V. 41

TIMROD, HENRY

Poems. Boston: 1860. V. 41

TINCKER, MARY AGNES

By the Tiber. London: 1881. V. 39

TINCTORIS, JOHANNES

Terminorvm Mvsicae Diffinitorivm. Treviso: 1494-95. V. 38

TINDAL, MATTHEW

Christianity as Old as the Creation. London: 1732. V. 38

New High Church Turn'd Old Presbyterian. London: 1709. V. 45

TINDAL, WILLIAM

The History and Antiquities of the Abbey and Borough of Evesham . . . Evesham: 1794. V. 41; 44

TINDALE, NORMAN B.

Aboriginal Tribes of Australia. 1974. V. 38

TINDALE, THOMAS KEITH

Handmade Papers of Japan. Rutland & Tokyo: 1952. V. 38

TING, WALASSE

Hot and Sour Soup. V. 45

Hot and Sour Soup. California: 1969? V. 41

1 Cent Life. Bern: 1964. V. 45

Rice Paper Painting. Paris: 1984. V. 45

Walasse Ting. Red Mouth. Hong Kong: 1977. V. 45

TINGLEY, H. F.

Incidents in the Life of Milton W. Streete, the Jealous and Infatuated Murder, Who Murdered His Young and Beautiful Wife, Elvira W. Streeter, at Southbrige, Mass. October 23, 1848. Pawticket: 1850. V. 43

TINGRY, P. F.

The Painter and Varnisher's Guide: or, a Treatise Both in Theory and Practice, on the Art of Making and Applying Varnishes . . . London: 1804. V. 37

TINGRY, P. F. continued

The Painter's and Colourman's Complete Guide . . . London: 1830. V. 43

TINKER, CHAUNCEY BREWSTER

Addresses Commemorating the One Hundredth Anniversary of the Birth of William Morris. Connecticut;: 1935. V. 41

Addresses Commemorating the One Hundredth Anniversary of the Birth of William Morris Delivered Before the Yale Library Associates . . . N.P.: 1935. V. 45

Addresses Commemorating the One Hundredth Anniversary of the Birth of William Morris Delivered Before the Yale Library Associates in the Sterling Memorial Library, XXIX October MCMXXXI . . . Stamford: 1935. V. 39

The Age of Johnson. New Haven: 1949. V. 45

The Wedgwood Medallion of Samuel Johnson. Cambridge: 1926. V. 42

Young Boswell. Boston: 1922. V. 39

TINKER, EDWARD LARACQUE

The Horsemen of the Americas, and the Literature They Inspired. New York: 1953. V. 37; 39

TINKHAM, GEORGE H.

The Half Century of California Odd Fellowship. Stockton: 1906. V. 37; 39

A History of Stockton from Its Organization Up to the Present Time Including a Sketch of San Joaquin County . . . San Francisco: 1880. V. 41; 44

TINKLE, LON

J. Frank Dobie: the Makings of an Ample Mind. Austin: 1968. V. 37; 38; 40; 45

TINMOUTH, NICHOLAS

An Inquiry Relative to Various Important Points of Seamanship, Considered as a Branch of Practical Science. London: 1845. V. 41

TINNEY, J.

Compendious Treatise of Anatomy. London: 1808. V. 44; 45; 46

TINSLEY, HENRY C.

Observations of a Retired Veteran. Staunton: 1904. V. 41

TINY Men and Maidens. London: 1885. V. 45

TIOMNADH, NUADH

Ar Tigheara Agus ar Slanmighir Iosa Criost. Eadar - Theagaithe on Ghrengais chum Gaelic Albanach. Dun-Eidin: 1796. V. 46

TIPHAIGNE DE LA ROCHE, CHARLES FRANCOIS

Giphantia. London: 1761-0. V. 38

TIPPING, H. AVRAY

English Homes. London: 1921-26. V. 44

English Gardens. London: 1925. V. 37; 39; 40; 44; 46

TIPPING, HENRY AVERY

English Homes. London: 1920-37. V. 42

TIPPING, HENRY AVRAY

English Homes of the Early Renaissance. London: 1930. V. 41

English Homes. London: 1921-37. V. 40

English Homes. Period II - Volume I: Early Tudor, 1485-1558. London: 1929. V. 37; 38; 39; 40; 41

English Homes. Period III. Volume 1. Late Tudor and Early Stuart 1558-1649. London: 1922. V. 41

English Homes Period IV. Volume I Late Stuart, 1649-1714. London: 1920. V. 37

English Homes. Period IV - Volume II. The Work of John Vanbrugh and His School 1699-1736. London: 1928. V. 37; 38

Gardens Old and New. London. V. 40

Grinling Gibbons and the Wood-Work of His Age. London: 1914. V. 37; 41

TIRABOSCHI, GIROLAMO

Storia Della Letteratura Italiana. Modena: 1787-1994. V. 40

TIRAQUEAU, ANDRE 1488-1558

Tratatus, Cessante Causa Effectus. Paris: 1551. V. 46

TIRAQVELLUS, ANDREAS

Commentariorvm de Vtroqve Retractv, et Mvnicipali, et Conventionali. Venice: 1561. V. 45

TISDALL, JOHN

Flora's Banquet. Belfast: 1782. V. 38; 40

TISSANDIER, GASTON 1843-1899

A History and Handbook of Photography. London: 1876. V. 40

A History and Handbook of Photography. London: 1876/1877. V. 38

Popular Scientific Recreations in Natural Philosophy, Astronomy, Geology, Chemistry, etc. London: 1880's. V. 45

TISSOT, ANDRE

An Essay on the Disorders of People of Fashion. London: 1771? V. 38

TISSOT, SAMUEL AUGUSTE ANDRE

Advice to the People in General with regard to their Health: but more particularly calculated for those, who, by their Distance from regular Physicians, ... *Translated from the French Edition* . . . . *by J. Kirkpatrick, M. D.* London: 1765. V. 39; 44

TISSOT, SAMUEL AUGUSTE ANDRE DAVID 1728-1797

Advice to the People in General, with Regard to Their Health . . . London: 1767. V. 45

Advice to the People in General, with Regard to Their Health. London: 1771. V. 41

Onaism: or, a Treatise upon the Disorders produced by Masturbation . . . *Translated from the last paris Edition by A. Hume.* London: 1766. V. 37

TISSOT, SIMON ANDRE

A Treatise on the Crime of Onan. London: 1766. V. 38; 40

TIT for Tat. London: 1890. V. 39

TITFORD, W. J.

Sketches Towards a Hortus Botanicus Americanus. London: 1811. V. 41

Sketches Towards a Hortus Botanicus Americanus . . . London: 1811-12. V. 42

TITI, FILIPPO

Studio di Pittura, Scoltura & Architecttura Nelle Chiese di Roma . . . Roma: 1675. V. 37

TITIS, PLACIDO DE

Primum Mobile . . . *the Nature and Extent of Celestial Influx Upon the Mental Faculties of Man* . . . London: 1800. V. 37

TITSWORTH, W. G.

Outskirt Episodes. Avoca: 1927. V. 46

TITTELMANS, FRANCISCUS

Paraphrastica Elucidatio in Librum D. Job, Priore Aeditione Multo Castigatior . . . Paris: 1550. V. 46

TITTSWORTH, W. G.

Outskirt Episodes. Des Moines: 1927. V. 41

TITUS, SILAS

Killing No Murder. London: 1743; V. 41

TIXER, JEAN

Epistolae. Lyon: 1559. V. 37

TJADER, RICHARD

The Big Game of Africa. New York: 1910. V. 45

TO Cataline (i. e. C. J. Fox). N.P.: 1784. V. 37

TO Churchmen. N.P.: 1863. V. 39

TO Doctor R.; Essays Here Collected and Published in Honor of the Seventieth Birthday of Dr. A.S.W. Rosenbach, July 22, 1946. Philadelphia: 1946. V. 39; 40; 45

TO Gibraltar and Back in the Eighteen Tonner by One of the Crew Crossing the Bay of Biscay and Portugal Coast Cruising in a Gaff-Rigged 52' Cutter. London: 1888. V. 42

TO Harvey Cushing, Master Surgeon and Teacher . . . Medical Essays and Papers Affectionately Dedicated by His Pupils on the Occasion of His Sixtieth Birthday. Chicago: 1929. V. 41

TO Hatti Hecht Sloss on Her Eightieth Birthday, June 12, 1954. San Francisco: 1954. V. 46

TO Mr. S----- M-----, on His Turning Evidence. London: 1747. V. 40; 41

TO Nursery Land. London: 1890. V. 46

TO the Alaska Gold Fields. San Francisco: 1912. V. 39

TO The Electors of Dutchess County. Poughkeepsie: 1797. V. 40

TO the Freemen, Freeholders and Other Inhabitants of the City and County of New York. New York: 1774. V. 45

TO the Friends of the Abolition of the Slave Trade. London: 1807. V. 40

TO the Honourable, the Knights, Citizens and Burgesses of the Commons House in Parliament Now Assembled, January 24, 1642. London: 1642. V. 42

TO the Marine Society, in praise of the Great and Good Work they have done by Clothing and Fitting out for the Sea-Service 2682 Men, and 1868 Boys, in the space of fifteen months, to the 6th of October last, ... in the Cause they have espoused. N.P.: 1757. V. 39

TO The Memory of Abraham Lincoln. Philadelphia: 1865. V. 40

TO the Merchants, Ship-Owners, Underwriters, and Others Concerned in the Commerce and Navigation of These Kingdoms. London: 1797. V. 42

TO The People of the United States. N.P.: 1827. V. 45

THE TOASTS of the Rump-Steak Club. London: 1734. V. 43

TOBIE, E. P.

History of the First Maine Cavalry 1861-1865. Boston: 1887. V. 39

TOBIN, AGNES

Love's Crucifix - Nine Sonnets and a Canzone from Petrarch. London: 1902. V. 44

TOBIN, CATHERINE

Shadows of the East; or Slight Sketches of Scenery, Persons and Customs ... London: 1855. V. 44; 45

TOBIN, LADY

The Land of Inheritance or Bible Scenes Revisited. London: 1863. V. 43; 46

TOBLER, JOHN

Pennsylvania Town and Country-Man's Almanack for 1771. Wilmington: 1770. V. 43

TOCKER, MARY ANN

The Trial of Mary Ann Tocker, for an Alledged Libel, on Mr. R. Gurney, Jun. London: 1818. V. 45

TOCQUEVILLE, ALEXIS CHARLES HENRI MAURICE CLEREL DE 1805-1859

L'Ancien Regime et la Revolution. Paris: 1856. V. 41

De La Democratie en Amerique. Bruxelles: 1840. V. 41

Democracy in America. New York: 1838. V. 38

Democracy in America. Translated by Henry Reeves. A New Edition, with an introductory notice by the translator. London: 1862. V. 37

Oeuvres. Paris: 1864-66. V. 42

The Old Regime and the Revolution. New York: 1856. V. 45

TOD, GEORGE

Plans, Elevations and Sections, of Hot-Houses, Green-Houses, an Aquariam, Conservatories &c. Recently Built in Different Parts of England ... London: 1807. V. 39

Plans, Elevations and Sections, of Hot-Houses, Green-Houses, and Aquarium Conservatories &c ... London: 1812. V. 45

TOD, THOMAS fl. 1781

Consolatory Thourghts on American Independence. Edinburgh: 1782. V. 38; 40; 45

TODA, KENJI

Descriptive Catalogue of Japanese and Chinese Illustrated Books in the Ryerson Library of the Art Institute of Chicago. Chicago: 1931. V. 42

TODD, CHARLES B.

A General History of the Burr Family. New York: 1891. V. 46

TODD, CHARLES S.

Sketches of the Civil and Military Services of William Henry Harrison. Cincinnati: 1840. V. 37

TODD, CHARLES W.

Woodville; or the Anchoret Reclaimed. Knoxville: 1832. V. 39; 40; 41

TODD, DOROTHY

Mortimer. The New Interior Decoration. New York: 1929. V. 44

The New Interior Decoration. New York: 1929. V. 38

TODD, ELIZABETH

The History of Lady Caroline Rivers in a Series of Letters in Two Volumes. London: 1788. V. 40

TODD, F. P.

Soldiers of the American Army 1775-1941. New York: 1941. V. 39

TODD, FRANK MORTON

The Story of the Exposition. New York: 1921. V. 37; 38; 39; 42; 46

TODD, FRANK S.

Waterfowl: Ducks, Geese and Swans of the World. New York: 1979. V. 42

TODD, GLENN

Shaped Poetry. San Francisco: 1981. V. 39; 41

TODD, HENRY

Memoirs of the Life and Writings of the Right Rev. Brian Walton, D.D. Lord Bishop of Chester ... London: 1821. V. 42

TODD, J. H.

The Book of Hymns of the Ancient Church in Ireland. Dublin: 1855. V. 43

Catalogue of the Valuable Library of the Late J. H. Todd, Ex-President of the R.I.A. and Precentor of St. Patrick's Cathedral, Dublin. Dublin: 1869. V. 43

Descriptive Remarks on Illuminations in Certain Ancient Irish Manuscripts. London: 1869. V. 43

The War of the Gaedhill with the Gael, or the Invasions of Ireland by the Danes and Other Norsemen. London: 1867. V. 43

TODD, J. S.

Great Western Railway. The Future of Paddington Station. London: 1928. V. 46

TODD, JAMES G.

Strila, or the Palace of Strife, a Poem in Four Cantos. Edinburgh: 1823. V. 42

TODD, JAMES HENTHORN

The Books of the Vaudois. London: 1865. V. 38; 44

Descriptive Remarks on Illuminations in Certain Ancient Irish Manuscript. London: 1869. V. 38

The Irish Version of Historia Britonum of Nennius. Dublin: 1848. V. 38

TODD, JOHN

The Daughter at School. Northampton: 1857. V. 37; 44; 45

TODD, JOHN HENRY

Historical Tablets and Medallions Illustrative of an Improved System of Artificial Memory ... London: 1827. V. 37

TODD, ROBERT

Clinical Lectures on Paralysis. Philadelphia: 1855. V. 46

TODD, ROBERT BENTLEY

Clinical Lectures on Paralysis, Disease of the Brain and Other Affections of the Nervous System. Philadelphia: 1855. V. 42; 44; 45

Clinical Lectures on Certain Diseases of the Urniary Organs; and On Dropsies. Philadelphia: 1857. V. 42

Clinical Lectures on Certain Acute Diseases. London: 1860. V. 37; 38; 39; 40; 41; 44

The Cyclopaedia of Anatomy and Physiology. London: 1835-59. V. 42

The Physiological Anatomy and Physiology of man. London: 1845-46. V. 41

The Physiological Anatomy and Physiology of Man. London: 1845-56. V. 44

TODD, THOMAS

The Gauger's Useful Companion ... Manchester: 1841. V. 43

TODD, W. E. CLYDE

Birds of the Labrador Peninsula. 1963. V. 39

Birds of Western Pennsylvania. Pittsburgh: 1940. V. 39

TODHUNTER, ISAAC

A History of the Progress of the Calculus of Variations During the Nineteenth Century. Cambridge: 1861. V. 38

A History of the Progress of the Calculus of Variations During the Nineteenth Century. London: 1861. V. 42

A History of the Mathematical Theories of Attraction and the Figure of the Earth from the Time of Newton to that of Laplace. London: 1873. V. 42

A History of the Theory of Elasticity and of the Strength of Materials from Galilei to the Present Time. Cambridge: 1886/93. V. 44

A History of the Theory of Elasticity and of the Strength of Materials from Galilei to the Present Time. London: 1886-93. V. 42

A History of the Progress of the Calculus of Variations During the Nineteenth Century. Cambridge: 1861. V. 37

Plane Trigonometry for the Use of Colleges and Schools With Numerous Examples. London: 1876. V. 38

Researches in the Calculus of Variations. London: 1871. V. 38

Spherical Trigonometry for the Use of Colleges and Schools with Numerous Examples. London: 1878. V. 38

William Whewell, D.D. Master of Trinity College, Cambridge. London: 1876. V. 43; 45

William Whewell ... an Account of His Writings with Selections from His Literary and Scientific Correspondence ... London: 1876. V. 45

TODHUNTER, JOHN

Ye Minutes of Ye CLXXVIIth Meeting of Ye Sette of Odd Volumes. Ashendene: 1896. V. 43; 45

TOESCA, PIETRO

Florentine Painting of the Trecento. Firenze & Paris: 1929. V. 42

TOESCA, PIETRO continued

Florentine Painting of the Trecento. Paris: 1929. V. 45

TOILERS in London; or, Inquiries Concerning Female Labour in the Metropolis. London: 1889. V. 40

THE TOILET. Washington: 1867. V. 38

THE TOILETTE of Health, Beauty and Fashion. L: 1832. V. 40

THE TOILETTE of Health, Beauty and Fashion . . . Boston: 1833. V. 43

TOKE, MONROE TSA

The Peyote Ritual: Visions and Descriptions of . . . San Francisco: 1957. V. 38

THE TOKEN and Atlantic Souvenir. Boston: 1833. V. 40

THE TOKEN and Atlantic Souvenir . . . for 1838. Boston: 1838. V. 40; 46

TOKLAS, ALICE B.

The Alice B. Toklas Cook Book. London: 1954. V. 38; 40

TOKUGAWA, YOSHINOBU

The Tokugawa Collection No Robes and Masks. New York: 1976. V. 41

TOLAND, JOHN

Anglia Libera; or the Limitation and Succession of the Crown of England . . . London: 1701. V. 42

The Art of Governing by Partys. London: 1701. V. 38

A Collection of Several Pieces, Now First Published from Original Manuscripts. London;: 1726. V. 37; 39

Dunkirk or Dover; or, the Queen's Honour, the Nation's Safety, the Liberties of Europe, and the Peace of the World, All at stake till that Fort and Port be Totally Demolish'd by the French. London: 1713. V. 45

Letters to Serena: Containing I. The Origin and Force of Prejudices. II. The History of the Soul's Immortality Among the Heathens. III. The Origin of Idolatry, and Reasons of Heathenism. IV. A Letter to a Gentleman in Holland . . . London: 1704. V. 40

The Life of Milton, Containing Besides the History of His Works, Several Extraordinary Characters of Men and Books, Sects, Parties, and Opinions. London: 1699. V. 41; 42

The Life of John Milton. London: 1761. V. 41; 42; 43; 45

No Man's Land. The Story of 1918. London: 1980. V. 45

Pantheisticon. Sive Formula Celebrandae Sodalitatis Socraticae, in Tres Particulas Divisa. Cosmopoli: 1720. V. 40

Vindicius Liberius, or M. Toland's Defence of Himself Against the Late Lower House of Convocation . . . London: 1702. V. 43

TOLD by Pioneers. Tales of Frontier Life as Told by Those Who Remember the Days of the Territory and Early Statehood of Washington. N.P.: 1937-38. V. 38

TOLD by the Pioneers. Tales of Frontier Life as Tol by Those Who Remember the Days of the Territory and Early Statehood of Washington. N.P.: 1937-8. V. 39

TOLD by the Pioneers. Tales of Frontier Life As Told by Those Who Remember The Days of the Territory and Early Statehood of Washington. Washington: 1937-38. V. 45

TOLDERVY, WILLIAM

Select Epitaphs. London: 1755. V. 38; 40

TOLET, FRANCOIS

Commentaria, una Cum Quaestionibus, in Universam Aristotelis Logicam . . . Coloniae Agrippinae, In: 1589. V. 37

Traite de la Lithotomie ou de l'Extraction de la Pierre Hors la Vessie. Paris: 1682. V. 37

TOLFREY, FREDERIC

The Sportsman in France . . . London: 1841. V. 39; 43

TOLKEIN, JEROME RONALD RUEL

The Lord of the Rings. London: 1969. V. 37

TOLKEIN, JOHN RONALD REUEL

Beowulf: and the Critics. London: 1936. V. 43

TOLKIEN, JOHN RONALD REUEL 1892-1973

The Adventures of Tom Bombadil and Other Verses from the Red Book. London: 1962. V. 42

The Devil's Coach-Houses. London: 1925. V. 40

Farmer Giles of Ham. London: 1949. V. 42

Farmer Giles of Ham. 1950. V. 44

The Fellowship of the Ring. 1954. V. 43; 44; 46

The Fellowship of the Ring. London: 1954. V. 40; 42

The Fellowship of the Ring. (with) The Two Towers. (with) The Return of the King. London: 1954-55. V. 42

The Fellowship of the Ring. The Two Towers. The Return of the King. London: 1974. V. 46

The History of the Middle-Earth. London: 1983-87. V. 43

The Hobbit. London: 1937. V. 39; 41; 42; 45; 46

The Hobbitt. 1938. V. 39

The Hobbit. Boston: 1938. V. 37; 41; 44; 45

The Lord of the Rings. London: 1954/54/55. V. 42

(The Lord of the Rings Triology). The Fellowship of the Ring. The Two Towers. The Return of the King. London: 1954/54/55. V. 41

The Lord of the Rings. London: 1954-55. V. 41; 42; 44

The Lord of the Rings. Boston: 1954/55/56. V. 42

The Lord of the Rings. 1955. V. 43

The Lord of the Rings. London: 1969. V. 40; 43; 45

The Lord of the Rings. 1966. V. 37

A Middle English Vocabulary. Oxford: 1922. V. 38

The Return of the King. 1955. V. 39

The Return of the King. London: 1955. V. 44

The Return of the King. 1956. V. 37

The Return of the King. Boston: 1956. V. 37

The Silmarillion. 1977. V. 37; 43; 44; 46

The Silmarillion. Boston: 1977. V. 41

Smith of Wootton Major. Boston: 1967. V. 40

Tree and Leaf. 1964. V. 37; 43

The Two Towers. Boston: 1955. V. 46

Unfinished Tales. 1980. V. 39; 46

TOLL, FREDERICK

a Plain and Proper Answer to This Question, Why Does Not the Bishop of Clogher, Supposing Him to be the Author of the Essay on Spirit, Resign His Preferments? London: 1753. V. 45

TOLL, NICHOLAS

The Green Glazed Pottery. New Haven: 1943. V. 40

TOLLEMACHE, JOHN

A Royal Historie of the Excellent Knight Generides. Hertford: 1865. V. 40

TOLLEMARCHE, STRATFORD

Reminiscences of the Yukon. Toronto: 1912. V. 40; 43; 45

TOLLER, ERNST

Brokenbrow: a Tragedy. London: 1926. V. 46

Brokenbrow. London: 1930. V. 42

Brokenbrow: A Tragedy, by Ernst Toller. Translated by Vera Mendel. London: (1926). V. 37

The Swallow Book. 1924. V. 44

A Tragedy by Ernst Toller. London: 1926. V. 43

TOLLER, ERNST BROKENBROW

George Grosz. London: 1930. V. 44

TOLLEY, CYRIL J. H.

The Modern Golfer. London: 1924. V. 43

TOLMER, A.

Mise en Page. The Theory and Practice of Lay-Out. London: 1931. V. 39; 45

TOLMIE, W. F.

Reply to Letter of 'Old Settler' Published in the 'Times' Newspaper, on the Selection of a Terminus on the Pacific Coast for the Proposed Canadian Pacific Railway. London: 1877. V. 42

TOLMIE, WILLIAM FRAZER

Comparative Vocabularies of the Indian Tribes of British Columbia. Montreal: 1884. V. 37; 38; 45

TOLNAY, CHARLES DE

H. Bosch. London: 1966. V. 40

Hieronymus Bosch. New York: 1966. V. 40

History and Technique of Old Master Drawings. New York. V. 44

History and Technique of Old Master Drawings. New York: 1943. V. 42

Michelangelo. Princeton: 1945-48. V. 42

TOLOMEI, CLAUDIO

De Le Lettere . . . Lib. Sette. Venice: 1547. V. 44

TOLSON, FRANCIS

The Battle of Dettingen. Northampton: 1743. V. 45

Hermathenae, or Moral Emblems, and Ethnick Tales, with Explanatory Notes. London: 1740. V. 45; 46

Octavius Prince of Syra, or, a Lash for Levi. London: 1719. V. 45

TOLSTOI, LEO 1828-1910

How Much Land Does a Man Need? 1986. V. 38

TOLSTOI, LEV NIKOLAEVICH 1828-1910

Anna Karenina. Moskva: 1878. V. 41; 46

Anna Karenina. New York: 1886. V. 38; 45

Anna Karenin: a Novel. London: 1901. V. 42

Anna Karenina. Moscow: 1933. V. 41; 43

Anna Karenina. Cambridge: 1951. V. 41

The Complete Works. London: 1904. V. 37

The Complete Works. Translated and Edited by Leo Wiener. Boston/New York: (1904). V. 37

How Much Land Does a Man Need? N.P.: 1986. V. 46

The Invaders and Other Stories. New York: 1887. V. 42

Katia. New York: 1888. V. 42; 44

'The Kingdom of God Is Within You' Christianity Not as a Mystic Religion But as a New Theory of Life. London: 1894. V. 38; 42

The Kingdom of God is Within You. New York: 1894. V. 45

Master and Man. New York: c. 1895. V. 37

My Religion. New York: 1885. V. 40

Novels and Other Writings of . . . New York: 1903. V. 44

The Novels and Other Works. New York: 1911. V. 42

The Novels and Other Works. New York: 1923. V. 40; 46

Popular Stories and Legends. First Series. Christchurch: 1901. V. 42

Preliminary Sketch of the 'Kreutzer Sonata'. 1965. V. 46

Resurrection. London: 1900. V. 38

A Russain Proprietor. New York: 1887. V. 46

The Slavery of Our Times. 1901. V. 43

Tolstoi's Love Letters. London: 1923. V. 42; 45

Viona I Mir. (War and Peace). Moscow: 1868-69. V. 42

War and Peace. New York: 1886. V. 37; 40; 43

War and Peace. New York: 1886-67. V. 44; 45

War and Peace. 1889. V. 43

War and Peace. Glasgow: 1938. V. 41; 45

War and Peace. New York: 1954. V. 45

War and Peace. London: 1959. V. 44

What I Believe. London: 1885. V. 45

What Men Live By. 1951. V. 44

What Men Live By. Belvedere: 1951. V. 40; 42; 46

Where God Is Love Is. Cantmarle: Dorset: 1924. V. 41

With wood engravings by Mallette Dean. Belvedere: 1951. V. 37

Works. New York: 1898. V. 42

Lev N. Tolstoy: His Writings. Cambridge: 1904. V. 42

TOLSTOI, LEV NIKOLAVEICH 1828-1910

Childhood, Boyhood, Youth. New York: 1886. V. 38

What Men Live By. Belvedere: 1951. V. 38

TOLSTOI, SOPHIE, COUNTESS

The Autobiography. London: 1922. V. 46

TOLSTOY, SERGE, COUNTESS

The Enchanted Garden. Tarrytown: 1948. V. 41

TOM, JOHN NICHOLS

The Eccentric and Singular Productions of Sir W. Courtenay, K.M. Alias Mr. Tom . . . Canterbury: 1833. V. 39

TOMALIN, MILES

Fool's Luck - Ten Poems. London: 1929. V. 44

TOMASINI, IACOPO FILIPPO

Petrarcha Redivivus. Padua: 1650. V. 37

TOMBES, JOHN

Praecursor: or a Forerunner to a Large Review of the Dispute . . . London: 1652. V. 39

TOMBLESON, W.

Upper Rhine. London: 1840. V. 45

Views of the Rhine. (with) Views of the Upper Rhine. London: 1832. V. 45

TOMBLESON, WILLIAM

Eighty Picturesque Views on the Thames and Medway. London: (1834). V. 37

Tombleson's Views of the Rhine. London: 1830-34. V. 37; 38; 39; 40; 42

Tombleson's Views of the Rhine. London: 1832. V. 39; 46

TOME, PHILIP

Pioneer Life; or, Thirty Years a Hunter, Being Scenes and Adventures in the Life of Philip Tome, Fifteen Years Interpreter for Cornplanter and Gov. Blacksnake, Chiefs of the Allegheny River. Buffalo: 1854. V. 42; 45

Pioneer Life; or, Thirty Years a Hunter . . . Harrisburg: 1928. V. 42

TOMES, ROBERT

Panama in 1855. New York: 1855. V. 43

The Prayer of the Book. Worcester: 1824. V. 38; 40; 44

TOMKINS, CHARLES

Eight Views of Reading Abbey, Drawn and Engraved . . . London: 1791. V. 37; 42

Six Views in the West of England. London: 1802. V. 44

Six Views in the West of England. London: 1802. V. 39

A Tour to the Isle of Wight. London: 1796. V. 40

TOMKINS, T.

A Tale of Midas the King. London: 1714. V. 41; 45

TOMKINS, THOMAS

The Beauties of Writing Exemplified in a Variety of Plain and Ornamental penmanship. London: 1777. V. 38

The Inconveniences of Toleration, or an Answer to a Late Book Intituled A Proposition Made to the King and Parliament . . . London: 1667. V. 38

Lingua: or The Combat of the Tongue, and The Five Senses for Superiority. London: 1657. V. 37

TOMKINSON, G. S.

A Select Bibliography of the Principal Modern Presses Public and Private in Great Britain and Ireland. 1928. V. 38

A Select Bibliography of the Principal Modern Presses Public and Private in Great Britain and Ireland. London: 1928. V. 39; 40; 42; 45

A Select bibliography of the principal modern presses public and private in Great Britain and Ireland. With an introduction by B.H. Newdigate. 1928. V. 37

TOMKIS, THOMAS

Lingua; or, The Combate of the Tonge, and the Five Sences for Superioritie. London: 1632. V. 42

Lingua; or the Combat of the Tongue and the Five Senses for Superiority. London: 1657. V. 46

TOMLIN, E. L.

Gleanings. London: 1891. V. 40

Rhymelets. London: 1891. V. 40

TOMLINSON, ABRAHAM

The Military Journals of Two Private Soldiers, 1758-1775. Poughkeepsie: 1855. V. 42

TOMLINSON, CHARLES

Cyclopaedia of Useful Arts . . . London: 1854. V. 42; 43

Cyclopedia of Useful Arts, Mechanical and Chemical, Manufactures, Mining and Engineering. London: 1852-54. V. 40

Cyclopaedia of Useful Arts, Mechanical and Chemical, Manufactures, Mining and Engineering. London: 1866. V. 42; 43

Illustrations of Useful Arts and Manufacture. London: 1858. V. 41

The Necklace. London: 1955. V. 45

The Necklace. Oxford: 1955. V. 38

The Necklace - Poems. Swinford: 1955. V. 44

Rudimentary Treatise on the Construction of Locks. London: 1853. V. 45

TOMLINSON, HENRY MAJOR 1873-1958

All Our Yesterdays. London: 1930. V. 41; 43; 44; 45; 46

All Our Yesterdays. New York: 1930. V. 42

Out of Soundings. New York: 1931. V. 44

The Sea and Jungle. London: 1912. V. 37; 38; 39; 40; 41; 42; 43; 44

South to Cadiz. London: 1934. V. 46

Under the Red Ensign. London: 1926. V. 41; 42

War Books . . . Cleveland: 1930. V. 45

TOMLINSON, JOHN

From Doncaster into Sherwood Forest; Passing through Bawtry, Blyth and Worksop. Doncaster: 1876? V. 38

TOMLINSON, RALPH

A Slang Pastoral Being a Parody of a Celebrated Poem of Dr. Bryon's (sic). London: 1780. V. 45

TOMLINSON, W. W.

The North Eastern Railway. Newcastle-upon-Tyne: 1914. V. 38; 40; 46

TOMMASI, FRANCESCO

Reggimento del Padre di Famiglia, di M. Francesco Tommasi da Colle di Val d'Elsa Toscano . . . Fiorenza: 1580. V. 39

TOMMY - 1916-1942. London: 1943. V. 45

TOMORY, PETER

The Life and Art of Henry Fuseli. London: 1972. V. 44

TOMPKINS, FRANK

Chasing Villa: the Story Behind the Story of Pershing's Expedition into Mexico. Harrisburg: 1934. V. 43

TOMPKINS, FRANK H.

Riparian Lands of the Mississippi River, Past, Present, Prospective. New Orleans: 1901. V. 42

TOMS, W.

Thirty Six New, Original and Practical Designs for Chairs, Adapted for the Drawing and Dining Room, Parlour and Hall. Bath: 1830. V. 42

TONE, WILLIAM THEOBALD WOLFE

The Life of Wolfe Tone, Founder of the United Irish Society. Washington: 1826. V. 38

TONER, J. M.

Address Before the Rocky Mountain Medical Association June 6, 1877 . . . Washington: 1877. V. 40; 43; 44

TONEY, MARCUS B.

The Privations of a Private. Nashville: 1907. V. 37

TONEYAMA, KOJIN

Popular Arts of Mexico. New York: 1974. V. 42

The Popular Arts of Mexico. New York & Tokyo: 1974. V. 38

Relief Sculpture of Ancient Mexico. Boston: 1971. V. 40

TONG, H. K.

Chiang Kai-Shek. 1953. V. 38

TONG, WILLIAM

An Account of the Life and Death of the Late Reverend Mr. Matthew Henry. London: 1718. V. 38

TONGE, ELIZA

Poetical Trifles. Cheltenham: 1832. V. 40

TONGUE, CORNELIUS

Hunting Tours: Descriptive of Various Fashionable Countries and Establishments . . . London: 1864. V. 43

TONGUE, MARGARET

A Book of Kinds. Iowa City: 1958. V. 45

TONKINSON, G. S.

A Select Bibliography of the Principal Modern Presses Public and Private in Great Britain and Ireland. With an introduction by B.H. Newdigate. London: 1928. V. 37

TONNA, CHARLOTTE ELIZABETH

Helen of Fleetwood. London: 1841. V. 44

Osric: a Missionary Tale; with the Garden and Other Poems. Dublin: 1825? V. 38; 42

The System: a Tale of the West Indies. London: 1827. V. 45

TONNA, CHARLOTTE ELIZABETH BROWNE

Izram, a Mexican Tale; and Other Poems. London: 1826. V. 41

Letters from Ireland, 1837. London: 1838. V. 38; 41

TONNIES, FERDINAND

Gemeinschaft und Gesellschaft Abhandlugen des Communismus und des Socialismus als Empirischer Kulturformen. Leipzig: 1887. V. 45

TONSBERG, CHRISTIAN

Norge Fremstillet I Tegninger . . . Christiania: 1846-48. V. 38

TONTI, HENRI DE

An Account of Monsieur de la Salle's Last Expedition and Discoveries in North America. London: 1698. V. 38

TONY'S Army. London: 1890. V. 45

TOOD, EDWIN

V. 42

TOOHEY, JOHN L.

A History of the Pulitzer Prize Plays. New York: 1967. V. 46

TOOK, WILLIAM

The Life of Catharine II, Empress of Russia. London: 1799. V. 39

TOOKE, JOHN HORNE 1736-1812

Eiiea Iltepoenta, or the Diversions of Purley. London: 1829. V. 39

Epea Pteroenta, or the Diversions of Purley. London: 1798-1805. V. 38

(Greek Title) Epea Pteroenta. Or the Diversions of Purley. London: 1829. V. 40

Facts Addressed to the Landholders, Stockholders, Merchants, Farmers, Manufacturerers, Tradesmen, Proprietors of Every Description and Generally to all the Subjectsw of Great Britain and Ireland. London: 1780. V. 38; 42

Or, The Diversions of Purley. London: 1786. V. 41

TOOKE, THOMAS

A History of Prices, and of the State of the Circulation from 1792 to the Present Time. London: 1838-1857. V. 42

Thoughts and Details on the High and Low Prices of the Last Thirty Years. London: 1823. V. 37

TOOKE, WILLIAM

History of Russia, from the Foundation of the Monarchy by Rurik, to the Accession of Catharine the Second. London: 1800. V. 37; 38; 41; 43

The Life of Catherine II, Empress of all the Russias . . . Philadelphia: 1802. V. 37; 44; 45

TOOKER, WILLIAM 1558?-1621

Charisma Sive Donum Santionis. London: 1597. V. 41

TOOKER, WILLIAM WALLACE

The Algonquin Series. New York: 1901. V. 41

John Eliot's First Indian Teacher and Interpreter Cockenoe-de-Long Island and the Story of His Career from the Early Records. New York: 1896. V. 37; 42

TOOLE, JOHN KENNEDY

A Confederacy of Dunces. 1980. V. 44

A Confederacy of Dunces. Baton Rouge: 1980. V. 42; 43; 45; 46

A Confederacy of Dunces. Baton Rouge & London: 1980. V. 37

TOOLE STOTT, R.

Circus and Allied Arts, a World Bibliography. Derby: 1958-71. V. 39; 42

TOOLE-STOTT, RAYMOND

Circus and Allied Arts. 1958-71. V. 46

TOOLEY, R. V.

An Atlas of England and Wales. The Maps of Christopher Saxton, Engraved 1574-1578. London: 1979. V. 42; 44; 45

English Books with Coloured plates 1790 to 1860. London: 1954. V. 43

TOOLEY, RONALD VERE

Dictionary of Mapmakers. New York: 1979. V. 39; 43

Tooley's Dictionary of Mapmakers. New York: 1979. V. 39

Landmarks of Mapmaking. Amsterdam: 1968. V. 39

Landmarks of Mapmaking, an Illustrated Survey of Maps and Mapmakers. New York: 1976. V. 40; 41

Some English Books with Coloured Plates. London: 1935. V. 42

Tooley's Dictionary of Mapmakers. New York: 1977. V. 40; 44

Tooley's Dictionary of Mapmakers. New York & Amsterdam: 1979. V. 40

TOOLY, THOMAS

Basia; or, the Charms of Kissing. London: 1719. V. 45

TOOMBS, ROBERT A.

The Address, Presented by Judge Nisbet, Chairman of the Committee of 17 Appointed to Draft Ordinance of Secession. Milledgeville: 1861. V. 42

TOOMER, JEAN

Essentials. Chicago: 1931. V. 43

The Flavor of Man. Philadelphia: 1949. V. 46

TOOMEY, D. F.

Paleoagology, Contemporary Research and Applications. Berlin: 1985. V. 37

TOONDER, MARTIN

Tom Puss Tales. London: 1930. V. 45

TOONE, WILLIAM

A Glossary and Etymological Dictionary . . . London: 1834. V. 45

A Practical Guide to the Duty and Authority of Overseers of the Poor. London: 1822. V. 37; 40

TOOR, FRANCES

Las Obras de Jose Guadalupe Posada . . . Mexico: 1930. V. 44

TOOROP, JAN

Gabrielle, door Marie Marx-Koning. Two Volumes. Bussum: 1902/1904. V. 37

TOOVEY, JAMES

A Catalogue of an Extensive and Extraordinary Assemblage of the Productions of the Aldine Press, From Its First Establishment at Venice in 1494 . . . London: 1880. V. 42

TOPHAM, EDWARD

The British Album. London: 1790. V. 45

TOPHAM, EDWARD continued

Letters from Edinburgh . . . Dublin: 1776? V. 42

The Life of the Late John Elwes, Esquire; Member in Three Successive Parliaments fro Berkshire. London. V. 38

TOPHAM, JOHN

The Life of the Late John Elwes, Esquire. London: 1790. V. 39

TOPHAM, ROBERT N.

Edward Randolph: Including His Letters and Official Papers from the New England, Middle and Soutehrn Colonies in America, with Other Documents Relating Chiefly to the Vacating of the Royal Charter of the Colony of Massachusetts Bay 1676-1703. Boston: 1898-1909. V. 42

TOPHAM, W. F.

The Lakes of England. London: 1869. V. 46

TOPLADY, AUGUSTUS

The Scheme of Christian and Philosophical Necessity Asserted. London: 1775. V. 45

TOPLADY, AUGUSTUS MONTAGUE

An Old Fox Tarr'd and Feather'd. London: 1775. V. 42

THE TOPOGRAPHER. London: 1789/71. V. 38

THE TOPOGRAPHER for the Years 1789, (1790 and 1791), Containing a Variety of Original Articles, Illustrative of Local History and Antiquities of England . . . London: 1789-91. V. 39

TOPOGRAPHICAL And Geological Atlas of the District of the High Plateus of Utah to Accompany the Report of Capt. C. E. Dutton, U.S. Ordnance Corps Assistant Geologists. New York: 1879. V. 46

THE TOPOLOBAMPO Pacific. N.P.: 1878. V. 41

TOPOLSKI, FELIKS

Portrait of G.B.S. with an Introduction by Herbert Pearson. London: 1946. V. 46

TOPONCE, ALEXANDER

Reminiscences of Alexander Toponce, 1839-1923. Ogden: 1923. V. 40; 42; 45

TOPPAN, ROBERT N.

Edward Randolph: Including His Letters and Official Papers from New England, Middle and Southern Colonies in America . . . Boston: 1898-1909. V. 40; 42; 45

TOPPING, E. S.

Chronicles of the Yellowstone. St. Paul: 1882. V. 42

The Chronicles of the Yellowstone. St. Paul: 1883. V. 45

TOPSELL, EDWARD d. 1638?

The Elizabethan Zoo: A Book of Beasts, Both Fabulous and Authentic. London: 1926. V. 43

The Historie of Foure-Footed Beastes. (with) The Historie of Serpents . . . London: 1607-08. V. 43

The History of Four Footed Beasts and Serpents and Insects . . . taken principally from the Historiae Animalium of Conrad Geener. New York: 1967. V. 37

The History of Four-footed Beasts and Serpents . . . . whereunto is now added The Theater of Insects . . . . by Mr. Muffet . . . London: 1658. V. 37; 38

TOPSY. New York: 1880. V. 46

TORBETT, D.

On Trial: the Story of a Woman at Bay . . . New York: 1928. V. 45

TORBUCK, JOHN

A Collection of Welsh Travels, and Memoirs of Wales. Containing I. The Briton Describ'd or a Journey thro' Wales: Being a Pleasant Relation of Dean Swift's Journey to that ancient Kingdom . . . II. A Trip to North Wales . . . London: (1740). V. 37

THE TORCH is Passed . . . The Associated Press Story of the Death of a President. N.P.: 1963. V. 37

TORCHE, ANTOINE DE

La Cassette Des Bijovx. Paris: 1668. V. 39

TORCHIANA, HENRY ALBERT VAN COENEN

Story of Mission Santa Cruz. San Francisco: 1933. V. 38

TORCYNER, HARRY

Lachish I (Tell ed. Duweir): The Lachish Letters. London: 1938. V. 37; 39; 42

Magritte: Ideas and Images. New York: 1977. V. 41; 43; 46

TORELLI, LELIO

Raguaglio della Marciata, e Comparsa a' Uso di Guerra con l'Artiglieria . . . Urbino: 1640. V. 46

TORELLI, POMPONIO

Trattao del Debito del Cavalliero. Parma: 1596. V. 37

TORESBY, R.

Vicaria Leodiensis: or, the History of the Church of Leedes in Yorkshire. London: 1724. V. 37

TORFEUS, THORMODO

Gronlandia Antiqua. Havniae: 1706. V. 40

Historia Vinlandiae Antiquae. Havniae: 1705. V. 40

THE TORIES' Great Doubts and Difficulties Fully Resolv'd by More Important Doubts and Difficulties. London: 1701. V. 45

TORIO DE LA RIVA Y HERRERO, TORQUATO

Arte de Escribir por Reglas y con Muestras, Segun la Doctrina de los Mejores Autores . . . Madrid: 1798. V. 38

Arte de Escribir por Reglas y sin Muestras. Madrid: 1802. V. 40

TORLESSE, J. Y. G.

The Antarctic Pilot. London: 1948. V. 39

TORMIO, ERIC OLAF

Disquisitionis Mechanicae Continuatio . . . Copenhagen: 1645. V. 45

TORNEL Y MENDIVEL, JOSE MARIA

Tejas Y Los Estados-Unidos de America, en Sus Relaciones con la Republica Mexicana. Mexico: 1837. V. 39; 41; 42; 45

TORONTO ARCHITECTURAL EIGHTEEN CLUB

Toronto: at Ontario Society of Artist's Galleries, 1901. Toronto: 1901. V. 44

THE TORONTO City Directory for 1889. Volume XXII. Toronto: 1888. V. 44

THE TORONTO City Directory of 1889. Toronto: 1888. V. 44

TORONTO HUMANE SOCIETY

Aims and Objects of the Toronto Humane Society. Toronto: 1888. V. 45

TORONTO PUBLIC LIBRARIES. BOYS & GIRLS SERVICES

The Osborne Collection of Early Children's Books 1566-1910. (Volume 2 dated 1476-1910). Toronto: 1975. V. 40

TORONTO PUBLIC LIBRARIES. BOYS & GRILS SERVICE

The Osborne Collection of Early Children's Books 1566-1910: a Catalogue Prepared at Boys and Girls House by Judith St. John. Toronto: 1958. V. 46

TORONTO. WATER WORKS

Annual Reports. 1875-1895 (lacking only 1876). In Three Bound Volumes. V. 37

TORP, OTTO

Instruction Book for the Spanish Guitar . . . New York: 1829. V. 44

THE TORPEDO, a Poem to the Electrical Eel. Addressed to Mr. John Hunter, Surgeon; and Dedicated to the Right Hon. Lord Cholmondeley. London: 1777. V. 40

TORQUATO, TASSO

Amyntas, a Tale of the Woods . . . London: 1820. V. 43

TORQUATUS, ANTONIUS

Prognosticon de Eversione Europae & Alia Quaedam. Antwerp: 1552. V. 38

TORQUEMADA, ANTONIO DE

Hexameron, ou Six Iournees, Contenans Plusieurs Doctes, Discours sur Aucuns Poincts Difficiles en Diverses Sciences . . . Rouen: 1610. V. 37

The Spanish Mandevile or Myracles. London: 1618. V. 41

TORQUEMADA, ANTONIO DI

Giardino di Fiori Curiosi in Forma di Dialogo . . . Venice: 1591. V. 39

TORQUEMADA, JUAN DE, CARDINAL 1388-1468

Quaestiones Evangeliorum de Tempore et Sancitis. Cologne: 1478. V. 45

TORR, JAMES

The Antiquities of York City. York: 1719. V. 37; 38; 40; 42; 44

TORRANCE, JARED SIDNEY

The Descendants of Lewis Hart and Anne Alliott with Additional Genealogical and Historical Data. Los Angeles: 1923. V. 38

TORRE BARRIO Y LIMA, D. LORENZO PHELIPE DE LA

Resumen Del Arte, O Cartilla Del Nuevo Beneficio de La Plata en Todo Cenero de Metales Frios Y Calientes . . . Madrid: 1743. V. 40; 43

TORRE, FILIPPO DE 1657-1717

Monumenta Veteris Antii . . . Rome: 1700. V. 46

TORRE, FRANCISCO DE LA

Obras del Bachiller Francisco de la Torre. Dalas a la Impression D. Francisco de Quevedo Villegas. Madrid: 1631. V. 41

TORREILLES, PIERRE

Errantes Graminees. Paris: 1971. V. 40

TORRENCE, RIDGELY

El Dorado; a Tragedy. New York: & London: 1903. V. 44

TORRENS, HENRY

Field Exercise and Evolutions of the Army. London: 1824. V. 38

TORRENS, HENRY WHITELOCK

Madame de Malguet: a Tale of 1820. London: 1848. V. 42

TORRENS, ROBERT RICHARD 1814-1884

Lectures on Dealings with Land by Registration of Title, as Proposed to Be Applied to Ireland. Dublin: 1864. V. 41

TORRENS, WILLIAM MC CULLAGH 1813-1894

History of Cabinets. London: 1894. V. 38

Memoirs of the Right Honourable William, Second Viscount Melbourne. London: 1878. V. 38

TORRENTIUS, LAEVINUS

Laevini Torrentii in C. Suetonii Tranquilli XII. Caesares Commentarii. Antwerp: 1578. V. 37

TORRES BOOLO, DIEGO DE

Relatione Breve del P. Diego de Torres . . . Procuratore della Prouincia del Peru, Circa il Frutto che si Raccoglie con Gli Indiani di Quel Regno. Rome: 1603. V. 40; 41

TORREY, EDWIN

Early Days in Dakota. Minneapolis: 1925. V. 38

TORREY, FRANKLIN P.

Journal of the Cruise of the United States Ship Ohio, Commodore Isaac Hull, Commander in the Mediterranean in the Years 1839, 40, 41. Boston: 1841. V. 40; 41

TORREY, JESSE

A Portraiture of Domestic Slavery, in the United States. Philadelphia: 1817. V. 40; 42

A Portraiture of Domestic Slavery in the United States, Proposing National Measures for the Education and Gradual Emancipation of the Slaves Without Impairing the Legal Privileges of the Professor . . . Ballston Spa: 1818. V. 38

TORREY, JOHN

A Flora of the State of New York, Comprising Full Descriptions of all the Indigenous and Naturalized Plants Hitherto . . . Albany: 1843. V. 44; 45

Plantae Fremontianae; or, Descriptions of Plants Collected by Col. J. C. Fremont in California. New York: 1853. V. 45

TORREY, WILLIAM

Torrey's Narrative; or, The Life and Adventures of William Torrey . . . Boston: 1848. V. 41

TORREY, WILLIAM T.

Memoirs and Letters of Mrs. Mary Dexter . . . of Plympton. Plymouth: 1823. V. 41

TORRIANO, GIOVANNI

The Italian Reviv'd: or, the Introduction to the Italian Tongue. London: 1689. V. 41

The Italian Reviv'd. Or, the Introduction to the Italian Tongue. Containing such Grounds as are most immediately useful, and necessary for the speedy and easier attaining of the same. London: 1673. V. 37

The Italina Reviv'd: or, the introduction to the Italian tongue. Containing such grounds as are most immediately useful and necessary for the speedy and easie attaining of the same. As also a new storehouse of proper and choice dialogues . . . London;: 1689. V. 37

TORRINGTON, GEORGE BYNG, 1ST VISCOUNT 1663-1733

An Account of the Expedition of the British Fleet to Sicilty in the Years 1718, 1719 and 1720. London: 1739. V. 39

Ceylon and the Government of Lord Torrington, Containing a Correction and Errors in an Article in the Quarterly Review for December, 1850, entitled 'The Mysteries of Ceylon'. London: 1851. V. 46

The Future of Ceylon in Connection with Its Railway System. London: 1860. V. 46

TORRINGTON, JOHN BYNG, 5TH VISCOUNT 1742?-1813

The Torrington Diaries. London: 1934-38. V. 38; 40; 42

TORRINGTON, OTTO M.

A Catalogue of the Etchings of Levon West. New York: 1930. V. 37; 39

TORRUBIA, F. G.

I Moscoviti Nella California . . . Venice: 1760. V. 38

TORTI, FRANCISCI

Therapeutice Specialis ad Febres Periodicas Perniciosas . . . Francofurt: 1756. V. 38

TORY, GEOFROY Ca. 1480-1533

L'Art et Science de la Vraye Proportion des Lettres. Paris: 1549. V. 38

Champ Fleury. New York: 1927. V. 37; 38; 39; 40; 41; 43; 44; 45

Champ Rose: Wherein May Be Discvoered the Roman Letters That Were Made by Geofroy Tory and printed by Him at Paris in His Book Called Champ Fleury. New Rochelle: 1933. V. 45

Champfelury: Auquel est Contenu L'Art & Science de la Deue & Vraye Proportion des Lettres Attiques, Quom dit Autrement Lettres Antiques & Fulgairement Lettres Romaines Proportionnees Selon de Corps & Visage Humain. Paris: 1529. V. 46

TOSCANELLA, ORAZIO DE 1510-1580

Il Dialogo Della Partitione Oratoria di Marco Tullio Cicerone; Tirato in Tavole da Oratio Toscanella della Famiglia di Maestro Luca Fiorentio. Venice: 1566. V. 43

TOSI, P.

L India Oriental . . . Dove si Tratta Della Parte Intra Gangem Contenente li Regni Soggetti all'Imperio del Gran Mogol . . . Rome: 1676. V. 39

TOSI, PIER FRANCESCO

Observations on the Florid Song; or, Sentiments on the Ancient and Modern Singers. London: 1742. V. 37; 42; 45

TOTANES, SEBASTIAN DE

Arte de la Lengua Tagala, Y Manual Tagalog, Para la Administracion de Los Santos Sacramentos . . . (with) Manual Tagalog Para Auxilio a Los Religiosos de Esta Santa Provincia . . . Manila: 1745. V. 40

TOTHILL, J. D.

The Coconut Moth in Fiji. London: 1930. V. 46

TOTHILL, WILLIAM

The Transactions of the High Court of Chancery, Both by Practice and President . . . London: 1671. V. 37; 39; 42

TOTT, FRANCIS, BARON DE

Memoirs of Baron De Tott, on the Turks and the Tartars. Dublin: 1785. V. 38

Memoirs . . . Containing the State of the Turkish Empire and the Crimea, During the Late War with Russia. London: 1786. V. 39; 42

Memoirs of Baron de Tott, containing the State of the Turkish Empire and the Crimea, during the late War with Russia, with numerous Anecdotes, Facts, and Observations, on the Manners and Customs of the Turks and Tartars. London: 1785. V. 37

TOTTEN, B. J.

Naval Textbook and Pictionary for the Use of the Midshipmen of the U.S. Navy. New York: 1863. V. 38

TOTTEN, CHARLES A. L.

Strategos; a Series of American Games of War Based Upon Miliary Principles and Designed for the Assistance Both of Beginners and Advanced Students in Prosecuting the Whole Study of Tactics . . . New York: 1880. V. 40

TOTTEN, GEORGE OAKLEY

Maya ARchitecture. Washington: 1926. V. 42; 43; 44

Maya Architecture. Washington: (1926). V. 37

Maya Architecture. Washington: (1928). V. 37

TOTTEN, J. G.

Essays on Hydraulic and Common Mortars and On Lime-Burning. Philadelhia: 1838. V. 44

Papers on Practical Engineering. Bitumen: Its Varieties, Properties and Uses . . . Washington: 1844. V. 41; 42; 44

TOTTENHAM, GEORGE L.

Terence McGowan, the Irish Tenant. London: 1870. V. 37; 41; 43; 45

TOUCH and Go: A Book fo Changing Pictures. London: 1895. V. 46

A TOUCH of the Times. N.P.: 1740. V. 45

THE TOUCH of the Times. A New Ballad. N.P., (Edinburgh): (1740?). V. 37

TOUCHSTONE, S. F.

History of Celebrated English and French Thorough-Bred Stallions and French Mares . . . London: 1890. V. 43

Racehorses: Pedigree - Description - History. London: 1890. V. 42

TOULET, PAUL JEAN

La Jeune Fille Verte. Monaco: 1946. V. 44

TOULMIN, HARRY

Digest of the Laws of the State of Alabama. Cahawba: 1823. V. 45

A Geographical and Statistical Sketch of the District of Mobile. V. 46

TOULMIN, JOSHUA

The History of Taunton, in the County of Somerset . . . Taunton: 1822. V. 37; 42

The History of the Town of Taunton, in the County of Somerset. Taunton: 1791. V. 37

Memoirs of the Life, Character, Sentiments and Writings, of Faustus Socinus. London: 1777. V. 43

TOULOUSE-LAUTREC, HENRI DE

Complete Lithographs and Drypoints. London: 1965. V. 39; 40

Elles. 1969. V. 38

A Sketch Book of Toulouse-Lautrec Owned by the Art Institute of Chicago. New York: 1952. V. 44

THE TOUR of Doctor Prosody. London: 1821. V. 41; 44

THE TOUR of Doctor Syntax through London, or the Pleasures and Miseries of the Metropolis, a Poem. London: 1820. V. 39; 45

THE TOUR of Valentine. London: 1786. V. 39

A TOUR through the Principal Provinces of Spain and Portugal, Performed in the Year 1803. London: 1806. V. 40

A TOUR to Cheltenham Spa, or Gloucestershire Display'd. Bath: 1783. V. 37; 40

TOUREAUX, LEON

Typographie Grammaire de la Composition. Chartres: 1884. V. 42

TOURIST'S Guide and Directory of the Truckee Basin. Truckee: 1883. V. 42

TOURIST'S Guide to Loch Lomond. London, Edinburgh & New York: 1860. V. 37

TOURNACHON, FELIX

A Terre & en L'Air . . . Memoires du Geant . . . Paris: 1865. V. 45

TOURNAY, THOMAS

The Cave of Eath. Canterbury: 1776. V. 43

TOURNEFORT, JOSEPH PITTON DE

Institutiones Rei Hebariae. Lugduni: 1719. V. 38

Institutiones Rei Herbariae. Lugduni juxta Exemplar: 1719. V. 40; 42; 44

Institutiones Rei Herbariae. Paris: 1719. V. 39; 41

Relation d'un Voyage du Levant, Fair par Ordre du Roy. Lyon: 1717. V. 40

Relation d'un Voyage au Levant. Amsterdam: 1718. V. 45

A Voyage into the Levant . . . London: 1741. V. 43

TOURNES, JEAN DE

Portraits Divers. Lyon: 1556. V. 46

Receuil de Figures de Bois Alternately Pourtraits Divers. Lyon: 1556. V. 37

TOURNEUR, CYRIL

Works. London: 1929. V. 39; 43; 44; 46

The Works of . . . 1930. V. 40; 45

The Works of Cyril Tourneur. London: 1930. V. 42; 43; 44

TOURNEUR, NIGEL

Hidden Witchery. London: 1898. V. 40

TOURNIER, MICHEL

A Garden of Hammamet. 1986. V. 42

TOURTEL, MARY

The Rabbit Book. London: 1904. V. 44

The Three Little Foxes. London: 1903. V. 46

TOUSSAINT, A.

Bibliography of Mauritius 1502-1954. 1956. V. 45

Bibliography of Mauritius (1502-1954). Port Louis, Mauritius: 1956. V. 38; 44; 45

TOUSSAINT, FRANZ 1879-

The Garden of Caresses. 1934. V. 40

The Garden of Caresses. London: 1934. V. 41

The Garden of Caresses. Waltham St. Lawrence: 1934. V. 37; 41

TOUSSAINT, MANUEL

Arte Colonial en Mexico. Mexico: 1948. V. 44

Colonial Art in Mexico. 1967. V. 42

Colonial Art in Mexico. Austin: 1967. V. 42

TOUT, THOMAS F.

Chapters in the Administrative History of Mediaeval England . . . Manchester: 1933-37-67. V. 44

TOUT, THOMAS FREDERICK

The Collected Papers of Thomas Frederick Tout, With Memoir and Bibliography. Manchester: 1932-34. V. 43

TOUZEAU, JAMES

The Rise and Progress of Liverpool from 1551 to 1835. Liverpool: 1910. V. 39

TOVEY, CHARLES

Champagne: Its History, Manufacture, Properties, &c. London: 1870. V. 40

A Free Library for Bristol. (with) The Bristol Library. London & Bristol: 1855-53. V. 38

TOWARDS a New American Poetics: Essays and Interviews. Santa Barbara: 1978. V. 43; 45

TOWER, CHARLEMAGNE

The Marquis de la Fayette in the American Revolution. Philadelphia: 1895. V. 46

THE TOWER of Babel: an Anthology. West Burke: 1974. V. 39; 44
THE TOWER of Babel: an Anthology. West Burke: 1975. V. 39

TOWERS, ALTON

Billy Bunce, or the Wanderings of A White Rabbit. London: 1911. V. 46

TOWERS, J. L.

The Expediency and Practicability of the Resumption of Cash-Pyments by the Bank of England, or Thoughts on the Present Serious State of the Circulating Medium of the Kingdom; and a Series of Measures Proposed . . . London: 1811. V. 38

TOWERS, JOSEPH

Observations on the Rights and Duty of Juries in Trials for Libels. London: 1784. V. 38

Thoughts on the Commencement of a New Parliament. Dublin: 1791. V. 42

TOWGOOD, MICAIJAH 1700-1792

An Essay Towards Attaining a True Idea of the Character and rEign of K. Charles the First and the Causes of the Civil War . . . . London: 1780. V. 39; 41

TOWGOOD, MICHAIJAH 1700-1792

An Essay Towards Attaining a True Idea of the Character and Reign of Charles the First, and the Causes of the Civil War. London: 1748. V. 40; 41; 43

THE TOWN and Country Toy Book. London: 1865. V. 44

TOWN, HAROLD

Enigmas, Enigmes. Toronto & Montreal: 1964. V. 39

TOWN, SALEM

An Analysis of the Derivative Words in the English Language. New York: 1836. V. 46

TOWN Swaps and Social Bridges. London: 1859. V. 37

TOWN, T.

The Complete Military Tutor Containing a System of Modern Tactics Applicable to Infantry in Company, Regiment or Line As Laid Down by Most Approved Authors and Now In Practice by Armies of the U.S. Philadelphia: 1809. V. 38

TOWN Talk. Pasadena: 1903. V. 37

TOWN Talk, or, Living Manners, July 1811-January 1814. London: 1811-14. V. 40

TOWNDROW, KENNETH ROMNEY

Alfred Stevens. A Biography with New Material. London: 1939. V. 39

TOWNE, BENJAMIN

New Year's Verses, Addressed to the King Customers of the Pennsylvania Evening Post, by the Printer's Lads Who Carry About the Same. Philadelphia: 1778. V. 46

TOWNE, H. R.

A Treatise on Cranes. Stamford: 1883. V. 43

TOWNE, JOHN

A Critical Inquiry into the Opinions and Practice of the Antient Philosophers Concerning the Nature of the Soul and a Future State, and Their Method of Double Doctrine. London: 1748. V. 39

TOWNE, R. M.

Plant Lore of Shakespeare. Louisville: 1975. V. 37

TOWNE, RICHARD

A Treatise of the Diseases Most Frequent in the West Indies, and Herein More Particularly of those Which Occur in Barbadoes. London: 1726. V. 40

TOWNELEY, JOHN 1731-1813

Catalogue of the Very Valuable Collection of British Portraits, Illustrative of Granger's Biographical History of England. London: 1828. V. 38

TOWNEND, JOSEPH

Autobiography . . . with Reminiscences of His Missionary Labours in Australia. London: 1869. V. 46

TOWNESEND, GEORGE

Tables to Most of the Printed Precedents of Pleadings, Writs and Retorn of Wirts, at the Common Law. London: 1667. V. 38

TOWNLEY, RICHARD

A Journal Kept in the Isle of Man, Giving an Account of the Wind and Weather, and Daily Occurrences, for Upwards of Eleven Months . . . Whitehaven: 1791. V. 42; 46

TOWNSEND, C. H.

Reports of . . . Condition of Seal Life on the Rookeries of the Pribilof Islands, and to Pelagie Sealing in Bering Sea and the North Pacific Ocean, in the years 1893-1895. (with) Illustrations Showing Condition of Fur-Seal Rookeries in 1892 & . . . Washington: 1896. V. 46

TOWNSEND, E. D.

Index of Principal Points from Which Mileage Distances Have Been Calculated: General Orders No. 98. Washington: 1870. V. 41

TOWNSEND, EARL C.

Birdstones of the North American Indian . . . Indianapolis: 1959. V. 38; 39; 42

TOWNSEND, GEORGE

Outram and Havelock's Persian Campaign. London: 1858. V. 42

Poems. London: 1810. V. 45

Tables to Most of the Printed Presidents of Pleadings, Writs and Retorn of writs, at the Common Law. London: 1667. V. 40

TOWNSEND, GEORGE ALFRED

Life, Crime and Capture of John Wilkes Booth . . . New York: 1865. V. 38

TOWNSEND, H. C.

Plain Facts About Arkansas and Texas. Chicago: 1883. V. 40

Statistics and Information Concerning the State of Texas, with Its Millions of Acres of Unoccupied Lands, for the Farmer and Stock Raiser. St. Louis: 1893. V. 38

TOWNSEND, HORATIO

A General and Statistical Survey of the County of Cork. Cork: 1815. V. 37; 43

TOWNSEND, J.

The Character of Moses Established for Veracity as an Historian. Bath: 1813. V. 38; 40

TOWNSEND, JOHN KIRK

Excursion to the Oregon. N.P.: 1846. V. 40

Excursion to the Oregon. (N.P.: 1846). V. 37

Narrative of a Journey Across the Rocky Mountains to the Columbia River, and a Visit to the Sandwich Islands, Chili &c. Philadelphia: 1839. V. 38; 39; 40; 42; 43; 45

Sporting Excursions in the Rocky Mountains, Including a Journey to the Columbia River . . . London: 1840. V. 42

TOWNSEND, JOHN SEALY EDWARD 1868-1957

Electricity in Gases. Oxford: 1915. V. 42

TOWNSEND, JOSEPH

Elements of Therapeutics. Boston: 1802. V. 40

Geological nd Mineralogical Researches, During a Period of More Than Fifty Years in England, Scotland, Ireland, Switzerland. Bath: 1824. V. 38

Select Essays on Agriculture and Rural Subjects, Wrote by a Society of Ingenious Gentleman. London: 1760-64. V. 40

TOWNSEND, LUTHER T.

History of the Sixteenth Regiment, New Hampshire Volunteers. Washington: 1897. V. 37; 39

TOWNSEND, MIRA SHARPLESS

Reports and Realities from the Sketch-Book of a Manager of the Rosine Association, Dec. 1855. Philadelphia: 1855. V. 45

TOWNSEND, PETER

An Account of the Yellow Fever as It Prevailed in the City of New York, in the Summer and Autumn of 1822. New York: 1823. V. 37; 38

TOWNSEND, RICHARD

Original Poems. Baltimore: 1809. V. 42

TOWNSEND, RICHARD EDWARD AUSTIN

Visions of the Western Railways. London: 1838. V. 46

TOWNSEND, RICHARD H.

Original Poems. Baltimore: 1809. V. 46

TOWNSEND, S. HUGENT

Our Indian Summer in the Far West. London: 1880. V. 46

TOWNSEND, W. G. PAULSON

Floral Forms in Historic Design, Mainly from Objects in the Victoria and Albert Museum, but Including Examples from Designs by William Morris and C.F.A. Voysey. London: 1922. V. 45

Modern Decorative Art in England. New York: 1922. V. 45

TOWNSEND, W. H.

A System of Foliage, with Hints on the Acquirement of a Touch, Being an Introduction to the Study of Nature . . . London: 1844. V. 44

TOWNSEND, W. PAULSON

Modern Decorative Art in England, Its Developments and Characteristics . . . Volume I (all published). Woven and Printed Fabrics, Wall-Papers, Lace and Embroidery. London: 1922. V. 37; 41

TOWNSEND, WILLIAM THOMPSON

The Cricket on the Hearth; a Fairy Tale of Home in Three Chirps . . . London: 1860. V. 43

TOWNSHED, GEORGE, MARQUIS OF

A Catalogue of the Magnificent Library, Books of Prints and Manuscripts of the Late Most Noble, George, Marquis of Townshed. London: 1812. V. 44

TOWNSHEND, CHARLES

National Thoughts, Recommended to the Serious Attention of the Public. London: 1749? V. 41; 45

Remarks on the Letter Adress'd to Two Great Men . . . London: 1760. V. 38

TOWNSHEND, CHARLES, 2ND VISCOUNT 1674-1738

The Barrier-Treaty Vindicated. London: 1712. V. 39

TOWNSHEND, CHAUNCEY HARE 1798-1868

Facts in Mesmerism, with Reasons for a Dispassionate Inquiry into It. London: 1844. V. 42; 46

TOWNSHEND, CHAUNCY HARE 1798-1868

Religious Opinions of the Late Reverend Chauncy Hare Townshend. London: 1869. V. 38; 40; 43

TOWNSHEND, F. TRENCH

A Cruise in Greek Waters, with a Hunting Excursion in Tunis. London: 1870. V. 45

TOWNSHEND, FREDERICK T.

Wild Life in Florida, with a Visit to Cuba. London: 1875. V. 41; 43; 46

TOWNSHEND, FREDERICK TRENCH

Ten Thousand Miles of Travel, Sport and Adventure. London: 1869. V. 38; 40

TOWNSHEND, GEORGE, 1ST MARQUIS

A Brief Narrative of the Late Campaigns in Germany and Flanders. London: 1751. V. 41

TOWNSHEND, HEYWOOD

Historical Collections; or, an Exact Account of the Proceedings of the Four Last Parliaments of Q. Elizabeth of Famous Memory. London: 1680. V. 37; 46

TOWNSHEND, S. NUGENT

Colorado: Its Agriculture, Stockfeeding, Scenery, and Shooting. London: 1879. V. 37

Our Indian Summer in the Far West, an Autumn Tour of 15,000 Miles in Kansas, Texas, New Mexico, Colorado and the Indian Territory. London: 1880. V. 37; 41; 43; 44; 45

TOWNSHEND, THOMAS

Poems. London: 1796. V. 40; 43; 45

A Summary Defence of the Right Hon. Edmund Burke. London: 1796. V. 42

TOWNSON, ROBERT

Travels in Hungary, with a Short Account of Vienna in the Year 1793. London: 1797. V. 39

TOWSEND, H. C.

Arkansas Statistics and Information Showing the Agricultural and Mineral Resources. St. Louis?: 1888. V. 41

TOWSEND, JOHN KIRK

Sporting Excursions in the Rocky Mountains, Including a Journey to the Columbia River, and a Visit to the Sandwich Islands, Chili &c. London: 1840. V. 38

TOY, H. SPENCER

The History of Helston. Oxford: 1936. V. 40

TOYNBEE, ARNOLD J.

Greek Policy Since 1882. London: 1914. V. 42

Hannibal's Legacy: The Hannibalic War's Effect on Roman Life. London: 1965. V. 40

Lectures on the Industrial Revolution in England, Popular Addresses, Notes and Other Fragments . . . London: 1884. V. 43; 45; 46

Nationality and the War. London: 1915. V. 40; 42

A Study of History. Oxford: 1934-61. V. 40; 41

A Study of History. Oxford: 1935-54. V. 42

TOYNBEE, J. M. C.

The Hadrianic School. Rome: 1967. V. 44

TOYNBEE, JOCELYN M. C.

The Hadrianic School. Cambridge: 1934. V. 40

TOYNBEE, JOSEPH

The Diseases of the Ear. Philadelphia: 1860. V. 42

TOYNBEE, PAGET

Journal of the Printing-Office at Strawberry Hill, Now First Printed from the Ms. of Horace Walpole, with Notes. London: 1923. V. 37

TOZER, HENRY F.

The Islands of the Aegean. Oxford: 1890. V. 44

Researches in the Highlands of Turkey. London: 1869. V. 37

TOZER, KATHERINE

Noah. London: 1940. V. 45

TOZZER, ALFRED M.

Chichen Itza and its Cenote of Sacrifice. Cambridge: 1957. V. 37

A Preliminary Study of the Prehistoric Ruins of Nakum Guatemala. Cambridge: 1913. V. 42; 44

TRABER, ZACHARIAS

Nervus Opticus sive Tractatus Theoricus, in tres Libros Opticam, Catoptricam, Dioptricam Distributus . . . Vienna: 1690. V. 40; 41

TRACEY, FRANCIS

The Sensational Tragedy in the New Orleans Parish Prison: a Startling Confession of Henri Romani, the King of the Mafia. Philadelphia: 1891. V. 43

TRACTATUS Contra Vicia. Strasbourg: 1498. V. 39

TRACTATUS De Martyrio Sanctorum. Basle: 1492. V. 38

A TRACTE Containing the Artes of Curious Paintinge, caruinge & buildinge . . . Englished by Richard Haydocke student in physick. Oxford: 1598. V. 37

TRACTS for the Times. London & Oxford: 1840-42. V. 38

TRACTS on the Oregon Question. New York: 1846. V. 38

TRACY, DESTUTT

A Treatise on Political Economy; to which is Prefixed a Supplement to a Preceding Work on the Understanding, or Element of Ideology. Georgetown: 1817. V. 38

TRACY, JOSEPH

History of American Missions to the Heathen, from Their Commencement to the Present Time. Worcester: 1840. V. 39

TRACY, L.

The Invaders. 1901. V. 44

TRACY, RUSSELL LORD

Some Experiences of Russell Lord Tracy. 1941. V. 42

TRACY, SUZY

Klondike Edition of Scientific Cookery. Seattle: 1898. V. 45

TRACY, URIAH

Scipio's Reflections on Monroe's View of the Conduct of the Executive on the Foreign Affairs of the United States. Boston: 1798. V. 42; 44

TRADE and Foreign Plantations Upon the Present State of the Laws for Regulating the Importation and Exporatation of Corn . . . London: 1800. V. 41

THE TRADE of Chimney-Sweeping Exhibited in Its True Light, Together with the State of Public Feeling on This Important Subject, as Shown By Evidence Before the House of Commons, etc. London: 1840. V. 42

TRADESCANT, JOHN

Musaeum Tradescantianum; or, a Collection of Rarities. London: 1656. V. 45

THE TRAGEDY of Nero. London: 1633. V. 37

TRAGER, PHILIP

Philip Trager: New York. Middletown: 1980. V. 41

TRAGOEDIAE Selectae Aeschyli, Sophoclis, Evripidis. Geneva: 1567. V. 42

TRAGOEDIARUM Graecarum Delectus. Oxonii: 1779. V. 44

TRAHERNE, THOMAS

Centuries of Meditations. London: 1908. V. 40

A Glimpse of Thomas Traherne . . . 1978. V. 45

The Poetical Works of Thomas Traherne, B.D. 1636?-1674. London: 1903. V. 40

The Poetical Works of . . . edited with Preface and Notes by Gladys I. Wade. London: 1932. V. 37

Roman Forgeries Or a True Account of False Records Discovering the Impostures and Counterfeit Antiquities of the Church of Rome. By a Faithful Son of the Church of England. London: 1673. V. 37

TRAICTE de la Sphere et de ses Parties. Rouen: 1631. V. 37; 42

THE TRAIL Makers Boys' Annual, Volume 1. Toronto: 1920. V. 44

THE TRAIL Makers Boys' Own Annual. Volume 3. Toronto: 1922. V. 44

TRAIL of the Assassins and Conspirators for the Murder of Abraham Lincoln, and the Attempted Assassination of Vice-President Johnson and the Whole Cabinet. Philadelphia: (1865). V. 37

TRAILL, CATHARINE PARR

Canadian Wild Flowers. Montreal: 1869. V. 44

The Canadian Crusoes. New York: 1853. V. 38

Pearls and Pebbles; or, Notes of an Old Naturalist. Toronto: 1894. V. 44

Studies of Plant Life in Canada. Toronto: 1906. V. 44

TRAILL, CATHERINE

The Backwoods of Canada. London: 1848. V. 41

TRAILL, CATHERINE PARR

The Backwoods of Canada . . . London: 1836. V. 37; 42; 43

Canada and Oregon. The Backwoods of Canada. London: 1846. V. 38

TRAILL, CATHERINE PARR STRICKLAND

Canada and Oregon. London: 1849. V. 42

Studies of Plant Life in Canada; or, Gleaning from Forest, Lake and Plain. Ottawa: 1885. V. 46

The Young Emigrants; or, Pictures of Canada, Calculated to Amuse and Instruct the Minds of Youth. London: 1826. V. 46

TRAILL, H. D.

The Building of Britain and the Empire. London: 1909. V. 42

TRAILL, THOMAS STEWART

A Memoir of William Roscoe. Liverpool: 1853. V. 44

TRAILL, THOMAS W.

Chain Cables and Chains. London: 1885. V. 44

Remarks of the Engineer Surveyor in Chief, and His Assistants, Respecting the Mild Steel Manufactured by the Steel Company of Scotland . . . London: 1878. V. 44

TRAILL, WILLIAM HENRY

A Queenly Colony. Brisbane: 1901. V. 39

TRAIN, GEORGE FRANCIS

The Great Epigram Campaign of Kansas. Leavenworth: 1867. V. 38

TRAIN, JOSEPH

An Historical and Statistical account of the Isle of Man, from the Earliest Times to the Present Date. 1845. V. 39; 46

An Historical and Statistical Account of the Isle of Man, from the Earliest Times to the Present Date. Douglas: 1845. V. 44

An Historical and Statistical Account of the Isle of Man, From the Earliest Times to the Present Date . . . Isle of Man: 1845. V. 38

An Historical and Statistical Account of the Isle of Man, From the Earliest Times to the Present Date . . . London: 1845. V. 41

TRAITE des Batiments Properes a Loger les Animaux, Qui Sont Necessaires a l'Economie Rurale. Leipzig: 1802. V. 42; 46

TRAITS of American Indian Life and Character. San Francisco: 1933. V. 39; 46

TRAKI, GEORG

Grodek. London: 1988. V. 40

TRALBAUT, MARC EDO

Vincent Van Gogh. London: 1969. V. 46

TRALL, RUSSELL T.

The Philosophy of the Temperance Reformation, or the Relations of Alcohol and the Human Organism . . . New York: 1845. V. 44

TRALL, RUSSELL THACHER

The Hydropathic Encyclopedia. New York: 1853. V. 40; 41

TRALLES, BALTHASAR LUDOVICUS 1708-1797

Exercitatione Physico-Medica Virtutem Camphorae Refrigerantem . . . Breslau and Leipzig: 1734. V. 42

Osus Opii. Breslau: 1756-62. V. 44

Usus Opii. Breslau: 1757-62. V. 42

TRANSCRIPTIONS of Manuscript Collections of Louisiana. No. 1. Favrot Papers, 1695-1812. New Orleans: 1940. V. 41

TRANSCRIPTIONS of Parish Records of Louisiana. No. 24. Iberville Parish (Plaquemine), 1850-1936. University of Louisiana: 1942. V. 41

TRANSCRIPTIONS of Parish Records of Louisiana. No. 26. Jefferson Parish (Gretna) Series 1. Police Jury Minutes. New Orleans: 1941. V. 41

TRANSCRIPTIONS of Parish Records of Louisiana. No. 44. St. Bernard Parish (St Bernard) Series I. Police Jury Minutes. 1870-1940. University of Louisiana: 1941. V. 41

TRANSITION. Paris &: 1927-1938. V. 40

A TRANSLATION of the Memorial to the Sovereigns of Europe Upon the Present State of Affairs, Bwteen the Old and the New World, into Common Sense and Intelligible English. London: 1781. V. 37

THE TRANSMIGRATION of the Seven Brahmans. New York: 1931. V. 46

TRANSTROMER, TOMAS

Baltics. Berkeley: 1973. V. 38; 40

TRAPANI, GAETANO

A Catalogue of the Different Kinds of Fish of Malta and Gozo, with Their Maltese, Latin, Italian, English and French Names, As Well as Their Season. Malta: 1838. V. 40

TRAPMAN, LEILA

The Spoofah and the Antidote. Edinburgh: 1898. V. 46

TRAPNELL, A.

A Catalogue of Bristol and Plymouth Porcelain with Examples of Bristol Glass and Pottery Forming the Collection Made by M. Alfred Trapnell. Bristol: 1905. V. 37

TRAPP, FRANK ANDERSON

The Attainmant of Delacroix. Baltimore: 1971. V. 43

TRAPP, JOSEPH

Abra-Mule. London: 1704. V. 37; 38; 39; 45

Proceedings of the French National Convetion on the Trial of Louis XVI. London: 1793. V. 37

Thoughts Upon the Four Last Things: Death, Judgment; Heaven; and Hell. London: 1745. V. 38

TRAPP, W. H.

Jefferyes Hamett O'Neale 1734-1801. London: 1938. V. 37

TRAQUAIR, RAMSAY

The Old Silver of Quebec. Toronto: 1940. V. 44

The Old Architecture of Quebec. Toronto: 1947. V. 44; 45

The Old Architecture of Quebec: A Study of the Buildings erected in New France from the Earliest Explorers to the Middle of the Nineteenth Century. Toronto: 1947. V. 37

The Old Silver of Quebec. Toronto: 1940. V. 37

TRASK, JOHN B.

Report on the Geology of the Coast Mountains, and Part of the Sierra Nevada, embracing Their Industrial Resources in Agriculture and Mining; Sacramento: 1854. V. 40

Report on the Geology of the Coast Mountains . . . Sacramento: 1855. V. 45

Report on the Geology of Northern & Southern California, Embracing the Mineral and Agricultural Resources of Those Sections. Sacramento: 1856/ V. 40

TRATTATELLO Della Umanita Di Gesu Cristo Stampata Dietro Un Ms. Del Sec. XV. Venezia: 1830. V. 38

TRAUBEL, HORACE L.

Camden's Compliment to Walt Whitman May 31, 1889. Philadelphia: 1889. V. 46

In Re Walt Whitman: Edited by His Literary Executors . . . Philadelphia: 1893. V. 41

TRAUTWINE, JOHN

Rough Notes of an Exploration for an Inter-Oceanic Canal Route . . . in New Granada, South America. Philadelphia: 1854. V. 37

TRAUX, CHARLES

The Mechanics of Surgery (1899). San Francisco: 1988. V. 41; 42; 44; 45; 46

TRAVASSOS VALDEZ, FRANCISCO

Six Years of a Traveller's Life in Western Africa. London: 1861. V. 42

A TRAVEL through Belgium, the Frontiers of France, Liege, Luxemburg and Along the Rhine in 1814. Amsterdam: 1815. V. 38

THE TRAVELLER; or, an Entertaining Journey Round the Habitable Globe . . . London: 1820. V. 44; 46

THE TRAVELLER Pausaniae de Tota Graecia Libri Decem . . . Basel: 1550. V. 44

THE TRAVELLERS Companion and Guide through France, Flanders, Brabant and Holland. London: 1753. V. 39

THE TRAVELLER'S Companion, from Holyhead to London. London:: 1796. V. 41

THE TRAVELLER'S Companion Through the City of Edinburgh and Suburbs . . . Edinburgh: 1794. V. 45

TRAVELLER'S Guide Through the State of Ohio, Michigan, Indiana, Illinois, Missouri, Iowa and Wisconsin . . . New York: 1855. V. 46

THE TRAVELLER'S Pocket Directory and Stranger's Guide . . . Schenectady: 1831. V. 42

THE TRAVELLER'S Pocket Directory and Stranger's Guide; Exhibiting Distances of the Principal Canal and Stage Routes in the State of New York. Schenectady: 1831. V. 37; 38

TRAVELS in America. (and) The Poetry of Pope. New York: 1851. V. 38

TRAVELS in Sweden, Denmark and Norway. Dublin: 1826. V. 40

TRAVELS in Tartary Thibet and China 1844-1846. Translated by William Hazlitt, now edited with an Introduction by Professor Paul Pelliot. London: (1928). V. 37

TRAVELS in the Interior Parts of America, Communicating Discoveries Made in Exploring the Missouri, Red River and Washita, By Captains Lewis and Clark, Dr. Sibley and Mr. Dunbar. London: 1807. V. 38

THE TRAVELS of Capts. Lewis & Clarke, from St. Louis, by Way of the Missouri and Columbia Rivers, to the Pacific Ocean; Performed in the Years 1804, 1805 and 1806 . . . London: 1809. V. 38; 40; 41; 43

THE TRAVELS of Mr. Drake Morris, Merchant. London: 1755. V. 39

TRAVELS of Several Learned Missioners of the Society of Jesus, into Divers Parts of the Archipelago, India, China and America. London: 1714. V. 38

TRAVELS of the Du Le Telle Family. Buffalo: 1869. V. 44

TRAVELS through Flanders, Holland, Germany, Sweden and Denmark. London: 1693. V. 42

TRAVEN, B.

The Bridge in the Jungle. New York: 1938. V. 45

The Bridge in the Jungle. London: 1940. V. 44

The Carreta. London: 1935. V. 45

The Death Ship; the Story of an American Sailor. New York: 1934. V. 38; 39; 44; 46

The Death Ship. London: 1940. V. 44

Der Karren. Berlin: 1931. V. 46

Government - a Novel. London: 1935. V. 42

Land des Fruhlings. Berlin: 1928. V. 42

The Rebellion of the Hanged. London. V. 40

The Rebellion of the Hanged. 1952. V. 44

The Rebellion of the Hanged. New York: 1952. V. 42

The Treasure of the Sierra Madre. New York: 1935. V. 39

TRAVER, ROBERT

Anatomy of a Murder. New York: 1958. V. 43

Trouble Shooter. New York: 1943. V. 37; 40; 42; 43; 44; 45

TRAVERS, BENJAMIN

An Inquiry Concerning the Distrubed State of the Vital Functions Usually Denominated Constitutional Irritation. New York: 1826. V. 42; 43; 44

TRAVERS, HENRY

Miscellaneous Poems and Translations. London: 1731. V. 37; 42; 45; 46

TRAVERS, PAMELA

Mary Poppins. New York: 1934. V. 39; 40; 43; 44

Mary Poppins Comes Back. London: 1935. V. 40

TRAVERS, PAMELA L.

Mary Poppins Comes Back. London: 1935. V. 38; 42

TRAVERS, W. T. LOCKE

From New Zealad to Lake Michigan. Wellington: 1889. V. 38; 46

TRAVESTIN, MR.

An Account of the Imperial Proceedings Against the Turks . . . London: 1685. V. 46

TRAVIES, EDOUARD

Types du Regne Animal . . . Paris: 1862, 1864. V. 42

TRAVLOS, JOHN

Pictorial Dictionary of Ancient Athens. V. 40

TREACY, WILLIAM P.

Irish Scholars of the Penal Days: Glimpses of Their Labours on the Continent of Europe. New York. V. 39

TREASURE Land. A story. Tuscon: 1897. V. 37

TREASURES of the Deep. London: 1851. V. 40

TREASURES of the Louvre. New York: 1966. V. 38; 42

TREAT, JOSEPH

The Vindication of Captain Joseph Treat, Late of the Twenty-First Regiment United States Infantry, Against the Atrocious Calumny Comprehended in Major Brown's Official Report of the Battle of Chippeway. Philadelphia: 1815. V. 42

A TREATISE Concerning Oaths and Perjury. London: 1750. V. 42

A TREATISE Explaining the Nature and Rules of the Several Sorts of Covenants: As, Express. In Law. Disjunctive. Copulataive. Several. Joint. Inherent. Collateral. Mutual or Reciprocal. Personal. Real . . . In the Savory: 1711. V. 37

A TREATISE of Destresses, Replevins, and Avowries . . . containing the common and statute law for securing the payment of rents . . . The fourth edition . . . To which is added, the office of a coroner. London: 1761. V. 37; 43

A TREATISE of Diseases of the Head, Brain and Nerves. London: 1721. V. 41

A TREATISE of Feme Coverts; or, the Lady's Law. London: 1732. V. 43; 45

A TREATISE of the Construction of Logarithms; to Which are Added Tables of Logarithms, Sines and Tangents. Philadelphia: 1802. V. 41

A TREATISE of the Description and Use of Globes. London: 1705. V. 39; 42

A TREATISE on Ackermann's Superfine Water Colours, With Directions How to Prepare and Use Them, Including Succint Hints on Drawing and Painting. London: 1801. V. 45

A TREATISE On Greyhounds, with Observations on the Treatment and Disorders of Them. London: 1819. V. 39; 41; 42; 43

A TREATISE on Soap-Making. Edinburgh: 1807. V. 39; 40

A TREATISE on the Art of Drawing; Containing Directions for Drawing Separate Parts of the Human Figure . . . London: 1814. V. 44

A TREATISE on the Powers and Duties of Executors and Administrators According to the Law of North Carolina. Newbern: 1803. V. 43; 45

A TREATISE on Virtue and Happiness. The Second Edition. London: 1736. V. 37

A TREATISE Upon the Herb Tobacco, Pointing Out Its Deleterious Pernicious Quality, and Its Fatal Effects Upon the Human Constitution. London: 1763. V. 40

TREBLE Almanack for 1791. Containing. 1. Watson's Irish Almanack. II. Exshaw's English Court Registry. III. Wilson's Dublin Directory . . . Dublin: 1791. V. 46

TREBLE Almanack for 1819. Containing. I. John Watson Stewarts Almanack. II. The English Court Registry. III. Wilson's Dublin Directory. Dublin: 1819. V. 44; 46

THE TREBLE Almanack for MDCCCII. Dublin: 1802. V. 44

THE TREBLE Almanack for MDCCXCI. Dublin: 1791. V. 44

THE TREBLE Almanack for the Year 1815. Dublin: 1815. V. 44

TREBY, GEORGE

Truth Vindicated . . . London: 1681. V. 43

TRECCO, GIOVANNI BATTISTA fl. 1782-1820

Coltivazione e Governo del Lino Marzulo. Vicenza: 1792. V. 44

TRECHSLIN, A. M.

Old Garden Roses. Switzerland: 1975. V. 40

TREDGOLD, THOMAS

Elementary Principles of Carpentry. London: 1820. V. 44

Elementary Principles of Carpentry. London: 1828. V. 40; 44

Elementary Principles of Carpentry. London: 1853. V. 44

Elementary Principles of Carpentry . . . London: 1886. V. 44

Elementary Principles of Carapentry. Philadelphia: 1837. V. 37

A Practical Treatise on Rail-roads and Carriages, Shewing the Principles of Estimating Their Strength, Proportions, Expense and Annual Produce . . . London: 1825. V. 46

A Practical Treatise on Rail-Roads and Carriages, Showing the Principles of Estimating Their Strength, Proportions, Expense and Annual Produce . . . New York: 1825. V. 42

A Practical Treatise on Rail-Roads and Carriages . . . London: 1835. V. 45

Practical Essay on the Strength of Cast Iron and Other Metals. London: 1842, 1846. V. 44

The Principles and Practice and Explanation of the Machinery of Locomotive Engines in Operation on the Several Lines of Railway. (with) The Principles and Practice and Explanation of the Machinery Used in Steam Navigation. London: 1850, 1851. V. 40

The Steam Engine, Comprising an Account of Its Invention and Progressive Improvement . . . London: 1827. V. 39

The Steam Engine: Its Invention and Progressive Improvement, an Investigation of Its Principles, and Its Aplication to Navigation, Manufactures and Railways. London: 1838/40. V. 46

The Steam Engine: Its Invention and Progressive Improvment, an Investigation of its Principles, and its Application to Navigation, Manufactures, and Railways. By Thomas Tredgold, Civil Engineer . . . A New (Second) Edition, enlarged . . . London: 1838. V. 37

Tracts on Hydraulics. London: 1836. V. 40

TREDWELL, DANIEL M.

A Monograph on Privately Illustrated Books: A Plea for Bibliomania. 1892. V. 42

A Monograph on Privately Illustrted Books. A Plean for Bibliomania. Flatbush, Long Island: 1892. V. 37

TREE, HERBERT BEERBOHM

The Imaginative Faculty. London: 1893. V. 41

Nothing Matters and Other Stories. Boston: 1917. V. 46

Thoughts and After-Thoughts. London: 1913. V. 46

TREE, IRIS

The Marsh Picnic. Cambridge: 1966. V. 42

Poems. Nassau: 1917. V. 38

TREE, VIOLA

Castles in the Air: the Story of My Singing Days. London: 1926. V. 40

TREECE, HENRY

Dylan Thomas 'Dog Among the Fairies'. London: 1949. V. 45; 46

TREGARTHEN, GREVILLE

A Sketch of the Progress and Resources of New South Wales. Sydney: 1893. V. 40

TREGASKIS, J.

International Bookbinding Exhibition by the Chief Craftsmen from all Parts of the World, at the 'Caxton Head.' 1894. V. 41

TREGASKIS, RICHARD

Vietnam Diary. New York: 1963. V. 45

TREGONING, JOSEPH

Laws of the Stannaries of Cornwall. Truro: 1808. V. 39; 44

TREHERNE, J.

Key Environments: Galapagos, Sahara Desert, Madagascar, Amazonia, Antarctica, Red Sea, Western Mediterranean, Malaysia. London: 1984-86. V. 37; 38

TREITZSAURWEIN, M.

Der Weiss Kunig, Eine Erzehlung von den Thaten Kaiser Maximilian des Ersten . . . Herausgegeben aus dem Manuscripte der Kaiserl. Vienna: 1775. V. 40

TRELAWNEY, DAYRELL

The King's Friend. London: 1890. V. 44

TRELAWNY, E. J.

Recollections of the Last Days of Shelley and Byron. London: 1858. V. 38; 40

TRELAWNY, EDWARD JOHN

Adventures of a Younger Son. London: 1831. V. 39; 40; 41

Records of Shelley, Byron and the Author. London: 1878. V. 37; 43

TREMAIN, HENRY EDWIN

Sailors' Creek to Appomattox Court House, 7th, 8th, 9th April, 1865. New York: 1885. V. 41

TREMAINE, JOHN

Placita Coronae; or Pleas of the Crown in Matters Criminal and Civil. London: 1723. V. 43

TREMAINE, MARIE

A Bibliography of Canadian Imprints 1751-1800. Toronto. V. 40

A Bibliography of Canadian Imprints, 1751-1800. Toronto: 1952. V. 39

TREMANONDO, DOMENICO ANGELO MALEVOLTI 1716-1802

L'Ecole des ARmes, Avec L'Expication Generale des Principales Attitudes et Positions Concerant l'Escrime. Londres: 1763. V. 44

TREMBLEY, A.

Memoires Pour Servir a lHistoire d'un Genre de Polypes d'eau Douce . . . Leiden: 1744. V. 38; 45

TREMEARNE, A. J. N.

Hausa Superstitions and Customs. London: 1913. V. 39

TREMELLIUS, IMMANUEL

Grammatica Chaldaea et Syra. Geneva: 1569. V. 37; 44

TREMENEERE, HUGH SEYMOUR

Notes on Public Subjects, Made During a Tour in the United States and Canada. London: 1852. V. 42; 44

TREMENHEERE, SEYMOUR

Observations on the Proposed Breakwater in Mount's Bay, and On Its Connection with a Railway Into Cornwall in a Letter to Richard Moyle . . . Penzance: 1839. V. 40

TRENCH, FREDERICK WILLIAM

A Collection of Papers Relating to the Thames Quay; With Hints for Some Further Improvements in the Metropolis . . . London: 1827. V. 38; 40; 45

A Lithographic Sketch of the North Bank of the Thames, from Westmisnter Bridge to London Brdige, Shewing the Proposed Quay, and Some Other Improvements Suggested by Lieut. Colonel Trench, to Which is Annexed, a Survey of that Part of the River . . . London: 1825. V. 37; 39

TRENCH GASCOIGNE, GWENDOLEN GALTON

The Handbook of Turning. London: 1842. V. 40

TRENCH, RICHARD CHENEVIX

Notes on the Parables of Our Lord. London: 1889. V. 38

Sacred Latin Poetry, Chiefly Lyrical . . . London: 1849. V. 42

TRENCHARD, JOHN

An Argument, Shewing, that a Standing Army is Inconsistent with a Free Government, and Absolutely Destructive to the Constitution of the English Monarchy. London: 1697. V. 39

Cato's Letters; or Essays on Liberty, Civil and Religious. London: 1733. V. 41

A Collection of all the Political Letters in the London Journal, to Dec. 17, Inclusive, 1720. London: 1721. V. 45

An History of Standing Armies in England . . . . London: 1739. V. 41

A Short History of Standing Armies in England. London: 1698. V. 42; 46

A Short History of Standing Armies in England. N.P.: 1698. V. 43

TRENCHFIELD, CALEB

A Cap of Grey Hairs for a Green Head. London: 1688. V. 38

TRENCK, FREDERIC

The Life of Baron Frederic Trenck Containing His Adventures . . . London: 1788. V. 42

TRENDALL, A. D.

The Red Figured Vases of Lucania, Campania and Sicily. Oxford: 1967. V. 44

The Red Figured Vases of Lucania, Campania and Sicily: Third Supplement. London: 1983. V. 44

TRENDALL, E. W.

Original Designs for Cottages and Villas, in the Grecian, Gothic and Italian Styles of Architecture . . . London: 1831. V. 39

TRENHOLM, VIRGINIA C.

Footprints on the frontier: Saga of a Laramie Reion of Wyoming. Douglas: 1945. V. 45

TRENT, COUNCIL OF, 1545-1563.

Canones Et Decreta Sacrosancti Oecumenici et Generalis Concilli Tridentini. Rome: 1564. V. 40

TRENT, WILLIAM

Journal of . . . From Logstown to Pickawillany A.D. 1752. Cincinnati: 1871. V. 42; 45

TRENTSENTSKY, M.

Exercises in Coloring - French Military. Vienna: (c. 1860). V. 37

TRES Vetustissimae Prophetiae, de Germania, Vivis Coloribus Tristem & Miserabilem Statum Omnium Rerum Depingentes . . . N.P.: 1579. V. 38

TRESEDER, N. G.

The Book of Magnolias. London: 1981. V. 45

TRETER, TOMASZ

In Quinti Horatii Flacci . . . Poemata Omnia Rerum ac Verborum Locupletissimus Index. Antwerp: 1576. V. 37

TRETYAKOV, N. A.

My Experiences at Nan Shan and Port Arthur with the fifth East Siberian Rifles. London: 1911. V. 46

TREUTLER, FREDERIC AUGUST

Observationes Pathologico-Anatomicae Auctarium ad Helminthologium Humani Corporis Continentes. (with) Joachim Diederich Brandis. Commentatio de Oleorum Unguinosorum Natura. Lipsiae: 1793/1785. V. 44

TREVATHAM, CHARLES E.

The American Thoroughbred. V. 43

TREVECCA COLLEGE, WALES.

Some Account of the Proceedings at the College of the Right Hon. the Countess of Huntingdon, in Wales. London: 1772. V. 46

TREVELYAN, GEORGE MACAULAY 1876-1962

Garibaldi's Defence of the Roman Republic 1848-49. London: 1914. V. 45

TREVELYAN, GEORGE OTTO

The V. 45

The American Revolution. George the Third and Charles Fox. The Concluding Part of 'The American Revolution'. The Early History of Charles James Fox. London: 1880-1914. V. 42

The American Revolution. George III and Charles Fox. Concluding Part of the American Revolution. London: 1899-1914. V. 39

The Life and Letters of Lord Macaulay. London: 1876. V. 41; 44; 46

TREVELYAN, R. C.

Meleager. London: 1927. V. 41

Polyphemus and Other Poems. London: 1901. V. 43

Poems and Fables. London: 1925. V. 41; 45

Rimeless Numbers. London: 1932. V. 40

TREVIGAR, LUKE

Sectionum Conicarum Elementa Methodo Facillima Demonstrata in Usum Juventutis Academicae. Cantabrigiae: 1731. V. 39; 41

TREVOR-BATTYE, AUBYN

Ice-Bound on Kolguev: a Chapter in the Exploration of Arctic Europe to Which is Added a Record of the Natural History of the Island. Westminster: 1895. V. 42

ice Bound on Kolguev. Westminster: 1895. V. 39; 41; 43; 46

TREVOR, WILLIAM 1928-

The Ballroom of Romance and Other Stories. London: 1972. V. 41

The Boarding House. London: 1965. V. 37

The Boarding House. London: 1965. V. 37

The Day We Got Drunk on Cake. London: 1967. V. 40

Dreaming - an Extract from Elizabeth Alone. London: 1973. V. 40

Elizabeth Alone. London: 1973. V. 38

Fools of Fortune. London: 1983. V. 38

The Last Lunch of the Season. London: 1973. V. 44

TREVOR, WILLIAM 1928- continued

Lovers of Their Time. London: 1978. V. 42; 44

Miss Gomez aand the Brethren. London: 1971. V. 38; 46

The Old Boys. London: 1964. V. 37; 38; 41

The Old Boys. New York: 1964. V. 46

Other People's Worlds. London: 1980. V. 38

The Silence in the Garden. London: 1988. V. 41; 42; 44

A Standard of Behaviour. London: 1958. V. 37

TREW, C. J.

Plantae Selectae Quarum Imagines ad Exemplaria Naturalia Londini in Hortis Curiosorum.. Nuremberg: 1750-73. V. 39

TREW, CHRISTOPH JACOB 1696-1769

Dissertatio Epistolica de Differentiis Quibusdam Inter Hominem Natum et Nascendum Intercedentibus . . . Nuremberg: 1736. V. 42

TREWMAN, ROBERT

The Principles of Free-Masonry Delineated. Exeter: 1777. V. 38

TRIAL for Murder: The People Vs. James K. Polk. Boston: 1847. V. 39

THE TRIAL Of a Black-Pudding. London: 1652. V. 42

THE TRIAL of Alpheus Livermore and Samuel Angler, Before the Supreme Judicial Court of the Commonwealth of Massachusetts, Upon an Indictment for the Murder of Nicholas John Crevay and Indian, Committed November 23, 1813. Boston: 1813. V. 42

THE TRIAL of Arthur O'Connor, Esq., John Binns, John Allen, Jeremiah Leary and James Coighley, for High Treason, Before Judge Buller, etc. Under a Special Commission, at Maidstone, in the County of Kent. London: 1798. V. 45

THE TRIAL of Boulton and Park, with Hurst and Fiske, a Complete and Accurate Report of the Proceedings (etc.). Manchester: 1871. V. 45

THE TRIAL of Frederick Calvert, Esq; Baron of Baltimore, in the Kingdom of Ireland, For a Rape on the Body of Sarah Woodcock; and of Eliz. Grissinburg and Ann Harvey, Otherwise Darby, as Accessories Before the Fact, for Procuring, Aiding and Abetting . . . Edinburgh: 1768. V. 43

TRIAL of Messrs. Lambert & Perry. To Which also is added, The Trial of William Cobbett for Libelling His Present Majesty, George III, King of England and His Government. New York: 1810. V. 45

TRIAL of the Assasins and Conspirators for the Murder of Abraham Lincoln. Philadelphia: 1865. V. 38; 39

THE TRIAL of Thomas Hunter, Peter Hacket, Richard M'Neil, James Gibb and William M'Lean, the Glasgow Cottonspinners, before the High Court of Justiciary at Edinburgh, on Charges of Murder . . . Edinburgh: 1838. V. 46

A TRIALL of the English Lyturgie. London: 1643. V. 42

TRIALS for Adultery; or, the History of Divorces. London: 1779-81. V. 43

THE TRIALS of Jeremiah Brandreth, William Turner, Isaac Ludlam, George Weightman and others, for High Treason, Under a Special Commission at Derby . . . October 1817. London: 1817. V. 46

TRIANA, JOSE MARIA MARTIN

Suite Lirica En Homenaje A Wallace Stevens. 1982. V. 38

TRIANOA, JOSE M. M.

Suite Lirica. Verona: 1982. V. 46

THE TRIBUTE: a Collection of Miscellaneous Unpublished Poems, By Various Authors. London: 1837. V. 40; 45

THE TRIBUTE of a London Publisher to His Printers: John Dunton's Sketches of the printers, Stationers and Binders of the City of London, 1689-1705. Cambridge: 1930. V. 40

TRIBUTE To Cecil Collins. Plymouth: 1983. V. 46

TRIBUTE to Walter de la Mare on His Seventy-Fifth Birthday. London: 1948. V. 39; 40; 41

TRIBUTES to Brooke Crutchley on His Retirement as University Printer. Cambridge: 1975. V. 39; 40; 44

TRIBUTES to Edward Johnston, Calligrapher. Kent: 1948. V. 40; 41

TRICASSO, PATRICIO

La Chiromance. Paris: 1546. V. 37

De la Derniere Reveue & Correction de l'Autheur & Naguères Fidelement Traduicte de l'Italien en Langaige Francoys. Paris: 1546. V. 45

THE TRICKS of London Laid Open, Being a Caution for Countrymen and Women. London: 1750-60. V. 46

THE TRICKS of London Laid Open: Being a True Caution To Both Sexes in Town and Country. I. A General Reflection on the Town . . . IX. Particular Observations and Reflections Upon Several Distinct Occurrences of the Town &c. London: 1785? V. 45

TRICKS of the Town Laid Open: or, a Companion for Country Gentlemen. London: 1747. V. 45

THE TRICKS of Trade in the Adulterations of Food and Physic with Directions for Their Detection and Counteraction. London: 1859. V. 41

THE TRIENNIAL Act Impartially Stated . . . London: 1716. V. 44

TRIER, EDUARD

The Sculpture of Marino Marini. New York: 1961. V. 46

TRIER, WALTER

Toys. London: 1922. V. 41

THE TRIFLER. London: 1788-89. V. 40

TRIFLES in Verse. Philadelphia: 1839. V. 45

TRIGG, HAIDEN C.

The American Fox-Hound. N.P.: 1895. V. 39

TRIGGS, HARRY INIGO 1876-1923

Formal Gardens in England and Scotland. London: 1902. V. 39; 44; 46

Some Architectural Works of Inigo Jones. London: 1901. V. 39

TRIGGS, J. H.

History of Cheyenne and Northern Wyoming Embracing the Gold Fields of the Black Hills, Powder River and Big Horn Mountains. Omaha: 1876. V. 41

TRIGGS, OSCAR LOVELL

Chapters in the History of the Arts and Crafts Movement. Chicago: 1902. V. 42

TRILLING, LIONEL

Matthew Arnold. London: 1939. V. 40

The Middle of the Journey. New York: 1954. V. 40

TRIMBLE, WILLIAM C.

The History of Enniskillen, with Reference to Some Manors in Co. Fermanagh and Other Local Subjects. Enniskillen: 1919-21. V. 43

TRIMEN, ROLAND

South African Butterflies: A Monograph of the Extra Tropical Species. London: 1887-89. V. 37; 45

TRIMMER, S.

A Description of a Set of Prints of Roman History . . . (with) A Series of Prints Designed to Illustrate the Roman History. London: 1817. V. 44

TRIMMER, SARAH

The Charity School Spelling Book. London: 1799-1800. V. 41

An Easy Introduction to the Knowledge of Nature and Reading the Holy Scriptures. Dublin: 1782. V. 42

An Easy Introduction to the Knowledge of Nature, and Reading the Holy Scriptures. London: 1793. V. 43

An Easy Introduction to the Knowledge of Nature. Boston: 1796. V. 39; 42

An Essay on Christian Education. London: 1812. V. 42

Fabulous Histories. London: 1786. V. 41

Fabulous Histories. Dublin: 1800. V. 40

The History of the Robins. London: 1869. V. 39

History of the Robins, Designed for the Instruction of Children Respecting Their Treatment of Animals. Dublin: 1819. V. 38

A New Series of Prints, Accompanied by Easy Lessons: Containing a General Outline of Antient History. London: 1811. V. 40

A Series of Prints of Ancient History, designed as Ornaments for Those Apartments, In Which Children Receive the First Rudiments of Their Education. London: 1788. V. 41

TRIMMER, SARAH KIRBY 1741-1810

Fabulous Histories: Designed for the Instruction of Children, Respecting Their Treatment of Animals. Dublin: 1800. V. 46

A Series of Prints of Scripture History, Designed as Ornaments for Those Apartments in Which Children Receive the First Rudiments of Their Education. London: 1786. V. 46

TRIMNELL, CHARLES

Partiality Detected; or, a Reply to a Late Pamphlet, entitled, Some Proceedings in the Convocation, A.D., 1705 . . . London: 1708. V. 39

TRINDER, WILLIAM MARTIN

The English Olive Tree; or, a Treatise on the Use of Oil and the Air Bath . . . London: 1812? V. 45

TRINIDAD. Short Stories, Articles and Poems. Port of Spain: 1929. V. 46

TRINITY HOUSE

A Descriptive Catalogue of the Charters, Deeds and Records of Trinity House, Newcastle Upon Tyne. Newcastle-Upon°Tyne: 1854-55. V. 40

TRINKA VON KRZOWITZ, WENZEL 1739-1791

Historia Cophoseos et Baryecoiae. Vienna: 1778. V. 42

TRINTIY CHURCH, NEW YORK.

The Charter of Trinity-Church in the City of New York. New York: 1788. V. 41

THE TRIP of the Steamer Oceanus to Fort Sumter and Charleston, S.C. . . . April 14th, 1865. Brooklyn: 1865. V. 40; 41

A TRIP to Mexico, being Notes of a Journey from Lake Erie to Lake Tuzcoco and Back, with an Appendix: (Ancient nations and races). Toronto: 1880. V. 37

A TRIP to Mexico or Recollections of a Ten Months' Ramble in 1849-50. London: 1851. V. 40

TRIPHOOK, ROBERT

Miscellanea Antiqua Anglicana . . . London: 1816. V. 45

TRIPLER, CHARLES

Hand-Book For the Military Surgeon. Cincinnati: 1862. V. 42

TRIPLETT, FRANK

The Life, Times and Treacherous Death of Jesse James. Chicago: 1882. V. 45

TRIPP, C. E.

Ace High, The 'Frisco Detective or, The Girl Sport's Double Game. A Story of the Sierra & The Golden Gate City. San Francisco: 1948. V. 37

TRIPP, F. E.

British Mosses; Their Homes, Aspects, Structures and Uses. London: 1874. V. 42; 43; 44; 45

British Mosses, Their Homes, Aspects, structure and Uses. London: 1888. V. 37; 38; 43; 45

TRIPP, WILLIAM HENRY

'Three Goes Fulkes.' The Story of New Bedford's Last Whaler, Being the Narrative of the Voyage of Schooner John R. Manta of (sic) Hatteras Grounds 1925 . . . New Bedford: 1938. V. 41

TRIPS in the Life of a Locomotive Engineer. New York: 1863. V. 44

TRIQUEL, R.

The Planters Manual. London: 1675. V. 39

TRISMOSIN, SALOMON

Aureum Vellus Oder Guldin Schatz und Kunst-Kammer, DArinnen der . . . Hamburg: 1708. V. 46

TRISMOSIN, SOLOMON

Splendor Solis. London: 1920. V. 38

TRISSEL, JAMES

Color for the Letterpress. 1987. V. 38; 40

TRISSINO, GIOVANNI GIORGIO

La Poetica. Vicenza: 1529. V. 38

La Swphnwnisba. Vicenza: 1529. V. 41; 43

TRISTAN

The Romance of Tristram of Lyonesse and La Belle Isoude. St. Albans: 1921. V. 39

Sir Tristrem: a Metrical Romance of the Thirteenth Century. Edinburgh: 1806. V. 43

Tristan et Iseut. Paris: 1914. V. 46

TRISTAN, FLORA

Promenades Dans Londres. Paris & London: 1840. V. 41

TRISTRAM, E. W.

English Medieval Wall Painting. The Thirteenth Century. London: 1950. V. 39

English Wall Painting of the Fourteenth Century. London: 1955. V. 39

TRISTRAM, H. B.

The Land of Israel; A Journal of Travels in Palestine, undertaken with Special Reference to Its Physical Character. London: 1866. V. 37

Scenes in the East . . . London: 1880. V. 44

TRISTRAM, HENRY B.

The Great Sahara. London: 1860. V. 41

Scenes in the East. London: 1887. V. 37; 41

TRISTRAM, O.

Coaching Days and Coaching Ways. London: 1893. V. 38

TRISTRAM, OUTRAM W.

Coaching Days and Coaching Ways. V. 44

TRISTRAM, R. W.

English Mediaeval Wall Painting. Oxford: 1944-50/55. V. 44

English Mediaeval Wall Paintings. Oxford: 1944-50-55. V. 42

TRISTRAM, W. OUTRAM

Coaching Days and Coaching Ways. London: 1888. V. 39; 41; 42

Coaching Days and Coaching Ways. London: 1894. V. 41

TRISTRAM, WILLIAM OUTRAM

Coaching Days and Coaching Ways. London: 1893. V. 42

TRITHEMIUS, JOANNES

Compendium Sive Breviarium Primi Voluminis Annalium Sive Historiarum, de Origine Regum et Gentis Francorum. Paris: 1539. V. 37

TRITHEMIUS, JOHANNES

De Origine Gentis Principvmqve Bavarorvm Commentarivs Per Qvam Elegans Nunc Primum in Lucem Aeditus. Frankfurt A.M.: 1549. V. 38

TRITTON, J. HERBERT

Tritton; the Place and the Family. London: 1907. V. 37

THE TRIUMPH of Goodnature, Exhibited in the History of Master Harry Fairborn and Master Trueworth. Boston: 1804. V. 39

TROCCHI, ALEXANDER

Invisible Insurrection of a Million Minds. Edinburgh: 1963. V. 42

TROELSCH, HENRY W.

The Kill Van Kull Bridge Between Bayonne, New Jersey and Port Richmond, New York Built by the Port of New York Authority. New York?: 1931. V. 43

TROGUS, POMPEIUS

Historiarvm Philippicarvm Epitoma: Ex Manuscriptis Codicibus Emendatior . . . Paris: 1851. V. 46

TROIL, UNO VON, ABP. OF UPSALA 1746-1803

Bref Rorande en Resa til Island 1772. Uppsala: 1777. V. 38

Letters on Iceland. Dublin: 1780. V. 38

Letters on Iceland; Containing Observations on the Civil, Liberary, Ecclesiastical and Natural History, Antiquities, Volcanos, Basaltes, Hot Springs, Customs, Dress, Manners of Inhabitants . . . London: 1780. V. 37; 38; 42; 43; 45

Letters on Iceland. London: 1783. V. 38

Lettres sur l'Islande. Paris: 1781. V. 38; 40

TROILI, GIULIO 1613-1685

Paradossi Per Pratticare a Prospettiva Senza Saperla . . . Bologna: 1683. V. 37; 40; 41

TROISE, GIUSTINO

Alfabeto Maiuscolo Ornato. Rome: 1858. V. 38; 40

TROJAN, JOHANNES

Speil und Leben. Bilderbuch fur Kinder. Meinhold: (ca. 1880). V. 37

TROLLOPE, ANTHONY 1815-1882

The American Senator. Detroit: 1877. V. 39

The American Senator. London: 1877. V. 37; 39; 42

The American Senator. London: 1877. V. 44; 45

The American Senator. Toronto: 1877. V. 39

The American Senator. London: 1878. V. 40

Australia and New Zealand. London: 1873. V. 43; 45

Australia and New Zealand. Melbourne: 1873. V. 38

An Autobiography. Edinburgh: 1883. V. 37; 38

An Autobiography. Edinburgh and London: 1883. V. 39; 44; 45

An Autobiography. Edinburgh/London: 1883. V. 37

An Autobiography. London: 1883. V. 38

An Autobiography. New York: 1883. V. 39; 41

Ayala's Angel. London: 1881. V. 37; 40; 44; 45

Ayala's Angel. London: 1882. V. 40

Barchester Towers. London: 1857. V. 42

The Barchester Novels. London: 1913. V. 42

Barchester Towers. Christiania;: 1882. V. 37

Barsetshire Novels. London: 1925 & n.d. V. 43

Barsetshire Novels. Oxford: 1929. V. 42

The Barsetshire Novels. Oxford: 1929. V. 42

The Barsetshire Novels. Oxford: 1929. V. 40

TROLLOPE, BARNARD

Leisure Moments. London: 1826. V. 40

TROLLOPE, FRANCES

Paris and the Parisians in 1835. London: 1836. V. 37

TROLLOPE, FRANCES ELEANOR TERNAN d. 1913

A Charming Fellow. London: 1876. V. 42

Frances Trollope: Her Life and Literary Work from George III to Victoria. London: 1895. V. 38; 40; 43

TROLLOPE, FRANCES MILTON 1780-1863

The Abbess, a Romance. London: 1833. V. 40

The Attractive Man. London: 1846. V. 45

The Barnabys in America. London: 1843. V. 42

Belgium and Western Germany in 1833 . . . Brussells: 1834. V. 42

Belgium and Western Germany in 1833. London: 1835. V. 39

Belgium and Western Germany in 1833. London: 1834. V. 38

Charles Chesterfield, or the Adventures of a Youth of Genius. London: 1841. V. 44

Charles Chesterfield; or, the Adventures of a Youth of Genius. Paris: 1841. V. 40

Domestic Manners of the Americans. London: 1832. V. 40

Gertrude, or Family Pride. London: 1855. V. 40

Jessie Phillips. A Tale of the Present Day. London: 1843. V. 46

Jesse Phillips. London: 1844. V. 38; 41; 42; 44; 46

The Life and Adventures of Jonathan Jefferson Whitlaw. London: 1836. V. 38

The Life and Adventures of Jonathan Jefferson Whitlaw; or, Scenes on the Mississippi. Paris: 1836. V. 44

Life and Adventures of Michael Armstrong, the Factory Boy. London: 1840. V. 37; 38; 42; 44

The Mother's Manual or Illustrations of Matrimonial Economy. London: 1833. V. 40; 44

The Old World and the New. Paris: 1850. V. 40

One Fault. Paris: 1840. V. 44

The Refugee in America. London: 1832. V. 41

Town and Country; or the Days of the Regency. London: 1848. V. 45

Tremordyn Cliff. Brussels: 1835. V. 45; 46

Tremordyn Cliff. London: 1835. V. 40; 44

The Vicar of Wrexhill. London: 1837. V. 37; 40; 41; 43; 44

Vienna and the Austrians. London: 1837. V. 38

Vienna and the Austrians; with some Account of a Journey through Swabia, Bavaria, the Ryrol, and the Salzbourg. London: 1838. V. 39

A Visit to Italy. London: 1842. V. 45

The Widow Barnaby. London: 1839. V. 38

The Widow Barnaby. London: 1840. V. 44

TROLLOPE, THEODOSIA

Social Aspects of the Italian Revolution, in a Series of Letters from Florence . . . London: 1861. V. 37; 39; 41

TROLLOPE, THOMAS ADOLPHUS 1810-1892

La Beata. London: 1862. V. 39

The Girlhood of Catherine De Medici. London: 1856. V. 37; 41

A History of the Commonwealth of Florence, from the Earliest Independence to the Fall of the Republic in 1531. London: 1865. V. 39; 43

Italy from the Alps to Mount Etna. London: 1877. V. 38

Italy, from the Alps to Mount Etna. New York: 1877. V. 41

Leonora Casaloni. London: 1868. V. 39

A Summer in Brittany. London: 1840. V. 37; 46

A Summer in Western France. London: 1841. V. 43

What I Remember. (with) The Further Reminiscenses of . . . London: 1887, 1889. V. 38; 40

What I Remember. (with) The Further Reminiscenses of . . . London: 1887/89. V. 41

TROLTSCH, ANTON FRIEDRICH

The Surgical Diseases of the Ear . . . London: 1874. V. 42

TROLTSCH, ANTON VON

Treatise on the Diseases of the Bar, Including the Anatomy of the Organ. New York: 1869. V. 42

TROMONIN, KORNILII YAKOLEVICH

Tromonin's Watermark Album, a Facsimile of the Moscow 1844 Edition. Hilversum: 1965. V. 38; 41; 45

TRONSON, JOHN M.

Personal Narrative of a Voyage to Japan, Kamtschatka, Siberia, Tartary and Various Parts of Coast of China; in H.M.S. Barracouta. London: 1859. V. 38; 45

TROPHIES of Wild Animal Life. Montreal: 1930's. V. 42

TROPPAU UND JAEGERNDORFF, ELEONORA MARIA ROSALIA, DUCHESS OF

Freywillig- Auffgesprungener Granat-Apffell Dess Chrsitlichen Samaritans. Vienna: 1695. V. 42; 44

TROTMAN, MISS

Catalogue of the Useful Household Furniture and a Small Library of Books . . . Removed from Wanstrow Rectory and Castle House, Frome . . . Frome: 1868. V. 45

TROTSKII, LEV 1879-1940

My Life the Rise and Fall of a Dictator. London: 1930. V. 45

TROTSKY, LEV 1879-1940

The History of the Russian Revolution to Brest-Litovsk. London: 1919. V. 38; 42

TROTTER, CATHERINE

Agnes de Castro, a Tragedy. London: 1696. V. 38

Fatal Friendship. London: 1698. V. 42

TROTTER, ELIZABETH HILL

Cindabright; or, the Fatal Flowers. Kensington: 1838. V. 40

TROTTER, ISABELLA S.

First Impressions of the New World on Two Travellers from the Old in the Autumn of 1858. London: 1859. V. 40

TROTTER, JOHN BERNARD

Memoirs of the Later Years of the Right Honourable Charles James Fox. London: 1811. V. 39

TROTTER, PHILIP DURHAM

Our Mission to the Court of Marocco in 1880 in 1880 Under Sir John Drummond Hay, K. C. B. Edinburgh: 1881. V. 46

TROTTER, THOMAS

An Essay, Medical, Philosophical and Chemical on Drunkenness and Its Effects on the Human Body. London: 1804. V. 45

An Essay, Medical, Philosophical and Chemical, on Drunkenness and Its Effects on the Human Body. Philadelphia: 1813. V. 37

A Proposal for Destroying the Fire and Choaking Damp of Coal-Mines . . . Newcastle: 1805. V. 45

A View of the Nervous Treatment . . . Troy: 1808. V. 43

A View of the Nervous Temperament. London: 1812. V. 39; 43

TROTTER, WILLIAM E.

Select Illustrated Topography of Thirty Miles Round London . . . London: 1839. V. 42; 44; 45

TROTTI, LAMAR

In Old Chicago. Beverley Hills: 1937. V. 45

TROTULA OF SALERNO

The Diseases of Women. Los Angeles: 1940. V. 38; 39

TROUP, ROBERT

A Letter to the Honorable Brockholst Livingston, Esq., One of the Justices of the Supreme Court of the U.S., on the Lake Canal Policy of the State of New York. Albany: 1822. V. 37; 42

A Vindication of the Claim of Elkanah Watson, Esq. to the merit of Projecting the Lake Canal Policy. Created by the Canal Act of March, 1792. Geneva, NY: 1821. V. 37

TROUSSEAU, A.

Lectures on Clinical Medicine Delivered at the Hotel Dieu. Paris: 1867-72. V. 40; 41

TROUSSEAU, ARMAND

Lectures on Clinical Medicine. London: 1868-72. V. 39

TROW, JAMES

Manitoba and North West Territories. Ottawa: 1878. V. 39; 42; 43

TROWBRIDGE, BERTHA CHADWICK

Old Houses of Connecticut, from Material Collected by the Committee on Old Housed of the Connecticut Society of the Colonial Dames of America. New Haven: 1923. V. 42

TROWBRIDGE, FRANCIS B.

The Hoadley Genealogy: a History of the Descendants of William Hoadley of Branford, Connecticut . . . New Haven: 1894. V. 46

TROWBRIDGE, J. T.

The South: a Tour of Its Battlefields and Ruined Cities . . . Hartford: 1866. V. 42

The Vagabonds. Boston: 1883. V. 44

TROWBRIDGE, JOHN TOWSEND

Neighbor Jackwood. Boston: 1857. V. 43

TROWBRIDGE, L. S.

A Brief History of the Tenth Michigan Cavalry. Detroit: 1905. V. 44

TROWBRIDGE, W. R. H.

Cagliostro. The Spendour and Misery of a Master of Magic. New York: 1910. V. 44

TROWELL, SAMUEL

The Farmer's Instructor; or, The Husbandman and Gardener's Useful and Necessary Companion . . . London: 1747. V. 37

A New Treatise of Husbandry, Gardening and Other Curious Matters Relating to Country Affairs. London: 1739. V. 38; 42; 45; 46

TROW'S New York City Directory for the Year Ending May 1, 1865. New York: 1864. V. 46

TROW'S New York City Directory for the Year Ending May 1, 1868. New York: 1867. V. 46

TROW'S New York City Directory for the Year Ending May 1, 1876. New York: 1875. V. 46

TROW'S New York City Directory for the Year Ending May 1, 1878. New York: 1877. V. 46

TROXELL, JANET CAMP 1828-1882

Three Rossettis. Cambridge: 1937. V. 39

TROY & BOSTON & WESTERN VERMONT RAILROADS

The Old Reliable All RailRoute Via Rutland & Bennington for Troy, Albany, & New York:. Montreal?: 1865. V. 45

TROYE, EDWARD

The Race Horses of America, 1832-1872. Saratoga Springs: 1981. V. 42

TRUAX, CHARLES

The Mechanics of Surgery. Chicago: 1899. V. 45

The Mechanics of Surgery. San Francisco: 1988. V. 40

TRUBLET DE VILLEJEGU, JACQUES J. A.

Relation Detaillee de la Campagne de M. Le Commandeur de Suffren, dans l'Indie du 1 er. Juin 1782 au 29 Septembre Suivant. Port Louis: 1783. V. 40

TRUBNER'S Bibliographical Guide to American Literature . . . London: 1855. V. 46

TRUCCHI, LORENZA

Francis Bacon. New York: 1975. V. 39; 43

TRUCHET, PERE SEBASTIEN

Methode Pour fair une Infinite de Desseins Differents, avec des Carreaux mi-Partis de Deux Coleurs para une Ligne Diagonale . . . Paris: 1722. V. 38; 45

A TRUE Account of the Most Considerable Occurrences That Have Hapned (sic) in the Warre Between the English and the Indians in New England . . . London: 1676. V. 42; 44; 45

A TRUE Account of the Royal Bagnio, with a Discourse of Its Vertues (sic). London: 1680. V. 45

A TRUE and Exact Relation of the Death of Two Catholicks, Who Suffered for Their Religion at the Summer Assizes Held at Lancaster in the Year 1628. London: 1737. V. 46

A TRUE and Full Account of the Late Bloody and Desperate Battle fought at Gladsmuir, Betwixt the Army Under the Command of His Royal Highness Charles Prince of Wales, Etc . . . N.P.: 1745. V. 39; 41

A TRUE and Impartial Account of the Blowing Up of the Church of St. Ninians on the 1st Day of February 1745-46. Edinburgh: 1746. V. 39

THE TRUE and Real Interest of Great Britain, Impartially Considered; with Regard to the Rupture Among the Northern Powers . . . In Order to Adjust the Material Point, How Far are We Bound to Assist Russia, in Case of a War in the North. London: 1749. V. 41; 46

THE TRUE Annals of Fairy Land: the Reign of King Herla. London. V. 46

TRUE Charity, an Example by San Bernardino of Stena. N.P.: 1979. V. 46

A TRUE Copie of the Master-Piece of All Those Petitions Which Have Formerly Beene Presented by the Major (sic), Aldermen and the Ret of the Common Counsell of the Citie of London . . . London: 1641(2). V. 43

TRUE Copies of I. The Agreement Between Lord Baltimore and Messieurs Penn, Dated 10 May, 1732. II. Between the Commissions Given to the Commissioners to Mark Out the Lines Between Maryland and Pensylvania and the Three Lower Counties on Delaware. III . . . London: 1734. V. 44

THE TRUE English Prophet; or Englands Happiness a Hundred Years Hence. London: 1697. V. 41

TRUE, FREDERICK M.

The Whalebone Whales of the Western North Atlantic Compared with Those Occurring in European Waters with some Observations On The Species of the North Pacific. Washington: 1904. V. 41

TRUE, FREDERICK W.

An Account of the Beaked Whales of the Family Ziphiidae in the Collection of the United States National Museum . . . Washington: 1910. V. 45

THE TRUE Narrative of the Five Years' Suffering and Perilous Adventures by Miss Barber, Wife of Squatting Bear . . . Philadelphia: 1873. V. 43

A TRUE Portrait of the E****** N******, drawn by M-----n Cavalier. To Which is Added, A Sketch of Some Great Alterations . . . London: 1757. V. 41

THE TRUE Portraiture of Iohn Wombergh, by Birth a Switzer, and by Religion a Protestant. London: 1690. V. 39

A TRUE Relation of His Majesties Reception and Royall Entertainment at Lincoln, by the Knights, Esquires, Gentlemen, and Free-Holders of the Said Countie. 1642. V. 43

THE TRUE Relation of the Queenes Departure from Falmouth Into the Breast in the West of France. London: 1644. V. 41

A TRUE Relation of the Wonderful Cure of Mary Maillard. London: 1694. V. 41

A TRUE Relation of the Wonderful Cure of Mary Maillard. On Sunday the 26the of November 1693. With the Affidavits and Certificates of the Girl, and several other Credible and Worthy Persons, who knew her both before . . . London: 1694. V. 37; 39

A TRUE State of Facts Relating to Ramsgate Harbour. N.P.: 1755. V. 41; 42; 46

A TRUE Translated Copy of a Writ of Prohibition, Granted by the Lord Chief Justice . . . N.P.: London: 1676. V. 43

TRUEFITT, HENRY PAUL

New Views of Baldness: Being a Treatise on the Hair and Skin. London: 1863. V. 44

TRUEHEART, JAMES L. 1815-1882

The Perote Prisoners, Being the Diary of James L. Truehart, Printed for the First Time. San Antonio: 1934. V. 39; 42

TRUETT, VELMA S.

On the Hoof in Nevada. Los Angeles: 1950. V. 43

TRUETTNER, WILLIAM H.

The Natural Man Observed. Kent: 1979. V. 41

TRUJILLO, TOMAS DE

Libro Llamado Reprobacion de Trajes, y Abuso de Juramentos. Con un Tratado de Lymosnas. Zaragoza: 1563. V. 41

THE TRULY Remarkable Life of the Beautiful Helen Jewett, Who Was So Mysteriously Murdered, The Strangest and Most Exciting Case Known in the Police Annals of Crimes and Mysteries in the Great City of New York. Philadelphia: 1882. V. 37

TRUMAN, BEN C.

From the Crescent City to the Golden Gate Via the Sunset Route of the Southern Pacific Company. New York: 1886. V. 40

Occidental Sketches. San Francisco: 1881. V. 39; 41; 42; 43; 45

TRUMAN, BENJAMIN C.

Semi-Tropical California: Its Climate, Healthfulness, Productiveness and Scenery . . . San Francisco: 1874. V. 42

Tourist's Illustrated Guide to the Celebrated Summer and Winter Resorts of California . . . San Francisco: 1883. V. 39; 40

TRUMAN, BENJAMIN CUMMINGS

Tiburcio Vasquez: the Life, Adventures and Capture of the Great California Bandit and Murderer. Los Angeles: 1941. V. 39; 41

TRUMAN, GEORGE

Narrative of a Visit to the West Indies in 1840 and 1841. Philadelphia: 1844. V. 42; 43

TRUMAN, HARRY S.

Memoirs. Garden City: 1955. V. 40; 46

Memoirs. New York: 1955/56. V. 45

Memoirs. Volume II. Years of Trial and Hope. Garden City: 1956. V. 43

Mr. Citizen. New York: 1960. V. 41; 46

Year of Decisions. Garden City: 1955. V. 45

TRUMAN, STELLA

A Romance of the Counting Room. New Orleans: 1896. V. 45

TRUMBELL, HENRY

History of the Discovery of America, of the Landing of Our Forefathers, at Plymouth. Boston: 1819. V. 44

TRUMBO, DALTON

Johnny Got His Gun. New York: 1939. V. 42

Johnny Got His Gun. Philadelphia: 1939. V. 42; 44; 46

Johnny Got His Gun. Beverly Hills: 1971. V. 44

Johnny Got His Gun. New York: 1939. V. 37

Washington Jitters. New York: 1936. V. 44

TRUMBULL, BENJAMIN

An Appeal to the Public, Especially to the Learned, with Respect to the Unlawfulness of Divorces . . . New Haven: 1788. V. 38

A Complete History of Connecticut, Civil and Ecclesiastical, from the Emigration of Its First Planters from England, From 1630 to 1713. Hartford: 1797. V. 42

A Plea, in Vindication of the Connecticut Title to the Contested Lands, Lying West of the Province of New York . . . New Haven: 1774. V. 38; 44

TRUMBULL, COLONEL

Catalogue of Paintings of Colonel Trumbull; Including Nine Subjects of the American Revolution, with Near Two Hundred and Fifty Portraits of Persons Distinguished in that Import Period. New York: 1831. V. 43; 45

Catalogue of Paintings, By Colonel Trumbull; Including Eight Subjects of the American Revolution . . . New Haven: 1835. V. 43; 45

TRUMBULL, H. CLAY

Kadesh-Barnea Its Importance and Probable Site Including Studies of the Route of the Exodus and the Southern Boundary of the Holy Land. London: 1884. V. 43

The Knightly Soldier; a Biography of Major Henry Ward Camp, Tenth Conn. Vols. Boston: 1865. V. 42

TRUMBULL, HENRY

History of . . . Our Forefathers . . . and Their Most Remarkable Engagements with the Indians . . . Braddock, Harmer & St. Clair. Norwich: 1812. V. 39; 42

History of the Discovery of America. Boston: 1833. V. 42

History of the Indian Wars . . . Philadelphia: 1851. V. 40

History of the Disocvery of America . . . Engagements with the Indians . . . 1620-1679 . . . Creek and Seminole War. Boston: 1831. V. 37

Life and Remarkable Adventures of Israel R. Potter, (A Native of Cranston, Rhode-Island), who was a Soldier in the American Revolution . . . Providence: 1824. V. 37; 38

TRUMBULL, JAMES HAMMOND

List of Books Printed in Connecticut, 1709-1800. N.P.: 1904. V. 43

Natick Dictionary. Washington: 1903. V. 46

TRUMBULL, JOHN 1756-1843

A Catalogue of a Most Superb and Distinguished Collection of Italian, French, Flemish, and Dutch Pictures, a Selection Formed with Peculiar Taste and Judgment by John Trumbull . . . London: 1797. V. 41

Catalogue of Paintings by Colonel Trumbull, Including Eight Subjects of the American Revolution . . . New Haven: 1835. V. 38; 40

The Poetical Works. Hartford: 1820. V. 45

The Progress of Dulness, Part First; or, the Rare Adventures of Tom Brainless, Shewing What His Father and Mother Said of Him . . . New Haven: 1773. V. 46

TRUMBULL, LEVI R.

History of Industrial Paterson. Being a compendium of the establishment, growth & present status of Paterson, N.J., of the silk, cotton, flax, locomotive, iron & miscellaneous industries. Paterson: 1882. V. 37; 38; 41

TRURAN, W.

The Iron Manufacture of Great Britain, Theoretically and Practically Considered . . . London: 1865. V. 44

TRURAN, WILLIAM

The Iron Manufacture of Great Britain, Theoretically and Practically Considered. London: 1855. V. 37; 45

TRUSLER, JOHN

Chronology; or, the Historian's Vade-Mecum. London: 1782. V. 44

The Difference Between Words, Esteemed Synonymous, in the English Language. Dublin: 1776. V. 43

The Habitable World, or the Present State of People in All Parts of the Globe, from North to South . . . London: 1788-97. V. 40; 46

Hogarth Moralized . . . London: 1768. V. 46

Hogarth Moralized. London: 1831. V. 46

The Honours of the Table, or Rules for Behaviour During Meals. London: 1788. V. 38; 40

The Honours of the Tables, or Rules for Behaviour During Meals . . . Bath: 1805. V. 46

The London Adviser and Guide: containing every instruction and information useful and necessary to persons living in London, and coming to reside there . . . London: 1786. V. 37

Modern Times; or, the Adventures of Gabriel Outcast. Dublin: 1785. V. 45

Poetic Endings; or, a Dictionary of Rhymes, Single and Double . . . London: 1783. V. 42; 45

Progress of Man and Society. London: 1791. V. 37; 46

Proverbs Exemplified, and Illustrated by Pictures from Real Life. London: 1790. V. 42

A System of Etiquette. Bath: 1820. V. 41

The Tablet of Memory, or Historian's Guide . . . Dublin: 1782. V. 42

The Works of Mr. Mogarth Moralized. London: 1840? V. 39

TRUSS, CHARLES

Considerations on the Present State of the Navigation of the River Thames, from Maidenhead to Isleworth, and Also on the Utility and Advantage of a Navigable Canal, from Boulter's Lock . . . to Isleworth . . . London?: 1791. V. 41

TRUSSLER, JOHN

The Economist. London: 1781. V. 38

TRUTH Christmas Numbers. London: 1892-1912. V. 40

THE TRUTH of the Case: or, Canning and Squires Fairly Opposed. London: 1753. V. 46

TRUTH Opposed to Fiction. Or, an Authentic and Impartial Review of the Life of the Late Honourable the Earl of Barrymore. London: 1793. V. 43; 45

THE TRUTH Seeker Company's Catalogue of Freethought Works. New York: 1925. V. 40

TRUTH, SOJOURNER

Narrative of Sojourner Truth, a Northern Slave, Emancipated from Bodily Servitude by the State of New York in 1828. Boston: 1850. V. 39

Narative of Sojourner Truth: a Bondswoman of Olden Time with a History of Her Labors and Correspondence . . . Boston: 1875. V. 45

TRUTH Triumphant; or, the Genuine Account of the Whole Proceedings Against Elizabeth Canning, Tried and Convicted of Perjury, at the Sessions House in the Old Bailey, Tuesday, May 7. London: 1754. V. 46

TRUTH Will Out! The Foul Charges of the Tories Against the Editor of the Aurora Repelled by Positive Proof and Plain Truth and His Base Calumniators Put to Shame. Philadelphia: 1798. V. 45

TRUXTON, THOMAS

Remarks, Instructions and Examples Relating to the Latitutde and Longitude; Also, the Variation of the Compass, &c . . . Philadelphia: 1794. V. 41

THE TRVE Copies of Svndrie Letters Concerning the Affaires of Bohemia. N.P.: 1620. V. 38; 44

THE TRYAL of Spencer Cowper, Esq. John Marson, Ellis Stevens and William Rogers, Gent . . . for the Murther of Mrs. Sarah Stout, a Quaker.. London: 1699. V. 44

THE TRYAL of Tho. Pilkington, Esq. Samuel Shute, Esq., Sheriffs, Henry Cornish, Alderman. Ford Lord Grey of Werk. Sir Tho. Player, Knt. Chamberlain of London, Slingsby Bethel Esq. (& 8 others) for the Riot at Guild-Hall, on Midsomer Day, 1682 . . . London: 1683. V. 44

TRYON, GEORGE W.

Structural and Systematic Conchology: an Introduction to the Study of the Mollusca. Philadelphia: 1882. V. 41

TRYON, R. M.

Ferns and Allied Plants with Special Reference to Tropical America. New York: 1982. V. 46

TRYON, THOMAS

Concerning Cats. San Francisco: 1959. V. 41

A New Art of Brewing Beer, Ale and Other Sorts of Liquors. London: 1691. V. 41

A New Method of Educating Children. London: 1695. V. 37

The Way to Health, Long Life and Happiness: Or, A Discourse of Temperance. London: 1691. V. 42

TRYPANIS, C. A.

The Elegies of a Glass Adonis. 1967. V. 38; 46

The Elegies of a Glass Adonis. New York: 1967. V. 39; 40

The Elegies of a Glass Adonis . . . With a Typographical Note by Will Carter. New York: (1967). V. 37

Medieval and Modern Greek Poetry: an Anthology. Oxford: 1951. V. 43

TSA TOKE, MONORE

The Peyote Ritual: Visions and Descriptions of Monore Tsa Toke. San Fransico: 1957. V. 38; 40; 41

TSCHICHOLD, JAN

Catalogue of the Egyptian Hieroglyphic Printing Type from Matrices Owned and Controlled by Dr. Alan Gardiner. Oxford: 1928. V. 40

Designing Books. New York: 1950. V. 41; 43; 44

TSCHICHOLJ, JAN

Hu-Cheng-Pen. A Chinese Wood-Engraver and Picture Printer. London: 1953. V. 46

TSCHIRNHAUS, EHRENFRIED WALTHER VON

Medicina Mentis, Sive Tentamen Genuinae Logicae, in Qua Disseritur de Methodo Detegendi Incognitas Veritates. Amsterdam: 1687-6. V. 40

Medicina Mentis, Sive Tentamen Genuinae Logicae, in Qua Disseritur de Methodo Detegendi Incognitas Veritates. Amsterdam: 1687-86. V. 42

TSCHUDI, J. J. VON

Travels in Peru, During the Years 1838-1842. London: 1847. V. 41

TSCHUDIN, W. F.

The Ancient Paper-Mills of Basle and Their Marks. Hilversum: 1958. V. 38; 41

TSENG, C. K.

Common Seaweeds of China. Beijing: 1983. V. 37

T'SERSTEVENS, A.

A la Danseuse. Paris: 1925. V. 38

TSOHSIN, CHENG

Synopsis of the Avifauna of China. 1987. V. 39

TSUDA, NORITAKE

Handbook of Japanese Art. Tokyo: 1935. V. 38; 41

TSUKADA, E.

Butterfiles of the South East Asian Islands. Volume I, Papilionidae. Tokyo: 1982. V. 37; 38

Butterflies of the South East Asian Islands: Volume 4: Nymphalidae. Tokyo: 1986. V. 37

TUBBS, E. M.

The New Hampshire Kitchen, Fruit and Floral Gardener. Peterboro: 1852. V. 42

TUBBY, A. H.

Deformities Including Diseases of the Bones and Joints. London: 1912. V. 42

Modern Methods in the Surgery of Paralyses with Special Reference to Muscle-Grafting, Tendon Transplantation & Arthrodesis. London: 1903. V. 42

TUBERVILLE, A. S.

Johnson's England, an Account of the Life and Manners of His Age. Oxford: 1933. V. 39

Johnson's England, an Account of the Life and Manners of His Age. Oxford: 1952. V. 39

TUCKER, ABRAHAM 1705-1774

An Abridgment of the Light of Nature Pursued, by Abraham Tucker, Esq. London: 1807. V. 39

The Light of Nature Pursued. London: 1805. V. 42; 43; 45

The Light of Nature Pursued. London: 1842. V. 38

TUCKER, ALAN

In Line, the Poems and In Line, the Collages. Stroud: 1988. V. 45

TUCKER, ALFRED R.

Eighteen Years in Uganda and East Africa. London: 1908. V. 42

TUCKER, B.

Observations on, a Pamphlet Which Has Been Privately Circulated, Said to be 'A' Concise Statement of Facts, and the Treatment Experienced by Sir Home Popham . . . London: 1805. V. 42

TUCKER, BEVERLEY

The Partisan Leader. Richmond: 1862. V. 38

TUCKER, CORINNE

Hawthorne Dale, and Miscellaneous Sketches, Chiefly Masonic. Chicago: 1869. V. 42

TUCKER, ELIZABETH S.

Little Grownups. London: 1897. V. 41; 46

Little Grown-Ups. London: 1897. V. 46

TUCKER, EPHRAIM W.

Five Months in Labrador and Newfoundland, During the Summer of 1838. Concord: 1839. V. 37; 45

TUCKER, GEORGE

Letters from Virginia. Baltimore: 1816. V. 43

Progress of the United States in Population and Wealth in Fifty Years, As Exhibited by the Decennial Census. New York: 1843. V. 38

The Theory of Money and Banks Investigated. Boston: 1839. V. 43

The Valley of Shenandoah; or Memoirs of the Graysons. New York: 1824. V. 40

TUCKER, GILBERT NORMAN

The Naval Service of Canada: Its Official History. Ottawa: 1952. V. 37; 44

TUCKER, J. C.

To the Golden Goal and Other Sketches. San Francisco: 1895. V. 37; 40

TUCKER, JOHN GOULSTON PRICE

A Narrative of the Operations of a Small British Force Under the Command of Brigadier-General Sir Samuel Auchmuty . . . London: 1807. V. 43

TUCKER, JOSIAH 1712-1799

A Brief Essay on the Advantages and Disadvantates Which Respectively Attend France and Great Britain . . . London: 1749. V. 41; 45

A Brief Essay on the Advantages and Disadvantages Which Respectively Attend France and Great Britain, with Regard to Trade. London: 1750. V. 41

A Brief Essay on the Advantages and Disadvantages Which Respectively Attend France and Great Britain with Regard to Trade. London: 1753. V. 39; 42

The Case of the Importation of Bar-Iron, from Our Own Colonies of North America . . . London: 1756. V. 37

Cui Bono? or, an Inquiry, What Benefits Can Arise Either to the English or the Americans, the French, Spaniards, or Dutch, from the Greatest Victories, or Successes, in the Present War? Glocester: (sic) 1781. V. 39

Four Tracts on Political and Commercial Subjects. Glocester: 1774. V. 42; 45

Four Tracts, on Political and Commercial Subjects. Gloucester: 1776. V. 38

Four Letters on Important National Subjects, Adressed to the Right Honourable the Earl of Shelburne . . . Glocester: 1783. V. 37

An Humble Address and Earnest Appeal to Those Respectable Personages in Great Britain and Ireland, Who, By Their Great and Permanent Interest in Landed Property, Their Liberal Education, Elevated Rank and Enlarged Views . . . Glocester: 1775. V. 38; 39; 40; 41

A Letter to Edmund Burke . . . in Answer to His Printed Speech, Said to be Spoken in the House of Commons on the Twenty-Second of March 1775. Glocester: 1775. V. 45

Letters to the Rev. Dr. Kippis Occasioned by His Treatise Intituled A Vindication of the Protestant Dissenting Ministers wit Regard to Their Late Application to Parliament. Glocester: 1773. V. 38

Reflections on the Expediency of a Law for the Naturalisation of Foreign Protestants. London: 1751-52. V. 38

Reflections on the Present Low Price of Coarse Wools, Its Immediate Causes and Its Probable Remedies. London: 1782. V. 37

A Series of Answers to Certain Popular Objections, Against Separating from the Rebellious Colonies, and Discarding Them Entirely . . . Glocester: 1776. V. 41

Tract V. The Respective Pleas and Arguments of the Mother Country, and of the Colonies, Distinctly Set Forth . . . Glocester: 1775. V. 42

A Treatise Concerning Civil Government, in Three Parts. London: 1781. V. 42

TUCKER, NATHANIEL

The Anchoret; a Poem. London: 1776. V. 37; 40; 42

The Bermudian: a Poem. Hull: 1808. V. 40

TUCKER, NATHANIEL B.

The Partisan Leader . . . Richmond: 1862. V. 43; 45

TUCKER, NATHANIEL BEVERLEY

George Balcombe. New York: 1836. V. 42; 43

TUCKER, PATRICK

Riding the High Country. Caldwell: 1933. V. 44

TUCKER, POMEROY

Origin, Rise and Progress of Mormonism Biography of Its Founders and History of the Church. New York: 1867. V. 39

TUCKER, S.

The Rainbow in the North. London: 1854. V. 40

TUCKER, ST. GEORGE 1752-1827

A Dissertation on Slavery; with a Proposal for the Gradual Abolition Of It, in the State of Virginia. Philadelphia: 1796. V. 42

The Probationary Odes of Jonathan Pindar, Esq. Cousin of Peter's and Candidate for the Post of Poet Laureat of the C.U.S. Philadelphia: 1796. V. 39

TUCKER, ST. GEORGE 1752-1827 continued

The Southern Cross Song. Richmond: 1863. V. 39

TUCKER, SARA JONES

Indian Vilalges of the Illinois Country. Springfield: 1942. V. 42

TUCKER, SARAH cc. 1859

Abbeokuta; or, Sunrise within the Tropics. London: 1853. V. 38; 41; 43

The Rainbow in the North: a Short Account of the First Establishment of Christianity in Rupert's Land by the Church of the Missionary Society. New York: 1854. V. 45

South Indian Sketches: Containing a Short Account of Some of the Missionary Stations, Connected with the Church Missionary Society in Southern India. London: 1842-43. V. 39

TUCKER, W.

Prison Planet. 1947. V. 44

TUCKER, WILLIAM

The Family Dyer and Scourer. Philadelphia: 1830. V. 39; 44

The Family Dyer and Scourer. Hartford: 1831. V. 42

The Family Dyer and Scourer. Philadelphia: 1831. V. 41

TUCKER, WRIGHT

An Inaugaral Dissertation on the Operation of Cold, Submitted to the Examination . . . of the University of Pennsylvania. Philadelphia: 1806. V. 37

TUCKERMAN, AFLRED

Index to the Literature of the Spectroscope. Washington: 1888-1902. V. 38; 40; 42

TUCKERMAN, E.

Genera Lichenum: an Arrangement of the North American Lichens. Amherst: 1872. V. 37

TUCKERMAN, EDWARD

Collected Lichenological Papers. V. 39

Synopsis of the North American Lichens. Boston & New Bedford. V. 39

TUCKERMAN, FREDERICK

Amherst Academy A New England School of the Past 1814-1861. Amherst: 1929. V. 45

TUCKERMAN, HENRY T.

The Life of Silas Talbot, a Commodore in the navy of the United States. New York: 1850. V. 46

TUCKERMAN, SAMUEL PARKMAN 1819-1890

The Episcopal Harp. Boston: 1844. V. 40

TUCKETT, ELIZABETH

Beaten Tracks or Pen and Pencil Sketches in Italy. London: 1866. V. 45

TUCKETT, FRANCIS

A Journey in the United States in the Years 1829 and 1830. Plymouth: 1976. V. 41

TUCKEY, J. H.

An Account of a Voyage to Establish a Colony at Port Philip in Bass's Strait, on teh South Coast of New South Wales, In His Majesty's Ship Calcutta, in the Years 1802-3-4. London: 1805. V. 41

TUCKEY, JAMES KINGSTON

Narrative of an Expedition to Explore the River Zaire, Usually Called the Congo in 1816 . . . London: 1818. V. 37; 43; 46

TUDOR-CRAIG, A.

Catalogue of Contents of the Museum at Freemasons' Hall. London: 1938. V. 38; 39

TUDOR-CRAIG, ALGERNON

Armorial Porcelain of the Eighteenth Century. London: 1925. V. 42; 46

Catalogue of Contents of the Museum at Freemason's Hall in the Possession of the United Grand Lodge of England. (with) Catalogue of Portraits and Prints . . . (and) Catalogue of Manuscripts and Library. London: 1938. V. 45

Catalogue of Contents of the Museum at Freemason's Hall in the Possession of the United Grand Lodge of England. London: (1938). V. 37

TUDOR, JOHN

Deacon Tudor's Diary, or 'Memorandoms (sic) from 1709, &c. by John Tudo to 1775 and 1778, 1780 and to '93. Boston: 1896. V. 46

TUDOR, TASHA

A is for Annabelle. New York: 1954. V. 46

Becky's Christmas. New York: 1961. V. 46

Edgar Allan Crow. New York: 1953. V. 38

Linsey Woolsey. New York: 1946. V. 38

The Springs of Joy. Chicago: 1979. V. 41

A Tale for Easter. New York: 1941. V. 38

Tasha Tudor Greeting Card Album. 1958. V. 42

Tudor's Favorite Stories. Philadelphia: 1965. V. 46

TUDOR, WILLIAM

Gebel Teir. Boston: 1829. V. 43

Letters on the Eastern STates. New York: 1820. V. 39

The Life of James Otis, of Massachusetts . . . Boston: 1823. V. 46

Miscellanies. Boston: 1821. V. 44

TUER, ANDREW W.

The Follies and Fashions of Our Grandfathers. London: 1886/7. V. 43

TUER, ANDREW WHITE

Bartollozzi and His Works. London: 1885. V. 37; 41

The Follies and Fashions of Our Grandfathers (1807). London: 1886/7. V. 45

Forgotten Children's Books. London: 1898-9. V. 38; 41

History of the Horn Book. London: 1896. V. 38; 39; 41; 46

History of the Horn Book. London: 1897. V. 38; 39

History of the Horn Book. New York: 1978. V. 39

London Cries. London: 1883. V. 38; 41

London Cries . . . London: 1885. V. 44

Luxurious Bathing: a Sketch. London: 1879. V. 42

1,000 Quaint Cuts from Books of Other Days. London: 1896. V. 38; 45

Pages and Pictures from Forgotten Children's Books. London: 1898-99. V. 37; 39; 42; 44

Quads within Quads For Authors, Editors, and Devils. London: 1984. V. 41

Stories from Old Fashioned Children's Books. London: 1899-1900. V. 44

TUFNELL, EDWARD CARLETON

Character, Object and Efforts of Trades' Unions . . . London: 1834. V. 43

TUFNELL, OLGA

Lachish IV (Tell ed Duweir). The Bronze Age. London: 1958. V. 44

TUFTS, JAMES

A Tract Descriptive of Montana Territory with a Sketch of Its Mineral and Agricultural Resources. New York: 1865. V. 37; 40; 41; 42; 43

TUFTS, MARSHALL

Arcana of Nature: a New Theory and Popular Explanation of the Causes of the More Mysterious, Though General and Fundamental, Pehnomena of the Physical world. Lexington: 1833. V. 45

Shores of Vespucci. Lexington: 1833. V. 39; 40

TUGWELL, GEORGE

The North-Devon Scenery-Book. 1863. V. 38; 43

TUGWELL, LT. COL.

History of the Bombay Pioneers. London: 1938. V. 42; 45; 46

TUKE, DANIEL HACK 1827-1895

Illustrations of the Influence of the Mind Upon the Body in Health and Disease. London: 1884. V. 43

Illustrations fo the Influence of the Mind upon the Body in Health and Disease, Designed to Elucidate the Action of the Imagination. Phildelphia: 1873. V. 37

Insanity in Ancient and Modern Life . . . London: 1878. V. 43

Sleep Walking and Hypnotism. London: 1884. V. 45; 46

Sleep-Walking and Hypnotism. London: 1884. V. 42

TUKE, SAMUEL

The Adventures of Five Hours. London: 1663. V. 37; 40; 44; 46

The Adventures of Five Hours. London: 1704. V. 45

Description of the Retreat, an Institution Near York, for Insane Persons of the Society of Friends. Philadelphia: 1813. V. 43

Description of the Retreat, an Institution Near York, for Insane Persons of the Society of Friends. York: 1813. V. 39; 45

Memoirs of the Life of Stepehn Crisp, With Selections from His Works. York: 1824. V. 45

TULASNE, L. R.

Selecta Fungorum Carpologia. London: 1931. V. 46

Selecta Fungorum Carpologia. Oxford: 1931. V. 37

TULL, J.

Horse-Hoeing Husbandry. London: 1751. V. 38

TULL, JETHRO

The Horse-Hoing Husbandry . . . (with) A Supplement . . . London: 1733, 1740. V. 42

Horse-Hoeing Husbandry: or, an Essay on the Principles of Vegetation and Tillage. London: 1762. V. 39

The Horse-Hoeing Husbandry. London: 1829. V. 37; 41; 43

TULL, JETHRO continued

The Horse-Hoing Husbandry. London: 1743. V. 37

TULLEY, SAMUEL

Life of . . . Who was executed at South-Boston, Dec. 10, 1812 for Piracy. written by Himself. Boston: 1812. V. 37

TULLIDGE, EDWARD W.

History of Salt Lake City. Salt Lake City: 1888. V. 42

Life of Brigham Young; or, Utah and Her Founders. New York: 1876. V. 42

Life of Brigham Young; or, Utah and Her Founders. New York: 1877. V. 42

The Western Galaxy. Salt Lake City: 1888. V. 42

The Women of Mormondom. New York: 1877. V. 42

TULLOCH, JOHN

Rational Theology and Christian Philosophy in England in the Seventeenth century . . . Edinburgh: 1874. V. 39; 40

TULLY, JIM

Beggards of Life. New York: 1924. V. 44

Emmett Lawler. New York: 1922. V. 38; 43; 46

TULLY, MISS

Letters Written During a Ten Years' Residence at the Court of Tripoli . . . London: 1819. V. 43

TULLY, RICHARD

Letters Written During a Ten Years' Residence at the Court of Tripoli . . . London: 1819. V. 38; 42

A Narrative of a Ten Year's Residence at Tripoli in Africa. London: 1816. V. 39

Narrative of a Ten Year's Residence at Tripoli in Africa . . . London: 1817. V. 38; 40; 46

TULLY, SAMUEL

The Life of Samuel Tully, Who Was Executed at South-Boston, Dec. 10, 1812, for Piracy. Boston: 1812. V. 42

A Report of the Trial of Samuel Tulley (sic) and John Dalton, on an Indictment for Piracy, Committed January 21st, 1812. Boston: 1812. V. 41

TULP, NICOLAS

Observarionum Medicarum. Amsterdam: 1641. V. 38

TUMBLETY, FRANCIS

A Few Passages in the Life of Dr. Francis Tumblety, the Indian Herb Doctor, Including His Experience in the Old Capitol Prison, to Which He was Consigned, With a Wanton Disregard to Justice and Liberty. Cincinnati: 1866. V. 37; 38; 40

THE TUNBRIDGE-MISCELLANY: Consisting of Poems, etc. Written at Tunbridge Wells, in the Year 1713. London: 1713. V. 41

THE TUNBRIDGE Wells Guide. Tunbridge Wells: 1834. V. 39

TUNDAL'S VISION

The Visions of Tundale; Together with Metrical Moralizations and Other Fragments of Early Poetry. Edinburgh: 1843. V. 44; 46

TUNIS, JOHN R.

American Girl. New York: 1930. V. 44

TUNISON, H. C.

Tunison's Peerless Universal Atlas of the World. New York: 1896. V. 45

TUNNARD, WILLIAM H.

A Southern Record, the History of the Third Louisiana Infantry Containing a Complete Record of the Campaigns in Arkansas and Missouri. Baton Rouge: 1866. V. 42; 46

TUNNICLIFFE, C. F.

Bird Portraiture. London: 1945. V. 45

Mereside Chronicle. London: 1948. V. 38; 39; 40; 44; 46

Shorelands Summer Diary. London: 1952. V. 38; 40; 42; 43; 44; 45; 46

TUNSTALL, CUTHBERT

De Arte Supputandi Libri Quatuor. Paris: 1538. V. 40

TUNSTALL, JAMES

Lectures on Natural and Revealed Religion, Read in the Chapel of St. John's College, Cambridge. London: 1765. V. 37

Observations on the Present Collection of Epistles Between Cicero and M. Brutus . . . London: 1744. V. 40

TUNSTALL, MARMADUKE

Ornithologia Britannica. London: 1771. V. 39

TUNSTALL, WILLIAM

Ballads and Some Other Occasion Poems. London: 1716. V. 46

TUOMEY, HONORIA

History of Sonoma County, California. San Francisco: 1926. V. 40

TUPINIER, M.

Observations on the Dimensions of the Ships of the Line and Frigates in the French Navy. London: 1830. V. 46

TUPPER, CHARLES HIBBERT

Supplement to the Life and Letters of the Right Hon. Sir Charles Tupper. Toronto: 1925. V. 43

TUPPER, F. B.

The Life and Correspondence of Major-General Sir Isaac Brock, K.B. Interspersed with notices of the Celebrated Indian Chief. London: 1845. V. 38

TUPPER, FERDINAND BROCK

Family Records . . . Guernsey: Ptd. & Pub. by: 1845. V. 43

TUPPER, MARTIN FAQUAHAR 1810-1889

Proverbial Philosophy. (First and Second Series). London: 1867. V. 39

TUPPER, MARTIN FARQIAJAR 1810-1889

Proverbial Philosophy. London: 1857. V. 37

TUPPER, MARTIN FARQUAHAR 1810-1889

Illustrative Tales. London: 1853. V. 40

A Modern Pyramid: To Commemorate a Septuagint of Worthies. London: 1839. V. 41

Proverbial Philosophy. London: 1838. V. 38

Proverbial Philosophy. Boston: 1851. V. 38; 40

Proverbial Philosophy. London: 1854. V. 38

Philosophie Proverbiale. London: 1851. V. 37

Sacra Poesis. London: 1832. V. 39

Stephen Langton. London: 1858. V. 39; 40

TURBAYNE, A. A.

Alphabets and Numerals Designed and Drawn by A. a. Turbayne. London: 1904. V. 40

TURBERVILLE, A. S.

English Men and Manners in the Eighteenth Century. Oxford: 1926. V. 46

Johnson's England. Oxford: 1933. V. 45; 46

Johnson's England. Oxford: 1965. V. 43

TURBERVILLE, H.

A Manuel of Controversies; Clearly Demonstrating the Truth of Catholique Religion.. Doawy: 1654. V. 44

TURBILLY, LOUIS FRANCOIS HENRI DE MENON, MARQUIS DE 1712-1776

A Discourse on the Cultivation of Waste and Barren Lands. London: 1762. V. 38; 42; 46

TURBYFILL, MARK

The Living Frieze. Evanston: 1921. V. 44

TURCICI Imperii Status, Seu Discursus Varii de Rebus Turcarum. Leyden: 1630. V. 37

TURELL, EBENEZER

The Life and Character of Rev. Benjamin Colman, D.D. Late of a Church in Boston New England, Who Deceased Aug. 29th 1747. Boston: 1749. V. 43; 44

THE TURF. London: 1831. V. 39

TURGENEV, IVAN

The Novels. New York: 1906-13. V. 38

TURGENEV, IVAN SERGEEVICH 1818-1883

Dimitri Roudine, Suivi du Journal d'un Homme de Trop. Paris: 1862. V. 43

Fathers and Sons. New York: 1867. V. 43

The Novels and Stories. New York: 1903. V. 38; 42

The Novels and Stories of . . . New York: 1903-04. V. 46

Novels and Stories. London: 1905. V. 42

Novels and Stories. New York: 1923. V. 39

Poems in Prose. Boston: 1883. V. 42

Russian Life in the Interior . . . Edinburgh: 1855. V. 46

Virgin Soil. New York: 1877. V. 39; 46

Virgin Soil. London: 1878. V. 42

The Works. New York: 1904. V. 41

TURGOT, MICHEL ETIENNE

Plan de Paris. Paris: 1739. V. 43

TURISANUS

Plusquam Commentum in Microtechni Galeni. Venetiis: 1517. V. 38

TURLEY, EDWARD ASTBURY

First Lines of Education: a Course of Four Lectures. Worcester: 1839. V. 43; 46

TURLINGTON, ROBERT

By Virtue of the King's Patent, Turlington's Balsam of Life Being a Specific Remedy for the Stone, Gravel, Cholic, Vomitting, and Spitting of Blood, and Other Inward Weaknesses and Decays . . . London: 1755. V. 40

TURNBRIDGE Epistles, from Lady Margaret to the Countess of B**. London: 1767. V. 40

TURNBULL, DAVID

Travels in the West Cuba; with Notices of Porto Rico, and the Slave Trade. London: 1840. V. 42; 45; 46

TURNBULL, GAEL

As From a Fleece; a Long Poem. 1990. V. 45

As From a Fleece. London: 1990. V. 45

TURNBULL, GEORGE

A Curious Collection of Ancient Paintings. London: 1744. V. 40; 41; 46

Observations Upon Liberal Education, In All Its Branches . . . London: 1742. V. 43

TURNBULL, JOHN

Turnbull's Voyage. A Voyage Round the World in the Years 1800, 1801, 1802, 1803 and 1804, in Which the author Visited the Principal Islands in the Pacific Ocean, and the English Settlements of Port Jackson and Norfolk Island. London: 1805. V. 40

A Voyage Round the World, in the Years 1800, 1801, 1802, 1803 and 1804. Philadelphia: 1810. V. 38

A Voyage Round the World in the Years 1800, 1801, 1802, 1803 and 1804. London: 1813. V. 38; 40; 41; 42; 43

TURNBULL, P.

A Cursory View of the Ancient and Present State of the Fieffs, Or Tenures, In Both Parts of the United Kingdom of Great Britain. London: 1747. V. 41

TURNBULL, PATRICK

Analogia Legum; or, a View of the Institutes of the Laws of England and Scotland, Set One Against the Other (etc.) London: 1725. V. 45

TURNBULL, ROBERT J.

A Visit to the Philadelphia Prison; being an accurate and particular Account of the Wise and Humae Administration adopted in every Part of that Building; containing also an Account of the gradual reformation and present improved . . . Phildelphia: 1797. V. 37

TURNBULL, THOMAS

T. Turnbull's Travels from the United States Across the Plains to California. Madison: 1914. V. 37; 40; 42

TURNBULL, WILLIAM

An Essay on the Air-Pump and Atmospheric Railway . . . London: 1847. V. 38; 46

A Treatise on the Strength, Flexure and Stiffness of Cast Iron Beams and Columns, Shewing Their Fitness to Resist Transverse Strains, Torsion, Compression, Tension and Impulsion . . . London: 1832. V. 44

TURNBULL, WILLIAM BARCLAY DAVID DONALD 1811-1863

The Romances of Sir Guy of Warwick and Rembrun His Son. Edinburgh: 1840. V. 44

THE TURNCOATS. London: 1750? V. 41; 45

TURNEBUS, ADRIANUS

Adversariorum Tomi III. Basel: 1581. V. 37

TURNER, A. A.

Villas on the Hudson. New York: 1860. V. 39

TURNER, A. J.

The Time Machine. Rockford: 1984-85. V. 43

TURNER & FISHER

Catalogue of Plays, Song Books and Juvenile Works, Offered to the Trade by Turner and Fisher, at Their Dramatic World and Song Repository, Almanack and Toy Book Warehouse, 52 Chatham Street, New York. New York: 1840. V. 40

TURNER, C.

An Inquiry into the Revenue, Credit and Commerce of France. London: 1742. V. 45

TURNER, CHARLES QUINCY

Yosemite Valley through the Stereoscope. New York: et al: 1908. V. 46

TURNER, CHIPMAN P.

The Pioneer Period of Western New York. Buffalo: 1885? V. 42

TURNER, DANIEL 1667-1741

The Art of Surgery. London: 1722. V. 38; 42; 45

The Art of Surgery. London: 1736. V. 44

De Morbo Gallico. A Treatise of the French Diseases published above 200 years past, by Sir Ulrich Hutten..Now again revised and recommended to the Press . . . and letter to Mr. James Fern, Surgeon . . . London: 1730. V. 37

A Discourse Concerning Fevers. In Two Letters to a Young Physician. London: 1739. V. 41

Letters Religious and Moral . . . London: 1766. V. 41; 43

De Morbis Cutaneis. London: 1736. V. 42; 45

De Morbo Gallico. A Treatise of the New French Diseases Published Above 200 Years Past, by Sir Ulrich Hutten. London: 1730. V. 38

Siphylis. London: 1732. V. 39; 40; 42; 43; 46

The United States Practical Receipt Book . . . Philadelphia: 1847. V. 45

TURNER, DAWSON 1775-1858

Account of a Tour in Normandy . . . London: 1820. V. 41; 44

The Botanist's Guide through England and Wales. London: 1805. V. 38

Catalogue of a Large and Highly Curious Collection of Autographs and Mss . . . , Duplicates & surplus samples . . . . From the Celebrated Collections of . . . London: 1860. V. 40

Fuci Sive Plantarum Fucorum Generi . . . Fuci . . . London: 1809. V. 42; 44

Muscologia Hibernica Spicilegium. Yarmouth: 1804. V. 43

Sketch of the History of Caister Castle, Near yarmouth . . . London: 1842. V. 44

TURNER, DECHERD

The Rhemes New Testament. Austin: 1990. V. 46

The Rhemes New Testament . . . Accomapnied by a Leaf from the Original Edition and Other Profitable Illustrations. San Francisco: 1990. V. 45

TURNER, E. B.

Reminiscences of Morris, and History of the Congregational Church . . . Chicago: 1865. V. 44

TURNER, EDWARD R.

The Negro in Pennsylvania Slavery-Servitude-Freedom. 1639-1861. Washington: 1911. V. 42

TURNER, ELIZABETH

The Daisy; or, Cautionary Stories in V(erse) . . . London: 1807. V. 46

TURNER, FRANCIS

Animadversions Upon a Late Pamphlet Entituled The Naked Truth; or the True State of the Primitive Church. London: 1676. V. 41

TURNER, FREDERICK JACKSON 1861-1932

The Character and Influence of the Indian Trade in Siconsin. Baltimore: 1891. V. 40; 42; 45

The Frontier in American History. New York: 1920. V. 44

The Significance of the Frontier in American History. Washington: 1894. V. 38

The Significance of the Frontier in American History. Ithaca: 1956. V. 38; 39; 40; 44; 45

TURNER, FREDERICK S.

British Opium Policy and Its Results to India and China. London: 1876. V. 42; 43

TURNER, G.

An Inquiry into the Revenue, Credit and Commerce of France. London: 1742. V. 41

TURNER, GEORGE

Nineteen Years in Polynesia. London: 1861. V. 38; 46

TURNER, HENRY GYLES

A History of the Colony of Victoria. London: 1904. V. 41

TURNER, J. A.

Remarks on the Linnaean Orders of Insects. London: 1828. V. 43

TURNER, J. B.

Mormonism in all Ages. New York: 1842. V. 38

TURNER, J. FOX

Sketches; Chiefly Contributed to the 'Manchester Examiner and Times.' Manchester: 1855. V. 41; 42

TURNER, J. HORSFALL

Ancient Bingley; or, Bingley, Its History and Scenery. Bingley: 1897. V. 45

TURNER, JAMES

Memoirs of His Own Life and Times 1632-1670. London: 1829. V. 45

TURNER, JIM

Lost Days. 1981. V. 44

TURNER, JOHN

Pioneers of the West: a True Narrative. Cincinnati: 1903. V. 46

TURNER, JOHN PETER

The North-West Mounted Police 1873-1893. Ottawa: 1950. V. 44

TURNER, JOSEPH MALLORD WILLIAM 1775-1851

An Antiquarian and Picturesque Tour Round the Southern Coast of England. London: 1849. V. 39

The Harbours of England. London. V. 39

The Harbours of England. London: 1856. V. 45

The Harbours of England. London: 1877. V. 39; 44

Liber Fluviorum. London: 1853. V. 37; 39; 40

Liber Fluviorum. London: 1857. V. 38

Turner's Liber Studiorum. London: 1861. V. 46

The Liber Studiorum. London: 1899. V. 44

Picturesque Views on the Southern Coast of England . . . London: 1826. V. 39

Picturesque Views in England and Wales, Reproduced in Permanent Photography with Descriptive and Historical Illustrations. Castles and Abbeys. London: 1873. V. 44; 46

Picturesque Views in England and Wales . . . London: 1832. V. 37

The Rivers of France. London: 1837. V. 41

The Water-Colour Drawings of . . . In the National Gallery . . . with Descriptive Text by T.A. Cook. London: 1904. V. 37

TURNER, LAURENCE

Decorative Plasterwork in Great Britain. London: 1927. V. 40

TURNER, LUCIEN McSHAW

Contributions to the Natural History of Alaska. Washington: 1886. V. 38; 39; 40; 41; 44

Ethnology of the Ungava District, Hudson Bay Territory. By L.M. Turner. (Washington: 1894). V. 37

TURNER, MARGARET

The Gentle Shepherd, a Scotch Pastoral. London: 1790. V. 40

TURNER, MARTHA ANNE

Clara Driscoll, an American Tradition. Austin: 1979. V. 40

TURNER, MARY HONEYMAN TEN EYCK

Into the West. Amarillo: 1938. V. 40

These High Plains. Amarillo: 1941. V. 39

TURNER, MATTHEW

An Account of an Extraordinary Medicinal Fluid Called Aether. Liverpool: 1761. V. 38

TURNER, NICHOLAS

An Essay on Draining and Improving Peat Bogs . . . London: 1774. V. 38

An Essay on Draining and Improving Peat Bogs . . . London: 1784. V. 41

TURNER, ORASMUS

History of the Pioneer Settlement of Phelps and Gorham's Purchase, and Morris' Reserve. Rochester: 1851. V. 44; 46

TURNER, PETER

Comhchruinneach do dh'Orain taghta Ghaidhealach. Edinburgh: 1813. V. 37

TURNER, RICHARD 1753-1788

An Easy Introduction to the Arts and Sciences . . . Dublin: 1783. V. 38

An Easy Introduction to the Arts and Sciences; Being a Short, but Comprehensive System of Useful and Polite Learning, Divided into Lessons. London: 1787. V. 39; 42

An Easy Introduction to the Arts and Sciences . . . London: 1791. V. 46

Universal History, Ancient and Modern. London: 1787. V. 38

TURNER, ROBERT

Maria Stuarta, Regina Scotiae, Dotaria Franciae, Haeres Angliae et Hyberniae, Martyr Ecclesiae, Innocens a Caede Darleana: Vindice Oberto Barnestapolio. Ingolstadt: 1588. V. 45

TURNER, SAMUEL

An Account of an Embassy to the Court of the Teshoo Lama, in Tibet. London: 1800. V. 38

The Conquest of the New Zealand Alps. London: 1922. V. 38

My Climbing Adventures in Four Continents. London: 1911. V. 40; 42; 46

TURNER, SAMUEL BLOIS

Turner Genealogy. London: 1884. V. 42

TURNER, SAMUEL H.

Biographical Notices of Some of the Most Distinguished Jewish Rabbies . . . New York: 1847. V. 42

TURNER, SHARON

The History of the Anglo-Saxons. London: 1823. V. 40

Prolusions on the Present Greatness, of Britain; on Modern Poetry . . . London: 1819. V. 45

The Sacred History of the World, Attempted to be Philosophically Considered in a Series of Letters to a Son. London: 1848. V. 40

A Vindication of the Genuineness of the Ancient British Poems of Aneurin, Taliesin, Llywarch Hen and Merdhin, With Specimens of Poems. London: 1803. V. 37; 40

TURNER, T.

Some Account of Domestic Architecture in England. Oxford and London: 1851/53/59/59. V. 38

TURNER, T. HUDSON

Some Account of Domestic Architecture in England . . . Oxford: 1851. V. 40

Some Account of Domestic Architecture in England from the Conquest to . . . . Henry VIII. London: 1851-59. V. 39

Some Account of the Domestic Architecture in England from the Conquest to the End of the Thirteenth Century, from Richard II to Henry VIII. Oxford: 1851-59. V. 37; 40

Some Account of Domestic Architecture in England, from the Conquest to the End of the Thirteenth Century . . . Oxford and London: 1859-82. V. 41

TURNER, THOMAS

The Case of the Bankers and Their Creditors. London: 1674. V. 41; 45

Narrative of a Journey, Associated with a Fly, from Gloucester to Aberystwith, and from Aberystwith through North Wales July 31st to September 8th 1837. London: 1840. V. 37; 42

TURNER, TIMOTHY G.

Gazetteer of the St. Joseph Valley, Michigan and Indiana with a View of Its Hydraulic and Business Capacities. Chicago: 1867. V. 42

Turner's Directory of the Inhabitants, Institutions and Manufactories of the City of South Bend, Indiana. South Bend: 1873. V. 46

Turner's Guide from the Lakes to the Rocky Mountains. Chicago: 1868. V. 40; 43

TURNER-TURNER, J.

Three Years Hunting and Trapping in America and the Great North West. London: 1888. V. 38; 43

TURNER, WILLIAM

The Ceramics of Swansea and Nantgarw . . . London: 1897. V. 37; 42; 46

A Compleat History of the msot Remarkable Providences, both of Judgement and mercy, Which have Happened in this Present Age . . . To which is added, whatever is Curious in the Works of Nature and Art. London: 1697. V. 37

An Essay Upon the Work of Creation and Providence. London: 1695. V. 41

The History of All Religions in the World. London: 1695. V. 40

Journal of a Tour in the Levant. London: 1820. V. 39

A New Herball, Wherein are Conteyned the Names of Herbes in Greke, Latin, Englysh, Duch, Frenche . . . London: 1562-1568. V. 45

Sound Anatomiz'd, in a Philosophical Essay on Musick. London: 1724. V. 37; 40; 42

Syllabus of a Course of Lectures on Mechanics, Hydrostatics, and Pneumataics. Newcastle-upon-Tyne: 1803. V. 39

William Adams, an Old English Potter, With Some Account of His Family and their Productions. London: 1904. V. 37

THE TURNER'S Companion; Containing Instructions in Concentric, Elliptic and Eccentric Turning . . . Philadelphia: 1902. V. 42

TURNER'S North Carolina Almanac, for the Year of Our Lord 1864. Raleigh: 1863. V. 37

TURNLEY, JOSEPH

The Language of the Eye: the Importance and Dignity of the Eye as Indicative of General Character, Female Beauty and Manly Genius. London: 1856. V. 40

TURNLEY, PARMENAS TAYLOR

Private Letters of Parmenas Taylor Tunrley . . . London: 1863. V. 43

Reminiscences of Parmenas Taylor Turnley from the Cradle to Three Score and Ten. Chicago: 1892. V. 37; 39; 42; 45

TURNOR, EDMUND

Collections for the History of the Town and Soke of Grantham. London: 1806. V. 38; 39; 41; 43; 44

A Short View of the Proceedings of the Several Committees and Meetings Held in Consequence of the Intended Petition to Parliament, from the County of Lincoln, for a Limited Exportation of Wool . . . London: 1782. V. 40; 43

TURNOR, HATTON

Astra Castra; Experiments and Adventures in the Atmosphere. London: 1865. V. 45

TURNOR, LEWIS

History of the Ancient Town and Borough of Hertford. Hertford: 1830. V. 39; 42

TURNPIKES and Toll-Bars. London. V. 44

TUROW, SCOTT

One L. New York: 1977. V. 46

TURPIN DE CRISSE, LANCELOT

Essai sur l'Art de la Guerre. Paris: 1754. V. 42

TURPIN, JEANNETTE

General William J. Palmer. N.P.: n.d. V. 37

TURRILL, CHARLES B.

California Notes. San Francisco: 1876. V. 38; 44; 45

TURRILL, GARDINER STILSON

A Tale of the Yellowstone. Jefferson: 1901. V. 37; 38; 42; 45

TURSTON, JOHN

Religious Emblems, Being a Series of Engravings on Wood, Executed by the Fine Artists in that Line, From Designs Drawn on the Blocks Themselves. London: 1809. V. 40

TURTON, JOHN

The Angler's Manual; or, Fly Fisher's Oracle. London: 1836. V. 39; 40; 43; 46

TURTON, WILLIAM

A Conchological Dictionary of the British Islands. London: 1819. V. 38; 43

A Manual of the Land and Fresh-Water Shells of the British Islands. London: 1831. V. 40

Manual of the Land and Fresh-Water Shells of the British Islands. London: 1860. V. 44

TURZAK, CHARLES

Abraham Lincoln. Chicago: 1933. V. 38

Abraham Lincoln. Biography in Woodcuts. 1933). V. 37

TUSHINGHAM, A. D.

Excavations in Jerusalem 1961-1967. Toronto: 1985. V. 44

TUSON, EDWARD WILLIAM

Myology, Illustrated by Plates. London: 1828. V. 38

A Supplement to Myology . . . London: 1828. V. 42

TUSSAUD, MARIE 1760-1850

Madame Tussaud's Memoirs and Reminiscences of France, Forming an Abridge History of the French Revolution. London: 1838. V. 44

TUSSER, THOMAS

Five Hundred Points of Good Husbandry. London: 1672. V. 38; 40

Five Hundred Points of Good Husbandry. London: 1812. V. 37; 40; 45; 46

Five Hundred Points of Good Husbandry. London: 1931. V. 37; 38; 40; 41; 42

A Selection from Five Hundred Points of Good Husbandry. 1981. V. 40

Tusser Redivivus. London: 1710. V. 37

Tusser Redivivus. London: 1770. V. 37

The United States Practical Receipt Book; or, Complete Book of Reference, for the Manufacturer, Tradesman, Agriculturist, or Housekeeper . . . Philadelphia: 1847. V. 45

TUTCHIN, JOHN

The Mouse Grown a Rat. London: 1702. V. 38

Pomes on Several Occasions. London: 1685. V. 40

The Western Martyrology: or, Bloodoy Assizes . . . Lives, Trials and Dying-Speeches of All Those Eminent Protestants that Suffer'd in the West of England . . . from 1678 . . . London: 1705. V. 38

TUTE, GEORGE

Guide to the Art of Wood Engraving. 1987. V. 40; 45

Leon Underwood: His wood engravings. With an introduction by George Tute. Wakefield: 1986. V. 37

TUTHILL, FRANKLIN

The History of California. San Francisco: 1866. V. 37; 44

The History of California. San Francisco: 1886. V. 45

TUTHILL, LOUIS CAROLINE

History of Architecture, from the Earliest Times . . . Philadelphia: 1848. V. 42; 45

TUTHILL, W. B.

The Suburban Cottage. Its Design and Construction. New York: 1891. V. 42

TUTHILL, WILLIAM B.

Interiors and Interior Details . . . New York: 1882. V. 41

Practical Lessons in Architectural Drawing . . . New York: 1891. V. 45

TUTIN, T. G.

Flora Europeaea. Cambridge: 1964-83. V. 38

Flora Europaea. Volume 1 - Lycopodiaceae to Platanaceae. 1964. V. 39

Flora Europaea. Volume 2 - Rosaceae to Umbelliferae. 1968. V. 39

Flora Europaea. Volume 3 - Diapensia to Myoporaceae. 1972. V. 39

Flora Europaea. Volume 4 - Plataginaceae to Compositae (U Rubiaceae). 1976. V. 39

Flora Europaea. Volume 5 - Alismataceae to Orchidaceae. 1978. V. 39

TUTTLE, CHARLES R.

An Illustrated History of the Dominion of Canada. Montreal: 1877/1879. V. 44

Tuttle's Popular History of the Dominion of Canada, with art illustrations. From the earliest settlement of the British-American colonies to the present time; together with portrait engravings and biographical sketches of the most . . . Montreal: 1877. V. 37

TUTTLE, CHARLES RICHARD

The Golden North: a Vast Country of Inexhaustible Gold Fields, & A Land of Illimitable Cereal & Stockraising Capabilities. Chicago: 1897. V. 37; 39

TUTTLE, CHARLES W.

Capt. John Mason, The Founder of New Hampshire. Boston: 1887. V. 45

Capt. Francis Champernowne, the Dutch Conquest of Acadie, and Other Historical Papers. Boston: 1889. V. 42

TUTTLE, EMERSON

Emerson Tuttle: Fifty Prints. New Haven: 1948. V. 45

TUTTLE, FRANCIS

Report of the Cruise of the U. S. Revenue Cutter Bear and the Overland Expedition for the Relief of the Whalers in the Arctic Ocean, from November 27, 1897, to September 13, 1898. Washington: 1899. V. 41; 43

TUTU, DESMOND

Hope and Suffering: Sermons & Speeches. Johannesburg: 1983. V. 46

TUVIL, DANIEL

The Dove and the Serpent. London: 1614. V. 46

TWEDDELL, JOHN

Remains of the Late John Tweddell, Fellow of Trinity College, Cambridge. London: 1815. V. 38; 42; 44; 45

Remains: a Selection of His Letters . . . London: 1815. V. 43

TWEED, JOHN

Popular Observations on Regimen and Diet. Chelmsford: 1820. V. 38

TWEEDALE, VIOLET

The Veiled Woman. London: 1918. V. 43

TWEEDDALE, ARTHUR, MARQUIS OF

Ornithological Works. London: 1881. V. 37; 38

TWEEDIE, W.

The Arabian Horse: His Country and People. London: 1894. V. 37

TWEEDIE, W. K.

The Rivers and Lakes of Scripture. London: 1857. V. 46

TWELVE Parables of Our Lord, Illustrated and Illuminated. London: 1870. V. 38; 43; 46

TWELVE Southerners. I'll Take My Stand: The South and the Agrarian Tradition. New York: 1930. V. 46

TWELVETREES, W. NOBLE

Concrete-Steel Buildings. London: 1907. V. 44

TWENEY, GEORGE H.

The Washington 89. Seattle: 1989. V. 43

THE TWENTIETH Century Bench and Bar of Pennsylvania. Chicago: 1903. V. 41

THE TWENTIETH Century Peerless Atlas and Pictorial Gazetteer of All Lands. Springfield;: 1901. V. 45

TWENTIETH Century Souvenir of the Fire Department of Seattle. Seattle: 1901. V. 38

TWENTIETH Crime and Mystery Writers. London: 1991. V. 45

TWENTY-FIVE Poems about Trees and Leaves. New York: 1959. V. 37

TWENTY Four Views of Eastbourne. Eastbourne: 1875. V. 41

TWENTY Four Views of Shepton-Mallet, & Neighbourhood. London: 1870. V. 45

TWENTY-FOURTH Anniversary of Society of California Pioneers. San Francisco: 1874. V. 46

TWENTY Scenes from the Works of Dickens. Sydney: 1883. V. 46

TWENTY Tales by Twenty Women from Real Life in Chicago. Chicago: 1903. V. 38

TWICE a Year. New York: 1938-46. V. 42

TWICI, WILLIAM
The Art of Hunting by . . . Huntsman to King Edward the Second. Daventry: 1843. V. 43

THE TWICKENHAM Tales. London: 1861. V. 43

TWIGDEN, B. L.
Pisces Tropicani. Melbourne: 1979. V. 37

TWINE, LAURENCE
The Patterne of Gainefull Adventures Gathered into English. New Rochelle: 1903. V. 43; 44; 46

TWINING, E.
Illustrations of the Natural Orders of Plants, With Groups and Descriptions. London: 1868. V. 37; 38

TWINING, HENRY
On the Elements of Picturesque Scenery, Considered with Reference to Landscape Painting . . . London: 1846. V. 45
On the Philosophy of Painting . . . London: 1849. V. 44

TWINING, LORD
European Regalia. London: 1967. V. 45

TWINING, LOUISA
Symbols and Emblems of Early and Mediaeval Christian Art. London: 1852. V. 38; 40

TWINING, RICHARD 1749-1824
An Answer to the Second Report of the East India Directors, Respecting the Sale and Prices of Tea. London: 1785. V. 45
Observations on the Tea and Window Acts, and on the Tea Trade. London: 1785. V. 39

TWINING, W. J.
Reports upon the Survey of the Boundary Between the Territory of the United States and the Possessions of Great Britain from the Lake of the Woods to the Summit of the Rocky Mountains . . . Washington: 1878. V. 37

TWISDEN, ROGER
An Historical Vindication of the Church of England in Point of Schism. London: 1675. V. 38

TWISS, FRANCIS
A Complete Verbal Index to the Plays of Shakespeare, Adapted to All the Editions. London: 1805. V. 42

TWISS, HORACE
Farewell Address Spoken by Mrs. Siddons, on Leaving the Stage, 29th of June, 1812. London: 1812. V. 42
The Public and Private Life of Lord Chancellor Eldon with Selections from His Correspondence. London: 1844. V. 37; 39

TWISS, RICHARD
An Herocik Answer (in verse) from Richard Twiss. Dublin: 1776. V. 40; 41; 45
A Tour in Ireland in 1775, with a Map and View of the Salmon Leap at Ballyshannon. London: 1776. V. 38
A Trip to Paris In July and August 1792 by Mr. Twiss. Dublin: 1793. V. 41

TWISS, TRAVERS 1809-1897
The Law of Nations Considered as Independent Political Communities. Oxford/London: 1861. V. 38; 40
On Certain Tests of a Thriving Population. London: 1845. V. 43
The Oregon Question Examined. London: 1846. V. 38; 39; 40; 41; 42; 43; 45
The Oregon Territory, Its History and Discovery . . . New York: 1846. V. 41; 45
The Oregon Territory, Its History and Discovery. New York & Philadelphia: 1846. V. 40; 41; 42
The Oregon Question, in Respect to Facts and the Law of Nations. London: 1846. V. 37

TWISSE, WILLIAM
Of the Morality of the Fourth Commandement, as Still in Force to Binde Christians Delivered by Way of Answer to the Translator of Doctor Prideaux His Lecture, Concerning the Doctrine of the Sabbath. London: 1641. V. 41

TWITCHELL, RALPH EMERSON
The History of the Military Occupation of the territory of New Mexico from 1846 to 1851 by the Government of the United States . . . Denver: 1909. V. 37; 41; 42; 45; 46
The Leading Facts of New Mexican History. Cedar Rapids: 1911-17. V. 40
The Leading Facts of New Mexican History. Cedar Rapids: 1911-17. V. 43
Leading Facts of New Mexican History. Alburquerque: 1963. V. 37; 38
The Leading Facts of New Mexican History. Cedar Rapids: 1911. V. 38
Old Santa Fe. The Story of New Mexico's ncient Capital. Santa Fe: 1925. V. 38
The Spanish Archives of New Mexico. Cedar Rapids: 1914. V. 37; 39; 40; 42; 43
The Spanish Archives of New Mexico by R.E. Twitchell. Cedar Rapids: 1914. V. 37

TWITCHETT, JOHN
The Old Derby Pattern Books. Worcester: 1971. V. 42

TWO Centuries of Song; or Lyrics, Madrigals, Sonnets & Other Occasional Verses of the English Poets of the Last Two Hundred Years. London: 1867. V. 43

THE TWO Cottages, or the Contrast Between Industry and Idleness, Truth and Falsehood. London: 1825. V. 41

TWO Epistles on Happiness: to a Young Lady. London: 1754. V. 46

TWO Essays: The One on the Origin of Evil; Wherein the Difficulties Arising From that Consideration, are Reconcciled with the Perfections of God . . . The Other on the Foundation of Morality . . . Newcastle upon Tyne: 1734. V. 42

TWO Letters Addressed to Sir Thomas Charles Bunbury, Member of Parliament for the County of Suffolk, in Feburary 1781 . . . Doncaster: 1782. V. 40

TWO Letters Concerning the Author of the Examiner. London: 1713. V. 42

TWO Letters to a Friend Concerning the Partition Treaty, Vindicating His Majesty, King William, from All Refelctions; and Answering the Arguments of a Late Designing Party, That Were for Surrendering to the French King the Whole Spanish Monarchy. London: 1702. V. 40

TWO Letters to a Friend Concerning the Partition Treaty, Vindicating His Majesty King William from all Reflections; and Answering the Arguments of a Late Designing Party That Were for Surrendering to the French King, the Whole Spanish Monarchy. Dublin: London: 1702. V. 43

TWO New and Curious Essays: I. Concerning the Best Methods of Pruning Fruit-Trees, Whether They are Trained Against Walls . . . II. A Discourse Concerning the Improvement of the Excellent Root the Potatoe . . . London: 1732. V. 41

TWO Papers on the Subject of Taxing the British Colonies in America . . . London: 1767. V. 42

TWO Reports on the Matter of Complaint of Mr. Livius Against Governor Wentworth; the Former a Report of the Board of Trade Recommending the Removal of Said Governor, the Latter a Report of the Privy Council on an Appeal, Wherein the Governor Stands . . . London: 1773. V. 41

TWO Thousand Miles in an Automobile, Being Desultory Narrative of a Trip through New England, New York, Canada and the West. Philadelphia and London: 1902. V. 38

TWO Years Adrift; the Story of a Rolling Stone. N.P.: 1875? V. 39; 45

TWOPENY, WILLIAM
Some Remarks on the Taste and Effects of Collecting Fragments of Ancient Architecture . . . London: 1832. V. 38

TWYMAN, MICHAEL
Lithography, 1800-1850, The Technique of Drawing on Stone in England and France and Their Application in Works of Topography. London: 1970. V. 46
Printing 1770-1970: An Illustrated History of Its Development and Uses in England. London: 1970. V. 38; 40
Printing 1770-1970, an Illustrated History of Its Development and Uses in England. London: 1970. V. 38

TWYNE, JOHN
De Rebvs Albionicis, Britannicis Atqve Anglicis, Commentarium Libri Duo. Londini: 1590. V. 37

TYAN, KENNETH
He That Plays the King: A View of the Theatre. London: (1950). V. 37

TYARD, PONTUS DE

Discovrs dv temps, de l'an, et de ses Parties. Paris: 1578. V. 44

Les Discovrs Philosophiqves de Pontvs de Tyard. Paris: 1587. V. 44

TYAS, ROBERT

Favourite Field Flowers . . . London: 1848. V. 43

Flower and Heraldry. London: 1851. V. 45

The Wild Flowers of England, or Favourite Field Flowers Popularly Described. London: 1860. V. 37

TYERMAN, DANIEL

Journal of Voyages and Travels by Rev. Daniel Tyerman and George Bennet, Esq. Deputed from the London Missionary Society to Visit Their Various Stations in the South Sea Islands, China, India &c. Boston: 1832. V. 40; 43

TYLER, ANNE 1941-

The Accidental Tourist. London: 1985. V. 42

The Accidental Tourist. New York: 1985. V. 37; 39; 41; 43; 44

Breathing Lessons. Franklin Center: 1988. V. 44

Breathing Lessons. New York: 1988. V. 39; 46

Celestial Navigation. New York: 1974. V. 39; 42; 45; 46

Celestial Navigation. London: 1975. V. 41; 42

The Clock Winder. New York: 1972. V. 37; 43; 44

The Clock Winder. London: 1973. V. 38; 40; 41; 42

Dinner at the Homesick Restaurant. New York: 1982. V. 37; 41; 42

Earthly Possessions. New York: 1977. V. 38; 40; 41; 42; 46

If Morning Ever Comes. New York: 1964. V. 42; 43; 44

If Morning Ever Comes. London: 1965. V. 41; 46

Morgan's Passing. London: 1980. V. 41

Morgan's Passing. New York: 1980. V. 41; 42; 44

Morgan's Passing. New York: London: 1980. V. 42

Saint Maybe. New York: 1991. V. 45

Searching for Caleb. New York: 1976. V. 44

Searching for Caleb. New York: 1976. V. 42; 45; 46

A Slipping Down Life. New York: 1970. V. 42; 43; 44; 46

The Tin Can Tree. New York: 1965. V. 42; 44; 45

The Tin Can Tree. London: 1966. V. 38; 42; 44; 46

A Visit with Eudora Welty. Chicago. V. 43

A Visit with Eudora Welty. Chicago: 1980. V. 43; 44; 46

A Visit With Eudora Welty. Chicago: (1980). V. 37

TYLER, DANIEL

A Concise History of the Mormon Battalion in the Mexican War 1846-1847. 1881. V. 42

A Concise History of the Mormon Battalion in the Mexican War 1846-1847. N.P.: 1881. V. 41

A Concise History of the Mormon Battalion in the Mexican War, 1846-1847. Salt Lake City: 1881. V. 42; 43; 45

A Concise History of the Mormon Battalion in the Mexican War, 1846-1847. Salt Lake City: 1882? V. 39

A Concise History of the Mormon Battalion in the Mexican War. 1846-1847. (Salt Lake City°: 1881. V. 37

TYLER, GEORGE W.

History of Bell County. San Antonio: 1936. V. 43

TYLER, J. O.

Shooting in Monmouthshire. 1729-1923. Pontypool: 1923. V. 39; 43

TYLER, JOHN

Message at the Commencement of the 28th Congress (With Accompanying Documents). Washington: 1844. V. 37

Message from the President . . . Proceedings of the Commissioner Appointed to Run the Boundary Line Between the U.S. and the Republic of Texas. Washington: 1842. V. 37

TYLER, JOSIAH

Forty Years Among the Zulus. Boston & Chicago: 1891. V. 42

TYLER, LYON G.

The Letters anfd Times of the Tylers. Richmond: 1884, 1885. V. 38

TYLER, PARKER

Florine Stettheimer - a Life in Art. New York: 1963. V. 44

The Granite Butterfly - a Poem in Nine Cantos. N.P.: 1945. V. 46

Magic and Myth of the Movies. New York: 1947. V. 41

TYLER, RON C.

The Mexican War. A Lithographic Record. Austin: 1973. V. 38

TYLER, ROYALL

The Algerine Captive; or, The Life and Adventures of Doctor Updike Underhill, Six Years a Prisoner Among the Algerines . . . Hartford: 1816. V. 38; 40; 43

A Book of Forms, with Occasional Notes. Brattleboro: 1845. V. 37

The Contrast: a Comedy in Five Acts . . . Boston: 1920. V. 44

The Yankey in London, Being the First Part of a Series of Letters Written by an American Youth, During Nine Months' residence in the City of London. New York: 1809. V. 40; 43

TYLER, S.

Advances in the Biology of Turbellerians and Related Platyhelminthes. 1986. V. 37

TYLER, W. S.

History of Amherst College During Its First Half Century 1821-1871. Springfield: 1873. V. 45

TYLOR, ALFRED

Paris Universal Exhibition. Report on General Metal Work. (with) Supplemental Report. London: 1857. V. 44

TYLOR, ALRED

Colouration in Animals and Plants. London: 1886. V. 42

TYLOR, EDWARD B.

Anahuac; or, Mexico and the Mexicans, Ancient and Modern. London: 1861. V. 37; 38; 39; 45

TYLOR, J. J.

The Tomb of Paheri. London: 1895. V. 40; 42; 44

TYMMS, A. R.

The Art of Illuminating as Practised in Europe from the Earliest Times. London: 1860. V. 37; 38; 39; 40; 41; 43; 44; 45; 46

TYMMS, W. R.

The Art of Illuminating as Practised in Europe from the Earliest Times. London: 1865. V. 38; 39

The Art of Illuminating as Practised in Europe from the Earliest Times. London: 1866. V. 39; 43; 44

The Art of Illuminating as practised in Europe from the Earliest Times. Illustrations by Borders, Initial Letters and Alphabets. (1866). V. 37

TYNAN, KATHARINE

Twenty One Poems by Katharine Tynan. Dundrum: 1907. V. 37

TYNDALE, JOHN WARRE

The Island of Sardinia, including pictures of the manners and customs of the Sardinians, and notes on the antiquities and modern objects of interest in the islands: to which is added some account of the House of Savoy. In Three Volumes. London: 1849. V. 37

TYNDALE, W.

Treatise on Military Equitation. London: 1797. V. 42

TYNDALE, WALTER

An Artist in Italy. London: 1913. V. 42

TYNDALE, WILLIAM d. 1536

The Whole Works of W. Tyndall, John Frith and Doct. Barnes, Three Worthy Martyrs and Principall Teachers of This Churche of England . . . London: 1573. V. 39

TYNDALL, JOHN

Contributions to Molecular Physics in the Domain of Radiant Heat . . . London: 1872. V. 38

Essays on the Floating Matter of the Air in Relation to Putrefaction and Infection. London: 1881. V. 37; 39; 44

Faraday as a Discoverer. London: 1868. V. 38; 40

The Forms of Water in Clouds and Rivers, Ice and Glaciers. London: 1872. V. 40

Fragments of Science of Unscientific People. London: 1871. V. 40; 41

The Glaciers of the Alps. London: 1860. V. 38; 41; 42; 44; 45; 46

The Glaciers of the Alps. Boston: 1861. V. 42; 45

Heat a Mode of Motion. London: 1868. V. 38; 41

Hours of Exercise in the Alps. London: 1871. V. 40

Mountaineering in 1861. London: 1862. V. 41; 43

Notes on Light. London: 1869. V. 45

Notes of a Course of Seven Lectures, on Electrical Phenomena and Theories, Delivered at the Royal Insitution of Great Britain, April 28-June 9, 1870. London: 1870. V. 39

The Optical Condition of the Atmosphere in the Bearings on Putrefaction and Infection. London: 1876. V. 37

Researches on Diamagnetism and Magne-Crystallic Action, Including the Question of Diamagnetic Polarity. London: 1870. V. 38; 40; 45

Researches on Diamagnetism and magne-Crystallic Action Including the Question of Diamagnetic Polarity. London: 1888. V. 40

TYNDALL, JOHN continued

Six Lectures on Light Delivered in America in 1872-1873. London: 1873.
V. 38

The United States Practical Receipt Book. Philadelphia: 1847. V. 40; 42

TYNER, GEORGE

*The Traveller's Guide through Ireland, Being Complete and Accurate
Companion to Capt. Alexnder Taylor's Map of Ireland.* Dublin: 1794. V. 38

TYNG, C. D.

The Stranger in the Tropics . . . New York: 1868. V. 42

TYPOGRAPHIA. An Ode, on Printing. Roanoke: 1926. V. 38; 43

TYPOGRAPHICA. London: 1949-1967. V. 40

A TYPOGRAPHICAL Commonplace Book. New York: 1932. V. 37
A TYPOGRAPHICAL Commonplace Book. Paris: 1932. V. 41

TYPOGRAPHY. London: 1936-39. V. 41

TYRELL, EDWARD

A Chronicle of London from 1809 to 1483 . . . London: 1827. V. 41

TYRELL, H.

*The History of Russia from the Foundation of the Empire to the Wars with
Turkey in 1877-78.* London: 1880. V. 40

TYRELL, HENRY

The History of the War with Russia . . . New York: 1856. V. 43

TYRELL, JAMES

*A Brief Disquisition of the Law of Nature, According to the Principles and
Method Laid Down in the Reverend Dr. Cumberland's* . . . London: 1692.
V. 40

A Brief Enquiry Into the Ancient Constitution and Government of England.
London: 1695. V. 45

TYRRELL, FREDERICK

*A Practical Work on the Diseases of the Eye, and Their Treatment
Medically, Topically and by Operation.* London: 1840. V. 42; 43; 44; 46

TYRRELL, HENRY

The History of the War with Russia. London & New York: 1854-56.
V. 39; 46

*The History of the War with Russia: Giving Full Details of the Operations of
the Allied Armies.* London: 1855-58. V. 39

*The History of the War with Russia; Giving Full Details of the Operations of
the Allied Armies.* London & New York: 1856. V. 40

TYRRELL, J. B.

Documents Relating to the Early History of Hudson Bay. Toronto: 1931.
V. 42; 43; 45

*Journals of Samuel Hearne and Philip Turnor Between the Years 1774 and
1792.* Toronto: 1934. V. 45

TYRRELL, J. W.

Across the Sub-Arctics of Canada . . . London: 1898. V. 44

Across the Sub-Arctics of Canada. Toronto: 1908. V. 43; 44

TYRRELL, JAMES

Bibliotheca Politica. London: 1694. V. 38; 40

*A Brief Disquisition of the Law of Nature, According to the Principles and
Method Laid Down in the Rev. Cumberland's (now Lord Bishop of
Peterborough's) Latin Treatise on that Subject.* London: 1701. V. 43

Patriarcha non Monarcha, the Patriarch Unmonarch'd . . . London: 1681.
V. 37; 46

TYRRELL, JAMES W.

Across the Sub-Arctics of Canada. Halifax: 1897. V. 44

Across the Sub-Arctics of Canada. Toronto: 1897. V. 42

Across the Sub-Arctics of Canada. New York: 1898. V. 44

TYRRELL, ROBERT YELERTON

Kottabos. Dublin: 1870-81. V. 40

TYRWHITT, THOMAS

*A Vindication of the Appendix to the Poems, Called Rowley's, in Reply to
the Answers of othe Dean of Exter, Jacob Bryant, Esquire, and a Third
Anonymous Writer.* London: 1782. V. 38; 41

TYSON, BRYAN

*Mr.------. Dear Sir:---I Hereby Send you a Book Which I Hope . . . to
Arrest the Farther Progress of this Terrible Civil War Now Upon
Us . . . Brower's Mill, N.C.; Sept. 24th, 1862.* Brower's Mill: 1862. V. 39

TYSON, EDWARD

*Orang-outang, Sive Homo Sylvestris; or the Anatomy of a Pygmie
Compared with that of a Monkey, an Ape and a Man.* London: 1699.
V. 46

A Philological Essay Concerning the Pygmies of the Ancients by . . .
London: 1894. V. 39

TYSON, EDWARD WILLIAM

Myology. London: 1828. V. 44

TYSON, JAMES

*A Brief Historical View of the Causes of the Decline of the Commerce of
Nations.* London: 1813. V. 39; 46

Letters, Poems and Miscellaneous Papers, of the Late James Tyson.
London: 1822. V. 37

TYSON, JAMES L.

Diary of a Physician in California. New York: 1850. V. 38; 40; 43

*Diary of the Physician in California; being the Results of Actual Experience,
Including Notes of the Journey by Land and Water, and Observations on
the Climate, Soil, Resources of the Country, etc* . . . New
York/Philadelphia: 1850. V. 37

TYSON, JERRY MERCHANT

Poems. San Francisco: 1963. V. 43

TYSON, JOHN S.

Life of Elisha Tyson, the Philanthropist. Baltimore: 1825. V. 41

TYSON, MARTHA E.

Banneker, the Afric-American Astronomer. Philadelphia: 1884. V. 43

TYSON, PHILIP T.

Geology and Industrial Resources of California. Baltimore: 1851.
V. 37; 40; 43

Information in Relation to the Geology and Topography of California.
Washington: 1850. V. 37; 39; 45

TYSSEN-AMHERST, ALICIA MARGARET

A History of Gardening in England. London: 1896. V. 37

TYTLER, ALEX FRASER

*Memoirs of the Life and Writings of the Hon. Henry Home of Kames, one
of the Senators of the College of Justice, and One of the Lords
Commissioners of Justiciary in Scotland.* Edinburgh: 1807. V. 45

TYTLER, ALEXANDER

*Plan and Outline of a Course of Lectures on the Universal History, Ancient
and Modern.* Edinburgh: 1782. V. 38; 44

TYTLER, ALEXANDER FRASER

Elements of General History, Ancient and Modern. Edinburgh: 1805. V. 38

Essay on the Life and Character of Petrarch. London: 1784. V. 42

Essay on the Principles of Translation. London: 1791. V. 39; 42; 44

TYTLER, JAMES

*An Interesting Account of the Dreadful Effects of the Plague and Yellow
Fever, at London, in 1695.* Boston: 1824. V. 38

A Treatise on the Plague and yellow Fever. Salem: 1799. V. 38; 40

TYTLER, PATRICK FRASER

*Historical Views of the Progress of Discovery on the More Northern Coasts
of America, from the Earliest Period to the Present Time* . . . Edinburgh:
1833. V. 45

*Historical View of the Progress of Discovery on the More Northern Coasts
of America.* Edinburgh & London: 1833. V. 40; 42

*Historical Notes on the Lennox of Darnley Jewel; the Property of the
Queen.* London: 1843. V. 44

*Historical View of the Progress of Discovery on the more Northern Coasts
of America . . . with Descriptive Sketches of the natural History . . . (by
James Wilson).* Edinburgh: 1832. V. 37; 40

History of Scotland (from 1249 to 1603). Edibnrugh: 1828-43. V. 39

History of Scotland. Edinburgh: 1841. V. 41

Life of the Admirable Crichton. Edinburgh: 1823. V. 40; 42

Life of Sir Walter Raleigh, found on Authentic and Original Documents.
Edinburgh: 1833. V. 44

TYTLER, WILLIAM

*An Historical and Critical Enquiry into the Evidence Produced by the Earls
of Murray and Morton, Against Mary Queen of Scots.* Edinburgh: 1760.
V. 46

*An Inquiry, Historical and Critical, Into the Evidence Against Mary Queen of
Scots* . . . London: 1790. V. 44

TZARA, TRISTAN

Juste Present. Paris: 1961. V. 39

Parler Seul. Poemes par Tristan Tzara. Paris: 1948-50. V. 39; 42

Parler Seul. Paris: 1955. V. 45; 46

U

UBALDINI, PETRUCCIO

Le Vite delle Donne illustri. Del Regno d'Inghilterra & del Regno de Scotia & di quelle, che d'altri paesi ne i due detti Regni sono stato maritate. Londra: 1591. V. 38

UBALDINUS, JOANNES PAULUS

Carmina Poetarum Nobilium. Milan: 1563. V. 41

UBERTINUS DE CASALI

Arbor Vitae Crucifixae Jesu Christi. Venice: 1485. V. 45

UCHARD, MARIO

My Uncle Barbassou. London: 1888. V. 43

UCHASTKINA, ZOYA VASIL-EVNA

A History of Russian Hand Paper-Mills and Their Watermarks. Hilversum: 1962. V. 38; 41

UCKO, PETER J.

Anthropomorphic Figurines of Predynastic Egypt and Nelithic Crete . . . London: 1968. V. 44

UDAL, JOHN SYMONDS

Dorsetshire Folk-lore. Hertford: 1922. V. 44

UDALL, JOHN

A Commentarie Upon the Lamentations of Ieremy . . . London: 1599. V. 42

UDALL, WILLIAM

The Historie of the Life and Death of Mary Stuart Queene of Scotland. London: 1624. V. 39

The Historie of the Life and Death of Mary Stuart, Queen of Scotland. London: 1636. V. 41

UDDERZOOK, WILLIAM E.

The Goss-Udderzook Tragedy: Being a History of a Strange Case of Deception and Murder, Including the Great Life Insurance Case, and the Trial of William E. Udderzook for the Murder of W. S. Goss. Baltimore: 1873. V. 37

UDE, LOUIS EUSTACHE

The French Book. London: 1829. V. 40

UDELL, JOHN

Incidents of Travel to California Across the Great Plains. Jefferson: 1856. V. 37; 38; 40; 41; 42

Journal Kept During a Trip Across the Plains Containing an Account of the Massacre of a Portion of His Party by the Mojave Indians in 1859. Los Angeles: 1946. V. 42; 45

UERBERWEG, FRIEDRICH

System der Logik und Geschichte der Logischen Lehren. Bonn: 1857. V. 38

UFANO, DIEGO

Tratado de la ARtilleria y uso Della . . . Brussels: 1612? V. 45

UFFENBACH, PHILIPP

De Quadratura Circuli Mechanici, Das ist ein Neuer . . . Mechanischer Bericht von der Vierung oder Quadratur dess Circkels . . . Nurnberg: 1653. V. 37

L'UFIZIOLO Visconteo Landau-Finaly: Facsimile of Selected Pages from the Codex. Florence: 1951. V. 40

UFJALVY-BOURDON, MARIE DE

De Paris a Samarkand, le Ferghanah, le Kouldja et la Siberie Occidentale. Paris: 1880. V. 45

UGERI, FRANCESCO

Componimenti Di Diversi In Occasione del Solenniss . . . Parma: 1604. V. 45

UGO DE S. VICTORE

Regula D. Aurelii Augustini Commentariis Doctissimis Illustrata. Dillingen: 1581. V. 37

UGONIUS, MATTHIAS

Libellus de Patriarchali Praestantia. Brescia: 1510. V. 37

UHLENBECK, C. C.

An English Blackfoot Vocabulary, Based on Material from the Southern Peigans. Amsterdam: 1930. V. 39

UHSEN, ERDMANN

Kirchen-Historie des XVI und XVII Jahr-Hunderts nach Christi Geburth, Worinnen Theils die Romis. Leipzig: 1710. V. 38

UKERS, WILLIAM H.

All About Coffee. New York: 1922. V. 42

All About Tea. New York: 1935. V. 37

UKIYO-E

The Floating World. San Francisco: 1962. V. 45

UKIYO-E. 'The Floating World.' San Francisco: 1962. V. 41

ULAM, S. M.

Adventures of a Mathematician. New York: 1976. V. 45

ULLAH, NEAMET

History of the Afghans. London: 1825-36. V. 38

ULLOA, ANTONIO DE

Conversaciones de Ulloa con sus Tres Hijos en Servicio de la Marina Instructivas y Curiosas, Sobre las Navegaciones, y Modo de Hacerlas, el Pilotage, y la maniobra . . . Madrid: 1795. V. 45

Noticias Americanas . . . Madrid: 1772. V. 38

A Voyage to South America. London: 1758. V. 37

A Voyage to South America . . . The Spanish Cities, Towns, Provinces, etc . . . London: 1760. V. 38; 39

A Voyage to South America . . . The Spanish Citites, Towns, Provinces, etc. Dublin: 1765. V. 38

A Voyage to South America . . . London: 1806. V. 40; 44

ULLOA, BERNARDO DE

Restablecimiento de las Fabricas, y Comerico Espanol . . . Madrid: 1740. V. 41

ULMANN, DORIS 1884-1934

A Portrait Gallery of American editors Being a group of XLIII Likenesses by Doris Ulmann. New York: 1925. V. 37; 43; 44; 45

ULREICH, NURA WOODSON

Nura's Garden of Betty & Booth. New York: 1935. V. 41

ULRICH, CAROLYN F.

Books and Printing. A Selected List of Periodicals 1800-1942. New York: 1943. V. 43

Books and Printing, a Selected List of Periodicals, 1800-1942. Woodstock: 1943. V. 43

Books and Printing, a Selected List of Periodicals 1800-1942. Woodstock: 1943. V. 44

ULSTADIUS, PHILIPPUS

Coelum Philosophorum, Seu Secreta Naturae . . . Paris: 1543. V. 37; 42; 44

THE ULSTER Journal of Archaeology. Belfast: 1853-62. V. 44

ULYANOV, VLADIMIR ILICH 1870-1924

La Mala die Infantile du Communisme. Paris: 1920. V. 38

UMAR IBN MUHAMMAD, AL NAFZAWI, 16th century

The Perfumed Garden of the Cheikh Nefzaoui. Cosmpoli: 1886. V. 40

UMBSTAETTER, H. D.

The Red Dollar and Other Stories from The Black Cat. Boston: 1911. V. 39

UMFREVILLE, EDWARD

Nipigon to Winnipeg. Ottawa: 1929. V. 44

The Present State of Hudson's Bay. London: 1790. V. 37

UMLAUFT, F.

The Alps. London: 1889. V. 40; 42

UNAMUNO Y JUGO, MIGUEL DE

Abel Sanchez, una Historia de Pasion. Madrid: 1917. V. 38

UNCERTAINTY of the Present Population of this Kindom; Deduced from a Candid Review of the Accounts Lately Given it by Dr. Price . . . London: 1781. V. 38; 39

UNCLE Buncle's Account of Tea in China. London: 1865. V. 46

UNCLE Buncle's Grandchildren. London: 1850. V. 46

UNCLE Frank's Fables for Children. New York: 1854. V. 38

UNCLE Remus. Joel Chandler Harris as Seen and Remembered by a Few of His Friends. 1908. V. 44

UNCLE True Songster. Philadelphia: 1850. V. 42

THE UNCLE'S Present, a New Battledoor. Philadelphia: 1810. V. 41; 45; 46

THE UNDER Sheriff; Containing the Office and Duty of High Sheriffs, Under Sheriffs and Bailiffs in the Following Order . . . London: 1766. V. 42; 45

UNDER the Union Jack. London: 1899-1900. V. 42

UNDERDOWN, EMILY
The Gateway to Spenser. London: 1911. V. 42

UNDERHILL, FRANCIS T.
Driving for Pleasure or the Harness Stable and Its Appointments. New York: 1896. V. 43; 44
Driving for Pleasure. New York: 1897. V. 37; 39

UNDERHILL, LONNIE E.
Outlaws in the Indian Territory: The Bill Cook Gang 1894-1895. Tucson: 1985. V. 38; 42

UNDERWOOD & UNDERWOOD
Yellowstone National Park. New York: 1904. V. 39

UNDERWOOD, E. ASHWORTH
Science, Medicine and History, Essays on the Evolution of Scientific Thought and Medical Practice, Written in Honour of Charles Singer. London: 1953. V. 37

UNDERWOOD, GEORGE C.
History of the Twenty-Sixth Regiment of North Carolina Troops in the Great War. Goldsboro: 1901. V. 43; 45

UNDERWOOD, J. L.
The Women of the Confederacy. New York and Washington: 1906. V. 37

UNDERWOOD, LEON
Leon Underwood: His Wood Engravings. 1986. V. 44
His Wood Engravings. London: 1986. V. 43
Leon Underwood: His Wood Engravings. Wakefield: 1986. V. 38; 42
Leon Underwood. His Wood Engravings. Wakefield, West Yorkshire: 1986. V. 38
His Wood Engravings. West Yorkshire: 1986. V. 43; 44; 46
Leon Underwood: His Wood Engravings. Woolley: 1986. V. 39
His Wood Engravings. 1987. V. 38; 40

UNDERWOOD, MICHAEL
A Treatise on the Diseases of Children with directions for the managements of Infants . . . from Sixth London Edition. Philadelphia: 1818. V. 37

UNDERWOOD, PAUL
The Kariye Djami. New York/Princeton: 1966/1975. V. 38

UNDERWOOD, PAUL A.
The Kariye Djami. New York: 1966. V. 39; 40

UNDERWOOD, PRISCILLA
When Christmas Comes Around. New York: 1915. V. 46

UNDERWOOD, THOMAS
Liberty, a Poem. London: 1768. V. 46
Poems. Bath: 1768. V. 40; 42
The Snarlers, a Poems. London: 1768. V. 42

THE UNEMBARRASSED Countenance, a New Ballad. London: 1746. V. 38

THE UNEXPECTED Wedding; in a series of Letters. London: 1768. V. 40

THE UNFORTUNATE Englishmen; or, a Faithful Narrative of the Distresses and Adventures of John Cockburn, and Five Other English Mariners . . . London: 1773. V. 46

THE UNFORTUNATE Maid Exemplified, in the Story of Elizabeth Canning Vindicated from Every Mean Aspersion Thrown Upon It. London: 1754. V. 46

UNGERER, TOMI
Fornicon. New York: 1969. V. 44
Fornicon. N.P.: 1969. V. 39

THE UNHAPPY Lovers; or, the History of James Welston, Gent. London: 1732. V. 46

UNIACKE, CROFTON
A Letter to Horace Twiss, Esq. M.P. Being an Answer to His 'Inquiry into the Means of Consolidating and Digesting the Laws of England.' London: 1826. V. 37

UNION COLONY OF COLORADO
First Annual Report of the Union Colony of Colorado Including a History of the Town of Greeley . . . New York: 1871. V. 45

THE UNION of the Roses, a Tale of the Fifteenth Century in Six Cantos, with Notes. London: 1821. V. 42

THE UNION. Or Select Scots and English Poems. London: 1759. V. 37

UNION PACIFIC RAILROAD
A Geological and Agricutlrual Survey of 100 Miles West of Omaha. New York: 1866. V. 39
Letter of John D. Perry, President of the Union Pacific Railway, (Eastern Division) Together with the Reports of the Engineer and the Geologist of the Road. Philadelphia: 1868. V. 39
The Policy of Extending Government Aid to Additional Railroads to the Pacific, by Guaranteeing Interest on Their Bonds. Washington: 1869. V. 39
Report of . . . Vice President and General Manager, to the Board of Directors, in Relation to the Operations of the Engineer Department, and the Construction of the Road, Up to the Close of the Year 1865. New York: 1866. V. 40; 45

UNION PACIFIC RAILROAD CO.
The Great Union Pacific Railroad Excursion, From New York City to the One-Hundredth Meridian of Longitude, October 1866. New York: 1866. V. 38

UNION PACIFIC RAILROAD COMPANY
Guide to the Union Pacific Railroad Lands . . . 3,000 Acres in Central and Eastern nebraska . . . Omaha: 1878. V. 37
Progress of the Union Pacific West from Omaha, Nebraska, Across the Continent, Making, With its Connections, an Unbroken Line from the Atlantic to the Pacific Ocean. Eight Hundred and Twenty Miles Completed Sept. 20, 1868. New York: 1868. V. 37
The Union Pacific Railroad Company, Chartered by the United States. Progress of their Road West from Omaha, Nebraska, across the Continent. New York: 1867. V. 37; 39; 41
Union Pacific Sketch Book: A Brief Description of Prominent Places of Interest Along the Line of the Union Pacific Railway and Connections. Omaha, Neb.: 1887. V. 37

UNION Pacific Railroad: The Great National Highway Between the Missouri River and California. The Direct Route to Colorado, Idaho, Utah, Montana, Nevada and California. Chicago: 1868. V. 41

THE UNITED Bowmen of Philadelphia 1828-1953. Philadelphia: 1953. V. 46

UNITED CHURCH OF CANADA
The V. 44

UNITED FIRE CLUB
Articles of the United Fire, Club, Instiued, Feb. 6, 1783. Newport: 1783? V. 39

UNITED NATIONS
Charter of the United Nations. New York: 1948. V. 37

UNITED STATES.
Annual Report of Supervising Architect to the Secretary of the Treasury for the Year 1873. Washington: 1873. V. 44
Instructions to the Envoys Extraordinary and Ministers Plenipotentiary from the United States of America, to the French Republic, Their Letters of Credence and Full Powers, and the Dispatches Received from them Relative to Their Mission. Philadelphia: 1798. V. 37
The United States: A Catalogue of Books Relating to the History of its Various States, Counties, and Cities. Cleveland: (1920). V. 37
The United States Biographical Dictionary and Portrait Gallery of Eminent and Self-Made Men: Wisconsin Volume. Chicago: 1877. V. 37

UNITED STATES. 6TH CENSUS, 1840.
COMPENDIUM of the Enumeration of the Inhabitants and Statistics of the United States . . . from the Returns of the Sixth Census. Washington: 1841. V. 41

UNITED STATES ANTI-MASONIC CONVENTION, PHILADELPHIA.
The Proceedings of the . . . Held at Philadelphia, September 11, 1830 . . . Philadelphia: 1830. V. 43

UNITED STATES. ARMY - 1856
Reports of Experiments on the Strength and Other Properties of Metals for Cannon. Phildelphia: 1856. V. 44

UNITED STATES. ARMY CORPS OF ENGINEERS - 1872
Preliminary Report Concerning Explorations and Surveys Principally in Nevada and Arizona . . . Washington: 1872. V. 39; 41; 42

UNITED STATES. ARMY CORPS OF ENGINEERS - 1874
Progress-Report Upon Geographical and Geological Explorations and Surveys West of the One Hundredth Meridian, in 1872 . . . Washington: 1874. V. 42

UNITED STATES. ARMY CORPS OF ENGINEERS - 1875

Report Upon Geographical and Geological Explorations and Surveys West of the One Hundredth Meridian . . . Washington: 1875. V. 42

UNITED STATES. ARMY CORPS OF ENGINEERS - 1889

Report Upon United States Geographical Surveys West of the One Hundredth Meridian, in Charge of Capt. Geo. M. Wheeler . . . Washington: 1889. V. 42

UNITED STATES. ARMY. CORPS OF TOPOGRAPHICAL ENGINEERS

Report of the Secretary of War Communicating . . . a Report and Map of the Examination of New Mexico, Made By . . . Washington: 1848. V. 39; 42; 43

Report of the Secretary of War, Communicating . . . Operations of the Army of the United States in Texas and the Adjacent Mexican States on the Rio Grande . . . Washington: 1850. V. 39

Report of the Secretary of War. Communicating . . . Captain Simpson's Report and Map of Wagon Road Routes in Utah Territory. Washington: 1859. V. 41

UNITED STATES. ARMY DEPARTMENT - 1856

Reports on Experiments with Small Arms for the Military Service. Washington: 1856. V. 38

UNITED STATES. ARMY. DEPT. OF OREGON

Report of the Secretary of War, Communicating . . . the Report of Captain H. D. Wallen of His Expedition in 1859 from Dalles City to Great Salt Lake and Back . . . Washington: 1860. V. 40

THE UNITED States Biographical Dictionary and Portrait Gallery of Eminent and Self-made Men: Wisconsin Volume. Chicago: 1877. V. 38

UNITED STATES. BUREAU OF AMERICAN ETHNOLOGY - 1879

Annual Reports. Washington: 1879/80-. V. 38

UNITED STATES. BUREAU OF AMERICAN ETHNOLOGY - 1884

Third Annual Report of the Bureau of Ethnology to the Secretary of the Smithsonian Institution 1881-82. Washington: 1884. V. 40

UNITED STATES. BUREAU OF AMERICAN ETHNOLOGY - 1886

Fourth Annual Report . . . Washington;: 1886. V. 37

Tenth Annual Report of the . . . (for) 1882-83. Washington: 1886. V. 38

UNITED STATES. BUREAU OF AMERICAN ETHNOLOGY - 1896

Fourteenth Annual Report of the . . . (for) 1892-93. Washington: 1896. V. 38

UNITED STATES. BUREAU OF AMERICAN ETHNOLOGY - 1901

18th Annual Report. Washington: 1901. V. 39

Twenty-Third Annual Report . . . Washington: 1904. V. 39

UNITED STATES. BUREAU OF AMERICAN ETHNOLOGY - 1903

Annual Report #21. Washington: 1903. V. 39

UNITED STATES. BUREAU OF AMERICAN ETHNOLOGY - 1928

43rd Annual Report. Washington: 1928. V. 39

UNITED STATES. BUREAU OF AMERICAN ETHNOLOGY - 1933

48th Annual Report: General Index: Annual reports Volumes 1-48. (1879-1931). Washington: 1933. V. 39

UNITED STATES. BUREAU OF AMERICAN ETHNOLOGY - 1946

Handbook of South American Indians. Washington: 1946-59. V. 39

UNITED STATES. BUREAU OF NAVIGATION - 1893

Merchant Vessels of the United States . . . Twenty-Fifth Annual List . . . for the Year Ended June 30, 1893. Washington: 1893. V. 40

UNITED STATES CARTRIDGE COMPANY

Where to Hunt American Game. Lowell: 1898. V. 39

UNITED STATES. CENSUS BUREAU - 1857

The Census Returns of the Different Counties of the State of Iowa for 1856. Showing in Detail, the Population, Place of Nativity, Agricultural Statistics, Domestic and General Manufactures, &c. Iowa City: 1857. V. 37

UNITED STATES. CENSUS OFFICE. 1ST CENSUS

Return of the Whole Number of Persons Withi the Several Districts of the United States. Washington: 1802. V. 40

UNITED STATES. CENSUS OFFICE. 1ST CENSUS - 1791

Return of the Whole Number of Persons Within the Several Districts of the United States. Philadelphia: 1791. V. 44

UNITED STATES. CENSUS OFFICE. 1ST CENSUS - 1801

Return of the Whole Number of Persons Within the Several Districts of the United States . . . Washington: 1801. V. 39

UNITED STATES. COAST AND GEODETIC SURVEY - 1870

Report of the Superintendent of the U.S. Coast Survey, Showing the Progress of the Survey During the Year 1870. Washington: 1873. V. 39

UNITED STATES. COAST AND GEODETIC SURVEY - 1897

Report of the Superintendent of the U.S. Coast and Geodetic Survey. Washington: 1897-1911. V. 42

UNITED States. Commission on the Assassination of President Kennedy - 1964 Hearings Before the President's Commission on the Assasination of President Kennedy. Washington: 1964. V. 39; 41; 46

UNITED STATES. COMMISSION TO THE FIVE TRIBES

Address of . . . Muskogee: 1894. V. 43

UNITED STATES. CONGRESS - 1776

Journal of the Proceedings of the Congress, Held at Philadelphia May 10, 1775. London: 1776. V. 45

UNITED STATES. CONGRESS - 1781

By the United States in Congress Assembled, April, 7, 1781. Be It Ordained . . . that the Following Instructions to be Observed by the Captains or Commanders of Private Armed Vessels, Commissioned by Letters of Marque or General Reprisals. Philadelphia: 1781. V. 45

UNITED STATES. CONGRESS - 1785

By the United States in Congress Assembled, November 2, 1785 . . . Resolved, That all Persons Having Claims for Services Performed in the Military Department, be Directed to Exhibit the Same for Liquidation . . . New York: 1785. V. 40

UNITED STATES. CONGRESS - 1789

The Committees of Both Houses of Congress, Appointed to Take Order for Conducting the Ceremonial of the Formal Reception . . . of the President of the United States, on Thursday Next . . . New York: 1789. V. 45

UNITED STATES. CONGRESS - 1794

Third Congress of the United States: at the First Session, Begun and Held at the City of Philadelphia, in the State of Pennsylvania, on Monday, the Second of December, One Thousand Seven Hundred and Ninety Three. Philadelphia. V. 40

UNITED STATES. CONGRESS - 1800

Journals of Congress: Containing Their Proceedings from September 5, 1774 to January 1, 1776. (-November 5, 1787 to November 3, 1788). Chiefly Philadelphia: 1800-01. V. 39

Journals of Congress: Containing their Proceedings from September 5, 1774 to January 1, 1776 (-November 5, 1787, to November 3, 1788). Philadelphia: 1800-1801. V. 41; 45

Report of the Committe of Commerce and Manufactures to Whom was Referred on the 17th of December Last, the Petition of Henry Stouffer, and Andrew Wallce, 10th February, 1800. Committed to the Whole House on Wednesday Next. Philadelphia: 1800. V. 46

UNITED STATES. CONGRESS - 1806

Report of the Committee Appointed on the Third Instant, On So Much of the Message of the President of the United States as Relates to the Farther Exploring of the Western Waters. December 22, 1806. Washington: 1806. V. 37

UNITED STATES. CONGRESS - 1813

Report of the Committee to Whom was Referred so Much of the Message of the President . . . as Relates to the Spirit and Manner in Which the War has Been Waged by the Enemy. Washington: 1813. V. 37; 38

UNITED STATES. CONGRESS - 1816

Journal of the Senate . . . (and) Journal of the House of Representatives of the United States at the Second Session of the Fourteenth Congress. Washington: 1816. V. 46

UNITED STATES. CONGRESS - 1817

Report of the Committee to Whom Was Referred a Memorial of a Convention of Delegates from Fifteen Counties in the Mississippi Territory . . . Washington: 1817. V. 39

UNITED STATES. CONGRESS - 1834

Investigation of the Department of the Interior and of the Bureau of Forestery. Washington: 1911. V. 41

UNITED STATES. CONGRESS. - 1845

. . . Memorial of Citizens of the U.S., Praying for the Establishment of a Distinct Territorial Government . . . Dec. 2, 1845. Washington: 1845. V. 37

UNITED STATES. CONGRESS - 1855

Documents and Other Papers Relating to the Boundary Line Between the States of Georgia and Florida Heretofore Laid Before Either House of Congress and the Reports of Committees . . . Washington: 1855. V. 39

UNITED STATES. CONGRESS - 1866

Report of the Joint Committee on Reconstruction. Washington: 1866. V. 39

UNITED STATES. CONGRESS - 1872

Report of the Joint Committee to Inquire into the Condition of Affairs in the Late Insurrectionary States. Washington: 1872. V. 38; 39

UNITED STATES. CONGRESS - 1877

Recent Election in Louisiana. Testimony Taken by the Select Committee on the Recent Election in the State of Louisiana (Parts 1-4 Complete). Washington: 1877. V. 38

UNITED STATES. CONGRESS - 1886

Organization of the Territory of Oklahoma. Washington: 1886. V. 39

UNITED STATES. CONGRESS - 1925

Northern Pacific Land Grants. Hearings Before the Joint Congressional Committee on the Investigation of the . . . Washington: 1925. V. 39

UNITED STATES. CONGRESS - 1946

Joint Committe on the Investigation of the Pearl Harbor Attack. Hearings . . . Washington: 1946. V. 38; 42; 44; 45

UNITED STATES. CONGRESS. HOUSE. COMMITTE ON JUDICIARY

Case of John C. Watrous . . . Report . . . by the Committee on the Judiciary, Touching the Charges Against the Hon. John C. Watrous, Judge of the District Court of the United States for the District of Texas. Washington: 1858. V. 38

UNITED STATES. CONGRESS. HOUSE. COMMITTE ON ROADS & CANALS

Railroad to the Pacific Ocean. Mr. Robert Smith, from the Committee on Roads & Canals . . . to whom Was Referred the Memorial of George Wilkes, with Numerous Petitions and Memorials, Upon the Subject of Constructing a Railroad or Other Method of Easy . . . Washington: 1846. V. 39

UNITED STATES. CONGRESS. HOUSE OF REPRESENATIVES - 1798

Journal of the House of Representatives of the United States, at the Third Dession of the Fifth Congress. Philadelphia: 1799. V. 45

UNITED STATES. CONGRESS. HOUSE OF REPRESENTATIVES - 1789

The Congressional Register: or, History of the Proceedings and Debates of the First House of Representatives of the United States. New York: 1789. V. 38

UNITED STATES. CONGRESS. HOUSE OF REPRESENTATIVES - 1792

Journal of the House of Representatives of the United States, at the First Session of the Second Congress. Philadelphia: 1792. V. 39; 43

UNITED STATES. CONGRESS. HOUSE OF REPRESENTATIVES - 1793

Journal of the House of Representatives, Saturday December 7, 1793. N.P.: 1793. V. 40

Journal of the House of Representatives of the United States; at the First Session of the Third Congress. Philadelphia: 1793. V. 42

UNITED STATES. CONGRESS. HOUSE OF REPRESENTATIVES - 1797

Journal of the House of Represenatives of the United States, at the Second Seesion of the Fourth Congress. Philadelphia: 1797. V. 45

UNITED STATES. CONGRESS. HOUSE OF REPRESENTATIVES - 1798

Report of the Committee of the House . . . Articles of Impeachment Against William Blount, a Senator . . . for High Crimes and Misdemeanors. Philadelphia: 1798. V. 38

UNITED STATES. CONGRESS. HOUSE OF REPRESENTATIVES - 1800

Report of the Committee of Commerce & Manufactures, to Whom Was Referred, on the 17th of December Last, the Petition of Henry Stouffer and Andrew Wallace, 10th February, 1800. Committed to the Whole Houe, on Wednesday next. Philadelphia: 1800. V. 37

UNITED STATES. CONGRESS. HOUSE OF REPRESENTATIVES - 1827

Report of the Committee Appointed on the 29th December, 1826, on a Letter of John C. Calhoun, Vice President of the United States, Asking an Investigation of His Conduct While Secretary of War, with Accompanying Documents. Washington: 1827. V. 38

Report of the Select Committee of the House of Representatives to Which Were Referred the Messages of the President of the U.S . . . Washington: 1827. V. 37; 42

UNITED STATES. CONGRESS. HOUSE OF REPRESENTATIVES - 1828

Report of the Committee on Military Affairs, to Which Were Referred The Correspondence and Documents from the War Department, In Relation to the Proceedings of a Court Martial Ordered for the Trial of Certain Tennessee Militiamen. Washington: 1828. V. 39

UNITED STATES. CONGRESS. HOUSE OF REPRESENTATIVES - 1845

Mr. Daniel, from the Committee on the Territories, Reported the Following Bill: a Bill Supplemental to the Bill for the Admission of the State of Iowa and Florida Into the Union. Washington. V. 46

UNITED STATES. CONGRESS. HOUSE OF REPRESENTATIVES - 1846

A Bill to Define the Boundaries of the State of Iowa and to Repeal So Much of the Act of the Third of March 1845, as Relates to the Boundaries of Iowa. Washington: 1846. V. 46

A Bill to Establish the Territorial Government of Oregon. Washington: 1846. V. 37

Railroad to the Pacific Ocean. Washington: 1846. V. 40; 41; 44

UNITED STATES. CONGRESS. HOUSE OF REPRESENTATIVES - 1848

House of Representatives. Manuel X. Harmony, March 30, 1848 . . . The Committee of Claims, to Who was Referred the Petition of Manuel X. Harmony, Report . . . Washington: 1848. V. 37

UNITED STATES. CONGRESS. HOUSE OF REPRESENTATIVES - 1856

Report Of the Special Committee Appointed to Investigate the Troubles in Kansas, With Views of the Minority of Said Committee. Washington: 1856. V. 41

UNITED STATES. CONGRESS. HOUSE OF REPRESENTATIVES - 1858

Claims in the Territory of New Mexico. Washington: 1858. V. 37

UNITED STATES. CONGRESS. HOUSE OF REPRESENTATIVES - 1862

Report of the Select Committee on Emancipation and Colonization. Washington. V. 39

Report of the Select Committee on Emancipation and Colonization, with an Appendix. Washington: 1862. V. 39

UNITED STATES. CONGRESS. HOUSE OF REPRESENTATIVES - 1866

Report of the Joint Committee on Reconstruction. Washington: 1866. V. 46

UNITED STATES. CONGRESS. HOUSE OF REPRESENTATIVES - 1867

Testimony Taken Before the Judiciary Committee on the House of Representatives in the Investigation of Charges Against Andrew Johnson. Washington: 1867. V. 39

UNITED STATES. CONGRESS. HOUSE OF REPRESENTATIVES - 1872

Depredations on the Frontiers of Texas. Washington: 1872. V. 41

Report of the Commissioners and Evidence Taken by the Committee on Mines and Mining of the House of Representatives of the United States in Regard to the Sutro Tunnel; Together with the Arguments and Report of the Committee. Washington: 1872. V. 37; 38; 40

UNITED STATES. CONGRESS. HOUSE OF REPRESENTATIVES - 1873

Report of the Select Committee to Investigate the Alleged Credit Mobilier Bribery, Made to the House of Representatives, February 18, 1873. Washington: 1873. V. 46

UNITED STATES. CONGRESS. HOUSE OF REPRESENTATIVES - 1876

Military Expedition Against the Sioux Indians 1876. 1876. V. 37

UNITED STATES. CONGRESS. HOUSE OF REPRESENTATIVES - 1878

Committee On Military Affairs. Testimony Taken by the Committee . . . In Relation to Texas Border Troubles. Washington: 1878. V. 38

Report and Accompanying Documents of the Committee on Foreign Affairs on the Relations of the United States with Mexico. Washington: 1878. V. 39

UNITED STATES. CONGRESS. HOUSE OF REPRESENTATIVES - 1880

Testimony in Relation to the Ute Indian Outbreak Taken by the Committee on Indian Affairs of the House of Representatives. Washington: 1880. V. 39

UNITED STATES. CONGRESS. HOUSE OF REPRESENTATIVES - 1889

Investigation of the Fur-Seal and Other Fisheries of Alaska. Washington: 1889. V. 37

UNITED STATES. CONGRESS. HOUSE OF REPRESENTATIVES - 1941

Report of the Select Committee of the House of Representatives, To Which Were Referred the Messages of the President U.S . . . with Accompanying Documents; and a Report and Resolutions of the Legislature of Georgia March 3, 1827. Washington: 1827. V. 39

UNITED STATES. CONGRESS. SENATE - 1789

Journal of the First Session of the Senate of the United States of America, Begun and Held at the City of New York, March 4th, 1789. New York: 1789. V. 42

UNITED STATES. CONGRESS. SENATE - 1793

Journal of the Senate of the United States of America, Being the First Session of the Third Congress, Begun and Held at the City of Philadelphia, December 2d, 1793. Philadelphia: 1793. V. 46

UNITED STATES. CONGRESS. SENATE - 1794

Journal of the Senate of the United States of America, Being the First Session of the Third Congress. Philadelphia: 1794. V. 42

UNITED STATES. CONGRESS. SENATE - 1796

Journal of the Senate of the United States of America, Being the First Session of the Fourth Congress, Begun . . . December 7th, 1795. Philadelphia: 1796. V. 45

UNITED STATES. CONGRESS. SENATE - 1797

Journal of the Senate of the United States of America Being the Second Session of the Fourth Congress, Begun . . . December 5th, 1796. Philadelphia: 1797. V. 45

Rules for Conducting Business in the Senate. Philadelphia: or Washington: 1797 or 1800. V. 37

UNITED STATES. CONGRESS. SENATE - 1798

Journal of the Senate of the United States of America, Being the Third Dession of the Fifth Congress, Begun . . . December 3D, 1798. Philadelphia: 1799. V. 45

UNITED STATES. CONGRESS. SENATE - 1799

Journal of the Senate of the United States of America, Being the First Session of the Sixth Congress, Began . . . December 2nd 1799. Philadelphia: 1800. V. 45

UNITED STATES. CONGRESS. SENATE - 1803

Journal of the Senate of the United States of America, Being the First Session of the Eighth Congress. Washington City: 1803. V. 39; 40; 41

Journal of the Senate of the United States of America, Being the First Session of the Eighth Congress, Begun October 17, 1803. (bound with) Journal of the Senate . . . Second Session of the Eighth Congress, Begun November 5, 1804- (March 3, 1805). Washington City: 1804-1805. V. 46

UNITED STATES. CONGRESS. SENATE - 1820

In Senate of the United States, February 16, 1820. Mr. Leake, from the Committee on Indian Affairs . . . Washington: 1820. V. 38

UNITED STATES. CONGRESS. SENATE - 1846

In the Senate of the United States . . . Executive Proceedings, Correspondence and Documents, Relating to Oregon, From Which the Injunction of Secrecy Has Been Removed. Washington: 1846. V. 37; 42

UNITED STATES. CONGRESS. SENATE - 1854

In the Senate of the U.S., July 10, 1854 . . . A Bill Authorizing the Construction of a Line of Telegraph from the Mississippi River to the Pacific Ocean. Washington: 1854. V. 37

UNITED STATES. CONGRESS. SENATE - 1869

In the Senate of the United States . . . Mr. Stewart Made the Following Report. Washington: 1869. V. 37

Policy of Extending Government Aid to Additional Railroads to the Pacific By Guaranteeing Interest on Their Bonds. Report of the Majority of the Sente Comittee on Pacific Railroad, Feb. 19, 1869. Washington: 1869. V. 38

UNITED STATES. CONGRESS. SENATE - 1872

Report of the Joint Committee to Inquire Into the Condition of Affairs in the Late Insurrectionary States. Washington: 1872. V. 45

UNITED STATES. CONGRESS. SENATE - 1878

Testimony Taken by the (Senate) Committee on Miltary Affairs in Relation to the Texas Border Troubles. Washington: 1878. V. 44

UNITED STATES. CONGRESS. SENATE - 1879

In the Senate of the United States . . . Mr. Patterson, from the Committee on Territories . . . Washington: 1879. V. 37

UNITED STATES. CONGRESS. SENATE - 1880

Report: the Committee on Privileges and Elections, to Whom was Referred the Memorial of Henry Spofford, Claiming to Be Entitled to the Seat in the Senate After the State of Louisiana Now Occupied by Henry P. Kellog. Washington: 1880. V. 37; 39

UNITED STATES. CONGRESS. SENATE - 1884

Report from the Select Committee to Examine the Conditions of the Sioux and Crow Indians. Washington: 1884. V. 38

UNITED STATES. CONGRESS. SENATE - 1889

Report on the La Abra Silver Mining Company. Washington: 1889. V. 38

UNITED STATES. CONGRESS. SENATE - 1894

Hawaiian Islands: Report of the Committee on Foreign Relations. Washington: 1894. V. 37

UNITED STATES. CONGRESS. SENATE - 1895

Report of the Committee on Agriculture and Forestry on the Condition of Cotton Growers . . . Prices of Cotton and the Remedy. Washington: 1985. V. 39

UNITED STATES. CONGRESS. SENATE - 1896

Reports . . . Condition of Seal Life on the Rookeries of Pribilof Islands Parts 1 and 2. Pelagic Sealing in Bering Sea and the North Pacific Ocean in the Years 1893-1895. Washington: 1896. V. 37

UNITED STATES. CONGRESS. SENATE - 1898

Report of the Boundary Commission Upon the Surveying and Re-Marking of the Boundary Between the United States and Mexico West of the Rio-Grande, 1891 to 1896. Parts I and II. Washington: 1898. V. 37

UNITED STATES. CONGRESS. SENATE - 1900

Report of the Committee on Privileges and Elections of the United States Senate Relative to the Right and Title of William A. Clark to a Seat as Senator from the State of Montana. Washington: 1900. V. 43

UNITED STATES. CONGRESS. SENATE - 1920

Investigation of Mexican Affairs. Preliminary Report and Hearings of the Committee on Foreign Relations. U. S. Senate Pursuant to S. Res. 106 Directing the Committee on Foreign Relations to Investigate the Matter of Outrges on Citizens of the U.S . . . Washington: 1920. V. 38

UNITED STATES. CONGRESS. SENATE - 1936

The Western Range, 74th Cong. 2nd Session. Doc. No. 199. Washington: 1936. V. 44

UNITED STATES. CONGRESSS - 1800

Journals of Congress: Containing their Proceedings from Sept. 5, 1774 to Jan. 1, 1776. (-November 5, 1787 to November 3, 1788). Philadelphia: 1800-01. V. 43

UNITED STATES. CONSTITUTION

The American's Guide. The Constitutions of the United States of America; with the latest Amendments: Also the Declaration of Independence, Articles of Confederation with the Federal Constitution, and Acts for the Government of the Territories. New York: 1813. V. 37

UNITED STATES. CONSTITUTION - 1781

The Constitutions of the Several Independent States of America; the Declaration of Indepdence . . . Philadelphia: 1781. V. 37; 42; 45

UNITED STATES. CONSTITUTION - 1783

The Constitutions of the Several Independent States of America: The Declaration of Independence, the Articles of Confederation Between Said States and the Treaties Between His Most Christian Majesty and the United States of America. Dublin: 1783. V. 45

Constitutions Des Treize Etats-Unis de L'Amerique. Philadelphie; et se trouve: 1783. V. 40; 41

UNITED STATES. CONSTITUTION - 1789

Acts Passed at a Congress of the United States of America. Begun and Held at the City of New York, on Wednesday the Fourth of March, in the Year MDCCLXXXIX. And of the Independence of the United States, The Thirteen. Being the Acts . . . New York: 1789. V. 42

UNITED STATES. CONSTITUTION - 1791

The Constitutions of the United States, According to the Latest Amendments: To Which are Annexed, the Declaration of Independence; and the Federal Constitution, with the Amendments Thereto. Philadelphia: 1791. V. 45

UNITED STATES. CONSTITUTION - 1795

The Federal Constitution of the United States of America . . . with The Alterations and Additions . . . and an Appendix Containing the Acts Passed by Congress Relative to the Constitution. London: 1795. V. 37

UNITED STATES. CONSTITUTION - 1802

The Federalist. New York: 1802. V. 37

UNITED STATES. CONSTITUTION - 1817

The Constitutions of all the United States, According to the Latest Amendments. To Which are Prefixed, the Declaration of Independence and the Federal Constitution. Lexington: 1817. V. 38

UNITED STATES. CONSTITUTION - 1819

The Constitution of the United States, and of the State of South Carolina, with the Amendments. Columbia: 1819. V. 40

UNITED STATES. CONSTITUTION - 1826

The Constitutions of the United States of America . . . Lexington: 1826. V. 40

UNITED STATES. CONSTITUTION - 1832

Constitution of the United States; and Washington's Farewell Address. Palmyra: 1832. V. 44

UNITED STATES. CONSTITUTION - 1852

Constitution of the United States of America as Proposed by the Convention Held at Philadelphia . . . with Amendment Thereto . . . Salt Lake City: 1852. V. 37; 45

UNITED STATES. CONSTITUTION - 1870

The Constitution of the United States and the Constitutions of California As Adopted in 1863 and 1879. San Francisco: 1879. V. 37

UNITED STATES. CONSTITUTION - 1911

The Constitution of the United States of America. Cambridge: 1911. V. 45

The Constitution of the United States of America. (Cambridge: 1911°. V. 37

UNITED STATES. CONSTITUTION - 1987

Constitution of the United States. San Francisco: 1987. V. 42; 44; 45

UNITED STATES. CONSTITUTIONAL CONVENTION

Secret Proceedings and Debates of the Convention Assembled in the Year 1787, for the Purpose of Forming the Constitution of the United States of America. From Notes Taken by the Late Robert Yates. (etc). Albany: 1821. V. 43

UNITED STATES. CONSTITUTIONAL CONVENTION - 1787

Journal, Acts and Proceedings of the Convention, Assembled at Philadelphia, Monday May 14, and Dissolved Monday, September 17, 1787, which Formed the Constitution of the United States. Boston: 1819. V. 38; 45

UNITED STATES. CONSTITUTIONS - 1852

The Constitutions of the Several States of the Union and United States Taken from Authentic Documents. New York: 1852. V. 37

UNITED STATES. CONTINENTAL CONGRESS - 1774

Extracts from the Votes and Proceedings of the American Continental Congress, Held at Philadelphia on the 5th of September, 1774. Boston: 1774. V. 38

Extracts from the Votes and Proceedings of the American Continental Congress, Held at Philadelphia, 5th September, 1774. Containing the Bill of Rights . . . New York: 1774. V. 44

Extracts from the Votes and Proceedings of the American Continental Congress, Held at Philadelphia on the Fifth Day of September, 1774, Containing the Bill of Rights, a List of Grievances, Occasional Resolves, the Association. Norwich: 1774. V. 40

Extracts from the Votes and Proceedings of the American Continental Congress Held at Philadelphia, on the Fifth of September, 1744 . . . Philadelphia: Printed,: 1774. V. 44

Journal of the Proceedings of the Congress, Held at Philadelphia, September 5th, 1774. London: 1775. V. 38

Journal of the Proceedings of the Congress, Held at Philadelphia, September 5, 1774. (with) Journal of the Proceedings of the Congress, Held at Philadelphia May 10, 1775. Philadelphia: 1774, 1775. V. 37

Letter from the General Congress at Philadelphia, September the 5th, 1774, to the People of Great Britain. N.P.: 1774? V. 37

UNITED STATES. CONTINENTAL CONGRESS - 1775

The Declaration by the Representatives of the United Colonies of North America, Now Met in General Congress in Philadelphia, Setting Forth the Causes and Necessity of Taking Up Arms. London: 1775. V. 37; 42; 46

A Declaration by the Representatives of the United Colonies of North America, Now Met in General Congress, at Philadelphia; Setting Forth the Causes and Necessity of their Taking up Arms. Newport: 1775. V. 39; 44; 45

Journal of the Proceedings of the Congress, Held at Philadelphia, September 5th, 1774. London: 1775. V. 40; 44; 46

Journal of the Proceedings of the Congress Held at Philadelphia. Mary 10, 1775. Philadelphia: 1776. V. 46

UNITED STATES. CONTINENTAL CONGRESS - 1776

Journal of the Proceedings of the Congress Held at Philadelphia May 10, 1775. Philadelphia: printed: 1776. V. 44

Rules and Articles for the Better Government of the Troops Raised, or to be Raised and Kept in Pay by and at the Expence of the United States of America. Philadelphia: 1776. V. 37

UNITED STATES. CONTINENTAL CONGRESS - 1778

Journal of the Proceedings of Congress, Held at Philadelphia, From September 5, 1775 to April 30, 1776. London: 1778. V. 38; 44

UNITED STATES. CONTINENTAL CONGRESS - 1783

Address and Recommendations to the States by the United States in Congress Assembled. Philadelphia: 1783. V. 40

Constitutions des Treize Etats-Unis de L'Amerique. Philadelphia: 1783. V. 40

UNITED STATES. CORPS OF TOPOGRAPHICAL ENGINEERS - 1848

Report of the Secretary of War Communicating . . . a Report and map of the Examination of New Mexico Made by Lieut. J. W. Abert . . . Washington: 1848. V. 46

UNITED STATES COURT OF PRIVATE LAND CLAIMS. SANTA FE DIST.

No. 110. United States Court of Private Land Claims. James Addison Peraltareavis and Dona Sofia Loreto Micaela de Peraltareavis, nee Maso y Silva de Peralta de la Cordoba (Husband and Wife) Plaintiffs vs. the United States of America. Santa Fe: 1895. V. 40

UNITED STATES. DECLARATION OF INDEPENDENCE - 1835

Declaration of Independence, in Congress, July 4, 1776. Boston: 1835. V. 39

UNITED STATES. DECLARATION OF INDEPENDENCE - 1837

In Congress July 4th, 1776. The Unanimous Declaration of Independence of the Thirteen United States of America. Boston: 1837. V. 45

UNITED STATES. DEPARTMENT OF AGRICULTURE - 1890

Letter from the Secretary of Agriculture . . . to Determine the Proper Location of Artesian Wells Within the Area of the Ninety-Seventh Meridian and East of the Foot-Hills of the Rocky Mountains. Washington: 1890. V. 39

UNITED STATES. DEPARTMENT OF AGRICULTURE - 1936

The Western Letter from the Secretary of Agriculture . . . A Report on the Western Range a Great but Neglected Natural Resource. Washington: 1936. V. 39

UNITED STATES. DEPARTMENT OF DEFENSE - 1961

Fallout Protection: What to Know and What to Do About Nuclear Attack. Washington: 1961. V. 39

UNITED STATES. DEPARTMENT OF INTERIOR - 1861

Report of the Commissioner of Indian Affairs Accompanying the Annual Report of the Secretary of the Interior, for the Year 1861. Washington: 1861. V. 37

UNITED STATES. DEPARTMENT OF INTERIOR - 1874

Statistical Atlas of the United States Based on the Results of the Ninth Census 1870 . . . New York: 1874. V. 45

UNITED STATES. DEPARTMENT OF INTERIOR - 1987

Report on the United States and Mexican Boundary Survey. Austin: 1987. V. 39

UNITED STATES. DEPARTMENT OF STATE

State Papers and Publick Documents . . . Exhibiting A Complete View of Our Foreign Relations, 1806-1808. Boston: 1815. V. 37; 39

UNITED STATES. DEPARTMENT OF STATE - 1798

Authentic Copies of the Correspondence of Charles Colesworth Pinckney, John Marshall and Elbridge Gerry, Esqrs. London: 1798. V. 40

UNITED STATES. DEPARTMENT OF STATE - 1806

State Papers and Publick Documents . . . Exhibiting a Complete View of Our Foreign Relations, 1806-1808. Boston: 1815. V. 39

UNITED STATES. DEPARTMENT OF STATE - 1839

Boundary Between Missouri & Iowa. Letter from the Secretary of State, Transmitting the Information . . . Respecting the Boundary-Line Between the State of Missouri and the Territory of Iowa. Washington: 1839. V. 39

UNITED STATES. DEPARTMENT OF STATE - 1878

Reports Upon the Survey of the Boundary Between the Territory of the United States and the Possessions of Great Britain from the Lake of the Woods to the Summit of the Rocky Mountains. Washington: 1878. V. 40

UNITED STATES. DEPARTMENT OF THE GULF - 1862

General Orders from the Headquarters Department of the Gulf from may 1st, 1862 to the Present Time (Nov. 9th, 1862). New Orleans: 1862. V. 39

UNITED STATES. DISTRICT ATTORNEY. CALIF. NORTHERN DISTRICT

Evidence in the Case of the United States, vs. Andres Castillero Introduced by the U. S. District Attorney, to Show Fraud and Forgery on the Part of the Claimant. San Francisco: 1857. V. 39

UNITED STATES. DISTRICT COURT. CALIF. NORTHERN DISTRICT

In the United States District Court, Northern District of California. The United States vs. Andrew Castillero on Cross Appeal. Claim for the Mine and Mines of New Almaden. Opening Argument by Archibald C. Peachy, for the Claimant. San Francisco: 1860. V. 39

UNITED STATES EXPLORING EXPEDITION, 1838-1842.

United States Exploring Expedition, 1838-42, under Command of C Wilkes. Botany. 1971. V. 38

UNITED STATES. GENERAL LAND OFFICE - 1837

Affairs of the General Land Office. Letter from the Secretary of the Treasury Transmitting Report of the Commissioner of the General Land Office . . . Washington: 1837. V. 39

UNITED STATES. GENERAL LAND OFFICE - 1841

Report from the Secretary of the Treasury Communicating the Annual of the Commissioner of the General Land Office. Washington: 1841. V. 39; 40; 44

Report from the Secretary of the Treasury Showing . . . the Quantity of Public Land Unsold on the 30th June, 1828. Washington: 1841. V. 41; 44

UNITED STATES. GENERAL LAND OFFICE - 1844

Report of the Secretary of the Treasury, Communicating the Annual Report of the Commissioner of the General Land Office. Washington: 1844. V. 39

UNITED STATES. GENERAL LAND OFFICE - 1848

Letter from the Secretary of the Treasury Transmitting the Annual Report of the Commissioner of the General Land Office. Washington: 1848. V. 39

UNITED STATES. GENERAL LAND OFFICE - 1850

Land Office Report. Letter from the Secretary of the Interior, Transmitting the Annual Report of the Commissioner of the General Land Office. Washington: 1850. V. 39

UNITED STATES. GENERAL LAND OFFICE - 1867

Report of the Commissioner of General Land Office, for the Year 1867. Washington: 1867. V. 39

UNITED STATES. GENERAL LAND OFFICE - 1882

Letter . . . in Response to Senate Resolution of January 6, 1882, the Report of the Commisioner of the General Land Office Upon the Survey of the United States and Texas Boundary Commission. Washington: 1882. V. 39

UNITED States. Geographical Surveys West of the 100th Meridian - 1878 Annual Report Upon the Geographical Surveys West of the 100th Meridian . . . Washington: 1878. V. 42

UNITED STATES. GEOLOGICAL & GEOGRAPHICAL SURVEY - 1872

Preliminary Report of the U.S. Geological Survey of Montana and Adjacent Territories. Washington: 1872. V. 42; 46

Preliminary Report of the United States geological Survey of Wyoming. Washington: 1872. V. 46

UNITED STATES. GEOLOGICAL & GEOGRAPHICAL SURVEY - 1874

Annual Report of the United States Geological and Geographical Survey of the Territories Embracing Colorado. Washington: 1874. V. 46

UNITED STATES. GEOLOGICAL & GEOGRAPHICAL SURVEY - 1876

Annual Report of the United States Geological and Geographical Survey of the Territories Embracing Colorado and Parts of Adjacent Territories. Washington: 1876. V. 41; 42; 46

UNITED STATES. GEOLOGICAL AND GEOGRAPHICAL SURVEY - 1878

Tenth Annual Report of the United States Geological and Geographic Survey of the Territories, Embracing Colorado and Parts of Adjacent Territories . . . Washington: 1878. V. 41; 42

UNITED STATES. GEOLOGICAL AND GEOGRAPHICAL SURVEY - 1879

Eleventh Annual Report of the United States and Geological and Geographical Survey of the Territories, Embracing Idaho and Wyoming . . . Washington: 1879. V. 42; 44

UNITED STATES. GEOLOGICAL AND GEOGRAPHICAL SURVEY - 1883

Twelfth Annual Report of the United States Geological and Geographical Survey . . . Washington: 1883. V. 42

UNITED STATES GEOLOGICAL AND GEOGRAPHICAL SURVEY OF THE TERRITORIES

Twelfth Annual Report of the United States Geological and Geographical Survey of the Territories. Washington: 1883. V. 43

UNITED STATES. GEOLOGICAL SURVEY - 1880

First Annual Report of the United States Geological Survey to the Hon. Carl Schurz, Secretary of the Interior. Washington: 1880. V. 42

UNITED STATES. GEOLOGICAL SURVEY - 1896

Eighteenth Annual Report of the United States Geological Survey . . . 1896-97. Washington: 1898. V. 39; 42

UNITED STATES. INTERIOR DEPARTMENT - 1802

Annual Reports of the Department of the Interior for the Fiscal year Ended June 30, 1901. Indian Affairs. Washington: 1902. V. 38

UNITED STATES. INTERIOR DEPARTMENT - 1850

Report of the Secretary of the Interior . . . Calling for Information in Relation to Operations on the Commission Appointed to Run and Mark the Boundary Between the United States and Mexico. Washington: 1850. V. 39; 40; 41; 42; 45

UNITED STATES. INTERIOR DEPARTMENT - 1851

Report of the Secretary of the Interior Communicating a Copy of the Report of William Carey Jones, Special Agent to Examine the Subject of Land Titles in California. Washington: 1851. V. 40

UNITED STATES. INTERIOR DEPARTMENT - 1852

Report of the Secretary of the Interior, Made in Compliance With a Resolution of the Senate Calling for Information in Relation to the Commission Appointed to Run and Mark the Boundary Between the United States and Mexico. Washington: 1852. V. 40; 41

UNITED STATES. INTERIOR DEPARTMENT - 1853

Report of the Secretary of the Interior . . . A Report from Mr. Bartlett on the Subject of the Boundary Line Between the United States and Mexico. Washington: 1853. V. 38; 40; 41

UNITED STATES. INTERIOR DEPARTMENT - 1855

Report of the Secretary of Interior . . . Communicating a Report and Map of A. B. Gray, Relative to the Mexican Boundary. Washington: 1855. V. 40

UNITED STATES. INTERIOR DEPARTMENT - 1859

Pacific Wagon Roads. Letter from the Secretary of Interior, Transmitting a Report Upon the Several Wagon Roads Constructed Under the Direction of the Interior Department. Washington: 1859. V. 40; 41; 43

UNITED STATES. INTERIOR DEPARTMENT - 1867

Letter of the Secretary of Interior . . . Information Touching the Origin and Progress of Indian Hostilities on the Frontier. Washington: 1867. V. 39

Massacre of Troops Near Fort Phil Kearney. Letter from the Secretary of the Interior. Washington: 1867. V. 37

UNITED STATES. INTERIOR DEPARTMENT - 1868

General Dodge's Report. Letter from the Secretary of the Interior Transmitting . . . a Copy of Gen. Dodge's Reprort. Washington: 1868. V. 40

UNITED STATES. INTERIOR DEPARTMENT - 1870

Report of the Board of Indian Commissioners . . . Being Results Obtained from Personal Observation and Inspection. Washington: 1870. V. 39

UNITED STATES. INTERIOR DEPARTMENT - 1871

Letter from the Secretary of the Interior Communicating . . . the Early Labors of the Missionaries of the American Board of Commissioners for Foreign Missions in Oregon Commencing in 1836. Washington: 1871. V. 39; 41

UNITED STATES. INTERIOR DEPARTMENT - 1885

Letter from the Secretary of the Interior Transmitting, in Answer to Senatae Resolution of Dec. 3, 1884, Report Relative to the Leasing of Indian Lands in the Indian Territory. Washington: 1885. V. 38

UNITED STATES. INTERIOR DEPARTMENT - 1890

Letter from the Secretary of Interior . . . Concerning the Legal Status of the Indians in Indian Territory. Washington: 1890. V. 38

UNITED STATES. INTERIOR DEPARTMENT - 1892

Letter from the Secretary of the Interior . . . Forwarding Report Made by the Hampton Instiute Regardings Its Returned Indian Students. Washington: 1892. V. 46

Report Upon the Location and Survey of Reservoir Sites During the Fiscal Year Ending June 30, 1891. Washington: 1892. V. 39

UNITED STATES. INTERIOR DEPARTMENT - 1905

Annual Repots of the Department of Interior for the Fiscal yeara Ended June 30, 1904. Indian Affairs. Washington: 1905. V. 38

UNITED STATES INTERNATIONAL EXHIBITION, PHILADELPHIA, 1876.

China. Catalogue of the Chinese Imperial Maritime Customs Collection, at the United States International Exhibition, Philadelphia, 1876. Shanghai: 1876. V. 40

UNITED STATES. JUSTICE DEPARTMENT - 1790

Report of the Attorney General Read in the House of Representatives, December 31, 1790. Philadelphia: 1790. V. 40

UNITED STATES. LAWS, STATUTES, ETC. - 1770

A Bill to Regulate the Consequences of the Expulsion of Members of This House. London: 1770. V. 46

UNITED STATES. LAWS, STATUTES, ETC. - 1787

Congress, October 1782. An Ordinance for Regulating the Post Office of the United States of America. New York: 1787. V. 44

UNITED STATES. LAWS, STATUTES, ETC. - 1790

An Act Providing for the Enumeration of the Inhabitants of the United States. New York: 1790. V. 39

UNITED STATES. LAWS, STATUTES, ETC. - 1791

An Act Giving Effect to the Laws of the United States Within the State of Vermont. Philadelphia: 1791. V. 46

An Act Repealing, After the Last Day of June Next, the Duties Heretofore Lid Upon Distilled Spirits, Imported from Abroad, and Laying Others in Their Stead; and also upon Spirits Distilled within the United States and for Approaching the Same. Philadelphia?: 1791. V. 37

Acts Concerning the Territory of Columbia and the City of Washington, Publishers, by Order of the House of Representatives. Philadelphia: 1791. V. 43

Acts Passed at the First Session of the Congress of the United States of America, Begun . . . the Fourth of March, in the Year MDCCLXXXIX. Bound with the Second and Third Sessions of Congress. Philadelphia: 1791. V. 37; 44

UNITED STATES. LAWS, STATUTES, ETC. - 1794

An Act in Addition to the Act for the Punishment of Certain Crimes Against the United States. Philadelphia: 1794. V. 45

An Act Laying Certain Duties Upon Snuff and Refined Sugar (Passed the House of Representatives May 24th, 1794). Philadelphia: 1794. V. 46

An Act to provide for the Defence of Certain Ports and Harbors in the United States . . . Passed the House of Representatives, March the 12th, 1794. Philadelphia?: 1794? V. 37

UNITED STATES. LAWS, STATUTES, ETC. - 1795

An Ordinance for the Government of the Territory of the United States, Northwest of the River Ohio. Cincinnati: 1795. V. 46

UNITED STATES. LAWS, STATUTES, ETC. - 1796

A Bill to Ascertain and Fix the Military Establishment of the United States. Philadelphia: 1796. V. 46

A Bill to Ascertain and Fix the Military Establishment of the United States. Philadelphia?: 1796. V. 37

UNITED STATES. LAWS, STATUTES, ETC. - 1803

An Act Supplementary to the Act Concerning, Consuls and Vice-Consuls and for the Furter Protection of American Seamen. New York: 1803. V. 41

Acts Passed At the First Session of the Eighth Congress of the United States of America . . . In the Year 1803. N.P.: n.d. V. 37

UNITED STATES. LAWS, STATUTES, ETC. - 1804

Acts Passed at the First Session of the Eighth Congress of the United States of America . . . in the Year 1803. Washington: 1804. V. 39; 40

UNITED STATES. LAWS, STATUTES, ETC. - 1805

Acts Passed at the First Session of the Ninth Congress of the United States. Washington: 1805. V. 39

UNITED STATES. LAWS, STATUTES, ETC. - 1806

Acts Passed at the First Session of the Ninth Congress of the United States. Washington: 1806. V. 38

UNITED STATES. LAWS, STATUTES, ETC. - 1807

Acts of Congress Relative to Land Claims in the Territory of New Orleans. New Orleans: 1807. V. 39; 40

Acts of Congress Relative to Land Claims, in the Territory of Orleans. (New Orleans): 1807). V. 37

UNITED STATES. LAWS, STATUTES, ETC. - 1808

An Act for Establishing Rules and Articles for the Government of the Armies of the United States; with Regulations Respecting the Same. Washington City: 1808. V. 37

UNITED STATES. LAWS, STATUTES, ETC. - 1813

An Act Supplementary to the Act, Entitled 'An Act for the More Perfect Organization of the Army of the United States. Washington City: 1813. V. 39

UNITED STATES. LAWS, STATUTES, ETC. - 1814

A Bill for Quieting and Adjusting Claims to Land in the Mississippi Territory. Washington: 1814. V. 39

UNITED STATES. LAWS, STATUTES, ETC. - 1815

An Act Laying a Direct Tax Upon the United States and to Provide for Assessing and Collecting the Same. An Act Laying Duties on Household Furniture, and On Gold and Silver Watches. Philadelphia: 1815. V. 37

Laws of the United States of America, from the 4th of March, 1789 to the 4th of March, 1815, Including the Constitution . . . Act of Confederation, Treaties and Many Other Valuable Ordinances and Documents. Philadelphia: 1815. V. 44

UNITED STATES. LAWS, STATUTES, ETC. - 1818

A Bill to Prohibit the Choctaw Tribe of Indians from Settling or Hunting on the Lands of the United States, West of the Mississippi. Washington: 1818. V. 39

UNITED STATES. LAWS, STATUTES, ETC. - 1821

Acts Passed at the Second Session of the Sixteenth Congress of the United States. Washington: 1821. V. 39; 43

UNITED STATES. LAWS, STATUTES, ETC. - 1822

An Act for the Establishment of a Territorial Government in Florida. Washington: 1822. V. 39

UNITED STATES. LAWS, STATUTES, ETC. - 1823

Acts Passed at the Second Session of the 17th Congress of the United States. Washington: 1823. V. 40

UNITED STATES. LAWS, STATUTES ETC. - 1826

Acts Passed at the First Session of the Nineteenth Congress of the United States. Washington: 1826. V. 38

A Bill for the Preservation and Civilization of the Indian Tribes, Within the United States. Washington: 1826. V. 38

UNITED STATES. LAWS, STATUTES, ETC. - 1827

A Bill to Establish a Uniform System of Bankruptcy Throughout the United States. Washington: 1827. V. 38

A Bill to Establish Sundry Post Roads. Washington: 1827. V. 38

A bill to Reform the Penal Laws of the District of Columbia, and for Other Purposes. Washington: 1827. V. 38

UNITED STATES. LAWS, STATUTES, ETC. - 1828

Acts Passed at the First Session of the Twentieth Congress of the United States. Washington: 1828. V. 38

UNITED STATES. LAWS, STATUTES, ETC. - 1836

An Act to Authorize the Location of the Leavenworth and Bloomington Railroad. Washington: 1836. V. 39

A Bill to Promote the Progress of Useful Arts. Washington: 1836. V. 38

UNITED STATES. LAWS, STATUTES, ETC. - 1838

A Bill to Prohibit the Giving or Accepting, Within the District of Columbia, of a Challenge to Fight a Duel. Washington: 1838. V. 39

UNITED STATES. LAWS, STATUTES, ETC. - 1839

A Bill to Enable the People of Iowa to Form a Constitution and State Government, for the Admission of Such State into the Union. Washington: 1839. V. 37; 39

UNITED STATES. LAWS, STATUTES, ETC. - 1846

A Bill to Establish the Territorial Government of Oregon. Washington: 1846. V. 42

In the Senate of the United States . . . An Act to Define the Boundaries of the State of Iowa, and to Repeal so Much of the Act of the Third of March, One Thousand Eight Hundred and Forty-Five, as Relates to the Boundaries of Iowa. Washington: 1846. V. 39

UNITED STATES. LAWS, STATUTES, ETC. - 1847

An Act to Amend an Act Entitled 'An Act to Provide for the Better Organization of the Department of Indian Affairs. Washington: 1847. V. 39; 45

UNITED STATES. LAWS, STATUTES, ETC. - 1848

A Bill Granting to the Alabama, Florida and Georgia Railroad Company, the Alternate Sections of the Public Land Along the Route of Their. Washington: 1848. V. 39

UNITED STATES. LAWS, STATUTES, ETC. - 1854

An Act to Organize the Territories of Nebraska and Kansas. Washington: 1854. V. 38; 39

UNITED STATES. LAWS, STATUTES, ETC. - 1862

An Act to Aid in the Construction of a Railroad and Telegraph Line from the Missouri River to the Pacific Ocean. Washington: 1862. V. 39; 42; 46

UNITED STATES. LAWS, STATUTES, ETC. - 1881

Existing Laws of the United States of a General and permanent Character and Relating to the Survey and Disposition of the Public Domain . . . , and Citations of Decisions from the Federal and the State Courts . . . Washington: 1881. V. 39

UNITED STATES. LAWS, STATUTES, ETC. - 1884

Laws of the United States of a Local or Temporary Character, and Exhibiting the Entire Legislation of Congress Upon Which the Public Land Titles in Each State and territory Have Depended . . . Also, a Digest of All Treaties Affecting the Title to Public . . . Washington: 1884. V. 39

UNITED STATES. LAWS, STATUTES, ETC. - 1892

An Act to Enable the People of New Mexico to Form a Constitutional and State Government . . . Washington: 1892. V. 43

UNITED STATES. LAWS, STATUTES, ETC. - 1894

A Bill to Increase the Present Military Establishment of the United States (and) Amendment. Washington: 1836. V. 39

UNITED STATES. LIBRARY OF CONGRESS - 1804

Catalogue of Books, Maps and Charts, Belonging to the Library of the Two Houses of Congress. Washington: 1804. V. 40

UNITED STATES. LIBRARY OF CONGRESS - 1815

Catalogue of the Library of the United States . . . Washington: 1815. V. 42

UNITED STATES. LIBRARY OF CONGRESS - 1901

A List of Maps of America in the Library of Congress. Washington: 1901. V. 39; 41; 43

UNITED STATES. LIBRARY OF CONGRESS - 1909

A List of Geographical Atlases in the Library of Congress with Bibliographical Notes. Washington: 1909/09/14/20. V. 43

A List of Geographical Atlases in the Library of Congress with Bibliographic Notes. Washington: 1909-14. V. 41

A List of Geographical Atlases in the Library of Congress. Washington: 1909-20. V. 39; 43

UNITED STATES. LIBRARY OF CONGRESS - 1912

The Lowery Collection. Washington: 1912. V. 44

UNITED STATES. LIBRARY OF CONGRESS - 1943

Catalog of the 1st National Exhibition of Prints Made During the Current Year, Held 1943 at the Library of Congress . . . Plus Similar Catalogues for the Second through Eighteenth Exhibitions. Washington: 1943-60. V. 41

UNITED STATES. LIBRARY OF CONGRESS - 1975

Children's Books in the Rare Book Division of the Library of Congress. 1975. V. 39

UNITED STATES. LIBRARY OF CONGRESS. MAP DIVISION - 1909

A List of Geographical Atlases in the Library of Congress . . . Washington: 1909-74. V. 40

THE UNITED States Literary Gazette. Boston: 1824. V. 43

UNITED STATES NATIONAL LAWN TENNIS ASSOCIATION

The Playing Rules of Lawn Tennis, as Adopted by the United States National Lawn Tennis Association. New York: 1884. V. 41

UNITED STATES. NATIONAL LIBRARY OF MEDICINE

Index-Catalogue of the Library of the Surgeon General's Office. All Published. Washington: 1880-1961. V. 41; 42

UNITED STATES. NATIONAL LIBRARY OF MEDICINE - 1972

Index Catalogue of the Library of the Surgeon's-General Office. 1st Series. New York: 1972. V. 39

UNITED States Naval Academy, Annapolis, Md. New York: 1887. V. 40

UNITED STATES. NAVAL ASTRONOMICAL EXPEDITION, 1849-1852.

The United States Naval Astronomical Expedition to the Southern Hemisphere, During the Years 1849-50-51-52. Washington: 1855. V. 42; 45

UNITED STATES. NAVAL ASTRONOMICAL EXPEDITION, 1849-
1852. continued

*The U. S. Naval Astronomical Expedition to the Southern Hemisphere
During the Years 1849-50-51-52..* Washington: 1855. V. 39; 41

*The United States Astronomical Expedition to the Southern Hemisphere,
During the Years 1849-50-51-51.* Washington: 1855-56. V. 39

*The U.S. Naval Astronomical Expedition to the Southern Hemisphere, During
the Years 1849-50-51-52 . . .* Philadelphia: 1856. V. 40

*The U.S. Naval Astronomical Expedition to the Southern Hemisphere, During
the Years 1849-50-51-52. Chile: Its Geography, Climate, Earthquakes,
Government, Social Condition, Mineral and Agricultural Resources
Commerce etc.* Philadelphia: 1856. V. 40

UNITED STATES. NAVY DEPARTMENT - 1814

*Letter from the Secretary of the Navy, Transmitting a List of All the
Commissioned Officers in the Navy of the United States.* Washington:
1814. V. 41

UNITED STATES. NAVY DEPARTMENT - 1815

*Naval Register. Printed by Order of the Secretary of Navy, August 1st,
1815.* Washington City: 1815. V. 37

UNITED STATES. NAVY DEPARTMENT - 1821

*Letter from the Secretary of the Navy, Transmitting . . . the Rules and
Regulations for the Naval Service . . . January 13, 1821.* Washington: 1821.
V. 38

UNITED STATES. NAVY DEPARTMENT - 1827

*Register of the Commissioned and Warrant Officers of the Navy of the
United States; Including Officers of the Marine Corps, &c. for the Year
1828.* City of Washington: 1827. V. 37

UNITED STATES. NAVY DEPARTMENT - 1876

*United States International Cetnennial Exhibition of 1876. Catalogue of the
Articles and Objects Exhibited by the United States Navy Department in
the United States Government Building, Fairmount Park, Philadelphia, Pa.*
Philadelphia: 1876. V. 46

UNITED STATES. ORDNANCE DEPARTMENT - 1861

*The Ordnance Manual for the Use of the Officers of the United States
Army.* Richmond: 1861. V. 42; 44

UNITED STATES. ORDNANCE DEPARTMENT - 1873

Report Chief of Ordnance Year 1873. Washington: 1873. V. 39

UNITED STATES. ORDNANCE DEPARTMENT - 1878

Report Chief of Ordnance Year 1878. Washington: 1879. V. 39

UNITED STATES. ORDNANCE DEPARTMENT - 1892

Report Chief of Ordnance Year 1892. Washington: 1892. V. 39

UNITED STATES. ORDNANCE DEPARTMENT - 1893

Report of Chief of Ordnance Year 1893. Washington: 1893. V. 39

THE UNITED States Patent Law. Instruction How to Obtain Letters
Patent for New Inventions: Including a Variety of Useful Information
Concerning the Rules and Practice of the Patent Office: How to Sell
Patents . . . by Munn and Co . . . . Solictors of Patents. New York: 1866.
V. 46

UNITED STATES. POSTAL SERVICE - 1798

*Letter from the Assistant Post-Master General, Accompanying a Specification
of the Various Post Offices and of the compensations, Which Have Been
Allowed to the Deputy Post Master . . . 26th March, 1798.* Philadelphia:
1798. V. 46

UNITED STATES. PRESIDENT - 1783

*Address and Recommendations to the States by the United States in
Congress Assembled.* Philadelphia: 1783. V. 45

UNITED STATES. PRESIDENT - 1786

Observations sur La Virginie. Paris: 1786. V. 46

UNITED STATES. PRESIDENT - 1790

*Plan for Establishing Uniformity in the Currency, Coins, Weights and
Measures of the United States.* Philadelphia: 1790. V. 43

UNITED STATES. PRESIDENT - 1793

*A Message from the President . . . to Congress Relative to France and
Great Britain Delivered December 5, 1793 with the Papers Therein
Referred to . . .* Philadelphia: 1793. V. 46

UNITED STATES. PRESIDENT - 1794

*A Message of the President to Congress, Enclosing Three Letters from the
Minister of the U.S. In London, and a Letter from the Minister of the
French Republic to the Secretary of State, with His Answer.* Philadelphia:
1794. V. 39; 41

Speech of the President of the United States to both Houses of Congress.
(caption title). Philadelphia: 1794. V. 37

UNITED STATES. PRESIDENT - 1795

*Message of the President . . . Relative to France and Great Britain,
December 5, 1793.* Philadelphia: 1795. V. 37; 39

UNITED STATES. PRESIDENT - 1796

*Message from the President of the United States, Accompanying a copy of
the Treaty of Friendship, Limits and Navigation, Between the United States
and the King of Spain.* Philadelphia: 1796. V. 37

UNITED STATES. PRESIDENT - 1797

*Message From the President of the United States, Accompanying a Report
to Him from the Secretary of State, Also, an Account of the Expenditures,
for the Prosecution of the Claims of Certain Citizens of the United
States . . .* 1798. V. 42

*Message from the President of the United States, Transmitting a Report
and Sundry Documents, from the Secretary of State, of the Depredations
Committed on the Commerce of the United States Since the First of
October, 1796 . . .* Philadelphia: 1797. V. 39

*A Message from the President to Congress Relative to the French
Republic . . . With Papers Therein Referred to.* Philadelphia: 1797. V. 39

UNITED STATES. PRESIDENT - 1798

*Message of the President of the United States. To Both Houses of
Congress. May 4th, 1798.* N.P.: 1798. V. 38; 39

*Message from the President of the United States, Accompanyin copies of
Two acts of the Parliament of Great Britain, Passed on the 4th & 19th of
July 1797, Relative to the Carrying into Execution the Treaty of Amity,
Commerce and Navigation Concluded . . .* Philadelphia: 1798. V. 39; 40

*Message of the President of the United States to Both Houses of
Congress, May 4th, 1798.* Philadelphia: 1798. V. 39; 40

UNITED STATES. PRESIDENT - 1799

*Message from the President of the United States, Accompanying a Report
of the Secretary of State.* Philadelphia: 1799. V. 38

*Message from the President . . . Accompanying Sundry Papers Relative to
the Affairs of the United States with the French Republic.* Philadelphia:
1799. V. 38; 40

UNITED STATES. PRESIDENT - 1800

*Message from the President of the United States Transmitting a report of
the Secretary of War, on Certain Measures Which Appear to Him to Be
Necessary for the Improvement of Our Military System.* Philadelphia: 1800.
V. 38; 40

UNITED STATES. PRESIDENT - 1801

*Documents Respecting Barbary, Accompanying the President's
Communications to Congress.* Washington: 1801. V. 39; 42

UNITED STATES. PRESIDENT - 1802

*Message from the President of the United States to Both Houses of
Congress, 15th December, 1802.* Washington City: 1802. V. 39; 42; 43

UNITED STATES. PRESIDENT - 1803

*An Account of Louisiana, Being an Abstract of Documents, in the Offices of
the Department of State, and of the Treasury.* Philadelphia: 1803. V. 39;
40; 41; 42; 45

*An Account of Louisiana, Laid Before Congress by Direction of the
President of the United States, November 14, 1803.* Providence: 1803.
V. 38

*An Account of Louisiana, Being an Abstract of Documents, in the Offices of
the Department of State, and of the Treasury (with) Appendix.* Washington:
1803. V. 39; 42

*Message from the President of the United States, to Both Houses of
Congress, at the Commencement of the Session, 17th October, 1803.*
Washington: 1803. V. 39

UNITED STATES. PRESIDENT - 1805

Message From the President of the Senate and House of Representatives.
New York: 1805. V. 40

UNITED STATES. PRESIDENT - 1806

*Message from the President of the United States, Communicating
Discoveries Made in Exploring the Missouri, Red River and Washita, by
Captains Lewis and Calrk, Doctor Silby and Mr. Dunbar . . .* Washington:
1806. V. 38; 39; 40; 41; 42; 44; 46

*Message from the President of the United States Transmitting as a
Memorial of the Merchants of the City of Baltimore on the Violation Of
Our Neutral Rights.* Washington: 1806. V. 42

*Message from the President . . . in Relation to Incursions by the Spanish
Troops into the Territory of Louisiana.* Washington: 1806. V. 45

*Message Respecting the Violation of Neutral Rights, the Depredations on
the Colonial Trade, and Impressments of American Seamen.* Washington:
1806. V. 39

UNITED STATES. PRESIDENT - 1807

*Message from the President . . . Communicating the Discoveries in Exploring
the Missouri, Red River and Washita.* Washington: 1807. V. 38

*Message from the President . . . Transmitting Further Information Touching
an Illegal Combination of Individuals Against the Peace and Safety of the
Union.* Washington: 1807. V. 37

*Travels in the Interior Parts of America; Communicating Discoveries Made in
Exploring the Missouri, Red River and Washita, by Captains Lewis and
Clark, Doctor Sibley and Mr. Dunbar . . .* London: 1807. V. 38; 40; 41; 42

UNITED STATES. PRESIDENT - 1808

*Letters from . . . to Messrs. Monroe and Pinkney on Subjects Committed to
their Joint Negotiation with Their Communications to the Secretary of
State.* Washington: 1808. V. 38

UNITED STATES. PRESIDENT - 1836 continued

Message at the Commencement of the 2nd Session of the 24th Congress. Washington: 1836. V. 43

Seminole Hostilities. Message from the President of the United States, Transmitting a Supplement Report Respecting the Causes of the Seminole Hostilities and the Measure Taken to Suprress them, June 3, 1836. Washington: 1836. V. 42; 46

UNITED STATES. PRESIDENT - 1837

Hostilities with Creek Indians. Message from the President. Washington: 1837. V. 39

Information Concerning the Boundary Between the U.S. and Mexico. Washington: 1837. V. 38; 39

Messages of Gen. Andrew Jackson, With a Short Sketch of His Life. Concord: 1837. V. 39

Mexico and Texas. Washington: 1837. V. 39

UNITED STATES. PRESIDENT - 1838

A Bill to Prohibit the Giving or Accepting, Within the District of Columbia, of a Challenge to Fight a Duel. Washington: 1838. V. 39

Maine. Boundary - Mr. Greely . . . Message from . . . In Relation to the Imprisonment of Mr. Greely, at Frederickton. Washington: 1838. V. 39; 41

Message from the President of the United States . . . Translation of a Pamphlet in the Spanish Language . . . Feb. 28, 1838. V. 44

Message From . . . to the Two Houses of Congress at the Commencement of the Third Session of the Twnety Fifth Congress. Washington: 1838. V. 39

Mexico--Texas--Canada. Washington: 1838. V. 38; 39

Speech . . . Relating to the Annexation of Texas. Washington: 1838. V. 39

United States and Mexico: Message From . . . Transmitting . . . A Report of the Secretary of State Upon the Existing Relations Between the United States and Mexico. Washington: 1838. V. 38; 42

UNITED STATES. PRESIDENT - 1840

Message From . . . Communicating . . . Copies of All Correspondence Between the War Department and Governor Call, Concerning the War in Florida. Washington: 1840. V. 42

Message From . . . to the Two Houses of Congress. At the Commencement of the Second Session of the Twenty Sixth Congress. Washington: 1840. V. 46

UNITED STATES. PRESIDENT - 1841

Attorneys General, Construction of Public Laws. Message from . . . . Transmitting Copies of Options Given by Attorneys General, Etc. Which Give Construction to the Public Laws Not of a Temporary Character. Washington: 1841. V. 39; 40; 42

UNITED STATES. PRESIDENT - 1842

Message from . . . Cumminicating . . . Proceedings of the Commissioner Appointed to Run the Boundary Line Between the United States and the Republic of Texas, March 21, 1842. 1842. V. 44

Message from the President of the United States . . . In Compliance with a Resolution . . . Between the United States and the Mexican Republic. Washington: 1842. V. 39

Message from the President . . . Communicating . . . Copies of Correspondence with the Government of Mexico. Washington: 1842. V. 40; 41

Message from the President . . . Proceedings of the Commissioner Appointed to Run the Boundary Line Between the United States and the Repubic of Texas. Washington: 1842. V. 38; 39; 40; 41; 42

UNITED STATES. PRESIDENT - 1843

Message from . . . to the Two Houses of Congress, at the Commencement of the First Session of the Twenty Eighth Congress . . . Washington: 1843. V. 39

Taking Possession of Monterey. Message from the President of the United States . . . Washington: 1843. V. 46

UNITED STATES. PRESIDENT - 1844

Message From . . . Transmitting the Rejected Treaty for the Annexation of the Republic of Texas to the United States. Washington: 1844. V. 42

Message from the President . . . Washington: 1844. V. 41

Message at the Commencement of the 28th Congress (with Accompanying Documents). Washington: 1844. V. 38; 39

UNITED STATES. PRESIDENT - 1845

Message from the President at the Commencement of the 1st Session of the 29th Congress. Washington: 1845. V. 39; 43; 46

Message from the President of the United States. Washington: 1845. V. 40; 43

Message from the President . . . Information Relative to the Operations of the United States Squadron on the Coast of Africa, the Condition of the American Colonies There, and the Commerce of the United States Therewith . . . Washington: 1845. V. 39; 42

Message of the President of the United States, December, 1845. Washington?: 1845. V. 39

UNITED STATES. PRESIDENT - 1846

Cherokee Disturbances. Message from the President . . . Relative to the Cherokee Difficulties. Washington: 1846. V. 37

Message from the President of the United States . . . Communicating a Report of an Expedition Led by Lieutenant Abert, on the Upper Arkansas and Through the Country of the Commanche Indians. Washington: 1846. V. 40

Message of . . . Relative to the Operations and Recent Engagements on the Mexican Frontier. Washington: 1846. V. 38; 39

Occupation of Mexican Territory. Washington: 1846. V. 41

UNITED STATES. PRESIDENT - 1847

Correspondence with General Taylor. Message from the President of the United States Transmitting the Correspondence With General Taylor Since the Commencement of Hostilities with Mexico. Washington: 1847. V. 39; 41

Message from the President . . . Washington: 1847. V. 39; 41

UNITED STATES. PRESIDENT - 1848

Lieuts. J. S. Pender and G. E. B. Singletery. Message of the President . . . A Report from the Secretary of War, Relative to the Dismissal from the Public Serivce of . . . Washington: 1848. V. 40

Message from the President of the United States to the Two Houses of Congress, at the Commencement of the Second Session of the Thirtieth Congress, Dec. 5, 1848 . . . Washington: 1818. V. 42

Message of . . . on the Subject of the Mexican War. Washington: 1848. V. 39; 43

Message from the President of the United States to the Two Houses of Congress at the Commencement of the Second Session of the Thirtieth Congress. Washington: 1848. V. 41

Message from the President . . . Proceedings of the Court of Inquiry Convened at Saltillo, Mexico, January 12, 1848 . . . Relative to An . . . Washington: 1848. V. 43

Message of the President of the United States, Communicating the Proceedings of the Court Martial in the Trial of Lieutenant Colonel Fremont. Washington: 1848. V. 38

New Mexico and California. Message from the President . . . in Answer to Resolutions of the House of Representatives . . . Washington: 1848. V. 37; 39

UNITED STATES. PRESIDENT - 1849

Treaty of Guadalupe Hidalgo. Message of the President of the United States . . . Washington: 1849. V. 42

UNITED STATES. PRESIDENT - 1850

California and New Mexico. Message from the President. Washington: 1850. V. 37; 39; 41; 45

Message from the President of the United States . . . Respecting Tigre Island and Central America. Washington: 1850. V. 39

Message From the President . . . In Relation to the Boundary of Texas . . . Washington: 1850. V. 39

Message from the President . . . Report of the Secretary of the Interior . . . (and) Report of the Secretary of War. Washington: 1850. V. 43

Message of the President of the United States. Washington: 1850. V. 38

Message from the President of the United States, Communicating Information, in Answer to a Resolution of the Seminole Indians in Florida, During the Past Year . . . Washington: 1850. V. 44

UNITED STATES. PRESIDENT - 1851

Message from the President of the United States to the Two Houses of Congress . . . Washington: 1851. V. 38; 39; 41

Opinions of the Attorneys General. Message from . . . Washington: 1851. V. 40

UNITED STATES. PRESIDENT - 1854

Message from . . . Communicating the Report of an Investigation of the Charges of Fraud and Misconduct in Office, Alleged Against Alexander Ramsey, Supt. of Indian Affairs in Minnesota . . . Washington: 1854. V. 38

UNITED STATES. PRESIDENT - 1855

Message of the President of The United States, Transmitting a Report of the Secretary of the navy, in Compliance with a Resolution of the Senate of December 6, 1854, Calling for Correspondence, &c., Relative to the Navel Expedition to Japan. January 31, 1855 - Read: 1855. V. 38

UNITED STATES. PRESIDENT - 1856

Council with the Sioux Indians at Fort Pierre. Message from the President of the United States Communicating Minutes of a Council Held at Fort Pierre with the Sioux Indians . . . Washington: 1856. V. 39

Indians on the Upper Missouri. Message from the President of the United States, Transmitting a Report In Regard to the Expedition Among the . . . Washington: 1856. V. 37

Message fo the President of the United States Communicating Sundry Documents in Relation to the Affairs Which the Government of Nicaragua, and Information That the New Minister from that Government Had Been Accredited by This Government. Washington: 1856. V. 39; 46

Message of the President of the United States, Communicating in Compliance with a Resolution of Senate of February 26, Calling for a Copy of the Report and Maps of Captain Marcy of His Explorations of the Big Wichita and Head Waters of the Brazos Rivers. Washington: 1856. V. 40; 42; 45

Message of the President of the United States, Communicating the Proceedings of the Commissioners for the Adjustment of Claims Under the Convention with Great Britain or February 8, 1853. Washington: 1856. V. 46

UNITED STATES. PRESIDENT - 1856 continued

Message of . . . Communicating . . . Information Relative to the Appropriation in the Civil and Diplomatic Bill of March 3, 1855, for Richard W. Thompson, on Account of Alledged Services to the Menomonee Indians. Washington: 1856. V. 39

UNITED STATES. PRESIDENT - 1857

Indian Affairs on the Pacific. Message from the President . . . Washington: 1857. V. 37; 42

UNITED STATES. PRESIDENT - 1858

By James Buchanan, President of the United States: A Proclamation. Washington: 1858. V. 40

Message from . . . Transmitting Reports from the Secretaries of State, of War, of the Interior, and of the Attorney General, Relative to the Military Expedition Ordered into the Territory of Utah. Washington: 1858. V. 39

The Utah Expedition. Washington: 1858. V. 38; 39

UNITED STATES. PRESIDENT - 1860

Difficulties on Southwestern Frontier. Washington: 1860. V. 39

Message of the President . . . Communicating . . . Information in Relation to the Massacre at Mountain Meadows, and Other Massacres in Utah Territory . . . Washington: 1860. V. 40; 41; 45

Message of the President . . . Concerning the Alleged Hostilities Existing on the Rio Grande . . . Washington: 1860. V. 39

Utah Territory. Washington: 1860. V. 39

UNITED STATES. PRESIDENT - 1862

Message of the President to the Two Houses of Congress at the Commencement of the 3rd Session of the 37th Congress. Washington: 1862. V. 39

Message from the President . . . Transmitting . . . Correspondence Relative to the Present Condition of Mexico. Washington: 1862. V. 39

UNITED STATES. PRESIDENT - 1863

By the President of the United States of America. A Proclamation. Washington: 1863. V. 40

Letter of the Secretary of War Communicating . . . A Copy of the Report and Journal of Captain Medorem Crawford, Commanding the Emigrant Escort to Oregon and Washington Territory in the Year 1862. Washington: 1863. V. 40

President Jackson's Proclamation Against the Nullification Ordinance of South Carolina, Dec. 11, 1832. Philadelphia: 1863. V. 44

President's Message, to the Senate and House of Representatives of the Confederate States. Richmond: 1863. V. 42

UNITED STATES. PRESIDENT - 1864

Emancipation Proclamation. Chicago: 1864. V. 39

Message of the President at the Commencement of the 1st Session of the 38th Congress. Washington: 1864. V. 39

President's Message to the Senate and House of Representatives of the Confederate States of America. Richmond: 1864. V. 42

UNITED STATES. PRESIDENT - 1865

Amnesty Proclamation. Washington: 1865. V. 40

By the President of the United States of America. A Proclamation. Washington: 1865. V. 39

Emancipation Proclamation. Davenport: 1865. V. 39

UNITED STATES. PRESIDENT - 1866

Message of . . . Communicating the Report of the Secretary of State, Made in Compliance with the Requirements of an Act Entitled 'An Act to Regulate the Diplomatic and Consular Systems of the United States' . . . Washington: 1866. V. 41

Message Transmitting from the State of Colorado and Other Information Relating to the Admission of that State into the Union. Washington: 1866. V. 39

UNITED STATES. PRESIDENT - 1867

George St. Leger Grenfel. Message of . . . Transmitting Papers Relative to the Late Case of . . . Washington: 1867. V. 39

UNITED STATES. PRESIDENT - 1868

Message of . . . Communicating . . . Information in Relation to the Occupation of the Island of San Juan, in Puet Sound. Washington: 1868. V. 41

Rights of American Citizens: Message from the President of the United States . . . Relative to Trial and Conviction of American Citizens in England for Fenianism. Washington: 1868. V. 44

UNITED STATES. PRESIDENT - 1871

By the President of the United States of America. A Proclamation. Washington: 1871. V. 39; 45

UNITED STATES. PRESIDENT - 1872

Depredations on the Frontiers of Texas. Washington: 1872. V. 38

UNITED STATES. PRESIDENT - 1873

Depredations on the Frontiers of Texas. Washington: 1873. V. 39

UNITED STATES. PRESIDENT - 1874

Depredations on the Frontiers of Texas. Washington: 1874. V. 39

UNITED STATES. PRESIDENT - 1876

Message Transmitting Information in Relation to the Hostile Demonstrations of the Sioux and the Disaster to the Forces Under General Custer. Washington: 1876. V. 39

UNITED STATES. PRESIDENT - 1879

Message from the President . . . Cumminicating the Report of the Commission Appointed . . . to Make Certain Negotiations With the Ute. Washington: 1879. V. 41

UNITED STATES. PRESIDENT - 1882

Message from the President of the United States, Transmitting a Communication from the Secretary of the Interiors, with a Draft of a Bill to Accept & Ratify an Agreement with the Crown Indians for the Sale of a Portion of Their Reservation . . . Washington: 1882. V. 39

Message from the President of the United States Transmitting a Communication from the Secretary of War . . . Recommending an Appropriation for the Purchase of a Site and the Erection of a Fire Proof Building to Contain the Records, Library & Museum . . . Washington: 1882. V. 39

UNITED STATES. PRESIDENT - 1883

Message From the President of the U.S., Transmitting a Communication . . . Submitting a Draft of a Bill 'To Accept & Ratify an Agreement with the Confederated Tribes of the Flathead, Kootenay, & Upper Pend D' Oreilles Indians for the Sale of . . . Washington: 1883. V. 37

UNITED STATES. PRESIDENT - 1884

Proceedings of the 'Proteus' Court of Inquiry on the Greely Relief Expediton of 1883. Message of . . . Transmitting . . . Records of the Court of Inquiry in Relation to the Loss of the Steamer Proteus in the Arctic Ocean. Washington: 1884. V. 38

UNITED STATES. PRESIDENT - 1885

Message from . . . Relative to Certain Lands in Indian Territory Acquired by Treaty from the Creek and Sminole Indians. Washington: 1885. V. 39

UNITED STATES. PRESIDENT - 1888

Message from . . . Transmitting Letter of the Secretary of the Interior with Draught of Bill to Forfeit Certain Lands Granted Oregon for Wagon Roads, and for Other Purposes. Washington: 1888. V. 39

Message from the President of the United States Transmitting the Reports of the United States Pacific Railway Commission and the Testimony. Washington: 1888. V. 46

UNITED STATES. PRESIDENT - 1890

Intrusions on Cherokee Strip, February 17, 1890 . . . a Proclamation. Washington: 1890. V. 39; 40

Message From . . . Transmitting Papers Relative to the Proposed Division of the Great Sioux Reservation, and Recommending Certain Legislation. Washington: 1890. V. 41

UNITED STATES. PRESIDENT - 1898

Equitable Distribution of the Waters of the Rio Grande. Message from the President of the U.S., transmitting . . . reports from the Secretary of State, the Secretary of War, the Secretary of the Interior and the Attorney General . . . Washington: 1898. V. 38

UNITED STATES. PRESIDENT - 1901

Message of the President at the Beginning of the First Session of the 57th Congress. Washington: 1901. V. 39

UNITED STATES. PRESIDENT - 1906

Report on the Transportation of Petroleum. Washington: 1906. V. 38

UNITED STATES. PRESIDENT - 1910

Coal Lands in Oklahoma. Message from the President . . . Transmitting Reports Rendered in Connection with the Investigation to Determine the Extent and Value of the Coal DEposits in and Under the Segegated Coal Lands of the Choctaw and Chickasaw Nations . . . Washington: 1910. V. 39

UNITED STATES. PRESIDENT - 1911

Message from the President of the U.S. Transmitting . . . All Papers & Information Relting to the Elimination from the Chugach National Forest of Certain Lands Fronting Upon Controller Bay, in Alaska. Washington: 1911. V. 38

UNITED STATES. PRESIDENT - 1944

Interregional Highways. Message from the President . . . Transmitting a Report of the National Interregional Highway Committee, Outlining and Recommending a National System of Interregional Highways. Washington: 1944. V. 40

UNITED STATES. QUARTERMASTER'S DEPT. - 1887

Flags of the Army of the United States Carried During the War of the Rebellion 1861-1865 . . . Philadelphia: 1887. V. 45

THE UNITED States Register for the Year 1795; Being the 19-20th National Sovereignty. Philadelphia: 1794. V. 46

THE UNITED States Register, or Blue Book for 1861-62, Containing a List of all the Principal Officers of the Federal Government. New York: 1861. V. 40

UNITED STATES. REVENUE CUTTER SERVICE - 1883

Cruise of the Revenue-Steamer Corwin in Alaska and the N.W. Arctic Ocean in 1881. Notes and Memoranda . . . Washington: 1883. V. 39

UNITED STATES. REVENUE CUTTER SERVICE - 1904

Report of the Operations of the U.S. Revenue Steamer Nunivak on the Yukon River Station, Alaska, 1899-1901. Washington: 1904. V. 39

THE UNITED States Sanitary Commission. A Sketch of Its Purposes and Its Work. Boston: 1863. V. 41; 42

UNITED States Service Magazine. New York: 1864. V. 38

UNITED STATES. SIXTH CENSUS - 1841

Compendium of the Enumeration of the Inhabitants and Statistics of the United States . . . from the Returns of the Sixth Census. Washington: 1841. V. 42

UNITED STATES. STATE DEPARTMENT - 1790

Report of the Secretary of State, on the Subject of Establishing a Uniformity in the Weights, Measures and Coins of the United States. New York: 1790. V. 37

UNITED STATES. STATE DEPARTMENT - 1791

Report of the Secretary of State, on the Subject of the Cod and Whale Fisheries. Philadelphia: 1791. V. 41

UNITED STATES. STATE DEPARTMENT - 1798

Letter from the Secretary of State. Accompanying a Report and Abstract of All the Return of Registered American Seamen and the Protests and Returns Respecting Impressed Seamen . . . Philadelphia: 1798. V. 37; 43

UNITED STATES. STATE DEPARTMENT - 1815

State Papers and Publick Documents . . . Exhibiting a Complete View of Our Foreign Relations, 1806-1808. Boston: 1815. V. 45

UNITED STATES. STATE DEPARTMENT - 1817

Letter from the Secretary of State Transmitting a List of the Names of Persons to Whom Patents Have Been Issued for the Invention of Any New or Useful Art, or Machine, Manufacture, or Composition of Matter, or Any Improvement Thereon, 1816-1817. Washington: 1817. V. 39

UNITED STATES. STATE DEPARTMENT - 1825

Documents from the Department of State, Intended to Accompany the President's Message to Congress of Seventh December Last. Washington: 1825. V. 39

UNITED STATES. STATE DEPARTMENT - 1828

Letter from the Secretary of State . . . . Washington: 1828. V. 41

UNITED STATES. STATE DEPARTMENT - 1862

Letter of the Secretary of State, Transmitting a Report of the Commercial Relations of the United States with Foreign Nations. Washington: 1862. V. 39

UNITED STATES. STATE DEPARTMENT - 1864

Communication of Hon. William H. Seward, Secretary of State, Upon the Subject of an Intercontinental Telegraph Connecting the Eastern and Western Hemispheres by Way of Behring's Strait, in Reply to Hon. Z. Chandler, Chairman of the Committee. Washington: 1864. V. 46

UNITED STATES. STATE DEPARTMENT - 1878

Reports Upon the Survey of the Boundary Between the Territory of the United States and the Possessions of Great Britain From the Lake of the Woods to the Summit of the Rocky Mountains . . . Washington: 1878. V. 42

UNITED STATES. STATE DEPARTMENT - 1889

Message from the President of the United States, Transmitting Report on the Boundary Line Between Alaska and British Columbia. Washington: 1889. V. 41

THE UNITED States Strategic Bombing Survey - The Effects of Atomic Bombs on Hiroshima and Nagasaki. 1946. V. 45

UNITED STATES. SUPREME COURT - 1793

A Case Decided in the Supreme Court of the United States, February 1793, in Which was Discussed the Question 'Whether a State be Liable to be Sued by a Private Person of Another State?' Philadelphia: 1793. V. 45

A Case Decided in the Supreme Court of the United States, In February, 1793, in Which is Discussed the Question, 'Whether a State be Liable to be Sued by a Private Citizen of Another State.' Boston: 1793. V. 38

UNITED STATES. SUPREME COURT - 1795

A Report of the Opinions of the Judges in the Important Cause of Penhallow et al, Against Doane's Administrators, Delivered in the Supreme Court of the United States at February Term, 1795. Philadelphia: 1795. V. 41

UNITED STATES. SUPREME COURT - 1806

Reports of Cases Argued and Adjudged in the Supreme Court of the United States, in February Term, 1804 and February Term 1805. New York: 1806. V. 43

UNITED STATES. SUPREME COURT - 1829

Opinion of the Supreme Court of the United States, Delivered by Mr. Chief Justice in the Case of Foster and Elam, Plantiffs in Error, vs. Neilson, Defendant in Error . . . N.P.: 1829. V. 39; 42; 45

UNITED STATES. SUPREME COURT - 1832

Opinion of the Supreme Court of the United States, at January Term, 1832, Delivered by Mr. Chief Justice Marshall, Together with the Opinion of Mr. Justice McLean. In the Case of Samuel A. Worcester, Plantiff in Error, Versus the State of Georgia . . . Washington: 1832. V. 38; 39; 44; 45

UNITED STATES. SUPREME COURT - 1852

The States of Louisiana and Maryland vs. the Executors of John McDonogh and the Citites of New Orleans and Baltimore; Argument for the Cities by Alex. Grailhe. New Orleans: 1852. V. 39

UNITED STATES. SUPREME COURT - 1882

Report of the Proceedings in the Case of the Unites States vs. Charles J. Guiteau Tried in the Supreme Court . . . of Columbia, November, 18881. Washington: 1882. V. 38

UNITED STATES. SURVEYOR GENERAL - 1871

Report of the Surveyor General of Wyoming. Washington: 1871. V. 39

UNITED STATES TOURING INFORMATION BUREAU

The Complete Camp Site Guide and Latest Highway Map of U.S.A. Waterloo: 1923. V. 39

UNITED STATES. TREASURY DEPARTMENT - 1791

Report of the Secretary of the Treasury of the United STates on the Subject of manufactures . . . December 5, 1791. Philadelphia: 1791. V. 44; 45

The Secretary of Treasury Having Attentively considered the Subject Referred to Him by the Order of the House of Representatives on the Fifteenth Day of April Last, Relative to the Estalbishment of a Mint, Most Respectfully Submits the Result . . . Philadelphia: 1791. V. 46

UNITED STATES. TREASURY DEPARTMENT - 1792

The Treasurer of the United States, Accounts of Payment and Receipts of the Public Monies from the 1st of January to the 30th of September, 1792. New York: 1792. V. 41

UNITED STATES. TREASURY DEPARTMENT - 1793

Report of the Secretary of the Treasury of the United States, on the Subject of Manufacutres. Presented to the House of Representatives. Dec. 5, 1791. London: 1793. V. 38

Treasury Department, February, 1793 . . . in Obedience to an Order of the President. Philadelphia: 1793. V. 39

UNITED STATES. TREASURY DEPARTMENT - 1795

Report of the Secretary of the Treasury . . . Containing a Plan for the Further Support of Public Credit. Philadelphia: 1795. V. 45

UNITED STATES. TREASURY DEPARTMENT - 1808

Report of the Secretary of the Treasury on the Subject of Public Roads and Canals made in Pursuance of a Resolution of Senate, of March 2, 1807. Washington: 1808. V. 46

UNITED STATES. TREASURY DEPARTMENT - 1814

Letter from the Comptroller of the Treasury, Transmitting the Annual List of Unsettled Balances on the Books of the Treasury and Navy Departments, April 5, 1814. Washington: 1814. V. 46

UNITED STATES. TREASURY DEPARTMENT - 1815

Letter from the Acting Comptroller of the Treasury Transmitting Statements of the Accounts in the Treasury and Navy Department, Which Have Remained More than Three Years Unsettled, or, on Which Balances Appear to Have Been Due . . . Washington: 1815. V. 46

Letter from the Secretary of the Treasury Transmitting Two Statements of the Importations of Goods, Wares & Merchandise in American & Foreign Vessels & an Aggregate View of Both from the first of Oc. 1813 to the 30th of September 1814. Washington: 1815. V. 46

UNITED STATES. TREASURY DEPARTMENT - 1817

Letter from the Comptroller of the Treasury Trnasmitting a List of Balances Which Appear to Have Been Due More Than Three Years Prior to the 13th of September Last . . . Washington: 1817. V. 46

Letter from the Secretary of the Treasury, Transmitting STatements of the Importations of Goods, Wares and Merchandise in American and Foreign Vessels and an Aggregate View of Both from the 1st of October, 1814 to the 30th of September 1815, Feb. 28, 1817. Washington: 1817. V. 46

Letter from the Secretary of the Treasury, Transmitting an Estimate of the Appropriations for the Service of the Year 1817. January 6, 1817. Washington: 1817. V. 46

Letter from the Secretary of the Treasury Transmitting Two Statements of the Importations of Goods, Wares & Merchandise in American & Foreign Vessels & an Aggregate View of Both from the First of Oct. 1813 to the 30th of Sept. 1814. Washington: 1817. V. 46

Letter from Thomas Tudor Tucker, Treasurer of the United States, Transmitting His Accounts for 1816, February 25, 1817. Washington: 1817. V. 46

UNITED STATES. TREASURY DEPARTMENT - 1846

Report of the Secretary of the Treasury Transmitting a Report from the Register of the Treasury on Commerce and Navigation. Washington: 1846. V. 42

UNITED STATES. TREASURY DEPARTMENT - 1848

Letter of the Secretary of the Treasury, Communicating a Report of a Geological Reconnaissance of the Chippewa Land District of Wisconsin, and the Northern Part of Iowa. Washington: 1848. V. 38

UNITED STATES. TREASURY DEPARTMENT - 1866

Petroleum. Letter from the Secretary of the Treasury, Transmitting a Report of S. S. Hays on Petroleum. Washington: 1866. V. 42

UNITED STATES. TREASURY DEPARTMENT - 1871

Report to the Secretary of the Treasury in Relation to the Foreign Commerce of the United States . . . Washington: 1871. V. 42

UNITED STATES. TREASURY DEPARTMENT - 1885

Letter from the Secretary of the Treasury, Transmitting a Report . . . in Regard to the Range and Ranch Cattle Traffic in the Western States and Territories. Washington: 1885. V. 38; 43; 46

Report on the Internal Commerce of the United States. Washington: 1885. V. 39; 40; 42; 43; 45

UNITED STATES. TREASURY DEPARTMENT - 1899

Cruise of the U. S. Revenue Cutter Bear and the Overland Expedition to . . . Washington: 1899. V. 37

UNITED STATES. TREASURY DEPTARTMENT - 1884

Report on the Internal Commerce of the United States, by Joseph Nimmo, Jr . . . . Washington: 1884. V. 42

UNITED STATES. TREATIES - 1796

The Laws of the United States of America, Volume II: The Treaties Made by the United States of America with Other Nations. Philadelhia: 1796. V. 37

UNITED STATES. TREATIES - 1867

A Treaty Between the United States and His Majesty the Emperor of all the Russias. Washington: 1867. V. 37

Treaty Between the United States of America and the Nez Perce Tribe of Indians. Concluded June 9, 1863. Ratification Advised, April 17, 1867. Proclaimed April 20. 1867. Washington: 1867. V. 37

UNITED STATES. TREATIES, ETC. - 1826

Commissioners Under the Treaty of Ghent: Proceedings of the Joint Commission of Indemnities. Washington: 1826. V. 39

Treaty with the Florida Indians. Letter from the Secretary of War. Transmitting the Information . . . in Relation to the Instructions Given to the Commissioners for Negotiating with the Florida Indians . . . 1826. Washington: 1826. V. 45

UNITED STATES. TREATIES, ETC. - 1828

Treaty of Amity, Commerce and Navigation Between the United States of America and the United Mexican States. Washington: 1828. V. 40

UNITED STATES. TREATIES, ETC. - 1834

Treaty Between the United States of America and the Cherokee Nation of Indians, West of the Mississippi. Concluded Feb. 14, 1833 - ratified April 12, 1834. Washington: 1834. V. 45

Treaty Between the United States of America and the Chickasaw Indians. Concluded May 24, 1834 - Ratified July 1, 1834. Washington: 1834. V. 45

UNITED STATES. TREATIES, ETC. - 1836

Treaty Between the United States of America and the Comanche and Witchetaw Nations, and Their Associated Bands or Tribes of Indians. Concluded August 24, 1835 - Ratified May 16, 1836. Washington: 1836. V. 39

UNITED STATES. TREATIES, ETC. - 1848

Tatado De Paz, Amistad, Limites Y Arreglo Definitivo Entre La Republica Mexicana Y Los Estados-Unidos de America . . . Mexico: 1848. V. 46

Treaty Between the United States and Mexico and the Proceedings of the Senate Thereon . . . From Which the Injunciton of Secresy Has Been Removed. Washington: 1848. V. 38

Treaty of Peace, Friendship, Limits, and Settlements Between the United States of America and the Mexican Republic. Dated at Guadalupe Hidalgo, 2nd February 1848. Washington: 1848. V. 40; 46

UNITED STATES. TREATIES, ETC. - 1849

Treaty of Guadalupe Hidalgo. Message of the President Transmitting a Communication from the Secretary of State . . . Relative to the Treaty of Peace Concluded at Guadalupe Hidalgo. Washington: 1849. V. 39

UNITED STATES. TREATIES, ETC. - 1854

Treaty Between the United States and the Ioway Indians. Washington: 1854. V. 39

UNITED STATES. TREATIES, ETC. - 1855

Treaty Between the United States and the Rogue River Indians. Washington: 1855. V. 39; 42; 46

Treaty (of Nebraska City) Between the United States and the Ottoe and Missouria Indians. Washington: 1855. V. 39

UNITED STATES. TREATIES, ETC. - 1859

Treaty Between the United States and the Flahead, Kootenay and Upper Pend d'oreilles Indians, July 16, 1855, Ratified April 18, 1859. Washington: 1859. V. 39

UNITED STATES. TREATIES, ETC. - 1860

Treaty Between the United States and the Confederated Tribes of the Sacs and Foxes of the Mississippi, Made October, 1859, Ratified July 9, 1860. Washington: 1860. V. 39; 41

UNITED STATES. TREATIES, ETC. - 1865

Treaty Between the United States and the Commanche and Kiowa Tribes of Indians, Concluded October 18, 1865. Washington: 1866. V. 39

UNITED STATES. TREATIES, ETC. - 1866

Treaty Between the United States and the (1) Blackfeet Band of Dakota or Sioux Indians (2) O'Gallala Band (3) Sans Arcs Band (4) Onk-Pah-Pah Band (5) Minneconjon Band (6) Two Kettles Band . . . Washington: 1866. V. 39; 41; 42; 45

Treaty Between the United States of America and the Woll-Pah-Pe Tribe of Snake Indians, Concluded August 12, 1865. Washington: 1866. V. 43

Treaty Between the United States and the Delaware Tribe of Indians, Concluded July 4, 1866. Washington: 1866. V. 39

Treaty Between the United States of America and the Comanche and Kiowa Tribes of Indians. Concluded October 18, 1865. Ratification Advised, May 22, 1866. Proclaimed May 26, 1866. Washington: 1866. V. 41

UNITED STATES. TREATIES, ETC. - 1867

A Treaty Between the United States and His Majesty the Emperor of All the Russias. Washington: 1867. V. 39; 43

Treaty Between the United States of America and the Nez Perce Tribe of Indians Concluded June 9, 1863 . . . Washington: 1867. V. 39; 41; 42

UNITED STATES. TREATIES, ETC. - 1870

Treaty Between the United States . . . and the Klamath and Modoc Tribes and Yahooskin Band of Snake Indians. Washington: 1870. V. 38; 45

UNITED STATES. TREATIES, ETC. - 1872

Papers Relating to the Treaty of Washington. Washington: 1872. V. 38

UNITED STATES. TREATIES, ETC. - 1899

A Treaty of Peace Between the United States and Spain. Washington: 1899. V. 42

UNITED STATES. WAR DEPARTMENT - 1798

Letter from the Secretary of War, Inclosing His Report on the Pteition of Stephen Cantrill. Philadelphia: 1798. V. 45

UNITED STATES. WAR DEPARTMENT - 1817

Rules and Regulations for the Field Exercise and Manoeuvres of Infantry, Compiled and Adapted to the Organization of the Army of the United States, Agreeable to a Resolve of Congress, Dated Dec. 1814 . . . Concord: 1817. V. 39

UNITED STATES. WAR DEPARTMENT - 1819

Letter from the Secretary of War, Transmitting . . . Information in Relation to the destruction of the Negro Fort, in East Florida, in the Month of July 1816 &c. Washington: 1819. V. 41

UNITED STATES. WAR DEPARTMENT - 1820

Report of the Secretary of War, or the Terms on Which Contracts Have Been Made for the Transportation of Troops Ordered on the Expedition. Washington: 1820. V. 39

UNITED STATES. WAR DEPARTMENT - 1823

Letter from the Secretary of War Transmitting Copies of the Accounts of Superintendents and Agents for Indian Affairs . . . Washington: 1823. V. 39

Letter from the Secretary of War . . . Upon the Subject of the Military Road Leading from Plattsburg to Sackett's Harbour. Washington: 1823. V. 42

Letter of the Secretary of War, Transmitting an Abstract of All Licenses Granted by Superindents of Indian Trade &c. Washington: 1823. V. 38

UNITED STATES. WAR DEPARTMENT - 1825

Letter from the Secretary of War, Transmitting Copies of the Report and Proceedings of the Commissioners Appointed to Treat with the Creek nation of Indians, for an Extinguishment of Their Claim to Land, Lying Within the State of Georgia, &c. Washington: 1825. V. 37

UNITED STATES. WAR DEPARTMENT - 1826

Canal--Buzzard and Barnstable Bays. Letter from the Secretary of War, Transmitting a Memoir of the Survey of the Route of a Canal, to Connect Buzzard and Barnstable Bays, in the State of Massachusetts, with Three Sheets of Drawings. Washington: 1826. V. 38

. . . Expedition Up the Missouri, Letter from the Secretary of War . . . Respecting the Movements of the Expedition Which Lately Ascended the Missouri River Mar. 6 1826. Washington: 1826. V. 37; 40; 41

UNITED STATES. WAR DEPARTMENT - 1828

Licenses Granted to Trade with Indians. Letter from the Secretary of Wara, Transmitting an Abstract of all Licenses Granted by the Uperintendents and Agents for Indian Affairs, to Trade with Indians. Washington: 1828. V. 37

Official Record from the War Department, of the Proceedings of the Court Martial which Tried, and the Orders of General Jackson for Shooting the Six Militia Men, Together with Official Letters from the War Department . . . Washington: 1828. V. 45

UNITED STATES. WAR DEPARTMENT - 1830

Indian Depredations in Georgia. Letter from the Secretary of War. Washington: 1830. V. 39

UNITED STATES. WAR DEPARTMENT - 1834

Report from the Secretary of War . . . Concerning the Location of Reservations Under the Choctaw Treaty of 1830. Washington: 1834. V. 38

UNITED STATES. WAR DEPARTMENT - 1836

Report of the Secretary of War, in Compliance with a Resolution of the Senate, Transmitting a Report of the Expedition of the Dragoons, Under the Command of Colonel Henry Dodge to the Rocky Mountains During the Summer of 1835 &c. Washington: 1836. V. 46

Report of the Secretary of War . . . Respecting the Enrollments, Emigration, and Improvements of the Cherokees Residing East of the Mississippi. Washington: 1836. V. 37

UNITED STATES. WAR DEPARTMENT - 1838

Report from the Secretary of War in Compliance with a Resolution . . . 1837, in Relation to the Cherokee Treaty of 1835. Washington: 1838. V. 37; 42

Report from the Secretary of War . . . in Relation to the Protection of the Western Frontier of the United States. Washington: 1838. V. 40; 41; 42

Report from the Secretary of War . . . in Relation to the Selection of a Site for a Fort on the Western Frontier Line of Arkansas. Washington: 1838. V. 42

Report from the Secretary of War . . . Transmitting Reports of the Surveys of . . . Milwaukie, Root, Manitowoc, Sheboygan and Kewaunee Rivers . . . Washington: 1838. V. 42

UNITED STATES. WAR DEPARTMENT - 1840

Defence of Western Frontier. Letter from the Secretary of War . . . Relative to the Plan Proposed for the Defence of the Western Frontier; Also, What Tribes of Indians Inhabit the Country Immediately West of Arkansas and Missouri. Washington: 1840. V. 41

Post-Frontier of Louisiana. Letter from the Secretary of War . . . Respecting the Non-Establishment of a Military Post on or Near the Western Boundary of the State of Louisiana. Washington: 1840. V. 40

UNITED STATES. WAR DEPARTMENT - 1847

Secretary of War Reprot. Washington: 1847. V. 37

UNITED STATES. WAR DEPARTMENT - 1848

Correspondence Between the Secretary of War and Generals Scott and Taylor, and Between General Scott and Mr. Trist. Washington: 1848. V. 38; 39

Mexican War Correspondence. Washington: 1848. V. 38

Report of the Secretary of War Communicating . . . a Report and Map of the Examination of New Mexico, Made by James W. Abert. Washington: 1848. V. 38; 40; 41

UNITED STATES. WAR DEPARTMENT - 1849

Report of the Secretary of War Communicating the Official Journal of Lieutenant Colonel Philip St. George Cooke, from Santa Fe to San Diego . . . Washington: 1849. V. 40

UNITED STATES. WAR DEPARTMENT - 1850

Ordnance Manual . . . Use Officers . . . United States Army. Washington: 1850. V. 37

Pembina Settlement. Letter from the Secretary of War, Transmitting Report of . . . Relative to His Expedition to Pembina Settlement, and the Condition of Affairs on the North Western Frontier of the Territory of Minnesota. Washington: 1850. V. 39

Report of the Secretary of War . . . an Exploration of the Territory of Minnesota, by Brevet Captain Pope. Washington: 1850. V. 40; 41

A Report of the Secretary of War, With Reconnaissances of Routes From San Antonio to El Paso . . . . Washington: 1850. V. 38; 39; 41; 43; 46

Report of the Secretary of War, Communicating . . . Operations of the Army of the United States in Texas and the Adjacent Mexican States on the Rio Grande. Washington: 1850. V. 39

Report of the Secretary of War, Communicating . . . a Map of the Valley of Mexico, from Surveys by Lieutenants Smith and Hardcastle. Washington: 1850. V. 42

UNITED STATES. WAR DEPARTMENT - 1851

Report of the Secretary of War Communicating . . . Colonel McCall's Reports in Relation to New Mexico. Washington: 1851. V. 39; 40

Report of the Secretary of War, Communicating a Copy of W. H. Sidell's Survey of a Route for a Railroad From the Great Bend, on the Red River, to Providence, on the Mississippi River. Washington: 1851. V. 39

UNITED STATES. WAR DEPARTMENT - 1852

Letter from the Secretary of War, Communicting . . . a Report of the Survey, Estimates &c. of a Route from St. Louis to the Big Bend of the Red River, By Joshua Barney . . . Washington: 1852. V. 38

Report of the Secretary of War, Communicating . . . The Report of Lieut. Colonel Graham on the Subject of the Boundary Line Between the United States and Mexico. Washington: 1852. V. 40; 41

Report of the Secretary of War, Communicating . . . a Reconnoissance of the Gulf of California and the Colorado River by Lieutenant Derby. Washington: 1852. V. 38

UNITED STATES. WAR DEPARTMENT - 1853

Reports of Explorations and Surveys, to Ascertain the Most Practicable and Economical Route for a Railroad from the Mississippi to the Pacific Ocean, Made Under the Directions of the Secretary of War in 1853-54. Washington: 1855-59/60/61. V. 46

UNITED STATES. WAR DEPARTMENT - 1854

Report of the Secretary of War, Communicating Copies of all Reports of the Engineers and Other Persons, Employed to Make Explorations and Surveys to Ascertain the Most Practicable and Economical Route for a Railroad from the Mississippi River . . . Washington: 1854. V. 38

UNITED STATES. WAR DEPARTMENT - 1855

Pacific Railroad Survey. Reports of Explorations and Surveys, to Ascertain the Most Practicable and Economical Route from the Mississippi River to the Pacific Ocean, 1853-54. Washington: 1855-61. V. 46

Report of the Secretary of War . . . Several Railroad Explorations. Washington: 1855. V. 38

Reports of Explorations and Surveys, to Ascertain the Most Practicable and economical Route for a Railroad from the Mississippi River to the Pacific Ocean . . . Volume 2. Washington: 1855. V. 38

Reports of Explorations and Surveys, to Ascertain the Most Practicable and Economical Route for a Railroad From the Mississippi River to the Pacific Ocean, Made Under the Direction of the Secretary of War . . . in 1853-4. Washington: 1855-60. V. 39; 40; 41; 42; 44; 45; 46

Reports of Explorations and Surveys, to Ascertain the Most Practicable and Economical Route for a Railroad from the Mississippi River to the Pacific Ocean. Washington: 1855-69. V. 45

Reports of Explorations and Surveys, to Ascertain the Most Practicable and Economical Route for a Railroad from the Mississippi Rover to the Pacific Ocean. Made Under the Direction of the Secretary of War. Washington: 1855-59. V. 39

UNITED STATES. WAR DEPARTMENT - 1856

Message of the President . . . Communicating . . . the Report and Maps of Captain Marcy of His Explorations of the Big Wichita and Head Waters of the Brazos Rivers. Washington: 1856. V. 41

UNITED STATES. WAR DEPARTMENT - 1857

Report of the Secretary of War, Communicatin . . . Information Respecting the Purchase of Camels for the Purposes of Military Transportation. Washington: 1857. V. 38; 39; 44

Report of the Secretary of War, Communicating the Report of Captain George B. McClellan . . . Washington: 1857. V. 42

UNITED STATES. WAR DEPARTMENT - 1859

Report of the Secretary of War, Communicating . . . Captain Simpson's Report and Map of Wagon Road Routes in Utah Territory. Washington: 1859. V. 40

UNITED STATES. WAR DEPARTMENT - 1860

Report of the Secretary of War, Communicating . . . the Report of Captain H. D. Wallen of His Expedition in 1859, from Dalles City to Great Salt Lake, and Back. Washington: 1860. V. 40; 41

Troubles on Texas Frontier. Letter from the Secretary of War, Communicating . . . Information in Relation to the Troubles of the Texas Frontier. Washington: 1860. V. 40

UNITED STATES. WAR DEPARTMENT - 1860 or PRESIDENT

Message from the President of the U.S., Communicating . . . . Washington: 1860. V. 42

UNITED STATES. WAR DEPARTMENT - 1863

General Orders. No. 100. War Department, Adjutant General's Office, Washington, April 24, 1863. Memphis: 1863. V. 40

Instructions for Heavy Artillery. Washington: 1863. V. 37; 38

Letter of the Secretary of War Communicating . . . a Copy of the Report of Major D. Fergusson on the Country, Its Resources, and the Route Between Tucson and Lobos Bay. Washington: 1863. V. 39; 42

Report of . . . Letter from the Secretary of War . . . Transmitting Copy of Report . . . concerning the Operations of the Army of Virginia, While Under His Command. Washington: 1863. V. 39

Report of the Judge Advocate General to the Secretary of War. Washington: 1863/1863. V. 44

UNITED STATES. WAR DEPARTMENT - 1864

Expedition of Captain Fisk to the Rocky Mountains. Letter From the Secretary of War . . . Washington: 1864. V. 40

Letter of the Secretary of War, Transmitting Report on the Organization of the Army of the Potomac and Of Its Campaigns in Virginia and Maryland, Under the Command of Maj. Gen. George B. McClellan. Washington: 1864. V. 45

UNITED STATES. WAR DEPARTMENT - 1865

Report of the Secretary of War, 1865. Washington: 1865. V. 39; 42; 43; 44; 45

UNITED STATES. WAR DEPARTMENT - 1866

Annual Report of the Secretary of War for the Year 1866. Washington: 1866. V. 37

Letter from the Secretary of War Transmitting a Report by the Commissioner of the Freedmen's Bureau, of All Orders by Him or any Assistant Commissioner. Washington: 1866. V. 39

UNITED STATES. WAR DEPARTMENT - 1867

Letter of the Secretary of War . . . Official Reports, Papers and Facts in Relation to the Causes and Extent of the Late Massacre of United States Troops by Indians At Fort Phil. Kearney. Washington: 1st edition; V. 45

Report of the Secretary of War of 1867. Part 1. Washington: 1867. V. 45

Report of the Secretary of War . . . a Copy of the Evidence Taken at Denver and Fort Lyon . . . to Inquire into the Sand Creek Massacre. Washington: 1867. V. 41; 42

UNITED STATES. WAR DEPARTMENT - 1871

Letter from the Secretary of War, Communiating the Report of Robert E. Strahorn Upon the So-Called Yellowstone Exepedition of 1870. Washington: 1871. V. 39

UNITED STATES. WAR DEPARTMENT - 1872

Letter from the Secretary of War, Communicating, in Compliance with a Resolution of the Senate of March 7, 1872, a Preliminary Report . . . of the Progress of the Engineer Exploration of the Public Domain in Nevada and Arizona. Washington: 1872. V. 40

UNITED STATES. WAR DEPARTMENT - 1876

H.R. 44th Cong. 2nd Sess. Ex. Doc. 1, Part II Report of the Secretary of War. Washington: 1876. V. 45

UNITED STATES. WAR DEPARTMENT - 1877

Annual Report of the Secretary of War on the Operations of the Department. Washington: 1877. V. 39; 41

UNITED STATES. WAR DEPARTMENT - 1878

El Paso Troubles in Texas. Letter from the Secretary of War. Washington: 1878. V. 38

UNITED STATES. WAR DEPARTMENT - 1881

Regulations Army . . . United States . . . General Orders in Force, Feb. 17l, 1881. Washington: 1881. V. 37

UNITED STATES. WAR DEPARTMENT - 1882

Uniform of the Army of the United States 1882. Prepared Under Instructions from the Quartermaster General. Philadelphia: 1882. V. 37

UNITED STATES. WAR DEPARTMENT - 1889

Letter from the Secretary of War Transmitting . . . Report of Capt. W. E. Birkhimer . . . Washington: 1889. V. 39; 41

UNITED STATES. WAR DEPARTMENT - 1890

Official Army Register for January, 1890. Published by Order of the Secretary of War. Washington: 1890. V. 41

Report of the Secretary of War - 1890. Washington: 1892. V. 37

UNITED STATES. WAR DEPARTMENT - 1898

Ship Canal at Sabine Pass, Texas. Letter from the Secretary of War, Transmitting a Letter from the Chief of Engineers in Response to the Joint Resolution of Congress, Approved May 28, 1898, Relating to a Ship Canal at Sabine Pass. Washington: 1898. V. 40

UNITED STATES. WAR DEPARTMENT - 1901

Annual Reports of the War Department for the Fiscal Year Ended June 30, 1901. Washington: 1901. V. 39

Report of the Military Governor of Cuba on Civil Affairs. Washington: 1901. V. 43

UNITED STATES. WAR DEPARTMENT - 1902

A Letter from the Secretary of War Transmitting Results of Preliminary Examinations & Surveys of Sites for Military Posts. Washington: 1902. V. 37

UNITED STATES. WAR DEPARTMENT - 1912

Claims Growing Out of Insurrection in Mexico. Letter from the Secretary of War . . . Report of . . . Claims of American Citizens for Damages Suffered Within American Territory and Growing Out of the Late Insurrection in Mexico. 1912. V. 44

UNITED STATES. WAR DEPARTMENT - 1917

War Surgery of the Nervous System. Washington: 1917. V. 45

UNITED STATES. WAR DEPARTMENT - 1918

Instruction on the Type 'R' Balloon. Washington: 1918. V. 39

UNITED STATES. WAR DEPARTMENT. INSEPCTOR GENERAL'S OFFICE

Regulations for the Order and Discipline of Troops of the United States. Part I. Hartford: 1782. V. 39

UNITED STATES. WAR DEPARTMENT. INSPECTOR GENERAL'S OFFICE

Regulations for the Order and Discipline of Troops of the United States. Part 1. Hartford: 1783? V. 39

THE UNIVERSAL Angler. London: 1766. V. 39; 40; 43; 45

UNIVERSAL Chronologist, and Historical Register. Comprehending the Period from the Year 1700 to the Close of the Year 1825. London: 1826. V. 41

THE UNIVERSAL Dream Book, Alphabetically Arranged. Baltimore: 1839. V. 40

UNIVERSAL Family Physician and Surgeon. Perth: 1796. V. 39

AN UNIVERSAL History from the Earliest Account of Time to the Present. (with) The Modern Part of the Universal History. London: 1736-44/59-65. V. 38

THE UNIVERSAL Instructor in the Art of Brewing Beer. London: 1820. V. 38; 40
THE UNIVERSAL Instructor in the Art of Brewing Beer. London: 1820. V. 40

THE UNIVERSAL Receipt Book; Being a Compendious Repository of Practical Information in Cookery . . . Philadelphia: 1818. V. 37

THE UNIVERSAL Songster. London: 1825. V. 40
THE UNIVERSAL Songster. London: 1832. V. 42

THE UNIVERSAL Songster; or, Museum of Mirth . . . London: 1834. V. 38; 42

THE UNIVERSAL Songster; or, Museum of Mirth, Forming the Most Complete Collection of Ancient and Modern Songs. London: 1832? V. 39
THE UNIVERSAL Songster; or, Museum of Mirth, Forming the Most Complete Collection of Ancient and Modern Songs. London: 1850. V. 39

THE UNIVERSITY Miscellany; or, More Burning Work for the Ox--f--d Convocation. London: 1713. V. 39

THE UNIVERSITY Printing Houses at Cambridge from the Sixteenth to the Twentieth Century. Cambridge: 1962. V. 39; 40; 41; 42; 43; 45

UNTERKIRCHER, FRANZ

European Illuminated Manuscripts in the Austrian National Library. London: 1967. V. 44

UNTERMEYER, JEAN STARR

Private Collection. New York: 1965. V. 40; 41; 42; 43; 44

UNTERMEYER, LOUIS

Heavens. New York: 1922. V. 37

James Branch Cabell: The Man and His Masks. Virginia: 1970. V. 41; 42; 43; 44

Modern American Poetry: a Critical Anthology. New York: 1942. V. 39; 42

Modern American Poetry. New York: 1950. V. 44

UNTERMYER, IRWIN

Bronzes Other Metalwork and Sculpture in the Irwin Untermyer Collection. New York: 1962. V. 42; 43; 46

Chelsea and Other English Porcelain Pottery and Enamel in the Irwin Untermyer Collection. Chambridge: 1957. V. 40

Chelsea and Other English Porcelain Pottery and Enamel in the Irwin Untermyer Collection. London: 1957. V. 39

English Furniture: With Some Furniture of Other Countries in the Irwin Untermyer Collection. Cambridge: 1958. V. 43

English and Other Needlework, Tapestries and Textiles in the Irwin Untermyer Collection. Cambridge: 1960. V. 40

English and Other Silver in the Irwin Untermyer Collection. New York: 1969. V. 39; 41

The Irwin Untermyer Collection. New York: 1956-1963. V. 40; 41

Meissen and Other Continental Porcelain, Faience and Enamel in the Irwin Untermyer Collection. Cambridge: 1936. V. 41

Meissen and Other Continental Porcelain, Faience and Enamel in the Irwin Untermyer Collection. Cambridge;: 1956. V. 38

Meissen and Other Continental Porcelain, Faience and Enamel in the Irwin Untermyer Collection. New York: 1956. V. 42

UNTEUTSCH, FRIEDRICH

Neues Zieratenbuch den Schreinern, Tischlern Oder Kunstlern und Bildhauern sehr Diestlich . . . Nuremberg: 1650. V. 44

UNTO the Right Honourable the Lords of Council and Session, the Petitition of the Clerks and Apprentices of Writers to the Signet, and Writers in Edinburgh: Humbly Sheweth . . . Edinburgh: 1795. V. 46

UNTRODDEN Fields of Anthropology. Paris: 1898. V. 41

UNWIN, A. HAROLD

West African Forests and Forestry. New York: 1920. V. 45

UNWIN, GEORGE

Letters, Remarks &c. London: 1790. V. 43; 46

unwin on Tin and Copper to India and China. London: 1812. V. 40

UNWIN, J. D.

Hopousia or the Sexual and Economic Foundations of a New Society. London: 1940. V. 39

UNWIN, JOSEPH

Materialism Refuted. Sheffield: 1829. V. 39

UNWIN, RAYMOND

Town Planning in Practice. London: 1909. V. 45

UNWIN'S Chap Book. London: 1899. V. 37

UNWIN'S Encyclopaedia of Animals Library. London: 1985-86. V. 38

UPCOTT, WILLIAM

A Bibliographical Account of the Principal Works Relating to English Topography. London: 1818. V. 38; 44

A Bibliographical Account of the PRIncipal Works Relating to English Topography. 1968. V. 40

A Bibliographical Account of the Principal Works Relating to English Topography. London: 1968. V. 41

Catalogue of the Library . . . London: 1856. V. 40

UPDIKE, DANIEL BERKELEY 1860-1941

Printing Types. Their History, Form and Use. 1922. V. 39

Printing Types; Their History, Forms and Use. Cambridge: 1922. V. 38; 40

Printing Types: Their History, Form and Use. Cambridge: 1927. V. 38

Printing Types. Their History, Forms and Use. 1937. V. 38

Printing Types, Their History, Forms and Use. Cambridge: 1937. V. 40; 42; 44; 46

Printing Types: Their History, Forms and Use, a Study in Survival. London: 1937. V. 42

UPDIKE, JOHN

The Afterlife; a Story. Leamington Spa: 1987. V. 40; 45

The Afterlife. London: 1987. V. 39

Assorted Prose. New York: 1963. V. 46

Assorted Prose. New York: 1965. V. 41; 43; 45

Bech is Back. V. 37

Bech. A Book. New York: 1970. V. 39; 41; 42; 43; 44; 45; 46

Bech is Back. New York: 1982. V. 37; 39; 40; 43; 44; 45; 46

The Beloved. 1982. V. 37

The Beloved. Northridge: 1982. V. 41; 42

Bottom's Dream. New York: 1969. V. 38; 39; 40; 42; 43

Brother Grasshopper. Worcester: 1990. V. 44; 46

Buchanan Dying. London: 1974. V. 46

Buchanan Dying. New York: 1974. V. 37

The Carpentered Hen. 1958. V. 43

The Carpentered Hen. New York: 1958. V. 39; 43; 44; 46

The Carpentered Hen and other Tame Creatures. New York: (1958). V. 37

The Centaur. London: 1963. V. 45

The Centaur. New York: 1963. V. 43; 44; 45; 46

The Chaste Planet. Worcester: 1980. V. 37; 40

The Coup. New York: 1978. V. 37; 38; 39; 40; 41; 42; 43; 45

Couples: a Short Story. Cambridge: 1976. V. 37; 38; 39; 40; 42; 43

Cunts. New York: 1974. V. 46

Cunts (Upon Receiving the Swingers Life Club Membership Solicitaion). New York: (1974). V. 37

Ego and Art in Walt Whitman. New York: 1980. V. 43; 45; 46

Essays and Criticism. New York: 1991. V. 44

Facing Nature. New York: 1985. V. 39; 44

Father Grasshopper. Worcester: 1990. V. 45

From the Journal of a Leper. Northridge: 1978. V. 45

Getting Older. Helsinki: 1986. V. 46

Going Abroad. Helsinki: 1988. V. 46

A Good Place. N.P.: 1973. V. 43

Hoping for a Hoopoe. London: 1959. V. 37; 45; 46

Hub Fans Bid Kid Adieu. Northridge: 1977. V. 43; 45

Hugging the Shore: Essays and Criticism. New York: 1983. V. 39

Hugging the Shore. New York: 1985. V. 39

Impressions. Hollywood: 1985. V. 46

Impressions. Los Angeles: 1985. V. 38; 40

Interviews with Insufficiently Famous Americans. Northridge: 1980. V. 45

Jester's Dozen. Northridge: 1984. V. 43

Just Looking. New York: 1989. V. 41; 42; 44; 45; 46

Marry me. New York: 1976. V. 37; 39; 41; 42; 43; 44; 45

Marry Me. 1976. V. 37

Midpoint and Other Poems. New York: 1969. V. 39; 40; 43; 44; 45; 46

A Month of Sundays. New York: 1975. V. 37; 38; 39; 40; 41; 42; 43; 44; 45; 46

More Stately Mansions. Jackson: 1987. V. 45

Museum and Women. New York: 1972. V. 37; 38; 39; 40; 42; 44; 46

The Music School. New York: 1966. V. 37; 38; 40; 42; 43; 45; 46

An Oddly Lovely Day Alone. London: 1978. V. 44

An Oddly Lovely Day Alone. Virginia: 1979. V. 37

Of the Farm. New York: 1965. V. 40; 42; 43; 45; 46

People One Knows. Northridge: 1980. V. 37; 39; 40; 42; 43; 46

People One Knows: Interviews with Insufficiently Famous Americans. Northridge, CA: 1908. V. 37

Picked Up Pieces. New York: 1975. V. 37; 38; 39; 40; 41; 42; 43; 44; 45; 46

Pigeon Feathers. New York: 1962. V. 40; 42; 43; 46

Pigeon Feathers and Other Stories. Franklin Center: 1981. V. 46

The Poorhouse Fair. New York: 1959. V. 37; 38; 40; 42; 43; 45

Problems and Other Stories. New York: 1970. V. 39

Problems. New York: 1979. V. 37; 38; 39; 40; 41; 42; 44; 46

Query. New York: 1974. V. 39

Rabbit, Run. New York: 1960. V. 40; 41; 42; 43; 44; 45

Rabbit, Run. London: 1961. V. 42; 45

Rabbit Redux. New York: 1971. V. 37; 39; 40; 45; 46

Rabbit is Rich. New York: 1981. V. 37; 39; 41; 44; 45; 46

Rabbit at Rest. New York: 1990. V. 43; 44; 45; 46

Rabbit is Rich. New York: 1976. V. 46

Rabbit is Rich. V. 37

The Ring. New York: 1964. V. 42; 43; 46

Roger's Version. New York: 1986. V. 37; 39; 44; 45; 46

S. London: 1988. V. 40; 43; 46

S. New York: 1988. V. 39; 41; 42; 43; 44; 45; 46

The Same Door. New York: 1959. V. 39; 42; 43; 44

The Same Door - Short Stories. London: 1962. V. 41

Self Consciousness. New York: 1989. V. 41; 43; 44; 45; 46

A Soft Spring Night in Shillington. Northridge: 1986. V. 41; 42

Spring Trio. 1982. V. 42; 44

Spring Trio. N.P.: 1982. V. 39

Styles of Bloom. 1982. V. 42

Styles of Bloom. 1985. V. 44

Talk from the Fifties. Northridge: 1978. V. 37; 38; 39; 40; 41; 42

Talk from the Fifties. Northridge: 1979. V. 37; 39; 43; 45

Trust Me. New York: 1987. V. 37; 38; 39; 42; 43; 44; 45

Two Sonnets Whose Titles Came to Me Simultaneously. 1983. V. 42

Warm Wine. New York: 1973. V. 38; 39; 43; 44; 45

Witches of Eastwick. London. V. 45

The Witches of Eastwick. New York: 1984. V. 37; 39; 41; 42; 45

UPDIKE, RICHARD

Witches of Eastwick. V. 38

UPDIKE, WILKINS

History of the Episcopal Church in Narragansett, Rhode Island . . . Boston: 1907. V. 38

UPFIELD, ARTHUR

Bony and the Mouse. London: 1959. V. 45

UPHAM, EDWARD

Rameses; an Egyptian Tale; with Historical Notes of the Era of the Pharaohs. London: 1824. V. 38; 41; 43; 45

UPHAM, J. W.

Views In and Near Weymouth. Weymouth: 1825. V. 39; 44

UPHAM, N. G.

Commission of Claims Report. Washington: 1856. V. 43

UPHAM, SAMUEL C.

Notes of a Voyage to California via Cape Horn, Together with Scenes in El Dorado, in the Years 1849-50. Philadelphia: 1878. V. 39; 42; 45

UPHAM, THOMAS C. 1799-1872

Elements of Mental Philosophy Embracing the Two Departments of the Intelelct and the Sensibilities. Portland: 1828. V. 42

Elements of Mental Philosophy, Embracing the two Departments of the Intellect and the Sensibilities. Portland: 1839. V. 37; 42; 43; 44

The Manual of Peace, Embracing: 1, Evils and Remedies of War, 2, Suggestions on the Law of Nations, 3, Consideration of a Congress of Nations. New York: 1836. V. 44

Outlines of Imperfect and Disordered Mental Action. New York: 1840. V. 42

URQUHART, DAVID HENRY

Commentaries on Classical Learning. London: 1803. V. 37

URQUHART, THOMAS

The Life and Death of the Admirable Crichtoun from the Discovery of a Most Exquisite Jewel. Paris: 1927. V. 44

URREA, JOSE

Diario de las Operaciones Militares . . . la Campana de Tejas . . . Victoria de Durango: 1838. V. 45

Mexico and Texas. Washington: 1838. V. 37

URRETA, LUIS DE

Historia Eclesiastica, Politica, Natural, y Moral, de los Grandes y Remotos Reynos de la Etiopia, Monarchia del Emperador, Llamado Preste Iuan de las Indias. Valencia: 1610. V. 41

URSIN, JOHANN HEINRICH

De Zoroastre Bactriano, Hermete Trismegisto, Sanchonithone Phoenicio, Eorumque, Scriptiis, & Aliis, Contra Mosaicae Scripturae Antiquitatem . . . Nuremberg: 1661. V. 37

URSINUS, FULVIUS

Illustrium Imagines, ex Antiquis Marmoribus, Nomismatibus, et Gemmis Expressae . . . Antwerp: 1606. V. 39; 45

URSINUS, ZACHARIAS

Doctrinae Christianae Compendium. Cambridge: 1585. V. 38

Doctrinae Christianae Compendium; Seu Commentarii Catechetici . . . Cum Indice. Londini: 1586. V. 38

The Summe of Christian Religion, Delivered by Zacharias Ursinus . . . London: 1633. V. 46

URUSOV, ALEXANDER

The Cry of Distant Ants. Toronto: 1978. V. 38

USARD d. ca. 875

Martyrologium . . . Louvain: 1568. V. 45

USBURNE, RICHARD

Wodehouse at Work. 1961. V. 42

USEFUL Hints to Single Gentlemen, Respecting Marriage, Concubinage, and Adultery. London: 1792. V. 38

THE USEFULNESS of the Edinburgh Theatre Seriously Considered. Edinburgh: 1757. V. 43

USHER, JAMES

The Dirge of Fauntleroy. London: 1824. V. 41; 42

USHER, JAMES WARD

An Art Collector's Treasures. 1916. V. 39

USHER, JOHN PALMER

In the Matter of the Resolution Touching the Operation of the Union Pacific Railroad and Branches: letter to the President. Washington: 1870. V. 39

USIMBARDUS, PETRUS

Constitutiones et Decreta Publicata in Synodo Diocesana Arretina. Anno Domini 1597. Florentiae: 1598. V. 38

USSELINCX, WILLEM 1567-1647?

Sweriges Rijkes General Handels Compagnies Contract, Dirigerat til Asiam, Africam, Americam och Magellanicam, sampt thess Conditioner och Wilkahr . . . Stockholm: 1625. V. 39

USSELINCX, WILLIAM

Vertoogh, Hoe Nootwendich, Nut Ende Profijtelick Het Fy Voor de Vereenighde Nederlanden Te Behouden de Vryheyt Van Te Handelen op West-Indien . . . Amsterdam: 1608. V. 41; 44

USSHER, ARLAND

An Alphabet of Aphorisms. Dublin: 1953. V. 40

The 22 Keys of the Tarot. Dublin: 1957. V. 40

USSHER, I.

Clio; or a Discourse on Taste. London: 1773. V. 40

USSHER, JAMES

The Annals of the World. London: 1658. V. 44

An Answer to a Challenge Made by a Jesuit in Ireland. Dublin: 1624. V. 43

An Answer to a Challenge Made by a Iesuite in Ireland . . . London: 1631. V. 40

An Answer to a Challenge Made by a Jesuite in Ireland. London: 1625. V. 37

A Body of Divinity, or the Sum and Substance of Christian Religion . . . London: 1670. V. 44

Britannicarum Ecclesiarum Antiquitates . . . Dublin: 1639. V. 43

Gravissimae Quaestionis. De Christianarum Ecclesiarum, In Occidentis Praesertim Partibus, ab Apostolicis Temporibus ad Nostram. Londini: 1613. V. 40

The Judgement of the Late ARch-Bishop of Armagh, and Primate of Ireland . . . London: 1657. V. 42

The Principles of Christian Religion . . . London: 1678. V. 39; 46

Veterum Epistolarum Hibernicarum Sylloge . . . Dublin: 1632. V. 40

USSHER, JAMES, ABP. OF ARMAGH 1581-1656

Britannicarum Ecclesiarum Antiquitates. London: 1687. V. 39

USSHER, RICHARD J.

The Birds of Ireland. London: 1900. V. 46

UTAH. CONSTITUTION

Constitution of the State of Utah. Adopted by the Convention April 27, 1882. Ratified by the People, May 22, 1882. Salt Lake City: 1881. V. 43

Constitution of the State of Utah. Adopted by the Convention, April 27, 1882. Salt Lake City: 1882. V. 38; 39; 45

UTAH. CONSTITUTION - 1852

Constitution of the United States of America, as Proposed by The Convention . . . wtih the Amendments Thereto . . . Also 'An Act to Establish A Territorial Government for Utah', Approved September 9, 1850. Salt Lake City: 1852. V. 37

UTAH. LAWS, STATUTES, ETC.

Resolutions, Acts and Memorials Passed at the Fifth Annual Session of the Legislative Assembly of the Territory of Utah . . . Great Salt Lake City: 1855. V. 40; 46

UTAH. LAWS, STATUTES, ETC. - 1852

Acts, Resolutions and Memoirals Passed by the First Annual and Special Sessions of the Legislative Assembly of Utah. Salt Lake City: 1852. V. 37

UTAH. LAWS, STATUTES, ETC. - 1855

Acts, Resolutions and Memorials, Passed at the Several Annual Sessions of the Legislative Assembly of the Territory of Utah. Great Salt Lake City: 1855. V. 37; 39; 46

UTAH. LAWS, STATUTES, ETC. - 1868

Acts, Resolutions and Memorials Passed and Adopted by the Legislative Assembly of the Territory of Utah, 17th Annual Session, 1868. Salt Lake City: 1868. V. 37

UTAH. (TERRITORY).

Rules for Conducting Business in the House of Representatives of the Territory of Utah. Salt Lake City: 1854-5. V. 40

UTAH. (TERRITORY). LAWS, STATUTES ETC.

Laws of the Territory of Utah Passed at the Twnety-Sixth Session of the Legislative Assembly. Salt Lake City: 1884. V. 46

UTAH. (TERRITORY). LAWS, STATUTES, ETC. - 1862

Acts, Resolutions and Memorials Passed by the Legislative Assembly of the Territory of Utah During the Twelfth Annual Session, for the Years 1862-63. Salt Lake City: 1863. V. 39

UTAMARO, KITAGAWA

Twelve Woodblock Prints of Kitagawa Utamaro, Illustrating the Process of Silk Culture. San Francisco: 1965. V. 38; 40; 41; 43; 44

AN UTILITARIAN Catechism. London: 1830. V. 37

UTLEY, ROBERT

Four Fighters of Lincoln County. Albuquerque: 1986. V. 42

UTLEY, ROBERT M.

Fort Union In Miniature. V. 44

Fort Union in Miniature. Santa Fe: 1963. V. 41

The Reno Court of Inquiry and Men with Custer. Ft. Collins: 1972. V. 45

The Reno Court of Inquiry. Bellevue: 1983. V. 38

UTTERSON, EDWARD VERNON

Select Pieces of Early Popular Poetry. London: 1817. V. 40

UTTLEY, ALISON

The Adventures of Peter and Judy in Bunnyland. London: 1935. V. 45

Ambush of Young Days. London: 1937. V. 40; 41

Little Grey Rabbit's Washing-Day. London: 1951. V. 45

Secret Places and Other Essays. London: 1972. V. 44

The Stuff of Dreams. London: 1953. V. 38

A Traveller in Time. London: 1939. V. 45

UVAROV, SERGEI SEMENOVICH, GRAF 1786-1855

Essay on the Mysteries of Eleusis. London: 1817. V. 40

UVEDALE, THOMAS

The Memoirs of Philip de Comines. London: 1712. V. 46

UXKULL, BORIS, BARON

Arms and the Woman. The Diaries of Baron Boris Uxkull 1812-1819. London: 1966. V. 41

UYEHARA, GEORGE ETSUJIRO

The Political Development of Japan 1867-1909. London: 1910. V. 40

UYNER, ROBERT T.

Notitia Venatica; A Treatise on Fox-Hunting embracing the General Management of Hounds. A new edition revised, corrected, and enlarged by William C.A. Blew. London: 1910. V. 37

UZANNE, OCTAVE

L'Art dans La Decoration Exterieure des Livres en France et a l'Etranger, les Couvertures Illustrees les Cartonnages d'Editeurs la Reliure d'Art. Paris: 1898. V. 39; 40; 44

The Book-Hunter in Paris. Chicago: 1893. V. 39; 46

Book-Hunter in Paris, Studies Among the Bookstalls and the Quays. London: 1893. V. 45

The Fan. London: 1884. V. 40; 41; 44

The French Bookbinders of the Eighteenth Century. Chicago: 1904. V. 38; 40; 41; 42

The Frenchwoman of the Century. London: 1886. V. 46

The Mirror of the World. London: 180. V. 44

The Mirror of the World . . . London: 1889. V. 46

The Sunshade - The Glove - The Muff. London: 1883. V. 39; 41; 44; 46

The Sunshade the Glove-The Muff/The Fan. London: 1884. V. 41; 42; 44

UZIELLI, MATTHEW

Catalogue of the Various Works of Art, Forming the Collection of Matthew Uzielli of Hanover Lodge. London: 1860. V. 40

UZTARIZ, DON GERONYMO DE

The Theory and Practice of Commerce and Maritime Affairs. London: 1751. V. 40; 42

UZZIAH and Jothan. A Poem. London: 1690. V. 42

V

V

A Sketch from Life. N.P.: 1820. V. 42

V., G.

Dinners and Dinner-Parties, or the Absurdities of Artificial Life. London: 1862. V. 42

V., L.

Choix de Quelques Memoires sur Les Colonies &c . . . Orleans: 1798. V. 41

V., MARY V.

A Dialogue, Between a Southern Delegate, and His Spouse, on His Return from the Grand Continental Congress. New York: 1774. V. 40

V., T.

A Dayly Exercise of the Devout Christian . . . London: 1688. V. 37

VACARESCO, HELENE

The Bard of the Dimbovitza. London: 1892. V. 43

the Bard of the Dimbovitza . . . (with) . . . . Second Series. London: 1892/94. V. 45

VACHER, S.

Fifteenth Century Italian Ornament Chiefly Taken from Brocades and Stuffs Found in Pictures in the National Gallery. London: 1886. V. 37

VACHSS, ANDREW

Flood. New York: 1985. V. 44

VACHTOVA, LUDMILA

Frank Kupka, Pioneer of Abstract Art. New York: 1968. V. 39; 43

VACUUM BRAKE CO.

The Vacuum Automatic Brake. London: 1890? V. 46

A VADE-MECUM from India to Europe, by Way of Egypt. London: 1827. V. 46

A VADE Mecum for Malt-Worms. London: 1880. V. 39

VADE Mecum, Piorum Sacerdotum, Sive Exercitia, et Preces Matutinae, Vespertinae . . . London: 1746. V. 39

VADIANUS, JOACHIM

Epitome Trium Terrae Partium. Aslae, Africae, et Europae. Zurich: 1534. V. 40; 43

Epitome Trium Terrae Partium, Asiae, Africae et Europae. Zurich: ager. V. 40

Ioachimi Vadiani . . . Aphorismorum Libri Sex de Consideratione Eucharistiae . . . Zurich: 1536. V. 43

VAENIUS, OTTO

Amorum Emblemata, Figuris Aeneis Incisa. Antwerp: 1608. V. 37; 38

VAHL, JENS

Alaska: Folket Og Missionen. Copenhagen: 1872. V. 37

VAHL, M.

Greenland. Copenhagen & London: 1928. V. 42

VAHLE, JOSEPH

The Jerico Papers. New York: 1893. V. 39

VAIL, DERRICK T.

Smith's Cataract Operation. Cincinnati: 1911. V. 42

VAIL, EUGENE A.

Notice Sur Les Indiens de l'Amerique Du Nord. Paris: 1840. V. 38

VAIL, I. N.

Alaska. The Land of the Nugget. Why? A Critical Examination of Geological and Other Testimony Showing How and Why Gold was Deposited in Polar Lands. Pasadena: 1897. V. 39

VAIL, ISRAEL E.

Three Years on the Blockade. New York: 1902. V. 44

VAILLANT, ANNETTE

Bonard. Greenwich: 1965. V. 43; 46

VAILLANT, AUGUSTE NICOLAS

Travels into the Interior Parts of Africa, By the Cape of Good Hope . . . Prth: 1791. V. 43

VAILLANT, S.

Botanicon Parisiense, ou Denombrement . . . Leyden & Amsterdam: 1727. V. 38; 40; 41

VAINES, DOM JEAN FRANCOIS DE

Dictionnaire Raissone de Diplomatique Contenant les Regles Principales & Essentielles Pour Sevir a Dechiffer les Anciens Thitres . . . Paris: 1774. V. 38

VAIRIUS, LEONARDUS

De Fascino, Libri Tres. Paris: 1583. V. 40; 45

VALADES, DIDACO

Rhetorica Christiana ad Concionandi, et Orandi Usum Accomodata . . . Rome: 1579. V. 46

VALANGIN, ALINE

Raum Ohne Kehrreim / Espace Sans Refrain, by Aline Valangin. St. Gallen: 1961. V. 37

VALCAREN, JOHN PETER A.

A Relation or Diary of the Siege of Vienna. London: 1684. V. 37; 40

VALE, JOSEPH G.

Minty and the Cavalry. Harrisburg: 1886. V. 43

VALENTI, ANGELO

Come Over and Stay Till Domesday. From the Cloister and the Hearth. New York: 1937. V. 39

VALENTI Angelo: Artist, Author, Illustrator and Printer. San Francisco: 1976. V. 39; 41; 45; 46

VALENTI Angelo: Author, Illustrator, Printer. A Checklist of His Work from 1926 to 1970. Bronxville: 1970. V. 45

VALENTIA, GEORGE, VISCOUNT

Voyages and Travels to India, Ceylon, the Red Sea, Abyssinia and Egypt in the Years 1802, 1803, 1804, 1805 and 1806. London: 1809. V. 40

Voyages and Travels to India, Ceylon The Red Sea, Abyssinia, and Egypt in the Years 1802, 1803, 1804, 1805 and 1806. London: 1811. V. 39

VALENTIN, CURT

The Drawings of Jacques Lipchitz. New York: 1944. V. 42

VALENTINE, BASIL

Last Will and Testament. (Of the aetherial liquor of Metals; A relation of Mines, Stones, Oars, etc. with their coherent powers and operations; of the Universal of the World and the XII Keys; The Manuals of Metals, of the Medicine . . . London: 1671-1670. V. 37

VALENTINE, EDWARD PLEASANTS

The Edward Pleasants Valentine Papers . . . Richmond: 1927. V. 40; 44

VALENTINE, LAURA BELINDA JEWRY

Aunt Louis'a Golden Gift. London. V. 45

Aunt Louisa's Book of Drolleries. London: 1876. V. 40

The Nobility of Life, Its Graces and Virtues. London: 1869. V. 38

VALENTINER, W. R.

Catalogue of Early Italian Paintings . . . New York: 1926. V. 44

Jacques Louis David and the French Revolution. New York: 1929. V. 44

Studies in Italian Renaissance Sculpture. London: 1950. V. 42; 46

VALENTINI, AGOSTINI

La Patriarcale Basilica Liberiana. Rome: 1839. V. 45

VALENTINI, CHRISTOPH BERNHARD

Tournefortius Contractus, Sub Forma Tabularum Sistens Institutiones Rei Herbie Juxta Methodum Modernorum, . . . Frankfurt: 1715. V. 38; 40; 44

VALENTINO, RUDOLPH

How You Can Keep Fit. New York: 1923. V. 44; 45

VALENTYN, FRANCOIS

Oud en Nieuw Oost-Indien, Vervattende een Naaukeurige en Uitvoerige Verhandelinge van Nederlands Mogentheyd in die Gewesten . . . Dordrecht & Amsterdamn: 1724-26. V. 45

VALERA, CIPRIANO DE

Dos Tratados. London: 1599. V. 45

VALERIANO BALZANI, GIOVANI PIERO

Castigationes et Variettes Virgilianae Lectionis. Rome: 1521. V. 45

VALERIANO BOLZANI, GIOVANNI PIERIO

Hieroglyphica, Sive de Sacris Aegyptiorum Literis Commentarii . . . Basel: 1567. V. 40

VALERIANUS, J. P.

Dissertatio pro Sacerdotum Barbis. Liege: 1643. V. 37

VALERIANUS, PIERIUS

Hexametri, Odae & Epigrammata. Venice: 1550. V. 40

VALERIUS FLACCUS, CAIUS

Argonautica Diligenter Accuratequ Emedata & Suo Nitori Reddita in Hoc Volumine Continentur. Venice: 1501. V. 40

Argonauticon Libri Octo . . . Paris: 1519. V. 41; 42; 43

Argonauticon Libri Octo. Paris: 1532. V. 44; 45

VALERIUS MAXIMUS

Dictorum Factorum Que Memorabilium Exempla. Lyon: 1536. V. 43

Dictorum Factorumque Memorabilium Libri IX. Lyon: 1613. V. 37; 40

Facta et Dicta Memorabilia. Venice: 1497. V. 40

Libri Novem Factorum Dictiorumque Memorabilium: cum Notis Integris . . . Leidae: 1726. V. 46

VALERY, PAUL

Le Cimetiere Marin. London: 1945. V. 44; 45

Le Cimetiere Marin. London: 1946. V. 46

Le Cimetierre Marin. Verona: 1946. V. 40

The Graveyard by the Sea. 1946. V. 38

The Graveyard by the Sea. Verona: 1946. V. 41; 42; 44; 46

Poesies. Paris: 1930. V. 39

The Collected Works. London: 1971-75. V. 41

VALESCO DE TARANTA

Philonium. Lyon: 1526. V. 38

VALESIO, FRANCESCO

Raccolta de 'Disegni et Compartimenti Diversi, Tratti da Marmie Bronzi de Gli Antichi Romani et Dedicate all. N.P. n.d. Italy. V. 44

VALIERO, AGOSTINO, CARDINAL 1531-1606

Libri Tres de Rehtorica Ecclesiastica . . . Paris: 1556. V. 40

VALIGNAN, P. ALEXANDRE

Advis de la Bien Heureuse Mort de Cinq Religeux de la Compagnie de Iesus, & d'Aucuns Autres Seculiers . . . Paris: 1584. V. 39

VALLA, GEORGIA

De Expedita Ratione Argumentandi. Parisiis: 1534. V. 37

VALLA, GIORGIO

De Corporis Commodis et Incommodis. Strassburg: 1530? V. 37

De Natura Oculorum. Strasburg: 1529. V. 42

De Physicis Quaestionibus. Strasburg: 1529. V. 42

VALLA, LAURENTIUS 1407-1457

Elegantiae Linguae Latinae. Paris: 1491. V. 45

Laurentii Vallae Elegantiarum Adeps, Ex Eius de Lingua Latina Libris per Bonum Accursium Pisanu Studiosissime Collectus. Antverpiae in Rapo: 1535. V. 40

Elegantiarum Libri Omnes Scholiis . . . Cologne: 1530. V. 40

Elegantiarum Libri Omnes. Cologne: 1534. V. 37

De Linguae Latinae Elegantia Libri Sex, Iam Nouissime de Integro Bona Fine Emaculati . . . Cologne: 1545. V. 39

De Lingua Latina Elegantia, Libri Sex. Cologne: 1563. V. 45

VALLANCE, AYMER

The Art of William Morris: a Record. London: 1897. V. 38; 39; 41

The Art of William Morris. London: 1898. V. 40

William Morris his art his writing and his public life. 1897. V. 37

William Morris: His Art and His Writings and His Public Life. London: 1897. V. 40; 42; 43; 44

William Morris: His Art, His Writings and His Public Life. London: 1898. V. 40

William Morris His Writings and His Public Life. London: 1909. V. 39

VALLANCEY, CHARLES

The Art of Tanning and Currying Leather . . . London: 1780. V. 41; 42

Collectanea de Rebus Hibernicis. Dublin: 1770. V. 38

An Essay on the Antiquity of the Irish Language. Dublin: 1772. V. 41; 42

A Grammar of the Ibero-Celtic or Irish Language. Dublin: 1773. V. 42

Prospectus of a Dictionary of the Language of the Aire Coti, or, Ancient Irish . . . Dublin: 1802. V. 44

VALLAVINE, PETER

Observations on the Present Condition of the Current Coin of This Kingdom. London: 1742. V. 41; 45

VALLE, JOSE CECILIO DE

Instruccion Sobre la Plaga de Langosta; Medios de Exterminaria, o de Disminuir sus Efectos, y Precaber la Escasez de Comestibles. N.G. (Nueva Guatemala): 1804. V. 45

VALLE, PIETRO DELLA

Les Fameux Voyages de Pietro Della Valle Gentil-Homme Romain, Surnomme Illustre Voyageur . . . Paris: 1664-65. V. 43

VALLE, ROBERTUS

Compendium Memorandum Vires Naturales & Commoda Comprehendens a Plinio Data. Paris: i.e. 1500. V. 43

VALLECILLO MINING COMPANY

Silver Mine Of 'Jesus Maria'. Situated Near the Rio Grande State of Nuevo Leon, Mexico. New York: 1855. V. 41

VALLEE, RUDY

Vagabond Dreams Come Ture. New York: 1930. V. 45; 46

VALLEIX, F. L. I.

Clinique des Maladies des Enfants Nouveau-Nes. Paris: 1838. V. 46

VALLEJO, MARIANO G.

'Ecspocision Que Hace el Comdanante (sic) General Interino de la Alta California al Governador de la Misma . . . Sonoma: 1837. V. 40

'Informe de la Comision Especial Sobre la Derivacion y Definicion de los Nombres de los Diferentes Condados del Estado de California &c.' San Jose: 1850. V. 40

Proclama. Mariano G. Vallejo Commandante General de la Alta California, a Sus Habiantes Conciudadanos: Convencidos los Hijos de Esta Preciosa Porsion del Territorio Mejicano de que los Gefes Destinados Para Regirla por Falta de Conocimientos Locales No.. Monterey: 1837. V. 42

VALLEMONT, PIERRE LE LORRAIN DE

Curiosities of Nature and Art in Husbandry and Gardening. London: 1707. V. 37

Description de l'Aimant, qui s'est forme a la pointe du Clocher neuf de N. Dmae de Chartres; avec plusieurs Experiences tres-curieuses, sur l'Aimant . . . Paris: 1692. V. 37

VALLET, PIERRE

Les Aventures Amoureuses de Theagenes et Cariclee . . . Paris: 1613. V. 46

VALLETTE, ELIE

The Deputy Commissary's Guide Within the Province of Maryland . . . Annapolis: 1774. V. 37; 40

VALLETTE-LAUDUN, M. DE

Journal d'un Voyage a la Louisiane, Fait en 1720. Hague & Paris: 1768. V. 41

THE VALLEY of Diamonds; or, Harlequin Sinbad. London: 1814. V. 37; 39

VALLIER, DORA

Henri Rousseau. London: 1979. V. 46

VALLINUS, NILS O.

De Oelandia. Holmiae: 1703. V. 38

VALLIS I SUBIRA, ORIOL

A Lively Book at Papermaking. North Hills: 1980. V. 38

VALLISNIERI, ANTONIO

Dialoghi . . . Sopra la curiosa origine di milti insetti. Venice: 1700. V. 37

Opere Fisico-Mediche Stampate e Manoscritte . . . Venice: 1733. V. 43

VALLS I SUBIRA, ORIOL

A Lively Look at Papermaking. North Hills: 1980. V. 42

VALMAYOR, H. L.

Orchidiana Philippiniana. 1984. V. 37

VALMIN, M. NATAN

The Swedish Messenia Expedition. Lund: 1938. V. 37; 44

VALNAY, N.

Connoissance et Culture Parfait des Tulipes Rares, des Anemones Extraordinaires des Oeillets Fins, et des Belles Oreilles d'Ours Panachees. Paris: 1688. V. 46

VALUABLE Secrets Concerning Arts and Trades or Approved Directions from the Best Artists. London: 1775. V. 44; 46

VALUABLE Secrets Concerning Arts and Trades; or, Approved Directions, from the Best Artists . . . Norwich: 1795. V. 39; 41; 42; 43

VALUABLE Secrets, Concerning Arts and Trades, or, Approved Directions from the Best Artists . . . Boston: 1798. V. 40

VALUABLE Secrets Concerning Arts and Trades; or Approved Directions, from the Best Artists, for the Various Methods of Engraving . . . Varnishes . . . of Colours and Painting . . . Dublin: 1778. V. 41; 46

VALUABLE Secrets in Arts, Trades, &c., Selected from the Best Authors, and Adapted to the Situation of the United States. New York: 1809. V. 37; 40; 41
VALUABLE Secrets in Arts, Trades &c. Selected from the Best Authors and Adapted to the Situation of the United States. New York: 1816. V. 45

VALVASONE, ERASMO DI

La Caccia. Venice: 1602. V. 37

VAMBERY, ARMINIUS

Travels in Central Asia. London: 1864. V. 40; 43

Travels in Central Asia . . . New York: 1865. V. 39; 40; 43

VAN ALSTYNE, LAWRENCE

Diary of an Enlisted Man. New Haven: 1910. V. 43

VAN ANTWERP, WILLIAM C.

A Collector's Comment on His First Editions of the Works of Sir Walter Scott. San Francisco: 1932. V. 38; 46

A Collector's Comment on his First Editions of the Works of Sir Walter Scott. San Francisco: V. 37

VAN BRAGT, TIELEMAN JANS

Der Blutige Schau-Platz oder Martyrer-Spiegel der Tauffs-Gesinnten oder Wehrlosen-Christen. Ephrata: 1748-49. V. 45

VANBRUGH, JOHN 1644-1720

Architectural Drawings in the Library of Elton Hall by Sir John Vanbrugh and Sir Edward Lovett Pearce. Oxford: 1964. V. 38; 43; 44

The Mistake. London: 1706. V. 38

Plays. London: 1735. V. 42

Plays. London: 1759. V. 37

Plays. London: 1776. V. 43

The Provok'd Husband. London: 1737. V. 46

The Provok'd Wife: a Comedy, as it is Acted at . . . Little Lincolns-Inn-Fields. By the Author of a New Comedy call'd the Relaps, or Virtue in Danger. Briscoe: 1697. V. 37; 46

The Relapse; or, Virtue in Danger; Being the Sequel of the Fool in Fashion. London: 1697. V. 42

A Short Vindication of the Relapse and the Provok'd Wife . . . London: 1697. V. 38

A Short Vindication of the Relapse and the Profok'd Wife, from Immorality and Prophaneness. By the Author. London: 1698. V. 37

The Complete Works. Bloomsbury: 1924. V. 46

The Complete Works of Sir John Vanbrugh. London: 1927. V. 40; 42; 45; 46

Complete Works. Soho: 1927. V. 39

The Complete Works of . . . Bloomsbury: 1927-28. V. 40; 41; 43; 44; 45

Complete Works of Sir John Vanbrugh. London: 1927-28. V. 43

VAN BUREN, E. DOUGLAS

Clay Figurines of Babylonia and Assyria. New Haven: 1930. V. 42

The Flowing Vase and the God with Streams. Berlin: 1933. V. 37

Foundation Figurines and Offerings. Berlin: 1931. V. 44

VAN BUREN, MARTIN

Exploring Expedition. Message from . . . in Relation to the Delay in the Outfit Etc. for the Exploring Expedition. Washington: 1838. V. 37

Maine. Boundary-Mr. Greely . . . Message from . . . Transmitting the Information Required . . . in Relation to the Imprisonment of Mr. Greely, at Frederickton . . . Washington: 1838. V. 37

Mexico-Texas-Canada. Washington: 1838. V. 37

Substance of Mr. Van Buren's Observations on Mr. Foot's Amendment to the Rules of the Senate, by Which It Was Proposed to Give the Vice President the Right to Call to Order for Words Spoken in Debate. Washington: 1828. V. 42

VAN BUREN, W. H.

Lectures on Diseases of the Rectum. New York: 1874. V. 42

VANCE, JOHN HOLBROOK

The Big Planet. 1957. V. 39

The Dying Earth. 1950. V. 39

Eight Fantasms and Magics. 1969. V. 43

Eight Fantasms and Magic. New York: 1969. V. 39

The Fox Valley Murders. Indianapolis, New York,: 1966. V. 43; 44

The Languages of Pao. 1958. V. 43

Light from a Lone Star. 1985. V. 39

The Man in the Cage. New York: 1960. V. 39

The Seventeen Virgins and The Bagful of Dreams. 1979. V. 39

To Live Forever. 1956. V. 39

To Live Forever. New York: 1956. V. 42

Vandals of the Void. 1953. V. 44

Vandals of the Void. Philadelphia/Toronto: (1953). V. 37

VANCE, WILSON J.

Stone's River. The Turning Point of the Civil War. New York: 1914. V. 37

VAN CLEVE, CHARLOTTE OUISCONSIN

Three Score Years and Ten. Minneapolis: 1888. V. 40; 42; 43

VANCOUVER, CHARLES 1758-1798

General View of the Agriculture of the County of Devon . . . London: 1808. V. 41; 46

VANCOUVER, GEORGE 1758-1798

Vancouver in California, 1792-1794. Los Angeles: 1953, 1954. V. 40

A Voyage of Discovery to the North Pacific Ocean and Round the World . . . London: 1798. V. 38; 40; 41; 42; 43; 44

Voyage de Decouvertes, a l'Ocean Pacifique du Nord, et Autour du Monde, Dans Lequel la Cote Nord-Ouest de l'Amerique. Paris: 1798. V. 38; 39

A Voyage of Discovery to the North Pacific Ocean, and Round the Worl; In Which the Coast of North-West America Has Been Carefully Examined . . . (with) Atlas du Voyage de Vancouver. London: Printed for G.G. &: 1798/1800. V. 45

Voyage de Decouvertes, a l'Ocean Pacifique du Nord, et Autour du Monde, dans Lequel la Cote Nord-Ouest de l'Amerique . . . Paris: 1798-1800. V. 37; 38

A Voyage of Discovery to the North Pacific Ocean, and Round the World . . . London: 1801. V. 37; 38

Voyage de Decouvertes, a l'Ocean Pacifique du Nord, et Autour du Monde. Paris: 1801-02. V. 40

A Voyage of Discovery, to the North Pacific Ocean and Round the World 1791-1795. London: 1948. V. 41

The Voyage of George Vancouver, 1791 - 1795. London: 1984. V. 37

VANCOUVER Island as a Home for Settlers. Victoria: 1896? V. 43

VANDAM, ALBERT V.

An Englishman in Paris . . . V. 42

VAN DE VELDE, M. S.

Cosmopolitan Recollections. London: 1889. V. 42

VAN DE WATER, FREDERIC

Glory Hunter, a Life of General Custer. Indianapolis: 1934. V. 45

VAN DELDEN LAERNE, C. F.

Brazil and Java. Report on Coffee-Culture in America, Asia and Africa, to H.E. the Minister of the Colonies. London: 1885. V. 40

VANDELLA'S Progress. In Eight Scenes. London: 1736. V. 39

VAN DEMAN, ESTHER BOISE

The Building of the Roman Aqueducts. Washington: 1934. V. 40

VAN DEN BERGH, LEONARD JOHN

On the Trail of the Pigmies. London: 1922. V. 41

VAN DER BENT, TEUNIS

The Problems of Hygiene in Man's Dwellings. New York: 1920. V. 46

VAN DER ELSKEN, ED

Love on the Left Bank. London: 1956. V. 37

VAN DER HEYDEN, HERMAANNUS

Speedy Help fro Rich and Poor, Etc. London: 1653. V. 37; 38; 41; 43

VAN DER KELLEN, D.

Illustrated International Architecture. The Hague: 1966. V. 46

VAN DER MEULEN, D.

Hadramaut Some Of Its Mysteries Unveiled. Edinburgh & London: 1854. V. 40

VAN DER OSTEN, HANS HENNING

The Alishar Huyuk Season of 1927. Chicago: 1932. V. 40

The Alishar Huyuk Seasons of 1930-32. Chicago: 1937. V. 44

Ancient Oriental Seals in the Collection of Mr. Edward T. Newell. Chicago: 1934. V. 44

Explorations in Central Anatolia: Aeason of 1926. Chicago: 1929. V. 44

VAN DER VIN, J. P. A.

Travaellers to Greece and Constantinople. Istanbul: 1980. V. 37

VANDERBILT, WILLIAM KISSAM

To Galapagos on the Ara. Mt. Vernon: 1927. V. 37; 42

VANDERBILT, WILLIAM KISSAM continued

To Galapagos on the Ara, 1926. The Events of a Pleasure Cruise to the Galapagos Islands and a Classification of a Few Rare Aquatic Findings . . . New York: 1927. V. 46

West Made East with the Loss of a Day. New York: 1933. V. 39

VANDERBORGHT, PAUL

Hommage a Rupert Brooke, 1887-1915. Bruxelles: 1931. V. 41

VANDERCOOK, JOHN W.

The Fool's Parade. New York: & London: 1930. V. 46

VANDERPOEL, GEORGE B.

Lineage of Richard Ely of Plymouth England, Who Came to Boston About 1655, and Settled at Lyme, Connecticut in 1660. New York: 1902. V. 41

VAN DEVENTER, C. I.

Sketches of Methodism in Northwest Missouri with Brief Semi-Centennial Notes. St. Joseph: 1894. V. 46

VAN DEVENTER, CORNELIUS

New Brunswick Collection of Sacred Music; a Selection of Tunes from the Most Approved Authors in Europe and America. Designed Principally for the Use of Churches . . . Seventh Edition, Enlarged and Improved. New Brunswick: 1835. V. 37

VANDEWATER, ROBERT J.

The Tourist, or Pocket Manual for Travellers on the Hudson River, the Western Canal and Stage Road, to Niagara Falls. New York: 1831. V. 42

VANDIANUS, JOACHIM VON WATT

Epitome Trivm Terre Partivm, Asiae, Africae et Evropae Compendiriam Locorum Descriptionem Continens . . . Zurich: 1534. V. 38

VAN DINE, S. S.

The John Riddell Murder Case. New York: 1930. V. 46

VANDIVEER, CLARENCE A.

The Fur Trade and Early Western Exploration. Cleveland: 1929. V. 40; 42; 44; 45

VAN DORE, WADE

Far Lake. New York: 1930. V. 38; 39

VAN DOREN, CARL

Benjamin Franklin. New York: 1938. V. 39

VAN DOREN, MARK

Collected Poems: 1922-1938. New York: 1939. V. 46

The Seven Sleepers. New York: 1944. V. 44

VAN DRUTEN, JOHN

Somebody Knows. London: 1932. V. 39

The Voice of the Turtle. New York: 1944. V. 39; 45

VAN DUSEN, CONRAD

The Indian Chief: an Account of the Labours, Losses, Sufferings and Oppressions of Ke-Zig-Ko-e-Ne-Ne (David Sawyer) a Chief of the Ojibbeway Indians in Canada West. London: 1867. V. 38

VAN DYCK, ANTHONY

Pictorial Notices a Memoir . . . London: 1844. V. 44

VAN DYKE, H. B.

The Physiology and Parmacology of the Pituitary Body. 1936-39. V. 44

The Physiology and Pharmacology of the Pituitary Body. Chicago: 1936-39. V. 42

VAN DYKE, HENRY

Little Masterpieces of English Poetry. Volume V. New York: 1907. V. 40

The Poetry of Tennyson. London: 1890. V. 38

The Story of the Other Wise Man. New York: 1920. V. 45

The Travel Diary of an Angler. New York: 1929. V. 37; 44

VAN DYKE, JOHN C.

Old Dutch and Flemish Masters. New York: 1895. V. 41

VAN DYKE, THEODORE S.

The City and County of San Diego. San Diego: 1888. V. 38

Southern California: Its Valley, Hills and Streams . . . New York: 1886. V. 42

The Still-Hunter. New York: 1904. V. 37

VAN DYKE, W. S. 1889-1943

Horning Into Africa. (Los Angeles: 1931). V. 37

VANE, C. W.

A Steam Voyage to Constantinople, by the Rhine and the Danube, in 1840-41. London: 1842. V. 37; 39

VANE, HENRY 1613-1662

A Healing Question Propounded and Resolved Upon Occasion of the Late Publique and Seasonable Call to Humiliation . . . London: 1656. V. 43

The Retired Mans Meditations of the Mysterie and Power of Godliness Shining Forth in the Living Word . . . London: 1655. V. 42

VANEGAS, ALEJO DE BUSTO

Primera Parte (all published) De Las Differencias de Libros que ay en el Universo. Madrid: 1569. V. 39

VAN EVRIE, JOHN H.

Negroes and Negro 'Slavery:' the First of an Inferior Race: the Latter is Normal Condition. New York: 1861. V. 45

Subgenation: The Theory of the Normal Relation of the Races; an Answer to 'Miscegenation'. New York: 1864. V. 42

VAN FLEET, J. A.

Old and New Mackinac. Ann Arbor: 1870. V. 38; 41; 44

VANGELDER, ARTHUR PINE

History of the Explosives Industry in America. New York: 1927. V. 46

VAN GOGH, VINCENT

The Letters of Vincent Van Gogh to His Brother. Together with Further Letters of Vincent Van Gogh to His Brother. London: 1927/29. V. 43

VAN GULIK, R. H.

Sexual Life in Ancient China. Leiden: 1961. V. 40

VAN GULIK, ROBERT

The Chinese Maze Murders - a Chinese Detective Story Suggested by Three Original Ancient Chinese Plots. The Hague and Bandung: 1956. V. 40

The Chinese Bell Murders. London: 1958. V. 43

The Chinese Gold Murders. London: 1959. V. 46

The Chinese Nail Murders - Judge Dee's Last Three Cases. London: 1961. V. 40

The Haunted Monastery - a Chinese Detective Story. London: 1963. V. 46

Judge Dee at Work - Eight Chinese Detective Stories. London: 1967. V. 46

New Year's Eve in Lan-Fang. Beirut: 1958. V. 40; 41; 42

The Phantom of the Temple - a Chinese Detective Story. London: 1966. V. 46

The Red Pavilion - a Chinese Detective Story. London: 1964. V. 46

VAN HALEN, DON JUAN

Narrative of Don Juan Van Halen's Imprisonment in the Dungeons of the Inquisition at Madrid, and His Escape in 1817 and 1818. New York: 1828. V. 39

VAN HEUMEN, JAN

Joseph Seomnians Complectens Falsas Variorum Imaginationes. Antwerp: 1660. V. 37

VAN HEURCK, H.

A Treatise on the Diatomaceae. London: 1896. V. 38

VAN HEUVEL, J. A.

El Dorado; Being a Narrative of The Circumstances Which Gave Rise to Reports, in the Sixteenth Century, of the Existence of a Rich and Splendid City in South America . . . New York: 1844. V. 38

VAN HEYTHUYSEN, F. M.

An Essay Upon Marine Evidence, in the Courts of Law and Equity, the Competency of a Marine Witness, the Legal Title to British Ships, the Proof and Construction of a Ship's Policy, and the Evidence Necessary to Establish a Variety of Nautical Subjects . . . London: 1819. V. 38

VAN HORN, ROBERT T.

Central Pacific Railway Route. Kansas City: 1858. V. 37; 40; 42

VAN HORNE, THOMAS B.

History of the Army of the Cumberland. Cincinnati: 1875. V. 37

THE VANISHED World. (Die Farshvundene Velt). New York: 1947. V. 41; 45

THE VANITY Fair Album. London: 1875. V. 41

VANITY Fair Book. New York: 1931. V. 42

THE VANITY of Human Life, a Monody. London: 1767. V. 41; 42

VAN KAMPEN, NICHOLAS

The Dutch Florist: or True Method of Managing All Sorts of Flowers with Bulbous Roots. London: 1764. V. 37

The History and Topography of Holland and Belgium . . . London: 1837. V. 40; 45

The History and Topography fo Holland and Belgium. London: 1840. V. 42

VAN KLEECK, MARY

Women in the Bookbinding Trade. New York: 1913. V. 40

VAN LAAR, G.

Magazijn van Tuin-Sieraaden. Amsterdam: 1802. V. 46

VAN LAER, A. J. F.

Documents Relating to New Netherland, 1624-1626 in the Henry E. Huntington Library. San Marino: 1924. V. 37; 38

VAN LAREN, A. J.

Cactus. Los Angeles: 1935. V. 42

Succulents. Los Angeles: 1935. V. 42

VAN LEAR, A. H. F.

Documents Relating to New Netherland 1624-1626. San Marino: 1924. V. 46

VAN LENNEP, HENRY JOHN

Bible Lands: Thei Modern Customs and Manners Illustrative of Scripture. New York: 1875. V. 37; 39; 45

Travels in Little-Known Parts of Asia Minor. London: 1870. V. 37; 39

VAN LENNEP, WILLIAM

The London Stage 1660-1800. 1965-68. V. 46

VAN LEYDEN, LUCAS

La Passion de Notre Seigneur Jesus Christ. Anvers: 1911. V. 44

VAN LIER, HELPERUS RITZEMA

The Power of Grace Illustrated. London: 1792. V. 37

VAN MARLE, RAIMOND

The Development of the Italian Schools of Painting. New York: 1970. V. 42

VAN METRE, ISAIAH

History of Black Hawk Country, Iowa. Chicago: 1904. V. 39

VAN MILLENGEN, ALEXANDER

Constantinople. London: 1906. V. 43; 44

VAN NECK, JACOB

Waerachtigh Verhael van de Schip-vaert op Oost-Indien, Ghedaen by de Acht Schepen, Warwijck, van Amsterdam Gezeylot in de Jare 1598. Amsterdam: 1648. V. 39

VAN NESS, C. P.

To the Public. Washington: 1848. V. 39

VAN NESS, WILLIAM PETER

An Examination of the Various Charges Exhibited Against Aaron Burr, Esq . . . . Virginia: 1803. V. 42

The Speeches at Full Length of Mr. Van Ness, Mr. Caines . . . and General Hamilton, in the Great Cause of the People Against Harry Croswell on an Indictment for a Libel on Thomas Jefferson. New York: 1804. V. 39; 42

VANNINI, GUIDO

Carminvm Libri Quattuor. Lyon: 1611. V. 39

VAN NORDEN, WARNER

Who's Who of the Chinese in New York. New York: 1918. V. 41

VAN NOSTRAND, JEANNE

Edward Vischer's California Drawings of the California Missions, 1861-1878. San Francisco: 1982. V. 45

The First Hundred Years of Painting in California, 1775-1875. San Francisco: 1980. V. 42

A Pictorial and Narrative History of Monterey, Adobe Capital of California, 1770-1847. San Francisco: 1968. V. 41; 44; 46

San Francisco, 1806-1906, in Contemporary Paintings, Drawings and Watercolors. San Francisco: 1975. V. 38; 39; 45; 46

VAN PATTEN, NORMAN

There are Some Who Mourn. Salem: 1948. V. 46

VANPELT & HEYER, DUBUQUE, IOWA.

1859-1860. Descriptive Catalogue of Fruit and Ornamental Trees, Shrubs, Vines and Roses, Cultivated and For Sale at the Commercial Nurseries, on the Delhi Road, Near West Dubuque, 3/4 Mile from the Post Office. Dubuque: 1859. V. 40

VAN PELT, GARRETT

Old Architecture of Southern Mexico. Cleveland: 1926. V. 44

VAN PRESSING, EDWARD R.

Dictionary and Grammar of the Chamorro Language of the Island of Guam. Washington: 1918. V. 44

VAN REGEMORTER, BERTHE

Some Oriental Bindings in the Chester Beatty Library. Dublin: 1961. V. 43; 46

VAN RENSSELAER, MARIANA GRISWOLD 1851-1934

The Devil's Picture Books: A History of Playing Cards. London: 1892. V. 45

Prophetical, Educational and Playing Cards. London: 1912. V. 45

VAN RENSSELAER, MARIANNA GRISWOLD 1851-1934

Prophetical, Educational and Playing Cards. Philadelphia: 1912. V. 43

VAN RENSSELAER, SOLOMON

A Narrative of the Affair of Queenstown: In the War of 1812. New York: 1836. V. 38; 42; 43

VAN RENSSELAER, STEPHEN

Geological and Agricultural Survey of the District Adjoining the Erie Canal, in the State of New York. Albany: 1824. V. 46

VAN ROYEN, P.

The Alpine Flora of New Guinea. Braunschweig: 1979-83. V. 37

VAN RYMSDYK, JOHN

Museum Brittanicum; or a Display in Thirty-Two Plates, in Antiquities and Natural Curiosities, in That Noble and Magnificent Cabinet, the British Museum. London: 1791. V. 41; 45

Museum Britannicum, Being an Exhibition of a Great Variety of Antiquities . . . Belonging to the British Museum. London: 1778. V. 38

VAN SANTVOORD, GEORGE

Sketches of the Lives and Judicial Services of the Chief Justices of the Supreme Court of the United States. New York: 1854. V. 40

VAN SCHAACK, HENRY CRUGER

The Life of Peter Van Schaack . . . During the American Revolution and His Exile in England. New York: 1842. V. 40

Memoirs of the Life of Henry Van Schaack embracing Selections from His Correspondence During the American Revolution. Chicago: 1892. V. 45; 46

VAN SICKEL, S. S.

A Story of Real Life on the Plains. Cedar Rapids: 1898. V. 42

VANSITTART, HENRY

A Letter to the Proprietors of East-India Stock, from Mr. Henry Vansittart. London: 1767. V. 38

A Narrative of the Transactions in Bengal, from the Year 1760 to the Year 1764, During the Government of . . . London: 1766. V. 38

VANSITTART, ROBERT

Certain Ancient Tracts Concerning the Management of Landed Property Reprinted. London: 1767. V. 38

The Singing Caravan. London: 1932. V. 40

The Singing Caravan. Newtown: 1932. V. 37; 38; 43; 44; 45

VAN STICKLEN, HELEN

A Sojourn in California by the King's Orphan. San Francisco: 1945. V. 46

VANSTON, GEORGE T. B.

The Law of Local Government in Ireland. Dublin: 1899/1919. V. 43

The Law Relating to Local Government in Ireland. Dublin: 1915-05-19. V. 40; 43; 46

VAN SWIETEN, GERARD

The Commentaries Upon the Aphorisms of Dr. Herman Boerhaave. London: 1744. V. 44

Commentaries Upon Boerhaave's Aphorisms Concerning the Knowledge and Curse of Diseases. Edinburgh: 1776. V. 40

VAN TASSEL, CHARLES SUMNER

The Book and Its 'Centennial' Or One Hundred Years of the Buckeye State. Bowling Green & Toledo: 1901. V. 42

Story of the Maumee Valley, Toledo & the Sandusky Region. Chicago: 1929. V. 46

VAN TRAMP, JOHN C.

Prairie and Rocky Mountain Adventures. Columbus: 1860. V. 39; 44

Prairie and Rocky Mountain Adventures, or, Life in the West. Columbus: 1867. V. 40

VAN URK, JOHN BLAN

The Horse. The Valley and the Chagrin Valley Hunt. New York: 1947. V. 37

The Story of American Foxhunting. New York: 1940. V. 39

The Story of Rolling Rock. New York: 1950. V. 42

VAN VECHTEN, CARL 1880-1964

The Blind Blow-Boy. New York: 1923. V. 42

C.V.V.: 101. New York: (1981). V. 37

Fifty Drawings. Introduction by Carl Van Vechten. New York: 1925. V. 37

VAN VECHTEN, CARL 1880-1964 continued

Fire Crackers. New York: 1925. V. 42

The Merry-Go-Round. New York: 1918. V. 46

Music After the Great War and Other Studies. New York: 1915. V. 39

The Tiger in the House. London: 1921. V. 40

VANVINIO, ONOFRIO

Fasti et Triumphi Rom. a Romulo Rege Usque a Carolum V. Venice: 1557. V. 41

VANVITELLI, LUIGI

Dichiarazione dei Disegni del Reale Palazzo di Caserta . . . Naples: 1756. V. 37; 42; 46

VAN VOGT, A. E.

The Book of Ptath. 1947. V. 44

Masters of Time. 1950. V. 44

Slan. Sauk City: 1946. V. 39; 45

VAN WAGENEN, G.

Embryology of the Ovary and the Testis Homo Sapiens and Macaca Mulatta. New Haven: 1965. V. 40

VAN WART, IRVING

A Recollection of Wondrous Wanderings. Fountainebleau: 1864. V. 46

VAN WIE, CARRIE

Wonderful City of Carrie Van Wie; Paintings of San Francisco At the Turn of the Century. With text by Oscar Lewis. San Francisco: 1963. V. 37

VAN WINKLE C. S.

The Printers' Guide. New York: 1818. V. 38

VAN WINKLE, H. E.

Nine Years of Democratic Rule in Mississippi: Being Notes Upon the Political History of the State, From the Beginning of the Year 1838, to the Present Time. Jackson: 1847. V. 45

VAN WINKLE, W. M.

Henry William Herbert (Frank Forester): A Bibliography of His Writings, 1832-1858. Portland: 1936. V. 40; 44

VAN WYCK, C. H.

An Address Delivered Before the Nebraska State Board of Agriculture, at the Fair Grounds . . . Sept. 14, 1881. Omaha: 1881. V. 44

VAN WYCK, WILLIAM

On the Terrasse. Paris: 1930. V. 39; 43

VAN ZANDT, FRANCES C. L.

Reminiscences of Frances Cooke Libscomb Van Zandt, Wife of Isaac Van Zandt. Forth Worth. V. 41

VAN ZANDT, NICHOLAS B.

A Full Description of the Soil, Water, Timber and Prairies of Each Lot, or Quarter Section of the Military Lands Between Mississippi and Illinois Rivers. Washington: 1818. V. 42

VAN ZANTEN, D. T.

Walter Burley Griffin: Selected Designs. Palos Park: 1970. V. 46

VARA, MADELEINE

Convalescent Conversations. London/Deya: (1936). V. 37

VARANO, ALFONSO 1705-1788

Giovanni di Giscala Tiranno del Tempio . . . Tragedia. Venice: 1754. V. 43

VARCHI, BENEDETTO

L'Hercolano, Dialogo nel Quale si Ragiona Generalmente delle Lingue & in Partaicolorae della Toscana, e della Fiorentina. Vinetia: 1570. V. 37

VARDON, ROGER

English Bloods. Ottawa: 1930. V. 44

VARDY, JOHN

Some Designs by Mr. Ingio Jones and Mr. William Kent. London: 1744. V. 38

VAREKAMP, MARJOLEIN

Francesco. Groningen: 1987. V. 45

VARELLA, AIRES

Sucessos Que Ouvve nas Fronteiras de Elvas, Olivenca, Campo Mayor & Ouguela, o Segundo Anno da Recuperacao de Portugal . . . Lisbon: 1643. V. 45

VAREN, BERNHARD

Geographia Generalis, in Qua Affectiones Generales Telluris Explicantur. Cambridge: 1712. V. 38

VARENIUS, BERNHARDUS

Descriptio Regni Iaponiae. Amsterdam: 1649. V. 41; 45

VARENNIUS, JOHANNES

Syntaxis Lingvae Graecae, Vna Cum Annotatiunculis Paucis . . . per Ioachimum Camerarium. Paris: 1546. V. 40

VARET, ALEXANDRE L.

The Nunns Complaint Against the Fryars. London: 1676. V. 37; 43; 44

VARGAS, ALFONSO DE

Relatio Ad Reges, & Principes Christianos De Stratagematis Et Sophismatis Politicis Societatis Jesu. N.P.: 1665. V. 37

VARGAS LLOSA, MARIO

Conversations in the Cathedral. New York: 1975. V. 44

The War of the End of the World. 1984. V. 43

VARIATIONS and Quotations. Laguna Beach: 1990. V. 45

VARICK, RICHARD 1753-1831

Varick Court of Inquiry to Investigate the Implication of Colonel Varick in the Arnold Treason. Boston: 1907. V. 40

VARIETY: a collection of original poems. By a Lady. London: 1802. V. 37; 39

VARIGNON, PIERRE 1654-1722

Nouvelle Mecanique or Statique, dont le Projet fut Donne en MDCLXXXVII. Paris: 1725. V. 38

Projet d'une Nouvelle Mechanique . . . Paris: 1687. V. 41; 45; 46

Traite du Mouvement, et de la Mesure des Eaux Coulantes et Jallissantes. Paris: 1725. V. 38; 41; 45

VARILLAS, ANTOINE, SIEUR DE 1624-1696

Les Anecdotes de Florence, ou l'Histoire Secrete de la Maison des Medicis. Hague: 1685. V. 38; 41

VARILLAS, ANTOINE, SIEUR OF 1624-1696

Reflexions on Dr. Gilbert Burnet's Travels Into Switzerland, Italy and Certain Parts of Germany and France &c . . . London: 1688. V. 44

VARIN, AMEDEE

Les Papillons Metamorphoses Terrestres de Peuples de l'Air. Paris: 1852. V. 41

VARINANA, GUGLIELMO

Ad Omnium Interiorum & Interiorum 7 Exteriorum Morbos Remediorum Praesidia . . . Basel: 1531. V. 38

THE VARIOUS Ages and Dgrees of Human Life, Explained by These Twelve Different Stages, from Our Birth to Our Grave. London. V. 43

VARIOUS Authors. A Martial Medley - Fact and Fiction. London: 1931. V. 40

VARLEY, CHARLES

A Treatise on Agriculture. Dublin: 1765. V. 38

VARLEY, JOHN

A Practical Treatise on Perspective. London: 1815. V. 46

A Treatise on the Principles of Landscape Design with General Observations and Instructions to Young Artists. London: 1849. V. 38

VARLEY, T.

Hampshire. London: 1909. V. 40

VARLEY, WILLIAM 1785-1856

Four Views in the Isle of Wight. London: 1816. V. 38; 44

Observations on Colouring and Sketching from Nature. London: 1820. V. 42

VARLO, CHARLES

Nature Display'd. London: 1793. V. 40

A New System of Husbandry. Philadelphia: 1785. V. 37; 40; 43; 45

VARLOT, LOUIS

Illustration de l'Ancienne Imprimerie Troyenne. Troyes: 1850. V. 45

VARNUM, JAMES M.

The Case, Trevett Against Weeden; on Information and Complaint, for Refusing Paper Bills in Payment . . . Providence: 1787. V. 41; 43

VARONA Y LOAYSA, JERONIMO

Sermon Que Predico Don Geronimo de Varona, Y Loaisa en La Festividad De La Concepcion Purissima de Maria Senora Nuestra; Y Concurrencia de Otras Solemnidades. Guatemala: 1660-61. V. 40

VARRO, MARCUS TERENTIUS

De Lingva Latina Libri Tres, & Totidem de Analogia. Paris: 1530. V. 38

VARTHEMA, LUDOVICO DI

The Itinerary of Ludovico di Varthema of Bologna from 1502-1508. London: 1928. V. 46

VARTY-SMITH, AUGUSTA A.

Matthew Tindale. London: 1891. V. 41

VASARELY, VICTOR

Octal. Traduction Allemand et Postface par/Ubertragung ins Deutsche und Nachwort von Helmut Scheffel. Munchen: 1972. V. 42

VASARI, GEORGIO

Capricci E Aneddoti di Artisti. Florence: 1864. V. 39

VASARI, GIORGIO

Lives of the Most Eminent Painters, Sculptors and Architects. London: 1885. V. 46

Lives of Seventy of the Most Eminent Painters, Scultpors and Architects. London: 1897. V. 45

Lives of the Most Eminent Painters, Sculptors and Architects. London: 1912-14. V. 45; 46

The Lives of the Most Eminent Painters. New York: 1966. V. 41; 43

Lives of the Most Eminent Painters. Verona: 1966. V. 37; 42

Opere De . . . Firenze: 1822-23. V. 45

Painting Illustrated in Three Dialogues . . . London: 1685. V. 41

Ragionamenti Sporza le Inuentioni da Lui Dipinte in Firenze nel Palazzo di Loro Altezze Serenissime. Florence: 1588. V. 37

Vite de Piu' Eccellenti Pittori, Scultori, ed Architetti . . . Livorno & Florence: 1767-1772. V. 42

VASCONCELLOS, P. SIMAO DE

Chronica da Companhia de Jesus do Estado do Brasil . . . Lisbon: 1663. V. 45

VASEY, GEORGE

Grasses of the Pacific Slope, Including Alaska and the Adjacent Islands. Washington: 1892-93. V. 42

Illustrations of North American Grasses. Washington: 1891-93. V. 37; 45

VASI, GIUSEPPE

Delle Magnificenze di Roma Antica e Moderna. Rome: 1747-61. V. 37

VASSAEUS, LADOICUS

In Anatomen Corporis Humani Tabulae Quatuor . . . Venice: 1544. V. 38; 41

VASSALL, SPENCER THOMAS

Memoir of the Life of Lieutenant-Colonel Vassall. Bristol: 1819. V. 38

VASSE, LOYS

In Anatomen Corporis Humani Tubulae Quatuor . . . Venice: 1544. V. 45

VASSEY, VERONICA

The Practical Paper Flower Maker. London: 1890. V. 42

VASSOS, JOHN

Contempo. Text by Ruth Vassos. New York: 1929. V. 37

Phobia. New York: 1931. V. 37

Salome. New York: (c. 1927). V. 37

VASSOS, RUTH

Humanities. New York: 1935. V. 38

Ultimo: An Imaginative Narration of Life Under the Earth . . . , by Ruth Vassos. New York: 1930. V. 37

VATICINIA Sive Prophetiae Abbatis Joanchimi & Anselmi Episcopi Marsicani . . . Venice: 1589. V. 39

VATSYAYANA, CALLED MALLA-NAGA

The Kama Sutra of Vatsyayana. London: 1883. V. 46

VATTEL, EMERICH DE

The Law of Nations; or, Principles of the Law of Nature. Dublin: 1792. V. 38; 40

The Law of Nations. London: 1797. V. 40

The Law of Nations; or Principles of the Law of Nature, Applied to the Conduct and Affairs of Nations and Sovereigns. Philadelphia: 1830. V. 43

The Law of Nations. London: 1834. V. 40

The Law of Nations; or Principles of the Law of Nature. London: 1760 & 1759. V. 37

VATTEL, EMMERICH DE

The Law of Nations: or, Principles of the Law of Nature . . . New York: 1796. V. 42; 45

VATTERMARE, ALEXANDER

International Exchanges: Letter to the Hon. Hannibal Hamlin with A Description of the Metrical Decimal System of William W. Mann . . . Paris: 1853. V. 38; 41

VAUBAN, SEBASTIEN LE PRESTRE DE

A Project for a Royal Tythe. London: 1708. V. 39; 40

Projet d'une Dixme Royale, qui Supprimant la Taille, les Aydes, les Douanes d'une Province a l'Autre . . . Paris: 1707. V. 38

VAUGHAN, BENJAMIN

Letters on the Subject of the Concert of Princes, and the Dismemberment of Poland and France . . . London: 1793. V. 38

New and Old Principles of Trade Compared . . . London: 1788. V. 46

VAUGHAN, DANIEL

The Destiny of the Solar System; Being an Epitome of Three Lectures Delivered in Cincinnati. Cincinnati: 1854. V. 41

VAUGHAN, HENRY

Poems. 1924. V. 40

Poems by Henry Vaughan. Newtown: 1924. V. 39; 42; 45

The Sacred Poems. London: 1897. V. 37; 42; 44; 46

Silex Scintillans &c. Sacred Poems and Pious Ejaculations. London: 1858. V. 46

The Works in Verse and Prose Complete. 1871. V. 46

Works in Verse and Prose . . . Edinburgh: 1871. V. 40

VAUGHAN, JOHN

The Reports and Arguments of that Learned Judge Sir John Vaughan Kt . . . Being All of Them Special Cases, and Many Wherein He Pronounced the Resolution of the Whole Court of Common Pleas . . . London: 1677. V. 45

VAUGHAN, MYRA MCALMON

David O. Dodd. N.P.: 1900. V. 40

VAUGHAN, RICE

A Discourse of Coin and Coinage: The First Invention, Use, Matter, Forms, Proportions and Differences, Ancient and Modern . . . London: 1675. V. 38

A Treatise of Money. London: 1675. V. 37

VAUGHAN, ROBERT

The Age of Great Cities; or, Modern Society Viewed In Its Relation to Intelligence, Morals and Religion. London: 1843. V. 42

Revolutions in English History. London: 1859. V. 39

St. John and the Seven Churches. London: 1877. V. 42; 43

VAUGHAN, T. WAYLAND

Recent Madreporaria of the Hawaiian Islands and Laysan. Washington: 1907. V. 37

VAUGHAN, W. E.

Autographica, with a Gossip on the (Lost) Art of Printing in Colours. N.P.: 1900. V. 38

A New History of Ireland V. Ireland Under the Union 1. 1801-70. Oxford: 1989. V. 43

VAUGHAN, WALTER

The Adventures of Five Englishmen from Pulo Condoro. London: 1714. V. 46

VAUGHAN, WALTER R.

Vaughan's 'Freedmen's Pension Bill.' Being an Appeal in Behalf of Men Released From Slavery. Omaha: 1890. V. 42

VAUGHAN, WATKINS M.

Paul Turner Vaughan, August 17, 1839 to September 17, 1916. Nashville: 1919. V. 44

VAUGHAN, WILLIAM 1752-1850

The Church Militant (in Verse) . . . London: 1640. V. 39; 42; 44; 46

Memoir of William Vaughan, Esq. F.R.S. with Miscellaneous Pieces Relative to Docks, Commerce, etc. London: 1839. V. 46

Tracts on Docks and Commerce, Printed Between the Years 1793 and 1800 . . . London: 1839. V. 43

VAUGHN, ALFRED

Personal Record of the Thirteenth Regiment. Tennessee Infantry. Memphis: 1897. V. 39; 42

VAUGHN, ROBERT

Then and Now. Minneapolis: 1900. V. 37; 38; 39; 40; 41

VAURIE, CHARLES

The Birds of the Palearctic Fauna. London: 1959-65. V. 37; 38

Birds of the Palearctic Fauna. London: 1965/69. V. 45

Tibet and Its Birds. London: 1972. V. 40

VAUX, CALVERT

Villas and Cottages. London: 1857. V. 41; 46

Villas and Cottages. New York: 1857. V. 38; 40; 41

Villas and Cottages. London: 1864. V. 38; 40

VAUX, CALVERT continued

Villas and Cottages, a Series of Designs Prepared for Execution in the United States. New York: 1867. V. 44

Villas and Cottages a Series of Designs Prepared for Execution in the United States. New York: 1869. V. 42; 46

Villas and Cottages. New York: 1872. V. 42

VAUX, FRANCIS

Detur Pulchriori; or, a Poem in Praise of the University of Oxford. N.P.: Oxford: 1658. V. 41

VAUX, JAMES HARDY

Memoirs of James Hardy Vaux. London: 1819. V. 39; 41; 42

VAUX, JOHN

A New Alamancke and Prognostication for the Yeere . . . 1636. London: 1635. V. 39

VAUX, ROBERTS

Memoirs of the Life of Anthony Benezet. Philadelphia: 1817. V. 37; 42

VAVON, ANTOINE

La Truite Sea Moeurs l'Art de la Pecher, Dessins De Causyn et Clerin Planches en Couleurs Hors Texte de Clerin . . . 1927. V. 40

VAVRA, JAROSLAU R.

5000 Years of Glass-Making. Prague: 1954. V. 37; 43

VAZ COUTINHO, GONCALO

Historia do Successo que na Ilha de S. Miguel Ovve com Armada Ingresa que Sobre a Ditta Ilha Foy, Sendo Gouernador della Goncalo Vaz Coutinho . . . Lisbon: 1630. V. 41

VEBLEN, THORSTEIN 1857-1929

Absentee Ownership and Business Enterprise in Recent Times. The Case of America. London: 1924. V. 41

The Engineers and the Price System. New York: 1921. V. 41

The Higher Learning in America. New York: 1918. V. 37

The Theory of the Leisure Class. New York: 1899. V. 37; 43; 45

The Theory of the Leisure Class. New York: 1902. V. 45

The Theory of Business Enterprise. New York: 1904. V. 41

VECELLIO, CESARE 1530-1606

Corona delle Nobili bt (sic) Virtuose donne Libro Primo (-Terzo). Nel Quale si Dimostra in Varii Dissegni . . . Venice: 1592. V. 41

De Gli Habiti Antichi et Moderni di Diverse Parti Del Mondo, Libri Due. Venice: 1590. V. 38; 40

VEDDER, DAVID

The Covenanters' Communion, and Other Poems. Edinburgh: 1828. V. 42

VEDDER, ELIHU 1836-1923

The Digressions of V. Boston: 1910. V. 42; 44; 46

The Digressions of V: Written for His Own Fun and That of His Friends. Boston and New York: 1910. V. 37

The Digressions of . . . New York: 1910. V. 40

Doubt and Other Things: Verse and Illustrations. Boston: 1922. V. 37; 38

Miscellaneous Moods in Verse. Boston: 1914. V. 41; 43

VEEN, JAN VAN DER

Zinne-Beelden, oft Adams Appel. Amsterdam: 1642. V. 40

VEEN, OCTAVIO VAN, KNOWN AS OTTO VAENIUS

Amoris Divini Emblemata . . . Antverpiae: 1615. V. 43; 46

Amorum Elblemata, Figuris Aeneis Incisa. Antwerp: 1608. V. 40

Qvinti Horatii Flacci Emblemata. Antverpiae: 1612. V. 39

Vita D. Thomae Aquinatis Othonis Vaeni Ingenio et Manu Delineata. Antwerp: 1610. V. 40

VEER, GERRIT

Verhael Van de Vier Eerste Schip-Vaerden der Hollantsche en Zeeuwsche Schepen. Amsterdam: 1663. V. 43; 44

VEER, GERRIT DE

The Three Voyages of William Barents to the Arctic Regions. London: 1876. V. 43; 45

VEGA, FELICIANO DE LA

Relectionvm Canonicarvm in Scvndvm Decretalivm Librvm. Lima: 1633. V. 40; 45

VEGA CARPIO, LOPE DE 1562-1635

Arcadia, Prosas, y Versos . . . con Una Exposicion de los Nombres Historicos, y Poeticos. Valencia: 1602. V. 40

Ierusalem Conquistada. Madrid: 1609. V. 38

VEGA CARPIO, LOPE FELIX DE 1562-1635

Pastores de Belen Prosas y Versos Divinos . . . Brussels: 1614. V. 41

Relacion de las Fiestas que la Insigne Villa de Madrid Hizo en la Canonicacion de su Bienaventurado Hijo y Patron San Isidro, con las Comedias que se Representaron y los Versos que en la Iusta Poetica se Escrivieron. Madrid: 1622. V. 41

The Star of Seville: A Drama in Three Acts and in Verse. Newtown: 1935. V. 45

VEGETIUS

Dell'arte Della Gverra, Tradotto de Francesco Ferrosi. Venetia: 1551-52. V. 42

VEGETIUS, RENATUS FLAVIUS

De Re Militari. Antuerpiae: 1585. V. 37

De Re Militari (and other works). Parisiis: 1535. V. 37; 38

God. Stewechii Commentarius ad Flavi Vegeti Renati Libros, De la Militari. Vesaliae: 1670. V. 39; 45

Military Institutions of Vegetius, in Five Books . . . London: 1676. V. 44

Military Instructions . . . London: 1767. V. 38

VEHLING, JOSEPH D.

America's Table. Chicago: 1950. V. 44

VEITCH, JAMES, & SONS

A Manual of the Coniferae, Containing a General Review of the Order, a Synopsis of the Hardy Kinds Cultivated in Great Britian . . . London: 1881. V. 41; 42

Manual of the Coniferae. London: 1900. V. 42; 43; 44; 46

VEITCH, JAMES H. 1868-1907

Hortus Veitchii. Chelsea: 1906. V. 45

Hortus Veitchii, a History of the Rise and Progress of the Nurseries . . . London: 1906. V. 39; 40; 42

VEITCH, JAMES HERBERT

A Traveller's Notes of a Tour through India, Malaysia, Japan, Corea, the Australian Colonies and New Zealand During the Years 1891-93. London: 1896. V. 43; 44; 46

VEITCH, JOHN

The History and Poetry of the Scottish Border. Edinburgh: 1893. V. 43

Memoir of Sir William Hamilton, Bart. Edinburgh & London: 1869. V. 41

VEITIA LINAGE, JOSE DE

The Spanish Rule of Trade to the West Indies . . . London: 1702. V. 43

VEITIA LINAJE, JOSE DE

Norte de la Contratacion de las Indias Occidentales . . . Seville: 1672. V. 45

VELASCO, JOSE FRANCISCO

Sonora: Its Extent, Population, Natural Productions, Indian Tribes, Mines, Mineral Lands, Etc. San Francisco: 1861. V. 40; 44

VELASQUEZ, JOSE ANTONIO

Le Qvalita Venere e Discorso Parenetico Morale . . . Naples: 1681. V. 43

VELASQUEZ, PEDRO

Illustrated Memoir of an Eventful Expedition into Central America Resulting in the Discovery of the Idodatrous (sic) City of Iximaya, in an Unexplored Region; and the Possession of Two Remarkable Aztec Children. Brighton. V. 37

Memoir of an Eventful Expedition in Central America; Resulting in the Discovery of the Idolatrous City of Iximaya, in an Unexplored Region and the Possession of Two Remarkable Aztec Children . . . New York: 1850. V. 37; 41

VELAZQUEZ DE VELASCO, LUIS JOSE, MARQUES DE VALDEFLORES

Ensayo Sobre los Alphabetos de las Letras Desconocidas, que se Encuentran en las mas Antiguas Medallas, y Monumentos de Espana. Madrid: 1752. V. 38

VELAZQUEZ, LORETA JANETA

The Woman in Battle. Hartford: 1876. V. 40

VELLEIUS PATERCULUS

Velleius Paterculus His Romane Historie . . . London: 1802. V. 46

VELLEZ GUERREIRO, JOAO TAVAREZ DE

Jornada, Que Antonio de Albuquerque Coelho, Governador, e Capitao General da Cidade de Nome de Deos de Macao na China, fez de Goa ate Chegar a Dita Cidade no Anno de 1718. Lisbon: 1732. V. 40

VELPEAU, ALFRED ARMAND LOUIS MARIE 1795-1867

An Elementary Treatise on Midwifery. Philadelphia: 1831. V. 42

Embryologie ou Ovologie Humaine . . . Paris: 1833. V. 45

New Elements of Operative Surgery . . . New York: 1847. V. 42

New Elements of Operative Surgery . . . New York: 1851. V. 42; 44

Traite Complet de l'Art des Accouchmens ou Tocologie Theorique et Pratique . . . Paris: 1835. V. 38

A Treatise on Surgical Anatomy, or the Anatomy of Regions. New York: 1830. V. 38; 39

VELPEAU, ALFRED ARMAND LOUIS MARIE 1795-1867 continued

A Treatise on the Diseases of the Breast. Philadelphia: 1841. V. 42

A Treatise on the Diseases of the Breast and Mammary Region . . . London: 1856. V. 42; 44

VENABLE, CHARLES SCOTT

The Campaign from the Wilderness to Petersburg. Richmond: 1879. V. 37; 44

VENABLE, WILLIAM HENRY

Beginnings of Literary Culture, in the Ohio Valley, Historical and Biographical Sketches. Cincinnati: 1891. V. 44

VENABLES, ROBERT

The Experienced Angler; or, Angling Improv'd. London: 1662. V. 45

The Experienced Angler . . . London: 1668. V. 44

The Experienced Angler; or Angling Improved. (and) Memoir of Col. Robert Venables. London: 1825. V. 39

The Experienced Angler. London: 1827. V. 37; 39; 42

VENEDEY, J.

Ireland and the Irish During the Repeal Year 1843 from the German of Herr J. Venedey. Dublin: 1844. V. 46

VENEGAS DE BUSTO, ALEJO

Primera Parte de Las Differencias de Libros Que Hay en El Universo. Madrid: 1569. V. 40

VENEGAS DE BUSTON, ALEJO

Primera Parte de las Diferencias de Libros que Hay en el Universo. Toledo: 1540. V. 38; 40; 43

VENEGAS, MIGUEL

Juan Maria de Salvatierra of the Company of Jesus, Missionary in the Province of New Spain, and Apostolic Conqueror of the Californias. Cleveland: 1920. V. 38

Juan Maria de Salvatierra of the Company of Jesus: Missionary in the Province of New Spain . . . Cleveland: 1929. V. 40; 42; 45; 46

A Natural and Civil History of California. London: 1759. V. 37; 39; 42; 43; 44; 45

Histoire Naturelle et Civile de la Californie . . . Paris: 1767. V. 42

Naturliche und Burgerliche Geschichte von Californien . . . von Johan Christoph Adelung . . . Lemgo: 1769-70. V. 38; 40; 42

Noticia de la California . . . Madrid: 1757. V. 38; 39

Obras Californianas del Padre Miguel Venegas. La Paz: 1977-83. V. 44

VENERIUS, MARCUS ANTONIUS

Physiologia. Aristotelis et Averois SEntentiae et Scita Theseque de Rebus naturae. Milan: 1525. V. 38

VENERONI, GIOVANNI

The Complete Italian Master . . . London: 1791. V. 41

The Italian Master: or, the Easiest and Best Method for Attaining that Language. London: 1729. V. 41; 43; 46

VENESS, WILLIAM T.

El Dorado; or, British Guiana as a Field for Colonization. London: 1866. V. 40

El Dorado; or British Guiana as a Field for Colonisation. London: 1867. V. 40; 46

VENETTE, NICHOLAS DE

The Mysteries of Conjugal Love Reveal'd. London: 1712. V. 38

VENETTE, NICOLAS 1633-1698

L'Art de Tailler les ARbres Fruitiers, avec un Dictionaire des Mots dont se Servent les Jardiniers, en Parlant des Arbres. Paris: 1683. V. 46

The Art of Pruning Fruit-Trees, With an Explanation of Some Words Which Gardiners Make Use of In Speaking of Trees, for Preserving Us in Health . . . London: 1685. V. 41

VENEZUELA

Interesting Official Documents Relating to the United Provinces of Venezuela, viz. Preliminary Remarks, the Act of Independence, Proclamation, Manifesto to the World of the Causes Which Have Impelled Said Provinces to separate from the Mother Country . . . London: 1812. V. 38

VENN, HENRY

The Duty of a Parish Priest . . . London: 1760. V. 42

VENN, JOHN 1834-1923

Catalogue of a Collection of Books on Logic Presented tot he Library by John Venn. Cambridge: 1889. V. 42

The Logic of Chance. London: 1888. V. 40; 41

The Principles of Empirical or Inductive Logic. London: 1907. V. 39; 41

VENN, SUSANNA CARNEGIE

The Gwillians of Bryn Gwillian. London: 1876/1875. V. 40

VENNE, ADRIEN VAN DE 1589-1665

Tafereel Van de Belacchende Werelt. The Hague: 1635. V. 44

VENNER, THOMAS

Via Recta and Ritam Longam. Or, a Treatise Wherein the Right Way and Best Manner of Living for Attaining to a Long and Heathful Life, Is Clearly Demonstrated and Punctually Applied to Every Age and Constitution of Body. London: 1650. V. 38

Via Recta ad Vitam Longam or a Treatise . . . Best Manner for Attaining to a Long and Healthy Life . . . London: 1660. V. 46

VENNER, TO.

A Briefe and Accurate Treatise of Tobacco. In which, the immoderate, irregular, & unseasonable use thereof is reprehended, and the true nature and best manner of using it, perspicously demonstrated, by To. Venner. San Francisco: 1931. V. 37

VENNING, MARY ANNE

A Geographical Present. London: 1817. V. 39; 43

VENNOR, HENRY G.

Our Birds of Prey, or the Eagles, Hawks, and Owls of Canada. Montreal: 1876. V. 42; 44

VENTENAT, ETIENNE PIERRE

Choix de Plantes, dont la Plupart Sont Cultivees dans le Jardin de Cels. Paris: 1803-08. V. 43

VENTH, CARL

My Memories. 1939. V. 42

VENTOUILLAC, L. T.

The French Librarian or Literary Guide . . . London: 1829. V. 46

Paris and Its Environs. London: 1831. V. 37; 46

VENTRIS, PEYTON 1645-1691

The Reports . . . 1668-1691 . . . with Learned Arguments By: Sir Francis North, Sir Matthew Hale, etc. London: 1696. V. 37; 38; 40; 45

The Reports of - Late One of the Justices of the Common-Pleas, in the Reign of Charles II & K. James II and in the Three First Years of the Reign of His Now Majesty K. William and the Late Queen Mary. London: 1701. V. 38

The Reports of Sir Peyton Ventris, Kt. Late One of the Justices of the Common Pleas. In the Savoy: 1726. V. 45

The Reports . . . 1668-1691 . . . with Learned Arguments By: Sir Francis North, Sir Matthew Hale, etc. London: 1726. V. 40

VENTURA, COMINO

Tresor Politique: Divise en Trois Livres; Contenant Les Relations, Instructions, Traictez, Et Divers Discours Appartenans a la Parfaicte Intelligence de la Raison D'Estat . . . Paris: 1608. V. 43

VENTURI, GIAMBATISTA

Commentari Sopra le Storia e Teorie dell'ottica . . . Tomo Primo. Bologna: 1814. V. 37

VENTURI, LIONELLO

Italian Painting: Creators of the Renaissance; The Renaissance from Caravaggio to Modigliani. Geneva;: 1950-52. V. 38

VENTURI, R.

Learning from Las Vegas. Cambridge: 1972. V. 37

VENUS Attiring the Graces. Addressed to -----. London: 1777. V. 40

VENUS Stirring the Graces. London: 1777. V. 42

VENUSTI, ANTONIO MARIA

Compendio Utilissimo di Quelle Cose, le Quali a Nobili e Christini Mercanti Appartengono. Milano: 1561. V. 38

VENUTI, NICCOLO MARCELLO, MARCHESE DI

Esequie di Luigi I. Cattolico Re delle Spagne . . . Delle Lodi di Luigi I . . . Orazione. Florence: 1724. V. 40; 46

VENUTI, RIDOLFINO

Collectanea Antiquitatum Romanarum Quas Centum Tabulis Aeneis Incisas et a Rodulphino Venuti . . . Rome: 1736. V. 44

A Collection of Some of the Finest Prospects in Italy, wth Short Remarks on Them, by Abbate R. Venuti Antiquarian to the Pope, and Fellow of the Royal Society of London. London: 1762. V. 37

VERANTIUS, FAUSTUS

Machinae Novae. Venice: 1616. V. 38

VER BECK, FRANK

Little Black Sambo and the Monkey People. 1935. V. 46

VERDE, FRANCISCUS

Ingenuae Observationes Apologeticae Physico-Legales, de Foetus Animationis & Nativitatis Tempore, &c. Lugduni: 1664. V. 37

VERDIER, P.

Catalogue of the Painted Enamels of the Renaissance. Baltimore: 1967. V. 37

VERE, CHARLES BROKE

The Danger of Opening the Ports to Foreign Corn at a fixed Duty, Considered. Ipswich: 1834. V. 42

VERE, FRANCIS

The Commentaries of Sir Francis Vere . . . Cambridge: 1657. V. 37; 38

VERE, PERCY

David Dalton, a Novel of Business Life. Edinburgh. V. 38; 40

VERELST, HARRY d. 1785

A View of the Rise, Progress, and Present State of the English Government in Bengal. London: 1772. V. 38; 42; 43; 45

VEREPAEUS, SIMON

Precationum Piarvm Enchiridion . . . Antwerp: 1586. V. 42

VEREY, ROSEMARY

A Country-woman's Notes. 1989. V. 44

VERGA, GIOVANNI

Cavalleria Rusticana. New York: 1928. V. 40; 41

Mastro-Don Gesualdo. London: 1925. V. 40

VERGILIUS

Picturae Antiquissimi Virgiliani Codicis Bibliothecae Vaticanae a Petro Sancte Bartoli Aere Incisae Accedunt ex Insignioribus Pinacotheeia Picturis Aliae Veteres Gemmae et Anaglypha. Rome: 1782. V. 40

VERGILIUS MARO, PUBLIUS 70-19 BC

The Seven First Books of the Eneidos of Virgill, converted in Englishe meter by THomas Phaer Esquier, sollicitour to the King and quenes maisetiees, attending their honorable counsaile in the Marchies of Wales. (London): 1558. V. 37

Dreyzehen Buecher Von Dem Tewren Helden Enea, Was der Wasser und Land Bestanden. Frankfurt: 1559. V. 41

Liber Quartus Aeneidos, & in Eum Commentarii Iacobi Heliae Marchiani. Paris: 1572. V. 37

L'Eneide di Virgilio, del Commendatore Annibal Caro. Venice: 1592. V. 45

The Thirteen Books of Aenidos. London: 1596. V. 40

The Thirteene Bookes of Aeneidos. London: 1607. V. 40

Virgils Aeneis. Edinburgh: 1710. V. 42

L'Eneide di Virgilio del Commendatore Annibal Caro. Paris: 1760. V. 45

The Aeneid of Virgil . . . London: 1794. V. 42

The Aeneis of Virgil. Chiswick: 1820. V. 39

The First Four Books of the Aeneid of Virgil in English Heroic Verse. With Other Translations and Poems. Edinburgh: 1836. V. 38

The Aneids of Virgil. London: 1876. V. 43

The Aeneid of Virgil. New York: 1906. V. 43; 44

Antiquissimi Virginiliani Codicis Fragmenta et Picturae ex Bibliotheca Vaticana . . . Romae: 1741. V. 44

Bvcolica, Georgica, Aeneis . . . 1531-32. V. 42

Bucolicorum, Georgicorum, et Aenidos, cum Accurata Simul & Fidei Servii Mauri Honorati Expositione, Pars Prima. Basle: 1534. V. 40

Les Bucoliques et Georgiques. Geneva: 1580. V. 37

Bucolica Argumentis Breviusculis Illustrata ac Diligentissime Recognita. Wittenberg: 1595. V. 37

Bucolica, Geogica, et Aeneis. Cambridge: 1701. V. 42

The Bucolicks of Virgil . . . The Georgicks . . . London: 1741-49. V. 42

Bucolica, Georgica et Aeneis. Edinburgh: 1743. V. 40

Bucolica, Georgica, et Aeneis. London: 1750. V. 39; 40; 41; 44; 46

Bucolica, Georgica, et Aeneis, ad Optimorum Exemplarium Fidem Recensita. Edinburgh: 1755. V. 45

Publii Virgilii Maronis. Bucolica, Georgica, et Aeneis. Birmingham: 1757. V. 37; 38; 41; 45; 46

Bucolica Georgia et Aeneis ex Cod. Mediceo-Laurentiano Descripta. Rome: 1763-65. V. 38; 40

Bucolica et Georgica. London: 1774. V. 45

Bucolica, Georgica et Aeneis. Glasgow: 1778. V. 38; 40; 43; 44; 45; 46

Bucolica, Georgica et Aeneis. Londini: 1800. V. 43

La Buccolica di P. Virgilio Marone in Rime Italiane. Parma: 1801. V. 41

Buccolica. London: 1810. V. 45

Les Bucoliques. Zurich: 1942. V. 46

Les Bucoliques de Virgile. Paris: 1953. V. 42

Les Bucoliques. Lausanne: 1960. V. 41

Bucolica, Georgica, et Aeneis. Glasgow: 1978. V. 42

Carmina Omnia. Paris: 1858. V. 45

A New Translation of Virgil's Eclogues. London: 1783. V. 45

The Eclogues of Virgil. London: 1883. V. 44

The Eclogues and Georgics of Virgil. London: 1889. V. 46

The Eclogues of Vergil. Weimar: 1926. V. 38; 43

The Eclogues of Vergil. London: 1927. V. 43

The Eclogues. New York: 1960. V. 41; 43

An English Version of the Eclogues of Virgil. London: 1883. V. 40

Eclogae et Georgica Latine et Germanice. Leipzig: 1926. V. 43

The Ecologues of Vergil. Weimar: 1927. V. 37

Virgil's Second Eclogue. Cambridge: 1958. V. 38

Les Georgicques de Virgille Maron. Paris: 1519. V. 37

La Georgica, Nuovamente di Latina in Thoscana Favella, per Bernardino Daniello tradotta e commentata. Venice: 1549. V. 37

Georgicorum Libri Quator. London: 1741. V. 45

Georgicum Libri Quatuor - the Georgicks of Virgil with and English Translation and Notes. (with) Bucolicorum Eclogae Decem. The Bucolics of Virgil. London: 1741/49. V. 41

Georgicorum . . . The Georgicks . . . with and English Translation and Notes (and) The Bucolicks . . . London: 1746/49. V. 45

The Georgics of Virgil. Cambridge: 1767. V. 39

The Farm and Fruit of Old. A Translation in Verse of the First and Second Georgics of Virgil. London: 1862. V. 40

The Georgics of Virgil. London: 1871. V. 42

The Georgics of Virgil. Boston: 1904. V. 37

Georgics. Cambridge: 1904. V. 45

The Georgics . . . London: 1931. V. 38; 46

The Georgics of Virgil in English Verse. New York: 1931. V. 41

Les Georgiques. Paris: 1937-43, 1950. V. 38

Les Georgiques. Paris: 1937-43-50. V. 41

The Georgics of Virgil. London: 1940. V. 41

Les Georgiques. Paris: 1947. V. 38

Les Georgiques. Paris: 1950. V. 41

The Georgics. 1952. V. 40

The Georgics. Verona: 1952. V. 40; 42

Oswald Belings Verdeutsche Waldlider/ Oder 10 + Hirten Gesprache Des . . . Poeten Virg. Marons/ In Deutsche Verse Ubersetzet/ . . . mit Schonen Kupfferstucken Gezieret . . . Schleswig: 1649. V. 41

The Pastorals of Virgil, with a Course of English Reading, Adapted for Schools . . . by Robert John Thornton. London: 1821. V. 39

Poemata Qvae Extant Omnia . . . Zurich: 1561. V. 43

Vniversum Poema vna cvm Emendatissimis Commentariis Servii Marii, et Tiberii Donati Multo Quam Antehac vnque Prodit . . . Venetiis: 1541. V. 39

Universum Poema cum Absoluta Servii Honorati Mauri, Grammatici & Badij Ascensii Interpretatione. Venice: 1566. V. 37

Vir Bonus. Est & Non. De Y Littera Pitagorica. De Rosa. Elegia in Obitu Mecenatis. Cologne: 1501. V. 45

Virgilius Maro Varietate Lectionis et Perpetua Adnotatione Illustratus a G.G. Heyne. Leipzig: 1800. V. 39

Virgilli Evangelisantis Christiados Libri XIII. London: 1638. V. 45

Virgil's Husbandry, or an Essay on the Georgics . . . London: 1724. V. 45

The Wonderful History of Virgilius the Sorcerer of Rome. London: 1913. V. 41

Opera. Lyons: 1517. V. 37

Opera. Parisiis: 1532. V. 41

L'Opere, Cioe la Bucolica, la Georgica, & l'Eneida Nvovamente . . . Florence: 1556. V. 45

Opera, in Locos Communes Digesta . . . in Gratiam Turnoniae Juventutis. Tournon: 1597. V. 37

Pvblii Virgilii Maronis Poetarvm Latinorvm Principis Opera Indvbitata Omnia. Iannoni: 1628. V. 44

Opera. Sedan: 1628. V. 38

Opera. Paris: 1641. V. 40

The Works of Publius Virgilius Maro. London: 1654. V. 46

The Works of Publius Virgilius Maro Translated, Adorned with Sculpture and Illustrated with Annotations. London: 1668. V. 39

Virgilii Maronis Opera Interpretatione et Notis Illustravit Carolus Ruaeus . . . Amstelodami: 1690. V. 46

Works. London: 1697. V. 41; 42

The Works of Virgil: Containing His Pastorals, Georgics and Aeneis. London: 1709. V. 42

The Works of Virgil. London: 1737. V. 46

The Works of Virgil Translated into English Prose . . . London: 1743. V. 41

Les Oeuvres . . . Traduites en Francois . . . Paris: 1743. V. 40

Opera. Paris: 1745. V. 38

The Works of Virgil. Tanslated into English Verse by Mr. Dryden. London: 1748. V. 39

The Works. London: 1753. V. 40; 41

The Works of Virgil. London: 1755. V. 44

The Works. London: 1763. V. 39

Opera Ex Cod. Medicea-Laurentianum Descripta. Rome: 1763-65. V. 40

Works. Brussels: 1765. V. 44; 46

The Works of Virgil. Birmingham: 1766. V. 42

The Works of Virgil, Translated by John Dryden. Glasgow: 1769. V. 38

VERGILIUS MARO, PUBLIUS 70-19 BC continued

Opera, Varietate Lectionis et Perpetua Adnotatione . . . London: 1793. V. 39

Opera. London: 1796. V. 38; 39

The Works. London: 1803. V. 44

The Works of Virgil. New York: 1803. V. 44

The Works. London: 1810. V. 39

P. Vergili Maronis Opera Omnia. Edited by John P. Postgate from the text of Henry Nettleship. 1912. V. 37

Opera Omnia. 1912. V. 39

Opera Omnia ex Recensione Henrici Nettleship. London: 1912. V. 45

VERGILIUS, POLYDORUS 1470-1555

An Abridgemente of the Notable Works of . . . London: 1560. V. 37

Anglicae Historiae Libri Vigintisex . . . Basel: 1546. V. 40; 41; 43; 45

Anglicae Historiae. Basle: 1555. V. 40

Urbinatis Anglicae Historiae . . . Gandavi: 1558. V. 43

De gli Inventori Delle Cose, Libri Otto. Fiorenza: 1587. V. 38; 39

De Gli Inventori Dell Cose, Libri Otto. Florence: 1592. V. 40

Polydori Vergilii Urbinatis. De Inventoribus Rerum Libri Tres. Strasburg: 1516. V. 40

De Rerum Inventoribus Libri Octo. Eiusdem in Dominicam Precem Commentariolum. Basle: 1550. V. 40

De Rerum Inventoribus Libri Octo. Romae: 1585. V. 45

De Inventoribus Rerum Libri VIII & De Prodigiis Libri III. Amsterdam: 1671. V. 38

A Pleasant and Compendious History of the First Inventers and Instituters of the Most Famous Arts, Misteries, Laws, Customs and Manners in the Whole World. London: 1686. V. 44

Polybii Histographi Historiarvm Libri Qvinque. Lugduni apud Seb. Gryphivm,: 1542. V. 39; 40

Proverbium Libellus. Venice: 1500. V. 40; 45

Proverbiroum et Adagiorum Veterum Libellus. Paris: 1510. V. 37

VERGNAUD, N.

L'Art de Creer les Jardins. Paris: 1835.. V. 38

L'Art de Creer les Jardins . . . Paris: 1839. V. 40; 44

VERHAER, FRANCISCUS

Annales Ducum seu Principum Brabantiae Totisque Belfii. Antwerp: 1623. V. 41

VERHAEREN, EMILE

Five Tales. New York: 1924. V. 43

Les Petits Vieux. London: 1901. V. 45

VERHEIDEN, JACOBUS

The History of the Moderne Protestant Divines, Containing Their Parents, Countries, Education, Studies, Lives and the Year of the Lord In Which They Dyed. London: 1637. V. 42

Praestantium Aliquot Theologorum qui Rom. Antichristum Praecipue Oppugnarunt Effigies. The Hague: 1602. V. 40

VERHEYEN, PHILIP

Anatomieae Liber Primus in quo tam Veterum, Quam Recentiorum Anatomicorum Inventa . . . (with) Supplementum Anatomicum. Brussels: 1710. V. 38; 41

VERINI, GIOVAN BAPTISTA

Luiminario; or, the Third Book of the Liber Elementorum Littearum on the Construction of Roman Capitals. Cambridge & Chicago: 1947. V. 41

Luminaro, or the Third Chapter of the Liber Elementorum Litterarum on the Construction of Roman Capitals. Cambridge: 1947. V. 37; 38; 41

VERINI, UGOLINO 1438-1516

Vita di Santa Chira Vergine. London: 1921. V. 38; 40; 42; 44

VERINO, UGOLINO 1438-1516

Vita di Santa Chiara Vergine. 1921. V. 39; 40

Vita di Santa Chiara Vergine. Chelsea: 1921. V. 40; 42; 44; 46

VERKAUF, WILLY

Dada. Monograph of a Movement . . . New York: 1961. V. 45

VERLAINE, PAUL MARIE 1844-1896

Beaute des Femmes. N.P.: 1977. V. 42

Confessions. Paris: 1895. V. 46

Elegies. Paris: 1893. V. 44

Epigrammes. Paris: 1894. V. 44; 46

Femmes/Hombres. Guildford: 1972. V. 45

Femmes/Hombres. London: 1972. V. 39

Fetes Galantes. Paris: 1928. V. 41

Fetes Galantes. Piazza: 1928. V. 41

Fetes Galantes. 1944. V. 45

Invectives. Paris: 1896. V. 46

Parallelement. Paris: 1900. V. 45

Parallelement. Paris: 1931. V. 38

VERLAINE, VALERY

The Graveyard by the Sea. Verona: 1946. V. 40

VERLANDIER, LUIS

Diario de Viage de la Comision de Limites que Puso el Gobierno de la Republica. Mexico: 1850. V. 40

VERLET, PIERRE

Great Tapestries: The Web of History from the 12th to the 20th Century. Lausanne: 1965. V. 38

VERMIGLI, PEITRO MARTIRE 1499-1562

In Librum Iudicum D. Petri Martyris Florentini . . . Commentarii Doctrissimi . . . Zurich: 1561. V. 38

VERMIGLIOLI, GIOVANNI BATTISTA

Saggio di Bronzi Etruschi Trovati Nell'agro Perugino L'Aprile del 1812. Perugia: 1813. V. 42; 44

VERMILLE, THOMAS E.

Funeral Discourse Occasioned by the Death of the Hon. Stephen Van Rensselaer. New York: 1839. V. 44

VERMONT, E. DE V.

America Heraldica: A Compilation of Coats of Arms, Crests & Mottoes of Prominent American Families settled in this country before 1800. New York: (1886). V. 37; 42

VERMONT. LAWS, STATUTES, ETC. - 1798

Laws of the State of Vermont; Revised and Passed by the Legislature in the Year of Our Lord Seventeen Hundred and Ninety Seven. Rutland: 1798. V. 40

VERNE, JULES 1828-1905

Adventures in the Land of the Behemoth. Boston: 1874. V. 40

Around the World in Eighty Days. London: 1873. V. 40

Around the World in Eighty Days. 1962. V. 40

Around the World in Eighty Days. Chicago: 1982. V. 45

At the North Pole. Philadelphia: 1874. V. 39

The Chase of the Golden Meteor. 1909. V. 44

Clovis Dardentor. London: 1897. V. 40

Dick Sand, or a Captain at Fifteen. New York: 1878. V. 46

Doctor Ox and Other Stories. 1874. V. 46

Doctor Ox, and Other Stories. Boston: 1874. V. 40

The Exploration of the World. New York: 1879. V. 40

The Exploration of the World. New York: 1875. V. 37

Five Weeks in a Balloon. 1869. V. 43

Five Weeks in a Balloon. New York: 1869. V. 39; 46

A Floating City and the Blockade Runners. London: 1874. V. 40

The Floating Island. (and) The Blockade Runners. London:k: 1874. V. 42

From the Clouds to the Moutains. Boston: 1874. V. 37; 40

From the Earth to the Moon and Around the Moon. New York: 1970. V. 43

The Fur Country; or, Seventy Degrees North Latitude. Montreal: 1876. V. 46

A Journey to the Center of the Earth. 1874. V. 43

Meridiana; the Adventures of Three Englishmen and Three Russians in South Africa. London: 1873. V. 41

Meridiana: The Adventures of the Englishmen and Three Russians in South Africa. New York: 1874. V. 39

Michael Strogoff. New York: 1877. V. 37

Michael Strogoff, a Courier of the Czar, by Jules Verne. New York: (1927). V. 37

Mistress Branican. 1891. V. 43

Mistress Branican. New York: 1891. V. 41

The Mysterious Island. New York: 1918. V. 41

The Tour of the World in 80 Days. 1873. V. 46

The Tour of the World in 80 Days. Baltimore: 1873. V. 46

The Tour of the World in Eighty Days. Boston: 1873. V. 37; 39; 40; 42; 45

The Tribulations of a Chinamen. London: 1880. V. 41

Twenty Thousand Leagues Under the Sea. 1873. V. 37; 39; 44

Twenty Thousand Leagues Under the Sea. Boston: 1875. V. 46

Twenty-Thousand Leagues Under the Sea. New York: 1956. V. 41

The Works. New York: 1911. V. 42

VERNER, COOLIE

The Northpart of North American. Toronto: 1979. V. 42; 43; 44; 45

VERNER, ELIZABETH O'NEILL

Prints and Impressions of Charleston. Columbia: 1939. V. 40

VERY, LYDIA L.

Goody Two Shoes. Boston: 1863. V. 45

Poems. Andover: 1856. V. 39

Red Riding Hood. (Boston): (1863). V. 37

Robinson Crusoe. Boston: 1863. V. 45

VERYARD, E.

An Account of Divers Choice Remarks, As Well Geographical as (sic) Historical, Political, Mathematical, Physical, and Moral . . . London: 1701. V. 43

VESALIUS, ANDREAS

Anatomia Deudsch, Ein Kurtzer Auszug der Beschreibung all Gilder Menschlichs Leybs aus den.. Nuremberg: 1551. V. 45

Anatomia. Venice: 1604. V. 46

Epitome anatomica. Opus redivivum, cui accessere, notae ac Commentariae.French . . . John W. Sterling. Leiden: 1616. V. 37

Anatomia Viri in Hoc Genere Princip. Andreae Vesalii Bruxellensis . . . Amstelodami: 1617. V. 41

The Blood-Letting Letter of 1539. V. 42

Chirurgia Magna in Septem Libros Digesta . . . Venice: 1568. V. 42

De Humani Corporis Fabrica Libris Septem. Basel (colophon): 1543. V. 38; 46

De Humani Corporis Fabrica . . . Venice: 1568. V. 37

Icones Anatomicae. New York & Munich: 1934. V. 43; 46

Andreae Vesalii Icones Anatomicae. Tabulae Selectae. Munich: 1935. V. 37

Opera Omnia Anatomica & Chirurgica. Leiden: 1725. V. 40

VESLING, JOHANNES 1598-1649

The Anatomy of the Body of Man. London: 1653. 37; 38; 42

The Anatomy of the Body of Man. London: 1653. V. 42

Syntagma Anatomicum, Locis Plurimis Auctum, Emendatum, Novisque Iconibus Diligenter Exornatum. Padua: 1647. V. 37; 42

Syntagma Anatomicum, Commentariis Illustratum a Gerardo Leonardi Blasio . . . Amsterdam: 1663. V. 45

Tavole Anatomiche Del Veslingio Spiegate in Lingua Italiana. Padua: 1745. V. 42

VESPUCCI, AMERIGO

Letters of . . . Describing His Four Voyages to the New World 1497-1504. San Francisco: 1926. V. 38; 45

VESSBERG, OLOF

The Hellenistic and Roman Periods in Cyprus. Lund: 1956. V. 42; 44

VEST, GEORGE GRAHAM

Man's Best Friend: a Plea to a Jury. New York: 1920. V. 44; 46

VESTAL, EMMIT

'Texas Slim', Gangster, Gangster Converted, Twice Condemned to Die. Baltimore: 1935. V. 46

VESTAL, STANLEY

Bigfoot Wallace. Boston: 1942. V. 42

Joe Meek, the Merry Mountain Man, a Biography. Caldwell: 1952. V. 42

New Sources of Indian History 1850-1891. The ghost Dance-The Prairie Sioux. Norman: 1934. V. 45

New Sources of Indian History, 1850-1891. Norman: 1943. V. 41

VESTEGAN, RICHARD

Theatrum Crudelitatum Haereticorum. Antuerpiae: 1587. V. 37

VETALAPANCAVIMASTI

Vikram and the Vampire. London: 1870. V. 39; 40

Vikram and the Vampire. London: 1870/69. V. 45

Vikram and the Vampire of Tales of Hindu Devilry. London: 1893. V. 41; 42

VETERINARIAE Medicinae Libri II. Paris: 1530. V. 39

VETH, CORNELIS

Comic Art in England. Amsterdam: 1930. V. 41; 42

VETHAKE, HENRY

The Principles of Political Economy. Philadelphia: 1838. V. 41

VETROMILE, EUGENE

The Abnakis and Their History; or, Historical Notes on the Aborigines of Acadia. New York: 1866. V. 46

VETTORI, PIETRO

Explicationes Suarum in Ciceronem Castigationum. Lugduni: 1540. V. 43

VEVER, HENRI

La Bijouterie Francaise du XIXe Siecle. Paris: H. Floury,: 1906-08. V. 39

Catalogue of Hightly Important Japanese Prints, Illustrated Books and Drawings; from the Henri Vever Collection. London: 1974-75. V. 41

VEZEY, FRANCIS

Cases Argued and Determined in the High Court of Chancery . . . In the Time of Lord Chancellor Hardwicke, from the Year 1746-7 to 1755. London: 1771. V. 45

VIA Viri in Adolescentia, Seu Juventutis In Avia Deviae. Munich: 1716. V. 42

VIAGGIO Pittorico Della Toscana. Florence: 1801. V. 37; 42; 46

VIARDEL, COSME

Observations sur la Pratique des Accouchemens Naturels, contre nature et Monstreux. Avec une Methodes tres-facile pour secourir les femmes en toutes sortes d'Accouchemens, sans . . . Paris: 1674. V. 37

VIBERT, LIONEL

The Rare Books of Freemasonry. 1923. V. 38; 40

VICAIRE, G.

Bibliographie Gastronomique. London: 1954. V. 39

THE VICAR of Bray. London: 1771. V. 38

VICARS, JOHN

A Discovery of the Rebels . . . London: 1643. V. 45

VICARY, THOMAS

The Anatomie of the Bodie of Man. London: 1888. V. 44

The English-Man's Treasure, with the True Anatomie of mans Body . . . London: 1641. V. 39; 41; 43

VICAT, L. J.

A Practical and Scientific Treatise on Calcareous Mortars and Cements, Artificial and Natural . . . London: 1837. V. 44

THE VICES of the Cities of London and Westminster. Dublin: 1751. V. 41

VICKARIS, A.

An Essay, for Regulating of the Coyn; Wherein also is Set Forth, First, How We Have Lost tht Import of Plate and Bullion We Formerly Hand. Secondly, What is Become of the Great Quantities of Money Coyned in the Reign of King Charles II . . . London: 1696. V. 38

VICKERS, HENRY

(Sale) Catalogue of Furniture . . . Library of Books . . . Oil Paintings and Engravings. Bridgnorth: 1865. V. 45

VICKERS, V. C.

The Google Book. London: 1913. V. 43

VICKERY, SUKEY

Emily Hamilton, a Novel. Worcester: 1803. V. 37; 45

VICO, ENEA 1523-1567

Ex Libris XXII Commentariorum in Vetera Imperatorum Romanorum Numismata. (with) Primorum XII Caesarum Verissimae Imagines ex Antiquis Numismatis Desumptae. Venice: 1562. V. 42

Le Imagini Delle Donne Auguste Intagliate in Istampa di Rame; con le Vite . . . Vinegia: 1557. V. 45

Sic Romae Antiqui Sculptores ex Aere et Marmore Faciebant. Rome: 1543 and 1552. V. 40; 44

VICO, GIOVANNI BATTISTA 1668-1744

De Antiquissima Italorum Sapientia . . . Naples: 1710. V. 40

Principi di Una Scienza Nuova Intorno alla Natura Delle Nazioni per la Quale si Ritruovano i Principi di Altro Sistema del Diritto Naturale delle Genti. Naples: 1725. V. 45

Principj di Scienza Nuova. Napoli: 1744. V. 39

De Rebus Gestis Antonj Caraphaei Libri Quatuor. Neapoli: 1716. V. 39

VICQ D'AZYR, FELIX

Oeuvres . . . Paris: 1805. V. 46

VICTOR, BENJAMIN

The History of the Theatres of London and Dublin,, from the Year 1730 to the Present Time. London: 1761. V. 37; 42

The History of the Theatres of London and Dublin, from the Year 1730 to the Present Time. London: 1771. V. 41; 42

The Widow of the Wood. London: 1755. V. 38; 39; 40; 44; 45

VICTOR, FRANCES FULLER

Eleven Years in the Rocky Mountains and Life on the Frontier. Hartford: 1881. V. 45

The River of the West. Hartford: 1870. V. 40; 41; 45

VICTOR, H. YOUNG

My Vimy Pilgrimage 1936. V. 46

VICTOR Hammer: Artist and Printer. Lexington: 1981. V. 40

VICTOR, ORVILLE J.

Prospectus of the Great National Work, History (Civil, Political and Military) of the Southern Rebellion. New York: 1862. V. 42

VICTOR, SARAH M.

The Life Story of . . . for Sixty Years. Cleveland: 1887. V. 45

VICTORIA & ALBERT MUSEUM

Catalogue of English Furniture and Woodwork. Volumes I and II Gothic and Early Tudor and Late Tudor and Early Stuart. Volume III Late Stuart to Queen Anne. Volume IV Georgian. London: 1929-31. V. 37

Catalogue of the Herbert Allen Collection of English Porcelain. London: 1917. V. 42

Catalogue of the Jones Collection. London: 1922-24. V. 42

Forster Collection. A Catalogue of the Printed Books Bequeathed by John Forster. London: 1888. V. 40

VICTORIA & ALBERT MUSUEM

Catalogue of the Jones Collection. Part I - Furniture by Oliver Brackett. Part II - Ceramics, Ormolu, Goldsmiths' Work, Enamels, Sculpture, Tapestry, Books and Prints. Part III - Paintings and Miniatures by Basil Long. London: 1930-23. V. 37

VICTORIA & ALBERT MUSUEM. DEPARTMENT OF WOODWORK

The Panelled Rooms: Volume I: The Bromley Room; Volume II: The Clifford's Inn Room Volume III: The Boudoir of Madame de Serilly; Volume IV: The Indlaid Room from Sizergh Castle; Volume V: The Hatton Garden Room. London: 1914-1922. V. 38

VICTORIA and Riverina, with Which is Incorporated Victoria 1930 . . . A Biographical Record of the Pioneer Families of Victoria and the Riverina. Melbourne: 1933. V. 41

VICTORIA County History of Surrey. London: 1905-14. V. 41

VICTORIA History of the County of Hertford. London: 1902-23. V. 41

VICTORIA History of the County of Sussex. London: 1905. V. 39

VICTORIA History of the County of York. London: 1907-13. V. 41

THE VICTORIA History of Yorkshire. Folkstone/London: 1974. V. 37

VICTORIA Illustrated: Published Under the Auspices of the Corporation of the City of Victoria. Victoria: 1891. V. 39; 45

VICTORIA, QUEEN OF GREAT BRITAIN 1819-1901

Leaves froma Journal of Our Life in the Highlands, from 1848 to 1861. London: 1868. V. 38; 39; 40; 41; 42; 44; 45; 46

Leaves from the Journal of Our Life in the Highlands, from 1848 to 1861. London: 1868, 1884. V. 38; 44

The Letters of Queen Victoria. London: 1907-32. V. 38

THE VICTORIA Regia. London: 1861. V. 38; 40

VICTORIA, R.I.: a Collection of Books, Manuscripts, Autograph Letters . . . San Francisco: 1969. V. 43; 45

VICTORIA, R.I.; a Collection of Books, Manuscripts, Autograph Letters, Original Drawgins, etc., by the Lady Herself & her Loyal Subjects, Produced During Her Long & Illustrious Reign. San Francisco: 1969-70. V. 39; 40

VICTORIA, R.I. a Collection of Books, Manuscripts, Autograph Letters, Original Drawings, ETc., by the Lady Herself and Her Loyal Subjects . . . San Francisco: 1968-69. V. 46

VICTORIA, R.I.: a Collection of Books, Manuscripts, Autographed Letters . . . by the Lady Herself . . . San Francisco: 1967-70. V. 46

VICTORIA UNIVERSITY OF MANCHESTER. LIBRARY

Catalogue of Medical Books in Manchester University Library 1480-1700. Manchester: 1972. V. 40; 41; 45; 46

VICTORIAN INSTITUTE FOR THE ADVANCEMENT OF SCIENCE

Transactions and Proceedings for the Sessions 1854-1855. Melbourne: 1855. V. 46

VICTORIUS, BENEDICTUS

Opus Theorice Latitudinum Medicine ad Libros Tegni Galleni. Bononiae: 1516. V. 38

VICTORY, JOHN P.

Compiled Laws of New Mexico. Santa Fe: 1897. V. 46

VICUNA-MACKENNA, BENJAMIN 1831-1878

Chile and Spain: the Whole Question Officially Stated. New York: 1865. V. 43

A Sketch of Chile, Expressly Prepared for the Use of Immigrants from the United States and Europe to that Country . . . (and the second part) Chile, The United States and Spain. New York: 1866. V. 38

VIDA, MARCO GIROLAMO, BP. OF ALBA d. 1566

Vida's Art of Poetry. London: 1725. V. 43; 44; 46

VIDA'S Art of Poetry. Translated into English Verse, By Mr. Pitt. The Second Edition. London: 1742. V. 37

Christiadis Libri Sex. Oxford: 1725. V. 38

Marci Hieronymi Vidae Cremonensis Albae Episcopi Christiados Libri Sex. (col:) Cremonae in aedibus: 1535. V. 38

Christiadis Libri Sex. Cremona: 1535. V. 38; 40

Christiados Libri Sex. Lyon: 1536. V. 37

The Game of Chess. London: 1921. V. 40; 41; 45; 46

VIDA, MARCUS HIERONYMOUS

The Poetics of Marcus Hieronymous Vida . . . Sunderland: 1793. V. 41

VIDA, MARCUS HIERONYMUS

De Arte Poetica lib. III. Eiusdem de Bombyce Lib. II. Eiusdem de Ludo Scacchorum Lib. I. Eiusdem Hymni. Eiusdem Bucolica. Rome: 1527. V. 41

De Arte Poetica Lib. III. Rome: 1527. V. 41

The Silkworm: a Poem. Dublin: 1750. V. 39; 41

VIDAL, EMERIC ESSEX

Picturesque Illustrations of Buenos Ayres and Monte Video . . . London: 1820. V. 39; 41; 45

Picturesque Illustrations of Buenos Ayres and Monte Video . . . Buenos Aires: 1944. V. 45

Picturesque Illustrations of Rio de Janeiro. Buenos Aires: 1967. V. 40

VIDAL, GORE

Creation. New York: 1981. V. 39; 43; 46

Dark Green, Bright Red. New York: 1950. V. 43

Death Before Bedtime. London: 1954. V. 41

Death Likes It Hot. London: 1955. V. 41

1876. New York: 1976. V. 39

Hollywood: A Novel of America in the Twenties. New York: 1990. V. 42

In A Yellow Wood. New York: 1947. V. 37; 39; 43; 46

The Judgement of Paris. New York: 1952. V. 43; 46

Lincoln, a Novel. New York: 1984. V. 38

Myra Breckinridge. London: 1968. V. 41

A Search for the King. New York: 1950. V. 46

Sex is Politics: and Vice Versa. Los Angeles: 1979. V. 44

A Thirsty Evil. New York: 1956. V. 45

Williwaw. New York: 1946. V. 37; 40; 42; 43

VIDIUS, VIDUS

Chirurgia e Graeco in Latinum Conversa, Vido Vidio Florentino Interprete, cum Nonnullis Eiusdem Vidii Commentariis. Paris: 1544. V. 37

VIEILLOT, LOUIS J. P.

Faune Francaise: Invertebrates. Paris: 1820-30. V. 41

La Galerie des Oiseaux. Paris: 1825. V. 40

Songbirds of the Torrid Zone. 1979. V. 45; 46

VIEIRA, ANTONIO

Arte de Furtar, Espelho de Enganos . . . Amsterdam: 1652. V. 38

VIEIRA, P. ANTONIO DE

Copia de Huma Carta para ElRey N. Senhor Sobre as Missoes do Seara, do Maranham, do Para, & do Grande Rio das Almasonas. Lisbon: 1660. V. 45

VIEL-CASTEL, HORACE, COMTE DE

Collection de Costumes, Armes et Meubles pour servir a l'Histoire de la Revolution Francaise et de l'Empire. Paris: 1870. V. 42

VIELE, EGBERT L.

The Arcade Under-Ground Railway. New York: 1868. V. 43; 46

Hand-Book of Field Fortifications and Artillery . . . Richmond: 1861. V. 37; 39

VIELE, TERESA

Following the Drum. New York: 1858. V. 39; 41; 42; 44; 45

VIELMIUS, HIERONIMUS

De Sex Diebus Conditi Orbis Liber . . . Adiecta sunt Praeterea Eiusdem Auctoris Libri Due de Thomae Doctrina et Scripta & Orationes Duae . . . Venetiis: 1575. V. 38

VIENNA. ORDINANCES & LAWS

Der Stat wienn Ordnug vnd Freyhaiten. Vienna: 1526. V. 43

VIERA, M. LAFFITTE

West Philadelphia Illustrated. Philadelphia: 1903. V. 42

VIERI, FRANCESCO

Trattato Delle Metheore Di . . . In Fiorenza: 1573. V. 38

VIET, ANTOINE

Voyage De La France Equinoxiale en L'Isle Cayenne, Entrepris par Les Francois en l'Annee MDCLII. Paris: 1664. V. 40

VIETE, FRANCOIS

In Artem Analyticam Isagoge, Seu Algebra Nova. Leyden: 1635. V. 41; 45

VIETIA LINAJE, JOSE DE

Norte de la Contratacion de Las Indias Occidentales. Seville: 1672. V. 40

VIETZ, F. B.

Icones Plantarum. Vienna: 1800-1820. V. 41

VIEUSSENS, RAYMOND

Neurographia Universalis . . . Editio Novissima. Lugduni: 1716. V. 37

Tractatus Duo Primus De Remotis et Proximis Mixti Principiis in Ordine and Corpus Humanum Spectatais. Lyons: 1688. V. 37; 42

VIEUSSEUX, A.

Italy and the Italians in the Nineteenth Century: A View of the Civil, Political and Moral State of That Country. London: 1824. V. 46

A **VIEW** of Paris and Places Adjoining. London: 1701. V. 37; 44

A **VIEW** of the Beau Monde: or, Memoirs of the Celebrated Coquetilla. London: 1731. V. 38

A **VIEW** of the Causes of Our Late Prosperity, and of Our Present Distress; and of the Means Which Have Been Proposed for Our Relief. Exter: 1816. V. 39

A **VIEW** of the Evidence Relative to the Conduct of the American War Under Wir William Howe, Lord Viscount Howe, and General Burgoyne; as Given Before a Committee of the House of Commons Last Sessaion of Parliament. London: 1779. V. 39; 42; 44

A **VIEW** of the History of Great-Britain, During the Administration of Lord North, to the Second Session of the Fifteenth Parliament. Dublin: 1782. V. 45

A **VIEW** of the Proceedings of the Assemblies of Jamaica, For Some Years Past. London: 1716. V. 40

A **VIEW** of the Proceedings of the Last Session of Congress. Portsmouth: 1802. V. 45

VIEW of the Works of the Gould & Curry Silver Mining Company, Virginia, N.T. San Francisco: 1863. V. 39

VIEWS & Descriptions of Burlington & Missouri River Railroad Lands, With Important Information Concerning Where & How to Select & Purchase Farms in Iowa & Nebraska, of Ten Years' Credit. Burlington, Iowa: (1872). V. 37

VIEWS at Risely, Derbyshire. Derby: 1860. V. 39

VIEWS in Boston. Boston: 1869. V. 41

VIEWS in Oxford. Oxford: 1850? V. 45

VIEWS of all the Colleges, Halls and Public Buildings in the University and City of Oxford, with Descriptions Which Point Out to Strangers All the Places and Curiosities More Particularly Deserving of Their Notice. Oxford: 1824. V. 41

VIEWS of all the Colleges, Halls and Public Buildings, in the University nd City of Oxford . . . Oford: 1823 or later. V. 38

VIEWS of Arizona and the Colorado River. San Francisco: 1868. V. 39

VIEWS of Bridlington Quay. No. 1 and No. 2. London: 1854-57. V. 41

VIEWS of Early New York with Illustrative Sketches Prepared for the New York Chapter of the Colonial Order of the Acorn. New York: 1904. V. 45

VIEWS of English Society. London. V. 38

VIEWS of Interesting Places in the Holy Land, with a Brief Sketch of the Principal Events Associated with Them in the Sacred Scriptures . . . Philadelphia: 1830. V. 43

VIEWS of St. Helena. St. Helena: 1863. V. 41

VIEWS of the English Lakes and Mountains. London: 1850's. V. 44

VIEWS of the Picturesque Scenery in the Isle of Man. London: 1860. V. 44

VIEYRA, ANTONIO

A Dictionary of the Portuguese and English Languages. London: 1794. V. 41; 42

VIGEE-LEBRUN, MARIE LOUISE ELISABETH

Souvenirs of Madame Vigee le Brun. New York: 1880. V. 39

VIGERIUS, MARCUS, CARDINAL

Decachordum Christianum. Fano: 1507. V. 45

Decachordum Christianum . . . Controversiaque de Instrumentis Dominicae Passionis. Paris: 1517. V. 37

VIGFUSSON, GUDBRANDUR

Corpus Poeticum Boreale. Oxford: 1883. V. 43; 46

Orkneyinga Saga and Magnus Saga, with Appendices. London: 1887. V. 43

VIGIER, JOAO

Historia das Plantas da Europa, e das Mais Uzadas que vem de Asia, de Affrica & da America . . . Lyon: 1718. V. 41

VIGNAL, PIERRE

Water Color Renderings, Gardens of Rome. Cleveland: 1926. V. 44

VIGNAUD, HENRY

Toscanelli and Columbus. The Letter and Chart of Toscanelli on the Route to the Indies by the Way of the West, Sent in 1474 to the Portuguese Fernam Martins . . . London: 1902. V. 42

VIGNE, GODFREY T.

A Personal Narrative of a Visit to Ghuzni, Kabul and Afghanistan, and of a Residence at the Court of Dost Mohamed: with Notices of Runjit Sing, Khiva, and the Russian Expedition. London: 1843. V. 39; 43

Six Months in America. Philadelphia: 1833. V. 41

Six Months in America. London: 1832. V. 37

Travels in Kashmir, Ladak, Iskardo The Countries Adjoining the Mountain Course of the Indus, and the Himalaya, North of the Punjab. London: 1842. V. 41

Travels in Mexico, South America, etc. London: 1863. V. 40

VIGNEY, ALFRED DE

Poemes Antiques et Modernes . . . Le Deluge, Moise, Dolorida, le Trapiste, la Neige, le Cor. Paris: 1826. V. 43

VIGNIER, fl. 1676

Le Chasteau de Richelieu, ou l'Histoire des Dieux est des Heros de l'Antiquite . . . Saumur: 1681. V. 38

VIGNIER, NICHOLAS 1530-1596

Rerum Burgundionum Chronicon. Basel: 1575. V. 46

VIGNIER, NICOLAS 1530-1596

Theatre de l'Antechrist. La Rohelle: 1610. V. 42; 46

Traicte de l'Estat et Origine des Anciens Francois. Troyes: 1582. V. 38

VIGNOLA, GIACOMO BAROZZIO 1507-1573

Il Vignola Illustrato Proposto da Giambattista Spampani e Carlo Antonini . . . Rome: 1770. V. 42; 44

Livre Nouveau ou Regles des Cinq Ordres d'Architecture. Paris: 1767. V. 39

Regola delli Cinque Ordini d'Architecttura. Rome. V. 38

Le Dve Regole Della Prospettiva Pratica . . . Con i Comentarij del R.P.M. Egnatio Danti. Rome: 1583. V. 41

Regola delli Cinque Ordini d'Architettvra con la Nuouo Agionta di Michelangelo Buonaroti di Carte Sette. Rome: 1610. V. 43

Le Dve Regola Delle Prospettiva Pratica . . . Roma: 1611. V. 41

Regola delli Cinque Ordini d'Architettvra. Amsterdam: 1631. V. 43

Regola delli Cinque Ordini d'Architettura . . . Bologna: 1635. V. 38; 40; 44

Regola Delli Cinque, Ordini d'Architattura. Siena: 1635. V. 38; 40; 44

Regola de Cinque Ordini . . . Amsterdam: 1641. V. 44

Regola Delli Cinque Ordini d'Architettura di M. Iacomo Barozzio da Vignola. Bologna: 1680. V. 41

La Due Regole della Prospettiva Pratica . . . Bologna: 1682. V. 37; 46

Regole della Prospettiva Prattica, con i Commentari del Egnatio Danti . . . Venice: 1743. V. 41; 44

Regles des Cinq Ordres d'Architecture. Paris: 1750. V. 40

Regras Cinco Ordens de Architectura . . . Lisbon: 1787. V. 38

The Regular Architect. London: 1669. V. 37; 39

Le Vignole de Poche ou memorial des Artistes . . . Paris: 1823. V. 40

VIGNOLA Revived; Wherein is Shewn the True and Most Elegant Proportions of the Five Orders. London: 1761. V. 38; 42

LE VIGNOLE de Poche ou Memorial des Artistes . . . Paris: 1823. V. 38

VIGNOLES, CHARLES

Two Reports Addressed to the Liverpool and Manchester Railway Co. on the Projected North Line of Railway From Liverpool to the Manchester, Bolton and Bury Canal, Near Manchester . . . Liverpool: 1835. V. 46

VIGNOLES, CHARLES B.

Observations Upon the Floridas. New York: 1823. V. 41; 42

VIGNY, ALFRED DE

Cinq-Mars. Une Conjuration Sous Louis XIII. Paris: 1855. V. 41

VIGO, GIOVANNI DE 1460-1520

La Practique et Cirurgie . . . Paris: 1542. V. 37; 39; 40; 41

Opera . . . Additur Chirurgia Marianisti Barolitani. Lyon: 1540. V. 38; 41

The Most Excellent Works of Chirurgerye. London: 1543. V. 38

The Most Excellent Worckes of Chirurgery, Made and Set Forth by Maister John Vignon, Head Chirurgien of Oure Tyme in Italy. London: 1550. V. 37; 42

The Whole Worke of that Famous Chirurgion Maister John Vigo. London: 1586. V. 40; 41

The Whole Worke of that Famous Chirurgion, Maister John Vigo. London: 1856. V. 41

VIGOUREUX, JEAN

Twenty-Eight Drawings of Paris. Los Angeles: 1942. V. 38

VIGUIER, PIERRE FRANCOIS

Elements de la Langue Turque. Constantinople: 1790. V. 40

VILALTA, JULIUS fl. c. 1545

Oratio pro Urbe Feltria Patria sua, ad Illustriss. Principem Venetiarum Franciscum Donatum. Venice: 1545. V. 37; 40

VILLA and Cottage Architecture: Select Examples of Country and Suburban Residences Recently Erected. London: 1871. V. 38

VILLA, JOSE GARCIA

Clay: a Literary Notebook - Numbers 1-3 (all published). Albuquerque and New York: 1931-32. V. 38

Footnote to Youth. New York: 1933. V. 40; 42

Have Come, am Here. New York: 1932. V. 42

Have Come, Am Here. New York: 1942. V. 41

VILLA, VINCENCIO

Orationes Magistri Vincentii Placentini . . . Bologna: 1553. V. 37

The VILLAGE Green; or Sports of Youth. New Haven: 1840. V. 40

VILLAGRA, GASPAR PEREZ DE

Historia de la Nueva Mexico. Mexico: 1900. V. 43

History of New Mexico. Los Angeles: 1933. V. 37; 38; 46

VILLALPANDO, J. BAPTISTA

In Ezechielem Explanationes et Apparatus Urbis ac Templi Hierosolymitani . . . Rome: 1606-07-04. V. 44

VILLANI, NICOLO

Ragionamento Dello Academico Aldeano Sopra la Poesia Giocosa de'Greci, de'Latini e de'Toscani . . . Venetia: 1643. V. 38

VILLARD, HENRY

Northern Pacific Railroad: Report of the President. New York: 1883. V. 38

VILLARI, L.

Giovanni Segantini: the Story of His Life. New York: 1901. V. 44

VILLARS, NICOLAS PIERRE HENRI MONTFAUCON 1635ca. - 1673

Antiquity Explained and Represented in Sculptures. London: 1721. V. 46

The Count of Gabalis; or, The Extravagnat Mysteries of the Cabalists, Exposed in Five Pleasant Discourses on the Secret Sciences. London: 1680. V. 40

The Count de Gabalis. London: 1714. V. 41

VILLASBOAS E SAMPAIO, ANTONIO DE

Nobiliarchia Portugueza, Tratado da Nobreza Hereditaria & Politica . . . Lisbon: 1676. V. 41

VILLAVICENCIO, MANUEL

Geografia De La Republica Del Ecuador. New York: 1858. V. 44; 46

VILLAVICENTIUS, LAURENTIUS DE

Conciones in Evangelia et Epistolas, quae Dominicis Diebus Populo in Ecclesia Proponi Solent. Lyons: 1568. V. 38

VILLEDIEU, MARIE CATHERINE HORTENSE DESJARDINS DE

Les Desordres de l'Amour. Paris: 1676. V. 37

VILLEGAGNON, NICHOLAS DURAND DE

D. Caroli V. Imperatoris Expeditio in Africam ad Argieram. Antwerp: 1542. V. 40; 43

VILLEGAS SELVAGO, ALONSO DE

Flos Sanctorum Segunda Parte y Historia General en que se Escrive la Vida de la Virgen Sacratissima Madre de Dios. Barcelona: 1587. V. 37

VILLENA, JOSEPH MANUEL DE

Instruccion Para los Cortes del Rey, Acordada con el Excmo. Sr. Comandante General de Marina . . . Havanna: 1790. V. 45

VILLENEUVE BARGEMONT, ALBAN DE

Histoire de l'Economie Politique. Brussels: 1839. V. 38

VILLENEUVE, N. DE

Le Voyageur Philosophe dans un pais Inconnu . . . Amsterdam: 1761. V. 40

VILLERME, LOUIS RENE

Des Prisons Telles qu'elles Sont, et Telles qu'elles Devraient Etre. Paris: 1820. V. 41; 45

VILLEROY, NICOLAS DE NEUFVILLE

Memoires. Paris: 1665. V. 37

VILLETARD DE PRUNERIES, EDMOND CHARLES

History of the International. New Haven: 1874. V. 37

VILLETTE, C. L. DE

Essay on the Happiness of the Life to Come. Bath: 1794. V. 42

VILLETTE, JOHN

A Genuine Account of the Behaviour and Dying Words of William Dodd, LL.D . . . London: 1777. V. 37

VILLIERS, BROUGHAM

The Case for Women's Suffrage. London: 1907. V. 39; 41

VILLIERS, CHARLES PELHAM 1802-1898

The Free Trade Speeches of . . . with a Political memoir. London: 1883. V. 46

VILLIERS, DAVID

A Winter Firework. Waltham St. Lawrence: 1937. V. 37; 40; 43; 45

A Winter Firework. N.P.: 1937. V. 37

VILLIERS DE L'ISLE-ADAM, JEAN MARIE MATTHIAS PHILIPPE

Axel. London: 1925. V. 39

VILLIERS, PIERRE DE

Reflections on Men's Prejudices Against Religion, and Their Mistakes in the Practice of It. London: 1709. V. 43

VILLIERS-STUART, H.

Adventures Amidst the Equatorial Forests and Rivers of South America. London: 1891. V. 40

VILLON, FRANCOIS

Autres Poesies de Maistre Francois Villon et de Son ecole. Hammersmith: 1901. V. 40

Autres Poesies de Maistre Francois Villon et de Son Ecole. London: 1901. V. 43

Les Ballades. London: 1900. V. 40; 43

The Ballads of Francois Villon. San Francisco: 1927. V. 43

Lyrical Poems. New York: 1979. V. 43

The Poems of Francois Villon. Boston: 1977. V. 39

Regrets de la Belle Heaulmiere. Paris: 1909. V. 45; 46

Sundry Ballades. San Francisco: 1922. V. 38; 42

VILLON, JACQUES

Cent Croquis 1894-1904. Paris: 1959. V. 46

VIMERCATI, CESAR

Constantinople et l'Egypte. Paris: 1856. V. 37

VINCARD, B.

L'Art du Typographe. Ouvrage Utile a MM. les Hommes de Lettres, Bibliographes, et Typographes. Paris: 1806. V. 41

VINCE, S.

A Confutation of Atheism, from the Laws and Constitution of the Heavenly Bodies . . . Cambridge: 1807. V. 41

A Treatise on Practical Astronomy. Cambridge: 1790. V. 40

VINCE, SAMUEL

The Principles of Fluxions: Designed for the Use of Students in the University . . . Philadelphia: 1812. V. 46

VINCENT, AUGUSTINE

A Discoverie of Errours in the first Edition of the Catalogue of Nobility . . . London: 1622. V. 37

VINCENT DE BEAUVAIS Ca. 1190-1264

Speculum Doctinale. Strassburg. V. 38

Speculum Naturale. Strassburg?: 1481. V. 38; 41; 42; 44

VINCENT, ETHEL GWENDOLINE MOFFATT, LADY

From China to Peru Over the Andes. London: 1894. V. 38

VINCENT, FRANK

Actual Africa or the Coming Continent a Tour of Exploration. London: 1895. V. 39

Through and Through the Tropics Thirty Thousand Miles of Travel in Oceanica, Australasia and India. New York: 1876. V. 40

VINCENT, HEBRON

A History of the Wesleyan Grove, Martha's Vineyard, Camp Meeting, from the First Meeting Held There in 1835, to that of 1858, Inclusvie. Boston: 1858. V. 39

VINCENT, JOHN

Fowling. A Poem. London: 1808. V. 39; 40; 41; 42

VINCENT, LEON H.

Dewitt Miller. A Biogrpahical Sketch. Cambridge: 1912. V. 44

VINCENT, SAINT OF LERINS

Peregrini, Id est. Vt Vvlgo Perhibetvr . . . Adversvs Prophanas Haereses, Commonitoria duo. Oxford: 1631. V. 37

Pro Catholicae Fidei Antiqvitate & Veritate, Aduersus Prophanas Omnium Haerese Nouationtinctus. London: 1591. V. 45

VINCENT, THOMAS

Christ's Sudden and Certain Appearance to Judgment. Wheeling: 1823. V. 44

God's Terrible Voice in the City. London: 1667. V. 41

VINCENT, WILLIAM

A Letter to the Reverend Dr. Richard Watson King's Professor of Divinity in the University of Cambridge. London: 1780. V. 39; 46

Public Education . . . London: 1817. V. 42

The Voyage of Nearchus from the Indus to the Euphrates . . . London: 1797. V. 44; 46

VINDEL, F.

Mapas de America en los Libros Espanoles de los Siglos XVI al XVIII (1503-1798). (with) . . . Apendice a los de America. Adicion de los de Filipinas (and): Portfolio: Mapas Espanoles de America Siglos XV-XVII. Madrid: 1951-59. V. 40

A **VINDICATION** of a Printed Paper, Entituled, an Ordinance Presented to the Honorable House of Commons for the Preventing of the Growth and Spreading of Heresies . . . London: 1646. V. 40

A **VINDICATION** of Edmund Randolph . . . Richmond: 1855. V. 42

A **VINDICATION** of Major General the Earl of Lucan from Lord Raglan's Reflections on His Conduct in the Action at Balaklava. London: 1855. V. 42

A **VINDICATION** of Our Present Royal Family Principally with Regard to Hanover. London: 1744. V. 41

A **VINDICATION OF THE** Conducy of Capt. M----n, and of the Court Martial. London: 1745. V. 41

A **VINDICATION** of the Court of Russia, From a False and Treasonable Attack in a Pamphlet, Intitled the State of the Negociation &c., &c. In an Address to the Public. London: 1807. V. 42

A **VINDICATION** of the Presbyteriall-Government and Ministry. London: 1650. V. 42

A **VINDICATION** of the Protestant Dissenters, from the Aspersions Cast Upon them in a Late Pamphlet, intitled, the Presbyterians Pleas of Merit. Dublin: 1733. V. 38

A **VINDICATION** of the Religious Society Called Quakers: Addressed to the Editors of the American Edition of Mosheim's Ecclesiastical History. Mount Holly: 1800. V. 45

VINDING, ERASMUS PAUL

Regia Academia Hauniensis in Regibus. Copenhagen: 1665. V. 37; 41; 46

VINE HALL, A.

Rainbow Houses for Boys and Girls. London: 1923. V. 45

VINES, ROBERT A.

Trees, Shrubs and Woody Vines of the Southwest. Austin: 1986. V. 44

Trees, Shrubs, and Woody Vines of the Southwest. Austin: 1960. V. 37; 42

VINES, SYDNEY HOWARD

Lecutres on Physiology of Plants. Cambridge: 1886. V. 37

VINGBOONS, PHILIP

Gronden en Afbeeldsels der Voornaamste Gebouwen, van alle die Philips Vingboons Geordineert Heeft. Amsterdam: 1665. V. 43

Gronden en Afbeeldsele . . . Amsterdam: 1688. V. 43

Oeuvres d'Architecture, Contenant les Desseins tant en Plans qu'en Elevations, des principaux et des Plus Nouveaux Betimens dans le Dernier Agrandissement de la Ville d'Amsterdam & Sutres Endroits de ces Provinces . . . Leiden: 1715. V. 43

VINGE, JOAN D.

The Snow Queen. New York: 1980. V. 42; 43; 44; 46

VINGUT, GERTRUDE FAIRFIELD

Irene; or, the Autobiography of an Artist's Daughter. Boston: 1853. V. 41

VINIUS, ARNOLD 1588-1657

In Quatuor Libros Institutionum Imperialium Commentarius. Amsterdam: 1665. V. 40

In Quatuor Libros Institutionum Imperialium Commentarius. Lyon: 1700. V. 40

VINNE, THEODORE LOW 1828-1914

The Invention of Printing. New York: 1876. V. 44

THE VINTNER'S, Brewer's, Spirit Merchant's and Licenced Victualler's Guide . . . London: 1838. V. 40

VINYCOMB, JOHN

Lambert (of Newcastle-upon-Tyne) as an Engraver of Bookplates. Newcastle-upon-Tyne: 1896. V. 38

VIO, TOMASSO DE, CAJETAN 1469-1534.

Epistolae Pauli et aliorum Apostolrum ad Gaecam veritatem castigatae. Paris: 1532. V. 37

VIOLA, JEROME

The Painting and Teaching of Philip Pearlstein. New York: 1982. V. 45

VIOLA Sanctorum. Strassburg: 1487. V. 40

VIOLA ZANINI, GIUSEPPE

Della Architettura . . . ne'Quali Con Nuoua Simmetria 7 Facilita si Monstrano le Giueste Regole de Gli Cinque Ordini di Detta Architettura. Padua: 1629. V. 37

VIOLET, THOMAS fl. 1634-1662

Narrative of Some Remarkable Proceedings Concerning the Ships Samson, Salvador and George, and Several Other Prize Ships Depending in the High Court of Admiraltie . . . London: 1653. V. 40

VIOLLET-LE-DUC, EUGENE EMMANUEL

Dictionnaire Raisonne du Mobilier Francaois de l'Epoque Carlovingienne a la Renaissance. Paris: 1858/1872-5. V. 41

Dictionnaire Raisonne de l'Architecture Francaise du XIe au XVI siecle. Paris: 1864-8. V. 42

Discourses on Archtiecture. New York: 1959. V. 41

How to Build a House: an Architectural Novelette. London: 1874. V. 46

Lectures on Architecture. London: 1877/1881. V. 42

VIRCHOW, RUDOLF

Cellular Pathology as Based Upon Physiological and Pathological Histology. Philadelphia: 1863. V. 44

Cellular Pathology As Based Upon Physiological and Pathological History . . . London: 1860. V. 42

Cellular Pathology as Based Upon the Physiological and Pathological Histology. New York: 1860. V. 45

Cellular Pathology as Based Upon Physiological and Pathological Histology. New York: 1867. V. 42

A Description and Explanation of the Method of Performing Post-Mortem Examinations in the Dead-House of the Berlin Charite Hospital, with Especial Reference to Medico-Legal Practice. Philadelphia: 1877. V. 42

Die Cellularpathologie . . . Zwanzig Vorlesungen . . . Berlin: 1858. V. 37

Die Krankhaften Geschwulste. Dreissig Vorlesungen, Gehalten Wahrend des Wintersemesters 1862-1863 an der Universitat zu Berlin. Berlin: 1863-65. V. 39

Die Krankhaften Geschulste. Dreisig Vorlesungen Gehalten . . . 1862 bis 1863 . . . Berlin: 1863-67. V. 44; 45; 46

VIRCHOW, RUDOLPH

A Description and Explanation of the Method of Performing Post-Mortem Examinations in the Dead-House of the Berlin Charite Hospital . . . Philadelphia: 1877. V. 43

VIREL, MATTHIEU

Regvlae Generaleas Et Perpetvaea, De Rebus Ad Calendarium Spectantaibus, Citraa Calendarium Cognoscendis, ad Vitae Vsum Accomodatissimae. Basle: 1579. V. 37; 40

THE VIRGIN Muse. London: 1717. V. 42

VIRGINIA. ADJUTANT GENERAL'S OFFICE

Military Laws: Containing Extracts from the Federal and State Constitutions, Synopsis of the Organization of the Militia, Militia Laws of Virginia, Militia Laws of the United States, Articles of War, Army Resolutions, Description of Uniform . . . . Richmond: 1820. V. 46

VIRGINIA CENTRAL RAILROAD

Address to the President of the Va. Central Railroad Co. To the Stockholders, on the Subject of Withdrawal of the Mails by the Postmaster General. Richmond: 1864. V. 45

VIRGINIA. (COLONY). COUNCIL

Executive Journals of the Council of Colonial Virginia 1680-1739. Richmond: 1925. V. 39

Journals of the Council of the State of Virginia: 1776-1791. Richmond: 1931-1982. V. 40

Legislative Journals of the Council of Colonial Virginia. Richmond: 1918. V. 38; 39; 44

Minutes of the Council and General Court of Colonial Virginia, 1622-1632, 1670-1676. Richmond: 1924. V. 38; 39

VIRGINIA. CONSTITUTION

Constitution of the State of Virginia, and the Ordinances Adopted by Convention with Assembled at Alexandria . . . February 1864. Alexandria: 1864. V. 45

VIRGINIA. CONSTITUTION - 1849

The Code of Virginia . . . and Constitution of Virginia. Richmond: 1849. V. 37

VIRGINIA. CONSTITUTION - 1863

The New Constitution of Virginia, with the Amended Bill of Rights as Adopted . . . and Amended by the Convention of 1860-61. Richmond: 1863. V. 37; 39

VIRGINIA. CONSTITUTION - 1864

Constitution of the State of Virginia, and the Ordinances Adopted by Convention Which Assembled at Alexanderia . . . February 1864. Alexandria: 1864. V. 39; 42

VIRGINIA. CONSTITUTION - 1868

The Constitution of Virginia, Framed by the Convention Which Met in Richmond on December 3, 1867. Richmond: 1868. V. 39

VIRGINIA. CONSTITUTIONAL CONVENTION - 1864

Journal of the Constitutional Convention Which Convened at Alexandria on the 13th Day of February, 1864. Alexandria: 1864. V. 37; 39

VIRGINIA. CONVENTION

Journal, Acts and Proceedings of a General Convention of the State of Virginia, Assembled at Richmond, On Monday, the Fourteenth Day of October, 1850. Richmond: 1850. V. 40; 41; 43; 44

VIRGINIA. CONVENTION, RICHMOND, 1861.

Bill of Rights and Proposed Amended Constitution Reported by the Committee Appointed to Consider and Report Amendments of the Constitution of Virginia, Presented June 19, 1861. Richmond: 1861. V. 41

VIRGINIA. CONVENTION, WHEELING, 1861.

Ordinances and Acts of the Restored Government of Virginia, Prior to the Formation of the State of West Virginia, with the Constitution and and Laws of the State of West Virginia to March, 1866. Wheeling: 1866. V. 39

VIRGINIA. COUNCIL - 1931

Journals of the Council of the State of Virginia, 1776-1791. Richmond: 1931-1982. V. 42

VIRGINIA. GENERAL ASSEMBLY - 1778

At A General Assembly Begun and Held at the Capitol, in the City of Williamsburg, on Monday the Fifth Day of October, In the Year of Our Lord One Thousand Seven Hundred and Seventy-Eight. Williamsburg: 1778. V. 40; 41

VIRGINIA. GENERAL ASSEMBLY - 1798

Proceedings of the Virginia Assembly, on the Answers of Sundry States to Their Resolutions Passed in December, 1798. Philadelphia: 1800. V. 42

VIRGINIA. GENERAL ASSEMBLY. HOUSE OF DELEGATES - 1816

Journal of the House of Delegates of the Commonwealth of . . . Begun and Held at the Capitol in the City of Richmond, on Monday the Eleventh Day of November, 1816. Richmond: 1816. V. 37; 42

VIRGINIA. GENERAL ASSEMBLY. SENATE - 1949

Journals of the Senate of Virginia: Nov. 1793-1802/3. Richmond: 1949-77. V. 42

VIRGINIA. LAWS, STATUTES, ETC. - 1794

A Collection of All Such Acts of the General Assembly of Virginia . . . as are Now in Force. Richmond: 1794. V. 37

VIRGINIA. LAWS, STATUTES, ETC. - 1803

A Collection of All Such Acts of the General Assembly of Virginia, of a Public and Permanent Nature . . . With a New and Complete Index. Richmond: 1803. V. 37; 39; 41

VIRGINIA. LAWS, STATUTES, ETC. - 1808

The Militia Laws of this Commonwealth, and of the United States, with the Articles of War. Richmond: 1808. V. 40

VIRGINIA. LAWS, STATUTES, ETC. - 1819

The Revised Code of the Laws of Virginia. Richmond: 1819. V. 39

VIRGINIA. LAWS, STATUTES, ETC. - 1849

The Code of Virginia . . . and Constitution of Virginia. Richmond: 1849. V. 39

VIRGINIA. LAWS, STATUTES, ETC. - 1861

Acts of the General Assembly of the State of Virginia, Passed in 1861, in the Eighty-Fifty Year of the Commonwealth. Richmond: 1861. V. 37; 42

VIRGINIA. LAWS, STATUTES, ETC. - 1862

Acts of the General Assembly of the State of Virginia Passed in 1861-2 . . . Richmond: 1862. V. 39; 42

VIRGINIA. LAWS, STATUTES, ETC. - 1863

Acts of the General Assembly of the State of Virginia . . . 1863 (&) 1863-4. Richmond: 1863-64. V. 37; 39

THE VIRGINIA Primer. Richmond: 1864. V. 39

VIRGINIA Richly Valued. London: 1609. V. 38; 39; 42; 45

VIRGINIA. SENATE

Journals of the Senate of Virginia: Nov. 1793-1802/3. Richmond: 1949-77. V. 44

VIRGINIA. STATE LIBRARY - 1975

Virginiana in the Printed Book Collection of the Virginia State Library. Richmond: 1975. V. 42

VIRTRUVIUS Britannicus, or the British Architect . . . London: 1725-71. V. 42

VIRTUE Triumphant, or, Elizabeth Canning in America . . . Boston: 1757. V. 46

THE VIS-A-VIS of Berkeley-Square; or, a Wheel Off Mrs. W*t**n's Carraige. London: 1783. V. 46

VISCHER, EDWARD

Edward Vischer's Drawings of California Missions, 1861-1878. San Francisco: 1982. V. 39; 41; 42

VISCHER, GEORG MATHAEUS

Topographia Austriae Superioris Modernae . . . Linz: 1709? V. 39

VISCHER, JOHANN

Enarratio Brevis Aphorismorum Hippocratis . . . Tubingae: 1591. V. 42

VISCONTI, ENNIO QUIRINO

Scultore del Palazzo della Villa Borghese Detta Pinciana; and Monumenti Gabinia dell Villa Pinciana. Rome: 1796, V. 44

VISCONTI, GASPARE

Di Paolo e daria Amanti. Milan: 1495. V. 37

VISCONTI, GIO BATTISTA

Il Museo Pio-Clementino. Rome: 1782-1807. V. 37

VISCONTI, LUDOVIC 1791-1853

Fontaines Monumentales Construites a Paris et Projetees Pour Bordeaux. Paris: 1860. V. 39

VISHNIAC, ROMAN

Polish Jews. New York: 1947. V. 45

A Vanished World. New York: 1983. V. 40

VISIAK, E. H.

Medusa. London: 1929. V. 38

THE VISIBLE Pursuit of a Foreign Interst, In Opposition to the Interests of England, Proved from Facts Stated in a Circular Rescript latedly Publish'd by the young Elector of Bavaria . . . London: 1745. V. 45

THE VISION and Creed of Piers Ploughman. London: 1856. V. 42

THE VISIONS of William Concerning Piers the Plowman. London: 1930. V. 46

VISIT of His Royal Highness The Prince of Wales to the Gold Coast Colony. 1915. Accra, Gold Coast Colony: 1925. V. 39

A VISIT to a Farmhouse or an Introduction to Various Subjects Connected with Rural Economy. London: 1815. V. 45; 46

VISIT to Portsmouth, May, 1907. V. 37

A VISIT to Texas, Being the Journal of a Traveller. New York: 1834. V. 37; 39; 40; 42; 45

A VISIT to Texas, Being the Journal of a Traveller . . . With a Sketch of the Late War. New York: 1836. V. 37

VISITATIO Heraldica Comitatus Wiltoniae. 1828. V. 38

VISSCHER, WILLIAM LIGHTFOOT

Black Mammy: a Song of the Sunny South, and Other Poems. Cheyenne: 1866. V. 40

Black Mammy: a Song of the Sunny South. Cheyenne: 1885. V. 38; 40

VISSCHER, WILLIAM LIGHTFOOT continued

Black Mammy: a Song of the Sunny South, and Other Poems. Cheyenne: 1886. V. 40; 44

Vissch. St. Joseph: 1873. V. 40

Vissch. St. Louis: 1873. V. 38

VISSER, H. F. E.

Asiatic Art. Amsterdam. V. 40

Asiatic Art in Private Collections of Holland and Belgium. New York: 1948. V. 42

VISSERING, G.

On Chinese Currency. Amsterdam: 1912-14. V. 43

VITA Del Padre Paolo, dell'Ordine de Servi e Theologo Della Serenissima Republica di Venetia. Leiden: 1646. V. 38

VITA P. Ignatii Loiolae Societatis Fundatoris. Rome: 1609. V. 43

VITALBA, GIOVANNI

A Collection of Landscapes, Containing Nine Original Subjects . . . London: 1792. V. 39

VITALINIS, BONIFACIOUS DE

Opus Super Maleficiis. Milan: 1503. V. 40

VITALIS, JANUS FRANCISCUS

Leonem X.P.M . . . Ingredientem Laetabundus Admiratur. Rome: 1513. V. 37

VITELO

Optica, id est de Natura, Ratione & Projectione Radiroum Visis, Luminum, Colorum atque Formarum, quam vulgo Perspectivam Vocant, Libri X . . . Nuremberg: 1535. V. 38

VITRUVIUS

De Architectura Libri Decem . . . Amsterdam: 1649. V. 43

VITRUVIUS Britannicus. London: 1765-71. V. 42

VITRUVIUS Britannicus. (with) The New Vitruvius Britannicus. London: 1725-1808. V. 42

VITRUVIUS POLLIO, MARCUS

An Abridgment of the Architecture of Vitruvius . . . . London: 1692. V. 38; 40

De Architectura Libri Dece. Como: 1521. V. 37; 38

M. L. Vitrvuio Pollione Di Architettura Dal Vero Esemplare Latino Nella Volgar Lingua . . . Venice: 1535. V. 45

De Architectura Libri Decem . . . Nunc Primum in Germania Qua Potuit Diligentia Excusi, Atque Hinc Inde Schermaataibus non Iniucundis Exornati . . . Strassburg: 1543. V. 37; 45

Nemlichen des Aller Namhafftigisten un Hocherfarnesten Romishcen Architecti und Kunstreichen Werck oder Bawmeisters Marci Vitruvii Pollionis Zehen Bucher von der Architectur and Kunstlichen Bawen . . . Nurnberg: 1548. V. 38

De Architectura Libri Decem . . . Accesserunt Gulielmi Philandri . . . Lyon: 1552. V. 45

De Architectura Libri Decem. Venice: 1567. V. 40; 44

I Dieci Libri Della'Architettura. Venice: 1567. V. 39; 40; 41; 44

I Dieci Libri dell'Architettura. Venice: 1629. V. 37

De Architectura Libri Decem, Cum Notis . . . Philandri Integris, Danieli Barbari Excerptis & Claudii Salmasii Passim Insertis . . . Amsterdam: 1649. V. 39

A New Treatise of Aarchitecture, According to Vitruvius . . . London: 1669. V. 38

Les Dix Livres d'Architecture. London: 1684. V. 44

Les Dix Livres d'Architecture Corrigez et Traduits Nouvellement en Francois avec des Notes et des Figures. Paris: 1684. V. 38; 42

L'Architettura Di M. Vitruvio Pollione . . . Napoli: 1758. V. 37; 44

The Architecture of M. Vitruvius Pollio. London: 1771-91. V. 38

L'Architettura, Colla Traduzione del Bernardo Galiani . . . Siena: 1790. V. 45

The Architecture. London: 1791. V. 42

The Civil Architecture of Vitruvius. London: 1812. V. 39

The Civil Architecture. London: 1812-14. V. 42

The Architecture of Marcus Vitruvius Pollio in Ten Books. London: 1826. V. 44

The Civil Architecture. London: 1912. V. 39

Iterum et Frontinus A Iocundoverisi Repurgatique ex Collatione Licuit. Florence: 1513. V. 44

Vitruvius Iterum et Frontinus a Iocundo Revisi Repurggatique Quantum ex Collatione Licuit. Florence: 1513. V. 44; 45

M. Vitruvius Per Iocundum Solito Castigatior Factus Cum Figuris et Tabula ut Iam Legi et Intelligi Possit. Venice: 1511. V. 44

Vetruuio in Volgar Lingua Raportato per M. Gianbatista Caporali di Perugia. Colophon: 1536. V. 37

VITRUVIVUS POLLIO, MARCUS

Los Diez Libros de Architectura. Madrid: 1797. V. 46

VITRY, PAUL

French Sculpture During the Reign of Saint Louis, 1226-1270. Florence: 1938. V. 44; 46

VITTORI, ANGELO

De Palpitatione Cordis, Fractura Costarum Aliisque Affectionibus B. Philippi Nerii . . . Rome: 1613. V. 45; 46

VITTORI, BENEDETTO

Commentaria in Hippocratis aphorismos nunc Primum in Lucem Edita. Venice: 1556. V. 43

Empirica Benedicti Victorii . . . Necnon Camilli Thomaii Ravennatis Morborum Humani Corporis Curandorum Rationalis Methodus, ac Trotulae . . . Lugduni: 1558. V. 40

VITZETELLY, HENRY

Glances Back Through Seventy Years . . . London: 1893. V. 45

VIVALDI, ANTONIO

The Four Seasons. New York: 1984. V. 46

VIVALDI, GIOVANNI LODOVICO

Aureum Opus de Veritate Contritionis in quo Mirifca Documenta Eterne Salutis Aperiuntur. Paris: 1517. V. 37

VIVALDUS, JOHANNES LUDOVICUS

Opus Regale i(n) quo Continentur Infrascripta Opuscula. Lyons: 1512. V. 37

VIVANCO, AURELIO DE

Baja California Al Dia - Lower California Up to Date. 1924. V. 38

VIVANI, VINCENZO 1622-1703

De Maximis et Minimis Geometrica Divinatio in Quintum Conicorum Apollonii Pergaei Adhuc Desideratum. Florence: 1659. V. 46

VIVAUD, PIERRE

The Destruction of the Boyne, First Rate Man of War, of Ninety-Eight Guns. London: 1801. V. 40

VIVES, JUAN LUIS

De Disciplinis Libri XX, in Tres Tomos Distincti . . . Cum Indice Novo . . . Cologne: 1536. V. 40

Ioannis Lodovici Vivis Valentini, Excitationes Animi in Deum. Basle: 1540. V. 40

De Veritate Fidei Christianae Libri Quinque . . . Basle: 1543. V. 45

Wie der Turck die Christen Haltet so Under im Leben . . . Strassburg: 1532. V. 45

VIVIAN, A. PENDARVES

Wanderings in the Western Land. London: 1879. V. 40

VIVIAN, CLAUD RICHARD HUSSEY VIVIAN, 1ST BARON

A Memoir. London: 1897. V. 40; 42

VIVIAN, H. HUSSEY

Notes on a Tour in America. London: 1878. V. 38; 42; 43; 44; 46

VIVIAN, JOHN

A Poem on the Countess of Pomfret's Benefaction to the Unversity of Oxford. Oxford: 1756. V. 38

VIVIAN, MARTIN

The Big Tree of California. Philadelphia: 1876. V. 39

VIVIANI, VINCENZIO

Discorso al Serenissimo Cosimo III Granduca di Toscana Intorno al Difendersi da'riempimenti, e Dalle Corrosioni de'Fiumi Applicato ad Arno in Vicinanza Della Citta di Firenze. Florence: 1688. V. 37

Quinto Libro Degli Elementi d'Euclide, Ovvero Scienza Universale delle Proporzioni Spiegata Colla Doctrina del Galileo.. Florence: 1674. V. 38

VIVIENNE, MAY

Travels in Western Australia Being a Description of the Various Cities and Towns, Goldfields and Agricultural Districts of the State. London: 1901. V. 46

Travels in Western Australia. London: 1902. V. 38; 41

VIZCAINO, SEBASTIAN

The Voyage of . . . to the Coast of California, Together with a Map . . . San Francisco: 1933. V. 37; 42; 45

VIZETELLY, ERNEST ALFRED

The True Story of the Chevalier D'eon: His Experiences and His Metamorphoses in France, Russia, Germany, and England . . . London: 1895. V. 38

VIZETELLY, HARRY

Christmas with the Poets: A Collection of Songs, Carols and Descriptive Verses, Relating to the Festival of Christmas, From the Anglo-Norman Period to the Present Time. London: 1851. V. 41

VIZETELLY, HENRY

Extracts Principally from English Classics. London: 1888. V. 37

Four Months Among the Gold Finders in Alta California. London: 1849. V. 37; 40; 45

History of Champagne. With Notes on the Other Sparkling Wines of France. London: 1882. V. 39

The Wines of the World Characterized and Classed. London: 1875. V. 40

VLEVE, P. I.

The Geology of the North-Eastern West India Islands. Stockholm: 1871. V. 42

VLIET, R. G.

Sand is the Tool. New York: 1953. V. 38

VOCABOLARIO Degli Accademia Della Crusca. Venice: 1729. V. 38

VOCABULARIUS Incipit: Registrum Vocabularii Sequentis. Augsburg: 1478. V. 38

A VOCABULARY, Or Pocket Dictionary. Birmingham: 1765. V. 38

A VOCABULORY of Such Words in the English Language as Are of Dubious or Unsettled Accentuation in Which the Pronunciation of Sheridan, Walker, and Other Orthoepists is Compared. London: 1797. V. 38

THE VOCAL Enchantress Presenting an Elegant Selection of the Most Favourite Hunting, Sea, Love and Miscellaneous Songs, Sung by Edwin, Bannister, Webster, Mrs. Cargill, Mrs. Kennedy, Mrs. Wrighten . . . London: 1783. V. 45

THE VOCAL Magazine; or, Complete British Songster, Consisting of Such English, Scotch and Irish Songs, Catches, Glees, Cantatas, Airs, Ballads, &c. London: 1784. V. 41

VOCAVULARIUS Ex Quo (Latin-German). Strassburg: 1483. V. 40

VOCAVULARIUS Juris. Strassburg: 1486. V. 40

VOET, LEON

The Plantin Press (1555-1589). A Bibliography of the Works Printed and Published by Christopher Plantin at Antwerp and Leiden in Collaboration with Jenny Voet-Grisolle. 1980-83. V. 39

The Plantin Press (1555-1589). Amsterdam: 1980-83. V. 44

The Plantin Press (1555-1589): a Bibliography of the Works Printed and Published by Christopher Plantin at Antwerp and Leiden. Amsterdam: 1980/1981. V. 37

VOGAN, A. J.

The Black Police: a Story of Modern Australia. London: 1890. V. 46

VOGEL, HERMANN

The Chemistry of Light and Photography in Their Application to Art, Science and Industry. London: 1892. V. 46

VOGEL, JOSEPH

Man's Courage. New York: 1938. V. 46

VOGEL, RUDOLF AUGUSTIN

Pratisches Mineralsystem. Leipzig: 1762. V. 46

VOGELENZANG, L.

Guide to the Prices of Antiquarian and Secondhand Botanical Books. Leiden: 1982 & 1983. V. 38; 44

VOGTS, M. M.

Proteas, Know Them and Grow Them. Johannesburg: 1959. V. 45

VOGUE, MELCHIOR DE

Le Temple de Jerusalem. Paris: 1864. V. 42

A VOICE from the Prison; Being a Narrative of Christian Experience . . . . Elgin: 1859. V. 40

THE VOICE of the Prophets: Messianic Prophecies. Flemington: 1970. V. 44

VOICES from the Southwest: a Gathering in Honor of Donald D. Dickinson. Flagstaff: 1976. V. 44

VOICES of the Garden, The Woods and the Fields. London: 1859. V. 40

VOIGHT COMPANY

Examples of Plastic Ornament. Philadelphia: 1928. V. 38

VOIGHT, H. H.

Forty-Three Drawings. London: 1914. V. 40

VOIGHT, HANS HENNING 1887-1969

Fifty Drawings. New York: 1925. V. 39

Fifty Drawings. New York: 1935. V. 43

VOIGT, JOHANN CARL WILHELM

Versuch Einer Geschichte der Steinkohlen, der Braunkohlen und des Torfes, Nebst Anleitung, Diese Fossilien Kennen und Unterscheiden zu Lernen . . . Weimar: 1802-05. V. 43

VOITURE, VINCENT DE

The Works . . . London: 1705. V. 42; 44; 46

The Works of the Celebrated Monsieur Voiture. London: 1715. V. 44

The Works of Monsieur Voiture. London: 1736. V. 46

VOKINS, JOAN

God's Might Power Magnified. London: 1691. V. 37

VOLBACH, WOLFGANG FRITZ

Early Christian Art. New York. V. 38; 42

Late Antique, Coptic and Islamic Textiles of Egypt. London: 1926. V. 37

VOLCABULARIUS Juris Utriusque. Nuremberg: 1496. V. 45

VOLCK, ADELBERT J.

The American Cyclops, The Hero of New Orleans and Spoiler of Silver Spoons. Baltimore: 1868. V. 39

Confederate War Etchings. Philadelphia?: 1880's. V. 39; 43

VOLK, ERNEST

The Archaeology of the Delaware Valley. Cambridge: 1911. V. 38; 41; 42; 44

VOLK, KURT H.

ABC Gem Box. A Display of Skill in Typography. New York: 1941. V. 41

VOLKER, JOHN DONALDSON

Trouble Shooter: the Story of Northwoods Prosecutor. New York: 1943. V. 39

VOLLARD, AMBROISE

Paul Cezanne. Paris: 1914. V. 41

VOLLARD, AMBROSE

La Vie & L'Oeuvre de Pierre-Auguste Renoir. 1919. V. 46

VOLLMANN, WILLIAM T.

The Convict Bird. 1987. V. 44

You Bright and Risen Angels. 1987. V. 44

VOLLMER, C. G. W.

Californien und das Goldfieber. Reisen in dem Wilden Westen Nord-Amerika's, Leben und Sitten der Goldgraber, Mormonen und Indianer . . . von W. F. A Zimmermann. Berlin: 1863. V. 37

VOLLMER, WILLIAM

United States Cook Book. Philadelphia: 1860. V. 37

VOLNEY, CONSTANTIN FRANCOIS 1757-1820

Common Sense; or, Natural Ideas Opposed to Supernatural. Philadelphia: 1795. V. 41

Considerations on the War with the Turks. London: 1788. V. 45

The Ruins; or a Survey of the Revolutions of Empires. Philadelphia: 1799. V. 42

Travels through Syria and Egypt in the years 1783, 1784 and 1785. London: 1787. V. 40

Travels through Syria and Egypt, in the Years 1783, 1784 and 1785. Dublin: 1788. V. 45

Travels through Syria and Egypt, in the Years 1783, 1784 and 1785. London: 1788. V. 42

Tableau du Climat et du Sol des Etats-Unis d'Amerique. Paris: 1803. V. 37; 38

View of the Climate and Soil of the United States of America. London: 1804. V. 38

A View of the Soil and Climate of the United States of America. Philadelphia: 1804. V. 38; 39; 42; 43; 45

VOLPI, CHARLES P.

Recueil Iconographique. A Pictorial Record. Montreal: 1963. V. 37

VOLPI, GIOVANNI ANTONIO

Rime. Padua: 1741. V. 43

VOLSUNGA SAGA

Volsunga Saga. London: 1870. V. 40

VOLTA, ALLESSANDRO

Le Opere. Milan: 1918-29. V. 46

VOLTAIRE, FRANCOIS MARIE AROUET DE 1694-1778

The Age of Lewis XIV. London: 1752. V. 39

Le Caffe, ou l'Ecossaise, Comedie, par Mr. Hume, Traduite en Francais. Londres (Geneva): 1760. V. 41

VOLTAIRE, FRANCOIS MARIE AROUET DE 1694-1778 continued

Candide. London. V. 41

Candide, ou l'Optimisme. N.P.: 1759. V. 37; 45

Candide . . . (with) Candide . . . Second partie. N.P.: 1761. V. 43

Candide, or the Optimist. London: 1814. V. 39; 42

Candide. London: 1898. V. 39

Candide. Munich: 1920. V. 41

Candide. New York: 1928. V. 43

Candide. New York: 1928. V. 37; 39; 40; 41; 42; 43; 44; 45

Candide Ou l'Optimisme. Paris: 1928. V. 40; 41

Candide by Voltaire. Introduction by Charles Merrill. New York: 1929. V. 37; 39

Candide. New York: 1944. V. 42

Candide. Stockholm: 1949. V. 40

Candide. Oxford: 1985. V. 37; 39

Collection Complete in Mr. de Voltaire. London: 1757-56. V. 46

La Defense de Mon Oncle. N.P.: London: 1767. V. 45

Elemens de la Philosophie Neuton. Amsterdam: 1738. V. 38; 42

The Elements of Sir Isaac Newton's Philosophy. London: 1738. V. 41

Epigrams. Chicago and Skokie: 1975. V. 41

Essay on Milton. 1954. V. 45

Essay on Milton. Cambridge: 1954. V. 40; 41; 45

The General History and State of Europe from the Time of Charlemain to Charles V . . . London: 1754. V. 38

The General History and State of Europe. London: 1754-7. V. 40

La Henriade. Londres: 1728. V. 39

Henriade. London: 1732. V. 40

Histoire d'Elizabeth Canning, et de Jean Calas. Londres: 1762. V. 46

The History of Charles XII . . . London: 1732. V. 40

Histoire de l'Empire de Russie Sous Pierre le Grand. N.P.: 1765. V. 46

The History of the Russian Empire Under Peter the Great. Edinburgh: 1769. V. 38

The History of the War of Seventeen Hundred and Forty-One. London: 1756. V. 37; 38; 40; 41; 42

The Ignorant Philosopher . . . London: 1779. V. 38; 40; 45

Letters Concerning the English Notion. London: 1733. V. 37; 38; 40; 42; 43; 44; 45

Letters Concerning the English Nation. London: 1773. V. 41

Letters Concerning the English Nation. London: 1783. V. 38

Letters Addressed to His Royal Highness the Prince of *****, Containing Comments on the Writings of the Most Eminent Authors, Who Have Been Accused of Attacking the Christian Religion . . . London: 1779. V. 37

Letters of M. De Voltaire to Several of His Friends. Glasgow: 1770. V. 40

Letters . . . to Several of His Friends. London: 1770. V. 42; 44

The Massacre of St. Bartholomew, from the Second Book of the Henriade. London: 1813. V. 40; 42

Memoirs of the Life of Voltaire. Written by Himself. London: 1784. V. 39; 41; 45; 46

Le Micromegas, avec une Histoire des Croisades & un Nouveaux Plan de l'Histoire de l'Espirt Humain . . . Londres: 1752. V. 45

Miscellaneous Poems . . . London: 1764. V. 38

The Philosophical Dictionary for the Pocket. London: 1765. V. 37; 41; 43; 46

The Philosophical Dictionary . . . London: 1786. V. 41; 45

The Philosophical Dictionary, for the Pocket. London: 1793. V. 45

The Philosophical Dictionary for the Pocket. Catskill: 1796. V. 37; 40

A Philosophical Dictionary . . . London: 1824. V. 39; 42

La Philosophie de l'Histoire. N.P.: 1765. V. 45

The Philosophy of History. London: 1766. V. 42; 45

Poem Upon the Lisbon Disaster. Lincoln: 1977. V. 39; 41; 44; 46

The Princess of Babylon. London: 1927. V. 40; 45; 46

La Pucelle, Poeme, Suivi des Contes et Satires. Kehl: 1789. V. 39; 45

La Pucelle D'Orleans, Poeme en Vingte Un Chants. Paris: 1795. V. 41; 45

La Pucelle. Dublin: 1796-97. V. 40

The Maid of Orleans, or La Pucelle of . . . London: 1822. V. 38; 46

La Pucelle: the Maid of Orleans: an Heroic-Comical Poem in Twenty One Cantos. London: 1899. V. 38; 39; 41; 43; 44; 45; 46

The Pupil of Nature: A True History, Found Amongst the Papers of Father Quesnel. London: 1771. V. 38; 44; 46

Romances, Tales and Smaller Pieces. London: 1794-92. V. 41

Select Pieces. London: 1754. V. 43

The Temple of Taste. Glasgow: 1751. V. 43

Therese. Cambridge: 1981. V. 42; 44; 46

A Treatise on Toleration; The Ignorant Philosopher; and a Commentary on the Marquis of Becaria's Treatise on Crimes and Punishments. London: 1779. V. 43

The White Bull, with Saul and Various Short Pieces. London: 1929. V. 46

Oeuvres. London: 1748. V. 38

The Dramatic Works. London: 1761-63. V. 38

The Works of . . . London: 1761-69. V. 46

The Works of . . . London: 1762-5. V. 38

Oeuvres Completes. Kehl: 1784-89. V. 39; 40; 43

Oeuvres Completes. Paris: 1784-89. V. 40; 46

Oeuvres Completes. Paris: 1785. V. 37

Oeuvres Completes de Voltaire. Paris: 1785-89. V. 46

Oeuvres Completes. De L'Imprimerie de La: 1823-28. V. 38

Oeuvres Completes. Paris: 1835-38. V. 39; 46

Works of . . . London: 1901. V. 46

The Works. New York: 1901. V. 42

Works of.. Paris, London, New York,: 1901. V. 40

Zadig or The Book of Fate. An Oriental History. Translated from the Frech Original . . . London;: 1749. V. 37; 41

Zadig, ou, la Destinee. N.P.: 1749. V. 40; 45

The History of Zadig; or, Destiny. New York: 1952. V. 44; 46

A VOLUME of Memoirs and Genealogy of Representative Citizens of Northern California. Chicago: 1901. V. 45

VOLUSPA; The Song of the Sybil. Iowa City: 1968. V. 46

VOLWILLER, ALBERT T.

George Croghan and the Westward Movement 1741-1782. Cleveland: 1926. V. 39; 41; 42; 44

VON BEZOLD, WILHELM

The Theory of Color in Its Relation to Art and Art-Industry. Boston: 1876. V. 38

VON BOEHN, MAX

Dolls and Puppets. London: 1932. V. 40; 46

VON BORCKE, HEROS

Colonel Heros Von Borcke's Journal, 26 April - October 1862. V. 42

Memoirs of the Confederate War for Independence. Edinburgh: 1866. V. 41

VON BOTHMER, DIETRICH

Amazons in Greek Art. Oxford: 1957. V. 42

VON BUCH, CHRISTIAN LEOPOLD 1774-1853

Travels through Norway and Lapland. London: 1813. V. 43

VONDEL, JOOST VAN DEN

Gijsbrecht van Aemstel. Haarlem: 1901. V. 43

VON DER OSTEN, HANS HENNING

The Alishar Huyuk. Season of 1927. Chicago: 1930. V. 44

The Alishar Huyuk Season of 1927. Chicago: 1930-32. V. 40

The Alishar Huyuk Seasons of 1930-32. Chicago: 1937. V. 42

Ancient Oriental Seals in the Collection of Mr. Edward T. Newell. Chicago: 1934. V. 42

Explorations in Central Anatolia: Season of 1926. Chicago: 1929. V. 40; 42

VON FEURBACH, ANSELM RITTER

Narratives of Remarkable Criminal Trials. London: 1846. V. 38

VON GRIMMELSHAUSEN, JOHANN JAKOB CHRISTOFFEL

The Adventures of Simplicissimus. New York: 1981. V. 38; 40; 46

VON GUMPACH, JOAHANNES

A Popular Inquiry into the Moon's Rotation on Her Axis. London: 1856. V. 41

VON HADELN, DETLEV

Titian's Drawings. London: 1927. V. 46

VON HAGEN, VICTOR WOLFGANG

The Aztec and Maya Papermakers. New York: 1943. V. 38; 41

The Aztec and Maya Papermakers. New York: 1944. V. 38; 40; 43

VON HARBOU, THEA

Metropolis. London: 1927. V. 42

VON HARTEN, GERARD

Trial of Gerard Von Harten, Late Merchant of Baltimore, For Forgeries, Committed to Amount of Fifty Thousand Dollars . . . Baltimore: 1807. V. 42

VON HELMONT, JOHN BAPTISTE

Deliramenta Catarrhi; or, The Incongruities, Impossibilities, and Absurdities Couched Under the Vulgar Opinion of Defluxions. London: 1650. V. 41

VON HERKOMER, HUBERT

A Certain Phase of Lithography. A Lecture Delivered at Lululaund, Bushey, Herts., on January 27, 1910, to a Number of Invited Artists. London: 1910. V. 38

VON HEUGLIN, T.

Reise Nach Abessinien, den Casa-Landern, Ost-Sudan und Chartum in den Jahren 1861-1862. Jena: 1868. V. 45

VON HIRSCH, ROBERT

The ... Collection ... Sold at Auction by Sotheby Parke Bernet & Co ... June 1978. London: 1979. V. 39

VON HOLST, H.

The Constitutional and Political History of the United States. Chicago: 1889. V. 44

VON HOLST, H. V.

Modern American Homes. Chicago: 1914. V. 46

VON HUMBOLDT, WILHELM

Thoughts and Opinions of a Statesman. London: 1850. V. 40

VON KARMAN, THEODORE

The wind and Beyond. Boston: 1967. V. 38

VON KOTZEBUE, AUGUSTUS

Travels through Italy in the Years 1804 and 1805. London: 1806. V. 43
Travels through Italy in the Years 1804 & 1805. London: 1807.. V. 45

VON MICHAELIS, H.

Birds of the Gauntlet. London: 1952. V. 40

VON MOE, EMILE A.

The Decorated Letter, From the VIIth to the XIIth Century. Paris: 1950. V. 41

VON MOLO, WALTER

Fugen Des Seins. Berlin: 1924. V. 40

VON MOLTKE, J.

Dutch and Flemish Old Masters in the Collection of Dr. C. J. K. Van Aalst Huis te Hoevalaken Holland. 1939. V. 45

VON MUFFLING, FRIEDRICH, BARON 1775-1851

Passages from My Life; Together with Memoirs of the Campaign of 1813 and 1814. London: 1853. V. 38

VONNEGUT, KURT

Between Time and Timbuktu or Promethus 5. 1972. V. 39
Bluebeard. New York: 1987. V. 41; 43
Cat's Cradle. 1963. V. 39
Cat's Cradle. London: 1963. V. 41; 42
Cat's Cradle. New York: (1963). V. 37; 45
Deadeye Dick. New York: 1982. V. 41; 44
Fates Worse than Death. New York: 1991. V. 46
Galapagos. New York: 1985. V. 45; 46
Galapagos. Pennsylvania: 1985. V. 41
God Bless You Mr. Rosewater. London: 1965. V. 41; 45
God Bless You Mr. Rosewater. New York: 1965. V. 42; 46
Hocus Pocus. New York: 1990. V. 43; 46
Jailbird. New York: 1979. V. 41; 42; 43; 45
Mother Night. Greenwich: 1962. V. 43
Mother Night. New York: 1966. V. 39; 42; 44; 45
Mother Night. London: 1968. V. 41; 42
Nothing is Lost Save Honor. Jackson: 1984. V. 45
Palm Sunday. New York: 1981. V. 39; 41; 42; 43
Player Piano. New York: 1952. V. 37; 39; 42; 43; 45; 46
The Sirens of Titan. New York: 1959. V. 42; 43; 45
Slapstick or Lonesome No More! New York: 1976. V. 41; 42; 45
Slaughterhouse-Five or the Children's Crusade. New York: 1969. V. 39; 41; 42; 45; 46
Slaughterhouse Five. New York: 1973. V. 43
Torture and Blubber. N.P.. V. 45
Wampeters, Foma and Granfalloons. New York: 1974. V. 44
Welcome to the Monkey House - a Collection of Short Works. New York: 1968. V. 41; 42; 45

VON NEUMANN, JOHN

Theory of Games and Economic Behavior. Princeton: 1944. V. 37

VON OETTINGEN, BURCHARD

Horse Breeding in Theory and Practice. London: 1909. V. 37; 42

VON RAUMER, FREDERIC

Italy and the Italians. London: 1840. V. 45

VON ROIL, UNO

Letters on Iceland: Containing Observations on the Civil, LIterary, Ecclesiastical and Natural History, Antiquities, Volcanoes, Basalts, Hot Springs, Customs, Dress, Manners ... 1783. V. 37

VON STEUBEN, BARON

Regulations for the Order and Discipline of the Troops of the United States ... to which is Added, The Manual Exercise and Evolution of the Cavalry, as Practiced in the Late American Army. Bennington: 1794. V. 38

VON TEMPSKY, C. F.

A Narrative of Incidents and Personal Adventures on a Journey in Mexico, Guatemala and Salvador in the Years 1853 to 1855 ... London: 1858. V. 39; 45

VON TSCHUDI, J. J.

Travels in Peru, During the Years 1838-1842, on the Coast, in the Sierra, Across the Cordilleras and the Andes, into the Primeval Forests. New York: 1849. V. 39; 45

VON VALENTINI, BARON

Military Reflections on Turkey. London: 1828. V. 39

VON WINNING, HASSO

Pre-Columbian Art of Mexico and Central America. New York: 1958/60. V. 40

Pre-Columbian Art of Mexico and Central America. New York: 1968. V. 39; 42; 46

VOORHEES, DANIEL W.

Speeches of Daniel W. Vorhees of Indiana Embracing His Most Prominent Forensic, Political, Occasional and Literary Addresses. Cincinnati: 1875. V. 44

VOORHEES, LUKE

Personal Recollections of Pioneer Life on the Mountains and Plains of the Great West. Cheyenne: 1920. V. 37; 45

VOORN, HENK

Old Ream Wrappers. An Essay on Early Ream Wrappers of Antiquarian Interest. North Hills: 1969. V. 38; 40; 44

VOORSANGER, JACOB

The Chronicles of Emanu-El ... San Francisco: 1900. V. 46

VORONOFF, SERGE

Rejuvenation by Grafting. London: 1925. V. 40

VORSE, MARY HEATON

Time and the Town. New York: 1942. V. 46

VOSBURGH, W. S.

Cherished Portraits of Thoroughbred Horses. London: 1929. V. 42

VOSBURGH, WALTER S.

'Cherry and Black' the Career of Mr. Pierre Lorilard on the Turf. New York: 1916. V. 43

Thoroughbred Types, 1900-1925. New York: 1926. V. 37

VOSE, REUBEN

Despotism; or the Last Days of the American Republic. New York: 1856. V. 43

Reuben Vose's Wealth of the World Displayed. New York: 1859. V. 43
Wealth of the World Displayed. New York: 1859. V. 38; 41

VOSMEER, MICHAEL

Principes Hollandiae et Zelandiae, Domini Frisiae ... cum Genuinis Ipsorum Iconibus ... Antwerp: 1578. V. 38

VOSS, JOHN CLAUS

Venturesome Voyages of Capt. Voss. Tokyo: 1913. V. 41; 42; 43

VOSSIUS, GERARDUS IOANNIS 1577-1649

De Arte Grammatica. Amsterdam: 1635. V. 46

VOSSIUS, GERARDUS JOANNES

De Cognitione Sui Libellus. Amsterdam: 1654. V. 42
Etymologicon Linguae Latinae ... Amsterdam: 1662. V. 45
Historiae de Controversiis Quas Pelagius Eiusque Reliquiae Moverunt. Amsterdam: 1655. V. 38

VOSSIUS, ISAAC 1618-1689

Variarum Observationum Liber. Londini: 1685. V. 37; 39

VOSSIUS, ISAC 1618-1689

De Poematum Cantu et Viribus Rythmi. Oxford: 1673. V. 38

VOSTELL, WOLF

De-collage Happenings. New York: 1966. V. 41

THE **VOTES** and Proceedings of the Freeholders and Other Inhabitants of the Town of Boston, in Town Meeting Assembled, According to Law. Boston: 1772. V. 37; 38

VOTES for Women. 1907-13. V. 45

VOTES of Parliament Touching Two Books: The One Entituled, the Accuser Sham'd Upon John Fry a Member of Parliament, by Colonel John Downs, Likewise a Member of Parliament; the Other Entiuled, The Clergy in Their Colours, or a Brief Character of Them . . . London: 1650. V. 44

VOTH, H. R.

   The Oraibi Summer Snake Ceremony. 1903. V. 39

   The Oraibi Summer Snake Ceremony. Chicago: 1903. V. 38

VOUGHT, JOHN G.

   A Treatise on Bowel Complaints. Rochester: 1823. V. 40

VOX Borealis, or the Northern Discoverie; by Way of Dialogue Between Jamie and Willie. London?: 1641. V. 40

VOYACHEK, W. E.

   Fundamentals of Aviation Medicine. Ottawa: 1943. V. 40

VOYAGE Aboard the Jupiter. Nappanee: 1967. V. 38

VOYAGE Force de Naples. Paris: 1801? V. 42

THE **VOYAGE** of St. Brendan: Journey to the Promised Land. 1976. V. 37

THE **VOYAGE** of Sebastian Vizcaino to the Coast of California, Together with a Map and Sebastian Vizcaino's Letter Written at Monterey, December 28, 1602. San Francisco: 1933. V. 44

THE **VOYAGE** of the Lady. London: 1860. V. 43

A VOYAGE to the Antipodes, a Simile, in a Dialouge Between Remarquo, a Member of the English Flying Squadron, and a Sayler . . . London: 1703. V. 45

A VOYAGE to the South-Seas, and To Many Other Parts of the World, Performed from the Month of September in the Year 1740 to June 1744. London: 1744. V. 43

VOYAGES IN the Arctic Seas, From 1821 to 1825, for the Discovery of a North-West Passage to the Pacific Ocean. Dublin: 1830. V. 37

VOYAGES Through the Northern Pacific Ocean, Indian Ocean, and Chinese Sea. Dublin: 1825. V. 41

VOYAGES to Vinland: the First American Saga. Chicago: 1941. V. 44

VOYER, J.

   The New Pocket Companion for the Modern Lute and Guitar Being a Collection of New Songs, Marches, etc. London: 1805. V. 39

VOYNICH, W. M.

   List of Books. (First-Ninth) London: 1902. V. 38

VOYSEY, CHARLES FRANCIS ANNESLEY

   Individuality. London: 1915. V. 42

VOZNESENSKY, ANDREI

   Nostalgia for the Present. New York: 1978. V. 44

   Selected Poems. 1964. V. 44

LA **VRAIE** Cronicque d'Escoce. Pretensions des Anglois a la Couronne de France. London: 1847. V. 46

VRANCKEN, CHARLES

   Exposition Picasso, 16 Juin - 30 Juillet 1932. Paris: 1932. V. 45

VREAM, WILLIAM

   A Description of the Air-Pump, According to the Late Mr. Hawksbee's Best and Last Improvements . . . London: 1717. V. 43

VREDEMAN, HANS

   Artis Perspectivae Plurium Generum Elegantissimae Formulae, Multigenis Fontibus . . . Antwerpen: 1568. V. 43

   Fountains. Antwerpen: 1573. V. 43

VREDENBURG, EDRIC

   Tinker Tailor. London. V. 45

VREELAND, DIANA

   Allure. New York: 1980. V. 43

VRIENTIUS, MAXIMILIAN

   Epigrammatum Libri IX. Antwerp: 1603. V. 38

VRIES, DAVID PETERSON DE

   Voyages from Holland to America, A.D. 1632 to 1644. New York: 1853. V. 42

VRIES, HUGO DE 1848-1935

   Intracellular Pangenesis, Including a Paper on Fertilization and Hybridization. Chicago: 1910. V. 42; 45; 46

   Die Mutationstheorie. Leipzig: 1901-03. V. 42

   The Mutation Theory. London: 1910-11. V. 38

   Species and Varities Their Origin by Mutation. Chicago: 1905. V. 45

VRIES, JAN VREDEMAN DE 1527-1606

   Architectura oder Bauung der Antiquen auss dem Vitruviuvs, Woeliches Sein Funff Collummen Orden . . . Antwerp: 1598. V. 46

VROMAN, ADAM CLARK

   Photographer of the Southwest: Adam Clark Vroman 1856-1916. Los Angeles: 1961. V. 45

VUES de Paris en Photographie (on front cover). Paris: 1869. V. 37

VUILLEUMIER, F.

   High Altitude Tropical Biogeography. Oxford: 1987. V. 38

   High Altitude Tropical Biogeography. London: 1986. V. 37

VULCANIUS, BONAVENTURA

   De Literis & Lingua Getarum sive Gothorum. Leiden: 1597. V. 37

VULLIAMY, LEWIS

   Examples of Ornamental Sculpture in Architecture. London: 1823. V. 39

   Examples of Ornamental Sculpture in Architecture, Drawn from the Originals of Bronze, Marble and Terra Cotta in Greece, Asia Minor and Italy in the Years 1818-21. London: 1823-7. V. 37; 40

VULLIER, GASTON

   A History of Dancing from the Earliest Ages to Present Times. New York: 1897. V. 39

VULSON, MARC DE

   Les Portraits des Hommes Illustres Francois qui sont Peints dans la Galerie du Palais Cardinal de Richelieu. Paris: 1655. V. 39

VYNER, R. T.

   Notitia Venatica: a Treataise on Fox-Hunting. London: 1871. V. 37

   Notitia Venatica: a Treatise on Fox-Hunting. London: 1892. V. 37

VYNER, ROBERT T.

   Notitia Venatica: a Treatise on Fox Hunting to Which is Added a Compendious Kennel Stud Book. London: 1841. V. 37; 39; 43

   Notitia Venatica: A Treatise on Fox Hunting. London: 1842. V. 39

   Notitia Venatica. London: 1910. V. 38; 39; 40; 46

VYSE, CHARLES

   The New London Spelling Book: or the Young Gentleman's and Lady's Guide to the English Tongue. London: 1796. V. 41

   The Tutor's Guide. London: 1779. V. 39

W

W., A.

Hieromachia; or, a True, Sincere, Impartial Account of a Certain Dispute That Happen'd August 1st 1717 Between K- a Presbyter of the Church of Engalnd, and C- a Presbyterian Teacher . . . London: 1719. V. 42

W., C.

A Summarie of Controuersies . . . 1616. V. 42

W. E. HILL & SONS

The Salabue Stradivari: A History and Critical Description of the Famous Violin Commonly Called 'Le Messie.' Illustrated with 3 coloured lithographs by Mr. Shirley Slocombe. London: 1891. V. 37

W., E. T.

The Baths of Bagnole, or the Juvenile Miscellany. London: 1826. V. 39

W., G.

A Rich Store-House, or Treasury of the Diseased . . . Many Approved Medicines . . . for . . . Poorer Sort of People. London: 1650. V. 37; 43; 44

W., J.

An O-Yes from the Court of Heaven to the Northern Nations, by the Streaming Lights That Have Appeared of Late Years in the Air. London: 1741. V. 39; 40

The Valiant Scot. London: 1637. V. 37

W., L.

An Englishman's Answer to a German Nobleman. London: 1743. V. 41

WAAGE, FREDERICK O.

Antioch On-The-Orontes IV. Part I: Ceramics and Islamic Coins. Princeton: 1948. V. 41

WAAGEN, G. F.

Works of Art and Artists in England. London: 1838. V. 44

WAAGEN, G. G.

Treasures of Art in Great Britain. London: 1854. V. 38

WACE, A. J. B.

Mediterranean and Near Eastern Embroideries from the Collection of Mrs. F. H. Cook. London: 1935. V. 37

WACE, ALAN J. B.

A Companion to Homer. London: 1962. V. 40

Prehistoric Thessaly, Being Some Account of Recent Excavations and Explorations in North-Eastern Greece from Lake Kopais tot he Borders of Macedonia. Cambridge: 1912. V. 40; 43; 44

WACK, HENRY WELLINGTON

The Story of the Congo Free State. New York: 1905. V. 40; 43

WACKEROW, CHARLES

Tables of Pedigrees of Thorough-bred Horses from the Earlaiest Accounts to the Year 1902 Inclusvie. Vienna: 1904. V. 37

WADD, WILLIAM

Comments on Corpulency Lineaments of Leanness Mems of Diet and Dietetics. London: 1829. V. 37

Mens, Maxims and Memoirs. London: 1827. V. 44

Nugae Chirurgicae; or, a Biographical Miscellany. London: 1824. V. 44; 45; 46

WADDELL, ALFRED M.

An Address Delivered to the Colored people, by Their Request, at the Wilimington Theatre, July 26, 1865. Wilmington: 1865. V. 38

WADDELL, ALFRED MOORE

A Colonial Officer and His Time, 1754-1773. Raleigh: 1890. V. 46

Gen. Francis Nash. An Address by Hon. A. M. Waddell Delivered at the Unveiling of a Monument to General Nash . . . July 4, 1906. Greensboro: 1906. V. 44

WADDELL, HELEN

New York City. Newtown: 1935. V. 46

WADDELL, HOPE MASTERTON

Twenty-Nine Years in the West Indies and Central Africa; a Review of Missionary Work and Adventure. 1829-1858. London: 1863. V. 40; 43

Twenty-Nine Years in the West Indies and Central Africa: A Review of Missionary Work and Adventure. London: 1892-1858. V. 39

WADDELL, I. A.

Among the Himalayas. Philadelphia: 1900. V. 44

WADDELL, JAMES D.

Biographical Sketch of Linton Stephens. Atlanta: 1877. V. 45

WADDELL, JOSEPH

Annals of Augusta County Virginia, from 1726 to 1871. Staunton: 1902. V. 40

WADDELL, LAWRENCE AUGUSTINE

Among the Himalayas . . . Westmisnter: 1899. V. 46

WADDILOVE, W. J. D.

The Stewart Missions: a Series of Letters and Journals Calculated to Exhibit to British Christians, the Spiritual Destitution of the Emigrants Settled in the Remote Parts of Upper Canada. London: 1838. V. 43

WADDINGTON, ALFRED

The Fraser Mines Vindicated or, The History of Four Months. Vancouver: 1949. V. 38

WADDINGTON, GEORGE

Journal of a Visit to Some Parts of Ethiopia. London: 1822. V. 40

WADDINGTON, ROBERT

A Practical Method for Finding the Longitude and Latitude of a Ship at Sea, by Observations of the Moon; with General Rules for Compurint the Same. London: 1763. V. 37

WADE, ALLAN

A Bibliography of the Writings of W. B. Yeats. London: 1958. V. 41

WADE-GERY, H. T.

Terpsichore and Other Poems. 1921. V. 42

WADE, H. T.

With Boat and Gun in the Yangtze Valley. Shanghai: 1910. V. 43

WADE, HENRY

Halcyon; or, Rod-Fishing with Fly, Minnow and Worm. London: 1861. V. 39

WADE, JOHN 1788-1875

The Black Book: or Corruption Unmasked . . . London: 1820. V. 38; 41; 44

The Cabinet Lawyer, or, Popular Digest of the Laws of England . . . with the Criminal Law of England. London: 1826. V. 40

The Extraordinary Black Book . . . With a Precis of the House of Commons, Past, Present and to Come. London: 1812. V. 41

The Extraordinary Black Book . . . London: 1831. V. 42

The Extraordinary Black Book. London: 1832. V. 40

History of the Middle and Working Classes . . . . London: 1833. V. 41; 42

History of the Middle and Working Classes. London: 1835. V. 42

A Political Dictionary; or Pocket Companion. London: 1821. V. 40

WADE, MARK SWEETEN

The Overlanders of '62. Victoria: 1931. V. 41; 44; 45; 46

The Thompson County. Kamloops: 1907. V. 43

WADE, T. F.

A Progressive Course . . . of Colloquial Chinese as Spoken in the Capital and the Metropolitan Department. Shanghai: Hongkong: 1903. V. 46

WADE, WILLIAM B.

Pursuant to the Above Orders All Officers and Men Belonging to the 8th Confederate Regiment of Cavalry Will Report to Me Immediately at Columbus, Mississippi. Columbus: 1864. V. 45

WADLEIGH, R. H.

Head-Gear, Antique and Modern. Boston: 1879. V. 40

WADSTROM, CARL BERNHARD

An Essay on Colonization, Particularly Applied to the Western Coast of Africa . . . London: 1794-95. V. 45

Obsevations on the Slave Trade and a Description of some Part of the Coast of Guinea, During a Voyage Made in 1787 and 1788, in Company . . . London: 1789. V. 43

WADSWORTH, BENJAMIN 1670-1737

The Benefits of God, and Mischiefs of an Evil Conscience. Boston: 1719. V. 38

WADSWORTH, CHARLES

The Address Delivered in Calvary Church, San Francisco on the Occasion of the Funeral Services of Gen. George Wright . . . San Francisco: 1865. V. 43

Historical Sketch of Calvary Presbyterian Church Together with a Full Report.. San Francisco: 1869. V. 43

WADSWORTH, CHARLES continued

Views from the Island. Poetry and Prints by . . . Boston: 1970. V. 44

WADSWORTH, EDWARD

The Black Country. London: 1920. V. 37

Sailing Ships & Barges of the Western Mediterranean & Adriatic Seas. London: 1926. V. 39; 45

Selection Chronique de la Vie Artistique: Cahier 13. Anvers: 1933. V. 42; 46

WADSWORTH, W. H.

Traduccion del Dictamen de Mr. Wadsworth, Sobre las Reclamaciones Mexicanas Procedentes de Depredaciones de los Indios . . . Mexico: 1873. V. 38

WAFER, LIONEL

A New Voyage and Description of the Isthmus of America, Giving an Account of the Author's Abode There, the Form and Make of the Country, the Coasts, Hills, Rivers . . . Soil, Weather &c . . . . London: 1699. V. 38; 40; 42

A New Voyage and Description of the Isthmus of America, Giving an Account of the Author's Abode There, the Form and Make of the Country, the Coasts, Hils, Rivers . . . London: 1704. V. 39; 40; 42

WAG, WALTER, PSEUD.

The Fudge Committee, or Creditors Wanting More . . . London: 1819. V. 42

WAGENAAR, JAN

'T Verheugd Amsterdam, ter Gelegenheid van het Plegtig Bezoek Hunner . . . Willem, Prinse van Oranje en Nassau . . . en zyne Gemaalinne Frederica Sophia Wilhelmina, Prinsesse van Pruissen, op . . . 30 May . . . 1768. Amsterdam: 1768. V. 37

WAGENAER, LUCAS JANSZ

Speculum Nuticum . . . Antwerp: 1591. V. 38

WAGENEN, G. VAN

Embryology of the Ovary and the Testis Homo Sapiens and Macaca Mulatta. New Haven: 1965. V. 39

WAGENSEIL, JOHANN CHRISTOF

Sota. Hoc Est: Liber Mischnicus de Uxore Adulterii Suspecta. Altdorf: 1674. V. 41

WAGENSEIL, JOHANN CHRISTOPH

De Hydraspide Sua, Sive Adversus Extrema Pericula Aquarum Munimento ac Praesidio, ad Petrum Valckenierium . . . Altdorfi Noricoum: 1690. V. 40

WAGENSEIL, JOHANN CHRISTOPHORUS

De Sacri Rom. Imperii Libera Civitate Noribergensi Commentatio. Altdorf: 1697. V. 40

WAGHORN, HENRY

Some Valuable Instructions and Receipts (Never Before Published) For Catching and Destroying the Following Vermin . . . London: 1722. V. 43

WAGNER, ANTHONY

Heralds of England. London: 1967. V. 39

WAGNER, ANTON

Los Angeles. Werden, Leben und Gestalt der Zweimillionenstadt in Sudkalifornien. Leipzig: 1935. V. 45

WAGNER, ARTHUR L.

The United States Army and Navy-Their Histories from the End of the Revolution to the Close of the Spanish-American War . . . Akron: 1899. V. 38

WAGNER, E.

Cut and Thrust Weapons. London: 1967. V. 38

WAGNER, GLENDOLIN D.

Old Neutriment. Boston: 1934. V. 38; 39; 45

WAGNER, H.

Economic and Medicinal Plant Research. New York: 1985. V. 37

Joaquin Miller and His Other Self. San Francisco: 1929. V. 46

Plant Drug Analysis. Berlin: 1984. V. 37

WAGNER, HENRY RAUP 1862-1957

A Bibliography of Original Narratives of Travel and Adventure 1800-1865. San Francisco: 1937. V. 45

Bullion to Books. Los Angeles: 1942. V. 42; 45

Bullion to Books, Fifty Years of Business and Pleasure. Los Angeles: 1962. V. 41

California Imprints. August 1846-June 1851. Berkeley: 1922. V. 42; 46

California Voyages 1539-1541. San Francisco: 1925. V. 42; 45

The Cartography of the Northwest Coast of America to the Year 1800. Berkeley: 1937. V. 38; 39; 40; 43; 45; 46

The Cartography of the Northwest Coast of America to the Year 1800. Amsterdam: 1968. V. 37; 40; 45

Juan Rodriguez Cabrillo, Discoverer of the Coast of California. San Francisco: 1941. V. 37; 38; 42; 45

Nueva Bibliografia Mexicana de Siglo XVI . . . Mexico: 1946. V. 40

Peter Pond, Fur Trader and Explorer. 1955. V. 38

Peter Pond Fur Trade & Explorer. New Haven: 1955. V. 37; 40; 42; 45

The Plains and the Rockies. San Francisco: 1921. V. 38; 41; 42

Henry R. Wagner's The Plains and the Rockies. San Francisco: 1937. V. 37; 38; 39; 40; 41; 42; 44; 45

Henry R. Wagner's The Plains and the Rockies. Columbus: 1953. V. 38; 39; 40; 41; 44

The Plains and the Rockies. N.P.: 1972. V. 40

The Plains and Rockies . . . San Francisco: 1982. V. 37; 38; 39; 40; 41; 42; 43; 44; 45; 46

The Rise of Fernando Cortes. Berkeley: 1944. V. 39

The Rise of Fernando Cortes. Los Angeles: 1944. V. 37

Sir Francis Drake's Voyage Around the World. San Francisco: 1926. V. 40; 42; 43; 44; 46

Sixty Years of Book Collecting. Los Angeles: 1952. V. 42

Sixty Years of Book Collecting. San Francisco: 1952. V. 39

The Spanish Southwest, 1542-1794 An Annotated Bibliography. Berkeley: 1924. V. 38; 42; 44; 45

Spanish Explorations in the Strait of Juan de Fuca. Santa Ana: 1933. V. 39; 41; 42; 45; 46

The Spanish Southwest 1542-1794. New York: 1967. V. 40

The Spanish Southwest 1542-1794. Albuquerque: 1937. V. 42

Spanish Voyages to the Northwest Coast of America in the Sixteenth Century. San Francisco: 1929. V. 39; 42; 45

Spanish Voyages to the Northwest Coast of America in the Sixteenth Century. Amsterdam: 1966. V. 37; 45

WAGNER, JOHANN JAKOB

Historia naturalis Helvetiae Curiosa, in VII. Sectiones Compendiose Digesta. Zurich: 1680. V. 46

WAGNER, MORITZ

Reisen in Nordamerika. Leipzig: 1854. V. 39

WAGNER, RICHARD 1813-1883

The Flying Dutchman. London: 1938. V. 40; 43; 45; 46

Mein Leben. Munich: 1911. V. 46

Parsifal. London: 1912. V. 46

The Rhinegold & the Valkyrie. London: 1910. V. 37; 38; 39; 40; 41; 44; 46

The Rhinegold & the Valkyrie. London & New York: 1910. V. 38; 39

The Rhinegold and the Valkryie. Siegfried and the Twilight of the Gods. London: 1910-11. V. 37; 40; 41; 43

The Rhinegold and the Valkyrie. London: 1912. V. 38

The Rhinegold and the Valkyrie. London: 1914. V. 38

The Rhinegold and the Valkyrie; Siegfried and the Twilight of the Gods. London: 1924/28. V. 45

The Rhinegold and the Valkyrie; Siegfried and the Twilight of the Gods. New York: 1925. V. 43

The Ring of the Niblung. The Rhinegold and the Valkyrie, Siegfried and the Twilight of the Gods. London: 1910-11. V. 44

The Ring of the Niblung. London: 1939. V. 40; 46

Siefried & The Twilight of the Gods. By Richard Wagner. Translated by Margaret Armour. London/New York: 1911. V. 37

Siegfied and the Twilight of the Gods. London: 1911. V. 37; 39; 40; 41; 42; 43; 44; 45; 46

Siegfried & the Twilight of the Gods. New York: 1911. V. 43

The Tale of Lohengrin. London: 1913. V. 39; 46

Tannhauser. London: 1911. V. 40; 46

Tannhauser. New York: 1911. V. 39; 42; 46

Tannhauser. A Dramatic Poem by Richard Wagner. Freely translated in poetic narrative form by T.W. Rolleston. London: (n.d.). V. 37

Tristan and Isolde. London: 1886. V. 42

Tristan and Isolde, Parsifal. Leipzig: 1900. V. 40

A Walk through Wales in August 1797. London: 1798. V. 46

WAGNER, RUDOLPHO

Prodromus Historiae Generationis Hominis Atque Animalium . . . Leipzig: 1836. V. 45

WAGNER, W. F.

Leonard's Narrative Adventures of Zenas Leonard Fur Trader and Trapper 183-1836. Cleveland: 1904. V. 42

WAGSTAFFE, THOMAS 1645-1712

A Vindication of King Charles the Martyr, Proving That His Majesty Was the Author of Eikon Basilika . . . London: 1693. V. 41

WAGSTAFFE, WILLIAM

The Character of Richard St--le, Esq., with Some Remarks. London: 1713. V. 43

A Comment Upon the History of Tom Thumb. London: 1711. V. 43; 46

WAGSTAFFE, WILLIAM continued

The Story of the St. Albans Ghost, or the Apparition of Mother Haggy. London: 1712. V. 37

Miscellaneous Works . . . To Which is Prefix'd His Life and an Account of His Writings . . . London: 1725. V. 40; 45; 46

Miscellaneous Works of Dr. William Wagstaffe . . . London: 1726/25. V. 46

Miscellaneous Works . . . To which is prefix'd his Life and an Account of his Writings . . . His Character writ by an eminent Physician soon after his Death. London: 1726 (ie 1725). V. 37

WAHRMUND, JACOB

Lob, Ruhm, Ursprung und Alterthum Des Lobl. Handwercks der Schmiede, Nebst Wahrhaften Bericht, Aller Derjenigen Ceremonien und Reden . . . Germany: 1620. V. 40

WAILES, B. L. C.

Report on the Agriculture and Geology of Mississippi. N.P.: 1854. V. 40

Report on the Agriculture and Geology of Mississippi. N.P.: 1854. V. 42

Report on the Agriculture and Geology of Mississippi. N.P.: 1854. V. 38

Report on the Agriculture and Geology of Mississippi. N.P.: 1854. V. 45

WAILES, LEVIN

Address to the Public, the Trustees of Jefferson College at Washington, Mississippi . . . Now Prepared for the Reception of Students. Washington: 1839. V. 41

WAIN, JOHN

Hurry on Down. London: 1953. V. 37; 40

Mixed Feelings. 1951. V. 41

Poems for the Zodiac. London: 1980. V. 41

Thinking About Mr. Person. Beckenham, Kent: 1980. V. 37; 39

WAIN, LOUIS

Cats! Cats!! Cats!!! London: 1901. V. 44

Cat's Cradle. A Picture-Book for Little Folk. Rhymes by May Byron. London: (1908). V. 37

Addy Cat. London: 1918. V. 46

Lous Wain's Cats and Dogs. London: 1902. V. 46

The Story of Tabbykin Town in School and a Play. London: 1920. V. 46

To Nursery Land with Louis Wain. London: n.d. V. 37

WAIN, LOUISE

Frolics in Fairyland, as Seen by Louise Wain. London, Paris, New York. V. 41

The Louis Wain Nursery Book. London: 1935. V. 41

WAINEWRIGHT, JEREMIAH

An Anatomical Treatise of the Liver, with the Diseases Incident To It. London: 1722. V. 41

A Mechanical Account of the Non-Naturals . . . London: 1718. V. 44

WAINEWRIGHT, LATHAM

The Literary and Scientific Pursuits Which are Encouraged and Enforced in the University of Cambridge . . . London: 1815. V. 41

WAINWRIGHT, A.

Westmorland Heritage. London: 1975. V. 40

WAINWRIGHT, J. W.

The Medical and Surgical Knowledge of William Shakespeare . . . New York: 1907. V. 39

WAINWRIGHT, JOHNATHAN M.

A Set of Chants Adapted to the Hymns in the Morning and Evening Prayer . . . Boston: 1819. V. 43

WAINWRIGHT, NICHOLAS B.

Philadelphia in the Romantic Age of Lithography. Philadlephia: 1958. V. 39; 41; 42; 46

WAISTELL, CHARLES

Designs for Agricultural Buildings, Including Labourers' Cottages, Farm Houses and Out-Offices. London: 1827. V. 39; 40; 41; 42; 45

WAIT, BENJAMIN

Letters from Van Dieman's Land, Written During Four Years Imprisonment for Political Offences Committed in Upper Canada. Buffalo: 1843. V. 37; 38; 40; 42; 43

WAIT, FIONA EUNICE

Yermah the Dorado. San Francisco: 1897. V. 39

WAIT, J. C.

The Car-Builder's Dictionay. New York: 1895. V. 40

WAIT, W. E.

Coloured Plates of the Birds of Ceylon. London: 1927-35. V. 43

WAIT, W. O.

Rugby: Past and Present, With an Historical Account of Neighboruing Parishes. Rugby: 1893. V. 41

WAITE, A. E.

A Book of Mystery and Vision. London: 1902. V. 41

A New Encycopaedia of Freemasonry. London: 1920. V. 40

WAITE, ARTHUR EDWARD

The Book of Black Magic and Pacts, Including the Rites and Mysteries of Goetic Theurgy, Sorcer and Infernal Necromancy . . . Chicago: 1910. V. 40

The hermetic and Alchemical Writings of 'Paracelsus' The Great . . . Now for the first time faithfully and accurately translated. Prepared under the editorship fo Dr. L.W. de Laurence. Chicago: 1910. V. 37

The Lamps of Western Mysticism. London: 1923. V. 42

Strange Houses of Sleep. London: 1906. V. 38; 42; 44

Strange Houses of Sleep. London: 1896. V. 37

The Turba Philosophorum or Assembly of the Sages. London: 1896. V. 42

WAITE, CATHARINE VAN VALKENBURG 1829-1913

The Mormon Prophet and His Harem; or, an Authentic History of Brigham Young, His Numerous Wives and Children. Cambridge: 1866. V. 42

WAITE, FRED

The Official History of Australia in the War 1914-1918. Volume I. The New Zealanders at Gallipoli. 1921. V. 45

WAITT, ERNEST

History of the Nineteenth Regiment Massachusetts Volunteer Infantry 1861-1965. Salem: 1906. V. 46

WAITT, M. W.

Views of British Columbia and Alaska. Victoria: 1890. V. 46

WAKE, RICHARD

A Selection of Sketches and Letters on Sport and Life in Morocco. London: 1889. V. 40; 43

WAKE, WILLIAM

The Missionaries Arts Discovered; or, An Account of Their Ways of Insinuation, Their Artifices and Several Methods of Which They Themselves in making Converts. London: 1688. V. 42

WAKEFIELD, D. R.

The Diary and Observations of a Tench Fisher. Tiverton: 1981. V. 37; 39

The Sporting Fishes of the British Isles. An Anthology compiled and illustrated by D.R. Wakefield. Tiverton: 1985. V. 37

WAKEFIELD, DANIEL

Observations on the Credit and Finances of Great Britain. London: 1797. V. 39

WAKEFIELD, EDWARD GIBBON 1796-1862

The British Colonization of New Zealand. London: 1837. V. 38; 41

England and America. London: 1833. V. 38

England and America. New York: 1834. V. 41

Facts Relating to the Punishment of Death in the Metropolis . . . London: 1832. V. 40

Facts Relating to the Punishment of Death in the Metropolis. London: 1833. V. 46

Facts Relating to the Punishment of Death in the Metropolis . . . London: 1834. V. 39

A View of the Art of Colonization with Present Reference to the British Empire . . . London: 1849. V. 43; 46

WAKEFIELD, EDWARD JENINGHAM

Adventure in New Zealand, from 1839 to 1844 With Some Account of the Beginning of the British Colonization of the Islands. London: 1845. V. 39

WAKEFIELD, EDWARD JERNINGHAM

Illustrations to Adventures in New Zealand. London: 1845. V. 46

WAKEFIELD, GILBERT

A Catalogue of the very elegant Classical and Critical Library of the late Rev. Gilbert Wakefield . . . the books are all in fine condition and a great number contain manuscript notes and corrections by the late . . . London: 1802. V. 37

Correspondence of the Late Gilbert Wakefield, B.A . . . London: 1813. V. 42

Memoirs of the Life of Gilbert Wakefield, B. A. London: 1804. V. 37

Observations on Pope. London: 1796. V. 38

Poetical Translations from the Ancients. London: 1795. V. 41

A Reply to the Letter of Edmund Burke, Esq. London: 1796. V. 41; 43

WAKEFIELD INDUSTRIAL AND FINE ART EXHIBITION, 1865.

Official Catalogue of the Wakefield Industrial and Fine Art exhibition, August 30 - October 19th, 1865. Huddersfield: 1865. V. 41

WAKEFIELD, JOHN A.

History of the War Between the United States and the Sac and Fox Nations of Indians . . . Jacksonville: 1834. V. 37; 39; 45

WAKEFIELD, JOSEPHUS

History of Waupaca County, Wisconsin. Waupaca: 1890. V. 37; 38

WAKEFIELD, PRISCILLA 1741-1832

Excursions in North America, Described in Letters from a Gentleman and His Young Companion, to Their Friends in England. London: 1806. V. 40; 44; 45; 46

Excursions in North America, Described in Letters from a Gentleman and His Young Companion, to Their Friends in England. London: 1810. V. 38

Excursions in North America, Described in letters from a Gentleman and His Companion to Their Friends in England. London: 1819. V. 37; 38; 42

An Introduction to Botany in a Series of Familiar Letters. London: 1812. V. 37; 41; 43

The Juvenile Travellers. London: 1802. V. 39

The Traveller in Asia. London: 1817. V. 42

WAKELEY, ANDREW

The Mariner's Compass Rectified. London: 1767. V. 38

WAKELING, T. G.

Forged Egyptian Antiquities. London: 1912. V. 40; 44

WAKELY, ANDREW

The Mariner's Compass Rectified. London: 1738. V. 41

The Mariner's Compass Rectified . . . . London: 1784. V. 43

The Mariner's Compass Rectified . . . London: 1787. V. 41; 42

WAKELY, CHARLES

Abstinence and Hard Work. London: 1894. V. 39; 44

WAKEMAN, EDGAR

The Log of an Ancient Mariner. San Francisco: 1878. V. 37; 38; 39; 41; 42

WAKEMAN, FRANCES

The Plough Press, 1967-1981, Fifteen Years Printing in a Loughborough Garage. Oxford: 1982. V. 37

WAKEMAN, GEOFFREY

The Art of Anastatic Printing, Three Mid 19th Century Accounts. Oxford: 1986. V. 37; 41; 43

Aspects of Victorian Lithography, Anastatic Printing and Photozincography. Wymondham: 1970. V. 37; 41

Bradbury & Evans, Colour Printers. Kidlington: 1984. V. 39

English Hand Made Papers Suitable for Bookwork. Loughborough: 1972. V. 38; 40

English Marbled Papers. Loughborough: 1975. V. 39

English Marbled Papers. Loughborough,: 1978. V. 38; 41; 45

Graphic Methods in Book Illustration. Leicestershire: 1981. V. 39

A Guide to Nineteenth Century Colour Printers. Loughborough: 1975. V. 40

A Leaf History of British Printing from 1610 to 1774. 1986. V. 38

A Leaf History of British Printing from 1610 to 1774. 1986. V. 45

A Leaf History of British Printing from 1610 to 1774. 1986. V. 40

A Leaf History of British Printing from 1610 to 1774. Kidlington: 1986. V. 38

A Leaf History of British Printing 1610-1774. Oxford: 1986. V. 37; 38; 39; 40

The Literature of Ltterpress Printing 1849-1900. 1986. V. 40

The Literature of Letterpress Printing 1849-1900. Oxford: 1986. V. 37; 39; 40; 41; 42

XIX Century Illustration, Some Methods Used in English Books. Loughborough: 1970. V. 44

Nineteenth Century Trade Binding. 1983. V. 40

Nineteenth Century Trade Binding. Oxford: 1983. V. 40; 41

The Plough Press 1967-1981. 1982. V. 40

The Plough Press 1967-1981: Fifteen Years Printing in a Loughborough Garage. N.P.: 1982. V. 39

Printing Relief Illustrations, Kirkall to the Line Block. Leicestershire: 1977. V. 38

Twentieth Century English Vat Paper Mills. Loughborough: 1980. V. 38; 39; 42

Victorian Book Illustration; the Technical Revolution. Newton Abbot: 1973. V. 40

Victorian Colour Printing. Loughborough: 1981. V. 38; 39; 40; 42; 43; 44

WAKEMAN, GEORGE

The Tryals of Sir George Wakeman, Baronet and William Marshall, William Rumley and James Corker, Benedictine Monks, for High Treason for Cospring the Death of the King, Subversion of the Government and Protestant Religiion. London: 1679. V. 41

WAKEMAN, STEPHEN H.

The Stephen H. Wakeman Collection of Books. New York: 1924. V. 46

WAKEMAN, W. F.

A Survey of the Antiquarian Remains on the Island of Inismurray. London: 1893. V. 38

WAKENHAM, WILLIAM

Report of the Expedition to Hudson Bay and Cumberland Gulf in the Steamship 'Diana' under Command of William Wakenham. Ottawa: 1898. V. 43

WAKOSKI, DIANE

Black Dream Ditty for Billy the Kid. 1970. V. 42

Cap of Darkness. Santa Barbara: 1980. V. 39

Coins and Coffins. New York: 1962. V. 39

The Collected Greed: Parts 1-13. 1984. V. 43

The Collected Greed: Parts 1-13. 1984. V. 44

George Washington's Camp Cuts. Madison: 1976. V. 42

Greed: parts One and Two. 1968. V. 42

Greed, Parts 5-7. Los Angeles: 1971. V. 39

The Lament of the Lady Bank Dick. Cambridge: 1969. V. 41; 42

The Magician's Feastletters. Santa Barbara: 1982. V. 39; 42; 46

Making a Sacher Torte: Nine Poems. 1981. V. 45

Making a Sacher Torte: Nine Poems. 1981. V. 40

Making a Sacher Torte. Mount Horeb: 1981. V. 38; 39; 42; 44; 45

The Managed World. New York: 1980. V. 42; 44

Overnight Projects With Wood. Madison: 1977. V. 42; 44

The Pumpkin Pie. 1972. V. 44

The Pumpkin Pie. 1972. V. 43

The Pumpkin Pie. 1972. V. 42

Smudging. 1972. V. 42

Thanking My Mother for Piano Lessons. Mount Horeb: 1969. V. 39; 40

Trophies. Santa Barbara: 1979. V. 46

The Wandering Tattler. Poems. Driftless: 1974. V. 40

The Wandering Tattler. Mt. Horeb: 1974. V. 46

WALAM Olum, or Red Score. The Migration of Legend of the Lenni Lenape or Delaware Indians. Indianapolis: 1954. V. 42

WALASSER, ADAM

Kunst Wol Zusterben. Ein gar Nutzlichs Buchlein Auss Hayliger Schifft . . . Dillingen. V. 41

Kunst wol Zusterben. Ein gar Nutzlichs Hochnotwendigs Buchlin auss Hayliger Schrifft . . . Dilingen: 1569. V. 42

WALBRAN, JOHN T.

British Columbia Coast Names 1592-1906. (To Which are Added a Few Names in Adjacent United States Territory) . . . Ottawa: 1909. V. 37; 39; 41; 46

WALCH, CHARLES EDWARD

The Story of the Life of Charles Edward Walch, with a Selection of His Writings. Hobart: 1908. V. 39

WALCH, JAN

De Vreesalyke Avonturen van Scholastica by Jan Walch. Bussum: 1933. V. 44

WALCH, JOHANN GEORG

Philosophisches Lexicon. Leipzig: 1726. V. 40

WALCHA, OTTO

Meissen Porcelain. New York: 1981. V. 44

WALCOT, JOHN

A Poetical and Congratulatory Epistle to James Boswell, Esq. on His Journal of a Tour to the Hebrides. London: 1786. V. 42

WALCOT, WILLIAM

Architectural Water-Colours and Etchings of W. Walcot, with an Introduction by Sir Reginald Blomfield, R. A. London: 1919. V. 38; 45

WALCOTT, BENJAMIN STUART

Above the French Lines, Letters of . . . Princeton: 1918. V. 42

WALCOTT, CHARLES H.

Archibald Campbell of Inverneill, Sometime Prisoner of War in the Jail at Concord, Massachusetts. Boston: 1898. V. 42

WALCOTT, DAVID

The Sea at Dauphin - a Play in One Act. Port of Spain: 1954. V. 44

WALCOTT, DEREK

Another Life. London: 1973. V. 38; 45

The Caribbean Poetry of Derek Walcott. 1983. V. 42

Caribbean Poetry. New York: 1983. V. 38; 43; 45

The Castaway: Poems. London: 1965. V. 46

WALKER, ALEXANDER

Colombia: Being a Geographical, Statistical, Agricultural, Commercial and Political Account of that Country. London: 1822. V. 41

Colombia: Siendo Una Relacion Geografica, Topografica, Agricultural, Commercial, Politica. London: 1822. V. 38

Hours Off and On Sentry. Montreal: 1859. V. 44

Jackson and New Orleans, an Authentic Narrative of the Memorable Achievements of the American Army Before New Orleans. New York: 1856. V. 39; 42

Physiognomy Founded on Physiology and Applied to Various Countries, Professions and Indivuals. London: 1834. V. 37; 38

Woman Physiologically Considered as to Mind, Morals, Marraige, Matrimonial Slavery, Infidelity and Divorce. London: 1840. V. 42

WALKER, ALEXANDER, MRS.

Female Beauty, as Preserved and Improved by Regimen, Cleanliness and Dress. London: 1837. V. 40; 41

WALKER, ALICE 1944-

The Clock Strikes Twice. Sauk City: 1946. V. 45

The Color Purple. 1982. V. 44

The Color Purple. New York: 1982. V. 38; 39; 42; 43; 44; 45; 46

Goodnight, Willie Lee, I'll See You in the Morning: Poems. New York: 1979. V. 45; 46

Her Blue Body, Everything We Know, Earthling Poems 1965-1990 Complete. San Diego: 1991. V. 45; 46

In Love & In Trouble: Stories of Black Women. New York: 1973. V. 45; 46

In Search of Our Mothers' Gardens. New York: 1983. V. 46

In Search of Our Mother's Gardens. San Diego: New York: 1983. V. 41

Meridian. 1976. V. 43

Meridian. 1976. V. 43

Meridian. 1976. V. 45

Meridian. London: 1976. V. 42

Meridian. New York: 1976. V. 38; 39; 42; 43; 44; 46

Once. New York: 1968. V. 37; 42; 46

Revolutionary Petunias and Other Poems. 1973. V. 43

Revolutionary Petunias & Other Poems. New York: 1973. V. 46

The Temple of My Familiar. New York: 1989. V. 43

The Temple of My Familiar. San Diego: 1989. V. 42; 45

The Third Life of Grange Copeland. New York: 1970. V. 37; 38; 39; 42; 43; 44; 45; 46

You Can't Keep a Good Woman Down. New York: 1981. V. 42; 43; 44; 45; 46

WALKER, ANTHONY

The Virtuous Woman found Her Loss Bewailed, and Character Exemplified in a Sermon Preached at Felsted in Essex, April 30, 1678. London: 1678. V. 43

WALKER, ARDIS MANLY

Sierra Nevada Sequence. 1968. V. 42

WALKER Art Center Reading Series 1979-1980. St. Paul: 1980. V. 41

WALKER Art Center Reading Series. 1980-1981. St. Paul: 1981. V. 44

WALKER Art Center Reading Series. 1981-1982. St. Paul: 1982. V. 44

WALKER Art Center Reading Series. 1982-1983. St. Paul: 1983. V. 44

WALKER, ARTHUR

The Rifle; Its Theory and Practice. London: 1864. V. 37

WALKER, ARTHUR N.

The Holcombe Hunt. Manchester: 1937. V. 42

WALKER, C. B.

The Mississippi Valley and Prehistoric Events. Burlington: 1880. V. 37; 41

WALKER, CHARLES EDWARD

The Rainbow Trout. London: 1898. V. 41

WALKER, CHARLES M.

History of Athens County, Ohio. Cincinnati: 1869. V. 45

WALKER, CLEMENT

Relations and Observations, Historical and Politick, Upon the Parliament Begun Anno Dom. 1640. London: 1648. V. 42; 43

Relations and Observations. Historicall and Politick Upon the Parliament, Begun Anno Dom 1640 . . . 1648/49/60. V. 38

WALKER, DANTON

Spooks Deluxe Some Excursions into the Supernatural, Watts Inc. New York: 1956. V. 37

WALKER, DAVID

Address of . . . Fayetteville, Arkansas, on the History and Resources of the State . . . Philadelphia: 1876. V. 40

Voiceprints. Portland: 1989. V. 41

WALKER, DONALD

Defensive Exercises. London: 1840. V. 39

Games and Spots . . . London: 1837. V. 46

Walker's Manly Exercises; Containing Rowing, Sailing, Riding, Driving, Racing, Hunting, Shooting and Other Manly Sports. Philadelphia: 1856. V. 39

WALKER, E. H.

Flora of Okinawa and the Southern Ryukyu Islands. Washington: 1976. V. 37

WALKER, EDWARD

The Art of Bookbinding, Its Rise and Progress; Including A Descriptive Account of the New York Book-Bindery. New York: 1850. V. 43

Historical Discourses Upon Several Occasions. London: 1705. V. 39; 42; 44; 46

Raphael, or the Pupil of Nature. London: 1805. V. 38; 40

WALKER, EMERY

Pageant of the Birth Life and Death of Richard Beauchamp Earl of Warwick 1389-1439. London: 1914. V. 46

WALKER, ERNEST P.

Mammals of the World. Baltimore: 1964. V. 39

Mammals of the World. Baltimore: 1975, 1964. V. 40

Mammals of the World. Baltimore: 1983. V. 37; 38

WALKER, FRANCIS A.

The Indian Question. Boston: 1874. V. 41

Money. London: 1878. V. 42

Political Economy. London: 1885. V. 37; 40

A Statistical Atlas of the United States. London: 1874. V. 38; 40; 46

A Statistical Atlas of the United States Based on the Results of the Ninth Census. Washington: 1874. V. 43

WALKER, FRANKLIN

Ambrose Bierce, the Wickedest Man in San Francisco. San Francisco: 1941. V. 46

The Seacoast of Bohemia. San Francisco: 1966. V. 37; 38; 40; 46

The Washoe Giant in San Francisco. San Francisco: 1938. V. 40

WALKER, FREDERICK

Aerial Navigation. New York: 1902. V. 38

Twenty Seven Illustrations. London: 1867. V. 39

WALKER, G. A.

The Book of the Seventh Service Battalion the Royal Inniskilling Fusiliers from Tipperary to Ypres. Dublin: 1920. V. 46

WALKER, G. GOULD

The Honourable Artillery Company, 1537-1926. With a Foreword by the Earl of Denbigh and Desmond. London: 1926. V. 37

WALKER, GEORGE 1772-1847

The Battle of Waterloo. London: 1815. V. 45

The Chess Player. Boston: 1841. V. 46

A Collection of Psalms and Hymns for Public Worship, Unmixed with the Disputed Doctrines of any Sect. Warrington: 1788. V. 44

The Costume of Yorkshire. London: 1814. V. 39; 40; 41

The Costume of Yorkshire in 1814. Leeds: 1885. V. 37; 38; 40; 45

Descriptive Catalogue of a Choice Assemblage of Original Pictures . . . Edinburgh: 1807. V. 44

The Life and Exploits of Theodore Cyphon; or the Benevolent Jew. London: 1824. V. 43

A True Account of the Siege of London-Derry. London: 1689. V. 38; 39

The Voyages and Cruises of Commodore Walker, During the Late Spanish and French Wars. London: 1760. V. 38

WALKER, GEORGE ALFRED

Lectures on the Actual Condition of the Metropolitan Grave Yards. London: 1847. V. 40

WALKER, GUILIELMO

De Argumentorum Inventione Libri Duo, Quorum Prior Agit de Inventione Logica . . . London: 1672. V. 43

WALKER, HORATIO

Walker's Buffalo City Directory (for) 1844 . . . Buffalo: 1844. V. 42

WALKER, HOVENDEN

A Journal; or Full Account of the Late Expedition to Canada. London: 1720. V. 37; 38; 39; 41; 42; 44; 46

WALKER, HOVENDEN continued

The Walker Expedition to Quebec, 1771. Toronto: 1953. V. 46

WALKER, J.

A Geological Map of England, Wales and part of Scotland, showing also the Inland Navigation by Means of Rivers & Canals, with their Elevation in Feet about the Sea. Together with the Rail Roads & Principal Roads. London: 1837. V. 37

This British Atlas . . . London: 1837. V. 42

WALKER, J. W.

Wakefield: Its History and People. Wakefield: 1934. V. 44

Wakefield, Its History and People. Wakefield: 1939. V. 37

WALKER, JAMES

Liverpool and Manchester Railway. Report to the Directors on the Comparative Merits of Loco-motive and Fixed Engines, as a Mowing Power. Liverpool: 1829. V. 46

A Sermon. Preached in Brooklyn, Connecticut at the Installation of Rev. Samuel Joseph May, Nov. 5, 1823. Boston: 1824. V. 43

WALKER, JAMES B.

Experiences of Pioneer Life in the Early Settlements and Citites of the West. Chicago: 1881. V. 42

The Living Question of the Age. Chicago: 1869. V. 37; 42

WALKER, JAMES M.

An Inquiry into the Use and Authority of Roman Jurisprudence, in the Law Concerning Real Estate. Charleston: 1850. V. 39

WALKER, JAMES P.

Book of Raphael's Madonnas. New York: 1860. V. 44

WALKER, JAMES SCOTT

An Accurate Descritpion of the Liverpool and Manchester Railway (sic) . . . Liverpool: 1830. V. 38

An Accurate Description of the Liverpool and Manchester Rail-way, The Tunnel, Bridges and Other Works . . . Liverpool: 1831. V. 46

The South American, a Metrical Tale, in Four Cantos . . . Edinburgh: 1816. V. 40; 42

WALKER, JEANIE MORT

Life of Capt. Joseph Fry, the Cuban Martyr . . . Hartford: 1875. V. 42

WALKER, JESSE

Queenston, a Tale of the Niagara Frontier. Buffalo: 1845. V. 40

WALKER, JOHN 1674-1747

An Attempt Towards Recovering an Account of the Numbers and Sufferings of the Clergy of England . . . of the Great Rebellion. London: 1714. V. 39; 40; 42; 46

A Critical Pronouncing Dictionary and Expositor of the English Language. Dublin: 1794. V. 42; 46

A Critical Pronouncing Dictionary . . . London: 1797. V. 41; 43

A Critical Pronouncing Dictionary, and Expositor of the English Language. London: 1806. V. 41

A Critical Pronouncing Dictionary, and Expositor of the English Language. London: 1810. V. 39

A Critical Pronouncing Dictionary and Exposition of the English Language. London: 1830. V. 38

A Critical Pronouncing Dictionary. Boston: 1845. V. 39

A Critical Pronouncing Dictionary and Expostior of the English Language. in which not only the Meaning of every word is clearly explained . . . To which are prefixed principles of English Pronunciation . . . London: 1791. V. 37

A Dictionary of the English Language. London: 1775. V. 38; 41

Elements of Elocution. London: 1799. V. 41

Elements of Elouction: In Which the Principles of Reading and Speaking are Investigated . . . London: 1806. V. 41

Fragments of Letters and Other Papers, Written in Different Parts of Europe, at Sea and on the Asiatic and African Coasts or Shores of the Medietrranean . . . London: 1802. V. 39

The Natural History and Antiquities of Northumberland . . . London: 1769. V. 38

Oxoniana. London: 1807? V. 39

The Philosophy of the Eye: Being a Familiar Exposition of Its Mechanism and of the Phenomena of Vision . . . London: 1837. V. 45

A Rehtorical Grammar. London: 1812. V. 39; 40; 41

A Rhetorical Grammar, or Course of Lessons in Elocution. London: 1787. V. 41

A Rhetorical Grammar in Which the Common Improprieties in Reading and Speaking are Detected, and the True Sources of Elegant Pronunciation are Pointed Out. London: 1816. V. 40

A Rhyming Dictionary. London: 1806. V. 41

The Universal Gazetteer. London: 1810. V. 45

WALKER, JOHN, farmer

Poems in English, Scotch and Gaelic, on Various Subjects. Glasgow: 1817. V. 43

WALKER, JOHN G.

General Orders, No. 4, Head Quarters, District of Texas, &c. Houston: 1865. V. 39

WALKER, JOHN, surgeon

The Occultist's Vade-Mecum . . . London: 1843. V. 41; 45

WALKER, JOSEPH COOPER 1761-1810

Historical Memoir on Italian Tragedy, from the Earliest Period to the Present Time. London: 1799. V. 39; 42

An Historical Essay on the Dress of the Ancient and Modern Irish. Dublin: 1788. V. 38; 44

WALKER, JUDSON ELLIOTT

Campaigns of General Custer in the North-West and the Final Surrender of Sitting Bull. New York: 1881. V. 37; 38; 42; 45

WALKER, LEWIS BURD

The Burd Papers. Pottsville: 1897. V. 45

The Burd Papers. Pottsville: 1899. V. 45

WALKER, MARY ADELAIDE

Through Macedonia to the Albanian Lakes. London: 1864. V. 37

Untrodden Paths in Romania. London: 1888. V. 45

WALKER, MARY E.

Hit. New York: 1871. V. 40

WALKER, OBADIAH

Of Education Especially of Young Gentlemen. Oxon: 1673. V. 40; 41; 42; 45; 46

Of Education, Especially of Young Gentlemen. Oxford: 1683. V. 42

A Paraphrase and Annotations Upon all the Epistles of St. Paul. Oxford: 1684. V. 39

WALKER, R.

Regency Portraits. 1985. V. 39

WALKER, R. A.

The Lithographs of Charles Shannon - with a Catalogue of Lithographs Issued Between the Years 1904 and 1918. London: 1920. V. 44

Some Unknown Drawings of Aubrey Beardsley, Collected and Annotated. London: 1923. V. 37; 40; 43

WALKER, R. C.

Catalogue of Books in the Free Public Library, Sydney, Relating to, or Published in, Austalia. Sydney: 1893. V. 44

WALKER, RALPH

A Treatise on Magnetism, with a Description and Explanation of a Meridional and Azimuth Compass, for Ascertaining the Quantity and Variation, Without any Calculations Whatever, at Any Time of the Day. London: 1794. V. 38

WALKER, ROBERT

An Inquiry into the Small-Pox Medical and Political Wherein a Successful Method of Treating That Disease is Proposed . . . London. V. 40

An Inquiry into the Small-pox Medical and Political Wherein a Successful Method of Treating that Disease is Prosposed . . . London. V. 41

An Inquiry into the Small-Pox Medical and Political . . . London: 1790. V. 44

Sermons on Practical Subjects. London & Edinburgh: 1792. V. 39

WALKER, ROBERT JAMES 1801-1869

Letter of Mr. Walker, of Mississippi, Relative to the Reannexation of Texas. Washington: 1844. V. 39

WALKER, ROBERT, M.D.

An Inquiry into the Small-Pox Medical and Political . . . London. V. 39

WALKER, SAMUEL

Forage Return for 51 Horses and 6 Mules of Capt. Walker's Company of Texian Rangers. Fort Brown: 1846. V. 42

WALKER, TACETTA B.

Stories of Early Days in Wyoming. Casper: 1936. V. 39; 43

WALKER, THOMAS

Aristology or the Art of Dying. Cambridge: 1965. V. 39; 41

Journal of an Exploration in the Spring of the Year 1750. Boston: 1888. V. 46

The Original. London: 1836. V. 39

A Treatise Upon the Art of Flying, by Mechanical Means . . . Yorkshire: 1810. V. 38

WALKER, THOMAS continued

The Whole Proceedings on the Trial of an Indictment Against Thomas Walker of Manchester, Merchant, William Paul, Samuel Jackson . . . (and others) For a Conspiracy to Overthrow the Constitution and Government and to Aid and Assist the French . . . Manchester: 1794. V. 46

WALKER, THOMAS A.

The Severn Tunnel: Its Construction and Difficulties, 1872-1887. London: 1891. V. 37; 42

WALKER, THOMAS LARKINS

An Historical Account of the Church of Saint Margaret, Stoke-Golding, Leicestershire. London: 1844. V. 44

The History and Antiquities of the Vicars' Close, Wells, Somersetshire. (with) The History and Antiquities of the Manor House and Church at Great Chalfield Wiltshire. (and) The History and Antiquities of the Manor House, at South Wraxhall . . . London: 1836-7-8. V. 41

WALKER, W.

Memoirs of the Distinguished Men of Science of Great Britain Living in the Years 1807-08. London: 1862. V. 43

WALKER, W. S.

Between the Tides Comprising Sketches, Tales, and Poems, Including H-U-N-G-R=Y L-A-N-D. Los Gatos: 1885. V. 40; 45

WALKER, W. W.

First Report of the President and Directors of the Cedar Rapids and Missouri River Rail Road (bound with) A Communication of the Board of Directors of the Galena and Chicago Union Rail Road Company . . . Relative to the Cedar Rapids & Missouri R.R . . . Chicago: 1860. V. 37; 38; 42

WALKER, WILLIAM 1623-1684

A Dictionary of English and Latin Idioms, Comprehending Whatsoever is Necessary and Most Useful in All Other Phraseological Books. London: 1712. V. 41

La Guerra de Nicaragua en 1860. Managua: 1884. V. 41

The Law of Cattle Plague in Scotland . . . for the Use of Justices, Inspectors, Farmers, Cattle-Salesmen and Others. Edinburgh: 1866. V. 45

A Treatise on English Particles. London: 1663. V. 38

A Treatise of English Particles: Shewing Much of the Variety of Their Significations and Uses in English . . . London: 1668. V. 39

A Treatise of English Particles, Shewing Much of the Variety of Their Significations and Uses in English . . . London: 1679. V. 46

A Treatise of English Particles. Shewing Much of the Variety of Their Significations and Uses in English . . . London: 1683. V. 41

The War in Nicaragua. Mobile: 1860. V. 37; 38; 45; 46

The War in Nicaragua. New York: 1860. V. 39

WALKER, WILLIAM CAREY

History of the Eighteenth Regiment Connecticut Volunteers in the War for the Union. Norwich: 1885. V. 42

WALKER, WILLIAM SIDNEY

Gustavus Vasa, and Other Poems. London: 1813. V. 42

WALKINGAME, FRANCIS

The Tutor's Assistant; Being a Compendium of Arithmetic and a Complete Question Book. Birmingham: 1797. V. 45

WALKINSHAW, LEWIS C.

Annals of Southwestern Pennsylvania. New York: 1939. V. 41; 42

WALKLEY, THOMAS

A New Catalogue of the Dukes, Marquesses, Earls, Viscounts . . . also the Baronets . . . the Knights . . . with the Dates and Places Where They Were Knighted. London: 1658. V. 39

WALKOWITZ, ABRAHAM

Improvisations of New York: A Symphony of Line. Girard, Kansas: 1948. V. 37

WALL, BARING

Lecture Delivered Before the Literary and Scientific Society of Salisbury. January, 1853. V. 38

WALL, BERNHARDT

Bits from Wall's Etched Books. N.P.: 1932. V. 45

Following General Sam Houston 1793-1863. Limerock: 1935. V. 39; 40; 45

General Robert E. Lee. Sierra Madre: 1949. V. 37; 43

Greenwich Village. Types Tenements & Temples. N.P.: 1920's. V. 41

WALL, CHARLES BARING

Thoughts on Parliamentary Independence in a Letter Addressed to the Electors of Guilford. London: 1839. V. 39

WALL, E. G.

Handbook of the State of Mississippi. Jackson: 1882. V. 44

WALL, E. J.

The History of Three Colour Photography. Boston: 1925. V. 37; 42

WALL, GARRET D.

An Address to the Legislature of New Jersey ont he Subject of Internal Improvements. N.P.: 1835. V. 44

WALL, JOHN F.

Thoroughbred Bloodlines. An Elementary Study. Baltimore: 1935. V. 37

Thoroughbred Bloodlines. An Elementary Study. Columbia: 1946. V. 37

WALL, JOHN P.

The Chronicles of New Brunswick, New Jersey 1667-1931. New Brunswick: 1931. V. 44

History of Middlesex County, N.J. 1664-1920. V. 41

WALL, JOSEPH

The Trial of Joseph Wall, Esq. Late Governor of Goree, for the Wilful Murder of Benjamin Armstrong, A Sergeant of the African Corps at the Old Bailey, on Wed. Jan. 20, 1802. V. 43

WALL, MARTIN

Dissertations on Select Subjects in Chemistry and Medicine. Oxford: 1783. V. 37; 38

WALL, O. A.

Sex and Sex Worship. St. Louis: 1919. V. 43

WALL, OSCAR G.

Recollections of the Sioux Massacre an Authentic History . . . Lake City: 1908. V. 44

Recollections of the Sioux Massacre, an Authentic History . . . with a Historical Sketch of the Sibley expedition of 1863. Lake City: 1909. V. 38; 42

WALL-TEX Fabric Wall Covering, Columbus Coated Fabrics Corporation, Columbus, Ohio. 1936. V. 46

WALL, THOMAS 1504-1536

The Voyage of Sir Nicholas Carewe to the Emperor Charles V in the Year 1529. Cambridge: 1959. V. 38; 40; 46

WALL, WILLIAM 1647-1728

The History of Infant-Baptism in Two Parts . . . London: 1705. V. 42

The History of Infant-Baptism. London: 1707. V. 39

WALLACE, ALFRED RUSSEL 1823-1913

Australasia with Ethnological Appendix by A. H. Keane. London: 1884. V. 38; 45

Contributions to the Theory of Natural Selection. London: 1870. V. 37; 42

Darwinism, an Exposition of the Theory of Natural Selection with Some of Its Applications. London: 1889. V. 37; 38; 39; 40; 45

Darwinism an Exposition of the Theory of Natural Selection with Some of Its Applicants. London: 1890. V. 37; 44

The Geographical Distribution of Animals. London: 1876. V. 37; 38; 42; 43

The Geographical Distribution of Animals. New York: 1876. V. 46

Is Mars Habitable? London: 1907. V. 38; 44

Island Life; or, the Phenomena and Causes of Insular Faunas and Floras, Including a Revision and Attempted Solution of the Problem of Geological Climates. London. V. 46

Island Life. London: 1880. V. 37; 38; 40; 43; 46

Island Life or the Phenomena and Causes of Insular Faunas and Floras . . . London: 1892. V. 42

Island Life or The Phenomena and Causes of Insular Faunas and Floras . . . Second and Revised Edition. London;: 1895. V. 37

The Malay Archipelago. London: 1869. V. 39; 40; 42; 45; 46

The Malay Archipelago. New York: 1869. V. 43

The Malay Archipelago. London: 1886. V. 40; 43

My Life, a Record of Events and Opinions. London: 1905. V. 38

A Narrative of Travels on the Amazon and Rio Negro. London: 1853. V. 39; 43

Natural Selection and Tropical Nature, Essays Descriptive and Theoretical Biology. London: 1891. V. 37

Palm Trees of the Amazon and Their Uses. London: 1853. V. 43

Social Environment and Moral Progress. London: 1913. V. 42

Stanford's Australasia . . . London: 1879. V. 39

Stanford's Compendium of Geography and Travel. Australasia. London: 1893. V. 38

Studies Scientific and Social. London: 1900. V. 37

Travels on the Amazon and Rio Negro, with an Account of the Native Tribes and Observations on the Climate, Geology and Natural History of the Amazon Valley. London: 1889. V. 45

Tropical Nature and Other Essays. London: 1878. V. 42

WALLACE, ARTHUR

The Trial of Arthur Wallace, Assistant Deputy Post Master of Carlow, for Stealing Notes Out of the Post Bag and for Forgery. Dublin: 1800. V. 46

WALLER, CATHARINE

The Medley. New York: 1810. V. 40

WALLER, EDMOND

Poems, &c. Written Upon Several Occasions . . . London: 1664. V. 43

WALLER, EDMUND

A Farther Vindication of the Case of the Hanover Troops. London: 1743. V. 41

Instructions (in verse) To a Painter, for the Drawing of the Posture & Progress of his Maties Forces at Sea, under the Command of His Highness Royal. Together with the Battel & Victory obtained over the Dutch, June 3, 1665. London: 1666. V. 37

The Maid's Tragedy Altered. London: 1690. V. 37

Poems &c. London: 1645. V. 37; 39

Poems, &c. Written Upon Several Occasions, and to Several Persons . . . London: 1686. V. 44

Poems, &c. Written Upon Several Occasions, and to Several Persons . . . (with) The Second Part of Mr. Waller's Poems. London: 1690. V. 46

Poems, &c. Written Upon Several Occasions, and to Several Persons . . . (with) The Second Part of Mr. Waller's Poems . . . London: for H. Herringman,: 1690. V. 39

Poems, &c Written Upon Several Occasions, and to Several Persons. London: 1693. V. 42

Poems &c. London: 1705. V. 46

Poems &c . . . . London: 1711. V. 39

Poems &c. Written Upon Several Occasions, and to Several Persons. London: 1682. V. 37

The Second Part of Mr. Waller's Poems. London: 1690. V. 37; 38; 45

Songs and Verses Selected from the Works. London: 1902. V. 40

Songs and Verse Selected from the Works of Edmund Waller. South Harting: 1902. V. 38; 44

Songs and Verses Selected from the Works of Edmund Waller. Sussex: 1902. V. 41; 45

Songs and Verses: Selected from the Works of . . . Shaftesbury: 1926. V. 39

The Works in Verse and Prose. London: 1729. V. 40; 44; 45

The Works.. London: 1730. V. 38; 41; 45; 46

The Works, in Verse and prose. London: 1758. V. 39

WALLER, ERIK

Bibliotheca Walleriana. The Books Illustrating the History of Medicine and Science. Collected by Dr. Erik Waller . . . Stockholm: 1955. V. 40

WALLER, J. F.

The Imperial Dictionary of Universal Biography. London: 1880. V. 39

WALLER, JOHN AUGUSTINUS

A Voyage in the West Indies. London: 1820. V. 39

WALLER, PICKFORD

Pickford Waller's Bookplates. London: 1922. V. 38

WALLER, WILLIAM

Divine Meditations Upon Several Occasions: with a Dayly Directory. London: 1680. V. 40

WALLEYS, THOMAS d. 1350

Divi Thomae Aqvinatis, In Beati Ioannis Apocalipsim Expositio, Nunc Primum e Tenebris Eruta. Florence: 1549. V. 40

WALLIHAN, A. G.

Hoofs, Claws and Antlers of the Rocky Mountains, By the Camera. Photographic Reproductions of Wild Game from Life. Denver: 1894. V. 38; 39

Hoofs, Claws & Antlers of the Rocky Mountains. Denver: 1902. V. 37

WALLIHAN, S. S.

The Rocky Mountain Directory and Colorado Gazetteer, for 1871 . . . with a complete and accurate Directory of Denver, Golden City, Black Hawk, Central City, Nevada, Idaho, Georgetown, Boulder, Greeley, Colorado City . . . Denver: (1870). V. 37; 44; 46

WALLING, EDNA

Cottage and Garden in Australia. Melbourne: 1947. V. 40

WALLING, HENRY FRANCIS

Atlas of the State of Michigan. Detroit: 1873. V. 41

Atlas of the Dominion of Canada. Montreal, Toronto & London: 1875. V. 37

Tackabury's Atlas of the Dominion of Canada. Montreal: 1875. V. 44

Tackabury's Atlas of the Dominion of Canada. Montreal: 1876. V. 42

Tackabury's Atlas of the Dominion of Canada. Montreal, Toronto & London: 1876. V. 41

WALLIS, E.

A New and Fashionable Mosaic Puzzle, Forming a Variety of Elegant Devices . . . London: and Sidmouth: 1830. V. 45

Two Letters to Mr. John Parkinson of Asgarby (Lincolnshire), Commissioner of Inclosures and Land-Valuer . . . London: 1795. V. 42

WALLIS, FRANK E.

The Georgian Period Being Measured Drawings of Colonial Work. N.P.: 1898. V. 46

WALLIS, GEORGE

The Art of Preventing Diseases and Restoring Health. London: 1793. V. 37; 38; 39; 40; 41; 44; 45; 46

The Art of Preventing Diseases and Restoring Health. New York: 1794. V. 39

WALLIS, H. M.

Bird Bolts Being Fugitive Papers, Poems, Articles and Lectures on Many Subjects 1890-1906. London: 1907. V. 45

WALLIS, HENRY

Eyyptian Ceramic Art: The MacGregor Collection. A contribution towards the history of Egyptian pottery, with illustrations by the author. London: 1898. V. 37; 44

WALLIS, JAMES

New Pocket Edition of the English Counties or Travellers Companion. London: 1810. V. 41

WALLIS, JOHANNEM

Institutio Logicae. Oxford: 1687. V. 43; 45

WALLIS, JOHN

The Beauties of Sidmouth Displayed. Sidmouth: 1810. V. 37; 40

A Brief Letter from a Young Oxonian to One of His Late Fellow-Pupils Upon the Subject of Magnetism. London: 1697. V. 41

Cono-Cuneus: or, The Shipwright's Circular Wedge. London: 1684. V. 40

The Doctrine of the Blessed Trinty Briefly Explained in a Letter to a Friend. London: 1690. V. 38

Grammatica Linguae Anglicanae. London: 1765. V. 38; 40; 43; 45

Grammatica Linguae Anglicanae. Cui praefigitur De Loquela . . . Editio Tertia, Prioribus Auctior. Hamburgi: 1672. V. 37

Institutio Logicae, Ad Communes Usus Accommodata. Oxford: 1715. V. 45

Institution Logicae, ad Communes Usus Accomodata. Oxford: 1687. V. 41

The Natural History and Antiquities of Northumberland . . . London: 1769. V. 37; 43

Opera Mathematica. Oxford: 1972. V. 39

Operum Mathematicorum Pars Prima (-Paras Altera) . . . Oxford: 1657, 1656. V. 38

WALLIS, JONNIE LOCKHART

Sixty Years on the Brazos: the Life and Letters of Dr. John Washington Lockhart. Los Angeles: 1930. V. 39

WALLIS, MARY DAVIS

Life in Feejee, or, Five Years Among the Cannibals. Boston: 1851. V. 37; 40

WALLIS, N.

The Carpenter's Treasure . . . London. V. 44

WALLIS, SEVERN TEACKLE

Reply of S. Teackle Wallis, Esq. to the Letter of Hon. John Sherman. Richmond?: 1863. V. 44

WALLIS, TALBOT H.

Catalogue of the California State Library. Law Department. Sacramento: 1886. V. 37

WALLIS, TAYLER, A. J.

Modern Cycles: a Practical Handbook on Their Construction and Repair. London: 1897. V. 45

WALLOP, DOUGLAS

The Year the Yankees Lost the Pennant. New York: 1954. V. 37; 45

WALLWORK, JAMES

The Modern Angler; Comprising Angling In All Its Branches. Manchester: 1847. V. 39

WALMSEY, EDWARD

Physiognomical Portraits. London: 1822-24. V. 38; 44

WALN, ROBERT

The Hermit in America on a Visit to Philadelphia. Philadelphia: 1819. V. 38; 43

The Hermit in America on a Visit to Philadelphia, Containing Some Account of the Beaux and Belles, Dandies and Coquettes, Cotillion Parties, Supper Parties, Tea Parties &c &c . . . (with) The Hermit in Philadelphia. Second Series. Philadelphia: 1819-1821. V. 41

The Hermit in America on a Visit to Philadelphia, Containing Some Account of the Beaux and Belles, dandies and Coquettes, Cotillion Parties, Supper Parties, Tea P. V. 41

WALPH, C. C.

Early Days on the Western Range. Boston: 1917. V. 44

WALPOLE-BOND, JOHN

A History of Sussex Birds. London: 1938. V. 37; 39; 41; 42; 43; 44; 46

WALPOLE, FREDERICK

The Ansayrii (or Assassins) with Travels in the Further East in 1840-51, including a Visit to Nineveh. London: 1851. V. 37; 41

Four Years in the Pacific. London: 1849. V. 38

Four Years in the Pacific in Her Majesty's Ship 'Collingwood' from 1844 to 1848. London: 1850. V. 46

WALPOLE, HORACE 1719-1797

Aedes Walpolianae; or, a Description of the Collection of Pictures at Houghton Hall in Nofolk. London: 1752. V. 41; 46

Aedes Walponianae. London: 1767. V. 40; 42; 43

Anecdotes of Painting in England. 1762. V. 40

Anecdotes of Painting in England . . . 1762-61. V. 45

Anecdotes of Painting in England. 1762-71. V. 38

Anecdotes of Painting in England. (with) A Catalogue of Engravers, Who Have Been Born, or Resided in England . . . Strawberry Hill: 1762-71/1763. V. 42

Anecdotes of Painting in England. 1762-73. V. 38

Anecdotes of Painting in England. 1765-71. V. 38

Anecdotes of Painting in England. London: 1782. V. 38

Anecdotes of Painting in England. London: 1786. V. 38; 39

Anecdotes of Painting in England. (and) A Catalog of Engravers Who Have Been Born or Resided in England . . . London: 1820-1828. V. 40

Anecdotes of Painting in England. London: 1826. V. 37

Anecdotes of Painting in England. London: 1828. V. 37; 38; 39; 40

Anecdotes of Painting in England. London: 1849. V. 41

Anecdotes of Painting in England. London: 1862. V. 39; 40

Anecdotes of Painting in England. London: 1888. V. 42

Anecdotes of Painting in England. London: 1826-28. V. 38

Anecdotes of Paintings in England. Strawberry Hill,: 1762-71, 1763. V. 38

The Beauties. London: 1746. V. 38; 41; 45

The Castle of Otranto. London: 1765. V. 38; 42; 43; 46

The Castle of Otranto. London: 1765-64. V. 45; 46

The Castle of Otranto, a Gothic Story. London: 1766. V. 45

The Castle of Otranto. London: 1769. V. 41

The Castle of Otranto. London: 1782. V. 43

The Castle of Otranto. Parma: 1791. V. 38; 39; 40; 41; 45; 46

Jeffery's Edition of the Castle of Otranto. London: 1796. V. 37; 44

The Castle of Otranto. Dublin: 1800. V. 38

Jeffrey's Edition of the Castle of Otranto, a Gothic Story. London: 1800. V. 37; 42

The Castle of Otranto and the Mysterious Mother. Boston: 1925. V. 43

The Castle of Otranto. Westerham: 1975. V. 46

A Catalogue of the Royal and Noble Authors of England . . . 1758. V. 41

A Catalogue of the Royal and Noble Authors of England. London: 1759. V. 37; 38; 39; 41; 43; 45

A Catalogue of the Royal and Noble Authors of England. London: 1759, 1758. V. 41; 45

A Catalogue of the Royal and Nobel Authors of England, Scotland and Ireland; with a List of Their Works. London: 1806. V. 38; 39; 42; 44; 46

Catalogue of the Royal and Noble Authors of England, Scotland and Ireland, With Lists of Their Works. London: 1807. V. 38; 43

A Catalogue of the Classic Contents of Strawberry Hill. London: 1842. V. 40; 44

A Catalogue of the Classic Contents of Strawberry Hill collected by Horace Walpole. London: 1842. V. 46

The (Collected) Letters. London: 1880. V. 46

A Description of the Villa of Mr. Horace Walpole, Youngest Son of Sir Robert Walpole Earl of Orford, at Strawberry-Hill Near Twickenham, Middlesex. Strawberry Hill: 1784. V. 37; 42

Essay on Modern Gardening . . . 1785. V. 40

Essay on Modern Gardening. (with) Essai sur l'Art des Jardins Modernes . . . Imprime a Strawberry Hill: 1785. V. 42

Essay on Modern Gardening. Strawberry Hill: 1785. V. 37; 40; 44; 45

Four Letters Publish'd in Old England; or, the Constitutional Journal. London: 1743. V. 41

Fugitive Pieces in Verse and Prose. Strawberry Hill: 1758. V. 43

Fugitive Pieces in Verse and Prose. 1768. V. 38

Fugitive Pieces in Verse and Prose. Strawberry Hill: 1768. V. 37

Gratulatio Academiae Cantabrigiensis Auspicatissimas Frederici Walliae Principis et Augustae Principissae Saxo-Gothae Nuptias Celbrantis. Cantabrigiae: 1736. V. 44

Head in Green Bronze and Other Stories. London: 1938. V. 45

Hieroglyphic Tales. London: 1926. V. 45

Hieroglyphic Tales. London. Montagnola: 1926. V. 40

Hieroglyphic Tales. Montagnola: 1926. V. 41

Historic Doubts On the Life and Reign of King Richard III. Dublin: 1768. V. 38; 46

Historic Doubts on the Life and Reign of King Richard the Third. London: 1768. V. 37; 41; 44; 45; 46

Horace Walpole's Letters to the Countess of Ossory. London: 1903. V. 41

Journal of the Printing-Office at Strawberry Hill. 1923. V. 44

Journal of the Printing-Office at Strawberry Hill. 1923. V. 41

Journal of Printing-Office at Strawberry Hill. London: 1923. V. 37; 39; 43; 44

Journal of the Printing Office at Strawberry Hill, Now Printed from the Ms. of Horace Walpole. N.P.: 1923. V. 40

A Letter to the Editor of the Miscellanies of Thomas Chatterton. Strawberry Hill: 1779. V. 38; 40; 41; 42

Letters . . . , to George Montague, Esq. from the Year 1736 to the Year 1770. London: 1818. V. 37; 39; 41

Letters to Sir Horace Mann, Published from the Originals in the Possession of the Earl of Waldegrave. London: 1833. V. 40

Letters of Horace Walpole Earl of Oxford to Sir Horace Man. New York: 1833. V. 37; 41; 43; 44

Letters of Horace Walpole to Sir Horace mann. London: 1843. V. 40; 41; 43; 44

The Letters of Horace Walpole, Earl of Oxford . . . (with) Letters to Sir Horace Mann . . . London: 1843-44. V. 46

Letters, Including Numerous Letters now First Published from the Original Manuscripts. London: 1846. V. 37

The Letters. London: 1857. V. 38; 42

The Letters. London: 1857-59. V. 38; 42

The Letters of . . . London: 1861-66. V. 44

Horace Walpole's Letters to the Countess of Ossory. London: 1903. V. 42; 44

The Letters. Oxford: 1903. V. 42

The Letters. Oxford: 1903-25. V. 38; 39; 40

The Letters. Edinburgh: 1906. V. 37; 38; 46

Letters Addressed to the Countess of Ossory, from the Year 1769 to 1797. London: 1848. V. 39

The Letters of Horace Walpole, Earl of Orford. London: 1840. V. 39

The Magpie and Her Brood, a Fable, from the Tales of Bonaventure des Periers . . . Strawberry Hill Press: 1764. V. 40; 42

Memoires of the Last Ten Years of the Reign of George the Second. London: 1822. V. 45

Memoirs of the Reign of King George the Second. London: 1846. V. 37; 40

Memoirs of the Reign of King George the Third. London: 1851. V. 37; 40

Memoirs of the Reign of King George the Third. London: 1894. V. 39

Memoirs of the Reign of George the Third. London: 1845. V. 38

Memoirs of the Reign of King George the Second. London: 1847. V. 38

Memoires of the Last Ten Years of the Reign of George the Second. London: 1822. V. 38; 41; 42; 45

Miscellaneous Antiquites . . . Strawberry Hill: 1772. V. 37; 38; 40; 41; 42; 45; 46

The Mysterious Mother. Strawberry Hill: 1768. V. 43

The Mysterious Mother. Dublin: 1791. V. 38; 41; 44

A Notebook of Horace Walpole. New York: 1927. V. 40; 43

On Modern Gardening; an Essay. 1987. V. 45

On Modern Gardening: an Essay. 1987. V. 40

Private Correspondence of Horace Walpole, Earl of Orford. London: 1820. V. 37; 46

Reminiscences, Written in MDCCLXXXVIII, for the Amusement of Miss Mary and Miss Agnes Berry. London: 1805. V. 42

Reminiscences Written in 1788 for the Amusement of Miss Mary and Miss Agnes Berry. Oxford: 1924. V. 40

A Second and Third Letter to the Whigs. London: 1748. V. 38

Three Letters to the Whigs. Occasion'd by the Letter to the Tories. London: 1748. V. 41

Walpoliana. London: 1799. V. 38

The Works. London: 1789. V. 38

Works. London: 1798. V. 37; 38; 42; 43; 46

The Works of Horatio Walpole, Earl of Oxford. (with) Letters from the Honorable Horace Walpole. London: 1798/1818. V. 38; 41

The Works. London: 1977. V. 39

WALPOLE, HORATIO WALPOLE, BARON 1678-1757

An Answer to the Latter Part of Lord Bolingbrooke's Letter on the Study of History. In a Series of letters to a Nobel Lord. Part I and II. (all published). London: 1762. V. 37; 40; 42; 44; 45

The Complaints of the Manufacturers, Relating to the Abuses in Marking the Sheep and Winding the Wool, Fairly Stated and Impartially Considered in a Letter to the Marquis of Rockingham. London: 1752. V. 46

The Convention Vindicated from the Misrepresentations of the Eneimies of Our Peace. London: 1739. V. 37; 39; 41; 42; 45

The Interest of Great Britain Steadily Pursued. London: 1743. V. 41; 42

WALPOLE, HUGH

Anthony Trollope. London: 1928. V. 38

WALPOLE, HUGH continued

The Apple Trees; Four Reminiscences. 1932. V. 42

The Apple Trees. London: 1932. V. 40; 41

The Apple Trees: Four Reminiscences. Waltham St. Lawrence: 1932. V. 44; 46

The Herries Chronicles. London: 1930-33. V. 44

The Joyful Delaneys. London: 1938. V. 44

The Old Ladies. London: 1924. V. 38; 40

The Silver Thorn. A Book of Stories. London: 1928. V. 38

The Wooden Horse. London: 1909. V. 39

WALPOLE, ROBERT

A Letter from a Member of Parliament to His Friends in the Country Concerning the Duties on Wine and Tobacco. London: 1733. V. 38; 40; 41; 45

Memoirs Relating to European and Asiatic Turkey, and Other Countries of the East. London: 1818. V. 37; 39

Mr. Walpole's Case, in a Letter from a Tory Member of Parliament to His Friend in the Country. London: 1712. V. 41

Obervations Upon the Treaty Between the Crowns of Great Britain, France and Spain, Concluded at Seville on the Ninth of November 1729. London: 1729. V. 41; 44

A Report from the Committee of Secrecy, Appointed by Order of the House of Commons to Examine Several Books and Papers . . . Relating to the Late Negotiations of Peace and Commerce. London: 1715. V. 45

A Short History of the Parliament . . . London: 1713. V. 45

WALPOLE SOCIETY

The Walpole Society Notebooks, 1926-1972. Topsfield: 1926-72. V. 42

The Walpole Society Notebooks, 1926-1972. Topsfield and Portland: 1926-72. V. 44

WALPOLE, WILLIAM RAY

Sophia, or the Girl of the Pine Woods; and the Golden Eagle. Paterson: 1834. V. 38

WALRAS, LEON

Etudes d'Economie Plitique Appliquee. Lausanne: 1898. V. 43

Etudes d'Economie Sociale. Lausanne: 1896. V. 43

WALSDORF, JOHN J.

William Morris in Private Press and Limited Editions. A Descriptive Bibliography of Books by and About William Morris 1891-1981. Phoenix: 1983. V. 40

WALSH, C. C.

Early Days on the Western Range. A Pastoral Narrative. Boston: 1917. V. 39; 45

WALSH, GEORGE

Contemporary Photographers. New York: 1982. V. 41

WALSH, J. H.

The Dogs of the British Islands, Being a Series of Articles and Letters by Various Contributors . . . London: 1872. V. 46

Every Horse Owners' (sic) Cyclopedia. Philadelphia: 1871. V. 46

The Greyhound. London: 1875. V. 46

The Modern Sportsman's Gun and Rifle; Including Game and Wilfowl Guns, Sporting and Match Rifles, and Revolvers. London: 1882. V. 39

The Shot-Gun and Sporting Rifle; and the Dogs, Ponies, Ferrets &c. Used with Them.. London: 1859. V. 37; 38; 46

The Shot-Gun and Sporting Rifle and the Dogs, Ponies, Ferrets &c. Used with Them in the Various Kinds of Shooting and Trapping. London: 1862. V. 46

WALSH, JAMES J.

History of Medicine in New York. New York: 1919. V. 38; 39

WALSH, LANGTON PRENDERGAST

Under the Flag and Somali Coast STories. London: 1912. V. 43

WALSH, PETER

A Prospect of the State of Ireland, from the Year of the World 1756. London: 1682. V. 42; 44

WALSH, ROBERT 1784-1859

The American Review of History and Politics. Philadelphia: 1811-12. V. 39

The American Register; or Summary Review of History, Politics and Literature. Philadelphia: 1817. V. 42

An Appeal from the Judgements of Great Britain Repsecting the United States of America. London: 1820. V. 42; 43; 46

The Jackson Wreath, or National Souvenir . . . Philadelphia: 1829. V. 39

A Letter on the Genius and Dispositions of the French Government Including a View of the Taxation of the French Empire. Baltimore: 1810. V. 41

A Letter on the Genius and Dispositions of the French Government . . . London: 1810. V. 40; 44

A Letter on the Genius and Dispositions of the French Government, Including a View of the Taxation of the French Empire. Philadelphia: 1810. V. 38

Narrative of a Journey from Constantinople to England. London: 1828. V. 37; 39; 45

Narrative of a Journey from Constainople to England. London: 1829. V. 45

WALSH, THEOBALD

George Sand. Paris: 1837. V. 41

WALSH, THOMAS

History of the Irish Hierarchy, with the Monasteries of Each County, Biographical Notes of Irish Stains, Prelates and Religious . . . New York: 1854. V. 39; 46

Journal of the Late Campaign in Egypt. London: 1803. V. 38; 41

WALSH, WILLIAM

A Dialogue Concerning Woman Being a Defence of Sex, Written to Eugenia. London: 1691. V. 37; 38; 44

A Funeral Elegy Upon the Death of the Queen. London: 1695. V. 38; 40; 41; 44; 45; 46

Ode for the Thanksgiving Day. London: 1706. V. 37; 45

Ode for the Thanksgiving Day. London: 1706, 1707? V. 40

WALSHE, WALTER

A Practical Treatise on the Diseases of the heart and Great Vessels, Including the Principles of Physical Diagnosis. Philadelphia: 1862. V. 42

WALSHE, WALTER HAYLE

The Anatomy, Physiology, Pathology and Treatment of Cancer. Boston: 1844. V. 38

WALSINGHAM, THOMAS

Historia Brevis . . . ad Henricum Quintum. (and) Ypodigma Neustriae. (and) Aelfridi Regis Res Gestae. London: 1574. V. 37

WALT Whitman's Workshop. Cambridge: 1928. V. 45

WALTER Browning; or, the Slave's Protector. Cincinnati: 1856. V. 45

WALTER, F. K.

Jesuit Relations and Other Americana in the Library of James F. Bell. Minneapolis: 1905. V. 41

Jesuit Relations and Other Americana in the Library of James F. Bell. Minneapolis: 1950. V. 40

WALTER, JOHANN GOTTLIEB

De Morbis Peritonaei et Apoplexia. (German title) Von den Krankheiten des Bauchfells und dem Schlagluss . . . Berlin: 1785. V. 43

WALTER, JOHN

First Impressions of America. London: 1867. V. 42

A Letter Addressed in 1834 to the Electors of Berkshire on the New System of Management of the Poor . . . Opinions Respecting the New Poor Law, Expressed Out of Parliament. London: 1839, 1841. V. 38

WALTER, L. EDNA

Spring Flowers. London: 1915. V. 42

WALTER OF COVENTRY

Memoriale Fratris Walteri de Coventria. The Historical Collections of Walter of Coventry. London: 1872-73. V. 44

WALTER, RICHARD 1716?-1785

Anson's Voyage Round the World. Boston: 1928. V. 44

A Voyage Round the World, in the Years MDCCXL, I, II, III, IV. London: 1748. V. 39; 40; 41; 43; 44; 45; 46

A Voyage Round the World in the Years MDCCXL, I, II, III, IV. By George Anson. London: 1749. V. 39

A Voyage Round the World in the Years MDCCXL, I, II, III, IV. London: 1756. V. 41

A Voyage Round the World in the Years MDCCXL, I, II, III, IV. London: 1776. V. 41; 42; 43

A Voyage Round the World in the Years 1740, 1741, 1742, 1743, 1744. Edinburgh: 1781. V. 39

WALTER, WEAVER

Letters from the Continent . . . Edinburgh: 1828. V. 43

WALTER, WILLIAM W.

The Great Understander True Life Story of the Last of the Wells Fargo Shotgun Express Messengers. Aurora: 1931. V. 37; 40

WALTERS ART GALLERY, BALTIMORE.

The History of Bookbinding 525-1950; an Exhibition Held at the Baltimore Museum of Art, November 12, 1957 to January 12, 1958. Baltimore: 1957. V. 41

WALTERS, EUROF

The Serpent's Presence. London: 1954. V. 40

WALTERS, H. B.

Catalogu of the Greek and Roman Lamps in the British Museum. London: 1914. V. 37; 42; 43

Catalogue of the Terracottas in the Department of Greek and Roman Antiquities, British Museum. London: 1903. V. 42

Catalogue of the Engraved Gems and Cameos . . . London: 1926. V. 44

Catalogue of the Silver Plate (Greek, Etruscan and Roman) in the British Museum. London: 1921. V. 37; 44

Catalogue of the Terracottas in the Department of Greek and Roman Antiquities, British Museum. London: 1903. V. 44

Church Bells of England. 1912. V. 44

History of Ancient Pottery: Greek, Etruscan and Roman . . . London: 1905. V. 44

Select Bronzes, Greek, Roman and Etruscan, in the Department of Antiquities. London: 1915. V. 44

WALTERS, HENRY

Incunabula Typographica. Baltimore: 1906. V. 38; 42; 43; 45

WALTERS, JOHN

An English and Welsh Dictionary . . . to Which is Subjointed a Dissertation on the Welsh Language . . . Denbigh: 1828. V. 40

WALTERS, L. D. O.

The Year's at the Spring. London: 1920. V. 40; 41; 42; 46

WALTERS, LORENZO D.

Tombstone's Yesterday. Tucson: 1928. V. 39; 41; 44

WALTERS, S. M.

The European Garden Flora. Volumes 1 and 2, Monocotyledons. Cambridge: 1984-86. V. 37; 38

WALTERS, W. T.

Oriental Ceramic Art: Collection of W. T. Walters. New York: 1899. V. 41

WALTHEN, JAMES

Journal of a Voyage in 1811 and 1812 to Madras and China . . . London: 1814. V. 46

WALTHER, JOANNES LUDOLF

Lexicon Diplomaticum Abbreviationes in Diplomatibus et Codicibus Seculo VIII ad SVI usque Occurentes Exponens. Ulm: 1756. V. 38; 45

WALTON, AUGUSTUS O.

A History of the Detection, Conviction, Life and Designs of John A. Murel, the Great Western Land Pirate; Together with His System of Villany, and Plan of Exciting a Negro Rebellion. Cincinnati: 1840's. V. 39

WALTON, AUGUSTUS Q.

A History of the Detection, Conviction, Life and Designs of John A Murel (sic) The Great Western Land Pirate . . . Cincinnati. V. 40

A History of the Detection, Conviction, Life and designs of John A. Murel, The Great Western Land Pirate! New York: 1839. V. 38

WALTON, ELIJAH

The Bernese Oberland, Twelve Scenes Among Its Peaks and Lakes. London: 1874. V. 39

Clouds: Their Forms and Combinations. London: 1869. V. 37

English Lake Scenery. London: 1876. V. 43

Peaks and Valleys of the Alps. London: 1867. V. 43

Welsh Scenery. London: 1875. V. 43

WALTON, EVANGELINE

The Virgin and the Swine. 1936. V. 43

The Virgin and the Swine: Fourth Branch of the Mabinogi. Chicago: 1936. V. 39

WALTON, H. HAYNES

A Treatise on the Surgical Diseases of the Eye. London: 1861. V. 44

WALTON, IZAAC 1593-1683

The Complete Angler. London: 1808. V. 38

The Complete Angler: Or The Contemplative Man's Recreation. With copious notes for the most part original, a bibliographical preface, giving an account of fishing and fishing books. With a note on Cotton . . . New York/London: 1847. V. 37

WALTON, IZAAK 1593-1683

The Compleat Angler. London. V. 40

The Complete Angler . . . London. V. 45

The Compleat Angler. Philadelphia. V. 37

The Compleat Angler. London: 1661. V. 39

The Life of Mr. Rich. Hooker. London: 1665. V. 37

The Complete Angler. London: 1668. V. 40; 42; 43

The Complete Angler. London: 1676. V. 40

The Compleat Angler. London: 1750. V. 37; 39; 43; 44; 45

The Complete Angler. London: 1760. V. 39; 42

The Complete Angler . . . London: 1766. V. 45

The Compleat Angler. London: 1772. V. 38

The Complete Angler. London: 1775. V. 38; 42; 44; 45

The Complete Angler. London: 1784. V. 39; 41

The Complete Angler . . . London: 1792. V. 37; 41

The Complete Angler. London: 1797. V. 37; 45

The Complete Angler. London: 1808. V. 37; 38; 39; 43; 46

The Compleat Angler; or, the Contemplative Man's Recreation. London: 1810. V. 39; 46

The Complete Angler. London: 1815. V. 39; 42

The Complete Angler . . . with The Lives of the Authors . . . London: 1822. V. 39

The Complete Angler. London: 1823. V. 40

The Complete Angler . . . with The Lives of Dr. John Donne, Sir Henry Wooton, Mr. Richard Hooker, Mr. George Herbert and Dr. Robert Sanderson. London: 1823-1825. V. 39

The Complete Angler. 1824. V. 37

The Complete Angler. Chiswick: 1824. V. 39

The Complete Angler. London: 1824. V. 39; 45; 46

The Complete Angler. London: 1825. V. 39; 41; 44; 46

The Complete Angler. Chiswick: 1826. V. 39

The Complete Angler. London: 1826. V. 38

The Complete Angler. London: 1826-27. V. 41

The Complete Angler. London: 1827. V. 39; 40

The Compleat Angler. London: 1835. V. 38; 39; 40; 44

The Compleat Angler, or the Contemplative Man's Recreation . . . 1836. V. 44

The Complete Angler. London: 1836. V. 39; 42; 46

The Complete Angler. London: 1837. V. 39

The Compleat Angler. London: 1844. V. 38; 46

The Complete Angler. New York: 1847. V. 39

The Complete Angler. New York: and London: 1847. V. 38; 39; 44; 45

The Complete Angler. New York: 1848. V. 44

The Complete Angler. New York: 1852. V. 44

The Complete Angler. London: 1854. V. 39

The Complete Angler or the Contemplative Man's Recreation . . . London: 1860. V. 41

The Complete Angler . . . London: 1861. V. 44

The Complete Angler. London: 1875. V. 40

The Complete Angler. London: 1876. V. 40

The Complete Angler; or, the Contemplative Man's Recreation. London: 1883. V. 44

The Complete Angler. London: 1885. V. 37; 43

The Compleat Angler. London: 1888. V. 39; 40; 43; 44; 45

The Compleat Angler. London: 1889. V. 40

The Complete Angler. Boston: 1892. V. 37; 39

The Complete Angler. London: 1893. V. 37; 39

The Complete Angler . . . London: 1896. V. 44

The Compleat Angler. London: 1897. V. 41

The Complete Angler. London: & New York: 1897. V. 41; 44

The Compleat Angler. 1905. V. 40

The Compleat Angler. Cambridge: 1909. V. 39; 45

The Compleat Angler. London: 1910. V. 44; 46

The Compleat Angler or the Contemplative Man's Recreation . . . London: 1911. V. 41

The Compleat Angler. The Lives of Donne, Wotton, Hooker, Herbert & Sanderson with Love and Truth and Miscellaneous Writings. London: 1925. V. 43; 45

The Complete Angler. London: 1926. V. 37

The Compleat Angler. London: 1927. V. 43

The Compleat Angler. Boston: 1928. V. 43; 46

The Compleat Angler. Bloomsbury: 1929. V. 37; 42; 43

The Compleat Angler. London: 1929. V. 37; 39; 40; 43; 44; 45

The Compleat Angler. London: 1930. V. 38; 40; 43

The Compleat Angler. London: 1931. V. 37; 38; 40; 41; 42; 44; 45; 46

The Compleat Angler. Philadelphia: 1931. V. 40

The Compleat Angler. New York: 1948. V. 39; 40; 44; 46

Extracts from the Compleat Angler. Oxford: 1988. V. 42

His Wallet Book. London: 1985. V. 41

Isaak Walton: His Wallet Book. London: 1885. V. 45

Izaak Walton's Life of George Herbert. Salisbury: 1988. V. 44

The Life of Mr. Rich. Hooker. London: 1665. V. 38; 44; 46

The Life of Dr. Sanderson, Late Bishop of Lincoln. London: 1678. V. 38; 41; 44; 45

The Lives of Dr. John Donne; Sir Henry Wotton; Mr. Richard Hooker; Mr. George Herbert; and Dr. Robert Sanderson. York: 1769. V. 38

WALTON, IZAAK 1593-1683 continued

The Lives of Dr. Donne; Sir Henry Wotton; Mr. Richard Hooker; Mr. George Herbert; and Dr. Robert Sanderson. York: 1796. V. 38; 39; 41; 43; 46

The Lives of Dr. John Donne, Sir Henry Wotton, Mr. Richard Hooker, Mr. George Herbert and Dr. Robert Sanderson. Oxford: 1824. V. 46

The Lives of Dr. John Donne, Sir Henry Wooton, Mr. Richard Hooker, Mr. George Herbert and Dr. Robert Sanderson . . . London: 1825. V. 39; 40; 41; 44; 45

The Lives . . . London: 1825. V. 45

The Lives of Dr. Donne, Sir Henry Wotton, Mr. Richard Hooker, Mr. George Herbert, Dr. Sanderson. London: 1847. V. 40

The Lives of Doctor John Donne, Sir Henry Wotton Knight, Mr. Richard Hooker, Mr. George Herbert and Doctor Robert Sanderson. New York: 1904. V. 43

The Lives of Dr. John Donne, Sir Henry Wootton, Mr. Richard Hooker, Mr. George Herbert and Dr. Robert Sanderson. The Autographs of These Eminent Men now first collected; An Index & Illustrative Notes. London: 1825. V. 37

The Universal Angler. London: 1676. V. 44; 45

Waltoniana: inedited Remains in Verse and Prose of Izaak Walton. London: 1878. V. 38

WALTON, JOHN

The Oxford Companion to Medicine. Oxford and New York: 1986. V. 45

WALTON, JOSEPH S.

Conrad Weiser and the Indian Policy of Colonial Pennsylvania. Philadlephia: 1900. V. 41; 42

WALTON, PAUL H.

The Drawings of John Ruskin. 1972. V. 46

WALTON, PETER

Creamware and other English Pottery at Temple Newsam House, Leeds. A Catalogue of the Leeds Collection. Bradfort/London: (1976). V. 37

WALTON, W. M.

Life and Adventures of Ben Thompson, the Famous Texan . . . by One Who Has Known Him since a child. Austin: 1884. V. 37

WALTON, WILLIAM

Army and Navy of the United States from the Period of the Revolution to the Present Day . . . Boston: 1889-1896. V. 45

The Army and Navy of the U.S. from the Period of the Revolution. Boston: 1889-95. V. 44

WALTON, WILLIAM A.

A Narrative of the Captivity and Sufferings of Benjamin Gilbert and His Family. Philadelphia. V. 41

A Narrative of the Captivity and Sufferings of Benjamin Gilbert and His Family. London: 1785. V. 41; 42

A Narrative of the Captivity and Sufferings of Benjamin Gilbert and His Family. Philadelphia printed: 1785. V. 38

A Narrative of the Captivity and Sufferings of Benjamin Gilbert and His Family. London: 1790. V. 40

A Narrative of the Captivity and Sufferings of Benjamin Gilbert and His Family . . . Philadelphia: 1790. V. 38

A Narrative of the Captivity and Sufferings of Benjamin Gilbert and His Family, Who Were Taken by the Indians in the Spring of 1780. Philadelphia: 1848. V. 38

A Narrative of the Captivity and Sufferings of Benjamin Gilbert and His Family. Philadelphia printed and: 1785. V. 37

WALTZ, NATHAN

A Specimen of Cubeo Indian Bark Cloth. Los Angeles: 1969. V. 38; 46

WALUM, OLUM

The Migration Legend of the Lenni Lenape or Delaware Indians. Indianapolis: 1954. V. 45

WALWORTH, REUBEN HYDE

Hyde Genealogy. Albany: 1864. V. 38

WAMPLER, JOSEPH CARSON

Tel en-Nasbeh Excavated Under the Direction of the Late William Frederic Bade. Berkeley and New Haven: 1947. V. 40

THE WANDERER. New York: 1821. V. 40

THE WANDERER: or, Memoirs of Charles Searle, Esq. Dublin: 1766. V. 46

THE WANDERER; or, Surprising Escape. Glasgow: 1752. V. 42

THE WANDERING Jew of Jerusalem's Chronicle; or, a Brief History of All the Kings and Queens of England, From William the Conqueror, to His Present Majesty's King George the Second. London: 1730-40? V. 42

WANDERINGS in the Land of Ham. By a Daughter of Japhet. London: 1858. V. 39; 45

WANDREI, DONALD

Dark Odyssey. St. Paul: 1931. V. 43; 45; 46

Ecstasy. Athol: 1928. V. 42; 43; 45; 46

The Eye and the Finger. 1944. V. 45

The Eye and the Finger. Sauk City: 1944. V. 40; 42; 43; 45

Poems for Midnight. With foru pen and ink drawings by Howard Wandrei. Sauk City: 1964. V. 37

The Web of Easter Island. Sauk City: 1948. V. 44; 45

WANG, HUI-MING

The Birds and the Animals. Northampton: 1969. V. 39

WANGERMEE, ROBERT

Flemish Music and Society in the Fifteenth and Sixteenth Centuries. New York: 1968. V. 39

WANKLYN, W. H. E.

The Australian Racehorse. Christchurch: 1949. V. 37

The Great Sire Lines. London: 1912. V. 37

WANLEY, NATHANIEL

The History of Man; or, the Wonders of Humane Nature, In Relation to the Virtues, Vices and Defects of Both Sexes. London: 1704. V. 41

The Wonders of the Little World; or, a General History of Man. London: 1678. V. 37; 41; 43

The Wonders of the Little World. London: 1774. V. 39

The Wonders of the Little World. London: 1806. V. 40; 46

WANN, PAULUS

Sermones de Tempore. Passau: 1491. V. 37

WANNAMAKER, J. SKOTTOWE

The Wannamaker, Salley, MacKay and Bellinger Families: Genealogies and Memoirs. Charleston: 1937. V. 42

WANSCHER, WILHELM

Raffaello Santi da Urbino: His Life and Works. London: 1926. V. 37

WANSEY, HENRY

An Excursion to the United States of America, in the Summer of 1794. Salisbury: 1798. V. 38; 42; 46

The Journal of an Excursion to the United States of North America, in the Summer of 1794 . . . Salisbury: 1796. V. 39; 40; 41; 42; 43

Wool Encouraged Without Exportation. London: 1791. V. 38; 42

WANSKAPS och Handels Tractat Emellan . . . Swerige och the Forente Staterne i Norra America . . . Traite d'Amitie et de Commerce entre . . . Suede et les Etats Unis de l'Amerique Septentrionale . . . Stockholm: 1785. V. 45

WANSLEBEN, JOHANN MICHAEL

The Present State of Egypt. London: 1678. V. 39

WANTLAND, C. E.

The Largest Suburban Tract in America. Salt Lake City: 1880's. V. 45

WANTRUP, JONATHAN

Australian Rare Books, 1788-1900. London: 1987. V. 38

Australian Rare Books, 1788-1900. Sydney: 1987. V. 40; 43

WAPLOCE, HORACE

Historic Doubts on the Life and Reign of King Richard III . . . Dublin: 1768. V. 44

WAR Horns, Make Room for the Bucks with Green Bowes. London: 1682. V. 46
THE WAR. New York: 1812-13. V. 37

WAR Against Peace: or, a New Attila. Contemporaneous Episodes of the Frontier of Texas. Rio Grande City: 1895. V. 39

WAR Horns, Make Room for the Bucks and Green Bowes. London: 1682. V. 40; 42

THE WAR of the Rebellion . . . Washington: 1880-1901. V. 45

WARBURDTON, G. D.

Hochelaga; or, England in the New World. London: 1846. V. 46

WARBURG, ADOLPH C.

Skizzer Fran Nord-merikanska Kriget 1861-1865. Stockholm: 1867. V. 38

WARBURG, OTTO HEINRICH 1883-1970

Heavy Metal Prosthetic Groups and Enzyme Action. Oxford: 1949. V. 42

WARBURG, PAUL M.

The Federal Reserve System, Its Origin and Growth. New York: 1930. V. 44

WARBURTON, A. B.

A History of Prince Edward Island. St. John: 1923. V. 44

WARBURTON, A. F.

Trial of the Officers and Crew of the Privateer Savannah on the Charge of Piracy. New York: 1862. V. 43; 45

WARBURTON, BARTHOLEMEW ELIOT

The Crescent and the Cross; or, Romance and Realities of Eastern Travel. London: 1845. V. 45

WARBURTON, EGERTON

Journey Across the Western Interior of Australia. London: 1875. V. 40

WARBURTON, ELIOT

Darien; or, the Merchant Prince. London: 1852. V. 43; 45

Hochelaga. London: 1846. V. 41; 44

Memoirs of Prince Rupert, and the Cavaliers. Including their private correspondence, now first published from the original manuscripts. By Eliot Warburton, author of 'The Crescent and the Cross.' In Three Volumes. London: 1849. V. 37

WARBURTON, GEORGE D.

The Conquest of Canada. By the Author of 'Hocholaga.' In Two Volumes. New York: 1850. V. 37

Hochelaga; or, England in the New World. Edited by Eliot Warburton . . . Fourth Edition, Revised. London: 1851. V. 37

WARBURTON, GEORGE DROUGH 1816-1857

Hochelaga. London: 1846. V. 37; 39

WARBURTON, GEORGE DROUGHT

The Conquest of Canada. London: 1850. V. 42

The Conquest of Canada. New York: 1850. V. 37; 42

WARBURTON, JOHN

History of the City of Dublin, from the Earliest Accounts to the Present Time. London: 1818. V. 38; 40

WARBURTON, PETER E.

Journey Across the Western Interior of Australia. London: 1875. V. 40

WARBURTON, R. E. EGERTON

Hunting Songs and Ballads. London: 1846. V. 38

Hunting Songs, Ballads, etc. Chester: 1834. V. 37; 39

Hunting Songs, Ballads, etc. Liverpool: 1912. V. 37

WARBURTON, ROBERT

Eighteen Years in the Khyber 1879-1898. London: 1900. V. 42

WARBURTON, THOMAS

The History of English Poetry, from the Close of the Eleventh to the Commencement of the Eighteenth Century. London: 1774-81. V. 38

WARBURTON, WILLIAM

A Critical and Philisophical Commentary on Mr. Pope's Essay on Man. London: 1742. V. 38; 42

Julian, or a Discourse Concerning the Earthquake and Firey Eruption Which Defeated the Emperor's Attempt to Rebuild the Temple at Jerusalem. London: 1751. V. 40

A Letter to the Editor of the Letters on the Spirit of Patriotism, the Idea of a Patriot-King, and the State of Parties, etc. London: 1749. V. 42

Letters from a Late Eminent Prelate to One of His Friends. London: 1809. V. 37; 40

Tracts by Warburton and a Warburtonian (i.e. Richard Hurd) not Admitted into the Collections of Their Respective Works. London: 1789. V. 38; 43

A View of Lord Bolingbroke's Philosophy. London: 1754-55. V. 41

The Works. London: 1978-80. V. 39

WARD, A. W.

The Cambridge History of English Literature. Cambridge: 1907. V. 46

The Cambridge History of English Literature. Cambridge: 1907-16. V. 46

The Cambridge History of English Literature. Cambridge: 1908-1916. V. 37

WARD, ADOLPHUS WILLIAM

Dickens. London: 1882. V. 43; 44

A History of English Dramatic Literature to the Death of Queen Anne. London: 1875. V. 42

WARD, AILEEN

John Keats. The Making of a Poet. London: 1963. V. 40

WARD And Lock's Book of Farm Management and Country Life. London: 1870-80. V. 38

WARD, BERNARD

The Eve of Catholic Emancipation. London: 1970. V. 41

WARD BROTHERS

Souvenir of El Paso, Texas & Paso del Norte, Mexico. Columbus, Ohio: 1887. V. 37

WARD, CATHERINE GEORGE

A Bachelor's Heiress. Lynn: 1814. V. 42; 44

Founded on Facts, the Orphan Boy, or, Test of Innocence. London: 1821. V. 40

The Rose of Claremont, or Daughter, Wife and Mother. London: 1821. V. 42; 45; 46

WARD, CHRISTOPHER

The Dutch and Swedes on the Delaware 1609-1664. Philadelphia: 1930. V. 41

The Triumph of the Nut and Other Parodies. New York: 1923. V. 37

WARD, CYRIL

Royal Gardens. London: 1912. V. 44

WARD, D. B.

Across the Plains in 1853. Seattle: 1911. V. 40

WARD, EDWARD 1667-1731

A Frolick to Horn-Fair. London: 1700. V. 38; 40; 42; 43

The History of the Grand Rebellion. London: 1713, 1715. V. 40

Hudibras Redivivus; or, a Burlesque Poem on the Times. London: 1705-1707. V. 37; 40; 44; 45

A Hue and Cry After a man Midwife, Who has Lately Deliver'd the Land-Bank of Their Money. Colophon: 1699. V. 40

The Island of Content. Or, a New Paradise Discover'd. In a Letter from Dr. Merryman of the same Country, to Dr. Dullman of Great Britain. By the Author of the Pleasures of a single Life. London: 1709. V. 39

The Merry Travellers: or, A Trip upon Ten-Toes, from Moorfields to Bromley. . . . . By the Author of the Cavalcade. London: 1724-22. V. 39; 40

Nuptial Dialogues and Debates . . . London: 1723. V. 42

Nuptial Dialogues and Debates; or, an Useful Prospect of the Felicities and Discomforts of Marry'd Life . . . London: 1710. V. 38; 43

Nuptial Dialogues and Debates; or, an Useful Prospect of the Felicities and Discomforts or a Marry'd Life, Incident to All Degrees, From the Throne to the Cottage. London: 1737. V. 41; 42

The Republican Procession. N.P.: 1714. V. 38

The Republican Procession; or, the Tumultuous Cavalcade. N.P.: 1714. V. 40

The Republican Procession: or, the Tumultuous Cavalcade. N.P.: 1714. V. 45

The Secret History of Clubs . . . London: 1709. V. 42; 43; 45

A Trip to Jamaica; with a True Character of the People and Island. Londod: (sic): 1700. V. 43; 46

A Vade Mecum for Malt-Worms. London: 1866. V. 37

The Vanity of Upstarts: or, an Honest Enquiry into Ignoble Greatness. An Ode. London: 1709. V. 39

Vulgus Britannicus; or, the British Hudibras. London: 1710. V. 40

The Whigs Unmask'd. London: 1713. V. 46

Wine and Wisdom. London: 1719? V. 38; 41

WARD, EMILY ELIZABETH SWINBURNE

Six Views of the Most Important Towns, and Mining Districts, Upon the Table Land of Mexico. London: 1829. V. 42

WARD, FRANCIS

An Account of Three Camp Meetings, Held by the Methodists, at Sharon in Litchfield County, Connecticut, at Rhinebeck, in Dutchess County and at Petersburgh in Rensselaer County, New York State. Brooklyn: 1806. V. 45

WARD, FREDERICK WILLIAM ORDE

Pessimus: A Rhapsody, and A Paradox. London: 1865. V. 37

WARD, GEORGE W.

History of the Second Pennsylvania Veteran Heavy Artillery (112th Regiment Pennsylvania Volunteers) from 1861 to 1866. Philadelphia: 1904. V. 42

WARD, H.

The Academic Reader. Whitehaven?: 1789. V. 46

WARD, H. G.

Mexico in 1827. London: 1828. V. 39

WARD, H. SNOWDEN

Photograms of the Year 1895, 1907 & 1909. London: 1909. V. 40

WARD, HARRY PARKER

Some American College Bookplates. Columbus: 1915. V. 38

WARD, HENRY DANA

Free Masonry: Its Pretension Exposed in Faithful Extracts of Its Standard Authors. New York: 1828. V. 46

WARD, HERBERT

L'Atelier de . . . Paris: 1900. V. 40

Five Years Among the Congo Cannibals. New York: 1890. V. 42; 43

Five Years with the Congo Cannibals. London: 1891. V. 45

Mr. Poilu. Notes and Sketches with the Fighting French. London: 1916. V. 46

WARD, HUMPHRY

Biographical and Critical Essay with a Cataloge Raisonne of His Works. London: 1904. V. 42; 44

A Biographical and Critical Essay with a Catalogue Raisonne of His Works. New York: 1904. V. 39

WARD, J.

Colour Harmony and Contrast. London: 1903. V. 46

Workmen and Wages at Home and Abroad or the Effects of STrikes, Combinations and Trades' Unions. London: 1868. V. 42; 46

WARD-JACKSON, PETER

English Furniture Designs of the Eighteenth Century. London: 1958. V. 44

WARD, JAMES

Perils, Pastimes and Pleasures of an Emigrant in Australia, Vancouver's Island and California. London: 1849. V. 41

WARD, JOHN

Diary of the Rev. John Ward, Vicar of Stratford-upon-Avon. Extending from 1648 to 1679. London: 1839. V. 39

New Zealand. Nelson, the Lastest Settlement of the New Zealand Company. London: 1842. V. 38; 43

The Sacred Beetle. London: 1902. V. 43; 44

Some Particulars Relating to the Somerset Hospital, at Foxfield in the County of Wilts, for Fifty Poor Widows. Marlborough: 1786. V. 45

The Young Mathematician's Guide. London: 1762. V. 40; 43

WARD, JOSEPH R. C.

History of the One-Hundred and Sixth Regiment Pennsylvania Volunteers 2nd Brigade, 2nd Divisions, 2nd Corps 1861-1865. Philadelphia: 1906. V. 46

WARD, JOSEPH R.C.

History of the 106th Pennsylvania Volunteers, 2nd Brigade, 2nd Division, 2nd Corps. 1861-1865. Philadelphia: 1883. V. 42

WARD, LESTER F.

Status of the Mesozoic Floras of the U.S. Washington: 1905. V. 44

WARD, LYND

The Biggest Bear. Boston: 1952. V. 39

God'd Man: Novel in Woodcuts. New York: (c. 1929). V. 37; 42

God's Man, A Novel in Woodcuts. New York: 1930. V. 37

Mad Man's Drum. London: 1930. V. 45

Mad Man's Drum: A Novel in Woodcuts. New York: 1930. V. 37; 39; 40; 43; 46

Song Without Words. New York: 1936. V. 37; 38; 43

Wild Pilgrimage. New York: 1932. V. 39; 40; 42; 43; 46

WARD, M. N.

Female Life Among the Mormons. London: 1855. V. 39

WARD, MARCUS 1807-1847

A Practical Treatise on the Art of Illuminating. London: 1873. V. 38

WARD, MARY AUGUSTA ARNOLD 1851-1920

Fenwick's Career by Mrs. Humphry Ward. London: 1906. V. 46

The History of David Grieve. London: 1892. V. 38; 41

Robert Elsmere. London: 1888. V. 37; 40; 41; 43; 45

Towards the Goal. London: 1917. V. 38

A World of Wonders Revealed by the Microscope. London: 1859. V. 38

The Writings of Mrs. Humphrey Ward. Boston: 1909. V. 44

The Writings. London: 1909-12. V. 38; 42

The Writings of Mrs. Humphrey Ward. London: 1911. V. 41

The Writings. London: 1911-12. V. 46

WARD, MARY JANE

The Tree Has Roots. New York: 1937. V. 42

WARD, MRS.

Recollections of an Old Soldier. London: 1849. V. 41

A World of Wonders Revealed by the Microscope. A Book for Young Students. London: 1859. V. 37

WARD, NATHANIEL

Mercurius Anti-Mechanicus. London: 1648. V. 40

A Religious Retreat Sounded to a Religious Army, by One that Desires to be Faithful to His Country, though Unworthy to be Named. London: 1647. V. 37

The Simple Cobler of Aggavvam in America. London: 1647. V. 38; 40; 42

The Simple Cobler of Aggavvam in America. London: 1847. V. 44

A Word to Mr. Peters, and Two Words for the Parliament and Kingdom. London: 1647. V. 45

WARD, NATHANIEL B.

Letter from Mr. N. B. Ward to Sir W. J. Hooker, on the Growth of Plants Without Open Exposure to Air. London: 1836. V. 39

WARD, NED

The London Spy Compleat. London: 1924. V. 37; 44

WARD-PERKINS, JOHN B.

Roman Architecture. New York: 1977. V. 44

WARD, R. GERARD

American Activities in the Central pacific 1790-1870. A History, Geography and Ethnography Pertaining to American Involvement and Americans in the Pacific, Taken from Contemporary Newspapers etc. Ridgewood: 1966-67. V. 41

WARD, ROBERT

Animadversions of Warre. or, A Militarie Magazine of the Truest Rules, and Ablest Instructions, for the Managing of Warre . . . London: 1639. V. 38; 44; 46

WARD, ROBERT ARTHUR

A Treatise on Investments. London: 1852. V. 38; 43

WARD, ROBERT PLUMER 1765-1846

De Clifford or, the Constant Man. London: 1841. V. 38; 40; 41; 43; 44; 45

De Vere; or, the Man of Independence. London: 1827. V. 37; 42; 46

Illustrations of Human Life. London: 1838. V. 41

Tremaine, or The Man of Refinement. London: 1825. V. 37; 38; 41; 42; 45

Tremaine. London: 1833. V. 43

WARD, ROBERT PLUMMER 1765-1846

De Vere: or the Man of Independence. Philadelphia: 1827. V. 40

WARD, ROWLAND

Records of Big Game. London: 1889. V. 40

Records of Big Game. London: 1896. V. 43; 45

Records of Big Game. London: 1899. V. 39; 43; 45

Records of Big Game. London: 1903. V. 39; 40; 43

Records of Big Game. London: 1907. V. 37; 38; 40; 43; 45

Records of Big Game. London: 1910. V. 38; 39; 40; 43

Records of Big Game. London: 1914. V. 40; 45

Records of Big Game. London: 1922. V. 37; 38

Records of Big Game. London: 1928. V. 38

Records of Big Game. London: 1973. V. 40

The Sportsman's Handbook to Practical Collecting, Preserving and Artistic Setting Up of Trophies and Specimens. London: 1894. V. 42

WARD, SAMUEL

Magnetis Redvctorivm Theolgicvm Tropologicum, in Quo Ejus Hovvs Vervs & Svpremvs Vsvs Indicatvr. London: 1639. V. 45

WARD, SETH

A Philosophical Essay Towards an Eviction of the Being and Attributes of God, immortality of the Souls of Men, Truth and Authority . . . Oxford: 1667. V. 41; 42

Vindicae Academiarum Containing, Some Brief Animadversions Upon Mr. Webster's Book, Stiled, the Examination of Academies. Oxford: 1654. V. 43; 45; 46

WARD, THOMAS

The Bird-Fancier's Recreation. London: 1770. V. 39

England Reformation from the Time of King Henry the VIIIth to the End of Oate's Plot. Hambourgh: 1710. V. 40

England's Reformation (in verse) from the Time of King Henry the VIIIth to the End of Oates Plot. London: 1710. V. 37; 42

England's Reformation. London: 1715. V. 43

England's Reformation . . . London: 1716. V. 42; 44

WARD, THOMAS HUMPHREY

The English Poets: Selections with Critical Introductions by Various Authors. London: 1880-1883. V. 37

WARD, VALENTINE

The Stage, a Dangerous and Irreconcilable, Enemy to Christianity . . . Aberdeen: 1819. V. 42

WARD, W. A.

Studies on Scarab Seals. Warminster: 1978-1984. V. 37; 42; 44

WARD, W. G.

Capital and Labour: a Paper Read Before the Literary and General Members of the Nottingham and County Liberal Club, and to Delegates from Operatives' Trade Socieities . . . Nottingham: 1874. V. 41

WARD, W. H.

The Architecture of the Renaissance in France. London: 1925. V. 44

The Architecture of the Renaissance in France . . . London: 1926. V. 42

WARD, WILLIAM

An Essay on Grammar, As It May Be Applied to the English Language. London: 1765. V. 43

Farewell Letters to a Few Friends in Britain and America, on Returning to Bengal in 1821. Lexington: 1822. V. 39

The Most Excellent, profitable & pleasant Book of the Famous Doctor, and expert Astrologian, Arcandam, or, Alcandrin: To find the fatal Destiny, Constellation, COmplexion, and Natural inclination of every Man and Child by His birth . . . London: 1670. V. 37

WARD, WILLIAM HAYES

The Seal Cylinders of Western Asia. Washington: 1910. V. 46

The Seal Cylinders of Western Asia. Washington: 1910, 1919. V. 44

WARDE, B.

Words in Their Hands. Cambridge: 1964. V. 39

WARDE, BEATRICE

The Shelter in Bedlem. A Story in Dialogue. 1937-38. V. 46

Supplement to 'Bombed But Unbeaten', Verses Composed After the Big Raid of April 1941. V. 41

This Is a Printing Office. N.P.: 1932. V. 42

Unjustified Lines. Middlesex: 1935. V. 46

WARDE, FREDERIC

Bruce Rogers Designer of Books. Cambridge: 1925. V. 37; 40; 41; 44; 45

Bruce Rogers Designer of Books. Cambridge: 1926. V. 46

Printers Ornaments Applied to the Composition of Decorative Borders, Panels and Patterns. London: 1928. V. 44; 46

WARDE, FREDERICK

The Silver Book of English Sonnets. Paris: 1927. V. 37; 42

WARDEN, ALEX J. 1810-1892

Burgh Laws of Dundee, with the History, Statutes and Proceedings of the Guild of Merchants and Fraternities of Craftsmen. London: 1872. V. 40

The Linen Trade, Ancient and Modern. London: 1867. V. 37; 42

WARDEN, DAVID BAILLIE

Bibliotheca America-Septentrionalis: Being a Choice Collection of Books in Various Languages . . . Paris: 1820. V. 39

Bibliotheca Americana, Being a Choice Collection of Books relating to North and South America and the West Indies. Paris: 1831. V. 39; 40

Bibliotheca Americana, Being a Choice Collection of Books Relating to North and South America and the West Indies . . . Paris: 1840. V. 39

Description Statiestisque, Historique, et Politique des Etats Unis. Paris: 1820. V. 38; 39

A Statistical, Political and Historical Account of the United States of North America. Edinburgh: 1819. V. 42

WARDEN, FLORENCE

My Child and I; a Woman's Story. London: 1894. V. 41

WARDER, JOSEPH

The True Amazons: or, the monarchy of Bees. Being a new discovery and improvement of those wonderful creatures. The Fourth Edition, Corrected. London: 1720. V. 37

WARDER, T. B.

Battle of Young's Branch, or Manassas Plain, Fought July 21, 1861. Richmond: 1862. V. 42; 44

WARDLAW, ELIZABETH

Hardykunte. London?: 1783. V. 46

WARDLE, FRANCIS

All Dogs. London: 1935. V. 39

WARDLE, G. L.

The Investigation of the Charges Brought Against His Royal Highness, the Duke of York, Commander in Chief . . . London: 1809. V. 42

WARDLE, THOMAS

Kashmir: Its New Silk Industry, with Some Account of Its Natural History, Geology, Sport, Etc . . . London: and Leek: 1904. V. 45

WARDMAN, GEORGE

A Trip to Alaska: a Narrative of What was Seen and Heard During a Summer Cruise in Alaskan Waters. San Francisco: 1884. V. 43

A Trip to Alaska. Boston: 1885. V. 45

WARDNER, JAMES F.

Wardner, British Columbia, the Omaha of Canada. Jennings, Montana?: 1896. V. 38

WARDNER, JIM

Jim Wardner, Idaho, by Himself. New York: 1900. V. 39; 42

THE WARDOUR Press Series of Armorial Bookplates: Baronets. London: 1895. V. 38

WARDROP, A. E.

Days and Nights with Indian Big Game. London: 1923. V. 42

WARDROP, JAMES

Essays on the Morbid Anatomy of the Human Eye. London: 1818. V. 42

History of James Mitchell, a Boy Born Blind and Deaf, with an Account of the Operation Performed for the Recovery of His Sight. London: 1813. V. 40; 43

On the Nature and Treatment of the Diseases of the Heart. London: 1851. V. 43

WARDROP, OLIVER

The Kingdom of Georgia Notes of Travel in a Land of Women, Wine and Song. London: 1888. V. 39

WARDWELL, JOSEPH

The Way of the World, or a Short Sketch of the Modern Customs of Mankind, Delineated, in a Variety of Methods, both Metaphorical, Ironical, Miscellaneous, Serious, Humorous, Entertaining, and Romantick. N.P.: (Bristol): 1813. V. 37

WARE, EUGENE FITCH

The Indian War of 1864, Being a Fragment of the Early History of Kansas, Nebraska, Colorado, and Wyoming. Topeka: 1911. V. 37; 38; 41; 42; 43; 45; 46

WARE, FABIAN

The Immortal Heritage. An Account of the Work and Policy of the Imperial War Graves Commission During Twenty Years 1917-1937. 1937. V. 46

The Immortal Heritage, an Account of the Work and Policy of the Imperial War Graves Commission During Twenty Years, 1917-37. Cambridge: 1937. V. 45

WARE, FRANCIS M.

Driving. New York: 1903. V. 39

First-Hand Bits of Stable Lore. Boston: 1903. V. 43

WARE, ISAAC d. 1766

A Complete Body of Architecture. London: 1756. V. 37; 38; 41

Designs of Inigo Jones and Others. London: 1733. V. 37; 44

Designs of Inigo Jones and Others. London: 1735. V. 39

Designs of Inigo Jones and Others. London: 1743. V. 38; 39

The Plans, Elevations, and Section; Chimney-Pieces and Ceilings of Houghton in Norfolk the seat of the Rt. Honourable Sir Robert Walpole. London: 1735. V. 38

WARE, JAMES

De Hibernia and Antiquitatibus, Disqisitiones. In Quibus, Prater ea Quae de Hiberniae Explicantur . . . London: 1654. V. 38

Observations on the Cataract, and Gutta Serena . . . London: 1812. V. 42

WARE, MAJOR

Squibs and Crackers, Serious, Comical and Tender. London: 1812. V. 43

WARE, MARY

Poems. London: 1809. V. 43

WARE, MARY CLEMENTINA HIBBERT

His Dearest Wish. London: 1883. V. 41

WARE, ROBERT

The Hunting of the Romish Fox, and the Quenching of Sectarian Fire-Brands . . . Dublin: 1683. V. 45

WARE, SAMUEL

A Treatise of Properties of Arches and Their Butment Piers. London: 1809. V. 38

WARE, THOMAS

Sketches of the Life and Travels of Rev. Thomas Ware . . . Written by Himself. New York: 1839. V. 38

WARE, W. H.

The Battle of Kelley's Ford, Fought March 17, 1863. Newport News: 1915. V. 44

WARE, WILLIAM

Probus: or Rome in the Third Century. New York: 1838. V. 37; 43

Zenobia; or the Fall of Palmyra. New York: 1838. V. 41

WARE, WILLIAM ROTCH

The Georgian Period, a Series of Measured Drawings. New York: 1898-1902. V. 44

The Georgian Period. New York: 1923. V. 42

WARFIELD, J. D.

The Founders of Anne Arundel and Howard Counties, Maryland. Baltimore: 1905. V. 46

WARHOL, ANDY

Andy Warhol's Index Book. New York: 1967. V. 45; 46

Andy Warhol's Exposures. London: 1979. V. 41

Andy Warhol's Exposures. New York: 1979. V. 45

Andy Warhol Prints. New York: 1985. V. 43

Andy Warhol: Portraits of the 70's. 1979. V. 37

Index Book. New York: 1967. V. 46

The Philosophy of Andy Warhol. 1975. V. 43

The Philosophy of Andy Warhol. New York: 1975. V. 45; 46

Popism. The Warhol '60 8. New York: 1980. V. 46

Popism. The Warhol '60 8. New York: 1983. V. 46

WARHURST, B. W.

A Colour Dictionary, Giving Two Hundred Names of Colours, Specially Prepared for Stamp Collectors. London. V. 42

WARING AND GILLOW, LTD.

The Artistic Evolution of the English Homes. London: 1900. V. 38; 40

Carpets of Quality by Waring & Gillow Ltd., Furnishers and Decorators to H. M. the King. London: 1920. V. 37

WARING, C.

The Minstrelsy of the Woods . . . London: 1832. V. 44

WARING, EDWARD 1734-1798

Bibliotheca Therapeutica or Bibliography of Therapeutics, Chiefly in Reference to Articles of the Materia Medica. London: 1878. V. 45

Meditationes Analyticae. Cambridge: 1785. V. 38

Miscellanea Analytica, de Aeqationibus Algebraicis, et Curvarum Proprietatibus. Cambridge: 1762. V. 43

WARING, EDWARD JOHN

Pharmacopoeia of India . . . India Office: 1868. V. 45

Pharmacopoeia of India. London: 1868. V. 42; 45

WARING, EDWARD SCOTT

A Tour to Sheeraz, by the Route of Kazroon and Feerozabad . . . V. 45

WARING, ELEANOR E.

Keble's Eveing Hymn. London: 1865. V. 38

WARING, GEORGE

Letters from Malta and Sicily. London: 1843. V. 45

WARING, GEORGE E.

The Bride of the Rhine, Two Hundred Miles in a Mosel Rowboat . . . Boston: 1878. V. 42

History and Present Condition of New Orleans . . . and Report of the City of Austin, Texas. Washington: 1881. V. 37; 38

Whip and Spur. New York: 1897. V. 46

WARING, JOHN BURLEY 1823-1875

Ceramic Art in Remote Ages. London: 1874. V. 41

Examples of Stained Glass, Fresco, Marble and Enamel Inlay and Wood Inlay. London: 1858. V. 40

Examples of Decorative Art in Furniture. Selected from the Royal and Other Collections. London: 1858. V. 38

Examples of Metal Work & Jewellry, Selected from the Royal and Other Collections. London: 1858. V. 38; 43

Examples of Pottery and Porcelain. London: 1858. V. 43

Masterpiece of Industrial Art and Sculpture at the International Exhibition 1862 . . . London: 1863. V. 37; 38; 46

WARING, S.

The Wild Garland. London: 1827. V. 42; 46

WARING, SARAH

The Minstrelsy of the Woods; or, Sketches and Songs Connected with the Natural History of Some of the Most Interesting British and Foreign Birds. London: 1832. V. 45

WARING, THOMAS

A Treatise on Archery, or the Art of Shooting with the Long Bow. London: 1827. V. 46

A Treatise on Archery, or the Art of Shooting with the Long Bow. London: 1828. V. 46

A Treatise on Archery or the Art of Shooting with the English Bow . . . London: 1847. V. 38

WARKWORTH Castle. London: 1851. V. 38

WARLAND, JOHN H.

The Plume: a Tuft of Literary Feathers. Boston: 1847. V. 43

WARLOCK, PETER

Songs of Gardens. Bloomsbury: 1925. V. 41

Songs of the Garden. London: 1925. V. 46

WARLOP, E.

The Flemish Nobility Before 1300. Kortrijk: 1975. V. 38; 46

WARLTIRE, JOHN

Analysis of a Course of Lectures in Experimental Philosophy . . . London: 1769. V. 46

Tales of the Various Combinations and Specific Attraction of the Substances Employed in Chemistry. London: 1769. V. 46

WARMAN, CY

The Story of the Railroad. New York: 1898. V. 38

WARMING, E.

Botany of the Faeroes. London: 1901-08. V. 37

WARNARS, G.

Histoire van den Amsterdamschen Schouwburg. Amsterdam: 1772. V. 45

WARNE, FREDERICK

Off We Go. London: 1910. V. 45

WARNER & BEERS

Atlas of Whiteside County and the State of Illinois, to Which is Added an Atlas of the United States . . . Chicago: 1872. V. 38

WARNER, CHARLES A.

Texas Oil and Gas Since 1543. 1939. V. 42

Texas Oil and Gas Since 1543. Austin: 1966. V. 43

Texas Oil and Gas Since 1543. Houston: (1939). V. 37; 38

WARNER, CHARLES DUDLEY

In the Wilderness. Boston: 1878. V. 43

In the Levant by Charles Dudley Warner. Boston: 1893. V. 40

In the Levant. Boston & New York: 1893. V. 44

Library of the World's Best Literature, Ancient and Modern. New York: 1896. V. 40

Library of the World's Best Literature. New York: 1896-97. V. 45

The Complete Writings. Hartford: 1904. V. 38; 42; 46

WARNER, ELISHA

The History of Spanish Fork. Spanish Fork, Utah: 1930. V. 37; 42

WARNER, ELLEN REBECCA

Herbert Lodge; a New Forest Story. N.P.: Bath,: 1808. V. 37

WARNER, FERDINANDO 1703-1768

A Full and Plain Account of the Gout. London: 1768. V. 39

A Full and Plain Account of the Gout . . . London: 1772. V. 45

The History of the Rebellion and Civil War in Ireland. London: 1768. V. 38; 41

Memoirs of the Life of Sir Thomas More, Lord High Chancellor of England in the Reign of Henry VIII. London: 1758. V. 41; 44

Remarks on the History of Fingal, and Other Poems of Ossian. London: 1762. V. 39

WARNER, FRANK

The Silk Industry of the United Kingdom: Its Origin and Development. London. V. 46

The Silk Industry of the United Kingdom, Its Origin and Development. London: 1921. V. 37; 42

WARNER, FRED

The History of the Rebellion and Civil War in Ireland (1641-1659). Dublin: 1768. V. 38

WARNER, GEORGE

Miniatures and Borders from a Flemish Horae. London: 1911. V. 40

WARNER, GEORGE E.

History of Hennepin County and the City of Minneapolis. Minneapolis: 1881. V. 46

History of Ramsey County and the City of St. Paul. Minneapolis: 1881. V. 46

WARNER, GEORGE FREDERIC 1845-1936

Queen Mary's Psalter Miniatures and Drawings by an English Artist of the 14th Century Reproduced from Royal MS. 2 B. VII in the British Museum. London: 1912. V. 37; 38; 42

Universal Classic Manuscripts. Washington: 1900. V. 38

WARNER, H. H.

Songs of the Spindle and Legends of the Loom. London: 1889. V. 38

WARNER, H. W.

Report of the Trail of Charles baldwin, for a Libel in Publishing Charges of Fraud and Swindling in the Management of N.Y. Lotteries. New York: 1818. V. 37

WARNER, I. W.

The Immigrant's Guide and Citizen's Manual. New York: 1848. V. 39

WARNER, JOSEPH

Cases in Surgery. London: 1760. V. 38

WARNER, JUAN J.

An Historical Sketch of Los Angeles, California, from the Spanish Occupancy, by the Founding of the Mission San Gabriel Archangel, Sept. 8, 1771 to July 4, 1876. Los Angeles: 1876. V. 37; 38; 39; 40; 42; 43; 44; 45

WARNER, LANGDON

The Craft of the Japanese Sculptor. New York: 1936. V. 42

WARNER, MATT

The Last of the Bandit Riders . . . As Told to Murray E. King. Caldwell: 1940. V. 41

WARNER, OPIE L.

A Pardoned Lifer: Life of George Sontag, Former Member, Notorious Evans-Sontag Gang of Train Robbers. San Bernardino: 1909. V. 38; 41; 42

WARNER, P. F.

Cricket in Many Climes. London: 1900. V. 41

Imperial Cricket. London: 1912. V. 41

WARNER, RALPH

The Dutch and Flemish Fruit and Flower Painters of the XVIITH and XVIIIth Centuries. London: 1928. V. 43

WARNER, REBECCA

Original Letters from Richard Baxter, Matthew Prior, Lord Bolingbroke, Alexander Pope, Dry Cheyne, Dr. Hartley, Dr. Samuel Johnson . . . Bath: 1817. V. 43

WARNER, REX

Views of Attica and Its Surroundings. London: 1950. V. 44

WARNER, RICHARD 1763-1857

Antiquitates Culinariae; or, Curious Tracts Relating to Culinary Affairs of the Old English. London: 1791. V. 39; 45

Collections for the History of Hampshire, and the Bishopric of Winchester, Including the Isles of Wight, Jersey, Guernesyand Sarke, by D. Y. London: 1795. V. 38

A Companion in a Tour Round Lymington. Southampton: 1789. V. 38; 45

The History of Bath. Bath: 1801. V. 38

An Illustration of the Roman Antiquities Discovered at Bath. Bath: 1797. V. 37

A Letter to David Garrick, Esq. London: 1768. V. 37; 38; 44; 45

Topographical Remarks Relating to the South-Western Parts of Hampshire . . . London: 1793. V. 44

A Tour through the Northern Counties of England and the Borders of Scotland. Bath: 1802. V. 39

A Tour Through Cornwall, in the Autumn of 1808. Bath: 1809. V. 38; 42

A Walk Through Wales, in August 1797. Bath: 1799. V. 38

A Walk Through Some of the Western Counties of England. Bath: 1800. V. 37; 39

A Walk through some of the Western Counties of England. (with) Excursions from Bath. Bath: 1800, 1801. V. 39

A Walk through some of the Western Counties of England. Bath: 1802. V. 39

A Walk through Wales, in August 1797. Bath: 1798. V. 37

WARNER, ROBERT BENJAMIN SAMUEL WILLIAMS

The Orchid Album. London: 1882-97. V. 44; 46

WARNER, SUSAN

Queechy. London: 1852. V. 44

Queechy. London: 1853. V. 45

WARNER, SYLVIA TOWNSEND

After the Death of Don Jun. London: 1938. V. 38

Elinor Barley. London: 1930. V. 39; 42; 43; 44; 46

The Espalier. London: 1925. V. 40; 43

A Garland of Straw and Other Stories. London: 1943. V. 38

King Duffus and Other Poems. London: 1968. V. 41

Lolly Willowes or the Loving Huntsman. London: 1926. V. 41

The Scapegoat. London. V. 44

Sketches from Nature. London: 1963. V. 40

Summer Will Show. London: 1936. V. 40

This Our Brother. London. V. 38

Time Importuned. London: 1928. V. 40

Whether a Dove or a Seagull - Poems. London: 1934. V. 38

WARNER, WORCESTER REED

Selections from Oriental Objects of Art Collected by Worcester Reed Warner, Most of Which Have Been Presented to the Cleveland Museum of Art. Tarrytown: 1921. V. 41

WARNERY, CHARLES EMMANUEL DE

Remarks on Cavalry. London: 1798. V. 42

WARNES, JOHN

On the Cultivation of Flax. London: 1846. V. 37

A **WARNING** Piece Against the Crime of Murder; or, an Account of Many Extraordinary and Most Providential Discoveries of Secret Murders. London: 1752. V. 46

A **WARNING-PIECE** to all Drunkards and Health Drinkers: Faithfully Collected from the Works of English and Foreign Learned Authors of Good Esteem . . . London: 1682. V. 40

WARR, G. FINDEN

Dynamics, Construction of Machinery, Equilibirum of Structures and the Strength of Materials. London: 1851. V. 44

WARR, GEORGE WINTER

Canada As It Is. London: 1847. V. 37

WARRE-CORNISH, BLANCHE

Alcestis. London: 1873. V. 37; 45

WARRE, HENRY

Sketches in North American and Oregon Territory. Barre: 1970. V. 44

WARREN, ALBERT HENRY

Arms of the Episcoptes of Great Britain and Ireland, with Heraldic Notes by Rev. John Woodward. N.P.: 1868. V. 38

WARREN, ANNE

Memoirs and Select Letters of Mrs. Anne Warren. London: 1827. V. 40

WARREN, ARTHUR

The Charles Whittinghams, Printers. New York: 1896. V. 37; 38; 40; 42; 44; 46

WARREN, BENJAMIN H.

Report on the Birds of Pennsylvania. Harrisburg: 1890. V. 38; 39; 41; 42; 44; 45

WARREN, BENJAMIN H. A.

Report on the Birds of Pennsylvania. Harrisburg: 1888. V. 43

WARREN, CHARLES

The Supreme Court in United States History. Boston: 1922. V. 44

Underground Jerusalem. London: 1876. V. 40

WARREN, EDWARD 1804-1878

An Epitome of Practical Surgery, for Field and Hospital. Richmond: 1863. V. 37; 38; 45

The Life of John Collins Warren. Boston: 1860. V. 43

Some Account of the Letheon; or, Who is the Discoverer? Boston: 1847. V. 45

WARREN, EDWARD PERRY

The Prince Who Did Not Exist. New York & London: 1900. V. 37

WARREN, ELIZA SPALDING

Memoirs of the West the Spaldings. Portland: 1916. V. 37; 42; 45

Memoirs of the West. Portland: 1917. V. 40; 43

WARREN, ERASMUS

Geologia; or, at Discourse Concerning the Earth Before the Deluge, Wherein the Form and Properties Ascribed to It, in a Book Intituled The Theory of the Earth . . . London: 1690. V. 45

WARREN, FREDERICK

Only One Other. A Novel. In Two Volumes. London: 1885. V. 37

WARREN, G. J. H.

A Century of Locomotive Building by Robert Stephenson & Co. Newcastle-upon-Tyne: 1923. V. 42

WARREN, GOUVERNEUR KEMBLE

Explorations in the Dacota Country, in the Year 1855 (34th Congress 1st Session. Senate Document 76). Washington: 1856. V. 37; 38; 40; 41; 43; 45

WARREN, GRENLIFFE

Olph: or the Wreckers of the Isle Shoals. Boston: 1846. V. 39

WARREN, HENRY

Hints Upon Tints, with Strokes Upon Copper and Canvas. London: 1833. V. 44

A Treatise Concerning the Malignant Fever in Barbados, and the Neighbouring Islands. London: 1741. V. 37; 39

WARREN, HENRY MATHER

To and Fro. Philadelphia: 1908. V. 37; 38; 39; 41; 42; 43

WARREN, J. G. H.

A Century of Locomotive Building by Robert Stephenson & Co. 1823-1923. Newcastle upon Tyne: 1923. V. 37; 46

A Century of Locomotive Building by Robert Stephenson & Co. 1823-1923. Newcastle: 1923. V. 37

WARREN, J. MASON

An Account of Two Remarkable Indian Dwarfs Exhibited in Boston Under the Name of Aztec Children. Boston: 1851. V. 38

Fissure of The Soft and Hard-Plate. Boston: 1848. V. 42

Surgical Observations, With Cases and Operations. New York: 1867. V. 42

WARREN, JANE S.

The Morning Star: History of the Children's Missionary Vessel and of the Marquesan and Micronesian Missions. Boston: 1860. V. 44

WARREN, JOHN C.

Remarks on Some Fossil Impressions in the Sandstone Rocks of Connecticut River. Boston: 1854. V. 39

WARREN, JOHN COLLIN

Etherization; with Surgical Remarks. Boston: 1848. V. 37

WARREN, JOHN COLLINS 1778-1856

Address to the Community of the Necessity of Legalizing the study of Anatomy. By order of the Massachusetts. Boston: 1829. V. 37

A Comparative View of the Sensorial and Nervous Systems of Men and Animals. Boston: 1822. V. 46

Description of a Skeleton of the Mastodon Giganteus of North America. Boston: 1855. V. 38; 40

Etherization; with Surgical Remarks. Boston: 1848. V. 37; 38; 40

Etherization; with Surgical Remarks. Boston: 1848. V. 41

The Healing of Arteries After Ligatures in Man and Animal. New York: 1886. V. 46

The Life of John Collins Warren, M.D. Boston: 1860. V. 40; 41; 44

The Mastodon Giganteus of North America. Boston: 1852. V. 40

The Physiological Effects of Alcoholic Drinks . . . Boston: 1848. V. 38; 39; 40

Surgical Observations on Tumours, with Cases and Operations. Boston: 1848. V. 44

WARREN, JOHN LEICESTER

Poems Dramatic and Lyrical. With Illustrations by C.S. Ricketts. London: 1893. V. 37

WARREN, JOSEPH

An Oration Delivered March 5th, 1772. At the Request of the Inhabitants of the Town of Boston to Commemorate the Bloody Tragedy of the Fifth of March, 1770. Boston: 1772. V. 39

WARREN, JOSEPH H.

A Plea for the Cure of Rupture; or, the Pathology of the Subcutaneous Operation by Injection for the Cure of Hernia. Boston: 1884. V. 45

WARREN, L.

Foundation Stone. New York: 1940. V. 43

WARREN, MERCY

Poems, Dramatic and Miscellaneous. Boston: 1790. V. 37; 38; 39

WARREN, ROBERT PENN 1905-

All the King's Men. New York: 1946. V. 37; 38; 39; 40; 44

All the King's Men. London: 1948. V. 43

All the King's Men. 1977. V. 41

All the King's Men. Franklin Center: 1977. V. 42

All the King's Men. New York: 1977. V. 46

All the King's Men. 1946. V. 37

American Prefaces. Iowa City: 1942. V. 40

At Heaven's Gate. New York: 1943. V. 44; 45

Audubon. New York: 1969. V. 39; 41; 42; 43; 44

Band of Angels. New York: 1955. V. 43

Being Here. New York: 1980. V. 39; 43; 45; 46

Blackberry Winter: A Story. 1946. V. 44

Blackberry Winter. Cummington: 1946. V. 41; 45

Blackberry Winter. Cummington: 1946. V. 37

Brother to Dragons. New York: 1953. V. 39; 41

Chief Joseph of the Nez Perce. New York: 1983. V. 39; 41; 42; 43

The Circus in the Attic. New York: 1947. V. 37; 38; 39; 40; 45; 46

Democracy and Poetry. Cambridge/London: 1975. V. 37

The Essential Melville. New York: 1987. V. 43

Flood. New York: 1964. V. 45

For Aaron Copeland on His 78th Birthday 14 November 1978. 1978. V. 39

The Gods of Mount Olympus. New York: 1959. V. 41; 42; 43

Homage to Theodore Dreiser. New York: 1971. V. 41; 42; 43; 44; 45

Incarnations. Poems 1966-1968. New York: 1968. V. 39; 42; 43; 44

Jefferson Davis Gets His Citizenship Back. Lexington: 1980. V. 43

John Brown. New York: 1929. V. 37; 38; 39; 40; 43

Love: Four Versions. 1981. V. 42

Love: Four Versions. N.P.: 1981. V. 41

Love: Four Versions. N.P.: 1981. V. 42

Love: Four Versions. N.P.: 1981. V. 43

Love: Four Versions. Winston-Salem: 1981. V. 39; 41

Meet Me in the Green Glen. New York: 1971. V. 39; 41; 42; 43; 45

Mountain Mystery. 1981. V. 42

Mountain Mystery. N.P.: 1981. V. 43

New and Selected Poems: 1923-1985. New York: 1985. V. 43

Night Rider. Boston: 1939. V. 38; 39; 44; 45

Night Rider. New York: 1939. V. 37

Now and Then. New York: 1978. V. 39; 41; 42; 43; 44

Old Flame. 1978. V. 42

Old Flame. 1978. V. 42

Old Flame. Winston Salem: 1978. V. 46

Or Else - Poem/Poems 1968-1974. New York: 1974. V. 37; 43

A Place to Come To. New York: 1977. V. 37; 39; 41; 42; 43; 44; 45; 46

Remember the Alamo. New York: 1958. V. 43; 44; 45; 46

Robert Penn Warren Talking. Interviews. 1950-1978. New York: 1980. V. 41; 45

A Robert Penn Warren Reader. New York: 1987. V. 39

Rumor Verified. Poems 1979-1980. New York: 1981. V. 39; 41; 46

Segregation: the Inner Conflict of the South. New York: 1956. V. 45

Selected Poems 1923-1943. London. V. 45

Selected Poems 1923-1943. London. V. 46

Selected Poems. New York: 1944. V. 38; 39; 40

Selected Essays. New York: 1958. V. 43

Selected Poems: New and Old, 1923-1966. New York: 1966. V. 39; 43; 45; 46

Selected Poems. 1923-1975. New York: 1975. V. 41; 42; 43

Selected Poems 1923-1975. New York: 1976. V. 39; 46

Snowfall. N.P.: 1984. V. 43

A Southern Harvest. Boston: 1937. V. 45

Thirty-Six Poems. New York: 1935. V. 37

Two Poems. 1979. V. 39

Two Poems. 1979. V. 42

Two Poems. Winston-Salem: 1979. V. 38

Who Speaks for the Negro? New York: 1965. V. 43

Wilderness: a Tale of the Civil War. New York: 1961. V. 45

William Faulkner and His South. Charlottesville: 1951. V. 41; 46

World Enough and Time. 1950. V. 46

World Enough and Time. New York: 1950. V. 37; 38; 39; 40; 41; 43; 45

WARREN, SAMUEL

Blackstone's Commentaries Systematically Abridges and Adapted to the Existing State of the Law and Constitution with Great Additions. London: 1855. V. 38

(Wrapper title) Labour: Its Rights, Difficulties, Dignity and Consolations. A Lecture. London: 1856. V. 43

The Merchant's Clerk and Other Tales. New York: 1836. V. 42

Passages from a Late Physician. Edinburgh: 1838. V. 39

Ten Thousand a Year. Philadelphia: 1840-41. V. 42; 44

Ten Thousand a Year. Edinburgh: 1841. V. 37; 39; 46

Ten Thousand a Year. London: 1841. V. 38

Ten Thousand a Year. Edinburgh: 1845. V. 39

The Works. Edinburgh: 1855-67. V. 38; 42

WARREN, SAMUEL continued

Works of Samuel Warren. London: 1867/54/55. V. 46

WARREN, T. ROBINSON

Dust and Foam; or, Three Oceans and Two Continents . . . New York: 1859. V. 40

WARREN, THOMAS HERBERT

By Severn Sea and Other Poems. Oxford: 1897. V. 46

WARREN, WILLIAM

These for Those. Portland: 1870. V. 44

WARREN, WILLIAM HENRY

Engineering Construction in Iron, Steel and Timber. London: 1894. V. 38; 44

WARREN, WILLIAM W.

history of the Ojibways, Based Upon Traditions and Oral Statements. St. Paul. V. 46

History of the Ojibway Nations. St. Paul: 1885. V. 45

WARRINER, FRANCIS

Cruise of the United States Frigate Potomac Round the World During the Years 1831-1834 Embracing the Attack on Quallah Battoo . . . New York: 1835. V. 37; 40; 41; 43

WARRINGTON, HENRY BOOTH, EARL OF

The Charge to the Grand Jury . . . Held for the County of Chester, 1693. London: 1694. V. 41

WARRINGTON, W.

The History of Stained Glass from the Earliest Period of the Art to the Present Time . . . London: 1848. V. 37

WARRINGTON, WILLIAM

The History of Wales. London: 1786. V. 39; 43

WARRS, ISAAC

The Improvement of the Mind, or a Supplement to the Art of Logic. Boston: 1793. V. 41

WARRUM, NOBEL

Utah Since Statehood: Historical and Biographical. Chicago/Salt Lake: 1919. V. 37

WARRUM, NOBLE

Utah Since Statehood Historical and Biographical. Chicago: 1919-20. V. 42

WARTHIN, ALDRED SCOTT

The Physician of the Dance of Death: A Historical Study of the Evolution of the Dance of Death Mythus in Art. New York: 1931. V. 38; 45

WARTON, JOSEPH

An Essay on the Writings and Genius of Mr. Pope. London: 1756, 1782. V. 40

An Essay on the Writings and Genius of Pope. London: 1772-82. V. 38; 45

An Essay on the Genius and Writings of Pope in Two Volumes. London: 1782. V. 38; 41

An Essay on the Genius and Writings of Pope. London: 1806. V. 41

Odes on Various Subjects. London: 1747. V. 40; 45

WARTON, THOMAS

An Enquiry into the Authenticity of the Poems, Attributed to Thomas Rowley. London: 1782. V. 38

The History of English Poetry, from the Close of the Eleventh, to the Commencement of the Eighteenth Century. London: 1774-85 & 1806. V. 44

The History of English Poetry. London: 1775. V. 38; 43

The History of English Poetry, from the Close of the Eleventh to the Commencement of the Eighteenth Century. London: 1775/78/81. V. 45

The History of English Poetry. London: 1775-81/1806. V. 42; 45

The History of English Poetry, from the Close of the Eleventh to the Commencement of the Eighteenth Century . . . London: 1775-81, 1806. V. 40

The History of English Poetry. London: 1824. V. 38; 40; 41; 43; 44

The History of English Poetry, from the Close of the Eleventh Century to the Commencement of the Eighteenth Century . . . London: 1840. V. 42; 43

History of English Poetry from the Twelfth to the Close of the Sixteenth Century. London: 1871. V. 45

The Life of Sir Thomas Pope, Founder of Trinity College Oxford. London: 1772. V. 45

New Market, a Satire. London: 1751. V. 38

Observations on the Faerie Queene of Spenser . . . London: 1754. V. 42

Observations on the Fairy Queen of Spencer. London: 1762. V. 44

Observations on the Fairy Queen of Spenser. The Second Edition, corrected and enlarged. London: 1762. V. 37

The Oxford Sausage or Select Poetical Pieces Written by the Most Celebrated Wits of the University of Oxford. London: 1764. V. 38; 40

The Oxford Sausage; or, Select Poetical Pieces . . . Dublin: 1766. V. 44

The Oxford Sausage. Oxford: 1772. V. 41

The Oxford Sausage. Oxford: 1777. V. 41

The Oxford Sausage. Oxford: 1797. V. 38

The Oxford Sausage; or, Select Poetical Pieces, written by the most celebrated wits of the University of Oxford. A New Edition, Adorn'd with Cuts, Engraved in a New Taste, and Designed by the Best Masters. Oxford: (c. 1798?) V. 37

The Pleasures of Melancholy. London: 1747. V. 37; 41; 45

Poems. London: 1777. V. 41

The Poems on Various Subjects . . . London: 1791. V. 43

Poetical Works, to which are Added Inscriptionum Romanarum Delectus and an Inaugural Speech, Together with Memoirs of His Life and Writings, and Notes . . . Oxford: 1802. V. 37; 38

Poetical Works. Oxford & London: 1802. V. 39

The Union; or Select Scots and English Poems. Edinburgh: 1753. V. 45

WARWICK, PHILIP 1609-1683

A Discourse Upon Government . . . Written in 1678. London: 1694. V. 38; 40; 45

WARWICK, ROBERT RICH, EARL OF

A Declaration of the Earl of Warwick, Lord High Admirall of England . . . London: 1648. V. 43

WARY, LYND

Wild Pilgrimage. New York: 1932. V. 37

WASE, CHRISTOPHER

Considerations Concerning Free Schools, as Settled in England. London: 1678. V. 39

WASER, CASPAR 1565-1625

Institutio Linguae Syrae. Leyden: 1594. V. 37; 38; 40

WASH, W. A.

Camp, Field and Prison Life. St. Louis: 1870. V. 42

WASHBURN, CEPHAS

Reminiscences of the Indians. Richmond: 1869. V. 37; 38; 39; 41; 42; 45

WASHBURN, CHARLES A.

The History of Paraguay with Notes of Personal Observations and Reminiscences of Diplomacy Under Difficulties. Boston: 1871. V. 42

WASHBURN, CHARLES G.

Theodore Roosevelt: The Logic of His Career. Boston/New York: 1916. V. 37

WASHBURN, EMORY

Lectures on the Study and Practice of Law. Boston: 1876. V. 43

WASHBURN, STANLEY

Trails, Trappers and Tender-Feet in the New Empire of Western Canada. London: 1912. V. 39

Trails, Trappers and Tender-Feet in the New Empire of Western Canada. New York: 1912. V. 44

WASHINGTON

Statement of the Oregon and Washington Delegation in Regard to the War Claims of Oregon and Washington. (Washington: 1857). V. 37

WASHINGTON, BOOKER T. 1856-1915

Frederick Douglas. London: 1906. V. 43

The Future of the American Negro. Boston: 1899. V. 37; 39

The Future of American Negro. Boston: 1907. V. 41

The Negro Problem. New York: 1903. V. 38

The Negro in the South. Philadelphia: 1907. V. 41

Putting the Most Into Life. New York: 1906. V. 42

Sowing and Reaping. Boston: 1900. V. 41

Tuskegee and Its People. New York: 1905. V. 43

Up From Slavery. 1901. V. 45

Up From Slavery. Up. New York: 1901. V. 43

Up from Slavery. New York: 1903. V. 44

Working With the Hands. New York: 1904. V. 41; 42

THE WASHINGTON Directory and National Register, for 1846. Washington: 1846. V. 39; 43

WASHINGTON, GEORGE 1732-1799

Address of the Late General George Washington to the Citizens of the Unites States, Declining a Re-Election to the Office of President . . . Hartford: 1796. V. 40

Address to the Citizens of the United States, on Decling a Re-election to the Office of President. Hartford: 1800. V. 39

WASHINGTON, GEORGE 1732-1799 continued

Calendar of the Correspondence of George Washington. Washington: 1915. V. 39; 41

A Circular Letter from George Washington . . . to His Excellency William Greene, Esq., Governor of the State of Rhode Island. London: 1783. V. 41

A Collection of Papers, Relative to Half-Pay and Commutation Thereof, Granted by Congress to the Officers of the Army, Together with a Circular Letter. From His Excellency General Washington, to the Several Legislatures of the United States. Boston: 1783. V. 41; 45

A Collection of the Speeches of the President of the United States to Both Houses of Congress, at the Opening of Every Session, with Their Answers, Also, The Addresses to the President, with His Answers, From the Time of His Election. Boston: 1796. V. 41

The Diaries of George Washington 1748-1799. Boston: 1925. V. 43

The Diary of George Washington from 1789 to 1791 . . . New York: 1860. V. 40

Epistles, Domestic, Confidential and Official from General Washington. New York: 1746. V. 40

Epistles Domestic, Confidential, and Official from General Washington, Written . . . in the American Revolution, 1776-1783. New York: 1796. V. 39; 42

George Washington's Accounts of Expenses While Commander-in-Chief of the Continental Army 1775-1783. Boston: 1917. V. 42

George Washington, Sportsman: From His Own Journals. Cambridge: 1928. V. 39

Head Quarters, Peeks-Kill, (New York), General Orders for the Army Under the Command of Brigadier General M'Dougall . . . Instructions for Soldiers in the Service of the United States Concerning the Means of Preserving Health, Of Cleanliness . . . Fishkill: 1777. V. 45

The Journal of Major George Washington, Sent by the Hon. Robert Dinwiddie, Esq . . . to the Commandant of the French Forces on Ohio . . . London: 1754. V. 39; 46

Journal of My Journey Over the Mountains in the Northern Neck of Virginia, Beyond the Blue Ridge in 1747-8. Albany: 1892. V. 39

Journal of Colonel George Washington, Commanding a Detachment of Virginia Troops Sent by Robert Dinwiddie, Lt. Governor of Virginia . . . Albany: 1893. V. 38; 42

The Journal of . . . . New York: 1865. V. 37

Legacies of Washington . . . Trenton: 1800. V. 37; 45

The Legacy of the Father of His Country: Address of George Washington to His Fellow Citizens, on Declining Being Considered a Candidate for Their Future Suffrages. Stockbridge: 1796. V. 38; 39

Letters from General Washington to Several of His Friends, 1776 . . . Philadelphia: 1795. V. 39; 42; 46

Letters from His Excellency George Washington . . . to Sir John Sinclair . . . on Agricultural and Other Interesting Topics. London: 1800. V. 37; 45

Letters from His Excellency George Washington to Arthur Young and Sir John Sinclair. Alexandria: 1803. V. 39; 40

Letters and Recollections of George Washington, Being Letters to Tobias Lear and Others, 1790-1799. New York: 1906. V. 39

Monuments of Washington's Patriotism . . . City of Washington: 1838. V. 41; 45

Official Letters to the Honorable American Congress, Written, During the War Between the United Colonies and Great Britain . . . London: 1795. V. 41; 45; 46

Official Letters to the Honourable American Congress, Written During the War Between the United Colonies and Great Britain . . . Boston: 1796. V. 39

Selections from the Correspondence of General Washington and James Anderson. London;: 1880. V. 39

Washington's Farewell Address in Facsimile. New York: 1935. V. 39

The Will of General George Washington. Alexandria: 1800. V. 37; 39; 40

Writings of George Washington. Boston: 1838. V. 38

The Writings of George Washington. New York & London: 1889. V. 41

Writings. Washington: 1931-44. V. 39; 40; 44; 45; 46

THE WASHINGTON Historical Quarterly. Seattle: 1906-35/36-43. V. 46

WASHINGTON, JOHN

Esquimaux and English Vocabulary, for the Use of the Arctic Expeditions. London: 1850. V. 40

WASHINGTON, JOSEPH

An Exact Abridgment of all the Statutes of King William and Queen Mary, and of King William III in Force and Use, Begun by Joseph Washington and Since His Death Revised and Continued to 1700. London: 1701. V. 40

WASHINGTON. LAWS, STATUTES, ETC. - 1868

Statutes of the Territory of Washington, Made and passed by the First Biennial Session. Olympia: 1868. V. 37

WASHINGTON. LAWS, STATUTES, ETC. - 1881

Code of Washington, Containing all Acts of a General Nature of the Territory of Washington. Olympia: 1881. V. 37

WASHINGTON SOCIETY OF MARYLAND

The Constitution of the Washington Society of Maryland. Baltimore: 1810. V. 46

WASHINGTON. SUPREME COURT - 1864

Opinions of the Supreme Court of the Territory of Washington. Olympia: 1864. V. 37

WASHINGTON. (TERRITORY). BAR, 3RD JUDICIAL DISTRICT

Proceedings of a Meeting of the Bar, 3rd Judicial District, Washington Territory, on the Arrest of the Hon. Edward Lander, Chief Justice of Said Territory . . . Steilacoom,: 1856. V. 40

WASHINGTON'S Political Legaces. (with) an Appendix. Boston: 1800. V. 41

WASHINGTON'S Reception by the Ladies of Trenton, Together with the Chorus Sung as He Passed Under the Triumphal Arch Raised on the Bridge Over the Assunpink, April Twenty-First MDCCLXXXIX. New York: 1903. V. 42

WASSERMANN, JAKOB

Die Geschichte des Grafen Erdmann Promnitz. Munchen: 1921. V. 46

WASSON, EDMUND ATWILL

That Gettysburg Address. Verona: 1965. V. 44

WASSON, JOHN MACAMY

Annals of Pioneer Settlers on the Whitewater and Its Tributaries, in the Vicinity of Richmond, Ind., from 1804 to 1830 . . . Richmond: 1875. V. 40

WASSON, JOSEPH

Bodie and Esmeralda. San Francisco: 1878. V. 37; 41

WASSON, PAVLOVNA VALENTINA

Mushrooms: Russia and History. New York: 1957. V. 45

WASSON, ROBERT GORDON

The Hall Carbine Affair: a Study in Contemporary Folklore. New York: 1941. V. 43; 44; 45

Hall Carbine Affair; an Essay in Historiography. Danbury: 1971. V. 38; 39; 41; 43; 46

Maria Sabina and Her Mazatec Mushroom Velada. New York: 1974. V. 44; 46

Maria Sabina and Her Mazatec Mushroom Velada. New York: & London: 1974. V. 40; 45

Maria Sabina and Her Mazatec Mushroom Velada. New York: 1975. V. 39

Soma, Divine Mushroom of Immortality. New York: 1968. V. 40; 41; 42; 43; 45; 46

Soma: Divine Mushroom of Immortality. The Hague: 1968. V. 38

The Wondrous Mushroom. New York: 1980. V. 37; 40; 44

WASSON, VALENTIA PAVLOVNA

Mushrooms, Russia and History. New York: 1957. V. 40; 42

Mushrooms, Russia and History. New York: 1974. V. 43

WATELET, CLAUDE HENRI

L'Art de Peindre. Poeme avec des Reflexions sur les differentes parties de la peinture. Paris: 1760. V. 37

THE WATER Cure Illustrated. London: 1870. V. 46

WATER, THOMAS WILLIAM RUSSELL

The Recollection of a Policeman. New York: 1853. V. 40

WATERFORD, LOUISA MARCHIONESS OF & TANKERVILLE, COUNTESS OF

Songs Being Original Poems Illustrated and Illuminated. London: 1884. V. 43

WATERHOSUE, ELLIS

Gainsborough. London: 1958. V. 46

WATERHOUS, EDWARD

An Humble Apologie for Learning and Learned Men. London: 1653. V. 42

WATERHOUSE, BENJAMIN

A Journal of a Young Man of Massachusetts, Late a Surgeon on Board an American Privateer, Who Was Captured by the British . . . and Was Confined First, at Melville Island, Halifax, Then at Chatham, in England and Last, at Dartmoor Prison . . . Boston: 1816. V. 38; 40

A Journal of a Young Man of Massachusetts, Late a Surgeon on Board an American Privateer. Milledgeville: 1816. V. 40; 42; 45

The Rise, Progress and Present State of Medicine. Boston: 1792. V. 40; 44; 45

WATERHOUSE, EDWARD

The Gentlemans Monitor. London: 1665. V. 40; 44; 46

An Humble Apologie for Learning and Learned Men. London: 1653. V. 46

WATERHOUSE, J.

Practical Notes on the Preparation of Drawings for Photographic Reproduction . . . London: 1890. V. 45

WATNEY, VERNON

Catalogue of the Library at Cornbury. Oxford: 1917. V. 38; 40

WATNEY, VERNON A.

Cornbury and the Forest of Wychwood. London: 1910. V. 44

WATROUS, ANSEL

History of Larimer County, Colorado. Fort Collins: 1911. V. 37; 38; 39; 43; 44

WATSON, A. G.

Catalogue of Dated and Datable Manuscripts c. 435-1600 in Oxford Libraries. Oxford: 1984. V. 39

WATSON, ALEXANDER

A Medico-Legal Treatise on Homicide by External Violence. Edinburgh: 1837. V. 39

WATSON, ALFRED E. T.

King Edward VII as a Sportsman. London: 1911. V. 38; 39; 40; 45

Lord Derby's Race-Horses. London: 1915. V. 37

WATSON & PRITCHETT

Plans, Elevations, Sections and Description of the Pauper Lunatic Asylum, Lately Erected at Wakefield, for the West Riding of Yorkshire . . . York: 1819. V. 45

WATSON, CHARLES J.

Catalogue of the Etched and Engraved Work of Charles J. Watson, R.E. Hammersmith: 1931. V. 39

WATSON, COLIN

Coffin Scarcely Used. London: 1958. V. 38

WATSON, DOUGLAS SLOANE

California in the Fifties. San Francisco: 1936. V. 37; 46

The Founding of the First California Missions Under the Spiritual Guidance of the Venerable Padre Fray Junipero Serra an Historical Account of the Expeditions Sent by Land and Sea in the Year 1769 . . . San Francisco: 1934. V. 42

The Santa Fe Trail to California 1849-1852. The Journal and Drawings of H.M.T. Powell. Edited by Douglas S. Watson. San Francisco: (1936). V. 37

Spanish Occupation of California. San Francisco: 1934. V. 38; 43; 45; 46

Trails of American Indian Life and Characters. San Francisco: 1933. V. 44; 46

West Wind, the Life Story of Joseph Reddedord Walker, Knight of the Golden Horseshoe. Los Angeles: 1934. V. 38; 40; 45

WATSON, E. T.

Fur, Feather and Fin Series. London: 1893-1906. V. 41

King Edward VII as a Sportsman. London: 1911. V. 37

WATSON, ELKANAH

History of the Rise, Progress and Existing Condition of the Western Canals in the State of New York . . . Albany: 1820. V. 43

Men and Times of the Revolution. New York: 1856. V. 38; 40; 46

A Tour in Holland in MDCCLXXXIV. Worcester: 1790. V. 37; 43

WATSON, F. J. B.

Watson Collection Catalogue; Furniture: Text with Historical Notes and Illustrations. By F.J.B Watson. London: 1956. V. 37

The Wrightsman Collection. New York: 1966-73. V. 43

WATSON, FRANCIS S.

Diseases and Surgery of the Genito Urinary System. Philadelphia: & New York: 1908. V. 45

WATSON, G.

Three Rolling Stones in Japan. London: 1904. V. 39; 44

WATSON, G. N.

A Treatise on the Theory of Bessel Functions. Cambridge: 1922. V. 37

WATSON, GAYLORD

New Indexed Family Atlas of the United States, with Maps of the World . . . Boston: 1885. V. 45

Watson's New and Complete Illustrated Atlas of the World. New York: 1891. V. 45

Watson's New and Complete Illustrated Atlas of the World . . . New York: 1892. V. 45

WATSON, GEORGE

The New Cambridge Bibliography of English Literature. Volume 3 1800-1900. Cambridge: 1969. V. 39

The New Cambridge Bibliography of English Literature. Volume 2 1660-1800. Cambridge: 1971. V. 39

The New Cambridge Bibliography of English Literature. Cambridge: 1971-77. V. 40

The New Cambridge Bibliography of English Literature. Volume 4, 1900-1950. Cambridge: 1972. V. 39

WATSON, IRVING

Physicians and Surgeons of America. Concord: 1896. V. 38; 41

Physicians and Surgeons of America. (Illustrated): A Collection of Biographical Sketches of the Regular Medical Profession. Concord: 1896. V. 37

WATSON, J. A. L.

Caste Differentiation in Social Insects. London: 1984. V. 37

WATSON, J. W.

Beautiful Snow and Other Poems. Philadelphia: 1869. V. 40

WATSON, JAMES

A V. 42

Choice Collection of Comic and Serious Scots Poems. Glasgow: 1869. V. 42

The Dog Book, a Popular History of the Dog, with Practical Information as to Care and Management of the House, Kennel and Exhibition Dogs . . . New York: 1905. V. 45

The Dog Book. London: 1906. V. 45

The Dog Book. New York: 1906. V. 45

The History of the Art of Printing . . . Edinburgh: 1713. V. 38

Observations in Some New Remedies. Edinburgh: 1864. V. 39; 41

Paramythia; or, Mental Pastimes. London: 1821. V. 43

The Spirit of the Doctor . . . Manchester: 1820. V. 42

The Structure of DNA. New York: 1953. V. 41

The Trial of James Watson, for High Treason at the Bar of the Court of King's Bench . . . June 1817. London: 1817. V. 46

WATSON, JAMES D.

The Double Helix. New York: 1968. V. 46

WATSON, JOHN

The History and Antiquities of the Parish of Halifax, in Yorkshire. London: 1765. V. 45

The History and Antiquities of the Parish of Halifax, in Yorkshire. London: 1775. V. 39

Memoires of the Family of the Stuarts and the Remarkable Providences of God Towards Them . . . London: 1683. V. 42

Memorals of the Ancient Earls of Warren and Surrey, and Their Descendants to the Present Time. Warrington: 1782. V. 40

Souvenir of a Tour in the United States of America and Canada in the Autumn of 1872. Glasgow: 1872. V. 38

WATSON, JOHN B.

Psychology from the Standpoint of the Behaviourist . . . Philadelphia & London: 1919. V. 37

WATSON, JOHN EDWARD

The Housewife's Directory. London: 1832. V. 39

WATSON, JOHN F.

Annals of Philadelphia and Pennsylvania, in the Olden Time. Philadelphia. V. 46

Annals of Philadelphia . . . Philadelphia: 1830. V. 42

Annals of Philadelphia and Pennsylvania in the Olden Time . . . Philadelphia: 1856. V. 42

Annals of Philadelphia and Pennsylvania in the Olden Time . . . Philadelphia: 1877. V. 42

Annals of Philadelphia and Pennsylvania, in the Olden Time . . . Philadelphia: 1877-79. V. 41; 42

Annals of Philadelphia and Pennsylvania, in the Olden Time: Memoirs. Philadelphia: 1927. V. 44

Historic Tales of Olden Time: COncerning the Early Settlement and Advancement of New York City and State. New York: 1832. V. 37

WATSON, JOHN FORBES

The Textile Manufactures and the Costumes of the People of India. London: 1866. V. 38; 41; 46

WATSON, JOSEPH YELLOLY

A Compendium of British Mining, with Statistical Notices of the Principal Mines in Cornwall; to which is Added, the History and Uses of Metals, and a Glossary of the Terms and Usages of Mining. London: 1843. V. 37; 42

WATSON, LEIGH F.

Hernia: Anatomy, Etiology, Symptoms, Diagnosis, Differential Diagnosis, Prognosis and the Operative and Injection Treatment. St. Louis: 1938. V. 42

WATSON, LILY

The Vicar of Langthwaite. London: 1893. V. 39; 41

WATSON, M. L.

Designs Illustrative of Samuel Roger's Poem 'Human Life.' London: 1851. V. 40

WATSON, MARY

People I Have Met. Short Sketches of Many Prominent Persons. San Francisco: 1890. V. 41

WATSON, MISS

Rosamund, Countess of Clarenstein. London: 1812. V. 41

WATSON, NORMAN

Round Mystery Mountian. London: 1935. V. 44; 45

WATSON, P. W.

Dendrologia Britannica, or Trees and Shrubs That Will Live in the Open Air of Britain . . . London: 1825. V. 37; 42; 43

WATSON, RICHARD, BP. OF LLANDAFF 1737-1816

Anecdotes of the Life of Richard Watson, Bishop of Landaff.. London: 1817. V. 37; 39; 40; 46

An Answer to the Disquisition on Government and Civil Liberty . . . London: 1782. V. 42

An Apology for the Bible, in a Series of Letters, Addressed to Thomas Paine. New York: 1796. V. 41

An Aplogy for Christianity, in a Series of Letters, Addressed to Edward Gibbon, Esq. Philadelphia: 1796. V. 45

Chemical Essays. London: 1784-87. V. 39

Chemical Essays. Cambridge: 1787. V. 46

Chemical Essays. London: 1800. V. 42; 43; 46

An Essay on Civil Liberty. Cambridge: 1776. V. 39

The Principles of Revolution Vindicated. Cambridge: 1776. V. 42

WATSON, ROBERT

Dreams of Fort Garry. Winnipeg: 1931. V. 41

The History of the Reign of Philip the Third, King of Spain. London: 1793. V. 38

The History of the Reign of Philip the Second, King of Spain. London: 1812. V. 46

The History of the Reign of Philip the Second, King of Spain. London: 1777, 1783. V. 37

WATSON, ROBERT SPENCE

A Visit to Wazan, the Sacred City of Morocco. London: 1880. V. 38; 40

WATSON, ROSAMUND MARRIO H.

Vespertilta and Other Verses. London: 1895. V. 41

WATSON, ROSAMUND MARRIOTT

Vespertilia and Other Verses. Chicago: 1895. V. 38

WATSON, SAMUEL

A Short Account of the Convincement, Gospell Labours, Sufferings and Service of that Faithful Servant . . . London: 1712. V. 44

WATSON, S.H., MRS.

A Folio of Old Songs. Waxahachie: 1912. V. 42

WATSON, THOMAS

Lectures on the Principles and Practice of Physic . . . Philadelphia: 1858. V. 42; 45

WATSON, THOMAS E.

The Life and Times of Andrew Jackson. Thomson, GA.: 1917. V. 37

WATSON, THOMAS WALLER

Report of the Trial of Thomas Jonathan Wooler, for a Libel on His Majesty's Ministers . . . Newcastle: 1823. V. 38

WATSON, WILBUR J.

Bridge Architecture. New York: 1927. V. 37

WATSON, WILLIAM

An Account of a Series of Experiments, Instituted with a View Ascertaining the Most Successful Method of Inoculating the Small-Pox. London: 1768. V. 40; 44

Art of Dynastic China. New York: 1981. V. 38; 41

The Clergy-Man's Law; or, the Compleat Incumbent. London: 1712. V. 40

The Clergy-Man's Law: Or, the Complete Incumbent. In the Savoy: 1725. V. 45

The Clergy-Man's Lw. London: 1725. V. 38

The Clergy-Man's Law, or, the Compleat Incumbent. London: 1747. V. 40

The Collected Poems of . . . New York & London: 1899. V. 42

Eloping Angels; a Caprice. London: 1893. V. 38; 41

Excursions in Criticism. London: 1893. V. 38; 41

Experiments and Observations Tending to Illustrate the Nature and Properties of Electricity. (with) A Sequel to the Experiments and Observations . . . London: 1746. V. 38

New Poems. London: 1909. V. 46

Orchids: Their Culture and Management . . . London: 1890. V. 37; 39

Orchids; their Culture and Management. London: 1893. V. 38

Orchids: Their Culture and Management. London: 1900. V. 41

Orchids: Their Culture and Management . . . London: 1903. V. 46

Paris Universal Exposition, 1889. Washington: 1802. V. 43

The Poems of William Watson. London: 1905. V. 42

The Prince's Quest. London: 1893. V. 40

Vienna International Exhibition, 1873. Washington: 1875. V. 43

Wordsworth's Grave and Other Poems. London: 1890. V. 43

WATSON, WILLIAM, F.A.S.

An Historical Account of the Ancient Town and Port of Wisbech, in the Isle of Ely, in the County of Cambridge, and of the Circumjacent Towns and Villages, the Drainage of the Great Level of the Fens, the Origin of the Royal Franchise to the Isle of Ely . . . London: 1827. V. 41

WATSON, WILLIAM, of Skelmorlie, Scotland

Life in the Confederate Army . . . New York: 1888. V. 42; 43

WATSON, WINSLOW C.

Military and Civil History of the County of Essex, New York. Albany: 1869. V. 38

WATT, ALEXANDER

The Art of Paper-Making. New York: 1907. V. 40; 44

WATT, G.

Dictionary of the Economic Products of India. London: & Calcutta,: 1889-93. V. 43

WATT, GEORGE

Indian Art at Delhi 1903. London: 1904. V. 44

The Pests and Blights of the Tea Plant, Being a Report of Investigations Conducted in Assam and . . . also in Kangra. Calcutta: 1898. V. 41

WATT, GERTRUDE BALMER

Town and Trail. Edmonton: 1908. V. 43; 45

WATT, JAMES

Correspondence of the Late James Watt On His Discovery of the Theory of the Composition of Water . . . London: 1846. V. 39

The Life of . . . with Selections from his Correspondence. By J.P. Muirhead. London;: 1858. V. 37

The Origin and Progress of the Mechanical Inventions of James Watt. London: 1854. V. 39

WATT, JOHN JAMES

Anatomical Chirurgical Views of the Nose, Mouth, Larygnx, Fauces with appropriate explanation. The Engravings executed by Hopwood, from original drawings by Baster: together with an additional anatomical description . . . London: 1809. V. 37

WATT, ROBERT 1774-1819

Bibliotheca Britannica. Edinburgh: 1824. V. 37; 38; 39; 40; 42; 43; 46

Cases of Diabetes, Consumption and with Observations on the History and Treatment of Disease in General. Edinburgh: 1808. V. 37; 38

The Declaration and Confession of Robert Watt, Written, Subscribed and Delivered by Himself, the Evening Before His Execution for High Treason. Edinburgh: 1794. V. 39

WATT, STUART, MRS.

In the Heart of Savagedom, Reminiscences of Life and Adventure During Quarter of a Century of Pioneering Missionary Labours in the Wilds of East Equatorial Africa. London. V. 43

WATTERS, WILLIAM

A Short Account of the Christian Experience and Ministereal Labours of William Watters. Alexandria: (1806). V. 37

WATTERSTON, GEORGE

Letters from Washington, on the Constitution and Laws; with Sketches of Some of the Prominent Public Characters of the United States. City of Washington: 1818. V. 45

WATTEVILLE, VIVIENNE DE

Out in the Blue. London: 1927. V. 44; 45

WATTS, ALAN

The Book: on the Taboo Against Knowing Who You Are. New York: 1966. V. 46

WATTS, ALAN W.

Zen. Stanford: 1948. V. 39

WATTS, ALARIC A.

Lyrics of the Heart; with other Poems. London: 1851. V. 37; 38

Poetical Sketches: The Profession; The Broken Heart, etc. London: 1823. V. 43

WATTS, ARTHUR

A Painter's Anthology. New York: 1924. V. 37

WATTS, GEORGE FREDERICK

Pictures By . . . New York: 1904. V. 42

WATTS, HENRY

A Dictionary of Chemistry and the Allied Branches of Other Sciences. London: 1866-81. V. 42

A Dictionary of Chemistry, and the Allied Branches of Other Sciences. London: 1874. V. 40

WATTS, ISAAC 1674-1748

Death and Heaven; or the Last Enemy Conquered . . . London: 1722. V. 41; 45

A Defense Against the Temptation to Self-Murther. London: 1726. V. 42

Divine Songs Attempted in Easy Language for Children. London: 1774. V. 39

Divine Songs for Children. Reading: 1800's. V. 38; 41

Divine and Moral Songs for Children. London: 1896. V. 40; 41

First Principles of Astronomy and Geography explained by the Use of Globes and maps, etc. London: 1765. V. 37

The Glory of Christ as God-Man Display', in Three Discourses . . . London: 1746. V. 42

A Guide to Prayer. London: 1715. V. 41; 45

Horae Lyricae. London: 1709. V. 41; 45

Hymns and Spiritual Songs. London: 1755. V. 43

Hymns and Spiritual Songs. London: 1774. V. 43

The Improvement of the Mind, or a Supplement to the Art of Logic. London: 1784. V. 37

Logick; or, the Right Use of Reason in the Enquiry after Truth, with a Variety of Rules to Guard Against Error, in the Affairs of Religion and Human Life . . . London: 1725. V. 43; 45

Logick; or, the Right Use of Reason in the Enquiry After Truth . . . London: 1726. V. 42

Logick; or, the Right Use of Reason in the Enquiry After Truth with a Variety of Rules to Guard Against Error, in the Affairs of Religion and Human Life. London: 1729. V. 40

Logick; or, the Right Use of Reason in the Inquiry After Truth. London: 1782. V. 41; 42

Memoirs of the Rev. Isaac Watts, D.D. London: 1780. V. 41

Philosophical Essays on Various Subjects, viz. Space, Substance, Body, Spirit, The Operations of the Soul in Union with the Body . . . London: 1733. V. 43

Philosophical Essays on Various Subjects . . . London: 1734. V. 39; 40

The Psalms of David Imitated in the Language of the New Testament, And Apply'd to the Christian State and Worship. London: 1719. V. 41; 42

The Psalms of David, Imitated in the Language of the New Testament and Subject to Christian State and Worship. London. V. 46

The Psalms of David, Imitated in the Language of the New Testament . . . Together with Hymns, and Spiritual Songs, in Three Books . . . Northampton: 1799. V. 37

Reliquiae Juveniles. London: 1734. V. 38; 40; 41; 45

Sermons on Various Subjects, Divine and Moral: with a Sacred Hymn Suited to each Subject. Designed for the use of Christian Families, as well as for the Hours of Devout Retirement. Boston/New England: 1746. V. 37

Shipbuilding, Theoretical and Practical. London: 1866. V. 38

Three Dissertations Relating to the Christian Doctrine of the Trinity . . . (with) Dissertations Relating to the Christian Doctrine of the Trinity . . . London: 1724-25. V. 45

A Wonderful Dream. Greenwich: 1804. V. 40

The Works of the Late Reverend and Learned Isaac Watts. London: 1753. V. 38; 41; 45

The Works of the Rev. Isaac Watts, D.D. Leeds: 1803. V. 41; 45

The Works . . . to Which are Prefixed, Memoirs of the Life of the author. London: 1810-11. V. 44

WATTS, ISSAC 1674-1748

The Improvement of the Mind: or a Supplement to the Art of Logic. Edinburgh: 1814. V. 46

WATTS, J. G.

Pictures of English Life. London: 1865. V. 43

WATTS, JANE ISABELLA

Memoirs of Early Days in South Australia. Adelaide: 1882. V. 37; 45

WATTS, JANE WALDIE

Sketches Descriptive of Italy in the Years 1816 and 1816. London: 1820. V. 44

WATTS, JOHN 1818-1887

The Facts of the Cotton Famine. London: & Manchester: 1866. V. 39; 42

WATTS, M. S.

George Frederic Watts. The Annals of an Artist's Life. London: 1912. V. 39; 46

George Frederic Watts. New York. V. 40

George Frederic Watts. New York. V. 44

George Frederic Watts. New York: (n.d.). V. 37

The Maid of the Alamo, or the Incarnation of Chivalry. Mineral Wells: 1913. V. 39

WATTS, W.

Select Views of the Principal Buildings and Other Interesting and Picturesque Objects in the Cities of Bath and Bristol, and Their Environs. London: 1819. V. 38; 41

WATTS, W. W.

Old English Silver. New York: 1924. V. 42; 45

WATTS, WILLIAM

The Seats of the Nobility and Gentry in a Collection of the Most Interesting and Picturesque Views. Chelsea: 1779-86. V. 39

Snioland: or, Iceland, Its Jokulls and Fjalls. London: 1875. V. 42

The Yahoo: a Satirical Rhapsody. (with) The Mohawks: a Satirical Poem with Notes. New York: 1922. V. 41

WATTS, WILLIAM W.

Works of Art in Silver and Other Metals Belonging to Viscount and Viscountess Lee of Fareham. London: 1936. V. 46

WAUCHOPE, A. G.

A History of the Black Watch (Royal Highlanders) in the Great War 1914-1918. London: 1925-26. V. 37; 42

WAUCHOPE, ROBERT

Handbook of Middle American Indians. Austin: 1964-76. V. 44

Modern Maya Houses: a Study of Their Archaeological Significance. Washington: 1938. V. 42

WAUGH, ALEC

Island in the Sun. London: 1965. V. 38

The Lipton Story. New York: 1950. V. 39

The Prisoners of Mainz. London: 1919. V. 46

Resentment - Poems. London: 1918. V. 38; 45

WAUGH, ARTHUR

The Square Book of Animals. London: 1899. V. 44

WAUGH, EDWIN

Home Life of the Lancashire Factory Folk During the Cotton Famine. London: 1867. V. 42; 43

The Works. Manchester: 1881. V. 41

WAUGH, EVELYN ARTHUR ST. JOHN 1903-1966

Basil Seal Rides Again. Boston: 1963. V. 37; 39; 40; 44; 46

Basil Seal Rides Again. London: 1963. V. 39; 40; 41; 42; 44

Black Mischief. London: 1932. V. 37; 38; 40; 41; 42; 43; 44; 46

Black Mischief. London: 1938. V. 40

Brideshead Revisited. Boston: 1945. V. 44; 45

Brideshead Revisited. London: 1945. V. 40; 42; 43; 46

Brideshead Revisited. Boston: 1946. V. 37; 40; 43

Bye-Bye Brevoort. Jackson: 1980. V. 44

Decline and Fall. London: 1928. V. 40; 42

Decline and Fall. London: 1937. V. 38

Edmund Campion. London: 1935. V. 39

A Handful of Dust. London: 1934. V. 38; 40; 42; 46

A Handful of Dust. New York: 1934. V. 42; 46

Helena, a Novel. London: 1950. V. 38; 41

Helena. Toronto: 1950. V. 39

The Holy Place. London: 1952. V. 44

The Holy Places. London: 1952. V. 37; 41; 42

The Holy Places. 1953. V. 42

The Holy Places. London: 1953. V. 38; 39; 41; 43; 45

The Holy Places. London: New York: 1953. V. 44

Labels, a Mediterranean Journal. London: 1930. V. 39; 40; 41; 46

A Little Learning. London: 1964. V. 38; 44

The Loom of Youth. London: 1917. V. 46

Love Among the Ruins. London: 1953. V. 39; 40; 41; 42

The Loved One. London: 1948. V. 37; 38; 40; 41; 45; 46

The Loved One. London. V. 37

Loveday's Little Outing. London: 1936. V. 42

WAUGH, EVELYN ARTHUR ST. JOHN 1903-1966 continued

The Mating Season. New York: 1949. V. 40

Men at Arms. London: 1952. V. 42; 43

Men at Arms; Officer and Gentlemen; the End of the Battle. Boston: 1952/55/61. V. 41; 42

Men at Arms, Officers and Gentlemen, Unconditional Surrender. London: 1952-61. V. 41

Mexico: an Object Lesson. Boston: 1939. V. 42; 44; 46

Mr. Loveday's Little Outing. 1936. V. 43

Mr. Loveday's Little Outing. Boston: 1936. V. 43

Mr. Loveday's Little Outing. London: 1936. V. 40; 42; 46

Ninety Two Days. London: 1934. V. 41; 42

Ninety-Two Days: a Tropical Journey. New York: 1934. V. 46

Officers and Gentlemen. London: 1955. V. 40; 45

The Ordeal of Gilbert Pinfold. London: 1957. V. 37; 40; 41

PRB. Kent: 1982. V. 43

P.R.B. An Essay on the Pre-Raphaelite Brotherhood: 1847-1854. London: 1982. V. 39

Put Out More Flags. Boston: 1942. V. 43

Put Out More Flags. London: 1942. V. 41; 42; 46

Remote People. London: 1931. V. 42

Retreat. 1981. V. 44

Robbery Under Law. London: 1939. V. 42

Rosetti His Life and Works. London: 1928. V. 37; 40; 42

Rossetti: His Life and Works. New York: 1928. V. 37; 40; 41; 42

Scoop. London: 1933. V. 37; 43; 45

Scoop. 1938. V. 43

Scoop. Boston: 1938. V. 37; 41; 44

Scoop. London: 1938. V. 38; 39; 40; 41; 43; 44; 45; 46

Scott-King's Modern Europe. London: 1947. V. 39; 40; 41

Scott-King's Modern Europe. London: 1947. V. 40

The Sword of Honour Trilogy. London: 1952-55-61. V. 42; 46

The Sword of Honour - a Final Version of Men at Arms, Officers and Gentlemen, Unconditional Surrender. London: 1965. V. 38

They Were Still Dancing. New York: 1932. V. 37; 40; 45

Unclouded Summer: a Love Story. New York: 1948. V. 44

Unconditional Surrender. London: 1961. V. 40; 41; 45

Vile Bodies. London: 1930. V. 40; 43; 46

Vile Bodies. London: 1931. V. 38

Waugh in Abyssinia. London: 1936. V. 41; 42

Waugh in Abyssinia. London & New York: 1936. V. 43

When the Going Was Good. London: 1946. V. 41

Wine in Peace and War. London: 1947. V. 39; 45

Wine in Peace and War. London: 1948. V. 45

Wine in Peace and War. London: 1949. V. 37

WAUGH, FREDERICK J.

The Clan of Munes. New York: 1916. V. 42

WAUGH, IDA

Ideal Heads. Philadelphia: 1890. V. 45

Over the Hills. London: 1882. V. 45

Tangles and Curls. New York: 1888. V. 44

WAUGH, LORENZO

Autobiography of Lorenzo Waugh. Oakland: 1883. V. 37; 40; 46

WAUGHBURTON, RICHARD

Innocence and Design. London: 1935. V. 42

WAUTERS, A. J.

Stanley's Emin Pasha Expedition. London: 1890. V. 45

WAVELL, ARCHIBALD PERCIVAL WAVELL, 1ST EARL OF 1883-1950

Other Men's Flowers. London: 1944. V. 43

WAWN, WILLIAM T.

The South Sea Islanders and the Queensland Labour Trade, a Record of Voyages and Experiences in the Western Pacific, from 1875 to 1891. London: 1893. V. 46

WAX Flowers; How to Make Them. Boston: 1864. V. 38

WAXEL, LEON DE

Receuil de Quelques Antiquites, Trouvees sur la Bords de la Mer Noire Appartenans a l'Empire de Russie . . . Berlin: 1803. V. 44

WAXHAM, F. E.

Intubation of the Larynx. Chicago: 1888. V. 39

THE WAY of the Cross. Ditchling: 1917. V. 41
THE WAY of the Cross. Ditchling: 1923. V. 45

THE WAY of the World, a Tale. London: 1798. V. 39

WAY, THOMAS ROBERT

The Lithographs by Whistler . . . New York: 1914. V. 41

Memories of James McNeill Whistler the Artist. London: 1912. V. 42; 45

Memories of James McNeill Whistler. London: and New York: 1912. V. 42

Mr. Whistler's Lithographs. London: 1905. V. 39; 41

THE WAY to True Peace, or a Calm, Seasonable and Modest Word in Love to the Independent, Phanaticks, Anabaptists, Presbyterians, Quakers, papists and Fifth Monarchists. London: 1660. V. 39

WAYLAND, FRANCIS 1796-1865

The Elements of Political Economy. New York: 1837. V. 43

The Elements of Political Economy. London: 1850. V. 42

A Memoir of the Life and Labors of the Rev. Adoniarum Judson, D.D. Boston: 1853. V. 44

WAYLAND, JOHN WALTER

The German Element of the Shenandoah Valley of Virginia. Charlottesville: 1907. V. 42

WAYLAND, VIRGINIA

Of Carving, Cards and Cookery or the Mode of Carving at the Table. Arcadia: 1962. V. 46

WAYLEN, EDWARD

Ecclesiastical Reminiscences of the United States. London: 1846. V. 43; 46

Ecclesiastical Reminiscences of the United States. New York: 1846. V. 42

WAYLETT, RICHARD

Puppy Tails. London. V. 45

WAYMENT, H.

The Windows of King's College Chapel, Cambridge. London: 1972. V. 37

WAYNE, T. G.

Morals and Marriage: the Catholic Background to Sex. London: 1936. V. 43

WAYS and Means; or an Easy Method to Raise the Supplies, in a Letter to an High-Constable. London: 1748. V. 41

WAYSIDE Posies: Original Poems of Country Life. London: 1867. V. 38; 42

WAYSS, G. A.

Das System Monier (Eisengerippe mit Cementumhullung) in Seiner Anwendung auf das Gesammte Bauwesen. Vienna: 1887. V. 44

WAYTE, SAMUEL C.

The Equestrian's Manual. London: 1850. V. 42

WAYWELL, G. B.

The Free Standing Sculptures of the Mausoleum at Halicarnasus in the British Museum. London: 1978. V. 40

WE Have All Been In the Wrong; or, Thoughts Upon the Dissolution of the late and Conduct of the Present Parliament, and Upon Mr. Fox's East India Bills. London: 1785. V. 41

WE Japanese, Being Descriptions of Many of the Customs, Manners, Ceremonies, Festivals, Arts and Crafts of the Japanese Besides Numerous Other Subjects. Mynoshita: 1935. V. 38

WEADOCK, JACK

Dust for the Desert. New York: 1936. V. 38

WEALE, JOHN

An Account of the Construction of the Iron Roof of the New Houses of Parliament. London: 1844. V. 43

Atlas of the Engravings to Illustrate and Practically Explain the Construction of Roofs of Iron, Intended to Further Elucidate this Particular Mode of Building with Iron for Public Edifices. London: 1859. V. 43

Divers Works of Early Masters in Christian Decoration . . . . London: 1846. V. 44

Ensamples of Railway Making; Which Although Not of English Practice are Submitted with Practical Illustrations, to the Civil Engineer, and the British and Irish. London: 1843. V. 46

London Exhibited in 1852. London: 1852. V. 40

Old English and French Ornament for the Interior Embellishment of Houses. London: 1846. V. 40

Quarterly Papers on Engineering. London: 1843-49. V. 42

Quarterly Papers on Architecture. London: 1844-45. V. 37; 42

Weale's Quarterly Papers on Architecture. London: 1843-45. V. 40

WEALE, W. H. JAMES

Bookbindings and Rubbings of Bindings in the National Art Library, South Kensington Museum. London: 1894-8. V. 41

WEALTH and Pedigree of the Wealthy Citizens of New York City. New York: 1842. V. 37

WEARE, W. K.

Songs of the Western Shore. San Francisco: 1879. V. 44

WEATHERBY, JAMES

The Racing Calendar . . . London: 1775-1899. V. 46

WEATHERHEAD, G. HUME

An Account of the Royal Beulah Saline Spar at Norwood, Surrey. London: 1835. V. 41

WEATHERHEAD, GEORGE HUME

An analysis of the Leamington Spa, in Warwickshire, with Remarks on Its Use and Medicinal Qualities. London: 1820. V. 42

WEATHERLEY, FRED E.

More Pleasant Surprises for Chicks of all Sizes. London: 1890. V. 40

WEATHERLY, F. E.

Peeps into Fairyland. London: 1880. V. 45

Peeps into Fairyland. A Panorama Picture Book of Fairy Stories. With an introduction by F.E. Weatherly. London: (n.d.). V. 37

Told in the Twilight. London: 1883. V. 45

WEATHERLY, FRED E.

Touch and Go. London & New York: 1895. V. 38

WEATHERLY, FREDERIC E.

Over the Hills, Away. London: 1880. V. 46

Over the Hills Away! Poems . . . London: 1892. V. 42

WEATHERS, J.

Commercial Gardening, a Practical and Scientific Treatise for Market Gardeners, Market Growers, Fruit, Flower and Vegetable Growers . . . London: 1913. V. 46

WEATHERWISE'S Almanack, for . . . 1797. Boston: 1797. V. 40

WEATHERWISE'S Almanack, for . . . 1797 . . . 1797. V. 44

WEAVER, ETHAN ALLEN

The Forks of the Delaware . . . Easton: 1900. V. 37; 42

WEAVER, FLAVE J.

Six Years in Bondage and Freedom at Last. N.P.. V. 39

Six Years in Bondage and Freedom at Last. Whitesboro: 1900. V. 44

WEAVER, HENRY

Hints on Cottage Architecture. Bath: 1850. V. 44

WEAVER, JOHN

Anatomical and Mechanical Lectures Upon Dancing. London: 1721. V. 38

WEAVER, LAURENCE

The House and Its Equipment. London: 1920. V. 46

Lutyens Houses and Gardens. London: 1921. V. 46

WEAVER, LAWRENCE

Exhibitions and the Art of Display. London: 1925. V. 37

Gas Fires and Their Settings. London: 1929. V. 38

Houses and Gardens by E. L. Lutyens. London: 1913. V. 37; 39; 44

Houses and Gardens by E. L. Lutyens. London: 1914. V. 40; 41; 44

Houses and Gardens by Sir Edwin Lutyens. London: 1925. V. 37; 38; 41

WEAVER, R.

Monumenta Antiqua. London: 1840. V. 39; 41; 45

WEAVER, RAYMOND M.

Herman Melville Mariner and Mystic. New York: 1921. V. 41

WEAVER, W. D.

Catalogue of the Wheeler Gift of Books, Pamphlets and Periodicals in the Library of the American Inst. of Electrical Engineers . . . New York: 1909. V. 39

WEAVER, WILLIAM AUGUSTUS

Examination of a Pamphlet Printed and Secretly Circulated by M. E. Gorostiza . . . Respecting the Passage of the Sabine by the Troops Under the Command of General Gaines. Washington: 1837. V. 41; 42

WEAVER, WILLIAM D.

Catalogue of the Wheeler Gift of Books, Pamphlets and Periodicals in the Library of the American Institute of Electrical Engineers, with Introduction, Descriptive and Critical Notes by Brother Potamian. New York: 1909. V. 37; 40

THE WEAVERS Pretences Examin'd. London: 1719. V. 46

WEBB, A. P.

A Bibliography of the Works of Thomas Hardy. London: 1916. V. 44

WEBB, ALFRED

A Compendium of Irish Biography, Comprising Sketches of Distinguished Irishmen and of Eminent Persons Connected with Ireland by Office or by their Writings. Dublin: 1878. V. 38

WEBB, BENJAMIN 1819-1885

Sketches of Continental Ecclesiology, or Church Notes on Belgium, Germany and Italy. London: 1848. V. 39

WEBB, CHARLES

Martin Chuzzlewit, a Drama in Three Acts. London: 1844. V. 40

WEBB, DANIEL

An Inquiry into the Beauties of Painting. London: 1761. V. 38; 39

An Inquiry Into the Beauties of Painting. (and) Remarks on the Beauty of Poetry. Dublin: 1764. V. 44

Observations on the Correspondence Between Poetry and Music. London: 1769. V. 39; 42; 43; 46

Remarks on the Beauties of Poetry. London: 1762. V. 40

Remarks on the Beauties of Poetry. (with) An Inquiry into the Beauties of Painting . . . Dublin: 1764. V. 41

Selections from M. Pauw, with Additions by Daniel Webb. Bath: 1795. V. 38

WEBB, DANIEL CARLESS

Observations and Remarks During Four Excursions Made to Various Parts of Great Britain . . . by Land, by Sea, by Various Modes of Conveyance and Partly in the Pedestrian Style. London: 1812. V. 37; 43

WEBB, DAVID

Old Paper Specimens of Three Centuries. Chillicothe: 1945. V. 38; 41

WEBB, E. B.

On Iron Breakwaters and Piers. London: 1862. V. 44

WEBB, F. C.

Up the Tigris to Bagdad. London: 1870. V. 45

WEBB, FRANCIS

Somerset. A Poem. London: 1811. V. 42

WEBB, FRANK J.

The Garies and their Friends. London/New York: 1857. V. 37

WEBB, GEORGE

Practical Hints to Young Sportsmen, on the Best method of Cleaning, Loading and Carrying the Gun; Training the Dogs for September &c. London: 1857. V. 46

WEBB, GEORGE W.

Chronological List of Engagements Between the Regular Army of the United States and Various Tribes of Hostile Indians which occured During the Years 1790 to 1898, Inclusive. St. Joseph: 1939. V. 37

WEBB, H. J.

Narrative of the Voyage of H. M. Floating Dock 'Bermunda' from England to Bermuda. London: 1870. V. 40

WEBB, HENRY

Dogs: Their Points, Whims, Instincts and Peculiarities. London: 1873. V. 45

WEBB, JAMES JOSIAH

Adventures in the Santa Fe Trade 1844-1847. Glendale: 1931. V. 42; 45

WEBB, JOHN

The Duty of Ministers to Work the Works of Him that Sent Them, While It Is Day . . . A Sermon Occasion'd by the Much Lamented Death of The Reverend Mr. William Waldron. Boston: 1727. V. 38

Some Plain and Necessary Directions to Obtain Eternal Salvation. Boston: 1741. V. 40

WEBB, LAURA S.

Custer's Immortality. New York. V. 39

Custer's Immortality: a Poem, with Biographical Sketches of the Chief Actors in the Late Tragedy of the Wilderness. New York: 1890. V. 39

WEBB, MARION ST. JOHN

The Seed Fairies. London: 1920. V. 44

WEBB, MARY

The Golden Arrow. London: 1916. V. 40; 41; 42; 43; 44

Gone to Earth. London: 1917. V. 39; 41; 42

Gone to Earth. London: 1971. V. 40

Memoir of Mrs. Chloe Spear, a Native of Africa, Who Was Enslaved in Childhood and Died in Boston, January 5, 1815. Boston: 1832. V. 42

Precious Bane. London: 1924. V. 38; 39; 40

WEBB, MARY continued

The Prize. By Mary Webb. With watercolor illustrations by Nicholas Parry. Shropshire: 1985. V. 37

WEBB, PHILIP CARTERET

The Bill Permitting the Jews to be Naturalized by Parliament, Having Been Misrepresented in the London Gazetteer of Friday the 18th of May . . . N.P.: 1753. V. 42

Remarks on the Pretender's Declaration and Commission. With Remarks on the Pretender's Son's Second Declaration. London: 1745. V. 41; 46

A Short Account of Some Particulars Concerning Domes-Day Book, with a View to Promote Its Being Published. London: 1756. V. 42

WEBB, RICHARD D.

The Life and Letters of Captain John Brown, Who was Executed at Charlestown, Virginia, Dec. 2, 1859, for an Armed Attack Upon American Slavery . . . London: 1861. V. 42

WEBB, SAMUEL

History of Pennsylvania Hall, Which was Destoryed by a Mob on the 17th of May, 1838. Philadelphia: 1838. V. 38; 41; 42; 46

WEBB, SAMUEL BLACHLEY

Correspondence and Journal of Samuel B. Webb. New York: 1893. V. 45

Correspondence and Journal of Samuel B. Webb. New York: 1893. V. 44

Correspondence & Journals of . . . 1772-1806. New York: 1893-94. V. 42

WEBB, SIDNEY

The History of Trade Unionism. London: 1894. V. 39

WEBB, T.

A New Select Collection of Epitaphs . . . London: 1775. V. 46

WEBB, THOMAS H.

Information for Kanzas Immigrants. Boston: 1856. V. 42

Organization, Objects and Plan of Operations, of the Emigrant Aid Company . . . Boston: 1854. V. 45

WEBB, THOMAS SMITH

The Freemason's Monitor; or, Illustrations of Masonry. Salem and Providence: 1808. V. 40

WEBB, VIRGINIA

Archaic Greek Faience: Miniature Scent Bottles and Related Objects from East Greece, 650-500 B.C. Warminster: 1978. V. 42; 44

WEBB, W. E.

Buffalo Land: An Authentic Account of the Discoveries, Adventures and Mishaps of a Scientific and Sporting Party in the Wild West . . . Philadelphia: 1872. V. 37; 38; 39

WEBB, WALTER PRESCOTT 1888-1963

Flat Top: A Story of Modern Ranching. El Paso: 1960. V. 46

The Great Plains. 1931. V. 43

The Great Plains. Boston: 1931. V. 46

The Handbook of Texas. Austin: 1952. V. 37; 38

The Handbook of Texas. Austin: 1952 & 1976. V. 38; 41

The Handbook of Texas. Austin: 1976. V. 38; 39

The Texas Rangers: a Century of Frontier Defense. Boston: 1935. V. 37; 42; 44

The Texas Rangers. New York: 1935. V. 40; 42

The Texas Rangers in the Mexican War. Austin: 1975. V. 37

Toward the Morning Sun. Austin: 1968. V. 37

WEBB, WILLIAM

Minutes of Remarks on Subjects Picturesque, Moral, and Miscellaneous, made in a course along the Rhine, and during a residence in Swisserland and Italy, in the years 1822 & 1823. London: 1827. V. 37

WEBB, WILLIAM HENRY

Standard Guide to Non-Poisonous Herbal Medicine. Southport: 1916. V. 46

WEBB, WILLIAM SEWARD

California and Alaska and Over the Canadian Pacific Railway. New York: 1890. V. 37; 38; 39; 42; 45

Shelburne Farms Stud (Shelburne, Chittenden County, Vermont) of English Hackneys, Harness and Saddle Horses, Ponies and Trotters. New York: 1893. V. 42

WEBBE, CAROLINE GARRETT

Nine Christmas Carols. London: 1981. V. 42; 46

WEBBE, SAMUEL

A Miscellaneous Collection of Songs, Ballads, Canzonets, Duets, Trios, Glees, & Elegies. London: 1798. V. 39

WEBBER, ALEXANDER

Wine. A Series of Notes on This Valuable Product . . . London: 1888. V. 38

WEBBER, BYRON

James Orrock, R. I. Painter, Connoisseur, Collector. London: 1903. V. 39; 46

WEBBER, CHARLES WILKINS

The Gold Mines of the Gila. New York: 1849. V. 42

The Hunter Naturalist. Philadelphia: 1851. V. 38; 46

The Hunter-Naturalist: Wild Scenes and Song-Birds. New York: 1854. V. 37; 39; 41

Old Hick the Guide; or Adventures in the Camanche Country in Search of a Gold Mine. New York: 1848. V. 40; 41; 42; 44; 45

Old Hicks the Guide; or, Adventures in the Camanche Country in Search of a Gold Mine. London: 1850's. V. 39

Romance of Natural History; or, Wild Scenes and Wild Hunters. Philadelphia: 1852. V. 40

Wild Scenes and Song Birds. New York: 1854. V. 38; 40

WEBBER, H. J.

The Citrus Industry. Berkeley: 1948-43-48. V. 46

WEBBER, SAMUEL

War, a Poem, in Three Parts. Cambridge: 1823. V. 45

WEBBER, SAMUEL G.

A Treatise on Nervous Diseases Their Symptoms and Treatment. New York: 1885. V. 40

WEBBER, WINSLOW L.

Books About Books: a Bio-Bibliography for Collectors. Boston: 1937. V. 39

WEBER, BRUCE

O Rio De Janeiro: a Photographic Journal. New York: 1988. V. 46

Photographs. Los Angeles: 1983. V. 41

WEBER, CARL J.

Fore-Edge Painting: a Historical Survey of A Curious Art in Book Decoration. Irvington-on-Hudson: 1966. V. 37; 42

Fore-Edge Painting. New York: 1966. V. 37; 39; 41; 42; 44; 45; 46

A Thousand and One Fore-Edge Paintings, With Notes on The Artists, Bookbinders, Publishers and Other Men and Women Connected with the History of a Curious Art. Waterville: 1949. V. 37; 41; 42; 45; 46

WEBER, CHARLES D.

Chinese Pictorial Bronze Vessels of the Late Chou Period. Ascona: 1968. V. 41

WEBER, FRIEDRICH CHRISTIAN

The Present State of Russia. London: 1723-2. V. 42; 43; 45; 46

WEBER, HENRY

Illustrations of Northern Antiquities from the Earlier Teutonic and Scandinavian Romances. Edinburgh: 1814. V. 39; 43

WEBER, HENRY WILLIAM

Popular Romances: Consisting of Imaginary Voyages and Travels. Edinburgh: 1812. V. 43

Tales of the East; Comprising the Most Popular Romances of Oriental Origin; and the Best Imitations by European Authors . . . Edinburgh: 1812. V. 46

WEBER, M.

The Fishes of the Indo-Australian Archipelago. Leyden: 1911-62. V. 37

WEBER, MAX 1864-1920

Cubist Poems. London: 1914. V. 40; 41; 42; 45

Essays on Art. New York: 1916. V. 37; 45

Primitives, Poems and Woodcuts. New York: 1926. V. 39

The Theory of Social and Economic Organisation. London: 1947. V. 41

Woodcuts and Linoleum Blocks by . . . New York: 1956. V. 41

WEBER, PARKS

Aspects of Death and Correlated Aspects of Life in Art, Epigram and Poetry. London: 1922. V. 45

WEBSTER, ALEXANDER

Divine Influence the True Sprint of the Extraordinary Work at Cambuslang and Other Places in the West of Scotland. Boston: 1743. V. 44

Divine Influence The True Srping of the Extraordinary Work at Cambuslang and Other Places in West of Scotland. Edinburgh: Printed: 1743. V. 43

WEBSTER, ALFRED, MRS.

Dancing, as a Means of Physical Education: with Remarks on Deformities, and Their Prevention and Cure. London: 1851. V. 41; 42

WEBSTER, BENJAMIN

Autobiography . . . to Which is Added Extracts from the Diary of Mrs. Benjamin Webster. Portland: 1900. V. 39; 41

WEBSTER, CHARLES

Facts Tending to Show the Connection of the Stomach With Life, Disease and Recovery. London: 1793. V. 41; 42

Facts tending to show the Connection of the Stomach with Life, Disease, and Recovery. London/Edinburgh: 1793. V. 37

WEBSTER, CHARLES A.

The Diocese of Cork. Cork: 1920. V. 37; 42

WEBSTER, DANIEL 1782-1852

Considerations on the Embargo Laws. Boston: 1808. V. 43

Considerations on the Embargo Laws. N.P.: 1808. V. 42

Mr. Webster's Speech on the Greek Revolution. Washington City: 1824. V. 37; 38; 40; 43

Speech of the Hon. Daniel Webster, Delivered in the House of Representatives of the United States, on the 14th January, 1814, on a Bill Making Further Provion for Filling the Ranks on the Regular Army . . . Alexandria: 1814. V. 44

Speech of . . . , in Reply to Mr. Hayne, of South Carolina: the Resolution of Mr. Foot, of Connecticut, Relative to the Public Lands . . . Washington: 1830. V. 40; 44; 46

Speech Delivered by Daniel Webster at Niblo's Saloon in New York, on the 15th of March, 1837. New York: 1837. V. 44

Speech on Mr. Clay's Resolutions. Washington: 1850. V. 38; 39; 40; 42

Speeches and Forensic Arguments. Boston: 1830. V. 37

The Works of . . . Boston: 1851. V. 37; 40; 42

The Works of Daniel Webster. (with) The Private Correspondence of Daniel Webster. Boston: 1851/57. V. 41

The Writings and Speeches of Daniel Webster. Boston: 1903. V. 40

WEBSTER, E. B.

Fishing in the Olympics. Salmon, Trout, Mud Shark, Bull Heads, Pike, Halibut, Dollies, Whale and Kippered Herrings. Port Angeles, Wa.: 1923. V. 37

WEBSTER, F. A. M.

The hill of Riches. London. V. 43

WEBSTER, G. WATMOUGH

Twenty Five Photographs (Printed in Platinotype) . . . of the Life History Group of Birds in the Grosvenor Museum, Chester . . . Chester: 1895. V. 43

WEBSTER, GEORGE G.

Around the Horn in '49: the Journal of the Hartford Union Mining and Trading Company December, 1948 to September 1949. San Francisco: 1928. V. 45

WEBSTER, HAROLD M.

Game Hawking . . . Denver: 1988. V. 45

WEBSTER, ISAAC

A Narrative of the Captivity of . . . Metuchen: 1927. V. 45

WEBSTER, J. CLARENCE

Wolfe and the Artists. Toronto: 1930. V. 43

WEBSTER, J. D.

Message from the President . . . Communicating the Report of Lieutenant Webster of a Survey of the Gulf Coast at the Mouth of the Rio Grande. Washington: 1850. V. 41

Report of a Survey of the Gulf Coast at the Mouth of the Rio Grande. Washington: 1850. V. 37; 41; 42

WEBSTER, JAMES

Travels through the Crimea, Turkey and Egypt: Performed During the Years 1825-1828. London: 1830. V. 37; 39

WEBSTER, JEAN 1878-1916

Daddy-Long Legs. New York: 1912. V. 39; 42; 45

WEBSTER, JOHN 1610-1682

Academiarum Examen, or the Examination of Academies. London: 1654. V. 45

The Displaying of Supposed Witchcraft Wherein is Affirmed that There Are Many Sorts of Deceivers and Imposters . . . London: 1677. V. 39; 46

Dramatic Works. London: 1857. V. 38; 42

The Duchess of Malfi and the White Devil. London: 1930. V. 40; 43

The Duchess of Malfi. London: 1945. V. 38

Elements of Chemistry. Taunton: 1811. V. 46

Metallographia; or an History of Metals. London: 1671. V. 42

Notes on a Recent Visit to Several Provincial Asylums for the Insane in France. London: 1850. V. 40

The Unfortunate Duchess of Malfy . . . London: 1708. V. 43

the Works of John Webster . . . London: 1830. V. 37; 45

WEBSTER, JOHN CLARENCE

Wolfiana. N.P.: 1927. V. 41

WEBSTER, JOHN W.

Report of the Trial of John W. Webster, Indicted for the Murder of Dr. George Parkman Before the Supreme Judicial Court of Massachusetts, Holden at Boston on Tuesday March 19, 1850. Boston: 1850. V. 39

Trial of Professor John W. Webster, for the Murder of Dr. George Parkman in the Medical College. Boston: 1850. V. 40

WEBSTER, JOHN WHITE

A Description of the Island of St. Michael, Comprising An Account of Its Geological Structure. Boston: 1821. V. 37; 40; 46

WEBSTER, KIMBALL

The Gold Seekers of '49. A Personal Narrative of the Overland Trail and Adventures in California and Oregon from 1849 to 1854. Manchester: 1917. V. 40; 44

WEBSTER, LYDIA GERTRUDE HAMILTON

When Dreams Come True. N.P.: 1925. V. 44

WEBSTER, MRS. M. M.

Pocahontas. Philadelphia: 1840. V. 41

WEBSTER, NOAH 1758-1843

An Address to the Freemen of Connecticut. Hartford: 1803. V. 45

An American Selection of Letters in Reading and Speaking. Hartford: 1796. V. 40

An American Dictionary of the English Language. New York: 1828. V. 37; 38; 39; 40; 43; 44

An American Dictionary of the English Language. New York: 1829. V. 41

An American Dictionary of the English Language. Springfield: 1854. V. 40

An American Dictionary of the English Language. New Haven: 1828. V. 37

A Brief History of Epidemic and Pestiential Diseases, etc. Hartford: 1799. V. 37

A Collection of Papers on Political, Literary and Moral Subjects. New York: 1843. V. 40; 43

A Dictionary for Primary Schools. New York: & New Haven: 1833. V. 45

A Dictionary of the English Language . . . London: 1856. V. 41

Dissertations on the English Language. Boston: 1789. V. 40

Dr. Webster's Complete Dictionary of the English Language. New York: 1902. V. 44

History of Animals. New Haven: 1812. V. 42

An Improved Grammar of the English Language. New Haven: 1831. V. 38

A Letter to Dr. David Ramsay, of Charleston Respecing the Errors in Johnson's Dictionary and Other Lexicons. New Haven: 1807. V. 40

A Letter to the Honourable John Pickering, on the Subject of His Vocabulary; or, Collection of Words and Phrases . . . Boston: 1817. V. 46

Letters to a Young Gentle Man Commencing His Education. New Haven: 1823. V. 37

Miscellaneous Papers on Political and Commercial Subjects . . . IV. A Sketch of the History and Present State of Banks and Insurance Companies, in the United States. New York: 1802. V. 37; 44

The Peculiar Doctrines of the Gospel, Explained and Defended. New York: 1809. V. 39

A Philosophical and Practical Grammar of the English Language. New Haven: 1807. V. 43

WEBSTER, P. C. G.

The Records of the Queen's Own Royal Regiment of Staffordshire Yeomanry. Lichfield: 1870. V. 37; 38

WEBSTER, SIDNEY 1828-1910

Duties of Neutrality. The United States vs. the Steamship 'Meteor', etc. Closing Argument on Behalf of the United States by Sidney Webster. New York: 1866. V. 40

WEBSTER, THOMAS

An Encyclopaedia of Domestic Economy. London: 1844. V. 40

An Encyclopaedia of Domestic Economy . . . New York: 1845. V. 39

History of the Methodist Episcopal Church in Canada. Hamilton: 1870. V. 37

Minutes of Evidence & of Proceedings on the Liverpool and Birkenhead Dock Bills in the Sessions of 1848, 1850, 1851 and 1852. London: 1853. V. 38

The Port and Docks of Birkenhead. London: 1848. V. 39

WEBSTER, WILLIAM

The Consequences of Trade, as to the Wealth and Strength of Any Nation . . . London: 1740. V. 46

An Essay on Book-Keeping, According to the True Italian Method of Debtor and Creditor, by Double Entry. London: 1726. V. 41

An Essay on Book-Keeping, According to the True Italian Method of Debtor and Creditor, by Double Entry. London: 1747. V. 39

The Life of General Monck: Late Duke of Albemarle . . . Dublin: 1724. V. 42

Narrative of a Voyage to the Southern Atlantic Ocean, in the years 1828, 29, 30, Performed in H.M. Sloop Chanticleer, Under the Command of the Late Capt. Henry Foster. London: 1834. V. 38; 41

WEBSTER, WILLIAM BULLOCK

Ireland Considered as A Field for Investment or Residence. Dublin: 1853. V. 40

WEBSTER, WILLIAM HENRY BAYLEY

Narrative of a Voyage to the Southern Atlantic Ocean in the Years 1828, 29, 30, performed in H.M. Sloop Chnanticleer.. London: 1834. V. 38

WEBSTER'S New Collegiate Dictionary. Springfield: 1953. V. 39

WEBSTER'S New International Dictionary of the English Language. 1937. V. 39

WEBSTER'S New International Dictionary of the English Language . . . London: 1924. V. 38

WECHER, JOHANN JACOB

Medicinae Virivsque Syntaxes, ex Graecorum, Latinoru, Arabumq. Basileae: 1576. V. 41

WECHSELMANN, WILHELM

The Treatment of Syphilis with Salvarsan. New York: 1911. V. 42

WECKER, JOHANN JACOB

Eighteen Books of the Secrets of Art and Nature . . . London: 1661. V. 46
Le Grand Thresor, ov Dispensaire, et Antidotaire . . . Cologny: 1616. V. 37

WEDDELL, A. W.

A Description of Virginia House, in Henrico County, Near Richmond Virginia . . . . Richmond: 1947. V. 44

WEDDELL, JAMES

A Voyage to the South Pole, Performed in the Years 1822-24. London: 1825. V. 39

THE WEDDING Present. London: 1839. V. 37

WEDDLE, ROBERT S.

The San Saba Mission Spanish Pivot in Texas. Austin: 1964. V. 42; 45

WEDEL, GEORG WOLFGANG

Specimen Experimenti Chimici Novi, De Sale Volatili Plantarum . . . (with) Experimentum Chimicum Novum de Sale Volatili Plantarum quo Latius Exponuntur . . . Jena: 1682. V. 38

WEDELII, GEORGII WOLFFGANGI

Opiologia . . . Jena: 1682. V. 37

WEDGE, JOHN

General View of the Agriculture of the County of Warwick. London: 1794. V. 41

WEDGWOOD, C. V.

New Poems 1965 - a P.E.N. Anthology of Contemporary Poetry. London: 1966. V. 44

WEDGWOOD, JOSEPH

Catalogue of Cameos, Intaglios, Medals, Bas Reliefs, Busts and Small Statues . . . Etruria: 1787. V. 39

WEDGWOOD, JOSIAH

An Address to the Young Inhabitants of the Pottery. 1783. V. 38
An Address to the Young Inhabitants of the Pottery. Printed at Newcastle: 1783. V. 37
Catalogue of Cameos, Intaglios, Medals, Bas-reliefs, Busts and Small Statues . . . Etruria: 1787. V. 43
Correspondence. London: 1903 and 1906. V. 38
The Life . . . from His Private Correspondence and Family Papers . . . London: 1865. V. 37

WEDGWOOD, MRS.

Wind Along the Waste; Poems. 1902. V. 45

WEDMORE, FREDERICK

Etching in England. London: 1895. V. 39
Etchings. London: 1911. V. 41
Renunciations. London: 1893. V. 37
Some of the Moderns. London: 1909. V. 44
Turner & Ruskin. London: 1900. V. 45

WEED, FRANK

Military Hospitals in the United States. Washington: 1923. V. 41; 42

WEED, JOHN

Brief and Argument for Count Joseph Telfener Vs. George W. Russ, the Defendant, in Supreme Court of the United States. Washington: 1891. V. 37

WEED, LEWIS H.

A Reconstruction of the Nuclear Masses in the Lower Portion of the Human Brain STem. Washington: 1914. V. 46

WEED, THOMAS

A Souvenir of the Trans-Continental Excursion of Railroad Agents, 1870, by One of the Party. Albany: 1871. V. 38

WEED, THURLOW

The Facts Stated. Hon. Thurlow Weed on the Morgan Abduction a Document for the People. Chicago: 1882. V. 39

WEED, WILLIAM H.

To Texas and Back. A Souvenir of the General Passenger & Ticket Agents' Excurison from St. Louis to Galveston, Houston, San Antonio, Austin and Other Points in the Lone Star State. March, 1877. New York: 1877. V. 37

WEEDEN, HOWARD

Shadows on the Wall. Huntsvile: 1899. V. 46

WEEDEN, WILLIAM B.

Economic and Social History of New England 1620-1789. Boston/New York: 1890. V. 41

WEEDON, GEORGE

Valley Forge Orderly Book of General George Weedon of the Continental Army Under General George Washington in the Campaign of 1777-78. New York: 1902. V. 42

WEEDON, L. L.

The Land of Long Ago: A Visit to Fairyland with Humpty Dumpty. London: 1890's. V. 45

WEEKS, DAVID

The Moisie Salmon Club. A Chronicle. Barre: 1971. V. 43

WEEKS, JOHN ELMER

A Treatise on Diseases of the Eye. New York: 1910. V. 44

WEEKS, JOHN H.

Among Congo Cannibals. Philadelphia: 1913. V. 45

WEEKS, LYMAN HORACE

The American Turf. New York: 1898. V. 39
A History of Paper-Manufacturing in the United States, 1690-1916. New York: 1916. V. 38

WEEMS, MASON LOCKE 1759-1825

The Bad Wife's Looking Glass, or, God's Revenge Against Cruelty to Husbands. Charleston: 1823. V. 40
The Drunkard's Looking Glass . . . Philadelphia: 1816. V. 45
The Drunkard's Looking Glass . . . Philadelphia: 1818. V. 43
God's Revenge Against Murder, Or the Drown'd Wife, a Tragedy. Philadelphia: 1808. V. 40; 44
God's Revenge Against Adultery, Awfully Exempolified in the Following Cases . . . Philadelphia: 1818. V. 43
God's Revenge Against Duelling; or the Duelist's Looking Glass. Georgetown: 1820. V. 38; 45
God's Revenge Against Gambling. Augusta: 1810. V. 38
God's Revenge Against Murder; or the Drown'd Wife of Stephen's Creek. Augusta: 1807. V. 38
A History of Life and Death, Virtues and Exploits, of General George Washington. Philadelphia: 1800. V. 40
Hymen's Recruiting=Sergant; or the New Matrimonial Tat-Too for Old Bachelors. Hartford: 1823. V. 44
The Life of Benjamin Franklin. Philadelphia: 1835. V. 40; 44
The Life of George Washignton; with Curious Anecodtes, Equally Honorable to Himself and Exemplary to His Young Countrymen. Philadelphia: 1809. V. 40; 44
Das Leben des Georg Washington, mit Sonderbaren Anecdoten, Sowohl Ehrenvoll fur ihn Selbst . . . Lebanon: 1810. V. 40; 41; 44
The Life of George Washington. Philadelphia: 1813. V. 40; 44
The Life of General Francis Marion . . . Baltimore: 1814. V. 45
The Life of Gen. Francis Marion. Baltimore: 1815. V. 41; 46
The Life of George Washington. Philadelphia: 1816. V. 40; 44
Das Leben des Georg Washington . . . Baltimore: 1817. V. 40; 44
The Life of George Washington . . . Philadelphia: 1820. V. 40
The Life of George Washington . . . Frankford near Philadelphia: 1826. V. 40; 44
The Life of Gen. Francis Marion. Philadelphia: 1831. V. 46
The Life of George Washington. Knoxville: 1842. V. 42
The Life of George Washington. Philadelphia: 1844. V. 40; 44
The Life of Washington. London: 1974. V. 46
The Life of William Penn. Philadelphia: 1829. V. 44
M. L. Weems Respectfully Solicits the Subscriptions of His Friends for Armstrong's Edition of Scott's Family Bible. Dumfries: 1818. V. 46
The Philanthropist. Dumfries: 1799. V. 38; 40; 41; 45

WEEMS, MASON LOCKE 1759-1825 continued

Three Discourses: Hymen's Recruiting Sergeant; The Drunkard's Looking Glass; God's Revenge Against Adultery. New York: 1929. V. 40

The True American, Shewing the Beauties and Blessings of the American Republic Contrasted with the Cruelties and Curses of the European Depotisms. Augusta: 1807. V. 38

WEEVER, JOHN

Ancient Funeral Monuments within the United Monarchie of Great Britaine, Ireland and the Islands Adjacent. London: 1631. V. 38; 39; 45; 46

WEGELIN, OSCAR

Early American Poetry. A Compilation of the Titles of Volumes of Verse and Broadsides by Writers Born or Residing in North America North of the Mexican Border . . . Volume I 1650 - 1799 (and) Volume II 1800 - 1820. New York: 1930. V. 37

WEGG-PROSSER, F. R.

Galileo and His Judges. London: 1889. V. 40

WEHMAN Bros: How to Box and Gymnastics Without a Teacher. New York: 1890. V. 43

WEIBEL, ADELE COULIN

Ten Thousand Years of Textiles. New York: 1952. V. 44

Two Thousand Years of Textiles. New York: 1952. V. 44; 46

WEIDEMEYER, J. W.

Illustrations of North American Lepidoptera, Sphingidae. Philadelphia: 1903. V. 38

WEIDENFELD, JOHANN SERGER VON

De Secretis Adeptorum, sive de Usu Spiritus Vini Lulliani Libri IV. London: 1684. V. 38

WEIDENMANN, J.

Beautifying Country Homes. New York: 1870. V. 39

WEIDLITZ, WOLDEMAR VON

A History of Japanese Colour-Prints. Philadelhia: 1910. V. 44

WEIDMAN, JEROME

I Can Get It for You Wholesale. New York: 1937. V. 46

WEIDNER, FREDERICK

Silver Mines of Mexico. New York: 1866. V. 37; 39; 41; 45

WEIDNER, PAUL

Loca Praecipua Fidei Christianae, Collecta et Explicata . . . Vienna: 1559. V. 45

WEIER, DEBRA

Between the Lines (Double Aquifer). New Jersey: 1980. V. 40

WEIGALL, ARTHUR E. P.

A Report of the Antiquities of Lower Nubia (The First Cataract to the Sudan Frontier). Oxford: 1907. V. 37; 40; 42; 44

WEIGHT, CAREL

The Curious Captain, War Artist 1939-1945. 1989. V. 45

WEIGHTMAN, R. H.

To the Congress of the United States . . . Requesting the Passage of a Bill Declaring New Mexico One of the United States of America on Certain Conditions. Washington: 1851. V. 40; 43

WEIL, E.

Albert Einstein 14th March 1879 (Ulm) - 18th April 1955 (Princeton). A Bibliography of His Scientific Papers. London: 1960. V. 37; 41; 44

WEIMAN, RITA

Footlights. New York: 1923. V. 45

WEIMANN, CHRISTOPHER

Marbled Papers. 1978. V. 44

Marbled Papers. Los Angeles: 1978. V. 42

Marbled Papers, Being a Collection of Twenty-two Contemporary Hand Marbled Papers, Showing a Variety of Patterns and Special Techinques, by Christopher Weimann. (North Hills): 1978. V. 37

Marbling in Miniature. Los Angeles: 1980. V. 42; 43

WEINBAUM, S.

Dawn of Flame and Other Stories. 1936. V. 43

The New Adam. 1939. V. 44

WEINBERGER, BERNARD W.

Dental Bibliography, a Reference . . . New York: 1929-32. V. 42

An Introduction to the History of Dentistry in America. St. Louis: 1948. V. 39

WEINBERGER, MARTIN

Michelangelo the Sculptor. London: New York: 1967. V. 40

WEINER, LEO

Mayan and Mexican Origins. Cambridge: 1926. V. 37

WEINER, NORBERT

The Human Use of Human Beings. Boston: 1950. V. 42

WEINGARTEN, JOANNES JACOBUS DE

Vindemiae Judicialis und Praejudicata Enthalten. Prag: 1692. V. 40

THE WEINREB Catalogues and Index. London: 1961-1968. V. 37

WEINRICH, MELCHIOR

Aerarium Poeticum, Hoc est, Phrases & Nomina Poetica, tam Propria . . . Leipzig: 1632. V. 42

WEIR, HARRISON

The Three Little Kittens. London: 1865. V. 39

WEIR, JAMES

Winter's Lodge; or, Vow Fulfilled. Philadelphia: 1854. V. 44; 45

WEIR, L. H.

Parks, a Manaul of Municipal and County Parks . . . New York: 1928. V. 45

WEIR, R. W.

The History of the 3rd. Batt. King's Own Scottish Borderers 1798-1907. Dumfries: 1907. V. 42

The History of the 3rd Batt. King's Own Scottish Borderers, 1798-1907. Dumfries: 1908. V. 38

WEIS, HENNING

Life of the Harrier in Denmark. London: 1923. V. 45

WEIS, J. M.

Representation des Fetes Donnees par la Ville de Strasbourg Pour la Convalescence du Roi . . . Paris: 1745. V. 45

WEISBACH, JULIUS

Principles of the Mechanics of Machinery and Engineering. Philadelphia: 1848-49. V. 37

WEISBERGER, EDWARD

City of Angels. New York: 1977. V. 45

WEISER, FREDERICK S.

The Pennsylvania German Fraktur of the Free Library of Philadelphia. Breinigsville: 1976. V. 39; 41

The Pennsylvania German Fraktur of the Free Library of Philadelphia . . . Philadelphia: 1976. V. 42

The Pennsylvania German Fraktur of the Free Library of Philadelphia. Breinigsville: 1978. V. 42

WEISHAUSM, JOEL

Ox Herding. San francisco: 1971. V. 44

WEISMANN, AUGUST

The Evolution Theory. London: 1904. V. 40

WEISMANN, ELIZABETH WILDER

The Unfinished Monument by Andrea del Verrocchio to Cardinal Niccolo Forteguerri at Pistola. Florence: 1932. V. 37; 40

WEISNER, WILLIAM

The Book of Magic. New York: 1944. V. 46

WEISS, JOHN

A Sermon Preached at the Ordination of Samuel Longfellow, at Fall River, Mass., Feb. 16th, 1848. Fall River: 1848. V. 43; 44

WEISSE, FRANZ

The Art of Marbling. V. 44

The Art of Marbling. New York: 1980. V. 41

The Art of Marbling. North Hills: 1980. V. 38; 41; 42; 44

WEISSE, MAXIMILIAN

Positiones Mediae Stellarum Fixarumin Zonis Regionmontanis a Besselio inter . . . Petersburg: 1846. V. 38

WEISSENBORN, HELLMUTH

Hellmuth Weissenborn: Engraver. Gloucestershire: 1983. V. 37; 39

Hellmuth Weissenborn Engraver . . . London: 1983. V. 45

Painter and Graphic Artist. London: 1976. V. 40

Signs of the Zodiac. Andoversford: 1978. V. 38

WEISSMULLER, JOHNNY

How He Does It! New York: 1930. V. 45

WEIST, JACOB R.

The Medical Department in the War. Cincinnati: 1886. V. 44

WEITENKAMPF, FRANK

The Etching of Contemporary Life. Marlborough-on-Hudson: 1916. V. 44

Famous Prints: Masterpieces of Graphic Art Reproduced from Rare Originals. New York: 1926. V. 41

The Illustrated Book. Cambridge: 1938. V. 40

WEITLANER-JOHNSON, IRMGARD

Design Motifs on Mexican Indian Textiles. Graz: 1976. V. 39; 41

WEITZMANN, KURT

The Fresco Cycle of S. Maria di Castelseprio. Princeton: 1951. V. 42

The Icon. New York: 1982. V. 46

Monastery of Saint Catherine at Mount Sinai. The Icons. Volume I: from the Sixth to the Tenth Century. Princeton: 1975. V. 39

The Monastery of Saint Catherine at Mount Sinai. Princeton: 1990. V. 45

A Treasury of Icons. New York: 1967. V. 42

WEIZMANN, CHAIM

The Letters and Papers. London: 1968-1980. V. 46

WELBY, T. EARLE

The Victorian Romantics 1850-1870. London: 1929. V. 40; 42

WELCH, ANDREW

A Narrative of Early Days and Remembrances of Oceola Nikkanochee, Prince of Econchatti, a Young Seminole Indian . . . London: 1841. V. 37; 38; 39

WELCH, CHARLES

History of Mount Union, Shirleysburg and Shirley Township. Mount Union: 1909-10. V. 42

History of the Big Horn Basin with Stories of Early Days, Sketches of Pioneers and Writings of the Author. Salt Lake City: 1940. V. 42

History of the Worshipful Company of Pewterers of the City of London, Based upon Their Own Records. London: 1902. V. 37

WELCH, CHARLES A.

History of the Big Horn Basin. Salt Lake City: 1940. V. 37; 38

WELCH, CHARLES H.

History of Mount Union, Shirleysburg and Shirley Township. Mount Union: 1909-1910. V. 41

WELCH, D'ALTE A.

A Bibligoraphy of American Children's Books Printed Prior to 1821. N.P.: 1821. V. 46

WELCH, DENTON

Brave and Cruel. London: 1948. V. 41

The Denton Welch Journals. London: 1952. V. 41

I Left My Grandfather's House. London: 1958. V. 40; 41

In Youth Is Pleasure. London: 1944. V. 44

A Voice Through a Cloud. London: 1950. V. 43

WELCH, F. G.

That Convention: or Five Days a Politician. New York: 1872. V. 43; 44

WELCH, GEORGE S.

The Ship Painter's Handbook with Useful Information For the General Painter and Decorator. London: 1916. V. 46

WELCH, JOSEPH

A List of Scholars of St. Peter's College, Westminster, as They Were Elected to Christ Church College, Oxford and Trinity College, Cambridge. London: 1788. V. 39; 42; 43; 46

WELCH, MOSES C.

The Gospel to be Preached to All men, Illustrated, in a Sermon, Delivered in Windham, (Conn). at the Execution of Samuel Freeman, a Mulatto, November 6, 1805 for the Murder of Hannah Simons. Windham: 1805. V. 45

WELCH, ROBERT H. W.

The Life of John Birch: In the Story of One American Boy, The Ordeal of His Age. Chicago: 1954. V. 37

WELCH, SPENCER GLASGOW

A Confederate Surgeon's Letters to His Wife. New York: 1911. V. 37; 42

WELCH, WILLIAM

Papers and Addresses. Baltimore: 1920. V. 37; 38; 39; 40; 41; 42; 44; 45; 46

A WELCOME; Original Contributions in Poetry and Prose. London: 1863. V. 42

WELCOME to Charles Dickens. The Boz Ball. New York: 1842. V. 39

WELD, CHARLES

A History of the Royal Society, With Memoirs of the Presidents. London: 1848. V. 41

WELD CHARLES RICHARD 1813-1869

Auvergne, Piedmont and Savoy: a Summer Ramble. London: 1850. V. 38

Continental Fragments. Dublin: 1839. V. 43; 45

A History of the Royal Society, with Memoirs of the Presidents . . . London: 1848. V. 42; 43

Last Winter in Rome. London: 1865. V. 39

WELD, ISAAC

Illustrations of the Scenery of Killarney and the Surrounding Country. London: 1802. V. 43

Travel through the Stages of North America and the Provinces of Upper and Lower Canada, During the Years 1795, 1796 and 1797. London: 1799. V. 38; 41; 42; 43; 45; 46

Travels through the States of North America, and the provinces of Upper and Lower Canda, During the Years 1795, 1796 and 1797. London: 1799. V. 41

Travels through the States of North America and the Provinces of Upper and Lower Canada, During the Years 1795, 1796 and 1797. London: 1800. V. 38; 42; 43; 44

Travels Through the States of North America and the Provinces of Upper and Lower Canada During the Years 1795, 1796 and 1797. London: 1807. V. 37; 40

WELD, T. D.

The Bible Against Slavery. New York: 1837. V. 42

WELD, THEODORE D.

American Slavery As It Is. New York: 1839. V. 39

WELDE, THOMAS

A Brief Narration of the Practices of the Churches in New England. London: 1645. V. 42

A Short Story of the Rise, Reign, and Ruin of the Antinomians, Familists & Libertines, That Infected the Churches of Nevv-England. London: 1644. V. 37; 41; 44

WELDON, ANTHONY

A Brief History of the Kings of England, Particularly Those of the Royal House of Stuart, of Blessed Memory. London: 1755. V. 46

The Court and Character of K. James. London: 1650. V. 38; 40; 45

History of the Court and Character of King James I, and of the Intrigues and Tragical Events of His Reign. London: 1817. V. 42

WELDON, FAY

The Fat Woman's Joke. London: 1967. V. 38

WELFORD, RICHARD

History of Newcastle and Gateshead. London: 1884-87. V. 45

WELFORD, RICHARD GRIFFITHS 1804-1852

The Influences of the Game Laws. London: 1846. V. 40

WELLARD, JAMES

The Affair in Arcady. New York: 1959. V. 46

WELLBELOVED, C.

Account of St. Mary's Abbey, York, with a Ground Plan of the Abbey, and Picturesque Views and Architectural Details. London: 1829. V. 41

WELLBURN, GERALD

The Postage Stamps and Postal History of Colonial Vancouver Island and British Columbia 1849-1871. Vancouver: 1987. V. 39

WELLBY, M. S.

Twixt Sirdar & Menelik, an Account of a Year's Expedition from Zeila to Cairo through Unknown Abyssinia. London: 1901. V. 46

WELLCOME, HENRY S.

The Story of Metlakahtla. London & New York: 1887. V. 41

The Story of Metlakahtla. New York: 1887. V. 39

WELLCOME HISTORICAL MEDICAL LIBRARY

A Catalogue of Printed Books in the Wellcome Historical Medical Library. 1962-76. V. 45

A Catalogue of Printed Books in the Wellcome Historical Medical Library. 1962-76. V. 46

WELLCOME LIBRARY

A Catalogue of Printed Books in the Wellcome Library . . . London: 1961-66/76. V. 41

WELLCOME LIBRARY continued

A Catalouge of Printed Books in the Wellcome Library. London: 1962/66/76. V. 40

WELLENDARFER, VIRGIL

Encenilogium Philophismata . . . Leipzig: 1516. V. 46

WELLER, SAM

The Beauties of Pickwick. London: 1838. V. 43

WELLER, SAMUEL

The Trial of Mr. Whitefield's Spirit. Boston: 1741. V. 43; 45

WELLES, C. BRADFORD

The Parchments and Papyri. New Haven: 1959. V. 40

WELLES, C. M.

Three Years' Wanderings of a Connecticut Yankee in South America, Africa, Australia and California. New York: 1859. V. 37; 41; 45; 46

WELLES, E. F.

Heads of Cattle, Exhibiting Bull and Cow of the Most Distinguished Breeds. 1830. V. 40

WELLES, GIDEON

The Diary of Gideon Welles, Secretary of the Navy Under Lincoln and Johnson . . . (1861-1869). New York: 1960. V. 39

Letter of . . . Transmitting the Official reports and Documents Connected with the Recent Engagements on the Mississippi River, Which Resulted in the Capture of Forts Jackson, St. Philip and the City of New Orleans . . . Washington: 1862. V. 39

Lincoln and Seward. New York: 1874. V. 46

WELLES, ORSON

Everybody's Shakespeare. Woodstock: 1934. V. 44

WELLESLEY, DOROTHY

Jupiter and the Nun. London: 1932. V. 38

Jupiter and the Nun. 1932. V. 37

WELLESLEY, MURIEL

The Man Wellington. Through the Eyes of Those Who Knew Him. London: 1937. V. 42

WELLESLEY, RICHARD COLLEY, MARQUESS

The Despatches, Minutes and Correspondence of the Marquess Wellesley, K.G. During His Administration in India. London: 1836-37. V. 38

WELLINGTON, ARTHUR WELLESLEY, 1ST DUKE OF 1769-1852

The Dispatches of Field Marshal the Duke of Wellington, K.G. During His Various Campaigns in India, Denmark, Portugal, Spain and the Low Countries and France from 1799 to 1818. London: 1834-39. V. 46

Dispatches, During His Various Campaigns in India, Denmark, Portugal, Spain the Low Countries and France, from 1799-1818 . . . London: 1837-38. V. 46

The Disptaches of Field Marshal the Duke of Wellinton, During His Various Compaigns in India, Denmark, Portugal, Spain and the Low Countries and France from 1799-1818. London: 1938. V. 38

A Selection from the Private Correspondence of . . . London: 1952. V. 44

WELLINGTON, DOROTHY WELLESLEY, DUCHESS OF

Beyond the Grave - Letters on Poetry to W. B. Yeats. Tunbridge Wells: 1950. V. 38

Poems of Ten Years - 1924-1934. London: 1934. V. 38

WELLINGTON, EVELYN

A Descriptive and Historical Catalogue of the Collection of Pictures and Sculpture at Apsley House. London: 1901. V. 40; 44

WELLMAN, FRANCIS L.

The Art of Cross-Examination. New York: 1903. V. 37; 43

WELLMAN, KLAUS F.

A Survey of North American Indian Rock Art. Graz: 1979. V. 38; 46

WELLMAN, MANLEY WADE

Who Fears the Devil. Sauk City: 1963. V. 43; 45; 46

WELLMAN, MANLY WADE

Giant in Gray; a Biography of Wade Hampton of South Carolina. New York: 1949. V. 42

The Invading Asteriod. New York: 1932. V. 39; 46

WELLMAN, PAUL I.

The Callaghan Yesterday and Today. Encinal: 1945. V. 42

WELLMAN, WALTER

The Aerial Age; A Thousand Miles by Airship Over the Atlantic Ocean . . . New York: 1911. V. 43

WELLS, CAROLYN

American Mystery Stories. New York: 1927. V. 42

The Happychaps. New York: 1908. V. 45

The Merry Go Round. New York: 1901. V. 37

Mother Goose's Menagerie. Boston: 1901. V. 43

The Seven Ages of Childhood. New York: 1909. V. 44; 46

WELLS, CHARLES

Ilm Tedbin Milk. 'The Science of the Administration of a State', or, an Essay on Political Economy, in Turkish, Being the First Ever Written in that Language. London: 1860. V. 42

WELLS, CHARLES JEREMIAH

Joseph and His Brethren, a Scriptural Drama. London: 1824. V. 40

WELLS, CHARLES K. POLK

Life and Adventures of Polk Wells, The Notorious Outlaw Whose Acts of Fearlessness and Chivalry Kept the Frontier Trails Alive with Excitement . . . Halls: 1907. V. 41

WELLS, CHARLES WESLEY

Frontier Life; Being a Description of My Experience on the Frontier the First Forty-Two Years of My Life. Cincinnati: 1902. V. 38; 40; 43; 46

WELLS, DAVID A.

The Relation of the Government to the Telegraph; or, a Review of the Two Propositions Now Pending Before Congress for Changing the Telegraphic Serivce of the Country. New York: 1873. V. 39; 42

WELLS, EDWARD 1667-1727

Elementa Arithmeticae Numerosae et Speiosae. Oxford: 1698. V. 45

An Historical Geography of the Old and New Testament. Oxford: 1801. V. 37; 40

A Treatise of Antient and Present Geography. London: 1706. V. 45

The Young Gentleman's Astronomy, Chronology and Dialing. London: 1712. V. 41; 43; 45

The Young Gentleman's Arithmetick and Geometry. London: 1713. V. 40

The Young Gentleman's Astronomy, Chronology and Dialling . . . . London: 1725. V. 38; 40; 45

The Young Gentleman's Astronomy. London: 1736. V. 40

The Young Gentleman's Astronomy, Chronology, and Dialling . . . London: 1736. V. 38

WELLS, EDWARD L.

Hampton and His Cavalry in '64. Richmond: 1899. V. 37; 40; 42; 43

Hampton and Reconstruction. Columbia: 1907. V. 37

WELLS, FARGO & CO.

Arrest Stage Robers. $1,800 Reward! Sacramento: 1881. V. 39

Shippers Guide and Wells, Fargo & Co.'s Express Directory Showing the Correct Way to Ship Freight and Express Matter to Over 10,000 Places on the Pacific Coast. San Francisco: 1882. V. 41

WELLS Fargo & Co. Express Official Directory. Chicago: 1915. V. 45

WELLS, HARRY L.

History of Nevada County California. Oakland: 1880. V. 46

WELLS, HENRY P.

City Boys in the Woods. London: 1890. V. 41

Fly-Rods and Fly-Tackle: Suggestions as to Their Manufacture and Use. New York: 1885. V. 37; 39

WELLS, HERBERT GEORGE 1866-1946

The Adventures of Tommy. London: 1929. V. 41

The Anatomy of Frustration - a Modern Synthesis. London: 1936. V. 46

Ann Veronica: a Modern Love Story. London: 1909. V. 40

Anticipations of the Reaction of Mechanical and Scientific Progress Upon Human Life and Thought. London: 1902. V. 46

Anticipations. New York & London: 1902. V. 38; 39

Apropos of Dolores. London: 1938. V. 46

Apropos of Dolores. New York: 1938. V. 44

The Autocracy of Mr. Parham. London: 1930. V. 41; 42

Certain Personal Matters. London: 1898. V. 39; 46

Christiana Alberta's FAther. London: 1925. V. 38; 39; 40

The Country of the Blind and Other Stories. London: 1911. V. 39; 41

The Country of the Blind. New York: 1915. V. 37; 38

The Country of the Blind. London: 1939. V. 37; 40; 41; 44

The Country of the Blind. Waltham St. Lawrence: 1939. V. 37; 44

The Croquet Player. London: 1936. V. 37

The Door in the Wall and Other Stories. New York: 1911. V. 38; 45

The Door in the Wall and Other Stories. New York/London: 1911. V. 37

The Dream. London: 1924. V. 39; 46

Experiment in Autobiography. 1934. V. 46

WELLS, HERBERT GEORGE 1866-1946 continued

Experiment in Autobiography. New York: 1934. V. 45

The First Men in the Moon. 1901. V. 37

The First Men in the Moon. London: 1901. V. 37; 38; 39; 40; 42; 44; 45; 46

First and Last Things. A Confession of Faith and Rule of Life. London: 1908. V. 39

First and Last Things. A Confession of Faith and Rule of Life. New York: 1908. V. 41

Floor Games. London: 1911. V. 37; 39; 46

Floor Games. London & Toronto: 1931. V. 39

The Food of the Gods and How It Came to Earth. London: 1904. V. 39; 43

God the Invisible King. London: 1917. V. 38

The Happy Turning a Dream of Life. London: 1945. V. 39

The History of Mr. Polly. London: 1910. V. 37

In the Days of the Comet. London: 1906. V. 42; 45

In the Country of the Blind. London: 1939. V. 38

The Invisible Man. 1897. V. 39

The Invisible Man. 1897. V. 46

The Invisible Man. London: 1897. V. 38; 39; 42; 44

The Invisible Man. 1897. V. 37

The Island of Dr. Moreau. 1896. V. 44

The Island of Dr. Moreau. 1896. V. 46

The Island of Doctor Moreau. London: 1896. V. 39; 40; 45

The Island of Doctor Moreau. New York: 1896. V. 40

The Labour Unrest. London: 1912. V. 39

Little Wars. London: 1913. V. 42; 45

Men Like Gods. 1923. V. 43

Men Like Gods. London: 1923. V. 38; 39; 40; 46

The Misery of Boots. London: 1907. V. 46

Mr. Britling Sees It Through. London: 1916. V. 39; 42

Mr. Britling Sees It Through. London, New York, Toronto: 1916. V. 40

New Worlds for Old. London: 1908. V. 38

The New America and the New World. New York: 1935. V. 37; 38; 40

The Outline of History. London: 1919-20. V. 37; 43

The Outline of History. New York: 1921. V. 40

The Plattner Story and Others. 1897. V. 39

The Plattner Story & Others. 1897. V. 37

A Quartette of Comedies. London: 1928. V. 42

The Research Magnificent. London: 1915. V. 39

Russia in the Shadows. New York: 1921. V. 41

The Salvaging of Civilization. London: 1921. V. 38; 40

The Science of Life. Garden City: 1931. V. 44

The Science of Life. New York: 1931. V. 41; 46

The Sea Lady. London: 1902. V. 45

The Secret Places of the Heart. London: 1922. V. 37; 38; 40

Select Conversations with an Uncle. London: 1895. V. 37; 42; 46

Select Conversations with an Uncle. London & New York: 1895. V. 40

Select Conversation with an Uncle. New York: 1895. V. 37; 41; 42; 43; 44

The Shape of Things to Come. London: 1933. V. 39; 40; 41; 43

The Shape of Things to Come. New York: 1933. V. 39

The Science of Life. New York: 1931. V. 41

The Stolen Bacillus. London: 1895. V. 42

Tales of Space and Time. New York: 1899. V. 38; 40

Tales of Space and Time. London: 1900. V. 39; 41

Tales of Space and Time. London: & New York: 1900. V. 42

Tales of Space & Time. 1899. V. 37

Things to Come - a Film Story Based on the Material Contained in His History of the Future 'The Shape of Things to Come'. London: 1935. V. 46

Thirty Strange Stories. New York: 1897. V. 39

The Time Machine. 1895. V. 46

The Time Machine. 1895. V. 43

The Time Machine. 1895. V. 37

The Time Machine. London: 1895. V. 37; 39; 40; 42; 43; 44; 45; 46

The Time Machine. New York: 1895. V. 39; 43; 46

The Time Machine. 1897. V. 39

The Time Machine. New York: 1931. V. 42

Tono-Bungay. London: 1909. V. 39; 40; 41

Tono-Bungay. New York: 1960. V. 38; 40

Twelve Stories and a Dream. London: 1903. V. 39

Twelve Stories & A Dream. 1903. V. 37

The War in the Air and Particularly How Mr. Bert Smallways Fared While It Lasted. 1908. V. 46

The War in the Air. London: 1908. V. 38; 40; 44; 45; 46

The War of the Worlds. London: 1898. V. 42; 43; 46

The War of the Worlds. New York: & London: 1898. V. 46

The War in the Air. 1908. V. 37

The War of the Worlds. New York: 1898. V. 40

The War of the Worlds. (and) The Time Machine. New York: 1964. V. 40

What Is Coming? London: 1916. V. 41; 42

The Wheels of Chance. London: 1896. V. 39; 46

When the Sleeper Wakes. London: 1899. V. 39; 42

When the Sleeper Wakes. New York: 1899. V. 39

When the Sleeper Wakes. New York: & London: 1899. V. 38; 46

The Wonderful Visit. 1895. V. 46

The Wonderful Visit. 1895. V. 39

The Wonderful Visit. London: 1895. V. 37; 42; 46

The Wonderful Visit. New York: 1895. V. 44

The Work, Wealth and Happiness of Mankind. New York: 1931. V. 42

Works. London: 1924. V. 46

The Works of . . . New York: 1924. V. 41; 42; 46

The Works of . . . London: 1924-27. V. 46

The Works. New York: 1924-27. V. 38; 42; 44; 46

The World Set Free. 1914. V. 43

The World of William Clissoid. London: 1926. V. 39; 40; 45; 46

The World of William Clissoid. New York: 1926. V. 40

The World Set Free. London: 1914. V. 38; 46

The World Set Free. New York: 1914. V. 46

.WELLS, J. R.

A New and Valuable Book Entitled the Family Companion . . . Boston: 1846. V. 45

WELLS, J. SOELBERG

A Treatise on the Diseases of the Eye. Philadlephia: 1880. V. 44

WELLS, JAMES L.

The Bronx and Its People: a History 1609-1927. New York: 1927. V. 46

WELLS, JAMES W.

Exploring and Travelling Three Thousand Miles Through Brazil from Rio de Janeiro to Maranhao. London: 1886. V. 38; 45

Exploring and Travelling Three Thousand Miles through Brazil from Rio de Janeiro to Maranaho. Philadelphia: 1886. V. 42

Three Thousand Miles through Brazil from Rio de Janeiro to Maranhao with an Appendix . . . London: 1886. V. 39

WELLS, JEREMIAH

Poems Upon Divers Occasions. London: 1667. V. 42

WELLS, JOHN G.

Wells Pocket Hand-Book of Nebraska. New York: 1857. V. 38; 42; 45

WELLS, JOHN SOELBERG

A Treatise on the Diseases of the Eye. Philadelphia: 1869. V. 41; 43

WELLS, LINTON

Around the World in Twenty-Eight Days. Boston: 1926. V. 46

WELLS, MARGARET

A Selection of Her Wood Engravings. 1985. V. 38

WELLS, MARY

Memoirs of the Life of Mrs. Sumbel, Late Wells; of the Theatres-Royal, Drury Lane, Covent-Garden and Haymarker. London: 1811. V. 39; 41

WELLS, NATHANIEL ARMSTRONG

The Picturesque Antiquities of Spain. London: 1846. V. 40; 45

WELLS, OLIVER

An Anthology of Younger Poets. Philadelphia: 1932. V. 38; 40; 42

WELLS, PERCY A.

Modern Cabinet Work. London: 1909. V. 42

WELLS, ROLLA

Episodes of My Life. St. Louis: 1933. V. 38; 39; 44

WELLS, SAMUEL

The History of the Drainage of the Great Level of the Fens, Called Bedford Level. London: 1830. V. 38

The True State of the National Finances, with Remedial Suggestions. London: 1842. V. 39

WELLS, SETH YOUNG

Millennial Praises, Containing a Collection of Gospel Hymns, in Fourt Parts . . . Hancock: 1813. V. 37; 46

WELLS, T. SPENCER

Eight Cases of Ovariotomy: with remarks on the means of diminishing the mortality after this operation. Reprint Dublin Quart J Med Sci. V. 37

On Ovarian and uterine Tumours, Their Diagnosis and Treatment. London: 1882. V. 42

WELLS, W. B.

Canadiana . . . London: 1837. V. 41

WELLS, WALTER

The Water Power of Maine. Augusta: 1869. V. 40

WELLS, WILLIAM

Catalogue of the Matchless Collection of Pictures by Old Masters. London: 1848. V. 38

WELLS, WILLIAM CHARLES

An Essay on Dew and Several Appearances Connected with it. London: 1814. V. 38; 39; 46

An Essay on Dew and Several Appearances Connected with It. Philadelphia: 1838. V. 38; 40; 42

Two Essays: One Upon Single Vision with 2 Eyes; the Other on Dew . . . London: 1818. V. 42

Two Essays: Upon Single Vision With Two Eyes: the Other on Dew . . . An Account of a Female of the White Race . . . London: 1818. V. 37

WELLS, WILLIAM HENRY

A Geographical Dictionary or Gazeteer of the Australian Colonies . . . Sydney: 1848. V. 39

WELLS, WILLIAM V.

Explorations and Adventures in Honduras, Comprising Sketches of Travel in the Gold Regions of Olancho, and a Review of the History and General Resouces of Central America. New York: 1857. V. 37; 38; 39; 44; 45

The Life and Public Services of Samuel Adams, Being a Narrative of His Acts and Opinions, and of His Agency in Producing and Forwarding the American Resolution. Boston: 1866. V. 42

Walker's Expedition to Nicaragua. New York: 1856. V. 39; 42; 43; 45

WELLSTEAD, JAMES RAYMOND

Travels to the City of the Caliphs, Along the Shores of the Persian Gulf and the Mediterranean. London: 1840. V. 40

WELLSTED, JAMES RAYMOND

Travels in Arabia. London: 1838. V. 41; 45

WELLWOOD, JAMES 1652-1727

Memoirs of the Most Material Transactions in England (1588-1688), Preceeding the Revolution in 1688. Glasgow: 1749. V. 41

WELSER, M.

Chronica der Reichsstadt Augusburg. Frankfurt: 1595. V. 41

WELSER, MARCUS 1558-1614

Rerum Boicarum Libri Quinque. Augsburg: 1602. V. 43

WELSH, DAVID

Account of the Life and Writings of Thomas Brown, M.D. Late Professor of Moral Philosophy in the University of Edinburgh. Edinburgh: 1825. V. 45

WELSH, DORIS VARNER

A Bibliography of Miniature Books (1470-1965). Cobleskill: 1989. V. 42

Following the Banyan Deer Taken from the Jataka. Chicago: 1963. V. 41

WELSH, HERBERT

The Apache Prisoners in Fort Marion, St. Augustine, Florida. Philadelphia: 1887. V. 39

Civilization Among the Sioux Indians: Report of a Visit to Some of the Sioux Reservations of South Dakota and Nebraska. Philadelphia: 1893. V. 37

Crow Creek Reservation, Dakota. Action of the Indian Rights Association, and Opinions of the Press, West and East, Regarding Its Recent Occupation by White Settlers, Together with the Proclamation of the President . . . Philadelphia: 1885. V. 37

Four Weeks Among Some of the Sioux Tribes of Dakota and Nebraska. Germantown, Philadelphia: 1882. V. 45

Report of a Visit to the Navajo, Pueblo and Hualapais Indians of New Mexico and Arizona. Philadelphia: 1885. V. 37; 39; 44; 46

Report of a Visit to the Great Sioux Reserve, Dakota, Made During the Months of May and June, 1883, in Behalf of the Indian Rights Association. Germantown: 1883. V. 37

WELSH, JAMES

Military Reminiscences, Extracted from a Journal of Nearly Forty Years' Active Service in the East Indies. London: 1830. V. 41; 43; 44

WELSH, WILLIAM

Poems, Songs and Anecdotes. Edinburgh: 1838. V. 42

Taopi and His Friends, or the Indians Wrongs and Rights. Philadelphia: 1869. V. 42

WELSTED, LEONARD

Epistles, Odes &c. Written on Several Subjects. With a Translation of Longinus's Treatise on the Sublime. To which is prefix'd, A Dissertation concerning the Perfection of the English Language, the State of Poetry &c. London: 1724. V. 37

Of Dulness and Scandal. London: 1732. V. 41; 45

WELTY, EUDORA 1909-

Acrobats in a Park. N.P.: 1977. V. 46

Acrobats in a Park. Northridge: 1980. V. 39; 42; 46

Black and White. Northridge: 1985. V. 43

The Bride of Innisfallen. New York: 1955. V. 38; 40; 41; 42; 43; 45; 46

By-Bye Trevoort. Jackson: 1980. V. 41; 42; 45

Bye-Bye Brevoort. A Skit. 1980. V. 37

The Collected Stories of Eudora Welty. New York: 1980. V. 38; 44; 46

The Collected Stories. New York & London: 1980. V. 37; 38; 39

A Curtain of Green. Garden City: 1941. V. 37; 39; 42; 45

A Curtain of Green. New York: 1941. V. 42; 46

A Curtain of Green. London: 1943. V. 46

A Curtain of Green. Stockholm/London: 1947. V. 42; 43; 44

Delta Wedding. New York: 1946. V. 37; 38; 39; 40; 42; 44; 45; 46

Eudora Welty: A Note on the Author and Her Work by Katherine Anne Porter, Together with 'The Key' one of Seventeen Stories from Miss Welty's Forthcoming 'A Curtain of Green'. Garden City: 1941. V. 45; 46

The Eye of the Story. New York: 1977. V. 37; 43; 44; 45

The Eye of the Story. New York: 1978. V. 41; 42; 45; 46

Fairy Tale of the Natchez Trace. Jackson: 1975. V. 42

A Flock of Guinea Hens Seen from a Car. 1970. V. 46

A Flock of Guinea Hens Seen From a Car. N.P.: 1970. V. 46

Four Photographs. Northridge: 1984. V. 39

The Golden Apples. New York: 1948. V. 45

The Golden Apples. 1949. V. 46

The Golden Apples. 1949. V. 43

The Golden Apples. New York: 1949. V. 37; 38; 39; 41; 42; 43; 44; 45

The Golden Apples. London: 1950. V. 45

Henry Green: a Novelist of the Imagination. N.P.: 1961. V. 46

Ida M'Toy. 1972. V. 46

Ida M'toy. 1972. V. 43

Ida M'Toy. Urbana: 1976. V. 46

Ida M'Toy. Urbana: 1979. V. 43; 44; 45

Ida M'Toy. Illinois: (1979). V. 37

Ida M'Toy. Urbana, Chicago, London: 1979. V. 38

In Black and White. 1985. V. 44

In Black and White. 1985. V. 43

In Black and White. 1985. V. 39

In Black and White. Northridge: 1985. V. 43; 44; 45; 46

The Key: One of Seventeen Stories from Miss Welty's Forthcoming 'A Curtain of Green.' Garden City: 1941. V. 40

Losing Battles. New York: 1970. V. 37; 39; 42; 43; 44

Morgana. Jackson: 1988. V. 42; 43; 45

Music from Spain. Greenville: 1948. V. 43; 46

The Norton Book of Friendship. New York: 1991. V. 46

On Short Stories. New York: 1949. V. 38; 39; 45

One Time, One Place. New York: 1971. V. 38; 39; 40; 42; 43; 46

One Writer's Beginning. Cambridge: 1984. V. 41; 42; 43; 45; 46

One Writer's Beginnings. Cambridge & London: 1984. V. 46

The Optimist's Daughter. New York: 1972. V. 38; 39; 40; 41; 42; 43; 45; 46

The Optimist's Daughter. Franklin Center: 1980. V. 39; 43

A Pageant of Birds. New York: 1974. V. 37; 38; 39; 40; 41; 42; 44

Percy Walker. New Orleans: 1986. V. 45

Photographs. V. 43

Photographs. Jackson. V. 41

Photographs. Jackson: 1989. V. 41; 42; 43; 44; 45; 46

Place in Fiction. New York: 1957. V. 38; 39; 42; 45; 46

The Ponder Heart. London: 1954. V. 38; 41

The Ponder Heart. New York: 1954. V. 39; 41; 42; 43; 44; 45

The Ponder Heart. New York: 1956. V. 43

Retreat. 1981. V. 41

Retreat. 1981. V. 42

Retreat. 1981. V. 42

Retreat. 1981. V. 42

Retreat. 1981. V. 42

Retreat. 1981. V. 42

Retreat. 1981. V. 37

Retreat. N.P.: 1981. V. 43

Retreat. N.P.: 1981. V. 41

WELTY, EUDORA 1909- continued

Retreat. N.P.: 1981. V. 42

Retreat. Winston-Salem: 1981. V. 37; 38; 39; 40

The Robber Bridegroom. New York: 1941. V. 39

The Robber Bridegroom. 1942. V. 39

the Robber Bridegroom. Garden City: 1942. V. 39; 42; 43; 44; 45; 46

The Robber Bridegroom. West Hatfield: 1987. V. 38; 39; 40; 44; 45

The Shoe Bird. New York: 1964. V. 37; 39; 42

Short Stories. New York: 1949. V. 37; 38; 39; 46

Some Notes on Time in Fiction. V. 45

Some Notes on Time in Fiction. Jackson: 1973. V. 46

A Sweet Devouring. New York: 1969. V. 37; 42

Three Papers on Fiction. Northampton: 1962. V. 46

Three Papers on Fiction. Smith College, Mass.: 1950. V. 37

Twenty Photographs. 1980. V. 42

Twenty Photographs. Winston-Salem: 1980. V. 38; 40

White Fruitcake. N.P.: 1980. V. 44

The Wide Net. New York: 1943. V. 38; 39; 42; 43; 44; 45; 46

The Wide Net. London: 1945. V. 38

Women! Make Turban in Own Home! 1979. V. 39

Women! Make Turban in Own Home! 1979. V. 42

Women!! Make Turban in Own Home! Winston Salem: 1979. V. 38; 40

Women! Make Turban in Own Home! Winston Salem: 1981. V. 39

WELTY, ROGER S.

Rent, Wages, and Capital: A Book for the Times. La Porte: 1886. V. 38

WELWITSCH, FRIEDRICH

Catalogue of the African Plants Collected by Dr. Friedrich Welwitsch in 1853-61. London: 1896-1901. V. 43

WEMBLEY in Colour Being Both an Impression and a Memento of the British Empire Exhibition of 1924 as Seen by Donald Maxwell . . . New York: 1924. V. 44

WEMORE, HELEN CODY

Last of the Great Scouts: The Life Story of 'Buffalo Bill'. Duluth: 1899. V. 39

WEMYSS, FRANCIS COURTNEY

Theatrical Biography or, the Life of an Actor and Manager. Glasgow: MDCCCLVIIII. V. 46

WEMYSS, JOHN 1579?-1636

An Exposition of the Morall Law or Ten Commandments of Almightie God . . . London: 1632. V. 45

WENBERG, THOMAS JAMES

The Violin Makers of the United States: Biographical Documentation of the Violin and Bow Makers Who Have Worked in the United States. Mt. Hood: 1986. V. 37; 38; 39

WENCKSTERN, F. V.

A Bibliography of the Japanese Empire. London: 1895-1928. V. 38

WENDEBORN, GEBHARDT FREDERICH AUGUST

A View of England Towards the Close of the Eighteenth Century . . . Dublin: 1791. V. 43; 46

WENDEHACK, CLIFFORD CHARLES

Golf & Country Clubs. A Survey of the Requirement of Planning, Construction and Equipment of the Modern Club House. New York: 1929. V. 42; 43; 46

WENDERBORN, GEBHARDT FRIEDRICH AUGUST

Der Zustand des Staats, der Religion, der Gelehrsamkeit und der Kunst in Grosbritannien Gegen das Ende des Achtzehnten Jahrhunderts. Berlin: 1785-88. V. 41

WENDINGEN. Amsterdam: 1924-31. V. 43

Maandblad voor Bouwen en Sieren. Amsterdam: 1918-31. V. 38

WENDORF, FRED

The Prehistory of Nubia. Dallas: (1968). V. 37

WENTINGHAM, CLIFFORD

Observations on Dr. Freind's History of Physick . . . London: 1726. V. 44

WENTWORTH DAY, J.

Sport in Egypt. London: 1938. V. 42

WENTWORTH, EDWARD NORRIS

America's Sheep Trails. Ames: 1948. V. 38; 39; 40

WENTWORTH, FRANK L.

Aspen on the Roaring Pork. PP: 1950. V. 46

WENTWORTH, JUDITH ANNE DOROTHEA WENTWORTH BLUNT-LYTTON 1873-

The Authentic Arabian Horse and His Descendants. London. V. 39

The Authentic Arabian Horse and His Descendants. London: 1945. V. 37; 40

Thoroughbred Racing Stock and Its Ancestors. London: 1938. V. 37; 39; 42; 43; 46

Thoroughbred Racing Stock and Its Ancestors. New York: 1960. V. 39

Thoroughbred Racking Stock and Its Ancestors. New York: 1962. V. 39

WENTWORTH, M.

James Tissot. Oxford: 1984. V. 39

WENTWORTH, PETER

A Pithie Exhortation to Her Maiestie for Establishing Her Successor to the Crowne. Edinburgh: 1598. V. 42

WENTWORTH, THOMAS

A Journal of the Expedition to Carthagena, with Notes. London: 1744. V. 41

WENTWORTH, THOMAS STRAFFORD, EARL OF

The Conclusion of the Earle of Straffords Defence. The Twelfth of April 1641. London: 1641. V. 40

The Earle of Straffords Speech, on the Scaffold Before He Was Beheaded on Tower-Hill May 12, 1641. London: 1641. V. 40

WENTZ, ROBY

The Grabhorn Press: A Bibliography. Aptos: 1981. V. 38

The Grabhorn Press. San Francisco: 1981. V. 37; 39; 40; 41; 43; 46

WENYON, C. M.

Protozoology. New York: 1926. V. 37

WENZEL, GOTTFRIED IMMANUEL

Neue auf Vernunft und Erfahrung Gegrundete Entdeckungen Uber die Sprache der Thiere. Vienaa: 1800. V. 43

WENZEL, JOSEPH

Uber die Schwammingen Auswuchse auf der Aussern Hirnhaut. Mainz: 1811. V. 43

WENZELL, ALBERT B.

The Passing Show. New York: 1903. V. 41

WEPFER, JOHANN JACOB

Cicutae Aquaticae Historiae et Noxae. Basel: 1679. V. 41; 45

Observationes Medico-Practicae, De Affectibvs Capitis Internis & Externis . . . 1727. V. 41

WEPFER, JOHANNES

Observationes Medico-Practicae. 1727. V. 46

Observationes Medico-Practicae, De Affectibus Capitis Internis & Externis, Nunc Demum Publici Juris Reddiate Studio & Opera Nepotum . . . Aiegleri: 1727. V. 45

WEPPNER, MARGARETHA

The North Star and the Southern Cross. London & Albany: 1876. V. 40; 42

WERGE, JOHN

The Evolution of Photography with a Chronological Record of Discoveries, Inventions, etc . . . London: 1890. V. 37

WERNER, ALFRED

Max Weber. New York: 1975. V. 39; 46

Pascin. New York: 1959. V. 41

WERNER, ARNO

Arno Werner, One Man's Work. Easthampton: 1982. V. 40; 41; 46

WERNER, BP. OF SANKT BLASIEN

Deflorationes Patrum. Basle: 1494. V. 41

WERNER, CARL

Nile-Sketches, Painted from Nature During His Travels through Egypt. Gustav W. Seitz, Pub.,: 1871-75. V. 42

WERNER, CHARLES J.

Eric Mullica and His Descendants. A Swedish Pioneer in New Jersey Together with a Description of the Mullica River Region. New Gretna: 1930. V. 41

WERNER, GEORG CHRISTOPH

Natur: und Kunstgemasse Vereinigung, dess Leichten und Schweren & Vice Versa. Augsburg: 1670. V. 37

WERNER, GEORGE

Queen Mary's Psalter. Miniatures and Drawings by an English Artist of the 14th Century Reproduced from the Royal MS 2B.VII in the British Museum. London: 1912. V. 40

WERNER, HERMAN

On the Western Frontier with the United States Cavalry Fifty Years Ago. Akron: 1934. V. 42

On the Western Frontier with the United States Cavalry Fifty Years Ago. N.P.: 1934. V. 45

On the Western Frontier with the United States Cavalry Fifty Years Ago. N.P.: 1934. V. 42

WERNER, J. C. 1798-1856

L'Orang Outang Arrive a Paris en 1836. Paris: 1836. V. 42

WERNER, J. R.

A Visit to Stanley's Rear Guard at Major Barttelot's Camp on the Aruhwimi With an Account of River-Life on the Congo. Edinburgh: 1889. V. 40

A Visit to Stanley's Rear-Guard at Major Barttelot's Camp on the Aruhwimi with an Account of River Life on the Congo. London: 1889. V. 39

WERNER, JOHANNES

Bericht/Regiment/ und Anordnung: Wie man sich in Itzo Schwebenden Sterbens Leufften/ Wider die Pest Praeseruirn Oder Bewahren. Leipzig: 1598. V. 43

WERNER OF ST. BLASIEN

Deflorationes Patrum. Basle: 1494. V. 37

WERNICKE, CARL

Lehrbuch der Gehirnkrankheten. Kassel: 1883. V. 41

WERRO, HENRY

'Ole Bull' Joseph Guarnerius del Gesu, 1744. Berne: 1971. V. 38

WERTH, JOHN J.

A Dissertation on the Resources and Policy of California. Benica: 1851. V. 40; 43

WERTHAM, FREDERIC

The Seduction of the Innocent. 1954. V. 39

Seduction of the Innocent. New York: 1954. V. 39

WERTHEIM, CHEVALIER FRANCOIS DE

Manuel de l'Outillage des Arts et Metiers . . . Vienna: 1869. V. 45

WERTHEIM, MAURICE

Salmon on the Dry Fly. New York: 1948. V. 39; 40

WESCHER, HERTA

Collage. New York: 1968. V. 44

WESCOTT, GLENWAY

Apartment in Athens. London: 1945. V. 41

Apartment in Athens. New York: 1945. V. 41; 46

The Apple of the Eye. New York: 1924. V. 38; 41

The Babe's Bed. N.P.: 1930. V. 41

The Babe's Bed. Paris: 1930. V. 37; 41

The Bitterns. Evanston: 1920. V. 37

A Calendar of Saints for Unbelievers. Paris: 1932. V. 37; 38; 40; 41; 42; 43; 44

A Calendar of Saints for Unbelievers. The Text by Glenway Wescott. The signs of the Zodiac by Pavel Tchelitchew. (Haarlem): 1932. V. 37

Good-Bye Wisconsin. New York & London: 1928. V. 42

The Grandmothers. New York: 1927. V. 45

The Grandmothers: a Family Portrait. New York & London: 1927. V. 39; 40; 41

Images of Truth - Remembrances and Criticism. London: 1962. V. 41

Like a Lover, by Glenway Wescott. France: 1926. V. 37

WESLEY, JOHN 1703-1791

The Beauties of Methodism . . . London: 1785. V. 42

The Beauties of the Rev. J. Wesley, M.A. Nottingham: 1802. V. 41; 45

A Calm Address to Our American Colonies. London: 1775. V. 42; 45

Christian's Pattern. London: 1735. V. 38

A Collection of Hymns for the Use of the People Called Methodists. London: 1815. V. 39

The Complete English Dictionary, Explaining Most of those Hard Words . . . Bristol: 1764. V. 43

The Doctrine of Original Sin . . . Bristol: 1757. V. 45

An Earnest Appeal to Men of Reason and Religion. Bristol: 1743. V. 44

An Extract of the Christian's Pattern. London: 1741. V. 44

A Farther Appeal to Men of Reason and Religion. London: 1745. V. 44

The Journal. London: 1827. V. 43

The Journal of the Rev. John Wesley. London: 1909. V. 38

The Journal. London: 1938. V. 37; 38; 46

The Journal of the Rev. John Wesley. New York: 1920. V. 37

A Letter to a Gentleman at Bristol. Bristol: 1758. V. 45

The Letters . . . Edited by John Telford. Standard Editions. 8 Volumes. London: 1931. V. 37

A Preservative Against Unsettled Notions in Religion. Bristol: 1770. V. 41; 45

Primitive Physic. London: 1781. V. 39

A Selection of the Most Important Passages in the Writings of Late Rev. John Wesley. London: 1825. V. 45

A Sermon on the Death of the Rev. Mr. George Whitefield. London: 1770. V. 45

A Short Account of the Life and Death of nathanael Othen, who was shot in Dover-Castle, October 26, 1757. The Second Edition. Bristol: (1758). V. 37

A Short Account of the Life and Death of the Rev. John Fletcher. London: 1786. V. 37

Some Remarks on Mr. Hill's Farrago Double-Distilled. Bristol: 1773. V. 45

Some Account of the Life and Death of Matthew Lee, Executed at Tyburn, October 11, 1752, in the 20th Year of His AGe. London: 1789. V. 46

Some Account of the Life and Death of Matthew Lee, Executed at Tyburn, October 11, 1752, in the 20th Year of His Age. Philadelphia: 1795. V. 42

The Works of Rev. John Wesley. London: 1809-1813. V. 39

WESLEY, SAMUEL

Maggots; or, Poems on Several Subjects, Never Before Handled. London: 1685. V. 45

Poems on Several Occasions. London: 1736. V. 37; 38; 40; 41

Poems on Several Occasions. Cambridge: 1743. V. 38; 42

WESSEL, NICKEL & GROSS

Illustrated Catalogue of Pianoforte Actions. New York: 1893. V. 39; 40; 46

WEST, ANTHONY

On a Dark Night. London: 1949. V. 46

WEST, ARTHUR

The Diary of a Dead Officer Being the Posthumous Papers of A. G. West. London: 1918. V. 45

WEST, B.

Melmoth, the Wanderer . . . London: 1823. V. 40; 43

WEST, BENJAMIN

Catalogue Raisonne of the Unequalled Collection of Historical Pictures. London: 1829. V. 38; 40

Catalogue of a Few Finished Original Pictures. London: 1829. V. 38; 40

Catalogue of the First Part of the Superb Collection of Prints and Drawings. London: 1820. V. 38; 44

A Discourse Delivered to the Students of the Royal Academy, on the Distribution of the Prizes, December 10, 1792 . . . London: 1793. V. 41

Miscellaneous Poems. Northampton: 1780. V. 41; 42

The New England Almanack, or Lady's and Gentleman's Diary, for the Year of Our Lord Christ 1770 . . . Providence: 1769. V. 42

West's Painting. Letter from the Sons of Benjamin West, Deceased, Late President of the Royal Academy of London, Offering to Sell to the Government of the United States Sundry Painting of that Artist. Washington: 1826. V. 45

WEST, CHARLES

Lectures on the Diseases of Infancy and Childhood. London: 1848. V. 43; 44

Lectures on the Diseases of Infancy and Childhood. London: 1854. V. 43

On Some Disorders of the Nervous System in Childhood. Philadelphia: 1871. V. 44; 45; 46

WEST, CHARLOTTE

A Ten Years' Residence in France, During the Severest Part of the Revolution, from . . . 1787 to 1797. London: 1821. V. 39

WEST, D. PORTER

Early History of Pope County. Russellville: 1906. V. 40

WEST, EDWARD

Multa Juncta in Uno. Emigration to British India. London: 1857. V. 43; 46

WEST, GILBERT

Education, a Poem: in Two Cantos. London: 1751. V. 45

The Institution of the Order of the Garter. London: 1742. V. 45; 46

WEST, H. A.

Six Views of Gibraltar. London: 1828. V. 40

WEST, HERBET FAULKNER

A Modern Conquistador: Robert Bontine Cunninghame Graham: His Life and Works. London: 1932. V. 46

WESTBY-GIBSON, JOHN

The Bibliography of Shorthand. London: 1887. V. 42

WESTCOTT, EDWARD NOYES

David Harum: A Story of American Life. New York: 1900. V. 43

WESTCOTT, THOMPSON 1820-1888

Centennial Portfolio. Philadelphia: 1876. V. 39; 40; 41; 42; 43; 44; 45

The Historic Mansions of Philadelphia . . . Philadelphia: 1877. V. 41; 42

Life of John Fitch, the Inventor of the Steam-Boat. Philadelphia: 1857. V. 44

Names of Persons Who Took the Oath of Allegiance to the State of Pennsylvania, 1777 & 1789. Philadelphia: 1865. V. 41; 42

WESTDROPP, M. S. DUDLEY

Irish Glass: an Account of Glass Making in IReland from the XVIth century to the Present Day . . . London: 1920. V. 41

WESTERMARCK, EDWARD

The History of Human Marriage. London: 1894. V. 42; 45

The History of Human Marriage. New York: 1922. V. 44

The History of Human Marriage. London: 1925. V. 44

Marriage Ceremonies in Morocco. London: 1914. V. 43; 45

The Origin and Development of the Moral Ideas. London: 1906-08. V. 39

Ritual and Beief in Morocco. London: 1926. V. 37; 40

WESTERN AND ATLANTIC RAILROAD CO.

Catalogue of Exhibits by the Western and Atlantic Railroad Company, Made at the International Cotton Exhibition. Atlanta: 1881. V. 42

WESTERN Canada and Its Great Resources: the Testimony of Settlers, Farmer Delegates and High Authorities with Preface and an Appendix on the Causes of Failure and Success in N.W. Farming. Ottawa: 1893. V. 39

WESTERN, CHARLES CALLIS, BARON 1767-1844

A Letter to the Earl of Liverpool on the Cause of Our Present Embarrassment and Distress. London: 1826. V. 41

WESTERN Frontier Library Series. Norman: 1953-84. V. 38

WESTERN Magazine. Chicago: 1845-46. V. 41

THE WESTERN Range. Letter from the Sec. of Agriculture, Report on the . . . , a Great but Neglected Natural Resource. Washington: 1939. V. 37

WESTERN Side-Saddle Scenes, and Young Lady's Equestrian Manual. Rochester: 1844. V. 45

WESTERNERS. CHICAGO CORRAL.

The Westerners Brand Book, 1944. Chicago: 1946. V. 40

THE WESTERNERS. DENVER POSSE. 1945 Brand Book Containing Twelve Original Papers Relating to Western and Rocky Mountain History. Denver: 1946. V. 39

THE WESTERNERS. Denver Posse. 1946 Brand Book: Twelve Original Papers Pertaining to the History of the West. Denver: 1947. V. 39

THE WESTERNERS. Denver Posse. 1949 Brand Book: A Baker's Dozen of Essays on the West: Its History, Places and People. Denver: 1950. V. 39

THE WESTERNERS. Denver Posse. Denver Prose, the Westerners Brand Book: Twelve Original Studies in Western and Rocky Mountain History. Denver: 1949. V. 39

WESTERNERS. LOS ANGELES CORRAL

The First Brand Book of the Los Angeles Corral. Los Angeles: 1947. V. 43

The Los Angeles Westerners Brand Book. Los Angeles: 1951. V. 45

The Westerners Brand Book 1950. Los Angeles: 1951. V. 43

The Westerners Brand Book: 1. Los Angeles: 1947. V. 40

The Westerners Brand Book: 2. Los Angeles: 1948. V. 40

WESTERNER'S. LOS ANGELES POSSE

The Westerner's Brand Book. Los Angeles: 1949-1950. V. 42; 45

WESTERNERS. SAN DIEGO CORRAL.

Brand Book Number One: The San Diego Corral of the Westerners. San Diego: 1968. V. 40

WESTERVELT, FRANCES A.

History of Bergen County, New Jersey, 1630-1923. New York: 1923. V. 41; 46

WESTGARTH, WILLIAM 1805-1889

The Colony of Victoria. London: 1864. V. 39

Personal Recollections of Early Melbourne & Victoria. Melbourne: 1888. V. 41

Victoria and the Australian Gold Mines in 1857 . . . London: 1857. V. 38; 40; 41; 43

WESTHEIM, PAUL

Prehispanic Mexican Art. New York: 1972. V. 39; 42

WESTHOLM, ALFRED

The Temples of Soli: Studies on Cypriote Art During Hellenistic and Roman Periods. Stockholm: 1936. V. 42

WESTIN, ALLAN F.

Privacy and Freedom. New York: 1967. V. 40

WESTLAKE, JOHN

A Treatise on Private International Law, or the Conflict of Laws, with Principal Reference to Its Practice in the English and Other Cognate Systems of Jurisprudence. London: 1858. V. 38

WESTLAKE, N. H. J.

History of Design in Painted Glass. London: 1881-1894. V. 43

WESTMACOTT, CHARLES

Points of Misery; or Fables for Mankind; Prose and Verse Chiefly Original. London: 1823. V. 40

WESTMACOTT, CHARLES MALLOY 1787-1868

The English Spy. London: 1825-26. V. 37; 38; 39; 41; 44; 45; 46

WESTMACOTT, CHARLES MOLLOY 1787?-1868

The Blue-Coat Boy; or Domestic Reminiscences of Mister Thomas Bounce . . . London: 1837. V. 43

The English Spy. London: 1825. V. 40; 44; 46

Fitzalleyne of Berkeley. A Romance of the present time. By Bernard Blackmantle, Author of the British Spy. London: 1825. V. 37

WESTMACOTT, WILLIAM

Historia Vegetabilium Sacra: or, A Scripture Herbal; . . . . Also their Medicinal Preparations, Vertues and Dose, . . . London: 1695. V. 39

WESTMINSTER ASSEMBLY OF DIVINES

The Larger Catechism . . . and Received by the Several Presbyterian Churches in America . . . Revised by Alex. M'Leod. New York: 1813. V. 38; 39

WESTMINSTER Kennel Club. New York: 1929. V. 43

WESTMINSTER, MATTHEW

Flores Historiarum per Matthaeum Westmonasteriensum Collecti . . . Frankfurt: 1601. V. 43

WESTMORELAND, J. FANE, EARL OF

Memoir of the Operations of the Allied Armies, Under Prince Schwarzenberg, and Marshal Blucher, During the Latter End of 1813, and the year 1814. London: 1822. V. 42

WESTMORLAND, MILDMAY FANE, 2ND EARL OF

Otia Sacra. Optima Fides. London: 1648. V. 43

WESTOFEN, W.

The Forth Bridge. London: 1890. V. 41

WESTON, CHARLES

California and the West. New York: 1940. V. 39; 41; 45

WESTON, EDWARD

50 Photographs. With Contributions by Robinson Jeffers, Merle Armitage, Donald Bear. New York: 1947. V. 37

The Art of Edward Weston. New York: 1932. V. 37

California and the West. New York: 1940. V. 40; 41

The Cats of Wildcat Hill. New York: 1947. V. 37; 39

The Daybooks of Edward Weston. Rochester: 1961. V. 41; 46

The Daybooks. New York: 1961, 1966. V. 41

The Daybooks of Edward Weston. Rochester: 1961-1966. V. 39

The Daybooks of Edward Weston. Volume I: Mexico. Volume II: California. Rochester & New York: 1961. V. 37

Edward Weston. New York: 1932. V. 38; 41

Edward Weston: His Life and Photographs. Millerton: 1979. V. 43

Enjoy Your Museum 11C: Photography. Pasadena: 1934. V. 46

50 Photographs. New York: 1947. V. 37; 40; 41; 44; 46

My Camera on Point Lobos. Boston: 1950. V. 37; 39; 40; 42

My Camera on Point Lobos. Yosemite and Boston: 1950. V. 37; 41

My Camera on Point Lobos. Yosemite National Park and: 1950. V. 41

My Camera on Point Lobos. 30 photographs and excepts from E.W.'s daybook. 1950. V. 37

Seeing California with Edward Weston. N.P.: 1939. V. 43

Seeing California with Edward Weston. N.P.: 1939. V. 41

Seeing California with Edward Weston. Westways: 1939. V. 44

WESTON, EDWARD P.

The Pedestrian; being a Correct Journal of 'Incidents' on a Walk from the State House, Boston, Mass., to the U.S. Capitol, at Washington, D.C . . . Also, an Account of His Adventures, while walking in Disguise through . . . New York: 1862. V. 37

WESTON, ELIZABETH JANE

Parthenicon Elisabethae Ioannae Westoniae, Virginis Nobilissimae Poetriae Fiorentissimae, Linguarum Plurimarum Pertissimae. Prague: 1606. V. 40

WESTON, GEORGE M.

The Progress of Slavery in the United States. Washington: 1857. V. 41

WESTON, JAMES

Stenography Compleated, or the Art of Short-Hand Brought to Perfection . . . London: 1727. V. 40; 42

WESTON, JESSIE L.

From Ritual to Romance. Cambridge: 1920. V. 37

Ico Meri or 'A Cycle of Cathay' - a Story of New Zealand Life. London: 1890. V. 44

Romance Vision and Satire. Boston: 1912. V. 42

Sir Gawain and the Green Knight: A Middle-English Arthurian Romance. London: 1898. V. 37

WESTON, MARIA D.

The Weldron Family; or, Vicissitudes of Fortune. Providence: 1848. V. 43

WESTON, PLOWDEN CHARLES JENNETT

Documents Connected with the History of South Carolina. London: 1856. V. 45

WESTON, R. HARCOURT

Letters and Important Documents Relative to the Edystone Lighthouse Selected Chiefly from the Correspondence of the Late Robert Weston . . . London: 1811. V. 41

WESTON, RICHARD

A Discourse of Husbandrie. London: 1652. V. 38

The Gardener's and Planter's Calendar. London: 1773. V. 38

The Gardener's Pocket-Calendar, On a New Plan . . . Nottingham: 1787. V. 38; 45

Tracts on Practical Agriculture and Gardening. London: 1769. V. 46

A Visit to the United States and Canada in 1833. Edinburgh: 1836. V. 39

WESTON, ROBERT HARCOURT

Letters and Important Documents Relative to the Edystone Lighthouse, Selected Chiefly from the Correspondence of the Late Robert Weston and from Other Manuscripts. London: 1811. V. 37; 39; 43

WESTON, SILAS

Four Months in the Mines of California; or Life in the Mountains. Providence: 1854. V. 40

Visit to a Volcano: or, What I Saw at the Western Island. Providence: 1856. V. 42

WESTON, STEPHEN

(Chinese characters.) Siao qu lin, or a Small Collection of Chinese Characters, Analysed and Decompunded, With the English Prefixed in the Order of the Alphabet, by the Way of Introduction to the Language of China . . . London: 1812. V. 41

Episodes from the Shah Nameh; or Annals of the Persian Kings. London: 1815. V. 41; 44

Persian Recreations. London: 1812. V. 37

The Praise of Paris. London: 1803. V. 43; 46

Remains of Arabic in the Spanish and Portuguese Languages . . . London: 1810. V. 38

La Scava; or Some Account of an Excavation of a Roman Town on the Hill of Chatelet in Champagne . . . London: 1818. V. 38

A Trimester in France and Swisserland; or, a Three Months' Journey . . . from Calais to Basle, through Lyons and from Basle to Paris, through Strasburg and Reims. London: 1821. V. 46

Viaggiana; or, Detached Remarks on the Buildings, Pictures, Statues, Inscriptions &c of Ancient and Modern Rome. London: 1776. V. 44

Viaggiana; or Detached Remarks on the Buildings, Pictures, Statues, Inscriptions &c. of Ancient and Modern Rome. London: 1797. V. 43

WESTON, WILLIAM

The Complete Merchant's Clerk. London: 1754. V. 37

Descriptive Pamphlet of Some of the Principal Mines and Prospects of Ourary County. Colorado in San Juan Gold and Silver Region. Denver: 1882. V. 37

An Enquiry into the Rejection of the Christian Miracles by the Heathens. Cambridge: 1746. V. 43; 44

WESTPHAL, JOHANN CASPAR

Pathologia Daemoniaca, id est Observationes & Meditationes Physiologico . . . Lipsiae. V. 46

WESTREENEN DE TIELLANDT, BARON DE

Rapport sur les Recherches Relatives a l'Invention Premiere et a lUsage le Plus Ancien de l'Imprimerie Stereotype. The Hague: 1833. V. 38

WESTROPP, HODDER M.

Ancient Symbol Worship. London: 1874. V. 38

WESTROPP, J. E., MRS.

Summer Experiences of Rome, Perugia and Siena in 1854, and Sketches of the Islands in the Bay of Naples. London: 1856. V. 46

WESTROPP, M. S. DUDLEY

Irish Glass. An Account of Glass Making in Ireland from the 16th Century to the Present Day. London: 1920. V. 39; 40

WESTROPP, T. J.

Illustrated Guide to the Northern, Western and Southern Islands and Coast of Ireland. Dublin: 1905. V. 38

THE WESTWARD March of Emigration in the United States, Considered In Its Bearing Upon the Near Future of Colorado and New Mexico. Lancaster: 1874. V. 39; 42; 45

WESTWOOD, JOHN OBADIAH 1805-1893

Arcana Entomologica or Illustrations of New, Rare and Interesting Insects. London: 1845. V. 38; 39

Arcana Entomolgica. London: 1841-45. V. 37

The Cabient of Oriental Entomology. London: 1848. V. 37

Illuminated Illustrations of the Bible. copies From Select Manuscripts of the Middle Ages. London: 1846. V. 39; 43

Illuminated Illustrations of the Bible. Copied from select MSS. of the Middle Ages. 1846. V. 37

An Introduction to the Modern Classification of Insects. London: 1839-40. V. 37; 39; 41; 43; 45

Palaeographia Sacra Pictoria . . . London: 1843-45. V. 38; 39; 43; 44; 45; 46

Palaeographia Sacra Pictoria: being a series of illustrations of the ancient versions fo the bible copied from Illuminated Manuscripts, executed between the 4th and 16the centuries. 1843-5. V. 37

Palaeographia Sacra Pictoria. London: 1845. V. 39

WESTWOOD, JOHN OBADIAN 1805-1893

An Introduction to the Modern Classification of Insects . . . London: 1840. V. 44

WESTWOOD, T.

Bibliotheca Piscatoria. London: 1966. V. 39

WETHERALD, R.

The Perpetual Calculator: or, time's universal standard. In three parts. I. A plain and easy introduction to chronology . . . II. An account of the solar system . . . the causes of eclipses . . . a synopsis of astronomy . . . Newcastle upon Tyne: 1760. V. 37

WETHERELL, ELIZABETH

The Old Helmet. London: 1864. V. 41

WETHEY, HAROLD E.

Alonso Cano: Painter, Sculptor, Architect. Princeton: 1955. V. 37

Colonial Architecture and Sculpture in Peru. Cambridge: 1949. V. 44

The Paintings of Titian. London: 1969. V. 44; 45

The Paintings of Titian. London: 1971. V. 40; 45

Titian. London: 1969-75. V. 46

WETMORE, A.

The Birds of the Republic of Panama. Washington: 1965-84. V. 37; 38

WETMORE, ALPHONSO

Gazetteer of Missouri, with an Appendix Containing Frontier Sketches and Illustrations of Indian Character. St. Louis: 1837. V. 37; 38; 39; 41; 42; 45

Petition of Sundry Inhabitants of the State of Missouri Upon the Subject of a Communication Between Said State and the Internal Provinces of Mexico. Washington: 1825. V. 43; 46

WETMORE, HELEN CODY

The Last of the Great Scouts. Chicago & Duluth: 1899. V. 43

Last of the Great Scouts. Duluth: 1899. V. 42

WETMORE, TIMOTHY FLETCHER

An Inaugural Dissertation on the Puerperal Fever. New York: 1795. V. 43; 45

WETTERSTRAND, OTTO GEORG

Hypnotism and Its Application to Practical Medicine . . . New York: 1897. V. 45

WETZEL, CHARLES

Trout Flies. Harrisburg: 1955. V. 39

WETZEL, CHARLES M.

American Fishing Books. Newark: 1950. V. 43

WETZEL, GEORGE

Howard Phillips Lovecraft - Memoirs, Critiques and Bibliographies. 1955. V. 44

Howard Phillips Lovecraft- Memoirs- Critiques and Bibliographies. 1955. V. 43

WEULE, KARL

Native Life in East Africa. The Results of an Ethnological Research Expedition. London: 1909. V. 41

WEXLEY, JOHN

The Last Mile. New York: 1934. V. 45

They Shall Not Die. New York: 1934. V. 39

WEY, FRANCIS

Rome. London. V. 41

Rome. London. V. 45

Rome. London: 1875. V. 39

WEYAND, L. R.

An Early History of Fayette County. LaGrange: 1936. V. 37

WEYER, JOHANN 1515-1588

De Praestigiis Daemonum & Incantationibus ac Veneficiis Libri Sex. Basileae: 1583. V. 45

Opera Omnia. Amstelodami: 1660. V. 43; 45

De Praestigiis. (On Magic). Basile: 1568. V. 43

WEYGAND, JAMES LAMAR

Afternoons with the Nappanee Bard. Dundee: 1963. V. 41

The Devout Tightwad and the Isfahan Columbian. Nappanee: 1975. V. 38; 44

Eastern European Papers, by James Lamar Weygand. (Nappanee): 1970. V. 37

The Hand Printing Press on Postage Stamps. Nappanee: 1954. V. 40; 44

Mountaineer; the Life and Times of Marvin Neel and the Blackwoods Press. Nappanee: 1969. V. 38

One Day in the Life of a Papermaker. Nappanee: 1972. V. 41

The Tightwads Guide to Gold Stamping. Nappanee: 1972. V. 38

Weygand Tightwad Beater, Its Design and Construction. N.P.: 1970. V. 41

WEYGAND, PHIL

An Eye Witness Account of the First Battle of Bull Run. 1967. V. 41

Murder on Beaver Island. Dundee: 1964. V. 41

WEYGAND, PHILIP

G. H. Petty and His Private Press. Dundee: 1962. V. 37; 41

THE WEYGAND Tightwad Beater. Its Design and Construction. Nappanee: 1970. V. 46

WEYLAND, JOHN

Observations on Mr. Whitbread's Poor Bill, and on the Population of England. London: 1807. V. 45

WEYMAN, STANLEY J.

A Gentleman of France. London: 1893. V. 37; 39; 41; 42

WEYMYSS, REID T.

The Life, Letters and Friendships of Richard Monckton Milnes, First Lord Houghton. London: 1890. V. 38

WHALEN, PHILIP

Memoirs of an Interglacial Age. San Francisco: 1960. V. 39

WHALEN, RICHARD J.

The Founding Father: the Story of Joseph P. Kennedy. New York: 1964. V. 37

WHALEY, JOHN

A Collection of Poems. London: 1732. V. 45

A Collection of Original Poems and Translations. London: 1745. V. 37; 39; 42; 44; 45

WHALLEY, JOYCE IRENE

The Art of Calligraphy, Western Europe and America. London: 1980. V. 38; 44

WHALLEY, PETER

Enquiry Into the Learning of Shakespeare. London: 1748. V. 42

WHARFDALE; or, a Description of the Several Delightful Features of that Extensive, Splendid and Fascinating Valley, Interspersed with Other Topographical Illustrations of Its Towns and Villages. Otley: 1813. V. 46

WHARNCLIFFE, LORD

Sketches in Egypt and the Holy Land . . . Taken During the Year 1855. London: 1855. V. 45

WHARTON, ANNE HOLLINGSWORTH

Salons, Colonial & Republican. Philadelphia: 1900. V. 37

WHARTON, CLARENCE

Santanta. The Great Chief of the Kiowas and His People. Dallas: 1935. V. 45

WHARTON, CLARENCE R.

History of Fort Bend County. Houston: 1939. V. 42

WHARTON, EDITH 1862-1937

The Age of Innocence. New York: 1920. V. 45; 46

The Age of Innocence. Avon: 1973. V. 44; 46

The Age of Innocence. London: 1973. V. 46

And Beyond. New York: 1926. V. 46

The Book of the Homeless. New York: 1916. V. 41; 43; 44

The Book of the Homeless. New York: & London: 1916. V. 43; 46

The Buccaneers. London: 1938. V. 41

Certain People. New York: 1930. V. 38; 39; 40; 42; 45

The Children. New York: 1928. V. 38; 42; 45

Crucial Instances. New York: 1901. V. 37; 44; 46

The Custom of the Country. London: 1913. V. 38

The Custom of the Country. New York: 1913. V. 39; 44

The Decoration of Houses. New York: 1897. V. 42; 43; 46

The Decoration of Houses. London: 1898. V. 37; 38

The Descent of Man. New York: 1904. V. 38

Ethan Frome. Stamford. V. 46

Ethan Frome. New York: 1911. V. 38; 39; 41; 43; 46

Ethan Frome. New York: 1922. V. 39; 44; 46

Ethan Frome. New York: 1922. V. 38

Ethan Frome. Stamford: 1967. V. 43

Fast and Loose: a Novelette. Charlottesville: 1977. V. 46

Fighting France from Dunkerque to Belfort. New York: 1915. V. 45

Fighting France from Dunkerque to Belfort. New York: 1925. V. 46

French Ways and Their Meaning. New York: 1919. V. 45

The Fruit of the Tree. New York: 1907. V. 44; 46

The Fruit of the Tree. New York: (1913). V. 37

Glimpses of the Moon. 1922. V. 46

The Glimpses of the Moon. New York: 1922. V. 38; 41; 44

The Glimpses of the Moon. New York & London: 1922. V. 38

The Gods Arrive. New York: 1932. V. 38; 43; 44; 45

The Greater Inclination. New York: 1899. V. 37; 38; 39; 40; 46

Here and Beyond. New York: 1926. V. 46

The Hermit and the Wild Woman. New York: 1908. V. 37; 38; 45

The House of Mirth. New York: 1905. V. 38; 39; 41; 44

The House of Mirth. Leipzig: 1906. V. 40

Hudson River Bracketed. New York: 1929. V. 44

Human Nature. New York: 1933. V. 39

Italian Villas and Their Gardens. London: 1904. V. 41

Italian Villas and Their Gardens. New York: 1904. V. 42; 43

Italian Back-Grounds. New York: 1905. V. 38; 39; 40

Italian Villas and Their Gardens. New York: 1910. V. 39; 43

Madame de treymes. New York: 1907. V. 44; 46

The Marne. New York: 1918. V. 39

The Mother's Recompense. New York: 1925. V. 41; 46

A Motor Flight through France. New York: 1908. V. 42; 46

Old New York False Dawn (The 'Forties). New York: 1924. V. 45

Old New York. New York: & London: 1924. V. 46

Quartet. 1975. V. 44

Quartet. Four Stories. Kentfield: 1975. V. 38; 41; 44

The Reef. New York: 1912. V. 38; 45

Sanctuary. New York: 1903. V. 44

A Son at the Front. New York: 1923. V. 37; 44; 45; 46

Summer. 1917. V. 46

Summer. New York: 1917. V. 40; 45

Tales of Men and Ghosts. New York: 1910. V. 45

The Touchstone. New York: 1900. V. 38; 44

Twilight Sleep. New York: 1927. V. 45; 46

The Valley of Decision. New York: 1902. V. 37; 38; 39; 40; 44; 45; 46

The World Over. New York: 1936. V. 45

The Writing of Fiction. New York: 1925. V. 40; 46

Xingu and Other Stories. New York: 1916. V. 46

WHARTON, EDITH 1862-1937 continued

Ximgu and Other Stories. New York: 1931. V. 45

WHARTON, FRANCIS

The Revolutionary Diplomatic Correspondence of the United States. Washington: 1889. V. 39; 41; 42; 44

A Treatise on Medical Jurisprudence. Philadelphia: 1855. V. 38

WHARTON, GRACE

The Queens of Society. London: 1900. V. 38

WHARTON, HENRY

Anglia Sacra, sive Collectio Historiarum . . . de Archiepiscopis & Episcopis Angliae, a Prima Fidei Christianae Suscepitione ad Annum MDXL. London: 1691. V. 41

A Defence of Pluralities, or Holding Two Benefices with Cure of Souls, as Now Practised in the Church of England. London: 1692. V. 39

WHARTON, HENRY E.

The Practice of Surgery . . . Philadelphia: 1890. V. 46

The Practice of Surgery . . . Philadelphia: 1899. V. 45

WHARTON, PHILIP, DUKE OF

Speech in the House of Lords, etc. (1723). V. 39

WHARTON, SAMUEL

Plain Facts: Being an Examination into the Rights of the Indian Nations of America, to Their Respective Countries . . . Philadelphia: 1781. V. 37

WHARTON, SARAH

The Cottage Minstrel; or, Verses on Various Subjects. Philadelphia: 1827. V. 40

WHARTON, T.

Essays on Gothic Architecture . . . London: 1802. V. 41

WHARTON, WILLIAM

Birdy. New York: 1978. V. 42

Birdy. New York: 1979. V. 39

WHARTON, WILLIAM H.

Address of the Honorable Wm. H. Wharton, Texas Commissioner, Delivered at Masonic Hall, New York, on the 26th of April, 1836. New York: 1836. V. 37

WHAT Farmers Say of Their Personal Experience in the Canadian North-West. Ottawa: 1881. V. 46
WHAT Farmers Say of Their Personal Experience in the Canadian North-West. Ottawa: 1884. V. 43; 45

WHAT Have We Got? or, All Our Glories: a Poetico-Political Morceau. Fragment I & II. London: 1820-21. V. 39

WHAT is Genius. A Poem. London: 1818. V. 37

WHAT Shall We Do With Canada? Leeds: 1836-37. V. 43

WHAT The Children Sing. London. V. 40

WHAT the Salt River Valley Offers to the Immigrant, Capitalist, and Invalid. Phoenix: 1887. V. 39

WHAT Things? Or, an Impartial Inquiry What Things Are So, and What Things ARe Not So. Occassioned by Two Late Poems, the One Intitled, Are These Thing So? And the Other Intitled, Yes, They Are. London: 1740. V. 40; 41

WHAT to Do with the Cold Mutton; a Book of Rechauffes. London: 1863. V. 39

WHATELEY, MARY

Original Poems on Several Occasions. London: 1764. V. 43

WHATELEY, RICHARD, ABP. OF DUBLIN 1787-1863

Elements of Logic. London: 1844. V. 38

WHATELEY, THOMAS d. 1772

L'Art de Former les Jardins Modernes, ou l'Art des Jardins anglois. Paris: 1771. V. 41

Observations on Modern Gardening, Illustrated by Descriptions. Dublin: 1770. V. 42; 43

Observations on Modern Gardening. Dublin: 1770. V. 38

Observations on Modern Gardening. London: 1770. V. 37; 40; 41; 43; 45

Observations on Modern Gardening. London: 1777. V. 44

Observations on Modern Gardening. London: 1793. V. 38; 39; 40; 41

Observations on Modern Gardening and Laying Out Pleasure-Grounds, Parks, Farms, Ridings . . . London: 1801. V. 44; 45

Observations on Modern Gardening, Illustrated by Descriptions. London: 1771. V. 37

WHATELEY, WILLIAM

A Bride-Bush. Or, a Direction for Married Persons. London: 1623. V. 45

WHATELY, RICHARD, ABP. OF DUBLIN 1787-1863

Address to the Clergy of the Dioceses of Dublin and Glandalagh and Kildare on the Recent Changes in the System of Irish National Education. Oxford: 1828. V. 45

Address to the Clergy of the Dioceses of Dublin and Glandalagh and Kildare on the Recent Changes in the System of Irish National Education. London: 1853. V. 45

Address to the Clergy of the Dioceses of Dublin and Glandalagh and Kildare on the Recent Changes in the System of Irish National Education. V. 45

Elements of Logic. London: 1826. V. 38; 41; 43; 45

Elements of Rhetoric. Oxford: 1828. V. 38; 45

Essays on Some of the Peculiarities of the Christian Religion. London: 1831. V. 43

Introductory Lectures on Political Economy. Oxford: 1831. V. 41

Introductory Lectures on Political economy, delivered at Oxford, 1831. London: 1847. V. 38

Miscellaneous Lectures and Reviews. London: 1861. V. 42; 45

Remarks on Transportation and on a Recent Defense of the System, in a Second Letter to Earl Grey. London: 1834. V. 43; 46

Thoughts on Secondary Punishments, in a Letter to Earl Grey. London: 1832. V. 42; 44

WHATELY, THOMAS

Considerations on the Trade and Finances of this Kingdom, and On the Measures of Administration, with Respect to Those Great National Objects Since the Conclusion of the Peace. London: 1766. V. 37; 42

An Improved Method of Treating Strictures in the Urethra. London: 1804. V. 38

The Regulations Lately Made Concerning the Colonies, and the Taxes Imposed Upon Them, Considered. London: 1765. V. 37; 38

Remarks on Some of the Characters of Shakespeare. V. 46

Remarks on the Budget, or a Candid Examination of the FActs and Arguments Offered to the Public in that Pamphlet. London: 1765. V. 42

WHATELY, WILLIAM

A Bride Bush. London: 1619. V. 40

WHATLEY, E. L.

The Southern Light, an Independent Religious and Literary Journal Set for the Defense of Truth and Devoted to the Difussion of Knowledge. Edgefield: 1856-57. V. 46

WHATMAN, J.

J. Whatman. Maidstone: 1931. V. 38; 41

WHATMAN, JAMES 1813-1887

Authentic Memoirs of William Wynne Ryland . . . London. V. 46

Catalogue of the Library at Vinters in Kent. London: 1841. V. 40

WHATMAN, SUSANNAH

Her Housekeeping Book. 1952. V. 40

Her Housekeeping Book. Cambridge: 1952. V. 41; 45

WHEAT, CARL I.

Books of the California Gold Rush. San Francisco: 1949. V. 37; 39; 40; 44; 45

Mapping the Transmissippi West. San Francisco: 1957-63. V. 37; 38; 39; 40; 42; 43; 45; 46

1540-1861 Mapping the Transmississippi West . . . Volume Three from the Mexican War to the Boundary Surveys 1846-1854. San Francisco: 1959. V. 40

The Maps of California Region 1848-1857. San Francisco: 1942. V. 37; 38; 39; 40; 41; 43; 44; 46

The Pioneer Press of California. Oakland: 1948. V. 39

Pioneers: The Engaging Tale of Three Early California Printing Presses and Their Strange Adventures. Los Angeles: 1934. V. 42

25 California Maps. San Francisco: 1948. V. 37; 42

WHEAT, MARVIN T.

Travels on the Western Slope of the Mexican Cordilera . . . Its Chief Cities and Towns . . . San Francisco: 1857. V. 39; 44

WHEATER, W.

The History of the Parishes of Sherburn and Cawood, With Notices of Wistow, Saxton, Towton &c. London: 1882. V. 39

Some Historic Mansions of Yorkshire and Their Associations. Leeds: 1888. V. 38

Some Historic Mansions of Yorkshire, and Their Associations . . . Leeds: 1888-89. V. 40

Some Historic Mansions of Yorkshire and Their Associations. Leeds: 1889. V. 38

Some Historic Mansions of Yorkshire and Their Associations . . . London:eeds: 1889-89. V. 37

WHEATLEY, DENNIS

Herewith the Clues! London: 1939. V. 43

The Malinsay Massacre. London: 1938. V. 43

Murder Off Miami. London: 1936. V. 43

Who Killed Robert Prentice? London: 1937. V. 43

WHEATLEY, H.

Remarkable Bindings in the British Museum Selected For Their Beauty or Historic Interest. London: 1889. V. 41

WHEATLEY, HENRY B.

Bookbinding Considered as a Fine Art, Mechanical Art and Manufacture. London: 1880. V. 39

Hogarth's London: Pictures and Manners of the Eighteenth Century. New York: 1909. V. 42

Les Reliures Remarquables du Musee Britannique . . . London: 1889. V. 40

Round About Piccadilly and Pall Mall. London: 1870. V. 38; 40

Samuel Pepys and the World He Lived in. London: 1880. V. 43

WHEATLEY, HEWITT

The Rod and Line; or Practical Hints and Dainty Devices. London: 1849. V. 43

WHEATLEY, JOHN

Remarks on Currency and Commerce. London: 1803. V. 42

WHEATLEY, PHILLIS ca. 1753-1784

Poems on Various Subjects, Religious and Moral. London: 1773. V. 37; 41; 43

Poems on Various Subjects, Religious and Moral. Walpole: 1802. V. 39; 40; 45

The Poems. Philadelphia: 1909. V. 45

WHEATLEY, RICHARD

Cathedrals and Abbeys in Great Britain and Ireland. New York: 1890. V. 44

WHEATLY, CHARLES 1686-1742

A Rational Illustration of the Book of Common Prayer. London: 1720. V. 39

WHEATON, HENRY

Enquiry Into the Validity of the British Claim to a Right of Visitation and Search of American Vessels Suspected to Be Engaged in the African Slave Trade . . . Lonon: 1842. V. 37

WHEELER, A.

The Westmorland Dialect . . . Kendal: 1821. V. 45

WHEELER, ALFRED

Land Titles in San Francisco, and the Laws Affecting the Same, with a Synopsis of all Grants and Sales of Land Within the Limits Claimed by the City. San Francisco: 1852. V. 39; 40; 43

WHEELER, ANDREW C.

The Chronicles of Milwaukee. Milwaukee: 1861. V. 42; 43

WHEELER, ANN COWARD

The Westmorland Dialect, in Three Familiar Dialogues. Kendal: 1790. V. 40

WHEELER, ARTHUR OLIVER

Eye-Witness; or, Life Scenes in the Old North State, Depciting the Trials and Sufferings of the Unionists During the Rebellion. Boston: 1865. V. 41; 44

The Selkirk Range by A. O. Wheeler. Ottawa: 1905. V. 37; 40; 42; 43; 44; 45

The Selkirk Mountains. A Guide for Moutain Climbers and Pilgrims. Winnipeg: 1912. V. 39

WHEELER, DANIEL

Extracts from the Letters and Journal of Daniel Wheeler Now Engaged in a Religious Visit to the Inhabitants of some of the Islands of the Pacific Ocean, Van Dieman's Land and New South Wales. London: 1839. V. 37; 40

Extracts from the Letters and Journal of Daniel Wheeler, While Engaged In a Religious Visit to the Inhabitants of Some of the Islands of the Pacific Ocean, Van Diemen's Land, New South Wales, and New Zealand . . . Philadelphia: 1840. V. 37; 40; 41; 42; 46

A Memoir of Daniel Wheeler with an Account of His Gospel Labours in the Islands of the Pacific. Philadelphia: 1859. V. 39; 40; 41

Memoirs of the Life and Gospel Labours of the Late Daniel Wheeler. London: 1842. V. 38; 41

Memoirs of the Life and Gospel Labours of the Late Daniel Wheeler, a Minister of the Society of Friends. London: 1842. V. 38; 42; 44

WHEELER, EDWARD L.

The Deadwood Dick Library. Cleveland: 1899. V. 41

WHEELER, ELLA

Shells. Milwaukee: 1873. V. 41

WHEELER, ETHEL ROLT

Famous Blue Stockings. London: 1910. V. 37; 39; 41; 43; 45

WHEELER, GEORGE MONTAGUE 1842-1905

Annual Report Upon the Geographical Surveys West of the One Hundreth Meiridan . . . Washington: 1876. V. 38

Letter from the Secretary of War, Communicating, in Compliance with a Resolution of the Senate of March 7, 1872, a Preliminary Report of Lieut. George M. Wheeler, Corps of Engineers, of he Progress of the Engineer Exploration of the Public Domain . . . Washington: 1872. V. 39; 44; 46

Preliminary report Concerning Explorations and Surveys Principally in Nevada and Arizona. Washington: 1872. V. 40; 43

Report Upon United States Geographical Surveys West of the One Hundredth Meridian. Washington: 1889. V. 42

WHEELER, GERVASE

Homes for the People in Suburb and Country . . . Adapted to American Climate and Wants. New York: 1855. V. 42

WHEELER, H. F. B.

Napoleon and the Invasion of England. London: 1908. V. 41

The War in Wexford. An Account of the Irish Rebellion in the South of Ireland in 1798 . . . London: 1910. V. 38

The War in Wexford. London & New York: 1910. V. 39

WHEELER, H. G., MRS.

Cupid's Little Game. Providence: 1881. V. 42

WHEELER, J. TALBOYS

Annals of James Macrae, Esq. Madras: 1862. V. 43

The History of the Imperial Assemblage at Delhi, Held on the 1st January 1877; to Celebrate the Assumption of the Title of 'Empress of India' by Her Majesty the Queen . . . London: 1877. V. 40

WHEELER, JACOB D.

A Practical Treatise on the Law of Slavery. New York & New Orleans: 1837. V. 38

WHEELER, JAMES

The Botantist's and Gardener's New Dictionary . . . London: 1763. V. 37; 45

WHEELER, JOHN

A Treatise of Commerce. New York: 1931. V. 38; 39

WHEELER, JOHN H.

Historical Sketches of North Carolina, from 1584 to 1851. Philadelphia: 1851. V. 44

WHEELER, JOSEPH

General Orders No. 7. Head Quarters, Wheeler's Cavalry Corps, June 3rd, 1863. N.P.: 1863. V. 45

General Orders No. 2. Head Q'rs Wheeler's Cavalry Corps. N.P.: 1864. V. 40

A Revised System of Cavalry Tactics, for the Use of the Cavalry and Mounted Infantry, C.S.A. Mobile: 1863. V. 38; 42

WHEELER, MONORE

A Typographical Commonplace Book. New York: 1932. V. 37; 40

WHEELER, MONROE

Soutine. New York: 1950. V. 44

A Typographical Commonplace Book. Paris & New York: 1932. V. 37

WHEELER, O. C.

The Chinese in America. Oakland: 1880. V. 38; 39; 41

WHEELER, OLIN D.

The Trail of Lewis and Clark 1804-1904. New York: 1904. V. 37; 40; 42

The Trail of Lewis and Clark 1804-1904. New York: 1926. V. 42; 46

WHEELER, STEVE

'Hello Steve.' New York: 1947. V. 37

WHEELER'S CAVALRY CORPS. (C.S.A.)

General Orders No. 2, Head Qu'rs Wheeler's Cavalry Corps, February 10th, 1864. N.P.: 1864. V. 39

General Orders, No. 4. 1863. V. 39

WHEELOCK, ELEAZAR 1711-1779

A Continuation of the Narrative of the Indian Charity School, Begun in Lebanon, in Connecticut; Now Incorporated with Dartmouth-College, in Hanover, in the Province of New Hampshire. Hartford: 1773. V. 39

WHEELOCK, ELEAZER 1711-1779

A Continuation of the Narrative of the Indian Charity School, in Lebanon, in Connecticut . . . Hartford: 1771. V. 41; 44

WHEELOCK, JOHN HALL

The Bright Doom. A Book of Poems. New York: 1927. V. 37

Dear Men and Women: New Poems. New York: 1966. V. 41

The Gardner and Other Poems. New York: 1961. V. 41

Love and Liberation. Boston: 1913. V. 38

Poems 1911-1936. New York: 1936. V. 38; 41

Poems Old and New. New York: 1956. V. 41

WHEELOCK, THOMPSON B.

Journal of Colonel Dodge's Expedition from Fort Gibson to the Pawnee Pict Village. V. 39

Journal of Colonel Dodge's Expedition from Fort Gibson to the Pawnee Pict Village. Washington. V. 44

Journal of Colonel Dodge's Expedition from Fort Gibson to the Pawnee Pict. Village. Washington: 1834. V. 42

WHEELS: An Anthology of Verse. Oxford: 1916. V. 37

WHEELWRIGHT, CHARLES

Poems, Original and Translated. London: 1811. V. 42

WHEELWRIGHT, CHARLES APTHORP

Poems, Original and Translated. London: 1810. V. 45

WHEELWRIGHT, H.

Ten Years in Sweden. London: 1865. V. 38

WHEELWRIGHT, HORACE WILLIAM

Bush Wanderings of a Naturalist . . . London: 1861. V. 45

A Spring and Summer in Lapland . . . London: 1864. V. 43

WHEELWRIGHT, JOHN BROOKS

Rock and Shell: Poems 1923-33. Boston: 1933. V. 37; 40

WHEILDON, WILLIAM

Sentry, or Beacon Hill; The Beacon and The Monument of 1635 and 1790. (with) New History of the Battle of Bunker Hill, June 17, 1775, . . . Concord: 1875, 1876. V. 38

WHELAN, EDWARD

The Union of the British Provinces. Charlottetown: 1865. V. 41; 43

WHELEN, TOWNSEND

Small Arms Design and Ballistics. Georgetown: 1955. V. 39

Wilderness Hunting and Wildcraft. Delaware: 1927. V. 39

WHELER, GEORGE

A Journey into Greece, in Company of Dr. Spon of Lyons. London: 1682. V. 39

Voyage de Dalmatie, de Grece, et du Levant . . . Amsterdam: 1689. V. 45

Voyage de Dalmatie, de Gece, et du Levant. La Haye: 1723. V. 38; 42

WHELER, ROBERT BELL 1785-1857

A Guide to Stratford-upon-Avon. Stratford-upon-Avon: 1814. V. 41

History and Antiquities of Stratford-upon-Avon . . . Stratford-upon-Avon: Printed. V. 37

History and Antiquities of Stratford-Upon-Avon. Stratford on Avon: 1804. V. 38

History and Antiquities of Stratford upon Avon. Comprising a description of the Collegiate Church, the Life of Shakespeare, etc. Stratford Upon Avon: 1806. V. 37; 41; 44

WHELLAN, T.

History and Topography of the City of York; the Ainsty Wapentake, and the East Riding of Yorkshire. Beverley: 1855. V. 38; 40

WHELLIER, ALEXANDER

The Complete English Lawyer. London: 1820. V. 40

The Complete English Lawyer. London: 1822. V. 40

The Complete English Lawyer. London: 1823. V. 40

The Complete English Lawyer. London: 1826. V. 40

WHERE the Two Came to Their Father; a Navaho War Ceremonial Given by Jeff King. New York: 1943. V. 41

WHERE to Recuperate During Summer Days; or, Spots in Northern Iowa and Minnesota, Where Health and Pleasure Can Be Found. Chicago: 1883. V. 43

WHERE to Recuperate During Summer Days. Or Spots in Northern Iowa and Minnesota, Where Health and Pleasure Cana be Found. Chicago: 1884. V. 37; 42

WHEREAS the General Court . . . Have Ordered . . . . Selectmen of the Several Towns . . . to Convene the Qualified Voters . . . for the Purpose of Collecting Their Sentiments on the Necessity of Expediency of Revising the Constitution. Boston: 1795. V. 43

WHERRY, GEORGE

Alpine Notes and Climbing Foot. Cambridge: 1896. V. 42

WHERRY, J. A.

List of Real Estate in the City of St. Louis, for Sale for the Taxes Due by the Owners This The Year Eighteen Hundred and Twenty-Seven. St. Louis: 1827. V. 39

WHEWELL, WILLIAM 1794-1866

Additional Lectures on the History of Moral Philosophy. Cambridge: 1862. V. 41

Astronomy and General Physics considered with reference to natural Theology. London: 1834. V. 37; 40

Astronomy and General Physics Considered with Reference to Natural Theology. London: 1833. V. 43; 45

The Elements of Morality, Including Polity. London: 1845. V. 38; 41; 43

The Elements of Morality, Including Polity. London: 1848. V. 43; 45

The Elements of Morality . . . London: 1854. V. 45

The Elements of Morality, Including Polity. Cambridge: 1864. V. 45

History of the Inductive Sciences, from the Earliest to the Present Times. London: 1837. V. 42; 43; 45

History of the Inductive Sciences, from the Earliest to the Present Time. London: 1847. V. 38; 40; 45

History of the Inductive Sciences, from the Earliest to the Present Time. London: 1857. V. 37; 42; 43; 45

History of Scientific Ideas. London: 1858. V. 43; 45

Indications of the Creator. London: 1845. V. 43

Lectures on Systematic Morality, Delivered in Lent Terms, 1846. London: 1846. V. 42; 43

Lectures on the History of Moral Philosophy in England. London: 1852. V. 38

Lectures on the History of Moral Philosophy. Cambridge: 1862. V. 43; 45

Of a Liberal Education in General. London: 1850. V. 39; 43

Of a Liberal Education in General; and with Particular Reference to the Leading Studies of the Univeristy of Cambridge . . . London: 1850. V. 45

Of the Plurality of Worlds: an Essay. London: 1853. V. 37; 43

On the Foundations of Morals. Cambridge: 1839. V. 45

On the Philosophy of Discovery, Chapters, Historical and Critical . . . London: 1860. V. 43

The Philosophy of the Inductive Sciences, Founded Upon Their History. London: 1840. V. 39; 43; 45

The Philosophy of Inductive Sciences, Founded Upon Their History . . . London: 1847. V. 42

The Platonic Dialogues for English Readers. Cambridge: 1859-61. V. 45

The Platonic Dialogues for English Readers. Cambridge: 1860/61. V. 43

Six Lectures on Political Economy Delivered at Cambridge, in Michaelmas Term 1861. Cambridge: 1862. V. 40; 43

Thoughts on the Study of Mathematics as a part of a Liberal Education. Cambridge: 1835. V. 38; 40; 43

A Treatise on Dynamics Containing a Considerable Collection of Mechanical Problems. Cambridge: 1823. V. 40

WHIBLEY, CHARLES

Cathedrals of England and Wales. London: 1888. V. 38

WHICHCOTE, BENJAMIN

Moral and Religious Aphorisms. Norwich: 1703. V. 41; 45

WHICHER, GEORGE MEASOM

From Muscatine - Verses. Muscatine: 1912. V. 37; 38; 40

WHIG Against Tory; or, the Military Adventures of a Shoemaker: a Tale of the Revolution for Children. Cincinnati: 1832/1831. V. 44

A WHIGG Ballad, or, a Summons to a Fresh Association. London: 1682. V. 41; 45

WHILLDIN, M. A.

A Description of Western Texas. Galveston: 1876. V. 37

WHINCOP, THOMAS

Scanderbeg; or, Love and Liberty. London: 1747. V. 37; 39; 40; 41; 43; 45

WHINNEY, MARGARET

Grinling Gibbons in Cambridge. Cambridge: 1948. V. 41

WHINYATES, F. A.

From Coruna to Sevastopol. The History of 'C' Battery, 'A' Brigade (Late C Troop), Royal Horse Artillary, with Succession of Officers from Its Formation to the Present Time. London: 1884. V. 38

WHIPPLE, A. W.

Report of Lieutenant Whipple's Expedition from San Diego to the Colorado. Washington: 1851. V. 41

Report of the Secretary of War . . . the Report of Lieutenant Whipple's Expedition from San Diego to Colorado. Washington: 1851. V. 37

WHIPPLE, AUGUSTUS OLIVER

Nine Letters, Particularly Addressed to the People of the Revolting Provinces of the Caraccas and to other Spanish Provinces in North and South America . . . Baltimore: 1811. V. 46

WHIPPLE, W.

Report of Explorations for a Railway Route, Near the Thirty-Fifth Parallel of Latitude from the Mississippi River to the Pacific Ocean. Washington: 1855. V. 45

WHISHAW, FRANCIS

Analysis of Railways: Consisting of a Series of Reports on the Railways Projected in England and Wales, in the Year MDCCCXXXVII. London: 1828. V. 46

Analysis of Railways. London: 1837. V. 40

The Railways of Great Britain and Ireland Practically Described and Illustrted. London: 1840. V. 38

WHISHAW, FRED J.

Out of Doors in Tsarland. London: 1893. V. 42

WHISTLER, HUGH

In the High Himalayas, Sport and Travel in the Rhotang and Baralecha, with Some Notes on the Natural History of that Area. London: 1924. V. 39

WHISTLER, JAMES ABBOT MAC NEILL

Nocturnes. Marines. Chevalet Pieces. London: 1892. V. 38

The Red Rag. Easthampton: 1970. V. 45

WHISTLER, JAMES ABBOT MC NEILL

Art and Art Critics. Whistler v. Ruskin. London: 1878. V. 41; 42

The Baronet and the Butterfly. 1899. V. 43

The Baronet and the Butterfly. New York: 1899. V. 40

Eden Versus Whistler; the Baronet and the Butterfly. Paris: 1869. V. 41

Eden Versus Whistler. The Baronet and the Butterfly. A Valentine with a Verdict. New York: 1899. V. 41

Eden Versus Whistler: The Baronet and the Butterfly: a Valentine with a Verdict. Paris: 1899. V. 37; 41; 43; 44

The Etchings of James McNeill Wistler. London: 1922. V. 38; 42

The Gentle Art of Making Enemies. Chelse: 1890. V. 43

The Gentle Art of Making Enemies. London: 1890. V. 39; 41; 42; 44; 45

The Gentle Art of Making Enemies. New York: 1890. V. 37; 38; 41; 42

The International Society of Sculptors, Painters & Gravers Memorial Exhibition of the Works of James McNeill Whistler . . . London: 1905. V. 38

Mr. Whistler's 'Ten O'Clock'. London: 1888. V. 40; 41

Ten O'Clock: A Lecture by . . . Foreword by Don C. Seitz. Portland, Maine: 1916. V. 37

Wilde V. Whistler: Being an Acrimonious Correspondence on Art Between Oscar Wilde and James A. Mc Neill Whistler. London: 1906. V. 37

Wilde vs. Whistler. Being an Acrimonious Correspondence on Art Between Oscar Wilde and James A. McNeill Whistler. London: 1904. V. 37

WHISTLER, LAURENCE

Armed Octover and Other Poems. London: 1932. V. 38

Children of Hertha and Other Poems. Oxford: 1929. V. 38

The Engraved Glass of Laurence Whistler. Hitchin: 1952. V. 39

Ioho! London: 1946. V. 40

Pictures on Glass. Ipswich: 1972. V. 41

Sir John Vanbrugh - Architect and Dramatist - 1664-1726. London: 1938. V. 38; 42; 44

The Work of Rex Whistler. London: 1960. V. 40

WHISTLER, LAWRENCE

The Image on the Glass. London: 1975. V. 46

WHISTLER, REX

Georgian Love Songs. Preston: 1949. V. 43

The Konigsmark Drawings. London: 1952. V. 37; 38; 40; 41

The Masque Library. Nos. 1-9. London: 1950. V. 41

The New Forget-Me-not. A Calendar. London: 1929. V. 40; 41

The New Keepsake. London: 1931. V. 41

Restoration Love Songs. Hitchin: 1950. V. 40

Rothman's Diamond Jubilee Portfolio. London: 1950. V. 44

Songs of Our Grandfathers - Reset in Guinness Time. Dublin: 1936. V. 41

Songs of Our Grandfathers. London: 1936. V. 45

The Work of Rex Whistler. London: 1960. V. 37; 38

WHISTON, WILLIAM

Astronomical Principles of Religion, Natural and Reveal'd. London: 1717. V. 38

The Calculation of Solar Eclipses without Parallaxes. With a specimen of the same in the total eclipse of the sun, May 11, 1724. Now first made publick. To which is added, a proposal how, with the latitude given, the geographical longitude of all the . . . London: 1724. V. 37

Historical Memoirs of the Life of Dr. Samuel Clarke Being a Supplement to Dr. Sykes's and Bishop Hoadleys Accounts . . . London: 1730. V. 37

The Literal Accomplishemnt of Scripture Prophecies Being a Full Answer to a Late Discourse. 1724. V. 38

Memoirs of the Life and Writings Containing Memoirs of Several of His Friends, Also. London: 1749. V. 37; 39; 40; 43

A New Theory of the Earth, from Its Original, to the Consummation of Things. London: 1696. V. 41; 43; 45

A New Theory of the Earth, from Its Original, to the Consummation of All Things, Wherein the Creation of the World in Six Days, the Universal Deluge, and the General Conflagration . . . London: 1722. V. 45

Reflexions on an Anonymous Pamphlet, Entitled a Discourse of Free Thinking. London: 1713. V. 41; 44

WHITAKER, A.

Atlas of Onshore Sedimentary Basins in England and Wales. Glasgow: 1985. V. 37

WHITAKER, ARTHUS PRESTON

Documents Relating to the Commerical Policy of Spain in the Floridas with Incidental Reference to Louisiana. Deland: 1931. V. 37; 42

WHITAKER, CHARLES HARRIS

Bertram Grosvenor Goodhue - Architect and Master of Many Arts. New York: 1925. V. 38; 39

WHITAKER, DANIEL K.

New Orleans Quarterly Review. New Orleans: 1878. V. 37; 43

WHITAKER, GEORGE

Two Letters to the Lord Bishop of Toronto, In Reply to Charges Brought by the Lord Bishop of Huron Against the Theological Teaching of Trinity College, Toronto . . . Toronto: 1860. V. 41; 44

WHITAKER, J.

The Deer Parks and Paddocks of England. London: 1892. V. 38

WHITAKER, J. I. S.

The Birds of Tunisia, Being a History of the Birds Found in the Regency of Tunis. London: 1905. V. 38; 39

WHITAKER, JARED I.

To the Justices of the Inferior Court of . . . . County, Gal . . . Head-Quarters, Commissary General's Office. Atlanta: 1863. V. 43

WHITAKER, JOHN

The Ancient Cathedral of Cornwall Historically Surveyed. London: 1804. V. 39; 43

The Course of Hannibal Over the Alps Ascertained. London: 1794. V. 39; 43

The History of Manchester. London: 1773. V. 38

Mary Queen of Scots Vindicated. London: 1787. V. 46

The Origin of Arianism Disclosed. London: 1791. V. 41

WHITAKER, JOSEPH

A Descriptive List of the Deer-Parks and Paddocks of England. London: 1892. V. 45; 46

WHITAKER, JOSEPH ISAAC SPADAFORCE

The Birds of Tunisia, Being a History of the Birds Found in the Regency of Tunis. London: 1905. V. 37

WHITAKER, MARY SCRIMZEOUR

Poems. Charleston: 1850. V. 46

WHITAKER, NATHANIEL

A Brief Narrative of the Indian Charity-School in Lebanaon in Connecticut, New England . . . London: 1767. V. 43; 46

WHITAKER T. D.

An Account of the Parish of Cartmell. London: 1818. V. 38

WHITAKER, T. H.

Victoria. Victoria: 1941. V. 45

WHITAKER, THOMAS D.

The History and Antiquities of the Deanery of Craven in the County of York. Leeds and London: 1878. V. 41

WHITAKER, THOMAS DUNHAM

The History and Antiquities of the Deanery of Craven, in the County of York. London: 1805. V. 38; 41; 42; 46

An History of the Original Parish of Whalley and Honor of Clitheroe, in the Counties of Lancaster and York. London: 1806. V. 38; 40

The History and Antiquities of the Deanery of Craven, in the County of York. Halifax: 1812. V. 44; 46

The History and Antiquities of the Deanery of Craven in the County of York. London: 1812. V. 39; 40; 44; 45

The History and Antiquities of Deanery of Craven in the County of York. Leeds: 1878. V. 37; 38; 40

WHITE, GILBERT 1720-1793 continued

The Natural Histoy and Antiquities of Selborne . . . London: 1789. V. 37

The Natural History and Antiquites of Selborne, in the County of Southampton. London: 1789. V. 37; 38; 39; 41; 43; 44

The Natural History of Selborne, To Which are Added the Naturalist's Calendar, Miscellaneous Observations and Poems. London: 1813. V. 43

The Natural History and Antiquities of Selborne in the County of Southampton. London: 1813. V. 37; 43; 46

The Natural History and Antiquities of Selbourne . . . London: 1818. V. 41

The Natural History of Selborne. By Gilbert White. To which are added The Naturalist's Calendar, Miscellaneous Observations, and Poems. London: 1822. V. 37; 38

The Natural History of Selborne . . . London: 1825. V. 38; 43

The Natural History of Selbourne. Edinburgh: 1829. V. 43

The Natural History of Selborne . . . London: 1842. V. 39

The Natural History of Selborne. London: 1861. V. 46

Natural History and Antiquities of Selborne. London: 1875. V. 43; 45; 46

Natural History and Antiquities of Selborne. London: 1876. V. 38

The Natural History of Selborne, in the County of Southampton. London: 1877. V. 45

The Natural History and Antiquities of Selborne, in the County of Southampton. London: 1877. V. 43; 46

The Natural History of Selborne. London: 1900. V. 38; 39; 40; 41

The Natural History and Antiquities of Selborne & A Garden Kalendar. London: 1900. V. 43; 45

The Natural History and Antiquities of Selborne and A Garden Kalendar. London & Philadelphia: 1900. V. 40

The Natural History of Selbourne. London: 1929. V. 39

The Natural History and Antiquities of Selborne . . . London: 1970. V. 40

The Natural History of Selborne. Ipswich: 1972. V. 45

A Naturalist's Calendar, with Observations in Various Branches of Natural History. London: 1795. V. 37; 40

The Works in Natural History (arranged by Dr. J. Aikin) Comprising The Natural History of Selborne; the Naturalist's Calendar; and Miscellaneous Observations, Extracted from His Papers. To Which is added A Calendar and Observations by W. Markwick. London: 1802. V. 39; 41

The Writings. London: 1938. V. 38; 41; 44; 45

WHITE, GLEESON

Book-Song, an Anthology of Poems of Books and Bookmen from Modern Authors. London: 1893. V. 43

Children's Books and Their Illustrations. London: 1897. V. 40

English Illustration. 'The Sixties': 1855-70. London: 1897. V. 42; 43

English Illustration: the Sixties 1855-1870. Westminster: 1897. V. 40; 42; 43

English Illustration, 'The Sixties', 1855-70. London: 1906. V. 39

English Illustration-'The Sixties': 1855-70. Westminster: 1903. V. 37

The Parade. London: 1897. V. 42

THE WHITE-HALL Prophecy, Lately Found Under the Ruins of That Royal Chapel. London: 1712. V. 41

WHITE, HENRY

Geology, Oil Fields and Minerals, of Canada West. Toronto: 1865. V. 43

WHITE, HENRY C.

Abraham Baldwin: One of the Founders of the Republic, and Father of the University of Georgia, the First of American State Universities. Athens: 1926. V. 42

The Life and Art of Dwight William Tryon. Boston and New York: 1930. V. 39; 41

WHITE, HENRY KIRKE 1785-1806

Clifton Grove, a Sketch in Verse with Other Poems. London: 1803. V. 37; 42

History of the Union Pacific Railway. Chicago: 1895. V. 38; 41; 45

The Life and Remains of Henry Kirke White, of Nottingham Late of St. John's College, Cambridge. London. V. 45

The Life and Remains of Henry Kirke White of Nottingham. London: 1838. V. 37

The Poetical Works. London: 1830. V. 42

The Poetical Works. London: 1853. V. 37; 42

WHITE, J.

Some Account of the Proposed Improvements of the Western Part of London, by the Formation of the Regent's Park, the New Street, the New Sewer, etc. London: 1815. V. 37

WHITE, J. G.

A Short History of Old London Bridge. London: 1900. V. 43

WHITE, J. P.

Garden Furniture and Ornament. Bedford & London: 1900. V. 38

WHITE, J. W.

Cases Illustrative of the Practical Application of the Rontgen Rays in Surgery. 1896. V. 46

Cases Illustrative of the Practical Application of the Rontgen Rays in Surgery. 1896. V. 41

WHITE, JAMES 1759-1799

The Adventures of John of Gaunt, Duke of Lancaster. London: 1790. V. 38; 40

A New Century of Inventions, Being Designs and Descriptions of One Hundred Machines, Relating to the Arts, Manufactures and Domestic Life. Manchester: 1822. V. 37; 43

A Treatise on Veterinary Medicine. London: 1807. V. 38; 40

WHITE, JAMES C.

The Autonomic Nervous System: Anatomy, Physiology, Surgical Treatment. New York: 1941. V. 44

WHITE, JOHN

American Drawings, 1577-1590 . . . London: 1964. V. 44

Art's Treasury of Rarities and Curious Inventions. London: 1700? V. 40

Charges Preferred by John White, of the City of New York, Pilot, Against Henry Cahoone, Esq. Late Commander of the Revenue Cutter Active, of This Port, and Now Commander of the Revenue Cutter Alert . . . New York: 1825. V. 41

Charges Preferred by John White, of the City of New York, Pilot, Against Henry Cahoone, Esq. Portland: 1959. V. 44

An Essay on the Indigenous Grasses. Dublin: 1808. V. 38

The First Century of Scandalous, Malignant Priests, Made and Admitted into Benefices of the Prelates, in Whose Hands the Ordination of Ministers and Government of the Church Hath Been. London: 1643. V. 38; 40

History of a Voyage to the China Sea. Boston: 1823. V. 42; 43

Journal of a Voyage to New South Wales with Sixty-Five Plates of Non Descript Animals, Birds, Lizards, Serpents, Curious Cones of Trees and Other Natural Productions. London: 1790. V. 40; 42

On Cementitious Architecture, as Applicable to the Construction of Bridges, with a Prefatory Notice on the First Introduction of Iron as the Constituent Material for ARches of a Large Span . . . London: 1832. V. 44

A Rich Cabinet with Variety of Inventions. London: 1677. V. 40

Rural Architecture Illustrated in a Series of Ornamental Cottages and Villas, Exemplified by Plans, Elevations, Sections and Details. Glasgow: 1845. V. 39

A Speech of . . . Counsellor at Law, made in the Commons House of Parliament Concerning Episcopacy. London: 1641. V. 45

Voyage a la Nouvelle Galles du Sud, a Botany-Bay, au Port Jackson en 1787 1788, 1789. Paris: 1795. V. 41; 43

A Voyage to Cochin China. London: 1824. V. 39; 42; 43; 46

The Workes. London: 1624. V. 39

WHITE, JOHN, architect

Rural Architecture: a Series of Designs, For Ornamental Cottages and Villas . . . Glasgow: 1856. V. 45

WHITE, JOHN NESBITT

Poems. Doncaster: 1806. V. 43

WHITE, JOHN, U.S.N.

History of a Voyage to the China sea. Boston: 1826. V. 41

WHITE, JOSEPH

A Statement of Dr. White's Literary Obligations to the Late Rev. Mr. Samuel Badcock and the Rev. Samuel Parr, LL.D. Oxford: 1790. V. 43

WHITE, JOSEPH BLANCO 1775-1841

The Life of Joseph Blanco White. London: 1845. V. 39

WHITE, JOSEPH M.

A New Collection of Laws, Charters, and Local Ordinances of Britain, France and Spain . . . Philadelphia: 1839. V. 44

WHITE, K.

A Narrative of the Life Occurences, Vicissitudes and Present Situation. Schenectady: 1809. V. 39

WHITE, KATHERINE KEOGH

The King's Mountain Men. The Story of the Battle with Sketches of the American Soldiers Who Took Part. Dayton: 1924. V. 42; 45

WHITE, KENNETH

Late August on the Coast. (1986). V. 37

Late August on the Coast. By Kenneth White. Illustrated with screenprints by Ronald King. Surrey: 1986. V. 37; 40

A Walk Along the Shore. Guildford: 1977. V. 37; 39

WHITE, LESLIE

Pioneers in American Anthrolpology. Albuquerque: 1940. V. 42

WHITE, LUKE

Henry William Herbert and the American Publishing Scene 1831-1858. Newark: 1943. V. 39

Irish Loan of 1800 . . . Speech of Isaac Corry, Chancellor of the Exchequer . . . with Documents. Dublin: 1800. V. 37

WHITE, MINOR

Mirror, Messages, Manifestations. New York: 1969. V. 37; 41; 44

WHITE, NEWPORT J.

A Short Catalogue of the English Books in ARchbishop Marsh's Library, Dublin. Dublin: 1905. V. 43

WHITE, OWEN

Out of the Desert, the Historical Romance of El Paso. El Paso: 1923. V. 42

WHITE, OWEN P.

The Autobiography of a Durable Sinner. New York: 1942. V. 37; 43

Just Me and Other Poems. El Paso: 1924. V. 37

WHITE, PATRICK 1912-

The Aunt's Story. London: 1948. V. 40; 42

The Aunt's Story. New York: 1948. V. 43

Big Toys. Sydney: 1978. V. 44

The Burnt Ones. London: 1964. V. 37; 38

The Cockatoos. London: 1974. V. 38

Eden-Ville. Paris: 1951. V. 42

The Eye of the Storm. London: 1973. V. 38; 39

Four Plays. London: 1965. V. 38; 39

Happy Valley. London: 1939. V. 38; 40; 41; 42

The Living and the Dead. New York: 1941. V. 37; 38; 41; 46

The Living and the Dead. London: 1962. V. 38

The Ploughman and Other Poems. Sydney: 1935. V. 38

Riders in the Chariot. London: 1961. V. 38

Riders in the Chariot. New York: 1961. V. 38

The Solid Mandala. London: 1966. V. 38

The Solid Mandala. New York: 1966. V. 38

The Tree of Man. New York: 1955. V. 38

The Tree of Man. London: 1956. V. 38; 46

The Twyborn Affair. London: 1979. V. 38

The Vivisector. New York. V. 38

The Vivisector. London: 1970. V. 38

The Vivisector. New York: 1970. V. 38

Voss. London: 1957. V. 38

Voss. New York: 1957. V. 38

THE WHITE Pine Series of Architectural Monographs. New York: 1916-28. V. 37

WHITE, R. E.

Padre Junipero Serra and the Mission of San Carlos De Carmelo. San Francisco: 1884. V. 39

WHITE, RICHARD G.

Revelations: a Companion to the 'New Gospel of Peace' According to Abraham. New York: 1863. V. 42

WHITE, RICHARD GRANT

The New Gospel of Peace According to St. Benjamin. New York: 1864. V. 38

WHITE, ROBERT

The Dukery Records Being Notes and Memoranda Illustrative of Nottinghamshire Ancient History Collected During Many Years. Worksop: 1904. V. 39

Practical Surgery. London: 1796. V. 38

To the Right Honourable The Lords of Trade and Plantations The Reply to His Majesty's Subjects, the Principal Inhabitants of the Mosquito-Shore in America . . . London: 1780. V. 40

WHITE, ROBERT W.

A History of the Cadiz Short Line Railroad. Chicago and Skokie: 1966. V. 41

A History of the Cadiz Short Line Railroad. Chicago: 1966. V. 38

WHITE-RODYNG, JOHN

The Night. London: 1900. V. 42

WHITE, SALLIE ELIZABETH

Business Openings for Girls. Boston: 1891. V. 45

WHITE, SAMUEL

History of the American Troops, During the Late War, Under the Command of Colonels Fenton and Campbell. Baltimore: 1829. V. 42; 45

WHITE, SAMUEL S.

Catalogue of Dental Materials, Furniture, Instruments, Etc. Philadelphia: 1867. V. 40

Catalogue of Dental Materials. Philadelphia: 1876. V. 40

THE WHITE Slaves of Monopolies; or John Fitz Patrick, the Miner, Soldier and Workingman's Friend. Harrisburg: 1884. V. 39

WHITE, STANFORD

Sketches and Designs by . . . with an Outline of His Career by His Son Lawrence Grant White . . . New York: 1920. V. 41

WHITE, STEPHEN

Collateral Bee-Boxes; or, a New Easy, and Advantageous Method of Managing Bees. London: 1764. V. 45

WHITE, STEPHEN VAN CULLEN

Address Upon the Race Question in the South, Delivered at Salisbury, N.C. Before the Literary Societies of Livingstone College, May 27, 1890. N.P.: 1890? V. 42

WHITE, STEWARD EDWARD

Arizona Nights. New York: 1907. V. 38; 39

WHITE, STEWART EDWARD

Arizona Nights. 1907. V. 46

The Claim Jumpers. New York: 1901. V. 41; 42

Conjuror's House. New York: 1903. V. 45

Dog Days. Garden City: 1930. V. 41; 42

The Forest. New York: 1903. V. 43

Gold: a Tale of the Forty-Niners. New York: 1913. V. 46

The Mystery. New York: 1908. V. 39

On Tiptoe. New York: 1922. V. 41; 42

WHITE, T. B.

A Portfolio of Seven Lithographs of the Colonial Mansions in Fairmont Park . . . Narberth: 1933. V. 42

WHITE, TERENCE HANBURY

Darkness at Pemberley. London: 1932. V. 46

The Elephant and the Kangaroo. London: 1948. V. 41; 43

Farewell Victoria. London: 1933. V. 38; 39

Farewell Victoria. New York: 1934. V. 37; 44

Gone to Ground. London: 1935. V. 42

The Green Bay Tree or The Wicked Man Touches Wood. Cambridge: 1929. V. 38; 44

The Ill Made Knight. London: 1941. V. 42; 44; 46

Loved Helen and Other Poems. London: 1929. V. 40; 41; 42; 44

The Master. London: 1957. V. 42

The Once and Future King. London: 1958. V. 39; 43; 46

The Once and Future King. 1958. V. 37

The Sword in the Stone. London: 1938. V. 39; 40; 41; 42; 43; 46

The Witch in the Wood. New York: 1939. V. 44

WHITE, THOMAS

Exetasis Scientiae Requisitae in Theologo and Censuras Sententiis Theologicis Inferendas. London: 1662. V. 45

Peripatieticall Institutions. London: 1656. V. 42

WHITE, W. C.

An Album of Chinese Bamboos. A Study of a Set of Ink-Bamboo Drawings AD 1725. Toronto: 1939. V. 46

Tomb Tile Pictures of Ancient China. Toronto: 1939. V. 46

WHITE, WALTER

A Londoner's Walk to the Land's End; and a Trip to the Scilly Isles. London: 1855. V. 46

WHITE, WILLIAM

A. E. Housman to Joseph Ishill: Five Unpublished Letters. Berkeley Heights: 1959. V. 37

A Babylonian Anthology. 1966. V. 40; 43

A Babylonian Anthology. North Hills: 1966. V. 46

An Essay on the Diseases of the Bile, More Particularly in Calculus Concretions, Called Gall-Stones. York: 1771. V. 40

History, Gazetteer and Directory of the West-Riding of Yorkshire, with the City of York and Port of Hull. Sheffield: 1837. V. 45

History Gazeteer and Directory of the West-Riding of Yorkshire . . . Sheffield: 1837-38. V. 44

The Principles of Art as Illustrated by Exmaples in the Ruskin Museum at Sheffield, with Passages by Permission, from the Writings of John Ruskin. London: 1895. V. 46

Thoughts on the Singing of Psalms and Anthems in Churches. Philadelphia: 1808. V. 45

WHITE, WILLIAM ALLEN

The Court of Boyville. New York: 1899. V. 41

The Court of Boyville by William Allen White, first edition, 1899. Six stories by the editor of the Emporia Gazette - one of th best and most famous of small U.S. Newspapers. V. 37

The Real Issue. Chicago: 1897. V. 41; 44; 46

WHITE, WILLIAM AUGUSTUS

Catalogue of Early English Books, Chiefly of the Elizabethan Period. Collected by . . . New York: 1926. V. 45

WHITE, WILLIAM CHARLES

Chinese Temple Frescoes. Toronto: 1940. V. 43

WHITE, WILLIAM HALE 1830-1913

The Autobiography of Mark Rutherford, Dissenting Minister. London: 1881. V. 38; 41

WHITEBREAD, SAMUEL 1758-1815

A Letter to . . . on the Late Occurrences in Spain and Portugal. London: 1809. V. 41

WHITECAR, WILLIAM B.

Four Years Aboard the Whaleship Embracing Cruises in the Pacific, Atlantic, Indian and Antarctic Oceans in the Years 1855, 6, 7, 8, 9. Philadelphia: 1860. V. 40; 41

WHITECROSS, JAMES WILLIAM

Sketches and Characters, or the Natural History of the Human Intellects. London: 1853. V. 41

WHITEFIELD, EDWIN

The Homes of Our Forefathers: Being a Collection of the Oldest and Most Interesting . . . Buildings in Massachusetts. Boston: 1879. V. 37

Homes of Our Forefathers in Boston, England and Homes of Our Forefathers in Boston, New England. Boston: 1889. V. 37

WHITEFIELD, GEORGE

The Benefits of an Early Piety. London: 1738. V. 45

A Continuation of the Account of the Orphan House in Georgia, From Jan. 1740/1 to January 1742/3. London: 1743. V. 43; 45

A Journal of a Voyage from Gibraltar to Georgia . . . London: 1738. V. 42; 45

A Letter to His Excellency Governor Wright, Giving an Account of the Steps Taken Relative to the Converting the Georgia Orphan-House into a College. London: 1768. V. 39

A Letter to the Reverend Dr. Durrell, Vicechancellor of the University of Oxford . . . London: 1768. V. 44

The Rev. Whitefield's Answer, to the Bishop of London's Last Pastoral Letter. London: 1739. V. 45

A Sermon by the Reverend Mr. George Whitefield, Being His Last Farewell to His Friends, Preached at the Tabernacle in Moorfields, at Seven in the Morning, August the 30th, 1769, Immediately Before His Departure for Georgia. London: 1769. V. 40

Sermons on Various Subjects. London: 1739. V. 44

WHITEFIELD, HENRY

Strength Out of Weakness; or a Glorious Manifestation of the Further Progresse of the Gospel Among the Indians in New England. London: 1652. V. 38

WHITEFORD, S. T.

A Guide to Porcelain Painting. London. V. 44

WHITEHAVEN-CARLISLE RAILWAY

Remarks on the Utility and Practicability of the Formation of a Rail Road, Between Whitehaven and Carlisle. Workington: 1830. V. 46

WHITEHEAD, ALFRED NORTH

An Enquiry Concerning the Principles of Natural Knowledge. Cambridge: 1919. V. 39

Principia Mathematica. Cambridge: 1910-13. V. 38; 40; 42

Principia Mathematica . . . Cambridge: 1925/27/27. V. 45

Principia Mathematica. Cambridge: 1950. V. 46

Symbolism Its Meaning and Effect. Cambridge: 1928. V. 46

A Treatise on Universal Algebra with Application. Cambridge: 1898. V. 41; 42; 45

WHITEHEAD, C.

Lives and Exploits of English Highwaymen, Pirates and Robbers . . . London: 1833-34. V. 42

Lives and Exploits of English Highwaymen, Pirates and Robbers, Drawn from the Earliest and Most Authentic Sources, and Brought Down to the Present Time. London: 1834. V. 42

WHITEHEAD, CHARLES

Richard Savage. London: 1844. V. 46

WHITEHEAD, CHARLES E.

The Adventures of Gerard, the Lion Killer . . . New York: 1856. V. 43

The Camp-Fires of the Everglades or Wild Sports in the South. Edinburgh: 1891. V. 37; 38; 46

The Camp-Fires of the Everglades. London: 1891. V. 38

Wild Sports in the South; or, the Campfires of the Everglades. New York: 1860. V. 38

WHITEHEAD, D. L.

Natural Products for Innovative Pest Management. London: 1983. V. 38

WHITEHEAD, G. K.

Deer and Their Management in the Deer Parks of Great Britain and Ireland. London: 1950. V. 39; 40; 43; 45; 46

The Deer Stalking Grounds of Great Britian and Ireland. London: 1960. V. 38

The Deer of Great Britain and Ireland. London: 1964. V. 38; 43

Deer of the World. London: 1972. V. 43

WHITEHEAD, HENRY S.

Jumbee and Other Uncanny Tales. Sauk City: 1944. V. 42; 43; 45

WHITEHEAD, JAMES

The Wife's Domain. London: 1860. V. 43

WHITEHEAD, JOHN

Exploration of Mount Kina Balu, North Boreno. London: 1893. V. 40; 42; 44; 46

The Judicial and Civil History of New Jersey. Boston?: 1897. V. 41

Materialism Philosophically Examined, or, the Immateriality of the Soul asserted and proved, on Philosophical Principles. London: 1778. V. 41; 42

The Passaic Valley, New Jersey. New York: 1901. V. 44; 46

WHITEHEAD, P. J. P.

Chinese Natural History Drawings Selected from the Reeves Collection in the British Museum. London: 1974. V. 38; 44; 46

Chinese Natural History Drawings Selected from the Reeves Collection in the British Museum (Natural History). British Museum: 1974. V. 43

WHITEHEAD, PAUL

The Case of the Hon. Alex. Murray, Esq. In an Appeal to the People of Great Britain. London: 1751. V. 40; 41; 45

The Gymnasiad, or Boxing Match. London: 1744. V. 38; 45

The History of An Old Lady and Her Family. London: 1754. V. 41

Manners; a Satire. London: 1739. V. 37; 38; 40; 41; 43; 45

The State Dunces. London: 1733. V. 37; 40; 41; 45

WHITEHEAD, RUSSELL F.

Architectural Monograph Series, volumes 2-16. New York: 1916-1931. V. 37

WHITEHEAD, SARAH

The Two Familes: an Episode in the History of Chapelton. London: 1852. V. 40; 44

WHITEHEAD, THOMAS

Original Anecdotes of the Late Duke of Kingston and Miss Chudleigh, Alias Mrs. Harvey, alias Countess of Bristol, alias Duchess of Kingston . . . London: 1792. V. 41; 42

WHITEHEAD, WILLIAM

Ann Boleyn to Henry the Eighth, an Epistle. London: 1743. V. 37; 40

A Charge to the Poets. London: 1762. V. 37

The Danger of Writing Verse: an Epistle. London: 1741. V. 43

The Danger of Writing Verse; an Epistle. London: 1741. V. 40

An Hymn to the Nymph of Bristol Spring. London: 1751. V. 37; 40; 45

On Nobility: an Epistle to the Right Honble. the Earl of ******. London: 1744. V. 37

Plays and Poems. (with) Memoirs of His Life and Writings by W. Mason. London: 1774, 1788. V. 38

A Poem on the Battle of Waterloo. London: 1820. V. 42

Poems on Several Occasions, with Roman Father, a Tragedy. London: 1744. V. 45

Poems on Several Occasions, with the Roman Father, a Tragdey. London: 1754. V. 37

Variety: a Tale, for Married People. London: 1776. V. 43

Verses to the People of England. London: 1758. V. 41

WHITEHEAD, WILLIAM A.

Contributions to the Early History of Perth Amboy and Adjoining Country, with Sketches of Men and Events in New Jersey During the Provincial Era . . . New York: 1856. V. 40; 41; 44

WHITEHILL, HENRY R.

Biennial Report of the State Mineralogist of the State of Nevada for the years 1875 and 1876. Carson City: 1876. V. 37

WHITEHILL, WALTER MUIR

The Club of Odd Volumes: Boston, 1887-1973. N.P.: 1973. V. 38; 42

WHITEHOUSE, HENRY J.

Eighth Annual Address of the Bishop of the Dioceses of Illinois. Chicago: 1859. V. 43

WHITEHOUSE, JOHN

An Elegiac Ode to the Memory of Sir Joshua Reynolds . . . London: 1792. V. 45

WHITEHOUSE, MARY

Whatever Happened to Sex? London: 1977. V. 44

WHITEHURST, FRED F.

On the Grampian Hills. London: 1882. V. 42

WHITEHURST, JOHN

An Attempt Towards Obtaining Invariable Measures of Length, Capacity and Weight, from the Mensuration of Time . . . London: 1787. V. 38; 41

An Inquiry Into the Original State and Formation of the EArth . . . London: 1778. V. 45

An Inquiry into the Original State and Formation of the Earth. London: 1786. V. 37; 41

An Inquiry into the Original state and Formation of the Earth . . . London: 1788. V. 45

An Inquiry Into the Original State and Formation of the Earth. London: 1792. V. 40; 42; 45

The Works, with Memoirs of His Life and Writings. London: 1792. V. 45

WHITELAW, ALEXANDER

The Casquet of Literary Gems. (also: Second Series). Glasgow: 1828-29. V. 46

WHITELAW, JAMES

An Essay on the Population of Dublin. Being the result of an actual survey taken in 1798, with great care and precision, and arranged in a manner entirely new . . . (ith) the general return of the District Committee in 1804, with . . . Dublin: 1805. V. 37

WHITELEY, IKE

Rural Life in Texas . . . Comically Illustrated. Atlanta: 1891. V. 37; 39

WHITELOCK, BULSTRODE

Memorials of the English Affairs. Oxford: 1853. V. 43; 44

WHITELOCK, JAMES

A Learned and Necessary Argument to Prove that Each Subject Hath a Propriety in His Goods. London: 1641. V. 38

WHITELOCK, METHUSELAH

The Peace Offering: an Essay, Shewing the Cession of Hanover to be the Only Probable Means for Extinguishing the Present Rebellion, Without Farther Bloodshed, and for Securing These Nations for ever, from Rebellions and Invasions in Favour of the Pretender.. London: 1746. V. 39; 41; 45

WHITELOCKE, BULSTRODE 1605-1676

A Journal of the Swedish Ambassy, in the Years 1653 and 1654 from the Commonwealth of England, Scotland and Ireland. London: 1772. V. 37; 40

Memorials of the English Affairs, from . . . Expedition of Brute to This Island, to the End of the Reign of James I. London: 1709. V. 37; 40; 41; 43

Memorials of the English Affairs: or, an Historical Account of What Passed from the Beginning of the Reign of King Charles the First, to King Charles the Second His Happy Restauration . . . London: 1732. V. 37; 39

Memorials of the English Affairs. Oxford: 1853. V. 40; 41

Memorials of the English Affairs: or, an Historical Account of what passed from the beginning of the Reign of King Charles the First, to King Charles the Second his Happy Restauration . . . London: 1682. V. 37

Monarchy Asserted, To Be the Best, Most Ancient and Legall Form of Government . . . London: 1660. V. 39; 40; 46

Notes Upon the King's Writ for Choosing Members Parliament, 13 Car. II, Being Disquisitions on the Government of England by King, Lords and Commons. London: 1766. V. 38; 40

WHITELOCKE, JOHN

Trial of Lieutenant General John Whitelocke, Commander in Chief of the Expedition Against Buenos Ayres. By Court-Martial, held in Chelsea College on Thursday the 28th January 1808 etc. London: 1808. V. 37

WHITELY, ISAAC H.

Rural Life in Texas. Atlanta: 1891. V. 40; 43

WHITER, JAMES SALTER

The Silk Industry of Great Britain, and Its Revival. London: 1882. V. 39

WHITER, LEONARD

Spade, a History of the Family, Factory and Wares from 1733 to 1833. London: 1970. V. 37

WHITER, WALTER

Etymologicon Magnum or Universal Etymological Dictionary, on a New Plan. Cambridge: 1800. V. 46

A Specimen of Commentary on Shakespeare. London: 1794. V. 45

WHITESIDE, JAMES 1804-1876

Italy in the Nineteenth Century Contrasted with Its Past Condition. London: 1848. V. 39

WHITFIELD, CHRISTOPHER

Lady from Yesterday. Waltham St. Lawrence: 1939. V. 40

Mr. Chambers and Persephone. London: 1937. V. 37; 39; 40; 41; 44

Mr. Chambers and Persephone. Waltham St. Lawrence: 1937. V. 45

Mr. Chambers and Persephone: A Tale, by Christopher Whitfield. 1937. V. 37

Together and Alone, Two Short Novels . . . 1945. V. 44

Together and Alone. London: 1945. V. 38; 43; 46

Together and Alone. Waltham St. Lawrence: 1945. V. 40; 45; 46

WHITFIELD, GEORGE

A Collection of Papers Lately printed in the Daily Advertiser . . . London: 1740. V. 42

WHITFIELD, HENRY

A Farther Discovery of the Present State of the Indians in New England, Concerning the Progress of the Gospel Among Them . . . New York: 1865. V. 42

WHITFIELD, WILLIAM

History of Snohomish County, Washington. Chicago: 1926. V. 45

WHITFORD, N.

History of the Canal System of State of New York . . . Histories of the Canals of the U.S. and Canada. 1906. V. 38

WHITFORD, WILLIAM CLARKE

Colorado Volunteers in the Civil War; the New Mexico Campaign of 1862. Denver: 1906. V. 38; 39; 42; 46

WHITING & Watson's American Edition of the New Edinburgh Encyclopedia . . . Philadelphia: 1832. V. 39

WHITING, GERTRUDE

A Lace Guide for Makers and Collectors. New York: 1920. V. 38; 41

Tools and Toys of Stitchery. New York: 1928. V. 37; 45

WHITING, HENRY

The Emigrant, a Poem. Detroit: 1819. V. 40

WHITING, JOHN 1656-1722

A Catalogue of Friend's Books: Written by Many of the People Called Quakers. London: 1708. V. 39; 44

WHITING, W. H. C.

March from Fredericksburg to El Paso Del Norte. Washington: 1905-06. V. 42; 44

WHITLEY, IKE

Rural Life in Texas . . . Comically Illustrated. Atlanta: 1891. V. 42; 43

WHITLEY, WILLIAM T.

Artists and Their Friends in England 1700-1799. London: 1928. V. 41

Artists and Their Friends in England. London & Boston: 1928. V. 39

WHITLOCK, ARNOLD

Eric Mendelsohn. London: 1940. V. 44

WHITLOCK, PAMELA

All Day Long. An Anthology of Poetry for Children. 1954. V. 45

All Day Long - an Anthology of Poetry for Children. London: 1954. V. 44

WHITLOCK, RICHARD

Zootomia, or Observations on the Present Manners of the English. London: 1654. V. 40

WHITLOCKE, JOHN

Trial of Lieutenant General John Whitlocke, Commander in Chief of the Expedition Against Buenos Ayres. London: 1808. V. 45

WHITMAN, ALFRED

Charles Turner. London: 1907. V. 38; 40; 42; 44

The Masters of Mezzotint: The Men and Their Work. London: 1898. V. 39

Samuel William Reynolds. London: 1903. V. 41

Samuel Cousins. London: 1904. V. 38; 39; 40

WHITMAN, BENJAMIN

An Index to the Laws of Massachusetts: from the Adoption of the Constitution to the Year MDCCXCVI. Worcester: 1797. V. 45

WHITMAN, JOHN W.

Report of a Trial in the Supreme Judicial Court, Holden at Boston, Dec. 16th and 17th. Boston: 1828. V. 43

WHITMAN, MALCOLM D.

Tennis Origins and Mysteries. New York: 1932. V. 39; 42

WHITMAN, SARAH HELEN

Edgar Poe and His Critics. New York: 1860. V. 39; 41; 46

Hours of Life, and Other Poems. Providence: 1853. V. 37; 43

WHITMAN, WALT 1819-1892

After All, Not to Create Only. Boston: 1871. V. 41

After All, Not to Create Only. New York: 1871. V. 43; 46

American Bard. Santa Cruz: 1981. V. 38

As a Strong Bird on Pinions Free. Washington: 1872. V. 40; 41; 46

Autobiographia. New York: 1892. V. 42; 43

The Book of Heavenly Death Compiled from Leaves of Grass by Horace Traubel. Portland: 1907. V. 46

Calamus. Boston: 1897. V. 45

Calamus. Geneva: 1919. V. 43

Criticism: an Essay. Newark: 1913. V. 46

Democratic Vistas, and Other Papers. London: 1888. V. 37

Walt Whitman's Drum Taps. New York: 1865. V. 37

Drum-Taps. New York: 1865. V. 43

Franklin Evans; or the Inebriate. New York: 1842. V. 39; 41

The Gathering of the Forces. New York/London: 1920. V. 37

Good-Bye My Fancy. Philadelphia: 1891. V. 38; 39; 44; 46

Walt Whitman's Hymn on the Death of Lincoln. 1900. V. 39

Leaves of Grass. V. 37

Leaves of Grass. Mt. Vernon. V. 46

Leaves of Grass. New York. V. 43

Leaves of Grass. Brooklyn: 1855. V. 38; 45

Leaves of Grass. Brooklyn: 1856. V. 37; 43; 44; 45; 46

Leaves of Grass Imprints. Boston: 1860. V. 43

Leaves of Grass. Boston: 1860. V. 41; 43

Leaves of Grass. Boston: 1860-61. V. 37; 40; 46

Leaves of Grass. Washington: 1872. V. 40

Leaves of Grass. Camden: 1876. V. 39

Leaves of Grass. Boston: 1881-2. V. 41; 42; 44; 45; 46

Leaves of Grass. Camden: 1882. V. 46

Leaves of Grass. Philadelphia: 1882. V. 38; 42; 44

Leaves of Grass. Philadelphia: 1884. V. 37

Leaves of Grass with Sands at Seventy & A Backward Glance O'er Travel'd Roads. Philadelphia: 1889. V. 45; 46

Leaves of Grass. Philadelphia: 1891-92. V. 42; 44; 45; 46

Leaves of Grass. Philadelphia: 1892. V. 37

Leaves of Grass. Philadelphia: 1894. V. 43; 45

Leaves of Grass. New York: 1903. V. 37

Leaves of Grass. Portland: 1919. V. 44

Leaves of Grass. New York: 1929. V. 37; 38; 40; 41; 43

Leaves of Grass. New York: 1930. V. 38; 39; 40; 41; 43; 44; 45

Leaves of Grass. New York: 1931. V. 37

Leaves of Grass. New York: 1942. V. 38; 40; 44

Leaves of Grass. New York: 1943. V. 43

Leaves of Grass. New York: 1950. V. 41

Leaves of Grass, by Walt Whitman. Mount Vernon: (1951). V. 37

Leaves of Grass. New York: 1867. V. 37

Memoranda During the War. Camden: 1875-76. V. 44

November Boughs. Philadelphia: 1888. V. 37; 38; 39; 40; 41; 43; 45; 46

Oh Captain! My Captain! San Francisco: 1935. V. 40

Out of the Cradle Endlessly Rocking. Santa Cruz and Torrance: 1976-78. V. 39

Out of the Cradle Endlessly Rocking. Torrance: 1977. V. 43

Pictures. An Unpublished Poem . . . New York: 1927. V. 44

'Pictures.' An Unpublished Poem. New York & London: 1927. V. 37; 40

A Poem, as Consequent, Etc., Written by Walt Whitman to Celebrate the Publication of Leaves of Grass in 1855. Northampton: 1955. V. 41

Poems. London: 1868. V. 38; 39; 40; 41; 42

Complete Poems and Prose of Walt Whitman. N.P.: 1889. V. 39

Poems from Leaves of Grass. London: 1913. V. 46

Complete Poems Prose 1855-1888. Philadelphia: 1888. V. 43; 44; 46

Complete Poems & Prose of Walt Whitman. (N.P.: 1888?). V. 43

Complete Poems and Prose of . . . N.P.: Philadelphia?: 1888? V. 39

Complete Poems and Prose, 1855-1888. Philadelphia: 1889. V. 37

Complete Poetry and Selected Prose and Letters. London: 1964. V. 46

The Uncollected Poetry and Prose of . . . Garden City: 1921. V. 39

Prose Works. Philadelphia: 1892. V. 37

Complete Prose Works. Philadelphia: 1892. V. 43; 46

Salut Au Monde! From 'Leaves of Grass.' New York: 1930. V. 42

Selected Poems. N.P. V. 46

Selected Poems. New York: 1892. V. 40

Selected Poems. Hove, Sussex: 1981. V. 38

The Song of the Broad Axe. Philadelphia: 1924. V. 42; 46

Song of the Redwood Tree. Mills College: 1934. V. 43

Specimen Days and Collect. Philadelphia: 1882-83. V. 38; 40; 43; 44

Specimen Days and Collect. Glasgow: 1883. V. 37

As Strong as Bird on Pinions Free. Washington: 1872. V. 41

There Was a Child Went Forth. Northampton: 1968. V. 37

Walt Whitman in Camden: a Selection of Prose from Specimen Days. Camden: 1938. V. 40

The Wound Dresser. A Series of Letters Written from the Hospitals in Washington During the War of the Rebellion. Edited by Richard Maurice Bucke. Boston: 1898. V. 37

The Complete Writings of . . . New York: 1902. V. 38; 41; 43; 46

The Complete Writings of Walt Whitman. New York & London: 1902. V. 41

The Complete Writings. New York & London: 1902. V. 40

WHITMAN, ZACHERIAH

An Historical Sketch of the Ancient and Honourable Artillery Company . . . Boston: 1820. V. 42

WHITMARCH, ESTHER

A Reed to the River. Verona: 1928. V. 40; 42

WHITMARSH, SAMUEL

Eight Years Experience and Observation in the Culture of the Mulberry Tree, and in the Care of the Silk Worm. Northampton: 1839. V. 42; 43

WHITMILL, BENJAMIN

Kalendarium Universale; or the Gardner's Universal Calendar . . . London: 1757. V. 41

WHITMORE, F. H. D. C.

The Tenth (P.W.O.) Royal Hussars and the Essex Yeomanry, during the European War, 1914-1918. Colchester: 1920. V. 37

WHITMORE, ROSA TULLOCH

Memoir of a Lady, Daughter of Major Francis Tulloch and Sister to the Marchioness of Stacpoole and Miss Ann Tulloch . . . Paris: 1827. V. 46

WHITMORE, WILLIAM H.

The American Genealogist. Albany: 1868. V. 42

WHITMORE, WILLIAM HENRY

A Memoir of Sir Edmund Andros, Knt., Governor of New England, New York, Virginia, etc. Boston: 1868. V. 38

WHITNEY, ADELINE DUTTON TRAIN

The Law of Woman Life. N.P.:,: 1889? V. 37

WHITNEY, ASA

Memorial of A. Whitney Praying a Grant of Public Land to Enable Him to Construct a Railroad from Lake Michigan to the Pacific Ocean. Washington: 1846. V. 38; 39; 40; 41; 43; 46

Memorial of Asa Whitney, of the City of New York, Praying a Grant of Land, to Enable Him to Construct a Railraod from Lake Michigan to the Pacific Ocean. Washington: 1845. V. 37

Railroad to Oregon, June 23, 1848 . . . The Select Committee to Who was Referred the Memorial of Asa Whitney . . . Report . . . Washington: 1848. V. 39; 42

Whitney's Railroad to the Pacific . . . The Committee on Roads and Canals, Made the Following Report . . . Washington: 1850. V. 39

WHITNEY, CARRIE WESTLAKE

Kansas City, Missouri: Its History and Its People 1808-1908. Chicago: 1908. V. 46

WHITNEY, CASPAR

Charles Adelbert Canfield. New York. V. 45

Charles Adelbert Canfield. New York: 1930. V. 37; 39; 41; 42; 43; 45

Jungle Trails and Jungle People. New York: 1905. V. 40

Musk-Ox, Bison, Sheep and Goat. New York: 1904. V. 37

On Snow Shoes to the Barren Grounds - 2800 Miles After Musk-Oxen and Wood-Bison. London: 1896. V. 38; 40; 46

On Snow-Shoes to the Barren Grounds. New York: 1896. V. 44

WHITNEY, CASPER

Hunt Clubs and Country Clubs in America. Boston: 1928. V. 39

WHITNEY, HARRY

Hunting with the Eskimos. London: 1910. V. 39

Hunting with the Eskimos . . . New York: 1910. V. 42

WHITNEY, HELEN HAY

The Bed-Time Book. New York: 1907. V. 42; 46

WHITNEY, JOEL P.

Colorado, in the United States of America. London: 1867. V. 37; 39; 42

Silver Mining Regions of Colorado. New York: 1865. V. 37; 38; 39; 41

WHITNEY, JOSIAH DWIGHT

The Yosemite Book. New York: 1868. V. 37; 41; 44

The Yosemite Guide-Book. Cambridge: 1869. V. 39

The Yosemite Guide-Book. Cambridge: 1871. V. 38; 44

WHITNEY, M. WILLIAM DWIGHT

The Century Dictionary. London: 1899. V. 42

WHITNEY, ORSON F.

History of Utah . . . Salt Lake City,: 1892-1904. V. 42

History of Utah. Salt Lake City: 1892-98. V. 39

Life of Hebert C. Kimball, an Apostle . . . Salt Lake City: 1888. V. 42

WHITNEY, PETER

The History of the County of Worcester. Worcester: 1793. V. 40

WHITNEY, W. D.

The Hayden Expedition. New Route to Yellowstone . . . New York. V. 43

WHITNEY, WILLIAM DWIGHT

The Century Dictionary. New York & London: 1889-91. V. 38

Century Dictionary and Cyclopedia. New York: 1899. V. 42

WHITROW, MAGDA

Isis Cumulative Bibliography. A Bibliography of the History of Science Formed for Isis Critical Bibliographies 1-90. 1913-1965. London: 1971-76. V. 41; 42

WHITSON, WILLIAM

Astronomical Lectures, Read in the Public Schools at Cambridge. London: 1728. V. 45

WHITTAKER, EDMUND T.

A History of the Theories of Aether and Electricity from the Age of Descartes to the Close of the Nineteenth Century. Dublin: 1910. V. 40; 46

WHITTAKER, FREDERICK

A Complete Life of Gen. George A. Custer. New York: 1876. V. 37; 39; 43; 45

A Popular Life of Gen George A. Custer. Chicago: 1876. V. 38; 39

A Popular life of Gen. George A. Custer. New York: 1963. V. 39

WHITTAKER, FREDRICK

Volunteer Cavalry, the Lessons of the Decade. New York: 1871. V. 44

WHITTAKER, MILO LEE

Pathbreakers and Pioneers of the Pueblo Region. Pueblo: 1917. V. 37; 40; 43

WHITTAKER, T. D.

The History and Antiquities of the Deanery of Craven, in the County of York. London: 1805. V. 40

WHITTEMORE, HENRY

History of Montclair Township, State of New Jersey, Including the History of the Families Who Have Been Identified With Its Growth and Prosperity. New York: 1894. V. 41; 42

WHITTEN, MARTHA E.

The Drunkard's Wife. Austin: 1887. V. 38

WHITTICK, ARNOLD

History of Cemetry Sculpture. London: 1938. V. 46

WHITTIER, JOHN GREENLEAF 1807-1892

Anti-Slavery Reporter. New York: 1833. V. 45

At Sundown. Cambridge: 1890. V. 37; 38; 39; 40; 41; 46

Ballads of New England. Boston: 1870. V. 38

The Branded Hand. Salem: 1845. V. 38; 39; 40; 42

Chapel of the Hermits, and Other Poems. Boston: 1853. V. 45

The Demon Lady. N.P.: 1894. V. 43

History of Pennsylvania Hall. Philadelphia: 1838. V. 37; 39

Home Ballads. Boston: 1860. V. 41

In War Time and Other Poems. Boston: 1864. V. 44

Justice and Expediency. New York: 1833. V. 46

The King's Missive and Other Poems. Boston: 1881. V. 45

Lays of My Home and Other Poems. Boston: 1843. V. 46

Leaves from Margaret Smith's Journal in the Province of Massachusetts Bay 1678-79. Boston: 1849. V. 45

Legends of New England. Hartford: 1831. V. 37; 42; 46

The Literary Remains of John G. C. Brainard with a Sketch of His Life. Hartford: 1832. V. 45

Literary Recreations and Miscellanies. Boston: 1854. V. 42; 45

Little Eva; Uncle Tom's Guardian Angel. Boston: 1852. V. 39; 43; 46

Mabel Martin a Harvest Idyl. Boston: 1876. V. 37; 40; 45

Mogg Megone, a Poem. Boston: 1836. V. 37; 38

Moll Pitcher, a Poem. Boston: 1832. V. 41

Moll Pitcher, and the Minstrel Girl. Philadelphia: 1840. V. 43

The Panorama and Other Poems. Boston: 1856. V. 43; 45

The Pennsylvania Pilgrim, and Other Poems. Boston: 1872. V. 40; 46

Poems Written During the Progress of the Abolition Question in the United States, Between the Years 1830 and 1838. Boston: 1837. V. 42

Poems. Philadelphia: 1838. V. 39; 41; 45; 46

Poems. Boston: 1849. V. 39; 43

Poems. Boston: 1874. V. 38

The Poetical Works. Boston: 1861. V. 44

The Poetical Works of John Greenleaf Whittier. Boston & New York: 1892. V. 39

The Poetical Works. London: 1890. V. 37

The Red River Voyageur. Winnipeg: 1892. V. 45

The Reunion. N.P.: 1885. V. 46

A Sabbath Scene. Boston: 1854. V. 42

Snow Bound: a Winter Idyl. Boston: 1866. V. 37; 39; 42; 43; 44; 45; 46

Snow-Bound A Winter Idyl. Boston: 1886. V. 39

Snowbound - a Winter Idyl. New York: 1930. V. 37; 40

Snowbound - A Winter Idyl. New York: 1930. V. 38

Songs of the Free. Boston: 1836. V. 41

The Stranger in Lowell. Boston: 1845. V. 39; 40; 46

The Supernaturalism of New England. London: 1847. V. 43

Supernaturalism in New England. New York: 1847. V. 41; 44; 46

The Tent on the Beach and Other Poems. Boston: 1867. V. 45

The Vision of Echard and Other Poems. Boston: 1878. V. 45

The Waif: a Collection of Poems and Lays of My Home and Other Poems. Cambridge: 1845. V. 46

The Works of . . . New York. V. 45

Works of . . . Boston & New York: 1892. V. 40; 46

The Writings of . . . Cambridge: 1888. V. 40

The Complete Writings. Boston: 1892. V. 42

WHITTIESEY, CHARLES

Railway Connections with Lake Superior. Cleveland: 1853. V. 46

WHITTINGHAM, FERDINAND

A Memoir of the Services of Lieutenant-General Sir Samuel Ford Whittingham, K.C.B., K.C.H., G.C.F., Colonel of the 71st Highland Infantry. London: 1868. V. 41

WHITTINGHAM, WILLIAM

Our Continental Tour, a trip made in twelve days and fifteen hours during which were visited the cities of Antwerp Brussels & Cologne . . . inclusive of two voyages up and down the Rhine . . . London: 1888. V. 37

WHITTINGTON, G. D.

An Historical Survey of the Ecclesiastical Antiquities of France . . . London: 1809. V. 44

WHITTINGTON PRESS

Matrix 1. Andoversford: (1985). V. 37

A Miscellany of Type. Manor Farm, Andoversford: 1990. V. 45

The Whittington Press: a Bibliography 1971-1981. Gloucestershire: 1982. V. 43

WHITTLE, W.

Journal of a Voyage to the River Plate; Including Observations Made During a Residence in the Republic of Monte Video. Manchester: 1846. V. 39

WHITTLE, WILLIAM C.

Cruises of the Confederate States Steamers 'Shenandoah' and 'Nashville'. Norfolk: 1910. V. 46

WHITTLESEY, AUSTIN

The Renaissance ARchitecture of Central and Northern Spain. New York: 1920. V. 39; 42

WHITTLESEY, CHARLES

Ancient Earth Forts of the Cuyahoga Valley, Ohio. Cleveland: 1871. V. 37

Descriptions of Ancient Works in Ohio and Ancient Mining on the Shores of Lake Superior. Washington: 1850/52. V. 42

Early History of Cleveland, Ohio. Cleveland: 1867. V. 38

Fugitive Essays, Upon Interesting and Useful Subjects Relating to the Early History of Ohio . . . Hudson: 1852. V. 42

War Memoranda. Cheat River to the Tennessee, 1861-62. Cleveland: 1884. V. 44

WHITTOCK, NATHANIEL

The Art of Drawing and Colouring from Nature, Flowers, Fruit and Shells . . . London: 1829. V. 41; 44

The Art of Drawing and Colouring from Nature, Birds, Beasts, Fishes and Insects. London: 1830. V. 41; 46

WHITTOCK, NATHANIEL continued

The Costumes of the Members of the University of Oxford. London: 1840.
V. 38

The Decorative Painters' and Glaziers' Guide . . . London: 1827. V. 42; 44

The Decorative Painters' and Glaziers' Guide. London: 1828. V. 46

The Microcosm of Oxford . . . Oxford: 1830. V. 39

*The Oxford Drawing Book, or the Art of Drawing, and the Theory and
Practice of Perspective, in a Series of Letters* . . . London: 1825. V. 45

The Youth's New London Self-Instructing Drawing Book . . . London: 1834.
V. 44

The Youth's New Lodnon Self-Instructing Drawing Book . . . London: 1836.
V. 39

WHITTON, JOHN M.

History of the Town of Antrim, N.H . . . . *1744-1844.* Concord: 1852. V. 39

WHITTROCK, WOLFGANG

Toulouse-Lautrec: the Complete Prints. London: 1985. V. 46

WHITTY, EDWARD MICHAEL

Friends of Bohemia; or, Phases of London Life. London: 1857. V. 43

WHITTY, J.

*Tales of Irish Life, Illustrative of the Manners, Customs and Condition of
the People.* London: 1824. V. 41; 42; 44

WHITWELL, CATHERINE VALE

*An Astronomical Catechism; or, Dialogues Between a Mother and Her
Daughter.* London: 1818. V. 43

WHITWORTH, CHARLES

An Account of Russia As It Was in 1710. V. 44

An Account of Russia As It Was In the Year 1710. 1758. V. 41

An Account of Russia as It Was in the Year 1710. 1758. V. 41

An Account of Russia, as It Was in the Year 1710. London: 1758. V. 45

An Account of Russia As It Was in the Year 1710. Strawberry Hill: 1758.
V. 44; 45; 46

An Account of Russia As it Was in the Year 1710. 1758. V. 37

*A Collection of the Supplies, and Ways and Means, from the Revolution to
the Present Time.* London: 1764. V. 38

*A Collection of the Supplies and Ways and Means: from the Revolution to
the Present Time.* London: 1765. V. 43

A List of the English, Scots and Irish Nobility. London: 1765. V. 38

WHITWORTH, GEOFFREY

The Art of Nijinsky. London: 1913. V. 40

WHITWORTH, JOSEPH 1803-1887

Miscellaneous Papers on Mechanical Subjects. London: 1873. V. 46

The Report of the Armstrong & Whitworth Committee. Manchester: 1866.
V. 40

THE WHOLE Art of Bookbinding. Oswestry: 1811. V. 38

THE WHOLE Art of Dress! London: 1830. V. 43

THE WHOLE Art of Fishing. London: 1714. V. 39

THE WHOLE Art of Legerdemain; or, Philosopher in Good Humour.
London: 1812. V. 44

THE WHOLE Duty of a Woman: or a Guide to the Female Sex from the
Age of Sixteen to Sixty . . . London: 1695. V. 38

THE WHOLE Family. New York: 1908. V. 41; 46

THE WHOLE Family. A Novel by Twelve Authors. New York: & London:
1908. V. 46

THE WHOLE Proceedings at the Assizes at Shrewsbury, on Friday
August the Sixth, 1784, in the Case of the King on the Prosecution of
William Jones . . . Against the Rev. William Davis Shipley, Dean of St.
Asaph. For Libel. London: 1784. V. 42

THE WHOLE Series of All That Hath Been Transacted in the House of
Peers, Concerning the Popish Plot, Wherein is Contained the Most
Material Passages in Both Houses of Parliament . . . London: 1681.
V. 42

WHOR, CORNELIUS

Village Musings on Moral and Religious Subjects. Norwich: 1837. V. 40

THE WHORE'S Rhetorick, MDCLXXXIII. Edinburgh: 1836. V. 42

WHO'S Who in Lebanon, 1986-1987. 1986. V. 37

WHO'S Who in the Arab World, 1986-1987. 1986. V. 37

WHYMPER, CHARLES

Egyptian Birds for the Most Part Seen in the Nile Valley. London: 1909.
V. 44; 46

WHYMPER, EDWARD

The Ascent of the Matterhorn. London: 1880. V. 38; 39; 43; 46

Chamonix and the Range of Mount Blanc. London: 1896. V. 44

A Guide to Chamonix and Mount Blanc. London: 1896. V. 40

Scrambles Amongst the Alps in the Years 1860-1869. London: 1871. V. 42;
44; 45; 46

Travels Amongst the Great Andes of the Equator. London: 1892. V. 37; 38;
40; 42; 43; 44; 45; 46

Travels Amongst the Great Andes of the Equator. New York: 1892. V. 42

Travels Amongst the Great Andes of the Equator. London: 1892-1.
V. 37; 39; 43

WHYMPER, FREDERICK

Travel and Adventure in the Territory of Alaska. London: 1868. V. 37; 41;
44; 46

Travel and Adventure in the Territory of Alaska. New York: 1869. V. 38

WHYTE, JAMES CHRISTIE

History of the British Tuf, from the Earliest Period to the Present Day.
London: 1840. V. 42

WHYTE-MELVILLE, GEORGE JOHN

The Brookes of Bridlemere. London: 1864. V. 38

Cerise: a Tale of the Last Century. London: 1866. V. 46

Contraband; or, a Losing Hazard. London: 1871. V. 40

General Bounce or the Lady and the Locust. London: 1855. V. 45

The Gladiators: a Tale of Rome and Judaea. London: 1863. V. 46

Good for Nothing; or, All Down Hill. London: 1861. V. 46

Market Harborough; or, How Mr. Sawyer Went to the Shires. London:
1861. V. 43

The Queen's Maries. London: 1862. V. 46

Roy's Wife. London: 1878. V. 41

Sarchedon; a Legend of the Great Queen. London: 1871. V. 38; 41; 44; 46

Tilbury Nogo; or, Passages in the Life of an Unsuccessful Man. London:
1854. V. 46

Works. London: 1898-1902. V. 38

WHYTE, SAMUEL 1733-1811

*A Collection of Poems, The Productions of the Kingdom of Ireland: Selected
from a Collection published in that Kingdom, intitled, the Shamrock, or
Hibernian Cresses.* London: 1773. V. 37; 39; 41

Miscellanea Nova . . . Dublin: 1800. V. 41

Miscellanea Nova . . . Dublin: 1801. V. 45

The Shamrock; or, Hiberian Cresses. Dublin: 1772. V. 38; 40; 45; 46

WHYTT, ROBERT 1714-1766

An Essay on the Virtues of Lime-Water and Soap in the Cure of the Stone.
Edinburgh: 1761. V. 40

*Observations on the Nature, Causes and Cure of Those Disorders Which
Have Been Commonly Called Nervous, Hypochondriac or Hysteric* . . .
Edinburgh: 1765. V. 37; 46

*Observations on the Nature, Causes and Cure to Those Disorders Which
Have Been Commonly Called Nervous, Hypochondriac, or Hysteric.*
Edinburgh: 1767. V. 43

The Works. Edinburgh: 1768. V. 42; 43

WICHMANN, SIEGFRIED

*Japonisme: the Japanese Influence on Western Art in the 19th and 20th
Centuries.* New York: 1981. V. 41

WICKERSHAM, JAMES

A Bibliography of Alaska Literature 1724-1924. Cordova: 1927. V. 37; 39;
40; 41; 43; 45; 46

Old Yukon. Tales - Trails - and Trials. Washington: 1938. V. 45; 46

WICKES, CHARLES

Illustrations of the Spires and Towers of the Medieval Churches of England.
London: 1853-59. V. 38

*Memorials of English Mediaeval Churches; Being Studies from the Finest
Exisiting Examples of the Ecclesiastical Steeples of Great Britain.* London:
1857. V. 38; 41

WICKES, STEPHEN

*History of Medicine in New Jersey and Of Its Medical Men from the
Settlement of the Province to 1800.* Newark: 1879. V. 41; 42; 46

WICKHAM, ANNA

The Man with a Hammer - Verses. London: 1916. V. 43

The Tired Man. London. V. 44

WICKHAM, GERTRUDE VAN RENSSELAER

Memorial to the Pioneer Women of the Western Reserve. Cleveland: 1896-
1924. V. 39

WICKHAM, GERTRUDE VAN RENSSELEAR

Pioneer Families of Cleveland, 1796-1840. Oil City: 1911. V. 44

WICKHOFF, FRANZ

Roman Art: Some Of Its Principles and Their Application to Early Christian Painting. London: 1900. V. 44

WICKLIFFE, ROBERT

Speech of Robert Wickliffe, Esq., in the House of Representatives of Kentucky, on the Property Bill, at the December Session, 1819. Frankfort: 1820. V. 44

WICKS, MARK

Organ Building for Amateurs. London: 1887. V. 46

WICKSELL, KNUT

Zur Lehre von der Steuerincidenz. Uppsala: 1895. V. 45

WICKSTED, CHARLES

The Cheshire Hunt: a Song. Chester: 1837. V. 42

WICKSTEED, JOHN HAMILTON

Memorials of John Hamilton Wicksteed: Being Passages from His Journal and Lettters. London: 1883. V. 41

WICKSTEED, JOSEPH

William Blake's Jerusalem. New York: 1955. V. 39

WICKSTEED, JOSEPH H.

Blake's Innocence and Experience. London: & Toronto: 1928. V. 43

WICKSTEED, P. H.

The Common Sense of Political Economy. London: 1910. V. 44

WICKSTEED, PHILIP

The Alphabet of Economic Science. London: 1888. V. 37

WICKSTEED, THOMAS

An Experimental Inquiry Concerning the Relative Power of, and Useful Effect Produced by, the Cornish and Boulton and Watt Pumping Engines, and Cylindrical and waggon-head boilers. By Thomas Wicksteed, Engineer to the East London . . . London;: 1841. V. 37

WICQUEFORT, ABRAHAM DE

Advis Fidele aux Veritables Hollandois, Touchant ce Qui s'est Passe dans les Villages de Bodegrave & Swammerdam, & les Cruautes Inouies, Que les Francois y ont Exercees . . . The Hague: 1673. V. 39

WIDDIFIELD, HANNAH

Widdifield's New Cook Book. Philadelphia: 1856. V. 38

WIDEMAN, JOHN EDGAR

A Glance Away. 1967. V. 43

The Lynchers. New York: 1973. V. 46

WIDENER, HARRY ELKINS

A Catalogue of the Writings of Charles Dickens in the Library of Harry Elkins Widener. Philadelphia: 1918. V. 40

WIDENER, JOSEPH

The Joseph Widener Collection. Tapestries, at Lynnewood Hall, Elkins Park Pennsylvania. Philadelphia: 1932. V. 39; 45

WIDENER, P. A. B.

Pictures in the Collection of P. A. B. Widener at Lynnewood Hall, Elkins Park, Pennsylvania. Philadelphia: 1913. V. 46

WIDMANN, OTTO

A Preliminary Catalog of the Birds of Missouri. St. Louis: 1907. V. 39

WISDOM in Miniature; or the Young Gentleman and Lady's Pleasing Instructor. Worcester: 1796. V. 42

THE WIDOW of Kent, or, the History of Mrs. Rowley. London: 1788. V. 40

THE WIDOW of Wallingford: A Comedy of Two Acts. London: 1775. V. 42

WIDUKIND

Witchindis Saxonis Rerum ab Henrico et Ottone 1 Impp. Gestarum Libri III . . . Basle: 1532. V. 45

WIED-NEUWIED, MAXIMILIAN ALEXANDER PHILIPP, PRINCE VON 1782-1867

Travels in Brazil, in the Years 1815, 1816, 1817. London: 1820. V. 40; 43

WIELAND, CHRISTOPH MARTIN

The History of Agathon. London: 1773. V. 40

The Republic of Fools. London: 1861. V. 39

Socrates Out of His Senses; or, Dialogues of Diogenes of Sinope. London: 1771. V. 40; 41

WIELAND, T.

Peptides of Poisonous Amanita Mushrooms. Berlin: 1986. V. 37

WIELHOSKI, or the Polish Sisters. Philadelphia: 1833. V. 37

WIENER, ALEXANDER

Rh-Hr Blood Types: Applications in Clinical and Legal Medicine and Anthropology . . . New York: 1954. V. 42; 45

WIENER, MEYER

Opthalmology in the War Years. Volume I: 1940-43. Chicago: 1946. V. 40

WIENER, NORBERT

Cybernetics of Control and Communication in the Animal and The Machine. New York: 1948. V. 43; 45; 46

Cybernetics of Control and Communication in the Animal and the Machine. Paris: 1948. V. 37; 39

WIENER, NORMAN

The Human Use of Human Beings, Cybernetics and Society. Boston: 1950. V. 46

DER WIENER Werkstatte 1903-1928. Modernes Kunstgewerbe und Sein Wg. Wien: 1929. V. 38

WIENERS, JOHN

Chinoiserie. San Francisco: 1965. V. 46

Measure: a Quarterly to the Poem. Boston. V. 46

Unhired. Mt. Horeb: 1968. V. 46

WIER, JOANNES

Medicarum Observatonum Rararum Liber I . . . . Basileae: 1567. V. 42

WIERZBICKI, FELIX P.

California As It Is and As It May Be or a Guide to the Gold Region. San Francisco: 1933. V. 38; 39; 42; 45

WIESE, KERT

The Original Crayon and Wash Illustrations for 'Midnight and Jeremiah'. Philadelphia: 1943. V. 39

WIESE, LUDWIG ADOLF

German Letters on English Education. London: 1854. V. 45

WIESER, FRIEDRICH VON

Natural Value . . . London: 1893. V. 37

WIETZ, J. K.

Sitten, Gebrauche und Trachten der Bewohner des Osmanischen oder Turkischen Reiches. Prague: 1828. V. 40

WIFFEN, J. H.

Historical Memoirs of the House of Russell, from the time of the Norman Conquest. London: 1833. V. 37

WIGFALL, LOUIS T.

Speech on the Pending Political Issues, Delivered at Tyler, Smith County, Texas, September 3, 1860. Washington: 1860. V. 37; 38

WIGGIN, KATE DOUGLAS

A Cathedral Courtship and Penelope's English Experiences. Boston and New York: 1896. V. 40

A Cathedral Courship. London: 1901. V. 40

The Diary of a Goose Girl. Toronto: 1902. V. 39

Love by Express. Hollis and Buxton, Maine: 1924. V. 42

My Garden of Memory. Boston & New York: 1923. V. 46

Penelope's English Experiences. Boston: 1900. V. 44

Penelope's Progress. Penelope's English Experiences and Penelope's Irish Experiences. Boston: 1900 & 1902. V. 39

Penelope's Postscripts: Switzerland, Venice, Walles, Devon Home. Boston: 1915. V. 44

Rebecca of Sunnybrook Farm. Boston & New York: 1903. V. 46

Rebecca of Sunnybrook Farm. New York: 1918. V. 41

The Story of Pasty by Kate Douglas Smith. San Francisco: 1883. V. 43; 44

Susanna and Sue. Boston: 1909. V. 42

The Writings of . . . Boston: 1917. V. 46

The Writings. Boston: 1917/23. V. 42

WIGGINS, JOHN

The 'Monster' Misery of Ireland. London: 1844. V. 38

WIGGINS, MARIANNE

Went South. New York: 1980. V. 46

WIGGINS, RICHARD

The New-York Expositor; or, Fifth Book . . . New York: 1825. V. 39

WIGGINS, WALT

Ernest Berke: Paintings and Sculptures of the Old West. Roswell: 1980. V. 42

WIGGLESWORTH, EDWARD

Calculations on American Population, with a Table for Estimating the Annual Increase of Inhabitants in the British Colonies . . . Boston: 1775. V. 45

Some Thoughts Upon the Spirit of Infallibility Claimed by the Church of Rome. Boston: 1757. V. 40

WIGGLESWORTH, MICHAEL

The Day of Doom; or, a Poetical Description of the Great and Last Judgment. Boston: 1715. V. 43; 45

The Day of Doom; or, a Poetical Description of the Great and Last Judgment, Abridged. Norwich: 1777. V. 40

The Day of Doom, or, A Political Description of the Great and Last Judgement. New York: 1929. V. 37; 45

WIGHT, ALEXANDER

An Inquiry into the Rise and Progress of Parliament, Chiefly in Scotland; and a Complete System of the Law Concerning the Elections of the Representatives from Scotland to the Parliament of Great Britian. Edinburgh: 1784. V. 41; 42

A Treatise on the Laws Concerning the Election of the Different Representatives Sent from Scotland to the Parliament of Great Britain. Edinburgh: 1773. V. 40; 43

WIGHT, ANDREW

A Catalogue of the Entire Library of Andrew Wight of Philadelphia. New York: 1864. V. 38; 44

WIGHT, FREDERICK S.

Hans Hoffman. Berkeley,: 1957. V. 37

WIGHT, JOHN

More Mornings at Bow Street. London: 1827. V. 38; 40

Mornings at Bow Street. London: 1824. V. 38; 41

Mornings at Bow Street, a Selection of the Most Humourous and Entertaining Reports Which Have Appeared in the Morning Herald. London: 1825. V. 42

Sunday in London. London: 1833. V. 39; 41

WIGHT, R.

Icones Plantarum Indiae Orientalis or Figures of Indian Plants. Madras: 1840-53. V. 43

Icones Plantarum Indiae Orientalis, or Figures of Indian Plants. London: 1963. V. 37

Illustrations of Indian Botany . . . Madras: 1838-1840-50. V. 43

WIGHT, SAMUEL F.

Adventures in California and Nicaragua, in Rhyme. Boston: 1860. V. 41; 42

WIGHT, THOMAS

A History of the Rise and Progress of the People Called Quakers in Ireland, etc. Dublin: 1751. V. 41; 43

WIGHT, WILLIAM

Cottage Poems. Edinburgh: 1820. V. 42

WIGHTMAN, FRANCIS

Little Leather Breeches and Other Southern Rhymes. New York: 1899. V. 43

WIGHTMAN, GEORGE

A Treatise on Roads. Halifax: 1845. V. 43

WIGHTMAN, WILLIAM M.

Life of William Capers, D.D., One of the Bishops of the Methodist Church. Nashville: 1858. V. 42

Life of William Capers, D. D. Nashville: 1859. V. 44

WIGHTWICK, GEORGE

Hints to Young Architects . . . with additional notes, and hints to persons about building in the country. By A. J. Downing. Second American Edition. New York: 1851. V. 37; 42

Select Views of the Roman Antiquities. London: 1827. V. 37; 40

WIGLEY, THOMAS B.

The Art of the Goldsmith and Jeweller. London: 1898. V. 41

WIGMORE, JOHN H.

The Australian Ballot System as Embodied in the Legislation of Various Countries. Boston: 1889. V. 37

WIGSTEAD, HENRY

Remarks on a Tour to North and South Wales. London: 1800. V. 46

WIJDEVELD, H. T.

The Life Work of the American Architect Frank Lloyd Wright. Santpoort: 1925. V. 38; 42; 44

Life Work of the American Architect Frank Lloyd Wright. 1965. V. 46

WIJNBLAD, CARL

Byggnings Konsten. Stockholm: 1775/56. V. 42

WIL, G. D.

Prehistoric Pottery in China. London: 1938. V. 42

WILBARGER, J. W.

Indian Depredations in Texas. Austin: 1890. V. 37; 45

WILBER, C. D.

The Great Valleys and Prairies of Nebraska and the Northwest. Omaha: 1881. V. 43

WILBER, E. J.

A Treatise on Counterfeit Altered, and Spurious Bank Notes, with Rules for the Dection of Frauds . . . Poughkeepsie: 1865. V. 38

WILBERFORCE, R. I.

The Life of William Wilberforce. London: 1838. V. 38; 40

WILBERFORCE, SAMUEL

Essays Contributed to the 'Quarterly Review' London: 1874. V. 42; 46

A History of the Protestant Episcopal Church in America. London;: 1844. V. 37

WILBERFORCE, WILLIAM

An Appeal to the Religion, Justice and Humanity of the Inhabitants of the British Empire in Behalf of the Negro Slaves in the West Indies. London: 1823. V. 37; 38; 42; 45

The Debate on a Motion for the Abolition of the Slave-Trade in the House of Commons on Monday and Tuesday, April 18 and 19, 1791, reported in Detail. London: 1791. V. 38

A Letter on the Abolition of the Slave Trade. Addressed to the Freeholders and Other Inhabitants of Yorkshire. London: 1807. V. 37; 38; 46

The Life (and Correspondence) of . . . London: 1838 & 1850. V. 39

A Practical View of the Prevailing Religious System of Professed Christians, in the Higher and Middle Classes in This Country . . . Dublin: 1797. V. 42

A Practical View of the Prevailing Religious System of Professed Christians in the Higher and Middle Classes . . . London: 1797. V. 44

A Practical View of the Prevailing Religious Systems of Professed Christians, in the Higher and Middle Classes in this Country . . . London: 1820. V. 41

WILBERT, C. D.

The Great Valleys and Prairies of Nebraska and the Northwest. Omaha: 1881. V. 40

WILBOUR, CHARLES EDWIN

Travels in Egypt (December 1880 to May 1891). Letters of . . . Brooklyn: 1936. V. 37; 44

WILBRAHAM, ROGER

An Attempt at a Glossary of Some Words Used in Cheshire. London: 1820. V. 41

An Attempt at a Glossary of Some Words Used in Cheshire. London: 1826. V. 46

WILBUR, RAY LYMAN

The Memoirs of Ray Lyman Wilbur, 1875-1949. Stanford: 1960. V. 45

WILBUR, RICHARD

The Beautiful Changes. New York: 1947. V. 43; 46

A Bestiary. New York: 1955. V. 39; 41; 42

A Bestiary. New York: 1959. V. 45

Ceremony and Other Poems. New York: 1950. V. 38; 40; 41

Pedestrian Flight. 1981. V. 42

Pedestrian Flight. 1981. V. 42

Poems 1943-1956. London: 1957. V. 44

Prince Souvanna Phouma: an Exchange Between Richard Wilbur and William Jay Smith. Williamstown: 1963. V. 42

Seed Leaves. 1974. V. 39

Seed Leaves. Boston: 1974. V. 38; 40; 45

Walking to Sleep. New York: 1969. V. 38

WILCOCK, JOHN

The Autobiography and Sex Life of Andy Warhol. New York: 1971. V. 46

WILCOCKE, SAMUEL HULL

History of the Vice Royalty of Buenos Ayres. London: 1807. V. 38

A Narrative of Occurrences in the Indian Counties of North America, Since the Connexion of the Right Hon. the Earl of Selkirk with the Hudson's Bay Co., and His Attempt to Establish a Colony on the Red River. London: 1817. V. 38; 41

A New and Complete Dictionary of the English and Dutch Languages . . . London: 1798. V. 41

WILCOX, CADMUS M.

History of the Mexican War. Washington: 1892. V. 40

WILCOX, ELLA WHEELER

Poems of Passion and Pleasure. London: 1912. V. 42

Poems and Passion & Pleasure. London: 1915. V. 40

Shells. Milwaukee: 1873. V. 41; 43; 45

WILCOX, H. S.

The Great Boo-Boo. 1892. V. 44

WILCOX, MICHAEL

Twelve Bindings. Austin: 1985. V. 38; 39; 40; 41; 44

WILCOX, WALTER DWIGHT

Camping in the Canadian Rockies. New York: 1897. V. 41

The Rockies of Canada. New York: 1900. V. 44

WILD, CHARLES

An Illustration of the Architecture of the Cathedral Church of Lichfield. (with) An Illustration of the Architecture of the Cathedral Church of Chester. London: 1813. V. 39

Illustration of the Architecture and Sculpture of the Cathedral Church at Lincoln. London: 1819. V. 38; 44

Select Examples of Architectural Grandeur in Belgium, Germany and France. (with) Select Examples of Architectural Grandeur . . . Second Series. London: 1827. V. 46

Select Examples of Architectural Grandeur in Belgium, Germany and France. London: 1837. V. 41

Select Examples of Architectural Grandeur in Belgium, Germany & France. London: 1843. V. 39; 41

Twelve Perspective Views of the Exterior and Interior Parts of the Metropolitical Church of York. London: 1809. V. 41

Twelve Select Examples from the Cathedrals of England of the Ecclesiastical Architecture of the Middle Ages . . . London: 1831. V. 39; 44

WILD Flowers. London. V. 46

WILD Flowers and Their Teachings. Bath & London: 1845. V. 43

WILD Flowers of America, Flowers of Every State in the American Union by a Corps of Special Artists and Botantists. New York: 1894. V. 45

WILD Flowers of Canada. Montreal: 1894. V. 44

WILD Flowers of Canada. By Special Artists and Botantists Endorsed by University Botantists of Both Continents. Montreal: (ca. 1910?). V. 37

WILD Flowers of the Rocky Mountains. New York: 1887. V. 43

WILD, FRANK

Shackleton's Last Voyage. London: 1923. V. 45; 46

Shackleton's Last Voyage . . . New York: 1923. V. 38; 42; 43

Shackelton's Last Voyage. London: New York: 1923. V. 43

Shackleton's Last Voyage. London: New York: 1928. V. 43

WILD, IOANNES

Postillae Siue Conciones in Epistollas et Euangelia Quae ab Adventu Usque ad Pascha in Ecclesia Legi Consueuerunt. Coloniae: 1555. V. 40

WILD, J. C.

The Valley of the Mississippi. St. Louis: 1948. V. 40

WILD, JOHN JAMES

At Anchor. London: 1878. V. 44; 46

A Letter to the Right Honourable Lord Brougham and Vaux. Containing Proposals for a Scientific Exploration of Egypt and Ethiopia. London: 1850. V. 43

WILD, ROBERT

Dr. Wild's Humble Thanks for His Majesties Gracious Declaration for Liberty of Conscience, March 15, 1672. London: 1672. V. 41; 45

Iter Boreale. With Other Select Poems: Being an Exact Collection of All Hitherto Extant. London: 1671. V. 40; 43; 45

WILDASH, WILLIAM

The History and Antiquities of Rochester and Its Environs . . . Rochester: 1817. V. 39

WILDE, FRANCESCA ELGEE

Poems by Speranza (Lady Wilde). V. 41

WILDE, JACOB DE

Signa Antiqua e Museo Jacobi de Wilde Veterum Poet14um Carminibus Illustrata et per Marium Filiam Aeri Inscripta . . . Amsterdam: 1703. V. 40

WILDE, JANE FRANCESCA ELGEE, LADY

Sidonia the Sorceress. Hammersmith: 1893. V. 42

WILDE, JANE FRANCESCA SPERANZA, LADY

Social Studies. London: 1893. V. 43

WILDE, OSCAR 1854-1900

The Works. London: 1908. V. 44

WILDE, OSCAR FINGALL O'FLAHERTIE WILLS 1854-1900

After Reading, Letters of Oscar Wilde to Robert Ross. 1921. V. 39

After Reading Letters of Oscar Wilde to Robert Ross. London: 1921. V. 37; 41

After Reading. Westminster: 1921. V. 37; 40; 41

After Berneval. Letters of Oscar Wilde to Robert Ross. London: 1922. V. 37; 38; 42; 43

L'Anniversaire de l'Infante. Paris: 1928. V. 46

Art and Decoration . . . L: 1920. V. 42

Ave Imperatrix. A Dirge of Empire. Snohomish: 1902. V. 42

The Ballad of Reading Gaol. V. 41

The Ballad of Reading Gaol. London: 1898. V. 37; 38; 39; 40; 42; 43; 45; 46

The Ballad of Reading Gaol. London: 1899. V. 43

The Ballad of Reading Gaol. New York: 1903. V. 41

The Ballad of Reading Gaol. Portland: 1904. V. 46

The Ballad of Reading Gaol. East Aurora: 1905. V. 37

The Ballad of Reading Gaol. London: 1924. V. 41

The Ballad of Reading Gaol. London: 1924, 1925. V. 38; 44

Ballad of Reading Gaol. London: 1925. V. 42; 46

The Ballad of Reading Gaol. New York: 1928. V. 37; 42; 45

The Ballad of Reading Gaol. New York: 1930, c. 1928. V. 41

The Ballad of Reading Goal. New York: 1936. V. 37

Ballad of Reading Goal/Ballade de la Geole de Reading. Paris: 1951. V. 37

The Ballad of Reading Gaol . . . New York: 1963. V. 42

The Birthday of the Infanta. Paris: 1928. V. 41; 46

The Birthday of the Infanta. New York: 1929. V. 46

Calendar. London: 1910. V. 40

Catalogue - DULAC & Company. A Collection of original manuscripts letters and books of Oscar Wilde including his letters written to Robert Ross from Reading Gaol and unpublished letters poems & plays formerly in . . . London;: (1928). V. 37

The Chameleon. London: 1894. V. 41

Children in Prison and Other Cruelties of Prison Life. London: 1898. V. 40

Les Cornes du Faune. Paris: 1890. V. 42

De Profundis. London: 1905. V. 37; 38; 39; 40; 41; 42; 43

De Profundis. London: 1908. V. 45

De Profundis. London: 1905. V. 41

De Profundis. London: 1905. V. 40

Decay of Lying. New York: 1902. V. 43; 44

The Duchess of Padua. New York. V. 39

The Duchess of Padua. London: 1908. V. 37; 38

The Duchess of Padua. London: 1909. V. 39

Essays, Criticism and Reviews. London: 1901. V. 37

The Fisherman and His Soul. San Francisco: 1939. V. 46

For Love of the King. London: 1902. V. 39

For Love of the King: A Burmese Masque. London: 1922. V. 38

For Love of the King. London: 1922. V. 37; 39; 40

Four Lettters, Which Were Not Included in the English Edition of 'De Profundis'. London: 1906. V. 45

The Happy Prince. London. V. 40

The Happy Prince and Other Tales. Boston: 1888. V. 42

The Happy Prince. London: 1888. V. 37; 41; 42; 44

The Happy Prince. London: 1913. V. 40; 43; 45; 46

The Happy Prince and Other Tales. Portland: 1919. V. 37

Oscar Wilde's Happy Prince. Seattle: 1931. V. 44

The Happy Prince and Other Tales. London: 1935. V. 46

The Harlot's House. London: 1903. V. 46

The Harlot's House. London: 1904. V. 40

The Harlot's House and Other Poems. New York: 1929. V. 37; 38; 41

Hellenism. 1979. V. 39

Hellenism. Edinburgh: 1979. V. 41

A House of Pomegranates. 1891. V. 45

A House of Pomegranates. London: 1891. V. 37; 38; 39; 40; 41; 42; 43; 44; 45; 46

A House of Pomegranates. London: 1891. V. 38

A House of Pomegranates. The Happy Prince and Other Tales. London: 1908. V. 42

A House of Pomegrantes. London: 1915. V. 43; 44; 46

The House of Judgement. Printed in Four Colours. Utrecht: 1986. V. 37

An Ideal Husband. London: 1899. V. 37; 38; 39; 41; 42; 43; 44; 45; 46

An Ideal Husband. London: 1902. V. 42

WILDE, OSCAR FINGALL O'FLAHERTIE WILLS 1854-1900 continued

The Importance of Being Earnest. A Trivial Comedy for Serious People. 'Copyright October 1893'. London: 1895. V. 37

The Importance of Being Earnest. London: 1899. V. 37; 40; 41; 42; 46

The Importance of Being Earnest. London: 1910. V. 38; 43

The Importance of Being Earnest. New York: 1956. V. 41

Impressions of America. 1906. V. 42

Impressions of America. Sunderland: 1906. V. 37; 41; 42; 43; 45

Intentions. London: 1891. V. 37; 39; 41; 42; 43; 44

Lady Windermere's Fan. London: 1893. V. 37; 38; 39; 40; 43; 46

Lady Windermere's Fan. A Play about a Good Woman. Paris: 1903. V. 37

Lady Windermere's Fan and the Importance of Being Earnest. London: 1973. V. 46

Lord Arthur Savile's Crime. London: 1891. V. 37; 43

Lord Arthur Savile's Crime. London: 1904. V. 43

Lord Arthur Savile's Crime. London: 1954. V. 44

Miscellanies. London: 1908. V. 37; 38

The Nightingale and the Rose, a Fairy Tale. 1961. V. 42

Le Nihilisme Sentimental-L'Entraine. Paris: 1892. V. 42

Oscariana. Epigrams. London: 1895. V. 44

Pan. A Double Villanelle, and Desespoir, A Sonnet. Boston: 1909. V. 40

Pan, a Double Villanelle and Desespoir, a Sonnet. Boston & London: 1909. V. 45; 46

Phrases and Philosophies for the Use of the Young. London: 1904, 1905. V. 43

The Picture of Dorian Gray. London and New York. V. 42

Picture of Dorian Gray. London & New York. V. 41

Picture of Dorian Gray. London/New York: n.d. V. 37

The Picture of Dorian Gray. London: 1890. V. 37

The Picture of Dorian Gray. New York: 1890. V. 37; 38; 42

The Picture of Dorian Gray. Philadelphia: 1890. V. 41

The Picture of Dorian Gray. London: 1891. V. 37; 39; 40; 43; 44

The Picture of Dorian Gray. Paris: 1908. V. 43

The Picture of Dorian Gray. Vienna: 1908. V. 37; 41; 43

The Picture of Dorian Gray. Paris: 1908, 1910. V. 41; 42

The Picture of Dorian Gray. Paris: 1910. V. 39; 41; 43

The Picture of Dorian Gray. London: 1925. V. 40

The Picture of Dorian Gray. London: 1968. V. 43

The Plays of Oscar Wilde. 1905-07. V. 42

Poems. Boston: 1881. V. 39

Poems. Boston: 1881. V. 37; 40; 41; 42; 43; 46

Poems. London: 1881. V. 37; 38; 41; 42; 46

Poems. London: 1892. V. 37; 40; 44

Poems Together with His Lecture on the English Reanissance. Paris: 1903. V. 39

Poems in Prose. Paris: 1905. V. 41

The Poems: Ravenna, Poems, the Sphinx, The Ballad of Reading Gaol, Uncollected Poems. Portland: 1905. V. 40

Poems in Prose. Portland: 1906. V. 41

Poems, by Oscar Wilde. London: 1909. V. 37

The Poems. New York: 1927. V. 37; 41

Poems in Prose. London: 1894. V. 37

Poems in Prose, by Oscar Wilde. 1905. V. 37

Poemes En Prose, by Oscar Wilde. French translation by Charles Grolleau. Paris: 1906. V. 37

Poems in Prose & The Preface to the Picture of Dorian Gray. (Pownal, VT): 1974. V. 37

Poetical Works of Oscar Wilde, Including Poems in Prose With Notes, Bibliographical Introduction, Index and Facsimiles of Title Pages. Portland, Maine: 1908. V. 37

The Portrait of Mr. W.H. London: 1904. V. 37; 38; 42

The Portrait of M. W. H. As Written by Oscar Wilde Sometime After the Publication of His Essay of the Same Title.. London: 1921. V. 41

The Portrait of Mr. W. H. New York: 1921. V. 46

The Portrait of Mr. W. H. V. 37

The Portrait of Mr. W.H., by Oscar Wilde. (London): (c.1907-1910). V. 37

The Portrait of Mr. W. H. London. V. 38

Prose Poems. Belfast: 1973. V. 39

Ravenna. V. 41

Ravenna. Oxford: 1878. V. 37; 38; 39; 40; 44; 45; 46

Newdigate Prize Poem. Ravenna. Recited in The Theatre, Oxford, June 26, 1878. Oxford: 1878. V. 37

Ravenna. London: 1904. V. 45

Ravenna. Newdigate Prize Poem, Recited in the Theatre, Oxford, by Oscar Wilde. Oxford: 1904. V. 37

The Rise of Historical Criticism. 1905. V. 43

The Rise of Historical Criticism. Hartford, Conn.: 1905. V. 37; 40; 42

Rose Leaf and Apple Leaf L'Envoi. London: 1904. V. 37; 41

Salome. Paris: 1893. V. 37; 40; 41; 44; 46

Salome, a Tragedy in One Act. London: 1894. V. 37

Salome. London: 1894. V. 37; 39; 40; 41; 42; 43; 46

Salome a Tragedy in One Act. London: and Boston: 1894. V. 44

Salome. London: 1906. V. 41

Salome. Boston: 1907. V. 42; 43

Salome, a Tragedy in One Act. London: 1907. V. 41

Salome. London: 1907. V. 37; 40; 41; 43

Salome, a Tragedy in One Act. London & New York: 1920. V. 38

Salome, a Tragedy in One Act. London & New York: 1920. V. 40

Salome. Paris: 1922. V. 40; 41; 43

Salome. Paris: 1923. V. 46

Salome. A Tragedy in One Act. Inventions by John Vassos. New York: 1927. V. 37

Salome. San Francisco: 1927. V. 38; 39; 42

Salome. New York: 1930. V. 39; 43

Salome. London & Paris: 1938. V. 37

Salome. New York: 1938. V. 41; 44

Salome. Paris: 1938. V. 40

Salome. Paris and London: 1938. V. 39; 45

Salome. Paris & London: 1938. V. 38

Salome: Tragoedie in Einem Akt, von Oscar Wilde. Leipzig: 1908. V. 37

Sen Artysty; or, The Artist's Dream. Translated from the Polish of madame Helena Modjeska, by Oscar Wilde. London: 1880. V. 37

Sixteen Letters from Oscar Wilde. London: 1930. V. 41

Some Letters from Oscar Wilde to Alfred Douglas. 1892-1897. San Francisco: 1924. V. 38; 39; 44

The Soul of Man. London;: 1895. V. 37

The Soul of Man Under Socialism, by Oscar Wilde. London: 1904. V. 37; 44

The Sphinx. London: 1894. V. 37; 40; 43; 44; 45; 46

The Sphinx. London: 1920. V. 37; 38; 45

The Sphinx. London & New York: 1920. V. 37; 40

Three Poems Printed In Kottabos. Dublin: 1877-79. V. 40

The Trial of Oscar Wilde from the Shorthand Reports. Paris: 1906. V. 37

Vera; or, The Nihilists. London: 1902. V. 37; 42

Vera, Or the Nihilists: A Drama in a Prologue and Four Acts, by Oscar Wilde. N.P.: 1902. V. 37

Wilde v. Whistler Being an Acrimonious Correspondence on Art Between Oscar Wilde and James A. McNeill Whistler. London: 1906. V. 38

A Woman of No Importance. London: 1894. V. 37; 38; 41; 42; 44

A Woman of No Importance. London: 1908. V. 42

Works. London: 1908. V. 44; 46

Works. (with) For Love the King: a Burmese Masque. London: 1908-22. V. 40

Complete Works of . . . New York: 1909. V. 39

The Complete Works. New York: 1923. V. 42; 44; 45

The Complete Works. New York: 1927. V. 42

The Writings. London: 1907. V. 38

The Writings of . . . London: 1907. V. 46

Complete Writings. New York, Philadelphia &: 1909. V. 39

The Writings. New York: 1925. V. 38

The Young King and Other Tales. Portland: 1922. V. 37

The Young King and Other Tales. Chelsea: 1924. V. 37

The Young King and Other tales. By Oscar Wilde. With a dedicatory poem from the printer to his daughter Rosamund M. Hornby on her tenth birthday. London: 1924. V. 37

The Young King and Other Stories. London: 1953. V. 41

WILDE, OSCAR FINGALL O'FLLAHERTIE WILLS 1854-1900

A House of Pomegranates. New York. V. 45

WILDE, WILLIAM ROBERT WILLS

The Beauties of the Boyne and Its Tributary, the Blackwater. Dublin: 1850. V. 43

The Closing of Dean Swift's Life. Dublin: 1849. V. 42

Memoir of Gabriel Beranger and His Labours in the Cause of Irish Art and Antiquities from 1760-1780. Dublin: 1880. V. 39

Narrative of a Voyage to Madeira, Teneriffe, and Along the Shores of the Mediterranean, Including a Visit to Algiers, Egypt, Palestine, Tyre, Rhodes, Telemessus, Cyprus and Greece. Dublin: 1840. V. 37; 41

Narrative of a Voyage to Madeira, Tenerife and Along the Shores of the Mediterranean . . . Dublin: 1844. V. 37; 41; 45

WILDENSTEIN, DANIEL

Claude Monet. Paris/Lausanne: 1947-85. V. 44

WILDENSTEIN, GEORGES

Chardin. Greenwich: 1969. V. 37; 40; 43; 45

Ingres. V. 46

WILDENSTEIN, GEORGES continued

Ingres. London: 1954. V. 37; 40; 41; 43; 45; 46

Ingres. London: 1956. V. 43

The Paintings of Fragonard. London: 1960. V. 42; 43

The Paintings of Fragonard. New York: 1960. V. 38

WILDER, ALEXANDER

History of Medicine. New Sharon: 1901. V. 39; 43

WILDER, AMOS NIVEN

Battle Retrospect and Other Poems. New Haven: 1923. V. 40

WILDER, BURT G.

What Young People Should Know. Boston: 1875. V. 40

WILDER, ELIZABETH

The Unfinished Monument by Andrea del Verrocchio to the Cardinal Niccolo Forteguerri at Pistoia. Florence: 1932. V. 38; 42

WILDER, L. B.

Colour in My Garden. Garden City: 1918. V. 45

WILDER, LAURA INGALLS

The Long Winter. New York: 1940. V. 38; 45

WILDER, MARSHALL P.

The Wit and Humor of America. New York: 1907, 1911. V. 38

WILDER, MITCHELL

Santos, The Religious Folk Art of New Mexico. Colorado Springs: 1943. V. 37

WILDER, THORNTON 1897-1976

American Characteristics and Other Essays. New York: 1979. V. 40

The Angel That Troubled the Waters. London: & New York: 1928. V. 38; 40; 45

The Angel that Troubled the Waters. New York: 1928. V. 39; 43; 46

The Bridge of Sain Luis Rey. New York: 1927. V. 38; 39; 40; 42; 46

The Bridge of San Luis Rey. London: 1927. V. 38

The Bridge of San Luis Rey. New York: 1929. V. 37; 38; 39; 42; 43; 44

The Bridge of San Luis Rey. New York: 1962. V. 39; 40; 44; 46

The Cabala. London: 1926. V. 38; 40; 42; 45

The Cabala. New York: 1926. V. 38

The Cabala. London: 1954. V. 44

Childhood: A Comedy in One Act. New York: 1960. V. 38

The Eighth Day. New York: 1967. V. 38; 40; 41; 43; 44; 45; 46

Heaven's My Destinaation. New York: 1935. V. 38; 40; 44; 45; 46

The Ides of March. New York: 1948. V. 44; 45; 46

Infancy: a Comedy in One Act. New York: 1961. V. 38

The Long Christmas Dinner and Other Plays. New Haven: 1931. V. 38; 39; 40; 41

The Long Christmas Dinner and Other Plays in One Act. New York: 1932/31. V. 44

Love and How to Cure It. London: 1932. V. 40

The Merchant of Yonkers. New York: 1939. V. 46

Our Town. V. 39

Our Town. New York: 1938. V. 39; 45

Our Century. N.P.: 1947. V. 45

Our Town. 1974. V. 38

Our Town. Avon: 1974. V. 46

The Skin of Our Teeth. New York: 1942. V. 37; 41; 42; 44

Theophilus North. New York: 1973. V. 38; 40; 44; 45

Three Plays: Our Town, The Skin of Our Teeth, The Matchmaker. New York: 1957. V. 38; 40

Three Plays: Our Town, the Skin of Our Teeth, the Matchmaker. London: 1958. V. 39; 45

The Woman of Andros. New York: 1830. V. 46

The Woman of Andros. London: 1930. V. 41

The Woman of Andros. London: & New York: 1930. V. 38; 40; 45

The Woman of Andros. New York: 1930. V. 38; 39; 40; 41; 42; 43; 45

WILDERSPIN, SAMUEL

Infant Education. London: 1829. V. 39

WILDFLOWERS of America. New York: 1894. V. 46

WILDMAN, THOMAS

A Treatise on the Management of Bees Wherein is Contained the Natural History of Those Insects . . . London: 1768. V. 37; 41; 43

WILDWOOD, WARREN

Thrilling Adventures Among the Early Settlers. Philadelphia: 1861. V. 43

WILEMAN, A. E.

Notes on Japanese Lepidoptera and Their Larvae. Manila: 1914-25. V. 38

WILENSKI, R. H.

Flemish Painters 1430-1830. New York: 1960. V. 46

WILEY & PUTNAM

Emigrant's Guide. London: 1845. V. 41

WILEY, C. H.

Adventures of Old Dan Tucker, and His Son Walter; A Tale of North Carolina. London: (1851). V. 37

WILEY, CALVIN HENDERSON

Address to the People of North CArolina. Raleigh?: 1861? V. 44

WILEY, SAMUEL T.

Biographical and Historical Cyclopedia of Delaware County . . . Comprising a Historical Sketch . . . Richmond & New York: 1894. V. 42

Biographical and Portrait Cyclopedia of the Third Congressional District of New Jersey . . . Philadelphia: 1896. V. 41; 42; 46

WILEY, SARA KING

The Yosemite, Alaska and the Yellowstone. London: 1893. V. 40; 41

The Yosemite, Alaska and Yellowstone. London & New York: 1893. V. 37

WILEY, WILLIAM H.

The Yosemite, Alaska & The Yellowstone. London/New York: 1894. V. 37

WILGUS, A. CURTIS

The Caribbean: Peoples, Problems and Prospects. Gainesville: 1952. V. 42

WILHELM, GOTTLIEB TOBIAS

Unterhaltungen aus der Naturgeschichte. Vienna: 1813. V. 42; 45

WILHELM, JOHANN

Architectura Civils, oder Beschreibung und Vorreifsung Vieler Vornehmer Dachwerck, als Hoher Helmen . . . Nurnberg: 1682. V. 44

WILHELM, JOSEPH

The Family of Grace; Pedigress and memoirs. London: 1911. V. 37

WILHELM, PAUL

Early Sacramento: Glimpses of John Augustus Sutter, the Hok Farm and Neighboring Indian Tribes from the Journals of Prince Paul H.R.H. Duke Paul Wilhelm of Wurttemberg. 1973. V. 45

WILHELM, RICHARD

The I Ching or Book of Changes. Princeton: 1952. V. 42

WILHELM, THOMAS

Synopsis of the History of the Eighth U.S. Infantry. New York: 1871. V. 43

WILHELM VIII

Mit der Allgemeinen Freude Hessens bey der Hoechsterwuenschten Wiederkunst . . . Kassel: 1758. V. 46

WILJDEVELD, H. T.

Life Work of the American Architect Frank Lloyd Wright. Santpoort: 1925. V. 46

WILKERSON, SAMUEL

Notes on Puget Sound. New York: 1870. V. 38

WILKES, CHARLES

Exploring Expedition: Message from the President of the United States Transmitting the Information Required by a Resolution of the House of Representatives of 7th Dec. Last, in Relation to the Delay in the Outfit &c. for the Exploring Expedition. Washington: 1838. V. 43

Exploring Expedition During the Years 1838, 1839, 1840, 1841, 1842. New York: 1858. V. 43

Narrative of the United Stateas Exploring Expedition During . . . Philadelphia: 1845. V. 37; 38; 40; 42; 45; 46

Narrative of the United States Exploring Expedition, During . . . 1838-1842. London: 1852. V. 42

Western America, Including California and Oregon . . . Philadelphia: 1849. V. 38

WILKES, GEORGE

The Great Battle, Fought at Manasas, Between Federal Forces, Under General McDowell and the Rebels, Under Gen. Beauregard, Sunday, July 21, 1861. New York: 1861. V. 43

The History of Oregon, Geographical and Political. New York: 1845. V. 37; 39; 40; 41; 42

Project of a National Railroad from the Atlantic to the Pacific Ocean. New York: 1845. V. 38; 40; 43; 44

Proposal for A National Rail-Road to the Pacific Ocean, for the Purpose of Obtaining a Short Route to Oregon and the Indies. New York: 1847. V. 37

WILKINSON, HENRY

Engines of War; or, Historical and Experimental Observations on Ancient and Modern Warlike Machines and Implements . . . London: 1841. V. 46

Sketches of Scenery in the Basque Provinces of Spain, with a Selection of Music . . . London: 1838. V. 40

WILKINSON, I. G.

Topography of thebes, and General View of Egypt, Being a Short Account of the Principal Objects Worthy of Notice in the Valley of the Nile . . . London: 1835. V. 39

WILKINSON, J.

A Treatise Collected Out of the Statutes of this Common-Wealth, and According to Common Experience of the Lawes, Concerning the Office and Authoritie of Coroners and Sherifes. London: 1657. V. 37

WILKINSON, JAMES

Hau Kiou Choaan, or the Pleasing History. London: 1761. V. 42; 44

Memoirs of My Own Times. Philadelphia: 1816. V. 37; 38; 39; 41; 42

Wilkinson, Soldier and Pioneer. New Orleans: 1935. V. 39

WILKINSON, JAMES VERE STEWART

The Lights of Canopus: Anvari i Suhaili. London: 1929. V. 41

The Shah-Namah of Firdausi: The Book of the Persian Kings. London: 1931. V. 41

WILKINSON, JOHN GARDNER

The Egyptians in the Time of the Pharaohs, Being a Companion to the Crystal Palace Egyptian Collections. London: 1857. V. 40

Manners and Customs of the Ancient Egyptians, Including Their Private Life, Government, Laws, Arts, Manufactures, Religion and Early History . . . London: 1837. V. 40

The Manners and Customs of the Ancient Egyptians. London: 1837-41. V. 40; 42

The Manners and Customs of the Ancient Egyptians. London: 1878. V. 42; 44

Modern Egypt and Thebes . . . London. V. 42

On Colour and on the Necessity for a General Diffusion of Taste Among All Classes. London: 1858. V. 38; 42; 43; 44; 45

A Popular Account of the Ancient Egyptians. New York: 1854. V. 40

Topography of Thebes, and General View of Egypt. London: 1835. V. 37; 44

WILKINSON, NEVILE R.

Wilton House Pictures. London: 1907. V. 44

WILKINSON, R. J.

A Malay-English Dictionary. Singapore: 1901-02. V. 38

A Malay-English Dictionary (Romanised). Mytilene: 1932. V. 38

WILKINSON, RIGHT REV. BISHOP

Saat: The Native Slave-Boy of Khartoum. London: 1878. V. 39

WILKINSON, ROBERT

An Ancient Atlas of the Principal Countries Mentioned by Antient Authors . . . Boston: 1812. V. 45

Atlas Classica Being a Collection of Maps of Countries Mentioned by the Ancient Authors, Both Sacred and Profane. London: 1817. V. 45

WILKINSON, S.

The Housekeeper's, Butcher's and Innkeeper's Guide . . . British Wines . . . Malt Liquors. London. V. 44

WILKINSON, SARAH

Love and Hymen; or, the Gentleman's and Ladies Polite and Original Valentine Writer. London: 1820? V. 44

WILKINSON, TATE

Memoirs of His Own Life. York: 1790. V. 38; 39; 41; 43; 44; 45; 46

The Wandering Pantentee; or, A History of the Yorkshire Theatres. York: 1795. V. 37; 38; 39; 41; 45

WILKINSON, WILLIAM 1819-1901

English Country Houses. London: 1870. V. 44

The Federal Calculator, and American Ready Reckoner. Providence: 1795. V. 39; 40

Memorials of Minnesota Forest Fires in the Year 1894 with a Chapter on the Forest Fires in Wisconsin the Same Year. Minneapolis: 1895. V. 37; 42

The Modern Veterinarian, with Several Receipts for Horned Cattle. Newcastle-upon-Tyne. V. 37

WILKS, CLAIRE WEISSMAN

The Magic Box: The Eccentric Genius of Hannah Maynard. Toronto: 1980. V. 45

WILL She Bear It? London: 1872. V. 43

WILL, WILLIAM

A View of the Establishment of the Royal Edinburgh Volunteers . . . Edinburgh: 1795. V. 38

WILLA Cather. A Biographical Sketch. An English Opinion and an Abridged Bibliography. (wrapper title). New York: 1926. V. 37

WILLAIMS, R. H.

With the Border Ruffians; Memories of the Far West, 1852-1868. London: 1907. V. 42

WILLAN, JOHN HENRY

A Manual of the Criminal Law of Canada. Quebec: 1861. V. 37; 39

WILLAN, ROBERT

On Vaccine Inoculation. London: 1806. V. 42

On Cutaneous Diseases. Volume I. Philadelphia: 1809. V. 42

WILLARD, BENJAMIN J.

Captain Ben's Book: a Record of the Things Which Happened to Capt. Benjamin J. Willard, Pilot and Stevedore, During Some Sixty Years on Sea and Land. Portland: 1895. V. 46

WILLARD, EMMA

Advancement of Female Education; or, a Series of Addresses in Favor of Establishing at Athens, in Greece, a Female Seminary . . . New York: 1833. V. 46

Journal and Letters from France and Great Britain. New York: 1833. V. 46

Journal and Letters from France and Great Britain. Troy: 1833. V. 37; 40; 45

Last Leaves of American History . . . New York: 1849. V. 45

WILLARD, JOSEPH

An Address in Commemoration of the Two Hundredth Anniversary of the Incorporation of Lancaster, Massachusetts. Boston: 1853. V. 40

WILLARD, MARGARET WHEELER

Letters on the American Revolution 1774-1776. Boston: 1925. V. 46

WILLARD, SAMUEL 1639-1707

The Peril of the Times Displayed. Boston: 1700. V. 38

Some Brief Sacramental Meditations Preparatory for the Great Ordinance of the Supper. Boston: 1743. V. 43

WILLARD, SIDNEY

A Hebrew Grammar. Cambridge: 1817. V. 43

WILLARD, THEODORE A.

The City of Sacred Well Being a Narrative of the Discoveries and Excavations of Edward Herbert Thompson in the Ancient City of ChiChen Itza with Some Discourse on the Culture and Development of the Mayan Civilisation as Revealed by Their Art . . . London: 1926. V. 40

The Lost Empires of the Itzaes and Mayas an American Civilization, Contemporary with Christ . . . Glendale: 1933. V. 42

WILLCOCKS, JAMES

From Kabul to Kumassi Twenty-Four Years of soldiering and Sport . . . . London: 1904. V. 45

WILLCOCKS, T.

Moral and Sacred Poetry. Devonport: 1834. V. 43

WILLCOCKS, W.

Egyptian Irrigation. London: 1899. V. 40

WILLCOX, R. N.

Reminiscences, Of California Life . . . Avery: 1897. V. 39

WILLCOX, W. T.

The Historical Records of the Fifth (Royal Irish) Lancers from their foundation as Wynne's Dragoons (in 1689) to the present day. London: 1908. V. 37

WILLDENOW, D. C.

The Principles of Botany and of Vegetable Physiology. Edinburgh: 1805. V. 39; 40; 42

WILLDENOW, KARL LUDWIG

Historia Amaranthorum. Zurich: 1790. V. 38; 40

WILLE, ELIZABETH DE

Johannes Olaf. London: 1873. V. 41

WILLEFORD, C.

High Priest of California and Wild Wives. 1987. V. 43

WILLEFORD, CHARLES

The Burnt Orange Heresy. New York: 1971. V. 41; 46

Cockfighter. Chicago: 1962. V. 39; 42

A Guide for the Undehemorrhoided. Boynton Beach: 1977. V. 45

WILLEFORD, CHARLES continued

I Was Looking for a Street. Woodstock: 1988. V. 45

Off the Wall. Montclair: 1980. V. 45

Proletaian Laughter: Poems. New York: 1948. V. 41; 42; 43; 44

WILLEM I, PRINCE OF ORANGE 1533-1584

Apologie ov Defense de Tresillvstre Prince Gvillavme par la Grace de Diev Prince d'Orange . . . Contre le Ban & Edict Publie par le Roi d'Espaigne . . . Leyden: 1581. V. 43

WILLEMENT, THOMAS

The Armorial Insignia of the Kings and Queens of England from Coeval Authorities. London: 1821. V. 38

Regal Heraldry. London: 1821. V. 46

WILLERT, JAMES

Little Big Horn Diary: Chronicle of the 1876 Indian War. La Mirada: 1977. V. 37

The Terry Letters. Montclair: 1980. V. 37

WILLES, JOHN

Reports of Adjudged Cases in the Court of Common Pleas, House of Lords, Court of Chancery, and Exchequer Chambers (1737-1758) . . . London: 1799. V. 38; 40

WILLES, THOMAS

A Word in Season, for Warning to England . . . London: 1659. V. 46

WILLET, ANDREW

Hexepla in Danielem. London: 1610. V. 42

WILLETS, GILSON

Greater America. Heroes, Battles, Camps, Dewey Islands, Cuba, Porto Rico. New York: 1898. V. 43

WILLETT, MARINUS

A Narrative of the Military Actions of Colonel Marinus Willett, Taken Chiefly from His Own Manuscript. New York: 1831. V. 38; 44

WILLETT, N. L.

Beaufort County, South Carolina: Its Shrines and Early History. Augusta: 1923/1927. V. 44

WILLETT, RALPH 1719-1785

A Memoir on the Origin of Printing. Newcastle: 1818. V. 38; 41

A Memoir On the Origin of Printing, In a Letter Addressed to John Topham, Esq . . . New Castle: 1820. V. 43

WILLETT, W. N.

Charles Vincent; or, the Two Clerks. New York: 1839. V. 43

WILLETT, WILLIAM M.

A Narrative of the Miltary Actions of Colonel Marinus Willett . . . New York: 1831. V. 45

Scenes in the Wilderness: an Authentic Narrative of the Labours and Sufferings of the Moravian Missionaries Among the North American Indians. New York: 1842. V. 42

WILLETTS, WILLIAM

Foundations of Chinese Art from Neolithic Pottery to Modern Architecture. New York: 1965. V. 38; 41

WILLEY, ELI B.

Six Poems, on Different Subjects, Relative to the Events of the Late War. N.P.: 1815. V. 42

WILLEY, GORDON R.

Archaeology of Southern Mesoamerica Parts I and II. Austin: 1965. V. 42

WILLEY, SAMUEL H.

An Historical Paper Relating to Santa Cruz, California. San Francisco: 1876. V. 40

A History of the College of California. San Francisco: 1887. V. 41

WILLEY, WORCESTER 1808-1899

A Tale of Home and War by E. P. H. Portland: 1888. V. 42

WILLIAM, EDWARD

Virgo Triumphans: or, Virginia Richly and Truly Valued; More Especially the South Part Thereof: Viz. The Fertile Carolina, and No Less Excellent Isle of Roanoak, of Latitude from 31 to 37 Degr. Relataing the Means of Raising Infinite Profits . . . London: 1650. V. 38

WILLIAM, FATHER, PSEUD.

Three Days on the Ohio River. New York: 1854. V. 45

WILLIAM FITZWILLIAM, VISCOUNT 1839-1877

British Columbia, by the Yellow Heas or Leather Pass. London: (1864). V. 37

WILLIAM I, PRINCE OF ORANGE

La Iustification du Prince d'Oranges, Contre les Faulx Blasmes, Que Ses Calumniateurs a luy Imposer a Tort. N.P.: 1568. V. 46

WILLIAM II, KING OF THE NETHERLANDS

Catalogue des Tableaux Anciens et Modernes . . . Dessins et Statues. Amsterdam: 1850. V. 38

WILLIAM IV, KING OF GREAT BRITAIN 1765-1837

The Speech of His Majesty to the Archbishops and Bishops, on their PResenting an Address of Congratulations on His Birthday. Oxford: 1834. V. 46

WILLIAM Lloyd Garrison, 1805-1879. The Story of This Life Told by His Children. New York: 1885-89. V. 39; 42

WILLIAM Morris and the Art of the Book. New York: 1976. V. 39; 40

WILLIAM OF MALMESBURY

Gesta Regum Anglorum, Atque Historia Novella. Londini: 1840. V. 45

Willelmi Malmesbiriensis Monachi. Gesta Regum Anglorum, atque Historia Novella. Londin: 1840. V. 39

WILLIAM, OF NEWBURGH 1136-1198?

Rerum Anglicarum Libri Quinque, Recens ceu e Tenebris Eruti, & in Studiosorum Gratiam in Lucem Dati . . . Antuerpiae: 1567. V. 39; 43

WILLIAM, PRINCE OF SWEDEN

Wild African Animals I Have Known. London: 1923. V. 38; 40

WILLIAM, WILLIAM CARLOS

Paterson (Book Two). New York: 1948. V. 37

WILLIAM Y-WORTH

Introitus Apertus ad Artem Distillationis; or the Whole Art of Distillation Practically Stated, and Adorned with All the New Modes of Working Now in Use. London: 1692. V. 45

WILLIAMS, A. BRYAN

Game Trails in British Columbia. London: 1925. V. 39

Game Trails in British Columbia: Big Game and Other Sport in the Wilds of British Columbia. New York: 1925. V. 37

Rod and Creel in British Columbia. Vancouver: 1919. V. 37; 41

WILLIAMS, AARON

Harmony Society at Economy, Penn'a. Pittsburg: 1866. V. 40; 41; 42; 44; 45

WILLIAMS, ALBERT

A Pioneer Pastorate and Times Embodying Contemporary Local Transactions and Events. San Francisco;: 1879. V. 39

WILLIAMS, ALFRED

A Wiltshire Village. London: 1912. V. 40

WILLIAMS, ALFRED M.

Sam Houston and the War of Independence in Texas. Boston and New York: 1893. V. 39

WILLIAMS, ALFRED MASON

Memorial of Alfred Mason Williams, Born October 23, 1840. Providence: 1898. V. 43

WILLIAMS, ALPHEUS F.

The Genesis of the Diamond. London: 1932. V. 40

WILLIAMS, AMELIA

Critical Study of the Siege of the Alamo and of the Personnel of Its Defenders. Austin: 1933. V. 44

WILLIAMS, ARCHIBALD

Petrol Peter. London: 1912. V. 40

WILLIAMS, B. S.

The Orchid Grower's Manual . . . London: 1894. V. 46

WILLIAMS, BASIL

The H.A.C. in South Africa. London: 1903. V. 41

WILLIAMS, BEN AMES

The Happy End. New York: 1942. V. 39

WILLIAMS' British Columbia Directory, 1891. Victoria,: 1890. V. 37

WILLIAMS, BROCK

The Earl of Chicago. Indianapolis: 1937. V. 44; 45

WILLIAMS, BUTLER

A Manual for Teaching Model-Drawing, from Solid Forms . . . London: 1843. V. 44

WILLIAMS, C.

A Brief Circular Relating to Rice County, Minnesota: Showing Its Resources, Advantages, and the Inducements it Offers to Those Seeking Homes in the West. Fairbault: 1860. V. 42

Child's Natural History of Birds. Philadelphia: 1850. V. 44

WILLIAMS, C. J. B.

Principles of Medicine. Philadelphia: 1857. V. 40; 41

WILLIAMS, C. W.

A Speech on the Improvement of the Shannon . . . London: 1835. V. 45

WILLIAMS, CAHTERINE READ ARNOLD

Fall River, An Authentic Narrative. Boston: 1833. V. 41

WILLIAMS, CARL M.

Silversmiths of New Jersey, 1700-1825. Philadelphia: 1949. V. 42; 44; 46

Silversmiths of New Jersey, 1700-1825, with some Notice of Clockmakers Who Were Also Silversmiths. Philadelphia: 1849. V. 38

WILLIAMS, CAROLINE RANSOM

The Decoration of the Tomb of Parneb. New York: 1932. V. 40; 42

Gold and Silver Jewelry and Related Objects. New York: 1924. V. 37; 42; 44

WILLIAMS, CATHERINE READ ARNOLD

Aristocracy or the Holbey Family: a National Tale. Providence: 1832. V. 43

Tales: National and Revolutionary. Providence: 1830. V. 43

WILLIAMS, CHARLES

All Hallows' Eve. New York: 1948. V. 42

A Carol of Amen House. London: 1927. V. 42; 44

Descent Into Hell. London: 1937. V. 40

The Descent of the Dove - a Short History of the Holy Spirit of the Church. London: 1939. V. 44

Divorce. London: 1920. V. 44

Flecker of Dean Close. London: 1946. V. 38; 40

He Came Down from Heaven. London: 1938. V. 38; 44

Heroes and Kings. London: 1930. V. 41; 44

Many Dimensions. London: 1931. V. 44

The Masque of the Manuscript. London: 1927. V. 42

The Moon - a Cantata Prepared and Arranged for Treble Voices from the Airs of Henry Purcell. London: 1923. V. 41

A Myth of Shakespeare. London: 1928. V. 44

Poems of Conformity. London: 1917. V. 38; 43; 44

Poetry at Present. London: 1930. V. 39; 44

Queen Elizabeth. London: 1936. V. 38

The Silver Stair. London: 1912. V. 38; 40; 41; 44

Thomas Cranmer of Canterbury. London: 1936. V. 38

Three Plays. London: 1931. V. 39; 40

War in Heaven. London: 1930. V. 44

The Way of Exchange. London: 1941. V. 40

Windows of Night. London: 1924. V. 38; 40; 44; 46

WILLIAMS, CHARLES HANBURY 1708-1759

A Dialogue Between G--s E---e and B--b D--n. London: 1741. V. 38

An Ode from the E---- of B---- to Ambition. London: 1746. V. 38

The Odes of . . . London: 1768. V. 37

Plain Thoughts in Plain Language. London: 1743. V. 38

S----s and J-----l. A New Ballad. London: 1743. V. 38

S---ys's Budget Open'd or, drink and be D---'d. London: 1743. V. 38

The Summer Miscellany; or a Present for the Country. London: 1742. V. 41; 45

The Wife and the Nurse: a Ballad. London: 1743. V. 38

WILLIAMS, CHAUNCEY P.

Lone Elk - Part I and II. Denver: 1935. V. 38

Lone Elk. The Life Story of Bill Williams, Trapper, and Guide of the Far West. Denver: 1935-36. V. 44

WILLIAMS, CLARA ANDREWS

The Stories that Glue Told. New York: 1907. V. 44

WILLIAMS, CYNRIC R.

The Philippines and Round About with Some Account of British Interests in These Waters. London: 1827. V. 44

A Tour through the Island of Jamaica, from the Western to the Eastern End in the Year 1823. London: 1827. V. 42; 44; 46

WILLIAMS, D. E.

The Life and Correspondence of Sir Thomas Lawrence. London: 1831. V. 39; 44

WILLIAMS, DANIEL

The Advancement of Christis Interests the Governing End of a Christians Life. London: 1688. V. 44

WILLIAMS, DAVID 1738-1816

The History of Monmouthshire . . . London: 1796. V. 38; 41

Lessons to a Young Prince, by an Old Statesman, on the Present Disposition in Europe to a General Revolution. London: 1790. V. 40

Lessons to a Young Prince, by an Old Statesman, on the Present Disposition in Europe to a General Revolution. New York: 1791. V. 40

Letters on Political Liberty. London: 1782. V. 40

WILLIAMS, E.

Early Holborn and the Legal Quarter of London. London: 1927. V. 40

WILLIAMS, EDWARD

Catalogue of the Elegant and Valuable Household Furniture . . . Library of Books . . . Shrewsbury: 1834. V. 45

Poems, Lyric and Pastoral. London: 1794. V. 41

Virginia's Discovery of Silk-Wormes, with Their Benefit and The Implanting of Mulberry Trees. London: 1650. V. 40

Virgo Triumphans; or, Virginia Richly and Truly Valued . . . London: 1650. V. 40; 44

WILLIAMS, EDWARD PEET

Extracts from Letters to A. B. T. from Edward P. Williams During His Service in the Civil War, 1862-64. New York: 1903. V. 44

WILLIAMS, EDWARD VAUGHAN

A Treatise on the Law of Executors and Administrators. London: 1841. V. 39

WILLIAMS, ELEAZER

Life of Te-Ho-Ra-Gwa-Ne-Gen, Alias, Thomas Williams, A Chief of the Caughnawaga Tribe of Indians In Canada. Albany: 1859. V. 38

WILLIAMS, ELISHA

The Essential Rights and Liberties of Protestants. Boston: 1744. V. 43; 45

WILLIAMS-ELLIS, CLOUGH

The Tank Corps. London: 1919. V. 43; 44

WILLIAMS, EMLYN

The Corn is Green. New York: 1941. V. 39

Night Must Fall - a Play in 3 Acts. London: 1935. V. 44

WILLIAMS, F. T.

The Angler's Pocket Diary, and Monthly Guide. London: 1867. V. 39

WILLIAMS, FRANCIS

A Method For More Fully Determining the Outline of the Heart by Means of the Fluorescope Together With Other Uses of this Instrument in Medicine. 1896. V. 42

WILLIAMS, FRANCIS EDGAR

Drama of Orokolo. The Social and Ceremonial Life of Elema. Oxford: 1940. V. 37

Orokaiva Society. London: 1930. V. 37

Papuans of the Trans-Fly. Oxford: 1936. V. 37

WILLIAMS, FRANKLIN B.

The Gardyners Passetaunce. London: 1985. V. 44

WILLIAMS, FREDERICK LAKE

An Historical and Topographical Description of the Municipium of Ancient Verulam; the Martyrdom of ST. Alban. St. Albans: 1822. V. 39

WILLIAMS, FREDERICK S.

The Midland Railway; It's Rise and Progress. London: 1876. V. 41; 45

Our Iron Roads: Their History, Construction and Social Influences. London: 1852. V. 40; 46

Our Iron Roads: Their History, Construction and Administration. London: 1883. V. 44

WILLIAMS, G. H.

The Land of the Soviets. A Western Farmer Sees the Russian Bear Change His Coat. Saskatoon: 1931. V. 39

WILLIAMS, GARDNER F.

The Diamond Mines of South Africa. New York: 1902. V. 38; 41

The Diamond Mines of South Africa. New York: 1905. V. 37; 38; 40; 44

The Diamond Mines of South Africa. London: 1906. V. 39; 40

The Diamond Mines of South Africa. New York: 1906. V. 43; 44; 46

WILLIAMS, GEORGE C.

English Conversation Pictues of the Eighteenth and Early Nineteenth Centuries. London: 1931. V. 39

WILLIAMS, GEORGE WHARTON

Sketches of Travel in the Old and New World. Charleston: 1871. V. 40

WILLIAMS, GODFREY TREVELYAN

The Historical Records of the Eleventh Hussars, Prince Albert's Own. London: 1908. V. 43

WILLIAMS, H.

Reminiscences of a Deceased Sister. Newbury: 1843. V. 42

WILLIAMS, H. C.

Gateway to Texas: The History of Orange County. Orange: 1986. V. 41

WILLIAMS, H. DWIGHT, MRS.

A Year In China: and a Narrative of Capture and Imprisonment, When Homeward Bound, on Board the Rebel Pirate Florida. New York: 1864. V. 46

WILLIAMS, H. M.

A Tour in Switzerland; or a View of the Present State of the Government and Manners of Those Cantons. Dublin: 1798. V. 38

WILLIAMS, H. NOEL

Madame Recamier and Her Friends. London & New York: 1901. V. 41

Madame du Barry. London: 1904. V. 38

WILLIAMS, H. S.

The History of the Art of Writing. Cambridge,. V. 38

WILLIAMS, HARCOURT

Tales from Ebony. London: 1934. V. 44; 46

WILLIAMS, HAROLD

Book Clubs & Printing Societies. London: 1929. V. 38; 39; 41

Dean Swift's Library, with Facsimile of the Original Sale Catalogue and Some Account of Two Manuscript Lits of His Books. 1932. V. 40

Dean Swift's Library. Cambridge: 1932. V. 42; 46

WILLIAMS, HELEN MARIA

Ambrose and Eleanor . . . Philadelphia: 1799. V. 40

Letters Written in France, in the Summer 1790, to a Friend in England, Containing Various Anecdotes Relative to the French Revolution . . . . London: 1790. V. 37; 41; 43

Letters Written in France. Dublin: 1794. V. 43

Letters Written in France in the Summer of 1790 to a Friend in England . . . London: 1794. V. 41

Letters Containing a Sketch of the Scenes Which Passed in Various Departments of France During the Tyranny of Robespierre . . . Philadelphia: 1796. V. 42

Letters on the Events Which Have Passed in France Since the Restoration in 1815. London: 1819. V. 40

Memoirs of Mons. and Madame du F. Boston: 1794. V. 42; 44; 45

A Narrative of the Events Which Have Taken Place in France, from the Landing of Napoleon Buonaparte, on the 1st of March, 1815 . . . London: 1815. V. 42

Peru, a Poem in Six Cantos. London: 1784. V. 40; 43

A Residence in France, during the Years 1792, 1793, 1794 and 1795; Described in a Series of Letters from an English Lady: with General and Incidental Remarks on the French character and manners. Prepared for the Press . . . Elizabeth Town: 1798. V. 37

A Tour in Switzerland. Dublin: 1798. V. 37; 45

A Tour in Switzerland; or, a View of the Present State of the Governments and Manners of Those Cantons; with Comparative Sketches of the Present State of Paris. London: 1798. V. 42; 43; 44; 46

WILLIAMS, HENRY

The Diagnosis and Treatment of Diseases of the Eye. Boston: 1882. V. 42

Elements of Drawing, Exemplified in a variety of Figures and Sketches of Parts of the Human Form. Boston: 1818. V. 40

Remarks on Banks and Banking. Boston: 1840. V. 38

WILLIAMS, HENRY SMITH

Manuscripts, Inscriptions and Muniments, Oriental, Classical, Medieval and Modern. London & New York: 1901-02. V. 37

WILLIAMS, HENRY T.

Beautiful Homes. Or Hints in Household Furnishing. New York: 1878. V. 42

The Pacific Toursit: Williams' Illustrated Trans-Continental Guide of Travel, from the Atlantic to the Pacific Ocean. New York: 1877. V. 40

The Pacific Tourist; Willians' Illustrated Trans-Continental Guide of Travel, from the Atlantic to the Pacific Ocean, Containing Full Descriptions of Railroad Routes . . . A Complete Traveller's Guide of the Union and Central Pacific Railroads. New York: 1879. V. 37

WILLIAMS, HENRY W.

A Practical Guide to the Study of the Diseases of the Eye . . . Boston: 1862. V. 42

A Practical Guide to the Study of the Diseases of the Eye: their Medical and Surgical Treatments. Boston: 1873. V. 44

WILLIAMS, HUGH WILLIAM 1773-1829

The History of North Carolina. Philadelphia: 1812. V. 42

Select Views in Greece. London: 1829. V. 37; 40; 42

Travels in Italy, Greece, and the Ionian Islands. Edinburgh: 1820. V. 39; 40; 45

WILLIAMS, HUNTINGTON

The World's First Text Printing on Paper - 770 A.D., by Huntingham Williams. (North Hills: 1965). V. 37

WILLIAMS, IOLO A.

Early English Watercolours and Some Cognate Drawings by Artists Born Not Later than 1785. London: 1952. V. 38; 40

Points in Eighteenth Century Verse. London: 1934. V. 37; 40; 44; 46

WILLIAMS, J. DAVID

America Illustrated. Boston: 1883. V. 42

WILLIAMS, J. E.

Forty-Eight Years in the Panhandle of Texas. Austin: 1944. V. 42

WILLIAMS, J. F.

The Guide to Minnesota. St. Paul: 1868. V. 38; 44

WILLIAMS, J. F. LAKE

An Historical Account of Inventions and Discoveries in Those Arts and Sciences Which are of Utility or Ornament to Man, Lend Assistance to Human Comfort . . . Traced From Their Origin . . . London: 1820. V. 37; 42

WILLIAMS, J. J.

Isthmus of Tehuantepec: Being the Results of a Survey for a Railroad to Connect the Atlantic and Pacific Oceans, Made by the Scientific Commission Under the Direction of Major J. G. Barnard . . . New York: 1852. V. 42

WILLIAMS, J. R.

Out Our Way. New York: 1943. V. 44

WILLIAMS, J. WHITTRIDGE

Obstetrics. New York: 1906. V. 42

WILLIAMS, JAMES

The Rise and Fall of 'The Model Republic.' London: 1863. V. 38; 42; 43

WILLIAMS, JAMES LEON 1852-1932

The Home and Haunts of Shakespeare. New York: 1894. V. 39; 41

WILLIAMS, JAMES ROBERT 1888-

Cowboys Out Our Way . . . New York: 1951. V. 39

WILLIAMS, JANE

The Literary Women of England. London: 1861. V. 37; 39

WILLIAMS, JOE

TV Boxing Book. New York: 1954. V. 45

WILLIAMS, JOHN

An Account of Some Remarkable Ancient Ruins, Lately Discovered in the Highlands, and Northern Parts of Scotland . . . Edinburgh: 1777. V. 37

Awstralia A'r Cloddfeydd Aur. Dinbych: 1852. V. 43; 46

the Crisis of The Colonies Considered; With Some Observations on the Necessity of Properly Connecting Their Commerical interest with Great Britain and America . . . London: 1785. V. 46

Doctor John Williams' Last Legacy, or the Useful Family Herbal. N.P.: 1826. V. 39

Dr. John Williams' Last Legacy, or the Useful Family Herbal. N.P.: 1826. V. 46

The Eccentricites of John Edwin, Comedian. Dublin: 1791. V. 38; 40; 43

The Eccentricities of John Edwin, Comedian. London: 1791. V. 46

An Enquiry into the Truth of the Tradition Concerning the Discovery of America by Prince Madog Ab Owen Gwynedd, About the Year 1170. (with) Farther Observations on the Discovery of America by Prince Madog Ab Owen Gwynedd, About the Year 1170. London: 1791, 1792. V. 38

The Hamiltoniad. New York: 1865. V. 39; 44

The Hamiltoniad, or, The Extinguisher for the Royal Faction of New England. Boston: 1804. V. 37

Letters from the Highlands of Scotland, Addressed to G. C. M. Esq. Edinburgh: 1777. V. 39

A Narrative of Missionary Enterprises in the South Sea Islands. London: 1837. V. 38; 41

A Narrative of Missionary Enterprises in the South Sea Islands; with Remarks Upon the Natural History. London: 1839. V. 38; 41

The Natural History of the Mineral Kingdom. Edinburgh: 1789. V. 41

The Natural History of the Mineral Kingdom Relative to the Strata of Coal, Mineral Veisn and the Prevailing Strata of the Globe. Edinburgh: 1810. V. 38; 46

The New Brighton Guide. London: 1796. V. 40; 41; 45; 46

Northern Governments. London: 1777. V. 45

WILLIAMS, JOHN continued

The Pin-Basket to the Children of Thespis. London: 1797. V. 45

A Postscript to the New Bath Guide. London: 1790. V. 41

The Redeemed Captive Returning to Zion, or a Faithful History of Remarkable Occurrences in the Captivity and Deliverance of Mr. John Williams. Greenfield: 1800. V. 38

The Rise, Progress and Present State of the Northern Governments. London: 1777. V. 38; 40; 43; 45; 46

The Royal Academicians. London. V. 39

Sacred Allegories; or Allegorical Poems, Illustrative of Subjects Moral and Divine; to Which is Added an Anacreontic, on the Discovery of Vaccination; with an Epilogue to the Same. London: 1810. V. 43; 46

Truth Opposed to Fiction. London: 1793. V. 38

WILLIAMS, JOHN A.

Leaves from a Trooper's Diary. Philadelphia: 1869. V. 42

Night Song. New York: 1961. V. 39; 40; 44; 45

WILLIAMS, JOHN CAMP

An Oneida County Printer, William Williams, Printer, Publisher, Editor with a Bibliography of the Press at Utica, Oneida County, New York, from 1803-1838. New York: 1906. V. 37

WILLIAMS, JOHN D.

Deadly Adulteration and Slow Poisoning. London: 1830. V. 37

WILLIAMS, JOHN EDWARD 1922-

Nothing but the Night. Denver: 1948. V. 40; 42

WILLIAMS, JOHN G.

Adventures of a Seventeen-Year Old Lad and the Fortunes He Might Have Won. Boston: 1894. V. 43

WILLIAMS, JOHN JAY 1818-1904

Isthmus of Tehuantepec: Being the Results of a Survey for a Railroad to Connect the Atlantic and Pacific Oceans, Made by the Scientific Commission Under the Direction of Major J. G. Barnard, U. S. Engineers. New York: 1852. V. 38; 39

WILLIAMS, JOHN LEE

The Territory of Florida; or Sketches of the Topography, Civil and Natural History . . . New York: 1837. V. 41

The Territory of Florida; or, Sketches of the Topography, Civil and Natural History. New York: 1839. V. 43

A View of West Florida, Embracing Its Geography, Topography, etc. Philadelphia: 1827. V. 42

WILLIAMS, JOHN, physician

Dr. John Williams' Last Legacy, and Useful Family Guide. Boston: 1841. V. 45

WILLIAMS, JOHN S.

The American Pioneer, a Monthly Periodical . . . Logan Historical Society . . . Volume I. With Volume II. Cincinnati: 1844, 1843. V. 38; 40

The American Pioneer. A Monthly Periodical, Devoted to the Objects of the Logan Historical Society; or to Collecting and Publishing Sketches Relative to the Early Settlement and Successive Improvements of the Country. Chillicothe, Ohio: 1842. V. 37

WILLIAMS, JONATHAN

Amen Huzza Selah. 1960. V. 42

Amen Huzza Selah. 1960. V. 40

Aposiopeses (Odds & Ends). Minneapolis: 1988. V. 39; 40

Elegies and Celebrations. Highlands: 1962. V. 42

Elite/Elate Poems. Highlands: 1979. V. 37; 40; 42; 44

The Empire Finals at Verona. Highlands: 1959. V. 40; 42

Lord Stodge's Good Thing Guide to Over 100 English Delights. Denver: 1985. V. 37; 42

The Lucidities: Sixteen in Visionary Company. London: 1967. V. 46

Pairidaeza. Dentdale: 1975. V. 45

The Paragonian Declaration of Independence. N.P.: 1958. V. 39

The Patagonian Declaration of Independence. Urbana: 1971. V. 46

Plan of . . . for Forifying the Narrows Between Long and Staten Islands. New York: Printed for the: 1807. V. 37

Ripostes. Aspen: 1968. V. 37

Thermometrical Navigation. Philadelphia: 1799. V. 45

Who Is Little Enis? Corn Close: 1974. V. 40; 42

Who is Little Enis? 1974. V. 37

WILLIAMS, JOSEPH

Crossing the Plains in 1853 the Diary of Joseph Williams. Lodi: 1941. V. 40

Insanity, Its Causes, Prevention and Cure. London: 1852. V. 39; 45

Narrative of a Tour from the State of Indiana to The Oregon Country in . . . 1841-42. New York: 1921. V. 38; 40

WILLIAMS, JOSEPH J.

Psychic Phenomena of Jamaica. New York: 1934. V. 46

WILLIAMS, JOSEPH VINCENT

James Tate Williams: His Family and Recollections. Kingsport: 1938. V. 44

WILLIAMS, KENNETH P.

Lincoln Finds a General. New York: 1949-49. V. 44

WILLIAMS, L. S.

Family Education and Government a Discourse in the Choctaw Language. Boston: 1835. V. 39

WILLIAMS, LT. COL.

The Life and Times of the Late Duke of Wellington: by Lieut. Colonel Williams. London: 1860. V. 40

WILLIAMS, M.

An Elementary Grammar of the Sanscrit Language, Partly in the Roman Character . . . London: 1846. V. 38

WILLIAMS, MARGERY

The Velveteen Rabbit. Mount Vernon: 1974. V. 46

WILLIAMS, MARTHA NOGES

A Year in China; and a Narrative of Capture and Imprisonment, When Homeward Bound, On Board the Rebel Pirate Florida. New York: 1864. V. 40; 43; 45

WILLIAMS, MARY FLOYD

History of the San Francisco Committee of Vigilance of 1851; A Study of Social Control on the California Frontier in the Days of the Gold Rush. Berkeley: 1921. V. 41

Papers of the San Francisco Committee of Vigilance of 1851. Berkeley: 1919. V. 42

WILLIAMS, MARY P.

History of the San Francisco Committee of Vigilance of 1861 . . . Berkeley: 1921. V. 44

WILLIAMS, MATILDA

The United Family of Characters Portrayed from Real Life for the Use of Children. 1829. V. 45

WILLIAMS, O. W.

Pioneer Surveyor, Frontier Lawyer: the Personal Narrative of O. W. Williams, 1877-1902. El Paso: 1966. V. 40

WILLIAMS, OSCAR 1900-1964

A Garland for Dylan Thomas. New York: 1963. V. 43

A Little Treasury of Modern Poetry. New York: 1946. V. 44

The Man Coming Toward You. New York: 1940. V. 39; 43

WILLIAMS, PETER

Letters Concerning Education: Addressed to a Gentleman Entering at the University. London: 1785. V. 42

WILLIAMS, R.

Bulmer's Pomona. Hereford: 1987. V. 38; 40

WILLIAMS, R. H.

Massacre on the Nueces River, The Story of a Civil War Tragedy. Grand Rapids: 1954. V. 44

With the Border Ruffians: Memories of the Far West, 1852-1868 . . . London: 1907. V. 42; 44

WILLIAMS, R. S.

Reports of Explorations and Surveys, to Ascertain the Most Practicable and Economic Route for a Railroad . . . Washington: 1856. V. 45

WILLIAMS, REEVE

A Letter from a Merchant to a Member of Parliament . . . London: 1718. V. 45

WILLIAMS, ROBERT FOLKSTONE

The Luttrells; or, the Two Marriages. London: 1850. V. 42

Shakespeare and His Friends; or, The Golden Age of Merry England. Paris: 1838. V. 46

The Youth of Shakespeare. London: 1839. V. 43; 46

WILLIAMS, ROGER

A Key Into the Language of America, or an Help to the Language of the Natives in that Part of America Called New-England. Providence: 1827. V. 42; 44; 46

WILLIAMS, SAMUEL

The Natural and Civil History of Vermont. Walpole: 1794. V. 40; 42; 43

Natural and Civil History of Vermont. Burlington: 1809. V. 37; 38

WILLIAMS, SAMUEL COLE

Beginnings of West Tennessee In the Land of the Chickasaws 1541-1841. Johnson City: 1930. V. 42

History of the Lost State of Franklin. Johnson City: 1924. V. 38

WILLIAMS, SAMUEL COLE continued

History of the Lost State of Franklin. New York: 1933. V. 42

WILLIAMS, SAMUEL WELLS 1812-1884

The Middle Kingdom; a Survey of the Geography, Government, Education, Social Life, Arts, Religion &c. of the Chinese Empire and Its Inhabitants. New York: 1853. V. 37; 39

The Middle Kingdom. London: 1883. V. 45

The Middle Kingdom. New York: 1883. V. 42; 44

A Tonic Dictionary of the Chinese Language. Canton: 1856. V. 40

WILLIAMS, SIDNEY HERBERT

A Bibliography of the Writings of Lewis Carroll. London: 1924. V. 37; 42; 46

A Handbook of the Literature of the Rev. C. L. Dodgson. Oxford: 1931. V. 42; 45

WILLIAMS, SOLOMON 1700-1776

The More Excellent Way. London: 1742. V. 43

A Vindication of the Gospel-doctrine of Justifying Faith. Boston: 1746. V. 40

WILLIAMS, STEPHEN

American Medical Biography. Greenfield,: 1845. V. 38; 41; 42; 45

An Experimental History of Road Water in Wiltshire. London: 1731. V. 38

WILLIAMS, STEPHEN H.

Report of the Proceedings and Evidence in the Arbitration Between the King and Government of the Hawaiian Islands and Messrs. Ladd & Co. Before Messrs. Stephen H. Williams and James F. B. Marshall, Arbitrators Under Compact, 13th of July 1846 . . . Honolulu: 1846. V. 44

WILLIAMS, STEPHEN W.

A Biographical Memoir of the Rev. John Williams, First Minister of Deerfield, Massachusetts . . . Greenfield: 1837. V. 38; 40

WILLIAMS, T.

Academical Stenography. London: 1826. V. 44

WILLIAMS, T. H.

Devonshire Scenery; or Directions for Visiting the Most Picturesque Spots on the Eastern and Southern Coast from Sidmouth to Plymouth. Exeter: 1827. V. 38; 42

Picturesque Excursions in Devonshire and Cornwall. London: 1804. V. 44

WILLIAMS, TENNESSEE 1911-1983

Androgyne, Mon Amour. New York: 1977. V. 37; 38; 39; 41; 42; 43; 45; 46

Battle of Angels. 1945. V. 43

Battle of Angels. Murray: 1945. V. 37; 38; 39; 45

Blue Mountain Ballads. New York: 1946. V. 42

Cat on a Hot Tin Roof. New York: 1955. V. 45

Cat on a Hot Tin Roof. London: 1956. V. 43

Dragon Country. New York: 1970. V. 46

Eight Mortal Ladies Possessed. New York: 1974. V. 46

The Glass Menagerie. New York: 1945. V. 43; 46

Grand. New York: 1964. V. 37; 38; 40; 41; 42; 45

Grand. New York: 1965. V. 42

Hard Candy: A Book of Stories. New York. V. 46

Hard Candy: A Book of Stories. 1954. V. 39

Hard Candy. New York: 1954. V. 38; 43; 46

In the Winter of Cities. New York: 1956. V. 37

It Happened the Day the Sun Rose. Los Angeles: 1981. V. 38

The Knightly Quest. New York: 1966. V. 46

Letters to Donald Windham 1940-1965. Verona: 1976. V. 43; 46

Memoirs. Garden City: 1975. V. 37; 43

Memoirs. New York: 1975. V. 39

The Milk Train Doesn't Stop Here Anymore. New York: 1964. V. 38

Moise and the World of Reason. New York: 1975. V. 37; 38; 39; 41; 43; 45; 46

The Night of the Iguana. New York: 1962. V. 43; 44

One Arm and Other Stories. New York: 1948. V. 44

One Arm and Other Stories. Norfolk: 1948. V. 38; 45; 46

The Remarkable Rooming-House of Mme. Le Monde. New York: 1984. V. 38

The Roman Spring of Mrs. Stone. 1950. V. 45

The Roman Spring of Mrs. Stone. New York: 1950. V. 37; 38; 39; 43; 44; 45; 46

The Rose Tattoo. Norfolk: 1950. V. 38; 40

The Rose Tattoo. New York: 1951. V. 39; 44; 46

Selected Plays. Franklin Center: 1980. V. 43

Steps Must Be Gentle. New York: 1980. V. 37; 39; 42; 43; 45; 46

A Streetcar Named Desire. New York: 1982. V. 39; 43; 46

A Street Car Named Desire. 1947. V. 46

A Streetcar Named Desire. 1947. V. 39

A Streetcar Named Desire. New York: 1947. V. 37; 38; 43; 45; 46

Suddenly Last Summer. New York: 1958. V. 46

Summer and Smoke. New York: 1948. V. 46

Tennessee Williams' Letters to Donald Wyndham: 1940-1965. V. 39

Tennessee Williams' Letters to Donald Windham 1940-1965. New York: (1977). V. 37

Tennessee Williams' Letters to Donald Wyndham. 1940-1965. V. 45

The Theatre of Tennessee Williams. New York: 1976. V. 39

This Property is Condemned. Beverley Hills. V. 37

Twenty-Seven Wagons Full of Cotton and other One-Act Plays. Norfolk: 1945. V. 38

The Two Character Play. 1969. V. 45

The Two Character Play. 1969. V. 46

The Two Character Play. 1969. V. 44

The Two Character Play. 1969. V. 42

The Two-Character Play. 1969. V. 40

The Two-Character Play. 1969. V. 41

The Two Character Play. New York: 1969. V. 38; 43; 46

Vieux Carre. New York: 1979. V. 43

Williams' Letters to Donald Windham. New York: 1977. V. 46

WILLIAMS, THEODORE

A Catalogue of the Spendid and Valuable Library of the Rev. Theodore Williams. London: 1827. V. 39

WILLIAMS, THOMAS

A Brief Memoir of Her Late Majesty Queen Charlotte. London: 1819. V. 37; 39

Fiji and the Fijians . . . and Missionary Labours Among the Cannibals . . . London: 1870. V. 43

WILLIAMS, THOMAS WALTER

Original Precedents in Conveyancing, Settled and Approved by the Most Eminent Conveyancers . . . London: 1788. V. 40

WILLIAMS, W.

Appleton's Southern and Western Traveller's Guide. New York: 1855. V. 46

WILLIAMS, WALTER

A History of Northeast Missouri. Chicago: 1913. V. 46

A History of Northwest Missouri. Chicago: 1915. V. 37

Missouri, Mother of the West. Chicago: 1930. V. 38

WILLIAMS, WELLINGTON

Appleton's Southern and Western Traveller's Guide. New York: 1850. V. 38

The Traveller's and Tourist's Guide Through the United States . . . By Railroad, Steamboat, Stage and Canal . . . Accompanied by an Entirely New and Authentic Map of the Untied States Including California, Oregon . . . Philadelphia: 1855. V. 37

WILLIAMS, WILLIAM 1800-1879

A Dictionary of the New Zealand Language. London: 1871. V. 39; 41

A Dictionary of the New Zealand Language. Auckland: 1892. V. 39

A Dictionary of the New Zealand Language. London: 1852. V. 37

The Duty and Interest of a People, Among Whom Religion Has Been Planted, to Continue Steadfast and Sincere in the Profession and Practice of It . . . Boston: 1736. V. 45

The Great Salvation Revealed and Offered in the Gospel Explained, and an Hearty Acceptance of It Urged in Several Sermons on hebrews II. 3. Boston: 1717. V. 41

The Head of the Rock, a Welsh Landskip. London: 1775. V. 40

Journal of the Life, Travels and Gospel Labours, of William Williams, Dec. A. Minister of the Society of Friends. Cincinnati: 1828. V. 38; 39; 40; 42

The Journal of Llewellin Penrose, A Seaman. London: 1815. V. 37

The Life and Times of the Late Duke of Wellington. London: 1853-56. V. 46

Oxonia Depicta Collegiorum.. Oxford: 1732-33. V. 38

WILLIAMS, WILLIAM, astrologer

Occult Physick, or the Three Principles in Nature Anatomized by a Philosophical Operation, Taken from Experience, in Three Books. London: 1660. V. 42

WILLIAMS, WILLIAM CARLOS 1883-1963

Al Que Auiere! Boston: 1917. V. 37; 38; 40; 41; 42; 43; 44; 46

The Autobiography. New York: 1951. V. 37; 46

The Broken Span. New York: 1941. V. 39

The Build-Up. New York: 1952. V. 46

The Clouds, Aigeltinger, Russia and Other Verses. 1948. V. 40

The Clouds, Aigeltinger, Russia &c. Poems. Aurora: 1948. V. 42

The Cod Head. San Francisco: 1932. V. 37; 39; 44; 46

The Complete Collected Poems of . . . 1906-1938. Norfolk: 1938. V. 37; 38; 39; 44

WILLIAMSON, HENRY continued

The Story of a Norfolk Farm. London: 1941. V. 46

Tarka the Otter, His Joyful Water-Life and Death in the Country of the Two Rivers. 1927. V. 44

Tarka the Otter. London: 1927. V. 37; 38; 40; 42

The Village Book. London: 1930. V. 37; 40; 46

The West Flanders Plain. London: 1929. V. 37

WILLIAMSON, HUGH

The Book. Numbers One to Six. London: 1954 & 1955. V. 40

The History of North Carolina. Philadelphia: 1812. V. 37; 41; 42; 44; 45

Observations on the Climate in Different Parts of America . . . . New York: 1811. V. 38; 45

WILLIAMSON, HUGH ROSS

Gods and Mortals in Love. London: 1936. V. 46

WILLIAMSON, J.

Darker than You Think. 1948. V. 44

The Girl from Mars. 1929. V. 39

The Legion of Space. 1947. V. 43

WILLIAMSON, J. A.

The Voyages of the Cabots and the English Discovery of North America . . . London: 1929. V. 39; 42; 44; 45; 46

WILLIAMSON, JOHN

The British Angler. London: 1740. V. 44

Ferns of Kentucky . . . Louisville: 1878. V. 44

The Narrative of a Commuted Pensioner. Montreal: 1838. V. 46

WILLIAMSON, JOHN P.

English Dakota Vocabulary. Santee Agency: 1871. V. 43

WILLIAMSON, JOSEPH

A Bibliography of the State of Maine from the Earliest Period to 1891. Portland: 1896. V. 37; 39; 43

WILLIAMSON, MARY LYNN HARRISON

The Life of Gen. Thomas J. Jackson. Richmond: 1899. V. 38; 42

WILLIAMSON, PASSMORE

Case of Passmore Williamson. Philadelphia: 1856. V. 42

WILLIAMSON, PETER

French and Indian Cruelty; Exemplified in the Life and Various Vicissitudes of Fortune, of Peter Williamson, a Disbanded Soldier, . . . York: 1758. V. 44

The Travels of Peter Williason, Among the Different Nations and Tribes of Savage Indians in America. Edinburgh: 1768. V. 38

WILLIAMSON, R. S.

Report Upon the Removal of Blossom Rock, in San Francisco Harbor, California. Washington: 1871. V. 38; 39

Reports of Explorations and Surveys, to Ascertain the Most Practicable and Economic Route for a Railroad. Washington: 1856. V. 44

WILLIAMSON, R. T.

Diseases of the Spinal Cord. London: 1911. V. 42

WILLIAMSON, ROBERT W.

The Social and Political Systems of Central Polynesia. Cambridge: 1924. V. 43

WILLIAMSON, THOMAS

The Complete Angler's Vade Mecum. London: 1808. V. 37; 39; 40

Foreign Field Sports, Fisheries, Sporting Anecdotes &c. from Drawings by Messrs. Howitt, Atkinson, Clark, Manskirch &c. London: 1818. V. 40

Illustrations of Indian Field Sports. London: 1892. V. 39; 40; 46

Oriental Field Sports . . . London: 1807. V. 44

Oriental Field Sports: Being a Complete, Detailed and Accurate Description of Wild Sports of the East. London: 1808. V. 39

Oriental Field Sports . . . London: 1819. V. 45

Oriental Field Sports . . . London: ?1828. V. 42

WILLIAMSON, WILLIAM CRAWFORD

On the Recent Foraminifera of Great Britain. London: 1848. V. 43

WILLIBALD, CHRISTOPH

Orfeo ed Euridice. Bangor: 1990. V. 44

WILLICH, ANTHONY FLORIAN MADIGNER

Lectures on Diet and Regimen; Being a Systematic Inquiry Into the Most Rational Means of Preserving Health and Prolonging Life. London: 1809. V. 41; 43

WILLICH, ANTHONY FLORIAN MADINGER

The Domestic Encyclopedia. London: 1802. V. 38; 41

The Domestic Encyclopaedia . . . Philadelphia: 1804. V. 43

The Domestic Encyclopedia . . . Philadelphia: 1804, 1803. V. 42

Elements of the Critical Philosophy . . . London: 1798. V. 45

Lectures on Diet and Regimen; Being a Systematic Inquiry Into the Most Rational Means of Preserving Health and Prolonging Life. London: 1799. V. 38; 40; 42; 45; 46

Lectures on Diet and Regimen: Being a Systematic Inquiry into the Most Rational Means of Preserving Health and Prolonging Life. London: 1800. V. 40

WILLINKS, DANIEL

Amsterdamsche Buitensingel Nevens de Omleggende Dorpen . . . Amsterdam: 1738. V. 38

WILLIS, ALFRED

London in Miniature. With Engravings of Its Public Buildings and Antiquities. With 47 full page engraved views. London: 1818. V. 37

WILLIS, B.

Notitia Parliamentaria; or, an History of the Counties, Cities and Boroughs in England and Wales. London: 1730. V. 45

WILLIS, BAILEY

Northern Patagonia Character and Resources. 1914. V. 39

Northern Patagonia, Character and Resources. 1914. V. 42

WILLIS, BROWNE 1682-1760

An History of the Mitred Parliamentary Abbies, and Conventual Cathedral Churches, Shewing the Times of Their Respective Foundations . . . Together with a Catalogue of Their Abbats, Priors &c. London: 1718-19. V. 41

Notitia Parliamentaria: or, an History of the Counties, Cities and Boroughs in England and Wales. London: 1715-16, 1750. V. 37

A Survey of the Cathedral Church of St Asaph. London: 1720. V. 38; 45

WILLIS, CHARLES WRIGHT

Army Life of an Illinois Soldier, Including a Day by Day Record of Sherman's March to the Sea. Washington: 1906. V. 38

WILLIS, H. PARKER

Foreign Banking Systems. London: 1929. V. 41

WILLIS, IRENE COOPER

The Authorship of Wurthering Heights. London: 1936. V. 45

WILLIS, JAMES

On the Poor Laws of England. The various Plans and Opinions of Judge Blackstone, Swift, Addison . . . Steward, Eden, Ptt . . . Colquhoun, Weyland, Bate, Rose, Monck, Malthus, Whitebread, and the . . . London: 1808. V. 37

The Universe: a Poem. London: 1821. V. 45

WILLIS, JOHN

Memonica; or, the Art Memory, Drained out of the pure Fountains of Art & Nature. Digested into Three Books. Also, a Physical Treatise of cherishing Natural Memory; diligently collected out of divers Learned Mens Writings. London: 1661. V. 37; 44

WILLIS, JOHN R.

Careton, a Tale of Seventeen Hundred and Seventy-Six. Philadlephia: 1841. V. 39

WILLIS, NATHANIEL PARKER 1806-1867

American Scenery; or Land, Lake and River Illustrations of a Transatlantic Nature. London: 1840. V. 37; 39; 42; 46

American Scenery; or Land, Lake, and River. London: 1840. V. 37

Canadian Scenery. London: 1840-42. V. 41; 42

Canadian Scenery Illustrated in a Series of Views. 1842. V. 41

Canadian Scenery Illustrated. London: 1842. V. 41; 42; 43; 44; 46

Canadian Scenery. Toronto: 1967. V. 44

The Corsair. New York: 1839-40. V. 45

Health Trip to the Tropics. New York: 1853. V. 37

Letters From Under a Bridge, and Poems. London: 1840. V. 42

Out-Doors at Idlewild, or the Shaping of a Home on the Banks of the Hudson. New York: 1855. V. 37

The Poems . . . of . . . New York: 1849. V. 38

Romance of Travel, Comprising Tales of Five Lands. New York: 1840. V. 43

Rural Letters and Other Records. New York: 1849. V. 42

Scenery and Antiquities of Ireland. London. V. 38

The Scenery and Antiquities of Ireland. London. V. 43

The Scenery and Antiquities of Ireland. London: 1841. V. 39; 41

Scenery & Antiquities of Ireland. Illustrated from drawings by W.H. Bartlett; the literary portion of the work by N.P. Willis, & J. Stirling Coyne. London: n.d. V. 37

WILLIS, NATHANIEL PARKER 1806-1867 continued

Sketches. Boston: 1827. V. 38

WILLIS, PETER

Charles Bridgeman and the English Landscape Garden. London: 1977. V. 41

WILLIS, R.

Remarks on the Architecture of the Middle AGes, Especially of Italy. Cambridge: 1835. V. 44

WILLIS, RICHARD

The Bishop of Salisbury's Speech in the House of Lords Upon the Third Reading of the Bill to Inflict Pains and Penalties on Francis (late) Bishop of Rochester, the 15 of May, 1723. London: 1723. V. 39

WILLIS, ROBERT

The Architectural History of the University of Cambridge and the Colleges of Cambridge and Eton. Cambridge: 1988. V. 39

An Attempt to Analyse the Automaton Chess Player, of Mr. De Kempelen. London: 1821. V. 45

Servetus and Calvin: London: 1877. V. 45

William Harvey: a History of the Discovery of the Circulation of the Blood. London: 1878. V. 42; 46

WILLIS, ROBERT DARLING

Philosophical Sketches of the Principles of Society and Government. London: 1796. V. 42

WILLIS, THOMAS

V. 37

Affectionum Quae dicuntur Hystericae et Hypochondriacae Patholgia Spasmodice Vindicata Contra Responsionem Epistolarem Nathanael, Highmori, M.D. Lvgd. Batav.: 1671. V. 45

Anatomy of the Brain and Nerves. Montreal: 1965. V. 39; 40; 42; 43

De Anima Brutorum Aquae Hominis Vitalis ac Sensitiva est, Exercitationes Duae. London: 1672. V. 39

De Anima Brutorum Quae Hominis Vitalis ac Sensitiva est, Exercitationes Duae. Oxford: 1672. V. 41; 45

De Anima Brutorum Quae Hominis Vitalis ac Sensitiva est, Exercitationes Duae. Oxonii: 1672. V. 37

De Anima Brutorum Quae Hominis Vitalis ac Sensitiva est, Exercitationes Duae . . . Amstelodami: 1674. V. 37

Dr. Willis's Practice of Physick, Being the Whole Works of . . . London: 1684-83. V. 42; 43

Dr. Willis's Practice of Physick, being the Whole Works of that Renowned and Famous Physician: containing these Eleven Several Treatises, viz. I. Of Fermentations. II. Of Fevers. III. Of Urines. IV. Of the Accension of the Blood . . . London: 1984-(1683). V. 37

The London Practice of Physick . . . London: 1685. V. 40; 41

Opera Omnia . . . Geneva: 1676. V. 42

Opera Omnia . . . Coloniae Allorrogum. Geneva: 1676-77. V. 43

Opera Omnia . . . Studio et Opera Geraldi Blassi. Amsterdam: 1682. V. 41; 44

Opera Omnia Nitidius Quam Unquam Hactenus Edita . . . Studio & Opera Gerardi Blasii . . . Venetiis: 1708. V. 46

The Remaining Medical Works . . . London: 1679-81. V. 40

WILLIS, THOMAS T.

De Anima Brutorum Quae Hominis Vitalis Ac Sensitiva est, Exercitationes Duae. Amsterdam: 1674. V. 40

WILLIS, W. A.

The Downfall of Lobengula: the Cause, History and Effect of the Matabeli War. V. 42

The Downfall of Lobengula: the Cause, History and Effect of the Matabelli War. 1894. V. 39

WILLIS, WILLIAM

A Business Directory of the Subscribers to the New Map of Maine, with a Brief History and Description of the State. Portland: 1862. V. 44

The History of Portland, from 1632 to 1864. Portland: 1865. V. 42

WILLISON, JOHN

A Sermon Preached Before His Majesty's High Commissioner to the General Assembly of the Church of Scotland, in the High Church of Edinburgh, On the 5th of May 1734. Edinburgh: 1734. V. 45

WILLIUS, FREDERICK A.

Cardiac Classics: a Collection of Classic Works in the Heart and Circulation . . . St. Louis: 1941. V. 38; 45

WILLLOCK, JOHN

The Voyages and Adventures of John Willock, Mariner. Philadelphis: 1798. V. 43

WILLMOTT, E.

The Genus Rosa. London: 1910-14. V. 40; 43

The Genus Rosa. London: 1911-14. V. 44

WILLMOTT, J. J.

Long Course of Instruction and Notes on Gunnery. Shoeburyness: 1867-68. V. 44

WILLMOTT, ROBERT ARIS

Conversations at Cambridge. London: 1836. V. 37

English Sacred Poetry of the 16th, 17th, 18th and 19th Centuries. London: 1862. V. 39

The Poets of the Nineteenth Century. London: 1857. V. 39; 40; 42

The Poets of the Nineteenth Century. London: 1866. V. 39

Summer Time in the Country. London: 1858. V. 42

WILLOCK, FRANKLIN J.

The Dalmation. New York: 1927. V. 43

WILLOCK, JOHN

Voyages to Various Parts of the World, and Remarks on Different Countries in Europe, Africa and America with the Customs and Manners of the Inhabitants. Penrith: 1789. V. 43

WILLOUGHBY, CHARLES C.

Antiquities of the New England Indians - With Notes on the Ancient Cultures of the Adjacent Territory. Cambridge: 1935. V. 39

WILLOUGHBY, EDWIN ELIOTT

The Making of the King James Bible. Los Angeles: 1956. V. 41; 43; 44; 46

WILLOUGHBY, HANNAH MARY RATHBONE

So Much of the Diary of Lady Willoughby as Relates to Her Domestic History . . . . (and) Some Further Portions of the Diary of Lady Willoughby Which do Relate to Her Domestic History . . . London: 1844-48. V. 45

WILLOUGHBY, HOWARD

Australian Pictures Drawn with Pen and Pencil. London: 1886. V. 39; 41

WILLOUGHBY, HUGH L.

Across the Everglades: a Canoe Journey of Exploration. Philadelphia: 1898. V. 41; 44

WILLOUGHBY, JOHN C.

East Africa and Its Big Game. London: 1889. V. 38

WILLOUGHBY, LADY

So Much of the Diary of Lady Willoughby as Relates ro Her Domestic History. London: 1844/48. V. 45

WILLS, ALFRED

'The Eagle's Nest' in the Valley of Sixth; a Summer Home Among the Alps; Together with Some Excursions Among the Great Glaciers. London: 1860. V. 40

Wanderings Among the High Alps. London: 1856. V. 40; 41; 44

WILLS, BROWNE

Notitia Parliamentaria. London: 1715. V. 40

WILLS, CHARLES JAMES

The Pit Town Coroner: a Family Mystery. London: 1888. V. 41

WILLS, JAMES

Letters on Philosophy of Unbelief. London: 1835. V. 43

WILLS, JESSE

Early and Late: Fugitive Poems and Others. Nashville: 1959. V. 45

WILLS, W. A.

The Downfall of Lobengula: The Cause, History and Effect of the Matabeli War. London & South Africa: 1894. V. 41

WILLS, W. H.

Poets Wit and Humour. London;: 1861. V. 39; 44

WILLS, WILLIAM

A Successful Exploration through the Interior of Australia, from Melbourne to the Gulf of Carpentaria. London: 1863. V. 41

WILLS, WILLIAM HENRY

Old Leaves; Gathered from Household Worlds. London: 1860. V. 40; 43

WILLSHIRE, WILLIAM HUGHES

An Introduction to the Study and Collection of Ancient Prints. London: 1874. V. 40

WILLSON, ARTHUR A.

Public Travel. The Law Relating To: Bicyclists, Horsemen, Pedestrians . . . Toronto: 1897. V. 45

WILLSON, BECKLES

The Great Company. Being a History of the Honourable Company of Merchants' Adventurers Trading into Hudson's Bay. Toronto: 1899. V. 40; 42; 45

WILLSON, BECKLES continued

The Great Company (1667-1871); Being a History of the Honourable Company of Merchants-Adventurers Trading into Hudson's Bay. London: 1900. V. 43

WILLSON, DAVID

The Impressions of the Mind. Toronto: 1835. V. 44; 45

WILLSON, HUGH BOWLBY

Currency, or the Fundamental Principles of Monetary Science Postulated, Explained and Applied. New York: 1882. V. 44

WILLSON, JAMES

Volunteer Chart. The Volunteer Army of 1806. London: 1807. V. 38

WILLUGHBY, FRANCIS

De Historia Piscium. Oxford: 1686. V. 40; 43

The Ornithology of Francis Willughby. London: 1678. V. 37; 39; 43; 45

WILLUGHBY SOCIETY

Publications. London: 1880-84. V. 37

WILLY, COLETTE

L'Ingenue Libertine. Paris: 1926. V. 38

WILLYAMS, COOPER

Account of the Campaign in the West Indies in the Year 1794. London: 1796. V. 41; 42

A Selection of Views in Egypt, Palestine, Rhodes, Italy, Inorca and Gibraltar . . . London: 1822. V. 37; 39; 42; 46

A Voyage Up the Mediterranean in His Majesty's Ship the Swiftshure, One of the Squadron Under the Command of Rear Admiral Sir Horatio Nelson . . . London: 1802. V. 37; 44; 45; 46

WILLYMOTT, WILLIAM

The Peculiar Use and Signification of Certain Words in the Latin Tongue; or a Collection of Observations, Wherein the Elegant and Commonly Unobserv'd Sense of Very Near Nine Hundred Common Latin Words . . . London: 1767. V. 46

The Peculiar Use and Signification of Certain Words in the Latin Tongue . . . Eton: 1790. V. 41

WILMAN, M.

The Rock Engravings of Griqualand West and Bechuanaland, South Africa. Cambridge: 1933. V. 37

WILMER, JOHN

The Case of John Wilmore Truly and Impartially Related. London: 1682. V. 37; 38; 40; 44

WILMER, L. ALLISTON

History and Roster of Maryland Volunteers, War of 1861-5. Baltimore: 1898. V. 42

WILMER, LAMBERT A.

The Life, Travels and Adventures of Ferdinand De Soto, Discoverer of the Mississippi. Philadelphia: 1859. V. 38

WILMER, WILLIAM HOLLAND

Atlas Fundus Oculi. New York: 1934. V. 40; 42

WILMINGTON. (NORTH CAROLINA). SAFETY COMMITTEE

Proceedings of the Safety Committee: for the Town of Wilmington, N.C. from 1774 to 1776. Raleigh: 1844. V. 45

WILMOT, A.

History of the Colony of the Cape of Good Hope From Its Discovery to the Year 1819 . . . from 1820 to 1868 . . . Cape town: 1869. V. 44

WILMOT, JOHN

Collected Works of John Wilmot, Earl of Rochester. London: 1926. V. 41

The Life of the Rev John Hough, D.D. London: 1812. V. 44

Memoirs of the Life of the Right Honourable Sir John Eardley Wilmot, Knt, Late Lord Chief Justice of the Court of Common Pleas, and One of His Majesty's Most Honourable Privy Council . . . London: 1811. V. 38; 42; 46

The Miscellaneous Works of the Right Honourable Earls of Rochester and Roscommon. With the Memoirs of the Life and Character of the late Earl of Rochester . . . by Mons. St. Evremont. To which is added, a curious collection of original . . . London: 1707. V. 37

WILMOT, JOHN EARDLEY

Memoirs of the Life with Some Original Letters. London: 1802. V. 38

WILMOT: or The Pupil of Folly. Dublin: 1782. V. 38

WILMOT, R. J.

American Camelia Yearbook. Gainsville: 1946-71. V. 37

WILNER, MERTON M.

Niagara Frontier, a Narrative and Documentary History. Chicago: 1931. V. 38; 42

WILSHIRE, WILLIAM HUGHES

An Introduction to the Study and Collection of Ancient Prints. London: 1877. V. 46

WILSHIRE'S Resolution, Presented with the Contributions of Divers Gentlemen to His Majesties Commisioners at Oxford. Oxford: 1642. V. 45

WILSON, A.

The Flora of Westmorland. London: 1938. V. 43; 45

WILSON, A. N.

Gentlemen in England. London: 1985. V. 40

Kindly Light. London: 1979. V. 40

The Sweets of Pimlico. London: 1977. V. 38

WILSON, ADRIAN

. . . Highest Form of Flatery . . . with a Leaf from the 1497 Edition of the Pirated Nuremberg Chronicle printed at Augsburg. Santa Cruz: 1982. V. 41; 46

The Making of the Nuremberg Chronicle. Amsterdam: 1976. V. 39; 46

The Making of the Nuremberg Chronicle . . . Amsterdam: 1978. V. 46

A Medieval Mirror. Berkeley: 1984. V. 40; 41

More Printing for Theater, a Portfolio of Ephemera. San Francisco: 1987. V. 37; 38; 40; 43; 45

Printing for Theater. San Francisco: 1957. V. 44; 45

The Stadium. Middletown: 1951. V. 44

The Work and Play of Adrian Wilson. Austin: 1983. V. 39; 40

WILSON, ALEXANDER 1766-1813

American Ornithology, or, the Natural History of the Birds of the United States. Philadelphia: 1808-14. V. 40

American Ornithology. Edinburgh: 1831. V. 39

American Ornithology; or, the Natural History of the Birds of the United States. London: 1832. V. 45

American Ornithology, or The Natural History of the Birds of the United States, with a Continuation by C. L. Bonaparte. London & Edinburgh: 1832. V. 41

American Ornithology or the Natural History of the Birds of the United States. London: 1875. V. 38

American Ornithology. London: 1876. V. 39; 41; 45

American Ornithology: Or the Natural History of the Birds of the United States. London: (c. 1875). V. 37

Poems, Chiefly in the Scottish Dialect. London: 1816. V. 39

Wilson's American Ornithology. Boston: 1840. V. 39

WILSON, ALEXANDER & SONS

A Specimen of Printing Type. Glasgow: 1783. V. 44

WILSON, ALEXANDER JOHNSTONE

The Resources of Modern Countries. London: 1878. V. 40; 43; 46

WILSON, AMOS

The Pennsylvania Hermit. Philadelphia: 1839. V. 40

The Sweets of Solitude! Boston: 1822. V. 45

WILSON & CHAMBERS

The Land of Burns. London: 1804. V. 44

WILSON & SONS

A Specimen of Printing Types. Glasgow: 1783. V. 40

WILSON, ANDREW

The Abode of Snow, Observations on a Journey from Chinese Tibet to the Indian Caucasus . . . Edinburgh: 1875. V. 45; 46

The 'Ever-Victorious Army': A History of the Chinese Campaign Under Lt. Col. C. G. Gordon, C. B., R. E. and of the Suppression of the Tai-Ping Rebellion. Edinburgh & London: 1868. V. 41

Naval History of the United Kingdom, Including an Account of the Naval and Martitime Transactions of the Phoenicians . . . Cork: 1807. V. 38; 41

WILSON, ANGUS

The World of Charles Dickens. London: 1970. V. 37

WILSON, ARNOLD T.

A Bibliography of Persia. Oxford: 1930. V. 45

Loyalties Mesopotamia 1914-1917. London: 1930. V. 44

Loyalties Mesopotamia 1914-1917. and Loyalties Mesopotamia 1917-1920. Oxford: 1936. V. 45

WILSON, ARTHUR

The Five Yearaes of King James, or the Condition of the State of England and the Relation it Had on Other Provinces. London: 1643. V. 37

The History of Great Britain, Being the Life and Reign of King James the First. London: 1653. V. 41

The Inconstant Lady . . . Oxford: 1814. V. 37; 46

The Swisser. Paris: 1904. V. 40

WILSON, AUGUSTA JANE EVANS

Inez: a Tale of the Alamo. New York: 1855. V. 37; 38; 40

WILSON, BENJAMIN

Observations Upon Lightning, and the Method of Securing Buildings from Its Effects, in a Letter to Sir Charles Frederick, etc. London: 1773. V. 46

WILSON, C. BARON, MRS.

Popularity; and the Destinies of Woman; (Tales of the World). London: 1842. V. 37

WILSON, C. H.

The Post Chaise Companion or Travellers Directory Through Ireland. Dublin: 1803. V. 37

WILSON, CARROLL A.

Thirteen Author Collections of the Nineteenth Century and Five Centuries of Familiar Quotations. New York: 1950. V. 38

WILSON, CHARIS

The Cats of Wildcat Hill. New York: 1947. V. 41

WILSON, CHARLES

The Survey of Western Palestine: Special Papers on Topography, Archaeology, Manners and Customs, etc. London: 1881. V. 44

The Survey of Western Palestine: Special Papers on Topography, Archaeology, Manners and Customs, etc. London: 1881. V. 37

WILSON, CHARLES H.

The Wanderer in America: or, Truth at Home.. V. 44

The Wanderer in America or Truth at Home. Thirsk: 1822. V. 38; 45

The Wanderer in America. Thirsk: 1872. V. 39

WILSON, CHARLES HENRY

Brookiana. London: 1804. V. 43

Swiftiana. London: 1804. V. 40; 41; 42; 45

WILSON, CHARLES WILLIAM 1836-1905

Picturesque Palestine, Sinai and Egypt. London. V. 40

Picturesque Palestine, Sinai and Egypt. London. V. 38

Picturesque Palestine: Sinai and Egypt. London: 1850. V. 38

Picturesque Palestine. New York: 1881. V. 40

Picturesque Palestine, Sinai and Egypt. 1880-1884. V. 37

The Recovery of Jerusalem. A Narrative of Exploration and Discovery in the City and the Holy Land. London: 1871. V. 37; 39

The Recovery of Jerusalem. New York: 1871. V. 43

Report on the Indian Tribes Inhabiting the Country in the Vicinity of the 49th Parallel of North Latitude. London: 1866. V. 45

WILSON, CLAUDE

Mountaineering. London: 1893. V. 39

WILSON, COLIN

Encyclopaedia of Murder. London: 1961. V. 41

Strange Powers. London: 1973. V. 44

Tree by Tolkien. London: 1973. V. 41

Tree by Tolkien. N.P.: 1973. V. 43

WILSON, COLONEL

Picturesque Palestine, Sinai and Egypt. New York: 1881-83. V. 43

WILSON, DANIEL

The Archaeology and Prehistoric Annals of Scotland. Edinburgh: 1851. V. 45

Letters from an Absent Brother, Containing Some Account of a Tour through Parts of the Netherlands, Switzerland, Northern Italy and France, in the Summer of 1823. London: 1824. V. 42; 44

Memorials of Edinburgh in the Olden Time. Edinburgh: 1872. V. 38

WILSON, DAVID

The Life of Jane McCrea, with an Account of Burgoyne's Expedition in 1777. New York: 1853. V. 42; 46

WILSON, EDMUND 1895-1972

Axel's Castle. New York: 1931. V. 44

The Boys in the Back Room. San Francisco: 1941. V. 37; 40; 41; 42; 44; 46

A Christmas Delirium. Boston: 1955. V. 38; 40

Devil Take the Hindmost - a Year of the Slump. New York & London: 1932. V. 38

Discordant Encounters. New York: 1926. V. 39

Europe Without Baedeker. New York: 1947. V. 38; 40

I Thought of Daisy. New York: 1929. V. 37; 39; 40; 41; 42

Memoirs of Hecate County. New York: 1946. V. 39; 40

Note-Books of Night. San Francisco: 1942. V. 41; 42

The Rats of Rutland Grange. New York: 1974. V. 39; 46

This Room and This Gin and These Sandwiches. New York: 1937. V. 39; 42

To the Finland Station - a Study in the Writing and Acting of History. London: 1941. V. 43

The Triple Thinkers: Ten Essays on Literture. New York: 1938. V. 39

The Undertaker's Garland. New York: 1922. V. 39

The Wound and the Bow. Boston: 1941. V. 42

The Wound and the Bow - Seven Studies in Literature. London: 1941. V. 40

WILSON, EDMUND BEECHER 1856-1939

The Cell in Development and Heredity. New York: 1925. V. 38

WILSON, EDWARD JAMES

The Artist's and Mechanic's Encyclopaedia. Newcastle-upon-Tyne: 1830? V. 41

WILSON, EDWARD L.

Wilson's Photographics: A series of Lessons Accompanied by Notes On all the Processes Which are Needful in the Art of Photography. New York: 1881. V. 39; 41; 44

Wilson's Photographics: A Series of Lessons . . . Philadelphia: 1881. V. 37; 44

Wilson's Quarter Century in Photography. New York: 1887. V. 39; 41; 44

WILSON, ELIJA N.

Among the Shoshones. Salt Lake City: 1910. V. 39; 40; 41; 42; 45

WILSON, ELIJAH N.

'Uncle Nick' Among the Shoshones. Salt Lake City: 1910. V. 38

WILSON, ENID

A Lakeland Diary. 1985. V. 38

WILSON, ERASMUS 1809-1884

The Eastern, or, Turkish Bath; with Its History, Revival in Britain and Appliation to the Purposes of Health. New York: 1867. V. 46

On Diseases of the Skin. London: 1847. V. 42

On Diseases of the Skin. Philadelphia: 1847. V. 46

On Diseases of the Skin. Philadelphia: 1847, 1863. V. 40

On Diseases of the Skin. Philadelphia: 1852. V. 44; 45; 46

A Practical and Theoretical Treatise on the Diagnosis, Pathology & Treatment of Diseases of the Skin, Arranged According to a Natural System of Classification, and Preceded by an Outline of the Anatomy and Physiology of the Skin. Philadelphia: 1843. V. 39

WILSON, ERNEST A.

Plant Hunting. Boston: 1927. V. 38

WILSON, ERNEST H.

Aristocrats of the Trees. Boston: 1930. V. 46

China, Mother of Gardens. Boston: 1939. V. 46

China Mother of Gardens. Boston: 1929. V. 37; 45

If I Were to Make a Garden. Boston: 1931. V. 45

The Lilies of Eastern Asia. London: 1929. V. 39

The Lilies of Eastern Asia. Dulau: 1925. V. 37

Plant Hunting. Boston: 1927. V. 39

WILSON, FRANCIS

Rare Books, Autographs, Manuscripts Comprising the Second Portion of the Library of the Late Francis Wilson, Actor Bibliophile. New York: 1940. V. 46

The Eugene Field I Knew. New York: 1898. V. 43

WILSON, FRANK CAMERON SEARES

Napanee and Norwood, Ontario, M.D., C.M. 1904 Trinity. V. 44

WILSON, FRANK I.

The Battle of Great Bethel. Raleigh: 1864. V. 44

WILSON, FREDERICK J. F.

A Practical Treatise Upon Modern Printing machinery and Letterpress Printing. London: 1888. V. 38; 45

Typographic Printing machines and Machine printing. A practical guide to the selection of bookwork, two colour, jobbing and rotary machines. London: (1879). V. 37

WILSON, FREDERICK RICHARD

An Architectural Survey of the Churches in the Archdeaconry of Lindisfarne, in the County of Northumberland. Newcastle-upon-Tyne: 1870. V. 38

WILSON, G.

Two Discourses Concerning Inspiration. London: 1713. V. 38

WILSON, G. H.

The Eccentric Mirror . . . London: 1807-13. V. 46

WILSON, G. MURRAY

Fighting Tanks. An Account of the Royal Tank Corps in Action. 1916-1919. London: 1929. V. 45; 46

WILSON, GEORGE

The Life of the Honorable Henry Cavendish Including Abstracts of His More Important Scientific Papers and a Critical Inquiry into the Claims of all the Alleged Discoverers of the Composition of Water. London: 1851. V. 38; 40; 46

Memoir of Edward Forbes, F.R.S. London: 1861. V. 39

A Practical Treatise on Fines and Recoveries. Dublin: 1792. V. 40

Reports of Cases in the King's Courts. London. V. 40

Reports of Cases in the King's Courts at Westminster. London: 1742-74. V. 38

Reports of Cases in the King's Courts. Dublin: 1784. V. 40

Reports of Cases Argued and Adjudged in the King's Courts at Westminster. London: 1799. V. 38

WILSON, H.

A Memorial of the Late J. D. Sedding . . . London: 1892. V. 37; 38; 45

WILSON, H. E., MRS.

Our Nig; or, Sketches from the Life of a Free Black in a Two-Story White House, North. Boston: 1859. V. 42

WILSON, H. L.

The Spenders. 1902. V. 43

WILSON, H. SCHUTZ

Alpine Ascent and Adventures . . . London: 1878. V. 43

WILSON, H. W.

The Great War the Standard History of the All-Europe Conflict. London: 1914-1919. V. 45

Ironclads in Action, a Sketch of Naval Warfare, from 1855-95 . . . London: 1896. V. 38; 41

Ironclads in Action. London: 1897. V. 39

Japan's Fight for Freedom. London: 1904-06. V. 41; 46

With the Flag to Pretoria and After Pretoria: The Guerilla War. London: 1900-02. V. 45

WILSON, HARDY

The Cow Pasture Road. Sydney: 1920. V. 37

WILSON, HARRIETTE

The Interesting Memoirs of . . . One of the Most Celebrated Women of the Present Day . . . London: 1826. V. 40

Memoirs of Harriette Wilson. London: 1825. V. 43; 46

WILSON, HARRY

The Use of a Box of Colours, in Practical Demonstration on Composition, Light and Shade and Colour. London: 1842. V. 44

WILSON, HARRY LEON

The Spenders. Boston: 1902. V. 39

WILSON, HENRY

Wonderful Characters . . . London. V. 43

WILSON, HORACE HAYMAN 1786-1860

Select Specimens of the Theatre of the Hindus. Translated from the Original Sanskrit. London: 1835. V. 37

WILSON, J.

A Descriptive Catalogue of the Prints of Rembrandt by an Amateur. London: 1836. V. 44

WILSON, J. C.

Television Engineering. London: 1937. V. 40

WILSON, J. FARLOW

A Few Personal Recollections. London: 1896. V. 38; 43; 44

WILSON, JAMES 1760-1839

Apostolic Church Government Displayed; and the Government and System of the Methodist Episcopal Church Investigated. Providence: 1798. V. 40

Capital Currency and Banking. London: 1847. V. 38; 39

Illustrations of Zooloy, Being Representations of New, Rare, Remarkable Subjects of the Animal Kingdom. Edinburgh: 1828-31. V. 38

An Introduction to the Natural History of Fishes (and) An Introduction to the Natural History of Birds. Edinburgh: 1838-39. V. 39

A Missionary Voyage to the Southern Pacific Ocean, Peformed in the Years 1796, 1797, 1798, In the Ship Duff, Commanded By . . . London: 1799. V. 38; 46

A Pamphlet Relating to the Claim of Sr. Don Jose Y. Limantour, To Purchase Four Leagues of Land in and Near San Francisco. San Francisco: 1853. V. 37

The Rod and the Gun, Being Two Treatises on Angling and Shooting . . . Edinburgh: 1840. V. 39; 41

The Works. Philadelphia: 1804. V. 40

WILSON, JAMES CORNELIUS 1847-1934

Address, Delivered in Gonzales, Texas, Nov. 17, 1860 by Rev . . . . at the Request of His Fellow Citizens, Without Distinction of Party. Gonzales: 1860. V. 37; 39

WILSON, JAMES GRANT

Biographical Sketches of Illinois Officers Engaged in the War Against the Rebellion of 1861. Chicago: 1862. V. 38

General Grant. New York: 1897. V. 38

Thackeray in the United States 1852-3, 1855-6. New York: 1904. V. 38

WILSON, JAMES H.

The Life of John A. Rawlins. New York: 1916. V. 37

Under the Old Flag. New York: 1912. V. 44

WILSON, JAMES HARRISON

Life and Services of Brevet Brigadier-General Andrew Jonathan Alexander, United States Army. New York: 1887. V. 38; 39; 42

WILSON, JAMES L.

The Metals in Canada: a Manual for Explorers . . . Montreal: 1861. V. 40; 46

WILSON, JEAN S.

Thirteen Author Collections of the 19th Century and Five Centuries of Familiar Quotations. New York: 1950. V. 38; 40; 42

WILSON, JEREMY

T. E. Lawrence. London: 1988. V. 42

WILSON, JOB

An Inquiry into othe Nature and Treatment of Prevailing Epidemic, Called Spotted Fever. Boston: 1815. V. 37

WILSON, JOHN

Belphegor, or the Marriage of the Devil. London: 1691. V. 37; 38; 44; 46

The English Martyrologye Conteyning a Summary of the Lives of the . . . Saintes of . . . England, Scotland and Ireland. St. Omer: 1608. V. 41; 45

The Foresters. Edinburgh: 1825. V. 37; 39; 42

A Genuine Narrative of the Transactions in Nova Scotia, Since the Settlement, June 1749, till August the 5th 1751. London: 1751. V. 40

The Isle of Palms, and Other Poems. Edinburgh. V. 43

The Isle of Palms, and Other Poems. Edinburgh: 1812. V. 38; 43; 44

The Land of Burns. London: 1840. V. 40

The Recreations of Christopher North. Edinburgh: 1842. V. 42; 43

The Recreations of Christopher North. Edinburgh & London: 1842. V. 40

The Royal Philatelic Collection. London: 1952. V. 39; 42

Shakespeariana. A Catalogue of all the Books, Pamphlets, Etc. Relating to Shakespeare. London: 1827. V. 40; 43

A Synopsis of British Plants, in Mr. Ray's Method. Newcastle upon Tyne: 1744. V. 41; 44

The Trials of Margaret Lyndsay. Edinburgh: 1823. V. 37; 39; 42

A Volume for All Libraries, Peculiarly Adapted to the Votaries of Correct Literature, and Beneficial to Every Class of Learners. Washington City: 1814. V. 44

WILSON, JOHN FARLOW

A Few Personal Recollections of an Old Printer. London: 1896. V. 38

WILSON, JOHN LYDE

The Code of Honor Its Rationale and Uses, by the Tests of Common Sense and Good Morals, with the Effects of Its Preventive Remedies. New Orleans: 1883. V. 38; 39; 42

The Code of Honor; or, Rules for the Governemnt of Principals and Second in Duelling. New Orleans: 1873. V. 37

WILSON, JOHN M.

The Rural Cyclopedia, or a General Dictionary of Agriculture, and of the Arts, Sciences, Instruments and Practice, Necessary to the Farmer, Stockfarmer, Gardener . . . Edinburgh: 1847-49. V. 46

WILSON, JOHN MARIUS

The Imperial Gazetteer of England and Wales. London: 1873. V. 40

WILSON, JOSEPH

Memorabilia Cantabrigiae; or an Account of the Different Colleges in Cambridge . . . London: 1803. V. 38

WILSON, JOSEPH T.

The Black Phalanx. A History of the Negro Soliders of the United States in the Wars of 1775-1812, 1861-'65. Hartford: 1888. V. 37

WILSON, JOYCE LANCASTER

The Work and Play of Adrian Wilson. Austin: 1983. V. 37; 38; 41; 45

WILSON, L. J.

The Confederate Soldier. Fayetteville: 1902. V. 39

WILSON, LAWRENCE 1842-1922

Itinerary of the 7th Ohio Vol. Inf. 1861-1864. New York: 1907. V. 39

WILSON, LILLIAN M.

Ancient Textiles from Egypt in the University of Michigan Collection. Ann Arbor: 1933. V. 44

WILSON, LIZZIE

Poems. Louisville: 1860. V. 40

WILSON, MARGARET HARRIES 1797-1846

Memoirs of Miss Mellon afterwards Duchess of St. Albans. London: 1887. V. 40

WILSON, MARGARET HARRIET 1797-1846

Popularity; and the Destinies of Woman. London: 1842. V. 39

WILSON, MATTHEW 1582-1656

Infidelity Unmasked, or the Confutation of a Booke Published by Mr. William Chillingworth Under this Title, The Religion of Protestants a Safe Way to Salvation. London: 1652. V. 45

Modesta ac Brevis Discussio. Antwerp: 1631. V. 38

WILSON, MEREDITH

And There I Stood with My Piccolo. New York: 1948. V. 45

WILSON, MONA

The Life of William Blake. London: 1927. V. 40; 41; 42; 43; 44

The Life of William Blake. London: 1928. V. 46

WILSON, OBED G.

My Adventures in the Sierras. Franklin: 1902. V. 40

WILSON, OWEN MEREDITH

A History of the Denver and Rio Grande Project 1870-1901. N.P.: 1941. V. 37

WILSON, PETER

The Letters of Peter Wilson Woldier, Explorer and Indian Agent West of the Mississippi River. Baltimore: 1940. V. 40

WILSON, PROFESSOR

The Land of Burns. London: 1840. V. 38

Noctes Ambrosianae. London: 1863-64. V. 39

WILSON, R.

A Second replie Against the Defensory and Apology of Sixtus the Fift Late Pope of Rome . . . London: 1592. V. 43; 46

WILSON, R. E.

The Recovery of Jerusalem. New York: 1871. V. 39

WILSON, R. L.

Antique Arms Annual . . . Waco: 1971. V. 42

Nimschke, Firearms Engraver. Preface by John J. McKendry. Teanceck: (1965). V. 37; 38

WILSON, RICHARD

The Russian Story Book, Tales from the Song Cycles of Kiev, Novgorod and Other Early Sources. London: 1916. V. 37; 45; 46

Studies and Designs, Done at Rome, in the Year 1752. Oxford: 1811. V. 38; 39

Twelve Original Views in Italy . . . London: 1776. V. 45

WILSON, RICHARD LUSH

Short Ravelings From a Long Yarn, or Camp March Sketches of the Santa Fe Trail. From the notes of Richard L. Wilson, by Benjamin F. Taylor. A Foreword for this edition by Henry R. Wagner. Santa Ana: 1936. V. 37; 38; 40; 45

WILSON, ROBERT

Ben K. Green: A Descriptive Bibliography of Writings by and About Him. Flagstaff: 1977. V. 37; 38; 39; 40; 42; 43

Brief Remarks on the Character and Composition of the Russian Army and a Sketch of the Campaigns in Poland, in 1806 and 1807. London: 1810. V. 40; 41

The Life and Times of Queen Victoria. London: 1887-88. V. 38

A Personal Narrative of the Action Fought at Villiers-En-Couche, April 24, 1794. London: 1889. V. 40

The Wilson Horticultural Colour Chart. London: 1939-41. V. 38

WILSON, ROBERT A.

Ben K. Green: A Bibliography of Writings by and About Him. Flagstaff: (1977). V. 37

Gertrude Stein: a Bibliography. New York: 1974. V. 46

Mexico and Its Religion. New York: 1855. V. 46

WILSON, ROBERT F.

The Wilson Colour Chart. London: 1939-42. V. 41

WILSON, ROBERT T.

History of the British Expedition to Egypt . . . London: 1802. V. 41; 45; 46

WILSON, ROBERT THOMAS

History of the British Expedition to Egypt. London: 1803. V. 40

WILSON, ROMER

Red Magic. London: 1930. V. 40; 42; 43; 45; 46

WILSON, RUFUS R.

A Noble Company of Adventures. New York: 1908. V. 43

WILSON, S. A. KINNIER

Neurology. Baltimore: 1955. V. 42

WILSON, SAMUEL

An Account of the Province of Carolina in America, Together with an Abstract of the Patent, and Several Other Necessary and Useful Particulars, to Such as Have Thoughts of Transporting Themselves Thither. London: 1682. V. 40; 42; 44; 45

WILSON, SAMUEL MAC KAY

Battle of Blue Licks August 19, 1782. Lexington: 1927. V. 46

WILSON, SAMUEL SHERIDAN

A Narrative of the Greek Mission. London: 1839. V. 37; 39

WILSON, SARAH ATKINS

Fruits of Enterprize Exhibited in the Travels of Belzoni in Egypt and Nubia . . . London: 1822. V. 44

A Visit to Grove Cottage: for the Entertainment and Instruction of Children. London: 1823. V. 44

WILSON, SCOT BARCHARD

Aves Hawaiiensis: the Birds of the Sandwich Islands. London: 1890-99. V. 43; 45; 46

WILSON, THEODORE D.

Shipbuilding - Theoretical and Practical - the Naval Architecture . . . New York: 1873. V. 38

WILSON, THOMAS

An Archaeological Dictionary. London: 1783. V. 38

An Archeological Dictionary; or, Classical Antiquities of the Jews, Greeks & Romans alphabetically arranged. London/Leeds: 1783. V. 37; 38

The Arte of Rhetorike, for the Use of All Suche as Are Studious of Eloqunce, Sette Forthe in Englishe by Thomas Wilson. London: 1584. V. 38; 44; 46

A Brief Journal of the Life, Travels and labour of Love in the Work of the Ministry of . . . Thomas Wilson, who departed this life at his own habitation near Edenderry in the Kingdom of Ireland, 20. 3. 1735. London: 1784. V. 37

A Catalogue Raisonne of the Seclect Collection of Engravings of An Amateur. London: 1828. V. 38

A Christian Dictionary. London: 1622. V. 45

The Complete System of English Country Dancing . . . London: 1820. V. 37; 38

Distilled Spirituous Liquours, the Bane of the Nation. London: 1736. V. 40; 43

The Knowledge and Practice of Christianity . . . London: 1751. V. 44

Pictures of Philadelphia, for 1824 . . . Philadelphia: 1823. V. 41

The Pitman's Pay, and Other Poems. 1843. V. 42

The Rule of Reason . . . London: 1567. V. 43; 45

Sermons. Bath: 1781. V. 39

The Works. With His Life . . . Bath: 1782. V. 39

WILSON, THOMAS A.

By Telegraph Direct! N. V. 44

WILSON, THOMAS, BP. OF SODOR & MAN 1663-1755

Knowledge and Practice of Christianity Made Easy to the Meanest Capacities . . . London: 1741. V. 45

The Knowledge and Practice of Christianity . . . or, an Essay Towards an Instruction for the Indians . . . London: 1751. V. 43; 45

The Life of the Right Reverend Father in God, Thomas Wilson, Lord Bishop Sodor and Man. Bath: 1782. V. 40

The Many Advantages of a Good Language to Any Nation . . . London: 1724. V. 42

The Principles of Duties of Christianity. Egham: 1791. V. 45

WILSON, THOMAS, dancing master

An Analysis of Country Dancing, Wherein the Figures Used in that Polite Amusement are Rendered Familiar by Engraved Lines. London: 1811. V. 40

WILSON, THOMAS L.

Sufferings Endured for a Free Government; or, a History of the Cruelties and Atrocities of the Rebellion. Washington: 1864. V. 42

WILSON, THOMAS, of Montreal

Transatlantic Sketches; or, Travelling Reminiscences of the West Indies and United States. Montreal: 1860. V. 42

WILSON, TOM MUIR

Photographs. N.P.: 1960. V. 37

WILSON, VIOLET

The Order of the Administration of the Lord's Supper, or Holy Communion. Surrey: 1951. V. 44

WILSON, WALTER

Memoirs of the Life and Times of Daniel Defoe. London: 1830. V. 41; 42; 43

WILSON, WILLIAM 1799-1871

Bryologia Britannica. London: 1855. V. 37; 38; 40; 44; 46

The Duties of Patriotism. N.P.: 1861. V. 42

Elements of Navigation; or the Practical Rules of the Art, Plainly Laid Down and Clearly Demonstrated from Their Principles . . . Edinburgh: 1773. V. 38; 46

The LBJ Brigade. Los Angeles: 1966. V. 44

A Missionary Voyage to the Southern Pacific Ocean, Performed in the Years 1796, 1797, 1798, in the Ship Duff, Commaned by Captain James Wilson . . . London: 1799. V. 37; 38; 41; 46

WILSON, WILLIAM B.

History of the Pennsylvania Railroad Company with Plan of Organization, Portraits of Officials and Biographical Sketches. Philadelphia: 1899. V. 37

WILSON, WILLIAM D.

Sketches of the Higher Classes of Colored Society in Philadelphia. Philadelphia: 1841. V. 41

WILSON, WILLIAM RAE 1772-1849

Records of a Route through France and Italy; with Sketches of Catholicism. London: 1835. V. 39; 44

Travels in Egypt and the Holy Land. London: 1824. V. 42

Travels in Norway, Sweden, Denmark, Hanover, Germany, Netherlands &c. London: 1826. V. 40

Travels. London: 1826-1835. V. 37

Travels in Russia &c . . . London: 1828. V. 39

WILSON, WILLIAM, topographer

The Post Chaise Companion, or Traveller's Directory through Ireland. Dublin: 1803. V. 43

WILSON, WOODROW

Constitutional Government in the United States. New York: 1917. V. 43

George Washington. New York: 1897. V. 44

History of the American People. New York: 1903. V. 42

A History of the American People. New York and London: 1902. V. 37

Mere Literature and Other Essays. Boston & New York: 1897. V. 39; 40; 41

Notes on Constitutional Government. 1894. V. 39

The President of the United States. New York: 1916. V. 46

Selected Addresses and Public Papers of Woodrow Wilson. New York: 1918. V. 44

Why We Are at War . . . New York: 1917. V. 43

Why We Are at War . . . New York & London: 1917. V. 40

WILSTACH, PAUL

Tidewater Virginia. Indianapolis: 1929. V. 41

WILSTON, ANDREW

J. M. W. Turner: His Art and Life. Secaucus: 1979. V. 39

WILTON, L. E.

Mary Browne. London: 1880. V. 37

WILTSE, CHARLES M.

John C. Calhoun. Indianapolis: 1944-51. V. 40

WILTSEE, ERNEST A.

Gold Rush Steamers. San Francisco: 1938. V. 37; 38; 41; 42; 44; 45; 46

The Pioneer Miner and Pack Mule Express. San Francisco: 1931. V. 40; 44

WIMER, JAMES

Events in Indian History, Beginning with An Account of the Origin of the American Indians, and Early Settlements in North America. Lancaster: 1841. V. 38; 45

Events in Indian History, Beginning with an Account of the Origina of the American Indians and Early Settlements in North America . . . Lancaster: 1841. V. 42

Events in Indian History, Beginning with an Account of the Origin of the American Indians, and Early Settlements in North America . . . Philadelphia: 1842. V. 45

WIMPEY, JOSEPH

Rural Improvements; or, Essays on the Most Rational Methods of Improving Estates. London: 1775. V. 40

WIMPHELING, JAKOB

Castigationes Locorum in Canticis Ecclesiasticis & Divinis Officiis Depravatorum. Strasbourg: 1513. V. 38

Elegantiarum Medulla, Oritoriaeque Precepta. Strasburg: 1506. V. 38; 40

De Integritate . . . Strassbourg: 1506. V. 46

WIMSATT, WILLIAM KURTZ

The Portraits of Alexander Pope. New Haven: 1965. V. 46

WINANS, ROSS

Address to the President and Directors of the Baltimore and Ohio Railroad Company, on the Subject of Locomotive Engines, and the Errors in Relation Thereto, Contained in a Pamphlet Recently Published by Authority of the Company. Address: 1857. V. 39

WINANS, WALTER

The Sporting Rifle. Shooting of Big and Little Game. 1908. V. 38

The Sporting Rifle. New York: 1908. V. 45

WINCHELL, ALEXANDER

Preadamites: or a Demonstration of the Existence of Men Before Adam. Chicago: 1880. V. 40

WINCHELL, N. H.

The Aborigines of Minnesota, 1906-1911: A Report based on the Collections of Jacob V. Bower and on the Field Surveys and Notes of Alfred J. Hill, and Theodore H. Lewis. St. Paul: 1911. V. 37; 39

WINCHELSEA AND NOTTINGHAM, GEORGE FINCH, EARL OF

Letter from the Earl of Winchelsea to the Board of Agriculture, on the Advantage of Cottagers Renting Land. London: 1796. V. 41

WINCHELSEA, ANNE FINCH, COUNTESS OF 1661-1720

Miscellaneous Poems, on Several Occasions. Written by a Lady. London: 1713. V. 37; 40; 43; 45

Poems on Several Occasions. London: 1714. V. 37

The Spleen. (with) A Prospect of Death. London: 1709. V. 38; 42

WINCHELSEA, ANNE KINGSMILL FINCH, COUNTESS OF 1661-1720

The Poems. Chicago: 1903. V. 42

WINCHESTER, BENJAMIN

The Gospel Reflector. Philadelphia: 1841. V. 40; 42

WINCHESTER, CHARLES

The Intruder. A Peridical paper, published at Aberdeen in the Year 1802. Aberdeen: 1802. V. 37

WINCHESTER, ELHANAN

The Process and Empire of Christ; from His Birth to the End of the Mediatorial Kingdom. Brattleboro: 1805. V. 40

WINCHESTER, J. D.

. . . Experience on a Voyage from Lynn, Massachusetts to San Francisco, California and to the Alaskan Gold Fields. Salem: 1900. V. 37; 39

WINCHESTER, JAMES D.

Capt. J. D. Winchester's Experience on a Voyage from Lynn, Massachusetts to San Francisco, California and to the Alaskan Gold Fields. Salem: 1900. V. 38; 42

WINCHESTER, S. G.

The Religion of the Bible, the Only Preservative of Our Civil Institutions. Natchez: 1838. V. 39

WINCHILSEA, HENEAGE FINCH, 2ND EARL OF

An Exact Relation of the Famous Earthquake and Eruption of Mount Aetna, or Mont-Gibello, A.D. 1669. London: 1775. V. 42

WINCKELMANN, JOHANN JOACHIM

Critical Account of the Situation and Destruction by the First Eruptions of Mount Vesuvius of Herculaneum, Pompeii, and Stavia. London: 1771. V. 42

WINCKELMANN, JOHANN JUST 1620-1699

Stam-Und Regentenbaum der Burch. V. 45

WINCKELMANN, JOHN J.

The History of Ancient Art Among the Greeks. London: 1850. V. 44

WINCKLER, DANIEL

De Opio Tractatus, in Quo Simul Liber de Opio D. Joh. Freitagii Examinatur. Leipzig: 1635. V. 38

WINDELER, B. C.

Elimus: a Story. Paris: 1923. V. 39; 41; 43; 46

WINDEN, TOBIAS

An Enquiry into the Nature and Place of Hell. London: 1714. V. 39

WINDHAM, DONALD

The Hitchhiker. Florence: 1950. V. 38

The Hitchhiker. 1950. V. 39

Tanaquil, or the Hardest Thing of All. Stamperia: 1972. V. 46

WINDHAM MINING & SMELTING CO.

Prospectus of the Windham Mining and Smelting Co. of Windham, Ouray Co., Colorado . . . New Haven: 1881. V. 38

WINDHAM, WILLIAM 1750-1810

A Plan of the Discipline for the Use of the Norfolk Militia. London: 1768. V. 41

Speeches in Parliament. (with) Some Account of His Life by Thomas Amyot. London: 1812. V. 39

THE WINDMILL. Stories, Essays, Poems and Pictures by Authors and Artists Whose Works are Published at the Sign of the Windmill. London: 1922. V. 41

WINDSOR, BESSIE WALLIS SIMPSON WARFIELD, DUCHESS OF 1896-

The Heart Has Its Reasons. London: 1956. V. 38

WINDSOR CASTLE. ROYAL LIBRARY

Specimens of Royal Fine and Historical Bookbinding, selected from the Royal Library, Windsor Castle. London: 1893. V. 39

WINDSOR, EDWARD, DUKE OF 1894-1972

Farewell Speech of King Edward the Eighth Broadcast from Windsor Castle the Tenth Day of December MCMXXXVI . . . 1938. V. 39

A King's Story. London: 1951. V. 45

A King's Story. New York: 1951. V. 39; 42

WINDSOR, EMMA S.

Babies' Crawling Rugs and How to Make Them . . . London: 1887. V. 38

THE WINDSOR Medley: Being a Choice Collection of several Curious and Valuable Pieces in prose and verse: that were handed about in Print and Manuscript, during the Stay of the Court at Windsor-Castle last Summer . . .* London: 1731. V. 37; 39; 40

WINDUS, JOHN

A Journey to Mequinez: The Residence of the Present Emperor of Fez and Morocco. London: 1725. V. 41

WINDUS, THOMAS

A New Elucidation of the Subjects on the Celebrated Portland Vase, Fromerly Called the Baberini. London: 1845. V. 38

WINE and Spirt Adulterations Unmasked, in a Treatise, setting Forth the Manner Employed, and the Various Ingredients Which Constitute, the Adulterations and Impositions . . .* London: 1828. V. 40

WINE, Beer, Ale, and Tobacco, Contending for Superiority. London: 1658. V. 40; 42

WINES, E. C.

Two Years and a Half in the American Navy. London: 1833. V. 37; 38; 39

Two Years and a Half in the American Navy: Comprising a Journal of a Cruise to England, in the Mediterranean, and in the Levant, on Board the U.S. Frigate Constellation, in the Years 1829, 1830 and 1831. Philadelphia: 1832. V. 37; 39

WINES, ENOCH C.

A Trip to Boston, in a Series of Letters to the Editor of the United States Gazette. Boston: 1838. V. 42

WINFIELD, CHARLES H.

History of the Land Titles in Hudson County, New Jersey, 1609-1871. New York: 1872. V. 41

History of the County of Hudson, New Jersey, from Its Earliest Settlement to the Present Time. New York: 1874. V. 44

WINFIELD, J.

History of Political Covnentions in California, 1849-1892. Sacramento: 1893. V. 45

WINFIELD, PERCY HENRY

The History of Conspiracy and Abuse of Legal Procedure. Cambridge: 1921. V. 43

WINFORD, MISS

Hobby-Horses; Read at Bath-Easton. London: 1780. V. 39; 40

WING, CONWAY P.

A Historical and Genealogical Register of John Wing, of Sandwich, Mass. and His Descendants, 1662-1881. Carlisle: 1881. V. 42

History of Cumberland County, Pennsylvania. Philadelphia: 1879. V. 41; 42

WING, DONALD

Short Title Catalogue of Books Printed in England, Scotland, Ireland, Wales and British America and of English Books Printed in Other Countries 1641-1700. New York: 1945, 1948. V. 40

Short-Title Catalogue of Books Printed in England, Scotland, Ireland, Wales and British America and of English Books Printed in Other Countries 1641-1700. New York: 1945/48/51. V. 40

Short Title Catalogue of Books Printed in England, Scotland, Ireland, Wales and British America . . . 1641-1700. New York: 1945-51. V. 38; 39; 42; 44

Short Title Catalogue of Books Printed in England, Scotland, Ireland, Wales and British America and of English Books Printed in Other Countries 1641-1700. New York: 1972. V. 42; 46

Short Title Catalogue of Books Printed in England. New York: 1972, 1982. V. 40

WING, DONALD G.

Short Title Catalogue of Books Printed in England (etc.). London: 1945-82. V. 39

WING, FRANK L.

The Book of Complete Information About Pianos. New York: 1914. V. 41

WING, J. M.

The Tunnels and Water System of Chicago. Under the Lake and Under the River. Chicago: 1874. V. 43

WING, JOHN

Geodoete Practicus Redivivus, The Art of Surveying . . . London: 1700. V. 44

WING, RUSSELL

Directions for the Prevention and Cure of the Scurvey. New Bedford: 1827. V. 39

WING, TALCOT E.

History of Monroe County Michigan. New York: 1890. V. 40; 42

WING, VINCENT

An Ephemerides of the Coelestiall Motions for VII Years, Beginning anno 1652, ending anno 1658. London: 1652. V. 38

Geodaetes Practicus Redivivus. The Art of Surveying . . . London: 1700. V. 45

WING, W. R.

Counterpoise Gun-Carriages and Platforms . . . for the Use of the Officers of the Corps of Engineers. Washington: 1869. V. 41

WINGATE, EDMUND 1596-1656

An Exact Abridgment of all Statutes in Force and Use, from the Beginning of Magna Charta Until 1641. London: 1684. V. 40

An Exact Abridgment of All the Statutes in Force and Use from the Beginning of the Magna Charta . . . London: 1700. V. 40

An Exact Abridgment of all Statutes in Force and Use. London: 1675. V. 38

Logarithmotechnica (Greek) or the Construction and Use of the Logarithmeticall Tables . . . Imprime a Londres,: 1635. V. 38

Maximes of Reason; or, the Reason of the Common Law. London: 1658. V. 38; 40

Mr. Wingate's Arithmetick, Containing a Plain and Vamiliar Method for Attaining the Knowledge and Practice of Common Arithmetick. London: 1678. V. 46

Mr. Wingate's Arithmetick, Containing a Plain and Familiar Method, for Attaining the Knowledge and Practice of Common Arithmetick. London: 1689. V. 40

WINGATE, F. REGINALD

Ten Years' Captivity in the Mahdi's Camp, 1882-1892. London: 1892. V. 39

WINGFIELD, C.

Historical Record of the Shropshire, Yeomanry Cavalry, from its fromation in 1795, up to the year 1887. Shrewsbury: 1888. V. 37

WINGFIELD, LEWIS

Lady Grizel. London: 1878. V. 42; 46

WINGFIELD, W.

The Poultry Book. London: 1853. V. 37

WINGLER, HANS M.

The Bauhaus, Weimar, Dessau, Berlin, Chicago: Cambridge: 1969. V. 45

Graphic Work from the Bauhaus. Greenwich: 1969. V. 46

WINGRAVE, MARION

The May Blossom, or The Princess and Her People. London: 1881. V. 39; 45

WINGROVE, BENJAMIN

    Remarks on a Bill Now Before Parliament . . . Regulating Turnpike Roads . . . Bath: 1821. V. 38; 45

WINHELSEA, HENEAGE FINCH, 2ND EARL OF

    An Exact Relation of the Famous Earthquake and Eruption of Mount Aetna, or Mont Gibello, A.D. 1669 . . . London: 1775. V. 44

WINKELMANN, JOHANN

    Geschichte der Kunst des Alter-Thums. Vienna: 1776. V. 38

WINKFIELD, TREVOR

    The Lewis Carroll Circular. Leeds: 1973. V. 45

WINKLER, A. V., MRS.

    The Confederate Capital and Hood's Brigade. Austin: 1894. V. 38

WINKLER, C.

    An Anatomical Guide to Experimental Researches on the Cat's Brain. Amsterdam: 1914. V. 45; 46

WINKLER, E. W.

    Manuscript Letters and Documents of Early Texians 1821-1845. Austin: 1937. V. 39; 40

WINKLER, ERNEST W.

    Platforms of Political Parties in Texas. Austin: 1916. V. 43; 46

WINKLER, HANS A.

    Rock-Drawings of Southern Upper Egypt, I-II. London: 1938-39. V. 37; 42; 44

WINKLER, MRS. A. V.

    The Confederate Capital and Hood's Brigade. Austin: 1894. V. 37

WINKLER, WILLIAM

    Journal of Secession Convention of Texas 1861. Austin: 1912. V. 45

WINKLE'S Architectural and Picturesque Illustrations of the Cathedral Churches of England and Wales . . . London: 1851. V. 44

WINKLES, BENJAMIN

    Cathedral Churches of England and Wales. London: 1851. V. 39

    Winkles's Architectural and Picturesque Illustrations of the Cathedral Churches of England and Wales. London: 1838-42. V. 39; 42; 46

    Winkles's Architectural and Picturesque Illustrations of the Cathedral Churches of England and Wales . . . London: 1851. V. 39; 41

WINKLES, M.

    Winkles's Architectural and Picturesque Illustrations of the Cathedral Chruches of England and Wales . . . London: 1860. V. 45

WINLOCK, H. E.

    Excavations at Deir el Bahri 1911-1931. New York: 1942. V. 40

    Models of Daily Life in Ancient Egypt from the Tomb of Meket Re' at Thebes. Cambridge: 1955. V. 40; 42; 44

    The Rise and Fall of the Middle Kingdom in Thebes. New York: 1947. V. 40; 42; 44

    The Tomb of Queen Meryet-Amun at Thebes. New York: 1932. V. 44

    The Tomb of Queen Meryet-Amun at Thebes. New York: 1973. V. 44

    The Treasure of Three Egyptian Princesses. New York: 1948. V. 40

WINNETT ORR, H.

    A Catalogue of the H. Winnett Orr Historical Collection and Other Rare Books in the Library of the American College of Surgeons. Chicago: 1960. V. 44

WINNING, HASSO VON

    Pre-Columbian Art of Mexico and Central America. New York. V. 42

    Pre-Columbian Art of Mexico and Central America. New York: (1968). V. 37

THE WINNING Post. London: 1904-11. V. 37

WINNINGTON, THOMAS

    An Apology for the Conduct of a Late Celebrated Second-Rate Minister, from the Year 17629, at Which Time He Commenc'd Courtier, till within a few Weeks of His Death, in 1746. London. V. 38

THE WINNIPEG and Northwest Petroleum Company. Incorporated Oct. 11th, 1883. Minneapolis: 1883. V. 42

THE WINNIPEG General Sympathetic Strike May-June 1919. Winnipeg: 1919. V. 39

WINSATT, W. K.

    Philosophic Words: a Study of Style and Meaning in the Rambler and Dictionary of Samuel Johnson. New York: 1948. V. 41

WINSER, HENRY J.

    The Great Northwest, a Guide Book and Itinerary for the Use of Tourists and Travellers over the Lines of the Northern Pacific Railroad. V. 40

    The Great Northwest. New York. V. 42

WINSHIP, GEORGE PARKER

    The Cambridge Press 1638-1692. A Reexamination of the Bay Psalm Book and the Eliot Indian Bible. Philaldelphia: 1945. V. 38

    The Coronado Expedition 1540-1542. Washington: 1896. V. 37; 42

    Journal of Madam Knight. Boston: 1920. V. 45

    The Journey of Francisco Vazquez de Coronado 1540-1542. San Francisco: 1933. V. 42; 45

    The Merrymount Press of Boston. Vienna: 1929. V. 37; 38; 41; 45

    The New England Company of 1649 and John Eliot, the Ledger for the Years 1650-1660 and the Record Book of Meetings Between 1656 and 1686 of the Corporation for the Propagation of the Gospel in New England . . . Boston: 1920. V. 46

    A Paper Read at the Club of Odd Volumes in Boston . . . January 1908. Hammersmith: 1909. V. 44

    A Paper Read at a Meeting of the Club of Odd Volumes in Boston. London: 1909. V. 43; 44; 46

    The Printing Press in South America. Providence: 1912. V. 40

    Sailors Narratives of Voyages Along the New England Coast 1524-1624. Boston: 1905. V. 42

    William Caxton. A Paper Read at a Meeting of the Club of Odd Volumes in Boston in January 1908. Hammersmith: 1909. V. 37; 38; 40; 43; 44; 46

    William Caxton and the First English Press. New York: 1938. V. 39; 40; 41; 42; 44

    William Caxton: a Paper Read at a Meeting of the Club of Odd Volumes Boston, Massachuseets, United STates of America in january 1908. Eugene: 1939. V. 46

    William Caxton. A Paper Read at the Meeting of the Club of Odd Volumes, Boston, Massachusetts, USA in January 1908. University of Oregon: 1939. V. 38

WINSLOW, ANNA GREEN

    Diary of A Boston School Girl of 1771. Boston: 1894. V. 42; 44

WINSLOW BROTHERS CO.

    Ornamental Iron and Bronze Executed by the Winslow Bros. Company, Chicago. Chicago: 1910. V. 38

WINSLOW, CHARLES FREDERICK

    Force and Nature. Attraction and Repulsion . . . London: 1869. V. 39

WINSLOW, FORBES BEIGNUS 1810-1874

    The Anatomy of Suicide. London: 1840. V. 37; 43; 45

WINSLOW, FORBES BENIGNUS 1810-1874

    The Case of Luigi Buranelli Medico-Legally Considered. London: 1855. V. 45

    Lettsomian Lectures on Insanity. London: 1854. V. 39

    Light: Its Influence on Life and Health. New York: 1868. V. 39

    Obscure Diseases of the Brain and Mind. Philadelphia: 1866. V. 39; 40; 43

    On the Obscure Dieseases of the Brain, and Disorders of the Mind. London: 1860. V. 43

    On Obscure Diseases of the Brain, and Disorders of the Mind: Their Incipient Symptoms, Pathology, Diagnosis, Treatment and Prophylaxis. Philadelphia: 1860. V. 42

    Physic and Physicians. London: 1839. V. 38

    The Plea of Insanity in Criminal Cases. London: 1842. V. 39

    The Plea Of Insanity in Criminal Cases. London: 1853. V. 40

    The Plea of Insanity in Criminal Cases. London: 1843. V. 37

WINSLOW, HENRY

    The Etching of Landscapes. Chicago: 1914. V. 41

WINSLOW, JACQUES BENIGNE

    Exposition Anatomique de la Structure du Corps Humain. Paris: 1732. V. 37; 38; 39; 40; 41; 44

WINSLOW, JAMES B.

    An Anatomical Expostition of the Structure of the Human Body. London: 1749. V. 37

WINSLOW, JAMES BENIGNUS

    An Anatomical Exposition of the Structure of the Human Body. London: 1733. V. 40

    An Anatomical Expostiion of the Structure of the Human Body. London: 1763. V. 40; 43

WINSLOW, W. H.

    Cruising and Blockading. Pittsburgh: 1885. V. 43

WINSLOW'S Roller Skates. Worcester: 1899. V. 44

WINSOR & NEWTON

    Specimen Tints of Artists' Oil Colours. London: 1870. V. 44

WINSOR, HENRY J.

The Great Northwest a Guide-Book and Itinerary for the Use of Tourists and Travelers Over the Lines of the Northern Pacific Railroad . . . St. Paul: 1886. V. 42

WINSOR, JUSTIN

Cartier to Frontenac. Boston, New York &: 1894. V. 37; 40

Cartier to Frontenac. New York: 1894. V. 43

The Kohl Collection . . . of Maps Relating to America . . . Washington: 1904. V. 37; 40

The Memorial History of Boston, Including Suffolk County, Mass. 1630-1880. Boston: 1880. V. 41; 42

Narrative and Critical History of America. Boston & New York: 1884-89. V. 43

Narrative and Critical History of America. Boston: 1889. V. 37; 38; 39; 44; 46

Narrative and Critical History of America. Boston & New York: 1889. V. 40

Narrative and Critical History of America. Boston: 1894-99. V. 42

Westward Movement: the Colonies and the Republic West of the Alleghenies, 1763-1798. Boston: 1897. V. 46

WINSOR, WILLIAM

The Poetic Art: a Poem. Providence: 1812. V. 40

WINSTANLEY, HENRY

Engravings of Audley End. V. 39

WINSTANLEY, JOHN

Poems Written Occasionally by . . . . Dublin: 1742. V. 43

Poems Written Occasionally by the Late John Winstanley . . . Dublin: 1751. V. 39; 45

WINSTANLEY, THOMAS

Observations on the Arts . . . Liverpool: 1828. V. 39

Observations on the Arts, with Tables of the Principal Painters of the Various Italian, Spanish, French, Flemish, Dutch and German School. Liverpool: 1830. V. 40; 44

Observations on the Arts, with Tables of the Principal Painters of the Various Italian, Spanish, French, Flemish, Dutch and German Schools. Liverpool: 1843? V. 38

WINSTANLEY, W.

A Visit to Abyssinia An Account of Travel in Modern Ethiopia. London: 1881. V. 41

WINSTANLEY, WILLIAM

England's Worthies. London: 1684. V. 43

The Lives of the Most Famous Poets. London: 1687. V. 45

WINSTON, CHARLES

An Enquiry Into the Differences of Style Observable in Ancient Glass Paintings . . . Oxford: 1867. V. 45

An Inquiry Into the Difference of Style Observable in Ancient Glass Paintings . . . Oxford: 1847. V. 46

An Inquiry Into the Difference of Style Observable in Ancient Glass Paintings, Especially in England with Hints on Glass Painting. Oxford and London: 1867. V. 40; 43

Memoirs Illustrative of the Art of Glass Painting. London: 1865. V. 37; 40

WINSTON, J.

The Theatric Tourist, Being a Genuine Collection of Correct Views . . . of All the Principal Provincial Theatres in the United Kingdom . . . London: 1805. V. 37

WINSTON, JAMES

Cora O'Kane; or, the Doom of the Rebel Guard. Claremont: 1868. V. 44

WINSTRUP, ELIAS

Manipulus stratagematum. Amsterdam: 1632. V. 37

WINT, PETER DE

Sicilian Scenery. London. V. 37

WINTER, ARCHDEACON

The Peep of Day in the Language of the Cree Indians. London: 1898. V. 38; 39

WINTER, DOUGLAS E.

Night Visions 5. Arlington Heights: 1988. V. 44

Prime Evil. 1988. V. 44

Prime Evil. West Kingston: 1988. V. 44; 46

WINTER, FERDINAND

The Combs of All Times. Leipzig: 1906. V. 43

WINTER, GEORGE

Animal Magnetism. Bath: 1801. V. 43

The Journals and Indian Paintings of George Winter 1837-1839. Indianapolis: 1948. V. 40; 44; 45

A New and Compendious System of Husbandry. Bristol: 1787. V. 38

WINTER, GEORGE B.

Principles of Exodontia as Applied to the Impacted Mandibular Third Molar, a Complete Treatise on the Operative Technique with Clinical Diagnoses and Radiographic Interpretations. St. Louis: 1926. V. 38

A WINTER in Paris; or Memoirs of Madame de C**** . . . London: 1811. V. 42

WINTER, JOHN

Narrative of the Sufferings of Massy Harbison, From Indian Barbarity, Giving an Account of Her Captivity, the Murder of Her Two Children . . . Pittsburgh;: 1829. V. 40

WINTER, JOHN PRATT

The Domestick Policy of the British Empire, Viewed in Connexion with Its Foreign Interests . . . London: 1824. V. 40

WINTER, JOHN STRANGE

Beautiful Jim, of the Blankshire Regiment. London: (1888). V. 37

Garrison Gossip Gathered in Blankhampton. A Novel. London: 1887. V. 37

WINTER, WILLIAM

David Belasco, His Life. New York: 1920. V. 46

George William Curtis - a Eulogy Delivered Before the People at Staten Island . . . New York: 1893. V. 42

WINTERBOTHAM, WILLIAM

An Historical, Geographical, Commercial and Philosophical View of the American States, and the European Settlements . . . London: 1795. V. 45

THE WINTERBOTTOM Book Cloth Co. Manchester: 1900? V. 45

WINTERBOTTOM BOOK CLOTH CO. LTD..

Art Fabrics. London: 1920's. V. 44

WINTERICH, JOHN T.

Early American Books and Printing. Boston: 1935. V. 42

The Grolier Club 1848-1950. New York: 1950. V. 41; 46

Pages from Earlier Editions of Horace From the Beginnings of Printing to the Present Century Selected to Accompany the Odes and Epodes. New York: 1961. V. 43

23 Books and the Stories Behind Them. Berkeley: 1938. V. 43

WINTERNITZ, MILTON CHARLES

Collected Studies on the Pathology of War Gas Poisoning. New Haven: 1920. V. 46

WINTERS, YVOR

Maule's Curse. Seven Studies in the History of American Obscurantism. Norfolk: 1938. V. 38

The Proof. New York: 1930. V. 38

WINTERTON, RALPH

Poetae Minores Graeci. Cantabrigiae: 1652. V. 40

WINTHER, OSCAR OSBURN

The Old Oregon Country. Bloomington: 1950. V. 45

The Story of San Jose, 1777-1869, California's First Pueblo. San Francisco: 1935. V. 40

WINTHROP, JOHN 1587-1649

A Journal of the Transactions and Occurrences in the Settlement of Massachusetts and the Other New-England Colonies, from the Year 1630 to 1644. Hartford: 1790. V. 38

A Lecture on Earthquakes; Read in the Chapel of Harvard College in Cambridge, N.E. November 26th 1755. Boston: 1755. V. 45

Relation of a Voyage from Boston to Newfoundland, for the Observation of the Transit of Venus, June 6, 1761. Boston: 1761. V. 38

A Short Story of the Rise, Reign and Ruin of the Antinomians, Ramilists and Libertines, that Infected the Churches of New England . . . London: 1644. V. 43; 45

Two Lectures on the Parallax and Distance of the Sun, as Deducible from the Transit of Venus. Read in Holden Chapel at Harvard College in Cambridge, New England, March 1769. Boston: 1769. V. 37

WINTHROP, THEODORE

The Canoe and the Saddle, Adventures Among the North Western Rivers and Forests and Isthmiana. Boston: 1863. V. 46

The Canoe and the Saddle or Klalam and Clickatat. Tacoma: 1913. V. 39; 44; 45

WINTON, JOHN G.

Modern Steam Practice and Engineering . . . London: 1883. V. 42

WINTON, N. W.

Pacific Railroad. Speech of the Hon. N. W. Winton, in the Nevada Senate, Febraruy 27th, 1865. Carson City: 1865. V. 39

WINTRHOP, R. C.

A Difference of Opinion Concerning the Reasons Why Katherine Winthrop Refused to Marry Chief Justice Sewall. Boston: 1885. V. 39

WINTRINGHAM, CLIFTON 1689-1748

Commentarium Nosologicum, Morbos Epidemicos et Aeris Variationes in Urbe Eboaracensi Locisque Vicinis per Decem Annos Grassantes Complectens. London: 1773. V. 39

WIRSING, ADAM LUDWIG

Marmora et Adfines Atiquos Lapides Coloribus Suis Exprimi . . . Nurnberg: 1775. V. 46

WIRSUNG, CHRISTOPH

The General Practice of Physicke. London: 1617. V. 42

WIRT, ELIZABETH WASHINGTON GAMBLE

Flora's Dictionary. Baltimore: (1855. V. 37

WIRT, WILLIAM

The Letters of the British Spy. Richmond: 1805. V. 46

Opinion on the Right of the State of Georgia to Extend Her Laws Over the Cherokee Nation. New Echota: 1830. V. 37

Sketches of the Life and Character of Patrick Henry. Philadelphia: 1817. V. 42

Sketches of the Life and Character of Patrick Henry. Philadelphia: 1818. V. 41; 44

The Two Principal Arguments of William Wirt, Esquire, on the Trial of Aaron Burr, for High Treason, and on the Motion to Commit Aaron Burr and Others, for Trial in Kentucky. Richmond: 1808. V. 41; 44

WIRTZUNG, CHRISTOPHER 1500-1571

The General Practise of Physick. London: 1654. V. 41

WISCHNITZER, RACHEL

Synagogue Architecture in the United States. Philadelphia: 1955. V. 45

WISCONSIN AND LAKE SUPERIOR MINING AND SMELTING CO.

THE Penokee Iron Range of Lake Superior, With Reports and Statistics, Showing Its Mineral Wealth and Prospects. Charter and Organization of the Wisconsin and Lake Superior Mining and Smelting Co. Milwaukee: 1860. V. 39

WISCONSIN. CONSTITUTION - 1846

Constitution of the State of Wisconsin. Madison: 1846. V. 40

WISCONSIN. CONSTITUTIONAL CONVENTION

Journal of the Convention to Form a Constitution for the State of Wisconsin, Begun and Held at Madison, on the Fifth Day of October, One Thousand Eight Hundred and Forty-Six. Madison: 1847. V. 37; 40; 42

THE WISCONSIN Farmer, and Northwestern Cultivator. Madison: 1856-57. V. 37

WISCONSIN. GOVERNOR - 1856

Annual Message of . . . Governor of the State of Wisconsin . . . January 11, 1856. Madison: 1856. V. 39

WISCONSIN: Its Natural Resources and Industrial Progress. Madison, Wisc.: 1862. V. 37

WISCONSIN. LEGISLATURE

Journal of the Council of the First Legislative Assembly of Wisconsin . . . Belmot: 1836. V. 44

WISDEN, JOHN

Wisden's Cricketers' Almanack for 1912. London: 1912. V. 41; 42

WISDOM in Miniature; or the Pleasing Instructor, Being a Collection of Sentences, Divine, Moral and Historical. London: 1804. V. 42

WISDOM in Miniature; or, the Young Gentleman and Lady's Pleasing Instructor. Coventry: 1791. V. 37

WISDOM In Miniature: or the Young Gentleman and Lady's Pleasing Instructor . . . London: 1794. V. 46

WISDOM in Miniature: or the Young Gentlemen and Lady's Pleasing Instructor . . . Brooklyn: 1800. V. 38

WISDOMITE CLUB

An Hour in the Study, by the Wisdomite Club. London: 1816. V. 41; 42

WISE, EDWARD

The Remarkable Tryal of Thomas Chandler, Late of Clifford's Inn, London, Gent. Reading: 1751. V. 38

WISE, FRANCIS 1695-1767

A Letter to Dr. Mead Concerning Some Antiquities in Berkshire . . . (with) Further Observations Upon the White Horse and Other Antiquities in Berkshire. Oxford: 1738-42. V. 39; 42

Nummorum Antiquorum Scriis Bodleianis Reconditorum Catalogus cum Commentario Tabrulis Aeneis et Appendice. Oxford: 1750. V. 46

Some Enquiries Concerning the First Inhabitants, Language, Religion, Learning and Letters of Europe. Oxford: 1758. V. 40; 45

WISE, GEORGE

History of the Seventeenth Virginia Infantry, C.S.A. Baltimore: 1870. V. 37

WISE, H. A.

Los Gringos: or, An Inside View of Mexico and California, with Wanderings in Peru, Chili, and Polynesia. New York: 1849. V. 37

WISE, H. D.

Tigers of the Sea. New York: 1937. V. 45

WISE, HENRY

An Analysis of One Hundred Voyages to and From India, China, etc., with Remarks on the Advantages of Steam-Power, and Suggestions for Improving Thereby the Communication with India. London: 1839. V. 38

WISE, HENRY AUGUSTUS 1819-1869

Los Gringos: or, an Inside View of Mexico and California, with Wanderings in Peur, Chili and Polynesia. New York. V. 38

Los Gringos: or, an Inside View of Mexico and California, with Wanderings in Peru, Chili and Polynesia. London: 1849. V. 42; 45

Los Gringos; or, an Inside View of Mexico and California, with Wanderings in Peru, Chili, and Polynesia. New York: 1849. V. 37; 40; 41; 43

Los Gringos or, an Inside View of Mexico and California, with Wanderings in Peru, Chili and Polynesia. New York: 1857. V. 45

Los Gringos. New York: 1850. V. 37

Scampavias from Gibel Tarek to Stamboul, by Harry Gringo. New York: 1857. V. 41

WISE, HUGH D.

Tigers of the Sea. New York: 1937. V. 37; 43; 46

WISE, ISAAC M.

History of the Israelitish Nation, from Abraham to the Present Time. Albany: 1854. V. 43; 46

A Lecture, Delivered Jan. 7, 1869 Before the Theological and Religious Library Association of Cincinnati. Cincinnati: 1869. V. 43

The Martyrdom of Jesus of Nazareth. Cincinnati: 1874. V. 37

WISE, JENNINGS CROPPER

The Long Arm of Lee: or the History of the ARtillery of the Army of Northern Virigina . . . Lynchburg: 1915. V. 44

WISE, JOHN

Full Particulars of the Greatest Aerial Voyage on Record. From St. Louis, Mo. to Adams, New York, in Nineteen Hours. New York: 1859. V. 37

A System of Aeronautics Comprehending Its Earliest Investigations, and Modern Practice and Art. Philadelphia: 1850. V. 37; 38; 42; 44; 45

A Vindiction of the Government of New-England Chruches. Boston. V. 46

A Vindication of the Government of New England Churches. Boston: 1772. V. 39; 41; 44

WISE, JOHN R.

The First of May, A Fairy Tale Masque: Presented in a Series of 52 Designs by Walter Crane. London. V. 41

The New Forest: Its History and Its Scenery. London: 1880. V. 41

WISE, JOSEPH

A Miscellany of Poems. London: 1775. V. 38

WISE, ROBERT

Remarks on Our Present Position with Affghanistan and China. Liverpool: 1842. V. 43

Remarks on Our Present Position with Affghanistan and China. Addressed to Rear Adrmiral Sir Edward Tucker, K.C.B. London: 1842. V. 38

WISE, T. A.

Commentary on the Hindu System of Medicine. Thacker, Calcutta: 1845. V. 39; 40; 41; 44; 45; 46

WISE, THOMAS, accountant

The Newest Young Man's Companion . . . London: 1773. V. 41

WISE, THOMAS JAMES 1859-1937

The Ashley Library. London: 1922-34. V. 39

The Ashley Library, a Catalogue of Printed Books, Manuscripts and Autograph Letters, Collected by Thomas J. Wise. Folkestone: 1971. V. 43

A Bibliographical List of the Scarcer Works and Uncollected Writings of Algernon Charles Swinburne. London: 1897. V. 41

A Bibliography of the Writings in Prose and Verse of Walter Savage Landor. London: 1919. V. 42; 44; 46

A Bibliography of the Writings in Prose and Verse of Algernon Charles Swinburne. London: 1919-20. V. 39

A Bibliography of the Writings of Joseph Conrad. London: 1920. V. 39

Bibliography of the Writings of Joseph Conrad. London: 1921. V. 39; 40

A Bibliography of the Writings in Verse and Prose of George Gordon Noel, Baron Byron. London: 1932. V. 38; 40; 42

WISE, THOMAS JAMES 1859-1937 continued

A Bibliography of the Writings in Verse and Prose of George Gordon Noel, Baron Byron. London: 1932/33. V. 37; 42; 44

A Bibliography of Writings in Verse and Prose of George Gordon Noel, Baron Byron. London: 1963. V. 42

A Biographical List of the Scarcer Works and Uncollected Writings of Algernon Charles Swinburne. London: 1897. V. 44

The Bronte Family: a Bibliography of the Writings in Prose and Verse. London: 1917. V. 41; 43

A Bronte Library. London: 1929. V. 39; 43

A Browning Library, a Catalogue of Printed Books, manuscripts and Autograph Letters by Robert Browning and Elizabeth Barrett Browning. London: 1929. V. 39; 41; 46

A Byron Library. London: 1928. V. 39; 41; 43

Two Lake Poets. A Catalogue of Printed Books, Manuscripts and Autograph Letters by William Wordsworth and Samuel Taylor Coleridge. London: 1927. V. 38

A Conrad Library. A Catalogue of Printed Books, Manuscripts, and Autograph Letters . . . Collected by Thomas James Wise. London: 1928. V. 41; 43

A Dryden Library. London: 1930. V. 39; 41; 42; 43; 46

A Landor Library. London: 1928. V. 39; 42

Letters of Thomas J. Wise to John Henry Wrenn. New York: 1944. V. 39; 40; 41

A Pope Library, a Catalogue of Plays, Poems and Prose Writings by Alexander Pope. London: 1931. V. 44

A Shelley Library. London: 1924. V. 39; 46

Spenser's Faerie Queene. Edited by Thomas J. Wise . . . Illustrated by Walter Crane. London: 1894-97. V. 37

A Swinburne Library. London: 1925. V. 38; 39; 40; 42

Two Lake Poets. London: 1927. V. 43

WISEMAN, D. J.

Catalogue of the Western Asiatic Seals in the British Museum. I: Cylinder Seals, Uruk-Early Dynastic Periods. London: 1962. V. 37; 44

WISEMAN, HENRY

The Highways of Peaceful Commerce Have Been the Highways of Art . . . Liverpool: 1853. V. 38

WISEMAN, JAMES

Studies in the Antiquities of Stobi. Beograd: 1973-81. V. 42; 44

WISEMAN, NICHOLAS P. S.

Fabiola; or the Church of the Catacombs. London: 1855. V. 43; 46

WISEMAN, RICHARD

Eight Chirurgical Treatises, On These Following Heads: I. Of Tumours. II. Of Ulcers. III of Diseases of the Anus. IV. of the Kings-Evil. V. Of Wounds. VI. Of Gun-shot Wounds. VII. Of Fractures and Luxations. VIII. Of the Lues Venera. London: 1705. V. 39; 42; 43

Several Chirurgical Treatises. London: 1686. V. 39; 42

WISHART, GEORGE

I)acobi) G(raemi) De Rebus Auspiciis . . . Caroli Magnae Britanniae . . . Regis . . . sub Imperie . . . Parisiis: 1648. V. 43

WISLIZENUS, FREDERICK ADOLPHUS 1810-1889

Denkschrift Uber Eine Reise nach Nord-Mexico . . . Braunschweig: 1850. V. 37; 38; 41; 42

A Journey to the Rocky Mountains in the Year 1839. St. Louis: 1912. V. 37; 40; 41; 42; 45

Memoir of a Tour to Northern Mexico, Connected with Col. Doniphan's Expedition in 1846 and 1847. Washington: 1848. V. 45

WISON, H. W.

With the Flag to Pretoria. A History of the Boer War of 1899-1900. By H.W. Wilson. Illustrated with numerous photos, and numerous sketches taken in South Africa. London: 1900. V. 37

WISS, M.

The Family Robinson Crusoe; or, Journal of a Father Shipwrecked with His Wife and Children on an Uninhabited Island. London: 1816. V. 39

WISSLER, CLARK

The Indians of Greater New York and the Lower Hudson. New York: 1909. V. 39

WISSMANN, HERMAN VON

My Second Journey Through Equatorial Africa from the Congo to the Zambesi in the Years 1886 & 1887. London: 1891. V. 38; 41; 42; 46

WISTAR, CASPAR

Dissertatio Medica Inauguralis. De Animo Demisso. Edinburgh: 1786. V. 45; 46

A System of Anatomy for the Use of Students of Medicine. Philadelphia: 1811-14. V. 42; 43; 45

A System of Anatomy. Philadelphia: 1817. V. 40; 41; 44; 45; 46

WISTAR, ISAAC JONES

Autobiography of Isaac Jones Wistar. Philadelphia: 1914. V. 37; 39; 40; 42

WISTER, FRANCIS

Recollections of the 12th U.S. Infantry and Regular Division, 1861-65. Philadelphia: 1887. V. 44

WISTER, OWEN 1860-1938

The Jimmyjohn Boss and Other Stories. New York: & London: 1901. V. 46

Mother. New York: 1907. V. 38

The New Swiss Family Robinson. New York: 1922. V. 40

Padre Ignacio of the Song of Temptation. New York: 1911. V. 38

The Pentecost of Calamity. New York: 1915. V. 38

Roosevelt, the Story of a Friendship 1880-1919. New York: 1930. V. 39

The Virginian. New York: 1902. V. 38; 41; 45; 46

The Virginian. New York: 1911. V. 39

The Virginian, a Horseman of the Plains. Los Angeles: 1951. V. 38

When West was West. New York: 1928. V. 43

WIT, FREDERICK DE

Atlas Containing 51 Double Page Engraved Maps. Amsterdam: 1670. V. 39; 42

WITCHER, WALTER C.

The Unveiling of the Ku Klux Klan. Fort Worth?: 1922. V. 45

WITEKIND

Saxonis Rerum ab Henrico et Ottone Ilmpp. Gestarum Libri III. Basle: 1532. V. 45

WITELO

Peri Optikes (Graece), id Est de Natura, Ratione & Proiectione Radiorum Visus, Luminum, Colorum Atque Formarum, Quam Vulgo Perspectivam Vocant, Libri X . . . Norimbergae: 1535. V. 42

WITH General Sheridan in Lee's Last Campaign. Philadelphia: 1866. V. 42

WITHAM, HENRY T. M.

The Internal Structure of Fossil Vegetables Found in the Carboniferous and Oolitic Deposits of Great Britain. Edinburgh: 1833. V. 45

WITHER, GEORGE

Abuses Stript, and Whipt. London: 1614. V. 37; 40; 42

Abuses Stript, and Whipt: or Satyricall Essayes. Diuided into two Books. Revised and enlarged. London: 1617. V. 37

Britain's Remembrancer Containing a Narration of the Plague Lately Past . . . London: 1628. V. 40

Campo-Musae. London: 1643. V. 37; 40; 42; 44; 46

A Collection of Emblemes, Ancient and Moderne . . . London: 1635. V. 42

A Collection of Emblemes, Ancient and Moderne; Quickened with Metricall Illustrations, Both Morall and Divine . . . London: 1635-34. V. 39; 46

Fair Virtue, the Mistress of Philarete. London: 1818. V. 38

Fides-Anglicana. London: 1660. V. 42

The Hymnes and Songs of the Church Divided into Two Parts. London: 1623. V. 38; 40

An Improvement of Imprisonment, Disgrace, Poverty, Into Real Freedom . . . London: 1661. V. 42

A Love Songs. Concord: 1903. V. 40; 41

Memorandum to London, Occasioned by the Pestilence There Begun this Present Year MDCLXV . . . London: 1665. V. 37

The Shepherd's Hunting. London: 1814. V. 45

Speculum Specualtivum . . . London. V. 46

Speculum Speculativm. London. V. 40

Speculum Speculativum; or, a Considering Glass. London. V. 42

Speculum Speculativum; or, a Considering-Glass (in verse) . . . London. V. 42

Speculum Speculativum . . . London. V. 44

Speculum Speculativum . . . London: 1660 i.e. 1661. V. 42

Speculum Speculativum: or, a Considering Glass; being an Inspection into the present and late sad Condition of these Nations; with some Cautional Expressions made thereon . . . London: (1661). V. 37

Speculum Speculativum: or, a Considering-Glass (in verse); being an Inspection into the Present and late sad Condition of these Nations. London. V. 37

WITHER, S. THOMAS

Observations on Chronic Weakness. York: 1777. V. 40

WITHERBY, H. F.

The Handbook of British Birds. London: 1938. V. 38; 40

The Handbook of British Birds. London: 1938-41. V. 37; 38; 39; 42; 43

The Handbook of British Birds. London: 1943-44. V. 37; 38; 39; 44

The Handbook of British Birds. London: 1945 or 1952. V. 46

Handbook of British Birds. London: 1946-48-49. V. 37; 38

WITHERBY, H. F. continued

The Handbook of British Birds. London: 1947/48. V. 42

The Handbook of British Birds. 1948. V. 37

The Handbook of British Birds. London: 1949. V. 39

The Handbook of British Birds. London: 1952. V. 37

The Handbook of British Lords. London: 1940, 1949. V. 39

WITHERING, WILLIAM

An Account of the Scarlet Fever and Sore Throat of Scarlatina Anginosa . . . London: 1779. V. 40

An Account of the Foxglove and Some Of Its Medical Uses . . . Tokyo: 1950. V. 41

An Arrangement of British Plants; According to the Latest Improvement of the Linnean System. Birmingham: 1796. V. 39

An Arrangement of British Plants. London: 1796. V. 39

An Arrangement of British Plants . . . London: 1818. V. 40; 42

The Miscellaneous Tracts. To which is prefixed a memoir of his Life, Character, and Writings. London: 1822. V. 37

A Systematic Arrangement of British Plants . . . London: 1801. V. 45

William Withering and the Foxglove. A Bicentennial Selection of Letters from the Osler Bequest to the Royal Society of Medicine . . . London: 1986. V. 37; 38

WITHERS, ALEXANDER SCOTT

Chronicles of Border Warfare, or a History of the Settlement by the Whites of North-Western Virginia . . . Clarksburg: 1831. V. 37; 38; 39; 42; 44; 45

WITHERS, PHILIP

History of the Royal Malady, with Variety of Entertaining Anecdotes, To Which are Added, Strictures on the Declaration of Horne Tooke, Esq., Respecting 'Her Royal Highness the Princess of Wales,' . . . London: 1789. V. 41; 43

WITHERS, ROBERT JEWELL 1823-1894

Church of the Resurrection (Anglican), Rue des Drapiers, Boulevard de Waterloo, Brussels. London: 1864. V. 38

WITHERS, THOMAS

A Letter to a Friend, Concerning the Epidemic Fever of April and May, 1778 in York and Its Neighbourhood . . . York: 1778. V. 42

Observations on Chronic Weakness. York: 1777. V. 41; 44; 45

WITHERS, W.

The Acacia Tree . . . . Holt: 1842. V. 45

WITHERS, WILLIAM BRAMWELL

The History of Ballarat, from the First Pastoral Settlement to the Present Time. Ballarat: 1887. V. 42

WITHERSPOON, JOHN

Christian Magnanimity: A Sermon, Preached at princeton, September, 1775 . . . and again with Additions, September 23, 1787. To which is added, an address to the Senior Class. Who were to Receive the Degree of Bachelor of Arts. Princeton: 1787. V. 37

Treatises on Justification and Regeneration. Glasgow: 1824. V. 44

The Works of . . . Late President of the College at Princeton, New-Jersey . . . Philadelphia: 1802. V. 38

The Works of the Rev. John Witherspoon . . . Late President of the College, at Princeton New Jersey. To which is prefixed an Account of the Author's Life . . . by Rev. Dr. John Rogers, of New York . . . Philadelphia: 1800. V. 37

WITHIN Fort Sumter; or, a View of Major Anderson's Garrison Family for One Hundred and Ten Days. By One of the Company. New York: 1861. V. 39

WITHINGTON, MARY C.

A Catalogue of Manuscripts in the Collection of Western Americana Founded by William Robertson Coe . . . New Haven: 1952. V. 37

WITKIN, JOEL PETER

Gods of Earth and Heaven. Altadena: 1989. V. 46

WITNESS: a Collection of Original and Selected Pieces on Various Religious Subjects. Boston: 1809. V. 43

WITS, HERMAN 1636-1708

The Oeconomy of the Convenants Between God and Man. London: 1763. V. 39

THE WIT'S Magazine; or Library of Momus. London: 1825. V. 40

THE WIT'S MUSEUM; or an Elegant Collection of Bon Mots, Repartees, etc., Rational and Entertaining. London: 1780. V. 41

THE WITS of Westminster. London: 1772. V. 43

WITSEN, N.

Scheeps - Bouw. Amsterdam: 1671. V. 41

WITT, HAROLD

Family in the Forest and Other Poems. San Francisco: 1956. V. 44

WITT, JAN DE

Fables Moral and Political with Large Explications. Translated from the Dutch. London: 1703. V. 37

WITTENBURG, MARY S. THERESE, SISTER

The Machados & Rancho La Balona: The story of the Land and Its Ranchero, Jose Agustin Antonio Machado. Los Angeles: 1973. V. 45

WITTENMYER, ANNIE

A Collection of Recipes for the Use of Special Diet Kitchens in Military Hospitals. St. Louis: 1864. V. 40

WITTER, DANIEL

The Land Laws of the United States. Denver: 1884. V. 39

The Settler's Guide to the Entry of Public Lands. Denver: 1884. V. 37; 38

WITTGENSTEIN, LUDWIG

Philosophical Investigations. Oxford: 1953. V. 39

Remarks on the Foundations of Mathematics. Oxford: 1956. V. 39; 40; 41

Tractatus Logico - Philosophicus. London: 1922. V. 41; 43; 45

Tractatus Logico-Philosophicus . . . New York: 1922. V. 37; 46

THE WITTICISMS, Anecdotes, Jests and Sayings of Dr. Samuel Johnson During the Whole Course of His Life. London: 1793. V. 40

WITTIE, ROBERT

Scarbrough-Spaw; or a Description of the Nature and Vertues of the Spaw at Scarbrough, Yorkshire. York: 1667. V. 45

WITTLIFF, WILLIAM D.

Selected Ephemera: William D. Wittliff & the Encino Press 1964-1973. Austin: 1973. V. 40; 41

Vaquero: Genesis of the Texas Cowboy. San Antonio: 1972. V. 37; 39; 45

WITTMAN, WILLIAM

Travels in Turkey, Asia-Minor, Syria and Across the Desert into Egypt During the Years 1799, 1800 and 1801, in Company with the Turkish Army, and British Military Mission. London: 1803. V. 38

Travels in Turkey, Asia Minor, Syria and Across the Desert into Egypt, During the Years 1799, 1800 and 1801 . . . Philadelphia: 1804. V. 40; 42; 46

WITTROCK, WOLFGANG

Toulouse-Lautrec. The Complete Prints. London: 1985. V. 39; 41

WITTWOR, L. O.

Notes Relating to Education. London: 1852. V. 42

WITTY Apophthegms Delivered At Several Times, and Upon Several Occasions, by King James, King Charles, the Marquess of Worcester, Francis Lord Bacon and Sir Thomas Moor . . . London: 1671. V. 41; 42

WITZEL, GEORG

Hagiologivm, Sev. De Sanctis Ecclesiae. Historiae Divorvm Toto Terravm Orbe Celeberrimorum, e Sacris Scriptoribus . . . Mogvntiae: 1541. V. 38; 44

WITZLEBEN, ELISABETH VON

Stained Glass in French Cathedrals. New York: 1968. V. 42

WIX, EDWARD

Six Months of a Newfoundland Missionary Journal, From February to August, 1835. London: 1836. V. 38

WLETY, EUDORA

Novel Writing in an Apocalyptic Time. V. 46

WODDERSPOON, JOHN

John Crome and His Works . . . Norwich: 1876. V. 39; 44

WODEHOUSE, E. A.

Minos. Oxford: 1902. V. 41

WODEHOUSE, PELHAM GRENVILLE 1881-1975

The Adventures of Sally. London: 1923. V. 43

America I Like You. New York: 1856. V. 41

America I Like You. New York: 1956. V. 45; 46

. . . And Guy Bolton. Bring on the Girls. London: 1954. V. 45

Angel Cake. Garden City: 1952. V. 44; 45

Angel Cake. New York: 1952. V. 42

Aunts Aren't Gentlemen. London: 1974. V. 46

Bachelors Anonymous. 1974. V. 37

Bertie Wooster Sees It Through. New York: 1955. V. 45; 46

Big Money. 19--? V. 42

WODEHOUSE, PELHAM GRENVILLE 1881-1975 continued

Big Money. London: 1931. V. 41; 43; 45
Big Money. Toronto: 1931. V. 37
Bill the Conqueror. London: 1924. V. 43
Bill the Conqueror. New York: 1924. V. 43; 45
Blandings Castle. Garden City: 1935. V. 41; 42
Blandings Castle and Elsewhere. London: 1935. V. 46
Bring on the Girls. London: 1954. V. 41
Brinkley Manor. 1934. V. 46
Brinkley Manor. Boston: 1934. V. 39; 45; 46
The Brinkmanship of Galahad Threepwood. New York: 1964. V. 46
The Butler Did It. New York: 1957. V. 46
Carry on Jeeves. London: 1925. V. 44; 45; 46
Carry on, Jeeves! Very Good Jeeves! The Inimitable Jeeves. Leipzig: 1930-35. V. 42
The Clicking of Cuthbert. London: 1922. V. 41; 43; 46
Cocktail Time. London: 1958. V. 45; 46
The Code of the Woosters. London: 1938. V. 37; 41; 46
The Crime Wave at Blandings. Garden City: 1937. V. 42
The Crime Wave at Blandings. New York: 1937. V. 39; 46
A Damsel in Distress. New York: 1919. V. 42
Doctor Sally. London: 1932. V. 46
Eggs, Beans and Crumpets. 1940. V. 42
Eggs, Beans and Crumpets. London: 1949. V. 45
Enter Psmith. London: 1935. V. 38; 43
A Few Quick Ones. London: 1959. V. 46
A Few Quick Ones. New York: 1959. V. 46
Fisher Preferred. 1929. V. 46
Full Moon. Garden City: 1947. V. 46
Full Moon. London: 1947. V. 41; 42; 43; 45; 46
The Gold Bat. London: 1904. V. 42
The Golden Moth. London: 1921. V. 38
Golf Without Tears. New York: 1924. V. 42; 43; 46
Good Morning Bill. London: 1928. V. 42; 43; 45
The Great Sermon Handicap. London. V. 40
The Great Sermon Handicap. London: 1933. V. 41; 42
The Head of Kay's. London: 1905. V. 42
The Heart of a Goof. London: 1926. V. 46
Heavy Weather. London: 1933. V. 40; 46
Heavy Weather. Toronto: 1933. V. 44; 45
Ice in the Bedroom. London: 1961. V. 45
The Ice in the Bedroom. New York: 1961. V. 46
If I Were You. London: 1931. V. 46
Indiscretions of Archie. 1921. V. 42
The Inimitable Jeeves. London: 1923. V. 41; 44; 46
The Intrusion of Jimmy. 1910. V. 43
The Intrusion of Jimmy. New York: 1910. V. 41; 42; 44; 45; 46
Jeeves. New York: 1923. V. 38; 46
Jeeves in the Offing. London: 1960. V. 43; 46
Joy in the Morning. London: 1945. V. 39
Joy in the Morning. Garden City: 1946. V. 46
Laughing Gas. Garden City: 1936. V. 46
Laughing Gas. London: 1936. V. 46
Leave it to Psmith. London: 1924. V. 45
The Little Nugget. New York: 1914. V. 46
Lord Emsworth and Others. London: 1937. V. 41
Love Among the Chickens. New York: 1909. V. 37; 38; 39; 41; 42; 46
The Luck of the Bodkins. London: 1935. V. 38
The Luck of the Bodkins. Boston: 1936. V. 42; 45
The Mating Season. New York: 194. V. 39
The Mating Season. London: 1949. V. 41; 45
The Mating Season. New York: 1949. V. 42; 46
Meet Mr. Mulliner. London: 1927. V. 43; 46
Meet Mr. Mulliner. 1930. V. 42
Mr. Mulliner Speaking. New York: 1930. V. 39; 46
Money for Nothing. 1930. V. 42
Money in the Bank. Garden City: 1942. V. 46
Much Obliged, Jeeves. London: 1971. V. 45
Mulliner Nights. Toronto: 1933. V. 46
My Man Jeeves. London. V. 40
My Man Jeeves: Stories. London: 1919. V. 41
Nothing Serious. Garden City: 1951. V. 41; 42; 46
The Old Reliable. Garden City: 1951. V. 46
The Old Reliable. London: 1951. V. 45

Over Seventy. London: 1957. V. 38
A Pelican at Blandings. London: 1969. V. 45
Performing Flea. 1953. V. 42
Performing Flea. London: 1953. V. 45
The Pothunters. 1902. V. 42
The Pothunters. London: 1902. V. 45; 46
The Pothunters. London: 1902/1905. V. 41
Prefects Uncle. 1903. V. 42
The Prince and Betty. New York: 1912. V. 38; 41; 42
Psmith in the City. London: 1910. V. 42; 43
Quick Service. New York: 1940. V. 46
Quck Service. Toronto: 1941. V. 39; 44; 45
Quick Service. 1949. V. 46
The Return of Jeeves. New York: 1954. V. 43; 46
Right Ho, Jeeves. London: 1935. V. 43
Right Ho Jeeves. 1940. V. 42
Ring for Jeeves. London: 1953. V. 38
Sam in the Suburbs. 1925. V. 42
Sam the Sudden. London: 1925. V. 41; 45; 46
Service with a Smile. London: 1962. V. 41; 42; 46
The Small Bachelor. 1927. V. 44
The Small Bachelor. London: 1927. V. 38; 40; 42; 43
Something New. 1915. V. 46
Something Fishy. 1957. V. 42
Spring Fever. Garden City: 1948. V. 46
Stiff Upper Lip, Jeeves. London: 1963. V. 39; 41; 42; 45; 46
Stiff Upper Lip, Jeeves. New York: 1963. V. 46
Summer Lightning. London: 1929. V. 45; 46
Summer Moonshine. 1937. V. 42
Summer Moonshine. Garden City: 1937. V. 42
Summer Moonshine. New York: 1937. V. 39; 44; 45
The Swoop! London: 1909. V. 40
Thank You, Jeeves. London: 1934. V. 43; 46
Thank You Jeeves. 1949. V. 42
Ukridge. London. V. 46
Ukridge. London: 1924. V. 43; 46
Uncle Dynamite. New York: 1948. V. 39
Uncle Dynamite. 1948. V. 42
Uncle Dynamite. London: 1948. V. 46
Uncle Fred in Springtime. 1939. V. 42
Uncle Fred in Springtime. New York: 1939. V. 42
Uncle Fred in the Springtime. 1939. V. 42
Uncle Fred in the Springtime. 1939. V. 37
Uncle Fred in the Springtime. London: 1939. V. 43; 46
Uneasy Money. 1916. V. 37
Very Good, Jeeves. Garden City: 1930. V. 41; 42; 46
The White Feather. London: 1914. V. 38; 42
William Tell Told Again. London: 1904. V. 38
William Tell Told Again. London: 1905. V. 43
Wodehouse on Crime. New Haven/New York: 1981. V. 46
Wodehouse on Golf. 1940. V. 46
Young Men in Spats. Garden City: 1936. V. 41; 44
Young Men in Spats. London: 1936. V. 43
Young Men in Spats. 1940. V. 42

WODHULL, MICHAEL

Poems. London: 1772. V. 38; 40
Poems. London: 1804. V. 38; 41

WOELLWARTH, MARY E.

Songs of Our Lady of Silence. Ditchling: 1921. V. 40; 41; 45; 46

WOGAN, CHARLES

Female Fortitude: Exemplify'd in an Impartial Narrative of the Seizure, Escape and Marriage of the Princess Clementina Sobieski. London: 1722. V. 38; 40; 45

WOGLOM, GILBERT TOTTEN

Parakites: a Treatise on the Making and Flying of Tailess Kites . . . New York: 1896. V. 38; 45

WOILLEZ, EUGENE J.

Archeologie des Monuments Religieux de l'Ancient Beauvoisis . . . Paris: 1839-49. V. 44

WOLBACH, S. BURT

Studies on Rocky Mountain Spotted Fever. Boston: 1919. V. 44

WOLCOT, JOHN 1738-1819

Bozzy & Piozzi: or, the British Biographers. London: 1788. V. 39

The Louisiad. London: 1791. V. 44

Pindariana; or Peter's Portfolio. London: 1794. V. 38

A Poetical and Congratulatory Epistle to James Boswell, Esq . . . London: 1788. V. 41

The Works. London: 1786-87. V. 40

The Works. London: 1789. V. 39

The Works of Peter Pindar. Dublin: 1793. V. 39; 40

The Works of Peter Pindar. London: 1794. V. 40; 43

The Works. London: 1794-1801. V. 40; 44; 45

Works. London: 1794-96. V. 40; 43; 46

The Works of Peter Pindar. Dublin: 1795. V. 38

The Works of Peter Pindar, Esq. Paris: 1800? V. 38

The Works of Peter Pindar, Esq. London: 1812. V. 38

WOLCOTT, OLIVER

An Address, to the People of the United States, on the Subject of the Report of a Committee of the House of Represenatives, Appointed to 'Examine . . . Whether Mones Drawn from the Treasury, Have Been Faithfully Applied to the Objects of Which They were . . . ' Boston: 1802. V. 44; 45

Remarks on the Present State of Currency, Credit, Commerce and National Industry . . . New York: 1820. V. 45

WOLCOTT, ROGER

Poetical Meditations, Being the Improvement of Some Vacant Hours. New London: 1725. V. 39; 44; 45

WOLCOTT, WALTER

The Military History of Yates County, New York. Penn Yan: 1895. V. 44

WOLF, CHRISTIAN

Epistolae et Vita Divi Thomae Martyris et Archi-Episcopi Cantuariensis. Brussels: 1682. V. 40

WOLF, E. C.

Rowlandson and His Illustrations of Eighteenth Century Literature. Copenhagen: 1945. V. 39

WOLF, EDWIN

A Descriptive Catalogue of the John Frederick Lewis Collection of European Manuscripts in the Free Library of Philadelphia. Philadelphia: 1937. V. 43

Rosenbach, a Biography. Cleveland: 1960. V. 38; 39; 41; 43; 46

Rosenbach, a Biography. Cleveland & New York: 1960. V. 39

WOLF-HUNTING and Wild Sport in Lower Brittany. London: 1875. V. 43

WOLF, JOSEPH

Heraldry. Chicago: 1956. V. 41

The Life of A. H. Palmer. London: 1895. V. 37

Monograph of the Pheasants (1872). The Original Charcoal Sketches. V. 45

Monograph of the Pheasants (1872). The Original Charcoal Sketches. V. 46

Monograph of the Pheasants. London: 1988. V. 40; 41; 43

WOLF, STEWART

Human Gastric Function, an Experimental study of a Man and His Stomach. New York: 1943. V. 42

WOLFE, BYRON B.

The Sketchbook of Byron B. Wolfe. Kansas City: 1972. V. 39; 41; 44

WOLFE, CHARLES

Remains, with a Brief Memoir. Dublin: 1825. V. 37

WOLFE, CHARLES W.

Catalogue of the Diocesan Library, Cashel, Co. Tipperary. Boston: 1973. V. 43

WOLFE, ELSIE DE

The House in Good Taste. New York: 1913. V. 45

WOLFE, G.

At the Point of Capricorn. 1983. V. 39

Bibliomen-Twenty Characters Waiting for a Book. 1983. V. 39

Bibliomen - Twenty Characters Waiting for a Book. 1984. V. 44

The Boy Who Hooked the Sun. 1985. V. 44

The Castle of the Otter. 1982. V. 44

The Castle of the Otter. 1982. V. 39

The Claw of the Conciliator. 1981. V. 44

The Sword of the Lictor. 1982. V. 43

The Urth of the New Sun. 1987. V. 39

The Urth of the New Sun. 1987. V. 43

WOLFE, GENE

The Fifth Head of Cerberus. New York: 1972. V. 41; 42

The Shadow of the Torturer. New York: 1980. V. 45

WOLFE, HUMBERT

The Craft of Verse. New York: 1928. V. 38; 40

The Silver Cat and Other Poems. London: 1928. V. 38

The Silver Cat and Other Poems. New York: 1928. V. 40; 44; 45; 46

WOLFE, J. H.

Our Heroes in the Great World War. Ottawa: 1919. V. 43

WOLFE, J. M.

Wolfe's Omaha City Directory, 1878-79. Omaha: 1878. V. 42; 45

WOLFE, JAMES

General Wolfe's Instructions to Young Officers: Also His Orders for a Battalion and an Army. London: 1768. V. 42; 44

General Wolfe's Instructions to Young Officers . . . Philadelphia: 1778. V. 45

General Wolfe's Instructions to Young Officers . . . London: 1780. V. 39; 44

WOLFE, JOSEPH

Journal . . . in a Series of Letters to Sir Thomas Baring. London: 1839. V. 37

WOLFE, MICHAEL

The Two-Star Pigeon. New York: 1975. V. 43

WOLFE-MURRAY, DAVID K.

Birds Through the Year. 1938. V. 46

WOLFE, OLIVER HOWARD

Back Log and Pine Knot. 1916. V. 39

WOLFE, RICHARD

Jacob Bigelow's American Medical Botany. North Hills: 1979. V. 38; 40

WOLFE, RICHARD J.

Jacob Bigelow's American Medical Botany, 1817-1821. 1979. V. 39

Jacob Bigelow's American Medical Botany. North Hills: 1979. V. 37; 38; 40; 41; 42; 44

Louis Herman Kinder and Fine Bookbining in America. 1985. V. 40

Louis Herman Kinder and Fine Bookbinding in America . . . 1985. V. 45

Louis Herman Kinder and Fine Bookbinding in America. 1985. V. 38

Louis Herman Kinder and Fine Bookbinding in America. Newtown: 1985. V. 37; 38; 39; 41; 42; 43; 44; 45

Marbled Paper. Its History, Techniques and Patterns. 1989. V. 41

On Improvements in Marbling the Edges of Books and Paper. Newtown: 1983. V. 37; 38; 41; 42; 44; 46

The Role of the Mann Family . . . in Marbling . . . and Other Booktrade Activities. Boston: 1981. V. 42; 44

Role of the Mann Family of Dedham, Massachusetts in the Marbling of Paper in Nineteenth century America. N.P.: 1981. V. 38

Secular Music in America, 1801-1825: A Bibliography. New York: 1964. V. 42

Three Early French Essays on Paper Marbling, 1642-1765. Newtown: 1987. V. 37; 38; 39; 40; 41; 45

WOLFE, THOMAS CLAYTON 1900-1938

The Crisis in Industry. Chapel Hill: 1919. V. 45; 46

The Crisis in Industry. Chapel Hill: 1919. V. 37

The Face of a Nation. New York: 1939. V. 39

From Death to Morning. New York: 1935. V. 37; 38; 39; 40; 41; 42; 43; 44; 45; 46

From Death to Morning. London: 1936. V. 39

From Death to Morning. New York: 1945. V. 45

Gentlemen of the Press. Chicago: 1942. V. 37; 39; 42; 44

The Hills Beyond. New York: 1941. V. 44; 45; 46

Look Homeward, Angel. New York: 1928. V. 40

Look Homeward Angel. New York: 1929. V. 37; 39; 41; 45; 46

Look Homeward Angel. London: 1930. V. 37; 39; 41; 42; 45; 46

Look Homeward Angel. New York: 1947. V. 43

Mannerhouse. New York: 1948. V. 37; 40; 44; 46

Mannerhouse. A Play in a Prologue and Three Acts. New York: 1948. V. 37

A Note on Experts: Dexter Vespasian Joyner. New York: 1939. V. 37; 38; 39; 40; 42; 45

Of Time and the River - a Legend of Man's Hunger in His Youth. London: 1935. V. 38

Of Time and the River. New York: 1935. V. 37; 39; 40; 41; 42; 43; 44; 45; 46

Au Fil Du Temps. Paris: 1951. V. 45

The Story of A Novel. New York: 1936. V. 37; 39; 44

The Story of a Novel. New York & London: 1936. V. 39

WOLFE, THOMAS CLAYTON 1900-1938 continued

To Rupert Brooke. Paris: 1948. V. 37; 39

The Web and the Rock. New York: 1939. V. 37; 39; 40; 41; 45; 46

The Web and the Rock. New York/London: 1939. V. 37; 38; 39; 40; 43

The Web and the Rock. London: 1947. V. 39; 42

A Western Journal. 1951. V. 39

The Years of Wandering in Many Lands and Cities. New York: 1949. V. 37; 39

You Can't Go Home Again. New York: 1940. V. 41; 43; 45; 46

You Can't Go Home Again. New York/London: (1940). V. 37

You Can't Go Home Again. London: 1947. V. 39

WOLFE, TOBIAS

In the Garden of the North American Martyrs. New York: 1981. V. 44

The Liar. Vineburg: 1989. V. 44

The Other Miller. 1900. V. 44

The Other Miller. 1990. V. 44

Ugly Rumours. London: 1975. V. 44

WOLFE, TOM

Bonfire of the Vanities. New York: 1987. V. 41; 42; 44; 45

From Bauhaus to Our House. New York: 1981. V. 42

In Our Time. New York: 1980. V. 44

The Purple Decades. New York: 1982. V. 44

The Right Stuff. New York: 1979. V. 45; 46

The Shadow of the Torturer. The Claw of the Conciliator. The Sword of the Lictor. The Citadel of the Autarch. The Urth of the New Sun. New York: 1980-87. V. 46

WOLFF, ALBERT

Notes Upon Certain Masters of the XIX Century. New York: 1886. V. 38; 44

WOLFF, CASPAR

Vues Remarquables des Montagnes de la Suisse avec Leur Description. Berne: 1776. V. 40

WOLFF, CHRISTIAN, FREIHERR VON

Der Anfangsgrunde aller Mathematischen Wissenschaften . . . (with) Kurzer Unterricht von den Vornehmsten Mathematischen Schriften . . . Vienna: 1763. V. 46

WOLFF, J. D.

Catalogus Variorum Librorum, Theologicorum, Juridicorum, Historicorum, Philosophicorum, ac Miscellaneorum, Quos Publica Auctione in Aedibus Joh. Dan. Wolfii, Stanni Fusoris in Platea Spiritus S. Prope Ecclesiam Nationis Britannicae Sitis . . . Dantzig: 1716. V. 39

WOLFF, JENS

Sketches on a Tour to Copenahgen, Through Norway and Sweden . . . London: 1814. V. 38; 40; 43; 44; 46

WOLFF, JOSEPH

Narrative of a Mission to Bokhara, in the Years 1843-1845, to Ascertain the Fate of Colonel Stoddart and Captain Conolly. London: 1845. V. 42

Narrative of a Mission to Bokhara, in the Years 1843-1845, to Ascertain the Fate of Colonel Stoddart and Captain Conolly. London: 1846. V. 39

Researches and Missionary Labours Among the Jews, Mohammedans, and Other Sects . . . Philadelphia: 1837. V. 43

Travels and Adventures of . . . London: 1860-61. V. 37; 45

WOLFF, JULIAN

The Sherlockian Atlas. New York: 1952. V. 46

WOLFF, O. L. B.

The British Museum. Bielefield: 1836-39. V. 45; 46

WOLFF, ROBERT LEE

Nineteenth Century Fiction. New York: 1981. V. 40

Nineteenth Century Fiction. New York: 1982. V. 40

Nineteenth Century Fiction. New York: 1984. V. 40

Nineteenth Century Fiction. New York: 1985. V. 40

Nineteenth Century Fiction. New York: 1986. V. 40

WOLFF, TOBIAS

In the Garden of the North American Martyrs. New York: 1981. V. 42

The Liar. Vineburg: 1989. V. 43

The Other Miller. Derry: 1986/90. V. 43

The Other Miller. 1990. V. 43

The Other Miller. 1990. V. 43

Ugly Rumours. London: 1975. V. 42; 45

WOLFF, W. A.

Behind the Screen. 1916. V. 37

WOLFF, W. J.

Ecology of the Wadden Sea. Rotterdam: 1983. V. 37; 38

WOLFFHART, KONRAD

Apophthegmatum Siue Responsorum Memorabilium, Ex Probatissimis Quibusqz tam Graecis Quam Latinis Autoribus, Priscis Pariter Atque Recentioribus Collectorum, Loci Commvnes ad Ordinem Alphabeticum Redacti. Basle: 1555. V. 38

WOLFKILL, GRANT

Reported to Be Alive. New York: 1965. V. 44

WOLL, ADRIAN

Expedicion Hecha en Tejas por Una Parte de la Za. Division del Cuerpo de Egercito del Norte. Monterey: 1842. V. 42; 45

WOLLASATON, GEORGE

The Life and History of a Pilgrim. Dublin: 1753. V. 37

WOLLASTON, A.

Reports on the Collections Made by the British Ornithologists' Union Expedition and the Wollaston Expedition in Dutch New Guinea, 1910-13. London: 1916. V. 40

WOLLASTON, A. F. R.

Pygmies and Papuans. London: 1912. V. 39

WOLLASTON, A. N.

The Sword of Islam. London: 1905. V. 44

WOLLASTON, FRANCIS

A Specimen of a General Astronomical Catalogue, Arranged in Zones of North Polar Distance, and Adapted to Jan. 1, 1790 . . . London: 1789. V. 38

WOLLASTON, GEORGE

The Life and History of a Pilgrim. Dublin: 1753. V. 38

WOLLASTON, WILLIAM

The Religion of Nature Delineated. London: 1724. V. 46

The Religion of Nature Delineated. London: 1725. V. 37; 38; 39; 40; 41; 45; 46

The Religion of Nature Delineated. London: 1726. V. 38; 44

The Religion of Nature Delineated. London: 1731. V. 38; 41

The Religion of Nature Delineated. London: 1738. V. 39

The Religion of Nature Delineated. London: 1738. V. 46

WOLLER, JOHANNES

Compendium Theologiae Christianae. Cambridge: 1648. V. 44

WOLLEY, HANNAH

The Accomplish'd Ladies Delight in Preserving, Physick, Beautifying and Cookery. London: 1683. V. 37

The Queen Like Closet, or Rich Cabinet: Stored with all manner of Rare Receipts for Reserving, Candying, and Cookery . . . to which is added a Supplement . . . London: 1681. V. 37

WOLLEY, J.

Ootheca Wolleyana: an Illustrated Catalogue of the Collection of Birds' Eggs, Begun by the Late John Wolley . . . London: 1864-1907. V. 37; 38; 42

WOLLSTONECRAFT, MARY 1759-1797

Letters Written During a Short Residence in Sweden, Noreay and Denmark. London: 1796. V. 40; 41; 42; 43; 44; 45; 46

Letters Written During a Short Residence in Sweden, Norway and Denmark. Wilmington: 1796. V. 42

Letters to Imlay. London: 1879. V. 41; 43; 44; 45

Original Stories, from Real Life, with Conversations, Calculated to Regulate the Affections and Form the Mind to Truth and Goodness. London: 1788. V. 40

Original Stories from Real Life, with Conversations Calculated to Regulate the Affections and Form the Mind to Truth and Goodness. London: 1791. V. 42

Original Stories, from Real Life, with Conversations, Calculated to Regulate the Affections and Form the Mind to Truth and Goodness . . . London: 1796. V. 40

Posthumous Works of the Author of a Vindication of the Rights of Woman. London: 1798. V. 41; 43; 45

A Vindication of the Rights of Men. London: 1790. V. 40; 41; 42; 44

A Vindation of the Rights of Woman. Boston: 1792. V. 44

A Vindication of the Rights of Woman. Boston: 1792. V. 42

A Vindication o the Rights of Woman, with Strictures on Political and Moral Subjects. London: 1792. V. 40; 41; 42; 43; 44; 46

A Vindication of the Rights of Woman. London: 1792. V. 42

A Vindication of the Rights of Woman; With Strictures on Moral and Political Subjects. Philadlphia: 1792. V. 42

Vindication of the Rights of Woman, with Strictures on Political and Moral Subjects. Philadelphia: 1794. V. 42

WOLLSTONECRAFT, MARY 1759-1797 continued

A Vindication of the Rights of Woman . . . London: 1844. V. 42

WOLPE, BERTHOLD

A Book of Fanfare Ornaments. London: 1939. V. 46

WOLPERIANA: An Illustrated Guide to Berthold L. Wolpe. London: 1960. V. 42

WOLSELEY, G. J.

Narrative of the War with China in 1860. London: 1862. V. 43

WOLSELEY, GARNET JOSEPH WOLSELEY, VISCOUNT 1833-1913

The Life of John Churchill Duke of Marlborough to the Accession of Queen Anne. London: 1894. V. 38; 41

The Story of A Soldier's Life. New York: 1903. V. 39; 42

WOLSELEY, VISCOUNT

The Story of a Solider's Life. Westminster: 1903. V. 37

WOLSEY, THOMAS 1475?-1530

An Enquiry into the Origin of Parliamentary Impeachments. London: 1770. V. 40

WOLVERTON, LORD

Five Months Sport in Somali Land. London: 1894. V. 37

THE WOMAN Turn'd Bully. London: 1675. V. 37

WOMAN'S Exchange of Texas, Austin, Texas. Austin: 1890's. V. 45

THE WOMAN'S Peace Festival, June 2, 1873. Boston: 1874. V. 43

THE WOMAN'S Peace Festival, June 2nd, 1874. Boston: 1874. V. 43

WOMEN of Worth. A Book of Girls. London: V. 40

THE WOMEN'S Union Journal: The Organ of the Women's Protective and Provident Legue. 1876-77. V. 38

THE WONDERFUL History of Virgilius the Sorcerer of Rome. London: 1893. V. 37

WONDERFUL London, Its Lights and Shadows of Humour and Sadness. London: 1878. V. 40

THE WONDERFUL Narrative: or, A Faithfull Account of the French Prophets, their Agitataions, Extasies, and Inspirations. Glasgaow: 1742. V. 37

THE WONDERFUL Prophecy of a Prophet Just Arrived from America to London. Edinburgh?: 1756? V. 42

THE WONDERS of Nature and Art. London: 1768. V. 38

THE WONDERS of Nature and Art . . . London: 1750. V. 45

THE WONDERS of the Telescope; or, a Display of the Wonders of the Heavens and of the System of the Universe. London: 1805. V. 40

WONG, GEORGE M.

Sagard's Long Journey to the Country of the Hurons. Toronto: 1939. V. 45

WONG, K.

History of Chinese Medicine Being a Chronicle of Medical Happenings in China from Ancient Times to the Present Period. Shanghai: 1936. V. 41

WONG-QUINCEY, J.

Chinese Hunter. New York: 1939. V. 45

WOOD, ANTHONY

Athenae Oxonienses. London: 1691-92. V. 37; 41; 44

Athenae Oxonienses. London: 1721. V. 38; 39; 40; 42; 43; 45

Athenae Oxonienses. London: 1813-20. V. 37; 39

Athenae Oxonienses. An Exact History of all the Writers and Bishops Who have had their Education in . . . Oxford, from . . . 1500 to the End of the year 1690 . . . London: 1691-2. V. 37

The History and Antiquities of the University of Oxford, in Two Books . . . Oxford: 1792-6. V. 39

The History and Antiquities of the Colleges and Halls in the University of Oxford . . . now first published in English, from the original manuscript in the Bodleian Library, with a continuation to the present time: by the editor, John Gutch, M.A. Oxford: 1786-90. V. 37

Modius Salium. A Collection of Such Pieces of Humour (not to be found in others of this kind) as Prevail'd at Oxford in the Time of Mr. Anthony a Wood. Oxford: 1751. V. 43

WOOD, ARNOLD

A Bibliography of the Complete Angler of Izaak Walton and Charles Cotton . . . New York: 1900. V. 39

WOOD, BASIL

The Duties of the Marriage State, a Pastoral Address . . . London: 1807. V. 43

WOOD, BENJAMIN

Benjamin Woods Ongelukkige Reys na Oost-Indien, met drie Schepen, Anno 1596. Leyden: 1706. V. 42

WOOD, C. F.

A Yachting Cruise in the South Seas. London: 1875. V. 38

WOOD, C. J.

Reminiscences of the War. N.P.: 1880. V. 46

Reminiscences of the War. N.P.: 1880. V. 41

Reminiscences of the War. N.P.: 1880. V. 43

WOOD, CASEY A.

An Introduction to the Literature of Vertebrate Zoology. 1931. V. 40

WOOD, CASEY ALBERT

The American Encyclopedia and Dictionary of Ophthalmology. Chicago: 1913-21. V. 37; 38; 41; 42; 45

The Fundus Oculi of Birds Especially as View by the Ophthalmoscope. Chicago: 1917. V. 42; 44

An Introduction to the Literature of Vertebrate Zoology. 1931. V. 39

An Introduction to the Literature of Vertebrate Zoology. London: 1931. V. 41

An Introduction to the Literature of Vertebrate Zoology. London: 1931. V. 37; 38; 45

A Physcian's Anthology of English and American Poetry. London: 1920. V. 41

A Physician's Anthology of English and American Poetry. London: 1920. V. 37; 38; 45

A System of Opthalmic Therapeutics . . . Chicago: 1909. V. 44

A System of Opthalmic Operations, Being a Complete Treatise on the Operative Conduct of Ocular Diseases and Some Extraocular Conditions Causing Eye Symptoms. Chicago: 1911. V. 44

A System of Opthalmic Operations, being a Complete Treatise on the Operative Condust of Ocular Diseases and Some Extraocular Conditions Causing Eye Symptoms. Chicago: 1911. V. 37

WOOD, CHARLES ERSKINE SCOTT

The Beautiful Wedding. San Francisco: 1929. V. 38; 46

Debs Has Visitors in Jail. 1964. V. 46

Maia. Portland: 1915. V. 38

A Masque of Love. Chicago: 1904. V. 38

Sonnets to Sappho. Los Gatos: 1939. V. 37

Souvenir: Edwin and Robert Grabhorn to Anne Cobden-Sanderson, San Francisco: June 26, 1926 At Coppa's Restaurant. San Francisco: 1926. V. 38; 46

WOOD, DE VOLSON

Treatise on the Theory of the Construction of Bridges and Roofs. New York: 1873. V. 38; 41

WOOD, EDWARD

A Complete Body of Conveyancing, In Theory and Practice. London: 1791. V. 45

Curiosities of Clocks and Watches from the Earliest Times. London: 1866. V. 44

WOOD, EDWIN

Historic Mckinac; the Historical, Picturesque and Legendary Features of the Mackinc Country. New York: 1918. V. 38

WOOD, ELLEN PRICE 1814-1887

Anne Hereford. London: 1868. V. 44; 45

Bessy Rane, a Novel. London: 1870. V. 41

The Channings. London: 1862. V. 39; 44

Court Netherleigh. London: 1881. V. 40

Dene Hollow. London: 1871. V. 41

East Lynne. London: 1861. V. 46

George Canterbury's Will. London: 1870. V. 44

The House of Halliwell. London: 1890. V. 41

Johnny Ludlow. London: 1874. V. 44

Johnny Ludlow. Second Series. London: 1880. V. 41

Johnny Ludlow. Third Series. London: 1885. V. 44

Lady Adelaide's Oath. London: 1867. V. 43; 44; 45

Lady Grace and Other Stories. London: 1887. V. 40; 44

Mrs. Halliburton's Troubles. London: 1862. V. 44

Mrs. Halliburton's Troubles. London: 1863. V. 39

Oswald Cray. Edinburgh: 1864. V. 41; 44

Pomeroy Abbey. London: 1878. V. 41

The Red Court Farm. London: 1868. V. 37; 44

WOOD, ELLEN PRICE 1814-1887 continued

The Shadow of Ashlydat. London: 1863. V. 41; 44

The Story of Charles Strange: a Novel. London: 1888. V. 44

Told in Twilight. London: 1875. V. 44

Trevlyn Hold; or, Squire Trevlyn's Heir. London: 1864. V. 44

Verner's Pride. London: 1863. V. 41; 44

WOOD, ESTHER

Dante Rossetti and the Pre-Raphaelite Movement. London: 1894. V. 37; 39; 40; 41

WOOD, EVELYN

From Midshipman to Field Marshal. London: 1906. V. 41

WOOD, G. ARNOLD

The Discovery of Australia. London: 1922. V. 46

WOOD, GEORGE

The Dispensatory of the United States of America. Philadelphia: 1849. V. 42

Peter Schlemihl in America. Philadelphia: 1848. V. 39

WOOD, GEORGE B.

An Address on the Occasion of the Centennial Celebration of the Founding of the Pennsylvania Hospital, Delivered June 10th 1851. Philadelphia: 1851. V. 45

The Dispensatory of the United States of America. Philadelphia: 1836. V. 41; 42

Syllabus of the Course of Lectures on Materia Medica & Pharmacy, Delivered in the University of Pennsylvania in the Winter in 1836-37. Philadelphia: 1836. V. 37

WOOD, H. S.

Shikar Memories. London: 1934. V. 45

WOOD, HARVEY

Personal Recollections. Pasadena: 1955. V. 37; 38; 41; 42; 45

WOOD, HENRY

Change for the American Notes: In Letters from London. V. 43

Change for the American Notes: in Letters from London to New York. 1843. V. 43

Change for the American Notes; In Letters from London to New York by an American Lady. London: 1843. V. 37; 38; 42

Change for American Notes: In Letters from London to New York by an American Lady. New York: 1843. V. 40; 43

Genealogical, Heraldic and Other Records, with Tables of Founder's Kin, of the Family of Woodd. London: 1886. V. 39

WOOD, HORATIO

Nervous Diseases and Their Diagnosis. Philadelphia: 1887. V. 42

WOOD, J. C.

Reminiscences of the War. N.P.: 1880. V. 39

WOOD, J. G.

Animate Creation. New York: 1898. V. 39

Bible Animals. London: 1869. V. 46

WOOD, J. M.

Natal Plants. 1970. V. 39

WOOD, J. N. PRICE

Travel and Sport in Turkestan . . . London: 1910. V. 45

WOOD, J. T.

Discoveries at Ephesus Including the Site and Remains of the Great Temple of Diana. London: 1877. V. 44

WOOD, JAMES

The Elements of Algebra Designed for the Use of Students in the University. Cambridge: 1825. V. 40

Memoir of Sylvester Scovel. D.D., Late President of Hanover College, Pa. New Albany: 1851. V. 44

WOOD, JAMES HARVEY

The War, 'Stonewall' Jackson, His Campaigns and Battles, the Regiment as I Saw Them. Cumberland: 1910. V. 37

WOOD, JOHN 1705?-1754

Choir Gaure, Vulgarly Called Stonehenge, on Salisbury Plain, Described, Restored and Explained . . . Oxford: 1747. V. 42

A Correct Statement of the Various Sources from Which the History of the Administration of John Adams was Compiled . . . New York: 1802. V. 42

An Elementary Treatise on Sketch from Nature with the Principles of Light and Shade, the Theory of Colours &c. London: 1850. V. 44; 46

Elements of Perspective: Containing the Nature of Light and Colours . . . London: 1799. V. 45

Full Exposition of the Clintonian Faction, and the Society of the Columbian Illuminati . . . Newark: 1802. V. 46

The History of the Administration of John Adams, Esq. New York: 1802. V. 44; 45

A Manual of Perspective . . . for the Use of Amateurs. London: 1843. V. 38

The Origin of Building; or, the Plagarism of the Heathens Detected. Bath: 1741. V. 39; 40; 42; 44

A Personal Narrative of a Journey to the source of the River Oxus by the Route of the Indus, Kabul, and Badakhshan, Performed Under the Sanction of the Supreme Government of India, in the Years 1836, 1837 and 1838. London: 1841. V. 40; 43

A Series of Plans for Cottages or Habitations of the Labourer . . . London: 1792. V. 39; 42

A Supplement to the New Compendious Treatise of Farriery. London: 1758. V. 45

WOOD, JOHN GEORGE

Lectures on the Principal and Practice of Perspective, as Delievered at the Royal Institution . . . London: 1809. V. 38; 44

The Principles and Practice of Sketching Landscape Scenery from Nature, Systematically Arranged. London: 1816. V. 44; 45

The Principles and Practice of Sketching Landscape Scenery from Nature, Systematically Arranged . . . London: 1820. V. 44

WOOD, JOHN, groom to the King of Sardinia

A New Compendious Treatise of Farriery. London: 1757. V. 43

WOOD, JOHN MEDLEY 1827-1914

Natal Plants. Durban: 1899-1912. V. 43

Natal Plants, Descriptions and Figures of Natal Indigenous Plants, with Notes on their Distribution, Economic value, Native Names, etc. 1970. V. 46

WOOD, JOHN S.

John Piper, Paintings, Drawings & Theatre Designs 1932-1954. London: 1955. V. 42

WOOD, L. INGLEBY

Scottish Pewter-Ware and Pewterers. Edinburgh. V. 46

WOOD, LAWSON

Granny Wumpus and How She Cleans Up for the Party. London. V. 40

The Lawson Wood Nursery Rhymes Book. London: 1920. V. 46

Mrs. Bear Goes to the Fair. London. V. 40

The Old Nursery Rhymes. London: 1920. V. 46

WOOD-MARTIN, W. G.

The Lake Dwellings of Ireland; or, Ancient Lacustrine Habitations of Erin, Commonly Called Crannogs. Dublin: 1886. V. 46

Pagan-Ireland. London: 1895. V. 43

The Rude Stone Monuments of Ireland, Co., Sligo and the Island of Achill. Dublin: 1888. V. 43

Traces of the Elder Faiths of Ireland, a Folklore Sketch. London: 1902. V. 43

WOOD, NEVILLE

The Ornithologist's Text Book. London: 1836. V. 39

WOOD, NICHOLAS

Address on the Two Late Eminent Engineers the Messrs. Stephenson, father and son. Newcastle-upon-Tyne: 1860. V. 43

A Practical Treatise on Rail-Roads and Interior Communication in General . . . London: 1825. V. 37; 39; 46

Practical Treatise on Railroads and Interior Communication in General. London: 1831. V. 37; 42; 46

A Practical Treatise on Rail-Roads and Internal Communication in General. London: 1832. V. 38; 42

A Practical Treatise on Rail-Roads and Interior Communication in General . . . Philadelphia: 1832. V. 40; 41; 42

A Practical Treatise on Rail-Roads, and Interior Communication in General . . . London: 1838. V. 39; 46

A Practical Treatise on Rail Road and Interior Communication in general with Orignal Experiments, and Tables of the Comparative Value of Canals and Rail Roads. London: 1825. V. 37

WOOD, R. E.

Life and Confessions of James Gilbert Jenkins. Napa City: 1864. V. 38; 39; 41; 42; 44

WOOD, ROBERT

An Essay on the Original Genius and Writings of Homer. London: 1775. V. 37; 39; 46

The Ruins of Palmyra, Otherwise Tedmor in the Desart. London: 1753. V. 43; 44; 46

The Ruins of Palmyra, otherwise Tedmor in the Desart. (with) The Ruins of Balbec, Otherwise Heliopolis in Coelosyria. London: 1753, 1757. V. 38

The Ruins of Balbec, Otherwise Heliopolis in Coelosyria. London: 1757. V. 39

WOOD, SALLY SAYWARD KEATING

Ferdinand and Elmira: a Russian Story. Baltimore: 1804. V. 39

WOOD, SAMUEL

Pembina Settlement . . . Washington: 1850. V. 40

WOOD, SAMUEL S.

Catalogue of Books on Medicine, Anatomy, Surgery, Midwifery, Chemistry, Agriculture &c. &c. for sale. New York: 1845. V. 38

WOOD, STANLEY

Over the Range to the Golden Gate. Chicago: 1903. V. 41

An Unattended Journey or Ten Thousand Miles by Rail a Tour by Four Young Ladies. Chicago: 1895. V. 39; 46

The White City (as It Was). Chicago: 1894. V. 38

WOOD, T. W.

Curiosities of Entomology. London: 1870. V. 43

WOOD, THOMAS fl. 1821

An Inquiry Concerning the Primitive Inhabitants of Ireland. London: 1821. V. 41; 42; 43; 46

An Institute of the Laws of England; or, the Laws of England in Their Natural Order . . . London: 1724. V. 40

An Institute of the Laws of England. London: 1738. V. 40

An Institute of the Laws of England. London: 1754. V. 38; 40

An Institute of the Laws of England; or, Laws of England in the Natural Order According to Common Use. London: 1763. V. 37; 38

An Institute of the Laws of England; or, the Laws of England In Their Natural Order . . . London: 1772. V. 45

A Vindication of the Historiographer of the University of Oxford and His Works . . . London: 1693. V. 41

WOOD, W. BIRKBECK

A History of the Civil War in the United States, 1861-65. London: 1908. V. 38

WOOD, WILLIAM 1774-1857

The Canadian War of 1812. Toronto: 1923-28. V. 45

The Capture of William Wood, by the Blackfoot Indians. N.P.: 1864. V. 42

General Conchology. London: 1835. V. 38

Illustrations of Linnaen Genera of Insects. London: 1821. V. 41; 43

Index Testaceologicus . . . London: 1825. V. 46

Index Testaceologicus; or a Catalogue of Shells . . . London: 1828. V. 43

Index Testaceologius. London: 1856. V. 37; 38

Index Entomologicus. London: 1845. V. 37

Index Entomologicus. London: 1854. V. 38

New Englands Prospect. London: 1639. V. 40; 44

A Survey of Trade. London: 1718. V. 41

Zoography; or the Beauties of Nature Displayed. London: 1807. V. 38; 40; 43

WOOD, WILLIAM C. H.

The Logs of the Conquest of Canada. Toronto: 1909. V. 37; 39; 45

WOOD, WILLIAM MAXWELL

Fankwei; or, The San Jacinto in the Seas of India, China and Japan. New York: 1859. V. 38

Wandering Sketches of People and Things in South America, Polynesia, California, and Other Places Visited During a Cruise on Board of the U.S. Ships Levant, Portsmouth and Savannah. Philadelphia: 1849. V. 37; 40

WOOD, WILLIAM NATHANIEL

Reminiscences of Big I. Charlottesville: 1907. V. 43

Reminiscences of Big I. Charlottesville: 1909. V. 44

WOODALL, MARY

Gainsborough's Landscape Drawings. London: 1939. V. 44; 45

WOODALL, R. G.

The Postal History of Yukon Territory. England: 1964. V. 45

WOODARD, DAVID

The Narrative of Captain David Woodard and Four Seamen, Who Lost Their Ship While in a Boat at Sea and Surrendered Themselves Up to the Malays in the Island of Celebes . . . London: 1804. V. 45

WOODARD, J. FLETCH

Fletch Woodard, His Fights With Those Bad, Bad Town Boys. Nashville: 1878-1902. V. 44

WOODBERRY, GEORGE E.

The Life of Edgar Allan Poe, Personal and Literary with His Chief Correspondence with Men of Letters. Boston and New York: 1909. V. 38

WOODBRIDGE, WILLIAM C.

Modern Atlas, Physical, Political and Statistical, Exhibiting on Separate Maps, the Physical and Political Characteristics of Countries . . . Hartford: 1845. V. 45

WOODBRIDGE, WILLIAM CHANNING

He Hoikehonua, He Mea ia e Hoakaka'ii Ke Ano O Ka Honua Nei, a Me na Mea Maluna Iho . . . Ohau: 1845. V. 41; 42

WOODBURN, SAMUEL

Catalogue of the First and Most Important Portion of the Highly Valuable Collection. London: 1853. V. 38; 40

Catalogue of . . . Capital Pictures by the Greatest Early Italian Masters. London: 1860. V. 38; 40

The Lawrence Gallery, First-(Tenth) Exhibtion. London: 1835-July 1836. V. 44

WOODBURY, FRANK S.

Tourist's Guide Book to Denver. 1882. Denver: 1882. V. 37

WOODBURY, LEVI

Condition of the State Banks. Letter from . . . Showing the Condition of the Several State Banks. Washington: 1841. V. 37

Letter of Hon. Levi Woodbury, on the Annexation of Texas. Washington: 1844. V. 38

Report . . . Transmitting a Report from the Register and Receiver of the Land Office at Quachita, with a Statement of the Claims Presented to Them, Together with the Opinion of the Commission of the General Land Office on the Validity of Said Claims. Washington: 1838. V. 37; 39; 42

WOODBURY, R. B.

The Ruins of Zaculeu, Guatemala. Boston: 1943. V. 38

WOODBURY, RICHARD B.

The Ruins of Zaculeu, Guatemala. Boston: 1953. V. 37; 42; 44

The Ruins of Zaculeu. Guatemala: 1953. V. 37

WOODCARVING: Original Designs . . . with Practical Instructions in the Art. London: 1867. V. 46

WOODCOCK, THOMAS

An Account of Some Remarkable Passages in the Life of a Private Gentleman; with Reflections Thereon. London: 1711. V. 43

WOODCROFT, BENNET

A Sketch of the Origin and Progress of Steam Navigation from Authentic Documents. London: 1848. V. 40

THE WOODCUT Annual for 1925. Kansas City: 1925. V. 41

WOODD, HENRY

Genealogical, Herldic and other Records, with tables of founder's kin, of the Family of Woodd. London: 1886. V. 37

WOODDESON, RICHARD 1745-1822

Elements of Jurisprudence Treated Of In the Preliminary Part of a Course of Lectures on the Laws of England. London: 1783. V. 38; 39; 40; 43

WOODFALL, WILLIAM

A Sketch of the Debate That Took Place at the India-House in Leadenhall-Street, on Wednesday, the 19th of October Inst . . . London: 1794. V. 37

WOODFORD, A. MONTAGUE

The Book of Sonnets. London: 1841. V. 39

WOODFORD, CHARLES MORRIS

A Naturalist Among the Head-Hunters. London: 1890. V. 43

WOODFORD, JAMES

The Diary of a Country Parson 1758-1802. Oxford: 1926. V. 38

WOODFORDE, JAMES

The Diary of a Country Parson. Oxford: 1981. V. 37

WOODGATE, WALTER BRADFORD

Tandem. A Novel. London: 1895. V. 37

WOODHEAD, ABRAHAM

A Compendious Discourse of the Eucharist. Oxford: 1688. V. 44

A Discourse of the Necessity of Church Guides . . . London: 1675. V. 45

Two Discourses. The First, Concerning the Spirit of Martin Luther, and the Original of the Reformation. The Second, Concerning the Celibacy of the Clergy. Oxford: 1687. V. 41; 42

WOODHOUSE, JAMES 1735-1820

Journeyman Shoemaker. London: 1766. V. 43

Poems on Sundry Occasions by James Woodhouse, a Journeyman Shoemaker. London: 1764. V. 40; 41; 43

Poems on Several Occasions. London: 1766. V. 37; 40; 41; 42; 45; 46

WOODHOUSE, JOHN

A New Almanacke and Prognostication for the Years . . . 1636. London: 1635. V. 39

WOODHOUSE, L. G. O.

The Butterfly Fauna of Ceylon. Colombo: 1950. V. 37; 38

The Butterfly Fauna of Ceylon. Colombo: 1951. V. 38

The Butterfly Fauna of Ceylon. Colombo: 1942. V. 37

WOODHOUSE, ROBERT 1773-1827

An Elementary Treatise on Astronomy. Volume II. Cambridge: 1818. V. 42

WOODHOUSE, WILLIAM J.

Aetolia. Its Geography, Topography and Antiquities. Oxford: 1897. V. 37; 39

WOODHULL, VICTORIA

The Human Body the Temple of God; or, the Philosohpy of Sociology . . . London: 1890. V. 42; 44

Woodhull & Claflin's Weekly Progress! Free Thought! Untrammeled Lives! New York: 1875. V. 37

WOODLAND Cottage. London: 1796. V. 40

WOODLEY, GEORGE

A View of the Present State of the Scilly Islands. London: 1822. V. 39; 41

A View of the Present State of the Scilly Islands . . . London: 1833. V. 41; 43

WOODMAN, ABBY JOHNSON

Picturesque Alaska: A Journal of a Tour Among the Mountains, Seas and Islands of the Northwest, from San Francisco to Sitka. Boston: & New York: 1889. V. 37

WOODMAN, DAVID

Guide to Texas Emigrants. Boston: 1835. V. 41

WOODMAN, FREDERICK

The House of Clarisford. London: 1877. V. :3

WOODRIDGE, KENNETH

Landscape and Antiquity Aspects of English Culture at Stourhead 1718 to 1838. London: 1970. V. 44

WOODROFFE, BENJAMIN

The Fall of Babylon. London: 1690. V. 40

WOODROOFE, ANNE

Shades of Character; or, the Infant Pilgrim. Bath: 1824. V. 44

WOODRUFF, HEZEKIAH H.

A Sermon. Preached at Scipio, N. Y. at the Execution of John Delaware, a Native; for the Murder of Ezekiel Crane . . . Albany: 1804. V. 41

WOODRUFF, HIRAM

The Trotting Horse of America: How to Train and Drive Him . . . London: 1876. V. 39

WOODRUFF, SETH D.

Methods of Working Coal and Metal Mines. Oxford: 1966. V. 38

WOODRUFF, W. E.

With the Light Guns in '61-'65; Reminiscences of Eleven Arkansas, Missouri and Texas Light Batteries in the Civil War. Little Rock: 1903. V. 37; 38; 39; 40

WOODRUFF, WILFORD

An Epistle of the Council of Twelve . . . Read October 10, 1887. Salt Lake City: 1887. V. 42

Leaves from My Journal. Salt Lake City: 1881. V. 42

WOODRUFF, WILLIAM EDWARD

With the Light Guns in '61-65 Reminiscences of Eleven Arkansas, Missouri and Texas Light Batteries in the Civil War. Little Rock: 1903. V. 46

WOODRUFFE-PEACOCK, E. A.

The Natural History of Lincolnshire. 1898. V. 46

WOODS, ALVA

Intellectual and Moral Culture: a Discourse Delivered at His Inauguration as President of Transylvania University. Lexington: 1828. V. 37; 39; 42

WOODS, C. E.

The Electric Automobile Its Construction, Care and Operation. Chicago & New York: 1900. V. 42

WOODS, DANIEL B.

Sixteen Months at the Gold Digging. New York: 1851. V. 38; 42

Sixteen Months at the Gold Diggings. London/New York: (ca. 1851). V. 37

WOODS, EDGAR

Albemarle County in Virginia. Charlottesville: 1901. V. 42

WOODS, GARY D.

The Hicks-Adams-Bass-Floyd-Pattillo and Collateral Lines, Together with Family Letters, 1840-1868. Salado: 1963. V. 42; 44

WOODS, GEORGE

An Account of the Past and Present State of the Isle of Man. London: 1811. V. 38; 42; 43; 46

Observations on the Present Price of Bullion, and Rates of Exchange . . . London: 1811. V. 38

WOODS, HENRY

Change for the American Notes. London: 1843. V. 37

WOODS, JOHN

Two Years' Residence in the Settlement on the English Prairie, in the Illinois Country. London: 1822. V. 37; 38; 39; 40; 42; 43

WOODS, JOSEPH 1776-1864

Letters of an Architect, from France, Italy and Greece. London: 1828. V. 37; 38; 39; 46

WOODS, JULIAN EDMUNDS

Geological Observations in South Australia. London: 1862. V. 40

WOODS, MARGARET LOUISA

Esther Vanhomrigh. London: 1891. V. 38; 41

Lyrics. Oxford: 1888. V. 40

Songs. Oxford: 1896. V. 37; 39

Songs. Oxford: 1986. V. 41

WOOD'S Medical and Surgical Monographs. Volume 10. New York: 1891. V. 42

WOODS' Medical and Surgical Monographs. Volume 11. New York: 1890. V. 42

WOODS, N. A.

The Past Campaign: A Sketch of the War in the West . . . London: 1855. V. 46

The Prince of Wales in Canada and the United States. London: 1861. V. 43

WOOD'S Plan of Telegraphic Instruction, Arranged by the Professors and Tutors of Morse's Telegraphic Institute, Syracuse, N.Y. Syracuse: 1864. V. 39

WOODS, R. S.

Harrison Hall and Its Association. Chatham: 1896. V. 42

WOODS, S. JOHN

John Piper - Paintings, Drawings, Theatre Designs - 1932-1954. London: 1955. V. 40

WOODSWORTH, J. S.

My Neighbor: a Study of City Conditions; a Plea for Social Justice. Toronto: 1913. V. 45

WOODTHORPE, R. G.

The Lushai Expedition, 1871-1872. London: 1873. V. 38

WOODVILLE; or, Interesting Memoirs of a Beggar Girl; Who, After a Series of Uncommon Events, Was Discovered to be Nearly Allied to a Noble Family and Restored to Her Parents. London: 1809. V. 46

WOODVILLE, WILLIAM

Medical Botany . . . London: 1810. V. 42

Medical Botany. London: 1832. V. 41; 42

Reports of a Series of Innoculations for the Variolae Vaccinae, or Cow-Pox . . . London: 1799. V. 42

WOODWARD, A. B.

Considerations on the Substance of the Sun. Washington: 1801. V. 42

WOODWARD, APOLLUS

A Brief Description of the Property Belonging to the Lycoming Coal Company, with Some General Remarks on the Subject of the Coal and Iron Business. Poughkeepsie: 1828. V. 39

WOODWARD, AUGUSTUS B.

Considerations on the Substance of the Sun. Washington: 1801. V. 40; 42

WOODWARD, BERNARD BOLINGBROKE

A General History of Hampshire, of the County of Southampton, Including the Isle of Wight. London: 1863. V. 41

The History of Wales, from the Earliest Times, to Its Final Incorporation with the Kingdom of England. London: 1853. V. 38; 42; 46

WOODWARD, CHARLES

Sacred Music in Miniature. Philadelphia: 1812. V. 40

WOODWARD, CHARLES L.

Bibliothica (sic) -- Scallawagiana. New York: 1880. V. 45

WOODWARD, E. M.

History of Burlington & Mercer Counties, New Jersey. Philadelphia: 1833. V. 41; 46

History of the 198th Pennsylvania Volunteers . . . Trenton: 1884. V. 42

WOODWARD, F. H.

The Genus Masdevallia . . . London: 1890-96/ V. 43

WOODWARD, GEORGE E.

Woodward's Architecture and Rural Art. New York: 1868. V. 37

Woodward's Architecture and Rural Art. No. 1. 1867. New York: 1867. V. 37; 42

Woodward's Country Homes. New York: 1865. V. 41; 42

WOODWARD, GEORGE MOUTARD 1760?-1809

Chesterfield Burlesqued, or, School for Modern Manners. London: 1811. V. 46

Chesterfield Travestie. Philadelphia: 1812. V. 37; 38; 39; 40; 42; 45

Grotesque Borders for Screens, Billiard Rooms, Dressing Rooms, etc., etc. London: 1799-1800. V. 39; 42

WOODWARD, H. B.

The History of the Geological Society of London. London: 1907. V. 40

WOODWARD, HENRY

A Letter from Henry Woodward, Comedian, the Meanest of All Characters to Dr. John Hill, Inspector General of Great Britain, the Greatest of all Characters. London: 1752. V. 42; 46

WOODWARD, J.

Fossils of all Kinds, Digested Into a Method, Suitable to Their Mutual Relation and Affinity . . . London: 1728. V. 45

WOODWARD, JOHN

Address of the Society of Tammany, or Columbian Order, to Its Absent Members and the Members of Its Several Branches Throughout the United States. New York: 1819. V. 45

The Empresario Rights in Texas of John Woodward, Late Consul General of That Republic. New York: 1841. V. 43

An Essay Toward a Natural History of the Earth and Terrestrial Bodies, Especially Minerals. London: 1695. V. 39; 42; 43; 44

An Essay Towards a Natural History of the Earth, and Terrestrial Bodies, Especially Minerals. London: 1702. V. 40

An Essay Towards a Natural History of the Earth, and Terrestrial Bodyes, Especially Minerals . . . . London: 1723. V. 40

The Natural History of the Earth, Illustrated, and Inlarged: as also Defended, and the Objections against it, particularly those lately published by Dr. Camerarius, answered. Written originally in Latin: And now first made . . . London: 1726. V. 37

A Treatise on Ecclesiastical Heraldry. Edinburgh and London: 1894. V. 41

A Treatise on Heraldry British and Foreign with english and French Glossaries. London: 1896. V. 44

WOODWARD, JOSEPH

The Medical and Surgical History of the War of Rebellion, 1861-65. The Three Medical Volumes. Washington: 1870-88. V. 45

Report on Epidemic Cholera and Yellow Fever in the Army of the United States During the Year 1867. Washington: 1868. V. 42

WOODWARD, JOSEPH JANIVER 1833-1884

The Medical and Surgical History of the War of the Rebellion. Washington: 1875-88. V. 46

WOODWARD, JOSEPH JANVIER 1833-1884

Diarrhoea and Dysentery. Washington: 1879. V. 38; 41; 42

The Hospital Steward's Manual: for the Instruction of Hospital Stewards, Ward-Masters, and Attendants, in Their Several Duties. Philadelphia: 1863. V. 42

The Medical and Surgical History of the War of Rebellion, 1861-65. The Three Surgical Volumes. Washington: 1870-83. V. 42; 45

The Medical and Surgical History of the War of the Rebellion, 1861-65. Washington: 1870-88. V. 37; 38; 41; 42; 44; 45; 46

The Medical and Surgical History of the War of the Rebellion. (1861-1865). Part First. Medical Volume and Appendix. Washington: 1870. V. 37

On the Structure of Cancerous Tumors and the Mode In Which Adjacent Parts are Invaded. Washington: 1873. V. 44; 46

WOODWARD, JOSIAH

An Account of the Societies for Reformation of Manners, in London and Westminster, and Other Parts of the Kingdom. London: 1699. V. 37; 41; 44

Some Thoughts Concerning the Stage in a Letter to a Lady. London: 1704. V. 37; 39; 42; 46

WOODWARD, R. B.

The History of Wales, from the Earliest Times to Its Final Incorporation with the Kingdom of England. London: 1863. V. 41

Natal Birds, Including the Species Belonging to Natal and the Eastern Districts of Cape Colony. Pietermaritzbug: 1899. V. 37; 38

WOODWARD, RICHARD

Considerations on the Immorality and Pernicious Effects of Dealing in Smuggled Goods. Cork: 1783. V. 41

The Present State of the Church of Ireland . . . Dublin: 1781. V. 38

WOODWARD, SAMUEL

The History and Antiquites of Norwich Castle. London: and Norwich: 1847. V. 37; 40; 44

The Norfolk Topographer's Manual. London: 1842. V. 40; 44

WOODWARD, THERON R.

Dodge Genealogy: Descendants of Tristam Dodge. Chicago: 1904. V. 46

WOODWARD, W. H.

Catalogue of a Collection of Pottery Belonging to W. H. Woodward. London: 1928. V. 37

WOODWARD, WILLIAM

Cherished Portraits of Thoroughbred Horses, from the Collection of William Woodward. New York: 1929. V. 43

WOODWARD, WILLIAM E.

Records of Salem Witchcraft Copied from the Original Documents. Roxbury: 1864-65. V. 42

WOODWORTH, JOHN M.

Cholera Epidemic of 1873 in the United States. Washington: 1875. V. 40; 42; 44

WOODWORTH, MARGUERITE

History of the Dominion Atlantic Railway. Kentville: 1936. V. 43

WOODWORTH, SAMUEL

The Champions of Freedom, or the Mysteious Chief, a Romance of the Nineteenth Century, Founded on the Events of the War, Between the United States and Great Britain . . . New York: 1816. V. 38; 40; 41; 43; 44; 46

The Heroes of the Lake. New York: 1814. V. 40; 45

The Poems, Odes, Songs and Metrical Effusions. New York: 1818. V. 44

WOODYATT, NIGEL

My Sporting Memories. London: 1923. V. 42

WOOLASTON, GEORGE

The Life and History of a Pilgrim. Dublin: 1753. V. 40

WOOLAVINGTON, JAMES BUCHANAN, BARON 1849-1935.

Sporting Pictures at Lavington Park (and) Supplementary Catalogue of Sporting Pictures. London: 1927. V. 37

WOOLEN, WILLIAM WATSON

The Inside Passage to Alaska, 1792-1920. Cleveland: 1924. V. 40; 41

WOOLER, T. J.

An Appeal to the Citizens of London Against the Alleged Lawful Mode of Packing Special Juries. London: 1817. V. 39

The Black Dwarf. London: V. 43

WOOLER, THOMAS JONATHAN

A Narrative of the Trial of Thomas Jonathan Wooler, for a Libel on His Majesty's Ministers. Glasgow: 1817. V. 38

WOOLEY, CHARLES LEONARD

The Development of Sumerian Art. New York: 1935. V. 38; 41

Palestine Exploration Fund, 1914. The Wilderness of Zin (Archaeological Report). London: 1915. V. 39

The Wilderness of Zin. London: 1914. V. 45

WOOLF, CECIL

A Bibliography of Norman Douglas. London: 1954. V. 39; 43

A Bibliography of Frederick Rolf (Baron Corvo). London: 1972. V. 38

A Bibliography of Frederick Rolfe Baron Corvo. London: 1957. V. 38

The Clerk Without a Benefice: a Study of Baron Corvo's Conversion and Vocation. Aylesford: 1964. V. 41

Corvo 1860-1960: Essays by Various Hands. Aylesford: 1961. V. 41

Notes on the Bibliography of Norman Douglas. Edinburgh: 1955. V. 42

WOOLF, DOUGLAS

Future Preconditional. Toronto: 1978. V. 46

WOOLF, L. S.

Quack, Quack! London: 1915. V. 41

WOOLF, LEONARD

Empire & Commerce in Africa. London: 1919. V. 43

Empire and Commerce in Africa. 1920. V. 42

Essays. London: 1927. V. 41; 42

Fear and Politics: a Debate at the Zoo. London: 1925. V. 37

The Future of International Government. London: 1941. V. 41

The Hotel. London: 1939. V. 38

Sowing. Growing. Beginning Again. Downhill All the Way. The Journey Not the Arrival Matters. London: 1960-69. V. 46

Stories of the East. Richmond: 1921. V. 45; 46

the Village in the Jungle. London: 1913. V. 37; 46

The Village in the Jungle. London: 1931. V. 38

WOOLF, VIRGINIA 1882-1941

Be Angry at the Sun. New York: 1941. V. 42

Beau Brummell. New York: 1930. V. 37; 38; 39; 41; 42; 45; 46

Between the Acts. London: 1941. V. 38; 40; 43; 45

Between the Acts. New York: 1941. V. 38; 43; 44; 46

The Captain's Death Bed and Other Essays. London: 1950. V. 37; 38; 39; 41; 42; 43; 44

The Captain's Death Bed and Other Essays. New York: 1950. V. 41

Collected Essays. London: 1966/67. V. 45

Collected Essays. New York: 1967. V. 40

The Common Reader. London: 1925. V. 37; 41; 45

The Common Reader. New York: 1925. V. 37; 41

The Common Reader. Second Series. London: 1932. V. 38; 41; 42; 45

The Common Reader. New York: 1948. V. 41

Contemporary Writers. London: 1965. V. 41

Dear Judas and Other Poems. New York: 1929. V. 42

The Death of the Moth. London: 1942. V. 37; 42

The Death of the Moth and Other Essays. New York: 1942. V. 39

The Diaries of . . . London: 1977/84. V. 43

The Diary. London: 1983. V. 38

Flush. London: 1933. V. 38; 39; 42; 43

Flush, a Biography. New York: 1933. V. 45

Grace after Meat by J.C. Ranson. London: 1924. V. 37

Granite and Rainbow. London: 1958. V. 41; 45

A Haunted Hosue and Other Short Stories. London: 1943. V. 37; 39; 40; 42; 46

A Haunted House and Other Stories. New York: 1944. V. 46

Hours in a Library. New York: 1958. V. 41

Jacob's Room. London: 1922. V. 40; 41; 42; 43

Jacob's Room. Richmond: 1922. V. 44

Kew Gardens. Richmond: 1919. V. 43; 46

Kew Gardens. London: 1927. V. 37; 38; 45

A Letter to a Young Poet. London: 1932. V. 41

Letters. London: 1956. V. 38

The Letters of Virginia Woolf. New York: 1975-80. V. 39; 43

The Mark on the Wall. Richmond: 1919. V. 40; 42; 44; 46

Mrs. Dalloway. London: 1925. V. 37; 39; 40; 41; 43; 44

Mr. Bennett and Mrs. Brown. London: 1924. V. 37; 38; 40; 41; 45; 46

The Moment and Other Essays. London: 1947. V. 37; 38; 41; 42; 44; 46

Monday or Tuesday. London: 1921. V. 41; 45; 46

Monday or Tuesday. Richmond: 1921. V. 37; 39; 41

Monday or Tuesday. New York: 1921. V. 37; 38; 42; 45

Mrs. Dalloway. Paris: 1929. V. 43; 45

Night and Day. London: 1919. V. 37; 38; 43; 44

Nurse Lugton's Golden Thimble. London: 1966. V. 46

On Being Ill. London: 1930. V. 37; 38; 44

Orlando. London: 1928. V. 38; 40; 41; 42; 45

Orlando. New York: 1928. V. 37; 38; 40; 41; 42; 43; 44; 46

Recent Paintings by Vanessa Bell. London: 1930. V. 37; 40

Recent Paintings by Vanessa Bell. February 4th to March 8th 1930. 1930. V. 37

Reviewing. London: 1939. V. 43

Roger Fry: A Biography. London: 1940. V. 37; 38; 39

Roger Fry: a Biography. New York: 1940. V. 44

A Room of One's Own. London: 1929. V. 37; 39; 40; 41; 42; 45

A Room of One's Own. London: 1929. V. 44

A Room of One's Own. New York: 1929. V. 38; 41; 46

A Room of One's Own. New York: and London: 1929. V. 46

Street Haunting. San Francisco: 1930. V. 37; 38; 39; 41; 42; 43; 45; 46

Three Guineas. London: 1938. V. 37; 38; 39; 40; 41; 42; 45; 46

Three Guineas. New York: 1938. V. 43; 45

Thurso's Landing and Other Poems. New York: 1932. V. 42

To the Light House. London: 1927. V. 37; 38; 39; 40; 43

To the Lighthouse. New York: 1927. V. 41

Two Stories. Richmond: 1917. V. 37; 41

The Voyage Out. London: 1915. V. 37; 38; 39; 40; 41; 42

The Voyage Out. London: 1920. V. 39; 45

The Voyage Out. New York: 1926. V. 46

Walter Sickert: a Conversation. London: 1934. V. 37; 38; 40; 41; 43; 44

The Waves. London: 1931. V. 37; 38; 39; 41; 44; 45

The Women at Point Sur. New York: 1927. V. 42

A Writer's Dairy. London: 1953. V. 38; 39; 41; 42; 43; 45

The Years. London: 1937. V. 38; 39; 41; 43; 45; 46

The Years. New York: 1937. V. 43

WOOLFE, JOHN

Vitruvius Britannicus, or the British Architect . . . London: 1767. V. 44

WOOLIAMS, N.

Cattle Ranch. The Story of the Dogulas Lake Cattle Company. Vancouver: 1979. V. 43

WOOLLCOTT, ALEXANDER

Enchanted Aisles: Essays. London: 1924. V. 41

Mrs. Fiske. New York: 1917. V. 40; 42; 45

Our Lady's Juggler: an Antique Legend as Retold for the Air. San Mateo: 1937. V. 46

Our Lady's Juggler. San Mateo: 1939. V. 38

The Woollcott Reader. New York: 1935. V. 43

Woollcott's Second Reader. New York: 1937. V. 43

WOOLLEN, WILLIAM WATSON

The Inside Passage to Alaska 1792-1920. Cleveland: 1924. V. 37; 38; 42

WOOLLETT, WILLIAM

Villas and Cottages or Homes for All Plans, Elevations and Views of Twelve Villas and Ten Cottages. New York: 1876. V. 40

WOOLLEY, CHARLES LEONARD 1880-1960

Alalakh: an Account of the Excavations at Tell Atchana in the Hatay, 1937-1949. Oxford: 1955. V. 40; 42

Carchemish. Report on the Excavations at Djerabis on Behalf of the British Museum. London: 1914. V. 38

The Development of Sumerian Art. New York: 1935. V. 40

Excavations at Ur. The Pottery of Tell Billa. Philadelphia: 1933. V. 37; 40; 42

The Neo-Babylonian and Persian Periods. London: 1962. V. 37

The Old Babylonian Period. London: 1976. V. 40

The Royal Cemetery. New York: 1934. V. 37; 40; 42

Ur Excavations: Volume II - The Royal Cemetery. London: 1934. V. 46

Ur Excavations. Volume II. The Royal Cemetry. A Report on the Predynastic and Sargonid Graves Excavated Between 1926 and 1931. London & New York. V. 37

The Wilderness of Zin. 1914-15. V. 38

The Wilderness of Zin. London: 1915. V. 40; 44

The Wilderness of Zin. New York: 1936. V. 45

The Ziggurat and His Surroundings. Oxford: 1939. V. 37; 40; 42; 44

WOOLLEY, JAMES, SON & CO.

Catalogue of Surgeons' Instruments and Medical Appliances. Manchester: 1894. V. 40

WOOLLEY, L. H.

California 1849-1913. Oakland: 1913. V. 40

WOOLLS, CHARLES

The Barrow Diggers. A Dialogue in Imitation of the Grave Diggers in Hamlet. London: 1839. V. 37

WOOLMAN, JOHN 1720-1772

A Journal of the Life, Gospel, Labours and Christian Experiences of that Faithful Minister of Jesus Christ, John Woolman, Late of Mount-Holly, in the Province of New Jersey, North America . . . Dublin: 1776. V. 42; 45

A Journal of the Life and Tavels of John Woolman in the Service of the Gospel. London: 1901. V. 40; 44; 46

A Journal of the Life, Gosepl, Labours and Christian Experiences of that Faithful minister of Jesus Christ . . . Late of Mt. Holly, in the Province of New Jersey, North America, to which are added his works . . . Philadelphia: 1778. V. 37

Serious Considerations on Various Subjects of Importance. London: 1773. V. 37; 40; 42; 46

Some Considerations on the Keeping of Negroes 1754. (with) Considerations on the Keeping of Negroes 1762. Northampton: 1975. V. 38; 44; 46

A Word of Remembrance and Caution to the Rich. Dublin: 1793. V. 40

The Works of.. Philadelphia: 1774. V. 39

Works. London: 1775. V. 39

WOOLNER, THOMAS

My Beautiful Lady. London: 1866. V. 38; 41; 43; 46

My Beautiful Lady. London: 1863. V. 37

WOOLNOTH, WILLIAM

Ancient Castles of England and Wales. London: 1825. V. 44

WOOLNOUGH, C. W.

The Whole Art of Marbling as Applied to Paper, Book Edges etc. London: 1881. V. 41; 44; 46

WOOLRICH, CORNELL

Black Alibi. New York: 1942. V. 43

The Black Path of Fear. Garden City: 1944. V. 39; 46

The Black Path of Fear. New York: 1944. V. 39

The Bride Wore Black. New York: 1940. V. 44

Cover Charge. New York: 1926. V. 43

The Dancing Detective. Philadelphia: 1946. V. 46

Dead Man Blues. Philadelphia: 1948. V. 46

Fright. 1950. V. 46

Hotel Room. New York: 1958. V. 46

I Married a Dead Man. Philadelphia & New York: 1948. V. 42; 44

Night Has a Thousand Eyes. 1945. V. 46

Night Has a Thousand Eyes. New York: 1945. V. 43

Night Has a Thousand Eyes. New York: & Toronto: 1945. V. 44

Nightmare. New York: 1956. V. 46

Rendezvous in Black. New York: 1948. V. 46

Violence. New York: 1958. V. 46

A Young Man's Heart. New York: 1930. V. 46

WOOLRIDGE, JOHN

Systema Horti-Cultruae: or, The Art of Gardening. London: 1688. V. 38

WOOLRYCH, HUMPHREY WILLIAM

The History and Results of the Present Capital Punishments in England. London: 1832. V. 37

WOOLRYCH, HUMPHRY WILLIAM

Our Island . . . London: 1832. V. 46

WOOLSEY, KATE

Republics Versus Woman, Contrasting the Treatment Accorded to Woman in Aristorcacies with that Meted Out to Her in Democracies. London: 1903. V. 39

WOOLSON, CONSTANCE FENIMORE

Castle Nowhere. Odessa. V. 39

WOOLWARD, F. H.

The Genus Masdevallia, Issued by the Marquess of Lothian. London: 1890-96. V. 37; 38; 40

WOOLWORTH, L. FOWLER

Littleton Folwer, Missionary to the Republic of Texas, 1837-1846. N.P.: 1936. V. 37

WOOSTER, DAVID

Alpine Plants, Figures and Descriptions of the Most Striking and Beautiful of the Alpine Flowers. London: 1872-74. V. 39; 43

Alpine Plants. London: 1874. V. 37; 38; 39; 40; 41; 42

WOOTEN, DUDLEY G.

A Comprehensive History of Texas 1685 to 1897. Dallas: 1898. V. 37

A Comprehensive History of Texas, 1685 to 1897. Austin: 1986. V. 37

WOOTEN, M. L.

Women Tell the Story of the Southwest. San Antonio: 1940. V. 39

WOOTON, W.

Cyrfeithjeu Hywel Dda ac Eraill, Seu Leges Wallicae Ecclesiasticae & Civiles Hoeli Boni et Aliorum Walliae Principum Qua ex Variis Codicibus Manuscriptis Eruit . . . London: 1730. V. 40

WOOTTEN, A. C.

Chronicles of Pharmacy. London: 1910. V. 43

WOOTTEN, BAYARD

Old Homes and Gardens of North Carolina. Chapel Hill,: 1941. V. 39

WOOTTON, A. C.

Chronicles of Pharmacy. London: 1910. V. 44

WORCESTER, DEAN CONANT

The Philippine Islands and Their People: A Record of Personal Observationa dn Experience . . . New York: 1899; V. 41

WORCESTER, EDWARD SOMERSET, 2ND MARQUIS OF

A Century of the Names and Scantlings of Such Inventions, as at Present I Can Call to Mind Have Tried and Perfected . . . London: 1663. V. 40

WORCESTER, G. R. G.

The Junks and Sampans of the Yangtze. Shanghai: 1947-48. V. 38; 42

WORCESTER, HENRY SOMERSET, MARQUIS OF

A Century of the Names and Scantlings of Such Inventions as at Present I Can Call to Mind to Have Tried and Perfected. Glasgow: 1767. V. 45

A Century of the Names and Scantlings of Such Inventions as at Present I Can Call to Mind to Have Tried and Perfected . . . London: 1767. V. 42

WORCESTER, JOSEPH EMERSON

A Dictionary of the English Language. Boston: 1864. V. 41

A Gross Literary Fraud Exposed; Relating to the Publication of Worcester's Dictionary in London. Boston: 1855. V. 38

WORCESTER, NOAH

The Friend of Peace, in a Series of Numbers: with a Solemn Review of the Custom War. Schenectady: 1817. V. 42

The Friend of Peace, in a Series of Numbers, Together with a Solemn Review of the Custom of War . . . Ballston Spa: 1822. V. 41

WORCESTER STATE HOSPITAL

By-Laws, Established by the Trustees of the State Lunatic Hospital, in Worcester. Worcester: 1845. V. 45

WORCESTERIANA. London: 1886. V. 39

WORCESTERSHIRE FURNISHING CO., LEICESTER.

Modern Furniture. Leicester: 1909. V. 43

A WORD in Behalf of the House of Commons; or, Remarks Upon a Speech Supposed to Have Been Delivered by a Right Honourable Gentleman, on the Motion for Expelling Mr. Wilkes, on Friday, Feb. 3, 1769. London: 1769. V. 41

A WORD to the Wise, Addressed to the Pillars of the Community. London: 1812. V. 43

WORDEN, EDWARD CHAUNCEY

Nitro-cellulose Industry. New York: 1911. V. 40

WORDS of Truth and Wisdom. London: 1848. V. 38

WORDSWORTH, CHARLES

Of Societies Called Clubs. London: 1841. V. 45

WORDSWORTH, CHRISTOPHER

Annals of My Early Life 1806-1846 with Occasional Compositions in Latin and English Verse. with Annals of My Life 1847-1856. London: 1891-93. V. 41

Athens and Attica: Journal of a Residence There. London: 1836. V. 37; 46

Athens and Attica: Journal of a Residence There. London: 1837. V. 45

Athens and Attica. Notes of a Tour . . . London: 1855. V. 39; 45

Ecclesiastical Biography; or, Lives of Eminent Men, Connected with the History of Religion in England from the Commencement of the Reformation to the Revolution . . . London: 1818. V. 37

Greece Pictorial, Descriptive and Historical . . . London: 1844. V. 45

Greece; Pictorial, Descriptive and Historical. London: 1849. V. 40

Greece: Pictorial, Descriptive and Historical. London: 1853. V. 37; 40

Greece: Pictorial, Descriptive, and Historical.. London: 1859. V. 45

Inscriptiones Pompeianae; or, Specimens and Facsimiles of Ancient Inscriptions Discovered on the Walls of the Buildings at Pompeii. London: 1837. V. 44

Memoirs of William Wordsworth, Poet-Laureate. Boston: 1851. V. 43

WORDSWORTH, DOROTHY

Journals of . . . London: 1897. V. 43; 45

Journals . . . London: 1941. V. 43; 45

WORDSWORTH, SAMUEL

Lyrical Ballads. London: 1800. V. 44

WORDSWORTH, WILLIAM 1770-1850

A Complete Guide to the Lakes . . . Kendal: 1842. V. 46

A Complete Guide to the English Lakes, with Minute Directions for Tourists, . . . London: 1859. V. 44

Concerning the Relations of Great Britain, Spain and Portugal To Each Other and to the Common Enemy . . . London: 1809. V. 40

A Decade of Years: Poems: 1798-1807. 1911. V. 46

A Decade of Years. Hammersmith: 1911. V. 39; 42; 43; 44

A Decade of Years. London: 1911. V. 37; 43; 45

A Description of the Scenery of the Lakes in the North of England. London: 1823. V. 39; 45

The Early Letters of William and Dorothy. Oxford: 1935/37/39. V. 45

THE WORLD Almanac for 1868. New York: 1867. V. 44

THE WORLD and Ourselves. London: 1938. V. 38

THE WORLD Display; or, a Curious Collection of Voyages and Travels Selected From Writers of All Nations. London: 1772-90. V. 42

THE WORLD in Miniature . . . Western Hemisphere. Toronto: 1861. V. 39; 41

WORLD SHIP SOCIETY. TORONTO BRANCH

Preliminary List of Canadian Merchant Steamships (Coastal and Inland) 1809-1930. Toronto: 1963. V. 45

A WORLD Unsuspected: Portraits of a Southern Childhood. Chapel Hill: 1987. V. 39

THE WORLD We Live In. A Pictorial Survey of the Universe . . . New York: 1893. V. 45

THE WORLD'S Best Fairy Stories. London: 1913. V. 45

WORLEY, E. D.

Iron Horses of the Santa Fe Trail. Dallas: 1965. V. 37

WORLIDGE, JOHN

Dictionarium Rusticum, Urbanicum & Botanicum; or, a Dictionary of Husbandry, Gardening, Trade, Commerce, and all Sorts of Country Affairs. London: 1726. V. 39

The Most Easie Method for Making Cider. London: 1687. V. 42

Systema Agriculturae. London: 1675. V. 40; 44

Systema Agricultrae . . . London: 1681. V. 37; 41; 43

Systema Horti-cultrae; or, the Art of Gardening. London: 1688. V. 39

Systema Agriculturae: the Mystery of Husbandry Discovered. London: 1697. V. 45

Systema Horti-Culturae: or, the Art of Gardening . . . The Fourth Edition. To which is added the Gardener's Monthly Directions. By J. Woolridge, (sic). London: 1700. V. 37; 44

Vinetum Britannicum: or a Treatise of Cider. London: 1678. V. 45

Vinetum Britannicum . . . London: 1691. V. 42

WORLIDGE, THOMAS

A Select Collection of Drawings from Curious Antique Gems. London: 1768. V. 37; 38; 39

WORMALD, FRANCIS 1904-1972

An Early Breton Gospel Book, a Ninth Century Manuscript from the Collection of H L Bradfer-Lawrence, 1887-1965. Cambridge: 1977. V. 37; 39; 46

An Early Breton Gospel Book, a Ninth Century Manuscript from the Collection of H. L. Bradfer-Lawrence. London: 1977. V. 39

WORMELEY, KATHARINE

The Other Side of the War with the Army of the Potomac. Boston: 1889. V. 41

WORMLEY, EDWARD

The Dunbar Book of Contemporary Furniture. Berne, Indiana: 1956. V. 37

WORMLEY, JUDITH

The Potomac River Muse. Richmond: 1825. V. 41

WORMS, HENRY DE

The Earl and Its Mechanism. London: 1862. V. 38

The Earth and Its Mechanism. London: 1862. V. 40

WORONOCO PAPER CO.

Woronoco Bond Manufactured by Woronoco Paper Co. Woronoco: 1930's. V. 41

Woronoco Bond Manufactured by Woronoco Paper Company. Woronoco: 1930's. V. 38

WORRALL, JOHN

Bibliotheca Legum Angliae, Part I. London: 1788, 1794. V. 40

WORRELL, JOHN

A Diamond in the Rough Embracing Anecdotes, Biography, Romance and History. Indianapolis: 1906. V. 40; 42

WORSAAE, JENS JACOB ASMUSSEN

The Primeval Antiquities of Denmark. London: 1849. V. 45

WORSDALE, JOHN

Genethliacal Astrology. Newark: 1796. V. 45

WORSDELL, W. C.

Principles of Plant-Teratology. London: 1915-16. V. 38

WORSHAM, JOHN H.

One of Jackson's Foot Cavalry. His Experience and what He saw during the war 1861-1865. New York: 1912. V. 37

WORSLEY, EDWARD

Protestancy Withovt Principles, or, Sectaries vnhappy Fall from Infallibility to Fancy. Antwerp: 1668. V. 42

Reason and Religion. Antwerp: 1672. V. 46

WORSLEY, ISRAEL

A View of the American Indians Their General Character, Customs, Language, Public Festivals, Religious Rites, and Traditions; Shewing them to be the Descendants of the Ten Tribes of Israel. London: 1828. V. 37; 42

WORSLEY, RICHARD

The History of the Isle of Wight. London: 1781. V. 38; 43

Museum Worsleyanum; or a collections of Antique Basso-Relievos, Bustos, Statues, and Gems; with Views in the Levant. Taken on the spot in the years MDCCLXXXV.VI and VII. London: 1824. V. 37

The Trial with the Whole of the Evidence Between the Right Hon. Sir Richard Worsley, Bart . . . and George Bissett . . . for Criminal Conversation with the Plantiff's Wife Before the Right Hon. William Earl of Mansfield . . . on Thursday the 21st of February 1782. London: 1782. V. 37

WORSNOP, THOMAS

History of the City of Adelaide from the Foundation of the Province of South Austrlaia in 1836 to the End of the Municipal Year 1877. Adelaide: 1878. V. 45

WORSTER, BENJAMIN

A Compendious and Methodical Account of the Principles of Natural Philosophy. London: 1722. V. 41; 45

A Compendious and Methodical Account of the Principles of Natural Philosophy. London: 1730. V. 38; 41; 44

WORSTER, W.

Eskimo Folk-Tales. Longon & Copenhagen: 1921. V. 45

WORTHAM, LOUIS J.

A History of Texas, from Wilderness to Commonwealth. Fort Worth: 1924. V. 38; 39; 42

WORTHINGTON, ELLIS

The Hunter of Monadnoc. Dedham: 1834. V. 44

WORTHINGTON, GREVILLE

A Bibliography of the Waverley Novels. London: 1931. V. 43

WORTHINGTON, RICHARD

An Invitation to the Inhabitants of England, to the Manufacture of Wines, from the Fruits of Their Own Country. Worcester: 1812. V. 40; 43

WORTHINGTON, W. H.

Portraits of the Sovereigns of England. London: 1824. V. 44

WORTIS, JOSEPH

Tricky Dick and His Pals. 1974. V. 41

WORTLEY, CHARLES JAMES STUART

Journal of an Excursion to Antwerp, During the Siege of the Citadel, in December 1832. London: 1832. V. 46

WORTLEY, EMMELINE STUART

Travels in the United States, etc. during 1849 and 1850. London: 1851. V. 38

Travels in the United States. New York: 1851. V. 38

WORTLEY, ROTHESAY STUART

Letters from a Flying Officer. London: 1928. V. 42

WOTTON, HENRY 1568-1639

The Elements of Architecture. 1624. V. 45

The Elements of Architecture, Collected from the Best Authors and Examples. London: 1624. V. 38; 42; 43

Letters and Dispatches from Sir Henry Wotton to James the First and His Ministers. London: 1850. V. 46

A Parallel Betweene Robert Late Earle of Essex, and George Late Duke of Buckingham. London: 1641. V. 46

Reliquiae Wottonianae, or, a Collection of Lives, Letter, Poems . . . London: 1651. V. 39; 45

Reliquiae Wottoniae; or, a Collection of Lives, Letters, Poems . . . London: 1672. V. 43

Reliquiae Wottonianae: A Collection of Lives, Letters, Poems, with Characters of Sundry Personages, etc. London: 1672. V. 44; 46

The State of Christendom . . . London: 1657. V. 38; 43; 45

The State of Christendome . . . London: 1679. V. 43

WOTTON, PHILIP HENRY

Views of the Ruins of the Principle Houses Destroyed During the Late Riots at Birmingham. London: 1792. V. 39

WOTTON, THOMAS

The English Baronetage. London: 1741. V. 44

WOTTON, WILLIAM

Reflections Upon Ancient and Modern Learning. London: 1694. V. 40; 42

Reflections Upon Ancient and Modern Learning. London: 1705. V. 38; 42

Reflections Upon Ancient and Modern Learning. L: 1694. V. 37

Wotton's Short View of George Hicke's Grammatico-Critical and Archaeological Treasure of the Ancient Northern Languages . . . London: 1735. V. 37

WOTY, WILLIAM

The Graces: a Poetical Epistle. London: 1774. V. 42

The Shrubs of Parnassus. London: 1760. V. 38; 45

WOUK, HERMAN

The Caine Mutiny. Garden City: 1951. V. 45

The Caine Mutiny. 1952. V. 39

The Caine Mutiny. Garden City: 1952. V. 41; 44

The Caine Mutiny. New York: 1952. V. 40; 43

The City Boy. New York: 1948. V. 42; 45

Inside, Outside. Boston: 1985. V. 46

The Main in the Trench Coat. 1941. V. 46

Marjorie Morningstar. New York: 1955. V. 46

Nature's Way. Garden City: 1958. V. 42

This is My God. Boston: (1987). V. 37

War and Remembrance. Boston: 1978. V. 38; 39; 40

WOULFE, STEPHEN 1787-1840

A Letter to a Protestant; or the Balance of Evils . . . Dublin: 1825. V. 43

WPA Historical Records Survey Project. American Imprints Inventory . . . No. 10. Checklist of Kansas Imprints. 1854-1876. Topeka: 1939. V. 44

WRAGG, ARTHUR

Alice Through the Paper Mill . . . Birmingham: 1940. V. 44

Jesus Wept. London: 1935? V. 42

WRANGELL, FERDINAND PETROVICH, BARON VON

Narrative of an Expedition to the Polar Sea, in the years 1820, 1821, 1822 & 1823 . . . Edited by Major Edward Sabine. London;: 1840. V. 37

WRANGHAM, FRANCIS 1769-1842

The British Plutarch, Containing the Lives of the Most Eminent Divies, Patriots, Statesmen, Warriors, Philosophers, Poets and Artists of Great Britain and Ireland from the Accession of Henry VIII to the Present Time. London: 1816. V. 37; 40

The English Portion of the Library of Francis Wrangham, Archdeacon of Cleveland. Malton: 1826. V. 41; 45

A Few Sonnets Attempted from Petrarch in Early Life. Kent: 1817. V. 40; 42; 46

The Pleiad; or, a Series of Abridgements of Seven Distinguished Writers, in Opposition to the Pernicious Doctrines of Deism. N.P.: 1820. V. 42

The Restoration of the Jews: a Poem. Cambridge: 1795. V. 38; 43

Sertum Cantabrigiensis; or, the Cambridge Garland. Malton: 1824. V. 40; 42; 46

WRATISLAW, THEODORE

Oscar Wilde: a Memoir. London: 1979. V. 41

WRAXALL, C. F.

The Backwoodsman; or, Life on the Indian Frontier. London: 1864. V. 37; 38

WRAXALL, C. F. LASCELLES

Life and Times of Her Majesty Caroline Matilda, Queen of Denmark and Norway and Sister of George III of England. London: 1864. V. 39

WRAXALL, FREDERICK CHARLES LASCELLES

Remarkable Adventures and Unrevealed Mysteries. London: 1863. V. 42

WRAXALL, NATHANIEL WILLIAM 1751-1831

The Correspondence Between a Traveller and a Minister of State, in October and November, 1792. London: 1796. V. 43

Historical Memoirs of My Own Time . . . from 1772 to 1784. London: 1815. V. 40

Historical Memoirs of My Own Time. London: 1818. V. 39

Historical Memoirs of His Own Time. London: 1836. V. 43

The Historical and the Posthumous Memoirs 1772-1784. London: 1884. V. 37; 40

The History of France, Under the Kings of the Race of Valois . . . London: 1785. V. 40

Memoirs of the Courts of Berlin, Dresden, Warsaw and Vienna in the Years 1777, 1778 and 1779. London: 1806. V. 41

Posthumous Memoirs of His Own Time. London: 1836. V. 39

A Short Review of the Political State of Great-Britain at the Commencement of the Year 1787. London: 1787. V. 39

A Tour through Some of the Northern Parts of Europe, Particularly Copenhagen, Stockholm, and Ptersburgh. London: 1775. V. 42; 43; 45

A Tour through Some of the Northern Parts of Europe, Particularly Copenhagen, Stockholm and Petersburgh. London: 1785. V. 41

WRAY, JOHN 1782-1869

Dangers of an Entire Repeal of the Bank Restriction Act: and a Plan Suggested for Obviating Them. London: 1818. V. 38

WRAY, MARY

The Ladies Library. London: 1732. V. 41; 43; 45

WRAY, W. J.

History of the Twenty Third Pennsylvania Volunteer Infantry Birney's Zouves . . . N.P.: 1903-04. V. 42

A WREATH for Edwin Markham: Tributes from the Poets of America on His Seventieth Birthday, April 23, 1922. Chicago: 1922. V. 39

WREDE, FRIEDRICH W. VON

Lebensbilder aus den Verenigten Staaten von Noradamerika und Texas. Cassel: 1844. V. 39; 42; 45

WREN, CHRISTOPHER

Parentalia; or, Memoirs of the Family of the Wrens. London: 1750. V. 45

WREN SOCIETY, LONDON.

Publications. Oxford: 1924-43. V. 38

WREN Society. The first (. . . twentieth) volume. Oxford: 1924-1943. V. 37; 40

WRENIUS Vuews des Nouveaux Etablissemens Publies, des Embelissemens, des Jeux et Promenades de Catherinehoff . . . (with Collection de Vues de Stain Petersbourg et de ses Environs . . . St. Petersburg: 1824. V. 46

WRENN, JOHN HENRY

A Catalogue of the Library of the Late John Henry Wrenn. Austin: 1920. V. 43

WRIFFORD, ALLISON

A New Plan of Writing Copies with Accompanying Explanations and Remarks. Boston: 1810. V. 40

WRIGHT, A. B.

An Essay Towards a History of Hexham . . . Alnwick: 1823. V. 45

WRIGHT, ABRAHAM

Delitiae Delitiarum sive Epigrammatum ex Optimis Poetis in Illa Bibliotheca Bodleiana. Oxford: 1637. V. 41

WRIGHT, ALBERT H.

Our Georgia-Florida Frontier: the Okefinokee Swamp, Its History and Cartography. New York: 1945. V. 42

WRIGHT, ALEXANDER

An Inquiry into the Rise and Progress of Parliament Chiefly in Scotland, etc, etc. Edinburgh: 1806. V. 37

WRIGHT, ALLEN KENDRICK

To the Poles by Airship, or Around the World Endways. Los Angeles: 1909. V. 37; 46

WRIGHT, ALMROTH E.

On Pharmaco-Therapy and Preventive Incolulation Applied to Pneumonia in the African Native with a Discourse on the Logical Methods Which Ought to be Employed in the Evaluation of Therapeutic Agents. London: 1914. V. 39

Researches from the Inoculation Department, St. Mary's Hospital. London: 1942-44. V. 37; 39

A Short Treatise on Anti-Typhoid Inoculation. Westminster: 1904. V. 37; 39

WRIGHT, ANDREW

Court Hand Restored; or, the Student's Assistant in Reading Old Deeds, Charters, etc. London: 1776. V. 38; 46

WRIGHT, ARNOLD

Parliament Past and Present Popular and Picturesque Account of a Thousand Years in the Palace of Westminster. London: 1900. V. 46

WRIGHT, ASHER

Gaa Nah Shoh ne De O Waah Sao Nyoh Gwah Na Wen Ni Yuh. 1843. V. 38

Go Wana Gwa Hi Sat Hah Yon Deyas Dah Gway. A Spelling Book in the Seneca Langauge. Buffalo-Creek Reservation: 1842. V. 40

WRIGHT, AUSTIN TAPPAN

Islandia. New York: 1492. V. 37; 44; 45; 46

Islandia. New York: 1958. V. 38

WRIGHT, BENJAMIN

Reports of Messrs. Benj. Wright and J. L. Sullivan, Engineers, Engaged int he Survey of the Route of the Proposed Canal from the Hudson. To the Headwaters of the Lackawaxen River Accompanied by Other Documents. Philadelphia: 1824. V. 46

WRIGHT, C.

The Antiquities and Description of Arundel Castle . . . with an Account of the Arundelian Marbles. Brighton: 1817. V. 37; 40

The History and Description of Arundel Castle. London: 1818. V. 37; 40

WRIGHT, C. T. HAGBERG

Catalogue of the London Library . . . . London: 1909-55. V. 46

Nicholas Fabri de Peiresc. London: 1926. V. 38; 45; 46

WRIGHT, CALEB

Lectures on India; also, Descriptions of Remarkable Customs and Personages in Other Pagan and Mohammadean Countries. Boston: 1849. V. 38; 45

WRIGHT, CALEB EARL

Wyoming. A Tale. New York: 1845. V. 40

WRIGHT, CHARLES

Dead Color: Poems. Salem: 1980. V. 46

Five Journals. New York: 1986. V. 42; 46

A History from the Founding of Lloyd's Coffee House to the Present Day. London: 1928. V. 39; 42

A Journal of the Year of the Ox. Iowa City: 1988. V. 46

The Venice Notebook. Boston: 1971. V. 46

WRIGHT, CHARLES W.

The Mammoth Cave, Kentucky. Vincennes, Ind.: 1858. V. 37

WRIGHT, CHAUNCEY 1830-1875

Essays. Leipzig: 1885. V. 42

Letters of Chauncey Wright with Some Account of His Life . . . Cambridge: 1878. V. 42

WRIGHT, DANIEL

History of Nepal. Cambridge: 1877. V. 39

WRIGHT, E. M.

Rustic Speech and Folk-Lore. London: 1913. V. 38

WRIGHT, E. PERCEVAL

The Book of Trinity College, Dublin 1591-1891. Belfast: 1892. V. 42

WRIGHT, EDGAR W.

Lewis & Dryden's Marine History of the Pacific Northwest. Portland: 1895. V. 38; 46

Lewis & Dryden's Marine History of the Pacific Northwest. Portland: 1895. V. 37; 39

Lewis & Dryden's Marine History of the Pacific Northwest: An Illustrated Review of the Growth and Development of the Maritime Industry. New York: 1961. V. 37; 39; 40; 44

Lewis and Dryden's Marine History of the Pacific Northwest. V. 38

WRIGHT, EDWARD

Some Observations Made in Travelling through France, Italy &c. in the Years 1720, 1721 and 1722. London: 1730. V. 43

Some Observations Made in Travelling through France, Italy, etc. in the Years 1720, 21 and 22. London: 1730. V. 41

Some Observations Made in Travelling through France, Italy &c. in the Years MDCCXX, MDCCXI and MDCCXXII . . . London: 1764. V. 40; 43

WRIGHT, EDWIN 1791-1859

Sketches in Bedlam; or Characteristic Traits of Insanity, as Displayed in the Cases of One Hundred and Forty Patients of Both Sexes . . . London: 1823. V. 43; 45

WRIGHT, ELIZUR

A Lecture on Tobacco, Delivered in the Chapel of the Western Reserve College, Hudson, Ohio, May 29, 1832. Cleveland: 1832. V. 44

WRIGHT, FRANCES

Altorf, a Tragedy. Philadelphia: 1819. V. 44

A Few Days in Athens: Being the Translation of a Greek Manuscript Discovered in Herculaneum. New York: 1825. V. 39

A Few Days in Athens. New York: 1831. V. 39

Views of Society and Manners in America. New York: 1821. V. 43

Views of Society and Manners in America . . . London: 1822. V. 42

WRIGHT, FRANK LLOYD 1869-1959

An American Architecture. New York: 1955. V. 38; 39; 40

Architecture and Modern Life. New York: London: 1937. V. 46

An Autobiography. V. 39

An Autobiography. New York: 1943. V. 41; 45; 46

Buildings, Plans and Designs. London: 1963. V. 42

Buildings, Plans and Designs. New York: 1963. V. 38; 43; 46

The Disappearing City. New York: 1932. V. 46

The Disappearing City. The Industrial Revolution Runs Away. New York: 1969. V. 37; 43

Drawings for a Living Architecture. New York: 1959. V. 42; 46

The Early Work. New York: 1968. V. 46

Falling Water 25 Years After. Milan: 1963. V. 44

Frank Lloyd Wright: The Early Work. New York: 1968. V. 43

Frank Lloyd Wright. Selected Drawings. Portfolio I, II, III. New York and Tokyo: 1977-82. V. 38

the Future of Arichtecture. New York: 1953. V. 43

Genius and Mobocracy. New York: 1949. V. 38; 40; 41; 44; 46

Greetings from Catherine and Frank Lloyd Wright, Oak Park, December Nineteen Hundred Seven. V. 44

The Industrial Revolution Runs Away. New York: 1969. V. 46

The Japanese Print/an Inerpretation. Chicago: 1912. V. 45; 46

The Japanese Print, an Interpretation. New York: 1967. V. 43; 46

The Life Works of . . . . Holland: 1925. V. 39

The Life Work of the American Architect Frank Lloyd Wright. Santpoort: 1925. V. 41; 45

The Living City. New York: 1958. V. 44; 46

The Living City. New York: 1958. V. 44

Modern Architecture, Being the Kahn Lectures for 1930. Princeton: 1931. V. 41

Modern Architecture, Being the Kahn Lectures for 1930. Princeton: 1931. V. 41

Modern Architecture. Princeton: 1931. V. 41; 42; 43

The Natural House. New York: 1954. V. 37; 43

A New House: on Bear Run Pennsylvania. New York: 1938. V. 41

On Architecture, Selected Writings 1894-1940. New York: 1941. V. 46

An Organic Architecture: the Architecture of Democracy. London: 1939. V. 46

Selected Drawings: Portfolio. New York: 1977. V. 46

Taliesin Drawings. New York: 1952. V. 44

A Testament. New York: 1957. V. 39; 42; 44; 46

A Testament. Tokyo: 1960. V. 41

A Testament. New York: 1975. V. 40

When Democracy Builds. Chicago: 1945. V. 44

The Work of Frank Lloyd Wright. New York: 1965. V. 41

WRIGHT, GEORGE

Pleasing Melancholy or a Walk Among the Tombs in a Country Church Yard in the Stile and Manner of Hervey's Meditations. London: 1793. V. 41

Topographical memoir and Map of Colonel Wright's Late Campaign Against the Indians in Oregon and Washington Territories. Washinton: 1859. V. 38

WRIGHT, GEORGE NEWENHAM 1790-1877

China, in a Series of Views . . . London: 1843. V. 40; 43; 44; 45

China, in a series of Views, Displaying the Scenery, Architecture, and Social Habits of that Ancient Empire. London and Paris: 1843. V. 40

France Illustrated, Exhibiting its Landscape Scenery, Antiquities, Military and Ecclesiastical Architecture & Drawings . . . London: 1845-47. V. 37; 43; 44; 46

The Gallery of Engravings. London: (1844-46). V. 37

An Historical guide to the city of Dublin, illustrated by engravings and a plan of the city. Second edition, with corrections and additional articles: also an itinerary, and various useful information for tourists and strangers. London: 1825. V. 37

Ireland Illustrated, from Original Drawings . . . London: 1831. V. 43

Ireland Illustrated, from Original Drawings. London: 1833. V. 41

Landscape-Historical Illustrations of Scotland and the Waverly Novels . . . London: 1836-38. V. 41

A New Comprehensive Gazetteer. London: 1838. V. 40

A New and Comprehnsive Gazetteer . . . London: 1838. V. 46

The Rhine, Italy and Greece. London: 1841. V. 40

The Shores and Islands of the Mediterranean. London and Paris: 1839. V. 38

The Shores and Islands of the Mediterranean. London: 1840. V. 40; 41; 43

WRIGHT, H.

Rehousing Urban AMerica. New York: 1935. V. 46

WRIGHT, HAROLD BELL

The Un-Crowned King. Chicago: 1910. V. 39

When a Man's a Man. New York: 1916. V. 39

The Winning of Barbara Worth. Chicago: 1911. V. 39; 44; 45

WRIGHT, HAROLD J. L.

The Etched Work of F. L. Griggs. London: 1941. V. 41

WRIGHT, HARRY

A Short History of Golf in Mexico and Mexico City Country Club. New York: 1938. V. 38; 40; 42

WRIGHT, HARRY ANDREW

Indian Deeds of Hampden County. Springfield: 1905. V. 38

WRIGHT, HENDRICK B.

Historical Sketches of Plymouth, Luzerne Co., Pennsylvania. Philadelphia: 1873. V. 37; 41; 42

WRIGHT, HENRY C.

Human Life: Illustrated in My Individual Experience as a Child, a Youth and a Man. Boston: 1849. V. 37

A Kiss for a Blow . . . Boston: 1842. V. 43

WRIGHT, J.

Mornings at Bow Street. London: 1824. V. 40

WRIGHT, J. L.

The Etched Work of F. I. Griggs. London: 1941. V. 40

WRIGHT, J. W.

No Gifts; The Doves of December . . . Carmel-by-the-Sea: 1924. V. 43

WRIGHT, JAMES

Country Conversations: Being an Account of Some Discourses that Happened in a Visit to the Country Last Summer, on Divers Subjects . . . London: 1694. V. 42

The Green Wall. New Haven: 1957. V. 37; 45

The Green Wall. New York: 1957. V. 45

The History and Antiquities of the County of Rutland. (with) Additions to the History and Antiquities of Rutlandshire. London: 1684-87. V. 42

The Temples in Nimes. Worcester: 1982. V. 44

Two Citizens. New York: 1973. V. 43

WRIGHT, JOHN fl. 1761-1765

The American Negotiator. London: 1763. V. 41; 45

The American Negotiator, or the Various Currencies of the British Colonies in America. London: 1765. V. 38; 40

The Flower Grower's Guide. London: 1896-1901. V. 42

The Fruit Grower's Guide. London: 1892-94. V. 42

Historic Bibles in America. New York: 1905. V. 43

Some Notable Altars in the Church of England and the American Episcopal Church. New York: 1908. V. 38

WRIGHT, JOHN A.

A Paper on the Character and Promise of the Country on the Southern Border, Along or Near the 32d Parallel, Its Adaptation to the Building and Support of a Railway . . . Philadelphia: 1876. V. 44

WRIGHT, JOHN C.

Chicago-Jig. The Tradition of the Happy Hunting Grounds. Alma, Michigan: 1934. V. 37

WRIGHT, JOHN, commander, R.N.

Memoir of the Mosquito Territory, as Respecting Voluntary Cession Of It to the Crown of Great Britain . . . London: 1808. V. 41

WRIGHT, JOHN LLOYD

My Father Who Is On Earth. New York: 1946. V. 46

WRIGHT, JOHN W.

Poems and Woodcuts. Omaha: 1976. V. 46

WRIGHT, JOSEPH

A Catalogue of Pictures, painted by J. Wright of Derby, and Exhibited at Mr. Robin's Rooms . . . London: 1785. V. 38; 40; 44

The English Dialect Dictionary . . . London: 1898-1905. V. 37; 42; 45

WRIGHT, LEWIS

The Illustrated Book of Poultry. London: 1873. V. 43

The Illustrated Book of Poultry . . . London: 1890. V. 43

The New Book of Poultry. London: 1902. V. 40

WRIGHT, MARCUS J.

General Officers of the Confederate Army, Officers of the Executive Departments of the Confederate States, members of the Confederate Congress by States. New York: 1911. V. 37; 45; 46

Reminiscences of the Early Settlement and Early Settlers of McNairy County, Tennessee. Washington: 1882. V. 44; 45

WRIGHT, MARCUS JOSEPH

General Scott. New York: 1893. V. 38

WRIGHT, MARIE ROBINSON

The New Brazil: Its Resources and Attractions, Historical, Descriptive and Industrial. Philadelphia: (1901). V. 37

The Old and the New Peru . . . Philadelphia: 1908. V. 42

WRIGHT, MARTIN

An Introduction to the Law of Tenures. London: 1734. V. 38

WRIGHT, MICHAEL

An Account of His Excellence Roger EArl of Castlemains's Embassy from His Sacred Majesty James the IId to His Holiness Innocent XI. London: 1688. V. 44

WRIGHT, NATHANIEL HILL

The Fall of Palmyra; and other Poems. Middlebury: 1817. V. 39; 40

The Fall of Palmyra and Other Poems. Fall: 1817. V. 43

WRIGHT, O. L.

Frank Lloyd Wright: His Life, His Work, His Words. New York: 1966. V. 46

WRIGHT, ORDON

MacDiarmid. An Illustrated Biography of Christopher Murray Grieve. Edinburgh: 1977. V. 38

WRIGHT, PAUL

The New and Complete Life of Our Blessed Lord and Saviour Jesus Christ. New York: 1795. V. 42

WRIGHT, R. G.

The Ducks of India. 1925. V. 40

The Ducks of India. London: 1925. V. 42

WRIGHT, R. PATRICK

The Standard Cyclopedia of Modern Agriculture and Rural Economy. London: 1908-11. V. 46

WRIGHT, RICHARD 1908-1960

How 'Bigger' was Born. New York: 1940. V. 38; 39; 41; 42

Native Son. New York: 1940. V. 38; 40; 45

Native Son: a Play . . . New York: 1941. V. 44

Native Son. New York: & London: 1940. V. 37

12 Million Black Voices. A Falk History of the Negro in the United States. New York: 1941. V. 37; 40; 41; 45

Uncle Tom's Children. New York: 1938. V. 44

When a man's a Man: a Novel. Chicago: 1916. V. 46

WRIGHT, ROBERT MARR

Dodge City. The Cowboy Capital and the Great Southwest in the Days of the Wild Indian, the Buffalo, the Cowboy, Dance Halls . . . N.P.. V. 45

Dodge City. The Cowboy Capital. Wichita: 1913. V. 39

Dodge City. The Cowboy Capital and the Great Southwest in the Days of The Wild Indian, the Buffalo, the Cowboy, Dance Halls, Gambling Halls and Bad Men. N.P.: 1930. V. 39

WRIGHT, S. F.

Dream or the Simian Maid. London: 1931. V. 44

Elfwin. 1930. V. 44

WRIGHT, SILAS

History of Perry County, Pennsylvania. Lancaster: 1873. V. 42

WRIGHT, THOMAS

The Anglo-Saxon Satirical Poets and Epigrammatists of the Twelfth Century. London: 1872. V. 44

The Antiquities of the Town of Halifax in Yorkshire. Leeds: 1738. V. 44

Arbors and Grottos. London: 1979. V. 45; 46

The Archaeological Album; or Museum of National Antiquities. London: 1845. V. 39

Caricature History of the Georges. London: 1867. V. 46

The Female Vertuoso's. London: 1683. V. 38

The Female Vertuoso's. London: 1693. V. 37; 41

A History of the Rise and Progress of the People Called Quakers in Ireland from 1653 to 1700 . . . and Continuation to 1751. Dublin: 1751. V. 38; 43; 46

The History and Topography of The County of Essex . . . London: 1836. V. 41

The History of Ludlow and Its Neighbourhood . . . Ludlow: 1852. V. 41

The History of Ireland, From the Earliest Period of the Irish Annals to the Present Time. London: 1854. V. 44

A History of Domestic Manners and Sentiments in England During the Middle Ages. London: 1862. V. 41

A History of Caricature and Grotesque in Literature and Art. London: 1875. V. 40

The History of Ireland: from the Earliest Period of the Irish Annals, to the Present Time. London. V. 41

Le Keux's Memorisl of Cambridge. Oxford: 1841-42. V. 41

The Life of Sir Richard Burton. London: 1906. V. 41; 45

The Life of Walter Pater. London: 1907. V. 40; 46

The Life of William Blake. London: 1929. V. 40

WYATT, BENJAMIN

Observations on the Design for the Theatre Royal, Drury Lane, as Executed in the Year 1812. London: 1813. V. 37

WYATT, EDITH

Every One His Own Way. New York: 1901. V. 37

WYATT, HORACE

Jersey in Jail - 1940-1945. Jersey: 1945. V. 40; 42

WYATT, HORACE M.

Alice in Motorland. London: 1904. V. 45

WYATT, JOHN

The Practical Register in Chancery. London: 1800. V. 40

WYATT, LEO

Engravings by Leo Wyatt. Cambridge: 1973. V. 37; 40; 41; 42

Leo Wyatt's Little Book of Alphabets. 1985. V. 44

Leo Wyatt's Little Book of Alphabets. Kent: 1985. V. 37; 42; 43

A Little Book of Alphabets. 1985. V. 38

A Suite of Little Alphabets Engraved in Wood. 1988. V. 45

A Suite of Little Alphabets. Kent: 1988. V. 42

WYATT, LEWIS WILLIAM

Prospectus of a Design for Various Improvements in the Metropolis; Principally about the Court. London: 1816. V. 37; 40

WYATT, MATTHEW DIGBY 1820-1877

The Art of Illuminating as Practised in Europe from the Earliest Times. London: 1860. V. 37; 38

Industrial Arts of the XIXth Century. London: 1851. V. 38

The Industrial ARts of the Nineteenth Century. London: 1851-53. V. 39

Notices of Sculpture in Ivory . . . London: 1856. V. 38; 40; 42; 44

Specimens of Ornamental Art Workmanship in Gold, Silver, Iron, Brass and Bronze . . . London: 1852. V. 39

WYATT, THOMAS

Memoirs of the Generals, Commodores and Other Commanders, Who Distinguished Themselves in the American Army and Navy During the Wars of the Revolution and 1812 . . . Philadelphia: 1848. V. 46

The Poetical Works of Sir Thomas Watt. London. V. 38

WYATVILLE, JEFFRY

Illustrations of Windsor Castle, by the Late Sir Jeffry Wyatville, R.A. London: 1841. V. 38

WYBERD, JOHN

An Almanacke and Prognostication, with the Forraine Computation, Serving for the Years . . . 1636. London: 1635. V. 39

WYCHE, WILLIAM

A Treatise on the Practice of the Supreme Court of Judicature of the State of New York in Civil Actions. New York: 1794. V. 37

WYCHERLEY, WILLIAM

Complete Works. London: 1924. V. 39; 46

The Complete Works of William Wycherley. Edited by Montague Summers. Soho: 1924. V. 37

The Country Wife. London: 1688. V. 40

Love in a Wood, Or, St. James's Park. London: 1672. V. 37

Love in a Wood, Or St. James's Park. London: 1694. V. 37; 40; 42; 44

Miscellaneous Poems: as Satyrs, Epistles, Love-Verses, Songs and Sonnets. London: 1704. V. 37; 38; 40; 41; 42; 43; 44; 45; 46

The Posthumous Works. London: 1728. V. 37; 38; 40; 45; 46

The Works of Mr. William Wycherley. London: 1713. V. 37; 38

The Complete Works. 1924. V. 45

The Complete Works. London: 1924. V. 42; 45

The Complete Works. Soho: 1924. V. 39; 40; 46

WYCHERLY, WILLIAM

Plays . . . London: 1720. V. 43

WYCOFF, EDITH

Biographical Contributions from the Lloyd Library. 1911-14. V. 42

WYETH, ANDREW

Andrew Wyeth. Boston: 1968. V. 37; 41; 42

Four Seasons. New York: 1962. V. 39

The Four Seasons. New York: 1963. V. 40

Wyeth at Kuerners. Boston: 1976. V. 41; 42; 45; 46

WYETH, JAMIE

Jamie Wyeth Paintings. Boston: 1982. V. 37

WYETH, JOHN

Wyeth's Repository of Sacred Music. Part Second. Harrisbugh: 1820. V. 44

WYETH, JOHN A.

A Text-Book on Surgery. New York: 1887. V. 40; 41; 44; 45

A Text-Book on Surgery. 1891. V. 42

WYETH, JOHN ALLAN

With Sabre and Scalpel. The Autobiography of a Soldier and Surgeon. New York/London: 1914. V. 37

WYETH, JOHN B.

Oregon: or a Short History of a Long Journey from the Atlantic Ocean to the Region of the Pacific by Land . . . Cambridge: 1883. V. 46

WYETH, JOSEPH 1663-1731

Anguis Falgellatus; or, a Switch for the Snake . . . London: 1699. V. 37; 43; 46

WYETH, N. C.

Robin Hood. Philadelphia: 1917. V. 37

WYGANT, L. J.

The Truman G. Blocker, Jr., History of Medicine Collections. London: 1987. V. 39

WYK, P. VAN

Trees of the Kruger National Park. Cape Town: 1972-74. V. 37

WYLD, GEORGE

Vaccination: Is It Worthy of National Support? London. V. 45

WYLD, JAMES

The London and Birmingham Railway Guide and Birmingham and London Railway Companion. (with) Wyld's Guide to the Grand Junction and Liverpool and Manchester Railways . . . London: 1838. V. 46

Maps & Plans, Showing the principal Movements, Battles & Sieges, in which the British Army was engaged during the war from 1808 to 1814 in the Spanish Peninsula and the South of France. London: (1840). V. 37

Memoir to an Atlas Containing Plans of the Principal Battles, Sieges, and Affairs, in Which the British Troops were Engaged During the War in the Spanish Peninsula and the South of France from 1808-1814. London: 1841. V. 38

A New Topographical Map of the Country in the Vincity of London, Describing all the new improvements, metropolitan boroughs and parish boundaries. (c. 1875). V. 37

Notes on the Distribution of Gold throughout the World, including Australia, California and Russia. London: 1852? V. 37

The South Western, or London, Southampton and Portsmouth Railway Guide . . . London: 1842? V. 46

WYLD, SAMUEL

The Practical Surveyor, or the Art of Land Measuring Made Easy. London: 1764. V. 39

WYLDE, HENRY, MRS.

Severed Ties. London: 1889. V. 41

WYLDE, JAMES

The Circle of the Sciences. London: 1875. V. 45

WYLIE, ANDREW

An Address Delivered at Bloomington, October 29, 1829 . . . on the Occasion of His Inauguration as President of Indiana College, Published by Order of the Board of Trustees. Indianapolis: 1829. V. 42

Sectarianism Is Heresy, in Three Parts, In Which Are Shewn Its Nature, Evils and Remedy. Bloomington: 1840. V. 46

WYLIE, ELINOR HOYT 1885-1928

Angels and Earthly Creatures. New York: 1929. V. 38; 40

Collected Poems. New York: 1932. V. 38; 39; 42; 44

Collected Prose of. New York: 1933. V. 42; 44; 46

Jennifer Lorn: a Sedate Extravaganza. New York: 1923. V. 42

Mr. Hodge & Mr. Hazard. New York: 1928. V. 39; 41; 42

Nets to Catch the Wind. New York: 1921. V. 39; 44

The Orphan Angel. New York: 1926. V. 38; 39; 42; 46

Trivial Breath. London: & New York: 1928. V. 43; 46

Trivial Breath (Poems). New York: 1928. V. 39; 42

The Venetian Glass Newphew. New York: 1925. V. 38

The Venetian Glass Nephew. New York: 1925. V. 40; 42; 46

WYLIE, J. A.

History of the Scottish Nations. 1886-90. V. 37

WYLIE, PHILIP

The Big Ones Get Away. New York: & Toronto: 1940. V. 45

Crunch and Des. New York & Toronto: 1948. V. 43

The Magic Animal. Garden City: 1968. V. 46

WYLIE, W. W.

Yellowstone National Park: or the Great American Wonderland. Kansas City: 1882. V. 39; 41

THE WYLL of the Devill, With His Detestable Commaundementes: Directed to His Obedient and Accursed Children and the Rewarde Promised to All Suche as Obediently Wyl Endeuer Themselves. London: 1825. V. 40

WYLLIE, W. L.

London to the Nore, Painted and Described. London: 1905. V. 41

WYLLY, H. C.

History of the 1st and 2nd Battalions The Sherwood Foresters, Nottinghamshire and Derbyshire Regiment, 1740-1914. London: 1929. V. 46

Neill's 'Blue Caps.' Being the Record of the Antecedents and Early History of the Regiment Variously Known as the East India Company's European Regiment, the Madras European Regiment, the 1st Madras Fuziliers . . . London: 1925. V. 37

WYLLYS, RUFUS KAY

Arizona: the History of a Frontier State. Phoenix: 1950. V. 37; 38; 39

WYMAN, MORRILL

Autumnal Catarrh (Hayfever) With Three Maps. New York: 1872. V. 38; 42

WYMAN, SETH

The Life and Adventures of Seth Wyman, Embodying the Principal Events of a Life Spent in Robbert, Theft, Gambling, Passing Counterfeit Money, &c. Written by Himself. Manchester, N.H.: 1843. V. 37

WYMAN, THOMAS B.

The Genealogies and Estates of Charlestown, in the County of Middlesex 1629-1818. Boston: 1879. V. 46

WYMBERLEY-JONES, GEORGE

Theory Concerning the Nature of Insanity. Wormsloe: 1847. V. 42

WYN, ELIS

Sleeping Bard; or Visions of the World, Death and Hell. London: 1860. V. 43; 46

WYNCH, ALEXANDER

A Catalogue of All the Genuine Stock of Excel-Wines, Consisting of About 400 Dozen of Oriental Madeira, Near 200 Dozen of Fine Old Red Port . . . Also Some Valuable Jewels, Two Gold Repeating Watches, Rich Snuff Boxes . . . London: 1781. V. 40

WYNDALE, WILLIAM

An Artist in Italy . . . London: 1913. V. 46

WYNDHAM, FRANCIS

Out of the War. London: 1974. V. 41

WYNDHAM, FRANCIS M.

Wild Life on the Fields of Norway. London: 1861. V. 39; 43; 46

WYNDHAM, HENRY PENRUDDOCKE

A Tour through Monmouthshire and Wales Made in the Months of June and July 1774 and in the Months of June, July and August 1777. Salisbury: 1781. V. 42

WYNDHAM, HENRY PENRYDDOCKE

A Gentleman's Tour through Monmouthshire and Wales, in the Months of June and July, 1774. London: 1775. V. 41

WYNDHAM, HENRY SAXE

The Annals of Covent Garden Theatre from 1732 to 1897. London: 1906. V. 42

WYNDHAM, JOHN

Chocky. London: 1969. V. 44

The Chrysalids. London: 1955. V. 40

The Day of the Triffids. 1951. V. 39

The Day of the Triffids. Garden City: 1951. V. 39

The Day of the Triffids. London: 1951. V. 44; 45

The Day of the Triffids. New York: 1951. V. 44

The Day of the Triffids. 1951. V. 37

The Kraken Wakes. 1953. V. 44

The Kraken Wakes. London: 1953. V. 40

The Midwich Cuckoos. New York: 1957. V. 39; 45

WYNDHAM, MARGARET

Catalogue of the Collection of Greek and Roman Antiquities in the Possession of Leconfield. London: 1915. V. 38

WYNDHAM, NEVILLE

Travels through Europe . . . Drawn from Unerring Sources of Information. Extracted from the United Productions of the following Celebrated Modern Travellers, viz. Coxe, Wraxall, Savary, Moroe, Baron Riesbeck . . . de Non, Mrs. Piozzi &c . . . London: (ca. 1792). V. 37

WYNDHAM QUIN, W. H.

The Yeomanry Cavalry of Gloucestershire and Monmouth. Cheltenham: 1898. V. 38

WYNDHAM, RICHARD

A Book of Towers and Other Buildings of Southern Europe - a Series of Dry-Points Engraved by Richard Wyndham. London: 1928. V. 38; 45

WYNN, CHARLES WATKIN WILLIAM 1775-1850

Argument Upon the Jurisdiction of the House of Commons to Commit in Cases of Breach of Privilege. London: 1810. V. 40

WYNN, MARCIA RITTENHOUSE

Pioneer Family of Whiskey Flat. Los Angeles: 1945. V. 43; 46

WYNNE, EDWARD 1734-1784

Eunomus; or, Dialogues Concerning the Law and Constitution of England. London: 1785. V. 42

Eunomus; or, Dialogues Concerning the Law and Constitution of England . . . London: 1821. V. 38; 40

WYNNE, ELLIS 1671-1734

Gweledigaethen Y Bardd Cwse, Visions of the Sleeping Bard. Newtown: 1940. V. 42; 45; 46

Gweledigaetheu y Bardd Cwcs (i.e.) Visions of the Sleeping Bard. 1940. V. 42

Gweledigaetheu Y Bardd Cwsc. (i.e.) Visions of the Sleeping Bards. 1940. V. 41

WYNNE, J. H.

A General History of the British Empire in American, an Historical, Political and Commercial View. London: 1770. V. 38

WYNNE, JAMES

Private Libraries of New York. New York: 1860. V. 40; 45; 46

WYNNE, JOHN

An Abridgment of Mr. Locke's Essay Concerning Humane Understanding. London: 1696. V. 41; 43; 45

An Abridgment of Mr. Locke's Essay Concerning Human Understanding. London: 1731. V. 42

A Sermon Preached to the Societies for the Reformation of Manners, at St. Mary-le-Bow on Monday January the 3d, 1725. London: 1727. V. 45

WYNNE, JOHN HUDDLESTONE 1743-1788

Choice Emblems, Natural, Historical, Fabulous, Moral and Divine. London: 1775. V. 38

Choice Emblems, Natural, Historical, Fabulous, Moral and Divine. London: 1793. V. 43

A General History of the British Empire in America. London: 1770. V. 42

A General History of Ireland. London: 1772. V. 40; 43

The Prostitute: a Poem. London: 1771. V. 40; 45

Riley's Emblems, Natural, Historical, Fabulous, Moral and Divine . . . London: 1781. V. 45; 46

Tales for Youth: in Thirty Poems; To Which are Annexed Historical Remarks and Moral Applications in Prose. London: 1800. V. 45

WYNNE, MADELENE YALE

The Little Room and Other Stories. Chicago: 1895. V. 38; 41

WYNNE, WILLIAM

The Defence of Francis, Late Lord Bishop of Rochester at the Bar of the House of Lords . . . 9 and 11 May, 1723, Against the Bill Then Depending for Inflicting Pains and Penalties on Him . . . London: 1723. V. 39

The Life of Sir Leoline Jenkins. London: 1724. V. 44

WYNTER, ANDREW

Fruit Between the Leaves. London: 1875. V. 41

WYNTOUN, ANDREW 1350?-1420?

De Orygynale Cronykil of Scotland, be Androw Wyntown, priowr of Sanct Serifis Ynche in Loch Levyn. London: 1795. V. 41

WYOMING. CONSTITUTION

Constitution of the Proposed State of Wyoming Adopted in Convention at Cheyenne, Wyoming. Cheyemme: 1889. V. 37; 42; 43

WYOMING. CONSTITUTIONAL CONVENTION

Journal and Debates of the Constitutional Convention of the State of Wyoming. Begun at the City of Cheyenne on September 2, 1889 and Concluded September 30, 1889. Cheyenne: 1893. V. 42

WYOMING. (TERRITORY). LAWS, STATUTES, ETC.

General Laws, Memorials and Resolutions of the Territory of Wyoming, Passed at the First Session of the Legislative Assembly Convened at Cheyenne, October 12th, 1869. Cheyenne: 1870. V. 39; 40; 46

WYRALL, EVERARD

The Gloucestershire Regiment in the War 1914-1918. London: 1931. V. 44

WYRLEY, WILLIAM

The True Use of Armorie, Shewed by Historie, and Plainy Proued by Example. London: 1592. V. 37

WYSE, FRANCIS

America, Its Realities and Resources . . . London: 1846. V. 42

WYSE, HENRY T.

Modern Type Display and the Use of Type Ornament. Edinburgh: 1911. V. 43

WYSE, THOMAS

An Excursion in the Peloponnesus in the Year 1858. London: 1865. V. 37

Historical Sketch of the Late Catholic Association of Ireland. London: 1829. V. 38; 43

Impressions of Greece. London: 1871. V. 45

WYSS, JOHANN DAVID 1743-1818

The Family Robinson Crusoe. London: 1814-16. V. 46

The Family Robinson Crusoe; or Journal of a Father Shipwrecked with His Wife and Children on an Uninhabited Island. London: 1816. V. 39

The Family Robinson Cruose; or, Journal of a Father Shipwrecked, With His Wife and Children, on an Uninhabited Island. London: 1814. V. 39; 40; 44

The Swiss Family Robinson. Ipswich: 1963. V. 44; 46

WYSTMAN, P.

Genera Avium. Brussels: 1905-14. V. 37

WYTFLIET, CORNELIUS

Histoire Universelle des Indes, Orientales et Occidentales . . . Douay: 1605. V. 43

Histoire Universelle des Indes Occidentales et Orientales, et de la Conversion des Indiens. Douay: 1611. V. 40

WYTH, JOHN

Graphic Sketches from Old an Authentic Works, Illustrating the Costume, Habits and Character of the Aborigines of America. New York: 1841. V. 38

WYTSMAN, P.

Genera Avium. 1905-14. V. 46

Genera Avium. London: 1905-14. V. 45

WYVILL, CHRISTOPHER

A Defence of Dr. Price and the Reformers of England. London: 1792. V. 42

A Defence of Dr. Price and the Reformers of England. York: 1792. V. 39

A State of the Representation of the People of England, on the Principles of Mr. Pitt in 1785. York: 1794. V. 39; 42

X

XANTUS, JANOS

Levelei Ejszakemirikabol . . . Budapest: 1858. V. 40

XARAMILLO, A.

Memorial al Rey Nuestro Senor, por la Provincia de la Compania de Jesus de la Islas Filipinas, en Satisfacion de Varios Escritos y Violentos Hechos . . . Madrid: 1689. V. 39

XAVIER, HIERONYMUS

Historia Christi Persice . . . Reddita & Amimadversionibus Notata a Ludovico de Dieu. Leiden: 1639. V. 40

XAVIER, JEROME

Historia S. Petri Persice Conscripta . . . Leiden: 1639. V. 37

XENEPHON c. 430 - 352 BC

The Ephesian Story. London: 1957. V. 37

Xenephon's History of the Affairs of Greece. London: 1760. V. 43

XENOPHON c. 430 -352 BC

Cyrupaedia. (The Institution and Life of Cyrus). 1936. V. 42

Cyrpuaedia. Newtown: 1936. V. 37; 38; 40; 46

The Ephesian Story. London: 1957. V. 40; 41; 43

(Greek title) Xenophontis De Cyri Institutione Libri Octo. Etonae: 1613. V. 43

Xenophon's History of the Affairs of Greece. London: 1685. V. 40

The History of the Affairs of Greece. London: 1770. V. 39

In Hoc Volvmine Continentvr Praedia Cyri Persarum Regis. De Venatione. De re Publica & de Legibus Lacedaemonioru. Lyon: 1511. V. 39

The Institution and the Life of Cyrus . . . London: 1936. V. 39; 41

Cyrupaedia. The Institution and Life of Cyrus. Newtown: 1936. V. 40; 42

Xenophon's Memoirs of Socrates. Bath: 1762. V. 38

Xenophon's Memoirs of Socrates. London: 1767. V. 38

Memorabilia. Glasgow: 1761. V. 39; 40

Oeuvres . . . Paris: 1795. V. 40

Omnia Quae Extant Opera. Geneva: 1561. V. 45

Opera, Graece & latine . . . Edinburgh: 1811. V. 45

L'Opere Morali . . . Venice: 1547. V. 40

Xenephon's History of the Affairs of Greece. London: 1760. V. 46

Xenophon's Ephesian History. London: 1727. V. 40

Xenophon's History of the Affairs of Greece. London: 1770. V. 46

Xenophon's Memoirs of Socrates. Bath: 1762. V. 40; 41; 46

Xenophontos' Apomnemoneymaton Proton. colophon: 1551. V. 45

XENOS, STEFANOS

Depredations; or, Overend, Gurney & Co. and the Greek & Oriental Steam Navigation Company. London: 1869. V. 39

East and West, a Diplomatic History of the Annexation of the Ionian Islands to the Kingdom of Greece. London: 1865. V. 39

XERES, FRANCISCO DE

Libro Primo de la Conquista del Peru & Provincia del Cuzco de le Indie Occidentali. Venice: 1535. V. 37

XIMENES, ANDRES

Descripcion del Real Monasterio de San Lorenzo del Escorial . . . Madrid: 1764. V. 40

XIMENES, LEONARDO 1716-1786

Piano di Operazioni Idrauliche per Ottenere la Massima Depressione del Lago di Sesto o sia di Bientina. Lucca: 1782. V. 39

XIMENEX DE VRREA, G.

Dialogo del Vero Honore Militar . . . Venetia: 1569. V. 42

THE XV Comforts of Rash and Inconsiderate Marriage; or Select Animadversions Upon the Miscarriage of a Wedded State. London: 1682. V. 44

Y

Y., M. U.

A History of the United Kingdom of Great Britain and Ireland, from the Earliest Ages to the treaty of Amiens in 1802. Cork: 1815. V. 37

Y-WORTH, WILLIAM

The Britannian Magazine . . . London: 1700? V. 43

Chymicus Rationalis; or, the Fundamental Grounds of the Chymical Art Rationally Stated and Demonstrated . . . London: 1692. V. 46

YAARI, A.

Bibliography of the Passover Haggadah from the Earliest Printed Edition to 1960. Jerusalem: 1960. V. 39

YABLON, G. ANTHONY

A Bronte Bibliography. London: 1978. V. 41; 42

YADIN, YIGAEL

The Art of Warfare in Biblical Lands in the Light of Archaeological Discovery. London: 1963. V. 40; 42; 44

The Art of Warfare in Biblical Lands in the Light of Archaeological Study. New York: 1963. V. 40; 42

The Art of Warfare in Biblical Lands in the light of archaeological study. New York: (1963). V. 37

The Finds from the Bar Kokhba Period in the Cave of Letters. Jerusalem: 1963. V. 37; 40; 42; 44

Hazor I. Jerusalem: 1958. V. 40

Hazor I-IV. Jerusalem: 1958-1961. V. 37; 40; 42; 44

YAHUDA, A. S.

The Language of the Pentateuch in Its Relation to Egyptian. London: 1933. V. 40; 42; 44

YAIR, JAMES

The Staple Contract Betwixt the Royal Burrows of Scotland and the City of Campvere in Zealand. Edinburgh: 1749. V. 46

YAKOV BEN ASHER

Tur Even Ha'Ezer. Venice: 1565. V. 45

YALDEN, JOHN

Compendium Politicum, or, the Distempers of Government. London: 1680. V. 38

YALE COLLEGE

The Laws of Yale College, in New Haven, in Connecticut, Enacted . . . the Sixth Day of October A.D. 1795. New Haven: 1795. V. 37

YALE UNIVERSITY

Papers in Anthropology. 1936-1954. V. 39

YALE UNIVERSITY. LIBRARY

Alchemy and the Occult. A Catalogue of Books and Manuscripts from the Collection of Paul and Mary Mellon, Given to Yale University Library. New Haven: 1968-77. V. 41; 42

YALE Verse: 1898-1908. New Haven;: 1909. V. 41; 42

THE YALLER Gal that Winked at Me! San Francisco: 1860. V. 45

YAMAAKI, AKIRA

Nippon Hand Weaves in 'Kusakizome' Dyes. 1960. V. 46

YAMADA, K.

Sense of Cooking. San Francisco: 1920s? V. 39

YAMATA, KIKOU

Les Huit Renommees. Paris: 1927. V. 40

YAMAZAKI, AKIRA

Nippon Hand Weaves in 'Kusakizome' Dyes. Kanagawa: 1959. V. 44

Nippon Hand Weaves in 'Kusakizome' Dyes. 1960. V. 40

YAMAZAKKI, AKIRA

Monograph of Plant-Dyeing Peculiar to Japan. Kanagawa: 1961. V. 40

THE YANKEE and Boston Literary Gazette. 1829. V. 37

THE YANKEE in London; or, A Short Trip to America. Philadelphia: 1826. V. 41

THE YANKEE Slave Dealer; or, an Abolitionist Down South. Nashville: 1860. V. 42; 43

A YANKEE Tale. Salt Lake City: 1857. V. 40

THE YANKEE Traveller; or, the Adventures of Hector Wigler. Concord: 1817. V. 43

YAPP, G. W.

Art Industy Metal-Work Illustrating the Chief Process of Art-Work Applied by the Goldsmith, Silversmith, Jeweller, Brass, Copper, Iron and Steel Worker, Bronzist, etc. London: 1890. V. 37

YARDLEY, EDWARD

The Supernatural in Romantic Fiction. London: 1880. V. 37

YARDLEY, HERBERT O.

The Education of a Poker Player. London: 1959. V. 38

YARMOLINSKI, AVRAHM

Picturesque United States of America. New York: 1930. V. 39

YARRANTON, ANDREW

England's Improvement by Sea and Land. London: 1677. V. 39; 42

YARRELL, WILLIAM

The Brotherton Library. A Catalogue of Ancient Manuscripts and Early Printed Books. Leeds: 1931. V. 46

A History of British Fishes. London: 1836-59. V. 46

A History of British Fishes. London: 1841, 1839. V. 39; 40

A History of British Birds. London: 1843. V. 37; 38; 39; 40; 45

A History of British Birds. London: 1843-45. V. 46

A History of British Birds. London: 1845. V. 38; 40

A History of British Birds. London: 1859. V. 43

A History of British Birds. London: 1843-56. V. 39

A History of British Birds. London: 1871-1885. V. 38; 39; 42; 44

A History of British Birds. London: 1871-75. V. 37

A History of British Birds. London: 1936-60. V. 42

A History of British Fishes. London: 1836. V. 42; 45

A History of British Fishes. Lodnon: 1836-39. V. 37; 39

A History of British Fishes. London: 1841. V. 39; 40

A History of British Fishes. London: 1859. V. 39; 42

On the Growth of the Salmon in Fresh Water. London: 1839. V. 39

YARROW, WILLIAM

Robert Henri, His Life and Works. New York: 1921. V. 46

YARSH, YOUSUF

Portraits of Greatness. London, Edinburgh & New York: 1959. V. 37

YASHIRO, YUKIO

Art Treasures of Japan. Tokyo: 1960. V. 41

Sandro Botticelli and the Florentine Renaissance. London: 1929. V. 44

2000 Years of Japanese Art. New York: 1958. V. 38; 39; 41

YATES, BARTHOLOMEW C.

The Detective Detected; or Detective Frauds Exposed. Chicago: 1883. V. 41

YATES, EDMUND

Edmund Yates: His Recollections and Experiences. London: 1884. V. 38

Land at Last. London: 1866. V. 38; 41

Our Miscellany. London: 1856. V. 38

YATES, EMMA WILLARD

Atlas to Accompany a System of Universal History. New York: 1839. V. 41

YATES, FREDERICK HENRY

Yates' Reminiscences; or, Etchings of Life and Character . . . London: 1827. V. 42

YATES, G.

The Ball; or, a Glance at Almack's in 1829. London: 1829. V. 39

YATES, J. MICHAEL

Contemporary Poets of British Columbia: Volume One. Vancouver: 1970. V. 37; 41

YATES, JAMES

An Account of the Art of Weaving Among the Ancients. London: 1843. V. 44; 46

YATES, LORENZO

Channel Islands: Stray Notes on the Geology . . . Mollusca . . . Insular Floras. (San Francisco: ca. 1890). V. 37

THE YELLOW Book. London: 1894-97, 1950. V. 37
THE YELLOW Book. London: 1894 - April 97. V. 40

THE YELLOWSTONE National Park. Chicago: 1883. V. 38

YELLOWSTONE National Park in Photogravure. Chicago: 1891. V. 41

YELVERTON, MARIA THERESA
Martyrs to Circumstance. London: 1861. V. 44

YELVERTON, MARIA THERESA LONGWORTH
Teresina Peregrina or, Fifty Thousand Miles of Travel Round the World. London: 1874. V. 38

YELVERTON, THERESE
Zanita. A Tale of the Yo-semite. New York: 1872. V. 37

YEO, JAMES
Omar and Zemira; an Eastern Tale. London: 1782. V. 38; 40

THE YEOMANRY Cavalry of Worcestershire. 1914-1922. Stourbridge: 1926. V. 46

YERBURY, F. R.
Georgian Details of Domestic Architecture. London: 1926. V. 42

YERKES, C. T.
Catalogue of Paintings and Sculpture in the Collection of . . . . New York: 1904. V. 45

YERKES, ROBERT
Psychological Examining in the United States Army. Washington: 1921. V. 42

YERUSHALMI, YOSEF
Haggadah and History. A Panorama in Facsimile of Five Centuries of the Printed Haggadah. Philadelphia: 1975. V. 41

YETKIN, SERARE
Early Caucasian Carpets in Turkey. London: 1978. V. 40

YETTS, W. PERCEVAL
The George Eumorfopoulos Collection. London: 1929. V. 40

YEVTUSHENKO, YEVGENY
The Poetry of . . . 1953 to 1965. New York: 1965. V. 45

YMITH, MICHAEL
A Geographical View of the British Possessions in North America . . . Baltimore: 1814. V. 44

Y MORNAY DE, SEIGNEUR DU PLESSIS-MARLY, CALLED DU PLESSIS-MORNA
Memoires. Le Forest-sur Sevre,: 1624-25. V. 37

YOAKUM, HENDERSON
History of Texas from Its First Settlement in 1685 to Its Annexation to the United States in 1846. New York: 1856. V. 38; 39; 41; 42
History of Texas from Its First Settlement in 1685 to Its Annexation to the United States in 1846. Austin: 1935. V. 44
History of Texas from its First Settlement in 1685 to its Annexation to the United States in 1846. New York: 1846. V. 37

YOLEN, JANE
The Lady and the Merman. Easthampton: 1977. V. 37

YONGE, CHARLOTTE MARY 1823-1901
The Armourer's Prentices. London: 1884. V. 41; 43
The Chaplet of Pearls. London: 1868. V. 37; 41; 42; 44
Heartsease; or The Brother's Wife. New York: 1871. V. 37; 39; 41; 43
The Heir of Redclyffe . . . Leipzig: 1855. V. 42
History of Christian Names. London: 1878. V. 41; 44
Life of John Coleridge Patterson. London: 1874. V. 41
Love and Life. London: 1880. V. 41
Magnum Bonum or Mother Carey's Brood. London: 1879. V. 37; 42; 46
A Parallel History of France and England. London: 1871. V. 39
The Pillars of the House; or, Under Wode, Under Rode. London: 1873. V. 46
The Three Brides. London: 1876. V. 41
The Two Sides of the Shield. London: 1885. V. 41; 44
Two Penniless Princesses. London: 1891. V. 41; 46

YONGE, JAMES
Wounds of the Brain Proved Curable, Not Only by the Opinion and Experience of Many . . . London: 1682. V. 38; 39

YONGE, WILLIAM
Sedition and Defamation Display'd: in a Letter to the Author of the Craftsman . . . London: 1731. V. 45

YORDAN, PHILIP
Anna Lucasta. New York: 1945. V. 45

YORK, DUKE OF
Speech of His Royal Highness the Duke of York for the House of Lords, April 25, 1825. London: 1825. V. 40

YORK, EDWARD, 2ND DUKE OF
The Master of Game. London: 1904. V. 45

YORK FIRE CLUB, BOSTON.
Rules and Orders to Be Observed by the York Fire-Club, Instituted at Boston the First Day of May, A.D. 1760. N.P.: 1760. V. 46

YORK, J. S.
Early Days in Texas. Corsicana: 1917. V. 38; 41; 42

YORK, JAMES, DUKE OF
Memoirs of the English Affairs, Chiefly Naval from the Year 1660 to 1673. London: 1729. V. 46

YORKE, CHARLES
Some Considerations on the Law of Forfeiture for High Treason. London: 1748. V. 37

YORKE, F. R. S.
The Modern Flat. London: 1937. V. 41

YORKE, HENRY REDHEAD
The Trial of Henry Yorke, for a Conspiracy, etc. Before the Hon. Mr. Justice Rooke, at the Assizes, Held for the County of York, on Sat. July 10, 1795. York: 1795. V. 42

YORKE, JAMES
The Union of Honour. London: 1640. V. 37; 40

YORKE, MALCOLM
Eric Gill: Man of Flesh and Spirit. London: 1981. V. 40

YORKSHIRE Castles. Helmsley, Scarborough, Skipton, Knaresborough, Ripley, Conisborough. Leeds. V. 45

YORKSHIRE PARISH REGISTER SOCIETY
Publications. Cambridge: 1899-1933. V. 44

YORKSHIRE RAMBLER'S CLUB
The Yorkshire Rambler's Club Journal. Leeds: 1902-13. V. 44

YORKSHIRE Ramblers' Club Journal. London: 1899-1949. V. 40

YORSKHIRE GEOLOGICAL SOCIETY
Proceedings of the Geological and Polytechnic Society of the West Riding of Yorkshire. Leeds: 1869. V. 45

YOSEMITE Illustrated in Colors. San Francisco: 1890. V. 38

YOSHINOBU, TOKUGAWA
The Tokugawa Collection: No Robes and Masks. New York: 1977. V. 41

YOSHIWARA: The Nightless City. Tokyo: 1907. V. 39

YOST, KARL
Bibliography of the Published Works of Charles M. Russell. Lincoln: 1971. V. 38
A Bibliography of the Works of Edna St. Vincent Millay. New York: 1937. V. 40
A Bibliography of the Published Works of Charles M. Russell by Karl Yost and Frederic Renner. 1971. V. 37

YOSY, A.
Switzerland, as Now Divided Into Nineteen Cantons . . . London: 1815. V. 44

YOUATT, WILLIAM
Cattle: Their Breed, Management and Diseases. London: 1843. V. 38; 40
Cattle: their Breeds, Management and Diseases. London: 1867. V. 45
The Dog. Philadelphia: 1852. V. 38; 39; 40
The Horse. Together with a General History of the Horse. Philadelphia: 1843. V. 43

YOUGHAL, IRELAND. CORPORATION
The Council Book of the Corporation of Youghal (Co. Cork) from 1610 to 1659, from 1666 to 1687 and from 1690 to 1800. Guildford,: 1878. V. 45
The Council Book of the Corporation of Youghal from 1610-1659, from 1666-1687 and from 1690-1800. Surrey: 1878. V. 39

YOULE, HENRY HIND

Narrative of the Canadian River Exploring Expedition of 1857 and of the Assinniboine and Saskatchewan Exploring Expedition of 1858. London: 1860. V. 39

YOUMANS, EDWARD L.

Chemical Atlas, or the Chemistry of Familiar Objects Exhibiting the General Principles of Science in a Series of Beautifully Colored Diagrams. New York: 1855. V. 40

Chemical Atlas; or, the Chemistry of Familiar Objects. New York: 1856. V. 41

Chemical Atlas, or the Chemistry of Familiar Objects Exhibiting the General Principles of Science in a Series of Beautifully Colored Diagrams. New York: 1855. V. 38

YOUMANS, JULIAN R.

Neurological Surgery: A Comprehensive Reference Guide to the Diagnosis and management of Neurosurgical Problems. Philadelphia: 1982. V. 42

YOUNCE, WILLIAM H.

The Adventures of Conscript. Cincinnati: 1901. V. 44

THE YOUNG Woman's Companion & Insturctor, in Grammar, Writing, Arithmetic, Geography, Drawing, Book-Keeping, Chronology, History, Letter-Writing, Cooking, Carving, Pickling, Preserving, Brewing, Wine Making &c . . . Manchester: 1806. V. 38

YOUNG, A.

The Paintings of James McNeill Whistler. New Haven & London: 1980. V. 39

YOUNG, A. W.

Introduction to the Science of Government, and Compend of Consitutional and Statutory Law. Warsaw: 1835. V. 45

YOUNG, AL

The Song Turning Back Into Itself. New York: 1971. V. 46

YOUNG, ALLEN

Cruise of the Pandora. London: 1876. V. 40

YOUNG, ANDREW

The Example of France a Warning to Britain. London: 1793. V. 42

Quiet as Moss - Thirty Six Poems. London: 1959. V. 41

Winter Harvest. London: 1933. V. 44

YOUNG, ANDREW JOHN 1885-1971

The Adversary. London: 1923. V. 38

The Bird-Cage. London: 1926. V. 38

Boaz and Ruth and Other Poems. London: 1920. V. 38

Collected Poems. London: 1936. V. 38

Collected Poems. London: 1950. V. 38; 40; 42

Collected Poems. London: 1960. V. 38; 40; 41; 44

The Cuckoo Clock. London: 1928. V. 38

The Death of Eli and Other Poems. London: 1921. V. 38

The New Shepherd. London: 1931. V. 38

Nicodemus - a Mystery. London: 1937. V. 38

Songs of Night. London: 1910. V. 38; 45; 46

Speak to the Earth. London: 1939. V. 38

Thirty-One Poems. London: 1922. V. 38

The White Blackbird. London: 1935. V. 38

Winter Harvest. London: 1933. V. 38

YOUNG, ANDREW W.

First Lessons in Civil Government, Including a Comprehensive View of the Government of the State of Ohio. Cleveland: 1846. V. 37

History of Wayne County, Indiana, From Its First Settlement to the Present Time . . . Cincinnati: 1872. V. 46

YOUNG, ANN ELIZA

Wife No. 19, or The Story of a Life in Bondage . . . Hartford: 1875. V. 45

YOUNG, ARTHUR

Annals of Agriculture and Other Useful Arts. Bury St. Edmunds: 1790-99. V. 39

A Course of Experimental Agriculture. London: 1770. V. 40; 43

An Enquiry Into the State of the Public Mind Amongst the Lower Clases . . . London: 1798. V. 39; 42; 45

The Example of France. Bury St. Edmund's: 1793. V. 37; 40; 45; 46

The Example of France a Warning to Britain. London: 1793. V. 39; 44

The Example of France, a warning to Britain. Dublin: 1793. V. 37

The Expediency of a Free Exportation of Corn at this Time; with Some Observtions on the Bounty and Its Effects. London: 1770. V. 38

The Farmer's Kalendar . . . London: 1771. V. 45

The Farmer's Kalendar; or, a Monthly directory for all sorts of country business: containing, plain instructions for perfoming the work of various kinds of farms . . . Dublin: 1772. V. 37

The Farmer's Calendar. London: 1804. V. 41

The Farmer's Calendar, Describing the Business Necessary to be Performed on VArious Kinds of Farms During Every Month in the Year . . . London: 1867. V. 44

The Farmer's Guide in Hring and Stocking Farms. London: 1770. V. 40; 42; 46

The Farmer's Letters to the People of England. London: 1767. V. 38; 46

The Farmer's Letters to the People of England. London: 1768. V. 39; 40; 42; 44

The Farmer's Tour through the East of England. London: 1771. V. 37; 39; 41; 42

General View of the Agriculture of the County of Sussex, with Observations on the Means of Its Improvement. London: 1793. V. 41; 43; 45

General View of the Agriculture of the County of Suffolk. London: 1794. V. 41

General View of the Agriculture of the County of Lincoln . . . London: 1799. V. 39; 40

General View of the Agriculture of Hertfordshire. London: 1804. V. 40

General View of the Agriculture of the County of Essex. London: 1807. V. 39; 41

General View of the Agriculture of Oxfordshire. London: 1813. V. 38

Political Arithmetic. London: 1774. V. 38

Rural Oeconomy. London: 1770. V. 42

A Six Months Tour Through the North of England. Containing an Account of the present state of Agriculture, Manufactories and Population, in Several Counties of this Kingdom . . . London: 1770. V. 37

A Six Months Tour through the North of England Containing an Account of the Present Stte of Agriculture, Manufactures and Population . . . London: 1771. V. 38; 40

A Six Weeks Tour, through the Southern Counties of England and Wales. London: 1768. V. 40; 44; 45

A Six Weeks Tour through the Southern Counties of England and Wales . . . Dublin: 1771. V. 41

A Tour in Ireland. Dublin: 1780. V. 38

A Tour in Ireland; with General Observations on the Present State of that Kingdom . . . London: 1780. V. 40; 41; 42; 44

A Tour in Ireland. London: 1892. V. 38; 43

Travels During the Years 1787, 1788 and 1789. Bury St. Edmund's: 1792. V. 37; 39; 40; 43

Travels During the Years 1787, 1788 and 1789 . . . Dublin: 1793. V. 43; 44; 46

Travels During the Years 1787, 1788 & 1789 . . . London: 1794. V. 37; 38; 39; 40; 42; 43

Travels During the Years 1787, 1788 and 1789, Undertaken More Particularly with a View to Ascertaining the Cultivation, Wealth, Resources and National Prosperity. London & Bury St. Edmunds,: 1794. V. 39; 43

The Works. London: 1792. V. 46

THE YOUNG Artist's Complete Magazine. London: 1780. V. 46

YOUNG, BENJAMIN SETH

Transcations of the Ohio Mob Called in the Public Papers 'An Expedition Against the Shakers.' Albany: 1810. V. 39

YOUNG, BENNETT H.

The Battle of the Thames in Which Kentuckians Defeated the British, French and Indians, October 5, 1813. Louisville: 1903. V. 37; 42

The Battle of the Thames, with a List of the Officers and Privates Who Won the Victory. Louisville: 1903. V. 46

The Prehistoric Men of Kentucky . . . Louisville: 1910. V. 42; 45

YOUNG Black Hawk. This Beautiful Young Horse, Will Stand the Present Season, to Improve the Breed of Horses, at J. S. Bowker's, in Gardner, Mass. Fitchburg: 1851. V. 44

THE YOUNG Brewer's Monitor, Comprising a Luminous and Scientific Summary of that Very Ancient and Important Art. London: 1824. V. 37

YOUNG, BRIGHAM

Proclamation by the Governor. Citizens of Utah - We Are Invaded by a Hostile Force. Salt Lake City: 1857. V. 40

YOUNG, CHARLES

Dangers of the Trail in 1865 - a Narrative of Actual Events. New York: 1912. V. 39

YOUNG, CHARLES E.

Dangers of the Trail in 1865. Geneva: 1912. V. 38; 41; 45

YOUNG, CHARLES FREDERIC T.

The Economy of Steam Power on Common Roads. London: 1861. V. 37; 40; 45

Fires, Fire Engines, and Fire Brigades. London: 1866. V. 38

THE YOUNG Chavalier, or, a Genuine Narrative of all that Befell that Unfortunate Adventurer. London: 1747. V. 39; 42

THE YOUNG Chevalier; or, a Genuine Narrative of All that Befell That Unfortunate Adventurer, From His Fatal Defeat to His Final Escape . . . London: 1750. V. 41

THE YOUNG Child's A, B, C; or First Book. New York: 1820. V. 44

YOUNG, CHRISTIE T.

The Black Princess and Other Fairy Tales from Brazil. London: 1916. V. 45

THE YOUNG Clerk's Magazine, or English Law Repository . . . London: 1772. V. 38; 40

THE YOUNG Clerk's Vade Mecum; or, Compleat Law Tudor. New York: 1776. V. 40

YOUNG, DAL

Apologia pro Oscar Wilde. London: 1895. V. 38; 40

YOUNG, DANIEL

Young's Demonstrative Translation of Scientific Secrets; or a Collection of Above 500 Useful Receipts on a Variety of Subjects. Toronto: 1861. V. 45

YOUNG, DAVID

Lectures on the Science of Astronomy, Explanatory and Demonstrative, which were First Delivered, at various Places in New Jersey, in the Year 1820 . . . Morris Town: 1821. V. 37

National Improvements Upon Agriculture in Twenty Seven Essays. Edinburgh: 1785. V. 38; 42; 46

Observations Upon Fire, with a View to the Best and Most Expeditious Methods of Extinguishing It, Upon a New Plan . . . Edinburgh: 1784. V. 38

The Wonderful History of the Morristown Ghost . . . Newark: 1826. V. 37; 41; 46

YOUNG, E. D.

Nyassa: a Journal of Adventures Whilst Exploring Lake Nyassa, Central Africa, and Establishing the Settlement of 'Livingstonia.' London: 1877. V. 39

The Search for Livingstone. London: 1868. V. 39

YOUNG, EDWARD

The Centaur Not Fabulous, in Six Letters to a Friend on the Life in Vogue. Dublin: 1755. V. 38; 43

The Complaint; or Night-Thoughts on Life, Death and Immortality. London: 1742-43. V. 41

The Complaint; or Night Thoughts on Life, Death and Immortality. London: 1742-44. V. 45

The Complaint . . . London: 1743. V. 45

The Complaint; or, Night Thoughts on Life, Death and Immorality. London: 1743-42-45. V. 42; 45

The Complaint; or, Night Thoughts on Life, Death and Immortality. London: 1743-45. V. 37; 46

The Complaint; or, Night Thoughts on Life, Death and Immortality. Dublin: 1747. V. 41

The Complaint; or, Night Thoughts on Life, Death and Immortality. Edinburgh: 1761. V. 45

The Complaint; or, Night-Thoughts . . . Dublin: 1766. V. 42

The Complaint; or, Night Thoughts. London: 1768. V. 46

The Complaint, and the Consolation; or, Night Thoughts . . . London: 1797. V. 45

The Complaint; or Night Thoughts on Life. London: 1822. V. 40

The Complaint, or Night Thoughts. London: 1817. V. 37; 39

Conjectures on Original Composition. London: 1759. V. 39

The Force of Religion; or, Vanquish'd Love. London: 1714. V. 38

Klagen, oder Nachtgedanken Uber Leben, Tod und Unsterblichkeit. Braunschweig: 69-74-69-71. V. 41

Labour in Europe and America; A Special Report on the Rates of Wages, the Cost of Subsistence, and the Condition of the Working Classes, in Great Britain, France, Belgium, Germany and other Countries in Europe, also in the United States . . . Philadelphia: 1875. V. 37

Love of Fame, the Universal Passion. London: 1728. V. 37; 39; 42; 43

Love of Fame, the Universal Passion. London: 1730. V. 38

Delle Notti di Young. Siena: 1775. V. 42

Night Thoughts on Life, Death & Immortality . . . London: 1793. V. 46

Night Thoughts. London: 1798. V. 37; 38; 40; 42

Night Thoughts on Life, Death and Immortality . . . London: 1862. V. 42

Ocean. London: 1728. V. 45

A Poem on the Last Day; with the Force of Religion, or Vanquished Love. (with) The Love of Fame, the Universal Passion. London: 1778. V. 41

A Poem on the Last Day. Oxford: 1713. V. 37

The Poetical Works. London: 1741. V. 37; 41; 42; 43; 46

Pre-Raffaelitism. London: 1857. V. 38

Resignation. London: 1762. V. 45

Two Epistles to Mr. Pope, Concerning the Authors of the Age. London: 1730. V. 46

The Universal Passion. London: 1725-28. V. 38; 45

The Universal Passion. Satire V. London: 1727. V. 45

The Works of the Author of Night Thoughts. London: 1767. V. 42

The Works of the Reverend Dr. Edward Young. Edinburgh: 1774. V. 41

Dr. Eduard Youngs Samtliche Werke. Mannheim: 1780. V. 41

The Works of the Author of Night Thoughts. London: 1792. V. 41; 46

The Works of Edward Young, D.D. London: 1813. V. 43

YOUNG, EDWARD, of Neath

The Ferns of Wales. Neath: 1856. V. 37; 39; 42; 44

YOUNG, ELLA

Celtic Wonder-Tales. London: 1910. V. 41

The Rose of Heaven. Dublin: 1920. V. 38

YOUNG, ERNEST A.

Harry Pinkurten, the King of Detectives. New York: 1884. V. 43

Wall Wheeler, the Scout Detective. New York: 1884. V. 44

YOUNG, FILSON

Venus and Cupid. An Impression in Prose After Velazquez in Colour. London: 1906. V. 38

YOUNG, FRANCIS

Every Man His Own Mechanic. London: 1893. V. 40

YOUNG, FRANCIS BRETT

The Cage Bird and Other Stories. Hamburg, Paris, Bologna: 1934. V. 38

My Brother Jonathan. London: 1928. V. 43

Portrait of Clare. London: 1927. V. 43

Portrait of a Village. London: 1937. V. 40

White Ladies. London: 1935. V. 41

YOUNG, FRANK C.

Across the Plains in '65. Denver: 1905. V. 37; 38; 40; 42

Echoes from Arcadia. Denver: 1903. V. 37; 42

YOUNG, FREDERICK

A Winter Tour in South Africa. London: 1890. V. 39; 40; 42

YOUNG, G. F.

The Medici. New York: 1926. V. 43

YOUNG, G. M.

Victorian England, 1830-1865. 1934. V. 46

YOUNG, GARY

A Single Day. Snata Cruz: 1991. V. 45

THE YOUNG Gentleman and Lady's Instructor, Being a Choice Collection of Pieces in Poetry and Prose . . . Lewes: 1808. V. 37; 44

YOUNG, GEOFFREY WINTHROP

Mountain Craft. London: 1920. V. 39; 44

On High Hills. Memories of the Alps. London: 1927. V. 39

YOUNG, GEORGE

A Geological Survey of the Yorkshire Coast. Whitby: 1822. V. 44

A Geological Survey of the Yorkshire Coast . . . Whitby: 1828. V. 37; 41; 45

A Treatise on Opium, Founded Upon Practical Observations. London: 1753. V. 37; 42; 46

YOUNG, H.

The Bentley Bedside Book. London: 1961. V. 38

YOUNG, H. H.

Saint Paul, the Commercial Emporium of the Northwest. St.Paul: 1886. V. 37

YOUNG, HARRY SAM

Hard Knocks, a Life Story of the Vanishing West. Portland: 1915. V. 37; 39

YOUNG, HUGH HAMPTON 1870-1945

Young's Practice of Urology. Based on a Study of 12,500 Cases. Philadelphia: 1926. V. 39; 42

YOUNG, HUGH HAMTPON 1870-1945

Genital Abnormalities, Hermaphroditism & related Adrenal Diseases. Baltimore: 1937. V. 44

YOUNG, J

A Catalogue of the Manuscripts in the Library of the Hunterian Museum in the University of Glasgow. Glasgow: 1908. V. 44

Instructions in the Syllabic Characters for the Use of the Cree Indians in the Diocese of Athabasca, 1896. Cheyenne: 1870. V. 46

YOUNG, J. H.

Caesarean Section: The History and Development of the Operation from Earliest Times. London: 1944. V. 45

YOUNG, J. P.

The Seventh Tennessee Cavalry. Nashville: 1890. V. 38

YOUNG, JAMES

A Manual and Atlas of Orthopedic Surgery Including the History, Etiology, Pathology, Diagnosis . . . Philadelphia: 1906. V. 42

A Practical Treatise on Orthopedic Surgery. Philadelphia: 1894. V. 42

YOUNG, JAMES FOSTER

Five Weeks in Greece. London: 1876. V. 39

YOUNG, JAMES WEBB

The Compleat Angler, or How to be an Advertising Man and Catch the Poor Fish. Coapa. V. 39

THE YOUNG Jewess: a Narrative Illustrative of the Polish and English Jews of the Present Century. Boston: 1827. V. 43

YOUNG, JOHN

A Catalogue of the Pictures at Gosvenor House . . . With Etchings from the Whole Collection . . . & Historical Notices of the Principal Works . . . London: 1820. V. 44

A Catalogue of the Pictures at Leigh Court; Near Bristol; the Seat of Philip John Miles, Esq. M.P. London: 1822. V. 38; 40; 44; 46

A Catalogue of the Collection of Pictures, of the Most Noble the Marquess of Stafford, at Cleveland House. London: 1825. V. 42

A Catalogue of Pictures by British Artists, in the Possession of Sir John Fleming Leicester, Bart. London: 1821. V. 40; 46

A Criticism on the Elegy Written in a Country Church-Yard. Edinburgh: 1810. V. 40; 41; 42; 46

A Criticism of the Elegy Written in a Country Churchyard. Being a continuation of Dr. Johnson's criticism of the poems of Gray. Edinburgh/London: 1810. V. 37

Essays on the Following Interesting Subjects. Glasgow: 1796. V. 41

Letters of Agricola on the Principles of Vegetation and Tillage, Written for Nova Scotia, and Published First in the Acadian Recorder. Halifax: 1822. V. 42; 46

The Province of Reason: a Criticism of the Bampton Lecture on 'The Limits of Religious Thought.' London: 1860. V. 41; 42

A Series of Portraits of the Emperors of Turkey . . . London: 1815. V. 39

A Series of Designs for Shop Fronts, Porticoes and Entrances to Buildings, Public and Private. London: 1835. V. 38

YOUNG, JOHN N.

San Diego 'Our Italy.' San Diego: 1895. V. 39

YOUNG, JOHN PHILIP

San Francisco, A History of the Pacific Coast Metropolis. San Francisco/Chicago: (1912). V. 37

YOUNG, JOHN R.

Memoirs of John R. Young Utah Pioneer 1847. Salt Lake City: 1920. V. 40; 42; 43

YOUNG, JOHN RADFORD 1799-1885

Modern Scepticism, Viewed in Relation to Modern Science. London: 1865. V. 40; 42; 43; 46

Modern Scepticism, Viewed in Relation to Modern Science . . . London: 1865. V. 42

YOUNG, JOHN RUSSELL

Around the World with General Grant . . . New York: 1979. V. 44; 46

YOUNG, JOSEPH

History of the Organization of the Seventies. Salt Lake City;: 1878. V. 41; 42; 44

A New Physical System of Astronomy; or, an Attempt to Explain the Operations of the Powers Which Impel the Planets and Comets to Perform Elliptical Revolutions Round the Sun, and Revolve on Their Own Axis . . . New York: 1800. V. 45

A New Physical System of Astronomy . . . New York: 1800. V. 42; 44

YOUNG Juba; or, The History of the Young Chevalier, From His Birth to His Escape From Scotland, After the Battle of Culloden. London: 1748. V. 40

YOUNG Ladies' Drawing Book, or Complete Instructor in Drawing and Colouring Flowers, Fruit and Shells . . . London: 1832. V. 42

THE YOUNG Lady's Book. N.P.: 1835. V. 42

THE YOUNG Lady's Book. A Manual of Elegant Recreations. London: 1844. V. 43

THE YOUNG Lady's Book: A Manual of Elegant Recreations, Exercise and Pursuits. London: 1829. V. 42; 44

THE YOUNG Lady's Companion in Cookery, and Pastry, Preserving, Pickling, Candying, &c. London: 1734. V. 38

YOUNG, LAFAYETTE

History of Cass County, Iowa, Together with Brief Mention of Old Settlers. Atlantic: 1877. V. 45

YOUNG, LUCIEN

The Boston at Hawaii or the Observations and Impressions of a Navl Officer Durin a Stay of Fourteen Months in Those Islands on a Man-Of-War. Washington: 1898. V. 38

YOUNG, LYMAN

Tim Tyler in the Jungle. The Illustrated Pop-Up Edition. Chicago: (c. 1935). V. 37

YOUNG, M.

The Complete Instructor in Boxing, Swimming, Gymnastics, Pedestrianisms, Horse Racing, Prize Fighting, Boat Racing and Other Sports . . . New York: 1881. V. 43

YOUNG, MARIANNE

The Moslem Noble: his land and people. With some notices of the Parsees, or ancient Persians. London: 1857. V. 37

YOUNG, MARTHA

Plantation Bird Legends. New York: 1902. V. 37

YOUNG, OTIS E.

The First Military Escort on the Santa Fe Trail, 1829 . . . Glendale: 1952. V. 40; 44

The West of Phillip St. George Cooke 1809-1895. Glendale: 1955. V. 44

YOUNG, PHILIP

The Hemingway Manuscripts. University Park: 1969. V. 45

San Francisco, a History of the Pacific Coast Metropolis. San Francisco & Chicago: 1912. V. 38

YOUNG, R. M.

Belfast and the Province of Ulster in the Twentieth Century, and Contemporary Biographies. Brighton Pike: 1909. V. 43

Historical Notices of Old Belfast and Its Vicinity. Belfast: 1896. V. 37; 38

The Town Book of the Corporation of Belfast, 1613-1816. Belfast: 1892. V. 37; 43

YOUNG, RICHARD M.

Argument of Richard M. Young as Attorney for the Occupants of Portage City, Against the State of Wisconsin. N.P.: 1857. V. 38

YOUNG, ROBERT

Timothy Hackworth and the Locomotive. London: 1923. V. 39; 46

YOUNG, ROLAND

Not for Children. Garden City: 1930. V. 37

YOUNG, S. GLENN, MRS.

Life and Exploits of S. Glenn Young. Herrin. V. 46

Life and Exploits of S. Glenn Young, World Famous Law Enforcement Officer. Herrin: 1924. V. 41

YOUNG, S. HALL

Alaska Days with John Muir. New York, etc: 1915. V. 40

YOUNG, SAMUEL

A Discourse Delivered at Schenectady . . . B(e)fore the New York Alpha of the Phia Beta Kappa. Ballston Spa: 1826. V. 45

THE YOUNG Shepherd; or, the Six Champions of the Castle Defeated; and the Triumph of Virtue and Sorcery and Oppression. London: 1810. V. 44

YOUNG, STANLEY

The Lace of a Thousand Trees. San Francisco: 1933. V. 39

Mr. Pickwick: a Comedy Freely Drawn from Charles Dickens' 'The Pickwick Papers'. New York: 1952. V. 44

YOUNG, STANLEY P.

The Wolves of North America. Washington, D.C.: 1944. V. 37

YOUNG, STARK

Addio. Madrette & Other Plays. Chicago: 1912. V. 39

The Blind Man at the Window and Other Poems. New York: 1906. V. 39

Guenevere: a Play in Five Acts. New York: 1906. V. 39

Immortal Shadows. New York: 1948. V. 46

YOUNG, T E.

On Centenrians & the Duration of the Human Race. London: 1899. V. 38

Z

Z., Y.

An Answer to the Author of Humble Thanks for His Majesties Gracious Declaration for Libery of Conscience. London: 1672. V. 41

ZABAGLIA, NICCOLA

Castelli, E Ponti (Latin title: Contignationes, Ac Pontes . . .) di Maestro Niccola Zabaglia con Alcune Ingegnose Pratiche, e con la Descrizione del Trasporto . . . Roma: 1743. V. 37; 41

ZABATA, CRISTOFORO

Diporto de Viandanti Nelquale si Legge Facetie, Motti & Burle. Trevico: 1599. V. 37

ZABRISKIE, F. N.

History of the Reformed P. D. Church of Claverack. A Centennial Address. Hudson: 1867. V. 39

ZABRISKIE, GEORGE A.

A Little About Washington Irving. Ormond Beach, Fl.: 1945. V. 37

ZACCARELLI, JOHN

Zaccarelli's Pictorial Souvenir Book of the Golden Northland. Dawson City: 1908. V. 42

ZACCHIA, PAOLO

Il Vitto Quaresimale . . . Ove Insegnasi, Come Senza Offender la Sanita si Possa Viver Nella Quaresima. Roma: 1637. V. 39

ZACH, FRANZ XAVER VON

Tabulae Motuum Solis Novae et Correctae ex Theoria Gravitatis et Observationibus Recentissimis Erutae. Gotha: 1792. V. 44

ZADKIEL, PSEUD.

The Horoscope. Liverpool: 1834. V. 45

ZAEHNSDORF, JOAEPH W.

A Short History of Bookbinding. 1895. V. 39

ZAEHNSDORF, JOSEPH W.

The Art of Bookbinding. London: 1880. V. 41; 42
The Art of Bookbinding. London: 1890. V. 40; 41

ZAHAV, ARI IBN

You, Jerusalem. Jerusalem: 1939. V. 41

ZAHN, JOHANN

Oculus Artificialis Teledioptricus sive Telescopium. Nuremberg: 1702. V. 45

ZAHN, O.

On Art Binding, a Monograph. Memphis: 1904. V. 41

ZAKANI, OBAID-E

The Pious Cat. London: 1986. V. 40

ZAMAGNA, BERNARD

Navis Aerea et Elegiarum Monobiblos. Rome: 1768. V. 45

THE ZAMORANO 80: a Selection of Distinguished California Books. Los Angeles: 1945. V. 37; 38; 39; 40; 41; 42; 44

THE ZAMORANO Club, 1929. Los Angeles?: 1929. V. 37

ZAMORANO CLUB, LOS ANGELES.

The Zamorano Club: The First Half Century. Los Angeles: 1978. V. 40; 46

ZAMPETTI, PIETRO

paintings from the Marches. Gentile to Raphael. London: 1971. V. 46

ZANETTI, ANTONIO MARIA

Delle Antiche Statue Greche e Romane, che Nell' Antisala Della Liberia di San Marco, e in Altri Luoghi Pubblici di Venezia si Trovano. Venice: 1740, 1743. V. 37

ZANGWILL, I.

The King of the Schnorrers. London: 1894. V. 40

ZANGWILL, ISRAEL

The Bachelor's Club. London: 1891. V. 37
Children of the Ghetto. Philadelphia: 1892. V. 37

The Complete Works. London: 1925. V. 37
Israel (a Poem). 1961. V. 46
Without Prejudice. London: 1896. V. 46
Works. V. 37

ZANONI, GIACOMO 1615-1682

Rariorum Stirpium Historia ex parte Olim Edita. Bologna: 1742. V. 38; 43

ZANOTTI, EUSTACIO 1709-1782

Ephemerides Motuum Coelestium ex Anno MDCCLI. In Annum MDCCLXII. Bologna: 1750. V. 38

ZANOTTI, GIAMPIETRO

Il Claustro di San Michele in Bosco di Bologna. Bologna: 1776. V. 44
Le Pitture di Pellegrino Tibaldi e di Niccolo Abbati, Eisetenti nell'Instituto di Bologna . . . Venice: 1756. V. 37; 40; 44

ZANOTTO, FRANCESCO

Il Palazzo Ducale di Venezia. Venice: 1842-61. V. 44

ZANZIBAR Blue Book. Further Correspondence Relating to Zanzibar. February, 1887. London: 1887. V. 41

ZANZIBAR Blue Book. Further Correspondence Relating to Zanzibar. March 1888. London: 1888. V. 41

ZANZOTTO, ANDREA

Circhi e Cene: Circuses and Suppers. 1979. V. 40
Circhi & Gene. Circuses and Suppers. Verona: 1979. V. 38; 45

ZAPATA, GIOVANNI BATTISTA

Maravigliosi Secreti di Medicina e Chirurgia . . . Nuovamente Ritrovati. Roma: 1586. V. 38

ZAPF, HERMAN 1918-

Manuale Typographicum. Frankfurt: 1954. V. 37

ZAPF, HERMANN 1918-

Das Blumen ABC. Frankfurt: 1962. V. 43
Feder un Stichel. Alphabete und Schriftblatter in Zeitgemasser Darstellung. Frankfurt am Main: 1949. V. 45
Hunt Roman: the Birth of a Type. Pittsburgh: 1965. V. 40
Manuale Typographicum. New York: 1954. V. 41
Manuale Typographicum. New York: 1968. V. 41; 42; 44
Orbis Typographicus. Kansas: 1980. V. 45
Orbis Typographicus. Prairie Villiage: 1980. V. 42
Pen and Graver. New York: 1952. V. 42; 45
Specimen Pages from the 'Manuale Typographicum'. Frankfurt: 1952. V. 45
Typographic Variations . . . New York: 1962. V. 45
Typographic Variations Designed by hermann Zapf on Themes in Contemporary Book Design and Typography in 78 Book and Title Pages. New York: 1964. V. 38; 39; 40; 44; 45; 46

ZARATE, DON AUGUSTIN DE

Histoire De la Decouverte et de La Conquete Du Perou. Paris: 1716. V. 38

ZATTA, A.

Basilica Di San Marco. New Jersey: 1964. V. 45

ZAVALA, LORENZO DE

Viage a Los Estados-Unidos Del Nortre De America. Paris: 1834. V. 45
Viaje a Los Estados-Unidos del Nortre de America . . . Merida: 1846. V. 39

ZAVALA Y AUNON, MIGUEL DE

Representacion al Rey N. Senor D. Phelipe V . . . . Dirigida al mas Seguro Aumento del Real Erario . . . N.P.: Madrid?: 1732. V. 41

ZAWAD, CHRISTINE

The Aging Ballerina. Maidson: 1977. V. 42

ZEGERS, T. N.

Scholion in Omnes Novi Testamenti Libros . . . Coloniae Agrippinae: 1553. V. 41

ZEIDLER, SEBASTIAN CHRISTIAN VON

Somatotomia Anthropologica, Seu, Corporus Humani Fabrica. Pragae: 1686. V. 37; 44

ZEIGLER, J. A.

The Last of the Bighams. Florence: 1925. V. 40

ZEIGLER, WILBUR G.

The Heart of the Alleghanies or Western North Carolina. Raleigh: 1883. V. 37

ZOCCHI, GIUSEPPE

Pitture del Salone Imperiale del Palazzo di Firenze. Florence: 1751. V. 37

Scelta di XXIV Vedute Delle Principali Contrade, Piazze, Chiese e Palazzi Della Citta di Firenze. Florence: 1754. V. 37

Vedute Delle Ville, e d'altri Luoghi Della Toscana. Florence: 1757. V. 37

ZOEGA, GIORGIO

De Origine et Usu Obeliscorum Rome. Lazzarini: 1797. V. 37

ZOGBAUM, RUFUS F.

Horse, Foot and Dragoons. Sketches of Army Life at Home and Abroad. New York: 188. V. 43

Horse, Foot and Dragoons. New York: 1888. V. 42; 43; 45

THE ZOHAR. London: 1931. V. 37

ZOHARY, M.

Flora Palaestina. Jerusalem: 1966-86. V. 37

Geobotanical Foundation of the Middle East. Stuttgart: 1973. V. 37

THE ZOIST: a Journal of a Cerebral Physiology and Mesmerism, and Their Applications to Human Welfare . . . London: 1844-56. V. 42; 46

ZOIST: a Journal of Cerebral Physiology and Mesmerism, and Their Applications to Human Welfare. London: 1843-56. V. 46

ZOLA, EMILE 1840-1902

Abbe Mouret's Transgression. London: 1886. V. 42

L'Affaire Dreyfus. Paris: 1901. V. 46

L'Assommoir. Paris: 1877. V. 46

The Assommoir. London: 1884. V. 42

L'Assommoir. London: 1928. V. 42

Etude GBiographique et Critique. Paris: 1867. V. 45

Fruitfulness. New York: 1900. V. 40

Germinal. London: 1885. V. 38

Germinal: a Realistic Novel. London: 1886. V. 42

The Ladies' Paradise. London: 1883. V. 41

Madeleine Ferat a Realistic Novel. London: 1888. V. 43

Nana. Paris: 1880. V. 37; 46

The Soil. London: 1888. V. 40

Stories from Emile Zola. Translated by Lafcadio Hearn. With a preface by Albert Modell. Tokyo: (1935). V. 37

Une Campagne 1880-1881. Paris: 1882. V. 46

L'Oeuvre. London: 1902. V. 39

Works. New York: 1924. V. 40

ZOLLERS, GEORGE D.

Thrilling Incidents on Sea and Land: the Prodigal's Return. Mount Morris: 1892. V. 41; 44

ZONARAS, JOHN

(Annales): Ioannis Zonarae Monachi, qui Olim Byzantii Magnus Drungarius Excubiaru seu Biglae . . . Basel: 1557. V. 39

ZONCA, VITTORIO

Nova Teatro di Machine (sic) et Edificii Per Varie et Sicure Operationi co'le Loro Figure Tagliate in Rame e la Dichiaratione e Dimostratione di Ciascuna. Padova: 1656. V. 39

Novo Teatro di Machine et Edificii per Varie et Sicure Operationi. Padua: 1607. V. 42; 44

Novo Teatro di Machine et Edificii per Uarie et Sicure Operationi. Padua: 1621. V. 38; 40

ZONGHI, AURELIO

Zonghi's Watermarks. Hilversum: 1953. V. 41

ZONGO-TEE-FOH-TCHI

Napoleon in the Other World. London: 1827. V. 39; 44

ZOOLOGICAL Record. London: 1864-1883. V. 37

ZOOLOGICAL SOCIETY

The Gardens and Menagerie of the Zoological Society Delineated. Chiswick: 1831. V. 44

ZOOLOGICAL SOCIETY OF LONDON

Transactions. Volume XXII: Zoological Results of the Cambridge Expedition to the Suez Canal, 1924. London: 1926-29. V. 40

ZORES, C. FERDINAND

Deuxieme Partie du Recueil. Paris: 1863. V. 44

Recueil de fers Speciaux des Experiences Faites sur Leur Resistance et de Leurs Diverses Applications dans les Constructions. Paris: 1853. V. 44

ZORN, BARTHOLOMAEUS

Botanologica Medica. Berlin: 1714. V. 45

ZORN, JOHANNES

Auswahl Schoener und Seltener Gewaechse, als Eine Fortsetzung der Americanischen Gewaechse. Nuernberg: 1795-96. V. 40

ZOTIKOV, I. A.

The Thermophysics of Glaciers. London: 1986. V. 37

ZOUCH, HENRY

An Account of the Present Practices of Night Hunters, and Poachers, with Some Hints Upon Which to Form a Law, As Well for Restraining These Offenders, as For the Preservation of the Game Throughout the Kingdom. London: 1783. V. 42

ZOUCH, RICHARD

Elementa Iurisprudentiae, Definitionibus, Regulis, et Sententiis Selectioribus Iuris Civilis Illustrata . . . Oxoniae: 1629. V. 37

The Sophister. London: 1639. V. 46

ZOUCH, THOMAS

The Life of Isaac Walton . . . London: 1823. V. 46

The Life of Izaak Walton . . . London: 1826. V. 45

ZOUCHE, ROBERT CURZON, BARON 1810-1873

Armenia; a Year at Erzeroom and on the Frontiers of Russia, Turkey, and Persia. London: 1854. V. 40

History of Printing in China and Europe. London: 1860. V. 40

The Lay of the Purple Falcon; a Metrical Romance . . . London: 1847. V. 46

Visits to the Monastries in the Levant. London: 1849. V. 46

ZSCHOKKE, HEINRICH

Abaellino, the Bravo of Venice. Baltimore: 1809. V. 46

Alamontade; or the Galley Slave. Philadelphia: 1845. V. 43

ZSCHOKKE, HENRY

The History of the Invasion of Switzerland by the French and the Destruction of the Democratical Republics of Schwitz, Eri and Unterwalden . . . London: 1803. V. 45

ZUALLART, JEAN

Le Tresdevot Voyage de Ierusalem. Antwerp: 1608. V. 37

ZUBLER, LEONHARD

Fabrica et Usus Instrumenti Chorographici, das ist Newe Planimetrische Beschreibung . . . Basel: 1614. V. 39

ZUCCHELLI DA GRADISCA, ANTONIO

Relazioni del Viaggio e Missione di Congo nell'Etiopia Inferiore Occidentale . . . Venice: 1712. V. 38

ZUCCOLO, GREGORIO

I Discorsi . . . Nei Quali si Tratta della Nobilita, Honore, Amore, Fortificationi et Antigaglie. Venice: 1575. V. 43

ZUCCOLO, LODOVICO

Discorsi dell'Honore, della Gloria, della Reputatione, del Buon Concetto. Venice: 1623. V. 37

ZUCCOLO, SIMEON

La Pazzia Del Ballo. Padua: 1549. V. 44

ZUCHETTA, GIOVANNI BATTISTA b. 1550.

Prima parte della Armmetica . . . Brescia: 1600. V. 37

ZUCKER, A. E.

The Chinese Theater. Boston: 1925. V. 43

ZUCKER, BENJAMIN

Islamic Rings and Gems: The Benjamin Zucker Collection. London: 1987. V. 40

ZUCKERMANN, WOLFGANG JOACHIM

The Modern Harpsichord; Twentieth Century Instruments and Their Makers. New York: (1969). V. 37

ZUGSMITH, LEANE

A Time to Remember. New York: 1936. V. 37; 46

ZUKOFSKY, LOUIS

'A' 1-12 With an Essay on Poetry by the Author and a Final Note By William Carlos Williams. Ashland: 1959. V. 37

'A-14'. London: 1967. V. 39; 42

Barely and Widley. New York: 1958. V. 39; 46

Initial. New York: 1970. V. 39

It Was. Ashland: 1961. V. 37

Little: a Fragment for Careenagers. Los Angeles: 1967. V. 38; 40

Little: a Fragment for Careenagers. San Francisco: 1967. V. 44

An Objectivists Anthology. Dijon: 1932. V. 43

ZUKOFSKY, LOUIS continued

A Test of Poetry. Brooklyn: 1948. V. 39

A Test of Poetry. New York: 1948. V. 39; 40; 42

ZUKOR, ADOLPH

The Public Is Never Wrong. New York: 1953. V. 45

ZUNZ, PAUL

The Crisis. A Celebrated Case at Manhattan Beach. First Direct Answer and Challenge to Corbin. War on Messrs. Corbin, Hilton & Co. and the New York Herlad. An Open Letter to the Public. New York: 1879. V. 39

ZURBRIGGEN, MATTIAS

From the Alps to the Andes. London: 1899. V. 43

ZURCHER, OTTO

Gerald Landon. New York: 1917. V. 46

ZUSTO, GIOVANNI

Descrizione Istorica dell' Estrazione della Pubblica Nave la Fenice dal Canale Spignon. Venice: 1789. V. 37

ZWEERTS, KORNELIS

Zinryke Dicht-Kunst, Getrokken uit Homerus, Heziodus, Anakreon . . . Amsterdam: 1712. V. 46

ZWEIG, PAUL

Images and Footsteps: a Poem. 1971. V. 40

Images & Footsteps. Verona: 1971. V. 43; 46

The River. Verona: 1981. V. 38; 39; 40; 45; 46

ZWEIG, STEFAN

George Frederick Handel's Resurrection. 1938. V. 40

ZWELFER, JOANNIS

Animadversiones in Pharmacopoeiam Avqvstanam et Annexam Ejus Mantissam Sive Pharmacopoeia Augustana Reformata . . . Maieslata: 1652. V. 37; 40

ZWINGLI, HULDREICH 1484-1531

Ain Christliche Fast Nutzliche und Trostliche Epistel . . . Augsburg: 1526. V. 43

In Evangelicam Historiam De Domino Nostro Iesu . . . Geneva: 1539. V. 40

The Latin Works and Correspondence of . . . Together with Selections from His German Works. New York: 1912/22/29. V. 37

ZWORYKIN, V. K.

Photocells and Their Application. New York: 1930. V. 46

ZYLBERZWEIG, ZALME

Album of Yiddish Theatre. New York: 1937. V. 46

ISBN 0-8103-9554-1

90000